The Red Book

2018–19

The Red Book

2018–19

Consultant Editors

Bill Dodwell LLB, LLM, CTA (Fellow), ACA

Kevin Prosser QC

Croner-i

HR • Tax • H&S • Audit & Accounting

Croner-i Ltd
240 Blackfriars Road
London SE1 8NW
Telephone: 0844 561 8166
Email: client.experience@croneri.co.uk
Website: croneri.co.uk

ISBN 978-1-78887-175-4

British Library Cataloguing-in-Publication Data.

A catalogue record for this book is available from the British Library.

Typeset by Innodata Inc., India

Printed and bound by L.E.G.O. S.p.A. – Italy.

The Red Book

Senior Technical Editor

PAUL ROBBINS BA(Hons.), ACA, CTA

Technical Editors

SARAH ARNOLD ACA, CTA

Foreword

Just four months after the 2017 edition, it falls to your consulting editors to pen an introduction to the 2018 edition of UK direct tax legislation.

We should start by celebrating the modest amount of additional legislation added by *Finance Act* 2018. The Act is a mere 187 pages, which compares favourably to over 800 pages added by the two 2017 Acts. There are no major new additions to the statute book. We should also celebrate the prospective nature of the legislation; with the exception of anti-avoidance and new reliefs, nothing takes effect from a date before enactment. Draft legislation on changes effective from the autumn Budget on 22 November was published on that date, with the full Bill being introduced to the House of Commons on 1 December 2017.

Corporate taxation

The UK has been at the forefront of adopting measures agreed by the Base Erosion and Profit Shifting (BEPS) project. The project was initiated by the G20 in November 2012. At the time of writing, 113 countries and jurisdictions have agreed to join the BEPS Inclusive Framework, each committing to adopt the four minimum standards of the project. Two of those standards – Treaty Abuse and Dispute Resolution – are part of the world's 3,000 double tax treaties and a Multilateral Convention is the best way to modify those treaties without individually negotiated protocols. This Act allows the UK to ratify the Convention, by providing that arrangements approved by statutory instrument may include arrangements which modify arrangements already made. The effect of the Multilateral Convention is to override existing treaties, which is why this change is needed. There are also minor changes to two other BEPS measures: anti-hybrid rules and the corporate interest restrictions. These latter measures are sufficiently complex that more changes may be needed in future Acts, to ensure that the policy goal is achieved without unintended consequences.

Employment taxation

Suppose that, with the agreement or acquiescence of the employee, an employer has made a payment to an EBT with a view to the trustees' "earmarking" the money for the employee's benefit, and/or making an interest-free loan to him. Prior to the decision in the *Rangers EBT* case (officially *RFC 2012 plc (in liquidation) (formerly Rangers Football Club plc) v Advocate General for Scotland* [2017] BTC 22), it was generally thought that the employee was not taxable in respect of the employer's payment (because it was made to the trustees, not to him), or in respect of the trustees' "earmarking" (because the trustees did not put the funds unreservedly at the employee's disposal), and so he could only be subject to the annual beneficial loan tax charge. In recognition of this analysis, in 2011 the Government introduced ITEPA 2003, Pt. 7A, which imposed a tax charge on the occasion of an "earmarking" or loan, as if the amount earmarked or lent had been paid outright to the employee. Following the *Rangers* decision, to the effect that the employer's payment was taxable earnings of the employee because he was party to it being "re-directed" to the EBT, it was argued by some that Pt. 7A could not apply as well: after all, if the payment was the employee's earnings, then he must be regarded as in effect having settled his own money, and so the "earmarking" or loan could not have anything to do with his employment. Unsurprisingly, HMRC did not agree with this argument, but FA 2018 puts the matter beyond any doubt by providing that the application of *Rangers* does not preclude the (past, present or future) application of Pt. 7A. Thus, there is potential for double charges, but changes made in 2017 are designed to prevent this.

Another change made by the Act is to introduce a new, and potentially very wide, disguised remuneration charge, to prevent avoidance of tax on benefits or loans received from close companies (including companies which would be close if UK resident) by employees or directors with a material interest in the company.

The third change is that, after many years, foreign service relief is removed on termination payments for UK residents. The Explanatory Notes state "This will ensure that all employees who are UK resident in the tax year their employment is terminated will be liable to income tax on their termination payment in the same way regardless of whether they have worked abroad." Whatever views there are on the principle, removing relief from someone who has worked abroad but who comes to the UK part-way through a tax year looks unfair. The issue is sharply in focus after the abolition of the so-called "split-year" concession on the introduction of the statutory residence test. Arguments that double tax treaties may provide an exemption aren't good enough.

Personal taxation

This Act introduces new partnership provisions. The aim is to cover how the law should apply where there are tiers of partnerships, or where partners are bare trustees for another person. The Act contains information and reporting requirements and now provides a new structured mechanism for the resolution of disputes about the allocation of profits between partners.

Changes are made to the requirements for investments to qualify for relief under the Enterprise Investment Scheme (EIS), the Seed Enterprise Investment Scheme (SEIS) or the Venture Capital Trusts scheme. There will be an overarching risk-to-capital condition to prevent investment in companies whose activities are mostly geared towards the preservation of the capital invested. There's also an enhanced relief for investment in knowledge-intensive companies. Parliament is starting to ask whether tax reliefs achieve their goal of supporting desired business investment. It would be helpful for HMRC to monitor whether the change boosts investment in innovative companies developing and exploiting new technologies, so that an informed decision may be taken on the benefits of these reliefs.

VAT

There are new VAT provisions covering joint and several liability of online marketplaces and the requirement on them to display valid VAT numbers. The background is an estimate by HMRC that up to £1.5 billion annually is lost to VAT evasion by sellers using marketplaces to sell their goods to UK customers, without accounting for VAT. These changes are part of a journey, where marketplaces may be required to take greater responsibility for VAT compliance of those who sell goods or services through a marketplace.

In the courts

It has been a relatively quiet period in the upper courts. Several attempts have been made by participants in tax schemes to challenge accelerated payment notices and follower notices, through judicial review. All have failed. Perhaps the most technical case is *Trigg (a partner in Tonnant LLP)* v *R & C Commrs* [2018] BTC 7; [2018] EWCA 17 Civ, where the Court of Appeal decided that clauses in bonds about the potential conversion from sterling to euro, in the event the UK adopted that currency, did not disqualify the bonds from being QCBs – and thus exempt from capital gains tax.

We congratulate the editors and publishers on speedily consolidating the provisions of the Finance Act into these volumes.

Bill Dodwell
Kevin Prosser QC

March 2018

Publisher's Note

Volume 1A contains the text of the *Taxes Management Act* 1970, the *Income and Corporation Taxes Act* 1988, the *Taxation of Chargeable Gains Act* 1992 and the *Capital Allowances Act* 2001. It also contains all other significant Acts affecting the imposition and collection of income tax, corporation tax and capital gains tax, up to and including the *Capital Allowances Act* 2001. Enactments are presented in chronological order.

Volume 1B includes the key personal tax Acts: *Income Tax (Earnings and Pensions) Act* 2003, *Finance Act* 2004, the *Income Tax (Trading and Other Income) Act* 2005 and the *Income Tax Act* 2007. It also contains all other significant Acts relating to income tax, corporation tax and capital gains tax up to and including the *Income Tax Act* 2007, presented in chronological order.

Volume 1C includes the key corporation tax Acts: the *Corporation Tax Act* 2009, the *Corporation Tax Act* 2010 and the *Taxation (International and Other Provisions) Act* 2010. It also contains all other significant Acts relating to income tax, corporation tax and capital gains tax up to and including the *Taxation (International and Other Provisions) Act* 2010, presented in chronological order.

Volume 1D includes contains all significant Acts relating to income tax, corporation tax and capital gains tax from the *Finance Act* 2010 to *Finance Act* 2018, presented in chronological order. This volume also includes the legislation for the bank levy (*Finance Act* 2011), the annual tax on enveloped dwellings (*Finance Act* 2013), the diverted profits tax (*Finance Act* 2015) and the apprenticeship levy (*Finance Act* 2016).

Volume 1E includes UK statutory instruments and Scottish statutory instruments relevant to the taxes covered in Volumes 1A, 1B, 1C and 1D. Volume 1E also includes EC directives and HMRC Directions.

Volume 1F includes extra-statutory concessions, statements of practice, HMRC Briefs and extensive *Tax Bulletin* extracts relevant to the taxes covered in Volumes 1A, 1B, 1C and 1D.

Also in Volume 1F, a considerable number of other HMRC materials are reproduced as well as selected extracts from ICAEW technical releases and selected releases from the Chartered Institute of Taxation. Selected Accounting Standards are also included.

The Index volume covers material in Volumes 1A, 1B, 1C, 1D, 1E and 1F. It contains the comprehensive topic index, list of definitions and meanings and a consolidated destination table where pre-consolidation enactments can be traced in the *Income and Corporation Taxes Act* 1988, the *Taxation of Chargeable Gains Act* 1992, the *Capital Allowances Act* 2001, the *Income Tax (Earnings and Pensions) Act* 2003, the *Income Tax (Trading and Other Income) Act* 2005, the *Income Tax Act* 2007, the *Corporation Tax Act* 2009, the *Corporation Tax Act* 2010 and the *Taxation (International and Other Provisions) Act* 2010. The table also includes destinations for PAYE and sub-contractor regulations following the consolidations in the *Income Tax (Sub-contractors in the Construction Industry) Regulations* 1993 (SI 1993/743) and the *Income Tax (Employments) Regulations* 2003 (SI 2003/2682).

The Index volume also includes the "Stop Press" section which contains material that was issued too late to go in its normal location. In the main, the items normally included here are statutory instruments, some of which have been formally laid, but some of which may be the latest draft available at the time of going to press. These drafts have been included because, when laid, they will form an important part of the 2018–19 legislative picture. Readers should, however, be aware that they are potentially subject to amendment.

Volume 1G includes all relevant material on National Insurance contributions, tax credits, inheritance tax and petroleum revenue tax.

Volume 1H includes all relevant material on stamp taxes (including the land and buildings transaction tax in Scotland and the land transaction tax in Wales).

Volume 2 includes all relevant material on value added tax.

The legislation is reproduced so as to show those provisions which are in force in 2018–19. The Acts have been abridged by the omission of the full text of provisions which either amend earlier enactments (unless the amendment is prospective) or have been repealed. However, the *Finance Act* 2018 appears in full text in Volume 1D, in so far as it relates to income tax, corporation tax and capital gains tax, and in the relevant parts of Volume 1G and in Volumes 1H and 2 for the taxes dealt with in those volumes.

Prospective changes for which no effective date in 2018–19 has been announced at the time of going to press, or where the effective date has been announced but is after 2018–19, are noted under the provisions to be amended or in the case of, for example, entirely new sections, at the place where they will appear when they enter into force, with reference made to the place where the text of the changes can be found. Prospective changes which enter into force during 2018–19 are made to the provisions amended, substituted, etc. with a "History" note setting out the "former" provisions in smaller type beneath. Where prospective legislation is amended before it takes effect it is shown in amended form at the place where it is introduced, but the "target" legislation to be amended carries only a brief description of the amendment.

Where, because of subsequent amendments, provisions do not appear as originally enacted, the former wording is reproduced only where it is either in force at some point in 2018–19 or likely to be of practical relevance to 2018–19 liabilities. Details of such amendments and, where appropriate, former wording in smaller type appear as "History" notes beneath the amended provisions. In some cases whole sections are involved and these appear in smaller type in their entirety.

Derivation notes under provisions of the *Income and Corporation Taxes Act* 1988, the *Taxation of Chargeable Gains Act* 1992, the *Capital Allowances Act* 2001, the *Income Tax (Earnings and Pensions) Act* 2003, the *Income Tax (Trading and Other Income) Act* 2005, the *Income Tax Act* 2007, the *Corporation Tax Act* 2009, the *Corporation Tax Act* 2010, and the *Taxation (International and Other Provisions) Act* 2010 indicate the former enactments.

Extensive cross references appear throughout, at the end of each section or paragraph, both to other provisions of the Taxes Acts and to extraneous legislation. Cross references under a section, paragraph, etc. mainly refer to provisions which explicitly mention that section, paragraph, etc. The order of cross references is first to list those involving the Act in point, then those involving the *Income and Corporation Taxes Act* 1988, then those involving other Taxes Acts in chronological order, and then those involving extraneous Acts, again in chronological order. Effective, or implicit, cross references are mentioned by way of editorial note (see below).

Relevant statutory instruments, extra-statutory concessions, statements of practice, *Tax Bulletin* decisions and interpretations (these are all reproduced) are noted. Other related materials (*Tax Bulletin* articles and special editions, HMRC press releases and booklets, releases from accountancy bodies and the Law Society, etc.) which affect particular provisions are also noted even if they are not reproduced. European material related to the provision in question is also noted, and editorial notes are inserted where additional comment is appropriate.

While Parliamentary materials or their equivalent had in other jurisdictions long been used as an aid to the interpretation of legislative acts, the decision of the House of Lords in *Pepper (HMIT) v Hart and related appeals* [1992] BTC 591 that ministerial statements may be so used in limited circumstances was an innovation in the UK. The cases in which such use can be made of Parliamentary material are at present limited to circumstances where: legislation is ambiguous, obscure or leads to an absurdity, the material relied upon consists of statements by a minister or other promoter of the Bill, and the statements relied upon are clear. A range of annotations covering Parliamentary material are grouped together under the generic heading of "Hansard Extracts" in the "Other materials" division. Editorial judgment has been used in selecting some of the more significant of such references, or those with the most widespread application; the coverage of Parliamentary material in the footnotes is by no means exhaustive.

As part of HMRC's response to the Government's code of practice on access to Government information, the HMRC guidance manuals have been made available to the public. The manuals provide HMRC staff with guidance on the interpretation of tax law and the operation of the tax system. References to useful material contained in the manuals appear under the heading "HMRC manuals". Editorial judgment has been used in selecting the references.

The publisher advises that the Acts, Regulations and other official material in this publication are not the authorised official versions. However, the greatest care has been taken to ensure exact conformity with the law as enacted and with the text of extra-statutory material. Some changes in printing style have been adopted for convenience and to improve readability. For example, marginal notes appearing in the official statutes have been reproduced in bold type in the first line of the section to which they relate. Many words and phrases have also been reproduced in bold where they are defined in the legislation so that the definitions can be located more easily.

Our role as publisher is not to guess which parts will be of greatest practical interest but rather to present all the legislation and related material accurately and to annotate it helpfully. We always welcome comments and suggestions from our readers and we thank those who have offered constructive thoughts over the past year.

ABBREVIATIONS

The following abbreviations are commonly used throughout this publication.

ACT	advance corporation tax
ADTSA 2017	Air Departure Tax (Scotland) Act 2017
AEA 1925	Administration of Estates Act 1925
AIM	Alternative Investment Market
AIS	accrued income scheme
AL	aggregates levy
App.	appendix
APR	annual percentage rate
APRT	advance petroleum revenue tax
ARPA 2004	Age-Related Payments Act 2004
art.	article(s)
ATCSA 2001	Anti-Terrorism, Crime and Security Act 2001
ATED	Annual tax on enveloped dwellings
BB	Customs and Excise Business Briefs
BEN	business economic note
BES	business expansion scheme
BN	Budget Notes
BRNAA 2011	Budget Responsibility and National Audit Act 2011
BSA 1986	Building Societies Act 1986
B(S)A 1985	Bankruptcy (Scotland) Act 1985
BTC	British Tax Cases, 1982–current (Croner-i)
CA 1985	Companies Act 1985
CA 2006	Companies Act 2006
C & E Commrs	Commissioners of Customs and Excise
CAA 1968	Capital Allowances Act 1968
CAA 1990	Capital Allowances Act 1990
CAA 2001	Capital Allowances Act 2001
CCBSA 2014	Co-operative and Community Benefit Societies Act 2014
CCL	climate change levy
CED(GR)A 1979	Customs and Excise Duties (General Reliefs) Act 1979
CEMA 1979	Customs and Excise Management Act 1979
CFA 2017	Criminal Finances Act 2017
CFC	controlled foreign company
CGT	capital gains tax
CGTA 1979	Capital Gains Tax Act 1979
Ch.	Chapter(s) (of a statute/SI etc.)
CHA 2011	Charities Act 2011
CIC	close investment-holding company
CICA 2013	Crime (International Co-Operation) Act 2003
CIOT	Chartered Institute of Taxation
CJPA 2001	Criminal Justice and Police Act 2001
cl.	clause(s)
col.	column(s)
Commr; Commrs	commissioner; commissioners
Conv.	convention
CPA 1947	Crown Proceedings Act 1947
CPA 2014	Childcare Payments Act 2014
CRCA 2005	Commissioners for Revenue and Customs Act 2005
CRGA 2010	Constitutional Reform and Governance Act 2010
CRSA 2014	Courts Reform (Scotland) Act 2014
CRT	composite rate tax
CSPSSA 2000	Child Support, Pensions and Social Security Act 2000
CT	corporation tax
CTA 2009	Corporation Tax Act 2009
CTA 2010	Corporation Tax Act 2010
CTD	certificates of tax deposits

CTFA 2004	Child Trust Funds Act 2004
CT(NI)A 2015	Corporation Tax (Northern Ireland) Act 2015
CTT	capital transfer tax
CTTA 1984	Capital Transfer Tax Act 1984
DDA(S)A 2002	Debt Arrangement and Attachment (Scotland) Act 2002
Dir.	EC directives
DLT	development land tax
DLTA 1976	Development Land Tax Act 1976
DPA 1998	Data Protection Act 1998
DPT	Diverted Profits Tax
DSS	Department of Social Security
DTI	Department of Trade and Industry
EA 2002	Employment Act 2002
EA 2004	Energy Act 2004
EC	European Community/Communities
edn.	edition
EEC	European Economic Community
EEIG	European Economic Interest Grouping
e.g.	(exempli gratia) for example
EIS	enterprise investment scheme
ELPA 2010	Equitable Life (Payments) Act 2010
EMPA 2003	Electricity (Miscellaneous Provisions) Act 2003
ERA 1996	Employee Rights Act 1996
ESC	extra-statutory concession
ESOP	employee stock ownership plan
ESOT	employee share ownership trust
etc.	(et cetera) and so on
et seq.	(et sequens) and the following
EU	European Union
FA	Finance Act
FA 2018	Finance Act 2018
FI 1985	Films Act 1985
FIA 2000	Freedom of Information Act 2000
FII	franked investment income
F(No. 2)A	Finance (No. 2) Act
F(No. 2)A 2017	Finance (No. 2) Act 2017
F(No. 3)A	Finance (No. 3) Act
F(No. 3)A 2010	Finance (No. 3) Act 2010
FSMA 2000	Financial Services and Markets Act 2000
FYA	first-year allowance
GAAP	generally accepted accounting practice
Grp.	Group (VAT legislation)
HA 1988	Housing Act 1988
HM	Her Majesty
HMIT	Her Majesty's Inspector of Taxes
HMRC	HM Revenue & Customs
HMSO	Her Majesty's Stationery Office
HRA 1998	Human Rights Act 1998
IA	initial allowance
IA 1986	Insolvency Act 1986
ICAEW	Institute of Chartered Accountants in England and Wales
ICAS	Institute of Chartered Accountants of Scotland
ICTA 1970	Income and Corporation Taxes Act 1970
ICTA 1988	Income and Corporation Taxes Act 1988
i.e.	*(id est)* that is
IHT	inheritance tax
IHTA 1984	Inheritance Tax Act 1984
IHTPA 2014	Inheritance and Trustee's Power's Act 2014
INA 1978	Interpretation Act 1978

IoT	Institute of Taxation
IPT	insurance premium tax
IR Commrs	Commissioners of Inland Revenue
IRDec.	Inland Revenue decision
IRInt.	Inland Revenue interpretation
IRRA 1890	Inland Revenue Regulation Act 1890
IT	income tax
ITA 2007	Income Tax Act 2007
ITEPA 2003	Income Tax (Earnings and Pensions) Act 2003
ITTOIA 2005	Income Tax (Trading and Other Income) Act 2005
LA 2011	Localism Act 2011
LAUTRO	Life Assurance and Unit Trust Regulatory Organisation
LBTTSA 2013	Land and Buildings Transaction Tax (Scotland) Act 2013
LBTTSA 2016	Land and Buildings Transaction Tax (Amendment) (Scotland) Act 2016
LDTWA 2017	Landfill Disposals Tax (Wales) Act 2017
LFT	landfill tax
LIFFE	London International Financial Futures and Options Exchange
LLPA 2000	Limited Liability Partnerships Act 2000
LPA 1907	Limited Partnerships Act 1907
LPA 1925	Law of Property Act 1925
LRRA 2006	Legislative and Regulatory Reform Act 2006
LSG	Law Society Gazette
LTTADA 2017	Land Transaction Tax and Anti-Avoidance of Devolved Taxes (Wales) Act 2017
MCT	mainstream corporation tax
MIRAS	mortgage interest relief at source
Misc.	miscellaneous items (denoted by number)
NB	(nota bene) note well
NHA 1980	National Heritage Act 1980
NI	Northern Ireland
NIC	National Insurance contributions
NICA 2002	National Insurance Contributions Act 2002
NICA 2004	National Insurance Contributions and Statutory Payments Act 2004
NICA 2006	National Insurance Contributions Act 2006
NICA 2008	National Insurance Contributions Act 2008
NICA 2014	National Insurance Contributions Act 2014
NICRCA 2015	National Insurance Contributions (Rate Ceilings) Act 2015
NICSPA 2004	National Insurance Contributions and Statutory Payments Act 2004
NR	Customs and Excise News Releases
O.	Order(s)
OJ	Official Journal of the European Communities
OJ "L" series	Official Journal of the European Communities, Legislation Series (cited by year, issue number and page, for example OJ 1989 L1/1 is the first page of the first issue of the legislation series of the Official Journal for 1989)
OPB	Occupational Pensions Board
Ors	others
OTA 1975	Oil Taxation Act 1975
OTA 1983	Oil Taxation Act 1983
p.; pp.	page; pages
PA 2004	Pensions Act 2004
PA 2007	Pensions Act 2007
PA 2011	Pensions Act 2011
PA 2014	Pensions Act 2014
PAA 2009	Perpetuities and Accumulations Act 2009
p.a.	per annum (each year)
PACE 1994	Police and Criminal Evidence Act 1994
para.	paragraph(s)
PAYE	pay as you earn
PCA 2002	Proceeds of Crime Act 2002
PCTA 1968	Provisional Collection of Taxes Act 1968
PEP	personal equity plan

PET	potentially exempt transfer
PLDA 1808	Probate and Legacy Duties Act 1808
PN	Customs and Excise Press Notices
PPS	personal pension scheme
PR	press release(s)
PRP	profit-related pay
PRT	petroleum revenue tax
PRTA 1980	Petroleum Revenue Tax Act 1980
PSA 1993	Pension Schemes Act 1993
PSA 2011	Postal Services Act 2011
PSA 2015	Pension Schemes Act 2015
PSO	Pensions Schemes Office
Pt.	Part(s)
QCB	qualifying corporate bond
r.	rule(s)
RA 1898	Revenue Act 1898 and similarly coded for appropriate subsequent years
RA 2005	Railways Act 2005
R & C Commrs	Revenue and Customs Commissioners
RDDA 1998	Regional Development Agencies Act 1998
reg.	regulations
Regulations	EC Regulations
RPI	retail prices index
RSC	Rules of the Supreme Court 1965
RSTPA 2014	Revenue Scotland and Tax Powers Act 2014
s.	section(s)
SA 1891	Stamp Act 1891
SAYE	save as you earn
SCA 1981	Supreme Court Act 1981
SCA 1998	Scotland Act 1998
SCA 2012	Scotland Act 2012
SCA 2016	Scotland Act 2016
SCDA 2012	Small Charitable Donations Act 2012
SCDCPA 2017	Small Charitable Donations and Childcare Payments Act 2017
Sch.	Schedule(s)
SDLT	stamp duty land tax
SDLTCN	Stamp Duty Land Tax Customer Newsletter
SDMA 1891	Stamp Duty Management Act 1891
SDRT	stamp duty reserve tax
SD(TP)A 1992	Stamp Duty (Temporary Provisions) Act 1992
SERPS	state earnings-related pension scheme
SFO	Superannuation Funds Office
SGCA 2017	Savings (Government Contributions) Act 2017
SI	statutory instrument
SMP	statutory maternity pay
SOCN	Stamp Office Customer Newsletter
SOCPA 2005	Serious Organised Crime and Police Act 2005
SP	Statement of practice
SPCA 2002	State Pension Credit Act 2002
SRO	self-regulating organisation
SR & O	statutory rules and orders
SSA 1975	Social Security Act 1975
SSA 1980	Social Security Act 1980
SSA 1986	Social Security Act 1986
SSA 1989	Social Security Act 1989
SSA 1998	Social Security Act 1998
SSAA 1992	Social Security Administration Act 1992
SSAP	Statement of Standard Accounting Practice
SSCBA 1992	Social Security Contributions and Benefits Act 1992
SS(CP)A 1992	Social Security (Consequential Provisions) Act 1992

SS(TF)A 1999	Social Security Contributions (Transfer of Functions, etc.) Act 1999
SSFA 2001	Social Security Fraud Act 2001
SSHBA 1982	Social Security Housing Benefits Act 1982
SS(MP)A 1977	Social Security (Miscellaneous Provisions) Act 1977
SSP	statutory sick pay
SSPA 1975	Social Security Pensions Act 1975
SSPA 1994	Statutory Sick Pay Act 1994
STA 1963	Stock Transfer Act 1963
STB	Stamp Taxes Bulletin
subcl.	subclause(s)
subpara.	subparagraph(s)
subs.	subsection(s)
TA 2000	Transport Act 2000
TAURUS	Transfer and Automated Registration of Uncertified Stock
TB	Tax Bulletin article
TBSE	Tax Bulletin special edition
TCA 2002	Tax Credits Act 2002
TCEA 2007	Tribunals, Courts and Enforcement Act 2007
TCGA 1992	Taxation of Chargeable Gains Act 1992
TCIA 2013	Trusts (Capital and Income) Act 2013
TCMWA 2016	Tax Collection and Management (Wales) Act 2016
TERA 2000	Terrorism Act 2000
TESSA	tax-exempt special savings account
TIOPA 2010	Taxation (International and Other Provisions) Act 2010
TMA 1970	Taxes Management Act 1970
TOPA 2014	Taxation of Pensions Act 2014
TR	technical release
TSA 2014	Tribunals (Scotland) Act 2014
TSBA 1985	Trustee Savings Bank Act 1985
TULR(C)A 1992	Trade Union and Labour Relations (Consolidation) Act 1992
TWDV	tax written-down value
UCITS	Undertakings for Collective Investment in Transferable Securities
UK	United Kingdom
USM	Unlisted Securities Market
VAT	value added tax
VATA 1983	Value Added Tax Act 1983
VATA 1994	Value Added Tax Act 1994
VCT	Venture Capital Trust
vol.	volume(s)
WA 2014	Wales Act 2014
WA 2017	Wales Act 2017
WDA	writing down allowance
WDV	written-down value
WFT	windfall tax
WRA 2012	Welfare Reform Act 2012
WRPA 1999	Welfare Reform and Pensions Act 1999
¶	Croner-i paragraph

About the Publisher

Croner-i Ltd is part of the international The Peninsula Group. Croner-i Ltd is the leading publisher specialising in tax, business and law publishing throughout Europe, the US and the Asia Pacific region. The group produces a wide range of information services in different media for the accounting and legal professions and for business.

All Croner-i Ltd publications are designed to be practical and authoritative reference works and guides and are written by our own highly qualified and experienced editorial team and specialist outside authors.

Croner-i Ltd publishes information packages including electronic products, loose-leaf reporting services, newsletters and books on UK and European legal topics for distribution world-wide.

Croner-i Ltd
240 Blackfriars Road
London SE1 8NW
Telephone: 0844 561 8166
Email: client.experience@croneri.co.uk
Website: croneri.co.uk

About the Consultant Editors

Bill Dodwell read law at King's College, London, and Queens' College, Cambridge. He became a partner in Deloitte in 2002, after 24 years with Arthur Andersen. He is a Fellow of the Chartered Institute of Taxation and a member of the ICAEW. Bill has been a CIOT Council member since 2008 and was CIOT President in 2016–17. He also chaired the CIOT's Technical Committee from 2010–16 and is a member of the International Taxes Sub-committee and Corporate Taxes Sub-committee. He is Head of Tax Policy at Deloitte, responsible for consultations with the OECD, the European Commission the HM Treasury and HMRC. He tweets as @BillDodwellTax.

Kevin Prosser QC read law at University College, London and St Edmund Hall, Oxford. He was called to the Bar in 1982, and has been a QC since 1996. He specialises in all forms of tax advice and litigation. He was Chairman of the Revenue Bar Association from 2008 to 2014, and is now head of Pump Court Tax Chambers. He was a Recorder from 2000 to 2015 and a Deputy High Court Judge from 2008 to 2015.

Acknowledgement

Croner-i Ltd gratefully acknowledges the endorsement of this publication by the Chartered Institute of Taxation.

THE
CHARTERED
INSTITUTE OF
TAXATION

Table of Contents

NATIONAL INSURANCE CONTRIBUTIONS

Table of Contents

NIC STATUTES

Table of Contents

continued over

TAXES MANAGEMENT ACT 1970

(1970 Chapter 9)

[*12th March 1970*]

ARRANGEMENT OF SECTIONS

PART II – RETURNS OF INCOME AND GAINS

PART IV – ASSESSMENT AND CLAIMS

PART V – APPEALS AND OTHER PROCEEDINGS

APPEALS

PART VA – PAYMENT OF TAX

INCOME TAX AND CAPITAL GAINS TAX

MANAGED PAYMENT PLANS

PART VI – COLLECTION AND RECOVERY

DISTRAINT AND POINDING

COURT PROCEEDINGS

SUPPLEMENTAL

PART X – PENALTIES, ETC.

This is an edited version of TMA 1970, generally containing only the provisions relevant to National Insurance contributions.

Cross references – SSCBA 1992, s. 16(1): provisions of the Income Tax Act, including provisions as to assessment, collection, repayment and recovery shall, with the necessary modifications, apply in relation to Class 4 contributions as if those contributions were income tax chargeable under ITTOIA 2005, Pt. 2, Ch. 2 in respect of the profits of a trade, profession or vocation which is not carried on wholly outside the UK.

PART II – RETURNS OF INCOME AND GAINS

Cross references – SSCBA 1992, s. 11A: Pt. II applies, with the necessary modifications, in relation to Class 2 contributions under s. 11(2) as if those contributions were income tax chargeable under ITTOIA 2005, Pt. 2, Ch. 2 in respect of profits of a trade, profession or vocation which is not carried on wholly outside the UK, with effect for the tax year 2015–16 and subsequent tax years.

INCOME TAX

7 Notice of liability to income tax and capital gains tax

7(1) Every person who–

(a) is chargeable to income tax or capital gains tax for any year of assessment, and

(b) falls within subsection (1A) or (1B),

shall, subject to subsection (3) below, within the notification period, give notice to an officer of the Board that he is so chargeable.

7(1A) A person falls within this subsection if the person has not received a notice under section 8 requiring a return for the year of assessment of the person's total income and chargeable gains.

7(1B) A person falls within this subsection if the person–

(a) has received a notice under section 8 requiring a return for the year of assessment of the person's total income and chargeable gains, and

(b) has received a notice under section 8B withdrawing the notice under section 8.

7(1C) In subsection (1) **"the notification period"** means–

(a) in the case of a person who falls within subsection (1A), the period of 6 months from the end of the year of assessment, or

(b) in the case of a person who falls within subsection (1B)–

(i) the period of 6 months from the end of the year of assessment, or

(ii) the period of 30 days beginning with the day after the day on which the notice under section 8 was withdrawn,

whichever ends later.

7(2) In the case of persons who are chargeable as mentioned in subsection (1) above as the relevant trustees of a settlement, that subsection and subsections (1A) to (1C) have effect as if references to a notice under section 8 were references to a notice under section 8A.

7(2A) A person who–

(a) falls within subsection (1A) or (1B), and

(b) is notified of a simple assessment for the year of assessment,

is not required to give notice under subsection (1) for that year unless the person is chargeable to income tax or capital gains tax for the year of assessment on any income or gain that is not included in the assessment.

7(3) A person shall not be required to give notice under subsection (1) above in respect of a year of assessment if for that year –

(a) the person's total income consists of income from sources falling within subsections (4) to (7) below,

(b) the person has no chargeable gains, and

(c) the person is not liable to a high income child benefit charge.

7(4) A source of income falls within this subsection in relation to a year of assessment if–

(a) all payments of, or on account of, income from it during that year, and

(b) all income from it for that year which does not consist of payments,

have or has been taken into account in the making of deductions or repayments of tax under PAYE regulations.

7(5) A source of income falls within this subsection in relation to any person and any year of assessment if all income from it for that year has been or will be taken into account–

(a) in determining that person's liability to tax, or

(b) in the making of deductions or repayments of tax under PAYE regulations.

7(6) A source of income falls within this subsection in relation to any person and any year of assessment if all income from it for that year is–

(a) income from which income tax has been deducted; or

(b) income from or on which income tax is treated as having been deducted or paid,

(c) [omitted by FA 2016, s. 5(9)(a)(iii),]

and that person is not for that year liable to tax at a rate other than the basic rate, the dividend nil rate, the Scottish basic rate, the dividend ordinary rate, the savings nil rate or the starting rate for savings.

7(6A) A source of income falls within this subsection in relation to any person and any year of assessment if for that year–

(a) all income from the source is dividend income (see section 19 of ITA 2007), and

(b) the person–

(i) is UK-resident,

(ii) is not liable to tax at the dividend ordinary rate,

(iii) is not liable to tax at the dividend upper rate,

(iv) is not liable to tax at the dividend additional rate, and

(v) is not charged to tax under section 832 of ITTOIA 2005 (relevant foreign income charged on remittance basis) on any dividend income.

In s. 8(1B) the words "the information filed in response to a notice to file" substituted for the words "a return under this section" and the word "partnership" inserted after the word "relevant" by F(No. 2)A 2017, s. 61 and Sch. 14, para. 3(6), with effect from a day to be appointed under F(No. 2)A 2017, s. 61(6).
In s. 8(1C) the word "partnership" inserted after the word "relevant" and after the words "means a" and the words ", or under regulations under paragraph 10 of Schedule A1," substituted for the words "of this Act" by F(No. 2)A 2017, s. 61 and Sch. 14, para. 3(7), with effect from a day to be appointed under F(No. 2)A 2017, s. 61(6).
S. 8(1D) substituted by F(No. 2)A 2017, s. 61 and Sch. 14, para. 3(8),with effect from a day to be appointed under F(No. 2)A 2017, s. 61(6).
In s. 8(1F) the words "the return" substituted for the words "a return" by F(No. 2)A 2017, s. 61 and Sch. 14, para. 3(9), with effect from a day to be appointed under F(No. 2)A 2017, s. 61(6).
In s. 8(1G) the words "the return" substituted for the words "a return" by F(No. 2)A 2017, s. 61 and Sch. 14, para. 3(10), with effect from a day to be appointed under F(No. 2)A 2017, s. 61(6).
S. 8(1HA) inserted by F(No. 2)A 2017, s. 61 and Sch. 14, para. 3(11), with effect from a day to be appointed under F(No. 2)A 2017, s. 61(6).
S. 8(2) substituted by F(No. 2)A 2017, s. 61 and Sch. 14, para. 3(12), with effect from a day to be appointed under F(No. 2)A 2017, s. 61(6).
S. 8(1D) substituted by F(No. 2)A 2017, s. 61 and Sch. 14, para. 3(8), with effect from a day to be appointed under F(No. 2)A 2017, s. 61(6).
In s. 8(3) the words "to file" substituted for the words "under this section" by F(No. 2)A 2017, s. 61 and Sch. 14, para. 3(13), with effect from a day to be appointed under F(No. 2)A 2017, s. 61(6).
In s. 8(4) the words "to file" substituted for the words "under this section" by F(No. 2)A 2017, s. 61 and Sch. 14, para. 3(13), with effect from a day to be appointed under F(No. 2)A 2017, s. 61(6).
S. 8(6) inserted by F(No. 2)A 2017, s. 61 and Sch. 14, para. 3(15), with effect from a day to be appointed under F(No. 2)A 2017, s. 61(6).
S. 8(7) inserted by F(No. 2)A 2017, s. 61 and Sch. 14, para. 3(15),with effect from a day to be appointed under F(No. 2)A 2017, s. 61(6).

History – In s. 8(1)(a), former words ", on or before the day mentioned in subsection (1A) below" which followed "to make and deliver to the officer" omitted by FA 2007, s. 88(2) and repealed by FA 2007, s. 114 and Sch. 27, Pt. 5(3), with effect in respect of a return for a year of assessment beginning on or after 6 April 2007.
S. 8(1) (together with s. 8(1A), (1B), (1C)) substituted for s. 8(1) by FA 1994, s. 178(1).
S. 8(1A) omitted by FA 2007, s. 88(3) and repealed by FA 2007, s. 114 and Sch. 27, Pt. 5(3), with effect in respect of a return for a year of assessment beginning on or after 6 April 2007.
S. 8(1A) amended by FA 1995, s. 104(1)–(3) and further amended by FA 1996, s. 121(1)–(3), s. 205 and Sch. 41, Pt. V(6) as respects the year 1996–97 and subsequent years of assessment.
S. 8(1A) (together with s. 8(1), (1B), (1C)) substituted for s. 8(1) by FA 1994, s. 178(1).
In s. 8(1AA)(b), the words " and any tax credits to which section 397(1) or 397A(1) of ITTOIA 2005 applies" (which appeared after the word "source") omitted by FA 2016, s. 5(11) and Sch. 1, para. 51(2), with effect for the tax year 2016–17 and subsequent tax years.
In s. 8(1AA)(b), "397A(1)" substituted for "397A(2)" by FA 2009, s. 40 and Sch. 19, para. 9 (a), with effect for:

- qualifying distributions arising on or after 22 April 2009;
- cash dividends paid over to a person under ITEPA 2003, Sch. 2, para. 68(4) on or after 22 April 2009;
- dividends treated under ITTOIA 2005, s. 407 as paid to a person on or after 22 April 2009; and
- manufactured overseas dividends that are representative of any of the above distributions (FA 2009, Sch. 19, para. 14(1)).

In s. 8(1AA)(b), the reference to ITTOIA 2005, s. 397A(2) inserted by FA 2008, s. 34 and Sch. 12, para. 8, with effect for 2008–09 and subsequent tax years.
In s. 8(1AA)(b) the reference to s. 397(1) ITTOIA 2005 substituted by ITTOIA 2005, s. 882(1) and Sch. 1, para. 359; effective for 2005–06 onwards (ITTOIA 2005, s. 883(1)).
S. 8(1AA) inserted by FA 1996, s. 121(1)–(3), s. 205 and Sch. 41, Pt. V(6) as respects the year 1996–97 and subsequent years of assessment.
S. 8(1B) amended by FA 1995, s. 104(1)–(3) as respects the year 1996–97 and subsequent years of assessment.
S. 8(1B) (together with s. 8(1), (1A), (1C)) substituted for s. 8(1) by FA 1994, s. 178(1).
S. 8(1C) (together with s. 8(1), (1A), (1B)) substituted for s. 8(1) by FA 1994, s. 178(1).
S. 8(1D)–(1H) inserted by FA 2007, s. 88(4), with effect in respect of a return for a year of assessment beginning on or after 6 April 2007.
S. 8(5) inserted by FA 1995, s. 104(1)–(3) by FA 1996, s. 121(1)–(3), s. 205 and Sch. 41, Pt. V(6) as respects the year 1996–97 and subsequent years of assessment.
S. 8 substituted by FA 1990, s. 90(1), (5), effective where a notice to deliver a return was, or fell to be, given after 5 April 1990.

8B Withdrawal by HMRC of notice under section 8 or 8A

Prospective amendments – In the heading the words "to file" inserted after the word "notice" by F(No. 2)A 2017, s. 61 and Sch. 14, para. 5, with effect from a day to be appointed under F(No. 2)A 2017, s. 61(6).

8B(1) This section applies to a person who is given a notice under section 8 or 8A.

8B(2) Before the end of the withdrawal period, HMRC may withdraw the notice (whether at the request of the person or otherwise).

8B(3) But the notice may not be withdrawn if–

(a) the person has made a return under section 8 or 8A in pursuance of the notice under that section, or

(b) the person has been served with notice of a determination under section 28C by virtue of the notice under section 8 or 8A having been given to the person.

8B(4) If HMRC decide to withdraw the notice under section 8 or 8A they must do so by giving the person a notice under this section.

8B(5) A notice under this section must specify the date on which the notice under section 8 or 8A is withdrawn.

8B(6) For the purposes of subsection (2) **"the withdrawal period"** means–

(a) the period of 2 years beginning with the end of the year of assessment to which the notice under section 8 or 8A relates, or

(b) in exceptional circumstances, such extended period as HMRC may determine.

8B(7) Withdrawal of a notice given to a person under section 8 or 8A in relation to a year of assessment does not prevent HMRC from giving the person a further notice under that section in relation to that year.

8B(8) See paragraph 17A of Schedule 55 to FA 2009 as to the cancellation of liability to a penalty under any paragraph of that Schedule by including provision in a notice under this section.

Prospective amendments – In s. 8B(1) the words "to file" inserted after the word ""notice"" by F(No. 2)A 2017, s. 61 and Sch. 14, para. 5, with effect from a day to be appointed under F(No. 2)A 2017, s. 61(6).

History – In s. 8B(2), the words "HMRC may withdraw the notice (whether at the request of the person or otherwise)" substituted for the words "the person may request HMRC to withdraw the notice" by FA 2016, s. 169(2), with effect in relation to any notice under TMA 1970, s. 8 or 8A given in relation to the 2014-15 tax year or any subsequent year (and it is immaterial whether the notice was given before or after 15 September 2016).

In s. 8B(3), the words "the notice may not be withdrawn" substituted for the words "no request may be made" by FA 2016, s. 169(3), with effect in relation to any notice under TMA 1970, s. 8 or 8A given in relation to the 2014-15 tax year or any subsequent year (and it is immaterial whether the notice was given before or after 15 September 2016).

In s. 8B(4), the words ", on receiving a request," (which appeared after the word "If") omitted by FA 2016, s. 169(4), with effect in relation to any notice under TMA 1970, s. 8 or 8A given in relation to the 2014-15 tax year or any subsequent year (and it is immaterial whether the notice was given before or after 15 September 2016).

In s. 8B(6)(b), the words "determine" substituted for the words "agree with the person" by FA 2016, s. 169(5), with effect in relation to any notice under TMA 1970, s. 8 or 8A given in relation to the 2014–15 tax year or any subsequent year (and it is immaterial whether the notice was given before or after 15 September 2016).

S. 8B inserted by FA 2013, s. 233 and Sch. 51, para. 3, with effect in relation to a return under TMA 1970, s. 12AA for a partnership which includes one or more companies, in respect of a return for a relevant period (a period in respect of which a return is required) beginning on or after 6 April 2012 and in relation to a return under that section for any other partnership, or a return under TMA 1970, s. 8 or 8A, in respect of a return for a year of assessment beginning on or after 6 April 2012.

9 Returns to include self-assessment

Prospective amendments – The heading "Self-assessment required by a notice to file" substituted for the heading by F(No. 2)A 2017, s. 61 and Sch. 14, para. 6(2), with effect from a day to be appointed under F(No. 2)A 2017, s. 61(6).

9(1) Subject to subsections (1A) and (2) below, every return under section 8 or 8A of this Act shall include a self-assessment, that is to say–

(a) an assessment of the amounts in which, on the basis of the information contained in the return and taking into account any relief or allowance a claim for which is included in the return, the person making the return is chargeable to income tax and capital gains tax for the year of assessment; and

(b) an assessment of the amount payable by him by way of income tax, that is to say, the difference between the amount in which he is assessed to income tax under paragraph (a) above and the aggregate amount of any income tax deducted at source

but nothing in this subsection shall enable a self-assessment to show as repayable any income tax treated as deducted or paid by virtue of section 246D(1) of the principal Act, section 626 of ITEPA 2003 or section 399(2) or 530(1) of ITTOIA 2005.

9(1A) The tax to be assessed on a person by a self-assessment shall not include any tax which–

(a) is chargeable on the scheme administrator of a registered pension scheme under Part 4 of the Finance Act 2004, or

(aa) is chargeable, on the scheme manager of a qualifying recognised overseas pension scheme or a former such scheme, under Part 4 of the Finance Act 2004,

(b) is chargeable on the person who is (or persons who are) the responsible person in relation to an employer-financed retirement benefits scheme under section 394(2) of ITEPA 2003.

9(2) A person shall not be required to comply with subsection (1) above if he makes and delivers his return for a year of assessment–

(a) on or before the 31st October next following the year, or

(b) where the notice under section 8 or 8A of this Act is given after the 31st August next following the year, within the period of two months beginning with the day on which the notice is given.

9(3) Where, in making and delivering a return, a person does not comply with subsection (1) above, an officer of the Board shall if subsection (2) above applies, and may in any other case–

(a) make the assessment on his behalf on the basis of the information contained in the return, and

(b) send him a copy of the assessment so made;

9(3A) An assessment under subsection (3) above is treated for the purposes of this Act as a self-assessment and as included in the return.

9(4) [Omitted by FA 2001, s. 88 and Sch. 29, para. 2.]

9(5) [Omitted by FA 2001, s. 88 and Sch. 29, para. 2.]

9(6) [Omitted by FA 2001, s. 88 and Sch. 29, para. 2.]

Prospective amendments – In s. 9(1) the words "Subject to subsection (1A), the self-assessment required by virtue of subsection (1AB)(a) of section 8 or 8A from a person given a notice to file for a year of assessment is–" substituted for the words "subject to subsections (1A) and (2) below, every return under section 8 or 8A of this Act shall include a self-assessment, that is to say–" by F(No. 2)A 2017, s. 61 and Sch. 14, para. 6(3), with effect from a day to be appointed under F(No. 2)A 2017, s. 61(6).

In s. 9(2) the words "by virtue of section 8 or 8A to make and file a self-assessment" substituted for the words "to comply with subsection (1) above" by F(No. 2)A 2017, s. 61 and Sch. 14, para. 6(4), with effect from a day to be appointed under F(No. 2)A 2017, s. 61(6).
In s. 9(3) the words "required by virtue of section 8 or 8A, a person does not include a self-assessment" substituted for the words ", a person does not comply with subsection (1) above" by F(No. 2)A 2017, s. 61 and Sch. 14, para. 6(5), with effect from a day to be appointed under F(No. 2)A 2017, s. 61(6).
In s. 9(3A) the words "under section 8 or 8A" inserted after the words "self-assessment" by F(No. 2)A 2017, s. 61 and Sch. 14, para. 6(6), with effect from a day to be appointed under F(No. 2)A 2017, s. 61(6).
History – In s. 9(1)(b), the words "and any tax credits to which section 397(1) or 397A(1) of ITTOIA 2005 applies" (which appeared after the word "source") omitted by FA 2016, s. 5(11) and Sch. 1, para. 51(4)(a), with effect for the tax year 2016–17 and subsequent tax years.
In s. 9(1)(b), "397A(1)" substituted for "397A(2)" by FA 2009, s. 40 and Sch. 19, para. 9(b), with effect for:

- qualifying distributions arising on or after 22 April 2009;
- cash dividends paid over to a person under ITEPA 2003, Sch. 2, para. 68(4) on or after 22 April 2009;
- dividends treated under ITTOIA 2005, s. 407 as paid to a person on or after 22 April 2009; and
- manufactured overseas dividends that are representative of any of the above distributions (FA 2009, Sch. 19, para. 14(1)(1)).

In s. 9(1)(b), the reference to ITTOIA 2005, s. 397A(2) inserted by FA 2008, s. 34 and Sch. 12, para. 10, with effect for 2008–09 and subsequent tax years.
In s. 9(1), ", 400(2), 414(1), 421(1)" (which appeared after "section 399(2)") omitted by FA 2016, s. 5(11)and Sch. 1 para. 51(4)(b), with effect for the tax year 2016–17 and subsequent tax years.
In s. 9(1), the words "or 547(5) of the principal Act or section 626 of ITEPA 2003" substituted by ITEPA 2003, Sch. 6, para. 125(2) which has effect for the tax year 2003–04 and subsequent tax years. The reference in para. (b) to ITTOIA 2005, s. 397(1) substituted by ITTOIA 2005, s. 882(1) and Sch. 1, para. 361(a); effective for 2005–06 onwards (ITTOIA 2005, s. 883(1)). References to ICTA 1988, s. 233(1), 249(4), 421(1) and 547(5) omitted by ITTOIA 2005, s. 882(1) and Sch. 1, para. 361(b) and repealed by ITTOIA 2005, s. 884, Sch. 3; effective for 2005–06 onwards (ITTOIA 2005, s. 883(1)). References to ITTOIA 2005, s. 399(2), 400(2), 414(1), 421(1) and 530(1) inserted by ITTOIA 2005, s. 882(1) and Sch. 1, para. 361; effective for 2005–06 onwards (ITTOIA 2005, s. 883(1)).
In s. 9(1A) the words after "any tax" substituted by FA 2004, s. 281 and Sch. 35, para. 1 with effect from 6 April 2006.
In s. 9(1A), the words "or under section 394(2) of ITEPA 2003" inserted by ITEPA 2003, Sch. 6, para. 125(3) which has effect for the tax year 2003–04 and subsequent tax years.
S. 9(1A) and reference to it in s. 9(1) inserted by FA 1998, s. 98(2) with effect for 1998–99 and subsequent years and with deemed effect for 1996–97 and 1997–98.
S. 9(1A)(aa) inserted by FA 2017, s. 10 and Sch. 4, para. 19, with effect in relation to transfers made on or after 9 March 2017.
In s. 9(2), the words "31st October" substituted for "30th September" and the words "31st August" substituted for "31st July" by FA 2007, s. 91(1), with effect in respect of a return for a year of assessment beginning on or after 6 April 2007.
In s. 9(3) the words "and references in this Act to a person's self-assessment include references to an assessment made on a person's behalf under this subsection" omitted by FA 2001, s. 88 and Sch. 29, para. 1, with effect from 11 May 2001 in relation to returns–
(a) whether made before or after 11 May 2001, and
(b) whether relating to periods before or after 11 May 2001.
S. 9(3A) inserted by FA 2001, s. 88 and Sch. 29, para. 1, with effect from 11 May 2001 in relation to returns–
(a) whether made before or after 11 May 2001, and
(b) whether relating to periods before or after 11 May 2001.
S. 9(4)–(6) omitted by FA 2001, s. 88 and Sch. 29, para. 2, with effect from 11 May 2001 in relation to returns–
(a) whether made before or after 11 May 2001, and
(b) whether relating to periods before or after 11 May 2001.
S. 9 substituted by FA 1994, s. 179 and amended by FA 1995, s. 104(4), 115(2), 162 and Sch. 29, Pt. VIII(14), and by FA 1996, s. 121(4), 122(1) as respects the year 1996–97 and subsequent years of assessment. S. 9 previously substituted by FA 1990, s. 90(1), (5), effective where a notice to deliver a return was, or falls to be, given after 5 April 1990.

9ZA Amendment of personal or trustee return by taxpayer

9ZA(1) A person may amend his return under section 8 or 8A of this Act by notice to an officer of the Board.

9ZA(2) An amendment may not be made more than twelve months after the filing date.

9ZA(3) In this section "the filing date", in respect of a return for a year of assessment (Year 1), means–

(a) 31st January of Year 2, or

(b) if the notice under section 8 or 8A is given after 31st October of Year 2, the last day of the period of three months beginning with the date of the notice.

History – S. 9ZA(3) substituted by FA 2007, s. 91(2), with effect in respect of a return for a year of assessment beginning on or after 6 April 2007.

9ZB Correction of personal or trustee return by Revenue

9ZB(1) An officer of the Board may amend a return under section 8 or 8A of this Act so as to correct–

(a) obvious errors or omissions in the return (whether errors of principle, arithmetical mistakes or otherwise), and

(b) anything else in the return that the officer has reason to believe is incorrect in the light of information available to the officer.

9ZB(2) A correction under this section is made by notice to the person whose return it is.

9ZB(3) No such correction may be made more than nine months after–

(a) the day on which the return was delivered, or

(b) if the correction is required in consequence of an amendment of the return under section 9ZA of this Act, the day on which that amendment was made.

9ZB(4) A correction under this section is of no effect if the person whose return it is gives notice rejecting the correction.

9ZB(5) Notice of rejection under subsection (4) above must be given–

(a) to the officer of the Board by whom the notice of correction was given,

(b) before the end of the period of 30 days beginning with the date of issue of the notice of correction.

History – S. 9ZB(1)(b) and the ", and" before it inserted (and s. 9ZB(1)(a) created from existing wording) by FA 2008, s. 119(1) with effect from 1 April 2010 (SI 2009/405).
S. 9ZB inserted by FA 2001, s. 88 and Sch. 29, para. 2 with effect from 11 May 2001 in relation to returns–
(a) whether made before or after 11 May 2001, and
(b) whether relating to periods before or after 11 May 2001.

9A Notice of enquiry

9A(1) An officer of the Board may enquire into a return under section 8 or 8A of this Act if he gives notice of his intention to do so (**"notice of enquiry"**)–

(a) to the person whose return it is (**"the taxpayer"**),

(b) within the time allowed.

9A(2) The time allowed is–

(a) if the return was delivered on or before the filing date, up to the end of the period of twelve months after the day on which the return was delivered;

(b) if the return was delivered after the filing date, up to and including the quarter day next following the first anniversary of the day on which the return was delivered;

(c) if the return is amended under section 9ZA of this Act, up to and including the quarter day next following the first anniversary of the day on which the amendment was made.

For this purpose the quarter days are 31st January, 30th April, 31st July and 31st October.

9A(3) A return which has been the subject of one notice of enquiry may not be the subject of another, except one given in consequence of an amendment (or another amendment) of the return under section 9ZA of this Act.

9A(4) An enquiry extends to–

(a) anything contained in the return, or required to be contained in the return, including any claim or election included in the return,

(b) consideration of whether to give the taxpayer a transfer pricing notice under section 168(1) of TIOPA 2010 (provision not at arm's length: medium-sized enterprise), but this is subject to the following limitation.

(c) consideration of whether to give the taxpayer a notice under section 81(2) of TIOPA 2010 (notice to counteract scheme or arrangement designed to increase double taxation relief).

9A(5) If the notice of enquiry is given as a result of an amendment of the return under section 9ZA of this Act–

(a) at a time when it is no longer possible to give notice of enquiry under subsection (2)(a) or (b) above,

(b) after a final closure notice has been issued in relation to an enquiry into the return, or

(c) after a partial closure notice has been issued in such an enquiry in relation to the matters to which the amendment relates or which are affected by the amendment,

the enquiry into the return is limited to matters to which the amendment relates or which are affected by the amendment.

9A(6) In this section **"the filing date"** means, in relation to a return, the last day for delivering it in accordance with section 8 or 8A.

History – In s. 9A(2)(a), the words "after the day on which the return was delivered" substituted by FA 2007, s. 96(1) and applicable to returns which relate to the tax year 2007–08 or a later tax year.
In s. 9A(4)(b), the words "section 168(1) of TIOPA 2010" substituted for the words "paragraph 5C of Schedule 28AA to the principal Act" by TIOPA 2010, s. 374 and Sch. 8, para. 107, with effect for corporation tax purposes for accounting periods ending on or after 1 April 2010, for income tax and capital gains tax purposes for the tax year 2010–11 and subsequent tax years, and for petroleum revenue tax purposes for chargeable periods beginning on or after 1 July 2010.
In s. 9A(4)(c), the words "section 81(2) of TIOPA 2010 (notice to counteract scheme or arrangement designed to increase double taxation relief)" substituted for the words "section 804ZA of the principal Act (schemes and arrangements designed to increase relief)" by TIOPA 2010, s. 374 and Sch. 8, para. 2, with effect for corporation tax purposes for accounting periods ending on or after 1 April 2010, for income tax and capital gains tax purposes for the tax year 2010–11 and subsequent tax years, and for petroleum revenue tax purposes for chargeable periods beginning on or after 1 July 2010.
S. 9A(4)(c) inserted by FA 2005, s. 88(1) with effect from 10 February 2005 (where credit for foreign tax is affected by a scheme to which ICTA 1988, Sch. 28AB, para. 5 applies) or 16 March 2005 (where that credit is affected by any other scheme or arrangement prescribed by ICTA 1988, Sch. 28AB.)
S. 9A(4) substituted by FA 2004 s. 30 and Sch. 5, para. 1, with effect in relation to chargeable periods beginning on or after 1 April 2004.
S. 9A(5)(b) and (c) substituted for former s. 9A(5)(b) (and the word "or" at the end of s. 9A(5)(a) omitted) by F(No. 2)A 2017, s. 63 and Sch. 15, para. 2, with effect in relation to an enquiry under TMA 1970, s. 9A, 12ZM or 12AC or FA 1998, Sch. 18 where the notice

of enquiry is given on or after 16 November 2017 (Royal Assent) or the enquiry is in progress immediately before that day. Former s. 9A(5)(b) read as follows:
"(b) after an enquiry into the return has been completed,"
In s. 9A(6), the words "means, in relation to a return, the last day for delivering it in accordance with section 8 or 8A" substituted for "means the day mentioned in section 8(1A) or, as the case may be, section 8A(1A) of this Act" by FA 2007, s. 91(3), with effect in respect of a return for a year of assessment beginning on or after 6 April 2007. See s. 8 or s. 8A History note as appropriate.
S. 9A substituted by FA 2001, s. 88 and Sch. 29, para. 4, with effect from 11 May 2001 in relation to return–
(a) whether made before or after 11 May 2001, and
(b) whether relating to periods before or after 11 May 2001.
Former s. 9A inserted by FA 1994, s. 180, with effect for the year 1996–97 and subsequent years of assessment.

9B Amendment of return by taxpayer during enquiry

9B(1) This section applies if a return is amended under section 9ZA of this Act (amendment of personal or trustee return by taxpayer), or in accordance with Chapter 2 of Part 4 of the Finance Act 2014 (amendment of return after follower notice), at a time when an enquiry into the return is in progress in relation to any matter to which the amendment relates or which is affected by the amendment.

9B(2) The amendment does not restrict the scope of the enquiry but may be taken into account (together with any matters arising) in the enquiry.

9B(3) So far as the amendment affects the amount stated in the self-assessment included in the return as the amount of tax payable, it does not take effect while the enquiry is in progress in relation to any matter to which the amendment relates or which is affected by the amendment and–

(a) if the officer states in a partial or final closure notice that he has taken the amendment into account and that–

(i) the amendment has been taken into account in formulating the amendments contained in the notice, or

(ii) his conclusion is that the amendment is incorrect,

the amendment shall not take effect;

(b) otherwise, the amendment takes effect when a partial closure notice is issued in relation to the matters to which the amendment relates or which are affected by the amendment or, if no such notice is issued, a final closure notice is issued.

9B(4) For the purposes of this section the period during which an enquiry is in progress in relation to any matter is the whole of the period–

(a) beginning with the day on which notice of enquiry is given, and

(b) ending with the day on which a partial closure notice is issued in relation to the matter or, if no such notice is issued, a final closure notice is issued.

History – In s. 9B(1) the words "into the return is in progress in relation to any matter to which the amendment relates or which is affected by the amendment" substituted for the words "is in progress into the return" by F(No. 2)A 2017, s. 63 and Sch. 15, para. 3(2), with effect in relation to an enquiry under TMA 1970, s. 9A, 12ZM or 12AC or FA 1998, Sch. 18 where the notice of enquiry is given on or after 16 November 2017 (Royal Assent) or the enquiry is in progress immediately before that day.
In s. 9B(1), the words ", or in accordance with Chapter 2 of Part 4 of the Finance Act 2014 (amendment of return after follower notice)," inserted by FA 2014, s. 233 and Sch. 33, para. 1, with effect from 17 July 2014.
In s. 9B(3) the words "in relation to any matter to which the amendment relates or which is affected by the amendment" inserted, in s. 9B(3)(a) the words "a partial or final closure notice" substituted for the words "the closure notice" and in s. 9A(3)b) the words "a partial closure notice is issued in relation to the matters to which the amendment relates or which are affected by the amendment or, if no such notice is issued, a final closure notice is issued" substituted for the words "the closure notice is issued" by F(No. 2)A 2017, s. 63 and Sch. 15, para. 3(3), with effect in relation to an enquiry under TMA 1970, s. 9A, 12ZM or 12AC or FA 1998, Sch. 18 where the notice of enquiry is given on or after 16 November 2017 (Royal Assent) or the enquiry is in progress immediately before that day.
In s. 9B(4) the words "in relation to any matter" inserted and the words "a partial closure notice is issued in relation to the matter or, if no such notice is issued, a final closure notice is issued" substituted for the words "the enquiry is completed" by F(No. 2)A 2017, s. 63 and Sch. 15, para. 3(4), with effect in relation to an enquiry under TMA 1970, s. 9A, 12ZM or 12AC or FA 1998, Sch. 18 where the notice of enquiry is given on or after 16 November 2017 (Royal Assent) or the enquiry is in progress immediately before that day.
S. 9B substituted with s. 9A, 9C and 9D for former s. 9A by FA 2001, s. 88, Sch. 29, para. 4, with effect from 11 May 2001 in relation to returns–
(a) whether made before or after 11 May 2001, and
(b) whether relating to periods before or after 11 May 2001.

9C Amendment of self-assessment during enquiry to prevent loss of tax

9C(1) This section applies where an enquiry into a return is in progress in relation to any matter as a result of notice of enquiry by an officer of the Board under section 9A(1) of this Act.

9C(2) If the officer forms the opinion–

(a) that the amount stated in the self-assessment contained in the return as the amount of tax payable is insufficient, and

(b) that unless the assessment is immediately amended there is likely to be a loss of tax to the Crown,

he may by notice to the taxpayer amend the assessment to make good the deficiency so far as it relates to the matter.

9C(3) In the case of an enquiry which under section 9A(5) of this Act is limited to matters arising from an amendment of the return, subsection (2) above only applies so far as the deficiency is attributable to the amendment.

9C(4) For the purposes of this section the period during which an enquiry is in progress in relation to any matter is the whole of the period–

(a) beginning with the day on which notice of enquiry is given, and

(b) ending with the day on which a partial closure notice is issued in relation to the matter or, if no such notice is issued, a final closure notice is issued.

History – In s. 9C(1) the words "into a return is in progress in relation to any matter" substituted for the words "is in progress into a return" by F(No. 2)A 2017, s. 63 and Sch. 15, para. 4(2), with effect in relation to an enquiry under TMA 1970, s. 9A, 12ZM or 12AC or FA 1998, Sch. 18 where the notice of enquiry is given on or after 16 November 2017 (Royal Assent) or the enquiry is in progress immediately before that day.

In s. 9C(2) the words "so far as it relates to the matter" inserted by F(No. 2)A 2017, s. 63 and Sch. 15, para. 4(3), with effect in relation to an enquiry under TMA 1970, s. 9A, 12ZM or 12AC or FA 1998, Sch. 18 where the notice of enquiry is given on or after 16 November 2017 (Royal Assent) or the enquiry is in progress immediately before that day.

In s. 9C(4) the words "in relation to any matter" inserted and the words "a partial closure notice is issued in relation to the matter or, if no such notice is issued, a final closure notice is issued" substituted for the words "the enquiry is completed" by F(No. 2)A 2017, s. 63 and Sch. 15, para. 4(4), with effect in relation to an enquiry under TMA 1970, s. 9A, 12ZM or 12AC or FA 1998, Sch. 18 where the notice of enquiry is given on or after 16 November 2017 (Royal Assent) or the enquiry is in progress immediately before that day.

S. 9C substituted with s. 9A, 9B and 9D for former s. 9A by FA 2001, s. 88, Sch. 29, para. 4, with effect from 11 May 2001 in relation to returns–

(a) whether made before or after 11 May 2001, and

(b) whether relating to periods before or after 11 May 2001.

RECORDS

12B Records to be kept for purposes of returns

12B(1) Any person who may be required by a notice under section 8, 8A or 12AA of this Act to make and deliver a return for a year of assessment or other period shall–

(a) keep all such records as may be requisite for the purpose of enabling him to make and deliver a correct and complete return for the year or period; and

(b) preserve those records until the end of the relevant day, that is to say, the day mentioned in subsection (2) below or, where a return is required by a notice given on or before that day, whichever of that day and the following is the latest, namely–

(i) where enquiries into the return are made by an officer of the Board, the day on which, by virtue of section 28A(1B) or 28B(1B) of this Act, those enquiries are completed; and

(ii) where no enquiries into the return are so made, the day on which such an officer no longer has power to make such enquiries.

12B(2) The day referred to in subsection (1) above is–

(a) in the case of a person carrying on a trade, profession or business alone or in partnership or a company, the fifth anniversary of the 31st January next following the year of assessment or (as the case may be) the sixth anniversary of the end of the period;

(b) otherwise, the first anniversary of the 31st January next following the year of assessment

or (in either case) such earlier day as may be specified in writing by the Commissioners for Her Majesty's Revenue and Customs (and different days may be specified for different cases).

12B(2A) Any person who–

(a) is required, by such a notice as is mentioned in subsection (1) above given at any time after the end of the day mentioned in subsection (2) above, to make and deliver a return for a year of assessment or other period; and

(b) has in his possession at that time any records which may be requisite for the purpose of enabling him to make and deliver a correct and complete return for the year or period,

shall preserve those records until the end of the relevant day, that is to say, the day which, if the notice had been given on or before the day mentioned in subsection (2) above, would have been the relevant day for the purposes of subsection (1) above.

12B(3) In the case of a person carrying on a trade, profession or business alone or in partnership–

(a) the records required to be kept and preserved under subsection (1) or (2A) above shall include records of the following, namely–

(i) all amounts received and expended in the course of the trade, profession or business and the matters in respect of which the receipts and expenditure take place, and

(ii) in the case of a trade involving dealing in goods, all sales and purchases of goods made in the course of the trade;

(b) [omitted by FA 2008, s. 115 and Sch. 37, para. 2(3).]

12B(3A) The Commissioners for Her Majesty's Revenue and Customs may by regulations–

(a) provide that the records required to be kept and preserved under this section include, or do not include, records specified in the regulations, and

(b) provide that those records include supporting documents so specified.

12B(4) The duty under subsection (1) or (2A) to preserve records may be discharged–

(a) by preserving them in any form and by any means, or

(b) by preserving the information contained in them in any form and by any means,

subject to subsection (4A) and any conditions or further exceptions specified in writing by the Commissioners for Her Majesty's Revenue and Customs.

12B(4A) Subsection (4)(b) does not apply in the case of the following kinds of records–

(a) any statement in writing such as is mentioned in–

(i) subsection (1) of section 1100 of CTA 2010 (amount of distribution, formerly amount of qualifying distribution and tax credit), or

(ii) section 495(1) or 975(2) or (4) of ITA 2007 (statements about deduction of income tax),

which is furnished by the company or person there mentioned, whether after the making of a request or otherwise;

(b) any record (however described) which is required by regulations under section 70(1)(c) of the Finance Act 2004 to be given to a sub-contractor (within the meaning of section 58 of that Act) on the making of a payment to which section 61 of that Act (deductions on account of tax) applies;

(c) any such record as may be requisite for making a correct and complete claim in respect of, or otherwise requisite for making a correct and complete return so far as relating to, an amount of tax–

(i) which has been paid under the laws of a territory outside the United Kingdom, or

(ii) which would have been payable under the law of a territory outside the United Kingdom ("territory F") but for a development relief.

12B(4B) In subsection (4A)(c) **"development relief"** means a relief–

(a) given under the law of territory F with a view to promoting industrial, commercial, scientific, educational or other development in a territory outside the United Kingdom, and

(b) about which provision is made in arrangements that have effect under section 2(1) of TIOPA 2010 (double taxation relief by agreement with territories outside the United Kingdom).

12B(5) Subject to subsections (5A) and (5B) below, any person who fails to comply with subsection (1) or (2A) above in relation to a year of assessment or accounting period shall be liable to a penalty not exceeding £3,000.

12B(5A) Subsection (5) above does not apply where the records which the person fails to keep or preserve are records which might have been requisite only for the purposes of claims, elections or notices which are not included in the return.

12B(5B) Subsection (5) above also does not apply where–

(a) the records which the person fails to keep or preserve are records falling within paragraph (a) of subsection (4A) above; and

(b) an officer of the Board is satisfied that any facts which he reasonably requires to be proved, and which would have been proved by the records, are proved by other documentary evidence furnished to him.

12B(5C) Regulations under this section may–

(a) make different provision for different cases, and

(b) make provision by reference to things specified in a notice published by the Commissioners for Her Majesty's Revenue and Customs in accordance with the regulations (and not withdrawn by a subsequent notice).

12B(6) For the purposes of this section–

(a) a person engaged in the letting of property shall be treated as carrying on a trade; and

(b) **"supporting documents"** includes accounts, books, deeds, contracts, vouchers and receipts.

Prospective amendments – S. 12B(1) and (1A) substituted for s. 12B(1) by F(No. 2)A 2017, s. 61 and Sch. 14, para. 14(2), with effect from a day to be appointed under F(No. 2)A 2017, s. 61(6).
In s. 12B(2) the words "relevant day is (subject to subsection (2ZB))" substituted for the words "day referred to in subsection (1) above is" by F(No. 2)A 2017, s. 61 and Sch. 14, para. 14(3), with effect from a day to be appointed under F(No. 2)A 2017, s. 61(6).
S. 12B(2ZA) and (2ZB) inserted by F(No. 2)A 2017, s. 61 and Sch. 14, para. 14(4), with effect from a day to be appointed under F(No. 2)A 2017, s. 61(6).
In s. 12B(2A)(a) the words "(1)(a) or (b)" substituted for the words "(1)" and in the end words to s. 12B(2A) the words "the relevant day, that is to say," omitted and "(1A)" substituted for "(1)" by F(No. 2)A 2017, s. 61 and Sch. 14, para. 14(5), with effect from a day to be appointed under F(No. 2)A 2017, s. 61(6).

In s. 12B(3)(a) "(1A)" substituted for "(1)" by F(No. 2)A 2017, s. 61 and Sch. 14, para. 14(6), with effect from a day to be appointed under F(No. 2)A 2017, s. 61(6).
In s. 12B(4) "(1A)" substituted for "(1)" and the words "and regulations under paragraph 11 of Schedule A1" inserted at the end by F(No. 2)A 2017, s. 61 and Sch. 14, para. 14(7), with effect from a day to be appointed under F(No. 2)A 2017, s. 61(6).
In s. 12B(5) "(1A)" substituted for "(1)" by F(No. 2)A 2017, s. 61 and Sch. 14, para. 14(8), with effect from a day to be appointed under F(No. 2)A 2017, s. 61(6).

History – In s. 12B(1), the words "(or under any of those sections as extended by section 12 of this Act)" omitted by SI 2009/2035, art. 2 and Schedule, para. 4, with effect from 13 August 2009.
In s. 12B(1)(b)(i) the words "28A(1B) or 28B(1B)" substituted for the words "28A(1) or 28B(1)" by F(No. 2)A 2017, s. 63 and Sch. 15, para. 9, with effect in relation to an enquiry under TMA 1970, s. 9A, 12ZM or 12AC or FA 1998, Sch. 18 where the notice of enquiry is given on or after 16 November 2017 (Royal Assent) or the enquiry is in progress immediately before that day.
In s. 12B(1)(b)(i) the words "or any amendment of the return" and "treated as" omitted and "28A(1) or 28B(1)" substituted by FA 2001, s. 88 and Sch. 29, para. 20 with effect from 11 May 2001.
In s. 12B(1)(b)(ii) the words "or any amendment of the return" omitted by FA 2001, s. 88 and Sch. 29, para. 20 with effect from 11 May 2001.
In s. 12B(1) reference to s. 11 omitted by FA 1998, s. 117(3), Sch. 19, para. 6, s. 165 and Sch. 27, Pt. III(28), with effect in relation to accounting periods ending on or after 1 July 1999, the self-assessment appointed day by virtue of FA 1994, s. 199(2) and SI 1998/3173 (C. 78).
In s. 12B(2) the word "otherwise" substituted for the words "in any other case" and the words "or (in either case) such earlier day as may be specified in writing by the Commissioners for Her Majesty's Revenue and Customs (and different days may be specified for different cases)." inserted by FA 2008, s. 115 and Sch. 37, para. 2(2) with effect from 1 April 2009 (SI 2009/402, art. 2).
S. 12B(3)(b), and the word "and" before it omitted by FA 2008, s. 115 and Sch. 37, para. 2(3) with effect from 1 April 2009 (SI 2009/402, art. 2).
S. 12B(3A) inserted by FA 2008, s. 115 and Sch. 37, para. 2(4) with effect from 1 April 2009 (SI 2009/402, art. 2).
S. 12B(4) substituted by FA 2008, s. 115 and Sch. 37, para. 2(5) with effect from 1 April 2009 (SI 2009/402, art. 2).
In s. 12B(4) the word "tribunal" substituted for the word "Commissioners" by SI 2009/56, art. 3(1) and Sch. 1, para. 7, operative from 1 April 2009, subject to transitional and saving provisions in SI 2009/56, Sch. 3.
In s. 12B(4A) the words "Subsection (4)(b) does not apply in the case of the following kinds of records" substituted for the words "The records that fall within this subsection are" by FA 2008, s. 115 and Sch. 37, para. 2(6) with effect from 1 April 2009 (SI 2009/402, art. 2).
In s. 12B(4A)(a)(i), the words "of distribution,formerly amount" inserted by FA 2016, s. 5(11) and Sch. 1, para. 51(7), with effect in relation to dividends paid or arising (or treated as paid), and other distributions made (or treated as made), in the tax year 2016–17 or at any later time.
In s. 12B(4A)(a)(i), the words "section 1100 of CTA 2010" substituted for the words "section 234 of the principal Act" by CTA 2010, s. 1177 and Sch. 1, para. 154, with effect for corporation tax purposes for accounting periods ending on or after 1 April 2010, and for income tax and capital gains tax purposes for the tax year 2010–11 and subsequent tax years.
S. 12B(4A)(a)(ii) substituted by ITA 2007, s. 1027 and Sch. 1, para. 246, with effect from 6 April 2007.
S. 12B(4A)(b) substituted by FA 2004, s. 76 and Sch. 12, para. 1, from 6 April 2007 (FA 2004, s. 77).
In s. 12B(4A)(c)(ii) substituted by TIOPA 2010, s. 374 and Sch. 8, para. 3(2), with effect for corporation tax purposes for accounting periods ending on or after 1 April 2010, for income tax and capital gains tax purposes for the tax year 2010–11 and subsequent tax years, and for petroleum revenue tax purposes for chargeable periods beginning on or after 1 July 2010.
S. 12B(4B) inserted by TIOPA 2010, s. 374 and Sch. 8, para. 3(3), with effect for corporation tax purposes for accounting periods ending on or after 1 April 2010, for income tax and capital gains tax purposes for the tax year 2010–11 and subsequent tax years, and for petroleum revenue tax purposes for chargeable periods beginning on or after 1 July 2010.
S. 12B(5C) inserted by FA 2008, s. 115 and Sch. 37, para. 2(7), with effect from 1 April 2009 (SI 2009/402, art. 2).
S. 12B inserted by FA 1994, s. 196 and Sch. 19, para. 3 and amended by FA 1995, s. 105, 162 and Sch. 29, Pt. VIII(14), and by FA 1996, s. 124(2)–(5), in so far as it relates to income tax or capital gains tax, as respects the year 1996–97 and subsequent years of assessment.

DIGITAL REPORTING AND RECORD-KEEPING

12C Digital reporting and record-keeping

12C [Prospectively inserted by F(No. 2)A 2017, s. 60(2).]

Prospective amendments – S. 12C inserted by F(No. 2)A 2017, s. 60(2), with effect from a day to be appointed under F(No. 2)A 2017, s. 60(4).

PART IV – ASSESSMENT AND CLAIMS

Cross references – SSCBA 1992, s. 11A: Pt. IV applies, with the necessary modifications, in relation to Class 2 contributions under s. 11(2) as if those contributions were income tax chargeable under ITTOIA 2005, Pt. 2, Ch. 2 in respect of profits of a trade, profession or vocation which is not carried on wholly outside the UK, with effect for the tax year 2015–16 and subsequent tax years.

28A Completion of enquiry into personal or trustee return or NRCGT return

History – In the heading, the words "or NRCGT return" inserted by FA 2015, s. 37 and Sch. 7, para. 44(2), with effect in relation to disposals made on or after 6 April 2015.

28A(1) This section applies in relation to an enquiry under section 9A(1) or 12ZM of this Act.

28A(1A) Any matter to which the enquiry relates is completed when an officer of Revenue and Customs informs the taxpayer by notice (a "partial closure notice") that the officer has completed his enquiries into that matter.

28A(1B) The enquiry is completed when an officer of Revenue and Customs informs the taxpayer by notice (a "final closure notice") –

(a) in a case where no partial closure notice has been given, that the officer has completed his enquiries, or

(b) a case where one or more partial closure notices have been given, that the officer has completed his remaining enquiries.

28A(2) A partial or final closure notice must state the officer's conclusions and–

(a) state that in the officer's opinion no amendment of the return is required, or

(b) make the amendments of the return required to give effect to his conclusions.

28A(3) A partial or final closure notice takes effect when it is issued.

28A(4) The taxpayer may apply to the tribunal for a direction requiring an officer of the Board to issue a partial or final closure notice within a specified period.

28A(5) Any such application is to be subject to the relevant provisions of Part 5 of this Act (see, in particular, section 48(2)(b)).

28A(6) The tribunal shall give the direction applied for unless satisfied that there are reasonable grounds for not issuing the partial or final closure notice within a specified period.

28A(7) In this section **"the taxpayer"** means the person to whom notice of enquiry was given.

28A(8) In the Taxes Acts, references to a closure notice under this section are to a partial or final closure notice under this section.

History – S. 28A(1), (1A) and (1B) substituted for former s. 28A(1) by F(No. 2)A 2017, s. 63 and Sch. 15, para. 12(2), with effect in relation to an enquiry under TMA 1970, s. 9A, 12ZM or 12AC or FA 1998, Sch. 18 where the notice of enquiry is given on or after 16 November 2017 (Royal Assent) or the enquiry is in progress immediately before that day. Former s. 28A(1) read as follows:

"**28A(1)** An enquiry under section 9A(1) or 12ZM of this Act is completed when an officer of the Board by notice (a **"closure notice"**) informs the taxpayer that he has completed his enquiries and states his conclusions.

In this section **"the taxpayer"** means the person to whom notice of enquiry was given."

In former s. 28A(1), the words "or 12ZM" inserted by FA 2015, s. 37 and Sch. 7, para. 44(3), with effect in relation to disposals made on or after 6 April 2015.

In s. 28A(2) the words "partial or final closure notice" substituted for the words "closure notice" and the words "state the officer's conclusions and" substituted for the word "either" by F(No. 2)A 2017, s. 63 and Sch. 15, para. 12(3), with effect in relation to an enquiry under TMA 1970, s. 9A, 12ZM or 12AC or FA 1998, Sch. 18 where the notice of enquiry is given on or after 16 November 2017 (Royal Assent) or the enquiry is in progress immediately before that day.

In s. 28A(4) the words "partial or final closure notice" substituted for the words "closure notice" by F(No. 2)A 2017, s. 63 and Sch. 15, para. 12(4), with effect in relation to an enquiry under TMA 1970, s. 9A, 12ZM or 12AC or FA 1998, Sch. 18 where the notice of enquiry is given on or after 16 November 2017 (Royal Assent) or the enquiry is in progress immediately before that day.

In s. 28A(4) the word "tribunal" substituted for the word "Commissioners" by SI 2009/56, art. 3(1) and Sch. 1, para. 17(2), operative from 1 April 2009, subject to transitional and saving provisions in SI 2009/56, Sch. 3.

S. 28A(5) substituted by SI 2009/56, art. 3(1) and Sch. 1, para. 17(3), operative from 1 April 2009, subject to transitional and saving provisions in SI 2009/56, Sch. 3.

In s. 28A(6) the words "the partial or final closure notice" substituted for the words "a closure notice" by F(No. 2)A 2017, s. 63 and Sch. 15, para. 12(5), with effect in relation to an enquiry under TMA 1970, s. 9A, 12ZM or 12AC or FA 1998, Sch. 18 where the notice of enquiry is given on or after 16 November 2017 (Royal Assent) or the enquiry is in progress immediately before that day.

In s. 28A(6) the word "tribunal" substituted for the words "Commissioners hearing the application" and the words "they are" omitted by SI 2009/56, art. 3(1) and Sch. 1, para. 17(2), operative from 1 April 2009,subject to transitional and saving provisions in SI 2009/56, Sch. 3.

S. 28A(7) inserted by F(No. 2)A 2017, s. 63 and Sch. 15, para. 12(6), with effect in relation to an enquiry under TMA 1970, s. 9A, 12ZM or 12AC or FA 1998, Sch. 18 where the notice of enquiry is given on or after 16 November 2017 (Royal Assent) or the enquiry is in progress immediately before that day.

S. 28A(8) inserted by F(No. 2)A 2017, s. 63 and Sch. 15, para. 12(6), with effect in relation to an enquiry under TMA 1970, s. 9A, 12ZM or 12AC or FA 1998, Sch. 18 where the notice of enquiry is given on or after 16 November 2017 (Royal Assent) or the enquiry is in progress immediately before that day.

s. 28A substituted by FA 2001, s. 88, Sch. 29, para. 8(1) with effect where the notice of enquiry is given after 11 May 2001, or where the enquiry is in progress immediately before that date (for these purposes, an "enquiry is in progress" until the officer's enquiries fall to be treated as completed under former s. 28A(5) prior to amendment).

28C Determination of tax where no return delivered

28C(1) This section applies where–

(a) a notice has been given to any person under section 8 or 8A of this Act (the relevant section), and

(b) the required return is not delivered on or before the filing date.

28C(1A) An officer of the Board may make a determination of the following amounts, to the best of his information and belief, namely–

(a) the amounts in which the person who should have made the return is chargeable to income tax and capital gains tax for the year of assessment; and

(b) the amount which is payable by him by way of income tax for that year;

and subsection (1AA) of section 8 or, as the case may be, section 8A of this Act applies for the purposes of this subsection as it applies for the purposes of subsection (1) of that section.

28C(2) Notice of any determination under this section shall be served on the person in respect of whom it is made and shall state the date on which it is issued.

28C(3) Until such time (if any) as it is superseded by a self-assessment made under section 9 of this Act (whether by the taxpayer or an officer of the Board) on the basis of information contained in a return under the relevant section, a determination under this section shall have effect for the purposes of Parts VA, VI, IX and XI of this Act as if it were such a self-assessment.

28C(4) Where–

(a) proceedings have been commenced for the recovery of any tax charged by a determination under this section; and

(b) before those proceedings are concluded, the determination is superseded by such a self-assessment as is mentioned in subsection (3) above,

those proceedings may be continued as if they were proceedings for the recovery of so much of the tax charged by the self-assessment as is due and payable and has not been paid.

28C(5) No determination under this section, and no self-assessment superseding such a determination, shall be made otherwise than–

(a) before the end of the period of 3 years beginning with the filing date; or

(b) in the case of such a self-assessment, before the end of the period of twelve months beginning with the date of the determination.

28C(6) In this section "the filing date" in respect of a return for a year of assessment (Year 1) means either–

(a) 31st January of Year 2, or

(b) if the notice under section 8 or 8A was given after 31st October of Year 2, the last day of the period of three months beginning with the day on which the notice is given.

Prospective amendments – In s. 28C(3) the words "section 8 or 8A" substituted for the words "section 9" by F(No. 2)A 2017, s. 61 and Sch. 14, para. 17, with effect from a day to be appointed under F(No. 2)A 2017, s. 61(6).

History – In s. 28C(4)(a) the words "proceedings have been commenced" substituted by FA 2001, s. 88, Sch. 29, para. 17(1) with effect in relation to proceedings begun after 11 May 2001.

In s. 28C(5)(a) "3 years" substituted for "five years" by FA 2008, s. 118 and Sch. 39, para. 2, with effect from 1 April 2010 (SI 2009/403, art. 2(2) subject to SI 2009/403, art. 3–10 – in particular art. 10).

S. 28C(6) substituted by FA 2007, s. 91(5), with effect in respect of a return for a year of assessment beginning on or after 6 April 2007. See s. 8 or s. 8A History note as appropriate.

S. 28C inserted by FA 1994 ss 190, 199 with effect for the tax year 1996–97 and subsequent tax years.

28H Simple assessments by HMRC: personal assessments

28H(1) HMRC may make a simple assessment for a year of assessment in respect of a person (other than a person to whom section 28I applies) if, when the assessment is made, the person is not excluded by subsection (2) in relation to that year.

28H(2) Subsection (1) does not apply to a person at any time in relation to that year of assessment if–

(a) the person has delivered a return under section 8 for that year, or

(b) the person is at that time subject to a requirement to make and deliver such a return by virtue of a notice under section 8.

but nothing in this subsection prevents HMRC from giving the person notice of a simple assessment at the same time as a notice withdrawing a notice under section 8.

28H(3) A simple assessment is–

(a) an assessment of the amounts in which the person is chargeable to income tax and capital gains tax for the year of assessment to which it relates, and

(b) an assessment of the amount payable by the person by way of income tax for that year, that is to say, the difference between the amount in which the person is assessed to income tax under paragraph (a) and the aggregate amount of any income tax deducted at source;

but nothing in this subsection enables an assessment to show as repayable any income tax which any provision of the Income Tax Acts provides is not repayable.

28H(4) The amounts in which a person is chargeable to income tax and capital gains are net amounts, taking into account any relief or allowance that is applicable.

28H(5) A simple assessment must be based on information relating to the person that is held by HMRC (whether or not supplied by the person to whom the assessment relates).

28H(6) The notice of a simple assessment required to be sent to the person by section 30A(3) must (among other things)–

(a) include particulars of the income and gains, and any relief or allowance, taken into account in the assessment, and

(b) state any amount payable by the person by virtue of section 59BA (with particulars of how it may be paid and the date by which it is payable).

28H(7) The tax to be assessed on a person by a simple assessment does not include any tax which–

(a) is chargeable on the scheme administrator of a registered pension scheme under Part 4 of Finance Act 2004,

(b) is chargeable on the sub-scheme administrator of a sub-scheme under Part 4 of the Finance Act 2004 as modified by the Registered Pension Schemes (Splitting of Schemes) Regulations 2006, or

(c) is chargeable on the person who is (or persons who are) the responsible person in relation to an employer-financed retirement benefits scheme under section 394(2) of ITEPA 2003.

28H(8) Nothing in this section prevents HMRC issuing more than one simple assessment to the same person in respect of the same year of assessment (whether or not any earlier simple assessment for that year is withdrawn).

28H(9) In this section references to a simple assessment are to an assessment under this section.

Prospective amendments – In s. 28H(2)(b) the word "imposed" substituted for the words "to make and deliver such a return" and the words "to file" inserted after the word "notice" by F(No. 2)A 2017, s. 61 and Sch. 14, para. 18, with effect from a day to be appointed under F(No. 2)A 2017, s. 61(6).

History – S. 28H inserted by FA 2016, s. 167(1) and Sch. 23, para. 3, with effect in relation to the 2016–17 tax year and subsequent years.

28I Simple assessments by HMRC: trustees

28I(1) HMRC may make a simple assessment for a year of assessment in respect of a settlement if, when the assessment is made, the relevant trustees of the settlement are not excluded by subsection (2) in relation to that year.

28I(2) Subsection (1) does not apply at any time in relation to that year of assessment if–

(a) a return under section 8A has been delivered for that year by the relevant trustees or any of them, or

(b) there is at that time a subsisting requirement to make and deliver such a return by virtue of a notice under section 8A;

but nothing in this subsection prevents HMRC from giving notice of a simple assessment at the same time as a notice withdrawing a notice under section 8A.

28I(3) A simple assessment is–

(a) an assessment of the amounts in which the relevant trustees are chargeable to income tax and capital gains tax for the year of assessment to which it relates, and

(b) an assessment of the amount payable by them by way of income tax for that year, that is to say, the difference between the amount in which they are assessed to income tax under paragraph (a) and the aggregate amount of any income tax deducted at source;

but nothing in this subsection enables an assessment to show as repayable any income tax which any provision of the Income Tax Acts provides is not repayable.

28I(4) The amounts in which the relevant trustees are chargeable to income tax and capital gains are net amounts, taking into account any relief or allowance that is applicable.

28I(5) A simple assessment must be based only on information relating to the settlement that is held by HMRC (whether or not supplied by the relevant trustees).

28I(6) The notice of a simple assessment required by section 30A(3) may be given to any one or more of the relevant trustees.

28I(7) That notice must (among other things)–

(a) include particulars of the income and gains, and any relief or allowance, taken into account in the assessment, and

(b) state any amount payable by the relevant trustees by virtue of section 59BA (with particulars of how it may be paid and the date by which it is payable).

28I(8) The tax to be assessed by a simple assessment does not include any tax which–

(a) is chargeable on the scheme administrator of a registered pension scheme under Part 4 of Finance Act 2004,

(b) is chargeable on the sub-scheme administrator of a sub-scheme under Part 4 of the Finance Act 2004 as modified by the Registered Pension Schemes (Splitting of Schemes) Regulations 2006, or

(c) is chargeable on the person who is (or persons who are) the responsible person in relation to an employer-financed retirement benefits scheme under section 394(2) of ITEPA 2003.

28I(9) Nothing in this section prevents HMRC issuing more than one simple assessment in respect of the same settlement and the same year of assessment (whether or not any earlier simple assessment for that year is withdrawn).

28I(10) In this section references to a **"simple assessment"** are to an assessment under this section.

28I(11) In this Act references to the person to whom a simple assessment relates are, in relation to one made under this section, to the relevant trustees of the settlement to which it relates.

Prospective amendments – In s. 28I(2)(b) the word "imposed" substituted for the words "to make and deliver such a return" and the words "to file" inserted after the word "notice" by F(No. 2)A 2017, s. 61 and Sch. 14, para. 19, with effect from a day to be appointed under F(No. 2)A 2017, s. 61(6).

28J Power to withdraw a simple assessment

28J(1) HMRC may withdraw a simple assessment by notice to the person to which it relates.

28J(2) An assessment that has been withdrawn ceases to have effect (and is to be taken as never having had any effect).

History – S. 28J inserted by FA 2016, s. 167(1) and Sch. 23, para. 3, with effect in relation to the 2016–17 tax year and subsequent years.

29 Assessment where loss of tax discovered

29(1) If an officer of the Board or the Board discover, as regards any person (the taxpayer) and a year of assessment–

(a) that any income which ought to have been assessed to income tax, or chargeable gains which ought to have been assessed to capital gains tax, have not been assessed, or

(b) that an assessment to tax is or has become insufficient, or

(c) that any relief which has been given is or has become excessive,

the officer or, as the case may be, the Board may, subject to subsections (2) and (3) below, make an assessment in the amount, or the further amount, which ought in his or their opinion to be charged in order to make good to the Crown the loss of tax.

29(2) Where–

(a) the taxpayer has made and delivered a return under section 8 or 8A of this Act in respect of the relevant year of assessment, and

(b) the situation mentioned in subsection (1) above is attributable to an error or mistake in the return as to the basis on which his liability ought to have been computed,

the taxpayer shall not be assessed under that subsection in respect of the year of assessment there mentioned if the return was in fact made on the basis or in accordance with the practice generally prevailing at the time when it was made.

29(3) Where the taxpayer has made and delivered a return under section 8 or 8A of this Act in respect of the relevant year of assessment, he shall not be assessed under subsection (1) above–

(a) in respect of the year of assessment mentioned in that subsection; and

(b) in the same capacity as that in which he made and delivered the return,

unless one of the two conditions mentioned below is fulfilled.

29(4) The first condition is that the situation mentioned in subsection (1) above was brought about carelessly or deliberately by the taxpayer or a person acting on his behalf.

29(5) The second condition is that at the time when an officer of the Board–

(a) ceased to be entitled to give notice of his intention to enquire into the taxpayer's return under section 8 or 8A of this Act in respect of the relevant year of assessment; or

(b) in a case where a notice of enquiry into the return was given–

(i) issued a partial closure notice as regards a matter to which the situation mentioned in subsection (1) above relates, or

(ii) if no such partial closure notice was issued, issued a final closure notice,

the officer could not have been reasonably expected, on the basis of the information made available to him before that time, to be aware of the situation mentioned in subsection (1) above.

29(6) For the purposes of subsection (5) above, information is made available to an officer of the Board if–

(a) it is contained in the taxpayer's return under section 8 or 8A of this Act in respect of the relevant year of assessment (the return), or in any accounts, statements or documents accompanying the return;

(b) it is contained in any claim made as regards the relevant year of assessment by the taxpayer acting in the same capacity as that in which he made the return, or in any accounts, statements or documents accompanying any such claim;

(c) it is contained in any documents, accounts or particulars which, for the purposes of any enquiries into the return or any such claim by an officer of the Board, are produced or furnished by the taxpayer to the officer; or

(d) it is information the existence of which, and the relevance of which as regards the situation mentioned in subsection (1) above–
   (i) could reasonably be expected to be inferred by an officer of the Board from information falling within paragraphs (a) to (c) above; or
   (ii) are notified in writing by the taxpayer to an officer of the Board.

29(7) In subsection (6) above–

(a) any reference to the taxpayer's return under section 8 or 8A of this Act in respect of the relevant year of assessment includes–
   (i) a reference to any return of his under that section for either of the two immediately preceding years of assessment;
   (ia) a reference to any NRCGT return made and delivered by the taxpayer which contains an advance self-assessment relating to the relevant year of assessment or either of the two immediately preceding chargeable periods; and
   (ii) where the return is under section 8 and the taxpayer carries on a trade, profession or business in partnership, a reference to any partnership return with respect to the partnership for the relevant year of assessment or either of those periods; and

(b) any reference in paragraphs (b) to (d) to the taxpayer includes a reference to a person acting on his behalf.

29(7A) The requirement to fulfil one of the two conditions mentioned above does not apply so far as regards any income or chargeable gains of the taxpayer in relation to which the taxpayer has been given, after any enquiries have been completed into the taxpayer's return, a notice under section 81(2) of TIOPA 2010 (notice to counteract scheme or arrangement designed to increase double taxation relief).

29(8) An objection to the making of an assessment under this section on the ground that neither of the two conditions mentioned above is fulfilled shall not be made otherwise than on an appeal against the assessment.

29(9) Any reference in this section to the relevant year of assessment is a reference to–

(a) in the case of the situation mentioned in paragraph (a) or (b) of subsection (1) above, the year of assessment mentioned in that subsection; and

(b) in the case of the situation mentioned in paragraph (c) of that subsection, the year of assessment in respect of which the claim was made.

29(10) [Repealed by FA 1998, s. 117(3) and Sch. 19, para. 12(6), s. 165 and Sch. 27, Pt. III(28).]

Prospective amendments – In s. 29(2) the words "(or, where the error or mistake is in an end of period statement forming part of the return, if that statement was provided on the basis of or in accordance with the practice generally prevailing at the time when it was provided)." inserted at the end by F(No. 2)A 2017, s. 61 and Sch. 14, para. 20(2), with effect from a day to be appointed under F(No. 2)A 2017, s. 61(6).

S. 29(6)(aa) inserted by F(No. 2)A 2017, s. 61 and Sch. 14, para. 20(3), with effect from a day to be appointed under F(No. 2)A 2017, s. 61(6).

History – In s. 29(1), words "income which ought … capital gains tax" substituted by FA 1998, s. 117(3) and Sch. 19 para. 12(2) with effect from 1 July 1999 (see note above).

In s. 29(2), (3), (5)(a), (6)(a) and (7)(a), words "section 8 or 8A" substituted by FA 1998, Sch. 19, para. 12(4) with effect from 1 July 1999 (see note above).

In s. 29(3)(b), words "in the case of a return under section 8 or 8A" repealed by FA 1998, s. 117(3), Sch. 19, para. 12(5), s. 165 and Sch. 27, Pt. III(28), with effect from 1 July 1999 (see note above).

In s. 29(4) the words "was brought about carelessly or deliberately by" substituted for the words "is attributable to fraudulent or negligent conduct on the part of" by FA 2008, s. 118 and Sch. 39, para. 3, with effect from 1 April 2010 (SI 2009/403, art. 2(2) subject to SI 2009/403, art. 3–10 – in particular art. 10).

S. 29(5)(b) substituted by F(No. 2)A 2017, s. 63 and Sch. 15, para. 14, with effect in relation to an enquiry under TMA 1970, s. 9A, 12ZM or 12AC or FA 1998, Sch. 18 where the notice of enquiry is given on or after 16 November 2017 (Royal Assent) or the enquiry is in progress immediately before that day. Former s. 29(5)(b) read as follows:

"(b) informed the taxpayer that he had completed his enquiries into that return,"

In s. 29(6)(c) the words omitted", whether in pursuance of a notice under section 19A of this Act or otherwise" by FA 2008, s. 113 and Sch. 36, para. 71, with effect from 1 April 2009 (SI 2009/404, art. 2, subject to savings at SI 2009/404, art. 3).

S. 29(7)(a)(ia) inserted (and the "and" after (i) omitted) by FA 2015, s. 37 and Sch. 7, para. 46, with effect in relation to disposals made on or after 6 April 2015.

In s. 29(7)(a)(ii), the words "any partnership return with respect to the partnership" substituted by FA 2001, s. 88, Sch. 29, para. 22 with effect from 11 May 2001 in relation to returns whether made before or after that date and whether relating to periods before or after then.

In s. 29(7A), the words "section 81(2) of TIOPA 2010 (notice to counteract scheme or arrangement designed to increase double taxation relief)" substituted for the words "section 804ZA of the principal Act" by TIOPA 2010, s. 374 and Sch. 8, para. 5, with effect for corporation tax purposes for accounting periods ending on or after 1 April 2010, for income tax and capital gains tax purposes for the tax year 2010–11 and subsequent tax years, and for petroleum revenue tax purposes for chargeable periods beginning on or after 1 July 2010.

S. 29(7A) inserted by FA 2005, s. 88(2) with effect from 10 February 2005 where credit for foreign tax is affected by a scheme to which ICTA 1988, Sch. 28AB, para. 5 applies or 16 March 2005 where that credit is affected by any other scheme or arrangement prescribed by ICTA 1988, Sch. 28AB (FA 2005, s. 87(3), (5)).

S. 29(10) repealed by FA 1998, s. 117(3) and Sch. 19, para. 12(6), s. 165 and Sch. 27, Pt. III(28), with effect from 1 July 1999 (see note above).

In s. 29, "year of assessment" substituted for "chargeable period", wherever it occured, by FA 1998, s. 117(3) and Sch. 19 para. 12(3) with effect from 1 July 1999 (see note above).

S. 29 substituted by FA 1994, s. 191(1), (2) with effect for income tax and capital gains tax from 1996–97 in respect of partnerships trading before 6 April 1994 and from 1997–98 in all other cases. (It was also to have had effect for corporation tax purposes for accounting periods ending on or after 1 July 1999, but was superseded by FA 1998, Sch. 18, para. 41. Consequential amendments were made to s. 29 with effect in relation to accountingperiods ending on or after 1 July 1999, the self-assessment appointed day by virtue of FA 1994, s. 199(2) and SI 1998/3173.)
S. 118(5)–(7): definition of carelessly and deliberately for purposes of s. 29(4).

30 Recovery of overpayment of tax, etc.

30(1) Where an amount of income tax or capital gains tax has been repaid to any person which ought not to have been repaid to him, that amount of tax may be assessed and recovered as if it were unpaid tax.

30(1A) Subsection (1) above shall not apply where the amount of tax which has been repaid is assessable under section 29 of this Act.

30(1B) Subsections (2) to (8) of section 29 of this Act shall apply in relation to an assessment under subsection (1) above as they apply in relation to an assessment under subsection (1) of that section; and subsection (4) of that section as so applied shall have effect as if the reference to the loss of tax were a reference to the repayment of the amount of tax which ought not to have been repaid.

30(2) In any case where–

(a) a repayment of tax has been increased in accordance with section 824 of the principal Act or section 283 of the 1992 Act (supplements added to repayments of tax, etc.) or section 102 of the Finance Act 2009 (repayment interest); and

(b) the whole or any part of that repayment has been paid to any person but ought not to have been paid to him; and

(c) that repayment ought not to have been increased either at all or to any extent;

then the amount of the repayment assessed under subsection (1) above may include an amount equal to the amount by which the repayment ought not to have been increased.

30(2A) [Repealed by FA 1998, s. 117(3) and Sch. 19, para. 13(4), s. 165 and Sch. 27, Pt. III(28), as respects accounting periods ending on or after 1 July 1999, the appointed day.]

30(3) In any case where–

(a) a payment, other than a repayment of tax to which subsection (2) above applies, is increased in accordance with section 824 or 825 of the principal Act or section 283 of the 1992 Act; and

(b) that payment ought not to have been increased either at all or to any extent;

then an amount equal to the amount by which the payment ought not to have been increased may be assessed and recovered as if it were unpaid income tax.

30(3A) [Repealed by FA 1998, s. 117(3) and Sch. 19, para. 13(6), s. 165 and Sch. 27, Pt. III(28) as respects accounting periods ending on or after 1 July 1999, the appointed day.]

30(4) [Omitted by ITTOIA 2005, s. 882(1) and Sch. 1, para. 369 and repealed by ITTOIA 2005, s. 884 and Sch. 3.]

30(4A) [Repealed by FA 1998, s. 117(3) and Sch. 19, para. 13(8), s. 165 and Sch. 27, Pt. III(28) as respects accounting periods ending on or after 1 July 1999, the appointed day.]

30(5) An assessment under this section shall not be out of time under section 34 of this Act if it is made before the end of whichever of the following ends the later, namely–

(a) the year of assessment following that in which the amount assessed was repaid or paid as the case may be, or

(b) where a return delivered by the person concerned is enquired into by an officer of the Board, the period ending with the day on which, by virtue of section 28A(1B) of this Act, the enquiry is completed.

30(6) Subsection (5) above is without prejudice to section 36 of this Act.

30(7) In this section any reference to an amount repaid or paid includes a reference to an amount allowed by way of set-off.

History – In s. 30(1), the words "income tax or capital gains tax" substituted for the word "tax" by FA 1998, s. 117(3) and Sch. 19, para. 13(2) with effect in relation to accounting periods ending on or after 1 July 1999, the self-assessment appointed day by virtue of FA 1994, s. 199(2) and SI 1998/3173 (C. 78).
The above amendment to s. 30(1), and the amendments by FA 1998 detailed in the notes below, effectively disapply s. 30 for the purposes of corporation tax for accounting periods ending on and after 1 July 1999, the appointed day. FA 1998, Sch. 18, which has effect in relation to accounting periods ending on or after 1 July 1999 and is construed and has effect as if it were contained in TMA 1970, contains equivalent provisions for corporation tax under self-assessment (FA 1998, s. 117(2)).
S. 30(1A) inserted by FA 1990, s. 105 in relation to amounts of tax repaid on or after 26 July 1990.
S. 30(1B) inserted by FA 1994, s. 196 and Sch. 19, para. 4, for income tax and capital gains tax, as respects the year 1996–97 and subsequent years of assessment, and originally also for corporation tax as respects accounting periods ending on or after 1 July 1999 (the appointed day: see above), but for corporation tax self-assessment see now FA 1998, Sch. 18.
In s. 30(2)(a), the words "or section 102 of the Finance Act 2009 (repayment interest)" inserted by SI 2014/992, art. 4(a), with effect from 6 May 2014 in relation to payments which are due and payable in respect of the tax year 2014–15 and subsequent tax years.

In s. 30(2)(a), reference to ICTA 1988, s. 825 omitted by FA 1998, s. 117(3) and Sch. 19, para. 13(3), s. 165 and Sch. 27, Pt. III(28) as respects accounting periods ending on or after 1 July 1999, the corporation tax self-assessment appointed day (see above).
In s. 30(2)(a) and (3)(a), references to "section 283 of the 1992 Act", substituted by TCGA 1992, s. 290 and Sch. 10, para. 2(6).
In s. 30(3), the words "or corporation tax" omitted by FA 1998, s. 117(3) and Sch. 19, para. 13(5), s. 165 and Sch. 27, Pt. III(27), with effect in relation to accounting periods ending on or after 1 July 1999, the corporation tax self-assessment appointed day (see above).
S. 30(2A) and (3A) repealed by FA 1998, s. 117(3) and Sch. 19, para. 13(4), (6) and (8), with effect in relation to accounting periods ending on or after 1 July 1999, the self-assessment appointed day (see above).
S. 30(4) omitted by ITTOIA 2005, s. 882(1) and Sch. 1, para. 369 and repealed by ITTOIA 2005, s. 884 and Sch. 3; effective for 2005–06 onwards.
S. 30(4A) repealed by FA 1998, s. 117(3) and Sch. 19, para. 13(4), (6) and (8),with effect in relation to accounting periods ending on or after 1 July 1999, the self-assessment appointed day (see above).
S. 30(4) substituted by FA 1998, s. 117(3) and Sch. 19, para. 13(5), with effect in relation to accounting periods ending on or after 1 July 1999, the corporation tax self-assessment appointed day (see above).
In s. 30(5)(b) the words "28A(1B)" substituted for the words "28A(1)" by F(No. 2)A 2017, s. 63 and Sch. 15, para. 16, with effect in relation to an enquiry under TMA 1970, s. 9A, 12ZM or 12AC or FA 1998, Sch. 18 where the notice of enquiry is given on or after 16 November 2017 (Royal Assent) or the enquiry is in progress immediately before that day.
In s. 30(5)(b), the words ", or an amendment of such a return," (which appeared after the words "the person concerned") omitted, "28A(1)" substituted for "28A(5)" and "the enquiry is" substituted for "the officer's enquiries are treated as", by FA 2001, s. 88, Sch. 29, para. 23, and the words omitted repealed by s. 110, Sch. 33, Pt. II(13), all with effect from 11 May 2001 in relation to returns whether made before or after that date and whether relating to periods before or after then.
S. 30(6) amended by FA 1989, s. 149(3)(a) omitting reference to s. 37 and 39 consequent to the repeal (with saving) of those sections.
S. 30 substituted by FA 1982, s. 149(1) in relation to any amount repaid or paid from 6 April 1982.

30A Assessing procedure

30A(1) Except as otherwise provided, all assessments to tax which are not self-assessments shall be made by an officer of the Board.

30A(2) All income tax which falls to be charged by an assessment which is not a self-assessment may, notwithstanding that it was chargeable under more than one Part or Chapter of ITEPA 2003 or ITTOIA 2005, be included in one assessment.

30A(3) Notice of any such assessment shall be served on the person assessed and shall state the date on which it is issued and the time within which any appeal against the assessment may be made.

30A(4) After the notice of any such assessment has been served on the person assessed, the assessment shall not be altered except in accordance with the express provisions of the Taxes Acts.

30A(5) Assessments to tax which under any provision in the Taxes Acts are to be made by the Board shall be made in accordance with this section.

History – In s. 30A(2) the words "Part or Chapter of ITEPA 2003 or ITTOIA 2005" substituted for the former word "Schedule" by ITTOIA 2005, s. 882(1) and Sch. 1, para. 370; effective for 2005–06 onwards (ITTOIA 2005, s. 883(1)).
S. 30A inserted by FA 1994, s. 196 and Sch. 19, para. 5(1) in respect of the year 1997–98 and subsequent years of assessment for partnerships whose trades, professions or businesses were set up or commenced before 6 April 1994 (FA 1994, Sch. 19, para. 5(2)) and otherwise in respect of the year 1996–97 and subsequent years of assessment (FA 1994, s. 199(2) and SI 1998/3173).

31 Appeals: right of appeal

31(1) An appeal may be brought against–

(a) any amendment of a self-assessment under section 9C of this Act (amendment by Revenue during enquiry to prevent loss of tax),

(b) any conclusion stated or amendment made by a closure notice under section 28A or 28B of this Act (amendment by Revenue on completion of enquiry into return),

(c) any amendment of a partnership return under section 30B(1) of this Act (amendment by Revenue where loss of tax discovered), or

(d) any assessment to tax which is not a self-assessment.

31(2) If an appeal under subsection (1)(a) above against an amendment of a self-assessment is made while an enquiry is in progress in relation to any matter to which the amendment relates or which is affected by the amendment none of the steps mentioned in section 49A(2)(a) to (c) may be taken in relation to the appeal until a partial closure notice is issued in relation to the matter or, if no such notice is issued, a final closure notice is issue.

31(3) [Omitted by CTA 2009, s. 1322 and Sch. 1, para. 301 and repealed by CTA 2009, s. 1326 and Sch. 3, Pt. 1.]

31(3A) In the case of a simple assessment, the right to appeal under subsection (1)(d) does not apply unless and until the person concerned has–

(a) raised a query about the assessment under section 31AA, and

(b) been given a final response to that query.

31(4) This section has effect subject to any express provision in the Taxes Acts, including in particular any provision making one kind of assessment conclusive in an appeal against another kind of assessment.

History – In s. 31(2) the words "in relation to any matter to which the amendment relates or which is affected by the amendment" inserted and the words "a partial closure notice is issued in relation to the matter or, if no such notice is issued, a final closure notice is issued" substituted for the words "the enquiry is completed" by F(No. 2)A 2017, s. 63 and Sch. 15, para. 18, with effect in

relation to an enquiry under TMA 1970, s. 9A, 12ZM or 12AC or FA 1998, Sch. 18 where the notice of enquiry is given on or after 16 November 2017 (Royal Assent) or the enquiry is in progress immediately before that day.
In s. 31(2) the word "If" and the word "is" (after "self-assessment") inserted and the words "none of the steps mentioned in section 49A(2)(a)–(c) may be taken in relation to the appeal" substituted for the words "shall not be heard and determined" by SI 2009/56, art. 3(1) and Sch. 1, para. 19, operative from 1 April 2009, subject to transitional and saving provisions in SI 2009/56, Sch. 3.
S. 31(3) omitted by CTA 2009, s. 1322 and Sch. 1, para. 301 and repealed by CTA 2009, s. 1326 and Sch. 3, Pt. 1, with effect for corporation tax purposes for accounting periods ending on or after 1 April 2009, and for income tax and capital gains tax purposes for the tax year 2009–10 and subsequent tax years.
In s. 31(3) the reference to TMA 1970, s. 9D omitted by ITTOIA 2005, s. 882(1) and Sch. 1, para. 371; effective 2005–06 onwards (ITTOIA 2005, s. 883(1)).
S. 31(3A) inserted by FA 2016, s. 167(1) and Sch. 23, para. 4, with effect in relation to the 2016–17 tax year and subsequent years.
S. 31–31D substituted for former s. 31 by FA 2001, Sch. 29, para. 11(1) with effect in relation to–
(a) amendments of a self assessment under s. 9C (as inserted by FA 2001, Sch. 29, para. 4, with effect from 11 May 2001);
(b) closure notices issued under s. 28A(1) or 28B(1) (as substituted by FA 2001, Sch. 29, para. 8 and 9, with effect from 11 May 2001);
(c) amendments of partnership returns under s. 30B(1) where notice of the amendment is issued after 11 May 2001, and
(d) assessments to tax which are not self assessments where the notice of the assessment is issued after 11 May 2001.

31A Appeals: notice of appeal

31A(1) Notice of an appeal under section 31 of this Act must be given–
(a) in writing,
(b) within 30 days after the specified date,
(c) to the relevant officer of the Board.

31A(2) In relation to an appeal under section 31(1)(a) or (c) of this Act–
(a) the specified date is the date on which the notice of amendment was issued, and
(b) the relevant officer of the Board is the officer by whom the notice of amendment was given.

31A(3) In relation to an appeal under section 31(1)(b) of this Act–
(a) the specified date is the date on which the closure notice was issued, and
(b) the relevant officer of the Board is the officer by whom the closure notice was given.

31A(4) In relation to an appeal under section 31(1)(d) of this Act (other than an appeal against a simple assessment)–
(a) the specified date is the date on which the notice of assessment was issued, and
(b) the relevant officer of the Board is the officer by whom the notice of assessment was given.

31A(4A) In relation to an appeal under section 31(1)(d) against a simple assessment–
(a) the specified date is the date on which the person concerned is given notice under section 31AA of the final response to the query the person is required by section 31(3A) to make, and
(b) the relevant officer of the Board is the officer by whom the notice of assessment was given.

31A(5) The notice of appeal must specify the grounds of appeal.

31A(6) [Omitted by SI 2009/56, art. 3(1) and Sch. 1, para. 20.]

History – In s. 31A(4), the words "(other than an appeal against a simple assessment)" inserted by FA 2016, s. 167(1) and Sch. 23, para. 5(2), with effect in relation to the 2016–17 tax year and subsequent years.
S. 31A(4A) inserted by FA 2016, s. 166(1) and Sch. 23, para. 5(3), with effect in relation to the 2016–17 tax year and subsequent years.
S. 31A(6) omitted by SI 2009/56, art. 3(1) and Sch. 1, para. 20, operative from 1 April 2009, subject to transitional and saving provisions in SI 2009/56, Sch. 3.
S. 31–31D substituted for former s. 31 by FA 2001, Sch. 29, para. 11(1) with effect in relation to–
(a) amendments of a self assessment under s. 9C (as inserted by FA 2001, Sch. 29, para. 4);
(b) closure notices issued under s. 28A(1) or 28B(1) (as substituted by FA 2001, Sch. 29, para. 8 and 9);
(c) amendments of partnership returns under s. 30B(1) where notice of the amendment is issued after 11 May 2001; and
(d) assessments to tax which are not self assessments where the notice of the assessment is issued after that date.

31AA Taxpayer's right to query simple assessment

31AA(1) This section applies where a person has been given notice of a simple assessment.

31AA(2) The person may query the simple assessment by notifying HMRC of–
(a) a belief that the assessment is or may be incorrect, and
(b) the reasons for that belief.

31AA(3) The person may exercise the power to query the simple assessment at any time within–
(a) the period of 60 days after the date on which the notice of assessment was issued, or
(b) such longer period as HMRC may allow.

31AA(4) If the simple assessment is queried, HMRC must–
(a) consider the query and the matters raised by it, and
(b) give a final response to the query.

31AA(5) The person may at any time withdraw a query (which terminates HMRC's duties under subsection (4)).

31AA(6) If it appears to HMRC that–

(a) they need time to consider the matters raised by the query, or

(b) further information (whether from the person or anyone else) is required,

HMRC may postpone the simple assessment in whole or part (according to how much of it is being queried by the person).

31AA(7) If the simple assessment is postponed in whole or part, HMRC must notify the person in writing–

(a) whether the assessment is postponed in whole or part, and

(b) if it is postponed in part, of the amount that remains payable under the assessment.

31AA(8) While the simple assessment is postponed the person is under no obligation to pay–

(a) the payable amount specified in the notice of assessment (if the whole assessment is postponed), or

(b) the postponed part of the payable amount so specified (if the assessment is postponed in part).

31AA(9) After considering the query the final response must be to–

(a) confirm the simple assessment,

(b) give the person an amended simple assessment (which supersedes the original assessment), or

(c) withdraw the simple assessment (without replacing it).

31AA(10) HMRC must notify the person in writing of their final response.

31AA(11) This section does not apply to an amended simple assessment given as a final response to the query.

31AA(12) Nothing in this section affects–

(a) a person's right to request an explanation from HMRC of a simple assessment or the information on which it is based, or

(b) HMRC's power to give a person such explanation or information as they consider appropriate,

whether as part of the querying process under this section or otherwise.

31AA(13) In subsection (12) **"person"** means a person who has been given notice of a simple assessment[.]

History – S. 31AA inserted by FA 2016, s. 167(1) and Sch. 23, para. 6, with effect in relation to the 2016–17 tax year and subsequent years.

OVERPAID TAX, EXCESSIVE ASSESSMENTS ETC

History – In the heading, the words "Overpaid tax, excessive assessments etc" substituted for "Relief for excessive assessments" by FA 2009, s. 100 and Sch. 52, para. 4 with effect in relation to claims made on or after 1 April 2010.

32 Double assessment

32(1) If on a claim made to the Board it appears to their satisfaction that a person has been assessed to tax more than once for the same cause and for the same chargeable period, they shall direct the whole, or such part of any assessment as appears to be an overcharge, to be vacated, and thereupon the same shall be vacated accordingly.

32(2) An appeal may be brought against the refusal of a claim under this section.

32(3) Notice of appeal under subsection (2) must be given–

(a) in writing;

(b) within 30 days after the day on which notice of the refusal is given;

(c) to the officer of Revenue and Customs by whom that notice was given.

History – S. 32(1) amended by FA 1985, Sch. 27, Pt. X, with effect from 19 March 1985 to remove references to development land tax. S. 32(2) and (3) substituted for former s. 32(2) by SI 2009/56, art. 3(1) and Sch. 1, para. 22, operative from 1 April 2009, subject to transitional and saving provisions in SI 2009/56, Sch. 3.

33 Recovery of overpaid tax etc

33 Schedule 1AB contains provision for and in connection with claims for the recovery of overpaid income tax and capital gains tax.

History – S. 33 substituted for former s. 33 and 33A by FA 2009, s. 100 and Sch. 52, para. 1 with effect in relation to claims made on or after 1 April 2010.

At the time of its substitution by FA 2009, s. 100 and Sch. 52, para. 1, former s. 33 was to have been amended prospectively: in former s. 33(1) the words "not more than 4 years after the end of" were to have been substituted for the words "not later than five years after the 31st January next following" by FA 2008, s. 118 and Sch. 39, para. 5, with effect from 1 April 2010 (SI 2009/403, art. 2(2) subject to SI 2009/403, art. 3–10 – in particular art. 10).

TIME LIMITS

34 Ordinary time limit of 4 years

History – In the heading to s. 34, "4 years" substituted for "six years" by FA 2008, s. 118 and Sch. 39, para. 7(3), with effect from 1 April 2010 (SI 2009/403, art. 2(2) subject to SI 2009/403, art. 3–10 – in particular art. 10).

34(1) Subject to the following provisions of this Act, and to any other provisions of the Taxes Acts allowing a longer period in any particular class of case, an assessment to income tax or capital gains tax may be made at any time not more than 4 years after the end of the year of assessment to which it relates.

34(1A) In subsection (1) the reference to an assessment to capital gains tax includes a determination under section 29A (non-resident CGT disposals: determination of amount which should have been assessed).

34(2) An objection to the making of any assessment on the ground that the time limit for making it has expired shall only be made on an appeal against the assessment.

34(3) In this section **"assessment"** does not include a self-assessment.

History – In s. 34(1) the words "not more than 4 years after the end of" substituted for the words "not later than five years after the 31st January next following" by FA 2008, s. 118 and Sch. 39, para. 7(2), with effect from 1 April 2010 (SI 2009/403, art. 2(2) subject to SI 2009/403, art. 3–10 – in particular art. 10).

In s. 34(1), the words from "an assessment to tax may be made" to the end of the subsection substituted by FA 1998, s. 117(3) and Sch. 19, para. 17(1), with effect in relation to accounting periods ending on or after 1 July 1999, the corporation tax self-assessment appointed day by virtue of FA 1994, s. 199(2) and SI 1998/3173 (C. 78).

The equivalent provisions under corporation tax self-assessment are to be found in FA 1998, Sch. 18, which has effect in relation to accounting periods ending on or after 1 July 1999 and is construed and has effect as if it were contained in TMA 1970 (FA 1998, 117(2)).

S. 34(1) formerly amended by FA 1994, s. 196 and Sch. 19, para. 10, in so far as it relates to income tax and capital gains tax, as respects the year 1996–97 and subsequent years of assessment, and originally also for corporation tax accounting periods ending on or after 1 July 1999, the appointed day (see notes above).

S. 34(1) formerly amended by FA 1985, Sch. 27, Pt. X, with effect from 19 March 1985, removing a reference to development land tax.

S. 34(1A) inserted by FA 2015, s. 37 and Sch. 7, para. 48, with effect in relation to disposals made on or after 6 April 2015.

S. 34(3) inserted by FA 2016, s. 168(2), with effect from 15 September 2016 (Royal Assent).

34A Ordinary time limit for self-assessments

34A(1) Subject to subsections (2) and (3), a self assessment contained in a return under section 8 or 8A may be made and delivered at any time not more than 4 years after the end of the year of assessment to which it relates.

34A(2) Nothing in subsection (1) prevents–

(a) a person who has received a notice under section 8 or 8A within that period of 4 years from delivering a return including a self-assessment within the period of 3 months beginning with the date of the notice,

(b) a person in respect of whom a determination under section 28C has been made from making a self-assessment in accordance with that section within the period allowed by subsection (5)(a) or (b) of that section.

34A(3) Subsection (1) has effect subject to the following provisions of this Act and to any other provisions of the Taxes Acts allowing a longer period in any particular class of case.

34A(4) This section has effect in relation to self-assessments for a year of assessment earlier than 2012–13 as if–

(a) in subsection (1) for the words from "not more" to the end there were substituted "on or before 5 April 2017", and

(b) in subsection (2)(a) for the words "within that period of 4 years" there were substituted "on or before 5 April 2017."

History – S. 34A inserted by FA 2016, s. 168(3), with effect from 15 September 2016 (Royal Assent).

35 Time limit: income received after year for which they are assessable

35(1) Where income to which this section applies is received in a year of assessment subsequent to that for which it is assessable, an assessment to income tax as respects that income may be made at any time not more than 4 years after the end of the year of assessment in which it was received.

35(2) This section applies to–

(a) employment income,

(b) pension income, and

(c) *social security income.*

History – In s. 35 the words "not more than 4 years after the end of" substituted for the words "within six years after" by FA 2008, s. 118 and Sch. 39, para. 8, with effect from 1 April 2010 (SI 2009/403, art. 2(2) subject to SI 2009/403, art. 3–10 – in particular art. 10).

S. 35 substituted by FA 2004, s. 92 and Sch. 17, para. 3(1) in relation to income assessable for 2004–05 and subsequent years of assessment. The previous version of the section had been repealed by FA 1998, s. 165 and Sch. 27, Pt. III(9) with effect from 6 April 1998.

36 Loss of tax brought about carelessly or deliberately etc

History – The heading to s. 36 substituted by FA 2008, s. 118 and Sch. 39, para. 9(6), with effect from 1 April 2010 (SI 2009/403, art. 2(2) subject to SI 2009/403, art. 3–10 – in particular art. 10). The former heading read: "Fraudulent or negligent conduct".

36(1) An assessment on a person in a case involving a loss of income tax or capital gains tax brought about carelessly by the person may be made at any time not more than 6 years after the end of the year of assessment to which it relates (subject to subsection (1A) and any other provision of the Taxes Acts allowing a longer period).

36(1A) An assessment on a person in a case involving a loss of income tax or capital gains tax–

(a) brought about deliberately by the person,

(b) attributable to a failure by the person to comply with an obligation under section 7,

(c) attributable to arrangements in respect of which the person has failed to comply with an obligation under section 309, 310 or 313 of the Finance Act 2004 (obligation of parties to tax avoidance schemes to provide information to Her Majesty's Revenue and Customs), or

(d) attributable to arrangements which were expected to give rise to a tax advantage in respect of which the person was under an obligation to notify the Commissioners for Her Majesty's Revenue and Customs under section 253 of the Finance Act 2014 (duty to notify Commissioners of promoter reference number) but failed to do so.

may be made at any time not more than 20 years after the end of the year of assessment to which it relates (subject to any provision of the Taxes Acts allowing a longer period).

36(1B) In subsections (1) and (1A), references to a loss brought about by the person who is the subject of the assessment include a loss brought about by another person acting on behalf of that person.

36(2) Where the person mentioned in subsection (1) or (1A) ("the person in default") carried on a trade, profession or business with one or more other persons at any time in the period for which the assessment is made, an assessment in respect of the profits or gains of the trade, profession or business in a case mentioned in subsection (1A) or (1B) may be made not only on the person in default but also on his partner or any of his partners.

36(3) If the person on whom the assessment is made so requires, in determining the amount of the tax to be charged for any chargeable period in any assessment made in a case mentioned in subsection (1) or (1A) above, effect shall be given to any relief or allowance to which he would have been entitled for that chargeable period on a claim or application made within the time allowed by the Taxes Acts.

36(3A) In subsection (3) above, **"claim or application"** does not include an election under any of sections 47 to 49 of ITA 2007 (tax reductions for married couples and civil partners: elections to transfer relief).

36(4) Any act or omission such as is mentioned in section 98B below on the part of a grouping (as defined in that section) or member of a grouping shall be deemed for the purposes of subsections (1) and (1A) above to be the act or omission of each member of the grouping.

History – S. 36(1A)(d) inserted (and the "or" at the end of s. 36(1A)(b) omitted, and the ", or" at the end of s. 36(1A)(c) inserted), by FA 2104, s. 277(1), with effect from 17 July 2014. It is assumed that the full stop at the end of s. 36(1A)(d) is included due to a parliamentary drafting error.

S. 36(1), (1A) and (1B) substituted for former s. 36(1) by FA 2008, s. 118 and Sch. 39, para. 9(2), with effect from 1 April 2010 (SI 2009/403, art. 2(2) subject to SI 2009/403, art. 3–10 – in particular art. 10).

In former s. 36(1) the words "income tax or capital gains tax" substituted for "tax", and words from "not later than" to the end of the subsection substituted, by FA 1998, s. 117(3) and Sch. 19 para. 18(1), with effect in relation to accounting periods ending on or after 1 July 1999, the corporation tax self-assessment appointed day by virtue of FA 1994, s. 199(2) and SI 1998/3173 (C.78).

The equivalent provisions under corporation tax self-assessment are to be found in FA 1998, Sch. 18, which has effect in relation to accounting periods ending on or after 1 July 1999 and is construed and has effect as if it were contained in TMA 1970 (FA 1998, 117(2)).

S. 36(1) formerly amended and s. 36(2) substituted, by FA 1994, s. 196 and Sch. 19, para. 11, in so far as it relates to income tax and capital gains tax, as respects the year 1996–97 and subsequent years of assessment, and originally also for corporation tax accounting periods ending on or after the self-assessment appointed day (see notes above).

In s. 36(2), the words "in a case" substituted for "for the purpose" by FA 2009, s. 99 and Sch. 51, para. 41 with effect from 1 April 2010 (SI 2010/867).

In s. 36(2), the words "Where the person mentioned in subsection (1) or (1A) ("the person in default")" substituted for the words "Where the person in default" and the words "subsection (1A) or (1B)" substituted for the words "subsection (1) above" by FA 2008, s. 118 and Sch. 39, para. 9(3), with effect from 1 April 2010 (SI 2009/403, art. 2(2) subject to SI 2009/403, art. 3–10 – in particular art. 10).

In s. 36(3), the words "in a case" substituted for "for the purpose" by FA 2009, s. 99 and Sch. 51, para. 41 with effect from 1 April 2010 (SI 2010/867).

In s. 36(3), "or (1A)" inserted by FA 2008, s. 118 and Sch. 39, para. 9(4), with effect from 1 April 2010 (SI 2009/403, art. 2(2) subject to SI 2009/403, art. 3–10 – in particular art. 10).

In s. 36(3A), the words "section 257BA of the principal Act or", which appeared after "election under", omitted by FA 2009, s. 5 and Sch. 1, para. 6(a)(i) with effect for the tax year 2010–11 and subsequent tax years.

In s. 36(3A), the words "or any of sections 47 to 49 of ITA 2007" inserted by ITA 2007, s. 1027 and Sch. 1, para. 251(a) and the words "(tax reductions for married couples and civil partners: elections to transfer relief)" substituted for the words "(elections as to transfer of married couple's allowance)" by ITA 2007, s. 1027 and Sch. 1, para. 251(b), with effect from 6 April 2007.

In s. 36(3A) the words "or under Schedule 13B to that Act (elections as to transfer of children's tax credit)" inserted by FA 1999, s. 30(4)(a) with effect for the year 2001–02 and subsequent years of assessment but then repealed by TCA 2002 s. 60 and Sch. 6 with effect from 6 April 2003 (SI 2003/962).

S. 36(3A) inserted, in relation to tax for 1993–94 and subsequent years of assessment, by F(No. 2)A 1992, s. 20 and Sch. 5, para. 9(1), (2).
In s. 36(4) the words "subsections (1) and (1A)" substituted for the words "subsection (1)" by FA 2008, s. 118 and Sch. 39, para. 9(5) with effect from 1 April 2010 (SI 2009/403, art. 2(2) subject to SI 2009/403, art. 3–10 – in particular art. 10).
S. 36(4) inserted by FA 1990, s. 69 and Sch. 11, para. 4(1), 5, deemed to have effect from 1 July 1989.
S. 36 substituted by FA 1989, s. 149(1), (7), with effect from 27 July 1989 but not affecting the making of assessments for any year before 1983–84 or for accounting periods which ended before 1 April 1983.

CLAIMS

42 Procedure for making claims etc.

42(1) Where any provision of the Taxes Acts provides for relief to be given, or any other thing to be done, on the making of a claim, this section shall, unless otherwise provided, have effect in relation to the claim.

42(1A) Subject to subsection (3) below, a claim for a relief, an allowance or a repayment of tax shall be for an amount which is quantified at the time when the claim is made.

42(2) Subject to subsections (3) to (3ZC) below, where notice has been given under section 8, 8A or 12AA of this Act, a claim shall not at any time be made otherwise than by being included in a return under that section if it could, at that or any subsequent time, be made by being so included.

42(3) [Not relevant to National Insurance contributions.]

42(3ZA) [Not relevant to National Insurance contributions.]

42(3ZB) [Not relevant to National Insurance contributions.]

42(3ZC) Subsection (2) also does not apply in relation to any claim under section 210 of the Finance Act 2013 (claims for consequential relieving adjustments after counteraction of tax advantage under the general anti-abuse rule).

42(3A)–(3B) [Repealed by FA 1996, s. 128(1)(a), s. 205 and Sch. 41, Pt. V(6).]

42(4)–(4A) [Repealed by FA 1998, s. 117(3) and Sch. 19, para. 20(3), s. 165 and Sch. 27, Pt. III(28).]

42(5) The references in this section to a claim being included in a return include references to a claim being so included by virtue of an amendment of the return.

42(6) [Not relevant to National Insurance contributions.]

42(7) [Not relevant to National Insurance contributions.]

42(8) [Omitted by FA 2012, s. 222(1)(a).]

42(9) Where a claim has been made (whether by being included in a return under section 8, 8A or 12AA of this Act or otherwise) and the claimant subsequently discovers that an error or mistake has been made in the claim, the claimant may make a supplementary claim within the time allowed for making the original claim.

42(10) This section (except subsection (1A) above and subject to subsection (10A) below) shall apply in relation to any elections as it applies in relation to claims.

42(10A) [Not relevant to National Insurance contributions.]

42(11) Schedule 1A to this Act shall apply as respects any claim or election which–

(a) is made otherwise than by being included in a return under section 8, 8A, 12ZB or 12AA of this Act.

(b) [repealed by FA 1995, s. 107(10).]

42(11A) Schedule 1B to this Act shall have effect as respects certain claims for relief involving two or more years of assessment.

42(12) [Repealed by FA 1996, s. 136 and Sch. 22, para. 6, s. 205 and Sch. 41, Pt. V(12).]

42(13) In this section **"profits"**–

(a) in relation to income tax, means income, and

(b) in relation to capital gains tax, means chargeable gains.

Prospective amendments – In s. 42(2) the words ", or where a partnership is required to provide a return by regulations under paragraph 10 of Schedule A1," inserted after the words "of this Act" and the words "or those regulations" inserted after the words "that section" by F(No. 2)A 2017, s. 61 and Sch. 14, para. 22(2), with effect from a day to be appointed under F(No. 2)A 2017, s. 61(6).
In s. 42(9) the words "or a Schedule A1 partnership return" inserted after the words "of this Act" by F(No. 2)A 2017, s. 61 and Sch. 14, para. 22(3), with effect from a day to be appointed under F(No. 2)A 2017, s. 61(6).
In s. 42(11)(a) the words "or a Schedule A1 partnership return" inserted after the words "of this Act" by F(No. 2)A 2017, s. 61 and Sch. 14, para. 22(4), with effect from a day to be appointed under F(No. 2)A 2017, s. 61(6).

History – In s. 42(2), "(3ZC)" substituted for "(3ZB)" by FA 2013, s. 213(2), with effect in relation to any tax arrangements entered into on or after 17 July 2013 (subject to provisions of FA 2013, s. 215(2) and (3)).
In s. 42(2), "to (3ZB)" substituted for "and (3ZA)" by FA 2012, s. 51 and Sch. 15, para. 11(2), in relation to claims whenever made.
In s. 42(2), "(3ZA)" substituted for "(3A)" by FA 2010, s. 32 and Sch. 8, para. 4(2), in relation to claims whenever made.
In s. 42(2), (9) and (11) references to TMA 1970, s. 11 omitted by FA 1998, s. 117(3) and Sch. 19, para. 20(2), s. 165 and Sch. 27, Pt. III(28), with effect in relation to accounting periods ending on or after 1 July 1999, the self-assessment appointed day by virtue of FA 1994, s. 199(2) and SI 1998/3173 (C. 78).

In s. 42(3), the words "PAYE regulations" substituted by ITEPA 2003, Sch. 6, para. 128 which has effect for the tax year 2003–04 and subsequent tax years.
S. 42(3ZC) inserted by FA 2013, s. 213(3), with effect in relation to any tax arrangements entered into on or after 17 July 2013 (subject to provisions of FA 2013, s. 215(2) and (3)).
S. 42(4), (4A) repealed by FA 1998, s. 117(3) and Sch. 19, para. 20(3), s. 165 and Sch. 27, Pt. III(28), with effect in relation to accounting periods ending on or after 1 July 1999, the corporation tax self-assessment appointed day (see notes above).
In s. 42(5), words at the end "and the reference in subsection (4) above to a claim for payment includes a reference to a claim resulting in payment" repealed by FA 1998, s. 117(3) and Sch. 19, para. 20(3), with effect in relation to accounting periods ending on or after 1 July 1999, the corporation tax self-assessment appointed day (see notes above).
(The repeals of s. 42(4), (4A), and the repeal in s. 42(5), noted above had already been made by F(No. 2)A 1997, s. 34 and Sch. 4, para. 3(1), s. 52 and Sch. 8, Pt. II(9) with effect in relation to tax credits in respect of distributions made on or after 6 April 1999.)
S. 42(8) omitted by FA 2012, s. 222(1)(a), with effect for the tax year 2012–13 and subsequent tax years.
In s. 42(10), the words "and subject to subsection (10A) below" inserted after the word "above" by FA 2014, s. 11(10)(a), with effect for the tax year 2015–16 and subsequent tax years.
In s. 42(11), "12ZB" inserted by FA 2015, s. 37 and Sch. 7, para. 49, with effect in relation to disposals made on or after 6 April 2015.
S. 42 substituted by FA 1994, s. 196 and Sch. 19, para. 13, and amended by FA 1995, s. 97(2), 107, 162 and Sch. 29, Pt. VIII(14),and by FA 1996, s. 128(1)(a), (c), 130(2)–(4), s. 136 and Sch. 22, para. 6 and s. 205 and Sch. 41, Pt. V(6), (7), and (12), in so far as it relates to income tax and capital gains tax, as respects the year 1996–97 and subsequent years of assessment, and originally also for corporation tax, as respects accounting periods ending on or after 1 July 1999, the day appointed by SI 1998/3173 for the purposes of FA 1994, s. 199(2), (3) (corporation tax self-assessment provisions now to be found in FA 1998, Sch. 18, Pt. VII: see notes above).

43 Time limit for making claims

43(1) Subject to any provision of the Taxes Acts prescribing a longer or shorter period, no claim for relief in respect of income tax or capital gains tax may be made more than 4 years after the end of the year of assessment to which it relates.

43(2) A claim (including a supplementary claim) which could not have been allowed but for the making of an assessment to income tax or capital gains tax after the year of assessment to which the claim relates may be made at any time before the end of the year of assessment following that in which the assessment was made.

43(3) [Repealed by FA 1985, Sch. 27, Pt. X, with effect from 19 March 1985.]

History – In s. 43(1), the words "4 years after the end of" substituted for the words "five years after the 31st January next following" by FA 2008, s. 118 and Sch. 39, para. 12, with effect from 1 April 2010 (SI 2009/403, art. 2(2) subject to SI 2009/403, art. 3–10 – in particular art. 10).
S. 43(1) substituted by FA 1998, s. 117(3) and Sch. 19, para. 21, with effect in relation to accounting periods ending on or after 1 July 1999, the self-assessment appointed day by virtue of FA 1994, s. 199(2) and SI 1998/3173 (C. 78). Corporation tax self-assessment provisions formerly in s. 43(1) are superseded by FA 1998, Sch. 18, which has effect in relation to accounting periods ending on or after 1 July 1999 and is construed and has effect as if it were contained in TMA 1970 (FA 1998, s. 115(2)).
Former s. 43(1) amended and s. 43(3) repealed by FA 1985, Sch. 27, Pt. X, removing references to development land tax.

43A Further assessments: claims etc.

43A(1) This section applies where–

(a) by virtue of section 29 of this Act an assessment to income tax or capital gains tax is made on any person for a year of assessment, and

(b) the assessment is not made for the purpose of making good to the Crown any loss of tax brought about carelessly or deliberately by that person or by someone acting on behalf of that person.

43A(2) Without prejudice to section 43(2) above but subject to section 43B below, where this section applies–

(a) any relevant claim, election, application or notice which could have been made or given within the time allowed by the Taxes Acts may be made or given at any time within one year from the end of the year of assessment in which the assessment is made, and

(b) any relevant claim, election, application or notice previously made or given may at any such time be revoked or varied–

(i) in the same manner as it was made or given, and

(ii) by or with the consent of the same person or persons who made, gave or consented to it (or, in the case of any such person who has died, by or with the consent of his personal representatives),

except where by virtue of any enactment it is irrevocable.

43A(2A) [Not relevant to National Insurance contributions.]

43A(2B) For the purposes of this section and section 43B below, a claim under Schedule 1AB is relevant in relation to an assessment for a year of assessment if it relates to that year of assessment.

43A(3) For the purposes of this section and section 43B below, any other claim, election, application or notice is relevant in relation to an assessment for a year of assessment if–

(a) it relates to that year of assessment or is made or given by reference to an event occurring in that year of assessment, and

(b) it or, as the case may be, its revocation or variation has or could have the effect of reducing any of the liabilities mentioned in subsection (4) below.

43A(4) The liabilities referred to in subsection (3) above are–

(a) the increased liability to tax resulting from the assessment,

(b) any other liability to tax of the person concerned for–

(i) the year of assessment to which the assessment relates, or

(ii) any year of assessment which follows that year of assessment and ends not later than one year after the end of the year of assessment in which the assessment is made.

43A(5) Where a claim, election, application or notice is made, given, revoked or varied by virtue of subsection (2) above, all such adjustments shall be made, whether by way of discharge or repayment of tax or the making of assessments or otherwise, as are required to take account of the effect of the taking of that action on any person's liability to tax for any year of assessment.

43A(6) The provisions of this Act relating to appeals against decisions on claims shall apply with any necessary modifications to a decision on the revocation or variation of a claim by virtue of subsection (2) above.

History – S. 43A(1)(a) substituted by FA 1998, s. 117(3) and Sch. 19, para. 22(2), and FA 1999, s. 139 and Sch. 20, Pt. III(20), with effect in relation to accounting periods ending on or after 1 July 1999, the self-assessment appointed day by virtue of FA 1994, s. 199(2) and SI 1998/3173 (C. 78). The corporation tax element of the former text is re-enacted in FA 1998, Sch. 18 as respects accounting periods ending on or after 1 July 1999.

In s. 43A(1)(b) the words "brought about carelessly or deliberately by that person or by someone acting on behalf of that person." substituted for the words "attributable to his fraudulent or negligent conduct or the fraudulent or negligent conduct of a person acting on his behalf." by FA 2008, s. 118 and Sch. 39, para. 13, with effect from 1 April 2010 (SI 2009/403, art. 2(2) subject to SI 2009/403, art. 3–10 – in particular art. 10).

Former s. 43A(1) amended, by substituting reference to s. 29 for previous reference to s. 29(3), by FA 1994, s. 196 and Sch. 19, para. 15(1):

- in so far as it relates to partnerships whose trades, professions or businesses are set up and commenced before 6 April 1994, as respects the year 1997–98 and subsequent years of assessment (FA 1994, Sch. 19, para. 15(2)); and
- in so far as it relates to income tax and capital gains tax, other than in relation to partnerships whose trades were set up and commenced after 6 April 1994, as respects the year 1996–97 and subsequent years of assessment; and
- also originally as respects corporation tax accounting periods ending on or after the day appointed under FA 1994, s. 199(2), but see now FA 1998, Sch. 18.

References to "chargeable periods" replaced by the phrase "year of assessment" in subsections (2), (3), (4) and (5) by FA 1998, s. 117(3) and Sch. 19, para. 22(3), with effect in relation to accounting periods ending on or after 1 July 1999, the self-assessment appointed day (see above).

S. 43A(2B) inserted by FA 2009, s. 100 and Sch. 52, para. 5(2) with effect in relation to claims made on or after 1 April 2010.

In s. 43A(3), the words "any other claim" to be substituted for the words "a claim" by FA 2009, s. 100 and Sch. 52, para. 5(3) with effect in relation to claims made on or after 1 April 2010.

S. 43A inserted by FA 1989, s. 150 for assessments notice of which is issued after 27 July 1989.

43B Limits on application of section 43A

43B(1) If the effect of the exercise by any person of a power conferred by section 43A(2) above–

(a) to make or give a claim, election, application or notice, or

(b) to revoke or vary a claim, election, application or notice previously made or given,

would be to alter the liability to tax of another person, that power may not be exercised except with the consent in writing of that other person or, where he has died, his personal representatives.

43B(2) Where–

(a) a power conferred by subsection (2) of section 43A above is exercised in consequence of an assessment made on a person, and

(b) the exercise of the power increases the liability to tax of another person,

that section shall not apply by reason of any assessment made because of that increased liability.

43B(3) In any case where–

(a) one or more relevant claims, elections, applications or notices are made, given, revoked or varied by virtue of the application of section 43A above in the case of an assessment, and

(b) the total of the reductions in liability to tax which, apart from this subsection, would result from the action mentioned in paragraph (a) above would exceed the additional liability to tax resulting from the assessment,

the excess shall not be available to reduce any liability to tax.

43B(4) Where subsection (3) above has the effect of limiting either the reduction in a person's liability to tax for more than one period or the reduction in the liability to tax of more than one person, the limited amount shall be apportioned between the periods or persons concerned–

(a) *except where paragraph* (b) *below applies*, in such manner as may be specified by the inspector by notice in writing to the person or persons concerned, or

(b) where the person concerned gives (or the persons concerned jointly give) notice in writing to the inspector within the relevant period, in such manner as may be specified in the notice given by the person or persons concerned.

43B(5) For the purposes of paragraph (b) of subsection (4) above the relevant period is the period of 30 days beginning with the day on which notice under paragraph (a) of that subsection is given to the person concerned or, where more than one person is concerned, the latest date on which such notice is given to any of them.

History – S. 43B inserted by FA 1989, s. 150 for assessments notice of which is issued on or after 27 July 1989.

43C Consequential claims etc.

43C(1) Where–

(a) a return is amended under section 28A(2)(b), 28B(2)(b) or 28B(4), and

(b) the amendment is made for the purpose of making good to the Crown any loss of tax brought about carelessly or deliberately by the taxpayer or a person acting on his behalf,

sections 36(3) and 43(2) apply in relation to the amendment as they apply in relation to any assessment under section 29.

43C(2) Where–

(a) a return is amended under section 28A(2)(b), 28B(2)(b) or 28B(4), and

(b) the amendment is not made for the purpose mentioned in subsection (1)(b) above,

sections 43(2), 43A and 43B apply in relation to the amendment as they apply in relation to any assessment under section 29.

43C(3) References to an assessment in sections 36(3), 43(2), 43A and 43B, as they apply by virtue of subsection (1) or (2) above, shall accordingly be read as references to the amendment of the return.

43C(4) Where it is necessary to make any adjustment by way of an assessment on any person–

(a) in order to give effect to a consequential claim, or

(b) as a result of allowing a consequential claim,

the assessment is not out of time if it is made within one year of the final determination of the claim.

For this purpose a claim is not taken to be finally determined until it, or the amount to which it relates, can no longer be varied, on appeal or otherwise.

43C(5) In subsection (4) above **"consequential claim"** means any claim, supplementary claim, election, application or notice that may be made or given under section 36(3), 43(2), 43A or 43D(6) (as it applies by virtue of subsection (1) or (2) above or otherwise).

History – In s. 43C(1)(b), the words "brought about carelessly or deliberately by" substituted for the words "attributable to fraudulent or negligent conduct on the part of" by FA 2008, s. 118 and Sch. 39, para. 14, with effect from 1 April 2010 (SI 2009/403, art. 2(2) subject to SI 2009/403, art. 3–10 – in particular art. 10).

In s. 43C(5), ", 43A or 43D(6)" substituted for "or 43A" by TIOPA 2010, s. 374 and Sch. 8, para. 6, with effect for corporation tax purposes for accounting periods ending on or after 1 April 2010, for income tax and capital gains tax purposes for the tax year 2010–11 and subsequent tax years, and for petroleum revenue tax purposes for chargeable periods beginning on or after 1 July 2010.

S. 43C inserted by FA 2003, s. 207(1) with effect from 10 July 2003. Where the section applies to an amendment to a return, it only does so where that amendment is issued after 10 July 2003

43E Making of income tax claims by electronic communications etc

43E(1) The Commissioners for Her Majesty's Revenue and Customs may, by publishing them in a manner the Commissioners consider appropriate, give any claims directions that the Commissioners consider appropriate.

43E(2) In subsection (1) **"claims directions"** means general directions for the purposes of income tax relating to–

(a) the circumstances in which, and

(b) the conditions subject to which,

claims by individuals under the Tax Acts may be made by the use of an electronic communications service or otherwise without producing a claim in writing.

43E(3) Directions under subsection (1)–

(a) may not relate to the making of a claim by an individual in the individual's capacity as a trustee, partner or personal representative, but

(b) subject to that, may relate to claims made by an individual through another person acting on the individual's behalf.

43E(4) Directions under subsection (1) may not relate to–

(a) the making of a claim to which Schedule 1B to this Act applies, or

(b) the making of a claim under any provision of the Capital Allowances Act 2001.

43E(5) Directions under subsection (1)–

(a) cannot modify any requirement imposed by or under any enactment as to the period within which any claim is to be made or as to the contents of any claim, but

(b) may include provision as to how any requirement as to the contents of a claim is to be met when the claim is not produced in writing.

43E(6) Directions under subsection (1) may make different provision in relation to the making of claims of different descriptions.

43E(7) A direction under subsection (1) may revoke or vary any previous direction given under that subsection.

43E(8) In subsection (2) **"electronic communications service"** has the same meaning as in the Communications Act 2003 (see section 32 of that Act).

43E(9) In subsections (1) to (6), references to the making of a claim include references to any of the following–

(a) the making of an election,

(b) the giving of a notification or notice,

(c) the amendment of any return, claim, election, notification or notice, and

(d) the withdrawal of any claim, election, notification or notice,

and in those subsections **"claim"** is to be read accordingly.

43E(10) For the purposes of subsection (9)(c)–

(a) **"return"** includes any statement or declaration under the Income Tax Acts, and

(b) the definition of **"return"** given by section 118(1) of this Act does not apply.

History – S. 43E inserted by TIOPA 2010, s. 374 and Sch. 7, para. 86, with effect for corporation tax purposes for accounting periods ending on or after 1 April 2010, for income tax and capital gains tax purposes for the tax year 2010–11 and subsequent tax years, and for petroleum revenue tax purposes for chargeable periods beginning on or after 1 July 2010.

43F Effect of directions under section 43E

43F(1) If directions under section 43E(1) are in force in relation to the making of claims of any description to the Commissioners for Her Majesty's Revenue and Customs, claims of that description may be made to the Commissioners in accordance with the directions.

43F(2) If directions under section 43E(1) are in force in relation to the making of claims of any description to an officer of Revenue and Customs, claims of that description may be made to an officer in accordance with the directions.

43F(3) Subsections (1) and (2) apply despite any enactment or subordinate legislation which requires claims of the description concerned to be made in writing or by notice.

43F(4) If directions under section 43E(1) are in force in relation to the making of claims of any description, claims of that description that are made without producing the claim in writing must be made in accordance with the directions.

43F(5) In subsection (3) **"subordinate legislation"** has the same meaning as in the Interpretation Act 1978.

43F(6) Section 43E(9) read with section 43E(10) (interpretation of references to making a claim, and meaning of **"claim"**) applies for the purposes of subsections (1) to (4) (as well as for those of section 43E(1) to (6)).

History – S. 43F inserted by TIOPA 2010, s. 374 and Sch. 7, para. 86, with effect for corporation tax purposes for accounting periods ending on or after 1 April 2010, for income tax and capital gains tax purposes for the tax year 2010–11 and subsequent tax years, and for petroleum revenue tax purposes for chargeable periods beginning on or after 1 July 2010.

PART V – APPEALS AND OTHER PROCEEDINGS

Cross references – SSCBA 1992, Sch. 2, para. 8: the provisions of Pt. V apply with the necessary modifications in relation to Class 4 contributions as they apply in relation to income tax.
SSCBA 1992, s. 11A: Pt. V applies, with the necessary modifications, in relation to Class 2 contributions under s. 11(2) as if those contributions were income tax chargeable under ITTOIA 2005, Pt. 2, Ch. 2 in respect of profits of a trade, profession or vocation which is not carried on wholly outside the UK, with effect for the tax year 2015–16 and subsequent tax years.

APPEALS

History – The above heading substituted by SI 2009/56, art. 3(1) and Sch. 1, para. 26, operative from 1 April 2009, subject to transitional and saving provisions in SI 2009/56, Sch. 3. Former heading was "PROCEEDINGS BEFORE COMMISSIONERS".

47C Meaning of tribunal

47C In this Act **"tribunal"** means the First-tier Tribunal or, where determined by or under Tribunal Procedure Rules, the Upper Tribunal.

History – S. 47C inserted by SI 2009/56, art. 3(1) and Sch. 1, para. 27, operative from 1 April 2009, subject to transitional and saving provisions in SI 2009/56, Sch. 3.

48 Application to appeals and other proceedings

48(1) In the following provisions of this Part of this Act, unless the context otherwise requires–

(a) **"appeal"** means any appeal under the Taxes Acts;

(b) a reference to notice of appeal given, or to be given, to HMRC is a reference to notice of appeal given, or to be given, under any provision of the Taxes Acts.

48(2) In the case of–

(a) an appeal other than an appeal against an assessment, the following provisions of this Part of this Act shall, in their application to the appeal, have effect subject to any necessary modifications, including the omission of sections 54A to 54C and 56 below;

(b) any proceedings other than an appeal which, under the Taxes Acts, are to be subject to the relevant provisions of this Part of this Act, the relevant provisions–

(i) shall apply to the proceedings as they apply to appeals;

(ii) but shall, in that application, have effect subject to any necessary modifications, including (except in the case of applications under section 55 below) the omission of section 56 below.

48(3) In subsection (2), a reference to the relevant provisions of this Part of this Act is a reference to the following provisions of this Part, except sections 49A to 49I and 54A to 54C.

History – In s. 48(2)(a), the words "sections 54A to 54C and 56" substituted for the words "section 56" by TIOPA 2010, s. 371 and Sch. 7, para. 31(2), with effect for corporation tax purposes for accounting periods ending on or after 1 April 2010, for income tax and capital gains tax purposes for the tax year 2010–11 and subsequent tax years, and for petroleum revenue tax purposes for chargeable periods beginning on or after 1 July 2010.

In s. 48(3), the words "and 54A to 54C" inserted by TIOPA 2010, s. 371 and Sch. 7, para. 31(3), with effect for corporation tax purposes for accounting periods ending on or after 1 April 2010, for income tax and capital gains tax purposes for the tax year 2010–11 and subsequent tax years, and for petroleum revenue tax purposes for chargeable periods beginning on or after 1 July 2010.

S. 48 substituted by SI 2009/56, art. 3(1) and Sch. 1, para. 28, operative from 1 April 2009, subject to transitional and saving provisions in SI 2009/56, Sch. 3.

Former s. 48(2) amended by F(No. 2)A 1975, s. 45(4).

Cross references – Social Security Contributions (Transfer of Functions, etc.) Act 1999, s. 13(2)(a)(ii): power of the Board, with the concurrence of the Lord Chancellor and the Lord Advocate, to make regulations making provision with respect to appeals on contributions matters, including any of the matters dealt with in s. 48.

49 Late notice of appeal

49(1) This section applies in a case where–

(a) notice of appeal may be given to HMRC, but

(b) no notice is given before the relevant time limit.

49(2) Notice may be given after the relevant time limit if–

(a) HMRC agree, or

(b) where HMRC do not agree, the tribunal gives permission.

49(3) If the following conditions are met, HMRC shall agree to notice being given after the relevant time limit.

49(4) Condition A is that the appellant has made a request in writing to HMRC to agree to the notice being given.

49(5) Condition B is that HMRC are satisfied that there was reasonable excuse for not giving the notice before the relevant time limit.

49(6) Condition C is that HMRC are satisfied that request under subsection (4) was made without unreasonable delay after the reasonable excuse ceased.

49(7) If a request of the kind referred to in subsection (4) is made, HMRC must notify the appellant whether or not HMRC agree to the appellant giving notice of appeal after the relevant time limit.

49(8) In this section **"relevant time limit"**, in relation to notice of appeal, means the time before which the notice is to be given (but for this section).

History – S. 49 substituted by SI 2009/56, art. 3(1) and Sch. 1, para. 29, operative from 1 April 2009, subject to transitional and saving provisions in SI 2009/56, Sch. 3.

49A Appeal: HMRC review or determination by tribunal

49A(1) This section applies if notice of appeal has been given to HMRC.

49A(2) In such a case–

(a) the appellant may notify HMRC that the appellant requires HMRC to review the matter in question (see section 49B),

(b) HMRC may notify the appellant of an offer to review the matter in question (see section 49C), or

(c) the appellant may notify the appeal to the tribunal (see section 49D).

49A(3) See sections 49G and 49H for provision about notifying appeals to the tribunal after a review has been required by the appellant or offered by HMRC.

49A(4) This section does not prevent the matter in question from being dealt with in accordance with section 54 (settling appeals by agreement).

History – S. 49A inserted by SI 2009/56, art. 3(1) and Sch. 1, para. 30, operative from 1 April 2009, subject to transitional and saving provisions in SI 2009/56, Sch. 3.

49B Appellant requires review by HMRC

49B(1) Subsections (2) and (3) apply if the appellant notifies HMRC that the appellant requires HMRC to review the matter in question.

49B(2) HMRC must, within the relevant period, notify the appellant of HMRC's view of the matter in question.

49B(3) HMRC must review the matter in question in accordance with section 49E.

49B(4) The appellant may not notify HMRC that the appellant requires HMRC to review the matter in question and HMRC shall not be required to conduct a review if–

(a) the appellant has already given a notification under this section in relation to the matter in question,

(b) HMRC have given a notification under section 49C in relation to the matter in question, or

(c) the appellant has notified the appeal to the tribunal under section 49D.

49B(5) In this section **"relevant period"** means–

(a) the period of 30 days beginning with the day on which HMRC receive the notification from the appellant, or

(b) such longer period as is reasonable.

History – S. 49B inserted by SI 2009/56, art. 3(1) and Sch. 1, para. 30, operative from 1 April 2009, subject to transitional and saving provisions in SI 2009/56, Sch. 3.

49C HMRC offer review

49C(1) Subsections (2) to (6) apply if HMRC notify the appellant of an offer to review the matter in question.

49C(2) When HMRC notify the appellant of the offer, HMRC must also notify the appellant of HMRC's view of the matter in question.

49C(3) If, within the acceptance period, the appellant notifies HMRC of acceptance of the offer, HMRC must review the matter in question in accordance with section 49E.

49C(4) If the appellant does not give HMRC such a notification within the acceptance period, HMRC's view of the matter in question is to be treated as if it were contained in an agreement in writing under section 54(1) for the settlement of the matter.

49C(5) The appellant may not give notice under section 54(2) (desire to repudiate or resile from agreement) in a case where subsection (4) applies.

49C(6) Subsection (4) does not apply to the matter in question if, or to the extent that, the appellant notifies the appeal to the tribunal under section 49H.

49C(7) HMRC may not notify the appellant of an offer to review the matter in question (and, accordingly, HMRC shall not be required to conduct a review) if–

(a) HMRC have already given a notification under this section in relation to the matter in question,

(b) the appellant has given a notification under section 49B in relation to the matter in question, or

(c) the appellant has notified the appeal to the tribunal under section 49D.

49C(8) In this section **"acceptance period"** means the period of 30 days beginning with the date of the document by which HMRC notify the appellant of the offer to review the matter in question.

History – S. 49C inserted by SI 2009/56, art. 3(1) and Sch. 1, para. 30, operative from 1 April 2009, subject to transitional and saving provisions in SI 2009/56, Sch. 3.

49D Notifying appeal to the tribunal

49D(1) This section applies if notice of appeal has been given to HMRC.

49D(2) The appellant may notify the appeal to the tribunal.

49D(3) If the appellant notifies the appeal to the tribunal, the tribunal is to decide the matter in question.

49D(4) Subsections (2) and (3) do not apply in a case where–

(a) HMRC have given a notification of their view of the matter in question under section 49B, or

(b) HMRC have given a notification under section 49C in relation to the matter in question.

49D(5) In a case falling within subsection (4)(a) or (b), the appellant may notify the appeal to the tribunal, but only if permitted to do so by section 49G or 49H.

History – S. 49D inserted by SI 2009/56, art. 3(1) and Sch. 1, para. 30, operative from 1 April 2009, subject to transitional and saving provisions in SI 2009/56, Sch. 3.

49E Nature of review etc

49E(1) This section applies if HMRC are required by section 49B or 49C to review the matter in question.

49E(2) The nature and extent of the review are to be such as appear appropriate to HMRC in the circumstances.

49E(3) For the purpose of subsection (2), HMRC must, in particular, have regard to steps taken before the beginning of the review–

(a) by HMRC in deciding the matter in question, and

(b) by any person in seeking to resolve disagreement about the matter in question.

49E(4) The review must take account of any representations made by the appellant at a stage which gives HMRC a reasonable opportunity to consider them.

49E(5) The review may conclude that HMRC's view of the matter in question is to be–

(a) upheld,

(b) varied, or

(c) cancelled.

49E(6) HMRC must notify the appellant of the conclusions of the review and their reasoning within–

(a) the period of 45 days beginning with the relevant day, or

(b) such other period as may be agreed.

49E(7) In subsection (6) **"relevant day"** means–

(a) in a case where the appellant required the review, the day when HMRC notified the appellant of HMRC's view of the matter in question,

(b) in a case where HMRC offered the review, the day when HMRC received notification of the appellant's acceptance of the offer.

49E(8) Where HMRC are required to undertake a review but do not give notice of the conclusions within the time period specified in subsection (6), the review is to be treated as having concluded that HMRC's view of the matter in question (see sections 49B(2) and 49C(2)) is upheld.

49E(9) If subsection (8) applies, HMRC must notify the appellant of the conclusion which the review is treated as having reached.

History – S. 49E inserted by SI 2009/56, art. 3(1) and Sch. 1, para. 30, operative from 1 April 2009, subject to transitional and saving provisions in SI 2009/56, Sch. 3.

49F Effect of conclusions of review

49F(1) This section applies if HMRC give notice of the conclusions of a review (see section 49E(6) and (9)).

49F(2) The conclusions are to be treated as if they were an agreement in writing under section 54(1) for the settlement of the matter in question.

49F(3) The appellant may not give notice under section 54(2) (desire to repudiate or resile from agreement) in a case where subsection (2) applies.

49F(4) Subsection (2) does not apply to the matter in question if, or to the extent that, the appellant notifies the appeal to the tribunal under section 49G.

History – S. 49F inserted by SI 2009/56, art. 3(1) and Sch. 1, para. 30, operative from 1 April 2009, subject to transitional and saving provisions in SI 2009/56, Sch. 3.

49G Notifying appeal to tribunal after review concluded

49G(1) This section applies if–

(a) HMRC have given notice of the conclusions of a review in accordance with section 49E, or

(b) the period specified in section 49E(6) has ended and HMRC have not given notice of the conclusions of the review.

49G(2) The appellant may notify the appeal to the tribunal within the post-review period.

49G(3) If the post-review period has ended, the appellant may notify the appeal to the tribunal only if the tribunal gives permission.

49G(4) If the appellant notifies the appeal to the tribunal, the tribunal is to determine the matter in question.

49G(5) In this section **"post-review period"** means–

(a) in a case falling within subsection (1)(a), the period of 30 days beginning with the date of the document in which HMRC give notice of the conclusions of the review in accordance with section 49E(6), or

(b) in a case falling within subsection (1)(b), the period that–

(i) begins with the day following the last day of the period specified in section 49E(6), and

(ii) ends 30 days after the date of the document in which HMRC give notice of the conclusions of the review in accordance with section 49E(9).

History – S. 49G inserted by SI 2009/56, art. 3(1) and Sch. 1, para. 30, operative from 1 April 2009, subject to transitional and saving provisions in SI 2009/56, Sch. 3.

49H Notifying appeal to tribunal after review offered but not accepted

49H(1) This section applies if–

(a) HMRC have offered to review the matter in question (see section 49C), and

(b) the appellant has not accepted the offer.

49H(2) The appellant may notify the appeal to the tribunal within the acceptance period.

49H(3) But if the acceptance period has ended, the appellant may notify the appeal to the tribunal only if the tribunal gives permission.

49H(4) If the appellant notifies the appeal to the tribunal, the tribunal is to determine the matter in question.

49H(5) In this section **"acceptance period"** has the same meaning as in section 49C.

History – S. 49H inserted by SI 2009/56, art. 3(1) and Sch. 1, para. 30, operative from 1 April 2009, subject to transitional and saving provisions in SI 2009/56, Sch. 3.

49I Interpretation of sections 49A to 49H

49I(1) In sections 49A to 49H–

(a) **"matter in question"** means the matter to which an appeal relates;

(b) a reference to a notification is a reference to a notification in writing.

49I(2) In sections 49A to 49H, a reference to the appellant includes a person acting on behalf of the appellant except in relation to–

(a) notification of HMRC's view under section 49B(2);

(b) notification by HMRC of an offer of review (and of their view of the matter) under section 49C;

(c) notification of the conclusions of a review under section 49E(6); and

(d) notification of the conclusions of a review under section 49E(9).

49I(3) But if a notification falling within any of the paragraphs of subsection (2) is given to the appellant, a copy of the notification may also be given to a person acting on behalf of the appellant.

History – S. 49I inserted by SI 2009/56, art. 3(1) and Sch. 1, para. 30, operative from 1 April 2009, subject to transitional and saving provisions in SI 2009/56, Sch. 3.

50 Procedure

50(1)–(5) [Omitted by SI 1994/1813, Sch. 1, para. 6(a), with effect from 1 September 1994.]

50(6) If, on an appeal notified to the tribunal, the tribunal decides–

(a) that the appellant is overcharged by a self-assessment;

(b) that any amounts contained in a partnership statement are excessive; or

(c) that the appellant is overcharged by an assessment other than a self-assessment,

the assessment or amounts shall be reduced accordingly, but otherwise the assessment or statement shall stand good.

50(7) If, on an appeal notified to the tribunal, the tribunal decides–

(a) that the appellant is undercharged to tax by a self-assessment;

(b) that any amounts contained in a partnership statement are insufficient; or

(c) that the appellant is undercharged by an assessment other than a self-assessment,

the assessment or amounts shall be increased accordingly.

50(7A) If, on an appeal notified to the tribunal, the tribunal decides that a claim or election which was the subject of a decision contained in a closure notice under section 28A of this Act should have been allowed or disallowed to an extent different from that specified in the notice, the claim or election shall be allowed or disallowed accordingly to the extent that the tribunal decides is appropriate, but otherwise the decision in the notice shall stand good.

50(8) Where, on an appeal notified to the tribunal against an assessment (other than a self-assessment) which–

(a) assesses an amount which is chargeable to tax, and

(b) charges tax on the amount assessed,

the tribunal decides as mentioned in subsection (6) or (7) above, the tribunal may, unless the circumstances of the case otherwise require, reduce or, as the case may be, increase only the amount assessed; and where any appeal notified to the tribunal is so determined the tax charged by the assessment shall be taken to have been reduced or increased accordingly.

50(9) Where any amounts contained in a partnership statement are reduced under subsection (6) above or increased under subsection (7) above, an officer of the Board shall by notice to each of the relevant partners amend–

(a) the partner's return under section 8 or 8A of this Act, or

(b) the partner's company tax return,

so as to give effect to the reductions or increases of those amounts.

50(10) Where an appeal is notified to the tribunal, the decision of the tribunal on the appeal is final and conclusive.

50(11) But subsection (10) is subject to–

(a) sections 9 to 14 of the TCEA 2007,

(b) Tribunal Procedure Rules, and

(c) the Taxes Acts.

History – S. 50(1)–(5) omitted by SI 1994/1813, Sch. 1, para. 6(a), Sch. 2, Pt. I, with effect from 1 September 1994.

In s. 50(6) the words "If, on an appeal notified to the tribunal, the tribunal decides–" substituted for the words "If, on an appeal, it appears to the majority of the Commissioners present at the hearing, by examination of the appellant on oath or affirmation, or by other evidence–" by SI 2009/56, art. 3(1) and Sch. 1, para. 31(2), operative from 1 April 2009, subject to transitional and saving provisions in SI 2009/56, Sch. 3.

In s. 50(6) the word "lawful" which appeared after the word "other" in the introductory paragraph omitted by SI 1994/1813, Sch. 1, para. 6(b), with effect from 1 September 1994.

In s. 50(6)–

- in para. (a), the words "by reason of an amendment under section 28A(2) or (4) of this Act or paragraph 30 or 34(2) of Schedule 18 to the Finance Act 1998", and
- in para. (b), the words "by reason of an amendment under section 28B(3) or 30B(1) of this Act,"

(both of which appeared after the word "that" in each para.) omitted and repealed by FA 2001, s. 88, Sch. 29, para. 30(2), (3) and s. 110, Sch. 33, Pt. 2(13) with effect from 11 May 2001 in relation to returns whether made before or after that date and whether relating to periods before or after then.

In s. 50(7) the words "If, on an appeal notified to the tribunal, the tribunal decides" substituted for the words "If, on an appeal, it appears to the Commissioners" by SI 2009/56, art. 3(1) and Sch. 1, para. 31(3), operative from 1 April 2009, subject to transitional and saving provisions in SI 2009/56, Sch. 3.

In s. 50(7)–

- in para. (a), the words "which has been amended under section 28A(2) or (4) of this Act or paragraph 30 or 34(2) of Schedule 18 to the Finance Act 1998", and
- in para. (b), the words "which has been amended under section 28B(3) or 30B(1) of this Act"

(which appeared after the words "self-assessment" and "partnership statement" respectively), omitted and repealed by FA 2001, s. 88, Sch. 29, para. 30(2), (3) and s. 110, Sch. 33, Pt. 2(13) with effect from 11 May 2001 in relation to returns whether made before or after that date and whether relating to periods before or after then.

Prior to the above repeal, in s. 50(6)(a) and (7)(a), the words "or paragraph 30 or 34(2) of Schedule 18 to the Finance Act 1998" had been inserted by FA 1998, s. 117(3) and Sch. 19, para. 27(4), with effect in relation to accounting periods ending on or after 1 July 1999, the corporation tax self-assessment appointed day by virtue of FA 1994, s. 199(2), (3) and SI 1998/3173 (C. 78).

Originally, s. 50(6), (7) had been substituted by FA 1994, s. 196 in so far as they relate to income tax and capital gains tax, as respects the year 1996–97 and subsequent years of assessment and, in so far as they relate to corporation tax, as respects accounting periods ending on or after 1 July 1999, the self-assessment appointed day (see above).

In s. 50(7A) the words "If, on an appeal notified to the tribunal, the tribunal decides" substituted for the words "If, on an appeal, it appears to the Commissioners" and the words "the tribunal decides is" substituted for the words "appears to them" by SI 2009/56, art. 3(1) and Sch. 1, para. 31(4), operative from 1 April 2009, subject to transitional and saving provisions in SI 2009/56, Sch. 3.

In s. 50(7A) the words "which was the subject of a decision contained in a closure notice under section 28A" substituted for the words "specified in a notice under section 28A(4A)" by FA 2001, s. 88, Sch. 29, para. 30(4) with effect from 11 May 2001 in relation to returns whether made before or after that date and whether relating to periods before or after then.
Originally, s. 50(7A) inserted by FA 1996, s. 133 and Sch. 19, para. 7, in so far as it relates to income tax and capital gains tax, as respects the year 1996–97 and subsequent years of assessment and, in so far as it relates to corporation tax, as respects accounting periods ending on or after 1 July 1999, the self-assessment appointed day (see above).
In s. 50(8) the words "notified to the tribunal" inserted twice; the words "the tribunal decides" substituted for the words "it appears to the Commissioners" and the words "the tribunal may" substituted for the words "they may" by SI 2009/56, art. 3(1) and Sch. 1, para. 31(5), operative from 1 April 2009, subjectto transitional and saving provisions in SI 2009/56, Sch. 3.
S. 50(8) amended, by the insertion of the words "(other than a self-assessment)" by FA 1994, s. 196 in so far as it relates to income tax and capital gains tax, as respects the year 1996–97 and subsequent years of assessment and, in so far as it relates to corporation tax, as respects accounting periods ending on or after 1 July 1999, the self-assessment appointed day (see above).
S. 50(8) originally inserted by F(No. 2)A 1975, s. 67(2).
S. 50(9)(a) substituted by FA 2001, s. 88, Sch. 29, para. 30(5) with effect from 11 May 2001 in relation to returns whether made before or after that date and whether relating to periods before or after then.
Former s. 50(9) substituted by FA 1998, s. 117(3) and Sch. 19, para. 27(4), with effect in relation to accounting periods ending on or after 1 July 1999, the self-assessment appointed day by virtue of FA 1994, s. 199(2), (3) and SI 1998/3173 (C. 78) (see above).
Former s. 50(9) originally inserted by FA 1994, s. 196 and Sch. 19, para. 17, in so far as it relates to income tax and capital gains tax, as respects the year 1996–97 and subsequent years of assessment and, in so far as it relates to corporation tax, as respects accounting periods ending on or after 1 July 1999, the self-assessment appointed day (see above).
S. 50(10) inserted by SI 2009/56, art. 3(1) and Sch. 1, para. 31(6), operative from 1 April 2009, subject to transitional and saving provisions in SI 2009/56, Sch. 3.
S. 50(11) inserted by SI 2009/56, art. 3(1) and Sch. 1, para. 31(6), operative from 1 April 2009, subject to transitional and saving provisions in SI 2009/56, Sch. 3.

Cross references – Social Security Contributions (Transfer of Functions, etc.) Act 1999, s. 13(2)(a)(ii): power of the Board, with the concurrence of the Lord Chancellor and the Lord Advocate, to make regulations making provision with respect to appeals on contributions matters, including any of the matters dealt with in s. 50.

54 Settling of appeals by agreement

54(1) Subject to the provisions of this section, where a person gives notice of appeal and, before the appeal is determined by the tribunal, the inspector or other proper officer of the Crown and the appellant come to an agreement, whether in writing or otherwise, that the assessment or decision under appeal should be treated as upheld without variation, or as varied in a particular manner or as discharged or cancelled, the like consequences shall ensue for all purposes as would have ensued if, at the time when the agreement was come to, the tribunal had determined the appeal and had upheld the assessment or decision without variation, had varied it in that manner or had discharged or cancelled it, as the case may be.

54(2) Subsection (1) of this section shall not apply where, within thirty days from the date when the agreement was come to, the appellant gives notice in writing to the inspector or other proper officer of the Crown that he desires to repudiate or resile from the agreement.

54(3) Where an agreement is not in writing–

(a) the preceding provisions of this section shall not apply unless the fact that an agreement was come to, and the terms agreed, are confirmed by notice in writing given by the inspector or other proper officer of the Crown to the appellant or by the appellant to the inspector or other proper officer; and

(b) the references in the said preceding provisions to the time when the agreement was come to shall be construed as references to the time of the giving of the said notice of confirmation.

54(4) Where–

(a) a person who has given a notice of appeal notifies the inspector or other proper officer of the Crown, whether orally or in writing, that he desires not to proceed with the appeal; and

(b) thirty days have elapsed since the giving of the notification without the inspector or other proper officer giving to the appellant notice in writing indicating that he is unwilling that the appeal should be treated as withdrawn,

the preceding provisions of this section shall have effect as if, at the date of the appellant's notification, the appellant and the inspector or other proper officer had come to an agreement, orally or in writing, as the case may be, that the assessment or decision under appeal should be upheld without variation.

54(5) The references in this section to an agreement being come to with an appellant and the giving of notice or notification to or by an appellant include references to an agreement being come to with, and the giving of notice or notification to or by, a person acting on behalf of the appellant in relation to the appeal.

History – In s. 54(1) the word "tribunal" substituted for the word "Commissioners" twice by SI 2009/56, art. 3(1) and Sch. 1, para. 33, operative from 1 April 2009, subject to transitional and saving provisions in SI 2009/56, Sch. 3.

Cross references – Social Security Contributions (Transfer of Functions, etc.) Act 1999, s. 13(2)(a)(ii): power of the Board, with the concurrence of the Lord Chancellor and the Lord Advocate, to make regulations making provision with respect to appeals on contributions matters, including any of the matters dealt with in s. 54.

55 Recovery of tax not postponed

55(1) This section applies to an appeal to the tribunal against–

(a) an amendment of a self-assessment–

(i) under section 9C of this Act, or

(ii) under paragraph 30 or 34 of Schedule 18 to the Finance Act 1998,

(aa) a conclusion stated or amendment made by a closure notice under section 28A or 28B of this Act,
(b) an assessment to tax other than a self-assessment,
(c) [omitted by ITA 2007, s. 1027 and Sch. 1, para. 257(a), and repealed by s. 1031 and Sch. 3, Pt. 1,]
(d) [omitted by FA 2012, s. 180 and Sch. 20, para. 11.]

55(2) Except as otherwise provided by the following provisions of this section, the tax charged–
(a) by the amendment or assessment, or
(b) where the appeal is against a conclusion stated by a closure notice, as a result of that conclusion,

shall be due and payable as if there had been no appeal.

55(3) If the appellant has grounds for believing that the amendment or assessment overcharges the appellant to tax, or as a result of the conclusion stated in the closure notice the tax charged on the appellant is excessive, the appellant may–
(a) first apply by notice in writing to HMRC within 30 days of the specified date for a determination by them of the amount of tax the payment of which should be postponed pending the determination of the appeal;
(b) where such a determination is not agreed, refer the application for postponement to the tribunal within 30 days from the date of the document notifying HMRC's decision on the amount to be postponed.

An application under paragraph (a) must state the amount believed to be overcharged to tax and the grounds for that belief.

55(3A) An application under subsection (3) above may be made more than thirty days after the specified date if there is a change in the circumstances of the case as a result of which the appellant has grounds for believing that he is over-charged to tax by the amendment or assessment, or as a result of the conclusion stated in the closure notice, or where the notice of appeal has been given after the relevant time limit (see section 49).

55(4) If, after any determination of the amount of tax the payment of which should be so postponed–
(a) there is a change in the circumstances of the case as a result of which either party has grounds for believing that the amount so determined has become excessive or, as the case may be, insufficient, and
(b) the parties cannot agree on a revised determination,

the party mentioned in paragraph (a) may, at any time before the determination of the appeal, apply to the tribunal for a revised determination of that amount.

55(5) Any such application is to be subject to the relevant provisions of Part 5 of this Act (see, in particular, section 48(2)(b)).

55(6) The amount of tax the payment of which shall be postponed pending the determination of the appeal shall be the amount (if any) in which it appears that there are reasonable grounds for believing that the appellant is overcharged to tax; and–
(a) in the case of a determination made on an application under subsection (3) above, other than an application made by virtue of subsection (3A) above, the date on which any tax the payment of which is not so postponed is due and payable shall be determined as if the tax were charged by an amendment or assessment notice of which was issued on the date of that determination and against which there had been no appeal; and
(b) in the case of a determination made on an application under subsection (4) above–
  (i) the date on which any tax the payment of which ceases to be so postponed is due and payable shall be determined as if the tax were charged by an amendment or assessment notice of which was issued on the date of that determination and against which there had been no appeal; and
  (ii) any tax overpaid shall be repaid.

55(6A) Notwithstanding the provisions of sections 11 and 13 of the TCEA 2007, the decision of the tribunal shall be final and conclusive.

55(7) If the appellant and HMRC reach an agreement as to the amount of tax the payment of which should be postponed pending the determination of the appeal, the agreement shall not have effect unless–
(a) the agreement is in writing, or
(b) the fact that the agreement has been reached, and the terms of the agreement, are confirmed by notice in writing given–
  (i) by the appellant to HMRC, or
  (ii) by HMRC to the appellant.

55(8) [Omitted by SI 2009/56, art. 3(1) and Sch. 1, para. 34(10).]

55(8A) Where an agreement is made which has effect under subsection (7), references in subsection (6)(a) and (b) above to the date of the determination shall be construed as references to the date that the agreement is confirmed in writing.

55(8B) Subsections (8C) and (8D) apply where a person has been given an accelerated payment notice or partner payment notice under Chapter 3 of Part 4 of the Finance Act 2014 and that notice has not been withdrawn.

55(8C) Nothing in this section enables the postponement of the payment of (as the case may be)–

(a) the understated tax to which the payment specified in the notice under section 220(2)(b) of that Act relates,

(b) the disputed tax specified in the notice under section 221(2)(b) of that Act,

(c) the understated partner tax to which the payment specified in the notice under paragraph 4(1)(b) of Schedule 32 to that Act relates, or

(d) the amount of tax specified in an assessment under paragraph 76 of Schedule 18 to the Finance Act 1998 where–

(i) an asserted surrenderable amount is specified in the notice under section 220(2)(d) of the Finance Act 2014 or under paragraph 4(1)(d) of Schedule 32 to that Act, and

(ii) the claimant company has failed to act in accordance with paragraph 75(6) of Schedule 18 to the Finance Act 1998.

55(8D) Accordingly, if the payment of an amount of tax within subsection (8C)(b) is postponed by virtue of this section immediately before the accelerated payment notice is given, it ceases to be so postponed with effect from the time that notice is given, and the tax is due and payable–

(a) if no representations were made under section 222 of that Act in respect of the notice, on or before the last day of the period of 90 days beginning with the day the notice or partner payment notice is given, and

(b) if representations were so made, on or before whichever is later of–

(i) the last day of the 90 day period mentioned in paragraph (a), and

(ii) the last day of the period of 30 days beginning with the day on which HMRC's determination in respect of those representations is notified under section 222 of that Act.

55(9) On the determination of the appeal–

(a) the date on which any tax payable in accordance with that determination is due and payable shall, so far as it is tax the payment of which had been postponed, or which would not have been charged by the amendment or assessment, or as a result of the conclusion stated in the closure notice, if there had been no appeal, be determined as if the tax were charged by an amendment or assessment–

(i) notice of which was issued on the date on which HMRC issue to the appellant a notice of the total amount payable in accordance with the determination, and

(ii) against which there had been no appeal; and

(b) any tax overpaid shall be repaid.

55(10) [Omitted by SI 2009/56, art. 3(1) and Sch. 1, para. 34(13).]

55(10A) In this section **"the specified date"** means the date of–

(a) the issue of the notice of amendment or assessment, or

(b) in the case of an appeal against a conclusion stated or amendment made by a closure notice, the issue of the closure notice.

55(10B) References in this section to agreements between an appellant and HMRC, and to the giving of notices between the parties, include references to agreements, and the giving of notices, between a person acting on behalf of the appellant in relation to the appeal and HMRC.

55(11) [Omitted by SI 2009/56, art. 3(1) and Sch. 1, para. 34(13).]

History – In s. 55(1) the word "tribunal" substituted for the word "Commissioners" twice by SI 2009/56, art. 3(1) and Sch. 1, para. 34(2), operative from 1 April 2009, subject to transitional and saving provisions in SI 2009/56, Sch. 3.
In s. 55(1)(a)(ii), "34" substituted for "34(2)" by FA 2008, s. 119(12)(a)(iv) with effect from 1 April 2010 (SI 2009/405).
S. 55(1)(a) and (aa) substituted for the previous version of subs. (1)(a) by FA 2001, s. 88, Sch. 29, para. 31(2) with effect from 11 May 2001 in relation to returns whether made before or after that date and whether relating to periods before or after then.
S. 55(1)(a) and (b) (previously) substituted by FA 1998, s. 117(3) and Sch. 19, para. 28 with effect in relation to accounting periods *ending on or after 1 July 1999, the corporation tax self-assessment appointed day by virtue of* FA 1994, s. 199(2), (3) and SI 1998/3173 (C. 78).
S. 55(1)(d) omitted by FA 2012, s. 180 and Sch. 20, para. 11 in relation to accounting periods of controlled foreign companies beginning on or after 1 January 2013.
S. 55(1) previously substituted and s. 55(2)–(11) amended, by the substitution of the words "amendment or assessment" for "assessment" in each place where it occurred, by FA 1994, s. 196 and Sch. 19, para. 18, in so far as it relates to income tax and capital gains tax, as respects the year 1996–97 and subsequent years of assessment, and also originally as respects corporation tax accounting periods

ending on or after 1 July 1999, the appointed day by virtue of SI 1998/3173 (but see now amendment made by FA 1998, s. 117(3) and Sch. 19, para. 28, above).
S. 55(1)(b) previously substituted by FA 1996, s. 132 and Sch. 18, para. 1:

- for the purposes of income tax and capital gains tax, as respects the year 1996–97 and subsequent years of assessment;
- for the purposes of corporation tax, as respects accounting periods ending on or after 1 July 1999, the appointed day by virtue of FA 1994, s. 199(2), (3) and SI 1998/3173 (C. 78); and
- so far as relating to partnerships whose trades, professions or businesses were set up and commenced before 6 April 1994, with effect as respects the year 1997–98 and subsequent years of assessment.

S. 55(1)(c) omitted by ITA 2007, s. 1027 and Sch. 1, para. 257(a), and repealed by s. 1031 and Sch. 3, Pt. 1 with effect from 6 April 2007.
In s. 55(1)(d), the words "the principal Act" substituted for "that Act" by ITA 2007, s. 1027 and Sch. 1, para. 257(b) with effect from 6 April 2007.
S. 55(1)(f) related to development land tax.
S. 55(1)(g) substituted by ICTA 1988, s. 844 and Sch. 29, para. 8(1) in relation to tax for 1988–89 and subsequent years of assessment, and for companies' accounting periods ending after 5 April 1988.
S. 55(2) amended, the amendment substituting subs. (2)(a), (b) for the words "by the amendment or assessment", by FA 2001, s. 88, Sch. 29, para. 31(3) with effect from 11 May 2001 in relation to returns whether made before or after that date and whether relating to periods before or after then.
S. 55(2), (6), (9) (previously in the case of (2)) amended by FA 1989, s. 156(2), (4) for tax charged by an assessment, notice of which is issued after 30 July 1982, to clarify wording consequent to previous amendments, see below.
S. 55(3) substituted by SI 2009/56, art. 3(1) and Sch. 1, para. 34(3), operative from 1 April 2009, subject to transitional and saving provisions in SI 2009/56, Sch. 3.
In former s. 55(3), the words "or as a result of the conclusion stated in the closure notice," inserted and the words "the specified date" substituted for the words "the date of the issue of the notice of amendment or assessment", by FA 2001, s. 88, Sch. 29, para. 31(4) with effect from 11 May 2001 in relation to returns whether made before or after that date and whether relating to periods before or after then.
In s. 55(3A) the words ", or where the notice of appeal has been given after the relevant time limit (see section 49)" inserted by SI 2009/56, art. 3(1) and Sch. 1, para. 34(4), operative from 1 April 2009, subject to transitional and saving provisions in SI 2009/56, Sch. 3.
In s. 55(3A), the words "the specified date" substituted for the words "the date of the issue of the notice of amendment or assessment" and the words "or as a result of the conclusion stated in the closure notice," inserted, by FA 2001, s. 88, Sch. 29, para. 31(5) with effect from 11 May 2001 in relation to returns whether made before or after that date and whether relating to periods before or after then.
S. 55(3A) originally inserted by FA 1982, s. 68(2) in relation to notices of assessment issued after 30 July 1982; s. 55(2), (6) amended accordingly by FA 1982, s. 68(1), (3).
S. 55(4) substituted by SI 2009/56, art. 3(1) and Sch. 1, para. 34(5), operative from 1 April 2009, subject to transitional and saving provisions in SI 2009/56, Sch. 3.
S. 55(5) substituted by SI 2009/56, art. 3(1) and Sch. 1, para. 34(6), operative from 1 April 2009, subject to transitional and saving provisions in SI 2009/56, Sch. 3.
In s. 55(6) the words "to the Commissioners, having regard to the representations made and any evidence adduced," omitted by SI 2009/56, art. 3(1) and Sch. 1, para. 34(7), operative from 1 April 2009, subject to transitional and saving provisions in SI 2009/56, Sch. 3.
In s. 55(6), the word "lawful" which appeared before the word "evidence" omitted by SI 1994/1813, Sch. 1, para. 9(a), Sch. 2, Pt. I, with effect from 1 September 1994.
S. 55(6A) substituted by SI 2009/56, art. 3(1) and Sch. 1, para. 34(8), operative from 1 April 2009, subject to transitional and saving provisions in SI 2009/56, Sch. 3.
Former s. 55(6A) inserted by ICTA 1988, s. 844 and Sch. 29, para. 8(2) in relation to tax for 1988–89 and subsequent years of assessment and for companies' accounting periods ending after 5 April 1988 – see previously FA 1984, s. 89(6).
S. 55(7) substituted by SI 2009/56, art. 3(1) and Sch. 1, para. 34(9), operative from 1 April 2009, subject to transitional and saving provisions in SI 2009/56, Sch. 3.
Former s. 55(7) amended by FA 1990, s. 104(2), (4), substituting "an inspector" for "the inspector", effective where notice of appeal is given on or after 26 July 1990.
S. 55(8) omitted by SI 2009/56, art. 3(1) and Sch. 1, para. 34(10), operative from 1 April 2009, subject to transitional and saving provisions in SI 2009/56, Sch. 3.
S. 55(8A) inserted by SI 2009/56, art. 3(1) and Sch. 1, para. 34(11), operative from 1 April 2009, subject to transitional and saving provisions in SI 2009/56, Sch. 3.
S. 55(8B), (8C) and (8D) inserted by FA 2014, s. 224(1), with effect from 17 July 2014.
S. 55(8C)(d) (and the ", or" before it) inserted (and the "or" after (b) omitted) by FA 2015, s. 118 and Sch. 18, para. 11, with effect from 26 March 2015.
In s. 55(9)(a)(i) the words "HMRC issue" substituted for the words "the inspector issues" by SI 2009/56, art. 3(1) and Sch. 1, para. 34(12), operative from 1 April 2009, subject to transitional and saving provisions in SI 2009/56, Sch. 3.
In s. 55(9)(a), the words "or as a result of the conclusion stated in the closure notice," inserted by FA 2001, s. 88, Sch. 29, para. 31(6) witheffect from 11 May 2001 in relation to returns whether made before or after that date and whether relating to periods before or after then.
S. 55(10) omitted by SI 2009/56, art. 3(1) and Sch. 1, para. 34(13), operative from 1 April 2009, subject to transitional and saving provisions in SI 2009/56, Sch. 3.
Former s. 55(10) substituted by FA 2001, s. 88, Sch. 29, para. 31(7) with effect from 11 May 2001 in relation to returns whether made before or after that date and whether relating to periods before or after then.
Former s. 55(10) previously amended by FA 1990, s. 104(2), (4), substituting "subsection (3) above" for "this section", effective where notice of appeal is given on or after 26 July 1990.
S. 55(10A) effectively inserted by FA 2001, s. 88, Sch. 29, para. 31(7) with effect from 11 May 2001 in relation to returns whether made before or after that date and whether relating to periods before or after then.
S. 55(10B) substituted by SI 2009/56, art. 3(1) and Sch. 1, para. 34(14), operative from 1 April 2009, subject to transitional and saving provisions in SI 2009/56, Sch. 3.
S. 55(10B) effectively inserted by FA 2001, s. 88, Sch. 29, para. 31(7) with effect from 11 May 2001 in relation to returns whether made before or after that date and whether relating to periods before or after then.
S. 55(11) omitted by SI 2009/56, art. 3(1) and Sch. 1, para. 34(15), operative from 1 April 2009, subject to transitional and saving provisions in SI 2009/56, Sch. 3.
In former s. 55(11), the words "or under regulations made pursuant to section 46A of this Act" inserted by SI 1994/1813, Sch. 1, para. 9(b), with effect from 1 September 1994.
Former s. 55(11) amended by FA 1984, Sch. 23, with effect, by virtue of SI 1984/1836, from 1 January 1985, removing a reference to s. 45(2) (repealed).
In s. 55 the word "tribunal" substituted for the word "Commissioners" twice by SI 2009/56, art. 3(1) and Sch. 1, para. 34(2), operative from 1 April 2009, subject to transitional and saving provisions in SI 2009/56, Sch. 3.

59A(9) If, at any time before the 31st January next following a year of assessment, an officer of the Board so directs–

(a) this section shall not apply, and shall be deemed never to have applied, as regards that year to any person specified in the direction; and

(b) there shall be made all such adjustments, whether by the repayment of amounts paid on account or otherwise, as may be required to give effect to the direction.

59A(10) PAYE regulations may provide that, for the purpose of determining the amount of any such excess as is mentioned in subsection (1) above, any necessary adjustments in respect of matters prescribed by the regulations shall be made to the amount of tax deducted at source under PAYE regulations.

Prospective amendments – In s. 59A(1)(a) the words "section 8 or 8A" substituted for the words "section 9" by F(No. 2)A 2017, s. 61 and Sch. 14, para. 23(2), with effect from a day to be appointed under F(No. 2)A 2017, s. 61(6).

In s. 59A(4A)(a) the words "section 8 or 8A" substituted for the words "section 9" by F(No. 2)A 2017, s. 61 and Sch. 14, para. 23(3), with effect from a day to be appointed under F(No. 2)A 2017, s. 61(6).

History – S. 59A(4B), and references to that subsection in s. 59A(2), (4A) and (5), inserted by FA 1996, s. 132 and Sch. 18, para. 2, generally as respects 1996–97 and subsequent years of assessment, and, so far as relating to partnerships whose trades, professions or businesses were set up or commenced before 6 April 1994, with effect as respects the 1997–98 and subsequent years of assessment.

S. 59A(7) omitted by FA 2015, s. 37 and Sch. 7, para. 50, with effect in relation to disposals made on or after 6 April 2015.

In s. 59A(8)(b), the words "or are tax credits to which section 397(1) or 397A(1) of ITTOIA 2005 applies," (which appeared after the words "subsequent years,") omitted by FA 2016, s. 5(11) and Sch. 1, para. 51(8), with effect in relation to dividends paid or arising (or treated as paid), and other distributions made (or treated as made), in the tax year 2016–17 or at any later time.

In s. 59A(8)(b), "397A(1)" substituted for "397A(2)" by FA 2009, s. 40 and Sch. 19, para. 9(d), with effect for:

- qualifying distributions arising on or after 22 April 2009;
- cash dividends paid over to a person under ITEPA 2003, Sch. 2, para. 68(4) on or after 22 April 2009;
- dividends treated under ITTOIA 2005, s. 407 as paid to a person on or after 22 April 2009; and
- manufactured overseas dividends that are representative of any of the above distributions (FA 2009, Sch. 19, para. 14(1)).

In s. 59A(8)(b), the reference to ITTOIA 2005, s. 397A(2) inserted by FA 2008, s. 34 and Sch. 12, para. 13, with effect for 2008–09 and subsequent tax years.

In s. 59A(8)(b), the reference to ITTOIA 2005, s. 397(1) substituted by ITTOIA 2005, s. 882(1) and Sch. 1, para. 376; effective for 2005–06 onwards (ITTOIA 2005, s. 883(1)).

In s. 59A(8), the words "PAYE regulations" substituted by FA 2003, s. 145(7)(a) with effect from 10 July 2003.

In s. 59A(8)(b), the words "PAYE regulations" substituted by ITEPA 2003, Sch. 6, para. 130(a) which has effect for the tax year 2003–04 and subsequent tax years. In addition the words "the principal Act" substituted for "that Act" by FA 2004, s. 92 and Sch. 17, para 10(1) with effect from 22 July 2004.

S. 59A(10) inserted by FA 1996, s. 119(1), as respects the year 1996–97 and subsequent years of assessment.

In s. 59A(10), the words "PAYE regulations" substituted by ITEPA 2003, Sch. 6, para. 130(b) which has effect for the tax year 2003–04 and subsequent tax years.

In s. 59A(10) the words "PAYE regulations" substituted by FA 2003, s. 145(7)(b) with effect from 10 July 2003.

S. 59A inserted by FA 1994, s. 192 with respect to 1996–97 and subsequent years. Subs. (1), (2) and (5) amended by FA 1995, s. 108(1), (2), (4), subs. (4A) inserted by FA 1995 s. 108(3) and subs. (8) and (9) substituted in order to correct deficiencies in original legislation.

59AB Amounts payable on account: recovery

59AB The provisions of the Taxes Acts as to the recovery of tax shall apply to an amount falling to be paid on account of tax in the same manner as they apply to an amount of tax.

History – S. 59AB inserted by FA 2015, s. 37 and Sch. 7, para. 51, with effect in relation to disposals made on or after 6 April 2015.

59B Payments of income tax and capital gains tax: assessments other than simple assessments

History – In the heading to s. 59B, the words ": assessments other than simple assessments" inserted by FA 2016, s. 167(1) and Sch. 23, para. 7(2), with effect in relation to the 2016–17 tax year and subsequent years.

59B(1) Subject to subsection (2) below, the difference between–

(a) the amount of income tax and capital gains tax contained in a person's self-assessment under section 9 of this Act for any year of assessment, and

(b) the aggregate of any payments on account made by him in respect of that year (whether under section 59A or 59AA of this Act or otherwise) and any income tax which in respect of that year has been deducted at source,

shall be payable by him or (as the case may be) repayable to him as mentioned in subsection (3) or (4) below but nothing in this subsection shall require the repayment of any income tax treated as deducted or paid by virtue of section 246D(1), of the principal Act, section 626 of ITEPA 2003 or section 399(2) or 530(1) of ITTOIA 2005.

59B(2) The following, namely–

(a) any amount which, in the year of assessment, is deducted at source under PAYE regulations in respect of a previous year, and

(b) any amount which, in respect of the year of assessment, is to be deducted at source under PAYE regulations in a subsequent year,

shall be respectively deducted from and added to the aggregate mentioned in subsection (1)(b) above.

59B(2A) The reference in subsection (1)(b) to payments on account under section 59AA does not include any amounts already repaid under section 59AA(5).

59B(3) In a case where the person–

(a) gave the notice required by section 7 of this Act within six months from the end of the year of assessment, but

(b) was not given notice under section 8 or 8A of this Act until after the 31st October next following that year,

the difference shall be payable or repayable at the end of the period of three months beginning with the day on which the notice under section 8 or 8A was given.

59B(4) In any other case, the difference shall be payable or repayable on or before the 31st January next following the year of assessment.

59B(4ZA) In a case in which the notice required by section 7 was given following the receipt of a notice under section 8B, subsections (3) and (4) apply as if–

(a) the reference to the notice required by section 7 were a reference to the original notice required by that section, and

(b) the references to notice under section 8 or 8A were references to the original notice under that section.

59B(4ZB) In subsection (4ZA) the references to original notices are to notices given before the notice under section 8B.

59B(4A) Where in the case of a repayment the return on the basis of which the person's self-assessment was made under section 9 of this Act is enquired into by an officer of the Board–

(a) nothing in subsection (3) or (4) above shall require the repayment to be made before the day on which, by virtue of section 28A(1B) of this Act, the enquiry is completed; but

(b) the officer may at any time before that day make the repayment, on a provisional basis, to such extent as he thinks fit.

59B(5) An amount of tax which is payable or repayable as a result of the amendment or correction of a self-assessment under–

(a) section 9ZA, 9ZB, 9C or 28A of this Act (amendment or correction of return under section 8 or 8A of this Act), or

(b) section 12ABA(3)(a), 12ABB(6)(a), 28B(4)(a), 30B(2)(a), 33A(4)(a) or 50(9)(a) of this Act (amendment of partner's return to give effect to amendment or correction of partnership return),

is payable (or repayable) on or before the day specified by the relevant provision of Schedule 3ZA to this Act.

59B(5A) Where a determination under section 28C of this Act which has effect as a person's self-assessment is superseded by his self-assessment under section 9 of this Act, any amount of tax which is payable or repayable by virtue of the supersession shall be payable or (as the case may be) repayable on or before the day given by subsection (3) or (4) above.

59B(6) Any amount of income tax or capital gains tax which is payable by virtue of an assessment made otherwise than under section 9, 28H or 28I of this Act shall, unless otherwise provided, be payable on the day following the end of the period of 30 days beginning with the day on which the notice of assessment is given.

59B(7) In this section any reference to income tax deducted at source is a reference to income tax deducted or treated as deducted from any income or treated as paid on any income.

But such a reference does not include income tax repaid on a claim for repayment of income tax which–

(a) is treated as having been paid by virtue of section 520(4) of ITA 2007 (gift aid relief: income tax treated as paid by trustees of charitable trust), or

(b) has been deducted at source from income to which section 532, 533, 536 or 537 of that Act (certain sources of income exempt from income tax) applies.

59B(8) PAYE regulations may provide that, for the purpose of determining the amount of the difference mentioned in subsection (1) above, any necessary adjustments in respect of matters prescribed by the regulations shall be made to the amount of tax deducted at source under PAYE regulations.

Prospective amendments – In s. 59B(1)(a) the words "section 8 or 8A" substituted for the words "section 9" by F(No. 2)A 2017, s. 61 and Sch. 14, para. 24(2), with effect from a day to be appointed under F(No. 2)A 2017, s. 61(6).
In s. 59B(4A) the words "section 8 or 8A" substituted for the words "section 9" by F(No. 2)A 2017, s. 61 and Sch. 14, para. 24(3), with effect from a day to be appointed under F(No. 2)A 2017, s. 61(6).
In s. 59B(5A) the words "section 8 or 8A" substituted for the words "section 9" by F(No. 2)A 2017, s. 61 and Sch. 14, para. 24(4), with effect from a day to be appointed under F(No. 2)A 2017, s. 61(6).
In s. 59B(6) the words "section 8 or 8A" substituted for the words "section 9" by F(No. 2)A 2017, s. 61 and Sch. 14, para. 24(5), with effect from a day to be appointed under F(No. 2)A 2017, s. 61(6).

History – In s. 59B(1), the final words beginning "but nothing in this subsection" inserted by FA 1996 s. 122(2) with respect to 1996–97 and subsequent years.

In s. 59B(1), the words "or 547(5) of the principal Act or section 626 of ITEPA 2003" substituted by ITEPA 2003, Sch. 6, para. 131(2) which has effect for the tax year 2003–04 and subsequent tax years.
In s. 59B(1), ", 400(2), 414(1), 421(1)" (which appeared after the words "section 399(2)") omitted by FA 2016, s. 5(11) and Sch. 1, para. 51(9)(a), with effect for the tax year 2016–17 and subsequent tax years.
In s. 59B(1) references to ICTA 1988, s. 233(1), 249(4), 421(1) and 547(5) omitted by ITTOIA 2005, s. 882(1) and Sch. 1, para. 377(2)(a) and repealed by ITTOIA 2005, s. 884 and Sch. 3; effective for 2005–06 onwards (ITTOIA 2005, s. 883(1)). References to ITTOIA 2005, s. 399(2), 400(2), 414(1), 421(1) and 530(1) substituted by ITTOIA 2005, s. 882(1) and Sch. 1, para. 377(2)(b); effective for 2005–06 onwards ((ITTOIA 2005, s. 883(1)).
In s. 59B(1)(b), the words "or 59AA" inserted by FA 2015, s. 37 and Sch. 7, para. 52(2), with effect in relation to disposals made on or after 6 April 2015.
In s. 59B(2)(b), the words "or is a tax credit to which section 397(1) or 397A(1) of ITTOIA 2005 applies," (which appeared after the words "subsequent year,") omitted by FA 2016, s. 5(11) and Sch. 1, para. 51(9)(b), with effect for the tax year 2016–17 and subsequent tax years.
In s. 59B(2)(b), "397A(1)" substituted for "397A(2)" by FA 2009, s. 40 and Sch. 19, para. 9(d), with effect for:

- qualifying distributions arising on or after 22 April 2009;
- cash dividends paid over to a person under ITEPA 2003, Sch. 2, para. 68(4) on or after 22 April 2009;
- dividends treated under ITTOIA 2005, s. 407 as paid to a person on or after 22 April 2009; and
- manufactured overseas dividends that are representative of any of the above distributions (FA 2009, Sch. 19, para. 14(1)).

In s. 59B(2)(a), the words "PAYE regulations" substituted by ITEPA 2003, Sch. 6, para. 131(3) which has effect for the tax year 2003–04 and subsequent tax years.
In s. 59B(2)(b), the reference to ITTOIA 2005, s. 397A(2) inserted by FA 2008, s. 34 and Sch. 12, para. 14, with effect for 2008–09 and subsequent tax years.
In s. 59B(2)(b), the words "PAYE regulations" substituted by FA 2003, s. 145(7)(b) with effect from 10 July 2003.
In s. 59B(2)(b), reference to ITTOIA 2005, s. 397(1) substituted by ITTOIA 2005, s. 882(1) and Sch. 1, para. 377(3); effective for 2005–06 onwards (ITTOIA 2005, s. 883(1)).
S. 59B(2A) inserted by FA 2015, s. 37 and Sch. 7, para. 52(3), with effect in relation to disposals made on or after 6 April 2015.
S. 59B(4ZA) and (4ZB) inserted by FA 2013, s. 233 and Sch. 51, para. 5, with effect in relation to a return under TMA 1970, s. 12AA for a partnership which includes one or more companies, in respect of a return for a relevant period (a period in respect of which a return is required) beginning on or after 6 April 2012 and in relation to a return under that section for any other partnership, or a return under TMA 1970, s. 8 or 8A, in respect of a return for a year of assessment beginning on or after 6 April 2012.
In s. 59B(4A)(a) the words "28A(1B)" substituted for the words "28A(1)" by F(No. 2)A 2017, s. 63 and Sch. 15, para. 20, with effect in relation to an enquiry under TMA 1970, s. 9A, 12ZM or 12AC or FA 1998, Sch. 18 where the notice of enquiry is given on or after 16 November 2017 (Royal Assent) or the enquiry is in progress immediately before that day.
In s. 59B(4A)(a), "28A(1)" substituted for "28A(5)" and "the enquiry is" substituted for "the officer's enquiries are treated as" and subs. (5) substituted, all by FA 2001, s. 88, Sch. 29, para. 14 with effect from 11 May 2001 in relation to returns whether made before or after that date and whether relating to periods before or after then.
S. 59B(4A) inserted by FA 1996, s. 127 with respect to 1996–97 and subsequent years.
S. 59B(5A) inserted by FA 1996, s. 125(4) with respect to 1996–97 and subsequent years.
In s. 59B(6), the words ", 28H or 28I" inserted by FA 2016, s. 167(1) and Sch. 23, para. 7(3), with effect in relation to the 2016–17 tax year and subsequent years.
In s. 59B(6) the words "otherwise than under section 9 of this Act shall, unless otherwise provided" substitutedfor "under section 29 of this Act shall" by FA 1995, s. 115(6) with respect to 1996–97 and subsequent years.
S. 59B(7) amended by FA 2012, s. 51 and Sch. 15, para. 9, with effect in relation to income tax repaid on gifts made or income received on or after 6 April 2006. Accordingly, any reference in that amendment to a provision of ITA 2007 is to be read as including a reference to any corresponding earlier enactment which was rewritten in that provision.
S. 59B(8) inserted by FA 1996, s. 126(2) with respect to 1996–97 and subsequent years.
In s. 59B(8), the words "PAYE regulations" substituted for the words "that section" by FA 2003, s. 145(7)(b) with effect from 10 July 2003.
In s. 59B(8), the words "PAYE regulations" substituted for the words "Regulations under section 203 of the principal Act (PAYE)" by ITEPA 2003, Sch. 6, para. 131(4) which has effect for the tax year 2003–04 and subsequent tax years.
S. 59B inserted by FA 1994, s. 193 with respect to 1996–97 and subsequent years, in order to correct deficiencies in original legislation.

59BA Payment of income tax and capital gains tax: simple assessments

59BA(1) This section applies where a person has been given a simple assessment in relation to a year of assessment.

59BA(2) Subject to subsection (3), the difference between–

(a) the amount of income tax and capital gains tax for that year contained in the simple assessment, and

(b) the aggregate of any payments on account made by the person in respect of that year (whether under section 59A or 59AA or otherwise) and any income tax which in respect of that year has been deducted at source,

is payable by that person as mentioned in subsection (4) or (5).

59BA(3) Nothing in subsection (2) is to be read as requiring the repayment of any income tax which any provision of the Income Tax Acts provides is not repayable.

59BA(4) In a case where the person is given notice of the simple assessment after the 31st October next after the year of assessment, the difference is payable at the end of the period of 3 months after the day on which that notice was given.

59BA(5) In any other case the difference is payable on or before the 31st January next after the end of the year of assessment.

59BA(6) *Section 59B(7) (which explains references to income tax deducted at source) applies for the purposes of this section.*

59BA(7) PAYE regulations may provide that, for the purpose of determining the amount of the difference mentioned in subsection (2), any necessary adjustments in respect of matters prescribed in the regulations shall be made to the amount of tax deducted at source under PAYE regulations.

History – S. 59BA inserted by FA 2016, s. 167(1) and Sch. 23, para. 8, with effect in relation to the 2016–17 tax year and subsequent years.

MANAGED PAYMENT PLANS

History – Heading inserted by FA 2013, s. 229 and Sch. 49, para. 3, with effect from 11 December 2012 in relation to an accounting period if the relevant day, in relation to that period, falls on or after 11 December 2012 (subject to provisions of FA 2013, Sch. 49, para. 8(2) and (3)).

59G Managed payment plans

59G(1) This section applies if a person (“P”) has entered into a managed payment plan in respect of–

(a) an amount on account of income tax which is to become payable in accordance with section 59A(2),

(b) an amount of income tax or capital gains tax which is to become payable in accordance with section 59B, or

(c) [not relevant to National Insurance contributions.]

59G(2) P enters into a managed payment plan in respect of an amount if–

(a) P agrees to pay, and an officer of Revenue and Customs agrees to accept payment of, the amount by way of instalments,

(b) the instalments to be paid before the due date are balanced by the instalments to be paid after it (see section 59H), and

(c) the agreement meets such other requirements as may be specified in regulations made by the Commissioners for Her Majesty’s Revenue and Customs.

59G(3) But this section does not apply, in the case of an amount of corporation tax, if an arrangement under section 59F has been made in relation to the amount.

59G(4) If P pays all of the instalments in accordance with the plan, P is to be treated as having paid, on the due date, the total of those instalments.

59G(5) If P–

(a) pays one or more instalments in accordance with the plan, but

(b) fails to pay one or more later instalments in accordance with it,

P is to be treated as having paid, on the due date, the total of the instalments paid before the failure (but this is subject to subsection (6)).

59G(6) If–

(a) subsection (5) applies in a case in which the first failure to pay an instalment occurs before the due date, and

(b) P would (in the absence of a managed payment plan) be entitled to be paid interest on any amount paid before that date,

then, despite that subsection, P is entitled to be paid that interest.

59G(7) If–

(a) subsection (5) applies,

(b) P makes one or more payments after the due date (whether or not in accordance with the plan), and

(c) an officer of Revenue and Customs gives P a notice specifying any or all of those payments,

P is not liable to a penalty or surcharge for failing to pay the amount of the specified payments on or before the due date.

59G(8) Regulations under this section may make different provision for different cases.

59G(9) In this section **“the due date”**, in relation to an amount mentioned in subsection (1), means the date on which it becomes payable.

History – S. 59G inserted by TIOPA 2010, s. 371 and Sch. 7, para. 80, with effect for corporation tax purposes for accounting periods ending on or after 1 April 2010, for income tax and capital gains tax purposes for the tax year 2010–11 and subsequent tax years, and for petroleum revenue tax purposes for chargeable periods beginning on or after 1 July 2010.

59H Balancing of instalments for the purposes of section 59G

59H(1) Subsection (2) applies for the purposes of section 59G(2)(b).

59H(2) The instalments to be paid before the due date are balanced by those to be paid after it if the time value of the instalments to be paid before that date is equal, or approximately equal, to the time value of the instalments to be paid after it.

59H(3) The time value of the instalments to be paid before the due date is the total of the time value of each of the instalments to be paid before that date (and the time value of the instalments to be paid after that date is to be read accordingly).

59H(4) The time value of an instalment is–

$$A \times T$$

where–

A is the amount of the instalment, and

T is the number of days before, or after, the due date that the instalment is to be paid.

59H(5) The Commissioners for Her Majesty's Revenue and Customs may by regulations make provision for the purpose of determining when an amount is approximately equal to another amount.

59H(6) Regulations under this section may make different provision for different cases.

History – S. 59H inserted by TIOPA 2010, s. 371 and Sch. 7, para. 80, with effect for corporation tax purposes for accounting periods ending on or after 1 April 2010, for income tax and capital gains tax purposes for the tax year 2010–11 and subsequent tax years, and for petroleum revenue tax purposes for chargeable periods beginning on or after 1 July 2010.

PART VI – COLLECTION AND RECOVERY

Cross references – SSCBA 1992, s. 11A: Pt. VI applies, with the necessary modifications, in relation to Class 2 contributions under s. 11(2) as if those contributions were income tax chargeable under ITTOIA 2005, Pt. 2, Ch. 2 in respect of profits of a trade, profession or vocation which is not carried on wholly outside the UK, with effect for the tax year 2015–16 and subsequent tax years.

60 Issue of demand notes and receipts

60(1) Every collector shall, when the tax becomes due and payable, make demand of the respective sums given to him in charge to collect, from the persons charged therewith, or at the places of their last abode, or on the premises in respect of which the tax is charged, as the case may require.

60(2) On payment of the tax, the collector shall if so requested give a receipt.

DISTRAINT AND POINDING

61 Distraint by collectors

61(1) If a person neglects or refuses to pay the sum charged, upon demand made by the collector, the collector may distrain upon the goods and chattels of the person charged (in this section referred to as **"the person in default"**).

61(1A) [Omitted by FA 2008, s. 129 and Sch. 43, para. 1(3).]

61(2) For the purpose of levying any such distress, a justice of the peace, on being satisfied by information on oath that there is reasonable ground for believing that a person is neglecting or refusing to pay a sum charged, may issue a warrant in writing authorising a collector to break open, in the daytime, any house or premises, calling to his assistance any constable.

Every such constable shall, when so required, aid and assist the collector in the execution of the warrant and in levying the distress in the house or premises.

61(3) A levy or warrant to break open shall be executed by, or under the direction of, and in the presence of, the collector.

61(4) A distress levied by the collector shall be kept for five days, at the costs and charges of the person in default.

61(5) If the person in default does not pay the sum due, together with the costs and charges, the distress shall be appraised by one or more independent persons appointed by the collector, and shall be sold by public auction by the collector for payment of the sum due and all costs and charges.

Any overplus coming by the distress, after the deduction of the costs and charges and of the sum due, shall be restored to the owner of the goods distrained.

61(6) The Treasury may by regulations make provision with respect to–

(a) the fees chargeable on or in connection with the levying of distress, and

(b) the costs and charges recoverable where distress has been levied;

and any such regulations shall be made by statutory instrument which shall be subject to annulment in pursuance of a resolution of the House of Commons.

61(7) This section extends only to Northern Ireland.

History – In s. 61(1), the words from "(a) in England and Wales, use the procedure in Schedule 12 to the Tribunals, Courts and Enforcement Act 2007 (taking control of goods) to recover that sum; (b) in Northern Ireland," omitted by FA 2008, s. 129 and Sch. 43, para. 1(2) with effect from 6 April 2014 (SI 2014/906, art. 2).

In s. 61(1), the words "– (a) in England and Wales, use the procedure in Schedule 12 to the Tribunals, Courts and Enforcement Act 2007 (taking control of goods) to recover that sum; (b) in Northern Ireland," inserted by TCEA 2007, s. 62(3) and Sch. 13, para. 33(2), with effect from 6 April 2014 (SI 2014/768, art. 2).

In s. 61(1), the words "the collector may … person in default)" substituted by FA 1989, s. 152 with effect from 1 February 1994 by virtue of SI 1994/87, the appointed day order for the purposes of FA 1989, s. 152(7).

S. 61(1A) omitted by FA 2008, s. 129 and Sch. 43, para. 1(3) with effect from 6 April 2014 (SI 2014/906, art. 2).
S. 61(1A) inserted by TCEA 2007, s. 62(3) and Sch. 13, para. 33(3), with effect from 6 April 2014 (SI 2014/768, art. 2).
In s. 61(2), the words "a justice of the peace … authorising a collector to" substituted by FA 1989, s. 152 with effect from 1 February 1994 by virtue of SI 1994/87, the appointed day order for the purposes of FA 1989, s. 152(7).
In s. 61(4), the words "in default" substituted by FA 1989, s. 152 with effect from 1 February 1994 by virtue of SI 1994/87, the appointed day order for the purposes of FA 1989, s. 152(7).
In s. 61(5), the words "in default" substituted; the words "within the said five days" which preceded the words ", the distress" omitted, the words "one or more independent … the collector" substituted and certain words which preceded "any overplus" omitted by FA 1989, s. 152 with effect from 1 February 1994 by virtue of SI 1994/87, the appointed day order for the purposes of FA 1989, s. 152(7).
S. 61(6) inserted by FA 1989, s. 152 with effect from 1 February 1994 by virtue of SI 1994/87, the appointed day order for the purposes of FA 1989, s. 152(7).
S. 61(7) inserted by FA 2008, s. 129 and Sch. 43, para. 1(4), with effect from 6 April 2014 (SI 2014/906, art. 2).

62 Priority of claim for tax

62(1) If at any time at which any goods or chattels belonging to any person (in this section referred to as "**the person in default**") are liable to be taken by virtue of any execution or other process, warrant, or authority whatever, or by virtue of any assignment, on any account or pretence whatever, except at the suit of the landlord for rent, the person in default is in arrears in respect of any such sums as are referred to in subsection (1A) below, the goods or chattels may not be so taken unless on demand made by the collector the person at whose suit the execution or seizure is made, or to whom the assignment was made, pays or causes to be paid to the collector, before the sale or removal of the goods or chattels, all such sums as have fallen due at or before the date of seizure.

62(1A) The sums referred to in subsection (1) above are–

(a) sums due from the person in default on account of deductions of income tax from taxable earnings (as defined by section 10 of ITEPA 2003) paid during the period of twelve months next before the date of seizure, being deductions which the person in default was liable to make under PAYE regulations less the amount of the repayments of income tax which he was liable to make during that period; and

(b) sums due from the person in default in respect of deductions required to be made by him for that period under section 61 of the Finance Act 2004 (sub-contractors in the construction industry).

62(2) If the sums referred to in subsection (1) above are not paid within ten days of the date of the demand referred to in that subsection, the collector may distrain the goods and chattels notwithstanding the seizure or assignment, and may proceed to the sale thereof, as prescribed by this Act, for the purpose of obtaining payment of the whole of those sums, and the reasonable costs and charges attending such distress and sale, and every collector so doing shall be indemnified by virtue of this Act.

62(3) [Repealed by FA 1985, Sch. 27, Pt. X, with effect from 19 March 1985 and (so far as unrepealed) by FA 1989, Sch. 17, Pt. VIII.]

62(4) This section does not extend to England and Wales.

History – In s. 62(1), the words from the beginning to first "are", from "the person in default" to "the collector", and "such sums" to the end substituted by FA 1989, s. 153.
In s. 62(1A)(a), the words "taxable earnings (as defined by section 10 of ITEPA 2003)" substituted by ITEPA 2003, Sch. 6, para. 132(a) which has effect for the tax year 2003–04 and subsequent tax years.
In s. 62(1A)(a), the words "PAYE regulations" substituted by ITEPA 2003, Sch. 6, para. 132(b) which has effect for the tax year 2003–04 and subsequent tax years.
In s. 62(1A)(b), the words "section 61 of the Finance Act 2004" substituted by FA 2004, s. 76 and Sch. 12, para. 4 with effect from 6 April 2007 (FA 2004, s. 77)
S. 62(1A) inserted by FA 1989, s. 153.
In s. 62(2) the words from the beginning to "the collector may", and the words "may proceed" and "those sums" substituted by FA 1989, s. 153.
S. 62(3) dealt with development land tax.
S. 62(4) inserted by TCEA 2007, s. 62(3) and Sch. 13, para. 34, with effect from 6 April 2014 (SI 2014/768, art. 2).

64 Priority of claim for tax in Scotland

64(1) If at any time at which any moveable goods and effects belonging to any person (in this section referred to as "**the person in default**") are liable to be taken by virtue of any diligence whatever, or by any assignation, the person in default is in arrears in respect of any such sums as are referred to in subsection (1A) below, the goods and effects may not be so taken unless on demand made by the collector the person proceeding to take the said goods and effects pays such sums as have fallen due at or before the date of poinding or, as the case may be, other diligence or assignation.

64(1A) The sums referred to in subsection (1) above are–

(a) sums due from the person in default on account of deductions of income tax from taxable earnings (as defined by section 10 of ITEPA 2003) paid during the period of twelve months next before the date of poinding, being deductions which the person in default was liable to make under PAYE regulations less the amount of the repayments of income tax which he was liable to make during that period; and

69(3) Those provisions are–

(a) sections 61, 63 and 65 to 68 of this Act;

(b) section 35(2)(g)(i) of the Crown Proceedings Act 1947 (rules of court: restriction of set-off or counterclaim where proceedings, or set-off or counterclaim, relate to tax) and any rules of court imposing any such restriction;

(c) section 35(2)(b) of that Act as set out in section 50 of that Act (which imposes corresponding restrictions in Scotland).

History – In the heading to s. 69, the word ", surcharge", which appeared after the word "penalty", omitted by SI 2011/702, art. 6(c), with effect from 1 April 2011, but subject to SI 2011/702, art. 20, which provides that the omission does not have effect in relation to a return or other document which is required to be made or delivered to HMRC, or an amount of tax which is payable, in relation to the tax year 2009–10 or any previous tax year.

S. 69(1)(b) substituted by SI 2011/702, art. 6(a), with effect from 1 April 2011, but subject to SI 2011/702, art. 20, which provides that the substitution does not have effect in relation to a return or other document which is required to be made or delivered to HMRC, or an amount of tax which is payable, in relation to the tax year 2009–10 or any previous tax year.

S. 69(1)(d) (and the word "; and" at the end of s. 69(1)(c)) inserted by SI 2011/701, art. 7, with effect from 31 October 2011.

In s. 69(2), the word ", surcharge", which appeared after the word "penalty", omitted by SI 2011/702, art. 6(b), with effect from 1 April 2011, but subject to SI 2011/702, art. 20, which provides that the omission does not have effect in relation to a return or other document which is required to be made or delivered to HMRC, or an amount of tax which is payable, in relation to the tax year 2009–10 or any previous tax year.

S. 69 substituted by FA 2001, s. 89(2) for proceedings begun (or a counterclaim made) after 11 May 2001 and to a set-off first claimed after that date.

In former s. 69 the words "or under Schedule 18 to the Finance Act 1998" inserted by FA 1998, s. 117(3) and Sch. 19, para. 31 with effect in relation to accounting periods ending on or after 1 July 1999, the corporation tax self-assessment appointed day by virtue of FA 1994, s. 199(2), (3) and SI 1998/3173 (C. 78).

In former s. 69 before paragraph (a) the words "or recoverable under section 826(8A) of the principal Act as if it were interest so charged" inserted by FA 1998, s. 35 and Sch. 4, para. 3 with effect in relation to accounting periods ending on or after 1 July 1999, the corporation tax self-assessment appointed day (see note above). Former s. 69 after paragraph (c) the words "or if it is interest recoverable under section 826(8A) of the principal Act," inserted by FA 1998, s. 35 and Sch. 4, para. 3 with effect in relation to accounting periods ending on or after 1 July 1999, the self-assessment appointed day (see note above).

In former s. 69 the words "A penalty imposed under … Part IX of this Act" substituted for the former words "Interest charged under Part IX of this Act", and the words "if it is a penalty or surcharge …interest on, tax" substituted for the former words "if it is interest on tax" by FA 1994, s. 196 and Sch. 19, para. 20, in so far as it relates to income tax and capital gains tax, as respects the year 1996–97 and subsequent years of assessment.

Former s. 69 previously amended by F(No. 2)A 1987, s. 86(1), with respect to accounting periods ending after 30 September 1993 (under Pay and File) by virtue of SI 1992/3066, art. 3.

70 Evidence

70(1) [Omitted by FA 2008, s. 138 and Sch. 44, para. 1.]

70(2) [Omitted by FA 2008, s. 138 and Sch. 44, para. 1.]

70(3) [Ceases to have effect by virtue of FA 1994, s. 196 and Sch. 19, para. 21(2).]

70(4) A written statement as to the wages, salaries, fees, and other earnings or amounts treated as earnings paid for any period to the person against whom proceedings are brought under section 65, 66 or 67 of this Act, purporting to be signed by his employer for that period or by any responsible person in the employment of the employer, shall in such proceedings be prima facie evidence that the wages, salaries, fees and other earnings or amounts treated as earnings therein stated to have been paid to the person charged have in fact been so paid.

70(5) In subsection (4) **"earnings or amounts treated as earnings"** means earnings or amounts treated as earnings which constitute employment income (see section 7(2)(a) or (b) of ITEPA 2003).

History – S. 70(1) omitted by FA 2008, s. 138 and Sch. 44, para. 1 with effect from 21 July 2008.

S. 70(2) omitted by FA 2008, s. 138 and Sch. 44, para. 1 with effect from 21 July 2008.

In former s. 70(2)(a), the words ", the principal Act or ITEPA 2003" substituted for the words "or the principal Act" by ITEPA 2003, Sch. 6, para. 135(2) which has effect for the tax year 2003–04 and subsequent tax years.

In former s. 70(2)(a), the words "payable under any provision of this Act or the principal Act" substituted for the words "payable under Part IX of this Act" by FA 2001, s. 89(3) applicable to certificates tendered in evidence after 11 May 2001.

In s. 70(2)(a), the words "or under Schedule 18 to the Finance Act 1998" inserted by FA 1998, s. 117(3) and Sch. 19, para. 19(32) with effect in relation to accounting periods ending on or after 1 July 1999, the corporation tax self-assessment appointed day by virtue of FA 1994, s. 199(2), (3) and SI 1998/3173 (C. 78).

S. 70(2)(a) and (b) substituted for the former words "that interest is payable under section 86 or 87 of this Act and that payment of the interest has not been made to him, or, to the best of his knowledge and belief, to any other collector, or to any person acting on his behalf or on behalf of another collector" by FA 1994, s. 196 and Sch. 19, para. 21(1), and s. 70(3) repealed by virtue of FA 1994, s. 196 and Sch. 19, para. 21(2), in relation to income tax and capital gains tax, as respects the year 1996–97 and subsequent years of assessment and in relation to corporation tax, as respects accounting periods ending on or after the appointed day (1 July 1999 by virtue of FA 1994, s. 199(2), (3) and SI 1998/3173 (C. 78)).

S. 70(3) substituted by FA 1989, s. 160(3).

In s. 70(4), the words "earnings or amounts treated as earnings" substituted for the words "emoluments" by ITEPA 2003, Sch. 6, para. 135(3) which has effect for the tax year 2003–04 and subsequent tax years.

S. 70(5) inserted by ITEPA 2003, Sch. 6, para. 135(4) which has effect for the tax year 2003–04 and subsequent tax years.

70A Payments by cheque

70A(1) For the purposes of this Act and the provisions mentioned in subsection (2) below, where–

(a) any payment to an officer of the Board or the Board is made by cheque, and

(b) the cheque is paid on its first presentation to the banker on whom it is drawn, the payment shall be treated as made on the day on which the cheque was received by the officer or the Board.

70A(2) The provisions are–

(a) sections 824 to 826 of the principal Act (repayment supplements and interest on tax overpaid);

(b) section 283 of the 1992 Act (repayment supplements); and

(c) section 102 of the Finance Act 2009 (repayment interest).

70A(3) This section is subject to regulations under section 95(1) of the Finance Act 2007 (payment by cheque).

History – S. 70A(2)(c) (and the "; and" before it) inserted (and the "and" after (a) omitted) by SI 2014/992, art. 4(b), with effect from 6 May 2014 in relation to payments which are due and payable in respect of the tax year 2014–15 and subsequent tax years.
S. 70A(3) inserted by FA 2007, s. 95(7), with effect from Royal Assent 19 July 2007.
S. 70A inserted by FA 1994, s. 196 and Sch. 19, para. 22, as respects cheques received on or after 6 April 1996.

PART X – PENALTIES, ETC.

Cross references – SSCBA 1992, s. 16(1)(b): Pt. X applies, with the necessary modifications, in relation to Class 4 contributions as if those contributions were income tax chargeable under ITTOIA 2005, Pt. 2, Ch. 2 in respect of the profits of a trade, profession or vocation which is not carried on wholly outside the UK.
SSCBA 1992, s. 11A: Pt. 10 applies, with the necessary modifications, in relation to Class 2 contributions under s. 11(2) as if those contributions were income tax chargeable under ITTOIA 2005, Pt. 2, Ch. 2 in respect of profits of a trade, profession or vocation which is not carried on wholly outside the UK, with effect for the tax year 2015–16 and subsequent tax years.

97A Two or more tax-geared penalties in respect of same tax

97A Where two or more penalties–

(a) are incurred by any person and fall to be determined by reference to any income tax or capital gains tax with which he is chargeable for a year of assessment,

(b) [Repealed by FA 1998, s. 117(3) and Sch. 19, para. 37, s. 165 and Sch. 27, Pt. III(28).]

each penalty after the first shall be so reduced that the aggregate amount of the penalties, so far as determined by reference to any particular part of the tax, does not exceed whichever is or, but for this section, would be the greater or greatest of them, so far as so determined.

History – S. 97A(b), and word "or" immediately preceding it, repealed by FA 1998, s. 117(3) and Sch. 19, para. 37, s. 165 and Sch. 27, Pt. III(28), with effect in relation to accounting periods ending on or after 1 July 1999, the appointed day by virtue of FA 1994, s. 199(2), (3) and SI 1998/3173 (C. 78).
S. 97A inserted by FA 1988, s. 129, with effect for 1988–89 and subsequent years of assessment, or for company accounting periods ending after 31 March 1989.

Cross references – FA 2016, Sch. 22, para. 21: disapplication of s. 97A in relation to an asset-based penalty imposed under FA 2016, Sch. 22.

98 Special returns, etc.

98(1) Subject to the provisions of this section and section 98A below, where any person–

(a) has been required, by a notice served under or for the purposes of any of the provisions specified in the first column of the Table below, to deliver any return or other document, to furnish any particulars, to produce any document, or to make anything available for inspection, and he fails to comply with the notice, or

(b) fails to furnish any information, give any certificate or produce any document or record in accordance with any of the provisions specified in the second column of the Table below,

he shall be liable, subject to subsections (3) and (4) below–

(i) to a penalty not exceeding £300, and

(ii) if the failure continues after a penalty is imposed under paragraph (i) above, to a further penalty or penalties not exceeding £60 for each day on which the failure continues after the day on which the penalty under paragraph (i) above was imposed (but excluding any day for which a penalty under this paragraph has already been imposed).

98(2) Subject to section 98A below, where a person fraudulently or negligently furnishes, gives, produces or makes any incorrect information, certificate, document, record or declaration of a kind mentioned in any of the provisions specified in either column of the Table below, he shall be liable to a penalty not exceeding £3,000.

98(3) No penalty shall be imposed under subsection (1) above in respect of a failure within paragraph (a) of that subsection at any time after the failure has been remedied.

98(4) No penalty shall be imposed under paragraph (ii) of subsection (1) above in respect of a failure within paragraph (b) of that subsection at any time after the failure has been remedied.

98(4A) [Not relevant to National Insurance contributions.]

98(4B) [Not relevant to National Insurance contributions.]

98(4C) [Not relevant to National Insurance contributions.]

98(4D) [Not relevant to National Insurance contributions.]

98(4DA) [Not relevant to National Insurance contributions.]

98(4E) [Not relevant to National Insurance contributions.]

98(4F) [Not relevant to National Insurance contributions.]

98(5) [Omitted by FA 2009, s. 37 and Sch. 17, para. 2(a).]

TABLE

1	2

Part III of this Act	In the principal Act–
	section 310(1), (2), (2A) and (3);
	regulations under section 333;
	section 375(5);
	regulations under section 444BB;
	regulations under section 444BD;
	section 552;
	regulations under section 552ZA(6);
	regulations under section 552ZB;
	regulations under paragraph 7 of Schedule 14;
	Schedule 15, paragraph 14(4);
	Regulations under section 151 of the 1992 Act.

Regulations under section 59E of this Act	Regulations 16 and 17 of the Income Tax (Interest Relief) Regulations 1982.
In the principal Act– section 310(4) and (5); regulations under section 333; Regulations under section 151 of the 1992 Act.	Sections 45B(5) and (6), 45G(4) and (5), 45I(5) and (6), 118–120, 145(2) and (3) and 203 of the Capital Allowances Act. section 12ADA of this Act
Paragraph 2(9) of Schedule 1 to the 1992 Act.	Paragraph 12 of Schedule 4ZA to the 1992 Act
Section 98 of the 1992 Act	Paragraphs 2 to 6 of Schedule 5A to the 1992 Act.
Section 73 of the Finance Act 1989.	Regulation 11(2) of the Income Tax (Manufactured Overseas Dividends) Regulations 1993.
Paragraph 1(7) of Schedule 1 to the 1992 Act	Regulations under section 73 of the Finance Act 1995.
Paragraph 66 of Schedule 15 to the Finance Act 2000.	Paragraph 64 or 65 of Schedule 15 to the Finance Act 2000.
Paragraph 10 of Schedule 34 to the Finance Act 2002.	Paragraph 93(2) of Schedule 22 to the Finance Act 2000.
Section 421J(4) of ITEPA 2003	Paragraph 129 of Schedule 22 to the Finance Act 2000.
Regulations under section 715 of ITEPA 2003	Paragraph 6 of Schedule 34 to the Finance Act 2002.
Paragraph 93 of Schedule 2 to ITEPA 2003	Regulations under section 589 of ITEPA 2003
Paragraph 45 of Schedule 3 to ITEPA 2003	Regulations under section 715 of ITEPA 2003
Paragraph 33 of Schedule 4 to ITEPA 2003	PAYE regulations
Paragraph 51 of Schedule 5 to ITEPA 2003	Regulations under section 65(2), 69(1), 70(1)(a) or (c) or 71 of the Finance Act 2004
Regulations under section 70(3) of the Finance Act 2004	Regulations under section 251(1)(a) or (4) of the Finance Act 2004
Section 401B of ITTOIA 2005	Section 75(4) of ITTOIA 2005
Section 421A of ITTOIA 2005	Regulations under Chapter 3 of Part 6 of ITTOIA 2005
Regulations under Chapter 3 of Part 6 of ITTOIA 2005	Section 37(3) of the Finance Act 2005

1	2
Section 40(1) of the Finance Act 2005	Section 37(6) of the Finance Act 2005
Regulations under section 17(3) of the Finance (No. 2) Act 2005.	Section 106 of FA 2006 as modified by Schedule 17 of that Act
Sections 242 and 243(1) and (2) of ITA 2007	Section 116 of FA 2006
Sections 257GG and 257GH(1) and (2) of ITA 2007	Regulations under section 116 of FA 2006
Sections 257SG and 257SH(1) and (2) of ITA 2007	Section 130 of FA 2006
Section 312A of ITA 2007	Sections 240 and 241 of ITA 2007
Regulations under Chapter 5 of Part 6 of ITA 2007	Sections 257GE and 257GF of ITA 2007
Section 748(1) and (2) of ITA 2007	Sections 257SE and 257SF of ITA 2007
Section 771 of ITA 2007	Section 271(1) of ITA 2007
Regulations under section 871(1) of ITA 2007	Regulations under Chapter 5 of Part 6 of ITA 2007
Regulations under section 969(1) of ITA 2007	Section 373 of ITA 2007
Regulations under section 971(1) of ITA 2007	Regulations under section 871(1) of ITA 2007
Regulations 21 and 22 of the Income Tax (Purchased Life Annuities) Regulations 2008.	Chapter 15 of Part 15 of ITA 2007
Section 31(3) and (4) of CTA 2010	Chapter 16 of Part 15 of ITA 2007
Section 465(3) and (4) of CTA 2010	Regulations under section 969(1) of ITA 2007
Section 832 of CTA 2010	Regulations under section 971(1) of ITA 2007
Section 1052(4) and (5) of CTA 2010	Regulations under section 973(1) of ITA 2007
Section 1101(5) and (6) of CTA 2010	Section 75(4) of CTA 2009
Section 1102(4) and (5) of CTA 2010	paragraph 4 of Schedule 17 to FA 2009.
Regulations under section 283, 284, 285, 295 or 297 of TIOPA 2010	Regulations 7, 23 and 25 of the Income Tax (Purchased Life Annuities) Regulations 2008
Regulations under section 61(5) of the Finance Act 2012	Section 1046(1) to (4) of CTA 2010
	Section 1095 of CTA 2010
	Section 1096 of CTA 2010
	Section 1052(1) to (3) of CTA 2010
	Section 1101(1), (2) and (4) of CTA 2010
	Section 228 of TIOPA 2010
	Regulations under paragraph 16 of Schedule 18 to the Finance Act 2011
	Regulations under section 61(5) of the Finance Act 2012
	Regulations under paragraph 3 of Schedule 22 to the Finance Act 2013
	Regulations under paragraph 8 of Schedule 6 to the Finance Act 2014
	paragraph 17 or 18 of Schedule 4 to FA 2016;

The references in this Table to regulations under section 602 have effect only for the purpose of giving effect to any provision mentioned in paragraphs (a) and (b) of subsection (2) of that section.

References in this Table to sections 240, 241, 242 and 243(1) and (2) of ITA 2007 are to provisions that apply only in relation to shares issued after 5 April 2007.

History – S. 98(1), (2) amended, (3) substituted and (4) inserted by FA 1989, s. 164(1)–(4), (7) adding "Subject to section 98A below," and reference to subs. (4) and increasing the level of penalties for offences on or after 27 July 1989.

S. 98(5) omitted by FA 2009, s. 37 and Sch. 17, para. 2(a) with effect in relation to events taking place and transactions carried out on or after 1 July 2009.

Former s. 98(5) inserted by FA 1990, s. 68(3)(b) and s. 98(1) accordingly amended.

NIC Statutes

In s. 98, in the Table, entry for "Regulations under section 283, 284, 285, 295 or 297 of TIOPA 2010" omitted by F(No. 2)A 2017, s. 20 and Sch. 5, para. 3(1), with effect in relation to periods of account of worldwide groups that begin on or after 1 April 2017 (but see provisions of F(No. 2)A 2017, Sch. 5, para. 25–36 for transitional provisions). The entry read as follows: "Regulations under section 283, 284, 285, 295 or 297 of TIOPA 2010 – Regulations 7, 23 and 25 of the Income Tax (Purchased Life Annuities) Regulations 2008"

In s. 98, in the Table, entry for "Section 1109 of CTA 2010" omitted by FA 2016, s. 5(11) and Sch. 1, para. 51(11), with effect in relation to dividends paid or arising (or treated as paid), and other distributions made (or treated as made), in the tax year 2016–17 or at any later time.

In s. 98, in the Table, entry for "paragraph 17 or 18 of Schedule 4 to FA 2016;" inserted by FA 2016, s. 19(8) and Sch. 4, para. 20, with effect from 15 September 2016 (Royal Assent).

Cross references – SSCBA 1992, Sch. 1, para. 6(7): s. 98 applies to regulations made under that paragraph as it applies to regulations under ICTA 1988, s. 203 (PAYE).

98A Special penalties in the case of certain returns

98A(1) PAYE regulations or regulations under section 70(1)(a) or 71 of the Finance Act 2004 (sub-contractors) may provide that this section shall apply in relation to any specified provision of the regulations.

98A(2) Where this section applies in relation to a provision of regulations, any person who fails to make a return in accordance with the provision shall be liable–

(a) to a penalty or penalties of the relevant monthly amount for each month (or part of a month) during which the failure continues, but excluding any month after the twelfth or for which a penalty under this paragraph has already been imposed, and

(b) if the failure continues beyond twelve months, without prejudice to any penalty under paragraph (a) above, to a penalty not exceeding

(i) in the case of a provision of PAYE regulations, so much of the amount payable by him in accordance with the regulations for the year of assessment to which the return relates as remained unpaid at the end of 19th April after the end of that year, or

(ii) in the case of a provision of regulations under section 70(1)(a) or 71 of the Finance Act 2004, £3,000

98A(3) For the purposes of subsection (2)(a) above, the relevant monthly amount in the case of a failure to make a return–

(a) where the number of persons in respect of whom particulars should be included in the return is fifty or less, is £100, and

(b) where that number is greater than fifty, is £100 for each fifty such persons and an additional £100 where that number is not a multiple of fifty.

98A(4) [Omitted by FA 2007, s. 97 and Sch. 24, para. 29(a) and repealed by FA 2007, s. 114 and Sch. 27, Pt. 5(5).]

History – In s. 98A(1), the words "section 70(1)(a) or 71 of the Finance Act 2004 (sub-contractors)" substituted for the words "section 566(1) (sub-contractors) of the principal Act" by FA 2004, s. 76 and Sch. 12, para. 8(2), with effect from 6 April 2007 (FA 2004, s. 77).

In s. 98A(1), the words "PAYE regulations or regulations under section" substituted for the words "Regulations under section 203(2) (PAYE) or" by ITEPA 2003, Sch. 6, para. 138 which has effect for the tax year 2003–04 and subsequent tax years.

In s. 98A(2)(b)(i) created from existing text and s. 98(2)(b)(ii) inserted by FA 2004 s. 76 and Sch. 12, para. 8(3), with effect from 6 April 2007 (FA 2004, s. 77).

S. 98A(4) omitted by FA 2007, s. 97 and Sch. 24, para. 29(a) and repealed by FA 2007, s. 114 and Sch. 27, Pt. 5(5), with effect as follows by virtue of SI 2008/568, art. 2:

- 1 April 2008 in relation to relevant documents relating to tax periods commencing on or after that date;
- 1 April 2008 in relation to assessments falling within paragraph 2 for tax periods commencing on or after that date;
- 1 July 2008 in relation to relevant documents relating to claims under the Thirteenth Council Directive (arrangements for the refund of value added tax to persons not established in Community territory) for years commencing on or after that date;
- 1 January 2009 in relation to relevant documents relating to claims under the Eighth Council Directive (arrangements for the refund of value added tax to taxable persons not established in the territory of the country) for years commencing on or after that date;
- 1 April 2009 in relation to documents relating to all other claims for repayments of relevant tax made on or after 1 April 2009 which are not related to a tax period; and
- in any other case, 1 April 2009 in relation to documents given where a person's liability to pay relevant tax arises on or after that date.

However, no person will be liable to a penalty under Sch. 24 in respect of any tax period for which a return is required to be made before 1 April 2009.

In s. 98A(4)(a) "(in the case of a provision of PAYE regulations) or a period (in the case of a provision of regulations under section 70(1)(a) or 71 of the Finance Act 2004)" inserted by FA 2004, s. 76 and Sch. 12, para. 8(4), with effect from 6 April 2007 (FA 2004, s. 77).

S. 98A inserted by FA 1989, s. 165 with effect from 27 July 1989, but with s. 98A(2)(a) modified as respects failures before 20 May 1995 (the day appointed by virtue of SI 1994/2503 (C. 50)).

Cross references – SSCBA 1992, Sch. 1, para. 7: application of s. 98A to returns of National Insurance contributions.

98C Notification under Part 7 of Finance Act 2004

98C(1) A person who fails to comply with any of the provisions of Part 7 of the Finance Act 2004 (disclosure of tax avoidance schemes) mentioned in subsection (2) below shall be liable–

(a) to a penalty not exceeding

(i) in the case of a provision mentioned in paragraph (a), (b), (c) or (ca) of that subsection, £600 for each day during the initial period (but see also subsections (2A), (2B) and (2ZC) below), and

(ii) in any other case, £5,000, and

(b) if the failure continues after a penalty is imposed under paragraph (a) above, to a further penalty or penalties not exceeding £600 for each day on which the failure continues after the day on which the penalty under paragraph (a) was imposed (but excluding any day for which a penalty under this paragraph has already been imposed).

98C(2) Those provisions are–

(a) section 308(1) and (3) (duty of promoter in relation to notifiable proposals and notifiable arrangements),

(b) section 309(1) (duty of person dealing with promoter outside United Kingdom),

(c) section 310 (duty of parties to notifiable arrangements not involving promoter),

(ca) section 310A (duty to provide further information requested by HMRC),

(cb) section 310C (duty of promoters to provide updated information),

(d) section 312(2) (duty of promoter to notify client of reference number),

(da) section 312A(2) and (2A) (duty of client to notify parties of reference number),

(daa) section 312B (duty of client to provide information to promoter),

(db) section 313ZA (duty of promoter to provide details of clients),

(dc) section 313ZB (enquiry following disclosure of client details),

(dca) section 313ZC (duty of employer to provide details of employees etc),

(e) sections 313A and 313B (duty of promoter to respond to inquiry),

(f) section 313C (duty of introducer to give details of persons who have provided information or have been provided with information), and

(g) section 316A (duty to provide additional information).

98C(2ZA) In this section **"the initial period"** means the period–

(a) beginning with the relevant day, and

(b) ending with the earlier of the day on which the penalty under subsection (1)(a)(i) is determined and the last day before the failure ceases;

and for this purpose **"the relevant day"** is the day specified in relation to the failure in the following table.

TABLE

Failure	*Relevant day*
A failure to comply with subsection (1) or (3) of section 308 in so far as the subsection applies by virtue of an order under section 306A	The first day after the end of the period prescribed under section 306A(6)
A failure to comply with subsection (1) or (3) of section 308 in so far as the subsection applies by virtue of an order under section 308A(2)	The first day after the end of the period prescribed under subsections (5) and (6)(a) of section 308A (as it may have been extended by a direction under subsection (6)(b) of that section)
Any other failure to comply with subsection (1) of section 308	The first day after the end of the period prescribed under that subsection
Any other failure to comply with subsection (3) of section 308	The first day after the end of the period prescribed under that subsection
A failure to comply with subsection (1) of section 309	The first day after the end of the period prescribed under that subsection
A failure to comply with section 310	The first day after the latest time by which section 310 must be complied with in the case concerned
A failure to comply with section 310A	The first day after the end of the period within which the person must comply with section 310A.

98C(2ZB) The amount of a penalty under subsection (1)(a)(i) is to be arrived at after taking account of all relevant considerations, including the desirability of its being set at a level which appears appropriate for deterring the person, or other persons, from similar failures to comply on future occasions having regard (in particular)–

(a) in the case of a penalty for a promoter's failure to comply with section 308(1) or (3) or section 310A, to the amount of any fees received, or likely to have been received, by the promoter in connection with the notifiable proposal (or arrangements implementing the notifiable proposal), or with the notifiable arrangements, and

(b) in the case of a penalty for a relevant person's failure to comply with section 309(1), 310 or 310A, to the amount of any advantage gained, or sought to be gained, by the relevant person in relation to any tax prescribed under section 306(1)(b) in relation to the notifiable arrangements.

98C(2ZBA) In subsection (2ZB)–

(a) **"promoter"** has the same meaning as in Part 7 of the Finance Act 2004, and

(b) **"relevant person"** means a person who enters into any transaction forming part of notifiable arrangements within the meaning of that Part.

98C(2ZC) If the maximum penalty under subsection (1)(a)(i) above appears inappropriately low after taking account of those considerations, the penalty is to be of such amount not exceeding £1 million as appears appropriate having regard to those considerations.

98C(2ZD) Where it appears to an officer of Revenue and Customs that a penalty under subsection (1)(a)(i) above has been determined on the basis that the initial period begins with a day later than that which the officer considers to be the relevant day, an officer of Revenue and Customs may commence proceedings for a re-determination of the penalty.

98C(2ZE) The Treasury may by regulations vary–

(a) any of the sums for the time being specified in subsection (1) above, and

(b) the sum specified in subsection (2ZC) above.

98C(2A) Where a failure to comply with a provision mentioned in subsection (2) concerns a proposal or arrangements in respect of which an order has been made under section 306A of the Finance Act 2004 (doubt as to notifiability), the amounts specified in subsection (1)(a)(i) and (b) above shall be increased to the prescribed sum in relation to days falling after the prescribed period.

98C(2B) Where a failure to comply with a provision mentioned in subsection (2) concerns a proposal or arrangements in respect of which an order has been made under section 314A of the Finance Act 2004 (order to disclose), the amounts specified in subsection (1)(a)(i) and (b) above shall be increased to the prescribed sum in relation to days falling after the prescribed period.

98C(2C) In subsection (2A) and (2B)–

(a) **"the prescribed sum"** means a sum prescribed by the Treasury by regulations, and

(b) **"the prescribed period"** means a period beginning with the date of the order under section 306A or 314A and prescribed by the Commissioners by regulations.

98C(2D) The making of an order under section 306A or 314A of that Act does not of itself mean that, for the purposes of section 118(2) of this Act, a person either did or did not have a reasonable excuse for non-compliance before the order was made.

98C(2E) Where an order is made under section 306A or 314A of that Act then for the purposes of section 118(2) of this Act–

(a) the person identified in the order as the promoter of the proposal or arrangements cannot, in respect of any time after the end of the period mentioned in subsection (2B), rely on doubt as to notifiability as an excuse for failure to comply with section 308 of that Act, and

(b) any delay in compliance with that section after the end of that period is unreasonable unless attributable to something other than doubt as to notifiability.

98C(2EA) Where a person fails to comply with–

(a) section 309 of that Act and the promoter for the purposes of that section is a monitored promoter for the purposes of Part 5 of the Finance Act 2014, or

(b) section 310 of that Act and the arrangements for the purposes of that section are arrangements of such a monitored promoter,

then for the purposes of section 118(2) of this Act legal advice which the person took into account is to be disregarded in determining whether the person had a reasonable excuse, if the advice was given or procured by that monitored promoter.

98C(2EB) In determining for the purpose of section 118(2) of this Act whether or not a person who is a monitored promoter within the meaning of Part 5 of the Finance Act 2014 had a reasonable excuse for a failure to do anything required to be done under a provision mentioned in subsection (2), reliance on legal advice is to be taken automatically not to constitute a reasonable excuse if either–

(a) the advice was not based on a full and accurate description of the facts, or

(b) the conclusions in the advice that the person relied on were unreasonable.

98C(2F) Regulations under this section–

(a) may include incidental or transitional provision,

(b) shall be made by statutory instrument,

(c) in the case of regulations under subsection (2C)(a), shall not be made unless a draft has been laid before and approved by resolution of the House of Commons, and

(d) in the case of regulations under subsection (2ZE) or (2C)(b), shall be subject to annulment in pursuance of a resolution of the House of Commons.

98C(3) A person who fails to comply with subsection (1) of section 313 of the Finance Act 2004 (duties of parties to notifiable arrangements to notify Board of reference number, etc.) or regulations under subsection (3) of that section shall be liable to a penalty not exceeding the relevant sum.

98C(4) In subsection (3) above **"the relevant sum"** means–

(a) in relation to a person not falling within paragraph (b) or (c) below, £5,000 in respect of each scheme to which the failure relates,

(b) in relation to a person who has previously failed to comply with subsection (1) of section 313 or regulations under subsection (3) of that section on one (and only one) occasion during the period of 36 months ending with the date on which the current failure to comply with that provision began, £7,500 in respect of each scheme to which the current failure relates (whether or not the same as the scheme to which the previous failure relates), or

(c) in relation to a person who has previously failed to comply with subsection (1) of section 313 or regulations under subsection (3) of that section on two or more occasions during the period of 36 months ending with the date on which the current failure to comply with that provision began, £10,000 in respect of each scheme to which the current failure relates (whether or not the same as the schemes to which any of the previous failures relates).

98C(5) In subsection (4) above **"scheme"** means any notifiable arrangements within the meaning of Part 7 of the Finance Act 2004.

History – In s. 98C(1)(a)(i), ", (c) or (ca)" substituted for "or (c)" by FA 2014, s. 284(6), with effect from 17 July 2014.
S. 98C(1)(a)(i) and (ii) substituted for "£5,000" in s. 98C(1)(a) by FA 2010, s. 56 and Sch. 17, para. 10(2), with effect from 1 January 2011 (SI 2010/3019).
S. 98C(2)(ca) inserted by FA 2014, s. 284(7), with effect from 17 July 2014.
S. 98C(2)(cb) inserted by FA 2015, s. 117 and Sch. 17, para. 3 with effect from 26 March 2015.
S. 98C(2)(daa) inserted by FA 2013, s. 223(4), with effect from 17 July 2013.
In s 98C(2)(da) the words "and (2A)" inserted by FA 2015, s. 117 and Sch. 17, para. 8 with effect from 26 March 2015.
In s. 98C(2)(da), the word "and" omitted from the end by FA 2010, s. 56 and Sch. 17, para. 10(3)(a), with effect from 1 January 2011 (SI 2010/3019).
S. 98C(2)(db) inserted by FA 2010, s. 56 and Sch. 17, para. 10(3)(b), with effect from 1 January 2011 (SI 2010/3019).
S. 98C(2)(dc) inserted by FA 2013, s. 223(4), with effect from 17 July 2013.
S. 98C(2)(dca) inserted by FA 2015, s. 117 and Sch. 17, para. 11 with effect from 26 March 2015.
In s 98C(2)(f) the words "or have been provided with information" inserted by FA 2015, s. 117 and Sch. 17, para. 13 with effect from 26 March 2015.
S. 98C(2)(f), and the word "and" before it, inserted by FA 2010, s. 56 and Sch. 17, para. 10(3)(c), with effect from 1 January 2011 (SI 2010/3019).
S. 98C(2)(g), and the word "and" before it, inserted (and the word "and" preceding it omitted) by FA 2015, s. 117 and Sch. 17, para. 15 with effect from 26 March 2015.
In s. 98C(2), the word "312(2)" substituted for the word "312(1)" in paragraph (d) and, after that paragraph (but before the word "and"), para. (da) inserted by FA 2008, s. 116 and Sch. 38, para. 7(2), with effect from 1 November 2008 for purposes other than stamp duty land tax (SI 2008/1935), and with effect from 1 April 2010, for stamp duty land tax purposes (SI 2010/409).
In s. 98C(2), the word "or" at the end of paragraph (c) repealed by FA 2007, s. 114 and Sch. 27, Pt. 6(4) and paragraph (e) and the word ", and" preceding it inserted by FA 2007, s. 108(9)(a), with effect from 19 July 2007.
In s. 98C(2ZA), in the table, the entry relating to a failure to comply with FA 2004, s. 310A inserted by FA 2014, s. 284(8), with effect from 17 July 2014.
S. 98C(2ZA) inserted by FA 2010, s. 56 and Sch. 17, para. 10(4), with effect from 1 January 2011 (SI 2010/3019).
In s. 98C(2ZB)(a), the word "promoter's" substituted for the word "person's" by FA 2014, s. 284(9)(a)(i), with effect from 17 July 2014.
In s. 98C(2ZB)(a), the words "or section 310A" inserted by FA 2014, s. 284(9)(a)(ii), with effect from 17 July 2014.
In s. 98C(2ZB)(a), the word "promoter" substitutedfor the word "person" by FA 2014, s. 284(9)(a)(iii), with effect from 17 July 2014.
In s. 98C(2ZB)(b), the word "relevant" inserted before the word "person's" by FA 2014, s. 284(9)(b)(i), with effect from 17 July 2014.
In s. 98C(2ZB)(b), ", 310 or 310A" substituted for "or 310" by FA 2014, s. 284(9)(b)(ii), with effect from 17 July 2014.
In s. 98C(2ZB)(b), the word "relevant" inserted before the word "person" inserted by FA 2014, s. 284(9)(b)(iii), with effect from 17 July 2014.
S. 98C(2ZB) inserted by FA 2010, s. 56 and Sch. 17, para. 10(4), with effect from 1 January 2011 (SI 2010/3019).
S. 98C(2ZBA) inserted by FA 2014, s. 284(10), with effect from 17 July 2014.
S. 98C(2ZC) inserted by FA 2010, s. 56 and Sch. 17, para. 10(4), with effect from 1 January 2011 (SI 2010/3019).
S. 98C(2ZD) inserted by FA 2010, s. 56 and Sch. 17, para. 10(4), with effect from 1 January 2011 (SI 2010/3019).
S. 98C(2ZE) inserted by FA 2010, s. 56 and Sch. 17, para. 10(4), with effect from 1 January 2011 (SI 2010/3019).
In s. 98C(2A), the words "amounts specified in subsection (1)(a)(i) and (b) above shall be increased to the prescribed sum in relation to days falling after the prescribed period" substituted for the words "amount specified in subsection (1)(b) above shall be increased to the prescribed sum" by FA 2010, s. 56 and Sch. 17, para. 10(5), with effect from 1 January 2011 (SI 2010/3019).

In s. 98C(2B), the words "amounts specified in subsection (1)(a)(i) and (b)" substituted for the words "amount specified in subsection (1)(b)" by FA 2010, s. 56 and Sch. 17, para. 10(6), with effect from 1 January 2011 (SI 2010/3019).
In s. 98C(2C)(b), the words "306A or" inserted by FA 2010, s. 56 and Sch. 17, para. 10(7), with effect from 1 January 2011 (SI 2010/3019).
In s. 98C(2D), the words "306A or" inserted by FA 2010, s. 56 and Sch. 17, para. 10(8), with effect from 1 January 2011 (SI 2010/3019).
In s. 98C(2E), the words "306A or" inserted by FA 2010, s. 56 and Sch. 17, para. 10(9), with effect from 1 January 2011 (SI 2010/3019).
S. 98C(2EA) and (2EB) inserted by FA 2014, s. 275, with effect from 17 July 2014.
In s. 98C(2F), in the opening words, the words "this section" substituted for the words "subsection (2C)" by FA 2010, s. 56 and Sch. 17, para. 10(10)(a), with effect from 1 January 2011 (SI 2010/3019).
In s. 98C(2F)(c), the words "(2ZE) or" inserted by FA 2010, s. 56 and Sch. 17, para. 10(10)(b), with effect from 1 January 2011 (SI 2010/3019).
S. 98C(2A)–(2F) inserted by FA 2007, s. 108(9)(b), with effect from 19 July 2007.
In s. 98C(3), the words "penalty not exceeding the relevant sum" substituted for the words "penalty of the relevant sum" by FA 2015, s. 117 and Sch. 17, para. 18(a), with effect from 26 March 2015.
In s. 98C(3), the words "subsection(1) of section 313" substituted for the words "section 313(1)" and the words "or regulations under subsection (3) of that section" inserted by FA 2008, s. 116 and Sch. 38, para. 7(3), with effect from 1 November 2008 for purposes other than stamp duty land tax (SI 2008/1935), and with effect from 1 April 2010, for stamp duty land tax purposes (SI 2010/409).
In s. 98C(4)(a), the figure "£5,000" substituted for "£100"; in (b), the figure "£7,500" substituted for "£500"; and in (c), the figure "£10,000" substituted for "£1,000" by FA 2015, s. 117 and Sch. 17, para. 18(b), with effect from 26 March 2015.
In s. 98C(4), the words "subsection (1) of section 313 or regulations under subsection (3) of that section" substituted (in both places) for the words "313(1)" by FA 2008, s. 116 and Sch. 38, para. 7(4), with effect from 1 November 2008 for purposes other than stamp duty land tax (SI 2008/1935), and with effect from 1 April 2010, for stamp duty land tax purposes (SI 2010/409).
S. 98C inserted by FA 2004, s. 315(1) with effect from 1 August 2004.

100 Determination of penalties by officer of Board

100(1) Subject to subsection (2) below and except where proceedings for a penalty have been instituted under section 100D below, an officer of the Board authorised by the Board for the purposes of this section may make a determination imposing a penalty under any provision of the Taxes Acts and setting it at such amount as, in his opinion, is correct or appropriate.

100(2) [Not relevant to National Insurance contributions.]

100(2A) [Not relevant to National Insurance contributions.]

100(3) Notice of a determination of a penalty under this section shall be served on the person liable to the penalty and shall state the date on which it is issued and the time within which an appeal against the determination may be made.

100(4) After the notice of a determination under this section has been served the determination shall not be altered except in accordance with this section or on appeal.

100(5) If it is discovered by an officer of the Board authorised by the Board for the purposes of this section that the amount of a penalty determined under this section is or has become insufficient the officer may make a determination in a further amount so that the penalty is set at the amount which, in his opinion, is correct or appropriate.

100(6) [Not relevant to National Insurance contributions.]

History – In s. 100(1), the words "or a penalty has been imposed by the Commissioners under section 53 of this Act" which appeared after the word "below" omitted by SI 1994/1813, Sch. 1, para. 14, with effect from 1 September 1994.
S. 100 substituted by FA 1989, s. 167.

Cross references – SSCBA 1992, Sch. 1, para. 7: application of s. 100 to returns of National Insurance contributions.
SI 2001/1004, reg. 82: application with respect to National Insurance returns.

100A Provisions supplementary to section 100

100A(1) [Omitted by FA 2007, s. 97 and Sch. 24, para. 29(b) and repealed by FA 2007, s. 114 and Sch. 27, Pt. 5(5).]

100A(2) A penalty determined under section 100 above shall be due and payable at the end of the period of thirty days beginning with the date of the issue of the notice of determination.

100A(3) A penalty determined under section 100 above shall for all purposes be treated as if it were tax charged in an assessment and due and payable.

History – S. 100A(1) omitted by FA 2007, s. 97 and Sch. 24, para. 29(b) and repealed by FA 2007, s. 114 and Sch. 27, Pt. 5(5), with effect as follows by virtue of SI 2008/568, art. 2:

- 1 April 2008 in relation to relevant documents relating to tax periods commencing on or after that date;
- 1 April 2008 in relation to assessments falling within paragraph 2 for tax periods commencing on or after that date;
- 1 July 2008 in relation to relevant documents relating to claims under the Thirteenth Council Directive (arrangements for the refund of value added tax to persons not established in Community territory) for years commencing on or after that date;
- 1 January 2009 in relation to relevant documents relating to claims under the Eighth Council Directive (arrangements for the refund of value added tax to taxable persons not established in the territory of the country) for years commencing on or after that date;
- 1 April 2009 in relation to documents relating to all other claims for repayments of relevant tax made on or after 1 April 2009 which are not related to a tax period; and
- in any other case, 1 April 2009 in relation to documents given where a person's liability to pay relevant tax arises on or after that date.

However, no person will be liable to a penalty under Sch. 24 in respect of any tax period for which a return is required to be made before 1 April 2009.
S. 100A inserted by FA 1989, s. 167.

Cross references – SSCBA 1992, Sch. 1, para. 7: application of s. 100A to returns of National Insurance contributions.

100B Appeals against penalty determinations

100B(1) An appeal may be brought against the determination of a penalty under section 100 above and, subject to the following provisions of this section, the provisions of this Act relating to appeals shall have effect in relation to an appeal against such a determination as they have effect in relation to an appeal against an assessment to tax, except that references to the tribunal shall be taken to be references to the First-tier Tribunal.

100B(2) On an appeal against the determination of a penalty under section 100 above section 50(6) to (8) of this Act shall not apply but–

(a) in the case of a penalty which is required to be of a particular amount, the First-tier Tribunal may–
  (i) if it appears that no penalty has been incurred, set the determination aside,
  (ii) if the amount determined appears to be correct, confirm the determination, or
  (iii) if the amount determined appears to be incorrect, increase or reduce it to the correct amount,

(b) in the case of any other penalty, the First-tier Tribunal may–
  (i) if it appears that no penalty has been incurred, set the determination aside,
  (ii) if the amount determined appears to be appropriate, confirm the determination,
  (iii) if the amount determined appears to be excessive, reduce it to such other amount (including nil) as it considers appropriate, or
  (iv) if the amount determined appears to be insufficient, increase it to such amount not exceeding the permitted maximum as it considers appropriate.

100B(3) In addition to any right of appeal on a point of law under section 11(2) of the TCEA 2007, the person liable to the penalty may appeal to the Upper Tribunal against the amount of the penalty which has been determined under subsection (2), but not against any decision which falls under section 11(5)(d) and (e) of the TCEA 2007 and was made in connection with the determination of the amount of the penalty.

100B(3A) Section 11(3) and (4) of the TCEA 2007 applies to the right of appeal under subsection (3) as it applies to the right of appeal under section 11(2) of the TCEA 2007.

100B(3B) On an appeal under this section the Upper Tribunal has the same powers as are conferred on the First-tier Tribunal by virtue of this section.

History – In s. 100B(1), the words "sections 93 and 93A of this Act and", which appeared after the words "subject to", omitted by SI 2011/702, art. 9(a), with effect from 1 April 2011, but subject to SI 2011/702, art. 20, which provides that the omission does not have effect in relation to a return or other document which is required to be made or delivered to HMRC, or an amount of tax which is payable, in relation to the tax year 2009–10 or any previous tax year.
In s. 100B(1) the words "sections 93 and 93A" substituted for the words "sections 93, 93A and 95A" by SI 2009/571, art. 8 and Sch. 1, para. 12, with effect from 1 April 2009.
In s. 100B(1) the words ", except that references to the tribunal shall be taken to be references to the First-tier Tribunal" inserted by SI 2009/56, art. 3(1) and Sch. 1, para. 45(2), operative from 1 April 2009, subject to transitional and saving provisions in SI 2009/56, Sch. 3.
In s. 100B(1), reference to TMA 1970, s. 93, 93A and 95A, and in s. 100B(2), reference to TMA 1970, s. 93(8) and 93A(7), inserted by FA 1994, s. 196 and Sch. 19, para. 31, FA 1995, s. 115(7), in so far as it relates to income tax and corporation tax, as respects the year 1996–97 and subsequent years of assessment and, in so far as it relates to corporation tax, as respects accounting periods ending on or after 1 July 1999, the appointed day for corporation tax self-assessment by virtue of FA 1994, s. 199(2), (3) and SI 1998/3173 (C. 78).
In s. 100B(2), the word "On" substituted for the words "Subject to sections 93(8) and 93A(7) of this Act on" by SI 2011/702, art. 9(b), with effect from 1 April 2011, but subject to SI 2011/702, art. 20, which provides that the substitution does not have effect in relation to a return or other document which is required to be made or delivered to HMRC, or an amount of tax which is payable, in relation to the tax year 2009–10 or any previous tax year.
In s. 100B(2) the words "First-tier Tribunal" substituted for the word "Commissioners" twice; the words "to them" omitted seven times and in para. (b)(iii) and (iv) the words"as it considers" substituted for the words "as they consider" by SI 2009/56, art. 3(1) and Sch. 1, para. 45(3), operative from 1 April 2009, subject to transitional and saving provisions in SI 2009/56, Sch. 3.
S. 100B(3), (3A) and (3B) substituted for former s. 100B(3) by SI 2009/56, art. 3(1) and Sch. 1, para. 45(4), operative from 1 April 2009, subject to transitional and saving provisions in SI 2009/56, Sch. 3.
In former s. 100B(3), thewords "any right to have a case stated under regulation 22 of the General Commissioners Regulations or any right of appeal under section 56A" substituted by SI 1994/1813, Sch. 1, para. 15, with effect from 1 September 1994.
S. 100B inserted by FA 1989, s. 167.

Cross references – SSCBA 1992, Sch. 1, para. 7: application of s. 100B to returns of National Insurance contributions.

100C Penalty proceedings before First-tier Tribunal

History – *In the heading to s. 100C the words "First-tier Tribunal"* substituted for the word "Commissioners" by SI 2009/56, art. 3(1) and Sch. 1, para. 46(2), operative from 1 April 2009, subject to transitional and saving provisions in SI 2009/56, Sch. 3.

100C(1) An officer of the Board authorised by the Board for the purposes of this section may commence proceedings before the First-tier Tribunal for any penalty to which subsection (1) of section 100 above does not apply by virtue of subsection (2) of that section.

100C(1A) [Omitted by SI 2009/56, art. 3(1) and Sch. 1, para. 45(4).]

100C(2) The person liable to the penalty shall be a party to the proceedings.

100C(3) Any penalty determined by the First-tier Tribunal in proceedings under this section shall for all purposes be treated as if it were tax charged in an assessment and due and payable.

100C(4) In addition to any right of appeal on a point of law under section 11(2) of the TCEA 2007, the person liable to the penalty may appeal to the Upper Tribunal against the determination of a penalty in proceedings under subsection (1), but not against any decision which falls under section 11(5)(d) and (e) of the TCEA 2007 and was made in connection with the determination of the amount of the penalty.

100C(4A) Section 11(3) and (4) of the TCEA 2007 applies to the right of appeal under subsection (4) as it applies to the right of appeal under section 11(2) of the TCEA 2007.

100C(5) On any such appeal the Upper Tribunal may–

(a) if it appears that no penalty has been incurred, set the determination aside,

(b) if the amount determined appears to be appropriate, confirm the determination,

(c) if the amount determined appears to be excessive, reduce it to such other amount (including nil) as the Upper Tribunal considers appropriate, or

(d) if the amount determined appears to be insufficient, increase it to such amount not exceeding the permitted maximum as the Upper Tribunal considers appropriate.

History – In s. 100C(1) the words "First-tier Tribunal" substituted for the words "General or Special Commissioners" by SI 2009/56, art. 3(1) and Sch. 1, para. 46(3), operative from 1 April 2009, subject to transitional and saving provisions in SI 2009/56, Sch. 3.
S. 100C(1A) omitted by SI 2009/56, art. 3(1) and Sch. 1, para. 46(4), operative from 1 April 2009, subject to transitional and saving provisions in SI 2009/56, Sch. 3.
Former s. 100C(1A) inserted by FA 2004, s. 315(3) with effect from 1 August 2004.
S. 100C(2) substituted by SI 2009/56, art. 3(1) and Sch. 1, para. 46(5), operative from 1 April 2009, subject to transitional and saving provisions in SI 2009/56, Sch. 3.
In s. 100C(3) the words "First-tier Tribunal" substituted for the words "General or Special Commissioners" by SI 2009/56, art. 3(1) and Sch. 1, para. 46(6), operative from 1 April 2009, subject to transitional and saving provisions in SI 2009/56, Sch. 3.
S. 100C(4) and (4A) substituted for former s. 100C(4) by SI 2009/56, art. 3(1) and Sch. 1, para. 46(7), operative from 1 April 2009, subject to transitional and saving provisions in SI 2009/56, Sch. 3.
In s. 100C(5) the words "Upper Tribunal" substituted for the word "court" three times by SI 2009/56, art. 3(1) and Sch. 1, para. 46(8), operative from 1 April 2009, subject to transitional and saving provisions in SI 2009/56, Sch. 3.
S. 100C inserted by FA 1989, s. 167.

Cross references – SSCBA 1992, Sch. 1, para. 7: application of s. 100C to returns of National Insurance contributions.

100D Penalty proceedings before court

100D(1) Where in the opinion of the Board the liability of any person for a penalty arises by reason of the fraud of that or any other person, proceedings for the penalty may be instituted before the High Court or, in Scotland, the Court of Session as the Court of Exchequer in Scotland.

100D(2) Proceedings under this section which are not instituted (in England, Wales or Northern Ireland) under the Crown Proceedings Act 1947 by and in the name of the Board as an authorised department for the purposes of that Act shall be instituted–

(a) in England and Wales, in the name of the Attorney General,

(b) in Scotland, in the name of the Lord Advocate, and

(c) in Northern Ireland, in the name of the Attorney General for Northern Ireland.

100D(3) Any proceedings under this section instituted in England and Wales shall be deemed to be civil proceedings by the Crown within the meaning of Part II of the Crown Proceedings Act 1947 and any such proceedings instituted in Northern Ireland shall be deemed to be civil proceedings within the meaning of that Part of that Act as for the time being in force in Northern Ireland.

100D(4) If in proceedings under this section the court does not find that fraud is proved but consider that the person concerned is nevertheless liable to a penalty, the court may determine a penalty notwithstanding that, but for the opinion of the Board as to fraud, the penalty would not have been a matter for the court.

History – S. 100D inserted by FA 1989, s. 167.

Cross references – SSCBA 1992, Sch. 1, para. 7: application of s. 100D to returns of National Insurance contributions.
SI 2001/1004, reg. 82: application with respect to National Insurance returns.

101 Evidence for purposes of proceedings relating to penalties

101 An assessment which can no longer be varied by the tribunal on an appeal notified to it or by order of any court is sufficient evidence, for the purposes of–

(a) the preceding provisions of this Part, and

(b) the provisions of Schedule 18 to the Finance Act 1998 relating to penalties,

that the amounts in respect of which tax is charged in the assessment arose or were received as stated in the assessment.

History – In s. 101 the words "the tribunal on an appeal notified to it" substituted for the words "any Commissioners on appeal" by SI 2009/56, art. 3(1) and Sch. 1, para. 47, operative from 1 April 2009, subject to transitional and saving provisions in SI 2009/56, Sch. 3.
S. 101 substituted by FA 1998, s. 117(3) and Sch. 19, para. 39, with effect in relation to accounting periods ending on or after 1 July 1999, the corporation tax self-assessment appointed day by virtue of FA 1994, s. 199(2), (3) and SI 1998/3173 (C. 78).
Former s. 101 amended by FA 1985, Sch. 27, Pt. X by removing a reference to development land tax, with effect from 19 March 1985.

102 Mitigation of penalties

102 The Board may in their discretion mitigate any penalty, or stay or compound any proceedings for a penalty, and may also, after judgment, further mitigate or entirely remit the penalty.

History – The words "a penalty" substituted for "recovery thereof" by FA 1989, s. 168(4), consequent to the substitution of s. 100 and the insertion of s. 100A–100D.

Cross references – SSCBA 1992, Sch. 1, para. 7: application of s. 102 to returns of National Insurance contributions.
SI 2001/1004, reg. 90K: application with respect to late payment of National Insurance Contributions due electronically.

103 Time limits for penalties

103(1) Subject to subsection (2) below, where the amount of a penalty is to be ascertained by reference to tax payable by a person for any period, the penalty may be determined by an officer of the Board, or proceedings for the penalty may be commenced before the tribunal or a court–

(a) at any time within six years after the date on which the penalty was incurred, or

(b) at any later time within three years after the final determination of the amount of tax by reference to which the amount of the penalty is to be ascertained.

103(2) [Omitted by FA 2007, s. 97 and Sch. 24, para. 29(b) and repealed by FA 2007, s. 114 and Sch. 27, Pt. 5(5).]

103(3) [Omitted by FA 2012, s. 223 and Sch. 38, para. 48(a).]

103(4) A penalty to which subsection (1) does not apply may be so determined, or proceedings for such a penalty may be commenced before the tribunal or a court, at any time within six years after the date on which the penalty was incurred or began to be incurred.

History – In s. 103(1) the word "tribunal" substituted for the word "Commissioners" by SI 2009/56, art. 3(1) and Sch. 1, para. 48, operative from 1 April 2009, subject to transitional and saving provisions in SI 2009/56, Sch. 3.
S. 103(2) omitted by FA 2007, s. 97 and Sch. 24, para. 29(b) and repealed by FA 2007, s. 114 and Sch. 27, Pt. 5(5), with effect as follows by virtue of SI 2008/568, art. 2:

- 1 April 2008 in relation to relevant documents relating to tax periods commencing on or after that date;
- 1 April 2008 in relation to assessments falling within paragraph 2 for tax periods commencing on or after that date;
- 1 July 2008 in relation to relevant documents relating to claims under the Thirteenth Council Directive (arrangements for the refund of value added tax to persons not established in Community territory) for years commencing on or after that date;
- 1 January 2009 in relation to relevant documents relating to claims under the Eighth Council Directive (arrangements for the refund of value added tax to taxable persons not established in the territory of the country) for years commencing on or after that date;
- 1 April 2009 in relation to documents relating to all other claims for repayments of relevant tax made on or after 1 April 2009 which are not related to a tax period; and
- in any other case, 1 April 2009 in relation to documents given where a person's liability to pay relevant tax arises on or after that date.

However, no person will be liable to a penalty under Sch. 24 in respect of any tax period for which a return is required to be made before 1 April 2009.
In former s. 103(2), the words "the 31st January next following the chargeable period" substituted for the previous words "the end of the chargeable period" by FA 1994, s. 196 and Sch. 19, para. 32, in so far as it relates to income tax and capital gains tax, as respects the year 1996–97 and subsequent years of assessment and, in so far as it relates to corporation tax, as respects accounting periods ending on or after 1 July 1999, the appointed day for corporation tax self-assessment by virtue of FA 1994, s. 199(2), (3) and SI 1998/3173 (C. 78).
S. 103(3) omitted by FA 2012, s. 223 and Sch. 38, para. 48(a), with effect from 1 April 2013 (SI 2013/279, art. 2).
In s. 103(4), the words "subsection (1) does not apply" substituted for the words "neither subsection (1) nor subsection (3) above applies" by FA 2012, s. 223 and Sch. 38, para. 48(b), with effect from 1 April 2013 (SI 2013/279, art. 2).
In s. 103(4) the word "tribunal" substituted for the word "Commissioners" by SI 2009/56, art. 3(1) and Sch. 1, para. 48, operative from 1 April 2009, subject to transitional and saving provisions in SI 2009/56, Sch. 3.
S. 103 substituted by FA 1989, s. 169 with effect from 27 July 1989, but not affecting the application of the former s. 103(4) to proceedings under s. 100 before substitution by that Act.

Cross references – SSCBA 1992, Sch. 1, para. 7: application of s. 103 to returns of National Insurance contributions.
SI 2001/1004, reg. 90P: application with respect to non-delivery of National Insurance Contributions due electronically.

103ZA Disapplication of sections 100 to 103 in the case of certain penalties

103ZA Sections 100 to 103 do not apply to a penalty under –

(a) Schedule 24 to FA 2007 (penalties for errors),

(b) Schedule 36 to FA 2008 (information and inspection powers),

(c) Schedule 41 to that Act (penalties for failure to notify and certain other wrongdoing),

(d) Schedule 55 to FA 2009 (penalties for failure to make returns etc),

(e) Schedule 56 to that Act (penalties for failure to make payments on time),

(f) Schedule 23 to FA 2011 (data-gathering powers),

(g) Schedule 38 to FA 2012 (tax agents: dishonest conduct),

(ga) section 212A of the Finance Act 2013 (general anti-abuse rule),

(h) Part 4 of the Finance Act 2014 (follower notices and accelerated payments),

(i) Part 5 of Schedule 18 to Finance Act 2016 (serial tax avoidance),

(j) Schedule 22 to the Finance Act 2016 (asset-based penalty),

(k) paragraph 1 or 45 of Schedule 16 to the Finance (No. 2) Act 2017 (enablers of defeated tax avoidance etc), or

(l) Schedule 18 to the Finance [(No. 2)] Act 2017.

History – In s. 103ZA(d), the word "or" at the end omitted by FA 2011, s. 86 and Sch. 23, para. 51(5)(a), with effect from 1 April 2012.
S. 103ZA(f) and the word "or" (at the end of s. 103ZA(e)) inserted by FA 2011, s. 86 and Sch. 23, para. 51(5)(b), with effect from 1 April 2012.
S. 103ZA(g) (and the ", or" before it) inserted (and the "or" in (e) omitted) by FA 2012, s. 223 and Sch. 38, para. 49, with effect from 1 April 2013 (SI 2013/279, art. 2).
S. 103ZA(ga) inserted (and the "or" at the end of (g) omitted) by FA 2016, s. 158(10), with effect in relation to tax arrangements (within the meaning of Pt. 5 of FA 2013) entered into on or after 15 September 2016 (Royal Assent).
S. 103ZA(h) inserted (and the "or" at the end of s. 103ZA(f) omitted, and the ", or" at the end of s. 103ZA(g) inserted), by FA 2014, s. 233 and Sch. 33, para. 2, with effect from 17 July 2014.
S. 103ZA(i) (and the "or" before it) inserted (and the "or" after (ga) omitted) by FA 2016, s. 159 and Sch. 18, para. 59, with effect in relation to relevant defeats incurred after 15 September 2016 (Royal Assent), subject to transitional provisions in Sch. 18, para. 64 and 65 (in relation to arrangements entered into before 15 September 2016 relevant defeats incurred before 6 April 2017 and certain relevant defeats incurred on or after 6 April 2017 are disregarded).
S. 103ZA(j) (and the word ", or" preceding it) inserted and the word "or" at the end of para. (h) omitted by FA 2016, s. 165 and Sch. 22, para. 20(1), with effect for income tax and capital gains tax purposes, in relation to tax years commencing on or after 6 April 2016 (SI 2017/277, reg. 2).
S. 103ZA(k) (and the word ", or" preceding it) inserted and the word "or" at the end of para. (i) omitted by F(No. 2)A 2017, s. 65 and Sch. 16, para. 58, with effect in relation to arrangements entered into on or after 16 November 2017 (Royal Assent) subject to F(No. 2)A 2017, Sch. 16, para. 62(2) and (3).
S. 103ZA(l) (and the word ", or" preceding it) inserted and the word "or" at the end of para. (j) omitted by F(No. 2)A 2017, s. 67 and Sch. 18, para. 29(2), with effect from 16 November 2017 (Royal Assent).
S. 103ZA inserted by FA 2009, s. 109 and Sch. 57, para. 13(3) with effect from 21 July 2009.

103A Interest on penalties

103A A penalty under any of the provisions of Part II, IV or VA or this Part of this Act, or Schedule 18 to the Finance Act 1998, shall carry interest at the rate applicable under section 178 of the Finance Act 1989 from the date on which it becomes due and payable until payment.

History – S. 103A amended by inserting the words ", or Schedule 18 to the Finance Act 1998,", by FA 1998, s. 117(3) and Sch. 19, para. 40, with effect in relation to accounting periods ending on or after 1 July 1999, the corporation tax self-assessment appointed day by virtue of FA 1994, s. 199(2), (3) and SI 1998/3173 (C. 78).
S. 103A inserted by FA 1994, s. 196 and Sch. 19, para. 33 and amended by FA 1995, s. 115(8), in so far as it relates to income tax and capital gains tax, as respects the year 1996–97 and subsequent years of assessment and, in so far as it relates to corporation tax, as respects accounting periods ending on or after 1 July 1999, the appointed day (see above).

Cross references – SI 2001/1004, reg. 90P: application with respect to non-delivery of National Insurance Contributions due electronically.

104 Saving for criminal proceedings

104 The provisions of the Taxes Acts shall not, save so far as is otherwise provided, affect any criminal proceedings for any misdemeanour.

Cross references – SSCBA 1992, Sch. 1, para. 7: application of s. 104 to returns of National Insurance contributions.
SI 2001/1004, reg. 82: application with respect to National Insurance returns.

105 Admissibility of evidence not affected by offer of settlement

History – Heading substituted for the words "Evidence in cases of fraud or wilful default" by FA 2003, s. 206(2).

105(1) Statements made or documents produced by or on behalf of a person shall not be inadmissible in any such proceedings as are mentioned in subsection (2) below by reason only that it has been drawn to his attention–

(a) that where serious tax fraud has been committed the Board may accept a money settlement and that the Board will accept such a settlement, and will not pursue a criminal prosecution, if he makes a full confession of all tax irregularities, or

(b) that the extent to which he is helpful and volunteers information is a factor that will be taken into account in determining the amount of any penalty,

105(2) The proceedings mentioned in subsection (1) above are–

(a) any criminal proceedings against the person in question for any form of fraudulent conduct in connection with or in relation to tax, and

(b) any proceedings against him for the recovery of any tax due from him, and

(c) any proceedings for a penalty or on appeal against the determination of a penalty.

History – In s. 105, the words "fraudulent conduct" substituted by FA 1989, s. 149(5) but not to affect the making of assessments for years of assessment before 1983–84 or for accounting periods ended before 1 April 1983.
In s. 105(1), para. (a) and (b) substituted by FA 2003, s. 206(1) in relation to statements made, or documents produced, on or after 10 July 2003. The previous paragraphs did not require a full confession to all tax irregularities for the acceptance of a money settlement in lieu of prosecution, it was merely a factor influencing the Board's decision.
S. 105(1)(a), the words "tax due from him, and" at the end of s. 105(2)(b) and s. 105(2)(c) substituted by FA 1989, s. 168(5).

Cross references – SI 2001/1004, reg. 82: application with respect to National Insurance returns.

106 Refusal to allow a deduction of income tax, and avoidance of agreements for payment without deduction

106(1) A person who refuses to allow a deduction of income tax authorised by the Taxes Acts to be made out of any payment shall incur a penalty of £50.

106(2) Every agreement for payment of interest, rent or other annual payment in full without allowing any such deduction shall be void.

EVASION

106A Offence of fraudulent evasion of income tax

106A(1) A person commits an offence if that person is knowingly concerned in the fraudulent evasion of income tax by that or any other person.

106A(2) A person guilty of an offence under this section is liable–

(a) on summary conviction, to imprisonment for a term not exceeding 12 months or a fine not exceeding the statutory maximum, or both, or

(b) on conviction on indictment, to imprisonment for a term not exceeding 7 years or a fine, or both.

106A(3) In the application of subsection (2)(a)–

(a) in England and Wales in relation to offences committed before the commencement of section 282(3) of the Criminal Justice Act 2003, and

(b) in Northern Ireland,

for "12 months" substitute "6 months".

106A(4) This section does not apply to things done or omitted before 1st January 2001.

History – S. 106A inserted by TIOPA 2010, s. 371 and Sch. 7, para. 95, with effect for corporation tax purposes for accounting periods ending on or after 1 April 2010, for income tax and capital gains tax purposes for the tax year 2010–11 and subsequent tax years, and for petroleum revenue tax purposes for chargeable periods beginning on or after 1 July 2010.

OFFSHORE INCOME, ASSETS AND ACTIVITIES

History – Heading inserted by FA 2016, s. 166(1), with effect in relation to the tax year commencing on 6 April 2017 and subsequent tax years, subject to the transitional provisions in FA 2016, s. 166(4) (SI 2017/970, reg. 2).

106B Offence of failing to give notice of being chargeable to tax

106B(1) A person who is required by section 7 to give notice of being chargeable to income tax or capital gains tax (or both) for a year of assessment and who has not given that notice by the end of the notification period commits an offence if–

(a) the tax in question is chargeable (wholly or in part) on or by reference to offshore income, assets or activities, and

(b) the total amount of income tax and capital gains tax that is chargeable for the year of assessment on or by reference to offshore income, assets or activities exceeds the threshold amount.

106B(2) It is a defence for a person accused of an offence under this section to prove that the person had a reasonable excuse for failing to give the notice required by section 7.

106B(3) In this section **"the notification period"** has the same meaning as in section 7 (see subsection (1C) of that section).

History – S. 106B inserted by FA 2016, s. 166(1), with effect in relation to the tax year commencing on 6 April 2017 and subsequent tax years, subject to the transitional provisions in FA 2016, s. 166(4) (SI 2017/970, reg. 2).

106C Offence of failing to deliver return

106C(1) A person who is required by a notice under section 8 to make and deliver a return for a year of assessment commits an offence if–

(a) the return is not delivered by the end of the withdrawal period,

(b) an accurate return would have disclosed liability to income tax or capital gains tax (or both) that is chargeable for the year of assessment on or by reference to offshore income, assets or activities, and

(c) the total amount of income tax and capital gains tax that is chargeable for the year of assessment on or by reference to offshore income, assets or activities exceeds the threshold amount.

106C(2) It is a defence for a person accused of an offence under this section to prove that the person had a reasonable excuse for failing to deliver the return.

106C(3) In this section **"the withdrawal period"** has the same meaning as in section 8B (see subsection (6) of that section).

"chargeable period" means a year of assessment or a company's accounting period,

"collector" means any collector of taxes,

"company" has the meaning given by section 1121(1) of CTA 2010 (with section 617 of that Act),

"CTA 2009" means the Corporation Tax Act 2009,

"CTA 2010" means the Corporation Tax Act 2010,

"HMRC" means Her Majesty's Revenue and Customs;

"inspector" means any inspector of taxes,

"ITEPA 2003" means the Income Tax (Earnings and Pensions) Act 2003,

"ITTOIA 2005" means the Income Tax (Trading and Other Income) Act 2005,

"ITA 2007" means the Income Tax Act 2007,

"NRCGT return" has the meaning given by section 12ZB;

"partnership return" has the meaning given by section 12AA(10A) of this Act,

"the principal Act" means the Income and Corporation Taxes Act 1988,

"the relevant trustees", in relation to a settlement, shall be construed in accordance with section 7(9) of this Act.

"return" includes any statement or declaration under the Taxes Acts,

"successor", in relation to a person who is required to make and deliver, or has made and delivered, a partnership return, and

"predecessor" and **"successor,"** in relation to the successor of such a person, shall be construed in accordance with section 12AA(11) of this Act;

"tax", where neither income tax nor capital gains tax nor corporation tax nor development land tax is specified, means any of those taxes,

"the Taxes Acts" means this Act and–

(a) the Tax Acts, and

(b) the Taxation of Chargeable Gains Act 1992 and all other enactments relating to capital gains tax,

"the TCEA 2007" means the Tribunals, Courts and Enforcement Act 2007;

"the 1992 Act" means the Taxation of Chargeable Gains Act 1992,

"TIOPA 2010" means the Taxation (International and Other Provisions) Act 2010,

"trade" includes every trade, manufacture, adventure or concern in the nature of trade,

"the tribunal" is to be read in accordance with section 47C;

118(2) For the purposes of this Act, a person shall be deemed not to have failed to do anything required to be done within a limited time if he did it within such further time, if any, as the Board or the tribunal or officer concerned may have allowed; and where a person had a reasonable excuse for not doing anything required to be done he shall be deemed not to have failed to do it unless the excuse ceased and, after the excuse ceased, he shall be deemed not to have failed to do it if he did it without unreasonable delay after the excuse had ceased.

118(3) [Repealed by FA 1994, s. 196 and Sch. 19, para. 34(2) and s. 258 and Sch. 26, Pt. V(23).]

118(4) For the purposes of this Act, the amount of tax covered by any assessment shall not be deemed to be finally determined until that assessment can no longer be varied, whether by the tribunal on an appeal notified to it or by the order of any court.

118(5) For the purposes of this Act a loss of tax or a situation is brought about carelessly by a person if the person fails to take reasonable care to avoid bringing about that loss or situation.

118(6) Where–

(a) information is provided to Her Majesty's Revenue and Customs,

(b) the person who provided the information, or the person on whose behalf the information was provided, discovers some time later that the information was inaccurate, and

(c) that person fails to take reasonable steps to inform Her Majesty's Revenue and Customs,

any loss of tax or situation brought about by the inaccuracy shall be treated for the purposes of this Act as having been brought about carelessly by that person.

118(7) In this Act, references to a loss of tax or a situation brought about deliberately by a person include a loss of tax or a situation that arises as a result of a deliberate inaccuracy in a document given to Her Majesty's Revenue and Customs by or on behalf of that person.

History – In s. 118(1):

(b) have been put to Her Majesty's Revenue and Customs in the course of an appeal by the claimant relating to that amount that is treated as having been determined by a tribunal (by virtue of section 54 (settling of appeals by agreement)).

2(6) Case E is where the claimant knew, or ought reasonably to have known, of the grounds for the claim before the latest of the following–

(a) the date on which an appeal by the claimant relating to the amount paid, or liable to be paid, in the course of which the ground could have been put forward (a "relevant appeal") was determined by a court or tribunal (or is treated as having been so determined),

(b) the date on which the claimant withdrew a relevant appeal to a court or tribunal, and

(c) the end of the period in which the claimant was entitled to make a relevant appeal to a court or tribunal.

2(7) Case F is where the amount in question was paid or is liable to be paid–

(a) in consequence of proceedings enforcing the payment of that amount brought against the claimant by Her Majesty's Revenue and Customs, or

(b) in accordance with an agreement between the claimant and Her Majesty's Revenue and Customs settling such proceedings.

2(8) Case G is where–

(a) the amount paid, or liable to be paid, is excessive by reason of a mistake in calculating the claimant's liability to income tax or capital gains tax (other than a mistake in a PAYE assessment or PAYE calculation), and

(b) liability was calculated in accordance with the practice generally prevailing at the time.

2(9) Case H is where–

(a) the amount paid, or liable to be paid, is excessive by reason of a mistake in a PAYE assessment or PAYE calculation, and

(b) the assessment or calculation was made in accordance with the practice generally prevailing at the end of the period of 12 months following the tax year for which the assessment or calculation was made.

2(9A) Cases G and H do not apply where the amount paid, or liable to be paid, is tax which has been charged contrary to EU law.

2(9B) For the purposes of sub-paragraph (9A), an amount of tax is charged contrary to EU law if, in the circumstances in question, the charge to tax is contrary to–

(a) the provisions relating to the free movement of goods, persons, services and capital in Titles II and IV of Part 3 of the Treaty on the Functioning of the European Union, or

(b) the provisions of any subsequent treaty replacing the provisions mentioned in paragraph (a).

2(10) For the purposes of Cases G and H–

(a) **"PAYE assessment"** means an assessment on the claimant made in accordance with section 709 of ITEPA 2003 (assessment in connection with PAYE deductions), and

(b) **"PAYE calculation"** means a calculation of the amount of a deduction or repayment made or to be made under PAYE regulations in respect of tax estimated to be payable by the claimant.

History – In para. 2(1), "paragraphs 3A and 4(5)" substituted for "paragraph 4(5)" by SI 2011/1037, art. 2(2), with effect from 1 April 2001, and in relation to determinations (within the meaning of s. 28C) made before 1 April 2011 (as in relation to determinations made on or after that date). But the substitution does not apply in relation to a determination made before that date if a claim for relief in respect of it has already been refused before that date.
Para. 2(9A) inserted by FA 2013, s. 231(1), with effect in relation to any claim (in respect of overpaid tax, excessive assessments etc) made after the end of the six month period beginning on 17 July 2013.
Para. 2(9B) inserted by FA 2013, s. 231(1), with effect in relation to any claim (in respect of overpaid tax, excessive assessments etc) made after the end of the six month period beginning on 17 July 2013.

MAKING A CLAIM

3(1) A claim under this Schedule may not be made more than 4 years after the end of the relevant tax year.

3(2) In relation to a claim made in reliance on paragraph 1(1)(a), the relevant tax year is–

(a) where the amount paid, or liable to be paid, is excessive by reason of a mistake in a return or returns under section 8, 8A or 12AA of this Act, the tax year to which the return (or, if more than one, the first return) relates, and

(b) otherwise, the tax year in respect of which the payment was made.

3(3) In relation to a claim made in reliance on paragraph 1(1)(b), the relevant tax year is–

(a) where the amount liable to be paid is excessive by reason of a mistake in a return or returns under section 8, 8A or 12AA, the tax year to which the return (or, if more than one, the first return) relates, and

(b) otherwise, the tax year to which the assessment, determination or direction relates.

3(4) A claim under this Schedule may not be made by being included in a return under section 8, 8A or 12AA of this Act.

3(5) Sub-paragraph (1) is subject to paragraph 3A.

Prospective amendments – In para. 3(2)(a) the words "or a Schedule A1 partnership return" inserted after the words "of this Act" by F(No. 2)A 2017, s. 61 and Sch. 14, para. 30(2), with effect from a day to be appointed under F(No. 2)A 2017, s. 61(6).
In para. 3(3)(a) the words "or a Schedule A1 partnership return" inserted after the words "12AA" by F(No. 2)A 2017, s. 61 and Sch. 14, para. 30(3), with effect from a day to be appointed under F(No. 2)A 2017, s. 61(6).
In para. 3(4) the words "or a Schedule A1 partnership return" inserted at the end by F(No. 2)A 2017, s. 61 and Sch. 14, para. 30(4), with effect from a day to be appointed under F(No. 2)A 2017, s. 61(6).

History – Para. 3(3)(a) and (b) (and the "–" before them) inserted by FA 2013, s. 232(1), with effect in relation to any claim (in respect of overpaid tax, excessive assessments etc.) made after the end of the six-month period beginning on 17 July 2013.
Para. 3(5) inserted by SI 2011/1037, art. 2(3), with effect from 1 April 2011, and in relation to determinations (within the meaning of s. 28C) made before 1 April 2011 (as in relation to determinations made on or after that date). But the insertion does not apply in relation to a determination made before that date if a claim for relief in respect of it has already been refused before that date.

Cross references – FA 2009, Sch. 52, para. 10: modification of para. 3(1) in relation to certain claims made before 1 April 2012.

DETERMINATIONS UNDER SECTION 28C: SPECIAL RULES

3A(1) This paragraph applies where–

(a) a determination has been made under section 28C of an amount that a person is liable to pay by way of income tax or capital gains tax, but the person believes the tax is not due or, if it has been paid, was not due,

(b) relief would be available under this Schedule but for the fact that–

(i) the claim falls within Case C (see paragraph 2(4)),

(ii) the claim falls within Case F(a) (see paragraph 2(7)(a)), or

(iii) more than 4 years have elapsed since the end of the relevant tax year (see paragraph 3(1)), and

(c) if the claim falls within Case F(a), the person was neither present nor legally represented during the enforcement proceedings in question.

3A(2) A claim under this Schedule for repayment or discharge of the amount may be made, and effect given to it, despite paragraph 2(4), paragraph 2(7)(a) or paragraph 3(1), as the case may be.

3A(3) But the Commissioners are not liable to give effect to a claim made in reliance on this paragraph unless conditions A, B and C are met.

3A(4) Condition A is that in the opinion of the Commissioners it would be unconscionable for the Commissioners to seek to recover the amount (or to withhold repayment of it, if it has already been paid).

3A(5) Condition B is that the person's affairs (as respects matters concerning the Commissioners) are otherwise up to date or arrangements have been put in place, to the satisfaction of the Commissioners, to bring them up to date so far as possible.

3A(6) Condition C is that either–

(a) the person has not relied on this paragraph on a previous occasion (whether in respect of the same or a different determination or tax), or

(b) the person has done so, but in the exceptional circumstances of the case should be allowed to do so again on the present occasion.

3A(7) For the purposes of sub-paragraph (6)–

(a) a person has relied on this paragraph on a previous occasion if the person has made a claim (or a composite set of claims involving one or more determinations, taxes and tax years) in reliance on this paragraph on a previous occasion, and

(b) it does not matter whether that claim (or set of claims) succeeded.

3A(8) A claim made in reliance on this paragraph must include (in addition to anything required by Schedule 1A) such information and documentation as is reasonably required for the purpose of determining whether conditions A, B and C are met.

History – Para. 3A inserted by SI 2011/1037, art. 2(4), with effect from 1 April 2011, and in relation to determinations (within the meaning of s. 28C) made before 1 April 2011 (as in relation to determinations made on or after that date). But the insertion does not apply in relation to a determination made before that date if a claim for relief in respect of it has already been refused before that date.

Notes – By virtue of SI 2011/1037, art. 4 (not reproduced), para. 3A(6) and (7) references to reliance "on this paragraph" include reliance before 1 April 2011 on the concession which para. 3A replaces (the "equitable liability" concession, described in TB 08/95-7).

THE CLAIMANT: ONE PERSON ACCOUNTABLE FOR AMOUNTS PAYABLE BY ANOTHER ETC

4(1) Sub-paragraph (2) applies where, under a relevant enactment, a person ("P") is accountable to the Commissioners for–

(a) an amount representing income tax or capital gains tax that is or is estimated to be payable by another person ("T"), or

(b) any other amount that, under a relevant enactment, has been or is to be set off against a liability of T.

4(2) A claim under this Schedule in respect of the amount may be made only by T.

4(3) Sub-paragraph (4) applies where–

(a) a person ("P") has paid an amount described in sub-paragraph (1)(a) or (b) in the belief that P was accountable to the Commissioners for the amount under a relevant enactment, but

(b) P was not so accountable.

4(4) A claim under this Schedule in respect of the amount may be made only by P.

4(5) The Commissioners are not liable to give effect to a claim under sub-paragraph (4) if or to the extent that the amount has been repaid to T or set against amounts payable to the Commissioners by T.

4(6) **"Relevant enactment"** means–

(a) PAYE regulations,

(b) Chapter 3 of Part 3 of the Finance Act 2004 or regulations under that Chapter (construction industry scheme), or

(c) any other provision of or made under the Taxes Acts.

THE CLAIMANT: PARTNERSHIPS

5(1) This paragraph applies where–

(a) a trade, profession or business is carried on by two or more persons in partnership,

(b) an amount is paid, or liable to be paid, by one or more of those persons in accordance with a self-assessment, and

(c) the amount is excessive by reason of a mistake in a partnership return.

5(2) A claim under this Schedule in respect of the amount–

(a) may be made by the relevant partner nominated to make the claim by all of the relevant partners, and

(b) may not be made by any other person.

5(3) In relation to such a claim, references in this Schedule to the claimant are to any of the relevant partners.

5(4) **"Relevant partner"** means–

(a) a person who was a partner in the partnership at any time during the period in respect of which the partnership return was made, or

(b) the personal representative of such a person.

ASSESSMENT OF CLAIMANT IN CONNECTION WITH CLAIM

6(1) This paragraph applies where–

(a) a claim is made under this Schedule,

(b) the grounds for giving effect to the claim also provide grounds for a discovery assessment or determination on the claimant in respect of any chargeable period, and

(c) such an assessment or determination could be made but for a relevant restriction.

6(2) **"Discovery assessment or determination"** means–

(a) an assessment under section 29(1), or

(b) a discovery assessment or discovery determination under Schedule 18 to the Finance Act 1998 (company tax return etc).

6(3) The following are relevant restrictions–

(a) the conditions in section 29(3) to (5),

(b) the restrictions in paragraphs 42 to 45 of Schedule 18 to the Finance Act 1998, and

(c) the expiry of a time limit for making a discovery assessment or determination.

6(4) Where this paragraph applies–

(a) the relevant restrictions are to be disregarded, and

(b) the discovery assessment or determination is not out of time if it is made before the final determination of the claim.

AMENDMENT OF PARTNERSHIP RETURN ETC IN CONNECTION WITH CLAIM

7(1) This paragraph applies where–

(a) a claim is made under this Schedule,

(b) the claimant is one of two or more persons carrying on a trade, profession or business in partnership,

(c) the grounds for giving effect to the claim also provide grounds for amending, under section 30B(1) (discovery of loss of tax from partnership), a return made by the partnership or any of the partners in respect of any period, and

(d) such an amendment could be made but for a relevant restriction.

7(2) The following are relevant restrictions–

(a) the conditions in section 30B(4) to (6), and

(b) the expiry of a time limit for making an assessment under that section.

7(3) Where this paragraph applies–

(a) the relevant conditions are to be disregarded, and

(b) the amendment is not out of time if it is made before the final determination of the claim.

CONTRACT SETTLEMENTS

8(1) In paragraph 1(1)(a), the reference to an amount paid by way of income tax or capital gains tax includes an amount paid under a contract settlement in connection with income tax or capital gains tax believed to be due from any person.

8(2) Sub-paragraphs (3) to (6) apply if the person who paid the amount under the contract settlement ("the payer") and the person from whom the tax was due ("the taxpayer") are not the same person.

8(3) In relation to a claim under this Schedule in respect of that amount–

(a) the references to the claimant in paragraph 2(5) to (7) (Cases D, E and F) have effect as if they included the taxpayer,

(b) the references to the claimant in paragraph 2(8) and (10) (Cases G and H) have effect as if they were references to the taxpayer,

(c) the references to the claimant in paragraphs 6(1)(b) and 7(1)(b) have effect as if they were references to the taxpayer, and

(d) references to tax in Schedule 1A (as it applies to a claim under this Schedule) include such an amount.

8(4) Sub-paragraph (5) applies where the grounds for giving effect to a claim by the payer in respect of the amount also provide grounds for a discovery assessment or determination on the taxpayer in respect of any chargeable period.

8(5) The Commissioners may set any amount repayable to the payer by virtue of the claim against any amount payable by the taxpayer by virtue of the assessment or determination.

8(6) The obligations of the Commissioners and the taxpayer are discharged to the extent of any set-off under sub-paragraph (5).

8(7) In this paragraph–

"contract settlement" means an agreement made in connection with any person's liability to make a payment to the Commissioners under or by virtue of an enactment;

"discovery assessment or determination" has the same meaning as in paragraph 6.

INTERPRETATION

9(1) In this Schedule **"the Commissioners"** means the Commissioners for Her Majesty's Revenue and Customs.

9(2) For the purposes of this Schedule, a claim is not finally determined until it, or the amount to which it relates, can no longer be varied (whether on appeal or otherwise).

SCHEDULE 1A – CLAIMS ETC. NOT INCLUDED IN RETURNS

Section 42

History – Sch. 1A inserted by FA 1994, s. 196 and Sch. 19, para. 35 and amended by FA 1995, s. 107(11) and Sch. 20 in so far as it relates to income tax and capital gains tax, as respects the year 1996–97 and subsequent years of assessment and, in so far as it relates to corporation tax, as respects accounting periods ending on or after 1 July 1999, the appointed day for the purposes of corporation tax self-assessment by virtue of FA 1994, s. 199(2), (3) and SI 1998/3173 (C. 78).

Cross references – CTA 2010, s. 9A: Sch. 1A does not apply to an election under CTA 2010, s. 9A made before 19 July 2011 (FA 2011, s. 34 and Sch. 7, para. 8(4)).
FA 1998, Sch. 18, para. 9, 10: company tax return under self assessment – claims or elections that cannot be made without a return and other claims, etc. to be included in a return.
FA 1998, Sch. 18, para. 59: Sch. 1A applies to claims or elections not within FA 1998, Sch. 18, para. 57 (claims or elections affecting a single accounting period) or 58 (claims or elections involving more than one accounting period) whether or not included in a company tax return.
CAA 2001, s. 201(5): Sch. 1A does not apply to an election under CAA 2001, s. 198 (election to apportion sale price on sale of qualifying interest) or 199 (election to apportion capital sum given by lessee on grant of lease).
CAA 2001, s. 227(5): Sch. 1A does not apply to an election under CAA 2001, s. 227 (special treatment for sale and leaseback cases).
SI 2003/282: regulations governing electronic delivery of information to or by the Board under this Schedule revoking SI 2000/945 with effect from 5 March 2003.

Statements of practice – SP 5/01: HMRC's approach to extending time limits for making claims for loss relief, capital allowances and group relief.

PRELIMINARY

1 In this Schedule–

"claim" means a claim or election as respects which this Schedule applies;

"partnership claim" means a claim made in accordance with section 42(6)(b) of, or paragraph 5 of Schedule 1AB to, this Act or paragraph 51D of Schedule 18 to the Finance Act 1998 (claims for overpaid corporation tax);

"profits"–

(a) in relation to income tax, means income,

(b) in relation to capital gains tax, means chargeable gains, and

(c) in relation to corporation tax, means profits as computed for the purposes of that tax;

"relevant partner", in relation to a partnership claim, means any person who was a partner at any time during the period in respect of which the claim is made;

"successor", in relation to a person who–

(a) has made a partnership claim, but

(b) is no longer a partner or is otherwise no longer available,

means such other partner who may at any time be nominated for the purposes of this paragraph by the majority of the partners at that time, and

"predecessor" and **"successor"**, in relation to a person so nominated, shall be construed accordingly.

History – In para. 1, in the definition of "partnership claim", the words ", or paragraph 5 of Schedule 1AB to," inserted by FA 2009, s. 100 and Sch. 52, para. 6 with effect in relation to claims made on or after 1 April 2010.
In para. 1, in the definition of "partnership claim", the words "or paragraph 51D of Schedule 18 to the Finance Act 1998 (claims for overpaid corporation tax)" added by FA 2009, s. 100 and Sch. 52, para. 17 with effect in relation to claims made on or after 1 April 2010.
Definition of "profits" substituted by FA 1998, s. 117(3) and Sch. 19, para. 42(2) with effect in relation to company accounting periods ending on or after 1 July 1999, the corporation tax self-assessment appointed day (FA 1998, s. 117(4), (5) and FA 1994, s. 199(2), (3)).
Definition of "claim" amended by FA 1996, s. 130(5).

Notes – Para. 1 rewritten as ITA 2007, s. 1020(1).

MAKING OF CLAIMS

2(1) Subject to any provision in the Taxes Acts for a claim to be made to the Board, every claim shall be made to an officer of the Board.

2(2) No claim requiring the repayment of tax shall be made unless the claimant has documentary proof that the tax has been paid by deduction or otherwise.

2(3) A claim shall be made in such form as the Board may determine.

2(4) The form of claim shall provide for a declaration to the effect that all the particulars given in the form are correctly stated to the best of the information and belief of the person making the claim.

2(5) The form of claim may require–

(a) a statement of the amount of tax which will be required to be discharged or repaid in order to give effect to the claim;

(b) such information as is reasonably required for the purpose of determining whether and, if so, the extent to which the claim is correct; and

(bb) the delivery with the claim of such accounts, statements and documents, relating to information contained in the claim, as are reasonably required for the purpose mentioned in paragraph (b) above;

(c) [omitted by SI 2009/2035, art. 2 and Schedule, para. 9.]

2(6) In the case of a claim made by or on behalf of a person who is not resident, or who claims to be not resident or not domiciled, in the United Kingdom, an officer of the Board or the Board may require a statement or declaration in support of the claim to be made by affidavit.

History – In para. 2(5)(b) the word "and" at end inserted and para. (c) (and the word "and" which preceded it) omitted by SI 2009/2035, art. 2 and Schedule, para. 9, with effect from 13 August 2009.

Para. 2(5)(c) amended by inserting the words "or paragraph 13 of Schedule 18 to the Finance Act 1998", by FA 1998, s. 117(3) and Sch. 19, para. 42(3) as respects company accounting periods ending on or after 1 July 1999, the corporation tax self-assessment appointed day by virtue of FA 1994, s. 199(2), (3) and SI 1998/3173 (C. 78).

Para. 2(5)(b) and (bb) substituted for former para. 2(5)(b) by FA 1995, s. 107(11) and Sch. 20, para. 1, with effect from the year 1996–97 as respects income tax and capital gains tax and, as respects corporation tax, with effect in relation to accounting periods ending after 30 June 1999 (SI 1998/3173 art 2).

In para. 2(6), the words "or not ordinarily resident" omitted by FA 2013, s. 219 and Sch. 46, para. 117, with effect from 17 July 2013.

Notes – Para. 2(3), (4) and (5) rewritten as ITA 2007, s. 1020(1).

KEEPING AND PRESERVING OF RECORDS

2A(1) Any person who may wish to make a claim in relation to a year of assessment or other period shall–

(a) keep all such records as may be requisite for the purpose of enabling him to make a correct and complete claim; and

(b) shall preserve those records until the end of the relevant day.

2A(2) In relation to a claim, the relevant day for the purposes of sub-paragraph (1) above is whichever of the following is the latest, namely–

(a) where enquiries into the claim or any amendment of the claim are made by an officer of the Board, the day on which, by virtue of paragraph 7(1) below, those enquiries are completed; and

(b) where no enquiries into the claim or any amendment of the claim are so made, the day on which such an officer no longer has power to make such enquiries.

2A(2A) The Commissioners for Her Majesty's Revenue and Customs may by regulations–

(a) provide that the records required to be kept and preserved under sub-paragraph (1) include, or do not include, records specified in the regulations, and

(b) provide that those records include supporting documents so specified.

2A(3) The duty under sub-paragraph (1) to preserve records may be discharged–

(a) by preserving them in any form and by any means, or

(b) by preserving the information contained in them in any form and by any means,

subject to sub-paragraph (3A) and any conditions or further exceptions specified in writing by the Commissioners for Her Majesty's Revenue and Customs.

2A(3A) Sub-paragraph (3)(b) does not apply in the case of records of the kinds specified in section 12B(4A) or paragraph 22(3) of Schedule 18 to the Finance Act 1998.

2A(4) Subject to sub-paragraph (5) below, any person who fails to comply with sub-paragraph (1) above in relation to any claim which is made for a year of assessment or accounting period shall be liable to a penalty not exceeding £3,000.

2A(5) Sub-paragraph (4) above does not apply where–

(a) the records which the person fails to keep or preserve are records falling within paragraph (a) of section 12B(4A) of this Act or paragraph 22(3) of Schedule 18 to the Finance Act 1998; and

(b) an officer of the Board is satisfied that any facts which he reasonably requires to be proved, and which would have been proved by the records, are proved by other documentary evidence furnished to him.

2A(6) Regulations under this paragraph may–

(a) make different provision for different cases, and

(b) make provision by reference to things specified in a notice published by the Commissioners for Her Majesty's Revenue and Customs in accordance with the regulations (and not withdrawn by a subsequent notice).

2A(7) In this paragraph **"supporting documents"** includes accounts, books, deeds, contracts, vouchers and receipts.

History – In para. 2A(2)(a), "7(1)" substituted for "7(4)" and the words "treated as" (which appeared before the word "completed") omitted, by FA 2001, s. 88, Sch. 29, para. 34(2), and the words omitted repealed by s. 110, Sch. 33, Pt. 2(13), all with effect from 11 May 2001 in relation to returns whether made before or after that date and whether relating to periods before or after then.
Para. 2A(2A) inserted by FA 2008, s. 115 and Sch. 37, para. 3 with effect from 1 April 2009 (SI 2009/402, art. 2).
Para. 2A(3) and (3A) substituted for para. 2A(3) by FA 2008, s. 115 and Sch. 37, para. 3 with effect from 1 April 2009 (SI 2009/402, art. 2).
In former para. 2A(3) the word "tribunal" substituted for the word "Commissioners" by SI 2009/56, art. 3(1) and Sch. 1, para. 54, operative from 1 April 2009, subject to transitional and saving provisions in SI 2009/56, Sch. 3.
In former para. 2A(3) and (5)(a) the words "or paragraph 22(3) of Schedule 18 to the Finance Act 1998" inserted by FA 1998, s. 117(3) and Sch. 19, para. 42(4) with effect in relation to company accounting periods ending on or after 1 July 1999, the corporation tax self-assessment appointed day by virtue of FA 1994, s. 199(2), (3) and SI 1998/3173 (C. 78).
In para. 2A(3) the words "Except in the case … 12B(4A) of this Act," inserted by FA 1996, s. 124(6) and in para. 2A(4) the words "Subject to sub-paragraph (5) below," inserted by FA 1996, s. 124(7), for the purposes of income tax and capital gains tax, as respects the year 1996–97 and subsequent years of assessment, and for the purposes of corporation tax, as respects accounting periods ending on or after 1 July 1999, the appointed day (FA 1994, s. 199(2), (3)). These amendments do not have effect in relation to any time before 29 April 1996, or any records which a person fails to preserve before 29 April 1996.
Para. 2A(5) inserted by FA 1996, s. 124(8), for the purposes of income tax and capital gains tax, as respects the year 1996–97 and subsequent years of assessment, and for the purposes of corporation tax, as respects accounting periods ending on or after 1 July 1999, the appointed day (FA 1994, s. 199(2), (3)). This amendment does not have effect in relation to any time before 29 April 1996, or anyrecords which a person fails to preserve before 29 April 1996.
Para. 2A(6) inserted by FA 2008, s. 115 and Sch. 37, para. 3(4) with effect from 1 April 2009 (SI 2009/402, art. 2).
Para. 2A(7) inserted by FA 2008, s. 115 and Sch. 37, para. 3(4) with effect from 1 April 2009 (SI 2009/402, art. 2).

AMENDMENTS OF CLAIMS

3(1) Subject to sub-paragraph (2) below–

(a) at any time before the end of the period of nine months beginning with the day on which a claim is made, an officer of the Board may by notice to the claimant so amend the claim as to correct any obvious errors or mistakes in the claim (whether errors of principle, arithmetical mistakes or otherwise); and

(b) at any time before the end of the period of twelve months beginning with the day on which the claim is made, the claimant may amend his claim by notice to an officer of the Board.

3(2) No amendment of a claim may be made under sub-paragraph (1) above at any time during the period–

(a) beginning with the day on which an officer of the Board gives notice of his intention to enquire into the claim, and

(b) ending with the day on which the officer's enquiries into the claim are completed.

Cross references – FA 2013, Sch. 24, para. 6(6): para. 3(1)(b) does not apply in relation to an election under FA 2013, Sch. 24, para. 6(3).

GIVING EFFECT TO CLAIMS AND AMENDMENTS

4(1) Subject to sub-paragraphs (1A), (3) to (5) below, an officer of the Board or the Board shall, as soon as practicable after a claim other than a partnership claim is made, or such a claim is amended under paragraph 3 above, give effect to the claim or amendment by discharge or repayment of tax.

4(1A) In relation to a claim which would otherwise fall to be taken into account in the making of deductions or repayments of tax under PAYE regulations, sub-paragraph (1) above shall apply as if for the word "shall" there were substituted the word "may".

4(2) Subject to sub-paragraphs (3) to (5) below, an officer of the Board or the Board shall, as soon as practicable after a partnership claim is made, or such a claim is amended under paragraph 3 above, give effect to the claim or amendment, as respects each of the relevant partners, by discharge or repayment of tax.

4(3) Where any such claim or amendment as is mentioned in sub-paragraph (1) or (2) above is enquired into by an officer of the Board–

(a) that sub-paragraph shall not apply until the day on which, by virtue of paragraph 7(1) below, the enquiry is completed; but

(b) the officer may at any time before that day give effect to the claim or amendment, on a provisional basis, to such extent as he thinks fit.

4(4) Nothing in this paragraph applies in relation to a claim or an amendment of a claim if the claim is not one for discharge or repayment of tax.

4(5) This paragraph has effect subject to any provision in the Taxes Acts that–

(a) requires or allows effect to be given to a claim by other means, or

(b) provides that an amount is not to be discharged or repaid.

History – In para. 4(1), "to (5)" substituted for "and (4)" by FA 2009, s. 100 and Sch. 52, para. 7(2)(a) with effect in relation to claims made on or after 1 April 2010.

In para. 4(1), the words "and to any other provision in the Taxes Acts which otherwise provides", which appeared before ", and officer of the Board", omitted by FA 2009, s. 100 and Sch. 52, para. 7(2)(b) with effect in relation to claims made on or after 1 April 2010.
In para. 4(1A), the words "PAYE regulations" substituted for the words "section 203 of the principal Act" by ITEPA 2003, Sch. 6, para. 141 which has effect, for income tax purposes, for the tax year 2003–04 and subsequent tax years and, for corporation tax purposes, for accounting periods ending after 5 April 2003.
In para. 4(2), "to (5)" substituted for "and (4)" by FA 2009, s. 100 and Sch. 52, para. 7(3) with effect in relation to claims made on or after 1 April 2010.
In para. 4(3)(a), "7(1)" substituted for "7(4)" and the words "the enquiry is" substituted for "the officer's enquiries are treated as", by FA 2001, s. 88 and Sch. 29, para. 34(3) with effect from 11 May 2001 in relation to returns whether made before or after that date and whether relating to periods before or after then.
Para. 4(4) inserted, and references to it in para. 4(1) and (2) inserted, by FA 1996, s. 133 and Sch. 19, para. 8, for the purposes of income tax and capital gains tax, as respects the year 1996–97 and subsequent years of assessment, and for the purposes of corporation tax, as respects accounting periods ending on or after 1 July 1999, the day appointed for the purposes of self-assessment by virtue of FA 1994, s. 199 and SI 1998/3173 (C. 78).
Para. 4(5) inserted by FA 2009, s. 100 and Sch. 52, para. 7(4) with effect in relation to claims made on or after 1 April 2010.

POWER TO ENQUIRE INTO CLAIMS

5(1) An officer of the Board may enquire into–

(a) a claim made by any person, or

(b) any amendment made by any person of a claim made by him,

if, before the end of the period mentioned in sub-paragraph (2) below, he gives notice in writing of his intention to do so to that person or, in the case of a partnership claim, any successor of that person.

5(2) The period referred to in sub-paragraph (1) above is whichever of the following ends the latest, namely–

(a) the period ending with the quarter day next following the first anniversary of the day on which the claim or amendment was made;

(b) where the claim or amendment relates to a year of assessment, the period ending with the first anniversary of the 31st January next following that year; and

(c) where the claim or amendment relates to a period other than a year of assessment, the period ending with the first anniversary of the end of that period;

and the quarter days for the purposes of this sub-paragraph are 31st January, 30th April, 31st July and 31st October.

5(3) A claim or amendment which has been enquired into under sub-paragraph (1) above shall not be the subject of–

(a) a further notice under that sub-paragraph; or

(b) if it is subsequently included in a return, a notice under section 9A(1) or 12AC(1) of this Act or paragraph 24 of Schedule 18 to the Finance Act 1998.

History – In para. 5(3)(b) the words "under section 9A(1) or 12AC(1) of this Act or paragraph 24 of Schedule 18 to the Finance Act 1998" substituted by FA 1998, s. 117(3) and Sch. 19, para. 42(5) with effect in relation to company accounting periods ending on or after 1 July 1999, the corporation tax self-assessment appointed day by virtue of FA 1994, s. 199(2), (3) and SI 1998/3173 (C. 78).
Cross references – ICTA 1988, s. 488(11A)(b), (12): enquiry into a claim by a housing association.
ICTA 1988, s. 489(9A): enquiry into a claim by a self-build society.

POWER TO CALL FOR DOCUMENTS FOR PURPOSES OF ENQUIRIES

6 [Omitted by FA 2008, s. 113 and Sch. 36, para. 77.]

History – Para. 6 omitted by FA 2008, s. 113 and Sch. 36, para. 77, with effect from 1 April 2009 (SI 2009/404, art. 2, subject to savings at SI 2009/404, art. 3).

APPEAL AGAINST NOTICE TO PRODUCE DOCUMENTS, ETC.

6A [Omitted by FA 2008, s. 113 and Sch. 36, para. 77.]

History – Para. 6A omitted by FA 2008, s. 113 and Sch. 36, para. 77, with effect from 1 April 2009 (SI 2009/404, art. 2, subject to savings at SI 2009/404, art. 3).

COMPLETION OF ENQUIRY INTO CLAIM

7(1) An enquiry under paragraph 5 above is completed when an officer of the Board by notice (a **"closure notice"**) informs the claimant that he has completed his enquiries and states his conclusions.

7(2) In the case of a claim for discharge or repayment of tax, the closure notice must either–

(a) state that in the officer's opinion no amendment of the claim is required, or

(b) if in the officer's opinion the claim is insufficient or excessive, amend the claim so as to make good or eliminate the deficiency or excess.

In the case of an enquiry falling within paragraph 5(1)(b) above, paragraph (b) above only applies so far as the deficiency or excess is attributable to the claimant's amendment.

7(3) In the case of a claim that is not a claim for discharge or repayment of tax, the closure notice must either–

(a) allow the claim, or

(b) disallow the claim, wholly or to such extent as appears to the officer appropriate.

7(4) A closure notice takes effect when it is issued.

7(5) The claimant may apply to the tribunal for a direction requiring an officer of the Board to issue a closure notice within a specified period.

7(6) Any such application is to be subject to the relevant provisions of Part 5 of this Act (see, in particular, section 48(2)(b)).

7(7) The tribunal shall give the direction applied for unless satisfied that there are reasonable grounds for not issuing a closure notice within a specified period.

7(8) In relation to a partnership claim, references in this paragraph to the claimant are to the person who made the claim or his successor.

History – In para. 7(5) the word "tribunal" substituted for the word "Commissioners" by SI 2009/56, art. 3(1) and Sch. 1, para. 56(2), operative from 1 April 2009, subject to transitional and saving provisions in SI 2009/56, Sch. 3.
Para. 7(6) substituted by SI 2009/56, art. 3(1) and Sch. 1, para. 56(3), operative from 1 April 2009, subject to transitional and saving provisions in SI 2009/56, Sch. 3.
In para. 7(7) the word "tribunal" substituted for the word "Commissioners hearing the application" and the words they are omitted by SI 2009/56, art. 3(1) and Sch. 1, para. 56(4), operative from 1 April 2009, subject to transitional and saving provisions in SI 2009/56, Sch. 3.
Para. 7 and the heading which precedes it substituted by FA 2001, s. 88 and Sch. 29, para. 10(2) with effect where the notice of enquiry is given after 11 May 2001, or where the enquiry is in progress immediately before that date (for these purposes, an "enquiry is in progress" until the officer's enquiries fall to be treated as completed under former para. 7(4) prior to substitution).
Former para. 7(3A), (3B) inserted, and in former para. 7(4)(b) the words "whether the claim … what amount (if any)" substituted for "the amount which" by FA 1996, s. 133 and Sch. 19, para. 9, for the purposes of income tax and capital gains tax, as respects the year 1996–97 and subsequent years of assessment, and for the purposes of corporation tax, as respects accounting periods ending on or after 1 July 1999, the day appointed for the purposes of self-assessment by virtue of FA 1994, s. 199 and SI 1998/3173 (C. 78).
Cross references – Para. 9: appeals against amendments under para. 7.
FA 2001, Sch. 29, para. 12(8): application of para. 9 (as amended by FA 2001) to closure notices issued under the substituted version of para. 7.

GIVING EFFECT TO SUCH AMENDMENTS

8(1) An officer of the Board or the Board shall, within 30 days after the date of issue of a closure notice amending a claim other than a partnership claim under paragraph 7(2) above, give effect to the amendment by making such adjustment as may be necessary, whether–

(a) by way of assessment on the claimant, or

(b) by discharge of tax or, on proof to the satisfaction of the officer or the Board that any tax has been paid by the claimant by deduction or otherwise, by repayment of tax.

8(2) An officer of the Board or the Board shall, within 30 days after the date of issue of a closure notice amending a partnership claim under paragraph 7(2) above, give effect to the amendment, as respects each of the relevant partners, by making such adjustment as may be necessary, whether–

(a) by way of assessment on the partner, or

(b) by discharge of tax or, on proof to the satisfaction of the officer or the Board that any tax has been paid by the partner by deduction or otherwise, by repayment of tax.

8(3) An assessment made under sub-paragraph (1) or (2) above shall not be out of time if it is made within the time mentioned in that sub-paragraph.

History – In para. 8(1), the words "after the date of issue of a closure notice amending a claim other than a partnership claim under paragraph 7(2)" substituted for the words "of a claim other than a partnership claim being amended under paragraph 7(2) or (3)" and, in 8(2), the words "after the date of issue of a closure notice amending a partnership claim under paragraph 7(2)" substituted for "of a [partnership] claim being amended under paragraph 7(2) or (3)", by FA 2001, s. 88, Sch. 29, para. 34(4) and (5) respectively, with effect from 11 May 2001 in relation to returns whether made before or after that date and whether relating to periods before or after then. (The amending legislation omits the word "partnership" from the text of the original words in para. 8(2) which are to be substituted, although it is clear that it is to be replaced along with the rest of the wording.)

APPEALS AGAINST SUCH AMENDMENTS

9(1) An appeal may be brought against–

(a) any conclusion stated or amendment made by a closure notice under paragraph 7(2) above, or

(b) any decision contained in a closure notice under paragraph 7(3) above.

9(1A) Notice of the appeal must be given–

(a) in writing,

(b) within 30 days after the date on which the closure notice was issued,

(c) to the officer of the Board by whom the closure notice was given.

9(2) Where, in the case of such an appeal, the issues arising include–

(a) any question arising under section 278 of the principal Act or section 56 or 460 of ITA 2007 (residence etc of claimants);

(b) any question of residence, ordinary residence or domicile; or

(c) the question whether a fund is one to which section 615(3) of the principal Act applies (pension funds for service abroad),

the time for bringing the appeal shall be three months from the date mentioned in sub-paragraph (1A)(b) above.

9(3) In the case of an appeal against an amendment made by a closure notice under paragraph 7(2) above, if an appeal is notified to the tribunal under section 49D, 49G or 49H, the tribunal may vary the amendment appealed against whether or not the variation is to the advantage of the appellant.

9(4) Where any such amendment is varied, whether by HMRC or by the tribunal or by the order of any court, paragraph 8 above shall (with the necessary modifications) apply in relation to the variation as it applied in relation to the amendment.

9(5) If, on an appeal notified to the tribunal, the tribunal decides that a claim which was the subject of a decision contained in a closure notice under paragraph 7(3) above should have been allowed or disallowed to an extent different from that specified in the notice, the claim shall be allowed or disallowed accordingly to the extent that appears appropriate, but otherwise the decision in the notice shall stand good.

History – Para. 9(1) and (1A) substituted for former para. 9(1) by FA 2001, s. 88, Sch. 29, para. 12(2), with effect in relation to closure notices issued under para. 7 (as substituted by FA 2001, Sch. 29, para. 10).

Former para. 9(1) substituted by FA 1996, s. 133 and Sch. 19, para. 10, for the purposes of income tax and capital gains tax, as respects the year 1996–97 and subsequent years of assessment, and for the purposes of corporation tax, as respects accounting periods ending on or after 1 July 1999, the day appointed for the purposes of self-assessment by virtue of FA 1994, s. 199(2), (3) and SI 1998/3173.

In para. 9(2)(a), the words "or section 56 or 460 of ITA 2007 (residence etc of claimants)" substituted for the words "(personal reliefs for non-residents)" by ITA 2007, s. 1027 and Sch. 1, para. 264(a), with effect from 6 April 2007.

In para. 9(2)(c), the words "of the principal Act" substituted for the words "of that Act" by ITA 2007, s. 1027 and Sch. 1, para. 264(b), with effect from 6 April 2007.

In para. 9(2), "(1A)(b)" substituted for "(1)" by FA 2001, s. 88, Sch. 29, para. 12(3), with effect in relation to closure notices issued under para. 7 (as substituted by FA 2001, Sch. 29, para. 10).

Previously, in para. 9(2), the words "date mentioned in sub-paragraph (1) above" substituted for "making of the amendment under paragraph 7(3) above" by FA 1996, s. 133 and Sch. 19, para. 10, for the purposes of income tax and capital gains tax, as respects the year 1996–97 and subsequent years of assessment, and for the purposes of corporation tax, as respects accounting periods ending on or after 1 July 1999 (see note further above).

In para. 9(3) the words "In the case of" substituted for the word "On" and the words "if an appeal is notified to the tribunal under section 49D, 49G or 49H, the tribunal" substituted for the words "the Commissioners" by SI 2009/56, art. 3(1) and Sch. 1, para. 57(2), operative from 1 April 2009, subject to transitional and saving provisions in SI 2009/56, Sch. 3.

In para. 9(3) the words "amendment made by a closure notice under paragraph 7(2) above" substituted for the words "amendment under paragraph 7(3) above" by FA 2001, s. 88, Sch. 29, para. 12(4), with effect in relation to closure notices issued under para. 7 (as substituted by FA 2001, Sch. 29, para. 10).

Previously, in para. 9(3), the words "againstan amendment under paragraph 7(3) above" substituted for "under this paragraph" by FA 1996, s. 133 and Sch. 19, para. 10, for the purposes of income tax and capital gains tax, as respects the year 1996–97 and subsequent years of assessment, and for the purposes of corporation tax, as respects accounting periods ending on or after 1 July 1999 (see note further above).

In para. 9(4) the words "HMRC or by the tribunal" substituted for the word "the Commissioners" by SI 2009/56, art. 3(1) and Sch. 1, para. 57(3), operative from 1 April 2009, subject to transitional and saving provisions in SI 2009/56, Sch. 3.

In para. 9(4) the words "any such amendment" substituted for the words "an amendment made under paragraph 7(3) above" by FA 2001, s. 88, Sch. 29, para. 12(5), with effect in relation to closure notices issued under para. 7 (as substituted by FA 2001, Sch. 29, para. 10).

In para. 9(5) the words "an appeal notified to the tribunal, the tribunal decides" substituted for the word "appeal, it appears to the Commissioners" and the words "to them" omitted by SI 2009/56, art. 3(1) and Sch. 1, para. 57(3), operative from 1 April 2009, subject to transitional and saving provisions in SI 2009/56, Sch. 3.

In para. 9(5) the words "which was the subject of a decision contained in a closure notice under paragraph 7(3)" substituted for the words "specified in a notice under paragraph 7(3A)" by FA 2001, s. 88, Sch. 29, para. 12(6), with effect in relation to closure notices issued under para. 7 (as substituted by FA 2001, Sch. 29, para. 10).

Para. 9(5) originally inserted by FA 1996, s. 133 and Sch. 19, para. 10, for the purposes of income tax and capital gains tax, as respects the year 1996–97 and subsequent years of assessment, and for the purposes of corporation tax, as respects accounting periods ending on or after 1 July 1999 (see note further above).

10 [Omitted by SI 2009/56, art. 3(1) and Sch. 1, para. 58.]

History – Para. 10 omitted by SI 2009/56, art. 3(1) and Sch. 1, para. 58, operative from 1 April 2009, subject to transitional and saving provisions in SI 2009/56, Sch. 3.

11 [Omitted by SI 2009/56, art. 3(1) and Sch. 1, para. 58.]

History – Para. 11 omitted by SI 2009/56, art. 3(1) and Sch. 1, para. 58, operative from 1 April 2009, subject to transitional and saving provisions in SI 2009/56, Sch. 3.

SCHEDULE 1B – CLAIMS FOR RELIEF INVOLVING TWO OR MORE YEARS

Section 42

History – Sch. 1B inserted by FA 1996, s. 128 and Sch. 17, with effect as respects claims made (or deemed to be made) in relation to the year 1996–97 or later years of assessment.

Cross references – ICTA 1988, Sch. 4A (creative artists relief for fluctuating profits): two or more claims made by the same person are associated if each of them are a claim under TMA 1970, Sch. 1B or a claim under Sch. 4A. See para. 1 below.

HMRC interpretations – IRInt. 211: HMRC's view on ability to make claims for an earlier year when, under self-assessment, a carry back claim is treated as a claim for the year in which the event occurs, not that to which the carry back is made (under TMA 1970, Sch. 1B) and the earlier year is not, as a consequence, reopened.

PRELIMINARY

1(1) In this Schedule–

(a) any reference to a claim includes a reference to an election or notice; and

(b) any reference to the amount in which a person is chargeable to tax is a reference to the amount in which he is so chargeable after taking into account any relief or allowance for which a claim is made.

1(2) For the purposes of this Schedule, two or more claims made by the same person are associated with each other if each of them is a claim to which this Schedule applies and the same year of assessment is the earlier year in relation to each of those claims.

1(3) In sub-paragraph (2) above, any reference to claims includes a reference to amendments and revocations to which paragraph 4 below applies.

History – In para. 1(2), the words "is a claim to which this Schedule applies and the same" substituted for the former wording by ITTOIA 2005, s. 882(1) and Sch. 1, para. 382(1)(a); effective for income tax purposes for 2005–06 onwards (ITTOIA 2005, s. 883(1)). In para. 1(3), the words "includes a reference to amendments and revocations to which paragraph 4 below applies." substituted for the former wording by ITTOIA 2005, s. 882(1) and Sch. 1, para. 382(1)(b); effective for income tax purposes for 2005–06 onwards (ITTOIA 2005, s. 883(1)).

Para. 1(2) and (3) substituted by FA 2001, s. 71, Sch. 24, para. 3(1) for the year 2000–01 and subsequent years of assessment.

LOSS RELIEF

2(1) This paragraph applies where a person makes a claim requiring relief for a loss incurred or treated as incurred, or a payment made, in one year of assessment (**"the later year"**) to be given in an earlier year of assessment (**"the earlier year"**).

2(2) Section 42(2) of this Act shall not apply in relation to the claim.

2(3) The claim shall relate to the later year.

2(4) Subject to sub-paragraph (5) below, the claim shall be for an amount equal to the difference between–

(a) the amount in which the person is chargeable to tax for the earlier year (**"amount A"**); and

(b) the amount in which he would be so chargeable on the assumption that effect could be, and were, given to the claim in relation to that year (**"amount B"**).

2(5) Where effect has been given to one or more associated claims, amounts A and B above shall each be determined on the assumption that effect could have been, and had been, given to the associated claim or claims in relation to the earlier year.

2(6) Effect shall be given to the claim in relation to the later year, whether by repayment or set-off, or by an increase in the aggregate amount given by section 59B(1)(b) of this Act, or otherwise.

2(7) For the purposes of this paragraph, any deduction made under section 62(2) of the 1992 Act (death: general provisions) in respect of an allowable loss shall be deemed to be made in pursuance of a claim requiring relief to be given in respect of that loss.

Cross references – ICTA 1988, s. 824(2C) (repayment supplement): application of ICTA 1988, s. 824(1) to repayment resulting from claim under para. 2.

FA 2009, Sch. 54, para. 7(a): repayment interest start date in respect of repaid following a claim under para. 2.

RELIEF FOR FLUCTUATING PROFITS OF FARMING ETC.

3(1) This paragraph applies where a person who is or has been carrying on a qualifying trade, profession or vocation (within the meaning of Chapter 16 of Part 2 of ITTOIA 2005) claims that Chapter 16 of Part 2 of ITTOIA 2005 shall have effect in relation to his profits from that trade, profession or vocation–

(a) in the case of a two-year claim, for two consecutive years of assessment, and

(b) in the case of a five-year claim, for five consecutive years of assessment.

3(2) The claim shall relate to the last of the two or five years.

3(3) Subject to sub-paragraph (4) below, in so far as the claim relates to the profits of an earlier year, the claim shall be for an amount equal to the difference between–

(a) the amount in which the person is chargeable to tax for the earlier year (**"amount A"**); and

(b) the amount in which he would be so chargeable on the assumption that effect could be, and were, given to the claim in relation to that year (**"amount B"**).

3(4) Where effect has been given to one or more associated claims, amounts A and B above shall each be determined on the assumption that effect could have been, and had been, given to the associated claim or claims in relation to the earlier year.

3(5) In so far as the claim relates to the profits of an earlier year, effect shall be given to the claim in relation to the last of the two or five years by an increase in the amount of tax payable or, as the case may require, in the aggregate amount given by section 59B(1)(b) of this Act.

3(6) Where this paragraph applies twice in relation to the same year of assessment, the increase or reduction in the amount of tax payable for that year which is required by sub-paragraph (5) above on the earlier application shall be disregarded in determining amounts A and B above for the purposes of the later application.

3(7) In this paragraph–

"two-year claim" means a claim under section 222 of ITTOIA 2005;

"five-year claim" means a claim under section 222A of ITTOIA 2005.

History – Para. 3(1)(a) and (b) substituted for the words "for two consecutive years of assessment (**"the earlier year"** and **"the later year"**)." by FA 2016, s. 25(10)(a), with effect for the tax year 2016–17 and subsequent tax years.
In para. 3(1), the words "a qualifying trade, profession or vocation (within the meaning of Chapter 16 of Part 2 of ITTOIA 2005) claims that Chapter 16 of Part 2 of ITTOIA 2005" substituted for the former words by ITTOIA 2005, s. 882(1) and Sch. 1, para. 382(3)(a); effective for income tax purposes for 2005–06 onwards (ITTOIA 2005, s. 883(1)); and the words "profession or vocation" inserted by ITTOIA 2005, s. 882(1) and Sch. 1, para. 382(3)(b); effective for income tax purposes for 2005–06 onwards (ITTOIA 2005, s. 883(1)).
In para. 3(2), the words "the last of the two or five years" substituted for the words "the later year" by FA 2016, s. 25(10)(b), with effect for the tax year 2016–17 and subsequent tax years.
In para. 3(3), the words "an earlier year" substituted for the words "the earlier year" by FA 2016, s. 25(10)(c), with effect for the tax year 2016–17 and subsequent tax years.
In para. 3(5), the words "an earlier year" substituted for the words "the earlier year" and the words "the last of the two or five years" substituted for the words "the later year" by FA 2016, s. 25(10)(d), with effect for the tax year 2016–17 and subsequent tax years.
Para. 3(7) inserted by FA 2016, s. 25(10)(e), with effect for the tax year 2016–17 and subsequent tax years.

Cross references – ICTA 1988, s. 824(2C) (repayment supplement): application of ICTA 1988, s. 824(1) to repayment resulting from claim under para. 3.

RELIEF CLAIMED BY VIRTUE OF SECTION 224(4) OF ITTOIA 2005

History – In the heading, the reference to ITTOIA 2005, s. 224(4) substituted for the former reference by ITTOIA 2005, s. 882(1) and Sch. 1, para. 382(5); effective for income tax purposes for 2005–06 onwards (ITTOIA 2005, s. 883(1)).

4(1) This paragraph applies where–

(a) a person who claims that Chapter 16 of Part 2 of ITTOIA 2005 shall have effect for two or five consecutive years of assessment makes or amends a claim for relief under any other provision of the Income Tax Acts for any of those years; and

(b) the making or amendment of the claim would be out of time but for section 224(4) of that Act.

4(2) The claim or amendment shall relate to the last of the two or five years.

4(3) Subject to sub-paragraph (4) below, in so far as the claim or amendment relates to income of an earlier year, the amount claimed, or (as the case may be) the increase or reduction in the amount claimed, shall be equal to the difference between–

(a) the amount in which the person is chargeable to tax for the earlier year (**"amount A"**); and

(b) the amount in which he would be so chargeable on the assumption that effect could be, and were, given to the claim or amendment in relation to that year (**"amount B"**).

4(4) Where effect has been given to one or more associated claims, amounts A and B above shall each be determined on the assumption that effect could have been, and had been, given to the associated claim or claims in relation to the earlier year.

4(5) In so far as the claim or amendment relates to income of an earlier year, effect shall be given to the claim or amendment in relation to the last of the two or five years by an increase in the amount of tax payable or, as the case may require, in the aggregate amount given by section 59B(1)(b) of this Act.

4(6) In this paragraph **"amend"** includes revoke and **"amendment"** shall be construed accordingly.

History – *In para. 4(1)(a), the words* "or five" inserted, the words "("the earlier year" and "the later year")" (which appeared after the words "years of assessment") omitted and the word "any" (before the words "of those years") substituted for the word "either" by FA 2016, s. 25(11)(a), with effect for the tax year 2016–17 and subsequent tax years.
In para. 4(1)(a), the words "claims that Chapter 16 of Part 2 of ITTOIA 2005" substituted for the former wording by ITTOIA 2005, s. 882(1) and Sch. 1, para. 382(4)(a); effective for income tax purposes for 2005–06 onwards (ITTOIA 2005, s. 883(1)).
In para. 4(1)(b), the words "section 224(4) of that Act" substituted for the former wording by ITTOIA 2005, s. 882(1) and Sch. 1, para. 382(4)(b); effective for income tax purposes for 2005–06 onwards (ITTOIA 2005, s. 883(1)).

In para. 4(2), the words "the last of the two or five years" substituted for the words "the later year" by FA 2016, s. 25(11)(b), with effect for the tax year 2016–17 and subsequent tax years.
In para. 4(3), the words "an earlier year" substituted for the words "the earlier year" by FA 2016, s. 25(11)(c), with effect for the tax year 2016–17 and subsequent tax years.
In para. 4(5), the words "an earlier year" substituted for the words "the earlier year" and the words "the last of the two or five years" substituted for the words "the later year" by FA 2016, s. 25(11)(d), with effect for the tax year 2016–17 and subsequent tax years.

CARRY-BACK OF POST-CESSATION ETC. RECEIPTS

5(1) This paragraph applies where a person who has received a sum to which section 257 of ITTOIA 2005 applies (election for carry-back) makes an election under that section requiring tax to he charged as if the sum were received on the date of cessation; and in this paragraph–

"the earlier year" means the year in which the sum is treated as received;

"the later year" means the year in which the sum is received.

5(2) The claim shall relate to the later year.

5(3) Subject to sub-paragraph (4) below, the claim shall be for an amount equal to the difference between–

(a) the amount in which the person is chargeable to tax for the earlier year (**"amount A"**); and

(b) the amount in which he would be so chargeable on the assumption that effect could be, and were, given to the claim in relation to that year (**"amount B"**).

5(4) Where effect has been given to one or more associated claims, amounts A and B above shall each be determined on the assumption that effect could have been, and had been, given to the associated claim or claims in relation to the earlier year.

5(5) In computing amount B for the purposes of this paragraph, no further deduction or relief shall be made or given in respect of any loss or allowance deducted in pursuance of section 254 of ITTOIA 2005.

5(6) Effect shall be given to the claim in relation to the later year by an increase in the amount of tax payable.

History – In para. 5(1), the reference to ITTOIA 2005, s. 254 substituted for the former reference to ICTA 1988, s. 108 and the words "the date of the cessation" substituted for the previous wording by ITTOIA 2005, s. 882(1) and Sch. 1, para. 382(6)(a); effective for income tax purposes for 2005–06 onwards (ITTOIA 2005, s. 883(1)).
In para. 5(5), the reference to ITTOIA 2005, s. 254 substituted for the former reference to ICTA 1988, s. 105 by ITTOIA 2005, s. 882(1) and Sch. 1, para. 382(6)(b); effective for income tax purposes for 2005–06 onwards (ITTOIA 2005, s. 883(1)).

BACKWARD SPREADING OF CERTAIN PAYMENTS

6 [Repealed by FA 2001, s. 110 and Sch. 33, Pt. 2(6).]

History – Para. 6 repealed by FA 2001, s. 110 and Sch. 33, Pt. 2(6) with effect in relation to payments actually receivable on or after 6 April 2001.

SCHEDULE 3ZA – DATE BY WHICH PAYMENT TO BE MADE AFTER AMENDMENT OR CORRECTION OF SELF-ASSESSMENT

History – Sch. 3ZA inserted by FA 2001, s. 88, Sch. 29, para. 15 with application where the "relevant day" is, or is after, 11 May 2001 (the "relevant day" being the first day of the period of 30 days specified in the relevant provision of Sch. 3ZA – i.e. the period beginning with the day on which the appropriate notice was given).

Cross references – FA 2001, s. 88, Sch. 29, para. 16(2): definition of "relevant day" for commencement of application of Sch. 3ZA.

GENERAL

1(1) This Schedule specifies the day by which tax has to be paid (or repaid) following the amendment or correction of a self-assessment or an advance self-assessment (see section 12ZE(1)).

1(2) If in any case the general rules in section 59AA(2) or 59B(3) and (4) of this Act give a later day, those rules apply instead.

1(3) The provisions of this Schedule have effect subject to section 55(6) and (9) of this Act (provisions as to postponement of payment, etc. in case of appeal).

History – In para. 1(1), the words "or an advance self-assessment (see section 12ZE(1))" inserted by FA 2015, s. 37 and Sch. 7, para. 55(2)(a), with effect in relation to disposals made on or after 6 April 2015.
In para. 1(2), the words "59AA(2) or" inserted by FA 2015, s. 37 and Sch. 7, para. 55(2)(b), with effect in relation to disposals made on or after 6 April 2015.

AMENDMENT OF PERSONAL OR TRUSTEE RETURN BY THE TAXPAYER

2(1) This paragraph applies where an amount of tax is payable or repayable as a result of the amendment of a self-assessment under section 9ZA of this Act (amendment of personal or trustee return by taxpayer) or an amendment of an advance self-assessment under section 12ZK (amendment of NRCGT return by taxpayer).

2(2) Subject to sub-paragraph (3) below, the amount is payable (or repayable) on or before the day following the end of the period of 30 days beginning with the day on which the notice of amendment was given.

2(3) If section 9B(3) or 12ZN(3) of this Act applies (amendment of self-assessment or advance self-assessment by taxpayer during enquiry: deferral of effect), then–

(a) if the amendment is taken into account as mentioned in paragraph (a)(i) of that subsection, paragraph 5 below (amendment of personal or trustee return by closure notice) applies accordingly; and

(b) if the amendment takes effect under paragraph (b) of that subsection on the issue of a partial or final closure notice, the amount is payable (or repayable) on or before the day following the end of the period of 30 days beginning with the relevant day.

2(4) In sub-paragraph (3)(b), **"the relevant day"** means–

(a) in the case of an amount of tax that is payable, the day on which the partial or final closure notice was given;

(b) in the case of an amount of tax that is repayable–

(i) if the closure notice was a final closure notice, the day on which that notice was given, and

(ii) if the closure notice was a partial closure notice, the day on which the final closure notice relating to the enquiry was given.

History – In para. 2(1), the words "or an amendment of an advance self-assessment under section 12ZK (amendment of NRCGT return by taxpayer)" inserted by FA 2015, s. 37 and Sch. 7, para. 55(3)(a), with effect in relation to disposals made on or after 6 April 2015.
In para. 2(3)(b) the words "a partial or final closure notice" substituted for the words "the closure notice" and the words "the relevant day" substituted for the words "the day on which the closure notice was given" by F(No. 2)A 2017, s. 63 and Sch. 15, para. 21(2), with effect in relation to an enquiry under TMA 1970, s. 9A, 12ZM or 12AC or FA 1998, Sch. 18 where the notice of enquiry is given on or after 16 November 2017 (Royal Assent) or the enquiry is in progress immediately before that day.
In para. 2(3), the words "or 12ZN(3)" and the words "or advance self-assessment" inserted by FA 2015, s. 37 and Sch. 7, para. 55(3)(b), with effect in relation to disposals made on or after 6 April 2015.
Para. 2(4) inserted by F(No. 2)A 2017, s. 63 and Sch. 15, para. 21(3), with effect in relation to an enquiry under TMA 1970, s. 9A, 12ZM or 12AC or FA 1998, Sch. 18 where the notice of enquiry is given on or after 16 November 2017 (Royal Assent) or the enquiry is in progress immediately before that day.

CORRECTION OF PERSONAL OR TRUSTEE RETURN BY REVENUE

3(1) This paragraph applies where an amount of tax is payable or repayable as a result of the correction of a self-assessment under section 9ZB or 12ZL of this Act (correction of personal or trustee return or NRCGT return by the Revenue).

3(2) The amount is payable (or repayable) on or before the day following the end of the period of 30 days beginning with the day on which the notice of correction was given.

History – In para. 3(1), the words "or 12ZL" and the words "or NRCGT return" inserted by FA 2015, s. 37 and Sch. 7, para. 55(4), with effect in relation to disposals made on or after 6 April 2015.

AMENDMENT OF PERSONAL OR TRUSTEE RETURN TO PREVENT LOSS OF TAX

4(1) This paragraph applies where an amount of tax is payable or repayable as a result of the amendment of a self-assessment under section 9C of this Act (amendment of personal or trustee return by Revenue to prevent loss of tax).

4(2) The amount is payable (or repayable) on or before the day following the end of the period of 30 days beginning with the day on which the notice of amendment was given.

AMENDMENT OF PERSONAL OR TRUSTEE RETURN BY CLOSURE NOTICE

5(1) This paragraph applies where an amount of tax or an amount on account of capital gains tax is payable or repayable as a result of the amendment of a self-assessment or advance self-assessment under section 28A of this Act (amendment of return by closure notice following enquiry).

5(2) The amount is payable (or repayable) on or before the day following the end of the period of 30 days beginning with the day on which the closure notice was given.

History – In para. 5(1), the words "or an amount on account of capital gains tax" and the words "or advance self-assessment" inserted and the words "personal or trustee" (which appeared before the word "return") by FA 2015, s. 37 and Sch. 7, para. 55(5), with effect in relation to disposals made on or after 6 April 2015.

AMENDMENT CONSEQUENTIAL ON AMENDMENT OF PARTNERSHIP RETURN BY TAXPAYER

6(1) This paragraph applies where an amount of tax is payable or repayable as a result of the amendment of a self-assessment under section 12ABA(3)(a) of this Act (consequential amendment of partner's personal or trustee return where partnership return amended by taxpayer).

6(2) The amount is payable (or repayable) on or before the day following the end of the period of 30 days beginning with the day on which the notice under section 12ABA(3)(a) of this Act was given.

AMENDMENT CONSEQUENTIAL ON CORRECTION OF PARTNERSHIP RETURN BY REVENUE

7(1) This paragraph applies where an amount of tax is payable or repayable as a result of the amendment of a self-assessment under section 12ABB(6)(a) of this Act (consequential amendment of partner's personal or trustee return where partnership return corrected by Revenue).

7(2) The amount is payable (or repayable) on or before the day following the end of the period of 30 days beginning with the day on which the notice under section 12ABB(6)(a) of this Act was given.

AMENDMENT CONSEQUENTIAL ON AMENDMENT OF PARTNERSHIP RETURN BY CLOSURE NOTICE

8(1) This paragraph applies where an amount of tax is payable or repayable as a result of the amendment of a self-assessment under section 28B(4)(a) of this Act (consequential amendment of partner's personal or trustee return where partnership return amended by closure notice).

8(2) The amount is payable (or repayable) on or before the day following the end of the period of 30 days beginning with the day on which the notice under section 28B(4)(a) of this Act was given.

AMENDMENT CONSEQUENTIAL ON AMENDMENT OF PARTNERSHIP RETURN TO PREVENT LOSS OF TAX

9(1) This paragraph applies where an amount of tax is payable or repayable as a result of the amendment of a self-assessment under section 30B(2)(a) of this Act (consequential amendment of partner's personal or trustee return where partnership return amended by Revenue to prevent loss of tax).

9(2) The amount is payable (or repayable) on or before the day following the end of the period of 30 days beginning with the day on which the notice under section 30B(2)(a) of this Act was given.

AMENDMENT CONSEQUENTIAL ON AMENDMENT OF PARTNERSHIP RETURN BY WAY OF ERROR OR MISTAKE RELIEF

10 [Omitted by FA 2009, s. 100 and Sch. 52, para. 8.]

History – Para. 10 omitted by FA 2009, s. 100 and Sch. 52, para. 8 with effect in relation to claims made on or after 1 April 2010.

AMENDMENT CONSEQUENTIAL ON REDUCTION OR INCREASE ON APPEAL OF AMOUNTS STATED IN PARTNERSHIP STATEMENT

11(1) This paragraph applies where an amount of tax is payable or repayable as a result of the amendment of a self-assessment under section 50(9)(a) of this Act (consequential amendment of partner's personal or trustee return where partnership statement amended by Revenue following decision on appeal).

11(2) The amount is payable (or repayable) on or before the day following the end of the period of 30 days beginning with the day on which the notice under section 50(9)(a) of this Act was given.

SOCIAL SECURITY PENSIONS ACT 1975

(1975 Chapter 60) [*7th August 1975*]

ARRANGEMENT OF SECTIONS

PART V – GENERAL

PART V – GENERAL

61B Orders and regulations (general provisions)

61B(1) Powers under this Act to make regulations or orders, are exercisable by statutory instrument.

61B(2) Except in so far as this Act otherwise provides, any power conferred thereby to make regulations or an order may be exercised–

(a) either in relation to all cases to which the power extends, or in relation to those cases subject to specified exceptions, or in relation to any specified cases or classes of case;

(b) so as to make, as respects the cases in relation to which it is exercised–

(i) the full provision to which the power extends or any less provision (whether by way of exception or otherwise),

(ii) the same provision for all cases in relation to which the power is exercised, or different provision for different cases or different classes of case or different provision as respects the same case or class of case for different purposes of this Act,

(iii) any such provision either unconditionally or subject to any specified condition;

and where such a power is expressed to be exercisable for alternative purposes it may be exercised in relation to the same case for any or all of those purposes; and powers to make regulations or an order for the purposes of any one provision of this Act are without prejudice to powers to make regulations or an order for the purposes of any other provision.

61B(3) Without prejudice to any specific provision in this Act, a power conferred by this Act to make regulations or an order includes power to make thereby such incidental, supplementary, consequential or transitional provision as appears to the authority making the regulations or order to be expedient for the purposes of the regulations or order.

61B(4) Without prejudice to any specific provisions in this Act, a power conferred by this Act to make regulations or an order includes power to provide for a person to exercise a discretion in dealing with any matter.

61B(5) A power conferred on the Secretary of State to make any regulations or order, where the power is not expressed to be exercisable with the consent of the Treasury, shall if the Treasury so direct be exercisable only in conjunction with them.

History – S. 61B inserted by SS(CP)A 1992, s. 4 and Sch. 2, para. 19, 37, with effect from 1 July 1992.
In s. 61B(1) the words "except any power of the Occupational Pensions Board to make orders" omitted by Pensions Act 1995, s. 126 and Sch. 4, para. 6(2) with effect from 6 April 1997 by virtue of SI 1997/664.

Cross references – SSA 1986, s. 83(1): orders and regulations (general provisions).

Notes – Interpretation Act 1978, Sch. 1: "Secretary of State" means one of HM's Principal Secretaries of State; "the Treasury" means the Commissioners of HM Treasury.

62 Other provisions about regulations and orders

62(1) [Repealed by SS(CP)A 1992, s. 3 and Sch. 1.]

62(2) A statutory instrument–

(a) which contains (whether alone or with other provisions) any order or regulations made under this Act by the Secretary of State, other than an order which, under any provision of this Act, is required to be laid before Parliament after being made; and

(b) which is not subject to any requirement that a draft of the instrument shall be laid before and approved by a resolution of each House of Parliament,

shall be subject to annulment in pursuance of a resolution of either House of Parliament.

62(3) [Repealed by SS(CP)A 1992, s. 3 and Sch. 1.]

62(4) [Repealed by PSA 1993, s. 188 and Sch. 5, Pt. I.]

Commencement Date – S. 62 came into force on 7 August 1975, by virtue of SI 1975/1318.

History – S. 62(1) repealed by SS(CP)A 1992, and Sch. 1, with effect from 1 July 1992.
S. 62(1), (2) substituted by SSA 1990, s. 21(1), 23(3) and Sch. 6, para. 8(2) with effect from 13 July 1990.
S. 62(2) substituted by SS(CP)A 1992, s. 4 and Sch. 2, para. 38, with effect from 1 July 1992.
S. 62(3) repealed by SS(CP)A 1992, s. 3 and Sch. 1, with effect from 1 July 1992.
S. 62(4) repealed by PSA 1993, s. 188 and Sch. 5, Pt. I, with effect from 7 February 1994.

Notes – Interpretation Act 1978, Sch. 1: "Secretary of State" means one of HM's Principal Secretaries of State.

67 Commencement

67 [Repealed by Statute Law (Repeals) Act 2004, Sch. 1, Pt. 11.]

History – S. 67 repealed by Statute Law (Repeals) Act 2004, Sch. 1, Pt. 11, with effect from 22 July 2004.

68 Short title, citation and extent

68(1) This Act may be cited as the Social Security Pensions Act 1975.

68(2) The Social Security Act 1975 and this Act may be cited together as the Social Security Acts 1975.

68(3) [Not relevant to National Insurance contributions.]

68(4) This Act extends to Northern Ireland so far as it–

(a) [repealed by PSA 1993, s. 188 and Sch. 5, Pt. I;]

(b) [repealed by PSA 1993, s. 188 and Sch. 5, Pt. I;]

(c) repeals Part III and section 89(3)(c) and (4) of that Act, and Schedules 18 to 20 to that Act;

(d) by section 65(2) and Part II of Schedule 4 amends the Social Security (Northern Ireland) Act 1975 and the Social Security (Consequential Provisions) Act 1975 and reinstates paragraph 1 of Schedule 5 to the Social Security Benefits Act 1975;

(e) repeals paragraphs 47 and (in part) 58 of Schedule 2 to the Social Security (Consequential Provisions) Act 1975;

(f) [repealed by the Statute Law (Repeals) Act 2004, Sch. 1, Pt. 11;]

(g) [repealed by the Statute Law (Repeals) Act 2004, Sch. 1, Pt. 11;]

(h) repeals provisions of the Public Records Act 1958, the Superannuation Act 1972, the Parliamentary and other Pensions Act 1972, the Pensions (Increase) Act 1974 and the House of Commons Disqualification Act 1975;

but subject to the foregoing provisions of this subsection and to subsection (3) above, this Act does not extend to Northern Ireland.

Commencement Date – S. 68 came into force on 7 August 1975, by virtue of SI 1975/1318.

History – S. 68(4)(f) and (g) repealed by the Statute Law (Repeals) Act 2004, Sch. 1, Pt. 11, with effect from 22 July 2004.
In s. 68(4), the opening words "The following provisions … Northern Ireland; and" repealed by PSA 1993, s. 188 and Sch. 5, Pt. I, with effect from 7 February 1994.
In s. 68(4), subpara. (a) and (b) repealed by PSA 1993, s. 188 and Sch. 5, Pt. I, with effect from 7 February 1994.

Notes – SSA 1975 was repealed by SS(CP)A 1992, Sch. 1.
In s. 68(4)(c), the references to "that Act" refer to SSA 1973; the subsection became unclear when s. 68(4)(a) (in which the Act was named) was repealed.

SOCIAL SECURITY ACT 1980

(1980 Chapter 30) [*23rd May 1980*]

ARRANGEMENT OF SECTIONS

COMMISSIONERS

12 Change of title of National Insurance Commissioners

12 National Insurance Commissioners shall, instead of being so called, be called Social Security Commissioners; and accordingly–

(a) any enactment or instrument passed or made before the coming into force of this section shall have effect, so far as may be necessary in consequence of the change of title made by this section, as if for any reference to a Chief or other National Insurance Commissioner there were substituted respectively a reference to a Chief or other Social Security Commissioner; and

(b) documents and forms printed or duplicated for use in connection with functions of National Insurance Commissioners may be used notwithstanding that they contain references to such Commissioners and those references shall be construed as references to Social Security Commissioners.

Commencement Date – S. 12 came into force on 23 May 1980, by virtue of SSA 1980, s. 21(5).

GENERAL

21 Supplemental

21(1) This Act may be cited as the Social Security Act 1980 and this Act and the Social Security Acts 1975 to 1979 may be cited together as the Social Security Acts 1975 to 1980.

21(2) In this Act **"the principal Act"** means the Social Security Act 1975 and **"the Pensions Act"** means the Social Security Pensions Act 1975.

21(3) Section 175(3) and (4) of the Social Security Contributions and Benefits Act 1992 (which among other things make provision about the extent of powers to make regulations and orders) shall apply to powers to make regulations and orders conferred by sections 8 and 20(2) of this Act and by subsection (5) of this section as extended by the said sections 8 and 20(2) as they apply to powers to make regulations and orders conferred by that Act but as if for references to that Act there were substituted references to the said sections 20(2) and the said subsection (5) as so extended.

21(4) [Repeals.]

21(5) The following provisions of this Act, namely, section 6 (except subsection (4)) and sections 7 to 10, 14 and 15, Part I and paragraphs 10 and 14 of Schedule 1, Schedules 2 to 4 and Part II of Schedule 5, shall come into force on such day as the Secretary of State may appoint by order made by statutory instrument, and different days may be appointed in pursuance of this subsection for different provisions of this Act; and accordingly the other provisions of this Act come into force on the passing of this Act.

21(6) The following provisions only of this Act shall extend to Northern Ireland, namely–

sections 9 to 16, except sections 11, 13(6) and 15;

[not relevant to National Insurance contributions];

this section;

Schedule 3; and

[not relevant to National Insurance contributions].

Commencement Date – S. 21 came into force on 23 May 1980, by virtue of SSA 1980, s. 21(5).

History – In s. 21(3) the words "Section 175(3) and (4) of the Social Security Contributions and Benefits Act 1992" substituted by SS(CP)A 1992, s. 4 and Sch. 2, para. 59, with effect from 1 July 1992.

Notes – The Social Security Act 1975 was repealed by SS(CP)A 1992, Sch. 1.

BANKRUPTCY (SCOTLAND) ACT 1985

(1985 Chapter 66)

[*30th October 1985*]

ARRANGEMENT OF SECTIONS

AWARD OF SEQUESTRATION AND APPOINTMENT AND RESIGNATION OF INTERIM TRUSTEE

12 When sequestration is awarded

12(1) Where a debtor application, other than an application under section 5(3)(a), is made and sections 11A and 11B do not apply, the Accountant in Bankruptcy shall award sequestration forthwith if he is satisfied–

(a) that the application has been made in accordance with the provisions of this Act and any provisions made under this Act;

(b) that either subsection (2B) of section 5 of this Act applies to the debtor; and

(c) that the provisions of subsection (6A) of that section have been complied with.

12(1A) [Repealed by Bankruptcy and Diligence etc. (Scotland) Act 2007, s. 226(2) and Sch. 6, Pt. 1.]

12(1B) Where a debtor application is made under section 5(3)(a) the Accountant in Bankruptcy must award sequestration forthwith if the Accountant is satisfied–

(a) that the application has been made in accordance with the provisions of this Act and any provision made under this Act, and

(b) that the provisions of subsection (6A) of section 5 have been complied with.

12(2) Where a petition for sequestration of a debtor's estate is presented by a creditor or a trustee acting under a trust deed, the sheriff to whom the petition is presented shall grant warrant to cite the debtor to appear before him on such date as shall be specified in the warrant, being a date not less than 6 nor more than 14 days after the date of citation, to show cause why sequestration should not be awarded.

12(3) Where, on a petition for sequestration presented by a creditor or a trustee acting under a trust deed, the sheriff is satisfied–

(a) that, if the debtor has not appeared, proper citation has been made of the debtor;

(b) that the petition has been presented in accordance with the provisions of this Act;

(c) that the provisions of subsection (6) of section 5 of this Act have been complied with;

(d) that, in the case of a petition by a creditor, the requirements of this Act relating to apparent insolvency have been fulfilled; and

(e) that, in the case of a petition by a trustee–

  (i) one or more of the conditions in section 5(2C)(a) applies, or

  (ii) the petition includes an averment in accordance with section 5(2C)(b),

he shall, subject to subsections (3A) to (3C) below, award sequestration forthwith.

12(3A) Sequestration shall not be awarded in pursuance of subsection (3) above if–

(a) cause is shown why sequestration cannot competently be awarded; or

(b) the debtor forthwith pays or satisfies, or produces written evidence of the payment or satisfaction of–

(i) the debt in respect of which he became apparently insolvent; and

(ii) any other debt due by him to the petitioner and any creditor concurring in the petition.

12(3B) Where the sheriff is satisfied that the debtor shall, before the expiry of the period of 42 days beginning with the day on which the debtor appears before the sheriff, pay or satisfy—

(a) the debt in respect of which the debtor became apparently insolvent; and

(b) any other debt due by the debtor to the petitioner and any creditor concurring in the petition,

the sheriff may continue the petition for a period of no more than 42 days.

12(3C) Where the sheriff is satisfied—

(a) that a debt payment programme (within the meaning of Part 1 of the Debt Arrangement and Attachment (Scotland) Act 2002 (asp 17)) relating to—

(i) the debt in respect of which the debtor became apparently insolvent; and

(ii) any other debt due by the debtor to the petitioner and any creditor concurring in the petition,

has been applied for and has not yet been approved or rejected; or

(b) that such a debt payment programme will be applied for,

the sheriff may continue the petition for such period as he thinks fit.

12(4) In this Act **"the date of sequestration"** means–

(a) where a debtor application is made, the date on which sequestration is awarded;

(b) where the petition for sequestration is presented by a creditor or a trustee acting under a trust deed and sequestration is awarded–

(i) the date on which the sheriff grants warrant under subsection (2) above to cite the debtor; or

(ii) where more than one such warrant is granted, the date on which the first such warrant is granted.

Commencement Date – S. 12 came into force on 1 April 1986, by virtue of SI 1985/1924.

History – In s. 12(1), the words ", other than an application under section 5(3)(a)," inserted after the first occurrence of the word "application" by Bankruptcy and Debt (Scotland) Act 2014, s. 11(4)(a) with effect from 1 April 2015 (SI 2014/261, art. 3).
In s. 12(1), the words "and sections 11A and 11B do not apply" inserted after the word "made" by Bankruptcy and Debt (Scotland) Act 2014, s. 56(1) and Sch. 3, para. 9(a), with effect from 1 April 2015 (SI 2014/261, art. 3).
In s. 12(1), the words "debtor application is made, the Accountant in Bankruptcy shall award sequestration forthwith if he is satisfied–" and para. (a) substituted for the words "petition for the sequestration of his estate is presented by the debtor, unless cause is shown why sequestration cannot competently be awarded, the court shall award sequestration forthwith if it is satisfied– (a) that the petition has been presented in accordance with the provisions of this Act;" by Bankruptcy and Diligence etc. (Scotland) Act 2007, s. 14(8), with effect from 1 April 2008 (SI 2008/115, art. 3).
In s. 12(1), the word "subsection" substituted for the words "subsections (6) and" by Bankruptcy and Diligence etc. (Scotland) Act 2007, s. 36 and Sch. 1, para. 10(a), with effect from 1 April 2008 (SI 2008/115, art. 3).
S. 12(1) substituted by B(S)A 1993, s. 4(2), with effect from 1 April 1993, by virtue of SI 1993/438, art. 3.
In s. 12(1)(b), the word "subsection" substituted for the words "either subsection (2A) or" by Home Owner and Debtor Protection (Scotland) Act 2010, s. 9(3), with effect from 15 November 2010 (SI 2010/314, art. 6).
S. 12(1A) repealed by Bankruptcy and Diligence etc. (Scotland) Act 2007, s. 226(2) and Sch. 6, Pt. 1, with effect from 1 April 2008 (SI 2008/115, art. 3).
S. 12(1A) inserted by B(S)A 1993, s. 4(3), with effect from 1 April 1993, by virtue of SI 1993/438, art. 3.
S. 12(1B) inserted by Bankruptcy and Debt (Scotland) Act 2014, s. 11(4)(b) with effect from 1 April 2015 (SI 2014/261, art. 3).
In s. 12(2), the words "sheriff to whom" substituted for the words "court to which" and the word "him" substituted for the word "it" by Bankruptcy and Diligence etc. (Scotland) Act 2007, s. 36 and Sch. 1, para. 10(b), with effect from 1 April 2008 (SI 2008/115, art. 3).
In s. 12(3), the words "subsections (3A) to (3C)" substituted for the words "subsection (3A)" by Bankruptcy and Diligence etc. (Scotland) Act 2007, s. 27(2), with effect from 1 April 2008 (SI 2008/115, art. 3).
In s. 12(3), the word "sheriff" substituted for the word "court" and the word "he" substituted for the word "it" by Bankruptcy and Diligence etc. (Scotland) Act 2007, s. 36 and Sch. 1, para. 10(c), with effect from 1 April 2008 (SI 2008/115, art. 3).
S. 12(3) substituted for s. 12(3) by B(S)A 1993, s. 4(4), witheffect from 1 April 1993, by virtue of SI 1993/438, art. 3.
S. 12(3)(e) substituted by Bankruptcy and Debt (Scotland) Act 2014, s. 47, with effect from 1 April 2015 (SI 2014/261, art. 3).
S. 12(3A) substituted for s. 12(3) by B(S)A 1993, s. 4(4), with effect from 1 April 1993, by virtue of SI 1993/438, art. 3.
In s. 12(3A)(b), the words ", or gives or shows that there is sufficient security for the payment of" repealed by Bankruptcy and Debt (Scotland) Act 2014, s. 56(2) and Sch. 4, with effect 1 April 2015 (SI 2014/261, art. 3).
S. 12(3B) and (3C) inserted by Bankruptcy and Diligence etc. (Scotland) Act 2007, s. 14(8), with effect from 1 April 2008 (SI 2008/115, art. 3).
In s. 12(4), the words "a debtor application is made" substituted for the words "the petition for sequestration is presented by the debtor" and the word "sheriff" substituted for the word "court" by Bankruptcy and Diligence etc. (Scotland) Act 2007, s. 36 and Sch. 1, para. 10(d), with effect from 1 April 2008 (SI 2008/115, art. 3).
S. 12(4) substituted by B(S)A 1993, s. 4(5), with effect from 1 April 1993, by virtue of SI 1993/438, art. 3.
In s. 12(4)(b), the words "and sequestration is awarded" inserted after the word "deed" by Bankruptcy and Debt (Scotland) Act 2014, s. 56(1) and Sch. 3, para. 9(b), with effect from 1 April 2015 (SI 2014/261, art. 3).

Cross references – SI 2013/1388, reg. 19(2): modification of s. 12 in its application to an authorised partnership.

DISTRIBUTION OF DEBTOR'S ESTATE

51 Order of priority in distribution

51(1) The funds of the debtor's estate shall be distributed by the trustee to meet the following debts in the order in which they are mentioned–

(a) the outlays and remuneration of the interim trustee in the administration of the debtor's estate;

(b) the outlays and remuneration of the trustee in the administration of the debtor's estate;

(c) where the debtor is a deceased debtor, deathbed and funeral expenses reasonably incurred and expenses reasonably incurred in administering the deceased's estate;

(d) the expenses reasonably incurred by a creditor who is a petitioner, or concurs in a debtor application, for sequestration;

(e) ordinary preferred debts (excluding any interest which has accrued thereon to the date of sequestration);

(ea) secondary preferred debts (excluding any interest which has accrued thereon to the date of sequestration);

(f) ordinary debts, that is to say a debt which is either a secured debt or a debt mentioned in any other paragraph of this subsection;

(g) interest at the rate specified in subsection (7) below on–

(i) the ordinary preferred debts;

(ia) the secondary preferred debts;

(ii) the ordinary debts,

between the date of sequestration and the date of payment of the debt;

(h) any postponed debt.

51(2) In this Act—

(a) **"preferred debt"** means a debt listed in Part I of Schedule 3 to this Act,

(b) **"ordinary preferred debt"** means a debt within any of paragraphs 4 to 6B of Part I of Schedule 3 to this Act,

(c) **"secondary preferred debt"** means a debt within paragraph 6C or 6D of Part 1 of Schedule 3 to this Act, and

Part II of that Schedule shall have effect for the interpretation of Part I.

51(3) In this Act **"postponed debt"** means–

(a) a loan made to the debtor, in consideration of a share of the profits in his business, which is postponed under section 3 of the Partnership Act 1890 to the claims of other creditors;

(b) a loan made to the debtor by the debtor's spouse or civil partner;

(c) a creditor's right to anything vesting in the trustee by virtue of a successful challenge under section 34 of this Act or to the proceeds of sale of such a thing.

51(4) Any debt falling within any of paragraphs (c) to (h) of subsection (1) above shall have the same priority as any other debt falling within the same paragraph and, where the funds of the estate are inadequate to enable the debts mentioned in the paragraph to be paid in full, they shall abate in equal proportions.

51(5) Any surplus remaining, after all the debts mentioned in this section have been paid in full, shall be made over to the debtor or to his successors or assignees; and in this subsection **"surplus"** includes any kind of estate but does not include any unclaimed dividend.

51(5A) Subsection (5) above is subject to Article 35 of the EC Regulation (surplus in secondary proceedings to be transferred to main proceedings).

51(6) Nothing in this section shall affect–

(a) the right of a secured creditor which is preferable to the rights of the trustee; or

(b) any preference of the holder of a lien over a title deed or other document which has been delivered to the trustee in accordance with a requirement under section 38(4) of this Act.

51(7) The rate of interest referred to in paragraph (g) of subsection (1) above shall be whichever is the greater of–

(a) the prescribed rate at the date of sequestration; and

(b) the rate applicable to that debt apart from the sequestration.

Commencement Date – S. 51(1), (3)–(7) came into force on 1 April 1986, by virtue of SI 1985/1924.
S. 51(2) came into force on 29 December 1986, by virtue of B(S)A 1985, s. 78(2) and SI 1986/1913.

History – In s. 51(1)(d), the words "a debtor application" substituted for the words "the petition" by Bankruptcy and Diligence etc. (Scotland) Act 2007, s. 36 and Sch. 1, para. 43, with effect from 1 April 2008 (SI 2008/115, art. 3).

S. 51(1)(e) and (ea) substituted for (e) by SI 2014/3486, art. 28(2)(a), with effect from 1 January 2015, subject to the transitional provision in SI 2014/3486, art. 3 (amendments have no effect in relation to any insolvency proceedings commenced before that date).
In s. 51(1)(g)(i), the word "ordinary" inserted by SI 2014/3486, art. 28(2)(a), with effect from 1 January 2015, subject to the transitional provision in SI 2014/3486, art. 3 (amendments have no effect in relation to any insolvency proceedings commenced before that date).
S. 51(1)(g)(ia) inserted by SI 2014/3486, art. 28(2)(a), with effect from 1 January 2015, subject to the transitional provision in SI 2014/3486, art. 3 (amendments have no effect in relation to any insolvency proceedings commenced before that date).
S. 51(2) substituted by SI 2014/3486, art. 28(2)(b), with effect from 1 January 2015, subject to the transitional provision in SI 2014/3486, art. 3 (amendments have no effect in relation to any insolvency proceedings commenced before that date).
In s. 51(3)(b) words "or civil partner" inserted at end by Civil Partnership Act 2004, Sch. 28, para. 39, with effect from 5 December 2005 (by virtue of Scottish SI 2005/604, art. 2(c)).
S. 51(5A) inserted by SI 2003/2109, reg. 14, with effect from 8 September 2003.
In s. 51 the word "permanent" which appeared before the word "trustee" in five places, omitted by the Bankruptcy and Diligence etc. (Scotland) Act 2007, s. 226(2) and Sch. 6, Pt. 1, with effect from 1 April 2008 (SSI 2008/115, art. 3 and Sch. 2, para. 8) subject to transitional provisions and savings at SSI 2008/115, art. 4–7, 10 and 15.

MISCELLANEOUS AND SUPPLEMENTARY

73 Interpretation

73(1) In this Act, unless the context otherwise requires–

"[Not relevant to National Insurance contributions]"

"date of sequestration" has the meaning assigned by section 12(4) of this Act;

"debtor" includes, without prejudice to the expression's generality, an entity whose estate may be sequestrated by virtue of section 6 of this Act, a deceased debtor or his executor or a person entitled to be appointed as executor to a deceased debtor;

"the EC Regulation" means Council Regulation (EC) No 1346/2000 of 29th May 2000 on insolvency proceedings;

"[Not relevant to National Insurance contributions]"

"interim trustee" shall be construed in accordance with section 2(5) of this Act;

"[Not relevant to National Insurance contributions]"

"ordinary debt" shall be construed in accordance with section 51(1)(f) of this Act;

"postponed debt" has the meaning assigned by section 51(3) of this Act;

"preferred debt" has the meaning assigned by section 51(2) of this Act;

"prescribed" means prescribed by regulations made by the Secretary of State;

"[Not relevant to National Insurance contributions]"

"secured creditor" means a creditor who holds a security for his debt over any part of the debtor's estate;

"[Not relevant to National Insurance contributions]"

73(2)–(6) [Not relevant to National Insurance contributions.]

Commencement Date – S. 73(1) came into force on 1 April 1986 and 29 December 1986, by virtue of SI 1985/1924 and 1986/1913.

History – The definition of "the EC Regulation" inserted by the Insolvency (Scotland) Regulations (SI 2003/2109), reg. 3 and 19 with effect from 8 September 2003.
In s. 73(1), in the definition of "interim trustee", "2(5)" substituted by Bankruptcy and Diligence etc (Scotland) Act 2007, s. 36 and Sch. 1, para. 60(2)(d).
The definition of "permanent trustee" omitted by Bankruptcy and Diligence etc. (Scotland) Act 2007, s. 226(2) and Sch. 6, Pt. 1, with effect from 1 April 2008 (SI 2008/115, art. 3).

78 Short title, commencement and extent

78(1) This Act may be cited as the Bankruptcy (Scotland) Act 1985.

78(2) This Act, except this section, shall come into force on such day as the Secretary of State may by order made by statutory instrument appoint; and different days may be so appointed for different purposes and for different provisions.

78(3), (4) [Transitional and saving provisions.]

78(5) This Act, except the provisions mentioned in subsection (6) below, extends to Scotland only.

78(6) [Not relevant to National Insurance contributions.]

Commencement Date – S. 78 came into force on 30 October 1985, by virtue of B(S)A 1985, s. 78(2).

SCHEDULES

SCHEDULE 3 – PREFERRED DEBTS

Section 51

Part I – List of Preferred Debts

SOCIAL SECURITY CONTRIBUTIONS

3 [Repealed by the Enterprise Act 2002, s. 251(2)(c), s. 278(2), and Sch. 26.]

Commencement Date – Sch. 3 came into force on 29 December 1986, by virtue of B(S)A 1985, s. 78(2) and SI 1986/1913.

History – Para. 3 repealed by the Enterprise Act 2002, s. 251(2)(c), s. 278(2), and Sch. 26, with effect from 15 September 2003, by virtue of SI 2003/2093, art. 2 and Sch. 1. Art. 4 contains transitional provisions.

Transitional – Enterprise Act 2002 (Commencement No. 4 and Transitional Provisions and Savings) Order 2003, SI 2003/2093, art. 4, contains transitional provisions so that the former rules remain in effect where insolvency arrangements are in place prior to 15 September 2003.

7 In Part I of the Schedule **"the relevant date"** means–

(a) in relation to a debtor (other than a deceased debtor), the date of sequestration; and

(b) in relation to a deceased debtor, the date of his death.

INSOLVENCY ACT 1986

(1986 Chapter 45) [*25th July 1986*]

ARRANGEMENT OF SECTIONS

THE FIRST GROUP OF PARTS – COMPANY INSOLVENCY; COMPANIES WINDING UP

PART IV – WINDING UP OF COMPANIES REGISTERED UNDER THE COMPANIES ACTS

Chapter VI – Winding Up by the Court

GROUNDS AND EFFECT OF WINDING-UP PETITION

126 Power to stay or restrain proceedings against company.

126(1) At any time after the presentation of a winding-up petition, and before a winding-up order has been made, the company, or any creditor or contributory, may–

(a) where any action or proceeding against the company is pending in the High Court or Court of Appeal in England and Wales or Northern Ireland, apply to the court in which the action or proceeding is pending for a stay of proceedings therein, and

(b) where any other action or proceeding is pending against the company, apply to the court having jurisdiction to wind up the company to restrain further proceedings in the action or proceeding;

and the court to which the application is so made may (as the case may be) stay, sist or restrain the proceedings accordingly on such terms as it thinks fit.

126(2) In the case of a company registered but not formed under the Companies Act 2006, where the application to stay, sist or restrain is by a creditor, this section extends to actions and proceedings against any contributory of the company.

126(3) Subsection (1) applies in relation to any action being taken in respect of the company under Part 1 of Schedule 8 to the Finance (No. 2) Act 2015 (enforcement by deduction from accounts) as it applies in relation to any action or proceeding mentioned in paragraph (b) of that subsection.

History – In s. 126(2), the words "a company registered but not formed under the Companies Act 2006" substituted for the words "a company registered under section 680 of the Companies Act (pre-1862 companies; companies formed under legislation other than the Companies Acts) or the previous corresponding legislation" by SI 2009/1941, art. 2(1) and Sch. 1, para. 75(14), with effect from 1 October 2009, subject to the transitional provisions in SI 2009/1941, art. 8.
S. 126(3) inserted by F(No. 2)A 2015, s. 51 and Sch. 8, para. 27, with effect from 18 November 2015 (Royal Assent).

127 Avoidance of property dispositions, etc.

127(1) In a winding up by the court, any disposition of the company's property, and any transfer of shares, or alteration in the status of the company's members, made after the commencement of the winding up is, unless the court otherwise orders, void.

127(2) This section has no effect in respect of anything done by an administrator of a company while a winding-up petition is suspended under paragraph 40 of Schedule B1.

History – S. 127(1) created from existing text and s. 127(2) inserted by Enterprise Act 2002, s. 248(3) and Sch. 17, para. 15, with effect from 15 September 2003, subject to transitional provisions in SI 2003/2093, art. 3 (amendments have no effect where a petition for an administration order has been presented before that date) (SI 2003/2093, art. 2(1)).

128 Avoidance of attachments, etc.

128(1) Where a company registered in England and Wales is being wound up by the court, any attachment, sequestration, distress or execution put in force against the estate or effects of the company after the commencement of the winding up is void.

128(2) This section, so far as relates to any estate or effects of the company situated in England and Wales, applies in the case of a company registered in Scotland as it applies in the case of a company registered in England and Wales.

128(3) In subsection (1) **"attachment"** includes a hold notice or a deduction notice under Part 1 of Schedule 8 to the Finance (No. 2) Act 2015 (enforcement by deduction from accounts) and, if subsection (1) has effect in relation to a deduction notice, it also has effect in relation to the hold notice to which the deduction notice relates (whenever the hold notice was given).

History – S. 128(3) inserted by F(No. 2)A 2015, s. 51 and Sch. 8, para. 28, with effect from 18 November 2015 (Royal Assent).

COMMENCEMENT OF WINDING UP

129 Commencement of winding up by the court

129(1) If, before the presentation of a petition for the winding up of a company by the court, a resolution has been passed by the company for voluntary winding up, the winding up of the company is deemed to have commenced at the time of the passing of the resolution; and unless the court, on proof of fraud or mistake, directs otherwise, all proceedings taken in the voluntary winding up are deemed to have been validly taken.

129(1A) Where the court makes a winding-up order by virtue of paragraph 13(1)(e) of Schedule B1, the winding up is deemed to commence on the making of the order.

129(2) In any other case, the winding up of a company by the court is deemed to commence at the time of the presentation of the petition for winding up.

History – S. 129(1A) inserted by Enterprise Act 2002, s. 248(3) and Sch. 17, para. 16, with effect from 15 September 2003, subject to transitional provisions in SI 2003/2093, art. 3 (amendments have no effect where a petition for an administration order has been presented before that date) (SI 2003/2093, art. 2(1)).

130 Consequences of winding-up order

130(1) On the making of a winding-up order, a copy of the order must forthwith be forwarded by the company (or otherwise as may be prescribed) to the registrar of companies, who shall enter it in his records relating to the company.

130(2) When a winding-up order has been made or a provisional liquidator has been appointed, no action or proceeding shall be proceeded with or commenced against the company or its property, except by leave of the court and subject to such terms as the court may impose.

130(3) When an order has been made for winding up a company registered but not formed under the Companies Act 2006, no action or proceeding shall be commenced or proceeded with against the company or its property or any contributory of the company, in respect of any debt of the company, except by leave of the court, and subject to such terms as the court may impose.

130(3A) In subsections (2) and (3), the reference to an action or proceeding includes action in respect of the company under Part 1 of Schedule 8 to the Finance (No. 2) Act 2015 (enforcement by deduction from accounts).

130(4) An order for winding up a company operates in favour of all the creditors and of all contributories of the company as if made on the joint petition of a creditor and of a contributory.

History – In s. 130(3), the words "registered but not formed under the Companies Act 2006" substituted for the words "registered under section 680 of the Companies Act" by SI 2009/1941, art. 2(1) and Sch. 1, para. 75(15), with effect from 1 October 2009, subject to the transitional provisions in SI 2009/1941, art. 8.
S. 130(3A) inserted by F(No. 2)A 2015, s. 51 and Sch. 8, para. 29, with effect from 18 November 2015 (Royal Assent)

Chapter VIII – Provisions of General Application in Winding Up

PREFERENTIAL DEBTS

175 Preferential debts (general provision)

175(1) In a winding up the company's preferential debts shall be paid in priority to all other debts.

175(1A) Ordinary preferential debts rank equally among themselves after the expenses of the winding up and shall be paid in full, unless the assets are insufficient to meet them, in which case they abate in equal proportions.

175(1B) Secondary preferential debts rank equally among themselves after the ordinary preferential debts and shall be paid in full, unless the assets are insufficient to meet them, in which case they abate in equal proportions.

175(2) Preferential debts–

(a) [omitted by SI 2014/3486, art. 5(4);]

(b) so far as the assets of the company available for payment of general creditors are insufficient to meet them, have priority over the claims of holders of debentures secured by, or holders of, any floating charge created by the company, and shall be paid accordingly out of any property comprised in or subject to that charge.

175(3) In this section **"preferential debts"**, **"ordinary preferential debts"** and **"secondary preferential debts"** each has the meaning given in section 386 in Part 12.

Commencement Date – IA 1986 came into force on 29 December 1986, by virtue of IA 1985, s. 236(2), IA 1986, s. 443 and SI 1986/1924.

History – In s. 175(1), the words "(within the meaning given by section 386 in Part XII)" (which appeared after the words "preferential debts ") omitted by SI 2014/3486, art. 5(2), with effect from 1 January 2015, subject to the transitional provision in SI 2014/3486, art. 3 (amendments have no effect in relation to any insolvency proceedings commenced before 1 January 2015).

S. 175(1A) and (1B) inserted by SI 2014/3486, art. 5(3), with effect from 1 January 2015, subject to the transitional provision in SI 2014/3486, art. 3 (amendments have no effect in relation to any insolvency proceedings commenced before 1 January 2015).

S. 175(2)(a) (and the "and" immediately following it) omitted by SI 2014/3486, art. 5(4), with effect from 1 January 2015, subject to the transitional provision in SI 2014/3486, art. 3 (amendments have no effect in relation to any insolvency proceedings commenced before 1 January 2015). Former s. 175(2) read as follows:

"(a) rank equally among themselves after the expenses of the winding up and shall be paid in full, unless the assets are insufficient to meet them, in which case they abate in equal proportions; and".

S. 175(3) inserted by SI 2014/3486, art. 5(5), with effect from 1 January 2015, subject to the transitional provision in SI 2014/3486, art. 3 (amendments have no effect in relation to any insolvency proceedings commenced before 1 January 2015).

176 Preferential charge on goods distrained, etc

176(1) This section applies where a company is being wound up by the court in England and Wales, and is without prejudice to section 128 (avoidance of attachments, etc.).

176(2) Subsection (2A) applies where–

(a) any person (whether or not a landlord or person entitled to rent) has distrained upon the goods or effects of the company, or

(b) Her Majesty's Revenue and Customs has been paid any amount from an account of the company under Part 1 of Schedule 8 to the Finance (No. 2) Act 2015 (enforcement by deduction from accounts),

in the period of 3 months ending with the date of the winding-up order.

176(2A) Where this subsection applies–

(a) in a case within subsection (2)(a), the goods or effects, or the proceeds of their sale, and

(b) in a case within subsection (2)(b), the amount in question,

is charged for the benefit of the company with the preferential debts of the company to the extent that the company's property is for the time being insufficient for meeting those debts.

176(3) Where by virtue of a charge under subsection (2A) any person surrenders any goods or effects to a company or makes a payment to a company, that person ranks, in respect of the amount of the proceeds of sale of those goods or effects by the liquidator or (as the case may be) the amount of the payment, as a preferential creditor of the company, except as against so much of the company's property as is available for the payment of preferential creditors by virtue of the surrender or payment.

History – In heading to s. 176, the words ", etc" inserted by F(No. 2)A 2015, s. 51 and Sch. 8, para. 30(4), with effect from 18 November 2015 (Royal Assent).

S. 176(2) and (2A) substituted for (2) by F(No. 2)A 2015, s. 51 and Sch. 8, para. 30(2), with effect from 18 November 2015 (Royal Assent). Former s. 176(2) read as follows:

"**176(2)** Where any person (whether or not a landlord or person entitled to rent) has distrained upon the goods or effects of the company in the period of 3 months ending with the date of the winding-up order, those goods or effects, or the proceeds of their sale, shall be charged for the benefit of the company with the preferential debts of the company to the extent that the company's property is for the time being insufficient for meeting them.".

In s. 176(3), "(2A)" substituted for "(2)" by F(No. 2)A 2015, s. 51 and Sch. 8, para. 30(3), with effect from 18 November 2015 (Royal Assent).

EXECUTION, ATTACHMENT AND THE SCOTTISH EQUIVALENTS

183 Effect of execution or attachment (England and Wales)

183(1) Where a creditor has issued execution against the goods or land of a company or has attached any debt due to it, and the company is subsequently wound up, he is not entitled to retain the benefit of the execution or attachment against the liquidator unless he has completed the execution or attachment before the commencement of the winding up.

183(2) However–

(a) if a creditor has had notice of a meeting having been called at which a resolution for voluntary winding up is to be proposed, the date on which he had notice is substituted, for the purpose of subsection (1), for the date of commencement of the winding up;

(b) a person who purchases in good faith under a sale by the enforcement officer or other officer charged with the execution of the writ any goods of a company on which execution has been levied in all cases acquires a good title to them against the liquidator; and

(c) the rights conferred by subsection (1) on the liquidator may be set aside by the court in favour of the creditor to such extent and subject to such terms as the court thinks fit.

183(3) For purposes of this Act–

(a) an execution against goods is completed by seizure and sale, or by making of a charging order under section 1 of the Charging Orders Act 1979;

(b) an attachment of a debt is completed by receipt of the debt; and

(c) an execution against land is completed by seizure, by the appointment of a receiver, or by the making of a charging order under section 1 of the Act above-mentioned.

183(4) In this section **"goods"** includes all chattels personal; and **"enforcement officer"** means an individual who is authorised to act as an enforcement officer under the Courts Act 2003.

183(4A) For the purposes of this section, Her Majesty's Revenue and Customs is to be regarded as having attached a debt due to a company if it has taken action under Part 1 of Schedule 8 to the Finance (No. 2) Act 2015 (enforcement by deduction for accounts) as a result of which an amount standing to the credit of an account held by the company is–

(a) subject to arrangements made under paragraph 6(3) of that Schedule, or

(b) the subject of a deduction notice under paragraph 13 of that Schedule.

183(5) This section does not apply in the case of a winding up in Scotland.

History – In s. 183(2)(b), the words "enforcement officer or other officer charged with the execution of the writ" substituted for the word "sheriff" by the Courts Act 2003, s. 109(1) and Sch. 8, para. 295(2), with effect from 15 March 2004, subject to the transitional provisions in SI 2004/401, art. 3 (SI 2004/401, art. 2(b)(vii)).

In s. 183(4), the words ""enforcement officer" means an individual who is authorised to act as an enforcement officer under the Courts Act 2003" substituted for the words ""the sheriff" includes any officer charged with the execution of a writ or other process." by the Courts Act 2003, s. 109(1) and Sch. 8, para. 295(3), with effect from 15 March 2004, subject to the transitional provisions in SI 2004/401, art. 3 (SI 2004/401, art. 2(b)(vii)).

S. 183(4A) inserted by F(No. 2)A 2015, s. 51 and Sch. 8, para. 31, with effect from 18 November 2015 (Royal Assent).

THE SECOND GROUP OF PARTS – INSOLVENCY OF INDIVIDUALS; BANKRUPTCY

PART IX – BANKRUPTCY

Chapter IV – Administration by Trustee

DISTRIBUTION OF BANKRUPT'S ESTATE

328 Priority of debts

328(1) In the distribution of the bankrupt's estate, his preferential debts shall be paid in priority to other debts.

328(1A) Ordinary preferential debts rank equally among themselves after the expenses of the bankruptcy and shall be paid in full, unless the bankrupt's estate is insufficient to meet them, in which case they abate in equal proportions between themselves.

328(1B) Secondary preferential debts rank equally among themselves after the ordinary preferential debts and shall be paid in full, unless the bankrupt's estate is insufficient to meet them, in which case they abate in equal proportions between themselves.

328(2)

328(3) Debts which are neither preferential debts nor debts to which the next section applies also rank equally between themselves and, after the preferential debts, shall be paid in full unless the bankrupt's estate is insufficient for meeting them, in which case they abate in equal proportions between themselves.

328(4) Any surplus remaining after the payment of the debts that are preferential or rank equally under subsection (3) shall be applied in paying interest on those debts in respect of the periods during which they have been outstanding since the commencement of the bankruptcy; and interest on preferential debts ranks equally with interest on debts other than preferential debts.

328(5) The rate of interest payable under subsection (4) in respect of any debt is whichever is the greater of the following–

(a) *the rate specified in* section 17 of the Judgments Act 1838 at the commencement of the bankruptcy, and

(b) the rate applicable to that debt apart from the bankruptcy.

328(6) This section and the next are without prejudice to any provision of this Act or any other Act under which the payment of any debt or the making of any other payment is, in the event of bankruptcy, to have a particular priority or to be postponed.

328(7) In this section **"preferential debts"**, **"ordinary preferential debts"** and **"secondary preferential debts"** each has the meaning given in section 386 in Part 12.

Commencement Date – IA 1986 came into force on 29 December 1986, by virtue of IA 1985, s. 236(2), IA 1986, s. 443 and SI 1986/1924.

History – In s. 328(1), the words "(within the meaning given by section 386 in Part XII)" (which appeared after the words "preferential debts" omitted by SI 2014/3486, art. 7(2), with effect from 1 January 2015, subject to the transitional provision in SI 2014/3486, art. 3 (amendments have no effect in relation to any insolvency proceedings commenced before 1 January 2015).

S. 328(1A) and (1B) inserted by SI 2014/3486, art. 7(3), with effect from 1 January 2015, subject to the transitional provision in SI 2014/3486, art. 3 (amendments have no effect in relation to any insolvency proceedings commenced before 1 January 2015).

S. 328(2) omitted by SI 2014/3486, art. 7(4), with effect from 1 January 2015, subject to the transitional provision in SI 2014/3486, art. 3 (amendments have no effect in relation to any insolvency proceedings commenced before 1 January 2015). Former s. 328(2) read as follows:

"**328(2)** Preferential debts rank equally between themselves after the expenses of the bankruptcy and shall be paid in full unless the bankrupt's estate is insufficient for meeting them, in which case they abate in equal proportions between themselves.".

S. 328(7) inserted by SI 2014/3486, art. 7(5), with effect from 1 January 2015, subject to the transitional provision in SI 2014/3486, art. 3 (amendments have no effect in relation to any insolvency proceedings commenced before 1 January 2015).

Chapter V – Effect of Bankruptcy on Certain Rights Transactions, Etc.

ADJUSTMENT OF PRIOR TRANSACTIONS, ETC.

346 Enforcement procedures

346(1) Subject to section 285 in Chapter II (restriction on proceedings and remedies) and to the following provisions of this section, where the creditor of any person who is made bankrupt has, before the commencement of the bankruptcy–

(a) issued execution against the goods or land of that person, or

(b) attached a debt due to that person from another person,

that creditor is not entitled, as against the official reciever or trustee of the bankrupt's estate, to retain the benefit of the execution or attachment, or any sums paid to avoid it, unless the execution or attachment was completed, or the sums were paid, before the commencement of the bankruptcy.

346(1A) For the purposes of this section, Her Majesty's Revenue and Customs is to be regarded as having attached a debt due to a person if it has taken action under Part 1 of Schedule 8 to the Finance (No. 2) Act 2015 (enforcement by deduction from accounts) as a result of which an amount standing to the credit of an account held by that person is–

(a) subject to arrangements made under paragraph 6(3) of that Schedule, or

(b) the subject of a deduction notice under paragraph 13 of that Schedule.

346(2) Subject as follows, where any goods of a person have been taken in execution, then, if before the completion of the execution notice is given to the enforcement officer or other officer charged with the execution that that person has been made bankrupt–

(a) the enforcement officer or other officer shall on request deliver to the official receiver or trustee of the bankrupt's estate the goods and any money seized or recovered in part satisfaction of the execution, but

(b) the costs of the execution are a first charge on the goods or money so delivered and the official receiver or trustee may sell the goods or a sufficient part of them for the purpose of satisfying the charge.

346(3) Subject to subsection (6) below, where–

(a) under an execution in respect of a judgment for a sum exceeding such sum as may be prescribed for the purposes of this subsection, the goods of any person are sold or money is paid in order to avoid a sale, and

(b) before the end of the period of 14 days beginning with the day of the sale or payment the enforcement officer or other officer charged with the execution is given notice that a bankruptcy application has been made or a bankruptcy petition has been presented in relation to that person, and

(c) a bankruptcy order is or has been made as a result of that application or,

the balance of the proceeds of sale or money paid, after deducting the costs of execution, shall (in priority to the claim of the execution creditor) be comprised in the bankrupt's estate.

346(4) Accordingly, in the case of an execution in respect of a judgment for a sum exceeding the sum prescribed for the purposes of subsection (3), the enforcement officer or other officer charged with the execution–

(a) shall not dispose of the balance mentioned in subsection (3) at any time within the period of 14 days so mentioned or while proceedings on a bankruptcy application are ongoing or (as the case may be) there is pending a bankruptcy petition of which he has been given notice under that subsection, and

(b) shall pay that balance, where by virtue of that subsection it is comprised, in the bankrupt's estate, to the official receiver or (if there is one) to the trustee or that estate.

346(5) For the purposes of this section–

(a) an execution against goods is completed by seizure and sale or by the making of a charging order under section 1 of the Charging Orders Act 1979;

(b) an execution against land is completed by seizure, by the appointment of a receiver or by the making of a charging order under that section;

(c) an attachment of a debt is completed by the receipt of the debt.

346(6) The rights conferred by subsections (1) to (3) on the official receiver or the trustee may, to such extent and on such terms as it thinks fit, be set aside by the court in favour of the creditor who has issued the execution or attached the debt.

346(7) Nothing in this section entitles the trustee of a bankrupt's estate to claim goods from a person who has acquired them in good faith under a sale by an enforcement officer or other officer charged with an execution.

346(8) Neither subsection (2) nor subsection (3) applies in relation to any execution against property which has been acquired by or has devolved upon the bankrupt since the commencement of the bankruptcy, unless, at the time the execution is issued or before it is completed–

(a) the property has been or is claimed for the bankrupt's estate under section 307 (after-acquired property), and

(b) a copy of the notice given under that section has been or is served on the enforcement officer or other officer charged with the execution.

346(9) In this section **"enforcement officer"** means an individual who is authorised to act as an enforcement officer under the Courts Act 2003.

History – In s. 346(1) and (2), the word "made" substituted for the word "adjudged" by the Enterprise and Regulatory Reform Act 2013, s. 71(3) and Sch. 19, para. 39(2), with effect from 6 April 2016, but subject to savings that amendment has no effect in respect of a petition for a bankruptcy order presented to the court by a debtor before 6th April 2016 (SI 2016/191).
S. 346(1A) inserted by F(No. 2)A 2015, s. 51 and Sch. 8, para. 32, with effect from 18 November 2015 (Royal Assent).
In s. 346(2), (3)(b), (4) and (8)(b), the words "enforcement officer" substituted for the word "sheriff" (in each place) by the Courts Act 2003, s. 109(1) and Sch. 8, para. 297(2), with effect from 15 March 2004, subject to the transitional provisions in SI 2004/401, art. 3 (SI 2004/401, art. 2(b)(vii)).
In s. 346(3)(b), the words "bankruptcy application has been made or a" inserted by the Enterprise and Regulatory Reform Act 2013, s. 71(3) and Sch. 19, para. 39(3)(a), with effect from 6 April 2016, but subject to savings that amendment has no effect in respect of a petition for a bankruptcy order presented to the court by a debtor before 6th April 2016 (SI 2016/191).
In s. 346(3)(c), the words "as a result of that application or" inserted by the Enterprise and Regulatory Reform Act 2013, s. 71(3) and Sch. 19, para. 39(3)(b), with effect from 6 April 2016, but subject to savings that amendment has no effect in respect of a petition for a bankruptcy order presented to the court by a debtor before 6th April 2016 (SI 2016/191).
In s. 346(4)(a), the words "proceedings on a bankruptcy application are ongoing or (as the case may be)" inserted by the Enterprise and Regulatory Reform Act 2013, s. 71(3) and Sch. 19, para. 39(4), with effect from 6 April 2016, but subject to savings that amendment has no effect in respect of a petition for a bankruptcy order presented to the court by a debtor before 6th April 2016 (SI 2016/191).
In s. 346(7), the words "an enforcement officer" substituted for the words "a sheriff" by the Courts Act 2003, s. 109(1) and Sch. 8, para. 297(3), with effect from 15 March 2004, subject to the transitional provisions in SI 2004/401, art. 3 (SI 2004/401, art. 2(b)(vii)).
S. 346(9) inserted by the Courts Act 2003, s. 109(1) and Sch. 8, para. 297(4), with effect from 15 March 2004, subject to the transitional provisions in SI 2004/401, art. 3 (SI 2004/401, art. 2(b)(vii)).

347 Distress, etc.

347(1) The right of any landlord or other person to whom rent is payable to distrain upon the goods and effects of an undischarged bankrupt for rent due to him from the bankrupt is available (subject to sections 252(2)(b) and 254(1) above and subsection (5) below) against goods and effects comprised in the bankrupt's estate, but only for 6 months' rent accrued due before the commencement of the bankruptcy.

347(2) Where a landlord or other person to whom rent is payable has distrained for rent upon the goods and effects of an individual to whom a bankruptcy application or a bankruptcy petition relates and a bankruptcy order is subsequently made on that petition as a result of that application or, any amount recovered by way of that distress which–

(a) is in excess of the amount which by virtue of subsection (1) would have been recoverable after the commencement of the bankruptcy, or

(b) is in respect of rent for a period or part of a period after the distress was levied,

shall be held for the bankrupt as apart of his estate.

347(3) Subsection (3A) applies where–

(a) any person (whether or not a landlord or person entitled to rent) has distrained upon the goods or effects of an individual who is made bankrupt before the end of the period of 3 months beginning with the distraint, or

(b) Her Majesty's Revenue and Customs has been paid any amount from an account of an individual under Part 1 of Schedule 8 to the Finance (No. 2) Act 2015 (enforcement by deduction from accounts) and the individual is adjudged bankrupt before the end of the period of 3 months beginning with the payment.

347(3A) Where this subsection applies–

(a) in a case within subsection (3)(a), the goods or effects, or the proceeds of their sale, and

(b) in a case within subsection (3)(b), the amount in question,

is charged for the benefit of the bankrupt's estate with the preferential debts of the bankrupt to the extent that the bankrupt's estate is for the time being insufficient for meeting them.

347(4) Where by virtue of any charge under subsection (3A) any person surrenders any goods or effects to the trustee of a bankrupt's estate or makes a payment to such a trustee, that person ranks, in respect of the amount of the proceeds of the sale of those goods or effects by the trustee or, as the case may be, the amount of the payment, as a preferential creditor of the bankrupt, except as against so much of the bankrupt's estate as is available for the payment of preferential creditors by virtue of the surrender or payment.

347(5) A landlord or other person to whom rent is payable is not at any time after the discharge of a bankrupt entitled to distrain upon any goods or effects comprised in the bankrupt's estate.

347(6) Where in the case of any execution–

(a) a landlord is (apart from this section) entitled under section 1 of the Landlord and Tenant Act 1709 or section 102 of the County Courts Act 1984 (claims for rent where goods seized in execution) to claim for an amount not exceeding one year's rent, and

(b) the person against whom the execution is levied is adjudged bankrupt before the notice of claim is served on the enforcement officer, or other officer charged with the execution,

the right of the landlord to claim under that section is restricted to a right to claim for an amount not exceeding 6 months' rent and does not extend to any rent payable in respect of a period after the notice of claim is so served.

347(7) Nothing in subsection (6) imposes any liability on an enforcement officer or other officer charged with an execution to account to the official receiver or the trustee of a bankrupt's estate for any sums paid by him to a landlord at any time before the enforcement officer or other officer was served with notice of the bankruptcy order in question.

But this subsection is without prejudice to the liability of the landlord.

347(8) Subject to sections 252(2)(b) and 254(1) above nothing in this Group of Parts affects any right to distrain otherwise than for rent; and any such right is at any time exerciseable without restriction against property comprised in a bankrupt's estate, even if that right is expressed by any enactment to be exerciseable in like manner as a right to distrain for rent.

347(9) Any right to distrain against property comprised in a bankrupt's estate is exerciseable notwithstanding that the property has vested in the trustee.

347(10) The provisions of this section are without prejudice to a landlord's right in a bankruptcy to prove for any bankruptcy debt in respect of rent.

347(11) In this section **"enforcement officer"** means an individual who is authorised to act as an enforcement officer under the Courts Act 2003.

History – In s. 347(1), the words "sections 252(2)(b) and 254(1) above and" inserted by the Insolvency Act 2003, s. 3 and Sch. 3, para. 14(a), with effect from 1 January 2003, subject to the transitional provisions in SI 2002/2711, art. 3–5 (SI 2002/2711, art. 2).

In s. 347(2), the words "a bankruptcy application or" and the words "as a result of that application or" inserted by the Enterprise and Regulatory Reform Act 2013, s. 71(3) and Sch. 19, para. 40(2), with effect from 6 April 2016, but subject to savings that amendment has no effect in respect of a petition for a bankruptcy order presented to the court by a debtor before 6th April 2016 (SI 2016/191).

In s. 347(3), the word "made" substituted for the word "adjudged" by the Enterprise and Regulatory Reform Act 2013, s. 71(3) and Sch. 19, para. 40(3), with effect from 6 April 2016, but subject to savings that amendment has no effect in respect of a petition for a bankruptcy order presented to the court by a debtor before 6th April 2016 (SI 2016/191).

S. 347(3) and (3A) substituted for (3) by F(No. 2)A 2015, s. 51 and Sch. 8, para. 33(1)(a), with effect from 18 November 2015 (Royal Assent). Former s. 347(3) read as follows:

"**347(3)** Where any person (whether or not a landlord or person entitled to rent) has distrained upon the goods or effects of an individual who is adjudged bankrupt before the end of the period of 3 months beginning with the distraint, so much of those goods or effects, or of the proceeds of their sale, as is not held for the bankrupt under subsection (2) shall be charged for the benefit of the bankrupt's estate with the preferential debts of the bankrupt to the extent that the bankrupt's estate is for the time being insufficient for meeting those debts.".

In s. 347(4), "(3A)" substituted for "(3)" by F(No. 2)A 2015, s. 51 and Sch. 8, para. 33(1)(b), with effect from 18 November 2015 (Royal Assent).

In s. 347(6), the words "enforcement officer," substituted for the word "sheriff" by the Courts Act 2003, s. 109(1) and Sch. 8, para. 298(2), with effect from 15 March 2004, subject to the transitional provisions in SI 2004/401, art. 3 (SI 2004/401, art. 2(b)(vii)).
In s. 347(7), the words "an enforcement officer" substituted for the words "a sheriff" and the words "the enforcement officer" substituted for the words "the sheriff" by the Courts Act 2003, s. 109(1) and Sch. 8, para. 298(3), with effect from 15 March 2004, subject to the transitional provisions in SI 2004/401, art. 3 (SI 2004/401, art. 2(b)(vii)).
In s. 347(8), the words "Subject to sections 252(2)(b) and 254(1) above." inserted by the Insolvency Act 2003, s. 3 and Sch. 3, para. 14(b), with effect from 1 January 2003, subject to the transitional provisions in SI 2002/2711, art. 3–5 (SI 2002/2711, art. 2).
S. 347(11) inserted by the Courts Act 2003, s. 109(1) and Sch. 8, para. 298(4), with effect from 15 March 2004, subject to the transitional provisions in SI 2004/401, art. 3 (SI 2004/401, art. 2(b)(vii)).

THE THIRD GROUP OF PARTS – MISCELLANEOUS MATTERS BEARING ON BOTH COMPANY AND INDIVIDUAL INSOLVENCY; GENERAL INTERPRETATION; FINAL PROVISIONS

PART XII – PREFERENTIAL DEBTS IN COMPANY AND INDIVIDUAL INSOLVENCY

386 Categories of preferential debts

386(1) A reference in this Act to the preferential debts of a company or an individual is to the debts listed in Schedule 6 to this Act (contributions to occupational pension schemes; remuneration, &c. of employees; levies on coal and steel production; deposits covered by Financial Services Compensation Scheme; other deposits); and references to preferential creditors are to be read accordingly.

386(1A) A reference in this Act to the **"ordinary preferential debts"** of a company or an individual is to the preferential debts listed in any of paragraphs 8 to 15B of Schedule 6 to this Act.

386(1B) A reference in this Act to the **"secondary preferential debts"** of a company or an individual is to the preferential debts listed in paragraph 15BA or 15BB of Schedule 6 to this Act.

386(2) In Schedule 6 **"the debtor"** means the company or the individual concerned.

386(3) Schedule 6 is to be read with Schedule 4 to the Pension Schemes Act 1993 (occupational pension scheme contributions).

Commencement Date – IA 1986 came into force on 29 December 1986, by virtue of IA 1985, s. 236(2), IA 1986, s. 443 and SI 1986/1924.

History – In s. 386(1), the words "; other deposits" inserted by SI 2014/3486, art. 8(2), with effect from 1 January 2015, subject to the transitional provision in SI 2014/3486, art. 3 (amendments have no effect in relation to any insolvency proceedings commenced before 1 January 2015).
In s. 386(1), the words "; deposits covered by Financial Services Compensation Scheme" inserted (after the word "production") by Financial Services (Banking Reform) Act 2013, s. 13(2), with effect from 31 December 2014 (SI 2014/3160, art. 2).
In s. 386(1) the words "(contributions to occupational pension schemes; remuneration, &c. of employees; levies on coal and steel production)" substituted by the Enterprise Act 2002, s. 251(3), with effect from 15 September 2003, by virtue of SI 2003/2093, art. 2 and Sch. 1. Art. 4 contains transitional provisions.
In s. 386(1), the words "aggregates levy" inserted by FA 2001, s. 27 and Sch. 5, para. 17.
In s. 386(1), the words "climate change levy" inserted by FA 2000, s. 30 and Sch. 7, para 3(1).
In s. 386(1), the words "landfill tax" inserted by FA 1996, s. 60 and Sch. 5, para. 12(1).
In s. 386(1), the words "air passenger duty" inserted by FA 1995, s. 17 with effect from 1 May 1995.
In s. 386(1), the words "insurance premium tax," inserted by FA 1994, s. 64 and Sch. 7, para. 7(2) consequential on the introduction of insurance premium tax from 1 October 1994.
In s. 386(1), the words "lottery duty" inserted by FA 1993, s. 36 with effect from 1 December 1993.
In s. 386(1), the words ", beer duty" inserted by FA 1991, s. 7 and Sch. 2, para. 21A, as inserted by F(No. 2)A 1992, s. 9(1), with effect from 16 July 1992.
In s. 386(1), the words "levies on coal and steel production" inserted by SI 1987/2093, reg. 2(2), with effect from 1 January 1988.
S. 386(1A) and (1B) inserted by SI 2014/3486, art. 8(3), with effect from 1 January 2015, subject to the transitional provision in SI 2014/3486, art. 3 (amendments have no effect in relation to any insolvency proceedings commenced before 1 January 2015).
In s. 386(2), the words "Schedule 6" substituted for the words "that Schedule" by SI 2014/3486, art. 8(4), with effect from 1 January 2015, subject to the transitional provision in SI 2014/3486, art. 3 (amendments have no effect in relation to any insolvency proceedings commenced before 1 January 2015).
In s. 386(3), the words "Schedule 4 to the Pension Schemes Act 1993" substituted by the Pension Schemes Act 1993, Sch. 8, para. 18, with effect from 7 February 1994.

Transitional – Enterprise Act 2002 (Commencement No. 4 and Transitional Provisions and Savings) Order 2003, SI 2003/2093, art. 4, contains transitional provisions so that the former rules remain in effect where insolvency arrangements are in place prior to 15 September 2003.

387 "The relevant date"

387(1) This section explains references in Schedule 6 to the relevant date (being the date which determines the existence and amount of a preferential debt).

387(2) For the purposes of section 4 in Part I (meetings to consider company voluntary arrangement), the relevant date in relation to a company which is not being wound up is–

(a) if the company is in administration, the date on which it entered administration, and
(b) if the company is not in administration, the date on which the voluntary arrangement takes effect.

387(2A) For the purposes of paragraph 31 of Schedule A1 (meetings to consider company voluntary arrangement where a moratorium under section 1A is in force), the relevant date in relation to a company is the date of filing.

387(3) In relation to a company which is being wound up, the following applies–

(a) if the winding up is by the court, and the winding-up order was made immediately upon the discharge of an administration order, the relevant date is the date on which the company entered administration;

(aa) if the winding up is by the court and the winding-up order was made following conversion of administration into winding up by virtue of Article 37 of the EC Regulation, the relevant date is the date on which the company entered administration;

(ab) if the company is deemed to have passed a resolution for voluntary winding up by virtue of an order following conversion of administration into winding up under Article 37 of the EC Regulation, the relevant date is the date on which the company entered administration;

(b) if the case does not fall within paragraph (a), (aa) or (ab) and the company–
  (i) is being wound up by the court, and
  (ii) had not commenced to be wound up voluntarily before the date of the making of the winding-up order,

the relevant date is the date of the appointment (or first appointment) of a provisional liquidator or, if no such appointment has been made, the date of the winding-up order;

(ba) if the case does not fall within paragraph (a), (aa), (ab) or (b) and the company is being wound up following administration pursuant to paragraph 83 of Schedule B1, the relevant date is the date on which the company entered administration;

(c) if the case does not fall within paragraph (a), (aa), (ab), (b) or (ba), the relevant date is the date of the passing of the resolution for the winding up of the company.

387(3A) In relation to a company which is in administration (and to which no other provision of this section applies) the relevant date is the date on which the company enters administration.

387(4) In relation to a company in receivership (where section 40 or, as the case may be, section 59 applies), the relevant date is–

(a) in England and Wales, the date of the appointment of the receiver by debenture-holders, and
(b) in Scotland, the date of the appointment of the receiver under section 53(6) or (as the case may be) 54(5).

387(5) For the purposes of section 258 in Part VIII (individual voluntary arrangements), the relevant date is, in relation to a debtor who is not an undischarged bankrupt, the date of the interim order made under section 252 with respect to his proposal.

(a) where an interim order has been made under section 252 with respect to his proposal, the date of that order, and
(b) in any other case, the date on which the voluntary arrangement takes effect.

387(6) In relation to a bankrupt, the following applies–

(a) where at the time the bankruptcy order was made there was an interim receiver appointed under section 286, the relevant date is the date on which the interim receiver was first appointed after the making of the bankruptcy application or (as the case may be) the presentation of the bankruptcy petition;

(b) otherwise, the relevant date is the date of the making of the bankruptcy order.

Commencement Date – IA 1986 came into force on 29 December 1986, by virtue of IA 1985, s. 236(2), IA 1986, s. 443 and SI 1986/1924.

History – S. 387(2)(a) and (b) substituted by the Enterprise Act 2002, s. 248(3) and Sch. 17, para. 34(2), with effect from 15 September 2003, by virtue of SI 2003/2093, art. 2 and Sch. 1. Art. 3 contains transitional provisions.
S. 387(2A) inserted by IA 2000, s. 1 and Sch. 1, para. 9, with effect from 1 January 2003, by virtue of SI 2002/2711, art. 2. Art. 3, 4, and 5 contain transitional provisions.
In s. 387(3)(a), (aa) and (ab) the words "the date on which the company entered administration" substituted by the Enterprise Act 2002, s. 248(3) and Sch. 17, para. 34(3)(a), with effect from 15 September 2003, by virtue of SI 2003/2093, art. 2 and Sch. 1. Art. 3 contains transitional provisions.
S. 387(3)(aa) and (ab) inserted by SI 2002/1240, reg. 16(a), with effect from 31 May 2002.
In s. 387(3)(b) the words ", (aa) or (ab)" inserted by SI 2002/1240, reg. 16(b), with effect from 31 May 2002.
S. 387(3)(ba) inserted by the Enterprise Act 2002, s. 248(3) and Sch. 17, para. 34(3)(b), with effect from 15 September 2003, by virtue of SI 2003/2093, art. 2 and Sch. 1. Art. 3 contains transitional provisions.
In s. 387(3)(c) the words "paragraph (a), (aa), (ab), (b) or (ba)" substituted by the Enterprise Act 2002, s. 248(3) and Sch. 17, para. 34(3)(c), with effect from 15 September 2003, by virtue of SI 2003/2093, art. 2 and Sch. 1. Art. 3 contains transitional provisions. Previously, in s. 387(3)(c) the words "paragraph (a), (aa), (ab) or (b)" substituted by SI 2002/1240, reg. 16(c), with effect from 31 May 2002.

S. 387(3)(3A) inserted by the Enterprise Act 2002, s. 248(3) and Sch. 17, para. 34(4), with effect from 15 September 2003, by virtue of SI 2003/2093, art. 2 and Sch. 1. Art. 3 contains transitional provisions.
In s. 387(5) para. (a) and (b) substituted for the words "the date of the interim order made under section 252 with respect to his proposal." by IA 2000, s. 3 and Sch. 3, para. 15, with effect from 1 January 2003, by virtue of SI 2002/2711, art. 2. Transitional provisions are contained in arts. 3, 4 and 5.
In s. 387(6)(a), the words "the making of the bankruptcy application or (as the case may be)" inserted by the Enterprise and Regulatory Reform Act 2013, s. 71(3) and Sch. 19, para. 39(2), with effect from 6 April 2016, but subject to savings that amendment has no effect in respect of a petition for a bankruptcy order presented to the court by a debtor before 6th April 2016 (SI 2016/191).

Transitional – Enterprise Act 2002 (Commencement No. 4 and Transitional Provisions and Savings) Order 2003, SI 2003/2093, art. 3, contains transitional provisions so that the former rules remain in effect where petition presented prior to 15 September 2003.
The Insolvency Act 2000 (Commencement No. 3 and Transitional Provisions) Order 2002, SI 2002/2711, art. 3, 4 and 5 contain transitional provisions in relation to proposals made before the appointed day.

PART XIX – FINAL PROVISIONS

440 Extent (Scotland)

440(1) Subject to the next subsection, provisions of this Act contained in the first Group of Parts extend to Scotland except where otherwise stated.

440(2) The following provisions of this Act do not extend to Scotland–

(a) [not relevant to National Insurance contributions;]

(b) the second Group of Parts;

(c), (d) [not relevant to National Insurance contributions.]

Commencement Date – IA 1986 came into force on 29 December 1986, by virtue of IA 1985, s. 236(2), IA 1986, s. 443 and SI 1986/1924.

Cross references – "the first Group of Parts" comprises s. 1–251, and "the second Group of Parts" comprises s. 252–385.

441 Extent (Northern Ireland)

441(1) [Not relevant to National Insurance contributions.]

441(2) Subject as above, and to any provision expressly relating to companies incorporated elsewhere than in Great Britain, nothing in this Act extends to Northern Ireland or applies to or in relation to companies registered or incorporated in Northern Ireland.

Commencement Date – IA 1986 came into force on 29 December 1986, by virtue of IA 1985, s. 236(2), IA 1986, s. 443 and SI 1986/1924.

442 Extent (other territories)

442 Her Majesty may, by Order in Council, direct that such of the provisions of this Act as are specified in the Order, being provisions formerly contained in the Insolvency Act 1985, shall extend to any of the Channel Islands or any colony with such modifications as may be so specified.

Commencement Date – IA 1986 came into force on 29 December 1986, by virtue of IA 1985, s. 236(2), IA 1986, s. 443 and SI 1986/1924.

Notes – See the Insolvency Act 1986 (Guernsey) Order 1989 (SI 1989/2409) (not reproduced).

443 Commencement

443 This Act comes into force on the day appointed under section 236(2) of the Insolvency Act 1985 for the coming into force of Part III of that Act (individual insolvency and bankruptcy), immediately after that Part of that Act comes into force for England and Wales.

Commencement Date – IA 1986 came into force on 29 December 1986, by virtue of IA 1985, s. 236(2), IA 1986, s. 443 and SI 1986/1924.

444 Citation

444 This Act may be cited as the Insolvency Act 1986.

Commencement Date – IA 1986 came into force on 29 December 1986, by virtue of IA 1985, s. 236(2), IA 1986, s. 443 and SI 1986/1924.

NIC Statutes

SCHEDULES

SCHEDULE 6 – THE CATEGORIES OF PREFERENTIAL DEBTS

Section 386

CATEGORY 3: SOCIAL SECURITY CONTRIBUTIONS

6 [Repealed by the Enterprise Act 2002, s. 251(1)(a), s. 278(2), and Sch. 26.]

Commencement Date – IA 1986 came into force on 29 December 1986, by virtue of IA 1985, s. 236(2), IA 1986, s. 443 and SI 1986/1924.

History – Sch. 6, para. 6 repealed by the Enterprise Act 2002, s. 251(1)(a), s. 278(2), and Sch. 26, with effect from 15 September 2003, by virtue of SI 2003/2093, art. 2 and Sch. 1. Art. 4 contains transitional provisions.

In para. 6, the words "Social Security Contributions and Benefits Act 1992" substituted by SS(CP)A 1992, s. 4 and Sch. 2, para. 73, with effect from 1 July 1992.

Transitional – Enterprise Act 2002 (Commencement No. 4 and Transitional Provisions and Savings) Order 2003, SI 2003/2093, art. 4, contains transitional provisions so that the former rules remain in effect where insolvency arrangements are in place prior to 15 September 2003.

7 [Repealed by the Enterprise Act 2002, s. 251(1)(a), s. 278(2), and Sch. 26.]

Commencement Date – IA 1986 came into force on 29 December 1986, by virtue of IA 1985, s. 236(2), IA 1986, s. 443 and SI 1986/1924.

History – Para. 7 repealed by the Enterprise Act 2002, s. 251(1)(a), s. 278(2), and Sch. 26, with effect from 15 September 2003, by virtue of SI 2003/2093, art. 2 and Sch. 1. Art. 4 contains transitional provisions.

Transitional – Enterprise Act 2002 (Commencement No. 4 and Transitional Provisions and Savings) Order 2003 (SI 2003/2093), art. 4 contains transitional provisions so that the former rules remain in effect where insolvency arrangements are in place prior to 15 September 2003.

SOCIAL SECURITY ACT 1986

(1986 Chapter 50) [*25th July 1986*]

ARRANGEMENT OF SECTIONS

PART VI – COMMON PROVISIONS

ADMINISTRATION

PART VII – MISCELLANEOUS, GENERAL AND SUPPLEMENTARY

SUPPLEMENTARY

PART VI – COMMON PROVISIONS

ADMINISTRATION

54 Breach of regulations

54(1) Regulations under any of the benefit Acts may provide for contravention of, or failure to comply with, any provision contained in regulations made under that Act to be an offence under that Act and for the recovery, on summary conviction of any such offence, of penalties not exceeding–

(a) for any one offence, level 3 on the standard scale; or

(b) for an offence of continuing any such contravention or failure after conviction, £40 for each day on which it is so continued.

54(2) [Repealed by SS(CP)A 1992 s. 3 and Sch. 1.]

Commencement Date – S. 54 came into force on 6 April 1987, by virtue of SI 1986/1959.

History – S. 54(2) repealed by SS(CP)A 1992, s. 3 and Sch. 1, with effect from 1 July 1992.

Notes – Level 3 on the standard scale is £1,000 in relation to offences committed after 1 October 1992. Criminal Justice Act 1982, s. 37(2); Criminal Justice Act 1991, s. 17(1); SI 1992/333.

56 Legal proceedings

56(1) Any person authorised by the Secretary of State in that behalf may conduct any proceedings under the benefit Acts before a magistrates' court.

56(2) Notwithstanding anything in any Act–

(a) proceedings for an offence under the benefit Acts may be begun at any time within the period of three months from the date on which evidence, sufficient in the opinion of the Secretary of State to justify a prosecution for the offence, comes to his knowledge or within a period of twelve months from the commission of the offence, whichever period last expires;

(b) [repealed by SS(CP)A 1992, s. 3 and Sch. 1.]

56(3) For the purposes of subsection (2) above–

(a) a certificate purporting to be signed by or on behalf of the Secretary of State as to the date on which such evidence as is mentioned in paragraph (a) of that subsection came to his knowledge shall be conclusive evidence of that date;

(b) [repealed by SS(CP)A 1992, s. 3 and Sch. 1.]

56(4)–(4B) [Repealed by SS(CP)A 1992, s. 3 and Sch. 1.]

56(5) In the application of this section to Scotland, the following provisions shall have effect in substitution for subsections (1) to (4A) above–

(a) proceedings for an offence under the benefit Acts may, notwithstanding anything in section 136 of the Criminal Procedure (Scotland) Act 1995, be commenced at any time within the period of three months from the date on which evidence sufficient in the opinion of the Lord Advocate to justify proceedings comes to his knowledge, or within the period of twelve months from the commission of the offence, whichever period last expires;

(b) for the purposes of this subsection–

(i) a certificate purporting to be signed by or on behalf of the Lord Advocate as to the date on which such evidence as is mentioned above came to his knowledge shall be conclusive evidence thereof;

(ii) subsection (3) of section 136 of the said Act of 1995 (date of commencement of proceedings) shall have effect as it has effect for the purposes of that section.

Commencement Date – S. 56 came into force on 6 April 1987, by virtue of SI 1986/1959.

History – In s. 56(1) the words "although not a barrister or solicitor", which appeared at the end, omitted by Legal Services Act 2007, s. 208 and Sch. 21, para. 68 and repealed by s. 210 and Sch. 23, with effect from 1 January 2010 (SI 2009/3250).
In s. 56(2)(a) the words "other than an offence relating to housing benefit or community charge benefit" repealed by SS(CP)A 1992, s. 3 and Sch. 1, with effect from 1 July 1992.
In s. 56(2)(a), the words "or community charge benefits" inserted by Local Government Finance Act 1988, s. 135 and Sch. 10, para. 9(2), with effect from 29 July 1988.
S. 56(2)(b), (3)(b), (4), (4A) and (4B) repealed by SS(CP)A 1992, s. 3 and Sch. 1, with effect from 1 July 1992.
In s. 56(5)(a) the words "section 136 of the Criminal Procedure (Scotland) Act 1995" and in s. 56(5)(b)(ii) the words "section 136 of the said Act of 1995" substituted by the Criminal Procedure (Consequential Amendments) (Scotland) Act 1995, Sch. 4, para. 64 with effect from 1 April 1996.

Notes – S. 84(1): meaning of "the benefit Acts".

57 Offences by bodies corporate

57(1) Where an offence under any of the benefit Acts which has been committed by a body corporate is proved to have been committed with the consent or connivance of, or to be attributable to any neglect on the part of, a director, manager, secretary or other similar officer of the body corporate, or any person who was purporting to act in any such capacity, he, as well as the body corporate, shall be guilty of that offence and be liable to be proceeded against accordingly.

57(2) Where the affairs of a body corporate are managed by its members, subsection (1) above applies in relation to the acts and defaults of a member in connection with his functions of management as if he were a director of the body corporate.

Commencement Date – S. 57 came into force on 6 April 1987, by virtue of SI 1986/1959.

Notes – SSAA 1992, s. 115: offences by bodies corporate under SSAA 1992.

PART VII – MISCELLANEOUS, GENERAL AND SUPPLEMENTARY

SUPPLEMENTARY

83 Orders and regulations (general provisions)

83(1) Section 61B(1) to (4) of the Social Security Pensions Act 1975 (extent of powers) shall apply to powers conferred by this Act to make regulations or orders as they apply to any power to make regulations or orders conferred by that Act but as if for references to that Act there were substituted references to this Act.

83(2) [Repealed by SS(CP)A 1992, s. 3 and Sch. 1.]

83(3) [Repealed by PSA 1993, s. 188 and Sch. 5, Pt. I.]

83(4) A statutory instrument–

(a) which contains (whether alone or with other provisions) orders or regulations under this Act, other than orders under section 88 below, and

(b) which is not subject to any requirement that a draft of the instrument be laid before and approved by a resolution of each House of Parliament,

shall be subject to annulment in pursuance of a resolution of either House of Parliament.

83(5) [Not relevant to National Insurance contributions.]

83(6) A power conferred by this Act to make any regulations or order, where the power is not expressed to be exercisable with the consent of the Treasury, shall if the Treasury so direct be exercisable only in conjunction with them.

Commencement Date – S. 83 came into force on 25 July 1986, by virtue of SSA 1986, s. 88(5).

History – In s. 83(1) the words "Section 61B(1) to (4) of the Social Security Pensions Act 1975" substituted by SS(CP)A 1992, s. 4 and Sch. 2, para. 84, with effect from 1 July 1992.
S. 83(2) repealed by SS(CP)A 1992, s. 3 and Sch. 1, with effect from 1 July 1992.
S. 83(3) repealed by PSA 1993, s. 188 and Sch. 5, Pt. I, with effect from 7 February 1994.
S. 83(4) substituted by SSA 1990, s. 21(1), 23(3) and Sch. 6, para. 8(9), with effect from 13 July 1990.

Cross references – SSPA 1975, s. 61B: general provisions on orders and regulations.

84 General interpretation

84(1) In this Act, unless the context otherwise requires–

"the benefit Acts" means–

(a) the Social Security Act 1973;

(b) the Social Security Acts 1975 to 1991;

"prescribed" means specified in or determined in accordance with regulations;

"regulations" means regulations made by the Secretary of State under this Act;

84(2) [Repealed by PSA 1993, s. 188 and Sch. 5, Pt. I.]

84(3) [Repealed by SS(CP)A 1992, s. 3 and Sch. 1.]

84(4) In this Act–

(a) references to the United Kingdom include references to the territorial waters of the United Kingdom; and

(b) references to Great Britain include references to the territorial waters of the United Kingdom adjacent to Great Britain.

Commencement Date – S. 84 came into force on 25 July 1986, by virtue of SSA 1986, s. 88(5).

History – In s. 84(1) in the definition of "the benefit Act", para. (c), (d) repealed by SS(CP)A 1992, s. 3 and Sch. 1, with effect from 1 July 1992.
In s. 84(1) in definition of "the benefit Acts", the words "the Social Security Acts 1975 to 1991" substituted by Statutory Sick Pay Act 1991, s. 3(1) and 4(2), with effect from 12 February 1991.
In s. 84(1), the definitions of "primary Class 1 contributions" and "secondary Class 1 contributions" repealed by SS(CP)A 1992 s. 3 and Sch. 1, with effect from 1 July 1992.
In s. 84(1), the definitions of "contract of service", "employed earner", "employee" and "employer" repealed by PSA 1993, s. 188 and Sch. 5, Pt. I, with effect from 7 February 1994.
S. 84(2) repealed by PSA 1993, s. 188 and Sch. 5, Pt. I, with effect from 7 February 1994.
S. 84(3) repealed by SS(CP)A 1992, s. 3 and Sch. 1, with effect from 1 July 1992.

Cross references – SS(C)A 1991, s. 6(5) (not reproduced): the 1991 Act included in those Acts that are cited as Social Security Acts 1975 to 1991.

Notes – Interpretation Act 1978, Sch. 1: "Secretary of State" means one of HM's Principal Secretaries of State.
The definitions reproduced in s. 84(1) are only those relevant to National Insurance contributions.

87 Extent

87(1) The following provisions of this Act extend to Northern Ireland–

(a) [repealed by PSA 1993, s. 188 and Sch. 5, Pt. I;]

(b) section 61 above;

(c), (d) [not specifically relevant to National Insurance contributions;]

(e) sections 83 to 86 above;

(f) this section;

(g) sections 88 to 90 below.

87(2), (3) [Not relevant to National Insurance contributions.]

87(4) Where any enactment repealed or amended by this Act extends to any part of the United Kingdom, the repeal or amendment extends to that part.

87(5) Except as provided by this section, this Act extends to England and Wales and Scotland, but not to Northern Ireland.

Commencement Date – S. 87 came into force on 25 July 1986, by virtue of SSA 1986, s. 88(5).

History – S. 87(1)(a) repealed by PSA 1993, s. 188 and Sch. 5, Pt. I, with effect from 7 February 1994.

88 Commencement

88(1) Subject to the following provisions of this section, the provisions of this Act shall come into force on such day as the Secretary of State may by order made by statutory instrument appoint, and different days may be appointed in pursuance of this section for different provisions or different purposes of the same provision.

88(2) In relation to section 52 above (including Schedule 5) and section 82 above (including Schedule 9) for the reference to the Secretary of State in subsection (1) above there shall be substituted a reference to the Lord Chancellor and the Secretary of State, acting jointly.

88(3), (4) [Not relevant to National Insurance contributions.]

88(5) The following provisions of this Act–

…

section 61;

…

section 83 to 85

…

section 87;

this section; and

sections 89 and 90;

shall come into force on the day this Act is passed.

Commencement Date – S. 88 came into force on 25 July 1986, by virtue of SSA 1986, s. 88(5).

90 Citation

90(1) This Act may be cited as the Social Security Act 1986.

90(2) This Act, except section 77 above, may be cited together with the Social Security Acts 1975 to 1985 as the Social Security Acts 1975 to 1986.

Commencement Date – S. 90 came into force on 25 July 1986, by virtue of SSA 1986, s. 88(5).

SOCIAL SECURITY ACT 1989

(1989 Chapter 24) [*21st July 1989*]

ARRANGEMENT OF SECTIONS

GENERAL AND SUPPLEMENTARY PROVISIONS

GENERAL AND SUPPLEMENTARY PROVISIONS

29 Regulations and orders: general provisions

29(1) Subject to the following provisions of this section, section 175(2) to (5) of the Social Security Contributions and Benefits Act 1992 shall apply in relation to any power conferred by any provision of this Act to make regulations or an order as they apply in relation to any power conferred by that Act to make regulations or an order, but as if for references to that Act there were substituted references to this Act.

29(2) [Repealed by SS(CP)A 1992, s. 3 and Sch. 1.]

29(3) A statutory instrument–

(a) which contains (whether alone or with other provisions) any regulations on orders under this Act, other than orders under section 33 below, and

(b) which is not subject to any requirement that a draft of the instrument be laid before and approved by a resolution of each House of Parliament,

shall be subject to annulment in pursuance of a resolution of either House of Parliament.

29(4) [Repealed by SSA 1990, s. 21(1), (2), Sch. 6, para. 8(12) and Sch. 7.]

29(5) [Repealed by SS(CP)A 1992, s. 3 and Sch. 1.]

29(6) A power conferred by this Act to make any regulations or order, where the power is not expressed to be exercisable with the consent of the Treasury, shall if the Treasury so direct be exercisable only in conjuction with them.

29(7) [Not relevant to National Insurance contributions.]

Commencement Date – S. 29 came into force on 21 July 1989, by virtue of SSA 1989, s. 33.

History – In s. 29(1) the words "section 175(2) to (5) of the Social Security Contributions and Benefits Act 1992" substituted by SS(CP)A 1992, s. 4 and Sch. 2, para. 106, with effect from 1 July 1992.
S. 29(2) repealed by SS(CP)A 1992, s. 3 and Sch. 1, with effect from 1 July 1992.
S. 29(3) substituted by SSA 1990, s. 21(1), 23(3) and Sch. 6, para. 8(12), with effect from 13 July 1990.
S. 29(5) repealed by SS(CP)A 1992, s. 3 and Sch. 1, with effect from 1 July 1992.

Cross references – SSCBA 1992, s. 175(2)–(5); powers to make orders and regulations apply to this Act.

30 Interpretation

30(1) In this Act unless the context otherwise requires–

…

"regulations" means regulations made by the Secretary of State.

30(2) [Not relevant to National Insurance contributions.]

Commencement Date – S. 30 came into force on 21 July 1989, by virtue of SSA 1989, s. 33.

31 Minor and consequential amendments, repeals and transitional provisions

31(1), (2) [Amending provisions only.]

31(3) The Secretary of State may by regulations make–

(a) such transitional provision,

(b) such consequential provision, or

(c) such savings,

as he considers necessary or expedient in preparation for or in connection with the coming into force of any provision of this Act or the operation of any enactment repealed or amended by a provision of this Act during any period when the repeal or amendment is not wholly in force.

Commencement Date – S. 31 (part) came into force on 21 July 1989, by virtue of SSA 1989, s. 33.

Statutory instruments – SI 1989/1677: s. 31(3).

33 Short title, commencement and extent

33(1) This Act may be cited as the Social Security Act 1989; and this Act, other than section 25, and the Social Security Acts 1975 to 1988 may be cited together as the Social Security Acts 1975 to 1989.

33(2) Apart from the provisions specified in subsection (3) below, this Act shall come into force on such day as the Secretary of State may by order appoint; and different days may be so appointed for different provisions or different purposes of the same provision.

33(3) The provisions referred to in subsection (2) above are the following–

(a) sections 2, 3, 4, 6, 14 to 20, 28, 29, 30, 31(3), 32 and this section;

(b)–(f) [Amending and repealing provisions, not reproduced.]

33(4) Where any enactment repealed or amended by this Act extends to any part of the United Kingdom, the repeal or amendment extends to that part.

33(5) [Not relevant to National Insurance contributions.]

33(6) Sections 25, 31(3), 32 and this section, and paragraph 20A of Schedule 4 extend to Northern Ireland.

33(7) Except as provided by this section, this Act does not extend to Northern Ireland.

Commencement Date – S. 33 came into force on 21 July 1989, by virtue of SSA 1989, s. 33.

History – In s. 33(6) the words ", and paragraph 20A of Schedule 4" inserted by SSA 1990, s. 7 and Sch. 1, para. 5(3), with effect from 13 July 1990.

SOCIAL SECURITY CONTRIBUTIONS AND BENEFITS ACT 1992

(1992 Chapter 4)

[*13th February 1992*]

ARRANGEMENT OF SECTIONS

PART I – CONTRIBUTIONS

PRELIMINARY

PART 12ZA – STATUTORY PATERNITY PAY

[ORDINARY STATUTORY PATERNITY PAY]

[ADDITIONAL STATUTORY PATERNITY PAY]

[ORDINARY AND ADDITIONAL STATUTORY PATERNITY PAY: ADDITIONAL PROVISIONS]

PART 12ZB – STATUTORY ADOPTION PAY

PART 12ZC – STATUTORY SHARED PARENTAL PAY

PART XIII – GENERAL

INTERPRETATION

SUBORDINATE LEGISLATION

PART I – CONTRIBUTIONS

Cross references – SSAA 1992, s. 61(1)(a)(iii): regulations pending determination of a person's liability for contributions under this part of this Act.
SSAA 1992, s. 110(2)(c)(i), (6)(a)(i): inspectors' powers of examination in relation to contravention of provisions of this Part of this Act.
SSAA 1992, s. 114(1): offences relating to contributions under this Part of this Act.
SSAA 1992, s. 141: annual review of contributions under this Part of this Act.
SSAA 1992, s. 143(1): power to alter contributions under this Part of this Act.
SI 2001/1004, reg. 154: application of this Part of this Act with modifications as respects volunteer development workers.

PRELIMINARY

1 Outline of contributory system

1(1) The funds required–

(a) for paying such benefits under this Act or any other Act as are payable out of the National Insurance Fund and not out of other public money; and

(b) for the making of payments under section 162 of the Administration Act towards the cost of the National Health Service,

shall be provided by means of contributions payable to the Inland Revenue by earners, employers and others, together with the additions under subsection (5) below and amounts payable under section 2 of the Social Security Act 1993.

1(2) Contributions under this Part of this Act shall be of the following classes–

(a) Class 1, earnings-related, payable under section 6 below, being–
  (i) primary Class 1 contributions from employed earners; and
  (ii) secondary Class 1 contributions from employers and other persons paying earnings;

(b) Class 1A, payable under section 10 below by persons liable to pay secondary Class 1 contributions and certain other persons;

(bb) Class 1B, payable under section 10A below by persons who are accountable to the Inland Revenue in respect of income tax on general earnings in accordance with a PAYE settlement agreement;

(c) Class 2, flat-rate, payable under section 11 below by self-employed earners;

(d) Class 3, payable under section 13 or 13A below by earners and others voluntarily with a view to providing entitlement to benefit, or making up entitlement; and

(da) Class 3A, payable by eligible people voluntarily under section 14A with a view to obtaining units of additional pension;

(e) Class 4, payable under section 15 below in respect of the profits or gains of a trade, profession or vocation, or under section 18 below in respect of equivalent earnings.

1(3) The amounts and rates of contributions in this Part of this Act and the other figures in it which affect the liability of contributors shall–

(a) be subject to regulations under sections 19(4) and 116 to 120 below; and

(b) to the extent provided for by Part IX of the Administration Act be subject to alteration by orders made by the Treasury from year to year under that Part,

1(3) [Omitted by PA 2014, s. 24 and Sch. 13, para. 49.]

1(4) Schedule 1 to this Act–

(a) shall have effect with respect to the computation, collection and recovery of contributions of Classes 1, 1A, 1B, 2, 3 and 3A, and otherwise with respect to contributions of those classes; and

(b) shall also, to the extent provided by regulations made under section 18 below, have effect with respect to the computation, collection and recovery of Class 4 contributions, and otherwise with respect to such contributions.

1(5) For each financial year there shall, by way of addition to contributions, be paid out of money provided by Parliament, in such manner and at such times as the Treasury may determine, amounts the total of which for any such year is equal to the aggregate of all statutory sick pay, statutory maternity pay, statutory paternity pay, statutory adoption pay and statutory shared parental pay recovered by employers and others in that year, as estimated by the Government Actuary or the Deputy Government Actuary.

1(6) No person shall–

(a) be liable to pay Class 1, Class 1A, Class 1B or Class 2 contributions unless he fulfils prescribed conditions as to residence or presence in Great Britain;

(b) be entitled to pay Class 3 contributions unless he fulfils such conditions; or

(c) be entitled to pay Class 1, Class 1A, Class 1B or Class 2 contributions other than those which he is liable to pay, except so far as he is permitted by regulations to pay them.

1(7) Regulations under subsection (6) above shall be made by the Treasury.

History – In s. 1 "Inland Revenue" substituted by SSC(TF)A 1999, s. 1; Sch. 1, para. 5(2) with effect from 1 April 1999 (SI 1999/527).
In s. 1(1), words after "below" inserted by SSA 1993, s. 2(9), with effect from 29 January 1993.
In s. 1(1)(a), the words "or any other Act" inserted after the words "this Act" by PA 2014, s. 23 and Sch. 12, para. 3, with effect from 6 April 2016 (as not brought into force by any earlier order under PA 2014, s. 56(1)).
In s. 1(2), the word "six" omitted by PA 2014, s. 25 and Sch. 15, para. 2(2)(a), with effect from 12 October 2015 (SI 2015/1475, art. 3).
In s. 1(2)(b) the words "in respect of cars made available for private use and car fuel" omitted by CSPSSA 2000, s. 74(1); s. 85(1), Sch. 9, Pt. VIII(1) with effect from 6 April 2000.
In s. 1(2)(bb) the words "general earnings" substituted by ITEPA 2003, Sch. 6, para. 170 which has effect for income tax purposes for the year 2003–04 and subsequent years.
In s. 1(2)(c) the word "weekly" (which appeared after the word "payable") omitted by NICA 2015, s. 2 and Sch. 1, para. 2, with effect for the tax year 2015–16 and subsequent tax years.
In s. 1(2)(d), "or 13A" inserted by Pensions Act 2008, s. 135(3) with effect from 6 April 2009.
S. 1(2)(da) inserted by PA 2014, s. 25 and Sch. 15, para. 2(2)(b), with effect from 12 October 2015 (SI 2015/1475, art. 3).
In s. 1(2), word "six" substituted and para. (bb) inserted by SSA 1998, s. 86(1) and Sch. 7, para. 56(1), with effect from 8 September 1998 for the purpose only of authorising the making of regulations or orders, and from 6 April 1999 for all other purposes (SI 1998/2209).
In s. 1(3), the words "Chapter II of Part III of the Pensions Act…members of certified schemes)" substituted by PSA 1993, Sch. 8, para. 32, with effect from 7 February 1994.
In s. 1(3)(b) "Treasury" substituted by SSC(TF)A 1999, s. 2; Sch. 3, para. 1(2) with effect from 1 April 1999 (SI 1999/527).
In s. 1(3), the words "and the provisions of this Part of this Act are subject to the provisions of Chapter II of Part III of the Pensions Act (reduction in state scheme contributions and benefits for members of certified schemes)." (which appeared after para. (b)) omitted by PA 2014, s. 24 and Sch. 13, para. 49, with effect from 6 April 2016 (as not brought into force by any earlier order under PA 2014, s. 56(1)).
In s. 1(4)(a), the words ", 3 and 3A" substituted for the words "and 3" by PA 2014, s. 25 and Sch. 15, para. 2(3), with effect from 12 October 2015 (SI 2015/1475, art. 3).
In s. 1(4)(a), (6), references to Class 1B inserted by SSA 1998, s. 86(1) and Sch. 7, para. 56(2), (3), with effect from 8 September 1998 for the purposeonly of authorising the making of regulations or orders, and from 6 April 1999 for all other purposes.
In s. 1(4)(b) words at the end omitted by SSC(TF)A 1999, s. 1; Sch. 1, para. 5(3) with effect from 1 April 1999 (SI 1999/527).
In s. 1(5), the words " statutory paternity pay, " substituted for the words "ordinary statutory paternity pay, additional statutory paternity pay and" by Children and Families Act 2014, s. 126(1) and Sch. 7, para. 7(a), with effect from 5 April 2015, subject to the transitional and saving provisions in SI 2014/1640, art. 16 (amendments do not have effect in relation to– (a) children whose expected week of birth ends on or before 4 April 2015; (b) children placed for adoption on or before 4 April 2015) (SI 2014/1640, art. 6 and 7).
In s. 1(5), the words "and statutory shared parental pay" inserted after the words "statutory adoption pay" by Children and Families Act 2014, s. 126(1) and Sch. 7, para. 7(b), with effect from 1 December 2014 (SI 2014/1640, art. 5).
In s. 1(5) the words "ordinary statutory paternity pay, additional statutory paternity pay" substituted for "statutory paternity pay" by the Work and Families Act 2006, s. 11 and Sch. 1, para. 3, with effect from 6 April 2010 (SI 2010/495).
In s. 1(5) words "statutory maternity pay, statutory paternity pay and statutory adoption pay" substituted by EA 2002, s. 6(3), with effect from 8 December 2002 (SI 2002/2866, art. 2(2), Sch. 1, Pt. 2).
S. 1(7) inserted by SSC(TF)A 1999, s. 2; Sch. 3, para. 1(3) with effect from 1 April 1999 (SI 1999/527).

Derivations – (as originally enacted) – SSA 1975, s. 1.

Cross references – S. 116: Her Majesty's forces.
S. 117: mariners, airmen etc.
S. 118: married women and widows.
S. 119: persons outside Great Britain.
S. 120: employment at sea (continental shelf provisions).
S. 172(a): "Great Britain" extends to adjacent territorial waters.
S. 174: "the Administration Act" means SSAA 1992.
SSAA 1992, Pt. IX: alteration of contributions.
SSAA 1992, s. 162: destination of contributions.
SSA 1993, s. 2 (not reproduced): payments into National Insurance Fund out of money provided by Parliament.
PSA 1993, Pt. III, Ch. II: reduction in state scheme contributions and social security benefits for members of certified schemes.
SI 2001/1004, reg. 145: conditions as to residence and presence in Great Britain.

Statutory instruments – SI 2013/622: partly made under s. 1(6).

2 Categories of earners

2(1) In this Part of this Act and Parts II to V below–

(a) **"employed earner"** means a person who is gainfully employed in Great Britain either under a contract of service, or in an office (including elective office) with earnings; and

(b) **"self-employed earner"** means a person who is gainfully employed in Great Britain otherwise than in employed earner's employment (whether or not he is also employed in such employment).

2(2) *Regulations may provide–*

(a) for employment of any prescribed description to be disregarded in relation to liability for contributions otherwise arising from employment of that description;

(b) for a person in employment of any prescribed description to be treated, for the purposes of this Act, as falling within one or other of the categories of earner defined in subsection (1) above, notwithstanding that he would not fall within that category apart from the regulations.

2(2ZA) Regulations under subsection (2)(b) may make provision treating a person ("P") as falling within one or other of the categories of earner in relation to an employment where arrangements have been entered into the main purpose, or one of the main purposes, of which is to secure–

(a) that P is not treated by other provision in regulations under subsection (2)(b) as falling within that category of earner in relation to the employment, or

(b) that a person is not treated as the secondary contributor in respect of earnings paid to or for the benefit of P in respect of the employment.

2(2ZB) In subsection (2ZA) **"arrangements"** include any scheme, transaction or series of transactions, agreement or understanding, whether or not legally enforceable, and any associated operations.

2(2A) Regulations under subsection (2)(a) above shall be made by the Treasury and, in the case of regulations under paragraph (b) of that subsection, with the concurrence of the Secretary of State.

2(3) Where a person is to be treated by reference to any employment of his as an employed earner, then he is to be so treated for all purposes of this Act; and references throughout this Act to employed earner's employment shall be construed accordingly.

2(4) [Not relevant to National Insurance contributions.]

2(5) For the purposes of this Act, a person shall be treated as a self-employed earner as respects any week during any part of which he is such an earner (without prejudice to his being also treated as an employed earner as respects that week by reference to any other employment of his).

History – In s. 2(1)(a) (definition of "employed earner") the word "general" omitted by NICA 2014, s. 15(1), with effect from 13 May 2014.
In s. 2(1)(a) the words "general earnings" substituted by ITEPA 2003, Sch. 6, para. 171 which has effect for income tax purposes for the year 2003–04 and subsequent years.
S. 2(2ZA) and (2ZB) inserted by NICA 2015, s. 6(3), with effect from 12 February 2015.
S. 2(2A) amended by WRPA 1999, s. 81 and Sch. 11, para. 2 with effect from 11 November 1999 (date of passing of WRPA 1999) as provided by WRPA 1999, s. 89(4)(d).
S. 2(2A) inserted by SSC(TF)A 1999, s. 2; Sch. 3, para. 2 with effect from 1 April 1999 (SI 1999/527).

Derivations – SSA 1975, s. 2.

Cross references – S. 122: "employed earner" to be construed in accordance with this section.
S. 172(a): "Great Britain" extends to adjacent territorial waters.
SSAA 1992, s. 17(1)(a): procedure relating to categorisation disputes.
ITEPA 2003, s. 7: meaning of "general earnings" for income tax purposes.
Diplomatic Privileges Act 1964, Sch. 1, art. 33: diplomats and certain persons employed by them exempt from contributions.
Consular Relations Act 1968, Sch. 1, art. 1, 48: members of consular posts and members of their families and private staff exempt from contributions.
Rent Act 1977, s. 63(3) (as amended by Housing Act 1988, Sch. 14, para. 4): rent officers included in category of employed earners.
SI 1978/1689: certain persons specifically categorised as employed earners, or not.
SI 2001/1004, reg. 11: modification of employed earner's employment in case of airmen.
SI 2001/1004, reg. 125: modification in relation to share fishermen.
SI 2001/1004, Pt. 9: modification of employed earner's employment for special classes of earner.

Statutory instruments – SI 1978/1689 partly made under s. 2(2).

Hansard – HC parliamentary statement, 13 November 1981 (HC 1981 vol. 12, col. 188): subcontractors holding a tax exemption certificate normally regarded as self-employed.
HC Written Answer (HC 1984 vol. 55, No. 108, col. 62–63) (not reproduced): if a person is reclassified as an employed earner with effect from a date earlier than the decision effecting that change then: (1) Class 2 contributions paid by contributor in error, because of change of status to employed, are reallocated as Class 1 contributions; (2) any balance of primary contributions, arrears in secondary contributions, are requested from employers; (3) any Class 2 contributions in excess of the Class 1 contributions are refundable; and (4) Class 4 contributions overpaid are dealt with by Inland Revenue.
Written Answer, 5 May 1993: term "self-employed" undefined.
847 HC Deb. 5th Series, col. 124 (not reproduced): the position of each category of earner was intended to be aligned for the purposes of National Insurance contributions and income tax.

Other material – IR press release, 19 March 1987 (not reproduced): procedures introduced by Revenue and (the then) DHSS to help individuals decide whether employed or self-employed.
Leaflet IR 56 (not reproduced): Employed or self-employed? A guide for tax and National Insurance.

3 "Earnings" and "earner"

3(1) In this Part of this Act and Parts II to V below–

(a) **"earnings"** includes any remuneration or profit derived from an employment; and

(b) **"earner"** shall be construed accordingly.

3(2) For the purposes of this Part of this Act and of Parts II to V below other than those of Schedule 8–

(a) the amount of a person's earnings for any period; or

(b) the amount of his earnings to be treated as comprised in any payment made to him or for his benefit,

shall be calculated or estimated in such manner and on such basis as may be prescribed by regulations made by the Treasury with the concurrence of the Secretary of State.

3(2A) Regulations made for the purposes of subsection (2) above may provide that, where a payment is made or a benefit provided to or for the benefit of two or more earners, a proportion (determined in such manner as may be prescribed) of the amount or value of the payment or benefit shall be attributed to each earner.

3(3) Regulations made for the purposes of subsection (2) above may prescribe that payments of a particular class or description made or falling to be made to or by a person shall, to such extent as may be prescribed, be disregarded or, as the case may be, be deducted from the amount of that person's earnings.

3(4) Subsection (5) below applies to regulations made for the purposes of subsection (2) above which make special provision with respect to the earnings periods of directors and former directors of companies.

3(5) Regulations to which this subsection applies may make provision–

(a) for enabling companies, and directors and former directors of companies, to pay on account of any earnings-related contributions that may become payable by them such amounts as would be payable by way of such contributions if the special provision had not been made; and

(b) for requiring any payments made in accordance with the regulations to be treated, for prescribed purposes, as if they were the contributions on account of which they were made.

History – In s. 3(2) the words "by regulations made by the Treasury with the concurrence of the Secretary of State." inserted by SSC(TF)A 1999, s. 2; Sch. 3, para. 3 with effect from 1 April 1999 (SI 1999/527).
S. 3(2A) inserted by SSA 1998, s. 48, with effect from 8 September 1998 (SI 1998/2209).
S. 3(4), (5) inserted by SSA 1998, s. 49, with effect from 8 September 1998 by virtue of SI 1999/2209.

Derivations – S. 3(1): SSA 1975, s. 3(1).
S. 3(2), (3): SSA 1975, s. 3(2), (3).

Cross references – S. 4: payments treated as earnings etc. for s. 3 purposes.
S. 112: regulations may provide for certain sums to be earnings.
S. 122: "earner" and "earnings" to be construed in accordance with this section.
SI 1978/1689, reg. 1(2): meaning of "remuneration".
SI 2001/1004, reg. 22: payments to be treated as earnings.
SI 2001/1004, reg. 14–16: aggregation of earnings.
SI 2001/1004, reg. 17: apportionment of single payment of earnings by different employers.
SI 2001/1004, reg. 24: calculation of earnings.
SI 2001/1004, reg. 25–27: payments disregarded in computing a person's earnings.

Statutory instruments – SI 2006/2003 made under s. 3(3) and (4).
SI 2006/2829 made under s. 3(2) and (3).
SI 2006/2924 made under s. 3(2) and (3).
SI 2007/2091: partly made under s. 3(2) and (3).
SI 2007/2905: partly made under s. 3(2) and (3).
SI 2008/1431: partly made under s. 3(2) and (3).
SI 2008/2624: partly made under s. 3(2) and (3).
SI 2013/622: partly made under s. 3(2) and (3).

Hansard – HC Written Answer, 28 July 1983, col. 589, (not reproduced): no Class 1 NI contributions payable for casual farm workers employed on a piecework basis. Employers' and employees' contributions payable in usual way for people employed as regular casual workers who are usually paid weekly. Under agreement between NFU and (the then) DHSS in 1978, no social security contributions will be sought in respect of workers in large gangs paid piecework, where it is impossible for employers to keep records on individuals (see Cyclo 918/74/78 Econ. Y. 57, 17 May 1978).

Other material – Tax Bulletin, Issue 18, August 1995, p. 245 (not reproduced): dispensations issued by an inspector of taxes also count for NICs.
ICAEW Technical Release TR 676 (not reproduced): Revenue confirm that total profit-related pay is part of pensionable emoluments (see also leaflet CA28 (NI 269), s. 15, para. 49).
ICAEW Tax Faculty Guidance Note TAX 21/92 December 1992, para. 6–39: directors' drawings.
Taxline 1993/85 (not reproduced): the cost of eyesight tests provided by employers for employees using display screen equipment and the cost of spectacles prescribed solely for VDU use does not give rise to a NIC liability.
Taxline 1993/107 (not reproduced): dividends paid to directors may be regarded as earnings when not paid in proportion to the paid up shares.
For special treatment of company cars available for private use and fuel similarly provided, see s. 10 below.

4 Payments treated as remuneration and earnings

4(1) For the purposes of section 3 above there shall be treated as remuneration derived from employed earner's employment–

(a) any sum paid to or for the benefit of a person in satisfaction (whether in whole or in part) of any entitlement of that person to–

(i) statutory sick pay; or

(ii) statutory maternity pay;

(iii) statutory paternity pay;

(iv) [repealed by Children and Families Act 2014, s. 126(1) and Sch. 7, para. 8(b);]

(v) statutory adoption pay; or

(vi) statutory shared parental pay; and

(b) any sickness payment made–
(i) to or for the benefit of the employed earner; and
(ii) in accordance with arrangements under which the person who is the secondary contributor in relation to the employment concerned has made, or remains liable to make, payments towards the provision of that sickness payment.

4(2) Where the funds for making sickness payments under arrangements of the kind mentioned in paragraph (b) of subsection (1) above are attributable in part to contributions to those funds made by the employed earner, regulations may make provision for disregarding, for the purposes of that subsection, the prescribed part of any sum paid as a result of the arrangements.

4(3) For the purposes of subsections (1) and (2) above **"sickness payment"** means any payment made in respect of absence from work due to incapacity for work.

4(4) For the purposes of section 3 above there shall be treated as remuneration derived from an employed earner's employment–

(a) the amount of any gain calculated under section 479 of ITEPA 2003 in respect of which an amount counts as employment income of the earner under section 476 of that Act (charge on acquisition of securities pursuant to option etc.), reduced by any amounts deducted under section 480(1) to (6) of that Act in arriving at the amount counting as such employment income;

(b) any sum paid (or treated as paid) to or for the benefit of the earner which is chargeable to tax by virtue of section 225 or 226 of ITEPA 2003 (taxation of consideration for certain restrictive undertakings).

4(5) For the purposes of section 3 above regulations may make provision for treating as remuneration derived from an employed earner's employment any payment made by a body corporate to or for the benefit of any of its directors where that payment would, when made, not be earnings for the purposes of this Act.

4(6) Regulations may make provision for the purposes of this Part–

(a) for treating any amount on which an employed earner is chargeable to income tax under the employment income Parts of ITEPA 2003 as remuneration derived from the earner's employment; and

(b) for treating any amount which in accordance with regulations under paragraph (a) above constitutes remuneration as an amount of remuneration paid, at such time as may be determined in accordance with the regulations, to or for the benefit of the earner in respect of his employment.

4(7) Regulations under this section shall be made by the Treasury with the concurrence of the Secretary of State.

History – In s. 4(1)(a)(iii), the word "ordinary" (which appeared before the words "statutory paternity pay") repealed by Children and Families Act 2014, s. 126(1) and Sch. 7, para. 8(a), with effect from 5 April 2015, subject to the transitional and saving provisions in SI 2014/1640, art. 16 (amendments do not have effect in relation to– (a) children whose expected week of birth ends on or before 4 April 2015; (b) children placed for adoption on or before 4 April 2015 (SI 2014/1640, art. 6 and 7).
S. 4(1)(a)(iii)–(v) substituted for former s. 4(1)(a)(iii)–(iv) by the Work and Families Act 2006, s. 11 and Sch. 1, para. 4, with effect from 6 April 2010 (SI 2010/495).
S. 4(1)(a)(iii), (iv) inserted by EA 2002, s. 53 and Sch. 7, para. 3, with effect from 8 December 2002 (SI 2002/2866, art. 2(2), Sch. 1. Pt. 2).
S. 4(1)(a)(iv) (and the "or" following it) repealed by Children and Families Act 2014, s. 126(1) and Sch. 7, para. 8(b), with effect from 1 December 2014 (SI 2014/1640, art. 5).
S. 4(1)(a)(vi) inserted (and the word "and" following (v) substituted for the word "or") by Children and Families Act 2014, s. 126(1) and Sch. 7, para. 8(c), with effect from 1 December 2014 (SI 2014/1640, art. 5).
In s. 4(3), the words ", within the meaning of section 57 below" omitted by the Social Security (Incapacity for Work Act) 1994, Sch. 1, para. 1 and Sch. 2, with effect from 13 April 1995 (SI 1994/2926).
S. 4(4)(a) substituted by ITEPA 2003, Sch. 6, para. 172(2) which has effect for income tax purposes for the year 2003–04 and subsequent years.
In s. 4(4)(a), words after "479" substituted by FA 2003, s. 140 and Sch. 22, para. 48 with effect on and after 16 April 2003 in relation to employment-related securities options which are not share options, and on and after 1 September 2003 in relation to employment-related securities options which are share options. For this purpose, "share options" means rights to acquire shares in a company or securities.
In s. 4(4)(b), the words "section 225 or 226 of ITEPA 2003" substituted by ITEPA 2003, Sch. 6, para. 172(3) which has effect for income tax purposes for the year 2003–04 and subsequent years.
S. 4(4) substituted by SSA 1998, s. 50(1) and 87(2)(b), with effect, so far as relating to a sum chargeable to tax under ICTA 1988, s. 313, in relation to any undertaking given on or after 10 July 1997, and for all other purposes with effect from 8 September 1998 by virtue of SI 1998/2209 (C. 47), art. 2(a) and Schedule, Pt. I.
In s. 4(6)(a), the words "the employment income Parts of ITEPA 2003" substituted by ITEPA 2003, Sch. 6, para. 172(4) which has effect for income tax purposes for the year 2003–04 and subsequent years.
S. 4(6) substituted by CSPSSA 2000, s. 74(3)with effect from 6 April 2000. The former s. 4(6) was inserted by SSA 1998, s. 50(2); with effect from 27 May 1998 (SSA 1998, s. 87(2)(b)).
S. 4(7) inserted by SSC(TF)A 1999, s. 2; Sch. 3, para. 4 with effect from 1 April 1999 (SI 1999/527).

Derivations – (as originally enacted) S. 4(1): SSA 1975, s. 3(1A); SSHBA 1982, s. 23; SSA 1986, s. 49, Sch. 4, para. 10.
S. 4(2), (3) (as originally enacted), (4): SSA 1975, s. 3(1B), (1C), (1D).
S. 4(5): SSA 1975, s. 3(4).

Cross references – SSA 1998, s. 50(6): regulations under s. 4(6) shall not be made before the passing of the Finance Act 1998 but may make provision having effect in relation to acquisitions on or after 6th April 1998.
S. 57 (not reproduced): determination of days for which benefit is provided.
S. 122: "earner" and "earnings" to be construed in accordance with this section.

Sch. 1, para. 11: power to make provision as to the manner in which, and the person through whom, any sickness payment which is to be treated as remuneration derived from an employed earner's employment is to be made.
ITEPA 2003, s. 225, 226: payments and valuable consideration for restrictive undertakings.
ITEPA 2003, s. 476, 479, 480: charge to tax following a chargeable event in relation to a securities option.
SI 2001/1004, reg. 23: manner of making sickness payments treated as remuneration.
SI 2001/1004, reg. 25 and Sch. 3: payments to be disregarded in the calculation of earnings for the purpose of earnings-related contributions.

Statutory instruments – SI 2007/1057 made partly under s. 4.

Other material – Taxline 1993/85 (not reproduced): the cost of eyesight tests provided by employers for employees using display screen equipment and the cost of spectacles prescribed solely for VDU use does not give rise to a NIC liability.

4A Earnings of workers supplied by service companies etc.

4A(1) Regulations may make provision for securing that where–

(a) an individual ("the worker") personally performs, or is under an obligation personally to perform, services for the purposes of a business carried on by another person ("the client"),

(b) the performance of those services by the worker is (within the meaning of the regulations) referable to arrangements involving a third person (and not referable to any contract between the client and the worker), and

(c) the circumstances are such that, were the services to be performed by the worker under a contract between him and the client, he would be regarded for the purposes of the applicable provisions of this Act as employed in employed earner's employment by the client,

relevant payments or benefits are, to the specified extent, to be treated for those purposes as earnings paid to the worker in respect of an employed earner's employment of his.

4A(2) For the purposes of this section–

(a) **"the intermediary"** means–

(i) where the third person mentioned in subsection (1)(b) above has such a contractual or other relationship with the worker as may be specified, that third person, or

(ii) where that third person does not have such a relationship with the worker, any other person who has both such a relationship with the worker and such a direct or indirect contractual or other relationship with the third person as may be specified; and

(b) a person may be the intermediary despite being–

(i) a person with whom the worker holds any office or employment, or

(ii) a body corporate, unincorporated body or partnership of which the worker is a member;

and subsection (1) above applies whether or not the client is a person with whom the worker holds any office or employment.

4A(3) Regulations under this section may, in particular, make provision–

(a) for the worker to be treated for the purposes of the applicable provisions of this Act, in relation to the specified amount of relevant payments or benefits (the worker's "attributable earnings"), as employed in employed earner's employment by the intermediary;

(b) for the intermediary (whether or not he fulfils the conditions prescribed under section 1(6)(a) above for secondary contributors) to be treated for those purposes as the secondary contributor in respect of the worker's attributable earnings;

(c) for determining–

(i) any deductions to be made, and

(ii) in other respects the manner and basis in and on which the amount of the worker's attributable earnings for any specified period is to be calculated or estimated,

in connection with relevant payments or benefits;

(d) for aggregating any such amount, for purposes relating to contributions, with other earnings of the worker during any such period;

(e) for determining the date by which contributions payable in respect of the worker's attributable earnings are to be paid and accounted for;

(f) for apportioning payments or benefits of any specified description, in such manner or on such basis as may be specified, for the purpose of determining the part of any such payment or benefit which is to be treated as a relevant payment or benefit for the purposes of the regulations;

(g) for disregarding for the purposes of the applicable provisions of this Act, in relation to relevant payments or benefits, an employed earner's employment in which the worker is employed (whether by the intermediary or otherwise) to perform the services in question;

(h) for otherwise securing that a double liability to pay any amount by way of a contribution of any description does not arise in relation to a particular payment or benefit or (as the case may be) a particular part of a payment or benefit;

(i) for securing that, to the specified extent, two or more persons, whether–

(i) connected persons (within the meaning of section 993 of the Income Tax Act 2007), or

(ii) persons of any other specified description,

are treated as a single person for any purposes of the regulations;

(j) (without prejudice to paragraph (i) above) for securing that a contract made with a person other than the client is to be treated for any such purposes as made with the client;

(k) for excluding or modifying the application of the regulations in relation to such cases, or payments or benefits of such description, as may be specified.

4A(4) Regulations made in pursuance of subsection (3)(c) above may, in particular, make provision–

(a) for the making of a deduction of a specified amount in respect of general expenses of the intermediary as well as deductions in respect of particular expenses incurred by him;

(b) for securing reductions in the amount of the worker's attributable earnings on account of–

(i) any secondary Class 1 contributions already paid by the intermediary in respect of actual earnings of the worker, and

(ii) any such contributions that will be payable by him in respect of the worker's attributable earnings.

4A(5) Regulations under this section may make provision for securing that, in applying any provisions of the regulations, any term of a contract or other arrangement which appears to be of a description specified in the regulations is to be disregarded.

4A(6) In this section–

"the applicable provisions of this Act" means this Part of this Act and Parts II to V below;

"business" includes any activity carried on–

(a) by a government department or public or local authority (in the United Kingdom or elsewhere), or

(b) by a body corporate, unincorporated body or partnership;

"relevant payments or benefits" means payments or benefits of any specified description made or provided (whether to the intermediary or the worker or otherwise) in connection with the performance by the worker of the services in question;

"specified" means prescribed by or determined in accordance with regulations under this section.

4A(7) Any reference in this section to the performance by the worker of any services includes a reference to any such obligation of his to perform them as is mentioned in subsection (1)(a) above.

4A(8) Regulations under this section shall be made by the Treasury with the concurrence of the Secretary of State.

4A(9) If, on any modification of the statutory provisions relating to income tax, it appears to the Treasury to be expedient to modify any of the preceding provisions of this section for the purpose of assimilating the law relating to income tax and the law relating to contributions under this Part of this Act, the Treasury may with the concurrence of the Secretary of State by order make such modifications of the preceding provisions of this section as the Treasury think appropriate for that purpose.

History – In s. 4A(3)(i)(i) the words "section 993 of the Income Tax Act 2007" substituted by ITA 2007, s. 1027 and Sch. 1, para. 289, with effect from 6 April 2007.
S. 4A inserted by WRPA 1999, s. 75 with effect from 22 December 1999 (SI 2000/3420, art. 3).

Cross references – SI 2003/1874: modification of s. 4A in respect of earnings of workers supplied by intermediaries.
SI 2007/2071, art. 2: modification of s. 4A so that the earnings of workers whose services are provided through a managed service company are treated as if the workers are employed by the managed service company.

Statutory instruments – SI 2000/727: partly made under s. 4A.
SI 2003/2079: partly made under s. 4A.
SI 2007/2071: made under s. 4A.

Notes – S. 4A and SI 2000/727 deal with the NIC aspects of the earnings of workers supplied by service companies from 6 April 2000; the income and corporation tax aspects and consequences of the regime are dealt with in Finance Act 2000.

4AA Limited liability partnerships

4AA(1) The Treasury may, for the purposes of this Act, by regulations–

(a) provide that, in prescribed circumstances–

(i) a person ("E") is to be treated as employed in employed earner's employment by a limited liability partnership (including where E is a member of the partnership), and

(ii) the limited liability partnership is to be treated as the secondary contributor in relation to any payment of earnings to or for the benefit of E as the employed earner;

(b) prescribe how earnings in respect of E's employed earner employment with the limited liability partnership are to be determined (including what constitutes such earnings);

(c) provide that such earnings are to be treated as being paid to or for the benefit of E at prescribed times.

4AA(2) Regulations under subsection (1) may modify the definition of "employee" or "employer" in section 163, 171, 171ZJ or 171ZS below as the Treasury consider appropriate to take account of any provision falling within subsection (1)(a) to (c).

4AA(3) If–

(a) a provision of the Income Tax Acts relating to limited liability partnerships or members of limited liability partnerships is passed or made, and

(b) in consequence, the Treasury consider it appropriate for provision to be made for the purpose of assimilating to any extent the law relating to income tax and the law relating to contributions under this Part,

the Treasury may by regulations make that provision.

4AA(4) The provision that may be made under subsection (3) includes provision modifying any provision made by or under this Act.

4AA(5) Regulations under this section are to be made with the concurrence of the Secretary of State.

4AA(6) Section 4(4) of the Limited Liability Partnerships Act 2000 does not limit the provision that may be made by regulations under this section.

History – S. 4AA inserted by NICA 2014, s. 14(2), with effect from 13 March 2014.

Statutory instruments – SI 2014/3159: made under s. 4AA.

4B Earnings: power to make retrospective provision in consequence of retrospective tax legislation

4B(1) This section applies where–

(a) a provision of the Income Tax Acts which relates to income tax chargeable under the employment income Parts of ITEPA 2003 is passed or made so as to have retrospective effect ("the retrospective tax provision"), and

(b) it appears to the Treasury to be appropriate to make regulations under a relevant power for the purpose of reflecting the whole or part of the provision made by the retrospective tax provision.

4B(2) Those regulations may be made so as to have retrospective effect if it appears to the Treasury to be expedient, in consequence of the retrospective tax provision, for the regulations to have that effect.

4B(3) A **"relevant power"** means a power to make regulations under any of the following provisions–

(a) section 3 (power to prescribe the manner and basis of the calculation or estimation of earnings);

(b) section 4(6) (power to treat amounts chargeable to income tax under the employment income Parts of ITEPA 2003 as earnings);

(c) section 4A (power to treat payments or benefits to workers supplied by service companies etc as earnings);

(d) section 4AA (power to make provision in relation to limited liability partnerships).

4B(4) It does not matter whether the retrospective tax provision in question was passed or made before the day on which the National Insurance Contributions Act 2006 was passed.

4B(5) But nothing in subsection (2) authorises regulations to be made which have effect in relation to any time before 2nd December 2004.

4B(6) Regulations under a relevant power made by virtue of subsection (2) may affect, for the purposes of any contributions legislation for the purposes of which the regulations are made, the earnings in respect of an employment paid to or for the benefit of an earner at a time before the regulations are made.

4B(7) In such a case, subsections (8) and (9) apply and in those subsections and this subsection–

"relevant contributions legislation" means any contributions legislation for the purposes of which the regulations have the effect mentioned in subsection (6);

"the relevant time" means the time before the regulations are made mentioned in that subsection;

"the revised earnings" means the earnings, in respect of the employment, paid to or for the benefit of the earner at the relevant time as determined after applying the regulations.

4B(8) References in any relevant contributions legislation, or any provision made under any such legislation, which relate to–

(a) the earnings, in respect of the employment, paid to or for the benefit of the earner at the relevant time, or

(b) the amount of such earnings so paid at that time,

are to be read, in so far as they so relate, as references which relate to the revised earnings or, as the case may be, the amount of those earnings.

4B(9) Any matter which, at the time when the regulations are made, has been determined for the purposes of any relevant contributions legislation, or any provision made under any such legislation, wholly or partly by reference to–

(a) the earnings, in respect of the employment, paid to or for the benefit of the earner at the relevant time, or

(b) the amount of such earnings so paid at that time,

is to be redetermined as it would have been determined at the time of the original determination if it had been determined wholly or partly, as the case may be, by reference to the revised earnings or the amount of those earnings.

4B(10) The matters referred to in subsection (9) may include–

(a) whether Class 1 contributions are payable in respect of earnings paid to or for the benefit of the earner in a tax week, and

(b) the amount of any such contribution.

4B(11) Subsections (7) to (10) are subject to any express provision to the contrary (including any such provision made by regulations under section 4C(1)).

4B(12) The power conferred by subsection (2) is without prejudice to any powers conferred by or by virtue of any other provision of this Act or of any other enactment (including any instrument made under an Act).

4B(13) For the purposes of this section **"contributions legislation"** means any Part of this Act or provision of such a Part.

History – S. 4B(3)(d) inserted by NICA 2014, s. 14(3), with effect from 13 March 2014.
S. 4B inserted by NICA 2006, s. 1(1), with effect from 30 March 2006.

Statutory instruments – SI 2007/1057 made partly under s. 4B.

4C Power to make provision in consequence of provision made by or by virtue of section 4B(2) etc

4C(1) The Treasury may by regulations made with the concurrence of the Secretary of State make such provision as appears to the Treasury to be expedient for any of the purposes mentioned in subsection (2) in consequence of any provision made by or by virtue of section 4B(2).

4C(2) Those purposes are–

(a) any purpose relating to any contributions;

(b) any purpose relating to any contributory benefit or contribution-based jobseeker's allowance;

(c) any purpose relating to any statutory payment;

(d) [repealed by PA 2007, s. 15(3)(a), s. 27(2), and Sch. 4, para. 42(2) and Sch. 7, Pt. 7;]

(e) any purpose of Chapter 2 of Part 3 of that Act (reduction in state scheme contributions and benefits for members of certified schemes);

(f) such other purposes as may be prescribed by regulations made by the Treasury with the concurrence of the Secretary of State.

4C(3) Regulations under subsection (1) may, in particular, make provision–

(a) modifying any provision of any enactment (including this Act and any enactment passed or made on or after the commencement day);

(b) for any provision of any such enactment to apply in such cases, and with such modifications (if any), as the regulations may prescribe.

4C(4) Regulations under subsection (1) may be made so as to have retrospective effect but must not have effect in relation to any time before 2nd December 2004.

4C(5) In particular, regulations under subsection (1) made by virtue of subsection (4) may affect any of the following matters–

(a) liability to pay contributions;

(b) the amount of any contribution;

(c) entitlement to a contributory benefit or contribution-based jobseeker's allowance;

(d) the amount of any such benefit or allowance;

(e) entitlement to a statutory payment;

(f) the amount of any such payment;

(g) [repealed by PA 2007, s. 15(3)(a), s. 27(2), and Sch. 4, para. 42(3)(b) and Sch. 7, Pt. 7;]

(h) [repealed by PA 2007, s. 15(3)(a), s. 27(2), and Sch. 4, para. 42(3)(b) and Sch. 7, Pt. 7;]

(i) liability to make payments under section 42A(3) of the Pensions Act or to pay minimum contributions under section 43 of that Act;

(j) the amount of any such payment or contribution.

4C(6) In such a case, where the matter has been determined before the time when the regulations are made, the regulations may provide for the matter to be redetermined accordingly.

4C(7) If (ignoring this subsection) the operative provisions would directly or indirectly have effect in any case so as–

(a) to remove a person's entitlement to a contributory benefit, contribution-based jobseeker's allowance or statutory payment, or

(b) to reduce the amount of any such benefit, allowance or payment to which a person has an entitlement,

those provisions are to be read with such modifications as are necessary to ensure that they do not have that effect.

4C(8) For the purposes of subsection (7)–

(a) **"the operative provisions"** are section 4B(7) to (10) and any provision made by virtue of section 4B(2) or under subsection (1) of this section;

(b) a person's "entitlement" includes any future entitlement which the person may have.

4C(9) The powers conferred by this section are without prejudice to any powers conferred by or by virtue of any other provision of this Act or any other enactment.

4C(10) In particular, any modification of any provision of an instrument by regulations made under subsection (1) is without prejudice to any other power to amend or revoke the provisions of the instrument (including the modified provision).

4C(11) For the purposes of this section–

"the commencement day" means the day on which the National Insurance Contributions Act 2006 was passed;

"enactment" includes an instrument made under an Act;

"statutory payment" means–

(a) statutory sick pay, statutory maternity pay, statutory paternity pay, statutory adoption pay or statutory shared parental pay; or

(b) any other payment prescribed by regulations made by the Treasury with the concurrence of the Secretary of State.

Prospective amendments – In s. 4C(2)(b), (5)(c) and (7a), the words "contribution-based" repealed by WRA 2012, s. 147 and Sch. 14, Pt. 1, with effect from a date to be set by order of the Secretary of State.
In s. 4C(5)(b) the words "or 42A(2C)" repealed by PA 2007, s. 15(3)(a), s. 27(2), and Sch. 4, para. 42(3)(a) and Sch. 7, Pt. 7, with effect from a date to be appointed, PA 2007, s. 30(2)(b).
S. 4C(5)(i) and (j) repealed by PA 2007, s. 15(3)(a), s. 27(2), and Sch. 4, para. 42(3)(c) and Sch. 7, Pt. 7, with effect from a date to be appointed, PA 2007, s. 30(2)(b).

History – S. 4C(2)(d) repealed by PA 2007, s. 15(3)(a), s. 27(2), and Sch. 4, para. 42(2) and Sch. 7, Pt. 7, with effect from 6 April 2015 (SI 2011/1267, art. 3(a)(ii) and (b)(i)).
In s. 4C(5)(a), the words ", including liability to pay Class 1 contributions at a reduced rate by virtue of Chapter 2 of Part 3 of the Pensions Act" (which appeared after the word "contributions" omitted by PA 2014, s. 24 and Sch. 13, para. 50, with effect from 6 April 2016 (as not brought into force earlier by any earlier order under PA 2014, s. 56(1)).
In s. 4C(5)(b), the words ", including the amount of any such reduced rate contribution and of any related rebate under section 41(1D) or 42A(2C) of that Act" (which appeared after the word "contribution" omitted by PA 2014, s. 24 and Sch. 13, para. 50, with effect from 6 April 2016 (as not brought into force by any earlier order under PA 2014, s. 56(1)).
S. 4C(5)(g) and (h) repealed by PA 2007, s. 15(3)(a), s. 27(2), and Sch. 4, para. 42(3)(b) and Sch. 7, Pt. 7, with effect from 6 April 2015 (SI 2011/1267, art. 3(a)(ii) and (b)(i)).
In s. 4C(11)(a), the words "statutory paternity pay," substituted for the words "ordinary statutory paternity pay, additional statutory paternity pay or" by Children and Families Act 2014, s. 126(1) and Sch. 7, para. 9(a), with effect from 5 April 2015, subject to the transitional and saving provisions in SI 2014/1640, art. 16 (amendments do not have effect in relation to–(a) children whose expected week of birth ends on or before 4 April 2015; (b) children placed for adoption on or before 4 April 2015) (SI 2014/1640, art. 6 and 7).
In s. 4C(11)(a), the words "or statutory shared parental pay" inserted (after the words "statutory adoption pay") by Children and Families Act 2014, s. *126(1) and* Sch. 7, para. 9(b), with effect from 30 June 2014 (SI 2014/1640, art. 3).
In s. 4C(11), in the definition of "statutory payment", the words "ordinary statutory paternity pay, additional statutory paternity pay" substituted for "statutory paternity pay" by the Work and Families Act 2006, s. 11, and Sch. 1, para. 5, with effect from 6 April 2010 (SI 2010/495).
S. 4C inserted by NICA 2006, s. 1(1), with effect from 30 March 2006.

Statutory instruments – SI 2007/1056: partly made under s. 4C.
SI 2007/1154: partly made under s. 4C(1) to (6).

CLASS 1 CONTRIBUTIONS

5 Earnings limits and thresholds for Class 1 contributions

5(1) For the purposes of this Act there shall for every tax year be–

(a) the following for primary Class 1 contributions–

(i) a lower earnings limit,

(ii) a primary threshold, and

(iii) an upper earnings limit; and

(b) a secondary threshold for secondary Class 1 contributions.

Those limits and thresholds shall be the amounts specified for that year by regulations.

5(2) The amount specified as the lower earnings limit for any tax year shall be an amount equal to or not more than 99p less than–

(a) the sum which at the beginning of that year is specified in section 44(4) below as the weekly rate of the basic pension in a Category A retirement pension; or

(b) that sum as increased by any Act or order passed or made before the beginning of that year and taking effect before 6th May in that year.

5(3) [Omitted by NICA 2008, s. 1(b).]

5(4) Regulations may, in the case of each of the limits or thresholds mentioned in subsection (1) above, prescribe an equivalent of that limit or threshold in relation to earners paid otherwise than weekly (and references in this or any other Act to "the prescribed equivalent", in the context of any of those limits or thresholds, are accordingly references to the equivalent prescribed under this subsection in relation to such earners).

5(5) The power conferred by subsection (4) above to prescribe an equivalent of any of those limits or thresholds includes power to prescribe an amount which exceeds, by not more than £1.00, the amount which is the arithmetical equivalent of that limit or threshold.

5(6) Regulations under this section shall be made by the Treasury.

Prospective amendments – S. 5(2) omitted by PA 2007, s. 7 and repealed by Sch. 7, Pt. 4, with effect in relation to the tax year following the designated tax year (such tax year as the Secretary of State may designate by an order made before 1st April 2011 (PA 2007, s. 5(4)) and subsequent tax years.

History – In s. 5(1), at the end, the words "which, in the case of those limits, shall be made in accordance with subsections (2) and (3) below" omitted by NICA 2008, s. 1(1)(a) and repealed by NICA 2008, s. 4 and Sch. 2, with effect from 21 September 2008.
S. 5(3) omitted by NICA 2008, s. 1(1)(b) and repealed by s. 4 and Sch. 2, with effect in relation to regulations specifying the upper earnings limit for 2009–10 or any subsequent tax year.
S. 5 substituted by WRPA 1999, s. 73, Sch. 9, para. 1 with effect from 6 December 1999 for the purpose of making regulations, and 6 April 2000 for all other purposes (SI 1999/3420, art. 2).

Derivations – S. 5(1) (as originally enacted): SSA 1975, s. 4(1); SSPA 1975, s. 1(1).
S. 5(2), (3) (as originally enacted): SSPA 1975, s. 1(2), (3).

Cross references – S. 44(4) (not reproduced): weekly rate of the basic pension in a Category A retirement pension.
S. 122: "current", in relation to lower and upper earnings limits, to be construed in accordance with this section.
SSAA 1992, Sch. 7, Pt. I, para. 4: regulations under this section do not require prior submission to Social Security Advisory Committee.
SI 2001/1004, reg. 10: lower and upper earnings limits; reg. 9: calculation of earnings-related contributions.
NICRCA 2015, s. 3: sets a ceiling on the upper earnings limit under s. 5(1) at the weekly equivalent of the "proposed higher rate threshold" for that tax year (as defined by NICRCA 2015, s. 5(3)–(4)), with effect for a tax year which begins after 17 December 2015 but before the date of the first parliamentary general election after that day.

Statutory instruments – SI 2007/118: made under s. 5.
SI 2009/111: partly made under s. 5(4), (5) and (6).

Other material – Revenue leaflet CA01 (not reproduced): National Insurance for Employees.

Notes – In s. 5(1), the words "in the case of the upper earnings limit shall be made in accordance with subsection (3) below." substituted for the words from "in the case of" to the end by PA 2007, s. 7, with effect in relation to the tax year following the designated tax year (such tax year as the Secretary of State may designate by an order made before 1st April 2011 (PA 2007, s. 5(4)) and subsequent tax years.

6 Liability for Class 1 contributions

6(1) Where in any tax week *earnings* are paid to or for the benefit of an earner over the age of 16 in respect of any one employment of his which is employed earner's employment–

(a) a primary Class 1 contribution shall be payable in accordance with this section and section 8 below if the amount paid exceeds the current primary threshold (or the prescribed equivalent); and

(b) a secondary Class 1 contribution shall be payable in accordance with this section and section 9 below if the amount paid exceeds the current secondary threshold (or the prescribed equivalent).

6(2) No primary or secondary Class 1 contribution shall be payable in respect of earnings if a Class 1B contribution is payable in respect of them.

6(3) Except as may be prescribed, no primary Class 1 contribution shall be payable in respect of earnings paid to or for the benefit of an employed earner after he attains pensionable age, but without prejudice to any liability to pay secondary Class 1 contributions in respect of any such earnings.

6(4) The primary and secondary Class 1 contributions referred to in subsection (1) above are payable as follows–

(a) the primary contribution shall be the liability of the earner; and

(b) the secondary contribution shall be the liability of the secondary contributor;

but nothing in this subsection shall prejudice the provisions of paragraphs 3 to 3B of Schedule 1 to this Act.

6(5) Except as provided by this Act, the primary and secondary Class 1 contributions in respect of earnings paid to or for the benefit of an earner in respect of any one employment of his shall be payable without regard to any other such payment of earnings in respect of any other employment of his.

6(6) Regulations may provide for reducing primary or secondary Class 1 contributions which are payable in respect of persons to whom Part XI of the Employment Rights Act 1996 (redundancy payments) does not apply by virtue of section 199(2) or 209 of that Act.

6(7) Regulations under this section shall be made by the Treasury.

History – In s. 6(4) reference to Sch. 1, para. 3B inserted and the words "relating to the manner in which the earner's liability falls to be discharged." at the end of the subsection omitted by CSPSSA 2000, s. 77(3), with effect from 28 July 2000 (date of Royal Assent).
S. 6 substituted by WRPA 1999, s. 73, Sch. 9, para. 2 with effect from 6 December 1999 for the purpose of making regulations, and 6 April 2000 for all other purposes (SI 1999/3420, art. 2).
Former s. 6(1) substituted by SSA 1998, s. 51(2) with effect from 23 February 1999 for the purposes of making regulations and for all other purposes, from 6 April 1999 (SI 1999/418).
Former s. 6(2A) inserted by SSA 1998, s. 86(1) and Sch. 7, para. 57, with effect from 6 April 1999 (SI 1998/2209).
In former s. 6(5), references to provisions of Employment Rights Act 1996 substituted by Sch. 1, para. 51(2) of that Act, with effect from 22 August 1996.
Former s. 6(7) inserted by SSC(TF)A 1999, s. 2; Sch. 3, para. 6 with effect from 1 April 1999 (SI 1999/527).

Derivations – S. 6(1) (as originally enacted): SSA 1975, s. 4(2).
S. 6(2) (as originally enacted): SSPA 1975, s. 4(1).
S. 6(3) (as originally enacted): SSA 1975, s. 4(3).
S. 6(4) (as originally enacted): SSA 1975, s. 4(2).
S. 6(5) (as originally enacted): SSA 1975, s. 4(7).
S. 6(6) (as originally enacted): SSA 1986, s. 74(5).

Cross references – S. 122(1): meaning of "tax week".
Employment Rights Act 1996, Pt. XI: general provisions as to right to redundancy payment.
Employment Rights Act 1996, s. 199(2): mariners remunerated only by share of gross earnings of vessel.
Employment Rights Act 1978, s. 209: general power of Secretary of State to amend Act.
PSA 1993, s. 8: meaning of "contracted-out employment".
PSA 1993, s. 36(6): surrender and cancellation of contracting-out certificates; ability to make regulations preventing an employer from recovering arrears payable by him under s. 6(3).
SI 1988/1409, art. 2: no primary or secondary contributions payable and no person liable to pay Class 1 contributions in respect of any person receiving a training premium during Employment Training.
SI 2001/1004, reg. 10: upper and lower earnings limit.
SI 2001/1004, reg. 11: prescribed equivalents of lower and upper earnings limits referred to in s. 6(1)(b).
SI 2001/1004, reg. 12: calculation of earnings-related contributions.
SI 2001/1004, reg. 17: apportionment of single payment of emoluments between different secondary contributors.
SI 2001/1004, reg. 29: liability of Class 1 contributions of persons over pensionable age.
SI 2001/1004, Sch. 4, reg. 4: employers' earnings related contributions.
SI 2001/1004, Sch. 4, reg. 7: calculation of deductions.

6A Notional payment of primary Class 1 contribution where earnings not less than lower earnings limit

6A(1) This section applies where in any tax week earnings are paid to or for the benefit of an earner over the age of 16 in respect of any one employment of his which is employed earner's employment and the amount paid–

(a) is not less than the current lower earnings limit (or the prescribed equivalent), but

(b) does not exceed the current primary threshold (or the prescribed equivalent).

6A(2) Subject to any prescribed exceptions or modifications–

(a) the earner shall be treated as having actually paid a primary Class 1 contribution in respect of that week, and

(b) those earnings shall be treated as earnings upon which such a contribution has been paid,

for any of the purposes mentioned in subsection (3) below.

6A(3) *The purposes are–*

(a) the purposes of section 14(1)(a) below;

(b) the purposes of the provisions mentioned in section 21(5A)(a) to (c) below;

(c) any other purposes relating to contributory benefits;

(d) any purposes relating to jobseeker's allowance; and

(e) any purposes relating to employment and support allowance.

6A(4) Regulations may provide for any provision of this Act which, in whatever terms, refers–

(a) to primary Class 1 contributions being payable by a person, or

(b) otherwise to a person's liability to pay such contributions,

to have effect for the purposes of this section with any prescribed modifications.

6A(5) Except as may be prescribed, nothing in this section applies in relation to earnings paid to or for the benefit of an employed earner after he attains pensionable age.

6A(6) Except as provided by this Act, this section applies in relation to earnings paid to or for the benefit of an earner in respect of any one employment of his irrespective of any other such payment of earnings in respect of any other employment of his.

6A(7) Regulations under this section shall be made by the Treasury.

History – In s. 6A(3)(c) the word "and" at the end repealed by the Welfare Reform Act 2007, s. 67 and Sch. 8, with effect from 27 October 2008 by virtue of SI 2008/787, art. 2(4)(g)(i).
S. 6A(3)(e) and the word "; and" preceding it inserted by the Welfare Reform Act 2007, s. 28 and Sch. 3, para. 9(2), with effect from 27 October 2008 by virtue of SI 2008/787, art. 2(4)(b) and (f).
S. 6A inserted by WRPA 1999, s. 73, Sch. 9, para. 3 with effect from 6 December 1999 for the purpose of making regulations, and 6 April 2000 for all other purposes (SI 1999/3420, art. 2).

Cross references – SI 2000/747: modifies s. 6A(2).

Statutory instruments – SI 2000/747: made under s. 6A(2) and (7).

7 "Secondary contributor"

7(1) For the purposes of this Act, the **"secondary contributor"** in relation to any payment of earnings to or for the benefit of an employed earner, is–

(a) in the case of an earner employed under a contract of service, his employer;

(b) in the case of an earner employed in an office with earnings, either–

(i) such person as may be prescribed in relation to that office; or

(ii) if no person is prescribed, the government department, public authority or body of persons responsible for paying the earnings of the office;

but this subsection is subject to subsection (2) below.

7(2) In relation to employed earners who–

(a) are paid earnings in a tax week by more than one person in respect of different employments; or

(b) work under the general control or management of a person other than their immediate employer,

and in relation to any other case for which it appears to the Treasury that such provision is needed, regulations may provide that the prescribed person is to be treated as the secondary contributor in respect of earnings paid to or for the benefit of an earner.

7(2A) Regulations under subsection (2) may make provision treating a person as the secondary contributor in respect of earnings paid to or for the benefit of an earner if arrangements have been entered into the main purpose, or one of the main purposes, of which is to secure that the person is not so treated by other provision in regulations under subsection (2).

7(2B) In subsection (2A) **"arrangements"** include any scheme, transaction or series of transactions, agreement or understanding, whether or not legally enforceable, and any associated operations.

7(3) Regulations under any provision of this section shall be made by the Treasury.

History – In s. 7(1) the word "general", which appeared before the word "earnings" (in each place), omitted by NICA 2014, s. 15 and Sch. 2, para. 2, with effect from 13 May 2014.
In s. 7(1)(b), "general earnings" substituted (twice) by ITEPA 2003, Sch. 6, para. 173 which has effect for income tax purposes for the year 2003–04 and subsequent years.
In s. 7(2) "Treasury" substituted by SSC(TF)A 1999, s. 21; Sch. 3, para. 7(2) with effect from 1 April 1999 (SI 1999/527).
S. 7(2A) and (2B) inserted by NICA 2015, s. 6(4), with effect from 12 February 2015.
S. 7(3) inserted by SSC(TF)A 1999, s. 2; Sch. 3, para. 7(3) with effect from 1 April 1999 (SI 1999/527).

Derivations – SSA 1975, s. 4(4), (5).

Cross references – ICTA 1988, s. 617(4): secondary Class 1 contributions deductible in computing profits or gains or expenses of management.
ICTA 1988, Sch. 8, para. 19(5), (6)(ff): secondary Class 1 contributions in respect of profit-related pay may be left out of profit and loss account prepared for the purpose of profit-related pay scheme.
SI 2001/1004, reg. 13: calculation of earnings-related contributions.

Statutory instruments – SI 1978/1689: partly made under s. 7(1).
SI 2003/2420: made under s. 7(2), (3).

8 Calculation of primary Class 1 contributions

8(1) Where a primary Class 1 contribution is payable as mentioned in section 6(1)(a) above, the amount of that contribution is the aggregate of–

(a) the main primary percentage of so much of the earner's earnings paid in the tax week, in respect of the employment in question, as–

(i) exceeds the current primary threshold (or the prescribed equivalent); but

(ii) does not exceed the current upper earnings limit (or the prescribed equivalent); and

(b) the additional primary percentage of so much of those earnings as exceeds the current upper earnings limit (or the prescribed equivalent).

8(2) For the purposes of this Act–

(a) the main primary percentage is 12 per cent; and

(b) the additional primary percentage is 2 per cent;

but the main primary percentage is subject to alteration under sections 143 and 145 of the Administration Act.

8(3) Subsection (1) above is subject to–

(a) regulations under section 6(6) above;

(b) regulations under sections 116 to 120 below; and

(c) [omitted by PA 2014, s. 24 and Sch. 13, para. 51.]

Prospective amendments – In s. 8(3)(c) the words "section 41" substituted for "sections 41 and 42A" by PA 2007, s. 15(3)(a), and Sch. 4, para. 43, with effect from a date to be appointed, PA 2007, s. 30(2)(b).

History – In s. 8(2)(a), "12" substituted for "11" by NICA 2011, s. 1(1)(a), with effect from 6 April 2011.
In s. 8(2)(b), "2" substituted for "1" by NICA 2011, s. 1(1)(b), with effect from 6 April 2011.
S. 8(3)(c) and the "and" before it omitted by PA 2014, s. 24 and Sch. 13, para. 51, with effect from 6 April 2016 (as not brought into force by any earlier order under PA 2014, s. 56(1)). Former s. 8(3)(c) read as follows:
"(c) sections 41 and 42A of the Pensions Act (reduced rates of Class 1 contributions for earners in contracted-out employment).".
S. 8 substituted by NICA 2002, s. 1(1), with effect for 2003–04 and subsequent tax years.
In former s. 8(1)(a) and (b) the words "(or the prescribed equivalent)"; at the end of each paragraph; omitted by WRPA 1999, s. 88, Sch. 13, Pt. VI, with effect 6 April 2000 (SI 1999/3420, art. 4(c), (e)).
S. 8 substituted by WRPA 1999, s. 73, Sch. 9, para. 4 with effect from 6 December 1999 for the purpose of making regulations, and 6 April 2000 for all other purposes (SI 1999/3420, art. 2).
Former s. 8(1) and (2) substituted by SSA 1998, s. 51(3) with effect from 23 February 1999 for the purposes of making regulations and for all other purposes, from 6 April 1999 (SI 1999/418).
Former s. 8(5) inserted by SSC(TF)A 1999, s. 2; Sch. 3, para. 8 with effect from 1 April 1999 (SI 1999/527).
In former s. 8(1), the words "section 41 of the Pensions Act…contracted-out employment" substituted by PSA 1993, s. 190 and Sch. 8, para. 33, with effect from 7 February 1994.
In former s. 8(2)(b), the words "10 per cent" substituted by the Social Security (Contributions) Act 1994, s. 1, with effect from 6 April 1994.

Derivations – S. 8(1)–(3) (as originally enacted): SSA 1975, s. 4(6), (6A), (6B).
S. 8(4) (as originally enacted): SSA 1986, s. 74(5).

Cross references – S. 116: treatment of serving members of Her Majesty's forces as employed earners, etc.
S. 117: mariners, airmen, etc.
S. 118: married women and widows.
S. 119: persons outside Great Britain.
S. 120: employment at sea (continental shelf operations).
S. 122: "initial percentage" and "main primary percentage" to be construed in accordance with this section.
SSAA 1992, Pt. IX: alteration of contributions.
SSAA 1992, s. 143: power to alter contributions with view to adjusting level of National Insurance Fund.
SSAA 1992, s. 145: power to alter primary and secondary contributions.
PSA 1993, s. 8(2): meaning of "contracted-out employment".
PSA 1993, s. 41: contracted-out rates of Class 1 contributions.
SI 2001/1004, reg. 52: return of contributions paid in error, etc.
SI 2001/1004, reg. 120: earnings periods for mariners and apportionment of earnings.
SI 2001/1004, Pt. 2: assessment of Class 1 contributions.
NICRCA 2015, s. 1: sets a ceiling on main primary percentage and additional primary percentage under s. 8(2)(a) and (b) of 12% and 2% respectively, with effect for a tax year which begins after 17 December 2015 but before the date of the first parliamentary general election after that day.

Other material – S. 122(1): meaning of "tax week".

9 Calculation of secondary Class 1 contributions

9(1) Where a secondary Class 1 contribution is payable as mentioned in section 6(1)(b) above, the amount of that contribution shall be the relevant percentage of so much of the earnings paid in the tax week, in respect of the employment in question, as exceeds the current secondary threshold (or the prescribed equivalent).

9(1A) For the purposes of subsection (1) "the relevant percentage" is–

(a) if section 9A below applies to the earnings, the age related secondary percentage;

(aa) if section 9B below (zero-rate secondary Class 1 contributions for certain apprentices) applies to the earnings, 0%;

(b) otherwise, the secondary percentage.

9(2) For the purposes of this Act the secondary percentage is 13.8 per cent; but that percentage is subject to alteration under sections 143 and 145 of the Administration Act.

9(3) Subsection (1) above is subject to–

(a) regulations under section 6(6) above;

(b) regulations under sections 116 to 120 below; and

(c) [omitted by PA 2014, s. 24 and Sch. 13, para. 52.]

Prospective amendments – In s. 9(3)(c) the words "section 41" substituted for "sections 41 and 42A" by PA 2007, s. 15(3)(a), and Sch. 4, para. 44, with effect from a date to be appointed, PA 2007, s. 30(2)(b).

History – S. 9(1A)(aa) inserted by NICA 2015, s. 1(2), with effect from 6 April 2016.
In s. 9(2), "13.8" substituted for "12.8" by NICA 2011, s. 1(2), with effect from 6 April 2011.
In s. 9(1) the words "the relevant percentage" substituted for the words "the secondary percentage" by NICA 2014, s. 9(2)(a) with effect from 6 April 2015.
In s. 9(1A) inserted by NICA 2014, s. 9(2)(b) with effect from 6 April 2015.
S. 9(2), (3) substituted by NICA 2002, s. 2(1) with effect for 2003–04 and subsequent tax years.
S. 9(3)(c) and the "and" before it omitted by PA 2014, s. 24 and Sch. 13, para. 52, with effect from 6 April 2016 (as not brought into force by any earlier order under PA 2014, s. 56(1)). Former s. 9(3)(c) read as follows:
"(c) sections 41 and 42A of the Pensions Act (reduced rates of Class 1 contributions for earners in contracted-out employment)."
S. 9 substituted by WRPA 1999, s. 73, Sch. 9, para. 5 with effect from 6 December 1999 for the purpose of making regulations, and 6 April 2000 for all other purposes (SI 1999/3420, art. 2).
Former s. 9 substituted by SSA 1998, s. 51(4) with effect from 23 February 1999 for the purposes of making regulations and for all other purposes, from 6 April 1999 (SI 1999/418).
Former s. 9(4) inserted by SSC(TF)A 1999, s. 2; Sch. 3, para. 9 with effect from 1 April 1999 (SI 1999/527).

Cross references – SSAA 1992, s. 143: power to alter contributions with view to adjusting level of National Insurance Fund.
SSAA 1992, s. 145: power to alter primary and secondary contributions.
PSA 1993, s. 41: contracted-out rates of Class 1 contributions.
Justices of the Peace Act 1997, s. 55(6): duties of local authorities.
SI 2001/1004, reg. 12: calculation of earnings-related contributions.
SI 2001/1004, reg. 119: modification of s. 9(3) in case of mariners.
SI 2001/1004, reg. 120: earnings periods for mariners and apportionment of income.
SI 2001/1004, Pt. 2: assessment of Class 1 contributions.
NICRCA 2015, s. 2: sets a ceiling on secondary percentage under s. 9(2) of 13.8%, with effect for a tax year which begins after 17 December 2015 but before the date of the first parliamentary general election after that day.

Notes – The "Administration Act" means SSAA 1992.

9A The age-related secondary percentage

9A(1) Where a secondary Class 1 contribution is payable as mentioned in section 6(1)(b) above, this section applies to the earnings paid in the tax week, in respect of the employment in question, if the earner falls within an age group specified in column 1 of the table in subsection (3).

9A(1A) But this section does not apply to those earnings so far as section 9B below (zero-rate secondary Class 1 contributions for certain apprentices) applies to them.

9A(2) For the purposes of section 9(1A)(a) above, the age-related secondary percentage is the percentage for the earner's age group specified in column 2 of the table.

9A(3) Here is the table—

Age group	*Age-related secondary percentage*
Under 21	0%

9A(4) The Treasury may by regulations amend the table—

(a) so as to add an age group in column 1 and to specify the percentage in column 2 for that age group;

(b) so as to reduce (or further reduce) the percentage specified in column 2 for an age group already specified in column 1 (whether for the whole of the age group or only part of it).

9A(5) A percentage specified under subsection (4)(a) must be lower than the secondary percentage.

9A(6) For the purposes of this Act a person is still to be regarded as being liable to pay a secondary Class 1 contribution even though the amount of the contribution is £0 because the age-related secondary percentage is 0%.

9A(7) The Treasury may by regulations provide that, in relation to an age group specified in the table, there is to be for every tax year an upper secondary threshold for secondary Class 1 contributions.

9A(8) Subsections (4) and (5) of section 5 above (which confer power to prescribe an equivalent of a secondary threshold in relation to earners paid otherwise than weekly), and subsection (6) of that section as it applies for the purposes of those subsections, apply for the purposes of an upper secondary threshold in relation to an age group as they apply for the purposes of a secondary threshold.

9A(9) Where—

(a) a secondary Class 1 contribution is payable as mentioned in section 6(1)(b) above,

(b) the earner falls within an age group in relation to which provision has been made under subsection (7), and

In s. 10(5) the words "secondary percentage" substituted by NICA 2002, s. 6 and Sch. 1, para. 2 with effect for 2003–04 and subsequent tax years.
S. 10(11) inserted by NICA 2014, s. 14(4), with effect from 13 March 2014.
In s. 10:

- in s. 10(6), the words "general earnings as are taken" substituted;
- s. 10(7), (7A), and (7B) substituted;
- s. 10(8)(a) substituted;
- in s. 10(8)(b), the words "subsections (7) to (7B)" and "on employment income" substituted;
- in s. 10(9)(a) "general earnings" substituted; and
- s. 10(10) omitted,

by ITEPA 2003, Sch. 6, para. 174, and the omitted subsection repealed by ITEPA 2003, Sch. 8, Pt. 1, both of which have effect, for income tax purposes, for the tax year 2003–04 and subsequent tax years.
S. 10 (including the heading) previously substituted by CSPSSA 2000, s. 74(2) with effect from 6 April 2000.

Derivations – (as originally enacted) – SSA 1975, s. 4A.

Cross references – Sch. 1, para. 5: regulations may modify s. 10 in relation to cases where a benefit was made available by reason of two or more employments under different employers.
Sch. 1, para. 8(1)(i): repayment of Class 1A contributions where too much has been paid.
ITEPA 2003, Pt. 2, Ch. 2: general charge on employment income.
ITEPA 2003, Pt. 3, Ch. 10: residual charge on benefits.
SI 2001/1004, reg. 55: repayment of Class 1A contributions.
SI 2001/1004, reg. 86: where employed earner's employer is exempt from Act by treaty, Class 1A contributions may be paid, if employer so wishes, in respect of car made available to earner.

Statutory instruments – SI 2007/799 (regulations made under s. 10(8)).
SI 2013/622: partly made under s. 10(9).

Other material – Misc. 204: HMRC position regarding NIC treatment of partial deductions under ITEPA 2003, s. 363–365 for years from 2003–04 to 2005–06.

Notes – Former s. 10(10) is unnecessary and so has not been rewritten into the provisions of ITEPA 2003 (see definitions in s. 122(1) instead).

10ZA Liability of third party provider of benefits in kind

10ZA(1) This section applies, where–

(a) a Class 1A contribution is payable for any tax year in respect of the whole or any part of general earnings received by an earner;

(b) the general earnings, in so far as they are ones in respect of which such a contribution is payable, consist in a benefit provided for the earner or a member of his family or household;

(c) the person providing the benefit is a person other than the person ("the relevant employer") by whom, but for this section, the Class 1A contribution would be payable in accordance with section 10(2) above; and

(d) the provision of the benefit by that other person has not been arranged or facilitated by the relevant employer.

10ZA(2) For the purposes of this Act if–

(a) the person providing the benefit pays an amount for the purpose of discharging any liability of the earner to income tax for any tax year, and

(b) the income tax in question is tax chargeable in respect of the provision of the benefit or of the making of the payment itself,

the amount of the payment shall be treated as if it were general earnings consisting in the provision of a benefit to the earner in that tax year and falling, for the purposes of Class 1 contributions, to be left out of account in the computation of the earnings paid to or for the benefit of the earner.

10ZA(3) Subject to subsection (4) below, the liability to pay any Class 1A contribution in respect of–

(a) the benefit provided to the earner, and

(b) any further benefit treated as so provided in accordance with subsection (2) above,

shall fall on the person providing the benefit, instead of on the relevant employer.

10ZA(4) Subsection (3) above applies in the case of a Class 1A contribution for the tax year beginning with 6th April 2000 only if the person providing the benefit in question gives notice in writing to the Inland Revenue on or before 6th July 2001 that he is a person who provides benefits in respect of which a liability to Class 1A contributions is capable of falling by virtue of this section on a person other than the relevant employer.

10ZA(5) The Treasury may by regulations make provision specifying the circumstances in which a person is or is not to be treated for the purposes of this Act as having arranged or facilitated the provision of any benefit.

10ZA(6) In this section references to a member of a person's family or household shall be construed in accordance with section 721(5) of ITEPA 2003.

History – In:

- s. 10ZA(1)(a), the words "general earnings" substituted;
- s. 10ZA (1)(b), "the general earnings, in so far as they are ones in respect of which" and "consist" substituted;

- s. 10ZA(2), in the words after paragraph (b), "general earnings" substituted; and
- s. 10ZA(6), the words "section 721(5) of ITEPA 2003" substituted,

by ITEPA 2003, Sch. 6, para. 175 which has effect, for income tax purposes, for the tax year 2003–04 and subsequent tax years.
S. 10ZA inserted by CSPSSA 2000, s. 75(1) with effect from 6 April 2000 (s. 76(3)).

10ZB Non-cash vouchers provided by third parties

10ZB(1) In section 10ZA above references to the provision of a benefit include references to the provision of a non-cash voucher.

10ZB(2) Where–

(a) a non-cash voucher is received by any person from employment which is lower-paid employment as a minister of religion, and

(b) the case would be one in which the conditions in section 10ZA(1)(a) to (d) above would be satisfied in relation to the provision of that voucher if that employment were not lower-paid employment as a minister of religion,

sections 10 and 10ZA above shall have effect in relation to the provision of that voucher, and to any such payment in respect of the provision of that voucher as is mentioned in section 10ZA(2) above, as if that employment were not an excluded employment.

10ZB(3) In this section **"non-cash voucher"** has the same meaning as in section 84 of ITEPA 2003.

History – In s. 10ZB(2)(a) the words "lower-paid employment as a minister of religion" substituted for the words "an excluded employment for the purposes of the benefits code" and in s. 10ZB(2)(b) the words "lower-paid employment as a minister of religion" substituted for the words "an excluded employment" by FA 2015, s. 13 and Sch. 1, para. 23(3), with effect for the tax year 2016–17 and subsequent tax years.
In:

- s. 10ZB(2)(a), the words "employment which is an excluded employment for the purposes of the benefits code, and" substituted;
- s. 10ZB(2)(b), the words "if that employment were not an excluded employment" substituted;
- s. 10ZB(2), in the words following para. (b), the words "as if that employment were not an excluded employment" substituted; and
- s. 10ZB(3), the words "section 84 of ITEPA 2003" substituted,

by ITEPA 2003, Sch. 6, para. 176 which has effect, for income tax purposes, for the tax year 2003–04 and subsequent tax years.
S. 10ZB inserted by CSPSSA 2000, s. 75(1) with effect from 6 April 2000 (s. 76(3)).

10ZC Class 1A contributions: power to make provision in consequence of retrospective tax legislation

10ZC(1) The Treasury may by regulations make such provision as appears to the Treasury to be expedient for any purpose of the law relating to Class 1A contributions in consequence of any relevant retrospective tax provision–

(a) which is passed or made at or before the time when the regulations are made, or

(b) which may be passed or made after that time.

10ZC(2) **"Relevant retrospective tax provision"** means a provision of the Income Tax Acts which–

(a) has retrospective effect, and

(b) affects the amount of general earnings received by an earner from an employment on which he is chargeable to income tax under the employment income Parts of ITEPA 2003 for a tax year.

10ZC(3) It does not matter whether the relevant retrospective tax provision was passed or made before the commencement day.

10ZC(4) Regulations under this section may, in particular, make provision–

(a) modifying any provision of any enactment (including this Act and any enactment passed or made on or after the commencement day);

(b) for any provision of any such enactment to apply in such cases, and with such modifications (if any), as the regulations may prescribe.

10ZC(5) Regulations under this section may be made so as to have retrospective effect but must not have effect in relation to any time before 2nd December 2004.

10ZC(6) *In particular*, regulations under this section made by virtue of subsection (5)–

(a) may affect matters determined before the time when the regulations are made, and

(b) may provide for those matters to be redetermined accordingly.

10ZC(7) Regulations under this section–

(a) may not impose any liability to pay a Class 1A contribution, and

(b) may not increase the amount of any Class 1A contribution.

10ZC(8) The powers conferred by this section are without prejudice to–

(a) any liability to pay a Class 1A contribution which arises by virtue of any relevant retrospective tax provision, and

(b) any powers conferred by or by virtue of any other provision of this Act or any other enactment.

10ZC(9) In particular, any modification of any provision of an instrument by regulations under this section is without prejudice to any other power to amend or revoke the provisions of the instrument (including the modified provision).

10ZC(10) For the purposes of this section–

"the commencement day" means the day on which the National Insurance Contributions Act 2006 was passed;

"enactment" includes an instrument made under an Act.

History – S. 10ZC inserted by NICA 2006, s. 3(1), with effect from 30 March 2006.

CLASS 1B CONTRIBUTIONS

10A Class 1B contributions

10A(1) Where for any tax year a person is accountable to the Inland Revenue in respect of income tax on general earnings of his employees in accordance with a PAYE settlement agreement, a Class 1B contribution shall be payable by him for that tax year in accordance with this section.

10A(2) The Class 1B contribution referred to in subsection (1) above is payable in respect of–

(a) the amount of any of the general earnings included in the PAYE settlement agreement which are chargeable emoluments; and

(b) the total amount of income tax in respect of which the person is accountable for the tax year in accordance with the PAYE settlement agreement.

10A(3) The amount of the Class 1B contribution referred to in subsection (1) above shall be the Class 1B percentage of the aggregate of the amounts mentioned in paragraphs (a) and (b) of subsection (2) above.

10A(4) General earnings are chargeable emoluments for the purposes of subsection (2) above if, apart from section 6(2) or 10(6) above, the person accountable in accordance with the PAYE settlement agreement would be liable or entitled to pay secondary Class 1 contributions or Class 1A contributions in respect of them.

10A(5) Where–

(a) the PAYE settlement agreement was entered into after the beginning of the tax year; and

(b) Class 1 contributions were due in respect of any general earnings before it was entered into,

those general earnings shall not be taken to be included in the PAYE settlement agreement.

10A(6) In subsection (3) above "the Class 1B percentage" means a percentage rate equal to the secondary percentage for the tax year in question.

10A(7) The Treasury may by regulations may provide for persons to be excepted in prescribed circumstances from liability to pay Class 1B contributions.

History – In:

- s. 10A(1) and (5) (twice), the words "general earnings" substituted;
- s. 10A(2)(a), the words "the general earnings included" substituted; and
- s. 10A(4), the words "General earnings are chargeable emoluments" substituted,

by ITEPA 2003, Sch. 6, para. 177 which has effect, for income tax purposes, for the tax year 2003–04 and subsequent tax years.

In s. 10A(4) the words "6(2) or 10(6)" substituted by NICSPA 2004, s. 11 and Sch. 1, para. 1(2) with effect from 1 September 2004 (by virtue of SI 2004/1943, reg. 5).

In s. 10A(6) the words "the secondary percentage" substituted by NICA 2002, s. 6 and Sch. 1, para. 3 with effect for 2003–04 and subsequent tax years.

S. 10A(6) previously substituted by WRPA 1999, s. 73 with effect from 6 April 2000 (SI 1999/3420, art. 4(a)).

S. 10A(7) amended; with insertion of reference to the Treasury; by SSC(TF)A 1999, s. 2; Sch. 3, para. 11 with effect from 1 April 1999 (SI 1999/527).

S. 10A inserted by SSA 1998, s. 53, with effect from 8 September 1998 for the purpose only of authorising the making of regulations and orders, and from 6 April 1999 for all other purposes (SI 1998/2209).

CLASS 2 CONTRIBUTIONS

11 Class 2 contributions

11(1) This section applies if an earner is in employment as a self-employed earner in a tax year (the "relevant tax year").

11(2) If the earner has relevant profits of, or exceeding, the small profits threshold, the earner is liable to pay Class 2 contributions for the relevant tax year at the rate of £2.95 in respect of each week in that year that the earner is in the employment.

(a) than the payment year;
(b) [omitted by NICA 2015, s. 2 and Sch. 1, para. 4(6).]

12(7) [Omitted by NICA 2015, s. 2 and Sch. 1, para. 4(7).]

12(8) In this section–

"ordinary contribution" means a contribution of the amount specified in section 11(6); and

"higher-rate contribution" means a contribution of an amount provided for in regulations under section 11(8).

History – In s. 12(1) the words "under section 11(6)" inserted after the words "Class 2 contribution" by NICA 2015, s. 2 and Sch. 1, para. 4(2), with effect in relation to a Class 2 contribution in respect of a week in the tax year 2015–16 or a subsequent tax year.
In s. 12(2) the words "and (4)" substituted for the words "to (5)" by NICA 2015, s. 2 and Sch. 1, para. 4(3), with effect in relation to a Class 2 contribution in respect of a week in the tax year 2015–16 or a subsequent tax year.
In s. 12(3) the words "(4) and (6)" substituted for the words "(4) to (6)" by NICA 2015, s. 2 and Sch. 1, para. 4(4), with effect in relation to a Class 2 contribution in respect of a week in the tax year 2015–16 or a subsequent tax year.
S. 12(4), (6) amended; with insertion of references to the Treasury; by SSC(TF)A 1999, s. 2; Sch. 3, para. 13 with effect from 1 April 1999 (SI 1999/527).
S. 12(5) omitted by NICA 2015, s. 2 and Sch. 1, para. 4(5), with effect in relation to a Class 2 contribution in respect of a week in the tax year 2015–16 or a subsequent tax year.
In s. 12(6) the words "or (5)" omitted, in para. (a) the words "in a case falling within subsection (3) above," omitted and para. (b) (and the word "and" preceding it) omitted by NICA 2015, s. 2 and Sch. 1, para. 4(6), with effect in relation to a Class 2 contribution in respect of a week in the tax year 2015–16 or a subsequent tax year.
S. 12(7) omitted by NICA 2015, s. 2 and Sch. 1, para. 4(7), with effect in relation to a Class 2 contribution in respect of a week in the tax year 2015–16 or a subsequent tax year.
In former s. 12(7), the words "the county court" substituted for the words "a county court" by Crime and Courts Act 2013, s. 17(5) and Sch. 9, para. 52(2), with effect from 22 April 2014 (SI 2014/954, art. 2).
S. 12(7)(aa) inserted by SSC(TF)A 1999, s. 26(2); Sch. 9, para. 3 with effect from 1 April 1999 (SI 1999/527).
In s. 12(8), in the definition of "ordinary contribution", the words "of the amount specified in section 11(6)" substituted for the words "under section 11(1) above" by NICA 2015, s. 2 and Sch. 1, para. 4(8), with effect in relation to a Class 2 contribution in respect of a week in the tax year 2015–16 or a subsequent tax year.
In s. 12(8), in the definition of "higher-rate contribution", the words "of an amount provided for in regulations under section 11(8)" substituted for the words "under regulations made under section 11(3) above" by NICA 2015, s. 2 and Sch. 1, para. 4(8), with effect in relation to a Class 2 contribution in respect of a week in the tax year 2015–16 or a subsequent tax year.

Derivations – SSA 1975, s. 7A.

Cross references – S. 174: "the Administration Act" means SSAA 1992.
SSAA 1992, s. 114: offences relating to failing to pay contributions.
SI 2001/769, reg. 4: treatment for purpose of contributory benefit of late paid contributions.
SI 2001/769, reg. 8: treatment for the purpose of any contributory benefit of contributions paid late through ignorance or error.
SI 2001/1004, reg. 61: voluntary Class 2 contributions not paid within a permitted period.
SI 2001/1004, reg. 89 and 90: method of, and time for, payment of Class 2 contributions, etc.
SI 2001/1004, reg. 63: Class 2 contributions paid late in accordance with a payment undertaking.
SI 2001/1004, reg. 100: annual maximum of Class 4 contributions due under s. 15.
SI 2001/1004, reg. 125: modification in relation to share fishermen.
SI 2001/1004, reg. 153: s. 12 disapplied in case of Class 2 contributions which a volunteer development worker is entitled to pay.

Statutory instruments – SI 2008/3099: made partly under s. 12(6).
SI 2013/622: partly made under s. 12(6).

CLASS 3 CONTRIBUTIONS

13 Class 3 contributions

13(1) The Treasury shall by regulations provide for earners and others, if over the age of 16, to be entitled if they so wish, but subject to any prescribed conditions, to pay Class 3 contributions; and, subject to the following provisions of this section, the amount of a Class 3 contribution shall be £14.65.

13(2) Payment of Class 3 contributions shall be allowed only with a view to enabling the contributor to satisfy conditions of entitlement to benefit by acquiring the requisite earnings factor for the purposes described in section 22 below.

13(3) The Secretary of State may by regulations provide for Class 3 contributions, although paid in one tax year, to be appropriated in prescribed circumstances to the earnings factor of another tax year.

13(4) The amount of a Class 3 contribution in respect of a tax year earlier than the tax year in which it is paid shall be the same as if it had been paid in the earlier year and in respect of that year, unless it falls to be calculated in accordance with subsection (6) below or regulations under subsection (7) below.

13(5) In this section–

"the payment year" means the tax year in which a contribution is paid; and

"the contribution year" means the earlier year mentioned in subsection (4) above.

13(6) Subject to subsection (7) below, in any case where–
(a) a Class 3 contribution is paid after the end of the next tax year but one following the contribution year; and
(b) the amount of a Class 3 contribution applicable had the contribution been paid in the contribution year differs from the amount of a Class 3 contribution applicable at the time of payment in the payment year,

Cross references – Interpretation Act 1978, Sch. 1: "Secretary of State" means one of HM's Principal Secretaries of State.
SSC(TF)A 1999, s. 8(2): determination by officers of Board of questions arising (i) under s. 17(1) as to whether the individual is exempt from Class 4 contributions or liability is deferred; or (ii) under regulations made by virtue of s. 17(3), (4), by the Inland Revenue.
SSAA 1992. s. 17(2): questions under s. 17(1), (3), (4) are determined by the Secretary of State.
SI 2001/1004, reg. 99: calculation of liability for, and recovery of, Class 4 contributions after issue of certificate of deferment.
SI 2001/1004, reg. 125: modification in relation to share fishermen.

18 Class 4 contributions recoverable under regulations

18(1) The Inland Revenue may by regulations make provision so that where–

(a) an earner, in respect of any one or more employments of his, is treated by regulations under section 2(2)(b) above as being self-employed; and

(b) in any tax year he has earnings from any such employment (one or more) which fall within paragraph (b)(i) of subsection (8) of section 11 above but is not liable for a higher weekly rate of Class 2 contributions by virtue of regulations under that subsection; and

(c) the total of those earnings exceeds £8,424,

he is to be liable, in respect of those earnings, to pay a Class 4 contribution.

18(1A) The amount of a Class 4 contribution payable by virtue of regulations under this section is equal to the aggregate of–

(a) the main Class 4 percentage of so much of the total of the earnings referred to in subsection (1)(b) above as exceeds £8,424 but does not exceed £46,350; and

(b) the additional Class 4 percentage of so much of that total as exceeds £46,350;

but the figures specified in this subsection are subject to alteration under section 141 of the Administration Act.

18(2) In relation to Class 4 contributions payable by virtue of regulations under this section, regulations made by the Inland Revenue may–

(a) apply any of the provisions of Schedule 1 to this Act (except a provision conferring power to make regulations); and

(b) make any such provision as may be made by regulations under that Schedule, except paragraph 6 or 7BZA.

History – In s. 18(1) and (1A), the figure "£8,424" substituted for the figure "£8,164" by SI 2018/337, reg. 5(a), with effect from 6 April 2018.
In s. 18(1A), the figure "£46,350" substituted for the figure "£45,000" by SI 2018/337, reg. 5(b), with effect from 6 April 2018.
In s. 18(1) and (1A), the figure "£8,164" substituted for the figure "£8,060" by SI 2017/415, reg. 5(a), with effect from 6 April 2017.
In s. 18(1A), the figure "£45,000" (in each place) substituted for the figure "£43,000" by SI 2017/415, reg. 5(b), with effect from 6 April 2017.
In s. 18(1), the figure "£8,060" substituted for "£7,956" by SI 2014/475, art. 3, with effect from 6 April 2015.
In s. 18(1), the figure "£7,956" substituted for "£7,755" by SI 2014/475, art. 4(a), with effect from 6 April 2014.
In s. 18(1), the figure "£7,755" substituted for "£7,605" by SI 2013/559, art. 4(a), with effect from 6 April 2013.
In s. 18(1), the figure "£7,605" substituted for "£7,225" by SI 2012/807, art. 4, with effect from 6 April 2012.
In s. 18(1), the figure of "£7,225" substituted by SI 2011/938, art. 4, with effect from 6 April 2011. Previously "£5,715" substituted by SI 2009/593, art. 4, with effect from 6 April 2009, "£5,435" substituted by SI 2008/579, art. 4, with effect from 6 April 2008, "£5,225" substituted by SI 2007/1052, art. 4, with effect from 6 April 2007, "£5,035" substituted by SI 2006/624, art. 4, with effect from 6 April 2006 and "£4,895" substituted by SI 2005/878, art. 4(a), with effect from 6 April 2005.
Words in s. 18(1) from "of an amount" onwards repealed by NICA 2002, s. 7 and Sch. 2 with effect for 2003–04 and subsequent tax years.
In s. 18(1)(b), the words "subsection (8)" substituted for the words "subsection (3)" by NICA 2015, s. 2 and Sch. 1, para. 5, with effect for the tax year 2015–16 and subsequent tax years.
In s. 18(1)(c), the percentage figure "7 per cent" substituted by SI 2000/755, art. 4(a), with effect from 6 April 2000; the previous percentage figure of "6 per cent" substituted by SI 1996/597, art. 5, with effect from 6 April 1996.
In s. 18(1A), the figure "£43,000" (in each place) substituted for the figure "£42,385" by SI 2016/343, reg. 3, with effect from 6 April 2016.
In s. 18(1A), the figures "£8,060" substituted for "£7,956" and "£42,385" substituted for "£41,865" by SI 2014/475, art. 3, with effect from 6 April 2015.
In s. 18(1A), the figure "£7,956" substituted for "£7,755" by SI 2014/475, art. 4(a), with effect from 6 April 2014.
In s. 18(1A), the figure "£41,865" substitutedfor "£41,450" by SI 2014/475, art. 4(b), with effect from 6 April 2014.
In s. 18(1A), the figure "£7,755" substituted for "£7,605" by SI 2013/559, art. 4(a), with effect from 6 April 2013.
In s. 18(1A), the figure "£41,450" substituted for "£42,475" by SI 2013/559, art. 4(b), with effect from 6 April 2013.
In s. 18(1A), the figure "£7,605" substituted for "£7,225" by SI 2012/807, art. 4, with effect from 6 April 2012.
In s. 18(1A), the figures of "£7,225" and "£42,475" (respectively) substituted by SI 2011/938, art. 4, with effect from 6 April 2011 (previously "£5,715" and "£43,875" (respectively) substituted by SI 2009/593, art. 4, with effect from 6 April 2009, "£5,435" and "£40,040" (respectively) substituted by SI 2008/579, art. 4, with effect from 6 April 2008, "£5,225" and "£34,840" (respectively) substituted by SI 2007/1052, art. 4, with effect from 6 April 2007, "£5,035" and "£33,540" (respectively) substituted by SI 2006/624, art. 4, with effect from 6 April 2006 and "£4,895" and "£32,760" (respectively) substituted by SI 2005/878, art. 4(a) and (b), with effect from 6 April 2005).
S. 18(1A) inserted by NICA 2002, s. 3(3) with effect for 2003–04 and subsequent tax years.
S. 18(1), (2) amended; with insertion of references to the Inland Revenue; by SSC(TF)A 1999, s. 2; Sch. 3, para. 18 with effect from 1 April 1999 (SI 1999/527).
In s. 18(2)(b) "or 7BZA" inserted after "6" by NICSPA 2004, s. 11 and Sch. 1, para. 1(3) with effect from 1 September 2004 (by virtue of SI 2004/1943, reg. 5).
S. 18(2) amended; with removal of references to the Secretary of State; by SSC(TF)A 1999, s. 1; Sch. 1, para. 7 with effect from 1 April 1999 (SI 1999/527).

Derivations – (as originally enacted) – SSA 1975, s. 10.

Cross references – S. 176(1): regulations made by way of statutory instrument under this section must be laid in draft before Parliament and approved by a resolution of each house.
Sch. 1: supplementary provisions relating to contributions.
Sch. 2, para. 6: application of TMA 1970, s. 86 and 88 and ICTA 1988, s. 824 to Class 4 contributions.
SSC(TF)A 1999, s. 8(2): determination by officers of Board of questions arising under regulations made by virtue of s. 18, by the Inland Revenue.
SSC(TF)A 1999, s. 4, Sch. 4: recovery of contributions where income tax recovery provisions not applicable.
SSAA 1992, s. 17(2)(b): determination by Secretary of State of questions arising under regulations made under this section.
SSAA 1992, s. 141(5): annual review of percentage rate of Class 4 contributions in line with alterations made to s. 15(3).
SSAA 1992, s. 143(2): alteration of percentage rate of Class 4 contributions with a view to adjusting the level of National Insurance Fund in line with alterations made to s. 15(3).
Interpretation Act 1978, Sch. 1: "Secretary of State" means one of HM's Principal Secretaries of State.
SI 2001/1004, Pt. 8: Class 4 contributions.
SI 2001/1004, reg. 103: Class 4 liability of earners treated as self-employed who otherwise would be employed earners.
SI 2001/1004, reg. 108: annual maximum of special Class 4 contributions.
SI 2001/1004, reg. 125(f): modification in relation to share fishermen.

18A Class 4 contributions: partnerships

18A(1) The Treasury may by regulations–

(a) modify the way in which liabilities for Class 4 contributions of a partner in a firm are determined, or

(b) otherwise modify the law relating to Class 4 contributions,

as they consider appropriate to take account of the passing or making of a provision of the Income Tax Acts relating to firms or partners in firms.

18A(2) **"Firm"** has the same meaning as in the Income Tax (Trading and Other Income) Act 2005 (and includes a limited liability partnership in relation to which section 863(1) of that Act applies); and **"partner"** is to be read accordingly and includes a former partner.

18A(3) Regulations under this section may have retrospective effect; but they may not have effect before the beginning of the tax year in which they are made.

History – S. 18A inserted by NICA 2014, s. 13(2), with effect from 13 May 2014.

GENERAL

19 General power to regulate liability for contributions

19(1) Regulations may provide either generally or in relation to–

(a) any prescribed category of earners; or

(b) earners in any prescribed category of employments,

that their liability in a particular tax year in respect of contributions of prescribed classes, or any prescribed part of such contributions, is not to exceed such maximum amount or amounts as may be prescribed.

19(2) Regulations made for the purposes of subsection (1) above may provide–

(a) for an earner whose liability is subject to a maximum prescribed under that subsection to be liable in the first instance for the full amount of any contributions due from him apart from the regulations, or to be relieved from liability for such contributions in prescribed circumstances and to the prescribed extent; and

(b) for contributions paid in excess of any such maximum to be repaid at such times, and in accordance with such conditions, as may be prescribed.

19(3) Regulations may provide, in relation to earners otherwise liable for contributions of any class or any part of such contributions, for excepting them from the liability for such periods, and in such circumstances, as may be prescribed.

19(4) As respects any woman who was married or a widow on 6th April 1977 (the date of the coming into force of the repeal of the old provisions that primary Class 1 contributions might be paid at a reduced rate and Class 2 contributions need not be paid by a married woman or a widow) regulations shall provide–

(a) for enabling her to elect that so much of her liability in respect of primary Class 1 contributions as is attributable to section 8(1)(a) above shall be a liability to contribute at such reduced rate as may be prescribed; and

(b) either for enabling her to elect that her liability in respect of Class 2 contributions shall be a liability to contribute at such reduced rate as may be prescribed or for enabling her to elect that she shall be under no liability to pay such contributions; and

(c) for enabling her to revoke any such election.

19(5) Regulations under subsection (4) above may–

(a) provide for the making or revocation of any election under the regulations to be subject to prescribed exceptions and conditions;

21(2) The class or classes of contribution which, for the purposes of subsection (1) above, are relevant in relation to each of those benefits are as follows–

	Short-term benefit
Short-term incapacity benefit under section 30A(1)(a) below	Class 1 or 2
	Other benefits
Widowed mother's allowance	Class 1, 2 or 3
Widowed parent's allowance	Class 1, 2 or 3
Widow's pension	Class 1, 2 or 3
Category A retirement pension	Class 1, 2 or 3
Category B retirement pension	Class 1, 2 or 3
Child's special allowance	Class 1, 2 or 3

21(3) The relevant contribution conditions in relation to the benefits specified in subsection (2) above are those specified in Part I of Schedule 3 to this Act.

21(4) [Omitted by PA 2014, s. 31 and Sch. 16, para. 4(3).]

21(5) In subsection (4) above and Schedule 3 to this Act–

(a) **"the contributor concerned"**, for the purposes of any contribution condition, means the person by whom the condition is to be satisfied;

(b) **"a relevant class"**, in relation to any benefit, means a class of contributions specified in relation to that benefit in subsection (2) above;

(c) **"the earnings factor"**–

(i) where the year in question is 1987–88 or any subsequent tax year, means, in relation to a person, the aggregate of his earnings factors derived from so much of his earnings as did not exceed the upper earnings limit and upon which primary Class 1 contributions have been paid or treated as paid and from his Class 2 and Class 3 contributions; and

(ii) where the year in question is any earlier tax year, means, in relation to a person's contributions of any class or classes, the aggregate of his earnings factors derived from all those contributions;

(d) except in the expression "benefit year", **"year"** means a tax year.

21(5A) Where primary Class 1 contributions have been paid or treated as paid on any part of a person's earnings, the following provisions, namely–

(a) subsection (5)(c) above;

(b) sections 22(1)(a), (2A) and (3)(a), 23(3)(a), 24(2)(a), 44(6)(za) and (a) below; and

(c) paragraphs 2(4)(a) and (5)(a), 4(2)(a), 5(2)(b) and (4)(a), 5A(3)(c) and 7(4)(a) of Schedule 3 to this Act,

shall have effect as if such contributions had been paid or treated as paid on so much of the earnings as did not exceed the upper earnings limit.

21(6) In this Part of this Act **"benefit year"** means a period–

(a) beginning with the first Sunday in January in any calendar year, and

(b) ending with the Saturday immediately preceding the first Sunday in January in the following calendar year;

but for any prescribed purposes of this Part of this Act **"benefit year"** may by regulations be made to mean such other period (whether or not a period of 12 months) as may be specified in the regulations.

Prospective amendments – In s. 21(1), the words from "short-term incapacity benefit" to "subsection (5) of that section" and the words "short-term or long-term incapacity benefit under section 40 or 41 below" repealed by the Welfare Reform Act 2007, s. 67 and Sch. 8, with effect from a date to be appointed, s. 70(2).

In s. 21(2), in the table, the words from "short-term benefit", the entry relating to short-term incapacity benefit, and the heading "Other benefits" repealed by the Welfare Reform Act 2007, s. 67 and Sch. 8, with effect from a date to be appointed, s. 70(2).

In s. 21(5A)(c), the words "2(4)(a) and (5)(a)" repealed by the Welfare Reform Act 2007, s. 67 and Sch. 8, with effect from a date to be appointed, s. 70(2).

History – In s. 21(1) words "short-term incapacity benefit under subsection (1)(b) of section 30A below" inserted and words "section 30A(1)(a)" substituted for words "section 30A" by WRPA 1999, s. 70 and Sch. 8, Pt. II, para. 20 and 21, with effect from 3 November 2000 (by virtue of SI 2000/2958).

In s. 21 (1) words", maternity allowance under section 35 below" inserted by WRPA 1999, s. 70 and 88 and Sch. 8, Pt. VI, para. 30, 31 and Sch. 13, Pt. V, with effect from 2 April 2000 (by virtue of SI 1999/3309 art 2(1)(b)(ii), (c)).

In s. 21(1) the words "or a shared pension under section 55A below" inserted by WRPA 1999, s. 84(1), Sch. 12, para. 16 with effect from 1 December 2000 (SI 2000/1047, art. 2(2)(d), Sch. Pt. IV).

In s. 21(1), the words "other than long-term incapacity benefit under section 30A below or short-term or long-term incapacity benefit under section 40 or 41 below" substituted by the Social Security (Incapacity for Work) Act 1994, Sch. 1, para. 3(2), with effect from 13 April 1995 (SI 1994/2926).

In s. 21(2), in the table, the entries for bereavement payment and bereavement allowance omitted by PA 2014, s. 31 and Sch. 16, para. 4(2), with effect from 6 April 2017, subject to SI 2017/297, art. 4 (later commencement for abolition of bereavement payment and bereavement allowance) and 5 (commencement for entitlement to bereavement payment and bereavement support payment) (SI 2017/297, art. 3(2)).
In the table at s. 21(2), the words "section 30A(1)(a)" substituted by WRPA 1999, s. 70 and Sch. 8, Pt. II, para. 20 and 21, with effect from 3 November 2000 (by virtue of SI 2000/2958).
In the table at s. 21(2), reference to "bereavement payment" substituted by WRPA 1999, s. 70 and Sch. 8, Pt. I, para. 2, 4(1), (2)(a) and (3), with effect from 9 April 2001 (by virtue of SI 2000/1047, art. 2(2)(a)(ii), Schedule, Pt. I).
In the table at s. 21(2), reference to "Widowed parent's allowance" and "Bereavement allowance" inserted by the WRPA 1999, s. 70, Sch. 8, Pt. I, para. 2, 4(1) and (2)(b), with effect from 9 April 2001 (by virtue of SI 2000/1047, art. 2(2)(a)(ii), Schedule, Pt. I).
In the table at s. 21(2), the former reference to "unemployment benefit" repealed by Jobseekers Act 1995, Sch. 3, with effect from 7 October 1996 (SI 1996/2208 (C. 54)).
In the table at s. 21(2), the reference to "maternity allowance" and at s. 21(4), the words "other than maternity allowance" repealed by WRPA 1999, s. 88, Sch. 13, Pt. V with effect from 2 April 2000 (SI 1999/3309, art. 2(1)(c)).
In the table at s. 21(2), the words "Short-term incapacity benefit under section 30A below" substituted by the Social Security (Incapacity for Work)Act 1994, Sch. 1, para. 3(3), with effect from 13 April 1995 (SI 1994/2926).
S. 21(4) omitted by PA 2014, s. 31 and Sch. 16, para. 4(3), with effect from 6 April 2017, subject to SI 2017/297, art. 4 (later commencement for abolition of bereavement payment and bereavement allowance) and 5 (commencement for entitlement to bereavement payment and bereavement support payment) (SI 2017/297, art. 3(2)). [Note: in s. 21(4), the words from "short-term benefit or" repealed by the Welfare Reform Act 2007, s. 67 and Sch. 8, with effect from a date to be appointed, s. 70(2). S. 21(4) omitted without this amendment having entered into force.]
In s. 21(4) the word "bereavement" substituted for the word "widow's" by WRPA 1999, s. 70 and Sch. 8, Pt. I, para. 2, 4(1), (2)(a) and (3), with effect from 9 April 2001 (by virtue of SI 2000/1047, art. 2(2)(a)(ii), Schedule, Pt. I).
In s. 21(5)(c)(i) words "so much of his earnings as did not exceed the upper earnings limit and " substituted by NICA 2002, s. 6 and Sch. 1, para. 6 with effect for 2003–04 and subsequent tax years.
In s. 21(5A)(b), words "and 45A(1)(a)" repealed by TCA 2002, s. 60 and Sch. 6, with effect from 6 April 2003 (SI 2003/962).
In s. 21(5A)(c), ", 5A(3)(c)" inserted by Pensions Act 2008, s. 104 and Sch. 4, para. 2 with effect from 3 January 2012 (SI 2011/3033, art. 2(c)).
S. 21(5A) inserted by SSA 1998, s. 86(1) and Sch. 7, para. 60, with effect from 6 April 1999 (SI 1999/418).

Derivations – S. 21(1), (2) (as originally enacted): SSA 1975, s. 13(1).
S. 21(3): SSA 1975, s. 13(6).
S. 21(4): SSA 1975, s. 13(8).
S. 21(5): SSA 1975, s. 13(6).
S. 21(6): SSA 1975, s. 13(7).

Cross references – S. 30A (not reproduced): incapacity benefit.
S. 40 (not reproduced): long-term incapacity benefit for widows.
S. 41 (not reproduced): long-term incapacity benefit for widowers.
Sch. 3 (not reproduced): contribution conditions for entitlement to benefit.

22 Earnings factors

22(1) A person shall, for the purposes specified in subsection (2) below, be treated as having annual earnings factors derived–

(a) in the case of 1987–88 or any subsequent tax year, from so much of his earnings as did not exceed the upper earnings limit and upon which primary Class 1 contributions have been paid or treated as paid and from Class 2 and Class 3 contributions; and

(b) in the case of any earlier tax year, from his contributions of any of Classes 1, 2 and 3;

but subject to the following provisions of this section and those of section 23 below.

22(2) The purposes referred to in subsection (1) above are those of–

(a) establishing, by reference to the satisfaction of contribution conditions, entitlement to a contribution-based jobseeker's allowance, to a contributory employment and support allowance or to any benefit specified in section 20(1) above, other than maternity allowance;

(b) calculating the additional pension in the rate of a long-term benefit.

(c) establishing entitlement to a state pension under Part 1 of the Pensions Act 2014 and, where relevant, calculating the rate of a state pension under that Part, and

(d) establishing entitlement to bereavement support payment under section 30 of the Pensions Act 2014.

22(2A) For the purposes specified in subsection (2)(b) above, in the case of the first appointed year or any subsequent tax year a person's earnings factor shall be treated as derived only from so much of his earnings as did not exceed the applicable limit and on which primary Class 1 contributions have been paid or treated as paid. This subsection does not affect the operation of sections 44A and 44B (deemed earnings factors).

22(2B) **"The applicable limit"** means–

(a) in relation to a tax year before 2009–10, the upper earnings limit;

(b) in relation to 2009–10 or any subsequent tax year, the upper accrual point; and

22(3) Separate earnings factors may be derived for 1987–88 and subsequent tax years–

(a) from earnings not exceeding the upper earnings limit upon which primary Class 1 contributions have been paid or treated as paid;

(b) from earnings which have been credited;

163 Interpretation of Part XI and supplementary provisions

163(1) In this Part of this Act–

"contract of service" (except in paragraph (a) of the definition below of "employee") includes any arrangement providing for the terms of appointment of an employee;

"employee" means a person who is–

(a) gainfully employed in Great Britain either under a contract of service or in an office (including elective office) with earnings (within the meaning of Parts 1 to 5 above); and

(b) over the age of 16;

but subject to regulations, which may provide for cases where any such person is not to be treated as an employee for the purposes of this Part of this Act and for cases where any person who would not otherwise be an employee for those purposes is to be treated as an employee for those purposes;

"employer", in relation to an employee and a contract of service of his, means a person who under section 6 above is, or but for the condition in subsection (1)(b) of that section would be, liable to pay secondary Class 1 contributions in relation to any earnings of the employee under the contract;

...

"prescribed" means prescribed by regulations;

...

163(2)–(7) [Not relevant to National Insurance contributions.]

History – In s. 163(1) in para. (a) of definition of "employee" the words "earnings (within the meaning of Parts 1 to 5 above)" substituted for the words "general earnings (as defined by section 7 of the Income Tax (Earnings and Pensions) Act 2003)" by NICA 2014, s. 15 and Sch. 2, para. 3, with effect from 13 May 2014.

In s. 163(1), in the definition of "employee", the words in paragraph (a) "general earnings (as defined by section 7 of the Income Tax (Earnings and Pensions) Act 2003)" substituted by ITEPA 2003, Sch. 6, para. 181 which has effect, for income tax purposes, for the tax year 2003–04 and subsequent tax years.

In s. 163(1) the definition of "employer" amended by SSA 1998, s. 86(1) and Sch. 7, para. 74, with effect from 6 April 1999 (SI 1999/418).

Derivations – S. 163(1): SSHBA 1982, s. 26(1).

Cross references – S. 172(a): "Great Britain" extends to adjacent territorial waters.

Notes – In s. 163(1), only those definitions of relevance to contributions have been included.

PART XII – STATUTORY MATERNITY PAY

166 Rate of statutory maternity pay

166(1) Statutory maternity pay shall be payable to a woman–

(a) at the earnings-related rate, in respect of the first 6 weeks in respect of which it is payable; and

(b) at whichever is the lower of the earnings-related rate and such weekly rate as may be prescribed, in respect of the remaining portion of the maternity pay period.

166(1A) In subsection (1) **"week"** means any period of seven days.

166(2) The earnings-related rate is a weekly rate equivalent to 90 per cent of a woman's normal weekly earnings for the period of 8 weeks immediately preceding the 14th week before the expected week of confinement.

166(3) The weekly rate prescribed under subsection (1)(b) above must not be less than the weekly rate of statutory sick pay for the time being specified in section 157(1) above or, if two or more such rates are for the time being so specified, the higher or highest of those rates.

166(4) Where for any purpose of this Part of this Act or of regulations it is necessary to calculate the daily rate of statutory maternity pay, the amount payable by way of statutory maternity pay for any day shall be taken as one seventh of the weekly rate.

History – S. 166 was substituted by EA 2002, s. 19 with effect from 6 April 2003, by virtue of SI 2002/2866, art. 2(3) and Sch. 1, Pt. 3; art. 3 and Sch. 3, para. 5, but does not have effect in relation to a woman–

- whose maternity pay period commences before 6 April 2003;
- who is entitled to statutory maternity pay at the rate of £75 a week immediately before that date; and
- who would be entitled to statutory maternity pay at a rate lower than £75 a week if the amendment had effect in relation to her.

S. 166(1A) inserted by the Work and Families Act 2006, s. 11, and Sch. 1, para. 8(2), with effect from 1 October 2006, by virtue of SI 2006/1682, art. 3(e).

S. 166(4) inserted by the Work and Families Act 2006, s. 11, and Sch. 1, para. 8(3), with effect from 1 October 2006, by virtue of SI 2006/1682, art. 3(e).

167 Funding of employers' liabilities in respect of statutory maternity pay

167(1) Regulations shall make provision for the payment by employers of statutory maternity pay to be funded by the Commissioners of Inland Revenue to such extent as may be prescribed.

167(2) Regulations under subsection (1) shall–

(a) make provision for a person who has made a payment of statutory maternity pay to be entitled, except in prescribed circumstances, to recover an amount equal to the sum of –

(i) the aggregate of such of those payments as qualify for small employers' relief; and

(ii) an amount equal to 92 per cent of the aggregate of such of those payments as do not so qualify; and

(b) include provision for a person who has made a payment of statutory maternity pay qualifying for small employers' relief to be entitled, except in prescribed circumstances, to recover an additional amount, determined in such manner as may be prescribed–

(i) by reference to secondary Class 1 contributions paid in respect of statutory maternity pay;

(ii) by reference to secondary Class 1 contributions paid in respect of statutory sick pay; or

(iii) by reference to the aggregate of secondary Class 1 contributions paid in respect of statutory maternity pay and secondary Class 1 contributions paid in respect of statutory sick pay.

167(3) For the purposes of this section a payment of statutory maternity pay which a person is liable to make to a woman qualifies for small employers' relief if, in relation to that woman's maternity pay period, the person liable to make the payment is a small employer.

167(4) For the purposes of this section **"small employer"**, in relation to a woman's maternity pay period, shall have the meaning assigned to it by regulations, and, without prejudice to the generality of the foregoing, any such regulations–

(a) may define that expression by reference to the amount of a person's contributions payments for any prescribed period; and

(b) if they do so, may in that connection make provision for the amount of those payments for that prescribed period–

(i) to be determined without regard to any deductions that may be made from them under this section or under any other enactment or instrument; and

(ii) in prescribed circumstances, to be adjusted, estimated or otherwise attributed to him by reference to their amount in any other prescribed period.

167(5) Regulations under subsection (1) may, in particular, make provision–

(a) for funding in advance as well as in arrear;

(b) for funding, or the recovery of amounts due under provision made by virtue of subsection (2)(b), by means of deductions from such amounts for which employers are accountable to the Commissioners of Inland Revenue as may be prescribed, or otherwise;

(c) for the recovery by the Commissioners of Inland Revenue of any sums overpaid to employers under the regulations.

167(6) Where in accordance with any provision of regulations under subsection (1) an amount has been deducted from an employer's contributions payments, the amount so deducted shall (except in such cases as may be prescribed) be treated for the purposes of any provision made by or under any enactment in relation to primary or secondary Class 1 contributions–

(a) as having been paid (on such date as may be determined in accordance with the regulations), and

(b) as having been received by the Commissioners of Inland Revenue,

towards discharging the employer's liability in respect of such contributions.

167(7) Regulations under this section must be made with the concurrence of the Commissioners of Inland Revenue.

167(8) In this section **"contributions payments"**, in relation to an employer, means any payments which the employer is required, by or under any enactment, to make in discharge of any liability in respect of primary or secondary Class 1 contributions.

History – S. 167 substituted by Employment Act 2002, s. 21, with effect from 6 April 2003 (SI 2002/2866, art. 2(3), Sch. 1, Pt. 3).
In former s. 167(1)(a), the words "an amount…qualify," substituted by SI 1994/1230 in relation to payments of statutory maternity pay due after 3 September 1994.
S. 167(1)(b), (e) amended by SSC(TF)A 1999, s. 1; Sch. 1, para. 13(2) with effect from 25 February 1999 regarding the power to make regulations transferring functions to the Revenue and 1 April 1999 for all other purposes (SI 1999/527).
In former s. 167(1)(b), the words "amounts…above" substituted by SI 1994/1230 in relation to payments of statutory maternity pay due after 3 September 1994.
In former s. 167(1)(c), the words "qualifying for small employers' relief" inserted by SI 1994/1230 in relation to payments of statutory maternity pay due after 3 September 1994.
Former s. 167(1A) and (1B) inserted by SI 1994/1230 in relation to payments of statutory maternity pay due after 3 September 1994.
Former s. 167(4)(b) amended by SSC(TF)A 1999, s. 1; Sch. 1, para. 13(3), substituting "Commissioners of Inland Revenue" for "Secretary of State", with effect from 25 February 1999 regarding the power to make regulations transferring functions to the Revenue and 1 April 1999 for all other purposes (SI 1999/527).

transitional and saving provision in SI 2014/1640, art. 16 (amendments do not have effect in relation to– (a) children whose expected week of birth ends on or before 4 April 2015; (b) children placed for adoption on or before 4 April 2015) (SI 2014/1640, art. 6 and 7). In s. 171ZD(2), the words "ordinary statutory paternity pay" substituted for "statutory paternity pay", and "liability for ordinary statutory paternity pay or additional statutory paternity pay (or both)" substituted for "liability for statutory paternity pay" by the Work and Families Act 2006, s. 11, and Sch. 1, para. 15(3), with effect from 6 April 2010 (SI 2010/495).
S. 171ZD inserted by EA 2002, s. 2, with effect from 8 December 2002, in relation to a person who satisfies the prescribed conditions of entitlement in respect of a child born on or after 6 April 2003, or whose expected week of birth begins on or after that date; or a child matched for the purposes of adoption with a person who is notified of having been matched on or after 6 April 2003, or placed for adoption on or after that date (SI 2002/2866, art. 2(2), Sch. 1, Pt. 2, Sch. 3, para. 1).

Statutory instruments – SI 2003/500: made under s. 171ZD(2), (3).
SI 2003/1194: made under s. 171ZD(2), (3).

171ZE Rate and period of pay

171ZE(1) Statutory paternity pay shall be payable at such fixed or earnings-related weekly rate as may be prescribed by regulations, which may prescribe different kinds of rate for different cases.

171ZE(2) Statutory paternity pay shall be payable in respect of–

(a) a period of two consecutive weeks within the qualifying period beginning on such date within that period as the person entitled may choose in accordance with regulations, or

(b) if regulations permit the person entitled to choose to receive statutory paternity pay in respect of–

(i) a period of a week, or

(ii) two non-consecutive periods of a week,

such week or weeks within the qualifying period as he may choose in accordance with regulations.

171ZE(3) For the purposes of subsection (2) above, the qualifying period shall be determined in accordance with regulations, which shall secure that it is a period of at least 56 days beginning–

(a) in the case of a person to whom the conditions in section 171ZA(2) above apply, with the date of the child's birth, and

(b) in the case of a person to whom the conditions in section 171ZB(2) above apply, with the date of the child's placement for adoption.

171ZE(3A) Statutory paternity pay is not payable to a person in respect of a statutory pay week if–

(a) statutory shared parental pay is payable to that person in respect of any part of that week or that person takes shared parental leave in any part of that week, or

(b) statutory shared parental pay was payable to that person or that person has taken shared parental leave in respect of the child before that week.

171ZE(4) Statutory paternity pay shall not be payable to a person in respect of a statutory pay week if it is not his purpose at the beginning of the week–

(a) to care for the child by reference to whom he satisfies the condition in sub-paragraph (i) of section 171ZA(2)(a) or 171ZB(2)(a) above, or

(b) to support the person by reference to whom he satisfies the condition in sub-paragraph (ii) of that provision.

171ZE(5) A person shall not be liable to pay statutory paternity pay to another in respect of a statutory pay week during any part of which the other works under a contract of service with him.

171ZE(6) It is immaterial for the purposes of subsection (5) above whether the work referred to in that subsection is work under a contract of service which existed immediately before the statutory pay week or a contract of service which did not so exist.

171ZE(7) Except in such cases as may be prescribed, statutory paternity pay shall not be payable to a person in respect of a statutory pay week during any part of which he works for any employer who is not liable to pay him statutory paternity pay.

171ZE(8) The Secretary of State may by regulations specify circumstances in which there is to be no liability to pay statutory paternity pay in respect of a statutory pay week.

171ZE(9) Where more than one child is born as a result of the same pregnancy, the reference in subsection (3)(a) to the date of the child's birth shall be read as a reference to the date of birth of the first child born as a result of the pregnancy.

171ZE(10) Where more than one child is placed for adoption as part of the same arrangement, the reference in subsection (3)(b) to the date of the child's placement shall be read as a reference to the date of placement of the first child to be placed as part of the arrangement.

171ZE(10A) Where for any purpose of this Part of this Act or of regulations it is necessary to calculate the daily rate of statutory paternity pay, the amount payable by way of statutory paternity pay for any day shall be taken as one seventh of the weekly rate.

171ZE(11) In this section–

"statutory pay week", in relation to a person entitled to statutory paternity pay, means a week chosen by him as a week in respect of which statutory paternity pay shall be payable;

"week" means any period of seven days.

171ZE(12) Where statutory paternity pay is payable to a person by virtue of section 171ZB(8), this section has effect as if–

(a) the references in subsections (3)(b) and (10) to placement for adoption were references to placement under section 22C of the Children Act 1989;

(b) the references in subsection (10) to being placed for adoption were references to being placed under section 22C.

171ZE(13) Where statutory paternity pay is payable to a person by virtue of section 171ZB(10), this section has effect as if–

(a) the references in subsections (3)(b) and (10) to placement for adoption were references to placement under section 81 of the Social Services and Wellbeing (Wales) Act 2014;

(b) the references in subsection (10) to being placed for adoption were references to being placed under section 81.

Prospective amendments – S. 171ZE(2), the following words substituted for the words "be payable in respect of– (a) a period of two consecutive weeks within the qualifying period beginning on such date within that period as the person entitled may choose in accordance with regulations, or (b) if regulations permit the person entitled to choose to receive ordinary statutory paternity pay in respect of– (i) a period of a week, or (ii) two non-consecutive periods of a week, such week or weeks within the qualifying period as he may choose in accordance with regulations." by Children and Families Act 2014, s. 123(3), with effect from a day to be appointed by order of the Secretary of State. Substituted words to read as follows:

"be payable in respect of–

(a) such week within the qualifying period, or

(b) such number of weeks, not exceeding the prescribed number of weeks, within the qualifying period,

as he may choose in accordance with regulations."

S. 171ZE(2A) and (2B) inserted by Children and Families Act 2014, s. 123(3), with effect from a day to be appointed by order of the Secretary of State. S. 171ZE(2A) to read as follows:

"171ZE(2A) Provision under subsection (2)(b) is to secure that the prescribed number of weeks is not less than two.

171ZE(2B) Regulations under subsection (2) may permit a person entitled to receive statutory paternity pay to choose to receive such pay in respect of non-consecutive periods each of which is a week or a number of weeks."

History – In s. 171ZE, the words "ordinary statutory paternity pay" substituted for "statutory paternity pay" throughout by the Work and Families Act 2006, s. 11, and Sch. 1, para. 16(2), with effect from 6 April 2010 (SI 2010/495)

In s. 171ZE(1), the word "Ordinary" (which appeared before the words "statutory paternity pay") repealed by Children and Families Act 2014, s. 126(1) and Sch. 7, para. 16(2), with effect from 5 April 2015, subject to the transitional and saving provision in SI 2014/1640, art. 16 (amendments do not have effect in relation to– (a) children whose expected week of birth ends on or before 4 April 2015; (b) children placed for adoption on or before 4 April 2015) (SI 2014/1640, art. 6 and 7).

In s. 171ZE(2), in the words preceding paragraph (a), the word "Ordinary" (which appeared before the words "statutory paternity pay") repealed by Children and Families Act 2014, s. 126(1) and Sch. 7, para. 16(3)(a), with effect from 5 April 2015, subject to the transitional and saving provision in SI 2014/1640, art. 16 (amendments do not have effect in relation to– (a) children whose expected week of birth ends on or before 4 April 2015; (b) children placed for adoption on or before 4 April 2015) (SI 2014/1640, art. 6 and 7).

In s. 171ZE(2)(b), the word "ordinary" (which appeared before the words "statutory paternity pay"), repealed by Children and Families Act 2014, s. 126(1) and Sch. 7, para. 16(3)(b), with effect from 5 April 2015, subject to the transitional and saving provision in SI 2014/1640, art. 16 (amendments do not have effect in relation to– (a) children whose expected week of birth ends on or before 4 April 2015; (b) children placed for adoption on or before 4 April 2015) (SI 2014/1640, art. 6 and 7).

S. 171ZE(3A) inserted by Children and Families Act 2014, s. 120(5), with effect from 30 June 2014 (SI 2014/1640, art. 3).

In s. 171ZE(4), the word "Ordinary" (which appeared before the words "statutory paternity pay") repealed by Children and Families Act 2014, s. 126(1) and Sch. 7, para. 16(4), with effect from 5 April 2015, subject to the transitional and saving provision in SI 2014/1640, art. 16 (amendments do not have effect in relation to– (a) children whose expected week of birth ends on or before 4 April 2015; (b) children placed for adoption on or before 4 April 2015) (SI 2014/1640, art. 6 and 7).

In s. 171ZE(5), the word "ordinary" (which appeared before the words "statutory paternity pay") repealed by Children and Families Act 2014, s. 126(1) and Sch. 7, para. 16(5), with effect from 5 April 2015, subject to the transitional and saving provision in SI 2014/1640, art. 16 (amendments do not have effect in relation to– (a) children whose expected week of birth ends on or before 4 April 2015; (b) children placed for adoption on or before 4 April 2015) (SI 2014/1640, art. 6 and 7).

Ins. 171ZE(7), the word "ordinary" (which appeared before the words "statutory paternity pay") (in both places it occurs) repealed by Children and Families Act 2014, s. 126(1) and Sch. 7, para. 16(6), with effect from 5 April 2015, subject to the transitional and saving provision in SI 2014/1640, art. 16 (amendments do not have effect in relation to– (a) children whose expected week of birth ends on or before 4 April 2015; (b) children placed for adoption on or before 4 April 2015) (SI 2014/1640, art. 6 and 7).

In s. 171ZE(8), the word "ordinary" (which appeared before the words "statutory paternity pay") repealed by Children and Families Act 2014, s. 126(1) and Sch. 7, para. 16(7), with effect from 5 April 2015, subject to the transitional and saving provision in SI 2014/1640, art. 16 (amendments do not have effect in relation to– (a) children whose expected week of birth ends on or before 4 April 2015; (b) children placed for adoption on or before 4 April 2015) (SI 2014/1640, art. 6 and 7).

In s. 171ZE(10A), the word "ordinary" (which appeared before the words "statutory paternity pay") (in both places it occurs) repealed by Children and Families Act 2014, s. 126(1) and Sch. 7, para. 16(8), with effect from 5 April 2015, subject to the transitional and saving provision in SI 2014/1640, art. 16 (amendments do not have effect in relation to– (a) children whose expected week of birth ends on or before 4 April 2015; (b) children placed for adoption on or before 4 April 2015) (SI 2014/1640, art. 6 and 7).

S. 171ZE(10A) inserted by the Work and Families Act 2006, s. 11, and Sch. 1, para. 16(3), with effect from 1 October 2006, by virtue of SI 2006/2232, art. 2.

In s. 171ZE(11), in the definition of "statutory pay week" the word "ordinary" (which appeared before the words "statutory paternity pay") (in both places it occurs) repealed by Children and Families Act 2014, s. 126(1) and Sch. 7, para. 16(9), with effect from 5 April 2015, subject to the transitional and saving provision in SI 2014/1640, art. 16 (amendments do not have effect in relation to– (a) children whose expected week of birth ends on or before 4 April 2015; (b) children placed for adoption on or before 4 April 2015) (SI 2014/1640, art. 6 and 7).

S. 171ZE(12) inserted by Children and Families Act 2014, s. 121(4), with effect from 30 June 2014 (SI 2014/1640, art. 3).

S. 171ZE(13) inserted by SI 2016/413, reg. 133, with effect from 6 April 2016.

171ZV(14) Regulations may provide that, where the conditions in subsection (15) are satisfied in relation to a person who is entitled to statutory shared parental pay under subsection (1) or (3) (**"V"**), V may vary the number of weeks in respect of which V intends to claim statutory shared parental pay.

171ZV(15) The conditions are–

(a) that V has given the person who will be liable to pay statutory shared parental pay to V notice of–

(i) the extent to which V has exercised an entitlement to statutory shared parental pay in respect of the child,

(ii) the extent to which V intends to claim statutory shared parental pay in respect of the child,

(iii) the extent to which another person has exercised an entitlement to statutory shared parental pay in respect of the child, and

(iv) the extent to which another person intends to claim statutory shared parental pay in respect of the child;

(b) that a notice under paragraph (a)–

(i) is given by such time as may be prescribed, and

(ii) satisfies prescribed conditions as to form and content;

(c) that the person who is X or, as the case may be, Y in relation to V consents to that variation.

171ZV(16) A person's entitlement to statutory shared parental pay under this section is not affected by the placement for adoption of more than one child as part of the same arrangement.

171ZV(17) Regulations are to provide for entitlement to statutory shared parental pay in respect of a child placed, or expected to be placed–

(a) under section 22C of the Children Act 1989 by a local authority in England, or

(b) under section 81 of the Social Services and Well-being (Wales) Act 2014 by a local authority in Wales,

with a local authority foster parent who has been approved as a prospective adopter.

171ZV(18) This section has effect in relation to regulations made by virtue of subsection (17) as if–

(a) references to a child being placed for adoption under the law of any part of the United Kingdom were references to being placed under section 22C of the Children Act 1989 or section 81 of the Social Services and Well-being (Wales) Act 2014 with a local authority foster parent who has been approved as a prospective adopter;

(b) references to a placement for adoption were references to placement under section 22C of the Children Act 1989 or section 81 of the Social Services and Well-being (Wales) Act 2014 with such a person.

History – S. 171ZV(17) and (18) substituted by SI 2016/413, reg. 138, with effect from 6 April 2016.
S. 171ZV inserted by Children and Families Act 2014, s. 119(1), with effect from 30 June 2014 (SI 2014/1640, art. 3).
Cross references – SI 2014/2866, reg. 5: modification of s. 171ZV for parental order parents (as defined at SI 2014/2866, reg. 2).

171ZW Entitlement: general

171ZW(1) Regulations may–

(a) provide that the following do not have effect, or have effect subject to prescribed modifications, in such cases as may be prescribed–

(i) section 171ZU(2)(a) to (o),

(ii) section 171ZU(4)(a) to (p),

(iii) section 171ZU(13)(a) and (b),

(iv) section 171ZU(15)(a) to (c),

(v) section 171ZV(2)(a) to (o),

(vi) section 171ZV(4)(a) to (p),

(vii) section 171ZV(13)(a) and (b), and

(viii) section 171ZV(15)(a) to (c);

(b) impose requirements about evidence of entitlement and procedures to be followed;

(c) specify in what circumstances employment is to be treated as continuous for the purposes of section 171ZU or 171ZV;

(d) provide that a person is to be treated for the purposes of section 171ZU or 171ZV as being employed for a continuous period of at least the prescribed period where–

(i) the person has been employed by the same employer for at least the prescribed period under two or more separate contracts of service, and

(ii) those contracts were not continuous;

(e) provide for amounts earned by a person under separate contracts of service with the same employer to be aggregated for the purposes of section 171ZU or 171ZV;

(f) provide that–

(i) the amount of a person's earnings for any period, or

(ii) the amount of the person's earnings to be treated as comprised in any payment made to the person or for the person's benefit,

are to be calculated or estimated for the purposes of section 171ZU or 171ZV in such manner and on such basis as may be prescribed and that for that purpose payments of a particular class or description made or falling to be made to or by a person are, to such extent as may be prescribed, to be disregarded or, as the case may be, to be deducted from the amount of the person's earnings.

171ZW(2) The persons upon whom requirements may be imposed by virtue of subsection (1)(b) include–

(a) a person who, in connection with another person's claim to be paid statutory shared parental pay, is required to satisfy conditions prescribed under section 171ZU(2)(b) or (4)(c) or 171ZV(2)(b) or (4)(c);

(b) an employer or former employer of such a person.

171ZW(3) In subsection (1)(d) **"the prescribed period"** means the period of the length prescribed by regulations under section 171ZU(2)(c) or (4)(d) or 171ZV(2)(c) or (4)(d), as the case may be.

History – S. 171ZW inserted by Children and Families Act 2014, s. 119(1), with effect from 30 June 2014 (SI 2014/1640, art. 3).

171ZX Liability to make payments

171ZX(1) The liability to make payments of statutory shared parental pay under section 171ZU or 171ZV is a liability of any person of whom the person entitled to the payments has been an employee as mentioned in section 171ZU(2)(c) or (4)(d) or 171ZV(2)(c) or (4)(d), as the case may be.

171ZX(2) Regulations must make provision as to a former employer's liability to pay statutory shared parental pay to a person in any case where the former employee's contract of service with the person has been brought to an end by the former employer solely, or mainly, for the purpose of avoiding liability for statutory shared parental pay.

171ZX(3) The Secretary of State may, with the concurrence of the Commissioners for Her Majesty's Revenue and Customs, by regulations specify circumstances in which, notwithstanding this section, liability to make payments of statutory shared parental pay is to be a liability of the Commissioners.

History – S. 171ZX inserted by Children and Families Act 2014, s. 119(1), with effect from 30 June 2014 (SI 2014/1640, art. 3).

171ZY Rate and period of pay

171ZY(1) Statutory shared parental pay is payable at such fixed or earnings-related weekly rate as may be prescribed by regulations, which may prescribe different kinds of rate for different cases.

171ZY(2) Subject to the following provisions of this section, statutory shared parental pay is payable to a person in respect of each week falling within a relevant period, up to the number of weeks determined in the case of that person in accordance with regulations under section 171ZU(5) or 171ZV(5).

171ZY(3) Except in such cases as may be prescribed, statutory shared parental pay is not payable to a person in respect of a week falling within a relevant period if it is not the person's intention at the beginning of the week to care for the child by reference to whom the person satisfies–

(a) the condition in section 171ZU(2)(a) or (4)(a), or

(b) the condition in section 171ZV(2)(a) or (4)(a).

171ZY(4) Except in such cases as may be prescribed, statutory shared parental pay is not payable to a person in respect of a week falling within a relevant period during any part of which week the person works for any employer.

171ZY(5) The Secretary of State may by regulations specify circumstances in which there is to be no liability to pay statutory shared parental pay in respect of a week falling within a relevant period.

171ZY(6) *Where for any purpose of this Part* or of regulations it is necessary to calculate the daily rate of statutory shared parental pay, the amount payable by way of statutory shared parental pay for any day shall be taken as one seventh of the weekly rate.

171ZY(7) For the purposes of this section a week falls within a relevant period if it falls within a period specified in a notice under–

(a) section 171ZU(2)(j), (4)(k) or (13)(a), or

(b) section 171ZV(2)(j), (4)(k) or (13)(a),

and is not afterwards excluded from such a period by a variation of the period or periods during which the person in question intends to claim statutory shared parental pay.

171ZY(8) In this section **"week"**, in relation to a relevant period, means a period of seven days beginning with the day of the week on which the relevant period starts.

History – S. 171ZY inserted by Children and Families Act 2014, s. 119(1), with effect from 30 June 2014 (SI 2014/1640, art. 3).

171ZZ Restrictions on contracting out

171ZZ(1) An agreement is void to the extent that it purports–

(a) to exclude, limit or otherwise modify any provision of this Part, or

(b) to require a person to contribute (whether directly or indirectly) towards any costs incurred by that person's employer or former employer under this Part.

171ZZ(2) For the avoidance of doubt, an agreement between an employer and an employee, authorising deductions from statutory shared parental pay which the employer is liable to pay to the employee in respect of any period, is not void by virtue of subsection (1)(a) if the employer–

(a) is authorised by that or another agreement to make the same deductions from any contractual remuneration which the employer is liable to pay in respect of the same period, or

(b) would be so authorised if the employer were liable to pay contractual remuneration in respect of that period.

History – S. 171ZZ inserted by Children and Families Act 2014, s. 119(1), with effect from 30 June 2014 (SI 2014/1640, art. 3).

171ZZ1 Relationship with contractual remuneration

171ZZ1(1) Subject to subsections (2) and (3), any entitlement to statutory shared parental pay is not to affect any right of a person in relation to remuneration under any contract of service ("contractual remuneration").

171ZZ1(2) Subject to subsection (3)–

(a) any contractual remuneration paid to a person by an employer of that person in respect of any period is to go towards discharging any liability of that employer to pay statutory shared parental pay to that person in respect of that period; and

(b) any statutory shared parental pay paid by an employer to a person who is an employee of that employer in respect of any period is to go towards discharging any liability of that employer to pay contractual remuneration to that person in respect of that period.

171ZZ1(3) Regulations may make provision as to payments which are, and those which are not, to be treated as contractual remuneration for the purposes of subsections (1) and (2).

History – S. 171ZZ1 inserted by Children and Families Act 2014, s. 119(1), with effect from 30 June 2014 (SI 2014/1640, art. 3).

171ZZ2 Crown employment

171ZZ2(1) The provisions of this Part apply in relation to persons employed by or under the Crown as they apply in relation to persons employed otherwise than by or under the Crown.

History – S. 171ZZ2 inserted by Children and Families Act 2014, s. 119(1), with effect from 30 June 2014 (SI 2014/1640, art. 3).

171ZZ3 Special classes of person

171ZZ3(1) The Secretary of State may with the concurrence of the Treasury make regulations modifying any provision of this Part in such manner as the Secretary of State thinks proper in its application to any person who is, has been or is to be–

(a) employed on board any ship, vessel, hovercraft or aircraft;

(b) outside Great Britain at any prescribed time or in any prescribed circumstances; or

(c) in prescribed employment in connection with continental shelf operations, as defined in section 120(2).

171ZZ3(2) Regulations under subsection (1) may, in particular, provide–

(a) for any provision of this Part to apply to any such person, notwithstanding that it would not otherwise apply;

(b) for any such provision not to apply to any such person, notwithstanding that it would otherwise apply;

(c) for excepting any such person from the application of any such provision where the person neither is domiciled nor has a place of residence in any part of Great Britain;

(d) for the taking of evidence, for the purposes of the determination of any question arising under any such provision, in a country or territory outside Great Britain, by a British consular official or such other person as may be determined in accordance with the regulations.

History – S. 171ZZ3 inserted by Children and Families Act 2014, s. 119(1), with effect from 30 June 2014 (SI 2014/1640, art. 3).

171ZZ4 Part 12ZC: supplementary

171ZZ4(1) In this Part–

"adoption pay period" has the meaning given in section 171ZN(2);

"employer", in relation to a person who is an employee, means a person who–

(a) under section 6 is liable to pay secondary Class 1 contributions in relation to any of the earnings of the person who is an employee, or

(b) would be liable to pay such contributions but for–

(i) the condition in section 6(1)(b), or

(ii) the employee being under the age of 16;

"local authority" has the same meaning as in the Children Act 1989 (see section 105(1) of that Act);

"local authority foster parent" has the same meaning as in the Children Act 1989 (see section 105(1) of that Act);

"maternity allowance period" has the meaning given in section 35(2);

"maternity pay period" has the meaning given in section 165(1);

"modifications" includes additions, omissions and amendments, and related expressions are to be read accordingly;

"prescribed" means prescribed by regulations.

171ZZ4(2) In this Part **"employee"** means a person who is gainfully employed in Great Britain either under a contract of service or in an office (including elective office) with general earnings (as defined by section 7 of the Income Tax (Earnings and Pensions) Act 2003).

171ZZ4(3) Regulations may provide–

(a) for cases where a person who falls within the definition in subsection (2) is not to be treated as an employee for the purposes of this Part, and

(b) for cases where a person who would not otherwise be an employee for the purposes of this Part is to be treated as an employee for those purposes.

171ZZ4(4) Without prejudice to any other power to make regulations under this Part, regulations may specify cases in which, for the purposes of this Part or of such provisions of this Part as may be prescribed–

(a) two or more employers are to be treated as one;

(b) two or more contracts of service in respect of which the same person is an employee are to be treated as one.

171ZZ4(5) In this Part, except where otherwise provided, **"week"** means a period of seven days beginning with Sunday or such other period as may be prescribed in relation to any particular case or class of cases.

171ZZ4(6) For the purposes of this Part, a person's normal weekly earnings are, subject to subsection (8), to be taken to be the average weekly earnings which in the relevant period have been paid to the person or paid for the person's benefit under the contract of service with the employer in question.

171ZZ4(7) For the purposes of subsection (6) **"earnings"** and **"relevant period"** have the meanings given to them by regulations.

171ZZ4(8) In such cases as may be prescribed, a person's normal weekly earnings are to be calculated in accordance with regulations.

171ZZ4(9) Where–

(a) in consequence of the establishment of one or more National Health Service trusts under the National Health Service Act 2006, the National Health Service (Wales) Act 2006 or the National Health Service (Scotland) Act 1978, a person's contract of employment is treated by a scheme under any of those Acts as divided so as to constitute two or more contracts, or

(b) an order under paragraph 26(1) of Schedule 3 to the National Health Service Act 2006 provides that a person's contract of employment is so divided,

regulations may make provision enabling the person to elect for all of those contracts to be treated as one contract for the purposes of this Part or such provisions of this Part as may be prescribed.

171ZZ4(10) Regulations under subsection (9) may prescribe–

(a) the conditions that must be satisfied if a person is to be entitled to make such an election;

(b) the manner in which, and the time within which, such an election is to be made;

(c) the persons to whom, and the manner in which, notice of such an election is to be given;

(d) the information which a person who makes such an election is to provide, and the persons to whom, and the time within which, the person is to provide it;

(e) the time for which such an election is to have effect;

(f) which one of the person's employers under two or more contracts is to be regarded for the purposes of statutory shared parental pay as the person's employer under the contract.

171ZZ4(11) The powers under subsections (9) and (10) are without prejudice to any other power to make regulations under this Part.

171ZZ4(12) Regulations under any of subsections (4) to (10) must be made with the concurrence of the Commissioners for Her Majesty's Revenue and Customs.

History – In s. 171ZZ4(1), in the definition of "local authority foster parent", the words "section 105(1)" substituted for the words "section 22C(12)" by SI 2016/413, reg. 139, with effect from 6 April 2016.
S. 171ZZ4 inserted by Children and Families Act 2014, s. 119(1), with effect from 30 June 2014 (SI 2014/1640, art. 3).

171ZZ5 Power to apply Part 12ZC

171ZZ5(1) The Secretary of State may by regulations provide for this Part to have effect in relation to cases which involve adoption, but not the placement of a child for adoption under the law of any part of the United Kingdom, with such modifications as the regulations may prescribe.

171ZZ5(2) The Secretary of State may by regulations provide for this Part to have effect in relation to cases which involve a person who has applied, or intends to apply, with another person for a parental order under section 54 of the Human Fertilisation and Embryology Act 2008 and a child who is, or will be, the subject of the order, with such modifications as the regulations may prescribe.

171ZZ5(3) Where section 171ZW(1)(b) has effect in relation to such cases as are described in subsection (2), regulations under section 171ZW(1)(b) may impose requirements to make statutory declarations as to–

(a) eligibility to apply for a parental order;

(b) intention to apply for such an order.

History – S. 171ZZ5 inserted by Children and Families Act 2014, s. 119(1), with effect from 30 June 2014 (SI 2014/1640, art. 3).

PART XIII – GENERAL

INTERPRETATION

172 Application of Act in relation to territorial waters

172 In this Act–

(a) any reference to **"Great Britain"** includes a reference to the territorial waters of the United Kingdom adjacent to Great Britain;

(b) any reference to **"the United Kingdom"** includes a reference to the territorial waters of the United Kingdom.

Derivations – SSA 1986, s. 84(4).

173 Age

173 For the purposes of this Act a person–

(a) is over or under a particular **"age"** if he has or, as the case may be, has not attained that age; and

(b) is between two particular ages if he has attained the first but not the second;

and in Scotland (as in England and Wales) the time at which a person attains a particular age expressed in years is the commencement of the relevant anniversary of the date of his birth.

Derivations – SSA 1975, s. 168(1), Sch. 20.

174 References to Acts

174 In this Act–

"the 1975 Act" means the Social Security Act 1975;

"the 1986 Act" means the Social Security Act 1986;

"the Administration Act" means the Social Security Administration Act 1992;

"the Consequential Provisions Act" means the Social Security (Consequential Provisions) Act 1992;

"the Northern Ireland Contributions and Benefits Act" means the Social Security Contributions and Benefits (Northern Ireland) Act 1992;

"the Old Cases Act" means the Industrial Injuries and Diseases (Old Cases) Act 1975; and

"the Pensions Act" means the Pension Schemes Act 1993.

History – In s. 174, in the definition of "the Pensions Act", the words "Pension Schemes Act 1993" substituted by PSA 1993, s. 190 and Sch. 8, para. 41, with effect from 7 February 1994.

SUBORDINATE LEGISLATION

175 Regulations, orders and schemes

175(1) Subject to subsection (1A) below, regulations and orders under this Act shall be made by the Secretary of State.

175(1A) Subsection (1) above has effect subject to–

(a) any provision providing for regulations or an order to be made by the Treasury or by the Commissioners of Inland Revenue.

(b) [Repealed by TCA 2002, s. 60 and Sch. 6.]

175(2) Powers under this Act to make regulations, orders or schemes shall be exercisable by statutory instrument.

175(3) Except in the case of an order under section 145(3) above and in so far as this Act otherwise provides, any power under this Act to make regulations or an order may be exercised–

(a) either in relation to all cases to which the power extends, or in relation to those cases subject to specified exceptions, or in relation to any specified cases or classes of case;

(b) so as to make, as respects the cases in relation to which it is exercised–

(i) the full provision to which the power extends or any less provision (whether by way of exception or otherwise),

(ii) the same provision for all cases in relation to which the power is exercised, or different provision for different cases or different classes of case or different provision as respects the same case or class of case for different purposes of this Act,

(iii) any such provision either unconditionally or subject to any specified condition;

and where such a power is expressed to be exercisable for alternative purposes it may be exercised in relation to the same case for any or all of those purposes; and powers to make regulations or an order for the purposes of any one provision of this Act are without prejudice to powers to make regulations or an order for the purposes of any other provision.

175(4) Without prejudice to any specific provision in this Act, any power conferred by this Act to make regulations or an order (other than the power conferred in section 145(3) above) includes power to make thereby such incidental, supplementary, consequential or transitional provision as appears to the person making the regulations or order to be expedient for the purposes of the regulations or order.

175(5) Without prejudice to any specific provisions in this Act, a power conferred by any provision of this Act except–

(a) sections 30, 25B(2)(a), 47(6) and 145(3) above and paragraph 3(9) of Schedule 7 to this Act;

(b) section 122(1) above in relation to the definition of "payments by way of occupational or personal pension"; and

(c) Part XI,

to make regulations or an order includes power to provide for a person to exercise a discretion in dealing with any matter.

175(6) [Not relevant to National Insurance contributions.]

175(7) Any power of the Secretary of State under any provision of this Act, except the provisions mentioned in subsection (5)(a) and (b) above and Part IX, to make any regulations or order, where the power is not expressed to be exercisable with the consent of the Treasury, shall if the Treasury so direct be exercisable only in conjunction with them.

175(8) Any power under any of sections 116 to 120 above to modify provisions of this Act or the Administration Act extends also to modifying so much of any other provision of this Act or that Act as re-enacts provisions of the 1975 Act which replaced provisions of the National Insurance (Industrial Injuries) Acts 1965 to 1974.

175(9) A power to make regulations under any of sections 116 to 120 above shall be exercisable in relation to any enactment passed after this Act which is directed to be construed as one with this Act; but this subsection applies only so far as a contrary intention is not expressed in the enactment so passed, and is without prejudice to the generality of any such direction.

175(10) Any reference in this section or section 176 below to an order or regulations under this Act includes a reference to an order or regulations made under any provision of an enactment passed after this Act and directed to be construed as one with this Act; but this subsection applies only so far as a contrary intention is not expressed in the enactment so passed, and without prejudice to the generality of any such direction.

Prospective amendments – S. 175(6) repealed by WRA 2012, s. 147 and Sch. 14, Pt. 1, with effect from a date to be set by order of the Secretary of State.

History – S. 175(6) repealed by WRA 2012, s. 147 and Sch. 14, Pt. 1, with effect from 1 April 2013 in so far as relating to the abolition of council tax benefit (SI 2013/358, art. 8(c)).
In s. 175, in relation to tax credit, references to the "Secretary of State" shall be construed, with effect from 5 October 1999, as if they were references to "the Treasury" or, as the case may be, "the Board" (TCA 1999, s. 20(2); s. 2 and Sch. 2, para. 20(a)).
In s. 175(1), reference to subsection (1A) substituted by SSC(TF)A 1999, s. 2; Sch. 3, para. 29(2) with effect from 1 April 1999 (SI 1999/527).
In s. 175(1A)(a), words "of Part 1 or Part 6 of this Act" and para. (b) and the word "and" immediately preceding it repealed by TCA 2002, s. 60 and Sch. 6, with effect from 1 April 2003 (SI 2003/392, art. 2).
S. 175(1A) previously inserted by SSC(TF)A 1999, s. 2; Sch. 3, para. 29(3) with effect from 1 April 1999 (SI 1999/527).
In s. 175(4), reference to the "Secretary of State" removed by SSC(TF)A 1999, s. 2; Sch. 3, para. 29(4) with effect from 1 April 1999 (SI 1999/527).
In s. 175(5)(a), "25B(2)(a)" substituted for "57(9)(a)" by the Social Security (Incapacity for Work) Act 1994, Sch. 1, para. 36, with effect from 13 April 1995 (SI 1994/2926).

Derivations – S. 175(1) (as originally enacted): SSA 1975, s. 168(1), Sch. 20 "regulations"; Child Benefit Act 1975, s. 22(1)(b); SS(MP)A 1977, s. 24(1) "regulations"; SS(No. 2)A 1980, s. 3(4), 5(3) "regulations"; SSHBA 1982, s. 47 "regulations"; SSA 1986, s. 84(1) "regulations"; SSA 1989, s. 30(1) "regulations".
S. 175(2): SSA 1975, s. 166(1); Industrial Injuries and Diseases (Old Cases) Act 1975, s. 4(8), 8(1); Child Benefit Act 1975, s. 22(3); SS(MP)A 1977, s. 24(3); SS(No. 2)A 1980, s. 7(3); SSHBA 1982, s. 45(2); SSA 1986, s. 83(1); SSA 1989, s. 29(1); SSA 1990, s. 21(1), Sch. 6, para. 8(7), 12.
S. 175(3): SSA 1975, s. 166(2); Child Benefit Act 1975, s. 22(6); SS(MP)A 1977, s. 24(3); SS(No. 2)A 1980, s. 7(3); SSHBA 1982, s. 45(1); SSA 1986, s. 83(1); SSA 1989, s. 29(1).
S. 175(4): SSA 1975, s. 166(3); Child Benefit Act 1975, s. 22(7); SS(MP)A 1977, s. 24(3); SS(No. 2)A 1980, s. 7(3); SSHBA 1982, s. 45(1); SSA 1986, s. 83(1); SSA 1989, s. 29(1), 31(1), Sch. 8, para. 10(1).
S. 175(5) (as originally enacted): SSA 1975, s. 166(3A); Child Benefit Act 1975, s. 22(7A); SS(MP)A 1977, s. 24(3); SSA 1986, s. 62(1), (2), 83(1); SSA 1989, s. 29(1).

section 10ZC;
section 11(8) or (9);
section 14A;
section 18;
section 18A;
section 19(4) to (6);
section 28(3);
section 45(2A);
section 104(3);
section 117;
section 118;
section 145;
section 171ZE(1);
any of sections 171ZU to 171ZY;

(aa) the first regulations made by virtue of section 23A(3)(c);

(b) regulations prescribing payments for the

S. 176(4) inserted by CSPSSA 2000, s. ... orders, SI 2000/2950, art. 6; with effect from 25 January 2001 for the purposes of making reports and orders ... 42B and 45A, SI 2001/153, art. 2(a)(i) and with effect from 6 April 2002 for the remaining purposes, art. 2(a)(ii).

Derivations – S. 176(1) (as originally enacted): SSA 1975, s. 167(1); SSPA 1975, s. 62(1); Child Benefit Act 1975, s. 22(3); SS(No. 2) A 1980, s. 5(4); SSHBA 1982, s. 7(1B), 9(1F); SSA 1986, s. 43(3)(b), 62(3), 67(1), 83(3)(e), 86, Sch. 10, para. 65; SSA 1989, s. 9(1); SSA 1990, s. 21(1), Sch. 6, para. 8(2), (3), (5), 15(2); SSPA 1991, s. 2(1).
S. 176(2) (as originally enacted): SSA 1975, s. 167(2); Child Benefit Act 1975, s. 22(4); SSA 1990, s. 21(2), Sch. 6, para. 8(1), (3).
S. 176(3) (as originally enacted): SSA 1975, s. 167(3); Industrial Injuries and Diseases (Old Cases) Act 1975, s. 4(8), 8(1); ChildBenefit Act 1975, s. 22(5); SS(MP)A 1977, s. 24(5); SS(No. 2)A, 1980, s. 7(4); SSHBA 1982, s. 45(2); SSA 1986, s. 83(4); SSA 1989, s. 29(3); SSA 1990, s. 21(1), Sch. 6, para. 8(1), (3), (4), (6), (7), (9), (12).

Cross references – S. 11(3): regulations may make provision for an earner to be liable for a higher rate of Class 2 contributions in certain cases.
S. 18: Class 4 contributions recoverable under regulations.
S. 19(4): election by women married or widowed before 6 April 1977 to pay reduced rate contributions.
S. 25B(1) (not reproduced): power to amend s. 25A (days of entitlement to unemployment benefit).
S. 28 (not reproduced): disqualifications from unemployment benefit.
S. 57 (not reproduced): determination of days for which child allowance payable.
S. 104 (not reproduced): increase in disablement pension where constant attendance needed.
S. 117: mariners, airmen etc.
S. 118: married women and widows.
S. 145 (not reproduced): rate of child benefit.
S. 148 (not reproduced): entitlement of pensioners to Christmas bonus.
S. 157 (not reproduced) rates of statutory sick pay.
S. 158: recovery by employers of amounts paid by way of statutory sick pay.
S. 159: power of Secretary of State to substitute provisions for s. 158(2).
S. 174: "the Administration Act" means SSAA 1992.
SSAA 1992, s. 141: annual review of contributions.

SSAA 1992, s. 143: power to alter contributions with a view to adjusting National Insurance Fund.
SSAA 1992, s. 145: power to alter primary and secondary contributions.
SSAA 1992, s. 146: power to alter number of secondary earnings brackets.
SSAA 1992, s. 162: destination of contributions.

SHORT TITLE, COMMENCEMENT AND EXTENT

177 Short title, commencement and extent

177(1) This Act may be cited as the Social Security Contributions and Benefits Act 1992.

177(2) This Act is to be read, where appropriate, with the Administration Act and the Consequential Provisions Act.

177(3) The enactments consolidated by this Act are repealed, in consequence of the consolidation, by the Consequential Provisions Act.

177(4) Except as provided in Schedule 4 to the Consequential Provisions Act, this Act shall come into force on 1st July 1992.

177(5) The following provisions extend to Northern Ireland–
section 16 and Schedule 2;
section 116(2); and
this section.

177(6) Except as provided by this section, this Act does not extend to Northern Ireland.

Cross references – S. 174: references to Acts.

SCHEDULES

SCHEDULE 1 – SUPPLEMENTARY PROVISIONS RELATING TO CONTRIBUTIONS OF CLASSES 1, 1A, 1B, 2, 3 and 3A

Section 1(4)

History – In heading to Sch. 1, the words ", 3 and 3A" substituted for the words "and 3" by PA 2014, s. 25 and Sch. 15, para. 12, with effect from 12 October 2015 (2015/1475, art. 3).
In heading to Sch. 1, the words "1B," inserted by SSA 1998, s. 86(1) and Sch. 7, para. 77(1), with effect from 6 April 1999 by virtue of SI 1998/2209 (C. 47), art. 2(c) and Sch., Pt. III.

CLASS 1 CONTRIBUTIONS WHERE EARNER EMPLOYED IN MORE THAN ONE EMPLOYMENT

1(1) For the purposes of determining whether Class 1 contributions are payable in respect of earnings paid to an earner in a given week and, if so, the amount of the contributions–

(a) all earnings paid to him or for his benefit in that week in respect of one or more employed earner's employments under the same employer shall, except as may be provided by regulations, be aggregated and treated as a single payment of earnings in respect of one such employment; and

(b) earnings paid to him or for his benefit in that week by different persons in respect of different employed earner's employments shall in prescribed circumstances be aggregated and treated as a single payment for earnings in respect of one such employment;

and regulations may provide that the provisions of this sub-paragraph shall have effect in cases prescribed by the regulations as if for any reference to a week there were substituted a reference to a period prescribed by the regulations.

1(2) [Omitted by PA 2014, s. 24 and Sch. 13, para. 54.]

1(3) [Omitted by PA 2014, s. 24 and Sch. 13, para. 54.]

1(4) [Repealed by WRPA 1999, s. 84(1), Sch. 12, para. 78(4) and s. 88, Sch. 13, Pt. VI.]

1(5) [Repealed by WRPA 1999, s. 84(1), Sch. 12, para. 78(4) and s. 88, Sch. 13, Pt. VI.]

1(6) [Omitted by PA 2014, s. 24 and Sch. 13, para. 54.]

1(7) Where any single payment of earnings is made in respect of two or more employed earner's employments under different employers, liability for Class 1 contributions shall be determined by apportioning the payment to such one or more of the employers as may be prescribed, and treating a part apportioned to any employer as a separate payment of earnings by him.

1(8) Where earnings are aggregated under sub-paragraph (1)(b) above, liability (if any) for the secondary contribution shall be apportioned, in such manner as may be prescribed, between the secondary contributors concerned.

1(8A) Regulations under any provision of this paragraph shall be made by the Inland Revenue.

1(9) [Omitted by PA 2014, s. 24 and Sch. 13, para. 54.]

1(10) [Omitted by PA 2014, s. 24 and Sch. 13, para. 54.]

1(11) [Omitted by PA 2014, s. 24 and Sch. 13, para. 54.]

Prospective amendments – Para. 1(3) (as amended by NICA 2008, Sch. 1, para. 6(2) and PA 2007, Sch. 4, para. 45(2)) amended by NICA 2008, s. 4 and Sch. 1, para. 6(3) and (as appropriate) repealed by s. 4 and Sch. 2, with effect from the day appointed by an order under PA 2007, s. 30(2) for the coming into force of PA 2007, Sch. 4, para. 45(2), as follows:

- omit para. (ba);
- in para. (c) omit the words "if some of the aggregated earnings are attributable to COSRS service,";
- in para. (c) substitute the words "the upper accrual point" for the words "the current upper earnings limit";
- in para. (ca) omit the words "if paragraph (c) applies" and ", when added to the APPS earnings or the part attributable to COMPS service (or both),";

Para. 1(3)(a) and (b) repealed by PA 2007, s. 15(3)(a), s. 27(2), and Sch. 4, para. 45(2)(a) and Sch. 7, Pt. 7, with effect from a date to be appointed, PA 2007, s. 30(2)(b).
In para. 1(3)(c) the words "to such part of the aggregated earnings attributable to COSRS service as exceeds the current primary threshold and does not exceed the current upper earnings limit" substituted for (i) and (ii) by PA 2007, s. 15(3)(a), and Sch. 4, para. 45(2)(b), with effect from a date to be appointed, PA 2007, s. 30(2)(b).
In para. 1(3)(d) the words "part attributable to COSRS service" substituted for "part or parts attributable to COMPS or COSRS service" by PA 2007, s. 15(3)(a), and Sch. 4, para. 45(2)(c), with effect from a date to be appointed, PA 2007, s. 30(2)(b).
Para. 1(6)(a) and (b) repealed by PA 2007, s. 15(3)(a), s. 27(2) and Sch. 4, para. 45(3) and Sch. 7, Pt. 7, with effect from a date to be appointed, PA 2007, s. 30(2)(b).
In para. 1(9), the definition of "COMPS service" repealed by PA 2007, s. 15(3)(a), and Sch. 4, para. 45(4), with effect from a date to be appointed, PA 2007, s. 30(2)(b).

History – In para. 1 the words "secondary threshold" and the words "primary threshold" substituted, wherever the terms occur, by WRPA 1999, s. 84(1), Sch. 12, para. 78(2), (3) with effect from 6 April 2000 (SI 2000/1047, art. 4(d)).
Para 1(2), (3), (6), and (9)–(11) omitted by PA 2014, s. 24 and Sch. 13, para. 54, with effect from 6 April 2016 (as not brought into force by any earlier order under PA 2014, s. 56(1)).
Para. 1(2) substituted and Sch. 1, para. 1(3), (6) amended by SSA 1998, s. 86(1) and Sch. 7, para. 77(2), (3), (4), with effect from 6 April 1999 (SI 1999/418).
In para. 1(2)(a) words "attributable to section 8(1)(a) above" inserted by NICA 2002, s. 6 and Sch. 1, para. 13 with effect for 2003–04 and subsequent tax years.
In para. 1(3)(b), the words "the upper accrual point" substituted for the words "the current upper earnings limit" (twice) by NICA 2008, s. 4 and Sch. 1, para. 6(2), with effect in relation to 2009–10 and subsequent tax years.
Para. 1(3)(ba) inserted by NICA 2008, s. 4 and Sch. 1, para. 6(2), with effect in relation to 2009–10 and subsequent tax years.
In para. 1(3)(c), the words "the upper accrual point" substituted for the words "the current upper earnings limit" (twice) by NICA 2008, s. 4 and Sch. 1, para. 6(2), with effect in relation to 2009–10 and subsequent tax years.
Para. 1(3)(ca) inserted by NICA 2008, s. 4 and Sch. 1, para. 6(2), with effect in relation to 2009–10 and subsequent tax years.
Para. 1(11) inserted by NICA 2008, s. 4 and Sch. 1, para. 6(4), with effect in relation to 2009–10 and subsequent tax years.
In para. 1(3) words "attributable to section 8(1)(a) above" inserted by NICA 2002, s. 6 and Sch. 1, para. 13 with effect for 2003–04 and subsequent tax years.
In para. 1(3) words "main primary percentage" substituted in each place by NICA 2002, s. 6 and Sch. 1, para. 13 with effect for 2003–04 and subsequent tax years.
Para. 1(3) and (6) substituted and para. 1(9) inserted by Pensions Act 1995, s. 148, with effect from 6 April 1996 SI 1996/778, art. 2(4), Sch., Pt. IV. Until the principal appointed day, s. 148(3), (6), (9) have effect with modifications as set out in Pensions Act 1995, s. 148(5). On and after the principal appointed day, s. 148(3), (6), (9) have effect as set out above. The principal appointed day is 6 April 1997 by virtue of SI 1996/778, art. 2(7).
Para. 1(4) and 1(5) repealed by WRPA 1999, s. 84(1), Sch. 12, para. 78(4) and s. 88, Sch. 13, Pt. VI with effect from 6 April 2000 (SI 2000/1047, art. 4(d), (e)).
Para. 1(8A) inserted by SSC(TF)A 1999, s. 2; Sch. 3, para. 31 with effect from 1 April 1999 (SI 1999/527).
Para. 1(10) inserted by WRPA 1999, s. 84(1), Sch. 12, para. 78(5) with effect from 6 April 2000 (SI 2000/1047, art. 4(d)).

Derivations – Para. 1(1): SSA 1975, s. 1(4), Sch. 1, para. 1(1); SS(MP)A 1977, s. 1(3).
Para. 1(2): SSA 1975, s. 1(4), Sch. 1, para. 1(1A).
Para. 1(3), (4): SSA 1975, s. 1(4), Sch. 1, para. 1(1B), (1C).
Para. 1(5): SSA 1986, s. 74(5).
Para. 1(6): SSA 1975, s. 1(4), Sch. 1, para. 1(1D).
Para. 1(7), (8): SSA 1975, s. 1(4), Sch. 1, para. 1(2), (3).

Cross references – SI 2001/1004, reg. 10, 11: earnings limits and thresholds and prescribed equivalents.
SI 2001/1004, reg. 13: references in para. 1 to "week" substituted by references to "earnings period" where whole or part of person's earnings from employed earner's employment not paid weekly.

EARNINGS NOT PAID AT NORMAL INTERVALS

2 Regulations made by the Inland Revenue may, for the purposes of Class 1 contributions, make provision as to the intervals at which payments of earnings are to be treated as made.

History – Para. 2 amended with the insertion of a reference to the Inland Revenue by SSC(TF)A 1999, s. 2; Sch. 3, para. 31 from 1 April 1999 (SI 1999/527).

Derivations – SSA 1975, s. 1(4), Sch. 1, para. 2.

METHOD OF PAYING CLASS 1 CONTRIBUTIONS

3(1) Where earnings are paid to an employed earner and in respect of that payment liability arises for primary and secondary Class 1 contributions, the secondary contributor shall (except in prescribed circumstances), as well as being liable for any secondary contribution of his own, be liable in the first instance to pay also the earner's primary contribution or a prescribed part of the earner's primary contribution, on behalf of and to the exclusion of the earner; and for the purposes of this Act and the Administration Act contributions paid by the secondary contributor on behalf of the earner shall be taken to be contributions paid by the earner.

3(2) [Repealed by CSPSSA 2000, s. 77(1); s. 85(1), Sch. 9, Pt. VIII(1).]

3(3) A secondary contributor shall be entitled, subject to and in accordance with regulations, to recover from an earner the amount of any primary Class 1 contribution paid or to be paid by him on behalf of the earner; and, subject to sub-paragraphs (3A) to (5) below but notwithstanding any other provision in any enactment, regulations under this sub-paragraph shall provide for recovery to be made by deduction from the earner's earnings, and for it not to be made in any other way.

3(3A) Sub-paragraph (3B) applies where a person ("the employee") who is employed by a particular employer ("the employer") receives earnings in a form other than money ("non-monetary earnings") from the employer in a tax year.

3(3B) If and to the extent that regulations so provide, the employer may recover from the employee, in the prescribed manner, any primary Class 1 contributions paid or to be paid by him on the employee's behalf in respect of those earnings.

3(4) Sub-paragraph (5) below applies in a case where–

(a) a person (**"the employee"**) ceases in a particular tax year ("the cessation year") to be employed by a particular employer (**"the employer"**); and

(b) the employee receives from the employer in the cessation year, after the cessation of the employment, or in the next year non-monetary earnings.

3(5) If and to the extent that regulations so provide, the employer may recover from the employee in such manner as may be prescribed any primary Class 1 contributions paid or to be paid by him on the employee's behalf in respect of–

(a) the non-monetary earnings mentioned in sub-paragraph (4) above.

3(6) Regulations under any provision of this paragraph shall be made by the Inland Revenue.

History – In para. 3(1) words "or a prescribed part of the earner's primary contribution" inserted by NICA 2002, s. 6 and Sch. 1, para. 13 with effect for 2003–04 and subsequent tax years.
In para. 3(1) the words "any secondary contribution of his own" substituted by SSA 1998, s. 86(1) and Sch. 7, para. 77(5), from 6 April 1999 (SI 1999/418).
Para. 3(2) repealed by CSPSSA 2000, s. 77(1); s. 85(1), Sch. 9, Pt. VIII(1); with effect from 6 April 2000.
In para. 3(3), the words "sub-paragraphs (3A) to (5)" substituted for the words "sub-paragraph (4)" by NICSPA 2004, s. 1(2) with effect from 1 September 2004 (by virtue of SI 2004/1943, reg. 2).
In para. 3(3), the words from "and, subject to" to "in any enactment" substituted by SSA 1998, s. 55, with effect from 8 September 1998 (SI 1998/2209).
Para. 3(3A) and (3B) inserted by NICSPA 2004, s. 1(3) with effect from 1 September 2004 (by virtue of SI 2004/1943, reg. 2).
In para. 3(4)(b) the words "or in the next year non-monetary earnings" substituted for the words "earnings in a form other than money (non-monetary earnings)" by NICSPA 2004, s. 1(4) with effect from 1 September 2004 (by virtue of SI 2004/1943, reg. 2).
Para. 3(4) inserted by SAA 1998, s. 55, with effect from 8 September 1998 (SI 1998/2209).
In para. 3(5) the word "or" at the end of para. 3(5)(a) and the text reproduced below omitted by NICSPA 2004, s. 1(5) and repealed by s. 12 and Sch. 2, with effect from 1 September 2004 (by virtue of SI 2004/1943, reg. 2 and 6).
Para. 3(5) inserted by SAA 1998, s. 55, with effect from 8 September 1998 (SI 1998/2209).
Para. 3(6) inserted by SSC(TF)A 1999, s. 2; Sch. 3, para. 33 with effect from 1 April 1999 (SI 1999/527).

Derivations – Para. 3(1) (as originally enacted): SSA 1975, s. 1(4), Sch. 1, para. 3(1).
Para. 3(2) (as originally enacted): SSA 1975, s. 1(4), Sch. 1, para. 3(2).
Para. 3(3) (as originally enacted): SSA 1975, s. 1(4), Sch. 1, para. 3(3).

Cross references – S. 174: "the Administration Act" means SSAA 1992.
SSAA 1992, s. 114: criminal offences relating to contributions.
SI 2001/1004, reg. 86: para. 3(1) disapplied in relation to culpable primary contributors and to secondary contributors/employers exempt from enforcement of Act or liability under it.

Notes – Manner in which earner's liability falls to be discharged under para. 3 unaffected by actual liability of earner (to primary contribution) and of secondary contributor (to secondary contribution) – see s. 6(4) above.

PROHIBITION ON RECOVERY OF EMPLOYER'S CONTRIBUTIONS

3A(1) Subject to sub-paragraph (2) below, a person who is or has been liable to pay any secondary Class 1 or any Class 1A or Class 1B contributions shall not–

(a) make, from earnings paid by him, any deduction in respect of any such contributions for which he or any other person is or has been liable;

(b) otherwise recover any such contributions (directly or indirectly) from any person who is or has been a relevant earner; or

(c) enter into any agreement with any person for the making of any such deduction or otherwise for the purpose of so recovering any such contributions.

3A(2) Sub-paragraph (1) above does not apply to the extent that an agreement between–
(a) a secondary contributor, and
(b) any person ("the earner") in relation to whom the secondary contributor is, was or will be such a contributor in respect of the contributions to which the agreement relates,
allows the secondary contributor to recover (whether by deduction or otherwise) the whole or any part of any secondary Class 1 contribution payable in respect of relevant employment income of that earner.

3A(2A) But an agreement in respect of relevant employment income is to be disregarded for the purposes of sub-paragraph (2) to the extent that it relates to–
(a) relevant employment income which is employment income of the earner by virtue of Chapter 3A of Part 7 of ITEPA 2003 (employment income: securities with artificially depressed market value), or
(b) any contribution, or any part of any contribution, liability to which arises as a result of regulations being given retrospective effect by virtue of section 4B(2) (earnings: power to make retrospective provision in consequence of retrospective tax legislation).

3A(2B) For the purposes of sub-paragraphs (2) and (2A) "relevant employment income", in relation to the earner, means–
(a) an amount that counts as employment income of the earner under section 426 of ITEPA 2003 (restricted securities: charge on certain post-acquisition events),
(b) an amount that counts as employment income of the earner under section 438 of that Act (convertible securities: charge on certain post-acquisition events), or
(c) a gain that is treated as remuneration derived from the earner's employment by virtue of section 4(4)(a) above.

3A(3) Sub-paragraph (2) above does not authorise any recovery (whether by deduction or otherwise)–
(a) in pursuance of any agreement entered into before 19th May 2000; or
(b) in respect of any liability to a contribution arising before the day of the passing of the Child Support, Pensions and Social Security Act 2000.

3A(4) In this paragraph–
"agreement" includes any arrangement or understanding (whether or not legally enforceable); and
"relevant earner", in relation to a person who is or has been liable to pay any contributions, means an earner in respect of whom he is or has been so liable.

History – Para. 3A inserted by CSPSSA 2000, s. 77(2) with effect from 28 July 2000 (date of Royal Assent).
In para. 3A(2) the words "relevant employment income of that earner" substituted for the words "a gain that is treated as remuneration derived from that earner's employment by virtue of section 4(4)(a) above" by NICSPA 2004, s. 3(2)(a) with effect in relation to agreements entered into from 1 September 2004 (by virtue of SI 2004/1943, reg. 2) which are in respect of post-commencement employment income and in relation to elections made after 1 September 2004 (by virtue of SI 2004/1943, reg. 2).
Para. 3A(2A)(a) created from existing content and para. 3A(2A)(b) inserted by NICA 2006, s. 5(2), with effect in relation to agreements and elections whether entered into or made before, or on or after, 30 March 2006 (including those entered into or made before 2 December 2004).
Para. 3A(2A) and (2B) inserted by NICSPA 2004, s. 3(2)(b) with effect in relation to agreements entered into from 1 September 2004 (by virtue of SI 2004/1943, reg. 2) which are in respect of post-commencement employment income and in relation to elections made after 1 September 2004 (by virtue of SI 2004/1943, reg. 2).

Cross references – ITEPA 2003, s. 428A: relief for secondary Class 1 contributions met by employee (restrictive securities).
ITEPA 2003, s. 442A: relief for secondary Class 1 contributions met by employee (convertible securities).
ITEPA 2003, s. 481: amounts deductible from charge on employee on gain on exercise, etc. of share option include certain amounts in respect of the gain recovered in accordance with an agreement effective under para. 3A.

TRANSFER OF LIABILITY TO BE BORNE BY EARNER

3B(1) This paragraph applies where–
(a) an election is jointly made by–
  (i) a secondary contributor, and
  (ii) a person ("the earner") in relation to whom the secondary contributor is or will be such a contributor in respect of contributions on relevant employment income of the earner, for the whole or a part of any liability of the secondary contributor to contributions on any such income to be transferred to the earner; and
(b) the election is one in respect of which the Inland Revenue have, before it was made, given by notice to the secondary contributor their approval to both–
  (i) the form of the election; and
  (ii) the arrangements made in relation to the proposed election for securing that liability transferred by the election will be met.

In para.3B(9) the words "that is notified to the tribunal, the tribunal may" substituted for the words "the Special Commissioners may"; and in para. (b) the words "tribunal thinks" substituted by SI 2009/56, art. 3 and Sch. 1, para. 169(4), with effect from 1 April 2009, subject to transitional and saving provisions in SI 2009/56, Sch. 3.
Para. 3B(10) substituted by NICSPA 2004, s. 3(3)(g) with effect in relation to agreements entered into from 1 September 2004 (by virtue of SI 2004/1943, reg. 2) that are in respect of post-commencement employment income and with effect in relation to elections made after 1 September 2004 (by virtue of SI 2004/1943, reg. 2).
Para. 3B(13) omitted by NICSPA 2004, s. 3(3)(h) and repealed by NICSPA 2004, s. 12 and Sch. 2 with effect in relation to agreements entered into from 1 September 2004 (by virtue of SI 2004/1943, reg. 2) that are in respect of post-commencement employment income and with effect in relation to elections made after 1 September 2004 (by virtue of SI 2004/1943, reg. 2 and 6).
Para. 3B(14) substituted by SI 2009/56, art. 3 and Sch. 1, para. 169(5), with effect from 1 April 2009, subject to transitional and saving provisions in SI 2009/56, Sch. 3.

Cross references – NICSPA 2004, s. 3(5): meaning of post-commencement employment income.
ITEPA 2003, s. 428A: relief for secondary Class 1 contributions met by employee (restrictive securities).
ITEPA 2003, s. 442A: relief for secondary Class 1 contributions met by employee (convertible securities).
ITEPA 2003, s. 481: amounts deductible from charge on employee on gain on exercise, etc. of share option include liability in respect of the gain transferred in accordance with an election under para. 3B.

Statutory instruments – SI 2007/1175: partly made under para. 3B(11).

Other material – HMRC template for transfers of NIC to a single employee is available at: https://www.gov.uk/government/uploads/system/uploads/attachment_data/file/367012/Single_NICs_joint_election.pdf.
HMRC template for transfers of NIC to multiple employees is available at: https://www.gov.uk/government/uploads/system/uploads/attachment_data/file/367014/2_part_NICs_joint_election.pdf.

GENERAL PROVISIONS AS TO CLASS 1 CONTRIBUTIONS

4 Regulations made by the Inland Revenue may, in relation to Class 1 contributions, make provision–

(a) for calculating the amounts payable according to a scale prepared from time to time by the Inland Revenue or otherwise adjusting them so as to avoid fractional amounts or otherwise facilitate computation;

(b) for requiring that the liability in respect of a payment made in a tax week, in so far as the liability depends on any conditions as to a person's age or retirement, shall be determined as at the beginning of the week or as at the end of it;

(c) for securing that liability is not avoided or reduced by a person following in the payment of earnings any practice which is abnormal for the employment in respect of which the earnings are paid; and

(d) without prejudice to sub-paragraph (c) above, for enabling the Inland Revenue, where they are satisfied as to the existence of any practice in respect of the payment of earnings whereby the incidence of Class 1 contributions is avoided or reduced by means of irregular or unequal payments, to give directions for securing that such contributions are payable as if that practice were not followed.

History – Para. 4 amended by SSC(TF)A 1999, s. 2; Sch. 3, para. 34 from 1 April 1999 (SI 1999/527) and para. 4(a), (d) amended, with the substitution of references to the Inland Revenue, by SSC(TF)A 1999, s. 1; Sch. 1, para. 16 from 1 April 1999 (SI 1999/527).

Derivations – SSA 1975, s. 1(4), Sch. 1, para. 4.

Cross references – Interpretation Act 1978, Sch. 1: "Secretary of State" means one of HM's Principal Secretaries of State.

CLASS 1A CONTRIBUTIONS

5 Regulations made by the Inland Revenue may–

(a) make provision for calculating the amount of Class 1A contributions so as to avoid fractional amounts;

(b) modify section 10 above in relation to cases where something is provided or made available by reason of two or more employed earner's employments under different employers.

History – Para. 5 amended, with the insertion of a reference to the Inland Revenue, by SSC(TF)A 1999, s. 2; Sch. 3, para. 34 from 1 April 1999 (SI 1999/527).
In para. 5(b) the words "something is provided or made available" substituted by CSPSSA 2000, s. 74(4) with effect from 6 April 2000 (s. 74(8)).
Para. 5 substituted by SSA 1998, s. 86(1) and Sch. 7, para. 77(6), with effect from 8 September 1998 by virtue of SI 1998/2209 (C. 47), art. 2(a) and Sch., Pt. I.

Derivations – (as originally enacted) SSA 1975, s. 1(4), Sch. 1, para. 4A.

Cross references – S. 10: Class 1A contributions

CLASS 1B CONTRIBUTIONS

5A Regulations made by the Inland Revenue may make provision for calculating the amount of Class 1B contributions so as to avoid fractional amounts.

History – Para. 5A inserted by SSA 1998, s. 86(1) and Sch. 7, para. 77(7), with effect from 8 September 1998 for the purpose only of authorising the making of regulations or orders, and 6 April 1999 for all other purposes (SI 1998/2209 (C. 47), art. 2(b), (c) and Sch., Pt. II, III).
Para. 5A amended, with the insertion of a reference to the Inland Revenue, by SSC(TF)A 1999, s. 2 and Sch. 3, para. 34 from 1 April 1999 (SI 1999/527).

POWER TO COMBINE COLLECTION OF CONTRIBUTIONS WITH TAX

6(1) Regulations made by of the Inland Revenue may–

(a) provide for Class 1, Class 1A, Class 1B or Class 2 contributions to be paid, accounted for and recovered in a similar manner to income tax in relation to which PAYE regulations have effect;

(b) apply or extend with or without modification in relation to such contributions any of the provisions of the Income Tax Acts or of PAYE regulations;

(c) make provision for the appropriation of the payments made by any person between his liabilities in respect of income tax and contributions.

6(2) Without prejudice to the generality of sub-paragraph (1) above, the provision that may be made by virtue of paragraph (a) of that sub-paragraph includes in relation to Class 1, Class 1A or Class 1B contributions–

(a) provision for requiring the payment of interest on sums due in respect of Class 1, Class 1A or Class 1B contributions which are not paid by the due date, for determining the date (being, in the case of Class 1 contributions, not less than 14 days after the end of the tax year in respect of which the sums are due) from which such interest is to be calculated and for enabling the repayment or remission of such interest;

(b) provision for requiring the payment of interest on sums due in respect of Class 1, Class 1A or Class 1B contributions which fall to be repaid and for determining the date from which such interest is to be calculated;

(c) provision for, or in connection with, the imposition and recovery of penalties in relation to any returns required to be made which relate to Class 1, Class 1A or Class 1B contributions, but subject to sub-paragraph (7) and paragraph 7 below;

and any reference to contributions or income tax in paragraph (b) or (c) of sub-paragraph (1) above shall be construed as including a reference to any interest or penalty in respect of contributions or income tax, as the case may be.

6(3) The rate of interest applicable for any purpose of this paragraph shall be the rate from time to time prescribed for that purpose under section 178 of the Finance Act 1989.

6(4) Where–

(a) a decision relating to contributions falls to be made under or by virtue of section 8, 10 or 11 of the Social Security Contributions (Transfer of Functions, etc.) Act 1999; and

(b) the decision will affect a person's liability for, or the amount of, any interest due in respect of those contributions,

regulations under sub-paragraph (1) above shall not require any such interest to be paid until the decision has been made.

6(4A) Regulations under sub-paragraph (1) above shall not require the payment of interest on a sum due in respect of a Class 1B contribution if a relevant tax appeal has been brought but not finally determined; and "a relevant tax appeal" means an appeal against a determination as to the amount of income tax in respect of which the person liable to pay the Class 1B contribution is accountable in accordance with the relevant PAYE settlement agreement.

6(4B) Interest required to be paid, by virtue of sub-paragraph (2)(a) or (b) above, by regulations under sub-paragraph (1) above shall be paid without any deduction of income tax and shall not be taken into account in computing any income, profits or losses for any tax purposes.

6(4C) Interest payable under section 101 of the Finance Act 2009 (late payment interest on sums due to HMRC) on sums due in respect of Class 1 contributions is not to be taken into account in computing any income, profits or losses for any tax purposes.

6(5) The Secretary of State may by regulations made with the concurrence of the Inland Revenue make such provision as the Secretary of State considers expedient in consequence of any provision made by or under section 4A, 159A or 167 above.

6(6) Provision made in regulations under sub-paragraph (5) above may in particular require the inclusion–

(a) in returns, certificates and other documents; or

(b) in any other form of record;

which the regulations require to be kept or produced or to which those regulations otherwise apply, of such particulars relating to relevant payments or benefits within the meaning of section 4A above or (as the case may be) to statutory sick pay, statutory maternity pay or deductions or payments made by virtue of section 167(1) above as may be prescribed by those regulations.

6(7) Section 98 of the Taxes Management Act 1970 shall apply in relation to regulations made under sub-paragraph (1) or (5) as it applies in relation to PAYE regulations.

METHOD OF COMPUTING PROFITS OR GAINS

2 Subject to the following paragraphs, Class 4 contributions shall be payable in respect of the full amount of all profits–

(a) which are the profits of any relevant trade, profession or vocation which is not carried on wholly outside the United Kingdom, and

(b) which are chargeable to income tax under Chapter 2 of Part 2 of ITTOIA 2005.

History – Para. 2(a) and (b) substituted for words "profits or gains of any relevant trade, profession or vocation chargeable to income tax under Case I or II of Schedule D" by virtue of ITTOIA 2005, s. 882 and Sch. 1, para. 422(3) which, in accordance with ITTOIA 2005, s. 883, have effect, for income tax purposes, for tax year 2005–06 and subsequent tax years.

In para. 2, words were omitted by CAA 2001, Sch. 2, para. 75(2) and repealed by CAA 2001, s. 580 and Sch. 4 for income tax chargeable periods ending on or after 6 April 2001, those words having previously been substituted by SSA 1998, s. 59(2), with effect from 8 September 1998 by virtue of SI 1998/2209 (C. 47), art. 2(a) and Schedule, Pt. I.

Derivations – SSA 1975, s. 9(4), Sch. 2, para. 2.

Cross references – ICTA 1988, s. 18: "profits or gains … chargeable to income tax under Case I or II of Schedule D" explained.

HMRC interpretations – IRInt. 44: deduction for personal pension contributions in arriving at Class 4 profit.

RELIEFS

3(1) For the purposes of computing the amount of profits in respect of which Class 4 contributions are payable, relief shall be available under, and in the manner provided by, the following provisions of ITA 2007–

(a) sections 64 and 72 (set-off of trade losses against general income), but only where loss arises from activities the profits of which would be brought into computation for the purposes of Class 4 contributions;

(b) [repealed by SSA 1998, s. 59(3), 86(2) and Sch. 8;]

(c) section 83 (carry-forward of loss against subsequent profits); and

(d) section 89 (carry-back of terminal losses).

3(2) The following relief provisions shall not apply, that is to say–

(a) Chapter I of Part VII of the Act of 1988 and Chapters 2 and 3 of Part 3 and sections 457, 458 and 459 of ITA 2007 (personal reliefs);

(b) section 383 of ITA 2007 (relief for payment of interest);

(c) [omitted by ITA 2007, s. 1027 and Sch. 1, para. 290(3)(b)(iv), and repealed by s. 1031 and Sch. 3, Pt. 1;]

(d) sections 88 and 94 of ITA 2007 (treatment of interest as a loss for purposes of carry-forward or carry-back);

(e) [repealed by FA 1996, s. 147(2) and s. 205 and Sch. 41, Pt. V(15).]

(f) sections 619 and 620 (premiums or other consideration under annuity contracts and trust schemes); and

(g) section 639 (personal pension contributions).

3(3) [Omitted by NICA 2014, s. 17(1)(a).]

3(4) Where in the year 1990–1991 or any subsequent year of assessment for which a person claims and is allowed relief by virtue of sub-paragraph (1) above there falls to be made in computing his net income for income tax purposes a deduction in respect of any loss in any relevant trade, profession or vocation–

(a) the amount of the deduction shall, as far as may be, be treated for the purpose of the charge to Class 4 contributions as reducing the person's profits for that year of any relevant trade, profession or vocation, and

(b) any excess shall be treated for that purpose as reducing such profits for subsequent years (being deducted as far as may be from those of the immediately following year, whether or not the person claims or is entitled to claim relief under this paragraph for that year, and, so far as it cannot be so deducted, then from those of the next year, and so on).

3(5) Relief shall be allowed, in respect of–

(a) [omitted by ITA 2007, s. 1027 and Sch. 1, para. 290(3)(d)(i), and repealed by s. 1031 and Sch. 3, Pt. 1;]

(b) payments under section 383 of ITA 2007 (relief for payment of interest), being payments for which relief from income tax is or can be given,

(c) payments from which a sum representing income tax must be deducted under–

  (i) section 900(2) of ITA 2007 (commercial payments made by individuals),

  (ii) section 903(5) of that Act (patent royalties), or

(iii) section 906(5) of that Act (certain royalties etc where usual place of abode of owner is abroad),

(d) so much of any payment from which a sum representing income tax must be deducted under section 910(2) of ITA 2007 (proceeds of a sale of patent rights: payments to non-UK residents) as is equal to the amount referred to in that provision as "the chargeable amount", or

(e) a payment from which a sum representing income tax must be deducted as a result of a direction under section 944(2) of ITA 2007 (tax avoidance: certain payments to non-UK residents)

so far as the payment is incurred wholly or exclusively for the purposes of any relevant trade, profession or vocation, by way of deduction from or set-off against profits chargeable to Class 4 contributions for the year in which the payments are made; and, in the case of any insufficiency of the profits or gains of that year, the payments shall be carried forward and deducted from or set off against the profits of any subsequent year (being deducted or set off as far as may be from or against the profits of the immediately following year, whether or not relief can be claimed under this paragraph for that year, and so far as it cannot be so deducted, from or against those of the next year, and so on).

History – In para. 3(1) the words "ITA 2007" substituted by ITA 2007, s. 1027 and Sch. 1, para. 290(3)(a)(i), with effect from 6 April 2007.
In para. 3(1), in opening sentence, words "or gains" omitted by ITTOIA 2005, s. 882 and Sch. 1, para. 422(4), and repealed by ITTOIA 2005, s. 884 and Sch. 3, which, in accordance with ITTOIA 2005, s. 883, have effect, for income tax purposes, for tax year 2005–06 and subsequent tax years.
In para. 3(1)(a) the words "sections 64 and 72" substituted by ITA 2007, s. 1027 and Sch. 1, para. 290(3)(a)(ii), with effect from 6 April 2007.
In para. 3(1)(a), words "or gains" omitted by ITTOIA 2005, s. 882 and Sch. 1, para. 422(4), and repealed by ITTOIA 2005, s. 884 and Sch. 3, which, in accordance with ITTOIA 2005, s. 883, have effect, for income tax purposes, for tax year 2005–06 and subsequent tax years.
Para. 3(1)(b) repealed by SSA 1998, s. 59(3), s. 86(2) and Sch. 8, with effect from 8 September 1998 by virtue of SI 1998/2209 (C. 47), art. 2(a) and Sch., Pt. I.
In para. 3(1)(c) the words "section 83" substituted by ITA 2007, s. 1027 and Sch. 1, para. 290(3)(a)(iii), with effect from 6 April 2007.
In para. 3(1)(d) the words "section 89" substituted by ITA 2007, s. 1027 and Sch. 1, para. 290(3)(a)(iv), with effect from 6 April 2007.
In para. 3(2) the words "of the Act of 1988" omitted by ITA 2007, s. 1027 and Sch. 1, para. 290(3)(b)(i), and repealed by s. 1031 and Sch. 3, Pt. 1, with effect from 6 April 2007.
In para. 3(2)(a) the words "of the Act of 1988 and Chapters 2 and 3 of Part 3 and sections 457, 458 and 459 of ITA 2007" inserted by ITA 2007, s. 1027 and Sch. 1, para. 290(3)(b)(ii), with effect from 6 April 2007.
In para. 3(2)(b) the words "section 383 of ITA 2007" substituted by ITA 2007, s. 1027 and Sch. 1, para. 290(3)(b)(iii), with effect from 6 April 2007.
Para. 3(2)(c) omitted by ITA 2007, s. 1027 and Sch. 1, para. 290(3)(b)(iv), and repealed by s. 1031 and Sch. 3, Pt. 1, with effect from 6 April 2007.
In para. 3(2)(d) the words "sections 88 and 94 of ITA 2007" substituted by ITA 2007, s. 1027 and Sch. 1, para. 290(3)(b)(v), with effect from 6 April 2007.
Para. 3(2)(e) (which referred to s. 617(5)) repealed by FA 1996, s. 147(2) and s. 205 and Sch. 41, Pt. V(15), with effect in relation to 1996–97 and subsequent tax years.
Para. 3(2)(g) and word "and" immediately preceding it inserted, and word "and" which formerly appeared at end of s. 3(2)(e) omitted, by SS(C)A 1994, s. 3, deemed to have had effect from 1 July 1992.
Para. 3(3) omitted by NICA 2014, s. 17(1)(a), with effect for 2014–15 and subsequent tax years.
In para. 3(4)the words "net income" substituted by ITA 2007, s. 1027 and Sch. 1, para. 290(3)(c), with effect from 6 April 2007.
In para. 3(4)(a), words "or gains" omitted by ITTOIA 2005, s. 882 and Sch. 1, para. 422(4), and repealed by ITTOIA 2005, s. 884 and Sch. 3, which, in accordance with ITTOIA 2005, s. 883, have effect, for income tax purposes, for tax year 2005–06 and subsequent tax years.
In para. 3(4)(b), words "or gains" omitted by ITTOIA 2005, s. 882 and Sch. 1, para. 422(4), and repealed by ITTOIA 2005, s. 884 and Sch. 3, which, in accordance with ITTOIA 2005, s. 883, have effect, for income tax purposes, for tax year 2005–06 and subsequent tax years.
Para. 3(5)(c), (d) and (e) inserted by SI 2010/588, reg. 2(3)(a), with effect for the tax year 2007–08 and subsequent tax years.
In reg. 3(5), the words "so far as the payment is incurred" substituted for the words "so far as incurred" by SI 2010/588, reg. 2(3)(b), with effect for the tax year 2007–08 and subsequent tax years.
Para. 3(5)(a) omitted by ITA 2007, s. 1027 and Sch. 1, para. 290(3)(d)(i), and repealed by s. 1031 and Sch. 3, Pt. 1, with effect from 6 April 2007.
In para. 3(5)(b) the words "section 383 of ITA 2007" substituted by ITA 2007, s. 1027 and Sch. 1, para. 290(3)(d)(ii), with effect from 6 April 2007.
In para. 3(5), words "or gains", in each place where occurring immediately after word "profits", were omitted by ITTOIA 2005, s. 882 and Sch. 1, para. 422(4), and were repealed by ITTOIA 2005, s. 884 and Sch. 3, which, in accordance with ITTOIA 2005, s. 883, have effect, for income tax purposes, for tax year 2005–06 and subsequent tax years.

Derivations – Para. 3(1), (2) (as originally enacted): SSA 1975, s. 9(4), Sch. 2, para. 3(1), (2).
Para. 3(3): SSA 1975, s. 9(4), Sch. 2, para. 3(3).
Para. 3(4): SSA 1975, s. 9(4), Sch. 2, para. 3(3).
Para. 3(5): SSA 1975, s. 9(4), Sch. 2, para. 3(4).

Cross references – ICTA 1988, s. 348: payment out of profits or gains brought into charge to income tax and deduction of tax.
ICTA 1988, s. 349(1): payments not out of profits or gains brought into charge to income tax, and annual interest.
ICTA 1988, s. 353: relief for payments of interest (excluding MIRAS).
ICTA 1988, s. 381: relief for losses in early years of a trade.
ICTA 1988, s. 387: carry forward as losses amounts taxed under ICTA 1988, s. 350.
ICTA 1988, s. 619: exemption from tax in respect of qualifying retirement annuity premiums.
ICTA 1988, s. 620: determination of "qualifying premiums".

PARTNERSHIPS

4(1) Where a trade or profession is carried on by two or more persons jointly, the liability of any one of them in respect of Class 4 contributions shall arise in respect of his share of the profits of that trade or profession (so far as immediately derived by him from carrying it on); and for this purpose his share shall be aggregated with his share of the profits of any other trade, profession or vocation (so far as immediately derived by him from carrying it on or exercising it).

4(2) Where sub-paragraph (1) above applies, the Class 4 contributions for which a person is liable in respect of the profits of the trade or profession carried on jointly (aggregated, where appropriate, as mentioned in that sub-paragraph) shall be charged on him separately.

History – In para. 4(1), words "or gains", in each place where occurring immediately after word "profits", were omitted by ITTOIA 2005, s. 882 and Sch. 1, para. 422(4), and were repealed by ITTOIA 2005, s. 884 and Sch. 3, which, in accordance with ITTOIA 2005, s. 883, have effect, for income tax purposes, for tax year 2005–06 and subsequent tax years.
In para. 4(2), words "or gains", occurring immediately after word "profits", were omitted by ITTOIA 2005, s. 882 and Sch. 1, para. 422(4), and were repealed by ITTOIA 2005, s. 884 and Sch. 3, which, in accordance with ITTOIA 2005, s. 883, have effect, for income tax purposes, for tax year 2005–06 and subsequent tax years.
In para. 4(2), words "shall be charged on him separately" substituted by SSA 1998, s. 59(4), with effect from 8 September 1998 by virtue of SI 1998/2209 (C. 47), art. 2(a) and Sch., Pt. I.

Derivations – SSA 1975, s. 9(4), Sch. 2, para. 5.

Cross references – ICTA 1988, s. 111–115, partnership taxation.

TRUSTEES, ETC.

5 In any circumstances in which apart from this paragraph a person would–

(a) [omitted by FA 2012, s. 220(4)(c)(i),]

(b) by virtue of section 8 of ITTOIA 2005 be assessed and charged to Class 4 contributions in respect of profits received or receivable by him in the capacity of trustee,

such contributions shall not be payable either by him or by any other person.

History – Para. 5(a) and the "or" after it, omitted by FA 2012, s. 222(4)(c)(i), with effect for the tax year 2012–13 and subsequent tax years.
In para. 5(b), the words "Class 4" substituted for "such" by FA 2012, s. 222(4)(c)(ii), with effect for the tax year 2012–13 and subsequent tax years.
In para. 5(a), words "or gains", occurring immediately after word "profits", were omitted by ITTOIA 2005, s. 882 and Sch. 1, para. 422(5)(a), and were repealed by ITTOIA 2005, s. 884 and Sch. 3, which, in accordance with ITTOIA 2005, s. 883, have effect, for income tax purposes, for tax year 2005–06 and subsequent tax years.
In para. 5(b), words "section 8 of ITTOIA 2005" substituted by ITTOIA 2005, s. 882 and Sch. 1, para. 422(5)(b)(i) which, in accordance with ITTOIA 2005, s. 883, have effect, for income tax purposes, for tax year 2005–06 and subsequent tax years.
In para. 5(b), words "or gains", occurring immediately after word "profits", were omitted by ITTOIA 2005, s. 882 and Sch. 1, para. 422(5)(b)(ii), and were repealed by ITTOIA 2005, s. 884 and Sch. 3, which, in accordance with ITTOIA 2005, s. 883, have effect, for income tax purposes, for tax year 2005–06 and subsequent tax years.

Derivations – SSA 1975, s. 9(4), Sch. 2, para. 6.

Cross references – TMA 1970, s. 72; persons chargeable to tax in a representative capacity – trustees etc. of incapacitated persons.
ICTA 1988, s. 59: persons chargeable to income tax under Sch. D.

OTHER PROVISIONS

6(1) Section 101 of the Finance Act 2009 (late payment interest on sums due to HMRC) shall apply in relation to any amount due in respect of Class 4 contributions as it applies in relation to income tax; and section 102 of the Finance Act 2009 (repayment interest on sums to be paid by HMRC) shall, with the necessary modifications, apply in relation to Class 4 contributions as it applies in relation to income tax.

6(2) [Repealed by SSC(TF)A 1999, s. 3(6) and s. 26(3); Sch. 10, Pt. I.]

History – In para. 6(1), the words "Section 101 of the Finance Act 2009 (late payment interest on sums due to HMRC)" substituted for the words "Section 86 of the Taxes Management Act 1970 (interest on overdue tax)" by SI 2011/702, art. 9(a), with effect from 31 October 2011.
In para. 6(1), the words "section 102 of the Finance Act 2009 (repayment interest on sums to be paid by HMRC)" substituted for the words "section 824 of the Act of 1988 (repayment supplements)" by SI 2011/702, art. 9(b), with effect from 31 October 2011.
In para. 6(1), the words "Section 86 of the Taxes Management Act 1970 (interest on overdue tax)", and the words " as it applies", substituted by SSA 1998, s. 59(5), with effect from 8 September 1998 by virtue of SI 1998/2209 (C. 47), art. 2(a) and Sch., Pt. I.
Para. 6(2) repealed by SSC(TF)A 1999, s. 3(6) and s. 26(3); Sch. 10, Pt. I, with effect from 1 April 1999 (SI 1999/527).
In para. 6(2), former reference to TMA 1970, s. 88 repealed by SSA 1998, s. 59(6) and s. 86(2); Sch. 8, and the words "that section on income tax" substituted, with effect from 8 September 1998 by virtue of SI 1998/2209 (C. 47), art. 2(a) and Sch., Pt. I.

Derivations – SSA 1975, s. 9(4), Sch. 2, para. 7.

Cross references – S. 16: application of Income Tax Acts and destination of Class 4 contributions.
S. 17(1): Secretary of State may, with concurrence with the Revenue, make regulations excepting persons from Class 4 liability or deferring any person's liability.
S. 18: Class 4 contributions recoverable by regulations under Sch. 2 other than para. 6.
TMA 1970, s. 86: interest on overdue tax.
ICTA 1988, s. 824: repayment supplement: individuals and others.
SS(CP)A 1992, Sch. 4, para. 8, 9 (not reproduced): interest under TMA 1970, s. 86 is only chargeable with effect from 19 April 1993.

7 Where an assessment has become final and conclusive for the purposes of income tax for any year, that assessment shall also be final and conclusive for the purposes of computing liability for Class 4 contributions; and no allowance or adjustment of liability, on the ground of diminution of income or loss, shall be taken into account in computing profits chargeable to Class 4 contributions unless that allowance or adjustment has previously been made on an application under the special provisions of the Income Tax Acts relating to it, or falls to be allowed under paragraph 3(5) of this Schedule.

History – In para. 7, words "or gains", occurring immediately after word "profits", were omitted by ITTOIA 2005, s. 882 and Sch. 1, para. 422(6), and were repealed by ITTOIA 2005, s. 884 and Sch. 3, which, in accordance with ITTOIA 2005, s. 883, have effect, for income tax purposes, for tax year 2005–06 and subsequent tax years.

Derivations – SSA 1975, s. 9(4), Sch. 2, para. 8.

8 The provisions of Part V of the Taxes Management Act 1970 (appeals, etc.) shall apply with the necessary modifications in relation to Class 4 contributions as they apply in relation to income tax; but nothing in this Schedule affects the extent to which the Income Tax Acts apply with respect to any decision falling to be made–

(a) under subsection (1) of section 17 above or subsection (1) of section 17 of the Northern Ireland Contributions and Benefits Act as to whether by regulations under that subsection a person is excepted from liability for Class 4 contributions, or his liability is deferred; or

(b) under regulations made by virtue of section 17(3) or (4) or 18 above or section 17(3) or (4) or 18 of the Northern Ireland Contributions and Benefits Act.

History – In para. 8 the words "but nothing in this Schedule affects the extent to which the Income Tax Acts apply with respect to any decision falling to be made–" substituted by SSC(TF)A 1999, s. 18 and Sch. 7, para. 11, with effect from 4 March 1999, for the purposes of making regulations (SI 1999/527) and 1 April 1999 for all other purposes (SI 1999/527).

Derivations – SSA 1975, s. 9(4), Sch. 2, para. 9.

Cross references – S. 17(1): Secretary of State may with concurrence with the Revenue make regulations excepting persons from Class 4 liability or deferring any person's liability.
S. 18: Class 4 contributions recoverable by regulations.

HUSBAND AND WIFE – 1989–90 AND PREVIOUS YEARS OF ASSESSMENT

9 [Omitted by NICA 2014, s. 17(1)(a).]

History – Para. 9 (and the heading immediately before it) omitted by NICA 2014, s. 17(1)(b), with effect from 13 March 2014.

SOCIAL SECURITY ADMINISTRATION ACT 1992

(1992 Chapter 5)

[*13th February 1992*]

ARRANGEMENT OF SECTIONS

PART XII – FINANCE

PART XIII – ADVISORY BODIES AND CONSULTATION

THE SOCIAL SECURITY ADVISORY COMMITTEE AND THE INDUSTRIAL INJURIES ADVISORY COUNCIL

PART XIV – SOCIAL SECURITY SYSTEMS OUTSIDE GREAT BRITAIN

CO-ORDINATION

PART XV – MISCELLANEOUS

TRAVELLING EXPENSES

OFFENCES

MISCELLANEOUS

PART XVI – GENERAL

SUBORDINATE LEGISLATION

SUPPLEMENTARY

SCHEDULES

PART I – CLAIMS FOR AND PAYMENTS AND GENERAL ADMINISTRATION OF BENEFIT

CHILD BENEFIT

13A Election not to receive child benefit

13A(1) A person ("P") who is entitled to child benefit in respect of one or more children may elect for all payments of the benefit to which P is entitled not to be made.

13A(2) An election may be made only if P reasonably expects that, in the absence of the election, P or another person would be liable to a high income child benefit charge in respect of the payments to which the election relates made for weeks in the first tax year.

13A(3) An election has effect in relation to payments made for weeks beginning after the election is made.

13A(4) But where entitlement to child benefit is backdated, an election may have effect in relation to payments for weeks beginning in the period of three months ending immediately before the claim for the benefit was made.

13A(5) An election may be revoked.

13A(6) A revocation has effect in relation to payments made for weeks beginning after the revocation is made.

13A(7) But if–

(a) P makes an election which results in all payments, in respect of child benefit, to which P is entitled for one or more weeks in a tax year not being paid, and

(b) had no election been made, neither P nor any other person would have been liable to a high income child benefit charge in relation to the payments,

P may, no later than two years after the end of the tax year, revoke the election so far as it relates to the payments.

13A(8) Subsections (2) to (7) are subject to directions under subsection (9).

13A(9) The Commissioners for Her Majesty's Revenue and Customs may give directions as to–

(a) the form of elections and revocations under this section, the manner in which they are to be made and the time at which they are to be treated as made, and

(b) the circumstances in which, if child benefit is not being paid to a person at the full rate or the Commissioners are satisfied that there are doubts as to a person's entitlement to child benefit for a child, an election or revocation is not to have effect or its effect is to be postponed.

13A(10) For the purposes of this section–

"child" includes a qualifying young person;

"first tax year", in relation to an election, means the tax year in which the first week beginning after the election is made falls;

"week" means a period of 7 days beginning with a Monday; and a week is in a tax year if (and only if) the Monday with which it begins is in the tax year.

History – S. 13A inserted by FA 2012, s. 8 and Sch. 1, para. 3, with effect for the tax year 2012–13 and subsequent tax years.

PART II – ADJUDICATION

Cross references – SSC(TF)A 1999, s. 15: until SSA 1998, Pt. I wholly in force the Secretary of State may make regulations modifying Part II of this Act.

SSC(TF)A 1999, s. 17: until SSA 1998, Pt. I commences the Secretary of State may arrange for adjudication functions under Pt. II to be discharged by the Board of Inland Revenue or one of their officers.

S. 117(1): Secretary of State's power to modify any provision of this Part of this Act in its application to mariners, airmen, etc. and which replaces a provision of SSA 1975, Pt. III.

S. 119: Secretary of State's power to modify any provision of this Part of this Act in its application to persons who are or who have been abroad and which replaces a provision of SSA 1975, Pt. III.

S. 120(1): Secretary of State's power to modify any provision of this Part of this Act in its application to persons employed in continental shelf operations and which replaces a provision of SSA 1975, Pt. III.

SSCBA 1992, s. 116(2): Secretary of State's power to modify any provision of this Part of this Act in its application to HM forces and which replaces a provision of SSA 1975, Pt. III.

ADJUDICATION BY THE SECRETARY OF STATE

17 Questions for the Secretary of State

17 [Repealed by SSA 1998, s. 86(2); Sch. 8.]

History – S. 17 repealed by SSA 1998, s. 86(2); Sch. 8 with effect from 29 November 1999 (except for the purposes of housing benefit, council tax benefit and decisions to which SI 1999/527, art. 4(6) applies; i.e. pre-1 April 1999 decisions under SSAA 1992, s. 17(1), s. 20(3) and PSA 1993, s. 170(1)) (SI 1999/3178 (C. 81), art. 2(1)(a); 2(2) and Sch. 1). The wording of the repealed section is as follows:

"17 Questions for the Secretary of State

17(1) Subject to this Part of this Act, any of the following questions shall be determined by the Secretary of State–
(a) a question whether a person is an earner and, if he is, as to the category of earners in which he is to be included;
(b) subject to subsection (2) below, a question whether the contribution conditions for any benefit are satisfied, or otherwise relating to a person's contributions or his earnings factor;
(c) a question whether a Class 1A contribution is payable or otherwise relating to a Class 1A contribution;
(d) [not relevant to National Insurance contributions];
(e) a question as to whether a person was, within the meaning of regulations, precluded from regular employment by responsibilities at home;
(f) [not relevant to National Insurance contributions];
(g) any question arising under any provision of Part XI of the Contributions and Benefits Act or this Act, or under any provision of regulations or an order under that Part, as to–
(i) whether a person is, or was, an employee or employer of another;
(ii) whether an employer is entitled to make any deduction from his contributions payments in accordance with an order under section 159A of the Contributions and Benefits Act;
(iii) whether a payment falls to be made to an employer in accordance with the regulations or order;
(iv) the amount that falls to be so deducted or paid;
(v) the amount of an employer's contributions payments for any period for the purposes of an order under section 159A of the Contributions and Benefits Act; or
(vi) whether two or more employers or two or more contracts of service are, by virtue of regulations made under section 163(5) of that Act, to be treated as one;
(h) any question arising under any provision of Part XII of that Act or this Act, or under any provision of regulations under that Part, as to–
(i) whether a person is, or was, an employee or employer of another;
(ii) whether an employer is entitled to make any deduction from his contributions payments in accordance with regulations under section 167 of the Contributions and Benefits Act;
(iii) whether a payment falls to be made to an employer in accordance with the regulations;
(iv) the amount that falls to be so deducted or paid; or
(v) whether two or more employers or two or more contracts of service are, by virtue of regulations made under section 171(2) of that Act, to be treated as one,
and any question arising under regulations made by virtue of paragraph (c), (d) or (f) of section 164(9) of that Act; and
(i) any question arising under section 27 of the Jobseekers Act 1995, or under any provision of regulations under that section, as to–
(i) whether a person is, or was, an employee or employer of another;
(ii) whether an employer is entitled to make any deduction from his contributions payments in accordance with regulations under section 27 of that Act;
(iii) whether a payment falls to be made to an employer in accordance with those regulations;
(iv) the amount that falls to be so deducted or paid; or
(v) whether two or more employers are, by virtue of regulations under section 27 of that Act, to be treated as one.

17(2) Subsection (1)(b) above includes any question arising–
(a) under section 17(1) of the Contributions and Benefits Act as to whether by regulations under that subsection a person is excepted from liability for Class 4 contributions, or his liability is deferred; or
(b) under regulations made by virtue of section 17(3) or (4) or 18 of that Act;
but not any other question relating to Class 4 contributions, nor any question within section 20(1)(c) below.

17(3) Regulations may make provision restricting the persons who may apply to the Secretary of State for the determination of any such question as is mentioned in subsection (1) above.

17(4) The Secretary of State may, if he thinks fit, before determining any such question as is mentioned in subsection (1) above, appoint a person to hold an inquiry into the question, or any matters arising in connection with it, and to report on the question, or on those matters, to the Secretary of State."

In s. 17(1)(g), references to an order, or to an order under SSCBA 1992, s. 159A, inserted/substituted by SI 1995/512, art. 6(2)(a), with effect from 6 April 1995.

In s. 17(1), para. (i) inserted by Jobseekers Act 1995, Sch. 2, para. 41, with effect from 6 April 1996 (SI 1995/3228) and in s. 17(1)(g), the word "and" at the end repealed by Sch. 3 of that Act.

Derivations – S. 17(1)(a), (b): SSA 1975, s. 93(1)(a), (b).
S. 17(1)(c): SSA 1975, s. 93(1)(bb).
S. 17(1)(e): SSA 1975, s. 93(1)(e).
S. 17(1)(g)(i)–(iv): SSA 1986, s. 52(2), Sch. 5, Pt. II, para. b(i)–(iv).
S. 17(1)(g)(v): SSA 1986, s. 52(2), Sch. 5, Pt. II, para. b(vi).
S. 17(1)(g)(vi): SSA 1986, s. 52(2), Sch. 5, Pt. II, para. b(v).
S. 17(1)(h): SSA 1986, s. 52(2), Sch. 5, Pt. II, para. (c).
S. 17(2): SSA 1975, s. 93(2).
S. 17(3): SSA 1975, s. 93(2A).
S. 17(4): SSA 1975, s. 93(3).

Cross references – S. 59(4): In proceedings for determination of a question relating to a Class 1A contribution, privilege against self-incrimination or against incrimination of a spouse, available to witnesses.
S. 117(1): conclusiveness of Secretary of State's decision on any question as mentioned in s. 17(1) arising in proceedings concerning an offence under the Act, payment of contributions (other than those recoverable by the Inland Revenue) or recovery of sums due to Secretary of State or National Insurance Fund.
SSCBA 1992, s. 17: exceptions, deferment and incidental matters relating to Class 4 contributions.
SSCBA 1992, s. 18: Class 4 contributions recoverable under regulations shall be recovered by the Secretary of State.
SSCBA 1992, s. 158: recovery by employers of amounts paid by way of statutory sick pay.
SSCBA 1992, s. 167: recovery of amounts paid by way of statutory maternity pay.
SSCBA 1992, s. 171(2): regulations may, for statutory maternity pay purposes, treat two or more employers as one or two or more contracts of service in respect of the same woman as one.
SSCBA 1992, Sch. 1, para. 6(4): interest on overdue contributions will not be sought until question is determined by Secretary of State.
SSCBA 1992, Sch. 1, para. 7(12): penalties will not be imposed under TMA 1970, s. 98A until question has been determined by the Secretary of State.
PSA 1993, s. 170: questions to which s. 17 applies.
PSA 1993, s. 171: questions arising in proceedings.

SI 1979/591, reg. 74: notification and payment of special Class 4 contributions.
SI 1979/591, Sch. 1, reg. 28D: remission of interest on Class 1 and 1A contributions.
SI 1995/1801, reg. 13: application for decision of Secretary of State on principal questions.
SI 1995/1801, reg. 14: procedure for inquiries.
SI 1995/1801, reg. 15: the Secretary of State's decision and statement of grounds.
SI 1995/1801, reg. 16: review or reference.
SI 1995/1801, Sch. 2: time limits for making applications, appeals or references.

Notes – SI 1978/1689, reg. 4: special provision with respect to persons declared by the High Court to fall within particular category of earners, where that ruling is inconsistent with previous determination of Secretary of State.
For form, procedure of, and locus standi to make, application for decision of Secretary of State on principal questions, see SI 1995/1801, reg. 13; for procedure of enquiries under s. 17(4), see SI 1995/1801, reg. 14; for contents of Secretary of State's decision, see reg. 15; and for application for review, see reg. 16.

18 Appeal on question of law

18 [Repealed by SSA 1998, s. 86(2); Sch. 8.]

History – S. 18 repealed by SSA 1998, s. 86(2); Sch. 8 with effect from 29 November 1999 (except for the purposes of housing benefit, council tax benefit and decisions to which SI 1999/527, art. 4(6) applies; i.e. pre-1 April 1999 decisions under SSAA 1992, s. 17(1), s. 20(3) and PSA 1993, s. 170(1)) (SI 1999/3178 (C. 81), art. 2(1)(a); 2(2) and Sch. 1).

19 Review of decisions

19 [Repealed by SSA 1998, s. 86(2); Sch. 8.]

History – S. 19 repealed by SSA 1998, s. 86(2); Sch. 8 with effect from 29 November 1999 (except for the purposes of housing benefit, council tax benefit and decisions to which SI 1999/527, art. 4(6) applies; i.e. pre-1 April 1999 decisions under SSAA 1992, s. 17(1), s. 20(3) and PSA 1993, s. 170(1)) (SI 1999/3178 (C. 81), art. 2(1)(a); 2(2) and Sch. 1).

APPEALS FROM ADJUDICATION OFFICERS – GENERAL

24 Appeal from Commissioners on point of law

24 [Repealed by SSA 1998, s. 86(2); Sch. 8.]

History – S. 24 repealed by SSA 1998, s. 86(2); Sch. 8 with effect from 29 November 1999 (except for the purposes of housing benefit, council tax benefit and decisions to which SI 1999/527, art. 4(6) applies; i.e. pre-1 April 1999 decisions under SSAA 1992, s. 17(1), s. 20(3) and PSA 1993, s. 170(1)) (SI 1999/3178 (C. 81), art. 2(1)(a); 2(2) and Sch. 1).

REFERENCES BY AUTHORITIES

53 Power of adjudicating authorities to refer matters to experts

53 [Repealed by SSA 1998, s. 86(2); Sch. 8.]

History – S. 53 repealed by SSA 1998, s. 86(2); Sch. 8 with effect from 29 November 1999 (except for the purposes of housing benefit, council tax benefit and decisions to which SI 1999/527, art. 4(6) applies; i.e. pre-1 April 1999 decisions under SSAA 1992, s. 17(1), s. 20(3) and PSA 1993, s. 170(1)) (SI 1999/3178 (C. 81), art. 2(1)(a); 2(2) and Sch. 1).

DETERMINATION OF QUESTIONS OF SPECIAL DIFFICULTY

56 Assessors

56 [Repealed by SSA 1998, s. 86(2); Sch. 8.]

History – S. 56 repealed by SSA 1998, s. 86(2); Sch. 8 with effect from 29 November 1999 (except for the purposes of housing benefit, council tax benefit and decisions to which SI 1999/527, art. 4(6) applies; i.e. pre-1 April 1999 decisions under SSAA 1992, s. 17(1), s. 20(3) and PSA 1993, s. 170(1)) (SI 1999/3178 (C. 81), art. 2(1)(a); 2(2) and Sch. 1).

57 Tribunal of three Commissioners

57 [Repealed by SSA 1998, s. 86(2); Sch. 8.]

History – S. 57 repealed by SSA 1998, s. 86(2); Sch. 8 with effect from 29 November 1999 (except for the purposes of housing benefit, council tax benefit and decisions to which SI 1999/527, art. 4(6) applies; i.e. pre-1 April 1999 decisions under SSAA 1992, s. 17(1), s. 20(3) and PSA 1993, s. 170(1)) (SI 1999/3178 (C. 81), art. 2(1)(a); 2(2) and Sch. 1).

REGULATIONS

58 Regulations as to determination of questions and matters arising out of, or pending, reviews and appeals

58 *[Repealed by SSA 1998, s. 86(2); Sch. 8.]*

History – S. 58 repealed by SSA 1998, s. 86(2); Sch. 8 with effect from 29 November 1999 (except for the purposes of housing benefit, council tax benefit and decisions to which SI 1999/527, art. 4(6) applies; i.e. pre-1 April 1999 decisions under SSAA 1992, s. 17(1), s. 20(3) and PSA 1993, s. 170(1)) (SI 1999/3178 (C. 81), art. 2(1)(a); 2(2) and Sch. 1).

59 Procedure

59 [Repealed by SSA 1998, s. 86(2); Sch. 8.]

History – S. 59 repealed by SSA 1998, s. 86(2); Sch. 8 with effect from 29 November 1999 (except for the purposes of housing benefit, council tax benefit and decisions to which SI 1999/527, art. 4(6) applies; i.e. pre-1 April 1999 decisions under SSAA 1992, s. 17(1), s. 20(3) and PSA 1993, s. 170(1)) (SI 1999/3178 (C. 81), art. 2(1)(a); 2(2) and Sch. 1).

60 Finality of decisions

60 [Repealed by SSA 1998, s. 86(2); Sch. 8.]

History – S. 60 repealed by SSA 1998, s. 86(2); Sch. 8 with effect from 29 November 1999 (except for the purposes of housing benefit, council tax benefit and decisions to which SI 1999/527, art. 4(6) applies; i.e. pre-1 April 1999 decisions under SSAA 1992, s. 17(1), s. 20(3) and PSA 1993, s. 170(1)) (SI 1999/3178 (C. 81), art. 2(1)(a); 2(2) and Sch. 1).

61 Regulations about supplementary matters relating to determinations

61 [Repealed by SSA 1998, s. 86(2); Sch. 8.]

History – S. 61 repealed by SSA 1998, s. 86(2); Sch. 8 with effect from 29 November 1999 (except for the purposes of housing benefit, council tax benefit and decisions to which SI 1999/527, art. 4(6) applies; i.e. pre-1 April 1999 decisions under SSAA 1992, s. 17(1), s. 20(3) and PSA 1993, s. 170(1)) (SI 1999/3178 (C. 81), art. 2(1)(a); 2(2) and Sch. 1).

Statutory instruments – SI 1986/2218.

CORRECTION OF ERRORS

70 Regulations as to correction of errors and setting aside of decisions

70 [Repealed by SSA 1998, s. 86(2); Sch. 8.]

History – S. 70 repealed by SSA 1998, s. 86(2); Sch. 8 with effect from 29 November 1999 (except for the purposes of housing benefit, council tax benefit and decisions to which SI 1999/527, art. 4(6) applies; i.e. pre-1 April 1999 decisions under SSAA 1992, s. 17(1), s. 20(3) and PSA 1993, s. 170(1)) (SI 1999/3178 (C. 81), art. 2(1)(a); 2(2) and Sch. 1).

PART VI – ENFORCEMENT

INSPECTION AND OFFENCES

109A Authorisations for investigators

109A(1) An individual who for the time being has the Secretary of State's authorisation for the purposes of this Part shall be entitled, for any one or more of the purposes mentioned in subsection (2) below, to exercise any of the powers which are conferred on an authorised officer by sections 109B and 109C below.

109A(2) Those purposes are–

(a) ascertaining in relation to any case whether a benefit is or was payable in that case in accordance with any provision of the relevant social security legislation;

(b) investigating the circumstances in which any accident, injury or disease which has given rise, or may give rise, to a claim for–

(i) industrial injuries benefit, or

(ii) any benefit under any provision of the relevant social security legislation,

occurred or may have occurred, or was or may have been received or contracted;

(c) ascertaining whether provisions of the relevant social security legislation are being, have been or are likely to be contravened (whether by particular persons or more generally);

(d) preventing, detecting and securing evidence of the commission (whether by particular persons or more generally) of benefit offences.

109A(3) An individual has the Secretary of State's authorisation for the purposes of this Part if, and only if, the Secretary of State has granted him an authorisation for those purposes and he is—

(a) an official of a Government department;

(b) an individual employed by an authority administering housing benefit or council tax benefit;

(c) an individual employed by an authority or joint committee that carries out functions relating to housing benefit or council tax benefit on behalf of the authority administering that benefit; or

(d) an individual employed by a person authorised by or on behalf of any such authority or joint committee as is mentioned in paragraph (b) or (c) above to carry out functions relating to housing benefit or council tax benefit for that authority or committee.

109A(4) An authorisation granted for the purposes of this Part to an individual of any of the descriptions mentioned in subsection (3) above–

(a) must be contained in a certificate provided to that individual as evidence of his entitlement to exercise powers conferred by this Part;

(b) may contain provision as to the period for which the authorisation is to have effect; and

(c) may restrict the powers exercisable by virtue of the authorisation so as to prohibit their exercise except for particular purposes, in particular circumstances or in relation to particular benefits or particular provisions of the relevant social security legislation.

109A(5) An authorisation granted under this section may be withdrawn at any time by the Secretary of State.

109A(6) Where the Secretary of State grants an authorisation for the purposes of this Part to an individual employed by a local authority, or to an individual employed by a person who carries out functions relating to housing benefit or council tax benefit on behalf of a local authority–

(a) the Secretary of State and the local authority shall enter into such arrangements (if any) as they consider appropriate with respect to the carrying out of functions conferred on that individual by or in connection with the authorisation granted to him; and

(b) the Secretary of State may make to the local authority such payments (if any) as he thinks fit in respect of the carrying out by that individual of any such functions.

109A(7) The matters on which a person may be authorised to consider and report to the Secretary of State under section 139A below shall be taken to include the carrying out by any such individual as is mentioned in subsection (3)(b) to (d) above of any functions conferred on that individual by virtue of any grant by the Secretary of State of an authorisation for the purposes of this Part.

109A(8) The powers conferred by sections 109B and 109C below shall be exercisable in relation to persons holding office under the Crown and persons in the service of the Crown, and in relation to premises owned or occupied by the Crown, as they are exercisable in relation to other persons and premises.

109A(9) This section and sections 109B to 109C below apply as if–

(a) the Tax Credits Act 2002 were relevant social security legislation, and

(b) accordingly, child tax credit and working tax credit were relevant social security benefits for the purposes of the definition of "benefit offence".

Prospective amendments – S. 109A(3)(b)–(d), (6) and (7) repealed by WRA 2012, s. 147 and Sch. 14, Pt. 1, with effect from a date to be set by order of the Secretary of State.

History – S. 109A(9) inserted by WRA 2012, s. 122, with effect from 6 June 2012 (SI 2012/1246).
S. 109A, 109B and 109C substituted for former s. 110 by CSPSSA 2000, Sch. 6, para. 2 with effect from 2 April 2001 (SI 2001/1252 (C. 45)).

109B Power to require information

109B(1) An authorised officer who has reasonable grounds for suspecting that a person–

(a) is a person falling within subsection (2) or (2A) below, and

(b) has or may have possession of or access to any information about any matter that is relevant for any one or more of the purposes mentioned in section 109A(2) above,

may, by written notice, require that person to provide all such information described in the notice as is information of which he has possession, or to which he has access, and which it is reasonable for the authorised officer to require for a purpose so mentioned.

109B(2) The persons who fall within this subsection are–

(a) any person who is or has been an employer or employee within the meaning of any provision made by or under the Contributions and Benefits Act;

(b) any person who is or has been a self-employed earner within the meaning of any such provision;

(c) any person who by virtue of any provision made by or under that Act falls, or has fallen, to be treated for the purposes of any such provision as a person within paragraph (a) or (b) above;

(d) any person who is carrying on, or has carried on, any business involving the supply of goods for sale to the ultimate consumers by individuals not carrying on retail businesses from retail premises;

(e) any person who is carrying on, or has carried on, any business involving the supply of goods or services by the use of work done or services performed by persons other than employees of his;

(f) any person who is carrying on, or has carried on, an agency or other business for the introduction or supply, to persons requiring them, of persons available to do work or to perform services;

(g) any local authority acting in their capacity as an authority responsible for the granting of any licence;

(h) any person who is or has been a trustee or manager of a personal or occupational pension scheme;

(i) any person who is or has been liable to make a compensation payment or a payment to the Secretary of State under section 6 of the Social Security (Recovery of Benefits) Act 1997 (payments in respect of recoverable benefits);

(ia) a person of a prescribed description; and

(j) the servants and agents of any such person as is specified in any of paragraphs (a) to (ia) above.

109B(2A) The persons who fall within this subsection are–

(a) any bank;

(aa) the Director of National Savings;

(b) any person carrying on a business the whole or a significant part of which consists in the provision of credit (whether secured or unsecured) to members of the public;

(c) any insurer;

(d) any credit reference agency (within the meaning given by section 145(8) of the Consumer Credit Act 1974 (c. 39));

(e) any body the principal activity of which is to facilitate the exchange of information for the purpose of preventing or detecting fraud;

(f) any person carrying on a business the whole or a significant part of which consists in the provision to members of the public of a service for transferring money from place to place;

(g) any water undertaker or sewerage undertaker, Scottish Water or any local authority which is to collect charges by virtue of an order under section 37 of the Water Industry (Scotland) Act 2002 (asp 3);

(h) any person who –

(i) is the holder of a licence under section 7 of the Gas Act 1986 (c. 44) to convey gas through pipes, or

(ii) is the holder of a licence under section 7A(1) of that Act to supply gas through pipes;

(i) any person who (within the meaning of the Electricity Act 1989 (c. 29)) distributes or supplies electricity;

(j) any person who provides a telecommunications service;

(k) any person conducting any educational establishment or institution;

(l) any body the principal activity of which is to provide services in connection with admissions to educational establishments or institutions;

(m) the Student Loans Company;

(n) any servant or agent of any person mentioned in any of the preceding paragraphs.

109B(2B) Subject to the following provisions of this section, the powers conferred by this section on an authorised officer to require information from any person by virtue of his falling within subsection (2A) above shall be exercisable for the purpose only of obtaining information relating to a particular person identified (by name or description) by the officer.

109B(2C) An authorised officer shall not, in exercise of those powers, require any information from any person by virtue of his falling within subsection (2A) above unless it appears to that officer that there are reasonable grounds for believing that the identified person to whom it relates is–

(a) a person who has committed, is committing or intends to commit a benefit offence; or

(b) a person who (within the meaning of Part 7 of the Contributions and Benefits Act) is a member of the family of a person falling within paragraph (a) above.

109B(2D) Nothing in subsection (2B) or (2C) above shall prevent an authorised officer who is an official of a Government department and whose authorisation states that his authorisation applies for the purposes of this subsection from exercising the powers conferred by this section for obtaining from–

(a) a water undertaker or Scottish Water,

(b) any person who (within the meaning the Gas Act 1986) supplies gas conveyed through pipes,

(c) any person who (within the meaning of the Electricity Act 1989) supplies electricity conveyed by distribution systems, or

(d) any servant or agent of a person mentioned in any of the preceding paragraphs,

any information which relates exclusively to whether and in what quantities water, gas or electricity are being or have been supplied to residential premises specified or described in the notice by which the information is required.

109B(2E) The powers conferred by this section shall not be exercisable for obtaining from any person providing a telecommunications service any information other than information which (within the meaning of section 21 of the Regulation of Investigatory Powers Act 2000 (c. 23)) is communications data but not traffic data.

109B(2F) Nothing in subsection (2B) or (2C) above shall prevent an authorised officer from exercising the powers conferred by this section for requiring information, from a person who provides a telecommunications service, about the identity and postal address of a person identified by the authorised officer solely by reference to a telephone number or electronic address used in connection with the provision of such a service.

109B(3) The obligation of a person to provide information in accordance with a notice under this section shall be discharged only by the provision of that information, at such reasonable time and in such form as may be specified in the notice, to the authorised officer who–

(a) is identified by or in accordance with the terms of the notice; or

(b) has been identified, since the giving of the notice, by a further written notice given by the authorised officer who imposed the original requirement or another authorised officer.

109B(4) The power of an authorised officer under this section to require the provision of information shall include a power to require the production and delivery up and (if necessary) creation of, or of copies of or extracts from, any such documents containing the information as may be specified or described in the notice imposing the requirement.

109B(5) No one shall be required under this section to provide–

(a) any information that tends to incriminate either himself or, in the case of a person who is married or is a civil partner, his spouse or civil partner; or

(b) any information in respect of which a claim to legal professional privilege or, in Scotland, confidentiality as between client and professional legal adviser, would be successful in any proceedings;

and for the purposes of this subsection it is immaterial whether the information is in documentary form or not.

109B(6) Provision maybe made by order–

(a) adding any person to the list of persons falling within subsection (2A) above;

(b) removing any person from the list of persons falling within that subsection;

(c) modifying that subsection for the purpose of taking account of any change to the name of any person for the time being falling within that subsection.

109B(7) In this section–

"bank" means–

(a) a person who has permission under Part 4A of the Financial Services and Markets Act 2000 (c. 8) to accept deposits;

(b) an EEA firm of the kind mentioned in paragraph 5(b) of Schedule 3 to that Act which has permission under paragraph 15 of that Schedule (as a result of qualifying for authorisation under paragraph 12 of that Schedule) to accept deposits or other repayable funds from the public; or

(c) a person who does not require permission under that Act to accept deposits, in the course of his business in the United Kingdom;

"credit" includes a cash loan or any form of financial accommodation, including the cashing of a cheque;

"insurer" means–

(a) a person who has permission under Part 4A of the Financial Services and Markets Act 2000 to effect or carry out contracts of insurance; or

(b) an EEA firm of the kind mentioned in paragraph 5(d) of Schedule 3 to that Act, which has permission under paragraph 15 of that Schedule (as a result of qualifying for authorisation under paragraph 12 of that Schedule) to effect or carry out contracts of insurance;

"residential premises", in relation to a supply of water, gas or electricity, means any premises which–

(a) at the time of the supply were premises occupied wholly or partly for residential purposes, or

(b) are premises to which that supply was provided as if they were so occupied; and

"telecommunications service" has the same meaning as in the Regulation of Investigatory Powers Act 2000 (c. 23).

109B(7A) The definitions of **"bank"** and **"insurer"** in subsection (7) must be read with;

(a) section 22 of the Financial Services and Markets Act 2000;

(b) any relevant order under that section; and

(c) Schedule 2 to that Act.

Prospective amendments – S. 109B(2A)(j) omitted by Investigatory Powers Act 2016, s. 12(1) and Sch. 2, para. 5(a), with effect from such day as the Secretary of State may by regulations appoint.
In s. 109B(2E), the words "so as to secure the disclosure by a telecommunications operator or postal operator of communications data without the consent of the operator." substituted for the words "for obtaining from any person providing a telecommunications service any information other than information which (within the meaning of section 21 of the Regulation of Investigatory Powers Act 2000 (c. 23)) is communications data but not traffic data." by Investigatory Powers Act 2016, s. 12(1) and Sch. 2, para. 5(b), with effect from such day as the Secretary of State may by regulations appoint.
S. 109B(2F) omitted by Investigatory Powers Act 2016, s. 12(1) and Sch. 2, para. 5(c), with effect from such day as the Secretary of State may by regulations appoint.
In s. 109B(7), definitions of "communications data", "postal operator" inserted and definition of "telecommunications operator" substituted for definition of "telecommunications service" by Investigatory Powers Act 2016, s. 12(1) and Sch. 2, para. 5(d), with effect from such day as the Secretary of State may by regulations appoint. New definitions to read as follows:

> "**"communications data"** has the same meaning as in the Investigatory Powers Act 2016 (see sections 261 and 262 of that Act);
> **"postal operator"** has the same meaning as in the Investigatory Powers Act 2016 (see section 262 of that Act);
> **"telecommunications operator"** has the same meaning as in the Investigatory Powers Act 2016 (see section 261 of that Act)."

History – In s. 109B(1), "or (2A)" inserted by SSFA 2001, s. 1(2) with effect from 30 April 2002 (SI 2002/1222 (C. 32)).
In s. 109B(2)(ia) (and the "and" after it) inserted (and the "and" before it omitted) by WRA 2012, s. 110(a), with effect from 17 June 2013 for the purpose of making regulations and from 1 October 2013 for all other purposes (SI 2013/1250).
In s. 109B(2)(j), "(ia)" substituted for "(i)" by WRA 2012, s. 110(b), with effect from 17 June 2013 for the purpose of making regulations and from 1 October 2013 for all other purposes (SI 2013/1250).
In s. 109B(2A)(g), the words "Scottish Water or any local authority which is to collect charges by virtue of an order under section 37 of the Water Industry (Scotland) Act 2002 (asp 3)" substituted by SI 2002/1822, art. 2 and Schedule, para. 16, with effect from 14 July 2004.
In s. 109B(2A), para. (aa) inserted and para. (c), (h) and (i) substituted by SI 2002/817, art. 2 with effect from 1 April 2002.
In s. 109B(2D)(a), the words "Scottish Water" substituted by SI 2002/1822, art. 2 and Schedule, para. 16, with effect from 14 July 2004.
S. 109B(2A)–(2F) inserted by SSFA 2001, s. 1(2) with effect from 30 April 2002 (SI 2002/1222 (C. 32)).
In s. 109B(5)(a) the words "married or is a civil partner, his spouse or civil partner" substituted by the Civil Partnership Act 2004, Sch. 24, para. 64, with effect from 5 December 2005 (by virtue of SI 2005/3175, art. 2(1)).
S. 109B(5) substituted by SSFA 2001, s. 1(3) with effect from 30 April 2002 (SI 2002/1222 (C. 32)).
S. 109B(6), (7) inserted by SSFA 2001, s. 1(4) with effect from 26 February 2002 (SI 2002/403 (C. 10)).
In s. 109B(7), the definition of "bank" substituted and the definition of "insurer" inserted by SI 2002/817, art. 3 with effect from 1 April 2002.
In s. 109B(7), in the definitions of "bank" and "insurer", the words "Part 4A" substituted for the words "Part IV" by Financial Services Act 2012, s. 114(1) and Sch. 18, para. 74(3), with effect from 1 April 2013 (SI 2013/423).
In s. 109B(7A) inserted by SI 2002/817, art. 3 with effect from 1 April 2002.
S. 109A, 109B and 109C substituted for former s. 110 by CSPSSA 2000, Sch. 6, para. 2 with effect from 2 April 2001 (SI 2001/1252 (C. 45)).

Cross references – SI 2013/1510 (not reproduced): prescribes persons for the purposes of s. 109B(2)(ia).

109BA Power of Secretary of State to require electronic access to information

109BA(1) Subject to subsection (2) below, where it appears to the Secretary of State–

(a) that a person falling within section 109B(2A) keeps any electronic records,

(b) that the records contain or are likely, from time to time, to contain information about any matter that is relevant for any one or more of the purposes mentioned in section 109A(2) above, and

(c) that facilities exist under which electronic access to those records is being provided, or is capable of being provided, by that person to other persons,

the Secretary of State may require that person to enter into arrangements under which authorised officers are allowed such access to those records.

109BA(2) An authorised officer–

(a) shall be entitled to obtain information in accordance with arrangements entered into under subsection (1) above only if his authorisation states that his authorisation applies for the purposes of that subsection; and

(b) shall not seek to obtain any information in accordance with any such arrangements other than information which relates to a particular person and could be the subject of a requirement under section 109B above.

109BA(3) The matters that may be included in the arrangements that a person is required to enter into under subsection (1) above may include–

(a) requirements as to the electronic access to records that is to be made available to authorised officers;

(b) requirements as to the keeping of records of the use that is made of the arrangements;

(c) requirements restricting the disclosure of information about the use that is made of the arrangements; and

(d) such other incidental requirements as the Secretary of State considers appropriate in connection with allowing access to records to authorised officers.

109BA(4) An authorised officer who is allowed access in accordance with any arrangements entered into under subsection (1) above shall be entitled to make copies of, and to take extracts from, any records containing information which he is entitled to require under section 109B.

History – S. 109BA inserted by SSFA 2001, s. 2(1) with effect from 30 April 2002 (SI 2002/1222 (C. 32)).

109C Powers of entry

109C(1) An authorised officer shall be entitled, at any reasonable time and either alone or accompanied by such other persons as he thinks fit, to enter any premises which–

(a) are liable to inspection under this section; and

(b) are premises to which it is reasonable for him to require entry in order to exercise the powers conferred by this section.

109C(2) An authorised officer who has entered any premises liable to inspection under this section may–

(a) make such an examination of those premises, and

(b) conduct any such inquiry there,

as appears to him appropriate for any one or more of the purposes mentioned in section 109A(2) above.

109C(3) An authorised officer who has entered any premises liable to inspection under this section may–

(a) question any person whom he finds there;

(b) require any person whom he finds there to do any one or more of the following–

(i) to provide him with such information,

(ii) to produce and deliver up and (if necessary) create such documents or such copies of, or extracts from, documents,

as he may reasonably require for any one or more of the purposes mentioned in section 109A(2) above; and

(c) take possession of and either remove or make his own copies of any such documents as appear to him to contain information that is relevant for any of those purposes.

109C(4) The premises liable to inspection under this section are any premises (including premises consisting in the whole or a part of a dwelling house) which an authorised officer has reasonable grounds for suspecting are–

(a) premises which are a person's place of employment;

(b) premises from which a trade or business is being carried on or where documents relating to a trade or business are kept by the person carrying it on or by another person on his behalf;

(c) premises from which a personal or occupational pension scheme is being administered or where documents relating to the administration of such a scheme are kept by the person administering the scheme or by another person on his behalf;

(d) premises where a person who is the compensator in relation to any such accident, injury or disease as is referred to in section 109A(2)(b) above is to be found;

(e) premises where a person on whose behalf any such compensator has made, may have made or may make a compensation payment is to be found.

109C(5) An authorised officer applying for admission to any premises in accordance with this section shall, if required to do so, produce the certificate containing his authorisation for the purposes of this Part.

109C(6) Subsection (5) of section 109B applies for the purposes of this section as it applies for the purposes of that section.

Prospective amendments – S. 109C(6) substituted by Investigatory Powers Act 2016, s. 12(1) and Sch. 2, para. 6, with effect from such day as the Secretary of State may by regulations appoint. S. 109C(6) to read as follows:

"**109C(6)** Subsections (2E) and (5) of section 109B apply for the purposes of this section as they apply for the purposes of that section."

History – S. 109A, 109B and 109C substituted for former s. 110 by CSPSSA 2000, Sch. 6, para. 2 with effect from 2 April 2001 (SI 2001/1252 (C. 45)).

110 Appointment and powers of inspectors

110 [S. 110 replaced by s. 109A, 109B, 109C with effect from 2 April 2001 by CSPSSA 2000, Sch. 6, para. 2 (SI 2001/1252 (C. 45)).]

110ZA Class 1, 1A, 1B or 2 contributions: powers to call for documents etc

110ZA(1) Schedule 36 to the Finance Act 2008 (information and inspection powers) applies for the purpose of checking a person's position as regards relevant contributions as it applies for the purpose of checking a person's tax position, subject to the modifications in subsection (2).

110ZA(2) That Schedule applies as if–

(a) references to any provision of the Taxes Acts were to any provision of this Act or the Contributions and Benefits Act or the National Insurance Contributions Act 2014 relating to relevant contributions,

(b) references to prejudice to the assessment or collection of tax were to prejudice to the assessment of liability for, and payment of, relevant contributions,

(c) the reference to information relating to the conduct of a pending appeal relating to tax were a reference to information relating to the conduct of a pending appeal relating to relevant contributions, and

(d) paragraphs 21, 21A, 35(4A)(c), 36, 37(2) and (2A), 37A and 37B of that Schedule (restrictions on giving taxpayer notice where taxpayer has made tax return) were omitted.

110ZA(2A) Part 3 of Schedule 38 to the Finance Act 2012 (power to obtain tax agent's files etc) applies in relation to relevant contributions as in relation to tax and, accordingly–

(a) the cases described in paragraph 7 of that Schedule (case A and case B) include cases involving conduct or an offence relating to relevant contributions,

(b) (whether the case involves conduct or an offence relating to tax or relevant contributions) the papers and other documents that may be sought under that Part include ones relating to relevant contributions, and

(c) the other Parts of that Schedule apply so far as necessary to give effect to the application of Part 3 by virtue of this subsection.

110ZA(3) In this section **"relevant contributions"** means Class 1, Class 1A, Class 1B or Class 2 contributions.

History – In s. 110ZA(2)(a) the words "or the National Insurance Contributions Act 2014" inserted by NICA 2014, s. 7(5), with effect from 6 April 2014.
In s. 110ZA(2)(d), ", 21A" inserted after "21" and "and (2A)" inserted after "37(2)" by SI 2009/3054, art. 3 and Schedule, para. 3, with effect from 1 April 2010.
In s. 110ZA(2)(d), "35(4)(c), 36, 37(2), 37A and 37B" substituted for "35(4)(b), 36 and 37(2)" by SI 2009/2035, art. 2 and Sch., para. 27, with effect from 13 August 2009.
S. 110ZA(1) and (2) substituted by FA 2008, s. 113 and Sch. 36, para. 84, with effect from 1 April 2009 (SI 2009/404, art. 2, subject to savings at SI 2009/404, art. 3).
S. 110ZA(2A) inserted by FA 2012, s. 223 and Sch. 38, para. 56, with effect from 1 April 2013 (SI 2013/279, art. 2).
S. 110ZA and section heading substituted by NICSPA 2004, s. 7 with effect from 6 April 2005 (by virtue of SI 2004/1943, reg. 4).
Former s. 110ZA(3A) inserted by CSPSSA 2000, s. 76(2) with effect from 28 July 2000 (date of Royal Assent).
Former s. 110ZA inserted by SSC(TF)A 1999, s. 5 and Sch. 5, para. 3, with effect from 1 April 1999 (SI 1999/527).

Cross references – NICA 2011, s. 9(5) (regional secondary contributions holiday for new businesses): for the purposes of FA 2008, Sch. 36 as applied by s. 110ZA, the duty to retain records imposed by NICA 2011, s. 9 is treated as if it were a duty imposed by SSCBA 1992.

111 Delay, obstruction etc. of inspector

111(1) If a person–

(a) intentionally delays or obstructs an authorised officer in the exercise of any power under this Act other than an Inland Revenue power;

(ab) refuses or neglects to comply with any requirement under section 109BA or with the requirements of any arrangements entered into in accordance with subsection (1) of that section, or

(b) refuses or neglects to answer any question or to furnish any information or to produce any document when required to do so under this Act otherwise than in the exercise of an Inland Revenue power,

he shall be guilty of an offence and liable on summary conviction to a fine not exceeding level 3 on the standard scale.

111(2) Where a person is convicted of an offence under subsection 1(ab) or (b) above and the refusal or neglect is continued by him after his conviction, he shall be guilty of a further offence and liable on summary conviction to a fine not exceeding £40 for each day on which it is continued.

111(3) In subsection (1) **"Inland Revenue power"** means any power conferred on an officer of the Inland Revenue by virtue of section 110ZA above or by virtue of an authorisation granted under section 109A above.

111(4) [Omitted by NICSPA 2004, s. 11 and Sch. 1, para. 3(2)(b) and repealed by s. 12 and Sch. 2.]

Prospective amendments – In s. 111(1)(ab), the words "or 110AA" repealed by WRA 2012, s. 147 and Sch. 14, Pt. 1, with effect (other than as noted in the History note below) from a date to be set by order of the Secretary of State.
In s. 111(3), the words "or 110A" repealed by WRA 2012, s. 147 and Sch. 14, Pt. 1, with effect (other than as noted in the History note below) from a date to be set by order of the Secretary of State.

History – In s. 111(1)(ab), the words "or 110AA" repealed by WRA 2012, s. 147 and Sch. 14, Pt. 1, with effect in so far as they relate to the abolition of council tax benefit from 1 April 2013 (SI 2013/358, art. 8(c) and Sch. 4).
In s. 111(1)(a) and (b) references to Inland Revenue power and its exercise inserted by SSC(TF)A 1999, s. 5 and Sch. 5 para. 4(2), with effect from 1 April 1999 (SI 1999/527).

In s. 111(3), the words "or 110A" repealed by WRA 2012, s. 147 and Sch. 14, Pt. 1, with effect in so far as they relate to the abolition of council tax benefit from 1 April 2013 (SI 2013/358, art. 8(c) and Sch. 4).
S. 111(3) and (4) inserted by SSC(TF)A 1999, s. 5 and Sch. 5, para. 4(3), with effect from 1 April 1999 (SI 1999/527).
In s. 111(1)(a), "authorised officer" substituted by SSFA 2001, s. 1(4) with effect from 30 April 2002 (SI 2002/1222 (C. 32)).
In s. 111, para. (ab) inserted by SSFA 2001, s. 2(3) with effect from 30 April 2002 (SI 2002/1222 (C. 32)).
In s. 111(2), "subsection (1)(ab) or (b)" substituted by SSFA 2001, s. 2(3) with effect from 30 April 2001 (SI 2002/1222 (C. 32)).
In s. 111(3), the words "virtue of" inserted by NICSPA 2004, s. 11 and Sch. 1, para. 3(2)(a) with effect from 6 April 2005 (by virtue of SI 2004/1943, reg. 5).
In s. 111(3), the words "an authorisation granted under section 109A or 110A" substituted by CSPSSA 2000, Sch. 6, para. 4(a) with effect from 2 April 2001 (SI 2001/1252 (C. 45)).
S. 111(4) omitted by NICSPA 2004, s. 11 and Sch. 1, para. 3(2)(b) and repealed by s. 12 and Sch. 2 with effect from 6 April 2005 (by virtue of SI 2004/1943, reg. 5 and 6).
In s. 111(4), the words "an authorisation granted under section 109A or 110A above, any power conferred by section 109B or 109C above" and the references to sections 109B and 109C at the end of that subsection substituted by CSPSSA 2000, Sch. 6, para. 4(b) with effect from 2 April 2001 (SI 2001/1252 (C. 45)).

Derivations – (as originally enacted) SSA 1986, s. 58(8), (9).

Cross references – TCA 1999, Sch. 2, para. 11: disapplication of s. 111 to the extent that it relates to tax credit.

Notes – Level 3 on standard scale is £1,000 in relation to offences committed after 1 October 1992 (Criminal Justice Act 1982, s. 37(2); Criminal Justice Act 1991, s. 17(1); SI 1992/333).

111A Dishonest representations for obtaining benefit etc.

111A(1) If a person dishonestly–

(a) makes a false statement or representation; or

(b) produces or furnishes, or causes or allows to be produced or furnished, any document or information which is false in a material particular;

111A(1A) A person shall be guilty of an offence if–

(a) there has been a change of circumstances affecting any entitlement of his to any benefit or other payment or advantage under any provision of the relevant social security legislation;

(b) the change is not a change that is excluded by regulations from the changes that are required to be notified;

(c) he knows that the change affects an entitlement of his to such a benefit or other payment or advantage; and

(d) he dishonestly fails to give a prompt notification of that change in the prescribed manner to the prescribed person.

111A(1B) A person shall be guilty of an offence if–

(a) there has been a change of circumstances affecting any entitlement of another person to any benefit or other payment or advantage under any provision of the relevant social security legislation;

(b) the change is not a change that is excluded by regulations from the changes that are required to be notified;

(c) he knows that the change affects an entitlement of that other person to such a benefit or other payment or advantage; and

(d) he dishonestly causes or allows that other person to fail to give a prompt notification of that change in the prescribed manner to the prescribed person.

111A(1C) This subsection applies where–

(a) there has been a change of circumstances affecting any entitlement of a person (**"the claimant"**) to any benefit or other payment or advantage under any provision of the relevant social security legislation;

(b) the benefit, payment or advantage is one in respect of which there is another person (**"the recipient"**) who for the time being has a right to receive payments to which the claimant has, or (but for the arrangements under which they are payable to the recipient) would have, an entitlement; and

(c) the change is not a change that is excluded by regulations from the changes that are required to be notified.

111A(1D) In a case where subsection (1C) above applies, the recipient is guilty of an offence if–

(a) he knows that the change affects an entitlement of the claimant to a benefit or other payment or advantage under a provision of the relevant social security legislation;

(b) the entitlement is one in respect of which he has a right to receive payments to which the claimant has, or (but for the arrangements under which they are payable to the recipient) would have, an entitlement; and

(c) he dishonestly fails to give a prompt notification of that change in the prescribed manner to the prescribed person.

111A(1E) In a case where that subsection applies, a person other than the recipient is guilty of an offence if–

(a) he knows that the change affects an entitlement of the claimant to a benefit or other payment or advantage under a provision of the relevant social security legislation;

(b) the entitlement is one in respect of which the recipient has a right to receive payments to which the claimant has, or (but for the arrangements under which they are payable to the recipient) would have, an entitlement; and

(c) he dishonestly causes or allows the recipient to fail to give a prompt notification of that change in the prescribed manner to the prescribed person.

111A(1F) In any case where subsection (1C) above applies but the right of the recipient is confined to a right, by reason of his being a person to whom the claimant is required to make payments in respect of a dwelling, to receive payments of housing benefit–

(a) a person shall not be guilty of an offence under subsection (1D) or (1E) above unless the change is one relating to one or both of the following–

(i) the claimant's occupation of that dwelling;

(ii) the claimant's liability to make payments in respect of that dwelling;

but

(b) subsections (1D)(a) and (1E)(a) above shall each have effect as if after "knows" there were inserted "or could reasonably be expected to know".

111A(1G) For the purposes of subsections (1A) to (1E) above a notification of a change is prompt if, and only if, it is given as soon as reasonably practicable after the change occurs.

111A(2) In this section **"the social security legislation"** means the Acts to which section 110 above applies and the Jobseekers Act 1995.

111A(3) A person guilty of an offence under this section shall be liable–

(a) on summary conviction, to imprisonment for a term not exceeding six months, or to a fine not exceeding the statutory maximum, or to both; or

(b) on conviction on indictment, to imprisonment for a term not exceeding seven years, or to a fine, or to both.

111A(4) In the application of this section to Scotland, in subsection (1) to (1E) for "dishonestly" substitute "knowingly".

History – In s. 111A(1), the word "relevant" immediately preceding "social security legislation" inserted by CSPSSA 1992, Sch. 6, para. 5 with effect from 2 April 2001 (SI 2001/1252 (C. 45)).
S. 111A(1)(c), (d) omitted by and the word "or" inserted by SSFA 2001, s. 16(1)(a) and Schedule with effect from 26 September 2001 for the purposes of making regulations and 18 October for all other purposes (SI 2001/3251 (C. 105)).
S. 111A(1A)–(1G) inserted by SSFA 2001, s. 16 with effect from 26 September 2001 for the purposes of making regulations and 18 October 2001 for all other purposes (SI 2001/3251 (C. 105)).
In s. 111A(4), the words "subsections (1) to (1E)" substituted by SSFA 2001, s. 16 with effect from 26 September 2001 for purposes of making regulations and from 18 October 2001 for all other purposes (SI 2001/3251 (C. 105)).
S. 111A inserted by Social Security Administration (Fraud) Act 1997, s. 13, with effect from 1 July 1997, by virtue of SI 1997/1577.
Cross references – TCA 1999, Sch. 2, para. 11: disapplication of section 111A to the extent that it relates to tax credit.

112 False representations for obtaining benefit etc.

112(1) If a person for the purpose of obtaining any benefit or other payment under the relevant social security legislation whether for himself or some other person, or for any other purpose connected with that legislation–

(a) makes a statement or representation which he knows to be false; or

(b) produces or furnishes, or knowingly causes or knowingly allows to be produced or furnished, any document or information which he knows to be false in a material particular,

he shall be guilty of an offence.

112(1A) A person shall be guilty of an offence if–

(a) there has been a change of circumstances affecting any entitlement of his to any benefit or other payment or advantage under any provision of the relevant social security legislation;

(b) the change is not a change that is excluded by regulations from the changes that are required to be notified;

(c) he knows that the change affects an entitlement of his to such a benefit or other payment or advantage; and

(d) he fails to give a prompt notification of that change in the prescribed manner to the prescribed person.

112(1B) A person is guilty of an offence under this section if–

(a) there has been a change of circumstances affecting any entitlement of another person to any benefit or other payment or advantage under any provision of the relevant social security legislation;

(b) the change is not a change that is excluded by regulations from the changes that are required to be notified;

(c) he knows that the change affects an entitlement of that other person to such a benefit or other payment or advantage; and

(d) he causes or allows that other person to fail to give a prompt notification of that change in the prescribed manner to the prescribed person.

112(1C) In a case where subsection (1C) of section 111A above applies, the recipient is guilty of an offence if–

(a) he knows that the change affects an entitlement of the claimant to a benefit or other payment or advantage under a provision of the relevant social security legislation;

(b) the entitlement is one in respect of which he has a right to receive payments to which the claimant has, or (but for the arrangements under which they are payable to the recipient) would have, an entitlement; and

(c) he fails to give a prompt notification of that change in the prescribed manner to the prescribed person.

112(1D) In a case where that subsection applies, a person other than the recipient is guilty of an offence if–

(a) he knows that the change affects an entitlement of the claimant to a benefit or other payment or advantage under a provision of the relevant social security legislation;

(b) the entitlement is one in respect of which the recipient has a right to receive payments to which the claimant has, or (but for the arrangements under which they are payable to the recipient) would have, an entitlement; and

(c) he causes or allows the recipient to fail to give a prompt notification of that change in the prescribed manner to the prescribed person.

112(1E) Subsection (1F) of section 111A above applies in relation to subsections (1C) and (1D) above as it applies in relation to subsections (1D) and (1E) of that section.

112(1F) For the purposes of subsections (1A) to (1D) above a notification of a change is prompt if, and only if, it is given as soon as reasonably practicable after the change occurs.

112(2) A person guilty of an offence under this section shall be liable on summary conviction to a fine not exceeding level 5 on the standard scale, or to imprisonment for a term not exceeding 3 months, or to both.

112(3) In this section **"the social security legislation"** means the Acts to which section 110 above applies and the Jobseekers Act 1995.

History – In s. 112(1), the words "social security legislation" substituted by the Social Security Administration (Fraud) Act 1997, s. 22 and Sch. 1, para. 4, with effect from 1 July 1997, by virtue of SI 1997/1577.

In s. 112(1), the word "relevant" immediately preceding the words "social security legislation" substituted by CSPSSA 1992, Sch. 6, para. 5.

S. 112(1A) inserted by the Social Security Administration (Fraud) Act 1997, s. 14, with effect from 1 July 1997, by virtue of SI 1998/1577.

S. 112(1A)–(1F) substituted for former s. 112(1A) with effect from 26 September 2001 for purposes of making regulations and from 18 October 2001 for all other purposes (SI 2001/3251 (C. 105)).

In s. 112(2), the words "this section" substituted by the Social Security Administration (Fraud) Act 1997, s. 22 and Sch. 1, para. 4, with effect from 1 July 1997, by virtue of SI 1997/1577.

S. 112(3) inserted by the Social Security Administration (Fraud) Act 1997, s. 22 and Sch. 1, para. 4, with effect from 1 July 1997, by virtue of SI 1997/1577.

Derivations – SSA 1986, s. 55.

Cross references – TCA 1999, Sch. 2, para. 11: disapplication of section 112 to the extent that it relates to tax credit.

Notes – Level 5 on standard scale is £5,000 in relation to offences committed after 1 October 1992 (Criminal Justice Act 1982, s. 37(2); Criminal Justice Act 1991, s. 17(1); SI 1992/333).

113 Breach of regulations

113(1) Regulations and schemes under any of the legislation to which this section applies may provide that any person who contravenes, or fails to comply with, any provision contained in regulations made *under that legislation*–

(a) in the case of a provision relating to contributions, shall be liable to a penalty;

(b) in any other case, shall be guilty of an offence under any enactment contained in the legislation in question.

113(1A) The legislation to which this section applies is–

(a) the relevant social security legislation; and

(b) the enactments specified in section 121DA(1) so far as relating to contributions.

113(2) Any regulations or scheme making such provision as is mentioned in subsection (1)(a) above shall–

(a) prescribe the amount or rate of penalty, or provide for how it is to be ascertained;

(b) provide for the penalty to be imposed by the Inland Revenue–

(i) within six years after the date on which the penalty is incurred; or

(ii) where the amount of the penalty is to be ascertained by reference to the amount of any contributions payable, at any later time within three years after the final determination of the amount of those contributions;

(c) provide for determining the date on which, for the purposes of paragraph (b) above, the penalty is incurred;

(d) prescribe the means by which the penalty is to be enforced; and

(e) provide for enabling the Inland Revenue, in their discretion, to mitigate or to remit any such penalty, or to stay or to compound any proceedings for a penalty.

113(3) A person guilty of such an offence as is mentioned in subsection (1)(b) above shall be liable on summary conviction–

(a) to a fine not exceeding level 3 on the standard scale;

(b) in the case of an offence of continuing a contravention or failure after conviction, to a fine not exceeding £40 for each day on which it is so continued.

113(4) Any provision contained in regulations which authorises statutory sick pay or statutory maternity pay to be set off against secondary Class 1 contributions is not a provision relating to contributions for the purposes of this section.

History – In s. 113(1) the following text substituted by CSPSSA 2000, s. 67 and Sch. 6, para. 7(1), with effect from 1 November 2000, by virtue of SI 2000/2950, art. 2(d)(i): "legislation to which this section applies" for "Acts to which section 110 above applies"; "that legislation " for "that Act" in the first place; and "any enactment contained in the legislation in question" for "that Act" in the second place.

In s. 113(1A)(b), the words ", statutory sick pay or statutory maternity pay" which followed "contributions" omitted by NICSPA 2004, s. 9(4) and repealed by s. 12 and Sch. 2 with effect from 6 April 2005 (by virtue of SI 2004/1943, reg. 4 and 6).

S. 113(1A) inserted by CSPSSA 2000, s. 67 and Sch. 6, para. 7(2) with effect from 1 November 2000, by virtue of SI 2000/2950, art. 2(d)(i).

In s. 113(2) references to "Inland Revenue" substituted for "Secretary of State" by SSC(TF)A 1999, s. 5 and Sch. 5, para. 5, with effect from 6 April 1999 (SI 1999/527).

S. 113 substituted by SSA 1998, s. 60 for the purposes of making regulations, with effect from 4 March 1999 and, for all other purposes, with effect from 6 April 1999 (SI 1999/526).

Cross references – TCA 1999, Sch. 2, para. 11: disapplication of section 113 to the extent that it relates to tax credit.

SSC(TF)A 1999, s. 8(1)(k) and (l): with effect from 6 April 1999 it is an officer of the Board's responsibility to decide on whether a person is liable to a penalty (and the amount thereof) under s. 13(1)(a).

SSA 1998, Sch. 3, para. 26: an appeal may be made against a decision under s. 113(1)(a).

Notes – Level 3 on standard scale is £1,000 in relation to offences committed after 1 October 1992 (Criminal Justice Act 1982, s. 37(2); Criminal Justice Act 1991, s. 17(1); SI 1992/333).

113A Statutory sick pay and statutory maternity pay: breach of regulations

113A(1) Where a person fails to produce any document or record, or provide any information, in accordance with–

(a) regulations under section 5(1)(i) and (5), so far as relating to statutory sick pay or statutory maternity pay,

(b) regulations under section 130 or 132, or

(c) regulations under section 153(5)(b) of the Contributions and Benefits Act,

that person is liable to the penalties mentioned in subsection (2).

113A(2) The penalties are–

(a) a penalty not exceeding £300, and

(b) if the failure continues after a penalty is imposed under paragraph (a), a further penalty or penalties not exceeding £60 for each day on which the failure continues after the day on which the penalty under that paragraph was imposed (but excluding any day for which a penalty under this paragraph has already been imposed).

113A(3) Where a person fails to maintain a record in accordance with regulations under section 130 or 132, he is liable to a penalty not exceeding £3,000.

113A(4) No penalty may be imposed under subsection (1) at any time after the failure concerned has been remedied.

113A(5) But subsection (4) does not apply to the imposition of a penalty under subsection (2)(a) in respect of a failure to produce any document or record in accordance with regulations under section 130(5) or 132(4).

113A(6) Where, in the case of any employee, an employer refuses or repeatedly fails to make payments of statutory sick pay or statutory maternity pay in accordance with any regulations under section 5, the employer is liable to a penalty not exceeding £3,000.

113A(7) Section 118(2) of the Taxes Management Act 1970 (extra time for compliance etc) applies for the purposes of subsections (1), (3) and (6) as it applies for the purposes of that Act.

113A(8) Schedule 1 to the Employment Act 2002 (penalties relating to statutory paternity pay and statutory adoption pay: procedures and appeals) applies in relation to penalties imposed under this section (with the modifications set out in subsection (9)).

113A(9) That Schedule applies as if–

(a) references to a penalty under section 11 or 12 of that Act were to a penalty under this section,

(b) in paragraph 1(2), the reference to section 11(2)(a) of that Act were to subsection (2)(a) of this section, and

(c) the provisions of the Taxes Management Act 1970 having effect in relation to an appeal mentioned in paragraph 3(2) of that Schedule did not include section 50(9) of that Act.

History – S. 113A inserted by NICSPA 2004, s. 9(5) with effect from 6 April 2005 (by virtue of SI 2004/1943, reg. 4).

113B Statutory sick pay and statutory maternity pay: fraud and negligence

113B(1) Where a person fraudulently or negligently–

(a) makes any incorrect statement or declaration in connection with establishing entitlement to statutory sick pay or statutory maternity pay, or

(b) produces any incorrect document or record or provides any incorrect information of a kind mentioned in–

- (i) regulations under 5(1)(i) and (5), so far as relating to statutory sick pay or statutory maternity pay,
- (ii) regulations under section 130 or 132, or
- (iii) regulations under section 153(5)(b) of the Contributions and Benefits Act,

he is liable to a penalty not exceeding £3,000.

113B(2) Where an employer fraudulently or negligently makes an incorrect payment of statutory sick pay or statutory maternity pay, he is liable to a penalty not exceeding £3,000.

113B(3) Where an employer fraudulently or negligently receives an overpayment in pursuance of regulations under section 167 of the Contributions and Benefits Act (statutory maternity pay: advance payments to employers), he is liable to a penalty not exceeding £3,000.

113B(4) Schedule 1 to the Employment Act 2002 (penalties relating to statutory paternity pay and statutory adoption pay: procedures and appeals) applies in relation to penalties imposed under this section (with the modifications set out in subsection (5)).

113B(5) That Schedule applies as if–

(a) references to a penalty under section 11 or 12 of that Act were to a penalty under this section, and

(b) the provisions of the Taxes Management Act 1970 having effect in relation to an appeal mentioned in paragraph 3(2) of that Schedule did not include section 50(9) of that Act.

History – S. 113B inserted by NICSPA 2004, s. 9(5) with effect from 6 April 2005 (by virtue of SI 2004/1943, reg. 4).

114 Offences relating to contributions

114(1) Any person who is knowingly concerned in the fraudulent evasion of any contributions which he or any other person is liable to pay shall be guilty of an offence.

114(2) A person guilty of an offence under this section shall be liable–

(a) on *conviction on indictment*, to imprisonment for a term not exceeding seven years or to a fine or to both;

(b) on summary conviction, to a fine not exceeding the statutory maximum.

History – S. 114 substituted by SSA 1998, s. 61 for the purposes of making regulations, with effect from 4 March 1999 and, for all other purposes, with effect from 6 April 1999 (SI 1999/526).

Cross references – SSCBA 1992, s. 12(7)(b): proceedings under this section for failure to pay Class 2 contributions.

SSCBA 1992, Sch. 1, para. 6: power to combine collection of contributions with tax.
Hansard – HC Written Answer, 22 February 1984, vol. 54, col. 543, (not reproduced): for payment which is less than an employers' full [PAYE] tax and NIC liability, collector is instructed to agree basis of apportionment.
Notes – Summary procedure (2)) governed by Magistrates' Court Act 1980.

115 Offences by bodies corporate

115(1) Where an offence under this Act, or under the Jobseekers Act 1995, which has been committed by a body corporate is proved to have been committed with the consent or connivance of, or to be attributable to any neglect on the part of, a director, manager, secretary or other similar officer of the body corporate, or any person who was purporting to act in any such capacity, he, as well as the body corporate, shall be guilty of that offence and be liable to be proceeded against accordingly.

115(2) Where the affairs of a body corporate are managed by its members, subsection (1) above applies in relation to the acts and defaults of a member in connection with his functions of management as if he were a director of the body corporate.

History – In s. 115(1) the words ", or under the Jobseekers Act 1995," inserted by Jobseekers Act 1995, Sch. 2, para. 55, with effect from 11 June 1996 by virtue of SI 1996/1509.
Derivations – SSA 1986, s. 57.

LEGAL PROCEEDINGS

116 Legal proceedings

116(1) Any person authorised by the Secretary of State in that behalf may conduct any proceedings under any provision of this Act other than section 114 or under any provision of the Jobseekers Act 1995 before a magistrates' court although not a barrister or solicitor.

116(2) Notwithstanding anything in any Act–

(a) proceedings for an offence under this Act (other than proceedings to which paragraph (b) applies), or for an offence under the Jobseekers Act 1995, may be begun at any time within the period of 3 months from the date on which evidence, sufficient in the opinion of the Secretary of State to justify a prosecution for the offence, comes to his knowledge or within a period of 12 months from the commission of the offence, whichever period last expires;

(b) [not relevant to National Insurance contributions.]

116(2A) Subsection (2) above shall not be taken to impose any restriction on the time when proceedings may be begun for an offence under section 111A above.

116(3) For the purposes of subsection (2) above–

(a) a certificate purporting to be signed by or on behalf of the Secretary of State as to the date on which such evidence as is mentioned in paragraph (a) of that subsection came to his knowledge shall be conclusive evidence of that date;

(b) [not relevant to National Insurance contributions.]

116(4) [Not relevant to National Insurance contributions.]

116(5) [Not relevant to National Insurance contributions.]

116(5A) In relation to proceedings for an offence under section 114 above, the references in subsections (2)(a) and (3)(a) to the Secretary of State shall have effect as references to the Inland Revenue.

116(6) [Repealed by SSA 1998, s. 86(2); Sch. 8.]

116(7) In the application of this section to Scotland, the following provisions shall have effect in substitution for subsections (1) to (5A) above–

(a) proceedings for an offence under this Act or the Jobseekers Act 1995 may, notwithstanding anything in section 136 of the Criminal Procedure (Scotland) Act 1995, be commenced at any time within the period of 3 months from the date on which evidence, sufficient in the opinion of the Lord Advocate to justify proceedings, comes to his knowledge, or within the period of 12 months from the commission of the offence, whichever period last expires;

(aa) this subsection shall not be taken to impose any restriction on the time when proceedings may be commenced for an offence under section 111A above;

(b) for the purposes of this subsection–

 (i) a certificate purporting to be signed by or on behalf of the Lord Advocate as to the date on which such evidence as is mentioned above came to his knowledge shall be conclusive evidence of that date; and

 (ii) subsection (3) of section 136 of the said Act of 1995 (date of commencement of proceedings) shall have effect as it has effect for the purposes of that section.

NIC Statutes

Prospective amendments – In s. 116(2)(a), the words "(other than proceedings to which paragraph (b) applies)" repealed by WRA 2012, s. 147 and Sch. 14, Pt. 1, with effect (other than as noted in the History note below) from a date to be set by order of the Secretary of State.
S. 116(2)(b) and the preceding "and" repealed by WRA 2012, s. 147 and Sch. 14, Pt. 1, with effect (other than as noted in the History note below) from a date to be set by order of the Secretary of State.
S. 116(3)(b) and the preceding "and" repealed by WRA 2012, s. 147 and Sch. 14, Pt. 1, with effect (other than as noted in the History note below) from a date to be set by order of the Secretary of State.
S. 116(4) and (5) repealed by WRA 2012, s. 147 and Sch. 14, Pt. 1, with effect (other than as noted in the History note below) from a date to be set by order of the Secretary of State.

History – In s. 116(2)(a), the words "(other than proceedings to which paragraph (b) applies)" repealed by WRA 2012, s. 147 and Sch. 14, Pt. 1, with effect in so far as they relate to the abolition of council tax benefit from 1 April 2013 (SI 2013/358, art. 8(c) and Sch. 4).
In s. 116(2)(a), the words "(other than proceedings to which paragraph (b) applies)" substituted for the words "other than an offence relating to housing benefit or council tax benefit" by WRA 2012, s. 111, with effect from 7 May 2012.
S. 116(2)(b) and the preceding "and" repealed by WRA 2012, s. 147 and Sch. 14, Pt. 1, in so far as they relate to the abolition of council tax benefit from 1 April 2013 (SI 2013/358, art. 8(c) and Sch. 4).
S. 116(3)(b) and the preceding "and" repealed by WRA 2012, s. 147 and Sch. 14, Pt. 1, with effect in so far as they relate to the abolition of council tax benefit from 1 April 2013 (SI 2013/358, art. 8(c) and Sch. 4).
S. 116(4) and (5) repealed by WRA 2012, s. 147 and Sch. 14, Pt. 1, with effect in so far as they relate to the abolition of council tax benefit from 1 April 2013 (SI 2013/358, art. 8(c) and Sch. 4).
In s. 116(7), para. (aa) inserted by SSFA 2001, s. 17 with effect from 30 April 2001.
In s. 116(1) the words "under any provision of this Act other than section 114 or under any provision of" substituted by SSC(TF)A 1999, s. 1 and Sch. 1, para. 21(2) for the purposes of making regulations, with effect from 25 February 1999 and for all other purposes, with effect from 1 April 1999 (SI 1999/527).
S. 116(1), (2)(a), (7)(a) amended by Jobseekers Act 1995, Sch. 2, para. 56, with effect from 11 June 1996 by virtue of SI 1996/1509, by inserting, in s. 116(1), "or the Jobseekers Act 1995"; in s. 116(2)(a), ", or for an offence under the Jobseekers Act 1995,", and in s. 116(7)(a), "or the Jobseekers Act 1995".
In s. 116(2) the words "council tax benefit" substituted by the Local Government Finance Act 1992, s. 103 and Sch. 9, para. 17(1) from 6 March 1992.
S. 116(2A) inserted by the Social Security Administration (Fraud) Act 1997, s. 22 and Sch. 1, para. 5 with effect from 1 July 1997, by virtue of SI 1997/1577.
S. 116(5A) inserted by SSC(TF)A 1999, s. 1 and Sch. 1, para. 21(3) for the purposes of making regulations, with effect from 25 February 1999 and for all other purposes, with effect from 1 April 1999 (SI 1999/527).
In s. 116(5A) the words "In relation to proceedings for an offence under section 114 above" substituted by WRPA 1999, s. 81, Sch. 11, para. 5 with effect from 11 November 1999 (date of passing of WRPA 1999) which is the commencement date provided for in WRPA 1999, s. 89(4)(d).
S. 116(6) repealed by SSA 1998, s. 86(2); Sch. 8, with effect from 29 November 1999(SI 1999/3178 (C. 81), art. 2(1)(a), Sch. 1).
In s. 116(7) the words "section 136 of the Criminal Procedure (Scotland) Act 1995" and the words "section 136 of the said Act of 1995" substituted by Criminal Procedure (Consequential Provisions) (Scotland) Act 1995, with effect from 1 April 1996.
In s. 116(7) reference to 116(5A) substituted by SSC(TF)A 1999, s. 1 and Sch. 1, para. 21(4) with effect from 1 April 1999 (SI 1999/527).

Derivations – (as originally enacted) – SSA 1986, s. 56.

Cross references – Criminal Procedure (Scotland) Act 1975, s. 331 (not reproduced): time limits for statutory offences.
PSA 1993, s. 167: application of general provisions relating to administration of social security.

117 Issues arising in proceedings

117(1) This section applies to proceedings before a court–

(a) for an offence under this Act or the Jobseekers Act 1995; or

(b) involving any question as to the payment of contributions (other than a Class 4 contribution recoverable by the Inland Revenue); or

(c) for the recovery of any sums due to the Secretary of State or the National Insurance Fund.

117(2) A decision of the Secretary of State which–

(a) falls within Part II of Schedule 3 to the Social Security Act 1998 ("the 1998 Act"); and

(b) relates to or affects an issue arising in the proceedings,

shall be conclusive for the purposes of the proceedings.

117(3) If–

(a) any such decision is necessary for the determination of the proceedings; and

(b) the decision of the Secretary of State has not been obtained or an application with respect to the decision has been made under section 9 or 10 of the 1998 Act,

the decision shall be referred to the Secretary of State to be made in accordance (subject to any necessary modifications) with Chapter II of Part I of that Act.

117(4) Subsection (2) above does not apply where, in relation to the decision–

(a) an appeal has been brought but not determined;

(b) an application for leave to appeal has been made but not determined;

(c) an appeal has not been brought (or, as the case may be, an application for leave to appeal has not been made) but the time for doing so has not yet expired; or

(d) an application has been made under section 9 or 10 of the 1998 Act.

117(5) In a case falling within subsection (4) above the court shall adjourn the proceedings until such time as the final decision is known; and that decision shall be conclusive for the purposes of the proceedings.

History – S. 117 (as amended by SSC(TF)A 1999, s. 18 and Sch. 7, para. 12; see previous version of text below) substituted by SSA 1998, s. 86(1) and Sch. 7, para. 84, with effect from 5 July 1999 for the purposes of any matter to which, by virtue of PSA 1993, s. 170, provisions of SSA 1998, Pt. I, Ch. II are to apply (SI 1999/1958 (C. 51), art. 2(1)(b)(iv)); and with effect from 29 November 1999 in so far as it was not already in force for all other purposes (except for housing benefit, council tax benefit and decisions to which SI 1999/527, art. 4(6) applies; i.e. pre-1 April 1999 decisions under SSAA 1992, s. 17(1), s. 20(3) and PSA 1993, s. 170(1)) (SI 1999/3178 (C. 81), art. 2(1)(a); 2(2) and Sch. 1).
The pre-SI 1999/1958 and 1999/3178 version of s. 117 that is still in force for the purposes of housing benefit, council tax benefit and decisions to which SI 1999/527, art. 4(6) applies (i.e. certain pre-1 April 1999 decisions) is as follows (together with appropriate History notes and other notes):

"117(5) Questions arising in proceedings

117(1) Where in any proceedings–

(a) for an offence under this Act or the Jobseekers Act 1995; or

(b) involving any question as to the payment of contributions (other than a Class 4 contribution recoverable by the Inland Revenue); or

(c) for the recovery of any sums due to the Secretary of State or the National Insurance Fund,

any such question arises as is mentioned in section 17(1) above, the decision of the Secretary of State shall be conclusive for the purposes of the proceedings.

117(2) If–

(a) a decision of any such question is necessary for the determination of proceedings; and

(b) the decision of the Secretary of State has not been obtained or a question has been raised with a view to a review of the decision obtained,

the question shall be referred to the Secretary of State for determination or review in accordance (subject to any necessary modifications) with Part II of this Act.

117(3) Subsection (1) above does not apply if–

(a) an appeal under section 18 above is pending; or

(b) the time for appealing has not expired; or

(c) a question has been raised with a view to a review of the Secretary of State's decision under section 19 above,

and the court dealing with the case shall adjourn the proceedings until such time as a final decision on the question has been obtained.

History – In s. 117(1)(a), the words "or the Jobseekers Act 1995" inserted by Jobseekers Act 1995, Sch. 2, para. 57, with effect from 11 June 1996 by virtue of SI 1996/1509.

Derivations – SSA 1975, s. 148.

Cross references – S. 17: questions to be determined by the Secretary of State.
S. 18: appeal or question of law.
S. 19: review of decisions.
S. 59: procedure.
SI 1986/2218, reg. 17: review or reference.

Hansard – HC Written Answer, 22 February 1984, vol. 54, col. 543 (not reproduced): for payment which is less than an employer's full [PAYE] tax and NIC liability, collector is instructed to agree basis of apportionment."

117A Issues arising in proceedings: contributions, etc.

117A(1) This section applies to proceedings before a court–

(a) for an offence under this Act or the Jobseekers Act 1995; or

(b) involving any question as to the payment of contributions (other than a Class 4 contribution recoverable in accordance with section 15 of the Contributions and Benefits Act); or

(c) for the recovery of any sums due to the inland Revenue or the National Insurance Fund.

117A(2) A decision of an officer of the Inland Revenue which–

(a) falls within section 8(1) of the Social Security Contributions (Transfer of Functions, etc.) Act 1999; and

(b) relates to or affects an issue arising in the proceedings,

shall be conclusive for the purposes of the proceedings.

117A(3) If–

(a) any such decision is necessary for the determination of the proceedings, and

(b) the decision of an officer of the Inland Revenue has not been obtained under section 8 of the Social Security Contributions (Transfer of Functions, etc.) Act 1999,

the decision shall be referred to such an officer to be made in accordance (subject to any necessary modifications) with Part II of the Social Security Contributions (Transfer of Functions, etc.) Act 1999.

117A(4) Subsection (2) above does not apply where, in relation to the decision–

(a) an appeal has been brought but not determined;

(b) an appeal has not been brought (or, as the case may be, an application for leave to appeal has not been made) but the time for doing so has not yet expired; or

(c) an application for variation of the decision has been made under regulations made under section 10 of the Social Security Contributions (Transfer of Functions, etc.) Act 1999.

117A(5) In a case falling within subsection (4) above the court shall adjourn the proceedings until such time as the final decision is known; and that decision shall be conclusive for the purposes of the proceedings.

History – S. 117A inserted by SSC(TF)A 1999, s. 18 and Sch. 7, para. 13, with effect from 1 April 1999 (SI 1999/527).

UNPAID CONTRIBUTIONS ETC.

118 Evidence of non-payment

118(1) [Omitted by FA 2008, s. 138 and Sch. 44, para. 4.]

118(2) [Repealed by SSC(TF)A 1999, s. 5; Sch. 5, para. 7(3) and s. 26(3); Sch. 10, Pt. I.]

118(3) [Omitted by FA 2008, s. 138 and Sch. 44, para. 4.]

118(4) A statutory declaration by an officer of the Inland Revenue that the searches specified in the declaration for a record of the payment of a particular contribution have been made, and that a record of the payment of the contribution in question has not been found, is admissible in any proceedings for an offence as evidence of the facts stated in the declaration.

118(5) Nothing in subsection (4) above makes a statutory declaration admissible as evidence in proceedings for an offence except in a case where, and to the extent to which, oral evidence to the like effect would have been admissible in those proceedings.

118(6) Nothing in subsections (4) and (5) above makes a statutory declaration admissible as evidence in proceedings for an offence–

(a) unless a copy of it has, not less than 7 days before the hearing or trial, been served on the person charged with the offence in any manner in which a summons or, in Scotland, a citation in a summary prosecution may be served; or

(b) if that person, not later than 3 days before the hearing or trial or within such further time as the court may in special circumstances allow, gives notice to the prosecutor requiring the attendance at the trial of the person by whom the declaration was made.

118(7) [Omitted by FA 2008, s. 138 and Sch. 44, para. 4.]

History – S. 118(1) omitted by FA 2008, s. 138 and Sch. 44, para. 4, with effect from 21 July 2008.
In s. 118(1) and (4) references to "Inland Revenue" substituted by SSC(TF)A 1999, s. 5; Sch. 5, para. 7(2) and s. 26(3); Sch. 10, Pt. I, with effect from 6 April 1999 (SI 1999/527).
S. 118(2) repealed by SSC(TF)A 1999, s. 5; Sch. 5, para. 7(3) and s. 26(3); Sch. 10, Pt. I, with effect from 6 April 1999 (SI 1999/527).
S. 118(3) omitted by FA 2008, s. 138 and Sch. 44, para. 4, with effect from 21 July 2008.
In s. 118(4) the words "for a particular contribution card or", and "the card in question or" omitted by SSA 1998, s. 62(3), with effect from 6 April 1999 (SI 1999/526).
S. 118(7) omitted by FA 2008, s. 138 and Sch. 44, para. 4, with effect from 21 July 2008.
S. 118(7) inserted by SSC(TF)A 1999, s. 5; Sch. 5, para. 7(6), with effect from 6 April 1999 (SI 1999/527).
S. 118(1) substituted by SSA 1998, s. 62(1), with effect from 6 April 1999 (SI 1999/526).

Derivations – SSA 1975, s. 149.

Hansard – HC Written Answer, 22 February 1984, vol. 54, col. 54 (not reproduced): for payment which is less than an employer's full [PAYE] tax and NIC liability, collector is instructed to agree basis of apportionment.

Notes – The reference in s. 118(1) above to SSCBA 1992, Sch. 1, para. 5(1) appears to be a Queen's printers' error as presumably the reference should be to SSCBA 1992, Sch. 1, para. 6(1).
SI 1979/591, reg. 46: deduction of contributions at source.

119 Recovery of unpaid contributions on prosecution

119(1) Where–

(a) a person has been convicted of an offence under section 114(1) above of failing to pay a contribution at or within the time prescribed for the purpose; and

(b) the contribution remains unpaid at the date of the conviction,

he shall be liable to pay to the Inland Revenue a sum equal to the amount which he failed to pay.

119(2) [Repealed by SSA 1998, s. 86(1) and Sch. 7, para. 85, s. 86(2) and Sch. 8.]

History – In s. 119 reference to "Inland Revenue" substituted for "Secretary of State" by SSC(TF)A 1999, s. 1 and Sch. 1 para. 22, with effect from 1 April 1999 (SI 1999/527).
S. 119(2) repealed by SSA 1998, s. 86(1) and Sch. 7, para. 85, s. 86(2) and Sch. 8, with effect from 6 April 1999 (SI 1999/526).

Derivations – SSA 1975, s. 150.

Cross references – SDMA 1891, s. 13: offences in relation to dies and stamp.
SSCBA 1992, Sch. 1, para. 7(3): persons liable to penalty under TMA 1970, s. 98A(2)(a) in consequence of a failure under a tax return shall not also be liable to a penalty in respect of any failure of the associated contributions return.
SI 1979/591, Sch. 2, Pt. I: regulation applying SDMA 1891, s. 13.

Hansard – 24 February 1978, vol. 944, no. 67, col. 386 (not reproduced): the DSS waives arrears by unpublished concession in various cases, e.g. where the contributor would have been entitled to the small earnings exception or where his financial circumstances would make recovery impractical.

120 Proof of previous offences

120(1) Subject to and in accordance with subsections (2) to (5) below, where a person is convicted of an offence mentioned in section 119(1) above, evidence may be given of any previous failure by him to pay contributions within the time prescribed for the purpose; and in those subsections **"the conviction"** and **"the offence"** mean respectively the conviction referred to in this subsection and the offence of which the person is convicted.

120(2) Such evidence may be given only if notice of intention to give it is served with the summons or warrant or, in Scotland, the complaint on which the person appeared before the court which convicted him.

120(3) If the offence is one of failure to pay a Class 1 contribution, evidence may be given of failure on his part to pay (whether or not in respect of the same person) such contributions or any Class 1A or Class 1B contributions or contributions equivalent premiums on the date of the offence, or during the 6 years preceding that date.

120(4) If the offence is one of failure to pay a Class 1A contribution, evidence may be given of failure on his part to pay (whether or not in respect of the same person or the same amount) such contributions, or any Class 1 or Class 1B contributions or contributions equivalent premiums, on the date of the offence, or during the 6 years preceding that date.

120(4A) If the offence is one of failure to pay a Class 1B contribution, evidence may be given of failure on his part to pay such contributions, or any Class 1 or Class 1A contributions or contributions equivalent premiums, on the date of the offence, or during the 6 years preceding that date.

120(5) If the offence–

(a) is one of failure to pay Class 2 contributions

(b) [repealed by SSA 1998, Sch. 7, para. 86(5)(a).]

evidence may be given of his failure to pay such contributions during those 6 years.

120(6) On proof of any matter of which evidence may be given under subsection (3), (4), (4A) or (5) above, the person convicted shall be liable to pay to the Inland Revenue a sum equal to the total of all amounts which he is so proved to have failed to pay and which remain unpaid at the date of the conviction.

History – In s. 120(1) the words "or (2)(a)" omitted by SSA 1998, s. 86(1) and Sch. 7, para. 86(1), with effect from 6 April 1999 by virtue of SI 1998/2209, art. 2(c) and Schedule, Pt. III.
In s. 120(3), reference to Class 1B contributions inserted, and the time period increased to 6 years from 2 years by SSA 1998, s. 86(1) and Sch. 7, para. 86(2), with effect from 6 April 1999 by virtue of SI 1999/526 and SI 1998/2209, art. 2(c) and Schedule, Pt. III.
In s. 120(3) and (4), the words "contributions equivalent premiums" substituted by Pensions Act 1995, Sch. 5, para. 15(3), with effect from 6 April 1997 by virtue of SI 1997/664, art. 2(3) and Schedule, Pt. II.
In s. 120(4), the word "amount" substituted by CSPSSA 2000, s. 75(6) with effect from 6 April 2000 (s. 75(8)).
In s. 120(4), reference to Class 1B contributions inserted, and the time period increased to 6 years from 2 years by SSA 1998, s. 86(1) and Sch. 7, para. 86(3), with effect from 6 April 1999 by virtue of SI 1999/526 and SI 1998/2209, art. 2(c) and Schedule, Pt. III.
S. 120(4A) and the reference to it in s. 120(6) inserted by SSA 1998, s. 86(1) and Sch. 7, para. 86(4)(a), (6), with effect from 6 April 1999 by virtue of SI 1998/2209, art. 2(c) and Schedule, Pt. III.
In s. 120(5) the time period is increased to 6 years from 2 years by SSA 1998, s. 86(1) and Sch. 7, para. 86(5)(b), with effect from 6 April 1999 by virtue of SI 1999/526.
S. 120(5)(b) repealed by SSA 1998, s. 86(1) and Sch. 7, para. 86(5)(a), with effect from 6 April 1999 by virtue of SI 1999/526.
In s. 120(6) reference to (4A) inserted by SSA 1998, s. 86(1) and Sch. 7, para. 86(6), with effect from 6 April 1999 by virtue of SI 1999/526 and reference to "Inland Revenue" substituted by SSC(TF)A 1999, s. 1 and Sch. 1, para. 23, with effect from 1 April 1999 (SI 1999/527).

Derivations – SSA 1975, s. 151.

121 Unpaid contributions – supplementary

121(1) Where in England and Wales a person charged with an offence mentioned in section 119(1) above is convicted of that offence in his absence under section 12(5) of the Magistrates' Courts Act 1980, then if–

(a) it is proved to the satisfaction of the court, on oath or in the manner prescribed by rules under section 144 of that Act, that notice under section 120(2) above has been duly served specifying the other contributions in respect of which the prosecutor intends to give evidence; and

(b) the clerk of the court has received a statement in writing purporting to be made by the accused or by a solicitor acting on his behalf to the effect that if the accused is convicted in his absence of the offence charged he desires to admit failing to pay the other contributions so specified or any of them,

section 120 above shall have effect as if the evidence had been given and the failure so admitted had been proved, and the court shall proceed accordingly.

121(2) In England and Wales, where a person is convicted of an offence mentioned in section 119(1) above and an order is made under section 12 of the Powers of Criminal Courts (Sentencing) Act 2000 discharging him *absolutely or conditionally*, sections 119 and 120 above, and subsection (1) above, shall apply as if it were a conviction for all purposes.

121(3) In Scotland, where a person is convicted on indictment of, or is charged before a court of summary jurisdiction with, any such offence, and an order is made under Part I of the Criminal Procedure (Scotland) Act 1975 discharging him absolutely or placing him on probation, sections 119 and 120 above shall apply as if–

(a) the conviction on indictment were a conviction for all purposes; or

(b) (as the case may be) the making of the order by the court of summary jurisdiction were a conviction.

121(4) In England and Wales, any sum which a person is liable to pay under section 119 or 120 above or under subsection (1) above shall be recoverable from him as a penalty.

121(5) Sums recovered by the Inland Revenue under the provisions mentioned in subsection (4) above, so far as representing contributions of any class, are to be treated for all purposes of the Contributions and Benefits Act and this Act (including in particular the application of section 162 below) as contributions of that class received by the Inland Revenue.

121(6) Without prejudice to subsection (5) above, in so far as such sums represent primary Class 1 or Class 2 contributions, they are to be treated as contributions paid in respect of the person in respect of whom they were originally payable; and enactments relating to earnings factors shall apply accordingly.

History – In s. 121(1) the words "section 12(5)" substituted by the Magistrates' Courts (Procedure) Act 1998.
In s. 121(2) the words "section 12 of the Powers of Criminal Courts (Sentencing) Act 2000" substituted by s. 165 and Sch. 9 para 150 of the Powers of Criminal Courts (Sentencing) Act 2000 with effect from 25 August 2000.
In s. 121(1), (2) references to SSAA 1992, s. 119(2)(a) repealed by SSA 1998, s. 86(1) and Sch. 7, para. 87 and s. 86(2) and Sch. 8, with effect from 6 April 1999 (SI 1999/526).
In s. 121(5) reference to "Inland Revenue" substituted by SSC(TF)A 1999, s. 1 and Sch. 1, para. 24, with effect from 1 April 1999 (SI 1999/527).

Derivations – SSA 1975, s. 152.

Cross references – Magistrates' Courts Act 1980, s. 12(2) (not reproduced): non-appearance of accused: plea of guilty.

121A Recovery of contributions etc. in England and Wales

121A [Omitted by FA 2008, s. 129 and Sch. 43, para. 2.]

History – S. 121A omitted by FA 2008, s. 129 and Sch. 43, para. 2, with effect from 6 April 2014 (SI 2014/906, art. 2).
In s. 121A(1), the words "use the procedure in Schedule 12 to the Tribunals, Courts and Enforcement Act 2007 (taking control of goods) to recover the sums due" substituted for "distrain upon the goods and chattels of that person ("the person in default")." by TCEA 2007, s. 62(3) and Sch. 13, para. 104(2)(b) with effect from 6 April 2014 (SI 2014/768, art. 2).
In s. 121A(1), the words "("the sums due")" inserted and the words "use the procedure in Schedule 12 to the Tribunals, Courts and Enforcement Act 2007 (taking control of goods) to recover the sums due." substituted for the words "distrain upon the goods and chattels of that person ("the person in default")." by TCEA 2007, s. 62(3) and Sch. 13, para. 104(2), with effect from 19 September 2007 (SI 2007/2709).
In s. 121A(1)(b) the words "("the sums due")" inserted by TCEA 2007, s. 62(3) and Sch. 13, para. 104(2)(a) with effect from 6 April 2014 (SI 2014/768, art. 2).
In s. 121A(1)(b) "7 days" substituted for "30 days" by NICSPA 2004, s. 5(1) with effect from 1 September 2004 (by virtue of SI 2004/1943, reg. 2).
S. 121A(2)–(8) repealed by TCEA 2007, s. 62(3) and Sch. 13, para. 104(3), and s. 146 and Sch. 23, Pt. 3, with effect from 6 April 2014 (SI 2014/768, art. 2).
In s. 121A(8) the words "The Inland Revenue may by regulations" substituted by WRPA 1999, s. 81, Sch. 11, para. 6, with effect from 11 November 1999 (date of passing of WRPA 1999) which is the commencement date provided for in WRPA 1999, s. 89(4)(d).
In s. 121A(9) "Inland Revenue" and "them" substituted by SSC(TF)A 1999, s. 5; Sch. 5, para. 8 with effect from 1 April 1999 (SI 1999/527).
S. 121A(10) repealed by TCEA 2007, s. 62(3) and Sch. 13, para. 104(3), and s. 146 and Sch. 23, Pt. 3, with effect from 6 April 2014 (SI 2014/768, art. 2).
S. 121A inserted by SSA 1998, s. 63 for the purposes of making regulations, with effect from 4 March 1999 and, for all other purposes, from 6 April 1999 (SI 1999/526).

121B Recovery of contributions etc. in Scotland

121B [Omitted by FA 2008, s. 129 and Sch. 43, para. 14.]

History – S. 121B omitted by FA 2008, s. 129 and Sch. 43, para. 14, from 23 November 2009 (SI 2009/3024, art. 3).

121C Liability of directors etc. for a company's contributions

121C(1) This section applies to contributions which a body corporate is liable to pay, where–

(a) the body corporate has failed to pay the contributions at or within the time prescribed for the purpose; and

(b) the failure appears to the Inland Revenue to be attributable to fraud or neglect on the part of one or more individuals who, at the time of the fraud or neglect, were officers of the body corporate (**"culpable officers"**).

121C(2) The Inland Revenue may issue and serve on any culpable officer a notice (a "personal liability notice")–

(a) specifying the amount of the contributions to which this section applies (**"the specified amount"**);

(b) requiring the officer to pay to the Inland Revenue–
   (i) a specified sum in respect of that amount; and
   (ii) specified interest on that sum; and

(c) where that sum is given by paragraph (b) of subsection (3) below, specifying the proportion applied by the Inland Revenue for the purposes of that paragraph.

121C(3) The sum specified in the personal liability notice under subsection (2)(b)(i) above shall be–

(a) in a case where there is, in the opinion of the Inland Revenue, no other culpable officer, the whole of the specified amount; and

(b) in any other case, such proportion of the specified amount as, in the opinion of the Inland Revenue, the officer's culpability for the failure to pay that amount bears to that of all the culpable officers taken together.

121C(4) In assessing an officer's culpability for the purposes of subsection (3)(b) above, the Inland Revenue may have regard both to the gravity of the officer's fraud or neglect and to the consequences of it.

121C(5) The interest specified in the personal liability notice under subsection (2)(b)(ii) above shall be at the Class 1 rate on the Class 1 element of the specified sum, and otherwise at the prescribed rate, and shall run from the date on which the notice is issued.

121C(6) An officer who is served with a personal liability notice shall be liable to pay to the Inland Revenue the sum and the interest specified in the notice under subsection (2)(b) above.

121C(7) Where, after the issue of one or more personal liability notices, the amount of contributions to which this section applies is reduced by a payment made by the body corporate–

(a) the amount that each officer who has been served with such a notice is liable to pay under this section shall be reduced accordingly;

(b) the Inland Revenue shall serve on each such officer a notice to that effect; and

(c) where the reduced liability of any such officer is less than the amount that he has already paid under this section, the difference shall be repaid to him together with interest on it at the Class 1 rate on the Class 1 element of it and otherwise at the prescribed rate.

121C(8) Any amount paid under a personal liability notice shall be deducted from the liability of the body corporate in respect of the specified amount.

121C(8A) The amount which an officer is liable to pay under this section is to be recovered in the same manner as a Class 1 contribution to which regulations under paragraph 6 of Schedule 1 to the Contributions and Benefits Act apply and for this purpose references in those regulations to Class 1 contributions are to be construed accordingly.

121C(9) In this section–

"the Class 1 rate"–

(a) in subsection (5) means the rate from time to time applicable under section 103(1) of the Finance Act 2009; and

(b) in subsection (7)(c) means the rate from time to time applicable under section 103(2) of that Act;

"the Class 1 element", in relation to any amount, means so much of that amount as is calculated by–

(a) multiplying that amount by so much of the specified amount as consists of Class 1 contributions; and

(b) dividing the product of that multiplication by the specified amount;

"contributions" includes any interest or penalty in respect of contributions (and accordingly, in the definition of "the Class 1 element" given by this subsection, "Class 1 contributions" includes any interest or penalty in respect of Class 1 contributions);

"officer", in relation to a body corporate, means–

(a) any director, manager, secretary or other similar officer of the body corporate, or any person purporting to act as such; and

(b) in a case where the affairs of the body corporate are managed by its members, any member of the body corporate exercising functions of management with respect to it or purporting to do so;

"the prescribed rate" means the rate from time to time prescribed by regulations under section 178 of the Finance Act 1989 for the purposes of the corresponding provision of Schedule 1 to the Contributions and Benefits Act, that is to say–

(a) in relation to subsection (5) above, paragraph 6(2)(a);

(b) in relation to subsection (7) above, paragraph 6(2)(b).

History – In s. 121C the words "Inland Revenue" substituted by SSC(TF)A 1999, s. 5 and Sch. 5, para. 10 with effect from 1 April 1999 (SI 1999/527).

In s. 121C(5), the words "at the Class 1 rate on the Class 1 element of the specified sum, and otherwise at the prescribed rate," substituted for the words "at the prescribed rate" by SI 2014/1283, art. 2 and Sch., para. 2(a), with effect in relation to payments in respect of Class 1 National Insurance contributions and construction industry scheme payments made on or after 20 May 2014 which are made for the tax year 2014–15 or for a subsequent tax year. "Construction industry scheme payments" for this purpose means any amount deducted by a contractor from a contract payment under FA 2004, s. 61 (SI 2014/1283, art. 1(3).

In s. 121C(7)(c), the words "at the Class 1 rate on the Class 1 element of it and otherwise" inserted by SI 2014/1283, art. 2 and Sch., para. 2(b), with effect in relation to payments in respect of Class 1 National Insurance contributions and construction industry scheme payments made on or after 20 May 2014 which are made for the tax year 2014–15 or for a subsequent tax year. "Construction industry scheme payments" for this purpose means any amount deducted by a contractor from a contract payment under FA 2004, s. 61 (SI 2014/1283, art. 1(3).

S. 121C(8A) inserted by NICSPA 2004, s. 5(3) with effect from 1 September 2004 (by virtue of SI 2004/1943, reg. 2).

In s. 121C(9), the definitions of "the Class 1 rate" and "the Class 1 element" inserted by SI 2014/1283, art. 2 and Sch., para. 2(c)(i), with effect in relation to payments in respect of Class 1 National Insurance contributions and construction industry scheme payments made on or after 20 May 2014 which are made for the tax year 2014–15 or for a subsequent tax year. "Construction industry scheme

payments" for this purpose means any amount deducted by a contractor from a contract payment under FA 2004, s. 61 (SI 2014/1283, art. 1(3).
In s. 121C(9), in the definition of "contributions", the words "(and accordingly, in the definition of "the Class 1 element" given by this subsection, "Class 1 contributions" includes any interest or penalty in respect of Class 1 contributions)" inserted by SI 2014/1283, art. 2 and Sch., para. 2(c)(ii), with effect in relation to payments in respect of Class 1 National Insurance contributions and construction industry scheme payments made on or after 20 May 2014 which are made for the tax year 2014–15 or for a subsequent tax year. "Construction industry scheme payments" for this purpose means any amount deducted by a contractor from a contract payment under FA 2004,s. 61 (SI 2014/1283, art. 1(3).
S. 121C inserted by SSA 1998, s. 64 with effect from 6 April 1999 (SI 1999/526).

Cross references – SSC(TF)A 1999, s. 8(1)(h): an officer of the Board to decide questions arising as to issue and content of notices under s. 121C(2).
TCA 1999, s. 11: application of directors liability to amounts representing tax credits.

121D Appeals in relation to personal liability notices

121D(1) No appeal shall lie in relation to a personal liability notice except as provided by this section.

121D(2) An individual who is served with a personal liability notice may appeal against the Inland Revenue's decision as to the issue and content of the notice on the ground that–

(a) the whole or part of the amount specified under subsection (2)(a) of section 121C above (or the amount so specified as reduced under subsection (7) of that section) does not represent contributions to which that section applies;

(b) the failure to pay that amount was not attributable to any fraud or neglect on the part of the individual in question;

(c) the individual was not an officer of the body corporate at the time of the alleged fraud or neglect; or

(d) the opinion formed by the Inland Revenue under subsection (3)(a) or (b) of that section was unreasonable.

121D(3) The Inland Revenue shall give a copy of any notice of an appeal under this section, within 28 days of the giving of the notice, to each other individual who has been served with a personal liability notice.

121D(4) On an appeal under this section, the burden of proof as to any matter raised by a ground of appeal shall be on the Inland Revenue.

121D(5) Where an appeal under this section–

(a) is brought on the basis of evidence not considered by the Inland Revenue, or on the ground mentioned in subsection (2)(d) above; and

(b) is not allowed on some other basis or ground,

and is notified to the tribunal, the tribunal shall either dismiss the appeal or remit the case to the Inland Revenue, with any recommendations the tribunal sees fit to make, for the Inland Revenue to consider whether to vary their decision as to the issue and content of the personal liability notice.

121D(6) In this section–

"officer", in relation to a body corporate, has the same meaning as in section 121C above;

"personal liability notice" has the meaning given by subsection (2) of that section;

"tribunal" means the First-tier Tribunal or, where determined under Tribunal Procedure Rules, the Upper Tribunal;

"vary" means vary under regulations made under section 10 of the Social Security Contributions (Transfer of Functions, etc.) Act 1999.

History – In s. 121D "Inland Revenue" substituted for "Secretary of State" wherever the words occur; by SSC(TF)A 1999, s. 5; Sch. 5, para. 11(2) with effect from 1 April 1999 (SI 1999/527).
In s. 121D(2) the words "to the Special Commissioners" omitted by SI 2009/56, art. 3 and Sch. 1, para. 171(2), with effect from 1 April 2009, subject to transitional and saving provisions in SI 2009/56, Sch. 3.
In s. 121D(2) "the Special Commissioners" substituted for "an appeal tribunal" by SSC(TF)A 1999, s. 5; Sch. 5, para. 11(3) with effect from 1 April 1999 (SI 1999/527).
In s. 121D(5) the words "and is notified to the tribunal, the tribunal shall" substituted for the words "the Special Commissioners shall" and the words "tribunal sees" substituted for the words "Special Commissioners see" by SI 2009/56, art. 3 and Sch. 1, para. 171(3), with effect from 1 April 2009, subject to transitional and saving provisions in SI 2009/56, Sch. 3.
In s. 121D(5) the words from "Special Commissioners shall either" to "whether to vary their" substituted by SSC(TF)A 1999, s. 5; Sch. 5, para. 11(4) with effect from 1 April 1999 (SI 1999/527).
In s. 121D(6) the definition of "tribunal" substituted for the definition of "the Special Commissioners" by SI 2009/56, art. 3 and Sch. 1, para. 171(4), with effect from 1 April 2009, subject to transitional and saving provisions in SI 2009/56, Sch. 3. Former definition read as follows:
""*the Special Commissioners*" means the Commissioners for the special purposes of the Income Tax Acts;"
In s. 121D(6) the definitions for "the Special Commissioners" and "vary" inserted by SSC(TF)A 1999, s. 5; Sch. 5, para. 11(5) with effect from 1 April 1999 (SI 1999/527).
S. 121D inserted by SSA 1998, s. 64 with effect from 6 April 1999 (SI 1999/526).

Cross references – SSC(TF)A 1999, s. 11(4): appeals against decisions of the Board.
SSC(TF)A 1999, s. 12(4): appeals normally directed to the General Commissioners.
TCA 1999, s. 11: application of appeals process, in respect of directors liability, to amounts representing tax credits.

121DA Interpretation of Part VI

121DA(1) In this Part **"the relevant social security legislation"** means the provisions of any of the following, except so far as relating to contributions, statutory sick pay or statutory maternity pay, that is to say–

(a) the Contributions and Benefits Act;
(b) this Act;
(c) the Pensions Act, except Part III;
(d) section 4 of the Social Security (Incapacity for Work) Act 1994;
(e) the Jobseekers Act 1995;
(f) the Social Security (Recovery of Benefits) Act 1997;
(g) Parts I and IV of the Social Security Act 1998;
(h) Part V of the Welfare Reform and Pensions Act 1999;
(hh) the State Pension Credit Act 2002;
(hi) Part 1 of the Welfare Reform Act 2007;
(hj) Part 1 of the Welfare Reform Act 2012;
(hk) Part 4 of that Act;
(hl) Part 1 of the Pensions Act 2014;
(hm) Part 5 of the Pensions Act 2014;
(i) the Social Security Pensions Act 1975;
(j) the Social Security Act 1973;
(k) any subordinate legislation made, or having effect as if made, under any enactment specified in paragraphs (a) to (j) above.

121DA(2) In this Part **"authorised officer"** means a person acting in accordance with any authorisation for the purposes of this Part which is for the time being in force in relation to him.

121DA(3) For the purposes of this Part–

(a) references to a document include references to anything in which information is recorded in electronic or any other form;
(b) the requirement that a notice given by an authorised officer be in writing shall be taken to be satisfied in any case where the contents of the notice–
   (i) are transmitted to the recipient of the notice by electronic means; and
   (ii) are received by him in a form that is legible and capable of being recorded for future reference.

121DA(4) In this Part **"premises"** includes–

(a) moveable structures and vehicles, vessels, aircraft and hovercraft;
(b) installations that are offshore installations for the purposes of the Mineral Workings (Offshore Installations) Act 1971; and
(c) places of all other descriptions whether or not occupied as land or otherwise;

and references in this Part to the occupier of any premises shall be construed, in relation to premises that are not occupied as land, as references to any person for the time being present at the place in question.

121DA(5) In this Part–

"benefit" includes any allowance, payment, credit or loan;

"benefit offence" means–

(a) any criminal offence in connection with a claim for a relevant social security benefit;
(b) any criminal offence in connection with the receipt or payment of any amount by way of such a benefit;
(c) any criminal offence committed for the purpose of facilitating the commission (whether or not by the same person) of a benefit offence;
(d) any attempt or conspiracy to commit a benefit offence;

"compensation payment" has the same meaning as in the Social Security (Recovery of Benefits) Act 1997.

121DA(6) [Repealed by WRA 2012, s. 147 and Sch. 14, Pt. 1.]

121DA(7) In this section **"relevant social security benefit"** means a benefit under any provision of the relevant social security legislation; and **"subordinate legislation"** has the same meaning as in the Interpretation Act 1978.

Prospective amendments – S. 121DA(6) repealed by WRA 2012, s. 147 and Sch. 14, Pt. 1, with effect (other than as noted in the History note below) from a date to be set by order of the Secretary of State.

History – In s. 121DA(1), the reference to working families' tax credit and disabled person's tax credit omitted by TCA 2002, s. 60 and Sch. 6, with effect from 8 April 2003 by virtue of SI 2003/962, art. 2(4)(e) and Sch. 2.
S. 121DA(1)(hi) inserted by the Welfare Reform Act 2007, s. 28 and Sch. 3, para. 10(12) with effect from 18 March 2008 for the purpose of making regulations by virtue of SI 2008/787, art. 2 and Sch., and for all other purposes from 27 October 2008 by virtue of art. 2(4)(b) and (f).
S. 121DA(1)(hj) inserted by WRA 2012, s. 31 and Sch. 2, para. 14, with effect from 29 April 2013 (SI 2013/983, art. 3(1)(b)).
S. 121DA(1)(hk) inserted by WRA 2012, s. 91 and Sch. 4, para. 12, with effect from 8 April 2013 in relation to a person whose only or principal residence is, on the date on which that person makes a claim for personal independence payment, located in an area to which one of the following postcodes corresponds: BL, CA, CH (except CH1, CH4, CH5, CH6, CH7 and CH8), CW, DH, DL (except DL6, DL7, DL8, DL9, DL10 and DL11), FY, L, LA (except LA2 7, LA2 8, LA6 2 and LA6 3), M, NE, PR, SR, TS (except TS9), WA and WN (SI 2013/358, art. 7(1) and (2)(k)), and from 10 June 2013 in relation to any other person (SI 2013/1250, art. 2).
S. 121DA(1)(hl) inserted by PA 2014, s. 23 and Sch. 12, para. 13, with effect from 6 April 2016 (as not brought into force by any earlier order under PA 2014, s. 56(1)).
S. 121DA(1)(hm) inserted by PA 2014, s. 31 and Sch. 16, para. 26, with effect from 6 April 2017, subject to SI 2017/297, art. 4 (later commencement for abolition of bereavement payment and bereavement allowance) and 5 (commencement for entitlement to bereavement payment and bereavement support payment) (SI 2017/297, art. 3(2)).
In s. 121DA(5), the definition of "benefit offence" substituted by SSFA 2001, s. 1(7) with effect from 30 April 2002.
In s. 121DA(1), the definition of "the relevant social security legislation", para. (hh) inserted by the State Pension Credit Act 2002, s. 14 and Sch. 2, para. 12 with effect from 2 July 2002 for the purposes of making regulations by virtue of SI 2002/1691.
S. 121DA(6) repealed by WRA 2012, s. 147 and Sch. 14, Pt. 1, with effect in so far as it relates to the abolition of council tax benefit from 1 April 2013 (SI 2013/358, art. 8(c) and Sch. 4). Former s. 121DA(6) read as follows:
"**121DA(6)** In this Part–
(a) any reference to a person authorised to carry out any function relating to housing benefit or council tax benefit shall include a reference to a person providing services relating to the benefit directly or indirectly to an authority administering it; and
(b) any reference to the carrying out of a function relating to such a benefit shall include a reference to the provision of any services relating to it.".
In s. 121DA(7), the words ""relevant social security benefit" means a benefit under any provision of the relevant social security legislation; and" inserted by SSFA 2001, s. 1(8) with effect from 30 April 2002 (SI 2002/1222 (C. 32)).
S. 121DA inserted by CSPSSA 2000, s. 67 and Sch. 6, para. 8, for the purposes of construing SSAA 1992, s. 113 as amended by CSPSSA 2000, Sch. 6, para. 7, with effect from 1 November 2000, by virtue of SI 2000/2950, art. 2(d)(ii).

PART VII – INFORMATION

INFORMATION RELATING TO, OR REQUIRED FOR PURPOSES OF, CONTRIBUTIONS, STATUTORY SICK PAY OR STATUTORY MATERNITY PAY

121E Supply of contributions etc. information held by Inland Revenue

121E(1) This section applies to information which is held for the purposes of functions relating to contributions, health in pregnancy grant, statutory sick pay or statutory maternity pay or functions under Part III of the Pensions Act–

(a) by the Inland Revenue, or

(b) by a person providing services to them, in connection with the provision of those services.

121E(2) Information to which this section applies may, and subject to subsection (2A), must if an authorised officer so requires, be supplied–

(a) to the Secretary of State, or

(b) to a person providing services to the Secretary of State,

for use for the purposes of functions relating to social security, war pensions or employment or training.

121E(2ZA) Information to which this section applies may, and subject to subsection (2A), must if an authorised officer so requires, be supplied–

(a) to the Northern Ireland Department, or

(b) to a person providing services to that Department,

for use for the purposes of functions relating to social security, child support, war pensions or employment or training.

121E(2A) An authorised officer may not require the supply under subsection (2) or (2ZA) of information for use for the purposes of functions relating to employment or training.

121E(3) In this section **"authorised officer"** means an officer of the Secretary of State or the Northern Ireland Department authorised for the purposes of this section by the Secretary of State or the Northern Ireland Department.

History – In s. 121E(1) the words "health in pregnancy grant," inserted by the Health and Social Care Act 2008, s. 132(6), with effect from 21 July 2008 (for certain purposes) and 1 January 2009 (for remaining purposes in relation to England and Wales) and from a day to be appointed (for remaining purposes in relation to Scotland).
In s. 121E(1) the words "or functions under Part III of the Pensions Act" inserted after "statutory maternity pay" by WRPA 1999, s. 81, Sch. 11, para. 7, with effect from 11 November 1999 (date of passing of WRPA 1999) which is the commencement date provided for in WRPA 1999, s. 89(4)(d).
S. 121E(2) and (2ZA) substituted for former s. 121E(2) by Child Maintenance and Other Payments Act 2008, s. 57 and Sch. 7, para. 2, with effect from 1 June 2009 (SI 2009/1314, art. 2(2)).

In s. 121E(2), the words "(subject to subsection (2A))" and the words "or employment training" inserted by EA 2002, Sch. 6, para. 11 with effect from 9 September 2002, by virtue of SI 2002/2256.
In s. 121E(2A), the words "or (2ZA)" inserted after the words "subsection (2)" by Child Maintenance and Other Payments Act 2008, s. 57 and Sch. 7, para. 2, with effect from 1 June 2009 (SI 2009/1314, art. 2(2)).
S. 121E(2A) inserted by the Employment Act 2002, Sch. 6, para. 11 with effect from 9 September 2002, by virtue of SI 2002/1192.
In s. 121E(4), the words "this section" substituted by EA 2002, Sch. 6, para. 11 with effect from 9 September 2002, by virtue of SI 2002/2256.
S. 121E and the heading preceding it inserted by SSC(TF)A 1999, s. 6 and Sch. 6, para. 1, with effect from 1 April 1999 (SI 1999/527).

121F Supply to Inland Revenue for purposes of contributions etc. of information held by Secretary of State

121F(1) This section applies to information which is held for the purposes of functions relating to social security, war pensions or employment or training–

(a) by the Secretary of State, or

(b) by a person providing services to the Secretary of State, in connection with the provision of those services.

121F(1A) This section also applies to information which is held for the purposes of functions relating to social security, child support, war pensions or employment or training–

(a) by the Northern Ireland Department, or

(b) by a person providing services to that Department, in connection with the provision of those services.

121F(2) Information to which this section applies may, and (subject to subsection (2A)) must if an officer of the Inland Revenue authorised by the Inland Revenue for the purposes of this section so requires, be supplied–

(a) to the Inland Revenue, or

(b) to a person providing services to the Inland Revenue,

for use for the purposes of functions relating to contributions, health in pregnancy grant, statutory sick pay or statutory maternity pay or functions under Part III of the Pensions Act.

121F(2A) An officer of the Inland Revenue may not require the supply under subsection (2) of information which is held for the purposes of functions relating to employment or training.

History – S. 121F(1) and (1A) substituted for former s. 121F(1) by Child Maintenance and Other Payments Act 2008, s. 57 and Sch. 7, para. 2, with effect from 1 June 2009 (SI 2009/1914, art. 2(2)).
In s. 121F(2) the words "Saving Gateway accounts", which appeared after the words "health in pregnancy grant," omitted by the Savings Accounts and Health in Pregnancy Grant Act 2010, with effect from 16 February 2010.
In s. 121F(2) the words "Saving Gateway accounts" inserted by the Saving Gateway Accounts Act 2009, s. 18(1), with effect from 1 January 2010 (SI 2009/3332, art. 2(c)).
In s. 121F(2) the words "health in pregnancy grant," inserted by the Health and Social Care Act 2008, s. 132(7), with effect from 21 July 2008 (for certain purposes) and 1 January 2009 (for remaining purposes in relation to England and Wales) and from a day to be appointed (for remaining purposes in relation to Scotland).
In s. 121F(2) the words "or functions under Part III of the Pensions Act" inserted at the end by WRPA 1999, s. 81, Sch. 11, para. 8, with effect from 11 November 1999 (date of passing of WRPA 1999) which is the commencement date provided for in WRPA 1999, s. 89(4)(d).
In s. 121F(2), the words "(subject to subsection (2A))" inserted by EA 2002, Sch. 6, para. 13 with effect from 9 September 2002 by virtue of SI 2002/2256.
S. 12F(2A) inserted by EA 2002, Sch. 6, para. 13 with effect from 9 September 2002 by virtue of SI 2002/2256.
In s. 121F, the words ", or employment or training" inserted by EA 2002, Sch. 6, para. 13 with effect from 9 September 2002, by virtue of SI 2002/2256.
S. 121F inserted by SSC(TF)A 1999, s. 6 and Sch. 6, para. 1, with effect from 1 April 1999 (SI 1999/527).

INFORMATION HELD BY TAX AUTHORITIES

122 Supply of information held by tax authorities for fraud prevention and verification

122 [Repealed by WRA 2012, s. 147 and Sch. 14, Pt. 13.]

History – S. 122 repealed by WRA 2012, s. 147 and Sch. 14, Pt. 13, with effect from 8 May 2012.

122ZA Supply of information held by tax authorities for fraud prevention and verification

122ZA [Repealed by WRA 2012, s. 147 and Sch. 14, Pt. 13.]

History – S. 122ZA repealed by WRA 2012, s. 147 and Sch. 14, Pt. 13, with effect from 8 May 2012.

122AA Disclosure of contributions etc. information by Her Majesty's Revenue and Customs

History – In the heading, the words "Her Majesty's Revenue and Customs" substituted for "Inland Revenue" by CRCA 2005, s. 50(6) and Sch. 4, para. 46(b) from 18 April 2005 by virtue of SI 2005/1126, art. 2.

122AA(1) No obligation as to secrecy imposed by statute or otherwise on Revenue and Customs officials (within the meaning of section 18 of the Commissioners for Revenue and Customs Act 2005 (confidentiality) shall prevent information held for the purposes of the functions of Her Majesty's Revenue and Customs in relation to contributions, statutory sick pay, statutory maternity pay, statutory paternity pay, statutory adoption pay or statutory shared parental pay from being disclosed–

(a) to any of the authorities to which this paragraph applies, or any person authorised to exercise any function of that authority, for the purposes of the functions of that authority, or

(b) in a case where the disclosure is necessary for the purpose of giving effect to any agreement to which an order under section 179(1) below relates.

122AA(2) The authorities to which subsection (1)(a) above applies are–

(a) the Health and Safety Executive,

(b) the Government Actuary's Department,

(c) the Statistics Board, and

(d) the Occupational Pensions Regulatory Authority.

History – In s. 122AA(1), the words "statutory paternity pay," substituted for the words "ordinary statutory paternity pay, additional statutory paternity pay or" by Children and Families Act 2014, s. 126(1) and Sch. 7, para. 25(a), with effect from 5 April 2015, subject to the transitional and saving provisions in SI 2014/1640, art. 16 (amendments do not have effect in relation to– (a) children whose expected week of birth ends on or before 4 April 2015; (b) children placed for adoption on or before 4 April 2015) (SI 2014/1640, art. 7).

In s. 122AA(1), the words "or statutory shared parental pay" inserted by Children and Families Act 2014, s. 126(1) and Sch. 7, para. 25(b), with effect from 1 December 2014 (SI 2014/1640, art. 5).

In s. 122AA(1) the words "ordinary statutory paternity pay" substituted for "statutory paternity pay" by the Work and Families Act 2006, s. 11 and Sch. 1, para. 25, with effect from 6 April 2010 (SI 2010/495).

In s. 122AA(1), the words "Revenue and Customs officials (within the meaning of section 18 of the Commissioners for Revenue and Customs Act 2005 (confidentiality)" substituted by CRCA 2005, s. 50(6) and Sch. 4, para. 46(a)(i) from 18 April 2005 by virtue of SI 2005/1126, art. 2.

In s. 122AA(1), the words "Her Majesty's Revenue and Customs" substituted by CRCA 2005, s. 50(6) and Sch. 4, para. 46(a)(ii) from 18 April 2005 by virtue of SI 2005/1126, art. 2.

In s. 122AA(1), the words ", statutory maternity pay, statutory paternity pay or statutory adoption pay" substituted by EA 2002, Sch. 7, para. 13 with effect from 8 December 2002, by virtue of SI 2002/2866.

In s. 122AA(2)(c) the words "Statistics Board" substituted by Statistics and Registration Services Act 2007, s. 46 and Sch. 2, para. 5, with effect from 1 April 2008.

S. 122AA inserted by SSC(TF)A 1999, s. 6 and Sch. 6, para. 3, with effect from 1 April 1999 (SI 1999/527).

Cross references – TCA 2002, s. 59 and Sch. 5: use and disclosure of information relating to tax credits, child benefit, guardian's allowance, etc. for specific purposes.

122A Supply of information by Inland Revenue for purposes of contributions

122A [Repealed by SSC(TF)A 1999, s. 6; Sch. 6, para. 4 and s. 26(3); Sch. 10, Pt. I, with effect from 1 April 1999 (SI 1999/527).]

OTHER GOVERNMENT DEPARTMENTS

122B Supply of other government information for fraud prevention and verification

122B(1) This section applies to information which is held by, or by a person providing services to, a Minister to the Crown or a government department (including a Northern Ireland department) and which relates to–

(a) passports, immigration and emigration, nationality or prisoners; or

(b) any other matter which is prescribed.

122B(2) Information to which this section applies may be supplied to, or to a person providing services to, the Secretary of State or the Northern Ireland Department–

(a) for use in the prevention, detection, investigation or prosecution of offences relating to social security or tax credits; or

(b) for use in checking the accuracy of information relating to benefits or national insurance numbers or to any other matter relating to social security and (where appropriate) amending or supplementing such information.

122B(3) Information supplied under subsection (2) above shall not be supplied by the recipient to any other person or body unless–

(a) it could be supplied to that person or body under that subsection;

(b) it is supplied for the purposes of any civil of criminal proceedings relating to the Contributions and Benefit Act, the Jobseekers Act 1995, the Tax Credits Act 2002, Part 1 of the Welfare Reform Act 2007, Part 1 of the Welfare Reform Act 2012, Part 4 of that Act, Part 1 of the Pensions Act 2014, section 30 of that Act or this Act to any provision or Northern Ireland legislation corresponding to any of them;

(c) it is supplied under section 122C below; or

(d) it is supplied under section 127 of the Welfare Reform Act 2012.

122B(4) But where information supplied under subsection (2) above has been used (in accordance with paragraph (b) of that subsection) in amending or supplementing other information, it is lawful for it to be–

(a) supplied to any person or body to whom that other information could be supplied; or

(b) used for any purpose for which that other information could be used.

122B(5) This section does not limit the circumstances in which information may be supplied apart from this section.

History – In s. 122B(2)(a) the words "or tax credits" inserted by WRA 2012, s. 123(2), with effect from 6 June 2012 (SI 2012/1246).
In s. 122B(2)(b) the word "contributions" omitted by the SSC(TF)A 1999, s. 6 and Sch. 6, para. 5, with effect from 1 April 1999 (SI 1999/527).
In s. 122B(3)(b), the words ", section 30 of that Act" inserted after the words ", Part 1 of the Pensions Act 2014" by PA 2014, s. 31 and Sch. 16, para. 27, with effect from 6 April 2017, subject to SI 2017/297, art. 4 (later commencement for abolition of bereavement payment and bereavement allowance) and 5 (commencement for entitlement to bereavement payment and bereavement support payment) (SI 2017/297, art. 3(2)).
In s. 122B(3)(b), the words ", Part 1 of the Pensions Act 2014" inserted after the words "Part 4 of that Act" by PA 2014, s. 23 and Sch. 12, para. 14, with effect from 6 April 2016 (as not brought into force by any earlier order under PA 2014, s. 56(1)).
In s. 122B(3)(b), after the words "Welfare Reform Act 2012", the words ", Part 4 of that Act" inserted by WRA 2012, s. 91 and Sch. 4, para. 13, with effect from 8 April 2013 in relation to a person whose only or principal residence is, on the date on which that person makes a claim for personal independence payment, located in an area to which one of the following postcodes corresponds: BL, CA, CH (except CH1, CH4, CH5, CH6, CH7 and CH8), CW, DH, DL (except DL6, DL7, DL8, DL9, DL10 and DL11), FY, L, LA (except LA2 7, LA2 8, LA6 2 and LA6 3), M, NE, PR, SR, TS (except TS9), WA and WN (SI 2013/358, art. 7(1) and (2)(k)), and from 10 June 2013 in relation to any other person (SI 2013/1250, art. 2).
In s. 122B(3)(b), the words ", Part 1 of the Welfare Reform Act 2012" inserted by WRA 2012, s. 31 and Sch. 2, para. 15, with effect 29 April 2013 (SI 2013/983, art. 3(1)(b)).
In s. 122B(3)(b) the words ", the Tax Credits Act 2002" inserted, and the "or" at the end repealed, by WRA 2012, s. 123(3)(a) and (b) respectively, with effect from 6 June 2012 (SI 2012/1246).
In s. 122B(3)(b) the words ", Part 1 of the Welfare Reform Act 2007" inserted by the Welfare Reform Act 2007, s. 28 and Sch. 3, para. 10(14) with effect from 27 October 2008 by virtue of art. 2(4)(b) and (f).
S. 122B(3)(d) (and the "or" at the end of s. 122B(3)(c)) inserted by WRA 2012, s. 123(3)(c), with effect from 6 June 2012 (SI 2012/1246).
S. 122B inserted by Social Security Administration (Fraud) Act 1997, s. 2(1), with effect from 1 July 1997, by virtue of SI 1997/1577.

PERSONS EMPLOYED OR FORMERLY EMPLOYED IN SOCIAL SECURITY ADMINISTRATION OR ADJUDICATION

123 Unauthorised disclosure of information relating to particular persons

123(1) A person who is or has been employed in social security administration or adjudication is guilty of an offence if he discloses without lawful authority any information which he acquired in the course of his employment and which relates to a particular person.

123(2) A person who is or has been employed in the audit of expenditure or the investigation of complaints is guilty of an offence if he discloses without lawful authority any information–

(a) which he acquired in the course of his employment;

(b) which is, or is derived from, information acquired or held by or for the purposes of any of the government departments or other bodies or persons referred to in Part I of Schedule 4 to this Act or Part I of Schedule 4 to the Northern Ireland Administration Act; and

(c) which relates to a particular person.

123(3) It is not an offence under this section–

(a) to disclose information in the form of a summary or collection of information so framed as not to enable information relating to any particular person to be ascertained from it; or

(b) to disclose information which has previously been disclosed to the public with lawful authority.

123(4) It is a defence for a person charged with an offence under this section to prove that at the time of the alleged offence–

(a) he believed that he was making the disclosure in question with lawful authority and had no reasonable cause to believe otherwise; or

(b) he believed that the information in question had previously been disclosed to the public with lawful authority and had no reasonable cause to believe otherwise.

123(5) A person guilty of an offence under this section shall be liable–

(a) on conviction on indictment, to imprisonment for a term not exceeding two years or a fine or both; or

(b) on summary conviction, to imprisonment for a term not exceeding six months or a fine not exceeding the statutory maximum or both.

123(6) For the purposes of this section, the persons who are **"employed in social security administration or adjudication"** are–

(a) any person specified in Part I of Schedule 4 to this Act or in any corresponding enactment having effect in Northern Ireland;

(b) any other person who carries out the administrative work of any of the government departments or other bodies or persons referred to in that Part of that Schedule or that corresponding enactment; and

(c) any person who provides, or is employed in the provision of, services to any of those departments, persons or bodies;

and **"employment"**, in relation to any such person, shall be construed accordingly.

123(6A) Subsection (6) above shall have effect as if any health care professional who, for the purposes of section 19 of the Social Security Act 1998, is provided by any person in pursuance of a contract entered into with the Secretary of State were specified in Part I of Schedule 4 to this Act.

123(7) For the purposes of subsections (2) and (6) above, any reference in Part I of Schedule 4 to this Act or any corresponding enactment having effect in Northern Ireland to a **"government department"** shall be construed in accordance with Part II of that Schedule or any corresponding enactment having effect in Northern Ireland, and for this purpose "government department" shall be taken to include–

(a) [repealed by SSC(TF)A 1999, s. 26(3); Sch. 10, Pt. I;]

(aa) the Scottish Administration;

(b) the Scottish Courts Administration.

123(8) For the purposes of this section, the persons who are **"employed in the audit of expenditure or the investigation of complaints"** are–

(a) the Comptroller and Auditor General;

(aa) any member or employee of the National Audit Office;

(ab) any other person who carries out the administrative work of the National Audit Office, or who provides, or is employed in the provision of, services to that Office;

(b) the Comptroller and Auditor General for Northern Ireland;

(ba) the Auditor General for Wales and any member of his staff;

(bb) any member of the staff of the Wales Audit Office, and any person providing services to that Office;

(c) the Parliamentary Commissioner for Administration;

(d) the Northern Ireland Parliamentary Commissioner for Administration;

(e) the Health Service Commissioner for England;

(f) [omitted and repealed by Public Services Ombudsman (Wales) Act 2005, s. 37 and Sch. 6, para. 26 and s. 39 and Sch. 7 respectively;]

(g) the Scottish Public Services Ombudsman;

(h) the Northern Ireland Commissioner for Complaints;

(ha) a member of the Local Commission for England;

(hb) [omitted and repealed by Public Services Ombudsman (Wales) Act 2005, s. 37 and Sch. 6, para. 26 and s. 39 and Sch. 7 respectively;]

(hc) [omitted by SI 2004/1823, art. 12(b);]

(hd) [omitted and repealed by Public Services Ombudsman (Wales) Act 2005, s. 37 and Sch. 6, para. 26 and s. 39 and Sch. 7 respectively;]

(he) the Public Services Ombudsman for Wales and any member of his staff;

(i) any member of the staff of the Northern Ireland Audit Office;

(j) any other person who carries out the administrative work of the Northern Ireland Audit Office, or who provides, or is employed in the provision of, services to that Office;

(jza) the following persons–

(i) any member of the staff of the National Audit Office that was established by section 3 of the National Audit Act 1983, or

(ii) any other person who carried out the administrative work of that Office, or who provided, or who was employed in the provision of, services to that Office;

(jzb) a local auditor within the meaning of the Local Audit and Accountability Act 2014;

(ja) [omitted by Local Audit and Accountability Act 2014, s. 45 and Sch. 12, para. 28;]

(jb) a member of the Accounts Commission for Scotland and any auditor within the meaning of Part VII of the Local Government (Scotland) Act 1973;

(jc) a Northern Ireland local government auditor; and

(k) any officer of any of the Commissioners, Ombudsman or Commissions referred to in paragraphs (c) to (ha), (ja) and (jb) above and any person assisting an auditor referred to in paragraph (a), (jb) or (jc) above.

and **"employment"**, in relation to any such person, shall be construed accordingly.

123(9) For the purposes of this section a disclosure is to be regarded as made with **"lawful authority"** if, and only if, it is made–

(a) in accordance with his official duty–

(i) by a civil servant; or

(ii) by a person employed in the audit of expenditure or the investigation of complaints, who does not fall within subsection (8)(j) above;

(b) by any other person either–

(i) for the purposes of the function in the exercise of which he holds the information and without contravening any restriction duly imposed by the person responsible; or

(ii) to, or in accordance with an authorisation duly given by, the person responsible;

(c) in accordance with any enactment or order of a court;

(d) for the purpose of instituting, or otherwise for the purposes of, any proceedings before a court or before any tribunal or other body or person referred to in Part I of Schedule 4 to this Act or Part I of Schedule 4 to the Northern Ireland Administration Act; or

(e) with the consent of the appropriate person:

and in this subsection **"the person responsible"** means the Secretary of State, the Lord Chancellor or any person authorised by the Secretary of State or the Lord Chancellor for the purposes of this subsection and includes a reference to **"the person responsibe"** within the meaning of any corresponding enactment having effect in Northern Ireland.

123(10) For the purposes of subsection (9)(e above, **"the appropriate person"** means the person to whom the information in question relates, excpt that if the affairs of that person are being dealt with–

(a) under a power of attorney;

(b) by a receiver appointed under sectior99 of the Mental Health Act 1983 or a controller appointed under Article 101 of the Mental Heah (Northern Ireland) Order 1986;

(c) by a Scottish mental health custodial, that is to say–

(i) a curator bonis, tutor or judical factor, or

(ii) the managers of a hospital acting on behalf of that person under section 94 of the Mental Health (Scotland) Act 1984 or

(d) by a mental health appointee, tlat is to say–

(i) a person directed or authorised as mentioned in sub-paragraph (a) of rule 41(1) of the Court of Protection Rules 1984 or sub-paragraph (a) of rule 38(1) of Order 109 of the Rules of the Supreme Court (Northern Ireland) 1980; or

(ii) a receiver ad interim appointed under sub-paragraph (b) of the said rule 41(1) or a controller ad interim appointed under sub-paragraph (b) of the said rule 38(1),

the appropriate person is the attorney, receiver, controller, custodian or appointee, as the case may be, or, in a case falling within paragraph (a) above, the person to whom the information relates.

History – In s. 123(2)(b) and (9)(d) "Schedule 4", in relation to the Northern Ireland Administration Act, substituted by the Social Security Administration (Fraud) Act 1997, s. 22 and Sch. 1, para. 6, with effect from 1 July 1997, by virtue of SI 1997/1577.
In s. 123(6A), the words "health care professional" substituted for the words "medical practitioner" by Welfare Reform Act 2007, s. 63 and Sch. 7, para. 3(3), with effect from 3 July 2007.
In s. 123(6A), the words "section 19 of the Social Security Act 1998" substituted for the words "section 54 above" by SSA 1998, s. 86 and Sch. 7, para. 88, with effect from dates in 1999.
S. 123(6A) inserted by the Deregulation and Contracting Out Act 1994, s. 76 and Sch. 16, para. 21, with effect from 3 January 1995.
S. 123(7)(a) repealed by SSC(TF)A 1999, s. 6; Sch. 6, para. 6, and s. 26(3); Sch. 10, Pt. I, with effect from 1 April 1999 (SI 1999/527).
S. 123(7)(aa) inserted by SI 1999/1820, Sch. 2, para. 195(2), with effect from 1 July 1999.
S. 123(8)(aa) and (ab) inserted after s. 123(8)(a) by the Budget Responsibility and National Audit Act 2011, s. 26 and Sch. 5, para. 15(2), with effect from 1 April 2012 (SI 2011/2576, art. 5).
S. 123(8)(ba) inserted by Government of Wales Act 1998, s. 125 and Sch. 12, para. 32, with effect from 1 February 1999 by virtue of SI 1999/118.
S. 123(8)(bb) inserted by Public Audit (Wales) Act 2013, s. 24 and Sch. 4, para. 3, with effect from 1 April 2014 (by virtue of Welsh SI 2013/1466, art. 3).
S. 123(8)(f), (hb) and (hd) omitted and repealed by Public Services Ombudsman (Wales) Act 2005, s. 37 and Sch. 6, para. 26 and s. 39 and Sch. 7 respectively, with effect from 1 April 2006.
In s. 123(8)(g), the words "the Scottish Public Services Ombudsman" substituted for the words "the Health Service Commissioner for Scotland" by SI 2004/1823, art. 12(a), with effect from 14 July 2004.

124B(4) **"Civil partnership register"** has the same meaning as in Part 3 of the Civil Partnership Act 2004.

History – In s. 124B(1), the words "and on payment of the sum of £8.50," inserted by the Local Electoral Administration and Registration Services (Scotland) Act 2006, s. 53(2) with effect from 1 October 2006 (by virtue of SI 2006/469).
S. 124B inserted by SI 2005/3129, Sch. 1, para. 4(1) with effect from 5 December 2005.

125 Regulations as to notification of deaths

125(1) Regulations made with the concurrence of the Inland Revenue may provide that it shall be the duty of any of the following persons–

(a) the Registrar General for England and Wales;

(b) the Registrar General of Births, Deaths and Marriages for Scotland;

(c) each registrar of births and deaths,

to furnish the Secretary of State, or the Inland Revenue, for the purposes of their respective functions under the Contributions and Benefits Act, the Jobseekers Act 1995, the Social Security (Recovery of Benefits) Act 1997, the Social Security Act 1998, the State Pension Credit Act 2002, Part 1 of the Welfare Reform Act 2007, Part 1 of the Welfare Reform Act 2012, Part 4 of that Act, Part 1 of the Pensions Act 2014, section 30 of that Act and this Act and the functions of the Northern Ireland Department under any Northern Ireland legislation corresponding to any of those Acts, with the prescribed particulars of such deaths as may be prescribed.

125(2) The regulations may make provision as to the manner in which and times at which the particulars are to be furnished.

History – In s. 125(1), the words ", section 30 of that Act" inserted after the words ", Part 1 of the Pensions Act 2014" by PA 2014, s. 31 and Sch. 16, para. 29, with effect from 6 April 2017, subject to SI 2017/297, art. 4 (later commencement for abolition of bereavement payment and bereavement allowance) and 5 (commencement for entitlement to bereavement payment and bereavement support payment) (SI 2017/297, art. 3(2)).
In s. 125(1), the words ", Part 1 of the Pensions Act 2014" inserted after the words "Part 4 of that Act" by PA 2014, s. 23 and Sch. 12, para. 16, with effect from 6 April 2016 (as not brought into force by any earlier order under PA 2014, s. 56(1)).
In s. 125(1), the words ", Part 1 of the Welfare Reform Act 2012" inserted by WRA 2012, s. 31 and Sch. 2, para. 18, with effect from 29 April 2013 (SI 2013/983, art. 3(1)(b)).
In s. 125(1), after the words "Welfare Reform Act 2012", the words ", Part 4 of that Act" inserted by WRA 2012, s. 91 and Sch. 4, para. 16, with effect from a 8 April 2013 in relation to a person whose only or principal residence is, on the date on which that person makes a claim for personal independence payment, located in an area to which one of the following postcodes corresponds: BL, CA, CH (except CH1, CH4, CH5, CH6, CH7 and CH8), CW, DH, DL (except DL6, DL7, DL8, DL9, DL10 and DL11), FY, L, LA (except LA2 7, LA2 8, LA6 2 and LA6 3), M, NE, PR, SR, TS (except TS9), WA and WN (SI 2013/358, art. 7(1) and (2)(k)), and from 10 June 2013 in relation to any other person (SI 2013/1250, art. 2).
In s. 125(1) the words ", Part 1 of the Welfare Reform Act 2007" inserted by the Welfare Reform Act 2007, s. 28 and Sch. 3, para. 10(17) with effect from 27 October 2008 by virtue of art. 2(4)(b) and (f).
In s. 125(1), the words ", the SSA 1998" inserted by SSA 1998, s. 86(1) and Sch. 7, para. 89, for the purposes of (i) decisions whether a person is entitled to be credited with earnings or contributions in accordance with regulations made under s. 22(5) of the Contributions and Benefits Act; and (ii) decisions whether a person was, within the meaning of regulations, precluded from regular employment by responsibilities at home; with effect from 18 October 1999 (SI 1999/2860 (C. 75), art. 2(c)(iv), (v) and Sch. 1); with effect from 6 September 1999, for the purposes of benefits under SSCBA 1992, Pt. II except child's special allowance (SI 1999/2422 (C. 61), art. 2(c)(i) and Sch. 1); and with effect from 29 November 1999 in so far as it was not already in force for all other purposes (except for housing benefit, council tax benefit and decisions to which SI 1999/527, art. 4(6) applies; i.e. pre-1 April 1999 decisions under SSAA 1992, s. 17(1), s. 20(3) and PSA 1993, s. 170(1)) (SI 1999/3178 (C. 81), art. 2(1)(a); 2(2) and Sch. 1).
In s. 125(1), the words ", the Social Security Act 1998" inserted by SSA 1998, s. 86(1) and Sch. 7, para. 89, with effect from 5 July 1999, for the purposes of any matter to which, by virtue of PSA 1993, s. 170, provisions of SSA 1998, Pt. I, Ch. II apply (SI 1999/1958 (C. 51), art. 2(1)(b)(iv)).
In s. 125(1) the words ", and the State Pension Credit Act 2002" inserted by the State Pension Credit Act 2002, s. 14 and Sch. 2, para. 14 with effect from 2 July 2002 for the purpose only of making regulations.
In s. 125(1) the words "made with the concurrence of the Inland Revenue" inserted and the words "or the Inland Revenue, for the purposes of their respective functions" substituted for "for the purposes of his functions" by SSC(TF)A 1999, s. 1; Sch. 1, para 25 from 25 February 1999, for the purposes of making regulations (SSC(TF)A 1999, s. 28(2)(b)), and for all other purposes, with effect from 1 April 1999 (SI 1999/527).
In s. 125(1), after "1995", the words "Social Security (Recovery of Benefits) Act 1997" inserted by the Social Security (Recovery of Benefits) Act 1997, s. 33(1) and Sch. 3, with effect from 6 October 1997, the date appointed by virtue of SI 1997/2085.
S. 125(1) amended by Jobseekers Act 1995, Sch. 2, para. 60, with effect from 11 June 1996 by virtue of SI 1996/1509, by inserting ", the Jobseekers Act 1995" and by substituting "any of those Acts".

Derivations – SSA 1986, s. 60.

Cross references – PSA 1993, s. 167: application of general provisions relating to administration of social security.

Notes – SI 1987/250 (not reproduced): duties of registrars to provide specified particulars of death to the Secretary of State for Social Services.

CONTRIBUTIONS AVOIDANCE ARRANGEMENTS

132A Disclosure of contributions avoidance arrangements

132A(1) The Treasury may by regulations make provision requiring, or relating to, the disclosure of information in relation to any notifiable contribution arrangements or notifiable contribution proposal.

132A(2) The only provision which may be made under subsection (1) is provision applying (with or without modification), or corresponding to, any of the following provisions–

(a) any provision of, or made under, Part 7 of the Finance Act 2004 (disclosure of tax avoidance schemes) so far as that provision relates to income tax;

(b) section 98C of the Taxes Management Act 1970 (penalties for failure to comply with Part 7 of the Finance Act 2004) and any other provision of the Taxes Management Act 1970 so far as it relates to a penalty under that section;

(c) any provision made under section 132 of the Finance Act 1999 or section 135 of the Finance Act 2002 (electronic communications);

(d) any provision of any other enactment or instrument (including any enactment or instrument passed or made on or after the day on which the National Insurance Contributions Act 2006 was passed) which requires, or relates to, the disclosure of information in relation to tax avoidance arrangements which relate in whole or in part to income tax.

132A(3) For the purposes of subsection (1)–

"notifiable contribution arrangements" means any arrangements which–

(a) enable, or might be expected to enable, any person to obtain an advantage in relation to a contribution, and

(b) are such that the main benefit, or one of the main benefits, that might be expected to arise from the arrangements is the obtaining of that advantage;

"notifiable contribution proposal" means a proposal for arrangements which, if entered into, would be notifiable contribution arrangements (whether the proposal relates to a particular person or to any person who may seek to take advantage of it).

132A(4) Where, at any time after the passing of the National Insurance Contributions Act 2006, a relevant tax provision is passed or made which changes the notifiable tax matters, the Treasury may, by regulations, amend the definitions in subsection (3) so as to make an analogous change to the matters in respect of which information may be required to be disclosed by virtue of this section.

132A(5) In subsection (4)–

"the notifiable tax matters" means the arrangements, proposals or other matters in respect of which information is or may be required to be disclosed under a relevant tax provision;

"relevant tax provision" means a provision mentioned in subsection (2).

132A(6) No provision made by regulations under this section may require any person to disclose to the Commissioners for Her Majesty's Revenue and Customs, or any other person, any information with respect to which a claim to legal professional privilege, or, in Scotland, to confidentiality of communications, could be maintained in legal proceedings.

132A(7) In this section–

"advantage", in relation to any contribution, means–

(a) the avoidance or reduction of a liability for that contribution, or

(b) the deferral of the payment of that contribution;

"arrangements" includes any scheme, transaction or series of transactions;

"contribution" means a contribution under–

(a) Part 1 of the Social Security Contributions and Benefits Act 1992, or

(b) Part 1 of the Social Security Contributions and Benefits (Northern Ireland) Act 1992;

"tax avoidance arrangements" includes arrangements which enable, or might be expected to enable, a person to obtain an advantage in relation to any tax (within the meaning of Part 7 of the Finance Act 2004).

History – S. 132A inserted by NICA 2006, s. 7(2), with effect from 30 March 2006.

Statutory instruments – SI 2012/1868: partly made under s. 132A(1).

PART IX – ALTERATION OF CONTRIBUTIONS ETC.

Cross references – SSCBA 1992, s. 1: contributory system.
SSCBA 1992, s. 9: calculation of secondary Class 1 contributions.

141 Annual review of contributions

141(1) In each tax year the Treasury shall carry out a review of the general level of earnings in Great Britain taking into account changes in that level which have taken place since their last review under this section, with a view to determining whether, in respect of Class 2, 3 or 4 contributions, an order should be made under this section, to have effect in relation to the next following tax year.

141(2) For the purposes of any review under this section, the Treasury –

(a) shall estimate the general level of earnings in such manner as they think fit; and

(b) shall take into account any other matters appearing to them to be relevant to their determination whether or not an order should be made under this section, including the current operation of the Contributions and Benefits Act.

141(3) If the Treasury determine, as a result of a review under this section, that having regard to changes in the general level of earnings which have taken place, and to any other matters taken into account on the review, an order under this section should be made for the amendment of Part I of the Contributions and Benefits Act, they shall prepare and lay before each House of Parliament a draft of such an order framed so as to give effect to their conclusions on the review.

141(4) An order under this section may amend Part I of the Contributions and Benefits Act by altering any one or more of the following figures–

(a) the figure specified in section 11(2) and (6) as the weekly rate of Class 2 contributions;

(b) the figure specified in section 11(4) as the small profits threshold for the purposes of Class 2 contributions;

(c) the figure specified in section 13(1) as the amount of a Class 3 contribution;

(d) the figures specified in subsection (3) of section 15 as the upper limit of profits or gains to be taken into account for the purposes of Class 4 contributions under that section and as the lower limit of profits or gains to be taken into account for those purposes under paragraph (a) of that subsection.

141(5) If an order under this section contains an amendment altering either of the figures referred to in subsection (4)(d) above it shall make the same alteration of the corresponding figure specified in section 18 of the Contributions and Benefits Act.

141(6) If the Treasury determine as a result of a review under this section that, having regard to their conclusions in respect of the general level of earnings and otherwise, no such amendments of Part I of the Contributions and Benefits Act are called for as can be made for the purposes of subsection (4) above, and determine accordingly not to lay a draft of an order before Parliament, they shall instead prepare and lay before each House of Parliament a report explaining their reasons for that determination.

141(7) In subsection (1) above in its application to the tax year 1992–93 the reference to the last review under this section shall be construed as a reference to the last review under section 120 of the 1975 Act.

History – In s. 141 references to "the Treasury", "they", "their", "them" and "determine" wherever the words occur substituted by SSC(TF)A 1999, s. 2; Sch. 3, para. 44 with effect from 1 April 1999 (SI 1999/527).

In s. 141(4)(a) the words "section 11(2) and (6)" substituted for the words "section 11(1)" and in para. (b) the words "small profits threshold for the purposes of Class 2 contributions" substituted for the words "amount of earnings below which regulations under that subsection may except an earner from liability for Class 2 contributions" by NICA 2015, s. 2 and Sch. 1, para. 20, with effect for the tax year 2015–16 and subsequent tax years.

In s. 141(4)(d), the words "subsection (3) of section 15 as the upper limit of profits or gains to be taken into account for the purposes of Class 4 contributions under that section and as the lower limit of profits or gains to be taken into account for those purposes under paragraph (a) of that subsection" substituted by NICA 2002, s. 6 and Sch. 1, para. 16(2) with effect for 2003–04 and subsequent tax years.

In s. 141(5), the words "referred to in subsection (4)(d) above" and the words "18 of the Contributions and Benefits Act" substituted by NICA 2002, s. 6 and Sch. 1, para. 16(3) with effect for 2003–04 and subsequent tax years.

Derivations – SSA 1975, s. 120(2)–(7).

Cross references – SSCBA 1992, s. 11(1), (4): Class 2 contributions: rate and small earnings exception.
SSCBA 1992, s. 13(1): amount of a Class 3 contribution.
SSCBA 1992, s. 15(3): rate of Class 4 contributions.
SSCBA 1992, s. 18(1): Class 4 contributions recoverable under regulations.
SSCBA 1992, s. 176(2)(a): subordinate legislation not requiring parliamentary control.

Notes – S. 170–174: procedure for consultation of Social Security Advisory Committee in drafting regulations and exclusions therefrom.

142 Orders under s. 141 – supplementary

142(1) Where the Treasury lay before Parliament a draft of an order under section 141 above, they shall lay with it a copy of a report by the Government Actuary or the Deputy Government Actuary on the effect which, in that Actuary's opinion, the making of such an order may be expected to have on the National Insurance Fund; and, where the Treasury determine not to lay a draft order, they shall with the report laid before Parliament under section 141(6) above lay a copy of a report by the Government Actuary or the Deputy Government Actuary on the consequences for the Fund which may, in that Actuary's opinion, follow from that determination.

142(2) Where the Treasury lay before Parliament a draft of an order under section 141 above, then if the draft is approved by a resolution of each House, the Treasury shall make an order in the form of the draft.

142(3) An order under section 141 above shall be made so as to be in force from the beginning of the tax *year following* that in which it receives Parliamentary approval, and to have effect for that year and any subsequent tax year (subject to the effect of any subsequent order under this Part of this Act); and for this purpose the order is to be taken as receiving Parliamentary approval on the date on which the draft of it is approved by the second House to approve it.

History – In s. 142(1) and (2) "Treasury", "they", "lays" and "the Treasury determine" wherever the words occur substituted by SSC(TF)A 1999, s. 2; Sch. 3, para. 44 with effect from 1 April 1999 (SI 1999/527).

Derivations – SSA 1975, s. 121.

143 Power to alter contributions with a view to adjusting level of National Insurance Fund

143(1) Without prejudice to section 141 above, the Treasury may at any time, if they think it expedient to do so with a view to adjusting the level at which the National Insurance Fund stands for the time being and having regard to the sums which may be expected to be paid from the Fund in any future period, make an order amending Part I of the Contributions and Benefits Act by altering any one or more of the following figures–

(a) the percentage rate specified as the main primary percentage in section 8(2)(a);

(b) the percentage rate specified as the secondary percentage in section 9(2);

(c) the figure specified in section 11(2) and (6) as the weekly rate of Class 2 contributions;

(d) the figure specified in section 13(1) as the amount of a Class 3 contribution;

(e) specified as the main Class 4 percentage in section 15(3ZA)(a).

143(2) [Repealed by NICA 2002, s. 7 and Sch. 2.]

143(3) An order under subsection (1) above may if it contains an amendment altering the figure specified in section 11(2) and (6) of the Contributions and Benefits Act as the weekly rate of Class 2 contributions and the Treasury think it expedient in consequence of that amendment, amend section 11(4) of that Act by altering the figure there specified as the small profits threshold for the purposes of Class 2 contributions.

143(4) No order shall be made under this section so as–

(a) to increase for any tax year the main primary percentage, or the secondary percentage, to a percentage rate more than 0.25 per cent higher than that applicable at the end of the preceding tax year; or

(b) to increase the main Class 4 percentage to more than 9.25 per cent.

History – In s. 143(1)(a), the words "main primary percentage in section 8(2)(a)" substituted by NICA 2002, s. 6 and Sch. 1, para. 17(2)(a) with effect for 2003–04 and subsequent tax years.
S. 143(1)(a) and (b) substituted by SSA 1998, s. 86(1) and Sch. 7, para. 90 with effect from 1 April 1999 (SI 1999/527).
In s. 143(1)(c) the words "section 11(2) and (6)" substituted for the words "section 11(1)" by NICA 2015, s. 2 and Sch. 1, para. 21(2), with effect for the tax year 2015–16 and subsequent tax years.
In s. 143(1)(e) the words "specified as the main Class 4 percentage in section 15(3ZA)(a)" substituted by NICA 2002, s. 6 and Sch. 1, para. 17(2)(b) with effect for 2003–04 and subsequent tax years.
In s. 143(1) and (3) references to "Treasury" substituted in place of "Secretary of State" and "they" and "think" for, respectively, "he" and "thinks" wherever the words occur; by SSC(TF)A 1999, s. 2; Sch. 3, para. 46 with effect from 1 April 1999 (SI 1999/527).
S. 143(2) repealed by NICA 2002, s. 7 and Sch. 2 with effect for 2003–04 and subsequent tax years.
In s. 143(3) the words "section 11(2) and (6)" substituted for the words "section 11(1)" and in para. (b) the words "small profits threshold for the purposes of Class 2 contributions" substituted for the words "amount of earnings below which regulations under that subsection may except an earner from liability for Class 2 contributions" by NICA 2015, s. 2 and Sch. 1, para. 21(3), with effect for the tax year 2015–16 and subsequent tax years.
S. 143(4)(a) substituted by SSA 1998, s. 86(1) and Sch. 7, para. 90 with effect from 1 April 1999 (SI 1999/527).
In s. 143(4)(b), "9.25" substituted for "8.25" by NICA 2011, s. 2(2), with effect from 6 April 2011.
In s. 143, in para. (a), the word "main", and in para. (b), the words "main Class 4 percentage" substituted by NICA 2002, s. 6 and Sch. 1, para. 17(3) with effect for 2003–04 and subsequent tax years.

Derivations – (as originally enacted) SSA 1975, s. 122.

Cross references – SSCBA 1992, s. 8(2)(a), (b): initial and main primary percentages for Class 1 contributions.
SSCBA 1992, s. 9(3): weekly earnings brackets for secondary Class 1 contributions.
SSCBA 1992, s. 11(1), (4): weekly rate of Class 2 contributions and small earnings exception.
SSCBA 1992, s. 13(1): amount of a Class 3 contribution.
SSCBA 1992, s. 15(3): rate of Class 4 contributions.
SSCBA 1992, s. 18(1): Class 4 contributions recoverable under regulations.
SSCBA 1992, s. 176(2)(a): subordinate legislation not requiring Parliamentary control.

Notes – S. 170–174: procedure for consultation of Social Security Advisory Committee in drafting regulations and exclusions therefrom.

143A Power to alter Class 1B contributions

143A [Repealed by WRPA 1999, s. 88; Sch. 13, Pt. VI, with effect from 6 April 2000 (SI 1999/3420 (C. 92), art. 4(c), (e)).]

History – S. 143A inserted by SSA 1998, s. 65(1), with effect from 8 September 1998 for the purpose only of authorising the making of regulations, and from 6 April 1999 for all other purposes (SI 1998/2209). S. 143A is indirectly repealed by WRPA 1999, s. 88; Sch. 13, Pt. VI; which repeals SSA 1998, s. 65(1) with effect from 6 April 2000 (SI 1999/3420 (C. 92), art. 4(c), (e)) when the NIC reforms introduced by WRPA 1999, Pt. V, Ch. II came into force.

144 Orders under s. 143 – supplementary

144(1) Where (in accordance with section 190 below) the Treasury lay before Parliament a draft of an order under section 143 above, they shall lay with it a copy of a report by the Government Actuary or the Deputy Government Actuary on the effect which, in that Actuary's opinion, the making of such an order may be expected to have on the National Insurance Fund.

144(2) An order under section 143 above shall be made so as to be in force from the beginning of the tax year following that in which it received Parliamentary approval, and to have effect for that year and any subsequent tax year (subject to the effect of any subsequent order under this Part of this Act); and for this purpose the order is to be taken as receiving Parliamentary approval on the date on which the draft of it is approved by the second House to approve it.

History – References to s. 143A inserted by SSA 1998, s. 86(1) and Sch. 7, para. 91, with effect from 8 September 1998 for the purpose only of making regulations and orders, and from 6 April 1999 for all other purposes (SI 1998/2209 (C. 47), art. 2(b), (c) and Schedule, Pt. II, III). References to s. 143A are omitted (since s. 143A is repealed) by WRPA 1999, s. 88; Sch. 13, Pt. VI, with effect from 6 April 2000 (SI 1999/3420 (C. 92), art. 4(c), (e)).
In s. 144(1) "Treasury" substituted in place of "Secretary of State" and "they think" for "he thinks" by SSC(TF)A 1999, s. 2; Sch. 3, para. 48 with effect from 1 April 1999 (SI 1999/527).
In s. 144(1), the words "under Part I of the Contributions and Benefits Act" repealed by Social Security Administration (Fraud) Act 1997 s. 22 and Sch. 2 with effect from 1 July 1997.

Derivations – (as originally enacted) SSA 1975, s. 123.

Cross references – S. 190: Parliamentary control of orders and regulations.

145 Power to alter primary and secondary contributions

145(1) For the purpose of adjusting amounts payable by way of primary Class 1 contributions, the Treasury may at any time make an order altering the percentage rate specified as the main primary percentage in section 8(2)(a) of the Contributions and Benefits Act.

145(2) For the purpose of adjusting amounts payable by way of secondary Class 1 contributions, the Treasury may at any time make an order altering the percentage rate specified as the secondary percentage in section 9(2) of the Contributions and Benefits Act.

145(3) No order shall be made under this section so as to increase for any tax year the primary percentage, or the secondary percentage, to a percentage rate more than 0.25 per cent higher than that applicable at the end of the preceding tax year.

145(4) Without prejudice to section 141 or 143 above, the Treasury may make such order–

(a) amending section 11(2) and (6) of the Contributions and Benefits Act by altering the figure specified as the weekly rate of Class 2 contributions;

(b) amending section 13(1) of that Act by altering the figure specified in that subsection as the amount of a Class 3 contribution,

as the Treasury think fit in consequence of the coming into force of an order made or proposed to be made under subsection (1) above.

History – In s. 145(1), the words "main primary percentage in section 8(2)(a)" substituted by NICA 2002, s. 6 and Sch. 1, para. 18(2) with effect for 2003–04 and subsequent tax years.
In s. 145 "Treasury" substituted and, in s. 145(4), "the Treasury think" by SSC(TF)A 1999, s. 2; Sch. 3, para. 49 with effect from 1 April 1999 (SI 1999/527).
S. 145(1)–(3) substituted by SSA 1998, s. 86(1) and Sch. 7, para. 92, with effect from 6 April 1999 (SI 1999/418).
In s. 145(3), the word "main" inserted by NICA 2002, s. 6 and Sch. 1, para. 18(3) with effect for 2003–04 and subsequent tax years.
In s. 145(4)(a) the words "section 11(2) and (6)" substituted for the words "section 11(1)" and the words "in that subsection" omitted by NICA 2015, s. 2 and Sch. 1, para. 22, with effect for the tax year 2015–16 and subsequent tax years.

Derivations – SSA 1975, s. 123A(1)–(4).

Cross references – SSCBA 1992, s. 8(2)(a), (b): initial and primary percentages for Class 1 contributions.
SSCBA 1992, s. 9(3): secondary earnings brackets for Class 1 contributions.
SSCBA 1992, s. 11(1): weekly rate of Class 2 contributions.
SSCBA 1992, s. 13(1): amount of a Class 3 contribution.
SSCBA 1992, s. 176(2)(a): subordinate legislation not requiring Parliamentary control.

Statutory instruments – SI 1996/597 (made under s. 145(2)): alteration of weekly earnings limits from 6 April 1996.

Notes – S. 170–174: procedure for consultation of Social Security Advisory Committee in drafting regulations and exclusions therefrom.

146 Power to alter number of secondary earnings brackets

146 [Repealed by SSA 1998, s. 86(1); Sch. 7, para. 93 and s. 86(2); Sch. 8.]

History – Repealed by SSA 1998, s. 86(1); Sch. 7, para. 93 and s. 86(2); Sch. 8 with effect from 6 April 1999 (SI 1999/418).

147 Orders under s. 145 and 146 – supplementary

147(1) An order under section 145 above may make such amendments of any enactment as appear to the Treasury to be necessary or expedient in consequence of any alteration made by it.

147(2) Where (in accordance with section 190 below) the Treasury lay before Parliament a draft of an order under section 145 above, they shall lay with it a copy of a report by the Government Actuary or the Deputy Government Actuary on the effect which, in that Actuary's opinion, the making of such an order may be expected to have on the National Insurance Fund.

147(3) An order under section 145 above shall be made so as to come into force–

(a) on a date in the tax year in which it receives Parliamentary approval; or

(b) on a date in the next tax year.

147(4) Such an order shall have effect for the remainder of the tax year in which it comes into force and for any subsequent tax year (subject to the effect of any subsequent order under this Part of this Act).

(d) in the case of Class 2 contributions, 15.5 per cent of the amount estimated to be the total of those contributions;

(e) in the case of Class 3 contributions, 15.5 per cent of the amount estimated to be the total of those contributions; and

(ea) in the case of Class 3A contributions, 15.5 per cent of the amount estimated to be the total of those contributions;

(f) in the case of Class 4 contributions, 2.15 per cent of the amount estimated to be that of so much of the profits or gains, or earnings, in respect of which those contributions were paid as exceeded the lower limit specified in paragraph (a) of subsection (3) of section 15, and in paragraph (a) of subsection (1A) of section 18, of the Contributions and Benefits Act but did not exceed the upper limit specified in those subsections.

162(5A) In subsection (5) above **"the product of the additional rate"** means the amount estimated to be the aggregate of–

(a) so much of the total of primary Class 1 contributions as is attributable to section 8(1)(b) of the Contributions and Benefits Act (additional primary percentage);

(b) so much of the total of Class 4 contributions under section 15 of that Act as is attributable to subsection (3)(b) of that section (additional Class 4 percentage); and

(c) so much of the total of Class 4 contributions payable by virtue of section 18 of that Act as is attributable to subsection (1A)(b) of that section (additional Class 4 percentage).

162(6) In subsections (5) and (5A) above **"estimated"** means estimated by the Inland Revenue in any manner which after consulting the Government Actuary or the Deputy Government Actuary the Inland Revenue consider to be appropriate and which the Treasury has approved.

162(6A) In the case of earners paid other than weekly, the reference in paragraph (a) of subsection (5) above to the primary threshold or the upper earnings limit shall be taken as a reference to the equivalent of that threshold or limit prescribed under section 5(4) of the Contributions and Benefits Act.

162(7) The Treasury may by order amend any of paragraphs (a) to (f) of subsection (5) above in relation to any tax year, by substituting for the percentage for the time being specified in that paragraph a different percentage.

162(8) No order under subsection (7) above shall substitute a figure which represents an increase or decrease in the appropriate national health service allocation of more than–

(a) 0.1 per cent of the relevant earnings, in the case of paragraph (a) or (b);

(b) 0.1 per cent of the relevant aggregate, in the case of paragraph (c) or (ca);

(c) 4 per cent of the relevant contributions, in the case of paragraph (d), (e) or (ea); or

(d) 0.2 per cent of the relevant earnings, in the case of paragraph (f).

162(9) From the national health service allocation in respect of contributions of any class there shall be deducted such amount as the Inland Revenue may estimate to be the portion of the total expenses incurred by them or any other government department in collecting contributions of that class which is fairly attributable to that allocation, and the remainder shall be paid by the Inland Revenue to the Secretary of State towards the cost–

(a) of the national health service in England;

(b) of that service in Wales; and

(c) of that service in Scotland,

in such shares as the Treasury may determine.

162(10) The Inland Revenue shall pay any amounts deducted in accordance with subsection (9) above into the Consolidated Fund.

162(11) [Repealed by SSC(TF)A 1999, s. 2; Sch. 3, para. 52(10) and s. 26(3) and Sch. 10, Pt. I. Any estimate by the Secretary of State for the purposes of subsection (9) above shall be made in accordance with any directions given by the Treasury.]

162(12) The Inland Revenue may make regulations modifying this section, in such manner as they think appropriate, in relation to the contributions of persons referred to in the following sections of the Contributions and Benefits Act–

(a) section 116(2) (H.M. forces);

(b) section 117(1) (mariners, airmen, etc.);

(c) section 120(1) (continental shelf workers),

and in relation to any contributions which are reduced under section 6(5) of that Act.

History – In s. 162(1), the words "from contributions of any class," and the words "in the case of contributions of that class" in s. 162(1) repealed by the NICA 2002 and Sch. 2 with effect for 2003–04 and subsequent tax years.

(b) the provisions of Part II of Schedule 3 to the Consequential Provisions Act, except as they apply to industrial injuries benefit; and

"the relevant Northern Ireland enactments" means–

(a) the provisions of the Northern Ireland Contributions and Benefits Act and the Northern Ireland Administration Act, except as they apply to Northern Ireland industrial injuries benefit and payments under Part I of Schedule 8 to the Northern Ireland Contributions and Benefits Act; and

(aa) any provisions in Northern Ireland which correspond to provisions of the Jobseekers Act 1995; and

(ab) any enactment corresponding to section 10 of the Child Support Act 1995 having effect with respect to Northern Ireland; and

(ac) any provisions in Northern Ireland which correspond to provisions of the Social Security (Recovery of Benefits) Act 1997;

(ad) any provisions in Northern Ireland which correspond to provisions of Chapter II of Part I of the Social Security Act 1998 and section 72 of that Act;

(ae) any provisions in Northern Ireland which correspond to sections 60, 72 and 79 of the Welfare Reform and Pensions Act 1999; and

(af) any provisions in Northern Ireland which correspond to section 42, any of sections 62 to 65, 69 and 70 of the Child Support, Pensions and Social Security Act 2000; and

(ag) any provisions in Northern Ireland which correspond to sections 7 to 11 of the Social Security Fraud Act 2001.

(ah) any provisions in Northern Ireland which correspond to provisions of the State Pension Credit Act 2002; and

(aia) any provisions in Northern Ireland which correspond to provisions of Part 1 of the Welfare Reform Act 2007;

(ak) any provisions in Northern Ireland which correspond to the provisions of Part 1 of the Welfare Reform Act 2012;

(al) any provisions in Northern Ireland which correspond to Part 4 of that Act;

(ala) any provisions in Northern Ireland which correspond to sections 96 to 97 of that Act;

(am) any provisions in Northern Ireland which correspond to the provisions of Part 1 of the Pensions Act 2014;

(an) any provisions in Northern Ireland which correspond to section 30 of the Pensions Act 2014;

(b) the provisions of Part II of Schedule 3 to the Social Security (Consequential Provisions) (Northern Ireland) Act 1992, except as they apply to Northern Ireland industrial injuries benefit; and

(c) [repealed by SI 1995/3213 (NI 22), Sch. 5, Pt. III;]

and in this definition–

(i) **"Northern Ireland Contributions and Benefits Act"** means the Social Security Contributions and Benefits (Northern Ireland) Act 1992;

(ii) **"Northern Ireland industrial injuries benefit"** means benefit under Part V of the Northern Ireland Contributions and Benefits Act other than under Schedule 8 to that Act.

Prospective amendments – In s. 170(5), in the definition of "the relevant enactments" para. (ao) inserted by Welfare Reform and Work Act 2016, s. 20(2)(a), with effect from a day to be appointed under s. 36(6). Para. (ao) to read as follows:

"(ao) sections 18, 19 and 21 of the Welfare Reform and Work Act 2016;"

In s. 170(5), in the definition of "the relevant Northern Ireland enactments" para. (ao) inserted by Welfare Reform and Work Act 2016, s. 20(2)(b), with effect from a day to be appointed under s. 36(6). Para. (ao) to read as follows:

"(ao) any provisions in Northern Ireland which correspond to sections 18, 19 and 21 of the Welfare Reform and Work Act 2016;"

In s. 170(5), para. (ab) of the definition of "the relevant enactments" repealed by CSPSSA 2000, Sch. 9, Pt. 1, with effect from 3 March 2003 for certain purposes (by virtue of SI 2003/192), and from a day to be appointed for remaining purposes.

In s. 170(5), in the definition of "the relevant enactments", para. (aj) repealed by WRA 2012, s. 147 and Sch. 14, Pt. 1, with effect from a date to be set by order of the Secretary of State.

History – In s. 170(5), in the definition of "the relevant enactments", the words ", this Act and the Social Security (Incapacity for Work) Act 1994" substituted for the words "and this Act" by the Social Security (Incapacity for Work) Act 1994, Sch. 1, para. 51, with effect from 13 April 1995 (SI 1994/2926).

In s. 170(5), in the definitions of "the relevant enactments" and "the relevant Northern Ireland enactments", para. (aa) in each definition inserted by Jobseekers Act 1995, Sch. 2, para. 67, with effect from 22 April 1996 by virtue of SI 1996/1126, art. 2, and para. (ab) in each definition inserted by Child Support Act 1995, Sch. 3, para. 20, with effect from 14 October 1996 by virtue of SI 1996/2630.

In s. 170(5), in the definition of "the relevant enactments" and "the relevant Northern Ireland enactments", para. (ac) in each definition inserted by the Social Security (Recovery of Benefits) Act 1997, s. 33(1) and Sch. 3, with effect from 6 October 1997 by virtue of SI 1997/2085.

In s. 170(5), in the definitions of "the relevant enactments" and "the relevant Northern Ireland enactments", para. (ad) inserted by SSA 1998, s. 86(1) and Sch. 7, para. 104, with effect from 4 March 1999 (SI 1999/528).

In s. 170(5), in the definitions of both “the relevant enactments” and “the relevant Northern Ireland enactments”, new para. (ae) inserted by the WRPA 1999, s. 84(1); Sch. 12, para. 81, with effect from 11 November 1999.
In s. 170(5), in the definition of “the relevant enactments”, in para. (af), the words “sections 69 and 70 of the Child Support, Pensions and Social Security Act 2000;” substituted for the words “sections 68 to 70 of the Child Support Pensions and Social Security Act 2000 and Schedule 7 to that Act” by WRA 2012, s. 31 and Sch. 2, para. 26(2)(a), with effect from 25 February 2013 (SI 2013/358, art. 3).
In s. 170(5), in the definition of “the relevant Northern Ireland enactments”, in para. (af), the words “sections 69 and 70 of the Child Support, Pensions and Social Security Act 2000;” substituted for the words “sections 68 to 70 of the Child Support Pensions and Social Security Act 2000 or Schedule 7 to that Act” by WRA 2012, s. 31 and Sch. 2, para. 26(3)(a), with effect from 25 February 2013 (SI 2013/358, art. 3).
In s. 170(5), in the definition of “relevant enactments” and “relevant Northern Ireland enactments”, para. (af) inserted by CSPSSA 2000, s. 73 with effect from 1 November 2000 in so far as it applies to s. 69 and Sch. 7 and with effect from December 2000 in so far as it applies in relation to s. 62 to 65.
In s. 170(5), in the definition of “relevant enactments” and “relevant Northern Ireland enactments”, para. (ag) inserted by SSFA 2001, s. 12(3) with effect from 1 April 2002 (SI 2001/3689) (C. 119).
In s. 170(5), in the definition of “relevant enactments” and “relevant Northern Ireland enactments” para. (ah) inserted by the State Pension Credit Act 2002, s. 14 and Sch. 2, para. 20 with effect from 2 July 2002 only for the purposes of making regulations or orders by virtue of SI 2002/1691.
In s. 170(5), in the definition of “relevant enactments” para. (ai) inserted by Age-related Payments Act 2004, s. 7(5), with effect from 8 July 2004.
In s. 170(5), in the definition of “the relevant enactments” para. (aia) inserted by Welfare Reform Act 2007, s. 28 and Sch. 3, para. 10(28) with effect from 18 March 2008 (for the purpose of making regulations) and 27 October 2008 (otherwise) (SI 2008/787).
In s. 170(5), in the definition of “the relevant Northern Ireland enactments” para. (aia) inserted by Welfare Reform Act 2007, s. 28 and Sch. 3, para. 10(28) with effect from 18 March 2008 (for the purpose of making regulations) and 27 October 2008 (otherwise) (SI 2008/787).
In s. 170(5), in the definition of “the relevant enactments”, para. (ak) inserted by WRA 2012, s. 31 and Sch. 2, para. 26(2)(b), with effect from 25 February 2013 (SI 2013/358, art. 3).
In s. 170(5), in the definition of “the relevant Northern Ireland enactments”, para. (ak) inserted by WRA 2012, s. 31 and Sch. 2, para. 26(3)(b), with effect from 25 February 2013 (SI 2013/358, art. 3).
In s. 170(5), in the definition of “the relevant enactments”, para. (al) inserted by WRA 2012, s. 91 and Sch. 4, para. 26(a), with effect from 25 February 2013 (SI 2013/358, art. 3).
In s. 170(5), in the definition of “the relevant enactments”, para. (ala) inserted by Welfare Reform and Work Act 2016, s. 10(1)(a), with effect from 9 June 2016 (SI 2016/610, reg. 2).
In s. 170(5), in the definition of “the relevant Northern Ireland enactments”, para. (al) inserted by WRA 2012, s. 91 and Sch. 4, para. 26(b), with effect from 25 February 2013 (SI 2013/358, art. 3).
In s. 170(5), in the definition of “the relevant Northern Ireland enactments” para. (ala) inserted by Welfare Reform and Work Act 2016, s. 10(1)(b), with effect from 9 June 2016 (SI 2016/610, reg. 2).
In s. 170(5), in the definition of “the relevant enactments” and the definition of “the relevant Northern Ireland enactments” para. (am) inserted by PA 2014, s. 23 and Sch. 12, para. 24, with effect from 6 April 2016 (as not brought into force by any earlier order under PA 2014, s. 56(1)).
In s. 170(5), in the definition of “the relevant enactments” and the definition of “the relevant Northern Ireland enactments”, para. (an) inserted by PA 2014, s. 31 and Sch. 16, para. 32, with effect from 6 April 2017, subject to SI 2017/297, art. 4 (later commencement for abolition of bereavement payment and bereavement allowance) and 5 (commencement for entitlement to bereavement payment and bereavement support payment) (SI 2017/297, art. 3(2)).
In s. 170(5) para. (c) of the definitionof “the relevant Northern Ireland enactments” repealed by SI 1995/3213 (NI 22), Sch. 5, Pt. III, with effect from 6 April 1997.
Derivations – S. 170(1)–(4): SSA 1980, s. 9(1)–(4).
S. 170(5) (as originally enacted): SSA 1980, s. 9(7).

172 Functions of Committee and Council in relation to regulations

172(1) Subject–

(a) to subsection (3) below; and

(b) to section 173 below,

where the Secretary of State proposes to make regulations under any of the relevant enactments, he shall refer the proposals, in the form of draft regulations or otherwise, to the Committee.

172(2) [Not relevant to National Insurance contributions.]

172(3) Subsection (1) above does not apply to the regulations specified in Part I of Schedule 7 to this Act.

172(4) [Not relevant to National Insurance contributions.]

172(5) In relation to regulations required or authorised to be made by the Secretary of State in conjunction with the Treasury, the reference in subsection (1) above to the Secretary of State shall be construed as a reference to the Secretary of State and the Treasury.

Derivations – S. 172(1): SSA 1980, s. 10(1).
S. 172(3): SSA 1980, s. 10(2).
S. 172(5): SSA 1980, s. 10(9).

173 Cases in which consultation is not required

173(1) Nothing in any enactment shall require any proposals in respect of regulations to be referred to the Committee or the Council if–

(a) it appears to the Secretary of State that by reason of the urgency of the matter it is inexpedient so to refer them; or

(b) the relevant advisory body have agreed that they shall not be referred.

173(2) Where by virtue only of subsection (1)(a) above the Secretary of State makes regulations without proposals in respect of them having been referred, then, unless the relevant advisory body agrees that this subsection shall not apply, he shall refer the regulations to that body as soon as practicable after making them.

173(3) Where the Secretary of State has referred proposals to the Committee or the Council, he may make the proposed regulations before the Committee have made their report or, as the case may be the Council have given their advice, only if after the reference it appears to him that by reason of the urgency of the matter it is expedient to do so.

173(4) Where by virtue of this section regulations are made before a report of the Committee has been made, the Committee shall consider them and make a report to the Secretary of State containing such recommendations with regard to the regulations as the Committee thinks appropriate; and a copy of any report made to the Secretary of State on the regulations shall be laid by him before each House of Parliament together, if the report contains recommendations, with a statement–

(a) of the extent (if any) to which the Secretary of State proposes to give effect to the recommendations; and

(b) in so far as he does not propose to give effect to them, of his reasons why not.

173(5) Except to the extent that this subsection is excluded by an enactment passed after 25th July 1986, nothing in any enactment shall require the reference to the Committee or the Council of any regulations contained in either–

(a) a statutory instrument made before the end of the period of 6 months beginning with the coming into force of the enactment under which those regulations are made; or

(b) a statutory instrument–

(i) which states that it contains only regulations made by virtue of, or consequential upon, a specified enactment; and

(ii) which is made before the end of the period of 6 months beginning with the coming into force of that specified enactment.

173(6) In relation to regulations required or authorised to be made by the Secretary of State in conjunction with the Treasury, any reference in this section to the Secretary of State shall be construed as a reference to the Secretary of State and the Treasury.

173(7) In this section **"regulations"** means regulations under any enactment, whenever passed.

Derivations – S. 173(1)–(5): SSA 1986, s. 61(1)–(5).
S. 173(6): SSA 1980, s. 10(9).
S. 173(7): SSA 1986, s. 61(10) "regulations".

Cross references – PSA 1993, s. 184: consultation with Social Security Advisory Committee about regulations under PSA 1993, s. 36(6).
PSA 1993, s. 185(6): s. 173 is to apply as if references to the Social Security Advisory Committee included references to the Occupational Pensions Board.

174 Committee's report on regulations and Secretary of State's duties

174(1) The Committee shall consider any proposals referred to it by the Secretary of State under section 172 above and shall make to the Secretary of State a report containing such recommendations with regard to the subject-matter of the proposals as the Committee thinks appropriate.

174(2) If after receiving a report of the Committee the Secretary of State lays before Parliament any regulations or draft regulations which comprise the whole or any part of the subject-matter of the proposals referred to the Committee, he shall lay with the regulations or draft regulations a copy of the Committee's report and a statement showing–

(a) the extent (if any) to which he has, in framing the regulations, given effect to the Committee's recommendations; and

(b) in so far as effect has not been given to them, his reasons why not.

174(3) In the case of any regulations laid before Parliament at a time when Parliament is not sitting, the requirements of subsection (2) above shall be satisfied as respects either House of Parliament if a copy of the report and statement there referred to are laid before that House not later than the second day on which the House sits after the laying of the regulations.

174(4) In relation to regulations required or authorised to be made by the Secretary of State in conjunction with the Treasury any reference in this section to the Secretary of State shall be construed as a reference to the Secretary of State and the Treasury.

Derivations – S. 174(1)–(3): SSA 1980, s. 10(3)–(5).
S. 174(4): SSA 1980, s. 10(9).

PART XIV – SOCIAL SECURITY SYSTEMS OUTSIDE GREAT BRITAIN

CO-ORDINATION

177 Co-ordination with Northern Ireland

177 [Repealed by the Northern Ireland Act 1998, Sch. 15.]

History – S. 177 repealed by the Northern Ireland Act 1998, Sch. 15 with effect from 2 December 1999 (SI 1999/3209, art. 2 and Schedule).

179 Reciprocal agreements with countries outside the United Kingdom

179(1) For the purpose of giving effect–

(a) to any agreement with the government of a country outside the United Kingdom providing for reciprocity in matters relating to payments for purposes similar or comparable to the purposes of legislation to which this section applies, or

(b) to any such agreement as it would be if it were altered in accordance with proposals to alter it which, in consequence of any change in the law of Great Britain, the government of the United Kingdom has made to the other government in question,

Her Majesty may by Order in Council make provision for modifying or adapting such legislation in its application to cases affected by the agreement or proposed alterations.

179(2) An Order made by virtue of subsection (1) above may, instead of or in addition to making specific modifications or adaptations, provide generally that legislation to which this section applies shall be modified to such extent as may be required to give effect to the provisions contained in the agreement or, as the case may be, alterations in question.

179(3) The modifications which may be made by virtue of subsection (1) above include provisions–

(a) for securing that acts, omissions and events having any effect for the purposes of the law of the country in respect of which the agreement is made have a corresponding effect for the purposes of this Act, the Jobseekers Act 1995, Chapter II of Part I of the Social Security Act 1998, the State Pension Credit Act 2002, Part 1 of the Welfare Reform Act 2007, Part 1 of the Welfare Reform Act 2012, Part 4 of that Act, Part 1 of the Pensions Act 2014, Part 5 of that Act and the Contributions and Benefits Act (but not so as to confer a right to double benefit);

(b) for determining, in cases where rights accrue both under such legislation and under the law of that country, which of those rights is to be available to the person concerned;

(c) for making any necessary financial adjustments.

179(4) This section applies–

(a) to the Contributions and Benefits Act;

(aa) to the Jobseekers Act 1995; and

(ab) to Chapter II of Part I of the Social Security Act 1998;

(ac) to Part II of the Social Security Contributions (Transfer of Functions, etc.) Act 1999; and

(ad) to Part III of the Social Security Contributions (Transfer of Functions, etc.) (Northern Ireland) Order 1999; and

(ae) to the State Pension Credit Act 2002; and

(af) to Part 1 of the Welfare Reform Act 2007;

(ag) to Part 1 of the Welfare Reform Act 2012; and

(ah) to Part 4 of that Act;

(ai) to Part 1 of the Pensions Act 2014;

(aj) to Part 5 of the Pensions Act 2014;

(b) to this Act, …

179(5) [Not relevant to National Insurance contributions.]

Prospective amendments – S. 179(4)(b)(i) repealed by WRA 2012, s. 147 and Sch. 14, Pt. 1, with effect from a date to be set by order of the Secretary of State.

History – In s. 179(3)(a) the words ", Part 5 of that Act" inserted after the words "Pensions Act 2014" by PA 2014, s. 31 and Sch. 16, para. 33(2), with effect from 8 February 2017 (SI 2017/111, reg. 5(c)).
In s. 179(3)(a), the words ", Part 1 of the Pensions Act 2014" inserted after the words "Part 4 of that Act" by PA 2014, s. 23 and Sch. 12, para. 25(2), with effect from 7 July 2015 (SI 2015/1475, art. 2(2)).
In s. 179(3)(a), after "2007", the words ", Part 1 of the Welfare Reform Act 2012" inserted by WRA 2012, s. 31 and Sch. 2, para. 27(2), with effect from 29 April 2013 (SI 2013/983, art. 3(1)(b)).
In s. 179(3)(a), the words ", Part 4 of that Act" inserted by WRA 2012, s. 91 and Sch. 9, para. 27(2), with effect from 8 April 2013 in relation to a person whose only or principal residence is, on the date on which that person makes a claim for personal independence

payment, located in an area to which one of the following postcodes corresponds: BL, CA, CH (except CH1, CH4, CH5, CH6, CH7 and CH8), CW, DH, DL (except DL6, DL7, DL8, DL9, DL10 and DL11), FY, L, LA (except LA2 7, LA2 8, LA6 2 and LA6 3), M, NE, PR, SR, TS (except TS9), WA and WN (SI 2013/358, art. 7(1) and (2)(k)), and from 10 June 2013 in relation to any other person (SI 2013/1250, art. 2).
In s. 179(3)(a), the words ", Part 1 of the Welfare Reform Act 2007" inserted by Welfare Reform Act 2007, s. 28 and Sch. 3, para. 10(29), with effect from 18 March 2008 (for the purpose of making regulations) and 27 October 2008 (otherwise) (SI 2008/787).
In s. 179(3)(a), the words ", Chapter II of Part I of the Social Security Act 1998" inserted by SSA 1998, s. 86(1) and Sch. 7, para. 107(1), with effect from 6 September 1999, for the purposes of (i) decisions whether a person is entitled to be credited with earnings or contributions in accordance with regulations made under s. 22(5) of the Contributions and Benefits Act; and (ii) decisions whether a person was, within the meaning of regulations, precluded from regular employment by responsibilities at home; with effect from 18 October 1999 (SI 1999/2860 (C. 75), art. 2(c)(iv), (v) and Sch. 1); for the purposes of benefits under SSCBA 1992, Pt. II except child's special allowance (SI 1999/2422 (C. 61), art. 2(c)(i) and Sch. 1) and, with effect from 5 July 1999, for the purposes of any matter to which, by virtue of PSA 1993, s. 170, provisions of SSA 1998, Pt. I, Ch. II are to apply (SI 1999/1958 (C. 51), art. 2(1)(b)(iv) and Sch. 1). In so far as it was not already in force (except for the purposes of housing benefit, council tax benefit and decisions to which SI 1999/527, art. 4(6) applies; i.e. pre-1 April 1999 decisions under SSAA 1992, s. 17(1), s. 20(3) and PSA 1993, s. 170(1)) it is effective from 29 November 1999 (SI 1999/3178 (C. 81), art. 2(1)(a); 2(2) and Sch. 1). The wording of s. 179(3)(a), as it continues to apply for purposes other than those mentioned above, reads as follows:
In s. 179(3), the words ", the State Pension Credit Act 2002" substituted by the State Pension Credit Act 2002, s. 14 and Sch. 2, para. 21 with effect from 2 July 2002 only for the purposes of making regulations.
In s. 179(4), para. (ae) inserted by the State Pension Credit Act 2002, s. 14 and Sch. 2, para. 21 with effect from 2 July 2002 only for the purposes of making regulations.
In s. 179(3)(a) reference to Pt. II of the Social Security Contributions (Transfer of Functions, etc.) Act 1999 inserted by SSC(TF)A 1999, s. 18; Sch. 7, para. 15(2) with effect from 1 April 1999 (SI 1999/527).
S. 179(3), (4) amended by Jobseekers Act 1995, Sch. 2, para. 70, with effect from 22 April 1996 by virtue of SI 1996/1126, art. 2, by inserting the reference to the Jobseekers Act 1995 in s. 179(3), and in s. 179(4) inserting para. (aa).
In s. 179(4) para. (ac) reference inserted by SSC(TF)A 1999, s. 18; Sch. 7, para. 15(3) with effect from 1 April 1999 (SI 1999/527).
S. 179(4)(ab) inserted by SSA 1998, s. 86(1) and Sch. 7, para. 107(2), for the purposes of (i) decisions whether a person is entitled to be credited with earnings or contributions in accordance with regulations made under s. 22(5) of the Contributions and Benefits Act and (ii) decisions whether a person was, within the meaning of regulations, precluded from regular employment by responsibilities at home, with effect from 18 October 1999 (SI 1999/2860 (C. 75), art. 2(c)(iv), (v) and Sch. 1); for the purposes of benefits under SSCBA 1992, Pt. II except child's special allowance, with effect from 6 September 1999 (SI 1999/2422 (C. 61), art. 2(c)(i) and Sch. 1) and, with effect from 5 July 1999, for the purposes of any matter to which, by virtue of PSA 1993, s. 170, provisions of SSA 1998, Pt. I, Ch. II are to apply (SI 1999/1958 (C. 51), art. 2(1)(b)(iv) and Sch. 1). In so far as it was not already in force (except for the purposes of housing benefit, council tax benefit and decisions to which SI 1999/527, art. 4(6) applies; i.e. pre-1 April 1999 decisions under SSAA 1992, s. 17(1), s. 20(3) and PSA 1993, s. 170(1)) it is effective from 29 November 1999 (SI 1999/3178 (C. 81), art. 2(1)(a); 2(2) and Sch. 1).
S. 179(4)(af) inserted by Welfare Reform Act 2007, s. 28 and Sch. 3, para. 10(29) with effect from 18 March 2008 (for the purpose of making regulations) and 27 October 2008 (otherwise) (SI 2008/787).
S. 179(4)(ag) inserted by WRA 2012, s. 31 and Sch. 2, para. 27(3), with effect from 29 April 2013 (SI 2013/983, art. 3(1)(b)).
S. 179(4)(ah) inserted by WRA 2012, s. 91 and Sch. 4, para. 27(3), with effect from 8 April 2013 in relation to a person whose only or principal residence is, on the date on which that person makes a claim for personal independence payment, located in an area to which one of the following postcodes corresponds: BL, CA, CH (except CH1, CH4, CH5, CH6, CH7 and CH8), CW, DH, DL (except DL6, DL7, DL8, DL9, DL10 and DL11), FY, L, LA (except LA2 7, LA2 8, LA6 2 and LA6 3), M, NE, PR, SR, TS (except TS9), WA and WN (SI 2013/358, art. 7(1) and (2)(k)), and from 10 June 2013 in relation to any other person (SI 2013/1250, art. 2).
S. 179(4)(ai) inserted by PA 2014, s. 23 and Sch. 12, para. 25(3), with effect from 7 July 2015 (SI 2015/1475, art. 2(2)).
In s. 179(4)(aj) inserted by PA 2014, s. 31 and Sch. 16, para. 33(3), with effect from 8 February 2017 (SI 2017/111, reg. 5(c)).

Derivations – S. 179(1)–(3): SSA 1975, s. 143(1), (1A), (2).
S. 179(4)(a), (b): SSA 1975, s. 143(1).

Cross references – S. 189(11): Secretary of State's extended powers of regulation.
SI 1979/591, reg. 82: modification of employed earner's employment in case of airmen.

Statutory instruments – SI 1995/767 and SI 1996/1928, made under s. 179(1)(b) and (2).

European Economic Area and European Community Countries

Austria	Italy
Belgium	Leichstenstein
Denmark	Luxembourg
Finland	Netherlands
France	Norway
Germany	Portugal
Gibraltar	Spain
Greece	Sweden
Iceland	Republic of Ireland

Reciprocal Agreement Countries

Barbados	SI 1992/812
Bermuda	SI 1969/1686
Bosnia–Herzegovina	
Croatia	
Canada	
Cyprus	SI 1983/1698
Guernsey	SI 1978/1527
Israel	SI 1957/1879 (amended SI 1984/354)
Jamaica	SI 1972/1587
Japan	SI 2000/3063
Jersey	SI 1978/1527

190 Parliamentary control of orders and regulations

190(1) Subject to the provisions of this section, a statutory instrument containing (whether alone or with other provisions)–

(za) regulations under section 132A(4);

(a) an order under section 141, 143, 145, 150, 150A, 151A, 152 or 162(7) above; or

(aza) any order containing provision adding any person to the list of persons falling within section 109B(2A) above;

(aa) the first regulations to be made under section 2A;

(ab) the first regulations to be made under section 2AA,

shall not be made unless a draft of the instrument has been laid before Parliament and been approved by a resolution of each House of Parliament;

(b) [not relevant to National Insurance contributions.]

190(2) [Not relevant to National Insurance contributions.]

190(3) A statutory instrument–

(a) which contains (whether alone or with other provisions) orders or regulations made under this Act by the Secretary of State, the Treasury or the Inland Revenue; and

(b) which is not subject to any requirement that a draft of the instrument be laid before and approved by a resolution of each House of Parliament,

shall be subject to annulment in pursuance of a resolution of either House of Parliament.

Prospective amendments – S. 190(1)(aa) and (ab) repealed by WRA 2012, s. 147 and Sch. 14, Pt. 1, with effect from a date to be set by order of the Secretary of State.

History – S. 190(1)(za) inserted by NICA 2006, s. 7(3), with effect from 30 March 2006.
In s. 190(1)(a), "151A," inserted by PA 2014, s. 23 and Sch. 12, para. 27, with effect from 6 April 2016 (as not brought into force by any earlier order under PA 2014, s. 56(1)).
In s. 190(1)(a), reference to s. 150A inserted by PA 2007, s. 5 and Sch. 1, para. 30, with effect in relation to purposes referred to in s. 5(7) and s. 30(1), for 2007–08 and subsequent years. For remaining purposes see s. 5(3)–(6).
In s. 190(1)(a), reference to s. 143A inserted by SSA 1998, s. 86(1) and Sch. 7, para. 110(1)(a), with effect from 8 September 1998 for the purpose only of authorising the making of regulations and orders, and from 6 April 1999 for all other purposes (SI 1998/2209 (C. 47), art. 2(b), (c) and Schedule, Pt. II, III). This reference to s. 143A was repealed (as is s. 143A) by WRPA 1999, s. 88; Sch. 13, Pt. VI, with effect from 6 April 2000 (SI 1999/3420 (C. 92), art. 4(c), (e).
In s. 190(1)(a), reference to s. 146 omitted by SSA 1998, s. 86(1) and Sch. 7, para. 110(1)(b), with effect from 6 April 1999 (SI 1999/418).
S. 190(1)(aza) inserted by SSFA 2001, s. 1(9) with effect from 26 February 2002 (SI 2002/403 (C. 10)).
S. 190(1)(aa) inserted by WRPA 1999, s. 84(1); Sch. 12, para. 83, with effect from 6 April 2000 (SI 1999/3420).
S. 190(1)(ab) inserted by the Employment Act 2002, s. 53 and Sch. 7, para. 15, with effect from 5 July 2003 (by virtue of SI 2003/1666).
In s. 190(3), in relation to tax credit, references to the "Secretary of State" shall be construed, with effect from 5 October 1999, as if they were references to "the Treasury" or, as the case may be, "the Board" (TCA 1999, s. 20(2); s. 2 and Sch. 2, para. 20(d)).
In s. 190(3)(a) the words, "the Treasury or the Inland Revenue" inserted by SSC(TF)A 1999, s. 2; Sch. 3, para. 58 with effect from 1 April 1999 (SI 1999/527).
S. 190(4) repealed by SSA 1998, s. 86(1) and Sch. 7, para. 110(2) and s. 86(2) and Sch. 8, with effect from 29 November 1999 (except for the purposes of housing benefit, council tax benefit and decisions to which SI 1999/527, art. 4(6) applies; i.e. pre-1 April 1999 decisions under SSAA 1992, s. 17(1), s. 20(3) and PSA 1993, s. 170(1)) (SI 1999/3178 (C. 81), art. 2(1)(a); 2(2) and Sch. 1). The text of s. 190(4), which is still effective for these purposes, is as follows:

"**190(4)** A statutory instrument–

(a) which contains (whether alone or with other provisions) regulations made under this Act by the Lord Chancellor; and

(b) which is not subject to any requirement that a draft of the instrument be laid before and approved by a resolution of each House of Parliament,

shall be subject to annulment in pursuance of a resolution of either House of Parliament."

Derivations – S. 190(1) (as originally enacted): SSA 1975, s. 167(1)(b); Child Benefit Act 1975, s. 22(3); SS(C)A 1981, s. 4(5)(b); SSA 1986, s. 62(3), 83(3)(d); SSA 1989, s. 17(2)(b), s. 29(2)(h).
S. 190(3): SSA 1975, s. 167(3); Child Benefit Act 1975, s. 22(5); SS(MP)A 1977, s. 24(5); SSHBA 1982, s. 45(2); SSA 1986, s. 83(4); SSA 1989, s. 29(3); SSA 1990, s. 21(1), Sch. 6, para. 8(1), (3), (4), (7), (9), (12); Disability Living Allowance and Disability Working Allowance Act 1991, s. 12(2).
S. 190(4): SSA 1975, s. 167(4); SSA 1980, s. 14(8); SSA 1990, s. 21(1), Sch. 6, para. 8(1).

SUPPLEMENTARY

191 Interpretation – general

191 In this Act, unless the context otherwise requires–

"the 1975 Act" means the Social Security Act 1975;

"the 1986 Act" means the Social Security Act 1986;

"benefit" means benefit under the Contributions and Benefits Act and includes universal credit, state pension under Part 1 of the Pensions Act 2014, a jobseeker's allowance state pension credit, an employment and support allowance, personal independence payment and bereavement support payment under section 30 of the Pensions Act 2014;

"claim" is to be construed in accordance with "claimant";

"claimant" (in relation to contributions under Part I and to benefit under Parts II to IV of the Contributions and Benefits Act) means–

(a) a person whose right to be excepted from liability to pay, or to have his liability deferred for, or to be credited with, a contribution, is in question;

(b) a person who has claimed benefit;

and includes, in relation to an award or decision a beneficiary under the award or affected by the decision;

…

"Commissioner" means the Chief Social Security Commissioner or any other Social Security Commissioner and includes a tribunal of 3 Commissioners constituted under section 57 above;

…

"the Consequential Provisions Act" means the Social Security (Consequential Provisions) Act 1992;

"contribution" means a contribution under Pt. I of the Contributions and Benefits Act;

"contribution-based jobseeker's allowance" has the same meaning as in the Jobseekers Act 1995;

…

"the Contributions and Benefits Act" means the Social Security Contributions and Benefits Act 1992;

…

"income-based jobseeker's allowance" has the same meaning as in the Jobseekers Act 1995;

…

"Inland Revenue" means the Commissioners of Inland Revenue;

…

"the Northern Ireland Department" means the Department for Social Development but

(a) in section 122 and sections 122B to 122E also includes the Department of Finance and Personnel; and

(b) in sections 121E, 121F, 122, 122ZA, 122C and 122D also includes the Department for Employment and Learning;

"the Northern Ireland Administration Act" means the Social Security (Northern Ireland) Administration Act 1992;

…

"the Old Cases Act" means the Industrial Injuries and Diseases (Old Cases) Act 1975;

"pensionable age" has the meaning given by the rules in paragraph 1 of Schedule 4 to the Pensions Act 1995;

…

"the Pensions Act" means the Pension Schemes Act 1993;

…

"prescribe" means prescribe by regulations and "prescribed" must be construed accordingly;

"state pension credit" means state pension credit under the State Pension Credit Act 2002;

…

"tax year" means the 12 months beginning with 6th April in any year.

…

Prospective amendments – In s. 191, the definitions of "billing authority", "contribution-based jobseeker's allowance", "contributory employment and support allowance", "council tax benefit scheme", "housing authority", "housing benefit scheme", "income-based jobseeker's allowance", "income-related benefit", "income-related employment and support allowance", "rent rebate" and "rent allowance" repealed by WRA 2012, s. 147 and Sch. 14, Pt. 1, with effect (other than as noted in the History note below) from a date to be set by order of the Secretary of State.

History – In s. 191, in the definition of "benefit", the words ", personal independence payment and bereavement support payment under section 30 of the Pensions Act 2014" substituted for the words "and personal independence payment" by PA 2014, s. 31 and Sch. 16, para. 35, with effect from 6 April 2017, subject to SI 2017/297, art. 4 (later commencement for abolition of bereavement payment and bereavement allowance) and 5 (commencement for entitlement to bereavement payment and bereavement support payment) (SI 2017/297, art. 3(2)).

In s. 191, in the definition of "benefit", the words "state pension under Part 1 of the Pensions Act 2014," inserted after the words "universal credit," by PA 2014, s. 23 and Sch. 12, para. 28, with effect from 6 April 2016 (as not brought into force by any earlier order under PA 2014, s. 56(1)).

In s. 191, in the definition of "benefit", the words "universal credit" inserted by WRA 2012, s. 31 and Sch. 2, para. 31, with effect from 29 April 2013 (SI 2013/983, art. 3(1)(b)).

In s. 191, in the definition of "benefit", the words " state pension credit, an employment and support allowance and personal independence payment" substituted for the words ", state pension credit and an employment and support allowance" by WRA 2012, s. 91 and Sch. 4, para. 32, with effect from 25 February 2013 for the purpose of making regulations (SI 2013/358, art. 2(1)), from

8 April 2013 in relation to a person whose only or principal residence is, on the date on which that person makes a claim for personal independence payment, located in an area to which one of the following postcodes corresponds: BL, CA, CH (except CH1, CH4, CH5, CH6, CH7 and CH8), CW, DH, DL (except DL6, DL7, DL8, DL9, DL10 and DL11), FY, L, LA (except LA2 7, LA2 8, LA6 2 and LA6 3), M, NE, PR, SR, TS (except TS9), WA and WN (SI 2013/358, art. 7(1) and (2)(k)), and from 10 June 2013 in relation to any other person (SI 2013/1250, art. 2).
In s. 191, in the definition of "benefit" the words ", state pension credit and an employment and support allowance" substituted by the Welfare Reform Act 2007, s. 28 and Sch. 3, para. 10(32)(a) with effect from 27 October 2008 by virtue of art. 2(4)(b) and (f).
In the definition of "benefit", the words "and state pension credit" inserted by the State Pension Credit Act 2002, s. 14 and Sch. 2, para. 24, with effect from 2 July 2002 only for the purpose of making regulations and orders.
In s. 191, the definition of "billing authority" repealed by WRA 2012, s. 147 and Sch. 14, Pt. 1, with effect in so far as it relates to the abolition of council tax benefit from 1 April 2013 (SI 2013/358, art. 8(c) and Sch. 4).
In s. 191, definitions of "Commissioner", "the disablement questions", "5 year general qualification", "President" and "10 year general qualification" repealed and definition of "claimant" amended by SSA 1998, s. 86(1) and Sch. 7, para. 111 and s. 86(2) and Sch. 8, with effect from 29 November 1999 (except for the purposes of housing benefit, council tax benefit and decisions to which SI 1999/527, art. 4(6) applies; i.e. pre-1 April 1999 decisions under SSAA 1992, s. 17(1), s. 20(3) and PSA 1993, s. 170(1)) (SI 1999/3178 (C. 81), art. 2(1)(a); 2(2) and Sch. 1)
In s. 191, the definition of "council tax benefit scheme" repealed by WRA 2012, s. 147 and Sch. 14, Pt. 1, with effect in so far as it relates to the abolition of council tax benefit from 1 April 2013 (SI 2013/358, art. 8(c) and Sch. 4).
In s. 191 the definition of "Inland Revenue" inserted by SSC(TF)A 1999, s. 1; Sch. 1, para. 31 with effect from 1 April 1999 (SI 1999/527).
In s. 191, in the definition of "benefit", reference to Jobseekers Act 1995 inserted, and definitions of "contribution-based jobseeker's allowance" and "income-based jobseeker's allowance" inserted, by Jobseekers Act 1995, Sch. 3, para. 73, with effect from 22 April 1996 by virtue of SI 1996/1126.
In s. 191, the definition of "pensionable age" substituted by Pensions Act 1995, Sch. 4, para. 14, with effect from the date of Royal Assent of that Act (19 July 1995) by virtue of s. 180(2)(a).
In s. 191, the former definition of "pensionable age" inserted by Pension Schemes Act 1993, Sch. 8, para. 31(a), with effect from 7 February 1994.
In s. 191, in the definition of "the Pensions Act", the words "Pension Schemes Act 1993" substituted by PSA 1993, Sch. 8, para. 31(c), with effect from 7 February 1994.
S. 191 amended by Social Security Administration (Fraud) Act 1997, s. 22 and Sch. 1, para. 12, with effect from 1 July 1997 (SI 1997/1577) by inserting the definition "contribution after the definition" of "the Consequential Provisions Act"– and in the former definition of "Northern Ireland Department", at the end inserting "but in section 122 and sections 122B to 122E also includes the Department of the Environment for Northern Ireland;".
In s. 191, in the definition of "prescribe" the words "and "prescribed" must be construed accordingly" inserted by the Welfare Reform Act 2007, s. 40 and Sch. 5, para. 10, with effect from 3 July 2007, by virtue of s. 70(1)(b).
In s. 191, the definition of "the Northern Ireland Department" substituted by EA 2002, s. 53 and Sch.7, para. 16, with effect from 9 September 2002 by virtue of SI 2002/2256.
Definition of "state pension credit" inserted by SPCA 2002, s. 14 and Sch. 2, para. 24, with effect from 2 July 2002 for the purposes only of making regulations and orders.
Derivations – "claim": SSA 1975, s. 168(1), Sch. 20.
"claimant": SSA 1975, s. 168(1), Sch. 20.
"prescribe": SSA 1975, s. 168(1), Sch. 20.
"tax year": SSA 1975, s. 168(1), Sch. 20.
Cross references – SSCBA 1992, s. 122: pensionable age means the age of 65 in the case of a man, and the age of 60 in the case of a woman.
Statutory instruments – SI 1994/1082 (amending SI 1986/2218).

192 Short title, commencement and extent

192(1) This Act may be cited as the Social Security Administration Act 1992.

192(2) This Act is to be read, where appropriate, with the Contributions and Benefits Act and the Consequential Provisions Act.

192(3) The enactments consolidated by this Act are repealed, in consequence of the consolidation, by the Consequential Provisions Act.

192(4) Except as provided in Schedule 4 to the Consequential Provisions Act, this Act shall come into force on 1st July 1992.

192(5) The following provisions extend to Northern Ireland–

section 24

section 132A (and sections 189 and 190, but only for the purposes of regulations under section 132A);

section 170 (with Schedule 5);

section 177 (with Schedule 8); and

this section.

192(6) Except as provided by this section this Act does not extend to Northern Ireland.

History – In s. 192(5) reference to section 132A etc. inserted by NICA 2006, s. 7(4), with effect from 30 March 2006.
In s. 192(5) reference to SSAA 1992, s. 24 repealed by SSA 1998, s. 86(2) and Sch. 8, with effect from 29 November 1999 (except for the purposes of housing benefit, council tax benefit and decisions to which SI 1999/527, art. 4(6) applies; i.e. pre-1 April 1999 decisions under SSAA 1992, s. 17(1), s. 20(3) and PSA 1993, s. 170(1)) (SI 1999/3178 (C. 81), art. 2(1)(a); 2(2) and Sch. 1).
In s. 192(5), reference to "section 101" repealed by the Social Security (Recovery of Benefits) Act 1997, s. 33(1) and Sch. 3, with effect from 6 October 1997, by virtue of SI 1997/2085.

SCHEDULES

SCHEDULE 2 – COMMISSIONERS, TRIBUNALS ETC. – SUPPLEMENTARY PROVISIONS

Sections 41, 43 and 50 to 52

TENURE OF OFFICES

1(1) Subject to the following provisions of this paragraph, the President and the regional and other full-time chairmen of social security appeal tribunals, medical appeal tribunals and disability appeal tribunals shall hold and vacate office in accordance with the terms of their appointment.

1(2) Commissioners, the President and the full-time chairmen shall vacate their offices at the end of the completed year of service in which they attain the age of 72.

1(3) [Repealed by Judicial Pensions and Retirement Act 1993, s. 31 and Sch. 9.]

1(4) A Commissioner, the President and a full-time chairman may be removed from office by the Lord Chancellor on the ground of incapacity or misbehaviour.

1(5) Where the Lord Chancellor proposes to exercise a power conferred on him by sub-paragraph (4) above, it shall be his duty to consult the [Secretary of State] with respect to the proposal.

1(6) Nothing in sub-paragraph (2) above or in section 13 or 32 of the Judicial Pensions Act 1981 (which relate to pensions for Commissioners) shall apply to a person by virtue of his appointment in pursuance of section 52(2) above.

1(7) Nothing in sub-paragraph (4) above applies to a Commissioner appointed before 23rd May 1980.

History – Para. 1(3) and in para. 1(5) the words "(3) or", in para. 1(6) the words "or (3)" and in para. 1(7) the words "(2) or" repealed by Judicial Pensions and Retirement Act 1993, s. 31 and Sch. 9, with effect from 31 March 1995 (SI 1995/631).
In para. 1(5) reference to "the Secretary of State" effectively substituted by Transfer of Functions (Lord Advocate and Secretary of State) Order 1999 (SI 1999/678), art. 7(4), with effect from 19 May 1999.

Derivations – Para. 1(1): SSA 1975, s. 97(4), Sch. 10, para. 1A(4); Health and Social Services and Social Security Adjudications Act 1983, s. 25, Sch. 8, para. 8.
Para. 1(2)–(4) (as originally enacted): SSA 1975, s. 97(4), Sch. 10, para. 1A(5)–(7); SSA 1980, s. 13(1)–(3); Health and Social Services and Social Security Adjudications Act 1983, s. 25, Sch. 8, para. 8.
Para. 1(6): SSA 1980, s. 13(5)(a); Judicial Pensions Act 1981, s. 36, Sch. 3, para. 10.
Para. 1(7): SSA 1980, s. 13(1).

Cross references – Transfer of Functions (Lord Advocate and Secretary of State) Order 1999 (SI 1999/678), art. 2: the function of the Lord Advocate originally specified in Sch. 1, para. 1(4) is transferred to the Secretary of State with effect from 19 May 1999.

2–8 [Not relevant to National Insurance contributions.]

SCHEDULE 3 – REGULATIONS AS TO PROCEDURE

Section 59

INTERPRETATION

1 In this Schedule **"competent tribunal"** means–

(a) a Commissioner;

(b) a social security appeal tribunal;

(c) a disability appeal tribunal;

(d) a medical appeal tribunal;

(e) an adjudicating medical practitioner.

Derivations – Para. 1: SSA 1975, s. 115(2), "competent tribunal"; Health and Social Services and Social Security Adjudications Act 1983, s. 25, Sch. 8, para. 5, 25; Disability Living Allowance and Disability Working Allowance Act 1991, s. 4, Sch. 1, para. 10.

PROVISION WHICH MAY BE MADE

2 Provision prescribing the procedure to be followed in connection with the consideration and determination of claims and questions by the Secretary of State, an adjudication officer and a competent *tribunal*, or in connection with the withdrawal of a claim.

3 Provision as to the striking out of proceedings for want of prosecution.

4 Provision as to the form which is to be used for any document, the evidence which is to be required and the circumstances in which any official record or certificate is to be sufficient or conclusive evidence.

5 Provision as to the time to be allowed–

(a) for producing any evidence; or

(b) for making an appeal.

6 Provision as to the manner in which, and the time within which, a question may be raised with a view to its decision by the Secretary of State under Part II of this Act or with a view to the review of a decision under that Part.

7 Provision for summoning persons to attend and give evidence or produce documents and for authorising the administration of oaths to witnesses.

8–11 [Not relevant to National Insurance contributions.]

12 Provision for requiring or authorising the Secretary of State to hold, or to appoint a person to hold, an inquiry in connection with the consideration of any question by the Secretary of State.

Derivations – Para. 2: SSA 1975, s. 115, Sch. 13, para. 1; SSA 1989, s. 21, Sch. 3, para. 4.
Para. 3: SSA 1975, s. 115, Sch. 13, para. 1A; SSA 1986, s. 52(1), Sch. 5, para. 19(a).
Para. 4–7: SSA 1975, s. 115, Sch. 13, para. 2–5.
Para. 12: SSA 1975, s. 115, Sch. 13, para. 11.

Cross references – S. 59: procedure.

Statutory instruments – SI 1979/676: para. 4.

SCHEDULE 4 – PERSONS EMPLOYED IN SOCIAL SECURITY ADMINISTRATION OR ADJUDICATION

Section 123

Prospective amendments – In Sch. 4, the paragraphs headed "Local authorities etc" repealed by WRA 2012, s. 147 and Sch. 14, Pt. 1, with effect from a date to be set by order of the Secretary of State.

Part I – The Specified Persons

GOVERNMENT DEPARTMENTS

A civil servant in–

(a) the Department of Social Security;

(b) the Department of Employment;

(c) the Ministry of Justice.

OTHER PUBLIC DEPARTMENTS AND OFFICES

A civil servant in the Scottish Administration or the Scottish Courts Administration.

LOCAL AUTHORITIES ETC.

History – Para. headed "Local Authorities etc" repealed by WRA 2012, s. 147 and Sch. 14, Pt. 1, with effect in so far as they relate to the abolition of council tax benefit from 1 April 2013 (SI 2013/358, art. 8(c) and Sch. 4).

A member, officer or employee of an authority administering housing benefit or council tax benefit.

A person authorised to exercise any function of such an authority relating to such a benefit or any employee of such a person.

A person authorised under section 139A(1) of this Act to consider and report to the Secretary of State on the administration of housing benefit or council tax benefit.

A member, officer or employee of a county council in England who exercises–

(a) any function conferred on the county council by regulations made under section 7A of this Act;

(b) any function in connection with a relevant purpose within the meaning of section 7B(3) of this Act.

A person authorised to exercise any such function of such a county council or an employee of such a person.

ADJUDICATING BODIES

The clerk to, or other officer or member of the staff of, any of the following bodies–

(a) [omitted by SI 2008/2833, art. 9 and Sch. 3, para. 104(3);]

(b) [omitted by the Social Security Act 1998, s. 86(1) and Sch. 7, para. 113(b) and s. 86(2) and Sch. 8;]

(c) [omitted by the Social Security Act 1998, s. 86(1) and Sch. 7, para. 113(b) and s. 86(2) and Sch. 8;]

(d) [omitted by the Social Security Act 1998, s. 86(1) and Sch. 7, para. 113(b) and s. 86(2) and Sch. 8;]

(e) a Pensions Appeal Tribunal constituted under the Pensions Appeal Tribunals Act 1943.

THE DISABILITY LIVING ALLOWANCE ADVISORY BOARD

A member of the Disability Living Allowance Advisory Board.

An officer or servant of that Board.

[THE SOCIAL FUND]

History – Heading omitted by WRA 2012, s. 147 and Sch. 14, Pt. 8, with effect from 1 August 2013 (SI 2012/3090, art. 2(2)).

[Omitted by WRA 2012, s. 147 and Sch. 14, Pt. 8.]

[Omitted by SSA 1998, s. 86(1) and Sch. 7, para. 113(c) and s. 86(2) and Sch. 8.]

[Omitted by WRA 2012, s. 147 and Sch. 14, Pt. 8.]

[Omitted by WRA 2012, s. 147 and Sch. 14, Pt. 8.]

FORMER OFFICERS

An officer or other member of the staff of–

(a) the former Supplementary Benefits Commission;

(b) the former National Assistance Board;

(c) the former Attendance Allowance Board.

A benefit officer.

An insurance officer.

A supplement officer.

A Chief Adjudication Officer.

An adjudication officer.

A social fund officer.

A clerk to, or other officer or member of the staff of, the former social security appeal tribunal, the former disability appeal tribunal or the former medical appeal tribunal.

The clerk to, or other officer or member of the staff of, an appeal tribunal.

The clerk to, or other officer or member of the staff of, a Pensions Appeal Tribunal for England and Wales.

History – In Pt. I, in the section headed "GOVERNMENT DEPARTMENTS", "Ministry of Justice" substituted for "Lord Chancellor's Department" by SI 2008/2833, art. 9 and Sch. 3, para. 104(2), with effect from 3 November 2008.

In Pt. I, after the heading "LOCAL AUTHORITIES ETC.", the entry relating to a member, officer or employee of a county council in England inserted by Welfare Reform Act 2007, s. 41(3) with effect from 3 July 2007.

In Pt. I, in the section headed "ADJUDICATING BODIES", para. (a) (reference to "a social security appeal tribunal") omitted by SI 2008/2833, art. 9 and Sch. 3, para. 104(3), with effect from 3 November 2008.

In Pt. I, in the section headed "FORMER OFFICERS", the entries for "The clerk to, or other officer or member of the staff of, an appeal tribunal" and "The clerk to, or other officer or member of the staff of, a Pensions Appeal Tribunal for England and Wales" inserted by SI 2008/2833, art. 9 and Sch. 3, para. 104(4), with effect from 3 November 2008.

In Pt. I, the words "the Scottish Administration or" inserted by SI 1999/1820, Sch. 2, para. 195(2), with effect from 1 July 1999.

In Pt. I, the section relating to "ADJUDICATION OFFICERS" is omitted (reference to "The Chief Adjudication Officer" and "An adjudication officer" thereby being removed) by the Social Security Act 1998, s. 86(1) and Sch. 7, para. 113(b) and s. 86(2) and Sch. 8, with effect from 29 November 1999 (except for the purposes of housing benefit, council tax benefit and decisions to which SI 1999/527, art. 4(6) applies; i.e. pre-1 April 1999 decisions under SSAA 1992, s. 17(1), s. 20(3) and PSA 1993, s. 170(1)) (SI 1999/3178 (C. 81), art. 2(1)(a); 2(2) and Sch. 1).

In Pt. I, in the section headed "ADJUDICATING BODIES" at para. (a) reference to "an appeal tribunal" is inserted by the Social Security Act 1998, s. 86(1) and Sch. 7, para. 113(b) and s. 86(2) and Sch. 8, with effect from 29 November 1999 (except for the purposes of housing benefit, council tax benefit and decisions to which SI 1999/527, art. 4(6) applies; i.e. pre-1 April 1999 decisions under SSAA 1992, s. 17(1), s. 20(3) and PSA 1993, s. 170(1)) (SI 1999/3178 (C. 81), art. 2(1)(a); 2(2) and Sch. 1).

In Pt. I, in the section headed "ADJUDICATING BODIES" para. (b) to (d) are omitted by the Social Security Act 1998, s. 86(1) and Sch. 7, para. 113(b) and s. 86(2) and Sch. 8, with effect from 29 November1999 (except for the purposes of housing benefit, council tax benefit and decisions to which SI 1999/527, art. 4(6) applies; i.e. pre-1 April 1999 decisions under SSAA 1992, s. 17(1), s. 20(3) and PSA 1993, s. 170(1)) (SI 1999/3178 (C. 81), art. 2(1)(a); 2(2) and Sch. 1). The omitted paragraphs refer to: "(b) a disability appeal tribunal; (c) a medical appeal tribunal; (d) a vaccine damage tribunal".

In Pt. I, in the section headed " THE SOCIAL FUND" reference to "A social fund officer" is omitted by the Social Security Act 1998, s. 86(1) and Sch. 7, para. 113(c) and s. 86(2) and Sch. 8, with effect from 29 November 1999 (except for the purposes of housing benefit, council tax benefit and decisions to which SI 1999/527, art. 4(6) applies; i.e. pre-1 April 1999 decisions under SSAA 1992, s. *17(1), s. 20(3) and PSA 1993*, s. 170(1)) (SI 1999/3178 (C. 81), art. 2(1)(a); 2(2) and Sch. 1).

In Pt. I, in the section headed "FORMER OFFICERS" the words "A Chief Adjudication Officer." "An adjudication officer." "A social fund officer." and "A clerk to, or other officer or member of the staff of, the former social security appeal tribunal, the former disability appeal tribunal or the former medical appeal tribunal." inserted by Social Security Act 1998, s. 86(1) and Sch. 7, para. 113(c) and s. 86(2) and Sch. 8, with effect from 29 November 1999 (except for the purposes of housing benefit, council tax benefit and decisions to which SI 1999/527, art. 4(6) applies; i.e. pre-1 April 1999 decisions under SSAA 1992, s. 17(1), s. 20(3) and PSA 1993, s. 170(1)) (SI 1999/3178 (C. 81), art. 2(1)(a); 2(2) and Sch. 1).

In Pt. I, in the section relating to “OTHER PUBLIC DEPARTMENTS AND OFFICES.” reference to “A member or officer of the Commissioners of Inland Revenue.” omitted by the SSC(TF)A 1999, s. 6 and Sch. 6, para. 6, with effect from 1 April 1999 (SI 1999/527).
In Pt. I, the section relating to “LOCAL AUTHORITIES ETC.” inserted by the Social Security Administration (Fraud) Act 1997, s. 4(1) with effect from 1 July 1997, by virtue of SI 1997/1577.
Pt. I amended by omitting the entries relating to the Occupational Pensions Board,by Pensions Act 1995, Sch. 5, para. 15(4), and Sch. 7, Pt. III, with effect from 6 April 1997 (SI 1996/778).
Derivations – SSA 1989, s. 19, Sch. 2, Pt. I; SSA 1990, s. 21(1), Sch. 6, para. 28(4), (5); Disability Living Allowance and Disability Working Allowance Act 1991, s. 4, Sch. 2, para. 19.
Cross references – S. 123: persons employed or formerly employed in social security administration or adjudication.

Part II – Construction of References to Government Departments etc.

1 The reference in Part I of this Schedule to **the Department of Social Security** includes a reference to–
(a) the former Department of Health and Social Security,
(b) the former Ministry of Pensions and National Insurance,
(c) the former Ministry of Social Security, and
(d) any other former government department,

but, in the case of paragraphs (a) and (d) above, only to the extent that the functions carried out in the former department related to social security to the investigation or prosecution of offences relating to tax credits, or to occupational or personal pension schemes or to war pensions.

History – In para. 1, the words “to the investigation or prosecution of offences relating to tax credits,” inserted by WRA 2012, s. 125, with effect from 6 June 2012 (SI 2012/1246, art. 2(2)).

2 The reference in Part I of this Schedule to **the Department of Employment** is a reference to that Department only to the extent that the functions carried out in it relate to a jobseeker’s allowance or to unemployment benefit or income support or related to the former supplementary benefit.

3 Any reference in Part I of this Schedule to **the Ministry of Justice**, the Scottish Administration or **the Scottish Courts Administration** is a reference to that Ministry or Administration only to the extent that the functions carried out by persons in its employ are, or are connected with–
(a) functions of the First-tier Tribunal or Upper Tribunal which relate to social security or to occupational or personal pension schemes or to war pensions or functions of the Chief, or any other, Social Security Commissioner;
(b) [omitted by SI 2013/2042, art. 7(a).]

[Omitted by SI 2013/2042, art. 7(b).]

History – In para. 3, “Ministry of Justice” substituted by SI 2008/2833, art. 9 and Sch. 3, para. 104(5)(a), with effect from 3 November 2008.
In para. 3, “that Ministry” substituted by SI 2008/2833, art. 9 and Sch. 3, para. 104(5)(b), with effect from 3 November 2008.
In para. 3(a), the words “the First-tier Tribunal or Upper Tribunal which relate to social security or to occupational or personal pension schemes or to war pensions or functions of” inserted by SI 2008/2833, art. 9 and Sch. 3, para. 104(5)(c), with effect from 3 November 2008.
Para. 3(b) (and the “or” before it) omitted by SI 2013/2042, art. 7(a), with effect from 19 August 2013.
In para. 3, words following (b) omitted by SI 2013/2042, art. 7(b), with effect from 19 August 2013.
In para. 3(b) the words “Administrative Justice and Tribunals Council or the Welsh or” substituted by TCEA 2007, s. 48(1) and Sch. 8, para. 18, with effect from 1 November 2007 to the extent that it relates to the Administrative Justice and Tribunals Council, by virtue of SI 2007/2709, art. 3(b)(iii), and with effect from 1 June 2008 for the remaining purposes, by virtue of SI 2007/2709, art. 6(b)(ii).
In para. 3, at the end, the words “The reference in paragraph (b) to the Administrative Justice and Tribunals Council and the Scottish Committee of that Council includes a reference to the former Council of Tribunals and the Scottish Committee of that former Council.” inserted by SI 2008/2833, art. 9 and Sch. 3, para. 104(5)(d), with effect from 3 November 2008.

3ZA Any reference in Part 1 of this Schedule to the Ministry of Justice includes a reference to–
(a) the former Lord Chancellor’s Department, and
(b) the former Department of Constitutional Affairs,

to the extent that the functions carried out by persons in its employ were, or were connected with, functions of the Chief, or any other, Social Security Commissioner (and paragraph 3 above does not apply for the purposes of this paragraph).

History – Para. 3ZA inserted by SI 2008/2833, art. 9 and Sch. 3, para. 104(6), with effect from 3 November 2008.

4 [Repealed by SSC(TF)A 1999, s. 6; Sch. 6, para 6, and s. 26(3); Sch. 10, Pt. I, with effect from 1 April 1999 (SI 1999/527).]

5 [Not relevant to National Insurance contributions.]

History – Pt. II, para. 2 amended by Jobseekers Act 1995, Sch. 2, para. 74, with effect from 11 June 1996 by virtue of SI 1996/1509, by inserting “a jobseeker’s allowance or to”.
In para. 3, the words “, the Scottish Administration” inserted by SI 1999/1820, art. 105(3)(b), with effect from 1 July 1999.
Part II, para. 4 repealed by SSC(TF)A 1999, s. 6; Sch. 6, para 6, and s. 26(3); Sch. 10, Pt. I, with effect from 1 April 1999 (SI 1999/527).
Derivations – SSA 1989, s. 19, Sch. 2, Pt. II; SSA 1990, s. 21(1), Sch. 6, para. 28(6).

SCHEDULE 5 – SOCIAL SECURITY ADVISORY COMMITTEE

Section 170

1 The Committee shall consist of a chairman appointed by the Secretary of State and not less than 10 nor more than 13 other members so appointed.

Derivations – SSA 1980, s. 9(2), Sch. 3, para. 1; SSHBA 1982, s. 48(5), Sch. 4, para. 32(2).

2(1) Each member of the Committee shall be appointed to hold office for such period of not more than 5 years, nor less than 3 years, as the Secretary of State shall determine.

2(2) The Secretary of State may, at any time before the expiration of the term of office of any member, extend or further extend that member's term of office; but no one extension shall be for a period of more than 5 years from the date when the term of office would otherwise expire.

2(3) Any member–

(a) shall be eligible for reappointment from time to time on or after the expiration of his term of office;

(b) may by notice in writing to the Secretary of State resign office at any time, while remaining eligible for reappointment.

Derivations – SSA 1980, s. 9(2), Sch. 3, para. 2; SSHBA 1982, s. 48(5), Sch. 4, para. 32(3).

3(1) Of the members of the Committee (other than the chairman) there shall be appointed–

(a) one after consultation with organisations representative of employers;

(b) one after consultation with organisations representative of workers; and

(c) one after consultation with the Head of the Northern Ireland Department;

and the Committee shall include at least one person with experience of work among, and of the needs of, the chronically sick and disabled.

3(2) In selecting a person with such experience regard shall be had to the desirability of having a chronically sick or disabled person.

Derivations – SSA 1980, s. 9(2), Sch. 3, para. 3.

4 The Secretary of State may remove a member of the Committee on the ground of incapacity or misbehaviour.

Derivations – SSA 1980, s. 9(2), Sch. 3, para. 4.

5 The Secretary of State shall appoint a secretary to the Committee and may appoint such other officers and such servants to the Committee, and there shall be paid to them by the Secretary of State such salaries and allowances, as the Secretary of State may with the consent of the Treasury determine.

Derivations – SSA 1980, s. 9(2), Sch. 3, para. 5.

6 The expenses of the Committee to such an amount as may be approved by the Treasury shall be paid by the Secretary of State.

Derivations – SSA 1980, s. 9(2), Sch. 3, para. 6.

7 There may be paid as part of the expenses of the Committee–

(a) to all or any of the members of the Committee, such salaries or other remuneration and travelling and other allowances; and

(b) to persons attending its meetings at the request of the Committee, such travelling and other allowances (including compensation for loss of remunerative time),

as the Secretary of State may with the consent of the Treasury determine.

Derivations – SSA 1980, s. 9(2), Sch. 3, para. 7.

8(1) The Secretary of State may pay or make provision for paying, to or in respect of any member of the Committee, such sums by way of pensions, superannuation allowances and gratuities as the Secretary of State may determine with the consent of the Treasury.

8(2) Where a person ceases to be a member of the Committee otherwise than on the expiry of his term of office and it appears to the Secretary of State that there are special circumstances which make it right for the person to receive compensation the Secretary of State may make to him a payment of such amount as the Secretary of State may determine with the consent of the Treasury.

Derivations – SSA 1980, s. 9(2), Sch. 3, para. 8.

9 The Committee may act notwithstanding any vacancy among the members.

Derivations – SSA 1980, s. 9(2), Sch. 3, para. 9.

10 The Committee may make rules for regulating its procedure (including the quorum of the Committee).

Derivations – SSA 1980, s. 9(2), Sch. 3, para. 10.

SCHEDULE 7 – REGULATIONS NOT REQUIRING PRIOR SUBMISSION

Section 172

Part I – Social Security Advisory Committee

1 [Not relevant to National Insurance contributions.]

2 [Not relevant to National Insurance contributions.]

UP-RATING ETC.

3 Regulations contained in a statutory instrument which states that it contains only provisions in consequence of an order under one or more of the following provisions–

(a) section 141, 143 or 145 above;

(b) section 150 or 150A above.

History – Para. 3(a) amended by SSA 1998, s. 86(1) and Sch. 7, para. 114(1), by adding the reference to s. 143A, with effect from September 1998 for the purpose only of authorising the making of regulations and orders, and from 6 April 1999 for all other purposes (SI 1998/2209 (C. 47), art. 2(b), (c) and Schedule, Pt. II, III). The reference to s. 143A was repealed by WRPA 1999, s. 88; Sch. 13, Pt. VI, with effect from 6 April 2000 (SI 1999/3420 (C. 92), art. 4(c), (e)).

In para. 3(b), reference to s. 150A inserted by PA 2007, s. 5 and Sch. 1, para. 31, with effect in relation to purposes referred to in s. 5(7) and s. 30(1), for 2007–08 and subsequent years. For remaining purposes see s. 5(3)–(6).

Derivations – SSA 1980, s. 10(2), Sch. 3, para. 12(2); SSA 1986, s. 86, Sch. 10, para. 99.

BENEFIT CAP

3A Regulations under section 96A of the Welfare Reform Act 2012.

History – Para. 3A inserted by Welfare Reform and Work Act 2016, s. 10(2), with effect from 9 June 2016 (SI 2016/610, reg. 2).

EARNINGS LIMITS

4 Regulations contained in a statutory instrument which states that it contains only regulations to make provision consequential on regulations under section 5 of the Contributions and Benefits Act.

History – Sch. 4, para. 4 substituted by SSC(TF)A 1999, s. 2; Sch. 3, para. 59, with effect from 1 April 1999 (SI 1999/527).

MARRIED WOMEN AND WIDOWS – REDUCED RATE CONTRIBUTIONS

5 [Repealed by SSC(TF)A 1999, s. 2; Sch. 3, para. 59 and s. 26(3); Sch. 10, Pt. I, with effect from 1 April 1999 (SI 1999/527).]

6, 7 [Not relevant to National Insurance contributions.]

STATUTORY MATERNITY PAY AND STATUTORY SICK PAY

8 Regulations under section 167 of the Contributions and Benefits Act.

History – The words "158 or", before "167" repealed by SI 1995/512, art. 6(2)(c), with effect from 6 April 1995.

Derivations – (as originally enacted) – SSA 1980, s. 10(2), Sch. 3, para. 15A, 15AA; SSHBA 1982, s. 48(5), Sch. 4, para. 33(3); SSA 1986, s. 86, Sch. 10, para. 107; SSA 1989, s. 31(1), Sch. 8, para. 12(6).

PROCEDURAL RULES FOR TRIBUNALS

9 [Omitted by SI 2013/2042, art. 8.]

History – Para. 9 omitted by SI 2013/2042, art. 8, with effect from 19 August 2013.

In former para. 9 the words "Administrative Justice and Tribunals Council is required by paragraph 24 of Schedule 7 to the Tribunals, Courts and Enforcement Act 2007" substituted for "Council on Tribunals is required by section 8(1) of the Tribunals and Inquiries Act 1992" by TCEA 2007, s. 48(1) and Sch. 8, para. 19, with effect from 1 November 2007, by virtue of SI 2007/2709, art. 3(b)(i).

In former para. 9, the words "section 8(1) of the Tribunal Inquiries Act 1992" substituted by Tribunals and Inquiries Act 1992, s. 18 and Sch. 3, para. 37 with effect from 1 October 1992.

Derivations – (as originally enacted) – SSA 1980, s. 10(2), Sch. 3, para. 19.

CONSOLIDATION

10 Regulations made for the purpose only of consolidating other regulations revoked by them.

Derivations – SSA 1980, s. 10(2), Sch. 3, para. 20.

SCHEDULE 8 – CONSTITUTION ETC. OF JOINT AUTHORITY FOR GREAT BRITAIN AND NORTHERN IRELAND

Section 177

1 The Joint Authority shall be a body corporate by the name of the National Insurance Joint Authority, and shall have an official seal which shall be officially and judicially noticed, and the seal of the Authority may be authenticated by either member of, or the secretary to, the Authority, or by any person authorised by the Authority to act on behalf of the secretary.

2 Either member of the Joint Authority shall be entitled, subject to and in accordance with any rules laid down by the Authority, to appoint a deputy to act for him at meetings of the Authority at which he is unable to be present.

3 The Documentary Evidence Act 1868 shall apply to the Joint Authority as if the Authority were included in the first column of the Schedule to that Act, and as if either member or the secretary, or any person authorised to act on behalf of the secretary, of the Authority were mentioned in the second column of that Schedule, and as if the regulations referred to in that Act included any document issued by the Authority.

Derivations – SSA 1975, s. 142(2), Sch. 17.

SOCIAL SECURITY (CONSEQUENTIAL PROVISIONS) ACT 1992

(1992 Chapter 6)

[13th February 1992]

ARRANGEMENT OF SECTIONS

SCHEDULES

1 Meaning of "the consolidating Acts"

1 In this Act–

"the consolidating Acts" means the Social Security Contributions and Benefits Act 1992 ("the Contributions and Benefits Act"), the Social Security Administration Act 1992 ("the Administration Act") and, so far as it reproduces the effect of the repealed enactments, this Act; and

"the repealed enactments" means the enactments repealed by this Act.

2 Continuity of the law

2(1) The substitution of the consolidating Acts for the repealed enactments does not affect the continuity of the law.

2(2) Anything done or having effect as if done under or for the purposes of a provision of the repealed enactments has effect, if it could have been done under or for the purposes of the corresponding provision of the consolidating Acts, as if done under or for the purposes of that provision.

2(3) Any reference, whether express or implied, in the consolidating Acts or any other enactment, instrument or document to a provision of the consolidating Acts shall, so far as the context permits, be construed as including, in relation to the times, circumstances and purposes in relation to which the corresponding provision of the repealed enactments has effect, a reference to that corresponding provision.

2(4) Any reference, whether express or implied, in any enactment, instrument or document to a provision of the repealed enactments shall be construed, so far as is required for continuing its effect, as including a reference to the corresponding provision of the consolidating Acts.

3 Repeals

3(1) The enactments mentioned in Schedule 1 to this Act are repealed to the extent specified in the third column of that Schedule.

3(2) Those repeals include, in addition to repeals consequential on the consolidation of provisions in the consolidating Acts, repeals in accordance with Recommendations of the Law Commission and the Scottish Law Commission, of section 30(6)(b) of the Social Security Act 1975, paragraphs 2 to 8 of Schedule 9 to that Act, paragraph 2(1) of Schedule 10 to that Act and section 10 of the Social Security Act 1988.

3(3) The repeals have effect subject to any relevant savings in Schedule 3 to this Act.

4 Consequential amendments

4 The enactments mentioned in Schedule 2 to this Act shall have effect with the amendments there specified (being amendments consequential on the consolidating Acts).

5 Transitional provisions and savings

5(1) The transitional provisions and savings in Schedule 3 to this Act shall have effect.

5(2) Nothing in that Schedule affects the general operation of section 16 of the Interpretation Act 1978 (general savings implied on repeal) or of the previous provisions of this Act.

6 Transitory modifications

6 The transitory modifications in Schedule 4 to this Act shall have effect.

Statutory instruments – SI 1993/1025.

7 Short title, commencement and extent

7(1) This Act may be cited as the Social Security (Consequential Provisions) Act 1992.

7(2) This Act shall come into force on 1st July 1992.

7(3) Section 2 above and this section extend to Northern Ireland.

7(4) Subject to subsection (5) below, where any enactment repealed or amended by this Act extends to any part of the United Kingdom, the repeal or amendment extends to that part.

7(5) The repeals–

(a) of provisions of sections 10, 13 and 14 of the Social Security Act 1980 and Part II of Schedule 3 to that Act;

(b) of enactments amending those provisions;

(c) of paragraph 2 of Schedule 1 to the Capital Allowances Act 1990; and

(d) of section 17(8) and (9) of the Social Security Act 1990,

do not extend to Northern Ireland.

7(6) Section 6 above and Schedule 4 to this Act extend to Northern Ireland in so far as they give effect to transitory modifications of provisions of the consolidating Acts which so extend.

7(7) Except as provided by this section, this Act does not extend to Northern Ireland.

7(8) Section 4 above extends to the Isle of Man so far as it relates to paragraphs 53 and 54 of Schedule 2 to this Act.

SCHEDULES

SCHEDULE 1 – REPEALS

Section 3

[Not reproduced here.]

SCHEDULE 2 – CONSEQUENTIAL AMENDMENTS

Section 4

Notes – Only those consequential amendments of relevance to statutes contained in *Tax Statutes and Statutory Instruments* have been included.

SOCIAL SECURITY PENSIONS ACT 1975

19 The Social Security Pensions Act 1975 shall be amended as follows.

37 [Inserts s. 61A, 61B.]

38 [Substitutes s. 62(2).]

SOCIAL SECURITY (MISCELLANEOUS PROVISIONS) ACT 1977

46 [Amends s. 24(3).]

CAPITAL GAINS TAX ACT 1979

52 [Amends Sch. 1, para. 5(2); since repealed.]

SOCIAL SECURITY ACT 1980

59 [Amends s. 21(3).]

VALUE ADDED TAX ACT 1983

65 [Amends Sch. 5, Grp. 14, note 7.]

INHERITANCE TAX ACT 1984

66(1) [Amends s. 74(4), 89(4).]

INSOLVENCY ACT 1986

73 [Repealed by the Enterprise Act 2002, s. 278(2), and Sch. 26.]

History – Sch. 2, para. 73 repealed by the Enterprise Act 2002, s. 278(2), and Sch. 26, with effect from 15 September 2003, by virtue of SI 2003/2093, art. 2 and Sch. 1. Art. 4 contains transitional provisions. Sch. 2, para. 73 originally amended Sch. 6, para. 6.

SOCIAL SECURITY ACT 1986

75 The Social Security Act 1986 shall be amended as follows.

83 [Amends s. 59(3)(c).]

84 [Amends s. 83(1).]

INCOME AND CORPORATION TAXES ACT 1988

93 [Repealed by ITEPA 2003, Sch. 8, Pt. 1 which has effect, for income tax purposes, for the tax year 2003–04 and subsequent tax years, and, for corporation tax purposes, for accounting periods ending after 5 April 2003.]

SOCIAL SECURITY ACT 1989

106 [Amends s. 29(1).]

FINANCE ACT 1989

107 [Amends s. 178(2)(gg).]

CAPITAL ALLOWANCES ACT 1990

109 [Amends s. 22(6)(a), 36(4)(a).]

SCHEDULE 3 – TRANSITIONAL PROVISIONS AND SAVINGS (INCLUDING SOME TRANSITIONAL PROVISIONS RETAINED FROM PREVIOUS ACTS)

Section 5

Notes – Only those provisions of relevance to statutes included in *Tax Statutes and Statutory Instruments* have been reproduced.

Part I – General and Miscellaneous

QUESTIONS RELATING TO CONTRIBUTIONS AND BENEFITS

1(1) A question other than a question arising under any of sections 1 to 3 of the Administration Act–

(a) whether a person is entitled to benefit in respect of a time before 1st July 1992;

(b) whether a person is liable to pay contributions in respect of such a time,

and any other question not arising under any of those sections with respect to benefit or contributions in respect of such a time is to be determined, subject to section 68 of the Administration Act, in accordance with provisions in force or deemed to be in force at that time.

1(2) Subject to sub-paragraph (1) above, the consolidating Acts apply to matters arising before their commencement as to matters arising after it.

GENERAL SAVING FOR OLD SAVINGS

2 The repeal by this Act of an enactment previously repealed subject to savings (whether or not in the repealing enactment) does not affect the continued operation of those savings.

DOCUMENTS REFERRING TO REPEALED ENACTMENTS

3 Any document made, served or issued after this Act comes into force which contains a reference to any of the repealed enactments shall be construed, except so far as a contrary intention appears, as referring or, as the context may require, including a reference to the corresponding provision of the consolidating Acts.

PROVISIONS RELATING TO THE COMING INTO FORCE OF OTHER PROVISIONS

4 The repeal by this Act of a provision providing for or relating to the coming into force of a provision reproduced in the consolidating Acts does not affect the operation of the first provision in so far as it remains capable of having effect, in relation to the enactment reproducing the second provision.

CONTINUING POWERS TO MAKE TRANSITIONAL ETC. REGULATIONS

5 Where immediately before 1st July 1992 the Secretary of State has power under any provision of the Social Security Acts 1975 to 1991 not reproduced in the consolidating Acts by regulations to make provision or savings in preparation for or in connection with the coming into force of a provision repealed by this Act but reproduced in the consolidating Acts, the power shall be construed as having effect in relation to the provision reproducing the repealed provision.

POWERS TO MAKE PREPARATORY REGULATIONS

6 The repeal by this Act of a power by regulations to make provision or savings in preparation for or in connection with the coming into force of a provision reproduced in the consolidating Acts does not affect the power, in so far as it remains capable of having effect, in relation to the enactment reproducing the second provision.

PROVISIONS CONTAINED IN ENACTMENTS BY VIRTUE OF ORDERS OR REGULATIONS

7(1) Without prejudice to any express provision in the consolidating Acts, where this Act repeals any provision contained in any enactment by virtue of any order or regulations and the provision is reproduced in the consolidating Acts, the Secretary of State shall have the like power to make orders or regulations repealing or amending the provision of the consolidating Acts which reproduces the effect of the repealed provision as he had in relation to that provision.

7(2) Sub-paragraph (1) above applies to a repealed provision which was amended by Schedule 7 to the Social Security Act 1989 as it applies to a provision not so amended.

AMENDING ORDERS MADE AFTER PASSING OF ACT

8 An order which is made under any of the repealed enactments after the passing of this Act and which amends any of the repealed enactments shall have the effect also of making a corresponding amendment of the consolidating Acts.

Part II – Specific Transitional Provisions and Savings (including some derived from previous Acts)

INTERPRETATION

9 In this Part of this Schedule–

"the 1965 Act" means the National Insurance Act 1965;

"the 1973 Act" means the Social Security Act 1973;

"the 1975 Act" means the Social Security Act 1975;

"the former Consequential Provisions Act" means the Social Security (Consequential Provisions) Act 1975; and

"the 1986 Act" means the Social Security Act 1986.

SOCIAL SECURITY PENSIONS ACT 1975

10 The repeal by this Act of any provision contained in the 1975 Act or any enactment amending such a provision does not affect the operation of that provision by virtue of section 66(2) of the Social Security Pensions Act 1975.

REGULATIONS AND ORDERS – SUPPLEMENTARY

23(1) Regulations under this Part of this Schedule shall be made by the Secretary of State.

23(2) Powers under this Part of this Schedule to make regulations or orders are exercisable by statutory instrument.

23(3) Any power conferred by this Part of this Schedule to make regulations or orders may be exercised–

(a) either in relation to all cases to which the power extends, or in relation to those cases subject to specified exceptions, or in relation to any specified cases or classes of case;

(b) so as to make, as respects the cases in relation to which it is exercised–

  (i) the full provision to which the power extends or any less provision (whether by way of exception or otherwise);

  (ii) the same provision for all cases in relation to which the power is exercised, or different provision for different cases or different classes of case or different provision as respects the same case or class of case for different purposes of this Part of this Schedule;

  (iii) any such provision either unconditionally or subject to any specified condition.

23(4) The powers to make regulations or orders conferred by any provision of this Part of this Schedule other than paragraph 22 above include powers to make thereby such incidental, supplementary, consequential or transitional provision as appears to the Secretary of State to be expedient for the purposes of the regulations.

23(5) A power conferred by this Part of this Schedule to make regulations or an order includes power to provide for a person to exercise a discretion in dealing with any matter.

23(6) If the Treasury so direct, regulations or orders under this Part of this Schedule shall be made only in conjunction with them.

23(7) A statutory instrument–

(a) which contains (whether alone or with other provisions) orders or regulations made under this Part of this Schedule, and

(b) which is not subject to any requirement that a draft of the instrument be laid before and approved by a resolution of each House of Parliament,

shall be subject to annulment in pursuance of a resolution of either House of Parliament.

PENSION SCHEMES ACT 1993

(1993 Chapter 48) [*5th November 1993*]

ARRANGEMENT OF SECTIONS

PART I – PRELIMINARY

PART III – SCHEMES THAT WERE CONTRACTED-OUT ETC AND EFFECTS ON MEMBERS' STATE SCHEME RIGHTS

CHAPTER I – SCHEMES THAT WERE CONTRACTED-OUT: GUARANTEED MINIMUM PENSIONS AND ALTERATION OF SCHEME RULES ETC

PRELIMINARY

[GENERAL REQUIREMENTS FOR CERTIFICATION]

CANCELLATION, VARIATION, SURRENDER AND REFUSAL OF CERTIFICATES

CHAPTER II – REDUCTION IN SOCIAL SECURITY BENEFITS FOR MEMBERS OF SCHEMES THAT WERE CONTRACTED-OUT

PRELIMINARY

[REDUCED RATES OF CONTRIBUTIONS FOR MEMBERS OF SALARY RELATED CONTRACTED-OUT SCHEMES]

REDUCED RATES OF CONTRIBUTIONS AND REBATES, FOR MEMBERS OF MONEY PURCHASE CONTRACTED-OUT SCHEMES

MINIMUM CONTRIBUTIONS: MEMBERS OF APPROPRIATE PERSONAL PENSION SCHEMES

PART XI – GENERAL AND MISCELLANEOUS PROVISIONS

INFORMATION ABOUT SCHEMES

PART I – PRELIMINARY

1 Categories of pension schemes

1(1) In this Act, unless the context otherwise requires–

"occupational pension scheme" means a pension scheme– or a pension scheme that is prescribed or is of a prescribed description;

(a) that–

(i) for the purpose of providing benefits to, or in respect of, people with service in employments of a description, or

(ii) for that purpose and also for the purpose of providing benefits to, or in respect of, other people,

is established by, or by persons who include, a person to whom subsection (2) applies when the scheme is established or (as the case may be) to whom that subsection would have applied when the scheme was established had that subsection then been in force, and

(b) that has its main administration in the United Kingdom or outside the member States,

"personal pension scheme" means a pension scheme that–

(a) is not an occupational pension scheme, and

(b) is established by a person within section 154(1) of the Finance Act 2004;

"public service pension scheme" means an occupational pension scheme established by or under an enactment or the Royal prerogative or a Royal charter, being a scheme–

(a) all the particulars of which are set out in, or in a legislative instrument made under, an enactment, Royal warrant or charter, or

(b) which cannot come into force, or be amended, without the scheme or amendment being approved by a Minister of the Crown or government department or by the Scottish Ministers,

1(2) This subsection applies–

(a) where people in employments of the description concerned are employed by someone, to a person who employs such people,

(b) to a person *in an employment* of that description, and

(c) to a person representing interests of a description framed so as to include–

(i) interests of persons who employ people in employments of the description mentioned in paragraph (a), or

(ii) interests of people in employments of that description.

1(3) For the purposes of subsection (2), if a person is in an employment of the description concerned by reason of holding an office (including an elective office) and is entitled to remuneration for holding it, the person responsible for paying the remuneration shall be taken to employ the office-holder.

1(4) In the definition in subsection (1) of "occupational pension scheme", the reference to a description includes a description framed by reference to an employment being of any of two or more kinds.

1(5) In subsection (1) **"pension scheme"** (except in the phrases "occupational pension scheme", "personal pension scheme" and "public service pension scheme") means a scheme or other arrangements, comprised in one or more instruments or agreements, having or capable of having effect so as to provide benefits to or in respect of people–

(a) on retirement,

(b) on having reached a particular age, or

(c) on termination of service in an employment.

1(6) The power of the Treasury under section 154(4) of the Finance Act 2004 (power to amend sections 154 and 155) includes power consequentially to amend–

(a) paragraph (a) of the definition in subsection (1) of "personal pension scheme", and

(b) any provision in force in Northern Ireland corresponding to that paragraph.

History – In s. 1(1) the words "any of the paragraphs of" omitted from the definition of "personal pension scheme" by FA 2007, s. 70 and Sch. 20, para. 23(1), and repealed by FA 2007, s. 114 and Sch. 27, Pt. 3(2) with effect from 6 April 2007.
The former provisions of s. 1 numbered as s. 1(1), and in that subsection, "definitions of occupational pension scheme" and "personal pension scheme" substituted; and s. 1(2)–(6) inserted, by Pensions Act 2004, s. 239 with effect from (a) for the purpose only of conferring power to make regulations, is 1 July 2005; and (b) for all other purposes– (i) in the case of an occupational pension scheme that has its main administration in the United Kingdom, is 22 September 2005; and (ii) in all other cases, is 6 April 2006 (by virtue of SI 2005/1720).
In former definition "personal pension scheme" the words "earners (whether employed or self-employed)" substituted by the Welfare Reform and Pensions Act 1999, s. 18 and Sch. 2, para. 3(1)(a), with effect from 25 April 2000 (by virtue of SI 2000/1047).
In definition of "public service pension scheme" the words "or established by or with the approval of the Scottish Ministers" inserted by the Scotland Act 1998 (Consequential Modifications) (No 2) Order (SI 1999/1820), art. 4 and Sch. 2, Pt. I, para. 113, with effect from 1 July 1999.

Derivations – SSPA 1975, s. 66(1).

PART III – SCHEMES THAT WERE CONTRACTED-OUT ETC AND EFFECTS ON MEMBERS' STATE SCHEME RIGHTS

History – In the heading to Pt. III, the words "SCHEMES THAT WERE CONTRACTED-OUT ETC" substituted for the words "CERTIFICATION OF PENSION SCHEMES", and the words "AND DUTIES" (which appeared after the words "STATE SCHEME RIGHTS") omitted, by PA 2014, s. 24 and Sch. 13, para. 3, with effect from 6 April 2016 (as not brought into force by any earlier order under PA 2014, s. 56(1)).

Chapter I – Schemes that were Contracted-out: Guaranteed Minimum Pensions and Alteration of Scheme Rules etc

History – Heading to Ch. I substituted by PA 2014, s. 24 and Sch. 13, para. 4, with effect from 6 April 2016 (as not brought into force by any earlier order under PA 2014, s. 56(1)). Former heading read "Chapter I – Certification".

PRELIMINARY

7 Issue of contracting-out

7 [Repealed by PA 2014, s. 24 and Sch. 13, para. 5.]

History – S. 7 repealed by PA 2014, s. 24 and Sch. 13, para. 5, with effect from 6 April 2016 (as not brought into force by any earlier order under PA 2014, s. 56(1)). Former s. 7 read as follows:

"**7 Issue of contracting-out**

7(1) Regulations shall provide for HMRC to issue certificates stating that the employment of an earner in employed earner's employment is contracted-out employment by reference to an occupational pension scheme.

7(1A) In this Act such a certificate is referred to as **"a contracting-out certificate"**.

7(2) The regulations shall provide for contracting-out certificates to be issued to employers and to specify–

(a) the employments which are to be treated, either generally or in relation to any specified description of earners, as contracted-out employments; and

(b) the occupational pension schemes by reference to which those employments are to be so treated.

7(2A) The regulations may provide, in the case of contracting-out certificates issued before the principal appointed day, for their cancellation by virtue of the regulations–

(a) at the end of a prescribed period beginning with that day, or

(b) if prescribed conditions are not satisfied at any time in that period,

but for them to continue to have effect until so cancelled; and the regulations may provide that a certificate having effect on and after that day by virtue of this subsection is to have effect, in relation to any earner's service on or after that day, as if issued on or after that day.

7(2B) In this Part, **"the principal appointed day"** means the day designated by an order under section 180 of the Pensions Act 1995 as the principal appointed day for the purposes of Part III of that Act.

7(3) An occupational pension scheme is a contracted-out scheme in relation to an earner's employment if it is for the time being specified in a contracting-out certificate in relation to that employment; and references in this Act to the contracting-out of a scheme are references to its inclusion in such a certificate.

7(4) [Repealed by PA 2007, s. 15 and Sch. 4, para. 4, and s. 27 and Sch. 7, Pt. 6.]

7(5) [Repealed by PA 2007, s. 15 and Sch. 4, para. 4, and s. 27 and Sch. 7, Pt. 6.]
7(6) [Repealed by PA 2007, s. 15 and Sch. 4, para. 4, and s. 27 and Sch. 7, Pt. 6.]
7(7) Except in prescribed circumstances, no contracting-out certificate shall have effect from a date earlier than that on which the certificate is issued.
7(8) References in this Act to a contracting-out certificate, a contracted-out scheme and to contracting-out in a context relating to a money purchase contracted-out scheme are to be construed in accordance with section 181A.".
In the heading to former s. 7 the words "and appropriate scheme" repealed by PA 2007, s. 15 and Sch. 4, para. 6, and s. 27 and Sch. 7, Pt. 6, with effect from 6 April 2012 (SI 2011/1267, art. 2(a)).
Former s. 7(1) and (1A) substituted for s. 7(1), by PA 2007, s. 15 and Sch. 4, para. 2, with effect from 6 April 2012 (SI 2011/1267, art. 2(a)).
In former s. 7(1), "Secretary of State" substituted by Pensions Act 1995, Sch. 5, para. 22(a), with effect from 6 April 1996 by virtue of SI 1996/778, art. 2(5)(a) and Schedule, Pt. V.
Former s. 7(2A) and (2B) inserted by Pensions Act 1995, s. 136(1), with effect from 6 April 1996 for the purpose only of authorising the making of regulations (SI 1996/778, art. 2(5)(a), Schedule, Pt. V), and for all other purposes with effect from 6 April 1997 by virtue of SI 1996/778, art. 2(7) (6 April 1997 is also the principal appointed day referred to in those subsections).
Former s. 7(4)–(6) repealed by PA 2007, s. 15 and Sch. 4, para. 4, and s. 27 and Sch. 7, Pt. 6, with effect from 6 April 2012 (SI 2011/1267, art. 2(a)).
In former s. 7(1) and (6) "Inland Revenue" substituted by SSC(TF)A 1999, s. 18 and Sch. 1, para. 33, with effect, from 25 February 1999 for the purpose making regulations, (SSC(TF)A 1999, s. 28(2)(b)) and 1 April 1999 for all other purposes (SI 1999/527).
In former s. 7(6) the words "Secretary of State" substituted and in s. 7(4) the words "by the Board" omitted by Pensions Act 1995, Sch. 5, para. 22 and Sch. 7, Pt. III, with effect from 6 April 1997 by virtue of SI 1997/664 (C. 23), art. 2(3) and Schedule, Pt. II.
In former s. 7(7) the words "or appropriate scheme certificate" repealed by PA 2007, s. 15 and Sch. 4, para. 3, and s. 27 and Sch. 7, Pt. 6, with effect from 6 April 2012 (SI 2011/1267, art. 2(a)).
Former s. 7(8) inserted by PA 2007, s. 15 and Sch. 4, para. 5, with effect from 6 April 2012 (SI 2011/1267, art. 2(a)).

Derivations – S. 7(1) (as originally enacted): SSPA 1975, s. 30(1) (in part), 31(1) (in part); SSA 1986, s. 1(8), 2(1)(a).
S. 7(2): SSPA 1975, s. 31(1) (in part).
S. 7(3): SSPA 1975, s. 32(1).
S. 7(4): SSA 1986, s. 1(8).
S. 7(5): SSA 1986, s. 2(6).
S. 7(6) (as originally enacted): SSA 1986, s. 2(1)(c).
S. 7(7): SSPA 1975, s. 31(7) (in part); SSA 1986, s. 2(5) (in part).

7A Meaning of "the first abolition date" and "the second abolition date"

7A In this Act–

"the first abolition date" means 6 April 2012 (the date appointed for the commencement of section 15(1) of the Pensions Act 2007 (abolition of contracting-out for defined contribution pension schemes));

"the second abolition date" means 6 April 2016 (the date on which section 56(4) of the Pensions Act 2014 provides for the commencement of section 24(1) of that Act (abolition of contracting-out for salary related schemes)).

History – S. 7A inserted by PA 2014, s. 24 and Sch. 13, para. 6, with effect from 6 April 2016 (as not brought into force by any earlier order under PA 2014, s. 56(1)).

7B Meaning of "contracted-out scheme" and "appropriate scheme" etc.

7B(1) This section applies for the interpretation of this Act.

7B(2) An occupational pension scheme was "contracted-out" at a time if, at that time, there was in force a certificate under section 7 (as it then had effect) stating that the employment of an earner in employed earner's employment was contracted-out employment by reference to the scheme.

7B(3) **"Contracting-out certificate"** means a certificate of the kind mentioned in subsection (2).

7B(4) An occupational pension scheme was a "salary related contracted-out scheme" at a time if, at that time, the scheme was contracted-out by virtue of satisfying section 9(2) (as it then had effect).

7B(5) An occupational pension scheme was a "money purchase contracted-out scheme" at a time if, at that time, the scheme was contracted-out by virtue of satisfying section 9(3) (as it then had effect).

7B(6) A personal pension scheme was an "appropriate scheme" at a time if, at that time, there was in force a certificate issued under section 7(1)(b) (as it then had effect) stating that the scheme was an appropriate scheme.

7B(7) **"Appropriate scheme certificate"** means a certificate of the kind mentioned in subsection (6).

7B(8) An appropriate scheme certificate that was in force in relation to a scheme is to be taken as conclusive that the scheme was, at that time, an appropriate scheme.

History – S. 7B inserted by PA 2014, s. 24 and Sch. 13, para. 6, with effect from 6 April 2016 (as not brought into force by any earlier order under PA 2014, s. 56(1)).

8 Meaning of "contracted-out employment", "guaranteed minimum pension" and "minimum payment"

8(1) In relation to any period before the second abolition date, the employment of an earner in employed earner's employment was "contracted-out employment" in relation to the earner during that period if–

(a) the earner was under pensionable age;

(b) the earner's service in the employment was service which qualified the earner for a pension provided by a salary related contracted-out scheme; and

(c) there was in force a contracting-out certificate issued in accordance with this Chapter (as it then had effect) stating that the employment was contracted-out employment by reference to the scheme.

8(1A) In addition, in relation to any period before the first abolition date, the employment of an earner in employed earner's employment was **"contracted-out employment"** in relation to him during that period if–

(a) he was under pensionable age;

(b) his employer made minimum payments in respect of his employment to a money purchase contracted-out scheme, and

(c) there was in force a contracting-out certificate issued in accordance with this Chapter (as it then had effect) stating that the employment was contracted-out employment by reference to the scheme.

8(1B) In the following provisions of this Act "earner", in relation to a scheme, means a person who was an earner in contracted-out employment by reference to the scheme.

8(2) In this Act–

"guaranteed minimum pension" means any pension which is provided, by a scheme that was a salary related contracted-out scheme, in accordance with the requirements of sections 13 and 17 to the extent to which its weekly rate is equal to the earner's or, as the case may be, the earner's widow's or widower's, surviving same sex spouse's guaranteed minimum as determined for the purposes of those sections respectively; and

"minimum payment", in relation to an earner's employment in any tax week, means the rebate percentage of so much of the earnings paid to or for the benefit of the earner in that week as exceeds the current lower earnings limit but not the applicable limit (or the prescribed equivalents if he is paid otherwise than weekly);

and for the purposes of this subsection **"rebate percentage"** means the appropriate flat rate percentage for the tax year in which the week falls as specified in an order made under section 42B (as it had effect before the first abolition date).

8(2A) In subsection (2) **"the applicable limit"** means–

(a) in relation to a tax year before 2009–10, the upper earnings limit;

(b) in relation to 2009–10 or any subsequent tax year, the upper accrual point.

8(3) [Repealed by PA 2007, s. 15 and Sch. 4, para. 47, and s. 27 and Sch. 7, Pt. 7.]

8(4) A contracting-out certificate that was in force in respect of an employed earner's employment is to be taken as conclusive that the employment was, at that time, contracted-out employment.

8(5) [Repealed by Pensions Act 1995, Sch. 5, para. 23(b) and Sch. 7, Pt. III.]

History – S. 8(1) substituted by PA 2014, s. 24 and Sch. 13, para. 7(2), with effect from 6 April 2016 (as not brought into force by any earlier order under PA 2014, s. 56(1)).

In s. 8, the words "the first abolition date" substituted for the words "the abolition date" (in each place) by PA 2014, s. 24 and Sch. 13, para. 2, with effect from 6 April 2016 (as not brought into force by any earlier order under PA 2014, s. 56(1)). Former s. 8(1) read as follows:

"**8(1)** The employment of an earner in employed earner's employment is **"contracted-out employment"** in relation to him during any period in which–

(a) he is under pensionable age;

(aa) his service in the employment is for the time being service which qualifies him for a pension provided by an occupational pension scheme contracted out by virtue of satisfying section 9(2) (in this Act referred to as "a salary related contracted-out scheme");

(b) there is in force a contracting-out certificate issued by the Inland Revenue in accordance with this Chapter stating that the employment is contracted-out employment by reference to the scheme.".

In former s. 8(1) para. (a) and (aa) substituted for the words "he is under pensionable age" to the end of para. (a), by PA 2007, s. 15 and Sch. 4, para. 3(2), with effect from 6 April 2012 (SI 2011/1267, art. 2(a)).

Former s. 8(1)(a)(i) substituted by Pensions Act 1995, s. 136(2), with effect from 6 April 1996 for the purpose only of authorising the making of regulations (SI 1996/778, art. 2(5)(a) and Schedule, Pt. V), and for all other purposes with effect from 6 April 1997 (SI 1996/778, art. 2(7)).

In former s. 8(1)(b), "Secretary of State" substituted by Pensions Act 1995, Sch. 22, para. 21(a), with effect from 6 April 1997 by virtue of SI 1997/664 (C.23), art. 2(3) and Schedule, Pt. II.

In former s. 8(1)(b) "Inland Revenue" substituted by SSC(TF)A 1999, s. 18 and Sch. 1, para. 34, with effect from 25 February 1999, for the purpose of making regulations (SSC(TF)A 1999, s. 28(2)(b)) and 1 April 1999 for all other purposes (SI 1999/527).

S. 8(1A) inserted by PA 2007, s. 15 and Sch. 4, para. 3(4), with effect from 6 April 2012 (SI 2011/1267, art. 2(a)).

S. 8(1B) inserted by PA 2014, s. 24 and Sch. 13, para. 7(3), with effect from 6 April 2016 (as not brought into force by any earlier order under PA 2014, s. 56(1)).

In s. 8(2), in the definition of "guaranteed minimum pension", the words ", surviving same sex spouse's" inserted by Marriage (Same Sex Couples) Act 2013, s. 11(4) and Sch. 4, para. 19, with effect from 13 March 2014 (SI 2014/93, art. 3).

In s. 8(2), in the definition of "guaranteed minimum pension", the words ", by a scheme that was a salary related contracted-out scheme," substituted for the words "by an occupational pension scheme" by PA 2014, s. 24 and Sch. 13, para. 7(4), with effect from 6 April 2016 (as not brought into force by any earlier order under PA 2014, s. 56(1)).

In s. 8(2) the words "for the tax year in which the week falls as specified in an order made under section 42B (as it had effect before the abolition date)" substituted for the words "for the purposes of section 42A", by PA 2007, s. 15 and Sch. 4, para. 3(4), with effect from 6 April 2012 (SI 2011/1267, art. 2(a)).
In s. 8(2) in the definition of "minimum payment", the words "the applicable limit" substituted by NICA 2008, s. 4 and Sch. 1, para. 8(2), with effect from 21 September 2008.
In s. 8(2) in the definition of "minimum payment"; reference to "section 42A" substituted by SSA 1998, s. 86(1) and Sch. 7, para. 126 with effect from 6 April 1999 (SI 1999/418).
In s. 8(2) the words following the definition of minimum payment substituted by Pensions Act 1995, Sch. 5, para. 23(a), with effect from 6 April 1997 by virtue of SI 1997/664 (C. 23), art. 2(3) and Schedule, Pt. II.
S. 8(2A) inserted by NICA 2008, s. 4 and Sch. 1, para. 8(3), with effect from 21 September 2008.
S. 8(3) repealed by PA 2007, s. 15 and Sch. 4, para. 47, and s. 27 and Sch. 7, Pt. 7, with effect from 6 April 2015 (SI 2011/ 1267, art. 3(a)(iv) and (b)(ii)).
In former s. 8(3)(f) "Inland Revenue" and "they are" substituted by SSC(TF)A 1999, s. 18 and Sch. 1, para. 34, with effect from 25 February 1999, for the purpose of making regulations, (SSC(TF)A 1999, s. 28(2)(b), and 1 April 1999 for all other purposes (SI 1999/527).
S. 8(4) substituted by PA 2014, s. 24 and Sch. 13, para. 7(5), with effect from 6 April 2016 (as not brought into force by any earlier order under PA 2014, s. 56(1)) Former s. 8(4) read as follows:
"8(4) Any contracting-out certificate for the time being in force in respect of an employed earner's employment shall be conclusive that the employment is contracted-out employment.".
S. 8(5) omitted by Pensions Act 1995, Sch. 5, para. 23(b) and Sch. 7, Pt. III, with effect from 6 April 1997 by virtue of SI 1997/664 (C. 23), art. 2(3) and Schedule, Pt. II.

Derivations – S. 8(1) (as originally enacted): SSPA 1975, s. 30(1), SSA 1986, Sch. 2, para. 4(a), Sch. 10, para. 15.
S. 8(2) (as originally enacted): SSPA 1975, s. 26(2), 30(1A), (1B); SSA 1986, s. 9(4), Sch. 2, para. 4(b), Sch. 10, para. 12(b).
S. 8(3) (as originally enacted): SSPA 1975, s. 30(1C); SSA 1986, Sch. 2, para. 4(b).
S. 8(4): SSPA 1975, s. 30(3).
S. 8(5) (as originally enacted): SSPA 1975, s. 30(4).

Cross references – S. 41: reduced rates of Class 1 contributions for earners in contracted-out employment.
SSCBA 1992, s. 6: liability for Class 1 contributions.
SSCBA 1992, s. 8: calculation of primary Class 1 contributions.
FA 2004, s. 188(6): registered pension schemes: members' contributions: relief for contributions.
FA 2004, s. 190(5): registered pension schemes: members' contributions: annual limit for relief.
FA 2004, s. 196(5): registered pension schemes: employers' contributions: relief for employers in respect of contributions paid.
FA 2004, s. 232(9): registered pension schemes: annual allowance charge: cash balance arrangements: adjustments of closing value.
FA 2004, s. 233(2): registered pension scheme: annual allowance charge: other money purchase arrangements.
FA 2004, s. 236(9): registered pension scheme: annual allowance charge: defined benefits arrangements: adjustments of closing value.
FA 2004, Sch. 36, para. 14(3): pre-commencement rights: lifetime allowance charge.

[GENERAL REQUIREMENTS FOR CERTIFICATION]

History – The above heading repealed by PA 2014, s. 24 and Sch. 13, para. 8, with effect from from 6 April 2016 (as not brought into force by any earlier order under PA 2014, s. 56(1)), subject to savings provision in SI 2015/1502, art. 2.

11 Elections as to employments covered by contracting-out certificates

11 [Repealed by PA 2014, s. 24 and Sch. 13, para. 9.]

History – S. 11 repealed by PA 2014, s. 24 and Sch. 13, para. 9, with effect from 6 April 2016 (as not brought into force by any earlier order under PA 2014, s. 56(1)), subject to savings provision in SI 2015/1502, art. 2. Former s. 11 read as follows:

"11 Elections as to employments covered by contracting-out certificates

11(1) Subject to the provisions of this Part, an employment otherwise satisfying the conditions for inclusion in a contracting-out certificate shall be so included if and so long as the employer so elects and not otherwise.
11(2) Subject to subsections (3) and (4), an election may be so made, and an employment so included, either generally or in relation only to a particular description of earners.
11(3) Except in such cases as may be prescribed, an employer shall not, in making or abstaining from making any election under this section, discriminate between different earners on any grounds other than the nature of their employment.
11(4) If the Inland Revenue consider that an employer is contravening subsection (3) in relation to any scheme, they may–
(a) refuse to give effect to any election made by him in relation to that scheme; or
(b) cancel any contracting-out certificate held by him in respect of it.
11(5) Regulations may make provision–
(a) for regulating the manner in which an employer is to make an election with a view to the issue, variation or surrender of a contracting-out certificate;
(b) for requiring an employer to give a notice of his intentions in respect of making or abstaining from making any such election in relation to any existing or proposed scheme–
 (i) to employees in any employment to which the scheme applies or to which it is proposed that it should apply;
 (ii) to any independent trade union recognised to any extent for the purpose of collective bargaining in relation to those employees;
 (iii) to the trustees and managers of the scheme; and
 (iv) to such other persons as may be prescribed;
(c) for requiring an employer, in connection with any such notice, to furnish such information as may be prescribed and to undertake such consultations as may be prescribed with any such trade union as is mentioned in paragraph (b)(ii);
(d) for empowering the Inland Revenue to refuse to give effect to an election made by an employer unless they are satisfied that he has complied with the requirements of the regulations;
(e) for referring to an employment tribunal any question–
 (i) whether an organisation is such a trade union as is mentioned in paragraph (b)(ii), or
 (ii) whether the requirements of the regulations as to consultation have been complied with.".
In former s. 11 the words "Secretary of State" substituted and in s. 11(4) the words "considers" and "he" substituted by Pensions Act 1995, Sch. 5, para. 21 with effect from 6 April 1997 by virtue of SI 1997/664 (C. 23), art. 2(3) and Schedule, Pt. II.
In former s. 11(4), "Inland Revenue consider" substituted and "they" by SSC(TF)A 1999, s. 1 and Sch. 1, para. 37(2) and in s. 11(5)(d), "Inland Revenue" and "they are" substituted by SSC(TF)A 1999, s. 1 and Sch. 1, para. 37(3), with effect from 25 February 1999, for the purpose making regulations, (SSC(TF)A 1999, s. 28(2)(b)) and 1 April 1999 for all other purposes (SI 1999/527).

In former s. 11(5)(d), "Secretary of State" and "he is" substituted by Pensions Act 1995, Sch. 5, para. 21 with effect from 6 April 1996 for the purpose only of making regulations (SI 1996/778, art. 2(5)(a), Schedule, Pt. V), and with effect from 6 April 1997 for all other purposes (SI 1997/664 (C. 23), art. 2(3) and Schedule, Pt. II).
In former s. 11(5)(e) the word "employment" substituted by the Employment Rights (Dispute Resolution) Act 1998, s. 1, with effect from 1 August 1998 (by virtue of SI 1998/1658).

Derivations – S. 11(1), (2): SSPA 1975, s. 31(3).
S. 11(3), (4) (as originally enacted): SSPA 1975, s. 31(4).
S. 11(5) (as originally enacted): SSPA 1975, s. 31(5).

CANCELLATION, VARIATION, SURRENDER AND REFUSAL OF CERTIFICATES

34 Cancellation, variation, surrender and refusal of certificates

34 [Repealed by PA 2014, s. 24 and Sch. 13, para. 22.]

History – S. 34 repealed by PA 2014, s. 24 and Sch. 13, para. 22, with effect from 6 April 2016 (as not brought into force by any earlier order under PA 2014, s. 56(1)), subject to savings provision in SI 2015/1502, art. 2. Former s. 34 read as follows:

"34 Cancellation, variation, surrender and refusal of certificates

34(1) Regulations shall provide for the cancellation, variation or surrender of a contracting-out certificate, or the issue of a new certificate–
(a) on any change of circumstances affecting the treatment of an employment as contracted-out employment; or
(b) where the certificate was issued on or after the principal appointed day, if any employer of persons in the description of employment to which the scheme in question relates, or the actuary of the scheme, fails to provide HMRC, at prescribed intervals, with such documents as may be prescribed for the purpose of verifying that the conditions of section 9(2B) are satisfied.

34(2) Regulations may enable the Inland Revenue to cancel or vary a contracting-out certificate where–
(a) they have reason to suppose that any employment to which it relates ought not to be treated as contracted-out employment in accordance with the certificate; and
(b) the employer does not show that it ought to be so treated.

34(3) Where by or by virtue of any provision of this Part the contracting-out of a scheme in relation to an employment depends on the satisfaction of a particular condition–
(a) [repealed by PA 2007, s. 15 and Sch. 4, para. 15(3)(a),]
(b) [repealed by PA 2007, s. 15 and Sch. 4, para. 15(3)(a),]
the continued contracting-out of the scheme shall be dependent on continued satisfaction of the condition; and if the condition ceases to be satisfied, that shall be a ground (without prejudice to any other) for the cancellation or variation of the contracting-out certificate.

34(4) A contracting-out certificate in respect of any employment may be withheld or cancelled by the Inland Revenue if they consider that there are circumstances which make it inexpedient that the employment should be or, as the case may be, continue to be, contracted-out employment by reference to the scheme, notwithstanding that the relevant scheme is one that they would otherwise treat as proper to be contracted-out in relation to all earners in that employment.

34(5) [Repealed by PA 2007, s. 15 and Sch. 4, para. 15(4), and s. 27 and Sch. 7, Pt. 6.]

34(6) [Omitted by Pensions Act 1995, Sch. 5, para. 37(b).]

34(7) Without prejudice to the previous provisions of this section, failure of a scheme to comply with any requirements prescribed by virtue of section 25(2) shall be a ground on which the Inland Revenue may, in respect of any employment to which the scheme relates, cancel a contracting-out certificate.

34(8) Except in prescribed circumstances, no cancellation, variation or surrender of a contracting-out certificate shall have effect from a date earlier than that on which the cancellation, variation or surrender is made.

34(9) A reference in this section to a contracting-out certificate does not include a reference to a contracting-out certificate issued in respect of a money purchase contracted-out scheme.".

Former s. 34(1) substituted by PA 2007, s. 15 and Sch. 4, para. 15(2), with effect from 6 April 2012 (SI 2011/1267, art. 2(a)).
In former s. 34 the words "Inland Revenue" substituted in each place that they appear; in s. 34(2)(a) the words "they have" substituted and in s. 34(4) and (5) the words "they consider" and "they" substituted by SSC(TF)A 1999, s. 1 and Sch. 1, para. 45, with effect from 25 February 1999, for the purpose of making regulations, (SSC(TF)A 1999, s. 28(2)(b)) and 1 April 1999 for all other purposes (SI 1999/527).
In former s. 34(1)(a)(ii) the words "or category" repealed by the Pensions Act 2004, s. 320 and Sch. 13, Pt. 1, with effect from 6 April 2005.
Former s. 34(1)(a) substituted by Pensions Act 1995, Sch. 5, para. 37(a), with effect from 6 April 1996 for the purpose only of making regulations (SI 1996/778, art. 2(5)(a), Schedule, Pt. V) and with effect from 6 April 1997 for all other purposes (SI 1997/664 (C. 23), art. 2(3) and Schedule, Pt. II).
In former s. 34(2), "Secretary of State" and "he has" substituted by Pension Schemes Act 1995, Sch. 5, para. 21, with effect from 6 April 1996 for the purpose only of making regulations (SI 1996/778, art. 2(5)(a), Schedule, Pt. V) and with effect from 6 April 1997 for all other purposes (SI 1997/664 (C. 23), art. 2(3) and Schedule, Pt. II).
Former s. 34(3)(a) and (b) repealed and the words "by or by virtue of any provision of this Part the contracting-out of a scheme in relation to an employment depends on the satisfaction of a particular condition" substituted by PA 2007, s. 15 and Sch. 4, para. 15(3)(a), with effect from 6 April 2012 (SI 2011/1267, art. 2(a)).
In former s. 34(3) the words "or, as the case may be, the scheme's continuing to be an appropriate scheme" and "or appropriate scheme" repealed by PA 2007, s. 15 and Sch. 4, para. 15(3)(b) and (c), and s. 27 and Sch. 7, Pt. 6, with effect from 6 April 2012 (SI 2011/1267, art. 2(a)).
In former s. 34(4)–(7), the words "Secretary of State" substituted throughout, and in s. 34(4), (5) the words "he considers" and "he" substituted by Pensions Act 1995, Sch. 5, para. 21, with effect from 6 April 1997 by virtue of SI 1997/664 (C. 23), art. 2(3) and Schedule, Pt. II.
Former s. 34(5) repealed by PA 2007, s. 15 and Sch. 4, para. 15(4), and s. 27 and Sch. 7, Pt. 6, with effect from 6 April 2012 (SI 2011/1267, art. 2(a)).
Former s. 34(6) omitted by Pensions Act 1995, Sch. 5, para. 37(b) and Sch. 7, Pt. III, with effect from 6 April 1996 for the purpose only ofmaking regulations (SI 1996/778, art. 2(5)(a), Schedule, Pt. V) and with effect from 6 April 1997 for all other purposes (SI 1997/664 (C. 23), art. 2(3) and Schedule, Pt. II).
Former s. 34(7) substituted by Pensions Act 1995, Sch. 5, para. 37(c), with effect from 6 April 1996 for the purpose only of making regulations (*SI 1996/778, art. 2(5)*(a), *Schedule*, Pt. V) and with effect from 6 April 1997 for all other purposes (SI 1997/664 (C. 23), art. 2(3) and Schedule, Pt. II).
In former s. 34(8) the words "or appropriate scheme certificate" repealed by PA 2007, s. 15 and Sch. 4, para. 15(5), and s. 27 and Sch. 7, Pt. 6, with effect from 6 April 2012 (SI 2011/1267, art. 2(a)).
Former s. 34(9) inserted by PA 2007, s. 15 and Sch. 4, para. 15(6), with effect from 6 April 2012 (SI 2011/1267, art. 2(a)).

Derivations – S. 34(1) (as originally enacted): SSPA 1975, s. 31(2); SSA 1986, s. 2(1)(b).
S. 34(2) (as originally enacted): SSPA 1975, s. 31(6).

S. 34(3): SSPA 1975, s. 32(3); SSA 1986, s. 2(4).
S. 34(4): SSPA 1975, s. 32(4).
Former s. 34(5): SSA 1986, s. 2(3).
S. 34(6) (as originally enacted): SSA 1980, s. 3(10) (in part).
S. 34(7): SSPA 1975, s. 41(2), (5).
S. 34(8): SSPA 1975, s. 31(7); SSA 1986, s. 2(5).

Cross references – SI 1982/1033, reg. 2: prevention of recovery by employers of Class 1 contributions.

35 Surrender and cancellation of contracting-out certificates: issue of further certificates

35 [Repealed by PA 2014, s. 24 and Sch. 13, para. 22.]

History – S. 35 repealed by PA 2014, s. 24 and Sch. 13, para. 22, with effect from 6 April 2016 (as not brought into force by any earlier order under PA 2014, s. 56(1)), subject to savings provision in SI 2015/1502, art. 2. Former s. 35 read as follows:

"35 Surrender and cancellation of contracting-out certificates: issue of further certificates

35(1) This section applies in any case where–
(a) a contracting-out certificate ("the first certificate") has been surrendered by an employer or cancelled by the Board; and
(b) at any time before the end of the period of 12 months beginning with the date of the surrender or cancellation, that or any connected employer makes an election under section 11 in respect of any employment which was specified by virtue of section 7(2)(a) in the first certificate, with a view to the issue of a further contracting-out certificate.

35(2) This section applies whether or not the scheme specified in the first certificate in relation to the employment concerned is the same as the scheme which would be specified in the further certificate if it were issued.

35(3) The Board shall not give effect to the election referred to in subsection (1) by issuing a further certificate unless they consider that, in all the circumstances of the case, it would be reasonable to do so.

35(4) Regulations may make such supplemental provision in relation to cases falling within this section as the Secretary of State considers necessary or expedient.

35(5) For the purposes of subsection (1)–
(a) an employment ("the second employment") in respect of which an election of the kind referred to in subsection (1)(b) has been made; and
(b) an employment ("the first employment") which was specified by virtue of section 7(2)(a) in the first certificate,
shall be treated as one employment if, in the opinion of the Board–
(i) they are substantially the same, however described; or
(ii) the first employment falls wholly or partly within the description of the second employment or the second employment falls wholly or partly within the description of the first employment.

35(6) Regulations shall prescribe the cases in which employers are to be treated as connected for the purposes of this section.".

Notes – SI 1996/1172, art. 75 modified former s. 35 and s. 36 with effect from 6 April 1997. SI 1996/1172, art. 75 reads as follows:

"**75** Transitional modifications to sections 35 and 36 of the 1993 Act.

75 Sections 35 and 36 of the 1993 Act (surrender and cancellation of contracting-out certificates: issue and cancellation of further certificates) shall be modified for transitional purposes until the coming into force of an order under section 180 of the 1995 Act repealing those provisions as follows–
(a) in paragraph (a) of subsection (1) of section 35 of the 1993 Act or the "Secretary of State" is added after "the Board";
(b) in each other place where the word appears, for "Board" there is substituted "Secretary of State";
(c) in subsection (3) of section 35 of the 1993 Act, for "they consider" there is substituted "he considers";
(d) in paragraph (c) of subsection (1) of section 36 of the 1993 Act, for "have formed" there is substituted "has formed", for "had they been aware" there is substituted "had he been aware" and for "they would have been prevented" there is substituted "he would have been prevented"; and
(e) in subsection (6) of section 36, for "have cancelled" there is substituted "has cancelled"."

36 Surrender and cancellation of contracting-out certificates: cancellation of further certificates

36 [Repealed by PA 2014, s. 24 and Sch. 13, para. 22.]

History – S. 36 repealed by PA 2014, s. 24 and Sch. 13, para. 22, with effect from 6 April 2016 (as not brought into force by any earlier order under PA 2014, s. 56(1)), subject to savings provision in SI 2015/1502, art. 2. Former s. 36 read as follows:

"36 Surrender and cancellation of contracting-out certificates: cancellation of further certificates

36(1) This section applies in any case where–
(a) a contracting-out certificate ("the first certificate") has been surrendered by an employer or cancelled by the Board;
(b) a further contracting-out certificate ("the further certificate") has been issued, after the surrender or cancellation of the first certificate but before the end of the period of 12 months beginning with the date of the surrender or cancellation, in respect of any employment which was specified by virtue of section 7(2)(a) in the first certificate; and
(c) the Board have formed the opinion that had they been aware of all the circumstances of the case at the time when the further certificate was issued they would have been prevented by section 35(3) from issuing it.

36(2) This section applies whether or not the scheme specified in the first certificate in relation to the employment concerned is the same as the scheme specified in the further certificate.

36(3) *The Board may*, before the end of the period of 12 months beginning with the date on which the further certificate was issued, cancel that certificate.

36(4) Where a contracting-out certificate is cancelled under subsection (3) the provisions of this Act and of any regulations and orders made under it shall have effect as if the certificate had never been issued.

36(5) Regulations may make such supplemental provision in relation to cases falling within this section as the Secretary of State considers necessary or expedient.

36(6) Without prejudice to subsection (5), regulations may make provision, in relation to any case in which the Board have cancelled a contracting-out certificate under subsection (3), preventing the recovery by the employer concerned (whether by deduction from emoluments or otherwise) of such arrears which he is required to pay to the Secretary of State in respect of an earner's liability under section 6(3) of the [1992 c. 4.] Social Security Contributions and Benefits Act 1992 as may be prescribed.

36(7) For the purposes of subsection (1)–
(a) an employment ("the second employment") in respect of which a further contracting-out certificate of the kind referred to in subsection (1)(b) has been issued; and
(b) an employment ("the first employment") which was specified by virtue of section 7(2)(a) in the first certificate,

shall be treated as one employment if, in the opinion of the Board–
(i) they are substantially the same, however described; or
(ii) the first employment falls wholly or partly within the description of the second employment or the second employment falls wholly or partly within the description of the first employment.".

Notes – SI 1996/1172, art. 75 modified former s. 35 and s. 36 with effect from 6 April 1997. SI 1996/1172, art. 75 reads as follows:

"75 Transitional modifications to sections 35 and 36 of the 1993 Act.

75 Sections 35 and 36 of the 1993 Act (surrender and cancellation of contracting-out certificates: issue and cancellation of further certificates) shall be modified for transitional purposes until the coming into force of an order under section 180 of the 1995 Act repealing those provisions as follows–
(a) in paragraph (a) of subsection (1) of section 35 of the 1993 Act or the "Secretary of State" is added after "the Board";
(b) in each other place where the word appears, for "Board" there is substituted "Secretary of State";
(c) in subsection (3) of section 35 of the 1993 Act, for "they consider" there is substituted "he considers";
(d) in paragraph (c) of subsection (1) of section 36 of the 1993 Act, for "have formed" there is substituted "has formed", for "had they been aware" there is substituted "had he been aware" and for "they would have been prevented" there is substituted "he would have been prevented"; and
(e) in subsection (6) of section 36, for "have cancelled" there is substituted "has cancelled"."

Chapter II – Reduction in Social Security Benefits for Members of Schemes that were Contracted-out

History – Heading to Ch. II substituted by PA 2014, s. 24 and Sch. 13, para. 26, with effect from 6 April 2016 (as not brought into force by any earlier order under PA 2014, s. 56(1)). Former heading read "Chapter II – Reduction in State Scheme Contributions and Social Security Benefits for Members of Certified Schemes".

Cross references – SI 2012/187: Social Security Revaluation Earnings Factor Order 2012.
SI 2013/527: Social Security Revaluation of Earnings Factors Order 2013.

PRELIMINARY

40 Scope of Chapter II

40 This Chapter has effect for the purpose–
(a) [omitted by PA 2014, s. 24 and Sch. 13, para. 27(a);]
(b) of providing for contributions to be paid by the Inland Revenue in respect of earners who are members of money purchase contracted-out schemes and members of appropriate personal pension schemes; and
(c) of making provision concerning the payment of certain social security benefits payable in respect of members and former members of schemes that were contracted-out pension schemes.

Prospective amendments – S. 40(b) repealed by PA 2007, s. 15 and Sch. 4, para. 50, and s. 27 and Sch. 7, Pt. 7, with effect from a date to be appointed under s. 30(2).

History – S. 40(a) omitted by PA 2014, s. 24 and Sch. 13, para. 27(a), with effect from 6 April 2016 (as not brought into force by any earlier order under PA 2014, s. 56(1)). Former s. 40(a) read as follows:
"(a) of reducing the rates at which certain national insurance contributions are payable by or in respect of earners whose employment is contracted-out by reference to contracted-out occupational pension schemes;".

In s. 40(b), words "money purchase contracted-out schemes and members of" inserted by Pensions Act 1995, s. 137(1), with effect from 13 March 1996 for the purpose only of authorising the making of orders (SI 1996/778, art. 2(1), Schedule, Pt. I), 6 April 1996 for the purpose only of authorising the making of regulations (SI 1996/778, art. 2(5)(a), Schedule, Pt. V, and 6 April 1997 for all other purposes (SI 1997/664, art. 2(3), Sch. Pt. II).

In s. 40(b), "Inland Revenue" substituted by Welfare Reform and Pensions Act 1999, Sch. 11, para. 21 with effect from 11 November 1999 (date of passing of WRPA 1998).

In s. 40(c), the words "schemes that were contracted-out pension schemes" substituted for the words "such schemes" by PA 2014, s. 24 and Sch. 13, para. 27(b), with effect from 6 April 2016 (as not brought into force by any earlier order under PA 2014, s. 56(1)).

Derivations – SSPA 1975, s. 26(1), (as originally enacted) (1A); SSA 1986, Sch. 2, para. 2, Sch. 10, para. 12; SS(CP)A 1992, Sch. 2, para. 20.

[REDUCED RATES OF CONTRIBUTIONS FOR MEMBERS OF SALARY RELATED CONTRACTED-OUT SCHEMES]

History – The above heading repealed by PA 2014, s. 24 and Sch. 13, para. 28, with effect from 6 April 2016 (as not brought into force by any earlier order under PA 2014, s. 56(1)), subject to savings provision in SI 2015/1502, art. 2.

41 Reduced rates of Class 1 contributions

41 [Repealed by PA 2014, s. 24 and Sch. 13, para. 29.]

History – S. 41 repealed by PA 2014, s. 24 and Sch. 13, para. 29, with effect from 6 April 2016 (as not brought into force by any earlier order under PA 2014, s. 56(1)). Former s. 41 read as follows:

"41 Reduced rates of Class 1 contributions

41(1) Subsections (1A) to (1E) apply where–
(a) the earnings paid to or for the benefit of an earner in any tax week are in respect of an employment which is contracted-out employment at the time of the payment, and
(b) the earner's service in the employment is service which qualifies him for a pension provided by a salary related contracted-out scheme;

and in subsections (1A) and (1B) **"the relevant part"**, in relation to those earnings, means so much of those earnings as exceeds the current lower earnings limit but not the upper accrual point (or the prescribed equivalents if the earner is paid otherwise than weekly).

41(1ZA) [Omitted by NICA 2008, s. 4 and Sch. 1, para. 10(3) and repealed by NICA 2008, s. 4 and Sch. 2.]
41(1A) The amount of any primary Class 1 contribution attributable to section 8(1)(a) of the Social Security Contributions and Benefits Act 1992 (c. 4) in respect of the earnings shall be reduced by an amount equal to 1.4 per cent of the relevant part of the earnings ("Amount R1").
41(1B) The amount of any secondary Class 1 contribution in respect of the earnings shall be reduced by an amount equal to 3.4 per cent of the relevant part of the earnings ("Amount R2").
41(1C) The aggregate of Amounts R1 and R2 shall be set off–
(a) first against the aggregate amount which the secondary contributor is liable to pay in respect of the contributions mentioned in subsections (1A) and (1B); and
(b) then (as to any balance) against any amount which the secondary contributor is liable to pay in respect of any primary or secondary Class 1 contribution in respect of earnings–
(i) paid to or for the benefit of any other employed earner (whether in contracted-out employment or not), and
(ii) in relation to which the secondary contributor is such a contributor;
and in this subsection any reference to a liability to pay an amount in respect of a primary Class 1 contribution is a reference to such a liability under paragraph 3 of Schedule 1 to the Social Security Contributions and Benefits Act 1992.
41(1D) If–
(a) any balance remains, and
(b) the secondary contributor makes an application for the purpose to the Inland Revenue,
the Inland Revenue shall, in such manner and at such time (or within such period) as may be prescribed, pay to the secondary contributor an amount equal to the remaining balance.
But regulations may make provision for the adjustment of an amount that would otherwise be payable under this subsection so as to avoid the payment of trivial or fractional amounts.
41(1E) If the Inland Revenue pay any amount under subsection (1D) which they are not required to pay, they may recover that amount from the secondary contributor in such manner and at such time (or within such period) as may be prescribed.
41(2) Where–
(a) an earner has ceased to be employed in an employment; and
(b) earnings are paid to him or for his benefit within the period of 6 weeks, or such other period as may be prescribed, from the day on which he so ceased,
that employment shall be treated for the purposes of subsection (1) as contracted-out employment at the time when the earnings are paid if it was contracted-out employment in relation to the earner when he was last employed in it.
41(3) This section shall not affect the amount of any primary Class 1 contribution which is payable at a reduced rate by virtue of regulations under section 19(4) of the Social Security Contributions and Benefits Act 1992 (reduced rates for married women and widows).".
In former s. 41(1), the words "the upper accrual point" substituted by NICA 2008, s. 4 and Sch. 1, para. 10(2), with effect in relation to 2009–10 and subsequent tax years.
In former s. 41(1) words "the applicable limit" substituted for "the current upper earnings limit" by PA 2007, s. 12 and Sch. 1, para. 37, with effect from 26 September 2007, s. 30(3).
Former s. 41(1), (1A) substituted and s. 41(1B), (1C) inserted by SSA 1998, s. 86(1) and Sch. 7, para. 127, with effect from 6 April 1999 (SI 1999/418).
In former s. 41(1A), "1.4 per cent" substituted for "1.6 per cent" by SI 2011/1036, art. 2(2), with effect from 6 April 2012.
In former s. 41(1B), "3.4 per cent" substituted for "3.7 per cent" by SI 2011/1036, art. 2(3), with effect from 6 April 2012.
Former s. 41(1) and 41(1A), including the sidenote and the preceding heading, substituted for former s. 41(1) by Pensions Act 1995, s. 137(2), with effect from 13 March 1996 for the purpose only of authorising the making of orders (SI 1996/778, art. 2(1) and Schedule, Pt. I), with effect from 6 April 1996 for the purpose only of authorising the making of regulations (SI 1996/778, art. 2(5), and Schedule, Pt. V), and with effect from 6 April 1997 for all other purposes (SI 1997/664 (C.23), art. 2(3) and Schedule, Pt. II).
Former s. 41(1ZA) omitted by NICA 2008, s. 4 and Sch. 1, para. 10(3) and repealed by NICA 2008, s. 4 and Sch. 2, with effect in relation to 2009–10 and subsequent tax years.
Former s. 41(1ZA) previously inserted by PA 2007, s. 12 and Sch. 1, para. 37, with effect from 26 September 2007, s. 30(3).
In former s. 41(1A), the words "attributable to section 8(1)(a) of the Social Security Contributions and Benefits Act 1992 (c. 4)" inserted by National Insurance Contributions Act 2002, s. 6 and Sch. 1, para. 36 with effect in relation to 2003–04 and subsequent tax years.
In former s. 41(1B) the figure "3.7" substituted for "3.5" by SI 2006/1009, art. 2, with effect from 6 April 2007.
Former s. 41(1A), (1B) and (1C) substituted and s. 41(1D) and (1E) inserted by WRPA 1999, Sch. 9, para. 6(3) with effect from 6 December 1999, only for the purpose of making regulations and 6 April 2000, for all other purposes (SI 1999/3420, art. 2). In s. 41(1), reference to s. 41(1E) inserted by WRPA 1999, Sch. 9, para. 6(2) with effect from the same dates.
In former s. 41(1A), percentages of 1.6 per cent specified by SI 1996/1054, art. 2, operative from 6 April 1997.
In former s. 41(1B), percentage of 3.5 percent specified by SI 2001/1356, art. 2, with effect from 6 April 2002.

Derivations – S. 41(1) (as originally enacted): SSPA 1975, s. 27(1)–(3); SSA 1985, Sch. 5, para. 17; SI 1992/795, art. 2.
S. 41(2): SSPA 1975, s. 27(4); SSA 1986, Sch. 10, para. 13.
S. 41(3): SSPA 1975, s. 27(5); SS(CP)A 1992, Sch. 2, para. 21.

Cross references – S. 45: prospective modification of PSA 1993, s. 45 by substituting a reference to the percentage mentioned in PSA 1993, s. 41(1A) (percentage used to reduce primary Class 1 contribution) for the reference to the age-related percentage in PSA 1993, s. 45(1) (amount of minimum contributions) by virtue of FA 2004, s. 202(3).
SSCBA 1992, s. 8: calculation of primary Class 1 contributions.
SSCBA 1992, s. 9: calculation of secondary Class 1 contributions.
SSCBA 1992, s. 19: general power to regulate liability for contributions.
FA 2004, s. 202(3): registered pension schemes: Inland Revenue contributions: minimum contributions under pensions legislation: modification of PSA 1993, s. 45 by substituting a reference to the percentage mentioned in PSA 1993, s. 41(1A) (percentage used to reduce primary Class 1 contribution) for the reference to the age-related percentage in PSA 1993, s. 45(1) (amount of minimum contributions).
SI 2001/1004, reg. 8: equivalent amounts.
SI 2001/1004, reg. 53: return of contributions.
SI 2001/1004, reg. 120: earnings periods for mariners and apportionment of earnings.

42 Review and alteration of rates of contributions applicable under s. 41

42 [Repealed by PA 2014, s. 24 and Sch. 13, para. 30.]

History – S. 42 repealed by PA 2014, s. 24 and Sch. 13, para. 30, with effect from 6 April 2016 (as not brought into force by any earlier order under PA 2014, s. 56(1)). Note that there was no duty, after 13 July 2014 and before the repeal of s. 42 comes into force, to lay before Parliament any reports under s. 42 (PA 2014, Sch. 13, para. 30(2) and s. 56(3)(e)). Former s. 42 read as follows:
"42 Review and alteration of rates of contributions applicable under s. 41
42(1) The Secretary of State may from time to time, and shall when required by subsection (2), lay before each House of Parliament–
(a) a report by the Government Actuary or the Deputy Government Actuary on–

(i) the percentages for the time being applying under section 41(1A) and (1B), and

(ii) any changes since the preparation of the last report under this paragraph in the factors in his opinion affecting the cost of providing benefits of an actuarial value equivalent to that of the benefits (or parts of benefits) which, in accordance with section 48A below and Schedules 4A and 4B to the Social Security Contributions and Benefits Act 1992, are foregone by or in respect of members of salary related contracted-out schemes; and

(b) a report by the Secretary of State stating whether he considers that, in view of the report of the Government Actuary or the Deputy Government Actuary, there should be an alteration in either or both of those percentages and, if so, what alteration is in his opinion required.

42(2) The Secretary of State shall lay such reports at intervals of not more than five years.

42(3) If in a report under subsection (1)(b) the Secretary of State states that he considers that there should be an alteration in either or both of the percentages mentioned in section 41(1A) and (1B), he shall prepare and lay before each House of Parliament with the report the draft of an order making that alteration; and if the draft is approved by resolution of each House the Secretary of State shall make the order in the form of the draft.

42(4) An order under subsection (3) shall have effect from the beginning of such tax year as may be specified in the order, but not a tax year earlier than the second after that in which the order is made.

42(5) No alteration of those percentages shall introduce any distinction on grounds of age or sex.

42(6) A draft of an order making alterations in either or both of those percentages may contain consequential provisions altering any percentage for the time being specified in paragraph 2(3) of Schedule 4 as that percentage applies in relation to earnings paid or payable on or after the day as from which the order is to have effect.".

In former s. 42(1)(a)(i) and (3) the words "41(1A) and (1B)" substituted by CSPSSA 2000, Sch. 5, para. 4, with effect from 28 July 2000.
In former s. 42(1)(a)(ii) words "Schedules 4A and 4B" substituted by PA 2007, s. 11 and Sch. 3, para. 12, with effect from 26 September 2007, s. 30(3).
In former s. 42(1)(a)(ii) words "(or parts of benefits) which, in accordance with section 48A below and Schedule 4A to the Social Security Contributions and Benefits Act 1992," substituted by the Child Support, Pensions and Social Security Act 2000, s. 34 and 86, with effect from 8 January 2001 for the purposes only of making regulations and orders, from 25 January 2001 for the purposes of making reports and orders under the Pension Schemes Act 1993, s. 42, 42B and 45A and from 6 April 2002 for all other purposes.
Former s. 42(1)(a) substituted by Pensions Act 1995, s. 137(3), with effect from 13 March 1996 for the purpose only of authorising the making of orders (SI 1996/778, reg. 2(1), Schedule, Pt. I), with effect from 6 April 1996 for the purpose only of authorising the making of regulations (SI 1996/778, reg. 2(5)(a), Schedule, Pt. V), and with effect from 6 April 1997 for all other purposes (SI 1997/664 (C. 23), art. 2(3), Schedule, Pt. II).
In former s. 42(3), the words "41(1A)(a)" substituted by Pensions Act 1995, Sch. 5, para. 41, with effect from 6 April 1997 by virtue of SI 1997/664 (C. 23), s. 2(3), Schedule, Pt. II.

Derivations – S. 42(1): SSPA 1975, s. 28(1), (2); SS(CP)A 1992, Sch. 2, para. 22.
S. 42(2)–(5): SSPA 1975, s. 28(3)–(6).
S. 42(6): SSPA 1975, s. 28(7); SSA 1985, Sch. 5, para. 18.

Cross references – Pensions Act 1995, s. 137(4): modification of s. 42 in relation to the first report under s. 42(1)(a) laid after the passing of the Pensions Act 1995.

Statutory instruments – SI 2006/1009: partly made under s. 42.
SI 2011/1036: partly made under s. 42.

Notes – The principal appointed day for the purposes of Pensions Act 1995, Pt. III, is 6 April 1997.

REDUCED RATES OF CONTRIBUTIONS AND REBATES, FOR MEMBERS OF MONEY PURCHASE CONTRACTED-OUT SCHEMES

42A Reduced rates of Class 1 contributions, and rebates

42A(1) Subsections (2) to (2D) and (3) apply where–

(a) the earnings paid to or for the benefit of an earner in any tax week are in respect of an employment which is contracted-out employment at the time of the payment, and

(b) the earner's service in the employment is service which qualifies him for a pension provided by a money purchase contracted-out scheme;

and in subsections (2) and (2A) **"the relevant part"**, in relation to those earnings, means so much of those earnings as exceeds the current lower earnings limit but not the upper accrual point (or the prescribed equivalents if the earner is paid otherwise than weekly).

42A(2) The amount of any primary Class 1 contribution attributable to section 8(1)(a) of the Social Security Contributions and Benefits Act 1992 in respect of the earnings shall be reduced by an amount equal to the appropriate flat-rate percentage of the relevant part of the earnings ("Amount R1").

42A(2A) The amount of any secondary Class 1 contribution in respect of the earnings shall be reduced by an amount equal to the appropriate flat-rate percentage of the relevant part of the earnings ("Amount R2").

42A(2B) The aggregate of Amounts R1 and R2 shall be set off–

(a) first against the aggregate amount which the secondary contributor is liable to pay in respect of the contributions mentioned in subsections (2) and (2A); and

(b) then (as to any balance) against any amount which the secondary contributor is liable to pay in respect of a primary or secondary Class 1 contribution in respect of earnings–

(i) paid to or for the benefit of any other employed earner (whether in contracted-out employment or not), and

(ii) in relation to which the secondary contributor is such a contributor;

and in this subsection any reference to a liability to pay an amount in respect of a primary Class 1 contribution is a reference to such a liability under paragraph 3 of Schedule 1 to the Social Security Contributions and Benefits Act 1992.

42A(2C) If–

(a) any balance remains, and

(b) the secondary contributor makes an application for the purpose to the Inland Revenue,

the Inland Revenue shall, in such manner and at such time (or within such period) as may be prescribed, pay to the secondary contributor an amount equal to the remaining balance.

But regulations may make provision for the adjustment of an amount that would otherwise be payable under this subsection so as to avoid the payment of trivial or fractional amounts.

42A(2D) If the Inland Revenue pay any amount under subsection (2C) which they are not required to pay, they may recover that amount from the secondary contributor in such manner and at such time (or within such period) as may be prescribed.

42A(3) Subject to subsection (5A) the Inland Revenue shall except in prescribed circumstances or in respect of prescribed periods pay in respect of that earner and that tax week to the trustees or managers of the scheme or, in prescribed circumstances, to a prescribed person the amount by which–

(a) the appropriate age-related percentage of that part of those earnings, exceeds

(b) the appropriate flat-rate percentage of that part of those earnings.

42A(4) Regulations may make provision–

(a) as to the manner in which and time at which or period within which payments under subsection (3) are to be made,

(b) for the adjustment of the amount which would otherwise be payable under that subsection so as to avoid the payment of trivial or fractional amounts,

(c) for earnings to be calculated or estimated in such manner and on such basis as may be prescribed for the purpose of determining whether any, and if so what, payments under subsection (3) are to be made.

42A(5) If the Inland Revenue pay an amount under subsection (3) which they are not required to pay or are not required to pay to the person to whom, or in respect of whom, they pay it, they may recover it from any person to whom, or in respect of whom, they paid it.

42A(5A) Where–

(a) a payment under subsection (3) is due in respect of an earner, and

(b) apart from this subsection, the payment would under regulations under subsection (3) be made to the earner,

HMRC are not required to make the payment if they determine that the cost to them of administering the payment would exceed the amount of the payment.".

42A(6) Where–

(a) an earner has ceased to be employed in an employment, and

(b) earnings are paid to him or for his benefit within the period of six weeks, or such other period as may be prescribed, from the day on which he so ceased,

that employment shall be treated for the purposes of this section as contracted-out employment at the time when the earnings are paid if it was contracted-out employment in relation to the earner when he was last employed in it.

42A(7) Subsection (3) of section 41 applies for the purposes of this section as it applies for the purposes of that.

42A(8) For the purposes of this section **"the appropriate age-related percentage"** and **"the appropriate flat-rate percentage"**, in relation to a tax year beginning before the first abolition date, are the percentages specified as such for that tax year in an order made under section 42B (as it had effect prior to that date).

Prospective amendments – S. 42A repealed by PA 2007, s. 15 and Sch. 4, para. 51, and s. 27 and Sch. 7, Pt. 7, with effect from a date to be appointed under s. 30(2).

History – In s. 42A(1), the words "the upper accrual point" substituted for "the current upper earnings limit for that week" by NICA 2008, s. 4 and Sch. 1, para. 11(1), with effect in relation to 2009–10 and subsequent tax years.

S. 42A(1), (2) substituted and s. 42A(2A), (2B) inserted by SSA 1998, s. 86(1) and Sch. 7, para. 128, with effect from 6 April 1999 (SI 1999/418).

In s. 42A(2), the words "attributable to section 8(1)(a) of the Social Security Contributions and Benefits Act 1992" inserted by the National Insurance Contributions Act 2002, s. 6 and Sch. 1, para. 37 with effect in relation to 2003–04 and subsequent tax years.

S. 42A(2), (2A) and (2B) substituted and s. 42A(2C) and (2D) inserted by WRPA 1999, Sch. 9, para. 7(3) with effect from 6 December 1999, only for the purpose of making regulations and 6 April 2000, for all other purposes (SI 1999/3420, art. 2). In s. 42A(1), reference to s. 42A(2D) inserted by WRPA 1999, Sch. 9, para. 7(2) with effect from the same dates.

In s. 42A(3) the words "Subject to subsection (5A)" inserted by SI 2012/1730, art. 5(8)(a), with effect from 6 April 2012.

In s. 42A(3) and (5) "Inland Revenue" substituted and in s. 42A(5) "pay", "they" and "are" substituted in each place where the words occur by SSC(TF)A 1999, s. 1 and Sch. 1, para. 46, with effect from 25 February 1999, for the purpose making regulations, (SSC(TF) A 1999, s. 28(2)(b)) and 1 April 1999 for all other purposes (SI 1999/527).

S. 42A(5A) inserted by SI 2012/1730, art. 5(8)(b), with effect from 6 April 2012.

In s. 42A(8), the words "the first abolition date" substituted for the words "the abolition date" by PA 2014, s. 24 and Sch. 13, para. 2, with effect from 6 April 2016 (as not brought into force by any earlier order under PA 2014, s. 56(1)).

S. 42A(8) inserted by PA 2007, s. 15 and Sch. 4, para. 17, with effect from 6 April 2012 (SI 2011/1267, art. 2(a)).
S. 42A inserted by Pensions Act 1995, s. 137(5), with effect from 13 March 1996 for the purpose only of authorising the making of orders (SI 1996/778, art. 2(1), Schedule, Pt. I), from 6 April 1996 for the purpose only of authorising the making of orders (SI 1996/778, art. 2(5)(a), Schedule, Pt. V), and from 6 April 1997 for all other purposes (SI 1997/664 (C. 23), art. 2(3), Schedule, Pt. II).

Cross references – FA 2004, s. 188(3): registered pension schemes: members' contributions: relief for contributions.
SI 1996/1055: specifies appropriate flat-rate percentage in respect of earners for the tax years 1997–98 to 2001–02 as follows:

- primary Class 1 contribution: 1.6 per cent;
- secondary Class 1 contribution: 1.5 per cent;

and appropriate age-related percentages in respect of earners in those tax years (Table in Schedule to Order).
SI 1998/945: reduced rates of Class 1 contributions, and rebates (money purchase contracted-out schemes.
SI 2006/1009: specifies appropriate flat-rate percentage in respect of earners for the tax years 2007–08 to 2011–12 as follows:

- primary Class 1 contribution: 1.6 per cent;
- secondary Class 1 contribution: 1.4 per cent

and appropriate age-related percentages in respect of earners in those tax years (Table in Schedule to Order).
SI 2011/1036, art. 3: specifies appropriate flat-rate percentage for the 2012–13 tax year as follows:

- primary Class 1 contribution: 1.4 per cent;
- secondary Class 1 contribution: 1.0 per cent

and appropriate age-related percentages in respect of earners in those tax years (Table in Schedule to Order).

42B Determination and alteration of rates of contributions, and rebates, applicable under section 42A

42B [Repealed by PA 2007, s. 15 and Sch. 4, para. 18, and s. 27 and Sch. 7, Pt. 6.]

History – S. 42B repealed by PA 2007, s. 15 and Sch. 4, para. 18, and s. 27 and Sch. 7, Pt. 6, with effect from 6 April 2012 (SI 2011/1267, art. 2(a)).

MINIMUM CONTRIBUTIONS: MEMBERS OF APPROPRIATE PERSONAL PENSION SCHEMES

43 Payment of minimum contributions to personal pension schemes.

43(1) Subject to the following provisions of this Part, the Inland Revenue shall, except in such circumstances or in respect of such periods as may be prescribed, pay minimum contributions in respect of an employed earner for any period during which the earner–

(a) is over the age of 16 but has not attained pensionable age;

(b) is not a married woman or widow who has made an election which is still operative that so much of her liability in respect of primary Class 1 contributions as is attributable to section 8(1)(a) of the Social Security Contributions and Benefits Act 1992 (c. 4) shall be a liability to contribute at a reduced rate; and

(c) is a member of an appropriate personal pension scheme which is for the time being the earner's chosen scheme.

43(2) Subject to subsection (3), minimum contributions in respect of an earner shall be paid to the trustees or managers of the earner's chosen scheme.

43(3) In such circumstances as may be prescribed minimum contributions shall be paid to a prescribed person.

43(4) Where the condition mentioned earlier in subsection (1)(a) or (c) ceases to be satisfied in the case of an earner in respect of whom the Inland Revenue is required to pay minimum contributions, the duty of the Inland Revenue to pay them shall cease as from a date determined in accordance with regulations.

43(5) If the Inland Revenue pays an amount by way of minimum contributions which he is not required to pay, he may recover it–

(a) from the person to whom he paid it, or

(b) from any person in respect of whom he paid it.

43(6) If the Inland Revenue pays in respect of an earner an amount by way of minimum contributions which he is required to pay, but does not pay it to the trustees or managers of the earner's chosen scheme, he may recover it from the person to whom he paid it or from the earner.

43(6A) Where–

(a) a payment under subsection (1) is due in respect of an earner, and

(b) apart from this subsection, the payment would under regulations under subsection (3) be made to the earner,

HMRC are not required to make the payment if they determine that the cost to them of administering the payment would exceed the amount of the payment.

43(7) In this section **"the earner's chosen scheme"** means the scheme which was immediately before the first abolition date the earner's chosen scheme in accordance with section 44 (as it had effect prior to that date).

Prospective amendments – S. 43 repealed by PA 2007, s. 15 and Sch. 4, para. 52, and s. 27 and Sch. 7, Pt. 7, with effect from a date to be appointed under s. 30(2).

History – In s. 43 "Inland Revenue" substituted in each place where the words occur and in s. 43(4) to (6) "pay", "they", "do" and "are" substituted in each place where the words occur by SSC(TF)A 1999, s. 1 and Sch. 1, para. 47, with effect from 25 February 1999, for the purpose making regulations, (SSC(TF)A 1999, s. 28(2)(b)) and 1 April 1999 for all other purposes (SI 1999/527).
In s. 43(1)(b), the words "so much of her liability in respect of primary Class 1 contributions as is attributable to section 8(1)(a) of the Social Security Contributions and Benefits Act 1992 (c. 4)" substituted by the National Insurance Contributions Act 2002, s. 6 and Sch. 1, para. 38 with effect in relation to 2003–04 and subsequent tax years.
In s. 43(1), words "or in respect of such periods" inserted by Pensions Act 1995, s. 151 and Sch. 5, para. 42, with effect from 6 April 1997 (SI 1997/664 (C. 23), art. 2(3) and Schedule, Pt. II).
S. 43(6A) inserted by SI 2012/1730, art. 5(9), with effect from 6 April 2012.
In s. 43(7), the words "the first abolition date" substituted for the words "the abolition date" by PA 2014, s. 24 and Sch. 13, para. 2, with effect from 6 April 2016 (as not brought into force by any earlier order under PA 2014, s. 56(1)).
S. 43(7) inserted by PA 2007, s. 15 and Sch. 4, para. 19, with effect from 6 April 2012 (SI 2011/1267, art. 2(a)).

Cross references – FA 2004, s. 188(3) (prospective provision which does not come into force until 6 April 2006): registered pension schemes: members' contributions: relief for contributions.
FA 2004, s. 202(1) (prospective provision which does not come into force until 6 April 2006): registered pension schemes: Inland Revenue contributions: minimum contributions under pensions legislation.

NIC Statutes

45 Amount of minimum contributions

45(1) In relation to any tax week falling within a period for which the Inland Revenue is required to pay minimum contributions in respect of an earner, the amount of those contributions shall be an amount equal to the appropriate age-related percentage of so much of the earnings paid in that week (other than earnings in respect of contracted-out employment) as exceeds the current lower earnings limit but not the upper accrual point (or the prescribed equivalents if he is paid otherwise than weekly).

45(2) [Repealed by Pensions Act 1995, s. 138(2), 177 and Sch. 7, Pt. III.]

45(3) Regulations may make provision–

(a) for earnings to be calculated or estimated in such manner and on such basis as may be prescribed for the purpose of determining whether any, and if so what, minimum contributions are payable in respect of them;

(b) for the adjustment of the amount which would otherwise be payable by way of minimum contributions so as to avoid the payment of trivial or fractional amounts;

(c) for the intervals at which, for the purposes of minimum contributions, payments of earnings are to be treated as made;

(d) [repealed by Pensions Act 1995, s. 151 and Sch. 5, para. 43, s. 177 and Sch. 7, Pt. III;]

(e) for this section to have effect in prescribed cases as if for any reference to a tax week there were substituted a reference to a prescribed period;

(f) as to the manner in which and time at which or period within which minimum contributions are to be made.

45(4) For the purposes of this section **"the appropriate age-related percentage"**, in relation to a tax year beginning before the first abolition date, is the percentage (or percentages) specified as such for that tax year in an order made under section 45A (as it had effect prior to that date).

Prospective amendments – S. 45 repealed by PA 2007, s. 15 and Sch. 4, para. 53, and s. 27 and Sch. 7, Pt. 7, with effect from a date to be appointed under s. 30(2).

History – In s. 45(1), the words "the upper accrual point" substituted for "the current upper earnings limit for that week" by NICA 2008, s. 4 and Sch. 1, para. 12(1), with effect in relation to 2009–10 and subsequent tax years.
In s. 45(1) "Inland Revenue are" substituted by SSC(TF)A 1999, s. 1 and Sch. 1, para. 49, with effect from 25 February 1999, for the purpose making regulations, (SSC(TF)A 1999, s. 28(2)(b)) and 1 April 1999 for all other purposes (SI 1999/527).
S. 45(1) substituted, and s. 45(2), 45(3)(d) and part of s. 45(3)(e), repealed by Pensions Act 1995, s. 138, 151, 177 and Sch. 5, para. 43, Sch. 7, Pt. III, with effect from 6 April 1997 (SI 1997/664, art. 2(3) and Schedule, Pt. II).
In s. 45(4), the words "the first abolition date" substituted for the words "the abolition date" by PA 2014, s. 24 and Sch. 13, para. 2, with effect from 6 April 2016 (as not brought into force by any earlier order under PA 2014, s. 56(1)).
S. 45(4) inserted by PA 2007, s. 15 and Sch. 4, para. 21, with effect from 6 April 2012 (SI 2011/1267, art. 2(a)).

Cross references – S. 41(1A): modification of PSA 1993, s. 45 by substituting a reference to the percentage mentioned in PSA 1993, s. 41(1A) (percentage used to reduce primary Class 1 contribution) for the reference to the age-related percentage in PSA 1993, s. 45(1) (amount of minimum contributions) by virtue of FA 2004, s. 202(3) (with effect from 1 6 April 2006.
FA 2004, s. 202(3) registered pension schemes: Inland Revenue contributions: minimum contributions under pensions legislation: modification of PSA 1993, s. 45 by substituting a reference to the percentage mentioned in PSA 1993, s. 41(1A) (percentage used to reduce primary Class 1 contribution) for the reference to the age-related percentage in PSA 1993, s. 45(1) (amount of minimum contributions), with effect from 6 April 2006.
SI 1998/944: minimum contributions to appropriate personal pension schemes.
SI 2006/1009, art. 4: age-related percentages for appropriate personal pension schemes with effect from 6 April 2007 for the tax years 2007–08 to 2011–12.
SI 2011/1036, art. 4: age-related percentages for appropriate personal pension schemes with effect from 6 April 2012 for the tax year 2012–13.

45A Determination and alteration of rates of minimum contributions under section 45

45A [Repealed by PA 2007, s. 15 and Sch. 4, para. 22, and s. 27 and Sch. 7, Pt. 6.]

History – S. 45A repealed by PA 2007, s. 15 and Sch. 4, para. 22, and s. 27 and Sch. 7, Pt. 6, with effect from 6 April 2012 (SI 2011/1267, art. 2(a)).

45B Money purchase and personal pension schemes: verification of ages

45B [Repealed by PA 2007, s. 15 and Sch. 4, para. 54, and s. 27 and Sch. 7, Pt. 7.]

History – S. 45B repealed by PA 2007, s. 15 and Sch. 4, para. 54, and s. 27 and Sch. 7, Pt. 7, with effect from 6 April 2015 (SI 2011/1267, art. 3(a)(iv)).

PART XI – GENERAL AND MISCELLANEOUS PROVISIONS

INFORMATION ABOUT SCHEMES

158 Disclosure of information between government departments etc.

158(1) No obligation as to secrecy imposed by statute or otherwise on Revenue and Customs officials shall prevent information obtained or held in connection with the assessment or collection of income tax from being disclosed–

(a) to the Secretary of State,

(b) to the Department of Health and Social Services for Northern Ireland, or

(c) to an officer of either of them authorised to receive such information, in connection with the operation of this Act (except Chapter II of Part VII and sections 157 and 161) or of any corresponding enactment of Northern Ireland legislation.

158(1A) No obligation as to secrecy imposed by statute or otherwise on Revenue and Customs officials shall prevent information obtained or held for the purposes of Part III of this Act from being disclosed–

(a) to the Secretary of State,

(b) to the Department of Health and Social Services for Northern Ireland, or

(c) to an officer of either of them authorised to receive such information,

in connection with the operation of this Act or of any corresponding enactment of Northern Ireland legislation.

158(2,3) [Omitted by Pensions Act 1995, Sch. 5, para. 66 and Sch. 7, Pt. III.]

158(4) In relation to persons who are carrying on or have carried on wholly or partly in the United Kingdom a trade, profession or vocation income from which is chargeable to tax under Part 2 of the Income Tax (Trading and Other Income) Act 2005 or Case I or II of Schedule D, disclosure under subsection (1) relating to that trade, profession or vocation shall be limited to information about the commencement or cessation of, and employed earners engaged in, that trade, profession or vocation, but sufficient information may also be given to identify the persons concerned.

158(5) Subsections (1) and (1A3) extend only to disclosure by or under the authority of the Inland Revenue.

158(6) Subject to subsection (7), information which is the subject of disclosure to any person by virtue of subsection (1) or (1A), shall not be further disclosed to any other person, except where the further disclosure is made–

(a) to a person to whom disclosure could by virtue of this section have been made by or under the authority of the Inland Revenue; or

(b) for the purposes of any civil or criminal proceedings in connection with the operation of this Act (except Chapter II of Part VII and sections 157 and 161); or

(c) for the purposes of Chapter II of Part I of the Social Security Act 1998 or any corresponding provisions of Northern Ireland legislation; or

(ca) for the purposes of Part II of the Social Security Contributions (Transfer of Functions, etc.) Act 1999 or any corresponding provisions of Northern Ireland legislation.

(d) [omitted by Pensions Act 1995, Sch. 5, para. 66 and Sch. 7, Pt. III].

158(7) The Secretary of State, and the Inland Revenue may provide the Registrar with such information as he may request for the purposes of the register; and no obligation as to secrecy or confidentiality imposed by statute or otherwise on–

(a) persons employed in the Department of Social Security, or

(b) Revenue and Customs officials,

(c) [omitted by Pensions Act 1995, Sch. 5, para. 66 and Sch. 7, Pt. III,]

shall prevent them from disclosing to the Registrar such information as is necessary for the purposes of the register.

158(8) [Omitted by Pensions Act 1995, Sch. 5, para. 66 and Sch. 7, Pt. III.]

158(9) In this section **"Revenue and Customs officials"** has the meaning given by section 18 of the Commissioners for Revenue and Customs Act 2005 (confidentiality).

History – In s. 158(1), (1A) and (7)(b), the words "Revenue and Customs officials" substituted by CRCA 2005, s. 50 and Sch. 4, para. 51(a), with effect from 18 April 2005 (by virtue of SI 2005/1126, art. 2).

S. 158(1A) inserted by SSC(TF)A 1999, s. 6 and Sch. 6, para. 7(2), with effect from 1 April 1999 (SI 1999/527).

In s. 158(4) the words "wholly or partly in the United Kingdom" and "Part 2 of the Income Tax (Trading and Other Income) Act 2005 or" inserted by ITTOIA 2005, s. 882(1) and Sch. 1, para. 468; effective for income tax purposes for 2005–06 onwards and for corporation tax purposes for accounting periods ending after 5 April 2005 (ITTOIA 2005, s. 883(1)).

In s. 158(5) reference to subsection (1A) substituted for (3) by SSC(TF)A 1999, s. 6 and Sch. 6, para. 7(3), with effect from 1 April 1999 (SI 1999/527).

In s. 158(6)(c) the words "Chapter II of Part I of the Social Security Act 1998" substituted by SSA 1998, s. 86(1) and Sch. 7, para. 129, with effect from 5 July 1999, for the purposes of any matter to which, by virtue of PSA 1993, s. 170, provisions of SSA 1998, Pt. I, Ch. II are to apply (SI 1999/1958 (C. 51), art. 2(1)(b)(iv)); and with effect from 29 November 1999 in so far as it was not already in force (except for the purposes of housing benefit, council tax benefit and decisions to which SI 1999/527, art. 4(6) applies; i.e. pre-1 April 1999 decisions under SSAA 1992, s. 17(1), s. 20(3) and PSA 1993, s. 170(1)) (SI 1999/3178 (C. 81), art. 2(1)(a); 2(2) and Sch. 1). The wording of s. 158(6)(c), as it continues to apply for purposes other than those mentioned above, reads as follows:

"(c) for the purposes of sections 17 to 62 of the Social Security Administration Act 1992 or any corresponding provisions of Northern Ireland legislation; or"

S. 158(6)(ca) inserted by SSC(TF)A 1999, s. 6 and Sch. 6, para. 7(4)(b), with effect from 1 April 1999 (SI 1999/527).

In s. 158(6) reference to subsection (1A) inserted by SSC(TF)A 1999, s. 6 and Sch. 6, para. 7(4)(a), with effect from 1 April 1999 (SI 1999/527).

S. 158(2), (3) and (8) omitted and s. 158(6) and (7) amended by omitting words "(2) or (3)", s. 158(6)(d) (and the "or" immediately preceding it) and s. 158(7)(c) (and the "or" immediately preceding it), and by substituting, in s. 158(7), the words "and the Inland Revenue" and inserting the word "or" after para. (a). These amendments were made by Pensions Act 1995, Sch. 5, para. 66 and Sch. 7, Pt. III, with effect from 6 April 1997 (SI 1997/664 (C. 23), art. 2(3), Schedule, Pt. II).

S. 158(9) added by CRCA 2005, s. 50 and Sch. 4, para. 51(b), with effect from 18 April 2005 (by virtue of SI 2005/1126, art. 2).

Derivations – S. 158(1): SSA 1973, s. 89(1), 99(1); SS(CP)A 1975, Sch. 2, para. 58; SSPA 1975, Sch. 4, para. 30; SSA 1986, s. 59(1); SSA 1989, s. 20(a).

S. 158(2) (as originally enacted): SSA 1973, s. 89(2).

S. 158(3): SSA 1973, s. 89(2A); SSA 1985, Sch. 5, para. 2(a); SSA 1982, s. 59(3); SS(CP)A 1992, Sch. 2, para. 83.

S. 158(4): SSA 1986, s. 59(2); SSA 1989, s. 20(b).

S. 158(5), (6) (as originally enacted): SSA 1973, s. 89(3); SSPA 1975, Sch. 4, para. 30; SSA 1985, Sch. 5, para. 2(b); SSA 1986, s. 59(3); SS(CP)A 1992, Sch. 2, para. 83.

S. 158(7): SSPA 1975, s. 59K(6).

S. 158(8): SSPA 1975, s. 57; SI 1987/1116, reg. 3(9).

158A Other disclosures by the Secretary of State

158A(1) The Secretary of State may, in spite of any obligation as to secrecy or confidentiality imposed by statute or otherwise on him or on persons employed in the Department for Work and Pensions, disclose any regulated information received by him in connection with his functions under this Act or the Pensions Act 1995 to any person specified in the first column of the following Table if he considers that the disclosure would enable or assist the person to discharge the functions specified in relation to the person in the second column of the Table.

TABLE

Persons	*Functions*
The Bank of England.	Any of its functions.
The Financial Services Authority.	Functions under the legislation relating to friendly societies, under the Building Societies Act 1986 or under the Financial Services and Markets Act 2000.
The Regulatory Authority.	Functions under this Act, the Pensions Act 1995, the Welfare Reform and Pensions Act 1999 or the Pensions Act 2004 or any enactment in force in Northern Ireland corresponding to any of those enactments.
The Pensions Ombudsman.	Functions conferred by or by virtue of this Act or any enactment in force in Northern Ireland corresponding to it.
The Board of the Pension Protection Fund.	Functions conferred by or by virtue of Part 2 of the Pensions Act 2004 or any enactment in force in Northern Ireland corresponding to that Part.
The Ombudsman for the Board of the Pension Protection Fund.	Functions conferred by or by virtue of Part 2 of the Pensions Act 2004 or any enactment in force in Northern Ireland corresponding to that Part.

NIC Statutes

Persons	*Functions*
A person appointed under– (a) section 167 of the Financial Services and Markets Act 2000, (b) subsections (3) or (5) of section 168 of that Act, or (c) section 284 of that Act,	Functions in relation to that investigation.
A body designated under section 326(1) of the Financial Services and Markets Act 2000	Functions in its capacity as a body designated under that section.
A recognised investment exchange, recognised clearing house, EEA central counterparty, third country central counterparty, recognised CSD, EEA CSD or third country CSD (as defined by section 285 of that Act).	Functions in its capacity as an exchange, clearing house or central securities depository recognised under that Act or as an EEA central counterparty or EEA CSD authorised by the competent authority of the EEA State in which it is established, or as a third country central counterparty or third country CSD recognised by the European Securities and Markets Authority established by Regulation (EU) No 1095/2010.

158A(1AA) In subsection (1), **"regulated information"** means information received by the Secretary of State in connection with his functions under–

(a) this Act,

(b) the Pensions Act 1995, or

(c) the Pensions Act 2004,

other than information supplied to him under section 235(2) of, or paragraph 2 of Schedule 10 to, the Pensions Act 2004 (supply of information for retirement planning purposes etc).

158A(1A) The Inland Revenue may, in spite of any obligation as to secrecy or confidentiality imposed by statute or otherwise on them or on their officers, disclose any information received by them in connection with their functions under Part III of this Act to any person specified in the first column of the Table in subsection (1) if they consider that the disclosure would enable or assist the person to discharge the functions specified in relation to the person in the second column of the Table.

158A(2) The Secretary of State may by order–

(a) amend the Table in subsection (1) by–

(i) adding any person exercising regulatory functions and specifying functions in relation to that person,

(ii) removing any person for the time being specified in the Table, or

(iii) altering the functions for the time being specified in the Table in relation to any person, or

(b) restrict the circumstances in which, or impose conditions subject to which, disclosure may be made to any person for the time being specified in the Table.

History – In s. 158A(1), in the Table, in the entry for " a recognised investment exchange", in the first column, the words ", recognised clearing house, EEA central counterparty, third country central counterparty, recognised CSD, EEA CSD or third country CSD" substituted for the words "or a recognised clearing house", and in the second column, the words ", clearing house or central securities depository" substituted for the words "or clearing house" and the words "or as an EEA central counterparty or EEA CSD authorised by the competent authority of the EEA State in which it is established, or as a third country central counterparty or third country CSD recognised by the European Securities and Markets Authority established by Regulation (EU) No 1095/2010" inserted by SI 2017/1064, reg. 10 and Sch., para. 7(3), with effect from 28 November 2017.

In s. 158A(1) the word "regulated" and the Table entries for "The Pensions Ombudsman", "The Board of the Pension Protection Fund" and "The Ombudsman for the Board of the Pension Protection Fund" inserted and various entries deleted by the Pensions Act 2004, s. 319(1) and Sch. 12, para. 9 and 26, with effect from 6 April 2005 (by virtue of SI 2005/275).

In s. 158A(1) the words "the Department for Work and Pensions" substituted by SI 2002/1397, art. 12 and Schedule, para. 9(1) and (3), with effect from 27 June 2002.

In s. 158A(1) the Table entries for "A person appointed under" various FSMA 2000 sections, "A body designated under section 326(1) of FSMA 2000" and "A recognised investment exchange or a recognised clearing house" inserted and various entries omitted by SI 2001/3649, art. 124, with effect from 1 December 2001.

In s. 158A(1), the words in the second column of the Table against "The Bank of England" substituted by Bank of England Act 1998 with effect from 23 April 1998.

S. 158A(1A) inserted by SSC(TF)A 1999, s. 6 and Sch. 6, para. 8, with effect from 1 April 1999 (SI 1999/527).

S. 158A(1AA) inserted by the Pensions Act 2004, s. 319(1) and Sch. 12, para. 9 and 26, with effect from 6 April 2005 (by virtue of SI 2005/275).

S. 158A inserted by Pensions Act 1995, Sch. 6, para. 9, with effect from 6 April 1996 by virtue of SI 1996/778, art. 2(4), Schedule, Pt. IV.

APPLICATION OF PROVISIONS RELATING TO SOCIAL SECURITY ADMINISTRATION

167 Application of general provisions relating to administration of social security

167(1) The Social Security Administration Act 1992 shall apply as if references to that Act in the provisions mentioned in subsection (2) included references to the provisions referred to in section 164(1)(b) of this Act (in this section referred to as **"the relevant provisions"**).

167(2) The provisions referred to in subsection (1) are the following provisions of the Social Security Administration Act 1992–

section 116 (legal proceedings)

section 125 (regulations as to notification of deaths)

section 177 (co-ordination with Northern Ireland)

section 180 (payment of travelling expenses by the Secretary of State)

section 180A (payment of travelling expenses by Inland Revenue).

167(3) [Repealed by SSC(TF)A 1999, s. 18 and Sch. 7, para. 18(3).]

167(4) [Repealed by SSA 1998, s. 86(2) and Sch. 8).]

167(5) Sections 124 to 124B of the Social Security Administration Act 1992 (provisions relating to age, death, marriage and civil partnership) shall apply as if information for the purposes mentioned in section 124(1) of that Act included information for the purposes of the relevant provisions.

167(6) Section 121 of the Social Security Contributions and Benefits Act 1992 (treatment of certain marriages) shall apply to the relevant provisions.

History – In s. 167(2) the reference to SSAA 1992, s. 180A inserted by SSC(TF)A 1999, s. 18 and Sch. 7, para. 18(2) with effect from 1 April 1999 (SI 1999/527).

S. 167(3) repealed by SSC(TF)A 1999, s. 18 and Sch. 7, para. 18(3) and s. 26(3); Sch. 10, Pt. I with effect from 5 July 1999 (SI 1999/1662).

S. 167(4) repealed by SSA 1998, s. 86(2) and Sch. 8, for the purposes of any matter to which, by virtue of PSA 1993, s. 170, provisions of SSA 1998, Pt. I, Ch. II are to apply, with effect from 5 July 1999 (SI 1999/1958 (C. 51), art. 2(1)(b)(iv)). It was repealed for most other purposes with effect from 29 November 1999 (SI 1999/3178, art. 2(1)(a)). It remains in force for the purposes of council tax benefit, housing benefit and certain decisions made before 1st April 1999 by the Secretary of State or an adjudication officer (SI 1999/3178, art. 2(2)).

S. 167(5) substituted by SI 2005/3129, Sch. 1, para. 5 with effect from 5 December 2005.

Derivations – SSA 1986, s. 66(2); SS(CP)A 1992, Sch. 2, para. 40, Sch. 3, para. 10.

Cross references – S. 41: reduced rates of Class 1 contributions for earners in contracted-out employment.
S. 42: review and alteration of rates of contributions applicable under s. 41.
S. 164(1) (not reproduced): provisions applicable to Crown employees.
SSCBA 1992, s. 121: treatment of certain marriages.
SSAA 1992, s. 58: regulations as to determination of questions and matters arising out of, or pending, reviews and appeals.
SSAA 1992, s. 116: legal proceedings.
SSAA 1992, s. 124: provisions relating to age, death and marriage.
SSAA 1992, s. 125: regulations as to notification of deaths.
SSAA 1992, s. 177: co-ordination with Northern Ireland.
SSAA 1992, s. 180: payment of travelling expenses by Secretary of State.

GENERAL PROVISIONS AS TO DETERMINATIONS AND APPEALS

170 Decisions and appeals

170(1) Section 2 (use of computers) of the Social Security Act 1998 ("the 1998 Act") applies as if, for the purposes of subsection (1) of that section, this Act were a relevant enactment.

170(2) It shall be for an officer of the Inland Revenue–

(a) to make any decision that falls to be made under or by virtue of Part III of this Act, other than a decision which under or by virtue of that Part falls to be made by the Secretary of State;

(b) to decide any issue arising in connection with payments under section 7 of the Social Security Act *1986* (occupational pension schemes becoming contracted-out between 1986 and 1993); and

(c) to decide any issue arising by virtue of regulations made under paragraph 15 of Schedule 3 to the Social Security (Consequential Provisions) Act 1992 (continuing in force of certain enactments repealed by the Social Security Act 1973).

170(3) In the following provisions of this section a **"relevant decision"** means any decision which under subsection (2) falls to be made by an officer of the Inland Revenue, other than a decision under section 53.

170(4) Sections 9 and 10 of the 1998 Act (revision of decisions and decisions superseding earlier decisions) apply as if–

(a) any reference in those sections to a decision of the Secretary of State under section 8 of that Act included a reference to a relevant decision; and

(b) any other reference in those sections to the Secretary of State were, in relation to a relevant decision, a reference to an officer of the Inland Revenue.

170(5) Regulations may make provision–

(a) generally with respect to the making of relevant decisions;

(b) with respect to the procedure to be adopted on any application made under section 9 or 10 of the 1998 Act by virtue of subsection (4); and

(c) generally with respect to such applications, revisions under section 9 and decisions under section 10;

but may not prevent a revision under section 9 or decision under section 10 being made without such an application.

170(6) Section 12 of the 1998 Act (appeal to First-tier Tribunal) applies as if, for the purposes of subsection (1)(b) of that section, a relevant decision were a decision of the Secretary of State falling within Schedule 3 to the 1998 Act.

170(7) The following provisions of the 1998 Act (which relate to decisions and appeals)–

sections 13 to 18,

sections 25 and 26,

section 28, and

Schedules 4 and 5,

shall apply in relation to any appeal under section 12 of the 1998 Act by virtue of subsection (6) above as if any reference to the Secretary of State were a reference to an officer of the Inland Revenue.

History – S. 170(1) substituted by SSA 1998, Sch. 7, para. 131, with effect from 4 March 1999, for the purposes of making regulations only (SI 1999/528) and with effect from 5 July 1999 for the purposes of any matter to which, by virtue of PSA 1993, s. 170, provisions of SSA 1998, Pt. I, Ch. II are to apply (SI 1999/1958).
In s. 170(3), the words "or 54" omitted from the end by SI 2012/1730, art. 5(19), with effect from 6 April 2012.
S. 170(2)–(7) substituted by SSC(TF)A 1999, s. 16(2), with effect from 14 June 1999, for the purposes of making regulations only, and 5 July 1999 for all other purposes (SI 1999/1662).
S. 170(2)–(7) was substituted for s. 170(2)–(4), itself substituted for the whole of s. 170 by SSA 1998, Sch. 7, para. 131, with effect from 4 March 1999 for the purposes of making regulations only (SI 1999/528).
The text of s. 170(1), as it continues to apply for purposes other than those mentioned above reads as follows (SSC(TF)A 1999, s. 16(1)) provides that the function of determining questions in s. 170(1) is transferred to an officer of the Board with effect from 5 July 1999 (SI 1999/1662)).

"170 Determination of questions by Secretary of State

170(1) The questions to which section 17(1) of the Social Security Administration Act 1992 (questions for determination by the Secretary of State) applies include–

(a) any question as to the amount of a person's guaranteed minimum for the purposes of section 13 or 17;

(b) any question–

(i) whether a contributions equivalent premium is payable or has been paid in any case or as to the amount of any such premium; or

(ii) otherwise arising in connection with any contributions equivalent premium;

(c) any question whether for the purposes of this Act a cash sum paid or an alternative arrangement made under the Policyholders Protection Act 1975 provides the whole or any part of the guaranteed minimum pension to which an earner or an earner's widow or widower was entitled under a contracted-out scheme;

(d) any question arising in connection with minimum contributions or payments under section 7 of the Social Security Act 1986; and

(e) any question whether an employment is, or is to be treated, for the purposes of the Pension Schemes Act 1993 as contracted-out employment or as to the persons in relation to whom, or the period for which, an employment is, or is to be treated, for the purposes of that Act as such employment,

other than a question such as is mentioned in paragraph (b)(ii) or (d) which is required by virtue of this Act to be determined by the Board."
In s. 170(1)(b) the words "contributions equivalent premium" substituted in both places, in s. 170(1)(c) the word "and" is omitted, s. 170(1)(e) and the word "and" immediately preceding it is inserted. by Pensions Act 1995, Sch. 5, para. 70(a) and (b) and Sch. 7, Pt. III, with effect from 6 April 1997 (SI 1997/664(C.23), art. 2(3), Schedule, Pt. II).
S. 170(2)–(7) substituted by SSC(TF)A 1999, s. 16(2), with effect from 14 June 1999, for the purposes of making regulations only, and 5 July 1999 for all other purposes (SI 1999/1662).
S. 170(2)–(7) was substituted for s. 170(2)–(4), itself substituted for the whole of s. 170 by SSA 1998, Sch. 7, para. 131, with effect from 4 March 1999 for the purposes of making regulations only (SI 1999/528).
S. 170(5), para. (a) and (b) substituted and a new para. (c) inserted by WRPA 1999, s. 81 and Sch. 11, para. 22(a) with effect from 11 November 1999 by virtue of WRPA 1999, s. 89(4)(d).
S. 170(5), the words "a revision under section 9 or decision under section 10" substituted for the words "such a revision or decision" by WRPA 1999, s. 81 and Sch. 11, para. 22(b) with effect from 11 November 1999 (date of passing of the WRPA 1999); this is the commencement date because of WRPA 1999, s. 89(4)(d).
In s. 170(6), "First-tier Tribunal" substituted for "appeal tribunal" by SI 2008/2833, art. 9 and Sch. 3, para. 112, with effect from 3 November 2008.

Derivations – S. 170(1): SSPA 1975, s. 52D(5), 60(1); SSA 1985, Sch. 1, para. 2, Sch. 5, para. 34; SSA 1986, s. 9(4)(h), 52(2), Sch. 5, *Pt. II(a); SS(CP)A 1992, Sch. 2,* para. 35(a), 82.

Cross references – SSC(TF)A 1999, s. 16(1): the function of determining questions in s. 170(1) transferred to an officer of the Board with effect from 5 July 1999 (SI 1999/1662).
SSAA 1992, s. 17: questions for the Secretary of State.
SI 1986/2218, reg. 13: adjudicating authorities.
SI 1986/2218, reg. 14: application for decision of the Secretary of State on principal questions.

171 Questions arising in proceedings

171(1) Where in any proceedings–

(a) for an offence under this Act;

(b) [omitted by PA 2014, s. 24 and Sch. 13, para. 41;]

any relevant decision as defined by section 170(3) is made by the Inland Revenue, the decision shall be conclusive for the purpose of the proceedings.

171(2) If–

(a) any such decision is necessary for the determination of the proceedings, and

(b) the decision of the Inland Revenue has not been obtained or an application with respect to the decision has been made under section 9 or 10 of the Social Security Act 1998,

the decision shall be referred to the Inland Revenue to be made in accordance (subject to any necessary modifications) with Chapter II of Part I of that Act.

171(3) Subsection (1) does not apply where, in relation to the decision–

(a) an appeal has been brought but not determined,

(b) an application for leave to appeal has been made but not determined,

(c) an appeal has not been brought (or, as the case may be, an application for leave to appeal has not been made) but the time for doing so has not yet expired, or

(d) an application has been made under section 9 or 10 of that Act.

171(4) In a case falling within subsection (3) the court shall adjourn the proceedings until such time as the final decision is known and that decision shall be conclusive for the purposes of the proceedings.

History – S. 171(1) amended, s. 171(2) and (3) substituted and s. 171(4) inserted by the SSC(TF)A 1999, Sch. 7, para. 19 with effect from 5 July 1999 (SI 1999/1662).

S. 171(1)(b) and the "or" before it omitted by PA 2014, s. 24 and Sch. 13, para. 41, with effect from 6 April 2016 (as not brought into force by any earlier order under PA 2014, s. 56(1)). Former s. 171(1)(b) read as follows:

"(b) involving any question as to the payment of a contributions equivalent premium;".

In former s. 171(1)(b) the words "contributions equivalent premium" substituted by Pensions Act 1995, Sch. 5, para. 71, with effect from 6 April 1997 (SI 1997/644 (C.23), art. 2(3), Schedule, Pt. II).

Derivations – SSPA 1975, s. 60ZC; SS(CP)A 1992, Sch. 2, para. 36.

Cross references – SSAA 1992, s. 17: questions for the Secretary of State.
SSAA 1992, s. 18: appeal on question of law.
SSAA 1992, s. 19: review of decisions.

171A Reports by Inland Revenue

171A(1) The Inland Revenue shall prepare, either annually or at such times or intervals as may be prescribed, a report on the standards achieved by their officers in the making of decisions against which, by virtue of section 170(6), the First-tier Tribunal.

171A(2) Any report under this section–

(a) may be included in any annual report by the Inland Revenue of which a copy is laid before each House of Parliament.

(b) [repealed by WRA 2012, s. 147 and Sch. 14, Pt. 13.]

171A(3) A copy of every report under this section shall be laid before each House of Parliament, unless the report is included in a report of which a copy is so laid.

History – In s. 171A(1), "the First-tier Tribunal" substituted for "an appeal tribunal constituted under Chapter I of Part I of the Social Security Act 1998" SI 2008/2833, art. 9 and Sch. 3, para. 113, with effect from 3 November 2008.

S. 171A(2)(b) and the preceding "or" repealed by WRA 2012, s. 147 and Sch. 14, Pt. 13, with effect from 8 May 2012 (SI 2012/863).

In s. 171A(3), the words ", or annexed to," repealed by WRA 2012, s. 147 and Sch. 14, Pt. 13, with effect from 8 May 2012 (SI 2012/863).

S. 171A inserted by SSC(TF)A 1999, s. 18 and Sch. 7, para. 20 with effect from 7 July 1999 (SI 1999/1662).

PART XII – SUPPLEMENTARY PROVISIONS

INTERPRETATION

181 General interpretation

181(1) In this Act, unless the context otherwise requires–

"appropriate scheme" and**" appropriate scheme certificate"** are to be construed in accordance with section 7B;

"Category A retirement pension" and **"Category B retirement pension"** mean the retirement pensions of those descriptions payable under Part II of the Social Security Contributions Benefits Act 1992;

"contract of service" has the same meaning as in section 122(1) of the Social Security Contributions and Benefits Act 1992;

"contracted-out employment" shall be construed in accordance with section 8;

"contracting-out certificate" and references to a contracted-out scheme and to contracting-out shall be construed in accordance with section 7 and section 7B;

"earner" and **"earnings"** shall be construed in accordance with section 8(1B) of this Act andsections 3, 4 and 112 of the Social Security Contributions and Benefits Act 1992;

"earnings factors" shall be construed in accordance with sections 22 and 23 of the Social Security Contributions and Benefits Act 1992;

"employed earner" has the same meaning as in section 2 of the Social Security Contributions and Benefits Act 1992;

"employee" means a person gainfully employed in Great Britain either under a contract of service or in an office (including an elective office) with earnings;

"employer" means–

(a) in the case of an employed earner employed under a contract of service, his employer;

(b) in the case of an employed earner employed in an office with emoluments–

(i) such person as may be prescribed in relation to that office; or

(ii) if no person is prescribed, the government department, public authority or body of persons responsible for paying the emoluments of the office;

"employment" includes any trade, business, profession, office or vocation and "employed" shall be construed accordingly except in the expression "employed earner";

"the first abolition date" has the meaning given by section 7A;

"guaranteed minimum pension" has the meaning given in section 8(2);

"HMRC" means the Commissioners for Her Majesty's Revenue and Customs;

"the Inland Revenue" means the Commissioners of Inland Revenue;

"lower earnings limit" and **"upper earnings limit"** shall be construed in accordance with section 5 of the Social Security Contributions and Benefits Act 1992 and "current", in relation to those limits, means for the time being in force;

"money purchase contracted-out scheme" is to be construed in accordance with section 7B

"occupational pension scheme" has the meaning given in section 1;

"pensionable age"

(a) so far as any provisions (other than sections 46 to 48) relate to guaranteed minimum pensions, means the age of 65 in the case of a man and the age of 60 in the case of a woman, and

(b) in any other case, has the meaning given by the rules in paragraph 1 of Schedule 4 to the Pensions Act 1995,

"pension debit" means a debit under section 29(1)(a) of the Welfare Reform and Pensions Act 1999;

"primary Class 1 contributions" and **"secondary Class 1 contributions"** have the same meanings as in the Social Security Contributions and Benefits Act 1992;

"the principal appointed day" means 6 April 1997 (which is the day designated as the principal appointed day for the purposes of Part 3 of the Pensions Act 1995);

"the Regulatory Authority" means the Occupational Pensions Regulatory Authority;

"salary related contracted-out scheme" is to be construed in accordance with section 7B;

"the second abolition date" has the meaning given by section 7A;

"the upper accrual point" has the meaning given by section 122 of the Social Security Contributions and Benefits Act 1992;

181(2)–(7) [Not relevant to National Insurance contributions.]

Prospective amendments – S. 181(1) amended by PSA 2015, s. 40 and Sch. 1, para. 5, with effect from a day to be appointed under PSA 2015, s. 89(4).

In s. 181(1) the definition of "minimum contributions" repealed by PA 2007, s. 15 and Sch. 4, para. 58, and s. 27 and Sch. 7, Pt. 7, with effect from a date to be appointed under s. 30(2).

In s. *181(4)* ", *43" repealed* by PA 2007, s. 15 and Sch. 4, para. 58, and s. 27 and Sch. 27, Pt. 7 with effect from a date to be appointed under s. 30(2).

History – In s. 181(1), the definition of "abolition date" omitted by PA 2014, s. 24 and Sch. 13, para. 43(3), with effect from 6 April 2016 (as not brought into force by any earlier order under PA 2014, s. 56(1)).

In s. 181(1) the definition of "abolition date" inserted by PA 2007, s. 15 and Sch. 4, para. 34, with effect from 6 April 2012 (SI 2011/1267, art. 2(a)).

In s. 181(1), in the definition of "appropriate scheme" and "appropriate scheme certificate", the words "section 7B" substituted for the words "section 181A" by PA 2014, s. 24 and Sch. 13, para. 43(4), with effect from 6 April 2016 (as not brought into force by any earlier order under PA 2014, s. 56(1)).
In s. 181(1) the definition of ""appropriate scheme" and "appropriate scheme certificate"" substituted for the definition of "appropriate scheme certificate" and references to "an appropriate scheme" by PA 2007, s. 15 and Sch. 4, para. 34, with effect from 6 April 2012 (SI 2011/1267, art. 2(a)).
The definition of "the Board" in s. 181(1) omitted by Pensions Act 1995, Sch. 5, para. 77, with effect from 6 April 1997 (SI 1997/664 (C.23), art. 2(3), Schedule, Pt. II).
In s. 181(1), in the definition of "contracting-out certificate", the words "section 7B" substituted for the words "section 7 and section 181A" by PA 2014, s. 24 and Sch. 13, para. 43(5), with effect from 6 April 2016 (as not brought into force by any earlier order under PA 2014, s. 56(1)).
In s. 181(1) in the definition of "contracting-out certificate" and references to "contracted-out scheme and to contracting-out", the words "and section 181A" inserted at the end by PA 2007, s. 15 and Sch. 4, para. 34, with effect from 6 April 2012 (SI 2011/1267, art. 2(a)).
In s. 181(1), in the definition of "earner" and "earnings", the words "section 8(1B) of this Act and" inserted after the words "in accordance with" by PA 2014, s. 24 and Sch. 13, para. 43(7), with effect from 6 April 2016 (as not brought into force by any earlier order under PA 2014, s. 56(1)).
In s. 181(1) in the definition of "employee" the word "earnings" substituted for the words "general earnings (as defined by section 7 of the Income Tax (Earnings and Pensions) Act 2003)" by NICA 2014, s. 15 and Sch. 2, para. 13, with effect from 13 May 2014.
In the definition of "employee" within PSA 1993, s. 181(1), the words "general earnings (as defined by section 7 of the Income Tax (Earnings and Pensions) Act 2003)" substituted by ITEPA 2003, Sch. 6, para. 222 which has effect, for the purposes of income tax, for the tax year 2003–04 and subsequent tax years, and, for the purposes of corporation tax, for accounting periods ending after 5 April 2003.
The definition of "equal access requirements" in s. 181(1) omitted by Pensions Act 1995, Sch. 3, para. 44(a)(i) witheffect from 1 January 1996 by virtue of SI 1995/3104.
In s. 181(1), the definition of "the first abolition date" inserted by PA 2014, s. 24 and Sch. 13, para. 43(2), with effect from 6 April 2016 (as not brought into force by any earlier order under PA 2014, s. 56(1)).
In s. 181(1), the definition of "the first abolition date" inserted by PA 2014, s. 24 and Sch. 13, para. 43(2), with effect from 6 April 2016 (as not brought into force by any earlier order under PA 2014, s. 56(1)).
In s. 181(1), the definition of "the flat rate introduction year" repealed by NICA 2008, s. 4 and Sch. 2, with effect in relation to 2009–10 and subsequent tax years.
In s. 181(1) the definition of "the flat rate introduction year" inserted by PA 2007, s. 12 and Sch. 1, para. 38, with effect from 26 September 2007, s. 30(3).
In s. 181(1) the definition of "HMRC" inserted by PA 2007, s. 15 and Sch. 4, para. 34, with effect from 6 April 2012 (SI 2011/1267, art. 2(a)).
In s. 181(1), in the definition of "money purchase contracted-out scheme", the words "section 7B" substituted for the words "section 181A" by PA 2014, s. 24 and Sch. 13, para. 43(8), with effect from 6 April 2016 (as not brought into force by any earlier order under PA 2014, s. 56(1)).
In s. 181(1) the definition of "money purchase contracted-out scheme" substituted by PA 2007, s. 15 and Sch. 4, para. 34, with effect from 6 April 2012 (SI 2011/1267, art. 2(a)).
In s. 181(1), definition of "pensionable age" inserted by Pensions Act 1995, Sch. 4, para. 17, with effect from 19 July 1995.
The definition of "pension debit" inserted by the Welfare Reform and Pensions Act 1999, s. 32(5), with effect from 11 November 1999, for the purpose of the exercise of any power to make regulations (s. 89(5)(a)) and 1 December 2000 for all other purposes (by virtue of SI 2000/1047).
In s. 181(1), the definition of "the principal appointed day" inserted by PA 2014, s. 24 and Sch. 13, para. 43(2), with effect from 6 April 2016 (as not brought into force by any earlier order under PA 2014, s. 56(1)).
In s. 181(1), definition of "the Regulatory Authority" inserted by Pensions Act 1995, Sch. 3, para. 44(a)(ii), with effect from 16 October 1996, for the purpose of making regulations, by virtue of SI 1996/2637, art. 3(d).
In s. 181(1), the definition of "salary related contracted-out scheme" inserted by PA 2014, s. 24 and Sch. 13, para. 43(2), with effect from 6 April 2016 (as not brought into force by any earlier order under PA 2014, s. 56(1)).
In s. 181(1), the definition of "the second abolition date" inserted by PA 2014, s. 24 and Sch. 13, para. 43(2), with effect from 6 April 2016 (as not brought into force by any earlier order under PA 2014, s. 56(1)).
In s. 181(1) the definition of "the upper accrual point" inserted by PA 2007, s. 12 and Sch. 1, para. 38,with effect from 26 September 2007, s. 30(3).
In s. 181(4) (not relevant to National Insurance contributions), ", 44" repealed by PA 2007, s. 15 and Sch. 4, para. 34, and s. 27 and Sch. 7, Pt. 6 with effect from 6 April 2012 (SI 2011/1267, art. 2(a)).

Derivations – S. 181(1): (as originally enacted) SSA 1973, s. 99(1); SSPA 1975, s. 31(1B), 66(1), 84(1); SSA 1986, s. 84(1).

181A Interpretation of references to money purchase contracted-out schemes or appropriate schemes after abolition date

181A [Repealed by PA 2014, s. 24 and Sch. 13, para. 44.]

History – S. 181A repealed by PA 2014, s. 24 and Sch. 13, para. 44, with effect from 6 April 2016 (as not brought into force by any earlier order under PA 2014, s. 56(1)). Former s. 181A read as follows:

"181A Interpretation of references to money purchase contracted-out schemes or appropriate schemes after abolition date

181A(1) This section applies for the interpretation of this Act on and after the abolition date.

181A(2) An occupational pension scheme was a money purchase contracted-out scheme at a time before the abolition date if, at that time, the scheme was contracted-out by virtue of satisfying section 9(3) (as it then had effect).

181A(3) A money purchase contracted-out scheme was, at a time before the abolition date, a contracted-out scheme in relation to an earner's employment if it was, at that time, specified in a contracting-out certificate in relation to that employment; and references to the contracting-out of a scheme are, in relation to a money purchase contracted-out scheme, references to its inclusion in such a certificate.

181A(4) Any reference to a contracting-out certificate is, in relation to a money purchase contracted-out scheme, a reference to a certificate issued by virtue of section 7, as it had effect before the abolition date, in relation to the employment of an earner in employed earner's employment which was contracted-out by reference to that scheme.

181A(5) Any certificate so issued that was, at a time before the abolition date, in force in respect of an employed earner's employment is to be taken as conclusive that the employment was, at that time, contracted-out employment.

181A(6) A personal pension scheme was an appropriate scheme at a time before the abolition date if, at that time, there was in force a certificate issued under section 7(1)(b) (as it then had effect) stating that the scheme was an appropriate scheme; and **"appropriate scheme certificate"** means such a certificate.

181A(7) Any appropriate scheme certificate in force in relation to a scheme at any time before the abolition date is to be taken as conclusive that the scheme was, at that time, an appropriate scheme.".

Former s. 181A inserted by PA 2007, s. 15 and Sch. 4, para. 35, with effect from 6 April 2012 (SI 2011/1267, art. 2(a)).

SUBORDINATE LEGISLATION ETC.

185 Consultations about other regulations

185(1) Subject to subsection (2), before the Secretary of State makes any regulations for the purposes of Parts I to VI, Chapter III of Part VII, Part VIII, IX or X or section 153, 154, 155, 156, 160, 162, 163, 174 or 175 of this Act he shall consult such persons as he may consider appropriate.

185(2) Subsection (1) does not apply to–

(a) regulations prescribing actuarial tables; or

(b) regulations made for the purpose only of consolidating other regulations revoked by them; or

(c) regulations under section 36(6); or

(d) regulations in the case of which the Secretary of State considers consultation inexpedient because of urgency; or

(e) regulations which–

(i) state that they are consequential upon a specified enactment, and

(ii) are made before the end of the period of six months beginning with the coming into force of that enactment.

185(3)–(4) [Omitted by Pensions Act 1995, Sch. 5, para. 80.]

185(5) In relation to any regulations required or authorised under this Act to be made by the Secretary of State in conjunction with the Treasury, any reference in subsection (1) to the Secretary of State shall be construed as a reference to him and the Treasury acting jointly.

185(5A) Subject to subsection (5C), before the Treasury (acting alone) make any regulations under section 95, 97A or 97C they shall consult such persons as they may consider appropriate.

185(5B) Subject to subsection (5C), before the Scottish Ministers make any regulations under section 97B(11) they shall consult such persons as they may consider appropriate.

185(5C) Subsections (5A) and (5B) do not apply to regulations in the case of which the Treasury or (as the case may be) the Scottish Ministers consider consultation inexpedient because of urgency or to regulations of the type described in subsection (2)(b) or (e).

185(6) [Omitted by Pensions Act 1995, Sch. 5, para. 80.]

185(7) The power of the Secretary of State to make regulations under section 162 of this Act shall be exercisable only after consultation with the Chief Registrar of Friendly Societies or the Friendly Societies Commission.

185(8) [Omitted by SI 2013/2042, art. 15.]

185(9) [Omitted by PA 2014, s. 24 and Sch. 13, para. 45.]

History – In s. 185(1), the words "I or" are omitted by Pensions Act 1995, Sch. 3, para. 46, with effect from 6 April 1997 (SI 1997/664 (C. 23), art. 2(3), Schedule, Pt. II).

In s. 185(1), the words "Subject to subsection (2), before the Secretary of State makes" and "consult such persons as he may consider appropriate" substituted, s. 185(d), (e) inserted and s. 185(3), (4) and (6) omitted, and in s. 185(5), the words "subsection (1)" substituted by Pensions Act, Sch. 5, para. 80, with effect from 6 April 1997 (SI 1997/664 (C. 23), art. 2(3), Schedule, Pt. II).

S. 185(5A) inserted by PSA 2015, s. 70(2), with effect from 6 April 2015.

S. 185(5B) inserted by PSA 2015, s. 70(2), with effect from 6 April 2015.

S. 185(5C) inserted by PSA 2015, s. 70(2), with effect from 6 April 2015.

S. 185(8) omitted by SI 2013/2042, art. 15, with effect from 19 August 2013.

In former s. 185(8) the words "Administrative Justice and Tribunals Council" substituted by TCEA 2007, s. 48 and Sch. 8, para. 32, with effect from 1 November 2007, by virtue of SI 2007/2709, art. 3(b)(i).

In former s. 185(8), reference to s. 170(5) substituted by WRPA 1999, s. 81 and Sch. 11, para. 23 with effect from 11 November 1999 (WRPA 1999, s. 89(4)(d)). Reference to s. 170(8) substituted by Pensions Act 1995, Sch. 5, para. 80(f) with effect from 16 October 1996, for the purpose of making regulations, by virtue of SI 1996/2637, art. 3(e).

S. 185(9) omitted by PA 2014, s. 24 and Sch. 13, para. 45, with effect from 6 April 2016 (as not brought into force by any earlier order under PA 2014, s. 56(1)). Former s. 185(9) read as follows:

"**185(9)** Before making any regulations under paragraph 7 of Schedule 2 the Secretary of State shall consult with such bodies concerned with employments of the class in question as appear to him fairly to represent the interests of the employers and earners in those employments.".

Derivations – S. 185(1), (2): SSA 1973, s. 68(1); SSPA 1975, s. 61(2); SSA 1979, Sch. 3, para. 3; SSHBA 1982, s. 40, Sch. 4, para. 21; SSA 1986, Sch. 10, para. 82, 94; SSA 1989, Sch. 8, para. 12.

S. 185(3), (4): SSA 1973, s. 68(2); SSPA 1975, s. 61(3).

S. 185(5): SSA 1973, s. 68(3); SSPA 1975, s. 61(4).

S. 185(6): SSA 1986, s. 61.

S. 185(7): SSA 1973, s. 71(1) (in part).

S. 185(8): SSA 1973, s. 67(5).

S. 185(9): SSPA 1975, Sch. 2, para. 8(2).

SUPPLEMENTAL PROVISIONS

193 Short title and commencement

193(1) This Act may be cited as the Pension Schemes Act 1993.

193(2) Subject to the provisions of Schedule 9, this Act shall come into force on such day as the Secretary of State may by order appoint.

193(3) As respects the coming into force of–

(a) Part II of Schedule 5 and section 188(1) so far as it relates to it; or

(b) Schedule 7 and section 190 so far as it relates to it,

an order under subsection (2) may appoint different days from the day appointed for the other provisions of this Act or different days for different purposes.

Commencement Date – PSA 1993 came into force on 7 February 1994 except for s. 188(1) (in part), 190 (in part) and Sch. 5, Pt. II (SI 1994/86).

FINANCE ACT 1997

(1997 Chapter 16) [*19th March 1997*]

PART VIII – MISCELLANEOUS AND SUPPLEMENTAL

MISCELLANEOUS

110 Obtaining information from social security authorities

110(1) This section applies to–

(a) any information held by the Secretary of State or the Department of Health and Social Services for Northern Ireland for the purposes of any of his or its functions relating to social security; and

(b) any information held by a person in connection with the provision by him to the Secretary of State or that Department of any services which that person is providing for purposes connected with any of those functions.

110(2) Subject to the following provisions of this section, the person holding any information to which this section applies shall be entitled to supply it to–

(a) the Commissioners of Customs and Excise or any person by whom services are being provided to those Commissioners for purposes connected with any of their functions; or

(b) the Commissioners of Inland Revenue or any person by whom services are being provided to those Commissioners for purposes connected with any of their functions.

110(3) Information shall not be supplied to any person under this section except for one or more of the following uses–

(a) use in the prevention, detection, investigation or prosecution of criminal offences which it is a function of the Commissioners of Customs and Excise, or of the Commissioners of Inland Revenue, to prevent, detect, investigate or prosecute;

(b) use in the prevention, detection or investigation of conduct in respect of which penalties which are not criminal penalties are provided for by or under any enactment;

(c) use in connection with the assessment or determination of penalties which are not criminal penalties;

(d) use in checking the accuracy of information relating to, or provided for purposes connected with, any matter under the care and management of the Commissioners of Customs and Excise or the Commissioners of Inland Revenue;

(e) use (where appropriate) for amending or supplementing any such information; and

(f) use in connection with any legal or other proceedings relating to anything mentioned in paragraphs (a) to (e) above.

110(4) An enactment authorising the disclosure of information by a person mentioned in subsection (2)(a) or (b) above shall not authorise the disclosure by such a person of information supplied to him under this section except to the extent that the disclosure is also authorised by a general or specific permission granted by the Secretary of State or by the Department of Health and Social Services for Northern Ireland.

110(5) In this section references to functions relating to social security include references to–

(a) functions in relation to social security benefits (whether contributory or not) or national insurance numbers; and

(b) functions under the Jobseekers Act 1995 or the Jobseekers (Northern Ireland) Order 1995.

110(5AA) [Repealed by TCA 2002, s. 60 and Sch. 6.]

110(5A) Nothing in this section affects any disclosure authorised by section 121F of the Social Security Administration Act 1992 (supply to Inland Revenue of information for purposes of contributions, statutory sick pay or statutory maternity pay of information held by Secretary of State), paragraph 3 of Schedule 5 to the Tax Credits Act 1999 (supply to Inland Revenue for purposes of tax credit of information so held) or *section* 14 of the Employment Act 2002 (supply to Inland Revenue for purposes of statutory paternity pay or statutory adoption pay of information so held).

110(6) In this section **"conduct"** includes acts, omissions and statements.

110(7) This section shall come into force on such day as the Treasury may by order made by statutory instrument appoint, and different days may be appointed under this subsection for different purposes.

Commencement Date – S. 110 came into effect on 2 July 1997 by virtue of SI 1997/1603.

History – In s. 110(5), former reference to social security contributions repealed by Social Security Contributions (Transfer of Functions, etc.) Act 1999, s. 6 and Sch. 6, para. 10(2) and s. 26(3) and Sch. 10, with effect from 1 April 1999 by virtue of SI 1999/527 (C. 11), art. 2(b).
In s. 110(5A) the words ", paragraph 3 of Schedule 5 to the Tax Credits Act 1999 (supply to Inland Revenue for purposes of tax credit of information so held) or section 14 of the Employment Act 2002 (supply to Inland Revenue for purposes of statutory paternity pay or statutory adoption pay of information so held).", substituted by EA 2002, s. 53 and Sch. 7, para. 50, with effect from 26 February 2003 for the purpose of making subordinate legislation in relation to child benefit and guardian's allowance (SI 2003/392); 1 April 2003 for certain other purposes (SI 2003/392); and 1 August 2002 for other purposes (SI 2002/1727).
In s. 110(5A), former words inserted by TCA 1999, s. 12(6) and Sch. 5, para. 7(3), with effect from 5 October 1999.
S. 110(5A) inserted by Social Security Contributions (Transfer of Functions, etc.) Act 1999, s. 6 and Sch. 6, para. 10(3), with effect from 1 April 1999 by virtue of SI 1999/527 (C. 11), art. 2(b).
S. 110(5AA) repealed by TCA 2002, s. 60 and Sch. 6, with effect from 8 April 2003 (SI 2003/962).
Former s. 110(5AA) inserted by Tax Credits Act 1999, s. 12(6) and Sch. 5, para. 7(2), with effect from 5 October 1999.

SOCIAL SECURITY ACT 1998

(1998 Chapter 14) [*21st May 1998*]

ARRANGEMENT OF SECTIONS

PART I – DECISIONS AND APPEALS

CHAPTER I – GENERAL

CHAPTER II – SOCIAL SECURITY DECISIONS AND APPEALS

PART II – CONTRIBUTIONS

Notes – The entry into force of the Social Security Act 1998 is effected piecemeal, over a prolonged period. Care should be taken to check for the commencement arrangements for each section or paragraph in the Commencement date notes.

PART I – DECISIONS AND APPEALS

Chapter I – General

DECISIONS

2 Use of computers

2(1) Any decision, determination or assessment falling to be made or certificate falling to be issued by the Secretary of State under or by virtue of a relevant enactment, or in relation to a war pension, may be made or issued not only by an officer of his acting under his authority but also–

(a) by a computer for whose operation such an officer is responsible; and

(b) in the case of a decision, determination or assessment that may be made or a certificate that may be issued by a person providing services to the Secretary of State, by a computer for whose operation such a person is responsible.

2(2) In this section **"relevant enactment"** means any enactment contained in–

(a) Chapter II of this Part;

(b) the Social Security Contributions and Benefits Act 1992 (**"the Contributions and Benefits Act"**);

(c) [not relevant to National Insurance contributions;]

(d) [not relevant to National Insurance contributions;]

(e) [not relevant to National Insurance contributions;]

(f) [not relevant to National Insurance contributions;]

(g) [not relevant to National Insurance contributions;]

(h) [not relevant to National Insurance contributions;]

(i) [not relevant to National Insurance contributions.]

(j) Part 1 of the Welfare Reform Act 2007;

(k) Part 1 of the Welfare Reform Act 2012;

(l) Part 4 of that Act.

(m) Part 1 of the Pensions Act 2014; or

(n) section 30 of the Pensions Act 2014;

2(3) [Not relevant to National Insurance contributions.]

Commencement Date – S. 2 (except for s. 2(2)(a)) entered into force with effect from 8 September 1998 (SI 1998/2209).
S. 2(2)(a) entered into force, for the purposes of any matter to which, by virtue of PSA 1993, s. 170, provisions of SSA 1998, Pt. I, Ch. II are to apply, with effect from 5 July 1999 (SI 1999/1958 (C. 51), art. 2(1)(b)(iv)).

Prospective amendments – S. 2(2)(o) inserted (and the "or" after (m) omitted) by Welfare Reform and Work Act 2016, s. 20(3), with effect from a day to be appointed by the Secretary of State under Welfare Reform and Work Act 2016, s. 36(6). S. 2(2)(o) to read as follows:
"(o) sections 18 to 21 of the Welfare Reform and Work Act 2016."

History – S. 2(2)(j) (and the "; or" before it) inserted by Welfare Reform Act 2007, s. 28(1) and Sch. 3, para. 17, with effect (for the purpose of making regulations) from 18 March 2008 and from 27 July 2008 for other purposes (SI 2008/787, art. 2 and Schedule).
S. 2(2)(k) inserted (and the "or" at the end of s. 2(2)(i) repealed) by WRA 2012, s. 31 and Sch. 2, para. 44, with effect from 29 April 2013 (SI 2013/983, art. 3(1)(b)).
S. 2(2)(l) (and the "; or" before it) inserted by WRA 2012, s. 91 and Sch. 9, para. 38, with effect from 8 April 2013, in relation to a person whose only or principal residence is, on the date on which that person makes a claim for personal independence payment, located in an area to which one of the postcodes listed in SI 2013/358, Sch. 3 corresponds (SI 2013/358, art. 7).
S. 2(2)(m) inserted (and the final "or" in s. 2(2)(k) omitted) by PA 2014, s. 23 and Sch. 12, para. 32, with effect from 6 April 2016 (as not brought into force by any earlier order under PA 2014, s. 56(1)).
S. 2(2)(n) (and the "or" before it) inserted by PA 2014, s. 31 and Sch. 16, para. 38, with effect from 6 April 2017, subject to SI 2017/297, art. 4 (later commencement for abolition of bereavement payment and bereavement allowance) and 5 (commencement for entitlement to bereavement payment and bereavement support payment) (SI 2017/297, art. 3(2)).

APPEALS

Cross references – SI 2008/2833, art. 3 and 4: transfer of Pt. 1, Ch. 1 appeal tribunal functions to the First-tier Tribunal, and abolition of the appeal tribunal, with effect from 3 November 2008, subject to transitional provisions in SI 2008/2833, Sch. 4.

4 Unified appeal tribunals

4 [Omitted by SI 2008/2833, art. 9 and Sch. 3, para. 144.]

History – S. 4 omitted by SI 2008/2833, art. 9 and Sch. 3, para. 144, with effect from 3 November 2008.

5 President of appeal tribunals

5 [Omitted by SI 2008/2833, art. 9 and Sch. 3, para. 145.]

History – S. 5 omitted by SI 2008/2833, art. 9 and Sch. 3, para. 145, with effect from 3 November 2008.

Cross references – SI 2008/2833, art. 5: the President of the appeal tribunal becomes a transferred-in judge of the First-tier Tribunal and deputy judge of the Upper Tribunal, with effect from 3 November 2008.

6 Panel for appointment to appeal tribunals

6 [Omitted by SI 2008/2833, art. 9 and Sch. 3, para. 146.]

History – S. 6 omitted by SI 2008/2833, art. 9 and Sch. 3, para. 146, with effect from 3 November 2008.

Cross references – SI 2008/2833, art. 5: a legally qualified member of the appeal tribunal becomes a transferred-in judge of the First-tier Tribunal, with effect from 3 November 2008.
SI 2008/2833, art. 5: a financially qualified or medically qualified panel member, or a panel member with a disability qualification, becomes a transferred-in other member of the First-tier Tribunal, with effect from 3 November 2008.

7 Constitution of appeal tribunals

7 [Omitted by SI 2008/2833, art. 9 and Sch. 3, para. 147.]

History – S. 7 omitted by SI 2008/2833, art. 9 and Sch. 3, para. 147, with effect from 3 November 2008.

Chapter II – Social Security Decisions and Appeals

History – In Ch. II, in relation to tax credit, references to decisions of the Secretary of State shall be construed, with effect from 5 October 1999, as if they were references to decisions of the Treasury or, as the case may be, the Board of Inland Revenue (TCA 1999, s. 20(2); s. 2 and Sch. 2, para. 21).

Cross references – SSC(TF)A 1999, s. 15: the Secretary of State may make regulations to modify enactments dealing with the appeals and decision making regime until Ch. II is fully in force.
SSC(TF)A 1999, s. 17: the Secretary of State may make arrangements with the Board of Inland Revenue for the Board to act as the Secretary's agent in carrying out some functions in relation to certain notional contribution attribution matters.
TCA 2002, s. 63(8) and (10): application (subject to Regulations) of Ch. 2 to appeals in respect of Tax Credit matters.
TCA 2002, s. 51 and Sch. 4, para. 15: References in Ch. 2 to a decision of the Secretary of State are, where the context so requires in consequence of TCA 2002, s. 50 (transfer of Secretary of State's functions relating to child benefit and guardian's allowance to the Board of Inland Revenue), to be construed as references to a decision of the Board or, where the power to decide is exercised by an officer of the Board, an officer of the Board.

DECISIONS

8 Decisions by Secretary of State

8(1) Subject to the provisions of this Chapter, it shall be for the Secretary of State–

(a) to decide any claim for a relevant benefit;

(b) [not relevant to National Insurance contributions;]

(c) subject to subsection (5) below, to make any decision that falls to be made under or by virtue of a relevant enactment.

(d) [omitted by SSC(TF)A 1999, s. 18 and Sch. 7, para. 22(2)(b).]

8(2) Where at any time a claim for a relevant benefit is decided by the Secretary of State–

(a) the claim shall not be regarded as subsisting after that time; and

(b) accordingly, the claimant shall not (without making a further claim) be entitled to the benefit on the basis of circumstances not obtaining at that time.

8(3) In this Chapter **"relevant benefit"** means any of the following, namely–

(a) benefit under Parts II to V of the Contributions and Benefits Act;

(aa) universal credit;

(ab) state pension or a lump sum under Part 1 of the Pensions Act 2014;

(ac) bereavement support payment under section 30 of the Pensions Act 2014;

(b) a jobseeker's allowance;

(ba) an employment and support allowance;

(baa) personal independence payment;

(bb) state pension credit;

(c) income support;

(d) [repealed by Tax Credits Act 2002, s. 60 and Sch. 6;]

(e) [repealed by Tax Credits Act 2002, s. 60 and Sch. 6;]

(f) a social fund payment mentioned in section 138(1)(a) or (2) of the Contributions and Benefits Act;

(g) child benefit;

(h) such other benefit as may be prescribed.

8(4) In this section **"relevant enactment"** means any enactment contained in this Chapter, the Contributions and Benefits Act, the Administration Act, the Social Security (Consequential Provisions) Act 1992, the Jobseekers Act, the State Pension Credit Act 2002, Part 1 of the Welfare Reform Act 2007, Part 1 of the Welfare Reform Act 2012, Part 4 of that Act or Part 1 of the Pensions Act 2014 or section 30 of that Act, other than one contained in–.

(a) Part VII of the Contributions and Benefits Act so far as relating to housing benefit and council tax benefit;

(b) Part VIII of the Administration Act (arrangements for housing benefit and council tax benefit and related subsidies)

8(5) Subsection (1)(c) above does not include any decision which under section 8 of the Social Security Contributions (Transfer of Functions, etc.) Act 1999 falls to be made by an officer of the Inland Revenue.

Commencement Date – S. 8 entered into force generally (except for the purposes of housing benefit, council tax benefit and decisions to which SI 1999/527, art. 4(6) applies; i.e. pre-1 April 1999 decisions under SSAA 1992, s. 17(1), s. 20(3) and PSA 1993, s. 170(1)) with effect from 29 November 1999 (SI 1999/3178 (C. 81), art. 2(1)(a); 2(2) and Sch. 1).

Prospective amendments – S. 8(3)(bc) inserted by Welfare Reform and Work Act 2016, s. 20(4)(a), with effect from a day to be appointed by the Secretary of State under Welfare Reform and Work Act 2016, s. 36(6). S. 8(3)(bc) to read as follows:
"(bc) a loan under section 18 of the Welfare Reform and Work Act 2016;"
S. 8(3)(c) repealed by WRA 2012, s. 147 and Sch. 14, Pt. 1, with effect from a date to be set by order of the Secretary of State.

In s. 8(4), the words ", section 30 of that Act or sections 18 to 21 of the Welfare Reform and Work Act 2016" substituted for the words "or section 30 of that Act" by Welfare Reform and Work Act 2016, s. 20(4)(b), with effect from a day to be appointed by the Secretary of State under Welfare Reform and Work Act 2016, s. 36(6).
In s. 8(5), the words from "other than" to the end repealed by WRA 2012, s. 147 and Sch. 14, Pt. 1, with effect from a date to be set by order of the Secretary of State.

History – S. 8(1)(bb) inserted by SPCA 2002, s. 11 and Sch. 1, para. 6(2), with effect from 2 July 2002 only for the purpose of making regulations or orders, by virtue of SI 2002/1691.
S. 8(1)(c), (4) and (5) entered into force; for the purposes of (i) decisions whether a person is entitled to be credited with earnings or contributions in accordance with regulations made under s. 22(5) of the Contributions and Benefits Act; and (ii) decisions whether a person was, within the meaning of regulations, precluded from regular employment by responsibilities at home; with effect from 18 October 1999 (SI 1999/2860 (C. 75), art. 2(c)(iv), (v) and Sch. 1).
S. 8(1)(a) and (1)(c), (4) and (5) entered into force, for the purposes of benefits under SSCBA 1992, Pt. II except child's special allowance, with effect from 6 September 1999 (SI 1999/2422 (C. 61), art. 2(c)(i) and Sch. 1).
S. 8(1)(c), (4) and (5) entered into force, for the purposes of any matter to which, by virtue of PSA 1993, s. 170, provisions of SSA 1998, Pt. I, Ch. II are to apply, with effect from 5 July 1999 (SI 1999/1958 (C. 51), art. 2(1)(b)(iv)).
S. 8(1)(d) omitted by SSC(TF)A 1999, s. 18 and Sch. 7, para. 22(2)(b), with effect from 1 April 1999 (SI 1999/527).
S. 8(3)(aa) inserted by WRA 2012, s. 31 and Sch. 2, para. 45(a), with effect (for the purpose of making regulations) from 25 February 2013 (SI 2013/358, art. 2 and Sch. 1) and from 29 April 2013 for other purposes (SI 2013/983, art. 3(1)(b)).
S. 8(3)(ab) inserted by PA 2014, s. 23 and Sch. 12, para. 33(a), with effect from 6 April 2016 (as not brought into force by any earlier order under PA 2014, s. 56(1)).
S. 8(3)(ac) inserted by PA 2014, s. 31 and Sch. 16, para. 39(2), with effect from 6 April 2017, subject to SI 2017/297, art. 4 (later commencement for abolition of bereavement payment and bereavement allowance) and 5 (commencement for entitlement to bereavement payment and bereavement support payment) (SI 2017/297, art. 3(2)).
S. 8(3)(ba) inserted by WRA 2007, s. 28(1) and Sch. 3, para. 17, with effect (for the purpose of making regulations) from 18 March 2008 and from 27 July 2008 for other purposes (SI 2008/787, art. 2 and Schedule).
S. 8(3)(baa) inserted by WRA 2012, s. 91 and Sch. 9, para. 39(a), with effect (for the purpose of making regulations) from 25 February 2013 (SI 2013/358, art. 2 and Sch. 1), from 8 April 2013 in relation to a person whose only or principal residence is, on the date on which that person makes a claim for personal independence payment, located in an area to which one of the following postcodes corresponds: BL, CA, CH (except CH1, CH4, CH5, CH6, CH7 and CH8), CW, DH, DL (except DL6, DL7, DL8, DL9, DL10 and DL11), FY, L, LA (except LA2 7, LA2 8, LA6 2 and LA6 3), M, NE, PR, SR, TS (except TS9), WA and WN, (SI 2013/358, art. 7(1) and (2)(k)) andfrom 10 June 2013 in relation to any other person (SI 2013/1250, art. 2).
In s. 8(3)(d) and (e) the words "working families' tax credit" and "disabled person's tax credit" substituted for the words "family credit" and "disability working allowance" respectively (TCA 1999, s. 1(2) and Sch. 1, para. 6(q)) with effect from 5 October 1999 (TCA 1999, s. 20(2)).
In s. 8(3) the words "subject to section 21(4) below", which followed the term "relevant benefit" omitted by WRPA 1999, s. 88 and Sch. 13, Part VI; with effect from 6 April 2000 (SI 1999/3420 (C. 75), art. 2(c)(iv), (v) and Sch. 1).
In s. 8(3)(d) and (e) the references to "working families' tax credit" and "disabled person's tax credit" repealed by TCA 2002, s. 60 and Sch. 6, with effect from 8 April 2003 (by virtue of SI 2003/968).
In s. 8(4), the words "or section 30 of that Act" inserted after the words "Part 1 of the Pensions Act 2014" by PA 2014, s. 31 and Sch. 16, para. 39(3), with effect from 6 April 2017, subject to SI 2017/297, art. 4 (later commencement for abolition of bereavement payment and bereavement allowance) and 5 (commencement for entitlement to bereavement payment and bereavement support payment) (SI 2017/297, art. 3(2)).
In s. 8(4), the words ", Part 4 of that Act or Part 1 of the Pensions Act 2014" substituted for the words "or Part 4 of that Act" by PA 2014, s. 23 and Sch. 12, para. 33(b), with effect from 6 April 2016 (as not brought into force by any earlier order under PA 2014, s. 56(1)).
In s. 8(4), after the words "Welfare Reform Act 2012", the words "or Part 4 of that Act" inserted by WRA 2012, s. 91 and Sch. 9, para. 39(b), with effect (for the purpose of making regulations) from 25 February 2013 (SI 2013/358, art. 2 and Sch. 1), from 8 April 2013 in relation to a person whose only or principal residence is, on the date on which that person makes a claim for personal independence payment, located in an area to which one of the following postcodes corresponds: BL, CA, CH (except CH1, CH4, CH5, CH6, CH7 and CH8), CW, DH, DL (except DL6, DL7, DL8, DL9, DL10 and DL11), FY, L, LA (except LA2 7, LA2 8, LA6 2 and LA6 3), M, NE, PR, SR, TS (except TS9), WA and WN, (SI 2013/358, art. 7(1) and (2)(k)) and from 10 June 2013 in relation to any other person (SI 2013/1250, art. 2).
In s. 8(4) the words ", Part 1 of the Welfare Reform Act 2007, Part 1 of the Welfare Reform Act 2012" substituted for the words "or Part 1 of the Welfare Reform Act 2007" by WRA 2012, s. 31 and Sch. 2, para. 45(b), with effect (for the purpose of making regulations) from 25 February 2013 (SI 2013/358, art. 2 and Sch. 1) and from 29 April2013 for other purposes (SI 2013/983, art. 3(1)(b)).
In s. 8(4) the words", the State Pension Credit Act 2002 or Part 1 of the Welfare Reform Act 2007" substituted for the words "or the State Pension Credit Act 2002" by WRA 2007, s. 28(1) and Sch. 3, para. 17, with effect (for the purpose of making regulations) from 18 March 2008 and from 27 July 2008 for other purposes (SI 2008/787, art. 2 and Schedule).
In s. 8(4), the words ", the Jobseekers Act or the State Pension Credit Act 2002" substituted by the State Pension Credit Act 2002, s. 11 and Sch. 1, para. 6(2), (3), with effect from 2 July 2002 only for the purposes of making regulations or orders by virtue of SI 2002/1691.
S. 8(5) substituted by SSC(TF)A 1999, s. 18 and Sch. 7, para. 22(3), with effect from 1 April 1999 (SI 1999/527).

Other material – HMRC guidance CA14F (2014 edn): contracted-out decision making and appeals is available at: https://www.gov.uk/government/publications/contracted-out-decision-making-and-appeals-ca14f/ca14f-contracted-out-decision-making-and-appeals.

9 Revision of decisions

9(1) Any decision of the Secretary of State under section 8 above or section 10 below may be revised by the Secretary of State–

(a) either within the prescribed period or in prescribed cases or circumstances; and

(b) either on an application made for the purpose or on his own initiative;

and regulations may prescribe the procedure by which a decision of the Secretary of State may be so revised.

9(2) In making a decision under subsection (1) above, the Secretary of State need not consider any issue that is not raised by the application or, as the case may be, did not cause him to act on his own initiative.

9(3) Subject to subsections (4) and (5) and section 27 below, a revision under this section shall take effect as from the date on which the original decision took (or was to take) effect.

9(4) Regulations may provide that, in prescribed cases or circumstances, a revision under this section shall take effect as from such other date as may be prescribed.

9(5) Where a decision is revised under this section, for the purpose of any rule as to the time allowed for bringing an appeal, the decision shall be regarded as made on the date on which it is so revised.

9(6) Except in prescribed circumstances, an appeal against a decision of the Secretary of State shall lapse if the decision is revised under this section before the appeal is determined.

Commencement Date – S. 9 entered into force generally (except for the purposes of housing benefit, council tax benefit and decisions to which SI 1999/527, art. 4(6) applies; i.e. pre-1 April 1999 decisions under SSAA 1992, s. 17(1), s. 20(3) and PSA 1993, s. 170(1)) with effect from 29 November 1999 (SI 1999/3178 (C.81), art. 2(1)(a); 2(2) and Sch. 1).
S. 9 entered into force; for the purposes of (i) decisions whether a person is entitled to be credited with earnings or contributions in accordance with regulations made under section 22(5) of the Contributions and Benefits Act; and (ii) decisions whether a person was, within the meaning of regulations, precluded from regular employment by responsibilities at home; with effect from 18 October 1999 (SI 1999/2860 (C. 75), art. 2(c)(iv), (v) and Sch. 1).
S. 9 entered into force, for the purposes of benefits under SSCBA 1992, Pt. II except child's special allowance, with effect from 6 September 1999 (SI 1999/2422 (C. 61), art. 2(c)(i) and Sch. 1).
S. 9 entered into force, for the purposes of any matter to which, by virtue of PSA 1993, s. 170, provisions of SSA 1998, Pt. I, Ch. II are to apply, with effect from 5 July 1999 (SI 1999/1958 (C. 51), art. 2(1)(b)(iv)).
S. 9(1), (4) and (6) entered into force, only for the purposes of making regulations, with effect from 4 March 1999 (SI 1999/528).

History – In s. 9(1), the words "Subject to section 36(3) below," at the start repealed by WRA 2012, s. 147 and Sch. 14, Pt. 8, with effect from 1 April 2013 (SI 2012/3090, art. 2).

Other material – HMRC guidance CA14F (2014 edn): contracted-out decision making and appeals is available at: https://www.gov.uk/government/publications/contracted-out-decision-making-and-appeals-ca14f/ca14f-contracted-out-decision-making-and-appeals.

10 Decisions superseding earlier decisions

10(1) Subject to subsection (3) below, the following, namely–

(a) any decision of the Secretary of State under section 8 above or this section, whether as originally made or as revised under section 9 above; and

(b) any decision under this Chapter of the First-tier Tribunal or any decision of the Upper Tribunal which relates to any such decision,

may be superseded by a decision made by the Secretary of State, either on an application made for the purpose or on his own initiative.

10(2) In making a decision under subsection (1) above, the Secretary of State need not consider any issue that is not raised by the application or, as the case may be, did not cause him to act on his own initiative.

10(3) Regulations may prescribe the cases and circumstances in which, and the procedure by which, a decision may be made under this section.

10(4) [Ceased to have effect by virtue of SSC(TF)A 1999, s. 18 and Sch. 7, para. 23.]

10(5) Subject to subsection (6) and section 27 below, a decision under this section shall take effect as from the date on which it is made or, where applicable, the date on which the application was made.

10(6) Regulations may provide that, in prescribed cases or circumstances, a decision under this section shall take effect as from such other date as may be prescribed.

Commencement Date – In so far as it was not already in force s. 10 entered into force (except for the purposes of housing benefit, council tax benefit and decisions to which SI 1999/527, art. 4(6) applies; i.e. pre-1 April 1999 decisions under SSAA 1992, s. 17(1), s. 20(3) and PSA 1993, s. 170(1)) with effect from 29 November 1999 (SI 1999/3178 (C. 81), art. 2(1)(a); 2(2) and Sch. 1).
S. 10 entered into force; for the purposes of (i) decisions whether a person is entitled to be credited with earnings or contributions in accordance with regulations made under s. 22(5) of the Contributions and Benefits Act; and (ii) decisions whether a person was, within the meaning of regulations, precluded from regular employment by responsibilities at home; with effect from 18 October 1999 (SI 1999/2860 (C. 75), art. 2(c)(iv), (v) and Sch. 1).
S. 10 entered into force, for the purposes of benefits under SSCBA 1992, Pt. II except child's special allowance, with effect from 6 September 1999 (SI 1999/2422 (C. 61), art. 2(c)(i) and Sch. 1).
S. 10 entered into force, for the purposes of any matter to which, by virtue of PSA 1993, s. 170, provisions of SSA 1998, Pt. I, Ch. II are to apply, with effect from 5 July 1999 (SI 1999/1958 (C. 51), art. 2(1)(b)(iv)).
S. 10(3) and (6) entered into force, only for the purposes of making regulations, with effect from 4 March 1999 (SI 1998/528).

History – In s. 10(1), the words "and section 36(3)" repealed by WRA 2012, s. 147 and Sch. 14, Pt. 8, with effect from 1 April 2013 (SI 2012/3090, art. 2).
In s. 10(1)(b), "of the First-tier Tribunal or any decision of the Upper Tribunal which relates to any such decision" substituted for "of an appeal tribunal or a Commissioner" by SI 2008/2833, art. 9 and Sch. 3, para. 148, with effect from 3 November 2008.
In s. 10(1) reference to s. 10(4) omitted by SSC(TF)A 1999, s. 18 and Sch. 7, para. 23(a) with effect from 1 April 1999 (SI 1999/527).
S. 10(4) ceased to have effect (never having entered into force), by virtue of SSC(TF)A 1999, s. 18 and Sch. 7, para. 23(b) from 1 April 1999 (SI 1999/527).

Other material – HMRC guidance CA14F (2014 edn): contracted-out decision making and appeals is available at: https://www.gov.uk/government/publications/contracted-out-decision-making-and-appeals-ca14f/ca14f-contracted-out-decision-making-and-appeals.

10A Reference of issues by Secretary of State to Inland Revenue

10A(1) Regulations may make provision requiring the Secretary of State, where on consideration of any claim or other matter he is of the opinion that there arises any issue which under section 8 of the Social Security Contributions (Transfer of Functions, etc.) Act 1999 falls to be decided by an officer of the Inland Revenue, to refer the issue to the Inland Revenue.

10A(2) Regulations under this section may–

(a) provide for the Inland Revenue to give the Secretary of State a preliminary opinion on any issue referred to them,

(b) specify the circumstances in which an officer of the Inland Revenue is to make a decision under section 8 of the Social Security Contributions (Transfer of Functions, etc.) Act 1999 on a reference by the Secretary of State,

(c) enable or require the Secretary of State, in specified circumstances, to deal with any other issue arising on consideration of the claim or other matter pending the decision on the referred issue, and

(d) require the Secretary of State to decide the claim or other matter in accordance with the decision of an officer of the Inland Revenue on the issue referred to them, or in accordance with any determination of the First-tier Tribunal or Upper Tribunal made on appeal from the tribunal's decision.

History – In s. 10A(2)(d), the words "First-tier Tribunal or Upper Tribunal" and the words "the tribunal's decision" substituted by SI 2009/56, art. 3(1) and Sch. 1, para. 248, operative from 1 April 2009, subject to transitional and saving provisions in SI 2009/56, Sch. 3.
S. 10A inserted by SSC(TF)A 1999, s. 18 and Sch. 7, para. 24 and brought into force with effect from 14 June 1999 for the purpose of making regulations and 5 July 1999 as respects all other matters (SI 1999/1662).

11 Regulations with respect to decisions

11(1) Subject to the provisions of this Chapter and the Administration Act, provision may be made by regulations for the making of any decision by the Secretary of State under or in connection with the current legislation, or the former legislation, including a decision on a claim for benefit.

11(2) Where it appears to the Secretary of State that a matter before him involves a question of fact requiring special expertise, he may direct that in dealing with that matter he shall have the assistance of one or more experts.

11(3) In this section–

"the current legislation" means the Contributions and Benefits Act, the Jobseekers Act, the Social Security (Recovery of Benefits) Act 1997, the State Pension Credit Act 2002, Part 1 of the Welfare Reform Act 2007, Part 1 of the Welfare Reform Act 2012 and, Part 4 of that Act and Part 1 of the Pensions Act 2014 and section 30 of that Act

"expert" means a person appearing to the Secretary of State to have knowledge or experience which would be relevant in determining the question of fact requiring special expertise;

"the former legislation" means the National Insurance Acts 1965 to 1974, the National Insurance (Industrial Injuries) Acts 1965 to 1974, the Social Security Act 1975 and Part II of the Social Security Act 1986.

Commencement Date – In so far as it was not already in force s. 11 entered into force (except for the purposes of housing benefit, council tax benefit and decisions to which SI 1999/527, art. 4(6) applies; i.e. pre-1 April 1999 decisions under SSAA 1992, s. 17(1), s. 20(3) and PSA 1993, s. 170(1)) with effect from 29 November 1999 (SI 1999/3178 (C. 81), art. 2(1)(a); 2(2) and Sch. 1).
S. 11(1), (2) and (3) (except the definition of "the current legislation" in so far as it relates to the Jobseekers Act 1995 and the Social Security (Recovery of Benefits) Act 1997, and the definition of "the former legislation") in so far as it relates to SSA 1986, Pt. II) entered into force; for the purposes of (i) decisions whether a person is entitled to be credited with earnings or contributions in accordance with regulations made under s. 22(5) of the Contributions and Benefits Act; and (ii) decisions whether a person was, within the meaning of regulations, precluded from regular employment by responsibilities at home; with effect from 18 October (SI 1999/2860 (C. 75), art. 2(c)(iv), (v) and Sch. 1).
S. 11(1) and (2), and (3) (except the definition of "the current legislation" in so far as it relates to the Jobseekers Act 1995 and the definition of "the former legislation" in so far as it relates to Pt. II of SSA 1986) entered into force, for the purposes of benefits under SSCBA 1992, Pt. II except child's special allowance, with effect from 6 September 1999 (SI 1999/2422 (C. 61), art. 2(c)(i) and Sch. 1).
S. 11(1), (2) and (3) (except the definition of "the current legislation" in so far as it relates to the Jobseekers Act 1995 and the Social Security (Recovery of Benefits) Act 1997, and the definition of "the former legislation") in so far as it relates to SSA 1986, Pt. II entered into force, for the purposes of any matter to which, by virtue of PSA 1993, s. 170, provisions of SSA 1998, Pt. I, Ch. II are to apply, with effect from 5 July 1999 (SI 1999/1958 (C. 51), art. 2(1)(b)(iv)).
S. 11(1), (2) and (3) (except the definition of "the current legislation" in so far as it relates to the Jobseekers Act 1995 and the Social Security (Recovery of Benefits) Act 1997, and the definition of "the formerlegislation") in so far as it relates to SSA 1986, Pt. II entered into force, for the purposes of benefits under SSCBA 1992, Pt. II except child's special allowance, with effect from 6 September 1999 (SI 1999/2422 (C. 61), art. 2(c)(i) and Sch. 1).

Prospective amendments – In s. 11(3), in the definition of "the current legislation", the words ", section 30 of that Act and sections 18 to 21 of the Welfare Reform and Work Act 2016" substituted for the words "and section 30 of that Act" by Welfare Reform and Work Act 2016, s. 20(5), with effect from a day to be appointed by the Secretary of State under Welfare Reform and Work Act 2016, s. 36(6).

History – In s. 11(3), in the definition of "the current legislation", the words "and section 30 of that Act" inserted after the words "Part 1 of the Pensions Act 2014" by PA 2014, s. 31 and Sch. 16, para. 40, with effect from 6 April 2017, subject to SI 2017/297, art. 4 (later commencement for abolition of bereavement payment and bereavement allowance) and 5 (commencement for entitlement to bereavement payment and bereavement support payment) (SI 2017/297, art. 3(2)).
In s. 11(3), in the definition of "the current legislation", the words ", Part 4 of that Act and Part 1 of the Pensions Act 2014" substituted for the words "and Part 4 of that Act" by PA 2014, s. 23 and Sch. 12, para. 34, with effect from 6 April 2016 (as not brought into force by any earlier order under PA 2014, s. 56(1)).
In s. 11(3), in the definition of "the current legislation", the words "and Part 4 of that Act" inserted by WRA 2012, s. 91 and Sch. 9, para. 40, with effect from 25 February 2013 (SI 2013/358, art. 2(2) and Sch. 2, para. 43).
In s. 11(3), in the definition of "the current legislation", the words ", Part 1 of the Welfare Reform Act 2007, Part 1 of the Welfare Reform Act 2012" substituted for the words "and Part 1 of the Welfare Reform Act 2007" by WRA 2012, s. 31 and Sch. 2, para. 46, with effect from 25 February 2013 (SI 2013/358, art. 2(2) and Sch. 2, para. 40).

In s. 11(3) in the definition of "the current legislation", the words", the State Pension Credit Act 2002 and Part 1 of the Welfare Reform Act 2007" substituted for the words "and the State Pension Credit Act 2002" by WRA 2007, s. 28(1) and Sch. 3, para. 17, with effect (for the purpose of making regulations) from 18 March 2008 and from 27 July 2008 for other purposes (SI 2008/787, art. 2 and Schedule).
In s. 11(3), in the definition of "current legislation" the words ", the Social Security (Recovery of Benefits) Act 1997 and the State Pension Credit Act 2002" substituted by the SPCA 2002, s. 11 and Sch. 1, para. 7 with effect from 2 July 2002 only for the purposes of making regulations and orders, by virtue of SI 2002/1691.
In s. 11(3), the definition of "current legislation" the word "and" in the second place that it occurs repealed by the SPCA 2002, s. 21 and Sch. 3 with effect from 7 April 2003 by virtue of SI 2003/966.
S. 11(1) entered into force, only for the purposes of making regulations, with effect from 4 March 1999 (SI 1998/528).

APPEALS

12 Appeal to First-tier Tribunal

12(1) This section applies to any decision of the Secretary of State under section 8 or 10 above (whether as originally made or as revised under section 9 above) which–

(a) is made on a claim for, or on an award of, a relevant benefit, and does not fall within Schedule 2 to this Act;

(b) is made otherwise than on such a claim or award, and falls within Schedule 3 to this Act.

(c) [omitted by SSC(TF)A 1999, s. 18 and Sch. 7, para. 25(2)(b).]

12(2) In the case of a decision to which this section applies, the claimant and such other person as may be prescribed shall have a right to appeal to the First-tier Tribunal, but nothing in this subsection shall confer a right of appeal

(a) in relation to a prescribed decision, or a prescribed determination embodied in or necessary to a decision, or

(b) where regulations under subsection (3A) so provide.

12(3) Regulations under subsection (2) above shall not prescribe any decision or determination that relates to the conditions of entitlement to a relevant benefit for which a claim has been validly made or for which no claim is required.

12(3A) Regulations may provide that, in such cases or circumstances as may be prescribed, there is a right of appeal under subsection (2) in relation to a decision only if the Secretary of State has considered whether to revise the decision under section 9.

12(3B) The regulations may in particular provide that that condition is met only where–

(a) the consideration by the Secretary of State was on an application,

(b) the Secretary of State considered issues of a specified description, or

(c) the consideration by the Secretary of State satisfied any other condition specified in the regulations

12(3C) The references in subsections (3A) and (3B) to regulations and to the Secretary of State are subject to any enactment under or by virtue of which the functions under this Chapter are transferred to or otherwise made exercisable by a person other than the Secretary of State.

12(3D) In the case of a decision relating to child benefit or guardian's allowance, the making of any appeal under this section against the decision as originally made must follow the Commissioners for Her Majesty's Revenue and Customs first deciding, on an application made for revision of that decision under section 9, not to revise the decision.

12(4) [Not relevant to National Insurance contributions.]

12(5) In any case where–

(a) the Secretary of State has made a decision in relation to a claim under Part V of the Contributions and Benefits Act; and

(b) the entitlement to benefit under that Part of that Act of any person other than the claimant is or may be, under Part VI of Schedule 7 to that Act, affected by that decision,

that other person shall have the same right of appeal to the First-tier Tribunal as the claimant.

12(6) A person with a right of appeal under this section shall be given such notice of a decision to which this section applies and of that right as may be prescribed.

12(7) Regulations may

(a) make provision as to the manner in which, and the time within which, appeals are to be brought

(b) provide that, where in accordance with regulations under subsection (3A) there is no right of appeal against a decision, any purported appeal may be treated as an application for revision under section 9.

12(8) In deciding an appeal under this section, the First-tier Tribunal–

(a) need not consider any issue that is not raised by the appeal; and

(b) shall not take into account any circumstances not obtaining at the time when the decision appealed against was made.

12(9) The reference in subsection (1) above to a decision under section 10 above is a reference to a decision superseding any such decision as is mentioned in paragraph (a) or (b) of subsection (1) of that section.

Commencement Date – In so far as it was not already in force s. 12 entered into force (except for the purposes of housing benefit, council tax benefit and decisions to which SI 1999/527, art. 4(6) applies; i.e. pre-1 April 1999 decisions under SSAA 1992, s. 17(1), s. 20(3) and PSA 1993, s. 170(1)) with effect from 29 November 1999 (SI 1999/3178 (C. 81), art. 2(1)(a); 2(2) and Sch. 1).
S. 12(1) entered into force on 4 March 1999, for the purposes of making regulations, but only so far as it relates to SSA 1998, Sch. 2, para. 9 and Sch. 3, para. 1, 4, and 9 (SI 1999/528).
S. 12(1)(b) (in so far as it relates to Sch. 3, para. 1–6, 8, 9, 16 and 17) entered into force; for the purposes of (i) decisions whether a person is entitled to be credited with earnings or contributions in accordance with regulations made under s. 22(5) of the Contributions and Benefits Act; and (ii) decisions whether a person was, within the meaning of regulations, precluded from regular employment by responsibilities at home; with effect from 18 October 1999 (SI 1999/2860 (C. 75), art. 2(c)(iv), (v) and Sch. 1).
S. 12(2) entered into force, for the purposes of making regulations, on 4 March 1999 (SSA (Commencement No. 5) Order 1999 (SI 1999/528)). The present wording was substituted by SSC(TF)A 1999, s. 18 and Sch. 7, para. 25(3), with effect from 1 April 1999 (SI 1999/527).
S. 12(2)–(4) and (6)–(9) entered into force; for the purposes of (i) decisions whether a person is entitled to be credited with earnings or contributions in accordance with regulations made under s. 22(5) of the Contributions and Benefits Act; and (ii) decisions whether a person was, within the meaning of regulations, precluded from regular employment by responsibilities at home; with effect from 18 October 1999 (SI 1999/2860 (C. 75), art. 2(c)(iv), (v) and Sch. 1).
S. 12(2)–(4) and (6)–(9) entered into force, for the purposes of benefits under SSCBA 1992, Pt. II except child's special allowance, with effect from 6 September 1999 (SI 1999/2422 (C. 61), art. 2(c)(i) and Sch. 1).
S. 12(2), (3), (5)–(9) entered into force, for the purposes of any matter to which, by virtue of PSA 1993, s. 170, provisions of SSA 1998, Pt. I, Ch. II are to apply, with effect from 5 July 1999, (SI 1999/1958 (C. 51), art. 2(1)(b)(iv)).
S. 12(3), (6) and (7) entered into force, for the purposes of making regulations, on 4 March 1999 (SI 1999/528).

History – In the heading to s. 12, "First-tier Tribunal" substituted by SI 2008/2833, art. 9 and Sch. 3, para. 149(a), with effect from 3 November 2008.
S. 12(1)(c) omitted by SSC(TF)A 1999, s. 18 and Sch. 7, para. 25(2)(b), with effect from 1 April 1999 (SI 1999/527).
S. 12(2)(b) inserted (and s. 12(2)(a) created from part of existing text of s. 12(2) and the word ", or") by WRA 2012, s. 102(2), with effect from 25 February 2013.
In s. 12(2), "the First-tier Tribunal" substituted by SI 2008/2833, art. 9 and Sch. 3, para. 149(b), with effect from 3 November 2008.
S. 12(3A), (3B) and (3C) inserted by WRA 2012, s. 102(3), with effect from 25 February 2013.
S. 12(3D) inserted by SI 2014/886, art. 4(1), with effect from 6 April 2014.
In s. 12(5), "the First-tier Tribunal" substituted by SI 2008/2833, art. 9 and Sch. 3, para. 149(b), with effect from 3 November 2008.
S. 12(7)(b) inserted (and s. 12(7)(a) created from part of existing text of s. 12(7)) by WRA 2012, s. 102(4), with effect from 25 February 2013.
In s. 12(8), "the First-tier Tribunal" substituted by SI 2008/2833, art. 9 and Sch. 3, para. 149(b), with effect from 3 November 2008.

Cross references – SI 2008/2685, Rule 25: medical and physical examination in appeals sunder s. 12.
SI 2005/191, reg. 6: modification of s. 12 for the purposes of appeals against Revenue decisions in respect of child trust funds.

13 Redetermination etc. of appeals by tribunal

13(1) This section applies where an application is made to the First-tier Tribunal for permission to appeal to the Upper Tribunal from any decision of the First-tier Tribunal under section 12 or this section.

13(2) [Omitted by SI 2008/2833, art. 9 and Sch. 3, para. 150(b).]

13(3) If each of the principal parties to the case expresses the view that the decision was erroneous in point of law, the First-tier Tribunal shall set aside the decision and refer the case for determination by a differently constituted First-tier Tribunal.

13(4) In this section and section 14 below **"the principal parties"** means–

(a) the persons mentioned in subsection (3)(a) and (b) of that section, and

(b) where applicable, the person mentioned in subsection (3)(d) and such a person as is first mentioned in subsection (4) of that section.

Commencement Date – In so far as it was not already in force s. 13 entered into force (except for the purposes of housing benefit, council tax benefit and decisions to which SI 1999/527, art. 4(6) applies; i.e. pre-1 April 1999 decisions under SSAA 1992, s. 17(1), s. 20(3) and PSA 1993, s. 170(1)) with effect from 29 November 1999 (SI 1999/3178 (C. 81), art. 2(1)(a), 2(2) and Sch. 1).
S. 13 entered into force; for the purposes of (i) decisions whether a person is entitled to be credited with earnings or contributions in accordance with regulations made under section 22(5) of the Contributions and Benefits Act; and (ii) decisions whether a person was, within the meaning of regulations, precluded from regular employment by responsibilities at home; with effect from 18 October 1999 (SI 1999/2860 (C. 75), art. 2(c)(iv), (v) and Sch. 1).
S. 13 entered into force, for the purposes of benefits under SSCBA 1992, Pt. II except child's special allowance, with effect from 6 September 1999 (SI 1999/2422 (C. 61), art. 2(c)(i) and Sch. 1).
S. 13 entered into force, for the purposes of any matter to which, by virtue of PSA 1993, s. 170, provisions of SSA 1998, Pt. I, Ch. II are to apply, with effect from 5 July 1999 (SI 1999/1958 (C. 51), art. 2(1)(b)(iv)).

History – In s. 13(1), the words "to the First-tier Tribunal for permission to appeal to the Upper Tribunal from any decision of the First-tier Tribunal under section 12 or this section" substituted by SI 2008/2833, art. 9 and Sch. 3, para. 150(a), with effect from 3 November 2008.
S. 13(2) omitted by SI 2008/2833, art. 9 and Sch. 3, para. 150(b), with effect from 3 November 2008.
In s. 13(3) "the First-tier Tribunal" in each place substituted, by SI 2008/2833, art. 9 and Sch. 3, para. 150(c), with effect from 3 November 2008.
S. 13(4) substituted by SSC(TF)A 1999, s. 18 and Sch. 7, para. 26, from 1 April 1999 (SI 1999/527).

Cross references – SI 2005/191, reg. 7: modification of s. 13 for the purposes of appeals against Revenue decisions in respect of child trust funds.

14 Appeal from First-tier Tribunal to Upper Tribunal

14(1) [Omitted by SI 2008/2833, art. 9 and Sch. 3, para. 151(b).]

14(2) [Omitted by SSC(TF)A 1999, s. 18 and Sch. 7, para. 27(a).]

14(3) An appeal to the Upper Tribunal under section 11 of the Tribunals, Courts and Enforcement Act 2007 from any decision of the First-Tier Tribunal under section 12 or 13 above lies at the instance of any of the following–

(a) the Secretary of State;

(b) the claimant and such other person as may be prescribed;

(c) in any of the cases mentioned in subsection (5) below, a trade union; and

(d) a person from whom it is determined that any amount is recoverable under or by virtue of section 71 or 74 of the Administration Act.

14(4) [Not relevant to National Insurance contributions.]

14(5) The following are the cases in which an appeal lies at the instance of a trade union–

(a) where the claimant is a member of the union at the time of the appeal and was so immediately before the matter in question arose;

(b) where that matter in any way relates to a deceased person who was a member of the union at the time of his death;

(c) where the case relates to industrial injuries benefit and the claimant or, in relation to industrial death benefit, the deceased, was a member of the union at the time of the relevant accident.

14(6) Subsections (2), (3) and (5) above, as they apply to a trade union, apply also to any other association which exists to promote the interests and welfare of its members.

14(7) [Omitted by SI 2008/2833, art. 9 and Sch. 3, para. 151(d).]

14(8) [Omitted by SI 2008/2833, art. 9 and Sch. 3, para. 151(d).]

14(9) [Omitted by SI 2008/2833, art. 9 and Sch. 3, para. 151(d).]

14(10) [Omitted by SI 2008/2833, art. 9 and Sch. 3, para. 151(d).]

14(11) [Omitted by SI 2008/2833, art. 9 and Sch. 3, para. 151(d).]

14(12) [Omitted by SI 2008/2833, art. 9 and Sch. 3, para. 151(d).]

Commencement Date – In so far as it was not already in force s. 14 entered into force (except for the purposes of housing benefit, council tax benefit and decisions to which SI 1999/527, art. 4(6) applies; i.e. pre-1 April 1999 decisions under SSAA 1992, s. 17(1), s. 20(3) and PSA 1993, s. 170(1)) with effect from 29 November 1999 (SI 1999/3178 (C. 81), art. 2(1)(a); 2(2) and Sch. 1).
S. 14 entered into force; for the purposes of (i) decisions whether a person is entitled to be credited with earnings or contributions in accordance with regulations made under s. 22(5) of the Contributions and Benefits Act; and (ii) decisions whether a person was, within the meaning of regulations, precluded from regular employment by responsibilities at home; with effect from 18 October 1999 (SI 1999/2860 (C. 75), art. 2(c)(iv), (v) and Sch. 1).
S. 14 entered into force, for the purposes of benefits under SSCBA 1992, Pt. II except child's special allowance, with effect from 6 September 1999 (SI 1999/2422 (C. 61), art. 2(c)(i) and Sch. 1).
S. 14 entered into force, for the purposes of any matter to which, by virtue of PSA 1993, s. 170, provisions of SSA 1998, Pt. I, Ch. II are to apply, with effect from 5 July 1999 (SI 1999/1958 (C. 51), art. 2(1)(b)(iv)).
S. 14(3), (10) and (11) in force, for the purposes of making regulations, from 4 March 1999 (SI 1999/528).
S. 14(12) in force, for the purposes of making regulations, from 4 March 1999 in so far as it relates to SSA 1998 Sch. 4, para. (6) and (8) (SSA (Commencement No. 5) Order 1999 (SI 1999/528)).

History – In the heading to s. 14, "First-tier Tribunal to Upper Tribunal" substituted for "tribunal to Commissioner" by SI 2008/2833, art. 9 and Sch. 3, para. 151(a), with effect from 3 November 2008.
S. 14(1) omitted by SI 2008/2833, art. 9 and Sch. 3, para. 151(b), with effect from 3 November 2008.
S. 14(2) omitted (without entering into force) by SSC(TF)A 1999, s. 18 and Sch. 7, para. 27(a), with effect from 1 April 1999 (SI 1999/527).
In s. 14(3), the words "to the Upper Tribunal under section 11 of the Tribunals, Courts and Enforcement Act 2007 from any decision of the First-Tier Tribunal under section 12 or 13 above lies" substituted for the words "lies under this section" by SI 2008/2833, art. 9 and Sch. 3, para. 151(c), with effect from 3 November 2008.
In s. 14(3) the words "In any other case", at the beginning of the subsection, omitted with effect from 1 April 1999, by SSC(TF)A 1999, s. 18 and Sch. 7, para. 27(b).
S. 14(7)–(12) omitted by SI 2008/2833, art. 9 and Sch. 3, para. 151(d), with effect from 3 November 2008.

Cross references – SI 2005/191, reg. 8: modification of s. 14 for the purposes of appeals against Revenue decisions in respect of child trust funds.
SI 2005/191, reg. 9: modification of s. 14(11) and (12) for the purposes of appeals against Revenue decisions in respect of child trust funds.

15 Applications for permission to appeal against a decision of the Upper Tribunal

15(1) [Omitted by SI 2008/2833, art. 9 and Sch. 3, para. 152(b).]

15(2) [Omitted by SI 2008/2833, art. 9 and Sch. 3, para. 152(b).]

15(3) An application for permission to appeal from a decision of the Upper Tribunal in respect of a decision of the First-tier Tribunal under section 12 or 13 may only be made by–

(a) a person who, before the proceedings before the Upper Tribunal were begun, was entitled to appeal to the Upper Tribunal from the decision to which the Upper Tribunal's decision relates;

(b) any other person who was a party to the proceedings in which the first decision mentioned in paragraph (a) above was given;

(c) any other person who is authorised by regulations to apply for permission.

15(4) [Omitted by SI 2008/2833, art. 9 and Sch. 3, para. 152(d).]

15(5) [Omitted by SI 2008/2833, art. 9 and Sch. 3, para. 152(b).]

Commencement Date – In so far as it was not already in force s. 15 entered into force (except for the purposes of housing benefit, council tax benefit and decisions to which SI 1999/527, art. 4(6) applies; i.e. pre-1 April 1999 decisions under SSAA 1992, s. 17(1), s. 20(3) and PSA 1993, s. 170(1)) with effect from 29 November 1999 (SI 1999/3178 (C. 81), art. 2(1)(a); 2(2) and Sch. 1).
S. 15 entered into force; for the purposes of (i) decisions whether a person is entitled to be credited with earnings or contributions in accordance with regulations made under s. 22(5) of the Contributions and Benefits Act; and (ii) decisions whether a person was, within the meaning of regulations, precluded from regular employment by responsibilities at home; with effect from 18 October 1999 (SI 1999/2860 (C. 75), art. 2(c)(iv), (v) and Sch. 1).
S. 15 entered into force, for the purposes of benefits under SSCBA 1992, Pt. II except child's special allowance, with effect from 6 September 1999 (SI 1999/2422 (C. 61), art. 2(c)(i) and Sch. 1).
S. 15 entered into force, for the purposes of any matter to which, by virtue of PSA 1993, s. 170, provisions of SSA 1998, Pt. I, Ch. II are to apply, with effect from 5 July 1999 (SI 1999/1958 (C. 51), art. 2(1)(b)(iv)).
S. 15(2) and (3) entered into force, only for the purposes of making regulations, with effect from 4 March 1999 (SI 1999/528).

History – Heading to s. 15 substituted by SI 2008/2833, art. 9 and Sch. 3, para. 152(a), with effect from 3 November 2008.
S. 15(1) and (2) omitted by SI 2008/2833, art. 9 and Sch. 3, para. 152(b), with effect from 3 November 2008.
In s. 15(3), the words "An application for permission to appeal from a decision of the Upper Tribunal in respect of a decision of the First-tier Tribunal under section 12 or 13" substituted by SI 2008/2833, art. 9 and Sch. 3, para. 152(c), with effect from 3 November 2008.
In s. 15(3)(a), "Upper Tribunal" substituted in both places, and "Upper Tribunal's" substituted, by SI 2008/2833, art. 9 and Sch. 3, para. 152(c), with effect from 3 November 2008.
In s. 15(3)(c), "permission" substituted by SI 2008/2833, art. 9 and Sch. 3, para. 152(c), with effect from 3 November 2008.
In s. 15(3), at the end, the words "and regulations may make provision with respect to the manner in which and the time within which applications must be made to a Commissioner for leave under this section and with respect to the procedure for dealing with such applications", omitted by SI 2008/2833, art. 9 and Sch. 3, para. 152(c), with effect from 3 November 2008.
S. 15(4) and (5) omitted by SI 2008/2833, art. 9 and Sch. 3, para. 152(d), with effect from 3 November 2008.

Cross references – SI 2005/191, reg. 10: modification of s. 15 for the purposes of appeals against Revenue decisions in respect of child trust funds.

15A Functions of Senior President of Tribunals

15A(1) The Senior President of Tribunals shall ensure that appropriate steps are taken by the First-tier Tribunal to secure the confidentiality, in such circumstances as may be prescribed, of any prescribed material, or any prescribed classes or categories of material.

15A(2) [Omitted by Deregulation Act 2015, s. 79.]

15A(3) [Omitted by Deregulation Act 2015, s. 79.]

History – S. 15A(2) and (3) omitted by Deregulation Act 2015, s. 79, with effect from the end of the period of 2 months beginning on 26 March 2015. Former s. 15A read as follows:
"**15A(2)** Each year the Senior President of Tribunals shall make to the Secretary of State a written report, based on the cases coming before the First-tier Tribunal, on the standards achieved by the Secretary of State in the making of decisions against which an appeal lies to the First-tier Tribunal.
15A(3) The Lord Chancellor shall publish the report.".
In former s. 15A(2), the words "and the Child Maintenance and Enforcement Commission" which appeared after the words "Secretary of State" (in both places) omitted by SI 2012/2007, art. 64(b), with effect from 31 July 2012.
S. 15A inserted by SI 2008/2833, art. 9 and Sch. 3, para. 153, with effect from 3 November 2008.

PROCEDURE ETC

16 Procedure

16(1) Regulations ("procedure regulations") may make any such provision as is specified in Schedule 5 to this Act.

16(2) [Omitted by SI 2008/2833, art. 9 and Sch. 3, para. 154.]

16(3) It is hereby declared–

(a) [omitted by SI 2008/2833, art. 9 and Sch. 3, para. 154;]

(b) that the power to provide for the procedure to be followed in connection with the making of decisions by the Secretary of State includes power to make provision with respect to the formulation of the matters to be decided, whether on a reference under section 117 of the Administration Act or otherwise.

16(4) [Ceased to have effect following SSC(TF)A 1999, s. 18 and Sch. 7 para. 28.]

16(5) [Ceased to have effect following SSC(TF)A 1999, s. 18 and Sch. 7 para. 28.]

16(6) [Omitted by SI 2008/2833, art. 9 and Sch. 3, para. 154.]

16(7) [Omitted by SI 2008/2833, art. 9 and Sch. 3, para. 154.]

16(8) [Omitted by SI 2008/2833, art. 9 and Sch. 3, para. 154.]

16(9) [Omitted by SI 2008/2833, art. 9 and Sch. 3, para. 154.]

Commencement Date – In so far as it was not already in force s. 16 entered into force (except for the purposes of housing benefit, council tax benefit and decisions to which SI 1999/527, art. 4(6) applies; i.e. pre-1 April 1999 decisions under SSAA 1992, s. 17(1), s. 20(3) and PSA 1993, s. 170(1)) with effect from 29 November 1999 (SI 1999/3178 (C. 81), art. 2(1)(a); 2(2) and Sch. 1).
S. 16 entered into force; for the purposes of (i) decisions whether a person is entitled to be credited with earnings or contributions in accordance with regulations made under section 22(5) of the Contributions and Benefits Act; and (ii) decisions whether a person was, within the meaning of regulations, precluded from regular employment by responsibilities at home; with effect from 18 October 1999 (SI 1999/2860 (C. 75), art. 2(c)(iv), (v) and Sch. 1).
S. 16 entered into force, for the purposes of benefits under SSCBA 1992, Pt. II except child's special allowance, with effect from 6 September 1999 (SI 1999/2422 (C. 61), art. 2(c)(i) and Sch. 1).
S. 16 entered into force, for the purposes of any matter to which, by virtue of PSA 1993, s. 170, provisions of SSA 1998, Pt. I, Ch. II are to apply, with effect from 5 July 1999 (SI 1999/1958 (C. 51), art. 2(1)(b)(iv)).
S. 16(1)–(3) and (9) in force, for the purposes of making regulations, with effect from 4 March 1999 (SI 1999/528).
S. 16(4) and (5) in force with effect from 8 September 1998 excepts. 16(4)(b) which entered into force on 6 April 1999 (SI 1998/2209).
History – S. 16(2) omitted by SI 2008/2833, art. 9 and Sch. 3, para. 154, with effect from 3 November 2008.
S. 16(3)(a) omitted by SI 2008/2833, art. 9 and Sch. 3, para. 154, with effect from 3 November 2008.
S. 16(4) and (5) ceased to have effect following Social Security (Transfer of Functions etc) Act 1999, s. 18 and Sch. 7 para. 28, with effect from 1 April 1999 (by virtue of SI 1999/527).
S. 16(6)–(9) omitted by SI 2008/2833, art. 9 and Sch. 3, para. 154, with effect from 3 November 2008.
Cross references – TCA 2002, s. 63(13): meaning of the term "Social Security Commissioner" by reference to s. 16.
SI 2005/191, reg. 11: modification of s. 16 for the purposes of appeals against Revenue decisions in respect of child trust funds.

17 Finality of decisions

17(1) Subject to the provisions of this Chapter and to any provision made by or under Chapter 2 of Part 1 of the Tribunals, Courts and Enforcement Act 2007, any decision made in accordance with the foregoing provisions of this Chapter shall be final; and subject to the provisions of any regulations under section 11 above, any decision made in accordance with those regulations shall be final.

17(2) If and to the extent that regulations so provide, any finding of fact or other determination embodied in or necessary to such a decision, or on which such a decision is based, shall be conclusive for the purposes of–

(a) further such decisions;

(b) [not relevant to National Insurance contributions;]

(c) [not relevant to National Insurance contributions.]

Commencement Date – In so far as it was not already in force s. 17 entered into force (except for the purposes of housing benefit, council tax benefit and decisions to which SI 1999/527, art. 4(6) applies; i.e. pre-1 April 1999 decisions under SSAA 1992, s. 17(1), s. 20(3) and PSA 1993, s. 170(1)) with effect from 29 November 1999 (SI 1999/3178 (C. 81), art. 2(1)(a); 2(2) and Sch. 1).
S. 17 entered into force, only for the purposes of making regulations, with effect from 4 March 1999 (SI 1999/528).
S. 17 entered into force, for the purposes of any matter to which, by virtue of PSA 1993, s. 170, provisions of SSA 1998, Pt. I, Ch. II are to apply, with effect from 5 July 1999 (SI 1999/1958 (C. 51), art. 2(1)(b)(iv)).
S. 17 entered into force, for the purposes of benefits under SSCBA 1992, Pt. II except child's special allowance, with effect from 6 September 1999 (SI 1999/2422 (C. 61), art. 2(c)(i) and Sch. 1).
S. 17 entered into force; for the purposes of (i) decisions whether a person is entitled to be credited with earnings or contributions in accordance with regulations made under section 22(5) of the Contributions and Benefits Act; and (ii) decisions whether a person was, within the meaning of regulations, precluded from regular employment by responsibilities at home; with effect from 18 October 1999 (SI 1999/2860 (C. 75), art. 2(c)(iv), (v) and Sch. 1).
History – In s. 17(1), the words "and to any provision made by or under Chapter 2 of Part 1 of the Tribunals, Courts and Enforcement Act 2007" inserted by SI 2008/2833, art. 9 and Sch. 3, para. 155, with effect from 3 November 2008.
Cross references – SI 2005/191, reg. 12: modification of s. 17 for the purposes of appeals against Revenue decisions in respect of child trust funds.
SI 2016/1078, reg. 3: modification of s. 17 for the purposes of decisions of an appropriate tribunal on a childcare payments appeal under CPA 2014, s. 56.

18 Matters arising as respects decisions

18(1) Regulations may make provision as respects matters arising–

(a) pending any decision under this Chapter of the Secretary of State, or the First-tier Tribunal, or any decision of the Upper Tribunal which relates to any decision under this Chapter of the First-Tier Tribunal, which relates to–

(i) [not relevant to National Insurance contributions;]

(ii) [not relevant to National Insurance contributions;]

(iii) [omitted by SSC(TF)A 1999, s. 18 and Sch. 7, para. 29, with effect from 1 April 1999;]

(iv) [omitted by SSC(TF)A 1999, s. 18 and Sch. 7, para. 29, with effect from 1 April 1999.]

(b) out of the revision under section 9 above or on appeal of any such decision.

18(2) [Not relevant to National Insurance contributions.]

Commencement Date – In so far as it was not already in force s. 18 entered into force (except for the purposes of housing benefit, council tax benefit and decisions to which SI 1999/527, art. 4(6) applies; i.e. pre-1 April 1999 decisions under SSAA 1992, s. 17(1), s. 20(3) and PSA 1993, s. 170(1)) with effect from 29 November 1999 (SI 1999/3178 (C. 81), art. 2(1)(a); 2(2) and Sch. 1).
S. 18(1) entered into force, for the purposes of making regulations, on 4 March 1999 (SI 1999/528).
S. 18(1) entered into force, for the purposes of any matter to which, by virtue of PSA 1993, s. 170, provisions of SSA 1998, Pt. I, Ch. II are to apply, with effect from 5 July 1999 (SI 1999/1958 (C. 51), art. 2(1)(b)(iv)).
S. 18(1) entered into force, for the purposes of benefits under SSCBA 1992, Pt. II except child's special allowance, with effect from 6 September 1999 (SI 1999/2422 (C. 61), art. 2(c)(i) and Sch. 1).

S. 18(1) entered into force; for the purposes of (i) decisions whether a person is entitled to be credited with earnings or contributions in accordance with regulations made under section 22(5) of the Contributions and Benefits Act; and (ii) decisions whether a person was, within the meaning of regulations, precluded from regular employment by responsibilities at home; with effect from 18 October 1999 (SI 1999/2860 (C. 75), art. 2(c)(iv), (v) and Sch. 1).

History – In s. 18(1)(a), the words "or the First-tier Tribunal, or any decision of the Upper Tribunal which relates to any decision under this Chapter of the First-Tier Tribunal," substituted for the words ", an appeal tribunal or a Commissioner" by SI 2008/2833, art. 9 and Sch. 3, para. 156, with effect from 3 November 2008.
S. 18(1)(a)(iii) and (1)(a)(iv) omitted by SSC(TF)A 1999, s. 18 and Sch. 7, para. 29, with effect from 1 April 1999 (SI 1999/527).

Cross references – TCA 2002, s. 51 and Sch. 4, para. 15: references in this Chapter to a decision of the Secretary of State are, where the context so requires in consequence of TCA 2002, s. 50 (functions transferred to the Board), to be construed as references to a decision of the Board, or, where the power to decide is exercised by an officer of the Board, an officer of the Board.

24A Appeals dependent on issues falling to be decided by Inland Revenue

24A(1) Regulations may make provision for the First-tier Tribunal or Upper Tribunal, where on any appeal there arises any issue which under section 8 of the Social Security Contributions (Transfer of Functions, etc.) Act 1999 falls to be decided by the Inland Revenue, to require the Secretary of State to refer the issue to the Inland Revenue.

24A(2) Regulations under this section may–

(a) provide for the appeal to be referred to the Secretary of State pending the decision by an officer of the Inland Revenue,

(b) enable or require the Secretary of State, in specified circumstances, to deal with any other issue arising on the appeal pending the decision on the referred issue, and

(c) enable the Secretary of State, on receiving the decision of an officer of the Inland Revenue, or any determination of the First-tier Tribunal or Upper Tribunal made on an appeal from his decision–

  (i) to revise his decision,

  (ii) to make a decision superseding his decision, or

  (iii) to refer the appeal to the First-tier Tribunal or Upper Tribunal for determination.

Commencement Date – In so far as it was not already in force s. 24A entered into force (except for the purposes of housing benefit, council tax benefit and decisions to which SI 1999/527, art. 4(6) applies; i.e. pre-1 April 1999 decisions under SSAA 1992, s. 17(1), s. 20(3) and PSA 1993, s. 170(1)) with effect from 29 November 1999 (SI 1999/3178 (C. 81), art. 2(1)(a); 2(2) and Sch. 1).
S. 24A entered into force; for the purposes of (i) decisions whether a person is entitled to be credited with earnings or contributions in accordance with regulations made under section 22(5) of the Contributions and Benefits Act; and (ii) decisions whether a person was, within the meaning of regulations, precluded from regular employment by responsibilities at home; with effect from 18 October 1999 (SI 1999/2860 (C. 75), art. 2(c)(iv), (v) and Sch. 1).
S. 24A entered into force, for the purposes of benefits under SSCBA 1992, Pt. II except child's special allowance, with effect from 6 September 1999 (SI 1999/2422 (C. 61), art. 2(c)(i) and Sch. 1).
S. 24A entered into force, for the purposes of any matter to which, by virtue of PSA 1993, s. 170, provisions of SSA 1998, Pt. I, Ch. II are to apply, with effect from 5 July 1999 (SI 1999/1958 (C. 51), art. 2(1)(b)(iv)).

History – In s. 24A(1), "the First-tier Tribunal or Upper Tribunal" substituted by SI 2008/2833, art. 9 and Sch. 3, para. 160(a), with effect from 3 November 2008.
In s. 24A(2)(c), the words "First-tier Tribunal or Upper Tribunal" substituted by SI 2009/56, art. 3(1) and Sch. 1, para. 249, operative from 1 April 2009, subject to transitional and saving provisions in SI 2009/56, Sch. 3.
In s. 24A(2)(c)(iii), "First-tier Tribunal or Upper Tribunal" substituted by SI 2008/2833, art. 9 and Sch. 3, para. 160(b), with effect from 3 November 2008.
S. 24A inserted by SSC(TF)A 1999, s. 18 and Sch. 7 para. 33.

DECISIONS AND APPEALS DEPENDENT ON OTHER CASES

25 Decisions involving issues that arise on appeal in other cases

25(1) This section applies where–

(a) a decision by the Secretary of State falls to be made under section 8, 9 or 10 above in relation to a particular case; and

(b) an appeal is pending against the decision given in another case by the Upper Tribunal or a court (whether or not the two cases concern the same benefit).

25(2) In a case relating to a relevant benefit, the Secretary of State need not make the decision while the appeal is pending if he considers it possible that the result of the appeal will be such that, if it were already determined, there would be no entitlement to benefit.

25(3) If the Secretary of State considers it possible that the result of the appeal will be such that, if it were already determined, it would affect the decision in some other way–

(a) he need not, except in such cases or circumstances as may be prescribed, make the decision while the appeal is pending;

(b) he may, in such cases or circumstances as may be prescribed, make the decision on such basis as may be prescribed.

25(4) Where the Secretary of State acts in accordance with subsection (3)(b) above, following the determination of the appeal he shall if appropriate revise his decision (under section 9 above) in accordance with that determination.

25(5) For the purposes of this section, an appeal against a decision is pending if–

(a) an appeal against the decision has been brought but not determined;

(b) an application for leave to appeal against the decision has been made but not determined; or

(c) in such circumstances as may be prescribed, an appeal against the decision has not been brought (or, as the case may be, an application for leave to appeal against the decision has not been made) but the time for doing so has not yet expired.

25(6) In paragraphs (a), (b) and (c) of subsection (5) above, any reference to an appeal, or an application for leave to appeal, against a decision includes a reference to–

(a) an application for, or for leave to apply for, judicial review of the decision under section 31 of the Supreme Court Act 1981; or

(b) an application to the supervisory jurisdiction of the Court of Session in respect of the decision.

Commencement Date – In so far as it was not already in force s. 25 entered into force (except for the purposes of housing benefit, council tax benefit and decisions to which SI 1999/527, art. 4(6) applies; i.e. pre-1 April 1999 decisions under SSAA 1992, s. 17(1), s. 20(3) and PSA 1993, s. 170(1)) with effect from 29 November 1999 (SI 1999/3178 (C. 81), art. 2(1)(a), 2(2) and Sch. 1).
S. 25 entered into force; for the purposes of (i) decisions whether a person is entitled to be credited with earnings or contributions in accordance with regulations made under section 22(5) of the Contributions and Benefits Act; and (ii) decisions whether a person was, within the meaning of regulations, precluded from regular employment by responsibilities at home; with effect from 18 October 1999 (SI 1999/2860 (C. 75), art. 2(c)(iv), (v) and Sch. 1).
S. 25 entered into force, for the purposes of any matter to which, by virtue of PSA 1993, s. 170, provisions of SSA 1998, Pt. I, Ch. II are to apply, with effect from 5 July 1999 (SI 1999/1958 (C. 51), art. 2(1)(b)(iv)).
S. 25 entered into force, for the purposes of benefits under SSCBA 1992, Pt. II except child's special allowance, with effect from 6 September 1999 (SI 1999/2422 (C. 61), art. 2(c)(i) and Sch. 1).
S. 25(3)(b) and (5)(c) entered into force, only for the purposes of making regulations, with effect from 4 March 1999 (SI 1999/528).

History – In s. 25(1)(b), "the Upper Tribunal" substituted for "a Commissioner" by SI 2008/2833, art. 9 and Sch. 3, para. 161, with effect from 3 November 2008.

26 Appeals involving issues that arise on appeal in other cases

26(1) This section applies where–

(a) an appeal (**"appeal A"**) in relation to a decision under section 8, 9 or 10 above is made to the First-tier Tribunal, or from the First-tier Tribunal to the Upper Tribunal; and

(b) an appeal (**"appeal B"**) is pending against a decision given in a different case by the Upper Tribunal or a court (whether or not the two appeals concern the same benefit).

26(2) If the Secretary of State considers it possible that the result of appeal B will be such that, if it were already determined, it would affect the determination of appeal A, he may serve notice requiring the First-tier Tribunal or Upper Tribunal–

(a) not to determine appeal A but to refer it to him; or

(b) to deal with the appeal in accordance with subsection (4) below.

26(3) Where appeal A is referred to the Secretary of State under subsection (2)(a) above, following the determination of appeal B and in accordance with that determination, he shall if appropriate–

(a) in a case where appeal A has not been determined by the First-tier Tribunal, revise (under section 9 above) his decision which gave rise to that appeal; or

(b) in a case where appeal A has been determined by the First-tier Tribunal, make a decision (under section 10 above) superseding the tribunal's decision.

26(4) Where appeal A is to be dealt with in accordance with this subsection, the First-tier Tribunal or Upper Tribunal shall either–

(a) stay appeal A until appeal B is determined; or

(b) if the First-tier Tribunal or Upper Tribunal considers it to be in the interests of the appellant to do so, determine appeal A as if–

  (i) appeal B had already been determined; and

  (ii) the issues arising on appeal B had been decided in the way that was most unfavourable to the appellant.

In this subsection **"the appellant"** means the person who appealed or, as the case maybe, first appealed against the decision mentioned in subsection (1)(a) above.

26(5) Where the First-tier Tribunal or Upper Tribunal acts in accordance with subsection (4)(b) above, following the determination of appeal B the Secretary of State shall, if appropriate, make a decision (under section 10 above) superseding the decision of the First-tier Tribunal or Upper Tribunal in accordance with that determination.

26(6) For the purposes of this section, an appeal against a decision is pending if–

(a) an appeal against the decision has been brought but not determined;

(b) an application for leave to appeal against the decision has been made but not determined; or

(c) in such circumstances as may be prescribed, an appeal against the decision has not been brought (or, as the case may be, an application for leave to appeal against the decision has not been made) but the time for doing so has not yet expired.

26(7) In this section–

(a) the reference in subsection (1)(a) above to an appeal to the Upper Tribunal includes a reference to an application for leave to appeal to the Upper Tribunal; and

(b) any reference in paragraph (a), (b) or (c) of subsection (6) above to an appeal, or to an application for leave to appeal, against a decision includes a reference to–

(i) an application for, or for leave to apply for, judicial review of the decision under section 31 of the Supreme Court Act 1981; or

(ii) an application to the supervisory jurisdiction of the Court of Session in respect of the decision.

26(8) Regulations may make provision supplementing that made by this section.

Commencement Date – In so far as it was not already in force s. 26 entered into force (except for the purposes of housing benefit, council tax benefit and decisions to which SI 1999/527, art. 4(6) applies; i.e. pre-1 April 1999 decisions under SSAA 1992, s. 17(1), s. 20(3) and PSA 1993, s. 170(1)) with effect from 29 November 1999 (SI 1999/3178 (C. 81), art. 2(1)(a); 2(2) and Sch. 1).
S. 26 (except s. 26(8)) entered into force; for the purposes of (i) decisions whether a person is entitled to be credited with earnings or contributions in accordance with regulations made under section 22(5) of the Contributions and Benefits Act; and (ii) decisions whether a person was, within the meaning of regulations, precluded from regular employment by responsibilities at home; with effect from 18 October 1999 (SI 1999/2860 (C. 75), art. 2(c)(iv), (v) and Sch. 1).
S. 26 entered into force, for the purposes of any matter to which, by virtue of PSA 1993, s. 170, provisions of SSA 1998, Pt. I, Ch. II are to apply, with effect from 5 July 1999 (SI 1999/1958 (C. 51), art. 2(1)(b)(iv)).
S. 26 (except s. 26(8)) entered into force, for the purposes of benefits under SSCBA 1992, Pt. II except child's special allowance, with effect from 6 September 1999 (SI 1999/2422 (C. 61), art. 2(c)(i) and Sch. 1).
S. 26(6)(c) entered into force, only for the purposes of making regulations, with effect from 4 March 1999 (SI 1999/528).
S. 26(8) entered into force with effect from 1 June 1999 (SI 1999/1510).

History – In s. 26(1)(a), the words "the First-tier Tribunal, or from the First-tier Tribunal to the Upper Tribunal" substituted by SI 2008/2833, art. 9 and Sch. 3, para. 162(2)(a), with effect from 3 November 2008.
In s. 26(1)(b), "the Upper Tribunal" substituted by SI 2008/2833, art. 9 and Sch. 3, para. 162(2)(b), with effect from 3 November 2008.
In s. 26(2), "First-tier Tribunal or Upper Tribunal" substituted by SI 2008/2833, art. 9 and Sch. 3, para. 162(3), with effect from 3 November 2008.
In s. 26(3)(a) and (b), "First-tier Tribunal" substituted by SI 2008/2833, art. 9 and Sch. 3, para. 162(4), with effect from 3 November 2008.
In s. 26(4), "First-tier Tribunal or Upper Tribunal" substituted by SI 2008/2833, art. 9 and Sch. 3, para. 162(5)(a), with effect from 3 November 2008.
In s. 26(4)(b), "First-tier Tribunal or Upper Tribunal" substituted by SI 2008/2833, art. 9 and Sch. 3, para. 162(5)(b), with effect from 3 November 2008.
In s. 26(5), "First-tier Tribunal or Upper Tribunal" (in the first place) substituted, and "First-tier Tribunal or Upper Tribunal" (in the second place) substituted by SI 2008/2833, art. 9 and Sch. 3, para. 162(6), with effect from 3 November 2008.
In s. 26(7)(a), "the Upper Tribunal" substituted in both places by SI 2008/2833, art. 9 and Sch. 3, para. 162(7), with effect from 3 November 2008.

CASES OF ERROR

27 Restrictions on entitlement to benefit in certain cases of error

27(1) Subject to subsection (2) below, this section applies where–

(a) the effect of the determination, whenever made, of an appeal to the Upper Tribunal or the court ("the relevant determination") is that the adjudicating authority's decision out of which the appeal arose was erroneous in point of law; and

(b) after the date of the relevant determination a decision falls to be made by the Secretary of State in accordance with that determination (or would, apart from this section, fall to be so made)–

(i) in relation to a claim for benefit;

(ii) as to whether to revise, under section 9 above, a decision as to a person's entitlement to benefit; or

(iii) on an application made under section 10 above for a decision as to a person's entitlement to benefit to be superseded.

27(2) This section does not apply where the decision of the Secretary of State mentioned in *subsection (1)(b) above*–

(a) is one which, but for section 25(2) or (3)(a) above, would have been made before the date of the relevant determination; or

(b) is one made in pursuance of section 26(3) or (5) above.

27(3) In so far as the decision relates to a person's entitlement to a benefit in respect of–

(a) a period before the date of the relevant determination; or

(b) in the case of a widow's payment, a death occurring before that date,

it shall be made as if the adjudicating authority's decision had been found by the Upper Tribunal or court not to have been erroneous in point of law.

27(4) In deciding whether a person is entitled to benefit in a case where his entitlement depends on his having been entitled to the same or some other benefit before attaining a particular age, subsection (3) above shall be disregarded for the purpose only of deciding whether he was so entitled before attaining that age.

27(5) Subsection (1)(a) above shall be read as including a case where–

(a) the effect of the relevant determination is that part or all of a purported regulation or order is invalid; and

(b) the error of law made by the adjudicating authority was to act on the basis that the purported regulation or order (or the part held to be invalid) was valid.

27(6) It is immaterial for the purposes of subsection (1) above–

(a) where such a decision as is mentioned in paragraph (b)(i) falls to be made, whether the claim was made before or after the date of the relevant determination;

(b) where such a decision as is mentioned in paragraph (b)(ii) or (iii) falls to be made on an application under section 9 or (as the case may be) 10 above, whether the application was made before or after that date.

27(7) In this section–

"adjudicating authority" means–

(a) the Secretary of State;

(b) any former officer, tribunal or body; or

(c) any officer, tribunal or body in Northern Ireland corresponding to a former officer, tribunal or body;

"benefit" means–

(a) benefit under Parts II to V of the Contributions and Benefits Act, other than Old Cases payments;

(b) benefit under Part II of the Social Security Act 1975 (in respect of a period before 1st July 1992 but not before 6th April 1975);

(c) benefit under the National Insurance Act 1946 or 1965, or the National Insurance (Industrial Injuries) Act 1946 or 1965 (in respect of a period before 6th April 1975);

(d) a jobseeker's allowance;

(dd) state pension credit;

(de) an employment and support allowance;

(df) personal independence payment;

(dg) bereavement support payment under section 30 of the Pensions Act 2014;

(e) any benefit corresponding to a benefit mentioned in paragraphs (a) to (dg) above; and

(f) universal credit;

(g) state pension or a lump sum under Part 1 of the Pensions Act 2014.

"the court" means the High Court, the Court of Appeal, the Court of Session, the High Court or Court of Appeal in Northern Ireland, the House of Lords or the Court of Justice of the European Community;

"former officer, tribunal or body" means any of the following, that is to say–

(a) an adjudication officer or, in the case of a decision given on a reference under section 21(2) or 25(1) of the Administration Act, a social security appeal tribunal, a disability appeal tribunal or a medical appeal tribunal;

(b) an adjudicating medical practitioner appointed under section 49 of that Act or a specially qualified adjudicating medical practitioner appointed in accordance with regulations under section 62(2) of that Act; or

(c) the National Assistance Board, the Supplementary Benefits Commission, the Attendance Allowance Board, a benefit officer, an insurance officer or a supplement officer.

27(8) For the purposes of this section, any reference to entitlement to benefit includes a reference to entitlement–

(a) to any increase in the rate of a benefit; or

(b) to a benefit, or increase of benefit, at a particular rate.

27(9) The date of the relevant determination shall, in prescribed cases, be determined for the purposes of this section in accordance with any regulations made for that purpose.

27(10) Regulations made under subsection (9) above may include provision–

(a) for a determination of a higher court to be treated as if it had been made on the date of a determination of a lower court or the Upper Tribunal; or

(b) for a determination of a lower court or the Upper Tribunal to be treated as if it had been made on the date of a determination of a higher court.

Commencement Date – In so far as it was not already in force s. 27 entered into force (except for the purposes of housing benefit, council tax benefit and decisions to which SI 1999/527, art. 4(6) applies; i.e. pre-1 April 1999 decisions under SSAA 1992, s. 17(1), s. 20(3) and PSA 1993, s. 170(1)) with effect from 29 November 1999 (SI 1999/3178 (C. 81), art. 2(1)(a); 2(2) and Sch. 1).

S. 27 entered into force; for the purposes of (i) decisions whether a person is entitled to be credited with earnings or contributions in accordance with regulations made under s. 22(5) of the Contributions and Benefits Act; and (ii) decisions whether a person was, within the meaning of regulations, precluded from regular employment by responsibilities at home; with effect from 18 October 1999 (SI 1999/2860 (C. 75), art. 2(c)(iv), (v) and Sch. 1).

S. 27 entered into force, for the purposes of any matter to which, by virtue of PSA 1993, s. 170, provisions of SSA 1998, Pt. I, Ch. II are to apply, with effect from 5 July 1999 (SI 1999/1958 (C. 51), art. 2(1)(b)(iv)).

S. 27 entered into force, for the purposes of benefits under SSCBA 1992, Pt. II except child's special allowance, with effect from 6 September 1999 (SI 1999/2422 (C. 61), art. 2(c)(i) and Sch. 1).

History – In s. 27(1)(a), "the Upper Tribunal" substituted by SI 2008/2833, art. 9 and Sch. 3, para. 163(a), with effect from 3 November 2008.

In s. 27(3), "the Upper Tribunal" substituted by SI 2008/2833, art. 9 and Sch. 3, para. 163(b), with effect from 3 November 2008.

In s. 27(7), in the definition of "benefit", para. (dd) inserted and in para. (e), the words "paragraphs (a) to (dd) above" substituted by the State Pension Credit Act 2002, s. 11 and Sch. 1, para. 9 with effect from 2 July 2002, only for the purpose of making regulations and orders, by virtue of SI 2002/1691.

In s. 27(7), in the definition of "benefit", para. (de) inserted by WRA 2007, s. 28(1) and Sch. 3, para. 17, with effect from 27 October 2008 (2008/787, art. 2).

In s. 27(7), in the definition of "benefit", para. (df) inserted by WRA 2012, s. 91 and Sch. 9, para. 41(a), with effect (for the purpose of making regulations) from 25 February 2013 (SI 2013/358, art. 2 and Sch. 1), from 8 April 2013 in relation to a person whose only or principal residence is, on the date on which that person makes a claim for personal independence payment, located in an area to which one of the following postcodes corresponds: BL, CA, CH (except CH1, CH4, CH5, CH6, CH7 and CH8), CW, DH, DL (except DL6, DL7, DL8, DL9, DL10 and DL11), FY, L, LA (except LA2 7, LA2 8, LA6 2 and LA6 3), M, NE, PR, SR, TS (except TS9), WA and WN (SI 2013/358, art. 7(1) and (2)(k)), and from 10 June 2013 in relation to any other person (SI 2013/1250, art. 2).

In s. 27(7), in the definition of "benefit", para. (dg) inserted by PA 2014, s. 31 and Sch. 16, para. 41(a), with effect from 6 April 2017, subject to SI 2017/297, art. 4 (later commencement for abolition of bereavement payment and bereavement allowance) and 5 (commencement for entitlement to bereavement payment and bereavement support payment) (SI 2017/297, art. 3(2)).

In s. 27(7), in the definition of "benefit", para. (e), the words "to (dg)" substituted for "to (df)" by PA 2014, s. 31 and Sch. 16, para. 41(b), with effect from 6 April 2017, subject to SI 2017/297, art. 4 (later commencement for abolition of bereavement payment and bereavement allowance) and 5 (commencement for entitlement to bereavement payment and bereavement support payment) (SI 2017/297, art. 3(2)).

In s. 27(7), in the definition of "benefit" in para. (e), "to (df)" substituted for "to (de)" by WRA 2012, s. 91 and Sch. 9, para. 41(b), with effect (for the purpose of making regulations) from 25 February 2013 (SI 2013/358, art. 2 and Sch. 1), from 8 April 2013 in relation to a person whose only or principal residence is, on the date on which that person makes a claim for personal independence payment, located in an area to which one of the following postcodes corresponds: BL, CA, CH (except CH1, CH4, CH5, CH6, CH7 and CH8), CW, DH, DL (except DL6, DL7, DL8, DL9, DL10 and DL11), FY,L, LA (except LA2 7, LA2 8, LA6 2 and LA6 3), M, NE, PR, SR, TS (except TS9), WA and WN (SI 2013/358, art. 7(1) and (2)(k)), and from 10 June 2013 in relation to any other person (SI 2013/1250, art. 2).

In s. 27(7), in the definition of "benefit" in para. (e), "to (de)" substituted for "to (dd)" by WRA 2007, s. 28(1) and Sch. 3, para. 17, with effect from 27 October 2008 (SI 2008/787, art. 2).

In s. 27(7), in the definition of "benefit", para. (f) substituted by WRA 2012, s. 91 and Sch. 4, para. 47, with effect (for the purpose of making regulations) from 25 February 2013 (SI 2013/358, art. 2 and Sch. 1) and from 29 April 2013 for other purposes (SI 2013/983, art. 3(1)(b)).

S. 27(7)(g) inserted by PA 2014, s. 23 and Sch. 12, para. 35, with effect from 6 April 2016 (as not brought into force by any earlier order under PA 2014, s. 56(1)).

In s. 27(10)(a) and (b), "the Upper Tribunal" substituted by SI 2008/2833, art. 9 and Sch. 3, para. 163(a), with effect from 3 November 2008.

28 Correction of errors and setting aside of decisions

28(1) Regulations may make provision with respect to–

(a) the correction of accidental errors in any decision of the Secretary of State or record of a decision of the Secretary of State made under any relevant enactment;

(b) [omitted by SI 2008/2833, art. 9 and Sch. 3, para. 164(a).]

28(1A) In subsection (1) **"decision"** does not include any decision of the First-tier Tribunal or any decision made by an officer of the Inland Revenue, other than a decision under or by virtue of Part III of the *Pension Schemes* Act 1993.

28(2) Nothing in subsection (1) above shall be construed as derogating from any power to correct errors which is exercisable apart from regulations made by virtue of that subsection.

28(3) In this section **"relevant enactment"** means any enactment contained in–

(a) this Chapter;

(b) the Contributions and Benefits Act;

(c) the Pension Schemes Act 1993;

(d) the Jobseekers Act;

(e) the Social Security (Recovery of Benefits) Act 1997;

(f) the State Pension Credit Act 2002;

(g) Part 1 of the Welfare Reform Act 2007

(h) Part 1 of the Welfare Reform Act 2012;

(i) Part 4 of that Act, or

(j) Part 1 of the Pensions Act 2014 or section 30 of that Act.

Commencement Date – In so far as it was not already in force s. 28 entered into force (except for the purposes of housing benefit, council tax benefit and decisions to which SI 1999/527, art. 4(6) applies; i.e. pre-1 April 1999 decisions under SSAA 1992, s. 17(1), s. 20(3) and PSA 1993, s. 170(1)) with effect from 29 November 1999 (SI 1999/3178 (C. 81), art. 2(1)(a); 2(2) and Sch. 1).
S. 28 (except subs. (3)(c), (d) and (e)) entered into force, for the purposes of benefits under SSCBA 1992, Pt. II except child's special allowance, with effect from 6 September 1999 (SI 1999/2422 (C. 61), art. 2(c)(i) and Sch. 1).
S. 28 (except s. 28 (3)(c) and (e)) entered into force; for the purposes of (i) decisions whether a person is entitled to be credited with earnings or contributions in accordance with regulations made under s. 22(5) of the Contributions and Benefits Act; and (ii) decisions whether a person was, within the meaning of regulations, precluded from regular employment by responsibilities at home; with effect from 18 October 1999 (SI 1999/2860 (C. 75), art. 2(c)(iv), (v) and Sch. 1).
S. 28 in force, for the purposes of making regulations, with effect from 4 March 1999 (SSA 1998 (Commencement No. 5) Order 1999 (SI 1999/528)).
S. 28 (except for s. 28(3)(d) and (e)) entered into force, for the purposes of any matter to which, by virtue of PSA 1993, s. 170, provisions of SSA 1998, Pt. I, Ch. II are to apply, with effect from 5 July 1999 (SI 1999/1958 (C. 51), art. 2(1)(b)(iv)).
S. 28 (except for s. 28(3)(c)–(e)) entered into force, for the purposes of benefits under SSCBA 1992, Pt. II except child's special allowance, with effect from 6 September 1999 (SI 1999/2422 (C. 61), art. 2(c)(i) and Sch. 1).

Prospective amendments – S. 28(3)(k) inserted (and the "or" after (i) omitted) by Welfare Reform and Work Act 2016, s. 20(6), with effect from a day to be appointed by the Secretary of State under Welfare Reform and Work Act 2016, s. 36(6). S. 28(3)(k) to read as follows:
"(k) sections 18 to 21 of the Welfare Reform and Work Act 2016."

History – In s. 28(1)(a), the words "of the Secretary of State" inserted in both places by SI 2008/2833, art. 9 and Sch. 3, para. 164(a), with effect from 3 November 2008.
S. 28(1)(b) (and the "and" immediately before it) omitted by SI 2008/2833, art. 9 and Sch. 3, para. 164(a), with effect from 3 November 2008.
In s. 28(1A), the words "any decision of the First-tier Tribunal or" inserted by SI 2008/2833, art. 9 and Sch. 3, para. 164(b), with effect from 3 November 2008.
S. 28(1A) inserted by SSC(TF)A 1999, s. 18 and Sch. 7, para. 34, with effect from 5 July 1999 (SI 1999/1662).
In s. 28(2), the words "or set aside decisions", which appeared after "correct errors", omitted by SI 2008/2833, art. 9 and Sch. 3, para. 164(c), with effect from 3 November 2008.
S. 28(3)(f) and word "or" immediately before it inserted by the State Pension Credit Act 2002, s. 11 and Sch. 1, para. 10 with effect from 2 July 2002 for the purpose only of making regulations and orders, by virtue of SI 2002/1691.
In s. 28(3), the word "or" immediately preceding para. (e) repealed by the State Pension Credit Act 2002, s. 21 and Sch. 3 with effect from 7 April 2003, by virtue of SI 2003/966.
S. 28(3)(g) and the word "or" preceding it inserted by WRA 2007, s. 28 and Sch. 3, para. 17, with effect (for purpose of making regulations) from 18 March 2008 and from 27 July 2008 for other purposes (SI 2008/787, art. 2 and Schedule).
In s. 28(3)(e) the word "or" immediately preceding para. (f) omitted by WRA 2007, s. 67 and Sch. 8, with effect from 27 October 2008 (SI 2008/787, art. 2).
S. 28(3)(h) inserted (and the "or" at the end of s. 28(3)(f) repealed) by WRA 2012, s. 31 and Sch. 2, para. 48, with effect from 25 February 2013 (SI 2013/358, art. 2 and Sch. 2, para. 40).
S. 23(3)(i) inserted by WRA 2012, s. 91 and Sch. 9, para. 42, with effect from 25 February 2013 (SI 2013/358, art. 2 and Sch. 2, para. 43).
S. 28(3)(j) inserted (and the final "or" in s. 28(3)(h) omitted, and a final "or" inserted in s. 23(3)(i)) by PA 2014, s. 23 and Sch. 12, para. 36, with effect from 6 April 2016 (as not brought into force by any earlier order under PA 2014, s. 56(1)).
In s. 28(3)(j), the words "or section 30 of that Act" inserted after the words "Part 1 of the Pensions Act 2014" by PA 2014, s. 31 and Sch. 16, para. 42, with effect from 6 April 2017, subject to SI 2017/297, art. 4 (later commencement for abolition of bereavement payment and bereavement allowance) and 5 (commencement for entitlement to bereavement payment and bereavement support payment) (SI 2017/297, art. 3(2)).

Cross references – SI 2005/191, reg. 13: modification of s. 28 for the purposes of appeals against HMRC decisions in respect of child trust funds.

SUPPLEMENTAL

39ZA Certificates

39ZA A document bearing a certificate which–

(a) is signed by a person authorised in that behalf by the Secretary of State, and

(b) states that the document, apart from the certificate, is a record of a decision of an officer of the Secretary of State,

shall be conclusive evidence of the decision; and a certificate purporting to be so signed shall be deemed to be so signed unless the contrary is proved.

History – S. 39ZA inserted by SI 2008/2833, art. 9 and Sch. 3, para. 166, with effect from 3 November 2008.

39 Interpretation etc. of Chapter II

39(1) In this Chapter–

"claimant", in relation to a joint-claim couple claiming a joint-claim jobseeker's allowance (within the meaning of the Jobseekers Act 1995), means the couple or either member of the couple;

"claimant", in relation to a couple jointly claiming universal credit, means the couple or either member of the couple;

"health care professional", means–

(a) a registered medical practitioner,

(b) a registered nurse,

(c) an occupational therapist or physiotherapist registered with a regulatory body established by an Order in Council under section 60 of the Health Care Act 1999, or

(d) a member of such other profession regulated by a body mentioned in section 25(3) of the National Health Service Reform and Health Care Professions Act 2002 as the Secretary of State may prescribe;

"relevant benefit" has the meaning given by section 8(3) above;

39(2) Expressions used in this Chapter to which a meaning is assigned by section 191 of the Administration Act have that meaning in this Chapter.

39(3) Part II of the Administration Act, which is superseded by the foregoing provisions of this Chapter, shall cease to have effect.

Commencement Date – In so far as it was not already in force s. 39 entered into force (except for the purposes of housing benefit, council tax benefit and decisions to which SI 1999/527, art. 4(6) applies; i.e. pre-1 April 1999 decisions under SSAA 1992, s. 17(1), s. 20(3) and PSA 1993, s. 170(1)) with effect from 29 November 1999 (SI 1999/3178 (C. 81), art. 2(1)(a); 2(2) and Sch. 1).
S. 39 entered into force; for the purposes of (i) decisions whether a person is entitled to be credited with earnings or contributions in accordance with regulations made under s. 22(5) of the Contributions and Benefits Act; and (ii) decisions whether a person was, within the meaning of regulations, precluded from regular employment by responsibilities at home; with effect from 18 October 1999 (SI 1999/2860 (C. 75), art. 2(c)(iv), (v) and Sch. 1).
S. 39 entered into force, for the purposes of any matter to which, by virtue of PSA 1993, s. 170, provisions of SSA 1998, Pt. I, Ch. II are to apply, with effect from 5 July 1999 (SI 1999/1958 (C. 51), art. 2(1)(b)(iv)).
S. 39 entered into force, for the purposes of benefits under SSCBA 1992, Pt. II except child's special allowance, with effect from 6 September 1999 (SI 1999/2422 (C. 61), art. 2(c)(i) and Sch. 1).
S. 39(3) entered into force on 18 October 1999 but only in so far as it provides for SSAA 1992, s. 63 (which is in Pt. II of the Administration Act) to cease to have effect (SI 1999/2860).

Prospective amendments – In s. 39(1), the definition of "claimant" repealed by WRA 2012, s. 147 and Sch. 14, Pt. 1, with effect from a date to be set by order of the Secretary of State.
S. 39(1A) inserted by Welfare Reform and Work Act 2016, s. 20(7), with effect from a day to be appointed by the Secretary of State under Welfare Reform and Work Act 2016, s. 36(6). S. 39(1A) to read as follows:
"39(1A) In this Chapter–

(a) a reference to a benefit includes a reference to a loan under section 18 of the Welfare Reform and Work Act 2016;

(b) a reference to a claim for a benefit includes a reference to an application for a loan under section 18 of the Welfare Reform and Work Act 2016;

(c) a reference to a claimant includes a reference to an applicant for Welfare Reform and Work Act 2016 (c. 7) a loan under section 18 of the Welfare Reform and Work Act 2016 or, in relation to a couple jointly applying for a loan under that section, a reference to the couple or either member of the couple;

(d) a reference to an award of a benefit to a person includes a reference to a decision that a person is eligible for a loan under section 18 of the Welfare Reform and Work Act 2016;

(e) a reference to entitlement to a benefit includes a reference to eligibility for a loan under section 18 of the Welfare Reform and Work Act 2016."

History – In s. 39(1), second definition of "claimant" inserted by WRA 2012, s. 31 and Sch. 2, para. 49, with effect (for the purpose of making regulations) from 25 February 2013 (SI 2013/358, art. 2) and from 29 April 2013 for other purposes (SI 2013/983, art. 3(1)(b)).
In s. 39(1) the definition of "health care professional" inserted by WRA 2007, s. 62, with effect from 3 July 2007.
In s. 39(1), the definition of "tax appeal Commissioners" omitted by SI 2009/56, art. 3(1) and Sch. 1, para. 250, operative from 1 April 2009, subject to transitional and saving provisions in SI 2009/56, Sch. 3.
In s. 39(1) the definitions of "appeal tribunal" and "Commissioner" omitted by SI 2008/2833, art. 9 and Sch. 3, para. 167, with effect from 3 November 2008.
In s. 39(1) the words "(except in the expression "tax appeal Commissioners")" inserted in the meaning of "Commissioner" and the former definition of "tax appeal Commissioners" added by SSC(TF)A 1999, s. 18 and Sch. 7, para. 35, with effect from 1 April 1999 (SI 1999/527).
In s. 39(1), the definition of "claimant" inserted by the WRPA1999, s. 59 and Sch. 7, para. 17, with effect from 19 March 2001 (by virtue of SI 2000/2958).

Cross references – TCA 2002, s. 51 and Sch. 4, para. 15: references in this Chapter to a decision of the Secretary of State are, where the context so requires in consequence of TCA 2002, s. 50 (functions transferred to the Board), to be construed as references to a decision of the Board, or, where the power to decide is exercised by an officer of the Board, an officer of the Board.
SI 2005/191, reg. 14: modification of s. 39 for the purposes of appeals against HMRC decisions in respect of child trust funds.

PART II – CONTRIBUTIONS

AMENDMENTS OF CONTRIBUTIONS AND BENEFITS ACT

48 Apportionment of payments etc. made for more than one earner

48(1) [Inserts SSCBA 1992, s. 3(2A).]

Commencement Date – S. 48 entered into force with effect from 8 September 1998 (SI 1998/2209).

49 Payments on account of directors' contributions

49(1) [Inserts SSCBA 1992, s. 3(4) and (5).]

Commencement Date – S. 49 entered into force with effect from 8 September 1998 (SI 1998/2209).

50 Payments treated as remuneration and earnings

50(1) [Substitutes SSCBA 1992, s. 4(4).]

50(2) [Repealed by CSPSSA 2000, s. 86(1), Sch. 9, Pt. VIII(1).]

50(3) Subsection (1) above, so far as relating to a sum which is chargeable to tax by virtue of section 313 of the Income and Corporation Taxes Act 1988, shall have effect in relation to any undertaking given on or after 10th July 1997.

50(4) Regulations under subsection (6) of section 4 of the Contributions and Benefits Act (as inserted by subsection (2) above)–

(a) shall not be made before the passing of the Finance Act 1998; but

(b) may make provision having effect in relation to acquisitions on or after 6th April 1998.

Commencement Date – S. 50(1) effective for undertakings given on or after 10 July 1997 in respect of sums chargeable under ICTA 1988, s. 313 (SSA 1998, s. 50(3) and s. 87(2)(b)) and 8 September 1998 in respect of all other matters (SSA 1998 (Commencement No. 1) Order 1998 (SI 1998/2209)).
S. 50(2)–(4) entered into force with effect from; the date of Royal Assent; 21 May 1998 (SSA 1998, s. 87(2)(b)).

History – S. 50(2) repealed by CSPSSA 2000, s. 86(1), Sch. 9, Pt. VIII(1); with effect from 6 April 2000.

51 Class 1 contributions

51 [Repealed by WRPA 1999, s. 88; Sch. 13, Pt. VI.]

Commencement Date – S. 51 entered into force, for the purposes of making regulations, with effect from 23 February 1999 and, for all other purposes, from 6 April 1999 (SI 1999/418).

History – S. 51 repealed by WRPA 1999, s. 88; Sch. 13, Pt. VI, with effect from 6 April 2000 (SI 1999/3420 (C. 92), art. 4(c), (e)).

52 Class 1A contributions

52(1) [Repealed by CSPSSA 2000, s. 86(1), Sch. 9, Pt. VIII(1).]

Commencement Date – S. 52 (which substituted the former SSCBA 1992, s. 10(2)(b)) entered into force with effect from 8 September 1998 (SI 1998/2209).

History – S. 52 repealed by CSPSSA 2000, s. 86(1), Sch. 9, Pt. VIII(1); with effect from 6 April 2000.

53 Class 1B contributions

53(1) [Inserts SSCBA 1992, s. 10A.]

Commencement Date – S. 53 entered into force, for purpose of making regulations, with effect from 8 September 1998 and for all other purposes with effect from 6 April 1999 (SI 1998/2209).

54 Contributions paid in error

54(1) [Inserts SSCBA 1992, s. 19A.]

Commencement Date – S. 54 entered into force, for the purposes of making regulations, with effect from 4 March 1999 and, for all other purposes, from 6 April 1999 (SI 1999/526).

55 Recovery of primary Class 1 contributions by secondary contributors

55(1) In paragraph 3 of Schedule 1 to the Contributions and Benefits Act (supplementary provisions as to contributions)–

(a) [amends SSCBA 1992, Sch. 1, para. 3(3);]

(b) [inserts SSCBA 1992, Sch. 1, para. 3(4) and (5).]

Commencement Date – S. 55 entered into force with effect from 8 September 1998 (SI 1998/2209).

56 Contributions returns

56(1) [Amends SSCBA 1992, Sch. 1, para. 7(3).]

56(2) [Inserts SSCBA 1992, Sch. 1, para. 7A(1), (2).]

Commencement Date – S. 56(1) entered into force with effect from 6 April 1999 (SI 1999/526).
S. 56(2) entered into force, for the purposes of making regulations, with effect from 4 March 1999 and, for all other purposes, with effect from 6 April 1999 (SI 1999/526).

57 Collection of contributions by Secretary of State

57(1) [Inserts SSCBA 1992, Sch. 1, para. 7B.]

Commencement Date – S. 57 entered into force, for the purposes of making regulations, with effect from 4 March 1999 and, for all other purposes, with effect from 6 April 1999 (SI 1999/526).

58 Interest and penalties chargeable concurrently with Inland Revenue

58 [Repealed by SSC(TF)A 1999, s. 26(3) and Sch. 10, Pt. I.]

History – S. 58 repealed (without entering into force) by SSC(TF)A 1999, s. 26(3) and Sch. 10, Pt. I, with effect from 1 April 1999 (SI 1999/527).

59 Levy of Class 4 contributions with income tax

59(1) Schedule 2 to the Contributions and Benefits Act (levy of Class 4 contributions with income tax) and Schedule 2 to the Social Security Contributions and Benefits (Northern Ireland) Act 1992 (corresponding provision for Northern Ireland) shall each be amended as follows.

59(2) [Amends SSCBA 1992, Sch. 2, para. 2.]

59(3) [Repeals SSCBA 1992, Sch. 2, para. 3(1)(b).]

59(4) [Amends SSCBA 1992, Sch. 2, para. 4(2).]

59(5) [Amends SSCBA 1992, Sch. 2, para. 6(1).]

59(6) [Repealed by SSC(TF)A 1999, s. 26(3) and Sch. 10, Part I.]

Commencement Date – S. 59 entered into force with effect from 8 September 1998 (SI 1998/2209).

History – S. 59(6) repealed by SSC(TF)A 1999, s. 26(3) and Sch. 10, Pt. I, with effect from 1 April 1999 (SI 1999/527).

Cross references – TMA 1970, s. 88: continued effect of interest provision in relation to pre-6 April 1994 partnership assessments for 1996–97 (SI 1998/2209, art. 3).

AMENDMENTS OF ADMINISTRATION ACT

60 Breach of regulations

60 [Substitutes SSAA 1992, s. 113.]

Commencement Date – S. 60 entered into force, for the purposes of making regulations, with effect from 4 March 1999 and, for all other purposes, with effect from 6 April 1999 (SI 1999/526).

61 Offences and penalties relating to contributions

61 [Substitutes SSAA 1992, s. 114.]

Commencement Date – S. 61 entered into force for the purposes of making regulations, with effect from 4 March 1999 and, for all other purposes, from 6 April 1999 (SI 1999/526).

62 Evidence of non-payment

62(1) [Omitted by FA 2008, s. 138 and Sch. 44.]

62(2) [Repealed by SSC(TF)A 1999, s. 26(3) and Sch. 7, Pt. I.]

62(3) [Amends SSAA 1992, s. 118(4).]

62(4) [Repealed by SSC(TF)A 1999, s. 26(3) and Sch. 7, Pt. I.]

Commencement Date – S. 62 entered into force with effect from 6 April 1999 (SI 1999/526).

History – S. 62(1) omitted by FA 2008, s. 138 and Sch. 44, with effect from 21 July 2008.
S. 62(2) and (4) repealed (without entering into force) by SSC(TF)A 1999, s. 26(3) and Sch. 7, Pt. I, with effect from 6 April 1999 (SI 1999/527).

63 Recovery of contributions etc

63 [Inserts SSAA 1992, s. 121A and s. 121B.]

Commencement Date – S. 63 entered into force for the purposes of making regulations, with effect from 4 March 1999 and, for all other purposes, from 6 April 1999 (SI 1999/526).

64 Liability of directors etc. for company's contributions

64 [Inserts SSAA 1992, s. 121C and s. 121D.]

Commencement Date – S. 64 entered into force with effect from 6 April 1999 (SI 1999/526).

65 Class 1B contributions: supplemental

65(1) [Repealed by WRPA 1999, s. 88; Sch. 13, Pt. VI).]

65(2) [Inserts SSAA 1992, s. 162(5)(ca).]

Commencement Date – S. 65 entered into force, for the purpose of making regulations, with effect from 8 September 1998 and for all other purposes, with effect from 6 April 1999 (SI 1998/2209).

History – S. 65(1) repealed by WRPA 1999, s. 88; Sch. 13, Pt. VI, with effect from 6 April 2000 (SI 1999/3420 (C. 92), art. 4(c), (e)).

66 Payments of certain contributions out of the Consolidated Fund

66(1) Subsection (4) of section 163 of the Administration Act (general financial arrangements) shall have effect, and shall be deemed always to have had effect, as if–

(a) for the words "a secondary contributor" there were substituted the words "any person"; and

(b) after the words "any secondary Class 1 contributions" there were inserted the words ", or any Class 1A contributions,".

66(2) Subsection (2) of section 1 of the Social Security (Miscellaneous Provisions) Act 1977 (from which subsection (4) of section 163 is derived) shall be deemed to have had effect with the same amendments as from the commencement of the Social Security (Contributions) Act 1991.

Commencement Date – S. 66 entered into force with effect from 21 May 1998 (SSA 1998, s. 87(2)).

PART IV – MISCELLANEOUS AND SUPPLEMENTAL

APPEALS IN RELATION TO PERSONAL LIABILITY NOTICES

78 Expenditure for facilitating transfer of functions etc

78(1) The Secretary of State and the Commissioners of Inland Revenue may incur expenditure in doing anything which in his or their opinion is appropriate for the purpose of facilitating either of the following things, namely–

(a) the transfer to the Commissioners of such of the functions of the Secretary of State as are exercisable by the Contributions Agency; and

(b) the exercise by the Commissioners of those functions.

78(2) The powers conferred by subsection (1) above–

(a) shall be exercisable whether or not Parliament has given any approval on which either of the things there mentioned depends; and

(b) shall be without prejudice to any power conferred otherwise than by virtue of that subsection.

78(3) Any expenditure incurred under this section shall be defrayed out of money provided by Parliament.

78(4) In its application to Northern Ireland, this section shall have effect with the following modifications, namely–

(a) for the first reference to the Secretary of State there shall be substituted a reference to the Department of Health and Social Services for Northern Ireland;

(b) for the reference to such of the functions of the Secretary of State as are exercisable by the Contributions Agency there shall be substituted a reference to such of the functions of that Department as correspond to those functions; and

(c) for the reference to money provided by Parliament there shall be substituted a reference to money appropriated by Measure of the Northern Ireland Assembly.

Commencement Date – S. 78 entered into force with effect from 21 May 1998 (SSA 1998, s. 87(2)(a)).

79 Regulations and orders

79(1) Subject to subsection (2A) below, regulations under this Act shall be made by the Secretary of State.

79(2) [Omitted by SI 2008/2833, art. 9 and Sch. 3, para. 168(b).]

79(2A) Subsection (1) has effect subject to any provision providing for regulations to be made by the Treasury or the Commissioners of Inland Revenue.

79(3) Powers under this Act to make regulations or orders are exercisable by statutory instrument.

79(4) Any power conferred by this Act to make regulations or orders may be exercised–

(a) either in relation to all cases to which the power extends, or in relation to those cases subject to specified exceptions, or in relation to any specified cases or classes of case;

(b) so as to make, as respects the cases in relation to which it is exercised–

(i) the full provision to which the power extends or any less provision (whether by way of exception or otherwise);

(ii) the same provision for all cases in relation to which the power is exercised, or different provision for different cases or different classes of case or different provision as respects the same case or class of case for different purposes of this Act;

(iii) any such provision either unconditionally or subject to any specified condition;

and where such a power is expressed to be exercisable for alternative purposes it may be exercised in relation to the same case for any or all of those purposes.

79(5) Powers to make regulations for the purposes of any one provision of this Act are without prejudice to powers to make regulations for the purposes of any other provision.

79(6) Without prejudice to any specific provision in this Act, a power conferred by this Act to make regulations includes power to make thereby such incidental, supplementary, consequential or transitional provision as appears to the authority making the regulations to be expedient for the purposes of those regulations.

79(6A) The provision referred to in subsection (6) includes, in a case where regulations under this Act require or authorise the use of electronic communications, provision referred to in section 8(4) and (5) and 9(5) of the Electronic Communications Act 2000.

79(6B) For the purposes of subsection (6A), references in section 8(4) and (5) and 9(5) of the Electronic Communications Act 2000 to an order under section 8 of that Act are to be read as references to regulations under this Act; and references to anything authorised by such an order are to be read as references to anything required or authorised by such regulations.

79(7) Without prejudice to any specific provisions in this Act, a power conferred by any provision of this Act to make regulations includes power to provide for a person to exercise a discretion in dealing with any matter.

79(8) [Repealed by WRA 2012, s. 147 and Sch. 14, Pt. 1.]

79(9) [Omitted by SI 2008/2833, art. 9 and Sch. 3, para. 168(b).]

Commencement Date – S. 79 entered into force with effect from 21 May 1998 (SSA 1998, s. 87(2)(a)).

Prospective amendments – S. 79(8) repealed by WRA 2012, s. 147 and Sch. 14, Pt. 1, with effect (other than as noted in the History note below) from a date to be set by order of the Secretary of State.

History – In s. 79(1) the words "Subject to subsection (2A) below," substituted for the words "Subject to subsections (2) and (2A) below and paragraph 6 of Schedule 4 to this Act," by SI 2008/2833, art. 9 and Sch. 3, para. 168(a), with effect from 3 November 2008.
In s. 79(1), in relation to tax credit, references to the "Secretary of State" shall be construed, with effect from 5 October 1999, as if they were references to "the Treasury" or, as the case may be, "the Board" (TCA 1999, s. 20(2); s. 2 and Sch. 2, para. 20(g)).
In s. 79(2) reference to "the Secretary of State" effectively substituted for "the Lord Advocate" by SI 1999/678, art. 7(4), with effect from 19 May 1999.
S. 79(2) omitted by SI 2008/2833, art. 9 and Sch. 3, para. 168(b), with effect from 3 November 2008.
S. 79(2A) added (and subsection 1 amended accordingly) by TCA 2002, s. 51 and Sch. 4, para. 13 with effect from 26 February 2003 (for the purposes of making subordinate legislation relating to child benefit and guardian's allowance), 1 April 2003 (for the purposes of the transfer of various functions) and 7 April 2003 (for the purposes of entitlement to payment) (all by virtue of SI 2003/392).
S. 79(6A) inserted by WRA 2012, s. 104(2), with effect from 25 February 2013 (SI 2013/358, art. 2 and Sch. 2).
S. 79(6B) inserted by WRA 2012, s. 104(2), with effect from 25 February 2013 (SI 2013/358, art. 2 and Sch. 2).
S. 79(8) repealed by WRA 2012, s. 147 and Sch. 14, Pt. 1, with effect in so far as it relates to the abolition of council tax benefit from 1 April 2013 (SI 2013/358, art. 8(c) and Sch. 4).
S. 79(9) omitted by SI 2008/2833, art. 9 and Sch. 3, para. 168(b), with effect from 3 November 2008.

Cross references – SI 1999/678, art. 2: the function of the Lord Advocate originally specified in s. 79(2) is transferred to the Secretary of State with effect from 19 May 1999.
SI 2005/191, reg. 15: modification of s. 79 for the purposes of appeals against HMRC decisions in respect of child trust funds.

Statutory instruments – SI 1998/2209.
SI 1998/2780.
SI 1999/418.
SI 1999/526.
SI 1999/528.
SI 1999/1055.
SI 1999/1510.
SI 1999/1958.
SI 1999/2422.
SI 1999/2739.
SI 1999/2860.
SI 1999/3178.

80 Parliamentary control of regulations

80(1) Subject to the provisions of this section, a statutory instrument containing (whether alone or with other provisions) regulations under–

(a) section 12(2) or (3A) or 72 above; or

(b) paragraph 9 of Schedule 2 to this Act,

shall not be made unless a draft of the instrument has been laid before Parliament and been approved by a resolution of each House of Parliament.

80(2) A statutory instrument–

(a) which contains (whether alone or with other provisions) regulations made under this Act by the Secretary of State, the Treasury or the Commissioners of Inland Revenue; and

(b) which is not subject to any requirement that a draft of the instrument be laid before and approved by a resolution of each House of Parliament,

shall be subject to annulment in pursuance of a resolution of either House of Parliament.

80(3) [Omitted by SI 2008/2833, art. 9 and Sch. 3, para. 169(c).]

Commencement Date – S. 80 entered into force with effect from 21 May 1998 (SSA 1998, s. 87(2)(a)).

History – In s. 80(1)(a), "or (3A)" inserted by WRA 2012, s. 102(5), with effect from 25 February 2013.
In s. 80(1)(a), "7, ", which appeared before "12(2)", omitted by SI 2008/2833, art. 9 and Sch. 3, para. 169(a), with effect from 3 November 2008.
In s. 80(1)(b), "paragraph 12 of Schedule 1," which appeared at the beginning, and "or paragraph 2 of Schedule 5" which appeared after "Schedule 2", omitted by SI 2008/2833, art. 9 and Sch. 3, para. 169(b), with effect from 3 November 2008.
In s. 80(2), the words ", the Treasury or the Commissioners of Inland Revenue" inserted by TCA 2002, s. 51 and Sch. 4, para. 14, with effect from 7 April 2003.
In s. 80(2), in relation to tax credit, references to the "Secretary of State" shall be construed, with effect from 5 October 1999, as if they were references to "the Treasury" or, as the case may be, "the Board" (TCA 1999, s. 20(2); s. 2 and Sch. 2, para. 20(h)).
S. 80(3) omitted by SI 2008/2833, art. 9 and Sch. 3, para. 169(c), with effect from 3 November 2008.

Cross references – SI 2005/191, reg. 15: modification of s. 80 for the purposes of appeals against HMRC decisions in respect of child trust funds.

81 Reports by Secretary of State

81(1) The Secretary of State shall prepare, either annually or at such times or intervals as may be prescribed, a report on the standards achieved by the Secretary of State in the making of decisions against which an appeal lies to the First-tier Tribunal.

81(1A) In its application to decisions against which an appeal lies under the Child Support Act 1991 or regulations made under section 6(5) of the Child Maintenance and Other Payments Act 2008, subsection (1) shall have effect as if the references to the Secretary of State were references to the Child Maintenance and Enforcement Commission.

81(2) A copy of every such report shall be laid before each House of Parliament.

Commencement Date – S. 81 entered into force with effect from 21 May 1998 (SSA 1998, s. 87(2)(a)).

History – In s. 81(1), the words "the First-tier Tribunal" substituted for the words "an appeal tribunal constituted under Chapter 1 of Part 1" by SI 2008/2833, art. 9 and Sch. 3, para. 170, with effect from 3 November 2008.
S. 81(1A) inserted by Child Maintenance and Other Payments Act 2008, s. 57 and Sch. 7, para. 3(3), with effect from 6 April 2010 (SI 2010/697).

84 Interpretation: general

84 In this Act–

"the Administration Act" means the Social Security Administration Act 1992;

"the Child Support Act" means the Child Support Act 1991;

"the Contributions and Benefits Act" means the Social Security Contributions and Benefits Act 1992;

"the Jobseekers Act" means the Jobseekers Act 1995;

"the Vaccine Damage Payments Act" means the Vaccine Damage Payments Act 1979;

"prescribe" means prescribe by regulations.

Commencement Date – S. 84 entered into force with effect from 21 May 1998 (SSA 1998, s. 87(2)(a)).

Cross references – SI 2005/191, reg. 15: modification of s. 84 for the purposes of appeals against HMRC decisions in respect of child trust funds.

86 Minor and consequential amendments and repeals

86(1) The enactments mentioned in Schedule 7 to this Act shall have effect subject to the amendments there specified, being minor amendments and amendments consequential on the provisions of this Act.

86(2) The enactments mentioned in Schedule 8 to this Act, which include some that are spent, are hereby repealed to the extent specified in the third column of that Schedule.

Commencement Date – S. 86 brought into force, to the extent required, for the purposes of the various commencement orders covering SSA 1998.

87 Short title, commencement and extent

87(1) This Act may be cited as the Social Security Act 1998.

87(2) This Act, except–

(a) sections 66, 69, 72 and 77 to 85, this section and Schedule 6 to this Act; and

(b) subsection (1) of section 50 so far as relating to a sum which is chargeable to tax by virtue of section 313 of the Income and Corporation Taxes Act 1988, and subsections (2) to (4) of that section,

shall come into force on such day as may be appointed by order made by the Secretary of State; and different days may be appointed for different provisions and for different purposes.

87(3) An order under subsection (2) above may make such savings, or such transitional or consequential provision, as the Secretary of State considers necessary or expedient–

(a) in preparation for or in connection with the coming into force of any provision of this Act; or

(b) in connection with the operation of any enactment repealed or amended by a provision of this Act during any period when the repeal or amendment is not wholly in force.

87(4) This Act, except–

(a) section 2 so far as relating to war pensions;

(b) sections 3, 15, 45 to 47, 59, 78 and 85 and this section; and

(c) section 86 and Schedules 7 and 8 so far as relating to enactments which extend to Northern Ireland,

does not extend to Northern Ireland.

87(5) The following provisions of this Act extend to the Isle of Man, namely–

(a) in section 4, subsections (1)(c) and (2)(c);

(b) sections 6 and 7 and Schedule 1 so far as relating to appeals under the Vaccine Damage Payments Act;

(c) sections 45 to 47 and this section;

(d) paragraphs 5 to 10 of Schedule 7 and section 86(1) so far as relating to those paragraphs; and

(e) section 86(2) and Schedule 8 so far as relating to the Vaccine Damage Payments Act.

Commencement Date – S. 87 entered into force with effect from 21 May 1998 (SSA 1998, s. 87(2)(a)).

Statutory instruments – SI 1998/2209.
SI 1998/2780.
SI 1999/418.
SI 1999/526.
SI 1999/528.
SI 1999/1055.
SI 1999/1510.
SI 1999/1958.
SI 1999/2422.
SI 1999/2739.
SI 1999/2860.
SI 1999/3178.

SCHEDULES

SCHEDULE 1 – APPEAL TRIBUNALS: SUPPLEMENTARY PROVISIONS

Section 5(3) and 7(7)

[Omitted by SI 2008/2833, art. 9 and Sch. 3, para. 171.]

History – Sch. 1 omitted by SI 2008/2833, art. 9 and Sch. 3, para. 171, with effect from 3 November 2008.

SCHEDULE 2 – DECISIONS AGAINST WHICH NO APPEAL LIES

Section 12(1)(a)

PERSONS TREATED AS IF PRESENT IN GREAT BRITAIN

5 A decision whether to certify, in accordance with regulations made under section 64(1), 71(6), 113(1) or 119 of the Contributions and Benefits Act, that it is consistent with the proper administration of that Act to treat a person as though he were present in Great Britain.

Commencement Date – Para. 5 entered into force (except for the purposes of housing benefit, council tax benefit and decisions to which SI 1999/527, art. 4(6) applies; i.e. pre-1 April 1999 decisions under SSAA 1992, s. 17(1), s. 20(3) and PSA 1993, s. 170(1)) with effect from 29 November 1999 (SI 1999/3178 (C. 81), art. 2(1)(a); 2(2) and Sch. 1).

POWER TO PRESCRIBE OTHER DECISIONS

9 Such other decisions as may be prescribed.

Commencement Date – Para. 9 entered into force, for the purpose of making regulations, with effect from 4 March 1999 (SI 1999/528). Para. 9 entered into force (except for the purposes of housing benefit, council tax benefit and decisions to which SI 1999/527, art. 4(6) applies; i.e. pre-1 April 1999 decisions under SSAA 1992, s. 17(1), s. 20(3) and PSA 1993, s. 170(1)) with effect from 29 November 1999 (SI 1999/3178 (C. 81), art. 2(1)(a); 2(2) and Sch. 1).

SCHEDULE 3 – DECISIONS AGAINST WHICH AN APPEAL LIES

Section 12(1)(b)

Part II – Contributions Decisions

RESPONSIBILITIES AT HOME

16 A decision whether a person was (within the meaning of regulations) precluded from regular employment by responsibilities at home.

Commencement Date – Para. 16 entered into force (except for the purposes of housing benefit, council tax benefit and decisions to which SI 1999/527, art. 4(6) applies; i.e. pre-1 April 1999 decisions under SSAA 1992, s. 17(1), s. 20(3) and PSA 1993, s. 170(1)) with effect from 29 November 1999 (SI 1999/3178 (C. 81), art. 2(1)(a); 2(2) and Sch. 1).

Cross references – SSC(TF)A 1999, s. 8(1)(m): decisions on contributions related issues, within the scope of para. 16, are not to be made by an officer of the Board.

EARNINGS AND CONTRIBUTIONS CREDITS

17 A decision whether a person is entitled to be credited with earnings or contributions in accordance with regulations made under section 22(5) or (5ZA) of the Contributions and Benefits Act.

Commencement Date – Para. 17 entered into force (except for the purposes of housing benefit, council tax benefit and decisions to which SI 1999/527, art. 4(6) applies; i.e. pre-1 April 1999 decisions under SSAA 1992, s. 17(1), s. 20(3) and PSA 1993, s. 170(1)) with effect from 29 November 1999 (SI 1999/3178 (C. 81), art. 2(1)(a); 2(2) and Sch. 1).

History – In para. 17, the words "or (5ZA)" inserted by SI 2016/931, art. 3, with effect from 16 September 2016.

Cross references – SSC(TF)A 1999, s. 8(1)(m): decisions on contributions related issues, within the scope of para. 17, are not to be made by an officer of the Board.

SCHEDULE 4 – SOCIAL SECURITY COMMISSIONERS

Section 14(12)

[Omitted by SI 2008/2833, art. 9 and Sch. 3, para. 172.]

History – Sch. 4 omitted by SI 2008/2833, art. 9 and Sch. 3, para. 172, with effect from 3 November 2008.

SCHEDULE 5 – REGULATIONS AS TO PROCEDURE: PROVISION WHICH MAY BE MADE

Section 16(1)

1 Provision prescribing the procedure to be followed in connection with–

(a) the making of decisions or determinations by the Secretary of State; and

(b) the withdrawal of claims, applications, appeals or references falling to be decided or determined by the Secretary of State.

Commencement Date – In so far as it was not already in force para. 1 entered into force (except for the purposes of housing benefit, council tax benefit and decisions to which SI 1999/527, art. 4(6) applies; i.e. pre-1 April 1999 decisions under SSAA 1992, s. 17(1), s. 20(3) and PSA 1993, s. 170(1)) with effect from 29 November 1999 (SI 1999/3178 (C. 81), art. 2(1)(a); 2(2) and Sch. 1).

Para. 1 entered into force; for the purposes of (i) decisions whether a person is entitled to be credited with earnings or contributions in accordance with regulations made under s. 22(5) of the Contributions and Benefits Act; and (ii) decisions whether a person was, within the meaning of regulations, precluded from regular employment by responsibilities at home; with effect from 18 October 1999 (SI 1999/2860 (C. 75), art. 2(c)(iv), (v) and Sch. 1).

Para. 1 entered into force, for the purposes of benefits under SSCBA 1992, Pt. II except child's special allowance, with effect from 6 September 1999 (SI 1999/2422 (C. 61), art. 2(c)(i) and Sch. 1).

Para. 1 entered into force, (in so far as not already in force), for the purposes of any matter to which, by virtue of PSA 1993, s. 170, provisions of SSA 1998, Pt. I, Ch. II are to apply, with effect from 5 July 1999 (SI 1999/1958 (C. 51), art. 2(1)(b)(iv)).

Para. 1 entered into force, for the purposes of making regulations, with effect from 4 March 1999 (SI 1999/528).

History – In para. 1(a) and 1(b), the words "an appeal tribunal or a Commissioner", which appeared after the words "Secretary of State" in both places, omitted by SI 2008/2833, art. 9 and Sch. 3, para. 173(a), with effect from 3 November 2008.

2 [Omitted by SI 2008/2833, art. 9 and Sch. 3, para. 173(b).]

History – Para. 2 omitted by SI 2008/2833, art. 9 and Sch. 3, para. 173(b), with effect from 3 November 2008.

3 Provision as to the form which is to be used for any document, the evidence which is to be required and the circumstances in which any official record or certificate is to be sufficient or conclusive evidence.

Commencement Date – In so far as it was not already in force para. 3 entered into force (except for the purposes of housing benefit, council tax benefit and decisions to which SI 1999/527, art. 4(6) applies; i.e. pre-1 April 1999 decisions under SSAA 1992, s. 17(1), s. 20(3) and PSA 1993, s. 170(1)) with effect from 29 November 1999 (SI 1999/3178 (C. 81), art. 2(1)(a); 2(2) and Sch. 1).
Para. 3 entered into force; for the purposes of (i) decisions whether a person is entitled to be credited with earnings or contributions in accordance with regulations made under s. 22(5) of the Contributions and Benefits Act; and (ii) decisions whether a person was, within the meaning of regulations, precluded from regular employment by responsibilities at home; with effect from 18 October 1999 (SI 1999/2860 (C. 75), art. 2(c)(iv), (v) and Sch. 1).
Para. 3 entered into force, for the purposes of benefits under SSCBA 1992, Pt. II except child's special allowance, with effect from 6 September 1999 (SI 1999/2422 (C. 61), art. 2(c)(i) and Sch. 1).
Para. 3 entered into force, (in so far as not already in force), for the purposes of any matter to which, by virtue of PSA 1993, s. 170, provisions of SSA 1998, Pt. I, Ch. II are to apply, with effect from 5 July 1999 (SI 1999/1958 (C. 51), art. 2(1)(b)(iv)).
Para. 3 entered into force, for the purposes of making regulations, with effect from 4 March 1999 (SI 1999/528).

4 Provision as to the time within which, or the manner in which–

(a) any evidence is to be produced; or

(b) any application, reference or appeal is to be made.

Commencement Date – In so far as it was not already in force para. 4 entered into force (except for the purposes of housing benefit, council tax benefit and decisions to which SI 1999/527, art. 4(6) applies; i.e. pre-1 April 1999 decisions under SSAA 1992, s. 17(1), s. 20(3) and PSA 1993, s. 170(1)) with effect from 29 November 1999 ((SI 1999/3178 (C. 81), art. 2(1)(a); 2(2) and Sch. 1).
Para. 4 entered into force; for the purposes of (i) decisions whether a person is entitled to be credited with earnings or contributions in accordance with regulations made under s. 22(5) of the Contributions and Benefits Act; and (ii) decisions whether a person was, within the meaning of regulations, precluded from regular employment by responsibilities at home; with effect from 18 October 1999 (SI 1999/2860 (C. 75), art. 2(c)(iv), (v) and Sch. 1).
Para. 4 entered into force, for the purposes of benefits under SSCBA 1992, Pt. II except child's special allowance, with effect from 6 September 1999 (SI 1999/2422 (C. 61), art. 2(c)(i) and Sch. 1).
Para. 4 entered into force, (in so far as not already in force), for the purposes of any matter to which, by virtue of PSA 1993, s. 170, provisions of SSA 1998, Pt. I, Ch. II are to apply, with effect from 5 July 1999 (SI 1999/1958 (C. 51), art. 2(1)(b)(iv)).
Para. 4 entered into force, for the purposes of making regulations, with effect from 4 March 1999 (SI 1999/528).

5 [Omitted by SI 2008/2833, art. 9 and Sch. 3, para. 173(b).]

History – Para. 5 omitted by SI 2008/2833, art. 9 and Sch. 3, para. 173(b), with effect from 3 November 2008.

6 [Omitted by SI 2008/2833, art. 9 and Sch. 3, para. 173(b).]

History – Para. 6 omitted by SI 2008/2833, art. 9 and Sch. 3, para. 173(b), with effect from 3 November 2008.

7 [Omitted by SI 2008/2833, art. 9 and Sch. 3, para. 173(b).]

History – Para. 7 omitted by SI 2008/2833, art. 9 and Sch. 3, para. 173(b), with effect from 3 November 2008.

8 [Omitted by SI 2008/2833, art. 9 and Sch. 3, para. 173(b).]

History – Para. 8 omitted by SI 2008/2833, art. 9 and Sch. 3, para. 173(b), with effect from 3 November 2008.

9 Provision for the non-disclosure to a person of the particulars of any medical advice or medical evidence given or submitted for the purposes of a determination.

Commencement Date – In so far as it was not already in force para. 9 entered into force (except for the purposes of housing benefit, council tax benefit and decisions to which SI 1999/527, art. 4(6) applies; i.e. pre-1 April 1999 decisions under SSAA 1992, s. 17(1), s. 20(3) and PSA 1993, s. 170(1)) with effect from 29 November 1999 (SI 1999/3178 (C. 81), art. 2(1)(a); 2(2) and Sch. 1).
Para. 9 entered into force; for the purposes of (i) decisions whether a person is entitled to be credited with earnings or contributions in accordance with regulations made under s. 22(5) of the Contributions and Benefits Act; and (ii) decisions whether a person was, within the meaning of regulations, precluded from regular employment by responsibilities at home; with effect from 18 October 1999 (SI 1999/2860 (C. 75), art. 2(c)(iv), (v) and Sch. 1).
Para. 9 entered into force, for the purposes of benefits under SSCBA 1992, Pt. II except child's special allowance, with effect from 6 September 1999 (SI 1999/2422 (C. 61), art. 2(c)(i) and Sch. 1).
Para. 9 entered into force, (in so far as not already in force), for the purposes of any matter to which, by virtue of PSA 1993, s. 170, provisions of SSA 1998, Pt. I, Ch. II are to apply, with effect from 5 July 1999 (SI 1999/1958 (C. 51), art. 2(1)(b)(iv)).
Para. 9 entered into force, for the purposes of making regulations, with effect from 4 March 1999 (SI 1999/528).

SCHEDULE 7 – MINOR AND CONSEQUENTIAL AMENDMENTS

Section 86(1)

SOCIAL SECURITY CONTRIBUTIONS AND BENEFITS ACT 1992 (C. 4)

56(1) [Amends SSCBA 1992, s. 1(2) and inserts s. 1(2)(bb).]

56(2) [Amends SSCBA 1992, s. 1(4)(a).]

56(3) [*Amends SSCBA 1992, s. 1(6).*]

Commencement Date – Para. 56 entered into force, for the purpose of making regulations, with effect from 8 September 1998 and for all other purposes, with effect from 6 April 1999 (SI 1998/2209).

57 [Repealed by WRPA 1999, s. 88; Sch. 13, Pt. VI, with effect from 6 April 2000 (SI 1999/3420 (C. 92), art. 4(c), (e)).]

Commencement Date – Para. 57, inserting SSCBA 1992, s. 6(2A), entered into force with effect from 6 April 1999 (SI 1998/2209).

58(1) [Repealed by CSPSSA 2000, s. 86(1), Sch. 9, Pt. VIII(1).]

58(2) [Repealed by CSPSSA 2000, s. 86(1), Sch. 9, Pt. VIII(1).]

Commencement Date – Para. 58(1) entered into force from 6 April 1999 (SI 1999/418).
Para. 58(2) entered into force with effect from 6 April 1999 (SI 1998/2209).

History – Para. 58 repealed by CSPSSA 2000, s. 86(1), Sch. 9, Pt. VIII(1); with effect from 6 April 2000.

59 [Inserts SSCBA 1992, s. 14(4).]

Commencement Date – Para. 59 entered into force from 6 April 1999 (SI 1999/418).

60 [Inserts SSCBA 1992, s. 21(5A).]

Commencement Date – Para. 60 entered into force from 6 April 1999 (SSA 1998 (Commencement No. 3) Order 1999 (SI 1999/418)).

61 [Amends SSCBA 1992, s. 22(4).]

Commencement Date – Para. 61 entered into force from 6 April 1999 (SI 1999/418).

67 [Amends SSCBA 1992, s. 116(2).]

Commencement Date – In so far as it was not already in force para. 67 entered into force (except for the purposes of housing benefit, council tax benefit and decisions to which SI 1999/527, art. 4(6) applies; i.e. pre-1 April 1999 decisions under SSAA 1992, s. 17(1), s. 20(3) and PSA 1993, s. 170(1)) with effect from 29 November 1999 (SI 1999/3178 (C. 81), art. 2(1)(a); 2(2) and Sch. 1).
Para. 67 entered into force; for the purposes of (i) decisions whether a person is entitled to be credited with earnings or contributions in accordance with regulations made under s. 22(5) of the Contributions and Benefits Act; and (ii) decisions whether a person was, within the meaning of regulations, precluded from regular employment by responsibilities at home; with effect from 18 October 1999 (SI 1999/2860 (C. 75), art. 2(c)(iv), (v) and Sch. 1).
Para. 67 entered into force, for the purposes of benefits under SSCBA 1992, Pt. II except child's special allowance, with effect from 6 September 1999 (SI 1999/2422 (C. 61), art. 2(c)(i) and Sch. 1).
Para. 67 entered into force, for the purposes of any matter to which, by virtue of PSA 1993, s. 170, provisions of SSA 1998, Pt. I, Ch. II are to apply, with effect from 5 July 1999 (SI 1999/1958 (C. 51), art. 2(1)(b)(iv)).

68 [Amends SSCBA 1992, s. 117(1).]

Commencement Date – In so far as it was not already in force para. 68 entered into force (except for the purposes of housing benefit, council tax benefit and decisions to which SI 1999/527, art. 4(6) applies; i.e. pre-1 April 1999 decisions under SSAA 1992, s. 17(1), s. 20(3) and PSA 1993, s. 170(1)) with effect from 29 November 1999 (SI 1999/3178 (C. 81), art. 2(1)(a); 2(2) and Sch. 1).
Para. 68 entered into force; for the purposes of (i) decisions whether a person is entitled to be credited with earnings or contributions in accordance with regulations made under s. 22(5) of the Contributions and Benefits Act; and (ii) decisions whether a person was, within the meaning of regulations, precluded from regular employment by responsibilities at home; with effect from 18 October 1999 (SI 1999/2860 (C. 75), art. 2(c)(iv), (v) and Sch. 1).
Para. 68 entered into force, for the purposes of benefits under SSCBA 1992, Pt. II except child's special allowance, with effect from 6 September 1999 (SI 1999/2422 (C. 61), art. 2(c)(i) and Sch. 1).
Para. 68 entered into force, for the purposes of any matter to which, by virtue of PSA 1993, s. 170, provisions of SSA 1998, Pt. I, Ch. II are to apply, with effect from 5 July 1999 (SI 1999/1958 (C. 51), art. 2(1)(b)(iv)).

69 [Amends SSCBA 1992, s. 119.]

Commencement Date – In so far as it was not already in force para. 69 entered into force (except for the purposes of housing benefit, council tax benefit and decisions to which SI 1999/527, art. 4(6) applies; i.e. pre-1 April 1999 decisions under SSAA 1992, s. 17(1), s. 20(3) and PSA 1993, s. 170(1)) with effect from 29 November 1999 (SI 1999/3178 (C. 81), art. 2(1)(a); 2(2) and Sch. 1).
Para. 69 entered into force; for the purposes of (i) decisions whether a person is entitled to be credited with earnings or contributions in accordance with regulations made under s. 22(5) of the Contributions and Benefits Act; and (ii) decisions whether a person was, within the meaning of regulations, precluded from regular employment by responsibilities at home; with effect from 18 October 1999 (SI 1999/2860 (C. 75), art. 2(c)(iv), (v) and Sch. 1).
Para. 69 entered into force, for the purposes of benefits under SSCBA 1992, Pt. II except child's special allowance, with effect from 6 September 1999 (SI 1999/2422 (C. 61), art. 2(c)(i) and Sch. 1).
Para. 69 entered into force, for the purposes of any matter to which, by virtue of PSA 1993, s. 170, provisions of SSA 1998, Pt. I, Ch. II are to apply, with effect from 5 July 1999 (SI 1999/1958 (C. 51), art. 2(1)(b)(iv)).

70 [Amends SSCBA 1992, s. 120(1).]

Commencement Date – In so far as it was not already in force para. 70 entered into force (except for the purposes of housing benefit, council tax benefit and decisions to which SI 1999/527, art. 4(6) applies; i.e. pre-1 April 1999 decisions under SSAA 1992, s. 17(1), s. 20(3) and PSA 1993, s. 170(1)) with effect from 29 November 1999 (SI 1999/3178 (C. 81), art. 2(1)(a); 2(2) and Sch. 1).
Para. 70 entered into force; for the purposes of (i) decisions whether a person is entitled to be credited with earnings or contributions in accordance with regulations made under s. 22(5) of the Contributions and Benefits Act; and (ii) decisions whether a person was, within the meaning of regulations, precluded from regular employment by responsibilities at home; with effect from 18 October 1999 (SI 1999/2860 (C. 75), art. 2(c)(iv), (v) and Sch. 1).
Para. 70 entered into force, for the purposes of benefits under SSCBA 1992, Pt. II except child's special allowance, with effect from 6 September 1999 (SI 1999/2422 (C. 61), art. 2(c)(i) and Sch. 1).
Para. 70 entered into force, for the purposes of any matter to which, by virtue of PSA 1993, s. 170, provisions of SSA 1998, Pt. I, Ch. II are to apply, with effect from 5 July 1999 (SI 1999/1958 (C. 51), art. 2(1)(b)(iv)).

71 [Amends SSCBA 1992, s. 122(1).]

Commencement Date – In so far as it was not already in force para. 71(a) entered into force (except for the purposes of housing benefit, council tax benefit and decisions to which SI 1999/527, art. 4(6) applies; i.e. pre-1 April 1999 decisions under SSAA 1992, s. 17(1), s. 20(3) and PSA 1993, s. 170(1)) with effect from 29 November 1999 (SI 1999/3178 (C. 81), art. 2(1)(a); 2(2) and Sch. 1).
Para. 71(a) entered into force, for the purposes of benefits under SSCBA 1992, Pt. II except child's special allowance, with effect from 6 September 1999 (SI 1999/2422 (C. 61), art. 2(c)(i) and Sch. 1).
Para. 71(a) entered into force; for the purposes of (i) decisions whether a person is entitled to be credited with earnings or contributions in accordance with regulations made under s. 22(5) of the Contributions and Benefits Act; and (ii) decisions whether a person was, within the meaning of regulations, precluded from regular employment by responsibilities at home; with effect from 18 October 1999 (SI 1999/2860 (C. 75), art. 2(c)(iv), (v) and Sch. 1).
Para. 71 entered into force, (in so far as not already in force), for the purposes of any matter to which, by virtue of PSA 1993, s. 170, provisions of SSA 1998, Pt. I, Ch. II are to apply, with effect from 5 July 1999 (SI 1999/1958 (C. 51), art. 2(1)(b)(iv)).
Para. 71(b), (c) and (e) entered into force from 6 April 1999 (SSA 1998 (Commencement No. 3) Order 1999 (SI 1999/418)). Sch. 7, para. 71(d) entered into force, for the purpose of making regulations, with effect from 8 September 1998 and for all other purposes, with effect from 6 April 1999 (SSA 1998 (Commencement No. 1) Order 1998 (SI 1998/2209)).
Para. 71(e) (which amends the definition of "primary percentage" in SSCBA 1992, s. 122(1)) repealed by National Insurance Contributions Act 2002, s. 7 and Sch. 2 with effect for 2003–04 and subsequent years of assessment.

74 [Amends SSCBA 1992, s. 163(1).]

Commencement Date – Sch. 7, para. 74 entered into force from 6 April 1999 (SSA 1998 (Commencement No. 3) Order 1999 (SI 1999/418)).

75 [Amends SSCBA 1992, s. 171(1).]

Commencement Date – Sch. 7, para. 75 entered into force from 6 April 1999 (SI 1999/418).

77(1) [Amends heading to SSCBA 1992, Sch. 1.]

77(2) [Substitutes SSCBA 1992, Sch. 1, para. 1(2).]

77(3) [Amends SSCBA 1992, Sch. 1, para. 1(3).]

77(4) [Amends SSCBA 1992, Sch.1, para. 1(6).]

77(5) [Amends SSCBA 1992. Sch. 1, para. 3(1).]

77(6) [Substitutes SSCBA 1992, Sch. 1, para. 5.]

77(7) [Inserts SSCBA 1992, Sch. 1, para. 5A.]

77(8) [Substitutes SSCBA 1992, Sch. 1, para. 6(10)(a).]

77(9) [Amends SSCBA 1992, Sch. 1, para. 6(2).]

77(10) [Repealed (without entering into force) by SSC(TF)A 1999, s. 26(3) and Sch. 10, Pt. I.]

77(11) [Inserts SSCBA 1992, Sch.1, para. 6(4A).]

77(12) [Amends SSCBA 1992, Sch. 1, para. 7(11)(a).]

77(13) [Repealed (without entering into force) by SSC(TF)A 1999, s. 26(3) and Sch. 10, Pt. I.]

77(14) [Amends SSCBA 1992, Sch. 1, para. 8(10)(b).]

77(15) [Inserts SSCBA 1992, Sch. 1, para. 8(10)(b)(ia).]

77(16) [Amends SSCBA 1992, Sch. 1, para. 8(l).]

Commencement Date – Para. 77(1) and (12) entered into force with effect from 6 April 1999 (SSA 1998 (Commencement No. 1) Order 1998 (SI 1998/2209)).
Para. 77(2), (3), (4) and (5) entered into force from 6 April 1999 (SI 1999/418).
Para. 77(6) entered into force with effect from 8 September 1998 (SI 1998/2209).
Para. 77(7), (8), (9), (11), (14), (15) and (16) entered into force, for the purpose of making regulations, with effect from 8 September 1998 and for all other purposes, with effect from 6 April 1999 (SI 1998/2209).

Prospective amendments – Para. 77(4)(a) repealed by PA 2007, s. 27 and Sch. 7, Pt. 7, with effect from a date to be appointed under PSA 2007, s. 30.

History – Para. 77(10) and (13) repealed (without entering into force) by SSC(TF)A 1999, s. 26(3) and Sch. 10, Pt. I, with effect from 1 April 1999 (SI 1999/527).

SOCIAL SECURITY ADMINISTRATION ACT 1992 (C. 5)

84 [Substitutes SSAA 1992, s. 117.]

Commencement Date – In so far as it was not already in force para. 84 entered into force (except for the purposes of housing benefit, council tax benefit and decisions to which SI 1999/527, art. 4(6) applies; i.e. pre-1 April 1999 decisions under SSAA 1992, s. 17(1), s. 20(3) and PSA 1993, s. 170(1)) with effect from 29 November 1999 (SI 1999/3178 (C. 81), art. 2(1)(a); 2(2) and Sch. 1).
Sch. 7, para. 84 entered into force, for the purposes of any matter to which, by virtue of PSA 1993, s. 170, provisions of SSA 1998, Pt. I, Ch. II are to apply, with effect from 5 July 1999 (SI 1999/1958 (C. 51), art. 2(1)(b)(iv)).

85 [Repeals SSAA 1992, s. 119(2).]

Commencement Date – Para. 85 entered into force with effect from 6 April 1999 (SI 1999/526).

86(1) [Amends SSAA 1992, s. 120(1).]

86(2) [Amends SSAA 1992, s. 120(3).]

86(3) [Amends SSAA 1992, s. 120(4).]

86(4) [Inserts SSAA 1992, s. 120(4A).]

86(5) [Amends SSAA 1992, s. 120(5).]

86(6) [Amends SSAA 1992, s. 120(6).]

Commencement Date – Para. 86 entered into force with effect from 6 April 1999 (SI 1998/2209 and SI 1999/526).

87 [Amends SSAA 1992, s. 121(1), (2).]

Commencement Date – Para. 87 entered into force with effect from 6 April 1999 (SI 1999/526).

89 [Amends SSAA 1992, s. 125(1).]

Commencement Date – In so far as it was not already in force para. 89 entered into force (except for the purposes of housing benefit, council tax benefit and decisions to which SI 1999/527, art. 4(6) applies; i.e. pre-1 April 1999 decisions under SSAA 1992, s. 17(1), s. 20(3) and PSA 1993, s. 170(1)) with effect from 29 November 1999 (SI 1999/3178 (C. 81), art. 2(1)(a); 2(2) and Sch. 1).
Para. 89 entered into force; for the purposes of (i) decisions whether a person is entitled to be credited with earnings or contributions in accordance with regulations made under s. 22(5) of the Contributions and Benefits Act; and (ii) decisions whether a person was, within the meaning of regulations, precluded from regular employment by responsibilities at home; with effect from 18 October 1999 (SI 1999/2860 (C. 75), art. 2(c)(iv), (v) and Sch. 1).
Sch. 7, para. 89 entered into force, for the purposes of benefits under SSCBA 1992, Pt. II except child's special allowance, with effect from 6 September 1999 (SI 1999/2422 (C. 61), art. 2(c)(i) and Sch. 1).

Sch. 7, para. 89 entered into force, for the purposes of any matter to which, by virtue of PSA 1993, s. 170, provisions of SSA 1998, Pt. I, Ch. II are to apply, with effect from 5 July 1999 (SI 1999/1958 (C. 51), art. 2(1)(b)(iv)).

90(1) [Substitutes SSAA 1992, s. 143(1)(a), (b).]

90(2) [Substitutes SSAA 1992, s. 143(4)(a).]

Commencement Date – Para. 90 entered into force from 6 April 1999 (SI 1999/418).

91 [Repealed by WRPA 1999, s. 88; Sch. 13, Pt. VI, with effect from 6 April 2000 (SI 1999/3420 (C. 92), art. 4(c), (e)).]

Commencement Date – Para. 91, amending SSAA 1992, s. 144, entered into force, for the purpose of making regulations, with effect from 8 September 1998 and for all other purposes, with effect from 6 April 1999 (SI 1998/2209).

92 [Substitutes SSAA 1992, s. 145(1)–(3).]

Commencement Date – Para. 92 entered into force from 6 April 1999 (SI 1999/418).

93 [Repeals SSAA 1992, s. 146.]

Commencement Date – Para. 93 entered into force from 6 April 1999 (SI 1999/418).

94 [Amends SSAA 1992, s. 147(1), (2), (3).]

Commencement Date – Para. 94 entered into force from 6 April 1999 (SI 1999/418).

99(1) [Inserts SSAA 1992, s. 162(2A).]

99(2) [Inserts SSAA 1992, s. 162(4A).]

99(3) [Amends SSAA 1992, s. 162(5)(b).]

99(4) [Amends SSAA 1992, s. 162(8).]

Commencement Date – Para. 99(1) entered into force with effect from 8 September 1998 (SI 1998/2209).
Para. 99(2) entered into force with effect from 6 April 1999 (SI 1999/526).
Para. 99(3) entered into force with effect from 6 April 1999 (SI 1999/418).
Para. 99(4) entered into force, for the purpose of making regulations, with effect from 8 September 1998 and for all other purposes, with effect from 6 April 1999 (SI 1998/2209).

104 [Amends SSAA 1992, s. 170.]

Commencement Date – Para. 104 entered into force with effect from 4 March 1999 (SI 1999/528).

105 [Amends SSAA 1992, s. 177(5).]

Commencement Date – Para. 105 entered into force with effect from 5 July 1999 (SI 1999/528).

107(1) [Amends SSAA 1992, s. 179(3)(a).]

107(2) [Inserts SSAA 1992, s. 179(40)(ab).]

Commencement Date – In so far as it was not already in force para. 107 entered into force (except for the purposes of housing benefit, council tax benefit and decisions to which SI 1999/527, art. 4(6) applies; i.e. pre-1 April 1999 decisions under SSAA 1992, s. 17(1), s. 20(3) and PSA 1993, s. 170(1)) with effect from 29 November 1999 (SI 1999/3178 (C. 81), art. 2(1)(a); 2(2) and Sch. 1).
Para. 107 entered into force; for the purposes of (i) decisions whether a person is entitled to be credited with earnings or contributions in accordance with regulations made under s. 22(5) of the Contributions and Benefits Act; and (ii) decisions whether a person was, within the meaning of regulations, precluded from regular employment by responsibilities at home; with effect from 18 October 1999 (SI 1999/2860 (C. 75), art. 2(c)(iv), (v) and Sch. 1).
Para. 107 entered into force, for the purposes of benefits under SSCBA 1992, Pt. II except child's special allowance, with effect from 6 September 1999 (SI 1999/2422 (C. 61), art. 2(c)(i) and Sch. 1).
Para. 107 entered into force, for the purposes of any matter to which, by virtue of PSA 1993, s. 170, provisions of SSA 1998, Pt. I, Ch. II are to apply, with effect from 5 July 1999 (SI 1999/1958 (C. 51), art. 2(1)(b)(iv)).

108 [Amends SSAA 1992, s. 180.]

Commencement Date – In so far as it was not already in force pPara. 108 entered into force (except for the purposes of housing benefit, council tax benefit and decisions to which SI 1999/527, art. 4(6) applies; i.e. pre-1 April 1999 decisions under SSAA 1992, s. 17(1), s. 20(3) and PSA 1993, s. 170(1)) with effect from 29 November 1999 (SI 1999/3178 (C. 81), art. 2(1)(a); 2(2) and Sch. 1).
Para. 108 entered into force; for the purposes of (i) decisions whether a person is entitled to be credited with earnings or contributions in accordance with regulations made under section 22(5) of the Contributions and Benefits Act; and (ii) decisions whether a person was, within the meaning of regulations, precluded from regular employment by responsibilities at home; with effect from 18 October 1999 (SI 1999/2860 (C. 75), art. 2(c)(iv), (v) and Sch. 1).
Para. 108 entered into force, for the purposes of benefits under SSCBA 1992, Pt. II except child's special allowance, with effect from 6 September 1999 (SI 1999/2422 (C. 61), art. 2(c)(i) and Sch. 1).
Para. 108 entered into force, for the purposes of any matter to which, by virtue of PSA 1993, s. 170, provisions of SSA 1998, Pt. I, Ch. II are to apply, with effect from 5 July 1999 (SI 1999/1958 (C. 51), art. 2(1)(b)(iv)).

109 [Amends SSAA 1992, s. 189(1), (4), (5), (6) and repeals SSAA 1992, s. 189(2), (10).]

Commencement Date – In so far as it was not already in force para. 109 entered into force (except for the purposes of housing benefit, council tax benefit and decisions to which SI 1999/527, art. 4(6) applies; i.e. pre-1 April 1999 decisions under SSAA 1992, s. 17(1), s. 20(3) and PSA 1993, s. 170(1)) with effect from 29 November 1999 (SI 1999/3178 (C. 81), art. 2(1)(a); 2(2) and Sch. 1).
Para. 109 entered into force; for the purposes of (i) decisions whether a person is entitled to be credited with earnings or contributions in accordance with regulations made under s. 22(5) of the Contributions and Benefits Act; and (ii) decisions whether a person was, within the meaning of regulations, precluded from regular employment by responsibilities at home; with effect from 18 October 1999 (SI 1999/2860 (C. 75), art. 2(c)(iv), (v) and Sch. 1).
Para. 109 entered into force, for the purposes of benefits under SSCBA 1992, Pt. II except child's special allowance, with effect from 6 September 1999 (SI 1999/2422 (C. 61), art. 2(c)(i) and Sch. 1).

110(1) In subsection (1)(a) of section 190 of that Act (instruments containing provisions under certain provisions to be subject to the affirmative Parliamentary procedure)–

(a) [repealed by WRPA 1999, s. 88; Sch. 13, Pt. VI;]

(b) [amends SSAA 1992, s. 190(1)(a).]

110(2) [Repeals SSAA 1992, s. 190(4).]

Commencement Date – In so far as it was not already in force para. 110 entered into force (except for the purposes of housing benefit, council tax benefit and decisions to which SI 1999/527, art. 4(6) applies; i.e. pre-1 April 1999 decisions under SSAA 1992, s. 17(1), s. 20(3) and PSA 1993, s. 170(1)) with effect from 29 November 1999 (SI 1999/3178 (C. 81), art. 2(1)(a); 2(2) and Sch. 1).
Para. 110(1)(a), amending SSAA 1992, s. 190, entered into force, for the purpose of making regulations, with effect from 8 September 1998 and for all other purposes, with effect from 6 April 1999 (SI 1998/2209). This amendment was only effective until 5 April 2000, after which the NIC reforms introduced by WRPA 1999, Pt. V, Ch. II came into force.
Para. 99(3) entered into force with effect from 6 April 1999 (SI 1999/418).

History – Para. 110(1)(a) repealed by WRPA 1999, s. 88; Sch. 13, Pt. VI, with effect from 6 April 2000 (SI 1999/3420 (C. 92), art. 4(c), (e)).

113 [Amends SSAA 1992, Sch. 4, Pt. I.]

Commencement Date – Para. 113 entered into force (except for the purposes of housing benefit, council tax benefit and decisions to which SI 1999/527, art. 4(6) applies; i.e. pre-1 April 1999 decisions under SSAA 1992, s. 17(1), s. 20(3) and PSA 1993, s. 170(1)) with effect from 29 November 1999 (SI 1999/3178 (C. 81), art. 2(1)(a); 2(2) and Sch. 1).

114(1) [Amends SSAA 1992, Sch. 7, Pt I.]

114(2) [Not relevant to National Insurance contributions.]

Commencement Date – Para. 114 entered into force, for the purpose of making regulations, with effect from 8 September 1998 and for all other purposes, with effect from 6 April 1999 (SI 1998/2209).

PENSION SCHEMES ACT 1993 (C. 48)

126 [Amends PSA 1993, s. 8(2).]

Commencement Date – Para. 126 entered into force from 6 April 1999 (SI 1999/418).

Prospective amendments – Para. 126 repealed by PA 2007, s. 27 and Sch. 7, Pt. 6, with effect from a date to be appointed under PSA 2007, s. 30.

127 [Substitutes PSA 1993, s. 41.]

Commencement Date – Para. 127 entered into force from 6 April 1999 (SI 1999/418).

128 [Substitutes PSA 1993, s. 42A(1)–(2B) for former subsection (1) and (2).]

Commencement Date – Para. 128 entered into force from 6 April 1999 (SI 1999/418).

Prospective amendments – Para. 128 repealed by PA 2007, s. 27 and Sch. 7, Pt. 7, with effect from a date to be appointed under PSA 2007, s. 30.

129 [Amends SSAA 1992, s. 158(6)(c).]

Commencement Date – In so far as it was not already in force para. 129 entered into force (except for the purposes of housing benefit, council tax benefit and decisions to which SI 1999/527, art. 4(6) applies; i.e. pre-1 April 1999 decisions under SSAA 1992, s. 17(1), s. 20(3) and PSA 1993, s. 170(1)) with effect from 29 November 1999 (SI 1999/3178 (C. 81), art. 2(1)(a); 2(2) and Sch. 1).
Para. 129 entered into force, for the purposes of any matter to which, by virtue of PSA 1993, s. 170, provisions of SSA 1998, Pt. I, Ch. II are to apply, with effect from 5 July 1999 (SI 1999/1958 (C. 51), art. 2(1)(b)(iv)).

130(1) [Repealed (without entering into force) by SSC(TF)A 1999, s. 26(3) and Sch. 10, Pt. I.]

130(2) [Repeals PSA 1993, s. 167(4).]

Commencement Date – Para. 130(2) entered into force, for the purposes of any matter to which, by virtue of PSA 1993, s. 170, provisions of SSA 1998, Pt. I, Ch. II are to apply, with effect from 5 July 1999 (SI 1999/1958 (C. 51), art. 2(1)(b)(iv)).

History – Para. 130(1) repealed (without entering into force) by SSC(TF)A 1999, s. 26(3) and Sch. 10, Pt. I, with effect from 5 July 1999 (SI 1999/1662).

Cross references – PSA 1993, s. 167: the section referred to in sub-paragraph (2) above.

131 [Substitutes PSA 1993, s. 170.]

Commencement Date – Para. 131 entered into force with effect from 4 March 1999, for the purposes of making regulations only (SI 1999/528), and with effect from 5 July 1999, for the purposes of any matter to which, by virtue of PSA 1993, s. 170, provisions of SSA 1998, Pt. I, Ch. II are to apply (SI 1999/1958 (C. 51), art. 2(1)(b)(iv)).

132 [Repealed by SSC(TF)A 1999, s. 26(3) and Sch. 10, Pt. I.]

History – Para. 132 repealed (without entering into force) by SSC(TF)A 1999, s. 26(3) and Sch. 10, Pt. I, with effect from 5 July 1999 (SI 1999/1662).

SOCIAL SECURITY CONTRIBUTIONS (TRANSFER OF FUNCTIONS, ETC.) ACT 1999

(1999 Chapter 2)

[25th February 1999]

ARRANGEMENT OF SECTIONS

PART I – GENERAL

PART II – DECISIONS AND APPEALS

PART III – MISCELLANEOUS AND SUPPLEMENTAL

SCHEDULES

PART I – GENERAL

TRANSFER OF FUNCTIONS

1 Transfer to Board of certain functions relating to contributions, etc.

1(1) Schedule 1 to this Act (which contains amendments transferring to the Board certain functions of the Secretary of State which have been exercised by the Contributions Agency and certain associated functions of the Secretary of State in relation to benefits, together with other amendments related to the transfer of those functions) shall have effect.

1(2) The functions of the Secretary of State under the provisions of subordinate legislation specified in Schedule 2 to this Act are hereby transferred to the Board.

Commencement Date – S. 1(1) (and Sch. 1 – see headnote to Schedule) entered into force on 25 February 1999, to enable subordinate legislation to be made for the purposes of transferring functions to the Board (s. 28(2)(a)), and for all other purposes, with effect from 1 April 1999 (SSC(TF)A 1999, s. 28(3) and SI 1999/527, art. 2(b), Sch. 2).
S. 1(2) (and Sch. 2 – see headnote to Schedule) entered into force with effect from 1 April 1999 (SSC(TF)A 1999, s. 28(3) and SI 1999/527, art. 2(b), Sch. 2).

Cross references – S. 28(5)(a): application of section to Northern Ireland as far as it amends ICTA 1988.

2 Transfer of other functions to Treasury or Board

2 Schedule 3 to this Act (which contains amendments transferring to the Treasury or the Board certain other functions of the Secretary of State, together with amendments related to the transfer of those functions) shall have effect.

Commencement Date – S. 2 entered into force (and Sch. 3 – see headnote to Schedule) with effect from 1 April 1999 (SSC(TF)A 1999, s. 28(3) and SI 1999/527, art. 2(b), Sch. 2).

Cross references – S. 28(5)(b): application of section to Northern Ireland so far as it amends SSAA 1992, s. 177 or the Northern Ireland Act 1998, s. 88.

EXERCISE BY BOARD OF FUNCTIONS TRANSFERRED TO THEM

3 General functions of Board

3(1) The Commissioners for Her Majesty's Revenue and Customs shall be responsible for the collection and management of contributions.

3(2)–(5) [Substituted by CRCA 2005, s. 50(6) and Sch. 4, para. 74.]

3(6) In Schedule 2 to the Social Security Contributions and Benefits Act 1992 (levy of Class 4 contributions with income tax) and Schedule 2 to the Social Security Contributions and Benefits (Northern Ireland) Act 1992, paragraph 6(2) (which is superseded by subsection (1) above) shall cease to have effect.

3(7) In this section **"contributions"** includes contributions under Part I of the Social Security Contributions and Benefits (Northern Ireland) Act 1992.

Commencement Date – S. 3 (except former s. 3(3)(c)) entered into force with effect from 1 April 1999 (SSC(TF)A 1999, s. 28(3) and SI 1999/527, art. 2(b), Sch. 2).

History – S. 3(1) substituted for s. 3(1)–(5) by CRCA 2005, s. 50(6) and Sch. 4, para. 74 with effect from 18 April 2005 by virtue of SI 2005/112, art. 2.
Former s. 3(3)(c) omitted by WRPA 1999, s. 81 and Sch. 11, para. 30 with effect from 11 November 1999 (date of passing of WRPA 1999) which is the commencement date provided for by WRPA 1999, S. 89(4)(d). This subsection was also repealed by WRPA 1999, S. 88 and Sch. 13, pt. VI.

Cross references – S. 28(5)(c): application of section to Northern Ireland

Statutory instruments – SI 2002/2366: made under s. 3(2) and s. 119.
SI 2002/2924 made under s. 3(2), (3).

4 Recovery of contributions where income tax recovery provisions not applicable

4 The provisions of Schedule 4 shall have effect with respect to the recovery of–

(a) those Class 1, Class 1A and Class 1B contributions to which regulations under paragraph 6 or 7BZA of Schedule 1 to the Social Security Contributions and Benefits Act 1992 or paragraph 6 or

7BZA of Schedule 1 to the Social Security Contributions and Benefits (Northern Ireland) Act 1992 (power to combine collection of contributions with income tax) do not apply,

(aa) those Class 2 contributions in relation to which–

(i) the regulations mentioned in paragraph (a), and

(ii) Part 6 of the Taxes Management Act 1970 (collection and recovery),

do not apply,

(b) [Omitted by NICSPA 2004, s. 11 and Sch. 1, para. 5(3) and s. 12 and Sch. 2.]

(c) interest or penalties payable under regulations made under paragraph 7A of Schedule 1 to the Social Security Contributions and Benefits Act 1992 or paragraph 7A of Schedule 1 to the Social Security Contributions and Benefits (Northern Ireland) Act 1992, and

(d) interest or penalties–

(i) payable under regulations made under paragraph 7B of Schedule 1 to the Social Security Contributions and Benefits Act 1992 and to which regulations under paragraph 7BZA of that Schedule do not apply, or

(ii) payable under regulations made under paragraph 7B of Schedule 1 to the Social Security Contributions and Benefits (Northern Ireland) Act 1992 and to which regulations under paragraph 7BZA of that Schedule do not apply.

Commencement Date – S. 4(a) (except as far as it relates to class 1B contributions), and s. 4(b), entered into force (and Sch. 4 – see headnote to Schedule) with effect from 1 April 1999 (SSC(TF)A 1999, s. 28(3) and SI 1999/527, art. 2(b), Sch. 2). As far as s. 4(a) (and Sch. 4) relates to class 1B contributions, it and s. 4(c) entered into force on 6 April 1999 (SSC(TF)A 1999, s. 28(3) and SI 1999/527, art. 2(c), Sch. 3).

History – In s. 4(a) the words "and Class 1B" substituted for the words ", Class 1B and Class 2" and para. (aa) inserted by NICA 2015, s. 2 and Sch. 1, para. 24, with effect for the tax year 2015–16 and subsequent tax years.

In s. 4(a), "or 7BZA" inserted twice by NICSPA 2004, s. 11 and Sch. 1, para. 5(2) with effect from 1 September 2004 (by virtue of SI 2004/1943, reg. 5).

In s. 4(a), the words or paragraph 6 of Schedule 1 to the Social Security Contributions and Benefits (Northern Ireland) Act 1992 inserted by WRPA 1999, Sch. 11, para. 31(a) with effect from 11 November 1999 (date of passing of WRPA 1999).

S. 4(b) and word "and" immediately after it omitted by NICSPA 2004, s. 11 and Sch. 1, para. 5(3) and repealed by s. 12 and Sch. 2 with effect from 1 September 2004 (by virtue of SI 2004/1943, reg. 5 and 6).

In s. 4(b), the words "the Social Security Contributions and Benefits Act 1992 or section 18 of the Social Security Contributions and Benefits (Northern Ireland) Act 1992" substituted by Welfare Reform and Pensions Act 1999, Sch. 11, para. 31(b) with effect from 11 November 1999 (date of passing of WRPA 1999).

In s. 4(c), two references to "or 7B" omitted by NICSPA 2004, s. 11 and Sch. 1, para. 5(4) and repealed by s. 12 and Sch. 2 with effect from 1 September 2004 (by virtue of SI 2004/1493, reg. 5 and 6).

In s. 4(c), the words "the Social Security Contributions and Benefits Act 1992 or paragraph 7A or 7B of Schedule 1 to the Social Security Contributions and Benefits (Northern Ireland) Act 1992" substituted by WRPA 1999, Sch. 11, para. 31(c) with effect from 11 November 1999 (date of passing of WRPA 1999).

S. 4(d) inserted by NICSPA 2004, s. 11 and Sch. 1, para. 5(4) with effect from 1 September 2004 (by virtue of SI 2004/1493, reg. 5).

Cross references – S. 28(5)(d): application of section to Northern Ireland.

5 Powers relating to enforcement

5 Schedule 5 to this Act (which relates to the enforcement powers of the Board in relation to functions transferred to them by this Act) shall have effect.

Commencement Date – S. 5 (and Sch. 5 – see the headnote to the Schedule) entered into force, except insofar as it relates to Sch. 5, para. 5 and 7, with effect from 1 April 1999 (SSC(TF)A 1999, s. 28(3) and SI 1999/527, art. 2(b), Sch. 2). As far as it relates to Sch. 5, para. 5 and 7, it is in force with effect from 6 April 1999 (SSC(TF)A 1999, s. 28(3) and SI 1999/527, art. 2(c), Sch. 3).

Cross references – S. 28(5)(e): application of section to Northern Ireland so far as it amends TMA 1970.

6 Disclosure of information

6 Schedule 6 to this Act (which contains amendments relating to the supply or disclosure of information) shall have effect.

Commencement Date – S. 6 (and Sch. 6 – see the headnote to the Schedule) entered into force with effect from 1 April 1999 (SSC(TF)A 1999, s. 28(3) and SI 1999/527, art. 2(b), Sch. 2).

7 Use of information by Board

7 [Ceased to have effect by CRCA 2005, s. 50 and Sch. 4, para. 75 and repealed by CRCA 2005, s. 52(2) and Sch. 5.]

Commencement Date – S. 7 entered into force with effect from 1 April 1999 (SSC(TF)A 1999, s. 28(3) and SI 1999/527, art. 2(b), Sch. 2).

History – S. 7 ceased to have effect by CRCA 2005, s. 50(6) and Sch. 4, para. 75 and repealed by s. 52(2) and Sch. 5 from 18 April 2005 by virtue of SI 2005/1126, art. 2. Former s. 7 read as follows:

"7 Use of information by Board

7(1) Information which is held–

(a) by the Board, or

(b) by a person providing services to the Board, in connection with the provision of those services, for the purposes of functions specified in any paragraph of subsection (2) below may be used for the purposes of, or for any purposes connected with, the exercise of functions specified in any other paragraph of that subsection, and may be supplied to any person providing services to the Board for those purposes.

7(2) The functions referred to in subsection (1) above are–

(a) the functions of the Board in relation to tax,

(b) their functions in relation to contributions, statutory sick pay and statutory maternity pay, and

(c) their functions under Part III of the Pension Schemes Act 1993 or Part III of the Pension Schemes (Northern Ireland) Act 1993.

7(3) In subsection (2)(b) above **"contributions"** includes contributions under Part I of the Social Security Contributions and Benefits (Northern Ireland) Act 1992."

PART II – DECISIONS AND APPEALS

Cross references – NICA 2011, s. 8(6)(a): decisions as to entitlement to refunds and deductions under NICA 2011, s. 8 (regional secondary contributions holiday for new businesses) treated for the purposes of SSCTFA 1999, Pt. II as decisions made under SSCTFA 1999, s. 8.

SI 1999/1027: regulations concerning decisions made by officers of the Board and the conduct etc. of appeals against such decisions.

8 Decisions by officers of Board

8(1) Subject to the provisions of this Part, it shall be for an officer of the Board–

(a) to decide whether for the purposes of Parts I to V of the Social Security Contributions and Benefits Act 1992 a person is or was an earner and, if so, the category of earners in which he is or was to be included,

(b) to decide whether a person is or was employed in employed earner's employment for the purposes of Part V of the Social Security Contributions and Benefits Act 1992 (industrial injuries),

(c) to decide whether a person is or was liable to pay contributions of any particular class and, if so, the amount that he is or was liable to pay,

(d) to decide whether a person is or was entitled to pay contributions of any particular class that he is or was not liable to pay and, if so, the amount that he is or was entitled to pay,

(e) to decide whether contributions of a particular class have been paid in respect of any period,

(ea) to decide whether a person is or was entitled to make a deduction under section 4 of the National Insurance Contributions Act 2014 (deductions etc of employment allowance) and, if so, the amount the person is or was entitled to deduct,

(eb) to decide whether a person is or was entitled to a repayment under that section and, if so, the amount of the repayment,

(f) subject to and in accordance with regulations made for the purposes of this paragraph by the Secretary of State with the concurrence of the Board, to decide any issue arising as to, or in connection with, entitlement to statutory sick pay, statutory maternity pay, statutory paternity pay, statutory adoption pay or statutory shared parental pay,

(g) to make any other decision that falls to be made under Parts 11 to 12ZC of the Social Security Contributions and Benefits Act 1992 (statutory sick pay, statutory maternity pay, statutory paternity pay, statutory adoption pay and statutory shared parental pay),

(ga) to make any decision that falls to be made under regulations under section 7 of the Employment Act 2002 (funding of employers' liabilities to make payments of statutory paternity pay, statutory adoption pay or statutory shared parental pay),

(h) to decide any question as to the issue and content of a notice under subsection (2) of section 121C of the Social Security Administration Act 1992 (liability of directors etc. for company's contributions),

(i) to decide any issue arising under section 27 of the Jobseekers Act 1995 (employment of long-term unemployed: deductions by employers), or under any provision of regulations under that section, as to–

  (i) whether a person is or was an employee or employer of another,

  (ii) whether an employer is or was entitled to make any deduction from his contributions payments in accordance with regulations under section 27 of that Act,

  (iii) whether a payment falls to be made to an employer in accordance with those regulations,

  (iv) the amount that falls to be so deducted or paid, or

  (v) whether two or more employers are, by virtue of regulations under section 27 of that Act, to be treated as one,

(ia) to decide whether to give or withdraw an approval for the purposes of paragraph 3B(1)(b) of Schedule 1 to the Social Security Contributions and Benefits Act 1992,

(j) [repealed by CSPSSA 2000, s. 77(6)(a); s. 86(1), Sch. 9, Pt. VIII(1).]

(k) to decide whether a person is liable to a penalty under–

(i) paragraph 7A(2) or 7B(2)(h) of Schedule 1 to the Social Security Contributions and Benefits Act 1992, or

(ii) section 113(1)(a) of the Social Security Administration Act 1992,

(l) to decide the penalty payable under any of the provisions mentioned in paragraph (k) above, and

(m) to decide such issues relating to contributions, other than the issues specified in paragraphs (a) to (l) above or in paragraphs 16 and 17 of Schedule 3 to the Social Security Act 1998, as may be prescribed by regulations made by the Board.

8(1A) No decision in respect of Class 2 contributions under section 11(2) of the Social Security Contributions and Benefits Act 1992 may be made under subsection (1) in relation to an issue specified in paragraph (c) or (e) of that subsection if the person to whom the decision would relate–

(a) has appealed under Part 5 of the Taxes Management Act 1970 in relation to that issue,

(b) can appeal under that Part in relation to that issue, or

(c) might in the future, without the agreement of Her Majesty's Revenue and Customs or permission of the tribunal, be able to appeal under that Part in relation to that issue.

8(2) Subsection (1)(c) and (e) above do not include any decision relating to Class 4 contributions other than a decision falling to be made–

(a) under subsection (1) of section 17 of the Social Security Contributions and Benefits Act 1992 as to whether by regulations under that subsection a person is or was excepted from liability for Class 4 contributions, or his liability is or was deferred, or

(b) under regulations made by virtue of subsection (3) or (4) of that section or section 18 of that Act.

8(3) Subsection (1)(g) above does not include–

(a) any decision as to the making of subordinate legislation, or

(b) any decision as to whether the liability to pay statutory sick pay, statutory maternity pay, statutory paternity pay, statutory adoption pay or statutory shared parental pay is a liability of the Board rather than the employer.

8(4) [Repealed by WRPA 1999, s. 88, Sch. 13, Pt. VI.]

Commencement Date – S. 8 entered into force, only for the purposes of making regulations, with effect from 25 February 1999 (SSC(TF)A 1999, s. 28(2)(b)). S. 8, except subsection (1)(h), (j), (k) and (l), entered into force for all other purposes on 1 April 1999 (SSC(TF)A 1999, s. 28(3) and SI 1999/527, art. 2(b), Sch. 2); subsection (1)(h), (j), (k) and (l), entered into force for all other purposes on 6 April 1999 (SI 1999/527, art. 2(c), Sch. 3).

History – S. 8(1)(ea) and (eb) inserted by NICA 2014, s. 6(1), with effect from 6 April 2014.
In s. 8(1)(f), the words "statutory paternity pay," substituted for the words "ordinary statutory paternity pay, additional statutory paternity pay or" by Children and Families Act 2014, s. 126(1) and Sch. 7, para. 45(2)(a), with effect from 5 April 2015, subject to the transitional and saving provisions in SI 2014/1640, art. 16 (amendments do not have effect in relation to– (a) children whose expected week of birth ends on or before 4 April 2015; (b) children placed for adoption on or before 4 April 2015) (SI 2014/1640, art. 7).
In s. 8(1)(f), the words "or statutory shared parental pay" inserted by Children and Families Act 2014, s. 126(1) and Sch. 7, para. 45(2)(b), with effect from 1 December 2014 (SI 2014/1640, art. 5).
In s. 8(1)(f) the words "ordinary statutory paternity pay, additional statutory paternity pay" substituted for "statutory paternity pay" by the Work and Families Act 2006, s. 11 and Sch. 1, para. 46(2)(a), with effect from 3 March 2010 (SI 2010/495).
In s. 8(1)(f), the words ", statutory maternity pay, statutory paternity pay or statutory adoption pay" substituted by the Employment Act 2002, s. 9(2)(a) with effect from 8 December 2002 by virtue of SI 2002/2866 (C. 91).
In s. 8(1)(g), the words "statutory paternity pay," substituted for the words "ordinary statutory paternity pay, additional statutory paternity pay and" by Children and Families Act 2014, s. 126(1) and Sch. 7, para. 45(2)(d), with effect from 5 April 2015, subject to the transitional and saving provisions in SI 2014/1640, art. 16 (amendments do not have effect in relation to– (a) children whose expected week of birth ends on or before 4 April 2015; (b) children placed for adoption on or before 4 April 2015) (SI 2014/1640, art. 7).
In s. 8(1)(g), the words "to 12ZC" substituted for the words "to 12ZB" and the words "and statutory shared parental pay" inserted by Children and Families Act 2014, s. 126(1) and Sch. 7, para. 45(2)(c) and (e), with effect from 1 December 2014 (SI 2014/1640, art. 5).
In s. 8(1)(g) the words "ordinary statutory paternity pay, additional statutory paternity pay" substituted for "statutory paternity pay" by the Work and Families Act 2006, s. 11 and Sch. 1, para. 46(2)(a), with effect from 3 March 2010 (SI 2010/495).
In s. 8(1)(g), the words "under Parts 11 to 12ZB of the Social Security Contributions and Benefits Act 1992 (statutory sick pay, statutory maternity pay, statutory paternity pay and statutory adoption pay)" substituted by the Employment Act 2002, s. 9(2)(b) with effect from 8 December 2002 by virtue of SI 2002/2866 (C. 91).
In para. 8(1)(ga), the words "statutory paternity pay," substituted forthe words "ordinary statutory paternity pay, additional statutory paternity pay or" by Children and Families Act 2014, s. 126(1) and Sch. 7, para. 45(2)(f), with effect from 5 April 2015, subject to the transitional and saving provisions in SI 2014/1640, art. 16 (amendments do not have effect in relation to– (a) children whose expected week of birth ends on or before 4 April 2015; (b) children placed for adoption on or before 4 April 2015) (SI 2014/1640, art. 7).
In para. 8(1)(ga), the words "or statutory shared parental pay" inserted by Children and Families Act 2014, s. 126(1) and Sch. 7, para. 45(2)(g), with effect from 1 December 2014 (SI 2014/1640, art. 5).
In s. 8(1)(ga) the words "ordinary statutory paternity pay, additional statutory paternity pay or statutory adoption pay" substituted for "statutory paternity pay or adoption pay" by the Work and Families Act 2006, s. 11 and Sch. 1, para. 46(2)(b), with effect from 3 March 2010 (SI 2010/495).
S. 8(1)(ga) inserted by the Employment Act 2002, s. 9(2)(c) with effect from 8 December 2002 by virtue of SI 2002/2866 (C. 91).
S. 8(1)(j) repealed by CSPSSA 2000, s. 77(6)(a); s. 86(1), Sch. 9, Pt. VIII(1); with effect in relation to interest accruing on sums becoming due for 2000–01 and subsequent tax years.
In s. 8(1)(l) reference to s. 8(1)(j) and the words "amount of interest or" omitted by CSPSSA 2000, s. 77(6)(b); s. 86(1), Sch. 9, Pt. VIII(1); with effect in relation to interest accruing on sums becoming due for 2000–01 and subsequent tax years.
S. 8(1)(ia) inserted by CSPSSA 2000, s. 78(5) with effect from 28 July 2000 (date of Royal Assent).
S. 8(1A) inserted by NICA 2015, s. 2 and Sch. 1, para. 25, with effect for the tax year 2015–16 and subsequent tax years.
In s. 8(3)(b), the words "statutory paternity pay," substituted for the words "ordinary statutory paternity pay, additional statutory paternity pay or" by Children and Families Act 2014, s. 126(1) and Sch. 7, para. 45(3)(a), with effect from 5 April 2015, subject to the

transitional and saving provisions in SI 2014/1640, art. 16 (amendments do not have effect in relation to– (a) children whose expected week of birth ends on or before 4 April 2015; (b) children placed for adoption on or before 4 April 2015) (SI 2014/1640, art. 7).
In s. 8(3)(b), the words "or statutory shared parental pay" inserted by Children and Families Act 2014, s. 126(1) and Sch. 7, para. 45(3)(b), with effect from 1 December 2014 (SI 2014/1640, art. 5).
In s. 8(3)(b), the words "ordinary statutory paternity pay, additional statutory paternity pay" substitutedfor "statutory paternity pay" by the Work and Families Act 2006, s. 11 and Sch. 1, para. 46(3), with effect from 3 March 2010 (SI 2010/495).
In s. 8(3)(b), the words ", statutory maternity pay, statutory paternity pay or statutory adoption pay" substituted by EA 2002, s. 9(3) with effect from 8 December 2002 by virtue of SI 2002/2866 (C. 91).
S. 8(4) repealed by WRPA 1999, s. 88, Sch. 13, Pt. VI with effect from 6 April 2000 (SI 1999/3420, art. 4(c), (e)).

Cross references – NICA 2011, s. 8(6)(a): decisions as to entitlement to refunds and deductions under NICA 2011, s. 8 (regional secondary contributions holiday for new businesses) treated for the purposes of SSCTFA 1999, Pt. II as decisions made under SSCTFA 1999, s. 8.
SI 1999/1027: regulations concerning decisions made by officers of the Board and the conduct etc. of appeals against such decisions.

Statutory instruments – SI 2003/1192: made under s. 8(1)(f).

9 Regulations with respect to decisions

9(1) Subject to the provisions of this Part and of the Social Security Administration Act 1992, provision may be made by the Board by regulations as to the making by their officer of any decision under or in connection with the Social Security Contributions and Benefits Act 1992, the Social Security Administration Act 1992 or the Jobseekers Act 1995 which falls to be made by such an officer.

9(2) Where it appears to an officer of the Board that a matter before him involves a question of fact requiring special expertise, he may direct that in dealing with that matter he shall have the assistance of one or more experts.

9(3) In subsection (2) above **"expert"** means a person appearing to the officer of the Board to have knowledge or experience which would be relevant in determining the question of fact requiring special expertise.

Commencement Date – S. 9 entered into force, only for the purposes of making regulations, with effect from 25 February 1999 (SSC(TF)A 1999, s. 28(2)(b)) and for all other purposes on 1 April 1999 (SSC(TF)A 1999, s. 28(3) and SI 1999/527, art. 2(b), Sch. 2.

Cross references – SI 1999/1027: regulations concerning decisions made by officers of the Board and the conduct etc. of appeals against such decisions.

Statutory instruments – SI 1999/1027.

10 Decisions varying or superseding earlier decisions

10(1) Subject to subsection (2A) below, the Board may by regulations make provision–

(a) for any decision of an officer of the Board under section 8 of this Act (including a decision superseding an earlier decision) to be varied either within the prescribed period or in prescribed cases or circumstances,

(b) for any such decision to be superseded, in prescribed circumstances, by a subsequent decision made by an officer of the Board, and

(c) for any such decision as confirmed or varied by the First-tier Tribunal or Upper Tribunal on appeal to be superseded, in the event of a material change of circumstances since the decision was made, by a subsequent decision made by an officer of the Board.

10(2) The date as from which–

(a) any variation of a decision, or

(b) any decision superseding an earlier decision,

is to take effect shall be determined in accordance with the regulations.

10(2A) The decisions in relation to which provision may be made by regulations under this section shall not include decisions falling within section 8(1)(ia) above.

10(3) In this section **"prescribed"** means prescribed by regulations under this section.

Commencement Date – S. 10 entered into force, only for the purposes of making regulations, with effect from 25 February 1999 (SSC(TF)A 1999, s. 28(2)(b)) and for all other purposes on 1 April 1999 (SSC(TF)A 1999, s. 28(3) and SI 1999/527, art. 2(b), Sch. 2.

History – In s. 10(1)(c), the words "First-tier Tribunal or Upper Tribunal" substituted for the words "tax appeal Commissioners" by SI 2009/56, art. 3(1) and Sch. 1, para. 269, operative from 1 April 2009, subject to transitional and saving provisions in SI 2009/56, Sch. 3.
In s. 10(1) the words "Subject to subsection (2A) below," inserted by CSPSSA 2000, s. 78(6); with effect from 28 July 2000 (date of Royal Assent).
S. 10(2A) inserted by CSPSSA 2000, s. 78(6); with effect from 28 July 2000 (date of Royal Assent).

Cross references – SI 1999/1027: regulations concerning decisions made by officers of the Board and the conduct etc. of appeals against such decisions.

Statutory instruments – SI 1999/1027.

11 Appeals against decisions of Board

11(1) This section applies to any decision of an officer of the Board under section 8 of this Act or under regulations made by virtue of section 10(1)(b) or (c) of this Act (whether as originally made or as varied under regulations made by virtue of section 10(1)(a) of this Act).

11(2) In the case of a decision to which this section applies–

(a) if it relates to a person's entitlement to statutory sick pay, statutory maternity pay, statutory paternity pay, statutory adoption pay or statutory shared parental pay, the employee and employer concerned shall each have a right to appeal to the tribunal, and

(b) in any other case, the person in respect of whom the decision is made and such other person as may be prescribed shall have a right to appeal to the tribunal.

11(3) In subsection (2)(b) above **"prescribed"** means prescribed by the Board by regulations.

11(4) This section has effect subject to section 121D of the Social Security Administration Act 1992 (appeals in relation to personal liability notices).

Commencement Date – S. 11 entered into force, only for the purposes of making regulations, with effect from 25 February 1999 (SSC(TF)A 1999, s. 28(2)(b)).
S. 11(1)–(3) entered into force for all other purposes on 1 April 1999 (SSC(TF)A 1999, s. 28(3) and SI 1999/527, art. 2(b), Sch. 2).
S. 11(4) entered into force for all other purposes on 6 April 1999 (SI 1999/527, art. 2(c), Sch. 3).

History – In s. 11(2)(a), the words "statutory paternity pay," substituted for the words "ordinary statutory paternity pay, additional statutory paternity pay or" by Children and Families Act 2014, s. 126(1) and Sch. 7, para. 46(a), with effect from 5 April 2015, subject to the transitional and saving provisions in SI 2014/1640, art. 16 (amendments do not have effect in relation to– (a) children whose expected week of birth ends on or before 4 April 2015; (b) children placed for adoption on or before 4 April 2015) (SI 2014/1640, art. 7).
In s. 11(2)(a), the words "or statutory shared parental pay" inserted (after the words "statutory adoption pay") by Children and Families Act 2014, s. 126(1) and Sch. 7, para. 46(b), with effect from 1 December 2014 (SI 2014/1640, art. 5).
In s. 11(2)(a) the words "ordinary statutory paternity pay, additional statutory paternity pay" substituted for "statutory paternity pay" by the Work and Families Act 2006, s. 11 and Sch. 1, para. 47, with effect from 6 April 2010 (SI 2010/495).
In s. 11(2), the word "tribunal" substituted for the words "tax appeal Commissioners" (twice) by SI 2009/56, art. 3(1) and Sch. 1, para. 270, operative from 1 April 2009, subject to transitional and saving provisions in SI 2009/56, Sch. 3.
In s. 11(2)(a), the words ", statutory maternity pay, statutory paternity pay or statutory adoption pay" substituted by EA 2002, s. 9(4) with effect from 8 December 2002 by virtue of SI 2002/2866 (C. 91).

Cross references – SI 1999/1027: regulations concerning decisions made by officers of the Board and the conduct etc. of appeals against such decisions.

Statutory instruments – SI 1999/1027.

12 Exercise of right of appeal

12(1) Any appeal against a decision must be brought by a notice of appeal in writing given within 30 days after the date on which notice of the decision was issued.

12(2) The notice of appeal shall be given to the officer of the Board by whom notice of the decision was given.

12(3) The notice of appeal shall specify the grounds of appeal.

12(4) [Omitted by SI 2009/56, art. 3(1) and Sch. 1, para. 271(3).]

12(5) [Omitted by SI 2009/56, art. 3(1) and Sch. 1, para. 271(3).]

Commencement Date – S. 12 entered into force, only for the purposes of making regulations, with effect from 25 February 1999 (SSC(TF)A 1999, s. 28(2)(b)). The remainder of s. 12, except for that part of subsection (4) dealing with SSAA 1992, s. 121D, entered into force for all other purposes on 1 April 1999 (SSC(TF)A 1999, s. 28(3) and SI 1999/527, art. 2(b), Sch. 2). The part of s. 12(4) dealing with SSAA 1992, s. 121D entered fully into force on 6 April 1999 (SI 1999/527, art. 2(c), Sch. 3).

History – S. 12(3) substituted by SI 2009/56, art. 3(1) and Sch. 1, para. 271(2), operative from 1 April 2009, subject to transitional and saving provisions in SI 2009/56, Sch. 3 Former s. 12(3) read as follows:
"12(3) The notice of appeal shall specify the grounds of appeal, but on the hearing of the appeal the tax appeal Commissioners may allow the appellant to put forward any ground not specified in the notice, and take it into consideration if satisfied that the omission was not wilful or unreasonable.".
S. 12(4) omitted by SI 2009/56, art. 3(1) and Sch. 1, para. 271(3), operative from 1 April 2009, subject to transitional and saving provisions in SI 2009/56, Sch. 3. Former s. 12(4) read as follows:
"12(4) Subject to paragraph 3B(8) of Schedule 1 to the Social Security Contributions and Benefits Act 1992 (which provides for appeals under that paragraph to be heard by the Special Commissioners), to section 121D of the Social Security Administration Act 1992 (which provides for an appeal against a decision under that section to be heard by the Special Commissioners) and to regulations under section 46A of the Taxes Management Act 1970 (regulations about jurisdiction), any appeal under this section shall be heard by the General Commissioners, except that the appellant may elect in accordance with section 46(1) of the Taxes Management Act 1970 to bring the appeal before the Special Commissioners instead of the General Commissioners.".
In former s. 12(4) the reference to SSCBA 1992, Sch. 1, para. 3B inserted by CSPSSA 2000, s. 78(7); with effect from 28 July 2000 (date of Royal Assent).
S. 12(5) omitted by SI 2009/56, art. 3(1) and Sch. 1, para. 271(3), operative from 1 April 2009, subject to transitional and saving provisions in SI 2009/56, Sch. 3. Former s. 12(5) read as follows:
"12(5) Subsections (2) to (7) of section 31D of the Taxes Management Act 1970 (which relate to an election to bring proceedings before the Special Commissioners) shall have effect in relation to an election under subsection (4) above as they have effect in relation to an election under subsection (1) of that section.".
In former s. 12(5) words "Subsections (2) to (7) of section 31D" substituted for words "(5A) to (5E) of section 31" and words "subsection (1) of that section" substituted for words "subsection (4) of that section" by FA 2001, s. 88 and Sch. 29, para. 39, with effect from 11 May 2001 in relation to returns whether made before or after 11 May 2001, and whether relating to periods before or after 11 May 2001.

Cross references – SI 1999/1027: regulations concerning decisions made by officers of the Board and the conduct etc. of appeals against such decisions.

13 Regulations with respect to appeals

13(1) The Board may, by regulations made with the concurrence of the Lord Chancellor and [the Secretary of State], make provision with respect to appeals to the tribunal under this Part.

13(2) Regulations under subsection (1) above may, in particular–

(a) make provision with respect to any of the matters dealt with in the following provisions of the Taxes Management Act 1970–

(i) [omitted by SI 2009/56, art. 3(1) and Sch. 1, para. 272(3),]

(ii) sections 48 to 54 (appeals to the tribunal under the Taxes Acts), and

(iii) section 56 (payment of tax where there is a further appeal), or

(b) provide for any of those provisions of that Act to apply, with such modifications as may be specified in the regulations, in relation to an appeal to the tribunal under this Part.

13(2A) Regulations under subsection (1) above may provide for sections 11(2) and 13(2) of the Tribunals, Courts and Enforcement Act 2007 to apply with such modifications as may be specified in the regulations in relation to an appeal to the tribunal under this Part.

13(3) [Omitted by SI 2009/56, art. 3(1) and Sch. 1, para. 272(4).]

13(4) [Omitted by SI 2009/56, art. 3(1) and Sch. 1, para. 272(4).]

13(5) [Omitted by SI 2009/56, art. 3(1) and Sch. 1, para. 272(4).]

Commencement Date – S. 13 entered into force, only for the purposes of making regulations, with effect from 25 February 1999 (SSC(TF)A 1999, s. 28(2)(b)) and for all other purposes on 1 April 1999 (SSC(TF)A 1999, s. 28(3) and SI 1999/527, art. 2(b), Sch. 2).

History – In s. 13(1), the word "tribunal" substituted for the words "tax appeal Commissioners" by SI 2009/56, art. 3(1) and Sch. 1, para. 272(2), operative from 1 April 2009, subject to transitional and saving provisions in SI 2009/56, Sch. 3.

In s. 13(1) reference to "the Secretary of State" effectively substituted by SI 1999/678, art. 7(4), with effect from 19 May 1999.

S. 13(2)(a)(i) omitted by SI 2009/56, art. 3(1) and Sch. 1, para. 272(3), operative from 1 April 2009, subject to transitional and saving provisions in SI 2009/56, Sch. 3. Former s. 13(2)(a)(i) read as follows:

"(i) section 44 and Schedule 3 (assigning proceedings to General Commissioners),".

In para. 13(2), the word "tribunal" substituted (in two places) for the words "tax appeal Commissioners", and the words "section 56 (payment of tax where there is a further appeal)" substituted for the words "for sections 56 and 56A (appeals from their decisions)" by SI 2009/56, art. 3(1) and Sch. 1, para. 272(3), operative from 1 April 2009, subject to transitional and saving provisions in SI 2009/56, Sch. 3.

S. 13(2A) inserted by SI 2009/777, art. 3, with effect from 1 April 2009.

S. 13(3) omitted by SI 2009/56, art. 3(1) and Sch. 1, para. 272(4), operative from 1 April 2009, subject to transitional and saving provisions in SI 2009/56, Sch. 3. Former s. 13(3) read as follows:

"**13(3)** In sections 56B and 56C of the Taxes Management Act 1970 (power of Lord Chancellor to make regulations about the practice and procedure to be followed in connection with appeals to the tax appeal Commissioners under the Taxes Acts), any reference to an appeal includes a reference to an appeal to the tax appeal Commissioners under this Part.".

S. 13(4) omitted by SI 2009/56, art. 3(1) and Sch. 1, para. 272(4), operative from 1 April 2009, subject to transitional and saving provisions in SI 2009/56, Sch. 3. Former s. 13(4) read as follows:

"**13(4)** Any regulations under section 56B of the Taxes Management Act 1970 which are in force immediately before the commencement of subsection (3) above shall apply in relation to appeals to the tax appeal Commissioners under this Part, subject to any necessary modifications, as they apply in relation to appeals to those Commissioners under the Taxes Acts.".

S. 13(5) omitted by SI 2009/56, art. 3(1) and Sch. 1, para. 272(4), operative from 1 April 2009, subject to transitional and saving provisions in SI 2009/56, Sch. 3. Former s. 13(5) read as follows:

"**13(5)** In this section **"the Taxes Acts"** has the same meaning as in the Taxes Management Act 1970.".

Cross references – SI 1999/678, art. 2: the function of the Lord Advocate originally specified in s. 13(1) is transferred to the Secretary of State with effect from 19 May 1999.

SI 1999/1027: regulations concerning decisions made by officers of the Board and the conduct etc. of appeals against such decisions.

Statutory instruments – SI 1999/1027.

14 Matters arising as respects decisions

14(1) The Board may by regulations make provision as respects matters arising–

(a) pending any decision of an officer of the Board under section 8 of this Act which relates to–

(i) statutory sick pay, statutory maternity pay, statutory paternity pay,r statutory adoption pay or statutory shared parental pay, or

(ii) any person's liability for contributions,

(b) pending the determination by the tribunal of an appeal against any such decision,

(c) out of the variation, under regulations made under section 10 of this Act or on appeal, of any such decision, or

(d) out of the making of a decision which, under regulations made under that section, supersedes an earlier decision.

14(2) Regulations under this section may, in particular–

(a) make provision making a person liable to pay contributions pending the determination by the tribunal of an appeal against a decision of an officer of the Board, and

(b) make provision as to the repayment in prescribed circumstances of contributions paid by virtue of the regulations.

14(3) Regulations under this section must be made with the concurrence of the Secretary of State in so far as they relate to statutory sick pay or, statutory maternity pay, statutory paternity pay, statutory adoption pay or statutory shared parental pay.

Commencement Date – S. 14 entered into force, only for the purposes of making regulations, with effect from 25 February 1999 (SSC(TF)A 1999, s. 28(2)(b)) and for all other purposes on 1 April 1999 (SSC(TF)A 1999, s. 28(3) and SI 1999/527, art. 2(b), Sch. 2).

History – In s. 14(1)(a)(i), the words "statutory paternity pay," substituted for the words "ordinary statutory paternity pay, additional statutory paternity pay or" by Children and Families Act 2014, s. 126(1) and Sch. 7, para. 47(2)(a), with effect from 5 April 2015, subject to the transitional and saving provisions in SI 2014/1640, art. 16 (amendments do not have effect in relation to– (a) children whose expected week of birth ends on or before 4 April 2015; (b) children placed for adoption on or before 4 April 2015) (SI 2014/1640, art. 7).

In s. 14(1)(a)(i), the words "or statutory shared parental pay" inserted (after the words "statutory adoption pay") by Children and Families Act 2014, s. 126(1) and Sch. 7, para. 47(2)(b), with effect from 30 June 2014 (SI 2014/1640, art. 3).

In s. 14(1)(a)(i) the words "ordinary statutory paternity pay, additional statutory paternity pay" substituted for "statutory paternity pay" by the Work and Families Act 2006, s. 11 and Sch. 1, para. 48, with effect from a 6 April 2010 (SI 2010/495).

In s. 14(1)(a)(i), (3), the words ", statutory maternity pay, statutory paternity pay or statutory adoption pay" substituted by EA 2002, s. 9(5) with effect from 8 December 2002, by virtue of SI 2002/2866 (C. 91).

In s. 14(1)(b), the word "tribunal" substituted for the words "tax appeal Commissioners" by SI 2009/56, art. 3(1) and Sch. 1, para. 273(2), operative from 1 April 2009, subject to transitional and saving provisions in SI 2009/56, Sch. 3.

In s. 14(2)(a), the word "tribunal" substituted for the words "tax appeal Commissioners" by SI 2009/56, art. 3(1) and Sch. 1, para. 273(2), operative from 1 April 2009, subject to transitional and saving provisions in SI 2009/56, Sch. 3.

In s. 14(3), the words "statutory paternity pay," substituted for the words "ordinary statutory paternity pay, additional statutory paternity pay or" by Children and Families Act 2014, s. 126(1) and Sch. 7, para. 47(3)(a), with effect from 5 April 2015, subject to the transitional and saving provisions in SI 2014/1640, art. 16 (amendments do not have effect in relation to– (a) children whose expected week of birth ends on or before 4 April 2015; (b) children placed for adoption on or before 4 April 2015) (SI 2014/1640, art. 7).

In s. 14(3), the words "or statutory shared parental pay" inserted (after the words "statutory adoption pay") by Children and Families Act 2014, s. 126(1) and Sch. 7, para. 47(3), with effect from 30 June 2014 (SI 2014/1640, art. 3).

In s. 14(3) the words "ordinary statutory paternity pay, additional statutory paternity pay" substituted for "statutory paternity pay" by the Work and Families Act 2006, s. 11 and Sch.1, para. 48, with effect from 6 April 2010 (SI 2010/495).

15 Power to make provision for period before commencement of new social security appeal provisions

15(1) The Secretary of State may by regulations modify any of the enactments to which this subsection applies during any period in which section 8 of this Act is in force but Chapter II of Part I of the Social Security Act 1998 (social security decisions and appeals) is not yet wholly in force.

15(2) Subsection (1) above applies to–

(a) Part II of the Social Security Administration Act 1992 (adjudication), and

(b) the Acts amended by section 16 of, and Schedule 7 to, this Act.

Commencement Date – S. 15 entered into force, only for the purposes of making regulations, with effect from 25 February 1999 (SSC(TF)A 1999, s. 28(2)(b)) and for all other purposes on 1 April 1999 (SSC(TF)A 1999, s. 28(3) and SI 1999/527, art. 2(b), Sch. 2).

Statutory instruments – SI 1999/978: made under s. 15(1).

16 Decisions under Pension Schemes Act 1993

16(1) The function of determining the questions referred to in subsection (1) of section 170 of the Pension Schemes Act 1993, as that section has effect before the commencement of paragraph 131 of Schedule 7 to the Social Security Act 1998, is hereby transferred to an officer of the Board.

16(2) [Substitutes PSA 1993, s. 170(2)–(4).]

Commencement Date – S. 16(2) entered into force, only for the purposes of making regulations for decisions and appeals under the Pension Schemes Act 1993, with effect from 14 June 1999 (SSC(TF)A 1999, s. 28(3) and SI 1999/1662, art. 2(a), Sch. Pt. I. The whole of s. 16 entered into force for all other purposes on 5 July 1999 (SSC(TF)A 1999, s. 28(3) and SI 1999/1662, art. 2(b), Sch. Pt. II).

17 Arrangements for discharge of decision-making functions

17(1) The Secretary of State may make arrangements with the Board for any of his functions under Chapter II of Part I of the Social Security Act 1998 in relation to–

(a) a decision whether a person was (within the meaning of regulations) precluded from regular employment by responsibilities at home, or

(b) a decision whether a person is entitled to be credited with earnings or contributions in accordance with regulations made under section 22(5) or (5ZA) of the Social Security Contributions and Benefits Act 1992,

to be discharged by the Board or by officers of the Board.

17(2) No such arrangements shall affect the responsibility of the Secretary of State or the application of Chapter II of Part I of the Social Security Act 1998 in relation to any decision.

17(3) Until the commencement of Chapter II of Part I of the Social Security Act 1998, the references to that Chapter in subsections (1) and (2) above shall have effect as references to Part II of the Social Security Administration Act 1992.

Commencement Date – S. 17 entered into force with effect from 25 February 1999 (SSC(TF)A 1999, s. 28(2)(c)).

History – In s. 17(1)(b), the words "or (5ZA)" inserted by SI 2016/224, art. 5, with effect from 6 April 2016 (immediately after PA 2014, Pt. 1 comes into force for all remaining purposes).

18 Amendments relating to decisions and appeals

18 Schedule 7 to this Act (which contains amendments relating to decisions and appeals) shall have effect.

Commencement Date – S. 18 entered into force over a period of time in relation to specific paragraphs, and specific purposes, of Sch. 7; see the headnotes at Sch. 7 for details.

19 Interpretation of Part II

19 In this Part–

"tribunal" means the First-tier Tribunal or, where determined by or under Tribunal Procedure Rules, the Upper Tribunal.

History – S. 19 substituted by SI 2009/56, art. 3(1) and Sch. 1, para. 274, operative from 1 April 2009, subject to transitional and saving provisions in SI 2009/56, Sch. 3. Former s. 19 read as follows:

"19 Interpretation of Part II

19 In this Part–

"the General Commissioners" means the Commissioners for the general purposes of the income tax appointed under section 2 of the Taxes Management Act 197;

"the Special Commissioners" means the Commissioners for the special purposes of the Income Tax Acts appointed under section 4 of the Taxes Management Act 197;

"the tax appeal Commissioners" means the General Commissioners or the Special Commissioners.".

Notes – Former s. 19 entered into force, only for the purposes of making regulations, with effect from 4 March 1999 (SSC(TF)A 1999, s. 28(3) and SI 1999/527, art. 2(a), Sch. 1) and for all other purpose, 1 April 1999 (SI 1999/527, art. 2(b), Sch. 2).

PART III – MISCELLANEOUS AND SUPPLEMENTAL

20 Payments in respect of money purchase contracted-out pension schemes to be made out of National Insurance Fund

20(1)–(5) [Not relevant to National Insurance contributions.]

21 Property, rights and liabilities

21(1) In this section a **"transfer provision"** means any of the following provisions of this Act–

(a) section 1 and Schedules 1 and 2,

(b) section 2 and Schedule 3,

(c) section 8, and

(d) section 16(1).

21(2) Any property, rights and liabilities to which the Secretary of State is entitled or subject immediately before the commencement of a transfer provision in connection with functions transferred to the Board or the Treasury by virtue of that provision are hereby transferred to the Board or, as the case may be, the Treasury on the commencement of that provision.

21(3) A certificate issued by the Board or the Treasury that any property vested in the Secretary of State immediately before the commencement of a transfer provision has been transferred by virtue of this Act to the Board or, as the case may be, the Treasury shall be conclusive evidence of the transfer.

Commencement Date – S. 21 entered into force with effect from 1 April 1999 (SSC(TF)A 1999, s. 28(3) and SI 1999/527, art. 2(b), Sch. 2).

Cross references – WRPA 1999, Sch. 11, para. 2, 3, 6, 21, 35: paragraphs to be treated as if specified in s. 21(1), with effect from 11 November 1999 (WRPA 1999, Sch. 11, para. 37).

22 Special provision for certain contracts

22(1) This section applies to–

(a) any contract for the supply of goods or services to the Secretary of State which relates partly to functions transferred by virtue of this Act to the Board (in this section referred to as "transferred functions") and partly to functions retained by the Secretary of State (in this section referred to as "retained functions"), and

(b) any contract for the supply of goods or services to the Secretary of State which relates only to transferred functions or only to retained functions, but whose terms are wholly or partly determined in accordance with a contract falling within paragraph (a) above.

22(2) Section 21 of this Act shall not apply in relation to any contract to which this section applies.

22(3) Subject to subsections (4) and (5) below, in any contract to which this section applies any term restricting the provision of goods or services under the contract to the Secretary of State or the Department of Social Security shall be treated as referring also to the Board, in connection with transferred functions.

22(4) If the Secretary of State so provides by order in relation to any specified contract or class of contracts to which this section applies, the provisions of subsection (5) below shall have effect in relation to that contract, or contracts falling within that class, in place of subsection (3) above.

22(5) Where this subsection applies, all rights and liabilities of the Secretary of State under the contract are by virtue of this subsection transferred to the Board on the commencement of this subsection, but any term restricting the provision of goods or services under the contract to the Secretary of State or the Department of Social Security shall be treated as referring both to the Board, in connection with transferred functions, and to the Secretary of State or that department.

Commencement Date – S. 22(4) entered into force, only for the purposes of making regulations, with effect from 25 February 1999 (SSC(TF)A 1999, s. 28(2)(e)). The rest of s. 22 came into force, for all other purposes, on 1 April 1999 (SSC(TF)A 1999, s. 28(3) and SI 1999/527, art. 2(b), Sch. 2).

Statutory instruments – SI 1999/979: made under s. 22(4).

23 Power to transfer functions by Order in Council

23(1) Her Majesty may by Order in Council–

(a) provide for the transfer from the Secretary of State to the Board, or from the Board to the Secretary of State, of any transferable function,

(b) provide that any transferable function of the Secretary of State is to be exercisable only with the concurrence of the Board or the Treasury, or is to cease to be exercisable only with that concurrence,

(c) provide that any transferable function of the Board is to be exercisable only with the concurrence of the Secretary of State, or is to cease to be exercisable only with that concurrence, and

(d) provide that any decision to which this paragraph applies–

(i) is to be made by the Secretary of State rather than the Board, or by the Board rather than the Secretary of State, and

(ii) is to be made subject to the provisions of Chapter II of Part I of the Social Security Act 1998, or subject to the provisions of Part II of this Act rather than the provisions of that Chapter.

23(2) In subsection (1) above

"transferable function" means–

(a) any function relating to contributions or the National Insurance Fund, other than functions under section 1(1) of the Social Security Contributions and Benefits Act 1992 (receipt of contributions) or section 161(1) of the Social Security Administration Act 1992 (control and management of National Insurance Fund),

(b) any function relating to statutory sick pay or statutory maternity pay,

(c) any function under section 7 of the Social Security Act 1986 (occupational pension schemes becoming contracted-out between 1986 and 1993), so far as that section remains in force by virtue of paragraph 22 of Schedule 6 to the Pension Schemes Act 1993, or

(d) any function under Part III of the Pension Schemes Act 1993.

23(3) The decisions to which subsection (1)(d) above applies are–

(a) any decision which is or has been specified–

(i) in section 8(1) of this Act,

(ii) in section 170(2) of the Pension Schemes Act 1993 (as amended by section 16(2) of this Act), or

(iii) in paragraph 16 or 17 of Schedule 3 to the Social Security Act 1998, and

(b) any other decision relating to contributions, the National Insurance Fund, statutory sick pay, statutory maternity pay or the subject-matter of Part III of the Pension Schemes Act 1993.

23(4) An Order in Council under this section may contain such supplemental, consequential or transitional provision as appears to Her Majesty to be expedient, including provision–

(a) for the transfer of any property, rights and liabilities held, enjoyed or incurred by the Secretary of State or the Board in connection with any functions transferred,

(b) for the carrying on and completion by or under the authority of the person to whom any functions are transferred of anything commenced by or under the authority of the person from whom they are transferred before the date when the Order takes effect,

(c) as to the effect of any provision made by virtue of subsection 1(d) above on decisions or proceedings made or commenced before the date when the Order takes effect,

(d) making such amendments of any enactment, including any enactment contained in this Act, as may be necessary for the purposes of the Order, and

(e) for the substitution of the person to whom any functions are transferred for the person from whom they are transferred in any instrument, contract or legal proceedings made or commenced before the date when the Order takes effect.

23(5) A certificate issued by a relevant authority that any property vested in the other relevant authority immediately before an Order under this section takes effect has been transferred by virtue of the Order to the relevant authority issuing the certificate shall be conclusive evidence of the transfer; and in this subsection **"relevant authority"** means the Secretary of State or the Board.

23(6) In the application of this section to Northern Ireland–

(a) references to the Secretary of State include references to the Department of Health and Social Services for Northern Ireland,

(b) **"contributions"** means contributions under Part I of the Social Security Contributions and Benefits (Northern Ireland) Act 1992,

(c) references to Chapter II of Part I of, and paragraphs 16 and 17 of Schedule 3 to, the Social Security Act 1998 have effect as references to Chapter II of Part II of, and paragraphs 16 and 17 of Schedule 3 to, the Social Security (Northern Ireland) Order 1998,

(d) the reference to the National Insurance Fund has effect as a reference to the Northern Ireland National Insurance Fund,

(e) references to section 1(1) of the Social Security Contributions and Benefits Act 1992 and section 161(1) of the Social Security Administration Act 1992 have effect as references to section 1(1) of the Social Security Contributions and Benefits (Northern Ireland) Act 1992 and section 141(1) of the Social Security Administration (Northern Ireland) Act 1992,

(f) references to section 7 of the Social Security Act 1986 and paragraph 22 of Schedule 6 to the Pension Schemes Act 1993 have effect as references to Article 9 of the Social Security (Northern Ireland) Order 1986 and paragraph 21 of Schedule 5 to the Pension Schemes (Northern Ireland) Act 1993, and

(g) the reference to Part III of the Pension Schemes Act 1993 has effect as a reference to Part III of the Pension Schemes (Northern Ireland) Act 1993;

and for the purposes of this section in its application to Northern Ireland any reference in section 8(1) of this Act or section 170(2) of the Pension Schemes Act 1993 to a decision is to be taken to be a reference to the corresponding decision under Northern Ireland legislation.

Commencement Date – S. 23 entered into force with effect from 1 April 1999 (SSC(TF)A 1999, s. 28(3) and SI 1999/527, art. 2(b), Sch. 2).

24 Provision for Northern Ireland

24(1) Her Majesty may by Order in Council do any of the following–

(a) make provision for transferring from the relevant Northern Ireland authority to the Board any function in relation to Northern Ireland corresponding to a function transferred to the Board by virtue of section 1 of this Act,

(b) make provision for transferring from the relevant Northern Ireland authority to the Secretary of State any other function in relation to Northern Ireland which relates to any of the matters specified in paragraph 10 of Schedule 2 to the Northern Ireland Act 1998 (excepted matters),

(c) make provision for transferring from the relevant Northern Ireland authority to the Board or the Treasury any function in relation to Northern Ireland corresponding to a function transferred to the Board or, as the case may be, the Treasury by virtue of section 2 of this Act, and

(d) make other provision for Northern Ireland for purposes corresponding to any or all of the purposes of those provisions of this Act which do not extend to Northern Ireland.

24(2) If an Order in Council made under this section by virtue of subsection (1)(b) above has transferred to the Secretary of State any function in relation to Northern Ireland which corresponds to a function transferred to the Board or the Treasury by virtue of section 2 of this Act, Her Majesty may by a further Order in Council under this section make provision for transferring that function from the Secretary of State to the Board or, as the case may be, the Treasury.

24(3) An Order in Council under this section may, for the purposes of the Order–

(a) amend any enactment, including any enactment contained in this Act,

(b) confer, extend or modify any power to legislate by means of an order or regulations, and

(c) contain such incidental, supplemental, consequential or transitional provision as appears to Her Majesty to be expedient, including–

(i) provision modifying references in any enactment to the Northern Ireland Assembly, to statutory rules for the purposes of the Statutory Rules (Northern Ireland) Order 1979 or to the Comptroller and Auditor General for Northern Ireland,

(ii) provision for the transfer of property, rights and liabilities, and

(iii) provision for the transfer to Her Majesty's Home Civil Service of persons employed in the Northern Ireland Civil Service.

24(4) A certificate issued by the Board, the Secretary of State or the Treasury that any property vested in a Northern Ireland department immediately before an Order under this section takes effect has been transferred by virtue of the Order to the Board, the Secretary of State or the Treasury, as the case may be, shall be conclusive evidence of the transfer.

24(5) A certificate issued by the Board or the Treasury that any property vested in the Secretary of State immediately before an Order under this section takes effect has been transferred by virtue of the Order to the Board or the Treasury, as the case may be, shall be conclusive evidence of the transfer.

24(6) Subsection (2) above does not limit the powers conferred by section 23 of this Act in relation to Northern Ireland.

24(7) In this section **"the relevant Northern Ireland authority"**, in relation to any function, means the Northern Ireland department by which the function is exercisable.

Commencement Date – S. 24 entered into force with effect from 25 February 1999 (SSC(TF)A 1999, s. 28(2)(f)).
Statutory instruments – SI 1999/1027.

25 Orders and regulations

25(1) Any power of the Secretary of State or the Board to make an order or regulations under this Act shall be exercisable by statutory instrument.

25(2) Any statutory instrument containing–

(a) an Order in Council under section 23 or 24 of this Act, or

(b) regulations under any provision of this Act,

shall be subject to annulment in pursuance of a resolution of either House of Parliament.

25(3) Any power conferred by this Act to make regulations may be exercised–

(a) either in relation to all cases to which the power extends, or in relation to those cases subject to specified exceptions, or in relation to any specified cases or classes of case;

(b) so as to make, as respects the cases in relation to which it is exercised–

(i) the full provision to which the power extends or any less provision (whether by way of exception or otherwise);

(ii) the same provision for all cases in relation to which the power is exercised, or different provision for different cases or different classes of case or different provision as respects the same case or class of case for different purposes of this Act;

(iii) any such provision either unconditionally or subject to any specified condition;

and where such a power is expressed to be exercisable for alternative purposes it may be exercised in relation to the same case for any or all of those purposes.

25(4) Powers to make regulations for the purposes of any one provision of this Act are without prejudice to powers to make regulations for the purposes of any other provision.

25(5) A power conferred by this Act to make regulations includes power to make thereby such incidental, supplementary, consequential or transitional provision as appears to the authority making the regulations to be expedient for the purposes of those regulations.

25(6) A power conferred by this Act to make regulations includes power to provide for a person to exercise a discretion in dealing with any matter.

Commencement Date – S. 25 entered into force with effect from 25 February 1999 (SSC(TF)A 1999, s. 28(2)(f)).
Statutory instruments – SI 2003/1192.
SI 1999/1027.

26 Savings, transitional provisions, consequential amendments, repeals and revocations

26(1) The provisions of this Act shall have effect subject to the savings and transitional provisions in Schedule 8 to this Act.

26(2) Schedule 9 to this Act (further consequential amendments) shall have effect.

26(3) Schedule 10 to this Act (repeals and revocations) shall have effect.

Commencement Date – S. 26(1) (and Sch. 8 – see the headnote to the Schedule) entered into force with effect from 25 February 1999 (SSC(TF)A 1999, s. 28(2)(g)).
S. 26(2) (and parts of Sch. 9 – see the headnote to the Schedule) entered into force, for various purposes, on several dates beginning with 4 March 1999; see separate commencement notes on Sch. 9.
S. 26(3) (and parts of the repeals Schedule; Sch. 10) entered into force on either 1 or 6 April 1999; see separate commencement headnotes on Sch. 10.

27 Interpretation

27 In this Act, unless a contrary intention appears–

"the Board" means the Commissioners of Inland Revenue;

"contributions" means contributions under Part I of the Social Security Contributions and Benefits Act 1992.

Commencement Date – S. 27 entered into force with effect from 25 February 1999 (SSC(TF)A 1999, s. 28(2)(h)).

28 Short title, commencement and extent

28(1) This Act may be cited as the Social Security Contributions (Transfer of Functions, etc.) Act 1999.

28(2) The following provisions of this Act–

(a) section 1(1) (with Schedule 1), so far as enabling the Secretary of State to make subordinate legislation conferring functions on the Board,

(b) sections 8 to 15, so far as conferring any power to make subordinate legislation,

(c) section 17,

(d) section 20,

(e) section 22(4), so far as conferring the power to make an order,

(f) sections 24 and 25,

(g) section 26(1) (with Schedule 8), and

(h) section 27 and this section,

shall come into force on the passing of this Act.

28(3) Except as provided by subsection (2) above, the provisions of this Act shall come into force on such day as the Secretary of State may by order appoint; and different days may be appointed for different purposes.

28(4) An order under subsection (3) above may make such savings, or such transitional or consequential provision, as the Secretary of State considers necessary or expedient–

(a) in preparation for or in connection with the coming into force of any provision of this Act, or

(b) in connection with the operation of any enactment repealed or amended by a provision of this Act during any period when the repeal or amendment is not wholly in force.

28(5) The following provisions of this Act extend to Northern Ireland–

(a) section 1 and Schedule 1, so far as they amend the Income and Corporation Taxes Act 1988,

(b) section 2 and Schedule 3, so far as they amend section 177 of the Social Security Administration Act 1992 or section 88 of the Northern Ireland Act 1998,

(c) section 3,

(d) section 4 and Schedule 4,

(e) section 5 and Schedule 5, so far as they amend the Taxes Management Act 1970,

(f) section 18 and Schedule 7, so far as they amend the Taxes Management Act 1970, Schedule 2 to the Social Security Contributions and Benefits Act 1992 or Schedule 2 to the Social Security Contributions and Benefits (Northern Ireland) Act 1992,

(g) section 6 and Schedule 6, so far as they amend the Finance Act 1989 or the Finance Act 1997,

(h) section 7,

(i) sections 23 to 25,

(j) section 26(3) and Schedule 10, so far as they relate to any enactment which extends to Northern Ireland, and

(k) section 27 and this section.

28(6) Section 20(2) and (4) of this Act extends to Northern Ireland only.

28(7) Except as provided by subsections (5) and (6) above, this Act does not extend to Northern Ireland.

Commencement Date – S. 28 entered into force with effect from 25 February 1999 (SSC(TF)A 1999, s. 28(2)(h)).

SCHEDULES

SCHEDULE 1 – TRANSFER OF CONTRIBUTIONS AGENCY FUNCTIONS AND ASSOCIATED FUNCTIONS

Section 1(1)

Commencement Date – Sch. 1 entered into force, only for the purposes of enabling the Secretary of State to make subordinate legislation conferring functions on the Board of Inland Revenue, with effect from 25 February 1999 (SSC(TF)A 1999, s. 28(2)(a)). The rest of Sch. 1 – except where indicated in footnotes to specific paragraphs – entered into force, for all other purposes, with effect from 1 April 1999 (SSC(TF)A 1999, s. 28(3) and SI 1999/527, art. 2(b), Sch. 2).

SOCIAL SECURITY ACT 1986 (C. 50)

1 [Not relevant to National Insurance contributions.]

2 [Not relevant to National Insurance contributions.]

INCOME AND CORPORATION TAXES ACT 1988 (C. 1)

3 [Repealed by FA 2004, s. 326 and Sch. 42, Pt. 3.]

History – Para. 3 repealed by FA 2004, s. 326 and Sch. 42, Pt. 3, with effect from 6 April 2006, subject to FA 2004, Sch. 36. Para. 3 was partially repealed by CSPSSA 2000, Sch. 9.

4 [Repealed by FA 2004, s. 326 and Sch. 42, Pt. 3.]

History – Para. 4 repealed by FA 2004, s. 326 and Sch. 42, Pt. 3, with effect from 6 April 2006, subject to FA 2004, Sch. 36. Former para. 4(6) omitted by WRPA 1999, S. 81 and Sch. 11, para. 32(a) with effect from 11 November 1999 (date of passing of WRPA 1999) which is the commencement date provided for by WRPA 1999, s. 89(4)(d). This subparagraph was also repealed by WRPA 1999, s. 88, Sch. 13, Pt. VI.

SOCIAL SECURITY CONTRIBUTIONS AND BENEFITS ACT 1992 (C. 4)

5(1) Section 1 of the Social Security Contributions and Benefits Act 1992 (outline of contributory system) is amended as follows.

5(2) [Amends SSCBA 1992, s. 1(1).]

5(3) [Amends SSCBA 1992, s. 1(4)(b).]

6 [Amends SSCBA 1992, s. 17.]

Statutory instruments – SI 2002/2929 (made under para. 6(1), (2)).

7 [Amends SSCBA 1992, s. 18(2).]

8 [Amends SSCBA 1992, s. 61A(2)(b), (4)(b). Partially repealed by CSPSSA 2000, Sch. 9.]

10 [Amends SSCBA 1992, s. 161(3).]

11 [Amends SSCBA 1992, s. 162(3).]

13 [Repealed by EA 2002, s. 54 and Sch. 8, para. 1.]

History – Para. 13 repealed by EA 2002, s. 54 and Sch. 8 para. 1, with effect from 6 April 2003 by virtue of SI 2002/2866 (C. 91), art. 2(5) and Sch. 2, Pt. 2.

14 [Amends SSCBA 1992, s. 170(1).]

15(1) Section 171 of the Social Security Contributions and Benefits Act 1992 (interpretation of Part XII and supplementary provisions) is amended as follows.

15(2) [Amends SSCBA 1992, s. 171(1).]

15(3) [Inserts SSCBA 1992, s. 171(7).]

16 [Amends SSCBA 1992, Sch. 1, para. 4.]

17 [Amends SSCBA 1992, Sch. 1, para. 6(5), (6), (7), (8)(a).]

History – Para. 17(c), to the extent that it deals with SSCBA 1992, Sch. 1, para. 6(8) did not enter into force with the rest of the Schedule (SSC(TF)A 1999, s. 28(3) and SI 1999/527, art. 2(b), Sch. 2).

18(1) Paragraph 7 of Schedule 1 to the Social Security Contributions and Benefits Act 1992 (special penalties in the case of certain returns) is amended as follows.

18(2) [Amends SSCBA 1992, Sch. 1, para. 7(1).]

18(3) [Amends SSCBA 1992, Sch. 1, para. 7(2).]

19(1) Paragraph 8 of Schedule 1 to the Social Security Contributions and Benefits Act 1992 (general regulation-making powers) is amended as follows.

19(2) [Repealed by CSPSSA 2000, s. 86(1), Sch. 9, Pt. VIII(1).]

19(3) [Repealed by WRPA 1999, s. 88, Sch. 13, Pt. VI.]

19(4) [Repealed by WRPA 1999, s. 88, Sch. 13, Pt. VI.]

History – Para. 19(2) repealed by CSPSSA 2000, s. 86(1), Sch. 9, Pt. VIII(1); with effect from 6 April 2000.
Para. 19(3), (4) repealed by WRPA 1999, s. 88, Sch. 13, Pt. VI with effect from 6 April 2000 (SI 1999/3420, art. 4(c), (e)).

SOCIAL SECURITY ADMINISTRATION ACT 1992 (C. 5)

21(1) Section 116 of the Social Security Administration Act 1992 (legal proceedings) is amended as follows.

21(2) [Amends SSAA 1992, s. 116(1).]

21(3) [Inserts SSAA 1992, s. 116(5A).]

21(4) [Amends SSAA 1992, s. 116(7).]

22 [Amends SSAA 1992, s. 119.]

23 [Amends SSAA 1992, s. 120(6).]

24 [Amends SSAA 1992, s. 121(5).]

25 [Amends SSAA 1992, s. 125(1).]

28(1) Section 162 of the Social Security Administration Act 1992 (payment of contributions into National Insurance Fund, etc.) is amended as follows.

28(2) [Inserts SSAA 1992, s. 162(4).]

28(3) [Amends SSAA 1992, s. 162(4A).]

32 [Amends SSAA 1992, s. 191.]

PENSION SCHEMES ACT 1993 (C. 48)

33 [Amends PSA 1993, s. 7.]

Prospective amendments – Para. 33 repealed by PA 2007, s. 27 and Sch. 7, Pt. 6, with effect from a date to be appointed under PA 2007, s. 30.

34 [Amends PSA 1993, s. 8.]

History – Para. 34(b) repealed by PA 2007, s. 27 and Sch. 7, Pt. 7, with effect from 6 April 2015 (SI 2011/1267, art. 3(b)(iv)).

37(1) [Amends PSA 1993, s. 11.]

45 [Amends PSA 1993, s. 34.]

46 [Repealed by PA 2007, s. 27 and Sch. 7, Pt. 7.]

History – Para. 46 repealed by PA 2007, s. 27 and Sch. 7, Pt. 7, with effect from 6 April 2015 (SI 2011/1267, art. 2(c)).

47 [Repealed by PA 2007, s. 27 and Sch. 7, Pt. 7.]

History – Para. 47 repealed by PA 2007, s. 27 and Sch. 7, Pt. 7, with effect from 6 April 2015 (SI 2011/1267, art. 2(c)).

49 [Repealed by PA 2007, s. 27 and Sch. 7, Pt. 7.]

History – Para. 49 repealed by PA 2007, s. 27 and Sch. 7, Pt. 7, with effect from 6 April 2015 (SI 2011/1267, art. 2(c)).

50 [Repealed by PA 2007, s. 27 and Sch. 7, Pt. 7.]

History – Para. 50 repealed by PA 2007, s. 27 and Sch. 7, Pt. 7, with effect from 6 April 2015 (SI 2011/1267, art. 2(c)).

61(1) Section 177 of the Pension Schemes Act 1993 (general financial arrangements) is amended as follows.

61(2) [Amends PSA 1993, s. 177(1).]

61(3) [Amends PSA 1993, s. 177(2).]

61(4) [Inserts PSA 1993, s. 177(3)(c).]

61(5) [Amends PSA 1993, s. 177(5).]

61(6) [Amends PSA 1993, s. 177(7)(d).]

History – Para. 61(3)(a) repealed by PA 2007, s. 27 and Sch. 7, Pt. 7, with effect from 6 April 2015 (SI 2011/1267, art. 2(c)).

SCHEDULE 2 – TRANSFER OF FUNCTIONS UNDER SUBORDINATE LEGISLATION

Section 1(2)

Commencement Date – Sch. 2 entered into force with effect from 1 April 1999 (SSC(TF)A 1999, s. 28(3) and SI 1999/527, art. 2(b), Sch. 2), except in relation to functions exerciseable under part of the Occupational Pension Schemes (Contracting-out) Regulations 1984 (*SI 1984/380, reg. 20(2)(b)*).

History – By WRPA 1999, s. 81 and Sch. 11, para. 33, which came into force on 11 November 1999 (the commencement date being the date of the passing of the WRPA 1999, by virtue of WRPA 1999, s. 89(4)(d)) the entry in the third column relating to the Pensions Act 1995 (Commencement No. 10) Order 1997 shall have effect, and be deemed always to have had effect, with the substitution for "Articles 4 and 13" of "In Article 4, paragraph (1), paragraph (2), except so far as relating to section 55(3) of the Pension Schemes Act 1993, to the making of regulations under section 64(1) of that Act and to section 64(3) and (5) to (9) of that Act, and paragraph (3) and Article 13".

Number	Title	Provisions conferring functions transferred
S.I. 1979/591.	The Social Security (Contributions) Regulations 1979.	All the regulations except regulations 36 to 39, 41 to 42 and 44.
S.I. 1982/894.	The Statutory Sick Pay (General) Regulations 1982.	Regulations 9A to 9C, 10 and 14.
S.I. 1983/376.	The Statutory Sick Pay (Compensation of Employers) and Miscellaneous Provisions Regulations 1983.	Regulation 3 (so far as remaining in force).
S.I. 1986/1960.	The Statutory Maternity Pay (General) Regulations 1986.	Regulations 7, 25, 30 and 31.
S.I. 1987/1115.	The Personal and Occupational Pension Schemes (Incentive Payments) Regulations 1987.	All the regulations (so far as remaining in force).
S.I. 1990/536.	The Social Security (Refunds) (Repayment of Contractual Maternity Pay) Regulations 1990.	Regulations 2 and 3.
S.I. 1992/796.	The State Scheme Premiums (Actuarial Tables) Regulations 1992.	All the regulations.
S.I. 1994/1882.	The Statutory Maternity Pay (Compensation of Employers) and Miscellaneous Amendment Regulations 1994.	Regulations 3 and 6.
S.I. 1995/512.	The Statutory Sick Pay Percentage Threshold Order 1995.	Article 4.
S.I. 1996/195.	The Employer's Contributions Re-imbursement Regulations 1996.	Regulations 7, 8 and 9.
S.I. 1996/1172.	The Occupational Pension Schemes (Contracting-out) Regulations 1996.	All the regulations except regulations 23 and 61.
S.I. 1996/1245.	The Social Security (Additional Pension) (Contributions Paid in Error) Regulations 1996.	All the regulations.
S.I. 1996/1537.	The Personal and Occupational Pension Schemes (Protected Rights) Regulations 1996.	All the regulations except regulation 4(3).
S.I. 1996/1977.	The Occupational Pension Schemes (Mixed Benefit Contracted-out Schemes) Regulations 1996.	Regulation 3.
S.I. 1997/38.	The Occupational Pension Schemes (Contracting-out) Transitional Regulations 1997.	All the regulations.
S.I. 1997/358.	The Occupational and Personal Pension Schemes (Contracting-out etc: Review of Determinations) Regulations 1997.	All the regulations.
S.I. 1997/470.	The Personal Pension Schemes (Appropriate Schemes) Regulations 1997.	All the regulations.
S.I. 1997/664 (C. 23).	The Pensions Act 1995 (Commencement No. 10) Order 1997.	In Article 4, paragraph (1), paragraph (2), except so far as relating to section 55(3) of the Pension Schemes Act 1993, to the making of regulations under section 64(1) of that Act and to section 64(3) and (5) to (9) of that Act, and paragraph (3) and Article 13.

Number	Title	Provisions conferring functions transferred
S.I. 1998/1397.	The Occupational Pension Schemes (Contracting-out) (Amount Required for Restoring State Scheme Rights and Miscellaneous Amendment) Regulations 1998.	All the regulations.
S.I. 1998/1846.	The Occupational Pension Schemes (validation of Rule Alterations) Regulations 1998.	Regulation 2.

Cross references – WRPA 1999, Sch. 11, para. 35 which provides for the transfer of certain functions under subordinate legislation (Great Britain) to the Commissioners of Inland Revenue.
WRPA 1999, Sch. 11, para. 36 which provides for the transfer of certain functions under subordinate legislation (Northern Ireland) to the Commissioners of Inland Revenue.

SCHEDULE 3 – TRANSFER OF OTHER FUNCTIONS TO TREASURY OR BOARD

Section 2

Commencement Date – Sch. 3 entered into force with effect from 1 April 1999 (SSC(TF)A 1999, s. 28(3) and SI 1999/527, art. 2(b), Sch. 2.

SOCIAL SECURITY CONTRIBUTIONS AND BENEFITS ACT 1992 (C. 4)

1(1) Section 1 of the Social Security Contributions and Benefits Act 1992 (outline of contributory system) is amended as follows.

1(2) [Amends SSCBA 1992, s. 1(3)(b).]

1(3) [Inserts SSCBA 1992, s. 1(7).]

2 [Repealed by WRPA 1999, s. 88, Sch. 13, Pt. VI.]

History – Para. 2 repealed by WRPA 1999, s. 88, Sch. 13, Pt. VI with effect from 6 April 2000 (SI 1999/3420, art. 4(c), (e)).

3 [Amends SSCBA 1992, s. 3.]

4 [Inserts SSCBA 1992, s. 4(4).]

5 [Repealed by WRPA 1999, s. 88, Sch. 13, Pt. VI.]

History – Para. 5 repealed by WRPA 1999, s. 88, Sch. 13, Pt. VI with effect from 6 April 2000 (SI 1999/3420, art. 4(c), (e)).

6 [Repealed by WRPA 1999, s. 88 and Sch. 13, Pt. VI.]

History – Para. 6 repealed by WRPA 1999, s. 88, Sch. 13, Pt. VI with effect from 6 April 2000 (SI 1999/3420, art. 4(c), (e)).

7(1) Section 7 of the Social Security Contributions and Benefits Act 1992 (definition of "secondary contributor") is amended as follows.

7(2) [Amends SSCBA 1992, s. 7(2).]

7(3) [Inserts SSCBA 1992, s. 7(3).]

8 [Repealed by WRPA 1999, s. 88 and Sch. 13, Pt. VI.]

History – Para 8 repealed by WRPA 1999, s. 88, Sch. 13, Pt. VI with effect from 6 April 2000 (SI 1999/3420, art. 4(c), (e)).

9 [Repealed by WRPA 1999, s. 88, Sch. 13, Pt. VI.]

History – Para. 9 repealed by WRPA 1999, s. 88, Sch. 13, Pt. VI with effect from 6 April 2000 (SI 1999/3420, art. 4(c), (e)).

10 [Repealed by CSPSSA 2000,s. 86(1), Sch. 9, Pt. VIII(1).]

History – Para. 10 repealed by CSPSSA 2000, s. 86(1), Sch. 9, Pt. VIII(1); with effect from 6 April 2000.

11 [Amends SSCBA 1992, s. 10A(7).]

12 [Omitted by NICA 2015, s. 2 and Sch. 1, para. 26.]

History – Para. 12 omitted by NICA 2015, s. 2 and Sch. 1, para. 26, with effect for the tax year 2015–16 and subsequent tax years.

13 [Amends SSCBA 1992, s. 13.]

14(1) Section 13 of the Social Security Contributions and Benefits Act 1992 (Class 3 contributions) is amended as follows.

14(2) [Amends SSCBA 1992, s. 13(1).]

14(3) [Amends SSCBA 1992, s. 13(3).]

14(4) [Amends SSCBA 1992, s. 13(7).]

15 [Inserts SSCBA 1992, s. 14(5).]

16 [Repealed by NICA 2002, s. 7 and Sch. 2.]

History – Para. 16 repealed by the National Insurance Contributions Act 2002, s. 7 and Sch. 2 with effect for 2003–04 and subsequent tax years.

17(1) Section 17 of the Social Security Contributions and Benefits Act 1992 (exceptions, deferment and incidental matters relating to Class 4 contributions) is amended as follows.

17(2) [Amends SSCBA 1992, s. 17(1).]

17(3) [Amends SSCBA 1992, s. 17(3), (4).]

17(4) [Repeals SSCBA 1992, s. 17(6).]

18(1) Section 18 of the Social Security Contributions and Benefits Act 1992 (Class 4 contributions recoverable under regulations) is amended as follows.

18(2) [Amends SSCBA 1992, s. 18(1).]

18(3) [Amends SSCBA 1992, s. 18(2).]

19(1) Section 19 of the Social Security Contributions and Benefits Act 1992 (general power to regulate liability for contributions) is amended as follows.

19(2) [Inserts SSCBA 1992, s. 19(5A).]

19(3) [Amends SSCBA 1992, s. 19(6).]

20 [Inserts SSCBA 1992, s. 19A(3).]

21(1) Section 112 of the Social Security Contributions and Benefits Act 1992 (certain sums to be earnings) is amended as follows.

21(2) [Amends SSCBA 1992, s. 112(1).]

21(3) [Inserts SSCBA 1992, s. 112(2A).]

22(1) Section 116 of the Social Security Contributions and Benefits Act 1992 (application of that Act and the Social Security Administration Act 1992 to Her Majesty's forces) is amended as follows.

22(2) [Amends SSCBA 1992, s. 116(2).]

22(3) [Amends SSCBA 1992, s. 116(3).]

23 [Amends SSCBA 1992, s. 117(1).]

24 [Amends SSCBA 1992, s. 118.]

25 [Amends SSCBA 1992, s. 119.]

26 [Amends SSCBA 1992, s. 120(1).]

27 [Amends SSCBA 1992, s. 121.]

29(1) Section 175 of the Social Security Contributions and Benefits Act 1992 (regulations, orders and schemes) is amended as follows.

29(2) [Amends SSCBA 1992, s. 175(1).]

29(3) [Inserts SSCBA 1992, s. 175(1A).]

29(4) [Amends SSCBA 1992, s. 175(4).]

30 [Amends SSCBA 1992, s. 176(3).]

31 [Inserts SSCBA 1992, Sch. 1, para. 1(8)(8A).]

32 [Amends SSCBA 1992, Sch. 1, para. 1(2).]

33 [Inserts SSCBA 1992, Sch. 1, para. 3(6).]

34 [Amends SSCBA 1992, Sch. 1, para. 4, 5, 5A.]

35(1) Paragraph 6 of Schedule 1 to the Social Security Contributions and Benefits Act 1992 (power to combine collection of contributions with tax) is amended as follows.

35(2) [Amends SSCBA 1992, Sch. 1, para. 6(1).]

35(3) [Omits SSCBA 1992, Sch. 1, para. 6(8).]

36(1) Paragraph 7 of Schedule 1 to the Social Security Contributions and Benefits Act 1992 (special penalties in the case of certain returns) is amended as follows.

36(2) [Amends SSCBA 1992, Sch. 1, para. 7(6).]

36(3) [Omits SSCBA 1992, Sch. 1, para. 7(7).]

36(4) [Amends SSCBA 1992, Sch. 1, para. 7(8).]

37 [Amends SSCBA 1992, Sch. 1, para. 7A(2).]

38 [Amends SSCBA 1992, Sch. 1, para. 7B(1).]

39(1) Paragraph 8 of Schedule 1 to the Social Security Contributions and Benefits Act 1992 (general regulation-making powers) is amended as follows.

39(2) [Amends SSCBA 1992, Sch. 1, para. 8(1).]

39(3) [Inserts SSCBA 1992, Sch. 1, para. 8(1A).]

39(4) [Repealed by WRPA 1999, s. 88, Sch. 13, Pt. VI.]

History – Para. 39(4) repealed by WRPA 1999, s. 88, Sch. 13, Pt. VI with effect from 6 April 2000 (SI 1999/3420, art. 4(c), (e)).

40 [Amends SSCBA 1992, Sch. 1, para. 9.]

41 [Amends SSCBA 1992, Sch. 1, para. 11(1).]

SOCIAL SECURITY ADMINISTRATION ACT 1992 (C. 5)

44(1) Section 141 of the Social Security Administration Act 1992 (annual review of contributions) is amended as follows.

44(2) [Amends SSAA 1992, s. 141(1).]

44(3) [Amends SSAA 1992, s. 141(2).]

44(4) [Amends SSAA 1992, s. 141(3).]

44(5) [Amends SSAA 1992, s. 141(6).]

45(1) Section 142 of the Social Security Administration Act 1992 (annual review: report of Government Actuary, etc.) is amended as follows.

45(2) [Amends SSAA 1992, s. 141(1).]

45(3) [Amends SSCBA 1992, s. 142(2).]

46(1) Section 143 of the Social Security Administration Act 1992 (alteration of contributions with a view to adjusting level of National Insurance Fund) is amended as follows.

46(2) [Amends SSAA 1992, s. 143(3).]

46(3) [Amends SSAA 1992, s. 143(3).]

47 [Repealed by WRPA 1999, s. 88, Sch. 13, Pt. VI.]

History – Para. 47 repealed by WRPA 1999, s. 88, Sch. 13, Pt. VI with effect from 6 April 2000 (SI 1999/3420, art. 4(c), (e)).

48 [Amends SSAA 1992, s. 144(1).]

49 [Amends SSAA 1992, s. 145.]

50 [Amends SSAA 1992, s. 147.]

52(1) Section 162 of the Social Security Administration Act 1992 (payment of contributions into National Insurance Fund, etc.) is amended as follows.

52(2) [Amends SSAA 1992, s. 162(1).]

52(3) [Repealed by NICA 2002, s. 7 and Sch. 2.]

52(4) [Amends SSAA 1992, s. 162(4).]

52(5) [Repealed by NICSPA 2004, s. 12 and Sch. 2.]

52(6) [Amends SSAA 1992, s. 162(6).]

52(7) [Amends SSAA 1992, s. 162(7).]

52(8) [Amends SSAA 1992, s. 162(9).]

52(9) [Amends SSAA 1992, s. 162(10).]

52(10) [Amends SSAA 1992, s. 162(11).]

History – Para. 52(3) repealed by the National Insurance Contributions Act 2002, s. 7 and Sch. 2 with effect for 2003–04 and subsequent tax years.

Para. 52(5) repealed by NICSPA 2004, s. 12 and Sch. 2 with effect from 1 September 2004 (by virtue of SI 2004/1493, reg. 6). Para. 52(5) previously amended SSAA 1992, s.162(4A).

56(1) [Amends SSAA 1992, s. 177(3)(a).]

56(2) This paragraph shall cease to have effect on the commencement of the repeal by the Northern Ireland Act 1998 of section 177 of the Social Security Administration Act 1992.

57(1) Section 189 of the Social Security Administration Act 1992 (general provision on regulations and orders) is amended as follows.

57(2) In subsection (1), after "and to" there is inserted "any provision providing for an order or regulations to be made by the Treasury or the Inland Revenue and to".

57(3) [Not relevant to National Insurance contributions.]

History – SSAA 1992, s. 177 repealed by the Northern Ireland Act 1998, Sch.15 with effect from a date to be appointed.

58 [Amends SSAA 1992, s. 190(3).]

59(1) Schedule 7 to the Social Security Administration Act 1992 (regulations not requiring prior submission to Social Security Advisory Committee) is amended as follows.

59(2) [Substitutes SSAA 1992, Sch. 7, para. 4.]

59(3) [Omits SSAA 1992, Sch. 7, para. 5.]

SCHEDULE 4 – RECOVERY OF CONTRIBUTIONS WHERE INCOME TAX RECOVERY PROVISIONS NOT APPLICABLE

Section 4

Commencement Date – Sch. 4 entered into force with effect from 1 April 1999 (SSC(TF)A 1999, s. 28(3) and SI 1999/527, art. 2(b), Sch. 2), except in relation to Class 1B contributions, and also any interest and penalties payable by regulations made under SSCBA 1992, Sch. 1, para. 7A and 7B; the Schedule entered into force in respect of these matters with effect from 6 April 1999 (SSC(TF)A 1999, s. 28(3) and SI 1999/527, art. 2(c), Sch. 3).

INTERPRETATION

1 In any provision of this Schedule **"authorised officer"** means an officer of the Board authorised by them for the purposes of that provision.

MAGISTRATES' COURTS

2(1) Any amount which–

(a) is due by way of contributions or by way of interest or penalty in respect of contributions, and

(b) does not exceed the prescribed sum,

shall, without prejudice to any other remedy, be recoverable summarily as a civil debt in proceedings commenced in the name of an authorised officer.

2(2) All or any of the sums due from any one person in respect of contributions, or interest or penalties in respect of contributions, (being sums which are by law recoverable summarily) may be included in the same complaint, summons, order, warrant or other document required by law to be laid before justices or to be issued by justices, and every such document shall, as respects each such sum, be construed as a separate document and its invalidity as respects any one such sum shall not affect its validity as respects any other such sum.

2(3) Proceedings under this paragraph in England and Wales may be brought–

(a) in the case of Class 2 contributions or interest or penalties in respect of such contributions, at any time before the end of the year following the tax year in which the contributor becomes liable to pay the contributions, and

(b) in any other case, not later than the first anniversary of the day on which the contributions became due.

2(4) In sub-paragraph (1) above, the expression **"recoverable summarily as a civil debt"** in respect of proceedings in Northern Ireland means recoverable in proceedings under Article 62 of the Magistrates' Courts (Northern Ireland) Order 1981.

2(5) In this paragraph–

"the prescribed sum" means the sum for the time being specified in section 65(1) of the Taxes Management Act 1970 (recovery of income tax, etc. in magistrates' courts);

"tax year" means the twelve months beginning with 6th April in any year.

COUNTY COURTS

3(1) Without prejudice to any other remedy, any sum which is due by way of contributions or by way of interest or penalty in respect of contributions may–

(a) in England and Wales, and

(b) in Northern Ireland, where the amount does not exceed the limit specified in Article 10(1) of the County Courts (Northern Ireland) Order 1980,

be sued for and recovered from the person liable as a debt due to the Crown by proceedings in England and Wales in the county court or in Northern Ireland in a county court.

3(2) [Omitted by FA 2008, s. 137(5)(b).]

3(3) In this paragraph as it applies in Northern Ireland, **"county court"** means a county court held for a division under the County Courts (Northern Ireland) Order 1980.

3(4) Sections 21 and 42(2) of the Interpretation Act (Northern Ireland) 1954 shall apply as if any reference in those provisions to any enactment included a reference to this paragraph, and Part III of the County Courts (Northern Ireland) Order 1980 (general civil jurisdiction) shall apply for the purposes of this paragraph in Northern Ireland.

History – In para. 3(1), the words "in England and Wales in the county court or in Northern Ireland" inserted after "proceedings" by Crime and Courts Act 2013, s. 17 and Sch. 9, para. 129, with effect from 22 April 2014 (SI 2014/954, art. 2).

In para. 3(1), the words "commenced in the name of an authorised officer" which appeared at the end omitted by FA 2008, s. 137(5)(a), with effect from 21 July 2008.
Para. 3(2) omitted by FA 2008, s. 137(5)(b), with effect from 21 July 2008.

SHERIFF COURTS IN SCOTLAND

4(1) In Scotland, any sum which is due by way of contributions or by way of interest or penalty in respect of contributions may, without prejudice to any other remedy, be sued for and recovered from the person liable as a debt due to the Crown by proceedings commenced in the sheriff court in the name of an authorised officer.

4(2) An authorised officer may conduct any proceedings under this paragraph, although not an advocate or solicitor.

4(3) Paragraphs 2 and 3 above shall not apply in Scotland.

GENERAL

5(1) Proceedings may be brought for the recovery of the total amount of Class 1 or Class 1A contributions which an employer has become liable to pay on a particular date and any sum due by way of interest or penalty in respect of those contributions without distinguishing the amounts which the employer is liable to pay in respect of each employee and without specifying the employees in question; and for the purposes of proceedings under any of paragraphs 2 to 4 above that total amount shall be one cause of action or one matter of complaint.

5(2) Nothing in sub-paragraph (1) above shall prevent the bringing of separate proceedings for the recovery of each of the several amounts of Class 1 or Class 1A contributions which the employer is liable to pay.

SCHEDULE 5 – ENFORCEMENT

Section 5

Commencement Date – Sch. 5 entered into force, except for paragraphs 5 and 7, with effect from 1 April 1999 (SSC(TF)A 1999, s. 28(3) and SI 1999/527, art. 2(b), Sch. 2). Paragraphs 5 and 7 entered into force with effect from 6 April 1999 (SI 1999/527, art. 2(c), Sch. 3).

1 [Repealed by NICSPA 2004, s. 12 and Sch. 2.]

History – Para. 1 repealed by NICSPA 2004, s. 12 and Sch. 2 with effect from 6 April 2005 (by virtue of SI 2004/1943, reg. 6).

2 [Repealed by CSPSSA 2000, Sch. 9, Pt. VI.]

History – Para. 2 repealed by CSPSSA 2000, Sch. 9, Pt. VI, with effect from 2 April 2001 (by virtue of SI 2001/1252).

3 [Repealed by NICSPA 2004, s. 12 and Sch. 2.]

History – Para. 3 repealed by NICSPA 2004, s. 12 and Sch. 2 with effect from 6 April 2005 (by virtue of SI 2004/1943, reg. 6).

4(1) Section 111 of the Social Security Administration Act 1992 (delay, obstruction etc. of inspector) is amended as follows.

4(2) [Amends SSAA 1992, s. 111(1).]

4(3) [Inserts SSAA 1992, s. 111(3).]

5 [Amends SSAA 1992, s. 113(2).]

6 [Repeals SSAA 1992, s. 114A.]

7(1) Section 118 of the Social Security Administration Act 1992 (evidence of non-payment) is amended as follows.

7(2) [Omitted by FA 2008, s. 138 and Sch. 44, para. 11(d).]

7(3) [Repeals SSAA 1992, s. 118(1A), (2).]

7(4) [Amends SSAA 1992, s. 118(3).]

7(5) [Amends SSAA 1992, s. 118(4).]

7(6) [Omitted by FA 2008, s. 138 and Sch. 44, para. 11(d).]

History – Para. 7(2) and (6) omitted by FA 2008, s. 138 and Sch. 44, para. 11(d), with effect from 21 July 2008.

8 [Omitted by FA 2008, s. 129 and Sch. 43, para. 11(a).]

History – Para. 8 omitted by FA 2008, s. 129 and Sch. 43, para. 11(a), with effect from 6 April 2014 (SI 2014/906, art. 2).

9 [Amends SSAA 1992, s. 121B(5), (6).]

10 [Amends SSAA 1992, s. 121C.]

11(1) Section 121D of the Social Security Administration Act 1992 (appeals in relation to personal liability notices) is amended as follows.

11(2) [Amends SSAA 1992, s. 121D.]

11(3) [Amends SSAA 1992, s. 121D(2).]

11(4) [Amends SSAA 1992, s. 121D(5).]

11(5) [Amends SSAA 1992, s. 121D(6).]

12 [Inserts SSAA 1992, s. 162(4ZA).]

SCHEDULE 6 – INFORMATION

Section 6

Commencement Date – Sch. 6 entered into force with effect from 1 April 1999 (SSC(TF)A 1999, s. 28(3) and SI 1999/527, art. 2(b), Sch. 2).

SUPPLY OF INFORMATION

1 [Inserts SSAA 1992, s. 121E, 121F.]

2 [Repealed by WRA 2012, s. 147 and Sch. 14, Pt. 13.]

History – Para. 2 repealed by WRA 2012, s. 147 and Sch. 14, Pt. 13, with effect from 8 May 2012. Former para. 2 read as follows:
"**2(1)** Section 122 of the Social Security Administration Act 1992 (supply of information held by tax authorities for fraud prevention and verification) is amended as follows.
2(2) [Substitutes SSAA 1992, s. 122(1).]
2(3) [Amends SSAA 1992, s. 122(2)(b).]".

3 [Inserts SSAA 1992, s. 122AA.]

4 [Repeals SSAA 1992, s. 122A.]

5 [Amends SSAA 1992, s. 122B(20)(b).]

6 [Amends SSAA 1992, Sch. 4.]

7(1) Section 158 of the Pension Schemes Act 1993 (disclosure of information between government departments) is amended as follows.

7(2) [Inserts PSA 1993, s. 158(1A).]

8 [Inserts PSA 1993, s. 158A(1A).]

UNAUTHORISED DISCLOSURE OF INFORMATION

9(1) Section 182 of the Finance Act 1989 (disclosure of information) is amended as follows.

9(2) [Amends FA 1989, s. 182(1).]

9(3) [Inserts FA 1989, s. 182(2A).]

9(4) [Amends FA 1989, s. 182(4).]

9(5) [Amends FA 1989, s. 182(5)(b).]

9(6) [Amends FA 1989, s. 182(10).]

OBTAINING INFORMATION FOR TAX PURPOSES FROM SOCIAL SECURITY AUTHORITIES

10 [Repealed by WRA 2012, s. 147 and Sch. 14, Pt. 13.]

History – Para. 10 repealed by WRA 2012, s. 147 and Sch. 14, Pt. 13, with effect from 8 May 2012.

SCHEDULE 7 – DECISIONS AND APPEALS

Section 18

Commencement Date – The paragraphs of Sch. 7 enter into force on different dates. The History note for each paragraph should be consulted for precise details of the date and scope of its entry into force. Where no date is given the paragraph has not entered into force.

Cross references – SI 1999/1027: regulations concerning decisions made by officers of the Board and the conduct etc. of appeals against such decisions.

TAXES MANAGEMENT ACT 1970 (C. 9)

1 [Repealed by TCEA 2007, s. 146 and Sch. 23, Pt. 1.]

Commencement Date – Para. 1 entered into force, only for the purposes of making regulations, with effect from 4 March 1999 (SSC(TF)A 1999, s. 28(3) and SI 1999/527, art. 2(a), Sch. 1), and for all other purposes, with effect from 1 April 1999 (SI 1999/527, art. 2(b), Sch. 2).

History – Para. 1 repealed by TCEA 2007, s. 146 and Sch. 23, Pt. 1, with effect from 1 April 2009 (SI 2008/2696, art. 6(c)(vi) – subject to transitional provisions of art. 3). Former para. 1 amended TMA 1970, s. 2(1).

2 [Omitted by SI 2009/56, art. 3(1) and Sch. 1, para. 275.]

Commencement Date – Para. 2 entered into force, only for the purposes of making regulations, with effect from 4 March 1999 (SSC(TF)A 1999, s. 28(3) and SI 1999/527, art. 2(a), Sch. 1), and for all other purposes, with effect from 1 April 1999 (SI 1999/527, art. 2(b), Sch. 2).

History – Para. 2 omitted by SI 2009/56, art. 3(1) and Sch. 1, para. 275, operative from 1 April 2009, subject to transitional and saving provisions in SI 2009/56, Sch. 3. Former para. 2 amended TMA 1970, s. 46(1).

3 [Omitted by SI 2009/56, art. 3(1) and Sch. 1, para. 275.]

Commencement Date – Para. 3 entered into force, only for the purposes of making regulations, with effect from 4 March 1999 (SSC(TF)A 1999, s. 28(3) and SI 1999/527, art. 2(a), Sch. 1), and for all other purposes, with effect from 1 April 1999 (SI 1999/527, art. 2(b), Sch. 2).

History – Para. 3 omitted by SI 2009/56, art. 3(1) and Sch. 1, para. 275, operative from 1 April 2009, subject to transitional and saving provisions in SI 2009/56, Sch. 3. Former para. 3 inserted TMA 1970, s. 46(1A).

SOCIAL SECURITY CONTRIBUTIONS AND BENEFITS ACT 1992 (C. 5)

5 [Amends SSCBA 1992, s. 116(2).]

Commencement Date – Para. 5 entered into force, only for the purposes of making regulations, with effect from 4 March 1999 (SSC(TF)A 1999, s. 28(3) and SI 1999/527, art. 2(a), Sch. 1), and for all other purposes, with effect from 1 April 1999 (SI 1999/527, art. 2(b), Sch. 2).

6 [Amends SSCBA 1992, s. 117(1).]

Commencement Date – Para. 6 entered into force, only for the purposes of making regulations, with effect from 4 March 1999 (SSC(TF)A 1999, s. 28(3) and SI 1999/527, art. 2(a), Sch. 1), and for all other purposes, with effect from 1 April 1999 (SI 1999/527, art. 2(b), Sch. 2).

7 [Amends SSCBA 1992, s. 119.]

Commencement Date – Para. 7 entered into force, only for the purposes of making regulations, with effect from 4 March 1999 (SSC(TF)A 1999, s. 28(3) and SI 1999/527, art. 2(a), Sch. 1), and for all other purposes, with effect from 1 April 1999 (SI 1999/527, art. 2(b), Sch. 2).

8 [Amends SSCBA 1992, s. 120(1).]

Commencement Date – Para. 8 entered into force, only for the purposes of making regulations, with effect from 4 March 1999 (SSC(TF)A 1999, s. 28(3) and SI 1999/527, art. 2(a), Sch. 1), and for all other purposes, with effect from 1 April 1999 (SI 1999/527, art. 2(b), Sch. 2).

9 [Substitutes SSCBA 1992, Sch. 1, para. 6.]

Commencement Date – Para. 9 entered into force, only for the purposes of making regulations, with effect from 4 March 1999 (SSC(TF)A 1999, s. 28(3) and SI 1999/527, art. 2(a), Sch. 1) and for all other purposes, from 6 April 1999 (SI 1999/527, art. 2(c), Sch. 3).

10 [Substitutes SSCBA 1992, Sch. 1, para. 7(12).]

Commencement Date – Para. 10 entered into force, only for the purposes of making regulations, with effect from 4 March 1999 (SSC(TF)A 1999, s. 28(3) and SI 1999/527, art. 2(a), Sch. 1) and for all other purposes, from 6 April 1999 (SI 1999/527, art. 2(c), Sch. 3).

11 [Amends SSCBA 1992, Sch. 2, para. 8.]

SOCIAL SECURITY ADMINISTRATION ACT 1992 (C. 5)

Commencement Date – Para. 11 entered into force, only for the purposes of making regulations, with effect from 4 March 1999 (SSC(TF)A 1999, s. 28(3) and SI 1999/527, art. 2(a), Sch. 1), and for all other purposes, with effect from 1 April 1999 (SI 1999/527, art. 2(b), Sch. 2).

12 [Amends SSAA 1992, s. 117.]

Commencement Date – Para. 12 entered into force with effect from 5 July 1999. (SSC(TF)A 1999, s. 28(3) and SI 1999/1662, art. 2(b), Sch. Pt. II).

13 [Inserts SSAA 1992, s. 117A.]

Commencement Date – Para. 13 entered into force with effect from 1 April 1999 (SSC(TF)A 1999, s. 28(3) and SI 1999/527, art. 2(b), Sch. 2).

15(1) Section 179 of the Social Security Administration Act 1992 (reciprocal agreements with countries outside the United Kingdom) is amended as follows.

15(2) [Amends SSAA 1992, s. 179(30)(a).]

15(3) [Inserts SSAA 1992, s. 179(40)(ac).]

Commencement Date – Para. 15 entered into force with effect from 1 April 1999 (SSC(TF)A 1999, s. 28(3) and SI 1999/527, art. 2(b), Sch. 2).

16 [Inserts SSAA 1992, s. 180A.]

Commencement Date – Para. 16 entered into force with effect from 1 April 1999 (SSC(TF)A 1999, s. 28(3) and SI 1999/527, art. 2(b), Sch. 2).

SOCIAL SECURITY CONTRIBUTIONS AND BENEFITS (NORTHERN IRELAND) ACT 1992

17 [Amends Social Security Contributions and Benefits (Northern Ireland) Act 1992, Sch. 2, para. 8.]

Commencement Date – Para. 17 entered into force, only for the purposes of making regulations, with effect from 4 March 1999 (SSC(TF)A 1999, s. 28(3) and SI 1999/527, art. 2(a), Sch. 1), and for all other purposes, with effect from 1 April 1999 (SI 1999/527, art. 2(b), Sch. 2).

PENSION SCHEMES ACT 1993 (C. 48)

18(1) Section 167 of the Pension Schemes Act 1993 (application of general provisions relating to administration of social security) is amended as follows.

18(2) [Amends PSA 1993, s. 167(2).]

18(3) [Omits PSA 1993, s. 167(3).]

Commencement Date – Para. 18(1) and (2) entered into force with effect from 1 April 1999 (SSC(TF)A 1999, s. 28(3) and SI 1999/527, art. 2(b), Sch. 2).

Para. 18(3) entered into force with effect from 5 July 1999 (SSC(TF)A 1999, s. 28(3) and SI 1999/1662, art. 2(b), Sch. Pt. II).

19(1) Section 171 of the Pension Schemes Act 1993 (questions arising in proceedings) is amended as follows.

19(2) [Amends PSA 1993, s. 171(1).]

19(3) [Substitutes PSA 1993, s. 171(2), (3) and inserts PSA 1993, s. 171(4).]

Commencement Date – Para. 19 entered into force with effect from 5 July 1999 (SSC(TF)A 1999, s. 28(3) and SI 1999/1662, art. 2(b), Sch. Pt. II.

20 [Inserts PSA 1993, s. 171A.]

Commencement Date – Para. 20 entered into force with effect from 5 July 1999 (SSC(TF)A 1999, s. 28(3) and SI 1999/1662, art. 2(b), Sch. Part II.

SOCIAL SECURITY ACT 1998 (C. 14)

22(1) Section 8 of the Social Security Act 1998 (decisions by Secretary of State) is amended as follows.

22(2) [Amends SSA 1998, s. 8(10).]

22(3) [Substitutes SSA 1998, s. 8(5).]

Commencement Date – Para. 22 entered into force with effect from 1 April 1999 (SSC(TF)A 1999, s. 28(3) and SI 1999/527, art. 2(b), Sch. 2).

23 [Amends SSA 1998, s. 10.]

Commencement Date – Para. 23 entered into force with effect from 1 April 1999 (SSC(TF)A 1999, s. 28(3) and SI 1999/527, art. 2(b), Sch. 2).

24 [Inserts SSA 1998, s. 10A.]

Commencement Date – Para. 24 entered into force, only for the purposes of making regulation, with effect from 14 June 1999 (SSC(TF)A 1999, s. 28(3) and SI 1999/1662, art. 2(b), Sch. Pt. I) and for all other purposes, from 5 July 1999 (SI 1999/1662, art. 2(c), Sch. Pt. II).

25(1) Section 12 of the Social Security Act 1998 (appeal to appeal tribunal) is amended as follows.

25(2) [Amends SSA 1998, s. 12(1).]

25(3) [Substitutes SSA 1998, s. 12(2).]

Commencement Date – Para. 25 entered into force with effect from 1 April 1999 (SSC(TF)A 1999, s. 28(3) and SI 1999/527, art. 2(b), Sch. 2).

26 [Substitutes SSA 1998, s. 13(4).]

Commencement Date – Para. 26 entered into force with effect from 1 April 1999 (SSC(TF)A 1999, s. 28(3) and SI 1999/527, art. 2(b), Sch. 2).

27 [Amends SSA 1998, s. 14(2), (3).]

Commencement Date – Para. 27 entered into force with effect from 1 April 1999 (SSC(TF)A 1999, s. 28(3) and SI 1999/527, art. 2(b), Sch. 2).

28 [Ceases SSA 1998, s. 14(2), (3) to have effect.]

29 [Amends SSA 1998, s. 18.]

Commencement Date – Para. 29 entered into force with effect from 1 April 1999 (SSC(TF)A 1999, s. 28(3) and SI 1999/527, art. 2(b), Sch. 2).

33 [Inserts SSA 1998, s. 24A.]

Commencement Date – Para. 33 entered into force, only for the purposes of making regulation, with effect from 14 June 1999 (SSC(TF)A 1999, s. 28(3) and SI 1999/1662, art. 2(b), Sch. Pt. I) and for all other purposes, from 5 July 1999 (SI 1999/1662, art. 2(c), Sch. Pt. II).

34 [Inserts SSA 1998, s. 28(1A).]

Commencement Date – Para. 34 entered into force with effect from 5 July 1999 (SSC(TF)A 1999, s. 28(3) and SI 1999/1662, art. 2(b), Sch. Pt. II.

35 [Amends SSA 1998, s. 39(1).]

Commencement Date – Para. 35 entered into force with effect from 1 April 1999 (SSC(TF)A 1999, s. 28(3) and SI 1999/527, art. 2(b), Sch. 2).

36 [Repeals SSA 1998, Sch. 3, para. 10.]

Commencement Date – Para. 36 entered into force, only to the extent that it relates to SSA 1998, Sch. 3, para. 23, with effect from 1 April 1999 (SSC(TF)A 1999, s. 28(3) and SI 1999/527, art. 2(b), Sch. 2).

SCHEDULE 8 – SAVINGS AND TRANSITIONAL PROVISIONS

Section 26(1)

Commencement Date – Sch. 8 entered into force with effect from 25 February 1999 (SSC(TF)A 1999, s. 28(2)(g)).

GENERAL SAVINGS

1(1) In this paragraph–

"transfer provision" has the meaning given by section 21(1) of this Act;

"instrument" includes in particular Royal Charters, Orders in Council, Letters Patent, judgments, decrees, orders, rules, regulations, schemes, bye-laws, awards, contracts and other agreements, memoranda and articles of association, warrants, certificates and other documents.

1(2) A transfer provision shall not affect the validity of anything done by or in relation to the Secretary of State before the commencement of the transfer provision; and anything which at that date is in the process of being done by or in relation to the Secretary of State may–

(a) if it relates to functions transferred by virtue of the transfer provision to the Board, be continued by or in relation to the Board, and

(b) if it relates to functions transferred by virtue of the transfer provision to the Treasury, be continued by or in relation to the Treasury.

1(3) Any authority, appointment, determination, approval, consent or direction given or made or other thing done, or having effect as if given, made or done, by the Secretary of State in connection with functions transferred by virtue of a transfer provision shall have effect as if given, made or done by the Board or, as the case requires, the Treasury in so far as that is required for continuing its effect after the commencement of the transfer provision.

1(4) Any instrument made before the commencement of a transfer provision shall have effect, so far as may be necessary for the purposes of or in consequence of that provision or section 21 or 22 of this Act, as if–

(a) any reference to the Secretary of State were or included a reference to the Board or the Treasury, as the case requires; and

(b) any reference to the Department of Social Security or any officer of that Department were or included a reference to the Board or any officer of theirs.

Notes – Para. 1 to have effect as if WRPA 1999, Sch. 11, para. 2, 3, 6, 21, 35 were provisions of SSC(TF)A 1999, specified in SSC(TF)A 1999, s. 21(1), with effect from 11 November 1999 (WRPA 1999, Sch. 11, para. 37).

DOCUMENTS AND FORMS

2 Documents or forms produced for use in connection with any function transferred by virtue of this Act to the Board may be used even though they contain references to the Secretary of State or to the Department of Social Security or to any officer of that Department; and those references shall be construed as far as necessary as references to the Board or to any officer of the Board.

Notes – Para. 2 to have effect as if WRPA 1999, Sch. 11, para. 2, 3, 6, 21, 35 were provisions of SSC(TF)A 1999, specified in SSC(TF)A 1999, s. 21(1), with effect from 11 November 1999 (WRPA 1999, Sch. 11, para. 37).

PAYMENT OF CONTRIBUTIONS ETC. TO SECRETARY OF STATE DURING TRANSITIONAL PERIOD

3 [Repealed by WRPA 1999, s. 88, Sch. 13, Pt. VI.]

History – Para. 3 repealed by WRPA 1999, s. 88, Sch. 13, Pt. VI with effect from 6 April 2000 (SI 1999/3420, art. 4(c), (e)).

SECTION 51 OF SOCIAL SECURITY ACT 1998

4 [Repealed by WRPA 1999, s. 88, Sch. 13, Pt. VI.]

History – Para. 4 repealed by WRPA 1999, s. 88, Sch. 13, Pt. VI with effect from 6 April 2000 (SI 1999/3420, art. 4(c), (e)).

SCHEDULE 9 – FURTHER CONSEQUENTIAL AMENDMENTS

Section 26(2)

Commencement Date – Sch. 9, para. 4, 5, 6, and 7 entered into force, only for the purposes of making regulations, with effect from 4 March 1999 (SSC(TF)A 1999, s. 28(3) and SI 1999/527, art. 2(a), Sch. 1).

The whole of Sch. 9, except for para. 1 and 2, entered into force generally with effect from 1 April 1999 (SSC(TF)A 1999, s. 28(3) and SI 1999/527, art. 2(b), Sch. 2).

Sch. 9, para. 1 and 2 entered into force generally with effect from 6 April 1999 (SSC(TF)A 1999, s. 28(3) and SI 1999/527, art. 2(c), Sch. 3).

SOCIAL SECURITY CONTRIBUTIONS AND BENEFITS ACT 1992 (C. 4)

3 [Omitted by NICA 2015, s. 2 and Sch. 1, para. 27.]

History – Para. 3 omitted by NICA 2015, s. 2 and Sch. 1, para. 27, with effect in relation to a class 2 contribution in respect of a week in the tax year 2015–16 or a subsequent tax year.

4 [Amends SSCBA 1992, s. 19A(1)(c).]

5 [Amends SSCBA 1992, Sch. 4, para. 6(4A).]

6(1) Paragraph 7A of Schedule 1 to the Social Security Contributions and Benefits Act 1992 (power to combine collection of contributions with tax) is amended as follows.

6(2) [Amends SSCBA 1992, Sch. 1, para. 7A(2).]

6(3) [Amends SSCBA 1992, Sch 1, para. 7A(3).]

7(1) Paragraph 7B of Schedule 1 to the Social Security Contributions and Benefits Act 1992 (collection of contributions) is amended as follows.

7(2) In the italic heading immediately preceding the paragraph, for "by Secretary of State" there is substituted "otherwise than through PAYE system".

7(3) [Amends SSCBA 1992, Sch. 1, para. 7B(1).]

7(4) [Amends SSCBA 1992, Sch. 1, para. 7B(2).]

7(5) [Omits SSCBA 1992, Sch. 1, para 7B(4), (6).]

7(6) [Amends SSCBA 1992, Sch. 1, para. 7B(2).]

7(7) [Omitted by NICA 2015, s. 2 and Sch. 1, para. 27.]

History – Para. 7(7) omitted by NICA 2015, s. 2 and Sch. 1, para. 27, with effect in relation to a class 2 contribution in respect of a week in the tax year 2015–16 or a subsequent tax year.

8 [Repeals SSCBA 1992, Sch. 1, para. 7C.]

FINANCE ACT 1999

(1999 Chapter 16)

[*27th July 1999*]

ARRANGEMENT OF SECTIONS

PART VIII – MISCELLANEOUS AND SUPPLEMENTAL

GENERAL ADMINISTRATION OF TAX

PART VIII – MISCELLANEOUS AND SUPPLEMENTAL

GENERAL ADMINISTRATION OF TAX

132 Power to provide for use of electronic communications

132(1) Regulations may be made, in accordance with this section, for facilitating the use of electronic communications for–

(a) the delivery of information the delivery of which is authorised or required by or under any legislation relating to a taxation matter;

(b) the making of payments under any such legislation.

132(2) The power to make regulations under this section is conferred–

(a) on the Commissioners of Inland Revenue in relation to matters which are under their care and management; and

(b) on the Commissioners of Customs and Excise in relation to matters which are under their care and management.

132(3) For the purposes of this section provision for facilitating the use of electronic communications includes any of the following–

(a) provision authorising persons to use electronic communications for the delivery of information to tax authorities, or for the making of payments to tax authorities;

(b) provision requiring electronic communications to be used for the making to tax authorities of payments due from persons using such communications for the delivery of information to those authorities;

(c) provision authorising tax authorities to use electronic communications for the delivery of information to other persons or for the making of any payments;

(d) provision as to the electronic form to be taken by any information that is delivered to any tax authorities using electronic communications;

(e) provision requiring persons to prepare and keep records of information delivered to tax authorities by means of electronic communications, and of payments made to any such authorities by any such means;

(f) provision for the production of the contents of records kept in accordance with any regulations under this section;

(g) provision imposing conditions that must be complied with in connection with any use of electronic communications for the delivery of information or the making of any payment;

(h) provision, in relation to cases where use is made of electronic communications, for treating information as not having been delivered, or a payment as not having been made, unless conditions imposed by any such regulations are satisfied;

(i) provision, in relation to such cases, for determining the time when information is delivered or a payment is made;

(j) provision, in relation to such cases, for determining the person by whom information is to be taken to have been delivered or by whom a payment is to be taken to have been made;

(k) provision, in relation to cases where information is delivered by means of electronic communications, for authenticating whatever is delivered.

132(4) The power to make provision under this section for facilitating the use of electronic communications shall also include power to make such provision as the persons exercising the power think fit (including provision for the application of conclusive or other presumptions) as to the manner of proving for any purpose–

(a) whether any use of electronic communications is to be taken as having resulted in the delivery of information or the making of a payment;

(b) the time of delivery of any information for the delivery of which electronic communications have been used;

(c) the time of the making of any payment for the making of which electronic communications have been used;

(d) the person by whom information delivered by means of electronic communications was delivered;

(e) the contents of anything so delivered;

(f) the contents of any records;

(g) any other matter for which provision may be made by regulations under this section.

132(5) Regulations under this section may–

(a) allow any authorisation or requirement for which such regulations may provide to be given or imposed by means of a specific or general direction given by the Commissioners of Inland Revenue or the Commissioners of Customs and Excise;

(b) provide that the conditions of any such authorisation or requirement are to be taken to be satisfied only where such tax authorities as may be determined under the regulations are satisfied as to specified matters;

(c) allow a person to refuse to accept delivery of information in an electronic form or by means of electronic communications except in such circumstances as may be specified in or determined under the regulations;

(d) allow or require use to be made of intermediaries in connection with–

(i) the delivery of information, or the making of payments, by means of electronic communications; or

(ii) the authentication or security of anything transmitted by any such means.

132(6) Power to make provision by regulations under this section shall include power–

(a) to provide for a contravention of, or any failure to comply with, a specified provision of any such regulations to attract a penalty of a specified amount not exceeding £1,000;

(b) to provide that specified enactments relating to penalties imposed for the purposes of any taxation matter (including enactments relating to assessments, review and appeal) are to apply, with or without modifications, in relation to penalties under such regulations;

(c) to make different provision for different cases;

(d) to make such incidental, supplemental, consequential and transitional provision in connection with any provision contained in any such regulations as the persons exercising the power think fit.

132(7) The power to make regulations under this section shall be exercisable by statutory instrument subject to annulment in pursuance of a resolution of the House of Commons.

132(8) References in this section to the delivery of information include references to any of the following (however referred to)–

(a) the production or furnishing to a person of any information, account, record or document;

(b) the giving, making, issue or surrender to, or service on, any person of any notice, notification, statement, declaration, certificate or direction;

(c) the imposition on any person of any requirement or the issue to any person of any request;

(d) the making of any return, claim, election or application;

(e) the amendment or withdrawal of anything mentioned in paragraphs (a) to (d) above.

132(9) References in this section to a taxation matter are references to any of the matters which are under the care and management of the Commissioners of Inland Revenue or of the Commissioners of Customs and Excise.

132(10) In this section–

"electronic communications" includes any communications by means of an electronic communications service;

"legislation" means any enactment, Community legislation or subordinate legislation;

"payment" includes a repayment;

"records" includes records in electronic form;

"subordinate legislation" has the same meaning as in the Interpretation Act 1978;

"tax authorities" means–

(a) the Commissioners of Inland Revenue or the Commissioners of Customs and Excise,

(b) any officer of either body of Commissioners; or

(c) any other person who for the purposes of electronic communications is acting under the authority of either body of Commissioners.

Commencement Date – S. 132 came into effect on 27 July 1999 (Royal Assent).

History – In s. 132(10), in the definition of "electronic communications", the words "an electronic communications service" substituted by the Communications Act 2003, s. 406(1) and Sch. 17, para. 156, with effect for the purpose only of enabling the networks and services functions and the spectrum functions to be carried out by the Director General of Telecommunications and the Secretary of State respectively, during the transitional period (as provided for by the Communications Act 2003, s. 408(6)) from 25 July 2003–29 December 2003 (by virtue of SI 2003/1900, art. 2(1), 3(1), Sch. 1 and the Communications Act 2003, s. 406(6), 408, Sch. 18, para. 2); and with effect for the purpose of conferring the networks and services functions and the spectrum functions on OFCOM from 29 December 2003 (by virtue of SI 2003/3142, art. 3(2)).

Cross references – FA 2000, Sch. 38, para. 1; power to make regulations for providing incentives to use electronic communications. Work and Families Act 2006, Sch. 1, para. 49 reads as follows:
"**49(1)** Sections 132 and 133 of the Finance Act 1999 shall have effect as if additional statutory paternity pay were a matter which is under the care and management of the Commissioners for Her Majesty's Revenue and Customs.
49(2) In this paragraph **"additional statutory paternity pay"** includes statutory pay under Northern Ireland legislation corresponding to the provisions of Part 12ZA of SSCBA 1992 relating to additional statutory paternity pay."

Statutory instruments – SI 2007/1077 made under s. 132.
SI 2007/792 made under s. 132.
SI 2006/570 made under s. 132.
SI 2005/3338 made under s. 132.
SI 2005/844 made under s. 132.
SI 2003/3143 made under s. 132.
SI 2003/2718 made under s. 132.
SI 2003/2682 made under s. 132.
SI 2003/493 made under s. 132.
SI 2003/492 made under s. 132.
SI 2003/282 made under s. 132.
SI 2002/3047 made under s. 132.
SI 2002/680 made under s. 132.
SI 2000/2315 made under s. 132.

133 Use of electronic communications under other provisions

133(1) Without prejudice to section 132 above, where any power to make subordinate legislation for or in connection with the delivery of information or the making of payments is conferred in relation to any taxation matter on–

(a) the Commissioners of Inland Revenue,

(b) the Commissioners of Customs and Excise, or

(c) the Treasury,

that power shall be taken (to the extent that it would not otherwise be so taken) to include power to make any such provision in relation to the delivery of that information or the making of those payments as could be made by any person by regulations in exercise of a power conferred by that section.

133(2) Provision made in exercise of the powers conferred by section 132 above or subsection (1) above shall have effect notwithstanding so much of any enactment or subordinate legislation as (apart from the provision so made) would require–

(a) any information to be delivered, or

(b) any amount to be paid,

in a form or manner that would preclude the use of electronic communications for its delivery or payment, or the use in connection with its delivery or payment of an intermediary.

133(3) Schedule 3A to the Taxes Management Act 1970 (electronic lodgment of tax returns etc.) shall cease to have effect.

133(4) Subsection (3) above shall come into force on such day as the Treasury may by order made by statutory instrument appoint; and different days may be appointed under this subsection for different purposes.

133(5) Expressions used in this section and section 132 above have the same meanings in this section as in that section.

Commencement Date – S. 133(1), (2), (4) and (5) came into effect on 27 July 1999 (Royal Assent).

Cross references – Work and Families Act 2006, Sch. 1, para. 49 reads as follows:
"**49(1)** Sections 132 and 133 of the Finance Act 1999 shall have effect as if additional statutory paternity pay were a matter which is under the care and management of the Commissioners for Her Majesty's Revenue and Customs.
49(2) In this paragraph **"additional statutory paternity pay"** includes statutory pay under Northern Ireland legislation corresponding to the provisions of Part 12ZA of SSCBA 1992 relating to additional statutory paternity pay."

Statutory instruments – SI 2007/1077 made under s. 133.
SI 2007/792 made under s. 133.
SI 2006/570 made under s. 133.
SI 2005/3338 made under s. 133.
SI 2005/844 made under s. 133.
SI 2003/2682 made under s. 133.
SI 2003/492 made under s. 133.
SI 2003/282 made under s. 133.
SI 2002/3047 made under s. 133.
SI 2002/3006 made under s. 133.
SI 2000/2315 made under s. 133.
SI 2000/2074 made under s. 133.

WELFARE REFORM AND PENSIONS ACT 1999

(1999 Chapter 30) [*11th November 1999*]

ARRANGEMENT OF SECTIONS

PART V – WELFARE

Chapter II – National Insurance Contributions

73 New threshold for primary Class 1 contributions

73 Schedule 9 (which amends the Contributions and Benefits Act, the Administration Act and the Pension Schemes Act 1993 so as to make provision for and in connection with the introduction of a new primary threshold for primary Class 1 contributions) shall have effect.

Commencement Date – S. 73 came into effect on 22 December 1999 for the purposes of making Regulations and on 6 April 2000 for all other purposes by virtue of SI 1999/3420, art. 2.

75 Earnings of workers supplied by service companies etc.

75 [Inserts SSCBA 1992, s. 4A.]

Commencement Date – S. 75 came into effect on 22 December 1999 by virtue of SI 1999/3420, art. 3.

Cross references – SI 2000/727: regulations dealing with personal services provided through intermediaries.

77 Class 1B contributions

77 [Inserts SSCBA 1992, s. 10A(6).]

Commencement Date – S. 77 came into effect on 6 April 2000 by virtue of SI 1999/3420, art. 4(a).

PART VI – GENERAL

MISCELLANEOUS

81 *Contributions* and pensions administration

81 Schedule 11 (which contains amendments dealing with administrative matters relating to contributions and pensions) shall have effect.

Commencement Date – S. 81 came into effect on 11 November 1999 (Royal Assent) by virtue of WRPA 1999, s. 89(4).

History – S. 81 and Sch. 11 in force with effect from 11 November 1999 (date of Royal Assent).

SCHEDULES

SCHEDULE 9 – NEW THRESHOLD FOR PRIMARY CLASS 1 CONTRIBUTIONS

Section 73

Commencement Date – Sch. 9 came into effect on 22 December 1999 for the purposes of making Regulations and on 6 April 2000 for all other purposes by virtue of SI 1999/3420, art. 2.

Part I – New Primary Threshold

EARNINGS LIMITS AND THRESHOLDS FOR CLASS 1 CONTRIBUTIONS

1 [Substitutes SSCBA 1992, s. 5.]

Commencement Date – Para. 1 in force with effect from 6 December 1999, only for the purpose of making regulations and 6 April 2000, for all other purposes (SI 1999/3420, art. 2).

LIABILITY FOR CLASS 1 CONTRIBUTIONS

2 [Substitutes SSCBA 1992, s. 66.]

Commencement Date – Para. 2 in force with effect from 6 December 1999, only for the purpose of making regulations and 6 April 2000, for all other purposes (SI 1999/3420, art. 2).

NOTIONAL PAYMENT OF PRIMARY CLASS 1 CONTRIBUTION WHERE EARNINGS NOT LESS THAN LOWER EARNINGS LIMIT

3 [Inserts SSCBA 1992, s. 6A.]

Commencement Date – Para. 3 in force with effect from 6 December 1999, only for the purpose of making regulations and 6 April 2000, for all other purposes (SI 1999/3420, art. 2).

CALCULATION OF PRIMARY CLASS 1 CONTRIBUTIONS

4 [Repealed by the National Insurance Contributions Act 2002, s. 7 and Sch. 2.]

Commencement Date – Para. 4 in force with effect from 6 December 1999 for the purpose of making regulations, and 6 April 2000 for all other purposes (SI 1999/3420, art. 2).

History – Para. 4 repealed by the National Insurance Contributions Act 2002, s. 7 and Sch. 2 with effect for 2003–04 and subsequent tax years.

CALCULATION OF SECONDARY CLASS 1 CONTRIBUTIONS

5 [Substitutes SSCBA 1992, s. 9.]

Commencement Date – Para. 5 in force with effect from 6 December 1999, for the purpose of making regulations and 6 April 2000, for all other purposes (SI 1999/3420, art. 2).

Part II – Reduced Contributions in Respect of Members of Contracted-out Schemes

REDUCED RATES FOR MEMBERS OF SALARY RELATED CONTRACTED-OUT SCHEMES

6(1) Section 41 of the Pension Schemes Act 1993 is amended as follows.

6(2) [Amends PSA 1993, s. 41(1).]

6(3) [Substitutes PSA 1993, s. 41(1A)–(1E) for former (1A)–(1C).]

Commencement Date – Para. 6 in force with effect from 6 December 1999, for the purpose of making regulations and 6 April 2000, for all other purposes (SI 1999/3420, art. 2).

REDUCED RATES FOR MEMBERS OF MONEY PURCHASE CONTRACTED-OUT SCHEMES

7(1) Section 42A of the Pension Schemes Act 1993 is amended as follows.

7(2) [Amends PSA 1993, s. 42A(1).]

7(3) [Substitutes PSA 1993, s. 42A(2)–(2D) for former (2)–(2B).]

Commencement Date – Para. 7 in force with effect from 6 December 1999, for the purpose of making regulations and 6 April 2000, for all other purposes (SI 1999/3420, art. 2).

Prospective amendments – Para. 7 repealed by PA 2007, s. 27 and Sch. 7, Pt. 7, with effect from a date to be appointed, s. 27(7).

PAYMENTS BY INLAND REVENUE OUT OF AND INTO NATIONAL INSURANCE FUND

8(1) Section 177 of the Pension Schemes Act 1993 is amended as follows.

8(2) [Amends PSA 1993, s. 177(2)(za).]

8(3) [Amends PSA 1993, s. 177(7)(a).]

Commencement Date – Para. 8 in force with effect from 6 December 1999, for the purpose of making regulations and 6 April 2000, for all other purposes (SI 1999/3420, art. 2).

Part III – National Health Service Allocation

9(1) Section 162 of the Administration Act is amended as follows.

9(2) [Amends SSAA 1992, s. 162(5).]

9(3) [Amends SSAA 1992, s. 162(6A).]

Commencement Date – Para. 9 in force with effect from 6 December 1999, for the purpose of making regulations and 6 April 2000, for all other purposes (SI 1999/3420, art. 2).

SCHEDULE 11 – CONTRIBUTIONS AND PENSIONS ADMINISTRATION

Section 81

SOCIAL SECURITY CONTRIBUTIONS AND BENEFITS ACT 1992 (c. 4)

1 The Contributions and Benefits Act is amended as follows.

Commencement Date – Para. 1 in force with effect from 11 November 1999 (date of Royal Assent).

2 [Substitutes SSCBA 1992, s. 2(2A).]

Commencement Date – Para. 2 in force with effect from 11 November 1999 (date of Royal Assent).

Cross references – SSC(TF)A 1999, Sch. 8, para. 1 and 2: has effect as if para. 2 were specified in SSC(TF)A 1999, s. 21(1) (WRPA 1999, Sch. 11, para. 37, with effect from 11 November 1999).

3 [Amends SSCBA 1992, Sch. 1, para. 8.]

Commencement Date – Para. 3 in force with effect from 11 November 1999 (date of Royal Assent).

Cross references – SSC(TF)A 1999, Sch. 8, para. 1 and 2: has effect as if para. 3 was specified in SSC(TF)A 1999, s. 21(1) (WRPA 1999, Sch. 11, para. 37, with effect from 11 November 1999).

SOCIAL SECURITY ADMINISTRATION ACT 1992 (c. 5)

4 The Administration Act is amended as follows.

Commencement Date – Para. 4 in force with effect from 11 November 1999 (date of Royal Assent).

5 [Amends SSAA 1992, s. 116(5A).]

Commencement Date – Para. 5 in force with effect from 11 November 1999 (date of Royal Assent).

6 [Omitted by FA 2008, s. 129 and Sch. 43, para. 11(b).]

History – Para. 6 omitted by FA 2008, s. 129 and Sch. 43, para. 11(b), with effect from 6 April 2014 (SI 2014/906, art. 2).

7 [Amends SSAA 1992, s. 121E(1).]

Commencement Date – Para. 7 in force with effect from 11 November 1999 (date of Royal Assent).

8 [Amends SSAA 1992, s. 121F(2).]

Commencement Date – Para. 8 in force with effect from 11 November 1999 (date of Royal Assent).

PENSION SCHEMES ACT 1993 (c. 48)

20 The Pension Schemes Act 1993 is amended as follows.

Commencement Date – Para. 20 in force with effect from 11 November 1999 (date of Royal Assent).

21 [Amends PSA 1993, s. 40.]

Commencement Date – Para. 21 in force with effect from 11 November 1999 (date of Royal Assent).

Prospective amendments – Para. 21 repealed by PA 2007, s. 27 and Sch. 7, Pt. 7, with effect from a date to be appointed, s. 27(7).

Cross references – SSC(TF)A 1999, Sch. 8, para. 1 and 2: has effect as if para. 21 was specified in SSC(TF)A 1999, s. 21(1) (WRPA 1999, Sch. 11, para. 37, with effect from 11 November 1999).

22 [Amends PSA 1993, s. 170(5).]

Commencement Date – Para. 22 in force with effect from 11 November 1999 (date of Royal Assent).

23 [Omitted by SI 2013/2042, art. 20.]

History – Para. 23 omitted by SI 2013/2042, art. 20, with effect from 19 August 2013.

SOCIAL SECURITY CONTRIBUTIONS (TRANSFER OF FUNCTIONS, ETC.) ACT 1999 (c. 2)

29 The Social Security Contributions (Transfer of Functions, etc.) Act 1999 is amended as follows.

Commencement Date – Para. 29 in force with effect from 11 November 1999 (date of Royal Assent).

30 [Omits SSC(TF)A 1999, s. 3(3)(c).]

Commencement Date – Para. 30 in force with effect from 11 November 1999 (date of Royal Assent).

31 [Amends SSC(TF)A 1999, s. 4. Partly repealed by NICSPA 2004, s. 12 and Sch. 2.]

Commencement Date – Para. 31 in force with effect from 11 November 1999 (date of Royal Assent).

History – Para. 31(b) repealed by NICSPA 2004, s. 12 and Sch. 2 with effect from 1 September 2004 (by virtue of SI 2004/1943, reg. 6).

32 [Omits SSC(TF)A 1999, Sch. 1, para. 4(6), 66(3).]

Commencement Date – Para. 32 in force with effect from 11 November 1999 (date of Royal Assent).

33 [Amends SSC(TF)A 1999, Sch. 2.]

Commencement Date – Para. 33 in force with effect from 11 November 1999 (date of Royal Assent).

TRANSFER OF CERTAIN FUNCTIONS UNDER SUBORDINATE LEGISLATION: GREAT BRITAIN

35 There are hereby transferred to the Commissioners of Inland Revenue–

(a) all functions of the Secretary of State under the Social Security (Contributions) Regulations 1979 which are not transferred to the Commissioners of Inland Revenue by virtue of section 1(2) of, and Schedule 2 to, the Social Security Contributions (Transfer of Functions, etc.) Act 1999, except his functions under regulation 44 of those regulations,

(b) the functions of the Secretary of State under those provisions of the Occupational Pension Schemes (Contracting-out) Regulations 1984 ("the 1984 regulations") which remain in force by virtue of regulation 77(a) of the Occupational Pension Schemes (Contracting-out) Regulations 1996 ("the 1996 regulations"), including his functions under the modifications of section 60(4) and (5) of the Pension Schemes Act 1993 made by regulation 23(10)(a)(iii) of the 1984 regulations, but excluding–

  (i) his functions under paragraph (2) of regulation 20 of the 1984 regulations so far as relating to any extension of the period first referred to in that paragraph by more than six months, and

  (ii) his functions under regulations 23(4) and 23A(4) of the 1984 regulations,

(c) the functions of the Secretary of State under regulation 2 of the Occupational Pension Schemes (Contracted-out Protected Rights Premiums) Regulations 1987 (so far as remaining in force by virtue of regulation 77(b) of the 1996 regulations), and

(d) the functions of the Secretary of State under the Personal Pension Schemes (Personal Pension Protected Rights Premiums) Regulations 1987 ("the 1987 regulations") (so far as remaining in force by virtue of regulation 4(2) of the Personal and Occupational Pension Schemes (Miscellaneous Amendments) Regulations 1997), except–

  (i) his functions under paragraph (3) of regulation 5 of the 1987 regulations so far as relating to any extension of the period first referred to in that paragraph by more than six months, and

  (ii) his functions under regulation 6(4) of the 1987 regulations.

Commencement Date – Para. 35 in force with effect from 11 November 1999 (date of Royal Assent).

Cross references – SSC(TF)A 1999, Sch. 8, para. 1 and 2: has effect as if para. 35 was specified in SSC(TF)A 1999, s. 21(1) (WRPA 1999, Sch. 11, para. 37, with effect from 11 November 1999).

SAVINGS

37 Paragraphs 1 and 2 of Schedule 8 to the Social Security Contributions (Transfer of Functions, etc.) Act 1999 (general provisions relating to transfers of functions) shall have effect as if paragraphs 2, 3, 6, 21 and 35 of this Schedule were provisions of that Act specified in section 21(1) of that Act.

Commencement Date – Para. 37 in force with effect from 11 November 1999 (date of Royal Assent).

CHILD SUPPORT, PENSIONS AND SOCIAL SECURITY ACT 2000

(2000 Chapter 19) [*28th July 2000*]

ARRANGEMENT OF SECTIONS

PART III – SOCIAL SECURITY

INVESTIGATION POWERS

PART IV – NATIONAL INSURANCE CONTRIBUTIONS

SCHEDULES

PART III – SOCIAL SECURITY

INVESTIGATION POWERS

67 Investigation powers

67 Schedule 6 to this Act (which amends the enforcement provisions contained in Part VI of the Social Security Administration Act 1992) shall have effect.

Commencement Date – S. 67 came into effect on 1 November 2000 by virtue of SI 2000/2950, art. 2(d).

PART IV – NATIONAL INSURANCE CONTRIBUTIONS

74 Contributions in respect of benefits in kind: Great Britain

74(1) [Amends SSCBA 1992, s. 1(2)(b).]

74(2) [Substitutes SSCBA 1992, s. 10.]

74(3) [Substitutes SSCBA 1992, s. 4(6).]

74(4) [Amends SSCBA 1992, Sch. 1, para. 5(b).]

74(5) [Amends SSCBA 1992, Sch. 1, para. 8(1)(ia).]

74(6) [Amends SSAA 1992, s. 120(4).]

74(7) [Amends SSAA 1992, s. 162(5)(c).]

74(8) This section shall have effect in relation to the tax year beginning with 6th April 2000 and subsequent tax years.

74(9) Regulations made by statutory instrument under any power conferred by virtue of this section may be made so as to have retrospective effect in relation to any time in the tax year in which they are made (including, in the case of regulations made in the tax year in which this Act is passed, any time in that tax year before the passing of this Act).

Commencement Date – S. 74 came into effect on 28 July 2000 (Royal Assent).

75 Third party providers of benefits in kind: Great Britain

75(1) [Inserts SSCBA 1992, s. 10ZA, 10ZB.]

75(2) [Repealed by NICSPA 2004, s. 12 and Sch. 2.]

75(3) Subsection (1) shall have effect in relation to the tax year beginning with 6th April 2000 and subsequent tax years.

75(4) Regulations made by virtue of this section under section 10ZA(5) of the Social Security Contributions and Benefits Act 1992 may be made so as to have retrospective effect in relation to any time in the tax year in which they are made (including, in the case of regulations made in the tax year in which this Act is passed, any time in that tax year before the passing of this Act).

Commencement Date – S. 75 came into effect on 28 July 2000 (Royal Assent).

History – S. 75(2) repealed by NICSPA 2004, s. 12 and Sch. 2 with effect from 6 April 2005 (by virtue of SI 2004/1943, reg. 6).

76 Collection etc. of NICs: Great Britain

76(1) Schedule 1 to the Social Security Contributions and Benefits Act 1992 (supplementary provisions relating to contributions) shall be amended in accordance with subsections (2) to (5).

76(2) [Amends SSCBA 1992, Sch. 1, para. 7(2)(b).]

76(3) [Substitutes SSCBA 1992, Sch. 1, para. 7B(2)(e).]

76(4) [Inserts SSCBA 1992, Sch. 1, para. 7B(5A).]

76(5) [Inserts SSCBA 1992, Sch. 1, para. 7BA.]

76(6) [Amends SSC(TF)A 1999, s. 8(1).]

76(7) Subsection (6) has effect in relation to interest accruing on sums becoming due in respect of the tax year beginning with 6th April 2000 or any subsequent tax year.

Commencement Date – S. 76 came into effect on 28 July 2000 (Royal Assent).

77 Liability of earner for secondary contributions: Great Britain

77(1) [Omits SSCBA 1992, Sch. 1, para. 3(2).]

77(2) [Inserts SSCBA 1992, Sch. 1, para. 3A, 3B.]

77(3) [Amends SSCBA 1992, s. 6(4).]

77(4) [Inserts SSCBA 1992, Sch. 1, para. 8(1)(ca).]

77(5) [Inserts SSC(TF)A 1999, s. 8(1)(ia).]

77(6) [Amends SSC(TF)A 1999, s. 10.]

77(7) [Amends SSC(TF)A 1999, s. 12(4).]

Commencement Date – S. 77 came into effect on 28 July 2000 (Royal Assent).

85 Repeals

85(1) The enactments mentioned in Schedule 9 (which include some spent provisions) are hereby repealed to the extent specified in the third column of that Schedule.

85(2) The repeals specified in that Schedule have effect subject to the commencement provisions and savings contained, or referred to, in the notes set out in that Schedule.

Commencement Date – S. 85 came into effect on 28 July 2000 (Royal Assent).

86 Commencement and transitional provisions

86(1) This section applies to the following provisions of this Act–

(a) [not relevant to National Insurance contributions;]

(b) [not relevant to National Insurance contributions;]

(c) [not relevant to National Insurance contributions;]

(d) [not relevant to National Insurance contributions;]

(e) Part III;

(f) [not relevant to National Insurance contributions;]

(g) [not relevant to National Insurance contributions;]

(h) [not relevant to National Insurance contributions.]

86(2) The provisions of this Act to which this section applies shall come into force on such day as may be appointed by order made by statutory instrument; and different days may be appointed under this section for different purposes.

86(3) The power to make an order under subsection (2) shall be exercisable–

(a) except in a case falling within paragraph (b), by the Secretary of State; and

(b) [not relevant to National Insurance contributions.]

86(4) [Not relevant to National Insurance contributions.]

86(5) [Not relevant to National Insurance contributions.]

86(6) [Not relevant to National Insurance contributions.]

86(7) Section 174(2) to (4) of the Pensions Act 1995 (supplementary provision in relation to powers to make subordinate legislation under that Act) shall apply in relation to the power to make regulations under subsection (5) as it applies to any power to make regulations under that Act.

86(8) In this section **"subordinate legislation"** has the same meaning as in the Interpretation Act 1978.

Commencement Date – S. 86 came into effect on 28 July 2000 (Royal Assent).

87 Short title and extent

87(1) This Act may be cited as the Child Support, Pensions and Social Security Act 2000.

87(2) The following provisions of this Act extend to Northern Ireland–

(a) so much of section 46 as amends section 21(3) of the Pensions Act 1995;

(b) sections 57 to 61 (except section 60(5));

(c) section 73;

(d) sections 78 to 81;

(e) in Schedule 3, paragraphs 8 and 9, and in paragraph 11, sub-paragraph (2) (and sub-paragraph (1) so far as it relates to that sub-paragraph);

(f) paragraph 6 of Schedule 5; and

(g) this Part, except–

(i) sections 82 and 83 and Schedule 8; and

(ii) so much of this Part as gives effect to any repeal other than the repeals mentioned in subsection (3).

87(3) The repeals mentioned in subsection (2)(g) (which extend to Northern Ireland) are–

(a) the repeals, in Part I of Schedule 9, that relate to the Tax Credits Act 1999;

(b) the repeals, in sections (1), (6) and (11) of Part III of that Schedule, that relate to–

(i) section 21(3) of the Pensions Act 1995;

(ii) paragraph 49(a)(ii) of Schedule 3 to the Pensions (Northern Ireland) Order 1995; and

(iii) section 52(5) of the Pension Schemes (Northern Ireland) Act 1993;

(c) the repeals in Part IV of that Schedule (except so far as relating to the Courts and Legal Services Act 1990); and

(d) the repeals in section (2) of Part VIII of that Schedule.

87(4) Subject to that, this Act does not extend to Northern Ireland.

Commencement Date – S. 87 came into effect on 28 July 2000 (Royal Assent).

SCHEDULES

SCHEDULE 3 – AMENDMENT OF ENACTMENTS RELATING TO CHILD SUPPORT

THE INCOME AND CORPORATION TAXES ACT 1988 (C. 1)

8(1) The Income and Corporation Taxes Act 1988 shall be amended as follows.

8(2) [Repealed by ITA 2007, s. 1031 and Sch. 3, Pt. 1.]

8(3) [Amends ICTA 1988, s. 617(2)(ae).]

History – Para. 8(2) repealed by ITA 2007, s. 1031 and Sch. 3, Pt. 1, with effect from 6 April 2007.

Notes – Para. 8(2) rewritten as ITA 2007, s. 454(7), (8), 455(1), (3).

THE FINANCE ACT 1988 (C. 39)

9 [Amends FA 1988, s. 36(5A) and 38(8A).]

SCHEDULE 5 – PENSIONS: MISCELLANEOUS AMENDMENTS AND ALTERNATIVE TO ANTI-FRANKING RULES

PART I – MISCELLANEOUS AMENDMENTS

REVIEW AND ALTERATION OF RATES OF CONTRIBUTION

4 [Amends PSA 1993, s. 42(1)(a)(i).]

SCHEDULE 6 – SOCIAL SECURITY INVESTIGATION POWERS

Section 67

Notes – Para. 1, 7, 8 came into force on 1 November 2000 (SI 2000/2950). The remainder of Sch. 6 came into force on 2 April 2001 (SI 2001/1252 (C. 45)).

PRELIMINARY

1 Part VI of the Social Security Administration Act 1992 (enforcement) shall be amended as follows.

Commencement Date – Para. 1, as far as it relates to the insertion by para. 8 of SSAA 1992, s. 121DA(1) and (7) for the purposes of construing SSAA 1992, s. 113 as amended by CSPSSA 2000, Sch. 6, para. 7, came into effect on 1 November 2000 by virtue of SI 2000/2950, art. 2(d). Otherwise it came into effect on 2 April 2001 by virtue of SI 2000/1252, art. 2(1)(a).

History – By virtue of SI 2000/2950, art. 2(d), CSPSSA 2000, Sch. 6, para. 1 has effect in so far as relating to CSPSSA 2000, Sch. 6, para. 7, and CSPSSA 2000, Sch. 6, para. 8 so far as para. 8 inserts SSAA 1992, s. 121DA(1) and (7) for the purposes of construing SSAA 1992, s. 113 as amended by CSPSSA 2000, Sch. 6, para. 7, from 1 November 2000.

REPLACEMENT FOR INSPECTOR'S POWERS

2 [Substitutes SSAA 1992, s. 109A, 109B and 109C for former s. 110.]

Commencement Date – Para. 2 came into effect on 2 April 2001 by virtue of SI 2000/1252, art. 2(1)(a).

History – Para. 2 has effect from 2 April 2001 (SI 2001/1252 (C. 45)).

CONSEQUENTIAL AMENDMENTS

4 [Amends SSAA 1992, s. 111(3), (4).]

Commencement Date – Para. 4 came into effect on 2 April 2001 by virtue of SI 2000/1252, art. 2(1)(a).

History – Para. 4(b) repealed by NICSPA 2004, s. 12 and Sch. 2 with effect from 6 April 2005 (by virtue of SI 2004/1943, reg. 6). Para. 4 has effect from 2 April 2001 (SI 2001/1252 (C. 45)).

5 [Amends SSAA 1992, s. 111A(1).]

Commencement Date – Para. 5 came into effect on 2 April 2001 by virtue of SI 2000/1252, art. 2(1)(a).

History – Para. 5 has effect from 2 April 2001 (SI 2001/1252 (C. 45)).

6 [Amends SSAA 1992, s. 112(1).]

Commencement Date – Para. 6 came into effect on 2 April 2001 by virtue of SI 2000/1252, art. 2(1)(a).

History – Para. 6 has effect from 2 April 2001 (SI 2001/1252 (C. 45)).

7(1) [Amends SSAA 1992, s. 113(1).]

7(2) [Inserts SSAA 1992, s. 113(1A).]

Commencement Date – Para. 7 came into effect on 1 November 2000 by virtue of SI 2000/2950, art. 2(d).

History – Para. 7 has effect from 1 November 2000 by virtue of SI 2000/2950, art. 2(d)(i).

8 [Inserts SSAA 1992, s. 121DA.]

Commencement Date – Para. 8, as far as it inserts SSAA 1992, s. 121DA(1) and (7) for the purposes of construing SSAA 1992, s. 113 as amended by CSPSSA 2000, Sch. 6, para. 7, came into effect on 1 November 2000 by virtue of SI 2000/2950, art. 2(d). Otherwise it comes into effect on 2 April 2001 by virtue of SI 2000/1252, art. 2(1)(a).

History – Para. 8, so far as it inserts SSAA 1992, s. 121DA (1) and (7) for the purposes of construing SSAA 1992, s. 113 as amended by CSPSSA 2000, Sch. 6, para. 7, has effect from 1 November 2000 by virtue of SI 2000/2950, art. 2(d)(ii).

9 [Not relevant to National Insurance contributions, tax credits, SSP and SMP.]

SCHEDULE 9 – REPEALS AND REVOCATIONS

PART I – CHILD SUPPORT

Chapter or Number	Citation	Extent of repeal or revocation
1992 c. 5.	The Social Security Administration Act 1992.	In section 170(5), in the definition of "the relevant enactments", paragraph (ab).

FINANCE ACT 2001

(2001 Chapter 9)

[*11th May 2001*]

PART 5 – MISCELLANEOUS AND SUPPLEMENTARY PROVISIONS

MISCELLANEOUS

107 Interest on unpaid tax, etc.: foot-and-mouth disease

107(1) This section applies in any case where, in exercise of their powers of care and management, the Commissioners of Inland Revenue agree that, by reason of circumstances arising as a result of the outbreak of foot-and-mouth disease, the payment of tax by a person may be deferred.

For this purpose **"tax"** includes any amount chargeable by way of tax, or as a result of the non-payment of tax, in respect of which interest would, apart from this section, be chargeable.

107(2) Where this section applies no interest on the amount deferred shall be chargeable in respect of the period–

(a) beginning with 31st January 2001 or, if the Commissioners so direct in any case, any later date from which the agreement for deferred payment has effect, and

(b) ending with the date on which the agreement for deferred payment ceases to have effect.

107(3) An agreement for deferred payment ceases to have effect at the end of the period of deferment specified in the agreement, subject as follows.

An agreement for deferred payment shall be treated as not ceasing to have effect if, or to the extent that, the Commissioners agree (whether before or after the end of the period of deferment specified in the agreement) to extend that period by reason of circumstances arising as a result of the outbreak of foot-and-mouth disease.

107(4) For the purposes of subsection (3) as it applies to an agreement for payment by instalments, the period of deferment in relation to each instalment ends with the date on or before which that instalment is to be paid.

But if any instalment is not paid by the agreed date and the Commissioners do not agree in accordance with that subsection to extend the period of deferment, the whole agreement shall be treated as ceasing to have effect on that date.

107(5) This section shall cease to have effect on a date specified by the Treasury by order made by statutory instrument.

This is without prejudice to its continued operation in relation to an agreement for deferred payment made by the Commissioners before the specified date.

107(6) This section applies–

(a) whether the agreement for deferred payment was made before or after the passing of this Act, and

(b) whether the agreement for deferred payment was made before or after the amount to which it relates became due and payable.

107(7) If in any case the Commissioners are satisfied that, although no agreement for deferred payment such as is mentioned in subsection (1) was made, such an agreement could have been made, this section shall apply as if such an agreement had been made.

The terms of the notional agreement shall be assumed to be such as the Commissioners are satisfied would have been agreed in the circumstances.

Commencement Date – S. 107 (as modified for NIC purposes) came into effect on 12 May 2001 by virtue of SI 2001/1818.

Cross references – SI 2001/1818: application of FA 2001, s. 107 for the purposes of Class 1, Class 1A and Class 1B contributions.

SOCIAL SECURITY FRAUD ACT 2001

(2001 Chapter 11) [*11th May 2001*]

ARRANGEMENT OF SECTIONS

OBTAINING AND SHARING INFORMATION

1 Additional powers to obtain information

1(1) The Administration Act shall be amended as follows.

1(2) [Amends SSAA 1992, s. 109B(1)(a) and inserts SSAA, 1992, s. 109B(2A) to (2F).]

1(3) [Substitutes SSAA 1992, s. 109B(5).]

1(4) [Inserts SSAA 1992, s. 109B (6), (7).]

1(5) [Not relevant to National Insurance contributions.]

1(6) [Amends SSAA 1992, s. 111(1)(a).]

1(7) [Amends SSAA 1992, s. 121DA(5).]

1(8) [Amends SSAA 1992, s. 121DA(7).]

1(9) [Inserts SSAA 1992, s. 190(1)(aza).]

Commencement Date – S. 1(1)–(3), (5)–(8) came into force on 30 April 2002 by virtue of SI 2002/1222.
S. 1(4) and (9) came into force on 26 February 2002 by virtue of SI 2002/403.

2 Electronic access to information

2(1) [Inserts SSAA 1992, s. 190BA.]

2(2) [Not relevant to National Insurance contributions.]

2(3) [Amends SSAA 1992, s. 111.]

Notes – S. 2 came into force on 30 April 2002 by virtue of SI 2002/1222.

3 Code of practice about use of information powers

3(1) The Secretary of State shall issue a code of practice relating to the exercise of–

(a) the powers that are exercisable by an authorised officer under section 109B of the Administration Act in relation to the persons mentioned in subsection (2A) of that section; and

(b) the powers conferred on an authorised officer by sections 109BA and 110AA of that Act.

3(2) The Secretary of State may from time to time–

(a) revise the whole or any part of the code for the time being in force under this section; and

(b) issue a revised code.

3(3) Before issuing or revising the code of practice under this section, the Secretary of State shall–

(a) prepare and publish a draft of the code, or of the revised code; and

(b) consider any representations made to him about the draft;

and the Secretary of State may incorporate in the code he issues any modifications made by him to his proposals after their publication.

3(4) The Secretary of State shall lay before each House of Parliament the code of practice, and every revised code, issued by him under this section.

3(5) The code of practice issued under this section and any revisions of the code shall come into force at the time at which the code or, as the case may be, the revised code is issued by the Secretary of State.

3(6) An authorised officer exercising any power in relation to which provision must be made by the code of practice under this section shall have regard, in doing so, to the provisions (so far as they are applicable) of the code for the time being in force under this section.

3(7) A failure on the part of any person to comply with any provision of the code of practice for the time being in force under this section shall not of itself render him liable to any civil or criminal proceedings.

3(8) The code of practice for the time being in force under this section shall be admissible in evidence in any civil or criminal proceedings.

3(9) In this section **"authorised officer"** has the same meaning as in Part 6 of the Administration Act.

Commencement Date – S. 3 came into force on 28 January 2002 by virtue of SI 2002/117.

4 Arrangements for payments in respect of information

4(1) It shall be the duty of the Secretary of State to ensure that such arrangements (if any) are in force as he thinks appropriate for requiring or authorising, in such cases as he thinks fit, the making of such payments as he considers appropriate in respect of compliance with relevant obligations by any of the following–

(a) a credit reference agency (within the meaning given by section 145(8) of the Consumer Credit Act 1974 (C. 39)) or any servant or agent of such an agency;

(b) a person providing a telecommunications service (within the meaning of the Regulation of Investigatory Powers Act 2000 (C. 23)) or any servant or agent of such a person;

(c) a water undertaker or a water and sewerage authority constituted under section 62 of the Local Government etc. (Scotland) Act 1994 (C. 39) or any servant or agent of such an undertaker or authority,

(d) any person who (within the meaning the Gas Act 1986 (C. 44)) supplies gas conveyed through pipes, or any servant or agent of such a person;

(e) any person who (within the meaning of the Electricity Act 1989 (C. 29)) supplies electricity conveyed by distribution systems, or any servant or agent of such a person;

(f) any person added to the list of persons falling within subsection (2A) of section 109B of the Administration Act by an order under subsection (6) of that section, or any person's servant or agent who falls within that subsection by virtue of such an order.

4(2) In subsection (1) **"relevant obligation"**–

(a) in relation to a person falling within paragraph (a), (b) or (f) of that subsection, means–

(i) an obligation to provide information in pursuance of a requirement imposed on that person under section 109B of the Administration Act by virtue only of his falling within subsection (2A) of that section; or

(ii) any obligation to comply, for the purpose of enabling an authorised officer to obtain information which might otherwise be obtained by the imposition of such a requirement, with any requirements imposed on that person under section 109BA or 110AA of that Act;

and

(b) in relation to a person falling within any of paragraphs (c) to (e) of that subsection, means any obligation to provide information in pursuance of a requirement imposed by such an exercise of the powers conferred by section 109BA of that Act as is mentioned in subsection (2D) of that section.

4(3) For the purpose of complying with his duty under this section, the Secretary of State may make arrangements for payments to be made out of money provided by Parliament.

4(4) It shall be the duty of an authority administering housing benefit or council tax benefit to comply with such general or specific directions as to the making of payments as may be given by the Secretary of State in accordance with any arrangements for the time being in force for the purposes of subsection (1).

Commencement Date – S. 4 came into force on 30 April 2002 by virtue of SI 2002/1222.

5 Exchange of information with overseas authorities

5(1) [Inserts SSAA 1992, s. 179A.]

5(2) [Not relevant to National Insurance contributions.]

Commencement Date – S. 5 came into force on 14 February 2003 by virtue of SI 2003/273.

12 Consequential amendments

12(1) [Not relevant to National Insurance contributions.]

12(2) [Not relevant to National Insurance contributions.]

12(3) [Amends SSAA 1992, s. 170(5).]

Commencement Date – S. 12 came into force on 1 April 2002 by virtue of SI 2001/3689.

OFFENCES

16 Offence of failing to notify a change of circumstances

16(1), (2) [Amends SSAA 1992, s. 111A(1); inserts SSAA 1992, s. 111A(1A)–(1G).]

16(3) [Substitutes SSAA 1992, s. 112(1A).]

Commencement Date – S. 16 came into force with effect from 26 September 2001 for the purposes of making regulations and 18 October 2001 for all other purposes by virtue of SI 2001/3251.

17 Time limit for proceedings in Scotland

17 [Inserts SSAA 1992, s. 116(7).]

Commencement Date – S. 17 came into force on 30 April 2002 by virtue of SI 2002/1222.

SUPPLEMENTAL

18 Meaning of "the Administration Act"

18 In this Act **"the Administration Act"** means the Social Security Administration Act 1992 (C. 5).

Commencement Date – S. 18 came into force on 30 April 2002 by virtue of SI 2002/1222.

19 Repeals

19 The enactments mentioned in the Schedule to this Bill (which include some spent provisions) are hereby repealed to the extent specified in the third column of that Schedule.

Commencement Date – S. 19 came into force on 30 April 2002 by virtue of SI 2002/1222.

20 Commencement

20(1) The preceding provisions of this Act shall come into force on such day as the Secretary of State may by order made by statutory instrument appoint.

20(2) Subject to subsection (3), different days may be appointed under this section for different purposes.

20(3) The power under this section to appoint a day for the coming into force of the provisions of sections 1 and 2 shall not authorise the appointment for those purposes of any day before the issue of the code of practice that must be issued under section 3.

Commencement Date – For commencement dates, see notes to individual sections.

21 Short title and extent

21(1) This Act may be cited as the Social Security Fraud Act 2001.

21(2) Sections 5(2), 7, 10, 11, 12(3), 13 and 20, and this section, extend to Northern Ireland; and the other provisions of this Act do not so extend.

SOCIAL SECURITY CONTRIBUTIONS (SHARE OPTIONS) ACT 2001

(2001 Chapter 20)

[*11th May 2001*]

ARRANGEMENT OF SECTIONS

1 Notices relating to share options acquired before 19th May 2000

1(1) Where–

(a) a right to acquire shares in a body corporate was obtained by any person in the period beginning with 6th April 1999 and ending with 19th May 2000,

(b) that right is one to which subsection (2) applies,

(c) a notice in respect of that right is given in accordance with the following provisions of this section to the Inland Revenue before the end of the period of ninety-two days beginning with the day on which this Act is passed,

liability to contributions in respect of gains realised after 7th November 2000 on the exercise, assignment or release of that right shall be determined in accordance with section 2.

1(2) This subsection applies to a right obtained by any person in the period mentioned in subsection (1)(a) if–

(a) were a gain to be realised after the passing of this Act on the exercise, assignment or release of that right, the gain would or (if circumstances changed) might be one falling, by virtue of section 4(4)(a) of the Contributions and Benefits Act, to be treated for the purposes of that Act as remuneration derived from that person's employment; or

(b) a gain that has been realised after 7th November 2000 and before the passing of this Act on any exercise, assignment or release of that right has fallen, by virtue of section 4(4)(a) of that Act, to be so treated.

1(3) The person who may give a notice under this section in respect of any right to which subsection (2) applies by virtue of paragraph (a) of that subsection is–

(a) where neither of the following paragraphs apply, the person who would be the secondary contributor in relation to any liability to pay secondary Class 1 contributions in respect of a gain realised on an exercise, assignment or release, of that right on the day of the notice;

(b) where an election for the purposes of paragraph 3B(1) of Schedule 1 to the Contributions and Benefits Act which is in force on the day of the notice would relate to the whole of any such gain–

(i) the person on whom (apart from this Act) any such liability would fall by virtue of the election; or

(ii) the secondary contributor on whom (apart from this Act) any such liability would fall were no election in force;

(c) where an election for the purposes of paragraph 3B(1) of that Schedule which is in force on the day of the notice would relate to only a part of any such gain, the persons mentioned in paragraph (b)(i) and (ii), acting jointly.

1(4) The person who may give a notice under this section in respect of any right to which subsection (2) applies by virtue of paragraph (b) of that subsection is–

(a) the person on whom (apart from this Act) the liability for secondary Class 1 contributions payable in respect of the gain mentioned in that paragraph did fall; and

(b) if different parts of that liability fell (apart from this Act) on different persons, those persons acting jointly.

1(5) A notice under this section in respect of any right–

(a) must be given in writing or by such electronic means as may be authorised by regulations made by the Inland Revenue;

(b) must contain such matters and be in such form as may be required by any such regulations; and

(c) once given, shall be irrevocable.

1(6) For the purposes of this Act where, in the case of any right to acquire shares, the person entitled or (if there is more than one) each of the persons entitled to give a notice under this section in respect of that right is a person whose liability by virtue of the giving of such a notice to pay a special contribution under section 2 in respect of that right would be nil, that person or, as the case may be, each of those persons acting jointly shall be deemed–

(a) to have given such a notice in respect of that right in accordance with this section and immediately before the end of the period specified in subsection (1)(c);

(b) to have accompanied that notice with a notification to the Inland Revenue that the liability arising by virtue of that notice was nil; and

(c) to have given that notification in the belief that the facts reasonably ascertainable by him at the time at which he is deemed to have given it were grounds for giving it.

Commencement Date – S. 1 came into effect on 11 May 2001 (Royal Assent).

Cross references – ITEPA 2003, s. 482(2): deductible amount in respect of special contribution made by employee.
SSCBA 1992, s. 4(4)(a): gain on unapproved share option charged to tax in accordance with ITEPA 2003, s. 479 and s. 480 treated as remuneration for Class 1 NIC purposes.
SSCBA 1992, Sch. 1, para. 3B: election to transfer all or part of legal liability for secondary NIC to employee.
SI 2001/1817, reg. 3: matters to be contained in notices under s.1.
SI 2001/1817, reg. 4: form and manner of giving notices under s. 1.
SI 2001/1817, reg. 10: records to be maintained where notice given under s.1.

2 Effect of notice under s. 1

2(1) Subject to subsections (3) and (4) and section 3, where liability to contributions in respect of gains realised after 7th November 2000 on the exercise, assignment or release of any right falls under section 1 to be determined in accordance with this section–

(a) no liability to pay any Class 1 contributions in respect of any gain realised after the passing of this Act shall arise on the exercise, assignment or release of that right;

(b) any liability to pay Class 1 contributions in respect of any gain realised after 7th November 2000 and before the passing of this Act on any exercise, assignment or release of that right shall be deemed never to have arisen; and

(c) the person who gave the notice under that section in respect of that right shall become liable to pay a special contribution in respect of that right under this section.

2(2) The amount of the special contribution in respect of any right shall be–

(a) 12.2 per cent. of the amount (if any) in respect of which Class 1 contributions would have been payable by virtue of section 4(4)(a) of the Contributions and Benefits Act if the right had been exercised in full on 7th November 2000 without the giving of any further consideration for the shares acquired by the exercise of that right; or

(b) where there is no such amount, nil.

2(3) Neither paragraph (a) nor paragraph (b) of subsection (1) shall apply in relation to any liability to pay Class 1 contributions in respect of so much of any gain realised on the assignment or release of a right as is equal to the amount (if any) by which the first of the following amounts exceeds the second, that is to say–

(a) the amount of any valuable consideration given for the assignment or release; and

(b) the amount which (in accordance with the provisions of section 479 of the Income Tax (Earnings and Pensions) Act 2003) would have been taken to be the amount of the gain realised by an exercise in full of that right immediately before the time of its assignment or release (less any deductible amounts under section 480(1) to (6) of that Act).

2(4) Subject to subsection (5), where–

(a) a person becomes liable to pay to the Inland Revenue a special contribution under this section in respect of any right, but

(b) *that liability is not discharged* before the end of the period of ninety-two days beginning with the day on which this Act is passed,

the Contributions and Benefits Act and this Act shall have effect as if no notice had been given under section 1 of this Act in respect of that right.

2(5) If it appears to the Inland Revenue that a person who has given a notice under section 1 in respect of any right and who would (but for subsection (4) of this section), be liable by virtue of that notice to pay a special contribution under this section–

(a) did, within the period of ninety-two days mentioned in that subsection, make a payment in respect of that liability to the Inland Revenue of an amount which he had reasonable grounds for believing was the correct amount of his liability,

(b) did, within that period, give notification to the Inland Revenue, in the belief on reasonable grounds that it was correct, that the liability arising by virtue of that notice was nil, or

(c) has a reasonable excuse for having failed to do either of those things within that period,

the Inland Revenue may, if they think fit, direct that, in relation to that notice, subsection (1) of section 1 and subsection (4) of this section are to be treated as having had effect with the period of ninety-two days mentioned in those subsections extended by such further period as they may determine.

2(6) A decision as to the giving or refusal of a direction under subsection (5) shall be made by an officer of the same description and be subject to the same rights of appeal as any decision, to which the giving of the direction is or would be relevant, as to whether a person is or has been liable to pay contributions of any particular class.

2(7) Where paragraph (b) of subsection (1) applies in relation to any liability to pay Class 1 contributions and amounts have already been paid to the Inland Revenue in respect of that liability before the passing of this Act–

(a) all such repayments shall be made as may be necessary by virtue of that paragraph; but

(b) any amount which it would otherwise be necessary to repay in respect of a secondary Class 1 contribution paid by a person who has become liable to pay a special contribution under this section may be retained and set against any undischarged liability of his to pay that special contribution.

Commencement Date – S. 2 came into effect on 11 May 2001 (Royal Assent).

History – In s. 2(3)(b), reference to ITEPA 2003, s. 479 substituted for reference to ICTA 1988, s. 135(3)(a) by ITEPA 2003, s. 722 and Sch. 6, para. 260, with effect for the year 2003–04 and subsequent tax years.
In s. 2(3)(b), words in parentheses after "release" inserted by FA 2003, Sch. 22, para. 56 with effect on and after 1 September 2003.

Cross references – ITEPA 2003, s. 479 and s. 480: gains by directors and employees from share options.
ITEPA 2003, s. 481(4): deductible amount in respect of secondary Class 1 contributions met by employee.
ITEPA 2003, s. 482: deductible amount in respect of special contribution made by employee.

3 Special provision for roll-overs

3(1) This section applies where–

(a) a right to acquire shares in a body corporate was obtained by any person in the period beginning with 6th April 1999 and ending with 19th May 2000 (**"the original right"**); and

(b) the original right is or has been assigned or released (whether before or after the passing of this Act) for a consideration that consists of or includes another right (**"the replacement right"**) to acquire shares in that or any other body corporate.

3(2) If the replacement right or any subsequent replacement right was obtained on or before 7th November 2000, that right shall be treated for the purposes of sections 1 and 2 and this section, but subject to subsection (5), as a right obtained in the period beginning with 6th April 1999 and ending with 19th May 2000.

3(3) Where the replacement right is or has been obtained after 7th November 2000 a notice may be given under section 1 in respect of the original right, notwithstanding that the assignment or release of that right was before the giving of the notice.

3(4) The liability by virtue of section 2(3) to pay Class 1 contributions in respect of a gain realised on the assignment or release of the original right shall be determined–

(a) as if (notwithstanding anything in section 483(1) to (4) of the Income Tax (Earnings and Pensions) Act 2003) the replacement right were or, as the case may be, were part of the valuable consideration given for the assignment or release; and

(b) as if the value of so much of that consideration as is represented by the replacement right were equal to whichever is the smaller of the following amounts–

  (i) the amounts which (in accordance with the provisions of section 479 of that Act) would have been taken to be the gain realised by an exercise in full of the original right immediately before the time of its assignment or release (less any deductible amounts under section 480(1) to (6) of that Act); and

  (ii) the amount which (in accordance with those provisions) would have been taken to be the amount of the gain realised by an exercise in full of the replacement right at that time which falls immediately after it is given in consideration of the assignment or release.

3(5) Paragraphs (a) and (b) of section 2(1) shall not, where this section applies–

(a) prevent a liability to pay Class 1 contributions from arising after the passing of this Act in respect of any gain realised on the exercise, assignment or release of the replacement right or of any subsequent replacement right, or

(b) have the effect of deeming any such liability not to have arisen on any such gain,

but those paragraphs shall have effect (instead) as if they provided for the amount of any such liability to be determined, or to be deemed to have been determined, or to be deemed to have been determined in accordance with the following provisions of this section.

3(6) Subject to subsection (7), in relation to the replacement right or any subsequent right, section 483(1) to (3) of the Income Tax (Earnings and Pensions) Act 2003 (application of Chapter 5 of Part 7 where share option exchanged for another) shall be deemed to have effect (or, as the case may be, to have had effect) for the purposes of the determination mentioned in subsection (5) of this section–

(a) as if that section had effect (or, as the case may be, had had effect) in relation to that right to the extent only that it is a right to acquire additional shares; and

(b) as if the value of the consideration for the grant of the original right had been nil.

3(7) Where–

(a) the whole or any part of any consideration given for the assignment or release of the replacement right or of any subsequent replacement right does not (or did not) comprise a subsequent replacement right, and

(b) as a consequence, a gain would (but for this Act) be taken for the purposes of Chapter 5 of Part 7 of the Income Tax (Earnings and Pensions) Act 2003 to be realised (or to have been realised) on that assignment or release,

that gain shall be taken for the purposes of the determination mentioned in subsection (5) to be (or, as the case may be, to have been) equal to the amount in respect of which liability to pay Class 1 contributions would have been preserved, on the assumptions mentioned in subsection (8), by virtue of section 2(3) (read with subsection (4) of this section) or, if no such liability would have been so preserved, to nil.

3(8) Those assumptions are–

(a) that (subject to paragraph (c)) the right assigned or released is a right the liability to pay Class 1 contributions in respect of which is a liability to which section 2(1)(a) or (b) applied;

(b) that references in subsection (4) of this section to the original right and to the replacement right are references, respectively, to the right comprised in the consideration for the assignment or release; and

(c) that so much of the right assigned or released as is a right to acquire additional shares is to be disregarded for the purposes of both section 2(3) and subsection (4) of this section.

3(9) Nothing in the preceding provisions of this section shall limit or remove, or be deemed to have limited or removed, any liability to pay Class 1 contributions in respect of a gain arising on the exercise, assignment or release of the replacement right, or of any subsequent replacement right, in any case in which the right in question or that gain derives (directly or indirectly) from a transaction the purpose, or one of the main purposes, of which was to make use of the provisions of this Act to avoid the payment of such contributions in respect of a benefit conferred after 19th May 2000.

3(10) For the purposes of this section shares are additional shares, in relation to any right (**"the new right"**) constituting or comprised in the consideration for the assignment or release of another right (**"the old right"**), to the extent that they are shares obtainable in exercise of the new right in addition to shares obtainable in exercise of the new right whose market value at the relevant time was, taken together, equal to that of all the shares (other than any that were themselves additional shares) which were obtainable by the exercise of the old right.

3(11) For the purposes of subsection (10) shares obtainable by the exercise of the new right shall be taken to have a value that matches the value of the shares obtainable in exercise of the old right to the extent, and to the extent only, that the following amounts are the same–

(a) the amount which (in accordance with the provisions of section 479 of the Income Tax (Earnings and Pensions) Act 2003) would be taken to be the amount of the gain realised by an exercise of the new right at the relevant time (assuming it to be exerciseable at that time) for obtaining the shares (less any deductible amounts under section 480(1) to (6)); and

(b) the amount which would have been taken (in accordance with those provisions) to be the gain realised by a full exercise of the old right immediately before the time of its assignment or release;

and in this subsection **"the relevant time"**, in relation to the new right, means the time which falls immediately after it is given in consideration of the assignment or release of the old right.

3(12) Where any question arises for the purposes of this Act, in relation to any partial exercise, assignment or release of any right, whether the shares obtainable under so much of the right as has been exercised, assigned or released were additional shares, it shall be assumed that the right in so far as it is a right to acquire additional shares must be exercised, assigned or released before the exercise, assignment or release of any part of that right that is a right to acquire shares that are not additional shares.

3(13) All such apportionments as may be necessary shall be made in determining for the purposes of this section, in a case in which the number of additional shares cannot be a whole number, to what extent a liability to pay Class 1 contributions arises in relation to the exercise, assignment or release of a right to acquire any such shares.

3(14) Nothing in this section shall apply (where the replacement right was granted on or before 7th November 2000) for determining the amount of any special contribution payable under section 2.

3(15) Where subsection (5) applies in relation to any liability to pay Class 1 contributions and amounts have already been paid to the Inland Revenue in respect of that liability before the passing of this Act–

(a) all such repayments shall be made as may be necessary by virtue of that subsection; but

(b) any amount which it would otherwise be necessary to repay in respect of a secondary Class 1 contribution paid by a person who has become liable to pay a special contribution under section 2 may be retained and set against any undischarged liability of his to pay that special contribution.

3(16) In this section references to a subsequent replacement right are references to any right to acquire shares in a body corporate which are or have been obtained by any person as, or as part of, the consideration for the assignment or release by him of the replacement right or of a subsequent replacement right.

Commencement Date – S. 3 came into effect on 11 May 2001 (Royal Assent).

History – In s. 3(4)(a), reference to ITEPA 2003, s. 485(1)–(4) substituted with effect for the year 2003–04 and subsequent tax years.
In s. 3(4)(a), as substituted by ITEPA 2003, reference to ITEPA 2003, s. 483(1)–(4) substituted with effect on and after 1 September 2003.
In s. 3(4)(b)(i) and s. 3(11)(a), reference to ITEPA 2003, s. 479 substituted with effect for the year 2003–04 and subsequent tax years.
In s. 3(4)(b)(i), words in parentheses after "release" inserted by FA 2003, s. 140 and Sch. 22, para. 57 with effect on and after 1 September 2003.
S. 3(6) substituted by ITEPA 2003, s. 722 and Sch. 6, para. 261(4), with effect for the year 2003–04 and subsequent tax years.
In s. 3(6), reference to ITEPA 2003, s. 483(1)–(3) substituted with effect on and after 1 September 2003.
In s. 3(7)(b), reference to ITEPA 2003, Ch. 5, Pt. 7 substituted with effect for the year 2003–04 and subsequent tax years.
In s. 3(11)(a), words in parentheses after "shares" inserted by ITEPA 2003, s. 140 and Sch. 22, para. 57 with effect on and after 1 September 2003.

Cross references – ITEPA 2003, s. 479 and s. 480: gains by directors and employees from share options.
ITEPA 2003, s. 483– s. 486; share option gains – supplementary provisions.

4 Consequential changes to tax relief provisions

4 [Repealed by ITEPA 2003, s. 724 and Sch. 8, Pt. 1.]

Commencement Date – S. 4 came into effect on 11 May 2001 (Royal Assent).

History – S. 4 repealed by ITEPA 2003, s. 724 and Sch. 8, Pt. 1, with effect for the year 2003–04 and subsequent tax years.

Notes – S. 4(1) was rewritten into the provisions of ITEPA 2003, s. 482(2)–(4).
S. 4(2) was rewritten into the provisions of ITEPA 2003, s. 482(1).
S. 4(3) was rewritten into the provisions of ITEPA 2003, s. 481(4) and s. 482(5).
S. 4(4) was unnecessary and was not rewritten into the provisions of ITEPA 2003.

5 Interpretation

5(1) In this Act–

"the Administration Act" means–

(a) in the application of this Act to Great Britain, the Social Security Administration Act 1992; and

(b) in the application of this Act to Northern Ireland, the Social Security Administration (Northern Ireland) Act 1992 (c. 8);

"the Contributions and Benefits Act" means–

(a) in the application of this Act to Great Britain, the Social Security Contributions and Benefits Act 1992 (c. 4); and

(b) in the application of this Act to Northern Ireland, the Social Security Contributions and Benefits (Northern Ireland) Act 1992 (c. 7).

5(2) In this Act–

(a) a reference to shares in a body corporate includes a reference to stock in that body corporate and to securities issued by that body corporate;

(b) a reference to the release of a right includes a reference to agreeing to a restriction of the exercise of the right; and

(c) references to the assignment or release of a right to acquire shares, and to gains realised on such an assignment or release, shall be construed as if section 477(6) of the Income Tax (Earnings and Pensions) Act 2003 applied for the purposes of this Act as it applies for the purposes of Chapter 5 of Part 7 of that Act.

5(3) Where any assumption that a right has been exercised at any time is made for the purposes of any provision of this Act, that assumption shall be taken to include the assumption that that right was capable of being exercised at that time.

5(4) A special contribution under section 2 shall be treated for the purposes of any provision made by or under any enactment–

(a) as a contribution of a class provided for by the Contributions and Benefits Act; and

(b) as due at the end of the period of ninety-two days beginning with the day on which this Act is passed;

and any reference in Schedule 1 to that Act or in any of the provisions of the Administration Act to a Class 1A contribution shall have effect as if it included a reference to a special contribution under section 2 of this Act.

5(5) This Act shall be construed, and the provisions of the Contributions and Benefits Act shall have effect, as if this section were contained in Part I of that Act.

Commencement Date – S. 5 came into effect on 11 May 2001 (Royal Assent).

History – In s. 5(2)(c), as originally enacted, reference to ITEPA 2003, s. 483(1) and Ch. 5, Pt. 7 substituted with effect for the year 2003–04 and subsequent tax years.

In s. 5(2)(c), as amended by ITEPA 2003, reference to ITEPA 2003, s. 477(6) substituted with effect on and after 1 September 2003.

Statutory instruments – SI 2001/1817: made under s. 5(3).

6 Short title and extent

6(1) This Act may be cited as the Social Security Contributions (Share Options) Act 2001.

6(2) This Act extends to Northern Ireland.

Commencement Date – S. 5 came into effect on 11 May 2001 (Royal Assent).

STATE PENSION CREDIT ACT 2002

(2002 Chapter 16)

[*25th June 2002*]

ARRANGEMENT OF SECTIONS

SCHEDULES

MISCELLANEOUS AND SUPPLEMENTARY

13 Transitional provisions

13(1) The Secretary of State may by regulations make such transitional provision, consequential provision or savings as he considers necessary or expedient for the purposes of, or in connection with,–

(a) the coming into force of any of the state pension credit provisions of this Act; or

(b) the operation of any enactment repealed or amended by any of those provisions during any period when the repeal or amendment is not wholly in force.

13(2) The provision that may be made by regulations under this section includes in particular–

(a) provision for a person who attains or has attained the qualifying age on or before the appointed day and who immediately before that day is entitled to income support–

(i) to be treated as having been awarded on, and with effect as from, that day state pension credit of an amount specified in or determined in accordance with the regulations; or

(ii) to be treated as having made a claim for state pension credit; and

(b) provision for an assessed income period under section 6 of such length as may be specified in or determined in accordance with the regulations (which may be longer than the maximum period provided for by section 9(1)) to have effect in the case of a person who attains or has attained the qualifying age on or before the appointed day.

13(3) In this section–

"the appointed day" means such day as the Secretary of State may by order appoint;

"the state pension credit provisions of this Act" means this Act other than section 18.

Commencement Date – S. 13 comes into force on 2 July 2002 for the purposes only of exercising any powers to make regulations and orders, by virtue of SI 2002/1691.

14 Minor and consequential amendments

14 Schedule 2 (which makes minor and consequential amendments relating to state pension credit) shall have effect.

Commencement Date – S. 14 (except in so far as it relates to Sch. 2, para. 3) came into force on 2 July 2002 for the purposes only of exercising any powers to make regulations and orders, by virtue of SI 2002/1691.

S. 14 (in so far as it relates to Sch. 2, para. 3) came into force on 27 January 2003 for the purposes only of exercising any powers to make regulations and orders, by virtue of SI 2003/83.

15 Income and capital

15 [Not relevant to National Insurance contributions.]

16 Retirement pension income

16 [Not relevant to National Insurance contributions.]

17 Other interpretation provisions

17(1) In this Act–

"the Administration Act" means the Social Security Administration Act 1992 (c. 5);

"assessed income period" shall be construed in accordance with sections 6 and 9;

"appropriate minimum guarantee" shall be construed in accordance with section 2(3);

"capital" shall be construed in accordance with section 15;

"claimant" means a claimant for state pension credit;

"the Contributions and Benefits Act" means the Social Security Contributions and Benefits Act 1992 (c. 4);

"couple" means–

(a) a man and woman who are married to each other and are members of the same household;

(b) a man and woman who are not married to each other but are living together as husband and wife otherwise than in prescribed circumstances;

(c) two people of the same sex who are civil partners of each other and are members of the same household; or

(d) two people of the same sex who are not civil partners of each other but are living together as if they were civil partners otherwise than in prescribed circumstances;

"earnings" has the same meaning as in Parts 1 to 5 of the Contributions and Benefits Act (see sections 3(1) and 112, and the definition of **"employment"** in section 122, of that Act);

"element", in relation to the claimant's retirement provision, shall be construed in accordance with section 7(6);

"entitled", in relation to state pension credit, shall be construed in accordance with–

(a) this Act,

(b) section 1 of the Administration Act (entitlement to be dependent on making of claim etc), and

(c) section 27 of the Social Security Act 1998 (c. 14) (restrictions on entitlement to benefit in certain cases of error),

(and, in relation to any other benefit within the meaning of section 1 of the Administration Act or section 27 of the Social Security Act 1998, in accordance with that section or (as the case may be) both of those sections in addition to any other conditions relating to that benefit);

"foreign social security benefit" means any benefit, allowance or other payment which is paid under the law of a country outside the United Kingdom and is in the nature of social security;

"foreign war disablement pension" means any retired pay, pension, allowance or similar payment granted by the government of a country outside the United Kingdom–

(a) in respect of disablement arising from forces' service or war injury; or

(b) corresponding in nature to any retired pay or pension to which section 641 of the Income Tax (Earnings and Pensions) Act 2003 applies;

"foreign war widow's or widower's pension" means any pension, allowance or similar payment granted to a widow or widower by the government of a country outside the United Kingdom–

(a) in respect of a death due to forces' service or war injury; or

(b) corresponding in nature to a pension or allowance for a widow or widower under any scheme mentioned in section 641(1)(e) or (f) of the Income Tax (Earnings and Pensions) Act 2003;

"guarantee credit" shall be construed in accordance with sections 1 and 2;

"income" shall be construed in accordance with section 15;

"married couple" means a man and a woman who are married to each other and are members of the same household;

"occupational pension scheme" has the meaning given by section 1 of the Pension Schemes Act 1993 (c. 48);

"pensionable age" has the meaning given by the rules in paragraph 1 of Schedule 4 to the Pensions Act 1995 (c. 26) (equalisation of pensionable ages for men and women);

"personal pension scheme" means a personal pension scheme–

(a) as defined in section 1 of the Pension Schemes Act 1993; or

(b) as defined in section 1 of the Pension Schemes (Northern Ireland) Act 1993 (c. 49);

"PPF periodic payments" means–

(a) any periodic compensation payments made in relation to a person, payable under the pension compensation provisions as specified in section 162(2) of the Pensions Act 2004 or Article 146(2) of the Pensions (Northern Ireland) Order 2005 (the pension compensation provisions); or

(b) any periodic payments made in relation to a person, payable under section 166 of the Pensions Act 2004 or Article 150 of the Pensions (Northern Ireland) Order 2005 (duty to pay scheme benefits unpaid at assessment date etc);

"prescribed" means specified in, or determined in accordance with regulations;

"the qualifying age" has the meaning given by section 1(6);

"regulations" means regulations made by the Secretary of State;

"retirement pension income" shall be construed in accordance with section 16;

"retirement provision" shall be construed in accordance with section 7(6);

"savings credit" shall be construed in accordance with sections 1 and 3;

"social security benefits" means benefits payable under the enactments relating to social security in any part of the United Kingdom;

"standard minimum guarantee" shall be construed in accordance with section 2(3) to (5) and (9);

"unmarried couple" means a man and a woman who are not married to each other but are living together as husband and wife otherwise than in prescribed circumstances;

"war disablement pension" means–

(a) any retired pay, pension or allowance granted in respect of disablement under powers conferred by or under–

(i) the Air Force (Constitution) Act 1917 (c. 51);

(ii) the Personal Injuries (Emergency Provisions) Act 1939 (c. 82);

(iii) the Pensions (Navy, Army, Air Force and Mercantile Marine) Act 1939 (c. 83);

(iv) the Polish Resettlement Act 1947 (c. 19); or

(v) Part 7 or section 151 of the Reserve Forces Act 1980 (c. 9); or

(b) without prejudice to paragraph (a), any retired pay or pension to which any of paragraphs (a) to (f) of section 641(1) of the Income Tax (Earnings and Pensions) Act 2003 applies;

"war widow's or widower's pension" means–

(a) any widow's or widower's pension or allowance granted in respect of a death due to service or war injury and payable by virtue of any enactment mentioned in paragraph (a) of the definition of "war disablement pension"; or

(b) a pension or allowance for a widow or widower granted under any scheme mentioned in section 641(1)(e) or (f) of the Income Tax (Earnings and Pensions) Act 2003;

"working tax credit" means a working tax credit under the Tax Credits Act 2002 to which a person is entitled whether alone or jointly with another.

17(1A) For the purposes of this Act, two people of the same sex are to be regarded as living together as if they were civil partners if, but only if, they would be regarded as living together as husband and wife were they instead two people of the opposite sex.

17(2) Regulations may make provision for the purposes of this Act–

(a) as to circumstances in which persons are to be treated as being or not being members of the same household;

(b) as to circumstances in which persons are to be treated as being or not being severely disabled.

17(3) The following provisions of the Contributions and Benefits Act, namely–

(a) section 172 (references to Great Britain or United Kingdom to include reference to adjacent territorial waters etc), and

(b) section 173 (meaning of attaining an age etc),

shall apply for the purposes of this Act as they apply for the purposes of that Act.

Commencement Date – S. 17 came into force on 2 July 2002 for the purposes only of exercising any powers to make regulations and orders, by virtue of SI 2002/1691.

Prospective amendments – In s. 17(1), definition of "housing credit" inserted by WRA 2012, s. 34 and Sch. 4, para. 7, with effect from a date to be set by order of the Secretary of State. The new definition reads as follows:

""**housing credit**" shall be construed in accordance with sections 1 and 3A;"

In s. 17(1), definition of "regular and substantial caring responsibilities" inserted by WRA 2012, s. 74, with effect from a date to be set by order of the Secretary of State. New definition reads as follows:

""**regular and substantial caring responsibilities**" has such meaning as may be prescribed;"

In s. 17(1), the definition of "working tax credit" repealed by WRA 2012, s. 147 and Sch. 14, Pt. 1, with effect from a date to be set by order of the Secretary of State.

History – In s. 17(1), the definition of "PPF periodic payments" inserted by SI 2006/343, art. 2 and Schedule, with effect from 14 February 2006.

In s. 17(1), the definition of "couple" inserted by the Civil Partnership Act 2004, Sch. 24, para. 142(2), with effect from 5 December 2005 (SI 2005/3175).

In s. 17(1), the definitions of "married couple" and "unmarried couple" omitted by the Civil Partnership Act 2004, Sch. 24, para. 142(4), with effect from 5 December 2005 (SI 2005/3175).

In s. 17(1), the definition of "war widow's or widower's pension" in para. (a) the words "any widow's, widower's or surviving civil partner's" substituted for the words "any widow's or widower's" and in para. (b) the words "widow, widower or surviving civil partner" substituted for the words "widow or widower" by the Civil Partnership Act 2004, Sch. 24, para. 142(5), with effect from 5 December 2005 (SI 2005/3175).

In s. 17(1), the definition of "foreign war widow's or widower's pension" the words "widow, widower or surviving civil partner" substituted for the words "widow or widower" by the Civil Partnership Act 2004, Sch. 24, para. 142(3), with effect from 5 December 2005 (SI 2005/3175).

In s. 17(1), in para. (b) of the definition of "foreign war disablement pension", the words "section 641 of the Income Tax (Earnings and Pensions) Act 2003" substituted for the words "subsection (1) of section 315 of the Income and Corporation Taxes Act 1988 (c. 1)" by ITEPA 2003, Sch. 6, para. 263(2) which has effect for the tax year 2003–04 and subsequent tax years.

In s. 17(1), in para. (b) of the definition of "foreign war widow's or widower's pension", the words "section 641(1)(e) or (f) of the Income Tax (Earnings and Pensions) Act 2003" substituted by ITEPA 2003, Sch. 6, para. 263(3) which has effect for the tax year 2003–04 and subsequent tax years.

In s. 17(1), in para. (b) of the definition of "war disablement pension", the words "any of paragraphs (a) to (f) of section 641(1) of the Income Tax (Earnings and Pensions) Act 2003" substituted for the words "subsection (1) of section 315 of the Income and Corporation Taxes Act 1988 (c. 1)" by ITEPA 2003, Sch. 6, para. 263(4) which has effect for the tax year 2003–04 and subsequent tax years.

In s. 17(1), in para. (b) of the definition of "war widow's or widower's pension", the words "section 641(1)(e) or (f) of the Income Tax (Earnings and Pensions) Act 2003" substituted by ITEPA 2003, Sch. 6, para. 263(5) which has effect for the tax year 2003–04 and subsequent tax years.

S. 17(1A) inserted by the Civil Partnership Act 2004, Sch. 24, para. 143, with effect from 5 December 2005 (SI 2005/3175).

FINAL PROVISIONS

19 Regulations and orders

19(1) Subject to the following provisions of this section, subsections (1), (2) to (5) and (10) of section 175 of the Contributions and Benefits Act (regulations and orders etc) shall apply in relation to any power conferred on the Secretary of State by any provision of this Act to make regulations or an order as they apply in relation to any power conferred on him by that Act to make regulations or an order, but as if for references to that Act (other than references to specific provisions of it) there were substituted references to this Act.

19(2) A statutory instrument containing (whether alone or with other provisions) the first regulations under–

(a) section 2(3)(b), (4) or (6),

(b) section 3(4), (5), (6), (7) or (8),

(c) section 4(3),

(d) section 12, or

(e) section 15(1)(e), (f) or (j), (2), (3), (4) or (6),

shall not be made unless a draft of the instrument has been laid before, and approved by a resolution of, each House of Parliament.

19(3) A statutory instrument–

(a) which contains regulations under this Act (whether alone or with other provisions), and

(b) which is not subject to any requirement that a draft of the instrument be laid before, and approved by a resolution of, each House of Parliament,

shall be subject to annulment in pursuance of a resolution of either House of Parliament.

20 Financial provisions

20(1) There shall be paid out of money provided by Parliament–

(a) any sums payable by way of state pension credit;

(b) any expenditure incurred by the Secretary of State or other government department under or by virtue of this Act; and

(c) any increase attributable to this Act in the sums payable out of money so provided under any other Act.

20(2) There shall be paid into the Consolidated Fund any increase attributable to this Act in the sums which under any other Act are payable into that Fund.

21 Enactments repealed

21 The enactments specified in Schedule 3 to this Act are repealed to the extent there specified.

History – Some repeals of SSA 1998 brought into effect by SI 2003/966 with effect from 6 April 2003.

22 Short title, commencement and extent

22(1) This Act may be cited as the State Pension Credit Act 2002.

22(2) This section and sections 19 and 20 come into force on the passing of this Act.

22(3) Except as provided by subsection (2), this Act shall come into force on such day as the Secretary of State may by order appoint; and different days may be so appointed for different purposes.

22(4) Any order under this section may make such transitional provision as appears to the Secretary of State to be necessary or expedient in connection with the provisions brought into force by the order.

22(5) Any amendment or repeal made by this Act has the same extent as the enactment to which it relates (unless otherwise provided).

22(6) Subject to that, this Act extends to England and Wales and Scotland only.

Notes – For commencement, see History notes at foot of each section.

SCHEDULES

SCHEDULE 1 – ADMINISTRATION

Section 11

Part 1 – Amendments of the Administration Act

INTRODUCTORY

1 Part 1 of the Administration Act (claims, evidence, and regulations about claims and payment) is amended as follows.

ENTITLEMENT DEPENDENT ON MAKING OF CLAIM ETC

2 [Not relevant to National Insurance contributions.]

POWER BY REGULATIONS TO MAKE RULES RELATING TO CLAIMS, TIME LIMITS, EVIDENCE ETC

3 [Not relevant to National Insurance contributions.]

Part 2 – Amendments of the Social Security Act 1998

INTRODUCTORY

4 Part 1 of the Social Security Act 1998 (c. 14) (decisions and appeals) is amended as follows.

USE OF COMPUTERS

5 [Not relevant to National Insurance contributions.]

DECISIONS BY SECRETARY OF STATE

6 [Amends SSA 1998, s. 8.]

Commencement Date – Para. 6 takes effect from 2 July 2002 only for the purposes of exercising any power to make regulations and orders (by virtue of SI 2002/1691) and from 6 April 2003 for all other purposes (by virtue of SI 2003/966).

REGULATIONS WITH RESPECT TO DECISIONS

7 [Amends SSA 1998, s. 11(3).]

Commencement Date – Para. 7 takes effect from 2 July 2002 only for the purposes of exercising any power to make regulations and orders (by virtue of SI 2002/1691) and from 6 April 2003 for all other purposes (by virtue of SI 2003/966).

SUSPENSION OF BENEFIT FOR FAILURE TO FURNISH INFORMATION ETC

8 [Not relevant to National Insurance contributions.]

RESTRICTIONS ON ENTITLEMENT TO BENEFIT IN CASES OF ERROR: DEFINITIONS

9 [Amends SSA 1998, s. 27(7).]

Commencement Date – Para. 9 takes effect from 2 July 2002 for the purpose only of exercising any power to make regulations or orders by virtue of SI 2002/1691.

CORRECTION OF ERRORS AND SETTING ASIDE OF DECISIONS

10 [Amends SSA 1998, s. 28.]

Commencement Date – Para. 10 takes effect from 2 July 2002 for the purpose only of exercising any power to make regulations or orders by virtue of SI 2002/1691 and from 6 April 2003 for all other purposes by virtue of SI 2003/966.

DECISIONS AGAINST WHICH NO APPEAL LIES

11–13 [Not relevant to National Insurance contributions.]

SCHEDULE 2 – MINOR AND CONSEQUENTIAL AMENDMENTS

Section 14

Part 1 – Amendments of the Contributions and Benefits Act

1–11 [Not relevant to National Insurance contributions.]

Part 2 – Amendments of Administration Act

INTERPRETATION OF PART 6: ENFORCEMENT

12 [Amends SSAA 1992, s. 122DA(1).]

Commencement Date – Para. 12 takes effect from 2 July 2002 for the purpose only of exercising any power to make regulations or orders by virtue of SI 2002/1691.

PROVISIONS RELATING TO AGE, DEATH OR MARRIAGE

13 [Amends SSAA 1992, s. 124.]

Commencement Date – Para. 13 takes effect from 2 July 2002 for the purpose only of exercising any power to make regulations or orders by virtue of SI 2002/1691.

REGULATIONS AS TO NOTIFICATION OF DEATH

14 [Amends SSAA 1992, s. 125(1).]

Commencement Date – Para. 14 takes effect from 2 July 2002 for the purpose only of exercising any power to make regulations or orders by virtue of SI 2002/1691.

15–18 [Not relevant to National Insurance contributions.]

ADJUSTMENTS BETWEEN SOCIAL FUND AND OTHER SOURCES OF FINANCE

19 [Amends SSAA 1992, s. 169(1).]

Commencement Date – Para. 19 takes effect from 2 July 2002 for the purpose only of exercising any power to make regulations or orders by virtue of SI 2002/1691.

THE SOCIAL SECURITY ADVISORY COMMITTEE

20 [Amends SSAA 1992, s. 170.]

Commencement Date – Para. 20 takes effect from 2 July 2002 for the purpose only of exercising any power to make regulations or orders by virtue of SI 2002/1691.

RECIPROCAL AGREEMENTS WITH COUNTRIES OUTSIDE THE UNITED KINGDOM

21 [Amends SSAA 1992, s. 179.]

Commencement Date – Para. 21 takes effect from 2 July 2002 for the purpose only of exercising any power to make regulations or orders by virtue of SI 2002/1691.

PAYMENT OF TRAVELLING EXPENSES BY SECRETARY OF STATE

22 [Amends SSAA 1992, s. 180.]

Commencement Date – Para. 22 takes effect from 2 July 2002 for the purpose only of exercising any power to make regulations or orders by virtue of SI 2002/1691.

CERTAIN BENEFITS TO BE INALIENABLE

23 [Not relevant to National Insurance contributions.]

Commencement Date – Para. 23 takes effect from 2 July 2002 for the purpose only of exercising any power to make regulations or orders by virtue of SI 2002/1691.

INTERPRETATION: GENERAL

24 [Amends SSAA 1992, s. 191.]

Commencement Date – Para. 24 takes effect from 2 July 2002 for the purpose only of exercising any power to make regulations or orders by virtue of SI 2002/1691.

NATIONAL INSURANCE CONTRIBUTIONS ACT 2002

(2002 Chapter 19)

[*8th July 2002*]

ARRANGEMENT OF SECTIONS

INCREASES IN CONTRIBUTIONS

1 Primary Class 1 contributions

1(1) [Substitutes SSCBA 1992, s. 8.]

1(2) [Substitues Social Security Contributions and Benefits (Northern Ireland) Act 1992, s. 8.]

2 Secondary Class 1 contributions

2(1) [Substitutes SSCBA 1992, s. 9(2), (3).]

2(2) [Substitutes Social Security Contributions and Benefits (Northern Ireland) Act 1992, s. 9(2), (3).]

3 Class 4 contributions

3(1) [Substitutes SSCBA 1992, s. 15(3).]

3(2) [Substitutes Social Security Contributions and Benefits (Northern Ireland) Act 1992, s. 15(3).]

3(3) [Inserts SSCBA 1992, s. 4(1A).]

3(4) [Inserts Social Security Contributions and Benefits (Northern Ireland) Act 1992, s. 18(1A).]

APPLICATION TOWARDS COST OF NATIONAL HEALTH SERVICE

4 Appropriate national health service allocation: Great Britain

4(1) Section 162 of the Social Security Administration Act 1992 (c. 5) (destination of contributions) is amended as follows.

4(2) [Amends SSAA 1992, s. 162(5).]

4(3) [Inserts SSAA 1992, s. 162(5A).]

5 Appropriate health service allocation: Northern Ireland

5(1) Section 142 of the Social Security Administration (Northern Ireland) Act 1992 (c. 8) (destination of contributions) is amended as follows.

5(2) [Amends Social Security Administration (Northern Ireland) Act 1992, s. 142(5).]

5(3) [Inserts Social Security Administration (Northern Ireland) Act 1992, s. 142(5A).]

SUPPLEMENTARY

6 Consequential amendments

6 Schedule 1 (consequential amendments) has effect.

7 Repeals and revocations

7 Schedule 2 (repeals and revocations) has effect.

8 Short title commencement and extent

8(1) This Act may be cited as the National Insurance Contributions Act 2002.

8(2) This Act has effect in relation to the tax year 2003–04 and subsequent tax years; and for this purpose **"tax year"** has the meaning given by section 122(1) of the Social Security Contributions and Benefits Act 1992 (c. 4).

8(3) The amendments, repeals and revocations made by this Act have the same extent as the provisions to which they relate.

8(4) Subject to that, this Act extends to Northern Ireland (as well as to England and Wales and Scotland).

SCHEDULES

SCHEDULE 1 – CONSEQUENTIAL AMENDMENTS

Section 6

SOCIAL SECURITY CONTRIBUTIONS AND BENEFITS ACT 1992 (C. 4)

1 The Social Security Contributions and Benefits Act 1992 has effect subject to the following amendments.

2 [Amends SSCBA 1992, s. 10(5).]

3 [Amends SSCBA 1992, s. 10A(6).]

4(1) Section 17 (Class 4 contributions: exceptions, deferment etc.) is amended as follows.

4(2) [Amends SSCBA 1992, s. 17(1).]

4(3) [Amends SSCBA 1992, s. 17(4).]

5(1) Section 19 (general power to regulate liability for contributions) is amended as follows.

5(2) [Amends SSCBA 1992, s. 19(1).]

5(3) [Amends SSCBA 1992, s. 19(3).]

5(4) [Amends SSCBA 1992, s. 19(4)(a).]

6 [Amends SSCBA 1992, s. 21(5)(c)(i).]

7(1) Section 22 (earnings factors) is amended as follows.

7(2) [Amends SSCBA 1992, s. 22(1)(a), (2A).]

7(3) [Amends SSCBA 1992, s. 22(3)(a).]

8 [Amends SSCBA 1992, s. 23(3)(a).]

9 [Amends SSCBA 1992, s. 24(2)(a).]

10 [Amends SSCBA 1992, s. 44(6)(za).]

11 [Amends SSCBA 1992, s. 44A(1)(a).]

12(1) Section 122(1) (interpretation) is amended as follows.

12(2) [Amends SSCBA 1992, s. 122(1).]

12(3) [Amends SSCBA 1992, s. 122(1).]

12(4) [Amends SSCBA 1992, s. 122(1).]

13(1) Schedule 1 (supplementary provisions relating to contributions) is amended as follows.

13(2) [Amends SSCBA 1992, Sch. 1, para. 1.]

13(3) [Amends SSCBA 1992, Sch. 1, para. 3(1).]

14(1) Schedule 3 (contribution conditions for entitlement to benefit) is amended as follows.

14(2) [Amends SSCBA 1992, Sch. 3, para. 2(4)(a)(i).]

14(3) [Amends SSCBA 1992, Sch. 3, para. 4(2)(a).]

14(4) [Amends SSCBA 1992, Sch. 3, para. 5(2)(b)(i).]

14(5) [Amends SSCBA 1992, Sch. 3, para. 5(4)(a)(i).]

14(6) [Amends SSCBA 1992, Sch. 3, para. 7(4)(a).]

SOCIAL SECURITY ADMINISTRATION ACT 1992 (C. 5)

15 The Social Security Administration Act 1992 has effect subject to the following amendments.

16 [Amends SSAA 1992, s. 141.]

17 [Amends SSAA 1992, s. 143.]

18 [Amends SSAA 1992, s. 145.]

19 [Amends SSAA 1992, s. 162.]

PENSION SCHEMES ACT 1993 (C. 48)

35 The Pension Schemes Act 1993 has effect subject to the following amendments.

36 [Amends PSA 1993, s. 41(1A).]

37 [Amends PSA 1993, s. 42A(2).]

Prospective amendments – Para. 37 repealed by PA 2007, s. 27 and Sch. 7, Pt. 7, with effect from a date to be appointed under PA 2007, s. 30(2).

38 [Amends PSA 1993, s. 43(1)(b).]

Prospective amendments – Para. 38 repealed by PA 2007, s. 27 and Sch. 7, Pt. 7, with effect from a date to be appointed under PA 2007, s. 30(2).

39 [Amends PSA 1993, s. 48A(1).]

EMPLOYMENT ACT 2002

(2002 Chapter 22)

[*8th July 2002*]

ARRANGEMENT OF SECTIONS

PART 1 – STATUTORY LEAVE AND PAY

CHAPTER 1 – PATERNITY AND ADOPTION

RIGHTS TO LEAVE AND PAY

ADMINISTRATION AND ENFORCEMENT: PAY

CHAPTER 2 – MATERNITY

PART 4 – MISCELLANEOUS AND GENERAL

MISCELLANEOUS

GENERAL

SCHEDULES

PART 1 – STATUTORY LEAVE AND PAY

Chapter 1 – Paternity and Adoption

RIGHTS TO LEAVE AND PAY

2 Statutory paternity pay

2 [Inserts SSCBA 1992, Pt. 12ZA.]

Commencement Date – S. 2 has effect from 8 December 2002, in relation to a person who satisfies the prescribed conditions of entitlement in respect of a child born on or after 6 April 2003, or whose expected week of birth begins on or after that date; or a child matched for the purposes of adoption with a person who is notified of having been matched on or after 6 April 2003, or placed for adoption on or after that date, by virtue of SI 2002/2866 (C. 91), art. 2(2) and Sch. 1, Pt. 2; art. 3 and Sch. 3, para. 1.

4 Statutory adoption pay

4 [Inserts SSCBA 1992, Pt. 12ZB.]

Commencement Date – S. 4 has effect from 8 December 2002, in relation to a person with whom a child is, or is expected to be placed for adoption on or after 6 April 2003, by virtue of SI 2002/2866 (C. 91), art. 2(2) and Sch. 1, Pt. 2; art. 3 and Sch. 3, para. 2.

ADMINISTRATION AND ENFORCEMENT: PAY

7 Funding of employers' liabilities

7(1) The Secretary of State shall by regulations make provision for the payment by employers of statutory paternity pay, statutory adoption pay and statutory shared parental pay to be funded by the Board to such extent as the regulations may specify.

7(2) Regulations under subsection (1) shall–

(a) make provision for a person who has made a payment of statutory paternity pay, statutory adoption pay or statutory shared parental pay to be entitled, except in such circumstances as the regulations may provide, to recover an amount equal to the sum of–

(i) the aggregate of such of those payments as qualify for small employers' relief; and

(ii) an amount equal to 92 per cent of the aggregate of such of those payments as do not so qualify; and

(b) include provision for a person who has made a payment of statutory paternity pay, statutory adoption pay or statutory shared parental pay qualifying for small employers' relief to be entitled, except in such circumstances as the regulations may provide, to recover an additional amount equal to the amount to which the person would have been entitled under section 167(2)(b) of the Social Security Contributions and Benefits Act 1992(corresponding provision for statutory maternity pay) had the payment been a payment of statutory maternity pay.

7(3) For the purposes of subsection (2), a payment of statutory paternity pay, statutory adoption pay or statutory shared parental pay qualifies for small employers' relief if it would have so qualified were it a payment of statutory maternity pay, treating–

(a) the period for which the payment of statutory paternity pay is made,

(b) the payee's adoption pay period, or

(c) the period for which the payment of statutory shared parental pay is made,

as the maternity pay period.

7(4) Regulations under subsection (1) may, in particular–

(a) make provision for funding in advance as well as in arrear;

(b) make provision for funding, or the recovery of amounts due under provision made by virtue of subsection (2)(b), by means of deductions from such amounts for which employers are accountable to the Board as the regulations may provide, or otherwise;

(c) make provision for the recovery by the Board of any sums overpaid to employers under the regulations.

7(5) Where in accordance with any provision of regulations under subsection (1) an amount has been deducted from an employer's contributions payments, the amount so deducted shall (except in such cases as the Secretary of State may by regulations provide) be treated for the purposes of any provision made by or under any enactment in relation to primary or secondary Class 1 contributions–

(a) as having been paid (on such date as may be determined in accordance with the regulations), and

(b) as having been received by the Board,

towards discharging the employer's liability in respect of such contributions.

7(6) Regulations under this section must be made with the concurrence of the Board.

7(7) In this section, **"contributions payments"**, in relation to an employer, means any payments which the employer is required, by or under any enactment, to make in discharge of any liability in respect of primary or secondary Class 1 contributions.

Commencement Date – S. 7 has effect from 8 December 2002, by virtue of SI 2002/2866 (C. 91), art. 2(2) and Sch. 1, Pt. 2.

History – In s. 7(1), the words "statutory paternity pay," substituted for the words "ordinary statutory paternity pay, additional statutory paternity pay and" by Children and Families Act 2014, s. 126(1) and Sch. 7, para. 51(2)(a), with effect from 5 April 2015, subject to the transitional and saving provisions in SI 2014/1640, art. 16 (amendments do not have effect in relation to– (a) children whose expected week of birth ends on or before 4 April 2015; (b) children placed for adoption on or before 4 April 2015) (SI 2014/1640, art. 7).
In s. 7(1), the words "and statutory shared parental pay" inserted by Children and Families Act 2014, s. 126(1) and Sch. 7, para. 51(2)(b), with effect from 30 June 2014 (SI 2014/1640, art. 3).
In s. 7(1), the words "ordinary statutory paternity pay, additional statutory paternity pay" substituted for the words "statutory paternity pay" by Work and Families Act 2006, s. 11 and Sch. 1, para. 50(2), with effect from 3 March 2010 (SI 2010/495, art. 3).
In s. 7(2)(a), the words "statutory paternity pay," substituted for the words "ordinary statutory paternity pay, additional statutory paternity pay or" by Children and Families Act 2014, s. 126(1) and Sch. 7, para. 51(3)(a)(i), with effect from 5 April 2015, subject to the transitional and saving provisions in SI 2014/1640, art. 16 (amendments do not have effect in relation to– (a) children whose expected week of birth ends on or before 4 April 2015; (b) children placed for adoption on or before 4 April 2015) (SI 2014/1640, art. 7).
In s. 7(2)(a), the words "or statutory shared parental pay" inserted by Children and Families Act 2014, s. 126(1) and Sch. 7, para. 51(3)(a)(ii), with effect from 30 June 2014 (SI 2014/1640, art. 3).
In s. 7(2)(b), the words "statutory paternity pay," substituted for the words "ordinary statutory paternity pay, additional statutory paternity pay or" by Children and Families Act 2014, s. 126(1) and Sch. 7, para. 51(3)(b)(i), with effect from 5 April 2015, subject to the transitional and saving provisions in SI 2014/1640, art. 16 (amendments do not have effect in relation to– (a) children whose expected week of birth ends on or before 4 April 2015; (b) children placed for adoption on or before 4 April 2015) (SI 2014/1640, art. 7).
In s. 7(2)(b), the words "or statutory shared parental pay" inserted by Children and Families Act 2014, s. 126(1) and Sch. 7, para. 51(3)(b)(ii), with effect from 30 June 2014 (SI 2014/1640, art. 3).
In s. 7(2), the words "ordinary statutory paternity pay, additional statutory paternity pay" substituted for the words "statutory paternity pay" (in both places) by Work and Families Act 2006, s. 11 and Sch. 1, para. 50(3), with effect from 3 March 2010 (SI 2010/495, art. 3).
In s. 7(3), the words "statutory paternity pay," substituted for the words "ordinary statutory paternitypay, additional statutory paternity pay or" by Children and Families Act 2014, s. 126(1) and Sch. 7, para. 51(4)(a), with effect from 5 April 2015, subject to the transitional and saving provisions in SI 2014/1640, art. 16 (amendments do not have effect in relation to– (a) children whose expected week of birth ends on or before 4 April 2015; (b) children placed for adoption on or before 4 April 2015) (SI 2014/1640, art. 7).
In s. 7(3), the words "or statutory shared parental pay" inserted by Children and Families Act 2014, s. 126(1) and Sch. 7, para. 51(4)(b), with effect from 30 June 2014 (SI 2014/1640, art. 3).
In s. 7(3), the words "treating– (a) the period for which the payment of statutory paternity pay is made, (b) the payee's adoption pay period, or (c) the period for which the payment of statutory shared parental pay is made, as the maternity pay period." substituted for the words "treating the period for which the payment is made, in the case of ordinary statutory paternity pay or additional statutory paternity pay, or the payee's adoption pay period, in the case of statutory adoption pay, as the maternity pay period." by Children and Families Act 2014, s. 126(1) and Sch. 7, para. 51(4)(c), with effect from 30 June 2014, subject to the transitional provisions in SI 2014/1640, art. 9 (amendments do not have effect in relation to– (a) children whose expected week of birth ends on or before 4 April 2015; (b) children placed for adoption on or before 4 April 2015) (SI 2014/1640, art. 3).
In s. 7(3), the words "a payment of ordinary statutory paternity pay, additional statutory paternity pay" substituted for the words "a payment of statutory paternity pay" and the words "in the case of ordinary statutory paternity pay or additional statutory paternity pay" substituted for the words "in the case of statutory paternity pay" by Work and Families Act 2006, s. 11 and Sch. 1, para. 50(4), with effect from 3 March 2010 (SI 2010/495, art. 3).

Statutory instruments – SI 2003/1192: made under s. 7(2)(a), (b), (4)(a), (b), (c), (5).

8 Regulations about payment

8(1) The Secretary of State may make regulations with respect to the payment by employers of statutory paternity pay, statutory adoption pay and statutory shared parental pay.

8(2) Regulations under subsection (1) may, in particular, include provision–

(a) about the records to be kept by employers in relation to payments of statutory paternity pay, statutory adoption pay and statutory shared parental pay, including the length of time for which they are to be retained;

(b) for the production of wages sheets and other documents and records to officers of the Board for the purpose of enabling them to satisfy themselves that statutory paternity pay, statutory adoption pay and statutory shared parental pay have been paid and are being paid, in accordance with the regulations, to employees who are entitled to them;

(c) for requiring employers to provide information to employees (in their itemised pay statements or otherwise);

(d) for requiring employers to make returns to the Board containing such particulars with respect to payments of statutory paternity pay, statutory adoption pay and statutory shared parental pay as the regulations may provide.

8(3) Regulations under subsection (1) must be made with the concurrence of the Board.

Commencement Date – S. 8 has effect from 8 December 2002, by virtue of SI 2002/2866 (C. 91), art. 2(2) and Sch. 1, Pt. 2.

History – In s. 8(1), the words "statutory paternity pay," substituted for the words "ordinary statutory paternity pay, additional statutory paternity pay and" by Children and Families Act 2014, s. 126(1) and Sch. 7, para. 52(2)(a), with effect from 5 April 2015, subject to the transitional and saving provisions in SI 2014/1640, art. 16 (amendments do not have effect in relation to– (a) children whose expected week of birth ends on or before 4 April 2015; (b) children placed for adoption on or before 4 April 2015) (SI 2014/1640, art. 7).
In s. 8(1), the words "and statutory shared parental pay" inserted by Children and Families Act 2014, s. 126(1) and Sch. 7, para. 52(2)(b), with effect from 30 June 2014 (SI 2014/1640, art. 3).
In s. 8(2)(a), the words "statutory paternity pay," substituted for the words "ordinary statutory paternity pay, additional statutory paternity pay and" by Children and Families Act 2014, s. 126(1) and Sch. 7, para. 52(3)(a)(i), with effect from 5 April 2015, subject to the transitional and saving provisions in SI 2014/1640, art. 16 (amendments do not have effect in relation to– (a) children whose

expected week of birth ends on or before 4 April 2015; (b) children placed for adoption on or before 4 April 2015) (SI 2014/1640, art. 7).
In s. 8(2)(a), the words "and statutory shared parental pay" inserted by Children and Families Act 2014, s. 126(1) and Sch. 7, para. 52(3)(a)(ii), with effect from 30 June 2014 (SI 2014/1640, art. 3).
In s. 8(2)(b), the words "statutory paternity pay," substituted for the words "ordinary statutory paternity pay, additional statutory paternity pay and" by Children and Families Act 2014, s. 126(1) and Sch. 7, para. 52(3)(b)(i), with effect from 5 April 2015, subject to the transitional and saving provisions in SI 2014/1640, art. 16 (amendments do not have effect in relation to– (a) children whose expected week of birth ends on or before 4 April 2015; (b) children placed for adoption on or before 4 April 2015) (SI 2014/1640, art. 7).
In s. 8(2)(b), the words "and statutory shared parental pay" inserted by Children and Families Act 2014, s. 126(1) and Sch. 7, para. 52(3)(b)(ii), with effect from 30 June 2014 (SI 2014/1640, art. 3).
In s. 8(2)(d), the words "statutory paternity pay," substituted for the words "ordinary statutory paternity pay, additional statutory paternity pay and" by Children and Families Act 2014, s. 126(1) and Sch. 7, para. 52(3)(c)(i), with effect from 5 April 2015, subject to the transitional and saving provisions in SI 2014/1640, art. 16 (amendments do not have effect in relation to– (a) children whose expected week of birth ends on or before 4 April 2015; (b) children placed for adoption on or before 4 April 2015) (SI 2014/1640, art. 7).
In s. 8(2)(d), the words "and statutory shared parental pay" inserted by Children and Families Act 2014, s.126(1) and Sch. 7, para. 52(3)(c)(ii), with effect from 30 June 2014 (SI 2014/1640, art. 3).
In s. 8, the words "ordinary statutory paternity pay, additional statutory paternity pay" substituted for the words "statutory paternity pay" (in all places) by Work and Families Act 2006, s. 11 and Sch. 1, para. 51, with effect from 3 March 2010 (SI 2010/495, art. 3).
Statutory instruments – SI 2003/1192: made under s. 8(1), (2)(a), (b), (c).

9 Decisions and appeals

9(1) Part 2 of the Social Security Contributions (Transfer of Functions, Etc.) Act 1999 (c. 2) (decisions and appeals) is amended as follows.

9(2) [Amends SSC(TF)A 1999, s. 8(1).]

9(3) [Amends SSC(TF)A 1999, s. 8(3)(b).]

9(4) [Amends SSC(TF)A 1999, s. 11.]

9(5) [Amends SSC(TF)A 1999, s. 14.]

Commencement Date – S. 9 has effect from 8 December 2002, by virtue of SI 2002/2866 (C. 91), art. 2(2) and Sch. 1, Pt. 2.

10 Powers to require information

10(1) The Secretary of State may by regulations make provision enabling an officer of the Board authorised by the Board for the purposes of this section to require persons of a description specified in the regulations to provide, or produce for inspection, within such period as the regulations may require, such information or documents as the officer may reasonably require for the purpose of ascertaining whether statutory paternity pay, statutory adoption pay or statutory shared parental pay is or was payable to or in respect of any person.

10(2) The descriptions of person which may be specified by regulations under subsection (1) include, in particular–

(a) any person claiming to be entitled to statutory paternity pay, statutory adoption pay or statutory shared parental pay,

(b) any person who is, or has been, the spouse or partner of such a person as is mentioned in paragraph (a),

(c) any person who is, or has been, an employer of such a person as is mentioned in paragraph (a),

(d) any person carrying on an agency or other business for the introduction or supply to persons requiring them of persons available to do work or to perform services, and

(e) any person who is a servant or agent of any such person as is specified in paragraphs (a) to (d).

10(3) Regulations under subsection (1) must be made with the concurrence of the Board.

Commencement Date – S. 10 has effect from 8 December 2002, by virtue of SI 2002/2866 (C. 91), art. 2(2) and Sch. 1, Pt. 2.

History – In s. 10(1), the words "statutory paternity pay," substituted for the words "ordinary statutory paternity pay, additional statutory paternity pay or" by Children and Families Act 2014, s. 126(1) and Sch. 7, para. 53(2)(a), with effect from 5 April 2015, subject to the transitional and saving provisions in SI 2014/1640, art. 16 (amendments do not have effect in relation to– (a) children whose expected week of birth ends on or before 4 April 2015; (b) children placed for adoption on or before 4 April 2015) (SI 2014/1640, art. 7).
In s. 10(1), the words "or statutory shared parental pay" inserted by Children and Families Act 2014, s. 126(1) and Sch. 7, para. 53(2)(b), with effect from 30 June 2014 (SI 2014/1640, art. 3).
In s. 10(2), the words "statutory paternity pay," substituted for the words "ordinary statutory paternity pay, additional statutory paternity pay or" by Children and Families Act 2014, s. 126(1) and Sch. 7, para. 53(3)(a), with effect from 5 April 2015, subject to the transitional and saving provisions in SI 2014/1640, art. 16 (amendments do not have effect in relation to– (a) children whose expected week of birth ends on or before 4 April 2015; (b) children placed for adoption on or before 4 April 2015) (SI 2014/1640, art. 7).
In s. 10(2), the words "or statutory shared parental pay" inserted by Children and Families Act 2014, s. 126(1) and Sch. 7, para. 53(3)(b), with effect from 30 June 2014 (SI 2014/1640, art. 3).
In s. 10, the words "ordinary statutory paternity pay, additional statutory paternity pay" substituted for the words "statutory paternity pay" (in both places) by Work and Families Act 2006, s. 11 and Sch. 1, para. 52, with effect from 3 March 2010 (SI 2010/495, art. 3).
Statutory instruments – SI 2003/1192: made under s. 10(1), (2).

11 Penalties: failures to comply

11(1) Where a person–

(a) fails to produce any document or record, provide any information or make any return, in accordance with regulations under section 8, or

(b) fails to provide any information or document in accordance with regulations under section 10,

he shall be liable to the penalties mentioned in subsection (2) below (subject to subsection (4)).

11(2) The penalties are–

(a) a penalty not exceeding £300, and

(b) if the failure continues after a penalty is imposed under paragraph (a), a further penalty or penalties not exceeding £60 for each day on which the failure continues after the day on which the penalty under that paragraph was imposed (but excluding any day for which a penalty under this paragraph has already been imposed).

11(3) Where a person fails to keep records in accordance with regulations under section 8, he shall be liable to a penalty not exceeding £3,000.

11(4) Subject to subsection (5), no penalty shall be imposed under subsection (2) or (3) at any time after the failure concerned has been remedied.

11(5) Subsection (4) does not apply to the imposition of a penalty under subsection (2)(a) in respect of a failure within subsection (1)(a).

11(6) Where, in the case of any employee, an employer refuses or repeatedly fails to make payments of statutory paternity pay, statutory adoption pay or statutory shared parental pay in accordance with any regulations under section 8, the employer shall be liable to a penalty not exceeding £3,000.

11(7) Section 118(2) of the Taxes Management Act 1970 (c. 9) (extra time for compliance etc) shall apply for the purposes of subsections (1), (3) and (6) as it applies for the purposes of that Act.

11(8) Schedule 1 to this Act (penalties: procedure and appeals) has effect in relation to penalties under this section.

Commencement Date – S. 11 has effect from 8 December 2002, by virtue of SI 2002/2866 (C. 91), art. 2(2) and Sch. 1, Pt. 2.

History – In s. 11(6), the words "statutory paternity pay," substituted for the words "ordinary statutory paternity pay, additional statutory paternity pay or" by Children and Families Act 2014, s. 126(1) and Sch. 7, para. 54(a), with effect from 5 April 2015, subject to the transitional and saving provisions in SI 2014/1640, art. 16 (amendments do not have effect in relation to– (a) children whose expected week of birth ends on or before 4 April 2015; (b) children placed for adoption on or before 4 April 2015) (SI 2014/1640, art. 7).
In s. 11(6), the words "or statutory shared parental pay" inserted by Children and Families Act 2014, s. 126(1) and Sch. 7, para. 54(b), with effect from 1 December 2014 (SI 2014/1640, art. 5).
In s. 11(6), the words "ordinary statutory paternity pay, additional statutory paternity pay" substituted for the words "statutory paternity pay" by Work and Families Act 2006, s. 11 and Sch. 1, para. 53, with effect from 6 April 2010 (SI 2010/495, art. 4).

12 Penalties: fraud etc.

12(1) Where a person fraudulently or negligently–

(a) makes any incorrect statement or declaration in connection with establishing entitlement to statutory paternity pay, or

(b) provides any incorrect information or document of a kind mentioned in regulations under section 10(1) so far as relating to statutory paternity pay,

he shall be liable to a penalty not exceeding £300.

12(2) Where a person fraudulently or negligently–

(a) makes any incorrect statement or declaration in connection with establishing entitlement to statutory adoption pay or statutory shared parental pay, or

(b) provides any incorrect information or document of a kind mentioned in regulations under section 10(1) so far as relating to statutory adoption pay or statutory shared parental pay,

he shall be liable to a penalty not exceeding £3,000.

12(3) Where an employer fraudulently or negligently makes incorrect payments of statutory paternity pay, he shall be liable to a penalty not exceeding £300.

12(4) Where an employer fraudulently or negligently makes incorrect payments of statutory adoption pay or statutory shared parental pay, he shall be liable to a penalty not exceeding £3,000.

12(5) Where an employer fraudulently or negligently–

(a) produces any incorrect document or record, provides any incorrect information or makes any incorrect return, of a kind mentioned in regulations under section 8, or

(b) receives incorrect payments in pursuance of regulations under section 7,

he shall be liable to a penalty not exceeding £3,000 or, if the offence relates only to statutory paternity pay, £300.

12(6) Schedule 1 (penalties: procedure and appeals) has effect in relation to penalties under this section.

Commencement Date – S. 12 has effect from 8 December 2002, by virtue of SI 2002/2866 (C. 91), art. 2(2) and Sch. 1, Pt. 2.

History – In s. 12(1)(a) and (b), the word "ordinary" repealed by Children and Families Act 2014, s. 126(1) and Sch. 7, para. 55(2), with effect from 5 April 2015, subject to the transitional and saving provisions in SI 2014/1640, art. 16 (amendments do not have effect in relation to– (a) children whose expected week of birth ends on or before 4 April 2015; (b) children placed for adoption on or before 4 April 2015) (SI 2014/1640, art. 7).
In s. 12(1), the words "ordinary statutory paternity pay" substituted for the words "statutory paternity pay" by Work and Families Act 2006, s. 11 and Sch. 1, para. 54(2), with effect from 6 April 2010 (SI 2010/495, art. 4).
In s. 12(2)(a), the words "statutory shared parental pay" substituted for the words "additional statutory paternity pay" by Children and Families Act 2014, s. 126(1) and Sch. 7, para. 55(3)(a), with effect from 1 December 2014, subject to the transitional provisions in SI 2014/1640, art. 12 (amendments do not have effect in relation to– (a) children whose expected week of birth ends on or before 4 April 2015; (b) children placed for adoption on or before 4 April 2015) (SI 2014/1640, art. 5).
In s. 12(2)(b), the words "statutory shared parental pay" substituted for the words "additional statutory paternity pay" by Children and Families Act 2014, s. 126(1) and Sch. 7, para. 55(3)(b), with effect from with effect from 1 December 2014, subject to the transitional provisions in SI 2014/1640, art. 12 (amendments do not have effect in relation to– (a) children whose expected week of birth ends on or before 4 April 2015; (b) children placed for adoption on or before 4 April 2015) (SI 2014/1640, art. 5).
In s. 12(2), the words "or additional statutory paternity pay" inserted by Work and Families Act 2006, s. 11 and Sch. 1, para. 54(3), with effect from 6 April 2010 (SI 2010/495, art. 4).
In s. 12(3), the word "ordinary" repealed by Children and Families Act 2014, s. 126(1) and Sch. 7, para. 55(4), with effect from 5 April 2015, subject to the transitional and saving provisions in SI 2014/1640, art. 16 (amendments do not have effect in relation to– (a) children whose expected week of birth ends on or before 4 April 2015; (b) children placed for adoption on or before 4 April 2015) (SI 2014/1640, art. 7).
In s. 12(3), the words "ordinary statutory paternity pay" substituted for the words "statutory paternity pay" by Work and Families Act 2006, s. 11 and Sch. 1, para. 54(2), with effect from 6 April 2010 (SI 2010/495, art. 4).
In s. 12(4), the words "statutory shared parental pay" substituted for the words "additional statutory paternity pay" by Children and Families Act 2014, s. 126(1) and Sch. 7, para. 55(5), with effect from 1 December 2014, subject to the transitional provisions in SI 2014/1640, art. 12 (amendments do not have effect in relation to– (a) childrenwhose expected week of birth ends on or before 4 April 2015; (b) children placed for adoption on or before 4 April 2015) (SI 2014/1640, art. 5).
In s. 12(4), the words "or additional statutory paternity pay" inserted by Work and Families Act 2006, s. 11 and Sch. 1, para. 54(3), with effect from 6 April 2010 (SI 2010/495, art. 4).
In s. 12(5), the word "ordinary" repealed by Children and Families Act 2014, s. 126(1) and Sch. 7, para. 55(6), with effect from 5 April 2015, subject to the transitional and saving provisions in SI 2014/1640, art. 16 (amendments do not have effect in relation to– (a) children whose expected week of birth ends on or before 4 April 2015; (b) children placed for adoption on or before 4 April 2015) (SI 2014/1640, art. 7).
In s. 12(5), the words "ordinary statutory paternity pay" substituted for the words "statutory paternity pay" by Work and Families Act 2006, s. 11 and Sch. 1, para. 54(4), with effect from 6 April 2010 (SI 2010/495, art. 4).

13 Supply of information held by the Board

13(1) This section applies to information which is held for the purposes of functions relating to statutory paternity pay, statutory adoption pay or statutory shared parental pay–

(a) by the Board, or

(b) by a person providing services to the Board, in connection with the provision of those services.

13(2) Information to which this section applies may be supplied–

(a) to the Secretary of State or the Department, or

(b) to a person providing services to the Secretary of State or the Department,

for use for the purposes of functions relating to social security, child support or war pensions.

Commencement Date – S. 13 has effect from 8 December 2002, by virtue of SI 2002/2866 (C. 91), art. 2(2) and Sch. 1, Pt. 2.

History – In s. 13(1), the words "statutory paternity pay," substituted for the words "ordinary statutory paternity pay, additional statutory paternity pay or" by Children and Families Act 2014, s. 126(1) and Sch. 7, para. 56(a), with effect from 5 April 2015, subject to the transitional and saving provisions in SI 2014/1640, art. 16 (amendments do not have effect in relation to– (a) children whose expected week of birth ends on or before 4 April 2015; (b) children placed for adoption on or before 4 April 2015) and art. 19 (transitional and saving provisions applicable where Northern Ireland legislation contains provision on additional statutory paternity pay) (SI 2014/1640, art. 7).
In s. 13(1), the words "or statutory shared parental pay" inserted by Children and Families Act 2014, s. 126(1) and Sch. 7, para. 56(b), with effect from 1 December 2014 (SI 2014/1640, art. 5).
In s. 13(1), the words "ordinary statutory paternity pay, additional statutory paternity pay" substituted for the words "statutory paternity pay" by Work and Families Act 2006, s. 11 and Sch. 1, para. 55, with effect from 6 April 2010 (SI 2010/495, art. 4).

14 Supply of information held by the Secretary of State

14(1) This section applies to information which is held for the purposes of functions relating to statutory paternity pay, statutory adoption pay or statutory shared parental pay–

(a) by the Secretary of State or the Department, or

(b) by a person providing services to the Secretary of State or the Department, in connection with the provision of those services.

14(2) Information to which this section applies maybe supplied–

(a) to the Board, or

(b) to a person providing services to the Board,

for use for the purposes of functions relating to statutory paternity pay, statutory adoption pay or statutory shared parental pay.

Commencement Date – S. 14 has effect from 8 December 2002, by virtue of SI 2002/2866 (C. 91), art. 2(2) and Sch. 1, Pt. 2.

History – In s. 14(1), the words "statutory paternity pay," substituted for the words "ordinary statutory paternity pay, additional statutory paternity pay or" by Children and Families Act 2014, s. 126(1) and Sch. 7, para. 57(2)(a), with effect from 5 April 2015, subject to the transitional and saving provisions in SI 2014/1640, art. 16 (amendments do not have effect in relation to– (a) children whose expected week of birth ends on or before 4 April 2015; (b) children placed for adoption on or before 4 April 2015) and art. 19 (transitional and saving provisions applicable where Northern Ireland legislation contains provision on additional statutory paternity pay) (SI 2014/1640, art. 7).

In s. 14(1), the words "or statutory shared parental pay" inserted by Children and Families Act 2014, s. 126(1) and Sch. 7, para. 57(2), with effect from 1 December 2014 (SI 2014/1640, art. 5).

In s. 14(2), the words "statutory paternity pay," substituted for the words "ordinary statutory paternity pay, additional statutory paternity pay or" by Children and Families Act 2014, s. 126(1) and Sch. 7, para. 57(3)(a), with effect from 5 April 2015, subject to the transitional and saving provisions in SI 2014/1640, art. 16 (amendments do not have effect in relation to– (a) children whose expected week of birth ends on or before 4 April 2015; (b) children placed for adoption on or before 4 April 2015) and art. 19 (transitional and saving provisions applicable where Northern Ireland legislation contains provision on additional statutory paternity pay) (SI 2014/1640, art. 7).

In s. 14(2), the words "or statutory shared parental pay" inserted by Children and Families Act 2014, s. 126(1) and Sch. 7, para. 57(3), with effect from 1 December 2014 (SI 2014/1640, art. 5).

In s. 14, the words "ordinary statutory paternity pay, additional statutory paternity pay" substituted for the words "statutory paternity pay" by Work and Families Act 2006, s. 11 and Sch. 1, para. 56, with effect from 6 April 2010 (SI 2010/495, art. 4).

15 Use of information by the Board

15(1) Information which is held–

(a) by the Board, or

(b) by a person providing services to the Board, in connection with the provision of those services,

for the purposes of any functions specified in any paragraph of subsection (2) below may be used for the purposes of, or for any purposes connected with, the exercise of any functions specified in any other paragraph of that subsection, and may be supplied to any person providing services to the Board for those purposes.

15(2) The functions referred to in subsection (1) above are–

(a) the functions of the Board in relation to statutory paternity pay;

(aa) [repealed by Children and Families Act 2014, s. 126(1) and Sch. 7, para. 58(b);]

(b) their functions in relation to statutory adoption pay;

(ba) their functions in relation to statutory shared parental pay; and

(c) their functions in relation to tax, contributions, statutory sick pay, statutory maternity pay or tax credits, or functions under Part 3 of the Pension Schemes Act 1993 (c. 48) (schemes that were contracted-out etc) or Part 3 of the Pension Schemes (Northern Ireland) Act 1993 (c. 49) (corresponding provisions for Northern Ireland).

15(3) In subsection (2)(c) above, **"contributions"** means contributions under Part 1 of the Social Security Contributions and Benefits Act 1992 (c. 4) or Part 1 of the Social Security Contributions and Benefits (Northern Ireland) Act 1992 (c. 7).

Commencement Date – S. 15 has effect from 8 December 2002, by virtue of SI 2002/2866 (C. 91), art. 2(2) and Sch. 1, Pt. 2.

History – In s. 15(2)(a), the word "ordinary" repealed by Children and Families Act 2014, s. 126(1) and Sch. 7, para. 58(a), with effect from 5 April 2015, subject to the transitional and saving provisions in SI 2014/1640, art. 16 (amendments do not have effect in relation to– (a) children whose expected week of birth ends on or before 4 April 2015; (b) children placed for adoption on or before 4 April 2015) and art. 19 (transitional and saving provisions applicable where Northern Ireland legislation contains provision on additional statutory paternity pay) (SI 2014/1640, art. 7).

In s. 15(2)(a), the word "ordinary" and para. (aa) inserted by Work and Families Act 2006, s. 11 and Sch. 1, para. 57, with effect from 6 April 2010 (SI 2010/495, art. 4).

S. 15(2)(aa) repealed by Children and Families Act 2014, s. 126(1) and Sch. 7, para. 58(b), with effect from 5 April 2015, subject to the transitional and saving provisions in SI 2014/1640, art. 16 (amendments do not have effect in relation to– (a) children whose expected week of birth ends on or before 4 April 2015; (b) children placed for adoption on or before 4 April 2015) and art. 19 (transitional and saving provisions applicable where Northern Ireland legislation contains provision on additional statutory paternity pay) (SI 2014/1640, art. 7).

S. 15(2)(ba) inserted (and the "and" following (b) repealed) by Children and Families Act 2014, s. 126(1) and Sch. 7, para. 58(c) and (d), with effect from 1 December 2014 (SI 2014/1640, art. 5).

In s. 15(2)(c), the words "(schemes that were contracted-out etc)" substituted for the words "(certification of pension schemes etc)" by PA 2014, s. 24 and Sch. 13, para. 72, with effect from 6 April 2016 (as not brought into force by any earlier order under PA 2014, s. 56(1)).

16 Interpretation

16 In sections 5 to 15–

"the Board" means the Commissioners of Inland Revenue;

"the Department" means the Department for Social Development or the Department for Employment and Learning;

"employer" and **"employee"** have the same meanings as in Parts 12ZA and 12ZB of the Social Security Contributions and Benefits Act 1992.

Commencement Date – S. 16 has effect from 8 December 2002, by virtue of SI 2002/2866 (C. 91), art. 2(2) and Sch. 1, Pt. 2.

Chapter 2 – Maternity

18 Maternity pay period

18 [Amends SSCBA 1992, s. 165(1).]

Notes – The day appointed under s. 55(2), (3) for the purposes of s. 18, with effect only in relation to those women whose expected week of confinement commences on or after 6 April 2003, is 24 November 2002 by virtue of SI 2002/2866 (C. 91), art. 2(1) and Sch. 1, Pt. 1; art. 3 and Sch. 3, para. 4.

19 Rate of statutory maternity pay

19 [Substitutes SSAA 1992, s. 166.]

Notes – The day appointed under s. 55(2), (3), by virtue of SI 2002/2866 (C. 91), art. 2(3) and Sch. 1, Pt. 3; art. 3 and Sch. 3, para. 5. is 6 April 2003 for the purposes of s.19, but does not have effect in relation to a woman–

- whose maternity pay period commences before 6 April 2003;
- who is entitled to statutory maternity pay at the rate of £75 a week immediately before that date; and
- who would be entitled to statutory maternity pay at a rate lower than £75 a week if the amendment had effect in relation to her.

20 Entitlement to statutory maternity pay

20 [Amends SSCBA 1992, s. 164.]

Notes – The day appointed under s. 55(2), (3) for the purposes of s. 20, with effect only in relation to those women whose expected week of confinement commences on or after 6 April 2003, is 24 November 2002 by virtue of SI 2002/2866 (C. 91), art. 2(1) and Sch. 1, Pt. 1; art. 3 and Sch. 3, para. 4.

21 Funding of employers' liabilities: statutory maternity pay

21(1) [Substitutes SSCBA 1992, s. 167.]

21(2) [Not reproduced here.]

Notes – The day appointed under s. 55(2), (3) for the purposes of s. 21 is 6 April 2003, by virtue of SI 2002/2866 (C. 91), art. 2(3) and Sch. 1, Pt. 3.

PART 4 – MISCELLANEOUS AND GENERAL

MISCELLANEOUS

48 Rate of maternity allowance

48(1) [Amends SSCBA 1992, s. 35A.]

48(2) In relation to any time before the coming into force of section 19, the reference to section 166(1)(b) of the Social Security Contributions and Benefits Act 1992 (c. 4) in section 35A(5)(c)(i) of that Act (as amended by subsection (1)(b) above) is a reference to section 166(3) of that Act.

Notes – The day appointed under s. 55(2), (3), by virtue of SI 2002/2866 (C. 91), art. 2(3) and Sch. 1, Pt. 3; art. 3 and Sch. 3, para. 6, is 6 April 2003 for the purposes of s.48(1)(a), but does not have effect in relation to a woman–

- whose maternity allowance period commences before 6 April 2003;
- who is entitled to maternity allowance at the rate of £75 a week immediately before that date; and
- who would be entitled to maternity allowance at a rate lower than £75 a week if the amendment had effect in relation to her.

The day appointed under s. 55(2), (3) for the purposes of s. 48(1)(b) and (2), with effect only in relation to those women whose expected week of confinement commences on or after 6 April 2003, is 24 November 2002 by virtue of SI 2002/2866 (C. 91), art. 2(1) and Sch. 1, Pt. 1; art. 3 and Sch. 3, para. 4.

The day appointed under s. 55(2) for the purposes of s. 48(1)(c) is 6 April 2003 by virtue of SI 2002/2866 (C. 91), art. 2(3) and Sch. 1, Pt. 3.

50 Use of information for, or relating to, employment and training

50 Schedule 6 (which contains provision for the use of information for, or relating to, employment and training) has effect.

Notes – The day appointed under s. 55(2) for the purposes of s. 50 and Sch. 6 is 9 September 2002 by virtue of SI 2002/2256 (C. 73), art. 2(a).

GENERAL

51 Orders and regulations

51(1) Any power of the Secretary of State to make orders or regulations under this Act includes power–

(a) *to make* different provision for different cases or circumstances;

(b) to make such incidental, supplementary, consequential or transitional provision as the Secretary of State thinks fit.

51(2) Any power of the Secretary of State to make orders or regulations under this Act is exercisable by statutory instrument.

51(3) No order may be made under this Act unless a draft of the order has been laid before and approved by resolution of each House of Parliament.

51(4) No regulations may be made under section 30, 31, 32, 33 or 45 unless a draft of the regulations has been laid before and approved by resolution of each House of Parliament.

51(5) A statutory instrument containing regulations under any other provision of this Act shall be subject to annulment in pursuance of a resolution of either House of Parliament.

51(6) This section does not apply to orders under section 55(2).

Statutory instruments – SI 2003/1192.

52 Financial provisions

52(1) There shall be paid out of money provided by Parliament–

(a) any expenses incurred by a Minister of the Crown or government department in consequence of this Act, and

(b) any increase attributable to this Act in the sums so provided under any other Act.

52(2) There shall be paid into the Consolidated Fund any increase attributable to this Act in the sums payable into that Fund under any other Act.

53 Minor and consequential amendments

53 Schedule 7 (which makes minor and consequential amendments) has effect.

Commencement Date – S. 53 came into force on 31 July 2002 by virtue of SI 2002/1989 in so far as it relates to Sch. 7, para. 50; on 9 September 2002 by virtue of SI 2002/2256 in so far as it relates to Sch. 7, para. 8, 16, 17; on 24 November 2002 by virtue of SI 2002/2866 in so far as it relates to Sch. 7, para. 8 (partially), 12, 24 (partially), 28, 52, 53; 8 December 2002 by virtue of SI 2002/2866 in so far as it relates to Sch. 7, para. 1, 2, 3, 7, 8 (partially), 11, 13, 24, 25, 26, 29–31, 33, 35, 48 and 49; on 6 April 2003 by virtue of SI 2002/2866 in so far as it relates to Sch. 7, para. 2 (partially), 4–6, 8 (partially), 14, 18 (partially), 22, 23(1), 23(2)(b), (c), (partially), 24 (partially), 27, 41–45, 47(1), (2), 49 (partially) and 54; 27 April 2003 by virtue of SI 2003/1190 in so far as it relates to Sch. 7, para. 18 (partially), 19–22, 23 (partially), 24 (partially) and 34.

54 Repeals and revocations

54 The enactments and instruments specified in Schedule 8 are hereby repealed or revoked to the extent specified there.

55 Short title etc.

55(1) This Act may be cited as the Employment Act 2002.

55(2) This Act, except sections 45, 46, 51 and 52 and this section, shall come into force on such day as the Secretary of State may by order made by statutory instrument appoint, and different days may be so appointed for different purposes.

55(3) An order under subsection (2) may contain such transitional provisions and savings as the Secretary of State considers necessary or expedient in connection with the coming into force of any of the provisions of this Act.

55(4) The Secretary of State may by regulations make such transitional provisions and savings as he considers necessary or expedient for the purposes of or in connection with–

(a) the coming into force of section 19 or 48, or Schedule 7 so far as relating to any amendment made in consequence of either of those sections; or

(b) the operation of any enactment amended by any of those provisions during any period when the amendment is not wholly in force.

55(5) Subject to subsections (6) and (7), this Act extends to England and Wales and Scotland only.

55(6) The following provisions also extend to Northern Ireland–

(a) section 5;

(b) sections 13 to 15, and section 16 so far as relating thereto;

(c) paragraphs 1, 4, 9 and 10 of Schedule 6, and section 50 so far as relating thereto;

(d) sections 51 and 52;

(e) paragraphs 1, 50, 52 and 53 of Schedule 7, and section 53 so far as relating thereto,

(f) Schedule 8, so far as relating to the repeal of section 3(3) of the Social Security Act 1998 (c. 14), and section 53 so far as relating thereto;

(g) this section.

55(7) The following provisions extend to Northern Ireland only–

(a) sections 21(2) and 46;

(b) paragraphs 7, 8, 12 and 14 of Schedule 6, and section 50 so far as relating thereto;

(c) paragraph 17 of Schedule 7, and section 53 so far as relating thereto;

(d) Schedule 8, so far as relating to–

(i) the repeal in the Social Security Administration (Northern Ireland) Act 1992 (c. 8), and

(ii) the revocations in the Social Security Administration (Fraud) (Northern Ireland) Order 1997 (S.I. 1997/1182 (N.I. 11)) and the Social Security Contributions (Transfer of Functions, etc.) (Northern Ireland) Order 1999 (S.I. 1999/671),

and section 54 so far as relating thereto.

55(8) In sections 5 and 13 to 15 and paragraph 53 of Schedule 7, references to statutory paternity pay, statutory adoption pay or statutory shared parental pay include statutory pay under Northern Ireland legislation corresponding to Part 12ZA, Part 12ZB or Part 12ZC of the Social Security Contributions and Benefits Act 1992 (c. 4).

History – In s. 55(8), the words "or statutory shared parental pay" inserted (after the words "statutory adoption pay") and the words ", Part 12ZB or Part 12ZC" substituted for the words "or Part 12ZB" by Children and Families Act 2014, s. 126(1) and Sch. 7, para. 59(b) and (c), with effect from 15 March 2015 (the day on which Northern Ireland legislation containing provision corresponding to SSCBA 1992, Pt. 12ZC (the Statutory Shared Parental Pay (General) Regulations (Northern Ireland) (S.R. (N.I.) 2015/94)) comes into force), subject to the transitional and saving provisions in SI 2014/1640, art. 18 (amendments do not have effect in relation to– (a) children whose expected week of birth ends on or before 4 April 2015; (b) children placed for adoption on or before 4 April 2015) (SI 2014/1640, art. 8).

In s. 55(8), the words "statutory paternity pay," substituted for the words "ordinary statutory paternity pay, additional statutory paternity pay or" by Children and Families Act 2014, s. 126(1) and Sch. 7, para. 59(a), with effect from 5 April 2015, subject to the transitional and saving provisions in SI 2014/1640, art. 16 (amendments do not have effect in relation to– (a) children whose expected week of birth ends on or before 4 April 2015; (b) children placed for adoption on or before 4 April 2015) (SI 2014/1640, art. 7).

In s. 55(8), the words "ordinary statutory paternity pay, additional statutory paternity pay" substituted for the words "statutory paternity pay" by Work and Families Act 2006, s. 11 and Sch. 1, para. 58, with effect from 6 April 2010 (SI 2010/495, art. 4).

Statutory instruments – SI 2002/1989 (C. 62) appointed day order made under s. 55(2).

SI 2002/2256 (C. 73) appointed day order made under s. 55(2).

SI 2002/2866 (C. 91) appointed day order made under s. 55(2) and (3).

SCHEDULES

SCHEDULE 1 – PENALTIES: PROCEDURE AND APPEALS

Sections 11 and 12

DETERMINATION OF PENALTIES BY OFFICER OF BOARD

Notes – Sch. 1 has effect from 8 December 2002, SI 2002/2866, art. 2(2), Sch. 1, Pt. 2.

1(1) Subject to sub-paragraph (2) and except where proceedings have been instituted under paragraph 5, an officer of the Board authorised by the Board for the purposes of this paragraph may make a determination–

(a) imposing a penalty under section 11 or 12, and

(b) setting it at such amount as, in his opinion, is correct or appropriate.

1(2) Sub-paragraph (1) does not apply to the imposition of such a penalty as is mentioned in section 11(2)(a).

1(3) Notice of a determination of a penalty under this paragraph shall be served on the person liable to the penalty and shall state the date on which it is issued and the time within which an appeal against the determination may be made.

1(4) After the notice of a determination under this paragraph has been served the determination shall not be altered except in accordance with this paragraph or on appeal.

1(5) If it is discovered by an officer of the Board authorised by the Board for the purposes of this paragraph that the amount of a penalty determined under this paragraph is or has become insufficient, the officer may make a determination in a further amount so that the penalty is set at the amount which, in his opinion, is correct or appropriate.

Commencement Date – Para. 1 has effect from 8 December 2002, SI 2002/2866, art. 2(2), Sch. 1, Pt. 2.

PROVISIONS SUPPLEMENTARY TO PARAGRAPH 1

2(1) A penalty determined under paragraph 1 above shall be due and payable at the end of the period of thirty days beginning with the date of the issue of the notice of determination.

2(2) Part 6 of the Taxes Management Act 1970 (c. 9) shall apply in relation to a penalty determined under paragraph 1 as if it were tax charged in an assessment and due and payable.

Notes – Para. 2 has effect from 8 December 2002, SI 2002/2866, art. 2(2), Sch. 1, Pt. 2.

APPEALS AGAINST PENALTY DETERMINATIONS

3(1) An appeal may be brought against the determination of a penalty under paragraph 1.

3(2) The provisions of the Taxes Management Act 1970 relating to appeals, except section 50(6) to (8), shall have effect in relation to an appeal against such a determination as they have effect in relation to an appeal against an assessment to tax except that references to the tribunal shall be taken to be references to the First-tier Tribunal.

3(3) On an appeal by virtue of sub-paragraph (2) against the determination of a penalty under paragraph 1, the First-tier Tribunal may–

(a) if it appears that no penalty has been incurred, set the determination aside;

(b) if the amount determined appears to be appropriate, confirm the determination;

(c) if the amount determined appears to be excessive, reduce it to such other amount (including nil) as the tribunal considers appropriate;

(d) if the amount determined appears to be insufficient, increase it to such amount not exceeding the permitted maximum as the tribunal considers appropriate.

3(4) In addition to any right of appeal on a point of law under section 11(2) of the Tribunals, Courts and Enforcement Act 2007, the person liable to the penalty may appeal to the Upper Tribunal against the amount of the penalty which had been determined under sub-paragraph (3), but not against any decision which falls under section 11(5)(d) or (e) of that Act and was made in connection with the determination of the amount of the penalty.

3(4A) Section 11(3) and (4) of the Tribunals, Courts and Enforcement Act 2007 applies to the right of appeal under sub-paragraph (4) as it applies to the right of appeal under section 11(2) of that Act.

3(4B) On an appeal under this paragraph the Upper Tribunal has the like jurisdiction as is conferred on the First-tier Tribunal by virtue of this paragraph.

History – In para. 3(2), the words "except that references to the tribunal shall be taken to be references to the First-tier Tribunal" inserted by SI 2009/56, art. 3(1) and Sch. 1, para. 322(2), operative from 1 April 2009, subject to transitional and saving provisions in SI 2009/56, Sch. 3.

In para. 3(3), the words "First-tier Tribunal" substituted, the words "to them" (which appeared after the word "appears" in sub-paragraphs (a)–(d)) omitted, and the words "the tribunal considers" substituted in sub-paragraphs (c) and (d) by SI 2009/56, art. 3(1) and Sch. 1, para. 322(3), operative from 1 April 2009, subject to transitional and saving provisions in SI 2009/56, Sch. 3.

Para. 3(4) (along with para. 3(4A) and 3(4B)) substituted for former para. 3(4) by SI 2009/56, art. 3(1) and Sch. 1, para. 322(4), operative from 1 April 2009, subject to transitional and saving provisions in SI 2009/56, Sch. 3.

Para. 3(4A) (along with para. 3(4) and 3(4B)) substituted for former para. 3(4) by SI 2009/56, art. 3(1) and Sch. 1, para. 322(4), operative from 1 April 2009, subject to transitional and saving provisions in SI 2009/56, Sch. 3.

Para. 3(4B) (along with para. 3(4) and 3(4A)) substituted for former para. 3(4) by SI 2009/56, art. 3(1) and Sch. 1, para. 322(4), operative from 1 April 2009, subject to transitional and saving provisions in SI 2009/56, Sch. 3.

Notes – Para. 3 has effect from 8 December 2002, SI 2002/2866, art. 2(2), Sch. 1, Pt. 2.

PENALTY PROCEEDINGS BEFORE FIRST-TIER TRIBUNAL

History – In the heading to para. 4, the words "FIRST-TIER TRIBUNAL" substituted by SI 2009/56, art. 3(1) and Sch. 1, para. 323(2), operative from 1 April 2009, subject to transitional and saving provisions in SI 2009/56, Sch. 3.

4(1) An officer of the Board authorised by the Board for the purposes of this paragraph may commence proceedings for any penalty to which sub-paragraph (1) of paragraph 1 does not apply by virtue of sub-paragraph (2) of that paragraph.

4(2) The person liable to the penalty shall be a party to the proceedings.

4(3) Part 6 of the Taxes Management Act 1970 (c. 9) shall apply in relation to a penalty determined in proceedings under this paragraph as if it were tax charged in an assessment and due and payable.

4(4) In addition to any right of appeal on a point of law under section 11(2) of the Tribunals, Courts and Enforcement Act 2007, the person liable to the penalty may appeal to the Upper Tribunal against the determination of a penalty in proceedings under sub-paragraph (1), but not against any decision which falls under section 11(5)(d) or (e) of that Act and was made in connection with the determination of the amount of the penalty.

4(4A) *Section 11(3) and (4) of the* Tribunals, Courts and Enforcement Act 2007 applies to the right of appeal under sub-paragraph (4) as it applies to the right of appeal under section 11(2) of that Act.

4(5) On any such appeal the Upper Tribunal may–

(a) if it appears that no penalty has been incurred, set the determination aside;

(b) if the amount determined appears to be appropriate, confirm the determination;

(c) if the amount determined appears to be excessive, reduce it to such other amount (including nil) as the Upper Tribunal considers appropriate;

(d) if the amount determined appears to be insufficient, increase it to such amount not exceeding the permitted maximum as the Upper Tribunal considers appropriate.

History – Para. 4(2) substituted by SI 2009/56, art. 3(1) and Sch. 1, para. 323(3), operative from 1 April 2009, subject to transitional and saving provisions in SI 2009/56, Sch. 3.
Para. 4(4) (along with para. 4(4A)) substituted for former para. 4(4) by SI 2009/56, art. 3(1) and Sch. 1, para. 323(4), operative from 1 April 2009, subject to transitional and saving provisions in SI 2009/56, Sch. 3.
In para. 4(5), the words "Upper Tribunal" substituted for the word "court" (in three places) by SI 2009/56, art. 3(1) and Sch. 1, para. 323(5), operative from 1 April 2009, subject to transitional and saving provisions in SI 2009/56, Sch. 3.

Notes – Para. 4 has effect from 8 December 2002, SI 2002/2866, art. 2(2), Sch. 1, Pt. 2.

PENALTY PROCEEDINGS BEFORE COURT

5(1) Where in the opinion of the Board the liability of any person for a penalty under section 11 or 12 arises by reason of the fraud of that or any other person, proceedings for the penalty may be instituted before the High Court or, in Scotland, the Court of Session as the Court of Exchequer in Scotland.

5(2) Subject to sub-paragraph (3), proceedings under this paragraph shall be instituted–

(a) in England and Wales, in the the name of the Attorney General, and

(b) in Scotland, in the name of the Advocate General for Scotland.

5(3) Sub-paragraph (2) shall not prevent proceedings under this paragraph being instituted in England and Wales under the Crown Proceedings Act 1947 (c. 44) by and in the name of the Board as an unauthorised department for the purposes of that Act.

5(4) Any proceedings under this paragraph instituted in England and Wales shall be deemed to be civil proceedings by the Crown within the meaning of Part 2 of the Crown Proceedings Act 1947.

5(5) If in proceedings under this paragraph the court does not find that fraud is proved but considers that the person concerned is nevertheless liable to a penalty, the court may determine a penalty notwithstanding that, but for the opinion of the Board as to fraud, the penalty would not have been a matter for the court.

Notes – Para. 5 has effect from 8 December 2002, SI 2002/2866, art. 2(2), Sch. 1, Pt. 2.

MITIGATION OF PENALTIES

6 The Board may in their discretion mitigate any penalty under section 11 or 12, or stay or compound any proceedings for a penalty, and may also, after judgment, further mitigate or entirely remit the penalty.

Notes – Para. 6 has effect from 8 December 2002, SI 2002/2866, art. 2(2), Sch. 1, Pt. 2.

TIME LIMITS FOR PENALTIES

7 A penalty under section 11 or 12 may be determined by an officer of the Board, or proceedings for the penalty may be commenced before the tribunal or the court, at any time within six years after the date on which the penalty was incurred or began to be incurred.

History – In para. 7, the word "tribunal" substituted by SI 2009/56, art. 3(1) and Sch. 1, para. 324, operative from 1 April 2009, subject to transitional and saving provisions in SI 2009/56, Sch. 3.

Notes – Para. 7 has effect from 8 December 2002 (SI 2002/2866, art. 2(2), Sch. 1, Pt. 2).

INTERPRETATION

9 In this Schedule–

"the Board" means the Commissioners of Inland Revenue;

History – In para. 9, the definition of "General Commissioners" and "Special Commissioners" omitted by SI 2009/56, art. 3(1) and Sch. 1, para. 325, operative from 1 April 2009, subject to transitional and saving provisions in SI 2009/56, Sch. 3.

Notes – Para. 9 has effect from 8 December 2002, SI 2002/2866, art. 2(2), Sch. 1 Pt. 2.

SCHEDULE 6 – USE OF INFORMATION FOR, OR RELATING TO, EMPLOYMENT AND TRAINING

Section 50

Notes – Sch. 6 has effect from 9 September 2002 by virtue of SI 2002/2256 (C. 73), art. 2(a).

SUPPLY OF TAX INFORMATION FOR EMPLOYMENT OR TRAINING PURPOSES

5 [Repealed by WRA 2012, s. 147 and Sch. 14, Pt. 13.]

History – Para. 5 repealed by WRA 2012, s. 147 and Sch. 14, Pt. 13, with effect from 8 May 2012.

6 [Repealed by WRA 2012, s. 147 and Sch. 14, Pt. 13.]

History – Para. 6 repealed by WRA 2012, s. 147 and Sch. 14, Pt. 13, with effect from 8 May 2012.

SUPPLY OF INLAND REVENUE TAX CREDITS INFORMATION FOR EMPLOYMENT OR TRAINING PURPOSES

9 [Repealed by TCA 2002, s. 60 and Sch. 6.]

History – Para. 9 repealed by TCA 2002, s. 60 and Sch 6, with effect from 8 April 2003 (by virtue of SI 2003/962).

SUPPLY TO INLAND REVENUE OF EMPLOYMENT OR TRAINING INFORMATION FOR PURPOSES OF TAX CREDITS

10 [Repealed by TCA 2002, s. 60 and Sch. 6.]

History – Para. 10 repealed by TCA 2002, s. 60 and Sch 6, with effect from 8 April 2003 (by virtue of SI 2003/962).

SUPPLY OF OTHER INLAND REVENUE INFORMATION FOR EMPLOYMENT OR TRAINING PURPOSES

11 [Amends SSAA 1992, s. 121E.]

Notes – The day appointed under s. 55(2) for the purposes of s. 50 and Sch. 6, para. 11 is 9 September 2002 by virtue of SI 2002/2256 (C. 73), art. 2(a).

SUPPLY TO INLAND REVENUE OF EMPLOYMENT OR TRAINING INFORMATION FOR OTHER PURPOSES

13 [Amends SSAA 1992, s. 121F.]

Notes – The day appointed under s. 55(2) for the purposes of s. 50 and Sch. 6, para. 13 is 9 September 2002 by virtue of SI 2002/2256 (C. 73), art. 2(a).

SCHEDULE 7 – MINOR AND CONSEQUENTIAL AMENDMENTS

Section 53

SOCIAL SECURITY CONTRIBUTIONS AND BENEFITS ACT 1992 (C. 4)

2 The Social Security Contributions and Benefits Act 1992 is amended as follows.

Notes – The day appointed under s. 55(2) for the purposes of Sch. 7, para. 2, so far as it relates to para. 3 and 7, is 8 December 2002, by virtue of SI 2002/2866 (C. 91), art. 2(2) and Sch. 1, Pt. 2.

3 [Amends SSCBA 1992, s. 4.]

Notes – The day appointed under s. 55(2) for the purposes of Sch. 7, para. 3, is 8 December 2002, by virtue of SI 2002/2866 (C. 91), art. 2(2) and Sch. 1, Pt. 2.

7 [Amends SSCBA 1992, s. 176.]

Notes – The day appointed under s. 55(2) for the purposes of Sch. 7, para. 7, is 8 December 2002, by virtue of SI 2002/2866 (C. 91), art. 2(2) and Sch. 1, Pt. 2.

SOCIAL SECURITY ADMINISTRATION ACT 1992 (C. 5)

8 The Social Security Administration Act 1992 is amended as follows.

Notes – The day appointed under s. 55(2) for the purposes of s. 53 and Sch. 7, para. 8, so far as it relates to para. 13, is 9 September 2002 by virtue of SI 2002/2256 (C. 73), art. 2(2) and Sch. 1, Pt. 2.

13 [Amends SSAA 1992, s. 122AA.]

History – Para. 13(b) and (c) repealed by WRA 2012, s. 147 and Sch. 14, Pt. 13, with effect from 8 May 2012.

15 [Inserts SSAA 1992, s. 190(1)(ab).]

SOCIAL SECURITY ACT 1998 (C. 14)

51 In paragraph 5A of Schedule 2 to the Social Security Act 1998 (no appeal against a decision made in consequence of a decision under regulations under section 2A of the Administration Act), after “section 2A” there is inserted “or 2AA”.

NATIONAL INSURANCE CONTRIBUTIONS AND STATUTORY PAYMENTS ACT 2004

(2004 Chapter 3)

[*13th May 2004*]

ARRANGEMENT OF SECTIONS

PAYMENT OF CLASS 1 CONTRIBUTIONS

1 Payment of Class 1 contributions: Great Britain

1(1) Paragraph 3 of Schedule 1 to the Social Security Contributions and Benefits Act 1992 (c. 4) (method of paying Class 1 contributions) is amended as follows.

1(2) [Amends SSCBA 1992, Sch.1, para. 3(3).]

1(3) [Inserts SSCBA 1992, Sch.1, para. 3(3A)–(3B).]

1(4) [Amends SSCBA 1992, Sch.1, para. 3(4).]

1(5) [Amends SSCBA 1992, Sch.1, para. 3(5).]

Commencement Date – S. 1 came into effect on 1 September 2004 by virtue of SI 2004/1943, reg. 2.

2 Payment of Class 1 contributions: Northern Ireland

2(1) Paragraph 3 of Schedule 1 to the Social Security Contributions and Benefits (Northern Ireland) Act 1992 (c. 7) (method of paying Class 1 contributions) is amended as follows.

2(2)–(5) [Amends SSCB(NI)A 1992, Sch.1, para. 3.]

Commencement Date – S. 2 came into effect on 1 September 2004 by virtue of SI 2004/1943, reg. 2.

3 Agreements and joint elections: Great Britain

3(1) Schedule 1 to the Social Security Contributions and Benefits Act 1992 (c. 4) (supplementary provisions relating to Class 1 contributions) is amended as follows.

3(2) In paragraph 3A (restrictions on recovery of employer's contributions)–

(a) [amends SSCBA 1992, Sch.1, para. 3A(2),]

(b) [inserts SSCBA 1992, Sch.1, para. 3A(2A)–(2B).]

3(3) In paragraph 3B (transfer of liability to be borne by the earner)–

(a) [amends SSCBA 1992, Sch.1, para. 3B(1)(a),]

(b) [inserts SSCBA 1992, Sch.1, para. 3B(1A),]

(c) [amends SSCBA 1992, Sch.1, para. 3B(2)(b),]

(d) [amends SSCBA 1992, Sch.1, para. 3B(3),]

(e) [amends SSCBA 1992, Sch.1, para. 3B(7)(b),]

(f) [inserts SSCBA 1992, Sch.1, para. 3B(7A)–(7B),]

(g) [substitutes SSCBA 1992, Sch.1, para. 3B(10),]

(h) [omits SSCBA 1992, Sch.1, para. 3B(13).]

3(4) The amendments made by this section have effect in relation to–

(a) agreements entered into after the date of commencement of this section which are in respect of post-commencement employment income, and

(b) elections made after that date.

3(5) For the purposes of subsection (4), **"post-commencement employment income"** means income which is relevant employment income within paragraph 3A(2B) of Schedule 1 to the Social Security Contributions and Benefits Act 1992 (c. 4) which, after the date of commencement of this section, counts as employment income for a tax year by virtue of Part 7 of the Income Tax (Earnings and Pensions) Act 2003 (c. 1).

Commencement Date – S. 3 came into effect on 1 September 2004 by virtue of SI 2004/1943, reg. 2.

4 Agreements and joint elections: Northern Ireland

4(1) Schedule 1 to the Social Security Contributions and Benefits (Northern Ireland) Act 1992 (c. 7) (supplementary provisions relating to Class 1 contributions) is amended as follows.

4(2)–(3) [Amends SSCB(NI)A 1992, Sch.1, para. 3A–3B.]

4(4) The amendments made by this section have effect in relation to–

(a) agreements entered into after the date of commencement of this section which are in respect of post-commencement employment income, and

(b) elections made after that date.

4(5) For the purposes of subsection (4), **"post-commencement employment income"** means income which is relevant employment income within paragraph 3A(2B) of Schedule 1 to the Social Security Contributions and Benefits (Northern Ireland) Act 1992 (c. 7) which, after the date of commencement of this section, counts as employment income for a tax year by virtue of Part 7 of the Income Tax (Earnings and Pensions) Act 2003 (c. 1).

Commencement Date – S. 4 came into effect on 1 September 2004 by virtue of SI 2004/1943, reg. 2.

METHOD OF RECOVERY OF CONTRIBUTIONS ETC

5 Recovery of contributions, etc: Great Britain

5(1) [Omitted by FA 2008, s. 129 and Sch. 43, para. 11(c).]

5(2) [Amends SSAA 1992, s. 121B(1).]

5(3) [Inserts SSAA 1992, s. 121C(8A).]

5(4) [Amends SSAA 1992, Sch. 1, para. 7BZA.]

Commencement Date – S. 5 came into effect on 1 September 2004 by virtue of SI 2004/1943, reg. 2.

History – S. 5(1) omitted by FA 2008, s. 129 and Sch. 43, para. 11(c), with effect from 6 April 2014 (SI 2014/906, art. 2).

Notes – In the HMSO copy, in s. 5(4), in inserted para. 7BZA(1) the wording "(2) Regulations under sub-paragraph (1) may apply or extend with or without modification in" removed as they were apparently inserted in error.

6 Recovery of contributions, etc: Northern Ireland

6(1)–(2) [Substitutes SSA(NI)A 1992.]

6(3) [Inserts SSCB(NI)A 1992, Sch.1, para. 7BZA.]

Commencement Date – S. 6 came into effect on 1 September 2004 by virtue of SI 2004/1943, reg. 2.

PROVISION OF INFORMATION

7 Class 1, 1A, 1B or 2 contributions: powers to call for documents etc: Great Britain

7 [Substitutes SSAA 1992, s. 110ZA.]

Commencement Date – S. 7 came into effect on 6 April 2005 by virtue of SI 2004/1943, reg. 4.

8 Class 1, 1A, 1B or 2 contributions: powers to call for documents etc: Northern Ireland

8 [Substitutes SSA(NI)A 1992, s. 104ZA.]

Commencement Date – S. 8 came into effect on 6 April 2005 by virtue of SI 2004/1943, reg. 4.

STATUTORY SICK PAY AND STATUTORY MATERNITY PAY

9 Compliance regime for statutory sick pay and statutory maternity pay: Great Britain

9(1) The Social Security Administration Act 1992 (c. 5) is amended as follows.

9(2) [Inserts SSAA 1992, s. 130(5).]

9(3) [Inserts SSAA 1992, s. 132(4).]

9(4) [Amends SSAA 1992, s. 113(1A)(b).]

9(5) [Inserts SSAA 1992, s. 113A–113B.]

Commencement Date – S. 9(1)–(3) came into effect on 1 January 2005 by virtue of SI 2004/1943, reg. 3. S. 9(4) and (5) came into effect on 6 April 2005 by virtue of SI 2004/1943, reg. 4.

10 Compliance regime for statutory sick pay and statutory maternity pay: Northern Ireland

10(1) The Social Security Administration (Northern Ireland) Act 1992 (c. 8) is amended as follows.

10(2)–(5) [Amends SSA(NI)A 1992.]

Commencement Date – S. 10(1)–(3) came into effect on 1 January 2005 by virtue of SI 2004/1943, reg. 3. S. 10(4) and (5) came into effect on 6 April 2005 by virtue of SI 2004/1943, reg. 4.

MISCELLANEOUS AND GENERAL

11 Minor and consequential amendments

11 Schedule 1 (which makes minor and consequential amendments) has effect.

Commencement Date – S. 11 came into effect variously from on 1 September 2004 and 6 April 2005 (by virtue of SI 2004/1943, reg. 5).

12 Repeals and revocations

12 The enactments and instruments mentioned in Schedule 2 are repealed or revoked to the extent specified.

Commencement Date – S. 12 came into effect variously from 1 September 2004 and 6 April 2005 (by virtue of SI 2004/1943, reg. 5). See Sch. 2 for details.

13 Commencement

13(1) The preceding provisions of this Act come into force in accordance with provision made by the Treasury by order.

13(2) The power to make an order under subsection (1) is exercisable by statutory instrument.

13(3) An order under this section–

(a) may include incidental, supplementary, consequential or transitional provision or savings;

(b) may make different provision for different purposes.

Statutory instruments – SI 2004/1943: The National Insurance Contributions and Statutory Payments Act 2004 (Commencement) Order 2004.

14 Extent

14(1) Sections 1, 3, 5, 7 and 9 extend to England and Wales and Scotland only.

14(2) Sections 2, 4, 6, 8 and 10 extend to Northern Ireland only.

14(3) An amendment, repeal or revocation contained in Schedule 1 or 2 has the same extent as the enactment or instrument to which it relates.

14(4) Subject to subsections (1) to (3) this Act extends to England and Wales, Scotland and Northern Ireland.

15 Short title

15 This Act may be cited as the National Insurance Contributions and Statutory Payments Act 2004.

SCHEDULES

SCHEDULE 1 – MINOR AND CONSEQUENTIAL AMENDMENTS

Section 11

Commencement Date – Sch. 1, para. 1, 2, 3 (part), 4 (part) and 5 came into effect on 1 September 2004 by virtue of SI 2004/1943, reg. 5(a).
Sch. 1, para. 3 (part) and 4 (part) came into effect on 6 April 2005 by virtue of SI 2004/1943, reg. 5(b).

1(1) The Social Security Contributions and Benefits Act 1992 (c. 4) is amended as follows.

1(2) [Amends SSCBA 1992, s. 10A(4).]

1(3) [Amends SSCBA 1992, s. 18(2)(b).]

2 [Amends SSCB(NI)A 1992.]

3(1) The Social Security Administration Act 1992 (c. 5) is amended as follows.

3(2) [Amends SSAA 1992, s. 111.]

3(3) [Amends SSAA 1992, s. 162.]

4 [Amends SSA(NI)A 1992.]

5(1) Section 4 of the Social Security Contributions (Transfer of Functions, etc.) Act 1999 (c. 2) (recovery of contributions where income tax recovery provisions not applicable) is amended as follows.

5(2) [Amends SSC(TF)A 1999, s. 4(a).]

5(3) [Omits SSC(TF)A 1999, s. 4(b).]

5(4) [Amends SSC(TF)A 1999, s. 4.]

INCOME TAX (TRADING AND OTHER INCOME) ACT 2005

(2005 Chapter 5)

[*24th March 2005*]

SCHEDULES

SCHEDULE 1 – CONSEQUENTIAL AMENDMENTS

SOCIAL SECURITY CONTRIBUTIONS AND BENEFITS ACT 1992 (C. 4)

419 The Social Security Contributions and Benefits Act 1992 is amended as follows.

420(1) Amend section 15 (Class 4 contributions recoverable under the Income Tax Acts) as follows.

420(2) [Amends SSCBA 1992, s. 15(1).]

420(3) [Amends SSCBA 1992, s. 15(2), (3) and (3A).]

420(4) [Omits SSCBA 1992, s. 15(4).]

421 [Amends SSCBA 1992, s. 16(1).]

422(1) Amend Schedule 2 (levy of Class 4 contributions with income tax) as follows.

422(2) [Inserts SSCBA 1992, Sch. 2, para. 1(ab).]

422(3) [Amends SSCBA 1992, Sch. 2, para. 2.]

422(4) [Amends SSCBA 1992, Sch. 2, para. 3(1), (4) and (5).]

422(5) [Amends SSCBA 1992, Sch. 2, para. 5.]

422(6) [Amends SSCBA 1992, Sch. 2, para. 7.]

PENSION SCHEMES ACT 1993 (C. 48)

467 The Pension Schemes Act 1993 is amended as follows.

468 [Amends PSA 1993, s. 158(4).]

COMMISSIONERS FOR REVENUE AND CUSTOMS ACT 2005

(2005 Chapter 11)

[*7th April 2005*]

Only those parts of CRCA 2005 which directly affect material in this division are reproduced here. The full text of CRCA 2005 is reproduced in the Income, Corporation and Capital Gains Taxes division (Vol. 1B).

SCHEDULES

SCHEDULE 4 – CONSEQUENTIAL AMENDMENTS, ETC.

SOCIAL SECURITY CONTRIBUTIONS AND BENEFITS ACT 1992 (C. 4)

43 [Amends SSCBA 1992, s. 171(1).]

SOCIAL SECURITY ADMINISTRATION ACT 1992 (C. 5)

44 The Social Security Administration Act 1992 shall be amended as follows.

45 [Amends SSAA 1992, s. 122ZA(4) and (5).]

46 [Amends SSAA 1992, s. 122AA(1).]

PENSION SCHEMES ACT 1993 (C. 48)

51 [Amends PSA 1993, s. 158.]

SOCIAL SECURITY CONTRIBUTIONS (TRANSFER OF FUNCTIONS, ETC.) ACT 1999 (C. 2)

73 The Social Security Contributions (Transfer of Functions etc.) Act 1999 shall be amended as follows.

74 [Substitutes SSC(TF)A 1999, s. 3(1).]

75 [Ceases SSC(TF)A 1999, s. 7 to have effect.]

NATIONAL INSURANCE CONTRIBUTIONS ACT 2006

(2006 Chapter 10) [*30th March 2006*]

ARRANGEMENT OF SECTIONS

POWER TO MAKE PROVISION IN CONSEQUENCE OF RETROSPECTIVE TAX LEGISLATION

1 Earnings: power to make provision in consequence of retrospective tax legislation: Great Britain

1(1) [Inserts SSCBA 1992, s. 4B and 4C.]

1(2) In section 176 of that Act (parliamentary control of statutory instruments)–

(a) [Amends SSCBA 1992, s. 176(1)(a).]

(b) [Inserts SSCBA 1992, s. 176(2A)–(2C).]

3 Class 1A contributions: power to make provision in consequence of retrospective tax legislation: Great Britain

3(1) [Inserts SSCBA 1992, s. 10ZC.]

3(2) [Amends SSCBA 1992, s. 176(1)(a).]

AGREEMENTS AND JOINT ELECTIONS

5 Agreements and joint elections: Great Britain

5(1) Schedule 1 to the Social Security Contributions and Benefits Act 1992 (c. 4) (supplementary provisions relating to Class 1 contributions) is amended as follows.

5(2) [Amends SSCBA 1992, Sch. 1, para. 3A(2A).]

5(3) [Amends SSCBA 1992, Sch. 1, para. 3B(7B).]

5(4) The amendments made by this section have effect in relation to agreements and elections whether entered into or made before, or on or after, the day on which this Act is passed (including those entered into or made before 2nd December 2004).

DISCLOSURE OF AVOIDANCE

7 Disclosure of contributions avoidance arrangements

7(1) The Social Security Administration Act 1992 (c. 5) is amended as follows.

7(2) [Inserts SSAA 1992, s. 132A.]

7(3) [Inserts SSAA 1992, s. 190(1)(za).]

7(4) [Amends SSAA 1992, s. 192(5).]

GENERAL

8 Extent

8(1) Sections 1, 3 and 5 extend to England and Wales and Scotland only.

8(2) Sections 2, 4 and 6 extend to Northern Ireland only.

8(3) The remaining provisions of this Act extend to England and Wales, Scotland and Northern Ireland.

9 Commencement

9 This Act comes into force on the day on which it is passed.

10 Short Title

10 This Act may be cited as the National Insurance Contributions Act 2006.

INCOME TAX ACT 2007

(2007 Chapter 3)

[*20th March 2007*]

ARRANGEMENT OF SECTIONS

PART 17 – DEFINITIONS FOR PURPOSES OF ACT AND FINAL PROVISIONS

FINAL PROVISIONS

SCHEDULES

PART 17 – DEFINITIONS FOR PURPOSES OF ACT AND FINAL PROVISIONS

FINAL PROVISIONS

1027 Minor and consequential amendments

1027 Schedule 1 (minor and consequential amendments) has effect.

Origin – S. 1027: Drafting.

1031 Repeals and revocations

1031 Schedule 3 (repeals and revocations, including of spent enactments) has effect.

Origin – S. 1031: Drafting.

1033 Extent

1033(1) This Act extends to England and Wales, Scotland and Northern Ireland (but see subsection (2)).

1033(2) An amendment, repeal or revocation contained in Schedule 1 or 3 has the same extent as the provision amended, repealed or revoked.

Origin – S. 1033: Drafting.

1034 Commencement

1034(1) This Act comes into force on 6 April 2007 and has effect–

(a) for income tax purposes, for the tax year 2007–08 and subsequent tax years, and

(b) for corporation tax purposes, for accounting periods ending after 5 April 2007.

1034(2) Subsection (1) is subject to subsections (3) and (4).

1034(3) The following–

(a) Part 5 (enterprise investment scheme),

(b) Part 3 of Schedule 1 (consequential amendment associated with Part 5), and

(c) Part 2 of Schedule 3 (repeals so associated),

do not have effect in relation to shares issued before 6 April 2007.

This is subject to Schedule 2 (transitional provisions and savings).

1034(4) Subsection (1) does not apply to the following provisions of this Act (which therefore come into force on the day on which this Act is passed)–

(a) in Part 15, section 852, and

(b) in this Part, sections 1017, 1018, 1028, 1029, 1030(2) to (4) and 1033, this section and section 1035.

Origin – S. 1034: Drafting.

1035 Short title

1035 This Act may be cited as the Income Tax Act 2007.

Origin – S. 1035: Drafting.

SCHEDULES

SCHEDULE 1 – MINOR AND CONSEQUENTIAL AMENDMENTS

Section 1027

Part 2 – Other enactments

SOCIAL SECURITY CONTRIBUTIONS AND BENEFITS ACT 1992 (C. 4)

288 The Social Security Contributions and Benefits Act 1992 (c. 4) is amended as follows.

289 [Amends SSCBA 1992, s. 4A(3)(i)(i).]

290(1) Amend Schedule 2 (levy of Class 4 contributions with income tax) as follows.

290(2) [Inserts SSCBA 1992, Sch. 2, para. 1(ac).]

290(3) [Amends SSCBA 1992, Sch. 2, para. 3.]

290(4) [Amends SSCBA 1992, Sch. 2, para. 9(4).]

FINANCE ACT 2007

(2007 Chapter 11) [*19th July 2007*]

ARRANGEMENT OF SECTIONS

PART 4 – PENSIONS

70 Miscellaneous

70 Schedule 20 contains miscellaneous provisions about registered pension schemes and employer-financed retirement benefits schemes.

PART 6 – INVESTIGATION, ADMINISTRATION ETC

OTHER ADMINISTRATION

97 Penalties for errors

97(1) Schedule 24 contains provisions imposing penalties on taxpayers who–

(a) make errors in certain documents sent to HMRC, or

(b) unreasonably fail to report errors in assessments by HMRC.

97(2) That Schedule comes into force in accordance with provision made by the Treasury by order.

97(3) An order–

(a) may commence a provision generally or only for specified purposes,

(b) may make different provision for different purposes, and

(c) may include incidental, consequential or transitional provision.

97(4) The power to make an order is exercisable by statutory instrument.

PART 8 – FINAL PROVISIONS

114 Repeals

114 Schedule 27 contains repeals.

115 Short title

115 This Act may be cited as the Finance Act 2007.

SCHEDULES

SCHEDULE 20 – PENSION SCHEMES ETC: MISCELLANEOUS

Section 70

CONSEQUENTIAL AMENDMENTS

23(1) [Amends PSA 1993, s. 1(1).]

COMMENCEMENT

24(1) The amendments made by paragraphs 2 to 4 and 23 are deemed to have come into force on 6th April 2007.

SCHEDULE 24 – PENALTIES FOR ERRORS

Section 97

Commencement Date – Sch. 24 has effect as follows by virtue of SI 2008/568, art. 2:

- 1 April 2008 in relation to relevant documents relating to tax periods commencing on or after that date;
- 1 April 2008 in relation to assessments falling within paragraph 2 for tax periods commencing on or after that date;
- 1 July 2008 in relation to relevant documents relating to claims under the Thirteenth Council Directive (arrangements for the refund of value added tax to persons not established in Community territory) for years commencing on or after that date;
- 1 January 2009 in relation to relevant documents relating to claims under the Eighth Council Directive (arrangements for the refund of value added tax to taxable persons not established in the territory of the country) for years commencing on or after that date;
- 1 April 2009 in relation to documents relating to all other claims for repayments of relevant tax made on or after 1st April 2009 which are not related to a tax period; and
- in any other case, 1 April 2009 in relation to documents given where a person's liability to pay relevant tax arises on or after that date.

However, no person will be liable to a penalty under Sch. 24 in respect of any tax period for which a return is required to be made before 1 April 2009.

Sch. 24 applies in relation to Class 2 contributions, with effect for the tax year 2015–16 and subsequent tax years (NICA 2015, Sch. 1, para. 35).

Notes – This is an edited version of Sch. 24, containing only the provisions relevant to national insurance.

Part 1 – Liability for Penalty

ERROR IN TAXPAYER'S DOCUMENT

1(1) A penalty is payable by a person (P) where–

(a) P gives HMRC a document of a kind listed in the Table below, and

(b) Conditions 1 and 2 are satisfied.

1(2) Condition 1 is that the document contains an inaccuracy which amounts to, or leads to–

(a) an understatement of a liability to tax,

(b) a false or inflated statement of a loss, or

(c) a false or inflated claim to repayment of tax.

1(3) Condition 2 is that the inaccuracy was careless (within the meaning of paragraph 3) or deliberate on P's part.

1(4) Where a document contains more than one inaccuracy, a penalty is payable for each inaccuracy.

Tax	**Document**
Income tax or capital gains tax	Return under section 8 of TMA 1970 (personal return).
Income tax or capital gains tax	Return under section 8A of TMA 1970 (trustee's return).
Income tax or capital gains tax	Return, statement or declaration in connection with a claim for an allowance, deduction or relief.
Income tax or capital gains tax	Accounts in connection with ascertaining liability to tax.

Tax	Document
Income tax	Return for the purposes of PAYE regulations.
Any of the taxes mentioned above	Any document which is likely to be relied upon by HMRC to determine, without further inquiry, a question about– (a) P's liability to tax, (b) payments by P by way of or in connection with tax, (c) any other payment by P (including penalties), or (d) repayments, or any other kind of payment or credit, to P.

1(5) [Not relevant to National Insurance contributions.]

Commencement Date – See headnote to Sch. 24.

History – In para. 1(2)(a) the word "a" substituted for the word "P's" and in para. (b) the words "by P" omitted by FA 2008, s. 122 and Sch. 40, para. 2(2), with effect from 1 April 2009 (SI 2009/571, art. 2).
In para. 1(3), the words "careless (within the meaning of paragraph 3) or deliberate on P's part" substituted for the words "careless or deliberate (within the meaning of paragraph 3)" by FA 2008, s. 122 and Sch. 40, para. 2(3), with effect from 1 April 2009 (SI 2009/571, art. 2).

ERROR IN TAXPAYER'S DOCUMENT ATTRIBUTABLE TO ANOTHER PERSON

1A(1) A penalty is payable by a person (T) where–

(a) another person (P) gives HMRC a document of a kind listed in the Table in paragraph 1,

(b) the document contains a relevant inaccuracy, and

(c) the inaccuracy was attributable to T deliberately supplying false information to P (whether directly or indirectly), or to T deliberately withholding information from P, with the intention of the document containing the inaccuracy.

1A(2) A **"relevant inaccuracy"** is an inaccuracy which amounts to, or leads to–

(a) an understatement of a liability to tax,

(b) a false or inflated statement of a loss, or

(c) a false or inflated claim to repayment of tax.

1A(3) A penalty is payable under this paragraph in respect of an inaccuracy whether or not P is liable to a penalty under paragraph 1 in respect of the same inaccuracy.

History – Para. 1A inserted by FA 2008, s. 122 and Sch. 40, para. 3, with effect from 1 April 2009 (SI 2009/571, art. 2).

UNDER-ASSESSMENT BY HMRC

2(1) A penalty is payable by a person (P) where–

(a) an assessment issued to P by HMRC understates P's liability to a relevant tax, and

(b) P has failed to take reasonable steps to notify HMRC, within the period of 30 days beginning with the date of the assessment, that it is an under-assessment.

2(2) In deciding what steps (if any) were reasonable HMRC must consider–

(a) whether P knew, or should have known, about the under-assessment, and

(b) what steps would have been reasonable to take to notify HMRC.

2(3) In sub-paragraph (1) **"relevant tax"** means any tax mentioned in the Table in paragraph 1.

2(4) In this paragraph (and in Part 2 of this Schedule so far as relating to this paragraph)–

(a) **"assessment"** includes determination, and

(b) accordingly, references to an under-assessment include an under-determination.

Commencement Date – See headnote to Sch. 24.

History – In para. 2(1)(a) the words "a relevant tax" substituted for the word "tax" by FA 2008, s. 122 and Sch. 40, para. 4(2), with effect from 1 April 2009 (SI 2009/571, art. 2).
Para. 2(3) substituted by FA 2008, s. 122 and Sch. 40, para. 4(3), with effect from 1 April 2009 (SI 2009/571, art. 2).
Para. 2(4) inserted by FA 2009. s. 109 and Sch. 57, para. 2, with effect from 21 July 2009.

DEGREES OF CULPABILITY

3(1) For the purposes of a penalty under paragraph 1, inaccuracy in a document given by P to HMRC is–

(a) "careless" if the inaccuracy is due to failure by P to take reasonable care,

(b) "deliberate but not concealed" if the inaccuracy is deliberate on P's part but P does not make arrangements to conceal it, and

(c) "deliberate and concealed" if the inaccuracy is deliberate on P's part and P makes arrangements to conceal it (for example, by submitting false evidence in support of an inaccurate figure).

3(2) An inaccuracy in a document given by P to HMRC, which was neither careless nor deliberate on P's part when the document was given, is to be treated as careless if P–

(a) discovered the inaccuracy at some later time, and

(b) did not take reasonable steps to inform HMRC.

Commencement Date – See headnote to Sch. 24.

History – In para. 3(1) the words "For the purposes of a penalty under paragraph 1, inaccuracy in" substituted for the words "Inaccuracy in" and the words "on P's part" inserted twice by FA 2008, s. 122 and Sch. 40, para. 5(2), with effect from 1 April 2009 (SI 2009/571, art. 2).

In para. 3(2) the words "on P's part" inserted by FA 2008, s. 122 and Sch. 40, para. 5(3), with effect from 1 April 2009 (SI 2009/571, art. 2).

Cross references – FA 2014, s. 276: promoters of tax avoidance schemes: limitation of defence of reasonable care under para. 3(1)(a) in relation to advice provided by monitored promoters and relating to relevant arrangements.

ERRORS RELATED TO AVOIDANCE ARRANGEMENTS

3A(1) This paragraph applies where a document of a kind listed in the Table in paragraph 1 is given to HMRC by a person ("P") and the document contains an inaccuracy which–

(a) falls within paragraph 1(2), and

(b) arises because the document is submitted on the basis that particular avoidance arrangements (within the meaning of paragraph 3B) had an effect which in fact they did not have.

3A(2) It is to be presumed that the inaccuracy was careless, within the meaning of paragraph 3, unless–

(a) the inaccuracy was deliberate on P's part, or

(b) P satisfies HMRC or (on an appeal notified to the tribunal) the tribunal that P took reasonable care to avoid inaccuracy.

3A(3) In considering whether P took reasonable care to avoid inaccuracy, HMRC and (on an appeal notified to the tribunal) the tribunal must take no account of any evidence of any reliance by P on advice where the advice is disqualified.

3A(4) Advice is **"disqualified"** if any of the following applies–

(a) the advice was given to P by an interested person;

(b) the advice was given to P as a result of arrangements made between an interested person and the person who gave the advice;

(c) the person who gave the advice did not have appropriate expertise for giving the advice;

(d) the advice took no account of P's individual circumstances;

(e) the advice was addressed to, or given to, a person other than P;

but this is subject to sub-paragraphs (5) and (7).

3A(5) Where (but for this sub-paragraph) advice would be disqualified under any of paragraphs (a) to (c) of sub-paragraph (4), the advice is not disqualified under that paragraph if at the relevant time P–

(a) has taken reasonable steps to find out whether the advice falls within that paragraph, and

(b) reasonably believes that it does not.

3A(6) In sub-paragraph (4) **"an interested person"** means–

(a) a person, other than P, who participated in the avoidance arrangements or any transaction forming part of them, or

(b) a person who for any consideration (whether or not in money) facilitated P's entering into the avoidance arrangements.

3A(7) Where (but for this sub-paragraph) advice would be disqualified under paragraph (a) of sub-paragraph (4) because it was given by a person within sub-paragraph (6)(b), the advice is not disqualified under that paragraph if–

(a) the person giving the advice had appropriate expertise for giving it,

(b) the advice took account of P's individual circumstances, and

(c) at the time when the question whether the advice is disqualified arises–

  (i) Condition E in paragraph 3B(5) is met in relation to the avoidance arrangements, but

  (ii) none of Conditions A to D in paragraph 3B(5) is or has at any time been met in relation to them.

3A(8) If the document mentioned in sub-paragraph (1) is given to HMRC by P as a personal representative of a deceased person ("D")–

(a) sub-paragraph (4) is to be read as if–

  (i) the references in paragraphs (a) and (b) to P were to P or D;

  (ii) the reference in paragraph (d) to P were to D, and

(iii) the reference in paragraph (e) to a person other than P were to a person who is neither P nor D,

(b) sub-paragraph (6) is to be read as if–

(i) the reference in paragraph (a) to P were a reference to the person to whom the advice was given, and

(ii) the reference in paragraph (b) to P were to D (or, where P also participated in the avoidance arrangements, P or D), and

(c) sub-paragraph (7) is to be read as if the reference in paragraph (b) to P were to D.

3A(9) In this paragraph–

"arrangements" includes any agreement, understanding, scheme, transaction or series of transactions (whether or not legally enforceable);

"the relevant time" means the time when the document mentioned in sub-paragraph (1) is given to HMRC;

"the tribunal" has the same meaning as in paragraph 17 (see paragraph 17(5A)).

History – Para. 3A inserted by F(No. 2)A 2017, s. 64(2), with effect in relation to any document of a kind listed in the Table in para. 1 which is given to HMRC on or after 16 November 2017 (Royal Assent) and relates to tax period which begins on or after 6 April 2017 and ends on or after 16 November (Royal Assent).

3B(1) In paragraph 3A **"avoidance arrangements"** means, subject to sub-paragraph (3), arrangements which fall within sub-paragraph (2).

3B(2) Arrangements fall within this sub-paragraph if, having regard to all the circumstances, it would be reasonable to conclude that the obtaining of a tax advantage was the main purpose, or one of the main purposes, of the arrangements.

3B(3) Arrangements are not avoidance arrangements for the purposes of paragraph 3A if (although they fall within sub-paragraph (2))–

(a) they are arrangements which accord with established practice, and

(b) HMRC had, at the time the arrangements were entered into, indicated its acceptance of that practice.

3B(4) If, at any time, any of Conditions A to E is met in relation to particular arrangements–

(a) for the purposes of this Schedule the arrangements are to be taken to fall within (and always to have fallen within) sub-paragraph (2), and

(b) in relation to the arrangements, sub-paragraph (3) (and the reference to it in sub-paragraph (1)) are to be treated as omitted.

This does not prevent arrangements from falling within sub-paragraph (2) other than by reason of one or more of Conditions A to E being met.

3B(5) Conditions A to E are as follows–

(a) Condition A is that the arrangements are DOTAS arrangements within the meaning given by section 219(5) and (6) of FA 2014;

(b) Condition B is that the arrangements are disclosable VAT arrangements or disclosable indirect tax arrangements for the purposes of Schedule 18 to FA 2016 (see paragraphs 8A to 9A of that Schedule);

(c) Condition C is that both of the following apply–

(i) P has been given a notice under a provision mentioned in sub-paragraph (6) stating that a tax advantage arising from the arrangements is to be counteracted, and

(ii) that tax advantage has been counteracted under section 209 of FA 2013;

(d) Condition D is that a follower notice under section 204 of FA 2014 has been given to P by reference to the arrangements (and not withdrawn) and–

(i) the necessary corrective action for the purposes of section 208 of FA 2014 has been taken in respect of the denied advantage, or

(ii) the denied advantage has been counteracted otherwise than as mentioned in sub-paragraph (i);

(e) Condition E is that a tax advantage asserted by reference to the arrangements has been counteracted (by an assessment, an amendment of a return or claim, or otherwise) on the basis that an avoidance-related rule applies in relation to P's affairs.

3B(6) The provisions referred to in sub-paragraph (5)(c)(i) are–

(a) paragraph 12 of Schedule 43 to FA 2013 (general anti-abuse rule: notice of final decision);

(b) paragraph 8 or 9 of Schedule 43A to that Act (pooled or bound arrangements: notice of final decision);

(c) paragraph 8 of Schedule 43B to that Act (generic referrals: notice of final decision).

3B(7) In sub-paragraph (5)(d) the reference to giving a follower notice to P includes giving a partnership follower notice in respect of a partnership return in relation to which P is a relevant partner; and for the purposes of this sub-paragraph–

(a) **"relevant partner"** has the meaning given by paragraph 2(5) of Schedule 31 to FA 2014;

(b) a partnership follower notice is given "in respect of" the partnership return mentioned in paragraph 2(2)(a) or (b) of that Schedule.

3B(8) For the purposes of sub-paragraph (5)(d) it does not matter whether the denied advantage has been dealt with–

(a) wholly as mentioned in one or other of sub-paragraphs (i) and (ii) of sub-paragraph (5)(d), or

(b) partly as mentioned in one of those sub-paragraphs and partly as mentioned in the other;

and **"the denied advantage"** has the same meaning as in Chapter 2 of Part 4 of FA 2014 (see section 208(3) of and paragraph 4(3) of Schedule 31 to that Act).

3B(9) For the purposes of sub-paragraph (5)(e) a tax advantage has been **"asserted by reference to"** the arrangements if a return, claim or appeal has been made by P on the basis that the tax advantage results from the arrangements.

3B(10) In this paragraph–

"arrangements" has the same meaning as in paragraph 3A;

"avoidance-related rule" has the same meaning as in Part 4 of Schedule 18 to FA 2016 (see paragraph 25 of that Schedule);

a **"tax advantage"** includes–

(a) relief or increased relief from tax,

(b) repayment or increased repayment of tax,

(c) avoidance or reduction of a charge to tax or an assessment to tax,

(d) avoidance of a possible assessment to tax,

(e) deferral of a payment of tax or advancement of a repayment of tax,

(f) avoidance of an obligation to deduct or account for tax, and

(g) in relation to VAT, anything which is a tax advantage for the purposes of Schedule 18 to FA 2016 under paragraph 5 of that Schedule.

History – Para. 3B inserted by F(No. 2)A 2017, s. 64(2), with effect in relation to any document of a kind listed in the Table in para. 1 which is given to HMRC on or after 16 November 2017 (Royal Assent) and relates to tax period which begins on or after 6 April 2017 and ends on or after 16 November (Royal Assent).

Part 2 – Amount of Penalty

STANDARD AMOUNT

4(1) This paragraph sets out the penalty payable under paragraph 1.

4(2) If the inaccuracy is in category 1, the penalty is–

(a) for careless action, 30% of the potential lost revenue,

(b) for deliberate but not concealed action, 70% of the potential lost revenue, and

(c) for deliberate and concealed action, 100% of the potential lost revenue.

4(3) If the inaccuracy is in category 2, the penalty is–

(a) for careless action, 45% of the potential lost revenue,

(b) for deliberate but not concealed action, 105% of the potential lost revenue, and

(c) for deliberate and concealed action, 150% of the potential lost revenue.

4(4) If the inaccuracy is in category 3, the penalty is–

(a) for careless action, 60% of the potential lost revenue,

(b) for deliberate but not concealed action, 140% of the potential lost revenue, and

(c) for deliberate and concealed action, 200% of the potential lost revenue.

4(5) Paragraph 4A explains the 3 categories of inaccuracy.

Commencement Date – See headnote to Sch. 24 for commencement date of former para. 4.

Prospective amendments – Para. 4(1A) inserted by FA 2015, s. 120 and Sch. 20, para. 2(2), with effect from a day to be appointed under FA 2015, s. 120(2).

In para. 4(2)(a) "37.5%" substituted for "30%", in para. 4(2)(b) "87.5%" substituted for "70%" and in para. 4(2)(c) "125%" substituted for "100%" by FA 2015, s. 120 and Sch. 20, para. 2(3), with effect from a day to be appointed under FA 2015, s. 120(2).

In para. 4(2)(a) "4" substituted for "3" by FA 2015, s. 120 and Sch. 20, para. 2(4), with effect from a day to be appointed under FA 2015, s. 120(2).

History – Para. 4, 4A, 4B, 4C and 4D substituted for former para. 4 by FA 2010, s. 35 and Sch. 10, para 2, with effect from 6 April 2011, but the substitution does not have effect in relation to documents given to HMRC and assessments issued by HMRC in relation to a tax period (as defined in para. 28(g)) commencing on or before 5 April 2011 (SI 2011/975).
Former para. 4(1A) inserted by FA 2008, s. 122 and Sch. 40, para. 6, with effect from 1 April 2009 (SI 2009/571, art. 2).

4A(1) An inaccuracy is in category 1 if–

(a) it involves a domestic matter, or

(b) it involves an offshore matter and–

(i) the territory in question is a category 1 territory, or

(ii) the tax at stake is a tax other than income tax or capital gains tax.

4A(2) An inaccuracy is in category 2 if–

(a) it involves an offshore matter or an offshore transfer,

(b) the territory in question is a category 2 territory, and

(c) the tax at stake is income tax, capital gains tax or inheritance tax.

4A(3) An inaccuracy is in category 3 if–

(a) it involves an offshore matter or an offshore transfer,

(b) the territory in question is a category 3 territory, and

(c) the tax at stake is income tax, capital gains tax or inheritance tax.

4A(4) An inaccuracy **"involves an offshore matter"** if it results in a potential loss of revenue that is charged on or by reference to–

(a) income arising from a source in a territory outside the UK,

(b) assets situated or held in a territory outside the UK,

(c) activities carried on wholly or mainly in a territory outside the UK, or

(d) anything having effect as if it were income, assets or activities of a kind described above.

4A(4A) Where the tax at stake is inheritance tax, assets are treated for the purposes of sub-paragraph (4) as situated or held in a territory outside the UK if they are so situated or held immediately after the transfer of value by reason of which inheritance tax becomes chargeable.

4A(4B) An inaccuracy **"involves an offshore transfer"** if–

(a) it does not involve an offshore matter,

(b) it is deliberate (whether or not concealed) and results in a potential loss of revenue,

(c) the tax at stake is income tax, capital gains tax or inheritance tax, and

(d) the applicable condition in paragraph 4AA is satisfied.

4A(5) An inaccuracy **"involves a domestic matter"** if it results in a potential loss of revenue and does not involve either an offshore matter or an offshore transfer.

4A(6) If a single inaccuracy is in more than one category (each referred to as a "relevant category")–

(a) it is to be treated for the purposes of this Schedule as if it were separate inaccuracies, one in each relevant category according to the matters or transfers that it involves, and

(b) the potential lost revenue is to be calculated separately in respect of each separate inaccuracy.

4A(7) **"Category 1 territory"**, **"category 2 territory"** and **"category 3 territory"** are defined in paragraph 21A.

4A(8) **"Assets"** has the meaning given in section 21(1) of TCGA 1992, but also includes sterling.

Prospective amendments – Para. 4A(1A) and (1) substituted for para. 4A(1) by FA 2015, s. 120 and Sch. 20, para. 3(2), with effect from a day to be appointed under FA 2015, s. 120(2).
In para. 4A(7) the words "Category 0 territory", "category 1" substituted for the words "Category 1" by FA 2015, s. 120 and Sch. 20, para. 3(8), with effect from a day to be appointed under FA 2015, s. 120(2).

History – In para. 4A(2)(a) the words "or an offshore transfer" inserted and in para. 4A(2)(c) the words ", capital gains tax or inheritance tax" substituted for the words "or capital gains tax" by FA 2015, s. 120 and Sch. 20, para. 3(3), with effect from 1 April 2016 (in relation to documents given to HMRC relating to a transfer of value made on or after that date for the purposes of inheritance tax; and a tax year commencing on or after 6 April 2016 for the purposes of income tax and capital gains tax) (SI 2016/456, art. 3).
In para. 4A(3)(a) the words "or an offshore transfer" inserted and in para. 4A(3)(c) the words ", capital gains tax or inheritance tax" substituted for the words "or capital gains tax" by FA 2015, s. 120 and Sch. 20, para. 3(4), with effect from 1 April 2016 (in relation to documents given to HMRC relating to a transfer of value made on or after that date for the purposes of inheritance tax; and a tax year commencing on or after 6 April 2016 for the purposes of income tax and capital gains tax) (SI 2016/456, art. 3).
Para. 4A(4A) and (4B) inserted by FA 2015, s. 120 and Sch. 20, para. 3(5), with effect from 1 April 2016 (in relation to documents given to HMRC relating to a transfer of value made on or after that date for the purposes of inheritance tax; and a tax year commencing on or after 6 April 2016 for the purposes of income tax and capital gains tax) (SI 2016/456, art. 3).
In para. 4A(5) the words "and does not involve either an offshore matter or an offshore transfer" substituted for the words "that is charged on or by reference to anything not mentioned in sub-paragraph (4)(a)–(d)" by FA 2015, s. 120 and Sch. 20, para. 3(6), with effect from 1 April 2016 (in relation to documents given to HMRC relating to a transfer of value made on or after that date for the purposes of inheritance tax; and a tax year commencing on or after 6 April 2016 for the purposes of income tax and capital gains tax) (SI 2016/456, art. 3).

In para. 4A(6)(a) the words "or transfers" inserted by FA 2015, s. 120 and Sch. 20, para. 3(7), with effect from 1 April 2016 (in relation to documents given to HMRC relating to a transfer of value made on or after that date for the purposes of inheritance tax; and a tax year commencing on or after 6 April 2016 for the purposes of income tax and capital gains tax) (SI 2016/456, art. 3).
Para. 4, 4A, 4B, 4C and 4D substituted for former para. 4 by FA 2010, s. 35 and Sch. 10, para 2, with effect from 6 April 2011, but the substitution does not have effect in relation to documents given to HMRC and assessments issued by HMRC in relation to a tax period (as defined in para. 28(g)) commencing on or before 5 April 2011 (SI 2011/975).

4AA(1) This paragraph makes provision in relation to offshore transfers.

4AA(2) Where the tax at stake is income tax, the applicable condition is satisfied if the income on or by reference to which the tax is charged, or any part of the income–

(a) is received in a territory outside the UK, or

(b) is transferred before the filing date to a territory outside the UK.

4AA(3) Where the tax at stake is capital gains tax, the applicable condition is satisfied if the proceeds of the disposal on or by reference to which the tax is charged, or any part of the proceeds–

(a) are received in a territory outside the UK, or

(b) are transferred before the filing date to a territory outside the UK.

4AA(4) Where the tax at stake is inheritance tax, the applicable condition is satisfied if–

(a) the disposition that gives rise to the transfer of value by reason of which the tax becomes chargeable involves a transfer of assets, and

(b) after that disposition but before the filing date the assets, or any part of the assets, are transferred to a territory outside the UK.

4AA(5) In the case of a transfer falling within sub-paragraph (2)(b), (3)(b) or (4)(b), references to the income, proceeds or assets transferred are to be read as including references to any assets derived from or representing the income, proceeds or assets.

4AA(6) In relation to an offshore transfer, the territory in question for the purposes of paragraph 4A is the highest category of territory by virtue of which the inaccuracy involves an offshore transfer.

4AA(7) **"Filing date"** means the date when the document containing the inaccuracy is given to HMRC.

4AA(8) **"Assets"** has the same meaning as in paragraph 4A.

History – Para. 4AA inserted by FA 2015, s. 120 and Sch. 20, para. 4, with effect from 1 April 2016 (in relation to documents given to HMRC relating to a transfer of value made on or after that date for the purposes of inheritance tax; and a tax year commencing on or after 6 April 2016 for the purposes of income tax and capital gains tax) (SI 2016/456, art. 3).

4B The penalty payable under paragraph 1A is 100% of the potential lost revenue.

History – Para. 4, 4A, 4B, 4C and 4D substituted for former para. 4 by FA 2010, s. 35 and Sch. 10, para 2, with effect from 6 April 2011, but the substitution does not have effect in relation to documents given to HMRC and assessments issued by HMRC in relation to a tax period (as defined in para. 28(g)) commencing on or before 5 April 2011 (SI 2011/975).

4C The penalty payable under paragraph 2 is 30% of the potential lost revenue.

History – Para. 4, 4A, 4B, 4C and 4D substituted for former para. 4 by FA 2010, s. 35 and Sch. 10, para 2, with effect from 6 April 2011, but the substitution does not have effect in relation to documents given to HMRC and assessments issued by HMRC in relation to a tax period (as defined in para. 28(g)) commencing on or before 5 April 2011 (SI 2011/975).

4D Paragraphs 5 to 8 define **"potential lost revenue"**.

History – Para. 4, 4A, 4B, 4C and 4D substituted for former para. 4 by FA 2010, s. 35 and Sch. 10, para 2, with effect from 6 April 2011, but the substitution does not have effect in relation to documents given to HMRC and assessments issued by HMRC in relation to a tax period (as defined in para. 28(g)) commencing on or before 5 April 2011 (SI 2011/975).

POTENTIAL LOST REVENUE: NORMAL RULE

5(1) **"The potential lost revenue"** in respect of an inaccuracy in a document (including an inaccuracy attributable to a supply of false information or withholding of information) or a failure to notify an under-assessment is the additional amount due or payable in respect of tax as a result of correcting the inaccuracy or assessment.

5(2) The reference in sub-paragraph (1) to the additional amount due or payable includes a reference to–

(a) an amount payable to HMRC having been erroneously paid by way of repayment of tax, and

(b) an amount which would have been repayable by HMRC had the inaccuracy or assessment not been corrected.

5(3) In sub-paragraph (1) **"tax"** includes national insurance contributions.

5(4) The following shall be ignored in calculating potential lost revenue under this paragraph–

(a) group relief, and

(b) any relief under section 458 of CTA 2010 (relief in respect of repayment etc of loan) which is deferred under subsection (5) of that section;

(but this sub-paragraph does not prevent a penalty being charged in respect of an inaccurate claim for relief).

Commencement Date – See headnote to Sch. 24.

History – In para. 5(1) the words "(including an inaccuracy attributable to a supply of false information or withholding of information)" inserted by FA 2008, s. 122 and Sch. 40, para. 7, with effect from 1 April 2009 (SI 2009/571, art. 2).
In para. 5(4)(b), the words "section 458 of CTA 2010" substituted for the words "subsection (4) of section 419 of ICTA", and "subsection (5)" substituted for "subsection (4A)", by CTA 2010, s. 1177 and Sch. 1, para. 575, with effect for corporation tax purposes for accounting periods ending on or after 1 April 2010, and for income tax and capital gains tax purposes for the tax year 2010–11 and subsequent tax years.
Para. 5(4)(b) substituted by FA 2009, s. 109 and Sch. 57, para. 3, with effect from 21 July 2009.

POTENTIAL LOST REVENUE: MULTIPLE ERRORS

6(1) Where P is liable to a penalty under paragraph 1 in respect of more than one inaccuracy, and the calculation of potential lost revenue under paragraph 5 in respect of each inaccuracy depends on the order in which they are corrected–

(a) careless inaccuracies shall be taken to be corrected before deliberate inaccuracies, and

(b) deliberate but not concealed inaccuracies shall be taken to be corrected before deliberate and concealed inaccuracies.

6(2) In calculating potential lost revenue where P is liable to a penalty under paragraph 1 in respect of one or more understatements in one or more documents relating to a tax period, account shall be taken of any overstatement in any document given by P which relates to the same tax period.

6(3) In sub-paragraph (2)–

(a) **"understatement"** means an inaccuracy that satisfies Condition 1 of paragraph 1, and

(b) **"overstatement"** means an inaccuracy that does not satisfy that condition.

6(4) For the purposes of sub-paragraph (2) overstatements shall be set against understatements in the following order–

(a) understatements in respect of which P is not liable to a penalty,

(b) careless understatements,

(c) deliberate but not concealed understatements, and

(d) deliberate and concealed understatements.

6(5) In calculating for the purposes of a penalty under paragraph 1 potential lost revenue in respect of a document given by or on behalf of P no account shall be taken of the fact that a potential loss of revenue from P is or may be balanced by a potential over-payment by another person (except to the extent that an enactment requires or permits a person's tax liability to be adjusted by reference to P's).

Commencement Date – See headnote to Sch. 24.

History – In para. 6(1) the words "under paragraph 1" inserted by FA 2008, s. 122 and Sch. 40, para. 8(2), with effect from 1 April 2009 (SI 2009/571, art. 2).
In para. 6(2) the words "under paragraph 1" inserted by FA 2008, s. 122 and Sch. 40, para. 8(2), with effect from 1 April 2009 (SI 2009/571, art. 2).
In para. 6(5) the words "for the purposes of a penalty under paragraph 1" inserted by FA 2008, s. 122 and Sch. 40, para. 8(3), with effect from 1 April 2009 (SI 2009/571, art. 2).

POTENTIAL LOST REVENUE: LOSSES

7(1) Where an inaccuracy has the result that a loss is wrongly recorded for purposes of direct tax and the loss has been wholly used to reduce the amount due or payable in respect of tax, the potential lost revenue is calculated in accordance with paragraph 5.

7(2) Where an inaccuracy has the result that a loss is wrongly recorded for purposes of direct tax and the loss has not been wholly used to reduce the amount due or payable in respect of tax, the potential lost revenue is–

(a) the potential lost revenue calculated in accordance with paragraph 5 in respect of any part of the loss that has been used to reduce the amount due or payable in respect of tax, plus

(b) 10% of any part that has not.

7(3) Sub-paragraphs (1) and (2) apply both–

(a) to a case where no loss would have been recorded but for the inaccuracy, and

(b) to a case where a loss of a different amount would have been recorded (but in that case sub-paragraphs (1) and (2) apply only to the difference between the amount recorded and the true amount).

7(4) *Where an inaccuracy* has the effect of creating or increasing an aggregate loss recorded for a group of companies–

(a) the potential lost revenue shall be calculated in accordance with this paragraph, and

(b) in applying paragraph 5 in accordance with sub-paragraphs (1) and (2) above, group relief may be taken into account (despite paragraph 5(4)(a)).

7(5) The potential lost revenue in respect of a loss is nil where, because of the nature of the loss or P's circumstances, there is no reasonable prospect of the loss being used to support a claim to reduce a tax liability (of any person).

Commencement Date – See headnote to Sch. 24.

POTENTIAL LOST REVENUE: DELAYED TAX

8(1) Where an inaccuracy resulted in an amount of tax being declared later than it should have been ("the delayed tax"), the potential lost revenue is–

(a) 5% of the delayed tax for each year of the delay, or

(b) a percentage of the delayed tax, for each separate period of delay of less than a year, equating to 5% per year.

8(2) This paragraph does not apply to a case to which paragraph 7 applies.

Commencement Date – See headnote to Sch. 24.

REDUCTIONS FOR DISCLOSURE

9(A1) Paragraph 10 provides for reductions in penalties–

(a) under paragraph 1 where a person discloses an inaccuracy that involves a domestic matter,

(b) under paragraph 1A where a person discloses a supply of false information or withholding of information, and

(c) under paragraph 2 where a person discloses a failure to disclose an under-assessment.

9(A2) Paragraph 10A provides for reductions in penalties under paragraph 1 where a person discloses an inaccuracy that involves an offshore matter or an offshore transfer.

9(A3) Sub-paragraph (1) applies where a person discloses–

(a) an inaccuracy that involves a domestic matter,

(b) a careless inaccuracy that involves an offshore matter,

(c) a supply of false information or withholding of information, or

(d) a failure to disclose an under-assessment.

9(1) A person discloses the matter by–

(a) telling HMRC about it,

(b) giving HMRC reasonable help in quantifying the inaccuracy, the inaccuracy attributable to the supply of false information or withholding of information, or the under-assessment, and

(c) allowing HMRC access to records for the purpose of ensuring that the inaccuracy, the inaccuracy attributable to the supply of false information or withholding of information, or the under-assessment is fully corrected.

9(1A) Sub-paragraph (1B) applies where a person discloses–

(a) a deliberate inaccuracy (whether concealed or not) that involves an offshore matter, or

(b) an inaccuracy that involves an offshore transfer.

9(1B) A person discloses the inaccuracy by–

(a) telling HMRC about it,

(b) giving HMRC reasonable help in quantifying the inaccuracy,

(c) allowing HMRC access to records for the purpose of ensuring that the inaccuracy is fully corrected, and

(d) providing HMRC with additional information.

9(1C) The Treasury must make regulations setting out what is meant by **"additional information"** for the purposes of sub-paragraph (1B)(d).

9(1D) Regulations under sub-paragraph (1C) are to be made by statutory instrument.

9(1E) An instrument containing regulations under sub-paragraph (1C) is subject to annulment in pursuance of a resolution of the House of Commons.

9(2) Disclosure–

(a) is "unprompted" if made at a time when the person making it has no reason to believe that HMRC have discovered or are about to discover the inaccuracy, the supply of false information or withholding of information, or the under assessment, and

(b) otherwise, is "prompted".

9(3) In relation to disclosure **"quality"** includes timing, nature and extent.

9(4) Paragraph 4A(4) to (5) applies to determine whether an inaccuracy involves an offshore matter, an offshore transfer or a domestic matter for the purposes of this paragraph.

Commencement Date – See headnote to Sch. 24.

History – Para. 9(A1)–(A3) substituted for (A1) by FA 2016, s. 163(1) and Sch. 21, para. 2(2), with effect from 1 April 2017 for all purposes and has effect for inheritance tax purposes (in relation to transfers of value on or after that date) and for income tax and capital gains tax purposes (in relation to any tax year commencing on or after 6 April 2016) (SI 2017/259, reg. 2). Former para. 9(A1) read as follows:

"**9(A1)** Paragraph 10 provides for reductions in penalties under paragraphs 1, 1A and 2 where a person discloses an inaccuracy, a supply of false information or withholding of information, or a failure to disclose an under-assessment.".

Para. 9(A1) inserted by FA 2008, s. 122 and Sch. 40, para. 9(2), with effect from 1 April 2009 (SI 2009/571, art. 2).

In para. 9(1)(b), the words "supply of false information" substituted for "supply or false information" by FA 2009, s. 109 and Sch. 57, para. 4, with effect from 21 July 2009.

In para. 9(1), the words "the matter" substituted for the words "an inaccuracy, a supply of false information or withholding of information, or a failure to disclose an under-assessment" by FA 2016, s. 163(1) and Sch. 21, para. 2(3), with effect from 1 April 2017 for all purposes and has effect for inheritance tax purposes (in relation to transfers of value on or after that date) and for income tax and capital gains tax purposes (in relation to any tax year commencing on or after 6 April 2016) (SI 2017/259, reg. 2).

In para. 9(1)(c), the words "supply of false information" substituted for "supply or false information" by FA 2009, s. 109 and Sch. 57, para. 4, with effect from 21 July 2009.

In para. 9(1) the words ", a supply of false information or withholding of information," inserted and in para. (b) and (c) the words ", the inaccuracy attributable to the supply or false information or withholding of information, or the" substituted for the word "or" by FA 2008, s. 122 and Sch. 40, para. 9(3), with effect from 1 April 2009 (SI 2009/571, art. 2).

Para. 9(1A)–(1E) inserted by FA 2016, s. 163(1) and Sch. 21, para. 2(4), with effect from 8 March 2017 for the purpose of making the regulations and from 1 April 2017 for all purposes and has effect for inheritance tax purposes (in relation to transfers of value on or after that date) and for income tax and capital gains tax purposes (in relation to any tax year commencing on or after 6 April 2016) (SI 2017/259, reg. 2 and 3).

In para. 9(2)(a) the words ", the supply of false information or withholding of information, or the under assessment" substituted for the word "or under-assessment" by FA 2008, s. 122 and Sch. 40, para. 9(3), with effect from 1 April 2009 (SI 2009/571, art. 2).

Para. 9(4) inserted by FA 2016, s. 163(1) and Sch. 21, para. 2(5), with effect from 1 April 2017 for all purposes and has effect for inheritance tax purposes (in relation to transfers of value on or after that date) and for income tax and capital gains tax purposes (in relation to any tax year commencing on or after 6 April 2016) (SI 2017/259, reg. 2).

10(1) If a person who would otherwise be liable to a penalty of a percentage shown in column 1 of the Table (a "standard percentage") has made a disclosure, HMRC must reduce the standard percentage to one that reflects the quality of the disclosure.

10(2) But the standard percentage may not be reduced to a percentage that is below the minimum shown for it–

(a) in the case of a prompted disclosure, in column 2 of the Table, and

(b) in the case of an unprompted disclosure, in column 3 of the Table.

Standard %	*Minimum % for prompted disclosure*	*Minimum % for unprompted disclosure*
30%	15%	0%
70%	35%	20%
100%	50%	30%

Commencement Date – See headnote to Sch. 24 for commencement of former para. 10.

Prospective amendments – The Table in para. 10(2) amended by FA 2015, s. 120 and Sch. 20, para. 5, with effect from a day to be appointed under FA 2015, s. 120(2).

History – The Table in para. 10(2) substituted by FA 2016, s. 163(1) and Sch. 21, para. 3, with effect from 1 April 2017 for all purposes and has effect for inheritance tax purposes (in relation to transfers of value on or after that date) and for income tax and capital gains tax purposes (in relation to any tax year commencing on or after 6 April 2016) (SI 2017/259, reg. 2). Former table read as follows:

"Standard %	*Minimum % for prompted disclosure*	*Minimum % for unprompted disclosure*
30%	15%	0%
45%	22.5%	0%
60%	30%	0%
70%	35%	20%
105%	52.5%	30%
140%	70%	40%
100%	50%	30%
150%	75%	45%
200%	100%	60%".

Para. 10 substituted by FA 2010, s. 35 and Sch. 10, para. 3, with effect from 6 April 2011, but the substitution does not have effect in relation to documents given to HMRC and assessments issued by HMRC in relation to a tax period (as defined in para. 28(g)) commencing on or before 5 April 2011 (SI 2011/975).

Cross references – FA 2009, s. 94(10)(a): no information may be published if the amount of the penalty is reduced to the full extent permitted.

10A(1) If a person who would otherwise be liable to a penalty of a percentage shown in column 1 of the Table (a "standard percentage") has made a disclosure, HMRC must reduce the standard percentage to one that reflects the quality of the disclosure.

10A(2) But the standard percentage may not be reduced to a percentage that is below the minimum shown for it–

(a) in the case of a prompted disclosure, in column 2 of the Table, and

(b) in the case of an unprompted disclosure, in column 3 of the Table.

Standard %	*Minimum % for prompted disclosure*	*Minimum % for unprompted disclosure*
30%	15%	0%
37.5%	18.75%	0%
45%	22.5%	0%
60%	30%	0%
70%	45%	30%
87.5%	53.75%	35%
100%	60%	40%
105%	62.5%	40%
125%	72.5%	50%
140%	80%	50%
150%	85%	55%
200%	110%	70%

History – Para. 10A inserted by FA 2016, s. 163(1) and Sch. 21, para. 4, with effect from 1 April 2017 for all purposes and has effect for inheritance tax purposes (in relation to transfers of value on or after that date) and for income tax and capital gains tax purposes (in relation to any tax year commencing on or after 6 April 2016) (SI 2017/259, reg. 2).

SPECIAL REDUCTION

11(1) If they think it right because of special circumstances, HMRC may reduce a penalty under paragraph 1, 1A or 2.

11(2) In sub-paragraph (1) **"special circumstances"** does not include–

(a) ability to pay, or

(b) the fact that a potential loss of revenue from one taxpayer is balanced by a potential over-payment by another.

11(3) In sub-paragraph (1) the reference to reducing a penalty includes a reference to–

(a) staying a penalty, and

(b) agreeing a compromise in relation to proceedings for a penalty.

Commencement Date – See headnote to Sch. 24.

History – In para. 11(1) ", (1A)" inserted by FA 2008, s. 122 and Sch. 40, para. 10, with effect from 1 April 2009 (SI 2009/571, art. 2).

INTERACTION WITH OTHER PENALTIES AND LATE PAYMENT SURCHARGES

History – In above heading the words "AND LATE PAYMENT SURCHARGES" inserted by FA 2008, s. 122 and Sch. 40, para. 11(4), with effect from 1 April 2009 (SI 2009/571, art. 2).

12(1) The final entry in the Table in paragraph 1 excludes a document in respect of which a penalty is payable under section 98 of TMA 1970 (special returns).

12(2) The amount of a penalty for which P is liable under paragraph 1 or 2 in respect of a document relating to a tax period shall be reduced by the amount of any other penalty incurred by P, or any surcharge for late payment of tax imposed on P, if the amount of the penalty or surcharge is determined by reference to the same tax liability.

12(2A) In sub-paragraph (2) **"any other penalty"** does not include a penalty under Part 4 of FA 2014 (penalty where corrective action not taken after follower notice etc) or Schedule 22 to FA 2016 (asset-based penalty).

12(3) In the application of section 97A of TMA 1970 (multiple penalties) no account shall be taken of a penalty under paragraph 1 or 2.

12(4) Where penalties are imposed under paragraphs 1 and 1A in respect of the same inaccuracy, the aggregate of the amounts of the penalties must not exceed the relevant percentage of the potential lost revenue.

12(5) The relevant percentage is–

(a) if the penalty imposed under paragraph 1 is for an inaccuracy in category 1, 100%,

(b) if the penalty imposed under paragraph 1 is for an inaccuracy in category 2, 150%, and

(c) if the penalty imposed under paragraph 1 is for an inaccuracy in category 3, 200%.

Commencement Date – See headnote to Sch. 24.

Prospective amendments – Para. 12(5)(za) inserted and in para. 12(5)(a) "125%" substituted for "100%" amended by FA 2015, s. 120 and Sch. 20, para. 6, with effect from a day to be appointed under FA 2015, s. 120(2).

History – In para. 12(2) the words "incurred by P, or any surcharge for late payment of tax imposed on P, if the amount of the penalty or surcharge is determined by reference to the same tax liability." substituted for the words "which P has incurred and the amount of which is determined by reference to P's tax liability for that period." by FA 2008, s. 122 and Sch. 40, para. 11(2), with effect from 1 April 2009 (SI 2009/571, art. 2).
In para. 12(2A), the words "or Schedule 22 to FA 2016 (asset-based penalty)" inserted by FA 2016, s. 165(1) and Sch. 22, para. 20(3), with effect for inheritance tax purposes, in relation to transfers of value made on or after 1 April 2017 and for income tax and capital gains tax purposes, in relation to tax years commencing on or after 6 April 2016 (SI 2017/277, reg. 2).
Para. 12(2A) inserted by FA 2014, s. 233 and Sch. 33, para. 3, with effect from 17 July 2014.
Para. 12(4) and (5) substituted for former para. 12(4) by FA 2010, s. 35 and Sch. 10, para. 4, with effect from 6 April 2011, but the substitution does not have effect in relation to documents given to HMRC and assessments issued by HMRC in relation to a tax period (as defined in para. 28(g)) commencing on or before 5 April 2011 (SI 2011/975).
Former para. 12(4) inserted by FA 2008, s. 122 and Sch. 40, para. 11(2), with effect from 1 April 2009 (SI 2009/571, art. 2).

Part 3 – Procedure

ASSESSMENT

13(1) Where a person becomes liable for a penalty under paragraph 1, 1A or 2 HMRC shall–

(a) assess the penalty,

(b) notify the person, and

(c) state in the notice a tax period in respect of which the penalty is assessed (subject to sub-paragraph (1ZB)).

13(1ZA) Sub-paragraph (1ZB) applies where–

(a) a person is at any time liable for two or more penalties relating to PAYE returns, or for two or more penalties relating to CIS returns, and

(b) the penalties ("the relevant penalties") are assessed in respect of more than one tax period ("the relevant tax periods").

13(1ZB) A notice under sub-paragraph (1) in respect of any of the relevant penalties may, instead of stating the tax period in respect of which the penalty is assessed, state the tax year or the part of a tax year to which the penalty relates.

13(1ZC) For that purpose, a relevant penalty relates to the tax year or the part of a tax year in which the relevant tax periods fall.

13(1ZD) For the purposes of sub-paragraph (1ZA)–

"a PAYE return" means a return for the purposes of PAYE regulations;

"a CIS return" means a return for the purposes of regulations under section 70(1)(a) of FA 2004 in connection with deductions on account of tax under the Construction Industry Scheme.

13(1A) A penalty under paragraph 1, 1A or 2 must be paid before the end of the period of 30 days beginning with the day on which notification of the penalty is issued.

13(2) An assessment–

(a) shall be treated for procedural purposes in the same way as an assessment to tax (except in respect of a matter expressly provided for by this Act),

(b) may be enforced as if it were an assessment to tax, and

(c) may be combined with an assessment to tax.

13(3) An assessment of a penalty under paragraph 1 or 1A must be made before the end of the period of 12 months beginning with–

(a) *the end of the appeal* period for the decision correcting the inaccuracy, or

(b) if there is no assessment to the tax concerned within paragraph (a), the date on which the inaccuracy is corrected.

13(4) An assessment of a penalty under paragraph 2 must be made before the end of the period of 12 months beginning with–

(a) the end of the appeal period for the assessment of tax which corrected the understatement, or

(b) if there is no assessment within paragraph (a), the date on which the understatement is corrected.

13(5) For the purpose of sub-paragraphs (3) and (4) a reference to an appeal period is a reference to the period during which–

(a) an appeal could be brought, or

(b) an appeal that has been brought has not been determined or withdrawn.

13(6) Subject to sub-paragraphs (3) and (4), a supplementary assessment may be made in respect of a penalty if an earlier assessment operated by reference to an underestimate of potential lost revenue.

13(7) In this Part of this Schedule references to an assessment to tax, in relation to inheritance tax and stamp duty reserve tax, are to a determination.

Commencement Date – See headnote to Sch. 24.

Prospective amendments – In para. 13(1ZA), the words "or for two or more penalties relating to apprenticeship levy returns," inserted (after the words "CIS returns,") by FA 2016, s. 113(3)(a), with effect in accordance with regulations made under FA 2016, s. 113(16).
In para. 13(1ZD), entry for "an apprenticeship levy return" inserted (after entry for "a CIS return") by FA 2016, s. 113(3)(b), with effect in accordance with regulations made under FA 2016, s. 113(16).

History – In s. 13(1)(c), the words "(subject to sub-paragraph (1ZB))" inserted by FA 2013, s. 230 and Sch. 50, para. 1(2), with effect in relation to any assessment of a penalty under FA 2007, Sch. 24 made on or after 17 July 2013.
In para. 13(1) the words "Where a person" substituted for the words "Where P", ", (1A)" inserted and the words "notify the person" substituted for the words "notify P" by FA 2008, s. 122 and Sch. 40, para. 12(2), with effect from 1 April 2009 (SI 2009/571, art. 2).
Para. 13(1ZA) inserted by FA 2013, s. 230 and Sch. 50, para. 1(3), with effect in relation to any assessment of a penalty under FA 2007, Sch. 24 made on or after 17 July 2013.
Para. 13(1ZB) inserted by FA 2013, s. 230 and Sch. 50, para. 1(3), with effect in relation to any assessment of a penalty under FA 2007, Sch. 24 made on or after 17 July 2013.
Para. 13(1ZC) inserted by FA 2013, s. 230 and Sch. 50, para. 1(3), with effect in relation to any assessment of a penalty under FA 2007, Sch. 24 made on or after 17 July 2013.
Para. 13(1ZD) inserted by FA 2013, s. 230 and Sch. 50, para. 1(3), with effect in relation to any assessment of a penalty under FA 2007, Sch. 24 made on or after 17 July 2013.
Para. 13(1A) inserted by FA 2008, s. 122 and Sch. 40, para. 12(3), with effect from 1 April 2009 (SI 2009/571, art. 2).
In para. 13(3) "or (1A)" inserted, the words "before the end of the" substituted for the words "within the" and the words "to the tax concerned" inserted by FA 2008, s. 122 and Sch. 40, para. 12(4), with effect from 1 April 2009 (SI 2009/571, art. 2).
In para. 13(4) the words from "before the end" to the end substituted for the words "within the period of 12 months beginning with the end of the appeal period for the assessment of tax which corrected the understatement." by FA 2008, s. 122 and Sch. 40, para. 12(5), with effect from 1 April 2009 (SI 2009/571, art. 2).
Para. 13(7) inserted by FA 2009, s. 109 and Sch. 57, para. 5, with effect from 21 July 2009.

SUSPENSION

14(1) HMRC may suspend all or part of a penalty for a careless inaccuracy under paragraph 1 by notice in writing to P.

14(2) A notice must specify–

(a) what part of the penalty is to be suspended,

(b) a period of suspension not exceeding two years, and

(c) conditions of suspension to be complied with by P.

14(3) HMRC may suspend all or part of a penalty only if compliance with a condition of suspension would help P to avoid becoming liable to further penalties under paragraph 1 for careless inaccuracy.

14(4) A condition of suspension may specify–

(a) action to be taken, and

(b) a period within which it must be taken.

14(5) On the expiry of the period of suspension–

(a) if P satisfies HMRC that the conditions of suspension have been complied with, the suspended penalty or part is cancelled, and

(b) otherwise, the suspended penalty or part becomes payable.

14(6) If, during the period of suspension of all or part of a penalty under paragraph 1, P becomes liable for another penalty under that paragraph, the suspended penalty or part becomes payable.

Commencement Date – See headnote to Sch. 24.

APPEAL

15(1) A person may appeal against a decision of HMRC that a penalty is payable by the person.

15(2) A person may appeal against a decision of HMRC as to the amount of a penalty payable by the person.

15(3) A person may appeal against a decision of HMRC not to suspend a penalty payable by the person.

15(4) A person may appeal against a decision of HMRC setting conditions of suspension of a penalty payable by the person.

Commencement Date – See headnote to Sch. 24.

History – In para. 15 the words "A person may" substituted for the words "P may" (four times) and the words "by the person" substituted for the words "by P" (four times) by FA 2008, s. 122 and Sch. 40, para. 13, with effect from 1 April 2009 (SI 2009/571, art. 2).

16(1) An appeal under this Part of this Schedule shall be treated in the same way as an appeal against an assessment to the tax concerned (including by the application of any provision about bringing the appeal by notice to HMRC, about HMRC review of the decision or about determination of the appeal by the First-tier Tribunal or Upper Tribunal).

16(2) Sub-paragraph (1) does not apply–

(a) so as to require P to pay a penalty before an appeal against the assessment of the penalty is determined, or

(b) in respect of any other matter expressly provided for by this Act.

Commencement Date – See headnote to Sch. 24.

History – Para. 16(2) substituted by FA 2009, s. 109 and Sch. 57, para. 6, with effect from 21 July 2009.

Para. 16 substituted by SI 2009/56, art. 3(1) and Sch. 1, para. 466, operative from 1 April 2009, subject to transitional and saving provisions in SI 2009/56, Sch. 3.

Para. 16 formerly substituted by FA 2008, s. 122 and Sch. 40, para. 14, with effect from 1 April 2009 (SI 2009/571, art. 2).

17(1) On an appeal under paragraph 15(1) the tribunal may affirm or cancel HMRC's decision.

17(2) On an appeal under paragraph 15(2) the tribunal may–

(a) affirm HMRC's decision, or

(b) substitute for HMRC's decision another decision that HMRC had power to make.

17(3) If the tribunal substitutes its decision for HMRC's, the appellate tribunal may rely on paragraph 11–

(a) to the same extent as HMRC (which may mean applying the same percentage reduction as HMRC to a different starting point), or

(b) to a different extent, but only if the appellate tribunal thinks that HMRC's decision in respect of the application of paragraph 11 was flawed.

17(4) On an appeal under paragraph 15(3)–

(a) the tribunal may order HMRC to suspend the penalty only if it thinks that HMRC's decision not to suspend was flawed, and

(b) if the tribunal orders HMRC to suspend the penalty–

(i) P may appeal against a provision of the notice of suspension, and

(ii) the tribunal may order HMRC to amend the notice.

17(5) On an appeal under paragraph 15(4) the tribunal–

(a) may affirm the conditions of suspension, or

(b) may vary the conditions of suspension, but only if the tribunal thinks that HMRC's decision in respect of the conditions was flawed.

17(5A) In this paragraph **"tribunal"** means the First-tier Tribunal or Upper Tribunal (as appropriate by virtue of paragraph 16(1)).

17(6) In sub-paragraphs (3)(b), (4)(a) and (5)(b) **"flawed"** means flawed when considered in the light of the principles applicable in proceedings for judicial review.

17(7) Paragraph 14 (see in particular paragraph 14(3)) is subject to the possibility of an order under this paragraph.

Commencement Date – See headnote to Sch. 24.

History – In para. 17(1), (2) and (3), the word "appellate", which appeared before the word "tribunal", omitted by SI 2009/56, art. 3(1) and Sch. 1, para. 467(2), operative from 1 April 2009, subject to transitional and saving provisions in SI 2009/56, Sch. 3.

In para. 17(4)(a) and (b), the word "appellate", which appeared before the word "tribunal", omitted by SI 2009/56, art. 3(1) and Sch. 1, para. 467(3)(a) and (b)(i), operative from 1 April 2009, subject to transitional and saving provisions in SI 2009/56, Sch. 3.

In para. 17(4)(b)(i), the words "to the appellate tribunal", which appeared after the word "appeal", omitted by SI 2009/56, art. 3(1) and Sch. 1, para. 467(3)(b)(ii), operative from 1 April 2009, subject to transitional and saving provisions in SI 2009/56, Sch. 3.

In para. 17(4)(b)(ii), the word "appellate", which appeared before the word "tribunal", omitted by SI 2009/56, art. 3(1) and Sch. 1, para. 467(3)(b)(iii), operative from 1 April 2009, subject to transitional and saving provisions in SI 2009/56, Sch. 3.

In para. 17(5), the word "appellate", which appeared before the word "tribunal" in each place, omitted by SI 2009/56, art. 3(1) and Sch. 1, para. 467(4), operative from 1 April 2009, subject to transitional and saving provisions in SI 2009/56, Sch. 3.

Para. 17(5A) inserted by SI 2009/56, art. 3(1) and Sch. 1, para. 467(5), operative from 1 April 2009, subject to transitional and saving provisions in SI 2009/56, Sch. 3.

Part 4 – Miscellaneous

AGENCY

18(1) P is liable under paragraph 1(1)(a) where a document which contains a careless inaccuracy (within the meaning of paragraph 3) is given to HMRC on P's behalf.

18(2) In paragraph 2(1)(b) and (2)(a) a reference to P includes a reference to a person who acts on P's behalf in relation to tax.

18(3) Despite sub-paragraphs (1) and (2), P is not liable to a penalty under paragraph 1 or 2 in respect of anything done or omitted by P's agent where P satisfies HMRC that P took reasonable care to avoid inaccuracy (in relation to paragraph 1) or unreasonable failure (in relation to paragraph 2).

18(4) In paragraph 3(1)(a) (whether in its application to a document given by P or, by virtue of sub-paragraph (1) above, in its application to a document given on P's behalf) a reference to P includes a reference to a person who acts on P's behalf in relation to tax.

18(5) In paragraph 3(2) a reference to P includes a reference to a person who acts on P's behalf in relation to tax.

18(6) Paragraph 3A applies where a document is given to HMRC on behalf of P as it applies where a document is given to HMRC by P (and in paragraph 3B(9) the reference to P includes a person acting on behalf of P).

Commencement Date – See headnote to Sch. 24.

History – In para. 18(3) the words "under paragraph 1 or 2" inserted by FA 2008, s. 122 and Sch. 40, para. 15, with effect from 1 April 2009 (SI 2009/571, art. 2).
Para. 18(6) inserted by F(No. 2)A 2017, s. 64(2), with effect in relation to any document of a kind listed in the Table in para. 1 which is given to HMRC on or after 16 November 2017 (Royal Assent) and relates to tax period which begins on or after 6 April 2017 and ends on or after 16 November (Royal Assent).

DOUBLE JEOPARDY

21 A person is not liable to a penalty under paragraph 1, 1A or 2 in respect of an inaccuracy or failure in respect of which the person has been convicted of an offence.

Commencement Date – See headnote to Sch. 24.

History – In para. 21 the words "A person is" substituted for the words "P is", ", 1A" inserted and the words "the person has" substituted for the words "P has" by FA 2008, s. 122 and Sch. 40, para. 17, with effect from 1 April 2009 (SI 2009/571, art. 2).

21ZA(1) A person is not liable to a penalty under paragraph 1 in respect of an inaccuracy if–

(a) the inaccuracy involves a claim by the person to exercise or rely on a VAT right (in relation to a supply) that has been denied or refused by HMRC as mentioned in subsection (4) of section 69C of VATA 1994, and

(b) the person has been assessed to a penalty under that section (and the assessment has not been successfully appealed against or withdrawn).

21ZA(2) In sub-paragraph (1)(a) **"VAT right"** has the same meaning as in section 69C of VATA 1994.

History – Para. 21ZA inserted by F(No. 2)A 2017, s. 68(6), with effect from 16 November 2017 (Royal Assent).

Part 5 – General

CLASSIFICATION OF TERRITORIES

21A(1) A category 1 territory is a territory designated as a category 1 territory by order made by the Treasury.

21A(2) A category 2 territory is a territory that is neither–

(a) a category 1 territory, nor

(b) a category 3 territory.

21A(3) A category 3 territory is a territory designated as a category 3 territory by order made by the Treasury.

21A(4) In considering how to classify a territory for the purposes of this paragraph, the Treasury must have regard to–

(a) the existence of any arrangements between the UK and that territory for the exchange of information for tax enforcement purposes,

(b) the quality of any such arrangements (in particular, whether they provide for information to be exchanged automatically or on request),

(c) the benefit that the UK would be likely to obtain from receiving information from that territory, were such arrangements to exist with it,

(d) the existence of any other arrangements between the UK and that territory for co-operation in the area of taxation, and

(e) the quality of any such other arrangements (in particular, the extent to which the co-operation provided for in them assists or is likely to assist in the protection of revenue raised from taxation in the UK).

21A(5) An order under this paragraph is to be made by statutory instrument.

21A(6) Subject to sub-paragraph (7), an instrument containing an order under this paragraph is subject to annulment in pursuance of a resolution of the House of Commons.

21A(7) If the order is–

(a) the first order to be made under sub-paragraph (1), or

(b) the first order to be made under sub-paragraph (3),

it may not be made unless a draft of the instrument containing it has been laid before, and approved by a resolution of, the House of Commons.

21A(8) An order under this paragraph does not apply to inaccuracies in a document given to HMRC (or, in a case within paragraph 3(2), inaccuracies discovered by P) before the date on which the order comes into force.

Prospective amendments – Para. 21A(A1) inserted by FA 2015, s. 120 and Sch. 20, para. 7(2), with effect from a day to be appointed under FA 2015, s. 120(2).
Para. 21A(2) substituted by FA 2015, s. 120 and Sch. 20, para. 7(3), with effect from a day to be appointed under FA 2015, s. 120(2).
Para. 21A(7) substituted by FA 2015, s. 120 and Sch. 20, para. 7(4), with effect from a day to be appointed under FA 2015, s. 120(2).

History – Para. 21A(4)(d) and (e) inserted (and the word "and" at the end of para. 21A(4)(b) omitted) by FA 2012, s. 219 with effect from 17 July 2012.
Para. 21A and the heading before it inserted by FA 2010, s. 35 and Sch. 10, para. 5, with effect from 6 April 2011, but the insertion does not have effect in relation to documents given to HMRC and assessments issued by HMRC in relation to a tax period (as defined in para. 28(g)) commencing on or before 5 April 2011 (SI 2011/975).

Statutory instruments – SI 2011/976: made under para. 21A(1)–(4).

LOCATION OF ASSETS ETC

21B(1) The Treasury may by regulations make provision for determining for the purposes of paragraph 4A where–

(a) a source of income is located,

(b) an asset is situated or held, or

(c) activities are wholly or mainly carried on.

21B(1A) The Treasury may by regulations make provision for determining for the purposes of paragraph 4AA where–

(a) income is received or transferred,

(b) the proceeds of a disposal are received or transferred, or

(c) assets are transferred.

21B(2) Different provision may be made for different cases and for income tax, capital gains tax and inheritance tax.

21B(3) Regulations under this paragraph are to be made by statutory instrument.

21B(4) An instrument containing regulations under this paragraph is subject to annulment in pursuance of a resolution of the House of Commons.

History – Para. 21B(1A) inserted by FA 2015, s. 120 and Sch. 20, para. 8(2), with effect from 1 April 2016 (in relation to documents given to HMRC relating to a transfer of value made on or after that date for the purposes of inheritance tax; and a tax year commencing on or after 6 April 2016 for the purposes of income tax and capital gains tax) (SI 2016/456, art. 3).
In para. 21B(2) the words ", capital gains tax and inheritance tax" substituted for the words "and capital gains tax" by FA 2015, s. 120 and Sch. 20, para. 8(3), with effect from 1 April 2016 (in relation to documents given to HMRC relating to a transfer of value made on or after that date for the purposes of inheritance tax; and a tax year commencing on or after 6 April 2016 for the purposes of income tax and capital gains tax) (SI 2016/456, art. 3).
Para. 21B and the heading before it inserted by FA 2010, s. 35 and Sch. 10, para. 5, with effect from 6 April 2011, but the insertion does not have effect in relation to documents given to HMRC and assessments issued by HMRC in relation to a tax period (as defined in para. 28(g)) commencing on or before 5 April 2011 (SI 2011/975).

TREATMENT OF CERTAIN PAYMENTS ON ACCOUNT OF TAX

21C In paragraphs 1(2) and 5 references to "tax" are to be interpreted as if amounts payable under section 59AA(2) of TMA 1970 (non-resident CGT disposals: payments on account of capital gains tax) were tax.

Prospective amendments – In para. 21C, the words "and amounts payable on account of apprenticeship levy" inserted (after the words "capital gains tax)") by FA 2016, s. 113(4), with effect in accordance with regulations made under FA 2016, s. 113(16).

History – Para. 21C inserted by FA 2015, s. 37 and Sch. 7, para. 56(3), with effect in relation to disposals made on or after 6 April 2015.

INTERPRETATION

22 Paragraphs 23 to 27 apply for the construction of this Schedule.

Commencement Date – See headnote to Sch. 24.

History – In para. 22 "27" substituted for "26" by FA 2008, s. 122 and Sch. 40, para. 18, with effect from 1 April 2009 (SI 2009/571, art. 2).

23 HMRC means Her Majesty's Revenue and Customs.

Commencement Date – See headnote to Sch. 24.

23A **"Tax"**, without more, includes duty.

History – Para. 23A inserted by FA 2008, s. 122 and Sch. 40, para. 19, with effect from 1 April 2009 (SI 2009/571, art. 2).

23B **"UK"** means the United Kingdom, including the territorial sea of the United Kingdom.

History – Para. 23B inserted by FA 2010, s. 35 and Sch. 10, para. 6, with effect from 6 April 2011, but the insertion does not have effect in relation to documents given to HMRC and assessments issued by HMRC in relation to a tax period (as defined in para. 28(g)) commencing on or before 5 April 2011 (SI 2011/975).

24 An expression used in relation to income tax has the same meaning as in the Income Tax Acts.

Commencement Date – See headnote to Sch. 24.

25 An expression used in relation to corporation tax has the same meaning as in the Corporation Tax Acts.

Commencement Date – See headnote to Sch. 24.

26 An expression used in relation to capital gains tax has the same meaning as in the enactments relating to that tax.

Commencement Date – See headnote to Sch. 24.

27 An expression used in relation to VAT has the same meaning as in VATA 1994.

Commencement Date – See headnote to Sch. 24.

28 In this Schedule–

(a) [not relevant to National Insurance contributions,]

(b) [not relevant to National Insurance contributions,]

(c) **"direct tax"** means–

   (i) income tax,

   (ii) [not relevant to National Insurance contributions,]

   (iii) [not relevant to National Insurance contributions,]

   (iv) [not relevant to National Insurance contributions.]

(d) [not relevant to National Insurance contributions,]

(da) [omitted by FA 2009, s. 109 and Sch. 57, para. 8,]

(e) a reference to a loss includes a reference to a charge, expense, deficit and any other amount which may be available for, or relied on to claim, a deduction or relief,

(f) a reference to repayment of tax includes a reference to allowing a credit against tax or to a payment of a corporation tax credit,

(fa) [not relevant to National Insurance contributions,]

(g) **"tax period"** means a tax year, accounting period or other period in respect of which tax is charged,

(h) a reference to giving a document to HMRC includes a reference to communicating information to HMRC in any form and by any method (whether by post, fax, email, telephone or otherwise),

(i) a reference to giving a document to HMRC includes a reference to making a statement or declaration in a document,

(j) a reference to making a return or doing anything in relation to a return includes a reference to amending a return or doing anything in relation to an amended return, and

(k) a reference to action includes a reference to omission.

Commencement Date – See headnote to Sch. 24.

History – Para. 28(c)(iv) and (da) and in para. (f) the words "against tax or to a payment of a corporation tax credit" and para. (fa) inserted by FA 2008, s. 122 and Sch. 40, para. 20, with effect from 1 April 2009 (SI 2009/571, art. 2).
Para. 28(da) omitted by FA 2009, s. 109 and Sch. 57, para. 8, with effect from 21 July 2009.
In para. 28(fa)(i) the words "Chapter 2 or 7 of Part 13 of CTA 2009" substituted for the words "Schedule 20 to FA 2000", in para. 28(fa)(ii) the words "Chapter 3 or 4 respectively of Part 14 of CTA 2009" substituted for the words "Schedule 22 to FA 2001", para. 28(fa)(iii) omitted and in para. 28(fa)(iv) the words "Chapter 3 of Part 15 of CTA 2009" substituted for the words "Schedule 5 to FA 2006" by CTA 2009, s. 1322 and Sch. 1, para. 727, with effect for corporation tax purposes for accounting periods ending on or after 1 April 2009, and for income tax and capital gains tax purposes for the tax year 2009–10 and subsequent tax years.

Para. 28(fa)(ia) inserted by FA 2013, s. 35 and Sch. 15, para. 8, with effect in relation to expenditure incurred on or after 1 April 2013.
Para. 28(fa)(iva) inserted (and the word "or" at the end of (iv) omitted) by FA 2013, s. 36 and Sch. 18, para. 7, with effect from 19 July 2013 (SI 2013/1817) in relation to accounting periods beginning on or after 1 April 2013 ("the relevant day" (as defined in FA 2013, Sch. 18, para. 23) for the purposes of CTA 2009, Pt. 15A (television production)).
Para. 28(fa)(ivb) inserted by FA 2013, s. 36 and Sch. 18, para. 7, with effect from 1 April 2014 (SI 2014/1962) in relation to accounting periods beginning on or after the day specified by order for the purposes of FA 2013, Sch. 17, para. 3 ("the relevant day" (as defined in FA 2013, Sch. 18, para. 23) for the purposes of CTA 2009, Pt. 15B (video games development)).
Para. 28(fa)(ivc) inserted by FA 2014, s. 36 and Sch. 4, para. 8, with effect from 22 August 2014, in relation to accounting periods beginning on or after 1 September 2014, subject to the transitional provisions in FA 2014, Sch. 4, para. 17.

CONSEQUENTIAL AMENDMENTS

29 The following provisions are omitted–

(a) sections 95, 95A, 97 and 98A(4) of TMA 1970 (incorrect returns and accounts),

(b) [not relevant to National Insurance contributions,]

(c) [not relevant to National Insurance contributions,]

(d) [not relevant to National Insurance contributions,]

Commencement Date – See headnote to Sch. 24.

30 In paragraphs 7 and 7B of Schedule 1 to the Social Security Contributions and Benefits Act 1992 (c. 4) (penalties) a reference to a provision of TMA 1970 shall be construed as a reference to this Schedule so far as is necessary to preserve its effect.

Commencement Date – See headnote to Sch. 24.

History – In para. 30, the words "paragraphs 7 and 7B" substituted for "paragraph 7" by FA 2009, s. 109 and Sch. 57, para. 9, with effect from 21 July 2009.

31 In paragraphs 7 and 7B of Schedule 1 to the Social Security Contributions and Benefits (Northern Ireland) Act 1992 (c. 7) (penalties) a reference to a provision of TMA 1970 shall be construed as a reference to this Schedule so far as is necessary to preserve its effect.

Commencement Date – See headnote to Sch. 24.

History – In para. 31, the words "paragraphs 7 and 7B" substituted for "paragraph 7" by FA 2009, s. 109 and Sch. 57, para. 9, with effect from 21 July 2009.

PENSIONS ACT 2007

(2007 Chapter 22)

[*26th July 2007*]

ARRANGEMENT OF SECTIONS

PART 1 – STATE PENSION

CREDITS FOR BASIC STATE PENSION

3 Contributions credits for relevant parents and carers

3(1) [Inserts SSCBA 1992, s. 23A.]

3(2) [Amends SSCBA 1992, Sch.3, para. 5.]

3(3) Part 3 of Schedule 1 contains consequential amendments.

UP-RATING OF BASIC STATE PENSION AND OTHER BENEFITS

5 Up-rating of basic pension etc. and standard minimum guarantee by reference to earnings

5(1) [Not reproduced.]

5(2) [Not reproduced.]

5(3) [Not reproduced.]

5(4) **"The designated tax year"** means such tax year as the Secretary of State may designate by an order made before 1st April 2011.

5(5) [Not reproduced.]

5(6) [Not reproduced.]

5(7) [Not reproduced.]

7 Removal of link between lower earnings limit and basic pension

7(1) Section 5 of the SSCBA (earnings limits and thresholds for Class 1 contributions) is amended as follows.

7(2) [Repealed by NICA 2008, s. 4 and Sch. 2.]

7(3) [Omits SSCBA 1992, s. 5(2).]

7(4) Subsections (2) and (3) have effect in relation to the tax year following the designated tax year (see section 5(4)) and subsequent tax years.

7(5) [Inserts SSCBA 1992, s. 176(1).]

History – S. 7(2) repealed by NICA 2008, s. 4 and Sch. 2, with effect from 21 September 2008. S. 7(2) amended SSCBA 1992, s. 5(1).

ADDITIONAL PENSION: SIMPLIFICATION OF ACCRUAL RATES

11 Additional pension: simplified accrual rates as from flat rate introduction year

11(1) Section 45 of the SSCBA (the additional pension in a Category A retirement pension) is amended as follows.

11(2)–(3) [Not relevant.]

11(4) [Amends SSCBA 1992, s. 122.]

11(5) In Schedule 2 to this Act–

(a) Part 1 inserts a new Schedule 4B into the SSCBA;

(b) Part 2 makes provision for up-rating the flat rate accrual amount introduced by the new Schedule 4B; and

(c) Part 3 contains consequential and related amendments.

12 Additional pension: upper accrual point

12(1) In section 22 of the SSCBA (earnings factors)–

(a) [Amends SSCBA 1992, s. 22(2A);]

(b) [Inserts SSCBA 1992, s. 22(2B).]

12(2) [Not relevant.]

12(3) [Amends SSCBA 1992, s. 122.]

12(4) Part 7 of Schedule 1 contains consequential amendments.

12(5) Subsection (6) applies if it appears to the Secretary of State that (apart from that subsection) he would be required to make an order under section 148A of the Administration Act (revaluation of low earnings threshold) by virtue of which the low earnings threshold for the following tax year would be an amount not less than the upper accrual point.

12(6) In that event the Secretary of State–

(a) is not required to make such an order under section 148A of the Administration Act, and

(b) instead must make an order abolishing the low earnings threshold and the upper accrual point as from the beginning of the following tax year.

12(7) An order under subsection (6) may make–

(a) such consequential, incidental or supplemental provision, and

(b) such transitional, transitory or saving provision,

as the Secretary of State thinks necessary or expedient in connection with, or in consequence of, the abolition of the low earnings threshold and the upper accrual point.

12(8) An order under subsection (6) may in particular amend, repeal or revoke any provision of any Act or subordinate legislation (whenever passed or made).

12(9) No order may be made under subsection (6) unless a draft of the order has been laid before and approved by a resolution of each House of Parliament.

12(10) In this section–

"the low earnings threshold" has the meaning given by section 44A(5) of the SSCBA;

"the upper accrual point" has the meaning given by section 122(7) and (8) of that Act.

PART 2 – OCCUPATIONAL AND PERSONAL PENSION SCHEMES

CONTRACTING-OUT

15 Abolition of contracting-out for defined contribution pension schemes

15(1) Any certificate which is either–

(a) a contracting-out certificate in relation to a money purchase contracted-out scheme, or

(b) an appropriate scheme certificate,

and is in force immediately before 6 April 2012, ceases to have effect on that date.

15(2) In this section–

"contracting-out certificate", **"money purchase contracted-out scheme"** and **"appropriate scheme certificate"** have the meanings given by section 181(1) of the Pension Schemes Act 1993 (c. 48) (as in force immediately before that day).

15(3) In Schedule 4–

(a) Parts 1 and 2 contain amendments which are consequential on, or related to, the provision made by subsection (1), and

(b) Part 3 contains savings relating to amendments made by Part 1.

15(4) The amendments made by Part 1 of that Schedule have effect as from 6 April 2012 (but any power to make regulations conferred by those amendments may be exercised at any time so as to make regulations having effect as from 6 April 2012).

15(5) The Secretary of State may by regulations make–

(a) such consequential, incidental or supplemental provision, and

(b) such transitional, transitory or saving provision,

as he thinks necessary or expedient in connection with, or in consequence of, the provisions of subsection (1) and Schedule 4.

15(6) Regulations under subsection (5) may in particular amend, repeal or revoke any provision of any Act or subordinate legislation (whenever passed or made).

15(7) No regulations which amend or repeal any provision of an Act may be made under this section unless a draft of the regulations has been laid before and approved by a resolution of each House of Parliament.

15(8) A statutory instrument containing regulations under this section that do not fall within subsection (7) is subject to annulment in pursuance of a resolution of either House of Parliament.

Commencement Date – S. 15(1) has effect from 6 April 2012 by virtue of SI 2011/1267, art. 2(a).

History – In s. 15(1), the words "6 April 2012" substituted for the words "the abolition date" by PA 2014, s. 24 and Sch. 13, para. 78(2), with effect from 6 April 2016 (as not brought into force by any earlier order under PA 2014, s. 56(1)).

In s. 15(2), the definition of "the abolition date" omitted by PA 2014, s. 24 and Sch. 13, para. 78(3), with effect from 6 April 2016 (as not brought into force by any earlier order under PA 2014, s. 56(1)).

In s. 15(4), the words "6 April 2012" substituted for the words "the abolition date" (in each place) by PA 2014, s. 24 and Sch. 13, para. 78(4), with effect from 6 April 2016 (as not brought into force by any earlier order under PA 2014, s. 56(1)).

PART 3 – PERSONAL ACCOUNTS DELIVERY AUTHORITY

20 Personal Accounts Delivery Authority

20(1) There is to be a body corporate known as the Personal Accounts Delivery Authority (referred to in this Part as the "Authority").

20(2) The Authority is not to be regarded as the servant or agent of the Crown or as enjoying any status, immunity or privilege of the Crown.

20(3) Schedule 6 makes provision about the Authority.

PART 4 – GENERAL

27 Consequential etc. provision, repeals and revocations

27(1) The Secretary of State may by order make–

(a) such supplementary, incidental or consequential provision, or

(b) such transitory, transitional or saving provision,

as he considers appropriate for the general purposes, or any particular purposes, of this Act, or in consequence of, or for giving full effect to, any provision made by this Act.

27(2) Schedule 7 contains repeals and revocations.

27(3) The following repeals have effect at the end of the period of 2 months beginning with the day on which this Act is passed–

(a) the repeals in Part 2 of Schedule 7 of the provisions of the Pensions Act 1995 (c. 26) other than paragraphs 19 and 20 of Schedule 4 to that Act;

(b) the repeal in Part 2 of Schedule 7 of paragraph 36 of Schedule 24 to the Civil Partnership Act 2004 (c. 33);

(c) the repeals in Parts 3 and 5 of Schedule 7.

27(4) The following repeals and revocations have effect on 6th April 2010–

(a) the repeals and revocations in Part 1 of Schedule 7;

(b) the repeals in Part 2 of that Schedule other than those falling within subsection (3).

27(5) The repeals in Part 4 of that Schedule have effect on 6th April in the tax year following the designated tax year (see section 5(4)).

27(6) The repeals and revocations in Part 6 of that Schedule have effect on 6 April 2012 (within the meaning of section 15).

27(7) The other repeals contained in that Schedule have effect on the date on which they come into force by virtue of an order made under section 30.

27(8) A statutory instrument containing an order under subsection (1) is subject to annulment in pursuance of a resolution of either House of Parliament.

History – In s. 27(6), the words "6 April 2012" substituted for the words "the abolition date (within the meaning of section 15)" by PA 2014, s. 24 and Sch. 13, para. 79, with effect from 6 April 2016 (as not brought into force by any earlier order under PA 2014, s. 56(1)).

30 Commencement

30(1) The following provisions of this Act come into force on the day on which it is passed–

(a) sections 5 and 6, and Part 5 of Schedule 1, so far as relating to the amounts mentioned in subsection (1)(d) of the new section 150A inserted into the Administration Act by section 5(1);

(b) sections 18(4) to (11) and 19;

(c) Part 3;

(d) this Part.

30(2) The following provisions of this Act come into force on such day as the Secretary of State may by order appoint–

(a) section 14;

(b) section 15(1), Part 2 of Schedule 4 and Part 7 of Schedule 7;

(c) section 17, Schedule 5 and Part 8 of Schedule 7;

(d) section 18(1) to (3).

30(3) The other provisions of this Act come into force at the end of the period of 2 months beginning with the day on which it is passed.

30(4) An order under subsection (2) may–

(a) appoint different days for different purposes;

(b) make such provision as the Secretary of State considers necessary or expedient for transitory, transitional or saving purposes in connection with the coming into force of any provision falling within subsection (2).

Statutory instruments – SI 2011/1267 (not reproduced): made under s. 30(2)(b) (gives commencement date of 6 April 2012).

31 Short title

31 This Act may be cited as the Pensions Act 2007.

SCHEDULES

SCHEDULE 1 – STATE PENSION: CONSEQUENTIAL AND RELATED AMENDMENTS

Sections 1–5, 9, 12 and 13

Part 3 – Contributions Credits for Relevant Parents and Carers

SOCIAL SECURITY CONTRIBUTIONS AND BENEFITS ACT 1992 (C. 4)

9 [Inserts SSCBA 1992, s. 22(5A).]

Part 6 – Deemed Earnings Factors for Purposes of Additional Pension

33 [Amends SSCBA 1992, s. 22(2A).]

34(1) Section 44A of the SSCBA (deemed earnings factors) is amended as follows.

34(2) [Inserts SSCBA 1992, s. 44A(A1).]

34(3) [Amends SSCBA 1992, s. 44A(1).]

34(4) [Inserts SSCBA 1992, s. 44A(4A).]

Part 7 – Additional Pension: Simplified Accrual Rates

SOCIAL SECURITY CONTRIBUTIONS AND BENEFITS ACT 1992 (C. 4)

35 In section 176 of the SSCBA (parliamentary control)–

(a) [repealed by NICA 2008, s. 4 and Sch. 2.]

(b) [amends SSCBA 1992, s. 176(4).]

History – Para. 35(a) repealed by NICA 2008, s. 4 and Sch. 2, with effect from 21 September 2008. Para. 35(a) amended SSCBA 1992, s. 176(1)(c).

PENSION SCHEMES ACT 1993 (C. 48)

37 [Repealed by NICA 2008, s. 4 and Sch. 2.]

History – Para. 37 repealed by NICA 2008, s. 4 and Sch. 2, with effect in relation to 2009–10 and subsequent tax years.

38 [Amends PSA 1993, s. 181(1).]

SCHEDULE 2 – ADDITIONAL PENSION: SIMPLIFIED ACCRUAL RATES

Section 11

Part 3 – Consequential and Related Amendments

PENSION SCHEMES ACT 1993 (C. 48)

12 [Amends PSA 1993, s. 42.]

SCHEDULE 4 – ABOLITION OF CONTRACTING-OUT FOR DEFINED CONTRIBUTION PENSION SCHEMES

Section 15

Part 1 – Amendments Having Effect as from Abolition Date

PENSION SCHEMES ACT 1993 (C. 48)

1 The Pension Schemes Act 1993 has effect subject to the following amendments.

2(1) Section 7 (issue of contracting-out and appropriate scheme certificates) is amended as follows.

2(2) [Substitutes PSA 1993, s. 7(1) and (1A).]

2(3) [Omits PSA 1993, s. 7(4)–(6).]

2(4) [Amends PSA 1993, s. 7(7).]

2(5) [Inserts PSA 1993, s. 7(8).]

2(6) In the sidenote, omit "and appropriate scheme".

3(1) Section 8 (definitions of certain terms) is amended as follows.

3(2) [Substitutes PSA 1993, s. 8(1)(a) and (aa).]

3(3) [Inserts PSA 1993, s. 8(1A).]

3(4) [Amends PSA 1993, s. 8(2).]

15(1) Section 34 (cancellation, variation, surrender and refusal of certificates) is amended as follows.

15(2) [Substitutes PSA 1993, s. 34(1).]

15(3) [Amends PSA 1993, s. 34(3).]

15(4) [Omits PSA 1993, s. 34(5).]

15(5) [Amends PSA 1993, s. 34(8).]

15(6) [Inserts PSA 1993, s. 34(9).]

17 [Inserts PSA 1993, s. 42A(8).]

18 [Omits PSA 1993, s. 42B.]

19 [Inserts PSA 1993, s. 43(7).]

21 [Inserts PSA 1993, s. 45(4).]

22 [Omits PSA 1993, s. 45A.]

34(1) Section 181 (general interpretation) is amended as follows.

34(2) [Amends PSA 1993, s. 181(1).]

34(3) [Amends PSA 1993, s. 181(4).]

35 [Inserts PSA 1993, s. 181A.]

Part 2 – Further Amendments

SOCIAL SECURITY CONTRIBUTIONS AND BENEFITS ACT 1992 (C. 4)

42(1) Section 4C of the SSCBA (power to make provision in consequence of provision made by or by virtue of section 4B(2) etc.) is amended as follows.

42(2) [Omits SSCBA 1992, s. 4C(2)(d).]

42(3) In subsection (5) (matters in respect of which regulations may have retrospective effect)–

(a) in paragraph (b) (amount of rebate under section 41(1D) or 42A(2C) of the Pension Schemes Act 1993 (c. 48)) omit "or 42A(2C)";

(b) [omits SSCBA 1992, s. 4C(5)(g) and (h);]

(c) omit paragraphs (i) and (j) (liability to make, and amount of, payments under section 42A(3) of that Act or minimum contributions).

Commencement Date – Para. 42(2) and (3)(b) (and para. 42(1) in so far as it relates to them) have effect from 6 April 2015 by virtue of SI 2011/1267, art. 3(a).

43 In section 8 of the SSCBA (calculation of primary Class 1 contributions) in subsection (3) (provisions to which calculation is subject) in paragraph (c), for "sections 41 and 42A" substitute "section 41".

44 In section 9 of the SSCBA (calculation of secondary Class 1 contributions) in subsection (3) (provisions to which calculation is subject) in paragraph (c), for "sections 41 and 42A" substitute "section 41".

45(1) In Schedule 1 to the SSCBA (supplementary provisions relating to contributions of Classes 1, 1A, 1B, 2 and 3) paragraph 1 (Class 1 contributions where earner is in more than one employment) is amended as follows.

45(2) In sub-paragraph (3) (determination of amount of primary Class 1 contributions where aggregate earnings include earnings from contracted-out employment)–

(a) omit paragraphs (a) and (b);

(b) in paragraph (c), for sub-paragraphs (i) and (ii) substitute "to such part of the aggregated earnings attributable to COSRS service as exceeds the current primary threshold and does not exceed the current upper earnings limit";

(c) in paragraph (d), for "part or parts attributable to COMPS or COSRS service" substitute "part attributable to COSRS service".

45(3) In sub-paragraph (6) (determination of amount of secondary Class 1 contributions where aggregate earnings include earnings from contracted-out employment) omit paragraphs (a) and (b).

45(4) In sub-paragraph (9) (interpretation) omit the definition of "COMPS service".

PENSION SCHEMES ACT 1993 (C. 48)

46 The Pension Schemes Act 1993 has effect subject to the following amendments.

Commencement Date – Para. 46, in so far as it relates to para. 47 and 54, has effect from 6 April 2015 by virtue of SI 2011/1267, art. 3(a).

47 In section 8 (meaning of, among other things, "minimum payment") omit subsection (3) (regulations may make provision about manner in which minimum payments to be made etc.).

Commencement Date – Para. 47 has effect from 6 April 2015 by virtue of SI 2011/1267, art. 3(a).

50 In section 40 (scope of Chapter 2 of Part 3) omit paragraph (b) (which relates to contributions to be paid by HMRC in respect of members of money purchase contracted-out schemes or of appropriate personal pension schemes).

51 Omit section 42A (reduced rates of contributions, and rebates, for members of money purchase contracted-out schemes etc.).

52 Omit section 43 (payment of minimum contributions to personal pension schemes).

53 Omit section 45 (amount of minimum contributions).

54 Omit section 45B (money purchase and personal pension schemes: verification of ages).

Commencement Date – Para. 54 has effect from 6 April 2015 by virtue of SI 2011/1267, art. 3(a).

58(1) Section 181 (interpretation) is amended as follows.

58(2) In subsection (1), omit the definition of **"minimum contributions"**.

58(3) In subsection (4) (regulations may prescribe the persons who are to be regarded as members or prospective members of an occupational scheme etc.) omit ", 43".

Part 3 – Savings

ISSUE AND CANCELLATION ETC. OF CERTIFICATES FOR PERIODS BEFORE THE ABOLITION DATE

61 Nothing in the relevant amendments and repeals affects the continued operation of any regulations in force under section 7(1) and (7) of the PSA 1993 (issue of certificates) immediately before the abolition date in relation to the issue of a certificate having effect for a period before 6 April 2012.

History – In para. 61, the words "6 April 2012" substituted for the words "the abolition date" in each place by PA 2014, s. 24 and Sch. 13, para. 80(2), with effect from 6 April 2016 (as not brought into force by any earlier order under PA 2014, s. 56(1)).

62(1) Nothing in the relevant amendments and repeals affects the continued operation of section 34 of the PSA 1993 (cancellation, variation, surrender and refusal of certificates), or any regulations in force under it immediately before 6 April 2012, for the purposes of a retrospective act.

62(2) In sub-paragraph (1) **"a retrospective act"** means the cancellation, variation, surrender or refusal of a certificate, or the issue of an amended certificate, where–

(a) the certificate was in force for a period beginning before 6 April 2012 (or, in the case of a refusal of a certificate, would have related to such a period if it had been issued), and

(b) the cancellation, variation, surrender, refusal or issue–

(i) is made after 6 April 2012, but

(ii) has effect from a date before that date.

62(3) An amended certificate issued by virtue of this paragraph must provide for it to cease to have effect as from 6 April 2012.

62(4) In this paragraph and paragraph 61 **"a certificate"** means an appropriate scheme certificate or a contracting-out certificate in respect of a money purchase contracted-out scheme, and each of those terms has the meaning given by section 181(1) of the PSA 1993.

History – In para. 62(1), (2)(a) and (b)(i) and (3), the words "6 April 2012" substituted for the words "the abolition date" in each place by PA 2014, s. 24 and Sch. 13, para. 80(2), with effect from 6 April 2016 (as not brought into force by any earlier order under PA 2014, s. 56(1)).

63 Nothing in the relevant amendments and repeals affects the continued operation of section 164(2) of the PSA 1993 (persons employed by or under the Crown to be treated as employed earners for the purposes of certain provisions) in relation to the provisions of that Act saved by paragraphs 61 and 62.

64 Nothing in the relevant amendments and repeals affects the continued operation of section 177(3)(b)(ii) of the PSA 1993 (administrative expenses of the Secretary of State, other than those arising out of certain provisions, to be paid out of the National Insurance Fund into the Consolidated Fund) in relation to the estimated administrative expenses of the Secretary of State in carrying into effect the provisions of that Act saved by paragraphs 61 and 62.

DETERMINATION OF QUESTION WHETHER SCHEME WAS APPROPRIATE SCHEME

65 Nothing in the relevant amendments and repeals affects the continued operation of any regulations in force under section 7(6) of the PSA 1993 (issue of certificates) immediately before 6 April 2012.

History – In para. 65, the words "6 April 2012" substituted for the words "the abolition date" by PA 2014, s. 24 and Sch. 13, para. 80(2), with effect from 6 April 2016 (as not brought into force by any earlier order under PA 2014, s. 56(1)).

PRESERVATION OF EARNER'S CHOSEN SCHEME

66(1) Nothing in the relevant amendments and repeals–

(a) prevents the giving of a preceding tax year notice, or

(b) otherwise affects the operation of section 44 of the PSA 1993 in relation to such a notice.

66(2) In sub-paragraph (1) a **"preceding tax year notice"** means a notice within section 44(1) of the PSA 1993 which is given on or after 6 April 2012 but in which the date specified in accordance with that provision falls before 6 April 2012.

History – In para. 66(2), the words "6 April 2012" substituted for the words "the abolition date" (in each place) by PA 2014, s. 24 and Sch. 13, para. 80(2), with effect from 6 April 2016 (as not brought into force by any earlier order under PA 2014, s. 56(1)).

INTERPRETATION ETC.

67(1) In this Part of this Schedule–

"the PSA 1993" means the Pension Schemes Act 1993 (c. 48);

"the relevant amendments and repeals" means–

(a) the amendments and repeals made by Part 1 of this Schedule, and

(b) the consequential repeals and revocations in Part 6 of Schedule 7.

67(2) Nothing in this Part of this Schedule is to be read as affecting the generality of section 16 of the Interpretation Act 1978 (c. 30) (general savings).

History – In para. 67(1), the definition of "the abolition date" omitted by PA 2014, s. 24 and Sch. 13, para. 80(3), with effect from 6 April 2016 (as not brought into force by any earlier order under PA 2014, s. 56(1)).

SCHEDULE 6 – THE PERSONAL ACCOUNTS DELIVERY AUTHORITY

Section 20

Part 4 – Supplementary

RECORDS AND FREEDOM OF INFORMATION

23 [Amends FOIA 2000, Sch. 1.]

SCHEDULE 7 – REPEALS AND REVOCATIONS

Section 27

Part 4 – Removal of Link Between Lower Earnings Limit and Basic Pension

Citation	*Extent of repeal*
Social Security Contributions and Benefits Act 1992	Section 5(2).

Part 6 – Abolition of Contracting-out for Defined Contribution Pension Schemes: Repeals and Revocations Having Effect on Abolition Date

Citation or reference	*Extent of repeal or revocation*
Pension Schemes Act 1993 (c. 48)	In section 7– (a) subsections (4) to (6); (b) in subsection (7), the words "or appropriate scheme certificate"; (c) in the sidenote, the words "and appropriate scheme". In section 9– (a) in subsection (1), "or (3)"; (b) subsections (3) and (5); (c) in subsection (6)(a), the words "or, as the case may be, appropriate"; (d) in subsection (6)(b), the words "or, as the case may be, of being an appropriate scheme,". Section 12. Sections 28 to 29. In section 34– (a) in subsection (3), the words "or, as the case may be, the scheme's continuing to be an appropriate scheme" and "or appropriate scheme"; (b) subsection (5); (c) in subsection (8), the words "or appropriate scheme certificate". Section 42B. Section 45A. In section 181(4) ", 44".
Social Security Act 1998 (c. 14)	In Schedule 7, paragraph 126.
Child Support, Pensions and Social Security Act 2000 (c. 19)	In Schedule 5, paragraphs 2(2) and 3(2).

Part 7 – Abolition of Contracting-out for Defined Contribution Pension Schemes: Further Repeals

Commencement Date – Sch. 7, Pt. 7 has effect from 6 April 2012 by virtue of SI 2011/1267, art. 2(c) in so far as it relates to the repeal of the specified provisions contained within PSA 1993, Sch. 4, para. 2.
Sch. 7, Pt. 7 has effect from 6 April 2015 by virtue of SI 2011/1267, art. 2(c) in so far as it relates to the repeal of:
(i) SSCBA 1992, s. 4C(2)(d) and (5)(g) and (h),
(ii) PSA 1993, s. 8(3) and 31,
(iii) PA 1995, Sch. 5, para. 36,
(iv) SSCTFA 1999, Sch. 1, para. 34(b) and 43.

Citation	*Extent of repeal*
Social Security Contributions and Benefits Act 1992 (c. 4)	In section 4C– (a) subsection (2)(d); (b) in subsection (5)(b), "or 42A(2C)"; (c) subsection (5)(g) to (j). In paragraph 1 of Schedule 1– (a) sub-paragraph (3)(a) and (b); (b) sub-paragraph (6)(a) and (b); (c) in sub-paragraph (9), the definition of "COMPS service".
Pension Schemes Act 1993 (c. 48)	Section 8(3). Section 40(b). Section 42A. Section 43. Section 45. Section 45B. In section 181– (a) in subsection (1), the definition of "minimum contributions"; (b) in subsection (4), ", 43".
Social Security Act 1998 (c. 14)	In Schedule 7, paragraphs 77(4)(a) and 128.
Social Security Contributions (Transfer of Functions, etc.) Act 1999 (c. 2)	In Schedule 1, paragraphs 34(b), 43, 46, 47, 49, 50 and 61(3)(a).
Welfare Reform and Pensions Act 1999 (c. 30)	In Part 2 of Schedule 9, paragraph 7. In Schedule 11, paragraph 21.

FINANCE ACT 2008

(2008 Chapter 9)

[*21st July 2008*]

ARRANGEMENT OF SECTIONS

PART 7 – ADMINISTRATION

Chapter 1 – Information etc

NEW INFORMATION ETC POWERS

113 Information and inspection powers

113(1) Schedule 36 contains provision about the powers of officers of Revenue and Customs to obtain information and to inspect businesses.

113(2) That Schedule comes into force on such day as the Treasury may by order made by statutory instrument appoint.

113(3) An order under subsection (2) may contain transitional provision and savings.

Chapter 5 – Payment and Enforcement

TAKING CONTROL OF GOODS ETC

129 Consequential provision and commencement

129(1) Part 1 of Schedule 43 contains provision consequential on section 127.

129(2) [Not relevant to National Insurance contributions.]

129(3) The extent of the amendments and repeals in Schedule 43 is the same as the provision amended or repealed.

129(4) Sections 127 and 128 and Schedule 43 come into force on such day as the Commissioners may by order made by statutory instrument appoint.

129(5) An order under subsection (4) may–

(a) make different provision for different purposes, and

(b) contain transitional provision and savings.

OTHER MEASURES

137 County court proceedings

137(1) [Not relevant to National Insurance contributions.]

137(2) [Not relevant to National Insurance contributions.]

137(3) [Not relevant to National Insurance contributions.]

137(4) [Not relevant to National Insurance contributions.]

137(5) [Amends SSC(TF)A 1999, Sch. 4, para. 3(1); amends para. 3(4).]

137(6) [Not relevant to National Insurance contributions.]

137(7) Nothing in subsections (2) to (6) affects proceedings commenced or brought in the name of a collector or authorised officer before this Act is passed.

138 Certificates of debt

138(1) [Not relevant to National Insurance contributions.]

138(2) Schedule 44 contains provisions consequential on this section.

PART 9 – FINAL PROVISIONS

165 Interpretation

165(1) In this Act–

"ALDA 1979" means the Alcoholic Liquor Duties Act 1979 (c. 4),

"BGDA 1981" means the Betting and Gaming Duties Act 1981 (c. 63),

"CAA 2001" means the Capital Allowances Act 2001 (c. 2),

"CEMA 1979" means the Customs and Excise Management Act 1979 (c. 2),

"CRCA 2005" means the Commissioners for Revenue and Customs Act 2005 (c. 11),

"CTA 2009" means the Corporation Tax Act 2009,

"CTTA 1984" means the Capital Transfer Tax Act 1984 (c. 51),

"HODA 1979" means the Hydrocarbon Oil Duties Act 1979 (c. 5),

"ICTA" means the Income and Corporation Taxes Act 1988 (c. 1),

"IHTA 1984" means the Inheritance Tax Act 1984 (c. 51),

"ITA 2007" means the Income Tax Act 2007 (c. 3),

"ITEPA 2003" means the Income Tax (Earnings and Pensions) Act 2003 (c. 1),

"ITTOIA 2005" means the Income Tax (Trading and Other Income) Act 2005 (c. 5),

"OTA 1975" means the Oil Taxation Act 1975 (c. 22),

"TCGA 1992" means the Taxation of Chargeable Gains Act 1992 (c. 12),

"TMA 1970" means the Taxes Management Act 1970 (c. 9),

"TPDA 1979" means the Tobacco Products Duty Act 1979 (c. 7),

"VATA 1994" means the Value Added Tax Act 1994 (c. 23), and

"VERA 1994" means the Vehicle Excise and Registration Act 1994 (c. 22).

165(2) In this Act–

"FA", followed by a year, means the Finance Act of that year, and

"F(No.2)A", followed by a year, means the Finance (No.2) Act of that year.

History – In s. 165(1), the definition of "CTA 2009" inserted by CTA 2009, s. 1322 and Sch. 1, para. 733, with effect for corporation tax purposes for accounting periods ending on or after 1 April 2009, and for income tax and capital gains tax purposes for the tax year 2009–10 and subsequent tax years.

166 Short title

166 This Act may be cited as the Finance Act 2008.

SCHEDULES

SCHEDULE 36 – INFORMATION AND INSPECTION POWERS

Section 113

Commencement Date – Sch. 36 came into effect from 1 April 2009 (SI 2009/404, art. 2, but subject to provisions of SI 2009/404, art. 3–12).

Part 10 – Consequential Provisions

SOCIAL SECURITY ADMINISTRATION ACT 1992 (C. 5)

84 [Substitutes SSAA 1992, s. 110ZA(1), (2).]

SCHEDULE 43 – TAKING CONTROL OF GOODS ETC: CONSEQUENTIAL PROVISION

Section 129

Part 1 – Consequential Provision: Taking Control of Goods

OTHER REPEALS

11 In consequence of the preceding provisions of this Schedule, omit–

(a) paragraph 8 of Schedule 5 to the Social Security Contributions (Transfer of Functions, etc.) Act 1999 (c. 2),

(b) paragraph 6 of Schedule 11 to the Welfare Reform and Pensions Act 1999 (c. 30),

(c) section 5(1) of the National Insurance Contributions and Statutory Payments Act 2004 (c. 3), and

(d) paragraphs 33, 104(2), 114, 116(2), 119, 123, 126(2), 136, 140 and 147(2) of Schedule 13 of the Tribunals, Courts and Enforcement Act 2007 (c. 15).

SCHEDULE 44 – CERTIFICATES OF DEBT: CONSEQUENTIAL PROVISION

Section 138

SOCIAL SECURITY ADMINISTRATION ACT 1992 (C. 5)

4 [Omits SSAA 1992, s. 118(1), (3) and (7).]

OTHER REPEALS

11 In consequence of the preceding provisions of this Schedule, omit–

(a) [Not relevant to National Insurance contributions.]

(b) [Omits SSA 1998, s. 62(1).]

(c) [Not relevant to National Insurance contributions.]

(d) [Omits SSC(TF)A 1999, Sch. 5, para. 7(2) and (6).]

(e) [Not relevant to National Insurance contributions.]

(f) [Not relevant to National Insurance contributions.]

NATIONAL INSURANCE CONTRIBUTIONS ACT 2008

(2008 Chapter 16)

[*21st July 2008*]

ARRANGEMENT OF SECTIONS

SCHEDULES

1 Amount to be specified as upper earnings limit: Great Britain

1(1) In section 5 of the Social Security Contributions and Benefits Act 1992 (c. 4) (earnings limits and thresholds for Class 1 contributions)–

(a) [amends SSCBA 1992, s. 5(1);]

(b) [omits SSCBA 1992, s. 5(3).]

1(2) [Inserts SSCBA 1992, s. 176(1)(zb).]

1(3) The amendments made by subsections (1)(b) and (2) have effect in relation to regulations specifying the upper earnings limit for 2009–10 or any subsequent tax year.

3 Additional pension: upper accrual point to replace upper earnings limit from 2009–10

3(1) The Social Security Contributions and Benefits Act 1992 (c. 4) is amended as follows.

3(2) [Amends SSCBA 1992, s. 22(2B).]

3(3) [Not reproduced.]

3(4) In section 122 (interpretation)–

(a) [amends SSCBA 1992, s. 122(1);]

(b) [inserts SSCBA 1992, s. 122(6A) and (6B);]

(c) [omits SSCBA 1992, s. 122(7) and (8).]

4 Consequential amendments and repeals

4(1) Schedule 1 contains consequential amendments.

4(2) Schedule 2 contains repeals.

5 Extent

5(1) Sections 1 and 3 extend only to England and Wales and Scotland.

5(2) Section 2 extends only to Northern Ireland.

5(3) Sections 4, 6 and 7 and this section extend to each part of the United Kingdom.

5(4) But an amendment or repeal contained in either Schedule has the same extent as the provision amended or repealed.

6 Commencement

6(1) Subject to subsection (2), this Act comes into force at the end of the period of two months beginning with the day on which it is passed.

6(2) Sub-paragraph (3) of paragraph 6 of Schedule 1, and Schedule 2 so far as relating to the repeals mentioned in that sub-paragraph, come into force on the day appointed by an order under section 30(2) of the Pensions Act 2007 (c. 22) for the coming into force of paragraph 45(2) of Schedule 4 to that Act.

7 Short title

7 This Act may be cited as the National Insurance Contributions Act 2008.

SCHEDULES

SCHEDULE 1 – CONSEQUENTIAL AMENDMENTS

Section 4

SOCIAL SECURITY CONTRIBUTIONS AND BENEFITS ACT 1992 (C. 4)

1 The Social Security Contributions and Benefits Act 1992 is amended as follows.

2 [Inserts SSCBA 1992, s. 22(9).]

3(1) Section 23 is amended as follows.

3(2) [Amends SSCBA 1992, s. 23(3)(a).]

3(3) [Inserts SSCBA 1992, s. 23(3A).]

6(1) Paragraph 1 of Schedule 1 (Class 1 contributions where earner employed in more than one employment) is amended as follows.

6(2) In sub-paragraph (3) (as it has effect without the amendments made by paragraph 45(2) of Schedule 4 to the Pensions Act 2007 (c. 22))–

(a) [amends SSCBA 1992, Sch. 1, para. 1(3)(b);]

(b) [inserts SSCBA 1992, Sch. 1, para. 1(3)(ba);]

(c) [amends SSCBA 1992, Sch. 1, para. 1(3)(c);]

(d) [inserts SSCBA 1992, s. 1(3)(ca).]

6(3) In sub-paragraph (3) (as amended by sub-paragraph (2) above and by paragraph 45(2) of Schedule 4 to the Pensions Act 2007 (c. 22))–

(a) omit paragraph (ba),

(b) in paragraph (c)–

  (i) omit “if some of the aggregated earnings are attributable to COSRS service,”, and

  (ii) for “the current upper earnings limit” substitute “the upper accrual point”, and

(c) in paragraph (ca), omit–

  (i) “if paragraph (c) applies”, and

  (ii) “, when added to the APPS earnings or the part attributable to COMPS service (or both),”.

6(4) [Inserts SSCBA 1992, Sch. 1, para. 1(11).]

6(5) The amendments made by sub-paragraphs (2) and (4) have effect in relation to 2009–10 and subsequent tax years.

PENSION SCHEMES ACT 1993 (C. 48)

7 The Pension Schemes Act 1993 is amended as follows.

8(1) Section 8 (meaning of “contracted-out employment” etc) is amended as follows.

8(2) [Amends PSA 1993, s. 8(2).]

8(3) [Inserts PSA 1993, s. 8(2A).]

10(1) Section 41 (reduced rates of Class 1 contributions for members of salary related contracted-out schemes) is amended as follows.

10(2) [Amends PSA 1993, s. 41(1).]

10(3) [Omits PSA 1993, s. 41(1ZA).]

10(4) The amendments made by this paragraph have effect in relation to 2009–10 and subsequent tax years.

11(1) [Amends PSA 1993, s. 42A(1).]

11(2) The amendment made by sub-paragraph (1) has effect in relation to 2009–10 and subsequent tax years.

12 [Amends PSA 1993, s. 45(1).]

12(2) The amendment made by sub-paragraph (1) has effect in relation to 2009–10 and subsequent tax years.

SCHEDULE 2 – REPEALS

Section 4

Short title and chapter	*Extent of repeal*
Social Security Contributions and Benefits Act 1992 (c. 4)	In Schedule 1, in paragraph 1(3)– (a) paragraph (ba), (b) in paragraph (c), the words "if some of the aggregated earnings are attributable to COSRS service,", and (c) in paragraph (ca), the words "if paragraph (c) applies" and ", when added to the APPS earnings or the part attributable to COMPS service (or both),".

PENSIONS ACT 2008

(2008 Chapter 30) [*26th November 2008*]

ARRANGEMENT OF SECTIONS

PART 5 – MISCELLANEOUS

STATE AND OFFICIAL PENSIONS

135 Additional Class 3 contributions

135(1) The Social Security Contributions and Benefits Act 1992 (c. 4) is amended as follows.

135(2) [Inserts SSCBA 1992, s. 13A.]

135(3) [Relevant to Northern Ireland only.]

135(4) [Amends SSCBA 1992, s. 1(2)(d).]

PART 6 – GENERAL

149 Commencement

149(1) Subject to the following provisions, this Act comes into force in accordance with provision made by order by the Secretary of State.

149(2) Subsection (1) does not apply to–

(a)–(f) [not relevant to National Insurance contributions;]

(g) sections 133 to 136;

(h)–(k) [not relevant to National Insurance contributions.]

149(3) [Not relevant to National Insurance contributions.]

149(4) Sections 105, 135 and 136 come into force on 6 April 2009.

149(5) [Not relevant to National Insurance contributions.]

149(6) An order under subsection (1) may appoint different days for different purposes.

150 Extent

150(1) Subject to the following provisions, this Act extends to England and Wales and Scotland.

150(2) [Relevant to Northern Ireland only.]

150(3) An amendment or repeal by this Act has the same extent as the enactment amended or repealed (subject to the provision made by section 63(3), section 64(2) and paragraph 9 of Schedule 10).

151 Short title

151 This Act may be cited as the Pensions Act 2008.

SCHEDULES

SCHEDULE 4 – ADDITIONAL PENSION ETC: MINOR AND CONSEQUENTIAL AMENDMENTS

Section 104

SOCIAL SECURITY CONTRIBUTIONS AND BENEFITS ACT 1992 (C. 4)

1 The Social Security Contributions and Benefits Act 1992 is amended as follows.

2 In section 21(5A)(c) (contribution conditions), after "5(2)(b) and (4)(a)" insert ", 5A(3)(a)".

3–13 [Not relevant to National Insurance contributions.]

14 [Repealed by PA 2014, s. 23 and Sch. 12, para. 96(c).]

History – Para. 14 repealed by PA 2014, s. 23 and Sch. 12, para. 96(c), with effect from 1 October 2014 under PA 2014, s. 56(1)).

15–22 [Not relevant to National Insurance contributions.]

FINANCE ACT 2009

(2009 Chapter 10)

[*21st July 2009*]

ARRANGEMENT OF SECTIONS

PART 7 – ADMINISTRATION

PART 9 – FINAL PROVISIONS

SCHEDULES

PART 7 – ADMINISTRATION

INTEREST

101 Late payment interest on sums due to HMRC

101(1) This section applies to any amount that is payable by a person to HMRC under or by virtue of an enactment.

101(2) But this section does not apply to–

(a) [not relevant to National Insurance contributions,]

(b) [not relevant to National Insurance contributions,]

(c) an amount of any description specified in an order made by the Treasury.

101(3) An amount to which this section applies carries interest at the late payment interest rate from the late payment interest start date until the date of payment.

101(4) The late payment interest start date in respect of any amount is the date on which that amount becomes due and payable.

101(5) In Schedule 53–

(a) Part 1 makes special provision as to the amount on which late payment interest is calculated,

(b) Part 2 makes special provision as to the late payment interest start date,

(c) [not relevant to National Insurance contributions,]

(d) Part 4 makes provision about the effect that the giving of a relief has on late payment interest.

101(6) Subsection (3) applies even if the late payment interest start date is a non-business day within the meaning of section 92 of the Bills of Exchange Act 1882.

101(7) Late payment interest is to be paid without any deduction of income tax.

101(8) Late payment interest is not payable on late payment interest.

101(9) For the purposes of this section any reference to the payment of an amount to HMRC includes a reference to its being set off against an amount payable by HMRC (and, accordingly, the reference to the date on which an amount is paid includes a reference to the date from which the set-off takes effect).

Commencement Date – S. 101 came into force on 31 October 2011 for the purposes of any self-assessment amount (as defined in SI 2011/701, art. 2) payable by a person to HMRC (SI 2011/701, art. 3). This is subject to transitional provisions in SI 2011/701, art. 4. The day appointed as the day on which s. 101 comes into force for the purposes of penalties assessed under FA 2012, Sch. 38, Pt. 3–5 (tax agents dishonest conduct) is 1 April 2013 (SI 2013/280).

6 May 2014 is the appointed day for the coming into force of s. 101 for the purposes of:

(a) any PAYE amount payable by a PAYE employer to HMRC,

(b) any Class 1 contributions amount payable by an employer to HMRC, and

(c) any CIS amount payable by a contractor to HMRC

which is due and payable for the tax year 2014–15 or for any subsequent tax year (SI 2014/992, art. 3(1)).

S. 101 applies in relation to Class 2 contributions, with effect for the tax year 2015–16 and subsequent tax years (NICA 2015, Sch. 1, para. 35).

Cross references – SI 2010/1879, reg. 3: sets late payment interest rate for the purposes of s. 101.

SSCBA 1992, s. 11A: s. 101 applies, with the necessary modifications, in relation to Class 2 contributions as if those contributions were income tax chargeable under ITTOIA 2005, Pt. 2, Ch. 2 in respect of profits of a trade, profession or vocation which is not carried on wholly outside the UK.

102 Repayment interest on sums to be paid by HMRC

102(1) This section applies to–

(a) any amount that is payable by HMRC to any person under or by virtue of an enactment, and

(b) a relevant amount paid by a person to HMRC that is repaid by HMRC to that person or to another person.

102(2) But this section does not apply to–

(a) [not relevant to National Insurance contributions,]

(b) [not relevant to National Insurance contributions,]

(c) an amount of any description specified in an order made by the Treasury.

102(3) An amount to which this section applies carries interest at the repayment interest rate from the repayment interest start date until the date on which the payment or repayment is made.

102(4) In Schedule 54–

(a) Parts 1 and 2 define the repayment interest start date, and

(b) Part 3 makes supplementary provision.

102(5) Subsection (3) applies even if the repayment interest start date is a non-business day within the meaning of section 92 of the Bills of Exchange Act 1882.

102(6) Repayment interest is not payable on an amount payable in consequence of an order or judgment of a court having power to allow interest on the amount.

102(7) Repayment interest is not payable on repayment interest.

102(8) For the purposes of this section–

(a) **"relevant amount"** means any sum that was paid in connection with any liability (including any purported or anticipated liability) to make a payment to HMRC under or by virtue of an enactment, and

(b) any reference to the payment or repayment of an amount by HMRC includes a reference to its being set off against an amount owed to HMRC (and, accordingly, the reference to the date on which an amount is paid or repaid by HMRC includes a reference to the date from which the set-off takes effect).

Commencement Date – S. 102 came into force on 31 October 2011 for the purposes of any self-assessment amount (as defined in SI 2011/701, art. 2) payable re repayable by HMRC to a person (SI 2011/701, art. 3). This is subject to transitional provisions in SI 2011/701, art. 4.

6 May 2014 is the day appointed for the coming into force of s. 102 for the purposes of:

(a) any PAYE amount repayable by HMRC to a PAYE employer,

(b) any Class 1 contributions amount which fall to be repaid by HMRC to an employer, and

(c) any CIS amount which falls to be repaid by HMRC to a contractor,

which was paid to HMRC for the tax year 2014–15 or any subsequent tax year (SI 2014/992, art. 3(2)).

S. 102 applies in relation to Class 2 contributions, with effect for the tax year 2015–16 and subsequent tax years (NICA 2015, Sch. 1, para. 35).

Cross references – SI 2010/1879, reg. 4: sets repayment interest rate for the purposes of s. 102.
SSCBA 1992, s. 11A: s. 101 applies, with the necessary modifications, in relation to Class 2 contributions as if those contributions were income tax chargeable under ITTOIA 2005, Pt. 2, Ch. 2 in respect of profits of a trade, profession or vocation which is not carried on wholly outside the UK.

103 Rates of interest

103(1) The late payment interest rate is the rate provided for in regulations made by the Treasury under this subsection.

103(2) The repayment interest rate is the rate provided for in regulations made by the Treasury under this subsection.

103(3) Regulations under subsection (1) or (2)–

(a) may make different provision for different purposes,

(b) may either themselves specify a rate of interest or make provision for such a rate to be determined (and to change from time to time) by reference to such rate, or the average of such rates, as may be referred to in the regulations,

(c) may provide for rates to be reduced below, or increased above, what they otherwise would be by specified amounts or by reference to specified formulae,

(d) may provide for rates arrived at by reference to averages to be rounded up or down,

(e) may provide for circumstances in which alteration of a rate of interest is or is not to be take place, and

(f) may provide that alterations of rates are to have effect for periods beginning on or after a day determined in accordance with the regulations in relation to interest running from before that day as well as from or from after that day.

Commencement Date – S. 103 came into force generally on 6 October 2011 (SI 2011/2401) (but see annotations to SI 2011/701, art. 3 and 4 in relation to self-assessment amounts (as defined in SI 2011/701, art. 2).
S. 103 came into force on 31 October 2011 for the purposes of any self-assessment amount (as defined in SI 2011/701, art. 2) payable by a person to HMRC or payable re repayable by HMRC to a person (SI 2011/701, art. 3). This is subject to transitional provisions in SI 2011/701, art. 4.
6 May 2014 is the day appointed for the coming into force of s. 102 for the purposes of:
(a) any PAYE amount repayable by HMRC to a PAYE employer,
(b) any Class 1 contributions amount which fall to be repaid by HMRC to an employer, and
(c) any CIS amount which falls to be repaid by HMRC to a contractor,
which was paid to HMRC for the tax year 2014–15 or any subsequent tax year (SI 2014/992, art. 3(2)).

Statutory instruments – SI 2011/2446: made under s. 103.

103A Further provision as to late payment interest and repayment interest

103A [Not relevant to National Insurance contributions.]

104 Supplementary

104(1) In sections 101 to 103–

"HMRC" means Her Majesty's Revenue and Customs;

"late payment interest" means interest payable under section 101;

"repayment interest" means interest payable under section 102;

"revenue" has the meaning given in section 5(4) of CRCA 2005.

104(2) A reference to the date on which an amount becomes due and payable is a reference to the date (however described) on or before which the amount must be paid.

104(3) Sections 101 to 103 come into force on such day as the Treasury may by order appoint.

104(4) An order under subsection (3)–

(a) may commence a provision generally or only for specified purposes, and

(b) may appoint different days for different provisions or for different purposes.

104(5) The Treasury may by order make any incidental, supplemental, consequential, transitional, transitory or saving provision which may appear appropriate in consequence of, or otherwise in connection with, those sections.

104(6) An order under subsection (5) may include provision amending, repealing or revoking any provision of any Act or subordinate legislation whenever passed or made (including this Act and any Act amended by it).

104(7) An order under subsection (5) may make different provision for different purposes.

104(8) The following are to be made by statutory instrument–

(a) orders under section 101(2) or 102(2),

(b) regulations under section 103(1) or (2), and

(c) orders under subsection (3) or (5).

104(9) A statutory instrument containing–

(a) an order under section 101(2) or 102(2),

(b) regulations under section 103(1) or (2),

(c) an order under subsection (5) which includes provision amending or repealing any provision of an Act,

is subject to annulment in pursuance of a resolution of the House of Commons.

Prospective amendments – In s. 104(1), "103A (and Schedules 53 to 54A)" substituted for "103" by F(No. 3)A 2010, s. 25 and Sch. 9, para. 5, with effect from a day to be appointed by Treasury order.

Statutory instruments – SI 2011/701: made under s. 104(3)–(7).
SI 2011/2391 (not reproduced): made partly under s. 104(3)–(5).
SI 2011/2401 (not reproduced): made partly under s. 104(3)–(5).
SI 2014/1283 (not reproduced): made under s. 104(4), (5) and (7).

105 Miscellaneous amendments

105 [Not relevant to National Insurance contributions.]

PENALTIES

109 Miscellaneous amendments

109 Schedule 57 contains amendments of Schedule 24 to FA 2007 (penalties for errors), Schedule 41 to FA 2008 (penalties for failure to notify and certain other wrongdoing) and certain other enactments relating to penalties.

PART 9 – FINAL PROVISIONS

127 Short title

127 This Act may be cited as the Finance Act 2009.

SCHEDULES

SCHEDULE 53 – LATE PAYMENT INTEREST

Section 101

Commencement Date – S. 101 and Sch. 53 came into force on 31 October 2011 for the purposes of any self-assessment amount (as defined in SI 2011/701, art. 2) payable by a person to HMRC (SI 2011/701, art. 3). This is subject to transitional provisions in SI 2011/701, art. 4.

The day appointed as the day on which s. 101 and Sch. 53 comes into force for the purposes of penalties assessed under FA 2012, Sch. 38, Pt. 3–5 (tax agents dishonest conduct) is 1 April 2013 (SI 2013/280).

6 May 2014 is the appointed day for the coming into force of s. 101 and Sch. 53 for the purposes of:

(a) any PAYE amount payable by a PAYE employer to HMRC,

(b) any Class 1 contributions amount payable by an employer to HMRC, and

(c) any CIS amount payable by a contractor to HMRC

which is due and payable for the tax year 2014–15 or for any subsequent tax year (SI 2014/992, art. 3(1)).

S. 101 and Sch. 53 apply in relation to Class 2 contributions, with effect for the tax year 2015–16 and subsequent tax years (NICA 2015, Sch. 1, para. 35).

Part 1 – Special Provision: Amount Carrying Late Payment Interest

PAYMENTS ON ACCOUNT AND BALANCING PAYMENT

1(1) This paragraph applies where as regards a tax year–

(a) payments on account are payable by a person ("P"),

(b) P makes a claim under section 59A(3) or (4) of TMA 1970 (reduction of payments on account) in respect of those amounts, and

(c) a balancing payment becomes payable by P.

1(2) Late payment interest is to be calculated as if each of the payments on account had been equal to the lesser of the following amounts–

(a) the aggregate of that payment on account and 50% of the balancing payment, and

(b) the amount which would have been payable as a payment on account if the claim under section 59A(3) or (4) had not been made.

1(3) In determining for the purposes of this paragraph what amount (if any) is payable by P as a balancing payment–

(a) it is to be assumed that both of the payments on account have been paid,

(b) no account is to be taken of any amount which has been paid on account otherwise than under section 59A(2) of TMA 1970, and

(c) no account is to be taken of any amount which is payable by way of capital gains tax.

1(4) In this paragraph–

"balancing payment" means an amount payable–

(a) in accordance with section 59B(3), (4) or (5) of TMA 1970, or

(b) in accordance with section 59B(6) of that Act in respect of income tax assessed under section 29 of that Act;

"payment on account" means an amount payable in accordance with section 59A(2) of TMA 1970.

PAYMENTS ON ACCOUNT AND OVERPAYMENT

2(1) This paragraph applies where as regards any person ("P") and a tax year–

(a) payments on account become payable by P, and

(b) an overpayment becomes repayable to P.

2(2) Late payment interest is payable only on the amount by which each of the payments on account exceeds 50% of the overpayment.

2(3) In determining for the purposes of this paragraph what amount (if any) is repayable to P as an overpayment–

(a) no account is to be taken of any amount which has been paid on account otherwise than under section 59A(2) of TMA 1970, and

(b) no account is to be taken of any amount which is payable by way of capital gains tax.

2(4) In this paragraph–

"overpayment" means an amount repayable in accordance with section 59B(3), (4) or (5) of TMA 1970;

"payment on account" means an amount payable in accordance with section 59A(2) of that Act.

CARRY BACK OF LOSSES ETC

2A–2D [Not relevant to National Insurance contributions.]

Part 2 – Special Provision: Late Payment Interest Start Date

AMENDMENTS AND DISCOVERY ASSESSMENTS ETC

3(1) This paragraph applies to any amount which is due and payable as a result of–

(a) an amendment or correction to an assessment or self-assessment ("assessment A"),

(b) an assessment made by HMRC in place of or in addition to an assessment ("assessment A") which was made by a taxpayer, or

(c) an assessment made by HMRC in place of an assessment ("assessment A") which ought to have been made by a taxpayer.

3(2) The late payment interest start date in respect of that amount is the date which would have been the late payment interest start date if–

(a) assessment A had been complete and accurate and had been made on the date (if any) by which it was required to be made, and

(b) accordingly, the amount had been due and payable as a result of assessment A.

3(3) In the case of a person ("P") who failed to give notice in accordance with a requirement under section 7 of TMA 1970 (notice of liability to tax) that arose by virtue of subsection (1A) of that section, the reference in sub-paragraph (1)(c) to an assessment which ought to have been made by P is a reference to the assessment which P would have been required to make if an officer of HMRC had given notice under section 8 of that Act.

3(3A) In the case of a person ("P") who failed to give notice in accordance with a requirement under section 7 of TMA 1970 that arose by virtue of subsection (1B) of that section, the reference in sub-paragraph (1)(c) to an assessment which ought to have been made by P is a reference to the assessment which P would have been required to make if no notice relating to the year of assessment concerned had been withdrawn under section 8B of that Act.

3(4) In this paragraph **"assessment"** means any assessment or determination (however described) of any amount due and payable to HMRC.

History – In para. 3(3), the words "in accordance with a requirement" substituted for the words "as required" and the words "that arose by virtue of subsection (1A) of that section" inserted by FA 2013, s. 233 and Sch. 51, para. 7(2), with effect in relation to a return under TMA 1970, s. 12AA for a partnership including one or more companies, in respect of a return for a relevant period beginning on or after 6 April 2012; and in relation to a return under TMA 1970, s. 12AA for any other partnership or a return under TMA 1970, s. 8 or 8A, in respect of a return for a year of assessment beginning on or after 6 April 2012.

Para. 3(3A) inserted by FA 2013, s. 233 and Sch. 51, para. 7(3), with effect in relation to a return under TMA 1970, s. 12AA for a partnership including one or more companies, in respect of a return for a relevant period beginning on or after 6 April 2012; and in relation to a return under TMA 1970, s. 12AA for any other partnership or a return under TMA 1970, s. 8 or 8A, in respect of a return for a year of assessment beginning on or after 6 April 2012.

AMOUNTS POSTPONED PENDING APPEAL UNDER TMA 1970

4(1) This paragraph applies to any amount if payment of the amount is postponed under section 55 of TMA 1970 pending the determination of an appeal against an assessment of income tax or capital gains tax.

4(2) The late payment interest start date in respect of that amount is the date which would have been the late payment interest start date if there had been no appeal.

OVERPAYMENT OF TAX

5(1) This paragraph applies to any amount of income tax or capital gains tax which is assessed and recoverable by virtue of an assessment under section 30 of TMA 1970 (recovery of overpayment of tax etc).

5(2) The late payment interest start date in respect of that amount is 31 January next following the tax year in respect of which the assessment under section 30 is made.

RECOVERY OF PAYMENT OF TAX CREDIT OR INTEREST

6 [Not relevant to National Insurance contributions.]

PAYMENT OF CORPORATION TAX BY PERSONS OTHER THAN COMPANY ASSESSED

6A [Not relevant to National Insurance contributions.]

INHERITANCE TAX PAYABLE BY INSTALMENTS

7 [Not relevant to National Insurance contributions.]

CERTAIN OTHER AMOUNTS OF INHERITANCE TAX

8–9 [Not relevant to National Insurance contributions.]

VAT DUE FROM PERSONS NOT REGISTERED AS REQUIRED

10 [Not relevant to National Insurance contributions.]

UNAUTHORISED VAT INVOICES

11 [Not relevant to National Insurance contributions.]

SOFT DRINKS INDUSTRY LEVY DUE FROM UNREGISTERED PERSONS

11C [Not relevant to National Insurance contributions.]

DEATH OF TAXPAYER

12(1) This paragraph applies if–

(a) a person chargeable to an amount of revenue dies before the amount becomes due and payable, and

(b) the executor or administrator is unable to pay the amount before obtaining probate or letters of administration or (in Scotland) the executor is unable to pay the amount before obtaining confirmation.

12(2) The late payment interest start date in respect of that amount is the later of the following–

(a) the date which would be the late payment interest start date apart from this paragraph, and

(b) the day after the end of the period of 30 days beginning with the grant of probate or letters of administration or (in Scotland) the grant of confirmation.

Part 3 – Special Provision: Date to Which Late Payment Interest Runs

DEDUCTION OF INCOME TAX AT SOURCE

13 [Not relevant to National Insurance contributions.]

PROPERTY ACCEPTED IN LIEU OF INHERITANCE TAX

14 [Not relevant to National Insurance contributions.]

Part 4 – Effect of Interest on Reliefs

15(1) Where conditions A and B are met–

(a) the appropriate adjustment is to be made of the amount of late payment interest payable, and

(b) accordingly, the appropriate repayment (if any) is to be made of any late payment interest previously paid.

15(2) Condition A is that any amount of late payment interest is payable on–

(a) any amount on account of income tax which is due and payable in accordance with section 59A(2) of TMA 1970, or

(b) any amount of income tax or capital gains tax which becomes due and payable in accordance with section 55 or 59B of TMA 1970.

15(3) Condition B is that relief from the tax is given by a discharge of any of that amount of tax. Paragraph 16 makes provision about the circumstances in which P is entitled to have a relief treated as being given by discharge.

15(4) In this paragraph–

"the appropriate adjustment" is such adjustment as is necessary to secure that the total amount of late payment interest, if any, paid or payable on the amount of tax in question is the same as it would have been if the tax discharged had never been charged;

"the appropriate repayment" is such repayment as is necessary to give effect to the appropriate adjustment.

16(1) Where–

(a) income tax or capital gains tax has been paid for a chargeable period ("period A"), and

(b) *relief* from any amount of that tax is given to a person ("P") by repayment,

P is entitled to require that the amount repaid be treated for the purposes of paragraph 15(3), so far as it will go, as if it were a discharge of a qualifying charge to tax.

16(2) A qualifying charge to tax is any amount of tax charged on P (whether alone or together with other persons) by or by virtue of any assessment for or relating to period A.

16(3) But sub-paragraph (1) does not permit an amount to be applied–

(a) to any assessment made after the relief was given, or

(b) to more than one assessment so as to reduce, without extinguishing, the amount of tax charged.

SCHEDULE 54 – REPAYMENT INTEREST

Section 102

Commencement Date – S. 102 and Sch. 54 came into force on 31 October 2011 for the purposes of any self-assessment amount (as defined in SI 2011/701, art. 2) payable re repayable by HMRC to a person (SI 2011/701, art. 3). This is subject to transitional provisions in SI 2011/701, art. 4.

6 May 2014 is the day appointed for the coming into force of s. 102 and Sch. 54 for the purposes of:

(a) any PAYE amount repayable by HMRC to a PAYE employer,

(b) any Class 1 contributions amount which fall to be repaid by HMRC to an employer, and

(c) any CIS amount which falls to be repaid by HMRC to a contractor,

which was paid to HMRC for the tax year 2014–15 or any subsequent tax year (SI 2014/992, art. 3(2)).

S. 102 and Sch. 54 applies in relation to Class 2 contributions, with effect for the tax year 2015–16 and subsequent tax years (NICA 2015, Sch. 1, para. 35).

Part A1 – Special Provision as to Amount Carrying Repayment Interest

A1–A4 [Not relevant to National Insurance contributions.]

Part 1 – Repayment Interest Start Date: General Rule

INTRODUCTORY

1(1) This Part sets out the general rule for determining the repayment interest start date.

1(2) The general rule is subject to the special provision made by Part 2.

REPAYMENT OF AMOUNTS PAID TO HMRC

2 In the case of an amount which has been paid to HMRC, the repayment interest start date is the later of date A and (where applicable) date B.

3 Date A is the date on which the amount was paid to HMRC.

4 Date B is, in the case of an amount which–

(a) has been paid in connection with a liability to make a payment to HMRC, and

(b) is to be repaid by them,

the date on which the payment became due and payable to HMRC.

PAYMENT OF AMOUNTS ON RETURN OR CLAIM

5(1) In the case of an amount which–

(a) has not been paid to HMRC, and

(b) is payable by virtue of a return having been filed or a claim having been made,

the repayment interest start date is the later of the dates mentioned in sub-paragraph (2).

5(2) The dates are–

(a) the date (if any) on which the return was required to be filed or the claim was required to be made, and

(b) the date on which the return was in fact filed or the claim was in fact made.

Part 2 – Special Provision as to Repayment Interest Start Date

INCOME TAX DEDUCTED AT SOURCE

6 [Not relevant to National Insurance contributions.]

CARRY BACK OF LOSSES AND AVERAGING

7 In the case of any amount which is to be repaid as a result of a claim for relief under–

(a) paragraph 2 of Schedule 1B to TMA 1970 (carry back of loss relief from later year to earlier year), or

(b) Chapter 16 of Part 2 of ITTOIA 2005 (claim for averaging of profits of farmers etc over two consecutive years),

the repayment interest start date is 31 January next following the year that is the later year in relation to the claim.

MIRAS

8 [Not relevant to National Insurance contributions.]

INCOME ACCUMULATED UNDER CERTAIN TRUSTS

9 [Not relevant to National Insurance contributions.]

TAX ON PAYMENTS OUT OF DISCRETIONARY TRUST TAXABLE AS EMPLOYMENT INCOME

9A [Not relevant to National Insurance contributions.]

COMPANIES: INCOME TAX AND CERTAIN TAX CREDITS

9B [Not relevant to National Insurance contributions.]

LOAN BY CLOSE COMPANY TO PARTICIPATOR

9C [Not relevant to National Insurance contributions.]

PAYMENTS IN CONNECTION WITH LIFE ASSURANCE PREMIUM RELIEF

9D [Not relevant to National Insurance contributions.]

CERTAIN OTHER AMOUNTS OF INHERITANCE TAX

10–12 [Not relevant to National Insurance contributions.]

Part 3 – Supplementary

ATTRIBUTION OF REPAYMENTS

13(1) This paragraph applies for the purpose of determining, for the purposes of this Schedule, how a repayment to a person ("P") in respect of income tax for a tax year is to be attributed to payments made in respect of that tax.

13(2) Such a repayment is to be attributed to payments in the following order–

(a) first, to so much of any payment made by P under section 59B of TMA 1970 as is a payment in respect of income tax for that year,

(b) second, in two equal parts to each of the payments (if any) made by P under section 59A of that Act on account of income tax for that year, and

(c) [not relevant to National Insurance contributions.]

13(3) In so far as it is attributable to a payment made in instalments, a repayment is to be attributed to a later instalment before being attributed to an earlier one.

INTERPRETATION

14 [Not relevant to National Insurance contributions.]

SCHEDULE 55 – PENALTY FOR FAILURE TO MAKE RETURNS ETC

Section 106

Commencement Date – 6 April 2011 is the day appointed for the coming into force of Sch. 55 in relation to a return or other document which is required to be made or delivered to HMRC in relation to the tax year 2010–11 or any subsequent tax year, and falls within item 1, 2 or 3 of the Table in para. 1 (SI 2011/702, art. 2). In consequence of the commencement of Sch. 55 for the purposes of returns and other documents falling within item 1, 2 or 3, the amendments by FA 2010, Sch. 10, para. 10 to 14 (increased penalties in respect of offshore income and gains) were also brought into effect (for the same purposes) from 6 April 2011 (SI 2011/975, art. 2). Similarly, the amendments to Sch. 55 by F(No.3)A 2010, Sch. 10, para. 1, 4 and 10 (relating to those provisions commenced from 6 April 2011) were also brought into effect (for the same purposes) from 6 April 2011 (SI 2011/703, art. 2(a)).
11 September 2014 is the day appointed for the coming into force of para. 6C(5), (7), (8), (9) and (10) (powers to make regulations) in relation to a return falling within item 4 (RTI returns) of the Table in para. 1 (SI 2014/2395, art. 2(a)).
6 October 2014 is the day appointed for the coming into force of para. 1, 6B, 6C(1) to (4), (6) and (10), 6D, 16 to 24, 26 and 27 in relation to a return falling within item 4 (RTI returns) of the Table in para. 1, which is required to be made or delivered on or after that date by a large existing employer (employs at least 50 employees as at 6 October 2014) (SI 2014/2395, art. 2(b)(i)).

6 March 2015 is the day appointed for the coming into force of para. 1, 6B, 6C(1) to (4), (6) and (10), 6D, 16 to 24, 26 and 27 in relation to a return falling within item 4 (RTI returns) of the Table in para. 1, which is required to be made or delivered on or after that date by a small existing employer (employs no more than 49 employees at 6 October 2014) or is a new employer after 6 October 2014 (2014/2395, art. 2(b)(ii)).
Sch. 55 applies in relation to Class 2 contributions, with effect for the tax year 2015–16 and subsequent tax years (NICA 2015, Sch. 1, para. 35).

Cross references – SSCBA 1992, s. 11A: Sch. 55 applies, with the necessary modifications, in relation to Class 2 contributions as if those contributions were income tax chargeable under ITTOIA 2005, Pt. 2, Ch. 2 in respect of profits of a trade, profession or vocation which is not carried on wholly outside the UK.

Notes – This is an edited version of Sch. 55, containing only the provisions relevant to national insurance contributions.

PENALTY FOR FAILURE TO MAKE RETURNS ETC

1(1) A penalty is payable by a person ("P") where P fails to make or deliver a return, or to deliver any other document, specified in the Table below on or before the filing date.

1(2) Paragraphs 2 to 13 set out–

(a) the circumstances in which a penalty is payable, and

(b) subject to paragraphs 14 to 17, the amount of the penalty.

1(3) If P's failure falls within more than one paragraph of this Schedule, P is liable to a penalty under each of those paragraphs (but this is subject to paragraph 17(3)).

1(4) In this Schedule–

"filing date", in relation to a return or other document, means the date by which it is required to be made or delivered to HMRC;

"penalty date", in relation to a return or other document falling within any of items 1 to 3 and 5 to 13 in the Table, means the date on which a penalty is first payable for failing to make or deliver it (that is to say, the day after the filing date).

1(4A) The Treasury may by order make such amendments to item 4 in the Table as they think fit in consequence of any amendment, revocation or re-enactment of the regulations mentioned in that item.

1(5) In the provisions of this Schedule which follow the Table–

(a) any reference to a return includes a reference to any other document specified in the Table, and

(b) any reference to making a return includes a reference to delivering a return or to delivering any such document.

	Tax to which return etc relates	*Return or other document*
1	Income tax or capital gains tax	(a) Return under section 8(1)(a) of TMA 1970 (b) Accounts, statement or document required under section 8(1)(b) of TMA 1970
4	Income tax	Return under any of the following provisions of the Income Tax (PAYE) Regulations 2003 (S.I. 2003/2682)– (a) regulation 67B (real time returns) (b) regulation 67D (exceptions to regulation 67B)

Commencement Date – 6 October 2014 is the day appointed for the coming into force of para. 1 in relation to a return falling within item 4 of the Table that is required to be delivered to HMRC on or after that date by a Real Time Information employer which is at 6 October 2014 a large existing employer (employs at least 50 employees) (SI 2014/2395, art. 2(b)(i)).
6 March 2015 is the day appointed for the coming into force of para. 1 in relation to a return falling within item 4 of the Table that is required to be delivered to HMRC on or after that date by a Real Time Information employer which is at 6 October 2014 a small existing employer (employs no more than 49 employees), or a person who becomes a new Real Time Information employer after 6 October 2014 (SI 2014/2395, art. 2(b)(ii)).

Prospective amendments – In para. 1(2), "13J" substituted for "13" by F(No. 3)A 2010, s. 26 and Sch. 10, para. 2(2), with effect from a day to be appointed by Treasury order.
In para. 1(4), in the definition of "penalty date", "13A" substituted for "13" by FA 2017, s. 56 and Sch. 11, para. 4(2), with effect from a day to be appointed under FA 2017, s. 61(1).
In para. 1(4), in the definition of "filing date", the words "(or, in the case of a return mentioned in item 7AA or 7AB of the Table, to the tax authorities to whom the return is required to be delivered)" inserted (at the end) by F(No.3A) 2010, s. 26 and Sch. 10, para. 2(2A) (as inserted by FA 2014, s. 103 and Sch. 22, para. 2(a)), with effect from a date to be appointed under F(No. 3)A 2010, s. 26(2).

History – In para. 1(4), in the definition of "penalty date", the words "falling within any of items 1 to 3 and 5 to 13 in the Table" inserted by FA 2013, s. 230 and Sch. 50, para. 3(a), with effect for the tax year 2014–15 and subsequent tax years in relation to failures to make returns with a filing date (as defined in para. 1(4)) on or after 6 April 2014.
Para. 1(4A) inserted by FA 2013, s. 230 and Sch. 50, para. 3(b), with effect for the tax year 2014–15 and subsequent tax years in relation to failures to make returns with a filing date (as defined in para. 1(4)) on or after 6 April 2014.
In para. 1, in the Table, in item 4, the words in the third column substituted by FA 2013, s. 230 and Sch. 50, para. 4, with effect for the tax year 2014–15 and subsequent tax years in relation to failures to make returns with a filing date (as defined in para. 1(4)) on or after 6 April 2014.

AMOUNT OF PENALTY: OCCASIONAL RETURNS AND ANNUAL RETURNS

2 Paragraphs 3 to 6 apply in the case of a return falling within any of items 1 to 3, 5 and 7 to 13 in the Table.

Prospective amendments – Para. 2 and the heading before it substituted by F(No. 3)A 2010, s. 26 and Sch. 10, para. 3, with effect from a day to be appointed by Treasury order. The substituted text reads as follows:

"AMOUNT OF PENALTY: OCCASIONAL RETURNS AND RETURNS FOR PERIODS OF 6 MONTHS OR MORE

22(1) Paragraphs 3 to 6 apply in the case of–
(a) a return falling within any of items 1 to 5, 7 and 8 to 13 in the Table,
(b) [not relevant to National Insurance contributions,]
(c) [not relevant to National Insurance contributions.]

2(2) [Not relevant to National Insurance contributions.]".

History – In para. 2, "1 to 3, 5" substituted for "1 to 5" by FA 2013, s. 230 and Sch. 50, para. 5, with effect for the tax year 2014–15 and subsequent tax years in relation to failures to make returns with a filing date (as defined in para. 1(4)) on or after 6 April 2014.

3 P is liable to a penalty under this paragraph of £100.

4(1) P is liable to a penalty under this paragraph if (and only if)–
(a) P's failure continues after the end of the period of 3 months beginning with the penalty date,
(b) HMRC decide that such a penalty should be payable, and
(c) HMRC give notice to P specifying the date from which the penalty is payable.

4(2) The penalty under this paragraph is £10 for each day that the failure continues during the period of 90 days beginning with the date specified in the notice given under sub-paragraph (1)(c).

4(3) The date specified in the notice under sub-paragraph (1)(c)–
(a) may be earlier than the date on which the notice is given, but
(b) may not be earlier than the end of the period mentioned in sub-paragraph (1)(a).

5(1) P is liable to a penalty under this paragraph if (and only if) P's failure continues after the end of the period of 6 months beginning with the penalty date.

5(2) The penalty under this paragraph is the greater of–
(a) 5% of any liability to tax which would have been shown in the return in question, and
(b) £300.

6(1) P is liable to a penalty under this paragraph if (and only if) P's failure continues after the end of the period of 12 months beginning with the penalty date.

6(2) Where, by failing to make the return, P deliberately withholds information which would enable or assist HMRC to assess P's liability to tax, the penalty under this paragraph is determined in accordance with sub-paragraphs (3) and (4).

6(3) If the withholding of the information is deliberate and concealed, the penalty is the greater of–
(a) the relevant percentage of any liability to tax which would have been shown in the return in question, and
(b) £300.

6(3A) For the purposes of sub-paragraph (3)(a), the relevant percentage is–
(a) for the withholding of category 1 information, 100%,
(b) for the withholding of category 2 information, 150%, and
(c) for the withholding of category 3 information, 200%.

6(4) If the withholding of the information is deliberate but not concealed, the penalty is the greater of–
(a) the relevant percentage of any liability to tax which would have been shown in the return in question, and
(b) £300.

6(4A) For the purposes of sub-paragraph (4)(a), the relevant percentage is–
(a) for the withholding of category 1 information, 70%,
(b) for the withholding of category 2 information, 105%, and
(c) for the withholding of category 3 information, 140%.

6(5) In any case not falling within sub-paragraph (2), the penalty under this paragraph is the greater of–
(a) 5% of any liability to tax which would have been shown in the return in question, and
(b) £300.

6(6) Paragraph 6A explains the 3 categories of information.

Prospective amendments – Para. 6(2) amended for certain purposes by F(No. 3)A 2010, s. 26 and Sch. 10, para. 4(2), with effect from a day or days to be appointed by Treasury order. See Note below for details.

Para. 6(3)(a) amended for certain purposes by FA 2010, s. 35 and Sch. 10, para. 11(2), with effect from a date to be appointed. See Note below for details.

Para. 6(3A)(za) inserted and in para. 6(3)(a) "125%" substituted for "100%" by FA 2015, s. 120 and Sch. 20, para. 15(2), with effect from a day to be appointed under FA 2015, s. 120(2).
Para. 6(3A) inserted for certain purposes by FA 2010, s. 35 and Sch. 10, para. 11(3), with effect from a date to be appointed. See Note below for details.
Para. 6(4)(a) amended for certain purposes by FA 2010, s. 35 and Sch. 10, para. 11(4), with effect from a date to be appointed. See Note below for details.
Para. 6(4A)(za) inserted and in para. 6(4A)(a) "87.5%" substituted for "70%" by FA 2015, s. 120 and Sch. 20, para. 15(3), with effect from a day to be appointed under FA 2015, s. 120(2).
Para. 6(4A) inserted for certain purposes by FA 2010, s. 35 and Sch. 10, para. 11(5), with effect from a date to be appointed. See Note below for details.
Para. 6(5) amended for certain purposes by F(No. 3)A 2010, s. 26 and Sch. 10, para. 4(3), with effect from a day or days to be appointed by Treasury order. See Note below for details.
In para. 6(6) "4" substituted for "3" by FA 2015, s. 120 and Sch. 20, para. 15(4), with effect from a day to be appointed under FA 2015, s. 120(2).
Para. 6(6) inserted for certain purposes by FA 2010, s. 35 and Sch. 10, para. 11(6), with effect from a date to be appointed. See Note below for details.

History – In para. 6(2), the word "deliberately" inserted by F(No. 3)A 2010, s. 26 and Sch. 10, para. 4(2), with effect from: 6 April 2011 in relation to a return or other document which is required to be made or delivered to HMRC in relation to the tax year 2010–11 or any subsequent tax year, and falls within item 1, 2 or 3 of the Table in para. 1; and 1 April 2011 in relation to a return under FA 2004, s. 254 (pension schemes; accounting for tax) to be made in respect of a return period ending on or after 31 March 2011 (where a "return period" means each period of three months ending with 31 March, 30 June, 30 September and 31 December for which a return must be made under FA 2004, s. 254) (SI 2011/703).
In para. 6(3)(a), the words "the relevant percentage" substituted for "100%" by FA 2010, s. 35 and Sch. 10, para. 11(2), with effect from 6 April 2011 in relation only to a return or other document which is required to be made or delivered to HMRC in relation to the tax year 2011–12 or any subsequent tax year, and which falls within item 1, 2 or 3 of the Table in para. 1 (SI 2011/975).
Para. 6(3A) inserted by FA 2010, s. 35 and Sch. 10, para. 11(3), with effect from 6 April 2011 in relation only to a return or other document which is required to be made or delivered to HMRC in relation to the tax year 2011–12 or any subsequent tax year, and which falls within item 1, 2 or 3 of the Table in para. 1 (SI 2011/975).
In para. 6(4)(a), the words "the relevant percentage" substituted for "70%" by FA 2010, s. 35 and Sch. 10, para. 11(4), with effect from 6 April 2011 in relation only to a return or other document which is required to be made or delivered to HMRC in relation to the tax year 2011–12 or any subsequent tax year, and which falls within item 1, 2 or 3 of the Table in para. 1 (SI 2011/975).
Para. 6(4A) inserted by FA 2010, s. 35 and Sch. 10, para. 11(5), with effect from 6 April 2011 in relation only to a return or other document which is required to be made or delivered to HMRC in relation to the tax year 2011–12 or any subsequent tax year, and which falls within item 1, 2 or 3 of the Table in para. 1 (SI 2011/975).
In para. 6(5), the words "any case not falling within sub-paragraph (2)" substituted for the words "any other case" by F(No. 3)A 2010, s. 26 and Sch. 10, para. 4(3), with effect from: 6 April 2011 in relation to a return or other document which is required to be made or delivered to HMRC in relation to the tax year 2010–11 or any subsequent tax year, and falls within item 1, 2 or 3 of the Table in para. 1; and 1 April 2011 in relation to a return under FA 2004, s. 254 (pension schemes; accounting for tax) to be made in respect of a return period endingon or after 31 March 2011 (where a "return period" means each period of three months ending with 31 March, 30 June, 30 September and 31 December for which a return must be made under FA 2004, s. 254) (SI 2011/703).
Para. 6(6) inserted by FA 2010, s. 35 and Sch. 10, para. 11(6), with effect from 6 April 2011 in relation only to a return or other document which is required to be made or delivered to HMRC in relation to the tax year 2011–12 or any subsequent tax year, and which falls within item 1, 2 or 3 of the Table in para. 1 (SI 2011/975).

Notes – The amendments made to para. 6(2) and (5) by F(No. 3)A 2010, s. 26 and Sch. 10, para. 4(2) and (3) currently have effect only for certain purposes (see History notes above). For other purposes the amendments remain prospective and, accordingly, para. 6(2) and (5) should be read as if the amendments had not been made.
The amendments to para. 6(3)(a) and (4)(a), and the insertion of para. 6(3A), (4A) and (6), made by FA 2010, s. 35 and Sch. 10, para. 11 currently have effect only for certain purposes (see History note above). For other purposes these amendments to para. 6 remain prospective and, accordingly, para. 6 should be read as if they had not been made.

6A(1) Information is category 1 information if–

(a) it involves a domestic matter, or

(b) it involves an offshore matter and–

(i) the territory in question is a category 1 territory, or

(ii) it is information which would enable or assist HMRC to assess P's liability to a tax other than income tax or capital gains tax.

6A(2) Information is category 2 information if–

(a) it involves an offshore matter or an offshore transfer,

(b) the territory in question is a category 2 territory, and

(c) it is information which would enable or assist HMRC to assess P's liability to income tax, capital gains tax or inheritance tax.

6A(3) Information is category 3 information if–

(a) it involves an offshore matter or an offshore transfer,

(b) the territory in question is a category 3 territory, and

(c) it is information which would enable or assist HMRC to assess P's liability to income tax, capital gains tax or inheritance tax.

6A(4) Information **"involves an offshore matter"** if the liability to tax which would have been shown in the return *includes a liability* to tax charged on or by reference to–

(a) income arising from a source in a territory outside the UK,

(b) assets situated or held in a territory outside the UK,

(c) activities carried on wholly or mainly in a territory outside the UK, or

(d) anything having effect as if it were income, assets or activities of a kind described above.

6A(4A) If the liability to tax which would have been shown in the return is a liability to inheritance tax, assets are treated for the purposes of sub-paragraph (4) as situated or held in a territory outside the UK if they are so situated or held immediately after the transfer of value by reason of which inheritance tax becomes chargeable.

6A(4B) Information **"involves an offshore transfer"** if–

(a) it does not involve an offshore matter,

(b) it is information which would enable or assist HMRC to assess P's liability to income tax, capital gains tax or inheritance tax,

(c) by failing to make the return, P deliberately withholds the information (whether or not the withholding of the information is also concealed), and

(d) the applicable condition in paragraph 6AA is satisfied.

6A(5) Information **"involves a domestic matter"** if it does not involve an offshore matter or an offshore transfer

6A(6) If the information which P withholds falls into more than one category–

(a) P's failure to make the return is to be treated for the purposes of this Schedule as if it were separate failures, one for each category of information according to the matters or transfers which the information involves, and

(b) for each separate failure, the liability to tax which would have been shown in the return in question is taken to be such share of the liability to tax which would have been shown in the return mentioned in paragraph (a) as is just and reasonable.

6A(7) For the purposes of this Schedule–

(a) paragraph 21A of Schedule 24 to FA 2007 (classification of territories) has effect, but

(b) an order under that paragraph does not apply to a failure if the filing date is before the date on which the order comes into force.

6A(8) [Omitted by FA 2015, s. 120 and Sch. 20, para. 16(8).]

6A(9) In this paragraph and paragraph 6AA–

"assets" has the meaning given in section 21(1) of TCGA 1992, but also includes sterling;

"UK" means the United Kingdom, including the territorial sea of the United Kingdom.

Prospective amendments – Para. 6A(A1) and (1) substituted for former para. 6A(1) by FA 2015, s. 120 and Sch. 20, para. 16(2), with effect from a day to be appointed under FA 2015, s. 120(2).

Para. 6A inserted for certain purposes by FA 2010, s. 35 and Sch. 10, para. 12, with effect from a date to be appointed. See Note below.

History – In para. 6A(2)(a) the words "or an offshore transfer" inserted and in para. 6A(2)(c) the words ", capital gains tax or inheritance tax" substituted for the words "or capital gains tax" by FA 2015, s. 120 and Sch. 20, para. 16(3), with effect from 6 April 2016 (and the amendments have effect in relation to a return or other document which: is required to be made or delivered to HMRC in relation to a tax year commencing on or after 6 April 2016; and falls within item 1, 2 or 3 of the Table in para. 1(5)) (SI 2016/456, art. 5).

In para. 6A(3)(a) the words "or an offshore transfer" inserted and in para. 6A(3)(c) the words ", capital gains tax or inheritance tax" substituted for the words "or capital gains tax" by FA 2015, s. 120 and Sch. 20, para. 16(4), with effect from 6 April 2016 (and the amendments have effect in relation to a return or other document which: is required to be made or delivered to HMRC in relation to a tax year commencing on or after 6 April 2016; and falls within item 1, 2 or 3 of the Table in para. 1(5)) (SI 2016/456, art. 5).

Para. 6A(4A) and (4B) inserted by FA 2015, s. 120 and Sch. 20, para. 16(5), with effect from 6 April 2016 (and the amendments have effect in relation to a return or other document which: is required to be made or delivered to HMRC in relation to a tax year commencing on or after 6 April 2016; and falls within item 1, 2 or 3 of the Table in para. 1(5)) (SI 2016/456, art. 5).

In para. 6A(5) the words "it does not involve an offshore matter or an offshore transfer" substituted for the words "the liability to tax which would have been shown in the return includes a liability to tax charged on or by reference to anything not mentioned in sub-paragraph (4)(a) to (d)" by FA 2015, s. 120 and Sch. 20, para. 16(6), with effect from 6 April 2016 (and the amendments have effect in relation to a return or other document which: is required to be made or delivered to HMRC in relation to a tax year commencing on or after 6 April 2016; and falls within item 1, 2 or 3 of the Table in para. 1(5)) (SI 2016/456, art. 5).

In para. 6A(6)(a) the words "or transfers" inserted by FA 2015, s. 120 and Sch. 20, para. 16(7), with effect from 6 April 2016 (and the amendments have effect in relation to a return or other document which: is required to be made or delivered to HMRC in relation to a tax year commencing on or after 6 April 2016; and falls within item 1, 2 or 3 of the Table in para. 1(5)) (SI 2016/456, art. 5).

Para. 6A(8) omitted by FA 2015, s. 120 and Sch. 20, para. 16(8), with effect from 6 April 2016 (and the amendments have effect in relation to a return or other document which: is required to be made or delivered to HMRC in relation to a tax year commencing on or after 6 April 2016; and falls within item 1, 2 or 3 of the Table in para. 1(5)) (SI 2016/456, art. 5).

In para. 6A(9) the words "and paragraph 6AA" insertedby FA 2015, s. 120 and Sch. 20, para. 16(9), with effect from 6 April 2016 (and the amendments have effect in relation to a return or other document which: is required to be made or delivered to HMRC in relation to a tax year commencing on or after 6 April 2016; and falls within item 1, 2 or 3 of the Table in para. 1(5)) (SI 2016/456, art. 5).

Para. 6A inserted by FA 2010, s. 35 and Sch. 10, para. 12, with effect from 6 April 2011 in relation only to a return or other document which is required to be made or delivered to HMRC in relation to the tax year 2011–12 or any subsequent tax year, and which falls within item 1, 2 or 3 of the Table in para. 1 (SI 2011/975).

Notes – The insertion of para. 6A by FA 2010, s. 35 and Sch. 10, para. 12 currently has effect only for certain purposes (see History note above). For other purposes the insertion remains prospective and, accordingly, Sch. 55 should be read as if it had not been made.

6AA(1) This paragraph makes provision in relation to offshore transfers.

6AA(2) Where the liability to tax which would have been shown in the return is a liability to income tax, the applicable condition is satisfied if the income on or by reference to which the tax is charged, or any part of the income–

(a) is received in a territory outside the UK, or

(b) is transferred before the relevant date to a territory outside the UK.

6AA(3) Where the liability to tax which would have been shown in the return is a liability to capital gains tax, the applicable condition is satisfied if the proceeds of the disposal on or by reference to which the tax is charged, or any part of the proceeds–

(a) are received in a territory outside the UK, or

(b) are transferred before the relevant date to a territory outside the UK.

6AA(4) Where the liability to tax which would have been shown in the return is a liability to inheritance tax, the applicable condition is satisfied if–

(a) the disposition that gives rise to the transfer of value by reason of which the tax becomes chargeable involves a transfer of assets, and

(b) after that disposition but before the relevant date the assets, or any part of the assets, are transferred to a territory outside the UK.

6AA(5) In the case of a transfer falling within sub-paragraph (2)(b), (3)(b) or (4)(b), references to the income, proceeds or assets transferred are to be read as including references to any assets derived from or representing the income, proceeds or assets.

6AA(6) In relation to an offshore transfer, the territory in question for the purposes of paragraph 6A is the highest category of territory by virtue of which the information involves an offshore transfer.

6AA(7) **"Relevant date"** means the date on which P becomes liable to a penalty under paragraph 6.

History – Para. 6AA inserted by FA 2015, s. 120 and Sch. 20, para. 17, with effect from 6 April 2016 (in relation to a return or other document which: is required to be made or delivered to HMRC in relation to a tax year commencing on or after 6 April 2016; and falls within item 1, 2 or 3 of the Table in para. 1(5)) (SI 2016/456, art. 5).

6AB Regulations under paragraph 21B of Schedule 24 to FA 2007 (location of assets etc) apply for the purposes of paragraphs 6A and 6AA of this Schedule as they apply for the purposes of paragraphs 4A and 4AA of that Schedule.

History – Para. 6AB inserted by FA 2015, s. 120 and Sch. 20, para. 17, with effect from 6 April 2016 (in relation to a return or other document which: is required to be made or delivered to HMRC in relation to a tax year commencing on or after 6 April 2016; and falls within item 1, 2 or 3 of the Table in para. 1(5)) (SI 2016/456, art. 5).

AMOUNT OF PENALTY: REAL TIME INFORMATION FOR PAYE AND APPRENTICESHIP LEVY

History – In heading before para. 6B, the words "and apprenticeship levy" inserted by FA 2016, s. 113(8), with effect from 15 September 2016 (Royal Assent).
Heading before para. 6B inserted by FA 2013, s. 230 and Sch. 50, para. 6, with effect for the tax year 2014–15 and subsequent tax years in relation to failures to make returns with a filing date (as defined in para. 1(4)) on or after 6 April 2014.

6B Paragraphs 6C and 6D apply in the case of a return falling within item 4 or 4A in the Table.

Commencement Date – 6 October 2014 is the day appointed for the coming into force of para. 6B in relation to a return falling within item 4 of the Table that is required to be delivered to HMRC on or after that date by a Real Time Information employer which is at 6 October 2014 a large existing employer (employs at least 50 employees) (SI 2014/2395, art. 2(b)(i)).
6 March 2015 is the day appointed for the coming into force of para. 6B in relation to a return falling within item 4 of the Table that is required to be delivered to HMRC on or after that date by a Real Time Information employer which is at 6 October 2014 a small existing employer (employs no more than 49 employees), or a person who becomes a new Real Time Information employer after 6 October 2014 (SI 2014/2395, art. 2(b)(ii)).

History – In para. 6B, the words "or 4A" inserted by FA 2016, s. 113(7), with effect from 15 September 2016 (Royal Assent). Note item 4A relates to apprenticeship levy and is therefore not reproduced at para. 1.
Para. 6B inserted by FA 2013, s. 230 and Sch. 50, para. 6, with effect for the tax year 2014–15 and subsequent tax years in relation to failures to make returns with a filing date (as defined in para. 1(4)) on or after 6 April 2014.

6C(1) If P fails during a tax month to make a return on or before the filing date, P is liable to a penalty under this paragraph in respect of that month.

6C(2) But this is subject to sub-paragraphs (3) and (4).

6C(3) P is not liable to a penalty under this paragraph in respect of a tax month as a result of any failure to make a return on or before the filing date which occurs during the initial period.

6C(4) P is not liable to a penalty under this paragraph in respect of a tax month falling in a tax year if the month is the first tax month in that tax year during which P fails to make a return on or before the filing date (disregarding for this purpose any failure which occurs during the initial period).

6C(5) In sub-paragraphs (3) and (4) **"the initial period"** means the period which–

(a) begins with the day in the first tax year on which P is first required to make a return, and

(b) is of such duration as is specified in regulations made by the Commissioners,

and for this purpose **"the first tax year"** means the first tax year in which P is required to make returns.

6C(6) P may be liable under this paragraph to no more than one penalty in respect of each tax month.

6C(7) The penalty under this paragraph is to be calculated in accordance with regulations made by the Commissioners.

6C(8) Regulations under sub-paragraph (7) may provide for a penalty under this paragraph in respect of a tax month to be calculated by reference to either or both of the following matters–

(a) the number of persons employed by P, or treated as employed by P for the purposes of PAYE regulations;

(b) the number of previous penalties incurred by P under this paragraph in the same tax year.

6C(9) The Commissioners may by regulations disapply sub-paragraph (3) or (4) in such circumstances as are specified in the regulations.

6C(10) If P has elected under PAYE regulations to be treated as different employers in relation to different groups of employees, this paragraph applies to P as if–

(a) in respect of each group P were a different person, and

(b) each group constituted all of P's employees.

6C(11) Regulations made by the Commissioners under this paragraph may–

(a) make different provision for different cases, and

(b) include incidental, consequential and supplementary provision.

Commencement Date – 11 September 2014 is the day appointed for the coming into force of para. 6C(5), (7), (8), (9) and (11) in relation to a return falling within item 4 of the Table in para. 1 (SI 2014/2395, art. 2).
6 October 2014 is the day appointed for the coming into force of para. 6C(1) to (4), (6) and (10) in relation to a return falling within item 4 of the Table that is required to be delivered to HMRC on or after that date by a Real Time Information employer which is at 6 October 2014 a large existing employer (employs at least 50 employees) (SI 2014/2395, art. 2(b)(i)).
6 March 2015 is the day appointed for the coming into force of para. 6C(1) to (4), (6) and (10) in relation to a return falling within item 4 of the Table that is required to be delivered to HMRC on or after that date by a Real Time Information employer which is at 6 October 2014 a small existing employer (employs no more than 49 employees), or a person who becomes a new Real Time Information employer after 6 October 2014 (SI 2014/2395, art. 2(b)(ii)).

History – Para. 6C inserted by FA 2013, s. 230 and Sch. 50, para. 6, with effect for the tax year 2014–15 and subsequent tax years in relation to failures to make returns with a filing date (as defined in para. 1(4)) on or after 6 April 2014.

6D(1) P may be liable to one or more penalties under this paragraph in respect of extended failures.

6D(2) In this paragraph an **"extended failure"** means a failure to make a return on or before the filing date which continues after the end of the period of 3 months beginning with the day after the filing date.

6D(3) P is liable to a penalty or penalties under this paragraph if (and only if)–

(a) HMRC decide at any time that such a penalty or penalties should be payable in accordance with sub-paragraph (4) or (6), and

(b) HMRC give notice to P specifying the date from which the penalty, or each penalty, is payable.

6D(4) HMRC may decide under sub-paragraph (3)(a) that a separate penalty should be payable in respect of each unpenalised extended failure in the tax year to date.

6D(5) In that case the amount of the penalty in respect of each failure is 5% of any liability to make payments which would have been shown in the return in question.

6D(6) HMRC may decide under sub-paragraph (3)(a) that a single penalty should be payable in respect of all the unpenalised extended failures in the tax year to date.

6D(7) In that case the amount of the penalty in respect of those failures is 5% of the sum of the liabilities to make payments which would have been shown in each of the returns in question.

6D(8) For the purposes of this paragraph, an extended failure is unpenalised if a penalty has not already been imposed in respect of it under this paragraph (whether in accordance with sub-paragraph (4) or (6)).

6D(9) The date specified in the notice under sub-paragraph (3)(b) in relation to a penalty–

(a) may be earlier than the date on which the notice is given, but

(b) may not be earlier than the end of the period mentioned in sub-paragraph (2) in relation to the relevant extended failure.

6D(10) In sub-paragraph (9)(b) **"the relevant extended failure"** means–

(a) the extended failure in respect of which the penalty is payable, or

(b) if the penalty is payable in respect of more than one extended failure (in accordance with sub-paragraph (6)), the extended failure with the latest filing date.

Commencement Date – 6 October 2014 is the day appointed for the coming into force of para. 6D in relation to a return falling within item 4 of the Table that is required to be delivered to HMRC on or after that date by a Real Time Information employer which is at 6 October 2014 a large existing employer (employs at least 50 employees) (SI 2014/2395, art. 2(b)(i)).
6 March 2015 is the day appointed for the coming into force of para. 6D in relation to a return falling within item 4 of the Table that is required to be delivered to HMRC on or after that date by a Real Time Information employer which is at 6 October 2014 a small existing employer (employs no more than 49 employees), or a person who becomes a new Real Time Information employer after 6 October 2014 (SI 2014/2395, art. 2(b)(ii)).

History – Para. 6D inserted by FA 2013, s. 230 and Sch. 50, para. 6, with effect for the tax year 2014–15 and subsequent tax years in relation to failures to make returns with a filing date (as defined in para. 1(4)) on or after 6 April 2014.

AMOUNT OF PENALTY: CIS RETURNS

7–13 [Not relevant to National Insurance contributions.]

AMOUNT OF PENALTY: RETURNS FOR PERIODS OF BETWEEN 2 AND 6 MONTHS

13A–13E [Not relevant to National Insurance contributions.]

AMOUNT OF PENALTY: RETURNS FOR PERIODS OF 2 MONTHS OR LESS

13F–13J [Not relevant to National Insurance contributions.]

REDUCTIONS FOR DISCLOSURE

14(A1) In this paragraph, **"relevant information"** means information which has been withheld by a failure to make a return.

14(1) Paragraph 15 provides for reductions in the penalty under paragraph 6(3) or (4) where P discloses relevant information that involves a domestic matter or 11(3) or (4) where P discloses relevant information.

14(1A) Paragraph 15A provides for reductions in the penalty under paragraph 6(3) or (4) where P discloses relevant information that involves an offshore matter or an offshore transfer.

14(1B) Sub-paragraph (2) applies where–

(a) P is liable to a penalty under paragraph 6(3) or (4) and P discloses relevant information that involves a domestic matter, or

(b) P is liable to a penalty under any of the other provisions mentioned in sub-paragraph (1) and P discloses relevant information.

14(2) P discloses relevant information by–

(a) telling HMRC about it,

(b) giving HMRC reasonable help in quantifying any tax unpaid by reason of its having been withheld, and

(c) allowing HMRC access to records for the purpose of checking how much tax is so unpaid.

14(2A) Sub-paragraph (2B) applies where P is liable to a penalty under paragraph 6(3) or (4) and P discloses relevant information that involves an offshore matter or an offshore transfer.

14(2B) P discloses relevant information by–

(a) telling HMRC about it,

(b) giving HMRC reasonable help in quantifying any tax unpaid by reason of its having been withheld,

(c) allowing HMRC access to records for the purpose of checking how much tax is so unpaid, and

(d) providing HMRC with additional information.

14(2C) The Treasury must make regulations setting out what is meant by **"additional information"** for the purposes of sub-paragraph (2B)(d).

14(2D) Regulations under sub-paragraph (2C) are to be made by statutory instrument.

14(2E) An instrument containing regulations under sub-paragraph (2C) is subject to annulment in pursuance of a resolution of the House of Commons.

14(3) Disclosure of relevant information–

(a) is "unprompted" if made at a time when P has no reason to believe that HMRC have discovered or are about to discover the relevant information, and

(b) otherwise, is "prompted".

14(4) In relation to disclosure **"quality"** includes timing, nature and extent.

14(5) Paragraph 6A(4) to (5) applies to determine whether relevant information involves an offshore matter, an offshore transfer or a domestic matter for the purposes of this paragraph.

Prospective amendments – In para. 14(1), ", 11(3) or (4), 13E(3) or (4) or 13J(3) or (4)" substituted for "or 11(3) or (4)" by F(No. 3)A 2010, s. 26 and Sch. 10, para. 8, with effect from a day to be appointed by Treasury Order.

History – Para. 14(A1) inserted by FA 2016, s. 163(1) and Sch. 21, para. 10(2), with effect from 1 April 2017 for all purposes and has effect for inheritance tax purposes (in relation to transfers of value on or after that date) and for income tax and capital gains tax purposes (in relation to any tax year commencing on or after 6 April 2016) (SI 2017/259, reg. 2).
In para. 14(1), the words "where P discloses relevant information that involves a domestic matter" inserted and the words "relevant information" substituted for the words "information which has been withheld by a failure to make a return ("relevant information")" by FA 2016, s. 163(1) and Sch. 21, para. 10(3), with effect from 1 April 2017 for all purposes and has effect for inheritance tax purposes (in relation to transfers of value on or after that date) and for income tax and capital gains tax purposes (in relation to any tax year commencing on or after 6 April 2016) (SI 2017/259, reg. 2).

Para. 14(1A) and (1B) inserted by FA 2016, s. 163(1) and Sch. 21, para. 10(4), with effect from 1 April 2017 for all purposes and has effect for inheritance tax purposes (in relation to transfers of value on or after that date) and for income tax and capital gains tax purposes (in relation to any tax year commencing on or after 6 April 2016) (SI 2017/259, reg. 2).
Para. 14(2A)–(2E) inserted by FA 2016, s. 163(1) and Sch. 21, para. 10(5), with effect from 8 March 2017 for the purpose of making the regulations and from 1 April 2017 for all purposes and has effect for inheritance tax purposes (in relation to transfers of value on or after that date) and for income tax and capital gains tax purposes (in relation to any tax year commencing on or after 6 April 2016) (SI 2017/259, reg. 2 and 3).
Para. 14(5) inserted by FA 2016, s. 163(1) and Sch. 21, para. 10(6), with effect from 1 April 2017 for all purposes and has effect for inheritance tax purposes (in relation to transfers of value on or after that date) and for income tax and capital gains tax purposes (in relation to any tax year commencing on or after 6 April 2016) (SI 2017/259, reg. 2).

15(1) If a person who would otherwise be liable to a penalty of a percentage shown in column 1 of the Table (a "standard percentage") has made a disclosure, HMRC must reduce the standard percentage to one that reflects the quality of the disclosure.

15(2) But the standard percentage may not be reduced to a percentage that is below the minimum shown for it–

(a) in the case of a prompted disclosure, in column 2 of the Table, and

(b) in the case of an unprompted disclosure, in column 3 of the Table.

Standard %	*Minimum % for prompted disclosure*	*Minimum % for unprompted disclosure*
70%	35%	20%
100%	50%	30%

15(3) [Omitted (for certain purposes only) by FA 2010, s. 35 and Sch. 10, para. 13(3).]

15(4) [Omitted (for certain purposes only) by FA 2010, s. 35 and Sch. 10, para. 13(3).]

15(5) But HMRC must not under this paragraph–

(a) reduce a penalty under paragraph 6(3) or (4) below £300, or

(b) reduce a penalty under paragraph 11(3) or (4) below the amount set by paragraph 11(3)(b) or (4)(b) (as the case may be).

Prospective amendments – Para. 15(1) substituted for certain purposes by FA 2010, s. 35 and Sch. 10, para. 13(2), with effect from a date to be appointed. See Note below.
The Table in para. 15(2) amended by FA 2015, s. 120 and Sch. 20, para. 18, with effect from a day to be appointed under FA 2015, s. 120(2).
Para. 15(2) substituted for certain purposes by FA 2010, s. 35 and Sch. 10, para. 13(2), with effect from a date to be appointed. See Note below.
Para. 15(3) omitted for certain purposes by FA 2010, s. 35 and Sch. 10, para. 13(3), with effect from a date to be appointed. See Note below.
Para. 15(4) omitted for certain purposes by FA 2010, s. 35 and Sch. 10, para. 13(3), with effect from a date to be appointed. See Note below.
In para. 15(5), the words "sub-paragraph (3) or (4) of any of paragraphs 11, 13E and 13J" substituted for the words "paragraph 11(3) or (4)" by F(No. 3)A 2010, s. 26 and Sch. 10, para. 9(a), with effect from a day to be appointed by Treasury order.
In para. 15(5), the words "paragraph (b) of that sub-paragraph" substituted for the words "paragraph 11(3)(b) or (4)(b) (as the case may be)" by F(No. 3)A 2010, s. 26 and Sch. 10, para. 9(b), with effect from a day to be appointed by Treasury order.
History – Para. 15(1) substituted by FA 2010, s. 35 and Sch. 10, para. 13(2), with effect from 6 April 2011 in relation only to a return or other document which is required to be made or delivered to HMRC in relation to the tax year 2011–12 or any subsequent tax year, and which falls within item 1, 2 or 3 of the Table in para. 1 (SI 2011/975).
The Table in para. 15(2) substituted by FA 2016, s. 163(1) and Sch. 21, para. 11, with effect from 1 April 2017 for all purposes and has effect for inheritance tax purposes (in relation to transfers of value on or after that date) and for income tax and capital gains tax (in relation to any tax year commencing on or after 6 April 2016) (SI 2017/259, reg. 2). Former Table read as follows:

Standard %	*Minimum % for prompted disclosure*	*Minimum % for unprompted disclosure*
70%	35%	20%
105%	52.5%	30%
140%	70%	40%
100%	50%	30%
150%	75%	45%
200%	100%	60%.

Para. 15(2) substituted by FA 2010, s. 35 and Sch. 10, para. 13(2), with effect from 6 April 2011 in relation only to a return or other document which is required to be made or delivered to HMRC in relation to the tax year 2011–12 or any subsequent tax year, and which falls within item 1, 2 or 3 of the Table in para. 1 (SI 2011/975).
Para. 15(3) omitted by FA 2010, s. 35 and Sch. 10, para. 13(3), with effect from 6 April 2011 in relation only to a return or other document which is required to be made or delivered to HMRC in relation to the tax year 2011–12 or any subsequent tax year, and which falls within item 1, 2 or 3 of the Table in para. 1 (SI 2011/975).
Para. 15(4) omitted by FA 2010, s. 35 and Sch. 10, para. 13(3), with effect from 6 April 2011 in relation only to a return or other document which is required to be made or delivered to HMRC in relation to the tax year 2011–12 or any subsequent tax year, and which falls within item 1, 2 or 3 of the Table in para. 1 (SI 2011/975).

Notes – The substitution of para. 15(1) and (2), and the omission of para. 15(3) and (4), made by FA 2010, s. 35 and Sch. 10, para. 13 currently have effect only for certain purposes (see History notes above). For other purposes these amendments remains prospective and, accordingly, para. 15 should be read as if they had not been made.

15A(1) If a person who would otherwise be liable to a penalty of a percentage shown in column 1 of the Table (a "standard percentage") has made a disclosure, HMRC must reduce the standard percentage to one that reflects the quality of the disclosure.

15A(2) But the standard percentage may not be reduced to a percentage that is below the minimum shown for it–

(a) in the case of a prompted disclosure, in column 2 of the Table, and

(b) in the case of an unprompted disclosure, in column 3 of the Table.

Standard %	*Minimum % for prompted disclosure*	*Minimum % for unprompted disclosure*
70%	45%	30%
87.5%	53.75%	35%
100%	60%	40%
105%	62.5%	40%
125%	72.5%	50%
140%	80%	50%
150%	85%	55%
200%	110%	70%

15A(3) But HMRC must not under this paragraph reduce a penalty below £300.

History – Para. 15A inserted by FA 2016, s. 163(1) and Sch. 21, para. 12, with effect from 1 April 2017 for all purposes and has effect for inheritance tax purposes (in relation to transfers of value on or after that date) and for income tax and capital gains tax purposes (in relation to any tax year commencing on or after 6 April 2016) (SI 2017/259, reg. 2).

SPECIAL REDUCTION

16(1) If HMRC think it right because of special circumstances, they may reduce a penalty under any paragraph of this Schedule.

16(2) In sub-paragraph (1) **"special circumstances"** does not include–

(a) ability to pay, or

(b) the fact that a potential loss of revenue from one taxpayer is balanced by a potential over-payment by another.

16(3) In sub-paragraph (1) the reference to reducing a penalty includes a reference to–

(a) staying a penalty, and

(b) agreeing a compromise in relation to proceedings for a penalty.

Commencement Date – 6 October 2014 is the day appointed for the coming into force of para. 16 to 24 in relation to a return falling within item 4 of the Table that is required to be delivered to HMRC on or after that date by a Real Time Information employer which is at 6 October 2014 a large existing employer (employs at least 50 employees) (SI 2014/2395, art. 2(b)(i)).

6 March 2015 is the day appointed for the coming into force of para. 16 to 24 in relation to a return falling within item 4 of the Table that is required to be delivered to HMRC on or after that date by a Real Time Information employer which is at 6 October 2014 a small existing employer (employs no more than 49 employees), or a person who becomes a new Real Time Information employer after 6 October 2014 (SI 2014/2395, art. 2(b)(ii)).

INTERACTION WITH OTHER PENALTIES AND LATE PAYMENT SURCHARGES

17(1) Where P is liable for a penalty under any paragraph of this Schedule which is determined by reference to a liability to tax, the amount of that penalty is to be reduced by the amount of any other penalty incurred by P, if the amount of the penalty is determined by reference to the same liability to tax.

17(2) In sub-paragraph (1) the reference to **"any other penalty"** does not include–

(a) a penalty under any other paragraph of this Schedule, or

(b) a penalty under Schedule 56 (penalty for late payment of tax), or

(c) a penalty under Part 4 of FA 2014 (penalty where corrective action not taken after follower notice etc), or

(d) a penalty under Schedule 22 to FA 2016 (asset-based penalty).

17(3) Where P is liable for a penalty under more than one paragraph of this Schedule which is determined by reference to a liability to tax, the aggregate of the amounts of those penalties must not exceed the relevant percentage of the liability to tax.

17(4) The relevant percentage is–

(a) if one of the penalties is a penalty under paragraph 6(3) or (4) and the information withheld is category 3 information, 200%,

(b) if one of the penalties is a penalty under paragraph 6(3) or (4) and the information withheld is category 2 information, 150%, and

(c) in all other cases, 100%.

Commencement Date – 6 October 2014 is the day appointed for the coming into force of para. 16 to 24 in relation to a return falling within item 4 of the Table that is required to be delivered to HMRC on or after that date by a Real Time Information employer which is at 6 October 2014 a large existing employer (employs at least 50 employees) (SI 2014/2395, art. 2(b)(i)).
6 March 2015 is the day appointed for the coming into force of para. 16 to 24 in relation to a return falling within item 4 of the Table that is required to be delivered to HMRC on or after that date by a Real Time Information employer which is at 6 October 2014 a small existing employer (employs no more than 49 employees), or a person who becomes a new Real Time Information employer after 6 October 2014 (SI 2014/2395, art. 2(b)(ii)).

Prospective amendments – Para. 17(3) amended for certain purposes by FA 2010, s. 35 and Sch. 10, para. 14(a), with effect from a date to be appointed. See Note below.
Para. 17(4)(ba) (and the words "and" at the end of it) inserted (and the words "and" at the end of para. (b) omitted) by FA 2015, s. 120 and Sch. 20, para. 19, with effect from a day to be appointed under FA 2015, s. 120(2).
Para. 17(4) inserted for certain purposes by FA 2010, s. 35 and Sch. 10, para. 14(b), with effect from a date to be appointed. See Note below.

History – Para. 17(2)(c) (and the ", or" before it) inserted by FA 2014, s. 233 and Sch. 33, para. 5, with effect from 17 July 2014.
Para. 17(2)(d) (and the ", or" before it) inserted by FA 2016, s. 165(1) and Sch. 22, para. 20(5), with effect for inheritance tax purposes, in relation to transfers of value made on or after 1 April 2017 and for income tax and capital gains tax purposes, in relation to tax years commencing on or after 6 April 2016 (SI 2017/277, reg. 2).
In para. 17(3), the words "the relevant percentage" substituted for "100%" by FA 2010, s. 35 and Sch. 10, para. 14(a), with effect from 6 April 2011 in relation only to a return or other document which is required to be made or delivered to HMRC in relation to the tax year 2011–12 or any subsequent tax year, and which falls within item 1, 2 or 3 of the Table in para. 1 (SI 2011/975).
Para. 17(4) inserted by FA 2010, s. 35 and Sch. 10, para. 14(b), with effect from 6 April 2011 in relation only to a return or other document which is required to be made or delivered to HMRC in relation to the tax year 2011–12 or any subsequent tax year, and which falls within item 1, 2 or 3 of the Table in para. 1 (SI 2011/975).

Notes – The amendment of para. 17(3), and the insertion of para. 17 (4), made by FA 2010, s. 35 and Sch. 10, para. 14 currently have effect only for certain purposes (see History notes above). For other purposes these amendments remains prospective and, accordingly, para. 17 should be read as if they had not been made.

CANCELLATION OF PENALTY

17A(1) This paragraph applies where–

(a) P is liable for a penalty under any paragraph of this Schedule in relation to a failure to make a return falling within item 1 or 2 in the Table, and

(b) HMRC decide to give P a notice under section 8B withdrawing a notice under section 8 or 8A of that Act.

17A(2) The notice under section 8B of TMA 1970 may include provision under this paragraph cancelling liability to the penalty from the date specified in the notice.

History – In para. 17A, the words "HMRC decide to give P a notice under section 8B withdrawing" substituted for the words "P makes a request under section 8B of TMA 1970 for HMRC to withdraw" by FA 2016, s. 169(6), with effect in relation to any notice under TMA 1970, s. 8 or 8A given in relation to the 2014–15 tax year or any subsequent year (and it is immaterial whether the notice was given before or after 15 September 2016).
Para. 17A inserted by FA 2013, s. 233 and Sch. 51, para. 8, with effect in relation to returns under TMA 1970, s. 12AA for partnerships which include one or more companies, in respect of returns for a relevant period (as defined by FA 2013, Sch. 51, para. 9(2)) beginning on or after 6 April 2012, and in relation to returns under TMA 1970, s. 12AA for any other partnership, or returns under TMA 1970, s. 8 or 8A, in respect of returns for a year of assessment beginning on or after 6 April 2012.

17B [Not relevant to National Insurance contributions.]

ASSESSMENT

18(1) Where P is liable for a penalty under any paragraph of this Schedule HMRC must–

(a) assess the penalty,

(b) notify P, and

(c) state in the notice the period in respect of which the penalty is assessed.

18(2) A penalty under any paragraph of this Schedule must be paid before the end of the period of 30 days beginning with the day on which notification of the penalty is issued.

18(3) An assessment of a penalty under any paragraph of this Schedule–

(a) is to be treated for procedural purposes in the same way as an assessment to tax (except in respect of a matter expressly provided for by this Schedule),

(b) may be enforced as if it were an assessment to tax, and

(c) may be combined with an assessment to tax.

18(4) A supplementary assessment may be made in respect of a penalty if an earlier assessment operated by reference to an underestimate of the liability to tax which would have been shown in a return.

18(5) Sub-paragraph (6) applies if–

(a) an assessment in respect of a penalty is based on a liability to tax that would have been shown in a return, and

(b) that liability is found by HMRC to be excessive.

18(6) HMRC may by notice to P amend the assessment so that it is based upon the correct amount.

18(7) An amendment under sub-paragraph (6)–

(a) does not affect when the penalty must be paid;

(b) may be made after the last day on which the assessment in question could have been made under paragraph 19.

Commencement Date – 6 October 2014 is the day appointed for the coming into force of para. 16 to 24 in relation to a return falling within item 4 of the Table that is required to be delivered to HMRC on or after that date by a Real Time Information employer which is at 6 October 2014 a large existing employer (employs at least 50 employees) (SI 2014/2395, art. 2(b)(i)).
6 March 2015 is the day appointed for the coming into force of para. 16 to 24 in relation to a return falling within item 4 of the Table that is required to be delivered to HMRC on or after that date by a Real Time Information employer which is at 6 October 2014 a small existing employer (employs no more than 49 employees), or a person who becomes a new Real Time Information employer after 6 October 2014 (SI 2014/2395, art. 2(b)(ii)).

History – Para. 18(5)–(7) substituted for (5) by FA 2013, s. 230 and Sch. 50, para. 7, with effect for the tax year 2014–15 and subsequent tax years in relation to failures to make returns with a filing date (as defined in para. 1(4)) on or after 6 April 2014.
Para. 18(5) inserted by F(No. 3)A 2010, s. 26 and Sch. 10, para. 10, with effect from:

- 6 April 2011 in relation to a return or other document which is required to be made or delivered to HMRC in relation to the tax year 2010–11 or any subsequent tax year, and falls within item 1, 2 or 3 of the Table in para. 1 (SI 2011/703);

Notes – The insertion of para. 18(5) by F(No. 3)A 2010, s. 27 and Sch. 10, para. 10, was brought into effect from 6 April 2011 in relation to items 1, 2 or 3 in the Table in para. 1 (which relate to income tax, capital gains tax and corporation tax) and from 1 April 2011 in relation to a return under FA 2004, s. 254 (pension schemes; accounting for tax) (SI 2011/703), and from 6 October 2011 in relation to item 6 (CIS returns) (SI 2011/2391) but remained prospectively inserted for other purposes. As a consequence of the substitution of para. 18(5)–(7) by FA 2013, s. 230 and Sch. 50, para. 7 (see history note above) (which applies for all purposes), F(No.3)A 2010, Sch. 10, para. 10 was repealed by FA 2013, s. 230 and Sch. 50, para. 15, with effect for the tax year 2014–15 and subsequent tax years in relation to failures to make returns with a filing date (as defined in para. 1(4)) on or after 6 April 2014.

19(1) An assessment of a penalty under any paragraph of this Schedule in respect of any amount must be made on or before the later of date A and (where it applies) date B.

19(2) Date A is–

(a) in the case of an assessment of a penalty under paragraph 6C, the last day of the period of 2 years beginning with the end of the tax month in respect of which the penalty is payable,

(b) in the case of an assessment of a penalty under paragraph 6D, the last day of the period of 2 years beginning with the filing date for the relevant extended failure (as defined in paragraph 6D(10)), and

(c) in any other case, the last day of the period of 2 years beginning with the filing date.

19(3) Date B is the last day of the period of 12 months beginning with–

(a) the end of the appeal period for the assessment of the liability to tax which would have been shown in the return or returns (as the case may be in relation to penalties under section 6C or 6D), or

(b) if there is no such assessment, the date on which that liability is ascertained or it is ascertained that the liability is nil.

19(4) In sub-paragraph (3)(a) **"appeal period"** means the period during which–

(a) an appeal could be brought, or

(b) an appeal that has been brought has not been determined or withdrawn.

19(5) Sub-paragraph (1) does not apply to a re-assessment under paragraph 24(2)(b).

Commencement Date – 6 October 2014 is the day appointed for the coming into force of para. 16 to 24 in relation to a return falling within item 4 of the Table that is required to be delivered to HMRC on or after that date by a Real Time Information employer which is at 6 October 2014 a large existing employer (employs at least 50 employees) (SI 2014/2395, art. 2(b)(i)).
6 March 2015 is the day appointed for the coming into force of para. 16 to 24 in relation to a return falling within item 4 of the Table that is required to be delivered to HMRC on or after that date by a Real Time Information employer which is at 6 October 2014 a small existing employer (employs no more than 49 employees), or a person who becomes a new Real Time Information employer after 6 October 2014 (SI 2014/2395, art. 2(b)(ii)).

History – In para. 19(2), the words " — (a) in the case of an assessment of a penalty under paragraph 6C, the last day of the period of 2 years beginning with the end of the tax month in respect of which the penalty is payable, (b) in the case of an assessment of a penalty under paragraph 6D, the last day of the period of 2 years beginning with the filing date for the relevant extended failure (as defined in paragraph 6D(10)), and (c) in any other case," inserted by FA 2013, s. 230 and Sch. 50, para. 8(2), with effect for the tax year 2014–15 and subsequent tax years in relation to failures to make returns with a filing date (as defined in FA 2009, Sch. 55, para. 1(4)) on or after 6 April 2014.
In para. 19(3)(a), the words "or returns (as the case may be in relation to penalties under section 6C or 6D)" inserted after the word "return", by FA 2013, s. 230 and Sch. 50, para. 8(3), with effect for the tax year 2014–15 and subsequent tax years in relation to failures to make returns with a filing date (as defined in para. 1(4)) on or after 6 April 2014.

APPEAL

20(1) P may appeal against a decision of HMRC that a penalty is payable by P.

20(2) P may appeal against a decision of HMRC as to the amount of a penalty payable by P.

Commencement Date – 6 October 2014 is the day appointed for the coming into force of para. 16 to 24 in relation to a return falling within item 4 of the Table that is required to be delivered to HMRC on or after that date by a Real Time Information employer which is at 6 October 2014 a large existing employer (employs at least 50 employees) (SI 2014/2395, art. 2(b)(i)).
6 March 2015 is the day appointed for the coming into force of para. 16 to 24 in relation to a return falling within item 4 of the Table that is required to be delivered to HMRC on or after that date by a Real Time Information employer which is at 6 October 2014 a small existing employer (employs no more than 49 employees), or a person who becomes a new Real Time Information employer after 6 October 2014 (SI 2014/2395, art. 2(b)(ii)).

21(1) An appeal under paragraph 20 is to be treated in the same way as an appeal against an assessment to the tax concerned (including by the application of any provision about bringing the appeal by notice to HMRC, about HMRC review of the decision or about determination of the appeal by the First-tier Tribunal or Upper Tribunal).

21(2) Sub-paragraph (1) does not apply–

(a) so as to require P to pay a penalty before an appeal against the assessment of the penalty is determined, or

(b) in respect of any other matter expressly provided for by this Act.

Commencement Date – 6 October 2014 is the day appointed for the coming into force of para. 16 to 24 in relation to a return falling within item 4 of the Table that is required to be delivered to HMRC on or after that date by a Real Time Information employer which is at 6 October 2014 a large existing employer (employs at least 50 employees) (SI 2014/2395, art. 2(b)(i)).
6 March 2015 is the day appointed for the coming into force of para. 16 to 24 in relation to a return falling within item 4 of the Table that is required to be delivered to HMRC on or after that date by a Real Time Information employer which is at 6 October 2014 a small existing employer (employs no more than 49 employees), or a person who becomes a new Real Time Information employer after 6 October 2014 (SI 2014/2395, art. 2(b)(ii)).

22(1) On an appeal under paragraph 20(1) that is notified to the tribunal, the tribunal may affirm or cancel HMRC's decision.

22(2) On an appeal under paragraph 20(2) that is notified to the tribunal, the tribunal may–

(a) affirm HMRC's decision, or

(b) substitute for HMRC's decision another decision that HMRC had power to make.

22(3) If the tribunal substitutes its decision for HMRC's, the tribunal may rely on paragraph 16–

(a) to the same extent as HMRC (which may mean applying the same percentage reduction as HMRC to a different starting point), or

(b) to a different extent, but only if the tribunal thinks that HMRC's decision in respect of the application of paragraph 16 was flawed.

22(4) In sub-paragraph (3)(b) **"flawed"** means flawed when considered in the light of the principles applicable in proceedings for judicial review.

22(5) In this paragraph **"tribunal"** means the First-tier Tribunal or Upper Tribunal (as appropriate by virtue of paragraph 21(1)).

Commencement Date – 6 October 2014 is the day appointed for the coming into force of para. 16 to 24 in relation to a return falling within item 4 of the Table that is required to be delivered to HMRC on or after that date by a Real Time Information employer which is at 6 October 2014 a large existing employer (employs at least 50 employees) (SI 2014/2395, art. 2(b)(i)).
6 March 2015 is the day appointed for the coming into force of para. 16 to 24 in relation to a return falling within item 4 of the Table that is required to be delivered to HMRC on or after that date by a Real Time Information employer which is at 6 October 2014 a small existing employer (employs no more than 49 employees), or a person who becomes a new Real Time Information employer after 6 October 2014 (SI 2014/2395, art. 2(b)(ii)).

REASONABLE EXCUSE

23(1) Liability to a penalty under any paragraph of this Schedule does not arise in relation to a failure to make a return if P satisfies HMRC or (on appeal) the First-tier Tribunal or Upper Tribunal that there is a reasonable excuse for the failure.

23(2) For the purposes of sub-paragraph (1)–

(a) an insufficiency of funds is not a reasonable excuse, unless attributable to events outside P's control,

(b) where P relies on any other person to do anything, that is not a reasonable excuse unless P took reasonable care to avoid the failure, and

(c) where P had a reasonable excuse for the failure but the excuse has ceased, P is to be treated as having continued to have the excuse if the failure is remedied without unreasonable delay after the excuse ceased.

Commencement Date – 6 October 2014 is the day appointed for the coming into force of para. 16 to 24 in relation to a return falling within item 4 of the Table that is required to be delivered to HMRC on or after that date by a Real Time Information employer which is at 6 October 2014 a large existing employer (employs at least 50 employees) (SI 2014/2395, art. 2(b)(i)).
6 March 2015 is the day appointed for the coming into force of para. 16 to 24 in relation to a return falling within item 4 of the Table that is required to be delivered to HMRC on or after that date by a Real Time Information employer which is at 6 October 2014 a small existing employer (employs no more than 49 employees), or a person who becomes a new Real Time Information employer after 6 October 2014 (SI 2014/2395, art. 2(b)(ii)).

Prospective amendments – Para. 23(1) substituted by F(No. 3)A 2010, s. 26 and Sch. 10, para. 11, with effect from a day to be appointed by Treasury order. The substituted para. 23(1) to read as follows:

"23(1) If P satisfies HMRC or (on appeal) the First-tier Tribunal or Upper Tribunal that there is a reasonable excuse for a failure to make a return–

(a) liability to a penalty under any paragraph of this Schedule does not arise in relation to that failure, and

(b) [not relevant to income tax, corporation tax or capital gains tax.]".

DETERMINATION OF PENALTY GEARED TO TAX LIABILITY WHERE NO RETURN MADE

24(1) References to a liability to tax which would have been shown in a return are references to the amount which, if a complete and accurate return had been delivered on the filing date, would have been shown to be due or payable by the taxpayer in respect of the tax concerned for the period to which the return relates.

24(2) In the case of a penalty which is assessed at a time before P makes the return to which the penalty relates–

(a) HMRC is to determine the amount mentioned in sub-paragraph (1) to the best of HMRC's information and belief, and

(b) if P subsequently makes a return, the penalty must be re-assessed by reference to the amount of tax shown to be due and payable in that return (but subject to any amendments or corrections to the return).

24(3) In calculating a liability to tax which would have been shown in a return, no account is to be taken of any relief under section 458 of CTA 2010 (relief in respect of repayment etc of loan) which is deferred under subsection (5) of that section.

Commencement Date – 6 October 2014 is the day appointed for the coming into force of para. 16 to 24 in relation to a return falling within item 4 of the Table that is required to be delivered to HMRC on or after that date by a Real Time Information employer which is at 6 October 2014 a large existing employer (employs at least 50 employees) (SI 2014/2395, art. 2(b)(i)).
6 March 2015 is the day appointed for the coming into force of para. 16 to 24 in relation to a return falling within item 4 of the Table that is required to be delivered to HMRC on or after that date by a Real Time Information employer which is at 6 October 2014 a small existing employer (employs no more than 49 employees), or a person who becomes a new Real Time Information employer after 6 October 2014 (SI 2014/2395, art. 2(b)(ii)).

History – In para. 24(3), the words "section 458 of CTA 2010" substituted for the words "subsection (4) of section 419 of ICTA" and the words "subsection (5)" substituted for the words "subsection (4A)" by CTA 2010, s. 1177 and Sch. 1, para. 723, with effect for corporation tax purposes for accounting periods ending on or after 1 April 2010, and for income tax and capital gains tax purposes for the tax year 2010–11 and subsequent tax years.

PARTNERSHIPS

25 [Not relevant to National Insurance contributions.]

DOUBLE JEOPARDY

26 P is not liable to a penalty under any paragraph of this Schedule in respect of a failure or action in respect of which P has been convicted of an offence.

Commencement Date – 6 October 2014 is the day appointed for the coming into force of para. 26 in relation to a return falling within item 4 of the Table that is required to be delivered to HMRC on or after that date by a Real Time Information employer which is at 6 October 2014 a large existing employer (employs at least 50 employees) (SI 2014/2395, art. 2(b)(i)).
6 March 2015 is the day appointed for the coming into force of para. 26 in relation to a return falling within item 4 of the Table that is required to be delivered to HMRC on or after that date by a Real Time Information employer which is at 6 October 2014 a small existing employer (employs no more than 49 employees), or a person who becomes a new Real Time Information employer after 6 October 2014 (SI 2014/2395, art. 2(b)(ii)).

INTERPRETATION

27(1) This paragraph applies for the construction of this Schedule.

27(2) The withholding of information by P is–

(a) **"deliberate and concealed"** if P deliberately withholds the information and makes arrangements to conceal the fact that the information has been withheld, and

(b) **"deliberate but not concealed"** if P deliberately withholds the information but does not make arrangements to conceal the fact that the information has been withheld.

27(2A) **"The Commissioners"** means the Commissioners for Her Majesty's Revenue and Customs.

27(3) **"HMRC"** means Her Majesty's Revenue and Customs.

27(3A) ***"Tax month"*** means the period beginning with the 6th day of a month and ending with the 5th day of the following month.

27(4) References to a liability to tax, in relation to a return falling within item 6 in the Table (construction industry scheme), are to a liability to make payments in accordance with Chapter 3 of Part 3 of FA 2004.

27(5) References to an assessment to tax, in relation to inheritance tax and stamp duty reserve tax, are to a determination.

Commencement Date – 6 October 2014 is the day appointed for the coming into force of para. 27 in relation to a return falling within item 4 of the Table that is required to be delivered to HMRC on or after that date by a Real Time Information employer which is at 6 October 2014 a large existing employer (employs at least 50 employees) (SI 2014/2395, art. 2(b)(i)).
6 March 2015 is the day appointed for the coming into force of para. 27 in relation to a return falling within item 4 of the Table that is required to be delivered to HMRC on or after that date by a Real Time Information employer which is at 6 October 2014 a small existing employer (employs no more than 49 employees), or a person who becomes a new Real Time Information employer after 6 October 2014 (SI 2014/2395, art. 2(b)(ii)).

History – Para. 27(2A) inserted by FA 2013, s. 230 and Sch. 50, para. 9(2), with effect for the tax year 2014–15 and subsequent tax years in relation to failures to make returns with a filing date (as defined in para. 1(4)) on or after 6 April 2014.
Para. 27(3A) inserted by FA 2013, s. 230 and Sch. 50, para. 9(3), with effect for the tax year 2014–15 and subsequent tax years in relation to failures to make returns with a filing date (as defined in para. 1(4)) on or after 6 April 2014.

SCHEDULE 56 – PENALTY FOR FAILURE TO MAKE PAYMENTS ON TIME

Section 107

Commencement Date – 6 April 2010 is the day appointed for the coming into force of Sch. 56 in respect of amounts of tax under items 2, 3 and 4 and items 17, 23 and 24 (but only insofar as the tax falls within items 2, 3 or 4) of the Table at para. 1, where those amounts of tax are:
"(a) chargeable in respect of a tax period starting on or after 6th April 2010, or
(b) chargeable in respect of a section 254 period ending on or after 30th September 2010"
(SI2010/466, art. 3).
The following relevant definitions provided at SI 2010/466, art. 2
""**tax quarter**" means any of the following (inclusive) periods–
6th April to 5th July, 6th July to 5th October, 6th October to 5th January and 6th January to 5th April;
"**tax month**" means the period beginning on the 6th day of a calendar month and ending on the 5th day of the following calendar month;
"**tax period**" means a tax quarter or tax month;
"**section 254 period**" means each period of three months ending with 31st March, 30th June, 30th September or 31st December as provided for in section 254(2) of the Finance Act 2004.".
Sch. 56 applies in relation to the late payment of Class 1, Class 1A and Class 1B contributions with effect from 6 April 2010 (but only in relation to 2010–11 and subsequent years) (SI 2001/1004, reg. 67A and 67B).
6 April 2011 is the day appointed for the coming into force of Sch. 56 in relation an amount of tax which is payable in relation to the tax year 2010–11 or any subsequent tax year, and falls within: item 1, 12, 18 or 19 of the Table in para. 1 (income tax self assessment); or, insofar as the tax falls within item 1 of that Table, item 17, 23 or 24 of that Table (SI 2011/702, art. 3). The amendments to Sch. 56 by F(No.3)A 2010, Sch. 11, para. 1 and 9 (only) were also brought into effect (for the same purposes) from 6 April 2011 (SI 2011/703, art. 3).
Sch. 56 applies in relation to Class 2 contributions, with effect for the tax year 2015–16 and subsequent tax years (NICA 2015, Sch. 1, para. 35).

Notes – This is an edited version of Sch. 56, containing only the provisions relevant to national insurance contributions.

PENALTY FOR FAILURE TO PAY TAX

1(1) A penalty is payable by a person ("P") where P fails to pay an amount of tax specified in column 3 of the Table below on or before the date specified in column 4.

1(2) Paragraphs 3 to 8 set out–

(a) the circumstances in which a penalty is payable, and

(b) subject to paragraph 9, the amount of the penalty.

1(3) If P's failure falls within more than one provision of this Schedule, P is liable to a penalty under each of those provisions.

1(4) In the following provisions of this Schedule, the **"penalty date"**, in relation to an amount of tax, means the day after the date specified in or for the purposes of column 4 of the Table in relation to that amount.

1(5) Sub-paragraph (4) is subject to paragraph 2A.

	Tax to which payment relates	*Amount of tax payable*	*Date after which penalty is incurred*
		PRINCIPAL AMOUNTS	
1	Income tax or capital gains tax	Amount payable under section 59B(3) or (4) of TMA 1970	The date falling 30 days after the date specified in section 59B(3) or (4) of TMA 1970 as the date by which the amount must be paid
2	Income tax	Amount payable under PAYE regulations	The date determined by or under PAYE regulations as the date by which the amount must be paid

	Tax to which payment relates	*Amount of tax payable*	*Date after which penalty is incurred*
3	Income tax	Amount shown in return under section 254(1) of FA 2004	The date falling 30 days after the date specified in section 254(5) of FA 2004 as the date by which the amount must be paid
		AMOUNTS PAYABLE IN DEFAULT OF A RETURN BEING MADE	
12	Income tax or capital gains tax	Amount payable under section 59B(5A) of TMA 1970	The date falling 30 days after the date specified in section 59B(5A) of TMA 1970 as the date by which the amount must be paid
17	Tax falling within any of items 1 to 6, 9, 10 or 10A	Amount (not falling within any of items 12 to 15A) which is shown in an assessment or determination made by HMRC in the circumstances set out in paragraph 2	The date falling 30 days after the date by which the amount would have been required to be paid if it had been shown in the return in question
		AMOUNTS SHOWN TO BE DUE IN OTHER ASSESSMENTS, DETERMINATIONS, ETC	
18	Income tax or capital gains tax	Amount payable under section 55 of TMA 1970	The date falling 30 days after the date determined in accordance with section 55(3), (4), (6) or (9) of TMA 1970 as the date by which the amount must be paid
19	Income tax or capital gains tax	Amount payable under section 59B(5) or (6) of TMA 1970	The date falling 30 days after the date specified in section 59B(5) or (6) of TMA 1970 as the date by which the amount must be paid
20	Income tax	Amount shown in determination made by HMRC where it appears that tax payable under PAYE regulations has not been paid	The date determined by or under PAYE regulations as the date by which the amount must be paid
23	Tax falling within any of items 1 to 6, 9 or 10	Amount (not falling within any of items 18 to 20) shown in an amendment or correction of a return showing an amount falling within any of items 1 to 6, 9 or 10	The date falling 30 days after– (a) the date by which the amount must be paid, or (b) the date on which the amendment or correction is made, whichever is later
24	Tax falling within any of items 1 to 6, 9 or 10	Amount (not falling within any of items 18 to 20) shown in an assessment or determination made by HMRC in circumstances other than those set out in paragraph 2	The date falling 30 days after– (a) the date by which the amount must be paid, or (b) the date on which the assessment or determination is made, whichever is later

Prospective amendments – In para. 1(2), "8J" substituted for "8" by F(No. 3)A 2010, s. 27 and Sch. 11, para. 2(2), with effect from a day to be appointed by Treasury order.
In para. 1, in the Table, item 1A inserted by FA 2016, s. 167(1) and Sch. 23, para. 9(2), with effect from a day to be appointed under FA 2016, s. 167(3).
In para. 1, in the Table, in item 23 in the second and third columns, "9 to 10A" substituted for "9, 10" by FA 2013, s. 164 and Sch. 34, para. 10(2)(a), with effect from the coming into force of F(No.3)A 2010, Sch. 11, para. 2(13)(a) and 2(14)(a).
In para. 1, in the Table, in item 23, in columns 2 and 3, "items 1 to 6A, 6C, 9, 10 or 11A to 11M" substituted for "items 1 to 6, 9 or 10" by F(No. 3)A 2010, s. 27 and Sch. 11, para. 2(13)(a), with effect from a day to be appointed by Treasury order.
In para. 1, in the Table, in item 23, in column 3, "item 18 or 19" substituted for "any of items 18 to 20" by F(No. 3)A 2010, s. 27 and Sch. 11, para. 2(13)(b), with effect from a day to be appointed by Treasury order.
In para. 1, in the Table, in item 24 in the second column, "9 to 10A" substituted for "9, 10" by FA 2013, s. 164 and Sch. 34, para. 10(2)(b), with effect from the coming into force of F(No.3)A 2010, Sch. 11, para. 2(13)(a) and 2(14)(a).

In para. 1, in the Table, in item 24, in column 2, "items 1 to 6A, 6C, 9, 10 or 11A to 11M" substituted for "items 1 to 6, 9 or 10" by F(No. 3)A 2010, s. 27 and Sch. 11, para. 2(14)(a), with effect from a day to be appointed by Treasury order.
In para. 1, in the Table, in item 24, in column 3, "item 18 or 19" substituted for "any of items 18 to 20" by F(No. 3)A 2010, s. 27 and Sch. 11, para. 2(14)(b), with effect from a day to be appointed by Treasury order.

History – In para. 1(4), the words "the day after the date specified in or for the purposes of column 4 of the Table in relation to that amount." substituted for the words "the date on which a penalty is first payable for failing to pay the amount (that is to say, the day after the date specified in or for the purposes of column 4 of the Table)." by FA 2013, s. 230 and Sch. 50, para. 11, with effect for defaults made (see para. 6(2), as amended by FA 2013, s. 230 and Sch. 50, para. 12(3)) in relation to the tax year 2014–15 and subsequent tax years.
Para. 1(5) inserted by F(No. 3)A 2010, s. 27 and Sch. 11, para. 2(3), with effect from 25 January 2011 (SI 2011/132, art. 2(a)).
In para. 1, in the Table, in item 2, in column 3, the words "(except an amount falling within item 20)" omitted from the end by F(No. 3)A 2010, s. 27 and Sch. 11, para. 2(5), with effect from 25 January 2011 (SI 2011/132, art. 2(a)).
In para. 1, in the Table, in item 17, in the second column, the words ", 10 or 10A" substituted for "or 10", and in the third column, the word "15A" substituted for "15" by FA 2013, s. 164 and Sch. 34, para. 9(4), with effect from 17 July 2013 (see FA 2013, Sch. 34, para. 12).
In para. 1, in the Table, item 20 omitted by F(No. 3)A 2010, s. 27 and Sch. 11, para. 2(12), with effect from 25 January 2011 (SI 2011/132, art. 2(a)).

Cross references – SI 2001/1004, reg. 67A: Sch. 56 applies in relation to the late payment of Class 1 contributions as if the Class 1 contribution were an amount of tax falling within item 2 of the Table in para. 1 and references to the PAYE regulations were references to SI 2001/1004, and references to "an assessment or determination" in item 24 of the Table were references to a decision made under SSCTFA 1999, s. 8(1)(c).
SI 2001/1004, reg. 67B: Sch. 56 applies in relation to the late payment of Class 1A and Class 1B contributions as if the Class 1A and Class 1B contributions were an amount of tax falling within item 3 of the Table in para. 1 and in the case of Class 1B contributions, the reference to "amount shown in return under section 254(1) of FA 2004" was a reference to the amount payable under SSCBA 1992, s. 10A.

ASSESSMENTS AND DETERMINATIONS IN DEFAULT OF RETURN

2 The circumstances referred to in items 14, 17, 21 and 24 are where–

(a) P or another person is required to make or deliver a return falling within any item in the Table in Schedule 55,

(b) that person fails to make or deliver the return on or before the date by which it is required to be made or delivered, and

(c) if the return had been made or delivered as required, the return would have shown that an amount falling within any of items 1 to 10 was due and payable.

Prospective amendments – In para. 2(c), "11M" substituted for "10" by F(No. 3)A 2010, s. 27 and Sch. 11, para. 3, with effect from a day to be appointed by Treasury order.

DIFFERENT PENALTY DATE FOR CERTAIN PAYE PAYMENTS

2A(1) PAYE regulations may provide that, in relation to specified payments of tax falling within item 2, the penalty date is a specified date later than that determined in accordance with column 4 of the Table.

2A(2) In sub-paragraph (1) **"specified"** means specified in the regulations.

History – Para. 2A and the heading before it inserted by F(No. 3)A 2010, s. 27 and Sch. 11, para. 4, with effect from 25 January 2011 (SI 2011/132, art. 2(b)).

AMOUNT OF PENALTY: OCCASIONAL AMOUNTS AND AMOUNTS IN RESPECT OF PERIODS OF 6 MONTHS OR MORE

3(1) This paragraph applies in the case of–

(a) a payment of tax falling within any of items 1, 3 and 7 to 24 in the Table,

(aa) a payment of tax falling within item 6ZB in the Table,

(b) a payment of tax falling within item 4A or item 2 or 4 which relates to a period of 6 months or more, and

(c) a payment of tax falling within item 2 which is payable under regulations under section 688A of ITEPA 2003 (recovery from other persons of amounts due from managed service companies).

(ca) an amount in respect of apprenticeship levy falling within item 4A which is payable by virtue of regulations under section 106 of FA 2016 (recovery from third parties).

3(2) P is liable to a penalty of 5% of the unpaid tax.

3(3) If any amount of the tax is unpaid after the end of the period of 5 months beginning with the penalty date, P is liable to a penalty of 5% of that amount.

3(4) If any amount of the tax is unpaid after the end of the period of 11 months beginning with the penalty date, P is liable to a penalty of 5% of that amount.

Prospective amendments – In para. 3(1)(a), "1A," inserted (after the words "items 1,") by FA 2016, s. 167(1) and Sch. 23, para. 9(3), with effect from a day to be appointed under FA 2016, s. 167(3).
In para. 3(1)(a), "items 1, 3, 6B, 7 to 11 and 12 to 24" substituted for "items 1, 3 and 7 to 24" by F(No. 3)A 2010, s. 27 and Sch. 11, para. 5(3), with effect from a day to be appointed by Treasury order.

In para. 3(1)(b), "any of items 2, 4, 6A, 6C and 11A to 11M" substituted for "item 2 or 4" by F(No. 3)A 2010, s. 27 and Sch. 11, para. 5(4)(a), with effect from a day to be appointed by Treasury order.
In para. 3(1)(b), the word "and" at the end omitted by F(No. 3)A 2010, s. 27 and Sch. 11, para. 5(4)(b), with effect from a day to be appointed by Treasury order.
Para. 3(1)(d) (and the word "and" at the end of para. 3(1)(c)) inserted by F(No. 3)A 2010, s. 27 and Sch. 11, para. 5(5), with effect from a day to be appointed by Treasury order. Para. 3(1)(d) is not relevant to income tax, corporation tax or capital gains tax.
Para. 3(1A) inserted by F(No. 3)A 2010, s. 27 and Sch. 11, para. 5(6), with effect from a day to be appointed by Treasury order. Para. 3(1A) relates to VAT and will not be reproduced here.
History – Para. 3(1)(aa) inserted by FA 2015, s. 104(2), with effect in relation to accounting periods beginning on or after 1 April 2015 (subject to the provisions of FA 2015, s. 116(2)–(5)).
In para. 3(1)(b), the words "item 4A or" inserted by FA 2016, s. 113(11)(a), with effect from 15 September 2016 (Royal Assent).
Para. 3(1)(ca) inserted by FA 2016, s. 113(11)(b), with effect from 15 September 2016 (Royal Assent).

4(1) This paragraph applies in the case of a payment of tax falling within item 5 or 6 in the Table.

4(2) P is liable to a penalty of 5% of the unpaid tax.

4(3) If any amount of the tax is unpaid after the end of the period of 3 months beginning with the penalty date, P is liable to a penalty of 5% of that amount.

4(4) If any amount of the tax is unpaid after the end of the period of 9 months beginning with the penalty date, P is liable to a penalty of 5% of that amount.

AMOUNT OF PENALTY: PAYE AND CIS AMOUNTS ETC.

History – In the heading before para. 5, the word "etc." inserted by FA 2016, s. 113(15), with effect from 15 September 2016 (Royal Assent).

5(1) Paragraphs 6 to 8 apply in the case of a payment of tax falling within item 2, 4 or 4A in the Table.

5(2) But those paragraphs do not apply in the case of a payment mentioned in paragraph 3(1)(b), (c) or (ca).

History – In para. 5(1), the words ", 4 or 4A" substituted for the words "or 4" by FA 2016, s. 113(12), with effect from 15 September 2016 (Royal Assent).
In para. 5(2), the words ", (c) or (ca)." substituted for the words "or (c)" by FA 2016, s. 113(13), with effect from 15 September 2016 (Royal Assent).

6(1) P is liable to a penalty under this paragraph, in relation to each tax, each time that P makes a default in relation to a tax year.

6(2) For the purposes of this paragraph, P makes a default in relation to a tax year when P fails to make one of the following payments (or to pay an amount comprising two or more of those payments) in full on or before the date on which it becomes due and payable–

(a) a payment under PAYE regulations of tax payable in relation to the tax year;

(b) a payment of earnings-related contributions within the meaning of the Social Security (Contributions) Regulations 2001 (S.I. 2001/1004) payable in relation to the tax year;

(ba) a payment under regulations under section 105 of FA 2016 of an amount in respect of apprenticeship levy payable in relation to the tax year;

(c) a payment due under the Income Tax (Construction Industry Scheme) Regulations 2005 (S.I. 2005/2045) payable in relation to the tax year;

(d) a repayment in respect of a student loan due under the Education (Student Loans) (Repayments) Regulations 2009 (S.I. 2009/470) or the Education (Student Loans) (Repayments) Regulations (Northern Ireland) 2000 (S.R. 2000 No. 121) and due for the tax year.

6(3) But where a failure to make one of those payments (or to pay an amount comprising two or more of those payments) would, apart from this sub-paragraph, constitute the first default in relation to a tax year, that failure does not count as a default in relation to that year for the purposes of a penalty under this paragraph.

6(4) The amount of the penalty for a default made in relation to a tax year is determined by reference to–

(a) the amount of the tax comprised in the default, and

(b) the number of previous defaults that P has made in relation to the same tax year.

6(5) If the default is P's 1st, 2nd or 3rd default in relation to the tax year, P is liable, at the time of the default, to a penalty of 1% of the amount of tax comprised in the default.

6(6) If the default is P's 4th, 5th or 6th default in relation to the tax year, P is liable, at the time of the default, to a penalty of 2% of the amount of tax comprised in the default.

6(7) If the default is P's 7th, 8th or 9th default in relation to the tax year, P is liable, at the time of the default, to a penalty of 3% of the amount of tax comprised in the default.

6(7A) If the default is P's 10th or subsequent default in relation to the tax year, P is liable, at the time of the default, to a penalty of 4% of the amount of tax comprised in the default.

6(8) For the purposes of this paragraph–

(a) the amount of a tax comprised in a default is the amount of that tax comprised in the payment which P fails to make;

(b) a previous default counts for the purposes of sub-paragraphs (5) to (7A) even if it is remedied before the time of the default giving rise to the penalty.

6(8A) Regulations made by the Commissioners for Her Majesty's Revenue and Customs may specify–

(a) circumstances in which, for the purposes of sub-paragraph (2), a payment of less than the full amount may be treated as a payment in full;

(b) circumstances in which sub-paragraph (3) is not to apply.

6(8B) Regulations under sub-paragraph (8A) may–

(a) make different provision for different cases, and

(b) include incidental, consequential and supplementary provision.

6(9) The Treasury may by order made by statutory instrument make such amendments to sub-paragraph (2) as they think fit in consequence of any amendment, revocation or re-enactment of the regulations mentioned in that sub-paragraph.

History – Para. 6(1) substituted by FA 2013, s. 230 and Sch. 50, para. 12(2), with effect for defaults made (see para. 6(2), as amended by FA 2013, s. 230 and Sch. 50, para. 12(3)) in relation to the tax year 2014–15 and subsequent tax years.
In para. 6(2), the words "in relation to a tax year" inserted by FA 2013, s. 230 and Sch. 50, para. 12(3)(a), with effect for defaults made (see para. 6(2), as amended by FA 2013, s. 230 and Sch. 50, para. 12(3)) in relation to the tax year 2014–15 and subsequent tax years.
In para. 6(2)(a), the words "of tax payable in relation to the tax year" inserted by FA 2013, s. 230 and Sch. 50, para. 12(3)(b), with effect for defaults made (see para. 6(2), as amended by FA 2013, s. 230 and Sch. 50, para. 12(3)) in relation to the tax year 2014–15 and subsequent tax years.
In para. 6(2)(b), the words payable in relation to the tax year inserted by FA 2013, s. 230 and Sch. 50, para. 12(3)(c), with effect for defaults made (see para. 6(2), as amended by FA 2013, s. 230 and Sch. 50, para. 12(3)) in relation to the tax year 2014–15 and subsequent tax years.
Para. 6(2)(ba) inserted by FA 2016, s. 113(14), with effect from 15 September 2016 (Royal Assent).
In para. 6(2)(c), the words "payable in relation to the tax year" inserted by FA 2013, s. 230 and Sch. 50, para. 12(3)(d), with effect for defaults made (see para. 6(2), as amended by FA 2013, s. 230 and Sch. 50, para. 12(3)) in relation to the tax year 2014–15 and subsequent tax years.
In para. 6(2)(d), the words "and due for the tax year" inserted by FA 2013, s. 230 and Sch. 50, para. 12(3)(e), with effect for defaults made (see para. 6(2), as amended by FA 2013, s. 230 and Sch. 50, para. 12(3)) in relation to the tax year 2014–15 and subsequent tax years.
Para. 6(3)–(7A) substituted for (3)–(7) by FA 2013, s. 230 and Sch. 50, para. 12(4), with effect for defaults made (see para. 6(2), as amended by FA 2013, s. 230 and Sch. 50, para. 12(3)) in relation to the tax year 2014–15 and subsequent tax years.
Para. 6(8)(b) substituted by FA 2013, s. 230 and Sch. 50, para. 12(5), with effect for defaults made (see para. 6(2), as amended by FA 2013, s. 230 and Sch. 50, para. 12(3)) in relation to the tax year 2014–15 and subsequent tax years.
Para. 6(8A) and 6(8B) inserted by FA 2013, s. 230 and Sch. 50, para. 12(6), with effect for defaults made (see para. 6(2), as amended by FA 2013, s. 230 and Sch. 50, para. 12(3)) in relation to the tax year 2014–15 and subsequent tax years.
Para. 6 substituted by F(No. 3)A 2010, s. 27 and Sch. 11, para. 6, with effect from 25 January 2011 (SI 2011/132, art. 2(b)).

7 If any amount of the tax is unpaid after the end of the period of 6 months beginning with the penalty date, P is liable to a penalty of 5% of that amount.

8 If any amount of the tax is unpaid after the end of the period of 12 months beginning with the penalty date, P is liable to a penalty of 5% of that amount.

AMOUNT OF PENALTY: AMOUNTS IN RESPECT OF PERIODS OF BETWEEN 2 AND 6 MONTHS

8A–8J [Not relevant to National Insurance contributions.]

CALCULATION OF UNPAID VAT: TREATMENT OF PAYMENTS ON ACCOUNT

8K [Prospectively inserted (see note below).]

Prospective amendments – Para. 8K inserted by F(No. 3)A 2010, s. 27 and Sch. 11, para. 8, with effect from a day to be appointed. Para. 8K relates to VAT and will not be reproduced here.

SPECIAL REDUCTION

9(1) If HMRC think it right because of special circumstances, they may reduce a penalty under any paragraph of this Schedule.

9(2) In sub-paragraph (1) **"special circumstances"** does not include–

(a) ability to pay, or

(b) the fact that a potential loss of revenue from one taxpayer is balanced by a potential over-payment by another.

9(3) In sub-paragraph (1) the reference to reducing a penalty includes a reference to–

(a) staying a penalty, and

(b) agreeing a compromise in relation to proceedings for a penalty.

INTERACTION WITH OTHER PENALTIES AND LATE PAYMENT SURCHARGES

9A In the application of the following provisions, no account shall be taken of a penalty under this Schedule–

(a) section 97A of TMA 1970 (multiple penalties),

(b) paragraph 12(2) of Schedule 24 to FA 2007 (interaction with other penalties), and

(c) paragraph 15(1) of Schedule 41 to FA 2008 (interaction with other penalties).

History – Heading inserted by FA 2013, s. 230 and Sch. 50, para. 13, with effect for defaults made (see para. 6(2), as amended by FA 2013, s. 230 and Sch. 50, para. 12(3)) in relation to the tax year 2014–15 and subsequent tax years.

Para. 9A inserted by FA 2013, s. 230 and Sch. 50, para. 13, with effect for defaults made (see para. 6(2), as amended by FA 2013, s. 230 and Sch. 50, para. 12(3)) in relation to the tax year 2014–15 and subsequent tax years.

SUSPENSION OF PENALTY DURING CURRENCY OF AGREEMENT FOR DEFERRED PAYMENT

10(1) This paragraph applies if–

(a) P fails to pay an amount of tax when it becomes due and payable,

(b) P makes a request to HMRC that payment of the amount of tax be deferred, and

(c) HMRC agrees that payment of that amount may be deferred for a period ("the deferral period").

10(2) If P would (apart from this sub-paragraph) become liable, between the date on which P makes the request and the end of the deferral period, to a penalty under any paragraph of this Schedule for failing to pay that amount, P is not liable to that penalty.

10(3) But if–

(a) P breaks the agreement (see sub-paragraph (4)), and

(b) HMRC serves on P a notice specifying any penalty to which P would become liable apart from sub-paragraph (2),

P becomes liable, at the date of the notice, to that penalty.

10(4) P breaks an agreement if–

(a) P fails to pay the amount of tax in question when the deferral period ends, or

(b) the deferral is subject to P complying with a condition (including a condition that part of the amount be paid during the deferral period) and P fails to comply with it.

10(5) If the agreement mentioned in sub-paragraph (1)(c) is varied at any time by a further agreement between P and HMRC this paragraph applies from that time to the agreement as varied.

ASSESSMENT

11(1) Where P is liable for a penalty under any paragraph of this Schedule HMRC must–

(a) assess the penalty,

(b) notify P, and

(c) state in the notice the period in respect of which the penalty is assessed.

11(2) A penalty under any paragraph of this Schedule must be paid before the end of the period of 30 days beginning with the day on which notice of the assessment of the penalty is issued.

11(3) An assessment of a penalty under any paragraph of this Schedule–

(a) is to be treated for procedural purposes in the same way as an assessment to tax (except in respect of a matter expressly provided for by this Schedule),

(b) may be enforced as if it were an assessment to tax, and

(c) may be combined with an assessment to tax.

11(4) A supplementary assessment may be made in respect of a penalty if an earlier assessment operated by reference to an underestimate of an amount of tax which was due or payable.

11(4A) If an assessment in respect of a penalty is based on an amount of tax due or payable that is found by HMRC to be excessive, HMRC may by notice to P amend the assessment so that it is based upon the correct amount.

11(4B) An amendment made under sub-paragraph (4A)–

(a) does not affect when the penalty must be paid;

(b) may be made after the last day on which the assessment in question could have been made under paragraph 12.

11(5) [Omitted by FA 2013, s. 230 and Sch. 50, para. 14(3).]

Prospective amendments – Para. 11(4) amended for certain purposes by F(No. 3)A 2010, s. 27 and Sch. 11, para. 9(2), with effect from a day or days to be appointed by Treasury order. See Note below for details.
Para. 11(4A) to be inserted for certain purposes by F(No. 3)A 2010, s. 27 and Sch. 11, para. 9(3), with effect from a day or days to be appointed by Treasury Order. See Note below.

History – In para. 11(4), the words "tax which was due or payable" substituted for the words "unpaid tax" by F(No. 3)A 2010, s. 27 and Sch. 11, para. 9(2), with effect from 6 April 2011 in relation an amount of tax which is payable in relation to the tax year 2010–11 or any subsequent tax year, and falls within: item 1, 12, 18 or 19 of the Table in para. 1; or, insofar as the tax falls within item 1 of that Table, item 17, 23 or 24 of that Table.
Para. 11(4A) and (4B) substituted for (4A) by FA 2013, s. 230 and Sch. 50, para. 14(2), with effect for defaults made (see para. 6(2), as amended by FA 2013, s. 230 and Sch. 50, para. 12(3)) in relation to the tax year 2014–15 and subsequent tax years.
Para. 11(4A) inserted by F(No. 3)A 2010, s. 27 and Sch. 11, para. 9(3), with effect from 6 April 2011 in relation an amount of tax which is payable in relation to the tax year 2010–11 or any subsequent tax year, and falls within: item 1, 12, 18 or 19 of the Table in para. 1; or, insofar as the tax falls within item 1 of that Table, item 17, 23 or 24 of that Table.
Para. 11(5) omitted by FA 2013, s. 230 and Sch. 50, para. 14(3), with effect for defaults made (see para. 6(2), as amended by FA 2013, s. 230 and Sch. 50, para. 12(3)) in relation to the tax year 2014–15 and subsequent tax years.

Notes – The amendment made to para. 11(4) by F(No. 3)A 2010, s. 27 and Sch. 11, para. 9(2) currently has effect only for certain purposes (see History note above). For other purposes the amendment remains prospective and, accordingly, para. 11(4) should be read as if the amendment had not been made.
The insertion of para. 11(4A) by F(No. 3)A 2010, s. 27 and Sch. 11, para. 9(3) currently has effect only for certain purposes (see History note above). For other purposes the insertion remains prospective and, accordingly, para. 11 should be read as if the insertion had not been made.

12(1) An assessment of a penalty under any paragraph of this Schedule in respect of any amount must be made on or before the later of date A and (where it applies) date B.

12(2) Date A is the last day of the period of 2 years beginning with the date specified in or for the purposes of column 4 of the Table (that is to say, the last date on which payment may be made without incurring a penalty).

12(3) Date B is the last day of the period of 12 months beginning with–

(a) the end of the appeal period for the assessment of the amount of tax in respect of which the penalty is assessed, or

(b) if there is no such assessment, the date on which that amount of tax is ascertained.

12(4) In sub-paragraph (3)(a) **"appeal period"** means the period during which–

(a) an appeal could be brought, or

(b) an appeal that has been brought has not been determined or withdrawn.

APPEAL

13(1) P may appeal against a decision of HMRC that a penalty is payable by P.

13(2) P may appeal against a decision of HMRC as to the amount of a penalty payable by P.

14(1) An appeal under paragraph 13 is to be treated in the same way as an appeal against an assessment to the tax concerned (including by the application of any provision about bringing the appeal by notice to HMRC, about HMRC review of the decision or about determination of the appeal by the First-tier Tribunal or Upper Tribunal).

14(2) Sub-paragraph (1) does not apply–

(a) so as to require P to pay a penalty before an appeal against the assessment of the penalty is determined, or

(b) in respect of any other matter expressly provided for by this Act.

15(1) On an appeal under paragraph 13(1) that is notified to the tribunal, the tribunal may affirm or cancel HMRC's decision.

15(2) On an appeal under paragraph 13(2) that is notified to the tribunal, the tribunal may–

(a) affirm HMRC's decision, or

(b) substitute for HMRC's decision another decision that HMRC had power to make.

15(3) If the tribunal substitutes its decision for HMRC's, the tribunal may rely on paragraph 9–

(a) to the same extent as HMRC (which may mean applying the same percentage reduction as HMRC to a different starting point), or

(b) to a different extent, but only if the tribunal thinks that HMRC's decision in respect of the application of paragraph 9 was flawed.

15(4) In sub-paragraph (3)(b) **"flawed"** means flawed when considered in the light of the principles applicable in proceedings for judicial review.

15(5) In this paragraph **"tribunal"** means the First-tier Tribunal or Upper Tribunal (as appropriate by virtue of paragraph 14(1)).

REASONABLE EXCUSE

16(1) If P satisfies HMRC or (on appeal) the First-tier Tribunal or Upper Tribunal that there is a reasonable excuse for a failure to make a payment–

(a) liability to a penalty under any paragraph of this Schedule does not arise in relation to that failure, and

(b) the failure does not count as a default for the purposes of paragraphs 6, 8B, 8C, 8G and 8H.

16(2) For the purposes of sub-paragraph (1)–

(a) an insufficiency of funds is not a reasonable excuse unless attributable to events outside P's control,

(b) where P relies on any other person to do anything, that is not a reasonable excuse unless P took reasonable care to avoid the failure, and

(c) where P had a reasonable excuse for the failure but the excuse has ceased, P is to be treated as having continued to have the excuse if the failure is remedied without unreasonable delay after the excuse ceased.

Prospective amendments – Para. 16(1) substituted for certain purposes by F(No. 3)A 2010, s. 27 and Sch. 11, para. 10, with effect from a day to be appointed by Treasury order. See Note below for details.

History – Para. 16(1) substituted by F(No. 3)A 2010, s. 27 and Sch. 11, para. 10, with effect from 25 January 2011 (SI 2011/132, art. 3), for the purposes of the following amounts of tax specified in column 3 of the Table in para. 1:

- item 2 (PAYE regulations), item 3 (returns under section 254(1) of the Finance Act 2004) and item 4 (section 62 of the Finance Act 2004); and
- items 17, 23 and 24 but only insofar as the tax falls within any of items 2, 3 or 4.

For the former wording of para. 16(1), which still applies for other purposes, see Note below.

Notes – The substitution of para. 16(1) by F(No. 3)A 2010, s. 27 and Sch. 11, para. 10, was brought into effect from 25 January 2011 for the purposes of item 2 (PAYE regulations), item 3 (returns under FA 2004, s. 254(1)) and item 4 (FA 2004, s. 62) of the Table in para. 1 and items 17, 23 and 24 but only insofar as the tax falls within any of items 2, 3 or 4 (SI 2011/132, art. 3). The former wording, which still applies for other purposes, was:

"**16(1)** Liability to a penalty under any paragraph of this Schedule does not arise in relation to a failure to make a payment if P satisfies HMRC or (on appeal) the First-tier Tribunal or Upper Tribunal that there is a reasonable excuse for the failure.".

DOUBLE JEOPARDY

17 P is not liable to a penalty under any paragraph of this Schedule in respect of a failure or action in respect of which P has been convicted of an offence.

INTERPRETATION

18(1) This paragraph applies for the construction of this Schedule.

18(2) **"HMRC"** means Her Majesty's Revenue and Customs.

18(3) References to tax include construction industry deductions under Chapter 3 of Part 3 of FA 2004.

18(4) References to a determination, in relation to an amount payable under PAYE regulations or under Chapter 3 of Part 3 of FA 2004, include a certificate.

18(5) References to an assessment to tax, in relation to inheritance tax and stamp duty reserve tax, are to a determination.

SCHEDULE 57 – AMENDMENTS RELATING TO PENALTIES

Section 109

Part 1 – Amendments of Schedule 24 to FA 2007

9 [Amends FA 2007, Sch. 24, para. 30.]

NATIONAL INSURANCE CONTRIBUTIONS ACT 2011

(2011 Chapter 3)

[22nd March 2011]

ARRANGEMENT OF SECTIONS

PART 1 – INCREASES IN RATES

PART 2 – REGIONAL SECONDARY CONTRIBUTIONS HOLIDAY FOR NEW BUSINESSES

PART 3 – GENERAL

PART 1 – INCREASES IN RATES

1 Class 1 contributions

1(1) [Amends SSCBA 1992, s. 8(2) and SSCB(NI)A 1992, s. 8(2).]

1(2) [Amends SSCBA 1992, s. 9(2) and SSCB(NI)A 1992, s. 9(2).]

2 Class 4 contributions

2(1) [Amends SSCBA 1992, s. 15(3ZA) and SSCB(NI)A 1992, s. 15(3ZA).]

2(2) [Amends SSAA 1992, s. 143(4)(b).]

3 Increased product of additional rates to be paid into National Insurance Fund

3 [Amends SSAA 1992, s. 162(5) and SSA(NI)A 1992, s. 142(5).]

PART 2 – REGIONAL SECONDARY CONTRIBUTIONS HOLIDAY FOR NEW BUSINESSES

4 Holiday for new businesses

4(1) This section applies where–

(a) a person, or a number of persons in partnership, ("P") starts a new business during the relevant period,

(b) the principal place at which the new business is carried on when it is started is not in any of the excluded regions, and

(c) one or more persons are qualifying employees in relation to the new business.

4(2) The appropriate amount in respect of each qualifying employee may be–

(a) deducted from Class 1 contributions payments which P is liable to make, or

(b) refunded to P.

4(3) Section 5 defines what is meant by **"starting a new business"**.

4(4) **"The relevant period"** is the period–

(a) beginning with 22 June 2010, and

(b) ending with 5 September 2013.

4(5) **"The excluded regions"** are Greater London, the South East Region and the Eastern Region.

4(6) Section 6 specifies when a person is a qualifying employee in relation to a new business.

4(7) Section 7 specifies what is the appropriate amount in respect of a qualifying employee.

4(8) Section 8 explains how a deduction or refund is made.

4(9) Section 9 makes provision requiring the retention of records.

4(10) Section 10 contains an anti-avoidance rule.

4(11) Section 11 makes provision for the interpretation of this Part.

5 Starting a new business

5(1) P "starts" a new business when P begins to carry on a new business.

5(2) A business is not a "new" business if–

(a) P has, at any time during the period of 6 months ending with the time when P begins to carry it on, carried on another business consisting of the activities of which the business consists (or most of them), or

(b) P carries it on as a result of a transfer (within the meaning of subsection (3)).

5(3) P carries on a business as a result of a transfer if P begins to carry on the business on another person ceasing to carry on the activities of which it consists (or most of them) in consequence of arrangements involving P and the other person.

5(4) For the purposes of subsection (3) P is to be taken to begin to carry on a business on another person ceasing to carry on such activities if–

(a) the business begins to be carried on by P otherwise than in partnership on such activities ceasing to be carried on by persons in partnership, or

(b) P is a number of persons in partnership who begin to carry on the business on such activities ceasing to be carried on–

(i) by a person, or a number of persons, otherwise than in partnership,

(ii) by persons in a partnership not consisting only of all the persons constituting P, or

(iii) partly as mentioned in sub-paragraph (i) and partly as mentioned in sub-paragraph (ii).

5(5) P is not to be regarded as starting a new business by beginning to carry on a business if–

(a) before P begins to carry on the business, P is a party to arrangements under which P may (at any time during the relevant period) carry on as part of the business activities carried on by any other person, and

(b) the business would have been prevented by subsection (2)(b) from being a new business had–

(i) P begun to carry on the activities when beginning to carry on the business, and

(ii) the other person at that time ceased to carry them on.

5(6) In this section **"business"** means something which is–

(a) a trade, profession or vocation for the purposes of the Income Tax Acts or the Corporation Tax Acts,

(b) a property business (within the meaning of section 263(6) of the Income Tax (Trading and Other Income) Act 2005), or

(c) an investment business (that is, a business consisting wholly or partly of making investments).

6 Qualifying employees

6(1) A person is a **"qualifying employee"** in relation to a new business if–

(a) the person first becomes employed as an employed earner for the purposes of the new business before the end of the initial period, and

(b) P is the secondary contributor in relation to any payment of earnings to or for the benefit of the person in respect of the employment at any time during the period that is the holiday period in relation to the person.

6(2) Where (apart from this subsection) there would be more than 10 qualifying employees, only the first 10 persons who become qualifying employees are qualifying employees.

6(3) The **"initial period"** means the period of one year beginning with–

(a) the date on which P starts the new business, or

(b) if earlier, the first date on which a person first becomes employed as an employed earner for the purposes of the new business,

but if the first date on which a person first becomes employed as an employed earner for the purposes of the new business is before 22 June 2010, the person is to be taken for the purposes of paragraph (b) as first so employed on that date.

6(4) The **"holiday period"**, in relation to a person, is the period–

(a) beginning with the day on which the person first becomes employed as an employed earner for the purposes of the new business or, if the person first becomes so employed before 6 September 2010, with that date, and

(b) ending with the earlier of–

(i) the end of the period of one year beginning with the day on which it begins, and

(ii) the end of the relevant period.

6(5) None of the following has effect for the purposes of this Part–

(a) the Social Security Contributions (Intermediaries) Regulations 2000 (S.I. 2000/727) and the Social Security Contributions (Intermediaries) (Northern Ireland) Regulations 2000 (S.I. 2000/728) (which provide in certain cases for an intermediary to be treated as the secondary contributor in relation to the payment of earnings), and

(b) the Social Security Contributions (Managed Service Companies) Regulations 2007 (S.I. 2007/2070) (which provide in certain cases for a managed service company to be treated as the secondary contributor in relation to the payment of earnings).

7 The appropriate amount

7(1) The appropriate amount in respect of a qualifying employee is the relevant amount of secondary Class 1 contributions.

7(2) **"The relevant amount of secondary Class 1 contributions"** is the amount of secondary Class 1 contributions which P is liable to pay in respect of relevant earnings.

7(3) **"Relevant earnings"** are earnings paid to or for the benefit of the qualifying employee, in respect of employment as an employed earner for the purposes of the new business, at any time during the holiday period when the principal place at which the business is carried on is not in any of the excluded regions.

7(4) But if (apart from this subsection) the relevant amount of secondary Class 1 contributions would exceed £5,000, it is the first £5,000 which P becomes liable to pay.

7(5) In the case of a qualifying employee who is a mariner, the reference in subsection (3) to earnings paid at any time during the holiday period includes, in relation to earnings paid for a voyage beginning in the holiday period but ending after it, earnings earned in the part of the voyage period falling within the holiday period.

"Mariner" and **"voyage period"** have the meaning given by regulation 115 of the 2001 Regulations.

7(6) If P is liable to pay secondary Class 1 contributions at the contracted-out rate, P is to be treated for the purposes of subsection (2) as liable to pay them at the non-contracted-out rate; and for this purpose **"contracted-out rate"** and **"non-contracted-out rate"** have the same meaning as in the 2001 Regulations.

8 Making of deductions or refunds

8(1) To the extent that the appropriate amount is attributable to secondary Class 1 contributions payable in respect of earnings paid in a tax year it may be deducted from any one or more Class 1 contributions payments made by P in respect of that tax year.

8(2) If the amount which P would be entitled to deduct under this section exceeds the amount of the payments from which it can be deducted, HMRC must instead refund the excess to P if P requests them to do so.

8(3) No deduction or refund may be made under this section until an application has been submitted to, and granted by, HMRC.

8(4) An application must contain such information, and must be made in such form and manner, as is specified by HMRC.

8(5) No application may be made for a refund in respect of a qualifying employee after the end of the period of 4 years beginning with the day on which the last deduction could be made in respect of the qualifying employee.

8(6) For the purposes of–

(a) Part 2 of the Social Security Contributions (Transfer of Functions, etc.) Act 1999, and

(b) Part 3 of the Social Security Contributions (Transfer of Functions, etc.) (Northern Ireland) Order 1999 (S.I. 1999/671),

(decisions and appeals), the decisions to which this subsection applies are decisions of an officer of Revenue and Customs under section 8 of that Act or Article 7 of that Order.

8(7) Subsection (6) applies to–

(a) a decision whether P is or was entitled to make a deduction under this section and, if so, the amount that P is or was entitled to deduct, and

(b) a decision whether P is entitled to a refund under this section and, if so, the amount of the refund.

9 Retention of records

9(1) This section applies where P is or was entitled to make a deduction under section 8 in respect of a qualifying employee.

9(2) P must keep and preserve any documents or records relating to–

(a) P's entitlement to make a deduction in respect of the employee, and

(b) the calculation of any amount that has been, or could have been, deducted,

for not less than 3 years beginning with the date on which the last deduction under section 8 is, or could be, made in respect of the employee.

9(3) Accordingly, the duty imposed by paragraph 26(1) of Schedule 4 to the 2001 Regulations (retention by employer of contribution and election records) does not apply to any such documents or records.

9(4) The duty imposed by this section may be discharged by preserving the documents or records in any form or by any means.

9(5) For the purposes of Schedule 36 to the Finance Act 2008 (information and inspection powers), as applied by section 110ZA of SSAA 1992 and section 104ZA of SSA(NI)A 1992, the duty imposed by this section is to be treated as if it were a duty imposed under or by virtue of SSCBA 1992 or SSCB(NI)A 1992.

10 Anti-avoidance

10(1) This Part does not apply if P starts the new business pursuant to avoidance arrangements.

10(2) Arrangements are **"avoidance arrangements"** if the main purpose, or one of the main purposes, of P in being a party to them is to secure that activities which might otherwise have been carried on as part of another business (whether by P or any other person) are carried on by P as part of the new business in order to obtain deductions or refunds (or increased deductions or refunds) under this Part.

11 Interpretation of Part 2

11(1) In this Part–

"the 2001 Regulations" means the Social Security (Contributions) Regulations 2001 (S.I. 2001/1004);

"the appropriate amount" is to be read in accordance with section 7;

"arrangements" includes any agreement, understanding, scheme, transaction or series of transactions (whether or not legally enforceable);

"Class 1 contributions payments" means payments under–

(a) paragraph 10 of Schedule 4 to the 2001 Regulations (monthly payments), or

(b) paragraph 11 of that Schedule (quarterly payments);

"the Eastern Region" means–

(a) the counties of Bedford, Cambridgeshire, Central Bedfordshire, Essex, Hertfordshire, Norfolk and Suffolk, and

(b) *the non-metropolitan* districts of Luton, Peterborough, Southend-on-Sea and Thurrock;

"the excluded regions" has the meaning given by section 4(5);

"HMRC" means the Commissioners for Her Majesty's Revenue and Customs;

"holiday period" has the meaning given by section 6(4);

"qualifying employee" has the meaning given by section 6;

"the relevant period" has the meaning given by section 4(4);

"the South East Region" means–

(a) the counties of Buckinghamshire, East Sussex, Hampshire, the Isle of Wight, Kent, Oxfordshire, Surrey and West Sussex, and

(b) the non-metropolitan districts of Bracknell Forest, Brighton and Hove, Medway, Milton Keynes, Portsmouth, Reading, Slough, Southampton, West Berkshire, Windsor and Maidenhead and Wokingham.

11(2) Expressions used in this Part and in Part 1 of SSCBA 1992 or SSCB(NI)A 1992 have the same meaning for the purposes of this Part as they have for the purposes of that Part.

PART 3 – GENERAL

12 Abbreviations of Acts

12 In this Act–

"SSAA 1992" means the Social Security Administration Act 1992;

"SSA(NI)A 1992" means the Social Security Administration (Northern Ireland) Act 1992;

"SSCBA 1992" means the Social Security Contributions and Benefits Act 1992;

"SSCB(NI)A 1992" means the Social Security Contributions and Benefits (Northern Ireland) Act 1992.

13 Commencement

13(1) Part 1 comes into force on 6 April 2011.

13(2) Part 2 and this Part come into force on the day on which this Act is passed.

Commencement Date – Under s. 13(2), Pt. 2 came into effect on 22 March 2011 (the date of Royal Assent).

14 Extent

14(1) The amendments made by Part 1 have the same extent as the provisions to which they relate.

14(2) Part 2 and this Part extend to England and Wales, Scotland and Northern Ireland.

15 Short title

15 This Act may be cited as the National Insurance Contributions Act 2011.

FINANCE ACT 2011

(2011 Chapter 11) [*19th July 2011*]

ARRANGEMENT OF SECTIONS

PART 2 – INCOME TAX, CORPORATION TAX AND CAPITAL GAINS TAX

ANTI-AVOIDANCE PROVISIONS

26 Employment income provided through third parties

26 Schedule 2 contains provision about steps which are taken in pursuance of, or which have some other connection with, arrangements concerned with the provision of rewards or recognition or loans in connection with current, former or prospective employments.

PART 9 – FINAL PROVISIONS

92 Interpretation

92(1) In this Act–

"ALDA 1979" means the Alcoholic Liquor Duties Act 1979,
"BGDA 1981" means the Betting and Gaming Duties Act 1981,
"CAA 2001" means the Capital Allowances Act 2001,
"CRCA 2005" means the Commissioners for Revenue and Customs Act 2005,
"CTA 2009" means the Corporation Tax Act 2009,
"CTA 2010" means the Corporation Tax Act 2010,
"FISMA 2000" means the Financial Services and Markets Act 2000,
"HODA 1979" means the Hydrocarbon Oil Duties Act 1979,
"ICTA" means the Income and Corporation Taxes Act 1988,
"IHTA 1984" means the Inheritance Tax Act 1984,
"ITA 2007" means the Income Tax Act 2007,
"ITEPA 2003" means the Income Tax (Earnings and Pensions) Act 2003,
"ITTOIA 2005" means the Income Tax (Trading and Other Income) Act 2005,
"OTA 1975" means the Oil Taxation Act 1975,
"PRTA 1980" means the Petroleum Revenue Tax Act 1980,
"TCGA 1992" *means* the Taxation of Chargeable Gains Act 1992,
"TIOPA 2010" means the Taxation (International and Other Provisions) Act 2010,
"TMA 1970" means the Taxes Management Act 1970,
"TPDA 1979" means the Tobacco Products Duty Act 1979,
"VATA 1994" means the Value Added Tax Act 1994, and

"VERA 1994" means the Vehicle Excise and Registration Act 1994.

92(2) In this Act–

"FA", followed by a year, means the Finance Act of that year;

"F(No. 2)A", followed by a year, means the Finance (No. 2) Act of that year.

93 Short title

93 This Act may be cited as the Finance Act 2011.

SCHEDULES

SCHEDULE 2 – EMPLOYMENT INCOME PROVIDED THROUGH THIRD PARTIES

Section 26

OTHER AMENDMENTS

50 [Amends SSCBA 1992, s. 122(1) and SSCB(NI)A 1992, s. 121(1).]

COMMENCEMENT AND TRANSITIONAL PROVISION RELATING TO PART 7A OF ITEPA 2003

52(1) Part 7A of ITEPA 2003 (as inserted by paragraph 1 of this Schedule) has effect in relation to relevant steps taken on or after 6 April 2011; and the other amendments made by this Schedule have effect accordingly.

52(2) Sub-paragraph (1) is subject to the following paragraphs.

53(1) This paragraph applies if–

(a) on or after 9 December 2010 but before 6 April 2011 a relevant step ("the early step") within section 554C(1)(a) of ITEPA 2003 is taken,

(b) Chapter 2 of Part 7A of ITEPA 2003 would have applied by reason of the early step had the reference in paragraph 52(1) of this Schedule to 6 April 2011 been a reference to 9 December 2010, and

(c) the early step is not chargeable to income tax by virtue of Schedule 34 to FA 2004 in whole or in part.

53(2) Subject to what follows, Chapter 2 of Part 7A of ITEPA 2003 is to apply by reason of the early step; and the amendments made by this Schedule have effect accordingly.

53(3) In determining the tax year for which the employment income of A counts for the purposes of section 554Z2(1) of ITEPA 2003, the early step is treated as having been taken on 6 April 2012; but otherwise Chapter 2 of Part 7A of that Act applies by reference to when the early step was actually taken.

53(4) The amount which (apart from this sub-paragraph) would count as employment income of A is to be reduced by an amount to reflect so much of the sum paid as has been repaid to P before 6 April 2012 by the person to whom the payment was made; and the Tax Acts are to apply in relation to the sum paid so far as repaid to P before that date by that person as if Chapter 2 of Part 7A of ITEPA 2003 had never applied by reason of the early step, with any adjustments that need to be made to any assessment to tax being made accordingly.

53(5) The amount of the reduction (if any) under sub-paragraph (4)–

(a) is to be determined on a just and reasonable basis, and

(b) may be the full amount of the employment income or nil or an amount in between (depending on the circumstances).

53(6) *Section 554Z5 of ITEPA 2003* does not apply in relation to the early step and, in the application of that section in relation to any other relevant step (whenever taken), the early step is to be ignored.

53(7) Section 554Z12 of ITEPA 2003 does not apply in relation to the early step.

53(8) For the purposes of section 687A(3)(a) of ITEPA 2003 (as inserted by paragraph 29 of this Schedule), the early step is treated as having been taken on 6 April 2012.

53(9) For the purposes of section 41(1A) of ITTOIA 2005 (as inserted by paragraph 38(3) of this Schedule), the early step is treated as having been taken on 6 April 2012; and for the purpose of determining whether section 41(1A) of that Act applies, section 41(1) is to be read as substituted by paragraph 38(2) of this Schedule.

53(10) For the purposes of section 1293(1A) of CTA 2009 (as inserted by paragraph 47(3) of this Schedule), the early step is treated as having been taken on 6 April 2012; and for the purpose of determining whether section 1293(1A) of that Act applies, section 1293(1) is to be read as substituted by paragraph 47(2) of this Schedule.

54(1) This paragraph applies if–

(a) on or after 9 December 2010 but before 6 April 2011 a relevant step ("the early step") within section 554C(1)(d) of ITEPA 2003 is taken,

(b) the relevant step does not involve a sum of money within the meaning of section 554Z(10) of ITEPA 2003,

(c) the asset which is the subject of the early step is a readily convertible asset which P makes available to secure the payment of a sum of money,

(d) Chapter 2 of Part 7A of ITEPA 2003 would have applied by reason of the early step had the reference in paragraph 52(1) of this Schedule to 6 April 2011 been a reference to 9 December 2010, and

(e) the early step is not chargeable to income tax by virtue of Schedule 34 to FA 2004 in whole or in part.

54(2) For the purposes of sub-paragraph (1)(a) section 554C(1)(d) of ITEPA 2003 is to be read as if the words "or makes it available under an arrangement which permits its use" were omitted.

54(3) In this paragraph **"readily convertible asset"** means anything mentioned in section 702(1)(a) to (c) of ITEPA 2003 (ignoring section 702(3)).

54(4) Subject to what follows, Chapter 2 of Part 7A of ITEPA 2003 is to apply by reason of the early step; and the amendments made by this Schedule have effect accordingly.

54(5) In determining the tax year for which the employment income of A counts for the purposes of section 554Z2(1) of ITEPA 2003, the early step is treated as having been taken on 6 April 2012; but otherwise Chapter 2 of Part 7A of that Act applies by reference to when the early step was actually taken.

54(6) The amount which (apart from this sub-paragraph) would count as employment income of A is to be reduced to nil if–

(a) before 6 April 2012 the readily convertible asset has been returned to P, and

(b) as at that date the asset is not being used to secure the payment of the sum of money (or any part of it),

and the Tax Acts are to apply in relation to the early step as if Chapter 2 of Part 7A of ITEPA 2003 had never applied by reason of it, with any adjustments that need to be made to any assessment to tax being made accordingly.

54(7) Section 554Z5 of ITEPA 2003 does not apply in relation to the early step and, in the application of that section in relation to any other relevant step (whenever taken), the early step is to be ignored.

54(8) Section 554Z8 of ITEPA 2003 applies in relation to the early step as if subsection (6)(b) were omitted.

54(9) Section 554Z12 of ITEPA 2003 does not apply in relation to the early step.

54(10) For the purposes of section 695A(3)(a) of ITEPA 2003 (as inserted by paragraph 31 of this Schedule), the early step is treated as having been taken on 6 April 2012.

54(11) For the purposes of section 41(1A) of ITTOIA 2005 (as inserted by paragraph 38(3) of this Schedule), the early step is treated as having been taken on 6 April 2012; and for the purpose of determining whether section 41(1A) of that Act applies, section 41(1) is to be read as substituted by paragraph 38(2) of this Schedule.

54(12) For the purposes of section 1293(1A) of CTA 2009 (as inserted by paragraph 47(3) of this Schedule), the early step is treated as having been taken on 6 April 2012; and for the purpose of determining whether section 1293(1A) of that Act applies, section 1293(1) is to be read as substitutedby paragraph 47(2) of this Schedule.

55(1) For the purpose of determining whether Chapter 2 of Part 7A of ITEPA 2003 would have applied by reason of the early step as mentioned in paragraph 53(1)(b) or 54(1)(d), section 554G of ITEPA 2003 is to be read–

(a) as if subsection (1)(a) were omitted, and

(b) as if the definition contained in sub-paragraph (2) applied for the purposes of the reference to a group of companies in subsection (4)(d) instead of section 554Z(5) of ITEPA 2003.

55(2) The definition referred to in sub-paragraph (1)(b) is–

""**group of companies**" means a company and any other companies of which it has control (as defined in section 995 of ITA 2007)".

55(3) For the purpose of determining whether Chapter 2 of Part 7A of ITEPA 2003 would have applied by reason of the early step, Chapter 1 of that Part is to be read as if section 554N(13) to (16) were omitted.

55(4) If, by virtue of section 554O of ITEPA 2003, Chapter 2 of Part 7A of that Act would not have applied by reason of the early step, section 554O(3) and (4) have effect in relation to the car loan.

55(5) But, for this purpose, if the repayment date is before 6 April 2012, in section section 554O(3) and (4) references to the repayment date are to be read as references to 6 April 2012.

56(1) This paragraph applies for the purposes of section 554Q of ITEPA 2003 in a case in which–

(a) the relevant step mentioned in subsection (2)(a) of that section was taken before 6 April 2011, and

(b) the requirement of subsection (2)(b) of that section would have been met had Part 7A of ITEPA 2003 had effect in relation to relevant steps within section 554B of that Act taken before that date.

56(2) The requirement of subsection (2)(b) of that section is to be treated as met in that case.

57(1) This paragraph applies for the purposes of section 554R of ITEPA 2003 in a case in which–

(a) the relevant step mentioned in subsection (6)(a) of that section was taken before 6 April 2011, and

(b) the requirement of subsection (6)(b) of that section would have been met had Part 7A of ITEPA 2003 had effect in relation to relevant steps within section 554B of that Act taken before that date.

57(2) The requirement of subsection (6)(b) of that section is to be treated as met in that case.

58(1) This paragraph applies if–

(a) B takes a step within section 554Z19 of ITEPA 2003 before 6 April 2011 by providing security ("the early security") for the performance of an undertaking ("the early undertaking"),

(b) on or after 6 April 2011 at a time when B is continuing to provide the early security, there is a change in the terms of the early undertaking which does not amount to the giving of a new undertaking, and

(c) as a result of the change, the amount to be paid as a contribution ("the early contribution") under the early undertaking increases, or will increase.

58(2) Chapter 3 of Part 7A of ITEPA 2003 has effect–

(a) as if the change in the terms of the early undertaking were a new undertaking to pay a contribution covering the increase in the amount of the early contribution as determined on a just and reasonable basis, and

(b) as if B, in continuing to provide the early security, provides security for the performance of the new undertaking at the time of the change in the terms.

58(3) Section 554Z17(7) of ITEPA 2003 applies for the purposes of this paragraph as it applies for the purposes of Chapter 3 of Part 7A of that Act.

59(1) This paragraph applies if–

(a) a relevant step within section 554C or 554D of ITEPA 2003 ("the chargeable step") is taken,

(b) Chapter 2 of Part 7A of ITEPA 2003 applies by reason of the chargeable step,

(c) in a tax year before 6 April 2011 ("the pre-6 April 2011 tax year") a relevant step ("the pre-6 April 2011 step") within section 554B of ITEPA 2003 was taken,

(d) before the chargeable step is taken–

(i) an agreement was made between Her Majesty's Revenue and Customs and either A or B (or both) under which it was agreed that the pre-6 April 2011 step was to be treated as giving rise to earnings of A from A's employment with B within Chapter 1 of Part 3 of ITEPA 2003 for the pre-6 April 2011 tax year, or

(ii) the tax payable by A for the pre-6 April 2011 tax year was otherwise decided on the basis that the pre-6 April 2011 step was to be treated as giving rise to earnings of A from A's employment with B within Chapter 1 of Part 3 of ITEPA 2003 for that tax year,

(e) before the chargeable step is taken, A or B has paid, or otherwise accounted for, any tax which A or B is required to pay or otherwise account for as a consequence of–

(i) the agreement mentioned in paragraph (d)(i), or

(ii) the tax payable by A for the pre-6 April 2011 tax year having otherwise been decided on the basis mentioned in paragraph (d)(ii), and

(f) after any reductions under sections 554Z4 to 554Z8 of ITEPA 2003, it is determined on a just and reasonable basis that the value of the chargeable step represents (or still represents after any such reductions) to any extent–

(i) the earnings treated as arising from the pre-6 April 2011 step as mentioned in paragraph (d)(i) or (ii), or

(ii) any return on those earnings since the taking of the pre-6 April 2011 step (whether income or capital, direct or indirect or realised or unrealised).

59(2) After any reductions under sections 554Z4 to 554Z8 of ITEPA 2003, the value of the chargeable step is to be reduced (but not below nil) by an amount reflecting the extent to which, as determined under sub-paragraph (1)(f), that value represents (or still represents) the earnings mentioned in sub-paragraph (1)(f)(i) or any return on those earnings mentioned in sub-paragraph (1)(f)(ii).

59(3) In sub-paragraph (1)(f)(ii) **"return"** does not include any return so far as, it is reasonable to suppose, the return exceeds the return which might have been expected applying the assumption that all relevant connected persons are acting at arm's length of each other.

59(4) In sub-paragraph (3) **"relevant connected person"** means a person with a connection (direct or indirect) to an arrangement (within the meaning of Part 7A of ITEPA 2003) by virtue of which the return arises.

Prospective amendments – In para. 59(1)(a) the words "or paragraph 1 of Schedule 11 to FA (No. 2) 2017" inserted after the words "ITEPA 2003" by F(No. 2)A 2017, s. 34 and Sch. 11, para. 47, with effect in relation to loans and quasi loans that are outstanding on 5 April 2019.

POWER TO MAKE PROVISION DEALING WITH INTERACTIONS ETC

64(1) The Treasury may by order made by statutory instrument make such provision as the Treasury consider appropriate dealing with the interaction between Part 7A of ITEPA 2003 (as inserted by paragraph 1 of this Schedule) and any other provision of the Tax Acts or any enactment relating to capital gains tax or inheritance tax.

64(2) The Treasury may by order made by statutory instrument make such provision as the Treasury consider appropriate in consequence of this Schedule.

64(3) An order under this paragraph may contain provision having retrospective effect, so long as it does not increase any person's liability to any tax.

64(4) An order under this paragraph may amend, repeal or revoke any provision made by or under an Act, including, in the case of an order under sub-paragraph (1), Part 7A of ITEPA 2003.

64(5) An order under this paragraph may contain incidental, supplemental, consequential and transitional provision and savings.

64(6) The powers conferred by this paragraph may not be exercised after 5 April 2015.

64(7) A statutory instrument containing an order under this paragraph is subject to annulment in pursuance of a resolution of the House of Commons.

PENSIONS ACT 2011

(2011 Chapter 19)

[*3rd November 2011*]

ARRANGEMENT OF SECTIONS

PART 1 – STATE PENSION

3 Consolidation of additional pension

3 Schedule 3 (consolidation of additional pension) has effect.

PART 6 – MISCELLANEOUS AND GENERAL

GENERAL

37 Extent

37 An amendment or repeal by this Act has the same extent as the enactment amended or repealed.

38 Commencement

38(1) Any provision of Part 2 that amends another Act so as–

(a) to modify a power to make an order or regulations, or

(b) to confer any such power,

comes into force, for the purposes of the exercise of the power, on the day on which this Act is passed.

38(2) The following provisions of this Act come into force on that day–

(a) sections 30 to 33;

(b) section 37;

(c) this section;

(d) section 39.

38(3) The following provisions of this Act come into force at the end of the period of 2 months beginning with that day–

(a) section 1 (and Schedule 1);

(b) section 25;

(c) section 27;

(d) section 28.

38(4) The other provisions of this Act come into force in accordance with provision made by order by the Secretary of State.

38(5) An order under subsection (4) may appoint different days for different purposes.

38(6) The Secretary of State may by order make transitional, transitory or saving provision in connection with the coming into force of any provision of this Act.

38(7) An order under subsection (4) or (6) is to be made by statutory instrument.

39 Short title

39 This Act may be cited as the Pensions Act 2011.

SCHEDULE 3 – CONSOLIDATION OF ADDITIONAL PENSION

Section 3

SOCIAL SECURITY CONTRIBUTIONS AND BENEFITS ACT 1992 (C. 4)

1 The Social Security Contributions and Benefits Act 1992 is amended as follows.

4 In section 122(1) (interpretation of Parts 1 to 6) insert at the appropriate place–

""**the additional pension consolidation year**" means such tax year as may be designated as such by order;".

5(1) Section 176 (Parliamentary control) is amended as follows.

5(2) After subsection (3) insert–

"**176(3A)** Subsection (3) above does not apply to a statutory instrument by reason only that it contains an order under section 45(2)."

5(3) In subsection (4) after "flat rate introduction year" insert "or the additional pension consolidation year".

SOCIAL SECURITY ADMINISTRATION ACT 1992 (C. 5)

8(1) Section 148AB of the Social Security Administration Act 1992 (revaluation of consolidated amount) (as inserted by paragraph 14 of Schedule 4 to the Pensions Act 2008) is amended as follows.

8(2) In subsections (1) and (2) for "flat rate introduction" substitute "additional pension consolidation".

8(3) After subsection (8) insert–

"**148AB(9)** In this section "the additional pension consolidation year" has the meaning given by section 122 of the Contributions and Benefits Act (interpretation of Parts 1 to 6 etc)."

WELFARE REFORM ACT 2012

(2012 Chapter 5)

[*8th March 2012*]

ARRANGEMENT OF SECTIONS

PART 1 – UNIVERSAL CREDIT

CHAPTER 3 – SUPPLEMENTARY AND GENERAL

PART 1 – UNIVERSAL CREDIT

Chapter 3 – Supplementary and General

SUPPLEMENTARY AND CONSEQUENTIAL

31 Supplementary and consequential amendments

31 Schedule 2 contains supplementary and consequential amendments.

UNIVERSAL CREDIT AND OTHER BENEFITS

33 Abolition of benefits

33(1) The following benefits are abolished–

(a) income-based jobseeker's allowance under the Jobseekers Act 1995;

(b) income-related employment and support allowance under Part 1 of the Welfare Reform Act 2007;

(c) income support under section 124 of the Social Security Contributions and Benefits Act 1992;

(d) housing benefit under section 130 of that Act;

(e) council tax benefit under section 131 of that Act;

(f) child tax credit and working tax credit under the Tax Credits Act 2002.

33(2) In subsection (1)–

(a) **"income-based jobseeker's allowance"** has the same meaning as in the Jobseekers Act 1995;

(b) **"income-related employment and support allowance"** means an employment and support allowance entitlement to which is based on section 1(2)(b) of the Welfare Reform Act 2007.

33(3) Schedule 3 contains consequential amendments.

Commencement Date – The days appointed for the coming into force of s. 33(1)(a), (b) and (2) in relation to claims for universal credit and the abolition of income-related employment and support allowance and income-based jobseeker's allowance were set initially in relation to persons falling within the "Pathfinder Group" (a person meeting the requirements of SI 2013/386, reg. 5–12) and subsequently by reference to the "Gateway conditions", (as introduced into SI 2013/983, Sch. 5 (by SI 2014/1452, art. 16) and modified by SI 2014/1661 and SI 2014/1923). Gateway conditions were removed by SI 2016/596 (by modification of earlier orders), with effect in relation to claims made on or after 25 May 2016, 29 June 2016 and 27 July 2016; by SI 2016/963 (by modification of earlier orders), with effect in relation to claims made on or after 5, 12, 19, 26 October 2016, 2, 9, 23, 30 November 2016 and 7 and 14 December 2016; by SI 2017/584 (by modification of earlier orders), with effect in relation to claims made on or after 3, 10, 17 and 24 May 2017 and 7, 14 and 28 June 2017;by SI 2017/664 (by modification of earlier orders), with effect in relation to claims made on or after 5, 12 and 19 July 2017 and 6, 13, 20 and 27 September 2017, and by SI 2017/952 (by modification of earlier orders), with effect in relation to claims made on or after 4, 11, 18 and 25 October 2017, 1, 8, 15, 22, and 29 November 2017, 6, 13 and 20 December 2017 and 10, 17 and 24 January 2018.

Commencement dates are staggered depending upon the claimant's postcode: 29 April 2013 (SI 2013/983, as amended by SI 2017/483 from 6 April 2017); 1 July 2013 and 29 July 2013 (SI 2013/1511); 28 October 2013 (SI 2013/2657); 25 November 2013 (SI 2013/2846); 24 February 2014 and 7 April 2014 (SI 2014/209); 23 June 2014 to 28 July 2014 (SI 2014/1583); 30 June 2014 (SI 2014/1661); 28 July 2014 (2014/1923); 15 September 2014 to 15 December 2014 (2014/2321); 24 November 2014 (SI 2014/3067); 26 November 2014 (SI 2014/3094), 26 January 2015 to 6 April 2015 (2015/32); 28 January 2015 (2015/33, as amended by SI 2017/483 from 6 April 2017); 16 February 2015 to 20 July 2015 (2015/101); 18 March 2015 to 4 November 2015 (2015/634); 21 September 2015 to 25 April 2016 (SI 2015/1537); 2 December 2015 (SI 2015/1930),27 January 2016 and 24 February 2016 (SI 2016/33) and 23 March and 27 April 2016 (SI 2016/407).

1 April 2013 is the day appointed for the coming into force of s. 33(1)(e) (SI 2013/358, art. 8(a)).

34 Universal credit and state pension credit

34 Schedule 4 provides for a housing element of state pension credit in consequence of the abolition of housing benefit by section 33.

PART 3 – OTHER BENEFIT CHANGES

STATE PENSION CREDIT

74 State pension credit: carers

74(1) The State Pension Credit Act 2002 is amended as follows.

74(2) [Not reproduced.]

74(3) In section 17 (interpretation), in subsection (1), in the appropriate place there is inserted–

""regular and substantial caring responsibilities" has such meaning as may be prescribed;"

PART 4 – PERSONAL INDEPENDENCE PAYMENT

GENERAL

91 Amendments

91 Schedule 9 contains amendments relating to this Part.

PART 5 – SOCIAL SECURITY: GENERAL

APPEALS

102 Power to require consideration of revision before appeal

102(1) The Social Security Act 1998 is amended as follows.

102(2) [Amends SSA 1998, s. 12(2).]

102(3) [Inserts SSA 1998, s. 12(3A)–(3C).]

102(4) [Amends SSA 1998, s. 12(7).]

102(5) [Amends SSA 1998, s. 80(1).]

102(6) Schedule 11 contains similar amendments to other Acts.

102(7) Subsection (8) applies where regulations under a provision mentioned in subsection (9) are made so as to have effect in relation to a limited area (by virtue of provision made under section 150(4)(b)).

102(8) Any power to make, in connection with those regulations, provision as respects decisions and appeals may be exercised so that that provision applies only in relation to the area mentioned in subsection (7).

102(9) The provisions referred to in subsection (7) are–

(a) section 12(3A) of the Social Security Act 1998;

(b) section 4(1B) of the Vaccine Damage Payments Act 1979;

(c) subsection (2A) of section 20 of the Child Support Act 1991 (as substituted by section 10 of the Child Support, Pensions and Social Security Act 2000);

(d) subsection (3A) of section 20 of the Child Support Act 1991 (as it has effect apart from section 10 of the Child Support, Pensions and Social Security Act 2000);

(e) section 11(2A) of the Social Security (Recovery of Benefits) Act 1997;

(f) paragraph 6(5A) of Schedule 7 to the Child Support, Pensions and Social Security Act 2000;

(g) section 50(1A) of the Child Maintenance and Other Payments Act 2008.

Commencement Date – 25 February 2013 is the day appointed for the coming into force of s. 102 for all purposes (SI 2013/358, art. 2(2) and Sch. 2, para. 37).

ELECTRONIC COMMUNICATIONS

104 Electronic communications

104(1) [Inserts SSAA 1992, s. 189(5A) and (5B).]

104(2) [Inserts SSA 1998, s. 79(6A) and (6B).]

Commencement Date – 25 February 2013 is the day appointed for the coming into force of s. 104 for all purposes (SI 2013/358, art. 2(2) and Sch. 2, para. 38).

ADMINISTRATION OF TAX CREDITS

122 Tax credit fraud: investigation

122 [Inserts SSAA 1992, s. 109A(9).]

Commencement Date – 6 June 2012 is the day appointed for the coming into force of s. 122 (SI 2012/1246, art. 2(2)).

123 Information-sharing for prevention etc of tax credit fraud

123(1) Section 122B of the Social Security Administration Act 1992 (supply of government information for fraud prevention etc) is amended as follows.

123(2) [Amends SSAA 1992, s. 122B(2)(a).]

123(3) [Amends SSAA 1992, s. 122B(3).]

Commencement Date – 6 June 2012 is the day appointed for the coming into force of s. 123 (SI 2012/1246, art. 2(2)).

125 Unauthorised disclosure of information relating to tax credit offences

125 [Amends SSAA 1992, Sch. 4, Pt. 2, para. 1.]

Commencement Date – 6 June 2012 is the day appointed for the coming into force of s. 125 (SI 2012/1246, art. 2(2)).

INFORMATION-SHARING: SECRETARY OF STATE AND HMRC

127 Information-sharing between Secretary of State and HMRC

127(1) This subsection applies to information which is held for the purposes of any HMRC functions–

(a) by the Commissioners for Her Majesty's Revenue and Customs, or

(b) by a person providing services to them.

127(2) Information to which subsection (1) applies may be supplied–

(a) to the Secretary of State, or to a person providing services to the Secretary of State, or

(b) to a Northern Ireland Department, or to a person providing services to a Northern Ireland Department,

for use for the purposes of departmental functions.

127(3) This subsection applies to information which is held for the purposes of any departmental functions–

(a) by the Secretary of State, or by a person providing services to the Secretary of State, or

(b) by a Northern Ireland Department, or by a person providing services to a Northern Ireland Department.

127(4) Information to which subsection (3) applies may be supplied–

(a) to the Commissioners for Her Majesty's Revenue and Customs, or

(b) to a person providing services to them,

for use for the purposes of HMRC functions.

127(5) Information supplied under this section must not be supplied by the recipient of the information to any other person or body without–

(a) the authority of the Commissioners for Her Majesty's Revenue and Customs, in the case of information supplied under subsection (2);

(b) the authority of the Secretary of State, in the case of information held as mentioned in subsection (3)(a) and supplied under subsection (4);

(c) the authority of the relevant Northern Ireland Department, in the case of information held as mentioned in subsection (3)(b) and supplied under subsection (4).

127(6) Where information supplied under this section has been used for the purposes for which it was supplied, it is lawful for it to be used for any purposes for which information held for those purposes could be used.

127(7) In this section–

"departmental functions" means functions relating to–

(a) social security,

(b) employment or training,

(c) the investigation or prosecution of offences relating to tax credits; or

(d) child support;

"HMRC function" means any function–

(a) for which the Commissioners for Her Majesty's Revenue and Customs are responsible by virtue of section 5 of the Commissioners for Revenue and Customs Act 2005,

(b) which relates to a matter listed in Schedule 1 to that Act, or

(c) which is conferred by or under the Childcare Payments Act 2014;

"Northern Ireland Department" means any of the following–

(a) the Department for Social Development;

(b) the Department of Finance and Personnel;

(c) the Department for Employment and Learning.

127(8) For the purposes of this section any reference to functions relating to social security includes a reference to functions relating to–

(a) statutory payments as defined in section 4C(11) of the Social Security Contributions and Benefits Act 1992;

(b) maternity allowance under section 35 of that Act;

(c) statutory payments as defined in section 4C(11) of the Social Security Contributions and Benefits (Northern Ireland) Act 1992;

(d) maternity allowance under section 35 of that Act.

127(9) This section does not limit the circumstances in which information may be supplied apart from this section.

127(10) In section 3 of the Social Security Act 1998 (use of information), in subsection (1A), after paragraph (d) there is inserted–

"(e) the investigation or prosecution of offences relating to tax credits."

History – In s. 127(7), in the definition of "HMRC function", para. (c) (and the ", or" before it) inserted (and the word "or" after (a) omitted) by CPA 2014, s. 27(6) with effect from 20 July 2016 (SI 2016/763, reg. 2(1)).
S. 127(7)(d) (and the "or" before it inserted (and the "or" after (b) omitted) by SI 2012/2007, art. 102, with effect from 31 July 2012.

PART 7 – FINAL

147 Repeals

147 Schedule 14 contains consequential repeals.

149 Extent

149(1) This Act extends to England and Wales and Scotland only, subject as follows.

149(2) The following provisions extend to England and Wales, Scotland and Northern Ireland–

(a) section 32 (power to make consequential and supplementary provision: universal credit);

(b) section 33 (abolition of benefits);

(c) section 76 (calculation of working tax credit);

(d) section 92 (power to make consequential and supplementary provision: personal independence payment);

(e) section 126(1) to (13) (tax credits: transfer of functions etc);

(f) section 127(1) to (9) (information-sharing between Secretary of State and HMRC);

(g) this Part, excluding Schedule 14 (repeals).

149(3) Sections 128 and 129 extend to England and Wales only.

149(4) Any amendment or repeal made by this Act has the same extent as the enactment to which it relates.

150 Commencement

150(1) The following provisions of this Act come into force on the day on which it is passed–

(a) section 76 (calculation of working tax credit);

(b) section 103 and Schedule 12 (supersession of decisions of former appellate bodies) (but see section 103(2));

(c) section 108 (application of Limitation Act 1980) (but see section 108(4));

(d) section 109 (recovery of fines etc by deductions from employment and support allowance) (but see section 109(3));

(e) section 126 (tax credits: transfer of functions etc);

(f) this Part, excluding Schedule 14 (repeals).

150(2) The following provisions of this Act come into force at the end of the period of two months beginning with the day on which it is passed–

(a) section 50 (dual entitlement to employment and support allowance and jobseeker's allowance);

(b) section 60 and Part 6 of Schedule 14 (claimants dependent on drugs etc);

(c) sections 71 and 72 (social fund: purposes of discretionary payments and determination of amount or value of budgeting loan);

(d) section 107 (recovery of child benefit and guardian's allowance);

(e) section 111 (time limit for legal proceedings);

(f) section 127 and Part 13 of Schedule 14 (information-sharing between Secretary of State and HMRC);

(g) section 134 (information-sharing for social security or employment purposes etc);

(h) section 135 (functions of registration service);

(i) section 142 (exclusion of child support maintenance from individual voluntary arrangements);

(j) section 145 and Schedule 13 (Social Mobility and Child Poverty Commission);

(k) Part 2 of Schedule 14 (entitlement to jobseeker's allowance without seeking employment).

150(3) The remaining provisions of this Act come into force on such day as the Secretary of State may by order made by statutory instrument appoint.

150(4) An order under subsection (3) may–

(a) appoint different days for different purposes;

(b) appoint different days for different areas in relation to—

(i) any provision of Part 1 (universal credit) or of Part 1 of Schedule 14;

(ii) section 61 or 62 (entitlement to work: jobseeker's allowance and employment and support allowance);

(iii) any provision of Part 4 (personal independence payment) or of Part 9 of Schedule 14;

(iv) section 102 (consideration of revision before appeal);

(c) make such transitory or transitional provision, or savings, as the Secretary of State considers necessary or expedient.

151 Short title

151 This Act may be cited as the Welfare Reform Act 2012.

SCHEDULES

SCHEDULE 2 – UNIVERSAL CREDIT: AMENDMENTS

Section 31

CHILDREN ACT 1989 (C. 41)

1 [Amends Children Act 1989, s. 17(9), 17A(5)(b), 29(3) and (3A) and Sch. 2, para. 21(4).]

Commencement Date – 29 April 2013 is the day appointed for the coming into force of para. 1 (and s. 31 so far as it relates to para. 1), in so far as not already in force (SI 2013/983, art. 3(1)(b)).

CHILD SUPPORT ACT 1991 (C. 48)

2 [Amends Child Support Act 1991, Sch. 1, para. 5(4).]

Commencement Date – 25 February 2013 is the day appointed for the coming into force of para. 2 (and s. 31 in so far as it relates to para. 2) for the purpose of making regulations (SI 2013/358, art. 2(1)).
29 April 2013 is the day appointed for the coming into force of para. 2 (and s. 31 so far as it relates to para. 2), in so far as not already in force (SI 2013/983, art. 3(1)(b)).

SOCIAL SECURITY ADMINISTRATION ACT 1992 (C. 5)

3 The Social Security Administration Act 1992 is amended as follows.

4 [Inserts SSAA 1992, s. 1(4)(za).]

Commencement Date – 25 February 2013 is the day appointed for the coming into force of para. 4 (and s. 31 and Sch. 2, para. 3 in so far as they relate to para. 4) for the purpose of making regulations (SI 2013/358, art. 2(1)).
29 April 2013 is the day appointed for the coming into force of para. 4 (and para. 3 in so far as it relates to para. 4), in so far as not already in force (SI 2013/983, art. 3(1)(b)).

5 [Amends SSAA 1992, s. 5(2)(a) and (6).]

Commencement Date – 25 February 2013 is the day appointed for the coming into force of para. 5 (and s. 31 and Sch. 2, para. 3 in so far as they relate to para. 5) for all purposes (SI 2013/358, art. 2(2) and Sch. 2, para. 40).

6 [Amends SSAA 1992, s. 15A(1) and (4).]

Commencement Date – 25 February 2013 is the day appointed for the coming into force of para. 6 (and s. 31 and Sch. 2, para. 3 in so far as they relate to para. 6) for all purposes (SI 2013/358, art. 2(2) and Sch. 2, para. 40).

7 [Amends SSAA 1992, s. 74(2)(b).]

Commencement Date – 25 February 2013 is the day appointed for the coming into force of para. 7 (and para. 3 in so far as it relates to para. 7 and s. 31 in so far as it relates to those paragraphs) (SI 2013/358, art. 5(1)).

8 [Amends SSAA 1992, s. 74A(7).]

Commencement Date – 29 April 2013 is the day appointed for the coming into force of para. 8 (and para. 3 in so far as it relates to para. 8), in so far as not already in force (SI 2013/983, art. 3(1)(b)).

9 [Amends SSAA 1992, s. 78.]

Commencement Date – 29 April 2013 is the day appointed for the coming into force of para. 9 (and para. 3 in so far as it relates to para. 9 and s. 31 in so far as it relates to those paragraphs) (SI 2013/358, art. 5(5)).

10 [Amends SSAA 1992, s. 105(1)(b).]

Commencement Date – 29 April 2013 is the day appointed for the coming into force of para. 10 (and para. 3 in so far as it relates to para. 10), in so far as not already in force (SI 2013/983, art. 3(1)(b)).

11 [Amends SSAA 1992, s. 106(1), (2), (3), (4)(a) and (b).]

Commencement Date – 29 April 2013 is the day appointed for the coming into force of para. 11 (and para. 3 in so far as it relates to para. 11), in so far as not already in force (SI 2013/983, art. 3(1)(b)).

12 [Amends SSAA 1992, s. 108(1)(a).]

Commencement Date – 29 April 2013 is the day appointed for the coming into force of para. 12 (and para. 3 in so far as it relates to para. 12), in so far as not already in force (SI 2013/983, art. 3(1)(b)).

13 [Amends SSAA 1992, s. 109(1).]

Commencement Date – 29 April 2013 is the day appointed for the coming into force of para. 13 (and para. 3 in so far as it relates to para. 13), in so far as not already in force (SI 2013/983, art. 3(1)(b)).

14 [Inserts SSAA 1992, s. 121DA(1)(hj).]

Commencement Date – 29 April 2013 is the day appointed for the coming into force of para. 14 (and para. 3 in so far as it relates to para. 14), in so far as not already in force (SI 2013/983, art. 3(1)(b)).

15 [Amends SSAA 1992, s. 122B(3)(b).]

Commencement Date – 29 April 2013 is the day appointed for the coming into force of para. 15 (and para. 3 in so far as it relates to para. 15), in so far as not already in force (SI 2013/983, art. 3(1)(b)).

16 [Amends SSAA 1992, s. 122F(1), (3)(a), (4) and heading.]

Commencement Date – 29 April 2013 is the day appointed for the coming into force of para. 16 (and para. 3 in so far as it relates to para. 16), in so far as not already in force (SI 2013/983, art. 3(1)(b)).

17 [Inserts SSAA 1992, s. 124(1)(ad).]

Commencement Date – 29 April 2013 is the day appointed for the coming into force of para. 17 (and para. 3 in so far as it relates to para. 17), in so far as not already in force (SI 2013/983, art. 3(1)(b)).

18 [Amends SSAA 1992, s. 125.]

Commencement Date – 29 April 2013 is the day appointed for the coming into force of para. 18 (and para. 3 in so far as it relates to para. 18), in so far as not already in force (SI 2013/983, art. 3(1)(b)).

19 [Amends SSAA 1992, s. 126(1).]

Commencement Date – 29 April 2013 is the day appointed for the coming into force of para. 19 (and para. 3 in so far as it relates to para. 19), in so far as not already in force (SI 2013/983, art. 3(1)(b)).

20 [Amends SSAA 1992, s. 130(1).]

Commencement Date – 29 April 2013 is the day appointed for the coming into force of para. 20 (and para. 3 in so far as it relates to para. 20), in so far as not already in force (SI 2013/983, art. 3(1)(b)).

21 [Amends SSAA 1992, s. 132(1).]

Commencement Date – 29 April 2013 is the day appointed for the coming into force of para. 21 (and para. 3 in so far as it relates to para. 21), in so far as not already in force (SI 2013/983, art. 3(1)(b)).

22 [Amends SSAA 1992, s. 150(1) and (7).]

Commencement Date – 29 April 2013 is the day appointed for the coming into force of para. 22 (and para. 3 in so far as it relates to para. 22), in so far as not already in force (SI 2013/983, art. 3(1)(b)).

23 [Inserts SSAA 1992, s. 159D.]

Commencement Date – 29 April 2013 is the day appointed for the coming into force of para. 23 (and para. 3 in so far as it relates to para. 23), in so far as not already in force (SI 2013/983, art. 3(1)(b)).

24 After section 160B there is inserted–

"160 Implementation of increases in universal credit due to attainment of a particular age

160C(1) This section applies where–

(a) an award of universal credit is in force in favour of a person ("the recipient"), and

(b) an element has become applicable, or applicable at a particular rate, because he or some other person has reached a particular age ("the qualifying age").

160C(2) If, as a result of the recipient or other person reaching the qualifying age, the recipient becomes entitled to an increased amount of universal credit, the amount payable to or for him under the award shall, as from the day on which he becomes so entitled, be that increased amount, without any further decision of the Secretary of State; and the award shall have effect accordingly.

160C(3) Subsection (2) does not apply where, in consequence of the recipient or other person reaching the qualifying age, a question arises in relation to the recipient's entitlement to–

(a) a benefit under the Contribution and Benefits Act, or

(b) personal independence payment.

160C(4) Subsection (2) does not apply where, in consequence of the recipient or other person reaching the qualifying age, a question arises in relation to the recipient's entitlement to universal credit, other than–

(a) the question whether the element concerned, or any other element, becomes or ceases to be applicable, or applicable at a particular rate, in the recipient's case, and

(b) the question whether, in consequence, the amount of his universal credit falls to be varied.

160C(5) In this section, **"element"**, in relation to universal credit, means any of the amounts specified in regulations under sections 9 to 12 of the Welfare Reform Act 2012 which are included in the calculation of an award of universal credit."

25 [Amends SSAA 1992, s. 165(1)(a)(iii) and (6)(a).]

Commencement Date – 29 April 2013 is the day appointed for the coming into force of para. 25 (and para. 3 in so far as it relates to para. 25), in so far as not already in force (SI 2013/983, art. 3(1)(b)).

26 [Amends SSAA 1992, s. 170(5).]

Commencement Date – 25 February 2013 is the day appointed for the coming into force of para. 26 (and s. 31 and Sch. 2, para. 3 in so far as they relate to para. 26) (SI 2013/358, art. 3(a) and (b)).

27(1) Section 179 (reciprocal agreements) is amended as follows.

27(2) [Amends SSAA 1992, s. 179(3)(a).]

27(3) [Inserts SSAA 1992, s. 179(4)(af).]

27(4) [Inserts SSAA 1992, s. 179(5)(za).]

Commencement Date – 29 April 2013 is the day appointed for the coming into force of para. 27 (and para. 3 in so far as it relates to para. 27), in so far as not already in force (SI 2013/983, art. 3(1)(b)).

28 [Amends SSAA 1992, s. 180(a) and (b)(i).]

Commencement Date – 29 April 2013 is the day appointed for the coming into force of para. 28 (and para. 3 in so far as it relates to para. 28), in so far as not already in force (SI 2013/983, art. 3(1)(b)).

29 [Amends SSAA 1992, s. 182B(5)(b).]

Commencement Date – 29 April 2013 is the day appointed for the coming into force of para. 29 (and para. 3 in so far as it relates to para. 29), in so far as not already in force (SI 2013/983, art. 3(1)(b)).

30 [Amends SSAA 1992, s. 187(1)(a).]

Commencement Date – 29 April 2013 is the day appointed for the coming into force of para. 30 (and para. 3 in so far as it relates to para. 30), in so far as not already in force (SI 2013/983, art. 3(1)(b)).

31 [Amends SSAA 1992, s. 191.]

Commencement Date – 25 February 2013 is the day appointed for the coming into force of para. 31 (and s. 31 in so far as it relates to para. 31) for the purpose of making regulations (SI 2013/358, art. 2(1)).
29 April 2013 is the day appointed for the coming into force of para. 31 (and para. 3 in so far as it relates to para. 31), in so far as not already in force (SI 2013/983, art. 3(1)(b)).

SOCIAL SECURITY ACT 1998 (C. 14)

43 The Social Security Act 1998 (decisions and appeals) is amended as follows.

44 [Inserts SSA 1998, s. 2(2)(k).]

Commencement Date – 29 April 2013 is the day appointed for the coming into force of para. 44 (and para. 43 in so far as it relates to para. 44), in so far as not already in force (SI 2013/983, art. 3(1)(b)).

45 In section 8 (decisions by Secretary of State)–

(a) [inserts SSA 1998, s. 8(3)(aa);]

(b) in subsection (4), for "or Part 1 of the Welfare Reform Act 2007" there is substituted ", Part 1 of the Welfare Reform Act 2007, Part 1 of the Welfare Reform Act 2012".

Commencement Date – 25 February 2013 is the day appointed for the coming into force of para. 45 (and s. 31 in so far as it relates to para. 45) for the purpose of making regulations (SI 2013/358, art. 2(1)).
29 April 2013 is the day appointed for the coming into force of para. 45 (and para. 43 in so far as it relates to para. 45), in so far as not already in force (SI 2013/983, art. 3(1)(b)).

46 [Amends SSA 1998, s. 11(3).]

Commencement Date – 25 February 2013 is the day appointed for the coming into force of para. 46 (and s. 31 in so far as it relates to para. 46) for all purposes (SI 2013/358, art. 2(2) and Sch. 2, para. 40).

47 [Inserts SSA 1998, s. 27(7)(f).]

Commencement Date – 25 February 2013 is the day appointed for the coming into force of para. 47 (and s. 31 in so far as it relates to para. 47) for the purpose of making regulations (SI 2013/358, art. 2(1)).
29 April 2013 is the day appointed for the coming into force of para. 47 (and para. 43 in so far as it relates to para. 47), in so far as not already in force (SI 2013/983, art. 3(1)(b)).

48 In section 28(3) (correction of errors in decisions etc)–

(a) in paragraph (f), the final "or" is repealed;

(b) after paragraph (g) there is inserted–

"(h) Part 1 of the Welfare Reform Act 2012;".

Commencement Date – 25 February 2013 is the day appointed for the coming into force of para. 48 (and s. 31 in so far as it relates to para. 48) for all purposes (SI 2013/358, art. 2(2) and Sch. 2, para. 40).

49 [Amends SSA 1998, s. 39(1).]

Commencement Date – 25 February 2013 is the day appointed for the coming into force of para. 49 (and s. 31 in so far as it relates to para. 49) for the purpose of making regulations (SI 2013/358, art. 2(1)).
29 April 2013 is the day appointed for the coming into force of para. 49 (and para. 43 in so far as it relates to para. 49), in so far as not already in force (SI 2013/983, art. 3(1)(b)).

50(1) Schedule 2 (decisions against which no appeal lies) is amended as follows.

50(2) [Amends SSA 1998, Sch. 2, para. 6(b).]

50(3) After paragraph 7 there is inserted–

"INCREASES IN UNIVERSAL CREDIT DUE TO ATTAINMENT OF PARTICULAR AGES

7A A decision as to the amount of benefit to which a person is entitled, where it appears to the Secretary of State that the amount is determined by the recipient's entitlement to an increased amount of universal credit in the circumstances referred to in section 160C(2) of the Administration Act."

Commencement Date – 29 April 2013 is the day appointed for the coming into force of para. 50 (2) (and para. 50(1) in so far as it relates to para. 50(2)), in so far as not already in force (SI 2013/983, art. 3(1)(b)).

51 [Inserts SSA 1998, Sch. 3, para. 3A]

Commencement Date – 1 April 2013 is the day appointed for the coming into force of para. 51 (and para. 43 in so far as it relates to para. 51 and s. 31 in so far as it relates to both those paragraphs) (SI 2013/358, art. 6(4)(d)(i)).

SCHEDULE 3 – ABOLITION OF BENEFITS: CONSEQUENTIAL AMENDMENTS

Section 33

SOCIAL SECURITY CONTRIBUTIONS AND BENEFITS ACT 1992 (C. 4)

1 The Social Security Contributions and Benefits Act 1992 is amended as follows.

2 In section 22 (earnings factors), in subsections (2)(a) and (5), for "a contributory" there is substituted "an".

SCHEDULE 4 – HOUSING CREDIT ELEMENT OF STATE PENSION CREDIT

Section 34

Part 1 – Amendments to State Pension Credit Act 2002

STATE PENSION CREDIT ACT 2002 (C. 16)

1 The State Pension Credit Act 2002 is amended as follows.

7 In section 17 (interpretation), in subsection (1), after the definition of "guarantee credit" there is inserted–

"**"housing credit"** shall be construed in accordance with sections 1 and 3A;".

SCHEDULE 9 – PERSONAL INDEPENDENCE PAYMENT: AMENDMENTS

Section 91

SOCIAL SECURITY ADMINISTRATION ACT 1992 (C. 5)

7 The Social Security Administration Act 1992 is amended as follows.

12 [Inserts SSAA 1992, s. 121DA(1)(hk).]

Commencement Date – The day appointed for the coming into force of para. 12 (and s. 91 in so far as it relates to para. 12) to the extent not already in force is 8 April 2013 in relation to a person whose only or principal residence is, on the date on which that person makes a claim for personal independence payment, located in an area to which one of the following postcodes corresponds: BL, CA, CH (except CH1, CH4, CH5, CH6, CH7 and CH8), CW, DH, DL (except DL6, DL7, DL8, DL9, DL10 and DL11), FY, L, LA (except LA2 7, LA2 8, LA6 2 and LA6 3), M, NE, PR, SR, TS (except TS9), WA and WN (SI 2013/358, art. 7(1) and (2)(k)).
The day appointed for the coming into force of para. 12 to the extent not already in force, in relation to a person other than a person referred to in SI 2013/358, art. 7(1) is 10 June 2013 (SI 2013/1250, art. 2).

13 [Amends SSAA 1992, s. 122B(3)(b).]

Commencement Date – The day appointed for the coming into force of para. 13 (and s. 91 in so far as it relates to para. 13) to the extent not already in force is 8 April 2013 in relation to a person whose only or principal residence is, on the date on which that person makes a claim for personal independence payment, located in an area to which one of the following postcodes corresponds: BL, CA, CH (except CH1, CH4, CH5, CH6, CH7 and CH8), CW, DH, DL (except DL6, DL7, DL8, DL9, DL10 and DL11), FY, L, LA (except LA2 7, LA2 8, LA6 2 and LA6 3), M, NE, PR, SR, TS (except TS9), WA and WN (SI 2013/358, art. 7(1) and (2)(k)).
The day appointed for the coming into force of para. 13 to the extent not already in force, in relation to a person other than a person referred to in SI 2013/358, art. 7(1) is 10 June 2013 (SI 2013/1250, art. 2).

15 [Inserts SSAA 1992, s. 124(1)(ae).]

Commencement Date – The day appointed for the coming into force of para. 15 (and s. 91 in so far as it relates to para. 15) to the extent not already in force is 8 April 2013 in relation to a person whose only or principal residence is, on the date on which that person makes a claim for personal independence payment, located in an area to which one of the following postcodes corresponds: BL, CA, CH (except CH1, CH4, CH5, CH6, CH7 and CH8), CW, DH, DL (except DL6, DL7, DL8, DL9, DL10 and DL11), FY, L, LA (except LA2 7, LA2 8, LA6 2 and LA6 3), M, NE, PR, SR, TS (except TS9), WA and WN (SI 2013/358, art. 7(1) and (2)(k)).
The day appointed for the coming into force of para. 15 to the extent not already in force, in relation to a person other than a person referred to in SI 2013/358, art. 7(1) is 10 June 2013 (SI 2013/1250, art. 2).

16 [Amends SSAA 1992, s. 125(1).]

Commencement Date – The day appointed for the coming into force of para. 16 (and s. 91 in so far as it relates to para. 16) to the extent not already in force is 8 April 2013 in relation to a person whose only or principal residence is, on the date on which that person makes a claim for personal independence payment, located in an area to which one of the following postcodes corresponds: BL, CA, CH (except CH1, CH4, CH5, CH6, CH7 and CH8), CW, DH, DL (except DL6, DL7, DL8, DL9, DL10 and DL11), FY, L, LA (except LA2 7, LA2 8, LA6 2 and LA6 3), M, NE, PR, SR, TS (except TS9), WA and WN (SI 2013/358, art. 7(1) and (2)(k)).
The day appointed for the coming into force of para. 16 to the extent not already in force, in relation to a person other than a person referred to in SI 2013/358, art. 7(1) is 10 June 2013 (SI 2013/1250, art. 2).

26 [Amends SSAA 1992, s. 170(5).]

Commencement Date – 25 February 2013 is the day appointed for the coming into force of para. 26 (and s. 91 and Sch. 9, para. 7 in so far as they relate to para. 26) (SI 2013/358, art. 3(c) and (d)).

Prospective amendments – Para. 26 repealed by WRA 2012, s. 147 and Sch. 14, Pt. 1, with effect from a date to be set by order of the Secretary of State.

27 [Amends SSAA 1992, s. 179(3)(a) and inserts (4)(ah).]

Commencement Date – The day appointed for the coming into force of para. 27 (and s. 91 in so far as it relates to para. 27) to the extent not already in force is 8 April 2013 in relation to a person whose only or principal residence is, on the date on which that person makes a claim for personal independence payment, located in an area to which one of the following postcodes corresponds: BL, CA, CH (except CH1, CH4, CH5, CH6, CH7 and CH8), CW, DH, DL (except DL6, DL7, DL8, DL9, DL10 and DL11), FY, L, LA (except LA2 7, LA2 8, LA6 2 and LA6 3), M, NE, PR, SR, TS (except TS9), WA and WN (SI 2013/358, art. 7(1) and (2)(k)).
The day appointed for the coming into force of para. 27 to the extent not already in force, in relation to a person other than a person referred to in SI 2013/358, art. 7(1) is 10 June 2013 (SI 2013/1250, art. 2).

Prospective amendments – Para. 27 repealed by WRA 2012, s. 147 and Sch. 14, Pt. 1, with effect from a date to be set by order of the Secretary of State.

28 [Amends SSAA 1992, s. 180(a) and (b)(i).]

Commencement Date – The day appointed for the coming into force of para. 28 (and s. 91 in so far as it relates to para. 28) to the extent not already in force is 8 April 2013 in relation to a person whose only or principal residence is, on the date on which that person makes a claim for personal independence payment, located in an area to which one of the following postcodes corresponds: BL, CA, CH (except CH1, CH4, CH5, CH6, CH7 and CH8), CW, DH, DL (except DL6, DL7, DL8, DL9, DL10 and DL11), FY, L, LA (except LA2 7, LA2 8, LA6 2 and LA6 3), M, NE, PR, SR, TS (except TS9), WA and WN (SI 2013/358, art. 7(1) and (2)(k)).
The day appointed for the coming into force of para. 28 to the extent not already in force, in relation to a person other than a person referred to in SI 2013/358, art. 7(1) is 10 June 2013 (SI 2013/1250, art. 2).

32 [Amends SSAA 1992, s. 191.]

Commencement Date – 25 February 2013 is the day appointed for the coming into force of para. 32 (and para. 7 in so far as it relates to para. 32 and s. 91 in so far as it relates to those paragraphs) for the purpose of making regulations (SI 2013/358, art. 2(1)).
The day appointed for the coming into force of para. 32 (and s. 91 in so far as it relates to para. 32) to the extent not already in force is 8 April 2013 in relation to a person whose only or principal residence is, on the date on which that person makes a claim for personal independence payment, located in an area to which one of the following postcodes corresponds: BL, CA, CH (except CH1, CH4, CH5, CH6, CH7 and CH8), CW, DH, DL (except DL6, DL7, DL8, DL9, DL10 and DL11), FY, L, LA (except LA2 7, LA2 8, LA6 2 and LA6 3), M, NE, PR, SR, TS (except TS9), WA and WN (SI 2013/358, art. 7(1) and (2)(k)).
The day appointed for the coming into force of para. 32 to the extent not already in force, in relation to a person other than a person referred to in SI 2013/358, art. 7(1) is 10 June 2013 (SI 2013/1250, art. 2).

SOCIAL SECURITY ACT 1998 (C. 14)

37 The Social Security Act 1998 is amended as follows.

39 [Inserts SSA 1998, s. 8(3)(baa) and amends (4).]

Commencement Date – 25 February 2013 is the day appointed for the coming into force of para. 39 (and para. 37 in so far as it relates to para. 39 and s. 91 in so far as it relates to those paragraphs) for the purpose of making regulations (SI 2013/358, art. 2(1)).
The day appointed for the coming into force of para. 39 (and s. 91 in so far as it relates to para. 39) to the extent not already in force is 8 April 2013 in relation to a person whose only or principal residence is, on the date on which that person makes a claim for personal independence payment, located in an area to which one of the following postcodes corresponds: BL, CA, CH (except CH1, CH4, CH5, CH6, CH7 and CH8), CW, DH, DL (except DL6, DL7, DL8, DL9, DL10 and DL11), FY, L, LA (except LA2 7, LA2 8, LA6 2 and LA6 3), M, NE, PR, SR, TS (except TS9), WA and WN, (SI 2013/358, art. 7(1) and (2)(k)).
The day appointed for the coming into force of para. 39 to the extent not already in force, in relation to a person other than a person referred to in SI 2013/358, art. 7(1) is 10 June 2013 (SI 2013/1250, art. 2).

40 [Amends SSA1998, s. 11(3).]

Commencement Date – 25 February 2013 is the day appointed for the coming into force of para. 40 (and para. 37 in so far as it relates to para. 40 and s. 31 in so far as it relates to those paragraphs) for all purposes (SI 2013/358, art. 2(2) and Sch. 2, para. 43).

41 [Inserts SSA 1998, s. 27(7)(df) and amends (e).]

Commencement Date – 25 February 2013 is the day appointed for the coming into force of para. 41 (and para. 37 in so far as it relates to para. 41 and s. 91 in so far as it relates to those paragraphs) for the purpose of making regulations (SI 2013/358, art. 2(1)).
The day appointed for the coming into force of para. 41 (and s. 91 in so far as it relates to para. 41) to the extent not already in force is 8 April 2013 in relation to a person whose only or principal residence is, on the date on which that person makes a claim for personal independence payment, located in an area to which one of the following postcodes corresponds: BL, CA, CH (except CH1, CH4, CH5, CH6, CH7 and CH8), CW, DH, DL (except DL6, DL7, DL8, DL9, DL10 and DL11), FY, L, LA (except LA2 7, LA2 8, LA6 2 and LA6 3), M, NE, PR, SR, TS (except TS9), WA and WN (SI 2013/358, art. 7(1) and (2)(k)).
The day appointed for the coming into force of para. 41 to the extent not already in force, in relation to a person other than a person referred to in SI 2013/358, art. 7(1) is 10 June 2013 (SI 2013/1250, art. 2).

42 [Inserts SSA 1998, s. 28(3)(i).]

Commencement Date – 25 February 2012 is the day appointed for the coming into force of para. 42 (and para. 37 in so far as it relates to para. 42 and s. 31 in so far as it relates to those paragraphs) for all purposes (SI 2013/358, art. 2(2) and Sch. 2, para. 43).

SCHEDULE 14 – REPEALS

Section 147

Part 1 – Abolition of Benefits Superseded by Universal Credit

Commencement Date – 1 April 2013 is the day appointed for the coming into force of the following repeals in so far as they relate to the abolition of council tax benefit: SSCBA 1992, s. 123 to 137, s. 175(6); SSAA 1992, s. 6, 7, 110A and 110AA, 111, 115A, 115B, 116, 116A, 121DA(6), 122C to 122E, 128A, 138 to 140G, 176(1)(a) and (b), 182A(3)(c), 182B(2), 189, 191 (definitions of billing authority and council-tax benefit scheme), and Sch. 4; SSA 1998, s. 34 and 79(8); SA 1998, Pt. 2; WRPA 1999, s. 57 and 58; CSPSSA 2000, s. 68, Sch. 6 and Sch. 7, SSFA 2001, s. 1(5), 2(2), 6, 6B, 7, 9 and 14; PA 2004, Sch. 10 and WRA 2012, s. 130(7)(b) and (c).
The day appointed for the coming into force of the repeals of WRPA 1999, Sch. 7, para. 2(3) and (4), 4, 5(3) and (4), 6, 9–11, 15 and 16 and Sch. 8, para. 29(2); SPCA 2002, Sch. 2, para. 36–38; and ITEPA 2003, Sch. 6, para. 228–230 in relation to claims for universal credit and the abolition of income-related employment and support allowance and income-based jobseeker's allowance are staggered from 29 April 2013 as set out at WRA 2012, s. 33.

Short title and chapter	*Extent of repeal*
Social Security Contributions and Benefits Act 1992 (c. 4)	In sections 4C(2)(b), (5)(c) and (7)(a), "contribution-based".
	In section 22– (a) in subsections (2)(a) and (5), "contribution-based"; (b) subsection (8).
	In section 44A(7), "contributory".
	In section 122(1), the definition of "contribution-based jobseeker's allowance".
	Sections 123 to 137.
	Section 175(6).
	In Schedule 3, in paragraph 5(6B), "or 4(2)(b)".
Social Security Administration Act 1992 (c. 5)	Section 1(4)(b).
	Sections 2A to 2H.
	In section 5– (a) subsection (2)(b) and (e); (b) in subsection (6), "or housing benefit".
	Section 6.

Short title and chapter	*Extent of repeal*
	In section 7– (a) in the heading, the words "community charge benefits and other"; (b) subsection (2), so far as not otherwise repealed; (c) subsection (3)(b) and the preceding "and".
	Section 7A(1) to (5).
	In section 15A– (a) in subsection (1)(a), the words from "income support" to "employment and support allowance"; (b) in subsection (1)(b), the words from "or the applicable" to "employment and support allowance""; (c) in subsection (1), in the words after paragraph (b), the words from "or applicable" to "employment and support allowance"; (d) in subsection (4), in the definition of "qualifying associate", "income support, an income-based jobseeker's allowance,", "or an income-related employment and support allowance,", "Part VII of the Contributions and Benefits Act or", "under the Jobseekers Act 1995," and "or Part 1 of the Welfare Reform Act 2007"; (e) in subsection (4), in the definition of "relevant benefits", paragraph (b).
	Section 71(11)(b).
	Section 71ZH(1)(c) and (d) (as inserted by section 105 of this Act).
	Section 71A.
	In section 73(1) and (4)(b), "contribution-based".
	In section 74– (a) in subsection (1)(b), "income support, an income-based jobseeker's allowance" and "or an income-related employment and support allowance"; (b) in subsection (2)(b), "income support, an income-based jobseeker's allowance," and "or an income-related employment and support allowance"; (c) subsection (3); (d) in subsection (4), "or (3)" and paragraph (b) and the preceding "and".
	In section 74A(7), the words from "income support" to "employment and support allowance".
	Section 75 (and the preceding cross-heading).
	Sections 76 and 77.
	In section 78(6)(d), "income support or an income-based jobseeker's allowance".
	In the heading to Part V, "Income support and".
	In section 105– (a) in subsection (1)(b), the words from "income support" to "support allowance"; (b) subsection (3)(b) and the preceding "or"; (c) subsection (4).
	In section 106(1), (2), (3) and (4)(a), "income support or".
	In section 108(1)(a), "income support or".
	In section 109(1), "or income support or an income-related employment and support allowance", in both places.

Short title and chapter	*Extent of repeal*
	In section 109A– (a) subsection (3)(b) to (d); (b) subsections (6) and (7).
	Sections 110A and 110AA.
	In section 111– (a) in subsection (1)(ab), "or 110AA"; (b) in subsection (3), "or 110A".
	In section 115A– (a) in subsection (1), "or an authority", "71A, 75 or 76" and "or authority"; (b) in subsection (1A) (as inserted by section 113 of this Act), "or an authority" in both places and "71A, 75 or 76"; (c) in subsection (2), "or authority", in both places; (d) in subsection (5), "or authority", in both places; (e) subsections (7A) and (7B).
	In section 115B– (a) in subsection (1), "or an authority that administers housing benefit or council tax benefit"; (b) in subsection (3), "or authority", in both places; (c) in subsection (4)(a) (as substituted by section 102 of this Act), "or authority"; (d) in subsection (4A) (as so substituted), the words from "(and, where" to the end; (e) in subsection (6), "or authority", in both places.
	In section 115C (as inserted by section 116 of this Act)– (a) in subsection (5), the words from "(and, where" to the end; (b) in subsection (6), in the definition of "appropriate authority", paragraph (b) and the preceding "or".
	In section 115D(5) (as inserted by section 116 of this Act), the words from "(and, where" to the end.
	In section 116– (a) in subsection (2)(a), "(other than proceedings to which paragraph (b) applies)" (as substituted by section 111(a) of this Act); (b) subsection (2)(b) and the preceding "and"; (c) subsection (3)(b) and the preceding "and"; (d) subsections (4) and (5).
	Section 116A.
	Section 121DA(6).
	Sections 122C to 122E.
	In section 122F, in subsection (3)(a) and (4), "housing benefit".
	Section 124(2)(b).
	In section 126(1)– (a) "income support, an income-based jobseeker's allowance"; (b) "an income-related employment and support allowance".
	Section 128A (and the preceding cross-heading).
	Section 134.
	Sections 138 to 140G.
	In section 150– (a) subsection (1)(h); (b) in subsection (1)(m) "or 4(2)(a) or (6)(c)"; (c) in subsection (7), "Part VII of the Contributions and Benefits Act or" and the words from "or which" to the end; (d) subsection (10)(b)(i) and (ii).

Short title and chapter	*Extent of repeal*
	Section 151(6).
	Section 159.
	In section 159B– (a) in subsection (1)(b)(iii), "contribution-based"; (b) in subsection (6), in the definitions of "alteration" and "component", "contribution-based".
	In section 159D (as inserted by Schedule 2 to this Act)– (a) in subsection (1)(b)(iv), "contribution-based"; (b) in subsection (6), in the definitions of "alteration" and "component", "contribution-based".
	Sections 160 and 160A.
	In section 160B(5), "or 4(2)(a)".
	Section 163(2)(d).
	In section 166– (a) in subsections (1)(c) and (2)(b), "relating to a contribution-based jobseeker's allowance"; (b) in subsection (2)(ba), "relating to a contributory employment and support allowance".
	In section 170(5), in the definition of "the relevant enactments"", paragraph (aj).
	Section 176(1)(a) and (b).
	Section 179(4)(b)(i) and (5)(a) and (d).
	Section 182A(3)(c).
	Section 182B(2).
	Section 187(1)(b).
	In section 189– (a) subsections (7) and (7A); (b) in subsection (8), "140B, 140C".
	Section 190(1)(aa) and (ab).
	In section 191, the definitions of– (a) "billing authority"; (b) "contribution-based jobseeker's allowance"; (c) "contributory employment and support allowance"; (d) "council tax benefit scheme"; (e) "housing authority"; (f) "housing benefit scheme"; (g) "income-based jobseeker's allowance"; (h) "income-related benefit"; (i) "income-related employment and support allowance"; (j) "rent rebate" and "rent allowance".
	In Schedule 4, the paragraphs headed "Local authorities etc".
Social Security Act 1998 (c. 14)	Section 8(3)(c).
	In section 8(5), the words from "other than" to the end.
	Section 34.
	In section 39(1), the definition of "claimant".
	Section 79(8).
	In Schedule 2– (a) paragraph 1 (and the preceding heading); (b) paragraph 5A (and the preceding heading); (c) paragraph 6(b)(i); (d) paragraph 7 (and the preceding heading).
	In Schedule 3, in paragraph 5, "or 71A".

Short title and chapter	*Extent of repeal*
	In Schedule 7, paragraphs 95, 97, 98, 139, 140 and 146.
Scotland Act 1998 (c. 46)	In Part 2 of Schedule 5, in Section F1, under the heading "Illustrations", "administration and funding of housing benefit and council tax benefit;".
Welfare Reform and Pensions Act 1999 (c. 30)	Sections 57 and 58.
	Section 72(3)(a).
	In Schedule 7, paragraphs 2(3) and (4), 4, 5(3) and (4), 6, 9 to 11, 15 and 16.
	In Schedule 8, paragraphs 28 and 29(2), (4), (5) and (7).
	In Schedule 12, paragraphs 79, 80, 82, 83 and 87.
Child Support, Pensions and Social Security Act 2000 (c. 19)	Section 68.
	Section 71.
	In Schedule 6, paragraph 3.
	Schedule 7.
Capital Allowances Act 2001 (c. 2)	In Schedule A1, in paragraph 17(1)– (a) in paragraph (a), the words from "disregarding any" to "working tax credit,"; (b) in paragraph (b), "child tax credit or working tax credit".
Social Security Fraud Act 2001 (c. 11)	Section 1(5).
	Section 2(2).
	Section 6.
	In section 6A(1), in the definition of "sanctionable benefit", paragraph (a).
	In section 6B– (a) in subsection (2)(b)(i), "or an authority which administers housing benefit or council tax benefit"; (b) subsections (6), (7), (9) and (10).
	In section 7– (a) subsections (3), (4), (4B) and (5); (b) in subsection (10), "8 or".
	Section 8.
	In section 9– (a) subsection (1)(a), (b), (bc), (c) and (d); (b) subsections (3), (4), (4B) and (5).
	In section 10(2), "8".
	In section 11(3)– (a) paragraph (b); (b) paragraph (d).
	In section 13, the definitions of– (a) "income-based jobseeker's allowance", "joint-claim jobseeker's allowance" and "joint-claim couple"; (b) "income-related allowance".
	Section 14.
State Pension Credit Act 2002 (c. 16)	Section 15(1)(b).
	In section 17(1), the definition of "working tax credit".
	Section 18A(7)(c) and the preceding "or".
	In Schedule 2, paragraphs 2 to 4 and 36 to 38.

Short title and chapter	*Extent of repeal*
Tax Credits Act 2002 (c. 21)	Part 1 (but not Schedule 1 or 3).
Employment Act 2002 (c. 22)	Section 49.
	In Schedule 6, paragraphs 2 and 3.
	In Schedule 7, paragraphs 9, 10, 12(a), 15 and 51.
Income Tax (Earnings and Payments) Act 2003 (c. 1)	In Schedule 6, paragraphs 179 and 228 to 230.
Pensions Act 2004 (c. 35)	In Schedule 10, paragraph 3.
Commissioners for Revenue and Customs Act 2005 (c. 11)	Section 5(1)(c) and the preceding "and".
	Section 44(3)(d) and the preceding "and".
	Section 54(4)(f) and the preceding "and".
	In Schedule 1, paragraphs 4 and 31.
Tribunals, Courts and Enforcement Act 2007 (c. 15)	In Schedule 13, paragraph 103.
Pensions Act 2007 (c. 22)	In Schedule 1, paragraph 25.
Corporation Tax Act 2009 (c. 4)	In section 1059– (a) subsection (3); (b) in subsection (5), "child tax credit or working tax credit".
	In section 1108– (a) subsection (3); (b) in subsection (5), "child tax credit or working tax credit".
Welfare Reform Act 2012 (c. 5)	Section 50(1).
	Section 52(2).
	Section 58(2).
	Section 59.
	Section 69.
	Section 105(5).
	Section 106(3).
	Section 111.
	Section 130(7)(b) and (c).
	In section 131– (a) in subsection (3), "or housing benefit"" in all three places; (b) in subsection (7)(a)(i), the words from "or a person engaged" to the end; (c) in subsection (9)(a)(i), the words from "or a person engaged" to the end; (d) subsection (11)(d) to (f); (e) in subsection (12), the definition of "person engaged in the administration of housing benefit".
	In Schedule 7, paragraphs 3 and 10(2).
	In Schedule 9, paragraphs 18, 22, 26 and 27.
	In Schedule 11, paragraphs 12 to 14.
	In Schedule 12, paragraph 5.

Part 3 – Jobseeker's Allowance: Responsibilities for Interim Period

Commencement Date – 22 October 2012 is the day appointed for the coming into force of Pt. 3 (save for the provisions in relation to the Jobseekers Act, s. 20(4), (6) and 35(1)) (SI 2012/2530, art. 2(2)(g)). Note: SI 2012/1246, art. 2(6) previously specified 14 October 2012 as the day appointed for the coming into force of Pt. 3 (save for the provision in relation to the Jobseekers Act 1995, s. 35(1)) but art. 2(6) was subsequently revoked by SI 2012/2530, art. 2(7).

Short title and chapter	*Extent of repeal*
Social Security Act 1998 (c. 14)	In Schedule 7, paragraph 141.
Welfare Reform and Pensions Act 1999 (c. 30)	In Schedule 7, paragraphs 12 and 13.
	In Schedule 8, paragraph 29(5).

Part 4 – Jobseeker's Allowance: Responsibilities After Introduction of Universal Credit

Commencement Date – The day appointed for the coming into force of the repeals in Pt. 4 in so far as they are not already in force, is, in relation to a particular case, the day on which the amending provisions come into force, under any secondary legislation, in relation to that case (SI 2013/983, art. 7).

Short title and chapter	*Extent of repeal*
Social Security Administration Act 1992 (c. 5)	Section 71ZH(1)(b) (as inserted by section 105 of this Act).
Social Security Act 1998 (c. 14)	In Schedule 3, paragraph 8 (and the preceding heading).
	In Schedule 7, paragraphs 134 and 135.
Welfare Reform Act 2012 (c. 5)	Section 44(3) to (5).
	Section 45.
	Section 46(1) and (2).
	In Schedule 7, paragraphs 2, 4, 5, 7, 8, 9, 10(1) and (3), 11, 14 and 16.

Part 5 – Employment and Support Allowance: Responsibilities After Introduction of Universal Credit

Commencement Date – The day appointed for the coming into force of the repeals in Pt. 5 in so far as they are not already in force, is, in relation to a particular case, the day on which the amending provisions come into force, under any secondary legislation, in relation to that case (SI 2013/983, art. 7).

Short title and chapter	*Extent of repeal*
Welfare Reform Act 2012 (c. 5)	Section 54(3) to (5).
	Sections 55 and 56.
	Section 58(1) and (3).

Part 6 – Claimants Dependent on Drugs etc

Short title and chapter	*Extent of repeal*
Social Security Act 1998 (c. 14)	In Schedule 3, in paragraph 3(da), ", or Schedule A1 to,".
Welfare Reform Act 2009 (c. 24)	In section 32, in the section 20E to be inserted into the Jobseekers Act 1995– (a) subsection (1)(d) to (f); (b) in subsections (3)(a) and (4)(a), "or Schedule A1".
	In Schedule 7, in Part 3, the entry relating to Schedule A1 to the Jobseekers Act 1995.

Part 7 – Industrial Injuries Arising Before 5 July 1948

Short title and chapter	*Extent of repeal*
Social Security Administration Act 1992 (c. 5)	Section 164(4) and (5). In section 166(1)(b), the words "(except Part 1 of Schedule 8)". Section 188(3). In section 191, in the definition of "industrial injuries benefit", the words "other than under Schedule 8". Schedule 9.
Social Security (Consequential Provisions) Act 1992 (c. 6)	In Schedule 2, paragraph 55(1)(b) and (2)(b).

Part 8 – Social Fund: Ending of Discretionary Payments

Commencement Date – 1 April 2013 is the day appointed for the coming into force of Pt. 8 in relation to the repeals relating to: SSCBA 1992, s. 138, 139 and 140; SSAA 1992, s. 12 and 168; and SSA 1998, s. 8(1)(b), 9(1), 10(1), 36 and 38 (SI 2012/3090, art. 2(1)(d)).
1 August 2013 is the day appointed for the coming into force of Pt. 8 in relation to the repeals relating to: SSAA 1992, Sch. 4, Pt. 1; SSA 1998, s. 37 and FOIA 2000, Sch. 1, Pt. 6 (SI 2012/3090, art. 2(2)(d).

Short title and chapter	*Extent of repeal*
Social Security Contributions and Benefits Act 1992 (c. 4)	In section 138– (a) in subsection (1), the "and" preceding paragraph (b); (b) subsections (3) and (5). Sections 139 and 140.
Social Security Administration Act 1992 (c. 5)	Section 12. Section 71ZA. Section 78(1) to (3E) and (5) to (9). Section 168. In Schedule 4, in Part 1– (a) the heading "The Social Fund"; (b) under that heading, the entries relating to the social fund Commissioner, a social fund inspector and a member of any staff employed in connection with the social fund.
Social Security Act 1998 (c. 14)	Section 8(1)(b) (but not the "and" following it). In section 9(1), "Subject to section 36(3) below,". In section 10(1), "and section 36(3)". Sections 36 to 38. Section 70(2). Section 71. Section 75. In Schedule 7, paragraphs 72, 73 and 103.
Freedom of Information Act 2000 (c. 36)	In Schedule 1, in Part 6, the entry relating to the social fund Commissioner appointed under section 65 of the Social Security Administration Act 1992.
Welfare Reform Act 2012 (c. 5)	Sections 71 and 72. Section 106(2) and (4).

Part 9 – Disability Living Allowance

Short title and chapter	*Extent of repeal*
Social Security Contributions and Benefits Act 1992 (c. 4)	Section 30B(4)(b).
	Section 64(1A)(b).
	In section 150(2), paragraph (b) of the definition of "attendance allowance".
Social Security Administration Act 1992 (c. 5)	In section 150– (a) subsection (1)(b), and (b) in subsection (3)(b), the word "(b),".
	In Schedule 7, paragraph 1.
Finance Act 1994 (c. 9)	In paragraph 3(4)(b) of Schedule 7A, the words "section 71 of the Social Security Contributions and Benefits Act 1992 or".
Value Added Tax Act 1994 (c. 23)	In Part 2 of Schedule 7A, in sub-paragraph (2)(b) of note 6 to Group 3, the words "Part III of the Contributions and Benefits Act or".
	In Part 2 of Schedule 8, in paragraph (a) of note (7) to Group 12, the words "section 71 of the Social Security Contributions and Benefits Act 1992, or".
Social Security Act 1998 (c. 14)	In Schedule 3, paragraph 3(b).
Welfare Reform and Pensions Act 1999 (c. 30)	Section 67.
Capital Allowances Act 2001 (c. 2)	Section 268D(2)(a)(i).
Social Security Fraud Act 2001 (c. 11)	In section 6A(1), paragraph (d) of the definition of "sanctionable benefit".
Income Tax (Earnings and Pensions) Act 2003 (c. 1)	In section 677(1), in Part 1 of Table B, in the entry relating to disability living allowance, the words "SSCBA 1992 Section 71" (in the second column).
Pensions Act 2007 (c. 22)	In Schedule 1, paragraph 42.

Part 10 – Powers to Require Information Relating to Claims and Awards

Short title and chapter	*Extent of repeal*
Social Security Administration Act 1992 (c. 5)	Section 126A.
Social Security Act 1998 (c. 14)	Section 22(4).
	Section 74.
Welfare Reform and Pensions Act 1999 (c. 30)	In Schedule 8, paragraph 34(2)(c).

Part 11 – Recovery of Benefit Payments

Commencement Date – 1 April 2013 is the day appointed for the coming into force of Pt. 11 in relation to the repeals of SSAA 1992, s. 7(2)(a), s. 71(7) and (8) (SI 2013/358, art. 4(1)).
29 April 2013 is the day appointed for the coming into force of Pt. 11 in relation to the repeals of SSAA 1992, s. 71(10A) and (10B), and 71(11)(aa) and (ac) (subject to savings in relation to benefits referred to in s. 71(11)(aa) and (ac) which remain benefits to which SSAA 1992, s. 71 applies to the extent that they relate to an old style JSA award and a new style ESA award) (SI 2013/358, art. 5(4) and (6) (as amended by SI 2013/983, art. 23(4) and (5))).

Short title and chapter	*Extent of repeal*
Social Security Administration Act 1992 (c. 5)	Section 7(2)(a). In section 71– (a) subsection (7); (b) in subsection (8), "or (7)"; (c) subsections (10A) and (10B); (d) subsection (11)(aa) and (ac).

Part 12 – Loss of Benefit: Cautions

Short title and chapter	*Extent of repeal*
Social Security Administration Act 1992 (c. 5)	In section 115C(1)(d) (as inserted by section 116 of this Act) "or cautioned". In section 115D(1)(c) and (2)(c) (as inserted by section 116 of this Act) "or cautioned".
Social Security Fraud Act 2001 (c. 11)	In section 6B– (a) in subsection (11A)(c), "or (c)"; (b) in subsection (13), the words from "or the caution" to the end. In section 6C, subsection (4)(a)(ii) and the preceding "or". In sections 8(8)(a) and 9(8)(a), "or M being cautioned in relation to the offence to which the old agreement relates". In section 13, the definition of "cautioned".
State Pension Credit Act 2002 (c. 16)	In Schedule 2, paragraph 49.
Tax Credits Act 2002 (c. 21)	In section 36A (as inserted by section 120 of this Act)– (a) in subsection (7)(c) "or (c)"; (b) in subsection (10), in the definition of "disqualifying event", paragraph (c). In section 36B (as so inserted), subsection (4)(a)(ii) and the preceding "or". In section 67, the definition of "cautioned".
Welfare Reform Act 2012 (c. 5)	Section 120(5).

Part 13 – Information-sharing Between Secretary of State and HMRC

Short title and chapter	*Extent of repeal*
Social Security Administration Act 1992 (c. 5)	In section 121E– (a) in subsections (2) and (2ZA), the words "subject to subsection (2A),", "social security," and "or employment or training"; (b) subsection (2A). In section 121F– (a) in subsections (1) and (1A), the words "social security," and "or employment or training"; (b) in subsection (2), "(subject to subsection (2A))"; (c) subsection (2A). Sections 122 and 122ZA.
Finance Act 1997 (c. 16)	Section 110.
Social Security Contributions (Transfer of Functions, etc.) Act 1999 (c. 2)	In Schedule 6, paragraphs 2 and 10.
Tax Credits Act 2002 (c. 21).	In Schedule 5– (a) in paragraph 4(2) "social security or"; (b) paragraph 4(3) (c) in paragraph 4(3A) "social security,"; (d) in paragraph 4(3B), "social security or"; (e) in paragraph 4(4), "(3) and"; (f) in paragraph 6(1), "social security,"; (g) in paragraph 6(1A), "social security," (h) in paragraph 6(3) "social security or"; (i) paragraph 12(a).
Commissioners for Revenue and Customs Act 2005 (c. 11)	In Schedule 4, paragraph 45.

Part 14 – Standards of Decision-making

Commencement Date – 8 May 2012 is the day appointed for the coming into force of Pt. 14 (SI 2012/863, art. 2(3)(j)).

Short title and chapter	*Extent of repeal*
Pension Schemes Act 1993 (c. 48)	In section 171A– (a) in subsection (2), paragraph (b) and the preceding "or"; (b) in subsection (3), ", or annexed to,".

FINANCE ACT 2012

(2012 Chapter 14)

[*17th July 2012*]

ARRANGEMENT OF SECTIONS

PART 1 – INCOME TAX, CORPORATION TAX AND CAPITAL GAINS TAX

Chapter 2 – Income Tax: General

CHILD BENEFIT

8 High income child benefit charge

8 Schedule 1 contains provision for and in connection with a high income child benefit charge.

PART 9 – MISCELLANEOUS MATTERS

INCAPACITATED PERSONS AND MINORS

222 Removal of special provision for incapacitated persons and minors

222(1) [Not relevant to National Insurance contributions.]

222(2) [Not relevant to National Insurance contributions.]

222(3) [Not relevant to National Insurance contributions.]

222(4) In consequence of the amendments made by subsections (1) and (2)–

(a) [not relevant to National Insurance contributions,]

(b) [not relevant to National Insurance contributions,]

(c) [amends SSCBA 1992, Sch. 2, para. 5.]

(d) [not relevant to National Insurance contributions,]

(e) [not relevant to National Insurance contributions.]

222(5) The amendments made by subsections (1) and (4)(a) to (d) have effect for the tax year 2012–13 and subsequent tax years.

222(6) The amendments made by subsections (2) and (4)(e) have effect in relation to land transactions of which the effective date is on or after the day on which this Act is passed.

ADMINISTRATION

223 Tax agents: dishonest conduct

223(1) Schedule 38 contains provision about tax agents who engage in dishonest conduct.

223(2) That Schedule comes into force on such day as the Treasury may by order appoint.

223(3) An order under subsection (2)–

(a) may make different provision for different purposes, and

(b) may include transitional provision and savings.

223(4) The Treasury may by order make any incidental, supplemental, consequential, transitional or saving provision in consequence of Schedule 38.

223(5) An order under subsection (4) may–

(a) make different provision for different purposes, and

(b) make provision amending, repealing or revoking any provision made by or under an Act (whenever passed or made).

223(6) An order under this section is to be made by statutory instrument.

223(7) A statutory instrument containing an order under subsection (4) is subject to annulment in pursuance of a resolution of the House of Commons.

Commencement Date – The day appointed as the day on which Sch. 38 comes into force is 1 April 2013 (SI 2013/279, made under s. 223(2) and (3)).

PART 10 – FINAL PROVISIONS

228 Interpretation

228(1) In this Act–

"ALDA 1979" means the Alcoholic Liquor Duties Act 1979,

"BGDA 1981" means the Betting and Gaming Duties Act 1981,

"CAA 2001" means the Capital Allowances Act 2001,

"CEMA 1979" means the Customs and Excise Management Act 1979,

"CRCA 2005" means the Commissioners for Revenue and Customs Act 2005,

"CTA 2009" means the Corporation Tax Act 2009,

"CTA 2010" means the Corporation Tax Act 2010,

"F(No.3)A 2010" means the Finance (No. 3) Act 2010,

"HODA 1979" means the Hydrocarbon Oil Duties Act 1979,

"ICTA" means the Income and Corporation Taxes Act 1988,

"IHTA 1984" means the Inheritance Tax Act 1984,

"ITA 2007" means the Income Tax Act 2007,

"ITEPA 2003" means the Income Tax (Earnings and Pensions) Act 2003,

"ITTOIA 2005" means the Income Tax (Trading and Other Income) Act 2005,

"OTA 1975" means the Oil Taxation Act 1975,

"PRTA 1980" means the Petroleum Revenue Tax Act 1980,

"TCGA 1992" means the Taxation of Chargeable Gains Act 1992,

"TIOPA 2010" means the Taxation (International and Other Provisions) Act 2010,

"TMA 1970" means the Taxes Management Act 1970,

"TPDA 1979" means the Tobacco Products Duty Act 1979,

"VATA 1994" means the Value Added Tax Act 1994, and

"VERA 1994" means the Vehicle Excise and Registration Act 1994.

228(2) In this Act–

"FA", followed by a year, means the Finance Act of that year;

"F(No.2)A", followed by a year, means the Finance (No. 2) Act of that year.

229 Short title

229 This Act may be cited as the Finance Act 2012.

SCHEDULES

SCHEDULE 1 – HIGH INCOME CHILD BENEFIT CHARGE

Section 8

CONSEQUENTIAL AMENDMENTS

3 [Inserts SSAA 1992, s. 13A.]

COMMENCEMENT

7(1) The amendments made by this Schedule have effect for the tax year 2012–13 and subsequent tax years.

7(2) In relation to the tax year 2012–13, references in section 681B of ITEPA 2003 (as inserted by paragraph 1) to an amount to which a person is entitled in respect of child benefit for a week in the tax year do not include any amount to which the person is entitled in respect of child benefit for a week beginning before 7 January 2013.

7(3) In sub-paragraph (2), **"week"** means a period of 7 days beginning with a Monday.

SCHEDULE 38 – TAX AGENTS: DISHONEST CONDUCT

Section 223

Commencement Date – The day appointed as the day on which Sch. 38 comes into force is 1 April 2013 (SI 2013/279). The provisions of Sch. 38 apply in relation to Class 1, Class 1A, Class 1B and Class 2 National Insurance contributions as in relation to tax to the extent that they do not already apply, with effect from 6 April 2013 in relation to the tax year 2013–14 and subsequent tax years (SI 2013/622, reg. 41).

Other material – HMRC Factsheet TA/FS1: Tax agents: dishonest conduct.

Part 1 – Introduction

OVERVIEW

1 This Schedule is arranged as follows–

(a) this Part explains who is a tax agent and what it means to engage in dishonest conduct,

(b) Part 2 sets out the process for establishing whether someone is engaging in or has engaged in dishonest conduct,

(c) Part 3 confers power on HMRC to obtain relevant documents,

(d) Part 4 sets out sanctions for engaging in dishonest conduct,

(e) Part 5 provides for assessment of and appeals against penalties, and

(f) Parts 6 and 7 contain miscellaneous provisions and consequential amendments.

TAX AGENT

2(1) A **"tax agent"** is an individual who, in the course of business, assists other persons ("clients") with their tax affairs.

2(2) Individuals can be tax agents even if they (or the organisations for which they work) are appointed–

(a) indirectly, or

(b) at the request of someone other than the client.

2(3) Assistance with a client's tax affairs includes–

(a) advising a client in relation to tax, and

(b) acting or purporting to act as agent on behalf of a client in relation to tax.

2(4) Assistance with a client's tax affairs also includes assistance with any document that is likely to be relied on by HMRC to determine a client's tax position.

2(5) Assistance given for non-tax purposes counts as assistance with a client's tax affairs if it is given in the knowledge that it will be, or is likely to be, used by a client in connection with the client's tax affairs.

DISHONEST CONDUCT

3(1) An individual **"engages in dishonest conduct"** if, in the course of acting as a tax agent, the individual does something dishonest with a view to bringing about a loss of tax revenue.

3(2) It does not matter whether a loss is actually brought about.

3(3) Nor does it matter whether the individual is acting on the instruction of clients.

3(4) A loss of tax revenue would be brought about for these purposes if clients were to–

(a) account for less tax than they are required to account for by law,

(b) obtain more tax relief than they are entitled to obtain by law,

(c) account for tax later than they are required to account for it by law, or

(d) obtain tax relief earlier than they are entitled to obtain it by law.

3(5) **"Tax"** is defined in Part 6 of this Schedule.

3(6) **"Tax relief"** includes–

(a) any exemption from or deduction or credit against or in respect of tax, and

(b) any repayment of tax.

3(7) A reference in this paragraph to doing something dishonest includes–

(a) dishonestly omitting to do something, and

(b) advising or assisting a client to do something that the individual knows to be dishonest.

Part 2 – Establishing Dishonest Conduct

CONDUCT NOTICE

4(1) This paragraph applies if HMRC determine that an individual is engaging in or has engaged in dishonest conduct.

4(2) An authorised officer (or an officer of Revenue and Customs with the approval of an authorised officer) may notify the individual of that determination.

4(3) The notice must state the grounds on which the determination was made.

4(4) For the effect of notifying the individual, see paragraphs 7(2) and 29(2).

4(5) A notice under this paragraph is referred to as a **"conduct notice"**.

4(6) In relation to a conduct notice, a reference to **"the determination"** is to the determination forming the subject of the notice.

APPEAL AGAINST DETERMINATION

5(1) An individual to whom a conduct notice is given may appeal against the determination.

5(2) Notice of appeal must be given–

(a) in writing to the officer who gave the conduct notice, and

(b) within the period of 30 days beginning with the day on which the conduct notice was given.

5(3) It must state the grounds of appeal.

5(4) On an appeal that is notified to the tribunal, the tribunal may confirm or set aside the determination.

5(5) Subject to this paragraph, the provisions of Part 5 of TMA 1970 relating to appeals have effect in relation to an appeal under this paragraph as they have effect in relation to an appeal against an assessment to income tax.

5(6) Setting aside a determination does not prevent a further conduct notice being given in respect of the same conduct if further evidence emerges.

OFFENCE OF CONCEALMENT ETC IN CONNECTION WITH CONDUCT NOTICE

6(1) A person ("P") commits an offence if, after a relevant event has occurred, P–
(a) conceals, destroys or otherwise disposes of a material document, or
(b) arranges for the concealment, destruction or disposal of a material document.

6(2) A **"relevant event"** occurs if–
(a) a conduct notice is given to an individual, or
(b) an individual is informed by an officer of Revenue and Customs that a conduct notice will be or is likely to be given to the individual.

6(3) A **"material document"** is any document that could be sought under paragraph 8 as a result of the giving of the conduct notice.

6(4) If P acts after the event described in sub-paragraph (2)(a), no offence is committed if P acts–
(a) after the determination has been set aside,
(b) more than 4 years after the conduct notice was given, or
(c) without knowledge of that event.

6(5) If P acts before that event but after the event described in sub-paragraph (2)(b), no offence is committed if P acts–
(a) more than 2 years after the individual was, or was last, so informed, or
(b) without knowledge of the event described in sub-paragraph (2)(b).

6(6) P acts without knowledge of an event if P–
(a) is not the individual with respect to whom the event has occurred, and
(b) does not know, and could not reasonably be expected to know, that the event has occurred.

6(7) A person guilty of an offence under this paragraph is liable–
(a) on summary conviction, to a fine not exceeding the statutory maximum, and
(b) on conviction on indictment, to imprisonment for a term not exceeding 2 years or to a fine, or both.

Part 3 – Power to Obtain Tax Agent's Files etc

CIRCUMSTANCES IN WHICH POWER IS EXERCISABLE

7(1) The power in paragraph 8 is exercisable only in case A or case B and only with the approval of the tribunal.

7(2) Case A is where a conduct notice has been given to an individual and either–
(a) the time allowed for giving notice of appeal against the determination has expired without any such notice being given, or
(b) notice of appeal against the determination was given within that time, but the appeal has been withdrawn or the determination confirmed.

7(3) Case B is where–
(a) an individual has been convicted of an offence relating to tax that involves fraud or dishonesty,
(b) the offence was committed after the individual became a tax agent (whether or not the individual was still a tax agent when it was committed and regardless of the capacity in which it was committed),
(c) either–
  (i) the time allowed for appealing against the conviction has expired without any such appeal being brought, or
  (ii) an appeal against the conviction was brought within that time, but the appeal has been withdrawn or the conviction upheld, and
(d) no more than 12 months have elapsed since the date on which paragraph (c) was satisfied.

7(4) *For the purposes* of this paragraph, a determination or conviction that is appealed is not considered to have been confirmed or upheld until–
(a) the time allowed for bringing any further appeal has expired, or
(b) if a further appeal is brought within that time, that further appeal has been withdrawn or determined.

7(5) In this Schedule, a reference to **"the tax agent"** is–

(a) in a case falling within case A, a reference to the individual mentioned in sub-paragraph (2), and

(b) in a case falling within case B, a reference to the individual mentioned in sub-paragraph (3).

7(6) It does not matter whether the individual is still a tax agent when the power in paragraph 8 is to be exercised.

FILE ACCESS NOTICE

8(1) Subject to paragraph 7, an officer of Revenue and Customs may by notice in writing require any person mentioned in sub-paragraph (2) to provide relevant documents.

8(2) The persons are–

(a) the tax agent, and

(b) any other person the officer believes may hold relevant documents.

8(3) **"Relevant documents"** is defined in paragraph 9.

8(4) A notice under this paragraph is referred to as a **"file access notice"**.

8(5) The person to whom a file access notice is given is referred to as **"the document-holder"**.

RELEVANT DOCUMENTS

9(1) **"Relevant documents"** means the tax agent's working papers (whenever acting as a tax agent) and any other documents received, created, prepared or used by the tax agent for the purposes of or in the course of assisting clients with their tax affairs.

9(2) It does not matter who owns the papers or other documents.

9(3) The reference in sub-paragraph (1) to clients–

(a) includes former clients, and

(b) is not limited to the clients with respect to whom the tax agent is engaging in or has engaged in dishonest conduct.

CONTENT OF NOTICE

10(1) A file access notice may require the provision of–

(a) particular relevant documents specified in the notice, or

(b) all relevant documents in the document-holder's possession or power.

10(2) A file access notice does not need to identify the clients of the tax agent.

10(3) A file access notice addressed to anyone other than the tax agent must name the tax agent.

COMPLIANCE

11 A file access notice may require documents to be provided–

(a) within such period,

(b) by such means and in such form, and

(c) to such person and at such place,

as is reasonably specified in the notice or in a document referred to in the notice.

12 Unless otherwise specified in the notice, a file access notice may be complied with by providing copies of the relevant documents.

APPROVAL BY TRIBUNAL

13(1) The tribunal may not approve the giving of a file access notice unless–

(a) the application for approval is made by or with the agreement of an authorised officer,

(b) the tribunal is satisfied that the case falls within case A or case B (see paragraph 7),

(c) the tribunal is satisfied that, in the circumstances, the officer giving the notice is justified in doing so,

(d) the document-holder and (where different) the tax agent have been told that relevant documents are to be required and given a reasonable opportunity to make representations to an officer of Revenue and Customs, and

(e) the tribunal has been given a summary of any representations so made.

13(2) Nothing in sub-paragraph (1) requires the tribunal to determine whether an individual is engaging in or has engaged in dishonest conduct.

13(3) A decision by the tribunal under this paragraph is final (despite the provisions of sections 11 and 13 of the Tribunals, Courts and Enforcement Act 2007).

DOCUMENTS NOT IN PERSON'S POSSESSION OR POWER

14 A file access notice only requires the document-holder to provide a document if it is in the document-holder's possession or power.

TYPES OF INFORMATION

15(1) A file access notice does not require the document-holder to provide–

(a) parts of a document that contain information relating to the conduct of a pending appeal relating to tax, or

(b) journalistic material (as defined in section 13 of the Police and Criminal Evidence Act 1984).

15(2) A file access notice does not require the document-holder to provide personal records (as defined in section 12 of the Police and Criminal Evidence Act 1984).

15(3) But a file access notice may require the document-holder to provide documents that are personal records, omitting any information whose inclusion (whether alone or with other information) makes the original documents personal records.

OLD DOCUMENTS

16(1) A file access notice does not require the document-holder to provide a relevant document if–

(a) the whole of the document originated before the back-stop day, and

(b) no part of it has a bearing on tax periods ending on or after that day.

16(2) **"The back-stop day"** is the first day of the period of 20 years ending with the day on which the file access notice is given.

PRIVILEGED COMMUNICATIONS BETWEEN PROFESSIONAL LEGAL ADVISERS AND CLIENTS

17(1) A file access notice does not require the document-holder to provide any part of a document that is privileged.

17(2) For the purposes of this paragraph a document is privileged if it is a document in respect of which a claim to legal professional privilege, or (in Scotland) to confidentiality of communications between client and professional legal adviser, could be maintained in legal proceedings.

17(3) Regulations under paragraph 23 of Schedule 36 to FA 2008 (information powers: privileged communications) apply (with any necessary modifications) to disputes under this paragraph as to whether a document is privileged.

POWER TO COPY DOCUMENTS

18 If a document is provided pursuant to a file access notice, an officer of Revenue and Customs may take copies of or make extracts from the document.

POWER TO RETAIN DOCUMENTS

19(1) If a document is provided pursuant to a file access notice, HMRC may retain the document for a reasonable period if an officer of Revenue and Customs thinks it necessary to do so.

19(2) While a document is retained–

(a) the document-holder may, if the document is reasonably required for any purpose, request a copy of it, and

(b) *an officer* of Revenue and Customs must comply with such a request without charge.

19(3) The retention of a document under this paragraph is not to be regarded as breaking any lien claimed on the document.

19(4) If a document retained under this paragraph is lost or damaged, the Commissioners are liable to compensate the owner of the document for any expenses reasonably incurred in replacing or repairing the document.

APPEAL AGAINST FILE ACCESS NOTICE

20(1) If the document-holder is a person other than the tax agent, the document-holder may appeal against the file access notice, or any requirement in it, on the ground that it would be unduly onerous to comply with the notice or requirement.

20(2) Notice of appeal must be given–

(a) in writing to the officer by whom the file access notice was given, and

(b) within the period of 30 days beginning with the day on which the file access notice was given.

20(3) It must state the grounds of appeal.

20(4) On an appeal that is notified to the tribunal, the tribunal may confirm, vary or set aside the file access notice or a requirement in it.

20(5) If the tribunal confirms or varies the notice or a requirement in it, the document-holder must comply with the notice or requirement–

(a) within such period as is specified by the tribunal, or

(b) if the tribunal does not specify a period, within such period as is reasonably specified in writing by an officer of Revenue and Customs following the tribunal's decision.

20(6) A decision by the tribunal under this paragraph is final (despite the provisions of sections 11 and 13 of the Tribunals, Courts and Enforcement Act 2007).

20(7) Subject to this paragraph, the provisions of Part 5 of TMA 1970 relating to appeals have effect in relation to an appeal under this paragraph as they have effect in relation to an appeal against an assessment to income tax.

OFFENCE OF CONCEALMENT ETC IN CONNECTION WITH FILE ACCESS NOTICE

21(1) A person ("P") commits an offence if P–

(a) conceals, destroys or otherwise disposes of a required document, or

(b) arranges for the concealment, destruction or disposal of a required document.

21(2) A **"required document"** is a document within sub-paragraph (3) or sub-paragraph (4).

21(3) A document is within this sub-paragraph if at the time when P acts–

(a) P is required to provide the document by a file access notice, and

(b) either–

  (i) the notice has not been complied with, or

  (ii) it has been complied with, but P has been notified in writing by an officer of Revenue and Customs that P must continue to preserve the document (and the notification has not been withdrawn).

21(4) A document is within this sub-paragraph if at the time when P acts–

(a) P is not required to provide the document by a file access notice,

(b) P has been informed by an officer of Revenue and Customs that P will be or is likely to be so required, and

(c) no more than 6 months have elapsed since P was, or was last, so informed.

21(5) A person guilty of an offence under this paragraph is liable–

(a) on summary conviction, to a fine not exceeding the statutory maximum, and

(b) on conviction on indictment, to imprisonment for a term not exceeding 2 years or to a fine, or both.

PENALTY FOR FAILURE TO COMPLY

22(1) A person who fails to comply with a file access notice is liable to a penalty of £300.

22(2) *Failing to comply with a file access notice also includes–*

(a) concealing, destroying or otherwise disposing of a required document, or

(b) arranging for any such concealment, destruction or disposal.

22(3) **"Required document"** has the same meaning as in paragraph 21.

DAILY PENALTY FOR FAILURE TO COMPLY

23 If the failure continues after notification of a penalty under paragraph 22 has been issued, the person is liable to a further penalty, for each subsequent day on which the failure continues, of an amount not exceeding £60 for each such day.

FAILURE TO COMPLY WITH TIME LIMIT

24 A failure to do anything required to be done within a limited period of time does not give rise to liability to a penalty under paragraph 22 or 23 if the thing was done within such further time (if any) as an officer of Revenue and Customs may have allowed.

REASONABLE EXCUSE

25(1) Liability to a penalty under paragraph 22 or 23 does not arise if the person satisfies HMRC or (on an appeal notified to the tribunal) the tribunal that there is a reasonable excuse for the failure.

25(2) For the purposes of this paragraph–

(a) an insufficiency of funds is not a reasonable excuse unless attributable to events outside the person's control,

(b) if the person relies on another person to do anything, that is not a reasonable excuse unless the first person took reasonable care to avoid the failure,

(c) if the person had a reasonable excuse for the failure but the excuse has ceased, the person is to be treated as having continued to have the excuse if the failure is remedied without unreasonable delay after the excuse ceased.

Part 4 – Sanctions for Dishonest Conduct

PENALTY FOR DISHONEST CONDUCT

26(1) An individual who engages in dishonest conduct is liable to a penalty.

26(2) Subject to paragraph 27, the penalty to which the individual is liable is to be–

(a) no less than £5,000, and

(b) no more than £50,000.

26(3) In assessing the amount of the penalty, regard must be had to–

(a) whether the individual disclosed the dishonest conduct,

(b) whether that disclosure was prompted or unprompted,

(c) the quality of that disclosure, and

(d) the quality of the individual's compliance with any file access notice in connection with the dishonest conduct.

26(4) An individual **"discloses"** dishonest conduct by–

(a) telling HMRC about it,

(b) giving HMRC reasonable help in identifying the client or clients concerned and in quantifying the loss of tax revenue (if any) brought about by it, and

(c) allowing HMRC access to records for the purpose of ensuring that any such loss is recovered or otherwise properly accounted for.

26(5) A disclosure is **"unprompted"** if it is made at a time when the individual has no reason to believe that HMRC have discovered or are about to discover the dishonest conduct.

26(6) Otherwise, a disclosure is **"prompted"**.

26(7) In relation to disclosure or compliance, **"quality"** includes timing, nature and extent.

SPECIAL REDUCTION

27(1) This paragraph applies if HMRC propose to assess an individual to a penalty under paragraph 26 of £5,000.

27(2) If they think it right because of special circumstances, HMRC may take one or more of the following steps–

(a) reduce the penalty to an amount below £5,000 (which may be nil),

(b) stay the penalty, or

(c) agree a compromise in relation to proceedings for the penalty.

27(3) **"Special circumstances"** does not include–

(a) ability to pay, or

(b) the fact that a loss of tax revenue from a client is balanced by an overpayment by another person (whether or not a client).

POWER TO PUBLISH DETAILS

28(1) The Commissioners may publish information about an individual if the individual incurs a penalty under paragraph 26.

28(2) The information that may be published is–

(a) the individual's name (including any trading name, previous name or pseudonym),

(b) the individual's address,

(c) the nature of any business carried on by the individual,

(d) the amount of the penalty,

(e) the periods or times to which the dishonest conduct relates,

(f) any other information the Commissioners consider it appropriate to publish in order to make clear the individual's identity, and

(g) the link (if there is one) between the dishonest conduct and any inaccuracy, failure or action as a result of which information is published under section 94 of FA 2009 (which relates to deliberate tax defaulters).

28(3) No information may be published under this paragraph if the penalty incurred by the individual is £5,000 or less.

28(4) Subsections (5) to (9) and (11) of section 94 of FA 2009 apply to publishing information about an individual under this paragraph as they apply to publishing information about a person under that section.

28(5) If, in acting as a tax agent, the individual works or worked for an organisation, sub-paragraph (2)(f) includes power to publish such information about that organisation as the Commissioners consider appropriate in order to make clear the individual's identity.

28(6) Before publishing information about the organisation, the Commissioners must–

(a) inform the organisation that they are considering doing so, and

(b) afford the organisation reasonable opportunity to make representations about whether it should be published.

Part 5 – Penalties: Assessment etc

ASSESSMENT OF PENALTIES

29(1) If a person becomes liable to a penalty under Part 3 or 4 of this Schedule, HMRC may assess the penalty.

29(2) But, in the case of a penalty under Part 4, they may only do so if a conduct notice has been given to the person and either–

(a) the time allowed for giving notice of appeal against the determination has expired without notice of appeal being given, or

(b) notice of appeal against the determination was given within the time allowed, but the appeal has been withdrawn or the determination confirmed.

29(3) Paragraph 7(4) applies for the purposes of sub-paragraph (2)(b).

29(4) If HMRC assess a penalty, they must notify the person.

30(1) HMRC may not assess a penalty under this Schedule after the applicable deadline.

30(2) For a penalty under Part 3, the applicable deadline is the end of the period of 12 months beginning with the day on which the person became liable to the penalty.

30(3) For a penalty under Part 4, the applicable deadline is the end of the period of 12 months beginning with the later of–

(a) the first day on which HMRC may assess the penalty (see paragraph 29(2)), and

(b) day X.

30(4) If a loss of tax revenue is brought about by the dishonest conduct, day X is–

(a) the day immediately following the end of the appeal period for the assessment or determination of the tax revenue lost (or, if more than one client is involved, the end of the last such period), or

(b) if there is no such assessment or determination, the day on which the amount of tax revenue lost is ascertained.

30(5) Otherwise, day X is the day on which HMRC ascertain that no loss of tax revenue has been brought about by the dishonest conduct.

30(6) In sub-paragraph (4), **"appeal period"** means the period during which–

(a) an appeal could be brought, or

(b) an appeal that has been brought has not been withdrawn or determined.

APPEAL AGAINST PENALTY

31(1) A person may appeal against a decision of HMRC–

(a) that a penalty is payable under Part 3 of this Schedule, or

(b) as to the amount of a penalty payable under Part 3 or 4 of this Schedule.

31(2) Notice of appeal must be given–

(a) in writing to HMRC, and

(b) before the end of the period of 30 days beginning with the day on which notification of the penalty was issued.

31(3) It must state the grounds of appeal.

31(4) On an appeal under sub-paragraph (1)(a) that is notified to the tribunal, the tribunal may confirm or cancel the decision.

31(5) On an appeal under sub-paragraph (1)(b) that is notified to the tribunal, the tribunal may–

(a) confirm the decision, or

(b) substitute for the decision another decision that HMRC had power to make.

31(6) If, in the case of an appeal against a penalty under Part 4, the tribunal substitutes its decision for HMRC's, the tribunal may rely on paragraph 27 (special reduction)–

(a) to the same extent as HMRC (which may mean applying the same reduction as HMRC to a different starting point), or

(b) to a different extent, but only if the tribunal thinks that HMRC's decision in respect of the application of that paragraph was flawed (when considered in the light of the principles applicable in proceedings for judicial review).

31(7) Subject to this paragraph and paragraph 32, the provisions of Part 5 of TMA 1970 relating to appeals have effect in relation to an appeal under this paragraph as they have effect in relation to an appeal against an assessment to income tax.

ENFORCEMENT OF PENALTY

32(1) A penalty under this Schedule must be paid–

(a) before the end of the period of 30 days beginning with the day on which notification of the penalty was issued, or

(b) if a notice of appeal under paragraph 31 is given, before the end of the period of 30 days beginning with the day on which the appeal is withdrawn or determined.

32(2) A penalty under this Schedule may be enforced as if it were income tax charged in an assessment and due and payable.

DOUBLE JEOPARDY

33 A person is not liable to a penalty under this Schedule in respect of anything in respect of which the person has been convicted of an offence.

34(1) A person is not liable to a penalty under this Schedule in respect of anything in respect of which the person is personally liable to a penalty under–

(a) Schedule 24 to FA 2007 (penalties for errors),

(b) Schedule 41 to FA 2008 (penalties for failure to notify etc), or

(c) Schedule 55 to FA 2009 (penalties for failure to make a return etc).

34(2) Sub-paragraph (1) applies where, for example, the person is personally liable by virtue of section 48(3) of VATA 1994 (VAT representatives).

POWER TO CHANGE AMOUNT OF PENALTIES

35(1) If it appears to the Treasury that there has been a change in the value of money since the last relevant day, they may by regulations substitute for the sums for the time being specified in paragraphs 22(1), 23, 26(2), 27(1) and (2)(a) and 28(3) such other sums as appear to them to be justified by the change.

35(2) **"Relevant day"**, in relation to a specified sum, means–
(a) the day on which this Act is passed, and
(b) each day on which the power conferred by sub-paragraph (1) has been exercised in relation to that sum.

35(3) Regulations under this paragraph do not apply to a failure or conduct that began before the day on which they come into force.

35(4) The power to make regulations under this paragraph is exercisable by statutory instrument.

35(5) A statutory instrument containing regulations under this paragraph is subject to annulment in pursuance of a resolution of the House of Commons.

Part 6 – Miscellaneous Provision and Interpretation

APPLICATION OF PROVISIONS OF TMA 1970

36 Subject to the provisions of this Schedule, the following provisions of TMA 1970 apply for the purposes of this Schedule as they apply for the purposes of the Taxes Acts–
(a) section 108 (responsibility of company officers),
(b) section 114 (want of form), and
(c) section 115 (delivery and service of documents).

TAX

37(1) **"Tax"** means–
(a) income tax,
(b) capital gains tax,
(c) corporation tax,
(d) construction industry deductions,
(e) VAT,
(f) insurance premium tax,
(g) inheritance tax,
(h) stamp duty land tax,
(i) stamp duty reserve tax,
(j) petroleum revenue tax,
(k) aggregates levy,
(l) climate change levy,
(la) apprenticeship levy,
(m) landfill tax, and
(n) any duty of excise other than vehicle excise duty.

37(2) **"Construction industry deductions"** means construction industry deductions under Chapter 3 of Part 3 of FA 2004.

37(3) **"Corporation tax"** includes an amount assessable or chargeable as if it were corporation tax.

37(4) **"VAT"** means–
(a) value added tax charged in accordance with VATA 1994,
(b) amounts recoverable under paragraph 5(2) of Schedule 11 to that Act (amounts shown on invoices as VAT), and
(c) amounts treated as VAT by virtue of regulations under section 54 of that Act (farmers etc).

History – S. 37(1)(la) inserted by FA 2016, s. 115, with effect from 15 September 2016 (Royal Assent).

GENERAL INTERPRETATION

38 In this Schedule–

"appointed" includes engaged;

"client" (except in paragraph 17)–
(a) has the meaning given in paragraph 2(1), and
(b) in relation to a particular tax agent, means a client of that tax agent;

"the Commissioners" means the Commissioners for Her Majesty's Revenue and Customs;

"conduct notice" has the meaning given in paragraph 4;

"the document-holder" has the meaning given in paragraph 8;

"document" includes a copy of a document (see also section 114 of FA 2008);

"file access notice" has the meaning given in paragraph 8;

"HMRC" means Her Majesty's Revenue and Customs;

"organisation" includes any person or firm carrying on a business;

"specify" includes describe;

"tax period" means a tax year, accounting period or other period in respect of which tax is charged;

"the tribunal" means the First-tier Tribunal or, where determined by or under the Tribunal Procedure Rules, the Upper Tribunal.

39(1) A reference in this Schedule to clients of a tax agent (or to a tax agent's clients) is a reference to the persons whom the agent assists with their tax affairs.

39(2) Sub-paragraph (1) applies even if–

(a) the agent works for an organisation, and

(b) it is the organisation that is appointed to give the assistance.

40 A loss of tax revenue is taken for the purposes of this Schedule to be (or to be capable of being) brought about by dishonest conduct despite the fact that the loss can be recovered or properly accounted for (following discovery of the conduct or otherwise).

41 A reference in this Schedule to working for an organisation includes being a partner or member of an organisation.

42 A reference in a provision of this Schedule to an authorised officer is to an officer of Revenue and Customs who is, or is a member of a class of officers who are, authorised by the Commissioners for the purposes of that provision.

RELATIONSHIP WITH OTHER ENACTMENTS

43 Nothing in this Schedule limits–

(a) any liability a person may have under any other enactment in respect of conduct in respect of which a person is liable to a penalty under this Schedule, or

(b) any power a person may have under any other enactment to obtain relevant documents.

Part 7 – Consequential Provisions

SOCIAL SECURITY CONTRIBUTIONS AND BENEFITS ACT 1992

53 [Amends SSCBA 1992, s. 16(1)(c).]

54 In paragraph 7B of Schedule 1 to that Act (collection of contributions other than through PAYE system), the reference in sub-paragraph (5A) to Part 10 of TMA 1970 includes a reference to this Schedule.

SOCIAL SECURITY ADMINISTRATION ACT 1992

56 [Inserts SSAA 1992, s. 110ZA.]

FINANCE ACT 2013

(2013 Chapter 29)

[*17th July 2013*]

ARRANGEMENT OF SECTIONS

PART 5 – GENERAL ANTI-ABUSE RULE

PART 6 – OTHER PROVISIONS

ADMINISTRATION

PART 7 – FINAL PROVISIONS

SCHEDULES

PART 5 – GENERAL ANTI-ABUSE RULE

Cross references – NICA 2014, s. 10(1): references in Pt. 5 to tax include references to national insurance contributions, where tax arrangements are entered into on or after 13 March 2014.

Other material – Misc. 02/2015: HMRC general anti-abuse rule (GAAR) guidance.

206 General anti-abuse rule

206(1) This Part has effect for the purpose of counteracting tax advantages arising from tax arrangements that are abusive.

206(2) The rules of this Part are collectively to be known as "the general anti-abuse rule".

206(3) The general anti-abuse rule applies to the following taxes–

(a) income tax,

(b) corporation tax, including any amount chargeable as if it were corporation tax or treated as if it were corporation tax,

(c) capital gains tax,

(d) petroleum revenue tax,
(da) diverted profits tax,
(db) apprenticeship levy,
(e) inheritance tax,
(f) stamp duty land tax, and
(g) annual tax on enveloped dwellings.

History – S. 206(3)(da) inserted by FA 2015, s. 115(1), with effect in relation to accounting periods beginning on or after 1 April 2015 (subject to the provisions of FA 2015, s. 116(2)–(5)).
S. 206(3)(db) inserted by FA 2016, s. 104(2), with effect from 15 September 2016 (Royal Assent).

Cross references – NICA 2014, s. 10(2): s. 206(3) has effect as if it included national insurance contributions, where tax arrangements are entered into on or after 13 March 2014.

207 Meaning of "tax arrangements" and "abusive"

207(1) Arrangements are **"tax arrangements"** if, having regard to all the circumstances, it would be reasonable to conclude that the obtaining of a tax advantage was the main purpose, or one of the main purposes, of the arrangements.

207(2) Tax arrangements are **"abusive"** if they are arrangements the entering into or carrying out of which cannot reasonably be regarded as a reasonable course of action in relation to the relevant tax provisions, having regard to all the circumstances including–
(a) whether the substantive results of the arrangements are consistent with any principles on which those provisions are based (whether express or implied) and the policy objectives of those provisions,
(b) whether the means of achieving those results involves one or more contrived or abnormal steps, and
(c) whether the arrangements are intended to exploit any shortcomings in those provisions.

207(3) Where the tax arrangements form part of any other arrangements regard must also be had to those other arrangements.

207(4) Each of the following is an example of something which might indicate that tax arrangements are abusive–
(a) the arrangements result in an amount of income, profits or gains for tax purposes that is significantly less than the amount for economic purposes,
(b) the arrangements result in deductions or losses of an amount for tax purposes that is significantly greater than the amount for economic purposes, and
(c) the arrangements result in a claim for the repayment or crediting of tax (including foreign tax) that has not been, and is unlikely to be, paid,

but in each case only if it is reasonable to assume that such a result was not the anticipated result when the relevant tax provisions were enacted.

207(5) The fact that tax arrangements accord with established practice, and HMRC had, at the time the arrangements were entered into, indicated its acceptance of that practice, is an example of something which might indicate that the arrangements are not abusive.

207(6) The examples given in subsections (4) and (5) are not exhaustive.

Cross references – NICA 2014, s. 10(3): s. 207(4)(a) has effect as if it included the words "earnings (within the meaning of Part 1 of the Social Security Contributions and Benefits Act 1992 or Part 1 of the Social Security Contributions and Benefits (Northern Ireland) Act 1992)," after the words "income", where tax arrangements are entered into on or after 13 March 2014.

208 Meaning of "tax advantage"

208 A **"tax advantage"** includes–
(a) relief or increased relief from tax,
(b) repayment or increased repayment of tax,
(c) avoidance or reduction of a charge to tax or an assessment to tax,
(d) avoidance of a possible assessment to tax,
(e) deferral of a payment of tax or advancement of a repayment of tax, and
(f) avoidance of an obligation to deduct or account for tax.

Cross references – NICA 2014, s. 10(1): references in Pt. 5 to tax include references to national insurance contributions, where tax arrangements are entered into on or after 13 March 2014.

209 Counteracting the tax advantages

209(1) If there are tax arrangements that are abusive, the tax advantages that would (ignoring this Part) arise from the arrangements are to be counteracted by the making of adjustments.

209(2) The adjustments required to be made to counteract the tax advantages are such as are just and reasonable.

209(3) The adjustments may be made in respect of the tax in question or any other tax to which the general anti-abuse rule applies.

209(4) The adjustments that may be made include those that impose or increase a liability to tax in any case where (ignoring this Part) there would be no liability or a smaller liability, and tax is to be charged in accordance with any such adjustment.

209(5) Any adjustments required to be made under this section (whether by an officer of Revenue and Customs or the person to whom the tax advantage would arise) may be made by way of an assessment, the modification of an assessment, amendment or disallowance of a claim, or otherwise.

209(6) But–

(a) no steps may be taken by an officer of Revenue and Customs by virtue of this section unless the procedural requirements of Schedule 43, 43A or 43B have been complied with, and

(b) the power to make adjustments by virtue of this section is subject to any time limit imposed by or under any enactment other than this Part.

209(7) Any adjustments made under this section have effect for all purposes.

209(8) Where a matter is referred to the GAAR Advisory Panel under paragraph 5 or 6 of Schedule 43, the taxpayer (as defined in paragraph 3 of that Schedule) must not make any GAAR-related adjustments in relation to the taxpayer's tax affairs in the period (the "closed period") which–

(a) begins with the 31st day after the end of the 45 day period mentioned in paragraph 4(1) of that Schedule, and

(b) ends immediately before the day on which the taxpayer is given the notice under paragraph 12 of Schedule 43 (notice of final decision after considering opinion of GAAR Advisory Panel).

209(9) Where a person has been given a pooling notice or a notice of binding under Schedule 43A in relation to any tax arrangements, the person must not make any GAAR-related adjustments in the period ("the closed period") that–

(a) begins with the 31st day after that on which that notice is given, and

(b) ends–

(i) in the case of a pooling notice, immediately before the day on which the person is given a notice under paragraph 8(2) or 9(2) of Schedule 43A, or a notice under paragraph 8(2) of Schedule 43B, in relation to the tax arrangements (notice of final decision after considering opinion of GAAR Advisory Panel), or

(ii) in the case of a notice of binding, with the 30th day after the day on which the notice is given.

209(10) In this section **"GAAR-related adjustments"** means–

(a) for the purposes of subsection (8), adjustments which give effect (wholly or in part) to the proposed counteraction set out in the notice under paragraph 3 of Schedule 43;

(b) for the purposes of subsection (9), adjustments which give effect (wholly or partly) to the proposed counteraction set out in the notice of pooling or binding (as the case may be).

History – In s. 209(6)(a), the words", 43A or 43B" inserted by FA 2016, s. 157(4), with effect in relation to tax arrangements (within the meaning of FA 2013, Pt. 5) entered into at any time (whether before or on or after 15 September 2016).
S. 209(8)–(10) inserted by FA 2016, s. 158(4), with effect in relation to tax arrangements (within the meaning of FA 2013, Pt. 5) entered into on or after 15 September 2016.

Cross references – NICA 2014, s. 10(4): s. 209 application in respect of national insurance contributions, where tax arrangements are entered into on or after 13 March 2014.

209A Effect of adjustments specified in a provisional counteraction notice

209A(1) Adjustments made by an officer of Revenue and Customs which–

(a) are specified in a provisional counteraction notice given to a person by the officer (and have not been cancelled: see sections 209B to 209E),

(b) are made in respect of a tax advantage that would (ignoring this Part) arise from tax arrangements that are abusive, and

(c) but for section 209(6)(a), would have effected a valid counteraction of that tax advantage under section 209,

are treated for all purposes as effecting a valid counteraction of the tax advantage under that section.

209A(2) A **"provisional counteraction notice"** is a notice which–

(a) specifies adjustments (the "notified adjustments") which the officer reasonably believes may be required under section 209(1) to counteract a tax advantage that would (ignoring this Part) arise to the person from tax arrangements;

(b) specifies the arrangements and the tax advantage concerned, and

(c) notifies the person of the person's rights of appeal with respect to the notified adjustments (when made) and contains a statement that if an appeal is made against the making of the adjustments–

(i) no steps may be taken in relation to the appeal unless and until the person is given a notice referred to in section 209F(2), and

(ii) the notified adjustments will be cancelled if HMRC fails to take at least one of the actions mentioned in section 209B(4) within the period specified in section 209B(2).

209A(3) It does not matter whether the notice is given before or at the same time as the making of the adjustments.

209A(4) In this section **"adjustments"** includes adjustments made in any way permitted by section 209(5).

History – S. 209A inserted by FA 2016, s. 156(1), with effect in relation to tax arrangements (within the meaning of FA 2013, Pt. 5) entered into at any time (whether before or on or after 15 September 2016).

209B Notified adjustments: 12 month period for taking action if appeal made

209B(1) This section applies where a person (the "taxpayer") to whom a provisional counteraction notice has been given appeals against the making of the notified adjustments.

209B(2) The notified adjustments are to be treated as cancelled with effect from the end of the period of 12 months beginning with the day on which the provisional counteraction notice is given unless an action mentioned in subsection (4) is taken before that time.

209B(3) For the purposes of subsection (2) it does not matter whether the action mentioned in subsection (4)(c), (d) or (e) is taken before or after the provisional counteraction notice is given (but if that action is taken before the provisional counteraction notice is given subsection (5) does not have effect).

209B(4) The actions are–

(a) an officer of Revenue and Customs notifying the taxpayer that the notified adjustments are cancelled;

(b) an officer of Revenue and Customs giving the taxpayer written notice of the withdrawal of the provisional counteraction notice (without cancelling the notified adjustments);

(c) a designated HMRC officer giving the taxpayer a notice under paragraph 3 of Schedule 43 which–

(i) specifies the arrangements and the tax advantage which are specified in the provisional counteraction notice, and

(ii) specifies the notified adjustments (or lesser adjustments) as the counteraction that the officer considers ought to be taken (see paragraph 3(2)(c) of that Schedule);

(d) a designated HMRC officer giving the taxpayer a notice of binding under paragraph 1 of Schedule 43A which–

(i) specifies the arrangements and the tax advantage which are specified in the provisional counteraction notice, and

(ii) specifies the notified adjustments (or lesser adjustments) as the counteraction that the officer considers ought to be taken (see paragraph 1(4)(c) of that Schedule);

(e) a designated HMRC officer giving the taxpayer a notice under paragraph 1(2) of Schedule 43B which–

(i) specifies the arrangements and the tax advantage which are specified in the provisional counteraction notice, and

(ii) specifies the notified adjustments (or lesser adjustments) as the counteraction that the officer considers ought to be taken.

209B(5) In a case within subsection (4)(c), (d) or (e), if–

(a) the notice under paragraph 3 of Schedule 43, or

(b) the pooling notice or notice of binding, or

(c) the notice under paragraph 1(2) of Schedule 43B,

(as the case may be) specifies lesser adjustments the officer must modify the notified adjustments accordingly.

209B(6) The officer may not take the action in subsection (4)(b) unless the officer was authorised to make the notified adjustments otherwise than under this Part.

209B(7) In this section **"lesser adjustments"** means adjustments which assume a smaller tax advantage than was assumed in the provisional counteraction notice.

History – S. 209B inserted by FA 2016, s. 156(1), with effect in relation to tax arrangements (within the meaning of FA 2013, Pt. 5) entered into at any time (whether before or on or after 15 September 2016).

209C Notified adjustments: case within section 209B(4)(c)

209C(1) This section applies if the action in section 209B(4)(c) (notice to taxpayer of proposed counteraction of tax advantage) is taken.

209C(2) If the matter is not referred to the GAAR Advisory Panel, the notified adjustments are to be treated as cancelled with effect from the date of the designated HMRC officer's decision under paragraph 6(2) of Schedule 43 unless the notice under paragraph 6(3) of Schedule 43 states that the adjustments are not to be treated as cancelled under this section.

209C(3) A notice under paragraph 6(3) of Schedule 43 may not contain the statement referred to in subsection (2) unless HMRC would have been authorised to make the adjustments if the general anti-abuse rule did not have effect.

209C(4) If the taxpayer is given a notice under paragraph 12 of Schedule 43 which states that the specified tax advantage is not to be counteracted under the general anti-abuse rule, the notified adjustments are to be treated as cancelled unless that notice states that those adjustments are not to be treated as cancelled under this section.

209C(5) A notice under paragraph 12 of Schedule 43 may not contain the statement referred to in subsection (4) unless HMRC would have been authorised to make the adjustments if the general anti-abuse rule did not have effect.

209C(6) If the taxpayer is given a notice under paragraph 12 of Schedule 43 stating that the specified tax advantage is to be counteracted–

(a) the notified adjustments are confirmed only so far as they are specified in that notice as adjustments required to give effect to the counteraction, and

(b) so far as they are not confirmed, the notified adjustments are to be treated as cancelled.

History – S. 209C inserted by FA 2016, s. 156(1), with effect in relation to tax arrangements (within the meaning of FA 2013, Pt. 5) entered into at any time (whether before or on or after 15 September 2016).

209D Notified adjustments: case within section 209B(4)(d)

209D(1) This section applies if the action in section 209B(4)(d) (notice of binding) is taken.

209D(2) If the taxpayer is given a notice under paragraph 8(2) or 9(2) of Schedule 43A which states that the specified tax advantage is not to be counteracted under the general anti-abuse rule, the notified adjustments are to be treated as cancelled, unless that notice states that those adjustments are not to be treated as cancelled under this section.

209D(3) A notice under paragraph 8(2) or 9(2) of Schedule 43A may not contain the statement referred to in subsection (2) unless HMRC would have been authorised to make the adjustments if the general anti-abuse rule did not have effect.

209D(4) If the taxpayer is given a notice under paragraph 8(2) or 9(2) of Schedule 43A stating that the specified tax advantage is to be counteracted–

(a) the notified adjustments are confirmed only so far as they are specified in that notice as adjustments required to give effect to the counteraction, and

(b) so far as they are not confirmed, the notified adjustments are to be treated as cancelled.

History – S. 209D inserted by FA 2016, s. 156(1), with effect in relation to tax arrangements (within the meaning of FA 2013, Pt. 5) entered into at any time (whether before or on or after 15 September 2016).

209E Notified adjustments: case within section 209B(4)(e)

209E(1) This section applies if the action in section 209B(4)(e) (notice of proposal to make generic referral) is taken.

209E(2) If the notice under paragraph 1(2) of Schedule 43B is withdrawn, the notified adjustments are to be treated as cancelled unless the notice of withdrawal states that the adjustments are not to be treated as cancelled under this section.

209E(3) The notice of withdrawal may not contain the statement referred to in subsection (2) unless HMRC was authorised to make the notified adjustments otherwise than under this Part.

209E(4) If the taxpayer is given a notice under paragraph 8(2) of Schedule 43B, which states that the specified tax advantage is not to be counteracted under the general anti-abuse rule, the notified adjustments are to be treated as cancelled, unless that notice states that those adjustments are not to be treated as cancelled under this section.

209E(5) A notice under paragraph 8(2) of Schedule 43B may not contain the statement referred to in subsection (4) unless HMRC was authorised to make the adjustments otherwise than under this Part.

209E(6) If the taxpayer is given a notice under paragraph 8(2) of Schedule 43B stating that the specified tax advantage is to be counteracted–

(a) the notified adjustments are confirmed only so far as they are specified in that notice as adjustments required to give effect to the counteraction, and

(b) so far as they are not confirmed, the notified adjustments are to be treated as cancelled.

History – S. 209E inserted by FA 2016, s. 156(1), with effect in relation to tax arrangements (within the meaning of FA 2013, Pt. 5) entered into at any time (whether before or on or after 15 September 2016).

209F Appeals against provisional counteractions: further provision

209F(1) Subsections (2) to (5) have effect in relation to an appeal by a person ("the taxpayer") against the making of adjustments which are specified in a provisional counteraction notice.

209F(2) No steps after the initial notice of appeal are to be taken in relation to the appeal unless and until the taxpayer is given–

(a) a notice under section 209B(4)(b),

(b) a notice under paragraph 6(3) of Schedule 43 (notice of decision not to refer matter to GAAR advisory panel) containing the statement described in section 209C(2) (statement that adjustments are not to be treated as cancelled),

(c) a notice under paragraph 12 of Schedule 43, or

(d) a notice under paragraph 8(2) or 9(2) of Schedule 43A,

(e) a notice under paragraph 8 of Schedule 43B,

in respect of the tax arrangements concerned.

209F(3) The taxpayer has until the end of the period mentioned in subsection (4) to comply with any requirement to specify the grounds of appeal.

209F(4) The period mentioned in subsection (3) is the 30 days beginning with the day on which the taxpayer receives the notice mentioned in subsection (2).

209F(5) In subsection (2) the reference to **"steps"** does not include the withdrawal of the appeal.

History – S. 209F inserted by FA 2016, s. 156(1), with effect in relation to tax arrangements (within the meaning of FA 2013, Pt. 5) entered into at any time (whether before or on or after 15 September 2016).

210 Consequential relieving adjustments

210(1) This section applies where–

(a) the counteraction of a tax advantage under section 209 is final, and

(b) if the case is not one in which notice of the counteraction was given under paragraph 12 of Schedule 43, paragraph 8 or 9 of Schedule 43A or paragraph 8 of Schedule 43B, HMRC have been notified of the counteraction by the taxpayer.

210(2) A person has 12 months, beginning with the day on which the counteraction becomes final, to make a claim for one or more consequential adjustments to be made in respect of any tax to which the general anti-abuse rule applies.

210(3) On a claim under this section, an officer of Revenue and Customs must make such of the consequential adjustments claimed (if any) as are just and reasonable.

210(4) Consequential adjustments–

(a) may be made in respect of any period, and

(b) may affect any person (whether or not a party to the tax arrangements).

210(5) But nothing in this section requires or permits an officer to make a consequential adjustment the effect of which is to increase a person's liability to any tax.

210(6) For the purposes of this section–

(a) if the claim relates to income tax or capital gains tax, Schedule 1A to TMA 1970 applies to it;

(b) if the claim relates to corporation tax, Schedule 1A to TMA 1970 (and not Schedule 18 to FA 1998) applies to it;

(c) if the claim relates to petroleum revenue tax, Schedule 1A to TMA 1970 applies to it, but as if the reference in paragraph 2A(4) of that Schedule to a year of assessment included a reference to a chargeable period within the meaning of OTA 1975 (see section 1(3) and (4) of that Act);

(d) if the claim relates to inheritance tax it must be made in writing to HMRC and section 221 of IHTA 1984 applies as if the claim were a claim under that Act;

(e) if the claim relates to stamp duty land tax or annual tax on enveloped dwellings, Schedule 11A to FA 2003 applies to it as if it were a claim to which paragraph 1 of that Schedule applies.

210(7) Where an officer of Revenue and Customs makes a consequential adjustment under this section, the officer must give the person who made the claim written notice describing the adjustment which has been made.

210(8) For the purposes of this section the counteraction of a tax advantage is final when the adjustments made to effect the counteraction, and any amounts arising as a result of those adjustments, can no longer be varied, on appeal or otherwise.

210(9) Any adjustments required to be made under this section may be made–

(a) by way of an assessment, the modification of an assessment, the amendment of a claim, or otherwise, and

(b) despite any time limit imposed by or under any enactment other than this Part.

210(10) In this section **"the taxpayer"**, in relation to a counteraction of a tax advantage under section 209, means the person to whom the tax advantage would have arisen.

History – In s. 210(1)(b), the words "paragraph 8 or 9 of Schedule 43A or paragraph 8 of Schedule 43B," inserted by FA 2016, s. 157(5), with effect in relation to tax arrangements (within the meaning of FA 2013, Pt. 5) entered into at any time (whether before or on or after 15 September 2016).

Cross references – NICA 2014, s. 10(5) and (6): s. 210 application in respect of national insurance contributions, where tax arrangements are entered into on or after 13 March 2014.

211 Proceedings before a court or tribunal

211(1) In proceedings before a court or tribunal in connection with the general anti-abuse rule, HMRC must show–

(a) that there are tax arrangements that are abusive, and

(b) that the adjustments made to counteract the tax advantages arising from the arrangements are just and reasonable.

211(2) In determining any issue in connection with the general anti-abuse rule, a court or tribunal must take into account–

(a) HMRC's guidance about the general anti-abuse rule that was approved by the GAAR Advisory Panel at the time the tax arrangements were entered into, and

(b) any opinion of the GAAR Advisory Panel given–

(i) under paragraph 11 of Schedule 43 about the arrangements or any tax arrangements which are, as a result of a notice under paragraph 1 or 2 of Schedule 43A, the referred or (as the case may be) counteracted arrangements in relation to the arrangements, or

(ii) under paragraph 6 of Schedule 43B in respect of a generic referral of the arrangements.

211(3) In determining any issue in connection with the general anti-abuse rule, a court or tribunal may take into account–

(a) guidance, statements or other material (whether of HMRC, a Minister of the Crown or anyone else) that was in the public domain at the time the arrangements were entered into, and

(b) evidence of established practice at that time.

History – S. 211(2)(b)(i) and (ii) and the words "Panel given–" before them substituted for the words "Panel about the arrangements (see paragraph 11 of Schedule 43)." by FA 2016, s. 157(6), with effect in relation to tax arrangements (within the meaning of FA 2013, Pt. 5) entered into at any time (whether before or on or after 15 September 2016).

Cross references – NICA 2014, s. 10(1): references in Pt. 5 to tax include references to national insurance contributions, where tax arrangements are entered into on or after 13 March 2014.

212 Relationship between the GAAR and priority rules

212(1) Any priority rule has effect subject to the general anti-abuse rule (despite the terms of the priority rule).

212(2) A **"priority rule"** means a rule (however expressed) to the effect that particular provisions have effect to the exclusion of, or otherwise in priority to, anything else.

212(3) Examples of priority rules are–

(a) the rule in section 464, 699 or 906 of CTA 2009 (priority of loan relationships rules, derivative contracts rules and intangible fixed assets rules for corporation tax purposes), and

(b) the rule in section 6(1) of TIOPA 2010 (effect to be given to double taxation arrangements despite anything in any enactment).

Cross references – NICA 2014, s. 10(1): references in Pt. 5 to tax include references to national insurance contributions, where tax arrangements are entered into on or after 13 March 2014.

212A Penalty

212A(1) A person (P) is liable to pay a penalty if–

(a) (P) has been given a notice under
  (i) paragraph 12 of Schedule 43,
  (ii) paragraph 8 or 9 of Schedule 43A, or
  (iii) paragraph 8 of Schedule 43B,

stating that a tax advantage arising from particular tax arrangements is to be counteracted,

(b) a tax document has been given to HMRC on the basis that the tax advantage arises to P from those arrangements,

(c) that document was given to HMRC–
  (i) by P, or
  (ii) by another person in circumstances where P knew, or ought to have known, that the other person gave the document on the basis mentioned in paragraph (c), and

(d) the tax advantage has been counteracted by the making of adjustments under section 209.

212A(2) The penalty is 60% of the value of the counteracted advantage.

212A(3) Schedule 43C–

(a) gives the meaning of **"the value of the counteracted advantage"**, and

(b) makes other provision in relation to penalties under this section.

212A(4) In this section **"tax document"** means any return, claim or other document submitted in compliance (or purported compliance) with any provision of, or made under, an Act.

212A(5) In this section the reference to giving a tax document to HMRC is to be interpreted in accordance with paragraph 11(g) and (h) of Schedule 43C.

History – S. 212A inserted by FA 2016, s. 158(2). with effect in relation to tax arrangements (within the meaning of FA 2013, Pt. 5) entered into on or after 15 September 2016.

213 Consequential amendment

213(1) Section 42 of TMA 1970 (procedure for making claims etc) is amended as follows.

213(2) [Amends TMA 1970, s. 42(2).]

213(3) [Inserts TMA 1970, s. 42(3ZC).]

Cross references – NICA 2014, s. 10(1): references in Pt. 5 to tax include references to national insurance contributions, where tax arrangements are entered into on or after 13 March 2014.

214 Interpretation of Part 5

214(1) In this Part–

"abusive", in relation to tax arrangements, has the meaning given by section 207(2) to (6);

"arrangements" includes any agreement, understanding, scheme, transaction or series of transactions (whether or not legally enforceable);

"the Commissioners" means the Commissioners for Her Majesty's Revenue and Customs;

"designated HMRC officer" has the meaning given by paragraph 2 of Schedule 43;

"the GAAR Advisory Panel" has the meaning given by paragraph 1 of Schedule 43;

"the general anti-abuse rule" has the meaning given by section 206;

"HMRC" means Her Majesty's Revenue and Customs;

"notice of binding" has the meaning given by paragraph 2(2) of Schedule 43A;

"notified adjustments", in relation to a provisional counteraction notice, has the meaning given by section 209A(2);

"pooling notice" has the meaning given by paragraph 1(4) of Schedule 43A;

"provisional counteraction notice" has the meaning given by section 209A(2);

"tax advantage" has the meaning given by section 208;

"tax appeal" has the meaning given by paragraph 1A of Schedule 43;

"tax arrangements" has the meaning given by section 207(1);

"tax enquiry" has the meaning given by section 202(2) of FA 2014.

214(2) In this Part references to any **"opinion of the GAAR Advisory Panel"** about any tax arrangements are to be interpreted in accordance with paragraph 11(5) of Schedule 43.

214(3) In this Part references to tax arrangements which are **"equivalent"** to one another are to be interpreted in accordance with paragraph 11 of Schedule 43A.

History – In s. 214(1), definitions of "notified adjustments" and "provisional counteraction notice" inserted by FA 2016, s. 156(2), with effect in relation to tax arrangements (within the meaning of FA 2013, Pt. 5) entered into at any time (whether before or on or after 15 September 2016).
In s. 214(1), definitions of "designated HMRC officer", "notice of binding", "pooling notice", "tax appeal" and "tax enquiry" inserted by FA 2016, s. 157(9), with effect in relation to tax arrangements (within the meaning of FA 2013, Pt. 5) entered into at any time (whether before or on or after 15 September 2016).
S. 214(1) created from existing text by FA 2016, s. 157(8), with effect in relation to tax arrangements (within the meaning of FA 2013, Pt. 5) entered into at any time (whether before or on or after 15 September 2016).
S. 214(2) and (3) inserted by FA 2016, s. 157(10), with effect in relation to tax arrangements (within the meaning of FA 2013, Pt. 5) entered into at any time (whether before or on or after 15 September 2016).

Cross references – NICA 2014, s. 10(1): references in Pt. 5 to tax include references to national insurance contributions, where tax arrangements are entered into on or after 13 March 2014.

215 Commencement and transitional provision

215(1) The general anti-abuse rule has effect in relation to any tax arrangements entered into on or after the day on which this Act is passed.

215(2) Where the tax arrangements form part of any other arrangements entered into before that day those other arrangements are to be ignored for the purposes of section 207(3), subject to subsection (3).

215(3) Account is to be taken of those other arrangements for the purposes of section 207(3) if, as a result, the tax arrangements would not be abusive.

Cross references – NICA 2014, s. 10(1): references in Pt. 5 to tax include references to national insurance contributions, where tax arrangements are entered into on or after 13 March 2014.

PART 6 – OTHER PROVISIONS

ADMINISTRATION

233 Self assessment: withdrawal of notice to file etc

233 Schedule 51 contains provision for, and in connection with, withdrawing a notice under section 8, 8A or 12AA of TMA 1970 and cancelling liability to a penalty under Schedule 55 to FA 2009.

PART 7 – FINAL PROVISIONS

235 Interpretation

235(1) In this Act–

"ALDA 1979" means the Alcoholic Liquor Duties Act 1979,

"BGDA 1981" means the Betting and Gaming Duties Act 1981,

"CAA 2001" means the Capital Allowances Act 2001,

"CEMA 1979" means the Customs and Excise Management Act 1979,

"CRCA 2005" means the Commissioners for Revenue and Customs Act 2005,

"CTA 2009" means the Corporation Tax Act 2009,

"CTA 2010" means the Corporation Tax Act 2010,

"F(No.3)A 2010" means the Finance (No. 3) Act 2010,

"HODA 1979" means the Hydrocarbon Oil Duties Act 1979,

"ICTA" means the Income and Corporation Taxes Act 1988,

"IHTA 1984" means the Inheritance Tax Act 1984,

"ITA 2007" means the Income Tax Act 2007,

"ITEPA 2003" means the Income Tax (Earnings and Pensions) Act 2003,

"ITTOIA 2005" means the Income Tax (Trading and Other Income) Act 2005,

"OTA 1975" means the Oil Taxation Act 1975,

"TCGA 1992" means the Taxation of Chargeable Gains Act 1992,

"TIOPA 2010" means the Taxation (International and Other Provisions) Act 2010,

"TMA 1970" means the Taxes Management Act 1970,

"TPDA 1979" means the Tobacco Products Duty Act 1979,

"VATA 1994" means the Value Added Tax Act 1994, and

"VERA 1994" means the Vehicle Excise and Registration Act 1994.

235(2) In this Act–

"FA", followed by a year, means the Finance Act of that year;

"F(No. 2)A", followed by a year, means the Finance (No. 2) Act of that year.

236 Short title

236 This Act may be cited as the Finance Act 2013.

SCHEDULES

SCHEDULE 43 – GENERAL ANTI-ABUSE RULE: PROCEDURAL REQUIREMENTS

Section 209

Other material – HMRC guidance: the general anti-abuse rule.

THE GAAR ADVISORY PANEL

1(1) In this Part **"the GAAR Advisory Panel"** means the panel of persons established by the Commissioners for the purposes of the general anti-abuse rule.

1(2) In this Schedule **"the Chair"** means any member of the GAAR Advisory Panel appointed by the Commissioners to chair it.

MEANING OF "TAX APPEAL"

1A In this Part **"tax appeal"** means–

(a) an appeal under section 31 of TMA 1970 (income tax: appeals against amendments of self-assessment, amendments made by closure notices under section 28A or 28B of that Act, etc), including an appeal under that section by virtue of regulations under Part 11 of ITEPA 2003 (PAYE),

(b) an appeal under paragraph 9 of Schedule 1A to TMA 1970 (income tax: appeals against amendments made by closure notices under paragraph 7(2) of that Schedule, etc),

(c) an appeal under section 705 of ITA 2007 (income tax: appeals against counteraction notices),

(d) an appeal under paragraph 34(3) or 48 of Schedule 18 to FA 1998 (corporation tax: appeals against amendment of a company's return made by closure notice, assessments other than self-assessments, etc),

(e) an appeal under section 750 of CTA 2010 (corporation tax: appeals against counteraction notices),

(f) an appeal under section 222 of IHTA 1984 (appeals against HMRC determinations) other than an appeal made by a person against a determination in respect of a transfer of value at a time when a tax enquiry is in progress in respect of a return made by that person in respect of that transfer,

(g) an appeal under paragraph 35 of Schedule 10 to FA 2003 (stamp duty land tax: appeals against amendment of self-assessment, discovery assessments, etc),

(h) an appeal under paragraph 35 of Schedule 33 to FA 2013 (annual tax on enveloped dwellings: appeals against amendment of self-assessment, discovery assessments, etc),

(i) an appeal under paragraph 14 of Schedule 2 to the Oil Taxation Act 1975 (petroleum revenue tax: appeal against assessment, determination etc),

(j) an appeal under section 102 of FA 2015 (diverted profits tax: appeal against charging notice etc),

(k) an appeal under section 114 of FA 2016 (apprenticeship levy: appeal against an assessment), or

(l) an appeal against any determination of–

  (i) an appeal within paragraphs (a) to (k), or

  (ii) an appeal within this paragraph.

History – Para. 1A (and the heading before it) inserted by FA 2016, s. 158(6), with effect in relation to tax arrangements (within the meaning of FA 2013, Pt. 5) entered into on or after 15 September 2016.

MEANING OF "DESIGNATED HMRC OFFICER"

2 In this Schedule a **"designated HMRC officer"** means an officer of Revenue and Customs who has been designated by the Commissioners for the purposes of the general anti-abuse rule.

NOTICE TO TAXPAYER OF PROPOSED COUNTERACTION OF TAX ADVANTAGE

3(1) If a designated HMRC officer considers–

(a) that a tax advantage has arisen to a person ("the taxpayer") from tax arrangements that are abusive, and

(b) that the advantage ought to be counteracted under section 209,

the officer must give the taxpayer a written notice to that effect.

3(2) The notice must–

(a) specify the arrangements and the tax advantage,

(b) explain why the officer considers that a tax advantage has arisen to the taxpayer from tax arrangements that are abusive,

(c) set out the counteraction that the officer considers ought to be taken,

(d) inform the taxpayer of the period under paragraph 4 for making representations, and

(e) explain the effect of–

(i) paragraphs 5 and 6, and

(ii) sections 209(8) and (9) and 212A.

3(3) The notice may set out steps that the taxpayer may take to avoid the proposed counteraction.

History – Para. 3(2)(e)(i) and (ii) and the word "of–" before them substituted for the words "of paragraphs 5 and 6" by FA 2016, s. 158(7), with effect in relation to tax arrangements (within the meaning of FA 2013, Pt. 5) entered into on or after 15 September 2016.

4(1) If a notice is given to the taxpayer under paragraph 3, the taxpayer has 45 days beginning with the day on which the notice is given to send written representations in response to the notice to the designated HMRC officer.

4(2) The designated officer may, on a written request made by the taxpayer, extend the period during which representations may be made.

CORRECTIVE ACTION BY TAXPAYER

4A(1) If the taxpayer takes the relevant corrective action before the beginning of the closed period mentioned in section 209(8), the matter is not to be referred to the GAAR Advisory Panel.

4A(2) For the purposes of this Schedule the "relevant corrective action" is taken if (and only if) the taxpayer takes the steps set out in sub-paragraphs (3) and (4).

4A(3) The first step is that–

(a) the taxpayer amends a return or claim to counteract the tax advantage specified in the notice under paragraph 3, or

(b) if the taxpayer has made a tax appeal (by notifying HMRC or otherwise) on the basis that the tax advantage specified in the notice under paragraph 3 arises from the tax arrangements specified in that notice, the taxpayer takes all necessary action to enter into an agreement with HMRC (in writing) for the purpose of relinquishing that advantage.

4A(4) The second step is that the taxpayer notifies HMRC–

(a) that the taxpayer has taken the first step, and

(b) of any additional amount which has or will become due and payable in respect of tax by reason of the first step being taken.

4A(5) Where the taxpayer takes the first step described in sub-paragraph (3)(b), HMRC may proceed as if the taxpayer had not taken the relevant corrective action if the taxpayer fails to enter into the written agreement.

4A(6) In determining the additional amount which has or will become due and payable in respect of tax for the purposes of sub-paragraph (4)(b), it is to be assumed that, where P takes the necessary action as mentioned in sub-paragraph (3)(b), the agreement is then entered into.

4A(7) No enactment limiting the time during which amendments may be made to returns or claims operates to prevent P taking the first step mentioned in sub-paragraph (3)(a) before the tax enquiry is closed (whether or not before the specified time).

4A(8) No appeal may be brought, by virtue of a provision mentioned in sub-paragraph (9), against an amendment made by a closure notice in respect of a tax enquiry to the extent that the amendment takes into account an amendment made by the taxpayer to a return or claim in taking the first step mentioned in sub-paragraph (3)(a).

4A(9) The provisions are–

(a) section 31(1)(b) or (c) of TMA 1970,

(b) paragraph 9 of Schedule 1A to TMA 1970,

(c) paragraph 34(3) of Schedule 18 to FA 1998,

(d) paragraph 35(1)(b) of Schedule 10 to FA 2003, and

(e) paragraph 35(1)(b) of Schedule 33 to FA 2013.

History – Para. 4A (and the heading before it) inserted by FA 2016, s. 158(8), with effect in relation to tax arrangements (within the meaning of FA 2013, Pt. 5) entered into on or after 15 September 2016.

REFERRAL TO GAAR ADVISORY PANEL

4B Paragraphs 5 and 6 apply if the taxpayer does not take the relevant corrective action (see paragraph 4A) by the beginning of the closed period mentioned in section 209(8).

History – Para. 4B inserted by FA 2016, s. 158(9), with effect in relation to tax arrangements (within the meaning of FA 2013, Pt. 5) entered into on or after 15 September 2016.

5 If no representations are made in accordance with paragraph 4, a designated HMRC officer must refer the matter to the GAAR Advisory Panel.

6(1) If representations are made in accordance with paragraph 4, a designated HMRC officer must consider them.

6(2) If, after considering them, the designated HMRC officer considers that the tax advantage ought to be counteracted under section 209, the officer must refer the matter to the GAAR Advisory Panel.

6(3) The officer must, as soon as reasonably practicable after deciding whether or not the matter is to be referred to the GAAR Advisory Panel, give the taxpayer written notice of the decision.

History – Para. 6(3) inserted by FA 2016, s. 157(11), with effect in relation to tax arrangements (within the meaning of FA 2013, Pt. 5) entered into at any time (whether before or on or after 15 September 2016).

7 If the matter is referred to the GAAR Advisory Panel, the designated HMRC officer must at the same time provide it with–

(a) a copy of the notice given to the taxpayer under paragraph 3,

(b) a copy of any representations made in accordance with paragraph 4 and any comments that the officer has on those representations, and

(c) a copy of the notice given to the taxpayer under paragraph 8.

8 If the matter is referred to the GAAR Advisory Panel, the designated HMRC officer must at the same time give the taxpayer a notice which–

(a) specifies that the matter is being referred,

(b) is accompanied by a copy of any comments provided to the GAAR Advisory Panel under paragraph 7(b), and

(c) informs the taxpayer of the period under paragraph 9 for making representations, and of the requirement under that paragraph to send any representations to the officer.

9(1) The taxpayer has 21 days beginning with the day on which a notice is given under paragraph 8 to send the GAAR Advisory Panel written representations about–

(a) the notice given to the taxpayer under paragraph 3, or

(b) any comments provided under paragraph 7(b).

9(2) The GAAR Advisory Panel may, on a written request made by the taxpayer, extend the period during which representations may be made.

9(3) The taxpayer must send a copy of any representations to the designated HMRC officer at the same time as the representations are sent to the GAAR Advisory Panel.

9(4) If no representations were made in accordance with paragraph 4, the designated HMRC officer–

(a) may provide the GAAR Advisory Panel with comments on any representations made under this paragraph, and

(b) if comments are provided, must at the same time send a copy of them to the taxpayer.

DECISION OF GAAR ADVISORY PANEL AND OPINION NOTICES

10(1) If the matter is referred to the GAAR Advisory Panel, the Chair must arrange for a sub-panel consisting of 3 members of the GAAR Advisory Panel (one of whom may be the Chair) to consider it.

10(2) The sub-panel may invite the taxpayer or the designated HMRC officer (or both) to supply the sub-panel with further information within a period specified in the invitation.

10(3) Invitations must explain the effect of sub-paragraph (4) or (5) (as appropriate).

10(4) If the taxpayer supplies information to the sub-panel under this paragraph, the taxpayer must at the same time send a copy of the information to the designated HMRC officer.

10(5) If the designated HMRC officer supplies information to the sub-panel under this paragraph, the officer must at the same time send a copy of the information to the taxpayer.

11(1) Where the matter is referred to the GAAR Advisory Panel, the sub-panel must produce–

(a) one opinion notice stating the joint opinion of all the members of the sub-panel, or

(b) two or three opinion notices which taken together state the opinions of all the members.

11(2) The sub-panel must give a copy of the opinion notice or notices to–

(a) the designated HMRC officer, and

(b) the taxpayer.

11(3) An opinion notice is a notice which states that in the opinion of the members of the sub-panel, or one or more of those members–

(a) the entering into and carrying out of the tax arrangements is a reasonable course of action in relation to the relevant tax provisions–

(i) having regard to all the circumstances (including the matters mentioned in subsections (2)(a) to (c) and (3) of section 207), and

(ii) taking account of subsections (4) to (6) of that section, or

(b) the entering into or carrying out of the tax arrangements is not a reasonable course of action in relation to the relevant tax provisions having regard to those circumstances and taking account of those subsections, or

(c) it is not possible, on the information available, to reach a view on that matter,

and the reasons for that opinion.

11(4) For the purposes of the giving of an opinion under this paragraph, the arrangements are to be assumed to be tax arrangements.

11(5) In this Part, a reference to any opinion of the GAAR Advisory Panel about any tax arrangements is a reference to the contents of any opinion notice about the arrangements.

NOTICE OF FINAL DECISION AFTER CONSIDERING OPINION OF GAAR ADVISORY PANEL

12(1) A designated HMRC officer who has received a notice or notices under paragraph 11 must, having considered any opinion of the GAAR Advisory Panel about the tax arrangements, give the taxpayer a written notice setting out whether the tax advantage arising from the arrangements is to be counteracted under the general anti-abuse rule.

12(2) If the notice states that a tax advantage is to be counteracted, it must also set out–

(a) the adjustments required to give effect to the counteraction, and

(b) if relevant, any steps that the taxpayer is required to take to give effect to it.

NOTICES MAY BE GIVEN ON ASSUMPTION THAT TAX ADVANTAGE DOES ARISE

13(1) A designated HMRC officer may give a notice, or do anything else, under this Schedule where the officer considers that a tax advantage might have arisen to the taxpayer.

13(2) Accordingly, any notice given by a designated HMRC officer under this Schedule may be expressed to be given on the assumption that the tax advantage does arise (without agreeing that it does).

SCHEDULE 43A – PROCEDURAL REQUIREMENTS: POOLING NOTICES AND NOTICES OF BINDING

History – *Sch. 43A inserted by FA 2016, s. 157(2),* with effect in relation to tax arrangements (within the meaning of FA 2013, Pt. 5) entered into at any time (whether before or on or after 15 September 2016).

POOLING NOTICES

1(1) This paragraph applies where a person has been given a notice under paragraph 3 of Schedule 43 in relation to any tax arrangements (the "lead arrangements") and the condition in sub-paragraph (2) is met.

1(2) The condition is that the period of 45 days mentioned in paragraph 4(1) of Schedule 43 has expired but no notice under paragraph 12 of Schedule 43 or paragraph 8 of Schedule 43B has yet been given in respect of the matter.

1(3) If a designated HMRC officer considers–

(a) that a tax advantage has arisen to a person ("R") from tax arrangements (other than the lead arrangements) that are abusive,

(b) that those tax arrangements ("R's arrangements") are equivalent to the lead arrangements, and

(c) that the advantage ought to be counteracted under section 209,

the officer may give R a notice (a "pooling notice") to that effect.

1(3A) For the purposes of this Schedule and Schedule 43B, all the tax arrangements in relation to which pooling notices have been served in respect of the same lead arrangements are to be regarded as being in a "pool" together.

1(4) [Omitted by SI 2017/1090, reg. 3(4).]

1(5) [Omitted by SI 2017/1090, reg. 3(4).]

1(6) The officer may not give R a pooling notice if R has been given in respect of R's arrangements a notice under paragraph 3 of Schedule 43.

History – In para. 1(3)(a), the word "a" substituted for the word "another" and the words "(other than the lead arrangements)" inserted by SI 2017/1090, reg. 3(2)(a), with effect from 5 December 2017.
In para. 1, the words "to that effect" substituted for the words "which places R's arrangements in a pool with the lead arrangements." by SI 2017/1090, reg. 3(2)(b), with effect from 5 December 2017.
Para. 1(3A) inserted by SI 2017/1090, reg. 3(3), with effect from 5 December 2017.
Para. 1(4) and (5) omitted by SI 2017/1090, reg. 3(4), with effect from 5 December 2017. Former para. 1(4) and (5) read as follows:
"**1(4)** There is one pool for any lead arrangements, so all tax arrangements placed in a pool with the lead arrangements (as well as the lead arrangements themselves) are in one and the same pool.
1(5) Tax arrangements which have been placed in a pool do not cease to be in the pool except where that is expressly provided for by this Schedule (regardless of whether or not the lead arrangements or any other tax arrangements remain in the pool).".

NOTICE OF PROPOSAL TO BIND ARRANGEMENTS TO COUNTERACTED ARRANGEMENTS

2(1) This paragraph applies where a counteraction notice has been given to a person in relation to any tax arrangements (the "counteracted arrangements").

2(2) If a designated HMRC officer considers–

(a) that a tax advantage has arisen to a person ("R") from tax arrangements (other than the counteracted arrangements) that are abusive,

(b) that those tax arrangements ("R's arrangements") are equivalent to the counteracted arrangements, and

(c) that the advantage ought to be counteracted under section 209,

the officer may give R a notice (a "notice of binding") in relation to R's arrangements.

2(3) The officer may not give R a notice of binding if R has been given in respect of R's arrangements a notice under–

(a) paragraph 1, or

(b) paragraph 3 of Schedule 43.

2(4) In this paragraph **"counteraction notice"** means a notice such as is mentioned in sub-paragraph (2) of paragraph 12 of Schedule 43 or sub-paragraph (3) of paragraph 8 of Schedule 43B (notice of final decision to counteract).

History – In para. 2(1), the words "which are in a pool created under paragraph 1" (which appeared after the words "(the "counteracted arrangements")") omitted by SI 2017/1090, reg. 4(2), with effect from 5 December 2017.
In para. 2(2)(a), the word "a" substituted for the word "another" and the words "(other than the counteracted arrangements)" inserted by SI 2017/1090, reg. 4(3), with effect from 5 December 2017.

3(1) The decision of a designated HMRC officer whether or not to give R a pooling notice or notice of binding must be taken, and any notice must be given, as soon as is reasonably practicable after the officer becomes aware of the relevant facts.

3(2) A pooling notice or notice of binding must–

(a) specify the tax arrangements in relation to which the notice is given and the tax advantage,

(b) explain why the officer considers R's arrangements to be equivalent to the lead arrangements or the counteracted arrangements (as the case may be),

(c) explain why the officer considers that a tax advantage has arisen to R from tax arrangements that are abusive,

(d) set out the counteraction that the officer considers ought to be taken, and

(e) explain the effect of–

 (i) paragraphs 4 to 10,

 (ii) subsection (9) of section 209, and

 (iii) section 212A.

3(3) A pooling notice or notice of binding may set out steps that R may (subject to subsection (9) of section 209) take to avoid the proposed counteraction.

History – In para. 3(1), the words "of a designated HMRC officer" inserted and the words "the officer" substituted for the word "HMRC" by SI 2017/1090, reg. 5, with effect from 5 December 2017.

CORRECTIVE ACTION BY A NOTIFIED TAXPAYER

4(1) If a person to whom a pooling notice or notice of binding has been given takes the relevant corrective action in relation to the tax arrangements and tax advantage specified in the notice before the beginning of the closed period mentioned in section 209(9), the person is to be treated for the purposes of paragraphs 6 to 8 and 9 and Schedule 43B (generic referral of tax arrangements) as not having been given the notice in question (and accordingly the tax arrangements in question are no longer in the pool).

4(2) For the purposes of this Schedule the **"relevant corrective action"** is taken if (and only if) the person takes the steps set out in sub-paragraphs (3) and (4).

4(3) The first step is that–

(a) the person amends a return or claim to counteract the tax advantage specified in the pooling notice or notice of binding, or

(b) P takes all necessary action to enter into an agreement with HMRC (in writing) for the purpose of relinquishing that advantage.

4(4) The second step is that the person notifies HMRC–

(a) that the first step has been taken, and

(b) of any additional amount which has or will become due and payable in respect of tax by reason of the first step being taken.

4(5) Where a person takes the first step described in sub-paragraph (3)(b), HMRC may proceed as if the person had not taken the relevant corrective action if the person fails to enter into the written agreement.

4(6) In determining the additional amount which has or will become due and payable in respect of tax for the purposes of sub-paragraph (4)(b), it is to be assumed that, where P takes the necessary action as mentioned in sub-paragraph (3)(b), the agreement is then entered into.

4(7) No enactment limiting the time during which amendments may be made to returns or claims operates to prevent P taking the first step mentioned in sub-paragraph (3)(a) before the tax enquiry is closed.

4(8) No appeal may be brought, by virtue of a provision mentioned in sub-paragraph (9), against an amendment made by a closure notice in respect of a tax enquiry to the extent that the amendment takes into account an amendment made by the taxpayer to a return or claim in taking the first step mentioned in sub-paragraph (3)(a).

4(9) The provisions are–

(a) paragraph 35(1)(b) of Schedule 33,

(b) section 31(1)(b) or (c) of TMA 1970,

(c) paragraph 9 of Schedule 1A to TMA 1970,

(d) paragraph 34(3) of Schedule 18 to FA 1998, and

(e) paragraph 35(1)(b) of Schedule 10 to FA 2003.

History – In para. 4(1), the words "6 to" inserted by SI 2017/1090, reg. 6(2), with effect from 5 December 2017.
In para. 4(3)(b), the words "if the person has made a tax appeal (by notifying HMRC or otherwise) on the basis that the tax advantage specified in the pooling notice or notice of binding arises from the tax arrangements specified in that notice," (which appeared before the words "P takes all ") omitted by SI 2017/1090, reg. 6(3), with effect from 5 December 2017.

CORRECTIVE ACTION BY LEAD TAXPAYER

5 [Omitted by SI 2017/1090, reg. 7.]

History – Para. 5 omitted by SI 2017/1090, reg. 7, with effect from 5 December 2017. Former para. 5 read as follows:
"**5** *If the person mentioned in paragraph 1(1) takes the relevant corrective action (as defined in paragraph 4A of Schedule 43) before the end of the period of 75 days beginning with the day on which the notice mentioned in paragraph 1(1) was given to that person, the lead arrangements are treated as ceasing to be in the pool.*".

OPINION NOTICES AND RIGHT TO MAKE REPRESENTATIONS

6(1) Sub-paragraph (2) applies where–

(a) a pooling notice is given to a person in relation to any tax arrangements, and

(b) an opinion notice (or opinion notices) under paragraph 11(2) of Schedule 43 aboutanother set of tax arrangements in the pool or the lead arrangements ("the referred arrangements") is subsequently given to a designated HMRC officer.

6(2) The officer must give the person a pooled arrangements opinion notice.

6(3) No more than one pooled arrangements opinion notice may be given to a person in respect of the same tax arrangements.

6(4) Where a designated HMRC officer gives a person a notice of binding, the officer must, at the same time, give the person a bound arrangements opinion notice.

History – In para. 6(1)(b), the words "or the lead arrangements" inserted by SI 2017/1090, reg. 8, with effect from 5 December 2017.

7(1) In relation to a person who is, or has been, given a pooling notice, **"pooled arrangements opinion notice"** means a written notice which–

(a) sets out a report prepared by HMRC of any opinion of the GAAR Advisory Panel about the referred arrangements,

(b) explains the person's right to make representations falling within sub-paragraph (3), and

(c) sets out the period in which those representations may be made.

7(2) In relation to a person who is given a notice of binding **"bound arrangements opinion notice"** means a written notice which–

(a) sets out a report prepared by HMRC of any opinion of the GAAR Advisory Panel about the counteracted arrangements (see paragraph 2(1)),

(b) explains the person's right to make representations falling within sub-paragraph (3), and

(c) sets out the period in which those representations may be made.

7(3) A person who is given a pooled arrangements opinion notice or a bound arrangements opinion notice has 30 days beginning with the day on which the notice is given to make representations in any of the following categories–

(a) representations that no tax advantage has arisen to the person from the arrangements to which the notice relates;

(b) representations as to why the arrangements to which the notice relates are or may be materially different from–

(i) the referred arrangements (in the case of a pooled arrangements opinion notice), or

(ii) the counteracted arrangements (in the case of a bound arrangements opinion notice).

7(4) In sub-paragraph (3)(b) references to **"arrangements"** include any circumstances which would be relevant in accordance with section 207 to a determination of whether the tax arrangements in question are abusive.

NOTICE OF FINAL DECISION

8(1) This paragraph applies where–

(a) further to a pooling notice given under paragraph 1(3), a set of tax arrangements is in a pool relating to any lead arrangements, and

(b) a designated HMRC officer has given a notice under paragraph 12 of Schedule 43 in relation to any other arrangements in the pool or the lead arrangements (the "referred arrangements").

8(2) The officer must, having considered any opinion of the GAAR Advisory Panel about the referred arrangements and any representations made under paragraph 7(3) in relation to the arrangements mentioned in sub-paragraph (1)(a), give the person a written notice setting out whether the tax advantage arising from those arrangements is to be counteracted under the general anti-abuse rule.

History – Para. 8(1)(a) substituted by SI 2017/1090, reg. 9(a), with effect from 5 December 2017.
In para. 8(1)(b), the words "or the lead arrangements" inserted by SI 2017/1090, reg. 9(b), with effect from 5 December 2017.

9(1) This paragraph applies where–

(a) a person has been given a notice of binding under paragraph 2, and

(b) the period of 30 days for making representations under paragraph 7(3) has expired.

9(2) A designated HMRC officer must, having considered any opinion of the GAAR Advisory Panel about the counteracted arrangements and any representations made under paragraph 7(3) in relation to the arrangements specified in the notice of binding, give the person a written notice setting out whether the tax advantage arising from the arrangements specified in the notice of binding is to be counteracted under the general anti-abuse rule.

10 If a notice under paragraph 8(2) or 9(2) states that a tax advantage is to be counteracted, it must also set out–

(a) the adjustments required to give effect to the counteraction, and

(b) if relevant, any steps the person concerned is required to take to give effect to it.

"EQUIVALENT ARRANGEMENTS"

11(1) For the purposes of paragraph 1, tax arrangements are **"equivalent"** to one another if they are substantially the same as one another having regard to–

(a) their substantive results,

(b) the means of achieving those results, and

(c) the characteristics on the basis of which it could reasonably be argued, in each case, that the arrangements are abusive tax arrangements under which a tax advantage has arisen to a person.

NOTICES MAY BE GIVEN ON ASSUMPTION THAT TAX ADVANTAGE DOES ARISE

12(1) A designated HMRC officer may give a notice, or do anything else, under this Schedule where the officer considers that a tax advantage might have arisen to the person concerned.

12(2) Accordingly, any notice given by a designated HMRC officer under this Schedule may be expressed to be given on the assumption that a tax advantage does arise (without conceding that it does).

HMRC OFFICERS

12A Anything that may or must be done by a given designated HMRC officer under this Schedule may be done instead by any other designated HMRC officer.

History – Para. 12A inserted by SI 2017/1090, reg. 10, with effect from 5 December 2017.

POWER TO AMEND

13(1) The Treasury may by regulations amend this Schedule (apart from this paragraph).

13(2) Regulations under sub-paragraph (1) may include–

(a) any amendment of this Part that is appropriate in consequence of an amendment by virtue of sub-paragraph (1);

(b) transitional provision.

13(3) Regulations under sub-paragraph (1) are to be made by statutory instrument.

13(4) A statutory instrument containing regulations under sub-paragraph (1) is subject to annulment in pursuance of a resolution of the House of Commons.

SCHEDULE 43B – PROCEDURAL REQUIREMENTS: GENERIC REFERRAL OF TAX ARRANGEMENTS

History – Sch. 43B inserted by FA 2016, s. 157(3), with effect in relation to tax arrangements (within the meaning of FA 2013, Pt. 5) entered into at any time (whether before or on or after 15 September 2016).

NOTICE OF PROPOSAL TO MAKE GENERIC REFERRAL OF TAX ARRANGEMENTS

1(1) Sub-paragraph (2) applies if–

(a) further to pooling notices given under paragraph 1(3) of Schedule 43A, two or more sets of tax arrangements are in a pool relating to any lead arrangements,

(b) the person to whom the notice mentioned in paragraph 1(1) of Schedule 43A was given takes the relevant corrective action (as defined in paragraph 4A of Schedule 43) before–

(i) the end of the period of 75 days beginning with the day on which that notice was given, or

(ii) such later time as that person and HMRC may agree, and

(c) no referral under paragraph 5 or 6 of Schedule 43 has been made in respect of any arrangements in the pool.

1(2) A designated HMRC officer may determine that, in respect of each of the tax arrangements that are in the pool, there is to be given (to the person to whom the pooling notice in question was given) a written notice of a proposal to make a generic referral to the GAAR Advisory Panel in respect of the arrangements in the pool.

1(3) Only one determination under sub-paragraph (2) may be made in relation to any one pool.

1(4) The persons to whom those notices are given are **"the notified taxpayers"**.

1(5) A notice given to a person ("T") under sub-paragraph (2) must–

(a) specify the arrangements (the "specified arrangements") and the tax advantage (the "specified advantage") to which the notice relates,

(b) inform T of the period under paragraph 2 for making a proposal.

History – Para. 1(1)(a) and (b) substituted by SI 2017/1090, reg. 12(2), with effect from 5 December 2017.

2(1) T has 30 days beginning with the day on which the notice under paragraph 1 is given to propose to HMRC that it–

(a) should give T a notice under paragraph 3 of Schedule 43 in respect of the arrangements to which the notice under paragraph 1 relates, and

(b) should not proceed with the proposal to make a generic referral to the GAAR Advisory Panel in respect of those arrangements.

2(2) If a proposal is made in accordance with sub-paragraph (1) a designated HMRC officer must consider it.

GENERIC REFERRAL

3(1) This paragraph applies where a designated HMRC officer has given notices to the notified taxpayers in accordance with paragraph 1(2).

3(2) If none of the notified taxpayers has made a proposal under paragraph 2 by the end of the 30 day period mentioned in that paragraph, the officer must make a referral to the GAAR Advisory Panel in respect of the notified taxpayers and the arrangements which are specified arrangements in relation to them.

3(3) If at least one of the notified taxpayers makes a proposal in accordance with paragraph 2, the designated HMRC officer must, after the end of that 30 day period, decide whether to–

(a) give a notice under paragraph 3 of Schedule 43 in respect of one set of tax arrangements in the relevant pool in relation to which such a proposal has been made, or

(b) make a referral to the GAAR Advisory Panel in respect of the tax arrangements in the relevant pool.

3(3A) If under sub-paragraph (3)(a) a notice is given under paragraph 3 of Schedule 43 in respect of one set of tax arrangements but (by virtue of paragraph 4A of that Schedule) the matter is not referred to the GAAR Advisory Panel, a designated officer must make a referral to the GAAR Advisory Panel in respect of the notified taxpayers and the arrangements which are specified arrangements in relation to them.

3(4) A referral under this paragraph is a **"generic referral"**.

History – In para. 3(3)(a), the words " in relation to which such a proposal has been made" inserted by SI 2017/1090, reg. 13(2), with effect from 5 December 2017.
Para. 3(3A) inserted by SI 2017/1090, reg. 13(3), with effect from 5 December 2017.

4(1) If a generic referral is made to the GAAR Advisory Panel, the designated HMRC officer must at the same time provide it with–

(a) a general statement of the material characteristics of the specified arrangements, and

(b) a declaration that–

 (i) the statement under paragraph (a) is applicable to all the specified arrangements, and

 (ii) as far as HMRC is aware, nothing which is material to the GAAR Advisory Panel's consideration of the matter has been omitted.

4(2) The general statement under sub-paragraph (1)(a) must–

(a) contain a factual description of the tax arrangements;

(b) set out HMRC's view as to whether the tax arrangements accord with established practice (when the arrangements were entered into);

(c) explain why it is the designated HMRC officer's view that a tax advantage of the nature described in the statement and arising from tax arrangements having the characteristics described in the statement would be a tax advantage arising from arrangements that are abusive;

(d) set out any matters the designated officer is aware of which may suggest that any view of HMRC or the designated HMRC officer expressed in the general statement is not correct;

(e) set out any other matters which the designated officer considers are required for the purposes of the exercise of the GAAR Advisory Panel's functions under paragraph 6.

5 If a generic referral is made the designated HMRC officer must at the same time give each of the notified taxpayers a notice which–

(a) specifies that a generic referral is being made, and

(b) is accompanied by a copy of the statement given to the GAAR Advisory Panel in accordance with paragraph 4(1)(a).

DECISION OF GAAR ADVISORY PANEL AND OPINION NOTICES

6(1) If a generic referral is made to the GAAR Advisory Panel under paragraph 3, the Chair must arrange for a sub-panel consisting of 3 members of the GAAR Advisory Panel (one of whom may be the Chair) to consider it.

6(2) The sub-panel must produce–

(a) one opinion notice stating the joint opinion of all the members of the sub-panel, or

(b) two or three opinion notices which taken together state the opinions of all the members.

6(3) The sub-panel must give a copy of the opinion notice or notices to the designated HMRC officer.

6(4) An opinion notice is a notice which states that in the opinion of the members of the sub-panel, or one or more of those members–

(a) the entering into and carrying out of tax arrangements such as are described in the general statement under paragraph 4(1)(a) is a reasonable course of action in relation to the relevant tax provisions,

(b) the entering into or carrying out of such tax arrangements is not a reasonable course of action in relation to the relevant tax provisions, or

(c) it is not possible, on the information available, to reach a view on that matter,

and the reasons for that opinion.

6(5) In forming their opinions for the purposes of sub-paragraph (4) members of the sub-panel must–

(a) have regard to all the matters set out in the statement under paragraph 4(1)(a),

(b) assume (unless the contrary is stated in the statement under paragraph 4(1)(a)) that the tax arrangements do not form part of any other arrangements,

(c) have regard to the matters mentioned in paragraphs (a) to (c) of section 207(2), and

(d) take account of subsections (4) to (6) of section 207.

6(6) For the purposes of the giving of an opinion under this paragraph, the arrangements are to be assumed to be tax arrangements.

6(7) In this Part, a reference to any opinion of the GAAR Advisory Panel in respect of a generic referral of any tax arrangements is a reference to the contents of any opinion notice given in relation to a generic referral in respect of the arrangements.

NOTICE OF RIGHT TO MAKE REPRESENTATIONS

7(1) Where a designated HMRC officer is given an opinion notice (or opinion notices) under paragraph 6, the officer must give each of the notified taxpayers a copy of the opinion notice (or notices) and a written notice which–

(a) explains the notified taxpayer's right to make representations falling within sub-paragraph (2), and

(b) sets out the period in which those representations may be made.

7(2) A notified taxpayer ("T") who is given a notice under sub-paragraph (1) has 30 days beginning with the day on which the notice is given to make representations in any of the following categories–

(a) representations that no tax advantage has arisen from the specified arrangements;

(b) representations that T has already been given a notice under paragraph 6 of Schedule 43A in relation to the specified arrangements;

(c) representations that any matter set out in the statement under paragraph 4(1)(a) is materially inaccurate as regards the specified arrangements (having regard to all circumstances which would be relevant in accordance with section 207 to a determination of whether the tax arrangements in question are abusive).

NOTICE OF FINAL DECISION AFTER CONSIDERING OPINION OF GAAR ADVISORY PANEL

8(1) A designated HMRC officer who has received a notice or notices under paragraph 6(3) in respect of a generic referral must consider the case of each notified taxpayer in accordance with sub-paragraph (2).

8(2) The officer must, having considered–

(a) any opinion of the GAAR Advisory Panel about the matters referred to it, and

(b) any representations made by the notified taxpayer under paragraph 7,

give to the notified taxpayer a written notice setting out whether the specified advantage is to be counteracted under the general anti-abuse rule.

8(3) If the notice states that a tax advantage is to be counteracted, it must also set out–

(a) the adjustments required to give effect to the counteraction, and

(b) if relevant, any steps that the taxpayer is required to take to give effect to it.

NOTICES MAY BE GIVEN ON ASSUMPTION THAT TAX ADVANTAGE DOES ARISE

9(1) A designated HMRC officer may give a notice, or do anything else, under this Schedule where the officer considers that a tax advantage might have arisen to the person concerned.

9(2) Accordingly, any notice given by a designated HMRC officer under this Schedule may be expressed to be given on the assumption that a tax advantage does arise (without conceding that it does).

HMRC OFFICERS

9A Anything that may or must be done by a given designated HMRC officer under this Schedule may be done instead by any other designated HMRC officer.

History – Para. 9A inserted by SI 2017/1090, reg. 14, with effect from 5 December 2017.

POWER TO AMEND

10(1) The Treasury may by regulations amend this Schedule (apart from this paragraph).

10(2) Regulations under sub-paragraph (1) may include–

(a) any amendment of this Part that is appropriate in consequence of an amendment by virtue of sub-paragraph (1);

(b) transitional provision.

10(3) Regulations under sub-paragraph (1) are to be made by statutory instrument.

10(4) A statutory instrument containing regulations under sub-paragraph (1) is subject to annulment in pursuance of a resolution of the House of Commons.

SCHEDULE 43C – PENALTY UNDER SECTION 212A: SUPPLEMENTARY PROVISION

History – Sch. 43C inserted by FA 2016, s. 158(3), with effect in relation to tax arrangements (within the meaning of FA 2013, Pt. 5) entered into on or after 15 September 2016.

VALUE OF THE COUNTERACTED ADVANTAGE: INTRODUCTION

1 Paragraphs 2 to 4 set out how to calculate the **"value of the counteracted advantage"** for the purposes of section 212A.

VALUE OF THE COUNTERACTED ADVANTAGE: BASIC RULE

2(1) The **"value of the counteracted advantage"** is the additional amount due or payable in respect of tax as a result of the counteraction mentioned in section 212A(1)(c).

2(2) The reference in sub-paragraph (1) to the additional amount due and payable includes a reference to–

(a) an amount payable to HMRC having erroneously been paid by way of repayment of tax, and

(b) an amount which would be repayable by HMRC if the counteraction were not made.

2(3) The following are ignored in calculating the value of the counteracted advantage–

(a) group relief, and

(b) any relief under section 458 of CTA 2010 (relief in respect of repayment etc of loan) which is deferred under subsection (5) of that section.

2(4) For the purposes of this paragraph consequential adjustments under section 210 are regarded as part of the counteraction in question.

2(5) If the counteraction affects the person's liability to two or more taxes, the taxes concerned are to be considered together for the purpose of determining the value of the counteracted advantage.

2(6) This paragraph is subject to paragraphs 3 and 4.

VALUE OF COUNTERACTED ADVANTAGE: LOSSES

3(1) To the extent that the tax advantage mentioned in section 212A(1)(b) ("the tax advantage") resulted in the wrong recording of a loss for the purposes of direct tax and the loss has been wholly used to reduce the amount due or payable in respect of tax, the value of the counteracted advantage is determined in accordance with paragraph 2.

3(2) To the extent that the tax advantage resulted in the wrong recording of a loss for purposes of direct tax and the loss has not been wholly used to reduce the amount due or payable in respect of tax, the value of the counteracted advantage is–

(a) the value under paragraph 2 of so much of the tax advantage as results (or would in the absence of the counteraction result) from the part (if any) of the loss which was used to reduce the amount due or payable in respect of tax, plus

(b) 10% of the part of the loss not so used.

3(3) Sub-paragraphs (1) and (2) apply both–

(a) to a case where no loss would have been recorded but for the tax advantage, and

(b) to a case where a loss of a different amount would have been recorded (but in that case sub-paragraphs (1) and (2) apply only to the difference between the amount recorded and the true amount).

3(4) To the extent that the tax advantage creates or increases (or would in the absence of the counteraction create or increase) an aggregate loss recorded for a group of companies–

(a) the value of the counteracted advantage is calculated in accordance with this paragraph, and

(b) in applying paragraph 2 in accordance with sub-paragraphs (1) and (2), group relief may be taken into account (despite paragraph 2(3)).

3(5) To the extent that the tax advantage results (or would in the absence of the counteraction result) in a loss, the value of it is nil where, because of the nature of the loss or the person's circumstances, there was no reasonable prospect of the loss being used to support a claim to reduce a tax liability (of any person).

VALUE OF COUNTERACTED ADVANTAGE: DEFERRED TAX

4(1) To the extent that the tax advantage mentioned in section 212A is a deferral of tax, the value of the counteracted advantage is–

(a) 25% of the amount of the deferred tax for each year of the deferral, or

(b) a percentage of the amount of the deferred tax, for each separate period of deferral of less than a year, equating to 25% per year,

or, if less, 100% of the amount of the deferred tax.

4(2) This paragraph does not apply to a case to the extent that paragraph 3 applies.

ASSESSMENT OF PENALTY

5(1) Where a person is liable for a penalty under section 212A, HMRC must assess the penalty.

5(2) Where HMRC assess the penalty, HMRC must–

(a) notify the person who is liable for the penalty, and

(b) state in the notice a tax period in respect of which the penalty is assessed.

5(3) A penalty under this paragraph must be paid before the end of the period of 30 days beginning with the day on which notification of the penalty is issued.

5(4) An assessment–

(a) is to be treated for procedural purposes as if it were an assessment to tax,

(b) may be enforced as if it were an assessment to tax, and

(c) may be combined with an assessment to tax.

5(5) An assessment of a penalty under this paragraph must be made before the end of the period of 12 months beginning with–

(a) the end of the appeal period for the assessment which gave effect to the counteraction mentioned in section 212A(1)(b), or

(b) if there is no assessment within paragraph (a), the date (or the latest of the dates) on which that counteraction becomes final.

5(6) The reference in sub-paragraph (5)(b) to the counteraction becoming final is to be interpreted in accordance with section 210(8).

ALTERATION OF ASSESSMENT OF PENALTY

6(1) After notification of an assessment has been given to a person under paragraph 5(2), the assessment may not be altered except in accordance with this paragraph or paragraph 7, or on appeal.

6(2) A supplementary assessment may be made in respect of a penalty if an earlier assessment operated by reference to an underestimate of the value of the counteracted advantage.

6(3) An assessment may be revised as necessary if it operated by reference to an overestimate of the value of the counteracted advantage.

REVISION OF ASSESSMENT FOLLOWING CONSEQUENTIAL RELIEVING ADJUSTMENT

7(1) Sub-paragraph (2) applies where a person–

(a) is notified under section 210(7) of a consequential adjustment relating to a counteraction under section 209, and

(b) an assessment to a penalty in respect of that counteraction of which the person has been notified under paragraph 5(2) does not take account of that consequential adjustment.

7(2) HMRC must make any alterations of the assessment that appear to HMRC to be just and reasonable in connection with the consequential amendment.

7(3) Alterations under this paragraph may be made despite any time limit imposed by or under an enactment.

AGGREGATE PENALTIES

8(1) Sub-paragraph (3) applies where–

(a) two or more penalties are incurred by the same person and fall to be determined by reference to an amount of tax to which that person is chargeable,

(b) one of those penalties is incurred under section 212A, and

(c) one or more of the other penalties are incurred under a relevant penalty provision.

8(2) But sub-paragraph (3) does not apply if section 212(2) of FA 2014 (follower notices: aggregate penalties) applies in relation to the amount of tax in question.

8(3) The aggregate of the amounts of the penalties mentioned in subsection (1)(b) and (c), so far as determined by reference to that amount of tax, must not exceed–

(a) the relevant percentage of that amount, or

(b) in a case where at least one of the penalties is under paragraph 5(2)(b) of, or sub-paragraph (3)(b), (4)(b) or (5)(b) of paragraph 6 of, Schedule 55 to FA 2009, £300 (if greater).

8(4) In the application of section 97A of TMA 1970 (multiple penalties) no account shall be taken of a penalty under section 212A.

8(5) **"Relevant penalty provision"** means–

(a) Schedule 24 to FA 2007 (penalties for errors),

(b) Schedule 41 to FA 2008 (penalties: failure to notify etc),

(c) Schedule 55 to FA 2009 (penalties for failure to make returns etc), or

(d) Part 5 of Schedule 18 to FA 2016 (penalty under serial tax avoidance regime).

8(6) **"The relevant percentage"** means–

(a) 200% in a case where at least one of the penalties is determined by reference to the percentage in–

  (i) paragraph 4(4)(c) of Schedule 24 to FA 2007,

  (ii) paragraph 6(4)(a) of Schedule 41 to FA 2008, or

  (iii) paragraph 6(3A)(c) of Schedule 55 to FA 2009,

(b) 150% in a case where paragraph (a) does not apply and at least one of the penalties is determined by reference to the percentage in–

  (i) paragraph 4(3)(c) of Schedule 24 to FA 2007,

  (ii) paragraph 6(3)(a) of Schedule 41 to FA 2008, or

  (iii) paragraph 6(3A)(b) of Schedule 55 to FA 2009,

(c) 140% in a case where neither paragraph (a) nor paragraph (b) applies and at least one of the penalties is determined by reference to the percentage in–
   (i) paragraph 4(4)(b) of Schedule 24 to FA 2007,
   (ii) paragraph 6(4)(b) of Schedule 41 to FA 2008, or
   (iii) paragraph 6(4A)(c) of Schedule 55 to FA 2009,
(d) 105% in a case where at none of paragraphs (a), (b) and (c) applies and at least one of the penalties is determined by reference to the percentage in–
   (i) paragraph 4(3)(b) of Schedule 24 to FA 2007,
   (ii) paragraph 6(3)(b) of Schedule 41 to FA 2008, or
   (iii) paragraph 6(4A)(b) of Schedule 55 to FA 2009, and
(e) in any other case, 100%.

Prospective amendments – Para. 8(6)(ba) inserted by FA 2015, s. 120 and Sch. 20, para. 20(2), with effect from a day to be appointed under s. 120(2).
In para. 8(6)(c), the words "none of paragraphs (a) to (ba) applies" substituted for the words "neither paragraph (a) nor paragraph (b) applies" by FA 2015, s. 120 and Sch. 20, para. 20(3), with effect from a day to be appointed under s. 120(2).
In para. 8(6)(d), the words "none of paragraphs (a) to (c) applies" substituted for the words "none of paragraphs (a), (b) and (c) applies" by FA 2015, s. 120 and Sch. 20, para. 20(4), with effect from a day to be appointed under s. 120(2).

APPEAL AGAINST PENALTY

9(1) A person may appeal against–
(a) the imposition of a penalty under section 212A, or
(b) the amount assessed under paragraph 5.

9(2) An appeal under sub-paragraph (1)(a) may only be made on the grounds that the arrangements were not abusive or there was no tax advantage to be counteracted.

9(3) An appeal under sub-paragraph (1)(b) may only be made on the grounds that the assessment was based on an overestimate of the value of the counteracted advantage (whether because the estimate was made by reference to adjustments which were not just and reasonable or for any other reason).

9(4) An appeal under this paragraph must be made within the period of 30 days beginning with the day on which notification of the penalty is given under paragraph 5(2).

9(5) An appeal under this paragraph is to be treated in the same way as an appeal against an assessment to the tax concerned (including by the application of any provision about bringing the appeal by notice to HMRC, about HMRC's review of the decision or about determination of the appeal by the First-tier Tribunal or Upper Tribunal).

9(6) Sub-paragraph (5) does not apply–
(a) so as to require a person to pay a penalty before an appeal against the assessment of the penalty is determined, or
(b) in respect of any other matter expressly provided for by this Part.

9(7) On an appeal against the penalty the tribunal may affirm or cancel HMRC's decision.

9(8) On an appeal against the amount of the penalty the tribunal may–
(a) affirm HMRC's decision, or
(b) substitute for HMRC's decision another decision that HMRC has power to make.

9(9) In this paragraph **"tribunal"** means the First-tier Tribunal or Upper Tribunal (as appropriate by virtue of sub-paragraph (5)).

MITIGATION OF PENALTIES

10(1) The Commissioners may in their discretion mitigate a penalty under section 212A, or stay or compound any proceedings for such a penalty.

10(2) *They may also, after judgment, further mitigate or entirely remit the penalty.*

INTERPRETATION

11 In this Schedule–
(a) a reference to an **"assessment"** to tax is to be interpreted, in relation to inheritance tax, as a reference to a determination;

(b) **"direct tax"** means–
  (i) income tax,
  (ii) capital gains tax,
  (iii) corporation tax (including any amount chargeable as if it were corporation tax or treated as corporation tax), and
  (iv) petroleum revenue tax;
  (v) diverted profits tax;

(c) a reference to a loss includes a reference to a charge, expense, deficit and any other amount which may be available for, or relied on to claim, a deduction or relief;

(d) a reference to a repayment of tax includes a reference to allowing a credit against tax or to a payment of a corporation tax credit;

(e) **"corporation tax credit"** means–
  (i) an R&D tax credit under Chapter 2 or 7 of Part 13 of CTA 2009,
  (ii) an R&D expenditure credit under Chapter 6A of Part 3 of CTA 2009,
  (iii) a land remediation tax credit or life assurance company tax credit under Chapter 3 or 4 respectively of Part 14 of CTA 2009,
  (iv) a film tax credit under Chapter 3 of Part 15 of CTA 2009,
  (v) a television tax credit under Chapter 3 of Part 15A of CTA 2009,
  (vi) a video game tax credit under Chapter 3 of Part 15B of CTA 2009,
  (vii) a theatre tax credit under section 1217K of CTA 2009,
  (viii) an orchestra tax credit under Chapter 3 of Part 15D of CTA 2009, or
  (ix) a first-year tax credit under Schedule A1 to CAA 2001;

(f) **"tax period"** means a tax year, accounting period or other period in respect of which tax is charged;

(g) a reference to giving a document to HMRC includes a reference to communicating information to HMRC in any form and by any method (whether by post, fax, email, telephone or otherwise),

(h) a reference to giving a document to HMRC includes a reference to making a statement or declaration in a document.

SCHEDULE 51 – WITHDRAWAL OF NOTICE TO FILE ETC

Section 233

FA 2009

7(1) Paragraph 3 of Schedule 53 to FA 2009 (late payment interest start date: amendments and discovery assessments etc) is amended as follows.

7(2) [Amends FA 2009, Sch. 53, para. 3(3).]

7(3) [Inserts FA 2009, Sch. 53, para. 3(3A).]

COMMENCEMENT

9(1) The amendments made by this Schedule have effect–

(a) in relation to a return under section 12AA of TMA 1970 for a partnership which includes one or more companies, in respect of a return for a relevant period beginning on or after 6 April 2012, and

(b) in relation to a return under that section for any other partnership, or a return under section 8 or 8A of that Act, in respect of a return for a year of assessment beginning on or after 6 April 2012.

9(2) In sub-paragraph (1)(a), **"relevant period"** means a period in respect of which a return is required.

NATIONAL INSURANCE CONTRIBUTIONS ACT 2014

(2014 Chapter 7)

[*13th March 2014*]

ARRANGEMENT OF SECTIONS

EMPLOYMENT ALLOWANCE

1 Employment allowance for national insurance contributions

1(1) A person qualifies for an employment allowance for a tax year if, in the tax year–

(a) the person is the secondary contributor in relation to payments of earnings to, or for the benefit of, one or more employed earners, and

(b) in consequence, the person incurs liabilities to pay secondary Class 1 contributions, under SSCBA 1992 or SSCB(NI)A 1992 (or both).

1(2) The person's employment allowance for the tax year is–

(a) £3,000, or

(b) if less, an amount equal to the total amount of the liabilities mentioned in subsection (1)(b) which are not excluded liabilities.

1(3) Subsection (1) is subject to sections 2 and 3 (and Schedule 1).

1(4) Sections 2 and 3 (and Schedule 1) set out cases in which a person cannot qualify for an employment allowance for a tax year.

1(5) Section 2 also sets out the cases in which liabilities to pay secondary Class 1 contributions are "excluded liabilities".

1(6) Section 4 provides for a person who qualifies for an employment allowance for a tax year to receive it by way of deductions or a repayment under that section.

1(7) In this Act references to "the employment allowance provisions" are to this section, sections 2 to 4 and Schedule 1.

1(8) In the employment allowance provisions and section 5 terms used which are also used in Part 1 of SSCBA 1992 or SSCB(NI)A 1992 have the same meaning as they have in that Part.

History – In s. 1(2)(a), the figure "£3,000" substituted for the figure "£2,000" by SI 2016/63, reg. 2, with effect from 6 April 2016.

Other material – HMRC guidance: employment allowance and further guidance at https://www.gov.uk/government/publications/employment-allowance-more-detailed-guidance.

2 Exceptions

Public authorities

2(1) A person cannot qualify for an employment allowance for a tax year if, at any time in the tax year, the person is a public authority which is not a charity.

2(2) In subsection (1)–

"charity" has the same meaning as in the Small Charitable Donations Act 2012 (see section 18(1) of that Act), and

"public authority" includes any person whose activities involve, wholly or mainly, the performance of functions (whether or not in the United Kingdom) which are of a public nature.

Personal, family or household affairs

2(3) Liabilities to pay secondary Class 1 contributions incurred by a person ("P") are "excluded liabilities" if they are incurred in respect of an employed earner who is employed (wholly or partly) for purposes connected with P's personal, family or household affairs.

2(3A) But the liabilities mentioned in subsection (3) are not 'excluded liabilities' by virtue of that subsection if all the duties of the employed earner's employment which relate to P's personal, family or household affairs are performed for an individual who needs those duties to be performed because of the individual's–

(a) old age,

(b) mental or physical disability,

(c) past or present dependence on alcohol or drugs,

(d) past or present illness, or

(e) past or present mental disorder.

Workers supplied by service companies etc

2(4) Liabilities to pay secondary Class 1 contributions are "excluded liabilities" if they are incurred by virtue of regulations made under section 4A of SSCBA 1992 or SSCB(NI)A 1992 (earnings of workers supplied by service companies etc).

Excluded companies

2(4A) A body corporate ("C") cannot qualify for an employment allowance for a tax year if–

(a) all the payments of earnings in relation to which C is the secondary contributor in that year are paid to, or for the benefit of, the same employed earner, and

(b) when each of those payments is made, that employed earner is a director of C.

Transfers of businesses

2(5) Subsection (6) applies if a business, or a part of a business, is transferred to a person ("P") in a tax year.

2(6) Liabilities to pay secondary Class 1 contributions incurred by P in the tax year are "excluded liabilities" if they are incurred in respect of an employed earner who is employed (wholly or partly) for purposes connected with the transferred business or part.

2(7) For the purposes of subsection (5) a business, or a part of a business, is transferred to P in a tax year if, in the tax year–

(a) another person ("Q") is carrying on the business or part, and

(b) in consequence of arrangements involving P and Q, P begins to carry on the business or part on or following Q ceasing to do so.

2(8) In subsection (7)(b) **"arrangements"** includes any agreement, understanding, scheme, transaction or series of transactions (whether or not legally enforceable).

2(9) In subsections (5) to (7) **"business"** includes–

(a) anything which is a trade, profession or vocation for the purposes of the Income Tax Acts or the Corporation Tax Acts;

(b) a property business (as defined in section 263(6) of the Income Tax (Trading and Other Income) Act 2005);

(c) any charitable or not-for-profit undertaking or any similar undertaking;

(d) functions of a public nature.

Anti-avoidance

2(10) A person cannot qualify for an employment allowance for a tax year if, apart from this subsection, the person would qualify in consequence of avoidance arrangements.

2(11) In a case not covered by subsection (10), liabilities to pay secondary Class 1 contributions incurred by a person ("P") in a tax year are "excluded liabilities" if they are incurred by P, or are incurred by P in that tax year (as opposed to another tax year), in consequence of avoidance arrangements.

2(12) In subsections (10) and (11) **"avoidance arrangements"** means arrangements the main purpose, or one of the main purposes, of which is to secure that a person benefits, or benefits further, from the application of the employment allowance provisions.

2(13) In subsection (12) **"arrangements"** includes any agreement, understanding, scheme, transaction or series of transactions (whether or not legally enforceable).

History – S. 2(4A) inserted by SI 2016/344, reg. 2, with effect from 6 April 2016.
S. 2(3A) inserted by SI 2015/578, reg. 2, with effect from 6 April 2015.

3 Connected persons

3(1) This section applies if–

(a) at the beginning of a tax year, two or more companies which are not charities are connected with one another, and

(b) apart from this section, two or more of those companies would qualify for an employment allowance for the tax year.

3(2) This section also applies if–

(a) at the beginning of a tax year, two or more charities are connected with one another, and

(b) apart from this section, two or more of those charities would qualify for an employment allowance for the tax year.

3(3) Only one of the companies or charities mentioned in subsection (1)(b) or (2)(b) (as the case may be) can qualify for an employment allowance for the tax year.

3(4) It is up to the companies or charities so mentioned to decide which of them that will be.

3(5) Part 1 of Schedule 1 sets out the rules for determining if two or more companies are "connected" with one another for the purposes of subsection (1).

3(6) Part 2 of Schedule 1 sets out the rules for determining if two or more charities are "connected" with one another for the purposes of subsection (2).

3(7) In this section and Schedule 1–

"charity" has the same meaning as in the Small Charitable Donations Act 2012 (see section 18(1) of that Act), subject to paragraph 8(5) of Schedule 1, and

"company" has the meaning given by section 1121(1) of the Corporation Tax Act 2010 (meaning of "company") and includes a limited liability partnership.

4 How does a person who qualifies for an employment allowance receive it?

4(1) Her Majesty's Revenue and Customs ("HMRC") must (from time to time) make such arrangements as HMRC consider appropriate for persons who qualify for an employment allowance for a tax year to receive it by making deductions from qualifying payments which they are required to make under regulations made under paragraph 6 of Schedule 1 to SSCBA 1992 or SSCB(NI)A 1992 (regulations combining collection of contributions with tax).

4(2) In this section **"qualifying payment"**, in relation to a person who qualifies for an employment allowance for a tax year, means a payment in respect of any of the person's liabilities mentioned in section 1(1)(b) which are not excluded liabilities (see section 2).

4(3) If under HMRC's arrangements a person is permitted to make a deduction from a qualifying payment, the person must make the deduction and must make it before any other deductions which the person is permitted to make from the payment under any other legislation.

4(4) HMRC's arrangements may (in particular)–

(a) require deductions to be made at the earliest opportunity in a tax year;

(b) provide that deductions may not be made in specified cases;

(c) place limits on the amounts of deductions;

(d) provide that a person is not permitted to make deductions unless the person has first given notice to HMRC in such form and manner, and containing such information, as HMRC may require.

4(5) Subsections (6) to (8) apply in relation to a person who qualifies for an employment allowance for a tax year if the person has not deducted under this section the full amount of the employment allowance by the end of the month of April in which the tax year ends.

4(6) The person may apply to HMRC for a repayment, up to the outstanding amount of the employment allowance, of qualifying payments made by the person; and HMRC must make the repayment.

4(7) The person's application must be made in such form and manner, and contain such information, as HMRC may require.

4(8) The person's application must be made before the end of the 4th tax year after the tax year mentioned in subsection (5).

4(9) In the application of section 102 of the Finance Act 2009 (repayment interest on sums to be paid by HMRC) in relation to a repayment under this section, the repayment interest start date is the date on which HMRC receive the person's application.

4(10) A repayment under this section, and any interest in respect of it under section 102 of the Finance Act 2009, are to be paid out of the National Insurance Fund or the Northern Ireland National Insurance Fund.

4(11) A person who qualifies for an employment allowance for a tax year may not receive it otherwise than by way of deductions or a repayment under this section.

5 Power to amend the employment allowance provisions

5(1) The Treasury may by regulations amend the employment allowance provisions–

(a) so as to increase or decrease a person's employment allowance for a tax year, or

(b) so as to add to, reduce or modify the cases in which a person cannot qualify for an employment allowance for a tax year or in which liabilities to pay secondary Class 1 contributions are "excluded liabilities".

5(2) Section 175(3) to (5) of SSCBA 1992 (various supplementary powers) applies to the power to make regulations conferred by this section.

5(3) The power conferred by section 175(4) of SSCBA 1992, as applied by subsection (2), includes (in particular) power to make the provision mentioned in section 175(4) by way of amendments to the employment allowance provisions.

5(4) Regulations under this section must be made by statutory instrument.

5(5) A statutory instrument containing (with or without other provision)–

(a) regulations falling within subsection (1)(a) which decrease a person's employment allowance for a tax year, or

(b) regulations falling within subsection (1)(b),

may not be made unless a draft has been laid before, and approved by a resolution of, each House of Parliament.

5(6) A statutory instrument–

(a) which contains regulations falling within subsection (1)(a) which increase a person's employment allowance for a tax year, and

(b) which does not have to be approved in draft under subsection (5),

must be laid before Parliament after being made.

5(7) Regulations contained in a statutory instrument which is required to be laid before Parliament under subsection (6) cease to have effect at the end of the period of 40 days after the day on which the instrument is made unless, before the end of that period, the instrument is approved by a resolution of each House of Parliament.

5(8) If regulations cease to have effect as a result of subsection (7), that does not–

(a) affect anything previously done by virtue of the regulations, or

(b) prevent the making of new regulations to the same or a similar effect.

5(9) In calculating the period of 40 days for the purposes of subsection (7), no account is to be taken of any time during which Parliament is dissolved or prorogued or during which either House is adjourned for more than 4 days.

6 Decisions and appeals about entitlements to make deductions etc

6(1) [Inserts SSCTFA 1999, s. 8(1)(ea) and (eb).]

6(2) [Inserts Social Security Contributions (Transfer of Functions, etc) (Northern Ireland) Order 1999 (SI 1999/671), art. 7(1)(ea) and (eb).]

7 Retention of records etc

7(1) [Inserts SSCBA 1992, Sch. 1, para. 8(1)(aa).]

7(2) [Inserts SSCB(NI)A 1992, Sch. 1, para. 8(1)(aa).]

7(3) [Inserts SI 2001/1004, Sch. 4, para. 26(4A) and (4B).]

7(4) The amendment made by subsection (3) is to be treated as having been made by the Treasury using the powers conferred by paragraph 8(1)(aa) of Schedule 1 to SSCBA 1992 (as inserted by subsection (1)) and paragraph 8(1)(aa) of Schedule 1 to SSCB(NI)A 1992 (as inserted by subsection (2)).

7(5) [Amends SSAA 1992, s. 110ZA(2)(a).]

7(6) [Amends SSA(NI)A 1992, s. 104ZA(2)(a).]

8 Commencement of the employment allowance provisions etc

8 Sections 1 to 7 and Schedule 1 come into force on 6 April 2014.

INTRODUCTION OF AGE-RELATED SECONDARY PERCENTAGE

9 Reduction of secondary Class 1 contributions for certain age groups

9(1) SSCBA 1992 is amended as follows.

9(2) In section 9 (calculation of secondary Class 1 contributions)–

(a) [amends SSCBA 1992, s. 9(1),]

(b) [inserts SSCBA 1992, s. 9(1A).]

9(3) [Inserts SSCBA 1992, s. 9A.]

9(4) [Amends SSCBA 1992, s. 122(1).]

9(5) [Amends SSCBA 1992, s. 176(1)(a).]

9(6) SSCB(NI)A 1992 is amended as follows.

9(7) [Amends SSCB(NI)A 1992, s. 9.]

9(8) [Inserts SSCB(NI)A 1992, s. 9A.]

9(9) [Amends SSCB(NI)A 1992, s. 121(1).]

9(10) [Amends SSCB(NI)A 1992, s. 172(11A).]

9(11) The following come into force at the end of the period of 2 months beginning with the day on which this Act is passed–

(a) any power conferred on the Treasury by virtue of this section to make regulations, and

(b) the amendments made by subsections (5) and (10).

9(12) So far as not already brought into force by subsection (11), the amendments made by this section come into force on 6 April 2015.

APPLICATION OF GENERAL ANTI-ABUSE RULE TO NATIONAL INSURANCE CONTRIBUTIONS

10 GAAR to apply to national insurance contributions

10(1) In Part 5 of the Finance Act 2013 (general anti-abuse rule)–

(a) references to tax, other than in references to particular taxes, include national insurance contributions, and

(b) references to a charge to tax include a liability to pay national insurance contributions.

10(2) Section 206(3) of that Act (list of taxes to which the general anti-abuse rule applies) has effect as if it included a reference to national insurance contributions.

10(3) Section 207 of that Act (meaning of "tax arrangements" and "abusive") has effect as if, in subsection (4)(a), after "income," there were inserted "earnings (within the meaning of Part 1 of the Social Security Contributions and Benefits Act 1992 or Part 1 of the Social Security Contributions and Benefits (Northern Ireland) Act 1992),".

10(4) Adjustments to be made in respect of national insurance contributions under section 209 of the Finance Act 2013 (counteracting the tax advantages) may be made by a notice given under paragraph 12 of Schedule 43 to that Act (notice of final decision), paragraph 8 or 9 of Schedule 43A to that Act (pooling of tax arrangements: notice of final decision) or paragraph 8 of Schedule 43B to that Act (generic referral of arrangements: notice of final decision).

10(5) For the purposes of section 210 of that Act (consequential relieving adjustments)–

(a) if a claim under that section relates to Class 4 national insurance contributions, Schedule 1A to the Taxes Management Act 1970 (as that Schedule applies in relation to such contributions) applies to it, and

(b) if a claim under that section relates to any other class of national insurance contributions, it must be made in such form and manner, and contain such information, as HMRC may require.

10(6) Adjustments to be made in respect of national insurance contributions under that section may be made by a notice given under subsection (7) of that section.

10(6A) Where, by virtue of this section, a case falls within paragraph 4A of Schedule 43 to the Finance Act 2013 (referrals of single schemes: relevant corrective action) or paragraph 4 of Schedule 43A to that Act (pooled schemes: relevant corrective action)–

(a) the person ("P") mentioned in sub-paragraph (1) of that paragraph takes the "relevant corrective action" for the purposes of that paragraph if (and only if)–

  (i) in a case in which the tax advantage in question can be counteracted by making a payment to HMRC, P makes that payment and notifies HMRC that P has done so, or

  (ii) in any case, P takes all necessary action to enter into an agreement in writing with HMRC for the purpose of relinquishing the tax advantage, and

(b) accordingly, sub-paragraphs (2) to (8) of that paragraph do not apply.

10(7) This section has effect in relation to tax arrangements (within the meaning of Part 5 of the Finance Act 2013 as modified by this section) entered into on or after the day on which this Act is passed.

10(8) Subsections (9) and (10) apply where the tax arrangements–

(a) would not have been tax arrangements but for the modifications made by this section, and

(b) form part of other arrangements entered into before the day on which this Act is passed.

10(9) The other arrangements are to be ignored for the purposes of section 207(3) of the Finance Act 2013, subject to subsection (10).

10(10) Account is to be taken of the other arrangements for the purposes of that section if, as a result, the tax arrangements would not be abusive.

10(11) In this section–

"abusive", **"arrangements"**, **"HMRC"** and **"tax advantage"** have the same meaning as in Part 5 of the Finance Act 2013 (as modified by this section);

"national insurance contributions" means contributions under either Part 1 of SSCBA 1992 or Part 1 of SSCB(NI)A 1992.

10(12) *See section* 10A for further modifications of Part 5 of the Finance Act 2013.

History – In s. 10(4), the words ", paragraph 8 or 9 of Schedule 43A to that Act (pooling of tax arrangements: notice of final decision) or paragraph 8 of Schedule 43B to that Act (generic referral of arrangements: notice of final decision)" inserted by FA 2016, s. 157(13), with effect in relation to tax arrangements (within the meaning of FA 2013, Pt. 5) entered into at any time (whether before or on or after 15 September 2016).

S. 10(6A) inserted by FA 2016, s. 157(14), with effect in relation to tax arrangements (within the meaning of FA 2013, Pt. 5) entered into at any time (whether before or on or after 15 September 2016).

In s. 10(11), the words ", "HMRC" and "tax advantage"" substituted for the words "and HMRC" and the words "(as modified by this section)" inserted by FA 2016, s. 157(15), with effect in relation to tax arrangements (within the meaning of FA 2013, Pt. 5) entered into at any time (whether before or on or after 15 September 2016).
S. 10(12) inserted by FA 2016, s. 157(16), with effect in relation to tax arrangements (within the meaning of FA 2013, Pt. 5) entered into at any time (whether before or on or after 15 September 2016).

10A Application of GAAR in relation to penalties

10A(1) For the purposes of this section a penalty under section 212A of the Finance Act 2013 is a **"relevant NICs-related penalty"** so far as the penalty relates to a tax advantage in respect of relevant contributions.

10A(2) A relevant NICs-related penalty may be recovered as if it were an amount of relevant contributions which is due and payable.

10A(3) Section 117A of the Social Security Administration Act 1992 or (as the case may be) section 111A of the Social Security Administration (Northern Ireland) Act 1992 (issues arising in proceedings: contributions etc) has effect in relation to proceedings before a court for recovery of a relevant NICs-related penalty as if the assessment of the penalty were a NICs decision as to whether the person is liable for the penalty.

10A(4) Accordingly, paragraph 5(4)(b) of Schedule 43C to the Finance Act 2013 (assessment of penalty to be enforced as if it were an assessment to tax) does not apply in relation to a relevant NICs-related penalty.

10A(5) In the application of Schedule 43C to the Finance Act 2013 in relation to a relevant NICs-related penalty, paragraph 9(5) has effect as if the reference to an appeal against an assessment to the tax concerned were to an appeal against a NICs decision.

10A(6) In paragraph 8 of that Schedule (aggregate penalties), references to a **"relevant penalty provision"** include–

(a) any provision mentioned in sub-paragraph (5) of that paragraph, as applied in relation to any class of national insurance contributions by regulations (whenever made);

(b) section 98A of the Taxes Management Act 1970, as applied in relation to any class of national insurance contributions by regulations (whenever made);

(c) any provision in regulations made by the Treasury under which a penalty can be imposed in respect of any class of national insurance contributions.

10A(7) The Treasury may by regulations–

(a) disapply, or modify the effect of, subsection (6)(a) or (b);

(b) modify paragraph 8 of Schedule 43C to the Finance Act 2013 as it has effect in relation to a relevant penalty provision by virtue of subsection (6)(b) or (c).

10A(8) Section 175(3) to (5) of SSCBA 1992 (various supplementary powers) applies to a power to make regulations conferred by subsection (7).

10A(9) Regulations under subsection (7) must be made by statutory instrument.

10A(10) A statutory instrument containing regulations under subsection (7) is subject to annulment in pursuance of a resolution of either House of Parliament.

10A(11) In this section **"NICs decision"** means a decision under section 8 of the Social Security Contributions (Transfer of Functions, etc) Act 1999 or Article 7 of the Social Security Contributions (Transfer of Functions, etc) (Northern Ireland) Order 1999 (SI 1999/671).

10A(12) In this section **"relevant contributions"** means the following contributions under Part 1 of SSCBA 1992 or Part 1 of SSCB(NI)A 1992–

(a) Class 1 contributions;

(b) Class 1A contributions;

(c) Class 1B contributions;

(d) Class 2 contributions which must be paid but in relation to which section 11A of the Act in question (application of certain provisions of the Income Tax Acts in relation to Class 2 contributions under section 11(2) of that Act) does not apply.

History – S. 10A inserted by FA 2016, s. 157(17), with effect in relation to tax arrangements (within the meaning of FA 2013, Pt. 5) entered into at any time (whether before or on or after 15 September 2016).

11 Power to modify application of GAAR to national insurance contributions

11(1) Where a modification is made to Part 5 of the Finance Act 2013 (general antiabuse rule) that does not apply in relation to national insurance contributions ("the tax only modification"), the Treasury may by regulations–

(a) make provision for the purpose of applying the tax only modification in relation to national insurance contributions (with or without modifications),

(b) make provision in relation to national insurance contributions corresponding to the tax only modification, or

(c) otherwise modify the general anti-abuse rule, as it has effect in relation to national insurance contributions, in consequence of, or for the purpose of making provision supplementary or incidental to, the tax only modification.

11(2) Regulations under this section–

(a) may amend, repeal or revoke any provision of an Act or instrument made under an Act (whenever passed or made),

(b) may make consequential, incidental, supplementary, transitional, transitory or saving provision, and

(c) may make different provision for different cases, classes of national insurance contributions or purposes.

11(3) Regulations under this section must be made by statutory instrument.

11(4) A statutory instrument containing (with or without other provision) regulations under this section that amend or repeal a provision of an Act may not be made unless a draft has been laid before, and approved by a resolution of, each House of Parliament.

11(5) A statutory instrument containing regulations under this section that does not have to be approved in draft under subsection (4) is subject to annulment in pursuance of a resolution of either House of Parliament.

11(6) In this section–

"general anti-abuse rule" has the same meaning as in Part 5 of the Finance Act 2013;

"national insurance contributions" means contributions under either Part 1 of SSCBA 1992 or Part 1 of SSCB(NI)A 1992.

OIL AND GAS WORKERS ON THE CONTINENTAL SHELF

12 Oil and gas workers on the continental shelf: secondary contributors etc

12(1) [Amends SSCBA 1992, s. 120.]

12(2) [Amends SSCBA 1992, s. 120(1).]

12(3) [Amends SSCBA 1992, s. 120(3).]

12(4) [Inserts SSCBA 1992, s. 120(4) and (5).]

PARTNERSHIPS

13 Class 4 contributions: partnerships

13(1) SSCBA 1992 is amended as follows.

13(2) [Inserts SSCBA 1992, s. 18A.]

13(3) [Amends SSCBA 1992, s. 176(1)(a).]

13(4) SSCB(NI)A 1992 is amended as follows.

13(5) [Inserts SSCB(NI)A 1992, s. 18A.]

13(6) [Amends SSCB(NI)A 1992, s. 172(11A).]

13(7) The amendments made by this section come into force at the end of the period of 2 months beginning with the day on which this Act is passed.

14 Limited liability partnerships

14(1) SSCBA 1992 is amended as follows.

14(2) [Inserts SSCBA 1992, s. 4AA.]

14(3) [Inserts SSCBA 1992, s. 4B(3)(d).]

14(4) [Inserts SSCBA 1992, s. 10(11).]

14(5) SSCB(NI)A 1992 is amended as follows.

14(6) [Inserts SSCB(NI)A 1992, s. 4AA.]

14(7) [Inserts SSCB(NI)A 1992, s. 4B(3)(d).]

14(8) [Inserts SSCB(NI)A 1992, s. 10(11).]

OTHER PROVISION

15 Office holders who receive "earnings" to be employed earners

15(1) [Amends SSCBA 1992, s. 2(1)(a).]

15(2) [Amends SSCB(NI)A 1992, s. 2(1)(a).]

15(3) Schedule 2 makes provision that is consequential upon office holders in receipt of "earnings" (as opposed to "general earnings") being employed earners.

15(4) The amendments made by this section and Schedule 2 come into force at the end of the period of 2 months beginning with the day on which this Act is passed.

16 Armed Forces early departure payments retrospectively disregarded

16 Paragraph 10A of Part 6 of Schedule 3 to the Social Security (Contributions) Regulations 2001 (S.I. 2001/1004) (payments under the Armed Forces Early Departure Payments Scheme Order 2005 (S.I. 2005/437) to be disregarded) also has effect for the tax years 2005–06 to 2012–13 inclusive.

17 Repeal of certain redundant reliefs relating to Class 4 contributions

17(1) In Schedule 2 to SSCBA 1992 (levy of Class 4 contributions with income tax)–

(a) [Omits SSCBA 1992, Sch. 2, para. 3(3).]

(b) [Omits SSCBA 1992, Sch. 2, para. 9 and the heading immediately before it.]

17(2) In Schedule 2 to SSCB(NI)A 1992 (levy of Class 4 contributions with income tax)–

(a) [Omits SSCB(NI)A 1992, Sch. 2, para. 3(3).]

(b) [Omits SSCB(NI)A 1992, Sch. 2, para. 9.]

17(3) The amendments made by subsections (1)(a) and (2)(a) have effect for the tax year after the one during which this Act is passed and for subsequent tax years.

18 Certain orders and regulations in respect of Northern Ireland

18(1) Section 172 of SSCB(NI)A 1992 (Assembly etc control of regulations and orders) is amended as follows.

18(2) [Omits SSCB(NI)A 1992, s. 172(11).]

18(3) [Omits SSCB(NI)A 1992, s. 172(11B).]

18(4) Section 165 of the Social Security Administration (Northern Ireland) Act 1992 (regulations and orders – general) is amended as follows.

18(5) [Omits SSA(NI)A 1992, s. 165(1).]

18(6) [Omits SSA(NI)A 1992, s. 165(3).]

18(7) The amendments made by this section come into force at the end of the period of 2 months beginning with the day on which this Act is passed.

GENERAL

19 HMRC administrative expenses: financial provision

19(1) [*Not relevant to National Insurance contributions.*]

19(2) [Amends SSA(NI)A 1992, s. 145(5)(a).]

20 Abbreviations of Acts

20 In this Act–

"SSCBA 1992" means the Social Security Contributions and Benefits Act 1992;

"SSCB(NI)A 1992" means the Social Security Contributions and Benefits (Northern Ireland) Act 1992.

21 Short title and extent

21(1) This Act may be cited as the National Insurance Contributions Act 2014.

21(2) Subject to subsection (3), this Act extends to England and Wales, Scotland and Northern Ireland.

21(3) An amendment or repeal made by this Act has the same extent as the provision amended or repealed.

SCHEDULE 1 – EMPLOYMENT ALLOWANCE: RULES FOR DETERMINING IF PERSONS ARE "CONNECTED"

Section 3

PART 1 – COMPANIES

APPLICATION

1 This Part applies for the purposes of section 3(1).

THE BASIC RULE

2(1) Two companies are **"connected"** with one another if–

(a) one of the two has control of the other, or

(b) both are under the control of the same person or persons.

2(2) In sub-paragraph (1) **"control"** has the same meaning as in Part 10 of CTA 2010 (see sections 450 and 451 of that Act) (and a limited liability partnership is to be treated as a company for the purposes of that Part as applied by this sub-paragraph).

2(3) For this purpose, where under section 450 of that Act **"C"** is a limited liability partnership, subsection (3) of that section has effect as if before paragraph (a) there were inserted–

"(za) rights to a share of more than half the assets, or of more than half the income, of C,".

2(4) Sub-paragraphs (1) to (3) are subject to paragraphs 3 to 6.

2(5) Paragraph 7 provides for further connections.

2(6) In this Part **"CTA 2010"** means the Corporation Tax Act 2010.

COMPANIES WHOSE RELATIONSHIP IS NOT ONE OF SUBSTANTIAL COMMERCIAL INTERDEPENDENCE

3(1) This paragraph applies for the purpose of determining under paragraph 2(1) if two companies are connected with one another if the relationship between the companies is not one of substantial commercial interdependence.

3(2) In the application of section 451 of CTA 2010 for the purposes of the determination, any person to whom rights and duties fall to be attributed under subsections (4) and (5) of that section is to be treated, for the purposes of those subsections, as having no associates.

3(3) In determining for the purposes of sub-paragraph (1) if two companies have a relationship of **"substantial commercial interdependence"**, the following factors are to be taken into account–

(a) the degree to which the companies are financially interdependent (see sub-paragraph (4)),

(b) the degree to which the companies are economically interdependent (see sub-paragraph (5)), and

(c) the degree to which the companies are organisationally interdependent (see sub-paragraph (6)).

3(4) Two companies are **"financially interdependent"** if (in particular)–

(a) one gives financial support (directly or indirectly) to the other, or

(b) each has (directly or indirectly) a financial interest in the other's activities.

3(5) Two companies are **"economically interdependent"** if (in particular)–

(a) they seek to realise the same economic objective,

(b) the activities of one benefit the other, or

(c) their activities involve common customers.

3(6) Two companies are **"organisationally interdependent"** if (in particular) they have–

(a) common management,

(b) common employees,

(c) common premises, or

(d) common equipment.

FIXED-RATE PREFERENCE SHARES

4(1) In determining for the purposes of paragraph 2(1) if a company is under the control of another, fixed-rate preference shares held by a company are ignored if the company holding them–

(a) is not a close company,

(b) takes no part in the management or conduct of the company which issued the shares, or in the management or conduct of its business, and

(c) subscribed for the shares in the ordinary course of a business which includes the provision of finance.

4(2) In sub-paragraph (1) **"fixed-rate preference shares"** means shares which–

(a) were issued wholly for new consideration,

(b) do not carry any right either to conversion into shares or securities of any other description or to the acquisition of any additional shares or securities, and

(c) do not carry any right to dividends other than dividends which–

(i) are of a fixed amount or at a fixed rate per cent of the nominal value of the shares, and

(ii) together with any sum paid on redemption, represent no more than a reasonable commercial return on the consideration for which the shares were issued.

4(3) In sub-paragraph (2)(a) **"new consideration"** has the meaning given by section 1115 of CTA 2010.

4(4) In sub-paragraph (1)(a) **"close company"** is to be read in accordance with Chapter 2 of Part 10 of CTA 2010 (see, in particular, section 439 of that Act).

CONNECTION THROUGH A LOAN CREDITOR

5(1) A company ("A") is not under the control of another company ("B") for the purposes of paragraph 2(1) if–

(a) B is a loan creditor of A,

(b) there is no other connection between A and B, and

(c) either–

(i) B is not a close company, or

(ii) B's relationship to A as a loan creditor arose in the ordinary course of a business which B carries on.

5(2) Sub-paragraph (3) applies if–

(a) two companies ("A" and "B") are under the control of the same person who is a loan creditor of each of them,

(b) there is no other connection between A and B, and

(c) either–

(i) the loan creditor is a company which is not a close company, or

(ii) the loan creditor's relationship to each of A and B as a loan creditor arose in the ordinary course of a business which the loan creditor carries on.

5(3) In determining under paragraph 2(1) if A and B are connected with one another, rights which the loan creditor has as a loan creditor of A, or as a loan creditor of B, are ignored.

5(4) In sub-paragraph (2)(a) **"control"** has the same meaning as in paragraph 2(1).

5(5) In this paragraph–

(a) **"close company"** is to be read in accordance with Chapter 2 of Part 10 of CTA 2010 (see, in particular, section 439 of that Act),

(b) **"connection"** includes a connection in the past as well as a connection in the present and references to a connection between two companies include any dealings between them, and

(c) references to a loan creditor of a company are to be read in accordance with section 453 of CTA 2010.

CONNECTION THROUGH A TRUSTEE

6(1) Sub-paragraph (2) applies if–

(a) two companies ("A" and "B") are under the control of the same person by virtue of rights or powers (or both) held in trust by that person, and

(b) there is no other connection between A and B.

6(2) In determining under paragraph 2(1) if A and B are connected with one another, the rights and powers mentioned in sub-paragraph (1)(a) are ignored.

6(3) In sub-paragraph (1)–

(a) **"control"** has the same meaning as in paragraph 2(1), and

(b) **"connection"** includes a connection in the past as well as a connection in the present and the reference to a connection between A and B includes any dealings between them.

FURTHER CONNECTIONS

7(1) This paragraph applies if–

(a) a company ("A") is connected with another company ("B"), and

(b) B is connected with another company ("C").

7(2) A and C are also connected with one another (if that would not otherwise be the case).

7(3) In sub-paragraph (1)(a) the reference to a company being connected with another company is to that company being so connected by virtue of paragraphs 2 to 6 or this paragraph, and in sub-paragraph (1)(b) the reference to a company being connected with another company is to that company being so connected by virtue of paragraphs 2 to 6.

PART 2 – CHARITIES

8(1) Two charities are connected with one another for the purposes of section 3(2) if–

(a) they are connected with one another in accordance with section 993 of the Income Tax Act 2007 (meaning of "connected" persons), and

(b) their purposes and activities are the same or substantially similar.

8(2) In the application of section 993 of the Income Tax Act 2007 for the purposes of sub-paragraph (1)(a)–

(a) a charity which is a trust is to be treated as if it were a company (and accordingly a person), including in this sub-paragraph;

(b) a charity which is a trust has **"control"** of another person if the trustees (in their capacity as trustees of the charity) have, or any of them has, control of the person;

(c) a person (other than a charity regulator) has **"control"** of a charity which is a trust if–

(i) the person is a trustee of the charity and some or all of the powers of the trustees of the charity could be exercised by the person acting alone or by the person acting together with any other persons who are trustees of the charity and who are connected with the person,

(ii) the person, alone or together with other persons, has power to appoint or remove a trustee of the charity, or

(iii) the person, alone or together with other persons, has any power of approval or direction in relation to the carrying out by the trustees of any of their functions.

8(3) A charity which is a trust is also connected with another charity which is a trust for the purposes of section 3(2) if at least half of the trustees of one of the charities are–

(a) trustees of the other charity,

(b) persons who are connected with persons who are trustees of the other charity, or

(c) a combination of both,

and the charities' purposes and activities are the same or substantially similar.

8(4) In determining if a person is connected with another person for the purposes of sub-paragraph (2)(c)(i) or (3)(b), apply section 993 of the Income Tax Act 2007 with the omission of subsection (3) of that section (and without the modifications in sub-paragraph (2)).

8(5) If a charity ("A") controls a company ("B") which, apart from this subparagraph, would not be a charity–

(a) B is to be treated as if it were a charity for the purposes of section 3 and this Part (including this sub-paragraph), and

(b) A and B are connected with one another for the purposes of section 3(2).

8(6) In sub-paragraph (5) **"control"** is to be read in accordance with–

(a) paragraph 2(2) and (3) (but ignoring paragraphs 3 to 6), and

(b) sub-paragraph (2)(b) of this paragraph.

9(1) This paragraph applies if–

(a) a charity ("A") is connected with another charity ("B") for the purposes of section 3(2), and

(b) B is connected with another charity ("C") for the purposes of section 3(2).

9(2) A and C are also connected with one another for the purposes of section 3(2) (if that would not otherwise be the case).

9(3) In sub-paragraph (1)(a) the reference to a charity being connected with another charity for the purposes of section 3(2) is to that charity being so connected by virtue of paragraph 8 or this paragraph, and in sub-paragraph (1)(b) the reference to a charity being connected with another charity for the purposes of section 3(2) is to that charity being so connected by virtue of paragraph 8.

SCHEDULE 2 – OFFICE HOLDERS IN RECEIPT OF "EARNINGS" TO BE EMPLOYED EARNERS: CONSEQUENTIAL PROVISION

Section 15

SSCBA 1992

1 SSCBA 1992 is amended as follows.

2 [Amends SSCBA 1992, s. 7(1).]

3 [Amends SSCBA 1992, s. 163(1).]

4 [Amends SSCBA 1992, s. 171(1).]

5 [Amends SSCBA 1992, s. 171ZJ(2)(a).]

6 [Amends SSCBA 1992, s. 171ZS(2)(a).]

SSCB(NI)A 1992

7 SSCB(NI)A 1992 is amended as follows.

8 [Amends SSCB(NI)A 1992, s. 7(1)(b).]

9 [Amends SSCB(NI)A 1992, s. 159(1).]

10 [Omits SSCB(NI)A 1992, s. 167(1).]

11 [Omits SSCB(NI)A 1992, s. 167ZJ(2)(a).]

12 [Omits SSCB(NI)A 1992, s. 167ZS(2)(a).]

PENSION SCHEMES ACT 1993 (C. 48)

13 [Amends PSA 1993, s. 181(3).]

PENSION SCHEMES (NORTHERN IRELAND) ACT 1993 (C. 49)

14 [Omits PS(NI)A 1993, s. 176(1).]

PENSIONS ACT 2014

(2014 Chapter 19)

[*14th May 2014*]

ARRANGEMENT OF SECTIONS

PART 1 – STATE PENSION

TRANSITION: PENSION SHARING ON DIVORCE ETC

15 Pension sharing: amendments

15 Schedule 11 contains amendments to do with pension sharing.

CONSEQUENTIAL AND OTHER AMENDMENTS

23 Amendments

23 In Schedule 12–

Part 1 contains amendments to do with state pensions under this Part;

Part 2 contains key amendments to do with the old state pension system;

Part 3 contains amendments to do with state pension credit;

Part 4 contains other amendments to do with this Part.

Commencement Date – S. 23 comes into force on 15 January 2016 for the purposes of making regulations only and only so far as it relates to Sch. 12, para. 6(3) (SI 2015/2058, art. 2).
S. 23 comes into force on 7 July 2015 but only in so far as it relates to Sch. 12, para. 25 and 90 (SI 2015/1475, art. 2(2)).
S. 23 comes into effect on 1 October 2014 in so far as it relates to Sch. 12, para. 96 (SI 2014/2377).

24 Abolition of contracting-out for salary related schemes etc

24(1) Schedule 13 contains amendments to abolish contracting-out for salary related schemes.

24(2) An employer may amend an occupational pension scheme in relation to some or all of its members to take account of increases in the employer's national insurance contributions in respect of some or all of the members to whom the amendments apply because of the repeal of section 41 of the Pension Schemes Act 1993 (by Schedule 13 to this Act).

24(3) The power may be used to make amendments that will apply in relation to future members and correspond to the amendments being made in relation to current members.

24(4) The power may not be used–

(a) to make amendments that apply to a member who is a protected person in relation to a scheme, or

(b) to amend a public service pension scheme or a scheme of a description specified in regulations under this paragraph.

24(5) Regulations must define what is meant by a protected person in relation to a scheme for the purposes of subsection (4)(a).

24(6) Schedule 14 contains more detail about the power.

24(7) In this section and Schedule 14–

"current member", in relation to a scheme, means a person who is a member of the scheme at the time that the power is used (and "future member" is to be read accordingly);

"employer", in relation to a scheme, means the employer of persons in the description of employment to which the scheme relates;

"member" has the meaning given by section 124(1) of the Pensions Act 1995;

"national insurance contributions", in relation to an employer, means secondary Class 1 national insurance contributions payable by the employer;

"occupational pension scheme" has the meaning given by section 1 of the Pension Schemes Act 1993;

"public service pension scheme" has the meaning given by that section.

24(8) Subsections (2) to (7) and Schedule 14 are repealed at the end of the period of 5 years beginning with 6 April 2016.

24(9) The Secretary of State may by order amend subsection (8) to extend the period for the time being mentioned there.

Commencement Date – S. 24(1) comes into force on 7 July 2015 but only in so far as it relates to Sch. 13. para 24 and 25 and for the purposes of making regulations only (SI 2015/1475, art. 2).
S. 24(2)–(9) comes into effect on 23 February 2015 (SI 2015/134, art. 2(2)).
Statutory instruments – SI 2015/118: partly made under s. 24(5).

PART 2 – OPTION TO BOOST OLD RETIREMENT PENSIONS

25 Option to boost old retirement pensions

25 In Schedule 15–

Part 1 contains amendments to allow certain people to pay additional contributions to boost their retirement pensions;

Part 2 contains amendments to allow corresponding legislation to be put in place for Northern Ireland.

Commencement Date – S. 25 comes into force on 12 October 2015 in so far as it relates to Sch. 15, para. 1–10 and 12–14 (SI 2015/1475, art. 3) and Sch. 15, para. 15 to 19, 21 and 22 (SI 2015/1670, art. 2).
S. 25 comes into effect on 1 October 2014 in so far as it relates to Sch. 15, para. 3 (SI 2014/2377).

PART 5 – BEREAVEMENT SUPPORT PAYMENT

Commencement Date – Pt. 5 comes into force on 8 March 2017 for the purposes of making regulations and 6 April 2017 for all other purposes (subject to SI 2017/297, art. 3(2)) (SI 2017/297, art. 3).

31 Bereavement support payment: contribution condition and amendments

31(1) For the purposes of section 30(1)(d) the contribution condition is that, for at least one tax year during the deceased's working life–

(a) he or she actually paid Class 1 or Class 2 national insurance contributions, and

(b) those contributions give rise to an earnings factor (or total earnings factors) equal to or greater than 25 times the lower earnings limit for the tax year.

31(2) For earnings factors, see sections 22 and 23 of the Social Security Contributions and Benefits Act 1992.

31(3) For the purposes of section 30(1)(d) the contribution condition is to be treated as met if the deceased was an employed earner and died as a result of–

(a) a personal injury of the kind mentioned in section 94(1) of the Social Security Contributions and Benefits Act 1992, or

(b) a disease or personal injury of the kind mentioned in section 108(1) of that Act.

31(4) In this section the following expressions have the meaning given by section 122(1) of the Social Security Contributions and Benefits Act 1992–

"employed earner",

"lower earnings limit",

"tax year", and

"working life".

31(5) Schedule 16 contains amendments to do with bereavement support payment.

Commencement Date – S. 31(5) comes into force on 8 February 2017 so far as it relates to Sch. 16, para. 20 and 33 (SI 2017/111, reg. 5(a)).
S. 31(5) comes into force on 6 April 2017, to the extent not already in force, subject to SI 2017/297, art. 4 (later commencement for abolition of bereavement payment and bereavement allowance) and 5 (commencement for entitlement to bereavement payment and bereavement support payment) (SI 2017/297, art. 3(2)).

PART 7 – FINAL PROVISIONS

53 Power to make consequential amendments etc

53(1) The Secretary of State or the Treasury may by order make consequential, incidental or supplementary provision in connection with any provision made by this Act.

53(2) An order under this section may amend, repeal, revoke or otherwise modify any enactment (whenever passed or made).

53(3) **"Enactment"** includes an enactment contained in subordinate legislation within the meaning of the Interpretation Act 1978.

Statutory instruments – SI 2016/252: partly made under s. 53(1) and (2).

54 Regulations and orders

54(1) Regulations and orders under this Act are to be made by statutory instrument.

54(2) A statutory instrument containing (whether alone or with other provisions)–

(a) regulations under section 3, 17, 18(3) or (5), 19, 20, 30, 32 or 34,

(b) the first regulations under section 10,

(c) an order under section 53 that amends or repeals a provision of an Act,

(d) regulations under Schedule 17,

(e) regulations under paragraph 2 of Schedule 18 or regulations under paragraph 7 of that Schedule that amend a provision of an Act, or

(e) *the first* regulations under paragraph 1 or 3 of that Schedule,

may not be made unless a draft of the instrument has been laid before and approved by a resolution of each House of Parliament.

54(3) Any other statutory instrument containing regulations or an order under this Act is subject to annulment in pursuance of a resolution of either House of Parliament.

54(4) Subsection (3) does not apply to a statutory instrument containing an order under section 56(1), (6) or (8) only.

54(5) A power to make regulations or an order under this Act may be used–

(a) to make different provision for different purposes;

(b) in relation to all or only some of the purposes for which it may be used.

54(6) Regulations or orders under this Act may include incidental, supplementary, consequential, transitional, transitory or saving provision.

Statutory instruments – SI 2015/118: partly made under s. 54(5) and (6).
SI 2016/252: partly made under s. 54(5) and (6).

55 Extent

55(1) This Act extends to England and Wales and Scotland only, subject to the following provisions of this section.

55(2) Any amendment or repeal made by this Act has the same extent as the enactment to which it relates.

55(3) This Part extends also to Northern Ireland.

56 Commencement

56(1) This Act comes into force on such day or days as the Secretary of State may by order appoint, subject as follows.

56(2) The following come into force on the day on which this Act is passed–

(a) section 29;

(b) section 51;

(c) this Part.

56(3) The following come into force at the end of the period of 2 months beginning with the day on which this Act is passed–

(a) Part 3;

(b) sections 34 and 35;

(c) section 41;

(d) sections 47 and 48;

(e) paragraph 30(2) of Schedule 13.

56(4) Part 1 comes into force on 6 April 2016, so far as not brought into force earlier by an order under subsection (1).

56(5) The Secretary of State may by order–

(a) amend subsection (4) so as to replace the reference to 6 April 2016 with a later date, and

(b) make corresponding amendments in Part 1 or any enactment amended by it.

56(6) Section 52 comes into force on such day or days as the Treasury may by order appoint.

56(7) An order under subsection (1) or (6) may appoint different days for different purposes.

56(8) The Secretary of State may by order make transitional, transitory or saving provision in connection with the coming into force of any provision of this Act.

Statutory instruments – SI 2015/1502: made under s. 56(8).
SI 2016/252: partly made under s. 56(8).

57 Short title

57 This Act may be cited as the Pensions Act 2014.

SCHEDULES

SCHEDULE 11 – PENSION SHARING: AMENDMENTS

Section 15

SOCIAL SECURITY ADMINISTRATION ACT 1992 (C. 5)

8 [Inserts SSAA 1992, s. 148AD.]

SCHEDULE 12 – STATE PENSION: AMENDMENTS

Section 23

Part 1 – Amendments to do with New State Pension System

SOCIAL SECURITY CONTRIBUTIONS AND BENEFITS ACT 1992 (C. 4)

2 The Contributions and Benefits Act is amended as follows.

3 [Amends SSCBA 1992, s. 1(1)(a).]

4 [Amends SSCBA 1992, s. 13(2).]

5 [Inserts SSCBA 1992, s. 19B.]

6(1) Section 22 (earnings factors) is amended as follows.

6(2) [Inserts SSCBA 1992, s. 22(2)(c).]

6(3) [Inserts SSCBA 1992, s. 22(5ZA) and (5ZB).]

Commencement Date – Para. 6(3) (and para. 6(1) so far as it relates to para. 6(3)) comes into force on 15 January 2016 but only for the purposes of making regulations (SI 2015/2058, art. 2).

7 [Amends SSCBA 1992, s. 122(1).]

SOCIAL SECURITY ADMINISTRATION ACT 1992 (C. 5)

8 The Administration Act is amended as follows.

13 [Inserts SSAA 1992, s. 121DA(1)(hl).]

14 [Amends SSAA 1992, s. 122B(3)(b).]

15 [Inserts SSAA 1992, s. 124(1)(af).]

16 [Amends SSAA 1992, s. 125(1).]

17 [Inserts SSAA 1992, s. 148AC.]

24 In section 170 (Social Security Advisory Committee), in subsection (5)–

(a) [amends SSAA 1992, s. 170(5),]

(b) [amends SSAA 1992, s. 170(5).]

25(1) Section 179 (reciprocal agreements) is amended as follows.

25(2) [Amends SSAA 1992, s. 179(3)(a).]

25(3) [Inserts SSAA 1992, s. 179(4)(ai).]

25(4) [Amends SSAA 1992, s. 179(5).]

Commencement Date – Para. 25 comes into force on 7 July 2015 (SI 2015/1475, art. 2(2)).

27 [Amends SSAA 1992, s. 190(1)(a).]

28 [Amends SSAA 1992, s. 191.]

SOCIAL SECURITY ACT 1998 (C. 14)

31 The Social Security Act 1998 is amended as follows.

32 [Inserts SSA 1998, s. 2(2)(m).]

33 In section 8 (decisions by Secretary of State)–

(a) [inserts SSA 1998, s. 8(3)(ab);]

(b) [amends SSA 1998, s. 8(4).]

34 [Amends SSA 1998, s. 11(3).]

35 [Amends SSA 1998, s. 27(7).]

36 [Inserts SSA 1998, s. 28(3)(j).]

37 [Not relevant to National Insurance contributions.]

STATE PENSION CREDIT ACT 2002 (C. 16)

42 The State Pension Credit Act 2002 is amended as follows.

44 [Amends SPCA 2002, s. 16(1).]

Part 2 – Amendments to do with Old State Pension System

CATEGORY B RETIREMENT PENSIONS

57 The Contributions and Benefits Act is amended as follows.

58 [Amends SSCBA 1992, s. 23A(1)(b).]

TRANSITION: SAME SEX MARRIAGES

87(1) If marriage of same sex couples is not lawful under the law of Scotland when the amendments made by this Part of this Schedule come into force then, under the law of Scotland, references in the amendments to a married person do not include a person married to someone of the same sex; and related expressions (such as "spouse") are to be read accordingly.

87(2) See also Part 1 of Schedule 2 to the Marriage (Same Sex Couples) Act 2013 (power to provide for English and Welsh marriages of same sex couples to be treated in Scotland as civil partnerships).

Part 4 – Other Amendments to do with Part 1

PENSIONS ACT 2008 (C. 30)

96 In the Pensions Act 2008, the following are repealed–

(a) [Not relevant to National Insurance contributions.]

(b) [Not relevant to National Insurance contributions.]

(c) [Repeals PA 2008, Sch. 4, para. 14. Other repeals made by this provision are not relevant to National Insurance contributions.]

Commencement Date – Para. 96 came into force on 1 October 2014 (SI 2014/2377, art. 2(3)(c)).

SCHEDULE 13 – ABOLITION OF CONTRACTING-OUT FOR SALARY RELATED SCHEMES

Section 24

Part 1 – Pension Schemes Act 1993: Amendments

1 The Pension Schemes Act 1993 is amended as follows.

2 [Amends PSA 1993.]

3 [Amends heading to PSA 1993, Pt. 3.]

4 [Amends heading to PSA 1993, Pt. 3, Ch. 1.]

5 [Repeals PSA 1993, s. 7.]

6 [Inserts PSA 1993, s. 7A and 7B.]

7(1) Section 8 (meaning of "contracted-out employment", "guaranteed minimum pension" and "minimum payment") is amended as follows.

7(2) [Substitutes PSA 1993, s. 8(1).]

7(3) [Inserts PSA 1993, s. 8(1B).]

7(4) [Amends PSA 1993, s. 8(2).]

7(5) [Substitutes PSA 1993, s. 8(4).]

8 [Repeals heading above PSA 1993, s. 9.]

9 [Repeals PSA 1993, s. 9 and 11.]

22 [Repeals PSA 1993, s. 34 to 36.]

26 [Substitutes heading to PSA 1993, Pt. 3, Ch. 2.]

27 In section 40 (scope of Chapter 2)–

(a) [omits PSA 1993, s. 40(a);]

(b) [amends PSA 1993, s. 40(c).]

28 [Repeals heading above PSA 1993, s. 41.]

29 [Repeals PSA 1993, s. 41.]

30(1) [Repeals PSA 1993, s. 42.]

30(2) There is no duty, before the repeal of section 42 comes into force, to lay before Parliament any reports under that section.

41 [Omits PSA 1993, s. 171(1)(b).]

43(1) Section 181(1) (general interpretation) is amended as follows.

43(2) [Amends PSA 1993, s. 181(1).]

43(3) [Amends PSA 1993, s. 181(1).]

43(4) [Amends PSA 1993, s. 181(1).]

43(5) [Amends PSA 1993, s. 181(1).]

43(6) [Amends PSA 1993, s. 181(1).]

43(7) [Amends PSA 1993, s. 181(1).]

43(8) [Amends PSA 1993, s. 181(1).]

44 [Repeals PSA 1993, s. 181A.]

45 [Omits PSA 1993, s. 185(9).]

Part 2 – Other Acts: Amendments

SOCIAL SECURITY CONTRIBUTIONS AND BENEFITS ACT 1992 (C. 4)

48 The Contributions and Benefits Act is amended as follows.

49 [Amends SSCBA 1992, s. 1(3).]

50 [Amends SSCBA 1992, s. 4C(5)(a) and (b).]

51 [Omits SSCBA 1992, s. 8(3)(c).]

52 [Omits SSCBA 1992, s. 9(3)(c).]

53 [Amends SSCBA 1992, s. 20(3).]

54 [Omits SSCBA 1992, Sch. 1, para. 1(2), (3), (6) and (9)–(11).]

SOCIAL SECURITY ADMINISTRATION ACT 1992 (C. 5)

55 The Administration Act is amended as follows.

57 [Amends SSAA 1992, s. 191.]

EMPLOYMENT ACT 2002 (C. 22)

72 [Amends EA 2002, s. 15(2)(c).]

PENSIONS ACT 2007 (C. 22)

77 The Pensions Act 2007 is amended as follows.

78(1) Section 15 (abolition of contracting-out for defined contribution pension schemes) is amended as follows.

78(2) [Amends PA 2007, s. 15(1).]

78(3) [Amends PA 2007, s. 15(2).]

78(4) [Amends PA 2007, s. 15(4).]

79 [Amends PA 2007, s. 27(6).]

80(1) Schedule 4 (abolition of contracting-out for defined contribution pension schemes) is amended as follows.

80(2) [Amends PA 2007, Sch. 4, para. 61, 62(1), (2)(a), (b)(i) and (3), 65 and 66(2).]

80(3) [Amends PA 2007, Sch. 4, para. 67.]

SCHEDULE 15 – OPTION TO BOOST OLD RETIREMENT PENSIONS

Section 25

Commencement Date – Sch. 15, para. 1–10 and 12–14 came into force on 12 October 2015 (SI 2015/1475, art. 3).

Part 1 – Great Britain

SOCIAL SECURITY CONTRIBUTIONS AND BENEFITS ACT 1992 (C. 4)

1 The Social Security Contributions and Benefits Act 1992 is amended as follows.

2(1) Section 1 (outline of contributory system) is amended as follows.

2(2) [Amends SSCBA 1992, s. 1(2).]

2(3) [Amends SSCBA 1992, s. 1(4)(a).]

3 [Inserts SSCBA 1992, s. 14A–14C.]

Commencement Date – Para. 3 came into force on 1 October 2014 (SI 2014/2377, art. 2(3)(d)).

4 If paragraph 3 comes into force before the day mentioned in section 56(4) of this Act, section 14A(2) as inserted by that paragraph has effect as if the reference to entitlement included the prospective entitlement of a person who–

(a) has not yet reached pensionable age, but

(b) will reach pensionable age before that day (assuming that the person lives until pensionable age).

10 [Amends SSCBA 1992, s. 122(1).]

11 [Amends SSCBA 1992, s. 176(1)(a).]

Commencement Date – Para. 11 came into force 13 October 2014 (SI 2014/2727, art. 2).

12 [Amends SSCBA 1992, Sch. 1, heading.]

SOCIAL SECURITY ADMINISTRATION ACT 1992 (C. 5)

13(1) Section 162 of the Social Security Administration Act 1992 (destination of contributions) is amended as follows.

13(2) [Inserts SSAA 1992, s. 162(5)(ea).]

13(3) [Amends SSAA 1992, s. 162(8)(c).]

SCHEDULE 16 – BEREAVEMENT SUPPORT PAYMENT: AMENDMENTS

Section 31

Commencement Date – Sch. 16 comes into force on 6 April 2017, to the extent not already in force, subject to SI 2017/297, art. 4 (later commencement for abolition of bereavement payment and bereavement allowance) and 5 (commencement for entitlement to bereavement payment and bereavement support payment) (SI 2017/297, art. 3(2)).

SOCIAL SECURITY CONTRIBUTIONS AND BENEFITS ACT 1992 (C. 4)

2 The Social Security Contributions and Benefits Act 1992 is amended as follows.

3(1) Section 20 (descriptions of contributory benefits) is amended as follows.

3(2) [Not relevant to National Insurance contributions.]

3(3) [Amends SSCBA 1992, s. 20(2).]

4(1) Section 21 (contribution conditions) is amended as follows.

4(2) *[Amends SSCBA 1992, s. 21(2).]*

4(3) [Omits SSCBA 1992, s. 21(4).]

5 [Inserts SSCBA 1992, s. 22(2)(d).]

6(1) Section 23A (contributions credits for relevant parents and carers) is amended as follows.

6(2) [Omits SSCBA 1992, s. 23A(1)(e).]

6(3) [Amends SSCBA 1992, s. 23A(6)(b).]

SOCIAL SECURITY ADMINISTRATION ACT 1992 (C. 5)

20 The Social Security Administration Act 1992 is amended as follows.

Commencement Date – Para. 20 comes into force on 8 February 2017 so far as it relates to Sch. 16, para. 33 (SI 2017/111, reg. 5(b)).

26 [Inserts SSAA 1992, s. 121DA(1)(hm).]

27 [Amends SSAA 1992, s. 122B(3)(b).]

28 [Inserts SSAA 1992, s. 124(1)(ag).]

29 [Amends SSAA 1992, s. 125(1).]

32 [Amends SSAA 1992, s. 170(5).]

33(1) Section 179 (reciprocal agreements) is amended as follows.

33(2) [Amends SSAA 1992, s. 179(3)(a).]

33(3) [Inserts SSAA 1992, s. 179(4)(aj).]

33(4) [Not relevant to National Insurance contributions.]

Commencement Date – Para. 33 comes into force on 8 February 2017 (SI 2017/111, reg. 5(c)).

35 [Amends SSAA 1992, s. 191]

SOCIAL SECURITY ACT 1998 (C. 14)

37 The Social Security Act 1998 is amended as follows.

38 [Inserts SSA 1998, s. 2(2)(n).]

39(1) Section 8 (decisions by Secretary of State) is amended as follows.

39(2) [Inserts SSA 1998, s. 8(3)(ac).]

39(3) [Amends SSA 1998, s. 8(4).]

40 [Amends SSA 1998, s. 11(3).]

41 [Amends SSA 1998, s. 27(7).]

42 [Amends SSA 1998, s. 28(3)(j).]

FINANCE ACT 2014

(2014 Chapter 26)

[*17th July 2014*]

ARRANGEMENT OF SECTIONS

PART 4 – FOLLOWER NOTICES AND ACCELERATED PAYMENTS

CHAPTER 1 – INTRODUCTION

CHAPTER 2 – FOLLOWER NOTICES

CHAPTER 3 – ACCELERATED PAYMENT

PART 4 – FOLLOWER NOTICES AND ACCELERATED PAYMENTS

Commencement Date – Pt. 4 applies to Class 1, 1A, 1B and certain Class 2 contributions with effect from the end of the period of 2 months beginning with 12 February 2015 (NICA 2015, s. 4(1) and Sch. 2, Pt. 1).
Pt. 4 applies to Class 4 contributions with effect from the end of the period of 2 months beginning with 12 February 2015 (SSCBA 1992, s. 16(1)(d)).

Cross references – NICA 2015, Sch. 2, para. 1–11: modified application of Pt. 4: references to tax or a relevant tax (other than references to particular taxes) include "relevant contributions" (Class 1, Class 1A, 1B and certain Class 2 contributions under SSCBA 1992, Pt. 1 (NICA 2015, Sch. 2, para. 22)) and references to charge to tax, assessment to tax, tax enquiry, tax appeal to be read accordingly.

Other material – Misc. 215: HMRC guidance – Ten things you need to know about accelerated payment notices (APNs).

Chapter 1 – Introduction

OVERVIEW

199 Overview of Part 4

199 In this Part–

(a) sections 200 to 203 set out the main defined terms used in the Part,

(b) Chapter 2 makes provision for follower notices and for penalties if account is not taken of judicial rulings which lay down principles or give reasoning relevant to tax cases,

(c) Chapter 3 makes–

(i) provision for accelerated payments to be made on account of tax,

(ii) provision restricting the circumstances in which payments of tax can be postponed pending an appeal,

(iii) provision to enable a court to prevent repayment of tax, for the purpose of protecting the public revenue, and

(iv) provision restricting the surrender of losses and other amounts for the purposes of group relief.

(d) Chapter 4–

(i) [not relevant to National Insurance contributions,]

(ii) confers a power to extend the provisions of this Part to other taxes, and

(iii) makes amendments consequential on this Part.

History – S. 199(c)(iv) (and the ", and" preceding it) inserted and the word "and" at the end of s. 199(c)(ii) omitted by FA 2015, s. 118 and Sch. 18, para. 2, with effect from 26 March 2015.

MAIN DEFINITIONS

200 "Relevant tax"

200 In this Part, **"relevant tax"** means–

(a) [not relevant to National Insurance contributions,]

(b) [not relevant to National Insurance contributions,]

(c) [not relevant to National Insurance contributions,]

(d) [not relevant to National Insurance contributions,]

(e) [not relevant to National Insurance contributions,]

(f) [not relevant to National Insurance contributions,]

(g) [not relevant to National Insurance contributions.]

Cross references – NICA 2015, Sch. 2, para. 12: the definition of "relevant tax" has effect as if "relevant contributions" (Class 1, Class 1A, 1B and certain Class 2 contributions under SSCBA 1992, Pt. 1 (NICA 2015, Sch. 2, para. 22)) were listed in it.

201 "Tax advantage" and "tax arrangements"

201(1) This section applies for the purposes of this Part.

201(2) **"Tax advantage"** includes–

(a) relief or increased relief from tax,

(b) repayment or increased repayment of tax,

(c) avoidance or reduction of a charge to tax or an assessment to tax,

(d) avoidance of a possible assessment to tax,

(e) deferral of a payment of tax or advancement of a repayment of tax, and

(f) avoidance of an obligation to deduct or account for tax.

201(3) Arrangements are **"tax arrangements"** if, having regard to all the circumstances, it would be reasonable to conclude that the obtaining of a tax advantage was the main purpose, or one of the main purposes, of the arrangements.

201(4) **"Arrangements"** includes any agreement, understanding, scheme, transaction or series of transactions (whether or not legally enforceable).

Cross references – NICA 2015, Sch. 2, para. 3 and 4: references to a charge to tax and assessment to tax include a liability to pay (and decisions relating a liability to pay) "relevant contributions" (Class 1, Class 1A, 1B and certain Class 2 contributions under SSCBA 1992, Pt. 1 (NICA 2015, Sch. 2, para. 22)).

202 "Tax enquiry" and "return"

202(1) This section applies for the purposes of this Part.

202(2) **"Tax enquiry"** means–

(a) an enquiry under section 9A or 12AC of TMA 1970 (enquiries into self-assessment returns for income tax and capital gains tax), including an enquiry by virtue of notice being deemed to be given under section 9A of that Act by virtue of section 12AC(6) of that Act,

(b) an enquiry under paragraph 5 of Schedule 1A to that Act (enquiry into claims made otherwise than by being included in a return),

(c) [not relevant to National Insurance contributions,]

(d) [not relevant to National Insurance contributions,]

(e) [not relevant to National Insurance contributions,]

(f) a deemed enquiry under subsection (6).

202(3) The period during which an enquiry is in progress–

(a) begins with the day on which notice of enquiry is given, and

(b) ends with the day on which the enquiry is completed.

202(4) Subsection (3) is subject to subsection (6).

202(5) [not relevant to National Insurance contributions,]

202(6) An enquiry is deemed to be in progress, in relation to a return to which subsection (5) applies, during the period which–

(a) begins with the time the account is delivered or (as the case may be) the statement, declaration, information or document is produced, and

(b) ends when the person is issued with a certificate of discharge under section 239 of that Act, or is discharged by virtue of section 256(1)(b) of that Act, in respect of the return (at which point the enquiry is to be treated as completed).

Cross references – NICA 2015, Sch. 2, para. 5: references to a tax enquiry include a "relevant contributions dispute" (as defined by NICA 2015, Sch. 2, para. 6; "relevant contributions" are Class 1, Class 1A, 1B and certain Class 2 contributions under SSCBA 1992, Pt. 1 (NICA 2015, Sch. 2, para. 22)).

203 "Tax appeal"

203 In this Part **"tax appeal"** means–

(a) an appeal under section 31 of TMA 1970 (income tax: appeals against amendments of self-assessment, amendments made by closure notices under section 28A or 28B of that Act, etc), including an appeal under that section by virtue of regulations under Part 11 of ITEPA 2003 (PAYE),

(b) an appeal under paragraph 9 of Schedule 1A to TMA 1970 (income tax: appeals against amendments made by closure notices under paragraph 7(2) of that Schedule, etc),

(c) [not relevant to National Insurance contributions,]

(d) [not relevant to National Insurance contributions,]

(e) [not relevant to National Insurance contributions,]

(ea) [not relevant to National Insurance contributions,]

(f) [not relevant to National Insurance contributions,]

(g) [not relevant to National Insurance contributions,]

(h) [not relevant to National Insurance contributions,]

(i) an appeal against any determination of–

(i) an appeal within paragraphs (a) to (h), or

(ii) an appeal within this paragraph.

Cross references – NICA 2015, Sch. 2, para. 9: references to a tax appeal include a "NICs appeal" (an appeal against a decision relating to relevant contributions (NICA 2015, Sch. 2, para. 10); "relevant contributions" are Class 1, Class 1A, 1B and certain Class 2 contributions under SSCBA 1992, Pt. 1 (NICA 2015, Sch. 2, para. 22)).

Chapter 2 – Follower Notices

GIVING OF FOLLOWER NOTICES

204 Circumstances in which a follower notice may be given

204(1) HMRC may give a notice (a "follower notice") to a person ("P") if Conditions A to D are met.

204(2) Condition A is that–

(a) a tax enquiry is in progress into a return or claim made by P in relation to a relevant tax, or

(b) P has made a tax appeal (by notifying HMRC or otherwise) in relation to a relevant tax, but that appeal has not yet been–

(i) determined by the tribunal or court to which it is addressed, or

(ii) abandoned or otherwise disposed of.

204(3) Condition B is that the return or claim or, as the case may be, appeal is made on the basis that a particular tax advantage ("the asserted advantage") results from particular tax arrangements ("the chosen arrangements").

204(4) Condition C is that HMRC is of the opinion that there is a judicial ruling which is relevant to the chosen arrangements.

204(5) Condition D is that no previous follower notice has been given to the same person (and not withdrawn) by reference to the same tax advantage, tax arrangements, judicial ruling and tax period.

204(6) A follower notice may not be given after the end of the period of 12 months beginning with the later of–

(a) the day on which the judicial ruling mentioned in Condition C is made, and

(b) the day the return or claim to which subsection (2)(a) refers was received by HMRC or (as the case may be) the day the tax appeal to which subsection (2)(b) refers was made.

Cross references – NICA 2015, Sch. 2, para. 13: modified application of s. 204 in relation to relevant contributions (Class 1, Class 1A, 1B and certain Class 2 contributions under SSCBA 1992, Pt. 1 (NICA 2015, Sch. 2, para. 22).

205 "Judicial ruling" and circumstances in which a ruling is "relevant"

205(1) This section applies for the purposes of this Chapter.

205(2) **"Judicial ruling"** means a ruling of a court or tribunal on one or more issues.

205(3) A judicial ruling is **"relevant"** to the chosen arrangements if–

(a) it relates to tax arrangements,

(b) the principles laid down, or reasoning given, in the ruling would, if applied to the chosen arrangements, deny the asserted advantage or a part of that advantage, and

(c) it is a final ruling.

205(4) A judicial ruling is a **"final ruling"** if it is–

(a) a ruling of the Supreme Court, or

(b) a ruling of any other court or tribunal in circumstances where–

(i) *no appeal* may be made against the ruling,

(ii) if an appeal may be made against the ruling with permission, the time limit for applications has expired and either no application has been made or permission has been refused,

(iii) if such permission to appeal against the ruling has been granted or is not required, no appeal has been made within the time limit for appeals, or

(iv) if an appeal was made, it was abandoned or otherwise disposed of before it was determined by the court or tribunal to which it was addressed.

205(5) Where a judicial ruling is final by virtue of sub-paragraph (ii), (iii) or (iv) of subsection (4)(b), the ruling is treated as made at the time when the sub-paragraph in question is first satisfied.

206 Content of a follower notice

206 A follower notice must–

(a) identify the judicial ruling in respect of which Condition C in section 204 is met,

(b) explain why HMRC considers that the ruling meets the requirements of section 205(3), and

(c) explain the effects of sections 207 to 210.

REPRESENTATIONS

207 Representations about a follower notice

207(1) Where a follower notice is given under section 204, P has 90 days beginning with the day that notice is given to send written representations to HMRC objecting to the notice on the grounds that–

(a) Condition A, B or D in section 204 was not met,

(b) the judicial ruling specified in the notice is not one which is relevant to the chosen arrangements, or

(c) the notice was not given within the period specified in subsection (6) of that section.

207(2) HMRC must consider any representations made in accordance with subsection (1).

207(3) Having considered the representations, HMRC must determine whether to–

(a) confirm the follower notice (with or without amendment), or

(b) withdraw the follower notice,

and notify P accordingly.

PENALTIES

208 Penalty if corrective action not taken in response to follower notice

208(1) This section applies where a follower notice is given to P (and not withdrawn).

208(2) P is liable to pay a penalty if the necessary corrective action is not taken in respect of the denied advantage (if any) before the specified time.

208(3) In this Chapter **"the denied advantage"** means so much of the asserted advantage (see section 204(3)) as is denied by the application of the principles laid down, or reasoning given, in the judicial ruling identified in the follower notice under section 206(a).

208(4) The necessary corrective action is taken in respect of the denied advantage if (and only if) P takes the steps set out in subsections (5) and (6).

208(5) The first step is that–

(a) in the case of a follower notice given by virtue of section 204(2)(a), P amends a return or claim to counteract the denied advantage;

(b) in the case of a follower notice given by virtue of section 204(2)(b), P takes all necessary action to enter into an agreement with HMRC (in writing) for the purpose of relinquishing the denied advantage.

208(6) The second step is that P notifies HMRC–

(a) *that P has taken the first step, and*

(b) of the denied advantage and (where different) the additional amount which has or will become due and payable in respect of tax by reason of the first step being taken.

208(7) In determining the additional amount which has or will become due and payable in respect of tax for the purposes of subsection (6)(b), it is to be assumed that, where P takes the necessary action as mentioned in subsection (5)(b), the agreement is then entered into.

208(8) In this Chapter–

"the specified time" means–

(a) if no representations objecting to the follower notice were made by P in accordance with subsection (1) of section 207, the end of the 90 day post-notice period;

(b) if such representations were made and the notice is confirmed under that section (with or without amendment), the later of–

(i) the end of the 90 day post-notice period, and

(ii) the end of the 30 day post-representations period;

"the 90 day post-notice period" means the period of 90 days beginning with the day on which the follower notice is given;

"the 30 day post-representations period" means the period of 30 days beginning with the day on which P is notified of HMRC's determination under section 207.

208(9) No enactment limiting the time during which amendments may be made to returns or claims operates to prevent P taking the first step mentioned in subsection (5)(a) before the tax enquiry is closed (whether or not before the specified time).

208(10) No appeal may be brought, by virtue of a provision mentioned in subsection (11), against an amendment made by a closure notice in respect of a tax enquiry to the extent that the amendment takes into account an amendment made by P to a return or claim in taking the first step mentioned in subsection (5)(a) (whether or not that amendment was made before the specified time).

208(11) The provisions are–

(a) section 31(1)(b) or (c) of TMA 1970,

(b) paragraph 9 of Schedule 1A to TMA 1970,

(c) [not relevant to National Insurance contributions,]

(d) [not relevant to National Insurance contributions,]

(e) [not relevant to National Insurance contributions.]

Cross references – NICA 2015, Sch. 2, para. 14: modified application of s. 208 in relation to relevant contributions (Class 1, Class 1A, 1B and certain Class 2 contributions under SSCBA 1992, Pt. 1 (NICA 2015, Sch. 2, para. 22).
NICA 2015, Sch. 2, para. 20: recovery of penalties under s. 208 imposed by virtue of NICA 2015, Sch. 2, Pt. 1.

209 Amount of a section 208 penalty

209(1) The penalty under section 208 is 50% of the value of the denied advantage.

209(2) Schedule 30 contains provision about how the denied advantage is valued for the purposes of calculating penalties under this section.

209(3) Where P before the specified time–

(a) amends a return or claim to counteract part of the denied advantage only, or

(b) takes all necessary action to enter into an agreement with HMRC (in writing) for the purposes of relinquishing part of the denied advantage only,

in subsections (1) and (2) the references to the denied advantage are to be read as references to the remainder of the denied advantage.

210 Reduction of a section 208 penalty for co-operation

210(1) Where–

(a) P is liable to pay a penalty under section 208 of the amount specified in section 209(1),

(b) the penalty has not yet been assessed, and

(c) P has co-operated with HMRC,

HMRC may reduce the amount of that penalty to reflect the quality of that co-operation.

210(2) In relation to co-operation, **"quality"** includes timing, nature and extent.

210(3) P has co-operated with HMRC only if P has done one or more of the following–

(a) provided reasonable assistance to HMRC in quantifying the tax advantage;

(b) counteracted the denied advantage;

(c) provided HMRC with information enabling corrective action to be taken by HMRC;

(d) provided HMRC with information enabling HMRC to enter an agreement with P for the purpose of counteracting the denied advantage;

(e) allowed HMRC to access tax records for the purpose of ensuring that the denied advantage is fully counteracted.

210(4) But nothing in this section permits HMRC to reduce a penalty to less than 10% of the value of the denied advantage.

211 Assessment of a section 208 penalty

211(1) Where a person is liable for a penalty under section 208, HMRC may assess the penalty.

211(2) Where HMRC assess the penalty, HMRC must–

(a) notify the person who is liable for the penalty, and

(b) state in the notice a tax period in respect of which the penalty is assessed.

211(3) A penalty under section 208 must be paid before the end of the period of 30 days beginning with the day on which the person is notified of the penalty under subsection (2).

211(4) An assessment–

(a) is to be treated for procedural purposes in the same way as an assessment to tax (except in respect of a matter expressly provided for by this Chapter),

(b) may be enforced as if it were an assessment to tax, and

(c) may be combined with an assessment to tax.

211(5) No penalty under section 208 may be notified under subsection (2) later than–

(a) in the case of a follower notice given by virtue of section 204(2)(a) (tax enquiry in progress), the end of the period of 90 days beginning with the day the tax enquiry is completed, and

(b) in the case of a follower notice given by virtue of section 204(2)(b) (tax appeal pending), the end of the period of 90 days beginning with the earliest of–

(i) the day on which P takes the necessary corrective action (within the meaning of section 208(4)),

(ii) the day on which a ruling is made on the tax appeal by P, or any further appeal in that case, which is a final ruling (see section 205(4)), and

(iii) the day on which that appeal, or any further appeal, is abandoned or otherwise disposed of before it is determined by the court or tribunal to which it is addressed.

211(6) In this section a reference to an assessment to tax, in relation to inheritance tax, is to a determination.

212 Aggregate penalties

212(1) Subsection (2) applies where–

(a) two or more penalties are incurred by the same person and fall to be determined by reference to an amount of tax to which that person is chargeable,

(b) one of those penalties is incurred under section 208, and

(c) one or more of the other penalties are incurred under a relevant penalty provision.

212(2) The aggregate of the amounts of the penalties mentioned in subsection (1)(b) and (c), so far as determined by reference to that amount of tax, must not exceed–

(a) the relevant percentage of that amount, or

(b) in a case where at least one of the penalties is under paragraph 5(2)(b) or 6(3)(b), (4)(b) or (5)(b) of Schedule 55 to FA 2009, £300 (if greater).

212(3) In the application of section 97A of TMA 1970 (multiple penalties), no account is to be taken of a penalty under section 208.

212(4) **"Relevant penalty provision"** means–

(a) Schedule 24 to FA 2007 (penalties for errors),

(b) Schedule 41 to FA 2008 (penalties: failure to notify etc),

(c) Schedule 55 to FA 2009 (penalties for failure to make returns etc),

(d) Part 5 of Schedule 18 to FA 2016 (serial tax avoidance), or

(e) section 212A of FA 2013 (general anti-abuse rule).

212(5) **"The relevant percentage"** means–

(a) 200% in a case where at least one of the penalties is determined by reference to the percentage in–

(i) paragraph 4(4)(c) of Schedule 24 to FA 2007,

(ii) paragraph 6(4)(a) of Schedule 41 to FA 2008, or

(iii) paragraph 6(3A)(c) of Schedule 55 to FA 2009,

(b) 150% in a case where paragraph (a) does not apply and at least one of the penalties is determined by reference to the percentage in–

(i) paragraph 4(3)(c) of Schedule 24 to FA 2007,
(ii) paragraph 6(3)(a) of Schedule 41 to FA 2008, or
(iii) paragraph 6(3A)(b) of Schedule 55 to FA 2009,

(c) 140% in a case where neither paragraph (a) nor paragraph (b) applies and at least one the penalties is determined by reference to the percentage in–
(i) paragraph 4(4)(b) of Schedule 24 to FA 2007,
(ii) paragraph 6(4)(b) of Schedule 41 to FA 2008,
(iii) paragraph 6(4A)(c) of Schedule 55 to FA 2009,

(d) 105% in a case where none of paragraphs (a), (b) and (c) applies and at least one of the penalties is determined by reference to the percentage in–
(i) paragraph 4(3)(b) of Schedule 24 to FA 2007,
(ii) paragraph 6(3)(b) of Schedule 41 to FA 2008,
(iii) paragraph 6(4A)(b) of Schedule 55 to FA 2009, and

(e) in any other case, 100%.

History – S. 212(4)(d) (and the ", or" before it) inserted (and the "or" after (b) omitted) by FA 2016, s. 159 and Sch. 18, para. 60, with effect in relation to relevant defeats incurred after 15 September 2016 (Royal Assent), subject to transitional provisions in Sch. 18, para. 64 and 65 (in relation to arrangements entered into before 15 September 2016 relevant defeats incurred before 6 April 2017 and certain relevant defeats incurred on or after 6 April 2017 are disregarded).
S. 212(4)(e) (and the ", or" before it) inserted (and the "or" after (c) omitted) by FA 2016, s. 158(11), with effect in relation to tax arrangements (within the meaning of FA 2013, Pt. 5) entered into on or after 15 September 2016.

Cross references – NICA 2015, Sch. 2, para. 15: modified application of s. 212 in relation to relevant contributions (Class 1, Class 1A, 1B and certain Class 2 contributions under SSCBA 1992, Pt. 1 (NICA 2015, Sch. 2, para. 22).

213 Alteration of assessment of a section 208 penalty

213(1) After notification of an assessment has been given to a person under section 211(2), the assessment may not be altered except in accordance with this section or on appeal.

213(2) A supplementary assessment may be made in respect of a penalty if an earlier assessment operated by reference to an underestimate of the value of the denied advantage.

213(3) An assessment or supplementary assessment may be revised as necessary if it operated by reference to an overestimate of the denied advantage; and, where more than the resulting assessed penalty has already been paid by the person to HMRC, the excess must be repaid.

214 Appeal against a section 208 penalty

214(1) P may appeal against a decision of HMRC that a penalty is payable by P under section 208.

214(2) P may appeal against a decision of HMRC as to the amount of a penalty payable by P under section 208.

214(3) The grounds on which an appeal under subsection (1) may be made include in particular–

(a) that Condition A, B or D in section 204 was not met in relation to the follower notice,
(b) that the judicial ruling specified in the notice is not one which is relevant to the chosen arrangements,
(c) that the notice was not given within the period specified in subsection (6) of that section, or
(d) that it was reasonable in all the circumstances for P not to have taken the necessary corrective action (see section 208(4)) in respect of the denied advantage.

214(4) An appeal under this section must be made within the period of 30 days beginning with the day on which notification of the penalty is given under section 211.

214(5) An appeal under this section is to be treated in the same way as an appeal against an assessment to the tax concerned (including by the application of any provision about bringing the appeal by notice to HMRC, about HMRC's review of the decision or about determination of the appeal by the First-tier Tribunal or Upper Tribunal).

214(6) Subsection (5) does not apply–

(a) so as to require a person to pay a penalty before an appeal against the assessment of the penalty is determined, or
(b) in respect of any other matter expressly provided for by this Part.

214(7) *In this section a reference* to an assessment to tax, in relation to inheritance tax, is to a determination.

214(8) On an appeal under subsection (1), the tribunal may affirm or cancel HMRC's decision.

214(9) On an appeal under subsection (2), the tribunal may–

(a) affirm HMRC's decision, or
(b) substitute for HMRC's decision another decision that HMRC had power to make.

214(10) The cancellation under subsection (8) of HMRC's decision on the ground specified in subsection (3)(d) does not affect the validity of the follower notice, or of any accelerated payment notice or partner payment notice under Chapter 3 related to the follower notice.

214(11) In this section **"tribunal"** means the First-tier Tribunal or Upper Tribunal (as appropriate by virtue of subsection (5)).

PARTNERS AND PARTNERSHIPS

215 Follower notices: treatment of partners and partnerships

215 [Not relevant to national insurance contributions.]

APPEALS OUT OF TIME

216 Late appeal against final judicial ruling

216(1) This section applies where a final judicial ruling ("the original ruling") is the subject of an appeal by reason of a court or tribunal granting leave to appeal out of time.

216(2) If a follower notice has been given identifying the original ruling under section 206(a), the notice is suspended until such time as HMRC notify P that–

(a) the appeal has resulted in a judicial ruling which is a final ruling, or

(b) the appeal has been abandoned or otherwise disposed of (before it was determined).

216(3) Accordingly the period during which the notice is suspended does not count towards the periods mentioned in section 208(8).

216(4) When a follower notice is suspended under subsection (2), HMRC must notify P as soon as reasonably practicable.

216(5) If the new final ruling resulting from the appeal is not a judicial ruling which is relevant to the chosen arrangements (see section 205), the follower notice ceases to have effect at the end of the period of suspension.

216(6) In any other case, the follower notice continues to have effect after the end of the period of suspension and, in a case within subsection (2)(a), is treated as if it were in respect of the new final ruling resulting from the appeal.

216(7) The notice given under subsection (2) must–

(a) state whether subsection (5) or (6) applies, and

(b) where subsection (6) applies in a case within subsection (2)(a), make any amendments to the follower notice required to reflect the new final ruling.

216(8) No new follower notice may be given in respect of the original ruling unless the appeal has been abandoned or otherwise disposed of before it is determined by the court or tribunal to which it is addressed.

216(9) Nothing in this section prevents a follower notice being given in respect of a new final ruling resulting from the appeal.

216(10) Where the appeal is abandoned or otherwise disposed of before it is determined by the court or tribunal to which it is addressed, for the purposes of the original ruling the period beginning when leave to appeal out of time was granted, and ending when the appeal is disposed of, does not count towards the period of 12 months mentioned in section 204(6).

TRANSITIONAL PROVISION

217 Transitional provision

217(1) In the case of judicial rulings made before the day on which this Act is passed, this Chapter has effect as if for section 204(6) there were substituted–

"**204(6)** A follower notice may not be given after–

(a) the end of the period of 24 months beginning with the day on which this Act is passed, or

(b) the end of the period of 12 months beginning with the day the return or claim to which subsection (2)(a) refers was received by HMRC or (as the case may be) with the day the tax appeal to which subsection (2)(b) refers was made,

whichever is later."

217(2) Accordingly, the reference in section 216(10) to the period of 12 months includes a reference to the period of 24 months mentioned in the version of section 204(6) set out in subsection (1) above.

DEFINED TERMS

218 Defined terms used in Chapter 2

218 For the purposes of this Chapter–

"arrangements" has the meaning given by section 201(4);

"the asserted advantage" has the meaning given by section 204(3);

"the chosen arrangements" has the meaning given by section 204(3);

"the denied advantage" has the meaning given by section 208(3);

"follower notice" has the meaning given by section 204(1);

"HMRC" means Her Majesty's Revenue and Customs;

"judicial ruling", and **"relevant"** in relation to a judicial ruling and the chosen arrangements, have the meaning given by section 205;

"relevant tax" has the meaning given by section 200;

"the specified time" has the meaning given by section 208(8);

"tax advantage" has the meaning given by section 201(2);

"tax appeal" has the meaning given by section 203;

"tax arrangements" has the meaning given by section 201(3);

"tax enquiry" has the meaning given by section 202(2);

"tax period" means a tax year, accounting period or other period in respect of which tax is charged;

"P" has the meaning given by section 204(1);

"the 30 day post-representations period" has the meaning given by section 208(8);

"the 90 day post-notice period" has the meaning given by section 208(8).

Chapter 3 – Accelerated Payment

ACCELERATED PAYMENT NOTICES

219 Circumstances in which an accelerated payment notice may be given

219(1) HMRC may give a notice (an "accelerated payment notice") to a person ("P") if Conditions A to C are met.

219(2) Condition A is that–

(a) a tax enquiry is in progress into a return or claim made by P in relation to a relevant tax, or

(b) P has made a tax appeal (by notifying HMRC or otherwise) in relation to a relevant tax but that appeal has not yet been–

(i) determined by the tribunal or court to which it is addressed, or

(ii) abandoned or otherwise disposed of.

219(3) Condition B is that the return or claim or, as the case may be, appeal is made on the basis that a particular tax advantage ("the asserted advantage") results from particular arrangements ("the chosen arrangements").

219(4) Condition C is that one or more of the following requirements are met–

(a) HMRC has given (or, at the same time as giving the accelerated payment notice, gives) P a follower notice under Chapter 2–

(i) in relation to the same return or claim or, as the case may be, appeal, and

(ii) by reason of the same tax advantage and the chosen arrangements;

(b) the chosen arrangements are DOTAS arrangements;

(c) a GAAR counteraction notice has been given in relation to the asserted advantage or part of it and the chosen arrangements (or is so given at the same time as the accelerated payment notice) in a case where the stated opinion of at least two of the members of the sub-panel of the GAAR Advisory Panel which considered the matter under paragraph 10 of Schedule 43 to FA 2013 was as *set out in paragraph 11*(3)(b) of that Schedule (entering into tax arrangements not reasonable course of action etc);

(d) a notice has been given under paragraph 8(2) or 9(2) of Schedule 43A to FA 2013 (notice of final decision after considering Panel's opinion about referred or counteracted arrangements) in relation to the asserted advantage or part of it and the chosen arrangements (or is so given at the same time as the accelerated payment notice) in a case where the stated opinion of at least two of the members of the sub-panel of the GAAR Advisory Panel about the other arrangements (see subsection (8)) was as set out in paragraph 11(3)(b) of Schedule 43 to FA 2013;

(e) a notice under paragraph 8(2) of Schedule 43B to FA 2013 (GAAR: generic referral of tax arrangements) has been given in relation to the asserted advantage or part of it and the chosen arrangements (or is so given at the same time as the accelerated payment notice) in a case where the stated opinion of at least two of the members of the sub-panel of the GAAR Advisory Panel which considered the generic referral in respect of those arrangements under paragraph 6 of Schedule 43B to FA 2013 was as set out in paragraph 6(4)(b) of that Schedule.

219(5) **"DOTAS arrangements"** means–

(a) notifiable arrangements to which HMRC has allocated a reference number under section 311 of FA 2004,

(b) notifiable arrangements implementing a notifiable proposal where HMRC has allocated a reference number under that section to the proposed notifiable arrangements, or

(c) arrangements in respect of which the promoter must provide prescribed information under section 312(2) of that Act by reason of the arrangements being substantially the same as notifiable arrangements within paragraph (a) or (b).

219(6) But the notifiable arrangements within subsection (5) do not include arrangements in relation to which HMRC has given notice under section 312(6) of FA 2004 (notice that promoters not under duty imposed to notify client of reference number).

219(7) **"GAAR counteraction notice"** means a notice under paragraph 12 of Schedule 43 to FA 2013 (notice of final decision to counteract under the general anti-abuse rule).

219(8) In subsection (4)(d) **"other arrangements"** means–

(a) in relation to a notice under paragraph 8(2) of Schedule 43A to FA 2013, the referred arrangements (as defined in that paragraph);

(b) in relation to a notice under paragraph 9(2) of that Schedule, the counteracted arrangements (as defined in paragraph 2 of that Schedule).

History – S. 219(4)(d) and (e) inserted by FA 2016, s. 157(19), with effect in relation to tax arrangements (within the meaning of FA 2013, Pt. 5) entered into at any time (whether before or on or after 15 September 2016).
S. 219(8) inserted by FA 2016, s. 157(20), with effect in relation to tax arrangements (within the meaning of FA 2013, Pt. 5) entered into at any time (whether before or on or after 15 September 2016).

Cross references – NICA 2015, Sch. 2, para. 16: modified application of s. 219 in relation to relevant contributions (Class 1, Class 1A, 1B and certain Class 2 contributions under SSCBA 1992, Pt. 1 (NICA 2015, Sch. 2, para. 22).

220 Content of notice given while a tax enquiry is in progress

220(1) This section applies where an accelerated payment notice is given by virtue of section 219(2)(a) (notice given while a tax enquiry is in progress).

220(2) The notice must–

(a) specify the paragraph or paragraphs of section 219(4) by virtue of which the notice is given,

(b) specify the payment (if any) required to be made under section 223 and the requirements of that section,

(c) explain the effect of sections 222 and 226, and of the amendments made by sections 224 and 225 (so far as relating to the relevant tax in relation to which the accelerated payment notice is given), and

(d) if the denied advantage consists of or includes an asserted surrenderable amount, specify that amount and any action which is required to be taken in respect of it under section 225A.

220(3) The payment required to be made under section 223 is an amount equal to the amount which a designated HMRC officer determines, to the best of that officer's information and belief, as the understated tax.

220(4) **"The understated tax"** means the additional amount that would be due and payable in respect of tax if–

(a) in the case of a notice given by virtue of section 219(4)(a) (cases where a follower notice is given)–

(i) it were assumed that the explanation given in the follower notice in question under section 206(b) is correct, and

(ii) the necessary corrective action were taken under section 208 in respect of what the designated HMRC officer determines, to the best of that officer's information and belief, as the denied advantage;

(b) in the case of a notice given by virtue of section 219(4)(b) (cases where the DOTAS requirements are met), such adjustments were made as are required to counteract what the designated HMRC officer determines, to the best of that officer's information and belief, as the denied advantage;

(c) in the case of a notice given by virtue of section 219(4)(c), (d) or (e) (cases involving counteraction under the general anti-abuse rule), such of the adjustments set out in the GAAR counteraction notice as have effect to counteract the denied advantage were made.

220(4A) "Asserted surrenderable amount" means so much of a surrenderable loss as a designated HMRC officer determines, to the best of that officer's information and belief, to be an amount–

(a) which would not be a surrenderable loss of P if the position were as stated in paragraphs (a), (b) or (c) of subsection (4), and

(b) which is not the subject of a claim by P for relief from corporation tax reflected in the understated tax amount (and hence in the payment required to be made under section 223).

220(4B) "Surrenderable loss" means a loss or other amount within section 99(1) of CTA 2010 (or part of such a loss or other amount).

220(5) "The denied advantage"–

(a) in the case of a notice given by virtue of section 219(4)(a), has the meaning given by section 208(3),

(b) in the case of a notice given by virtue of section 219(4)(b), means so much of the asserted advantage as is not a tax advantage which results from the chosen arrangements or otherwise, and

(c) in the case of a notice given by virtue of section 219(4)(c), (d) or (e), means so much of the asserted advantage as would be counteracted by making the adjustments set out in the GAAR counteraction notice.

220(6) If a notice is given by reason of two or all of the requirements in section 219(4) being met, any payment specified under subsection (2)(b) or amount specified under subsection (2)(d) is to be determined as if the notice were given by virtue of such one of them as is stated in the notice as being used for this purpose.

220(7) "The GAAR counteraction notice" means the notice under–

(a) paragraph 12 of Schedule 43 to FA 2013,

(b) paragraph 8 or 9 of Schedule 43A to that Act, or

(c) paragraph 8 of Schedule 43B to that Act,

as the case may be.

History – In s. 220(2)(b) the words "(if any)" inserted and s. 220(2)(d) (and the word ", and" preceding it) inserted and the word "and" at the end of s. 220(2)(b) omitted by FA 2015, s. 118 and Sch. 18, para. 3(2), with effect from 26 March 2015.

In s. 220(4)(c), the words ", (d) or (e)" inserted by FA 2016, s. 157(21)(a), with effect in relation to tax arrangements (within the meaning of FA 2013, Pt. 5) entered into at any time (whether before or on or after 15 September 2016).

S. 220(4A) and (4B) inserted by FA 2015, s. 118 and Sch. 18, para. 3(3), with effect from 26 March 2015.

In s. 220(5)(c), the words ", (d) or (e)" inserted by FA 2016, s. 157(21)(b), with effect in relation to tax arrangements (within the meaning of FA 2013, Pt. 5) entered into at any time (whether before or on or after 15 September 2016).

In s. 220(6) the words "any payment specified under subsection (2)(b) or amount specified under subsection (2)(d)" substituted for the words "the payment specified under subsection (2)(b)" by FA 2015, s. 118 and Sch. 18, para. 3(4), with effect from 26 March 2015.

S. 220(7)(a)–(c) and the word "under–" before them substituted for the words "under paragraph 12 of Schedule 43 to FA 2013 (notice of final decision to counteract under the general anti-abuse rule)." by FA 2016, s. 157(21)(c), with effect in relation to tax arrangements (within the meaning of FA 2013, Pt. 5) entered into at any time (whether before or on or after 15 September 2016).

221 Content of notice given pending an appeal

221(1) This section applies where an accelerated payment notice is given by virtue of section 219(2)(b) (notice given pending an appeal).

221(2) The notice must–

(a) specify the paragraph or paragraphs of section 219(4) by virtue of which the notice is given,

(b) specify the disputed tax (if any),

(c) explain the effect of section 222 and of the amendments made by sections 224 and 225 so far as relating to the relevant tax in relation to which the accelerated payment notice is given, and

(d) if the denied advantage consists of or includes an asserted surrenderable amount (within the meaning of section 220(4A)), specify that amount and any action which is required to be taken in respect of it under section 225A.

221(3) "The disputed tax" means so much of the amount of the charge to tax arising in consequence of–

(a) the amendment or assessment to tax appealed against, or

(b) where the appeal is against a conclusion stated by a closure notice, that conclusion,

as a designated HMRC officer determines, to the best of the officer's information and belief, as the amount required to ensure the counteraction of what that officer so determines as the denied advantage.

221(4) **"The denied advantage"** has the same meaning as in section 220(5).

221(5) If a notice is given by reason of two or all of the requirements in section 219(4) being met, the denied advantage is to be determined as if the notice were given by virtue of such one of them as is stated in the notice as being used for this purpose.

221(6) In this section a reference to an assessment to tax, in relation to inheritance tax, is to a determination.

History – In s. 221(2)(b) the words "(if any)" inserted and s. 221(2)(d) (and the word ", and" preceding it) inserted and the word "and" at the end of s. 221(2)(b) omitted by FA 2015, s. 118 and Sch. 18, para. 4(2), with effect from 26 March 2015.

222 Representations about a notice

222(1) This section applies where an accelerated payment notice has been given under section 219 (and not withdrawn).

222(2) P has 90 days beginning with the day that notice is given to send written representations to HMRC–

(a) objecting to the notice on the grounds that Condition A, B or C in section 219 was not met,

(b) objecting to the amount specified in the notice under section 220(2)(b) or section 221(2)(b), or

(c) objecting to the amount specified in the notice under section 220(2)(d) or section 221(2)(d).

222(3) HMRC must consider any representations made in accordance with subsection (2).

222(4) Having considered the representations, HMRC must–

(a) if representations were made under subsection (2)(a), determine whether–

(i) to confirm the accelerated payment notice (with or without amendment), or

(ii) to withdraw the accelerated payment notice, and

(b) if representations were made under subsection (2)(b) (and the notice is not withdrawn under paragraph (a)), determine whether a different amount (or no amount) ought to have been specified under section 220(2)(b) or section 221(2)(b), and then–

(i) confirm the amount specified in the notice,

(ii) amend the notice to specify a different amount, or

(iii) remove from the notice the provision made under section 220(2)(b) or section 221(2)(b), and

(c) if representations were made under subsection (2)(c) (and the notice is not withdrawn under paragraph (a)), determine whether a different amount (or no amount) ought to have been specified under section 220(2)(d) or 221(2)(d), and then–

(i) confirm the amount specified in the notice,

(ii) amend the notice to specify a different amount, or

(iii) remove from the notice the provision made under section 220(2)(d) or section 221(2)(d),

and notify P accordingly.

History – S. 222(2)(c) (and the word ", or" preceding it) inserted and the word "or" at the end of s. 222(2)(a) omitted by FA 2015, s. 118 and Sch. 18, para. 5(2), with effect from 26 March 2015.
In s. 222(4)(b) the words "(or no amount)" inserted, the word "and" at the end of para. (4)(a) omitted, the word or at the end of para. (4)(b)(i) omitted and para. (4)(b)(iii) (and the word ", or" preceding it) and (4)(c) inserted by FA 2015, s. 118 and Sch. 18, para. 5(3), with effect from 26 March 2015.

FORMS OF ACCELERATED PAYMENT

223 Effect of notice given while tax enquiry is in progress: accelerated payment

History – In the heading to s. 223 the words ": accelerated payment" inserted by FA 2015, s. 118 and Sch. 18, para. 6(4), with effect from 26 March 2015.

223(1) This section applies where–

(a) an accelerated payment notice is given by virtue of section 219(2)(a) (notice given while a tax enquiry is in progress) (and not withdrawn), and

(b) *an amount is stated in the notice in accordance with section 220(2)(b).*

223(2) P must make a payment ("the accelerated payment") to HMRC of that amount.

223(3) The accelerated payment is to be treated as a payment on account of the understated tax (see section 220).

223(4) The accelerated payment must be made before the end of the payment period.

223(5) **"The payment period"** means–

(a) if P made no representations under section 222, the period of 90 days beginning with the day on which the accelerated payment notice is given, and

(b) if P made such representations, whichever of the following periods ends later–

(i) the 90 day period mentioned in paragraph (a);

(ii) the period of 30 days beginning with the day on which P is notified under section 222 of HMRC's determination.

223(6) [Not relevant to National Insurance contributions.]

223(7) If P pays any part of the understated tax before the accelerated payment in respect of it, the accelerated payment is treated to that extent as having been paid at the same time.

223(8) Any tax enactment which relates to the recovery of a relevant tax applies to an amount to be paid on account of the relevant tax under this section in the same manner as it applies to an amount of the relevant tax.

223(9) **"Tax enactment"** means provisions of or made under–

(a) the Tax Acts,

(b) [not relevant to National Insurance contributions,]

(c) [not relevant to National Insurance contributions,]

(d) [not relevant to National Insurance contributions,]

(e) [not relevant to National Insurance contributions.]

History – S. 223(1) substituted by FA 2015, s. 118 and Sch. 18, para. 6(2), with effect from 26 March 2015.
In s. 223(2) the words "that amount" substituted for the words "the amount specified in the notice in accordance with section 220(2)(b)" by FA 2015, s. 118 and Sch. 18, para. 6(3), with effect from 26 March 2015.

Cross references – NICA 2015, Sch. 2, para. 17: disapplication of s. 223(3) and (7) to (9) in relation to relevant contributions (Class 1, Class 1A, 1B and certain Class 2 contributions under SSCBA 1992, Pt. 1 (NICA 2015, Sch. 2, para. 22).
NICA 2015, Sch. 2, para. 18: effect of accelerated payment notice in respect of an appeal in relation to relevant contributions (Class 1, Class 1A, 1B and certain Class 2 contributions under SSCBA 1992, Pt. 1 (NICA 2015, Sch. 2, para. 22).

224 Restriction on powers to postpone tax payments pending initial appeal

224(1) [Inserts TMA 1970, s. 55(8B)–(8D).]

224(2) [Not relevant to National Insurance contributions.]

224(3) [Not relevant to National Insurance contributions.]

224(4) [Not relevant to National Insurance contributions.]

224(5) [Not relevant to National Insurance contributions.]

224(6) [Not relevant to National Insurance contributions.]

225 Protection of the revenue pending further appeals

225(1) [Inserts TMA 1970, s. 56(4)–(6).]

225(2) [Not relevant to National Insurance contributions.]

225(3) [Not relevant to National Insurance contributions.]

PREVENTION OF SURRENDER OF LOSSES

225A Effect of notice: surrender of losses ineffective, etc

225A [Not relevant to National Insurance contributions.]

PENALTIES

226 Penalty for failure to pay accelerated payment

226(1) This section applies where an accelerated payment notice is given by virtue of section 219(2)(a) (notice given while tax enquiry is in progress) (and not withdrawn).

226(2) If any amount of the accelerated payment is unpaid at the end of the payment period, P is liable to a penalty of 5% of that amount.

226(3) If any amount of the accelerated payment is unpaid after the end of the period of 5 months beginning with the penalty day, P is liable to a penalty of 5% of that amount.

226(4) If any amount of the accelerated payment is unpaid after the end of the period of 11 months beginning with the penalty day, P is liable to a penalty of 5% of that amount.

226(5) **"The penalty day"** means the day immediately following the end of the payment period.

226(6) [Not relevant to National Insurance contributions.]

226(7) Paragraphs 9 to 18 (other than paragraph 11(5)) of Schedule 56 to FA 2009 (provisions which apply to penalties for failures to make payments of tax on time) apply, with any necessary modifications, to a penalty under this section in relation to a failure by P to pay an amount of the accelerated payment as they apply to a penalty under that Schedule in relation to a failure by a person to pay an amount of tax.

Cross references – NICA 2015, Sch. 2, para. 19: modified application of s. 226(7) in relation to a penalty under s. 226 imposed by virtue of NICA 2015, Sch. 2, Pt. 1.
NICA 2015, Sch. 2, para. 20: recovery of penalties under s. 226 imposed by virtue of NICA 2015, Sch. 2, Pt. 1.

WITHDRAWAL ETC OF ACCELERATED PAYMENT NOTICE

227 Withdrawal, modification or suspension of accelerated payment notice

227(1) In this section a **"Condition C requirement"** means one of the requirements set out in Condition C in section 219.

227(2) Where an accelerated payment notice has been given, HMRC may, at any time, by notice given to P–

(a) withdraw the notice,

(b) where the notice is given by virtue of more than one Condition C requirement being met, withdraw it to the extent it is given by virtue of one of those requirements (leaving the notice effective to the extent that it was also given by virtue of any other Condition C requirement and has not been withdrawn),

(c) reduce the amount specified in the accelerated payment notice under section 220(2)(b) or 221(2)(b), or

(d) reduce the amount specified in the accelerated payment notice under section 220(2)(d) or 221(2)(d).

227(3) Where–

(a) an accelerated payment notice is given by virtue of the Condition C requirement in section 219(4)(a), and

(b) the follower notice to which it relates is withdrawn,

HMRC must withdraw the accelerated payment notice to the extent it was given by virtue of that requirement.

227(4) Where–

(a) an accelerated payment notice is given by virtue of the Condition C requirement in section 219(4)(a), and

(b) the follower notice to which it relates is amended under section 216(7)(b) (cases where there is a new relevant final judicial ruling following a late appeal),

HMRC may by notice given to P make consequential amendments (whether under subsection (2)(c) or (d) or otherwise) to the accelerated payment notice.

227(5) Where–

(a) an accelerated payment notice is given by virtue of the Condition C requirement in section 219(4)(b), and

(b) HMRC give notice under section 312(6) of FA 2004 with the result that promoters are no longer under the duty in section 312(2) of that Act in relation to the chosen arrangements,

HMRC must withdraw the notice to the extent it was given by virtue of that requirement.

227(6) Subsection (7) applies where–

(a) an accelerated payment notice is withdrawn to the extent that it was given by virtue of a Condition C requirement,

(b) that requirement is the one stated in the notice for the purposes of section 220(6) or 221(5) (calculation of amount of the accelerated payment or of the denied advantage etc), and

(c) the notice remains effective to the extent that it was also given by virtue of any other Condition C requirement.

227(7) HMRC must, by notice given to P–

(a) modify the accelerated payment notice so as to state the remaining, or one of the remaining, Condition C requirements for the purposes of section 220(6) or 221(5),

(b) if the amount of the accelerated payment or (as the case may be) the amount of the disputed tax determined on the basis of the substituted Condition C requirement is less than the amount specified in the notice, amend that notice under subsection (2)(c) to substitute the lower amount, and

(c) if the amount of the asserted surrenderable amount is less than the amount specified in the notice, amend the notice under subsection (2)(d) to substitute the lower amount.

227(8) If a follower notice is suspended under section 216 (appeals against final rulings made out of time) for any period, an accelerated payment notice in respect of the follower notice is also suspended for that period.

227(9) Accordingly, the period during which the accelerated payment notice is suspended does not count towards the periods mentioned in the following provisions–

(a) section 223;

(b) section 55(8D) of TMA 1970;

(c) [not relevant to National Insurance contributions,]

(d) [not relevant to National Insurance contributions,]

227(10) But the accelerated payment notice is not suspended under subsection (8) if it was also given by virtue of section 219(4)(b) or (c) and has not, to that extent, been withdrawn.

227(11) In a case within subsection (10), subsections (6) and (7) apply as they would apply were the notice withdrawn to the extent that it was given by virtue of section 219(4)(a), except that any change made to the notice under subsection (7) has effect during the period of suspension only.

227(12) Where an accelerated payment notice is withdrawn, it is to be treated as never having had effect (and any accelerated payment made in accordance with, or penalties paid by virtue of, the notice are to be repaid).

227(12A) Where, as a result of an accelerated payment notice specifying an amount under section 220(2)(d) or 221(2)(d), a notice of consent by P to a claim for group relief in respect of the amount specified (or part of it) became ineffective by virtue of section 225A(3), nothing in subsection (12) operates to revive that notice.

227(13) If, as a result of a modification made under subsection (2)(c), more than the resulting amount of the accelerated payment has already been paid by P, the excess must be repaid.

227(14) If the accelerated payment notice is amended under subsection (2)(d) or withdrawn–

(a) section 225A(2) and (3) (which prevents consent being given to group relief claims) cease to apply in relation to the released amount, and

(b) a claim for group relief may be made in respect of any part of the released amount within the period of 30 days after the day on which the notice is amended or withdrawn.

227(15) The time limits otherwise applicable to amendment of a company tax return do not apply to the extent that it makes a claim for group relief within the time allowed by subsection (14).

227(16) **"The released amount"** means–

(a) in a case where the accelerated payment notice is amended under subsection (2)(d), the amount represented by the reduction, and

(b) in a case where the accelerated payment notice is withdrawn, the amount specified under section 220(2)(d) or 221(2)(d).

History – S. 227(2)(d) (and the word ", or" preceding it) inserted and the word "or" at end para. (b) omitted FA 2015, s. 118 and Sch. 18, para. 8(2), with effect from 26 March 2015.
In s. 227(4) the words "or (d)" inserted d FA 2015, s. 118 and Sch. 18, para. 8(3), with effect from 26 March 2015.
In s. 227(6)(b) the word "etc" inserted d FA 2015, s. 118 and Sch. 18, para. 8(4), with effect from 26 March 2015.
S. 227(7)(c) (and the word ", and" preceding it) inserted and the word "and" at end para. (a) omitted FA 2015, s. 118 and Sch. 18, para. 8(5), with effect from 26 March 2015.
S. 227(12A) inserted FA 2015, s. 118 and Sch. 18, para. 8(6), with effect from 26 March 2015.
S. 227(14)–(16) inserted FA 2015, s. 118 and Sch. 18, para. 8(7), with effect from 26 March 2015.

Cross references – NICA 2015, Sch. 2, para. 21: modified application of s. 227(9) to include NICA 2015, Sch. 2, para. 18(2).

GROUP RELIEF CLAIMS AFTER ACCELERATED PAYMENT NOTICES

227A Group relief claims after accelerated payment notices

227A [Not relevant to National Insurance contributions.]

PARTNERS AND PARTNERSHIPS

228 Accelerated partner payments

228 [Not relevant to National Insurance contributions.]

DEFINED TERMS

229 Defined terms used in Chapter 3

229 In this Chapter–

"the accelerated payment" has the meaning given by section 223(2);

"accelerated payment notice" has the meaning given by section 219(1);

"arrangements" has the meaning given by section 201(4);

"the asserted advantage" has the meaning given by section 219(3);

"the chosen arrangements" has the meaning given by section 219(3), except in Schedule 32 where it has the meaning given by paragraph 3(3) of that Schedule;

"the denied advantage" has the meaning given by section 220(5), except in paragraph 4 of Schedule 32 where it has the meaning given by paragraph 4(4) of that Schedule;

"designated HMRC officer" means an officer of Revenue and Customs who has been designated by the Commissioners for the purposes of this Part;

"follower notice" has the meaning given by section 204(1);

"HMRC" means Her Majesty's Revenue and Customs;

"P" has the meaning given by section 219(1);

"partner payment notice" has the meaning given by paragraph 3 of Schedule 32;

"relevant tax" has the meaning given by section 200;

"tax advantage" has the meaning given by section 201(2);

"tax appeal" has the meaning given by section 203;

"tax enquiry" has the meaning given by section 202(2).

Chapter 4 – Miscellaneous and General Provision

EXTENSION OF PART BY ORDER

232 Extension of this Part by order

232(1) The Treasury may by order amend section 200 (definition of "relevant tax") so as to extend this Part to any other tax.

232(2) An order under this section may include–

(a) provision in respect of that other tax corresponding to the provision made by sections 224 and 225,

(b) consequential and supplemental provision, and

(c) transitional and transitory provision and savings.

232(3) For the purposes of subsection (1) or (2) an order under this section may amend this Part (other than this section) or any other enactment whenever passed or made.

232(4) The power to make orders under this section is exercisable by statutory instrument.

232(5) An order under this section may only be made if a draft of the instrument containing the order has been laid before and approved by a resolution of the House of Commons.

232(6) In this section **"tax"** includes duty.

CONSEQUENTIAL AMENDMENTS

233 Consequential amendments

233 [Not relevant to National Insurance contributions.]

PART 5 – PROMOTERS OF TAX AVOIDANCE SCHEMES

Commencement Date – Pt. 5 applies to Class 1, 1A, 1B and certain Class 2 contributions with effect from 12 February 2015 for the purposes of making regulations under Pt. 5 and at the end of the period of 2 months beginning with 12 February 2015 for remaining purposes (NICA 2015, s. 4(2) and Sch. 2, Pt. 2).

Pt. 5 applies to Class 4 contributions with effect from the end of the period of 2 months beginning with 12 February 2015 (SSCBA 1992, s. 16(1)(d)).

Cross references – NICA 2015, Sch. 2, para. 23 to 26: modified application of Pt. 5: references to tax, other than references to particular taxes, include "relevant contributions" (Class 1, Class 1A, 1B and certain Class 2 contributions under SSCBA 1992, Pt. 1 (NICA 2015, Sch. 2, para. 31)) and references to tax advantage includes the avoidance or reduction of a liability to pay relevant contributions.

INTRODUCTION

234 Meaning of "relevant proposal" and "relevant arrangements"

234(1) **"Relevant proposal"** means a proposal for arrangements which (if entered into) would be relevant arrangements (whether the proposal relates to a particular person or to any person who may seek to take advantage of it).

234(2) Arrangements are **"relevant arrangements"** if–

(a) they enable, or might be expected to enable, any person to obtain a tax advantage, and

(b) the main benefit, or one of the main benefits, that might be expected to arise from the arrangements is the obtaining of that advantage.

234(3) **"Tax advantage"** includes–

(a) relief or increased relief from tax,

(b) repayment or increased repayment of tax,

(c) avoidance or reduction of a charge to tax or an assessment to tax,

(d) avoidance of a possible assessment to tax,

(e) deferral of a payment of tax or advancement of a repayment of tax, and

(f) avoidance of an obligation to deduct or account for tax.

234(4) **"Arrangements"** includes any agreement, scheme, arrangement or understanding of any kind, whether or not legally enforceable, involving a single transaction or two or more transactions.

235 Carrying on a business "as a promoter"

235(1) A person carrying on a business in the course of which the person is, or has been, a promoter in relation to a relevant proposal or relevant arrangements carries on that business "as a promoter".

235(2) A person is a **"promoter"** in relation to a relevant proposal if the person–

(a) is to any extent responsible for the design of the proposed arrangements,

(b) makes a firm approach to another person in relation to the relevant proposal with a view to making the proposal available for implementation by that person or any other person, or

(c) makes the relevant proposal available for implementation by other persons.

235(3) A person is a **"promoter"** in relation to relevant arrangements if the person–

(a) is by virtue of subsection (2)(b) or (c), a promoter in relation to a relevant proposal which is implemented by the arrangements, or

(b) is responsible to any extent for the design, organisation or management of the arrangements.

235(4) For the purposes of this Part a person makes a firm approach to another person in relation to a relevant proposal if–

(a) the person communicates information about the relevant proposal to the other person at a time when the proposed arrangements have been substantially designed,

(b) the communication is made with a view to that other person or any other person entering into transactions forming part of the proposed arrangements, and

(c) the information communicated includes an explanation of the tax advantage that might be expected to be obtained from the proposed arrangements.

235(5) For the purposes of subsection (4) proposed arrangements have been substantially designed at any time if by that time the nature of the transactions to form them (or part of them) has been sufficiently developed for it to be reasonable to believe that a person who wished to obtain the tax advantage mentioned in subsection (4)(c) might enter into–

(a) transactions of the nature developed, or

(b) transactions not substantially different from transactions of that nature.

235(6) A person is not a promoter in relation to a relevant proposal or relevant arrangements by reason of anything done in prescribed circumstances.

235(7) Regulations under subsection (6) may contain provision having retrospective effect.

Statutory instruments – SI 2015/130: partly made under s. 235(6) and (7).

236 Meaning of "intermediary"

236 For the purposes of this Part a person ("A") is an intermediary in relation to a relevant proposal if–

(a) A communicates information about the relevant proposal to another person in the course of a business,

(b) the communication is made with a view to that other person, or any other person, entering into transactions forming part of the proposed arrangements, and

(c) A is not a promoter in relation to the relevant proposal.

CONDUCT NOTICES

237 Duty to give conduct notice

237(1) Subsections (5) to (9) apply if an authorised officer becomes aware at any time that a person ("P") who is carrying on a business as a promoter–

(a) has, in the period of 3 years ending with that time, met one or more threshold conditions, and

(b) was carrying on a business as a promoter when P met that condition.

237(1A) Subsections (5) to (9) also apply if an authorised officer becomes aware at any time ("the relevant time") that–

(a) a person has, in the period of 3 years ending with the relevant time, met one or more threshold conditions,

(b) at the relevant time another person ("P") meets one or more of those conditions by virtue of Part 2 of Schedule 34 (meeting the threshold conditions: bodies corporate and partnerships), and

(c) P is, at the relevant time, carrying on a business as a promoter.

237(2) Part 1 of Schedule 34 sets out the threshold conditions and describes how they are met.

237(3) Part 2 of that Schedule contains provision about when a person is treated as meeting a threshold condition.

237(4) See also Schedule 36 (which contains provision about the meeting of threshold conditions and other conditions by partnerships).

237(5) The authorised officer must determine–

(a) in a case within subsection (1), whether or not P's meeting of the condition mentioned in subsection (1)(a) (or, if more than one condition is met, the meeting of all of those conditions, taken together) should be regarded as significant in view of the purposes of this Part, or

(b) in a case within subsection (1A), whether or not–

(i) the meeting of the condition by the person as mentioned in subsection (1A)(a) (or, if more than one condition is met, the meeting of all of those conditions, taken together), and

(ii) P's meeting of the condition (or conditions) as mentioned in subsection (1A)(b),

should be regarded as significant in view of those purposes.

237(6) Subsection (5) does not apply if a conduct notice or a monitoring notice already has effect in relation to P.

237(7) If the authorised officer determines under subsection (5)(a) that P's meeting of the condition or conditions in question should be regarded as significant, the officer must give P a conduct notice, unless subsection (8) applies.

237(7A) If the authorised officer determines under subsection (5)(b) that both–

(a) the meeting of the condition or conditions by the person as mentioned in subsection (1A)(a), and

(b) P's meeting of the condition or conditions as mentioned in subsection (1A)(b),

should be regarded as significant, the officer must give P a conduct notice, unless subsection (8) applies.

237(8) This subsection applies if the authorised officer determines that, having regard to the extent of the impact that P's activities as a promoter are likely to have on the collection of tax, it is inappropriate to give P a conduct notice.

237(9) The authorised officer must determine under subsection (5) that the meeting of the condition (or all the conditions) should be regarded as significant if the condition (or any of the conditions) is in any of the following paragraphs of Schedule 34–

(a) paragraph 2 (deliberate tax defaulters);

(b) paragraph 3 (breach of Banking Code of Practice);

(c) paragraph 4 (dishonest tax agents);

(d) paragraph 6 (persons charged with certain offences);

(e) paragraph 7 (opinion notice of GAAR Advisory Panel).

237(10) If, as a result of subsection (1A), subsections (5) to (9) apply to a person, this does not prevent the giving of a conduct notice to the person mentioned in subsection (1A)(a).

History – S. 237(1A) inserted by FA 2015, s. 119 and Sch. 19, para. 2(2), with effect for the purposes of determining whether a person meets a threshold condition in a period of three years ending on or after 26 March 2015 (Royal Assent).

In s. 237(3) the words "when a person is treated as meeting a threshold condition" substituted for the words "the meeting of threshold conditions by bodies corporate" by FA 2015, s. 119 and Sch. 19, para. 2(3), with effect for the purposes of determining whether a person meets a threshold condition in a period of three years ending on or after 26 March 2015 (Royal Assent).
S. 237(5) substituted by FA 2015, s. 119 and Sch. 19, para. 2(4), with effect for the purposes of determining whether a person meets a threshold condition in a period of three years ending on or after 26 March 2015 (Royal Assent).
In s. 237(7) the words "subsection (5)(a)" substituted for the words "subsection (5)" by FA 2015, s. 119 and Sch. 19, para. 2(5), with effect for the purposes of determining whether a person meets a threshold condition in a period of three years ending on or after 26 March 2015 (Royal Assent).
S. 237(7A) inserted by FA 2015, s. 119 and Sch. 19, para. 2(6), with effect for the purposes of determining whether a person meets a threshold condition in a period of three years ending on or after 26 March 2015 (Royal Assent).
In s. 237(9) the words "mentioned in subsection (1)(a)" omitted by FA 2015, s. 119 and Sch. 19, para. 2(7), with effect for the purposes of determining whether a person meets a threshold condition in a period of three years ending on or after 26 March 2015 (Royal Assent).
S. 237(10) inserted by FA 2015, s. 119 and Sch. 19, para. 2(8), with effect for the purposes of determining whether a person meets a threshold condition in a period of three years ending on or after 26 March 2015 (Royal Assent).

237A Duty to give conduct notice: defeat of promoted arrangements

237A(1) If an authorised officer becomes aware at any time ("the relevant time") that a person ("P") who is carrying on a business as a promoter meets any of the conditions in subsections (11) to (13), the officer must determine whether or not P's meeting of that condition should be regarded as significant in view of the purposes of this Part.

But see also subsection (14).

237A(2) An authorised officer must make the determination set out in subsection (3) if the officer becomes aware at any time ("the section 237A(2) relevant time") that–

(a) a person meets a condition in subsection (11), (12) or (13), and

(b) at the section 237A(2) relevant time another person ("P"), who is carrying on a business as a promoter, meets that condition by virtue of Part 4 of Schedule 34A (meeting the section 237A conditions: bodies corporate and partnerships).

237A(3) The authorised officer must determine whether or not–

(a) the meeting of the condition by the person as mentioned in subsection (2)(a), and

(b) P's meeting of the condition as mentioned in subsection (2)(b),

should be regarded as significant in view of the purposes of this Part.

237A(4) Subsections (1) and (2) do not apply if a conduct notice or monitoring notice already has effect in relation to P.

237A(5) Subsection (1) does not apply if, at the relevant time, an authorised officer is under a duty to make a determination under section 237(5) in relation to P.

237A(6) Subsection (2) does not apply if, at the section 237A(2) relevant time, an authorised officer is under a duty to make a determination under section 237(5) in relation to P.

237A(7) But in a case where subsection (1) does not apply because of subsection (5), or subsection (2) does not apply because of subsection (6), subsection (5) of section 237 has effect as if–

(a) the references in paragraph (a) of that subsection to "subsection (1)", and "subsection (1)(a)" included subsection (1) of this section, and

(b) in paragraph (b) of that subsection the reference to "subsection (2)(a)" included a reference to subsection (2)(a) of this section and the reference to subsection (2)(b) included a reference to subsection (2)(b) of this section.

237A(8) If the authorised officer determines under subsection (1) that P's meeting of the condition in question should be regarded as significant, the officer must give P a conduct notice, unless subsection (10) applies.

237A(9) If the authorised officer determines under subsection (3) that–

(a) the meeting of the condition by the person as mentioned in subsection (2)(a), and

(b) P's meeting of the condition as mentioned in subsection (2)(b),

should be regarded as significant in view of the purposes of this Part, the officer must give P a conduct notice, unless subsection (10) applies.

237A(10) This subsection applies if the authorised officer determines that, having regard to the extent of the impact that P's activities as a promoter are likely to have on the collection of tax, it is inappropriate to give P a conduct notice.

237A(11) The condition in this subsection is that in the period of 3 years ending with the relevant time at least 3 relevant defeats have occurred in relation to P.

237A(12) The condition in this subsection is that at least two relevant defeats have occurred in relation to P at times when a single defeat notice under section 241A(2) or (6) had effect in relation to P.

237A(13) The condition in this subsection is that at least one relevant defeat has occurred in relation to P at a time when a double defeat notice under section 241A(3) had effect in relation to P.

237A(14) A determination that the condition in subsection (12) or (13) is met cannot be made unless–

(a) the defeat notice in question still has effect when the determination is made, or

(b) the determination is made on or before the 90th day after the day on which the defeat notice in question ceased to have effect.

237A(15) Schedule 34A sets out the circumstances in which a **"relevant defeat"** occurs in relation to a person and includes provision limiting what can amount to a further relevant defeat in relation to a person (see paragraph 6).

History – S. 237A inserted by FA 2016, s. 160(2), with effect from 15 September 2016 (Royal Assent).

Cross references – FA 2016, s. 160(20)–(25): defeats treated as not having occurred.

237B Duty to give further conduct notice where provisional notice not complied with

237B(1) An authorised officer must give a conduct notice to a person ("P") who is carrying on a business as a promoter if–

(a) a conduct notice given to P under section 237A(8)–

(i) has ceased to have effect otherwise than as a result of section 237D(2) or 241(3) or (4), and

(ii) was provisional immediately before it ceased to have effect,

(b) the officer determines that P had failed to comply with one or more conditions in the conduct notice,

(c) the conduct notice relied on a Case 3 relevant defeat,

(d) since the time when the conduct notice ceased to have effect, one or more relevant defeats falling within subsection (2) have occurred in relation to–

(i) P, and

(ii) any arrangements to which the Case 3 relevant defeat also relates, and

(e) had that relevant defeat or (as the case may be) those relevant defeats, occurred before the conduct notice ceased to have effect, an authorised officer would have been required to notify the person under section 237C(3) that the notice was no longer provisional.

237B(2) A relevant defeat falls within this subsection if it occurs by virtue of Case 1 or Case 2 in Schedule 34A.

237B(3) Subsection (1) does not apply if the authorised officer determines that, having regard to the extent of the impact that the person's activities as a promoter are likely to have on the collection of tax, it is inappropriate to give the person a conduct notice.

237B(4) Subsection (1) does not apply if a conduct notice or monitoring notice already has effect in relation to the person.

237B(5) For the purposes of this Part a conduct notice **"relies on a Case 3 relevant defeat"** if it could not have been given under the following condition.

The condition is that paragraph 9 of Schedule 34A had effect with the substitution of "100% of the tested arrangements" for "75% of the tested arrangements".

History – S. 237B inserted by FA 2016, s. 160(2), with effect from 15 September 2016 (Royal Assent).

237C When a conduct notice given under section 237A(8) is "provisional"

237C(1) This section applies to a conduct notice which–

(a) is given to a person under section 237A(8), and

(b) relies on a Case 3 relevant defeat.

237C(2) The notice is **"provisional"** at all times when it has effect, unless an authorised officer notifies the person that the notice is no longer provisional.

237C(3) An authorised officer must notify the person that the notice is no longer provisional if subsection (4) or (5) applies.

237C(4) This subsection applies if–

(a) the condition in subsection (5)(a) is not met, and

(b) a full relevant defeat occurs in relation to P.

237C(5) This subsection applies if–

(a) two, or all three, of the relevant defeats by reference to which the conduct notice is given would not have been relevant defeats if paragraph 9 of Schedule 34A had effect with the substitution of "100% of the tested arrangements" for "75% of the tested arrangements", and

(b) the same number of full relevant defeats occur in relation to P.

237C(6) A **"full relevant defeat"** occurs in relation to P if–

(a) a relevant defeat occurs in relation to P otherwise than by virtue of Case 3 in paragraph 9 of Schedule 34A, or

(b) circumstances arise which would be a relevant defeat in relation to P by virtue of paragraph 9 of Schedule 34A if that paragraph had effect with the substitution of "100% of the tested arrangements" for "75% of the tested arrangements".

237C(7) In determining under subsection (6) whether a full relevant defeat has occurred in relation to P, assume that in paragraph 6 of Schedule 34A (provision limiting what can amount to a further relevant defeat in relation to a person) the first reference to a **"relevant defeat"** does not include a relevant defeat by virtue of Case 3 in paragraph 9 of Schedule 34A.

History – S. 237C inserted by FA 2016, s. 160(2), with effect from 15 September 2016 (Royal Assent).

237D Judicial ruling upholding asserted tax advantage: effect on conduct notice which is provisional

237D(1) Subsection (2) applies if at any time–

(a) a conduct notice which relies on a Case 3 relevant defeat (see section 237B(5)) is provisional, and

(b) a court or tribunal upholds a corresponding tax advantage which has been asserted in connection with any of the related arrangements to which that relevant defeat relates (see paragraph 5(2) of Schedule 34A).

237D(2) The conduct notice ceases to have effect when that judicial ruling becomes final.

237D(3) An authorised officer must give the person to whom the conduct notice was given a written notice stating that the conduct notice has ceased to have effect.

237D(4) For the purposes of this section, a tax advantage is **"asserted"** in connection with any arrangements if a person makes a return, claim or election on the basis that the tax advantage arises from those arrangements.

In relation to the arrangements mentioned in paragraph (b) of subsection (1) **"corresponding tax advantage"** means a tax advantage corresponding to any tax advantage the counteraction of which contributed to the relevant defeat mentioned in that paragraph.

237D(5) For the purposes of this section a court or tribunal **"upholds"** a tax advantage if–

(a) the court or tribunal makes a ruling to the effect that no part of the tax advantage is to be counteracted, and

(b) that judicial ruling is final.

237D(6) For the purposes of this Part of this Act a judicial ruling is **"final"** if it is–

(a) a ruling of the Supreme Court, or

(b) a ruling of any other court or tribunal in circumstances where–

(i) no appeal may be made against the ruling,

(ii) if an appeal may be made against the ruling with permission, the time limit for applications has expired and either no application has been made or permission has been refused,

(iii) if such permission to appeal against the ruling has been granted or is not required, no appeal has been made within the time limit for appeals, or

(iv) if an appeal was made, it was abandoned or otherwise disposed of before it was determined by the court or tribunal to which it was addressed.

237D(7) In this section references to **"counteraction"** include anything referred to as a counteraction in any of Conditions A to F in paragraphs 11 to 16 of Schedule 34A.

History – S. 237D inserted by FA 2016, s. 160(2), with effect from 15 September 2016 (Royal Assent).

238 Contents of a conduct notice

238(1) A conduct notice is a notice requiring the person to whom it has been given ("the recipient") to comply with conditions specified in the notice.

238(2) Before deciding on the terms of a conduct notice, the authorised officer must give the person to whom the notice is to be given an opportunity to comment on the proposed terms of the notice.

238(3) A notice may include only conditions that it is reasonable to impose for any of the following purposes–

(a) to ensure that the recipient provides adequate information to its clients about relevant proposals, and relevant arrangements, in relation to which the recipient is a promoter;

(b) to ensure that the recipient provides adequate information about relevant proposals in relation to which it is a promoter to persons who are intermediaries in relation to those proposals;

(c) to ensure that the recipient does not fail to comply with any duty under a specified disclosure provision;

(d) to ensure that the recipient does not discourage others from complying with any obligation to disclose to HMRC information of a description specified in the notice;

(e) to ensure that the recipient does not enter into an agreement with another person ("C") which relates to a relevant proposal or relevant arrangements in relation to which the recipient is a promoter, on terms which–

(i) impose a contractual obligation on C which falls within paragraph 11(2) or (3) of Schedule 34 (contractual terms restricting disclosure), or

(ii) impose on C obligations within both paragraph 11(4) and (5) of that Schedule (contractual terms requiring contribution to fighting funds and restricting settlement of proceedings);

(f) to ensure that the recipient does not promote relevant proposals or relevant arrangements which rely on, or involve a proposal to rely on, one or more contrived or abnormal steps to produce a tax advantage;

(g) to ensure that the recipient does not fail to comply with any stop notice which has effect under paragraph 12 of Schedule 34.

238(4) References in subsection (3) to ensuring that adequate information is provided about proposals or arrangements include–

(a) ensuring the adequacy of the description of the arrangements or proposed arrangements;

(b) ensuring that the information includes an adequate assessment of the risk that the arrangements or proposed arrangements will fail;

(c) ensuring that the information does not falsely state, and is not likely to create a false impression, that HMRC have (formally or informally) considered, approved or expressed a particular opinion in relation to the proposal or arrangements.

238(5) In subsection (3)(c) **"specified disclosure provision"** means a disclosure provision that is specified in the notice; and for this purpose **"disclosure provision"** means any of the following–

(a) section 308 of FA 2004 (disclosure of tax avoidance schemes: duties of promoter);

(b) section 312 of FA 2004 (duty of promoter to notify client of number);

(c) sections 313ZA and 313ZB of FA 2004 (duties to provide details of clients and certain others);

(d) Part 1 of Schedule 36 to FA 2008 (duties to provide information and produce documents).

238(6) In subsection (4)(b) **"fail"**, in relation to arrangements or proposed arrangements, means not result in a tax advantage which the arrangements or (as the case may be) proposed arrangements might be expected to result in.

238(7) The Treasury may by regulations amend the definition of **"disclosure provision"** in subsection (5).

239 Section 238: supplementary

239(1) In section 238 the following expressions are to be interpreted as follows.

239(2) **"Adequate"** means adequate having regard to what it might be reasonable for a client or (as the case may be) an intermediary to expect; and **"adequacy"** is to be interpreted accordingly.

239(3) A person ("C") is a **"client"** of a promoter, if at any time when a conduct notice has effect, the promoter–

(a) makes a firm approach to C in relation to a relevant proposal with a view to the promoter making the proposal available for implementation by C or another person;

(b) makes a relevant proposal available for implementation by C;

(c) takes part in the organisation or management of relevant arrangements entered into by C.

239(4) The recipient of a conduct notice **"promotes"** a relevant proposal if it–

(a) takes part in designing the proposal,

(b) makes a firm approach to a person in relation to the proposal with a view to making the proposal available for implementation by that person or another person, or

(c) makes the proposal available for implementation by persons (other than the recipient).

239(5) The recipient of a conduct notice **"promotes"** relevant arrangements if it takes part in designing, organising or managing the arrangements.

240 Amendment or withdrawal of conduct notice

240(1) This section applies where a conduct notice has been given to a person.

240(2) An authorised officer may at any time amend the notice.

240(3) An authorised officer–

(a) may withdraw the notice if the officer thinks it is not necessary for it to continue to have effect, and

(b) in considering whether or not that is necessary must take into account the person's record of compliance, or failure to comply, with the conditions in the notice.

241 Duration of conduct notice

241(1) A conduct notice has effect from the date specified in it as its commencement date.

241(2) A conduct notice ceases to have effect–

(a) at the end of the period of two years beginning with its commencement date, or

(b) if an earlier date is specified in it as its termination date, at the end of that day.

241(3) A conduct notice ceases to have effect if withdrawn by an authorised officer under section 240.

241(4) A conduct notice ceases to have effect in relation to a person when a monitoring notice takes effect in relation to that person.

241(5) See also section 237D(2) (provisional conduct notice affected by judicial ruling).

History – S. 241(5) inserted by FA 2016, s. 160(6), with effect from 15 September 2016 (Royal Assent).

DEFEAT NOTICES

History – Heading inserted by FA 2016, s. 160(3), with effect from 15 September 2016 (Royal Assent).

241A Defeat notices

241A(1) This section applies in relation to a person ("P") only if P is carrying on a business as a promoter.

241A(2) An authorised officer, or an officer of Revenue and Customs with the approval of an authorised officer, may give P a notice if the officer concerned has become aware of one (and only one) relevant defeat which has occurred in relation to P in the period of 3 years ending with the day on which the notice is given.

241A(3) An authorised officer, or an officer of Revenue and Customs with the approval of an authorised officer, may give P a notice if the officer concerned has become aware of two (but not more than two) relevant defeats which have occurred in relation to P in the period of 3 years ending with the day on which the notice is given.

241A(4) A notice under this section must be given by the end of the 90 days beginning with the day on which the matters mentioned in subsection (2) or (as the case may be) (3) come to the attention of HMRC.

241A(5) Subsection (6) applies if–

(a) a single defeat notice which had been given to P (under subsection (2) or (6)) ceases to have effect as a result of section 241B(1), and

(b) in the period when the defeat notice had effect a relevant defeat ("the further relevant defeat") occurred in relation to P.

241A(6) An authorised officer or an officer of Revenue and Customs with the approval of an authorised officer may give P a notice in respect of the further relevant defeat (regardless of whether or not it occurred in the period of 3 years ending with the day on which the notice is given).

241A(7) In this Part–

(a) **"single defeat notice"** means a notice under subsection (2) or (6);

(b) **"double defeat notice"** means a notice under subsection (3);

(c) **"defeat notice"** means a single defeat notice or a double defeat notice.

241A(8) A defeat notice must–

(a) set out the dates on which the look-forward period for the notice begins and ends;

(b) in the case of a single defeat notice, explain the effect of section 237A(12);

(c) in the case of a double defeat notice, explain the effect of section 237A(13).

241A(9) HMRC may specify what further information must be included in a defeat notice.

241A(10) "Look-forward period"–

(a) in relation to a defeat notice under subsection (2) or (3), means the period of 5 years beginning with the day after the day on which the notice is given;

(b) in relation to a defeat notice under subsection (6), means the period beginning with the day after the day on which the notice is given and ending at the end of the period of 5 years beginning with the day on which the further relevant defeat mentioned in subsection (6) occurred in relation to P.

241A(11) A defeat notice has effect throughout its look-forward period unless it ceases to have effect earlier in accordance with section 241B(1) or (4).

History – S. 241A inserted by FA 2016, s. 160(3), with effect from 15 September 2016 (Royal Assent).

Cross references – FA 2016, s. 160(20) to (25): defeats treated as not having occurred.

241B Judicial ruling upholding asserted tax advantage: effect on defeat notice

241B(1) If the relevant defeat to which a single defeat notice relates is overturned (see subsection (5)), the notice has no further effect on and after the day on which it is overturned.

241B(2) Subsection (3) applies if one (and only one) of the relevant defeats in respect of which a double defeat notice was given is overturned.

241B(3) The notice is to be treated for the purposes of this Part (including this section) as if it had always been a single defeat notice given (in respect of the other of the two relevant defeats) on the date on which the notice was in fact given.

The look-forward period for the notice is accordingly unchanged.

241B(4) If both the relevant defeats to which a double defeat notice relates are overturned (on the same date), that notice has no further effect on and after that date.

241B(5) A relevant defeat specified in a defeat notice is **"overturned"** if–

(a) the notice could not have specified that relevant defeat if paragraph 9 of Schedule 34A had effect with the substitution of "100% of the tested arrangements" for "75% of the tested arrangements", and

(b) at a time when the notice has effect a court or tribunal upholds a corresponding tax advantage which has been asserted in connection with any of the related arrangements to which the relevant defeat relates (see paragraph 5(2) of Schedule 34A).

Accordingly the relevant defeat is overturned on the day on which the judicial ruling mentioned in paragraph (b) becomes final.

241B(6) If a defeat notice ceases to have effect as a result of subsection (1) or (4) an authorised officer, or an officer of Revenue and Customs with the approval of an authorised officer, must notify the person to whom the notice was given that it has ceased to have effect.

241B(7) If subsection (3) has effect in relation to a defeat notice, an authorised officer, or an officer of Revenue and Customs with the approval of an authorised officer, must notify the person of the effect of that subsection.

241B(8) For the purposes of this section, a tax advantage is **"asserted"** in connection with any arrangements if a person makes a return, claim or election on the basis that the tax advantage arises from those arrangements.

241B(9) In relation to the arrangements mentioned in paragraph (b) of subsection (5) **"corresponding tax advantage"** means a tax advantage corresponding to any tax advantage the counteraction of which contributed to the relevant defeat mentioned in that paragraph.

241B(10) For the purposes of this section a court or tribunal **"upholds"** a tax advantage if–

(a) the court or tribunal makes a ruling to the effect that no part of the tax advantage is to be counteracted, and

(b) that judicial ruling is final.

241B(11) In this section references to **"counteraction"** include anything referred to as a counteraction in any of Conditions A to F in paragraphs 11 to 16 of Schedule 34A.

History – S. 241B inserted by FA 2016, s. 160(3), with effect from 15 September 2016 (Royal Assent).

MONITORING NOTICES: PROCEDURE AND PUBLICATION

242 Monitoring notices: duty to apply to tribunal

242(1) If–

(a) a conduct notice has effect in relation to a person who is carrying on a business as a promoter, and

(b) an authorised officer determines that the person has failed to comply with one or more conditions in the notice,

the authorised officer must apply to the tribunal for approval to give the person a monitoring notice.

242(2) An application under subsection (1) must include a draft of the monitoring notice.

242(3) Subsection (1) does not apply if–

(a) the condition (or all the conditions) mentioned in subsection (1)(b) were imposed under subsection (3)(a), (b) or (c) of section 238, and

(b) the authorised officer considers that the failure to comply with the condition (or all the conditions, taken together) is such a minor matter that it should be disregarded for the purposes of this section.

242(4) Where an authorised officer makes an application to the tribunal under subsection (1), the officer must at the same time give notice to the person to whom the application relates.

242(5) The notice under subsection (4) must state which condition (or conditions) the authorised officer has determined under subsection (1)(b) that the person has failed to comply with and the reasons for that determination.

242(6) At a time when a notice given under section 237A is provisional, no determination is to be made under subsection (1) in respect of the notice.

242(7) If a promoter fails to comply with conditions in a conduct notice at a time when the conduct notice is provisional, nothing in subsection (6) prevents those failures from being taken into account under subsection (1) at any subsequent time when the conduct notice is not provisional.

History – S. 242(6) and (7) inserted by FA 2016, s. 160(4), with effect from 15 September 2016 (Royal Assent).

243 Monitoring notices: tribunal approval

243(1) On an application under section 242, the tribunal may approve the giving of a monitoring notice only if–

(a) the tribunal is satisfied that, in the circumstances, the authorised officer would be justified in giving the monitoring notice, and

(b) the person to whom the monitoring notice is to be given ("the affected person") has been given a reasonable opportunity to make representations to the tribunal.

243(2) The tribunal may amend the draft notice included with the application under section 242.

243(3) If the representations that the affected person makes to the tribunal include a statement that in the affected person's view it was not reasonable to include the condition mentioned in section 242(1)(b) in the conduct notice, the tribunal must refuse to approve the giving of the monitoring notice if it is satisfied that it was not reasonable to include that condition (but see subsection (4)).

243(4) If the representations made to the tribunal include the statement described in subsection (3) and the determination under section 242(1)(b) is a determination that there has been a failure to comply with more than one condition in the conduct notice–

(a) subsection (3) does not apply, but

(b) in deciding whether or not to approve the giving of the monitoring notice, the tribunal is to assume, in the case of any condition that the tribunal considers it was not reasonable to include in the conduct notice, that there has been no failure to comply with that condition.

244 Monitoring notices: content and issuing

244(1) Where the tribunal has approved the giving of a monitoring notice, the authorised officer must give the notice to the person to whom it relates.

244(2) A monitoring notice given under subsection (1) or paragraph 9 or 10 of Schedule 36 must–

(a) explain the effect of the monitoring notice and specify the date from which it takes effect;

(b) inform the recipient of the right to request the withdrawal of the monitoring notice under section 245.

244(3) In addition, a monitoring notice must–

(a) if given under subsection (1), state which condition (or conditions) it has been determined the person has failed to comply with and the reasons for that determination;

(b) if given under paragraph 9 or 10 of Schedule 36, state the date of the original monitoring notice and name the partnership to which that notice was given.

244(4) The date specified under subsection (2)(a) must not be earlier than the date on which the monitoring notice is given.

244(5) In this Part, a person in relation to whom a monitoring notice has effect is called a **"monitored promoter"**.

245 Withdrawal of monitoring notice

245(1) A person in relation to whom a monitoring notice has effect may, at any time after the end of the period of 12 months beginning with the end of the appeal period, request that the notice should cease to have effect.

245(2) The **"appeal period"** means–

(a) the period during which an appeal could be brought against the approval by the tribunal of the giving of the monitoring notice, or

(b) where an appeal mentioned in paragraph (a) has been brought, the period during which that appeal has not been finally determined, withdrawn or otherwise disposed of.

245(3) A request under this section is to be made in writing to an authorised officer.

245(4) Where a request is made under this section, an authorised officer must within 30 days beginning with the day on which the request is received determine either–

(a) that the monitoring notice is to cease to have effect, or

(b) that the request is to be refused.

245(5) The matters to be taken into account by an authorised officer in making a determination under subsection (4) include–

(a) whether or not the person subject to the monitoring notice has, since the time when the notice took effect, engaged in behaviour of a sort that conditions included in a conduct notice in accordance with section 238(3) could be used to regulate;

(b) whether or not it appears likely that the person will in the future engage in such behaviour;

(c) the person's record of compliance, or failure to comply, with obligations imposed on it under this Part, since the time when the monitoring notice took effect.

245(6) An authorised officer–

(a) may withdraw a monitoring notice if the officer thinks it is not necessary for it to continue to have effect, and

(b) in considering whether or not that is necessary, the officer must take into account the matters in paragraphs (a) to (c) of subsection (5).

245(7) If the authorised officer makes a determination under subsection (4)(a), or decides to withdraw a monitoring notice under subsection (6), the officer must also determine that the person is, or is not, to be given a follow-on conduct notice.

245(8) **"Follow-on conduct notice"** means a conduct notice taking effect immediately after the monitoring notice ceases to have effect.

245(9) Where the monitoring notice mentioned in subsection (1) is a replacement monitoring notice–

(a) in subsection (1) the reference to the end of the appeal period is to be read as a reference to whichever is the later of the end of the appeal period for the original monitoring notice and the date the replacement monitoring notice takes effect, and

(b) in subsection (5)(a) and (c) the time referred to is to be read as the time when the original monitoring notice (see paragraph 11(2) of Schedule 36) took effect.

246 Notification of determination under section 245

246(1) Where an authorised officer makes a determination under section 245(4), that officer, or an officer of Revenue and Customs with that officer's approval, must notify the person who made the request of the determination.

246(2) If the determination is that the monitoring notice is to cease to have effect, the notice must–

(a) specify the date from which the monitoring notice is to cease to have effect, and

(b) inform the person of the determination made under section 245(7).

246(3) If the determination is that the request is to be refused, the notice must inform the person who made the request–

(a) of the reasons for the refusal, and

(b) of the right to appeal under section 247.

247 Appeal against refusal to withdraw monitoring notice

247(1) A person may appeal against a refusal by an authorised officer of a request that a monitoring notice should cease to have effect.

247(2) Notice of appeal must be given–

(a) in writing to the officer who gave the notice of the refusal under section 245, and

(b) within the period of 30 days beginning with the day on which notice of the refusal was given.

247(3) The notice of appeal must state the grounds of appeal.

247(4) On an appeal that is notified to the tribunal, the tribunal may–

(a) confirm the refusal, or

(b) direct that the monitoring notice is to cease to have effect.

247(5) Subject to this section, the provisions of Part 5 of TMA 1970 relating to appeals have effect in relation to an appeal under this section.

248 Publication by HMRC

248(1) An authorised officer may publish the fact that a person is a monitored promoter.

248(2) Publication under subsection (1) may also include the following information about the monitored promoter–

(a) its name;

(b) its business address or registered office;

(c) the nature of the business mentioned in section 242(1)(a);

(d) any other information that the authorised officer considers it appropriate to publish in order to make clear the monitored promoter's identity.

248(3) The reference in subsection (2)(a) to the monitored promoter's name includes any name under which it carries on a business as a promoter and any previous name or pseudonym.

248(4) Publication under subsection (1) may also include a statement of which of the conditions in a conduct notice it has been determined that the person (or, in the case of a replacement monitoring notice, the person to whom the original monitoring notice was given) has failed to comply with.

248(5) Publication may not take place before the end of the appeal period (or, in the case of a replacement monitoring notice, the appeal period for the original monitoring notice).

248(6) The **"appeal period"**, in relation to a monitoring notice, means–

(a) the period during which an appeal could be brought against the approval by the tribunal of the giving of the notice, or

(b) where an appeal mentioned in paragraph (a) has been brought, the period during which that appeal has not been finally determined, withdrawn or otherwise disposed of.

248(7) Publication under this section is to be in such manner as the authorised officer thinks fit; but see subsection (8).

248(8) If an authorised officer publishes the fact that a person is a monitored promoter and the monitoring notice is withdrawn, the officer must publish the fact of the withdrawal in the same way as the officer published the fact that the person was a monitored promoter.

249 Publication by monitored promoter

249(1) A person who is given a monitoring notice ("the monitored promoter") must give the persons mentioned in subsection (6) a notice stating–

(a) that it is a monitored promoter, and

(b) which of the conditions in a conduct notice it has been determined that it (or, if the monitoring notice is a replacement monitoring notice, the person to whom that notice was given) has failed to comply with.

249(2) If the monitoring notice is a replacement monitoring notice, the notice under subsection (1) must also identify the original monitoring notice.

249(3) If regulations made by the Commissioners so require, the monitored promoter must publish on the internet–

(a) the information mentioned in paragraph (a) and (b) of subsection (1), and

(b) its promoter reference number (see section 250).

249(4) Subsection (1) and any duty imposed under subsection (3) or (10) do not apply until the end of the period of 10 days beginning with the end of the appeal period (and also see subsection (9)).

249(5) The **"appeal period"** means–

(a) the period during which an appeal could be brought against the approval by the tribunal of the giving of the monitoring notice, or

(b) where an appeal mentioned in paragraph (a) has been brought, the period during which that appeal has not been finally determined, withdrawn or otherwise disposed of.

249(6) The notice under subsection (1) must be given–

(a) to any person who becomes a client of the monitored promoter while the monitoring notice has effect, and

(b) (except in a case where the monitoring notice is a replacement monitoring notice) any person who is a client of the monitored promoter at the time the monitoring notice takes effect.

249(7) A person ("C") is a client of a monitored promoter at the time a monitoring notice takes effect if during the period beginning with the date the conduct notice mentioned in subsection (1)(b) takes effect and ending with that time the promoter–

(a) made a firm approach to C in relation to a relevant proposal with a view to the promoter making the proposal available for implementation by C or another person;

(b) made a relevant proposal available for implementation by C;

(c) took part in the organisation or management of relevant arrangements entered into by C.

249(8) A person becomes a client of a monitored promoter if the promoter does any of the things mentioned in paragraph (a) to (c) of subsection (7) in relation to that person.

249(9) In the case of a person falling within subsection (6)(a), notice under subsection (1) may be given within the period of 10 days beginning with the day on which the person first became a client of the monitored promoter if that period would expire at a later date than the date on which notification would otherwise be required by virtue of subsection (4).

249(10) A monitored promoter must also include in any prescribed publication or prescribed correspondence–

(a) the information mentioned in paragraph (a) and (b) of subsection (1), and

(b) its promoter reference number (see section 250).

249(11) Notification under subsection (1), publication under subsection (3) or inclusion of the information required by subsection (10) is to be in such form and manner as is prescribed.

249(12) Where the monitoring notice mentioned in subsection (1) is a replacement monitoring notice, the reference in subsection (4) to the end of the appeal period is to be read as a reference to whichever is the later of the end of the appeal period for the original monitoring notice and the date the replacement monitoring notice takes effect.

Statutory instruments – SI 2015/549: partly made under s. 249(3), (10) and (11).

ALLOCATION AND DISTRIBUTION OF PROMOTER REFERENCE NUMBER

250 Allocation of promoter reference number

250(1) Where a monitoring notice is given to a person ("the monitored promoter") HMRC must as soon as practicable after the end of the appeal period–

(a) allocate the monitored promoter a reference number, and

(b) notify the relevant persons of that number.

250(2) **"Relevant persons"** means–

(a) the monitored promoter, and

(b) if the monitored promoter is resident outside the United Kingdom, any person who HMRC know is an intermediary in relation to a relevant proposal of the monitored promoter.

250(3) The **"appeal period"** means–

(a) the period during which an appeal could be brought against the approval by the tribunal of the giving of the monitoring notice, or

(b) where an appeal mentioned in paragraph (a) has been brought, the period during which that appeal has not been finally determined, withdrawn or otherwise disposed of.

250(4) The duty in subsection (1) does not apply if the monitoring notice is set aside following an appeal.

250(5) A number allocated to a person under this section is referred to in this Part as a **"promoter reference number"**.

250(6) Where the monitoring notice mentioned in subsection (1) is a replacement monitoring notice–

(a) in subsection (1) the reference to the end of the appeal period is to be read as a reference to whichever is the later of the end of the appeal period for the original monitoring notice and the date the replacement monitoring notice takes effect, and

(b) in subsection (4) the reference to the monitoring notice is to be read as a reference to the original monitoring notice.

251 Duty of monitored promoter to notify clients and intermediaries of number

251(1) This section applies where a person who is a monitored promoter ("the monitored promoter") is notified under section 250 of a promoter reference number.

251(3) The monitored promoter must, within the relevant period, notify the promoter reference number to–

(a) any person who has become its client at any time in the period beginning with the day on which the monitoring notice in relation to the monitored promoter took effect and ending with the day on which the monitored promoter was notified of that number,

(b) any person who becomes its client after the end of the period mentioned in paragraph (a) but while the monitoring notice has effect,

(c) any person who the monitored promoter could reasonably be expected to know falls within subsection (4), and

(d) any person who the monitored promoter could reasonably be expected to know is a relevant intermediary in relation to a relevant proposal of the monitored promoter.

251(3) A person ("C") becomes a client of a monitored promoter if the promoter does any of the following in relation to C–

(a) makes a firm approach to C in relation to a relevant proposal with a view to the promoter making the proposal available for implementation by C or another person;

(b) makes a relevant proposal available for implementation by C;

(c) takes part in the organisation or management of relevant arrangements entered into by C.

251(4) A person falls within this subsection if during the period beginning with the date the conduct notice took effect and ending with the date on which the monitoring notice took effect the person has entered into transactions forming part of relevant arrangements and those arrangements–

(a) enable, or are likely to enable, the person to obtain a tax advantage during the time a monitoring notice has effect, and

(b) are either relevant arrangements in relation to which the monitored promoter is or was a promoter or implement a relevant proposal in relation to which the monitored promoter was a promoter.

251(5) A person is a relevant intermediary in relation to a relevant proposal of a monitored promoter if the person meets the conditions in section 236(a) to (c) (meaning of "intermediary") at any time while the monitoring notice in relation to the monitored promoter has effect.

251(6) The **"relevant period"** means–

(a) in the case of a person falling within subsection (2)(a), the period of 30 days beginning with the day of the notification mentioned in subsection (1),

(b) in the case of a person falling within subsection (2)(b), the period of 30 days beginning with the day on which the person first became a client in relation to the monitored promoter,

(c) in the case of a person falling within subsection (2)(c), the period of 30 days beginning with the later of the day of the notification mentioned in subsection (1) and the first day on which the monitored promoter could reasonably be expected to know that the person fell within subsection (4), and

(d) in the case of a person falling within subsection (2)(d), the period of 30 days beginning with the later of the day of the notification mentioned in subsection (1) and the first day on which the monitored promoter could reasonably be expected to know that the person was a relevant intermediary in relation to a relevant proposal of the monitored promoter.

251(7) In this section **"the conduct notice"** means the conduct notice that the monitored promoter failed to comply with which resulted in the monitoring notice being given to the monitored promoter.

251(8) Subsection (2)(c) is to be ignored in a case where the monitoring notice is a replacement monitoring notice.

252 Duty of those notified to notify others of promoter's number

252(1) In this section **"notified client"** means–

(a) a person who is notified of a promoter reference number under section 250 by reason of being a person falling within subsection (2)(b) of that section, and

(b) a person who is notified of a promoter reference number under section 251.

252(2) A notified client must, within 30 days of being notified as described in subsection (1), provide the promoter reference number to any other person who the notified client might reasonably be expected to know has become, or is likely to have become, a client in relation to the monitored promoter concerned at a time when the monitoring notice in relation to that monitored promoter had effect.

252(3) A person ("C") becomes a client of a monitored promoter if the promoter does any of the following in relation to C–

(a) makes a firm approach to C in relation to a relevant proposal with a view to the promoter making the proposal available for implementation by C or another person;

(b) makes a relevant proposal available for implementation by C;

(c) takes part in the organisation or management of relevant arrangements entered into by C.

252(4) Where the notified client is an intermediary in relation to a relevant proposal of the monitored promoter concerned, the notified client must also, within 30 days, provide the promoter reference number to–

(a) any person to whom the notified client has, since the monitoring notice in relation to the monitored promoter concerned took effect, communicated in the course of a business information about a relevant proposal of the monitored promoter, and

(b) any person who the notified client might reasonably be expected to know has, since that monitoring notice took effect, entered into, or is likely to enter into, transactions forming part of relevant arrangements in relation to which that monitored promoter is a promoter.

252(5) Subsection (2) or (4) does not impose a duty on a notified client to notify a person of a promoter reference number if the notified client reasonably believes that the person has already been notified of the promoter reference number (whether as a result of a duty under this section or as a result of any of the other provision of this Part).

253 Duty of persons to notify the Commissioners

253(1) If a person ("N") is notified of a promoter reference number under section 250, 251 or 252, N must report the number to the Commissioners if N expects to obtain a tax advantage from relevant arrangements in relation to which the monitored promoter to whom the reference number relates (whether that is N or another person) is the promoter.

253(2) A report under this section–

(a) must be made in (or, if prescribed circumstances exist, submitted with) each tax return made by N for a period that is or includes a period for which the arrangements enable N to obtain a tax advantage (whether in relation to the tax to which the return relates or another tax);

(b) if no tax return falls within paragraph (a), or in the case mentioned in subsection (3), must contain such information, and be made in such form and manner and within such time, as is prescribed.

253(3) The case is that the tax return in which the report would (apart from this subsection) have been made is not submitted–

(a) by the filing date, or

(b) if there is no filing date in relation to the tax return concerned, by such other time that the tax return is required to be submitted by or under any enactment.

253(4) Where N expects to obtain the tax advantage referred to in subsection (1) in respect of inheritance tax, stamp duty land tax, stamp duty reserve tax or petroleum revenue tax–

(a) subsection (2) does not apply in relation to that tax advantage, and

(b) a report under this section in respect of that tax must be in such form and manner and contain such information and be made within such time as is prescribed.

253(5) Where the relevant arrangements referred to in subsection (1) give rise to N making a claim under section 261B of TCGA 1992 (treating trade loss as CGT loss) or for loss relief under Part 4 of ITA 2007 and that claim is not contained in a tax return, a report under this section must also be made in that claim.

253(6) In this section **"tax return"** means any of the following–

(a) a return under section 8 of TMA 1970 (income tax and capital gains tax: personal return);

(b) [not relevant to National Insurance contributions;]

(c) [not relevant to National Insurance contributions;]
(d) [not relevant to National Insurance contributions;]
(da) [not relevant to National Insurance contributions;]
(e) [not relevant to National Insurance contributions;]
(f) [not relevant to National Insurance contributions.]

Prospective amendments – In s. 253(6)(c) the words ", or regulations under paragraph 10 of Schedule A1 to," inserted after the words "section 12AA of" by F(No. 2)A 2017, s. 61 and Sch. 14, para. 44, with effect from a day to be appointed under F(No. 2)A 2017, s. 61(6).

History – S. 253(6)(da) inserted by FA 2016, s. 104(7), with effect from 15 September 2016.

Cross references – NICA 2015, Sch. 2, para. 27: references in s. 253 to a tax return include a return relating to "relevant contributions" (Class 1, Class 1A, 1B and certain Class 2 contributions under SSCBA 1992, Pt. 1 (NICA 2015, Sch. 2, para. 31).

Statutory instruments – SI 2015/549: partly made under s. 253(2) and (4).

OBTAINING INFORMATION AND DOCUMENTS

254 Meaning of "monitored proposal" and "monitored arrangements"

254(1) For the purposes of this Part a relevant proposal in relation to which a person ("P") is a promoter is a **"monitored proposal"** in relation to P if any of the following dates fell on or after the date on which a monitoring notice took effect–

(a) the date on which P first made a firm approach to another person in relation to the relevant proposal;
(b) the date on which P first made the relevant proposal available for implementation by any other person;
(c) the date on which P first became aware of any transaction forming part of the proposed arrangements being entered into by any person.

254(2) For the purposes of this Part relevant arrangements in relation to which a person ("P") is a promoter are "monitored arrangements" in relation to P if–

(a) P was by virtue of section 235(2)(b) or (c) a promoter in relation to a relevant proposal which was implemented by the arrangements and any of the following fell on or after the date on which the monitoring notice took effect–
  (i) the date on which P first made a firm approach to another person in relation to the relevant proposal;
  (ii) the date on which P first made the relevant proposal available for implementation by any other person;
  (iii) the date on which P first became aware of any transaction forming part of the proposed arrangements being entered into by any person,
(b) the date on which P first took part in designing, organising or managing the arrangements fell on or after the date on which a monitoring notice took effect, or
(c) the arrangements enable, or are likely to enable, the person who has entered into transactions forming them to obtain the tax advantage by reason of which they are relevant arrangements, at any time on or after the date on which a monitoring notice took effect.

255 Power to obtain information and documents

255(1) An authorised officer, or an officer of Revenue and Customs with the approval of an authorised officer, may by notice in writing require any person ("P") to whom this section applies–

(a) to provide information, or
(b) to produce a document,

if the information or document is reasonably required by the officer for any of the purposes in subsection (3).

255(2) This section applies to–

(a) any person who is a monitored promoter, and
(b) any person who is a relevant intermediary in relation to a monitored proposal of a monitored promoter,

and in either case that monitored promoter is referred to below as **"the relevant monitored promoter"**.

255(3) The purposes mentioned in subsection (1) are–

(a) considering the possible consequences of implementing a monitored proposal of the relevant monitored promoter for the tax position of persons implementing the proposal,
(b) checking the tax position of any person who the officer reasonably believes has implemented a monitored proposal of the relevant monitored promoter, or

(c) checking the tax position of any person who the officer reasonably believes has entered into transactions forming monitored arrangements of the relevant monitored promoter.

255(4) A person is a **"relevant intermediary"** in relation to a monitored proposal if the person meets the conditions in section 236(a) to (c) (meaning of "intermediary") in relation to the proposal at any time after the person has been notified of a promoter reference number of a person who is a promoter in relation to the proposal.

255(5) In this section **"checking"** includes carrying out an investigation or enquiry of any kind.

255(6) In this section **"tax position"**, in relation to a person, means the person's position as regards any tax, including the person's position as regards–

(a) past, present and future liability to pay any tax,

(b) penalties and other amounts that have been paid, or are or may be payable, by or to the person in connection with any tax,

(c) claims, elections, applications and notices that have been or may be made or given in connection with the person's liability to pay any tax,

(d) deductions or repayments of tax, or of sums representing tax, that the person is required to make–

  (i) under PAYE regulations, or

  (ii) by or under any other provision of the Taxes Acts, and

(e) the withholding by the person of another person's PAYE income (as defined in section 683 of ITEPA 2003).

255(7) In this section the reference to the tax position of a person–

(a) includes the tax position of a company that has ceased to exist and an individual who has died, and

(b) is to the person's tax position at any time or in relation to any period.

255(8) A notice under subsection (1) which is given for the purpose of checking the tax position of a person mentioned in subsection (3)(b) or (c) may not be given more than 4 years after the person's death.

255(9) A notice under subsection (1) may specify or describe the information or documents to be provided or produced.

255(10) Information or a document required as a result of a notice under subsection (1) must be provided or produced within–

(a) the period of 10 days beginning with the day on which the notice was given, or

(b) such longer period as the officer who gives the notice may direct.

Cross references – NICA 2015, Sch. 2, para. 28: references in s. 255 to a persons tax position include a person's position as regards "relevant contributions" (Class 1, Class 1A, 1B and certain Class 2 contributions under SSCBA 1992, Pt. 1 (NICA 2015, Sch. 2, para. 31).

256 Tribunal approval for certain uses of power under section 255

256(1) An officer of Revenue and Customs may not, without the approval of the tribunal, give a notice under section 255 requiring a person ("A") to provide information or produce a document which relates (in whole or in part) to a person who is neither A nor an undertaking in relation to which A is a parent undertaking.

256(2) An officer of Revenue and Customs may apply to the tribunal for the approval required by subsection (1); and an application for approval may be made without notice.

256(3) The tribunal may approve the giving of the notice only if–

(a) the application for approval is made by, or with the agreement of, an authorised officer,

(b) the tribunal is satisfied that, in the circumstances, the officer giving the notice is justified in doing so,

(c) the person to whom the notice is to be given has been informed that the information or documents referred to in the notice are required and given a reasonable opportunity to make representations to *an officer of Revenue and Customs*, and

(d) the tribunal has been given a summary of any representations made by that person.

256(4) Where a notice is given under section 255 with the approval of the tribunal, it must state that it is given with that approval.

256(5) Paragraphs (c) and (d) of subsection (3) do not apply to the extent that the tribunal is satisfied that taking the action specified in those paragraphs might prejudice the assessment or collection of tax.

256(6) In subsection (1) **"parent undertaking"** and **"undertaking"** have the same meaning as in the Companies Acts (see section 1161 and 1162 of, and Schedule 7 to, the Companies Act 2006).

256(7) A decision of the tribunal under this section is final (despite the provisions of sections 11 and 13 of the Tribunals, Courts and Enforcement Act 2007).

257 Ongoing duty to provide information following HMRC notice

257(1) An authorised officer, or an officer of Revenue and Customs with the approval of an authorised officer, may give a notice to a person ("P") in relation to whom a monitoring notice has effect.

257(2) A person to whom a notice is given under subsection (1) must provide prescribed information and produce prescribed documents relating to–

(a) all the monitored proposals and all the monitored arrangements in relation to which the person is a promoter at the time of the notice, and

(b) all the monitored proposals and all the monitored arrangements in relation to which the person becomes a promoter after that time.

257(3) The duty under subsection (2)(b) does not apply in relation to any proposals or arrangements in relation to which the person first becomes a promoter after the monitoring notice ceases to have effect.

257(4) A notice under subsection (1) must specify the time within which information must be provided or a document produced and different times may be specified for different cases.

Statutory instruments – SI 2015/549: partly made under s. 257(2).

258 Duty of person dealing with non-resident monitored promoter

258(1) This section applies where a monitored promoter who is resident outside the United Kingdom has failed to comply with a duty under section 255 or 257 to provide information about a monitored proposal or monitored arrangements.

258(2) An authorised officer, or an officer of Revenue and Customs with the approval of an authorised officer, may give a notice to a relevant person which–

(a) specifies or describes the information which the monitored promoter has failed to provide, and

(b) requires the person to provide the information.

258(3) A **"relevant person"** means–

(a) any person who is an intermediary in relation to the monitored proposal concerned, and

(b) any person ("A") to whom the monitored promoter has made a firm approach in relation to the monitored proposal concerned with a view to making the proposal available for implementation by a person other than A.

258(4) If an authorised officer is not aware of any person to whom a notice could be given under subsection (2) the authorised officer, or an officer of Revenue and Customs with the approval of the authorised officer, may give a notice to any person who has implemented the proposal which–

(a) specifies or describes the information which the monitored promoter has failed to provide, and

(b) requires the person to provide the information.

258(5) If the duty mentioned in subsection (1) relates to monitored arrangements an authorised officer, or an officer of Revenue and Customs with the approval of an authorised officer, may give a notice to any person who has entered into any transaction forming part of the monitored arrangements concerned which–

(a) specifies or describes the information which the monitored promoter has failed to provide, and

(b) requires the person to provide the information.

258(6) A notice under this section may be given only if the officer giving the notice reasonably believes that the person to whom the notice is given is able to provide the information requested.

258(7) Information required as a result of a notice under this section must be provided within–

(a) the period of 10 days beginning with the day on which the notice was given, or

(b) such longer period as the officer who gives the notice may direct.

259 Monitored promoters: duty to provide information about clients

259(1) An authorised officer, or an officer of Revenue and Customs with the approval of an authorised officer, may give notice to a person in relation to whom a monitoring notice has effect ("the monitored promoter").

259(2) A person to whom a notice is given under subsection (1) must, for each relevant period, give the officer who gave the notice the information set out in subsection (9) in respect of each person who was its client with reference to that relevant period (see subsections (5) to (8)).

259(3) Each of the following is a **"relevant period"**–

(a) the calendar quarter in which the notice under subsection (1) was given but not including any time before the monitoring notice takes effect,

(b) the period (if any) beginning with the date the monitoring notice takes effect and ending immediately before the beginning of the period described in paragraph (a), and

(c) each calendar quarter after the period described in paragraph (a) but not including any time after the monitoring notice ceases to have effect.

259(4) Information required as a result of a notice under subsection (1) must be given–

(a) within the period of 30 days beginning with the end of the relevant period concerned, or

(b) in the case of a relevant period within subsection (3)(b), within the period of 30 days beginning with the day on which the notice under subsection (1) was given if that period would expire at a later time than the period given by paragraph (a).

259(5) A person ("C") is a client of the monitored promoter with reference to a relevant period if–

(a) the promoter did any of the things mentioned in subsection (6) in relation to C at any time during that period, or

(b) the person falls within subsection (7).

259(6) Those things are that the monitored promoter–

(a) made a firm approach to C in relation to a relevant proposal with a view to the promoter making the proposal available for implementation by C or another person;

(b) made a relevant proposal available for implementation by C;

(c) took part in the organisation or management of relevant arrangements entered into by C.

259(7) A person falls within this subsection if the person has entered into transactions forming part of relevant arrangements and those arrangements–

(a) enable the person to obtain a tax advantage either in that relevant period or a later relevant period, and

(b) are either relevant arrangements in relation to which the monitored promoter is or was a promoter, or implement a relevant proposal in relation to which the monitored promoter was a promoter.

259(8) But a person is not a client of the monitored promoter with reference to a relevant period if–

(a) the person has previously been a client of the monitored promoter with reference to a different relevant period,

(b) the promoter complied with the duty in subsection (2) in respect of the person for that relevant period, and

(c) the information provided as a result of complying with that duty remains accurate.

259(9) The information mentioned in subsection (2) is–

(a) the person's name and address, and

(b) such other information about the person as may be prescribed.

259(10) Where the monitoring notice mentioned in subsection (1) is a replacement monitoring notice, subsection (5)(b) does not impose a duty on the monitored promoter concerned to provide information about a person who has entered into transactions forming part of relevant arrangements (as described in subsection (7)) if the monitored promoter reasonably believes that information about that person has, in relation to those arrangements, already been provided under the original monitoring notice.

Statutory instruments – SI 2015/549: partly made under s. 259(9).

260 Intermediaries: duty to provide information about clients

260(1) An authorised officer, or an officer of Revenue and Customs with the approval of an authorised officer, may give notice to a person ("the intermediary") who is an intermediary in relation to a relevant proposal which is a monitored proposal of a person in relation to whom a monitoring notice has effect ("the monitored promoter").

260(2) A person to whom a notice is given under subsection (1) must, for each relevant period, give the officer who gave the notice the information set out in subsection (7) in respect of each person who was its client with reference to that relevant period (see subsections (5) to (6)).

260(3) Each of the following is a **"relevant period"**–

(a) the calendar quarter in which the notice under subsection (1) was given but not including any time before the intermediary was first notified under section 250, 251 or 252 of the promoter reference number of the monitored promoter,

(b) the period (if any) beginning with the date of the notification under section 250, 251 or 252 and ending immediately before the beginning of the period described in paragraph (a), and

(c) each calendar quarter after the period described in paragraph (a) but not including any time after the monitoring notice mentioned in subsection (1) ceases to have effect.

260(4) Information required as a result of a notice under subsection (1) must be given–

(a) within the period of 30 days beginning with the end of the relevant period concerned, or

(b) in the case of a relevant period within subsection (3)(b), within the period of 30 days beginning with the day on which the notice under subsection (1) was given if that period would expire at a later time than the period given by paragraph (a).

260(5) A person ("C") is a client of the intermediary with reference to a relevant period if during that period–

(a) the intermediary communicated information to C about a monitored proposal in the course of a business, and

(b) the communication was made with a view to C, or any other person, entering into transactions forming part of the proposed arrangements.

260(6) But a person is not a client of the intermediary with reference to a relevant period if–

(a) the person has previously been a client of the intermediary with reference to a different relevant period,

(b) the intermediary complied with the duty in subsection (2) in respect of the person for that relevant period, and

(c) the information provided as a result of complying with that duty remains accurate.

260(7) The information mentioned in subsection (2) is–

(a) the person's name and address, and

(b) such other information about the person as may be prescribed.

Statutory instruments – SI 2015/549: partly made under s. 260(7).

261 Enquiry following provision of client information

261(1) This section applies where–

(a) a person ("the notifying person") has provided information under section 259 or 260 about a person who was a client of the notifying person with reference to a relevant period (within the meaning of the section concerned) in connection with a particular relevant proposal or particular relevant arrangements, and

(b) an authorised officer suspects that a person in respect of whom information has not been provided under section 259 or 260–

(i) has at any time been, or is likely to be, a party to transactions implementing the proposal, or

(ii) is a party to a transaction forming (in whole or in part) particular relevant arrangements.

261(2) The authorised officer may by notice in writing require the notifying person to provide prescribed information in relation to any person whom the notifying person might reasonably be expected to know–

(a) has been, or is likely to be, a party to transactions implementing the proposal, or

(b) is a party to a transaction forming (in whole or in part) the relevant arrangements.

261(3) But a notice under subsection (2) does not impose a requirement on the notifying person to provide information which the notifying person has already provided to an authorised officer under section 259 or 260.

261(4) The notifying person must comply with a requirement under subsection (2) within–

(a) 10 days of the notice, or

(b) such longer period as the authorised officer may direct.

Statutory instruments – SI 2015/549: partly made under s. 261(2).

262 Information required for monitoring compliance with conduct notice

262(1) *This section applies where a conduct notice has effect in relation to a person.*

262(2) An authorised officer, or an officer of Revenue and Customs with the approval of an authorised officer, may (as often as is necessary for the purpose mentioned below) by notice in writing require the person–

(a) to provide information, or

(b) to produce a document,

if the information or document is reasonably required for the purpose of monitoring whether and to what extent the person is complying with the conditions in the conduct notice.

263 Duty to notify HMRC of address

263 If, on the last day of a calendar quarter, a monitoring notice has effect in relation to a person ("the monitored promoter") the monitored promoter must within 30 days of the end of the calendar quarter inform an authorised officer of its current address.

264 Failure to provide information: application to tribunal

264(1) This section applies where–

(a) a person ("P") has provided information or produced a document in purported compliance with section 255, 257, 258, 259, 260, 261 or 262, but

(b) an authorised officer suspects that P has not provided all the information or produced all the documents required under the section concerned.

264(2) The authorised officer, or an officer of Revenue and Customs with the approval of the authorised officer, may apply to the tribunal for an order requiring P to–

(a) provide specified information about persons who are its clients for the purposes of the section to which the application relates,

(b) provide specified information, or information of a specified description, about a monitored proposal or monitored arrangements,

(c) produce specified documents relating to a monitored proposal or monitored arrangements.

264(3) The tribunal may make an order under subsection (2) in respect of information or documents only if satisfied that the officer has reasonable grounds for suspecting that the information or documents–

(a) are required under section 255, 257, 258, 259, 260, 261 or 262 (as the case may be), or

(b) will support or explain information required under the section concerned.

264(4) A requirement by virtue of an order under subsection (2) is to be treated as part of P's duty under section 255, 257, 258, 259, 260, 261 or 262 (as the case may be).

264(5) Information or a document required as a result of subsection (2) must be provided, or the document produced, within the period of 10 days beginning with the day on which the order under subsection (2) was made.

264(6) An authorised officer may, by direction, extend the 10 day period mentioned in subsection (5).

265 Duty to provide information to monitored promoter

265(1) This section applies where a person has been notified of a promoter reference number–

(a) under section 250 by reason of being a person falling within subsection (2)(b) of that section, or

(b) under section 251 or 252.

265(2) The person notified ("C") must within 10 days notify the person whose promoter reference number it is of–

(a) C's national insurance number (if C has one), and

(b) C's unique tax reference number (if C has one).

265(3) If C has neither a national insurance number nor a unique tax reference number, C must within 10 days inform the person whose promoter reference number it is of that fact.

265(4) A unique tax reference number is an identification number allocated to a person by HMRC.

265(5) Subsection (2) or (3) does not impose a duty on C to provide information which C has already provided to the person whose promoter reference number it is.

OBTAINING INFORMATION AND DOCUMENTS: APPEALS

266 Appeals against notices imposing information etc requirements

266(1) This section applies where a person is given a notice under section 255, 257, 258, 259, 260, 261 or 262.

266(2) The person to whom the notice is given may appeal against the notice or any requirement under the notice.

266(3) Subsection (2) does not apply–

(a) to a requirement to provide any information or produce any document that forms part of the person's statutory records, or

(b) if the tribunal has approved the giving of the notice under section 256.

266(4) For the purposes of this section, information or a document forms part of a person's statutory records if it is information or a document which the person is required to keep and preserve under or by virtue of–

(a) the Taxes Acts, or

(b) any other enactment relating to a tax.

266(5) Information and documents cease to form part of a person's statutory records when the period for which they are required to be preserved by the enactments mentioned in subsection (4) has expired.

266(6) Notice of appeal must be given–

(a) in writing to the officer who gave the notice, and

(b) within the period of 30 days beginning with the day on which the notice was given.

266(7) The notice of appeal must state the grounds of the appeal.

266(8) On an appeal that is notified to the tribunal, the tribunal may–

(a) confirm the notice or a requirement under the notice,

(b) vary the notice or such a requirement, or

(c) set aside the notice or such a requirement.

266(9) Where the tribunal confirms or varies the notice or a requirement, the person to whom the notice was given must comply with the notice or requirement–

(a) within such period as is specified by the tribunal, or

(b) if the tribunal does not specify a period, within such period as is reasonably specified in writing by an officer of Revenue and Customs following the tribunal's decision.

266(10) A decision of the tribunal on an appeal under this section is final (despite the provisions of sections 11 and 13 of the Tribunals, Courts and Enforcement Act 2007).

266(11) Subject to this section, the provisions of Part 5 of TMA 1970 relating to appeals have effect in relation to an appeal under this section.

OBTAINING INFORMATION AND DOCUMENTS: SUPPLEMENTARY

267 Form and manner of providing information

267(1) The Commissioners may specify the form and manner in which information required to be provided or documents required to be produced by sections 255 to 264 must be provided or produced if the provision is to be complied with.

267(2) The Commissioners may specify that a document must be produced for inspection–

(a) at a place agreed between the person and an officer of Revenue and Customs, or

(b) at such place (which must not be a place used solely as a dwelling) as an officer of Revenue and Customs may reasonably specify.

267(3) The production of a document in compliance with a notice under this Part is not to be regarded as breaking any lien claimed on the document.

268 Production of documents: compliance

268(1) Where the effect of a notice under section 255, 257 or 262 is to require a person to produce a document, the person may comply with the requirement by producing a copy of the document, subject to any conditions or exceptions that may be prescribed.

268(2) Subsection (1) does not apply where–

(a) the effect of the notice is to require the person to produce the original document, or

(b) an authorised officer, or an officer of Revenue and Customs with the approval of an authorised officer, subsequently makes a request in writing to the person for the original document.

268(3) Where an officer requests a document under subsection (2)(b), the person to whom the request is made must produce the document–

(a) within such period, and

(b) at such time and by such means,

as is reasonably requested by the officer.

Statutory instruments – SI 2015/549: partly made under s. 268(1).

269 Exception for certain documents or information

269(1) Nothing in this Part requires a person to provide or produce–

(a) information that relates to the conduct of a pending appeal relating to tax or any part of a document containing such information,

(b) journalistic material (as defined in section 13 of the Police and Criminal Evidence Act 1984) or information contained in such material, or

(c) personal records (as defined in section 12 of the Police and Criminal Evidence Act 1984) or information contained in such records (but see subsection (2)).

269(2) A notice under this Part may require a person–

(a) to produce documents, or copies of documents, that are personal records, omitting any information whose inclusion (whether alone or with other information) makes the original documents personal records ("personal information"), and

(b) to provide any information contained in such records that is not personal information.

270 Limitation on duty to produce documents

270 Nothing in this Part requires a person to produce a document–

(a) which is not in the possession or power of that person, or

(b) if the whole of the document originates more than 6 years before the requirement to produce it would, if it were not for this section, arise.

271 Legal professional privilege

271(1) Nothing in this Part requires any person to disclose to HMRC any privileged information.

271(2) **"Privileged information"** means information with respect to which a claim to legal professional privilege by the person who would (ignoring the effect of this section) be required to disclose it, could be maintained in legal proceedings.

271(3) In the case of legal proceedings in Scotland, the reference in subsection (2) to legal professional privilege is to be read as a reference to confidentiality of communications.

272 Tax advisers

272(1) This section applies where a notice is given under section 258(4) or (5) and the person to whom the notice is given is a tax adviser.

272(2) The notice does not require a tax adviser–

(a) to provide information about relevant communications, or

(b) to produce documents which are the tax adviser's property and consist of relevant communications.

272(3) Subsection (2) does not have effect in relation to–

(a) information explaining any information or document which the person to whom the notice is given has, as tax accountant, assisted any person in preparing for, or delivering to, HMRC, or

(b) a document which contains such information.

272(4) But subsection (2) is not disapplied by subsection (3) if the information in question has already been provided, or a document containing the information has already been produced, to an officer of Revenue and Customs.

272(5) In this section–

"relevant communications" means communications between the tax adviser and–

(a) a person in relation to whose tax affairs the tax adviser has been appointed, or

(b) any other tax adviser of such a person,

the purpose of which is the giving or obtaining of advice about any of those tax affairs, and

"tax adviser" means a person appointed to give advice about the tax affairs of another person (whether appointed directly by that person or by another tax adviser of that person).

273 Confidentiality

273(1) No duty of confidentiality or other restriction on disclosure (however imposed) prevents the voluntary disclosure by a relevant client or a relevant intermediary to HMRC of information or documents about–

(a) a monitored promoter, or

(b) relevant proposals or relevant arrangements in relation to which a monitored promoter is a promoter.

273(2) **"Relevant client"** means a person in relation to whom the monitored promoter mentioned in subsection (1)(a) or (b)–

(a) has made a firm approach in relation to a relevant proposal with a view to making the proposal available for implementation by that person or another person;

(b) has made a relevant proposal available for implementation by that person;

(c) took part in the organisation or management of relevant arrangements entered into by that person.

273(3) **"Relevant intermediary"** means a person who is an intermediary in relation to a relevant proposal in relation to which the monitored promoter mentioned in subsection (1)(a) or (b) is a promoter.

273(4) The relevant proposal or relevant arrangements mentioned in subsection (2) or (3) need not be the relevant proposals or relevant arrangements to which the disclosure relates.

PENALTIES

274 Penalties

274 Schedule 35 contains provision about penalties for failure to comply with provisions of this Part.

275 Failure to comply with Part 7 of the Finance Act 2004

275 [Inserts TMA 1970, s. 98C(2EA)–(2EB).]

276 Limitation of defence of reasonable care

276 [Omitted by F(No. 2)A 2017, s. 64(4).]

History – Omitted by F(No. 2)A 2017, s. 64(4), with effect in relation to any document of a kind listed in the Table at FA 2007, Sch. 24, para. 1 which is given to HMRC on or after 16 November 2017 (Royal Assent) and relates to a tax period that begins on or after 6 April 2017 and ends on or after 16 November 2017 (Royal Assent). Former s. 276 read as follows:

"276 Limitation of defence of reasonable care

276(1) Subsection (2) applies where–

(a) a person gives HMRC a document of a kind listed in the Table in paragraph 1 of Schedule 24 to FA 2007 (penalties for providing inaccurate documents to HMRC), and

(b) the document contains an inaccuracy.

276(2) In determining whether or not the inaccuracy was careless for the purposes of paragraph 3(1)(a) of Schedule 24 to FA 2007, reliance by the person on legal advice relating to relevant arrangements in relation to which a monitored promoter is a promoter is to be disregarded if the advice was given or procured by a person who was a monitored promoter in relation to the arrangements."

277 Extended time limit for assessment

277(1) [Inserts TMA 1970, s. 36(1A)(d).]

277(2) [Not relevant to National Insurance contributions.]

277(3) [Not relevant to National Insurance contributions.]

277(4) [Not relevant to National Insurance contributions.]

277(5) [Not relevant to National Insurance contributions.]

277(6) [Not relevant to National Insurance contributions.]

OFFENCES

278 Offence of concealing etc documents

278(1) A person is guilty of an offence if–

(a) the person is required to produce a document by a notice given under section 255,

(b) the tribunal approved the giving of the notice under section 256, and

(c) the person conceals, destroys or otherwise disposes of, or arranges for the concealment, destruction or disposal of, that document.

278(2) Subsection (1) does not apply if the person acts after the document has been produced to an officer of Revenue and Customs in accordance with section 255, unless the officer has notified the person in writing that the document must continue to be available for inspection (and has not withdrawn the notification).

278(3) *Subsection (1) does* not apply, in a case to which section 268(1) applies, if the person acts after the end of the expiry of 6 months beginning with the day on which a copy of the document was produced in accordance with that section unless, before the expiry of that period, an officer of Revenue and Customs makes a request for the original document under section 268(2)(b).

279 Offence of concealing etc documents following informal notification

279(1) A person is guilty of an offence if the person conceals, destroys or otherwise disposes of, or arranges for the concealment, destruction or disposal of, a document after an officer of Revenue and Customs has informed the person in writing that–

(a) the document is, or is likely, to be the subject of a notice under section 255, and

(b) the officer of Revenue and Customs intends to seek the approval of the tribunal to the giving of the notice.

279(2) A person is not guilty of an offence under this section if the person acts after–

(a) at least 6 months has expired since the person was, or was last, informed as described in subsection (1), or

(b) a notice has been given to the person under section 255, requiring the document to be produced.

280 Penalties for offences

280(1) A person who is guilty of an offence under section 278 or 279 is liable–

(a) on summary conviction, to–

(i) in England and Wales, a fine, or

(ii) in Scotland or Northern Ireland, a fine not exceeding the statutory maximum, or

(b) on conviction on indictment, to imprisonment for a term not exceeding 2 years or to a fine or both.

280(2) In relation to an offence committed before section 85(1) of the Legal Aid, Sentencing and Punishment of Offenders Act 2012 comes into force, subsection (1)(a)(i) has effect as if the reference to "a fine" were a reference to "a fine not exceeding the statutory maximum".

SUPPLEMENTAL

281 Partnerships

281 [Not relevant to National Insurance contributions.]

281A VAT and other indirect taxes

History – In the heading to s. 281A the words "and other indirect taxes" inserted by F(No. 2)A 2017, s. 66 and Sch. 17, para. 53(2), with effect so far as necessary for enabling the making of regulations under that Schedule from 16 November 2017 (Royal Assent) and from 1 January 2018 for all other purposes.

281A [Not relevant to National Insurance contributions.]

History – S. 281A inserted by FA 2016, s. 160(7), with effect from 15 September 2016 (Royal Assent).

282 Regulations under this Part

282(1) Regulations under this Part are to be made by statutory instrument.

282(2) Apart from an instrument to which subsection (3) applies, a statutory instrument containing regulations made under this Part is subject to annulment in pursuance of a resolution of the House of Commons.

282(3) A statutory instrument containing (whether alone or with other provision) regulations made under–

(a) section 238(7),

(b) paragraph 31 of Schedule 34,

(ba) paragraph 31 of Schedule 34A,

(c) paragraph 5(1) of Schedule 35, or

(d) paragraph 21 of Schedule 36,

may not be made unless a draft of the instrument has been laid before and approved by a resolution of the House of Commons.

282(4) Regulations under this Part–

(a) may make different provision for different purposes;

(b) may include transitional provision and savings.

History – S. 282(3)(ba) inserted by FA 2016, s. 160(8), with effect from 15 September 2016 (Royal Assent).

Statutory instruments – SI 2015/549: partly made under s. 282(4).

283 Interpretation of this Part

283(1) In this Part–

"arrangements" has the meaning given by section 234(4);

"the Commissioners" means the Commissioners for Her Majesty's Revenue and Customs;

"calendar quarter" means a period of 3 months beginning with 1 January, 1 April, 1 July or 1 October;

"conduct notice" means a notice of the description in section 238 that is given under–

(a) section 237(7) or (7A)),

(aa) section 237A(8),

(ab) section 237B(1),

(b) section 245(7), or

(c) paragraph 8(2) or (3) or 10(3)(a) or (4)(a) of Schedule 36;

"contract settlement" means an agreement in connection with a person's liability to make a payment to the Commissioners under or by virtue of an enactment;

"defeat", in relation to arrangements, has the meaning given by paragraph 10 of Schedule 34A;

"defeat notice" has the meaning given by section 241A(7);

"double defeat notice" has the meaning given by section 241A(7);

"final", in relation to a judicial ruling, is to be interpreted in accordance with section 237D(6);

"HMRC" means Her Majesty's Revenue and Customs;

"firm approach" has the meaning given by section 235(4);

"judicial ruling" means a ruling of a court or tribunal on one or more issues;

"look-forward period", in relation to a defeat notice, has the meaning given by section 241A(10);

"monitored promoter" has the meaning given by section 244(5);

"monitored proposal" and **"monitored arrangements"** have the meaning given by section 254;

"monitoring notice" means a notice given under section 244(1) or paragraph 9(2) or (3) or 10(3)(b) or (4)(b) of Schedule 36;

"the original monitoring notice" has the meaning given by paragraph 11(2) of Schedule 36;

"prescribed" means prescribed, or of a description prescribed, in regulations made by the Commissioners;

"promoter reference number" has the meaning given by section 250(5);

"provisional", in relation to a conduct notice given under section 237A(8), is to be interpreted in accordance with section 237C;

"related", in relation to arrangements, is to be interpreted in accordance with paragraph 2 of Schedule 34A;

"relevant arrangements" has the meaning given by section 234(2);

"relevant defeat", in relation to a person, is to be interpreted in accordance with Schedule 34A;

"relevant proposal" has the meaning given by section 234(1);

"relies on a Case 3 relevant defeat" is to be interpreted in accordance section 237B(5);

"replacement conduct notice" has the meaning given by paragraph 11(1) of Schedule 36;

"replacement monitoring notice" has the meaning given by paragraph 11(1) of Schedule 36;

"single defeat notice" has the meaning given by section 241A(7);

"tax" (except in provisions to which section 281A applies) means–

(a) [not relevant to National Insurance contributions,]

(b) [not relevant to National Insurance contributions,]

(c) [not relevant to National Insurance contributions,]

(d) [not relevant to National Insurance contributions,]

(e) [not relevant to National Insurance contributions,]

(f) [not relevant to National Insurance contributions,]

(g) [not relevant to National Insurance contributions,]

(h) [not relevant to National Insurance contributions,]

(i) [not relevant to National Insurance contributions,]

"tax advantage" has the meaning given by section 234(3) (but see also section 281A);

"Taxes Acts" has the same meaning as in TMA 1970 (see section 118(1) of that Act);

"the tribunal" means the First-tier Tribunal or, where determined by or under Tribunal Procedure Rules, the Upper Tribunal.

283(2) A reference in a provision of this Part to an authorised officer is to an officer of Revenue and Customs who is, or is a member of a class of officers who are, authorised by the Commissioners for the purposes of that provision.

283(3) A reference in a provision of this Part to meeting a threshold condition is to meeting one of the conditions described in paragraphs 2 to 12 of Schedule 34.

History – In s. 283(1), in the definition of "conduct notice", para. (aa) and (ab) inserted by FA 2016, s. 160(9)(a), with effect from 15 September 2016 (Royal Assent).

In s. 283(1), in the definition of "conduct notice", the words "or (7A)" inserted by FA 2015, s. 119 and Sch. 19, para. 3, with effect for the purposes of determining whether a person meets a threshold condition in a period of three years ending on or after 26 March 2015 (Royal Assent).

In s. 283(1), definitions of "contract settlement", "defeat", "defeat notice", "double defeat notice", "final", "judicial ruling", "look-forward period", "provisional", "relevant defeat", "related", "relies on a Case 3 relevant defeat" and "single defeat notice" inserted by FA 2016, s. 160(9)(d), with effect from 15 September 2016 (Royal Assent).

In s. 283(1), in the definition of "tax", the words "(except in provisions to which section 281A applies)" inserted by FA 2016, s. 160(9)(b), with effect from 15 September 2016 (Royal Assent).

In s. 283(1), in the definition of "tax advantage", the words "(but see also section 281A)" inserted by FA 2016, s. 160(9)(c), with effect from 15 September 2016 (Royal Assent).

Cross references – NICA 2015, Sch. 2, para. 30: definition of "tax" in s. 283(1) has effect as if "relevant contributions" (Class 1, Class 1A, 1B and certain Class 2 contributions under SSCBA 1992, Pt. 1 (NICA 2015, Sch. 2, para. 31) were listed in it.

Statutory instruments – SI 2015/130: partly made under s. 283(1).
SI 2015/131: partly made under s. 283(1).
SI 2015/549: partly made under s. 283(1).

PART 7 – FINAL PROVISIONS

301 Power to update indexes of defined terms

301(1) The Treasury may by order amend any index of defined expressions contained in an Act relating to taxation, so as to make amendments consequential on any enactment.

301(2) In this section–

"enactment" means any provision made by or under an Act (whether before or after the passing of this Act);

"index of defined expressions" means a provision contained in an Act relating to taxation which lists where expressions used in the Act, or in a particular part of the Act, are defined or otherwise explained.

301(3) The power to make an order under this section is exercisable by statutory instrument.

301(4) An order under this section is subject to annulment in pursuance of a resolution of the House of Commons.

302 Interpretation

302(1) In this Act–

"ALDA 1979" means the Alcoholic Liquor Duties Act 1979,

"BGDA 1981" means the Betting and Gaming Duties Act 1981,

"CAA 2001" means the Capital Allowances Act 2001,

"CEMA 1979" means the Customs and Excise Management Act 1979,

"CRCA 2005" means the Commissioners for Revenue and Customs Act 2005,

"CTA 2009" means the Corporation Tax Act 2009,

"CTA 2010" means the Corporation Tax Act 2010,

"F(No.3)A 2010" means the Finance (No. 3) Act 2010,

"IHTA 1984" means the Inheritance Tax Act 1984,

"ITA 2007" means the Income Tax Act 2007,

"ITEPA 2003" means the Income Tax (Earnings and Pensions) Act 2003,

"ITTOIA 2005" means the Income Tax (Trading and Other Income) Act 2005,

"OTA 1975" means the Oil Taxation Act 1975,

"TCGA 1992" means the Taxation of Chargeable Gains Act 1992,

"TIOPA 2010" means the Taxation (International and Other Provisions) Act 2010,

"TMA 1970" means the Taxes Management Act 1970,

"TPDA 1979" means the Tobacco Products Duty Act 1979,

"**VATA 1994**" means the Value Added Tax Act 1994, and

"**VERA 1994**" means the Vehicle Excise and Registration Act 1994.

302(2) In this Act–

"**FA**", followed by a year, means the Finance Act of that year, and

"**F(No. 2)A**", followed by a year, means the Finance (No. 2) Act of that year.

303 Short title

303 This Act may be cited as the Finance Act 2014.

SCHEDULES

SCHEDULE 34 – PROMOTERS OF TAX AVOIDANCE SCHEMES: THRESHOLD CONDITIONS

Section 237

Part 1 – Meeting the Threshold Conditions: General

MEANING OF "THRESHOLD CONDITION"

1 Each of the conditions described in paragraphs 2 to 12 is a "**threshold condition**".

DELIBERATE TAX DEFAULTERS

2 A person meets this condition if the Commissioners publish information about the person in reliance on section 94 of FA 2009 (publishing details of deliberate tax defaulters).

BREACH OF THE BANKING CODE OF PRACTICE

3 A person meets this condition if the person is named in a report under section 285 as a result of the Commissioners determining that the person breached the Code of Practice on Taxation for Banks by reason of promoting arrangements which the person cannot have reasonably believed achieved a tax result which was intended by Parliament.

DISHONEST TAX AGENTS

4 A person meets this condition if the person is given a conduct notice under paragraph 4 of Schedule 38 to FA 2012 (tax agents: dishonest conduct) and either–

(a) the time period during which a notice of appeal may be given in relation to the notice has expired, or

(b) an appeal against the notice has been made and the tribunal has confirmed the determination referred to in sub-paragraph (1) of paragraph 4 of that Schedule.

NON-COMPLIANCE WITH PART 7 OF FA 2004

5(1) A person meets this condition if the person fails to comply with any of the following provisions of Part 7 of FA 2004 (disclosure of tax avoidance schemes)–

(a) section 308(1) and (3) (duty of promoter in relation to notifiable proposals and notifiable arrangements);

(b) section 309(1) (duty of person dealing with promoter outside the United Kingdom);

(c) section 310 (duty of parties to notifiable arrangements not involving promoter);

(d) section 313ZA (duty of promoter to provide details of clients).

5(2) For the purposes of sub-paragraph (1), a person ("P") fails to comply with a provision mentioned in that sub-paragraph if and only if any of conditions A to C are met.

5(3) Condition A is met if–

(a) the tribunal has determined that P has failed to comply with the provision concerned,

(b) the appeal period has ended, and

(c) the determination has not been overturned on appeal.

5(4) Condition B is met if–

(a) the tribunal has determined for the purposes of section 118(2) of TMA 1970 that P is to be deemed not to have failed to comply with the provision concerned as P had a reasonable excuse for not doing the thing required to be done,

(b) the appeal period has ended, and

(c) the determination has not been overturned on appeal.

5(5) Condition C is met if P has admitted in writing to HMRC that P has failed to comply with the provision concerned.

5(6) The **"appeal period"** means–

(a) the period during which an appeal could be brought against the determination of the tribunal, or

(b) where an appeal mentioned in paragraph (a) has been brought, the period during which that appeal has not been finally determined, withdrawn or otherwise disposed of.

History – Para. 5(2)–(6) substituted for former para. 5(2) by FA 2015, s. 119 and Sch. 19, para. 6, with effect for the purposes of determining whether a person meets a threshold condition in a period of three years ending on or after 26 March 2015 (Royal Assent).

CRIMINAL OFFENCES

6(1) A person meets this condition if the person is charged with a relevant offence.

6(2) The fact that a person has been charged with an offence is disregarded for the purposes of this paragraph if–

(a) the person has been acquitted of the offence, or

(b) the charge has been dismissed or the proceedings have been discontinued.

6(3) An acquittal is not taken into account for the purposes of sub-paragraph (2) if an appeal has been brought against the acquittal and has not yet been disposed of.

6(4) **"Relevant offence"** means any of the following–

(a) an offence at common law of cheating in relation to the public revenue;

(b) in Scotland, an offence at common law of–

(i) fraud;

(ii) uttering;

(c) an offence under section 17(1) of the Theft Act 1968 or section 17 of the Theft Act (Northern Ireland) 1969 (c. 16 (N.I.)) (false accounting);

(d) an offence under section 106A of TMA 1970 (fraudulent evasion of income tax);

(e) an offence under section 107 of TMA 1970 (false statements: Scotland);

(f) an offence under any of the following provisions of CEMA 1979–

(i) section 50(2) (improper importation of goods with intent to defraud or evade duty);

(ii) section 167 (untrue declarations etc);

(iii) section 168 (counterfeiting documents etc);

(iv) section 170 (fraudulent evasion of duty);

(v) section 170B (taking steps for the fraudulent evasion of duty);

(g) an offence under any of the following provisions of VATA 1994–

(i) section 72(1) (being knowingly concerned in the evasion of VAT);

(ii) section 72(3) (false statement etc);

(iii) section 72(8) (conduct involving commission of other offence under section 72);

(h) an offence under section 1 of the Fraud Act 2006 (fraud);

(i) an offence under any of the following provisions of CRCA 2005–

(i) section 30 (impersonating a Commissioner or officer of Revenue and Customs);

(ii) section 31 (obstruction of officer of Revenue and Customs etc);

(iii) section 32 (assault of officer of Revenue and Customs);

(j) an offence under regulation 86(1) of the Money Laundering, Terrorist Financing and Transfer of Funds (Information on the Payer) Regulations 2017;

(k) an offence under section 49(1) of the Criminal Justice and Licensing (Scotland) Act 2010 (asp 13) (possession of articles for use in fraud).

History – In para. 6(4)(j), the words "regulation 86(1) of the Money Laundering, Terrorist Financing and Transfer of Funds (Information on the Payer) Regulations 2017" substituted for the words "regulation 45(1) of the Money Laundering Regulations 2007 (S.I. 2007/2157)" by SI 2017/692, Sch. 7, para. 10, with effect from 26 June 2017.

OPINION NOTICE OF GAAR ADVISORY PANEL

7 A person meets this condition if–

(a) arrangements in relation to which the person is a promoter–

(i) have been referred to the GAAR Advisory Panel under Schedule 43 to FA 2013 (referrals of single schemes),

(ii) are in a pool in respect of which a referral has been made to that Panel under Schedule 43B to that Act (generic referrals), or

(iii) have been referred to that Panel under paragraph 26 of Schedule 16 to F(No. 2)A 2017 (referrals in relation to penalties for enablers of defeated tax avoidance),

(b) one or more opinion notices are given in respect of the referral under (as the case may be)–

(i) paragraph 11(3)(b) of Schedule 43 to FA 2013,

(ii) paragraph 6(4)(b) of Schedule 43B to that Act, or

(iii) paragraph 34(3)(b) of Schedule 16 to F(No. 2)A 2017,

(opinion of sub-panel of GAAR Advisory Panel that arrangements are not reasonable), and

(c) the notice, or the notices taken together, either–

(i) state the joint opinion of all the members of the sub-panel arranged under that Schedule, or

(ii) state the opinion of two or more members of that sub-panel.

History – Para. 7(a)(i)–(iii) (and the "–" preceding them) substituted for the words "have been referred to the GAAR Advisory Panel under Schedule 43 to FA 2013, (referrals of single schemes) or are in a pool in respect of which a referral has been made to that Panel under Schedule 43B to that Act (generic referrals)," by F(No. 2)A 2017, s. 65 and Sch. 16, para. 61(a), with effect in relation to arrangements entered into on or after 16 November 2017 (Royal Assent).
In para. 7(a), the words "(referrals of single schemes) or are in a pool in respect of which a referral has been made to that Panel under Schedule 43B to that Act (generic referrals)," inserted by FA 2016, s. 157(29)(a), with effect in relation to tax arrangements (within the meaning of FA 2013, Pt. 5) entered into at any time (whether before or on or after 15 September 2016).
Para. 7(b)(i)–(iii) (and the "under (as the case may be)–" preceding them and the end words after them) substituted for the words " under paragraph 11(3)(b) or (as the case may be) 6(4)(b) of that Schedule (opinion of sub-panel of GAAR Advisory Panel that arrangements are not reasonable), and" by F(No. 2)A 2017, s. 65 and Sch. 16, para. 61(b), with effect in relation to arrangements entered into on or after 16 November 2017 (Royal Assent).
In para. 7(b), the words "in respect of the referral" substituted for the words "in relation to the arrangements" and the words "or (as the case may be) 6(4)(b)" inserted by FA 2016, s. 157(29)(b), with effect in relation to tax arrangements (within the meaning of FA 2013, Pt. 5) entered into at any time (whether before or on or after 15 September 2016).
In para. 7(c), the words "paragraph 10 of" (which appeared before the words "that Schedule") omitted by FA 2016, s. 157(29)(c), with effect in relation to tax arrangements (within the meaning of FA 2013, Pt. 5) entered into at any time (whether before or on or after 15 September 2016).

DISCIPLINARY ACTION AGAINST A MEMBER OF A TRADE OR PROFESSION

History – In the heading the words "AGAINST A MEMBER OF A TRADE OR PROFESSION" substituted for the words "BY A PROFESSIONAL BODY" by FA 2015, s. 119 and Sch. 19, para. 7(3), with effect for the purposes of determining whether a person meets a threshold condition in a period of three years ending on or after 26 March 2015 (Royal Assent).

8(1) A person who carries on a trade or profession that is regulated by a professional body meets this condition if all of the following conditions are met–

(a) the person is found guilty of misconduct of a prescribed kind,

(b) action of a prescribed kind is taken against the person in relation to that misconduct, and

(c) a penalty of a prescribed kind is imposed on the person as a result of that misconduct.

8(2) Misconduct may only be prescribed for the purposes of sub-paragraph (1)(a) if it is misconduct other than misconduct in matters (such as the payment of fees) that relate solely or mainly to the person's relationship with the professional body.

8(3) A **"professional body"** means–

(a) the Institute of Chartered Accountants in England and Wales;

(b) the Institute of Chartered Accountants of Scotland;

(c) the General Council of the Bar;

(d) the Faculty of Advocates;

(e) the General Council of the Bar of Northern Ireland;

(f) the Law Society;

(g) the Law Society of Scotland;

(h) the Law Society of Northern Ireland;

(i) the Association of Accounting Technicians;

(j) the Association of Chartered Certified Accountants;

(k) the Association of Taxation Technicians;

(l) any other prescribed body with functions relating to the regulation of a trade or profession.

History – Para. 8(1) substituted by FA 2015, s. 119 and Sch. 19, para. 7(2), with effect for the purposes of determining whether a person meets a threshold condition in a period of three years ending on or after 26 March 2015 (Royal Assent).
In para. 8(3)(h) the word "of" substituted for the word "for" by FA 2015, s. 119 and Sch. 19, para. 7(2)4 with effect for the purposes of determining whether a person meets a threshold condition in a period of three years ending on or after 26 March 2015 (Royal Assent).
Statutory instruments – SI 2015/131: partly made under para. 8(1) and (3).

DISCIPLINARY ACTION BY A REGULATORY AUTHORITY

9(1) A person meets this condition if a regulatory authority imposes a relevant sanction on the person.

9(2) A **"relevant sanction"** is a sanction which is–

(a) imposed in relation to misconduct other than misconduct in matters (such as the payment of fees) that relate solely or mainly to the person's relationship with the regulatory authority, and

(b) prescribed.

9(3) The following are regulatory authorities for the purposes of this paragraph–

(a) the Financial Conduct Authority;

(b) the Financial Services Authority;

(c) any other authority that may be prescribed.

9(4) Only authorities that have functions relating to the regulation of financial institutions may be prescribed under sub-paragraph (3)(c).

Statutory instruments – SI 2015/131: partly made under para. 9(2).

EXERCISE OF INFORMATION POWERS

10(1) A person meets this condition if the person fails to comply with an information notice given under any of paragraphs 1, 2, 5 and 5A of Schedule 36 to FA 2008.

10(2) For the purposes of section 237, the failure to comply is taken to occur when the period within which the person is required to comply with the notice expires (without the person having complied with it).

RESTRICTIVE CONTRACTUAL TERMS

11(1) A person ("P") meets this condition if P enters into an agreement with another person ("C") which relates to a relevant proposal or relevant arrangements in relation to which P is a promoter, on terms which–

(a) impose a contractual obligation on C which falls within sub-paragraph (2) or (3), or

(b) impose on C both obligations within sub-paragraph (4) and obligations within sub-paragraph (5).

11(2) A contractual obligation falls within this sub-paragraph if it prevents or restricts the disclosure by C to HMRC of information relating to the proposals or arrangements, whether or not by referring to a wider class of persons.

11(3) A contractual obligation falls within this sub-paragraph if it requires C to impose on any tax adviser to whom C discloses information relating to the proposals or arrangements a contractual obligation which prevents or restricts the disclosure of that information to HMRC by the adviser.

11(4) A contractual obligation falls within this sub-paragraph if it requires C to–

(a) meet (in whole or in part) the costs of, or contribute to a fund to be used to meet the costs of, any proceedings relating to arrangements in relation to which P is a promoter (whether or not implemented by C), or

(b) take out an insurance policy which insures against the risk of having to meet the costs connected with proceedings relating to arrangements which C has implemented and in relation to which P is a promoter.

11(5) A contractual obligation falls within this paragraph if it requires C to obtain the consent of P before–

(a) entering into any agreement with HMRC regarding arrangements which C has implemented and in relation to which P is a promoter, or

(b) withdrawing or discontinuing any appeal against any decision regarding such arrangements.

11(6) In sub-paragraph (5)(b), the reference to withdrawing or discontinuing an appeal includes any action or inaction which results in an appeal being discontinued.

11(7) In this paragraph–

"proceedings" includes any sort of proceedings for resolving disputes (and not just proceedings in court), whether commenced or contemplated;

"tax adviser" means a person appointed to give advice about the tax affairs of another person (whether appointed directly by that person or by another tax adviser of that person).

CONTINUING TO PROMOTE CERTAIN ARRANGEMENTS

12(1) A person ("P") meets this condition if P has been given a stop notice and after the end of the notice period P–

(a) makes a firm approach to another person ("C") in relation to an affected proposal with a view to making the affected proposal available for implementation by C or another person, or

(b) makes an affected proposal available for implementation by other persons.

12(2) **"Affected proposal"** means a relevant proposal that is in substance the same as the relevant proposal specified in the stop notice in accordance with sub-paragraph (4)(c).

12(3) An authorised officer may give a person ("P") a notice (a "stop notice") if each of these conditions is met–

(a) a person has been given a follower notice under section 204 (circumstances in which a follower notice may be given) in relation to particular relevant arrangements;

(b) P is a promoter in relation to a relevant proposal that is implemented by those arrangements;

(c) 90 days have elapsed since the follower notice was given and–

(i) the follower notice has not been withdrawn, and

(ii) if representations objecting to the follower notice were made under section 207 (representations about a follower notice), HMRC have confirmed the follower notice.

12(4) A stop notice must–

(a) specify the arrangements which are the subject of the follower notice mentioned in sub-paragraph (3)(a),

(b) specify the judicial ruling identified in that follower notice,

(c) specify a relevant proposal in relation to which the condition in sub-paragraph (3)(b) is met, and

(d) explain the effect of the stop notice.

12(5) An authorised officer may determine that a stop notice given to a person is to cease to have effect.

12(6) If an authorised officer makes a determination under sub-paragraph (5) the officer must give the person written notice of the determination.

12(7) The notice must specify the date from which it takes effect, which may be earlier than the date on which the notice is given.

12(8) In this paragraph–

"the notice period" means the period of 30 days beginning with the day on which a stop notice is given;

"judicial ruling" means a ruling of a court or tribunal.

Part 2 – Meeting the Threshold Conditions: Bodies Corporate and Partnerships

History – In the heading the words "and Partnerships" inserted by FA 2015, s. 119 and Sch. 19, para. 4(2), with effect for the purposes of determining whether a person meets a threshold condition in a period of three years ending on or after 26 March 2015 (Royal Assent).

13 [Para. 13A–13D substituted for para. 13 by FA 2015, s. 119 and Sch. 19, para. 4(3).]

History – Para. 13 substituted by former para 13A–13D by FA 2015, s. 119 and Sch. 19, para. 432), with effect for the purposes of determining whether a person meets a threshold condition in a period of three years ending on or after 26 March 2015 (Royal Assent).

INTERPRETATION

13A(1) This paragraph contains definitions for the purposes of this Part of this Schedule.

13A(2) Each of the following is a **"relevant body"**–

(a) a body corporate, and

(b) a partnership.

13A(3) **"Relevant time"** means the time referred to in section 237(1A) (duty to give conduct notice to person treated as meeting threshold condition).

13A(4) "Relevant threshold condition" means a threshold condition specified in any of the following paragraphs of this Schedule–

(a) paragraph 2 (deliberate tax defaulters);
(b) paragraph 4 (dishonest tax agents);
(c) paragraph 6 (criminal offences);
(d) paragraph 7 (opinion notice of GAAR advisory panel);
(e) paragraph 8 (disciplinary action against a member of a trade or profession);
(f) paragraph 9 (disciplinary action by regulatory authority);
(g) paragraph 10 (failure to comply with information notice).

13A(5) A person controls a body corporate if the person has power to secure that the affairs of the body corporate are conducted in accordance with the person's wishes–

(a) by means of the holding of shares or the possession of voting power in relation to the body corporate or any other relevant body,
(b) as a result of any powers conferred by the articles of association or other document regulating the body corporate or any other relevant body, or
(c) by means of controlling a partnership.

13A(6) Two or more persons together control a body corporate if together they have the power to secure that the affairs of the body corporate are conducted in accordance with their wishes in any way specified in sub-paragraph (5)(a) to (c).

13A(7) A person controls a partnership if the person is a member of the partnership and–

(a) has the right to a share of more than half the assets, or more than half the income, of the partnership, or
(b) directs, or is on a day-to-day level in control of, the management of the business of the partnership.

13A(8) Two or more persons together control a partnership if they are members of the partnership and together they–

(a) have the right to a share of more than half the assets, or of more than half the income, of the partnership, or
(b) direct, or are on a day-to-day level in control of, the management of the business of the partnership.

13A(9) Paragraph 19(2) to (5) of Schedule 36 (connected persons etc) applies to a person referred to in sub-paragraph (7) or (8) as if references to "P" were to that person.

13A(10) A person has significant influence over a body corporate or partnership if the person–

(a) does not control the body corporate or partnership, but
(b) is able to, or actually does, exercise significant influence over it (whether or not as the result of a legal entitlement).

13A(11) Two or more persons together have significant influence over a body corporate or partnership if together those persons–

(a) do not control the body corporate or partnership, but
(b) are able to, or actually do, exercise significant influence over it (whether or not as the result of a legal entitlement).

13A(12) References to a person being a promoter are to the person carrying on business as a promoter.

History – Para. 13A(6)–(12) substituted for para. 13A(6)–(8) by FA 2017, s. 24(1), with effect for the purposes of determining whether a person meets a threshold condition in a period of three years ending on or after 8 March 2017. Former para. 13A(6)–(8) read as follows:

"**13A(6)** A person controls a partnership if the person is a controlling member or the managing partner of the partnership.
13A(7) "Controlling member" has the same meaning as in Schedule 36 (partnerships).
13A(8) "Managing partner", in relation to a partnership, means the member of the partnership who directs, or is on a day-to-day level in control of, the management of the business of the partnership.".

Para. 13A–13D substituted for former para 13 by FA 2015, s. 119 and Sch. 19, para. 4(3), with effect for the purposes of determining whether a person meets a threshold condition in a period of three years ending on or after 26 March 2015 (Royal Assent).

RELEVANT BODIES CONTROLLED ETC BY OTHER PERSONS TREATED AS MEETING A THRESHOLD CONDITION

13B(1) A relevant body is treated as meeting a threshold condition at the relevant time if any of Conditions A to C is met.

13B(2) Condition A is that–

(a) a person met the threshold condition at a time when the person was a promoter, and
(b) the person controls or has significant influence over the relevant body at the relevant time.

13B(3) Condition B is that–

(a) a person met the threshold condition at a time when the person controlled or had significant influence over the relevant body,

(b) the relevant body was a promoter at that time, and

(c) the person controls or has significant influence over the relevant body at the relevant time.

13B(4) Condition C is that–

(a) two or more persons together controlled or had significant influence over the relevant body at a time when one of those persons met the threshold condition,

(b) the relevant body was a promoter at that time, and

(c) those persons together control or have significant influence over the relevant body at the relevant time.

13B(5) Where the person referred to in sub-paragraph (2)(a) or (3)(a) or (4)(a) as meeting a threshold condition is an individual, sub-paragraph (1) only applies if the threshold condition is a relevant threshold condition.

13B(6) For the purposes of sub-paragraph (2) it does not matter whether the relevant body existed at the time referred to in sub-paragraph (2)(a).

History – Para. 13B substituted by FA 2017, s. 24(2), with effect for the purposes of determining whether a person meets a threshold condition in a period of three years ending on or after 8 March 2017. Former para. 13B read as follows:

"TREATING PERSONS UNDER ANOTHER'S CONTROL AS MEETING A THRESHOLD CONDITION

13B(1) A relevant body ("RB") is treated as meeting a threshold condition at the relevant time if–

(a) the threshold condition was met by a person ("C") at a time when–

(i) C was carrying on a business as a promoter, or

(ii) RB was carrying on a business as a promoter and C controlled RB, and

(b) RB is controlled by C at the relevant time.

13B(2) Where C is an individual sub-paragraph (1) applies only if the threshold condition mentioned in sub-paragraph (1)(a) is a relevant threshold condition.

13B(3) For the purposes of determining whether the requirements of sub-paragraph (1) are met by reason of meeting the requirement in sub-paragraph (1)(a)(i), it does not matter whether RB existed at the time when the threshold condition was met by C.".

Para. 13A and former para. 13B–13D substituted for former para. 13 by FA 2015, s. 119 and Sch. 19, para. 4(3), with effect for the purposes of determining whether a person meets a threshold condition in a period of three years ending on or after 26 March 2015 (Royal Assent).

PERSONS WHO CONTROL ETC A RELEVANT BODY TREATED AS MEETING A THRESHOLD CONDITION

13C(1) If at a time when a person controlled or had significant influence over a relevant body–

(a) the relevant body met a threshold condition, and

(b) the relevant body, or another relevant body which the person controlled or had significant influence over, was a promoter,

the person is treated as meeting the threshold condition at the relevant time.

13C(2) It does not matter whether any relevant body referred to sub-paragraph (1) exists at the relevant time.

History – Para. 13C substituted by FA 2017, s. 24(2), with effect for the purposes of determining whether a person meets a threshold condition in a period of three years ending on or after 8 March 2017. Former para. 13C read as follows:

"TREATING PERSONS IN CONTROL OF OTHERS AS MEETING A THRESHOLD CONDITION

13C(1) A person other than an individual is treated as meeting a threshold condition at the relevant time if–

(a) a relevant body ("A") met the threshold condition at a time when A was controlled by the person, and

(b) at the time mentioned in paragraph (a) A, or another relevant body ("B") which was also at that time controlled by the person, carried on a business as a promoter.

13C(2) For the purposes of determining whether the requirements of sub-paragraph (1) are met it does not matter whether A or B (or neither) exists at the relevant time."

Para. 13A and former para. 13B–13D substituted for former para. 13 by FA 2015, s. 119 and Sch. 19, para. 4(3), with effect for the purposes of determining whether a person meets a threshold condition in a period of three years ending on or after 26 March 2015 (Royal Assent).

RELEVANT BODIES CONTROLLED ETC BY THE SAME PERSON TREATED AS MEETING A THRESHOLD CONDITION

13D(1) If–

(a) a person controlled or had significant influence over a relevant body at a time when it met a threshold condition, and

(b) at that time that body, or another relevant body which the person controlled or had significant influence over, was a promoter,

any relevant body which the person controls or has significant influence over at the relevant time is treated as meeting the threshold condition at the relevant time.

13D(2) If–

(a) two or more persons together controlled or had significant influence over a relevant body at a time when it met a threshold condition, and

(b) at that time that body, or another relevant body which those persons together controlled or had significant influence over, was a promoter,

any relevant body which those persons together control or have significant influence over at the relevant time is treated as meeting the threshold condition at the relevant time.

13D(3) It does not matter whether–

(a) a relevant body referred to in sub-paragraph (1)(a) or (b) or (2)(a) or (b) exists at the relevant time, or

(b) a relevant body existing at the relevant time existed at the time referred to in sub-paragraph (1)(a) or (2)(a).

History – Para. 13D substituted by FA 2017, s. 24(2), with effect for the purposes of determining whether a person meets a threshold condition in a period of three years ending on or after 8 March 2017. Former para. 13D read as follows:

"TREATING PERSONS CONTROLLED BY THE SAME PERSON AS MEETING A THRESHOLD CONDITION

13D(1) A relevant body ("RB") is treated as meeting a threshold condition at the relevant time if–

(a) RB or another relevant body met the threshold condition at a time ("time T") when it was controlled by a person ("C"),

(b) at time T, there was a relevant body controlled by C which carried on a business as a promoter, and

(c) RB is controlled by C at the relevant time.

13D(2) For the purposes of determining whether the requirements of sub-paragraph (1) are met it does not matter whether–

(a) RB existed at time T, or

(b) any relevant body (other than RB) by reason of which the requirements of sub-paragraph (1) are met exists at the relevant time.".

Para. 13A and former para. 13B–13D substituted for former para. 13 by FA 2015, s. 119 and Sch. 19, para. 4(3), with effect for the purposes of determining whether a person meets a threshold condition in a period of three years ending on or after 26 March 2015 (Royal Assent).

Part 3 – Power to Amend

14(1) The Treasury may by regulations amend this Schedule.

14(2) An amendment made by virtue of sub-paragraph (1) may, in particular–

(a) vary or remove any of the conditions set out in paragraphs 2 to 12;

(b) add new conditions.

(c) vary any of the circumstances described in paragraphs 13B to 13D in which a person is treated as meeting a threshold condition (including by amending paragraph 13A);

(d) add new circumstances in which a person will be so treated.

14(3) Regulations under sub-paragraph (1) may include any amendment of this Part of this Act that is appropriate in consequence of an amendment made by virtue of sub-paragraph (1).

History – Para. 14(2)(c) and (d) inserted by FA 2015, s. 119 and Sch. 19, para. 8 with effect from 26 March 2015 (Royal Assent).

SCHEDULE 34A – PROMOTERS OF TAX AVOIDANCE SCHEMES: DEFEATED ARRANGEMENTS

History – Sch. 34A inserted by FA 2016, s. 160(5), with effect from 15 September 2016 (Royal Assent).

Part 1 – Introduction

1 In this Schedule–

(a) Part 2 is about the meaning of **"relevant defeat"**;

(b) Part 3 contains provision about when a relevant defeat is treated as occurring in relation to a person;

(c) Part 4 contains provision about when a person is treated as meeting a condition in subsection (11), (12) or (13) of section 237A;

(d) Part 5 contains definitions and other supplementary provisions.

Part 2 – Meaning of "Relevant Defeat"

"RELATED" ARRANGEMENTS

2(1) For the purposes of this Part of this Act, separate arrangements which persons have entered into are **"related"** to one another if (and only if) they are substantially the same.

2(2) Sub-paragraphs (3) to (6) set out cases in which arrangements are to be treated as being **"substantially the same"** (if they would not otherwise be so treated under sub-paragraph (1)).

2(3) Arrangements to which the same reference number has been allocated under Part 7 of FA 2004 (disclosure of tax avoidance schemes) are treated as being substantially the same.
For this purpose arrangements in relation to which information relating to a reference number has been provided in compliance with section 312 of FA 2004 are treated as arrangements to which that reference number has been allocated under Part 7 of that Act.

2(4) Arrangements to which the same reference number has been allocated under paragraph 9 of Schedule 11A to VATA 1994 (disclosure of avoidance schemes) or paragraph 22 of Schedule 17 to F[(No. 2)]A 2017 (disclosure of avoidance schemes: VAT and other indirect taxes) are treated as being substantially the same.

2(5) Any two or more sets of arrangements which are the subject of follower notices given by reference to the same judicial ruling are treated as being substantially the same.

2(6) Where a notice of binding has been given in relation to any arrangements ("the bound arrangements") on the basis that they are, for the purposes of Schedule 43A to FA 2013, equivalent arrangements in relation to another set of arrangements (the "lead arrangements")–

(a) the bound arrangements and the lead arrangements are treated as being substantially the same, and

(b) the bound arrangements are treated as being substantially the same as any other arrangements which, as a result of this sub-paragraph, are treated as substantially the same as the lead arrangements.

History – In para. 2(4) the words "or paragraph 22 of Schedule 17 to FA 2017 (disclosure of avoidance schemes: VAT and other indirect taxes)" inserted by F(No. 2)A 2017, s. 66 and Sch. 17, para. 54(2), with effect so far as necessary for enabling the making of regulations under that Schedule from 16 November 2017 (Royal Assent) and from 1 January 2018 for all other purposes.

"PROMOTED ARRANGEMENTS"

3(1) For the purposes of this Schedule arrangements are **"promoted arrangements"** in relation to a person if–

(a) they are relevant arrangements or would be relevant arrangements under the condition stated in sub-paragraph (2), and

(b) the person is carrying on a business as a promoter and–

(i) the person is or has been a promoter in relation to the arrangements, or

(ii) that would be the case if the condition in sub-paragraph (2) were met.

3(2) That condition is that the definition of **"tax"** in section 283 includes, and has always included, value added tax.

RELEVANT DEFEAT OF SINGLE ARRANGEMENTS

4(1) A defeat of arrangements (entered into by any person) which are promoted arrangements in relation to a person ("the promoter") is a **"relevant defeat"** in relation to the promoter if the condition in sub-paragraph (2) is met.

4(2) The condition is that the arrangements are not related to any other arrangements which are promoted arrangements in relation to the promoter.

4(3) For the meaning of **"defeat"** see paragraphs 10 to 16.

RELEVANT DEFEAT OF RELATED ARRANGEMENTS

5(1) This paragraph applies if arrangements (entered into by any person) ("Set A")–

(a) are promoted arrangements in relation to a person ("P"), and

(b) are related to other arrangements which are promoted arrangements in relation to P.

5(2) If Case 1, 2 or 3 applies (see paragraphs 7 to 9) a relevant defeat occurs in relation to P and each of the related arrangements.

5(3) **"The related arrangements"** means Set A and the arrangements mentioned in sub-paragraph (1)(b).

LIMIT ON NUMBER OF SEPARATE RELEVANT DEFEATS IN RELATION TO THE SAME, OR RELATED, ARRANGEMENTS

6 In relation to a person, if there has been a relevant defeat of arrangements (whether under paragraph 4 or 5) there cannot be a further relevant defeat of–

(a) those particular arrangements, or

(b) arrangements which are related to those arrangements.

CASE 1: COUNTERACTION UPHELD BY JUDICIAL RULING

7(1) Case 1 applies if–

(a) any of Conditions A to E is met in relation to any of the related arrangements, and

(b) in the case of those arrangements the decision to make the relevant counteraction has been upheld by a judicial ruling (which is final).

7(2) In sub-paragraph (1) **"the relevant counteraction"** means the counteraction mentioned in paragraph 11(d), 12(1)(b), 13(1)(d), 14(1)(d) or 15(1)(d) (as the case requires).

CASE 2: JUDICIAL RULING THAT AVOIDANCE-RELATED RULE APPLIES

8 Case 2 applies if Condition F is met in relation to any of the related arrangements.

CASE 3: PROPORTION-BASED RELEVANT DEFEAT

9(1) Case 3 applies if–

(a) at least 75% of the tested arrangements have been defeated, and

(b) no final judicial ruling in relation to any of the related arrangements has upheld a corresponding tax advantage which has been asserted in connection with any of the related arrangements.

9(2) In this paragraph **"the tested arrangements"** means so many of the related arrangements (as defined in paragraph 5(3)) as meet the condition in sub-paragraph (3) or (4).

9(3) Particular arrangements meet this condition if a person has made a return, claim or election on the basis that a tax advantage results from those arrangements and–

(a) there has been an enquiry or investigation by HMRC into the return, claim or election, or

(b) HMRC assesses the person to tax on the basis that the tax advantage (or any part of it) does not arise, or

(c) a GAAR counteraction notice has been given in relation to the tax advantage or part of it and the arrangements.

9(4) Particular arrangements meet this condition if HMRC takes other action on the basis that a tax advantage which might be expected to arise from those arrangements, or is asserted in connection with them, does not arise.

9(5) For the purposes of this paragraph a tax advantage has been **"asserted"** in connection with particular arrangements if a person has made a return, claim or election on the basis that the tax advantage arises from those arrangements.

9(6) In sub-paragraph (1)(b) **"corresponding tax advantage"** means a tax advantage corresponding to any tax advantage the counteraction of which is taken into account by HMRC for the purposes of sub-paragraph (1)(a).

9(7) For the purposes of this paragraph a court or tribunal **"upholds"** a tax advantage if–

(a) the court or tribunal makes a ruling to the effect that no part of the tax advantage is to be counteracted, and

(b) that judicial ruling is final.

9(8) In this paragraph references to **"counteraction"** include anything referred to as a counteraction in any of Conditions A to F in paragraphs 11 to 16.

9(9) In this paragraph **"GAAR counteraction notice"** means–

(a) a notice such as is mentioned in sub-paragraph (2) of paragraph 12 of Schedule 43 to FA 2013 (notice of final decision to counteract),

(b) a notice under paragraph 8(2) or 9(2) of Schedule 43A to that Act (binding of arrangements to lead arrangements) stating that the tax advantage is to be counteracted under the general anti-abuse rule, or

(c) a notice under paragraph 8(2) of Schedule 43B to that Act (generic referrals) stating that the tax advantage is to be counteracted under the general anti-abuse rule.

"DEFEAT" OF ARRANGEMENTS

10 For the purposes of this Part of this Act a **"defeat"** of arrangements occurs if any of Conditions A to F (in paragraphs 11 to 16) is met in relation to the arrangements.

11 Condition A is that–

(a) a person has made a return, claim or election on the basis that a tax advantage arises from the arrangements,

(b) a notice given to the person under paragraph 12 of Schedule 43 to, paragraph 8(2) or 9(2) of Schedule 43A to or paragraph 8(2) of Schedule 43B to FA 2013 stated that the tax advantage was to be counteracted under the general anti-abuse rule,

(c) the tax advantage has been counteracted (in whole or in part) under the general anti-abuse rule, and

(d) the counteraction is final.

12(1) Condition B is that a follower notice has been given to a person by reference to the arrangements (and not withdrawn) and–

(a) the person has complied with subsection (2) of section 208 of FA 2014 by taking the action specified in subsections (4) to (6) of that section in respect of the denied tax advantage (or part of it), or

(b) the denied tax advantage has been counteracted (in whole or in part) otherwise than as mentioned in paragraph (a) and the counteraction is final.

12(2) In this paragraph **"the denied tax advantage"** is to be interpreted in accordance with section 208(3) of FA 2014.

12(3) In this Schedule **"follower notice"** means a follower notice under Chapter 2 of Part 4 of FA 2014.

13(1) Condition C is that–

(a) the arrangements are DOTAS arrangements,

(b) a person ("the taxpayer") has made a return, claim or election on the basis that a relevant tax advantage arises,

(c) the relevant tax advantage has been counteracted, and

(d) the counteraction is final.

13(2) For the purposes of sub-paragraph (1) **"relevant tax advantage"** means a tax advantage which the arrangements might be expected to enable the taxpayer to obtain.

13(3) For the purposes of this paragraph the relevant tax advantage is **"counteracted"** if adjustments are made in respect of the taxpayer's tax position on the basis that the whole or part of that tax advantage does not arise.

14(1) Condition D is that–

(a) the arrangements are disclosable VAT or other indirect tax arrangements to which a person is a party,

(b) the person has made a return or claim on the basis that a relevant tax advantage arises,

(c) the relevant tax advantage has been counteracted, and

(d) the counteraction is final.

14(2) For the purposes of sub-paragraph (1) **"relevant tax advantage"** means a tax advantage which the arrangements might be expected to enable the person to obtain.

14(3) For the purposes of this paragraph the relevant tax advantage is **"counteracted"** if adjustments are made in respect of the person's tax position on the basis that the whole or part of that tax advantage does not arise.

History – In para. 14(1)(a) the words "or other indirect tax" inserted by F(No. 2)A 2017, s. 66 and Sch. 17, para. 54(3)(a), with effect so far as necessary for enabling the making of regulations under that Schedule from 16 November 2017 (Royal Assent) and from 1 January 2018 for all other purposes.

In para. 14(1)(a) and (b) the word "taxable" (which appeared before the word "person") omitted by F(No. 2)A 2017, s. 66 and Sch. 17, para. 54(3)(b), with effect so far as necessary for enabling the making of regulations under that Schedule from 16 November 2017 (Royal Assent) and from 1 January 2018 for all other purposes.

In para. 14(2) the word "taxable" (which appeared before the word "person") omitted by F(No. 2)A 2017, s. 66 and Sch. 17, para. 54(3)(b), with effect so far as necessary for enabling the making of regulations under that Schedule from 16 November 2017 (Royal Assent) and from 1 January 2018 for all other purposes.

In para. 14(3) the word "taxable" (which appeared before the word "person") omitted by F(No. 2)A 2017, s. 66 and Sch. 17, para. 54(3)(b), with effect so far as necessary for enabling the making of regulations under that Schedule from 16 November 2017 (Royal Assent) and from 1 January 2018 for all other purposes.

15(1) Condition E is that the arrangements are disclosable VAT arrangements to which a taxable person ("T") is a party and–

(a) the arrangements relate to the position with respect to VAT of a person other than T ("S") who has *made supplies* of goods or services to T,

(b) the arrangements might be expected to enable T to obtain a tax advantage in connection with those supplies of goods or services,

(c) the arrangements have been counteracted, and

(d) the counteraction is final.

15(2) For the purposes of this paragraph the arrangements are **"counteracted"** if–

(a) HMRC assess S to tax or take any other action on a basis which prevents T from obtaining (or obtaining the whole of) the tax advantage in question, or

(b) adjustments are made on a basis such as is mentioned in paragraph (a).

16(1) Condition F is that–

(a) a person has made a return, claim or election on the basis that a relevant tax advantage arises,

(b) the tax advantage, or part of the tax advantage would not arise if a particular avoidance-related rule (see paragraph 25) applies in relation to the person's tax affairs,

(c) it is held in a judicial ruling that the relevant avoidance-related rule applies in relation to the person's tax affairs, and

(d) the judicial ruling is final.

16(2) For the purposes of sub-paragraph (1) **"relevant tax advantage"** means a tax advantage which the arrangements might be expected to enable the person to obtain.

Part 3 – Relevant Defeats: Associated Persons

ATTRIBUTION OF RELEVANT DEFEATS

17(1) Sub-paragraph (2) applies if–

(a) there is (or has been) a person ("Q"),

(b) arrangements ("the defeated arrangements") have been entered into,

(c) an event occurs such that either–

(i) there is a relevant defeat in relation to Q and the defeated arrangements, or

(ii) the condition in sub-paragraph (i) would be met if Q had not ceased to exist,

(d) at the time of that event a person ("P") is carrying on a business as a promoter (or is carrying on what would be such a business under the condition in paragraph 3(2)), and

(e) Condition 1 or 2 is met in relation to Q and P.

17(2) The event is treated for all purposes of this Part of this Act as a relevant defeat in relation to P and the defeated arrangements (whether or not it is also a relevant defeat in relation to Q, and regardless of whether or not P existed at any time when those arrangements were promoted arrangements in relation to Q).

17(3) Condition 1 is that–

(a) P is not an individual,

(b) at a time when the defeated arrangements were promoted arrangements in relation to Q–

(i) P was a relevant body controlled by Q, or

(ii) Q was a relevant body controlled by P, and

(c) at the time of the event mentioned in sub-paragraph (1)(c)–

(i) Q is a relevant body controlled by P,

(ii) P is a relevant body controlled by Q, or

(iii) P and Q are relevant bodies controlled by a third person.

17(4) Condition 2 is that–

(a) P and Q are relevant bodies,

(b) at a time when the defeated arrangements were promoted arrangements in relation to Q, a third person ("C") controlled Q, and

(c) C controls P at the time of the event mentioned in sub-paragraph (1)(c).

17(5) For the purposes of *sub-paragraphs* (3)(b) and (4)(b), the question whether arrangements are promoted arrangements in relation to Q at any time is to be determined on the assumption that the reference to **"design"** in paragraph (b) of section 235(3) (definition of "promoter" in relation to relevant arrangements) is omitted.

DEEMED DEFEAT NOTICES

18(1) This paragraph applies if–

(a) an authorised officer becomes aware at any time ("the relevant time") that a relevant defeat has occurred in relation to a person ("P") who is carrying on a business as a promoter,

(b) there have occurred, more than 3 years before the relevant time–

(i) one third party defeat, or

(ii) two third party defeats, and

(c) conditions A1 and B1 (in a case within paragraph (b)(i)), or conditions A2 and B2 (in a case within paragraph (b)(ii)), are met.

18(2) Where this paragraph applies by virtue of sub-paragraph (1)(b)(i), this Part of this Act has effect as if an authorised officer had (with due authority), at the time of the time of the third party defeat, given P a single defeat notice under section 241A(2) in respect of it.

18(3) Where this paragraph applies by virtue of sub-paragraph (1)(b)(ii), this Part of this Act has effect as if an authorised officer had (with due authority), at the time of the second of the two third party defeats, given P a double defeat notice under section 241A(3) in respect of the two third party defeats.

18(4) Section 241A(8) has no effect in relation to a notice treated as given as mentioned in subsection (2) or (3).

18(5) Condition A1 is that–

(a) a conduct notice or a single or double defeat notice has been given to the other person (see sub-paragraph (9)) in respect of the third party defeat,

(b) at the time of the third party defeat an authorised officer would have had power by virtue of paragraph 17 to give P a defeat notice in respect of the third party defeat, had the officer been aware that it was a relevant defeat in relation to P, and

(c) so far as the authorised officer mentioned in sub-paragraph (1)(a) is aware, the conditions for giving P a defeat notice in respect of the third party defeat have never been met (ignoring this paragraph).

18(6) Condition A2 is that–

(a) a conduct notice or a single or double defeat notice has been given to the other person (see sub-paragraph (9)) in respect of each, or both, of the third party defeats,

(b) at the time of the second third party defeat an authorised officer would have had power by virtue of paragraph 17 to give P a double defeat notice in respect of the third party defeats, had the officer been aware that either of the third party defeats was a relevant defeat in relation to P, and

(c) so far as the authorised officer mentioned in sub-paragraph (1)(a) is aware, the conditions for giving P a defeat notice in respect of those third party defeats (or either of them) have never been met (ignoring this paragraph).

18(7) Condition B1 is that, had an authorised officer given P a defeat notice in respect of the third party defeat at the time of that relevant defeat, that defeat notice would still have effect at the relevant time (see sub-paragraph (1)).

18(8) Condition B2 is that, had an authorised officer given P a defeat notice in respect of the two third party defeats at the time of the second of those relevant defeats, that defeat notice would still have effect at the relevant time.

18(9) In this paragraph **"third party defeat"** means a relevant defeat which has occurred in relation to a person other than P.

MEANING OF "RELEVANT BODY" AND "CONTROL"

19(1) In this Part of this Schedule **"relevant body"** means–

(a) a body corporate, or

(b) a partnership.

19(2) For the purposes of this Part of this Schedule a person controls a body corporate if the person has power to secure that the affairs of the body corporate are conducted in accordance with the person's wishes–

(a) by means of the holding of shares or the possession of voting power in relation to the body corporate or any other relevant body,

(b) as a result of any powers conferred by the articles of association or other document regulating the body corporate or any other relevant body, or

(c) by means of controlling a partnership.

19(3) For the purposes of this Part of this Schedule a person controls a partnership if the person is a controlling member or the managing partner of the partnership.

19(4) In this paragraph **"controlling member"** has the same meaning as in Schedule 36 (partnerships).

19(5) In this section **"managing partner"**, in relation to a partnership, means the member of the partnership who directs, or is on a day-to-day level in control of, the management of the business of the partnership.

Part 4 – Meeting Section 237A Conditions: Bodies Corporate and Partnerships

RELEVANT BODIES CONTROLLED ETC BY OTHER PERSONS TREATED AS MEETING SECTION 237A CONDITION

20(1) A relevant body is treated as meeting a section 237A condition at the section 237A(2) relevant time if any of Conditions A to C is met.

20(2) Condition A is that–

(a) a person met the section 237A condition at a time when the person was a promoter, and

(b) the person controls or has significant influence over the relevant body at the section 237A(2) relevant time.

20(3) Condition B is that–

(a) a person met the section 237A condition at a time when the person controlled or had significant influence over the relevant body,

(b) the relevant body was a promoter at that time, and

(c) the person controls or has significant influence over the relevant body at the section 237A(2) relevant time.

20(4) Condition C is that–

(a) two or more persons together controlled or had significant influence over the relevant body at a time when one of those persons met the section 237A condition,

(b) the relevant body was a promoter at that time, and

(c) those persons together control or have significant influence over the relevant body at the section 237A(2) relevant time.

20(5) Sub-paragraph (1) does not apply where the person referred to in sub-paragraph (2)(a), (3)(a), or (4)(a) as meeting a section 237A condition is an individual.

20(6) For the purposes of sub-paragraph (2) it does not matter whether the relevant body existed at the time referred to in sub-paragraph (2)(a).

History – Para. 20 substituted by FA 2017, s. 24(3), with effect for the purposes of determining whether a person meets a FA 2014, s. 237A condition in a period of three years ending on or after 8 March 2017. Former para. 20 read as follows:

"TREATING PERSONS UNDER ANOTHER'S CONTROL AS MEETING SECTION 237A CONDITION

20(1) A relevant body ("RB") is treated as meeting a section 237A condition at the section 237A(2) relevant time if–

(a) that condition was met by a person ("C") at a time when–

(i) C was carrying on a business as a promoter, or

(ii) RB was carrying on a business as a promoter and C controlled RB, and

(b) RB is controlled by C at the section 237A(2) relevant time.

20(2) Sub-paragraph (1) does not apply if C is an individual.

20(3) For the purposes of determining whether the requirements of sub-paragraph (1) are met by reason of meeting the requirement in sub-paragraph (1)(a)(i), it does not matter whether RB existed at the time when C met the section 237A condition.".

PERSONS WHO CONTROL ETC A RELEVANT BODY TREATED AS MEETING A SECTION 237A CONDITION

21(1) If at a time when a person controlled or had significant influence over a relevant body–

(a) the relevant body met a section 237A condition, and

(b) the relevant body, or another relevant body which the person controlled or had significant influence over, was a promoter,

the person is treated as meeting the section 237A condition at the section 237A(2) relevant time.

21(2) It does not matter whether any relevant body referred to sub-paragraph (1) exists at the section 237A(2) relevant time.

History – Para. 21 substituted by FA 2017, s. 24(3), with effect for the purposes of determining whether a person meets a FA 2014, s. 237A condition in a period of three years ending on or after 8 March 2017. Former para. 21 read as follows:

"TREATING PERSONS IN CONTROL OF OTHERS AS MEETING SECTION 237A CONDITION

21(1) A person other than an individual is treated as meeting a section 237A condition at the section 237A(2) relevant time if–

(a) a relevant body ("A") met the condition at a time when A was controlled by the person, and

(b) at the time mentioned in paragraph (a) A, or another relevant body ("B") which was also at that time controlled by the person, carried on a business as a promoter.

21(2) For the purposes of determining whether the requirements of sub-paragraph (1) are met it does not matter whether A or B (or neither) exists at the section 237A(2) relevant time.".

RELEVANT BODIES CONTROLLED ETC BY THE SAME PERSON TREATED AS MEETING A SECTION 237A CONDITION

22(1) If–

(a) a person controlled or had significant influence over a relevant body at a time when it met a section 237A condition, and

(b) at that time that body, or another relevant body which the person controlled or had significant influence over, was a promoter,

any relevant body which the person controls or has significant influence over at the section 237A(2) relevant time is treated as meeting the section 237A condition at the section 237A(2) relevant time.

22(2) If–

(a) two or more persons together controlled or had significant influence over a relevant body at a time when it met a section 237A condition, and

(b) at that time that body, or another relevant body which those persons together controlled or had significant influence over, was a promoter,

any relevant body which those persons together control or have significant influence over at the section 237A(2) relevant time is treated as meeting the section 237A condition at the section 237A(2) relevant time.

22(3) It does not matter whether–

(a) a relevant body referred to in sub-paragraph (1)(a) or (b) or (2)(a) or (b) exists at the section 237A(2) relevant time, or

(b) a relevant body existing at the section 237A(2) relevant time existed at the time referred to in sub-paragraph (1)(a) or (2)(a).

History – Para. 22 substituted by FA 2017, s. 24(3), with effect for the purposes of determining whether a person meets a FA 2014, s. 237A condition in a period of three years ending on or after 8 March 2017. Former para. 22 read as follows:

"TREATING PERSONS CONTROLLED BY THE SAME PERSON AS MEETING SECTION 237A CONDITION

22(1) A relevant body ("RB") is treated as meeting a section 237A condition at the section 237A(2) relevant time if–

(a) another relevant body met that condition at a time ("time T") when it was controlled by a person ("C"),

(b) at time T, there was a relevant body controlled by C which carried on a business as a promoter, and

(c) RB is controlled by C at the section 237A(2) relevant time.

22(2) For the purposes of determining whether the requirements of sub-paragraph (1) are met it does not matter whether–

(a) RB existed at time T, or

(b) any relevant body (other than RB) by reason of which the requirements of sub-paragraph (1) are met exists at the section 237A(2) relevant time.".

INTERPRETATION

23(1) In this Part of this Schedule–

"control" and **"significant influence"** have the same meanings as in Part 4 of Schedule 34 (see paragraph 13A(5) to (11));

references to a person being a promoter are to the person carrying on business as a promoter;

"relevant body" has the same meaning as in Part 3 of this Schedule;

"section 237A(2) relevant time" means the time referred to in section 237A(2);

"section 237A condition" means any of the conditions in section 237A(11), (12) and (13).

23(2) For the purposes of paragraphs 20 to 22, the condition in section 237A(11) (occurrence of 3 relevant defeats in the 3 years ending with the relevant time) is taken to have been met by a person at any time if at least 3 relevant defeats have occurred in relation to the person in the period of 3 years ending with that time.

History – In para. 23(1), definition of "control" substituted by FA 2017, s. 24(4)(a), with effect for the purposes of determining whether a person meets a FA 2014, s. 237A condition in a period of three years ending on or after 8 March 2017.

In para. 23(2), the words "20 to 22" substituted for the words "20(1)(a), 21(1)(a) and 22(1)(a)" by FA 2017, s. 24(4)(b), with effect for the purposes of determining whether a person meets a FA 2014, s. 237A condition in a period of three years ending on or after 8 March 2017.

Part 5 – Supplementary

"ADJUSTMENTS"

24 In this Schedule **"adjustments"** means any adjustments, whether by way of an assessment, the modification of an assessment or return, the amendment or disallowance of a claim, the entering into of a contract settlement or otherwise (and references to **"making"** adjustments accordingly include securing that adjustments are made by entering into a contract settlement).

MEANING OF "AVOIDANCE-RELATED RULE"

25(1) In this Schedule **"avoidance-related rule"** means a rule in Category 1 or 2.

25(2) A rule is in Category 1 if–

(a) it refers (in whatever terms) to the purpose or main purpose or purposes of a transaction, arrangements or any other action or matter, and

(b) to whether or not the purpose in question is or involves the avoidance of tax or the obtaining of any advantage in relation to tax (however described).

25(3) A rule is also in Category 1 if it refers (in whatever terms) to–

(a) expectations as to what are, or may be, the expected benefits of a transaction, arrangements or any other action or matter, and

(b) whether or not the avoidance of tax or the obtaining of any advantage in relation to tax (however described) is such a benefit.

For the purposes of paragraph (b) it does not matter whether the reference is (for instance) to the **"sole or main benefit"** or **"one of the main benefits"** or any other reference to a benefit.

25(4) A rule falls within Category 2 if as a result of the rule a person may be treated differently for tax purposes depending on whether or not purposes referred to in the rule (for instance the purposes of an actual or contemplated action or enterprise) are (or are shown to be) commercial purposes.

25(5) For example, a rule in the following form would fall within Category 1 and within Category 2–

"Example rule

Section X does not apply to a company in respect of a transaction if the company shows that the transaction meets Condition A or B.

Condition A is that the transaction is effected–

(a) for genuine commercial reasons, or

(b) in the ordinary course of managing investments.

Condition B is that the avoidance of tax is not the main object or one of the main objects of the transaction."

"DOTAS ARRANGEMENTS"

26(1) For the purposes of this Schedule arrangements are **"DOTAS arrangements"** at any time if at that time a person–

(a) has provided, information in relation to the arrangements under section 308(3), 309 or 310 of FA 2004, or

(b) has failed to comply with any of those provisions in relation to the arrangements.

26(2) But for the purposes of this Schedule **"DOTAS arrangements"** does not include arrangements in respect of which HMRC has given notice under section 312(6) of FA 2004 (notice that promoters not under duty to notify client of reference number).

26(3) For the purposes of sub-paragraph (1) a person who would be required to provide information under subsection (3) of section 308 of FA 2004–

(a) but for the fact that the arrangements implement a proposal in respect of which notice has been given under subsection (1) of that section, or

(b) but for subsection (4A), (4C) or (5) of that section,

is treated as providing the information at the end of the period referred to in subsection (3) of that section.

DISCLOSABLE VAT OR OTHER INDIRECT TAX ARRANGEMENTS

26A(1) For the purposes of this Schedule arrangements are **"disclosable VAT or other indirect tax arrangements"** at any time if at that time–

(a) the arrangements are disclosable Schedule 11A arrangements, or

(b) sub-paragraph (2) applies.

26A(2) This sub-paragraph applies if a person–

(a) has provided information in relation to the arrangements under paragraph 12(1), 17(2) or 18(2) of Schedule 17 to F[(No. 2)]A 2017, or

(b) has failed to comply with any of those provisions in relation to the arrangements.

26A(3) But for the purposes of this Schedule arrangements in respect of which HMRC have given notice under paragraph 23(6) of that Schedule (notice that promoters not under duty to notify client of reference number) are not to be regarded as disclosable VAT or other indirect tax arrangements.

26A(4) For the purposes of sub-paragraph (2) a person who would be required to provide information under paragraph 12(1) of that Schedule–

(a) but for the fact that the arrangements implement a proposal in respect of which notice has been given under paragraph 11(1) of that Schedule, or

(b) but for paragraph 13, 14 or 15 of that Schedule,

is treated as providing the information at the end of the period referred to in paragraph 12(1).

History – Para. 26A inserted by F(No. 2)A 2017, s. 66 and Sch. 17, para. 54(4), with effect so far as necessary for enabling the making of regulations under that Schedule from 16 November 2017 (Royal Assent) and from 1 January 2018 for all other purposes.

"DISCLOSABLE SCHEDULE 11A VAT ARRANGEMENTS"

History – In the heading the words "Schedule 11A" inserted by F(No. 2)A 2017, s. 66 and Sch. 17, para. 54(5), with effect so far as necessary for enabling the making of regulations under that Schedule from 16 November 2017 (Royal Assent) and from 1 January 2018 for all other purposes.

27 For the purposes of paragraph 26A arrangements are **"disclosable Schedule 11A VAT arrangements"** at any time if at that time–

(a) a person has complied with paragraph 6 of Schedule 11A to VATA 1994 in relation to the arrangements (duty to notify Commissioners),

(b) a person under a duty to comply with that paragraph in relation to the arrangements has failed to do so, or

(c) a reference number has been allocated to the scheme under paragraph 9 of that Schedule (voluntary notification of avoidance scheme which is not a designated scheme).

History – In para. 27 the words "paragraph 26A" substituted for the words "this Schedule" and the words "Schedule 11A" inserted by F(No. 2)A 2017, s. 66 and Sch. 17, para. 54(6), with effect so far as necessary for enabling the making of regulations under that Schedule from 16 November 2017 (Royal Assent) and from 1 January 2018 for all other purposes.

PARAGRAPHS 26 TO 27: SUPPLEMENTARY

History – In the heading the words "to 27" substituted for the words "and 27" by F(No. 2)A 2017, s. 66 and Sch. 17, para. 54(7), with effect so far as necessary for enabling the making of regulations under that Schedule from 16 November 2017 (Royal Assent) and from 1 January 2018 for all other purposes.

28(1) A person **"fails to comply"** with any provision mentioned in paragraph 26(1)(a), 26A(2)(a) or 27(b) if and only if any of the conditions in sub-paragraphs (2) to (4) is met.

28(2) The condition in this sub-paragraph is that–

(a) the tribunal has determined that the person has failed to comply with the provision concerned,

(b) the appeal period has ended, and

(c) the determination has not been overturned on appeal.

28(3) The condition in this sub-paragraph is that–

(a) the tribunal has determined for the purposes of section 118(2) of TMA 1970 that the person is to be deemed not to have failed to comply with the provision concerned as the person had a reasonable excuse for not doing the thing required to be done,

(b) the appeal period has ended, and

(c) the determination has not been overturned on appeal.

28(4) The condition in this sub-paragraph is that the person admitted in writing to HMRC that the person has failed to comply with the provision concerned.

28(5) In this paragraph **"the appeal period"** means–

(a) the period during which an appeal could be brought against the determination of the tribunal, or

(b) where an appeal mentioned in paragraph (a) has been brought, the period during which that appeal has not been finally determined, withdrawn or otherwise disposed of.

History – In para. 28(1) the words ", 26A(2)(a)" (the comma assumed by Croner-i) inserted by F(No. 2)A 2017, s. 66 and Sch. 17, para. 54(8), with effect so far as necessary for enabling the making of regulations under that Schedule from 16 November 2017 (Royal Assent) and from 1 January 2018 for all other purposes.

"FINAL" COUNTERACTION

29 For the purposes of this Schedule the counteraction of a tax advantage or of arrangements is **"final"** when the assessment or adjustments made to effect the counteraction, and any amounts arising as a result of the assessment or adjustments, can no longer be varied, on appeal or otherwise.

INHERITANCE TAX, STAMP DUTY RESERVE TAX, VAT AND PETROLEUM REVENUE TAX

30(1) In this Schedule, in relation to inheritance tax, each of the following is treated as a return–

(a) an account delivered by a person under section 216 or 217 of IHTA 1984 (including an account delivered in accordance with regulations under section 256 of that Act);

(b) a statement or declaration which amends or is otherwise connected with such an account produced by the person who delivered the account;

(c) information or a document provided by a person in accordance with regulations under section 256 of that Act;

and such a return is treated as made by the person in question.

30(2) In this Schedule references to an assessment to tax, in relation to inheritance tax, stamp duty reserve tax and petroleum revenue tax, include a determination.

30(3) In this Schedule an expression used in relation to VAT has the same meaning as in VATA 1994.

POWER TO AMEND

31(1) The Treasury may by regulations amend this Schedule (apart from this paragraph).

31(2) An amendment by virtue of sub-paragraph (1) may, in particular, add, vary or remove conditions or categories (or otherwise vary the meaning of "avoidance-related rule").

31(3) Regulations under sub-paragraph (1) may include any amendment of this Part of this Act that is appropriate in consequence of an amendment made by virtue of sub-paragraph (1).

SCHEDULE 35 – PROMOTERS OF TAX AVOIDANCE SCHEMES: PENALTIES

Section 274

INTRODUCTION

1 In this Schedule a reference to an **"information duty"** is to a duty arising under any of the following provisions to provide information or produce a document–

(a) section 255 (duty to provide information or produce document);

(b) section 257 (ongoing duty to provide information);

(c) section 258 (duty of person dealing with non-resident promoter);

(d) section 259 (monitored promoter: duty to provide information about clients);

(e) section 260 (intermediaries: duty to provide information about clients);

(f) section 261 (duty to provide information about clients following enquiry);

(g) section 262 (information required for monitoring compliance with conduct notice);

(h) section 263 (information about monitored promoter's address).

PENALTIES FOR FAILURE TO COMPLY

2(1) A person who fails to comply with a duty imposed by or under this Part mentioned in column 1 of the Table is liable to a penalty not exceeding the amount shown in relation to that provision in column 2 of the Table.

Column 1	*Column 2*
Provision	*Maximum penalty (£)*
Section 249(1) (duty to notify clients of monitoring notice)	5,000
Section 249(3) (duty to publicise monitoring notice)	1,000,000
Section 249(10) (duty to include information on correspondence etc)	1,000,000
Section 251 (duty of promoter to notify clients and intermediaries of reference number)	5,000
Section 252 (duty of those notified to notify others of promoter's number)	5,000

Column 1 *Provision*	*Column 2* *Maximum penalty (£)*
Section 253 (duty to notify HMRC of reference number)	the relevant amount (see sub-paragraph (3))
Section 255 (duty to provide information or produce document)	1,000,000
Section 257 (ongoing duty to provide information or produce document)	1,000,000
Section 258 (duty of person dealing with non-resident promoter)	1,000,000
Section 259 (monitored promoter: duty to provide information about clients)	5,000
Section 260 (intermediaries: duty to provide information about clients)	5,000
Section 261 (duty to provide information about clients following an enquiry)	10,000
Section 262 (duty to provide information required to monitor compliance with conduct notice)	5,000
Section 263 (duty to provide information about address)	5,000
Section 265 (duty to provide information to promoter)	5,000

2(2) In relation to a failure to comply with section 249(1), 251, 252, 259 or 260 the maximum penalty specified in column 2 of the Table is a maximum penalty which may be imposed in respect of each person to whom the failure relates.

2(3) In relation to a failure to comply with section 253, the **"relevant amount"** is–

(a) £5,000, unless paragraph (b) or (c) applies;

(b) £7,500, where a person has previously failed to comply with section 253 on one (and only one) occasion during the period of 36 months ending with the date on which the current failure occurred;

(c) £10,000, where a person has previously failed to comply with section 253 on two or more occasions during the period mentioned in paragraph (b).

2(4) The amount of a penalty imposed under sub-paragraph (1) is to be arrived at after taking account of all relevant considerations, including the desirability of setting it at a level which appears appropriate for deterring the person, or other persons, from similar failures to comply on future occasions having regard (in particular)–

(a) in the case of a penalty imposed for a failure to comply with section 255 or 257, to the amount of fees received, or likely to have been received, by the person in connection with the monitored proposal, arrangements implementing the monitored proposal or monitored arrangements to which the information or document required as a result of 255 or 257 relates;

(b) in the case of a penalty imposed in relation to a failure to comply with section 258(4) or (5), to the amount of any tax advantage gained, or sought to be gained, by the person in relation to the monitored arrangements or the arrangements implementing the monitored proposal.

DAILY DEFAULT PENALTIES FOR FAILURE TO COMPLY

3(1) If the failure to comply with an information duty continues after a penalty is imposed under paragraph 2(1), the person is liable to a further penalty or penalties not exceeding the relevant sum for each day on which the failure continues after the day on which the penalty under paragraph 2(1) was imposed.

3(2) In sub-paragraph (1) **"the relevant sum"** means–

(a) £10,000, in a case where the maximum penalty which could have been imposed for the failure was £1,000,000;

(b) £600, in cases not falling within paragraph (a).

PENALTIES FOR INACCURATE INFORMATION AND DOCUMENTS

4(1) If–

(a) in complying with an information duty, a person provides inaccurate information or produces a document that contains an inaccuracy, and

(b) condition A, B or C is met,

the person is liable to a penalty not exceeding the relevant sum.

4(2) Condition A is that the inaccuracy is careless or deliberate.

4(3) An inaccuracy is careless if it is due to a failure by the person to take reasonable care.

4(4) For the purpose of determining whether or not a person who is a monitored promoter took reasonable care, reliance on legal advice is to be disregarded if either–

(a) the advice was not based on a full and accurate description of the facts, or

(b) the conclusions in the advice that the person relied on were unreasonable.

4(5) For the purpose of determining whether or not a person who complies with a duty under section 258 took reasonable care, reliance on legal advice is to be disregarded if the advice was given or procured by the monitored promoter mentioned in subsection (1) of that section.

4(6) Condition B is that the person knows of the inaccuracy at the time the information is provided or the document produced but does not inform HMRC at that time.

4(7) Condition C is that the person–

(a) discovers the inaccuracy some time later, and

(b) fails to take reasonable steps to inform HMRC.

4(8) The **"relevant sum"** means–

(a) £1,000,000, where the information is provided or document produced in compliance with a duty under section 255, 257 or 258;

(b) £10,000, where the information is provided in compliance with a duty under section 261;

(c) £5,000, where the information is provided or document produced in compliance with a duty under section 259, 260, 262 or 263.

4(9) If the information or document contains more than one inaccuracy, one penalty is payable under this paragraph whatever the number of inaccuracies.

POWER TO CHANGE AMOUNT OF PENALTIES

5(1) If it appears to the Treasury that there has been a change in the value of money since the last relevant date, they may by regulations substitute for the sums for the time being specified in paragraph 2, 3 or 4 such other sums as appear to them to be justified by the change.

5(2) Regulations under sub-paragraph (1) may include any amendment of paragraph 10(b) that is appropriate in consequence of an amendment made by virtue of sub-paragraph (1).

5(3) The **"relevant date"**, in relation to a specified sum, means–

(a) the date on which this Act is passed, and

(b) each date on which the power conferred by sub-paragraph (1) has been exercised in relation to that sum.

CONCEALING, DESTROYING ETC DOCUMENTS FOLLOWING IMPOSITION OF A DUTY TO PROVIDE INFORMATION

6(1) A person must not conceal, destroy or otherwise dispose of, or arrange for the concealment, destruction or disposal of, a document which is subject to a duty under section 255, 257 or 262.

6(2) Sub-paragraph (1) does not apply if the person acts after the document has been produced to an officer of Revenue and Customs in accordance with the duty, unless the officer has notified the person in writing that the document must continue to be available for inspection (and has not withdrawn the notification).

6(3) Sub-paragraph (1) does not apply, in a case to which section 268(1) applies, if the person acts after the expiry of the period of 6 months beginning with the day on which a copy of the document was produced in accordance with that section unless, before the expiry of that period, an officer of Revenue and Customs makes a request for the original document under section 268(2)(b).

6(4) A person who conceals, destroys or otherwise disposes of, or arranges for the concealment, destruction or disposal of, a document in breach of sub-paragraph (1), is taken to have failed to comply with the duty to produce the document under the provision concerned (but see sub-paragraph (5)).

6(5) If a person conceals, destroys or otherwise disposes of, or arranges for the concealment, destruction or disposal of, a document which is subject to a duty under more than one of the provisions mentioned in sub-paragraph (1) then–

(a) in a case where a duty under section 255 applies, the person will be taken to have failed to comply only with that provision, or

(b) in a case where a duty under section 255 does not apply, the person will be taken to have failed to comply only with section 257.

CONCEALING, DESTROYING ETC DOCUMENTS FOLLOWING INFORMAL NOTIFICATION

7(1) A person must not conceal, destroy or otherwise dispose of, or arrange for the concealment, destruction or disposal of, a document if an officer of Revenue and Customs has informed the person in writing that the person is, or is likely, to be given a notice under 255, 257 or section 262 the effect of which will, or is likely to, require the production of the document.

7(2) Sub-paragraph (1) does not apply if the person acts–

(a) at least 6 months after the person was, or was last, informed as described in sub-paragraph (1), or

(b) after the person becomes subject to a duty under 255, 257 or section 262 which requires the document to be produced.

7(3) A person who conceals, destroys or otherwise disposes of, or arranges for the concealment, destruction or disposal of, a document in breach of sub-paragraph (1), is taken to have failed to comply with the duty to produce the document under the provision concerned (but see sub-paragraph (4)).

7(4) If a person conceals, destroys or otherwise disposes of, or arranges for the concealment, destruction or disposal of, a document which is subject to a duty under more than one of the provisions mentioned in sub-paragraph (1) then–

(a) in a case where a duty under section 255 applies, the person will be taken to have failed to comply only with that provision, or

(b) in a case where a duty under section 255 does not apply, the person will be taken to have failed to comply only with section 257.

FAILURE TO COMPLY WITH TIME LIMIT

8 A failure to do anything required to be done within a limited period of time does not give rise to liability to a penalty under this Schedule if the person did it within such further time, if any, as an officer of Revenue and Customs or the tribunal may have allowed.

REASONABLE EXCUSE

9(1) Liability to a penalty under this Schedule does not arise if there is a reasonable excuse for the failure.

9(2) For the purposes of this paragraph–

(a) an insufficiency of funds is not a reasonable excuse unless attributable to events outside the person's control,

(b) if the person relies on any other person to do anything, that is not a reasonable excuse unless the first person took reasonable care to avoid the failure,

(c) if the person had a reasonable excuse for the failure but the excuse has ceased, the person is to be treated as having continued to have the excuse if the failure is remedied without unreasonable delay after the excuse ceased,

(d) reliance on legal advice is to be taken automatically not to constitute a reasonable excuse where the person is a monitored promoter if either–

  (i) the advice was not based on a full and accurate description of the facts, or

  (ii) the conclusions in the advice that the person relied on were unreasonable, and

(e) reliance on legal advice is to be taken automatically not to constitute a reasonable excuse in the case of a penalty for failure to comply with section 258, if the advice was given or procured by the monitored promoter mentioned in subsection (1) of that section.

ASSESSMENT OF PENALTY AND APPEALS

10 Part 10 of TMA 1970 (penalties, etc) has effect as if–

(a) the reference in section 100(1) to the Taxes Acts were read as a reference to the Taxes Acts and this Schedule,

(b) in subsection (2) of section 100, there were inserted a reference to a penalty under this Schedule, other than a penalty under paragraph 3 of this Schedule in respect of which the relevant sum is £600.

INTEREST ON PENALTIES

11(1) A penalty under this Schedule is to carry interest at the rate applicable under section 178 of FA 1989 from the date it is determined until payment.

11(2) [Inserts FA 1989, s. 178(2)(u).]

DOUBLE JEOPARDY

12 A person is not liable to a penalty under this Schedule in respect of anything in respect of which the person has been convicted of an offence.

OVERLAPPING PENALTIES

13 A person is not liable to a penalty under–

(a) Schedule 24 to the FA 2007 (penalties for errors),

(b) Part 7 of FA 2004, or

(c) any other provision which is prescribed,

by reason of any failure to include in any return or account a reference number required by section 253.

NATIONAL INSURANCE CONTRIBUTIONS ACT 2015

(2015 Chapter 5) [*12th February 2015*]

ARRANGEMENT OF SECTIONS

SECONDARY CLASS 1 CONTRIBUTIONS: APPRENTICES UNDER 25

1 Zero-rate secondary Class 1 contributions for apprentices under 25

1(1) SSCBA 1992 is amended as follows.

1(2) [Inserts SSCBA 1992, s. 9(1A)(aa).]

1(3) [Inserts SSCBA 1992, s. 9A(1A).]

1(4) [Inserts SSCBA 1992, s. 9B.]

1(5) [Amends SSCBA 1992, s. 176(1)(a).]

1(6) SSCB(NI)A 1992 is amended as follows.

1(7) [Inserts SSCB(NI)A 1992, s. 9(1A)(aa).]

1(8) [Inserts SSCB(NI)A 1992, s. 9A(1A).]

1(9) [Inserts SSCB(NI)A 1992, s. 9B.]

1(10) [Amends SSCB(NI)A 1992, s. 172(11A).]

1(11) The amendments made by this section come into force–

(a) for the purposes of making regulations under section 9B of SSCBA 1992 or section 9B of SSCB(NI)A 1992, at the end of the period of 2 months beginning with the day on which this Act is passed, and

(b) for remaining purposes, on 6 April 2016.

CLASS 2 CONTRIBUTIONS

2 Reform of Class 2 contributions

2 Schedule 1 contains provision relating to Class 2 national insurance contributions.

3 Consequential etc power

3(1) The Treasury may by regulations make consequential, incidental or supplementary provision in connection with the provision made in Schedule 1.

3(2) Regulations under this section may modify any provision of an Act or an instrument made under an Act.

3(3) In subsection (2) **"modify"** includes amend, repeal or revoke.

3(4) Section 175(3) to (5) of SSCBA 1992 (various supplementary powers) applies to the power to make regulations conferred by this section.

3(5) Regulations under this section must be made by statutory instrument.

3(6) A statutory instrument containing (with or without other provision) regulations under this section that amend or repeal a provision of an Act may not be made unless a draft of the instrument has been laid before, and approved by a resolution of, each House of Parliament.

3(7) A statutory instrument containing regulations under this section that does not have to be approved in draft under subsection (6) is subject to annulment in pursuance of a resolution of either House of Parliament.

FOLLOWER NOTICES, ACCELERATED PAYMENTS AND PROMOTERS OF AVOIDANCE

4 Application of Parts 4 and 5 of FA 2014 to national insurance contributions

4(1) Part 1 of Schedule 2 applies Part 4 of FA 2014 (follower notices and accelerated payments) to Class 1, 1A, 1B and certain Class 2 contributions.

4(2) Part 2 of that Schedule applies Part 5 of that Act (promoters of tax avoidance schemes) to Class 1, 1A, 1B and certain Class 2 contributions.

4(3) Part 3 of that Schedule applies Parts 4 and 5 of that Act to Class 4 contributions.

4(4) Part 4 of that Schedule contains commencement and transitory provision.

5 Provision in consequence etc of tax-only changes to Part 4 or 5 of FA 2014

5(1) Where a modification is made to Part 4 of FA 2014 (follower notices and accelerated payments) or Part 5 of that Act (promoters of tax avoidance schemes) that does not apply in relation to national insurance contributions ("the tax-only modification"), the Treasury may by regulations–

(a) make provision for the purpose of applying the tax-only modification in relation to national insurance contributions (with or without modifications),

(b) make provision in relation to national insurance contributions corresponding to the tax-only modification, or

(c) otherwise modify the Part concerned, as it has effect in relation to national insurance contributions, in consequence of, or for the purpose of making provision supplementary or incidental to, the tax-only modification.

5(2) Regulations under this section–

(a) may amend, repeal or revoke any provision of an Act or instrument made under an Act (whenever passed or made),

(b) may make consequential, incidental, supplementary, transitional, transitory or saving provision, and

(c) may make different provision for different cases, classes of national insurance contributions or purposes.

5(3) Regulations under this section must be made by statutory instrument.

5(4) A statutory instrument containing (with or without other provision) regulations under this section that amend or repeal a provision of an Act may not be made unless a draft of the instrument has been laid before, and approved by a resolution of, each House of Parliament.

5(5) A statutory instrument containing regulations under this section that does not have to be approved in draft under subsection (4) is subject to annulment in pursuance of a resolution of either House of Parliament.

5(6) In this section **"national insurance contributions"** means contributions under Part 1 of SSCBA 1992 or Part 1 of SSCB(NI)A 1992.

5(7) This section comes into force at the end of the period of 2 months beginning with the day on which this Act is passed.

ANTI-AVOIDANCE

6 Categorisation of earners etc: anti-avoidance

6(1) [Inserts SI 1978/1689, reg. 5A.]

6(2) [Inserts S.R. (NI) 1978 No. 401, reg. 5A.]

6(3) [Inserts SSCBA 1992, s. 2(2ZA) and (2ZB).]

6(4) [Inserts SSCBA 1992, s. 7(2A) and (2B).]

6(5) [Inserts SSCB(NI)A 1992, s. 2(2ZA) and (2ZB).]

6(6) [Inserts SSCB(NI)A 1992, s. 7(2A) and (2B).]

6(7) Subsections (1) and (2)–

(a) are to be treated as having come into force on 6 April 2014 for the purposes of inserting regulation 5A(1) to (5), (6)(a) and (7), and

(b) come into force for the purposes of inserting regulation 5A(6)(b) on the day on which this Act is passed.

6(8) Paragraphs (4) and (5) of regulation 5A have effect in relation to arrangements entered into on or after 6 April 2014 the main purpose, or one of the main purposes of which, is to secure that a person is not treated, under a provision mentioned in paragraph (6)(b) of that regulation, as the secondary Class 1 contributor in respect of payments of earnings to or for the benefit of an employed earner in respect of an employment.

6(9) But regulation 5A(5) only applies as a result of arrangements mentioned in subsection (8) in relation to payments of earnings that are made on or after the day on which this Act is passed.

6(10) In subsections (7) to (9) references to regulation 5A are to regulation 5A–

(a) inserted by subsection (1) into the 1978 GB regulations;

(b) inserted by subsection (2) into the 1978 NI regulations.

6(11) The amendments made by subsections (1) and (2) are without prejudice to any power to make regulations amending or revoking the provision inserted.

GENERAL

7 HMRC administrative expenses: financial provision

7(1) [Not relevant to National Insurance contributions.]

7(2) [Not relevant to National Insurance contributions.]

8 Abbreviations of Acts

8 In this Act–

"CRCA 2005" means the Commissioners for Revenue and Customs Act 2005;

"FA", followed by a year, means the Finance Act of that year;

"JA 1995" means the Jobseekers Act 1995;

"PA 2014" means the Pensions Act 2014;

"SSAA 1992" means the Social Security Administration Act 1992;

"SSA(NI)A 1992" means the Social Security Administration (Northern Ireland) Act 1992;

"SSCBA 1992" means the Social Security Contributions and Benefits Act 1992;

"SSCB(NI)A 1992" means the Social Security Contributions and Benefits (Northern Ireland) Act 1992;

"SSC(TF)A 1999" means the Social Security Contributions (Transfer of Functions, etc) Act 1999;

"TMA 1970" means the Taxes Management Act 1970;

"WRA 2007" means the Welfare Reform Act 2007;

"WRA 2012" means the Welfare Reform Act 2012.

9 Short title and extent

9(1) This Act may be cited as the National Insurance Contributions Act 2015.

9(2) Subject to subsection (3), this Act extends to England and Wales, Scotland and Northern Ireland.

9(3) An amendment, repeal or revocation made by this Act has the same extent as the provision amended, repealed or revoked.

SCHEDULES

SCHEDULE 1 – REFORM OF CLASS 2 CONTRIBUTIONS

Section 2

SSCBA 1992

1 SSCBA 1992 is amended as follows.

2 [Amends SSCBA 1992, s. 1(2)(c).]

3 [Substitutes SSCBA 1992, s. 11 and inserts 11A.]

4(1) Section 12 (late paid Class 2 contributions) is amended as follows.

4(2) [Amends SSCBA 1992, s. 12(1).]

4(3) [Amends SSCBA 1992, s. 12(2).]

4(4) [Amends SSCBA 1992, s. 12(3).]

4(5) [Omits SSCBA 1992, s. 12(5).]

4(6) [Amends SSCBA 1992, s. 12(6) and (a) and omits (b).]

4(7) [Omits SSCBA 1992, s. 12(7).]

4(8) [Amends SSCBA 1992, s. 12(8).]

5 [Amends SSCBA 1992, s. 18(1)(b).]

6 [Not relevant to National Insurance contributions.]

7 [Not relevant to National Insurance contributions.]

8 [Amends SSCBA 1992, s. 176(1)(a).]

9(1) Schedule 1 (supplementary provisions) is amended as follows.

9(2) [Omits SSCBA 1992, Sch. 1, para. 7B(7).]

9(3) [Inserts SSCBA 1992, Sch. 1, para. 7BB.]

9(4) [Omits SSCBA 1992, Sch. 1, para. 8(1)(j) and (k).]

SSCB(NI)A 1992

10 SSCB(NI)A 1992 is amended as follows.

11 [Amends SSCB(NI)A 1992, s. 1(2)(c).]

12 [Substitutes SSCB(NI)A 1992, s. 11 and inserts 11A.]

13(1) Section 12 (late paid Class 2 contributions) is amended as follows.

13(2) [Amends SSCB(NI)A 1992, s. 12(1).]

13(3) [Amends SSCB(NI)A 1992, s. 12(2).]

13(4) [Amends SSCB(NI)A 1992, s. 12(3).]

13(5) [Omits SSCB(NI)A 1992, s. 12(5).]

13(6) [Amends SSCB(NI)A 1992, s. 12(6) and (a) and omits (b).]

13(7) [Omits SSCB(NI)A 1992, s. 12(7).]

13(8) [Omits SSCB(NI)A 1992, s. 12(8).]

14 [Amends SSCB(NI)A 1992, s. 18(1)(b).]

15 [Amends SSCB(NI)A 1992, s. 35A(5)(c).]

16 [Amends SSCB(NI)A 1992, s. 35B(1)(c).]

17 [Amends SSCB(NI)A 1992, s. 172(11A).]

18(1) Schedule 1 (supplementary provisions) is amended as follows.

18(2) [Omits SSCB(NI)A 1992, Sch. 1, para. 7B(7).]

18(3) [Inserts SSCB(NI)A 1992, Sch. 1, para. 7BB.]

18(4) [Omits SSCB(NI)A 1992, Sch. 1, para. 8(1)(j) and (k).]

SSAA 1992

19 SSAA 1992 is amended as follows.

20 [Amends SSAA 1992, s. 141(4)(a) and (b).]

21(1) Section 143 (power to alter contributions with a view to adjusting the level of the National Insurance Fund) is amended as follows.

21(2) [Amends SSAA 1992, s. 143(1)(c).]

21(3) [Amends SSAA 1992, s. 143(3).]

22 [Amends SSAA 1992, s. 145(4)(a).]

SSC(TF)A 1999

23 SSC(TF)A 1999 is amended as follows.

24 [Amends SSC(TF)A 1999, s. 4(a) and inserts (aa).]

25 [Inserts SSC(TF)A 1999, s. 8(1A).]

26 [Omits SSC(TF)A 1999, Sch. 3, para. 12.]

27 [Omits SSC(TF)A 1999, Sch. 9, para. 3 and 7(7).]

SOCIAL SECURITY CONTRIBUTIONS (TRANSFER OF FUNCTIONS, ETC) (NORTHERN IRELAND) ORDER 1999 (S.I. 1999/671)

28 The Social Security Contributions (Transfer of Functions, etc) (Northern Ireland) Order 1999 is amended as follows.

29 [Inserts SI 1999/671, art. 7(1A).]

30 [Omits SI 1999/671, Sch. 3, para. 13.]

31 [Omits SI 1999/671, Sch. 8, para. 1 and 5(7).]

SOCIAL SECURITY (CONTRIBUTIONS) REGULATIONS 2001 (S.I. 2001/1004)

32 The Social Security (Contributions) Regulations 2001 are amended as follows.

33(1) [Amends SI 2001/1004, reg. 125.]

33(2) The amendment made by sub-paragraph (1) is without prejudice to any power to make regulations amending or revoking the provision amended.

34 [Amends SI 2001/1004, reg. 127(3)(b).]

34(2) The amendment made by sub-paragraph (1) is without prejudice to any power to make regulations amending or revoking the provision inserted.

COMMENCEMENT

35 The amendments made by this Schedule, other than those mentioned in paragraph 36, have effect for the tax year 2015–16 and subsequent tax years.

36 The amendments made by paragraphs 4, 9(2), 13, 18(2), 27 and 31 have effect in relation to a Class 2 contribution in respect of a week in the tax year 2015–16 or a subsequent tax year.

37 The Treasury may by regulations made by statutory instrument make transitional or transitory provision or savings in connection with the coming into force of any of the amendments made by this Schedule.

SCHEDULE 2 – APPLICATION OF PARTS 4 AND 5 OF FA 2014 TO NATIONAL INSURANCE CONTRIBUTIONS

Section 4

Part 1 – Follower Notices & Accelerated Payments: Class 1, 1A, 1B and certain Class 2

INTRODUCTION

1 Part 4 of FA 2014 (follower notices and accelerated payments) has effect with the following modifications.

GENERAL

2 References to tax or a relevant tax, other than references to particular taxes, include relevant contributions.

3 References to a charge to tax include a liability to pay relevant contributions and references to a person being chargeable to tax, or to tax being charged, are to be construed accordingly.

4 References to an assessment to tax include a NICs decision relating to a person's liability for relevant contributions.

5 References to a tax enquiry include a relevant contributions dispute.

6 A "relevant contributions dispute" arises if–

(a) without making a NICs decision, HMRC notifies a person in writing that HMRC considers the person to be liable to pay an amount of relevant contributions, and

(b) the person notifies HMRC in writing (a "notification of dispute") that the person disputes liability for some or all of the contributions ("the disputed contributions").

7 The relevant contributions dispute is in progress, in relation to the notification of dispute, during the period which–

(a) begins with the day on which the person gives the notification of dispute, and

(b) ends (at which point it is to be treated as completed) with the day on which–

  (i) the disputed contributions are paid in full,

  (ii) HMRC and the person enter into an agreement in writing as to the person's liability for the disputed contributions and any amount of those contributions that the person is to pay under that agreement is paid,

  (iii) an officer of Revenue and Customs makes a NICs decision in relation to the person's liability for the disputed contributions, or

  (iv) without making a NICs decision, HMRC notifies the person in writing that HMRC no longer considers the person to be liable to pay the disputed contributions.

8 References to a return into which a tax enquiry is in progress include a notification of dispute in relation to which a relevant contributions dispute is in progress.

9 References to a tax appeal include a NICs appeal.

10 A **"NICs appeal"** means–

(a) an appeal, under section 11 of SSC(TF)A 1999 or Article 10 of the Social Security Contributions (Transfer of Functions, etc) (Northern Ireland) Order 1999 (S.I. 1999/671), against a NICs decision relating to relevant contributions, or

(b) an appeal against any determination of–

  (i) an appeal within paragraph (a), or

  (ii) an appeal within this paragraph.

11(1) A reference to a provision of Part 7 of FA 2004 (disclosure of tax avoidance schemes) (a "DOTAS provision") includes a reference to–

(a) that DOTAS provision as applied by regulations under section 132A of SSAA 1992 (disclosure of contributions avoidance arrangements);

(b) any provision of regulations under that section that corresponds to that DOTAS provision,

whenever the regulations are made.

11(2) Regulations under section 132A of SSAA 1992 may disapply, or modify the effect of, sub-paragraph (1).

LIST OF RELEVANT TAXES

12 The definition of "relevant tax" in section 200 ("relevant tax") has effect as if relevant contributions were listed in it.

CIRCUMSTANCES IN WHICH FOLLOWER NOTICE MAY BE GIVEN

13 For the purposes of section 204 (circumstances in which a follower notice may be given), Condition B is also met if, in a relevant contributions dispute, a person disputes liability for relevant contributions on the basis mentioned in subsection (3) of that section (regardless of whether the notification of dispute was given on that basis).

FOLLOWER NOTICES: CORRECTIVE ACTION AND PENALTIES

14(1) This paragraph applies in a case in which, by virtue of this Part of this Schedule, a follower notice is given by virtue of section 204(2)(a).

14(2) For the purposes of section 208 (penalty if corrective action not taken in response to follower notice), the necessary corrective action is taken in respect of the denied advantage if (and only if)–

(a) in a case in which the denied advantaged can be counteracted by making a payment to HMRC, P makes that payment and notifies HMRC that P has done so, or

(b) in any case, P takes all necessary action to enter into an agreement in writing with HMRC for the purpose of relinquishing the denied advantage.

14(3) Accordingly–

(a) subsections (4) to (7) and (9) to (11) of section 208 do not apply, and

(b) the reference in section 209(3)(a) to P amending a return or claim is to be treated as a reference to P making a payment mentioned in sub-paragraph (2)(a).

14(4) Terms used in this paragraph that are defined for the purposes of section 208 have the same meaning as in that section.

FOLLOWER NOTICES: AGGREGATE PENALTIES

15(1) In section 212 (aggregate penalties), references to a "relevant penalty provision" include–

(a) any provision mentioned in subsection (4) of that section, as applied in relation to relevant contributions by regulations (whenever made);

(b) section 98A of TMA 1970, as applied in relation to relevant contributions by regulations (whenever made);

(c) any provision specified in regulations made by the Treasury under which a penalty can be imposed in respect of relevant contributions.

15(2) The Treasury may by regulations disapply, or modify the effect of, sub-paragraph (1)(a) or (b).

15(3) The Treasury may by regulations modify section 212 as it has effect in relation to a relevant penalty provision by virtue of sub-paragraph (1)(b) or (c).

15(4) Section 175(3) to (5) of SSCBA 1992 (various supplementary powers) applies to a power to make regulations conferred by this paragraph.

15(5) Regulations under this paragraph must be made by statutory instrument.

15(6) A statutory instrument containing regulations under this paragraph is subject to annulment in pursuance of a resolution of either House of Parliament.

CIRCUMSTANCES IN WHICH ACCELERATED PAYMENT NOTICE MAY BE GIVEN

16 For the purposes of section 219 (circumstances in which an accelerated payment notice may be given), Condition B is also met if, in a relevant contributions dispute, a person disputes liability for relevant contributions on the basis mentioned in subsection (3) of that section (regardless of whether the notification of dispute was given on that basis).

NATURE AND RECOVERY OF ACCELERATED PAYMENT

17(1) This paragraph applies in relation to an accelerated payment (see section 223(2)) so far as (but only so far as) it represents understated tax (see section 220) that consists of an additional amount that would be due and payable in respect of relevant contributions ("the understated contributions").

17(2) The accelerated payment is a payment of the understated contributions (and not a payment on account of them).

17(3) Accordingly, subsections (3) and (7) to (9) of section 223 do not apply in relation to the accelerated payment.

17(4) The accelerated payment must be paid before the end of the payment period regardless of whether P brings a NICs appeal that relates to the understated contributions.

17(5) Section 117A of SSAA 1992 and section 111A of SSA(NI)A 1992 (issues arising in proceedings: contributions etc) do not apply to proceedings for the recovery of any amount of the accelerated payment that is unpaid at the end of the payment period.

17(6) A certificate of an officer of Revenue and Customs under section 25A of CRCA 2005 (certificates of debt) that the accelerated payment has not been paid is to be treated as conclusive evidence that the amount is unpaid.

17(7) If some or all of the understated contributions are subsequently repaid to P–

(a) the contributions repaid are to be treated, for the purposes of determining a person's entitlement to benefit, or the amount of a person's benefit, as not having been paid, but

(b) that does not affect any payments of benefit made to a person before the repayment.

17(8) In sub-paragraph (7) **"benefit"** means a contributory benefit or a statutory payment.

17(9) Terms used in this paragraph that are defined for the purposes of section 223 have the same meaning as in that section.

EFFECT OF ACCELERATED PAYMENT NOTICE IN RESPECT OF APPEAL

18(1) This paragraph applies where–

(a) a person ("P") has been given an accelerated payment notice by virtue of section 219(2)(b) (notice given when appeal pending), which has not been withdrawn, and

(b) the appeal by virtue of which the notice could be given was a NICs appeal in relation to relevant contributions.

18(2) P must pay the disputed contributions (see sub-paragraph (8))–

(a) if no representations were made under section 222 in respect of the notice, on or before the last day of the period of 90 days beginning with the day the notice is given, and

(b) if representations were so made, on or before whichever is later of–

  (i) the last day of the 90 day period mentioned in paragraph (a), and

  (ii) the last day of the period of 30 days beginning with the day on which HMRC's determination in respect of those representations is notified under section 222.

18(3) Subsections (4) and (5) of section 117A of SSAA 1992 or (as the case may be) of section 111A of SSA(NI)A 1992 (decision of officer of HMRC not conclusive if subject to appeal and proceedings for recovery to be adjourned pending appeal) do not apply to proceedings before a court for recovery of the disputed contributions.

18(4) Accordingly, if proceedings have been adjourned under subsection (5) of either of those sections, they cease to be adjourned, so far as they relate to the recovery of the disputed contributions, from the end of the applicable period under sub-paragraph (2).

18(5) A certificate of an officer of Revenue and Customs under section 25A of CRCA 2005 (certificates of debt) that the disputed contributions have not been paid is to be treated as conclusive evidence that the disputed contributions are unpaid.

18(6) If some or all of the disputed contributions are subsequently repaid to P–

(a) the contributions repaid are to be treated, for the purposes of determining a person's entitlement to benefit, or the amount of a person's benefit, as not having been paid, but

(b) that does not affect any payments of benefit made to a person before the repayment.

18(7) In sub-paragraph (6) **"benefit"** means a contributory benefit or a statutory payment.

18(8) In this paragraph **"the disputed contributions"** means the relevant contributions to which the NICs appeal relates so far as they are disputed tax specified in the notice under section 221(2)(b).

PENALTY FOR FAILURE TO PAY ACCELERATED PAYMENT

19(1) Subsection (7) of section 226 (penalty for failure to pay accelerated payment) applies in relation to a penalty under that section imposed by virtue of this Part of this Schedule, but the reference in that subsection to tax does not include relevant contributions.

19(2) But in their application by virtue of sub-paragraph (1), the provisions of Schedule 56 to FA 2009 mentioned in that subsection have effect–

(a) as if references to an assessment to tax were to a NICs decision relating to a person's liability for relevant contributions,

(b) as if a reference to an appeal against an assessment to the tax concerned were a reference to an appeal against a NICs decision,

(c) as if sub-paragraph (3)(b) of paragraph 11 were omitted (but see paragraph 20 of this Schedule), and

(d) with any other necessary modifications.

RECOVERY OF PENALTIES UNDER PART 4 OF FA 2014

20(1) A penalty under section 208 or 226 imposed by virtue of this Part of this Schedule may be recovered as if it were an amount of relevant contributions which is due and payable.

20(2) Section 117A of SSAA 1992 or (as the case may be) section 111A of SSA(NI)A 1992 (issues arising in proceedings: contributions etc) has effect in relation to proceedings before a court for recovery of the penalty as if the assessment of the penalty were a NICs decision as to whether the person is liable for the penalty.

20(3) Accordingly, section 211(4)(b) (assessment of penalty to be enforced as if it were an assessment to tax) does not apply in relation to a penalty under section 208 imposed by virtue of this Part of this Schedule.

WITHDRAWAL, MODIFICATION OR SUSPENSION OF ACCELERATED PAYMENT NOTICE

21 In section 227 (withdrawal, modification or suspension of accelerated payment notice), subsection (9) has effect as if the provisions mentioned there included paragraph 18(2) of this Schedule.

INTERPRETATION

22 In this Part of this Schedule–

"accelerated payment notice" means an accelerated payment notice under Chapter 3 of Part 4 of FA 2014;

"contributory benefit" means–

(a) a contributory benefit under Part 2 of SSCBA 1992,

(b) a jobseeker's allowance under JA 1995,

(c) an employment and support allowance under Part 1 of WRA 2007,

(d) state pension or a lump sum under Part 1 of PA 2014,

(e) bereavement support payment under section 30 of that Act, or

(f) any corresponding benefit in Northern Ireland;

"the disputed contributions", other than in paragraph 18, has the meaning given by paragraph 6(b);

"HMRC" means Her Majesty's Revenue and Customs;

"NICs appeal" has the meaning given by paragraph 10;

"NICs decision" means a decision under section 8 of SSC(TF)A 1999 or Article 7 of the Social Security Contributions (Transfer of Functions, etc) (Northern Ireland) Order 1999 (S.I. 1999/671);

"notification of dispute" has the meaning given by paragraph 6(b);

"relevant contributions" means the following contributions under Part 1 of SSCBA 1992 or Part 1 of SSCB(NI)A 1992–

(a) *Class 1 contributions;*

(b) Class 1A contributions;

(c) Class 1B contributions;

(d) Class 2 contributions which a person is, or is alleged to be, liable to pay but in relation to which section 11A of the Act in question (application of certain provisions of the Income Tax Acts in relation to Class 2 contributions under section 11(2) of that Act) does not, or would not, apply;

"relevant contributions dispute" has the meaning given by paragraphs 6 and 7;

"statutory payment" means a statutory payment for the purposes of section 4C of SSCBA 1992 or section 4C of SSCB(NI)A 1992;

and references to sections are to sections of FA 2014, unless otherwise indicated.

Part 2 – Promoters of Avoidance Schemes: Class 1, 1A, 1B and certain Class 2

INTRODUCTION

23 Part 5 of FA 2014 (promoters of tax avoidance schemes) has effect with the following modifications.

GENERAL

24 References to tax, other than in references to particular taxes, include relevant contributions.

25 References to a tax advantage include the avoidance or reduction of a liability to pay relevant contributions.

26(1) A reference to a provision of Part 7 of FA 2004 (disclosure of tax avoidance schemes) (a "DOTAS provision") includes a reference to–

(a) that DOTAS provision as applied by regulations under section 132A of SSAA 1992 (disclosure of contributions avoidance arrangements);

(b) any provision of regulations under that section that corresponds to that DOTAS provision, whenever the regulations are made.

26(2) Regulations under section 132A of SSAA 1992 may disapply, or modify the effect of, sub-paragraph (1).

DUTY TO NOTIFY COMMISSIONERS

27 In section 253 (duty of persons to notify the Commissioners), references to a tax return include a return relating to relevant contributions that is required to be made by or under an enactment.

POWER TO OBTAIN INFORMATION AND DOCUMENTS

28 In section 255 (power to obtain information and documents), references to a person's tax position include the person's position as regards deductions or repayments of relevant contributions, or of sums representing relevant contributions, that the person is required to make by or under an enactment.

LIMITATION OF DEFENCE OF REASONABLE CARE

29 In section 276 (limitation of defence of reasonable care), the reference in subsection (1) to a document of a kind listed in the Table in paragraph 1 of Schedule 24 to FA 2007 includes a document, relating to relevant contributions, in relation to which that Schedule applies (and, accordingly, the reference to that Schedule in subsection (2) of that section includes that Schedule as it so applies).

LIST OF TAXES

30 The definition of **"tax"** in section 283(1) (interpretation) has effect as if relevant contributions were listed in it.

THRESHOLD CONDITIONS

30A(1) In paragraph 5 of Schedule 34 (non-compliance with Part 7 of FA 2004), in sub-paragraph (4)–

(a) paragraph (a) includes a reference to a decision having been made for corresponding NICs purposes that P is to be deemed not to have failed to comply with the provision concerned as P had a reasonable excuse for not doing the thing required to be done, and

(b) the reference in paragraph (c) to a determination is to be read accordingly.

30A(2) In this paragraph **"corresponding NICs purposes"** means the purposes of any provision of regulations under section 132A of SSAA 1992.

History – Para. 30A inserted by FA 2016, s. 160(18), with effect from 15 September 2016 (Royal Assent).

RELEVANT DEFEATS

30B(1) Schedule 34A (promoters of tax avoidance schemes: defeated arrangements) has effect with the following modifications.

30B(2) References to an assessment (or an assessment to tax) include a NICs decision relating to a person's liability for relevant contributions.

30B(3) References to adjustments include a payment in respect of a liability to pay relevant contributions (and the definition of "adjustments" in paragraph 24 accordingly has effect as if such payments were included in it).

30B(4) In paragraph 9(3) the reference to an enquiry into a return includes a relevant contributions dispute (as defined in paragraph 6 of this Schedule).

30B(5) In paragraph 28(3)–

(a) paragraph (a) includes a reference to a decision having been made for corresponding NICs purposes that the person is to be deemed not to have failed to comply with the provision concerned as the person had a reasonable excuse for not doing the thing required to be done, and

(b) the reference in paragraph (c) to a determination is to be read accordingly.

"Corresponding NICs purposes" means the purposes of any provision of regulations under section 132A of SSAA 1992.

History – Para. 30B inserted by FA 2016, s. 160(18), with effect from 15 September 2016 (Royal Assent).

INTERPRETATION

31 In this Part of this Schedule–

(za) **"NICs decision"** means a decision under section 8 of SSC(TF)A 1999 or Article 7 of the Social Security Contributions (Transfer of Functions, etc) (Northern Ireland) Order 1999 (SI 1999/671);

(a) **"relevant contributions"** means the following contributions under Part 1 of SSCBA 1992 or Part 1 of SSCB(NI)A 1992–

(i) Class 1 contributions;

(ii) Class 1A contributions;

(iii) Class 1B contributions;

(iv) Class 2 contributions which must be paid but in relation to which section 11A of the Act in question (application of certain provisions of the Income Tax Acts in relation to Class 2 contributions under section 11(2) of that Act) does not apply;

(b) references to sections or Schedules are to sections of, or Schedules to FA 2014, unless otherwise indicated.

History – Para. 31(za) inserted by FA 2016, s. 160(19)(a), with effect from 15 September 2016 (Royal Assent).
In para. 31(b), the words "or Schedules are to sections of, or Schedules to" substituted for the words "are to sections of" by FA 2016, s. 160(19)(b), with effect from 15 September 2016 (Royal Assent).

Part 3 – Application of Parts 4 and 5 of FA 2014: Class 4

32 [Inserts SSCBA 1992, s. 16(1)(d).]

Part 4 – Commencement and Transitory Provision

33(1) Parts 1 and 3 of this Schedule come into force at the end of the period of 2 months beginning with the day on which this Act is passed.

33(2) Part 2 of this Schedule comes into force–

(a) for the purposes of making regulations under Part 5 of FA 2014, on the day on which this Act is passed, and

(b) for remaining purposes, at the end of the period of 2 months beginning with the day on which this Act is passed.

34 Before the coming into force of the repeals in section 4C of SSCBA 1992 made by Part 1 of Schedule 14 to WRA 2012 (abolition of benefits superseded by universal credit), the reference in paragraph 22 to a jobseeker's allowance is to be treated as a reference to a contribution-based jobseeker's allowance (within the meaning of JA 1995).

35 Before the coming into force of the repeal of section 22(8) of SSCBA 1992 made by Part 1 of Schedule 14 to WRA 2012 (abolition of benefits superseded by universal credit), the reference in paragraph 22 to an employment and support allowance is to be treated as a reference to a contributory allowance (within the meaning of Part 1 of WRA 2007).

PENSION SCHEMES ACT 2015

(2015 Chapter 8)

[*3rd March 2015*]

ARRANGEMENT OF SECTIONS

PART 1 – CATEGORIES OF PENSION SCHEME

PART 4 – PENSIONS FLEXIBILITIES

CHAPTER 4 – TRANSFERS

GREAT BRITAIN

PART 6 – GENERAL

SCHEDULES

PART 1 – CATEGORIES OF PENSION SCHEME

1 Introduction

1(1) This Part defines some key expressions used in pensions legislation–

(a) defined benefits scheme – see section 2;

(b) shared risk scheme (sometimes known as "defined ambition") – see section 3;

(c) defined contributions scheme – see section 4.

1(2) The definitions–

(a) do not apply in any public service pensions legislation;

(b) apply in other legislation only where legislation expressly provides for the definitions to apply.

2 Defined benefits scheme

2 A pension scheme is a **"defined benefits scheme"** if–

(a) the scheme provides for all members to be paid retirement income beginning at normal pension age and continuing for life,

(b) there is a full pensions promise in relation to the retirement income and any other retirement benefits that may be provided to members,

(c) the normal pension age in relation to the retirement income and any other retirement benefits that may be provided to members is fixed, and

(d) such other requirements as may be specified in regulations are met.

3 Shared risk scheme (sometimes known as "defined ambition")

3 A pension scheme is a **"shared risk scheme"** if–

(a) there is a pensions promise in relation to at least some of the retirement benefits that may be provided to each member, but

(b) the scheme is not a defined benefits scheme.

4 Defined contributions scheme

4 A pension scheme is a **"defined contributions scheme"** if there is no pensions promise in relation to any of the retirement benefits that may be provided to the members.

5 Meaning of "pensions promise" etc

5(1) For the purposes of section 2 there is a "full pensions promise" in relation to a retirement benefit if–

(a) the scheme provides for there to be a promise, at all times before the benefit comes into payment, about the level of the benefit, and

(b) the level of the benefit is to be determined wholly by reference to that promise in all circumstances.

5(2) For the purposes of sections 3 and 4 there is a **"pensions promise"** in relation to a retirement benefit if the scheme provides for there to be a promise, at a time before the benefit comes into payment, about the level of the benefit.

5(3) A reference in this section to a promise about the level of a retirement benefit–

(a) includes a promise about factors, other than longevity, that will be used to calculate the level of the benefit,

(b) does not include a promise if, or to the extent that, it consists merely of a promise that the level of the benefit will be calculated by reference to an amount available for its provision, and

(c) in the case of a benefit the level of which depends on the amount available for the provision of benefits to or in respect of the member and one or more other members collectively, does not include a promise about the factors used to determine what proportion of that amount is available for the provision of the particular benefit.

5(4) A scheme provides for there to be a promise if the scheme–

(a) sets out the promise, or

(b) requires the promise to be obtained from a third party.

5(5) A scheme also provides for there to be a promise for the purposes of subsection (2) if the scheme provides for the member to be given–

(a) the option of a promise from the scheme, or

(b) the option of requiring a promise to be obtained from a third party,

(whether or not the option is subject to conditions).

5(6) A benefit does not fail the test in subsection (1)(b) just because the scheme confers a discretion to vary the benefit so long as the discretion–

(a) is capable of being used only for reasons related to a member's individual circumstances and meets any other requirements that may be specified in regulations, or

(b) is of a description specified in regulations.

5(7) A promise about the level of retirement income is not to be treated as a pensions promise if–

(a) the promise is conditional on the retirement income coming into payment by a particular date,

(b) the scheme provides for the member to be first given the promise during such period ending on that date as may be specified in regulations, and

(c) the promise is not of a description specified in regulations.

5(8) When working out for the purposes of sections 2 to 4 what benefits "may be provided" to a member, take into account–

(a) benefits that may be provided only if the member has been a member for a certain length of time, and

(b) any other benefits that, at a future time, are benefits that may be provided to the member.

6 Treatment of a scheme as two or more separate schemes

6(1) Regulations must provide for a pension scheme that does not fit within any of the categories to be treated, for the purposes of this Part and any other specified legislation, as if it were two or more separate schemes each of which then fits within one of the categories.

6(2) Regulations may provide for other circumstances in which a scheme is to be treated, for the purposes of this Part and any other specified legislation, as two or more separate schemes each of which fits within one of the categories.

6(3) In this section **"category"** means a category of scheme defined by section 2, 3 or 4.

7 Interpretation of Part 1

7 In this Part–

"fixed", in respect of normal pension age in relation to a benefit, means incapable of changing except by an amendment to the scheme rules;

"full pensions promise" has the meaning given by section 5;

"legislation" means–

(a) an Act, or

(b) subordinate legislation as defined by section 21(1) of the Interpretation Act 1978;

"level", in relation to a retirement benefit, means–

(a) in the case of retirement income, the rate of that income, and

(b) in the case of a retirement lump sum, the amount of that lump sum;

"normal pension age", in relation to a benefit for a member of a pension scheme, means–

(a) the earliest age at which, or earliest occasion on which, the member is entitled to receive the benefit without adjustment for taking it early or late (disregarding any special provision as to early payment on the grounds of ill health or otherwise), or

(b) if there is no such age or occasion, normal minimum pension age as defined by section 279(1) of the Finance Act 2004;

"pensions promise" has the meaning given by section 5;

"pension scheme" has the meaning given by section 1(5) of the Pension Schemes Act 1993;

"public service pensions legislation" means–

(a) the Public Service Pensions Act 2013,

(b) the Superannuation Act 1972, and

(c) any other provision by or under which a public service pension scheme is established;

"public service pension scheme" has the meaning given by section 1(1) of the Pension Schemes Act 1993;

"regulations" means regulations made by the Secretary of State;

"retirement benefit", in relation to a member of a pension scheme, means–

(a) retirement income, or

(b) a retirement lump sum;

"retirement income", in relation to a member of a pension scheme, means a pension or annuity payable to the member on reaching normal pension age;

"retirement lump sum", in relation to a member of a pension scheme, means a lump sum payable to the member on reaching normal pension age or available for the provision of other retirement benefits for the member on or after reaching normal pension age.

PART 4 – PENSIONS FLEXIBILITIES

Chapter 4 – Transfers

GREAT BRITAIN

70 Sections 68 and 69: consequential amendments

70(1) [Not relevant to National Insurance contributions.]

70(2) [Inserts PSA 1993, s. 185(5A)–(5C).]

70(3) [Not relevant to National Insurance contributions.]

70(4) [Not relevant to National Insurance contributions.]

70(5) [Not relevant to National Insurance contributions.]

PART 6 – GENERAL

83 Power to make consequential amendments

83(1) The appropriate national authority may by regulations make provision that is consequential on any provision made by this Act.

83(2) Regulations under this section may amend, repeal, revoke or otherwise modify any primary or subordinate legislation (whenever passed or made).

83(3) In this section–

"appropriate national authority" means–

(a) in relation to provision which could be made by an Act of the Northern Ireland Assembly without the consent of the Secretary of State (see sections 6 to 8 of the Northern Ireland Act 1998), the Department for Social Development in Northern Ireland, and

(b) in relation to any other provision, the Secretary of State or the Treasury;

"primary legislation" means–

(a) an Act;

(b) Northern Ireland legislation;

"subordinate legislation" means–

(a) subordinate legislation as defined by section 21(1) of the Interpretation Act 1978;

(b) an instrument made under Northern Ireland legislation.

84 Regulations

84(1) Regulations made by the Secretary of State or the Treasury under this Act are to be made by statutory instrument.

84(2) A statutory instrument containing–

(a) the first regulations under section 8(3)(b), 9, 10, 11 or 21,

(b) regulations under section 48(3)(b), or

(c) regulations under section 83 that amend, repeal or otherwise modify a provision of primary legislation,

(whether alone or with other provision) may not be made unless a draft of the instrument has been laid before and approved by a resolution of each House of Parliament.

84(3) Any other statutory instrument containing regulations under this Act is subject to annulment in pursuance of a resolution of either House of Parliament.

84(4) Subsection (3) does not apply to a statutory instrument containing regulations under section 89(4) or (6) only.

85 Regulations: Northern Ireland

85(1) A power of the Department for Social Development in Northern Ireland to make regulations under this Act is exercisable by statutory rule for the purposes of the Statutory Rules (Northern Ireland) Order 1979 (S.I. 1979/1573 (N.I. 12)).

85(2) Subsection (3) applies where regulations made by the Department for Social Development in Northern Ireland contain–

(a) provision made under section 51(3)(b), or

(b) provision made under section 83 that amends, repeals, revokes or otherwise modifies a provision of primary legislation,

(whether alone or with other provision).

85(3) Where this subsection applies, the regulations–

(a) must be laid before the Northern Ireland Assembly after being made;

(b) take effect on such date as may be specified in the regulations but (without prejudice to the validity of anything done under them or to the making of new regulations) cease to have effect on the expiry of a period of 6 months from that date unless at some time before the expiry of that period the regulations are approved by a resolution of the Northern Ireland Assembly.

85(4) Any other regulations made by the Department for Social Development in Northern Ireland under this Act are subject to negative resolution within the meaning of section 41(6) of the Interpretation Act (Northern Ireland) 1954 (c. 33 (N.I.)).

85(5) Subsection (4) does not apply to regulations containing provision under section 89(6) only.

86 Regulations: supplementary

86(1) A power to make regulations under this Act may be used–

(a) to make different provision for different purposes;

(b) in relation to all or only some of the purposes for which it may be used.

86(2) Regulations under this Act may include incidental, supplementary, consequential, transitional, transitory or saving provision.

87 Crown application

87(1) In this section **"the relevant provisions"** means–

(a) Part 2,

(b) section 36,

(c) section 37,

(d) in Chapter 2 of Part 4, sections 48, 49, 51 and 52, and

(e) in Chapter 3 of Part 4, sections 55 to 57 and 61 to 63.

87(2) The relevant provisions apply to a pension scheme managed by or on behalf of the Crown as they apply to other pension schemes.

87(3) Accordingly, references in those provisions to a person in the person's capacity as a trustee or manager of a pension scheme include the Crown, or a person acting on behalf of the Crown, in that capacity.

87(4) References in the relevant provisions to a person in the person's capacity as an employer include the Crown, or a person acting on behalf of the Crown, in that capacity.

87(5) Nothing in the relevant provisions applies to Her Majesty in Her private capacity (within the meaning of the Crown Proceedings Act 1947).

88 Extent

88(1) This Act extends to England and Wales and Scotland only, subject to the following provisions of this section.

88(2) Any amendment or repeal made by this Act has the same extent as the enactment to which it relates.

88(3) Section 81 extends to Scotland only.

88(4) The following extend also to Northern Ireland–

(a) section 54(3);

(b) Chapter 5 of Part 4;

(c) this Part.

88(5) The following extend to Northern Ireland only–

(a) in Chapter 2 of Part 4, sections 51 and 52;

(b) in Chapter 3 of Part 4, sections 61 to 63;

(c) section 71(8) and (9).

89 Commencement

89(1) The following come into force on the day on which this Act is passed–

(a) section 47 and Schedule 3;

(b) any other provision of Part 4 so far as is necessary for enabling the exercise on or after the day on which this Act is passed of any power to make provision by regulations;

(c) sections 78 and 79 and Schedule 5;

(d) section 80;

(e) this Part.

89(2) Section 82 comes into force on 1 April 2015.

89(3) The following come into force on 6 April 2015–

(a) paragraphs 24, 30, 33 and 36 of Schedule 2 (and section 46 so far as relating to those provisions);

(b) Part 4, so far as not already in force.

89(4) The following come into force on such day or days as may be appointed by regulations made by the Secretary of State–

(a) Parts 1 to 3 other than paragraphs 24, 30, 33 and 36 of Schedule 2 (and section 46 so far as relating to those provisions);

(b) sections 77 and 81.

89(5) Regulations under subsection (4) may appoint different days for different purposes.

89(6) The Secretary of State or the Department for Social Development in Northern Ireland may by regulations make transitional, transitory or saving provision in connection with the coming into force of any provision of this Act.

90 Short title

90 This Act may be cited as the Pension Schemes Act 2015.

SCHEDULES

SCHEDULE 2 – OTHER AMENDMENTS TO DO WITH PARTS 1 AND 2

Section 46

PENSION SCHEMES ACT 1993 (C. 48)

5(1) In section 181 (interpretation), subsection (1) is amended as follows.

5(2) At the appropriate places insert–

"**"collective benefit"** has the meaning given by section 8 of the Pension Schemes Act 2015;"

"**"defined benefits scheme"** has the meaning given by section 2 of the Pension Schemes Act 2015;"

"**"defined contributions scheme"** has the meaning given by section 4 of the Pension Schemes Act 2015;"

"**"shared risk scheme"** has the meaning given by section 3 of the Pension Schemes Act 2015;".

5(3) Omit the definition of **"money purchase scheme"**.

FINANCE ACT 2015

(2015 Chapter 11)

[*26th March 2015*]

ARRANGEMENT OF SECTIONS

PART 1 – INCOME TAX, CORPORATION TAX AND CAPITAL GAINS TAX

Chapter 2 – Income Tax: General

13 Extension of benefits code except in relation to certain ministers of religion

13(1) [Not relevant to National Insurance contributions.]

13(2) [Not relevant to National Insurance contributions.]

13(3) Schedule 1 contains amendments relating to subsections (1) and (2).

13(4) The amendments made by this section and Schedule 1 have effect for the tax year 2016–17 and subsequent tax years.

PART 4 – OTHER PROVISIONS

ANTI-AVOIDANCE

120 Penalties in connection with offshore matters and offshore transfers

120(1) Schedule 20 contains provisions amending–

(a) Schedule 24 to FA 2007 (penalties for errors),

(b) Schedule 41 to FA 2008 (penalties for failure to notify),

(c) Schedule 55 to FA 2009 (penalties for failure to make returns etc), and

(d) Schedule 43C to FA 2013 (as amended by FA 2016).

120(2) That Schedule comes into force on such day as the Treasury may by order appoint.

120(3) An order under subsection (2)–

(a) may commence a provision generally or only for specified purposes, and

(b) may appoint different days for different provisions or for different purposes.

120(4) The power to make an order under this section is exercisable by statutory instrument.

History – S. 120(1)(d) (and the ", and" before it) inserted (and the "and" after (b) omitted) by FA 2016, s. 158(13), with effect in relation to tax arrangements (within the meaning of FA 2013, Pt. 5) entered into on or after 15 September 2016.

PART 5 – FINAL PROVISIONS

126 Interpretation

126(1) In this Act–

"ALDA 1979" means the Alcoholic Liquor Duties Act 1979,

"CAA 2001" means the Capital Allowances Act 2001,

"CTA 2009" means the Corporation Tax Act 2009,

"CTA 2010" means the Corporation Tax Act 2010,

"IHTA 1984" means the Inheritance Tax Act 1984,

"ITA 2007" means the Income Tax Act 2007,

"ITEPA 2003" means the Income Tax (Earnings and Pensions) Act 2003,

"ITTOIA 2005" means the Income Tax (Trading and Other Income) Act 2005,

"OTA 1975" means the Oil Taxation Act 1975,

"TCGA 1992" means the Taxation of Chargeable Gains Act 1992,

"TIOPA 2010" means the Taxation (International and Other Provisions) Act 2010,

"TMA 1970" means the Taxes Management Act 1970,

"TPDA 1979" means the Tobacco Products Duty Act 1979,

"VATA 1994" means the Value Added Tax Act 1994, and

"VERA 1994" means the Vehicle Excise and Registration Act 1994.

126(2) In this Act **"FA"**, followed by a year, means the Finance Act of that year.

127 Short title

127 This Act may be cited as the Finance Act 2015.

SCHEDULES

SCHEDULE 1 – EXTENSION OF BENEFITS CODE EXCEPT IN RELATION TO CERTAIN MINISTERS OF RELIGION

Section 13

Part 2 – Amendments of Other Enactments

23(1) The Social Security Contributions and Benefits Act 1992 is amended as follows.

23(2) In section 10 (Class 1A contributions: benefits in kind etc), in subsection (1)(b)(ii), for "an excluded employment" substitute "lower-paid employment as a minister of religion".

23(3) In section 10ZB (non-cash vouchers provided by third parties), in subsection (2)–

(a) in paragraph (a), for "an excluded employment for the purposes of the benefits code" substitute "lower-paid employment as a minister of religion", and

(b) in paragraph (b) and in the words following that paragraph, for "an excluded employment" substitute "lower-paid employment as a minister of religion".

23(4) In section 122 (interpretation of Parts 1 to 6), in subsection (1)–

(a) omit the entry relating to "excluded employment", and

(b) at the appropriate place insert–

""**lower-paid employment as a minister of religion"** has the meaning given by section 290D of ITEPA 2003;".

SCHEDULE 20 – PENALTIES IN CONNECTION WITH OFFSHORE MATTERS AND OFFSHORE TRANSFERS

Section 120

Commencement Date – 1 April 2016 is the day appointed for the coming into force of Sch. 20, para. 3(3)–(7), 4 and 8, and 6 April 2016 is the day appointed for the coming into force of Sch. 20, para. 11(3)–(9), 12, 16(3)–(9) and 17 (SI 2016/456).

PENALTIES FOR ERRORS

1 Schedule 24 to FA 2007 is amended as follows.

2(1) Paragraph 4 (penalties payable under paragraph 1) is amended as follows.

2(2) After sub-paragraph (1) insert–

"**4(1A)** If the inaccuracy is in category 0, the penalty is–

(a) for careless action, 30% of the potential lost revenue,

(b) for deliberate but not concealed action, 70% of the potential lost revenue, and

(c) for deliberate and concealed action, 100% of the potential lost revenue."

2(3) In sub-paragraph (2)–

(a) in paragraph (a), for "30%" substitute "37.5%",

(b) in paragraph (b), for "70%" substitute "87.5%", and

(c) in paragraph (c), for "100%" substitute "125%".

2(4) In sub-paragraph (5), for "3" substitute "4".

3(1) Paragraph 4A (categorisation of inaccuracies) is amended as follows.

3(2) For sub-paragraph (1) substitute–

"**4A(A1)** An inaccuracy is in category 0 if–

(a) it involves a domestic matter,

(b) it involves an offshore matter or an offshore transfer, the territory in question is a category 0 territory and the tax at stake is income tax, capital gains tax or inheritance tax, or

(c) it involves an offshore matter and the tax at stake is a tax other than income tax, capital gains tax or inheritance tax.

4A(1) An inaccuracy is in category 1 if–

(a) it involves an offshore matter or an offshore transfer,

(b) the territory in question is a category 1 territory, and

(c) the tax at stake is income tax, capital gains tax or inheritance tax."

3(3) [Amends FA 2007, Sch. 24, para. 4A(2)(a) and (c).]

3(4) [Amends FA 2007, Sch. 24, para. 4A(3)(a) and (c).]

3(5) [Inserts FA 2007, Sch. 24, para. 4A(4A) and (4B).]

3(6) [Amends FA 2007, Sch. 24, para. 4A(5).]

3(7) [Amends FA 2007, Sch. 24, para. 4A(6)(a).]

3(8) In sub-paragraph (7), for "Category 1" substitute "Category 0 territory", "category 1".

Commencement Date – 1 April 2016 is the appointed day for the coming into force of para. 3(3)–(7) (and the amendments have effect in relation to documents given to HMRC relating to: a transfer of value made on or after that date for the purposes of inheritance tax; and a tax year commencing on or after 6 April 2016 for the purposes of income tax and capital gains tax) (SI 2016/456, art. 3).

4 [Inserts FA 2007, Sch. 24, para. 4AA.]

Commencement Date – 1 April 2016 is the appointed day for the coming into force of para. 4 (and the amendments have effect in relation to documents given to HMRC relating to: a transfer of value made on or after that date for the purposes of inheritance tax; and a tax year commencing on or after 6 April 2016 for the purposes of income tax and capital gains tax) (SI 2016/456, art. 3).

5 In paragraph 10 (standard percentage reductions for disclosure), in the Table in sub-paragraph (2), at the appropriate places insert–

"37.5%	18.75%	0%",
"87.5%	43.75%	25%", and
"125%	62.5%	40%".

6 In paragraph 12(5) (interaction with other penalties and late payment surcharges: the relevant percentage)–

(a) before paragraph (a) insert–

"(za) if the penalty imposed under paragraph 1 is for an inaccuracy in category 0, 100%,", and

(b) in paragraph (a), for "100%" substitute "125%".

7(1) Paragraph 21A (classification of territories) is amended as follows.

7(2) Before sub-paragraph (1) insert–

"**21A(A1)** A category 0 territory is a territory designated as a category 0 territory by order made by the Treasury."

7(3) For sub-paragraph (2) substitute–

"**21A(2)** A category 2 territory is a territory that is not any of the following–

(a) a category 0 territory;

(b) a category 1 territory;

(c) a category 3 territory."

7(4) For sub-paragraph (7) substitute–

"**21A(7)** An instrument containing (whether alone or with other provisions) the first order to be made under sub-paragraph (A1) may not be made unless a draft of the instrument has been laid before, and approved by a resolution of, the House of Commons."

8(1) Paragraph 21B (location of assets etc) is amended as follows.

8(2) [Inserts FA 2007, Sch. 24, para. 21B(1A).]

8(3) [Amends FA 2007, Sch. 24, para. 21B(2).]

Commencement Date – 1 April 2016 is the appointed day for the coming into force of para. 8 (and the amendments have effect in relation to documents given to HMRC relating to: a transfer of value made on or after that date for the purposes of inheritance tax; and a tax year commencing on or after 6 April 2016 for the purposes of income tax and capital gains tax) (SI 2016/456, art. 3).

PENALTIES FOR FAILURE TO MAKE RETURNS ETC

14 Schedule 55 to FA 2009 is amended as follows.

15(1) Paragraph 6 (penalty for failure continuing 12 months after penalty date) is amended as follows.

15(2) In sub-paragraph (3A)–

(a) before paragraph (a) insert–

"(za) for the withholding of category 0 information, 100%,", and

(b) in paragraph (a), for "100%" substitute "125%".

15(3) In sub-paragraph (4A)–

(a) before paragraph (a) insert–

"(za) for the withholding of category 0 information, 70%,", and

(b) in paragraph (a), for "70%" substitute "87.5%".

15(4) In sub-paragraph (6), for "3" substitute "4".

16(1) Paragraph 6A (categorisation of information) is amended as follows.

16(2) For sub-paragraph (1) substitute–

"**6A(A1)** Information is category 0 information if–

(a) it involves a domestic matter,

(b) it involves an offshore matter or an offshore transfer, the territory in question is a category 0 territory and it is information which would enable or assist HMRC to assess P's liability to income tax, capital gains tax or inheritance tax, or

(c) it involves an offshore matter and it is information which would enable or assist HMRC to assess P's liability to a tax other than income tax, capital gains tax or inheritance tax.

6A(1) Information is category 1 information if–

(a) it involves an offshore matter or an offshore transfer,

(b) the territory in question is a category 1 territory, and

(c) it is information which would enable or assist HMRC to assess P's liability to income tax, capital gains tax or inheritance tax."

16(3) [Amends FA 2009, Sch. 55, para. 6A(2)(a) and (c).]

16(4) [Amends FA 2009, Sch. 55, para. 6A(3)(a) and (c).]

16(5) [Inserts FA 2009, Sch. 55, para. 6A(4A) and (4B).]

16(6) [Amends FA 2009, Sch. 55, para. 6A(5).]

16(7) [Amends FA 2009, Sch. 55, para. 6A(6)(a).]

16(8) [Omits FA 2009, Sch. 55, para. 6A(8).]

16(9) [Amends FA 2009, Sch. 55, para. 6A(9).]

Commencement Date – 6 April 2016 is the day appointed for the coming into force of para. 16(3)–(9) (and the amendments have effect in relation to a return or other document which: is required to be made or delivered to HMRC in relation to a tax year commencing on or after that date; and falls within item 1, 2 or 3 of the Table in Sch. 55, para. 1(5) (penalty for failure to make returns etc)) (SI 2016/456, art. 5).

17 [Inserts FA 2009, Sch. 55, para. 6AA and 6AB.]

Commencement Date – 6 April 2016 is the day appointed for the coming into force of para. 17 (and the amendments have effect in relation to a return or other document which: is required to be made or delivered to HMRC in relation to a tax year commencing on or after that date; and falls within item 1, 2 or 3 of the Table in Sch. 55, para. 1(5) (penalty for failure to make returns etc)) (SI 2016/456, art. 5).

18 In paragraph 15 (standard percentage reductions for disclosure), in the Table in sub-paragraph (2), at the appropriate places insert–

"87.5%	43.75%	25%", and
"125%	62.5%	40%".

19 In paragraph 17(4) (interaction with other penalties and late payment surcharges), omit the "and" at the end of paragraph (b) and after that paragraph insert–

"(ba) if one of the penalties is a penalty under paragraph 6(3) or (4) and the information withheld is category 1 information, 125%, and".

GENERAL ANTI-ABUSE RULE: AGGREGATE PENALTIES

20(1) In Schedule 43C to FA 2013 (general anti-abuse rule: supplementary provision about penalty), sub-paragraph (6) of paragraph 8 is amended as follows.

20(2) After paragraph (b) insert–

"(ba) 125% in a case where neither paragraph (a) nor paragraph (b) applies and at least one of the penalties is determined by reference to the percentage in–

(i) paragraph 4(2)(c) of Schedule 24 to FA 2007,

(ii) paragraph 6(2)(a) of Schedule 41 to FA 2008,

(iii) paragraph 6(3A)(a) of Schedule 55 to FA 2009,".

20(3) In sub-paragraph (c) for "neither paragraph (a) nor paragraph (b) applies" substitute "none of paragraphs (a) to (ba) applies".

20(4) In sub-paragraph (d) for "none of paragraphs (a), (b) and (c) applies" substitute "none of paragraphs (a) to (c) applies".

History – Para. 20 (and the heading before it) inserted by FA 2016, s. 158(14), with effect in relation to tax arrangements (within the meaning of FA 2013, Pt. 5) entered into on or after 15 September 2016.

FINANCE (NO. 2) ACT 2015

(2015 Chapter 33)

[*18th November 2015*]

ARRANGEMENT OF SECTIONS

PART 6 – ADMINISTRATION AND ENFORCEMENT

51 Enforcement by deduction from accounts

51(1) Schedule 8 contains provision about the enforcement of debts owed to the Commissioners for Her Majesty's Revenue and Customs by making deductions from accounts held with deposit-takers.

51(2) The Treasury may, by regulations made by statutory instrument, make consequential, incidental or supplementary provision in connection with any provision made by that Schedule.

51(3) Regulations under subsection (2) may amend, repeal or revoke any enactment (whenever passed or made).

51(4) **"Enactment"** includes an enactment contained in subordinate legislation within the meaning of the Interpretation Act 1978.

51(5) A statutory instrument containing (whether alone or with other provision) provision amending or repealing an Act may not be made unless a draft of the instrument has been laid before and approved by a resolution of the House of Commons.

51(6) Any other statutory instrument containing regulations under subsection (2) is subject to annulment in pursuance of a resolution of the House of Commons.

52 Rate of interest applicable to judgment debts etc in taxation matters

52(1) This section applies if a sum payable to or by the Commissioners under a judgment or order given or made in any court proceedings relating to a taxation matter (a "tax-related judgment debt") carries interest as a result of a relevant enactment.

52(2) The **"relevant enactments"** are–

(a) section 17 of the Judgments Act 1838 (judgment debts to carry interest), and

(b) any order under section 74 of the County Courts Act 1984 (interest on judgment debts etc).

52(3) The relevant enactment is to have effect in relation to the tax-related judgment debt as if for the rate specified in section 17(1) of the Judgments Act 1838 and any other rate specified in an order under section 74 of the County Courts Act 1984 there were substituted–

(a) in the case of a sum payable to the Commissioners, the late payment interest rate provided for in regulations made by the Treasury under section 103(1) of FA 2009, and

(b) in the case of a sum payable by the Commissioners, the special repayment rate.

52(4) Subsection (3) does not affect any power of the court under the relevant enactment to prevent any sum from carrying interest or to provide for a rate of interest which is lower than (and incapable of exceeding) that for which the subsection provides.

52(5) If section 44A of the Administration of Justice Act 1970 (interest on judgment debts expressed otherwise than in sterling), or any corresponding provision made under section 74 of the County Courts Act 1984 in relation to the county court, applies to a tax-related judgment debt–

(a) subsection (3) does not apply, but

(b) the court may not specify in an order under section 44A of the Administration of Justice Act 1970, or under any provision corresponding to that section which has effect under section 74 of the County Courts Act 1984, an interest rate which exceeds (or is capable of exceeding)–

(i) in the case of a sum payable to the Commissioners, the rate mentioned in subsection (3)(a), or

(ii) in the case of a sum payable by the Commissioners, the special repayment rate.

52(6) The **"special repayment rate"** is the percentage per annum given by the formula–

$$BR + 2$$

where BR is the official Bank rate determined by the Bank of England Monetary Policy Committee at the operative meeting.

52(7) **"The operative meeting"**, in relation to the special repayment rate applicable in respect of any day, means the most recent meeting of the Bank of England Monetary Policy Committee apart from any meeting later than the 13th working day before that day.

52(8) The Treasury may by regulations made by statutory instrument–

(a) repeal subsections (6) and (7), and

(b) provide that the **"special repayment rate"** for the purposes of this section is the rate provided for in the regulations.

52(9) Regulations under subsection (8)–

(a) may make different provision for different purposes,

(b) may either themselves specify a rate of interest or make provision for such a rate to be determined (and to change from time to time) by reference to such rate, or the average of such rates, as may be referred to in the regulations,

(c) may provide for rates to be reduced below, or increased above, what they would otherwise be by specified amounts or by reference to specified formulae,

(d) may provide for rates arrived at by reference to averages to be rounded up or down,

(e) may provide for circumstances in which the alteration of a rate of interest is or is not to take place, and

(f) may provide that alterations of rates are to have effect for periods beginning on or after a day determined in accordance with the regulations ("the effective date") regardless of–

(i) the date of the judgment or order in question, and

(ii) whether interest begins to run on or after the effective date, or began to run before that date.

52(10) A statutory instrument containing regulations under subsection (8) is subject to annulment in pursuance of a resolution of the House of Commons.

52(11) To the extent that a tax-related judgment debt consists of an award of costs to or against the Commissioners, the reference in section 24(2) of the Crown Proceedings Act 1947 (which relates to interest on costs awarded to or against the Crown) to the rate at which interest is payable upon judgment debts due from or to the Crown is to be read as a reference to the rate at which interest is payable upon tax-related judgment debts.

52(12) This section has effect in relation to interest for periods beginning on or after 8 July 2015, regardless of–

(a) the date of the judgment or order in question, and

(b) whether interest begins to run on or after 8 July 2015, or began to run before that date.

52(13) Subsection (14) applies where, at any time during the period beginning with 8 July 2015 and ending immediately before the day on which this Act is passed ("the relevant period")–

(a) a payment is made in satisfaction of a tax-related judgment debt, and

(b) the payment includes interest under a relevant enactment in respect of any part of the relevant period.

52(14) The court by which the judgment or order in question was given or made must, on an application made to it under this subsection by the person who made the payment, order the repayment of the amount by which the interest paid under the relevant enactment in respect of days falling within the relevant period exceeds the interest payable under the relevant enactment in respect of those days in accordance with the provisions of this section.

52(15) In this section–

"the Commissioners" means the Commissioners for Her Majesty's Revenue and Customs;

"taxation matter" means anything the collection and management of which is the responsibility of the Commissioners (or was the responsibility of the Commissioners of Inland Revenue or Commissioners of Customs and Excise);

"working day" means any day other than a non-business day as defined in section 92 of the Bills of Exchange Act 1882.

52(16) This section extends to England and Wales only.

History – In s. 52(15), in the definition of "taxation matter", the words ", other than national insurance contributions," (which appeared after the words "means anything") omitted by FA 2016, s. 172(1), with effect (in England and Wales only) in relation to interest for periods beginning on or after 15 September 2016, regardless of– (a) the date of the judgment or order in question, and (b) whether interest begins to run on or after 15 September 2016, or began to run before that date.

PART 7 – FINAL

53 Interpretation

53 In this Act–

"CAA 2001" means the Capital Allowances Act 2001,

"CTA 2009" means the Corporation Tax Act 2009,

"CTA 2010" means the Corporation Tax Act 2010,

"FA", followed by a year, means the Finance Act of that year,

"IHTA 1984" means the Inheritance Tax Act 1984,

"ITA 2007" means the Income Tax Act 2007,

"ITEPA 2003" means the Income Tax (Earnings and Pensions) Act 2003,

"ITTOIA 2005" means the Income Tax (Trading and Other Income) Act 2005,

"TCGA 1992" means the Taxation of Chargeable Gains Act 1992,

"TIOPA 2010" means the Taxation (International and Other Provisions) Act 2010,

"TMA 1970" means the Taxes Management Act 1970,

"VATA 1994" means the Value Added Tax Act 1994, and

"VERA 1994" means the Vehicle Excise and Registration Act 1994.

54 Short title

54 This Act may be cited as the Finance (No. 2) Act 2015.

SCHEDULES

SCHEDULE 8 – ENFORCEMENT BY DEDUCTION FROM ACCOUNTS

Section 51

Part 1 – Scheme for Enforcement by Deduction from Accounts

INTRODUCTION

1 This Part of this Schedule contains provision about the collection of amounts due and payable to the Commissioners by the making of deductions from accounts held with deposit-takers.

"RELEVANT SUM"

2(1) In this Part of this Schedule **"relevant sum"**, in relation to a person, means a sum that is due and payable by the person to the Commissioners–

(a) under or by virtue of an enactment, or

(b) under a contract settlement,

and in relation to which Conditions A to C are met.

2(2) Condition A is that the sum is at least £1,000.

2(3) Condition B is that the sum is–

(a) an established debt (see sub-paragraph (5)),

(b) due under section 223 of, or paragraph 6 of Schedule 32 to, FA 2014 (accelerated payment notice or partner payment notice), or

(c) the disputed tax specified in a notice under section 221(2)(b) of FA 2014 (accelerated payment of tax: notice given pending appeal).

2(4) Condition C is that HMRC is satisfied that the person is aware that the sum is due and payable by the person to the Commissioners.

2(5) A sum that is due and payable to the Commissioners is an **"established debt"** if there is no possibility that the sum, or any part of it, will cease to be due and payable to the Commissioners on appeal.

2(6) For the purposes of sub-paragraph (5) it does not matter whether the reason that there is no such possibility is–

(a) that there is no right of appeal in relation to the sum,

(b) that a period for bringing an appeal has expired without an appeal having been brought, or

(c) that an appeal which was brought has been finally determined or withdrawn;

and any power to grant permission to appeal out of time is to be disregarded.

INFORMATION NOTICE

3(1) This paragraph applies if it appears to HMRC that–

(a) a person has failed to pay a relevant sum, and

(b) that person holds one or more accounts with a deposit-taker.

3(2) HMRC may give the deposit-taker a notice under this paragraph (an "information notice") requiring the deposit-taker to provide HMRC with–

(a) prescribed information about accounts held by the person with the deposit-taker,

(b) in relation to any joint account held by the person with the deposit-taker, prescribed information about the other holder or holders of the account, and

(c) any other prescribed information.

3(3) HMRC may exercise the power under sub-paragraph (2) only for the purposes of determining whether to give a hold notice to the deposit-taker in respect of the person concerned (see paragraph 4).

3(4) Where a deposit-taker is given an information notice, it must comply with the notice as soon as reasonably practicable and, in any event, within the period of 10 working days beginning with the day on which the notice is given to it.

3(5) An information notice must explain the effect of–

(a) sub-paragraph (4), and

(b) paragraph 14 (penalties).

Statutory instruments – SI 2015/1986: partly made under para. 3(2).

HOLD NOTICE

4(1) If it appears to HMRC that–

(a) a person ("P") has failed to pay a relevant sum, and

(b) P holds one or more accounts with a deposit-taker,

HMRC may give the deposit-taker a notice under this paragraph (a "hold notice").

4(2) The hold notice must–

(a) specify P's name and last known address,

(b) specify as the "specified amount" an amount that meets the conditions in sub-paragraph (4),

(c) specify as the "safeguarded amount" an amount that meets the requirements set out in sub-paragraphs (6) to (8),

(d) set out any rules which are to apply for the purposes of paragraph 7(5)(b) (priority of accounts subject to a hold notice),

(e) explain the effect of–

 (i) paragraphs 6 to 13 (effect of hold notice, duty to notify account holders etc),

 (ii) paragraph 14 (penalties), and

 (iii) any regulations under paragraph 20(2)(c) or (d) (powers to restrict the accounts or amounts in relation to which a hold notice may have effect, in addition to the powers to make provision in the hold notice under sub-paragraph (3)(b) and (c)), and

(f) contain a statement about HMRC's compliance with paragraph 5 in relation to the notice.

For provision about the particular relevant sums to which a hold notice relates see paragraph 8(6)(a)(ii) and (7) (notice to be given by HMRC to P).

4(3) The hold notice may–

(a) specify any other information which HMRC considers might assist the deposit-taker in identifying accounts which P holds with it;

(b) specify an account, or description of account, which is to be treated for the purposes of the hold notice and this Part of this Schedule as not being an account held by P with the deposit-taker;

(c) require that an amount specified in the notice is to be treated for the purposes of the hold notice and this Part of this Schedule as if it were not an amount standing to the credit of a specified account held by P.

4(4) The amount specified as the specified amount in the hold notice ("the current hold notice") must not exceed so much of the notified sum (see paragraph 8(6) to (8)) as remains after deducting–

(a) the amount specified as the **"specified amount"** in any hold notice which relates to the same debts as the current hold notice (see sub-paragraph (5)) and is given to another deposit-taker on the same day as that notice, and

(b) the amount specified as the **"specified amount"** in any hold notice which relates to the same debts as the current hold notice and is given to a deposit-taker on an earlier day, (unless HMRC has received a notification under paragraph 8(4) in relation to that earlier hold notice).

4(5) For the purposes of this paragraph, any two hold notices given in respect of the same person **"relate to the same debts"** if at least one relevant sum specified in relation to one of those notices by virtue of paragraph 8(7)(a) is the same debt as a relevant sum so specified in relation to the other notice.

4(6) The amount specified in the hold notice as the safeguarded amount must be at least £5,000; but this is qualified by sub-paragraphs (7) and (8).

4(7) The safeguarded amount must be nil if–

(a) HMRC has previously given a deposit-taker a hold notice ("the earlier hold notice") relating to the same debts as the hold notice mentioned in sub-paragraph (2) ("the new hold notice"), and

(b) within the period of 30 days ending with the day on which the new hold notice is given to the deposit-taker, HMRC has received a notice under paragraph 8which states that there is a held amount as a result of the earlier hold notice.

4(8) HMRC may (in a case not falling within sub-paragraph (7)) determine that an amount less than £5,000 (which may be nil) is to be the safeguarded amount if HMRC considers it appropriate to do so having regard to the value (or aggregate value) in sterling at the relevant time of any amounts which at that time stand to the credit of a qualifying non-sterling account or accounts.

4(9) In sub-paragraph (8) **"qualifying non-sterling account"** means an account which, but for paragraph 6(6)(b) (account not denominated in sterling), would be a relevant account in relation to the hold notice.

4(10) For the purposes of sub-paragraph (8), the value in sterling of any amount is to be determined in the prescribed manner; and regulations for the purposes of this sub-paragraph may specify circumstances in which the exchange rate is to be determined in accordance with a notice published by the Commissioners.

4(11) In sub-paragraph (8) **"the relevant time"** means the time when the Commissioners determine the amount to be specified as the **"safeguarded amount"** under sub-paragraph (2)(c).

4(12) HMRC must not on any one day give to a single deposit-taker more than one hold notice relating to the same debts.

PERSONS AT A PARTICULAR DISADVANTAGE IN DEALING WITH REVENUE AND CUSTOMS AFFAIRS

5(1) Before deciding whether or not to exercise the power under paragraph 3(2) or 4(1) in relation to a person, HMRC must consider whether or not, to the best of HMRC's knowledge, there are any matters as a result of which the person is, or may be, at a particular disadvantage in dealing with the person's Revenue and Customs affairs.

5(2) If HMRC determines that there are any such matters, HMRC must take those matters into account in deciding whether or not to exercise the power concerned in relation to the person.

5(3) The Commissioners must publish guidance as to the factors which are relevant to determining whether or not a person is at a particular disadvantage in dealing with the person's Revenue and Customs affairs for the purposes of this Schedule.

5(4) In this paragraph **"Revenue and Customs affairs"**, in relation to a person by whom a relevant sum is payable, means any affairs of the person which relate to the relevant sum.

EFFECT OF HOLD NOTICE

6(1) A deposit-taker to whom a hold notice is given under paragraph 4 must, for each relevant account (see sub-paragraph (6))–

(a) determine whether or not there is a held amount (greater than nil) in relation to that account, and

(b) if there is such a held amount in relation to that account, take the first or second type of action (see sub-paragraph (3)) in respect of that account.

See paragraph 7 for how to determine the held amount in relation to any relevant account.

6(2) The deposit-taker must comply with sub-paragraph (1) as soon as is reasonably practicable and, in any event, within the period of 5 working days beginning with the day on which the hold notice is given.

6(3) In relation to each affected account (see sub-paragraph (7))–

(a) the first type of action is to put in place such arrangements as are necessary to ensure that the deposit-taker does not do anything, or permit anything to be done, that would reduce the amount standing to the credit of that account below the held amount in relation to that account;

(b) the second type of action is to–

  (i) transfer an amount equal to the held amount from the affected account into an account created by the deposit-taker for the sole purpose of containing that transferred amount (a "suspense account"), and

  (ii) put in place such arrangements as are necessary to ensure that the deposit-taker does not do anything, or permit anything to be done, that would reduce the amount standing to the credit of that suspense account below the amount that is the held amount in relation to the affected account.

6(4) The deposit-taker must maintain any arrangements made under sub-paragraph (3) until the hold notice ceases to be in force.

6(5) A hold notice ceases to be in force when–

(a) the deposit-taker is given a notice cancelling it under paragraph 9 or 11 or the hold notice is cancelled under paragraph 12, or

(b) the deposit-taker is given a deduction notice in relation to the hold notice (see paragraph 13).

6(6) In this Part of this Schedule **"relevant account"**, in relation to a hold notice, means an account held with the deposit-taker by P, but not including–

(a) an account excluded under paragraph 4(3)(b) or by regulations under paragraph 20(2)(c),

(b) an account not denominated in sterling, or

(c) any suspense account.

6(7) For the purposes of this Part of this Schedule, a relevant account is an **"affected account"** if, as a result of the hold notice, an amount is the held amount in relation to that account (see paragraph 7(1) and (2)).

DETERMINATION OF HELD AMOUNTS

7(1) If there is only one relevant account (see paragraph 6(6)) in existence at the time the deposit-taker complies with paragraph 6(1), **"the held amount"** in relation to that account is–

(a) if the available amount in respect of the account (see sub-paragraph (3)) exceeds the safeguarded amount, so much of the amount of the excess as does not exceed the specified amount, and

(b) if the available amount does not exceed the safeguarded amount, nil.

For the meaning of **"the safeguarded amount"** and **"the specified amount"** see paragraph 23(1).

7(2) If there is more than one relevant account in existence at the time the deposit-taker complies with paragraph 6(1), "the held amount" in relation to each relevant account is determined as follows–

Step 1

Determine the available amount in respect of each relevant account.

Step 2

Determine the total of the available amounts in respect of all of the relevant accounts.

If that total does not exceed the safeguarded amount, the held amount in relation to each relevant account is nil (and no further steps are to be taken). In any other case, go to Step 3.

Step 3

Match the safeguarded amount against the available amounts in respect of the relevant accounts, taking those accounts in reverse priority order (see sub-paragraph (6)).

Step 4

Match the specified amount against what remains of the available amounts in respect of the relevant accounts by taking each relevant account in priority order (see sub-paragraph (5)) and matching the specified amount (or, as the case may be, what remains of the specified amount) against the available amount for each account until either–

(a) the specified amount has been fully matched, or

(b) what remains of the available amounts is exhausted.

Where this sub-paragraph applies, **"the held amount"**, in relation to a relevant account–

(i) is so much of the amount standing to the credit of the account as is matched against the specified amount under Step 4, and

(ii) accordingly, is nil if no amount standing to the credit of the account is so matched against the specified amount.

7(3) In this paragraph **"the available amount"** means–

(a) in the case of an account other than a joint account, the amount standing to the credit of that account at the time the deposit-taker complies with paragraph 6(1), or

(b) in the case of a joint account, the appropriate fraction of the amount standing to the credit of that account at that time;

so, if no amount stands to the credit of an account at that time, **"the available amount"** is nil.

7(4) In this paragraph **"the appropriate fraction"**, in relation to a joint account, means–

$$\frac{1}{N}$$

where N is the number of persons who together hold the joint account.

7(5) In this paragraph **"priority order"** means such order as the deposit-taker considers appropriate, but the deposit-taker must ensure–

(a) that accounts other than joint accounts always have a higher priority than joint accounts, and

(b) subject to paragraph (a), that any rule set out in the hold notice under paragraph 4(2)(d) is adhered to.

7(6) In this paragraph **"reverse priority order"** means the reverse of the order determined under sub-paragraph (5).

7(7) In this paragraph references to an amount standing to the credit of an account are to be read subject to any regulations under paragraph 20(2)(d).

DUTY TO NOTIFY HMRC AND ACCOUNT HOLDERS ETC

8(1) This paragraph applies where a deposit-taker receives a hold notice.

8(2) If the deposit-taker determines that there are one or more affected accounts (see paragraph 5(7)) as a result of the hold notice, the deposit-taker must give HMRC a notice which sets out–

(a) prescribed information about each of the affected accounts held by P,

(b) the amount of the held amount in relation to each such account,

(c) if any of the affected accounts is a joint account held by P and one or more other persons, prescribed information about the other person or persons, and

(d) any other prescribed information.

8(3) The notice under sub-paragraph (2) must be given within the period of 5 working days beginning with the day on which the deposit-taker complies with paragraph 6(1).

8(4) If the deposit-taker determines that there are no affected accounts as a result of the hold notice, it must give HMRC a notice which–

(a) states that this is the case, and

(b) sets out any other prescribed information.

8(5) The notice under sub-paragraph (4) must be given within the period of 5 working days beginning with the day on which the deposit-taker makes that determination.

8(6) If HMRC receives a notice under sub-paragraph (2) it must as soon as reasonably practicable–

(a) give P–

(i) a copy of the hold notice, and

(ii) a notice under sub-paragraph (7), and

(b) in relation to each affected account, give a notice to each person within sub-paragraph (9) explaining that a hold notice has been given in respect of the account, the effect of the hold notice so far as it relates to the account and the effect of paragraphs 10 to 12.

8(7) A notice under this sub-paragraph must comply with the following requirements–

(a) the notice must specify the particular relevant sums (see paragraph 2) to which the hold notice relates;

(b) the details given for that purpose must include a statement, to the best of HMRC's knowledge, of the amount of each of those sums (that is, the unpaid amount) at the date of the notice;

(c) the notice must state the total of the amounts stated under paragraph (b) (if more than one), and

(d) the notice must state that the notified sum for the purposes of the hold notice (see paragraph 4(4)) is equal to–

(i) the total amount specified under paragraph (c) or,

(ii) if paragraph (c) is not applicable, the amount specified under paragraph (b) as the amount of the relevant sum to which the hold notice relates.

8(8) In this Part of this Schedule **"the notified sum"**, in relation to a hold notice, means the amount identified as such (or that is to be identified as such) in the notice under sub-paragraph (7).

8(9) The persons mentioned in sub-paragraph (6)(b) are–

(a) in the case of a joint account, any holder of the account other than P, and

(b) any person (not falling within paragraph (a)) who is an interested third party in relation to the affected account,

in respect of whom prescribed information has been provided under sub-paragraph (2)(c) or sufficient information has otherwise been given in the notice under sub-paragraph (2) to enable HMRC to give a notice.

8(10) After the deposit-taker has complied with paragraph 6(1), the deposit-taker may, in relation to any affected account, give a notice to–

(a) P,

(b) if the account is a joint account, any other holder of the account, and

(c) any person (not falling within paragraph (b)) who is an interested third party in relation to the account,

which states that a hold notice has been received by the deposit-taker in respect of the account and the effect of that notice so far as it relates to that account.

8(11) In this Part of this Schedule **"interested third party"**, in relation to a relevant account, means a person other than P who has a beneficial interest in–

(a) an amount standing to the credit of the account, or

(b) an amount which has been transferred from that account to a suspense account.

8(12) But, in relation to a hold notice, an interest which comes into existence after any arrangements under paragraph 6(3) have been put into place is treated as not being a beneficial interest for the purposes of sub-paragraph (11).

Statutory instruments – SI 2015/1986: partly made under para. 8(2)(a), (2)(c), (2)(d) and 8(4)(b).

CANCELLATION OR VARIATION OF EFFECTS OF HOLD NOTICE

9(1) Where a hold notice has been given to a deposit-taker HMRC may, by a notice given to the deposit-taker (a "notice of cancellation or variation")–

(a) cancel the hold notice,

(b) cancel the effect of the hold notice in relation to one or more accounts, or

(c) cancel the effect of the hold notice in relation to any part of the held amount standing to the credit of a particular account or accounts.

In this sub-paragraph references to the effect of a hold notice are to its effect by virtue of paragraph 6(4).

9(2) Where HMRC gives a notice under sub-paragraph (1) it must give a copy of that notice to–

(a) P, and

(b) any other person who HMRC considers is affected by the giving of the notice of cancellation or variation and is–

(i) a person who holds a relevant account of which P is also a holder and in respect of whom prescribed information is provided under paragraph 8(2)(c), or

(ii) an interested third party in relation to a relevant account in respect of whom sufficient information has been given in the notice under paragraph 8(2) to enable HMRC to give a notice.

9(3) Where the deposit-taker is given a notice under sub-paragraph (1), it must as soon as reasonably practicable and, in any event, within the period of 5 working days beginning with the day the notice is given–

(a) if the notice is given under sub-paragraph (1)(a), cancel the arrangements made under paragraph 6(3) as a result of the notice, and

(b) if the notice is given under sub-paragraph (1)(b) or (c), make such adjustments to those arrangements as are necessary to give effect to the notice.

MAKING OBJECTIONS TO HOLD NOTICE

10(1) Where a hold notice is given to a deposit-taker, a person within sub-paragraph (2) may by a notice given to HMRC (a "notice of objection") object against the hold notice.

10(2) The persons who may object are–

(a) P,

(b) any interested third party in relation to an affected account, and

(c) any person (not falling within paragraph (a) or (b)) who is a holder of an affected account which is a joint account,

but only P may object on the ground in sub-paragraph (3)(a).

10(3) An objection may only be made on one or more of the following grounds–

(a) that the debts to which the hold notice relates (see paragraph 8(7)(a)) have been wholly or partly paid,

(b) that at the time when the hold notice was given, either there was no sum that was a relevant sum in relation to P or P did not hold any account with the deposit-taker,

(c) that the hold notice is causing or will cause exceptional hardship to the person making the objection or another person, or

(d) that there is an interested third party in relation to one or more of the affected accounts.

10(4) A notice of objection must state the grounds of the objection.

10(5) Objections under this paragraph may only be made within the period of 30 days beginning with–

(a) in the case of–

(i) P, or

(ii) a person within sub-paragraph (2)(b) or (c) who has not been given a notice under paragraph 8(6)(b),

the day on which a copy of the hold notice is given to P under paragraph 8(6)(a), and

(b) in the case of a person given a notice under paragraph 8(6)(b), the day on which that notice is given.

10(6) Sub-paragraph (5) does not apply if HMRC agree to the notice of objection being given after the end of the period mentioned in that sub-paragraph.

10(7) HMRC must agree to a notice of objection being given after the end of that period if the following conditions are met–

(a) the person seeking to make the objection has made a request in writing to HMRC to agree to the notice of objection being given;

(b) HMRC is satisfied that there was reasonable excuse for not giving the notice before the relevant time limit, and

(c) HMRC is satisfied that the person complied with paragraph (a) without unreasonable delay after the reasonable excuse ceased.

10(8) If a request of the kind referred to in sub-paragraph (7)(a) is made, HMRC must by a notice inform the person making the request whether or not HMRC agrees to the request.

10(9) Nothing in Part 5 of TMA 1970 (appeals and other proceedings) applies to an objection under this paragraph.

CONSIDERATION OF OBJECTIONS

11(1) HMRC must consider any objections made under paragraph 10 within 30 working days of being given the notice of objection.

11(2) Having considered the objections, HMRC must decide whether–

(a) to cancel the hold notice,

(b) to cancel the effect of the hold notice in relation to the held amount, or any part of the held amount, in respect of a particular account or accounts, or

(c) to dismiss the objection.

11(3) HMRC must give a notice stating its decision to–

(a) P,

(b) each person other than P who objected, and

(c) any other person who HMRC considers is affected by the decision and is–

(i) a person who holds a relevant account of which P is also a holder and in respect of whom prescribed information is provided under paragraph 8(2)(c), or

(ii) an interested third party in relation to a relevant account in respect of whom sufficient information has been given in the notice under paragraph 8(2) to enable HMRC to give a notice.

11(4) HMRC must, by a notice to the deposit-taker–

(a) if it makes a decision under sub-paragraph (2)(a), cancel the hold notice;

(b) if it makes a decision under sub-paragraph (2)(b), cancel the effect of the hold notice in relation to the accounts or amounts in question.

11(5) HMRC must give each person to whom HMRC is required to give a notice under sub-paragraph (3) a copy of any notice given to the deposit-taker under sub-paragraph (4).

11(6) Where the deposit-taker is given a notice under sub-paragraph (4), it must as soon as reasonably practicable and, in any event, within the period of 5 working days beginning with the day the notice is given–

(a) if the notice is given under sub-paragraph (4)(a), cancel the arrangements mentioned in paragraph 6(3), or

(b) if the notice is given under sub-paragraph (4)(b), make such adjustments to those arrangements as are necessary to give effect to the notice.

11(7) In this paragraph references to the effect of a hold notice are to its effect by virtue of paragraph 6(4).

APPEALS

12(1) Where HMRC makes a decision under paragraph (b) or (c) of paragraph 11(2), a person within sub-paragraph (2) may appeal against the hold notice.

12(2) The persons who may appeal are–

(a) P,

(b) any interested third party in relation to an affected account, and

(c) any person not falling within paragraph (a) or (b) who is a holder of an affected account which is a joint account.

12(3) An appeal may only be made on one or more of the grounds set out in paragraph 10(3) (and for this purpose the reference in paragraph 10(3)(c) to **"the objection"** is to be read as a reference to the appeal).

12(4) An appeal under sub-paragraph (1) must be made–

(a) in England and Wales, to the county court, and

(b) in Northern Ireland, to a county court.

12(5) An appeal under this paragraph may only be made within the period of 30 days beginning–

(a) in the case of a person given a notice of HMRC's decision under paragraph 11(3), with the day on which that notice is given to that person, and

(b) in the case of any person within sub-paragraph (2)(b) or (c) to whom such a notice has not been given, the day on which P is given such a notice.

12(6) A notice of appeal must state the grounds of appeal.

12(7) On an appeal under this paragraph, the court may–

(a) cancel the hold notice,

(b) cancel the effect of the hold notice in relation to the held amount, or any part of the held amount, in respect of a particular account or accounts, or

(c) dismiss the appeal.

12(8) Where the deposit-taker is served with an order made by the court under sub-paragraph (7)(a) or (b), the deposit-taker must as soon as reasonably practicable and, in any event, within the period of 5 working days beginning with the day the notice is given take such steps as are necessary to give effect to the order.

12(9) Where an appeal on the ground that the hold notice is causing or will cause the person making the appeal or another person exceptional hardship (or a further appeal following such an appeal) is pending, the court to which the appeal is made may, on an application made by the person who made the appeal–

(a) suspend the effect of the hold notice if adequate security is provided in respect of so much of the notified sum as remains unpaid,

(b) suspend the effect of the hold notice in relation to a particular account if adequate security is provided in respect of the held amount in relation to that account, or

(c) suspend the effect of the hold notice in relation to any part of the held amount standing to the credit of a particular account, if adequate security is provided in respect of that part.

12(10) In this paragraph references to the effect of a hold notice are to its effect by virtue of paragraph 6(4).

12(11) Nothing in Part 5 of TMA 1970 (appeals and other proceedings) applies to an appeal under this paragraph.

DEDUCTION NOTICE

13(1) If it appears to HMRC that a person in respect of whom a hold notice given to a deposit-taker is in force–

(a) has failed to pay a relevant sum, and

(b) holds an account (or more than one account) with the deposit-taker in respect of which there is a held amount in relation to that sum,

HMRC may give the deposit-taker a deduction notice in respect of that person.

13(2) A **"deduction notice"** is a notice which–

(a) specifies the name of the person concerned,

(b) specifies one or more affected accounts held by that person with the deposit-taker, and

(c) in relation to each such specified account requires the deposit-taker to deduct and pay a qualifying amount (see sub-paragraph (6)) to the Commissioners by a day specified in the notice.

13(3) Where a deduction notice specifies a particular affected account–

(a) the deduction required to be made in relation to that account by virtue of sub-paragraph (2)(c) must be made from the appropriate account, that is to say–

  (i) if the deposit-taker has by virtue of the hold notice transferred an amount from the specified account into a suspense account, that suspense account, or

  (ii) otherwise, the specified account, and

(b) the deposit-taker must not during the period in which the deduction notice is in force do anything, or permit anything to be done (except in accordance with paragraph (a)) that would reduce the amount standing to the credit of the appropriate account below the balance required for the purpose of making that deduction.

13(4) A deduction notice must explain the effect of sub-paragraph (3)(b) and paragraph 14 (penalties).

13(5) A deduction notice may not be given in respect of an account unless–

(a) the period for making an objection under paragraph 10 has expired and either no objections were made or any objection made has been decided or withdrawn, and

(b) if objections were made and decided, the period for appealing under paragraph 12 has expired and any appeal or further appeal has been finally determined.

13(6) In this paragraph **"qualifying amount"**, in relation to an affected account, means an amount not exceeding the held amount in relation to that account (as modified, where applicable, under paragraph 9(3)(b), 11(6)(b) or 12(7)(b)).

13(7) The total of the qualifying amounts specified in the deduction notice must not exceed the unpaid amount of the notified sum (see paragraph 8(8)).

13(8) HMRC must–

(a) give a copy of the deduction notice to the person in respect of whom it is given, and

(b) in the case of each account in respect of which the notice is given, give a notice to each person within sub-paragraph (9) explaining that a deduction notice has been given in respect of that account and the effect of the deduction notice so far as it relates to that account.

13(9) The persons mentioned in sub-paragraph (8)(b) are–

(a) if the account is a joint account, each person other than P who is a holder of the account, and

(b) any person (not falling within paragraph (a))–

  (i) who is an interested third party in relation to the account whom HMRC knows will be affected by the deduction notice, and

  (ii) about whom HMRC has sufficient information to enable it to give the notice under sub-paragraph (8)(b).

13(10) HMRC may, by a notice given to the deposit-taker, amend or cancel the deduction notice, and where it does so it must–

(a) give a copy of the notice under this sub-paragraph to the person in respect of whom the deduction notice was given, and

(b) in the case of each account affected by the amendment or cancellation, give a notice to each person within sub-paragraph (9) explaining the effect of the amendment or cancellation so far as it relates to that account.

13(11) The deduction notice–

(a) comes into force at the time it is given to the deposit-taker, and

(b) ceases to be in force at the time–

(i) the deposit-taker is given a notice cancelling it under sub-paragraph (10), or

(ii) the deposit-taker makes the final payment required by virtue of sub-paragraph (2)(c).

PENALTIES

14(1) This paragraph applies to a deposit-taker who–

(a) fails to comply with an information notice,

(b) fails to comply with a hold notice or a deduction notice,

(c) fails to comply with an obligation under paragraph 8(2) in accordance with paragraph 8(3) (obligation to notify HMRC of effects of hold notice),

(d) fails to comply with an obligation under paragraph 8(4) in accordance with paragraph 8(5) (obligation to notify HMRC if no affected accounts),

(e) fails to comply with an obligation under paragraph 9(3) (obligation to cancel or modify effects of hold notice),

(f) fails to comply with an obligation under paragraph 11(6) (obligation to cancel or adjust arrangements to give effect to HMRC's decision of objection), or

(g) following receipt of an information notice or hold notice in relation to an account or accounts held with the deposit-taker by a person ("the affected person"), makes a disclosure of information to the affected person or any other person in circumstances where that disclosure is likely to prejudice HMRC's ability to use the provisions of this Part of this Schedule to recover a relevant sum owed by the affected person.

14(2) In sub-paragraph (1)(g), the reference to a disclosure of information does not include the giving of a notice in accordance with paragraph 8(10) to the affected person in respect of a hold notice.

14(3) The deposit-taker is liable to a penalty of £300.

14(4) If a failure within sub-paragraph (1)(a) to (f) continues after the day on which notice is given under paragraph 15(1) of a penalty in respect of the failure, the deposit-taker is liable to a further penalty or penalties not exceeding £60 for each subsequent day on which the failure continues.

14(5) A failure by a deposit-taker to do anything required to be done within a limited period of time does not give rise to liability to a penalty under this paragraph if the deposit-taker did it within such further time, if any, as HMRC may have allowed.

14(6) Liability to a penalty under this paragraph does not arise if the person satisfies HMRC or (on an appeal notified to the tribunal) the tribunal that there is a reasonable excuse for the failure or (as the case may be) disclosure.

14(7) For the purposes of this paragraph–

(a) where the deposit-taker relies on any other person to do anything, that is not a reasonable excuse unless the deposit-taker took reasonable care to avoid the failure or disclosure, and

(b) where the deposit-taker had a reasonable excuse for the failure but the excuse has ceased, the deposit-taker is to be treated as having continued to have the excuse if the failure is remedied without unreasonable delay after the excuse ceased.

ASSESSMENT OF PENALTY

15(1) Where a deposit-taker becomes liable to a penalty under paragraph 14–

(a) HMRC must assess the penalty, and

(b) if HMRC does so, it must notify the deposit-taker in writing.

15(2) An assessment of a penalty by virtue of paragraph (a) of paragraph 14(1) must be made within the period of 12 months beginning with the day on which the deposit-taker becomes liable to the penalty.

15(3) An assessment of a penalty under any of paragraphs (b) to (g) of paragraph 14(1) must be made within the period of 12 months beginning with the latest of the following–

(a) the day on which the deposit-taker became liable to the penalty,

(b) the end of the period in which notice of an appeal in respect of the hold notice could have been given, and

(c) if notice of such an appeal is given, the day on which the appeal is finally determined or withdrawn.

APPEAL AGAINST PENALTY

16(1) A deposit-taker may appeal against–

(a) a decision that a penalty is payable by the deposit-taker under paragraph 14, or

(b) a decision as to the amount of such a penalty.

16(2) Notice of an appeal must be given to HMRC before the end of the period of 30 days beginning with the day on which the notification under paragraph 15 was given.

16(3) Notice of an appeal must state the grounds of appeal.

16(4) On an appeal under sub-paragraph (1)(a) that is notified to the tribunal (in accordance with Part 5 of TMA 1970: see below) the tribunal may confirm or cancel the decision.

16(5) On an appeal under sub-paragraph (1)(b) that is notified to the tribunal, the tribunal may–

(a) confirm the decision, or

(b) substitute for the decision another decision that HMRC had power to make.

16(6) Subject to this paragraph and paragraph 17, the provisions of Part 5 of TMA 1970 relating to appeals have effect in relation to appeals under this paragraph as they have effect in relation to an appeal against an assessment to income tax.

ENFORCEMENT OF PENALTY

17(1) A penalty under paragraph 14 must be paid–

(a) before the end of the period of 30 days beginning with the day on which the notification under paragraph 15 was given, or

(b) if notice of an appeal against the penalty is given, before the end of the period of 30 days beginning with the day on which the appeal is finally determined or withdrawn.

17(2) A penalty under paragraph 14 may be enforced as if it were income tax charged in an assessment and due and payable.

PROTECTION OF DEPOSIT-TAKERS ACTING IN GOOD FAITH

18 A deposit-taker is not liable for damages in respect of anything done in good faith for the purposes of complying with a hold notice or a deduction notice.

POWER TO MODIFY AMOUNTS AND TIME LIMITS

19(1) The Commissioners may by regulations amend any of the following provisions by substituting a different amount for the amount for the time being specified there–

(a) paragraph 2(2) (requirement that relevant sum is a minimum amount);

(b) paragraph 4(6) and (8) (threshold for safeguarded amount);

(c) paragraph 14(3) or (4) (level of penalties).

19(2) The Commissioners may by regulations amend any of the following provisions by substituting a different period for the period for the time being specified there–

(a) paragraph 3(4) (time limit for complying with information notices);

(b) paragraph 6(2) (time limit for complying with hold notices);

(c) paragraph 8(3) or (5) (time limit for notifying HMRC of effects of hold notice);

(d) paragraph 9(3) (cancellation etc of hold notice: time limit for cancelling or adjusting arrangements);

(e) paragraph 10(5) (time limit for making objections);

(f) paragraph 11(1) (time limit for consideration of objections);

(g) paragraph 11(6) (consideration of objections: time limit for cancelling or adjusting arrangements);

(h) paragraph 12(8) (appeals: time limit for compliance with court order).

POWER TO MAKE FURTHER PROVISION

20(1) The Commissioners may by regulations make provision supplementing this Part of this Schedule.

20(2) The regulations may, in particular, make provision–

(a) about the manner in which a notice or a copy of a notice is to be given under this Part of this Schedule, or the circumstances in which a notice or a copy of a notice is to be treated as given, for the purposes of this Part of this Schedule;

(b) specifying circumstances in which a notice under this Part of this Schedule may not be given;

(c) specifying descriptions of account in respect of which a hold notice or deduction notice has no effect;

(d) specifying circumstances in which amounts standing to the credit of an account are to be treated as not standing to the credit of the account for the purposes of a hold notice or deduction notice;

(e) about fees a deposit-taker may charge a person in respect of whom a notice is given under this Part of this Schedule towards administrative costs in complying with that notice;

(f) with respect to priority as between a notice under this Part of this Schedule and–

(i) any other such notice, or

(ii) any notice or order under any other enactment.

Statutory instruments – SI 2016/44: made under para. 20(2)(e).

REGULATIONS

21(1) Regulations under this Part of this Schedule may–

(a) make different provision for different purposes,

(b) include supplementary, incidental and consequential provision, or

(c) make transitional provision and savings.

21(2) Regulations under this Part of this Schedule are to be made by statutory instrument.

21(3) A statutory instrument containing only regulations within sub-paragraph (4) is subject to annulment in pursuance of a resolution of the House of Commons.

21(4) The regulations within this sub-paragraph are–

(a) regulations which prescribe information for the purposes of paragraph 3(2) or any provision of paragraph 8,

(b) regulations under paragraph 4(10),

(c) regulations under paragraph (a), (b), (c), (d), (g) or (h) of paragraph 19(2), or

(d) regulations under paragraph 20(2).

21(5) Any other statutory instrument containing regulations under this Part of this Schedule may not be made unless a draft of the instrument has been laid before, and approved by a resolution of, the House of Commons.

JOINT ACCOUNTS

22 In this Part of this Schedule a reference to an account held by a person includes a reference to a joint account held by that person and one or more other persons.

DEFINED TERMS

23(1) In this Part of this Schedule–

"affected account" has the meaning given by paragraph 6(7);

"the Commissioners" means the Commissioners for Her Majesty's Revenue and Customs;

"contract settlement" means an agreement made in connection with any person's liability to make a payment to the Commissioners under or by virtue of an enactment;

"deduction notice" has the meaning given by paragraph 13;

"deposit-taker" means a person who may lawfully accept deposits in the United Kingdom in the course of a business (see sub-paragraph (2));

"HMRC" means Her Majesty's Revenue and Customs;

"hold notice" has the meaning given by paragraph 4;

"information notice" has the meaning given by paragraph 3;

"interested third party", in relation to a relevant account, has the meaning given by paragraph 8(11);

"joint account", in relation to a person, means an account held by the person and one or more other persons;

"notice" means notice in writing;

"notified sum", in relation to a hold notice, has the meaning given by paragraph 8(8);

"prescribed" means prescribed by regulations made by the Commissioners;

"relevant account" (in relation to a hold notice) has the meaning given by paragraph 6(6);

"relevant sum", in relation to a person, has the meaning given by paragraph 2(1);

"the safeguarded amount" (in relation to a hold notice) means the amount specified as the safeguarded amount in the notice (see paragraph 4(2)(c));

"the specified amount" (in relation to a hold notice) means the amount specified as such in the notice (see paragraph 4(2)(b));

"suspense account" has the meaning given by paragraph 6(3)(b)(i);

"the tribunal" means the First-tier Tribunal;

"working day" means a day other than–

(a) Saturday or Sunday,

(b) Christmas Eve, Christmas Day or Good Friday, or

(c) a day which is a bank holiday under the Banking and Financial Dealings Act 1971 in England and Wales or Northern Ireland.

23(2) The definition of **"deposit-taker"** in sub-paragraph (1) is to be read with–

(a) section 22 of the Financial Services and Markets Act 2000 (regulated activities),

(b) any relevant order under that section, and

(c) Schedule 2 to that Act.

Statutory instruments – SI 2015/1986: partly made under para. 23(1).

EXTENT

24 This Part of this Schedule extends to England and Wales and Northern Ireland.

NATIONAL INSURANCE CONTRIBUTIONS (RATE CEILINGS) ACT 2015

(2015 Chapter 35) [*17th December 2015*]

ARRANGEMENT OF SECTIONS

RATE CEILINGS

RATE CEILINGS

1 Main and additional primary percentages

1(1) In relation to primary Class 1 contributions payable in respect of any period in a tax year to which this section applies–

(a) the main primary percentage shall not exceed 12%, and

(b) the additional primary percentage shall not exceed 2%.

1(2) This section applies to a tax year which begins after the day on which this Act comes into force but before the date of the first parliamentary general election after that day.

1(3) In this section, **"main primary percentage"** and **"additional primary percentage"** are to be construed in accordance with section 8(2)(a) and (b) of SSCBA 1992 and SSCB(NI)A 1992.

2 Secondary percentage

2(1) In relation to secondary Class 1 contributions payable in respect of any period in a tax year to which this section applies, the secondary percentage shall not exceed 13.8%.

2(2) This section applies to a tax year which begins after the day on which this Act comes into force but before the date of the first parliamentary general election after that day.

2(3) In this section, **"secondary percentage"** is to be construed in accordance with section 9(2) of SSCBA 1992 and SSCB(NI)A 1992.

3 Upper earnings limit

3(1) The upper earnings limit specified in regulations under section 5(1) of SSCBA 1992 and SSCB(NI)A 1992 for any tax year to which this section applies shall not exceed the weekly equivalent of the proposed higher rate threshold for that tax year.

3(2) This section applies to a tax year–

(a) which begins after the day on which this Act comes into force but before the date of the first parliamentary general election after that day, and

(b) for which income tax is charged.

3(3) For the purposes of this section, the **"proposed higher rate threshold"** for a tax year is the sum of–

(a) the basic rate limit for income tax for the tax year as proposed in the pre-budget proposals for that year, and

(b) the personal allowance for income tax for the tax year as so proposed.

3(4) For the purposes of this section, the weekly equivalent of a proposed higher rate threshold for a tax year is the amount produced by dividing that threshold by 52 and rounding up or down to the nearest pound.

3(5) In this section **"pre-budget proposals"** means the government's pre-budget fiscal proposals for a tax year which are contained in a document presented to Parliament by the Chancellor of the Exchequer by Command of Her Majesty.

FINAL

4 Interpretation

4 In this Act–

"SSCBA 1992" means the Social Security Contributions and Benefits Act 1992;

"SSCB(NI)A 1992" means the Social Security Contributions and Benefits (Northern Ireland) Act 1992.

5 Extent, commencement and short title

5(1) This Act extends to England and Wales, Scotland and Northern Ireland.

5(2) This Act comes into force on the day on which it is passed.

5(3) This Act may be cited as the National Insurance Contributions (Rate Ceilings) Act 2015.

FINANCE ACT 2016

(2016 Chapter 24)

[*15th September 2016*]

ARRANGEMENT OF SECTIONS

PART 1 – INCOME TAX

RATE STRUCTURE

PENSIONS

TRADING AND OTHER INCOME

PART 6 – APPRENTICESHIP LEVY

ANTI-AVOIDANCE

INFORMATION AND PENALTIES

GENERAL

PART 10 – TAX AVOIDANCE AND EVASION

GENERAL ANTI-ABUSE RULE

TACKLING FREQUENT AVOIDANCE

OFFSHORE ACTIVITIES

PART 11 – ADMINISTRATION, ENFORCEMENT AND SUPPLEMENTARY POWERS

ASSESSMENT AND RETURNS

JUDGMENT DEBTS

PART 1 – INCOME TAX

RATE STRUCTURE

4 Savings allowance, and savings nil rate etc

4(1)–(14) [Not relevant to National Insurance contributions.]

4(15) [Amends TMA 1970, s. 7(6).]

4(16) [Not relevant to National Insurance contributions.]

4(17) Subject to subsection (18), the amendments made by this section have effect for the tax year 2016–17 and subsequent tax years.

4(18) The amendments in section 669 of ITTOIA 2005, and the repeals made by subsection (14), have effect where the tax year mentioned in section 669(1)(b) of ITTOIA 2005 is the tax year 2016–17 or a later tax year.

4(19) The Treasury may, by regulations made by statutory instrument, make such provision amending, repealing or revoking any provision made by or under the Taxes Acts as the Treasury considers appropriate in consequence of the amendments made by this section; and regulations under this subsection that have effect for the tax year 2016–17 may be made at any time before the end of that tax year.

4(20) In subsection (19) **"the Taxes Acts"** means–

(a) the Tax Acts,

(b) TMA 1970, and

(c) TCGA 1992 and all other enactments relating to capital gains tax.

4(21) A statutory instrument containing regulations under subsection (19) is subject to annulment in pursuance of a resolution of the House of Commons.

5 Rates of tax on dividend income, and abolition of dividend tax credits etc

5(1)–(8) [Not relevant to National Insurance contributions.]

5(9) In section 7 of TMA 1970 (duty to notify HMRC of liability to tax)–

(a) [amends TMA 1970, s. 7(6),]

(b) [inserts TMA 1970, s. 7(6A).]

5(10) The amendments made by the preceding provisions of this section have effect for the tax year 2016–17 and subsequent tax years.

5(11) Schedule 1 contains provision for, and connected with, the abolition of dividend tax credits etc.

PENSIONS

19 Standard lifetime allowance from 2016–17

19(1)–(9) [Not relevant to National Insurance contributions.]

19(10) Schedule 4 contains transitional and connected provision (including provision for "fixed protection 2016" and "individual protection 2016").

TRADING AND OTHER INCOME

25 Averaging profits of farmers etc

25(1)–(9) [Not relevant to National Insurance contributions.]

25(10) In paragraph 3 of Schedule 1B to TMA 1970 (relief for fluctuating profits of farmers etc)–

(a) [inserts TMA 1970, Sch. 1B, para. 3(1)(a) and (b);]

(b) [amends TMA 1970, Sch. 1B, para. 3(2);]

(c) [amends TMA 1970, Sch. 1B, para. 3(3);]

(d) [amends TMA 1970, Sch. 1B, para. 3(5);]

(e) [inserts TMA 1970, Sch. 1B, para. 3(7).]

25(11) In paragraph 4 of Schedule 1B to TMA 1970 (relief claimed by virtue of section 224(4) of ITTOIA 2005)–

(a) [amends TMA 1970, Sch. 1B, para. 4(1);]

(b) [amends TMA 1970, Sch. 1B, para. 4(2);]

(c) [amends TMA 1970, Sch. 1B, para. 4(3);]

(d) [amends TMA 1970, Sch. 1B, para. 4(5).]

25(12) The amendments made by this section have effect for the tax year 2016–17 and subsequent tax years.

PART 6 – APPRENTICESHIP LEVY

ANTI-AVOIDANCE

104 Application of other regimes to apprenticeship levy

104(1) [Not relevant to National Insurance contributions.]

104(2) [Inserts FA 2013, s. 206(3)(db).]

104(3) Part 4 of FA 2014 (follower notices and accelerated payments) is amended in accordance with subsections (4) and (5).

104(4) [Inserts FA 2014, s. 200(ca).]

104(5) [Inserts FA 2014, s. 203(ea).]

104(6) Part 5 of FA 2014 (promoters of tax avoidance schemes) is amended in accordance with subsections (7) and (8).

104(7) [Not relevant to National Insurance contributions.]

104(8) [Inserts FA 2014, s. 283(1)(da).]

INFORMATION AND PENALTIES

113 Penalties

113(1) Schedule 24 to FA 2007 (penalties for errors) is amended in accordance with subsections (2) to (4).

113(2) [Not relevant to National Insurance contributions.]

113(3) [Amends FA 2007, Sch. 24, para. 13(1ZA) and (1ZD).]

113(4) [Amends FA 2007, Sch. 24, para. 21C.]

113(5) Schedule 55 to FA 2009 (penalty for failure to make returns etc) is amended in accordance with subsections (6) to (8).

113(6) [Not relevant to National Insurance contributions.]

113(7) In paragraph 6B, after "item 4" insert "or 4A".

113(8) In the italic heading before paragraph 6B, at the end insert "and apprenticeship levy".

113(9) Schedule 56 to FA 2009 (penalty for failure to make payments on time) is amended in accordance with subsections (10) to (15).

113(10) [Not relevant to National Insurance contributions.]

113(11) In paragraph 3(1)–

(a) in paragraph (b) after "within" insert "item 4A or";

(b) after paragraph (c) insert–

"(ca) an amount in respect of apprenticeship levy falling within item 4A which is payable by virtue of regulations under section 106 of FA 2016 (recovery from third parties)."

113(12) In paragraph 5(1), for "or 4" substitute ", 4 or 4A".

113(13) In paragraph 5(2), for "or (c)" substitute ", (c) or (ca)."

113(14) In paragraph 6(2), after paragraph (b) insert–

"(ba) a payment under regulations under section 105 of FA 2016 of an amount in respect of apprenticeship levy payable in relation to the tax year;".

113(15) In the italic heading before paragraph 5, at the end insert "etc.".

113(16) The amendments made by subsections (1) to (4) of this section come into force in accordance with provision made by the Treasury by regulations.

113(17) In subsections (2) and (4) of section 106 of FA 2009 (penalties for failure to make returns: commencement etc) references to Schedule 55 to that Act have effect as references to that Schedule as amended by subsections (5) to (8) of this section.

113(18) Schedule 56 to FA 2009, as amended by this section, is taken to come into force for the purposes of apprenticeship levy on the date on which this Act is passed.

Commencement Date – S. 113(1) to (4) comes into force on 6 April 2017 (SI 2017/355, reg. 2).

GENERAL

115 Tax agents: dishonest conduct

115 [Inserts FA 2012, Sch. 38, para. 37(1)(la).]

PART 10 – TAX AVOIDANCE AND EVASION

GENERAL ANTI-ABUSE RULE

156 General anti-abuse rule: provisional counteractions

156(1) [Inserts FA 2013, s. 209A–209F.]

156(2) [Amends FA 2013, s. 214(1).]

156(3) The amendments made by this section have effect in relation to tax arrangements (within the meaning of Part 5 of FA 2013) entered into at any time (whether before or on or after the day on which this Act is passed).

157 General anti-abuse rule: binding of tax arrangements to lead arrangements

157(1) Part 5 of FA 2013 (general anti-abuse rule) is amended in accordance with subsections (2) to (11).

157(2) [Inserts FA 2013, Sch. 43A.]

157(3) [Inserts FA 2013, Sch. 43B.]

157(4) [Amends FA 2013, s. 209(6)(a).]

157(5) [Inserts FA 2013, s. 210(1)(b).]

157(6) [Substitutes FA 2013, s. 211(2)(b).]

157(7) Section 214 (interpretation of Part 5) is amended in accordance with subsections (8) to (10).

157(8) [Amends FA 2013, s. 214(1).]

157(9) [Amends FA 2013, s. 214(1).]

157(10) [Inserts FA 2013, s. 214(2) and (3).]

157(11) [Inserts FA 2013, Sch. 43, para. 6(3).]

157(12) Section 10 of the National Insurance Contributions Act 2014 (GAAR to apply to national insurance contributions) is amended in accordance with subsections (13) to (16).

157(13) [Amends NICA 2014, s. 10(4).]

157(14) [Inserts NICA 2014, s. 10(6A).]

157(15) [Amends NICA 2014, s. 10(11).]

157(16) [Inserts NICA 2014, s. 10(12).]

157(17) [Inserts NICA 2014, s. 10A.]

157(18) Section 219 of FA 2014 (circumstances in which an accelerated payment notice may be given) is amended in accordance with subsections (19) and (20).

157(19) [Inserts FA 2014, s. 219(4)(d) and (e).]

157(20) [Inserts FA 2014, s. 219(8).]

157(21) In section 220 of FA 2014 (content of notice given while a tax enquiry is in progress)–

(a) [amends FA 2014, s. 220(4)(c);]

(b) [amends FA 2014, s. 220(5)(c);]

(c) [amends FA 2014, s. 220(7).]

157(22)–(28) [Not relevant to National Insurance contributions.]

157(29) In Schedule 34 to FA 2014 (promoters of tax avoidance schemes: threshold conditions), in paragraph 7–

(a) [amends FA 2014, Sch. 34, para. 7(a);]

(b) [amends FA 2014, Sch. 34, para. 7(b);]

(c) [amends FA 2014, Sch. 34, para. 7(c).]

157(30) The amendments made by this section have effect in relation to tax arrangements (within the meaning of Part 5 of FA 2013) entered into at any time (whether before or on or after the day on which this Act is passed).

158 General anti-abuse rule: penalty

158(1) Part 5 of FA 2013 (general anti-abuse rule) is amended as follows.

158(2) [Inserts FA 2013, s. 212A.]

158(3) [Inserts FA 2013, Sch. 43C.]

158(4) [Inserts FA 2013, s. 209(8)–(10).]

158(5) Schedule 43 (general anti-abuse rule: procedural requirements) is amended in accordance with subsections (6) to (9).

158(6) [Inserts FA 2013, Sch. 43, para. 1A.]

158(7) [Amends FA 2013, Sch. 43, para. 3(2)(e).]

158(8) [Inserts FA 2013, Sch. 43, para. 4A.]

158(9) [Inserts FA 2013, Sch. 43, para. 4B.]

158(10) [Inserts TMA 1970, s. 103ZA(ga).]

158(11) [Inserts FA 2014, s. 212(4)(e).]

158(12) FA 2015 is amended in accordance with subsections (13) and (14).

158(13) [Inserts FA 2015, s. 120(1)(d).]

158(14) [Inserts FA 2015, Sch. 20, para. 20.]

158(15) The amendments made by this section have effect in relation to tax arrangements (within the meaning of Part 5 of FA 2013) entered into on or after the day on which this Act is passed.

TACKLING FREQUENT AVOIDANCE

159 Serial tax avoidance

159 Schedule 18 contains provision about the issue of warning notices to, and further sanctions for, persons who incur a relevant defeat in relation to arrangements.

160 Promoters of tax avoidance schemes

160(1) Part 5 of FA 2014 (promoters of tax avoidance schemes) is amended as follows.

160(2) [Inserts FA 2014, s. 237A–237D.]

160(3) [Inserts FA 2014, s. 241A and 241B.]

160(4) [Inserts FA 2014, s. 242(6) and (7).]

160(5) [Inserts FA 2014, Sch. 34A.]

160(6) [Inserts FA 2014, s. 241(5).]

160(7) [Inserts FA 2014, s. 281A.]

160(8) [Inserts FA 2014, s. 282(3)(ba).]

160(9) [Amends FA 2014, s. 283(1).]

160(10) Schedule 36 (promoters of tax avoidance schemes: partnerships) is amended in accordance with subsections (11) to (16).

160(11) [Inserts FA 2014, Sch. 36, para. 4A.]

160(12) [Amends FA 2014, Sch. 36, para. 7(1)(b).]

160(13) [Amends FA 2014, Sch. 36, para. 7(2).]

160(14) [Inserts FA 2014, Sch. 36, para. 7A.]

160(15) In paragraph 10–

(a) [amends FA 2014, Sch. 36, para. 10(1)(b);]

(b) [inserts FA 2014, Sch. 36, para. 10(3)(za);]

(c) [inserts FA 2014, Sch. 36, para. 10(4)(za);]

(d) [inserts FA 2014, Sch. 36, para. 10(5A).]

160(16) [Inserts FA 2014, Sch. 36, para. 11A.]

160(17) Part 2 of Schedule 2 to the National Insurance Contributions Act 2015 (application of Part 5 of FA 2014 to national insurance contributions) is amended in accordance with subsections (18) and (19).

160(18) [Inserts NICA 2015, Sch. 2, para. 30A and 30B.]

160(19) In paragraph 31 (interpretation)–

(a) [inserts NICA 2015, Sch. 2, para. 31(za).]

(b) [amends NICA 2015, Sch. 2, para. 31(b).]

160(20) For the purposes of sections 237A and 241A of FA 2014, a defeat (by virtue of any of Conditions A to F in Schedule 34A to that Act) of arrangements is treated as not having occurred if–

(a) there has been a final judicial ruling on or before the day on which this Act is passed as a result of which the counteraction referred to in paragraph 11(d), 12(1)(b), 13(1)(d), 14(1)(d) or 15(1)(d) (as the case may be) is final for the purposes of Schedule 34A of that Act, or

(b) (in the case of a defeat by virtue of Condition F in Schedule 34A) the judicial ruling mentioned in paragraph 16(1)(d) of that Schedule becomes final on or before the day on which this Act is passed.

160(21) Subsection (20) does not apply in relation to a person (who is carrying on a business as a promoter) if at any time after 17 July 2014 that person or an associated person takes action as a result of which the person taking the action–

(a) becomes a promoter in relation to the arrangements, or arrangements related to those arrangements, or

(b) would have become a promoter in relation to arrangements mentioned in paragraph (a) had the person not already been a promoter in relation to those arrangements.

160(22) For the purposes of sections 237A and 241A of FA 2014, a defeat of arrangements is treated as not having occurred if it would (ignoring this sub-paragraph) have occurred–

(a) on or before the first anniversary of the day on which this Act is passed, and

(b) by virtue of any of Conditions A to E in Schedule 34A to FA 2014, but otherwise than as a result of a final judicial ruling.

160(23) For the purposes of subsection (21) a person ("Q") is an "associated person" in relation to another person ("P") at any time when any of the following conditions is met–

(a) P is a relevant body which is controlled by Q;

(b) Q is a relevant body, P is not an individual and Q is controlled by P;

(c) P and Q are relevant bodies and a third person controls P and Q.

160(24) In subsection (23) "relevant body" and "control" are to be interpreted in accordance with paragraph 19 of Schedule 34A to FA 2014.

160(25) In subsections (20) to (22) expressions used in Part 5 of FA 2014 (as amended by this section) have the same meaning as in that Part.

161 Large businesses: tax strategies and sanctions for persistently unco-operative behaviour

161(1) Schedule 19 contains provisions relating to–

(a) the publication of tax strategies by bodies which are or are part of a large business,

(b) the imposition of sanctions for such bodies where there has been persistent unco-operative behaviour.

161(2) That Schedule, so far as relating to the publication of a tax strategy for a financial year of a relevant body or other entity, has effect only where the financial year begins on or after the day on which this Act is passed.

161(3) An officer of HMRC may not give a warning notice under Part 3 of that Schedule to a relevant body or other entity before the beginning of its first financial year beginning on or after the day on which this Act is passed.

161(4) In this section and Schedule 19 **"HMRC"** means Her Majesty's Revenue and Customs.

OFFSHORE ACTIVITIES

163 Penalties in connection with offshore matters and offshore transfers

163(1) Schedule 21 contains provisions amending–

(a) Schedule 24 to FA 2007 (penalties for errors in tax returns etc),

(b) Schedule 41 to FA 2008 (penalties for failure to notify etc), and

(c) Schedule 55 to FA 2009 (penalties for failure to make return etc).

163(2) That Schedule comes into force on such day as the Treasury may by regulations made by statutory instrument appoint.

163(3) Regulations under this section may–

(a) commence a provision generally or only for specified purposes,

(b) appoint different days for different provisions or for different purposes, and

(c) make supplemental, incidental and transitional provision.

165 Asset-based penalties for offshore inaccuracies and failures

165(1) Schedule 22 contains provision imposing asset-based penalties on certain taxpayers who have been charged a penalty for deliberate offshore inaccuracies and failures.

165(2) That Schedule comes into force on such day as the Treasury may by regulations made by statutory instrument appoint.

165(3) Regulations under subsection (2) may–

(a) commence a provision generally or only for specified purposes,

(b) appoint different days for different provisions or for different purposes, and

(c) make supplemental, incidental and transitional provision.

166 Offences relating to offshore income, assets and activities

166(1) [Inserts TMA 1970, s. 106A–106H.]

166(2) The amendment made by this section comes into force on such day as the Treasury may by regulations made by statutory instrument appoint.

166(3) The regulations–

(a) may appoint different days for different purposes, and

(b) may include incidental, supplemental, consequential and transitional provision and savings.

166(4) The amendment made by this section does not have effect in relation to–

(a) a failure to give a notice required by section 7 of TMA 1970,

(b) a failure to make and deliver a return required by section 8 of TMA 1970, or

(c) a return required by section 8 that contains an inaccuracy,

if the notice or return relates to a tax year before that in which the amendment comes into force.

Commencement Date – The amendment to TMA 1970 made by s. 166 comes into force on 7 October 2017 and has effect in relation to the tax year commencing on 6 April 2017 and subsequent tax years (SI 2017/970, reg. 2).

PART 11 – ADMINISTRATION, ENFORCEMENT AND SUPPLEMENTARY POWERS

ASSESSMENT AND RETURNS

167 Simple assessments

167(1) Schedule 23 contains provisions about simple assessments by HMRC.

167(2) Paragraphs 1 to 8 of that Schedule have effect in relation to the 2016–17 tax year and subsequent years.

167(3) Paragraph 9 of that Schedule comes into force on such day as the Treasury may appoint by regulations made by statutory instrument.

167(4) Regulations under subsection (3) may–

(a) commence paragraph 9 generally or only for specified purposes, and

(b) appoint different days for different purposes.

168 Time limit for self assessment tax returns

168(1) TMA 1970 is amended as follows.

168(2) [Inserts TMA 1970, s. 34(3).]

168(3) [Inserts TMA 1970, s. 34A.]

169 HMRC power to withdraw notice to file a tax return

169(1) Section 8B of TMA 1970 (withdrawal of notice under section 8 or 8A) is amended as follows.

169(2) [Amends TMA 1970, s. 8B(2).]

169(3) [Amends TMA 1970, s. 8B(3).]

169(4) [Amends TMA 1970, s. 8B(4).]

169(5) [Amends TMA 1970, s. 8B(6)(b).]

169(6) [Amends FA 2009, Sch. 55, para. 17A(1)(b).]

169(7) The amendments made by this section have effect in relation to any notice under section 8 or 8A of TMA 1970 given in relation to the 2014–15 tax year or any subsequent year (and it is immaterial whether the notice was given before or after the passing of this Act).

JUDGMENT DEBTS

170 Rate of interest applicable to judgment debts etc: Scotland

170(1) This section applies if–

(a) a sum is payable to or by the Commissioners under a decree or extract issued in any court proceedings relating to a taxation matter (a "tax-related judgment debt"), and

(b) interest in relation to the tax-related judgment debt is included in or payable under the decree or extract.

170(2) In a case where the rate of interest in relation to the tax-related judgment debt is stated in the decree or extract, the rate stated in relation to that debt may not exceed (and may not be capable of exceeding)–

(a) in the case of a sum payable to the Commissioners, the late payment interest rate, and

(b) in the case of a sum payable by the Commissioners, the special repayment rate.

170(3) In a case where the rate of interest in relation to the tax-related judgment debt is not stated in the decree or extract but provided for by an enactment or rule of court (whenever passed or made), that enactment or rule is to have effect in relation to the debt as if for the rate for which it provides there were substituted–

(a) in the case of a sum payable to the Commissioners, the late payment interest rate, and

(b) in the case of a sum payable by the Commissioners, the special repayment rate.

170(4) This section has effect in relation to interest for periods beginning on or after the day on which this Act is passed, regardless of–

(a) the date of the decree or extract in question, and

(b) whether interest begins to run on or after the day on which this Act is passed, or began to run before that date.

170(5) In this section–

"the Commissioners" means the Commissioners for Her Majesty's Revenue and Customs;

"enactment" includes an Act of the Scottish Parliament or an instrument made under such an Act;

"late payment interest rate" means the rate provided for in regulations made by the Treasury under section 103(1) of FA 2009;

"special repayment rate" has the same meaning as in section 52 of F(No. 2)A 2015 (and subsections (7) to (10) of that section apply for the purposes of this section as they apply for the purposes of that section);

"taxation matter" means anything the collection and management of which is the responsibility of the Commissioners (or was the responsibility of the Commissioners of Inland Revenue or Commissioners of Customs and Excise);

"working day" means any day other than a non-business day as defined in section 92 of the Bills of Exchange Act 1882.

170(6) This section extends to Scotland only.

171 Rate of interest applicable to judgment debts etc: Northern Ireland

171(1) This section applies if a sum payable to or by the Commissioners under a judgment or order given or made in any court proceedings relating to a taxation matter (a "tax-related judgment debt") carries interest.

171(2) In a case where the rate of interest is specified in the judgment (in the case of the High Court) or directed by the judge (in the case of a county court), the rate specified or directed in relation to that debt may not exceed (and may not be capable of exceeding)–

(a) in the case of a sum payable to the Commissioners, the late payment interest rate, and

(b) in the case of a sum payable by the Commissioners, the special repayment rate.

171(3) In a case where the rate of interest in relation to the tax-related judgment debt is not specified in the judgment or directed by the judge but provided for by an enactment or rule of court (whenever passed or made), that enactment or rule is to have effect in relation to the debt as if for the rate for which it provides there were substituted–

(a) in the case of a sum payable to the Commissioners, the late payment interest rate, and

(b) in the case of a sum payable by the Commissioners, the special repayment rate.

171(4) This section has effect in relation to interest for periods beginning on or after the day on which this Act is passed, regardless of–

(a) the date of the judgment or order in question, and

(b) whether interest begins to run on or after the day on which this Act is passed, or began to run before that date.

171(5) In this section–

"the Commissioners" means the Commissioners for Her Majesty's Revenue and Customs;

"enactment" includes Northern Ireland legislation or an instrument made under such legislation;

"late payment interest rate" means the rate provided for in regulations made by the Treasury under section 103(1) of FA 2009;

"special repayment rate" has the same meaning as in section 52 of F(No.2)A 2015 (and subsections (7) to (10) of that section apply for the purposes of this section as they apply for the purposes of that section);

"taxation matter" means anything the collection and management of which is the responsibility of the Commissioners (or was the responsibility of the Commissioners of Inland Revenue or Commissioners of Customs and Excise);

"working day" means any day other than a non-business day as defined in section 92 of the Bills of Exchange Act 1882.

171(6) This section extends to Northern Ireland only.

172 Rate of interest applicable to judgment debts etc: England and Wales

172(1) [Amends F(No. 2)A 2015, s. 52(15).]

172(2) This section has effect in relation to interest for periods beginning on or after the day on which this Act is passed, regardless of–

(a) the date of the judgment or order in question, and

(b) whether interest begins to run on or after the day on which this Act is passed, or began to run before that date.

172(3) This section extends to England and Wales only.

PART 13 – FINAL

190 Interpretation

190 In this Act–

"ALDA 1979" means the Alcoholic Liquor Duties Act 1979;

"CAA 2001" means the Capital Allowances Act 2001;

"CEMA 1979" means the Customs and Excise Management Act 1979;

"CTA 2009" means the Corporation Tax Act 2009;

"CTA 2010" means the Corporation Tax Act 2010;

"FA", followed by a year, means the Finance Act of that year;

"F(No. 2)A", followed by a year means the Finance (No. 2) Act of that year;

"F(No. 3)A", followed by a year, means the Finance (No. 3) Act of that year;

"HODA 1979" means the Hydrocarbon Oil Duties Act 1979;

"ICTA" means the Income and Corporation Taxes Act 1988;

"IHTA 1984" means the Inheritance Tax Act 1984;

"ITA 2007" means the Income Tax Act 2007;

"ITEPA 2003" means the Income Tax (Earnings and Pensions) Act 2003;

"ITTOIA 2005" means the Income Tax (Trading and Other Income) Act 2005;

"OTA 1975" means the Oil Taxation Act 1975;

"TCGA 1992" means the Taxation of Chargeable Gains Act 1992;

"TIOPA 2010" means the Taxation (International and Other Provisions) Act 2010;

"TMA 1970" means the Taxes Management Act 1970;

"TPDA 1979" means the Tobacco Products Duty Act 1979;

"VATA 1994" means the Value Added Tax Act 1994;

"VERA 1994" means the Vehicle Excise and Registration Act 1994.

191 Short title

191 This Act may be cited as the Finance Act 2016.

SCHEDULES

SCHEDULE 1 – ABOLITION OF DIVIDEND TAX CREDITS ETC

Section 5

OTHER AMENDMENTS

51(1) TMA 1970 is amended as follows.

51(2) [Amends TMA 1970, s. 8(1AA)(b).]

51(3) [Not relevant to National Insurance contributions.]

51(4) In section 9(1) (self-assessment)–

(a) [amends TMA 1970, s. 9(1)(b),]

(b) [amends TMA 1970, s. 9(1).]

51(5) [Not relevant to National Insurance contributions.]

51(6) [Not relevant to National Insurance contributions.]

51(7) [Amends TMA 1970, s. 12B(4A)(a)(i).]

51(8) [Amends TMA 1970, s. 59A(8)(b).]

51(9) In section 59B (payment of income tax and capital gains tax)–

(a) [amends TMA 1970, s. 59B(1),]

(b) [amends TMA 1970, s. 59B(2)(b).]

51(10) [Omits TMA 1970, s. 87A(5).]

51(11) [Amends table in TMA 1970, s. 98.]

COMMENCEMENT

73(1) Subject to the following sub-paragraphs of this paragraph, the amendments made by this Schedule have effect in relation to dividends paid or arising (or treated as paid), and other distributions made (or treated as made), in the tax year 2016–17 or at any later time.

73(2) The following have effect for the tax year 2016–17 and subsequent tax years–

(a) the amendments in sections 8 to 9, 12AA and 59B of TMA 1970,

(b) the amendments in section 854(6) of ITTOIA 2005,

(c) the amendments in section 425 except the amendment in section 425(5)(b), and the amendments in section 498, 745 and 1026 of ITA 2007,

(d) the repeals of paragraphs 359, 360, 361(a), 363 and 377(3) of Schedule 1 to ITTOIA 2005,

(e) the repeals of paragraphs 8 to 11 and 14 of Schedule 12 to FA 2008, and

(f) the repeals of the following provisions of Schedule 19 to FA 2009–

(i) paragraph 9(a) and (b),

(ii) paragraph 9(c) so far as relating to section 12AA of TMA 1970, and

(iii) paragraph 9(d) so far as relating to section 59B of TMA 1970.

73(3) The amendment in paragraph 23 of Schedule 6 to F(No. 2)A 1997 has effect in relation to foreign income dividends received on or after 6 April 2016.

73(4) The amendments in sections 393 and 406 of ITTOIA 2005, and the repeal of paragraph 19 of Schedule 12 to FA 2008, have effect in relation to cash dividends paid over in the tax year 2016–17 or at any later time.

73(5) The amendment in section 396A of ITTOIA 2005 has effect in relation to things received on or after 6 April 2016 (even if the choice to receive them was made before that date).

73(6) The amendments in section 401 of ITTOIA 2005 have effect where the subsequent distribution is made in the tax year 2016–17 or at any later time, even if the prior distribution is made before 6 April 2016.

73(7) The amendments in sections 411 and 414 of ITTOIA 2005, and the repeal of paragraph 520 of Schedule 1 to ITA 2007, have effect in relation to stock dividend income treated as arising in the tax year 2016–17 or at any later time.

73(8) The amendments in sections 651 to 680A of ITTOIA 2005 (but not the repeal of section 680(3)(a) of that Act) and the amendment in section 425(5)(b) of ITA 2007–

(a) so far as they relate to income within section 664(2)(c) of ITTOIA 2005 (stock dividends), have effect in relation to stock dividend income treated as arising in the tax year 2016–17 or at any later time, and

(b) so far as they relate to income within section 664(2)(d) of ITTOIA 2005 (release of loans), have effect in relation to amounts released or written off in the tax year 2016–17 or at any later time.

73(9) The amendments in Chapter 6 of Part 4 of ITTOIA 2005 and in section 463 of CTA 2010, and the repeal of paragraph 522 of Schedule 1 to ITA 2007, have effect in relation to amounts released or written off in the tax year 2016–17 or at any later time.

73(10) The amendments in section 614ZD of ITA 2007 have effect in relation to manufactured payments made on or after 6 April 2016.

73(11) The amendments in section 687 of ITA 2007 have effect where the relevant consideration is received in the tax year 2016–17 or at any later time.

73(12) The amendments in section 1222 of CTA 2009 have effect in relation to income arising in the tax year 2016–17 or at any later time.

73(13) The amendment in section 1026(1) of CTA 2010 has effect where the bonus share capital is issued *on or after 6 April 2016.*

73(14) Sub-paragraph (1) does not apply in relation to–

(a) the amendments in section 401B of ITTOIA 2005;

(b) the amendment in paragraph 14 of Schedule 19 to FA 2009.

SCHEDULE 4 – PENSIONS: LIFETIME ALLOWANCE: TRANSITIONAL PROVISION

Section 19

Part 3 – Reference Numbers Etc

PENALTIES FOR NON-SUPPLY, OR FRAUDULENT ETC SUPPLY, OF INFORMATION UNDER PARAGRAPH 17 OR 18

20 [Amends table in TMA 1970, s. 98.]

SCHEDULE 18 – SERIAL TAX AVOIDANCE

Section 159

Part 1 – Contents of Schedule

1 In this Schedule–

(a) Part 2 provides for HMRC to give warning notices to persons who incur relevant defeats and includes–

(i) provision about the duration of warning periods under warning notices (see paragraph 3), and

(ii) definitions of "relevant defeat" and other key terms;

(b) Part 3 contains provisions about persons to whom a warning notice has been given, and in particular–

(i) imposes a duty to give information notices, and

(ii) allows the Commissioners to publish information about such persons in certain cases involving repeated relevant defeats;

(c) Part 4 contains provision about the restriction of reliefs;

(d) Part 5 imposes liability to penalties on persons who incur relevant defeats in relation to arrangements used in warning periods;

(e) Part 6 contains provisions about corporate groups, associated persons and partnerships;

(f) Part 7 contains definitions and other supplementary provisions.

Part 2 – Entry into the Regime and Basic Concepts

DUTY TO GIVE WARNING NOTICE

2(1) This paragraph applies where a person incurs a relevant defeat in relation to any arrangements.

2(2) HMRC must give the person a written notice (a "warning notice").

2(3) The notice must be given within the period of 90 days beginning with the day on which the relevant defeat is incurred.

2(4) The notice must–

(a) set out when the warning period begins and ends (see paragraph 3),

(b) specify the relevant defeat to which the notice relates, and

(c) explain the effect of paragraphs 3 and 17 to 46.

2(5) A warning notice given by virtue of paragraph 49 must also explain the effect of paragraph 51 (information in certain cases involving partnerships).

2(6) In this Schedule **"arrangements"** includes any agreement, understanding, scheme, transaction or series of transactions (whether or not legally enforceable).

2(7) For the meaning of "relevant defeat" and provision about when a relevant defeat is incurred see paragraph 11.

WARNING PERIOD

3(1) If a person is given a warning notice with respect to a relevant defeat (and sub-paragraph (2) does not apply) the period of 5 years beginning with the day after the day on which the notice is given is a **"warning period"** in relation to that person.

3(2) If a person incurs a relevant defeat in relation to arrangements during a period which is a warning period in relation to that person, the warning period is extended to the end of the 5 years beginning with the day after the day on which the relevant defeat occurs.

3(3) In relation to a warning period which has been extended under this Schedule, references in this Schedule (including this paragraph) to the warning period are to be read as references to the warning period as extended.

MEANING OF "TAX"

4(1) In this Schedule **"tax"** includes any of the following taxes–

(a) income tax,

(b) corporation tax, including any amount chargeable as if it were corporation tax or treated as if it were corporation tax,

(c) capital gains tax,

(d) petroleum revenue tax,

(e) diverted profits tax,

(f) apprenticeship levy,

(g) inheritance tax,

(h) stamp duty land tax,

(i) annual tax on enveloped dwellings,

(j) VAT and other indirect taxes, and

(k) national insurance contributions.

4(2) [Not relevant to National Insurance contributions.]

History – Para. 4(1) created from existing text (with the insertion of the words "and other indirect taxes") by F(No. 2)A 2017, s. 66 and Sch. 17, para. 55(2) with effect so far as is necessary for enabling the making of regulations under that Schedule on 16 November 2017 (Royal Assent) and on 1 January 2018 for all other purposes.

Para. 4(2) inserted by F(No. 2)A 2017, s. 66 and Sch. 17, para. 55(2) with effect so far as is necessary for enabling the making of regulations under that Schedule on 16 November 2017 (Royal Assent) and on 1 January 2018 for all other purposes.

MEANING OF "TAX ADVANTAGE" IN RELATION TO VAT

5 [Not relevant to National Insurance contributions.]

MEANING OF "NON-DEDUCTIBLE TAX"

6 [Not relevant to National Insurance contributions.]

"TAX ADVANTAGE": OTHER TAXES

7 In relation to taxes other than VAT, **"tax advantage"** includes–

(a) relief or increased relief from tax,

(b) repayment or increased repayment of tax,

(c) receipt, or advancement of a receipt, of a tax credit,

(d) avoidance or reduction of a charge to tax, an assessment of tax or a liability to pay tax,

(e) avoidance of a possible assessment to tax or liability to pay tax,

(f) deferral of a payment of tax or advancement of a repayment of tax, and

(g) avoidance of an obligation to deduct or account for tax.

"DOTAS ARRANGEMENTS"

8(1) For the purposes of this Schedule arrangements are **"DOTAS arrangements"** at any time if they are notifiable arrangements at the time in question and a person–

(a) has provided information in relation to the arrangements under section 308(3), 309 or 310 of FA 2004, or

(b) has failed to comply with any of those provisions in relation to the arrangements.

8(2) But for the purposes of this Schedule **"DOTAS arrangements"** does not include arrangements in respect of which HMRC has given notice under section 312(6) of FA 2004 (notice that promoters not under duty to notify client of reference number).

8(3) For the purposes of sub-paragraph (1) a person who would be required to provide information under subsection (3) of section 308 of FA 2004–

(a) but for the fact that the arrangements implement a proposal in respect of which notice has been given under subsection (1) of that section, or

(b) but for subsection (4A), (4C) or (5) of that section,

is treated as providing the information at the end of the period referred to in subsection (3) of that section.

8(4) In this paragraph **"notifiable arrangements"** has the same meaning as in Part 7 of FA 2004.

"DISCLOSABLE SCHEDULE 11A VAT ARRANGEMENTS"

History – In the heading the words "SCHEDULE 11A" inserted by F(No. 2)A 2017, s. 66 and Sch. 17, para. 55(4) with effect so far as is necessary for enabling the making of regulations under that Schedule on 16 November 2017 (Royal Assent) and on 1 January 2018 for all other purposes.

8A [Not relevant to National Insurance contributions.]

History – Para. 8A inserted by F(No. 2)A 2017, s. 66 and Sch. 17, para. 55(3) with effect so far as is necessary for enabling the making of regulations under that Schedule on 16 November 2017 (Royal Assent) and on 1 January 2018 for all other purposes.

9 [Not relevant to National Insurance contributions.]

DISCLOSABLE INDIRECT TAX ARRANGEMENTS

9A [Not relevant to National Insurance contributions.]

History – Para. 9A inserted by F(No. 2)A 2017, s. 66 and Sch. 17, para. 55(6) with effect so far as is necessary for enabling the making of regulations under that Schedule on 16 November 2017 (Royal Assent) and on 1 January 2018 for all other purposes.

PARAGRAPHS 8 TO 9A: "FAILURE TO COMPLY"

History – In the heading the words "TO 9A" substituted for the words "AND 9" by F(No. 2)A 2017, s. 66 and Sch. 17, para. 55(7) with effect so far as is necessary for enabling the making of regulations under that Schedule on 16 November 2017 (Royal Assent) and on 1 January 2018 for all other purposes.

10(1) A person **"fails to comply"** with any provision mentioned in paragraph 8(1), 8A(2)(c), 9(a) or 9A(1)(c) if and only if any of the conditions in sub-paragraphs (2) to (4) is met.

10(2) The condition in this sub-paragraph is that–

(a) the tribunal has determined that the person has failed to comply with the provision concerned,

(b) the appeal period has ended, and

(c) the determination has not been overturned on appeal.

10(3) The condition in this sub-paragraph is that–

(a) the tribunal has determined for the purposes of section 118(2) of TMA 1970 that the person is to be deemed not to have failed to comply with the provision concerned as the person had a reasonable excuse for not doing the thing required to be done,

(b) the appeal period has ended, and

(c) the determination has not been overturned on appeal.

10(4) The condition in this sub-paragraph is that the person admitted in writing to HMRC that the person has failed to comply with the provision concerned.

10(5) In this paragraph **"the appeal period"** means–

(a) the period during which an appeal could be brought against the determination of the tribunal, or

(b) where an appeal mentioned in paragraph (a) has been brought, the period during which that appeal has not been finally determined, withdrawn or otherwise disposed of.

10(6) In this paragraph **"the tribunal"** means the First-tier tribunal or, where determined by or under Tribunal Procedure Rules, the Upper Tribunal.

History – In para. 10(1) the words ", 8A(2)(c), 9(a) or 9A(1)(c)" substituted for the words "or 9(a)" by F(No. 2)A 2017, s. 66 and Sch. 17, para. 55(8) with effect so far as is necessary for enabling the making of regulations under that Schedule on 16 November 2017 (Royal Assent) and on 1 January 2018 for all other purposes.

"RELEVANT DEFEAT"

11(1) A person ("P") incurs a **"relevant defeat"** in relation to arrangements if any of Conditions A to F is met in relation to P and the arrangements.

11(2) The relevant defeat is incurred when the condition in question is first met.

History – In para. 11(1) "F" substituted for "E" by F(No. 2)A 2017, s. 66 and Sch. 17, para. 55(9) with effect so far as is necessary for enabling the making of regulations under that Schedule on 16 November 2017 (Royal Assent) and on 1 January 2018 for all other purposes.

CONDITION A

12(1) Condition A is that–

(a) P has been given a notice under paragraph 12 of Schedule 43 to FA 2013 (general anti-abuse rule: notice of final decision), paragraph 8 or 9 of Schedule 43A to that Act (pooled arrangements: notice of final decision) or paragraph 8 of Schedule 43B to that Act (generic referrals: notice of final decision)stating that a tax advantage arising from the arrangements is to be counteracted,

(b) that tax advantage has been counteracted under section 209 of FA 2013, and

(c) the counteraction is final.

12(2) For the purposes of this paragraph the counteraction of a tax advantage is **"final"** when the adjustments made to effect the counteraction, and any amounts arising as a result of those adjustments, can no longer be varied, on appeal or otherwise.

CONDITION B

13(1) Condition B is that (in a case not falling within Condition A above) a follower notice has been given to P by reference to the arrangements (and not withdrawn) and–

(a) the necessary corrective action for the purposes of section 208 of FA 2014 has been taken in respect of the denied advantage, or

(b) the denied advantage has been counteracted otherwise than as mentioned in paragraph (a) and the counteraction of the denied advantage is final.

13(2) In sub-paragraph (1) the reference to giving a follower notice to P includes a reference to giving a partnership follower notice in respect of a partnership return in relation to which P is a relevant partner (as defined in paragraph 2(5) of Schedule 31 to FA 2014).

13(3) For the purposes of this paragraph it does not matter whether the denied advantage has been dealt with–

(a) wholly as mentioned in one or other of paragraphs (a) and (b) of sub-paragraph (1), or

(b) partly as mentioned in one and partly as mentioned in the other of those paragraphs.

13(4) In this paragraph **"the denied advantage"** has the same meaning as in Chapter 2 of Part 4 of FA 2014 (see section 208(3) of and paragraph 4(3) of Schedule 31 to that Act).

13(5) For the purposes of this paragraph the counteraction of a tax advantage is **"final"** when the adjustments made to effect the counteraction, and any amounts arising as a result of those adjustments, can no longer be varied, on appeal or otherwise.

13(6) In this Schedule **"follower notice"** means a follower notice under Chapter 2 of Part 4 of FA 2014.

13(7) For the purposes of this paragraph a partnership follower notice is given "in respect of" the partnership return mentioned in paragraph (a) or (b) of paragraph 2(2) of Schedule 31 to FA 2014.

CONDITION C

14(1) Condition C is that (in a case not falling within Condition A or B)–

(a) the arrangements are DOTAS arrangements,

(b) P has relied on the arrangements (see sub-paragraph (2))–

(c) the arrangements have been counteracted, and

(d) the counteraction is final.

14(2) For the purposes of sub-paragraph (1), P **"relies on the arrangements"** if–

(a) P makes a return, claim or election, or a partnership return is made, on the basis that a relevant tax advantage arises, or

(b) P fails to discharge a relevant obligation ("the disputed obligation") and there is reason to believe that P's failure to discharge that obligation is connected with the arrangements.

14(3) For the purposes of sub-paragraph (2) **"relevant tax advantage"** means a tax advantage which the arrangements might be expected to enable P to obtain.

14(4) For the purposes of sub-paragraph (2) an obligation is a **"relevant obligation"** if the arrangements might be expected to have the result that the obligation does not arise.

14(5) For the purposes of this paragraph the arrangements are **"counteracted"** if–

(a) adjustments, other than taxpayer emendations, are made in respect of P's tax position–

(i) on the basis that the whole or part of the relevant tax advantage mentioned in sub-paragraph (2)(a) does not arise, or

(ii) on the basis that the disputed obligation does (or did) arise, or

(b) an assessment to tax other than a self-assessment is made, or any other action is taken by HMRC, on the basis mentioned in paragraph (a)(i) or (ii) (otherwise than by way of an adjustment).

14(6) For the purposes of this paragraph a counteraction is **"final"** when the assessment, adjustments or action in question, and any amounts arising from the assessment, adjustments or action, can no longer be varied, on appeal or otherwise.

14(7) For the purposes of sub-paragraph (1) the time at which it falls to be determined whether or not the arrangements are DOTAS arrangements is when the counteraction becomes final.

14(8) The following are **"taxpayer emendations"** for the purposes of sub-paragraph (5)–

(a) an adjustment made by P at a time when P had no reason to believe that HMRC had begun or were about to begin enquiries into P's affairs relating to the tax in question;

(b) an adjustment (by way of an assessment or otherwise) made by HMRC with respect to P's tax position as a result of a disclosure made by P which meets the conditions in sub-paragraph (9).

For the purposes of paragraph (a) a payment in respect of a liability to pay national insurance contributions is not an adjustment unless it is a payment in full.

14(9) The conditions are that the disclosure–

(a) is a full and explicit disclosure of an inaccuracy in a return or other document or of a failure to comply with an obligation, and

(b) was made at a time when P had no reason to believe that HMRC were about to begin enquiries into P's affairs relating to the tax in question.

14(10) For the purposes of this paragraph a contract settlement which HMRC enters into with P is treated as an assessment to tax (other than a self-assessment); and in relation to contract settlements references in sub-paragraph (5) to the basis an which any assessment or adjustments are made, or any other action is taken, are to be read with any necessary modifications.

CONDITION D

15 [Not relevant to National Insurance contributions.]

CONDITION E

16 [Not relevant to National Insurance contributions.]

CONDITION F

16A [Not relevant to National Insurance contributions.]

History – Para. 16A inserted by F(No. 2)A 2017, s. 66 and Sch. 17, para. 55(10) with effect so far as is necessary for enabling the making of regulations under that Schedule on 16 November 2017 (Royal Assent) and on 1 January 2018 for all other purposes.

Part 3 – Annual Information Notices and Naming

ANNUAL INFORMATION NOTICES

17(1) A person ("P") who has been given a warning notice under this Schedule must give HMRC a written notice (an "information notice") in respect of each reporting period in the warning period (see sub-paragraph (11)).

17(2) An information notice must be given not later than the 30th day after the end of the reporting period to which it relates.

17(3) An information notice must state whether or not P–

(a) has in the reporting period delivered a return, or made a claim, election, declaration or application for approval, on the basis that a relevant tax advantage arises, or has since the end of the reporting period delivered on that basis a return which P was required to deliver before the end of that period,

(b) has in the reporting period failed to take action which P would be required to take under or by virtue of an enactment relating to tax but for particular disclosable arrangements to which P is a party,

(c) has in the reporting period become a party to arrangements which–

(i) relate to the position with respect to VAT of another person ("S") who has made supplies of goods or services to P, and

(ii) might be expected to enable P to obtain a relevant tax advantage ("the expected tax advantage") in connection with those supplies of goods or services,

(d) has failed to deliver a return which P was required to deliver by a date falling in the reporting period.

17(4) In this paragraph **"relevant tax advantage"** means a tax advantage which particular disclosable arrangements enable, or might be expected to enable, P to obtain.

17(5) If P has, in the reporting period concerned, made a return, claim, election, declaration or application for approval on the basis mentioned in sub-paragraph (3)(a) or failed to take action as mentioned in sub-paragraph (3)(b) the information notice must–

(a) explain (on the assumptions made by P in so acting or failing to act) how the disclosable arrangements enable P to obtain the tax advantage, or (as the case may be) have the result that P is not required to take the action in question, and

(b) state (on the same assumptions) the amount of the relevant tax advantage mentioned in sub-paragraph (3)(a) or (as the case may be) the amount of any tax advantage which arises in connection with the absence of a requirement to take the action mentioned in sub-paragraph (3)(b).

17(6) If P has, in the reporting period, become a party to arrangements such as are mentioned in sub-paragraph (3)(c), the information notice–

(a) must state whether or not it is P's view that the expected tax advantage arises to P, and

(b) if that is P's view, must explain how the arrangements enable P to obtain the tax advantage and state the amount of the tax advantage.

17(7) If the time by which P must deliver a return falls within a reporting period and P fails to deliver the return by that time, HMRC may require P to give HMRC a written notice (a "supplementary information notice") setting out any matters which P would have been required to set out in an information notice had P delivered the return in that reporting period.

17(8) A requirement under sub-paragraph (7) must be made by a written notice which states the period within which P must comply with the notice.

17(9) If P fails to comply with a requirement of (or imposed under) this paragraph HMRC may by written notice extend the warning period to the end of the period of 5 years beginning with–

(a) the day by which the information notice or supplementary information notice should have been given (see sub-paragraphs (2) and (8)) or, as the case requires,

(b) the day on which P gave the defective information notice or supplementary information notice to HMRC,

or, if earlier, the time when the warning period would have expired but for the extension.

17(10) HMRC may permit information notices given by members of the same group of companies (as defined in paragraph 46(9)) to be combined.

17(11) For the purposes of this paragraph–

(a) the first reporting period in any warning period begins with the first day of the warning period and ends with a day specified by HMRC ("the specified day"),

(b) the remainder of the warning period is divided into further reporting periods each of which begins immediately after the end of the preceding reporting period and is twelve months long or (if that would be shorter) ends at the end of the warning period.

17(12) In this paragraph **"disclosable arrangements"** means any of the following–

(a) DOTAS arrangements,

(b) disclosable VAT arrangements, and

(c) disclosable indirect tax arrangements.

History – In para. 17(3)(a) the words ", election, declaration or application for approval," (initial comma assumed by Croner-i) substituted for the words "or election," by F(No. 2)A 2017, s. 66 and Sch. 17, para. 55(11)(a) with effect so far as is necessary for enabling the making of regulations under that Schedule on 16 November 2017 (Royal Assent) and on 1 January 2018 for all other purposes.

In para. 17(3)(b) the words "disclosable" (initial comma assumed by Croner-i) substituted for the words "DOTAS arrangements or [disclosable] VAT" by F(No. 2)A 2017, s. 66 and Sch. 17, para. 55(11)(b) with effect so far as is necessary for enabling the making of regulations under that Schedule on 16 November 2017 (Royal Assent) and on 1 January 2018 for all other purposes.

In para. 17(4) the words "disclosable" (initial comma assumed by Croner-i) substituted for the words "DOTAS arrangements or [disclosable] VAT" by F(No. 2)A 2017, s. 66 and Sch. 17, para. 55(11)(b) with effect so far as is necessary for enabling the making of regulations under that Schedule on 16 November 2017 (Royal Assent) and on 1 January 2018 for all other purposes.

In para. 17(5)(a) the words "disclosable" (initial comma assumed by Croner-i) substituted for the words "DOTAS arrangements or [disclosable] VAT" by F(No. 2)A 2017, s. 66 and Sch. 17, para. 55(11)(b) with effect so far as is necessary for enabling the making of regulations under that Schedule on 16 November 2017 (Royal Assent) and on 1 January 2018 for all other purposes.

In para. 17(5) the words ", election, declaration or application for approval" (initial comma assumed by Croner-i) substituted for the words "or election" by F(No. 2)A 2017, s. 66 and Sch. 17, para. 55(11)(c) with effect so far as is necessary for enabling the making of regulations under that Schedule on 16 November 2017 (Royal Assent) and on 1 January 2018 for all other purposes.

Para. 17(12) inserted by F(No. 2)A 2017, s. 66 and Sch. 17, para. 55(11)(d) with effect so far as is necessary for enabling the making of regulations under that Schedule on 16 November 2017 (Royal Assent) and on 1 January 2018 for all other purposes.

NAMING

18(1) The Commissioners may publish information about a person if the person–

(a) incurs a relevant defeat in relation to arrangements which the person has used in a warning period, and

(b) has been given at least two warning notices in respect of other defeats of arrangements which were used in the same warning period.

18(2) Information published for the first time under sub-paragraph (1) must be published within the 12 months beginning with the day on which the most recent of the warning notices falling within that sub-paragraph has been given to the person.

18(3) No information may be published (or continue to be published) after the end of the period of 12 months beginning with the day on which it is first published.

18(4) The information that may be published is–

(a) the person's name (including any trading name, previous name or pseudonym),

(b) the person's address (or registered office),

(c) the nature of any business carried on by the person,

(d) information about the fiscal effect of the defeated arrangements (had they not been defeated), for instance information about total amounts of tax understated or total amounts by which claims, or statements of losses, have been adjusted,

(e) the amount of any penalty to which the person is liable under paragraph 30 in respect of the relevant defeat of any defeated arrangements,

(f) the periods in which or times when the defeated arrangements were used, and

(g) any other information the Commissioners may consider it appropriate to publish in order to make clear the person's identity.

18(5) If the person mentioned in sub-paragraph (1) is a member of a group of companies (as defined in paragraph 46(9)), the information which may be published also includes–

(a) any trading name of the group, and

(b) information about other members of the group of the kind described in sub-paragraph (4)(a), (b) or (c).

18(6) If the person mentioned in sub-paragraph (1) is a person carrying on a trade or business in partnership, the information which may be published also includes–

(a) any trading name of the partnership, and

(b) information about other members of the partnership of the kind described in sub-paragraph (4)(a) or (b).

18(7) The information may be published in any manner the Commissioners may consider appropriate.

18(8) Before publishing any information the Commissioners–

(a) must inform the person that they are considering doing so, and

(b) afford the person reasonable opportunity to make representations about whether or not it should be published.

18(9) Arrangements are **"defeated arrangements"** for the purposes of sub-paragraph (4) if the person used them in the warning period mentioned in sub-paragraph (1) and a warning notice specifying the defeat of those arrangements has been given to the person before the information is published.

18(10) If a person has been given a single warning notice in relation to two or more relevant defeats, the person is treated for the purposes of this paragraph as having been given a separate warning notice in relation to each of those relevant defeats.

18(11) Nothing in this paragraph prevents the power under sub-paragraph (1) from being exercised on a subsequent occasion in relation to arrangements used by the person in a different warning period.

Part 4 – Restriction of Reliefs

DUTY TO GIVE A RESTRICTION RELIEF NOTICE

19(1) HMRC must give a person a written notice (a "restriction of relief notice") if–

(a) the person incurs a relevant defeat in relation to arrangements which the person has used in a warning period,

(b) the person has been given at least two warning notices in respect of other relevant defeats of arrangements which were used in that same warning period, and

(c) the defeats mentioned in paragraphs (a) and (b) meet the conditions in sub-paragraph (2).

19(2) The conditions are–

(a) that each of the relevant defeats is by virtue of Condition A, B or C,

(b) that each of the relevant defeats relates to the misuse of a relief (see sub-paragraph (5)), and

(c) in the case of each of the relevant defeats, either–

(i) that the relevant counteraction (see sub-paragraph (7)) was made on the basis that a particular avoidance-related rule applies in relation to a person's affairs, or

(ii) that the misused relief is a loss relief.

19(3) In sub-paragraph (2)(c)–

(a) the **"misused relief"** means the relief mentioned in sub-paragraph (5), and

(b) **"loss relief"** means any relief under Part 4 of ITA 2007 or Part 4 or 5 of CTA 2010.

19(4) A restriction of relief notice must–

(a) explain the effect of paragraphs 20, 21 and 22, and

(b) set out when the restricted period is to begin and end.

19(5) For the purposes of this Part of this Schedule, a relevant defeat by virtue of Condition A, B or C **"relates to the misuse of a relief"** if–

(a) the tax advantage in question, or part of the tax advantage in question, is or results from (or would but for the counteraction be or result from) a relief or increased relief from tax, or

(b) it is reasonable to conclude that the making of a particular claim for relief, or the use of a particular relief, is a significant component of the arrangements in question.

19(6) In sub-paragraph (5) **"the tax advantage in question"** means–

(a) in relation to a defeat by virtue of Condition A, the tax advantage mentioned in paragraph 12(1)(a),

(b) in relation to a defeat by virtue of Condition B, the denied advantage (as defined in paragraph 13(4)), or

(c) in relation to a defeat by virtue of Condition C–

(i) the tax advantage mentioned in paragraph 14(2)(a), or, as the case requires,

(ii) the absence of the relevant obligation (as defined in paragraph 14(4)).

19(7) In this paragraph **"the relevant counteraction"**, in relation to a relevant defeat means–

(a) in the case of a defeat by virtue of Condition A, the counteraction referred to in paragraph 12(1)(c);

(b) in the case of a defeat by virtue of Condition B, the action referred to in paragraph 13(1);

(c) in the case of a defeat by virtue of Condition C, the counteraction referred to in paragraph 14(1)(d).

19(8) If a person has been given a single warning notice in relation to two or more relevant defeats, the person is treated for the purposes of this paragraph as having been given a separate warning notice in relation to each of those relevant defeats.

RESTRICTION OF RELIEF

20(1) Sub-paragraphs (2) to (15) have effect in relation to a person to whom a relief restriction notice has been given.

20(2) The person may not, in the restricted period, make any claim for relief.

20(3) Sub-paragraph (2) does not have effect in relation to–

(a) a claim for relief under Schedule 8 to FA 2003 (stamp duty land tax: charities relief);

(b) a claim for relief under Chapter 3 of Part 8 of ITA 2007 (gifts of shares, securities and real property to charities etc);

(c) a claim for relief under Part 10 of ITA 2007 (special rules about charitable trusts etc);

(d) a claim for relief under double taxation arrangements;

(e) an election under section 426 of ITA 2007 (gift aid: election to treat gift as made in previous year).

20(4) Claims under the following provisions in Part 4 of FA 2004 (registered pension schemes: tax reliefs etc) do not count as claims for relief for the purposes of this paragraph–

section 192(4) (increase of basic rate limit and higher rate limit);

section 193(4) (net pay arrangements: excess relief);

section 194(1) (relief on making of a claim).

20(5) The person may not, in the restricted period, surrender group relief under Part 5 of CTA 2010.

20(6) No deduction is to be made under section 83 of ITA 2007 (carry forward against subsequent trade profits) in calculating the person's net income for a relevant tax year.

20(7) No deduction is to be made under section 118 of ITA 2007 (carry-forward property loss relief) in calculating the person's net income for a relevant tax year.

20(8) The person is not entitled to relief under section 448 (annual payments: relief for individuals) or 449 (annual payments: relief for other persons) of ITA 2007 for any payment made in the restricted period.

20(9) No deduction of expenses referable to a relevant accounting period is to be made under section 1219(1) of CTA 2009 (expenses of management of a company's investment business).

20(10) No reduction is to be made under section 45(4) of CTA 2010 (carry-forward of trade loss relief) in calculating the profits for a relevant accounting period of a trade carried on by the person.

20(11) In calculating the total amount of chargeable gains accruing to a person in a relevant tax year (or part of a relevant tax year), no losses are to be deducted under subsections (2) to (2B) of section 2 of TCGA 1992 (persons and gains chargeable to capital gains tax, and allowable losses).

20(12) In calculating the total amount of ATED-related chargeable gains accruing to a person in a relevant tax year, no losses are to be deducted under subsection (3) of section 2B of TCGA 1992 (persons chargeable to capital gains tax on ATED-related gains).

20(13) In calculating the total amount of chargeable NRCGT gains accruing to a person in a relevant tax year on relevant high value disposals, no losses are to be deducted under subsection (2) of section 14D of TCGA 1992 (persons chargeable to capital gains tax on NRCGT gains).

20(14) If the person is a company, no deduction is to be made under section 62 of CTA 2010 (relief for losses made in UK property business) from the company's total profits of a relevant accounting period.

20(15) No deduction is to be made under regulation 18 of the Unauthorised Unit Trusts (Tax) Regulations 2013 (S.I. 2013/2819) (relief for deemed payments by trustees of an exempt unauthorised unit trust) in calculating the person's net income for a relevant tax year.

20(16) In this paragraph **"relevant tax year"** means any tax year the first day of which is in the restricted period.

20(17) In this paragraph **"relevant accounting period"** means an accounting period the first day of which is in the restricted period.

20(18) In this paragraph **"double taxation arrangements"** means arrangements which have effect under section 2(1) of TIOPA 2010 (double taxation relief by agreement with territories outside the UK).

THE RESTRICTED PERIOD

21(1) In paragraphs 19 and 20 (and this paragraph) **"the restricted period"** means the period of 3 years beginning with the day on which the relief restriction notice is given.

21(2) If during the restricted period (or the restricted period as extended under this sub-paragraph) the person to whom a relief restriction notice has been given incurs a further relevant defeat meeting the conditions in sub-paragraph (4), HMRC must give the person a written notice (a "restricted period extension notice").

21(3) A restricted period extension notice extends the restricted period to the end of the period of 3 years beginning with the day on which the further relevant defeat occurs.

21(4) The conditions mentioned in sub-paragraph (2) are that–

(a) the relevant defeat is incurred by virtue of Condition A, B or C in relation to arrangements which the person used in the warning period mentioned in paragraph 19(1)(a), and

(b) the warning notice given to the person in respect of the relevant defeat relates to the misuse of a relief.

21(5) If the person to whom a relief restriction notice has been given incurs a relevant defeat which meets the conditions in sub-paragraph (4) after the restricted period has expired but before the end of a concurrent warning period, HMRC must give the person a restriction of relief notice.

21(6) In sub-paragraph (5) **"concurrent warning period"** means a warning period which at some time ran concurrently with the restricted period.

REASONABLE EXCUSE

22(1) If a person who has incurred a relevant defeat satisfies HMRC or, on an appeal under paragraph 24, the First-tier Tribunal or Upper Tribunal that the person had a reasonable excuse for the matters to which that relevant defeat relates, then–

(a) for the purposes of paragraph 19(1)(a) and 21(2) and (5), the person is treated as not having incurred that relevant defeat, and

(b) for the purposes of paragraph 19(1)(b) and (c) any warning notice given to the person which relates to that relevant defeat is treated as not having been given to the person.

22(2) For the purposes of this paragraph, in the case of a person ("P")–

(a) an insufficiency of funds is not a reasonable excuse unless attributable to events outside P's control,

(b) where P relies on another person to do anything, that is not a reasonable excuse unless P took reasonable care to avoid the relevant failure, and

(c) where P had reasonable excuse for the relevant failure but the excuse had ceased, P is to be treated as having continued to have the excuse if the failure is remedied without unreasonable delay after the excuse ceased.

22(3) In determining for the purposes of this paragraph whether or not a person ("P") had a reasonable excuse for any action, failure or inaccuracy, reliance on advice is to be taken automatically not to constitute a reasonable excuse if the advice is addressed to, or was given to, a person other than P or takes no account of P's individual circumstances.

22(4) In this paragraph **"relevant failure"**, in relation to a relevant defeat, is to be interpreted in accordance with sub-paragraphs (2) to (7) of paragraph 43.

MITIGATION OF RESTRICTION OF RELIEF

23(1) The Commissioners may mitigate the effects of paragraph 20 in relation to a person ("P") so far as it appears to them that there are exceptional circumstances such that the operation of that paragraph would otherwise have an unduly serious impact with respect to the tax affairs of P or another person.

23(2) For the purposes of sub-paragraph (1) the Commissioners may modify the effects of paragraph 20 in any way they think appropriate, including by allowing P access to the whole or part of a relief to which P would otherwise not be entitled as a result of paragraph 20.

APPEAL

24(1) A person may appeal against–

(a) a relief restriction notice, or

(b) a restricted period extension notice.

24(2) An appeal under this paragraph must be made within the period of 30 days beginning with the day on which the notice is given.

24(3) An appeal under this paragraph is to be treated in the same way as an appeal against an assessment to income tax (including by the application of any provision about bringing the appeal by notice to HMRC, about HMRC's review of the decision or about determination of the appeal by the First-tier Tribunal or Upper Tribunal).

24(4) On an appeal the tribunal may–

(a) cancel HMRC's decision, or

(b) affirm that decision with or without any modifications in accordance with sub-paragraph (5).

24(5) On an appeal the tribunal may rely on paragraph 23 (mitigation of restriction of relief)–

(a) to the same extent as HMRC (which may mean applying the same mitigation as HMRC to a different starting point), or

(b) to a different extent, but only if the tribunal thinks that HMRC's decision in respect of the application of paragraph 23 was flawed.

24(6) In this paragraph **"tribunal"** means the First-tier Tribunal or Upper Tribunal (as appropriate by virtue of sub-paragraph (3)).

MEANING OF "AVOIDANCE-RELATED RULE"

25(1) In this Part of this Schedule **"avoidance-related rule"** means a rule in Category 1 or 2.

25(2) A rule is in Category 1 if it refers (in whatever terms)–

(a) to the purpose or main purpose or purposes of a transaction, arrangements or any other action or matter, and

(b) to whether or not the purpose in question is or involves the avoidance of tax or the obtaining of any advantage in relation to tax (however described).

25(3) *A rule is also in Category 1 if it* refers (in whatever terms) to–

(a) expectations as to what are, or may be, the expected benefits of a transaction, arrangements or any other action or matter, and

(b) whether or not the avoidance of tax or the obtaining of any advantage in relation to tax (however described) is such a benefit.

For the purposes of paragraph (b) it does not matter whether the reference is (for instance) to the "sole or main benefit" or "one of the main benefits" or any other reference to a benefit.

25(4) A rule falls within Category 2 if as a result of the rule a person may be treated differently for tax purposes depending on whether or not purposes referred to in the rule (for instance the purposes of an actual or contemplated action or enterprise) are (or are shown to be) commercial purposes.

25(5) For example, a rule in the following form would fall within Category 1 and within Category 2–

"Example rule

Section X does not apply to a company in respect of a transaction if the company shows that the transaction meets Condition A or B.

Condition A is that the transaction is effected–

(a) for genuine commercial reasons, or

(b) in the ordinary course of managing investments.

Condition B is that the avoidance of tax is not the main object or one of the main objects of the transaction."

MEANING OF "RELIEF"

26 The following are **"reliefs"** for the purposes of this Part of this Schedule–

(a) any relief from tax (however described) which must be claimed, or which is not available without making an election,

(b) relief under section 1219 of CTA 2009 (expenses of management of a company's investment business),

(c) any relief (not falling within paragraph (a)) under Part 4 of ITA 2007 (loss relief) or Part 4 or 5 of CTA 2010 (loss relief and group relief), and

(d) any relief (not falling within paragraph (a) or (b)) under a provision listed in section 24 of ITA 2007 (reliefs deductible at Step 2 of the calculation of income tax liability).

"CLAIM" FOR RELIEF

27 In this Part of this Schedule **"claim for relief"** includes any election or other similar action which is in substance a claim for relief.

VAT AND INDIRECT TAXES

History – In the heading the words "and indirect taxes" inserted by F(No. 2)A 2017, s. 66 and Sch. 17, para. 55(12) with effect so far as is necessary for enabling the making of regulations under that Schedule on 16 November 2017 (Royal Assent) and on 1 January 2018 for all other purposes.

28 In this Part of this Schedule **"tax"** does not include VAT or any other indirect tax.

History – In para. 28 the words "or any other indirect tax" inserted by F(No. 2)A 2017, s. 66 and Sch. 17, para. 55(13) with effect so far as is necessary for enabling the making of regulations under that Schedule on 16 November 2017 (Royal Assent) and on 1 January 2018 for all other purposes.

POWER TO AMEND

29(1) The Treasury may by regulations amend–

(a) amend paragraph 20;

(b) amend paragraph 26.

29(2) Regulations under sub-paragraph (1)(a) may, in particular, alter the application of paragraph 20 in relation to any relief, exclude any relief from its application or extend its application to further reliefs.

29(3) Regulations under sub-paragraph (1)(b) may amend the meaning of "relief" in any way (including by extending or limiting the meaning).

29(4) Regulations under this paragraph may–

(a) make supplementary, incidental and consequential provision;

(b) make transitional provision.

29(5) Regulations under this paragraph are to be made by statutory instrument.

29(6) A statutory instrument containing regulations under this Part may not be made unless a draft of the instrument has been laid before and approved by a resolution of the House of Commons.

Part 5 – Penalty

PENALTY

30(1) A person is liable to pay a penalty if the person incurs a relevant defeat in relation to any arrangements which the person has used in a warning period.

30(2) The penalty is 20% of the value of the counteracted advantage if neither sub-paragraph (3) nor sub-paragraph (4) applies.

30(3) The penalty is 40% of the value of the counteracted advantage if before the relevant defeat is incurred the person has been given, or become liable to be given, one (but not more than one) relevant prior warning notice.

30(4) The penalty is 60% of the value of the counteracted advantage if before the current defeat is incurred the person has been given, or become liable to be given, two or more relevant prior warning notices.

30(5) In this paragraph **"relevant prior warning notice"** means a warning notice in relation to the defeat of arrangements which the person has used in the warning period mentioned in sub-paragraph (1).

30(6) For the meaning of "the value of the counteracted advantage" see paragraphs 32 to 37.

SIMULTANEOUS DEFEATS ETC

31(1) If a person incurs simultaneously two or more relevant defeats in relation to different arrangements, sub-paragraphs (2) to (4) of paragraph 30 have effect as if the relevant defeat with the lowest value was incurred last, the relevant defeat with the next lowest value immediately before it, and so on.

31(2) For this purpose the **"value"** of a relevant defeat is taken to be equal to the value of the counteracted advantage.

31(3) If a person has been given a single warning notice in relation to two or more relevant defeats, the person is treated for the purposes of paragraph 30 as having been given a separate warning notice in relation to each of those relevant defeats.

VALUE OF THE COUNTERACTED ADVANTAGE: BASIC RULE FOR TAXES OTHER THAN VAT

32(1) In relation to a relevant defeat incurred by virtue of Condition A, B, C or F, the **"value of the counteracted advantage"** is–

(a) in the case of a relevant defeat incurred by virtue of Condition A, the additional amount due or payable in respect of tax as a result of the counteraction mentioned in paragraph 12(1)(c);

(b) in the case of a relevant defeat incurred by virtue of Condition B, the additional amount due or payable in respect of tax as a result of the action mentioned in paragraph 13(1);

(c) in the case of a relevant defeat incurred by virtue of Condition C, the additional amount due or payable in respect of tax as a result of the counteraction mentioned in paragraph 14(1)(d);

(d) in the case of a relevant defeat incurred by virtue of Condition F, the additional amount due or payable in respect of tax as a result of the counteraction mentioned in paragraph 16A(1)(d).

32(2) The reference in sub-paragraph (1) to the additional amount due and payable includes a reference to–

(a) an amount payable to HMRC having erroneously been paid by way of repayment of tax, and

(b) an amount which would be repayable by HMRC if the counteraction mentioned in paragraph (a), (c) or (d) of sub-paragraph (1) were not made or the action mentioned in paragraph (b) of that sub-paragraph were not taken (as the case may be).

32(3) The following are ignored in calculating the value of the counteracted advantage–

(a) group relief, and

(b) any relief under section 458 of CTA 2010 (relief in respect of repayment etc of loan) which is deferred under subsection (5) of that section.

32(4) This paragraph is subject to paragraphs 33 and 34.

History – In para. 32(1) the words ", C or F" (comma assumed by Croner-i) substituted for the words "or C" and para. 32(1)(d) inserted by F(No. 2)A 2017, s. 66 and Sch. 17, para. 55(14)(a) with effect so far as is necessary for enabling the making of regulations under that Schedule on 16 November 2017 (Royal Assent) and on 1 January 2018 for all other purposes.

In para. 32(2)(b) the words ", (c) or (d)" (comma assumed by Croner-i) substituted for the words "or (c)" and para. 32(1)(d) inserted by F(No. 2)A 2017, s. 66 and Sch. 17, para. 55(14)(b) with effect so far as is necessary for enabling the making of regulations under that Schedule on 16 November 2017 (Royal Assent) and on 1 January 2018 for all other purposes.

VALUE OF COUNTERACTED ADVANTAGE: LOSSES FOR PURPOSES OF DIRECT TAX

33(1) This paragraph has effect in relation to relevant defeats incurred by virtue of Condition A, B or C.

33(2) To the extent that the counteracted advantage (see paragraph 35) has the result that a loss is wrongly recorded for the purposes of direct tax and the loss has been wholly used to reduce the amount due or payable in respect of tax, the value of the counteracted advantage is determined in accordance with paragraph 32.

33(3) To the extent that the counteracted advantage has the result that a loss is wrongly recorded for purposes of direct tax and the loss has not been wholly used to reduce the amount due or payable in respect of tax, the value of the counteracted advantage is–

(a) the value under paragraph 32 of so much of the counteracted advantage as results from the part (if any) of the loss which is used to reduce the amount due or payable in respect of tax, plus

(b) 10% of the part of the loss not so used.

33(4) Sub-paragraphs (2) and (3) apply both–

(a) to a case where no loss would have been recorded but for the counteracted advantage, and

(b) to a case where a loss of a different amount would have been recorded (but in that case sub-paragraphs (2) and (3) apply only to the difference between the amount recorded and the true amount).

33(5) To the extent that a counteracted advantage creates or increases an aggregate loss recorded for a group of companies–

(a) the value of the counteracted advantage is calculated in accordance with this paragraph, and

(b) in applying paragraph 32 in accordance with sub-paragraphs (2) and (3), group relief may be taken into account (despite paragraph 32(3)).

33(6) To the extent that the counteracted advantage results in a loss, the value of it is nil where, because of the nature of the loss or the person's circumstances, there is no reasonable prospect of the loss being used to support a claim to reduce a tax liability (of any person).

VALUE OF COUNTERACTED ADVANTAGE: DEFERRED TAX

34(1) To the extent that the counteracted advantage (see paragraph 35) is a deferral of tax (other than VAT), the value of that advantage is–

(a) 25% of the amount of the deferred tax for each year of the deferral, or

(b) a percentage of the amount of the deferred tax, for each separate period of deferral of less than a year, equating to 25% per year,

or, if less, 100% of the amount of the deferred tax.

34(2) This paragraph does not apply to a case to the extent that paragraph 33 applies.

MEANING OF "THE COUNTERACTED ADVANTAGE" IN PARAGRAPHS 33 AND 34

35(1) In paragraphs 33 and 34 **"the counteracted advantage"** means–

(a) in relation to a relevant defeat incurred by virtue of Condition A, the tax advantage mentioned in paragraph 12(1)(b);

(b) in relation to a relevant defeat incurred by virtue of Condition B, the denied advantage in relation to which the action mentioned in paragraph 13(1) is taken;

(c) in relation to a relevant defeat incurred by virtue of Condition C, means any tax advantage in respect of which the counteraction mentioned in paragraph 14(1)(c) is made;

(d) in relation to a relevant defeat incurred by virtue of Condition F, means any tax advantage in respect of which the counteraction mentioned in paragraph 16A(1)(c) is made.

35(2) In sub-paragraph (1)(c) **"counteraction"** is to be interpreted in accordance with paragraph 14(5).

History – Para. 35(1)(d) inserted by F(No. 2)A 2017, s. 66 and Sch. 17, para. 55(15) with effect so far as is necessary for enabling the making of regulations under that Schedule on 16 November 2017 (Royal Assent) and on 1 January 2018 for all other purposes.

VALUE OF THE COUNTERACTED ADVANTAGE: CONDITIONS D AND E

36 [Not relevant to National Insurance contributions.]

VALUE OF COUNTERACTED ADVANTAGE: DELAYED VAT

37 [Not relevant to National Insurance contributions.]

ASSESSMENT OF PENALTY

38(1) Where a person is liable for a penalty under paragraph 30, HMRC must assess the penalty.

38(2) Where HMRC assess the penalty, HMRC must–

(a) notify the person who is liable for the penalty, and

(b) state in the notice a tax period in respect of which the penalty is assessed.

38(3) A penalty under this paragraph must be paid before the end of the period of 30 days beginning with the day on which the person is notified of the penalty under sub-paragraph (2).

38(4) An assessment–

(a) is to be treated for procedural purposes as if it were an assessment to tax,

(b) may be enforced as if it were an assessment to tax, and

(c) may be combined with an assessment to tax.

38(5) An assessment of a penalty under this paragraph must be made before the end of the period of 12 months beginning with the date of the defeat mentioned in paragraph 30(1).

ALTERATION OF ASSESSMENT OF PENALTY

39(1) After notification of an assessment has been given to a person under paragraph 38(2), the assessment may not be altered except in accordance with this paragraph or on appeal.

39(2) A supplementary assessment may be made in respect of a penalty if an earlier assessment operated by reference to an underestimate of the value of the counteracted advantage.

39(3) An assessment may be revised as necessary if operated by reference to an overestimate of the value of the counteracted advantage.

AGGREGATE PENALTIES

40(1) The amount of a penalty for which a person is liable under paragraph 30 is to be reduced by the amount of any other penalty incurred by the person, or any surcharge for late payment of tax imposed on the person, if the amount of the penalty or surcharge is determined by reference to the same tax liability.

40(2) In sub-paragraph (1) **"any other penalty"** does not include a penalty under section 212A of FA 2013 (GAAR penalty) or Part 4 of FA 2014 (penalty where corrective action not taken after follower notice etc).

40(3) In the application of section 97A of TMA 1970 (multiple penalties) no account shall be taken of a penalty under paragraph 30.

APPEAL AGAINST PENALTY

41(1) A person may appeal against a decision of HMRC that a penalty is payable under paragraph 30.

41(2) A person may appeal against a decision of HMRC as to the amount of a penalty payable by P under paragraph 30.

41(3) An appeal under this paragraph must be made within the period of 30 days beginning with the day on which notification of the penalty is given under paragraph 38.

41(4) An appeal under this paragraph is to be treated in the same way as an appeal against an assessment to the tax concerned (including by the application of any provision about bringing the appeal by notice to HMRC, about HMRC's review of the decision or about determination of the appeal by the First-tier Tribunal or Upper Tribunal).

41(5) Sub-paragraph (4) does not apply–

(a) so as to require a person to pay a penalty before an appeal against the assessment of the penalty is determined, or

(b) in respect of any other matter expressly provided for by this Part of this Schedule.

41(6) On an appeal under sub-paragraph (1) or (2) the tribunal may–

(a) affirm HMRC's decision, or

(b) substitute for HMRC's decision another decision that HMRC has power to make.

41(7) *In this paragraph* **"tribunal"** means the First-tier Tribunal or Upper Tribunal (as appropriate by virtue of sub-paragraph (4)).

PENALTIES: REASONABLE EXCUSE

42(1) A person is not liable to a penalty under paragraph 30 in respect of a relevant defeat if the person satisfies HMRC or (on appeal) the First-tier Tribunal or Upper Tribunal that the person had a reasonable excuse for the relevant failure to which that relevant defeat relates (see paragraph 43).

42(2) Sub-paragraph (3) applies if–

(a) a person has incurred a relevant defeat in respect of which the person is liable to a penalty under paragraph 30, and

(b) before incurring that defeat the person had been given, or become liable to be given, an excepted warning notice.

42(3) The person is treated for the purposes of sub-paragraphs (2) to (4) of paragraph 30 (rate of penalty) as not having been given, and not having become liable to be given, the excepted notice (so far as it relates to the relevant defeat in respect of which the person had a reasonable excuse).

42(4) A warning notice is **"excepted"** for the purposes of this paragraph if the person was not liable to a penalty in respect of the defeat specified in it because the person had a reasonable excuse for the relevant failure in question.

42(5) For the purposes of this paragraph, in the case of a person ("P")–

(a) an insufficiency of funds is not a reasonable excuse unless attributable to events outside P's control,

(b) where P relies on another person to do anything, that is not a reasonable excuse unless P took reasonable care to avoid the relevant failure, and

(c) where P had a reasonable excuse for the relevant failure but the excuse had ceased, P is to be treated as having continued to have the excuse if the failure is remedied without unreasonable delay after the excuse ceased.

42(6) In determining for the purposes of this paragraph whether or not a person ("P") had a reasonable excuse for any action, failure or inaccuracy, reliance on advice is to be taken automatically not to constitute a reasonable excuse if the advice is addressed to, or was given to, a person other than P or takes no account of P's individual circumstances.

PARAGRAPH 42: MEANING OF "THE RELEVANT FAILURE"

43(1) In paragraph 42 **"the relevant failure"**, in relation to a relevant defeat, is to be interpreted in accordance with sub-paragraphs (2) to (7).

43(2) In relation to a relevant defeat incurred by virtue of Condition A, **"the relevant failure"** means the failures or inaccuracies as a result of which the counteraction under section 209 of FA 2013 was necessary.

43(3) In relation to a relevant defeat incurred by virtue of Condition B, **"the relevant failure"** means the failures or inaccuracies in respect of which the action mentioned in paragraph 13(1) was taken.

43(4) In relation to a relevant defeat incurred by virtue of Condition C, **"the relevant failure"** means the failures of inaccuracies as a result of which the adjustments, assessments, or other action mentioned in paragraph 14(5) are required.

43(5) In relation to a relevant defeat incurred by virtue of Condition D, **"the relevant failure"** means the failures or inaccuracies as a result of which the adjustments, assessments or other action mentioned in paragraph 15(5) are required.

43(6) In relation to a relevant defeat incurred by virtue of Condition E, **"the relevant failure"** means P's actions (and failures to act), so far as they are connected with matters in respect of which the counteraction mentioned in paragraph 16(1) is required.

43(7) In sub-paragraph (6) **"counteraction"** is to be interpreted in accordance with paragraph 16(2).

43(8) In relation to a relevant defeat incurred by virtue of Condition F, **"the relevant failure"** means the failures or inaccuracies as a result of which the adjustments, assessments, or other actions mentioned in paragraph 16A(5) are required.

History – Para. 43(8) inserted by F(No. 2)A 2017, s. 66 and Sch. 17, para. 55(16) with effect so far as is necessary for enabling the making of regulations under that Schedule on 16 November 2017 (Royal Assent) and on 1 January 2018 for all other purposes.

MITIGATION OF PENALTIES

44(1) The Commissioners may in their discretion mitigate a penalty under paragraph 30, or stay or compound any proceedings for such a penalty.

44(2) They may also, after judgment, further mitigate or entirely remit the penalty.

Part 6 – Corporate Groups, Associated Persons and Partnerships

REPRESENTATIVE MEMBER OF A VAT GROUP

45 [Not relevant to National Insurance contributions.]

CORPORATE GROUPS

46(1) Sub-paragraphs (2) and (3) apply if HMRC has a duty under paragraph 2 to give a warning notice to a company ("C") which is a member of a group.

46(2) That duty has effect as a duty to give a warning notice to each current group member (see sub-paragraph (8)).

46(3) Any warning notice which has been given (or is treated as having been given) previously to any current group member is treated as having been given to each current group member (and any provision in this Schedule which refers to a **"warning period"** in relation to a person is to be interpreted accordingly). But see sub-paragraphs (4) and (5).

46(4) In relation to a company which incurs a relevant defeat, paragraph 19(1) (duty to give relief restriction notice) does not have effect unless the warning period mentioned in that sub-paragraph would be a warning period in relation to the company regardless of sub-paragraph (3).

46(5) A company which incurs a relevant defeat is not liable to pay a penalty under paragraph 30 unless the warning period mentioned in sub-paragraph (1) of that paragraph would be a warning period in relation to the company regardless of sub-paragraph (3).

46(6) HMRC may discharge any duty to give a warning notice to a current group member in accordance with sub-paragraph (2) by delivering the notice to C (and if it does so may combine one or more warning notices in a single notice).

46(7) If a company ceases to be a member of a group, and–

(a) immediately before it ceases to be a member of the group, a warning period has effect in relation to the company, but

(b) no warning period would have effect in relation to the company at that time but for sub-paragraph (2) or (3),

that warning period ceases to have effect in relation to the company when it ceases to be a member of that group.

46(8) In this paragraph **"current group member"** means a company which is a member of the group concerned at the time when the warning notice mentioned in sub-paragraph (1) is given.

46(9) For the purposes of this paragraph two companies are members of the same group of companies if–

(a) one is a 75% subsidiary of the other, or

(b) both are 75% subsidiaries of a third company.

46(10) In this paragraph **"75% subsidiary"** has the meaning given by section 1154 of CTA 2010.

46(11) In this paragraph **"company"** has the same meaning as in the Corporation Tax Acts (see section 1121 of CTA 2010).

ASSOCIATED PERSONS TREATED AS INCURRING RELEVANT DEFEATS

47(1) Sub-paragraph (2) applies if a person ("P") incurs a relevant defeat in relation to any arrangements (otherwise than by virtue of this paragraph).

47(2) Any person ("S") who is associated with P at the relevant time is also treated for the purposes of paragraphs 2 (duty to give warning notice) and 3(2) (warning period) as having incurred that relevant defeat in relation to those arrangements (but see sub-paragraph (3)).
For the meaning of "associated" see paragraph 48.

47(3) Sub-paragraph (2) does not apply if P and S are members of the same group of companies (as defined in paragraph 46(9)).

47(4) In relation to a warning notice given to S by virtue of sub-paragraph (2), paragraph 2(4)(c) (certain *information to be included in* warning notice) is to be read as referring only to paragraphs 3, 17 and 18.

47(5) A warning notice which is given to a person by virtue of sub-paragraph (2) is treated for the purposes of paragraphs 19(1) (duty to give relief restriction notice) and 30 (penalty) as not having been given to that person.

47(6) In sub-paragraph (2) **"the relevant time"** means the time when P is given a warning notice in respect of the relevant defeat.

MEANING OF "ASSOCIATED"

48(1) For the purposes of paragraph 47 two persons are associated with one another if–

(a) one of them is a body corporate which is controlled by the other, or

(b) they are bodies corporate under common control.

48(2) Two bodies corporate are under common control if both are controlled–

(a) by one person,

(b) by two or more, but fewer than six, individuals, or

(c) by any number of individuals carrying on business in partnership.

48(3) For the purposes of this section a body corporate ("H") is taken to control another body corporate ("B") if–

(a) H is empowered by statute to control B's activities, or

(b) H is B's holding company within the meaning of section 1159 of and Schedule 6 to the Companies Act 2006.

48(4) For the purposes of this section an individual or individuals are taken to control a body corporate ("B") if the individual or individuals, were they a body corporate, would be B's holding company within the meaning of those provisions.

PARTNERS TREATED AS INCURRING RELEVANT DEFEATS

49(1) Where paragraph 50 applies in relation to a partnership return, each relevant partner is treated for the purposes of this Part of this Act as having incurred the relevant defeat mentioned in paragraph 50(1)(b), (2) or (3)(b) (as the case may be).

49(2) In this paragraph **"relevant partner"** means any person who was a partner in the partnership at any time during the relevant reporting period (but see sub-paragraph (3)).

49(3) The **"relevant partners"** do not include–

(a) the person mentioned in sub-paragraph (1)(b), (2) or (3)(b) (as the case may be) of paragraph 50, or

(b) any other person who would, apart from this paragraph, incur a relevant defeat in connection with the subject matter of the partnership return mentioned in sub-paragraph (1).

49(4) In this paragraph the **"relevant reporting period"** means the period in respect of which the partnership return mentioned in sub-paragraph (1), (2) or (3) of paragraph 50 was required.

PARTNERSHIP RETURNS TO WHICH THIS PARAGRAPH APPLIES

50(1) This paragraph applies in relation to a partnership return if–

(a) that return has been made on the basis that a tax advantage arises to a partner from any arrangements, and

(b) that person has incurred, in relation to that tax advantage and those arrangements, a relevant defeat by virtue of Condition A (final counteraction of tax advantage under general anti-abuse rule).

50(2) Where a person has incurred a relevant defeat by virtue of sub-paragraph (2) of paragraph 13 (Condition B: case involving partnership follower notice) this paragraph applies in relation to the partnership return mentioned in that sub-paragraph.

50(3) This paragraph applies in relation to a partnership return if–

(a) that return has been made on the basis that a tax advantage arises to a partner from any arrangements, and

(b) that person has incurred, in relation to that tax advantage and those arrangements, a relevant defeat by virtue of Condition C (return, claim or election made in reliance on DOTAS arrangements).

50(4) The references in this paragraph to a relevant defeat do not include a relevant defeat incurred by virtue of paragraph 47(2).

PARTNERSHIPS: INFORMATION

51(1) If paragraph 50 applies in relation to a partnership return, the appropriate partner must give HMRC a written notice (a "partnership information notice") in respect of each sub-period in the information period.

51(2) The **"information period"** is the period of 5 years beginning with the day after the day of the relevant defeat mentioned in paragraph 50.

51(3) If, in the case of a partnership, a new information period (relating to another partnership return) begins during an existing information period, those periods are treated for the purposes of this paragraph as a single period (which includes all times that would otherwise fall within either period).

51(4) An information period under this paragraph ends if the partnership ceases.

51(5) A partnership information notice must be given not later than the 30th day after the end of the sub-period to which it relates.

51(6) A partnership information notice must state–

(a) whether or not any relevant partnership return which was, or was required to be, delivered in the sub-period has been made on the basis that a relevant tax advantage arises, and

(b) whether or not there has been a failure to deliver a relevant partnership return in the sub-period.

51(7) In this paragraph–

(a) **"relevant partnership return"** means a partnership return in respect of the partnership's trade, profession or business;

(b) **"relevant tax advantage"** means a tax advantage which particular DOTAS arrangements enable, or might be expected to enable, a person who is or has been a partner in the partnership to obtain.

51(8) If a partnership information notice states that a relevant partnership return has been made on the basis mentioned in sub-paragraph (6)(a) the notice must–

(a) explain (on the assumptions made for the purposes of the return) how the DOTAS arrangements enable the tax advantage concerned to be obtained, and

(b) describe any variation in the amounts required to be stated in the return under section 12AB(1) of TMA 1970 which results from those arrangements.

51(9) HMRC may require the appropriate partner to give HMRC a notice (a "supplementary information notice") setting out further information in relation to a partnership information notice.
In relation to a partnership information notice **"further information"** means information which would have been required to be set out in the notice by virtue of sub-paragraph (6)(a) or (8) had there not been a failure to deliver a relevant partnership return.

51(10) A requirement under sub-paragraph (9) must be made by a written notice and the notice must state the period within which the notice must be complied with.

51(11) If a person fails to comply with a requirement of (or imposed under) this paragraph, HMRC may by written notice extend the information period concerned to the end of the period of 5 years beginning with–

(a) the day by which the partnership information notice or supplementary information notice was required to be given to HMRC or, as the case requires,

(b) the day on which the person gave the defective notice to HMRC,

or, if earlier, the time when the information period would have expired but for the extension.

51(12) For the purposes of this paragraph–

(a) the first sub-period in an information period begins with the first day of the information period and ends with a day specified by HMRC,

(b) the remainder of the information period is divided into further sub-periods each of which begins immediately after the end of the preceding sub-period and is twelve months long or (if that would be shorter) ends at the end of the information period.

51(13) In this paragraph **"the appropriate partner"** means the partner in the partnership who is for the time being nominated by HMRC for the purposes of this paragraph.

Prospective amendments – In para. 51(8)(b) the words ", or under equivalent provision made by regulations under paragraph 10 of Schedule A1 to that Act," inserted after the words "TMA 1970" by F(No. 2)A 2017, s. 61 and Sch. 14, para. 48(2), with effect from a day to be appointed under F(No. 2)A 2017, s. 61(6).

PARTNERSHIPS: SPECIAL PROVISION ABOUT TAXPAYER EMENDATIONS

52(1) Sub-paragraph (2) applies if a partnership return is amended at any time under section 12ABA of TMA 1970 (amendment of partnership return by representative partner etc) on a basis that–

(a) results in an increase or decrease in, or

(b) otherwise affects the calculation of,

any amount stated under subsection (1)(b) of section 12AB of that Act (partnership statement) as a partner's share of any income, loss, consideration, tax or credit for any period.

52(2) For the purposes of paragraph 14 (Condition C: counteraction of DOTAS arrangements), the partner is treated as having at that time amended–

(a) the partner's return under section 8 or 8A of TMA 1970, or

(b) the partner's company tax return,

so as to give effect to the amendments of the partnership return.

52(3) Sub-paragraph (4) applies if a partnership return is amended at any time by HMRC as a result of a disclosure made by the representative partner or that person's successor on a basis that–

(a) results in an increase or decrease in, or

(b) otherwise affects the calculation of,

any amount stated under subsection (1)(b) of section 12AB (partnership statement) as the share of a particular partner (P) of any income, loss, consideration, tax or credit for any period.

52(4) If the conditions in sub-paragraph (5) are met, P is treated for the purposes of paragraph 14 as having at that time amended–

(a) P's return under section 8 or 8A of TMA 1970, or

(b) P's company tax return,

so as to give effect to the amendments of the partnership return.

52(5) The conditions are that the disclosure–

(a) is a full and explicit disclosure of an inaccuracy in the partnership return, and

(b) was made at a time when neither the person making the disclosure nor P had reason to believe that HMRC was about to begin enquiries into the partnership return.

Prospective amendments – In para. 52(1) the words "section 12AB(1)(b) of that Act or under equivalent provision made by regulations under paragraph 10 of Schedule A1 to that Act (partnership statement)" substituted for the words "subsection (1)(b) of section 12AB of that Act (partnership statement)" by F(No. 2)A 2017, s. 61 and Sch. 14, para. 48(3)(a), with effect from a day to be appointed under F(No. 2)A 2017, s. 61(6).

In para. 52(3)(a) the words "(in the case of a section 12AA partnership return) or the nominated partner (in the case of a Schedule A1 partnership return)" inserted after the words "that person's successor" and in the end words to para. 52(3) the words "section 12AB(1)(b) of TMA 1970 or under equivalent provision made by regulations under paragraph 10 of Schedule A1 to that Act (partnership statement)" substituted for the words "subsection (1)(b) of section 12AB of TMA 1970 (partnership statement)" by F(No. 2)A 2017, s. 61 and Sch. 14, para. 48(3)(b), with effect from a day to be appointed under F(No. 2)A 2017, s. 61(6).

SUPPLEMENTARY PROVISION RELATING TO PARTNERSHIPS

53(1) In paragraphs 49 to 52 and this paragraph–

"partnership" is to be interpreted in accordance with section 12AA of TMA 1970 (and includes a limited liability partnership);

"the representative partner", in relation to a partnership return, means the person who was required by a notice served under or for the purposes of section 12AA(2) or (3) of TMA 1970 to deliver the return;

"successor", in relation to a person who is the representative partner in the case of a partnership return, has the same meaning as in TMA 1970 (see section 118(1) of that Act).

53(2) For the purposes of this Part of this Act a partnership is treated as the same partnership notwithstanding a change in membership if any person who was a member before the change remains a member after the change.

Prospective amendments – In para. 53(1), in the definition of "the representative partner" the words "section 12AA" inserted after the words "in relation to a" by F(No. 2)A 2017, s. 61 and Sch. 14, para. 48(4)(a), with effect from a day to be appointed under F(No. 2)A 2017, s. 61(6).

In para. 53(1) the definition of "the nominated partner" inserted by F(No. 2)A 2017, s. 61 and Sch. 14, para. 48(4)(b), with effect from a day to be appointed under F(No. 2)A 2017, s. 61(6).

Part 7 – Supplemental

MEANING OF "ADJUSTMENTS"

54(1) In this Schedule **"adjustments"** means any adjustments, whether by way of an assessment, the modification of an assessment or return, amendment or disallowance of a claim, a payment, the entering into of a contract settlement, or otherwise (and references to "making" adjustments accordingly include securing that adjustments are made by entering into a contract settlement).

54(2) **"Adjustments"** also includes a payment in respect of a liability to pay national insurance contributions.

TIME OF "USE" OF DEFEATED ARRANGEMENTS

55(1) With reference to a particular relevant defeat incurred by a person in relation to arrangements, the person is treated as having "used" the arrangements on the dates set out in this paragraph.

55(2) If the person incurs the relevant defeat by virtue of Condition A, the person is treated as having **"used"** the arrangements on the following dates–

(a) the filing date of any return made by the person on the basis that the tax advantage mentioned in paragraph 12(1)(a) arises from the arrangements;

(b) the date on which the person makes any claim or election on that basis;

(c) the date of any relevant failure by the person to comply with an obligation.

55(3) For the purposes of sub-paragraph (2) a failure to comply with an obligation is a **"relevant failure"** if the whole or part of the tax advantage mentioned in paragraph 12(1)(b) arose as a result of, or in connection with, that failure.

55(4) If the person incurs the relevant defeat by virtue of Condition B, the person is treated as having **"used"** the arrangements on the following dates–

(a) the filing date of any return made by the person on the basis that the asserted advantage (see section 204(3) of FA 2014) results from the arrangements,

(b) the date on which any claim is made by the person on that basis,

(c) the date of any failure by the person to comply with a relevant obligation.

In this sub-paragraph **"relevant obligation"** means an obligation which would not have fallen on the person (or might have been expected not to do so), had the denied advantage arisen (see section 208(3) of FA 2014).

55(5) If the person incurs the relevant defeat by virtue of Condition C, the person is treated as having **"used"** the arrangements on the following dates–

(a) the filing date of any return made by the person on the basis mentioned in paragraph 14(2)(a);

(b) the date on which the person makes any claim or election on that basis;

(c) the date of any failure by the person to comply with a relevant obligation (as defined in paragraph 14(4)).

55(6) If the person incurs the relevant defeat by virtue of Condition D, the person is treated as having **"used"** the arrangements on the following dates–

(a) the filing date of any return made by the person on the basis mentioned in paragraph 15(2)(a);

(b) the date on which the person makes any claim on that basis;

(c) the date of any failure by the person to comply with a relevant obligation (as defined in paragraph 15(4)).

55(7) If the person incurs the relevant defeat by virtue of Condition E, the person is treated as having **"used"** the arrangements on the following dates–

(a) the filing date of any return made by S to which the counteraction mentioned in paragraph 16(1)(c) relates;

(b) the date on which S made any claim to which that counteraction relates;

(c) the date of any relevant failure by S to which that counteraction relates.

55(8) In sub-paragraph (7) **"relevant failure"** means a failure to comply with an obligation relating to VAT.

55(8A) If the person incurs the relevant defeat by virtue of Condition F, the person is treated as having **"used"** the arrangements on the following dates–

(a) the filing date of any return made by the person on the basis mentioned in paragraph 16A(2)(a);

(b) the date on which the person makes any claim, declaration or application for approval;

(c) the date of any failure by the person to comply with a relevant obligation (as defined in paragraph 16A(4)).

55(9) In this paragraph **"filing date"**, in relation to a return, means the earlier of–

(a) the day on which the return is delivered, or

(b) the last day of the period within which the return must be delivered.

55(10) References in this paragraph to the date on which a person fails to comply with an obligation are to the date on which the person is first in breach of the obligation.

History – Para. 55(8A) inserted by F(No. 2)A 2017, s. 66 and Sch. 17, para. 55(17) with effect so far as is necessary for enabling the making of regulations under that Schedule on 16 November 2017 (Royal Assent) and on 1 January 2018 for all other purposes.

INHERITANCE TAX

56 [Not relevant to National Insurance contributions.]

NATIONAL INSURANCE CONTRIBUTIONS

57(1) In this Schedule references to an assessment to tax include a NICs decision relating to a person's liability for relevant contributions.

57(2) In this Schedule a reference to a provision of Part 7 of FA 2004 (disclosure of tax avoidance schemes) (a "DOTAS provision") includes a reference to–

(a) that DOTAS provision as applied by regulations under section 132A of the Social Security Administration Act 1992 (disclosure of contributions avoidance arrangements);

(b) any provision of regulations under that section that corresponds to that DOTAS provision,

whenever the regulations are made.

57(3) Regulations under section 132A of that Act may disapply, or modify the effect of, sub-paragraph (2).

57(4) In this paragraph **"NICs decision"** means a decision under section 8 of the Social Security Contributions (Transfer of Functions, etc) Act 1999 or Article 7 of the Social Security Contributions (Transfer of Functions, etc) (Northern Ireland) Order 1999 (S.I. 1999/671).

GENERAL INTERPRETATION

58(1) In this Schedule–

"arrangements" has the meaning given by paragraph 2(6);

"the Commissioners" means the Commissioners for Her Majesty's Revenue and Customs;

"contract settlement" means an agreement in connection with a person's liability to make a payment to the Commissioners under or by virtue of an enactment;

"disclosable indirect tax arrangements" is to be interpreted in accordance with paragraph 9A;

"disclosable Schedule 11A VAT arrangements" is to be interpreted in accordance with paragraph 9;

"disclosable VAT arrangements" is to be interpreted in accordance with paragraph 8A;

"DOTAS arrangements" is to be interpreted in accordance with paragraph 8 (and see also paragraph 57(2));

"follower notice" has the meaning given by paragraph 13(6);

"HMRC" means Her Majesty's Revenue and Customs;

"indirect tax" has the meaning given by paragraph 4(2);

"national insurance contributions" means contributions under Part 1 of the Social Security Contributions and Benefits Act 1992 or Part 1 of the Social Security Contributions and Benefits (Northern Ireland) Act 1992;

"net income" has the meaning given by section 23 of ITA 2007 (see Step 2 of that section);

"partnership follower notice" has the meaning given by paragraph 2(2) of Schedule 31 to FA 2014;

"partnership return" means a return under section 12AA of TMA 1970;

"relevant contributions" means the following contributions under Part 1 of the Social Security Contributions and Benefits Act 1992 or Part 1 of the Social Security Contributions and Benefits (Northern Ireland) Act 1992–

(a) Class 1 contributions;

(b) Class 1A contributions;

(c) Class 1B contributions;

(d) Class 2 contributions which must be paid but in relation to which section 11A of the Act in question (application of certain provisions of the Income Tax Acts in relation to Class 2 contributions under section 11(2) of that Act) does not apply;

"relevant defeat" is to be interpreted in accordance with paragraph 11;

"tax" has the meaning given by paragraph 4(1);

"tax advantage" has the meaning given by paragraph 7;

"warning notice" has the meaning given by paragraph 2.

58(2) In this Schedule an expression used in relation to VAT has the same meaning as in VATA 1994.

58(3) In this Schedule (except where the context requires otherwise) references, however expressed, to a person's affairs in relation to tax include the person's position as regards deductions or repayments of, or of sums representing, tax that the person is required to make by or under an enactment.

58(4) For the purposes of this Schedule a partnership return is regarded as made on the basis that a particular tax advantage arises to a person from particular arrangements if–

(a) it is made on the basis that an increase or reduction in one or more of the amounts mentioned in section 12AB(1) of TMA 1970 (amounts in the partnership statement in a partnership return) results from those arrangements, and

(b) that increase or reduction results in that tax advantage for the person.

Prospective amendments – In para. 58(1) the definition of "partnership return" substituted by F(No. 2)A 2017, s. 61 and Sch. 14, para. 48(5), with effect from a day to be appointed under F(No. 2)A 2017, s. 61(6).

History – In para. 58(1) the definition of "disclosable indirect tax arrangements" inserted by F(No. 2)A 2017, s. 66 and Sch. 17, para. 55(18)(a) with effect so far as is necessary for enabling the making of regulations under that Schedule on 16 November 2017 (Royal Assent) and on 1 January 2018 for all other purposes.

In para. 58(1) the definition of "disclosable Schedule 11A VAT arrangements" inserted by F(No. 2)A 2017, s. 66 and Sch. 17, para. 55(18)(a) with effect so far as is necessary for enabling the making of regulations under that Schedule on 16 November 2017 (Royal Assent) and on 1 January 2018 for all other purposes.

In para. 58(1) the definition of "indirect tax" inserted by F(No. 2)A 2017, s. 66 and Sch. 17, para. 55(18)(b) with effect so far as is necessary for enabling the making of regulations under that Schedule on 16 November 2017 (Royal Assent) and on 1 January 2018 for all other purposes.

In para. 58(1), in the definition of "disclosable VAT arrangements" ,"8A" substituted for "9" by F(No. 2)A 2017, s. 66 and Sch. 17, para. 55(18)(c) with effect so far as is necessary for enabling the making of regulations under that Schedule on 16 November 2017 (Royal Assent) and on 1 January 2018 for all other purposes.

In para. 58(1), in the definition of "tax" ,"4(1)" substituted for "4" by F(No. 2)A 2017, s. 66 and Sch. 17, para. 55(18)(d) with effect so far as is necessary for enabling the making of regulations under that Schedule on 16 November 2017 (Royal Assent) and on 1 January 2018 for all other purposes.

CONSEQUENTIAL AMENDMENTS

59 [Inserts TMA 1970, s. 103ZA(i).]

60 [Inserts FA 2014, s. 212(4)(d).]

61(1) The Social Security Contributions and Benefits Act 1992 is amended as follows.

61(2) [Inserts SSCBA 1992, s. 11A(1)(ea).]

61(3) [Inserts SSCBA 1992, s. 16(1)(e).]

62 [Inserts SSCB(NI)A 1992, s. 11A(1)(ea).]

COMMENCEMENT

63 Subject to paragraphs 64 and 65, paragraphs 1 to 62 of this Schedule have effect in relation to relevant defeats incurred after the day on which this Act is passed.

64(1) A relevant defeat is to be disregarded for the purposes of this Schedule if it is incurred before 6 April 2017 in relation to arrangements which the person has entered into before the day on which this Act is passed.

64(2) A relevant defeat incurred on or after 6 April 2017 is to be disregarded for the purposes of this Schedule if–

(a) the person entered into the arrangements concerned before the day on which this Act is passed, and

(b) before 6 April 2017–

 (i) the person incurring the defeat fully discloses to HMRC the matters to which the relevant counteraction relates, or

 (ii) that person gives HMRC notice of a firm intention to make a full disclosure of those matters and makes such a full disclosure within any time limit set by HMRC.

64(3) In sub-paragraph (2) **"the relevant counteraction"** means–

(a) in a case within Condition A, the counteraction mentioned in paragraph 12(1)(c);

(b) in a case within Condition B, the action mentioned in paragraph 13(1);

(c) in a case within Condition C, the counteraction mentioned in paragraph 14(1)(c);

(d) in a case within Condition D, the counteraction mentioned in paragraph 15(1)(d);

(e) in a case within Condition E, the counteraction mentioned in paragraph 16(1)(c).

64(4) In sub-paragraph (3)–

(a) in paragraph (c) **"counteraction"** is to be interpreted in accordance with paragraph 14(5);

(b) in paragraph (d) **"counteraction"** is to be interpreted in accordance with paragraph 15(5);

(c) in paragraph (e) **"counteraction"** is to be interpreted in accordance with paragraph 16(2).

64(5) See paragraph 11(2) for provision about when a relevant defeat is incurred.

65(1) A warning notice given to a person is to be disregarded for the purposes of–

(a) paragraph 18 (naming), and

(b) Part 4 of this Schedule (restriction of reliefs),

if the relevant defeat specified in the notice relates to arrangements which the person has entered into before the day on which this Act is passed.

65(2) Where a person has entered into any arrangements before the day on which this Act is passed–

(a) a relevant defeat incurred by a person in relation to the arrangements, and

(b) any warning notice specifying such a relevant defeat,

is to be disregarded for the purposes of paragraph 30 (penalty).

SCHEDULE 19 – LARGE BUSINESSES: TAX STRATEGIES AND SANCTIONS

Section 161

Part 1 – Interpretation

PURPOSE OF PART 1

1 This Part defines terms for the purposes of this Schedule.

"RELEVANT BODY"

2(1) **"Relevant body"** means a UK company or any other body corporate (wherever incorporated), but does not include a limited liability partnership.

2(2) A relevant body is a **"foreign"** relevant body (or member of a group or subgroup) if it is incorporated outside the United Kingdom.

"UK COMPANY"

3(1) **"UK company"** means a company which is (or is treated as if it is) formed and registered under the Companies Act 2006, unless it falls within sub-paragraph (2).

3(2) The term **"UK company"** does not include a company which is–

(a) an open-ended investment company within the meaning of section 613 of CTA 2010, or

(b) an investment trust within the meaning of section 1158 of CTA 2010.

"UK PERMANENT ESTABLISHMENT"

4(1) **"UK permanent establishment"** means a permanent establishment in the United Kingdom of a foreign relevant body.

4(2) In sub-paragraph (1) **"permanent establishment"** has the same meaning as it has for the purposes of the Corporation Tax Acts (see section 1141 to 1144 of CTA 2010).

"QUALIFYING COMPANY"

5(1) A UK company is a **"qualifying company"** in any financial year (subject to any regulations under sub-paragraph (5)) if sub-paragraph (2) or (3) applies to it.

5(2) This sub-paragraph applies to the company if, at the end of the previous financial year–

(a) it satisfied the qualification test for a UK company, and

(b) was not a member of a UK group or a UK sub-group.

5(3) This sub-paragraph applies to the company if, at the end of the previous financial year–

(a) it was a member of a foreign group,

(b) the group met the qualification test for a group, and

(c) it was not a member of a UK sub-group of that foreign group.

5(4) The qualification test for a UK company is that the company satisfied either or both of the following conditions (by reference to the previous financial year)–

1. The company's turnover	More than £200 million
2. The company's balance sheet total	More than £2 billion.

5(5) The Treasury may by regulations provide that a company of a description specified in the regulations is not a qualifying company for the purposes of this Schedule (or any such purpose specified in the regulations).

5(6) For the purposes of this paragraph a UK permanent establishment of a foreign relevant body is to be treated as if it were–

(a) a UK company, and

(b) if the foreign relevant body is a member of a UK group or a UK subgroup, a member of that group or sub-group.

"GROUP" AND RELATED EXPRESSIONS

6(1) **"Group"** means two or more relevant bodies which together constitute–

(a) an MNE Group (see paragraph 7), or

(b) a group other than an MNE group (see paragraph 8).

6(2) **"UK group"** means a group whose head is a relevant body incorporated in the United Kingdom.

6(3) **"Foreign group"** means a group whose head is a foreign relevant body.

6(4) For the purposes of sub-paragraphs (2) and (3) it is immaterial where other members of the group are incorporated.

7(1) **"MNE Group"** has the same meaning (subject to sub-paragraph (2) below) as in the OECD Model Legislation in the OECD Country-by-Country Reporting Implementation Package as contained in the OECD's Guidance on Transfer Pricing Documentation and Country-by-Country Reporting published in 2014.

7(2) Paragraph (ii) (excluded MNE Group) of the Implementation Package is not part of the definition applied by sub-paragraph (1) above for the purposes of this Schedule.

7(3) In sub-paragraph (1) **"OECD"** means the Organisation for Economic Cooperation and Development.

8(1) A **"group other than an MNE group"** means a group consisting of two or more relevant bodies–

(a) each of which is a member of the group by virtue of sub-paragraph (3) or (4),

(b) at least two of which are UK companies,

which is not an MNE Group.

8(2) For the purposes of the condition in sub-paragraph (1)(b) a UK permanent establishment of a foreign member of a group is to be treated as if it were a UK company and a member of the group.

8(3) A relevant body is a member of a group if–

(a) another relevant body is its 51% subsidiary, or

(b) it is a 51% subsidiary of another relevant body.

8(4) Two relevant bodies are members of the same group if–

(a) one is a 51% subsidiary of the other, or

(b) both are 51% subsidiaries of another relevant body.

8(5) Chapter 3 of Part 24 of CTA 2010 (meaning of 51% subsidiary) applies for the purposes of this Schedule as it applies for the purposes of the Corporation Tax Acts (but with the modification in sub-paragraph (6)).

8(6) It applies as if references to a body corporate were references to a relevant body.

9 A group is headed by whichever relevant body within the group is not a 51% subsidiary of another relevant body within the group (and **"head"**, in relation to the group, means that body).

"QUALIFYING GROUP"

10(1) A group is a **"qualifying group"** in any financial year if, at the end of the previous financial year–

(a) in the case of a group other than an MNE Group, the group satisfied the qualification test for such a group (subject to any regulations under sub-paragraph (6)), or

(b) in the case of an MNE Group–
  (i) there was a mandatory reporting requirement in respect of the group under regulations made under section 122 of FA 2015 (country-by-country reporting), or
  (ii) there would have been such a requirement if the head of the group were resident in the United Kingdom for tax purposes.

10(2) The qualification test for a group other than an MNE Group is that the group satisfied either or both of the following conditions (by reference to the previous financial year)–

1. Group turnover	More than £200 million
2. Group balance sheet total	More than £2 billion.

10(3) In sub-paragraph (2)–

(a) **"group turnover"** means the aggregate turnover of the UK companies that are members of the group at the end of the previous financial year, and

(b) **"group balance sheet total"**, means the aggregate balance sheet totals for all those UK companies.

10(4) Where the financial year of a UK company within in the group does not end on the same day as the previous financial year of the head of the group, the figures from the company that are to be included in the aggregate figures are those for the company's financial year ending last before the end of the previous financial year of the head of the group.

10(5) For the purposes of assessing the turnover or balance sheet total of the group, sub-paragraphs (3) and (4) apply as if a UK permanent establishment of a foreign member of the group were a UK company and a member of the group.

10(6) The Treasury may by regulations provide–

(a) that a group other than an MNE Group which is of a specified description is not a qualifying group for the purposes, or any specified purpose, of this Schedule, or

(b) that a relevant body, or a UK permanent establishment, of a specified description is to be disregarded in determining whether the qualification test is satisfied by a group other than an MNE Group;

and in this sub-paragraph **"specified"** means specified in the regulations.

10(7) In this paragraph **"financial year"**, in relation to a group, means a financial year of the head of the group.

"UK SUB-GROUP" AND "HEAD" (IN RELATION TO A UK SUB-GROUP)

11(1) A **"UK sub-group"** consists of two or more relevant bodies that would be a UK group, but for the fact that they are members of a larger group headed by a relevant body incorporated outside the United Kingdom.

11(2) A UK sub-group is headed by the company or other relevant body incorporated in the United Kingdom that is not a 51% subsidiary of another member of the UK sub-group (and **"head"**, in relation to the sub-group, means that company or body).

"UK PARTNERSHIP", "QUALIFYING PARTNERSHIP" AND "REPRESENTATIVE PARTNER"

12(1) **"UK partnership"** means a body of any of the following descriptions which is carrying on a trade, business or profession with a view to profit–

(a) a partnership within the meaning of the Partnership Act 1890,

(b) a limited partnership registered under the Limited Partnerships Act 1907, or

(c) a limited liability partnership incorporated in the United Kingdom.

12(2) A UK partnership is a **"qualifying partnership"** in a financial year, if it satisfied the qualification test for a UK partnership at the end of the previous financial year (subject to any regulations under sub-paragraph (4)).

12(3) The qualification test for a UK partnership is that the partnership satisfied either or both of the following conditions (by reference to the previous financial year)–

1. The partnership's turnover	More than £200 million
2. The partnership's balance sheet total	More than £2 billion.

12(4) The Treasury may by regulations provide that a UK partnership of a description specified in the regulations is not a qualifying partnership for the purposes of this Schedule (or any such purpose specified in the regulations).

12(5) "Representative partner", in relation to a UK partnership, means the partner who is required by a notice served under or by virtue of section 12AA(2) or (3) of TMA 1970 to make and deliver returns to an officer of HMRC.

Prospective amendments – Para. 12(5)(a) created from existing text and para. 12(5)(b) (and the word ", or" preceding it) inserted by F(No. 2)A 2017, s. 61 and Sch. 14, para. 49(2), with effect from a day to be appointed under F(No. 2)A 2017, s. 61(6).

"FINANCIAL YEAR"

13 "Financial year"–

(a) in relation to a UK company, has the meaning given by the Companies Act 2006 (see section 390 of that Act),

(b) in relation to any other relevant body, means any period in respect of which a profit and loss account for the body's undertaking is required to be made up (whether by its constitution or by the law under which it is established), whether that period is a year or not,

(c) in relation to a UK partnership, means any period of account for which its representative partner has provided or is required to provide a partnership statement under a return issued under section 12AB TMA 1970.

Prospective amendments – In para. 13(c) the words "within the meaning of" substituted for the words "under a return issued under section 12AB" by F(No. 2)A 2017, s. 61 and Sch. 14, para. 49(3), with effect from a day to be appointed under F(No. 2)A 2017, s. 61(6).

"TURNOVER" AND "BALANCE SHEET TOTAL"

14(1) "Turnover"–

(a) in relation to a UK company, has the same meaning as in Part 15 of the Companies Act 2006 (see section 474 of that Act), and

(b) in relation to a UK partnership or a UK permanent establishment, has a corresponding meaning.

14(2) "Balance sheet total", in relation to a UK company, UK partnership or UK permanent establishment and a financial year, means the aggregate of the amounts shown as assets in its balance sheet at the end of the financial year.

"UK TAXATION"

15(1) "UK taxation" means–

(a) income tax,

(b) corporation tax, including any amount assessable or chargeable as if it were corporation tax or treated as if it were corporation tax,

(c) value added tax,

(d) amounts for which the company is accountable under PAYE regulations,

(e) diverted profits tax,

(f) insurance premium tax,

(g) annual tax on enveloped dwellings,

(h) stamp duty land tax,

(i) stamp duty reserve tax,

(j) petroleum revenue tax;

(k) customs duties,

(l) excise duties,

(m) national insurance contributions.

15(2) In relation to a tax strategy required to be published by Part 2, **"UK taxation"** refers to the taxes or duties mentioned above so far as relating to or affecting the bodies or body to which the required tax strategy relates.

Part 2 – Publication of Tax Strategies

QUALIFYING UK GROUPS: DUTY TO PUBLISH A GROUP TAX STRATEGY

16(1) This paragraph applies in relation to a UK group which is a qualifying group in any financial year ("the current financial year").

16(2) The head of the group must ensure that a group tax strategy for the group, containing the information required by paragraph 17, is prepared and published on behalf of the group in accordance with this paragraph.

16(3) The group tax strategy–

(a) must be published before the end of the current financial year, and

(b) if the group was a qualifying group in the previous financial year, must not be published more than 15 months after the day on which its previous group tax strategy was published.

16(4) The group tax strategy–

(a) must be published on the internet by any of the UK companies that are members of the group so as to be accessible to the public free of charge (whether or not it is also published in any other way), and

(b) may be published as a separate document or as a self-contained part of a wider document.

16(5) The head of the group must ensure that the group tax strategy published on the internet remains accessible to the public free of charge–

(a) if a group tax strategy for the group's next financial year is required by this paragraph to be published, until that tax strategy is published, or

(b) if paragraph (a) does not apply, for at least one year.

16(6) For the purposes of this paragraph–

(a) a group tax strategy is published when it is first published on the internet as mentioned in paragraph (4)(a),

(b) the identity of the group is not to be regarded as altered by any change in its membership during the current financial year resulting from a relevant body–

(i) becoming a 51% subsidiary of a member of the group, or

(ii) ceasing to be a 51% subsidiary of another member of the group; and

(c) if the group becomes a UK sub-group of a foreign group during the current financial year, it is to be treated for the rest of that year as if it were still a UK group.

16(7) In this paragraph and paragraph 17 **"financial year"**, in relation to a UK group, means a financial year of the head of the group.

CONTENT OF GROUP TAX STRATEGY

17(1) A group tax strategy required to be published on behalf of a UK group by paragraph 16 must set out–

(a) the approach of the group to risk management and governance arrangements in relation to UK taxation,

(b) the attitude of the group towards tax planning (so far as affecting UK taxation),

(c) the level of risk in relation to UK taxation that the group is prepared to accept, and

(d) the approach of the group towards its dealings with HMRC.

17(2) The group tax strategy may–

(a) include other information relating to taxation (whether UK taxation or otherwise), and

(b) deal with a matter mentioned in sub-paragraph (1) by reference to the group as a whole or to individual members of the group (or to both).

17(3) The information required by sub-paragraph (1) to be included in the group tax strategy does not include any information about activities of any member of the group that consists of the provision of tax advice or related professional services to persons who are not members of the group.

17(4) The publication of information as the group tax strategy does not constitute publication of the strategy for the purposes of paragraph 16 unless the UK company publishing it makes clear (in a way that will be readily apparent to anyone accessing the information online) that the company regards its publication as complying with the duty under paragraph 16(2) in the current financial year.

17(5) For the purposes of this paragraph a UK permanent establishment of a foreign member of the group is to be treated as if it were a member of the group.

17(6) The Treasury may by regulations require the group tax strategy to include a country-by-country report.

17(7) In this paragraph **"country-by-country report"** has the meaning given by the Taxes (Base Erosion and Profit Shifting) (Country-by-Country Reporting) Regulations 2016.

PENALTY FOR NON-COMPLIANCE WITH PARAGRAPH 16

18(1) This paragraph applies where paragraph 16 requires a group tax strategy to be published for a UK group in any financial year of the head of the UK group.

18(2) The head of the group is liable to a penalty of £7,500 if–

(a) there is a failure to publish a group tax strategy for the group that complies with paragraph 16(2), or

(b) where a group tax strategy has been published, there is a failure to comply with paragraph 16(5).

18(3) Subject to sub-paragraph (5) the head of the group is only liable to one penalty by virtue of sub-paragraph (2) in respect of a group tax strategy required for the financial year in question.

18(4) Sub-paragraph (5) applies where–

(a) the head of the group is liable to a penalty under this paragraph in respect of a failure mentioned in sub-paragraph (2)(a), and

(b) no group tax strategy for the group that complies with paragraph 16(2) (disregarding paragraph 16(3)) is published within the period of 6 months after the last day on which the duty under paragraph 16(2) could have been complied with.

18(5) At the end of that period, the head of the group–

(a) is liable to a further penalty of £7,500, and

(b) where the failure mentioned in sub-paragraph (4)(b) continues, is liable to a further penalty of £7,500 at the end of each subsequent month in which no such group tax strategy is published.

UK SUB-GROUPS: DUTY TO PUBLISH A SUB-GROUP TAX STRATEGY

19(1) This paragraph applies to a UK sub-group of a foreign group if in any financial year ("the current financial year") the foreign group is a qualifying group.

19(2) The head of the sub-group must ensure that a sub-group tax strategy for the sub-group, giving the information required by paragraph 20, is prepared and published in accordance with this paragraph.

19(3) The sub-group tax strategy–

(a) must be published before the end of the current financial year, and

(b) if the group of which the sub-group is part was a qualifying group in the previous financial year, must not be published more than 15 months after the day on which its sub-group tax strategy for that year was published;

19(4) The sub-group tax strategy–

(a) must be published on the internet by any of the UK companies that are members of the foreign group so as to be accessible to the public free of charge (whether or not it is also published in any other way), and

(b) may be published as a separate document or as a self-contained part of a wider document.

19(5) The head of the sub-group must ensure that the sub-group tax strategy published on the internet remains accessible to the public free of charge–

(a) if a sub-group tax strategy for the sub-group's next financial year is required by this paragraph to be published, until that tax strategy is published, or

(b) if paragraph (a) does not apply, for at least one year.

19(6) For the purposes of this paragraph–

(a) a sub-group tax strategy is published when it is first published on the internet as mentioned in sub-paragraph (4)(a),

(b) the identity of the sub-group is not affected by any change in its membership in the current financial year resulting from a relevant body becoming or ceasing to be a 51% subsidiary of a member of the sub-group, and

(c) if the sub-group becomes a UK sub-group of another foreign group during the current financial year, for the rest of that year it is to be treated as if it were still a UK sub-group of the original foreign group (but only a UK company within the sub-group may publish a subgroup tax strategy for the sub-group after that change).

19(7) In this paragraph **"financial year"**, in relation to a UK sub-group, means a financial year of the *head of the group of which it is a sub-group.*

CONTENT OF A SUB-GROUP TAX STRATEGY

20(1) Paragraph 17 applies in relation to a sub-group tax strategy required to be published on behalf of a UK sub-group by paragraph 19 as it applies to a group tax strategy required to be published by a qualifying UK group.

20(2) In the application of paragraph 17 to a sub-group tax strategy, references to the group or members of the group are to be read as references to the UK sub-group or members of the UK sub-group.

20(3) In the application of paragraph 17 as modified by this paragraph to a subgroup tax strategy, a UK permanent establishment of a foreign member of the UK sub-group is to be treated as if it were a member of the sub-group.

PENALTY FOR NON-COMPLIANCE WITH REQUIREMENTS OF PARAGRAPH 19

21(1) This paragraph applies where paragraph 19 requires a sub-group tax strategy to be published for a UK sub-group in any financial year of the head of the sub-group.

21(2) The head of the sub-group is liable to a penalty of £7,500 if–

(a) there is a failure to publish a sub-group tax strategy for the subgroup that complies with paragraph 19(2), or

(b) where a sub-group tax strategy has been published, there is a failure to comply with paragraph 19(5).

21(3) Subject to sub-paragraph (5), the head of the sub-group is only liable to one penalty by virtue of sub-paragraph (2) in respect of a sub-group tax strategy required for the financial year in question.

21(4) Sub-paragraph (5) applies where–

(a) the head of the sub-group is liable to a penalty under this paragraph in respect of a failure mentioned in sub-paragraph (2)(a), and

(b) no sub-group tax strategy for the sub-group that complies with paragraph 19(2) (disregarding paragraph 19(3)) is published within the period of 6 months after the last day on which the duty under paragraph 19(2) could have been complied with.

21(5) At the end of that period, the head of the sub-group is liable–

(a) to a further penalty of £7,500, and

(b) where the failure mentioned in sub-paragraph (4)(b) continues, to a further penalty of £7,500 at the end of each subsequent month in which no such sub-group tax strategy is published.

QUALIFYING COMPANIES: DUTY TO PUBLISH A COMPANY TAX STRATEGY

22(1) This paragraph applies in relation to a UK company which in any financial year ("the current financial year") is a qualifying company.

22(2) The company must prepare and publish a company tax strategy, containing the information required by paragraph 23, in accordance with this paragraph.

22(3) The duty under sub-paragraph (2) applies even if the company becomes a member of a UK group or a UK sub-group during the current financial year.

22(4) The company tax strategy–

(a) must be published by the company before the end of the current financial year, and

(b) if the company was a qualifying company in the previous financial year, must not be published more than 15 months after the day on which its company tax strategy was published in the previous financial year.

22(5) The company tax strategy–

(a) must be published on the internet so as to be accessible to the public free of charge (whether or not published in any other way), and

(b) *may be published* as a separate document or a self-contained part of a wider document.

22(6) The company must ensure that the company tax strategy published on the internet remains accessible to the public free of charge–

(a) if a company tax strategy for the next financial year is required by this paragraph to be published, until that tax strategy is published, or

(b) if paragraph (a) does not apply, for at least one year.

22(7) For the purposes of this paragraph a company tax strategy is published when it is first published as mentioned in sub-paragraph (5)(a).

22(8) A UK permanent establishment which in any financial year is by virtue of paragraph 5(6) to be treated as a qualifying company is to be treated for the purposes of this paragraph and paragraphs 23 and 24 as if it were a UK company which in that financial year is a qualifying company.

CONTENT OF A COMPANY TAX STRATEGY

23(1) The company tax strategy must set out–

(a) the company's approach to risk management and governance arrangements in relation to UK taxation,

(b) the company's attitude towards tax planning (so far as affecting UK taxation),

(c) the level of risk in relation to UK taxation that the company is prepared to accept,

(d) the company's approach towards its dealings with HMRC.

23(2) The company tax strategy may include other information relating to taxation (whether UK taxation or otherwise).

23(3) The information required by sub-paragraph (1) to be included in a company tax strategy does not include any information about activities of the company that consist of the provision of tax advice or related professional services to other persons.

23(4) The publication of information as a company tax strategy does not constitute publication of the strategy for the purposes of paragraph 22 unless the company makes clear (in a way that will be readily apparent to anyone accessing the information online) that the company regards its publication as complying with the duty under paragraph 22(2) in the current financial year.

PENALTY FOR NON-COMPLIANCE WITH PARAGRAPH 22

24(1) This paragraph applies where paragraph 22 requires a company tax strategy to be published for a UK company in any financial year.

24(2) The company is liable to a penalty of £7,500 if–

(a) there is a failure to publish a company tax strategy for the company that complies with paragraph 22(2), or

(b) where a company tax strategy has been published, there is a failure to comply with paragraph 22(6).

24(3) Subject to sub-paragraph (5), the company is only liable to one penalty by virtue of sub-paragraph (2) in respect of a company tax strategy required for the financial year in question.

24(4) Sub-paragraph (5) applies where–

(a) a penalty is imposed under this paragraph in respect of a failure mentioned in sub-paragraph (2)(a), and

(b) no company tax strategy that complies with paragraph 22(2) (disregarding paragraph 22(4)) is published within the period of 6 months after the last day on which the duty under paragraph 22(2) could have been complied with.

24(5) At the end of that period, the company is liable–

(a) to a further penalty of £7,500, and

(b) where the failure mentioned in sub-paragraph (4)(b) continues, to a further penalty of £7,500 at the end of each subsequent month in which no such company tax strategy is published.

QUALIFYING PARTNERSHIPS: DUTY TO PUBLISH A PARTNERSHIP TAX STRATEGY

25(1) Paragraphs 22 to 24 apply in relation to a UK partnership which is (in any financial year of the partnership) a qualifying partnership as they apply to a UK company which is (in any financial year of the company) a qualifying company.

25(2) Those paragraphs have effect in their application to a qualifying partnership–

(a) with the omission of paragraph 22(3) and (8),

(b) as if for "company tax strategy" (in each place) there were substituted "partnership tax strategy", and

(c) as if for "company" and "company's" (in each place) there were substituted respectively "partnership" and "partnership's".

PENALTIES UNDER THIS PART: GENERAL PROVISIONS

26(1) Paragraphs 27 to 33 apply in relation to the liability of any person to a penalty under this Part and, accordingly, in those paragraphs–

"failure", in relation to a liability for a penalty, means a failure which could give rise to that liability,

"liability to a penalty" means a liability under paragraph 18, 21 or 24 (including paragraph 24 as applied to a qualifying UK partnership), and

"penalty" means a penalty under any of those paragraphs.

26(2) In those paragraphs **"tribunal"** means the First-tier Tribunal or, where determined by or under the Tribunal Procedure Rules, the Upper Tribunal.

FAILURE TO COMPLY WITH A TIME LIMIT

27 A failure to do anything required by this Part to be done within a limited period of time goes not give rise to liability to a penalty if it is done within such further time (if any) as an officer of Revenue and Customs may have allowed.

REASONABLE EXCUSE

28(1) Liability to a penalty for a failure does not arise if the person who would otherwise be liable to that penalty satisfies HMRC or (on an appeal notified to the tribunal) the tribunal that the person had a reasonable excuse for that failure.

28(2) For the purposes of this paragraph–

(a) an insufficiency of funds is not a reasonable excuse unless attributable to events outside the person's control,

(b) where the person relies on another person to do anything, that cannot be a reasonable excuse–

(i) unless the first person took reasonable care to avoid the failure, or

(ii) if the first person is a UK group or UK sub-group, where the person relied on is another member of the group or subgroup,

(c) where the person had a reasonable excuse but the excuse has ceased, the person is to be treated as having continued to have the excuse if the failure is remedied without unreasonable delay after the excuse ceased.

ASSESSMENT OF PENALTIES

29(1) Where a person becomes liable to a penalty–

(a) HMRC may assess the penalty, and

(b) if they do so, HMRC must notify the person of the assessment.

29(2) An assessment of a penalty may not be made–

(a) more than 6 months after the failure first comes to the attention of an officer of Revenue and Customs, or

(b) more than 6 years after the end of the financial year in which the tax strategy to which the failure relates was (or was originally) required to be published.

APPEAL

30(1) A person may appeal against a decision of HMRC that a penalty is payable by that person.

30(2) Notice of an appeal must be given–

(a) in writing,

(b) before the end of the period of 30 days beginning with the date on which the notification under paragraph 29(1)(b) was issued,

30(3) Notice of an appeal must state the grounds of appeal.

30(4) On an appeal that is notified to the tribunal, the tribunal may confirm or cancel the decision.

30(5) Subject to this paragraph and paragraph 31, the provisions of Part 5 of TMA 1970 relating to appeals have effect in relation to appeals under this Schedule as they have effect in relation to an appeal against an assessment to income tax.

ENFORCEMENT

31(1) A penalty must be paid–

(a) before the end of the period of 30 days beginning with the date on which the notification under paragraph 29(1)(b) was issued, or

(b) if a notice of appeal is given, before the end of 30 days beginning with the day on which the appeal is determined or withdrawn.

31(2) A penalty may be enforced as if it were corporation tax charged in an assessment and due and payable.

POWER TO CHANGE AMOUNT OF PENALTIES

32(1) If it appears to the Treasury that there has been a change in the value of money since the last relevant date, they may by regulations substitute for any sums for the time being specified in paragraph 18, 21 or 24 such other sum as appear to them to be justified by the change.

32(2) In sub-paragraph (1) **"relevant date"** means–

(a) the date on which this Act is passed, and

(b) each date on which the power conferred by that sub-paragraph has been exercised.

32(3) Regulations under this paragraph do not apply to a failure that occurs in respect of a financial year (of the body or partnership responsible for the failure) that begins before the date on which they come into force.

APPLICATION OF PROVISIONS OF TMA 1970

33 Subject to the provisions of this Part, the following provisions of TMA 1970 apply for the purposes of this Part as they apply for the purposes of the Taxes Acts–

(a) section 108 (responsibility of company officers),

(b) section 114 (want of form), and

(c) section 115 (delivery and service of documents).

MEANING OF "TAX STRATEGY"

34 In this Part **"tax strategy"** means–

(a) a group tax strategy (see paragraphs 16 to 18),

(b) a sub-group tax strategy (see paragraphs 19 to 21),

(c) a company tax strategy (see paragraphs 22 to 24), or

(d) a partnership tax strategy (see paragraph 25).

Part 3 – Sanctions for Persistently Unco-operative Large Businesses

LARGE GROUPS FALLING WITHIN PART 3

35 A UK group falls within this Part of this Schedule ("this Part") if–

(a) the group has persistently engaged in unco-operative behaviour (see paragraphs 36 to 38),

(b) some or all of the unco-operative behaviour has caused there to be, or contributed to there being, two or more significant tax issues in respect of the group or members of the group which are unresolved (see paragraph 39), and

(c) there is a reasonable likelihood of further instances of the group engaging in unco-operative behaviour in a manner which causes there to be, or contributes to there being, significant tax issues in respect of the group or members of the group.

36(1) A UK group has **"engaged in unco-operative behaviour"** if–

(a) a member of the group has satisfied either or both of the conditions listed in sub-paragraph (2), or

(b) two or more of the members of the group, taken together, have satisfied either or both of those conditions.

36(2) Those conditions are–

(a) the behaviour condition (see paragraph 37);

(b) the arrangements condition (see paragraph 38).

36(3) A UK group has engaged in unco-operative behaviour **"persistently"** if–

(a) a member of the group has done so persistently, or

(b) two or more members of the group, taken together, have done so persistently.

36(4) References in this Part to doing something **"persistently"** include doing it on a sufficient number of occasions for it to be clear that it represents a pattern of behaviour.

37(1) A member of a UK group has, or two or more members of a UK group (taken together) have, **"satisfied the behaviour condition"** if it has, or they have, behaved in a manner which has delayed or otherwise hindered HMRC in the exercise of their functions in connection with determining the liability to UK taxation of the group or a member of the group.

37(2) Factors which may indicate that a member of a UK group has behaved as described in sub-paragraph (1) include–

(a) the extent to which HMRC have used statutory powers to obtain information relating to the UK group or members of the group;

(b) the reasons why those powers have been used;

(c) the number and seriousness of inaccuracies in, and omissions from, documents given to HMRC by or on behalf of the UK group or members of the group;

(d) the extent to which, in dealings with HMRC, members of the group (or people acting on their behalf) have relied on interpretations of legislation relating to UK taxation which, at the time, are speculative.

37(3) An interpretation of legislation relating to UK taxation is **"speculative"** if it is likely that a court or tribunal would disagree with it.

38(1) A member of a UK group has **"satisfied the arrangements condition"** if it is a party to a tax avoidance scheme.

38(2) **"Tax avoidance scheme"** means–

(a) arrangements in respect of which a notice of final decision has been given under–

(i) paragraph 12 of Schedule 43 to FA 2013,

(ii) paragraph 5 or 6 of Schedule 43A to FA 2013, or

(iii) paragraph 9 of Schedule 43B to FA 2013,

stating that a tax advantage arising from the arrangements is to be counteracted;

(b) arrangements which are notifiable arrangements for the purposes of Part 7 of FA 2004 (disclosure of tax avoidance schemes), other than arrangements in relation to which HMRC have given notice under section 312(6) of FA 2004 (notice that promoters not under duty to provide clients with prescribed information);

(c) a scheme which is a notifiable scheme for the purposes of Schedule 11A to VATA 1994 (disclosure of avoidance schemes).

39(1) There is a significant tax issue in respect of a UK group or a member of a UK group where–

(a) there is a disagreement between HMRC and a member of the group about an issue affecting the amount of the liability of the group or a member of the group to UK taxation,

(b) the issue has been, or could be, referred to a court or tribunal to determine, and

(c) as regards the amount of the liability, the difference between HMRC's view and the view of the member is, or is likely to be, not less than £2 million.

39(2) The reference in sub-paragraph (1)(a) to circumstances in which there is a disagreement include circumstances in which there is a reasonable likelihood of a disagreement.

39(3) The Treasury may by regulations substitute a higher amount for the amount for the time being specified in sub-paragraph (1)(c).

40 The references in paragraphs 36 to 39 to things done by a member of a UK group ("the group in question")–

(a) include acts and omissions of a relevant body that is not a member of the group in question if they took place at a time when the relevant body was a member of a group headed by the body that is the head of the group in question;

(b) do not include acts or omissions of a relevant body that is a member of the group in question if they took place at a time when the relevant body was not a member of a group headed by the body that is the head of the group in question.

WARNING NOTICES

41(1) A designated HMRC officer may give the head of a UK group a notice under this paragraph (a "warning notice") if the officer considers that the group is a qualifying group that falls within this Part.

41(2) The notice must set out the reasons why the officer considers that the group falls within this Part.

41(3) The notice–

(a) may be withdrawn by a designated HMRC officer at any time by giving a further notice to the head of the group, and

(b) expires (if not previously withdrawn) at the end of the period of 15 months beginning with the day on which it was given.

41(4) Once a warning notice has been given–

(a) it is immaterial for the purposes of this Part whether the group remains a qualifying group,

(b) the identity of the group is not to be regarded as altered by any change in its membership resulting from a relevant body–

(i) becoming a 51% subsidiary of a member of the group, or

(ii) ceasing to be a 51% subsidiary of another member of the group; and

(c) if the group becomes a UK sub-group of a foreign group it is to be treated as if it were still a UK group.

41(5) Sub-paragraph (4) applies while the group is subject to–

(a) the warning notice, or

(b) any other notice under this Part issued as a result of the group having been given the warning notice.

SPECIAL MEASURES NOTICES

42(1) This paragraph applies to a UK group if–

(a) the head of the group has been given a warning notice in relation to the group that has not been withdrawn,

(b) the period of 12 months beginning with the day on which the warning notice was given has elapsed, and

(c) the period of 15 months beginning with that day has not elapsed.

42(2) If a designated HMRC officer considers that the group falls within this Part, the officer may give the head of the group a notice under this paragraph (a "special measures notice").

42(3) When considering whether the group falls within this Part, the officer may take into account any relevant behaviour, whether or not it is mentioned in the warning notice.

42(4) When deciding whether to give a special measures notice, the designated HMRC officer must consider any representations made by a member of the group before the end of the period of 12 months beginning with the day on which the warning notice was given.

42(5) The special measures notice must set out the reasons why the officer considers that the group falls within this Part.

42(6) Paragraph 45 deals with other circumstances in which a UK group may be given a special measures notice.

43(1) A special measures notice–

(a) may be withdrawn by a designated HMRC officer at any time by giving a further notice to the head of the UK group, and

(b) expires, if not previously withdrawn, at the end of the period of 27 months beginning with the relevant day.

43(2) **"The relevant day"** means the later of–

(a) the day on which the special measures notice was given, and

(b) the day on which it was last confirmed under paragraph 44.

44(1) This paragraph applies to a UK group if–

(a) the head of the group has been given a special measures notice in relation to the group which has not been withdrawn,

(b) the period of 24 months beginning with the relevant day has elapsed, and

(c) the period of 27 months beginning with that day has not elapsed.

44(2) If a designated HMRC officer considers that the group falls within this Part, the officer may give the head of the group a notice under this paragraph (a "confirmation notice") confirming the special measures notice given in relation to the group.

44(3) When considering whether the group falls within this Part, the officer may take into account any relevant behaviour, whether or not it is mentioned in the special measures notice which is to be confirmed, in any previous confirmation notice or in the warning notice.

44(4) **"The relevant day"** has the same meaning as in paragraph 43(2).

44(5) The confirmation notice must set out the reasons why the officer considers that the group falls within this Part.

44(6) When deciding whether to give a confirmation notice, a designated HMRC officer must consider any representations made by a member of the group before the end of the period of 24 months beginning with the relevant day.

44(7) A confirmation notice–

(a) may be withdrawn by a designated HMRC officer at any time by giving a further notice to the head of the group, and

(b) expires, if not previously withdrawn, at the end of the period of 27 months beginning with the day on which it is given.

45(1) This paragraph applies in relation to a UK group where–

(a) the head of the group has been given a warning notice or a special measures notice in relation to the group, and

(b) that notice has expired.

45(2) A designated HMRC officer may give the head of a UK group a special measures notice if–

(a) it appears to the officer that–

(i) during the period of 6 months beginning with the day on which the notice mentioned in sub-paragraph (1)(a) expired ("the expiry day"), the group has engaged in unco-operative behaviour (see paragraphs 36 to 38), and

(ii) there is a reasonable likelihood that, if it had engaged in the behaviour before the notice expired, a designated HMRC officer would have considered that the group fell within this Part (so that a special measures notice or confirmation notice could have been given to the head of the group),

(b) during the period of 7 months beginning with the expiry day, a designated HMRC officer has notified the head of the group that the power under this paragraph may be exercised in relation to the group, and

(c) the period of 9 months beginning with that day has not elapsed.

45(3) When deciding whether to give a special measures notice under this paragraph, the officer must consider any representations made by a member of the group before the end of the period of 8 months beginning with the expiry day.

CIRCUMSTANCES IN WHICH WARNING AND SPECIAL MEASURES NOTICES ARE TREATED AS HAVING BEEN GIVEN

46(1) Sub-paragraphs (2) and (3) apply where–

(a) a relevant body ("B1") is given a warning notice, and

(b) before the notice ceases to have effect, B1 becomes a member of a group headed by another relevant body ("H1").

46(2) H1 is to be treated as having been given a warning notice on the day on which the warning notice was given to B1.

46(3) A warning notice treated as given under sub-paragraph (2) is valid whether or not, on the day mentioned in that sub-paragraph, H1 was the head of a qualifying UK group that fell within this Part.

46(4) Sub-paragraphs (5) to (7) apply where–

(a) a relevant body ("B2") is given a special measures notice, and

(b) before the notice ceases to have effect, B2 becomes a member of a group headed by another relevant body ("H2").

46(5) H2 is to be treated as having been given a special measures notice on the day on which the special measures notice was given to B2.

46(6) A special measures notice treated as given under sub-paragraph (5) is valid whether or not, on the day mentioned in that sub-paragraph, H2 was the head of a qualifying UK group that fell within this Part.

46(7) Paragraph 47(1) does not by virtue of sub-paragraphs (5) and (6) of this paragraph apply to an inaccuracy in a document given to HMRC by or on behalf of a person–

(a) at a time when the person was a member of a group headed by H2, but

(b) before the day B2 becomes a member of H2.

46(8) Sub-paragraphs (9) and (10) apply where–

(a) a relevant body ("B3") is given a confirmation notice, and

(b) before the notice ceases to have effect, B3 becomes a member of a group headed by another relevant body ("H3").

46(9) H3 is to be treated as having been given a confirmation notice on the day on which the confirmation notice was given to B3.

46(10) A confirmation notice treated as given under sub-paragraph (9) is valid whether or not, on the day mentioned in that sub-paragraph, H3 was the head of a qualifying UK group that fell within this Part.

46(11) The Treasury may by regulations make provision for warning notices, special measures notices and confirmation notices to be treated as having been given to relevant bodies in other circumstances described in the regulations.

46(12) Regulations under this paragraph may, in particular–

(a) make provision about the validity of notices treated as given by virtue of the regulations;

(b) make provision about the effect of paragraph 47(1) in cases involving such notices.

SANCTIONS: LIABILITY FOR PENALTIES FOR ERRORS IN DOCUMENTS GIVEN TO HMRC

47(1) For the purposes of Schedule 24 to FA 2007 (penalties for errors), an inaccuracy in a document given to HMRC by or on behalf of a person is to be treated as being due to failure by the person to take reasonable care if–

(a) the document was given to HMRC at a time when the person was a member of a group subject to a special measures notice, and

(b) the inaccuracy–

 (i) relates to a tax avoidance scheme (as defined in paragraph 38) entered into by the person at a time when the person was a member of a group subject to a special measures notice, or

 (ii) is, entirely or partly, attributable to an interpretation of legislation relating to UK taxation which, at the time the document was given to HMRC, was speculative.

47(2) A group is **"subject to a special measures notice"** if a special measures notice–

(a) has been given to the head of the group in relation to the group, and

(b) is in force.

47(3) An interpretation of legislation relating to UK taxation is **"speculative"** if it is likely that a court or tribunal would disagree with it.

47(4) Sub-paragraph (1) does not apply to an inaccuracy if–

(a) it is deliberate on the part of the person or someone acting on the person's behalf,

(b) it is in fact due to a failure by the person or someone acting on the person's behalf to take reasonable care, or

(c) it is treated as due to such a failure by virtue of another enactment.

48 In Schedule 24 to FA 2007 (penalties for errors), at the end of paragraph 3 (meaning of "careless" etc) insert–

> "**3(3)** Paragraph 47 of Schedule 19 to FA 2016 (special measures for persistently unco-operative large businesses) provides for certain inaccuracies to be treated, for the purposes of this Schedule, as being due to a failure by P to take reasonable care."

SANCTIONS: COMMISSIONERS PUBLISHING INFORMATION

49(1) If a group is subject to a confirmed special measures notice, the Commissioners for Her Majesty's Revenue and Customs ("the Commissioners") may publish the following information–

(a) *the name of the group, including* any previous name;

(b) the address or registered office of the head of the group;

(c) any other information that the Commissioners consider it appropriate to publish in order to identify the group;

(d) the fact that the group is subject to a confirmed special measures notice.

49(2) A group is **"subject to a confirmed special measures notice"** if sub-paragraph (3) or (4) is satisfied.

49(3) This sub-paragraph is satisfied if–

(a) a special measures notice has been given to the head of the group and confirmed under paragraph 44, and

(b) the special measures notice is in force.

49(4) This sub-paragraph is satisfied if–

(a) a special measures notice has been given to the head of the group and confirmed under paragraph 44,

(b) that notice has ceased to have effect,

(c) a further special measures notice has been given to the head of the group under paragraph 45 in the period of 9 months beginning with the day on which the special measures notice mentioned in paragraph (a) ceased to have effect, and

(d) that notice is in force.

49(5) Before publishing the information, the Commissioners must–

(a) inform the head of the group that they are considering doing so, and

(b) allow the head of the group a reasonable opportunity to make representations about whether the information should be published.

49(6) If, after information about a group is published under this paragraph, the group ceases to be subject to a confirmed special measures notice, the Commissioners must publish a notice stating that the group is no longer subject to a confirmed special measures notice.

49(7) A notice under sub-paragraph (6) must be published before the end of the period of 30 days beginning with the day on which the special measures notice is withdrawn or has expired.

49(8) The Commissioners may publish information and notices under this paragraph in any manner they consider appropriate.

APPLICATION OF PART 3 TO LARGE UK SUB-GROUPS

50(1) A UK sub-group of a foreign group falls within this Part if–

(a) the sub-group has persistently engaged in unco-operative behaviour (see paragraphs 36 to 38),

(b) some or all of the unco-operative behaviour has caused there to be, or contributed to there being, two or more significant tax issues in respect of the sub-group or members of the sub-group which are unresolved (see paragraph 39), and

(c) there is a reasonable likelihood of further instances of the sub-group engaging in unco-operative behaviour in a manner which causes there to be, or contributes to there being, significant tax issues in respect of the sub-group or members of the sub-group.

50(2) Paragraphs 36 to 40 apply in relation to a UK sub-group as they apply in relation to a UK group.

50(3) Paragraphs 41 to 45 apply in relation to the head of a UK sub-group of a foreign group that is a qualifying group at the material time as they apply in relation to the head of a UK group.

50(4) In the application of paragraph 41 in the case of a UK sub-group, sub-paragraph (4) has effect in relation to a UK sub-group as if for paragraphs (b) and (c) there were substituted–

"(b) the identity of the sub-group is not to be regarded as altered by any change in its membership resulting from a relevant body–

(i) becoming a 51% subsidiary of a member of the sub-group, or

(ii) ceasing to be a 51% subsidiary of another member of the sub-group; and

(c) if the sub-group becomes a UK sub-group of another foreign group, it is to be treated as if it were still a UK subgroup of the original foreign group."

50(5) As applied by this paragraph, paragraphs 36 to 45 have effect as if references to a UK group (including in references to the head of a UK group or members of a UK group) were references to a UK sub-group.

50(6) In paragraphs 40, 41, 46, 47 and 49, references to a group (including in references to the head of a group or members of a group) include a UK sub-group.

50(7) In paragraph 46, references to the head of a UK group include the head of a UK sub-group.

APPLICATION OF PART 3 TO LARGE COMPANIES

51(1) A UK company falls within this Part if–

(a) the company has persistently engaged in unco-operative behaviour (see paragraphs 36 to 38),

(b) some or all of the unco-operative behaviour has caused there to be, or contributed to there being, two or more significant tax issues in respect of the company which are unresolved (see paragraph 39), and

(c) there is a reasonable likelihood of further instances of the company engaging in unco-operative behaviour in a manner which causes there to be, or contributes to there being, significant tax issues in respect of the company.

51(2) Paragraphs 36 to 39 apply in relation to a company as they apply in relation to a UK group.

51(3) Paragraphs 41 to 45 apply in relation to a company as they apply in relation to the head of a UK group.

51(4) As applied by this paragraph, paragraphs 36 to 39 and 41 to 45 have effect as if references to a UK group, the head of a UK group or a member of a UK group were references to a company.

51(5) Paragraph 47 applies in relation to a company as it applies in relation to a member of a group.

51(6) Paragraph 49 applies in relation to a company as it applies in relation to a group.

51(7) As applied by this paragraph, paragraphs 47 and 49 have effect as if references to a group, the head of a group or a member of a group were references to a company.

APPLICATION OF PART 3 TO LARGE PARTNERSHIPS

52(1) A UK partnership falls within this Part if–

(a) the partnership has persistently engaged in unco-operative behaviour (see paragraphs 36 to 38),

(b) some or all of the unco-operative behaviour has caused there to be, or contributed to there being, two or more significant tax issues in respect of the partnership which are unresolved (see paragraph 39), and

(c) there is a reasonable likelihood of further instances of the partnership engaging in unco-operative behaviour in a manner which causes there to be, or contributes to there being, significant tax issues in respect of the partnership.

52(2) Paragraphs 36 to 39 of this Schedule apply in relation to a UK partnership as they apply in relation to a UK group.

52(3) Paragraphs 41 to 45 of this Schedule apply in relation to the representative partner of a UK partnership as they apply in relation to the head of a UK group.

52(4) As applied by this paragraph, paragraphs 36 to 39 and 41 to 45 have effect as if–

(a) references to a UK group were references to a UK partnership;

(b) references to the head of a UK group were references to the representative partner of a UK partnership;

(c) references to a member of a UK group were references to a partner of a UK partnership, acting in the person's capacity as such.

52(5) The Treasury may by regulations make provision for warning notices, special measures notices and confirmation notices to be treated as having been given to the representative partner of a UK partnership in circumstances described in the regulations.

52(6) Paragraph 46(12) applies to regulations under this paragraph.

52(7) Paragraph 47 applies in relation to an inaccuracy in a document given to HMRC by a partner of a UK partnership, acting in the person's capacity as such, as if–

(a) references to a group were references to a partnership;

(b) references to the head of a group were references to the representative partner of a partnership;

(c) references to a member of a group were references to a partner of a partnership.

52(8) Paragraph 47 applies in relation to an inaccuracy in any other document given to HMRC on behalf of a UK partnership as if–

(a) references to a person included a UK partnership;

(b) references to a group, or a member of a group, were references to a UK partnership;

(c) references to the head of a group were references to the representative partner of a UK partnership.

52(9) Paragraph 49 applies in relation to a UK partnership as it applies in relation to a group.

52(10) As applied by this paragraph, paragraph 49 has effect as if–
(a) references to a group were references to a UK partnership;
(b) references to the head of a group were references to the representative partner of a UK partnership.

MEANING OF "DESIGNATED HMRC OFFICER"

53 In this Part **"designated HMRC officer"** means an officer of Revenue and Customs who has been designated by the Commissioners for Her Majesty's Revenue and Customs for the purposes of this Part.

Part 4 – Supplementary

AMENDMENT OF POWER UNDER SECTION 122 OF FA 2015

54 The power to make regulations under section 122(6)(c) of FA 2015 (country-by-country reporting: incidental etc provision that may be included in regulations) includes power to amend paragraph 7 above.

REGULATIONS

55(1) Regulations under this Schedule are to be made by statutory instrument.

55(2) A statutory instrument containing regulations under this Schedule is subject to annulment in pursuance of a resolution of the House of Commons.

Terms defined for purposes of more than one paragraph of this Schedule

Term	*Paragraph*
balance sheet total	paragraph 14(2)
confirmation notice (in Part 3)	paragraph 44
designated HMRC officer (in Part 3)	paragraph 53
engaged in unco-operative behaviour (in Part 3)	paragraph 36
failure (in paragraphs 27 to 33)	paragraph 26(1)
financial year (in relation to a UK group) (in paragraphs 16 and 17)	paragraph 16(7)
foreign (in relation to a relevant body)	paragraph 2(2)
foreign (in relation to a group)	paragraph 6(3)
group	paragraph 6(1)
group other than an MNE Group	paragraph 8
head (in relation to a group)	paragraph 9
head (in relation to a UK sub-group)	paragraph 11(2)
"liability to a penalty" (in paragraphs 27 to 33)	paragraph 26(1)
MNE Group	paragraph 7(1)
member (in relation to a group)	paragraph 8(2) and (3)
penalty (in paragraphs 27 to 33)	paragraph 26(1)
qualifying company	paragraph 5
qualifying group	paragraph 10
qualifying UK partnership	paragraph 12(2)
relevant body	paragraph 2(1)
representative partner	paragraph 12(5)
satisfied the arrangements condition (in Part 3)	paragraph 38
satisfied the behaviour condition (in Part 3)	paragraph 37
special measures notice	paragraphs 42 and 45
tax strategy (in Part 2)	paragraph 34
tribunal (in paragraphs 27 to 33)	paragraph 26(2)
turnover	paragraph 14(1)

Term	Paragraph
UK company	paragraph 3
UK group	paragraph 6(2)
UK partnership	paragraph 12(1)
UK permanent establishment	paragraph 4(1)
UK sub-group	paragraph 11(1)
UK taxation	paragraph 15
warning notice	paragraph 41.

SCHEDULE 21 – PENALTIES RELATING TO OFFSHORE MATTERS AND OFFSHORE TRANSFERS

Section 163

Commencement Date – 1 April 2017 is the day appointed for the coming into force of amendments by Sch. 21 for all purposes except as noted below and the amendments have effect for inheritance tax purposes, in relation to transfers of value made on or after that day; and for income tax and capital gains tax purposes, in relation to any tax year commencing on or after 6 April 2016 (SI 2017/259, reg. 2–3). Excepted commencement dates as follows:

- para. 2(4) comes into force on 8 March 2017 for the purpose of making the regulations required by FA 2007, Sch. 24, para. 9(1C) (penalties for errors);
- para. 10(5) comes into force on 8 March 2017 for the purpose of making the regulations required by FA 2009, Sch. 55, para. 14(2C) (penalty for failure to make returns etc).

AMENDMENTS TO SCHEDULE 24 TO THE FINANCE ACT 2007 (C. 11)

1 Schedule 24 to FA 2007 (penalties for errors) is amended as follows.

2(1) Paragraph 9 (reductions for disclosure) is amended as follows.

2(2) [Substitutes FA 2007, Sch. 24, para. 9(A1)–(A3).]

2(3) [Amends FA 2007, Sch. 24, para. 9(1).]

2(4) [Inserts FA 2007, Sch. 24, para. 9(1A)–(1E).]

2(5) [Inserts FA 2007, Sch. 24, para. 9(4).]

Commencement Date – Para. 2(4) comes into force on 8 March 2017 for the purpose of making the regulations required by FA 2007, Sch. 24, para. 9(1C) (penalties for errors) (SI 2017/259, reg. 3(a)).

3 [Substitutes Table in FA 2007, Sch. 24, para. 10(2).]

4 [Inserts FA 2007, Sch. 24, para. 10A.]

AMENDMENTS TO SCHEDULE 55 TO THE FINANCE ACT 2009 (C. 10)

9 Schedule 55 to FA 2009 (penalty for failure to make returns etc) is amended as follows

10(1) Paragraph 14 (reductions for disclosure) is amended as follows.

10(2) [Inserts FA 2009, Sch. 55, para. 14(A1).]

10(3) [Amends FA 2009, Sch. 55, para. 14(1).]

10(4) [Inserts FA 2009, Sch. 55, para. 14(1A) and (1B).]

10(5) [Inserts FA 2009, Sch. 55, para. 14(2A)–(2E).]

10(6) [Inserts FA 2009, Sch. 55, para. 14(5).]

History – Para. 10(5) comes into force on 8 March 2017 for the purpose of making the regulations required by FA 2009, Sch. 55, para. 14(2C) (penalty for failure to make returns etc) (SI 2017/259, reg. 3(c)).

11 [Substitutes Table in FA 2009, Sch. 55, para. 15(2).]

12 [Inserts FA 2009, Sch. 55, para. 15A.]

SCHEDULE 22 – ASSET-BASED PENALTY FOR OFFSHORE INACCURACIES AND FAILURES

Section 165

Commencement Date – Sch. 22 comes into force on 1 April 2017 and has effect for inheritance tax purposes, in relation to transfers of value made on or after 1 April 2017 and for income tax and capital gains tax purposes, in relation to tax years commencing on or after 6th April 2016 (SI 2017/277, reg. 2).

Part 5 – General

CONSEQUENTIAL AMENDMENTS ETC

20(1) [Inserts TMA 1970, s. 103ZA(j).]

20(2) [Not relevant to National Insurance contributions.]

20(3) [Amends FA 2007, Sch. 24, para. 12(2A).]

20(4) [Not relevant to National Insurance contributions.]

20(5) [Inserts FA 2009, Sch. 55, para. 17(2)(d).]

SCHEDULE 23 – SIMPLE ASSESSMENTS

Section 167

1 TMA 1970 is amended in accordance with paragraphs 2 to 8 of this Schedule.

2 [Inserts TMA 1970, s. 7(2A).]

3 [Inserts TMA 1970, s. 28H–28J.]

4 [Inserts TMA 1970, s. 31(3A).]

5(1) Section 31A (appeals: notice of appeal) is amended as follows.

5(2) [Amends TMA 1970, s. 31A(4).]

5(3) [Inserts TMA 1970, s. 31A(4A).]

6 [Inserts TMA 1970, s. 31AA.]

7(1) Section 59B (payment of income tax and capital gains tax) is amended as follows.

7(2) [Amends heading to TMA 1970, s. 59B.]

7(3) [Amends TMA 1970, s. 59B(6).]

8 [Inserts TMA 1970, s. 59BA.]

9(1) Schedule 56 to FA 2009 (penalty for failure to make payments on time) is amended as follows.

9(2) In the Table in paragraph 1, after item 1 insert–

"1A	Income tax or capital gains tax	Amount payable under section 59BA(4) or (5) of TMA 1970	The date falling 30 days after the date specified in section 59BA(4) or (5) of TMA 1970 as the date by which the amount must be paid."

9(3) In paragraph 3(1)(a), after "items 1," insert "1A,".

FINANCE ACT 2017

(2017 Chapter 10)

[*27th April 2017*]

ARRANGEMENT OF SECTIONS

PART 1 – DIRECT AND INDIRECT TAXES

INCOME TAX: GENERAL

10 Pensions: offshore transfers

10 Schedule 4 contains provision about charging income tax–

(a) where payments are made in respect of overseas pensions, and

(b) on transfers to qualifying recognised overseas pension schemes.

AVOIDANCE

24 Promoters of tax avoidance schemes: threshold conditions etc

24(1) [Substitutes FA 2014, Sch. 34, para. 13A(6)–(12).]

24(2) [Substitutes FA 2014, Sch. 34, para. 13B–13D.]

24(3) [Substitutes FA 20014, Sch. 34A, para. 20–22.]

24(4) [Amends FA 2014, Sch. 34A, para. 23.]

24(5) The amendments made by subsections (1) and (2) have effect for the purposes of determining whether a person meets a threshold condition in a period of three years ending on or after 8 March 2017.

24(6) The amendments made by subsections (3) and (4) have effect for the purposes of determining whether a person meets a section 237A condition in a period of three years ending on or after 8 March 2017.

PART 3 – FINAL

62 Interpretation

62 In this Act the following abbreviations are references to the following Acts.

ALDA 1979	Alcoholic Liquor Duties Act 1979
CAA 2001	Capital Allowances Act 2001
CTA 2009	Corporation Tax Act 2009
CTA 2010	Corporation Tax Act 2010
FA, followed by a year	Finance Act of that year

ICTA	Income and Corporation Taxes Act 1988
IHTA 1984	Inheritance Tax Act 1984
ITA 2007	Income Tax Act 2007
ITEPA 2003	Income Tax (Earnings and Pensions) Act 2003
ITTOIA 2005	Income Tax (Trading and Other Income) Act 2005
TCGA 1992	Taxation of Chargeable Gains Act 1992
TMA 1970	Taxes Management Act 1970
TPDA 1979	Tobacco Products Duty Act 1979
VATA 1994	Value Added Tax Act 1994
VERA 1994	Vehicle Excise and Registration Act 1994

63 Short title

63 This Act may be cited as the Finance Act 2017.

SCHEDULES

SCHEDULE 4 – PENSIONS: OFFSHORE TRANSFERS

Section 10

Part 2 – Income Tax on Pension Transfers: Overseas Transfer Charge

OTHER AMENDMENTS

19 [Inserts TMA 1970, s. 9(1A)(aa).]

COMMENCEMENT AND TRANSITIONAL PROVISION

25(1) Subject to sub-paragraphs (2) to (4), the amendments made by this Part of this Schedule have effect in relation to transfers made on or after 9 March 2017.

25(2)–(5) [Not relevant to National Insurance contributions.]

SCHEDULE 11 – SOFT DRINKS INDUSTRY LEVY: SUPPLEMENTARY AMENDMENTS

Section 56

PENALTIES: FAILURE TO COMPLY WITH REQUIREMENTS RELATING TO RETURNS

4(1) Schedule 55 to FA 2009 (penalty for failure to make returns etc) is amended in accordance with this paragraph.

4(2) In paragraph 1(4), in the definition of "penalty date", for "13" substitute "13A".

4(3) [Not relevant to National Insurance contributions.]

4(4) In subsections (2) and (4) of section 106 of FA 2009 (penalties for failure to make returns: commencement) references to Schedule 55 to that Act have effect as references to that Schedule as amended by this paragraph.

FINANCE (NO. 2) ACT 2017

(2017 Chapter 32)

[*16th November 2017*]

ARRANGEMENT OF SECTIONS

PART 1 – DIRECT TAXES

CORPORATION TAX

20 Corporate interest restriction

20 Schedule 5 makes provision about the amounts that may be brought into account for the purposes of corporation tax in respect of interest and other financing costs.

DISGUISED REMUNERATION

34 Employment income provided through third parties

34(1) [Not relevant to National Insurance contributions.]

34(2) [Not relevant to National Insurance contributions.]

34(3) Schedule 11 makes provision about the application of Part 7A of ITEPA 2003 in relation to loans and quasi-loans that are outstanding on 5 April 2019.

PART 4 – ADMINISTRATION, AVOIDANCE AND ENFORCEMENT

REPORTING AND RECORD-KEEPING

60 Digital reporting and record-keeping for income tax etc

60(1) TMA 1970 is amended as set out in subsections (2) and (3).

60(2) After section 12B insert–

"DIGITAL REPORTING AND RECORD-KEEPING

12 Digital reporting and record-keeping

12C Schedule A1 (digital reporting and record-keeping) has effect."

60(3) Before Schedule 1AA insert–

"SCHEDULE A1 – DIGITAL REPORTING AND RECORD-KEEPING

Section 12C

Part 1 – Application

APPLICATION: PERSONS

1(1) This Schedule applies to a person within the charge to income tax who, otherwise than in partnership, carries on (or has carried on)–

(a) a trade, profession or vocation the profits of which are chargeable to income tax under Part 2 of ITTOIA 2005,

(b) a property business the profits of which are chargeable to income tax under Part 3 of ITTOIA 2005, or

(c) any other activity which may give rise to profits or other income chargeable to income tax under Part 2 or 3 of ITTOIA 2005.

1(2) This is subject to paragraph 2.

2(1) This Schedule does not apply to–

(a) the trustees of a charitable trust, or

(b) the trustees of an exempt unauthorised unit trust (within the meaning of the Unauthorised Unit Trusts (Tax) Regulations 2013 (S.I. 2013/2819)),

unless the trustees elect for this Schedule to apply to them.

2(2) This Schedule does not apply to a person in respect of an excluded activity unless the person elects for this Schedule to apply to the person in respect of the excluded activity.

2(3) The following are excluded activities–

(a) the underwriting business of a member of Lloyd's (within the meaning of section 184 of the Finance Act 1993),

(b) holding shares in respect of which a distribution may be made which is chargeable to income tax under Part 3 of ITTOIA 2005 by virtue of section 548(6) of CTA 2010 (distributions to shareholders in real estate investment trusts), and

(c) participating in an open-ended investment company which may make distributions chargeable to income tax under Part 3 of ITTOIA 2005 by virtue of regulation 69Z18 of the Authorised Investment Funds (Tax) Regulations 2006 (S.I. 2006/964) (property income distributions).

2(4) The Commissioners may by regulations make provision about elections under this paragraph and the withdrawal of such elections, including provision–

(a) about how an election may be made or withdrawn, and

(b) about the period for which an election or withdrawal has effect.

APPLICATION: PARTNERSHIPS

3(1) This Schedule applies to a partnership if one or more of the partners is within the charge to income tax.

3(2) This is subject to paragraph 4.

4(1) If all the activities of a partnership which may give rise to profits or income are excluded activities, this Schedule does not apply to the partnership unless the partnership elects for this Schedule to apply to it.

4(2) The following are excluded activities–

(a) the underwriting business of a Lloyd's partnership (as defined in section 184(1) of the Finance Act 1993),

(b) holding shares in respect of which a distribution may be made which is chargeable to income tax under Part 3 of ITTOIA 2005 by virtue of section 548(6) of CTA 2010 (distributions to shareholders in real estate investment trusts), and

(c) participating in an open-ended investment company which may make distributions chargeable to income tax under Part 3 of ITTOIA 2005 by virtue of regulation 69Z18 of the Authorised Investment Funds (Tax) Regulations 2006 (S.I. 2006/964) (property income distributions).

4(3) The Commissioners may by regulations make provision about elections under this paragraph and the withdrawal of such elections, including provision–

(a) about how an election may be made or withdrawn, and

(b) about the period for which an election or withdrawal has effect.

NOMINATED PARTNERS

5(1) Requirements imposed by regulations under this Schedule on a partnership are to be met by a nominated partner.

5(2) A **"nominated partner"** is a partner nominated for the purposes of this Schedule–

(a) by the partners, or

(b) by the Commissioners.

5(3) A nomination, or a revocation of a nomination, by the partners does not have effect until notice of the revocation or nomination is given to HMRC.

5(4) The Commissioners may by regulations make provision about nominations and the revocation of nominations, including provision about the circumstances in which the Commissioners may nominate a partner.

5(5) In this Act references to a nominated partner are to a partner nominated for the purposes of this Schedule.

Part 2 – Digital Reporting and Record-keeping

INTERPRETATION

6 In this Part of this Schedule **"business"**–

(a) in relation to a person to whom this Schedule applies (see paragraphs 1 and 2), means the activity by virtue of which this Schedule applies to the person (and if more than one, means each of them), and

(b) in relation to a partnership to which this Schedule applies (see paragraphs 3 and 4), means any activity of the partnership.

PERIODIC UPDATES

7(1) The Commissioners may by regulations require a person or partnership to whom this Schedule applies to provide to HMRC, by electronic communications, specified information about the business of the person or partnership.

7(2) The information which may be specified includes any information ("financial information") relevant to calculating profits, losses or income of the business, including information about receipts and expenses.

7(3) The regulations may require information to be provided at or for specified intervals, times or periods.

7(4) The regulations may not require financial information about the business to be provided more often than once every 3 months.

END OF PERIOD STATEMENT

8(1) The Commissioners may by regulations require a person to whom this Schedule applies to provide to HMRC, by electronic communications, a statement containing specified information about the person's business in relation to each relevant period.

8(2) **"Relevant period"** means–

(a) in relation to a business the profits or income of which are chargeable to income tax under Chapter 2 of Part 2 of ITTOIA 2005, a basis period (see Chapter 15 of that Part), and

(b) otherwise, a tax year.

8(3) The information which may be specified includes any information relevant to calculating profits, losses or income of the business for the relevant period, including information about receipts and expenses.

8(4) Regulations under this paragraph may require the statement to include a declaration to the effect that the information included in it is correct and complete.

8(5) An end of period statement for a tax year must be provided to HMRC at or before–

(a) the time at which the person delivers a return under section 8 or 8A for the tax year (see section 8(7)(c) and 8A(7)(c)), or

(b) if earlier, the end of 31 January following the tax year.

8(6) In this Act–

(a) references to an end of period statement are to a statement required by regulations under this paragraph;

(b) references to an end of period statement for a tax year are to an end of period statement for that tax year or, where the relevant period is a basis period, for the basis period for that tax year.

FACILITY FOR COMPLYING WITH NOTICE TO FILE UNDER SECTION 8 OR 8A

9 The Commissioners may by regulations make provision for the establishment and use of a facility enabling a person to whom this Schedule applies to file or deliver, by electronic communications–

(a) anything which under section 8(1AB) may be required to be filed or delivered by a notice to file under section 8;

(b) anything which under section 8A(1AB) may be required to be filed or delivered by a notice to file under section 8A.

PARTNERSHIP RETURN

10(1) The Commissioners may by regulations require a partnership to which this Schedule applies to provide to HMRC, by electronic communications, a return containing specified information about the partnership's business in relation to each tax year.

10(2) The information which may be specified includes any information which is or may be required to be included in a section 12AA partnership return, including information in respect of any partners within the charge to corporation tax.

10(3) In particular, the information which may be specified includes the information required to be included in a section 12AA partnership return by section 12AB (partnership statements).

10(4) Regulations under this paragraph may require the return to include a declaration to the effect that the information included in it is correct and complete.

10(5) A Schedule A1 partnership return for a tax year must be provided to HMRC on or before 31 January following the tax year.

10(6) In this Act–

(a) references to a Schedule A1 partnership return are to a return required by regulations under this paragraph, and

(b) references to a partnership statement, in relation to a Schedule A1 partnership return, are to information required to be included in the return by virtue of sub-paragraph (3).

10(7) In the Taxes Acts, unless the contrary intention appears, a reference (whether general or specific) to a return under, or a return required under, this Act includes a reference to a Schedule A1 partnership return.

RECORD-KEEPING

11(1) The Commissioners may by regulations require a person or partnership to whom this Schedule applies to–

(a) keep specified records relating to the business in electronic form, and

(b) preserve those records in electronic form for a specified period.

11(2) The records which may be specified are any records the Commissioners consider relevant to ascertaining information required to be provided by regulations under this Part of this Schedule.

11(3) A requirement imposed by regulations under this paragraph is in addition to, and not in place of, any other requirement that the person or partnership keep and preserve records (or keep and preserve records in a particular form).

11(4) Paragraph 5(1) (requirements imposed on partnership to be met by nominated partner) does not apply to requirements imposed by regulations under this paragraph.

12(1) This paragraph applies where requirements imposed by regulations under paragraph 11 for any period are not complied with.

12(2) The person, or in the case of a partnership each relevant partner, is liable for a penalty.

12(3) **"Relevant partner"** means any person who was a partner in the partnership at any time during the period in question.

12(4) The amount of the penalty must not exceed £3,000.

12(5) A person or relevant partner is not liable to a penalty under this paragraph in relation to a period if the person or relevant partner is liable to a penalty under section 12B(5) in relation to that period.

ELECTRONIC COMMUNICATIONS AND RECORDS: SUPPLEMENTARY POWERS

13(1) This paragraph applies to regulations under paragraphs 7, 8, 9, 10 and 11.

13(2) The regulations may (amongst other things) make provision–

(a) as to the electronic form to be taken by information provided and records kept or preserved,

(b) requiring persons to prepare and keep records of information provided by means of electronic communications,

(c) for the production of the contents of records kept or preserved in accordance with regulations under this Part of this Schedule,

(d) as to conditions that must be complied with in connection with the use of electronic communications or the keeping or preservation of electronic records,

(e) for treating information as not having been provided or records as not having been kept or preserved unless conditions are complied with,

(f) for determining the time at which and person by whom information is taken to have been delivered, and

(g) for authenticating information or records.

13(3) The regulations may also make provision (which may include provision for the application of conclusive or other presumptions) about the manner of proving for any purpose–

(a) whether any use of electronic communications is to be taken as having resulted in the provision of information,

(b) the time at which information was provided,

(c) the person by whom information was provided,

(d) the contents of any information provided,

(e) the contents of any records, and

(f) any other matter for which provision may be made by the regulations.

13(4) The regulations may allow or require use to be made of intermediaries in connection with–

(a) the provision of information by means of electronic communications, and

(b) the authentication or security of anything transmitted by any such means.

13(5) The regulations may–

(a) allow any authorisation or requirement for which the regulations may provide to be given by means of a specific or general direction given by the Commissioners, and

(b) provide that the conditions of an authorisation or requirement are to be taken to be satisfied only where the Commissioners are satisfied as to specified matters.

13(6) The regulations may provide–

(a) that information provided must meet standards of accuracy and completeness set by specific or general directions given by the Commissioners, and

(b) that failure to meet those standards may be treated as a failure to provide the information, or as a failure to comply with the requirements of the regulations.

Part 3 – Exemptions

EXEMPTION FOR THE DIGITALLY EXCLUDED

14(1) The Commissioners must by regulations make provision–

(a) for a person to be exempt from requirements imposed by regulations under paragraphs 7, 8 and 11 if the Commissioners are satisfied that the person is digitally excluded, and

(b) for a partnership to be exempt from requirements imposed by regulations under paragraphs 7, 10 and 11 if the Commissioners are satisfied that the partnership is digitally excluded.

14(2) A person is digitally excluded if the digital exclusion condition is met in relation to the person.

14(3) A partnership is digitally excluded if the digital exclusion condition is met in relation to each partner.

14(4) The digital exclusion condition is met in relation to a person or partner if–

(a) the person or partner is a practising member of a religious society or order whose beliefs are incompatible with using electronic communications or keeping electronic records, or

(b) for any reason (including age, disability or location) it is not reasonably practicable for the person or partner to use electronic communications or to keep electronic records.

FURTHER EXEMPTIONS

15(1) The Commissioners may by regulations make provision for further exemptions.

15(2) The exemptions for which provision may be made include exemptions based on income or other financial criteria.

Part 4 – Supplementary Provision

APPEALS

16(1) An appeal may be brought against any decision made by the Commissioners, or by an officer of Revenue and Customs, under regulations under this Schedule.

16(2) Notice of an appeal under this paragraph must be given to HMRC within 30 days after the day on which notice of the decision is given.

16(3) The notice of appeal must–

(a) be in writing, and

(b) specify the grounds of appeal.

INTERPRETATION

17 Any power in this Schedule to require the provision of information includes power to require the provision of accounts, statements and documents relating to that information.

REGULATIONS

18(1) Regulations under this Schedule may–

(a) make provision which applies generally or only for specified cases or purposes;

(b) make different provision for different cases or purposes;

(c) include incidental, supplemental, consequential, saving, transitional or transitory provision;

(d) make provision for matters to be specified by the Commissioners in accordance with the regulations.

18(2) Sub-paragraph (1)(d) does not apply to any interval, time or period specified by virtue of paragraph 7(3) (which may be specified only by the regulations).

18(3) Regulations under this Schedule may make provision for a person or partnership to whom this Schedule applies, but who would not otherwise be subject to a requirement imposed by the regulations, to elect to be subject to that requirement.

18(4) Regulations under this Schedule may provide that, for the purposes of any provision of this Schedule or of the regulations, a change in the accounting date of a business is to be disregarded (and its period of account determined accordingly).

18(5) The power to make regulations under this Schedule is exercisable by statutory instrument.

18(6) A statutory instrument containing regulations under this Schedule is subject to annulment in pursuance of a resolution of the House of Commons."

60(4) Subsections (1) to (3) come into force on such day as the Treasury may by regulations made by statutory instrument appoint.

60(5) Regulations under subsection (4) may appoint different days for different purposes.

61 Digital reporting and record-keeping for income tax etc: further amendments

61(1) Schedule 14 contains provision amending TMA 1970 and other Acts.

61(2) The Commissioners for Her Majesty's Revenue and Customs may by regulations amend or modify any provision of the Taxes Acts in consequence of the provision made by section 60 or Schedule 14.

61(3) Regulations under subsection (2) may make transitional, transitory or saving provision.

61(4) Regulations under subsection (2) must be made by statutory instrument.

61(5) A statutory instrument containing regulations under subsection (2) may not be made unless a draft of the instrument has been laid before, and approved by a resolution of, the House of Commons.

61(6) Subsections (1) to (5) and Schedule 14 come into force on such day as the Treasury may by regulations made by statutory instrument appoint.

61(7) Regulations under subsection (6) may appoint different days for different purposes.

ENQUIRIES

63 Partial closure notices

63 Schedule 15 makes provision for partial closure notices in respect of enquiries under sections 9A, 12ZM and 12AC of TMA 1970 and Schedule 18 to FA 1998.

AVOIDANCE ETC

64 Errors in taxpayers' documents

64(1) Schedule 24 to FA 2007 (penalties for errors) is amended as set out in subsections (2) and (3).

64(2) [Inserts FA 2007, Sch. 24, para. 3A and 3B.]

64(3) [*Inserts* FA 2007, Sch. 24, para. 18(6).]

64(4) [Omits FA 2014, s. 276.]

64(5) The amendments made by this section have effect in relation to any document of a kind listed in the Table in paragraph 1 of Schedule 24 to FA 2007 which–

(a) is given to HMRC on or after the day on which this Act is passed, and

(b) relates to a tax period that–
 (i) begins on or after 6 April 2017, and
 (ii) ends on or after the day on which this Act is passed.

64(6) In subsection (5) **"tax period"**, and the reference to giving a document to HMRC, have the same meaning as in Schedule 24 to FA 2007 (see paragraph 28 of that Schedule).

65 Penalties for enablers of defeated tax avoidance

65 Schedule 16 makes provision for penalties for persons who enable tax avoidance which is defeated.

66 Disclosure of tax avoidance schemes: VAT and other indirect taxes

66(1) Schedule 17 contains provision about the disclosure of tax avoidance schemes involving VAT or other indirect taxes.

66(2) In consequence of the provision made by Schedule 17, section 58A of, and Schedule 11A to, VATA 1994 (disclosure of VAT avoidance schemes) cease to have effect to require a person to disclose any scheme which–

(a) is first entered into by that person on or after 1 January 2018,

(b) constitutes notifiable arrangements under Schedule 17,

(c) implements proposals which are notifiable proposals under Schedule 17.

66(3) No scheme or proposed scheme may be notified to the Commissioners under paragraph 9 of Schedule 11A to VATA 1994 (voluntary notification of schemes) on or after 1 January 2018.

66(4) This section and Schedule 17 come into force–

(a) so far as is necessary for enabling the making of regulations under that Schedule, on the passing of this Act, and

(b) for all other purposes, on 1 January 2018.

67 Requirement to correct certain offshore tax non-compliance

67 Schedule 18 makes provision for and in connection with requiring persons to correct any offshore tax non-compliance subsisting on 6 April 2017.

68 Penalty for transactions connected with VAT fraud etc

68(6) [Inserts FA 2007, Sch. 24, para. 21ZA.]

PART 5 – FINAL

71 Interpretation

71 In this Act the following abbreviations are references to the following Acts.

CAA 2001	Capital Allowances Act 2001
CEMA 1979	Customs and Excise Management Act 1979
CTA 2009	Corporation Tax Act 2009
CTA 2010	Corporation Tax Act 2010
CT(NI)A 2015	Corporation Tax (Northern Ireland) Act 2015
FA, followed by a year	Finance Act of that year
F(No. 2)A, followed by a year	Finance (No. 2) Act of that year
F(No. 3)A, followed by a year	Finance (No. 3) Act of that year
ICTA	Income and Corporation Taxes Act 1988
IHTA 1984	Inheritance Tax Act 1984
ITA 2007	Income Tax Act 2007
ITEPA 2003	Income Tax (Earnings and Pensions) Act 2003
ITTOIA 2005	Income Tax (Trading and Other Income) Act 2005
OTA 1975	Oil Taxation Act 1975

TCGA 1992	Taxation of Chargeable Gains Act 1992
TIOPA 2010	Taxation (International and Other Provisions) Act 2010
TMA 1970	Taxes Management Act 1970
TPDA 1979	Tobacco Products Duty Act 1979
VATA 1994	Value Added Tax Act 1994

72 Short title

72 This Act may be cited as the Finance (No. 2) Act 2017.

SCHEDULES

SCHEDULE 5 – CORPORATE INTEREST RESTRICTION

Section 20

Part 3 – Consequential Amendments

TMA 1970

3(1) [Amends TMA 1970, s. 98.]

3(2) [Not relevant to National Insurance contributions.]

Part 4 – Commencement and Transitional Provision

COMMENCEMENT: NEW PART 10 OF TIOPA

25(1) The corporate interest restriction amendments have effect in relation to periods of account of worldwide groups that begin on or after 1 April 2017.

25(2) In this paragraph **"the corporate interest restriction amendments"** means the amendments made by Parts 1 to 3 of this Schedule, apart from those made by paragraph 11 (repeal of Part 7 of TIOPA 2010).

25(3) Any regulations made by the Treasury or Commissioners under Part 10 of TIOPA 2010 before 1 April 2018 may have effect in relation to periods of account of worldwide groups that begin on or after 1 April 2017.

25(4) Sub-paragraphs (6) to (11) apply if–

(a) financial statements of a worldwide group are drawn up by or on behalf of the ultimate parent in respect of a period that begins before, and ends on or after, 1 April 2017,

(b) the period in respect of which the financial statements are drawn up is 18 months or less, and

(c) the financial statements are drawn up before the end of the period of 30 months beginning with the beginning of the period in respect of which they are drawn up.

25(5) In sub-paragraphs (6) to (11)–

(a) **"the group's actual financial statements"** means the financial statements mentioned in sub-paragraph (4);

(b) **"the straddling period of account"** means the period in respect of which those financial statements are drawn up.

25(6) For the purposes of Part 10 of TIOPA 2010, the group's actual financial statements are treated as not having been drawn up.

25(7) Instead, financial statements of the worldwide group are treated for those purposes as having been drawn up in respect of each of the following periods–

(a) the period beginning at the time the straddling period of account begins and ending with 31 March 2017, and

(b) the period beginning with 1 April 2017 and ending at the time the straddling period of account ends.

25(8) Where condition C or D in section 481 of TIOPA 2010 is met in relation to the group's actual financial statements, the financial statements treated as drawn up by sub-paragraph (7) are treated as drawn up in accordance with the generally accepted accounting principles and practice with which the group's actual financial statements were drawn up.

25(9) Where neither of those conditions is met in relation to the group's actual financial statements, the financial statements treated as drawn up by sub-paragraph (7) are IAS financial statements.

25(10) Where, for the purpose of determining amounts recognised in the financial statements treated as drawn up by sub-paragraph (7), it is expedient to apportion any amount that is recognised in the group's actual financial statements, the apportionment is to be made in accordance with section 1172 of CTA 2010 (apportionment on a time basis).

25(11) But if it appears that apportionment in accordance with that section would work unjustly or unreasonably, the apportionment is to be made on a just and reasonable basis.

25(12) Expressions used in this paragraph and in Part 10 of TIOPA 2010 have the same meaning in this paragraph as they have in that Part.

COMMENCEMENT: REPEAL OF PART 7 OF TIOPA 2010

26(1) The repeals and revocations made by paragraph 11 of this Schedule have effect in relation to periods of account of the worldwide group that begin on or after 1 April 2017.

26(2) Sub-paragraphs (4) to (10) apply if financial statements of the worldwide group are drawn up in respect of a period that begins before, and ends on or after, 1 April 2017.

26(3) In sub-paragraphs (4) to (10)–

(a) **"the group's actual financial statements"** means the financial statements mentioned in sub-paragraph (2);

(b) **"the straddling period of account"** means the period in respect of which those financial statements are drawn up.

26(4) For the purposes of Part 7 of TIOPA 2010, the group's actual financial statements are treated as not having been drawn up.

26(5) Instead, financial statements of the worldwide group are treated for those purposes as having been drawn up in respect of each of the following periods–

(a) the period beginning at the time the straddling period of account begins and ending with 31 March 2017, and

(b) the period beginning with 1 April 2017 and ending at the time the straddling period of account ends.

26(6) Where condition B, C or D in regulation 2 of the Acceptable Financial Statements Regulations is met in relation to the group's actual financial statements, the financial statements treated as drawn up by sub-paragraph (5) are treated as drawn up in accordance with the generally accepted accounting principles and practice with which the group's actual financial statements were drawn up.

26(7) Where none of those conditions is met in relation to the group's actual financial statements, the financial statements treated as drawn up by sub-paragraph (5) are IAS financial statements.

26(8) Where, for the purpose of determining amounts recognised in the financial statements treated as drawn up by sub-paragraph (5), it is expedient to apportion any amount that is recognised in the group's actual financial statements, the apportionment is to be made in accordance with section 1172 of CTA 2010 (apportionment on a time basis).

26(9) But if it appears that apportionment in accordance with that section would work unjustly or unreasonably, the apportionment is to be made on a just and reasonable basis.

26(10) In sub-paragraph (6), **"the Acceptable Financial Statements Regulations"** means the Corporation Tax (Tax Treatment of Financing Costs and Income) (Acceptable Financial Statements) Regulations 2009 (S.I. 2009/3217).

26(11) Expressions used in this paragraph and in Part 7 of TIOPA 2010 have the same meaning in this paragraph as they have in that Part.

TIME LIMITS FOR ELECTIONS RELATING TO FINANCIAL STATEMENTS OF A WORLDWIDE GROUP

27(1) In section 484 of TIOPA 2010, subsection (5) (which requires the date specified in an election under subsection (3) of that section to be on or after the day on which the election is made) does not apply in relation to an election made on or before 31 March 2018.

27(2) In section 486 of that Act, subsection (5)(a) (which requires an election under that section to be made before the end-day of the new period of account) does not apply in relation to an election made on or before 31 March 2018.

TIME LIMIT RELATING TO APPOINTMENT OF REPORTING COMPANY OR FILING INTEREST RESTRICTION RETURN

28(1) Paragraph 1(4)(a) of Schedule 7A to TIOPA 2010 (notice of the appointment of reporting company ineffective if given outside the period specified in that provision) does not apply to a notice that–

(a) is given on or before 31 March 2018, and

(b) would otherwise be of no effect by reason only of the expiry of the period specified in that provision.

28(2) Paragraph 2(4)(a) of that Schedule (notice of the revocation of the appointment of reporting company ineffective if given outside the period specified in that provision) does not apply to a notice that–

(a) is given on or before 31 March 2018, and

(b) would otherwise be of no effect by reason only of the expiry of the period specified in that provision.

28(3) Where the date determined under paragraph 7(5) of that Schedule as the filing date in relation to a period of account of a worldwide group would (apart from this sub-paragraph) be a date before 30 June 2018, that provision has effect as if it provided for the filing date in relation to the period to be 30 June 2018.

CHANGE OF ACCOUNTING POLICY

29(1) For the purposes of Part 10 of TIOPA 2010 a debit or credit to which this paragraph applies is to be ignored.

29(2) This paragraph applies to a debit or credit if–

(a) it is brought into account under the Loan Relationships and Derivative Contracts (Change of Accounting Practice) Regulations 2004 (S.I. 2004/3271), and

(b) the later period, in relation to the change of accounting policy to which the debit or credit relates, begins before 1 April 2017.

29(3) In sub-paragraph (2) **"the later period"** has the same meaning as in the regulations mentioned in that sub-paragraph.

ADJUSTMENTS UNDER SCHEDULE 7 TO F(NO. 2)A 2015

30(1) For the purposes of Part 10 of TIOPA 2010 a debit or credit to which this paragraph applies is to be ignored.

30(2) This paragraph applies to a debit or credit if–

(a) it is brought into account for the purposes of Part 5 of CTA 2009 by virtue of paragraphs 115 and 116 of Schedule 7 to F(No. 2)A 2015 (transitional adjustments relating to loan relationships), or

(b) it is brought into account for the purposes of Part 7 of CTA 2009 by virtue of paragraphs 119 and 120 of that Schedule (transitional adjustments relating to derivative contracts).

POWER TO MAKE ELECTIONS UNDER DISREGARD REGULATIONS FOR PRE-1 APRIL 2020 DERIVATIVE CONTRACTS

31(1) A company which is a UK group company of a worldwide group on 1 April 2017 may elect for the Disregard Regulations to have effect as if–

(a) the company had made an election ("the disregard election") under regulation 6A of those Regulations for the purposes of regulation 6(1)(a) of those Regulations,

(b) the disregard election applied to regulations 7, 8 and 9 of those Regulations, and

(c) the disregard election had effect in relation to derivative contracts entered into by the company before 1 April 2020.

31(2) The election has effect for the calculation under Part 10 of TIOPA 2010 of–

(a) the tax-interest expense amounts and tax-interest income amounts of the company and any relevant transferee company, and

(b) the adjusted corporation tax earnings under section 406 of that Act of the company and any relevant transferee company.

31(3) A company is a **"relevant transferee company"** if regulation 6B or 6C of the Disregard Regulations applies in relation to the company as the transferee mentioned in the regulation (on the assumption that an election has been made before the transfer under this paragraph).

31(4) An election under this paragraph has effect only if every company which was a UK group company of the worldwide group on 1 April 2017 (other than one which was dormant on that date or at the time the election is made) also makes an election under this paragraph.

31(5) An election under this paragraph–

(a) must be made before 1 April 2018, and

(b) is irrevocable.

31(6) Section 457 of TIOPA 2010 is to apply in relation to debits resulting from an election under this paragraph.

31(7) In this paragraph **"the Disregard Regulations"** means the Loan Relationships and Derivative Contracts (Disregard and Bringing into Account of Profits and Losses) Regulations 2004 (S.I. 2004/3256).

31(8) Expressions used in this paragraph and in Part 10 of TIOPA 2010 have the same meaning in this paragraph as they have in that Part.

QUALIFYING INFRASTRUCTURE COMPANIES

32(1) In the case of an accounting period of a company beginning before 1 April 2018, the company may make an election under section 433 or 444 of TIOPA 2010 before that date.

32(2) Companies making an election under section 435 of TIOPA 2010 before 1 April 2018 may specify a date in the election from which it has effect which is before the date on which the election is made.

33(1) This paragraph applies in the case of an accounting period of a company beginning before 1 April 2018 ("the transitional accounting period") if–

(a) the company does not meet the public infrastructure assets test, or the public infrastructure income test, for the transitional accounting period, but

(b) in the case of each test that it does not meet as mentioned in paragraph (a), the company would meet the test for an accounting period that includes that date and is at least 3 months long.

33(2) For the purposes of section 433 of TIOPA 2010 the company is treated as meeting the test (or tests) for the transitional accounting period.

33(3) For the purposes of sections 438 and 440 to 442 of TIOPA 2010 such adjustments to the relevant amounts are to be made as are just and reasonable, having regard to the extent to which, but for this paragraph, the company would not have met the public infrastructure assets test, or the public infrastructure income test, for the transitional accounting period.

33(4) For this purpose **"the relevant amounts"** means–

(a) amounts that would otherwise have qualified as exempt amounts under section 438,

(b) amounts that would otherwise have been treated as mentioned in section 440,

(c) the tax-EBITDA of the company, and

(d) the amounts that would otherwise have been left of account as a result of section 442.

33(5) Expressions used in this paragraph and in section 433 of TIOPA 2010 have the same meaning in this paragraph as they have in that section.

COUNTERACTING EFFECT OF AVOIDANCE ARRANGEMENTS

34(1) This paragraph applies in relation to section 461 of TIOPA 2010.

34(2) Section 461 applies in relation to arrangements whenever entered into.

34(3) Arrangements are not **"relevant avoidance arrangements"** for the purposes of section 461 so far as–

(a) they secure that an amount paid before 1 April 2017 is brought into account in an accounting period ending before that date, and

(b) directly in consequence of the amount being brought into account as mentioned in paragraph (a), there is a reduction in the tax-interest expense amounts that could otherwise have been left out of account under Part 10 of TIOPA 2010.

34(4) If an accounting period begins before 1 April 2017 and ends on or after that date, sub-paragraph (3) is to have effect as if so much of the accounting period as falls before that date, and so much of that period as falls on or after that date, were treated as separate accounting periods.

34(5) Arrangements are not **"relevant avoidance arrangements"** for the purposes of section 461 if the obtaining of any tax advantages that would otherwise arise from them can reasonably be regarded as arising wholly from commercial restructuring arrangements entered into in connection with the commencement of Part 10 of TIOPA 2010.

34(6) For this purpose **"commercial restructuring arrangements"** means–

(a) arrangements that, but for that Part, would have resulted in significantly more corporation tax becoming payable as a result of one or more loan relationships being brought within the charge to corporation tax, or

(b) arrangements that–

(i) are designed to secure, in a way that is wholly consistent with its policy objectives, the benefit of a relief expressly conferred by a provision of that Part, and

(ii) are effected by taking only ordinary commercial steps in accordance with a generally prevailing commercial practice.

34(7) This paragraph is to be read as if it formed part of section 461.

COMMENCEMENT OF ORDERS OR REGULATIONS CONTAINING CONSEQUENTIAL PROVISION

35(1) This paragraph applies in relation to any order or regulations made before 1 April 2018 by the Treasury or Commissioners containing provision that is consequential on provision made by this Schedule.

35(2) Any order or regulations to which this paragraph applies may contain provision (however expressed) for securing that the consequential provision made by the order or regulations has effect in accordance with paragraph 25 (commencement) as if the consequential provision were included in the corporate interest restriction amendments mentioned in that paragraph.

INTERPRETATION

36 References in this Part of this Schedule to Part 10 of TIOPA 2010 are to Part 10 of that Act as inserted by Parts 1 and 2 of this Schedule.

SCHEDULE 11 – EMPLOYMENT INCOME PROVIDED THROUGH THIRD PARTIES: LOANS ETC OUTSTANDING ON 5 APRIL 2019

Section 34

Part 5 – Consequential Amendments

FA 2011

47 In paragraph 59 of Schedule 2 to FA 2011 (transitional provision relating to Part 7A of ITEPA 2003), in sub-paragraph (1)(a), after "ITEPA 2003" insert "or paragraph 1 of Schedule 11 to FA (No. 2) 2017".

SCHEDULE 14 – DIGITAL REPORTING AND RECORD-KEEPING FOR INCOME TAX ETC: FURTHER AMENDMENTS

Section 61

Part 1 – Amendments of TMA 1970

1 TMA 1970 is amended as follows.

2(1) Section 7 (notice of liability) is amended as follows.

2(2) In subsection (1A) for the words from "under section 8" to the end substitute "to file under section 8 for the year of assessment".

2(3) In subsection (1B)(a) for the words from "under section 8" to "gains" substitute "to file under section 8 for the year of assessment".

2(4) In subsection (7) for "section 9" substitute "section 8 or 8A".

3(1) Section 8 (personal return) is amended as follows.

3(2) For the heading substitute "Notices to file: persons other than trustees".

3(3) For subsection (1) substitute–

"**8(1)** For the purpose of establishing–

(a) the amounts in which a person is chargeable to income tax and capital gains tax for a year of assessment, and

(b) the amount payable by the person by way of income tax for the year,

an officer of Revenue and Customs may give the person a notice to file for the year of assessment."

3(4) In subsection (1AA)(a) for "return" substitute "information filed in response to the notice to file or in any end of period statement for the year of assessment provided to HMRC by the person".

3(5) After subsection (1AA) insert–

"**8(1AB)** A notice to file for a year of assessment is a notice requiring the person concerned–

(a) to file the following for that year (in addition to any end of period statement for the year that may be required by regulations under paragraph 8 of Schedule A1)–

(i) such information as may reasonably be required in pursuance of the notice for the purpose mentioned in subsection (1),

(ii) a self-assessment (but see section 9(2)), and

(iii) a final declaration, and

(b) to deliver to HMRC such accounts, statements, or other documents (relating to the information filed as mentioned in paragraph (a)(i) and (ii)) as may reasonably be required for the purpose mentioned in subsection (1).

8(1AC) The duty to file the things mentioned in subsection (1AB)(a) is to be complied with–

(a) where the person is not required to provide an end of period statement for the year, by making and delivering to HMRC a return containing those things, and

(b) where the person is required to provide such a statement, by–

(i) making and delivering to HMRC a return containing those things, or

(ii) providing those things to HMRC using the facility to file mentioned in paragraph 9 of Schedule A1.

8(1AD) It is immaterial that any of the information required as mentioned in subsection (1AB)(a)(i) in response to a notice to file has been provided to HMRC before the date of the notice."

3(6) In subsection (1B)–

(a) for "a return under this section" substitute "the information filed in response to a notice to file";

(b) after "relevant" insert "partnership".

3(7) In subsection (1C)–

(a) after "relevant" insert "partnership";

(b) after "means a" insert "partnership";

(c) for "of this Act" substitute ", or under regulations under paragraph 10 of Schedule A1,".

3(8) For subsection (1D) substitute–

"**8(1D)** Where the method to be used for complying with a notice to file for a year of assessment (Year 1) is filing a return–

(a) if the return is a non-electronic return, the person must comply with the notice on or before 31 October in Year 2, and

(b) if the return is an electronic return, the person must comply with the notice on or before 31 January in Year 2."

3(9) In subsection (1F) for "a return" substitute "the return".

3(10) In subsection (1G) for "a return" substitute "the return".

3(11) After subsection (1H) insert–

"**8(1HA)** Where the method to be used for complying with a notice to file for a year of assessment (Year 1) is using the facility mentioned in paragraph 9 of Schedule A1, the person must comply with the notice on or before–

(a) 31 January in Year 2, or

(b) if later, the last day of the period of 3 months beginning with the date of the notice."

3(12) For subsection (2) substitute–

"**8(2)** The final declaration required by a notice to file is a declaration by the person concerned to the effect that to the best of the person's knowledge the information and self-assessment filed in response to the notice are (taken together) correct and complete."

3(13) In subsections (3), (4) and (4A) for "under this section" substitute "to file".

3(14) In subsection (4B) for the words from "may" to "income" substitute "to file may require the information filed in response".

3(15) After subsection (5) insert–

"**8(6)** In this section **"notice to file"** means a notice to file under this section.

8(7) In the Taxes Acts, unless the contrary intention appears, a reference (whether specific or general)–

(a) to a return under this section for a year of assessment, is to–

(i) the information, self-assessment and final declaration filed for the year under this section, and

(ii) any end of period statement for the year provided to HMRC;

(b) to anything required to be included in a return under this section for a year of assessment, is to–

(i) the information, self-assessment and final declaration required to be filed for the year under this section, and

(ii) any end of period statement for the year required to be provided to HMRC, and

(c) to making or delivering a return under this section, is to–

(i) making or delivering a return as mentioned in subsection (1AC)(a) or (b)(i), or

(ii) if the response to a notice to file is made using the facility mentioned in paragraph 9 of Schedule A1, making the final declaration required by the notice."

5 In section 8B (withdrawal of notice under section 8 or 8A)–

(a) in the heading after "notice" insert "to file";

(b) in subsection (1) after "notice" insert "to file".

6(1) Section 9 (returns to include self-assessment) is amended as follows.

6(2) For the heading substitute "Self-assessment required by a notice to file".

6(3) In subsection (1) for the words from the beginning to "say–" substitute "Subject to subsection (1A), the self-assessment required by virtue of subsection (1AB)(a) of section 8 or 8A from a person given a notice to file for a year of assessment is–".

6(4) In subsection (2) for "to comply with subsection (1) above" substitute "by virtue of section 8 or 8A to make and file a self-assessment".

6(5) In subsection (3) for the words from ", a person" to "above" substitute "required by virtue of section 8 or 8A, a person does not include a self-assessment".

6(6) In subsection (3A) after "self-assessment" insert "under section 8 or 8A".

14(1) Section 12B (records to be kept for purposes of returns) is amended as follows.

14(2) For subsection (1) substitute–

"**12B(1)** This section applies to any person who may–

(a) be given a notice to file under section 8 or 8A in respect of a year of assessment,

(b) be required by a notice under section 12AA to make and deliver a partnership return in respect of a year of assessment or other period, or

(c) be required by regulations under paragraph 10 of Schedule A1 to provide a partnership return for a year of assessment.

12B(1A) The person must–

(a) keep all such records as may be requisite for the purpose of enabling the person to make and deliver a correct and complete return, under that section or those regulations, for that year of assessment or period, and

(b) preserve those records until the end of the relevant day (see subsections (2) to (2ZB))."

14(3) In subsection (2) for "day referred to in subsection (1) above is" substitute "relevant day is (subject to subsection (2ZB))".

14(4) After subsection (2) insert–

"**12B(2ZA)** Subsection (2ZB) applies where, before the day mentioned in subsection (2), the person–

(a) is given a notice under section 8, 8A or 12AA, or

(b) becomes subject to a requirement imposed by regulations under paragraph 10 of Schedule A1.

12B(2ZB) Where this subsection applies the relevant day is the later of the day mentioned in subsection (2), and–

(a) if enquiries are made into the return, the day on which under section 28A(1B) or 28B(1B) those enquiries are completed, or

(b) if no such enquiries are made, the day on which an officer no longer has power to make them."

14(5) In subsection (2A)–

(a) in paragraph (a) for "(1)" substitute "(1)(a) or (b)";

(b) in the words after paragraph (b)–

(i) omit "the relevant day, that is to say,";

(ii) for "(1)" substitute "(1A)".

14(6) In subsection (3)(a) for "(1)" substitute "(1A)".

14(7) In subsection (4)–

(a) for "(1)" substitute "(1A)";

(b) at the end insert "and regulations under paragraph 11 of Schedule A1".

14(8) In subsection (5) for "(1)" substitute "(1A)".

17 In section 28C(3) (determination of tax where no return delivered) for "section 9" substitute "section 8 or 8A".

18 In section 28H(2)(b) (simple assessments)–

(a) for the words "to make and deliver such a return" substitute "imposed";

(b) after "notice" insert "to file".

19 In section 28I(2)(b) (simple assessments for trustees)–

(a) for the words "to make and deliver such a return" substitute "imposed";

(b) after "notice" insert "to file".

20(1) Section 29 (assessment where loss of tax discovered) is amended as follows.

20(2) In subsection (2) at the end insert "(or, where the error or mistake is in an end of period statement forming part of the return, if that statement was provided on the basis of or in accordance with the practice generally prevailing at the time when it was provided)."

20(3) In subsection (6) after paragraph (a) insert–

"(aa) it is contained in any information provided by the taxpayer to HMRC under regulations under paragraph 7 of Schedule A1 (periodic updates);".

22(1) Section 42 (procedure for making claims) is amended as follows.

22(2) In subsection (2)–

(a) after "of this Act" insert ", or where a partnership is required to provide a return by regulations under paragraph 10 of Schedule A1,";

(b) after "that section" insert "or those regulations".

22(3) In subsection (9) after "of this Act" insert "or a Schedule A1 partnership return".

22(4) In subsection (11)(a) after "of this Act" insert "or a Schedule A1 partnership return".

23(1) Section 59A (payments on account of income tax) is amended as follows.

23(2) In subsection (1)(a) for "section 9" substitute "section 8 or 8A".

23(3) In subsection (4A)(a) for "section 9" substitute "section 8 or 8A".

24(1) Section 59B (payment of income tax and capital gains tax: assessments other than simple assessments) is amended as follows.

24(2) In subsection (1)(a) for "section 9" substitute "section 8 or 8A".

24(3) In subsection (4A) for "section 9" substitute "section 8 or 8A".

24(4) In subsection (5A) for "section 9" substitute "section 8 or 8A".

24(5) In subsection (6) for "section 9" substitute "section 8 or 8A".

25(1) Section 106C (offence of failing to deliver a return) is amended as follows.

25(2) In subsection (1)–

(a) for "required by a notice under section 8 to make and deliver a return" substitute "given a notice to file under section 8";

(b) in paragraph (a) for "the return" substitute "a return under that section".

25(3) In subsection (2) for "the return" substitute "a return under section 8".

26 In section 106D(1) (offence of making inaccurate return)–

(a) for "required by a notice under section 8 to make and deliver a return" substitute "given a notice to file under section 8";

(b) in paragraph (a) after "return" insert "under that section".

27 In section 106E (exclusions from offences under sections 106B to 106D) for "or make and deliver the return" substitute "under section 7, or is given the notice to file under section 8,".

30(1) Paragraph 3 of Schedule 1AB (recovery of overpaid tax) is amended as follows.

30(2) In sub-paragraph (2)(a) after "of this Act" insert "or a Schedule A1 partnership return".

30(3) In sub-paragraph (3)(a) after "12AA" insert "or a Schedule A1 partnership return".

30(4) In sub-paragraph (4) at the end insert "or a Schedule A1 partnership return".

Part 2 – Amendments of Other Acts

FA 2014

43 FA 2014 is amended as follows.

44 In section 253(6)(c) (definition of "tax return") after "section 12AA of" insert ", or regulations under paragraph 10 of Schedule A1 to,".

FA 2016

47 FA 2016 is amended as follows.

48(1) Schedule 18 (serial tax avoidance) is amended as follows.

48(2) In paragraph 51(8)(b) (partnerships: information) after "TMA 1970" insert ", or under equivalent provision made by regulations under paragraph 10 of Schedule A1 to that Act,".

48(3) In paragraph 52 (partnerships: special provision about taxpayer emendations)–

(a) in sub-paragraph (1) for "subsection (1)(b) of section 12AB of that Act (partnership statement)" substitute "section 12AB(1)(b) of that Act or under equivalent provision made by regulations under paragraph 10 of Schedule A1 to that Act (partnership statement)";

(b) in sub-paragraph (3)–

(i) in the words before paragraph (a), after "that person's successor" insert "(in the case of a section 12AA partnership return) or the nominated partner (in the case of a Schedule A1 partnership return)";

(ii) for "subsection (1)(b) of section 12AB of TMA 1970 (partnership statement)" substitute "section 12AB(1)(b) of TMA 1970 or under equivalent provision made by regulations under paragraph 10 of Schedule A1 to that Act (partnership statement)".

48(4) In paragraph 53(1) (supplementary provision relating to partnerships)–

(a) in the definition of "the representative partner" after "in relation to a" insert "section 12AA";

(b) after the definition of "successor" insert–

""**the nominated partner**", in relation to a Schedule A1 partnership return, has the meaning given by paragraph 5 of Schedule A1 to TMA 1970."

48(5) In paragraph 58(1) (general interpretation), for the definition of "partnership return" substitute–

""**partnership return**" means a return–

(a) under section 12AA of TMA 1970 (a "section 12AA partnership return"), or

(b) required by regulations made under paragraph 10 of Schedule A1 to TMA 1970 (a "Schedule A1 partnership return");".

49(1) Schedule 19 (large businesses: tax strategies and sanctions) is amended as follows.

49(2) In paragraph 12(5) (definition of "representative partner")–

(a) the words from "the partner" to the end become paragraph (a);

(b) at the end of that paragraph insert ", or";

(c) after that paragraph insert–

"(b) the nominated partner within the meaning of paragraph 5 of Schedule A1 to TMA 1970."

49(3) In paragraph 13 (definition of "financial year") in paragraph (c) for "under a return issued under section 12AB" substitute "within the meaning of".

SCHEDULE 15 – PARTIAL CLOSURE NOTICES

Section 63

TMA 1970

1 TMA 1970 is amended as follows.

2 [Amends TMA 1970, s. 9A.]

3(1) Section 9B (amendment of return by taxpayer during enquiry) is amended as follows.

3(2) [Amends TMA 1970, s. 9B(1).]

3(3) [Amends TMA 1970, s. 9B(3).]

3(4) [Amends TMA 1970, s. 9B(4).]

4(1) Section 9C (amendment of self-assessment during enquiry to prevent loss of tax) is amended as follows.

4(2) [Amends TMA 1970, s. 9C(1).]

4(3) [Amends TMA 1970, s. 9C(2).]

4(4) [Amends TMA 1970, s. 9C(4).]

9 [Amends TMA 1970, s. 12B(1).]

12(1) Section 28A (completion of enquiry into personal, trustee or NRCGT return) is amended as follows.

12(2) [Amends TMA 1970, s. 28.]

12(3) [Amends TMA 1970, s. 28A(2).]

12(4) [Amends TMA 1970, s. 28A(3) and (4).]

12(5) [Amends TMA 1970, s. 28A(6).]

12(6) [Inserts TMA 1970, s. 28A(7) and (8).]

14 [Amends TMA 1970, s. 29(5).]

16 [Amends TMA 1970, s. 30(5).]

18 [Amends TMA 1970, s. 31(2).]

20 [Amends TMA 1970, s. 59B(4A).]

21(1) In Schedule 3ZA (date by which payment to be made after amendment etc of self-assessment), paragraph 2 is amended as follows.

21(2) [Amends TMA 1970, Sch. 3ZA, para. 2(3).]

21(3) [Inserts TMA 1970, Sch. 3ZA, para. 2(4).]

COMMENCEMENT

44 The amendments made by this Schedule have effect in relation to an enquiry under section 9A, 12ZM or 12AC of TMA 1970 or Schedule 18 to FA 1998 where–

(a) notice of the enquiry is given on or after the day on which this Act is passed, or

(b) the enquiry is in progress immediately before that day.

SCHEDULE 16 – PENALTIES FOR ENABLERS OF DEFEATED TAX AVOIDANCE

Section 65

Part 12 – General

CONSEQUENTIAL AMENDMENTS

58 [Amends TMA 1970, s. 103ZA.]

61 [Amends FA 2014, Sch. 34, para. 7.]

COMMENCEMENT

62(1) Subject to sub-paragraphs (2) and (3), paragraphs 1 to 61 of this Schedule have effect in relation to arrangements entered into on or after the day on which this Act is passed.

62(2) In determining in relation to any particular arrangements whether a person is a person who enabled the arrangements, any action of the person carried out before the day on which this Act is passed is to be disregarded.

62(3) The amendments made by paragraph 61 do not apply in relation to a person who is a promoter in relation to arrangements if by virtue of sub-paragraph (2) above that person is not a person who enabled the arrangements.

SCHEDULE 17 – DISCLOSURE OF TAX AVOIDANCE SCHEMES: VAT AND OTHER INDIRECT TAXES

Section 66

Part 3 – Consequential Amendments

PROMOTERS OF TAX AVOIDANCE SCHEMES

52 Part 5 of FA 2014 (promoters of tax avoidance schemes) is amended as follows.

53 [Amends FA 2014, s. 281A.]

54(1) Schedule 34A (defeated arrangements) is amended as follows.

54(2) [Amends FA 2014, Sch. 34A, para. 2.]

54(3) [Amends FA 2014, Sch. 34A, para. 14.]

54(4) [Inserts FA 2014, Sch. 34A, para. 26A.]

54(5) [Amends heading before FA 2014, Sch. 34A, para. 27.]

54(6) [Amends FA 2014, Sch. 34A, para. 27.]

54(7) [Amends the heading before FA 2014, Sch. 34A, para. 28.]

54(8) [Amends FA 2014, Sch. 34A, para. 28.]

SERIAL TAX AVOIDANCE

55(1) Schedule 18 to FA 2016 (serial tax avoidance) is amended as follows.

55(2) [Amends FA 2016, Sch. 18, para. 4.]

55(3) [Inserts FA 2016, Sch. 18, para. 8A.]

55(4) [Amends heading before FA 2016, Sch. 18, para. 9.]

55(5) [Amends FA 2016, Sch. 18, para. 9.]

55(6) [Inserts FA 2016, Sch. 18, para. 9A.]

55(7) [Amends heading before FA 2016, Sch. 18, para. 10.]

55(8) [Amends FA 2016, Sch. 18, para. 10.]

55(9) [Amends FA 2016, Sch. 18, para. 11.]

55(10) [Inserts FA 2016, Sch. 18, para. 16A.]

55(11) [Amends FA 2016, Sch. 18, para. 17.]

55(12) [Amends heading before FA 2016, Sch. 18, para. 28.]

55(13) [Amends FA 2016, Sch. 18, para. 28.]

55(14) [Amends FA 2016, Sch. 18, para. 32.]

55(15) [Amends FA 2016, Sch. 18, para. 35.]

55(16) [Inserts FA 2016, Sch. 18, para. 43(8).]

55(17) [Inserts FA 2016, Sch. 18, para. 55(8A).]

55(18) [Amends FA 2016, Sch. 18, para. 58(1).]

Part 4 – Supplemental

REGULATIONS

56(1) Any power of the Treasury or the Commissioners to make regulations under this Schedule is exercisable by statutory instrument.

56(2) Regulations made under any such power may make different provision for different cases and may contain transitional provisions and savings.

56(3) A statutory instrument containing regulations made by the Treasury under paragraph 2(2) or 42(1) may not be made unless a draft of the instrument has been laid before and approved by a resolution of the House of Commons.

56(4) Any other statutory instrument containing regulations made under this Schedule, if made without a draft having been approved by a resolution of the House of Commons, is subject to annulment in pursuance of a resolution of the House of Commons.

INTERPRETATION

57 In this Schedule–

"arrangements" includes any scheme, transaction or series of transactions;

"the Commissioners" means the Commissioners for Her Majesty's Revenue and Customs;

"company" has the meaning given by section 1121 of the Corporation Tax Act 2010;

"HMRC" means Her Majesty's Revenue and Customs;

"indirect tax" has the meaning given by paragraph 2(1);

"introducer" is to be construed in accordance with paragraph 9;

"makes a firm approach" has the meaning given by paragraph 10(1);

"makes a marketing contact" has the meaning given by paragraph 10(2);

"marketing contact" has the meaning give by paragraph 10(2);

"notifiable arrangements" has the meaning given by paragraph 3(1);

"notifiable proposal" has the meaning given by paragraph 3(3);

"prescribed" (except in or in references to paragraph 3(1)(a)), means prescribed by regulations made by HMRC;

"promoter" is to be construed in accordance with paragraph 8;

"reference number", in relation to notifiable arrangements, has the meaning given by paragraph 22(4);

"TCEA 2007" means the Tribunals, Courts and Enforcement Act 2007;

"tax advantage" means a tax advantage within the meaning of–

(a) paragraph 6 (in relation to VAT), or

(b) paragraph 7 (in relation to indirect taxes other than VAT);

"trade" includes every venture in the nature of a trade;

"tribunal" means the First-tier tribunal, or where determined by or under Tribunal Procedure Rules, the Upper Tribunal;

"working day" means a day which is not a Saturday or a Sunday, Christmas Day, Good Friday or a bank holiday under the Banking and Financial Dealings Act 1971 in any part of the United Kingdom.

NIC STATUTORY INSTRUMENTS

Table of Contents

Those statutory instruments listed below which contain substantive provisions are reproduced in the following pages. Statutory instruments which do no more than amend other instruments are not reproduced; the amendments made by them have been consolidated in the relevant amended regulations. They are, however, listed below for convenience.

continued over

STATUTORY INSTRUMENTS **Page**

continued over

continued over

continued over

STATUTORY INSTRUMENTS		Page
1992/3210	Social Security (Finland) Order 1992 (amends SI 1984/125). Not reproduced.	
1992/3211	Social Security (Iceland) Order 1992 (amends SI 1985/1202). Not reproduced.	
1992/3212	Social Security (Norway) Order 1992 (amends SI 1991/767). Not reproduced.	
1992/3213	Social Security (Sweden) Order 1992 (amends SI 1988/590). Not reproduced.	
1993/280	Social Security (Contributions) (Re-rating) Order 1993 (amends SSCBA 1992, s. 9, 11, 13, 15, 18). Not reproduced.	
1993/1025	Social Security (Consequential Provisions) Act 1992 Appointed Day Order 1993 (appoints day from which SS(CP)A 1992, Sch. 4, para. 8, 9 cease to have effect). Not reproduced.	
1994/544	Social Security (Contributions) (Re-rating and National Insurance Fund Payments) Order 1994 (amends SSCBA 1992, s. 9, 11, 13, 15 and 18). Not reproduced.	
1994/561	Statutory Sick Pay (Small Employers' Relief) Amendment Regulations 1994 (amends SI 1991/428, reg. 2(1), (3)). Not reproduced.	
1994/726	Social Security (Categorisation of Earners) Amendment Regulations 1994 (amends SI 1978/1689, reg. 1(2), Sch. 1, Pt. III, Sch. 3). Not reproduced.	
1994/730	Statutory Sick Pay Act 1994 (Consequential) Regulations 1994 (amends SI 1993/376, reg. 2(1)). Not reproduced.	
1994/1082	Social Security (Adjudication) Amendment Regulations 1994 (amends SI 1986/2218, reg. 7, Sch. 2; inserts reg. 1(6), 5(1A)). Not reproduced.	
1994/1367	Social Security Maternity Benefits and Statutory Sick Pay (Amendment) Regulations 1994 (amends SI 1986/1960, reg. 2, 4, 6, 21 and 23). Not reproduced.	
1994/1646	Social Security (Cyprus) Order 1994. Not reproduced.	
1994/1882	Statutory Maternity Pay (Compensation of Employers) and Miscellaneous Amendment Regulations 1994	24,873
1994/2802	Social Security (Jersey and Guernsey) Order 1994. Not reproduced.	
1994/2926	Social Security (Incapacity for Work) Act 1994 (Commencement) Order. Not reproduced.	
1995/512	Statutory Sick Pay Percentage Threshold Order 1995. Not reproduced.	
1995/561	Social Security (Contributions) (Re-rating and National Insurance Fund Payments) Order 1995 (amends SSCBA 1992, s. 9, 11, 13, 15 and 18). Not reproduced.	
1995/566	Statutory Maternity Pay (Compensation of Employers) Amendment Regulations 1995 (amends SI 1994/1882). Not reproduced.	

continued over

continued over

STATUTORY INSTRUMENTS

continued over

continued over

continued over

continued over

continued over

continued over

continued over

STATUTORY INSTRUMENTS Page

continued over

STATUTORY INSTRUMENTS

continued over

continued over

continued over

continued over

STATUTORY INSTRUMENTS **Page**

continued over

continued over

continued over

continued over

STATUTORY INSTRUMENTS

continued over

continued over

continued over

continued over

STATUTORY INSTRUMENTS

continued over

ALPHABETICAL LISTING

continued over

continued over

continued over

STATUTORY INSTRUMENTS

continued over

continued over

STATUTORY INSTRUMENTS Page

continued over

continued over

STATUTORY INSTRUMENTS Page

2005/728	Social Security (Contributions) (Amendment No. 2) Regulations 2005 (amends SI 2001/1004, reg. 40 and Sch. 3, Pt. 7). Not reproduced.	
2007/1057	Social Security (Contributions) (Amendment No. 2) Regulations 2007 (amends SI 2001/1004). Not reproduced.	
2008/607	Social Security (Contributions) (Amendment No. 2) Regulations 2008 (amends SI 2001/1004). Not reproduced.	
2009/591	Social Security (Contributions) (Amendment No. 2) Regulations 2009 (amends SI 2001/1004). Not reproduced.	
2010/188	Social Security (Contributions) (Amendment No. 2) Regulations 2010 (amends SI 2001/1004). Not reproduced.	
2011/940	Social Security (Contributions) (Amendment No. 2) Regulations 2011 (amends SI 2001/1004). Not reproduced.	
2012/817	Social Security (Contributions) (Amendment No. 2) Regulations 2012 (amends SI 2001/1004). Not reproduced.	
2013/1142	Social Security (Contributions) (Amendment No. 2) Regulations 2013 (amends SI 2001/1004). Not reproduced.	
2014/572	Social Security (Contributions) (Amendment No. 2) Regulations 2014 (amends SI 2001/1004). Not reproduced.	
2018/257	Social Security (Contributions) (Amendment No. 2) Regulations 2018 (amends SI 2001/2004). Not reproduced.	
2002/2366	Social Security (Contributions) (Amendment No. 3) Regulations 2002 (amends SI 2001/1004, reg. 3, 30, 31, 50, 52, 54, 55, 60, 61, 110 and 149 and inserts reg. 155A, and amends SI 2001/769, reg. 5 and 6). Not reproduced.	
2003/1059	Social Security (Contributions) (Amendment No. 3) Regulations 2003 (amends SI 2003/1004, Sch. 2, para. 10, 11, Sch. 3, Pt. 9, para. 16; inserts Sch. 2, para. 11A, Sch. 3, Pt. 9, para. 17). Not reproduced.	
2004/1362	Social Security (Contributions) (Amendment No. 3) Regulations 2004 (amends SI 2001/1004, reg. 50; inserts reg. 50A, 65A). Not reproduced.	
2005/778	Social Security (Contributions) (Amendment No. 3) Regulations 2005 (amends SI 2001/1004, Sch. 2, para. 14 and Sch. 3, Pt. 5 and 6 and inserts reg. 65B). Not reproduced.	
2006/883	Social Security (Contributions) (Amendment No. 3) Regulations 2006 (amends SI 2001/1004, Sch. 3, para. 7(3)). Not reproduced.	

continued over

STATUTORY INSTRUMENTS Page

2007/1175	Social Security (Contributions) (Amendment No. 3) Regulations 2007 (amends SI 2001/1004). Not reproduced.	
2008/636	Social Security (Contributions) (Amendment No. 3) Regulations 2008 (amends SI 2001/1004). Not reproduced.	
2009/600	Social Security (Contributions) (Amendment No. 3) Regulations 2009 (amends SI 2001/1004). Not reproduced.	
2010/646	Social Security (Contributions) (Amendment No. 3) Regulations 2010 (amends SI 2001/1004). Not reproduced.	
2011/797	Social Security (Contributions) (Amendment No. 3) Regulations 2011 (amends SI 2001/1004). Not reproduced.	
2012/821	Social Security (Contributions) (Amendment No. 3) Regulations 2012 (amends SI 2001/1004). Not reproduced.	
2013/1907	Social Security (Contributions) (Amendment No. 3) Regulations 2013 (amends SI 2001/1004). Not reproduced.	
2014/1016	Social Security (Contributions) (Amendment No. 3) Regulations 2014 (amends SI 2001/1004, Sch. 4). Not reproduced.	
2016/647	Social Security (Contributions) (Amendment No. 3) Regulations 2016 (substitutes SI 2001/1004, Sch. 3, Pt. 8, para. 6ZB(a)). Not reproduced.	
2001/2187	Social Security (Contributions) (Amendment No. 4) Regulations 2001 (amends SI 2001/1004, reg. 80; inserts reg. 80A). Not reproduced.	
2002/2924	Social Security (Contributions) (Amendment No. 4) Regulations 2002 (amends SI 2001/1004, reg. 43 and Sch. 3). Not reproduced.	
2003/1337	Social Security (Contributions) (Amendment No. 4) Regulations 2003 (amends Sch. 4, para. 7(5), 9(2); inserts Sch. 4, para. 7(5A), (5B)). Not reproduced.	
2004/2096	Social Security (Contributions) (Amendment No. 4) Regulations 2004 (amends SI 2001/1004, reg. 1 and 69; Sch. 2, para. 7; Sch. 3, Pt. 10, para. 3; Sch. 4, para. 6, 8, 21 and 23; Sch. 5, heading and para. 1). Not reproduced.	
2005/1086	Social Security (Contributions) (Amendment No. 4) Regulations 2005 (amends SI 2005/778). Not reproduced.	
2006/2003	Social Security (Contributions) (Amendment No. 4) Regulations 2006 (amends SI 2001/1004). Not reproduced.	
2007/1838	Social Security (Contributions) (Amendment No. 4) Regulations 2007 (amends SI 2001/1004). Not reproduced.	

continued over

continued over

continued over

STATUTORY INSTRUMENTS		Page
2002/238	Social Security (Contributions) (Amendment) Regulations 2002 (amends SI 2001/1004, reg. 10, 11(3)). Not reproduced.	
2003/193	Social Security (Contributions) (Amendment) Regulations 2003 (amends SI 2001/1004, reg. 1(2), 9, 10, 90(4), 94, 95, 99, 103, Sch. 4, para. 7(13), 9(1), 11(4), 22, 26; substitutes reg. 21, 84, 100; omits reg. 85). Not reproduced.	
2004/173	Social Security (Contributions) (Amendment) Regulations 2004 (amends SI 2001/1004, Sch. 3, Pt. 10, para. 5). Not reproduced.	
2005/166	Social Security (Contributions) (Amendment) Regulations 2005 (amends SI 2001/1004, reg. 10, 11). Not reproduced.	
2006/127	Social Security (Contributions) (Amendment) Regulations 2006 (amends SI 2001/1004, reg. 10 and 11(3)). Not reproduced.	
2007/118	Social Security (Contributions) (Amendment) Regulations 2007 (amends SI 2001/1004). Not reproduced.	
2009/111	Social Security (Contributions) (Amendment) Regulations 2009 (amends SI 2001/1004). Not reproduced.	
2010/834	Social Security (Contributions) (Amendment) Regulations 2010 (amends SI 2001/1004). Not reproduced.	
2011/25	Social Security (Contributions) (Amendment) Regulations 2011 (amends SI 2001/1004). Not reproduced.	
2012/573	Social Security (Contributions) (Amendment) Regulations 2012 (amends SI 2001/1004). Not reproduced.	
2013/718	Social Security (Contributions) (Amendment) Regulations 2013 (amends SI 2001/1004). Not reproduced.	
2014/608	Social Security (Contributions) (Amendment) Regulations 2014 (amends SI 2001/1004). Not reproduced.	
2015/543	Social Security (Contributions) (Amendment) Regulations 2015 (amends SI 2001/1004, Sch. 3, Pt. 6). Not reproduced.	
2016/117	Social Security (Contributions) (Amendment) Regulations 2016 (inserts SI 2001/1004, Case Head H and reg. 154A). Not reproduced.	
2018/120	Social Security (Contributions) (Amendment) Regulations 2018 (amends SI 2001/1004). Not reproduced.	
2006/576	Social Security (Contributions) (Amendments No. 2) Regulations 2006 (amends SI 2001/1004). Not reproduced.	

continued over

continued over

continued over

continued over

STATUTORY INSTRUMENTS

continued over

continued over

continued over

STATUTORY INSTRUMENTS Page

continued over

continued over

continued over

continued over

continued over

continued over

STATUTORY INSTRUMENTS **Page**

continued over

STATUTORY INSTRUMENTS		Page
	Commencement No. 9 and Transitional and Transitory Provisions (Amendment)) Order 2014. Not reproduced.	
2015/33	Welfare Reform Act 2012 (Commencement No. 21 and Transitional and Transitory Provisions) Order 2015. Not reproduced.	
2015/101	Welfare Reform Act 2012 (Commencement No. 22 and Transitional and Transitory Provisions) Order 2015. Not reproduced.	
2015/740	Welfare Reform Act 2012 (Commencement No. 23 and Transitional and Transitory Provisions) (Amendment) Order 2015. Not reproduced.	
2015/634	Welfare Reform Act 2012 (Commencement No. 23 and Transitional and Transitory Provisions) Order 2015. Not reproduced.	
2015/1537	Welfare Reform Act 2012 (Commencement No. 24 and Transitional and Transitory Provisions and Commencement No. 9 and Transitional and Transitory Provisions (Amendment)) Order 2015. Not reproduced.	
2015/1930	Welfare Reform Act 2012 (Commencement No. 25 and Transitional and Transitory Provisions) Order 2015. Not reproduced.	
2016/33	Welfare Reform Act 2012 (Commencement No. 26 and Transitional and Transitory Provisions and Commencement No. 22, 23 and 24 and Transitional and Transitory Provisions (Modification)) Order 2016. Not reproduced.	
2016/407	Welfare Reform Act 2012 (Commencement No. 27 and Transitional and Transitory Provisions and Commencement No. 22, 23 and 24 and Transitional and Transitory Provisions (Modification)) Order 2016. Not reproduced.	
2017/664	Welfare Reform Act 2012 (Commencement No. 29 and Commencement No. 17, 19, 22, 23 and 24 and Transitional and Transitory Provisions (Modification)) Order 2017. Not reproduced.	
2012/1651	Welfare Reform Act 2012 (Commencement No. 3, Savings Provision) Order 2012. Not reproduced.	
2012/2530	Welfare Reform Act 2012 (Commencement No. 4) Order 2012. Not reproduced.	
2012/2946	Welfare Reform Act 2012 (Commencement No. 5) Order 2012. Not reproduced.	
2012/3090	Welfare Reform Act 2012 (Commencement No. 6 and Savings Provisions) Order 2012. Not reproduced.	
2013/178	Welfare Reform Act 2012 (Commencement No. 7) Order 2013. Not reproduced.	
2013/358	Welfare Reform Act 2012 (Commencement No. 8 and Savings and Transitional Provisions) Order 2013. Not reproduced.	

continued over

STATUTORY INSTRUMENTS		Page
2017/483	Welfare Reform Act 2012 (Commencement No. 9 and 21 and Transitional and Transitory Provisions (Amendment)) Order 2017. Not reproduced.	
2013/983	Welfare Reform Act 2012 (Commencement No. 9 and Transitional and Transitory Provisions and Commencement No. 8 and Savings and Transitional Provisions (Amendment)) Order 2013. Not reproduced.	
2014/3067	Welfare Reform Act 2012 (Commencement No. 9, 11, 13 14, 16, 17 and 19 and Transitional and Transitory Provisions (Amendment)) Order 2014. Not reproduced.	
2014/1452	Welfare Reform Act 2012 (Commencement No. 9, 11, 13, 14 and 16 and Transitional and Transitory Provisions (Amendment)) Order 2014 (amends SI 2013/983, SI 2013/1511, SI 2013/2657, SI 2013/2846 and SI 2014/209). Not reproduced.	
2014/1923	Welfare Reform Act 2012 (Commencement No. 9, 11, 13, 14, 16 and 17 and Transitional and Transitory Provisions (Amendment) (No. 2)) Order 2014. Not reproduced.	
2014/1661	Welfare Reform Act 2012 (Commencement No. 9, 11, 13, 14, 16 and 17 and Transitional and Transitory Provisions) (Amendment) Order 2014. Not reproduced.	
2015/32	Welfare Reform Act 2012 (Commencement No. 9, 11, 13, 14, 16, 17 and 19 and Transitional and Transitory Provisions (Amendment)) Order 2015. Not reproduced.	
2016/610	Welfare Reform and Work Act 2016 (Commencement No. 2) Regulations 2016 (sets 9 June 2016 for the coming into force of the Welfare Reform and Work Act 2016, s. 10). Not reproduced.	

SOCIAL SECURITY (CONTRIBUTIONS) (EMPLOYMENT PROTECTION) REGULATIONS 1977

(SI 1977/622)

Regulations made on 31 March 1977 by the Secretary of State for Social Services, in exercise of the powers conferred upon him by s. 18 of the Social Security (Miscellaneous Provisions) Act 1977 [SSCBA 1992, s. 112] and of all other powers so enabling him.

CITATION, INTERPRETATION AND COMMENCEMENT

1(1) These regulations may be cited as the Social Security (Contributions) (Employment Protection) Regulations 1977 and shall come into operation on 6th April 1977.

1(2) In these regulations, unless the context otherwise requires–

"the Act" means the Social Security Act 1975 [SSCBA 1992; SSAA 1992];

"maternity pay" has the meaning assigned to it by section 126(1) of the Employment Protection Act 1975;

and other expressions have the same meanings as in the Act.

1(3) The rules for the construction of Acts of Parliament contained in the Interpretation Act 1889 [1978] shall apply for the purposes of the interpretation of these regulations as they apply for the purposes of the interpretation of any Act of Parliament.

CERTAIN SUMS TO BE EARNINGS

2 For the purposes of the Act–

(a) any such sum as is referred to in section 18(2)(a) or (b) of the Social Security (Miscellaneous Provisions) Act 1977 [now repealed] (certain sums to be earnings for social security purposes) shall be deemed to be earnings payable by the person liable to pay the maternity pay, to the person entitled to receive such sum and to be so payable in respect of the period for which it is paid;

(b) any such sum as is referred to in section 18(2)(c) to (e) of the said Act [SSCBA 1992, s. 112(3)] shall be deemed to be earnings payable by the person liable to make such payment to the person entitled to receive it and to be so payable in respect of the period to which the order or as the case may be award relates;

(c) any amount (save where such amount is a payment of earnings from another employment) taken into account for the purpose of calculating the amount payable by way of any such sum as is referred to in sub-paragraph (b) above so as to reduce the amount payable shall be treated as related to such sum and shall be deemed to be earnings payable by and to the persons referred to in the said sub-paragraph (b) and to be so payable in respect of the period referred to in that sub-paragraph;

(d) any period referred to in this regulation shall, so far as it is not a period of employment, be deemed to be a period of employment.

Cross references – SSCBA 1992, s. 112: sums deemed to be earnings.
SI 2001/1004, reg. 5: earnings period for sums deemed to be earnings by virtue of regulations made under the Social Security (Miscellaneous Provisions) Act 1977, s. 18 [SSCBA 1992, s. 112].

Notes – SS(MP)A 1977, s. 18(2)(a), (b) repealed by SSA 1986, s. 86 and Sch. 11, with effect from 6 April 1987.

SOCIAL SECURITY (CATEGORISATION OF EARNERS) REGULATIONS 1978

(SI 1978/1689, as amended by SI 1980/1713, SI 1984/350, SI 1990/1894, SI 1994/726, SI 1998/1728, SI 1999/3, SI 2003/736, SI 2003/2420, SI 2004/770, SI 2005/3133, SI 2006/1121, SI 2006/1530, SI 2012/816, SI 2014/635, NICA 2015, SI 2015/478 and SI 2017/307)

Regulations made on 24 November 1978 by the Secretary of State for Social Services in exercise of the powers conferred upon him by s. 2(2), 4(4) and (5) of, and para. 6(1)(k) of Sch. 1 to, the Social Security Act 1975 [SSCBA 1992, s. 2(2), 7(1), (2) and Sch. 1, para. 8(1)(o)] and of all other powers so enabling him.

Other material – HMRC Brief 10/11: National Insurance implications of the decision in *ITV Services Ltd* [2011] TC 00836.

HMRC Brief 19/12: National Insurance Contributions: HMRC's position following the Upper Tribunal decision in the case of ITV Services Ltd.

HMRC Brief 29/13: National Insurance Contributions: HMRC position following the Court of Appeal decision in the case of *ITV Services Ltd* [2013] BTC 633.

HMRC Brief 35/13: National Insurance Contributions: repeal of Social Security (Categorisation of Earners) Regulations 1978 in respect of entertainers from 6 April 2014.

ARRANGEMENT OF REGULATIONS

SCHEDULES

CITATION, COMMENCEMENT AND INTERPRETATION

1(1) These regulations may be cited as the Social Security (Categorisation of Earners) Regulations 1978 and shall come into operation on 27th December 1978.

1(2) In these regulations, unless the context otherwise requires–

"the Act" means the Social Security Act 1975 [SSCBA 1992; SSAA 1992];

"an agency" in paragraph 2 of Schedule 1 and paragraphs 2 and 9 of Schedule 3 to these regulations means either a UK agency or a foreign agency;

"category A, B, C or D waters" has the meaning given in the Merchant Shipping (Categorisation of Waters) Regulations 1992;

"end client" in paragraph 2 of Schedule 1 and paragraphs 2 and 9 of Schedule 3 to these regulations means a person (including any connected person within the meaning given by section 993 of the Income Tax Act 2007) who has a place of business, residence or presence in Great Britain and to whom the worker personally provides services;

"foreign agency" in paragraph 2 of Schedule 1 and paragraphs 2 and 9 of Schedule 3 to these regulations means a person (including a body of persons unincorporate of which the employed person is a member) who does not have a place of business, residence or presence in Great Britain;

"foreign employer" in paragraph 9 of Schedule 3 to these regulations means a person–

(a) who does not fulfil the conditions as to residence or presence in Great Britain prescribed under section 1(6)(a) of the Social Security Contributions and Benefits Act 1992; and

(b) who, if he did fulfil those conditions as to residence or presence in Great Britain referred to in (a) above, would be the secondary contributor in relation to any payment of earnings to or for the benefit of the person employed;

"host employer" in paragraph 9 of Schedule 3 to these regulations means a person having a place of business, residence or presence in Great Britain;

"mariner" has the meaning given in regulation 115 of the Social Security (Contributions) Regulations 2001;

"remuneration"–

(a) in paragraph 2 of Schedule 1 and paragraphs 2 and 9 of Schedule 3 to these regulations means–

(i) every form of payment, profit, gratuity or benefit, but

(ii) does not include anything that would not have constituted employed earner's earnings if it had been receivable in connection with an employment but for those paragraphs; and

(b) in paragraph 8 of Schedule 3 to these regulations includes any payment in respect of stipend or salary and excludes–

(i) any payment disregarded or, as the case may be, deducted from the amount of a person's earnings by virtue of regulations made under section 3(3) of the Act; or

(ii) any specific and distinct payment made towards the maintenance or education of a dependent of the person receiving the payment;

"UK agency" in paragraph 2 of Schedule 1 and paragraphs 2 and 9 of Schedule 3 to these regulations means a person (including a body of persons unincorporate of which the employed person is a member) who has a place of business, residence or presence in Great Britain;

"worker" in paragraph 2 of Schedule 1 and paragraphs 2 and 9 of Schedule 3 to these regulations means the person providing services under or in consequence of the contract;

and other expressions have the same meaning as in the Act.

1(3) Any reference in these regulations to any provision made by or contained in any enactment or instrument shall, except in so far as the context otherwise requires, be construed as including a reference to that provision as amended or extended by any enactment or instrument, and as including a reference to any provision which it re-enacts or replaces with or without modification.

1(4) The rules for the construction of Acts of Parliament contained in the Interpretation Act 1889 [1978] shall apply for the purposes of the interpretation of these regulations as they apply for the purposes of the interpretation of an Act of Parliament.

History – In reg. 1(2), the definition of "an agency" inserted by SI 2014/635, reg. 2(2)(a), with effect from 6 April 2014.
In reg. 1(2), the definitions of "entertainer" and "entertainment" omitted by SI 2014/635, reg. 2(2)(b), with effect from 6 April 2014.
In reg. 1(2), the definitions of "end client" and "foreign agency" inserted by SI 2014/635, reg. 2(2)(c), with effect from 6 April 2014.
In reg. 1(2), in the definition of "host employer", the words ", residence or presence" inserted by SI 2014/635, reg. 2(2)(d), with effect from 6 April 2014.
In reg. 1(2), the definition of "remuneration" substituted by SI 2014/635, reg. 2(2)(e), with effect from 6 April 2014.
In reg. 1(2), the definitions of "UK agency" and "worker" inserted by SI 2014/635, reg. 2(2)(f), with effect from 6 April 2014.
In reg. 1(2), the definition of "educational establishment" omitted by SI 2012/816, reg. 3, with effect from 6 April 2012.
In reg. 1(2) the definition of "category A, B, C or D waters" and "mariner" inserted by SI 2003/2420, reg. 3, with effect from 13 October 2003.
In reg. 1(2) the definition of "entertainer" and "entertainment" inserted by SI 1998/1728, reg. 2, operative from 17 July 1998 and continuing in effect beyond 1 February 1999 by virtue of SI 1999/3, reg. 2.
In reg. 1(2), the definitions of "foreign employer" and "host employer" inserted by SI 1994/726, reg. 2, operative 6 April 1994.

Cross references – SSCBA 1992, s. 3(3): certain payments may be disregarded in determining a person's earnings.

TREATMENT OF EARNERS IN ONE CATEGORY OF EARNERS AS FALLING WITHIN ANOTHER CATEGORY AND DISREGARD OF EMPLOYMENTS

2(1) For the purposes of the Act an earner in one category of earners shall be treated as falling within another category in accordance with the following provisions of this regulation.

2(2) Subject to the provisions of paragraph (4) of this regulation, every earner shall, in respect of any employment described in any paragraph in column (A) of Part I of Schedule 1 to these regulations, be treated as falling within the category of an employed earner in so far as he is gainfully employed in such employment and is not a person specified in the corresponding paragraph in column (B) of that Part, notwithstanding that the employment is not under a contract of service, or in an office (including elective office) with earnings.

2(3) Subject to the provisions of paragraph (4) of this regulation, every earner shall, in respect of any employment described in any paragraph in column (A) of Part II of the said Schedule 1, be treated as falling within the category of a self-employed earner in so far as he is gainfully employed in such employment and is not a person specified in the corresponding paragraph in column (B) of that Part, notwithstanding that the employment is under a contract of service, or in an office (including elective office) with earnings.

2(4) Every employment described in any paragraph in column (A) of Part III of the said Schedule 1 shall, in relation to liability for contributions otherwise arising from employment of that description, be disregarded, except in so far as it is employment of a person specified in the corresponding paragraph in column (B) of that Part.

History – In reg. 2(2) and (3), the word "general" (which appeared before the word "earnings") omitted by SI 2015/478, reg. 25(2), with effect from 6 April 2015.

In reg. 2(2) and (3) "general earnings" substituted for "emoluments chargeable to income tax under Schedule E" by SI 2004/770, reg. 34, with effect from 6 April 2004.

EMPLOYMENTS TREATED AS CONTINUING

3 For the purposes of the Act with respect to the computation, collection and recovery of, and otherwise with respect to, contributions (other than Class 4 contributions which under section 9 of the Act [SSCBA 1992, s. 15, 16] are to be recovered by the Inland Revenue), the employment of a person shall be treated as continuing in the circumstances specified in Schedule 2 to these regulations.

Cross references – SSCBA 1992, s. 15: Class 4 contributions recoverable under Income Tax Acts.
SSCBA 1992, s. 16: application of Income Tax Acts and destination of Class 4 contributions.

SPECIAL PROVISIONS WITH RESPECT TO PERSONS DECLARED BY THE HIGH COURT TO BE PERSONS FALLING WITHIN A PARTICULAR CATEGORY OF EARNERS

4(1) Where, under the provisions of the Act relating to references and appeals to the High Court, the High Court decides any question whether in respect of any employment a person is an earner and, if so, as to the category of earners in which he is to be included, and that decision is inconsistent with some previous determination of the Secretary of State, then, if the Secretary of State is satisfied that contributions appropriate to another category of earners have been paid by or in respect of any person by reason of that determination or in the reasonable belief that that determination was applicable, the Secretary of State may, if it appears to him that it would be in the interests of the person by or in respect of whom such contributions have been paid, or of any claimant or beneficiary by virtue of that person's contributions, so to do, direct that that person shall be treated as though he had been included in the category of earners corresponding to the contributions paid during the period for which contributions appropriate to that other category were so paid before the date on which the decision of the High Court was given, and, if such a direction is given, that person shall be deemed to have been included in that category accordingly for such period.

4(2) Where the Secretary of State, on review under section 96(1) of the Act [SSAA 1992, s. 19], has revised a determination of a question previously given by him, the provisions of this regulation shall apply with the necessary modifications in the same manner as they apply where the High Court has given a decision inconsistent with a determination previously given by the Secretary of State.

4(3) In the application of this regulation to Scotland, for any reference to the High Court, there shall be substituted a reference to the Court of Session.

Cross references – SSAA 1992, s. 19: review of decisions.

PERSONS TO BE TREATED AS SECONDARY CONTRIBUTORS

5(1) For the purposes of section 4 of the Act [SSCBA 1992, s. 7, 9] (Class 1 contributions), in relation to any payment of earnings to or for the benefit of an employed earner in any employment described in any paragraph in column (A) of Schedule 3 to these regulations, the person specified in the corresponding paragraph in column (B) of that Schedule shall be treated as the secondary Class 1 contributor in relation to that employed earner.

5(2) Paragraph 9 of Schedule 3 applies to mariners notwithstanding anything in regulations 122 and 124(1) of the Social Security (Contributions) Regulations 2001.

History – Original reg. 5 renumbered as reg. 5(1) and reg. 5(2) inserted by SI 2003/2420, reg. 4, with effect from 13 October 2003.

Cross references – SSCBA 1992, s. 7: meaning of "secondary contributor".
SSCBA 1992, s. 9: calculation of secondary Class 1 contributions.

ANTI-AVOIDANCE

5A(1) Paragraph (2) applies if–

(a) an earner has an employment in which the earner personally provides services to a person who is resident or present or has a place of business in Great Britain

(b) a third person enters into relevant avoidance arrangements, and

(c) but for paragraph (2), the earner would not be, and would not be treated as falling within the category of, an employed earner in relation to the employment.

5A(2) The earner is to be treated as falling within the category of an employed earner in relation to the employment.

5A(3) In paragraph (1)(b) **"relevant avoidance arrangements"** means arrangements the main purpose, or one of the main purposes, of which is to secure–

(a) that the earner is not treated under paragraph 2 of Schedule 1 as falling within the category of employed earner in relation to the employment, or

(b) that a person is not treated under paragraph 2 or 9(b) or (d) of Schedule 3 as the secondary Class 1 contributor in respect of payments of earnings to or for the benefit of the earner in respect of the employment.

5A(4) Paragraph (5) applies if–

(a) a person ("P") enters into arrangements the main purpose, or one of the main purposes, of which is to secure that P is not treated under a relevant provision as the secondary Class 1 contributor in respect of payments of earnings to or for the benefit of an employed earner in respect of an employment, and

(b) but for paragraph (5), no person who is resident or present or has a place of business in Great Britain would–

(i) be the secondary Class 1 contributor in respect of such payments, or

(ii) be treated, under a provision other than paragraph 2(a) or (b) or 9(g) or (h) in column (B) of Schedule 3, as the secondary Class 1 contributor in respect of such payments.

5A(5) If P is resident or present or has a place of business in Great Britain, P is to be treated as the secondary Class 1 contributor in respect of such payments.

5A(6) In paragraph (4)(a) a **"relevant provision"** means any provision of–

(a) paragraph 2 of Schedule 3, other than sub-paragraphs (a) and (b) of that paragraph in column (B), or

(b) paragraph 9(a) to (d) of that Schedule.

5A(7) In this regulation **"arrangements"** include any scheme, transaction or series of transactions, agreement or understanding, whether or not legally enforceable, and any associated operations.

History – Reg. 5A inserted by NICA 2015, s. 6(1), with effect as follows:

- para. (1)–(3), (6)(a) and (7) are treated as having come into force on 6 April 2014;
- para. (4) and (5) with effect in relation to arrangements entered into on or after 6 April 2014 the main purpose, or one of the main purposes of which, is to secure that a person is not treated, under a provision mentioned in para. (6)(b), as the secondary Class 1 contributor in respect of payments of earnings to or for the benefit of an employed earner in respect of an employment but para. (5) only applies as a result of such arrangements in relation to payments of earnings that are made on or after 12 February 2015; and
- para. (6)(b) with effect from 12 February 2015.

REVOCATION AND GENERAL SAVINGS

6(1) The regulations specified in column (1) of Schedule 4 to these regulations are hereby revoked to the extent mentioned in column (3) of that Schedule.

6(2) Anything whatsoever done or by virtue of any regulation revoked by these regulations shall be deemed to have been done under or by virtue of the corresponding provision of these regulations and anything whatsoever begun under any such regulation may be continued under these regulations as if begun thereunder.

SCHEDULES

SCHEDULE 1

Regulation 2

Part I

Column (A) Employments in respect of which, subject to the provisions of regulation 2 and to the exceptions in column (B) of this Part, earners are treated as falling within the category of employed earner	Column (B) Persons excepted from operation of column (A)
1 Employment– (a) as an office cleaner or as an operative in any similar capacity in any premises other than those used as a private dwelling-house; or (b) as a cleaner of any telephone apparatus and associated fixtures, other than of apparatus and fixtures in premises used as a private dwelling-house.	**1** None.
2 Employment (not being an employment in which the employed earner is treated as an employed earner under the provisions of paragraph 1, 3 or 5 of this Schedule) where– (a) the worker personally provides services to the end client; (b) there is a contract between the end client and an agency under or in consequence of which– (i) the services are provided, or (ii) the end client pays, or otherwise provides consideration for the services, and (c) remuneration is receivable by the worker (from any person) in consequence of providing the services.	**2** Any employed person described in paragraph 2 of column (A)– (a) where the worker carries out the employment wholly in their own home or on other premises not under the control or management of the end client (except where the other premises are premises at which the employed person is required, by reason of working for the client, to work); or (b) who works for the end client as an actor, singer, musician or other entertainer, or as a fashion, photographic or artist's model; or (c) where it is shown that the manner in which the worker provides the services is not subject to (or to the right of) supervision, direction or control by any person.
3 Employment of a person by his or her spouse or civil partner for the purposes of the employment of the spouse or civil partner.	**3** None.
4 [Omitted by SI 2012/816, reg. 4.]	**4** [Omitted by SI 2012/816, reg. 4.]
5 Employment as a minister of religion, not being *employment under a contract of service* or in an office with earnings.	**5** Any person in employment described in paragraph 5 of column (A) whose remuneration in respect of that employment (disregarding any payment in kind) does not consist wholly or mainly of stipend or salary.

History – Para. 2, column (A) substituted by SI 2014/635, reg. 2(3)(a), with effect from 6 April 2014.
Para. 2, column (B) substituted by SI 2014/635, reg. 2(3)(b), with effect from 6 April 2014.

Para. 5A, columns (A) and (B) omitted by SI 2014/635, reg. 2(3)(c), with effect from 6 April 2014.
Para. 1, column (A) substituted by SI 1990/1894, reg. 2, with effect from 16 October 1990.
Para. 2(b) in col. (B) amended and para. 5A, columns (A) and (B) inserted with effect from 17 July 1998 and continuing in effect beyond 1 February 1999 by virtue of SI 1999/3, reg. 2.
Para. 2(b), column (B) amended by SI 1998/1728, reg. 3(a), by omitting words from "actor" to "other", operative from 17 July 1998 and continuing in effect beyond 1 February 1999 by virtue of SI 1999/3, reg. 2.
In para. 3, column (A) the words "or civil partner" inserted and the words "employment of the spouse or civil partner" substituted by SI 2005/3133, reg. 3(2), with effect from 5 December 2005.
Para. 4, column (A) and (B) omitted by SI 2012/816, reg. 4, with effect from 6 April 2012.
Para. 4, column (B) substituted by SI 1984/350, reg. 2(b), with effect from 6 April 1984.
In para. 5, column (A), the word "general" (which appeared before the word "earnings") omitted by SI 2015/478, reg. 25(3), with effect from 6 April 2015.
In para. 5 and 5A, column (A) "general earnings" substituted by SI 2004/770, reg. 34, with effect from 6 April 2004.
In para. 5A, entry in column (B) substituted by SI 2003/736 reg. 3, with effect from 6 April 2003.
Para. 5A inserted by SI 1998/1728, reg. 3(b), operative from 17 July 1998 and continuing in effect beyond 1 February 1999 by virtue of SI 1999/3, reg. 2.

Other material – HMRC Brief 29/13: National Insurance contributions: HMRC position following the Court of Appeal decision in the case of *ITV Services Ltd* [2013] BTC 633.

Part II

Column (A) Employments in respect of which, subject to the provisions of regulation 2 and to the exceptions in column (B) of this Part, earners are treated as falling within the category of self-employed earner	Column (B) Persons excepted from operation of column (A)
6 Employment (not being employment described in paragraph 2 in column (A) of this Schedule) by any person responsible for the conduct or administration of any examination leading to any certificate, diploma, degree or professional qualification– under a contract where the whole of the work to be performed is to be performed in less than twelve months.	**6** None. (a) as an examiner, moderator or invigilator or in any similar capacity; or (b) in which the person employed is engaged to set questions or tests for any such examination,

Other material – DSS leaflet CA26 (NI222) (not reproduced): National Insurance for examiners, teachers, lecturers.

Part III

Column (A) Employments which, subject to the exceptions in column (B) of this Part, are to be disregarded	Column (B) Employments excepted from the operation of column (A)
7 Employment by the father, mother, grandfather, grandmother, stepfather, stepmother, son, daughter, grandson, granddaughter, stepson, stepdaughter, brother, sister, half-brother, half-sister of the person employed, in so far as the employment–	**7** None. (a) is employment in a private dwelling-house in which both the person employed and the employer reside; and (b) is not employment for the purposes of any trade or business carried on there by the employer.
8 Employment (whether or not under a contract of service) of a person by his or her spouse or civil partner otherwise than for the purposes of the employment of the spouse or civil partner.	**8** None.

Column (A)	Column (B)
Employments which, subject to the exceptions in column (B) of this Part, are to be disregarded	Employments excepted from the operation of column (A)
9 Any employment or employments as a self-employed earner (including any employment in respect of which a person is, under these regulations, treated as falling within the category of a self-employed earner) where the earner is not ordinarily employed in such employment or employments.	**9** None.
10 Employment for the purpose of any election or referendum authorised by Act of Parliament–	**10** None. (a) as a returning officer or acting returning officer; or (b) as a Chief Counting Officer or counting officer; or (c) of any person by any officer referred to in (a) or (b) above.
11 Employment: (a) as a member of the naval, military or air forces of a country to which a provision of the Visiting Forces Act 1952 applies by virtue of section 1 thereof; (b) as a civilian by any such force.	**11** Any employment described in paragraph 11(b) in column (A) of a person who is ordinarily resident in the United Kingdom.
12 Employment as a member of any international headquarters or defence organisation designated under section 1 of the International Headquarters and Defence Organisations Act 1964.	**12** Any employment described in paragraph 12 in column (A) of a person who is– (a) a serving member of the regular naval, military or air forces of the Crown– (i) raised in the United Kingdom; or (ii) having its depot or headquarters in the United Kingdom; or (b) a civilian ordinarily resident in the United Kingdom who is not a member of a scheme providing a pension, lump sum, gratuity or like benefit on cessation of the employment which is established under arrangements made by the international headquarters or, as the case may be, defence organisation of which he is a member.
13 [Omitted by SI 2006/1530, reg. 2(3).]	**13** [Omitted by SI 2006/1530, reg. 2(3).]
14. Employment by the International Finance Corporation ("IFC") of a person who is– (a) exempt from tax by virtue of article 3 of, and section 9 of article 6 of the Agreement establishing the IFC as set out in the Schedule to, the International Finance Corporation Order 1955 (b) a member of a scheme established by or on behalf of the IFC which provides for a pension or any *other benefit on cessation* of the employment.	**14.** None.

Column (A) Employments which, subject to the exceptions in column (B) of this Part, are to be disregarded	Column (B) Employments excepted from the operation of column (A)
15. Employment by the Asian Infrastructure Investment Bank ("AIIB") of a person who is– (a) exempt from tax by virtue of regulation 18(2) of the Asian InfrastructureInvestment Bank (Immunities and Privileges) Order 2015, and (b) a member of a scheme established by or on behalf of the AIIB which provides for a pension or any other benefit on cessation of the employment.	**15.** None.

History – In para. 8, column (A) the words "or civil partner" inserted and the words "employment of the spouse or civil partner" substituted by SI 2005/3133, reg. 3(3), with effect from 5 December 2005.
Para. 11, columns (A) and (B) inserted by SI 1980/1713, reg. 2, with effect from 1 December 1980.
Para. 12(a)(i) and (ii), column (B), substituted by SI 2006/1530, reg. 2(2), with effect from 5 July 2006.
In para. 12, column (B), subpara. (b), the words "scheme providing … employment which is" substituted by SI 1984/350, reg. 3, with effect from 6 April 1984.
Para. 12, columns (A) and (B), inserted by SI 1980/1713, reg. 2, with effect from 1 December 1980.
Para. 13 omitted by SI 2006/1530, reg. 2(3), with effect from 5 July 2006.
Para. 13, columns (A) and (B) inserted by SI 1994/726, reg. 3, with effect from 6 April 1994.
Para. 14 inserted by SI 2017/307, reg. 5(2), with effect from 6 April 2017.
Para. 15 inserted by SI 2017/307, reg. 5(2), with effect from 6 April 2017.

Cross references – SI 2006/1121: s. 246 of the Civil Partnership Act 2004 (interpretation of statutory references to stepchildren etc.) applies to the entry in para. 7, column (A).

SCHEDULE 2 – CIRCUMSTANCES IN WHICH EMPLOYMENT IS TREATED AS CONTINUING

Regulation 3

Where a person is employed as a self-employed earner or in an employment in respect of which he is, under these regulations, treated as falling within the category of a self-employed earner, the employment shall in either case be treated as continuing unless and until he is no longer ordinarily employed in that employment.

SCHEDULE 3 – EMPLOYMENTS IN RESPECT OF WHICH PERSONS ARE TREATED AS SECONDARY CLASS 1 CONTRIBUTORS

Regulation 5

Column (A) Employments	Column (B) Persons treated as secondary Class 1 contributors
1 Employment– (a) as an office cleaner or as an operative in any similar capacity in any premises other than those used as a private dwelling-house; or	1(a) Where the person employed is supplied by, or through the agency of some third person and receives his remuneration from, or through the agency of, that third person;
(b) as a cleaner of any telephone apparatus and associated fixtures, other than of apparatus and fixtures in premises used as a private dwelling-house.	(b) in any other case, except where the employment is also one described in paragraph 4 in column (A) of this Schedule, the person with whom the person employed contracted to do the work.

Column (A) Employments	Column (B) Persons treated as secondary Class 1 contributors
2 Employment (not being an employment described in paragraph 2 of column (B) of Schedule 1 to these regulations or an employment to which paragraph 1, 4, 5, 7 or 8 of this Schedule applies) where–	2 The UK agency who is party to the contract with the end client; or–
(a) the worker personally provides services to the end client;	(a) where, at any time, the end client provides to the UK agency fraudulent documents in connection with the control, direction or supervision which is to be exercised over the employed person, the end client; or
(b) there is a contract between the end client and a UK agency under or in consequence of which– (i) the services are provided, or (ii) the end client pays, or otherwise provides consideration for the services, and	(b) where, at any time, a person (other the end client) who is resident in Great Britain and who has a contractual relationship with the UK agency provides to the UK agency fraudulent documents in connection with the purported deduction or payment of contributions in connection with the employed person, the person who provides the fraudulent documents.
(c) remuneration is receivable by the worker (from any person) in consequence of providing the services.	
3 Employment of a person by his or her spouse or civil partner for the purposes of the employment of the spouse or civil partner.	3 The spouse or civil partner.
4 Employment (not being employment in respect of which a secondary contributor, in any particular case, is prescribed in paragraph 1(a) in column (B) of this Schedule, and not being employment described in paragraph 2 in column (A) of that Schedule) by a company, being a company within the meaning of the Companies Act 1948 [1985] and in voluntary liquidation but carrying on business under a liquidator.	4 The person who at the time of the employment holds the office of liquidator.
5 Employment in chambers as a barrister's clerk.	5 The head of chambers.
6 [Omitted by SI 2012/816, reg. 5.]	6 [Omitted by SI 2012/816, reg. 5.]
7 Employment as a minister of the Church of England, not being employment under a contract of service.	7 The Church Commissioners for England.
8 Employment as a minister of religion not being employment–	8(a) Where the remuneration in respect of the employment is paid from one fund, the person responsible for the administration of that fund;
(a) as a minister of the Church of England; or	
(b) under a contract of service; or	
(c) described in paragraph 5 in column (B) of Schedule 1 to these regulations.	(b) where the remuneration in respect of the employment is paid from more than one fund and– (i) remuneration is also paid from one of those funds to other ministers of religion, the person responsible

Column (A) Employments	Column (B) Persons treated as secondary Class 1 contributors
	for the administration of that fund; (ii) remuneration is also paid from two or more of those funds to other ministers of religion, the person responsible for the administration of the fund from which remuneration is paid to the greatest number of ministers of religion who carry out their duties in Great Britain; (iii) no person falls to be treated as secondary contributor by virtue of sub-paragraph (b)(i) or (ii) or this paragraph, the person responsible for the administration of the fund from which the minister of religion first receives a payment of remuneration in the tax year.
9 "Employment"–	**9** Where the employment is–
(a) (not being an employment described in sub-paragraphs (b) to (f)) by a foreign employer where the employed person, under an arrangement involving the foreign employer and the host employer, provides, or is personally involved in the provision of services, to a host employer;	(a) employment within paragraph 9(a) of column (A), the host employer;
(b) under or in consequence of a contract between a foreign agency and an end client where the worker provides services to that end client;	(b) employment within paragraph 9(b) of column (A), the end client;
(c) by a foreign employer where the worker provides services to an end client under or in consequence of a contract between that end client and a UK agency;	(c) employment within paragraph 9(c) of column (A), the UK agency who has the contractual relationship with the end client;
(d) by a foreign agency where the worker provides services to an end client under or in consequence of a contract between that end client and a UK agency;	(d) employment within paragraph 9(d) of column (A), the UK agency who has the contractual relationship with the end client;
(e) by a UK employer where the worker provides services to a person outside the United Kingdom under or in consequence of a contract between that person and a UK agency and the worker is eligible to pay contributions in the United Kingdom in relation to that employment; or	(e) employment within paragraph 9(e) of column (A), the UK employer or UK agency who has the contractual relationship with the person outside the United Kingdom; or
(f) by a foreign employer where the worker provides services to a person outside the United Kingdom under or in consequence of a contract between that person and a UK agency and the worker is eligible to pay contributions in the United Kingdom in relation to that employment.	(f) employment within paragraph 9(f) of column (A), the UK agency who has the contractual relationship with the person outside the United Kingdom;

Column (A) Employments	Column (B) Persons treated as secondary Class 1 contributors
	(g) employment within paragraphs 9(c) or (d) of column (A) and the end client provides at any time to the UK agency fraudulent documents in connection with the control, direction or supervision which is to be exercised over the employed person, the end client; or
	(h) employment within paragraphs 9(c) or (d) of column (A) and a person who is resident in Great Britain (who is not the end client) with a contractual relationship with the UK agency provides at any time to the UK agency fraudulent documents in connection with the purported deduction or payment of contributions in connection with the employed person, the person who provides the fraudulent documents.
Where the employment is as a mariner, this paragraph only applies where the duties of the employment are performed wholly or mainly in category A, B, C or D waters.	

History – Para. 1, column (A) substituted by SI 1990/1894, reg. 3(1), with effect from 16 October 1990.
Para. 2, column (A) substituted by SI 2014/635, reg. 2(4)(a), with effect from 6 April 2014.
Para. 2, column (B) substituted by SI 2014/635, reg. 2(4)(b), with effect from 6 April 2014.
In para. 2(c), column (B), the words "regulation 119(1)(b) of the Social Security (Contributions) Regulations 1979" substituted by SI 1990/1894, reg. 3(2), with effect from 16 October 1990.
In para. 3, column (A) the words "or civil partner" inserted and the words "employment of the spouse or civil partner" substituted by SI 2005/3133, reg. 4(2), with effect from 5 December 2005.
In para. 3, column (B) the words "or civil partner" inserted by SI 2005/3133, reg. 4(3), with effect from 5 December 2005.
Para. 6, column (A) and (B) omitted by SI 2012/816, reg. 5, with effect from 6 April 2012.
In para. 6, column (A), para. (a) revoked by SI 1984/350, reg. 4, with effect from 6 April 1984.
Para. 9, column (A) substituted by SI 2014/635, reg. 2(4)(c), with effect from 6 April 2014.
In para. 9, column (A), the words from "Where the employment" to "A, B, C or D waters." inserted by SI 2003/2420, reg. 5, with effect from 13 October 2003.
Para. 9, column (B) substituted by SI 2014/635, reg. 2(4)(d), with effect from 6 April 2014.
Para. 9, columns (A) and (B) inserted by SI 1994/726, reg. 4, operative 6 April 1994.
Para. 10, columns (A) and (B) omitted by SI 2014/635, reg. 2(4)(e), with effect from 6 April 2014.
In para. 10, entry in column (B) substituted by SI 2003/736 reg. 4, with effect from 6 April 2003.
In para. 10, column A "general earnings" substituted by SI 2004/770, reg. 34, with effect from 6 April 2004.
Para. 10, columns (A) and (B) inserted by SI 1998/1728, reg. 4, operative from 17 July 1998 and continuing in effect beyond 1 February 1999 by virtue of SI 1999/3, reg. 2.

SCHEDULE 4 – REVOCATIONS

Regulation 6(1)

[This Schedule revokes the regulations listed below.]

Notes – Sch. 4 revokes the following regulations: SI 1975/528; SI 1976/404; SI 1977/1015; SI 1977/1987, reg. 1(2)(a), 2–7; SI 1978/1462.

SOCIAL SECURITY (EARNINGS FACTOR) REGULATIONS 1979

(SI 1979/676 as amended by SI 1987/411, SI 1988/429, SI 1991/1165, SI 2003/608, SI 2015/1985)

Regulations made on 18 June 1979 by the Secretary of State for Social Services, in exercise of the powers conferred on him by s. 13(5) and 115(1) of, and para. 2 of Sch. 13 to, the Social Security Act 1975 [SSCBA 1992, s. 23(1); SSAA 1992, s. 59(1) and Sch. 3, para. 4], s. 35(3) of the Social Security Pensions Act 1975 and s. 1(5) of the Social Security (Miscellaneous Provisions) Act 1977 and of all other powers so enabling him.

CITATION, COMMENCEMENT AND INTERPRETATION

1(1) These regulations may be cited as the Social Security (Earnings Factor) Regulations 1979 and shall come into operation on 16th July 1979.

1(2) In these regulations–

"the Act" means the Social Security Act 1975 [SSCBA 1992; SSAA 1992];

"the Contributions Regulations" means the Social Security (Contributions) Regulations 1979; [Social Security (Contributions) Regulations 2001]

"year" means tax year;

and other expressions have the same meanings as in the Act.

1(3) In these regulations references to contributions of any class are to contributions actually of that class notwithstanding that for the purposes of any benefit they may be treated as or be deemed to be contributions of another class.

History – Reg. 1(2) amended by SI 1987/411, reg. 2(2), with effect from 6 April 1987 (continued by virtue of SI 1988/429, reg. 3(2)(b).) Reg. 1(3) inserted by SI 1987/411, reg. 2(2), with effect from 6 April 1987, and, following revocation of SI 1987/411, preserved by SI 1988/429, reg. 3(2)(b).

ASCERTAINMENT OF EARNINGS FACTORS

2(1) The earnings factors derived from a person's earnings paid in, or from earnings credited or Class 2 or Class 3 contributions in respect of, any year shall, subject to paragraph (2) of this regulation, be ascertained in accordance with the rules contained in Schedule 1 to these regulations.

2(2) A person's earnings factors in respect of the year commencing on 6th April 1988, or any subsequent year, shall not in respect of any such year together exceed an amount equal to 58 times the upper earnings limit of that year.

History – Reg. 2 substituted by SI 1988/429, reg. 2(2), with effect from 4 April 1988.

EVIDENCE OF OFFICIAL RECORDS

3 For the purposes of Part III of the Act (determinations of claims and questions) a certificate signed by a duly authorised officer of the Department of Health and Social Security, as to the manner in which any contributions paid or treated as having been paid or as not repaid have been or are to be recorded in the records of that Department, shall be sufficient evidence of the facts so certified; and any document purporting to be so signed shall be deemed to be so signed unless the contrary is proved.

Notes – Social security functions of Department of Health and Social Security transferred to Department of Social Security, with effect from 28 November 1988 (SI 1988/1843).

CONTRIBUTIONS TO BE TREATED AS HAVING BEEN PAID OR AS NOT REPAID

4 For the purposes of paragraph 5 of Schedule 1 to these regulations–

(a) any contributions which would have been payable by the person in question but for the fact that they are not payable by virtue of regulation 49 of the Contributions Regulations, or

(b) any contributions repayable or repaid to him under regulation 32 of those regulations as having been paid in excess of the amount prescribed in regulation 17 of those regulations (annual maximum)

shall be treated as having been paid and in the case of repaid contributions as not repaid.

History – In reg. 4, the reference to "paragraph 5" substituted by SI 1991/1165, reg. 2, with effect from 6 June 1991.

REVOCATIONS

5 The regulations specified in Schedule 2 to these regulations are hereby revoked.

SCHEDULES

SCHEDULE 1 – RULES FOR THE ASCERTAINMENT OF EARNINGS FACTORS

Regulation 2

Part I – Class 1 Contributions

History – Sch. 1, Pt. I substituted in consolidated form by SI 1991/1165, reg. 3 and Schedule, with effect from 6 June 1991, applying to ascertainment of earnings factors in respect of tax years beginning on or after 6 April 1987. These rules replace the previous Pt. I of the Schedule, as amended by SI 1985/1417, SI 1987/316, SI 1987/411 and SI 1988/429. Paragraphs 4 and 5 replace the previous para. 6 and 7.

1(1) In this Part of this Schedule–

"Class 1 contributions" means primary Class 1 contributions paid or treated as paid on so much of a person's earnings as do not exceed the current upper earnings limit or the prescribed equivalent if he is paid otherwise than weekly;

"contracted-out contributions" means primary Class 1 contributions paid or treated as paid on so much of a person's earnings in respect of any contracted-out employment as exceed the current lower earnings limit but do not exceed the current upper earnings limit or the prescribed equivalents if he is paid otherwise than weekly;

"the standard level" in relation to any year means that year's lower earnings limit for primary Class 1 contributions multiplied by 50; and

each paragraph has effect subject to the provisions of all later paragraphs.

1(2) Paragraphs 2, 3 and 4 below shall apply for the purposes specified in section 13(2) of the Act or section 2(4) of the Pensions Act 2014 [SSCBA 1992, s. 22(2)], and paragraph 5 below for the purposes of section 35 of the Social Security Pensions Act 1975 (earner's guaranteed minimum).

History – In para. 1, the definition of "Class 1 contributions" and "contracted-out contributions" substituted, and in the definition of "the standard level", the word "primary" inserted after the words "lower earnings limit for" by SI 2003/608, reg. 2 with effect from 6 April 2003. The changes do not apply for the purposes of ascertaining a person's earnings factors in respect of the year commencing on 6 April 2002 or any preceding year.

In para. 1(2), the words "or section 2(4) of the Pensions Act 2014" inserted by SI 2015/1985, art. 6(a), with effect from 6 April 2016 immediately after the State Pension Regulations 2015 (SI 2015/173).

Cross references – SSCBA 1992, s. 22(2): purposes for which earnings factors may be derived.

2(1) Subject to sub-paragraph (2) below, a person's earnings factor derived in respect of the year commencing on 6th April 1987, or any subsequent year, from–

(a) those of his earnings paid in that year upon which Class 1 contributions have been paid or treated as paid in respect of that year, and

(b) earnings with which he has been credited in respect of that year,

shall be equal to the amount of those actual and credited earnings.

2(2) Any earnings factor ascertained under sub-paragraph (1) above shall be rounded down to the nearest whole pound.

3 Where a person's earnings paid in the year commencing on 6th April 1987, or in any subsequent year, are earnings upon which Class 1 contributions have been paid or treated as paid in respect of that year and are, or are to be, recorded as separate sums in the records of the Department of Social Security, the earnings factor derived from those earnings shall be equal to the aggregate of the amounts ascertained by rounding down each sum separately to the nearest whole pound.

4 Where Class 1 contributions have been paid or treated as paid in respect of the year commencing on 6th April 1987, or any subsequent year, upon a person's earnings paid in that year and, but for this paragraph, the ascertainment of any earnings factor of his in respect of such year by the application of paragraphs 2 or 3 above would have the effect that–

(a) his earnings factor derived from those earnings, or

(b) the aggregate of his earnings factors derived from those earnings, and any earnings credited in respect of the same year, together with any derived from Class 2 or Class 3 contributions paid or credited in that year

would fall short of–

(i) the qualifying earnings factor, by an amount not exceeding £50, or

(ii) the standard level, by an amount not exceeding £50, or

(iii) one-half of the standard level, by an amount not exceeding £25, the amount of that earnings factor so ascertained shall, for the purpose of section 13(2)(a) of the Act or section 2(4) of the Pensions Act 2014, be increased by the amount of the shortfall, and the amount resulting shall be rounded up to the next whole pound.

History – In para. 4, the words "or section 2(4) of the Pensions Act 2014" inserted by SI 2015/1985, art. 6(b), with effect from 6 April 2016 immediately after the State Pension Regulations 2015 (SI 2015/173).

5(1) Subject to sub-paragraphs (2) and (3) below, a person's earnings factor derived in respect of the year commencing on 6th April 1987, or any subsequent year, from those of his earnings in contracted-out employment upon which contracted-out contributions have been paid, or treated as paid, in respect of such year, shall be equal to the amount of those earnings.

5(2) Any earnings factor ascertained under sub-paragraph (1) above shall be rounded down to the nearest whole pound.

5(3) Where a person's earnings paid in the year commencing on 6th April 1987, or in any subsequent year, are earnings upon which contracted-out contributions have been paid or treated as paid in respect of that year and are, or are to be, recorded as separate sums in the records of the Department of Social Security, the earnings factor derived from those earnings shall be equal to the aggregate of the amounts ascertained by rounding down each sum separately to the nearest whole pound.

Part II – Class 2 and Class 3 Contributions

8 Subject to the provisions of paragraph 9, the earnings factor derived from a person's Class 2 or Class 3 contributions, being in each case contributions actually paid or contributions paid or credited, in respect of any year shall be that year's lower earnings limit for Class 1 contributions multiplied by the number of the contributions from which the earnings factor is to be derived.

9 Where any earnings factor ascertained by applying the rule contained in paragraph 8 above would not, but for this paragraph, be expressed as a whole number of pounds, it shall be so expressed by the rounding down of any fraction of a pound less than one-half and the rounding up of any other fraction of a pound.

SCHEDULE 2 – REVOCATIONS

Regulation 5

[This Schedule revokes statutory instruments noted below.]

Notes – Sch. 2 revokes the following regulations: SI 1975/468; SI 1977/1706; and SI 1977/1707.

SOCIAL SECURITY (EMPLOYMENT TRAINING: PAYMENTS) ORDER 1988

(SI 1988/1409, as amended by SI 1991/387)

Order made on 8 August 1988 by the Secretary of State for Social Security, in exercise of the powers conferred upon him by s. 26(1)(d), (2) and (4) of the Employment Act 1988 and of all other powers so enabling him.

CITATION, COMMENCEMENT AND INTERPRETATION

1(1) This Order may be cited as the Social Security (Employment Training: Payments) Order 1988 and shall come into force on 4th September 1988.

1(2) In this Order, **"Class 1 contributions"**, **"primary Class 1 contributions"**, **"secondary Class 1 contributions"** and **"Class 2 contributions"** shall have the same meanings as in the Social Security Act 1975.

TREATMENT OF PAYMENTS FOR PURPOSES OF THE SOCIAL SECURITY ACT 1975

2 No primary or secondary Class 1 contributions shall be payable, and no person shall be liable to pay Class 1 or Class 2 contributions, in respect of payments to any person in receipt of a training premium under provision made under section 2 of the Employment and Training Act 1973 or section 2 of the Enterprise and New Towns (Scotland) Act 1990, being payments under provision made under either of those sections in connection with his use of facilities provided in pursuance of arrangements, known by the name of Employment Training, under either of those sections; and Part I (Contributions) of the Social Security Act 1975 shall be modified accordingly.

History – In art. 2, words "or section 2 of the Enterprise and New Towns (Scotland) Act 1990" inserted and words "either of those sections" substituted twice by SI 1991/387, art. 2, Schedule, with effect from 1 April 1991 (by virtue of SI 1991/387, art. 1).

SOCIAL SECURITY (REFUNDS) (REPAYMENT OF CONTRACTUAL MATERNITY PAY) REGULATIONS 1990

(SI 1990/536, as amended by SI 1990/2208, SSC(TF)A 1999 and SI 2001/1004)

Regulations made on 8 March 1990 by the Secretary of State for Social Security in exercise of the powers conferred upon him by s. 166(2) of, and para. 6(1)(gg) and (m) of Sch. 1 to, the Social Security Act 1975 [SSCBA 1992, s. 175(3); SSAA 1992, s. 189(4); SSCBA 1992, Sch. 1, para. 8(1)(i), (q)] and of all other powers so enabling him.

CITATION, COMMENCEMENT AND INTERPRETATION

1(1) These Regulations may be cited as the Social Security (Refunds) (Repayment of Contractual Maternity Pay) Regulations 1990 and shall come into force on 31st March 1990.

1(2) In these Regulations **"the Act"** means the Social Security Act 1975 [SSCBA 1992; SSAA 1992] and **"the Contributions Regulations"** means the Social Security (Contributions) Regulations 1979.

REFUNDS OF CONTRIBUTIONS

2(1) Where contractual maternity pay becomes repayable after 31st March 1990 and–

(a) subject to paragraph (2) below, an application for refund of contributions paid in respect of that pay is made in accordance with paragraph (3) below; and

(b) the net amount of the refund which would, but for this sub-paragraph, be payable exceeds the amount of one fifteenth of a standard rate primary Class 1 contribution payable on earnings at the upper limit in respect of primary Class 1 contributions prescribed in regulation 7 of the Contributions Regulations (lower and upper earnings limits) for the last or only year in respect of which the contributions were paid,

the Commissioners of Inland Revenue shall refund the whole of any primary or secondary Class 1 contributions paid in respect of that pay or, as the case may be, such part of those contributions as is prescribed in regulation 3 below.

2(2) No application under this regulation may be made unless–

(a) where the application is by the employee, the contractual maternity pay has been repaid; or

(b) where the application is by the employer, he has been repaid the contractual maternity pay or can satisfy the Commissioners of Inland Revenue that he has taken all reasonable steps to recover it.

2(3) A person desiring to apply for the refund of any contribution under this regulation shall make the application in writing and within the period of 6 years from the end of the year in which that contribution was paid or, if the Commissioners of Inland Revenue are satisfied that the person making the application had good cause for not making it within the said period, within such longer period as the Commissioners of Inland Revenue may allow.

2(4) In this regulation–

(a) **"contractual maternity pay"** means earnings payable under a contract of service by reason of pregnancy or confinement and repayable to the employer in the event of the employee failing to resume that employment after the birth or confinement; and

(b) **"standard rate"** means the appropriate percentage rate specified in section 4(6A) of the Act [SSCBA 1992, s. 8(2)] for primary Class 1 contributions.

History – In reg. 2(1), 2(2)(b) and 2(3) the words "Commissioners of Inland Revenue" substituted and in reg. 2(3) the words "Commissioners of Inland Revenue are" substituted by SSC(TF)A 1999, s. 1(2), Sch. 2, with effect from 1 April 1999 (SI 1999/527, art. 2(b), Sch. 2).

Cross references – SSCBA 1992, s. 8(2): from 6 April 1994, initial primary percentage is two per cent and main primary percentage is ten per cent.

REFUND OF PART OF CONTRIBUTIONS

3 Where there has been paid an amount by way of any of the contributory benefits (as described in section 12(1) of the Act [SSCBA 1992, s. 20(1)]) which would not have been paid had any of the contributions (in respect of which an application for their refund is duly made in accordance with regulation 2 above) not been paid in the first instance, the Commissioners of Inland Revenue shall refund that part of the contributions remaining after the deduction of that amount paid by way of such benefits.

History – In reg. 3, the words "that amount" substituted by SI 1990/2208, reg. 19, with effect from 5 December 1990.
In reg. 3 the words "Commissioners of Inland Revenue" substituted and in reg. 2(3) the words "Commissioners of Inland Revenue are" substituted by SSC(TF)A 1999, s. 1(2), Sch. 2, with effect from 1 April 1999 (SI 1999/527, art. 2(b), Sch. 2).

CONSEQUENTIAL AMENDMENT OF SCHEDULE 1 TO THE CONTRIBUTIONS REGULATIONS

4 [Repealed by SI 2001/1004, reg. 157 and Sch. 8 with effect from 6 April 2001.]

STATUTORY MATERNITY PAY (COMPENSATION OF EMPLOYERS) AND MISCELLANEOUS AMENDMENT REGULATIONS 1994

(SI 1994/1882 as amended by SI 1995/566, SI 1998/522, SI 2003/672, SI 2002/225, SI 2003/672 and SI 2004/698)

Regulations made on 14 July 1994 by the Secretary of State for Social Security, in exercise of powers conferred on him by s. 35(3), 167(1), (1A), (1B) and (4), 171(1) and 175(1) to (4) of the Social Security Contributions and Benefits Act 1992 and of all other powers enabling him in that behalf after agreement by the Social Security Advisory Committee that proposals in respect of reg. 9 should not be referred to it. Operative for 31 July 1994 (reg. 1, 9) and from 4 September 1994 (reg. 2–8).

CITATION, COMMENCEMENT AND INTERPRETATION

1(1) These Regulations may be cited as the Statutory Maternity Pay (Compensation of Employers) and Miscellaneous Amendment Regulations 1994 and regulations 2 to 7 shall have effect in relation to payments of statutory maternity pay due on or after 4th September 1994.

1(2) This regulation and regulation 9 shall come into force on 31 July 1994.

1(3) Regulations 2 to 8 shall come into force on 4 September 1994.

1(4) In these Regulations–

"the Contributions and Benefits Act" means the Social Security Contributions and Benefits Act 1992;

"the Maternity Allowance Regulations", means the Social Security (Maternity Allowance) Regulations 1987;

"the Board" means the Commissioners of Inland Revenue;

"contributions payments" has the same meaning as in section 167(8) of the Contributions and Benefits Act;

"the Contributions Regulations" means the Social Security (Contributions) Regulations 2001;

"employer" shall include a person who was previously an employer of a woman to whom a payment of statutory maternity pay was made, whether or not that person remains her employer at the date any deduction from contributions payments is made by him in accordance with regulation 5 or, as the case may be, any payment is received by him in accordance with regulation 6;

"the Employment Act" means the Employment Act 2002;

"income tax month" means the period beginning on the 6th day of any calendar month and ending on the 5th day of the following calendar month;

"income tax quarter" means, in any tax year, the period beginning on 6th April and ending on 5th July, the period beginning on 6th July and ending on 5th October, the period beginning on 6th October and ending on 5th January, or the period beginning on 6th January and ending on 5th April;

"qualifying day" means the first day in the week immediately preceding the 14th week before the expected week of confinement in which a woman who is or has been an employee first satisfies the conditions of entitlement to statutory maternity pay for which a deduction from a contributions payment is made by her employer in respect of a payment of statutory maternity pay made by him;

"qualifying tax year" means the tax year preceding the tax year in which the qualifying day in question falls.

"statutory adoption pay" means any payment under section 171ZL of the Contributions and Benefits Act;

"statutory paternity pay" means any payment under section 171ZA or 171ZB of the Contributions and Benefits Act;

"tax year" means the period of 12 months beginning on 6th April in any year;

"writing" includes writing delivered by means of electronic communications approved by directions issued by the Board pursuant to regulations made under section 132 of the Finance Act 1999;

1(5) Any reference in these Regulations to the employees of any employer includes, where the context permits, a reference to his former employees.

1(6) [Omitted by SI 2003/672, reg. 2(4).]

History – In reg. 1(4), the former definition of "contributions payment" and the definition of "payment of statutory maternity pay" omitted, and the definitions of "the Board", "contributions payments", "the Contributions Regulations", "the Employment Act", "income tax quarter", "statutory adoption pay", "statutory paternity pay", "tax year" and "writing" inserted by SI 2003/672, reg. 2 with effect from 6 April 2003.

Reg. 1(5) substituted by SI 2003/672, reg. 2(3) with effect from 6 April 2003.
Reg. 1(6) omitted by SI 2003/672, reg. 2(4) with effect from 6 April 2003.

MEANING OF "SMALL EMPLOYER"

2(1) Subject to the following provisions of this regulation, a small employer is an employer whose contributions payments for the qualifying tax year do not exceed £45,000.

2(2) For the purposes of this regulation, the amount of an employer's contributions payments shall be determined without regard to any deductions that may be made from them under any enactment or instrument.

2(3) Where in the qualifying tax year an employer has made contributions payments in one or more, but less than 12, of the income tax months, the amount of his contributions payments for that tax year shall be estimated by adding together all of those payments, dividing the total amount by the number of those months in which he has made those payments and multiplying the resulting figure by 12.

2(4) Where in the qualifying tax year an employer has made no contributions payments, but does have such payments in one or more income tax months which fall both–

(a) in the tax year in which the qualifying day falls, and

(b) before the qualifying day or, where there is more than one such day in that tax year, before the first of those days,

then the amount of his contributions payments for the qualifying tax year shall be estimated in accordance with paragraph (3) but as if the amount of the contributions payments falling in those months had fallen instead in the corresponding tax months in the qualifying tax year.

History – In reg. 2(1), "£45,000" substituted for "£40,000" by SI 2004/698, reg. 2, with effect from 6 April 2004.
In reg. 2(1), "£40,000" substituted for "£20,000" by SI 2002/225, reg. 2(2) with effect from 6 April 2002.

DETERMINATION OF THE AMOUNT OF ADDITIONAL PAYMENT TO WHICH A SMALL EMPLOYER SHALL BE ENTITLED

3 In respect of any payment of statutory maternity pay made in the tax year commencing 6th April 2002, or in any subsequent tax year, a small employer shall be entitled to recover an additional amount being an amount equal to 4.5 per cent of such payment, that percentage being the total amount of secondary Class 1 contributions estimated by the Commissioners of Inland Revenue as to be paid in respect of statutory maternity pay by all employers in that year, expressed as a percentage of the total amount of statutory maternity pay estimated by him to be paid by all employers in that year.

History – In reg. 3, "6th April 2002" and "4.5 per cent" substituted by SI 2002/225. Previous figures substituted by SI 1999/363 and by SI 1998/522, reg. 2.
In reg. 3, the words "entitled to recover an additional amount" substituted by SI 2003/672, reg. 3 with effect from 6 April 2003.
In reg. 3 the words "Commissioners of Inland Revenue" substituted by SSC(TF)A 1999, s. 1(2), Sch. 2, with effect from 1 April 1999 (SI 1999/527, art. 2(b), Sch. 2).
In reg. 3, words "made in the tax year … subsequent tax year" inserted by SI 1995/566, reg. 2, operative from 6 April 1995.

RIGHT OF EMPLOYERS TO PRESCRIBED AMOUNT

4 An employer who has made, or is liable to make, any payment of statutory maternity pay shall be entitled to recover–

(a) an amount equal to 92 per cent. of such payment; or

(b) if he is a small employer–

(i) an amount equal to such payment, and

(ii) an additional amount under regulation 3,

in accordance with the provisions of these Regulations.

History – Reg. 4 substituted by SI 2003/672, reg. 4 with effect from 6 April 2003.

APPLICATION FOR ADVANCE FUNDING FROM THE BOARD

5(1) If an employer is entitled to recover an amount determined in accordance with regulation 4 in respect of statutory maternity pay which he is required to pay to an employee or employees in any income tax month or income tax quarter and the amount exceeds the aggregate of–

(a) the total amount of tax which the employer is required to pay to the collector of taxes in respect of deductions from the emoluments of his employees in accordance with the Income Tax (Employments) Regulations 1993 for that income tax month or income tax quarter;

(b) the total amount of deductions made by the employer from the emoluments of his employees for that income tax month or income tax quarter in accordance with regulations made under section 22(5) of the Teaching and Higher Education Act 1998 or section 73B of the Education (Scotland) Act 1980 or in accordance with Article 3(5) of the Education (Student Support) (Northern Ireland) Order 1988;

(c) the total amount of contributions payments which the employer is required to pay to the collector of taxes in respect of the emoluments of his employees (whether by means of deduction or otherwise) in accordance with the Contributions Regulations for that income tax month or income tax quarter;

(d) the total amount of payments which the employer is required to pay to the collector of taxes in respect of deductions made on account of tax from payments to sub-contractors in accordance with section 559 of the Income and Corporation Taxes Act 1988 for that income tax month or income tax quarter; and

(e) the statutory paternity pay, statutory adoption pay and statutory maternity pay which the employer is required to pay to his employees in that income tax month or income tax quarter,

the employer may apply to the Board in accordance with paragraph (2) for funds ("advance funding") to pay that excess (or so much of it as remains outstanding) to the employee or employees.

5(2) Where–

(a) the conditions in paragraph (1) are satisfied; or

(b) the employer considers that the conditions in paragraph (1) will be satisfied on the date of any subsequent payment of emoluments to one or more employees who are entitled to a payment of statutory maternity pay,

the employer may apply to the Board for advance funding on a form approved for that purpose by the Board.

5(3) An application by an employer under paragraph (2) shall be for an amount not exceeding the amount of statutory maternity pay which the employer is entitled to recover in accordance with regulation 4 and which he is required to pay to an employee or employees for the income tax month or income tax quarter to which the payment of emoluments relates.

History – Reg. 5 substituted by SI 2003/672, reg. 4 with effect from 6 April 2003.

PAYMENTS TO EMPLOYERS BY THE SECRETARY OF STATE

6 An employer who is entitled to recover an amount under regulation 4 may do so by making one or more deductions from the aggregate of the amounts specified in sub-paragraphs (a) to (e) of regulation 5(1), except where and insofar as–

(a) those amounts relate to earnings paid before the beginning of the income tax month or income tax quarter in which the payment of statutory maternity pay was made;

(b) those amounts are paid by him later than six years after the tax year in which the payment of statutory maternity pay was made;

(c) the employer has received advance funding from the Board in accordance with an application under regulation 5; or

(d) the employer has made a request in writing under regulation 5 that the amount which he is entitled to recover under regulation 4 be paid to him and he has not received notification by the Board that such request is refused.

History – Reg. 6 substituted by SI 2003/672, reg. 4 with effect from 6 April 2003.

PAYMENTS TO EMPLOYERS BY THE BOARD

6A If, in an income tax month or an income tax quarter–

(a) the total amount that the employer is entitled to deduct under regulation 6 is less than the amount which the employer is entitled to recover under regulation 4;

(b) the Board is satisfied that this is so; and

(c) the employer has so requested in writing,

the Board shall pay to the employer the sum that the employer is unable to deduct under regulation 6.

History – Reg. 6A substituted (along with reg. 4, 5, 6) for former reg. 4, 5, 6, by SI 2003/672, reg. 4 with effect from 6 April 2003.

DATE WHEN CERTAIN CONTRIBUTIONS ARE TO BE TREATED AS PAID

7 Where an employer has made a deduction from a contributions payment under regulation 6, the date on which it is to be treated as having been paid for the purposes of section 167(6) of the Contributions and Benefits Act (amount deducted to be treated as paid and received towards discharging liability in respect of Class 1 contributions) is–

(a) in a case where the deduction did not extinguish the contributions payment, the date on which the remainder of the contributions payment or, as the case may be, the first date on which any part of the remain[d]er of the contributions payment was paid; and

(b) in a case where the deduction extinguished the contributions payment, the 14th day after the end of the income tax month during which there were paid the earnings in respect of which the contributions payment was payable.

History – In reg. 7, the words "regulation 6" and the words "section 167(6)" substituted by SI 2003/672, reg. 5 with effect from 6 April 2003.

OVERPAYMENTS

7A(1) Where advance funding has been provided to an employer in accordance with an application under regulation 5, the Board may recover any part of it not used to pay statutory maternity pay ("the overpayment").

7A(2) An officer of the Board shall decide to the best of his judgement the amount of the overpayment and shall give notice in writing of his decision to the employer.

7A(3) A decision under paragraph (2) may be in respect of funding provided in accordance with regulation 5 for one or more income tax months or income tax quarters in a tax year–

(a) in respect of one or more classes of employees specified in a decision notice (where a notice does not name any individual employee); or

(b) in respect of one or more individual employees named in a decision notice.

7A(4) Subject to paragraphs (5), (6) or (7), Part 6 of the Taxes Management Act 1970 (collection and recovery) shall apply with any necessary modifications to a decision under this regulation as if the amount specified were an assessment and as if the amount set out in the notice were income tax charged on the employer.

7A(5) Where a decision under paragraph (2) relates to more than one employee, proceedings may be brought to recover the amount overpaid without distinguishing the sum to be repaid in respect of each employee and without specifying the employee in question.

7A(6) A decision to recover an amount made in accordance with this regulation shall give rise to one cause of action or matter of complaint for the purpose of proceedings under section 65, 66 or 67 of the Taxes Management Act 1970.

7A(7) Nothing in paragraph (5) shall prevent separate proceedings being brought for the recovery of any amount which the employer is liable to repay in respect of each employee to whom the decision relates.

History – Reg. 7A inserted by SI 2003/672, reg. 6 with effect from 6 April 2003.

REVOCATION

8 [Revokes SI 1987/91.]

AMENDMENT OF REGULATION 3 OF THE MATERNITY ALLOWANCE REGULATIONS

9 [Amends SI 1987/416.]

EMPLOYER'S CONTRIBUTIONS RE-IMBURSEMENT REGULATIONS 1996

(SI 1996/195 as amended by SI 1999/286, SSC(TF)A 1999 and SI 2001/1004)

Made on 1 February 1996 by the Secretary of State for Social Security, in exercise of the powers conferred by s. 27, 34(3) and (7), 35(1) and (3) and 36 of the Jobseekers Act 1995 and of all other powers so enabling him.

ARRANGEMENT OF REGULATIONS

CITATION AND COMMENCEMENT AND INTERPRETATION

1(1) These Regulations may be cited as the Employer's Contributions Re-imbursement Regulations 1996 and shall come into force on 6th April 1996.

1(2) In these Regulations–

"benefit week" means a period of 7 days (including Sundays) ending on the week-day corresponding to the particular week-day specified in a written notice last given to a person by the Secretary of State for the purposes of claiming unemployment benefit;

"breaking period" means–

(a) any period of not more than 12 consecutive weeks in respect of which a person is not entitled to a qualifying benefit; or

(b) a period in respect of which a person is summoned to jury service;

"carer" means a person of the description specified in paragraph 4(1) of Schedule 1 to the Income Support Regulations;

"contracted-out rate" means in relation to Class 1 contributions payable in respect of earnings paid to or for the benefit of an earner in contracted-out employment the percentages for the time being applying in section 41(1)(b) of the Pension Schemes Act 1993 for the calculation of the amount of those contributions;

"the Contributions Regulations" means the Social Security (Contributions) Regulations 1979;

"*deductions certificate*" means a certificate obtained from the Secretary of State in accordance with regulation 7;

"earnings" is to be construed in accordance with section 3 of the Benefits Act;

"employee" means a person who is–

(a) an employed earner within the meaning of section 2(1)(a) of the Benefits Act; or

(b) treated as such under section 116 of the Benefits Act or by regulations made under section 2(2), 117, 119 or 120 of that Act; and

(c) over the age of 16;

"employer" means a person who in relation to an employee is a secondary contributor within the meaning of section 7(1) of the Benefits Act or who is treated as such under section 116 of the Benefits Act or by regulations made under section 7(2), 117, 119 or 120 of the Benefits Act;

"the Income Support Regulations" means the Income Support (General) Regulations 1987;

"income tax period" has the meaning specified in Regulation 2(1) of Schedule 1 to the Contributions Regulations;

"the Jobseekers Act" means the Jobseekers Act 1995;

"lone parent" has the meaning specified in regulation 2(1) of the Income Support Regulations;

"mariner" has the meaning specified in regulation 86 of the Contributions Regulations;

"non-contracted-out rate" has the meaning specified in regulation 1(2) of the Contributions Regulations;

"pensionable age" has the meaning given under the rules in paragraph 1 of Schedule 4 to the Pensions Act 1995;

"qualifying benefit" means–

(a) unemployment benefit;

(b) in the case of a person–

(i) who is treated as available for employment under regulation 9 of the Income Support Regulations; or

(ii) to whom paragraph 1, 4 or 11 of Schedule 1 to the Income Support Regulations applies,

income support;

"training allowance" means an allowance (whether by way of periodical grants or otherwise) payable–

(a) out of public funds by a Government department or by or on behalf of the Secretary of State for Education and Employment, Scottish Enterprise or Highlands and Islands Enterprise; and

(b) to a person for his maintenance or in respect of a member of his family; and

(c) for the period, or part of the period, during which he is following a course of training or instruction provided by, or in pursuance of arrangements made with, that department or approved by that department in relation to him or so provided or approved by or on behalf of the Secretary of State for Education and Employment, Scottish Enterprise or Highlands and Islands Enterprise,

but it does not include an allowance paid by any Government department to or in respect of a person by reason of the fact that he is following a course of full-time education, other than under arrangements made under section 2 of the Employment and Training Act 1973, or is training as a teacher;

"tax week" has the meaning specified in section 122(1) of the Benefits Act;

"the Unemployment Regulations" means the Social Security (Unemployment, Sickness and Invalidity Benefit) Regulations 1983;

"voyage period" has the meaning specified in regulation 86 of the Contributions Regulations;

"week" means a period of 7 consecutive days;

"year" except in regulation 5(4) means a period of 365 days or where that period includes 29th February, 366 days.

1(3) In these Regulations, unless the context otherwise requires, any reference–

(a) to a numbered regulation is to the regulation in these Regulations bearing that number;

(b) in a regulation to a numbered paragraph is to the paragraph in that regulation bearing that number;

(c) in a paragraph to a lettered or numbered sub-paragraph is to the sub-paragraph in that paragraph bearing that letter or number.

1(4) [Revoked by SSC(TF)A 1999, s 26(3), Sch 10, Pt II.]

History – Reg. 1(4) revoked by SSC(TF)A 1999, s. 26(3), Sch. 10, Pt. II, with effect from 1 April 1999 (by virtue of SI 1999/527, art. 2(b), Sch. 2).

CIRCUMSTANCES IN WHICH A PERSON IS TREATED AS ENTITLED TO A *JOBSEEKER'S ALLOWANCE* FOR A CONTINUOUS PERIOD OF 2 YEARS IMMEDIATELY BEFORE HIS EMPLOYMENT

2(1) Where this regulation applies, a person who would not otherwise satisfy the relevant condition shall be treated as satisfying that condition.

2(2) This regulation applies where a person would have satisfied the relevant condition had the reference to "two years" been a reference to a period of two years within the meaning of regulation 1(2).

2(3) This regulation applies where a person is entitled to a jobseeker's allowance for periods (in this regulation referred to as **jobseeker's allowance periods**) separated by breaking periods; and the jobseeker's allowance periods excluding the intervening breaking periods form in aggregate a period of not less than two years.

2(4) This regulation applies where–

(a) a person has any one or more jobseeker's allowance periods; and

(b) he is also entitled to a qualifying benefit for one or more other periods (the additional periods) throughout which he is a person of a specified description; and

(c) the jobseeker's allowance periods plus the additional periods, form a continuous period of not less than two years.

2(5) This regulation applies where, but for a breaking period occurring immediately after a jobseeker's allowance period, or an additional period a person would have satisfied the relevant condition.

2(6) For the purposes of paragraph (4)(b) in determining whether a person has been entitled to a qualifying benefit for any period any benefit week on any day of which that person was entitled to unemployment benefit shall be treated as a period throughout which that person was entitled to a qualifying benefit.

2(7) For the purposes of paragraph (4)(b) a person is a person of a specified description if he is–

(a) undergoing a course of training for which a training allowance is payable;

(b) available or treated as available for employment under regulation 9 of the Income Support Regulations or under regulations made under section 25A(1)(a) of the Benefits Act;

(c) a carer; or

(d) a lone parent.

2(8) For the purposes of paragraph (4)(c) in determining whether there has been a continuous period of not less than two years where a person has jobseeker's allowance periods or additional periods separated by breaking periods, the jobseeker's allowance periods and the additional periods shall be aggregated together and treated as a single period and the intervening breaking periods shall be excluded in the computation of that single period.

2(9) In this regulation **"the relevant condition"** means the condition in subsection (1) of section 27 of the Jobseekers Act.

CIRCUMSTANCES IN WHICH A PERSON IS TO BE TREATED AS UNEMPLOYED FOR A CONTINUOUS PERIOD OF 2 YEARS IMMEDIATELY BEFORE HIS EMPLOYMENT

3(1) Where this regulation applies, a person who would not otherwise satisfy the relevant condition shall be treated as satisfying that condition.

3(2) This regulation applies where a person would have satisfied the relevant condition had the reference to "two years" been a reference to a period of two years within the meaning of regulation 1(2).

3(3) This regulation applies where, but for a breaking period occurring immediately after the period of unemployment, a person would have satisfied the relevant condition.

3(4) This regulation applies where a person has periods of unemployment separated by breaking periods and those periods of unemployment excluding the intervening breaking periods form in aggregate a period of not less than two years.

3(5) This regulation applies where a person would have satisfied the relevant condition but for his engagement in employment which is not treated as remunerative work for the purposes of regulation 5(1) of the Income Support Regulations.

3(6) This regulation applies where–

(a) a person would have satisfied the relevant condition but for his engagement in employment for any day; and

(b) that day would not be excluded as a day of unemployment in relation to him by the application of regulation 7(1)(o) of the Unemployment Regulations.

3(7) In this regulation **"the relevant condition"** means the condition in subsection (2)(a) of section 27 of the Jobseekers Act.

PRESCRIBED DESCRIPTION OF A PERSON FOR THE PURPOSES OF SECTION 27(2)(c) OF THE JOBSEEKERS ACT

4(1) For the purposes of section 27(2)(c) of the Jobseekers Act a person falls within a prescribed description of person if–

(a) he is in receipt of a qualifying benefit for a continuous period of not less than two years; and

(b) continuously for the whole of that period he satisfied any one or more of the following conditions–

(i) he is undergoing a course of training for which a training allowance is payable;

(ii) he is available or treated as available for employment under regulation 9 of the Income Support Regulations or under regulations made under section 25A(1)(a) of the Benefits Act;

(iii) he is a carer;

(iv) he is a lone parent.

4(2) For the purposes of paragraph (1)(a) in determining whether a person has been entitled to a qualifying benefit for any period, any benefit week on any day of which that person was entitled to unemployment benefit shall be treated as a period throughout which he was entitled to a qualifying benefit.

4(3) For the purposes of paragraph (1) in determining whether there has been a continuous period of not less than two years, where a person has periods throughout which he is a qualifying person separated by breaking periods the periods throughout which the person is a qualifying person shall be aggregated together and treated as a single period and the intervening breaking periods shall be excluded in the computation of that single period.

4(4) In this regulation **"qualifying person"** means a person who is entitled to a qualifying benefit and is of a description specified in paragraph (1).

DEDUCTIONS FROM EMPLOYER'S CONTRIBUTIONS PAYMENTS

5(1) An employer–

(a) who employs a person who is a qualifying employee in relation to him for a continuous period of at least 13 weeks commencing on or before 31st March 1999; and

(b) who has obtained a deductions certificate, in accordance with regulation 7; and

(c) who is liable to pay Class 1 contributions in respect of earnings paid to or for the benefit of that qualifying employee in the relevant period,

shall be entitled to deduct an amount determined in accordance with this regulation from his contributions payments.

5(2) The amount which an employer is entitled to deduct shall be where the Class 1 contributions specified in paragraph (1)(c) are payable–

(a) at the contracted-out rate, an amount equal to the amount of secondary Class 1 contributions which would be payable by that employer in respect of the earnings paid in the relevant period were those contributions payable at the non-contracted-out rate;

(b) at any other rate, an amount equal to the amount of secondary Class 1 contributions which would be payable by that employer in respect of the earnings paid in the relevant period.

5(3) For the purposes of determining an amount which an employer is entitled to deduct under paragraph (2) no account shall be taken of any earnings paid to or for the benefit of the qualifying employee after the relevant period.

5(4) In this regulation **"the relevant period"** means the period commencing with the first day of that qualifying employee's employment with that employer and ending–

(a) on the last day of such employment;

(b) on the day the qualifying employee reaches pensionable age; or

(c) in the following year on the day preceding the day corresponding to that first day of employment,

whichever shall first occur.

History – In reg. 5(1)(a) words "commencing on or before 31st March 1999" inserted by SI 1999/286, reg. 2, with effect from 8 March 1999.

DEDUCTIONS FROM EMPLOYER'S CONRIBUTIONS PAYMENTS WHERE A MARINER'S EARNINGS ARE PAID FOR A VOYAGE PERIOD

6(1) An employer–

(a) who employs a person who is a qualifying employee in relation to him as a mariner for a continuous period of at least 13 weeks commencing on or before 31st March 1999; and

(b) who has obtained a deductions certificate in accordance with regulation 7; and

(c) who is liable to pay Class 1 contributions in accordance with regulation 90 of the Contributions Regulations in respect of earnings paid to or for the benefit of that mariner for a voyage period commencing in the relevant period but ending after it,

shall be entitled to deduct an amount determined in accordance with this regulation from his contributions payments.

6(2) The amount which an employer is entitled to deduct shall be where the Class 1 contributions specified in paragraph (1)(c) are payable–

(a) at the contracted-out rate, an amount equal to the amount of secondary Class 1 contributions which would be payable by that employer in respect of the earnings earned in the part of the voyage period falling within the relevant period were those contributions assessed at the non-contracted-out rate;

(b) at any other rate, an amount equal to the amount of secondary Class 1 contributions which would be payable by that employer in respect of the earnings earned in the part of the voyage period falling within the relevant period.

6(3) For the purposes of determining an amount which an employer is entitled to deduct under paragraph (2) no account shall be taken of any earnings earned or treated as earned under regulation 90 of the Contributions Regulations in that part of the voyage period falling after the end of the relevant period.

6(4) In this regulation **"the relevant period"** has the same meaning as in regulation 5(4).

History – In reg. 6(1)(a) words "commencing on or before 31st March 1999" inserted by SI 1999/286, reg. 2, with effect from 8 March 1999.

DEDUCTIONS CERTIFICATE

7(1) An application for a deductions certificate must be in writing and shall contain the particulars specified in paragraph (2).

7(2) For the purposes of paragraph (1) the particulars required are–

– the name and address of the person employing the qualifying employee;

– the name and national insurance number of the qualifying employee;

– the date the qualifying employee's employment with that person commenced.

7(3) An application for a deductions certificate must be made to the Commissioners of Inland Revenue before the end of the period commencing with the first day of the qualifying employee's employment with the employer and ending on the expiry of 52 weeks after that date.

7(4) The Commissioners of Inland Revenue on receipt of an application from a person employing a qualifying employee shall issue a deductions certificate and shall certify on the deductions certificate that the person to whom it is issued is the employer entitled to make deductions in accordance with these Regulations.

7(5) Where an application is made after the period specified in paragraph (3) it may be accepted by the Commissioners of Inland Revenue if the person applying for it proves that there was good cause for his failure to make the application within the period specified.

7(6) A deductions certificate remains at all times the property of the Commissioners of Inland Revenue.

7(7) A person who has been issued with a deductions certificate shall be responsible for its custody.

7(8) A person to whom a deductions certificate has been issued shall, within 28 days of receiving a request from the Commissioners of Inland Revenue to do so, return the certificate to the Commissioners of Inland Revenue unless he has reasonable cause for not so doing.

7(9) Where a deductions certificate has been lost or destroyed the Commissioners of Inland Revenue may, at their discretion, issue a duplicate.

History – In reg. 7(3), (4), (5), (6), (8) and (9), words "Commissioners of Inland Revenue" substituted and in reg. 7(9) the word "their" substituted by SSC(TF)A 1999, s. 1(2) and Sch. 2, with effect from 1 April 1999 (by virtue of SI 1999/527, art. 2(b), Sch. 2).

DEDUCTIONS FROM CONTRIBUTIONS PAYMENTS

8 An employer who is entitled to deduct an amount determined in accordance with regulation 5 or 6 may do so by making one or more deductions from his contributions payments except where and insofar as–

(a) those contributions payments are made more than six years after the end of the year in which he first became entitled to make the deduction;

(b) that amount has been repaid to him by the Commissioners of Inland Revenue;

(c) he has made a request in writing under regulation 9 that an amount be paid to him and he has not received notification by the Commissioners of Inland Revenue that the request is refused.

History – In reg. 8, words "Commissioners of Inland Revenue" substituted twice by SSC(TF)A 1999, s. 1(2) and Sch. 2, with effect from 1 April 1999 (by virtue of SI 1999/527, art. 2(b), Sch. 2).

PAYMENTS TO EMPLOYERS BY THE SECRETARY OF STATE

9(1) If the amount an employer is or would otherwise be entitled to deduct under regulation 8 exceeds the amount of his contributions payments in respect of earnings paid in an income tax period the Commissioners of Inland Revenue shall, if the employer requests them to do so in writing, pay the employer an amount equal to such excess.

9(2) If an employer is not liable to pay any contributions payments in an income tax period but would otherwise be entitled to deduct an amount under regulation 8 and the Commissioners of Inland Revenue are satisfied that this is the case the Commissioners of Inland Revenue shall, if the employer requests them to do so in writing, pay the employer such amount.

History – In reg. 9(1), words "Commissioners of Inland Revenue" substituted and the word "them" substituted by SSC(TF)A 1999, s. 1(2) and Sch. 2, with effect from 1 April 1999 (by virtue of SI 1999/527, art. 2(b), Sch. 2).
In reg. 9(2), words "Commissioners of Inland Revenue" substituted, the words "Commissioners of Inland Revenue are" substituted and the word "them" substituted by SSC(TF)A 1999, s. 1(2) and Sch. 2, with effect from 1 April 1999 (by virtue of SI 1999/527, art. 2(b), Sch. 2).

QUALIFYING EMPLOYEES WITH MORE THAN ONE EMPLOYMENT

10 Where an employee is a qualifying employee in relation to more than one employer at the same time, the right to make deductions shall be confined to the employer–

(a) with whom the qualifying employee's employment began first; and

(b) certified on the deductions certificate as the employer entitled to make the deductions.

TREATMENT OF 2 OR MORE EMPLOYERS AS ONE

11(1) Where this regulation applies, the employers concerned are to be treated as one for the purposes of determining the amount which may be deducted in accordance with regulation 5 or 6.

11(2) This regulation applies where–

(a) an employer is entitled to make deductions in accordance with these Regulations in relation to a qualifying employee; and

(b) earnings paid to or for the benefit of that employee are for the purposes of determining the amount of Class 1 contributions payable aggregated by virtue of regulation 12(1)(a) of the Contributions Regulations.

OFFENCES

12(1) A person who contravenes or fails to comply with the requirements of regulation 7(8) is guilty of an offence.

12(2) Subsection (7) of section 34 of the Jobseekers Act shall apply in relation to the original offence; and **"the original offence"** has the meaning given to it in that subsection.

AMENDMENT OF SCHEDULE 1 TO THE CONTRIBUTIONS REGULATIONS

13(1) [Repealed by SI 2001/1004, reg. 157 and Sch. 8 with effect from 6 April 2001.]

SOCIAL SECURITY CONTRIBUTIONS (DECISIONS AND APPEALS) REGULATIONS 1999

(SI 1999/1027 as amended by SI 2001/4023, SI 2002/3120, SI 2009/56, SI 2009/777, SI 2010/2451, SI 2015/174 and SI 2015/521)

Made on 30 March 1999 by the Commissioners of Inland Revenue, in exercise of the powers conferred on them by s. 9, 10, 11, 13, 24 and 25 of the Social Security Contributions (Transfer of Functions, etc.) Act 1999 and by art. 8, 9, 10, 12 and 23 of the Social Security Contributions (Transfer of Functions, etc.) (Northern Ireland) Order 1999 and, in relation to Pt. III of this instrument, with the concurrence of the Lord Chancellor and the Lord Advocate.

PART I – INTRODUCTORY

CITATION AND COMMENCEMENT

1 These Regulations may be cited as the Social Security Contributions (Decisions and Appeals) Regulations 1999 and shall come into force on 1st April 1999.

INTERPRETATION

2 In these Regulations unless the context otherwise requires–

"the Board" means the Commissioners of Inland Revenue;

"the Management Act" means the Taxes Management Act 1970;

"notice" means notice in writing and

"notify" and **"notification"** shall be construed accordingly;

"the Transfer Act" means the Social Security Contributions (Transfer of Functions, etc.) Act 1999;

"the Transfer Order" means the Social Security Contributions (Transfer of Functions, etc.) (Northern Ireland) Order 1999.

PART II – DECISIONS

DECISIONS – GENERAL

3(1) A decision which, by virtue of section 8 of the Transfer Act or Article 7 of the Transfer Order, falls to be made by an officer of the Board under or in connection with the Social Security Contributions and Benefits Act 1992, the Social Security Administration Act 1992, the Social Security Contributions and Benefits (Northern Ireland) Act 1992, the Social Security Administration (Northern Ireland) Act 1992, the Jobseekers Act 1995 or the Jobseekers (Northern Ireland) Order 1995–

(a) must be made to the best of his information and belief, and

(b) must state the name of every person in respect of whom it is made and–

(i) the date from which it has effect, or

(ii) the period for which it has effect.

3(2) Where an officer of the Board has resolved to make a decision of a kind referred to in paragraph (1), he may entrust to some other officer of the Board responsibility for completing the procedure for making the decision, whether by means involving the use of a computer or otherwise, including responsibility for serving notice of the decision on any person named in it.

3(3) In the case of a decision to which section 11 of the Transfer Act or Article 10 of the Transfer Order applies, other than one which relates to a person's entitlement to statutory sick pay, statutory maternity pay, statutory paternity pay, statutory shared parental pay or statutory adoption pay each person who is named in the decision has a right to appeal.

History – In reg. 3(3), the words "statutory paternity pay" substituted for the words "ordinary statutory paternity pay, additional statutory paternity pay" by SI 2015/174, reg. 2(a), with effect from 5 April 2015, subject to the transitional provision in SI 2015/174, reg. 3 (amendments do not have effect where an appeal under reg. 3 or settlement under reg. 11 relates to a person's entitlement to ordinary statutory paternity pay or additional statutory paternity pay).

In reg. 3(3), the words ", statutory shared parental pay" inserted by SI 2015/174, reg. 2(b), with effect from 5 March 2015.

In reg. 3(3), the words "ordinary statutory paternity pay, additional statutory paternity pay" substituted for the words "statutory paternity pay" by SI 2010/2451, reg. 2, with effect from 14 November 2010.

In reg. 3(3), the words "to the tax appeal Commissioners", which appeared after "appeal", omitted by SI 2009/56, art. 3(2) and Sch. 2, para. 60, operative from 1 April 2009 subject to transitional and saving provisions in SI 2009/56, Sch. 3.

In reg. 3(3) words "statutory sick pay, statutory maternity pay, statutory paternity pay or statutory adoption pay" inserted by SI 2002/3120, reg. 3(2)(a), with effect from 7 January 2003.

NOTICE OF DECISION

4(1) Notice of a decision by an officer of the Board referred to in regulation 3(1) must be given–

(a) in the case of a decision relating to a person's entitlement to statutory sick pay, statutory maternity pay, statutory paternity pay, statutory shared parental pay or statutory adoption pay, to the employee and employer concerned, and

(b) in any other case, to every person named in the decision.

4(2) A notice under this regulation must state the date on which it is issued and may be served by post addressed to any person to whom it is to be given at his usual or last known place of residence, or his place of business or employment.

4(3) Where notice is to be given to a company, it may be served by post addressed to its registered office or its principal place of business.

History – In reg. 4(1)(a), the words "statutory paternity pay" substituted for the words "ordinary statutory paternity pay, additional statutory paternity pay" by SI 2015/174, reg. 2(a), with effect from 5 April 2015, subject to the transitional provision in SI 2015/174, reg. 3 (amendments do not have effect where an appeal under reg. 3 or settlement under reg. 11 relates to a person's entitlement to ordinary statutory paternity pay or additional statutory paternity pay).
In reg. 4(1)(a), the words ", statutory shared parental pay" inserted by SI 2015/174, reg. 2(b), with effect from 5 March 2015.
In reg. 4(1)(a), the words "ordinary statutory paternity pay, additional statutory paternity pay" substituted for the words "statutory paternity pay" by SI 2010/2451, reg. 2, with effect from 14 November 2010.
In reg. 4(1)(a) words "statutory sick pay, statutory maternity pay, statutory paternity pay or statutory adoption pay " inserted by SI 2002/3120, reg. 3(2)(b), with effect from 7 January 2003.

VARIATION OF DECISION

5(1) An officer of the Board may vary a decision under section 8 of the Transfer Act or Article 7 of the Transfer Order if he has reason to believe that it was incorrect at the time that it was made.

5(2) Notice of a variation of a decision must be given to the same persons and in the same manner as notice of the decision was given.

5(3) A variation of a decision may state that it has effect for any period in respect of which the decision could have had effect, if the reason for the variation had been known to the person making the decision at the time that it was made.

5(4) A decision which is under appeal may be varied at any time before the tribunal determines the appeal.

History – In reg. 5(4), the words "tribunal determines" substituted for the words "tax appeal Commissioners determine" by SI 2009/56, art. 3(2) and Sch. 2, para. 61, operative from 1 April 2009 subject to transitional and saving provisions in SI 2009/56, Sch. 3.

DECISION SUPERSEDING EARLIER DECISION

6(1) An officer of the Board may make a decision superseding an earlier decision, whether as originally made or as varied in accordance with regulation 5, which has become inappropriate for any reason.

6(2) A decision superseding an earlier decision which is made in these circumstances has effect from the date of the change in circumstances which rendered the earlier decision inappropriate and the earlier decision ceases to have effect as soon as the superseding decision has effect.

PART III – APPEALS

APPLICATION OF THE TAXES MANAGEMENT ACT 1970IN RELATION TO REVIEWS AND APPEALS WITH MODIFICATIONS

7(1) In this regulation reference to a section alone is reference to the section so numbered in the Management Act.

7(2) For the purposes of these regulations, sections 49A to 49I of the Management Act shall apply to appeals with the following modifications–

(a) in section 49A(4) for "in accordance with section 54" substitute "in accordance with regulation 11 of the Social Security Contributions (Decisions and Appeals) Regulations 1999",

(b) in section 49C(4) for "agreement in writing under section 54(1)" substitute "agreement under regulation 11 of the Social Security Contributions (Decisions and Appeals) Regulations 1999",

(c) omit section 49C(5),

(d) in section 49F(2) for "agreement in writing under section 54(1)" substitute "agreement under regulation 11 of the Social Security Contributions (Decisions and Appeals) Regulations 1999",

(e) omit section 49F(3)

History – Reg. 7 substituted by SI 2009/56, art. 3(2) and Sch. 2, para. 62, operative from 1 April 2009 subject to transitional and saving provisions in SI 2009/56, Sch. 3. Former reg. 7 read as follows:

"ASSIGNMENT OF APPEALS TO GENERAL COMMISSIONERS

7(1) An appeal to the General Commissioners under Part II of the Transfer Act or Part III of the Transfer Order must be brought before the Commissioners for the division in which the place given by the provisions of this regulation (in this regulation referred to as "the relevant place") is situated.

7(2) The relevant place is whichever of the places specified in paragraph (3) is identified by an election made by the appellant.

7(3) Those places are–

(a) the place (if any) in the United Kingdom which, at the time when the election is made, is the appellant's place of residence;

(b) the place (if any) which at that time is the appellant's place of business in the United Kingdom;

(c) the place (if any) in the United Kingdom which at that time is the appellant's place of employment;

and, in the case of a place of employment, it is immaterial for the purposes of this regulation whether the appeal relates to matters connected with the employment of the appellant.

7(4) Where the appellant fails to make an election for the purposes of this regulation before the time limit given in paragraph (5) an officer of the Board may elect which of the places specified in paragraph (3) is to be the relevant place.

7(5) An election by an appellant for the purposes of this regulation–

(a) must be made by notice to an officer of the Board;

(b) must be made at the time when notice of appeal is given or before such later date as the Board allow; and

(c) is irrevocable.

7(6) Where there is no place falling within paragraph (3) an officer of the Board may give directions for determining the relevant place.

7(7) A direction given under paragraph (6) does not have effect in relation to an appeal unless the officer of the Board has served on the appellant a notice stating the effect of the direction in relation to the appeal.

7(8) In paragraph (3)(a) **"place of residence"** means the appellant's usual place of residence.

7(9) In paragraph (3)(b)

"place of business" means–

(a) the place where the trade, profession, vocation or business with which the appeal is concerned is carried on, or

(b) if the trade, profession, vocation or business is carried on at more than one place, the head office or place where it is mainly carried on.".

MULTIPLE APPEALS

8 [Omitted by SI 2009/56, art. 3(2) and Sch. 2, para. 63.]

History – Reg. 8 omitted by SI 2009/56, art. 3(2) and Sch. 2, para. 63, operative from 1 April 2009 subject to transitional and saving provisions in SI 2009/56, Sch. 3. Former reg. 8 read as follows:

"**8(1)** This regulation applies where there is more than one appeal under Part II of the Transfer Act or Part III of the Transfer Order against the same decision and none of the appellants has elected in accordance with section 46(1) of the Management Act to bring the appeal before the Special Commissioners instead of before the General Commissioners.

8(2) Where none of the appellants has made an election under regulation 7(2), an officer of the Board may, after taking account of the factors which appear to him to be relevant, give directions for determining the division of General Commissioners who are to hear the appeals.

8(3) Where different places have been identified by the appellants in elections under regulation 7(2), paragraphs (4) to (7) of this regulation apply for the purpose of determining the division of General Commissioners before whom the appeals are to be brought.

8(4) Any election by an appellant who is liable under section 6 of the Social Security Contributions and Benefits Act 1992 or the Social Security Contributions and Benefits (Northern Ireland) Act 1992, or would be liable but for subsection (1)(b) of that section, to pay secondary Class 1 contributions in relation to–

(a) in the case of an appeal relating to a person's entitlement to statutory sick pay, statutory maternity pay, statutory paternity pay or statutory adoption pay, the earnings of that person, or

(b) in any other case, the earnings of another person named in the decision, must be ignored.

8(5) If, applying the rule in paragraph (4), it appears to an officer of the Board that only one appellant has made an election under regulation 7(2), he may direct that the General Commissioners for the division in which the place for which that appellant elected is situated must, after considering any representations made to them orally or in writing by any of the appellants, determine the division of General Commissioners who are to hear the appeals.

8(6) If, applying the rule in paragraph (4), it appears to an officer of the Board that more than one of the appellants have made elections, he may give directions as to the division of General Commissioners who, after considering any representations made to them orally or in writing by any of the appellants, are to determine the division of General Commissioners who are to hear the appeals.

8(7) If, applying the rule in paragraph (4), it appears to an officer of the Board that none of the appellants has made an election, he may, after taking into account the factors which appear to him to be relevant, give directions for determining the division of General Commissioners who are to hear the appeals.

8(8) Directions given under paragraph (2), (5), (6) or (7) do not have effect in relation to any appeals unless the officer of the Board has served on each of the appellants a notice stating the effect of the directions in relation to the appeals.".

Former reg. 8(1) substituted by SI 2001/4023, reg. 3, effective from 31 January 2002.

In former reg. 8(4)(a) words "statutory sick pay, statutory maternity pay, statutory paternity pay or statutory adoption pay " inserted by SI 2002/3120, reg. 3(2)(c), with effect from 7 January 2003.

TRANSFER OF PROCEEDINGS TO THE SPECIAL COMMISSIONERS ETC.

8A [Omitted by SI 2009/56, art. 3(2) and Sch. 2, para. 63.]

History – *Reg. 8A omitted by SI 2009/56, art. 3(2) and Sch. 2, para. 63, operative from 1 April 2009 subject to transitional and saving provisions in SI 2009/56, Sch. 3. Former reg. 8A read as follows:*

"**8A(1)** Subsections (2), (3), (3A), (4) and (5) of section 44 of the Management Act apply to appeals to the tax appeal Commissioners under Part II of the Transfer Act and Part III of the Transfer Order as they apply to proceedings relating to income tax with the modifications specified in this regulation.

8A(2) In those subsections **"the Taxes Acts"** includes Part II of the Transfer Act and Part III of the Transfer Order.

8A(3) In the said subsection (2) for "the said rules" substitute "the rules relating to the assignment of appeals given in the Social Security Contributions (Decisions and Appeals) Regulations 1999".

8A(4) In the said subsection (4) after "this section" insert "or the Social Security Contributions (Decisions and Appeals) Regulations 1999".".

Former reg. 8A inserted by SI 2001/4023, reg. 4, effective from 31 January 2002.

PROCEEDINGS BROUGHT OUT OF TIME

9(1) Section 49 of the Management Act applies to appeals to the tribunal under Part II of the Transfer Act and Part III of the Transfer Order which are brought out of time with the modifications specified in this regulation.

9(2) In that section **"the Taxes Acts"** includes Part II of the Transfer Act and Part III of the Transfer Order and **"inspector or the Board"** includes an officer of the Board.

History – In reg. 9(1), the word "tribunal" substituted for the words "tax appeal Commissioners" by SI 2009/56, art. 3(2) and Sch. 2, para. 64, operative from 1 April 2009 subject to transitional and saving provisions in SI 2009/56, Sch. 3.

DETERMINATION OF APPEALS BY THE TRIBUNAL

10 If, on an appeal under Part II of the Transfer Act or Part III of the Transfer Order that is notified to the tribunal, it appears to the tribunal that the decision should be varied in a particular manner, the decision shall be varied in that manner, but otherwise shall stand good.

History – In the heading to reg. 10, the words "the tribunal" substituted for the words "tax appeal Commissioners" by SI 2009/56, art. 3(2) and Sch. 2, para. 65(2), operative from 1 April 2009 subject to transitional and saving provisions in SI 2009/56, Sch. 3.
In reg. 10, the words "to the tax appeal Commissioners", which appeared after "appeal", omitted by SI 2009/56, art. 3(2) and Sch. 2, para. 65(3), operative from 1 April 2009 subject to transitional and saving provisions in SI 2009/56, Sch. 3.
In reg. 10, the words "that is notified to the tribunal" inserted by SI 2009/56, art. 3(2) and Sch. 2, para. 65(4), operative from 1 April 2009 subject to transitional and saving provisions in SI 2009/56, Sch. 3.
In reg. 10, the word "tribunal" substituted for the words "majority of the Commissioners present at the hearing, by examination of the appellant on oath or affirmation or by other evidence," by SI 2009/56, art. 3(2) and Sch. 2, para. 65(5), operative from 1 April 2009 subject to transitional and saving provisions in SI 2009/56, Sch. 3.

SETTLING OF APPEALS BY AGREEMENT

11(1) Subject to the provisions of this regulation, where before an appeal is determined by the tribunal, an officer of the Board and every person who has appealed against the decision come to an agreement, whether in writing or otherwise, that the decision under appeal should be treated as upheld without variation, as varied in a particular manner or as superseded by a further decision, the like consequences ensue for all purposes as would have ensued if, at the time when the agreement was come to, the officer of the Board had made a decision in the same terms as the decision under appeal, had varied the decision in that manner or had made a decision superseding the decision under appeal in the same terms as that further decision, as the case may be.

11(2) Where an agreement is come to in the manner described in paragraph (1) the appeals of all persons who have appealed against the decision lapse.

11(3) Notice of the agreement must be given by the officer of the Board to the persons named in the decision who have not appealed against it.

11(4) Where an agreement is not in writing–

(a) the preceding provisions of this regulation do not apply unless the fact that an agreement was come to, and the terms agreed, are confirmed by notice given by the officer of the Board to the appellant and any other person who has appealed against the decision or by the appellant or any other person who has appealed against the decision to the officer of the Board; and

(b) the references in those provisions to the time when the agreement was come to shall be construed as references to the time of the giving of the notice of confirmation.

11(5) Where before an appeal is determined by the tribunal–

(a) a person who has appealed against a decision notifies the officer of the Board and every other person named in the decision, whether orally or in writing, that he does not wish to proceed with the appeal, and

(b) thirty days have elapsed since the giving of the notification without the officer of the Board or any other person named in the decision giving notice to the appellant and any other person named in the decision or the officer of the Board, as the case may be, indicating that he is unwilling that the appeal should be treated as withdrawn,

the preceding provisions of this regulation have effect as if, at the date of the appellant's notification, the appellant and the officer of the Board and every other person named in the decision had come to an agreement, orally or in writing, as the case may be, that the decision under appeal should be upheld without variation.

11(6) *The references in* this regulation to an agreement being come to with an appellant and other persons named in the decision and the giving of notice or notification to or by an appellant or any other person named in the decision include references to an agreement being come to with, and the giving of notice or notification to or by, a person acting on behalf of the appellant or any of the other persons named in the decision in relation to the appeal.

11(7) In this regulation **"any other person named in the decision"** includes, in the case of a decision relating to a person's entitlement to statutory sick pay, statutory maternity pay, statutory paternity pay, statutory shared parental pay or statutory adoption pay, the employee and the employer concerned.

History – In reg. 11(1), the word "tribunal" substituted for the words "tax appeal Commissioners" by SI 2009/56, art. 3(2) and Sch. 2, para. 66, operative from 1 April 2009 subject to transitional and saving provisions in SI 2009/56, Sch. 3.
In reg. 11(5), the word "tribunal" substituted for the words "tax appeal Commissioners" by SI 2009/56, art. 3(2) and Sch. 2, para. 66, operative from 1 April 2009 subject to transitional and saving provisions in SI 2009/56, Sch. 3.
In reg. 11(7), the words "statutory paternity pay" substituted for the words "ordinary statutory paternity pay, additional statutory paternity pay" by SI 2015/174, reg. 2(a), with effect from 5 April 2015, subject to the transitional provision in SI 2015/174, reg. 3 (amendments do not have effect where an appeal under reg. 3 or settlement under reg. 11 relates to a person's entitlement to ordinary statutory paternity pay or additional statutory paternity pay).
In reg. 11(7), the words ", statutory shared parental pay" inserted by SI 2015/174, reg. 2(b), with effect from 5 March 2015.
In reg. 11(7), the words "ordinary statutory paternity pay, additional statutory paternity pay" substituted for the words "statutory paternity pay" by SI 2010/2451, reg. 2, with effect from 14 November 2010.
In reg. 11(7) words "statutory sick pay, statutory maternity pay, statutory paternity pay or statutory adoption pay " inserted by SI 2002/3120, reg. 3(2)(d), with effect from 7 January 2003.

APPEALS FROM TAX APPEALS COMMISSIONERS

12(1) Section 56 of the Management Act (payment of tax where there is a further appeal) shall apply to appeals from the tribunal under Part II of the Transfer Act and Part III of the Transfer Order.

12(2) For the purposes of sections 11(2) and 13(2) of the Tribunals, Courts and Enforcement Act 2007 a party to the case includes–

(a) the appellant and HMRC;

(b) in the case of an appeal against a decision relating to a person's entitlement to statutory sick pay, statutory maternity pay, statutory paternity pay, statutory shared parental pay or statutory adoption pay, the employee or employer concerned; and

(c) in any other case, any other person named in the decision.

12(3) The reference to section 56 of the Taxes Management Act 1970 in this regulation includes a reference to that section as amended by section 225(1) of the Finance Act 2014 (protection of the revenue pending further appeals).

History – In reg. 12(2)(b), the words "statutory paternity pay" substituted for the words "ordinary statutory paternity pay, additional statutory paternity pay" by SI 2015/174, reg. 2(a), with effect from 5 April 2015, subject to the transitional provision in SI 2015/174, reg. 3 (amendments do not have effect where an appeal under reg. 3 or settlement under reg. 11 relates to a person's entitlement to ordinary statutory paternity pay or additional statutory paternity pay).
In reg. 12(2)(b), the words ", statutory shared parental pay" inserted by SI 2015/174, reg. 2(b), with effect from 5 March 2015.
In reg. 12(2)(b), the words "ordinary statutory paternity pay, additional statutory paternity pay" substituted for the words "statutory paternity pay" by SI 2010/2451, reg. 2, with effect from 14 November 2010.
Reg. 12 substituted by SI 2009/777, art. 6, with effect from 1 April 2009. (Reg. 12 had previously been substituted with effect from the same date by SI 2009/56, art. 3(2) and Sch. 2, para. 67, but that provision is omitted by SI 2009/777, art. 7 and therefore the substitution under SI 2009/56 must be taken as never having taken effect.)
In former reg. 12(2)(a) and 3(a) words "statutory sick pay, statutory maternity pay, statutory paternity pay or statutory adoption pay" inserted by SI 2002/3120, reg. 3(2)(e), with effect from 7 January 2003.
Reg. 12(3) inserted by SI 2015/521, reg. 2, with effect from 12 April 2015.

FORFEITURE REGULATIONS 1999

(SI 1999/1495 as amended by SI 2000/2854, SI 2001/1095, SI 2005/207, SI 2005/870 and SI 2008/2683)

Made on 26 May 1999 by the Lord Chancellor, in exercise of the powers conferred by s. 14–16, 28, 79(2) and 84 of, and Sch. 4 and 5 to, the Social Security Act 1998, s. 4(2) of the Forfeiture Act 1982 and of all other powers enabling him in that behalf, after consultation with the Lord Advocate and, in accordance with s. 8 of the Tribunals and Inquiries Act 1992, with the Council on Tribunals. Operative from 1 June 1999.

History – In the title to the Regulations, the word "Forfeiture" substituted for the words "Social Security Commissioners (Procedure)" by SI 2008/2683, art. 6 and Sch. 1, para. 131, with effect from 3 November 2008.

PART I – GENERAL PROVISIONS

CITATION AND COMMENCEMENT

1 These Regulations may be cited as the Forfeiture Regulations 1999 and shall come into force on 1st June 1999.

History – In reg. 1, the word "Forfeiture" substituted by SI 2008/2683, art. 6 and Sch. 1, para. 131, with effect from 3 November 2008.

REVOCATION

2 [Omitted by SI 2008/2683, art. 6 and Sch. 1, para. 132.]

History – Reg. 2 omitted by SI 2008/2683, art. 6 and Sch. 1, para. 132, with effect from 3 November 2008.

TRANSITIONAL PROVISIONS

3 [Omitted by SI 2008/2683, art. 6 and Sch. 1, para. 132.]

History – Reg. 3 omitted by SI 2008/2683, art. 6 and Sch. 1, para. 132, with effect from 3 November 2008.

INTERPRETATION

4(1) In these Regulations, unless the context otherwise requires–

"the 1998 Act" means the Social Security Act 1998.

4(2) [Omitted by SI 2008/2683, art. 6 and Sch. 1, para. 133(b).]

4(3) [Omitted by SI 2008/2683, art. 6 and Sch. 1, para. 133(b).]

History – In reg. 4(1), all definitions except the definition of "the 1998 Act" omitted by SI 2008/2683, art. 6 and Sch. 1, para. 133(a), with effect from 3 November 2008.
In former reg. 4(1) definition of "the 1943 Act" inserted by SI 2005/870, reg. 2(a), with effect from 6 April 2005.
In former reg. 4(1) definition of "appeal tribunal" substituted by SI 2005/870, reg 2(b), with effect from 6 April 2005.
In former reg. 4(1) definition of "Commissioner" substituted by SI 2005/870, reg 2(e), with effect from 6 April 2005.
In former reg. 4(1) the definitions of "child benefit", "funding notice", "guardian's allowance", "legal aid certificate", "Legal Services Commission", "live television link" and "Scottish Legal Aid Board" inserted by SI 2005/207, reg. 2(3), with effect from 28 February 2005.
In former reg. 4(1) in the definition of "the chairman", in para. (ii), the words "section 14 of the 1998 Act or paragraph 8 of Schedule 7 to the 2000 Act" substituted by SI 2001/1095, reg. 3(f), with effect from 2 July 2001.
In former reg. 4(1) in the definitions of "the Act", "appeal tribunal", "authorised officer", "Commissioner" the word "1998" inserted before "Act" by SI 2001/1095, reg. 3, with effect from 2 July 2001.
In former reg. 4(1) the definitions of "the 2000 Act", "persons affected" and "relevant authority" inserted by SI 2001/1095, reg. 3, with effect from 2 July 2001.
In former reg. 4(1) the definitions of "the Board" and "tax credits" inserted, the word "and" at the end of the definition of "respondent" omitted and the full stop at the end of the definition of "summons" substituted by SI 2000/2854, reg. 3, with effect from 10 November 2000.
Reg. 4(1) created from existing content and reg. 4(2) inserted by SI 2001/1095, reg. 3(a) and (k), with effect from 2 July 2001.
Reg. 4(2) omitted by SI 2008/2683, art. 6 and Sch. 1, para. 133(b), with effect from 3 November 2008.
Reg. 4(3) omitted by SI 2008/2683, art. 6 and Sch. 1, para. 133(b), with effect from 3 November 2008.
Former reg. 4(3) inserted by SI 2005/870, reg. 2(g), with effect from 6 April 2005.

GENERAL POWERS OF A COMMISSIONER

5 [Omitted by SI 2008/2683, art. 6 and Sch. 1, para. 134.]

History – Reg. 5 omitted by SI 2008/2683, art. 6 and Sch. 1, para. 134, with effect from 3 November 2008.

TRANSFER OF PROCEEDINGS BETWEEN COMMISSIONERS

6 [Omitted by SI 2008/2683, art. 6 and Sch. 1, para. 134.]

History – Reg. 6 omitted by SI 2008/2683, art. 6 and Sch. 1, para. 134, with effect from 3 November 2008.

DELEGATION OF FUNCTIONS TO AUTHORISED OFFICERS

7 [Omitted by SI 2008/2683, art. 6 and Sch. 1, para. 134.]

History – Reg. 7 omitted by SI 2008/2683, art. 6 and Sch. 1, para. 134, with effect from 3 November 2008.

MANNER OF AND TIME FOR SERVICE OF NOTICES, ETC.

8 [Omitted by SI 2008/2683, art. 6 and Sch. 1, para. 134.]

History – Reg. 8 omitted by SI 2008/2683, art. 6 and Sch. 1, para. 134, with effect from 3 November 2008.

FUNDING OF LEGAL SERVICES

8A [Omitted by SI 2008/2683, art. 6 and Sch. 1, para. 134.]

History – Reg. 8A omitted by SI 2008/2683, art. 6 and Sch. 1, para. 134, with effect from 3 November 2008.

PART II – APPLICATIONS FOR LEAVE TO APPEAL, APPEALS AND REFERENCES

APPLICATION TO A COMMISSIONER FOR LEAVE TO APPEAL

9 [Omitted by SI 2008/2683, art. 6 and Sch. 1, para. 134.]

History – Reg. 9 omitted by SI 2008/2683, art. 6 and Sch. 1, para. 134, with effect from 3 November 2008.

NOTICE OF APPLICATION TO A COMMISSIONER FOR LEAVE TO APPEAL

10 [Omitted by SI 2008/2683, art. 6 and Sch. 1, para. 134.]

History – Reg. 10 omitted by SI 2008/2683, art. 6 and Sch. 1, para. 134, with effect from 3 November 2008.

DETERMINATION OF APPLICATION

11 [Omitted by SI 2008/2683, art. 6 and Sch. 1, para. 134.]

History – Reg. 11 omitted by SI 2008/2683, art. 6 and Sch. 1, para. 134, with effect from 3 November 2008.

NOTICE OF APPEAL

12 [Omitted by SI 2008/2683, art. 6 and Sch. 1, para. 134.]

History – Reg. 12 omitted by SI 2008/2683, art. 6 and Sch. 1, para. 134, with effect from 3 November 2008.

TIME LIMIT FOR APPEALING AFTER LEAVE OBTAINED

13 [Omitted by SI 2008/2683, art. 6 and Sch. 1, para. 134.]

History – Reg. 13 omitted by SI 2008/2683, art. 6 and Sch. 1, para. 134, with effect from 3 November 2008.

REFERENCES UNDER THE FORFEITURE ACT 1982

14(1) For the purposes of section 4(5) of the Forfeiture Act 1982, the 1998 Act shall be prescribed as a relevant enactment.

14(2) [Omitted by SI 2008/2683, art. 6 and Sch. 1, para. 135.]

14(3) [Omitted by SI 2008/2683, art. 6 and Sch. 1, para. 135.]

History – In reg. 14(1) "1998" inserted by SI 2001/1095, reg. 5(b), with effect from 2 July 2001.
Reg. 14(2) omitted by SI 2008/2683, art. 6 and Sch. 1, para. 135, with effect from 3 November 2008.
In former reg. 14(2)(a) the words "child benefit or guardian's allowance" substituted for the words "tax credits" by SI 2005/207, reg. 2(6)(a), with effect from 28 February 2005.
Former reg. 14(2) substituted by SI 2001/1095, reg. 5(b), with effect from 2 July 2001.
Former reg. 14(2) substituted by SI 2000/2854, reg. 5(a), with effect from 10 November 2000.
Reg. 14(3) omitted by SI 2008/2683, art. 6 and Sch. 1, para. 135, with effect from 3 November 2008.
In former reg. 14(3) the words "A reference under this regulation or under regulation 15(2) shall" substituted by SI 2005/207, reg. 2(6)(b), with effect from 28 February 2005.
In former reg. 14(3)(c) the words "the Secretary of State, the Board or the relevant authority" substituted for the words "the Secretary of State or the Board" by SI 2001/1095, reg. 5(b), with effect from 2 July 2001.
In former reg. 14(3)(c) the words "or the Board, as appropriate" inserted by SI 2000/2854, reg. 5(b), with effect from 10 November 2000.

FURTHER PROVISIONS RELATING TO REFERENCES UNDER THE FORFEITURE ACT 1982

15 [Omitted by SI 2008/2683, art. 6 and Sch. 1, para. 136.]

History – Reg. 15 omitted by SI 2008/2683, art. 6 and Sch. 1, para. 136, with effect from 3 November 2008.

ACKNOWLEDGEMENT OF A NOTICE OF APPEAL OR A REFERENCE AND NOTIFICATION TO EACH RESPONDENT

16 [Omitted by SI 2008/2683, art. 6 and Sch. 1, para. 136.]

History – Reg. 16 omitted by SI 2008/2683, art. 6 and Sch. 1, para. 136, with effect from 3 November 2008.

PART III – PROCEDURE

REPRESENTATION

17 [Omitted by SI 2008/2683, art. 6 and Sch. 1, para. 136.]

History – Reg. 17 omitted by SI 2008/2683, art. 6 and Sch. 1, para. 136, with effect from 3 November 2008.

RESPONDENT'S WRITTEN OBSERVATIONS

18 [Omitted by SI 2008/2683, art. 6 and Sch. 1, para. 136.]

History – Reg. 18 omitted by SI 2008/2683, art. 6 and Sch. 1, para. 136, with effect from 3 November 2008.

WRITTEN OBSERVATIONS IN REPLY

19 [Omitted by SI 2008/2683, art. 6 and Sch. 1, para. 136.]

History – Reg. 19 omitted by SI 2008/2683, art. 6 and Sch. 1, para. 136, with effect from 3 November 2008.

DIRECTIONS

20 [Omitted by SI 2008/2683, art. 6 and Sch. 1, para. 136.]

History – Reg. 20 omitted by SI 2008/2683, art. 6 and Sch. 1, para. 136, with effect from 3 November 2008.

PROCEDURE ON LINKED CASE NOTICE FROM THE SECRETARY OF STATE

21 [Omitted by SI 2008/2683, art. 6 and Sch. 1, para. 136.]

History – Reg. 21 omitted by SI 2008/2683, art. 6 and Sch. 1, para. 136, with effect from 3 November 2008.

NON-DISCLOSURE OF MEDICAL EVIDENCE

22 [Omitted by SI 2008/2683, art. 6 and Sch. 1, para. 136.]

History – Reg. 22 omitted by SI 2008/2683, art. 6 and Sch. 1, para. 136, with effect from 3 November 2008.

REQUESTS FOR HEARINGS

23 [Omitted by SI 2008/2683, art. 6 and Sch. 1, para. 136.]

History – Reg. 23 omitted by SI 2008/2683, art. 6 and Sch. 1, para. 136, with effect from 3 November 2008.

HEARINGS

24 [Omitted by SI 2008/2683, art. 6 and Sch. 1, para. 136.]

History – Reg. 24 omitted by SI 2008/2683, art. 6 and Sch. 1, para. 136, with effect from 3 November 2008.

SUMMONING OF WITNESSES

25 [Omitted by SI 2008/2683, art. 6 and Sch. 1, para. 136.]

History – Reg. 25 omitted by SI 2008/2683, art. 6 and Sch. 1, para. 136, with effect from 3 November 2008.

WITHDRAWAL OF APPLICATIONS FOR LEAVE TO APPEAL, APPEALS AND REFERENCES

26 [Omitted by SI 2008/2683, art. 6 and Sch. 1, para. 136.]

History – Reg. 26 omitted by SI 2008/2683, art. 6 and Sch. 1, para. 136, with effect from 3 November 2008.

IRREGULARITIES

27 [Omitted by SI 2008/2683, art. 6 and Sch. 1, para. 136.]

History – Reg. 27 omitted by SI 2008/2683, art. 6 and Sch. 1, para. 136, with effect from 3 November 2008.

PART IV – DECISIONS

DETERMINATIONS AND DECISIONS OF A COMMISSIONEr

28 [Omitted by SI 2008/2683, art. 6 and Sch. 1, para. 136.]

History – Reg. 28 omitted by SI 2008/2683, art. 6 and Sch. 1, para. 136, with effect from 3 November 2008.

PROCEDURE AFTER DETERMINATION OF A FORFEITURE RULE QUESTION

29 [Omitted by SI 2008/2683, art. 6 and Sch. 1, para. 136.]

History – Reg. 29 omitted by SI 2008/2683, art. 6 and Sch. 1, para. 136, with effect from 3 November 2008.

CORRECTION OF ACCIDENTAL ERRORS IN DECISIONS

30 [Omitted by SI 2008/2683, art. 6 and Sch. 1, para. 136.]

History – Reg. 30 omitted by SI 2008/2683, art. 6 and Sch. 1, para. 136, with effect from 3 November 2008.

SETTING ASIDE DECISIONS ON CERTAIN GROUNDS

31 [Omitted by SI 2008/2683, art. 6 and Sch. 1, para. 136.]

History – Reg. 31 omitted by SI 2008/2683, art. 6 and Sch. 1, para. 136, with effect from 3 November 2008.

PROVISIONS COMMON TO REGULATIONS 30 AND 31

32 [Omitted by SI 2008/2683, art. 6 and Sch. 1, para. 136.]

History – Reg. 32 omitted by SI 2008/2683, art. 6 and Sch. 1, para. 136, with effect from 3 November 2008.

PART V – APPLICATIONS FOR LEAVE TO APPEAL TO THE APPELLATE COURT

APPLICATION TO A COMMISSIONER FOR LEAVE TO APPEAL TO THE APPELLATE COURT

33 [Omitted by SI 2008/2683, art. 6 and Sch. 1, para. 136.]

History – Reg. 33 omitted by SI 2008/2683, art. 6 and Sch. 1, para. 136, with effect from 3 November 2008.

SOCIAL SECURITY CONTRIBUTIONS (INTERMEDIARIES) REGULATIONS 2000

(SI 2000/727 as amended by SI 2000/2084, SI 2002/703, SI 2003/2079, SI 2004/770, SI 2005/3131, SI 2014/3159, SI 2017/373 and SI 2017/613)

Made on 13 March 2000 by the Treasury, in exercise of the powers conferred on them by sections 4A, 122(1) and 175(1A), (2) to (4) of the Social Security Contributions and Benefits Act 1992. Operative from 6 April 2000.

Cross references – NICA 2011, s. 6(5)(a): disapplication of SI 2000/727 for the purposes of NICA 2011, Pt. 2 (regional secondary contributions holiday for new businesses).

Notes – SI 2000/727 deals with the NIC aspects of personal services provided through intermediaries. The corresponding IR35 income tax legislation is in ITEPA 2003, Pt. 2, Ch. 8; business tax deductions (under Sch. D and corporation tax) are given by FA 2000, Sch. 12, para. 17 and 18.

Unamended references to income tax legislation repealed and re-enacted by ITEPA 2003 refer to the rewritten equivalents: ITEPA 2003, Sch. 7, Pt. 1.

ARRANGEMENT OF REGULATIONS

REGULATION

CITATION, COMMENCEMENT AND EFFECT

1(1) These Regulations may be cited as the Social Security Contributions (Intermediaries) Regulations 2000 and shall come into force on 6th April 2000.

1(2) These Regulations have effect for the tax year 2000–01 and subsequent years and apply in relation to services performed, or to be performed, on or after 6th April 2000.

1(3) Payments or other benefits in respect of such services received before that date shall be treated as if received in the tax year 2000–01.

Cross references – SSCBA 1992, s. 4A: inserted by WRPA 1999, s. 75 with effect from 22 December 1999 (SI 1999/3420, art. 3); provides authority for making regulations dealing with workers supplied by service companies.

Part 1: Intermediaries - General Provisions

History – Pt. 1 created from existing provisions and heading inserted by SI 2017/373, reg. 2(2), with effect from 6 April 2017.

INTERPRETATION

2(1) In these Regulations unless the context otherwise requires–

"associate" has the meaning given by regulation 3;

"attributable earnings" in relation to a worker shall be construed in accordance with regulation 6(3)(a);

"the Board" means the Commissioners for Her Majesty's Revenue and Customs;

"Class 1A contributions" has the meaning given by section 10 of the Contributions and Benefits Act;

"company" means any body corporate or unincorporated association, but does not include a partnership;

"the Contributions and Benefits Act" means the Social Security Contributions and Benefits Act 1992;

"the Contributions Regulations" means the Social Security (Contributions) Regulations 2001

"CTA 2010" means the Corporation Taxes Act 2010;

"public authority" has the meaning given by regulation 3A;

"relevant benefit" means any benefit falling within regulation 4 that is provided to the intermediary or to or on behalf of the worker under the arrangements;

"relevant payment" means any payment made to an intermediary or to or on behalf of the worker under the arrangements;

"secondary Class 1 contributions" has the meaning given by section 6 of the Contributions and Benefits Act;

"secondary contributor" has the meaning given by section 7 of the Contributions and Benefits Act;

"statutory auditor" has the meaning given by Part 42 of the Companies Act 2006;

"the Taxes Act" means the Income and Corporation Taxes Act 1988;

"tax year" means year of assessment;

2(2) References in these Regulations to payments or benefits received or receivable from a partnership or unincorporated association include payments or benefits to which a person is or may be entitled in his capacity as a member of the partnership or association.

2(3) For the purposes of these Regulations–

(a) anything done by or in relation to an associate of an intermediary is treated as done by or in relation to the intermediary, and

(b) a payment or other benefit provided to a member of an individual's family or household is treated as provided to the individual.

2(4) The reference in paragraph (3)(b) to an individual's family or household shall be construed in accordance with sections 721(4) and (5) of ITEPA 2003.

2(5) For the purposes of these Regulations a man and a woman living together as husband and wife are treated as if they were married to each other.

2(6) For the purposes of these Regulations two people of the same sex living together as if they were civil partners of each other are treated as if they were civil partners of each other; and, for the purposes of these Regulations, two people of the same sex are to be regarded as living together as if they were civil partners if, but only if, they would be regarded as living together as husband and wife were they instead two people of the opposite sex.

2(7) For the purposes of these Regulations "connected" shall be construed in accordance with section 993 of the Income Tax Act 2007.

2(8) For the purposes of these Regulations "controlled" shall be construed in accordance with section 995 of the Income Tax Act 2007.

History – In reg. 2(1), definitions of "arrangements", "client", "intermediary" and "worker" omitted by SI 2017/373, reg. 2(3)(a), with effect from 6 April 2017.

In reg. 2(1) the definition of "the Board" substituted by SI 2005/3131, reg. 4(2), with effect for the tax year 2005–06 and subsequent tax years, and applies in relation to services performed, or to be performed, on or after 5 December 2005.

In reg. 2(1) the definition of "business" omitted by SI 2003/2079, reg. 4, with effect for 2003–04 and subsequent tax years and in relation to services performed or due to be performed on or after 1 September 2003.

In reg. 2(1), the definition of "the Contributions Regulations" was substituted by SI 2002/703, reg. 3 with effect for 2002–03 and subsequent years of assessment, applying in relation to services performed, or to be performed, on or after 6 April 2002.
In reg. 2(1), definition of "CTA 2010" inserted by SI 2017/373, reg. 2(3)(b), with effect from 6 April 2017.
In reg. 2(1), definition of "public authority" inserted by SI 2017/373, reg. 2(3)(c), with effect from 6 April 2017.
In reg. 2(1), definition of "statutory auditor" inserted by SI 2017/373, reg. 2(3)(d), with effect from 6 April 2017.
In reg. 2(4) "sections 721(4) and (5) of ITEPA 2003" substituted by SI 2004/770, reg. 35, with effect from 6 April 2004.
Reg. 2(6) inserted by SI 2005/3131, reg. 4(3), with effect for the tax year 2005–06 and subsequent tax years, and applies in relation to services performed, or to be performed, on or after 5 December 2005.
Reg. 2(7) and (8) inserted by SI 2017/373, reg. 2(4), with effect from 6 April 2017.

Cross references – SI 2001/1004: the Social Security (Contributions) Regulations 2001 (the "Contributions Regulations").

DEFINITIONS FOR THE PURPOSES OF PART 1

2A In this Part–

"arrangements" means the arrangements referred to in regulation 6(1)(b);

"client" shall be construed in accordance with regulation 6(1)(b);

"intermediary" has the meaning given by regulation 5; and

"worker" means the individual referred to in regulation 6(1)(a).

History – Reg. 2A inserted by SI 2017/373, reg. 2(5), with effect from 6 April 2017.

MEANING OF ASSOCIATE

3(1) In these Regulations **"associate"**–

(a) in relation to an individual, has the meaning given by section 417(3) and (4) of the Taxes Act, subject to the following provisions of this regulation;

(b) in relation to a company, means a person connected with the company within the meaning of section 839 of the Taxes Act; and

(c) in relation to a partnership, means any associate of a member of the partnership.

3(2) Where an individual has an interest in shares or obligations of the company as a beneficiary of an employee benefit trust, the trustees are not regarded as associates of his by reason only of that interest except in the following circumstances.

3(3) The exception is where–

(a) the individual, either on his own or with one or more of his associates, or

(b) any associate of his, with or without other such associates, has been the beneficial owner of, or able (directly or through the medium of other companies or by any other indirect means) to control, more than 5 per cent. of the ordinary share capital of the company.

3(4) In paragraph (2) **"employee benefit trust"** has the same meaning as in sections 550 and 551 of ITEPA 2003.

History – In reg. 3(4) "sections 550 and 551 of ITEPA 2003" substituted by SI 2004/770, reg. 35, with effect from 6 April 2004.

MEANING OF PUBLIC AUTHORITY

3A(1) In these Regulations **"public authority"** means–

(a) a public authority as defined by the Freedom of Information Act 2000,

(b) a Scottish public authority as defined by the Freedom of Information (Scotland) Act 2002,

(c) the Corporate Officer of the House of Commons,

(d) the Corporate Officer of the House of Lords,

(e) the National Assembly for Wales Commission, or

(f) the Northern Ireland Assembly Commission.

3A(2) An authority within paragraph (1)(a) or (b) is a public authority for the purposes of these Regulations in relation to all its activities even if provisions of the Act mentioned in that paragraph do not apply to all information held by the authority.

3A(3) Paragraph (1) is subject to paragraph (4).

3A(4) A primary-healthcare provider is a public authority for the purposes of these Regulations only if the primary-healthcare provider–

(a) has a registered patient list for the purposes of relevant medical-services regulations,

(b) is within paragraph 43A in Part 3 of Schedule 1 to the Freedom of Information Act 2000 (providers of primary healthcare services in England and Wales) by reason of being a person providing primary dental services,

(c) is within paragraph 51 in that Part of that Schedule (providers of healthcare services in Northern Ireland) by reason of being a person providing general dental services, or

(d) is within paragraph 33 in Part 4 of Schedule 1 to the Freedom of Information (Scotland) Act 2002 (providers of healthcare services in Scotland) by reason of being a person providing general dental services.

3A(5) In paragraph (4)–

"primary-healthcare provider" means an authority that is within paragraph (1)(a) or (b) only because it is within a relevant paragraph,

"relevant paragraph" means–

(a) any of paragraphs 43A to 45A and 51 in Part 3 of Schedule 1 to the Freedom of Information Act 2000, or

(b) any of paragraphs 33 to 35 in Part 4 of Schedule 1 to the Freedom of Information (Scotland) Act 2002, and

"relevant medical-services regulations" means any of the following–

(a) the Primary Medical Services (Sale of Goodwill and Restrictions on Sub-contracting) Regulations 2004,

(b) the Primary Medical Services (Sale of Goodwill and Restrictions on Sub-contracting) (Wales) Regulations 2004,

(c) the Primary Medical Services (Sale of Goodwill and Restrictions on Sub-contracting) (Scotland) Regulations 2004, and

(d) the Primary Medical Services (Sale of Goodwill and Restrictions on Sub-contracting) Regulations (Northern Ireland) 2004.

History – Reg. 3A substituted by SI 2017/613, reg. 2(2), with effect from 18 May 2017. Former reg. 3A read as follows:

"MEANING OF PUBLIC AUTHORITY

3A In these Regulations **"public authority"** means–

(a) a public authority as defined by the Freedom of Information Act 2000,
(b) a Scottish public authority as defined by the Freedom of Information (Scotland) Act 2002,
(c) the Corporate Officer of the House of Commons,
(d) the Corporate Officer of the House of Lords,
(e) the National Assembly for Wales Commission, or
(f) the Northern Ireland Assembly Commission.

An authority within paragraph (a) or (b) is a public authority for the purposes of these Regulations in relation to all its activities even if provisions of the Act mentioned in that paragraph do not apply to all information held by the authority.".
Former reg. 3A inserted by SI 2017/373, reg. 2(6), with effect from 6 April 2017.

MEANING OF BENEFIT

4(1) For the purposes of these Regulations a **"benefit"** means anything that, if received by an employee for performing the duties of an employment, would be general earnings of the employment.

4(2) The amount of a benefit is taken to be–

(a) in the case of a cash benefit, the amount received, and

(b) in the case of a non–cash benefit, the cash equivalent of the benefit.

4(3) The cash equivalent of a non–cash benefit is taken to be whichever is the greater of–

(a) the amount that would, for income tax purposes, be general earnings if the benefit were general earnings from an employment, and

(b) the cash equivalent determined in accordance with section 398(2)(b) of ITEPA 2003.

4(4) For the purposes of these Regulations a benefit is treated as received–

(a) in the case of a cash benefit, when payment is made of or on account of the benefit; and

(b) in the case of an non–cash benefit, when it is used or enjoyed.

History – Reg. 4(1) substituted by SI 2004/770, reg. 35, with effect from 6 April 2004.
Reg. 4(3)(a) and (b) substituted by SI 2004/770, reg. 35, with effect from 6 April 2004.
Cross references – ITEPA 2003, s. 55: IR35 income tax: benefits.

MEANING OF INTERMEDIARY

5(1) In this Part **"intermediary"** means any person, including a partnership or unincorporated association of which the worker is a member–

(a) whose relationship with the worker in any tax year satisfies the conditions specified in paragraph (2), (6), (7) or (8), and

(b) from whom the worker, or an associate of the worker–

(i) receives, directly or indirectly, in that year a payment or benefit that is not chargeable to tax as employment income under ITEPA 2003, or

(ii) is entitled to receive, or in any circumstances would be entitled to receive, directly or indirectly, in that year any such payment or benefit.

5(2) Where the intermediary is a company the conditions are that–

(a) the intermediary is not an associated company of the client, within the meaning of section 416 of the Taxes Act, by reason of the intermediary and the client both being under the control of the worker, or under the control of the worker and another person; and

(b) either–

(i) the worker has a material interest in the intermediary, or

(ii) the payment or benefit is received or receivable by the worker directly from the intermediary, and can reasonably be taken to represent remuneration for services provided by the worker to the client.

5(3) A worker is treated as having a material interest in a company for the purposes of paragraph (2)(a) if–

(a) the worker, alone or with one or more associates of his, or

(b) an associate of the worker, with or without other such associates,

has a material interest in the company.

5(4) For this purpose a material interest means–

(a) beneficial ownership of, or the ability to control, directly or through the medium of other companies or by any other indirect means, more than 5 per cent of the ordinary share capital of the company; or

(b) possession of, or entitlement to acquire, rights entitling the holder to receive more than 5 per cent of any distributions that may be made by the company; or

(c) where the company is a close company, possession of, or entitlement to acquire, rights that would in the event of the winding up of the company, or in any other circumstances, entitle the holder to receive more than 5 per cent of the assets that would then be available for distribution among the participators.

In sub-paragraph (c) **"close company"** has the meaning given by sections 414 and 415 of the Taxes Act, and **"participator"** has the meaning given by section 417(1) of that Act.

5(5) Where the intermediary is a partnership the conditions are as follows.

5(6) In relation to payments or benefits received or receivable by the worker as a member of the partnership, the conditions are–

(a) that the worker, alone or with one or more relatives, is entitled to 60 per cent or more of the profits of the partnership; or

(b) that most of the profits of the partnership derive from the provision of services under the arrangements–

(i) to a single client or

(ii) to a single client together with an associate or associates of that client; or

(c) that under the profit sharing arrangements the income of any of the partners is based on the amount of income generated by that partner by the provision of services under the arrangements.

In sub-paragraph (a) **"relative"** means spouse or civil partner, parent or child or remoter relation in the direct line, or brother or sister.

5(7) In relation to payments or benefits received or receivable by the worker otherwise than as a member of the partnership, the conditions are that the payment or benefit–

(a) is received or receivable by the worker directly from the intermediary, and

(b) can reasonably be taken to represent remuneration for services provided by the worker to the client.

5(8) Where the intermediary is an individual the conditions are that the payment or benefit–

(a) is received or receivable by the worker directly from the intermediary, and

(b) can reasonably be taken to represent remuneration for services provided by the worker to the client.

History – In reg. 5(1), the words "In this Part" substituted for the words "In these Regulations" by SI 2017/373, reg. 2(7), with effect from 6 April 2017.

In reg. 5(1)(b)(i) "as employment income under ITEPA 2003" substituted by SI 2004/770, reg. 35, with effect from 6 April 2004.

In reg. 5(6), the words "or child or remoter relation in the direct line, or brother or sister." substituted for the words "or remoter forebear, child or remoter issue, or brother or sister." by SI 2017/373, reg. 2(8), with effect from 6 April 2017.

In reg. 5(6) the words "spouse or civil partner" substituted for the words "husband and wife" by SI 2005/3131, reg. 5, with effect for the tax year 2005–06 and subsequent tax years, and apply in relation to services performed, or to be performed, on or after 5 December 2005.

Cross references – ITEPA 2003, s. 50: IR35 income tax: worker treated as receiving earnings from employment.

PROVISION OF SERVICES THROUGH INTERMEDIARY

6(1) This Part applies where–

(a) an individual ("the worker") personally performs, or is under an obligation personally to perform, services for another person ("the client"),

(aa) the client is not a public authority,

(b) the performance of those services by the worker is carried out, not under a contract directly between the client and the worker, but under arrangements involving an intermediary, and

(c) the circumstances are such that, had the arrangements taken the form of a contract between the worker and the client, the worker would be regarded for the purposes of Parts I to V of the Contributions and Benefits Act as employed in employed earner's employment by the client.

6(2) Paragraph (1)(b) has effect irrespective of whether or not–

(a) there exists a contract between the client and the worker, or

(b) the worker is the holder of an office with the client.

6(2A) Holding office as a statutory auditor of the client does not count as the worker being the holder of an office with the client for the purposes of paragraph 6(2)(b).

6(3) Where these Regulations apply–

(a) the worker is treated, for the purposes of Parts I to V of the Contributions and Benefits Act, and in relation to the amount deriving from relevant payments and relevant benefits that is calculated in accordance with regulation 7 ("the worker's attributable earnings"), as employed in employed earner's employment by the intermediary, and

(b) the intermediary, whether or not he fulfils the conditions prescribed under section 1(6)(a) of the Contributions and Benefits Act for secondary contributors, is treated for those purposes as the secondary contributor in respect of the worker's attributable earnings,

and Parts I to V of that Act have effect accordingly.

6(4) Any issue whether the circumstances are such as are mentioned in paragraph (1)(c) is an issue relating to contributions that is prescribed for the purposes of section 8(1)(m) of the Social Security Contributions (Transfer of Functions, etc.) Act 1999 (decision by officer of the Board).

History – In reg. 6(1), the words "This Part applies" substituted for the words "These Regulations apply" by SI 2017/373, reg. 2(9), with effect from 6 April 2017.

In reg. 6(1)(a) the words "for another person" substituted by SI 2003/2079, reg. 5, with effect for 2003–04 and subsequent tax years in relation to services performed or due to be performed on or after 1 September 2003.

Reg. 6(1)(aa) inserted by SI 2017/373, reg. 2(10), with effect from 6 April 2017.

Reg. 6(2A) inserted by SI 2017/373, reg. 2(11), with effect from 6 April 2017.

WORKER'S ATTRIBUTABLE EARNINGS – CALCULATION

7(1) For the purposes of regulation 6(3)(a) the amount of the worker's attributable earnings for a tax year is calculated as follows:

Step One

Find the total amount of all payments and benefits received by the intermediary in that year under the arrangements but excluding amounts on which Class 1 or Class 1A contributions are payable by virtue of regulation 3 or 4 of the Social Security Contributions (Limited Liability Partnership) Regulations 2014, and reduce that amount by 5 per cent.

Step Two

Add the amount of any payments and benefits received by the worker in that year under the arrangements, otherwise than from the intermediary, that–

(a) are not chargeable to income tax as employment income under ITEPA 2003, and

(b) would be so chargeable if the worker were employed by the client.

Step Three

Deduct the amount of any expenses met in that year by the intermediary that under ITEPA 2003 would have been deductible from the taxable earnings of the employment, within the meaning of section 10 of ITEPA 2003, in accordance with section 327(3) to (5) of that Act if the worker had been employed by the client and the expenses had been met by the worker out of those earnings.

Step Four

Deduct the amount of any capital allowances in respect of expenditure incurred by the intermediary in that year that could have been claimed by the worker under Part 2 of the Capital Allowances Act 2001 (plant and machinery allowances) by virtue of section 15(1)(i) of that Act (which provides that employment is a qualifying activity for the purposes of that Part) if the worker had been employed by the client and had incurred the expenditure.

Step Five

Deduct any contributions made in that year for the benefit of the worker by the intermediary to a registered pension scheme for the purposes of Part 4 of the Finance Act 2004 that if made by an employer for the benefit of an employee would not be chargeable to income tax as income of the employee, and any payments made in that year in respect of the worker by the intermediary in respect of any of the Pensions Act levies.

This does not apply to excess contributions made and later repaid.

Step Six

Deduct the amount of secondary Class 1 contributions and Class 1A contributions paid by the intermediary for that year in respect of earnings of the worker.

Step Seven

Deduct–

(a) the amount of any payments made by the intermediary to the worker in that year that constitute remuneration derived from the worker's employment by that intermediary including, where the intermediary is a body corporate and the worker is a director of that body corporate, payments treated as remuneration derived from that employment by virtue of regulation 22(2) of the Contributions Regulations (payments to directors to be treated as earnings), but excluding payments which represent items in respect of which a deduction was made under Step Three and payments within paragraph 25 of Part 10 of Schedule 3 to the Contributions Regulations, and

(b) the amount of any benefits provided by the intermediary to the worker in that year, being benefits that constitute amounts of general earnings in respect of which Class 1A contributions are payable, but excluding any benefits which represent items in respect of which a deduction was made under Step Three.

If the result at this point is nil or a negative amount, there are no worker's attributable earnings for that year.

Step Eight

Find the amount that, together with the amount of secondary Class 1 contributions payable in respect of it, is equal to the amount resulting from Step Seven (if that amount is a positive amount).

Step Nine

The result is the amount of the worker's attributable earnings for that year.

7(2) Where section 559 of the Taxes Act applies (sub-contractors in the construction industry: payments to be made under deduction) the intermediary is treated for the purposes of Step One of the calculation in paragraph (1) as receiving the amount that would have been received had no deduction been made under that section.

7(3) For the purpose of calculating the amount of deductible expenses referred to in Step Three of the calculation in paragraph (1) it shall be assumed that all engagements of the worker under the arrangements involving the intermediary are undertaken in the course of the same employment.

7(4) For the purposes of this regulation any necessary apportionment shall be made on a just and reasonable basis of amounts received by the intermediary that are referable–

(a) to the services of more than one worker, or

(b) partly to the services of the worker and partly to other matters.

7(5) For the purposes of this regulation the time when payments are received by the intermediary or the worker under the arrangements shall be found in accordance with the rules contained in sections 18 and 19 of ITEPA 2003, subject to the qualification that the worker shall not be treated, by virtue of Rule 2 in section 18, as receiving a payment prior to the time of its actual receipt.

7(6) The reference in Step Three of the calculation in paragraph (1) to expenses met by the intermediary includes expenses met by the worker and reimbursed by the intermediary.

7(7) Where the intermediary is a partnership and the worker is a member of the partnership, expenses met by the worker for and on behalf of the intermediary shall be treated for the purposes of paragraph (6) as expenses met by the worker and reimbursed by the intermediary.

7(8) Where

(a) the intermediary provides a vehicle for the worker, and

(b) the worker would have been entitled to an amount of mileage allowance relief under section 231 of ITEPA 2003 for a tax year in respect of the use of the vehicle if the worker had been employed by the client, or would have been so entitled if the worker had been employed by the client and the vehicle had not been a company vehicle,

Step Three of the calculation in paragraph (1) shall have effect as if that amount were an amount of expenses deductible under that Step.

7(9) Where

(a) the intermediary is a partnership,

(b) the worker is a member of the partnership, and

(c) the worker provides a vehicle for the purposes of the business of the partnership,

then for the purposes of paragraph (8) the vehicle shall be regarded as provided by the intermediary for the worker.

7(10) Where the intermediary makes payments to the worker that are exempt from income tax as employment income under ITEPA 2003 by virtue of section 229 or 233 of ITEPA 2003 (mileage allowance payments and passenger payments), paragraph (a) of Step Seven of the calculation in paragraph (1) shall have effect as if the intermediary had made payments to the worker that constituted remuneration derived from the worker's employment by the intermediary.

7(11) In this regulation **"the Pensions Act levies"** means–

(a) the administration levy referred to in section 117(1) of the Pensions Act 2004;

(b) the initial levy referred to in section 174(1) of that Act;

(c) the risk-based pension protection levy referred to in section 175(1)(a) of that Act;

(d) the scheme-based pension protection levy referred to in section 175(1)(b) of that Act;

(e) the fraud compensation levy referred to in section 189(1) of that Act;

(f) a levy in respect of eligible schemes imposed by regulations made under section 209(7) of that Act (the Ombudsman for the Board of the Pension Protection Fund).

History – In reg. 7(1) in Step One the words "but excluding amounts on which Class 1 or Class 1A contributions are payable by virtue of regulation 3 or 4 of the Social Security Contributions (Limited Liability Partnership) Regulations 2014" inserted by SI 2014/3159, reg. 6(2)(a), with effect for the tax year 2014–15 and subsequent tax years.
In reg. 7(1) in Step Two the words "as employment income under ITEPA 2003" substituted by SI 2003/2079, reg. 6(2)(a), with effect for 2003–04 and subsequent tax years in relation to services performed or due to be performed on or after 1 September 2003.
In reg. 7(1) in Step Three the words "ITEPA 2003"; "taxable earnings of the employment, within the meaning of section 10 of ITEPA 2003, in accordance with section 327(3) to (5) of that Act" and "those earnings" substituted by SI 2003/2079, reg. 6(2)(b), with effect for 2003–04 and subsequent tax years in relation to services performed or due to be performed on or after 1 September 2003.
In reg. 7(1) in Step Four the words "under Part 2 of the Capital Allowances Act 2001 (plant and machinery allowances) by virtue of section 15(1)(i) of that Act (which provides that employment is a qualifying activity for the purposes of that Part)" substituted by SI 2003/2079, reg. 6(2)(c), with effect for 2003–04 and subsequent tax years in relation to services performed or due to be performed on or after 1 September 2003.
In reg. 7(1) in Step Five the words ", and any payments made in that year in respect of the worker by the intermediary in respect of any of the Pensions Act levies" inserted by SI 2005/3131, reg. 6(2), with effect for the tax year 2005–06 and subsequent tax years, and apply in relation to services performed, or to be performed, on or after 5 December 2005.
In reg. 7(1) in Step Five the words "a registered pension scheme for the purposes of Part 4 of the Finance Act 2004" substituted for the words "a scheme approved under Chapter I or Chapter IV of Part XIV of the Taxes Act" by SI 2005/3131, reg. 8(2), with effect for the tax year 2006–07 and subsequent tax years, and apply in relation to services performed, or to be performed, on or after 6 April 2006.
In reg. 7(1), para. (a) of Step Seven, the words "and payments within paragraph 25 of Part 10 of Schedule 3 to the Contributions Regulations" inserted by SI 2014/3159, reg. 6(2)(b), with effect for the tax year 2014–15 and subsequent tax years.
In reg. 7(1) in para. (a) of Step Seven, "22(2)" substituted by SI 2002/703, reg. 4 with effect for the year of assessment 2002–03 and subsequent tax years and applying in relation to services performed, or to be performed, on or after 6 April 2002.
In reg. 7(1), para. (a) of Step Seven, former reference to "17A(2)" substituted by SI 2000/2084, reg. 10, with effect from 4 August 2000.
In reg. 7(1), para.(b) of Step Seven, "general earnings" substituted by SI 2004/770, reg. 35, with effect from 6 April 2004.
In reg. 7(5) the words "sections 18 and 19 of ITEPA 2003, subject to the qualification that the worker shall not be treated, by virtue of Rule 2 in section 18, as receiving a payment prior to the time of its actual receipt" substituted by SI 2003/2079, reg. 6(3), with effect for 2003–04 and subsequent tax years in relation to services performed or due to be performed on or after 1 September 2003.
Reg. 7(6), (7), (8), (9) and (10) inserted by SI 2002/703, reg. 5 with effect for 2002–03 and subsequent years of assessment, applying in relation to services performed, or to be performed, on or after 6 April 2002.
In reg. 7(8)(b) the words "section 231 of ITEPA 2003" substituted by SI 2003/2079, reg. 6(2)(c), with effect for 2003–04 and subsequent tax years in relation to services performed or due to be performed on or after 1 September 2003.
In reg. 7(10) the words "as employment income under ITEPA 2003" substituted by SI 2003/2079, reg. 6(5)(a), with effect for 2003–04 and subsequent tax years in relation to services performed or due to be performed on or after 1 September 2003.
In reg. 7(10) the words "section 229 or 233 of ITEPA 2003" substituted by SI 2003/2079, reg. 6(5)(b), with effect for 2003–04 and subsequent tax years in relation to services performed or due to be performed on or after 1 September 2003.
Reg. 7(11) inserted by SI 2005/3131, reg. 6(3), with effect for the tax year 2005–06 and subsequent tax years, and apply in relation to services performed, or to be performed, on or after 5 December 2005.

WORKER'S ATTRIBUTABLE EARNINGS – DEEMED PAYMENT

8(1) The amount referred to in Step Nine of the calculation in regulation 7(1) is treated, for the purposes of Parts I to V of the Contributions and Benefits Act, as a single payment of the worker's attributable earnings made by the intermediary on the 5th April in the tax year concerned or, as the case may be, on the date found in accordance with paragraphs (4) to (7), and those Parts of that Act shall have effect accordingly.

8(2) The worker's attributable earnings shall be aggregated with any other earnings paid to the worker by the intermediary in the year concerned to or for the benefit of the worker in respect of employed earner's employment, and the amount of earnings–related contributions payable in respect of that aggregate amount shall be assessed in accordance with the appropriate earnings period specified in regulation 8 of the Contributions Regulations (earnings period for directors), whether or not the worker is a director of a company during that year.

8(3) Where the intermediary is a partnership or unincorporated association, the amount referred to in Step Nine of the calculation in regulation 7(1) is treated, for the purposes of Parts I to V of the Contributions and Benefits Act, as received by the worker in his personal capacity and not as income of the partnership or association.

8(4) If in a tax year–

(a) an amount of the worker's attributable earnings is treated as made under paragraph (1), and

(b) before the date on which the payment would be treated as made under that paragraph any relevant event (as defined below) occurs in relation to the intermediary,

that amount is treated, for the purposes of Parts I to V of the Contributions and Benefits Act, as having been made immediately before that event or, if there is more than one, immediately before the first of them.

8(5) Where the intermediary is a company the following are relevant events–

(a) where the worker is a member of the company, his ceasing to be such a member;

(b) where the worker holds an office with the company, his ceasing to hold such an office;

(c) where the worker is employed by the company, his ceasing to be so employed.

(d) the company ceasing to trade.

8(6) Where the intermediary is a partnership the following are relevant events–

(a) the dissolution of the partnership or the partnership ceasing to trade or a partner ceasing to act as such;

(b) where the worker is employed by the partnership, his ceasing to be so employed.

8(7) Where the intermediary is an individual and the worker is employed by him, it is a relevant event if the worker ceases to be so employed.

8(8) The fact that an amount of the worker's attributable earnings is treated as made under paragraph (1) before the end of the tax year concerned does not affect what payments and benefits are taken into account in calculating that amount.

History – In reg. 8(2), the reference to regulation 8 substituted by SI 2002/703, reg. 6(1)(a) with effect for 2002-03 and subsequent tax years, applying in relation to services performed, or to be performed, on or after 6 April 2002.
In reg. 8(5), para. (d) inserted by SI 2002/703, reg. 6(1)(b) with effect in relation to 2002–03 and subsequent years of assessment, applying in relation to services performed, or to be performed, on or after 6 April 2002.

MULTIPLE INTERMEDIARIES – GENERAL

9(1) Regulations 10 and 11 apply where in any tax year the arrangements involve more than one intermediary.

9(2) Except as provided by regulations 10 and 11, the provisions of this Part applies separately in relation to each intermediary.

History – In reg. 9(2), the words "this Part applies" substituted for the words "these regulations apply" by SI 2017/373, reg. 2(12), with effect from 6 April 2017.

MULTIPLE INTERMEDIARIES – AVOIDANCE OF DOUBLE–COUNTING

10(1) This regulation applies where a payment or benefit has been made or provided, directly or indirectly, from one intermediary to another intermediary under the arrangements.

10(2) In that case, the amount taken into account in relation to any intermediary in Step One or Step Two of the calculation in regulation 7(1) shall be reduced to such extent as is necessary to avoid double-counting having regard to the amount so taken into account in relation to any other intermediary.

MULTIPLE INTERMEDIARIES – JOINT AND SEVERAL LIABILITY

11(1) Where the arrangements involve more than one intermediary, all the intermediaries are jointly and severally liable, subject to paragraph (3), to pay contributions in respect of the amount of the worker's attributable earnings treated in accordance with regulation 8(1) as paid by any of them–

(a) under those arrangements, or

(b) *under those arrangements* together with other arrangements.

11(2) For the purposes of paragraph (1), each amount of the worker's attributable earnings shall be aggregated, and the aggregate amount shall be treated for the purposes of regulation 8(1) as a single payment of the worker's attributable earnings, but so that the total liability of the intermediaries to pay contributions in respect of that aggregate amount is not less than it would have been if the arrangements had involved a single intermediary and that aggregate amount had been an amount treated as paid in accordance with regulation 8(1) by a single intermediary.

11(3) An intermediary is not jointly and severally liable as mentioned in paragraph (1) if the intermediary has not received any payment or benefit under the arrangements concerned or under any such other arrangements as are mentioned in sub-paragraph (b) of that paragraph.

SOCIAL SECURITY (CATEGORISATION OF EARNERS) REGULATIONS 1978 – SAVING

12 Nothing in these Regulations affects the operation of regulation 2 of the Social Security (Categorisation of Earners) Regulations 1978 (treatment of earners in one category of earners as falling within another category and disregard of employments) as that regulation applies to employment listed in paragraph 2 in column (A) of Part I of Schedule 1 to those Regulations (earner supplied through a third person treated as employed earner).

Cross references – SI 1978/1689: the Social Security (Categorisation of Earners) Regulations 1978.

Part 2 – Intermediaries – Worker's Services Provided to Public Authorities

History – Pt. 2 inserted by SI 2017/373, reg. 2(13), with effect from 6 April 2017.

ENGAGEMENTS TO WHICH THIS PART APPLIES

13(1) Regulations 14 to 18 apply where–

(a) an individual ("the worker") personally performs, or is under an obligation personally to perform, services for another person ("the client"),

(b) the client is a public authority,

(c) the services are provided not under a contract directly between the client and the worker but under arrangements involving a third party ("the intermediary"), and

(d) the circumstances are such that–

(i) if the services were provided under a contract directly between the client and the worker, the worker would be regarded for the purposes of Parts I to V of the Contributions and Benefits Act as employed in employed earner's employment by the client, or

(ii) the worker is an office-holder who holds that office under the client and the services relate to that office.

13(2) The references in sub-paragraph (1)(c) to "third party" includes a partnership or unincorporated association of which the worker is a member.

13(3) The circumstances referred to in sub-paragraph (1)(d) includes the terms on which the services are provided, having regard to the terms of the contracts forming part of the arrangements under which the services are provided.

13(4) Holding office as a statutory auditor of the client does not count as holding office under the client for the purposes of sub-paragraph (1)(d).

History – Reg. 13 inserted by SI 2017/373, reg. 2(13), with effect from 6 April 2017.

WORKER TREATED AS RECEIVING EARNINGS FROM EMPLOYMENT

14(1) If one of conditions A to C in paragraphs (9) to (11) is met, identify the chain of two or more persons where–

(a) the highest person in the chain is the client,

(b) the lowest person in the chain is the intermediary, and

(c) each person in the chain above the lowest makes a chain payment to the person immediately below them in the chain.

(See regulation 21 for cases where one of conditions A to C is treated as being met).

14(2) In this Part–

(a) **"chain payment"** means a payment, or money's worth that can reasonably be taken to be for the worker's services to the client,

(b) **"make"** in relation to a chain payment that is money's worth, means transfer, and

(c) **"the fee-payer"** means the person in the chain immediately above the lowest.

14(3) The fee-payer is treated as making to the worker, and the worker is treated as receiving, a payment ("the deemed direct earnings") which is to be treated for the purposes of Parts 1 to 5 of the Contributions and Benefits Act as earnings from an employed earner's employment, but this is subject to paragraphs (5) to (7) and regulations 20 and 22.

14(4) The deemed direct earnings are treated as paid at the same time as the chain payment made by the fee-payer.

14(5) Paragraphs (6) and (7) apply, subject to regulations 20 and 22, if the fee-payer–

(a) is not the client, and

(b) is not a qualifying person.

14(6) If there is no person in the chain below the highest and above the lowest who is a qualifying person, paragraphs (3) and (4) have effect as if for any reference to the fee-payer there were substituted a reference to the client.

14(7) Otherwise, paragraphs (3) and (4) have effect as if for any reference to the fee-payer there were substituted a reference to the person in the chain who–

(a) is above the lowest,

(b) is a qualifying person, and

(c) is lower in the chain than any other person in the chain who–

 (i) is above the lowest, and

 (ii) is a qualifying person.

14(8) In paragraphs (5) to (7) a **"qualifying person"** is a person who–

(a) is resident in the United Kingdom or has a place of business in the United Kingdom,

(b) is not a person who is controlled by–

 (i) the worker, alone or with one or more associates of the worker, or

 (ii) an associate of the worker, with or without other associates of the worker, and

(c) if a company, is not one in which–

 (i) the worker, alone or with one or more associates of the worker, or

 (ii) an associate of the worker, with or without other associates of the worker,

has a material interest (within the meaning given by section 51(4) and (5) of ITEPA 2003 (meaning of material interest)).

14(9) Condition A is that–

(a) the intermediary is a company, and

(b) the conditions in regulation 15 are met in relation to the intermediary.

14(10) Condition B is that–

(a) the intermediary is a partnership,

(b) the worker is a member of the partnership,

(c) the provision of the services is by the worker as a member of the partnership, and

(d) the condition in regulation 16 is met in relation to the intermediary.

14(11) Condition C is that the intermediary is an individual.

14(12) Where a payment or money's worth can reasonably be taken to be for both–

(a) the worker's services to the client, and

(b) anything else,

then, for the purposes of this Part, so much of it as can, on a just and reasonable apportionment, be taken to be for the worker's services is to be treated as (and the rest is to be treated as not being) a payment or money's worth, that can reasonably be taken to be for the worker's services.

History – Reg. 14 inserted by SI 2017/373, reg. 2(13), with effect from 6 April 2017.

CONDITIONS WHERE INTERMEDIARY IS A COMPANY

15(1) The conditions mentioned in regulation 14(9)(b) are that–

(a) the intermediary is not an associated company of the client that falls within sub-paragraph (2), and

(b) the worker has a material interest in the intermediary.

15(2) An associated company of the client falls within this paragraph if it is such a company by reason of the intermediary and the client being under the control–

(a) of the worker, or

(b) of the worker and other persons.

15(3) The worker is treated as having a material interest in the intermediary if–

(a) the worker, alone or with one or more associates of the worker, or

(b) an associate of the worker, with or without other associates of the worker,

has a material interest in the intermediary.

15(4) For this purpose **"material interest"** has the meaning given by section 51(4) and (5) of ITEPA 2003.

15(5) In this regulation **"associated company"** has the meaning given by section 449 of CTA 2010.

History – Reg. 15 inserted by SI 2017/373, reg. 2(13), with effect from 6 April 2017.

CONDITIONS WHERE INTERMEDIARY IS A PARTNERSHIP

16(1) The condition mentioned in regulation 14(10)(d) is–

(a) that the worker, alone or with one or more relatives, is entitled to 60 per cent or more of the profits of the partnership, or

(b) that most of the profits of the partnership derive from the provision of services under engagements to which one or other of this Part and Part 1 applies–

(i) to a single client, or

(ii) to a single client together with associates of that client, or

(c) that under the profit sharing arrangements the income of any of the partners is based on the amount of income generated by that partner by the provision of services under engagements to which one or other of this Part and Part 1 applies.

16(2) In sub-paragraph (1)(a) **"relative"** means spouse or civil partner, parent or child or remoter relation in the direct line, or brother or sister.

16(3) For the purposes of this regulation section 61(4) and (5) of ITEPA 2003 apply as they apply for the purposes of Chapter 8 of that Act.

History – Reg. 16 inserted by SI 2017/373, reg. 2(13), with effect from 6 April 2017.

CALCULATION OF DEEMED DIRECT EARNINGS

17(1) The amount of the deemed direct earnings is the amount resulting from the following steps–

Step 1

Identify the amount or value of the chain payment made by the person who is treated as making the deemed direct earnings, and deduct from that amount so much of it (if any) as is in respect of value added tax.

Step 2

Deduct, from the amount resulting from Step 1, so much of that amount as represents the direct cost to the intermediary of materials used, or to be used, in the performance of the services.

Step 3

Deduct, at the option of the person treated as making the deemed direct earnings, from the amount resulting from Step 2, so much of that amount as represents expenses met by the intermediary that under ITEPA 2003 would have been deductible from the taxable earnings of the employment under section 10 ITEPA 2003, in accordance with section 327(3) to (5) of that Act, if–

(a) the worker had been employed by the client, and

(b) the expenses had been met by the worker out of those earnings.

Step 4

If the amount resulting from the preceding Steps is nil or negative, there are no deemed direct earnings. Otherwise, that amount is the amount of the deemed direct earnings.

17(2) For the purposes of Step 1 of paragraph (1), exclude amounts on which Class 1 or Class 1A contributions are payable by virtue of regulation 3 or 4 of the Social Security Contributions (Limited Liability Partnership) Regulations 2014.

17(3) In paragraph (1), the reference to the amount or value of the chain payment means the amount or value of that payment before the deduction (if any) permitted under regulation 19.

17(4) If the actual amount or value of the chain payment mentioned in Step 1 of paragraph (1) is such that its recipient bears the cost of amounts due under the Income Tax (Pay As You Earn) Regulations 2003 or the Contributions Regulations in respect of the deemed direct earnings, that Step applies as if the amount or value of the chain payment were what it would be if the burden of that cost were not being passed on through the setting of the level of the payment.

17(5) In Step 3 of paragraph (1), the reference to "expenses met by the intermediary" includes–

(a) expenses met by the worker and reimbursed by the intermediary, and

(b) where the intermediary is a partnership and the worker is a member of the partnership, expenses met by the worker for and on behalf of the partnership.

17(6) The deemed direct earnings are to be assessed on the amount of such earnings paid, or treated as paid, in the earnings period specified in regulations 3 to 6 or 8 of the Contributions Regulations.

17(7) For the purposes of paragraph (6), the definition of "regular interval" in regulation 1(2) of the Contributions Regulations is to be read as if "employed earner" were replaced with "intermediary" and the words "of earnings" were deleted.

History – Reg. 17 inserted by SI 2017/373, reg. 2(13), with effect from 6 April 2017.

APPLICATION OF SOCIAL SECURITY CONTRIBUTIONS AND BENEFITS (NORTHERN IRELAND) ACT 1992 TO DEEMED EMPLOYMENT

18(1) This Regulation applies where deemed direct earnings are treated as having been paid in any tax year under regulation 14.

18(2) For the purposes of Parts 1 to 5 of the Contributions and Benefits Act–

(a) the amount of any deemed direct earnings calculated under regulation 17 shall be treated as remuneration derived from an employed earner's employment,

(b) the worker shall be treated, in relation to the deemed direct earnings as employed in employed earner's employment by the person treated as making the payment of deemed direct earnings,

(c) the services were performed, or are to be performed, by the worker in the course of performing the duties of that employment, and

(d) the person treated as making the payment of deemed direct earnings shall be treated as the secondary contributor in relation to the deemed direct earnings.

History – Reg. 18 inserted by SI 2017/373, reg. 2(13), with effect from 6 April 2017.

DEDUCTIONS FROM CHAIN PAYMENTS

19(1) This regulation applies if, as a result of regulation 18, a person who is treated as making a payment of deemed direct earnings is required under the Contributions Regulations to pay primary Class 1 contributions to the Commissioners for Her Majesty's Revenue and Customs (the Commissioners) in respect of the payment.

(But see paragraph (4)).

19(2) The person may deduct from the underlying chain payment an amount which is equal to the amount payable to the Commissioners in respect of primary Class 1 contributions, but where the amount or value of the underlying chain payment is treated by regulation 17(4) as increased by the cost of any amount due under the Contributions Regulations, the amount that may be deducted is limited to the difference (if any) between the amount of primary Class 1 contributions payable to the Commissioners and the amount of that increase.

19(3) Where a person in the chain other than the intermediary receives a chain payment from which an amount has been deducted in reliance on paragraph (2) or this paragraph, that person may deduct the same amount from the chain payment made by them.

19(4) This regulation does not apply in a case to which regulation 22(2) applies.

19(5) In paragraph (2) **"the underlying chain payment"** means the chain payment whose amount is used at Step 1 of regulation 17(1) as the starting point for calculating the amount of the deemed direct earnings.

History – Reg. 19 inserted by SI 2017/373, reg. 2(13), with effect from 6 April 2017.

INFORMATION TO BE PROVIDED BY CLIENTS AND CONSEQUENCES OF FAILURE

20(1) If the conditions in regulation 13(1)(a) to (c) are met in any case, and a person as part of the arrangements mentioned in regulation 13(1)(c) enters into a contract with the client, the client must inform that person (in the contract or otherwise) of which one of the following is applicable–

(a) the client has concluded that the condition in regulation 13(1)(d) is met in the case;

(b) the client has concluded that the condition in regulation 13(1)(d) is not met in the case.

20(2) If the contract is entered into on or after 6th April 2017, the duty under paragraph (1) must be complied with–

(a) on or before the time of entry into the contract, or

(b) if the services begin to be performed at a later time, before that later time.

20(3) If the contract is entered into before 6th April 2017, the duty under paragraph (1) must be complied with on or before the date the first payment is made under the contract on or after 6th April 2017.

20(4) If the information which paragraph (1) requires the client to give to a person has been given (whether in the contract, as required by paragraph (2) or (3) or otherwise), the client must, on a written request by the person, provide the person with a written response to any questions raised by the person about the client's reasons for reaching the conclusion identified in the information.

20(5) A response required by paragraph (4) must be provided before the end of 31 days beginning with the day the request for it is received by the client.

20(6) If–

(a) the client fails to comply with the duty under paragraph (1) within the time allowed by paragraph (2) or (3), or

(b) the client fails to provide a response required by paragraph (4) within the time allowed by paragraph (5), or

(c) the client complies with the duty under paragraph (1) but fails to take reasonable care in coming to its conclusion as to whether the condition in regulation 13(1)(d) is met in the case,

regulations 14(3) and (4) have effect in the case as if for any reference to the fee-payer there were substituted a reference to the client, but this is subject to regulation 22.

History – Reg. 20 inserted by SI 2017/373, reg. 2(13), with effect from 6 April 2017.

INFORMATION TO BE PROVIDED BY WORKER AND CONSEQUENCES OF FAILURE

21(1) In the case of an engagement to which this Part applies, the worker must inform the potential deemed employer of which one of the following is applicable–

(a) that one of conditions A to C in regulation 14 is met in the case,

(b) that none of conditions A to C in regulation 14 is met in the case.

21(2) If the worker has not complied with paragraph (1), then for the purposes of regulation 14(1), one of conditions A to C in regulation 14 is to be treated as met.

21(3) In this regulation, **"the potential deemed employer"** is the person who, if one of conditions A to C in regulation 14 were met, would be treated as making a payment of deemed direct earnings to the worker under regulation 14(3).

History – Reg. 21 inserted by SI 2017/373, reg. 2(13), with effect from 6 April 2017.

CONSEQUENCES OF PROVIDING FRAUDULENT INFORMATION

22(1) Paragraph (2) applies if in any case–

(a) a person ("the deemed employer") would, but for this paragraph, be treated by regulation 14(3) as making a payment to another person ("the services-provider"), and

(b) the fraudulent documentation condition is met.

22(2) Regulation 14(3) has effect in the case as if the reference to the fee-payer were a reference to the services-provider, but

(a) regulation 14(4) continues to have effect as if the reference to the fee-payer were a reference to the deemed employer, and

(b) Step 1 of regulation 17(1) continues to have effect as referring to the chain payment to be made by the deemed employer.

22(3) Paragraph (2) has effect even though that involves the services-provider being treated as both employer and employee in relation to the deemed employment under regulation 14(3).

22(4) **"The fraudulent documentation condition"** is that a relevant person provided any person with a fraudulent document intended to constitute evidence–

(a) that the case is not an engagement to which this Part applies, or

(b) that none of the conditions A to C in regulation 14 is met in the case.

22(5) For the purposes of this regulation a **"relevant person"** is–

(a) the services-provider,

(b) a person connected with the services-provider,

(c) if the intermediary in the case is a company, an office-holder in that company.

History – Reg. 22 inserted by SI 2017/373, reg. 2(13), with effect from 6 April 2017.

PREVENTION OF DOUBLE LIABILITY TO NATIONAL INSURANCE CONTRIBUTIONS AND ALLOWANCE OF CERTAIN DEDUCTIONS

23(1) Paragraph (2) applies where–

(a) a person ("the payee") receives a payment ("the end-of-line remuneration") from another person ("the paying intermediary"),

(b) the end-of-line remuneration can reasonably be taken to represent remuneration for services of the payee to a public authority,

(c) a payment ("the deemed payment") has been treated by regulation 14(3) as paid to the payee,

(d) the underlying chain payment can reasonably be taken to be for the same services of the payee to that public authority, and

(e) the recipient of the underlying chain payment has (whether by deduction from that payment or otherwise) borne the cost of any amounts due, under Income Tax (Pay As You Earn) Regulations 2003 and Contributions Regulations in respect of the deemed payment from the person treated by regulation 14(3) as making the deemed payment.

23(2) For national insurance contributions purposes, the paying intermediary may treat the amount of the end-of-line remuneration as reduced (but not below nil) by the amount (see regulation 17) of the deemed payment less the amount of income tax and primary Class 1 national insurance contributions deducted from that amount.

23(3) Nothing in paragraph (2) shall be read as removing a worker's entitlement to Statutory Maternity Pay which would have existed but for the operation of that paragraph.

History – Reg. 23 inserted by SI 2017/373, reg. 2(13), with effect from 6 April 2017.

SOCIAL SECURITY CONTRIBUTIONS (NOTIONAL PAYMENT OF PRIMARY CLASS 1 CONTRIBUTION) REGULATIONS 2000

(SI 2000/747 as amended by SI 2001/1004)

Made on 13 March 2000 by the Treasury, in exercise of the powers conferred on them by s. 3(2), 6A(2) and (7), 119, 122(1) and 175(3) and (4) of the Social Security Contributions and Benefits Act 1992. Operative from 6 April 2000.

ARRANGEMENT OF REGULATIONS

CITATION AND COMMENCEMENT

1 These Regulations may be cited as the Social Security Contributions (Notional Payment of Primary Class 1 Contribution) Regulations 2000 and shall come into force on 6th April 2000.

INTERPRETATION

2 In these Regulations unless the context otherwise requires-

"the Contributions and Benefits Act" means the Social Security Contributions and Benefits Act 1992;

"the principal Regulations" means the Social Security (Contributions) Regulations 1979;

"section 6A(2)" means section 6A(2) of the Contributions and Benefits Act.

INTRODUCTORY

3 Section 6A(2) (notional payment of primary Class 1 contribution where in any tax week payment of earnings is not less than the current lower earnings limit but does not exceed the current primary threshold) has effect subject to the modifications and exceptions prescribed by regulations 4 to 6 of these Regulations.

PRESCRIBED MODIFICATIONS AND EXCEPTIONS

4 The modification prescribed by this regulation is that section 6A(2) has effect to the extent only that, if the amount of earnings paid in the tax week concerned had exceeded the current primary threshold, the earner would have been liable or entitled under the Contributions and Benefits Act and the principal Regulations to pay a primary Class 1 contribution in respect of those earnings.

5 The exception prescribed by this regulation is that section 6A(2) does not have effect for the purposes of regulation 32 of the principal Regulations (return of contributions).

6 The modification prescribed by this regulation is that, where the earner is a woman who has made an election under regulation 100 of the principal Regulations (elections by married women and widows for liability to pay primary Class 1 contributions at the reduced rate) and that election has not ceased to have effect, section 6A(2) has effect as if the primary Class 1 contribution there referred to had been paid at the reduced rate.

CONSEQUENTIAL AMENDMENTS TO THE PRINCIPAL REGULATIONS

7–9 [Repealed by SI 2001/1004, reg. 157 and Sch. 8 with effect from 6 April 2001.]

SOCIAL SECURITY REVALUATION OF EARNINGS FACTORS ORDER 2001

(SI 2001/631)

Made on 28 February 2001 by the Secretary of State for Social Security, in exercise of the powers conferred on him by s. 148(3) and (4) and 189(5) of the Social Security Administration Act 1992 and of all other powers enabling him in that behalf, having on a review under the said s. 148 concluded, having had regard to earlier orders under that section, that earnings factors for the relevant previous tax years have not, during the period taken into account for that review, maintained their value in relation to the general level of earnings obtaining in Great Britain. Operative from 6 April 2001.

CITATION AND COMMENCEMENT

1 This Order may be cited as the Social Security Revaluation of Earnings Factors Order 2001 and shall come into force on 6th April 2001.

REVALUATION OF EARNINGS FACTORS

2 The earnings factors for tax years specified in the Schedule to this Order, in so far as they are relevant–

(a) to the calculation–

(i) of the additional pension in the rate of any long-term benefit; or

(ii) of any guaranteed minimum pension; or

(b) to any other calculation required under Part III of the Pension Schemes Act 1993 (including that Part as modified by or under any other enactment),

are directed to be increased for those tax years by the percentage of their amount shown opposite those tax years in that Schedule.

ROUNDING OF FRACTIONAL AMOUNTS

3 Where any earnings factor relevant to the calculation specified in article 2(a)(i) of this Order, as increased in accordance with this Order, would not but for this article be expressed as a whole number of pounds, it shall be so expressed by the rounding down of any fraction of a pound less than one half and the rounding up of any other fraction of a pound.

SCHEDULE

Article 2

Tax Year	*Percentage*
1978/79	475.9
1979/80	408.3
1980/81	324.6
1981/82	255.6
1982/83	223.0
1983/84	199.9
1984/85	177.7
1985/86	160.5
1986/87	139.2
1987/88	122.7
1988/89	104.9
1989/90	84.9
1990/91	72.4
1991/92	56.5
1992/93	47.0
1993/94	40.0
1994/95	35.8
1995/96	30.1

Tax Year	*Percentage*
1996/97	26.5
1997/98	20.5
1998/99	15.2
1999/2000	10.6
2000/2001	4.0

SOCIAL SECURITY (CREDITING AND TREATMENT OF CONTRIBUTIONS, AND NATIONAL INSURANCE NUMBERS) REGULATIONS 2001

(SI 2001/769 as amended by SI 2001/1004, SI 2002/2366, SI 2004/1361, SI 2006/2897, SI 2007/1154, SI 2007/2582, SI 2008/223, SI 2008/1554, SI 2008/2683, SI 2009/659, SI 2013/630, SI 2013/3165, SI 2015/67, SI 2015/1828 and SI 2016/1145)

Made on 7 March 2001 by the Secretary of State for Social Security, with the concurrence of the Inland Revenue in so far as required, in exercise of powers conferred by s. 13(3), 22(5), 122(1) and 175(1) to (4) of, and para. 8(1)(d) and (1A) and 10 of Sch. 1 to, the Social Security Contributions and Benefits Act 1992 and s. 182C and 189(1) and (3) to (6) of the Social Security Administration Act 1992 and of all other powers enabling him in that behalf and for the purpose only of consolidating other regulations hereby revoked. Operative from 6 April 2001.

CITATION, COMMENCEMENT AND INTERPRETATION

1(1) These Regulations may be cited as the Social Security (Crediting and Treatment of Contributions, and National Insurance Numbers) Regulations 2001 and shall come into force on 6th April 2001.

1(2) In these Regulations, including this regulation–

"the Act" means the Social Security Contributions and Benefits Act 1992;

"the Contributions Regulations" means the Social Security (Contributions) Regulations 2001;

"contribution week" means a period of seven days beginning with midnight between Saturday and Sunday;

"contribution-based jobseeker's allowance" means an allowance under the Jobseekers Act 1995 as amended by the provisions of Part 1 of Schedule 14 to the Welfare Reform Act 2012 that remove references to an income-based allowance, and a contribution-based allowance under the Jobseekers Act 1995 as that Act has effect apart from those provisions;

"contributory benefit" includes a contribution-based jobseeker's allowance but not an income-based jobseeker's allowance and includes a contributory employment and support allowance but not an income-related employment and support allowance;

"contributory employment and support allowance" means an allowance under Part 1 of the Welfare Reform Act as amended by the provisions of Schedule 3, and Part 1 of Schedule 14, to the Welfare Reform Act 2012 that remove references to an income-related allowance, and a contributory allowance under Part 1 of the Welfare Reform Act as that Part has effect apart from those provisions;

"due date" (subject to regulation 4(11)) means, in relation to–

(a) any Class 1 contribution, the date by which payment falls to be made;

(b) any Class 2 contribution which a person is liable or entitled to pay, the 31st January following the end of the year in respect of which it is payable;

(c) any Class 3 contribution, the date 42 days after the end of the year in respect of which it is paid;

"earnings factor" has the meaning assigned to it in section 21(5)(c) of the Act;

"income-based jobseeker's allowance" has the same meaning as in the Jobseekers Act 1995;

"income-related employment and support allowance" means an income-related allowance under Part 1 of the Welfare Reform Act (employment and support allowance);

"relevant benefit year" has the meaning assigned to it in–

(a) section 2(4)(b) of the Jobseekers Act 1995, in relation to a contribution-based jobseeker's allowance;

(b) paragraph 2(6)(b) of Schedule 3 to the Act (contribution conditions for entitlement to short-term incapacity benefit), in relation to short-term incapacity benefit;

(c) paragraph 3(1)(f) of Schedule 1 to the Welfare Reform Act (conditions relating to national insurance), in relation to a contributory employment and support allowance.

"relevant time", in relation to short-term incapacity benefit, has the meaning assigned to it in *paragraph 2(6)(a)* of Schedule 3 to the Act;

"the Welfare Reform Act" means the Welfare Reform Act 2007;

"year" means tax year.

1(3) In these Regulations, **"official error"** means an error made by–

(a) an officer of the Department for Work and Pensions or an officer of Revenue and Customs acting as such which no person outside the Department or Her Majesty's Revenue and Customs caused or to which no person outside the Department or Her Majesty's Revenue and Customs materially contributed; or

(b) a person employed by a service provider and to which no person who was not so employed materially contributed,

but excludes any error of law which is shown to have been an error by virtue of a subsequent decision of the Upper Tribunal or the court.

1(4) In paragraph (3)–

"service provider" means a person providing services to the Secretary of State for Work and Pensions or to Her Majesty's Revenue and Customs.

History – In reg. 1(1), in the definition of "contributory benefit" the words "and includes a contributory employment and support allowance but not an income-related employment and support allowance" inserted, the definitions of "contributory employment and support allowance", "income-related employment and support allowance" and "the Welfare Reform Act" inserted and in the definition of "relevant benefit year" para. (c) inserted by SI 2008/1554, reg. 49(2), with effect from 27 October 2008.
In reg. 1(1), definition of "contributory employment and support allowance" substituted by SI 2013/630, reg. 71(2)(b), with effect from 29 April 2013.
In reg. 1(1), definition of "income-based jobseeker's allowance" substituted by SI 2013/630, reg. 71(2)(b), with effect from 29 April 2013.
In reg. 1(2), in the definition of "the Contributions Regulations", the year "2001" substituted for the year "1979" by SI 2016/1145, reg. 5(2)(a), with effect from 1 January 2017.
In reg. 1(2), definition of "contribution-based jobseeker's allowance" substituted for the definition of ""contribution-based jobseeker's allowance" and "income-based jobseeker's allowance"" by SI 2013/630, reg. 71(2)(a), with effect from 29 April 2013.
In reg. 1(2), definition of "due date" substituted by SI 2016/1145, reg. 5(2)(b), with effect from 1 January 2017.
In reg. 1(2) the words "(subject to regulation 4(11))" inserted in the definition of "due date" by SI 2007/1154, reg. 2(2), operative from 6 April 2007, with effect from 2 December 2004.
In reg. 1(3), the words "the Upper Tribunal" substituted by SI 2008/2683, art. 6 and Sch. 1, para. 147(a), with effect from 3 November 2008.
Reg. 1(3) inserted by SI 2007/2582, reg. 4(2), with effect from 1 October 2007.
In reg. 1(4), the definition of "Commissioner" omitted by SI 2008/2683, art. 6 and Sch. 1, para. 147(b), with effect from 3 November 2008.
Reg. 1(4) inserted by SI 2007/2582, reg. 4(2), with effect from 1 October 2007.

APPROPRIATION OF CLASS 3 CONTRIBUTIONS

2 Any person paying Class 3 contributions in one year may appropriate such contributions to the earnings factor of another year if such contributions are payable in respect of that other year or, in the absence of any such appropriation, the Inland Revenue may, with the consent of the contributor, make such appropriation.

CREDITING OF CLASS 3 CONTRIBUTIONS

3 Where, for any year, a contributor's earnings factor derived from–

(a) earnings upon which primary Class 1 contributions have been paid or treated as paid;

(b) credited earnings;

(c) Class 2 or Class 3 contributions paid by or credited to him; or

(d) any or all of such earnings and contributions,

falls short of a figure which is 52 times that year's lower earnings limit for Class 1 contributions by an amount which is equal to, or less than, half that year's lower earnings limit, that contributor shall be credited with a Class 3 contribution for that year.

TREATMENT FOR THE PURPOSE OF ANY CONTRIBUTORY BENEFIT OF LATE PAID CONTRIBUTIONS

4(1) Subject to the provisions of regulations 5 to 6C below and regulation 61 of the Contributions Regulations (voluntary Class 2 contributions not paid within permitted period), for the purpose of entitlement to any contributory benefit, paragraphs (1B) to (9) below shall apply to contributions (**"relevant contributions"**)–

(a) paid after the due date; or

(b) treated as paid after the due date under regulation 7(2) below.

4(1A) Any relevant contribution which is paid–

(a) by virtue of an official error; and

(b) more than six years after the end of the year in which the contributor was first advised of that error,

shall be treated as not paid.

4(1B) Where contributions are paid in accordance with regulation 63A of the Social Security (Contributions) Regulations 2001 (collection of unpaid Class 2 contributions through PAYE code), any relevant contributions are to be treated as paid on 5th April of the tax year in which they are paid.

4(2) Subject to the provisions of paragraph (4) below, any relevant contribution other than one referred to in paragraph (3) below–

(a) if paid after the end of the second year–

(i) following the year in which liability for that contribution arises, or

(ii) following the year in respect of which a person is entitled, but not liable, to pay the contribution,

shall be treated as not paid;

(b) if paid before the end of the said second year, shall, subject to paragraphs (7) and (8) below, be treated as paid on the date on which payment of the contribution is made.

4(3) Subject to the provisions of paragraph (4) below, any relevant Class 2 contribution payable in respect of a contribution week after 5th April 1983 or any relevant Class 3 contribution payable in respect of a year after 5th April 1982–

(a) if paid after the end of the sixth year–

(i) following the year in which liability for that contribution arises, or

(ii) following the year in respect of which a person is entitled, but not liable, to pay the contribution,

shall be treated as not paid;

(b) if paid before the end of the said sixth year, shall, subject to paragraphs (7) or (8) below, be treated as paid on the date on which payment of the contribution is made.

4(4) A Class 3 contribution payable by a person to whom regulation 48(3)(b)(ii) or (iii) of the Contributions Regulations (which specify the conditions to be complied with before a person may pay a Class 3 contribution) applies in respect of a year which includes a period of education, apprenticeship, training, imprisonment or detention in legal custody such as is specified in that regulation–

(a) if paid after the end of the sixth year specified in that regulation, shall be treated as not paid;

(b) if paid before the end of the said sixth year shall, subject to the provisions of paragraphs (7) and (8) below, be treated as paid on the date on which payment of the contribution is made.

4(5) Notwithstanding the provisions of paragraph (4) above, for the purpose of entitlement to any contributory benefit, where–

(a) a Class 3 contribution other than one referred to in sub-paragraph (b) below which is payable in respect of a year specified in that sub-paragraph, is paid after–

(i) the due date, and

(ii) the end of the second year following the year preceding that in which occurred the relevant time or, as the case may be, the relevant event,

that contribution shall be treated as not paid;

(b) in respect of a year after 5th April 1982, a Class 3 contribution which is payable in respect of a year specified in paragraph (4) above, is paid after–

(i) the due date, and

(ii) the end of the sixth year following the year preceding that in which occurred the relevant time or, as the case may be, the relevant event,

that contribution shall be treated as not paid.

4(6) For the purposes of paragraph (5) above, **"relevant event"** means the date on which the person concerned attained pensionable age or, as the case may be, died under that age.

4(7) Notwithstanding the provisions of paragraphs (2), (3) and (4) above, in determining whether the relevant contribution conditions are satisfied in whole or in part for the purpose of entitlement to any contributory benefit, any relevant contribution which is paid within the time specified in paragraph (2)(b), (3)(b) or, as the case may be, (4)(b) above shall be treated–

(a) for the purpose of entitlement in respect of any period before the date on which the payment of the contribution is made, as not paid; and

(b) subject to the provisions of paragraph (8) below, for the purpose of entitlement in respect of any other period, as paid on the date on which the payment of the contribution is made.

4(7A) In determining whether the relevant contribution conditions are satisfied in whole or in part for the purpose of entitlement to any contributory benefit, any relevant contribution which is treated as paid on the date specified in paragraph (1B) shall be treated–

(a) for the purpose of entitlement in respect of any period before the date on which payment of the contribution is treated as paid, as not paid; and

(b) subject to the provisions of paragraph (8) below, for the purpose of entitlement in respect of any other period, as paid on the date specified in paragraph (1B).

4(8) For the purpose of determining whether the second contribution condition for entitlement to a contribution-based jobseeker's allowance or a contributory employment and support allowance is satisfied in whole or in part a relevant contribution is to be treated–

(a) if a Class 1 contribution paid before the beginning of the relevant benefit year, as paid on the due date;

(b) if, subject to paragraph (2)(a), a Class 1 contribution paid after the end of the benefit year immediately preceding the relevant benefit year or, subject to paragraph (3)(a), a Class 2 contribution–

(i) as not paid in relation to the benefit claimed in respect of any day before the expiry of a period of 42 days (including Sundays) commencing with the date on which the payment of that contribution is made; and

(ii) as paid at the expiry of that period in relation to entitlement to such benefit in respect of any other period.

(a) if paid before the beginning of the relevant benefit year, as paid on the due date;

(b) if paid after the end of the benefit year immediately preceding the relevant benefit year, as not paid in relation to the benefit claimed in respect of any day before the expiry of a period of 42 days (including Sundays) commencing with the date on which the payment of that contribution is made, and, subject to the provisions of paragraphs (2)(a) and (3)(a) above, as paid at the expiry of that period in relation to entitlement to such benefit in respect of any other period.

4(9) For the purposes of paragraph (8) above, **"second contribution condition"** in relation to–

(a) a contribution-based jobseeker's allowance is a reference to the condition specified in section 2(1)(b) of the Jobseekers Act 1995;

(b) short-term incapacity benefit is a reference to the condition specified in paragraph 2(3) of Schedule 3 to the Act.

(c) a contributory employment and support allowance is a reference to the condition specified in paragraph 2(1) of Schedule 1 to the Welfare Reform Act

4(10) This regulation shall not apply to Class 4 contributions.

4(11) Where an amount is retrospectively treated as earnings ("retrospective earnings") by regulations made by virtue of section 4B(2) of the Act, the "due date" for earnings-related contributions in respect of those earnings is the date given by paragraph 11A of Schedule 4 to the Social Security (Contributions) Regulations 2001, for the purposes of this regulation and regulations 5 and 5A.

History – In reg. 4(1), "61" substituted for "40" by SI 2016/1145, reg. 5(3)(a), with effect from 1 January 2017.
In reg. 4(1), the words "paragraphs (1B)" substituted for the words "paragraphs (2)" by SI 2013/3165, reg. 2(a), with effect from 6 April 2014.
In reg. 4(1), "to 6C" substituted by SI 2009/659, reg. 3(2), with effect from 6 April 2009.
In reg. 4(1), the reference to "6B" substituted by SI 2007/2582, reg. 4(3)(a), with effect from 1 October 2007.
In reg. 4(1), words "to 6A" substituted by SI 2004/1361, reg. 2(a), with effect from 17 May 2004.
Reg. 4(1A) inserted by SI 2007/2582, reg. 4(3)(b), with effect from 1 October 2007.
Reg. 4(1B) inserted by SI 2013/3165, reg. 2(b), with effect from 6 April 2014.
In reg. 4(2)(a), the words "after the end of the second year" inserted by SI 2016/1145, reg. 5(3)(b)(i), with effect from 1 January 2017.
In reg. 4(2)(a)(i), the words "after the end of the second year" (which appeared before the words "following the year") omitted by SI 2016/1145, reg. 5(3)(b)(ii), with effect from 1 January 2017.
Reg. 4(2)(a)(ii) substituted (and the "or" after (i) inserted) by SI 2016/1145, reg. 5(3)(b)(iii)–(iv), with effect from 1 January 2017.
Former reg. 4(2)(a)(ii) read as follows:
"(ii) following the due date for that contribution in the case of a contribution which a person is entitled, but not liable, to pay,".
In reg. 4(3)(a), the words "after the end of the sixth year" inserted by SI 2016/1145, reg. 5(3)(c)(i), with effect from 1 January 2017.
In reg. 4(3)(a)(i), the words "after the end of the sixth year" (which appeared before the words "following the year") omitted by SI 2016/1145, reg. 5(3)(c)(ii), with effect from 1 January 2017.
Reg. 4(3)(a)(ii) substituted (and the "or" after (i) inserted) by SI 2016/1145, reg. 5(3)(c)(iii)–(iv), with effect from 1 January 2017.
Former reg. 4(3)(a)(ii) read as follows:
"(ii) following the due date for that contribution in the case of a contribution which a person is entitled, but not liable, to pay,".
In reg. 4(3)(b), the word "or" substituted for the word "and" by SI 2016/1145, reg. 5(3)(c)(v), with effect from 1 January 2017.
In reg. 4(4), the words "48(3)(b)(ii) or (iii)" substituted for the words "27(3)(b)(ii) or (iii)" by SI 2016/1145, reg. 5(3)(d), with effect from 1 January 2017.
Reg. 4(7A) inserted by SI 2013/3165, reg. 2(c), with effect from 6 April 2014.
Reg. 4(8) substituted by SI 2016/1145, reg. 5(3)(e), with effect from 1 January 2017. Former reg. 4(8) read as follows:

"**4(8)** For the purpose of determining whether the second contribution condition for entitlement to a contribution-based jobseeker's allowance, short-term incapacity benefit or a contributory employment and support allowance is satisfied in whole or in part, any relevant contribution shall be treated–

(a) if paid before the beginning of the relevant benefit year, as paid on the due date;

(b) if paid after the end of the benefit year immediately preceding the relevant benefit year, as not paid in relation to the benefit claimed in respect of any day before the expiry of a period of 42 days (including Sundays) commencing with the date on which the payment of that contribution is made, and, subject to the provisions of paragraphs (2)(a) and (3)(a) above, as paid at the expiry of that period in relation to entitlement to such benefit in respect of any other period. ".

In reg. 4(8), the words ", short-term incapacity benefit or a contributory employment and support allowance" substituted by SI 2008/1554, reg. 49(3), with effect from 27 October 2008.
Reg. 4(9)(c) inserted by SI 2008/1554, reg. 49(3), with effect from 27 October 2008.
Reg. 4(11) inserted by SI 2007/1154, reg. 2(3), operative from 6 April 2007, with effect from 2 December 2004.

TREATMENT FOR THE PURPOSE OF ANY CONTRIBUTORY BENEFIT OF LATE PAID PRIMARY CLASS 1 CONTRIBUTIONS WHERE THERE WAS NO CONSENT, CONNIVANCE OR NEGLIGENCE BY THE PRIMARY CONTRIBUTOR

5(1) This regulation applies where a primary Class 1 contribution which is payable on a primary contributor's behalf by a secondary contributor–

(a) is paid after the due date; or

(b) in relation to any claim for–

(i) a contribution-based jobseeker's allowance, is not paid before the beginning of the relevant benefit year,

(ii) short-term incapacity benefit, is not paid before the relevant time, or

(iii) a contributory employment and support allowance, is not paid before the beginning of the relevant benefit year,

and the delay in making payment is shown to the satisfaction of an officer of the Inland Revenue not to have been with the consent or connivance of, or attributable to any negligence on the part of, the primary contributor.

5(2) Where paragraph (1) above applies, the primary Class 1 contribution shall be treated–

(a) for the purpose of the first contribution condition of entitlement to a contribution-based jobseeker's allowance or short-term incapacity benefit, as paid on the day on which payment is made of the earnings in respect of which the contribution is payable; and

(b) for any other purpose relating to entitlement to any contributory benefit, as paid on the due date.

5(3) For the purposes of this regulation–

(a) **"first contribution condition"** in relation to–

(i) a contribution-based jobseeker's allowance is a reference to the condition specified in section 2(1)(a) of the Jobseekers Act 1995,

(ii) short-term incapacity benefit is a reference to the condition specified in paragraph 2(2) of Schedule 3 to the Act;

(b) **"primary contributor"** means the person liable to pay a primary Class 1 contribution in accordance with section 6(4)(a) of the Act (liability for Class 1 contributions);

(c) **"secondary contributor"** means the person who, in respect of earnings from employed earner's employment, is liable to pay a secondary Class 1 contribution in accordance with section 6(4)(b) of the Act.

History – In reg. 5(1)(b), the word "or" repealed in para. (i) and inserted in para. (ii) and para. (iii) inserted by SI 2008/1554, reg. 49(4), with effect from 27 October 2008.
In reg. 5(1) the words "an officer of" inserted by SI 2002/2366, reg. 19(2), with effect from 8 October 2002.

TREATMENT FOR THE PURPOSE OF ANY CONTRIBUTORY BENEFIT OF DULY PAID PRIMARY CLASS 1 CONTRIBUTIONS IN RESPECT OF RETROSPECTIVE EARNINGS

5A Where a primary Class 1 contribution payable in respect of retrospective earnings is paid by the due date, it shall be treated–

(a) for the purposes of the first contribution condition of entitlement to a contribution-based jobseeker's allowance, short-term incapacity benefit or a contributory employment and support allowance, as paid on the day on which payment is made of the retrospective earnings in respect of which the contribution is payable; and

(b) for any other purpose relating to entitlement to any contributory benefit, as paid on the due date.

History – In reg. 5A(a), the words ", short-term incapacity benefit or a contributory employment and support allowance" substituted by SI 2008/1554, reg. 49(5), with effect from 27 October 2008.
Reg. 5A inserted by SI 2007/1154, reg. 2(4), operative from 6 April 2007, with effect from 2 December 2004.

TREATMENT FOR THE PURPOSE OF ANY CONTRIBUTORY BENEFIT OF CONTRIBUTIONS UNDER THE ACT PAID LATE THROUGH IGNORANCE OR ERROR

6(1) In the case of a contribution paid by or in respect of a person after the due date, where–

(a) the contribution is paid after the time when it would, under regulation 4 or 5 above, have been treated as paid for the purpose of entitlement to contributory benefit; and

(b) it is shown to the satisfaction of an officer of the Inland Revenue that the failure to pay the contribution before that time is attributable to ignorance or error on the part of that person or the person making the payment and that that ignorance or error was not due to any failure on the part of such person to exercise due care and diligence

an officer of the Inland Revenue may direct that, for the purposes of those regulations, the contribution shall be treated as paid on such earlier day as the officer considers appropriate in the circumstances, and those regulations shall have effect subject to any such direction.

6(2) This regulation shall not apply to a Class 4 contribution.

History – In reg. 6(1)(b) the words "an officer of" inserted by SI 2002/2366, reg. 19(3)(a), with effect from 8 October 2002.
In reg. 6(1) the words "an officer of the Inland Revenue may direct" substituted by SI 2002/2366, reg. 19(3)(b), with effect from 8 October 2002.
In reg. 6(1) the words "the officer considers" substituted by SI 2002/2366, reg. 19(3)(c), with effect from 8 October 2002.

TREATMENT FOR THE PURPOSES OF ANY CONTRIBUTORY BENEFIT OF CERTAIN CLASS 3 CONTRIBUTIONS

6A(1) For the purposes of entitlement to any contributory benefit, this regulation applies in the case of a Class 3 contribution paid after the due date–

(a) which would otherwise under regulation 4–

(i) have been treated as paid on a day other than on the day on which it was actually paid; or

(ii) have been treated as not paid; and

(b) which is paid in respect of a year after 5th April 1996 but before 6th April 2002.

6A(2) A contribution referred to in paragraph (1), where it is paid on or before 5th April 2009 by or in respect of a person who attains pensionable age on or after 6th April 2008, shall be treated as paid on the day on which it is paid.

6A(3) A contribution referred to in paragraph (1), where it is paid on or before 5th April 2009 by or in respect of a person who attains pensionable age on or after 24th October 2004 but before 6th April 2008, shall be treated as paid on–

(a) the day on which it is paid; or

(b) the date on which the person attained pensionable age,

whichever is the earlier.

6A(4) A contribution referred to in paragraph (1), where it is paid on or before 5th April 2010 by or in respect of a person who attains pensionable age on or after 6th April 1998 but before 24th October 2004, shall be treated as paid on–

(a) 1st October 1998; or

(b) the date on which the person attained pensionable age,

whichever is the later.

History – Reg. 6A inserted by SI 2004/1361, reg. 2(b), with effect from 17 May 2004.

TREATMENT FOR THE PURPOSE OF ANY CONTRIBUTORY BENEFIT OF CERTAIN CLASS 2 OR CLASS 3 CONTRIBUTIONS

6B For the purpose of entitlement to any contributory benefit, a Class 2 or a Class 3 contribution paid after the due date–

(a) which would otherwise under regulation 4 (apart from paragraph (1A) of that regulation)–

(i) have been treated as paid on a day other than the day on which it was actually paid; or

(ii) have been treated as not paid; and

(b) which was paid after the due date by virtue of an official error,

shall be treated as paid on the day on which it is paid.

History – Reg. 6B inserted by SI 2007/2582, reg. 4(4), with effect from 1 October 2007.

TREATMENT OF CLASS 3 CONTRIBUTIONS PAID UNDER SECTION 13A OF THE ACT

6C(1) This regulation applies to a Class 3 contribution paid by an eligible person under section 13A (right to pay additional Class 3 contributions in certain cases) of the Act.

6C(2) A contribution paid after 5th April 2009 but before 6th April 2011 shall be treated as paid on–

(a) the day on which it is paid; or

(b) the date on which the person attained pensionable age,

whichever is the earlier.

6C(3) A contribution paid after 5th April 2011 shall be treated as paid on the day on which it is paid.

History – Reg. 6C inserted by SI 2009/659, reg. 3(3), with effect from 6 April 2009.

TREATMENT FOR THE PURPOSE OF ANY CONTRIBUTORY BENEFIT OF CONTRIBUTIONS PAID UNDER CERTAIN PROVISIONS RELATING TO THE PAYMENT AND COLLECTION OF CONTRIBUTIONS

History – Heading substituted by SI 2016/1145, reg. 5(4)(a), with effect from 1 January 2017.

7(1) Subject to the provisions of paragraph (2), for the purpose of entitlement to any contributory benefit except a contribution-based jobseeker's allowance or a contributory employment and support allowance, where–

(a) a person pays a Class 2 contribution under section 11(2) or (6) of the Act, or a Class 3 contribution in accordance with regulation 89, 89A, 90 or 148C of the Contributions Regulations (provisions relating to the method of, and time for, payment of Class 2 and Class 3 contributions etc.); and

(b) the due date for payment of that contribution is a date after the relevant day,

that contribution is treated as paid by the relevant day.

7(2) Where, in respect of any part of a late notification period, a person pays a Class 2 contribution which he is liable or entitled to pay, that contribution shall be treated as paid after the due date, whether or not it was paid by the due date.

7(3) For the purposes of this regulation–

(a) **"late notification period"** means the period beginning with the day a person liable or entitled to pay a Class 2 contribution was first required to notify the Inland Revenue in accordance with the provisions of regulation 87, 87A or 87AA of the Contributions Regulations (notification of commencement or cessation of payment of Class 2 or Class 3 contributions) and ending on the day on which he gives that notification;

(b) **"relevant day"** means the first day in respect of which a person would have been entitled to receive the contributory benefit in question if any contribution condition relevant to that benefit had already been satisfied;

(c) [omitted by SI 2016/1145, reg. 5(4)(e).]

History – Reg. 7(1) substituted by SI 2016/1145, reg. 5(4)(b), with effect from 1 January 2017. Former reg. 7(1) read as follows:

"**(1)** Subject to the provisions of paragraph (2) below, for the purpose of entitlement to any contributory benefit, where–

(a) a person pays a Class 2 or Class 3 contribution in accordance with regulation 54 of the Contributions Regulations (method of, and time for, payment of Class 2 and Class 3 contributions etc.); and

(b) the due date for payment of that contribution is a date after the relevant day,

that contribution shall be treated as paid by the relevant day.".

In reg. 7(2), the words "or entitled" inserted by SI 2016/1145, reg. 5(4)(c), with effect from 1 January 2017.

In reg. 7(3)(a), the words "or entitled" inserted, the words "87, 87A or 87AA" substituted for "53A", and the words "day on" substituted for the words "last day of the contribution quarter immediately before the contribution quarter in" by SI 2016/1145, reg. 5(4)(d), with effect from 1 January 2017.

Reg. 7(3)(c) omitted by SI 2016/1145, reg. 5(4)(e), with effect from 1 January 2017. Former reg. 7(3)(c) read as follows:

"(c) **"contribution quarter"** means one of the four periods of not less than 13 contribution weeks commencing on the first day of the first, fourteenth, twenty-seventh or fortieth contribution week, in any year.".

TREATMENT FOR THE PURPOSE OF A CONTRIBUTION-BASED JOBSEEKER'S ALLOWANCE OR A CONTRIBUTORY EMPLOYMENT AND SUPPORT ALLOWANCE OF CLASS 2 CONTRIBUTIONS PAID IN ACCORDANCE WITH THE ACT

7A(1) For the purpose of entitlement to a contribution-based jobseeker's allowance or a contributory employment and support allowance, a Class 2 contribution is to be treated as paid as set out in paragraph (2) if the contribution is paid–

(a) in relation to–

(i) a contribution-based jobseeker's allowance, on or after the first day of the week for which the jobseeker's allowance is claimed; or

(ii) a contributory employment and support allowance, on or after the first day of the relevant benefit week; and

(b) by the due date.

7A(2) The contribution is treated as paid–

(a) in relation to a contribution-based jobseeker's allowance, before the week for which the jobseeker's allowance is claimed; or

(b) in relation to a contributory employment and support allowance, before the relevant benefit week.

"Relevant benefit week" has the meaning given in paragraph 5 of Schedule 1 to the Welfare Reform Act.

History – Reg. 7A inserted by SI 2016/1145, reg. 5(5), with effect from 1 January 2017.

TREATMENT FOR THE PURPOSE OF ANY CONTRIBUTORY BENEFIT OF CONTRIBUTIONS PAID UNDER AN ARRANGEMENT

8 For the purposes of regulations 4 to 7A above and regulation 61 of the Contributions Regulations (voluntary Class 2 contributions not paid within permitted period)–

(a) where a contribution is paid under an arrangement to which regulations 68 and 84 or, as the case may be, regulation 90 of the Contributions Regulations (other methods of collection and recovery of earnings-related contributions; special provisions relating to primary Class 1 contributions and arrangements approved by the Inland Revenue for method of, and time for, payment of Class 2 and Class 3 contributions respectively) apply, the date by which, but for the said regulations 4 to 7A and 61, the contribution would have fallen due to be paid shall, in relation to that contribution, be the due date;

(b) any payment made of, or as on account of, a contribution in accordance with any such arrangement shall, on and after the due date, be treated as a contribution paid on the due date.

History – In reg. 8, "7A" substituted for "7" (in both places); "61" substituted for "40 " (in both places); "68 and 84" substituted for "46A and 48", and "90" substituted for "54A" by SI 2016/1145, reg. 5(6), with effect from 1 January 2017.

APPLICATION FOR ALLOCATION OF NATIONAL INSURANCE NUMBER

9(1) Subject to the provisions of paragraphs (2) and (2A) below, every person, who is over the age of 16 and satisfies the conditions specified in regulation 87 or 119 of the Contributions Regulations (conditions of domicile or residence and conditions as to residence or presence in Great Britain respectively), shall, unless he has already been allocated a national insurance number under the Act, the Social Security Act 1975 or the National Insurance Act 1965, apply either to the Secretary of State or to the Inland Revenue for the allocation of a national insurance number and shall make such application at such time and in such manner as the Secretary of State shall direct.

9(1A) An application under paragraph (1) shall be accompanied by a document of a description specified in Schedule 1.

9(2) As respects any person who is neither an employed earner nor a self-employed earner the provisions of paragraph (1) above shall not apply unless and until that person wishes to pay a Class 3 contribution.

9(2A) The provisions of paragraph (1) shall not apply to a person in respect of whom the Secretary of State or the Commissioners for Her Majesty's Revenue and Customs are notified that a biometric immigration document is to be issued pursuant to regulation 13 or 13A of the Immigration (Biometric Registration) Regulations 2008.

9(3) The Secretary of State may authorise arrangements for the allocation of a national insurance number to any person during the 12 months before that person reaches the age of 16, and in particular may direct that a person who will attain the age of 16 within 12 months after such direction shall apply for the allocation of a national insurance number before attaining the age of 16, and any such person shall accordingly comply with such direction.

9(4) Where a person–

(a) qualifies for a loan made in accordance with regulations made under section 22 of the Teaching and Higher Education Act 1998 (new arrangements for giving financial support to students) or sections 73 to 74(1) of the Education (Scotland) Act 1980 in connection with an academic year beginning on or after 1st September 2007; and

(b) has been required as a condition of entitlement to payment of the loan to provide his national insurance number,

he shall, unless he has already been allocated a national insurance number, apply to the Secretary of State or the Commissioners for Her Majesty's Revenue and Customs for one to be allocated to him, and the Secretary of State or, as the case may be, the Commissioners may direct how the application is to be made.

History – In reg. 9(1), the words "paragraphs (2) and (2A)" substituted for "paragraph (2)" by SI 2015/67, reg. 5(a), with effect from 23 February 2015.
In reg. 9(1A), the words "in Schedule 1" substituted by SI 2008/223, with effect from 29 February 2008.
Reg. 9(1A) inserted by SI 2006/2897, reg. 2(a), with effect from 11 December 2006.
In reg. 9(2A), the words "or 13A" inserted by SI 2015/1828, reg. 2, with effect from 30 November 2015.
Reg. 9(2A) inserted by SI 2015/67, reg. 5(b), with effect from 23 February 2015.
Reg. 9(4) inserted by SI 2006/2897, reg. 2(b), with effect from 1 March 2007.

DEDUCTION OF CONTRIBUTION FROM PENSIONS ETC. – PRESCRIBED ENACTMENTS AND INSTRUMENTS UNDER WHICH PAYABLE

10 For the purposes of paragraph 10 of Schedule 1 to the Act (power to deduct contributions from a pension or allowance payable by the Secretary of State by virtue of any prescribed enactment or instrument), the enactments and instruments are–

(a) Order in Council 19th December 1881;
(b) The Royal Warrant 27th October 1884;
(c) The Naval and Military War Pensions Act 1915;
(d) The War Pensions Act 1920;
(e) The War Pensions Act 1921;
(f) Order by His Majesty 14th January 1922;
(g) The War Pensions (Coastguards) Scheme 1944;
(h) The Royal Warrant 1964;
(i) The Order by Her Majesty 1964;
(j) The War Pensions (Naval Auxiliary Personnel) Scheme 1964;
(k) The Pensions (Polish Forces) Scheme 1964;
(l) The War Pensions (Mercantile Marine) Scheme 1964;
(m) The Order by Her Majesty (Ulster Defence Regiment) 1971;
(n) The Personal Injuries (Civilians) Scheme 1983;
(o) The Naval, Military and Air Forces Etc. (Disablement and Death) Service Pensions Order 1983.

CONSEQUENTIAL AMENDMENTS TO THE CONTRIBUTIONS REGULATIONS

11 [Revoked by SI 2001/1004, reg. 157(1), Sch. 8, Pt. I.]

History – Reg. 11 revoked by SI 2001/1004, reg. 157(1), Sch. 8, Pt. I, with effect from 6 April 2001.

REVOCATIONS

12 The regulations set out in column (1) of Schedule 2 to these Regulations are hereby revoked to the extent mentioned in column (3) of that Schedule.

History – In reg. 12, the words "Schedule 2" substituted by SI 2008/223, reg. 2(4), with effect from 29 February 2008.

SCHEDULE 1

Regulation 9(1A)

DOCUMENTS TO ACCOMPANY AN APPLICATION FOR A NATIONAL INSURANCE NUMBER

1 Any document specified for the time being in paragraphs 1 to 6 of List A of the Schedule to the Immigration (Restrictions on Employment) Order 2007.

2 Any document specified for the time being in paragraphs 1 to 6 of List B of the Schedule to the Immigration (Restrictions on Employment) Order 2007.

3 Any of the following documents–

(a) a full birth certificate issued in the United Kingdom which includes the name(s) of at least one of the holder's parents;
(b) a full adoption certificate issued in the United Kingdom which includes the name(s) of at least one of the holder's adoptive parents;
(c) a birth certificate issued in the Channel Islands, the Isle of Man or Ireland;
(d) an adoption certificate issued in the Channel Islands, the Isle of Man or Ireland;
(e) a certificate of registration or naturalisation as a British Citizen;
(f) an Immigration Status Document issued by the Home Office or the Border and Immigration Agency to the holder with an endorsement indicating that the person named in it is allowed to stay indefinitely in the United Kingdom or has no time limit on their stay in the United Kingdom;
(g) a letter issued by the Home Office or the Border and Immigration Agency to the holder which indicates that the person named in it is allowed to stay indefinitely in the United Kingdom;
(h) an Immigration Status Document issued by the Home Office or the Border and Immigration Agency to the holder with an endorsement indicating that the person named in it can stay in the United Kingdom, and is allowed to do the type of work in question;
(i) a letter issued by the Home Office or the Border and Immigration Agency to the holder or the employer or prospective employer, which indicates that the person named in it can stay in the United Kingdom and is allowed to do the work in question.

History – Schedule 1 inserted by SI 2008/223, reg. 2(5), with effect from 29 February 2008.

SCHEDULE 2 – REGULATIONS REVOKED

Regulation 12

History – Schedule renumbered as "Schedule 2" by SI 2008/223, reg. 2(3), with effect from 29 February 2008.

Column (1)	*Column (2)*	*Column (3)*
Citation	*Statutory Instrument*	*Extent of Revocation*
The Social Security (Contributions) Regulations 1979	SI 1979/591	Regulations 30, 36, 38, 38A, 41, 41A, 42, 44 and 55
The Social Security (Contributions) Amendment Regulations 1980	SI 1980/1975	Regulation 4
The Social Security (Contributions) Amendment Regulations 1984	SI 1984/77	Regulation 13
The Social Security (Contributions) Amendment (No. 2) Regulations 1987	SI 1987/413	Regulations 8 and 9
The Social Security (Contributions) Amendment (No. 5) Regulations 1992	SI 1992/669	Regulations 2 and 4
The Social Security (Contributions) Amendment (No. 6) Regulations 1993	SI 1993/2094	Regulations 3, 4 and 5
The Social Security (Contributions) Amendment (No. 2) Regulations 1994	SI 1994/1553	Regulation 3
The Social Security (Incapacity Benefit) (Consequential and Transitional Amendments and Savings) Regulations 1995	SI 1995/829	Regulation 13(4)
The Social Security (Credits and Contributions) (Jobseeker's Allowance Consequential and Miscellaneous Amendments) Regulations 1996	SI 1996/2367	Regulation 3(4)
The Social Security (Contributions, Statutory Maternity Pay and Statutory Sick (Miscellaneous Amendments) Regulations 1999	SI 1999/567	Regulation 7
The Social Security (Contributions and Credits (Miscellaneous Amendments) Regulations 1999	SI 1999/568	Regulation 13
The Social Security (Contributions) (Amendment No. 8) Regulations 2000	SI 2000/2207	Regulation 6

SOCIAL SECURITY (CONTRIBUTIONS) REGULATIONS 2001

(SI 2001/1004, as variously amended)

Made on 15 March 2001.

Notes – Unamended references to income tax legislation repealed and re-enacted by ITEPA 2003 refer to the rewritten equivalents: ITEPA 2003, Sch. 7, para. 1–7.

ARRANGEMENT OF REGULATIONS

REGULATION

PART 7A – ELECTRONIC COMMUNICATIONS

PART 8 – CLASS 4 CONTRIBUTIONS

SCHEDULES

SCHEDULE

PART 1 – GENERAL

CITATION, COMMENCEMENT AND INTERPRETATION

1(1) These Regulations may be cited as the Social Security (Contributions) Regulations 2001 and shall come into force on 6th April 2001 immediately after–

(a) the Social Security (Contributions) (Amendment No. 2) Regulations 2001;

(b) the Social Security (Contributions) (Amendment No. 2) (Northern Ireland) Regulations 2001;

(c) the Social Security (Contributions) (Amendment No. 3) Regulations 2001;

(d) the Social Security (Contributions) (Amendment No. 3) (Northern Ireland) Regulations 2001;

(e) the Social Security (Crediting and Treatment of Contributions, and National Insurance Numbers) Regulations 2001); and

(f) the Social Security (Crediting and Treatment of Contributions, and National Insurance Numbers) Regulations (Northern Ireland) 2001.

1(2) In these Regulations, unless the context otherwise requires–

"the acquired gender" has the same meaning as it has in the Gender Recognition Act 2004;

"the Act" means the Social Security Contributions and Benefits Act 1992;

"the Administration Act" means the Social Security Administration Act 1992;

"aggregation" means the aggregating and treating as a single payment under paragraph 1(1) of Schedule 1 to the Act (Class 1 contributions; more than one employment) of two or more payments or earnings and **"aggregated"** shall be construed accordingly;

"apportionment" means the apportioning under paragraph 1(7) of Schedule 1 to the Act to one or more employers of a single payment of earnings made to or for the benefit of an employed earner in respect of two or more employments, or, as the case may be, the apportioning under paragraph 1(8) of that Schedule of contribution liability between two or more employers in respect of earnings which have been aggregated under paragraph 1(1)(b) of that Schedule, and in either case **"apportioning"** and **"apportioned"** shall be construed accordingly;

"approved method of electronic communications" in relation to the delivery of information or the making of a payment in accordance with a provision of these Regulations, means a method of electronic communications which has been approved, by specific or general directions issued by the Board, for the delivery of information of that kind or the making of a payment of that kind under that provision;

"the Board" means the Commissioners of Inland Revenue, and subject to section 4A of the Inland Revenue Regulation Act 1890, includes any officer or servant of theirs;

"business travel" has the meaning given in section 236(1) of ITEPA 2003 and includes journeys which are treated as business travel by section 235A of ITEPA 2003 (journeys made by members of local authorities etc);

"cash voucher" has the meaning given to it in section 75 of ITEPA 2003;

"company" means a company within the meaning of section 1 of the Companies Act 2006 or a body corporate to which, by virtue of regulations made under section 1043 of that Act, any provision of that Act applies;

"conditional interest in shares" means an interest which is conditional for the purposes of Chapter 2 of Part 7 of ITEPA 2003 as originally enacted;

"contribution week" means a period of seven days beginning with midnight between Saturday and Sunday;

"contribution year" *shall* be construed in accordance with section 12(1) or (as the case requires) section 13(5) of the Act (late paid Class 2 or Class 3 contributions);

"contribution-based jobseeker's allowance" means an allowance under the Jobseekers Act 1995 as amended by the provisions of Part 1 of Schedule 14 to the Welfare Reform Act 2012 that removes references to an income-based allowance, and a contribution-based allowance under the Jobseekers Act 1995 as that Act has effect apart from those provisions;

"contributory benefit" includes a contribution-based jobseeker's allowance but not an income-based jobseeker's allowance;

"director" means–

(a) in relation to a company whose affairs are managed by a board of directors or similar body, a member of that board or similar body;

(b) in relation to a company whose affairs are managed by a single director or similar person that director or person; and

(c) any person in accordance with whose directions or instructions the company's directors as defined in paragraphs (a) and (b) above are accustomed to act, and for this purpose a person is not to be treated as such a person by reason only that the directors act on advice given by him in his professional capacity;

"due date" in Part 6 means, in relation to–

(a) any Class 1 contribution, the date by which payment falls to be made;

(b) any Class 2 contribution which a person is liable or entitled to pay, the 31st January following the end of the tax year in respect of which it is paid or payable; and

(c) any Class 3 contribution, the date 42 days after the end of the year in respect of which it is paid.

"earnings period" means the period referred to in regulation 2;

"earnings-related contributions" means contributions payable under the Act in respect of earnings paid to or for the benefit of an earner in respect of employed earner's employment;

"employment and support allowance" has the same meaning as in the Welfare Reform Act 2007;

"electronic communications" includes any communications conveyed by means of an electronic communications network;

"full gender recognition certificate" means a certificate issued under section 4 of the Gender Recognition Act 2004;

"HMRC" means Her Majesty's Revenue and Customs;

"an income-based jobseeker's allowance" has the same meaning as in the Jobseekers Act 1995;

"national insurance number" means the national insurance number allocated within the meaning of regulation 9 of the Social Security (Crediting and Treatment of Contributions, and National Insurance Numbers) Regulations 2001;

"non-cash voucher" has the meaning given to it in section 84 of ITEPA 2003;

"official computer system" means a computer system maintained by or on behalf of the Board;

"optional remuneration arrangements" has the meaning given in section 69A of ITEPA 2003;

"the PAYE regulations" means the Income Tax (Pay As You Earn) Regulations 2003;

"profits or gains" for the purposes of Part 8 means profits or gains which, subject to the provisions of Schedule 2 to the Act, are chargeable to income tax under Case I or Case II of Schedule D;

"readily convertible asset" has the meaning given in section 702 of ITEPA 2003 as amended by the Finance Act 2003;

"regular interval" for the purposes of regulations 3, 4 and 7 includes only such interval as is in accordance with an express or implied arrangement between the employed earner and the secondary contributor as to the intervals at which payments of earnings normally fall to be made, being intervals of substantially equal length;

"registered pension scheme" has the meaning given in section 150(2) of the Finance Act 2004;

"relevant employment income" has the meaning given in paragraph 3B(1A) of Schedule 1 to the Act;

"restricted securities" and **"restricted interest in securities"** have the meanings given in sections 423 and 424 of ITEPA 2003 as substituted by the Finance Act 2003;

"retirement benefits scheme" has the meaning given in section 611 of the Taxes Act;

"retrospective contributions regulations" means regulations made by virtue of section 4B(2) of the Act and, in relation to an amount of retrospective earnings, **"the relevant retrospective contributions regulations"** means the regulations which treat that amount as earnings;

"retrospective earnings" means an amount retrospectively treated as earnings by retrospective contributions regulations;

"retrospective contributions", in relation to an amount of retrospective earnings, means the amount of earnings-related contributions based on those earnings which the employee is liable to pay under section 6(4)(a) of the Act (primary contributions);

"secondary contributor" means the person who, in respect of earnings from employed earner's employment, is liable to pay a secondary Class 1 contribution under section 6(4)(b) of the Act (liability for Class 1 contributions);

"securities" and **"securities option"** have the meaning given by section 420 of ITEPA 2003 as substituted by the Finance Act 2003;

"serving member of the forces" means a person, other than one mentioned in Part 2 of Schedule 6, who, being over the age of 16, is a member of any establishment or organisation specified in Part I of that Schedule (being a member who gives full pay service) but does not include any such person while absent on desertion;

"the Taxes Act" means the Income and Corporation Taxes Act 1988;

"tax month" has the meaning given in paragraph 1(2) of Schedule 4;

"training" means full-time training at a course approved by the Board;

"the Transfer Act" means the Social Security Contributions (Transfer of Functions, etc.) Act 1999;

"tribunal" means the First-tier tribunal or, where determined by or under Tribunal Procedure Rules, the Upper Tribunal;

"week" means tax week, except in relation to Case C of Part 9, where **"week"** and **"weekly"** have the meanings given in regulation 115;

"the Welfare Reform Act" means the Welfare Reform and Pensions Act 1999;

"year" means tax year;

"year of assessment" has the meaning given to it in section 832(1)of the Taxes Act.

1(3) For the purposes of regulations 52, 57, 67, and 116, references to **"contributions"**, **"Class 1 contributions"** and **"earnings-related contributions"** shall, unless the context otherwise requires, include any amount paid on account of earnings-related contributions in accordance with regulation 8(6).

1(3A) In these Regulations, references to–

(a) Schedule 24 to the Finance Act 2007 (penalties for errors); and

(b) Schedule 55 to the Finance Act 2009 (penalties for failure to make a return)

include references to these Schedules as amended by paragraphs 3 and 5 of Schedule 33 to the Finance Act 2014 (Part 4: Consequential Amendments).

1(4) Where, by any provision of these Regulations–

(a) any notice or other document is required to be given or sent to the Board, that notice or document shall be treated as having been given or sent on the day that it is received by the Board; and

(b) any notice or other document is required to be given or sent by the Board to any person, that notice or document shall, if sent by post to that person's last known address, be treated as having been given or sent on the day that it was posted.

1(5) Unless the context otherwise requires–

(a) any reference in these Regulations to a numbered regulation is a reference to the regulation bearing that number in these Regulations;

(b) any reference in these Regulations to a numbered Part or Schedule is to the Part of, or Schedule to, these Regulations bearing that number;

(c) any reference in a regulation or a Schedule to a numbered paragraph is a reference to the paragraph bearing that number in that regulation or Schedule;

(d) any reference in paragraph of a regulation or a Schedule to a numbered or lettered sub-paragraph is a reference to the sub-paragraph bearing that number or letter in that paragraph; and

(e) any reference in a sub-paragraph to a numbered head is a reference to the head in that sub-paragraph bearing that number.

History – In reg. 1(2):

- definition of "the acquired gender" inserted by SI 2005/778, reg. 3, with effect from 6 April 2005.
- definition of "approved method of electronic communications" inserted and the definition of "business travel" substituted by SI 2004/770, reg. 3, with effect from 6 April 2004.
- in the definition of "business travel", the words *"and includes journeys which are treated as business travel by section 235A of ITEPA 2003 (journeys made by members of local authorities etc)."* inserted by SI 2016/352, reg. 3, with effect from 6 April 2016.
- former definition of "business travel" inserted by SI 2002/307, reg. 3 (repealed by SI 2004/770, Sch. from 6 April 2004), operative from 6 April 2002.
- definition of "cash voucher" substituted by SI 2004/770, reg. 3, with effect from 6 April 2004.
- definition of "the Commissioner" omitted by SI 2008/2683, art. 6 and Sch. 1, para. 164(a), with effect from 3 November 2008.
- definition of "the Commissioner" inserted by SI 2007/2520, reg. 3(2), with effect from 1 October 2007.

- in the definition of "company", "1" substituted for "735", "2006" substituted for "1985", and the words "that Act" substituted for the words "the Companies Act 2006" and "those Acts" by SI 2009/1890, art. 3(9), with effect from 1 October 2009.
- in the definition of "company" the words "regulations made under section 1043 of the Companies Act 2006, any provision of those Acts" substituted by SI 2008/954, art. 50 with effect from 6 April 2008.
- definition of "COMPS employment" omitted by SI 2012/817, reg. 3(a), with effect from 6 April 2012, subject to savings provisions in relation to obligations arising in connection with tax years beginning prior to 6 April 2012 (the operation of SI 2001/1004 is unaffected by the amendments made by SI 2012/817, reg. 3 to 6, and the reference to s. 9(3) of the Pensions Act in the former definition of "COMPS employment" in SI 2001/1004, reg. 1(2), is to be read as though that section were still in force). Former definition of "COMPS employment" read as follows:
  "**"COMPS employment"** means employment in respect of which minimum payments are made to a money purchase pension scheme contracted out under section 9(3) of the Pensions Act;".
- in the definition of "conditional interest in shares" the words "Chapter 2 of Part 7 of ITEPA 2003 as originally enacted;" substituted by SI 2004/770, reg. 3, with effect from 6 April 2004.
- definitions of "contracted-out employment" and "contracted-out rate"omitted by SI 2016/352, reg. 8, with effect from 6 April 2016, subject to savings in relation to rights or obligations arising in connection with tax years beginning before 6 April 2016 (and for savings purposes, references to repealed provisions of the Pension Schemes Act 1993 are to be read as though such provisions were still in force). Former definitions read as follows:

  "**"contracted-out employment"** has the same meaning as in section 8(1) of the Pensions Act;

  "contracted-out rate" means, in relation to Class 1 contributions payable in respect of earnings paid to or for the benefit of an earner who is in–

  (a) COSRS employment, the reduced amount for the time being applying in accordance with section 41(1) to (1B) of the Pensions Act (which specifies the percentage reduction of primary and secondary Class 1 contribution in respect of that part of an employed earner's earnings which exceed the current lower earnings limit, but not the current upper accrual point, in respect of members of a COSRS);

  (b) [omitted by SI 2012/817, reg. 3(b)(ii).]".
- in the definition of "contracted-out rate", the words "upper accrual point" substituted for the words "upper earnings limits" by SI 2012/817, reg. 3(b)(i), with effect from 6 April 2012, subject to savings provisions in relation to obligations arising in connection with tax years beginning prior to 6 April 2012 (the operation of SI 2001/1004 is unaffected by the amendments made by SI 2012/817, reg. 3–6, and the reference to s. 9(3) of the Pensions Act in the former definition of "COMPS employment" in SI 2001/1004, reg. 1(2), is to be read as though that section were still in force).
- in the definition of "contracted-out rate", para. (b) omitted by SI 2012/817, reg. 3(b)(ii), with effect from 6 April 2012, subject to savings provisions in relation to obligations arising in connection with tax years beginning prior to 6 April 2012 (the operation of SI 2001/1004 is unaffected by the amendments made by SI 2012/817, reg. 3–6 and the reference to s. 9(3) of the Pensions Act in the former definition of "COMPS employment" in SI 2001/1004, reg. 1(2), is to be read as though that section were still in force).
- definition of "contribution-based jobseeker's allowance" substituted by SI 2013/630, reg. 72(2), with effect from 29 April 2013.
- definition of "convertible shares" omitted by SI 2003/2085, reg. 4, with effect from 1 September 2003.
- definition of "COSRS employment" omitted by SI 2016/352, reg. 8, with effect from 6 April 2016, subject to savings in relation to rights or obligations arising in connection with tax years beginning before 6 April 2016 (and for savings purposes, references to repealed provisions of the Pension Schemes Act 1993 are to be read as though such provisions were still in force). Former definition read as follows:
  "**"COSRS employment"** means employment which qualifies an earner for a pension provided by a salary related scheme contracted out under section 9(2) of the Pensions Act;".
- definition of "due date" substituted by SI 2015/478, reg. 3(2), with effect from 6 April 2015.
- definition of "electronic communications" substituted by SI 2003/2155, art. 3(1) and Sch. 1, Pt. 5, para. 23(1)(d), (2), with effect from 17 September 2003.
- definition of "employment and support allowance" inserted by SI 2015/478, reg. 3(3), with effect from 6 April 2015.
- definition of "full gender recognition certificate" inserted by SI 2005/778, reg. 3, with effect from 6 April 2005.
- definition of "HMRC" inserted by SI 2009/600, reg. 3, with effect from 1 April 2009.
- definition of "income tax month" omitted by SI 2004/770, reg. 3 and Schedule, with effect from 6 April 2004.
- definition of "month" omitted by SI 2004/770, reg. 3 and Schedule, with effect from 6 April 2004.
- definitions of "non-contracted-out employment" and "non-contracted out rate" omitted by SI 2016/352, reg. 8, with effect from 6 April 2016, subject to savings in relation to rights or obligations arising in connection with tax years beginning before 6 April 2016 (and for savings purposes, references to repealed provisions of the Pension Schemes Act 1993 are to be read as though such provisions were still in force). Former definitions read as follows:

  "**"non-contracted-out employment"** means employed earner's employment which is not contracted-out employment;

  "non-contracted-out rate" means, in relation to Class 1 contributions payable in respect of earnings paid to or for the benefit of an earner in non-contracted-out employment, the main primary percentage for the time being specified in section 8(2)(a) of the Act;".
- in the definition of "non-contracted out rate", words "the main primary percentage for the time being specified in section 8(2)(a) of the Act" substituted by SI 2003/193, reg. 3 with effect from 6 April 2003.
- definition of "normal rate" omitted by SI 2016/352, reg. 8, with effect from 6 April 2016, with effect from 6 April 2016, subject to savings in relation to rights or obligations arising in connection with tax years beginning before 6 April 2016 (and for savings purposes, references to repealed provisions of the Pension Schemes Act 1993 are to be read as though such provisions were still in force). Former definition read as follows:

  "**"normal rate"** means the amount of a Class 1 contribution which would be payable in respect of earnings paid to or for the benefit of an employed earner in any week if the employment were not contracted-out employment;".
- definition of "normal rate" omitted and then inserted after "non-contracted out rate" by SI 2007/1056, reg. 4(b), with effect from 6 April 2007.
- definition of "official computer system" inserted by SI 2004/770, reg. 3, with effect from 6 April 2004.
- definition of "official error" omitted by SI 2015/478, reg. 24(1)(a), with effect from 6 April 2015.
- definition of "optional remuneration arrangements" inserted by SI 2018/120, reg. 3, with effect from 6 April 2018.
- in the former definition of "official error", "the Upper Tribunal" substituted for "a Commissioner" by SI 2008/2683, art. 6 and Sch. 1, para. 164(b), with effect from 3 November 2008.
- former definition of "official error" inserted by SI 2007/2520, reg. 3(3), with effect from 1 October 2007.
- definition of "the PAYE regulations" inserted by SI 2004/770, reg. 3, with effect from 6 April 2004.
- definition of "the Pensions Act" omitted by SI 2016/352, reg. 8, with effect from 6 April 2016, subject to savings in relation to rights or obligations arising in connection with tax years beginning before 6 April 2016 (and for savings purposes, references to repealed provisions of the Pension Schemes Act 1993 are to be read as though such provisions were still in force). Former definition read as follows:
- in the definition of "readily convertible asset" the words from "section 702" to the end substituted by SI 2003/2085, reg. 4, with effect from 1 September 2003.
- definition of "registered pension scheme" inserted by SI 2006/576, reg. 3, with effect from 6 April 2006.

- definition of "relevant employment income" inserted by SI 2004/2096, reg. 3, with effect in relation to–
  - agreements entered into after 1 September 2004 which are in respect of post-commencement employment income (presumably as defined in NICSPA 2004, s. 3(5)), and
  - elections made after that date.
- definition of "restricted securities" inserted by SI 2003/2085, reg. 4, with effect from 1 September 2003.
- definition of "restricted interest in securities" inserted by SI 2003/2085, reg. 4, with effect from 1 September 2003.
- definition of "retrospective contributions regulations" inserted by SI 2007/1056, reg. 4(a), with effect from 6 April 2007.
- definition of "retrospective earnings" inserted by SI 2007/1056, reg. 4(a), with effect from 6 April 2007.
- definition of "retrospective contributions" inserted by SI 2007/1056, reg. 4(a), with effect from 6 April 2007.
- definition of "securities" inserted by SI 2003/2085, reg. 4, with effect from 1 September 2003.
- definition of "securities option" inserted by SI 2003/2085, reg. 4, with effect from 1 September 2003.
- definition of "service provider" omitted by SI 2015/478, reg. 24(1)(a), with effect from 6 April 2015.
- former definition of "service provider" inserted by SI 2007/2520, reg. 3(4), with effect from 1 October 2007.
- definition of "tax month" inserted by SI 2004/770, reg. 3, with effect from 6 April 2004.
- definition of "tribunal" inserted by SI 2009/600, reg. 3, with effect from 1 April 2009.

Reg. 1(3A) inserted by SI 2015/521, reg. 3, with effect from 12 April 2015.

Derivations – Reg. 1(2): SI 1979/591, reg. 1(2).

Cross references – HMRC Direction of 4 April 2011 made under reg. 1(2).

PART 2 – ASSESSMENT OF EARNINGS RELATED CONTRIBUTIONS

EARNINGS PERIODS

2 Except where regulation 8 applies, the amount, if any, of earnings-related contributions payable or, where section 6A of the Act applies, treated as having been paid, in respect of earnings paid to or for the benefit of an earner in respect of an employed earner's employment shall, subject to regulations 7 and 12 to 19, be assessed on the amount of such earnings paid, or treated as paid, in the earnings period specified in regulation 3, 4, 5, 6 or 9.

Derivations – SI 1979/591, reg. 2.

EARNINGS PERIOD FOR EARNINGS NORMALLY PAID OR TREATED AS PAID AT REGULAR INTERVALS

3(1) If any part of earnings paid to or for the benefit of an earner is normally paid, or is treated under regulation 7 as paid, at regular intervals, the earnings period in respect of those earnings shall be the period found in accordance with the following Table, subject to paragraphs (2) to (6).

Earnings Periods

Case	*Applicable earnings period*
Earnings paid at an interval of 7 days or more.	The length of the interval.
Earnings paid at intervals of different lengths, each of which is 7 days or more.	The length of the shorter or shortest of those intervals.
Earnings paid at one or more intervals of less than 7 days.	A week.
Earnings paid at one or more intervals of less than 7 days and at one or more intervals of more than 7 days.	A week.

3(2) In any year, the earnings period for the earnings mentioned in paragraph (1) shall only be that found by the Table in that paragraph if the period in which the earnings are paid is one of a succession of periods and–

(a) the periods are the same length;

(b) the first period begins on the first day of the year; and

(c) the subsequent periods begin immediately after the end of the preceding period.

For the purpose of this paragraph, if all the periods in the succession mentioned above, apart from the last in the year in question, are the same length, the last period in the year shall be treated as if it were the same length as the others.

This paragraph is subject to the following qualification.

3(2A) Paragraph (2B) applies if it appears to an officer of the Board that–

(a) it is the employer's practice to pay the greater part of the earnings referred to in paragraph (2) at intervals of greater length than the shorter or shortest of the earnings periods produced by the application of that paragraph; and

(b) that practice is likely to continue.

3(2B) If this paragraph applies the officer may, and if requested to do so by the earner or the secondary contributor shall, decide whether to give a notice to the earner and the secondary contributor specifying the longer or longest of the earnings periods produced by the application of paragraph (2) to be the earnings period applicable to those earnings.

3(2C) A notice under paragraph (2B) shall–

(a) be given to both the earner and the secondary contributor; and

(b) specify the date from which the change of earnings period is to take effect.

The date specified shall not be earlier than that on which the notice is given.

3(2D) A notice given under paragraph (2B) shall have effect until an officer of the Board decides (either of his own motion or on an application by the earner or the secondary contributor) that the practice to which it relates has ceased.

If an officer of the Board decides that a notice is to cease to have effect, he shall notify the earner and the secondary contributor accordingly.

3(3) If the length of the earnings period determined in accordance with paragraph (2B) is a year, then notwithstanding paragraph (2), where the change in the length of the earnings period takes effect during the course of a year, the length of the earnings period in respect of any earnings in that year which are paid or treated as paid on or after the change shall be the number of weeks remaining in that year commencing with the week in which the change takes effect.

3(4) [Repealed by SI 2002/2366, reg. 4(4).]

3(5) Where–

(a) the employment in respect of which the earnings are paid has ended;

(b) the employment in respect of which the earnings are paid was one in which, during its continuance, earnings were paid or treated under regulation 7 as paid at a regular interval; and

(c) after the end of the employment, a payment of earnings is made which satisfies either or both of the conditions specified in paragraph (6),

the earnings period in respect of such payment of earnings shall, notwithstanding regulation 7, be the week in which the payment is made.

3(6) The conditions referred to in paragraph (5) are that the payment is–

(a) by way of addition to a payment made before the end of the employment; and

(b) not in respect of a regular interval.

History – Reg. 3(1), (2), (2A)–(2D) substituted for reg. 3(1), (2) by SI 2002/2366, reg. 4(2), with effect from 8 October 2002. In reg. 3(3) words "paragraph (2B)" and words "paragraph (2)" substituted by SI 2002/2366, reg. 4(3), with effect from 8 October 2002. Reg. 3(4) repealed by SI 2002/2366, reg. 4(4), with effect from 8 October 2002.

Derivations – SI 1979/591, reg. 3.

EARNINGS PERIOD FOR EARNINGS NORMALLY PAID OTHERWISE THAN AT REGULAR INTERVALS AND NOT TREATED AS PAID AT REGULAR INTERVALS.

4 Subject to regulation 3(5) or regulation 5, where earnings are paid to or for the benefit of an earner in respect of an employed earner's employment, but no part of those earnings is normally paid or treated under regulation 7 as paid at regular intervals, the earnings period in respect of those earnings shall be a period of one of the following lengths–

(a) the length of the period of that part of the employment for which the earnings are paid or a week, whichever is the longer; or

(b) where it is not reasonably practicable to determine that period under paragraph (a)–

(i) the length of the period from the date on which the last payment of earnings, before the payment in question, was paid during the employment in respect of the employment (or, if there has been no such payment, from the date on which the employment began) to the date of the payment in question, unless the period so calculated would be of a length less than that of a week, in which case the earnings period shall be a week, or

(ii) where the payment is made before the employment begins or after it ends, a week.

Derivations – SI 1979/591, reg. 4.

EARNINGS PERIOD FOR SUMS DEEMED TO BE EARNINGS BY VIRTUE OF REGULATIONS MADE UNDER SECTION 112 OF THE ACT

5 Where any sum or amount is deemed to be earnings by virtue of any regulations made under section 112 of the Act (sums to be earnings for the purposes of Parts I to V of the Act)–

(a) the earnings period in respect of any payment of those earnings shall be the length of the protected period (as referred to in section 189 of the Trade Union and Labour Relations (Consolidation) Act 1992) or, as the case may be, that part of it in respect of which the sum is paid, or a week whichever is the longer;

(b) contributions paid in respect of such earnings shall, if the employed earner so requests–

(i) if the period to which the payment of earnings relates falls wholly in a year other than the year in which they are paid, be treated as paid in respect of the year in which the period to which the payment of earnings relates falls, or

(ii) if the period to which the payment of earnings relates falls partly in the year in which they are paid and partly in one or more other years, be treated as paid proportionately in respect of each of the years in which the period to which the payment of earnings relates falls, or

(iii) if the period to which the payment of earnings relates falls wholly in two or more years other than the year in which they are paid, be treated as paid proportionately in respect of each of the years in which the period to which the payment of earnings relates falls.

Derivations – SI 1979/591, reg. 5.

EARNINGS PERIOD FOR EARNINGS TO BE AGGREGATED WHERE THE EARNINGS PERIODS FOR THOSE EARNINGS OTHERWISE WOULD BE OF DIFFERENT LENGTHS

6(1) Paragraphs (2) and (3) apply where–

(a) earnings paid in respect of two or more employed earner's employments fall to be aggregated; and

(b) the earnings periods in respect of those earnings are, by virtue of regulation 3, 4 or 5, of different lengths.

6(2) In a case to which this regulation applies, where (but for its provisions) the earnings period in respect of earnings derived from any of the employments is of a different length from the designated earnings period, the earnings period in respect of any payment of those earnings shall be the designated earnings period.

6(3) In this regulation **"the designated earnings period"** means the shorter, or as the case may be the shortest, of the earnings periods in respect of earnings derived from such employments.

History – Reg. 6(3) substituted by SI 2016/352, reg. 9, with effect from 6 April 2016, subject to savings in relation to rights or obligations arising in connection with tax years beginning before 6 April 2016 (and for savings purposes, references to repealed provisions of the Pension Schemes Act 1993 are to be read as though such provisions were still in force). Former reg. 6(3) read as follows:

"**6(3)** In this regulation **"the designated earnings period"** means–

(a) where the earnings are derived from employments which include any contracted-out employment and any non-contracted out employment, the earnings period in respect of earnings derived from the contracted-out employment or, if there is more than one such employment, the shorter, or as the case may be the shortest, of the earnings periods in respect of the earnings derived from such employments; and

(b) in any other case, the shorter, or as the case may be the shortest, of the earnings periods in respect of the earnings derived from such employments.

History – Reg. 6(3) substituted by SI 2012/817, reg. 4, with effect from 6 April 2012, subject to savings provisions in relation to obligations arising in connection with tax years beginning prior to 6 April 2012 (the operation of SI 2001/1004 is unaffected by the amendments made by SI 2012/817, reg. 3–6, and the reference to s. 9(3) of the Pensions Act in the former definition of "COMPS employment" in SI 2001/1004, reg. 1(2), is to be read as though that section were still in force). Former reg. 6(3) read as follows:

"**6(3)** In this regulation **"the designated earnings period"** means–

(a) where the earnings are derived from employments which include any contracted-out employment and any non-contracted-out employment and the employed earner is a person in respect of whom minimum contributions are paid by the Board in accordance with section 43 of the Pensions Act (payment of minimum contributions to personal pension schemes), the earnings period in respect of earnings which are derived from such non-contracted-out employment or, if there is more than one such employment, the shorter, or as the case may be the shortest, of the earnings periods derived from such employments; or

(b) where the earnings are derived from employments which include any contracted-out employment and any non-contracted-out employment and the employed earner is not a person in respect of whom minimum contributions are paid by the Board in accordance with section 43 of the Pensions Act, and–

(i) any of the contracted-out employments is COMPS employment, the earnings period in respect of the earnings derived from that COMPS employment or, if there is more than one such employment, the shorter, or as the case may be the shortest, of the earnings periods derived from such employments,

(ii) the contracted-out employment is COSRS employment only, the earnings period in respect of the earnings derived from that COSRS employment or, if there is more than one such employment, the shorter, or (as the case may be) the shortest, of the earnings periods derived from such employments, or

(c) where the earnings are derived from employments which are contracted-out employment only and–

(i) any of the employments is COMPS employment, the earnings period in respect of the earnings derived from that COMPS employment or, if there is more than one such employment, the shorter, or as the case may be the shortest, of the earnings periods derived from such employments,

(ii) all of those employments are COSRS employment, the shorter or shortest of the earnings periods derived from such employments, and

(d) in any other case, the shorter or shortest of the earnings periods in respect of the earnings derived from the employments.".".

Derivations – SI 1979/591, reg. 5A.

TREATMENT OF EARNINGS PAID OTHERWISE THAN AT REGULAR INTERVALS

7(1) Subject to regulation 3(5) and paragraphs (2) and (3), for the purposes of assessing earnings-related contributions–

(a) if on any occasion a payment of earnings which would normally fall to be made at a regular interval is made otherwise than at the regular interval, it shall be treated as if it were a payment made at that regular interval;

(b) if payments of earnings are made at irregular intervals which secure that one and only one payment is made in each of a succession of periods consisting of the same number of days, weeks or calendar months, those payments shall be treated as if they were payments made at the regular interval of one of those periods of days, weeks or, as the case may be, calendar months;

(c) if payments of earnings, other than those specified in sub-paragraph (b), are made in respect of regular intervals, but otherwise than at regular intervals, each such payment shall be treated as made at the regular interval in respect of which it is due.

7(2) Where under paragraph (1) a payment of earnings is treated as made at a regular interval, it shall for the purposes of assessment under these regulations of earnings-related contributions also be treated as paid–

(a) in a case falling within paragraph (1)(a), on the date on which it would normally have fallen to be made;

(b) in any other case, on the last day of the regular interval at which it is treated as paid.

7(3) Paragraphs (1) and (2) shall not apply to a payment of earnings made in one year where by virtue of those paragraphs that payment would be treated as made in another year.

7(4) Notwithstanding regulation 15, a payment to which paragraph (3) applies (**"the relevant payment"**) shall not be aggregated with any other earnings unless–

(a) other earnings to which paragraphs (1) and (2) do not apply by virtue only of paragraph (3) are paid in the earnings period in which the relevant payment falls; and

(b) those other earnings would have been aggregated with the relevant payment had paragraph (3) not applied.

7(5) A relevant payment shall be aggregated only with the other earnings specified in paragraph (4).

Derivations – SI 1979/591, reg. 6.

EARNINGS PERIODS FOR DIRECTORS

8(1) Where a person is, or is appointed, or ceases to be a director of a company during any year the amount, if any, of earnings-related contributions payable in respect of earnings paid to or for the benefit of that person in respect of any employed earner's employment with that company shall, subject to regulations 12 and 14 to 17, be assessed on the amount of all such earnings paid (whether or not paid weekly) in the earnings periods specified in paragraphs (2) to (5).

8(2) Where on one or more than one occasion a person is appointed a director of a company during the course of a year the earnings period in respect of such earnings as are paid in so much of the year as remains in the period commencing with the week in which he is appointed or, as the case may be, first appointed shall be the number of weeks in that period.

8(3) Where a person is a director of a company at the beginning of a year the earnings period in respect of such earnings shall be that year, whether or not he remains such a director throughout that year.

8(4) Where the earnings paid in respect of two or more employed earner's employments fall to be aggregated and the earnings periods in respect of those earnings would be of different lengths, then–

(a) if those periods are determined only by paragraphs (1) to (3); or

(b) if the length of one or more of those periods is determined by those paragraphs and the length of one or more of the others is determined by any other provision of these Regulations,

the earnings period in respect of all those earnings shall be the period determined by those paragraphs or, where there is more than one such period, the longer or longest period so determined.

8(5) Where a person is no longer a director of a company and, in any year after that in which he ceased to be a director of that company, he is paid earnings in respect of any period during which he was such a director, then–

(a) notwithstanding regulation 15, those earnings shall not be aggregated with any other earnings with which they would otherwise fall to be aggregated; and

(b) the earnings period in respect of those earnings shall be the year in which they are paid.

8(6) Without prejudice to paragraphs (1) to (5), a director and any company employing him may pay on account of any earnings-related contributions that may become payable by them such amounts as would be payable by way of such contributions if those paragraphs did not apply.

8(7) If a full gender recognition certificate is issued under the Gender Recognition Act 2004 to a person aged at least 60 but not more than 64–

(a) whose gender before its issue was female; and

(b) whose acquired gender is male;

the periods in the year of issue respectively falling before and after its issue shall be treated, for the purpose of computing liability for primary Class 1 contributions, as separate earnings periods.

History – Reg. 8(7) inserted by SI 2005/778, reg. 4 with effect from 6 April 2005.

Derivations – SI 1979/591, reg. 6A.

EARNINGS PERIOD FOR STATUTORY MATERNITY PAY, STATUTORY PATERNITY PAY, STATUTORY ADOPTION PAY, STATUTORY SHARED PARENTAL PAY AND STATUTORY SICK PAY PAID BY THE BOARD

History – In the heading, the words "statutory paternity pay" substituted for "ordinary and additional statutory paternity pay" by SI 2015/175, reg. 3(2)(a), with effect from 5 April 2015, subject to the transitional provisions in SI 2015/175, reg. 9 (amendments do not have effect where they relate to additional statutory paternity pay or ordinary statutory paternity pay and payments of either on or after 5 April 2015).
In reg. 9 heading, the words ", statutory shared parental pay" inserted by SI 2015/175, reg. 3(2)(b), with effect from 5 March 2015.
In the heading to reg. 9, the words "ordinary and additional statutory paternity pay," substituted for the words "statutory paternity pay," by SI 2010/2450, reg. 3(2), with effect from 14 November 2010.
Words "statutory paternity pay, statutory adoption pay" inserted into heading to reg. 9 by SI 2003/193, reg. 4(2) with effect from 6 April 2003.

9(1) In this regulation the expression **"week"**–

(a) in paragraph (2)(a); and

(b) in paragraph (2)(b) where it first occurs, has the same meaning as in section 171(1) of the Act.

9(2) If the Board make a payment of statutory maternity pay, statutory paternity pay, statutory shared parental pay or statutory adoption pay under regulations made under the relevant provision–

(a) that payment of statutory maternity pay, statutory paternity pay, statutory shared parental pay or statutory adoption pay (as the case may be) shall not be aggregated with any other earnings; and

(b) the earnings period in respect of that payment for any week shall be a week.

9(2A) In paragraph (2) **"the relevant provision"** means–

(a) in relation to statutory maternity pay, section 164(9)(b),

(b) in relation to statutory paternity pay, section 171ZD(3),

(ba) omitted by SI 2015/175, reg. 3(4)(b),

(c) in relation to statutory adoption pay, section 171ZM(3) and

(d) in relation to statutory shared parental pay, section 171ZX(3),

of the Act (liability to make payments of the relevant statutory pay to be that of the Board).

9(3) If the Board make a payment of statutory sick pay under regulations made under section 151(6) of the Act (circumstances in which the Board are liable to pay statutory sick pay), the earnings period for that payment shall be–

(a) a period of the same length as the period in respect of which the payment is made, or

(b) a week,

whichever is the longer.

History – In reg. 9(2), the words "statutory paternity pay" substituted for "ordinary statutory paternity pay, additional statutory paternity pay" (in both places) by SI 2015/175, reg. 3(3)(a), with effect from 5 April 2015, subject to the transitional provisions in SI 2015/175, reg. 9 (amendments do not have effect where they relate to additional statutory paternity pay or ordinary statutory paternity pay and payments of either on or after 5 April 2015).
In reg. 9(2), the words ", statutory shared parental pay" (in both places) inserted by SI 2015/175, reg. 3(3)(b), with effect from 5 March 2015.
In reg. 9(2) introductory words, the words "ordinary statutory paternity pay, additional statutory paternity pay" substituted for the words "statutory paternity pay" by SI 2010/2450, reg. 3(3), with effect from 14 November 2010.
In reg. 9(2)(a), the words "ordinary statutory paternity pay, additional statutory paternity pay" substituted for the words "statutory paternity pay" by SI 2010/2450, reg. 3(3), with effect from 14 November 2010.
Reg. 9(2), (2A) substituted for former reg. 9(2) by SI 2003/193, reg. 4(3) with effect from 6 April 2003.
In reg. 9(2A)(b), the word "ordinary" omitted by SI 2015/175, reg. 3(4)(a), with effect from 5 April 2015, subject to the transitional provisions in SI 2015/175, reg. 9 (amendments do not have effect where they relate to additional statutory paternity pay or ordinary statutory paternity pay and payments of either on or after 5 April 2015).
Reg. 9(2A)(ba) omitted by SI 2015/175, reg. 3(4)(b), with effect from 5 April 2015, subject to the transitional provisions in SI 2015/175, reg. 9 (amendments do not have effect where they relate to additional statutory paternity pay or ordinary statutory paternity pay and payments of either on or after 5 April 2015).
Reg. 9(2A)(b) and (ba) substituted for former reg. 9(2A)(b) by SI 2010/2450, reg. 3(4), with effect from 14 November 2010.
Reg. 9(2A)(d) (and the word "and" immediately preceding it) inserted (and the "and" at the end of (ba) omitted) by SI 2015/175, reg. 3(4), with effect from 5 March 2015.

Derivations – SI 1979/591, reg. 6B.

EARNINGS LIMITS AND THRESHOLDS

10 For the purposes of sections 5(1), 9A and 9B of the Act (earnings limits and thresholds to be specified for each tax year in respect of Class 1 contributions), for the tax year which begins on 6th April 2018–

(a) the lower earnings limit (for primary Class 1 contributions) shall be £116;

(b) the upper earnings limit (for primary Class 1 contributions) shall be £892;

(c) the primary threshold (for primary Class 1 contributions) shall be £162;

(d) the secondary threshold (for secondary Class 1 contributions) shall be £162;

(e) the upper secondary threshold for secondary Class 1 contributions in relation to the Under 21 group (for the upper limit of the age-related secondary percentage) shall be £892; and

(f) the upper secondary threshold for secondary Class 1 contributions in relation to relevant apprentices (for the upper limit of zero-rate secondary Class 1 contributions) shall be £892.

History – In reg. 10(a), the figure "£116" substituted for the figure "£113"; in (b), the figure "£892" substituted for the figure "£866"; in (c), the figure "£162" substituted for the figure "£157"; in (d), the figure "£162" substituted for the figure "£157", and in (e) and (f), the figure "£892" substituted for the figure "£866" by SI 2018/337, reg. 7, with effect from 6 April 2018.

In reg. 10(a), the figure "£113" substituted for the figure "£112"; in (b), the figure "£866" substituted for the figure "£827"; in (c), the figure "£157" substituted for the figure "£155"; in (d), the figure "£157" substituted for the figure "£156", and in (e) and (f), the figure "£866" substituted for the figure "£827" by SI 2017/415, reg. 7, with effect from 6 April 2017. Note: in what appears to be a drafting error, the year "2017" in the text before para. (a) was not substituted for the year "2016" by SI 2017/415. This amendment has been reflected on the presumption this was an error.

In reg. 10, the words ", 9A and 9B" substituted for the words "and 9A" and "2016" substituted for "2015" by SI 2016/343, reg. 4(a), with effect from 6 April 2016.

In reg. 10, the words "sections 5(1) and 9A" substituted for "section 5(1)"; "2015" substituted for "2014"; "£112" substituted for "£111"; "£815" substituted for "£805"; "£155" substituted for "£153"; "£156" substituted for "£153" by SI 2015/577, reg. 3, with effect from 6 April 2015.

In reg. 10(b), the figure "£827" substituted for the figure "£815" by SI 2016/343, reg. 4(b), with effect from 6 April 2016.

Reg. 10(e) (and the word "; and" preceding it) inserted by SI 2015/577, reg. 3(h), with effect from 6 April 2015.

Reg. 10(f) (and the word "; and" before it) inserted (and the "and" after (d) omitted by SI 2016/343, reg. 4(c)–(d), with effect from 6 April 2016.

In reg. 10, "2014" substituted for "2013"; "£111" substituted for "£109"; "£805" substituted for "£797"; "£153" substituted for "£149"; "£153" substituted for "£148" by SI 2014/569, reg. 3, with effect from 6 April 2014.

In reg. 10, "2013" substituted for "2012"; "£109" substituted for "£107"; "£797" substituted for "£817"; "£149" substituted for "£146"; and "£148" substituted for "£144" by SI 2013/558, reg. 3, with effect from 6 April 2013.

In reg. 10, "2012" substituted for "2011"; "£107" substitutedfor "£102"; "£146" substituted for "£139"; and "£144" substituted for "£136" by SI 2012/804, reg. 3, with effect from 6 April 2012.

In reg. 10, "2011" substituted for "2010"; "£102" substituted for "£97"; "£817" substituted for "£844"; "£139" substituted for "£110"; and "£136" substituted for "£110", by SI 2011/940, reg. 3, with effect from 6 April 2011.

In reg. 10, "2010" substituted for "2009" and "£97" substituted for "£95" by SI 2010/834, reg. 3 with effect from 6 April 2010.

In reg. 10, "2009" substituted for "2008"; "£95" substituted for "£90"; "£844" substituted for "£770"; and "£110" substituted for "£105" in both places, by SI 2009/591, reg. 3 with effect from 6 April 2009.

In reg. 10, "2008" substituted for "2007"; "£90" substituted for "£87"; "£770" substituted for "£670"; and "£105" substituted for "£100" in both places, by SI 2008/133, reg. 3 with effect from 6 April 2008.

In reg. 10, "2007" substituted for "2006"; "£87" substituted for "£84"; "£670" substituted for "£645"; and "£100" substituted for "£97" in both places, by SI 2007/118, reg. 4 with effect from 6 April 2007.

In reg. 10, "2006" substituted for "2005"; "£84" substituted for "£82"; "£645" substituted for "£630"; and "£97" substituted for "£94" in both places, by SI 2006/127, reg. 3 with effect from 6 April 2006.

In reg. 10, "2005" substituted for "2004"; "£82" substituted for "£79"; "£630" substituted for "£610"; and "£94" substituted for "£91" in both places, by SI 2005/166, reg. 3 with effect from 6 April 2005.

In reg. 10, "2004" substituted for "2003"; "79" substituted for "77"; "610" substituted for "595"; and "91" substituted for "89" in both places, by SI 2004/220, reg. 3 with effect from 6 April 2004.

Derivations – SI 1979/591, reg. 7.

PRESCRIBED EQUIVALENTS

11(1) The prescribed equivalents of the lower and upper earnings limits, the primary and secondary thresholds and the upper secondary thresholds, for the purposes of–

(a) sections 6(1), 6A(1), 8(1), 9(1), 9A(9), and 9B(6) of the Act (which provide for liability for Class 1 contributions, notional payment of primary Class 1 contribution where earnings are not less than the lower earnings limit, the calculation of primary Class 1 contributions, the calculation of secondary Class 1 contributions, the calculation of secondary Class 1 contributions in relation to the Under 21 age group and the calculation of secondary Class 1 contributions in relation to relevant apprentices respectively); and

(aa) section 22 of the Act (earnings factors);

(b) [omitted by SI 2016/352, reg. 10(a).]

shall be determined in accordance with paragraphs (2) to (5).

11(1A) [Omitted by SI 2016/352, reg. 10(b).]

11(2) Subject to paragraphs (4) and (5), the prescribed equivalents of the lower earnings limit shall be–

(a) where the earnings period is a multiple of a week, the amount calculated by multiplying the lower earnings limit by the corresponding multiple;

(b) where the earnings period is a month, the amount calculated by multiplying the lower earnings limit by 4 1/3;

(c) where the earnings period is a multiple of a month, the amount calculated by multiplying the lower earnings limit by 4 1/3 and multiplying the result by the corresponding multiple;

(d) in any other case, the amount calculated by dividing the lower earnings limit by 7 and multiplying the result by the number of days in the earnings period concerned.

11(2A) Subject to paragraphs (4) and (5), the prescribed equivalents of the upper earnings limit shall be–

(a) where the earnings period is a month, £3,863;

(b) where the earnings period is a year, £46,350;

(c) where the earnings period is a multiple of a week, the amount calculated by dividing the figure in sub-paragraph (b) by 52 and multiplying the result by the corresponding multiple;

(d) where the earnings period is a multiple of a month, the amount calculated by dividing the figure in sub-paragraph (b) by 12 and multiplying the result by the corresponding multiple;

(e) in any other case, the amount calculated by dividing the figure in sub-paragraph (b) by 365 and multiplying the result by the number of days in the earnings period concerned.

11(3) Subject to paragraphs (4) and (5), the prescribed equivalents of the primary threshold shall be–

(a) where the earnings period is a month, £702;

(b) where the earnings period is a year, £8,424;

(c) where the earnings period is a multiple of a week, the amount calculated by dividing the figure in sub-paragraph (b) by 52 and multiplying the result by the corresponding multiple;

(d) where the earnings period is a multiple of a month, the amount calculated by dividing the figure in sub-paragraph (b) by 12 and multiplying the result by the corresponding multiple;

(e) in any other case, the amount calculated by dividing the figure in sub-paragraph (b) by 365 and multiplying the result by the number of days in the earnings period concerned.

11(3A) Subject to paragraphs (4) and (5), the prescribed equivalents of the secondary threshold shall be–

(a) where the earnings period is a month, £702;

(b) where the earnings period is a year, £8,424;

(c) where the earnings period is a multiple of a week, the amount calculated by dividing the figure in sub-paragraph (b) by 52 and multiplying the result by the corresponding multiple;

(d) where the earnings period is a multiple of a month, the amount calculated by dividing the figure in sub-paragraph (b) by 12 and multiplying the result by the corresponding multiple;

(e) in any other case, the amount calculated by dividing the figure in sub-paragraph (b) by 365 and multiplying the result by the number of days in the earnings period concerned.

11(3B) Subject to paragraphs (4) and (5), the prescribed equivalents of the upper secondary threshold for secondary Class 1 contributions in relation to the Under 21 age group shall be–

(a) where the earnings period is a month, £3,863;

(b) where the earnings period is a year, £46,350;

(c) where the earnings period is a multiple of a week, the amount calculated by dividing the figure in sub-paragraph (b) by 52 and multiplying the result by the corresponding multiple;

(d) where the earnings period is a multiple of a month, the amount calculated by dividing the figure in sub-paragraph (b) by 12 and multiplying the result by the corresponding multiple;

(e) in any other case, the amount calculated by dividing the figure in sub-paragraph (b) by 365 and multiplying the result by the number of days in the earnings period concerned.

11(3C) Subject to paragraphs (4) and (5), the prescribed equivalents of the upper secondary threshold for secondary Class 1 contributions in relation to relevant apprentices shall be–

(a) where the earnings period is a month, £3,863;

(b) where the earnings period is a year, £46,350;

(c) where the earnings period is a multiple of a week, the amount calculated by dividing the figure in sub-paragraph (b) by 52 and multiplying the result by the corresponding multiple;

(d) where the earnings period is a multiple of a month, the amount calculated by dividing the figure in sub-paragraph (b) by 12 and multiplying the result by the corresponding multiple;

(e) in any other case, the amount calculated by dividing the figure in sub-paragraph (b) by 365 and multiplying the result by the number of days in the earnings period concerned.

11(4) The amounts determined in accordance with paragraphs (2)(b) and (c), paragraph (2A)(c) and (d), paragraph (3)(c) and (d), paragraph (3A)(c) and (d), paragraph (3B)(c) and (d) and paragraph (3C)(c) and (d) if not whole pounds, shall be rounded up to the next whole pound.

11(5) The amounts determined in accordance with paragraph (2)(d), paragraph (2A)(e), paragraph (3)(e), paragraph (3A)(e), paragraph (3B)(e) and paragraph (3C)(e) shall be calculated to the nearest penny, and any amount of a halfpenny or less shall be disregarded.

11(6) [Omitted by SI 2016/352, reg. 10(d).]

History – In reg. 11(1), the words ", the primary and secondary thresholds and the upper secondary thresholds" substituted for the words "and the primary and secondary thresholds" by SI 2016/343, reg. 5(a)(i), with effect from 6 April 2016.

In reg. 11(1)(a), the words "9(1), 9A(9), and 9B(6)" substituted for the words "and 9(1)" and the words ", the calculation of secondary Class 1 contributions, the calculation of secondary Class 1 contributions in relation to the Under 21 age group and the calculation of secondary Class 1 contributions in relation to relevant apprentices" substituted for the words "and the calculation of secondary Class 1 contributions" by SI 2016/343, reg. 5(a)(ii), with effect from 6 April 2016.

Reg. 11(1)(aa) inserted, and the word "and" at the end of reg. 11(1)(a) omitted, by SI 2009/111, reg. 3(2)(a) and (b), with effect from 6 April 2009.

Reg. 11(1)(b) (and the "and" before it) omitted (and the "and" after (a) inserted) by SI 2016/352, reg. 10(a), with effect from 6 April 2016, subject to savings in relation to rights or obligations arising in connection with tax years beginning before 6 April 2016 (and for savings purposes, references to repealed provisions of the Pension Schemes Act 1993 are to be read as though such provisions were still in force). Former reg. 11(1)(b) read as follows:

"(b) sections 41(1) (reduced rates of Class 1 contributions), 42A(1) (reduced rates of Class 1 contributions and rebates) and 45(1) (amount of minimum contributions) of the Pensions Act,".

Former reg. 11(1)(b) substituted by SI 2009/111, reg. 3(2)(c), with effect from 6 April 2009.

Reg. 11(1A) omitted by SI 2016/352, reg. 10(b), with effect from 6 April 2016, subject to savings in relation to rights or obligations arising in connection with tax years beginning before 6 April 2016 (and for savings purposes, references to repealed provisions of the Pension Schemes Act 1993 are to be read as though such provisions were still in force). Former reg. 11(1A) read as follows:

"**11(1A)** The prescribed equivalents of the upper accrual point for the purposes of–

(a) section 22 of the Act (earnings factors); and

(b) sections 41(1) (reduced rates of Class 1 contributions), 42A(1) (reduced rates of Class 1 contributions and rebates) and 45(1) (amount of minimum contributions) of the Pensions Act,

shall be determined in accordance with paragraphs (2), (4) and (5).".

Former reg. 11(1A) inserted by SI 2009/111, reg. 3(3), with effect from 6 April 2009.

In reg. 11(2), the words "and the upper accrual point" (which appeared after the words "lower earnings limit") omitted by SI 2016/352, reg. 10(c)(i), with effect from 6 April 2016, subject to savings in relation to rights or obligations arising in connection with tax years beginning before 6 April 2016 (and for savings purposes, references to repealed provisions of the Pension Schemes Act 1993 are to be read as though such provisions were still in force).

Reg. 11(2) opening words and reg. 11(2)(a) substituted by SI 2009/111, reg. 3(4), with effect from 6 April 2009.

In reg. 11(2)(a), the words "or the upper accrual point ("the weekly limits")" (which appeared after the words "lower earnings limit") omitted by SI 2016/352, reg. 10(c)(ii), with effect from 6 April 2016, subject to savings in relation to rights or obligations arising in connection with tax years beginning before 6 April 2016 (and for savings purposes, references to repealed provisions of the Pension Schemes Act 1993 are to be read as though such provisions were still in force).

In reg. 11(2)(a)–(d), the word "amount" substituted for the word "amounts" (in each place) by SI 2016/352, reg. 10(c)(iii)(aa), with effect from 6 April 2016, subject to savings in relation to rights or obligations arising in connection with tax years beginning before 6 April 2016 (and for savings purposes, references to repealed provisions of the Pension Schemes Act 1993 are to be read as though such provisions were still in force).

In reg. 11(2)(b)–(d), the words "the lower earnings limit" substituted for the words "each of the weekly limits" (in each place) by SI 2016/352, reg. 10(c)(iii)(bb), with effect from 6 April 2016, subject to savings in relation to rights or obligations arising in connection with tax years beginning before 6 April 2016 (and for savings purposes, references to repealed provisions of the Pension Schemes Act 1993 are to be read as though such provisions were still in force).

In reg. 11(2)(c)–(d), the words "the result" substituted for the words "each result" (in each place) by SI 2016/352, reg. 10(c)(iii)(cc), with effect from 6 April 2016, subject to savings in relation to rights or obligations arising in connection with tax years beginning before 6 April 2016 (and for savings purposes, references to repealed provisions of the Pension Schemes Act 1993 are to be read as though such provisions were still in force).

In reg. 11(2A), the figure "£3,863" substituted for the figure "£3,750" and the figure "£46,350" substituted for the figure "£45,000" by SI 2018/337, reg. 8(a), with effectfrom 6 April 2018.

In reg. 11(2A), the figure "£3,750" substituted for the figure "£3,583" and the figure "£45,000" substituted for the figure "£43,000" by SI 2017/415, reg. 8(a), with effect from 6 April 2017.

In reg. 11(2A), the figure "£3,583" substituted for "£3,532" and "£43,000" substituted for "£42,385" by SI 2016/343, reg. 5(b), with effect from 6 April 2016.

In reg. 11(2A), the figure "£3,532" substituted for "£3,489" and "£42,385" substituted for "£41,865" by SI 2015/577, reg. 4(a), with effect from 6 April 2015.

In reg. 11(2A), the figure "£3,489" substituted for "£3,454" and "£41,865" substituted for "£41,450" by SI 2014/569, reg. 4(a), with effect from 6 April 2014.

In reg. 11(2A), the figure "£3,454" substituted for "£3,540" and the figure "£41,450" substituted for "£42,475" by SI 2013/558, reg. 4(a), with effect from 6 April 2013.

In reg. 11(2A), "£3,540" substituted for "£3,656" and "£42,475" substituted for "£43,875" by SI 2011/940, reg. 4(2), with effect from 6 April 2011.

Reg. 11(2A) inserted by SI 2009/111, reg. 3(5), with effect from 6 April 2009.

In reg. 11(3), the figure "£702" substituted for the figure "£680" and the figure "£8,424" substituted for the figure "£8,164" by SI 2018/337, reg. 8(b), with effect from 6 April 2018.

In reg. 11(3), the figure "£680" substituted for the figure "£672" and the figure "£8,164" substituted for the figure "£8,060" by SI 2017/415, reg. 8(b), with effect from 6 April 2017.

In reg. 11(3), the figure "£672" substituted for "£663" and "£8,060" substituted for "£7,956" by SI 2015/577, reg. 4(b), with effect from 6 April 2015.

In reg. 11(3), the figure "£663" substituted for "£646" and "£7,956" substituted for "£7,755" by SI 2014/569, reg. 4(b), with effect from 6 April 2014.

In reg. 11(3), the figure "£646" substituted for "£634" and the figure "£7,755" substituted for "£7,605" by SI 2013/558, reg. 4(b), with effect from 6 April 2013.

In reg. 11(3), the figure "£634" substituted for "£602" and the figure "£7,605" substituted for "£7,225" by SI 2012/804, reg. 4(a), with effect from 6 April 2012.

In reg. 11(3), the words "the prescribed equivalents of the primary threshold" substituted for the words "the prescribed equivalents of the primary and secondary thresholds" by SI 2011/940, reg. 4(3)(a), with effect from 6 April 2011.

In reg. 11(3), "£602" substituted for "£476" and "£7,225" substituted for "£5,715" by SI 2011/940, reg. 4(3)(b) and (c), with effect from 6 April 2011.

In reg. 11(3), "£476" substituted for "£453", and "£5,715" substituted for "£5,435" by SI 2009/111, reg. 3(6), with effect from 6 April 2009.

In reg. 11(3), "£453" substituted for "£435", and "£5,435" substituted for "£5,225" by SI 2008/133, reg. 4 with effect from 6 April 2008.

In reg. 11(3), "£435" substituted for "£420", and "£5,225" substituted for "£5,035" by SI 2007/118, reg. 4 with effect from 6 April 2007.

In reg. 11(3), "£420" substituted for "£408", and "£5,035" substituted for "£4,895" by SI 2006/127, reg. 4 with effect from 6 April 2006.

In reg. 11(3), "£408" substituted for "£395", and "£4,895" substituted for "£4,745" by SI 2005/166, reg. 4 with effect from 6 April 2005.
In reg. 11(3), "395" substituted for "385", and "4,745" substituted for "4,615" by SI 2004/220, reg. 4 with effect from 6 April 2004.
In reg. 11(3A), the figure "£702" substituted for the figure "£680" and the figure "£8,424" substituted for the figure "£8,164" by SI 2018/337, reg. 8(c), with effect from 6 April 2018.
In reg. 11(3A), the figure "£680" substituted for the figure "£676" and the figure "£8,164" substituted for the figure "£8,112" by SI 2017/415, reg. 8(c), with effect from 6 April 2017.
In reg. 11(3A), the figure "£676" substituted for "£663" and "£8,112" substituted for "£7,956" by SI 2015/577, reg. 4(c), with effect from 6 April 2015.
In reg. 11(3A), the figure "£663" substituted for "£641" and "£7,956" substituted for "£7,696" by SI 2014/569, reg. 4(c), with effect from 6 April 2014.
In reg. 11(3A), the figure "£641" substituted for "£624" and the figure "£7,696" substituted for "£7,488" by SI 2013/558, reg. 4(c), with effect from 6 April 2013.
In reg. 11(3A), the figure "£624" substituted for "£589" and the figure "£7,488" substituted for "£7,072" by SI 2012/804, reg. 4(b), with effect from 6 April 2012.
Reg 11(3A) inserted by SI 2011/940, reg. 4(4), with effect from 6 April 2011.
In reg. 11(3B), the figure "£3,863" substituted for the figure "£3,750" and the figure "£46,350" substituted for the figure "£45,000" by SI 2018/337, reg. 8(d), with effect from 6 April 2018.
In reg. 11(3B), the figure "£3,750" substituted for the figure "£3,583" and the figure "£45,000" substituted for the figure "£43,000" by SI 2017/415, reg. 8(d), with effect from 6 April 2017.
In reg. 11(3B)(a), the figure "£3,583" substituted for "£3,532" by SI 2016/343, reg. 5(c), with effect from 6 April 2016.
In reg. 11(3B)(b), the figure "£43,000" substituted for "£42,385" by SI 2016/343, reg. 5(c), with effect from 6 April 2016.
Reg 11(3B) inserted by SI 2015/577, reg. 4(d), with effect from 6 April 2015.
In reg. 11(3C), the figure "£3,863" substituted for the figure "£3,750" and the figure "£46,350" substituted for the figure "£45,000" by SI 2018/337, reg. 8(e), with effect from 6 April 2018.
In reg. 11(3C), the figure "£3,750" substituted for the figure "£3,583" and the figure "£45,000" substituted for the figure "£43,000" by SI 2017/415, reg. 8(e), with effect from 6 April 2017.
Reg. 11(3C) inserted by SI 2016/343, reg. 5(d), with effect from 6 April 2016.
In reg. 11(4), the words ", paragraph (3B)(c) and (d) and paragraph (3C)(c) and (d)" substituted for the words "and paragraph (3B)(c) and (d)" by SI 2016/343, reg. 5(e), with effect from 6 April 2016.
In reg. 11(4), the words ", paragraph (3A)(c) and (d) and paragraph (3B)(c) and (d)" substituted for the words "and paragraph (3A)(c) and (d)" by SI 2015/577, reg. 4(e), with effect from 6 April 2015.
In reg. 11(4), the words ", paragraph (3)(c) and (d) and paragraph (3A)(c) and (d)" substituted for the words "and paragraph (3)(c) and (d)" by SI 2011/940, reg. 4(4), with effect from 6 April 2011.
Reg. 11(4) substituted by SI 2009/111, reg. 3(7), with effect from 6 April 2009.
In reg. 11(5), the words ", paragraph (3A)(e) and paragraph (3B)(e)" substituted for the words "and paragraph (3A)(e)" by SI 2015/577, reg. 4(f), with effect from 6 April 2015.
In reg. 11(5), the words ", paragraph (3)(e) and paragraph (3A)(e)" substituted for the words "and paragraph (3)(e)" by SI 2011/940, reg. 4(5), with effect from 6 April 2011.
In reg. 11(5), the words "paragraph (2)(d), paragraph (2A)(e) and paragraph (3)(e)" substituted for the words "paragraph (2)(d) and paragraph (3)(e)" by SI 2009/111, reg. 3(8), with effect from 6 April 2009.
Reg. 11(6) omitted by SI 2016/352, reg. 10(d), with effect from 6 April 2016, subject to savings in relation to rights or obligations arising in connection with tax years beginning before 6 April 2016 (and for savings purposes, references to repealed provisions of the Pension Schemes Act 1993 are to be read as though such provisions were still in force). Former reg. 11(6) read as follows:

"**11(6)** The following provisions of this regulation do not apply to Northern Ireland–
(a) paragraph (1A), and
(b) both references to "the upper accrual point" in paragraph (2), so that the term "the weekly limits" shall be read as referring only to the lower earnings limit in relation to Northern Ireland.".

Former reg. 11(6) inserted by SI 2009/111, with effect from 6 April 2009.
Derivations – SI 1979/591, reg. 8.

CALCULATION OF EARNINGS-RELATED CONTRIBUTIONS

12(1) Subject to paragraphs (3) and (4), primary and secondary Class 1 contributions under section 6 of the Act (liability for Class 1 contributions) shall be calculated to the nearest penny and any amount of a halfpenny or less shall be disregarded.

12(2) In the alternative, but subject to paragraphs (3) to (5), the contributions specified in paragraph (1) may be calculated in accordance with the appropriate scale or, for contributions payable on earnings above the upper earnings limit or the prescribed equivalent of that limit, a contributions calculator prepared by the Board.

12(3) Where the amount of earnings to which–

(a) the appropriate scale is to be applied does not appear in the scale, the amount of contributions payable shall be calculated by reference to the next smaller amount of earnings in the appropriate column in the scale;

(b) the appropriate contributions calculator is to be applied does not appear in the calculator, the amount of contributions payable shall be calculated–

  (i) by obtaining from the calculator the amounts of contributions payable on the largest components of the earnings provided for in the calculator, and

  (ii) by adding together the amounts so obtained.

12(4) Where a scale or a contributions calculator would, but for the period to which it relates, be appropriate and the earnings period in question is a multiple of the period in the scale or, as the case may be, calculator, the scale or calculator shall be applied by dividing the earnings in question so as to obtain the equivalent earnings for the period to which the scale or calculator relates and–

(a) in the case of the scale, by multiplying the amount of contributions shown in the scale as appropriate to those equivalent earnings by the same factor as the earnings were divided;

(b) in the case of the calculator, by multiplying the amount of contributions shown in the calculator as appropriate to those equivalent earnings or, where no equivalent earnings are shown, the amount of contributions calculated in accordance with paragraph (3)(b), by the same factor as the earnings were divided.

12(5) Unless the Board agree to the contrary, all the contributions payable in a year in respect of the earnings paid to or for the benefit of an earner in respect of his employed earner's employment or, where he has more than one such employment and the earnings from those employments are aggregated under paragraph 1(1) of Schedule 1 to the Act (Class 1 contributions where more than one employment), in respect of those employments, shall be calculated either in accordance with paragraph (1) or paragraph (2) but not partly in accordance with one and partly in accordance with the other of those paragraphs, save that the contributions calculator may also be used where the contributions have been calculated in accordance with paragraph (1).

History – Reg. 12(1) substituted by SI 2016/352, reg. 11, with effect from 6 April 2016, subject to savings in relation to rights or obligations arising in connection with tax years beginning before 6 April 2016 (and for savings purposes, references to repealed provisions of the Pension Schemes Act 1993 are to be read as though such provisions were still in force). Former reg. 12(1) read as follows;

"**12(1)** Subject to paragraphs (3) and (4), earnings-related contributions shall be calculated as follows–

(a) primary and secondary Class 1 contributions under section 6 of the Act (liability for Class 1 contributions) and any primary and secondary Class 1 contributions at the normal rate and at the contracted-out rate shall each be calculated separately; and

(b) as regards the calculation referred to in sub-paragraph (a) primary and secondary Class 1 contributions shall be calculated to the nearest penny and any amount of a halfpenny or less shall be disregarded.".

Derivations – SI 1979/591, reg. 9.

GENERAL PROVISIONS AS TO AGGREGATION

13 Where on one or more occasions the whole or any part of a person's earnings in respect of employed earner's employment is not paid weekly (whether or not it is treated for the purpose of earnings-related contributions as paid weekly), paragraph 1 of Schedule 1 to the Act (Class 1 contributions where more than one employment) shall have effect as if for the references to "week" there were substituted references to "earnings period".

Derivations – SI 1979/591, reg. 10.

AGGREGATION OF EARNINGS PAID IN RESPECT OF SEPARATE EMPLOYED EARNER'S EMPLOYMENTS UNDER THE SAME EMPLOYER

14 For the purpose of earnings-related contributions, where an earner is concurrently employed in more than one employed earner's employment under the same employer, the earnings paid to or for the benefit of the earner in respect of those employments shall not be aggregated if such aggregation is not reasonably practicable because the earnings in the respective employments are separately calculated.

Derivations – SI 1979/591, reg. 11.

AGGREGATION OF EARNINGS PAID IN RESPECT OF DIFFERENT EMPLOYED EARNER'S EMPLOYMENTS BY DIFFERENT PERSONS AND APPORTIONMENT OF CONTRIBUTION LIABILITY

15(1) Subject to regulation 7, for the purposes of determining whether earnings-related contributions are payable in respect of earnings paid to or for the benefit of an earner in a given earnings period, and, if so, the amount of the contributions, where in that period earnings in respect of different employed earner's employments are paid to or for the benefit of the earner–

(a) by different secondary contributors who in respect of those employments carry on business in association with each other;

(b) by different employers, one of whom is, by virtue of Schedule 3 to the Social Security (Categorisation of Earners) Regulations 1978, treated as the secondary contributor in respect of each of those employments; or

(c) by different persons, in respect of work performed for those persons by the earner in those employments and in respect of those earnings, some other person is, by virtue of that Schedule, treated as the secondary contributor,

the earnings paid in respect of each of the employments referred to in this paragraph shall, unless in a case falling under sub-paragraph (a) it is not reasonably practicable to do so, be aggregated and treated as a single payment of earnings in respect of one such employment.

15(2) Where, under paragraph (1), earnings are aggregated, liability for the secondary contributions payable in respect of those earnings shall, in a case falling within paragraph (1)(a), be apportioned between the secondary contributors in such proportions as they shall agree amongst themselves, or, in default of agreement, in the proportions which the earnings paid by each bearer to the total amount of the aggregated earnings.

Derivations – SI 1979/591, reg. 12.

AGGREGATION OF EARNINGS PAID AFTER PENSIONABLE AGE

16 Notwithstanding regulation 15, a payment of earnings to which regulation 28 applies shall not be aggregated with any other earnings.

Derivations – SI 1979/591, reg. 12A.

APPORTIONMENT OF SINGLE PAYMENT OF EARNINGS IN RESPECT OF DIFFERENT EMPLOYED EARNER'S EMPLOYMENTS BY DIFFERENT SECONDARY CONTRIBUTORS

17 Where any single payment of earnings is made in respect of two or more employed earner's employments under different secondary contributors, liability for earnings-related contributions shall be determined by apportioning the payment as follows–

(a) where the secondary contributors are, in respect of those employments, carrying on business in association with each other, to the secondary contributor who makes the payment;

(b) where the secondary contributors are not so carrying on business in association with each other, to each of those secondary contributors in the proportion which the earnings due in respect of that secondary contributor's employment bears to the total of the single payment.

Derivations – SI 1979/591, reg. 13.

CHANGE OF EARNINGS PERIOD

18(1) Paragraphs (2) and (3) apply where, by reason of a change in the regular interval at which any part of an earner's earnings is paid or treated as paid in respect of employed earner's employment (**"the regular interval of payment"**), that person's earnings period in any employment or employments under the same secondary contributor is, or is in the process of being, changed.

18(2) Subject to paragraph (3), in relation to any payments made on or after the date of change the earnings period shall be determined in accordance with the new interval.

18(3) Where the new period is longer than the old period and during the first new period any payment has also been made at the old interval, the earnings-related contributions payable on any payment made on or after the date of change shall not exceed in amount the total which would have been payable if all the payments during the new period had been made at the new interval.

18(4) In this regulation–

(a) the regular interval of payment which has been discontinued is referred to as **"the old interval"** and the interval which has, or is to, become the regular interval of payment is referred to as **"the new interval"**;

(b) the earnings period determined according to the old interval is referred to as **"the old period"** and that determined according to the new interval is referred to as **"the new period"**;

(c) reference to payment means payment of earnings actually made or, as the case may be, treated under regulation 7 as made, at an interval or date; and

(d) **"date of change"** means the date on which the first payment of earnings at the new interval is made.

Derivations – SI 1979/591, reg. 14.

HOLIDAY PAYMENTS

19 Where, as respects an employed earner's employment in which the earner is paid or would, but for paragraph (b), be treated under regulation 7 as paid at a regular interval of a week or a fixed number of weeks, a payment of earnings includes or comprises a payment in respect of a period of holiday entitlement other than such a payment made to an earner in respect of a period of holiday entitlement outstanding on termination of that employment, for the purposes of calculating the earnings-related contributions payable in respect of that payment of earnings–

(a) the earnings period may be the length of the period in respect of which the payment is made, but where the length of that earnings period includes a fraction of a week that fraction shall be treated as a whole week; and

(b) where the earnings period is so determined, regulation 7 shall not apply.

Derivations – SI 1979/591, reg. 15.

JOINT EMPLOYMENT OF SPOUSES OR CIVIL PARTNERS

History – The heading of reg. 20 substituted by SI 2005/3130, reg. 3(2), with effect from 5 December 2005.

20 For the purposes of earnings-related contributions, where spouses or civil partners are jointly employed in employed earner's employment and earnings in respect of the employment are paid to them jointly, the amount of the earnings of each shall be calculated upon the same basis as that upon which those earnings are calculated for the purposes of income tax and, in the absence of such calculation, upon such basis as may be approved by the Board.

History – In reg. 20 the words "spouses or civil partners" substituted by SI 2005/3130, reg. 3(3), with effect from 5 December 2005.

Derivations – SI 1979/591, reg. 16.

ANNUAL MAXIMA FOR THOSE WITH MORE THAN ONE EMPLOYMENT

21(1) For the purposes of section 19(1) and (2) of the Act (power to prescribe maximum amounts of contributions and repayments of excess) if an earner is employed in more than one employment his liability in any year–

(a) for primary Class 1 contributions; or

(b) where both primary Class 1 contributions and Class 2 contributions are payable by him, for both primary Class 1 contributions and Class 2 contributions,

shall not exceed an amount which equals the amount found in accordance with paragraph (2).

21(2) The amount is found as follows.

Step One

Calculate–

53 × (UEL − PT)

Here *UEL* is the upper earnings limit, and *PT* the primary threshold, specified for the year.

Step Two

Multiply the result of Step One by 12 per cent.

Step Three

Add together, in respect of all of the employed earner's employments, so much of the earnings in each of those employments as exceeds the primary threshold and does not exceed the upper earnings limit.

Step Four

From the sum produced by Step Three subtract the amount found by the formula in Step One.

Step Five

If the result produced by Step Four is a positive value, multiply it by 2 per cent.

If that result is nil or a negative value, it is treated for the purposes of Step Eight as nil.

Step Six

Add together, in respect of all of the employed earner's employments, so much of the earnings in each of those employments as exceeds the upper earnings limit.

Step Seven

Multiply the sum produced by Step Six by 2 per cent.

Step Eight

Add together the amounts produced by Steps Two, Five and Seven.

The result of Step Eight is the annual maximum, subject to the further qualifications in paragraphs (3) and (4).

21(3) For the purpose only of determining the extent of the earner's liability for contributions under paragraph (2), the amount of a primary Class 1 contribution which is paid at a rate less than 12 per cent because the earner is a married woman who has made an election to pay contributions at the reduced rate as mentioned in regulation 127, shall be treated as equal to the amount of the primary Class 1 contribution which would be payable if the election had not been made.

21(4) Paragraph (2) is subject to–

(a) section 12 of the Act (late paid Class 2 contributions); and

(b) regulations 63 to 65 (special provisions about Class 2 and Class 3 contributions paid late).

21(5) Notwithstanding paragraphs (1) to (4), an earner shall be liable, in the first instance, for the full amount of the contributions which would have been payable but for this regulation.

History – In reg. 21(2), in Step Two, the words "12 per cent" substituted for the words "11 per cent" by SI 2012/573, reg. 2(a)(i), which came into force on 26 March 2012, with effect in relation to contributions paid in respect of the tax year 2011–12 and subsequent tax years.

In reg. 21(2), in Step Five, the words "2 per cent" substituted for the words "1 per cent" by SI 2012/573, reg. 2(a)(ii), which came into force on 26 March 2012, with effect in relation to contributions paid in respect of the tax year 2011–12 and subsequent tax years.

In reg. 21(2), in Step Seven, the words "2 per cent" substituted for the words "1 per cent" by SI 2012/573, reg. 2(a)(iii), which came into force on 26 March 2012, with effect in relation to contributions paid in respect of the tax year 2011–12 and subsequent tax years.

Reg. 21(3) substituted by SI 2016/352, reg. 12, with effect from 6 April 2016, subject to savings in relation to rights or obligations arising in connection with tax years beginning before 6 April 2016 (and for savings purposes, references to repealed provisions of the Pension Schemes Act 1993 are to be read as though such provisions were still in force). Former reg. 21(3) read as follows:

"**21(3)** For the purpose only of determining the extent of the earner's liability for contributions under paragraph (2), the amount of a primary Class 1 contribution which is paid at a rate less than 12 per cent –

(a) because the earner is in contracted-out employment, or

(b) because the earner is a married woman who has made an election to pay contributions at the reduced rate as mentioned in regulation 127,

shall be treated as equal to the amount of the primary Class 1 contribution which would be payable if the employment were not contracted-out or the election had not been made.".

In former reg. 21(3), the words "12 per cent" substituted for the words "11 per cent" by SI 2012/573, reg. 2(b), which came into force on 26 March 2012, with effect in relation to contributions paid in respect of the tax year 2011–12 and subsequent tax years.

Reg. 21 substituted by SI 2003/193, reg. 6 with effect from 6 April 2003.

Derivations – SI 1979/591, reg. 17.

AMOUNTS TO BE TREATED AS EARNINGS

22(1) For the purposes of section 3 of the Act (earnings), the amounts specified in paragraphs (2) to (14) shall be treated as remuneration derived from an employed earner's employment.

22(2) The amount specified in this paragraph is the amount of any payment by a company to or for the benefit of any of its directors if–

(a) apart from this paragraph the payment would, when made, not be earnings for the purposes of the Act; and

(b) the payment is made on account of or by way of an advance on a sum which would be earnings for those purposes.

22(3) The amount specified in this paragraph is the amount equal to the cash equivalent in respect of car fuel which is treated as earnings from the employment of the earner for income tax purposes by virtue of section 149 of ITEPA 2003.

22(4) The amount specified in this paragraph is the amount which is treated as earnings from the employment of the employed earner by virtue of section 222(2) of ITEPA 2003.

22(5) The amount specified in this paragraph is the amount which counts as employment income of the employed earner under Chapter 2 of Part 7 of ITEPA 2003 computed in accordance with section 428 of ITEPA 2003 in respect of conditional shares or interests in conditional shares acquired before 16th April 2003.

References in this paragraph and paragraph (6) to ITEPA 2003 are to that Act as originally enacted.

22(6) The amount specified in this paragraph is the amount which counts as employment income of the employed earner by virtue of Chapter 4 of Part 7 of ITEPA 2003 (shares: post-acquisition charges) in respect of shares or interests in shares acquired before 16th April 2003.

22(7) The amounts specified in this paragraph are those–

(a) which count as employment income of the employed earner in relation to employment-related securities (within the meaning given by section 421B(8) of ITEPA 2003; and

(b) to which section 698 of ITEPA 2003 (PAYE: special charges on employment-related securities) applies.

References in this paragraph and paragraphs (9) and (10) to ITEPA 2003 are to that Act as amended.

22(8) The amount specified in this paragraph is the amount–

(a) which counts as employment income of the employed earner by virtue of sections 500 to 508 of ITEPA 2003; and

(b) in respect of which income tax is recoverable in accordance with PAYE regulations.

22(9) The amount specified in this paragraph is any amount–

(a) which, by reason of the operation of Schedule 2 to the Finance (No. 2) Act 2005, counts as employment income of the employed earner under any of Chapters 2 to 4 of Part 7 of ITEPA 2003; and

(b) where the relevant date for that income determined under section 698(6) of ITEPA 2003 (whether or not the PAYE Regulations apply to that income) is on or after 2nd December 2004 and before 20th July 2005.

22(10) The amount specified in this paragraph is any amount–

(a) which by virtue of the operation of section 92 of the Finance Act 2006 counts as employment income of the employed earner under any of Chapters 2 to 4 of Part 7 of ITEPA 2003; and

(b) where the relevant date for that income determined under section 698(6) of ITEPA 2003 (whether or not the PAYE Regulations apply to that income) is on or after 2nd December 2004 and before 19th July 2006.

22(11) The amount specified in this paragraph is the amount treated as earnings from the employment by virtue of section 226A of ITEPA 2003 (amount treated as earnings).

22(12) The amount specified in this paragraph is any amount–

(a) paid or reimbursed to an employed earner in respect of expenses;

(b) provided pursuant to relevant salary sacrifice arrangements within the meaning of section 289A(5) of ITEPA 2003; and

(c) which is not a payment or reimbursement of relevant motoring expenditure within the meaning of paragraph (3) of regulation 22A.

22(13) The amount specified in this paragraph is any amount paid or reimbursed to an employed earner in respect of expenses which is calculated according to a set rate rather than by reference to the actual amount incurred in respect of the expenses where such a rate is not–

(a) contained in regulations made by the Commissioners for Her Majesty's Revenue and Customs under section 289A(6)(a); or

(b) approved under section 289B of ITEPA 2003.

22(14) The amount specified in this paragraph is the amount of a termination award which is treated as earnings from the employment of the employed earner by virtue of section 402B of ITEPA 2003.

History – In reg. 22(1), the words "(14)" substituted for "(13)" by SI 2018/257, reg. 2(2)(a), with effect from 6 April 2018.
In reg. 22(1), the words "(2) to (13)" substituted for "(2) to (11)" by SI 2016/352, reg. 4(2), with effect from 6 April 2016.
In reg. 22(1), the figure "(11)" substituted for "(10)" by SI 2013/1907, reg. 3(a), with effect from 1 September 2013.
In reg. 22(1) the figure "(10)" substituted for "(8)" by SI 2007/1057, reg. 2(2), with effect from 6 April 2007, in relation to times on and after 2 December 2004.
In the heading to reg. 22 the word "Amounts" substituted by SI 2003/2085, reg. 5(2), with effect from 1 September 2003.
In reg. 22(1) the words "(2) to (8)" substituted by SI 2003/2085, reg. 5(3), with effect from 1 September 2003.
In reg. 22, para. (3) to (8) substituted for para. (3) to (5) by SI 2003/2085, reg. 5(4), with effect from 1 September 2003.
In reg. 22(1) words "(2) to (5)" substituted by SI 2002/307, reg. 3 (repealed by SI 2004/770, Sch. from 6 April 2004), operative from 6 April 2002.
Reg. 22(5) inserted by SI 2002/307, reg. 4, operative from 6 April 2002.
In reg. 22(7) the words "and paragraphs (9) and (10)" inserted by SI 2007/1057, reg. 2(3)(a), with effect from 6 April 2007, in relation to times on and after 2 December 2004.
In reg. 22(7) the words "by Schedule 22" to the end omitted by SI 2007/1057, reg. 2(3)(b), with effect from 6 April 2007, in relation to times on and after 20 July 2005.
Reg. 22(9) inserted by SI 2007/1057, reg. 2(4), with effect from 6 April 2007, in relation to times on and after 2 December 2004.
Reg. 22(10) inserted by SI 2007/1057, reg. 2(4), with effect from 6 April 2007, in relation to times on and after 2 December 2004.
Reg. 22(11) inserted by SI 2013/1907, reg. 3(b), with effect from 1 September 2013.
Reg. 22(12) and (13) inserted by SI 2016/352, reg. 4(3), with effect from 6 April 2016.
Reg. 22(14) inserted by SI 2018/257, reg. 2(2)(b), with effect from 6 April 2018.
Derivations – SI 1979/591, reg. 17A.

AMOUNTS TO BE TREATED AS EARNINGS IN CONNECTION WITH THE USE OF QUALIFYING VEHICLES OTHER THAN CYCLES

22A(1) To the extent that it would not otherwise be earnings, the amount specified in paragraph (2) shall be so treated.

22A(2) The amount is that produced by the formula–

$$RME - QA$$

Here–

RME is the aggregate of relevant motoring expenditure within the meaning of paragraph (3) in the earnings period; and

QA is the qualifying amount calculated in accordance with paragraph (4).

22A(2A) But the amount in paragraph (2) is taken to be RME (without the subtraction of QA) so far as the aggregate of relevant motoring expenditure is paid pursuant to optional remuneration arrangements.

22A(3) A payment is relevant motoring expenditure if–

(a) it is a mileage allowance payment within the meaning of section 229(2) of ITEPA 2003;

(b) it would be such a payment but for the fact that it is paid to another for the benefit of the employee; or

(c) it is any other form of payment, except a payment in kind, made by or on behalf of the employer, and made to, or for the benefit of, the employee in respect of the use by the employee of a qualifying vehicle.

Here **"qualifying vehicle"**means a vehicle to which section 235 of ITEPA 2003 applies, but does not include a cycle within the meaning of section 192(1) of the Road Traffic Act 1988.

22A(4) The qualifying amount is the product of the formula–

$$M \times R$$

Here–

M is the sum of–

(a) the number of miles of business travel undertaken, at or before the time when the payment is made–

(i) in respect of which the payment is made, and

(ii) in respect of which no other payment has been made; and

(b) the number of miles of business travel undertaken–

(i) since the last payment of relevant motoring expenditure was made, or, if there has been no such payment, since the employment began, and

(ii) for which no payment has been, or is to be, made; and

R is the rate applicable to the vehicle in question, at the time when the payment is made, in accordance with section 230(2) of ITEPA 2003, and, if more than one rate is applicable to the class of vehicle in question, is the higher or highest of those rates.

History – Reg. 22A(2A) inserted by SI 2018/120, reg. 4, with effect from 6 April 2018.
In reg. 22A(3) words "section 229(2) of ITEPA 2003" substituted by SI 2004/770, reg. 4, with effect from 6 April 2004.
In reg. 22A(3) words "Here **"qualifying vehicle"** means a vehicle to which section 235 of ITEPA 2003 applies," substituted by SI 2004/770, reg. 4, with effect from 6 April 2004.
In reg. 22A(4) words "section 230(2) of ITEPA 2003," substituted by SI 2004/770, reg. 4, with effect from 6 April 2004.
Reg. 22A inserted by SI 2002/307, reg. 5, operative from 6 April 2002.

Cross references – ITEPA 2003, s. 229(2) rewrites ICTA 1988, s. 197AD(2).
ITEPA 2003, s. 235 rewrites ICTA 1988, Sch. 12AA ("qualifying vehicle").
ITEPA 2003, s. 230(2)–(5) rewrite ICTA 1988, Sch. 12AA, para. 4(2) (applicable rates).

AMOUNTS TO BE TREATED AS EARNINGS: PART 7A OF ITEPA 2003

22B(1) For the purposes of section 3 of the Act (earnings), the amount specified in paragraph (2) shall be treated as remuneration derived from an employed earner's employment.

22B(2) The amount is the amount which counts as employment income of the employed earner by virtue of Chapter 2 of Part 7A of ITEPA 2003.

22B(3) Paragraph (2) does not apply if the relevant step which gives rise to the amount which counts as employment income by virtue of Chapter 2 of Part 7A of ITEPA 2003 would otherwise give rise to earnings for the purposes of the Act.

22B(4) In paragraph (3) **"relevant step"** means a relevant step for the purposes of Part 7A of ITEPA 2003.

Prospective amendments – In reg. 22B(2), the words "This paragraph is subject to paragraphs (3) and (3A)." inserted after the words "Part 7A of ITEPA 2003." by SI 2018/257, reg. 2(3)(a), with effect from 5 April 2019.
Reg. 22B(3A) inserted by SI 2018/257, reg. 2(3)(b), with effect from 5 April 2019. New reg. 22B(3A) reads as follows:

"**22B(3A)** Paragraph (2) does not apply if–

(a) the amount would count as employment income by virtue of Part 7A ITEPA 2003 by reason of a relevant step within paragraph 1 of Schedule 11 (employment income provided through third parties: loans etc outstanding on 5 April 2019) to the Finance (No. 2) Act 2017, and

(b) the secondary contributor in relation to that amount would have been a person treated as a secondary contributor by virtue of regulation 5(1)(d) of, and any of sub-paragraphs (a) to (f) of paragraph 9 of Column (B) of Schedule 3 (employments in respect of which persons are treated as secondary class 1 contributors) to, the Social Security (Categorisation of Earners) Regulations 1978."

In reg. 22B(4), the words "paragraphs (3) and (3A)" substituted for the words "paragraph (3)" by SI 2018/257, reg. 2(3)(c), with effect from 5 April 2019.

History – Reg. 22B inserted by SI 2011/2700, reg. 3, with effect from 6 December 2011.

MANNER OF MAKING SICKNESS PAYMENTS TREATED AS REMUNERATION

23 Where by virtue of section 4(1) of the Act (payments treated as remuneration and earnings) a sickness payment is treated as remuneration derived from an employed earner's employment, that payment shall be made through the person who is the secondary contributor in relation to the employment concerned except where–

(a) the payment is payable by another person;

(b) that person has agreed with the secondary contributor to make the payment; and

(c) arrangements have been made between them for the person who has agreed to make the payment to furnish the secondary contributor with the information specified in paragraph 3(5)(a) of Schedule 4 (intermediate employers).

Derivations – SI 1979/591, reg. 17B.

CALCULATION OF EARNINGS FOR THE PURPOSES OF EARNINGS-RELATED CONTRIBUTIONS

24 For the purpose of determining the amount of earnings-related contributions, the amount of a person's earnings from employed earner's employment shall be calculated on the basis of his gross earnings from the employment or employments in question.

This is subject to the provisions of Schedule 2 (calculation of earnings for the purposes of earnings-related contributions in particular cases) and Schedule 3 (payments to be disregarded in the calculation of earnings for the purposes of earnings-related contributions).

Derivations – SI 1979/591, reg. 18.

PAYMENTS TO BE DISREGARDED IN THE CALCULATION OF EARNINGS FOR THE PURPOSES OF EARNINGS-RELATED CONTRIBUTIONS

25 Schedule 3 specifies payments which are to be disregarded in the calculation of earnings from employed earner's employment for the purpose of earnings-related contributions.

Derivations – SI 1979/591, reg. 19.

CERTAIN PAYMENTS BY TRUSTEES TO BE DISREGARDED

26(1) For the purposes of earnings-related contributions, there shall be excluded from the calculation of a person's earnings in respect of any employed earner's employment any payment, or any part of a payment–

(a) which is made by trustees before 6th April 1990;

(b) the amount of which is or may be dependent upon the exercise by the trustees of a discretion or the performance by them of a duty arising under the trust;

(c) not being a sickness payment which by virtue of section 4(1) of the Act (payments treated as remuneration and earnings) is treated as remuneration derived from an employed earner's employment,

and in respect of which either paragraph (2) or (3) is satisfied.

26(2) This paragraph is satisfied if the trust, under which the payment is made, was created before 6th April 1985.

26(3) This paragraph is satisfied if–

(a) the trust, under which the payment is made, was created on or after 6th April 1985;

(b) that trust took effect immediately on the termination of a trust created before 6th April 1985;

(c) the person to whom the payment is made either–

(i) was a beneficiary under the earlier trust, or

(ii) would have been such a beneficiary if, while the earlier trust was subsisting, he had held the employment in respect of which the payment is made; and

(d) there were or are payments under the earlier trust which in the case of payments made on or after 6th October 1987, are payments made in circumstances to which sub-paragraphs (a), (b) and (c) apply.

Derivations – SI 1979/591, reg. 19A.

PAYMENTS TO DIRECTORS WHICH ARE TO BE DISREGARDED

27(1) For the purposes of earnings-related contributions, there shall be excluded from the calculation of a person's earnings any payment in so far as it is a payment–

(a) by a company;

(b) to or for the benefit of a director of that company;

(c) in respect of any employed earner's employment of that director with that company; and

(d) in respect of which paragraph (2), (3) or (4) is satisfied.

27(2) This paragraph is satisfied if–

(a) the director is a partner in a firm carrying on a profession;

(b) being a director of a company is a normal incident of membership of that profession and of membership of the firm of the director;

(c) the director is required by the terms of his partnership to account to his firm for the payment; and

(d) the payment forms an insubstantial part of that firm's gross returns.

27(3) This paragraph is satisfied if–

(a) the director was appointed to that office by a company having the right to do so by virtue of its shareholding in, or an agreement with, the company making the payment;

(b) by virtue of an agreement with the company that appointed him, the director is required to account for the payment to that company; and

(c) the payment forms part of the profits brought into charge to corporation tax or income tax of the company that appointed the director.

27(4) This paragraph is satisfied if–

(a) the director was appointed to that office by a company other than the company making the payment;

(b) by virtue of an agreement with the company that appointed him, the director is required to account for the payment to that company;

(c) the payment forms part of the profits brought into charge to corporation tax of the company that appointed the director; and

(d) the company that appointed the director is not one over which–

(i) the director has, or

(ii) any person connected with the director has, or

(iii) the director and any persons connected with him together have, control.

27(5) In this regulation–

(a) **"company"** has the meaning given by section 832(1) of the Taxes Act (interpretation of the Tax Acts) and Part 2 of Schedule 1 to ITEPA 2003;

(b) **"the director"** means the director to or for the benefit of whom the payment referred to in paragraph (1) is made; and

(c) in paragraph (4)(d)–

(i) **"control"** has the same meaning as in section 840 of the Taxes Act,

(ii) **"any person connected with the director"** means any of the following, namely the spouse, civil partner, parent, child, son-in-law or daughter-in-law of the director.

History – In reg. 27(5)(a) words "and (2)" following the words "section 832(1)" omitted and the words "and Part 2 of Schedule 1 to ITEPA 2003" added by SI 2004/770, reg. 5, with effect from 6 April 2004.
In reg. 27(5)(c)(ii) the words "civil partner," inserted by SI 2005/3130, reg. 4(2), with effect from 5 December 2005.

Derivations – SI 1979/591, reg. 19B.

LIABILITY FOR CLASS 1 CONTRIBUTIONS IN RESPECT OF EARNINGS NORMALLY PAID AFTER PENSIONABLE AGE

28 Where in the year in which an earner attains pensionable age a payment of earnings is made to or for his benefit before the date he reaches pensionable age, and those earnings would normally fall to be paid in a year following that year, he shall be excepted from liability for primary Class 1 contributions payable in respect of those earnings.

Derivations – SI 1979/591, reg. 20.

LIABILITY FOR CLASS 1 CONTRIBUTIONS OF PERSONS OVER PENSIONABLE AGE

29 If–

(a) earnings are paid to or for the benefit of an earner after he attains pensionable age; and

(b) those earnings would normally fall to be paid before the date on which he reaches pensionable age,

section 6(3) of the Act (liability for Class 1 contributions) shall not operate to except him from liability for primary Class 1 contributions in respect of those earnings.

Derivations – SI 1979/591, reg. 20A.

ABNORMAL PAY PRACTICES

30(1) If an officer of the Board is satisfied that–

(a) a secondary contributor has followed or is following a practice in the payment of earnings which is abnormal for the employment in question (**"an abnormal pay practice"**); and

(b) by reason of that practice the liability for earnings-related contributions is or has been avoided or reduced,

paragraph (2) applies.

30(2) If this paragraph applies the officer may, and if requested to do so by the earner or the secondary contributor shall, decide any question relating to a person's earnings-related contributions as if the secondary contributor had not followed an abnormal pay practice, but had followed a practice normal for the employment in question.

30(3) A decision under this regulation shall not apply to contributions based on payments made more than one year before the beginning of the year in which that decision is given.

History – Reg. 30 substituted by SI 2002/2366, reg. 5, with effect from 8 October 2002.

PRACTICES AVOIDING OR REDUCING LIABILITY FOR CONTRIBUTIONS

31(1) If an officer of the Board is satisfied that–

(a) a practice exists as to the making of irregular or unequal payments of earnings; and

(b) by reason of the practice the liability for earnings-related contributions is avoided or reduced, he may, and if requested to do so by either the earner or the secondary contributor shall, decide whether to issue a direction to secure that the same contributions are payable as would be payable if the practice were not followed.

31(2) A direction under paragraph (1)–

(a) shall specify the date from which it is to have effect, which shall not be earlier than that on which it is given;

(b) shall have effect until–

(i) the direction is superseded by the giving of a further direction, or

(ii) an officer of the Board is satisfied that the practice has ceased, or has ceased to have the effect mentioned in paragraph (1)(b); and

(c) shall be given to the earner and the secondary contributor concerned.

This is subject to the qualification in paragraph (3).

31(3) A direction under paragraph (1) need not be given to an earner if the officer of the Board is for any reason unable to ascertain his identity or whereabouts.

31(4) This regulation does not limit the operation of regulation 30.

History – Reg. 31 substituted by SI 2002/2366, reg. 6, with effect from 8 October 2002.

PART 3 – CLASS 1A CONTRIBUTIONS

INTERPRETATION FOR THE PURPOSES OF THIS PART

32 [Omitted by SI 2004/770, reg. 6 and revoked by reg. 36 and Sch. 1.]

History – Reg. 32 omitted by SI 2004/770, reg. 6 and revoked by reg. 36 and Sch. 1, with effect from 6 April 2004.

EXCEPTION FROM LIABILITY TO PAY CLASS 1A CONTRIBUTIONS IN RESPECT OF CARS MADE AVAILABLE TO MEMBERS OF AN EMPLOYED EARNER'S FAMILY OR HOUSEHOLD IN CERTAIN CIRCUMSTANCES

33 [Omitted by SI 2004/770, reg. 6 and revoked by reg. 36 and Sch. 1.]

History – Reg. 33 omitted by SI 2004/770, reg. 6 and revoked by reg. 36 and Sch. 1, with effect from 6 April 2004.

CLASS 1A CONTRIBUTIONS PAYABLE WHERE TWO OR MORE CARS ARE MADE AVAILABLE CONCURRENTLY

34 [Omitted by SI 2004/770, reg. 6 and revoked by reg. 36 and Sch. 1.]

History – Reg. 34 omitted by SI 2004/770, reg. 6 and revoked by reg. 36 and Sch. 1, with effect from 6 April 2004.

REDUCTION OF CERTAIN CLASS 1A CONTRIBUTIONS IN THE CASE OF A CAR PROVIDED OR MADE AVAILABLE BY REASON OF TWO OR MORE EMPLOYMENTS OR TO TWO OR MORE EMPLOYED EARNERS

35 [Omitted by SI 2004/770, reg. 6 and revoked by reg. 36 and Sch. 1.]

History – Reg. 35 omitted by SI 2004/770, reg. 6 and revoked by reg. 36 and Sch. 1, with effect from 6 April 2004.

REDUCTION OF CERTAIN CLASS 1A CONTRIBUTIONS ON ACCOUNT OF THE NUMBER OF EMPLOYMENTS IN THE CASES OF SOMETHING PROVIDED OR MADE AVAILABLE BY REASON OF TWO OR MORE EMPLOYMENTS AND OF SOMETHING PROVIDED OR MADE AVAILABLE TO TWO OR MORE EMPLOYED EARNERS

36(1) This regulation applies if something is provided or made available to–

(a) an employed earner by reason of two or more employed earner's employments, whether under the same employer or different employers; or

(b) two or more employed earners concurrently by reason of their respective employed earner's employments under the same employer, and all of those employed earner's employments are employments other than excluded employments within the meaning of the benefits code (see Chapter 2 of Part 3 of ITEPA 2003).

36(2) If this regulation applies the amount of any Class 1A contribution payable for the year by the person liable to pay such contribution shall be reduced by deducting from that amount an amount equal to the fraction–

$$\frac{X-1}{X}$$

of the amount which would be payable but for this regulation.

Here X is the total number of employments in respect of which the thing is provided or made available.

History – In reg. 36(1) words "other than excluded employments within the meaning of the benefits code (see Chapter 2 of Part 3 of ITEPA 2003)" substituted by SI 2004/770, reg. 7, with effect from 6 April 2004.

In reg. 36(2) words "(or, where regulation 35 applies, shall be further reduced)" omitted by SI 2004/770, reg. 7, with effect from 6 April 2004.

Derivations – SI 1979/591 reg. 22E.

Cross references – ICTA 1988, Pt. V, Ch. II: see ITEPA 2003, Pt. 3, Ch. 2 (the benefits code) and Ch. 11 (exclusion of lower-paid employments from parts of the benefits code).

REDUCTION OF CERTAIN CLASS 1A CONTRIBUTIONS IN RESPECT OF CARS MADE AVAILABLE TO DISABLED EMPLOYED EARNERS

37 [Omitted by SI 2004/770, reg. 8 and revoked by reg. 36 and Sch. 1.]

History – Reg. 37 omitted by SI 2004/770, reg. 8 and revoked by reg. 36 and Sch. 1, with effect from 6 April 2004.

EXCEPTION FROM LIABILITY TO PAY CLASS 1A CONTRIBUTIONS IN RESPECT OF CARS MADE AVAILABLE TO DISABLED EMPLOYED EARNERS ONLY FOR BUSINESS AND HOME TO WORK TRAVEL

38(1) If the conditions mentioned in paragraphs (2) to (5) are satisfied, the person who would otherwise be liable to pay the Class 1A contribution for that year in respect of the employer earner and the car mentioned in those paragraphs shall be excepted from that liability.

38(2) The first condition is that the car is made available to an earner who is disabled.

38(3) The second condition is that the car is made available to the earner by reason of his employment.

38(4) The third condition is that the car is made available on account of the earner's disability for the purposes of, or for purposes which include assisting, the earner's travelling between the earner's home and place of employment.

38(5) The fourth condition is that the terms on which the car is made available to the earner prohibit private use other than–

(a) by the earner to whom it is made available; and

(b) in travelling between the earner's home and place of employment.

38(6) The fifth condition is that no prohibited private use of the car has been made in the year.

Derivations – SI 1979/591 reg. 22G.

CALCULATION OF CLASS 1A CONTRIBUTIONS

39 Where a person is liable to pay a Class 1A contribution in accordance with section 10 of the Act (Class 1A contributions: benefits in kind etc.) the amount of that contribution shall be calculated to the nearest penny, and any amount of a halfpenny or less shall be disregarded.

Derivations – SI 1979/591 reg. 22H.

PRESCRIBED GENERAL EARNINGS IN RESPECT OF WHICH CLASS 1A CONTRIBUTIONS NOT PAYABLE

40(1) Class 1A contributions shall not be payable in respect of the general earnings prescribed by paragraphs (2) to (7).

40(2) The general earnings prescribed by this paragraph are those which are excluded from the calculation of a person's earnings in respect of any employed earner's employment by virtue of the following provisions of Schedule 3–

(za) [omitted by SI 2013/622, reg. 33,]

(a) in Part VI, paragraphs 2(b), 3 to 5, 7, 10 and 11;

(ab) in Part 7, paragraph 12;

(b) in Part VIII, paragraphs 4 to 5 and 13;

(c) *in Part IX*, paragraphs 3 to 7A; and

(d) in Part X, paragraphs 5, 9, 11 to 13 and 15.

40(3) The general earnings prescribed by this paragraph are those which are payments which are not excluded from the calculation of a person's earnings in respect of any employed earner's employment by virtue of paragraph 1 of Part II of Schedule 3 (payments in kind), but which are so excluded by virtue of paragraph 3 of Part VIII of Schedule 3 (qualifying travelling expenses) or paragraph 9 of that Part (specific and distinct expenses).

40(4) [Omitted by SI 2012/817, reg. 7(1).]

40(5) [Omitted by SI 2005/778, reg. 5.]

40(6) [Omitted by SI 2006/576, reg. 4(b).]

40(6A) [Omitted by SI 2006/576, reg. 4(b).]

40(7) The general earnings prescribed by this paragraph are so much of any general earnings as are not charged to income tax as employment income by virtue of any of the following extra-statutory concessions published by the Board as at 1st September 2000–

(a) [omitted by SI 2001/2412, reg. 3;]

(b) [omitted by SI 2003/2085, reg. 6(7);]

(c) A11 (residence in the United Kingdom: year of commencement or cessation of residence);

(d) [omitted by SI 2003/2085, reg. 6(7);]

(e) A37 (tax treatment of directors' fees received by partnerships and other companies);

(f) A56 (benefits in kind: tax treatment of accommodation in Scotland provided for employees);

(g) [omitted by SI 2003/2085, reg. 6(7);]

(h) [omitted by SI 2003/2085, reg. 6(7);]

(i) [omitted by SI 2003/2085, reg. 6(7);]

(j) [omitted by SI 2003/2085, reg. 6(7);]

(k) [omitted by SI 2003/2085, reg. 6(7);]

(l) [omitted by SI 2003/2085, reg. 6(7);]

(m) [omitted by SI 2003/2085, reg. 6(7);]

(n) [omitted by SI 2003/2085, reg. 6(7);]

(o) [omitted by SI 2003/2085, reg. 6(7);]

(p) A91 (living accommodation provided by reason of employment);

(q) A97 (Jobmatch programme).

Sub-paragraph (f) applies only to Scotland and sub-paragraph (q) does not apply to Northern Ireland.

40(8) [Omitted by SI 2005/778, reg. 5.]

40(9) [Omitted by SI 2005/778, reg. 5.]

History – In the heading to reg. 40 and in para. (1) the words "general earnings" substituted by SI 2003/2085, reg. 6(2) with effect from 1 September 2003.

In reg. 40(2)(a) the words "paragraphs 2(b), 3 to 4, 7, 10 and 11;" substituted by SI 2006/576, reg. 4(a), with effect from 6 April 2006.

Reg. 40(2)(ab) inserted by SI 2005/728, reg. 3, with effect from 6 April 2005 in respect of the academic year beginning on 1 September 2005 and subsequent academic years.

In reg. 40(2)(b), the words "4 to 5" substituted for the words "4, 5" by SI 2016/1067, reg. 3, with effect from 28 November 2016.

In reg. 40(2)(c) words "3 to 7A" substituted by SI 2004/770, reg. 9, with effect from 6 April 2004.

In reg. 40(2)–(6) the words "general earnings" substituted where first occurring and the word "those" substituted for "emoluments" in the second instance where it occurs, by SI 2003/2085, reg. 6(3) with effect from 1 September 2003.

Reg. 40(2)(za) omitted by SI 2013/622, reg. 33, with effect from 6 April 2013 in relation to the tax year 2013–14 and subsequent tax years.

Reg. 40(2)(za) inserted by SI 2001/2412, reg. 3, operative from 26 July 2001.

In reg. 40(2)(d) the words "9,11 to 13 and 15" substituted by SI 2001/2412, reg. 3, operative from 26 July 2001.

Reg. 40(4) omitted by SI 2012/817, reg. 7(1), with effect from 6 April 2012.

Reg. 40(4)(b) substituted by SI 2003/2085, reg. 6(4) with effect from 1 September 2003.

Reg. 40(5) omitted by SI 2005/778, reg. 5 with effect from 6 April 2005.

Reg. 40(6) omitted by SI 2006/576, reg. 4(b), with effect from 6 April 2006.

Reg. 40(6)(a) omitted by SI 2003/2085, reg. 6(5) with effect from 1 September 2003.

In reg. 40(6)(c) words "or sections 590 (annuities) and 591 (taxable pension income)" inserted by SI 2004/770, reg. 9, with effect from 6 April 2004.

Reg. 40(6A) omitted by SI 2006/576, reg. 4(b), with effect from 6 April 2006.

Former reg. 40(6A) inserted by SI 2003/2085, reg. 6(3) with effect from 1 September 2003.

In reg. 40(7) the words from the beginning of the para. to "by virtue of" substituted by SI 2003/2085, reg. 6(7) with effect from 1 September 2003.

Reg. 40(7)(a) omitted by SI 2001/2412, reg. 3, operative from 26 July 2001.

Reg. 40(7)(b), (d) and (g)–(o) omitted by SI 2003/2085, reg. 6(7) with effect from 1 September 2003.

In reg. 40(7) the final sentence substituted by SI 2003/2085, reg. 6(7)(c) with effect from 1 September 2003. It formerly read "Sub-paragraphs (b) and (q) do not apply to Northern Ireland and sub-paragraph (f) applies only to Scotland."

Reg. 40(8) omitted by SI 2005/778, reg. 5 with effect from 6 April 2005.

In reg. 40(8)(a) words "Part 10 or 10A" substituted by SI 2004/770, reg. 9, with effect from 6 April 2004.

In reg. 40(8) definition of emolument omitted by SI 2003/2085,reg. 6(8) with effect from 1 September 2003.

Reg. 40(9) omitted by SI 2005/778, reg. 5 with effect from 6 April 2005.

Derivations – SI 1979/591 reg. 22HA.

EXCEPTION FROM LIABILITY TO PAY CLASS 1A CONTRIBUTIONS IN RESPECT OF AN AMOUNT REPRESENTING AN AMOUNT ON WHICH CLASS 1 OR CLASS 1A CONTRIBUTIONS HAVE ALREADY BEEN PAID PURSUANT TO THE SOCIAL SECURITY CONTRIBUTIONS (LIMITED LIABILITY PARTNERSHIP) REGULATIONS 2014

40A Class 1A contributions shall not be payable in respect of a benefit in kind provided by an employer to an employed earner which represents an amount on which Class 1 or Class 1A contributions are payable by a limited liability partnership in respect of that earner by virtue of regulation 3 or 4 of the Social Security Contributions (Limited Liability Partnership) Regulations 2014.

History – Reg. 40A inserted by SI 2014/3159, reg. 5(2), with effect for the tax year 2014–15 and subsequent tax years.

EXCEPTION FROM LIABILITY TO PAY CLASS 1A CONTRIBUTIONS IN RESPECT OF SPORTING TESTIMONIALS PAYMENTS

History – In the heading the words "FOR TAX YEAR 2017–18" omitted by SI 2018/120, reg. 8(2), with effect from 6 April 2018.

40B(1) Paragraph (2) applies to Class 1A contributions payable for the tax year 2017–18 and subsequent tax years where–

(a) the whole or part of the general earnings in respect of which the Class 1A contribution is payable consists of a sporting testimonial payment, and

(b) the person making the sporting testimonial payment is the controller of the independent sporting testimonial committee.

40B(2) Class 1A contributions shall not be payable by the secondary contributor in respect of the sporting testimonial payment.

40B(3) In this regulation–

(a) **"controller"** means the person who controls the disbursement of any money raised by the independent sporting testimonial committee for or for the benefit of an individual who is or has been employed as a professional sports person,

(b) **"independent sporting testimonial committee"** means a committee which acts independently of the secondary contributor in organising a sporting testimonial and making the sporting testimonial payment, and

(c) **"sporting testimonial"** and **"sporting testimonial payment"** have the meaning given in section 226E of ITEPA 2003 (sporting testimonial payments).

History – In reg. 40B(1) the words "and subsequent tax years" inserted by SI 2018/120, reg. 8(3), with effect from 6 April 2018.
In reg. 40B(2) the words "for the tax year 2017–18" omitted by SI 2018/120, reg. 8(4), with effect from 6 April 2018.
Reg. 40B inserted by SI 2017/307, reg. 3, with effect from 6 April 2017.

PART 4 – CLASS 1B CONTRIBUTIONS

CALCULATION OF CLASS 1B CONTRIBUTIONS

41 Where a person is liable to pay a Class 1B contribution in accordance with section 10A of the Act (Class 1B contributions), the amount of that contribution shall be calculated to the nearest penny, and any amount of a halfpenny or less shall be disregarded.

Derivations – SI 1979/591 reg. 22I.

EXCEPTION FROM LIABILITY TO PAY CLASS 1B CONTRIBUTIONS

42(1) A person shall be excepted from liability to pay a Class 1B contribution for any year in respect of

(a) the amount of any general earnings which are chargeable emoluments under section 10A(4) of the Act of an employee included in a PAYE settlement agreement; and

(b) the total amount of income tax in respect of which that person is accountable to the Board in relation to general earnings of such an employee in accordance with a PAYE settlement agreement;

where the employee is a person falling within paragraph (2) or (3).

42(2) The employee falls within this paragraph if he is subject to the legislation of a contracting party, other than the United Kingdom, to the Agreement on the European Economic Area signed at Oporto on 2nd May 1992 as adjusted by the Protocol signed at Brussels on 17th March 1993.

42(3) The employee falls within this paragraph if he is subject to the legislation of a country outside the United Kingdom in respect of which there is an Order in Council under section 179 of the Administration Act (reciprocal agreements with countries outside the United Kingdom) giving effect to a reciprocal agreement.

42(4) If a person is excepted from liability to pay a Class 1B contribution for any year under paragraphs (1) to (3), he shall be entitled, if he so wishes, to pay that contribution for that year.

History – In reg. 42(1)(a) words "general earnings which are chargeable emoluments" substituted by SI 2004/770, reg. 10, with effect from 6 April 2004.

In reg. 42(1)(b) words "general earnings" substituted by SI 2004/770, reg. 10, with effect from 6 April 2004.

Derivations – SI 1979/591 reg. 22J.

PART 5 – EXCEPTION FROM LIABILITY FOR CLASS 2 CONTRIBUTIONS, PROVISIONS ABOUT CLASS 3 CONTRIBUTIONS, AND REALLOCATION AND REFUND OF CONTRIBUTIONS (OTHER THAN CLASS 4)

EXCEPTION FROM CLASS 2 CONTRIBUTIONS

History – In heading, the words "liability for" (which appeared before the words "Class 2") omitted by SI 2015/478, reg. 4(2), with effect from 6 April 2015.

43(1) Subject to paragraphs (2) and (3), a self-employed earner shall be excepted from paying a Class 2 contribution for any contribution week

(a) in respect of the whole of which the earner is in receipt of incapacity benefit;

(ab) in respect of the whole of which the earner is in receipt of employment and support allowance;

(b) throughout the whole of which the earner is incapable of work;

(c) in respect of which the earner is in receipt of maternity allowance;

(d) throughout the whole of which he is undergoing imprisonment or detention in legal custody; or

(e) in respect of any part of which the earner is in receipt of carer's allowance or an unemployability supplement.

43(2) For the purposes of paragraph (1), in computing the period of a contribution week

(a) subject to sub-paragraph (b), Sunday shall be disregarded;

(b) in the case of a self-employed earner who objects on religious grounds to working on a specific day in each contribution week other than Sunday, and does not object to working on Sunday, that specific day shall be disregarded instead of Sunday.

43(3) If a self-employed earner is excepted from paying a Class 2 contribution for any contribution week by virtue of paragraph (1), he shall be entitled, subject to Part 6, to pay a contribution for that week if he so wishes.

History – Reg. 43(1)(ab) inserted by SI 2015/478, reg. 4(3), with effect from 6 April 2015.

In reg. 43(1)(e) words "carer's allowance" substituted by SI 2002/2924, reg. 3(1), with effect from 1 April 2003.

In reg. 43(1) and (3), the word "paying" substituted for the words "liability to pay" by SI 2015/478, reg. 4(4), with effect from 6 April 2015.

Derivations – SI 1979/591 reg. 23.

APPLICATION FOR, AND DURATION AND CANCELLATION OF, CERTIFICATES OF EXCEPTION

44 [Omitted by SI 2015/478, reg. 24(1)(b).]

History – Reg. 44 omitted by SI 2015/478, reg. 24(1)(b), with effect from 6 April 2015.

EARNINGS FOR THE PURPOSES OF CERTIFICATES OF EXCEPTION

45 [Omitted by SI 2015/478, reg. 24(1)(b).]

History – Reg. 45 omitted by SI 2015/478, reg. 24(1)(b), with effect from 6 April 2015.

CERTIFICATES OF EXCEPTION – EXCEPTION FROM LIABILITY FOR, AND ENTITLEMENT TO PAY, CLASS 2 CONTRIBUTIONS

46 [Omitted by SI 2015/478, reg. 24(1)(b).]

History – Reg. 46 omitted by SI 2015/478, reg. 24(1)(b), with effect from 6 April 2015.

RETURN OF CLASS 2 CONTRIBUTIONS PAID BY LOW EARNERS

47 [Omitted by SI 2015/478, reg. 24(1)(b).]

History – Reg. 47 omitted by SI 2015/478, reg. 24(1)(b), with effect from 6 April 2015.

CLASS 3 CONTRIBUTIONS

48(1) Subject to sections 13(2) and 14(1) of the Act (Class 3 contributions only payable for purposes of satisfying certain conditions and circumstances in which persons shall not be entitled to pay Class 3 contributions) and these Regulations, any person who is over the age of 16 and fulfils the conditions as to residence or presence in Great Britain or in Northern Ireland prescribed in regulation 145 may, if he so wishes, pay Class 3 contributions.

48(2) It shall be a condition of a person's right to pay a Class 3 contribution that he

(a) complies with Part 7 in so far as it applies to persons paying such a contribution, and

(b) complies with either of the two conditions specified in paragraph (3).

48(3) The conditions are that the person specified in paragraph (1) shall either

(a) pay the contribution not later than 42 days after the end of the year in respect of which it is paid; or

(b) subject to regulations 50, 50A and 50C and Part 6, pay the contribution

(i) where the contribution is payable in respect of any year before 6th April 1982, before the end of the second year following the year in respect of which it is paid; and where the contribution is payable in respect of any year after 5th April 1982, before the end of the sixth year following the year in respect of which it is paid; or

(ii) where the year in respect of which it is paid includes a period of at least 6 months throughout which the contributor has been undergoing full-time education, or full-time apprenticeship or training for which, in either case, any earnings are less than the lower earnings limit, or has been undergoing imprisonment or detention in legal custody, before the end of the sixth year following the year in which the education, or apprenticeship or training, or imprisonment or detention terminated; and

(iii) where the year first mentioned in head (ii) is immediately preceded or followed by a year in which the conditions specified in that head are not satisfied in respect only of the length of the period specified in that head, in respect of that preceding or following year, before the end of the sixth year following the year in which the education, apprenticeship, training, imprisonment or detention described in that head terminated.

History – In reg. 48(1), the word "contribution" (which appeared after the words "satisfying certain") omitted by SI 2015/1985, art. 21(2), with effect from 6 April 2016 immediately after the State Pension Regulations 2015 (SI 2015/173).
In reg. 48(3)(b), ", 50B" omitted by SI 2015/478, reg. 24(2), with effect from 6 April 2015.
In reg. 48(3)(b), the words ", 50B and 50C" substituted for the words "and 50B" by SI 2013/622, reg. 34, with effect from 6 April 2013 in relation to the tax year 2013–14 and subsequent tax years.
In reg. 48(3)(b) the words "regulations 50, 50A and 50B" substituted by SI 2007/2520, reg. 4, with effect from 1 October 2007.
In reg. 48(3)(b) former words "regulations 50 and 50A" substituted by SI 2004/1362, reg. 3, with effect from 17 May 2004.

Derivations – SI 1979/591 reg. 27.

PRECLUDED CLASS 3 CONTRIBUTIONS

49(1) Subject to paragraph (2), no person shall be entitled to pay a Class 3 contribution

(a) in respect of any year if he would, but for the payment of such a contribution, be entitled to be credited with a contribution;

(b) in respect of any year in which the aggregate of his earnings factors derived from earnings in respect of which primary Class 1 contributions, payable at the main primary percentage have been paid, credited earnings, or Class 2 or Class 3 contributions paid or credited is less than 25 times the lower earnings limit and either the period has passed within which any Class 3 contributions may be treated as paid for that year under regulation 4 of the Social Security (Crediting and Treatment of Contributions, and National Insurance Numbers) Regulations 2001 or he has sooner, in accordance with regulation 56, applied for the return of any Class 3 contributions paid in respect of that year;

(c) in respect of any year if the aggregate of his earnings factors derived from earnings in respect of which primary Class 1 contributions, payable at the main primary percentage have been paid, credited earnings, or Class 2 or Class 3 contributions paid or credited is more than 25 times the lower earnings limit but less than the qualifying earnings factor and either

(i) the period referred to in sub-paragraph (b) has passed, or

(ii) he has sooner applied under regulation 56 for the return of any Class 3 contributions paid in respect of that year;

(d) in respect of any year if it causes the aggregate of his earnings factors derived from earnings in respect of which primary Class 1 contributions, payable at the main primary percentage have been paid, credited earnings, or Class 2 or Class 3 contributions paid or credited to exceed the qualifying earnings factor by an amount which is half or more than half that year's lower earnings limit;

(e) [omitted by SI 2005/778, reg. 6(2);]

(f) in respect of the year in which he attains 17 or 18 years of age if in an earlier year he has satisfied the first contribution condition for retirement pension or widow's pension or widowed mother's allowance.

Sub-paragraphs (a), (b) and (c) are subject to the following qualification.

49(2) A person shall be entitled to pay a Class 3 contribution in respect of any year if it would enable him to satisfy

(a) the first contribution condition for retirement pension or widowed mother's allowance, widowed parent's allowance or widow's pension and he has not satisfied that condition at the beginning of that year; or

(b) the contribution condition for widow's payment and he has not satisfied that condition at the beginning of that year.

49(2A) No person shall be entitled to pay a Class 3 contribution in respect of the year in which he attains pensionable age or any subsequent year.

This is subject to the following qualification.

49(2B) A person–

(a) who has attained the age of 60;

(b) to whom a full gender recognition certificate is issued; and

(c) whose acquired gender is male;

is not precluded from paying Class 3 contributions for the relevant years.

49(2C) For the purposes of paragraph (2B) the relevant years are–

(a) the year in which the person attains the age of 60;

(b) any subsequent year before that in which the full gender recognition certificate is issued; and

(c) the year in which the full gender recognition certificate is issued.

49(3) In this regulation **"credited"** means credited for the purposes of retirement pension, a state pension under section 2 or 4 of the Pensions Act 2014 widowed mother's allowance, widowed parent's allowance and widow's pension.

History – Reg. 49(1)(e) omitted by SI 2005/778, reg. 6(2) with effect from 6 April 2005.
In reg. 49(1), the words "primary Class 1 contributions, payable at the main primary percentage" substituted, in each place that they occur, by SI 2003/193, reg. 7 with effect from 6 April 2003.
In reg. 49(1), the words "Sub-paragraphs (a), (b) and (c) are subject to the following qualification." inserted by SI 2001/3728, reg. 2(2) with effect from 12 December 2001.
In reg. 49(2), the words "Notwithstanding paragraph (1)(a), (b) or (c)," deleted by SI 2001/3728, reg. 2(3)(a) with effect from 12 December 2001.
In reg. 49(2)(a), the words ", bereavement allowance" (which appeared after the words "widowed parent's allowance") omitted by SI 2017/422, art. 18(a)(i), with effect from 6 April 2017 (the day on which PA 2014, s. 30 comes into force for all purposes (SI 2017/297, art. 3(b)), subject to SI 2017/422, art. 2 (later commencement for abolition of bereavement payment and bereavement allowance) and 3 (commencement for entitlement to bereavement payment and bereavement support payment).
In reg. 49(2)(b), the words "bereavement payment or" (which appeared before the words "widow's payment") omitted by SI 2017/422, art. 18(a)(ii), with effect from 6 April 2017 (the day on which PA 2014, s. 30 comes into force for all purposes (SI 2017/297, art. 3(b)), subject to SI 2017/422, art. 2 (later commencement for abolition of bereavement payment and bereavement allowance) and 3 (commencement for entitlement to bereavement payment and bereavement support payment).
In reg. 49(2)(a), the words "widowed mother's allowance, widowed parent's allowance, bereavement allowance or widow's pension" inserted by SI 2001/3728, reg. 2(3)(b) with effect from 12 December 2001.
In reg. 49(2)(b), the words " bereavement payment or" inserted by SI 2001/3728, reg. 2(3)(c) with effect from 12 December 2001.
Reg. 49(2A) inserted by SI 2005/778, reg. 6(3) with effect from 6 April 2005.
Reg. 49(2B) inserted by SI 2005/778, reg. 6(3) with effect from 6 April 2005.
Reg. 49(2C) inserted by SI 2005/778, reg. 6(3) with effect from 6 April 2005.
In reg. 49(3), the words "bereavement allowance" (which appeared after the words "widowed parent's allowance") omitted by SI 2017/422, art. 18(b), with effect from 6 April 2017 (the day on which PA 2014, s. 30 comes into force for all purposes (SI 2017/297, art. 3(b)), subject to SI 2017/422, art. 2 (later commencement for abolition of bereavement payment and bereavement allowance) and 3 (commencement for entitlement to bereavement payment and bereavement support payment).
In reg. 49(3), the words "a state pension under section 2 or 4 of the Pensions Act 2014" inserted by SI 2015/1985, art. 21(3), with effect from 6 April 2016 immediately after the State Pension Regulations 2015 (SI 2015/173).
In reg. 49(3),the words ", widowed parent's allowance, bereavement allowance" inserted by SI 2001/3728, reg. 2(4) with effect from 12 December 2001.

Derivations – SI 1979/591 reg. 28.

CONDITIONS RELATING TO CLASS 3 CONTRIBUTIONS: TRANSFERS TO THE COMMUNITIES' PENSION SCHEME

49A(1) The entitlement of a person to pay a Class 3 contribution is subject to the condition set out in paragraph (2).

49A(2) The condition is that a person may not pay a Class 3 contribution for any part of the period to which that person's Communities transfer relates.

49A(3) For the purposes of this regulation, paragraph (3) of regulation 148A applies to determine the meaning of a Communities transfer in the same way as it applies to determine the meaning of that expression for the purposes of that regulation.

History – Reg. 49A inserted by SI 2007/1838, reg. 3, with effect from 18 July 2007.

CLASS 3 CONTRIBUTIONS NOT PAID WITHIN PRESCRIBED PERIODS

50(1) If–

(a) a person (**"the contributor"**)–

(i) was entitled to pay a Class 3 contribution under regulation 48, 146(2)(b) or 147; and

(ii) failed to pay that contribution in the appropriate period specified for its payment; and

(b) the condition in paragraph (2) is satisfied,

the contributor may pay the contribution within such further period as an officer of the Board may direct.

50(2) The condition is that an officer of the Board is satisfied that–

(a) the failure to pay is attributable to the contributor's ignorance or error; and

(b) that ignorance or error was not the result of the contributor's failure to exercise due care and diligence.

History – Reg. 50 substituted by SI 2002/2366, reg. 7, with effect from 8 October 2002.

CLASS 3 CONTRIBUTIONS: TAX YEARS 1996–97 TO 2001–02

50A(1) This regulation applies to Class 3 contributions payable in respect of the tax years 1996–97 to 2001–02 ("the relevant years").

50A(2) If a person ("the contributor")–

(a) was entitled to pay a Class 3 contribution in respect of any of the relevant years under regulation 48, 146(2)(b) or 147;

(b) had not, before the coming into force of these Regulations, paid that contribution; and

(c) had not, before 1st November 2003, received notice–

(i) in the case of a contributor in Great Britain, from the Department for Work and Pensions, the former Department of Social Security or the Board, or

(ii) in the case of a contributor in Northern Ireland, from the Department for Social Development, the former Department for Health and Social Services for Northern Ireland or the Board,

that he was entitled to pay a Class 3 contribution for that relevant year;

he may pay the contribution within the period specified in paragraph (3).

50A(3) The period within which the contribution may be paid is the period beginning with the coming into force of these Regulations and ending–

(a) in the case of a contributor who has reached or will reach pensionable age before 24th October 2004, on 5th April 2010; and

(b) in the case of a contributor who will reach pensionable age on or after 24th October 2004, on 5th April 2009.

50A(4) Nothing in this regulation limits the application of regulation 50 or 50B.

History – In reg. 50A(4) the words "regulations 50 or 50B" substituted for words "regulation 50" by SI 2007/2520, reg. 5, with effect from 1 October 2007.

Reg. 50A inserted by SI 2004/1362, reg. 4, with effect from 17 May 2004.

CLASS 3 CONTRIBUTIONS: TAX YEARS 1993–94 TO 2007–08

50B [Omitted by SI 2015/478, reg. 24(1)(c).]

History – Reg. 50B omitted by SI 2015/478, reg. 24(1)(c), with effect from 6 April 2015.

CLASS 3 CONTRIBUTIONS: TAX YEARS 2006–07 TO 2015–16: UNAVAILABILITY OF PENSION STATEMENTS 2013–14 TO 2016–17

50C(1) This regulation applies to Class 3 contributions payable in respect of one or more of the tax years 2006–07 to 2015–16 ("the relevant contribution years").

50C(2) *Paragraph (3) applies if* a person ("the contributor")–

(a) was entitled under regulation 48, 146(2)(b) or 147(1)(b) to pay a Class 3 contribution in respect of one or more of the relevant contribution years;

(b) had not, before the coming into force of this regulation, paid that contribution; and

(c) will reach pensionable age on or after 6th April 2016.

50C(3) The contributor may pay a Class 3 contribution under this regulation, in respect of any of the relevant contribution years, within the period specified in paragraph (4).

50C(4) The period within which the contribution may be paid is the period beginning on 6th April 2013 and ending on 5th April 2023.

50C(5) Notwithstanding section 13(6) of the Act, the amount of a Class 3 contribution payable under this regulation shall be–

(a) in respect of contribution years 2006–07 to 2009–10, the amount payable in relation to tax year 2012–13; or

(b) in respect of contribution years 2010–11 to 2015–16, the amount payable in the contribution year to which the payment relates.

50C(6) Paragraph (5) does not apply to a Class 3 contribution paid on or after 6th April 2019.

50C(7) Nothing in this regulation limits the application of regulations 50, 50A and 50B.

History – In reg. 50C(2)(c), "2016" substituted for "2017" by SI 2013/718, reg. 2(2), with effect from 18 April 2013.
Reg. 50C inserted by SI 2013/622, reg. 35, with effect from 6 April 2013 in relation to the tax year 2013–14 and subsequent tax years.

Notes – Where the contributor reaches pensionable age on or after 6 April 2016 but before 6 April 2017 the reference to 6th April 2013 in reg. 50C(4) is to be read as a reference to 18th April 2013 (SI 2013/718, reg. 3).

DISPOSAL OF CONTRIBUTIONS NOT PROPERLY PAID

51(1) Where contributions (other than Class 1A, Class 1B or Class 4 contributions) are paid which are of the wrong class, or at the wrong rate, or of the wrong amount, HMRC may treat them as paid on account of contributions properly payable under the Act.

51(2) Where the whole or any part of a Class 1A contribution or a Class 1B contribution falls to be returned by HMRC to any person under regulation 52 or 52A or any part of a Class 1A contribution falls to be repaid by HMRC to any person under regulation 55(1), or regulation 55A, HMRC may treat

(a) the amount of the Class 1A contribution or, as the case may be, any part of such a contribution, as a payment on account of any secondary Class 1 contributions, Class 1B contributions or Class 2 contributions;

(b) the amount of that Class 1B contribution or, as the case may be, any part of such a contribution, as a payment on account of any secondary Class 1 contributions, Class 1A contribution or Class 2 contributions, properly payable by that person.

History – In reg. 51, in each place it occurs, "HMRC" substituted for the words "the Board" by SI 2011/797, reg. 4(a), with effect from 6 April 2011.
In reg. 51(2) words "regulation 52 or 52A" substituted by SI 2004/770, reg. 11, with effect from 6 April 2004, in respect of contributions payable in respect of the year 2003–04 and subsequent years.
In reg. 51(2), the words "to any person under regulation 55(1), or regulation 55A" substituted for the words "to any person under regulation 55(1)" by SI 2011/797, reg. 4(b), with effect from 6 April 2011.

Derivations – SI 1979/591 reg. 31.

RETURN OF CONTRIBUTIONS PAID IN ERROR

52(1) This regulation applies if a contribution other than a Class 4 contribution has been paid in error.

This regulation is subject to regulations 51 and 57.

52(2) If this regulation applies, an application may be made to the Board for the return of the contribution paid in error.

52(3) An application under paragraph (2) shall be made to the Board–

(a) in writing, or in such form and by such means of electronic communications as are approved; and

(b) within the time permitted by paragraph (8).

52(4) On the making of an application under paragraph (2) the Board shall return the contribution paid in error.

This is subject to paragraphs (5) and (6).

52(5) Paragraph (4) does not require the return of contributions unless the amount to be returned exceeds–

(a) in the case of Class 1 contributions, 1/15 of a contribution at the main primary percentage payable on earnings at the upper earnings limit in respect of primary Class 1 contributions prescribed in regulation 10 for the last or only year in respect of which the contributions were paid; or

(b) in the case of a Class 1A or Class 1B contribution, 50 pence.

52(6) Paragraph (4) does not require the return of a primary Class 1 contribution which is treated as properly paid by regulation 3 of the Social Security (Additional Pension) (Contributions Paid in Error) Regulations 1996.

52(7) Contributions paid by a secondary contributor on behalf of any person in error–

(a) if they are not recovered from that person by the secondary contributor, may be returned to the secondary contributor; and

(b) if they are recovered by the secondary contributor from that person may be returned–

(i) to that person; or

(ii) with that person's consent given in writing or in such form and by such means of electronic communications as may be approved, to the secondary contributor.

52(8) An application for the return of any contribution paid in error shall be made within the period of six years from the end of the year in which the contribution was due to be paid.

This is subject to the following qualification.

If the application is made after the end of that period, an officer of the Board shall admit it if satisfied that–

(a) the person making the application had reasonable excuse for not making the application within that period; and

(b) the application was made without unreasonable delay after the excuse had ceased.

52(9) In this regulation **"error"** means, and means only, an error which–

(a) is made at the time of the payment; and

(b) relates to some past or present matter.

History – Reg. 52 substituted by SI 2004/770, reg. 12, with effect from 6 April 2004, in respect of contributions payable in respect of the year 2003–04 and subsequent years.
Reg. 52 substituted by SI 2002/2366, reg. 8, with effect from 8 October 2002.

RETURN OF CONTRIBUTIONS PAID IN EXCESS OF MAXIMA PRESCRIBED IN REGULATION 21

52A(1) This regulation applies if there has been a payment of contributions in excess of the maximum determined in accordance with regulation 21 (annual maxima for those with more than one employment) in the particular case.

This regulation is subject to regulations 51, 52 and 57.

52A(2) If this regulation applies, an application may be made to the Board, in writing or in such form and by such means of electronic communications as may be approved for the return of so much of the payment of contributions as exceeds the maximum determined in accordance with regulation 21 in the particular case.

52A(3) On the making of an application under paragraph (2) the Board shall, subject to the following provisions of this regulation, return so much of the contributions actually paid by the earner as exceeds the maximum determined in accordance with regulation 21 in the particular case.

52A(4) Paragraph (3) does not require the return of–

(a) a payment of Class 1 or Class 2 contributions unless the amount to be returned exceeds 1/15 of a contribution at the primary percentage payable on earnings at the upper-earnings limit in respect of main primary Class 1 contributions prescribed in regulation 10 for the last or only year in respect of which the contributions were paid;

(b) a primary Class 1 contribution to which regulation 3 of the Social Security (Additional Pension) (Contributions Paid in Error) Regulations 1996 (purposes for which primary Class 1 contributions paid in error are to be treated as properly paid) applies.

52A(5) Contributions to which this regulation applies shall be returned in the following order–

(a) primary Class 1 contributions at the reduced rate;

(b) Class 2 contributions;

(c) primary Class 1 contributions at the main primary percentage.

(d) [omitted by SI 2016/352, reg. 13(b)–(c),]

(e) [omitted by SI 2016/352, reg. 13(b)–(c).]

52A(6) [Omitted by SI 2016/352, reg. 13(d).]

52A(7) [Omitted by SI 2016/352, reg. 13(d).]

52A(8) [Omitted by SI 2016/352, reg. 13(d).]

52A(9) Contributions paid by a secondary contributor on behalf of any person in excess of the amount *specified in regulation 21*–

(a) if they are not recovered from that person by the secondary contributor, may be returned to the secondary contributor; and

(b) if they are recovered by the secondary contributor from that person may be returned–

(i) to that person; or

(ii) with that person's consent given in writing or in such form and by such means of electronic communications as may be approved, to the secondary contributor.

History – In reg. 52A(3), the words "contributions actually paid by the earner" substituted for the words "payment of contributions" by SI 2016/352, reg. 13(a), with effect from 6 April 2016, subject to savings in relation to rights or obligations arising in connection with tax years beginning before 6 April 2016 (and for savings purposes, references to repealed provisions of the Pension Schemes Act 1993 are to be read as though such provisions were still in force).

Reg. 52A(5)(d) and (e) omitted (and the "." after (c) substituted for ";") by SI 2016/352, reg. 13(b)–(c), with effect from 6 April 2016, subject to savings in relation to rights or obligations arising in connection with tax years beginning before 6 April 2016 (and for savings purposes, references to repealed provisions of the Pension Schemes Act 1993 are to be read as though such provisions were still in force). Former reg. 52A(5)(d) and (e) read as follows:

"(d) any amount of primary Class 1 contributions reduced in accordance with section 41(1) and (1A) of the Pensions Act in respect of COSRS employment;

(e) any amount of primary Class 1 contributions reduced in accordance with section 42A(1) and (2) of the Pensions Act in respect of COMPS employment.".

In reg. 52A(6), "10.6%" substituted for "10.4%" in each place where it appears by SI 2013/622, reg. 36, with effect in relation to contributions paid in respect of the tax year 2012–13 and subsequent tax years.

In reg. 52A(6), "12%" substituted for "11%" in each place where it appears by SI 2012/817, reg. 8(a), with effect in relation to contributions paid in respect of the tax year 2011–12 and subsequent tax years.

In reg. 52A(6), "10.4%" substituted for "9.4%" in each place where it appears by SI 2012/817, reg. 8(b), with effect in relation to contributions paid in respect of the tax year 2011–12 and subsequent tax years.

In reg. 52A(6) the word "and" at the end of the definition of "an APP employment" omitted, and the definition of "UAP" inserted and Rules 2 and 3 substituted by SI 2010/646, reg. 2, with effect from 6 April 2010 in relation to contributions paid in respect of 2009–10 and subsequent years.

Reg. 52A(6)–(8) omitted by SI 2016/352, reg. 13(d), with effect from 6 April 2016, subject to savings in relation to rights or obligations arising in connection with tax years beginning before 6 April 2016 (and for savings purposes, references to repealed provisions of the Pension Schemes Act 1993 are to be read as though such provisions were still in force). Former reg. 52A(6)–(8) read as follows:

"**52A(6)** The amount to be refunded is determined in accordance with the following Rules.

In this paragraph–

"a valid personal pension notice" means a notice given under subsection (1) of section 44 of the Pensions Act (approved personal pension arrangements) which has not been rejected by the Board;

"an APP employment" means an employment in respect of which a valid personal pension notice has been given;

"UAP" means the upper accrual point; and

"UEL" means the upper earnings limit for the year in respect of which the contributions were due to be paid and **"PT"** means the primary threshold for that year.

Rule 1 applies where none of the employments is contracted-out.

Rule 2 applies where at least one employment is contracted-out and no valid personal pension notice has been given in respect of another employment.

Rule 3 applies where at least one of the employments is contracted-out and a valid personal pension notice has been given in respect of another employment.

Rule 1

The amount to be returned is the excess of the contributions actually paid by the earner over the maximum prescribed by regulation 21 in the particular case.

Rule 2

If the amount of contributions paid in respect of contracted-out employments exceeds the amount found by the following formula, the amount to be returned is the excess.

The formula is–

$53 \times [((UAP - PT) \times 10.6\%) + ((UEL - UAP) \times 12\%)]$

In any other case to which this Rule applies take the following Steps: the amount to be returned is the excess of the contributions actually paid by the earner over the amount found by Step 5 in the following sequence.

Step 1

Determine the amount of earnings between the PT and UAP in respect of contracted-out employments held in the year.

Step 2

Multiply the amount found at Step 1 by 10.6%.

Step 3

Subtract the amount found at Step 1 from that found by the formula–

$53 \times (UEL - PT)$

Step 4

Multiply the result found at Step 3 by 12%.

Step 5

Add together the results of Steps 2 and 4.

Rule 3

If the amount of contributions paid in respect of APP employments exceeds the amount produced by the formula below, the amount to be refunded is the excess. The formula is–

$53 \times (UEL - PT) \times 12\%$

In any other case to which this Rule applies take the following Steps: the amount to be returned is the excess of the contributions actually paid by the earner over the amount found by Step 7 in the following sequence.

Step 1

Determine the amount of earnings between the PT and UEL in respect of APP employments held in the year.

Step 2

Multiply the amount found at Step 1 by 12%.

Step 3

Subtract the amount found at Step 1 from that found by the formula–

$53 \times (UAP - PT)$

If the result is a positive amount go to Step 4, otherwise go to Step 5.

Step 4

Multiply the amount found at Step 3 by 10.6%.

Step 5

Subtract the amount found at Step 1 together with any positive amount found at Step 3 from the amount found by the formula–

53 × (*UEL* – *PT*)

Step 6

Multiply the amount found at Step 5 by 12%.

Step 7

Add together the results of Steps 2, 4 (if completed) and 6.

52A(7) From the amount otherwise falling to be returned under Rule 2 or Rule 3 in paragraph (6) there shall be deducted so much of any payment of contributions as is attributable to the application of Steps Five and Seven in regulation 21(2).

52A(8) If–

(a) an application has been made under paragraph (2) for the return of contributions in excess of the amount specified in regulation 21, and

(b) the Board have been given notice under section 44(1) of the Pensions Act and have not rejected it,

the contributions shall be returned in the order specified in paragraph (5) save that the contributions specified in sub-paragraph (c) shall be returned after those in sub-paragraphs (d) and (e).".

Reg. 52A inserted by SI 2004/770, reg. 12, with effect from 6 April 2004, in respect of contributions payable in respect of the year 2003–04 and subsequent years.

RETURN OF CONTRIBUTIONS: FURTHER PROVISIONS

53 [Omitted by SI 2006/576, reg. 5.]

History – Reg. 53 omitted by SI 2006/576, reg. 5, with effect from 6 April 2006.

Derivations – SI 1979/591 reg. 32A.

RETURN OF CLASS 1 CONTRIBUTIONS PAID AT THE NON-CONTRACTED OUT RATE INSTEAD OF AT THE CONTRACTED-OUT RATE

54 [Omitted by SI 2016/352, reg. 14.]

History – Reg. 54 omitted by SI 2016/352, reg. 14, with effect from 6 April 2016, subject to savings in relation to rights or obligations arising in connection with tax years beginning before 6 April 2016 (and for savings purposes, references to repealed provisions of the Pension Schemes Act 1993 are to be read as though such provisions were still in force). Former reg. 54 read as follows:

"**54(1)** Subject to paragraphs (2) and (3) and without prejudice to paragraph 13(2) and (3) of Schedule 4, where a secondary contributor has paid an amount on account of contributions at the non-contracted-out rate in respect of any employed earner's employment which amount he would have been liable to pay but for that employment being or becoming contracted-out employment, the Board shall, on application of the secondary contributor, return to him the amount so paid after deducting the amount of Class 1 contributions payable at the contracted-out rate in respect of that employment.

54(2) Any amount falling to be returned under paragraph (1) which has been paid by the secondary contributor on behalf of an earner and recovered from him shall be returned to the earner, or with the earner's consent given–

(a) in writing; or

(b) in such form and by such means of electronic communications as are approved,

to the secondary contributor.

54(3) An application under paragraph (1) shall be made in such manner as the Board shall approve and within the period of 6 years from the end of the year in which the contracting-out certificate in respect of the employment was issued.

This is subject to the following qualification.

If the application is made after the end of that period, an officer of the Board shall admit it if satisfied that–

(a) the secondary contributor had reasonable excuse for not making the application within that period; and

(b) the application was made without unreasonable delay after the excuse had ceased.".

In former reg. 54(3) words from "was issued." to the end substituted by SI 2002/2366, reg. 9, with effect from 8 October 2002.

Derivations – SI 1979/591 reg. 33.

REPAYMENT OF CLASS 1A CONTRIBUTIONS

55(1) Subject to regulations 51 and 57and paragraphs (2) and (3), where, in a case specified in paragraph (2), in the light of information provided to the Board, it appears that too much has been paid in respect of a Class 1A contribution, they shall repay to the person paying that contribution the amount which has been overpaid, unless that amount does not exceed 50 pence.

55(2) The cases to which paragraph (1) applies are those in which a person has paid a Class 1A contribution and –

(a) in calculating the amount of that contribution the person used information which later proves to have been inaccurate or incomplete; or

(b) the employee who received the general earnings in respect of which the contribution was payable is later found to have been a person not residing in the United Kingdom for the purposes of income tax at the time of receipt.

55(3) *The repayment of part of a Class 1A* contribution under paragraph (1) is subject to the condition that the person referred to in that paragraph (**"the applicant"**) shall make an application to that effect in writing to the Board and within the period of 6 years from the end of the year in which the Class 1A contribution was due to be paid.

This is subject to the following qualification.

If the application is made after the end of that period, an officer of the Board shall admit it if satisfied that–

(a) the applicant had reasonable excuse for not making the application within that period; and

(b) the application was made without unreasonable delay after the excuse had ceased.

History – In reg. 55(2)(b) "general earnings" substituted by SI 2004/770, reg. 13, with effect from 6 April 2004.
In reg. 55(3) "("the applicant")" inserted and words from "was due to be paid." to the end, substituted by SI 2002/2366, reg.10, with effect from 8 October 2002.

Derivations – SI 1979/591 reg. 33A.

REPAYMENT OF CLASS 1A CONTRIBUTIONS: CERTAIN EARNINGS NO LONGER TREATED AS EARNINGS FOR INCOME TAX PURPOSES

55A(1) Subject to regulations 51 and 57 and to paragraph (2), where an officer of Revenue and Customs is satisfied that an amount treated as earnings in respect of which a Class 1A contribution was paid is no longer treated as earnings in accordance with the provisions of sections 100A and 100B of the Income Tax (Earnings and Pensions) Act 2003 (homes outside UK owned through company etc), the amount paid shall be repaid to the person who paid that contribution.

55A(2) The repayment of all or part of a Class 1A contribution under paragraph (1) is subject to the condition that an application shall be made in writing to HMRC on or before 6th April 2015.

History – Reg. 55A inserted by SI 2011/797, reg. 3, with effect from 6 April 2011.

Other material – Misc. 206: guidance on applications for refunds under reg. 55A.

RETURN OF PRECLUDED CLASS 3 CONTRIBUTIONS

56(1) Subject to regulations 51 and 57 and to paragraph (2), where a contributor has paid a Class 3 contribution which by virtue of section 14(1) of the Act (restriction on the right to pay Class 3 contributions) or regulation 49 he was not entitled to pay, the Board shall, on application of the contributor, return that contribution to the contributor.

56(2) A contributor wishing to apply for the return of a contribution falling within paragraph (1) shall make an application to the Board either–

(a) in writing; or

(b) in such form, and by such means of electronic communications, as are approved.

Derivations – SI 1979/591 reg. 34.

REPAYMENT OF CLASS 3A CONTRIBUTIONS

56A(1) Where a Class 3A contribution has been paid, the contribution shall be repaid if one or more of the following conditions are satisfied–

(a) the person who paid the contribution ("the contributor") dies within the period of 90 days beginning with the date of payment of the contribution, or

(b) the contributor makes an application to HMRC for repayment within the period of 90 days beginning with the date of payment of the contribution.

56A(2) Where a Class 3A contribution is repaid, any amounts received under section 45(1)(b) or (2)(e) of the Act in return for that contribution shall be deducted from the repayment.

History – Reg. 56A and the heading preceding it inserted by SI 2014/2746, reg. 4(2), with effect from 12 October 2015.

CALCULATION OF RETURN OF CONTRIBUTIONS

57(1) In calculating the amount of any return of contributions to be made under regulation 52, 52A, 55, 55A or 56, there shall be deducted

(a) the amount of any contribution which has under regulation 51 been treated as paid on account of other contributions;

(b) in the case of such contributions paid in error in respect of any person, the amount, if any, paid to that person (and to any other person on the basis of that error) by way of contributory benefit which would not have been paid had any of the contributions (in respect of which an application for their return is duly made in accordance with regulation 52(8)) not been paid in the first instance;

(c) the amount of any contributions equivalent premium payable under Chapter III of Part III of the Pensions Act;

(d) the amount of any minimum contributions paid by the Board under section 43 of the Pensions Act (minimum contributions to personal pension schemes);

(e) the amount of any payment made by the Board under section 7 of the Social Security Act 1986 (schemes becoming contracted-out between 1986 and 1993); and

(f) in the case of such contributions paid in error in respect of any person, the amount of any payment made by the Board under section 42A(3) of the Pensions Act (age-related rebates).

57(2) Paragraph (1)(b) is subject to the qualification that, if the Secretary of State certifies that a deduction of an additional amount of income support or income-based job-seeker's allowance has been made under regulation 13 of the Social Security (Payments on account, Overpayments and Recovery) Regulations 1988 ("the 1988 Regulations") (sums to be deducted in calculating the recoverable amount), paragraph (3) applies.

57(3) If this paragraph applies, the amount to be returned shall be reduced by applying the formula

$$CB - IS$$

here

CB is the amount of contributory benefit specified in paragraph (1)(b) and

IS is the amount of income support or income-based job-seeker's allowance specified in regulation 13(b) of the 1988 Regulations.

57(4) In this regulation the expression **"contributions equivalent premium"** has the same meaning as in section 55(2) of the Pensions Act.

History – In reg. 57(1), ", 55, 55A" inserted by SI 2011/797, reg. 5, with effect from 6 April 2011.
In reg. 57(1) "regulation 52, 52A or 56" substituted, and "regulation 52(8)" substituted by SI 2004/770, reg. 14, with effect from 6 April 2004, in respect of contributions payable in respect of the year 2003–04 and subsequent years.

Derivations – SI 1979/591 reg. 35.

REALLOCATION OF CONTRIBUTIONS FOR BENEFIT PURPOSES

58(1) Where any payment of earnings is made in one year which, but for regulation 7(3), would by virtue of that regulation have been treated as paid at an interval falling within another year, the contributions paid in respect of those earnings shall, on the application of the employed earner or the direction of the Secretary of State, be treated, for the purposes of entitlement to benefit, as paid in respect of that other year.

58(2) Where

(a) an employed earner's employment commences in one year;

(b) the first payment of earnings in respect of that employment is made in the following year; and

(c) earnings in respect of that employment which fall to be paid in that later year are paid at regular intervals,

the contributions paid in respect of the first payment of earnings shall, on the application of the employed earner to the Secretary of State, be treated, for the purposes of entitlement to benefit, as paid in respect of the year in which the employment commenced.

Derivations – SI 1979/591 reg. 37

CIRCUMSTANCES IN WHICH TWO-YEAR LIMIT FOR REFUNDS OF CLASS 1, 1A OR 1B CONTRIBUTIONS NOT TO APPLY

59(1) Section 19A(1) of the Act (repayment of Class 1, 1A or 1B contributions paid in error) does not apply where the three circumstances prescribed in paragraphs (2), (3) and (4) exist.

59(2) The first circumstance is that, in respect of the earnings derived in year 1 from an employment of the earner, Class 1, 1A or 1B contributions have been paid.

59(3) The second circumstance is that in respect of that employment and before the end of year 2

(a) an application for the determination of a question as to the category of earners in which the earner is or was to be included ("the categorisation question") has been made under section 17(1)(a) of the Administration Act in accordance with regulation 13(1) of the Social Security (Adjudication) Regulations 1995;

(b) a question of law arising in connection with the categorisation question has been referred by the Secretary of State to a court under section 18 of the Administration Act;

(c) a request in writing has been made that an officer of the Board

(i) decide the categorisation question under section 8(1)(a) of the Transfer Act, or

(ii) vary a decision made under that section; or

(d) the amount of income tax, which is liable to be paid in respect of year 1 and in respect of which the person liable to pay a Class 1B contribution is accountable, has been the subject of a relevant tax appeal.

59(4) The third circumstance is that the question, reference, request or appeal referred to in paragraph (3) has not been determined or finally disposed of, as the case may be, at the end of year 2.

59(5) For the purposes of this regulation

"relevant tax appeal" has the meaning given by paragraph 6(4A) of Schedule 1 to the Act,

"year 1" and **"year 2"** have the meanings given by section 19A(1) of the Act,

and a question, reference, request or appeal shall only be taken to be determined or finally disposed of when the time for appealing against it has expired or no further appeal is possible.

Derivations – SI 1979/591 reg. 37A.

PART 6 – LATE PAID AND UNPAID CONTRIBUTIONS (OTHER THAN CLASS 4 CONTRIBUTIONS)

TREATMENT FOR THE PURPOSE OF CONTRIBUTORY BENEFIT OF UNPAID PRIMARY CLASS 1 CONTRIBUTIONS WHERE NO CONSENT, CONNIVANCE OR NEGLIGENCE ON THE PART OF THE PRIMARY CONTRIBUTOR

60(1) If a primary Class 1 contribution payable on a primary contributor's behalf by a secondary contributor is not paid, and the failure to pay that contribution is shown to the satisfaction of an officer of the Board not to have been with the consent or connivance of, or attributable to any negligence on the part of the primary contributor, that contribution shall be treated–

(a) for the purpose of the first contribution condition of entitlement to a contribution-based jobseeker's allowance or short-term incapacity benefit, as paid on the date on which payment is made of the earnings in respect of which the contribution is payable; and

(b) for any other purpose of entitlement to contributory benefit, as paid on the due date.

60(2) In paragraph (1)(a) **"the first contribution condition"**, in relation to a contribution-based jobseeker's allowance means the condition specified in section 2(1)(a) of the Jobseekers Act 1995.

60(3) Where–

(a) an amount is retrospectively treated as earnings by retrospective contributions regulations, and

(b) the primary Class 1 contribution payable in respect of those earnings is not paid, and the failure to pay that contribution is shown to the satisfaction of an officer of the Board not to have been with the consent or connivance of, or attributable to any negligence on the part of the primary contributor,

that contribution shall be treated in accordance with paragraph (1)(a) and (b).

History – Reg. 60(3) inserted by SI 2007/1056, reg. 5, with effect from 6 April 2007.
In reg. 60(1) "of an officer of the Board" substituted by SI 2002/2366, reg. 11, with effect from 8 October 2002.

Derivations – SI 1979/591 reg. 39.

Other material – HMRC Brief 11/14: social security (categorisation of earners) regulations in relation to entertainers: reg. 60 of the Social Security (Contributions) Regulations 2001; invitation to specified entertainers to apply to have Class 1 employee's national insurance contributions (NIC) treated as paid.

VOLUNTARY CLASS 2 CONTRIBUTIONS NOT PAID WITHIN PERMITTED PERIOD

61(1) If a person who was entitled, but not liable, to pay a Class 2 contribution (**"the contributor"**) fails to pay that contribution within the period within which it may be paid, and the condition in paragraph (2) is satisfied, the contribution may be paid within such further period as an officer of the Board may direct.

61(2) The condition is that an officer of the Board is satisfied that–

(a) the failure was attributable to the contributor's ignorance or error; and

(b) that ignorance or error was not the result of the contributor's failure to exercise due care and diligence.

History – Reg. 61 substituted by SI 2002/2366, reg.12, with effect from 8 October 2002.

VOLUNTARY CLASS 2 CONTRIBUTIONS: TAX YEARS 1993–94 TO 2007–08

61A [Omitted by SI 2015/478, reg. 24(1)(d).]

History – Reg. 61A omitted by SI 2015/478, reg. 24(1)(d), with effect from 6 April 2015.

VOLUNTARY CLASS 2 CONTRIBUTIONS: TAX YEARS 2006–07 TO 2015–16: UNAVAILABILITY OF PENSION STATEMENTS 2013–14 TO 2016–17

61B(1) This regulation applies to Class 2 contributions which a person ("the contributor") was entitled, but not liable, to pay in respect of one or more of the tax years 2006–07 to 2015–16 ("the relevant contribution years").

61B(2) Paragraph (3) applies if the contributor–

(a) was entitled to pay a Class 2 contribution in respect of one or more of the relevant contribution years;

(b) had not, before the coming into force of this regulation, paid that contribution; and

(c) will reach pensionable age on or after 6th April 2016.

61B(3) The contributor may pay a Class 2 contribution under this regulation, in respect of any of the relevant contribution years, within the period specified in paragraph (4).

61B(4) The period within which the contribution may be paid is the period beginning on 6th April 2013 and ending on 5th April 2023.

61B(5) Notwithstanding section 12(3) of the Act, the amount of a Class 2 contribution payable under this regulation shall be–

(a) in respect of contribution years 2006–07 to 2010–11, the amount payable in relation to tax year 2012–13; or

(b) in respect of contribution years 2011–12 to 2015–16, the amount payable in the contribution year to which the payment relates.

61B(6) Paragraph (5) does not apply to a Class 2 contribution paid on or after 6th April 2019.

61B(7) Nothing in this regulation limits the application of regulation 61.

History – In reg. 61B(2)(a), the words "under regulation 46 or 147(1)(a)" (which appeared after the words "was entitled") omitted by SI 2015/478, reg. 5(2), with effect from 6 April 2015.
In reg. 61B(2)(c), "2016" substituted for "2017" by SI 2013/718, reg. 2(2), with effect from 18 April 2013.
In reg. 61B(7), the word "regulation" substituted for the word "regulations" and the words "and 61A" (which appeared after the words "regulation 61") omitted by SI 2015/478, reg. 5(3), with effect from 6 April 2015.
In reg. 61B(7), the words "regulation 61" substituted for "regulations 61 and 61A" by SI 2015/478, reg. 24(3), with effect from 6 April 2015. Note: the text of s. 61B(7) already reflected the substituted words by virtue of the amendments by SI 2015/478, reg. 5(3) (see above).
Reg. 61B inserted by SI 2013/622, reg. 37, with effect from 6 April 2013 in relation to the tax year 2013–14 and subsequent tax years.
Notes – Where the contributor reaches pensionable age on or after 6 April 2016 but before 6 April 2017 the reference to 6th April 2013 in reg. 61B(4) is to be read as a reference to 18th April 2013 (SI 2013/718, reg. 3).

PAYMENT OF CONTRIBUTIONS AFTER DEATH OF CONTRIBUTOR

62 If a person dies, any contributions which, immediately before his death he was entitled, but not liable, to pay, may be paid, notwithstanding his death, subject to the same provisions with respect to the time for payment as were applicable to that person.

Derivations – SI 1979/591 reg. 43.

CLASS 2 CONTRIBUTIONS PAID LATE IN ACCORDANCE WITH A PAYMENT UNDERTAKING

63(1) This regulation applies to any Class 2 contributions which–

(a) the earner has failed to pay on or by the due date and which, after that date, is payable in accordance with the provisions of an undertaking to pay such a contribution entered into after that date; and

(b) would when paid fall to be computed in accordance with section 12(3) of the Act.

63(2) In the case of a contribution to which this regulation applies

(a) which is paid in accordance with the provisions of an undertaking entered into in the contribution year or the year immediately following that year, the amount of such a contribution shall be computed by reference to the weekly rate applicable in the contribution year;

(b) which is paid in accordance with the provisions of an undertaking entered into in any year other than a year specified in sub-paragraph (a), the amount of such a contribution shall be computed by reference to the highest weekly rate of such a contribution in the period beginning with the contribution week in respect of which the contribution is paid and ending with the day on which the undertaking was entered into;

(c) which is not paid in accordance with the provisions of the undertaking, the amount of such a contribution shall be computed by reference to the highest weekly rate of such a contribution

  (i) where the contribution is paid in accordance with a further undertaking, in the period beginning with the contribution week in respect of which the contribution is paid and ending with the day on which the further undertaking was entered into, or

  (ii) where the contribution is paid otherwise than in accordance with a further undertaking, in the period beginning with the contribution week in respect of which the contribution is paid and ending with the day on which it is paid.

63(3) In this regulation **"undertaking"** means an arrangement between the Board and an earner under which the Board have agreed to accept payment of arrears of Class 2 contributions by instalments.

Derivations – SI 1979/591 reg. 43B.

COLLECTION OF UNPAID CLASS 2 CONTRIBUTIONS THROUGH PAYE CODE

63A(1) Where–

(a) the amount of any Class 2 contributions ("relevant debt") would fall to be computed in accordance with section 12(3) of the Act (late paid Class 2 contributions), and

(b) paragraph (2) applies,

the amount of the relevant debt must be computed in accordance with paragraph (4).

63A(2) This paragraph applies where–

(a) the code ("the PAYE code") required by regulation 13 of the PAYE Regulations (determination of code by Inland Revenue) for use by an employer for a year in respect of the person liable to pay the relevant debt is determined in accordance with regulation 14A of the PAYE Regulations (determination of code in respect of recovery of relevant debts) so as to effect recovery of the relevant debt;

(b) the determination of the PAYE code is made assuming the amount of the relevant debt is the amount computed in accordance with paragraph (4); and

(c) the relevant debt is paid in the year in respect of which the PAYE code is determined for use by an employer of the person liable to pay the relevant debt.

63A(3) For the purpose of determining whether a relevant debt is paid in accordance with paragraph (2)(c), the amount of the relevant debt must be assumed to be the amount computed in accordance with paragraph (4).

63A(4) The amount referred to in paragraphs (1), (2)(b) and (3) is the highest weekly rate of a Class 2 contribution in the period beginning with the week to which the relevant debt relates and ending with the day the PAYE code mentioned in paragraph (2)(a) is determined.

History – In reg. 63A(4), the word "contribution" (which appeared after the words "in the period beginning with the") omitted by SI 2015/478, reg. 6, with effect from 6 April 2015.
Reg. 63A inserted by SI 2013/622, reg. 38, with effect from 6 April 2013 in relation to the tax year 2013–14 and subsequent tax years.

CLASS 2 AND CLASS 3 CONTRIBUTIONS PAID WITHIN A MONTH FROM NOTIFICATION OF AMOUNT OF ARREARS

64(1) This regulation applies to any Class 2 or Class 3 contribution

(a) which would when paid fall to be computed in accordance with section 12(3) or 13(6) of the Act; and

(b) the amount of that contribution has been notified to the contributor by the Board in the last month of a year.

64(2) Where a contribution to which this regulation applies is paid

(a) within one calendar month from the date of such notification; and

(b) in the year following that in which the amount was so notified;

the amount of that contribution shall be computed by reference to the weekly rate or, as the case may be, amount of such a contribution calculated in accordance with section 12 or 13 of the Act as if the contribution had been paid on the last day of the year in which the notification was given.

Derivations – SI 1979/591 reg. 43C.

CLASS 2 AND CLASS 3 CONTRIBUTIONS PAID LATE THROUGH IGNORANCE OR ERROR

65(1) This regulation applies to any Class 2 or Class 3 contribution which would when paid fall to be computed at a rate or, as the case may be, an amount, other than that applicable in the contribution year in accordance with section 12(3) or 13(6) of the Act.

65(2) Where

(a) it is shown to the satisfaction of an officer of the Board that, by reason of ignorance or error on the part of the earner, not being ignorance or error due to any failure on his part to exercise due care and diligence, he has failed to pay a Class 2 contribution to which this regulation applies for any period on or by the due date; and

(b) payment of that contribution is made in a year later than that in which the period commenced;

the amount of that contribution shall be calculated by reference to the weekly rate at which a contribution paid under section 12 of the Act would have been payable if it had been paid at the time when the period began.

65(3) Where a Class 3 contribution would otherwise fall to be calculated in accordance with section 13(6) of the Act, but it is shown to the satisfaction of an officer of the Board that the contributor has not paid that contribution before the end of the second year following the contribution year by reason of ignorance or error on the part of the earner, not being ignorance or error due to any failure on his part to exercise due care and diligence, the amount of that contribution shall be computed by reference to the amount of such a contribution applicable to the period for which the contribution is paid.

65(4) Where

(a) a Class 3 contribution would when paid fall to be computed in accordance with section 13(6) of the Act,

(b) such a contribution remains unpaid for a period commencing at any time after the end of the second year following the contribution year ("the relevant period"), and

(c) it is shown to the satisfaction of an officer of the Board that the contributor has not, during the relevant period only, paid such a contribution by reason of ignorance or error not being ignorance or error due to any failure on the contributor's part to exercise due care and diligence,

paragraph (5) applies.

65(5) If this paragraph applies to a contribution, the amount of that contribution shall be calculated in accordance with section 13(6) of the Act as if the contribution had been paid at the time when the relevant period commenced.

History – In reg. 65(2)(a), (3), (4)(c) words "to the satisfaction of an officer of the Board" substituted for "to the satisfaction of the Board" by SI 2002/2366, reg.13, with effect from 8 October 2002.

Derivations – SI 1979/591 reg. 43D.

AMOUNTS OF CLASS 2 AND CLASS 3 CONTRIBUTIONS IN CERTAIN CASES WHERE EARNINGS REMOVED

65ZA [Omitted by SI 2015/478, reg. 24(1)(e).]

History – Reg. 65ZA omitted by SI 2015/478, reg. 24(1)(e), with effect from 6 April 2015.

AMOUNT OF CLASS 3 CONTRIBUTIONS PAYABLE BY VIRTUE OF REGULATION 50A

65A The amount of a contribution payable by virtue of regulation 50A during the period mentioned in paragraph (3) of that regulation shall, notwithstanding section 13(6) of the Act, be calculated by reference to the weekly rate which would have been applicable if it had been paid during the contribution year to which it relates.

History – Reg. 65A inserted by SI 2004/1362, reg. 5, with effect from 17 May 2004.

AMOUNT OF CLASS 3 CONTRIBUTIONS PAYABLE AFTER ISSUE OF A FULL GENDER RECOGNITION CERTIFICATE

65B The amount of a contribution payable by virtue of regulation 49(2B) (Class 3 contributions not precluded where gender recognition certificate issued) which is paid in the year in which the full gender recognition certificate is issued or the following year shall, notwithstanding section 13(6) of the Act, be calculated by reference to the weekly rate which would have been applicable if it had been paid during the contribution year to which it relates.

History – Reg. 65B inserted by SI 2005/778, reg. 7 with effect from 6 April 2005.

LATE PAYMENT OF VOLUNTARY CLASS 2 AND 3 CONTRIBUTIONS FOR TAX YEAR 2005–06

65C [Omitted by SI 2015/478, reg. 24(1)(f).]

History – Reg. 65C omitted by SI 2015/478, reg. 24(1)(f), with effect from 6 April 2015.

LATE PAYMENT OF VOLUNTARY CLASS 2 AND 3 CONTRIBUTIONS FOR TAX YEAR 2006–07

65D [Omitted by SI 2015/478, reg. 24(1)(g).]

History – Reg. 65D omitted by SI 2015/478, reg. 24(1)(g), with effect from 6 April 2015.

PART 7 – COLLECTION OF CONTRIBUTIONS (OTHER THAN CLASS 4 CONTRIBUTIONS) AND RELATED MATTERS

NOTIFICATION OF NATIONAL INSURANCE NUMBERS TO SECONDARY CONTRIBUTORS

66 Every employed earner, in respect of whom any person is liable to pay an earnings-related contribution, shall, on request, supply his national insurance number to that person.

Derivations – SI 1979/591 reg. 45.

COLLECTION AND RECOVERY OF EARNINGS-RELATED CONTRIBUTIONS AND CLASS 1B CONTRIBUTIONS

67(1) Subject to regulations 68 and 70, earnings-related contributions and Class 1B contributions shall be paid, accounted for and recovered in like manner as income tax deducted from PAYE income by virtue of regulations under section 684 of ITEPA 2003 (PAYE Regulations).

67(1A) PAYE income has the meaning given in section 683 of ITEPA 2003.

67(2) The provisions contained in Schedule 4 (which contains provisions derived from the Income Tax Acts and the PAYE Regulations with extensions and modifications) shall apply to and for the purposes of earnings-related contributions and Class 1B contributions.

67(3) Schedules 4A (real time returns) and 4B (additional information about payments) apply to and for the purposes of earnings related contributions.

History – In reg. 67(1), the words "PAYE income" substituted for the words "the general earnings from an office or employment" by SI 2015/478, reg. 7(a), with effect from 6 April 2015.
In reg. 67(1) the words "general earnings from an office or employment by virtue of regulations under section 684 of ITEPA 2003 (PAYE Regulations)." substituted by SI 2004/770, reg. 15, with effect from 6 April 2004.
Reg. 67(1A) inserted by SI 2015/478, reg. 7(b), with effect from 6 April 2015.
In reg. 67(2), the introductory words "In any case to which this regulation applies," omitted by SI 2008/636, reg. 3, with effect from 1 April 2008.
In reg. 67(2) the words "the PAYE Regulations" substituted by SI 2004/770, reg. 15, with effect from 6 April 2004.
Reg. 67(3) inserted by SI 2012/821, reg. 3, with effect from 6 April 2012.

Derivations – SI 1979/591 reg. 46.

Cross references – ITEPA 2003, s. 684 rewrites ICTA 1988, s. 203 (PAYE regulations).
SI 2003/2682 rewrites the Income Tax (Employments) Regulations 1993.

PENALTY FOR FAILURE TO MAKE PAYMENTS ON TIME: CLASS 1 CONTRIBUTIONS

67A(1) Schedule 56 to the Finance Act 2009 ("Schedule 56 FA 2009") (penalty for failure to make payments on time) shall apply in relation to the late payment of Class 1 contributions, as if–

(a) the Class 1 contributions were an amount of tax falling within item 2 of the Table in paragraph 1 of Schedule 56 FA 2009 ("the Table"),

(b) references to the PAYE Regulations were references to these Regulations, and

(c) references to "an assessment or determination" in item 24 of the Table were references to a decision made under section 8(1)(c) of the Social Security Contributions (Transfer of Functions, etc) Act 1999.

67A(2) Regulation 69A of the PAYE Regulations (circumstances in which payment of a lesser amount is to be treated as payment in full for the purposes of paragraph 6(2) of Schedule 56 to the Finance Act 2009) applies in relation to the late payment of Class 1 contributions as if–

(a) the Class 1 contributions were an amount of tax falling within item 2 of the Table in paragraph 1 of that Schedule,

(b) references to regulations 67G and 67H(2) were references to paragraphs 10 and 11 of Schedule 4 to these Regulations, and

(c) references to earnings-related contributions were references to tax deducted under the PAYE Regulations.

History – Reg. 67A renumbered as reg. 67A(1) and reg. 67A(2) inserted by SI 2014/608, reg. 3, with effect in relation to a payment made in relation to the tax year 2014–15 and subsequent tax years.
Reg. 67A inserted by SI 2010/721, reg. 3, with effect from 6 April 2010 (but only in relation to 2010–11 and subsequent tax years).

PENALTY FOR FAILURE TO MAKE PAYMENTS ON TIME: CLASS 1A AND CLASS 1B CONTRIBUTIONS

67B Schedule 56 to the Finance Act 2009 ("Schedule 56 FA 2009") shall apply in relation to the late payment of Class 1A and Class 1B contributions, as if–

(a) the Class 1A and Class 1B contributions were an amount of tax falling within item 3 of the table in paragraph 1 of Schedule 56 FA 2009,

(b) in the case of Class 1B contributions, the reference to "amount shown in return under section 254(1) of FA 2004" was a reference to the amount payable under section 10A of the Act, and

(c) the reference to section 254(5) of the Finance Act 2004 was a reference to these Regulations.

History – Reg. 67B inserted by SI 2010/721, reg. 3, with effect from 6 April 2010 (but only in relation to 2010–11 and subsequent tax years).

OTHER METHODS OF COLLECTION AND RECOVERY OF EARNINGS-RELATED CONTRIBUTIONS

68(1) The Board may authorise arrangements under which earnings-related contributions are to be paid in a different manner from that prescribed by regulation 67.

68(2) The provisions of regulation 67 shall be in addition to any remedy otherwise available for the recovery of earnings-related contributions.

Derivations – SI 1979/591 reg. 46A.

TRANSFER OF LIABILITY FROM SECONDARY CONTRIBUTOR TO EMPLOYED EARNER: RELEVANT EMPLOYMENT INCOME

69 Schedule 5 contains provisions which have effect with respect to elections made jointly by a secondary contributor and an employed earner that the liability of the secondary contributor in respect of relevant employment income shall be transferred to the employed earner.

History – In reg. 69 and the heading preceding it, the words "relevant employment income" substituted by SI 2004/2096, reg. 4, with effect in relation to–

- agreements entered into after 1 September 2004 which are in respect of post-commencement employment income (presumably as defined in NICSPA 2004, s. 3(5)), and
- elections made after that date.

Derivations – SI 1979/591 reg. 46B.

PAYMENT OF CLASS 1A CONTRIBUTIONS

70(1) In the cases prescribed by paragraph (2), contributions shall be paid to the Board in accordance with regulations 71 to 83.

70(2) The cases prescribed by this paragraph are cases where an employer is liable to pay a Class 1A contribution to the Board.

70(3) For the purposes of this regulation and regulations 71 to 83 where–

(a) any payment to the Board is made by cheque; and

(b) the cheque is paid on its first presentation to the banker on whom it is drawn, the payment shall be treated as made on the day on which the cheque was received by the Board, and related expressions shall be construed accordingly.

70(4) In this regulation, and in regulations 71 to 83, **"employer"** means the person liable, in accordance with section 10(2) or 10ZA of the Act, to pay a Class 1A contribution.

History – In reg. 70(4) words from "means the person liable" to the end, substituted by SI 2002/2929, reg. 3, with effect from 28 November 2002.

Derivations – SI 1979/591 reg. 47.

DUE DATE FOR PAYMENT OF A CLASS 1A CONTRIBUTION

71(1) Subject to regulation 72(2) or 73(2), as the case may be, an employer who is liable to pay a Class 1A contribution to the Board shall pay that contribution to them not later than 19th July or, where payment is made by an approved method of electronic communications in respect of earnings paid after 5th April 2004, not later than 22nd July in the year immediately following the end of the year in respect of which it is payable.

71(2) *A Class 1A contribution paid* to the Board in accordance with paragraph (1) shall be shown in a return made to them in accordance with regulation 80(1).

History – In reg. 71(1) the words "or, where payment is made by an approved method of electronic communications in respect of earnings paid after 5th April 2004, not later than 22nd July" inserted by SI 2004/770, reg. 16, with effect from 6 April 2004.

Derivations – SI 1979/591 reg. 47A.

Cross references – Direction of the Board, 5 April 2004: direction consolidating various directions in respect of the electronic delivery of information and specifying approved methods of electronic payments of sums due.

PROVISIONS RELATING TO A CLASS 1A CONTRIBUTION DUE ON SUCCESSION TO BUSINESS

72(1) Paragraphs (2) and (3) apply in relation to the payment of a Class 1A contribution if

(a) there is a change in the employer who is liable to pay earnings to or for the benefit of all the persons who are employed in a business in respect of their employment in that business; and

(b) the employees in question are those who ceased to be employed in that business before the change of employer occurred.

72(2) Not later than 14 days or, where payment is made by an approved method of electronic communications in respect of earnings paid after 5th April 2004, 17 days after the end of the relevant final tax month, the employer shall pay to the Board

(a) any Class 1A contribution referred to in paragraph (1) in respect of the relevant final year; and

(b) where the relevant final tax month is the month beginning on 6th April, 6th May or 6th June, any Class 1A contribution referred to in paragraph (1) in respect of the year immediately preceding the relevant final year.

72(3) The employer shall include the amount of any Class 1A contribution which is payable in accordance with paragraph (2)(a) in the return required by regulation 80(1) for the relevant final year.

72(4) In this regulation

"business" includes any trade, concern or undertaking;

"employer" means the employer before the change referred to in paragraph (1)(a);

"relevant final tax month" means the tax month in which the employer has made any payments of emoluments which were, by reason of the change of employer referred to in paragraph (1)(a) in respect of the employment of all those persons who were employed by him in that tax month, the final payments of earnings to be made by him in the year in which those payments were made;

"relevant final year" means the year in which the relevant final tax month occurs.

History – In reg. 72(1)(a), the word "general" (which appeared before the word "earnings") omitted by SI 2015/478, reg. 8(a), with effect from 6 April 2015.
In reg. 72(1)(a) the words "general earnings" substituted by SI 2004/770, reg. 17(a), with effect from 6 April 2004.
In reg. 72(2) the words "tax month" substituted in both places and "or, where payment is made by an approved method of electronic communications in respect of earnings paid after 5th April 2004, 17 days" inserted by SI 2004/770, reg. 17(b), with effect from 6 April 2004.
In reg. 72(4), the definition of "general earnings" omitted by SI 2015/478, reg. 8(b)(i), with effect from 6 April 2015.
Inreg. 72(4) the former definition of "general earnings" inserted by SI 2004/770, reg. 17(c), with effect from 6 April 2004.
In reg. 72(4), in the definition of "relevant tax month", the word "general" (which appeared before the word "earnings") omitted by SI 2015/478, reg. 8(b)(ii), with effect from 6 April 2015.
In reg. 72(4) the words "tax month" substituted in each place, and "final payment[s] of general earnings" substituted by SI 2004/770, reg. 17(c), with effect from 6 April 2004.
In reg. 72(4) the words "and for these purposes **"emoluments"** means so much of a person's remuneration or profits derived from employed earner's employment as constitutes earnings for the purposes of the Act; and" omitted by SI 2004/770, reg. 17(c) and revoked by reg. 36 and Sch. 1, with effect from 6 April 2004.

Derivations – SI 1979/591 reg. 47B.

Cross references – Direction of the Board, 5 April 2004: direction consolidating various directions in respect of the electronic delivery of information and specifying approved methods of electronic payments of sums due.

PROVISIONS RELATING TO A CLASS 1A CONTRIBUTION DUE ON CESSATION OF BUSINESS

73(1) Paragraphs (2) and (3) apply in relation to the payment of a Class 1A contribution if

(a) an employer ceases to carry on business and upon that cessation no other person becomes liable to pay earnings to or for the benefit of any employee in respect of his employment in that business; and

(b) the employees are all those who were employed in that business at any time in the relevant final year or the year immediately preceding the relevant final year.

73(2) Not later than 14 days or where payment is made by an approved method of electronic communications in respect of earnings paid after 5th April 2004, 17 days after the end of the relevant final tax month, the employer shall pay to the Board

(a) any Class 1A contribution referred to in paragraph (1) in respect of the relevant final year; and

(b) where the relevant final tax month is the month beginning on 6th April, 6th May or 6th June any Class 1A contribution referred to in paragraph (1) in respect of the year immediately preceding the relevant final year.

73(3) The employer shall include the amount of any Class 1A contribution which is payable in accordance with paragraph (2)(a) in the return required by regulation 80 for the relevant final year.

73(4) In this regulation

"business" includes any trade, concern or undertaking;

"employer" means the employer before the cessation of business referred to in paragraph (1)(a);

"relevant final tax month" means the tax month in which the employer has made any payments of emoluments which were, by reason of the cessation of business referred to in paragraph (1)(a) in respect of the employment of all those persons who were employed by him in that tax month, the final payments of earnings to be made by him in the year in which those payments were made;

"relevant final year" means the year in which the relevant final tax month occurs.

History – In reg. 73(1)(a), the word "general" (which appeared before the word "earnings") omitted by SI 2015/478, reg. 9(a), with effect from 6 April 2015.

In reg. 73(1) the words "general earnings" substituted by SI 2004/770, reg. 18(a), with effect from 6 April 2004.

In reg. 73(2) the words "or where payment is made by an approved method of electronic communications in respect of earnings paid after 5th April 2004, 17 days" inserted and "tax month" substituted in each place by SI 2004/770, reg. 18(b), with effect from 6 April 2004.

In reg. 73(4), the definition of "general earnings" omitted by SI 2015/478, reg. 9(b)(i), with effect from 6 April 2015.

In reg. 73(4), former definition of "general earnings" inserted by SI 2004/770, reg. 18(c), with effect from 6 April 2004.

In reg. 73(4), in the definition of "relevant final tax month", the word "general" (which appeared before the word "earnings") omitted by SI 2015/478, reg. 9(b)(ii), with effect from 6 April 2015.

In reg. 73(4) the words "tax month" substituted in each place by SI 2004/770, reg. 18(c) and Schedule, with effect from 6 April 2004.

In reg. 73(4) the words "final payment[s] of general earnings" substituted in each place by SI 2004/770, reg. 18(c), with effect from 6 April 2004.

In reg. 73(4) the words "and for these purposes **"emoluments"** means so much of a person's remuneration or profits derived from employed earner's employment as constitutes earnings for the purposes of the Act;" omitted by SI 2004/770, reg. 18(c), with effect from 6 April 2004.

Derivations – SI 1979/591 reg. 47C.

Cross references – Direction of the Board, 5 April 2004: direction consolidating various directions in respect of the electronic delivery of information and specifying approved methods of electronic payments of sums due.

EMPLOYER FAILING TO PAY A CLASS 1A CONTRIBUTION

74(1) If

(a) the employer has paid no amount of a Class 1A contribution to the Board by the date which applies to him under regulation 71(1), 72(2), or 73(2) (as the case may be); and

(b) the Board are unaware of the amount, if any, which the employer is liable so to pay, they may give notice to the employer requiring him to render, within 14 days, a return in the prescribed form showing the amount of a Class 1A contribution which the employer is liable to pay to them under that regulation in respect of the year in question.

74(2) A notice may be given by the Board under paragraph (1) notwithstanding that an amount of a Class 1A contribution has been paid to them by the employer under regulation 71(1), 72(2), or 73(2), in respect of the year in question, if they are not satisfied that the amount so paid is the full amount which the employer is liable to pay to them for that year and the provisions of this regulation shall have effect accordingly.

74(3) Upon receipt of a return made by an employer under paragraph (1) the Board may prepare a certificate showing the amount of a Class 1A contribution which the employer is liable to pay to them for the year in question.

74(4) The production of the return made by the employer under paragraph (1) and of the certificate of the Board under paragraph (3) shall be sufficient evidence that the amount shown in the certificate is the amount of a Class 1A contribution which the employer is liable to pay to the Board in respect of the year in question.

74(5) Any document purporting to be a certificate under paragraph (3) shall be presumed to be such a certificate until the contrary is proved.

Derivations – SI 1979/591 reg. 47D.

SPECIFIED AMOUNT OF A CLASS 1A CONTRIBUTION

75(1) If, following the date which applies to him under regulation 71(1), 72(2) or 73(2) (as the case may be), the employer has paid no amount of a Class 1A contribution to the Board in respect of the year in question and there is reason to believe that the employer is liable so to pay, the Board

(a) in the case of the first year in which the employer is liable to pay such a contribution, upon consideration of any information which has been provided to them by the employer relating to his *liability to pay such contributions*; or

(b) in the case of any later year, upon consideration of the employer's record of past payments; may to the best of their judgment specify the amount of a Class 1A contribution which they consider the employer is liable to pay and give notice to him of that amount.

75(2) If, on the expiration of the period of 7 days allowed in the notice, the specified amount of a Class 1A contribution or any part of that amount is unpaid, the amount so unpaid

(a) shall be treated for the purposes of these Regulations to be an amount of a Class 1A contribution which the employer was liable to pay in respect of the year in question in accordance with regulation 71(1), 72(2) or 73(2); and

(b) may be certified by the Board.

75(3) Paragraph (2) does not apply if, during the period allowed in the notice

(a) the employer pays to the Board the full amount of a Class 1A contribution which he is liable to pay under regulation 71(1), 72(2) or 73(2) in respect of the year in question; or

(b) the employer satisfies the Board that no amount of such a contribution is due.

75(4) The production of a certificate such as is mentioned in paragraph (2)(b) shall, until the contrary is established, be sufficient evidence that the employer is liable to pay to the Board the amount shown in the certificate, and any document purporting to be such a certificate shall be presumed to be such a certificate until the contrary is proved.

75(5) A notice may be given by the Board under paragraph (1) notwithstanding that an amount of a Class 1A contribution has been paid to them by the employer under regulation 71(1), 72(2) or 73(2) in respect of the year in question, if, after seeking the employer's explanation as to the amount of a Class 1A contribution paid, they are not satisfied that the amount so paid is the full amount which the employer is liable to pay to them in respect of that year, and this regulation shall have effect accordingly, but paragraph (2) shall not apply if, during the period allowed in the notice, the employer satisfies the Board that no further amount of a Class 1A contribution is due in respect of that year.

75(6) Where, during the period allowed in a notice given by the Board under paragraph (1), the employer claims, but does not satisfy the Board, that the payment of a Class 1A contribution made in respect of the year specified in the notice is the full amount of a Class 1A contribution which he is liable to pay to the Board in respect of that year, the employer may require the Board to inspect his documents and records as if they had called upon him to produce those documents and records in accordance with Schedule 36 to the Finance Act 2008 (information and inspection powers).

75(7) If the employer does require the Board to inspect his documents and records in accordance with paragraph (6), the provisions of paragraph 26A of Schedule 4 shall apply in relation to that inspection and the notice given by the Board under paragraph (1) shall be disregarded.

History – In reg. 75(6), the words "Schedule 36 to the Finance Act 2008 (information and inspection powers)" substituted by SI 2009/600, reg. 4(a), with effect from 1 April 2009.
In reg. 75(7), "paragraph 26A" substituted by SI 2009/600, reg. 4(b), with effect from 1 April 2009.

Derivations – SI 1979/591 reg. 47E.

INTEREST ON AN OVERDUE CLASS 1A CONTRIBUTION

76(1) Where an employer has not paid a Class 1A contribution, which he is liable to pay, by the date which applies to him under regulation 71(1), 72(2) or 73(2) (as the case may be), any contribution not so paid shall carry interest at the rate applicable under paragraph 6(3) of Schedule 1 to the Act from the reckonable date until payment.

76(2) Interest payable under this regulation shall be recoverable as if it were a Class 1A contribution which an employer is liable to pay to the Board under regulation 71(1), 72(2) or 73(2) (as the case may be).

76(3) A contribution to which paragraph (1) applies shall carry interest from the reckonable date even if that date is a non-business day within the meaning of section 92 of the Bills of Exchange Act 1882.

76(4) A certificate of the Board that any amount of interest payable under this regulation has not been paid to the Board or, to the best of the Board's knowledge and belief, to any person acting on their behalf, shall be sufficient evidence that the employer is liable to pay to the Board the amount of interest shown on the certificate and that the sum is unpaid and due to be paid, and any document purporting to be such a certificate shall be deemed to be a certificate until the contrary is proved.

76(5) For the purposes of this regulation, **"the reckonable date"** means the 19th July or where payment is made by an approved method of electronic communications in respect of earnings paid after 5th April 2004, the 22nd July in the year immediately following the end of the year in respect of which the Class 1A contribution is payable to the Board.

History – In reg. 76(5) the words "or where payment is made by an approved method of electronic communications in respect of earnings paid after 5th April 2004, the 22nd July" inserted by SI 2004/770, reg. 19, with effect from 6 April 2004.

Derivations – SI 1979/591 reg. 47F.

Cross references – Direction of the Board, 5 April 2004: direction consolidating various directions in respect of the electronic delivery of information and specifying approved methods of electronic payments of sums due.

PAYMENT OF INTEREST ON A REPAID CLASS 1A CONTRIBUTION

77(1) Where

(a) a Class 1A contribution paid by an employer to the Board in respect of the year ended 5th April 1999 or any subsequent year is repaid to him; and

(b) that repayment is made after the relevant date,

any such repaid contribution shall carry interest at the rate applicable under paragraph 6(3) of Schedule 1 to the Act from the relevant date until the order for the repayment is issued.

77(2) For the purposes of this regulation, **"the relevant date"** means–

(a) the 14th day after the end of the year in respect of which the Class 1A contribution was paid; or

(b) if later than that day, the date on which that contribution was paid.

Derivations – SI 1979/591 reg. 47G.

REPAYMENT OF INTEREST PAID ON A CLASS 1A CONTRIBUTION

78 If an employer has paid interest on a Class 1A contribution, that interest shall be repaid to him where

(a) the interest paid is found not to have been due to be paid, although the contribution in respect of which it was paid was due to be paid;

(b) the Class 1A contribution in respect of which interest was paid is returned or repaid to the employer in accordance with the provisions of regulation 52 or 55.

Derivations – SI 1979/591 reg. 47H.

REMISSION OF INTEREST ON A CLASS 1A CONTRIBUTION

79(1) Where interest is payable in accordance with regulation 76 it shall be remitted for the period commencing on the first relevant date and ending on the second relevant date in the circumstances specified in paragraph (2).

79(2) For the purposes of paragraph (1), the circumstances are that the liability, or a greater liability, to pay interest in respect of a Class 1A contribution arises as the result of an official error being made.

79(3) For the purposes of this regulation

"official error" means a mistake made, or something omitted to be done, by an officer of, or person employed in relation to, the Board acting as such, where the employer or any person acting on his behalf has not caused, or materially contributed to, that mistake or omission;

"the first relevant date" means the date defined in regulation 76(5) or, if later, the date on which the official error occurs; and

"the second relevant date" means the date 14 days after the date on which the official error is rectified and the employer is advised of its rectification.

Derivations – SI 1979/591 reg. 47I.

RETURN BY EMPLOYER

80(1) Where a Class 1A contribution is payable to the Board in accordance with regulation 71(1), 72(2) or 73(2), the employer shall render to them a return, not later than 6th July following the end of the year, showing

(a) such particulars as they may require for the identification of the employer;

(b) the year to which the return relates;

(c) the amounts which are general earnings in respect of which a Class 1A contribution is payable; and

(d) the amount of any Class 1A contribution payable in respect of that year.

80(1A) The employer must render the return required by paragraph (1)–

(a) by sending it to the Board; or

(b) arranging for the information which it would contain to be delivered to an official computer system by an approved method of electronic communications.

80(1B) [Omitted by SI 2004/770, reg. 20 and Schedule.]

80(1C) [Omitted by SI 2004/770, reg. 20 and Schedule.]

80(1D) [Omitted by SI 2004/770, reg. 20 and Schedule.]

80(1E) [Omitted by SI 2004/770, reg. 20 and Schedule.]

80(1F) [Omitted by SI 2004/770, reg. 20 and Schedule.]

80(2) The return shall include a declaration by the person making the return to the effect that the return is, to the best of his knowledge, correct and complete.

80(3) The declaration must be–

(a) signed by the employer; or,

(b) where the employer is a body corporate, signed either by the secretary or by a director.

80(3A) Where the return referred to in this regulation is rendered as mentioned in paragraph (1A)(b) the declaration must, instead of being signed, be authenticated by or on behalf of the employer in such a manner as may be approved by HMRC.

80(4) If, by the date which applies to him under regulation 71(1), 72(2) or 73(2) (as the case may be), an employer has failed to pay a Class 1A contribution which he is liable to pay, the Board may prepare a certificate showing the total amount of a Class 1A contribution remaining unpaid in respect of the year in question, and regulation 76(1) and (2) shall, with any necessary modifications, apply to the amount shown in that certificate.

History – In reg. 80(1)(c) the words "general earnings" substituted by SI 2004/770, reg. 20, with effect from 6 April 2004.
Reg. 80(1A) substituted by SI 2004/770, reg. 20, with effect from 6 April 2004.
Former reg. 80(1A) inserted by SI 2001/2187, reg. 3(2), operative from 6 July 2001.
Reg. 80(1B)–(1F) omitted by SI 2004/770, reg. 20 and Schedule, with effect from 6 April 2004.
Reg. 80(1B)–(1F) were inserted by SI 2001/2187, reg. 3(2), operative from 6 July 2001; SI 2001/2187, reg. 3(2), to the extent that it inserts SI 2001/1004, reg. 80(1B)–(1F), is repealed by SI 2004/770, Schedule.
Reg. 80(3) substituted by SI 2012/821, reg. 19(a), with effect from 6 April 2012.
In former reg. 80(3), words from "shall" to the end substituted by SI 2001/2187, reg. 3(3), operative from 6 July 2001.
Reg. 80(3A) inserted by SI 2012/821, reg. 19(b), with effect from 6 April 2012.

Derivations – SI 1979/591 reg. 47J

Cross references – Direction of the Board, 5 April 2004: direction consolidating various directions in respect of the electronic delivery of information and specifying approved methods of electronic payments of sums due.

RETURNS RENDERED ELECTRONICALLY ON ANOTHER'S BEHALF

80A [Omitted by SI 2004/770, reg. 21 and Schedule.]

History – Reg. 80A omitted by SI 2004/770, reg. 21 and Schedule, with effect from 6 April 2004.
Reg. 80A previously inserted by SI 2001/2187, reg. 4 (repealed by SI 2004/770, Schedule from 6 April 2004), operative from 6 July 2001.

PENALTIES FOR FAILURE TO MAKE A RETURN AND INCORRECT RETURNS

81(1) Schedule 24 to the Finance Act 2007 (penalties for errors) applies to the return of contributions referred to in regulation 80(1) (return by employer) as if–

(a) Class 1A contributions were a tax; and

(b) that tax and the return of contributions in relation to it were listed in the table in paragraph 1 of that Schedule.

81(1A) That Schedule also applies to decisions made under section 8(1)(c) of the Social Security Contributions (Transfer of Functions, etc) Act 1999 regarding Class 1A contributions and for that purpose a reference in the Schedule to an assessment is to be treated as if it included a reference to a decision and "under-assessment" shall be construed accordingly.

81(1B) Paragraphs (6) to (9) do not apply in relation to penalties under paragraphs (1) and (1A).

81(2) Any person who fails to make a return referred to in paragraph (1), by the date which applies to him under regulation 71(1), 72(2) or 73(2), may be liable

(a) within 6 years after the date of that failure, to a penalty of the relevant monthly amount for each month (or part of a month) during which the failure continues but excluding any month after the twelfth, or for which a penalty under this paragraph has already been imposed; and

(b) if the failure continues beyond 12 months, to a penalty not exceeding so much of the amount payable by him in accordance with the regulations for the year to which the return relates as remains unpaid at the end of 19th July after the end of that year.

81(3) The penalty referred to in paragraph (2)(b) is without prejudice to any penalty which may be imposed under paragraph (2)(a) and may be imposed within six years after the date of the failure referred to in paragraph (2) or at any later time within three years of the final determination of the amount of a Class 1A contribution by reference to which the amount of that penalty is to be ascertained.

81(4) For the purposes of paragraph (2), **"the relevant monthly amount"** in the case of a failure to make a return is–

(a) where the number of earners in respect of whom particulars of the amount of any Class 1A contribution payable should be included in the return is 50 or less, £100; or

(b) where that number is greater than 50, £100 for each 50 such earners and an additional £100 where that number is not a multiple of 50.

81(5) The total penalty payable under paragraph (2)(a) shall not exceed the total amount of Class 1A contributions payable in respect of the year to which the return in question relates.

81(6) Any penalty imposed in accordance with this regulation shall be recoverable as if it were a Class 1A contribution which the employer is liable to pay to the Board under regulation 71.

81(7) A penalty imposed in accordance with this regulation shall be due and payable at the end of 30 days beginning with the date on which notice of the decision to impose it was issued.

81(8) The Board may, in their discretion, mitigate any penalty, or stay or compound any proceedings for any penalty, imposed in accordance with the provisions of this regulation, and may also, after judgment, further mitigate or entirely remit such a penalty.

81(9) For the purposes of this regulation a person shall be deemed not to have failed to have done anything required to be done within a limited time if he–

(a) did it within such further time as the Board allowed; or

(b) had a reasonable excuse for the failure and if that excuse ceased, did it without unreasonable delay after that excuse ceased.

History – Reg. 81(1)–(1B) substituted for reg. 81(1) by SI 2010/721, reg. 4, with effect from 6 April 2010 (but only in relation to 2010–11 and subsequent tax years).

Derivations – SI 1979/591 reg. 47K.

APPLICATION OF THE MANAGEMENT ACT TO PENALTIES FOR FAILURE TO MAKE A RETURN AND INCORRECT RETURNS

82(1) Section 100 of the Management Act (determination of penalties by an officer of the Board) shall apply with any necessary modifications in relation to the determination of any penalty under regulation 81 as it applies to the determination of a penalty under the Taxes Acts.

82(2) Section 100D of the Management Act (penalty proceedings before court) shall apply with any necessary modifications in relation to any proceedings for a penalty under regulation 81 as it applies to proceedings for a penalty under the Taxes Acts.

82(3) Section 104 of the Management Act (saving for criminal proceedings) shall apply with any necessary modifications in relation to the provisions of regulation 81 as it applies to the provisions of the Taxes Acts.

82(4) Section 105 of the Management Act (evidence in cases of fraudulent conduct) shall apply with any necessary modifications in respect of any proceedings for a penalty under regulation 81, or on appeal against the determination of such a penalty, as it applies in relation to any proceedings for a penalty, or on appeal against the determination of a penalty, under the Management Act.

82(5) In this regulation–

"the Management Act" means the Taxes Management Act 1970; and

"the Taxes Acts" has the same meaning as in section 118(1) of the Management Act (interpretation).

Derivations – SI 1979/591 reg. 47L.

SET-OFF OF CLASS 1A CONTRIBUTIONS FALLING TO BE REPAID AGAINST EARNINGS-RELATED CONTRIBUTIONS

83(1) In the circumstance prescribed in paragraph (2), an amount in respect of a Class 1A contribution that falls to be repaid in accordance with these Regulations may be set off against liabilities under them to the extent prescribed in paragraph (3).

83(2) The circumstance is that an employer has paid to the Board in accordance with regulations 70 to 82 an amount, in respect of Class 1A contributions, which he was not liable to pay.

83(3) The extent of the set-off is that the employer shall be entitled to deduct the amount which he was not liable to pay in respect of Class 1A contributions from any payment in respect of secondary earnings-related contributions which he is subsequently liable to pay to a Collector under paragraph 10 or 11 of Schedule 4 for any income tax period in the same year.

83(4) In this regulation **"Collector"**, **"income tax period"** and **"year"** have the meanings given in paragraph 1(2) of Schedule 4.

Derivations – SI 1979/591 reg. 47M.

REQUIREMENT TO GIVE SECURITY OR FURTHER SECURITY FOR AMOUNTS OF CLASS 1A CONTRIBUTIONS

83A Paragraphs 29M to 29X of Schedule 4 (security for payment of Class 1 contributions) apply in relation to Class 1A contributions as they apply in relation to Class 1 contributions but as if–

(a) in paragraph 29N–

(i) the reference to **"Class 1 contributions"** were a reference to "Class 1A contributions"; and

(ii) the reference to **"paragraph 10, 11 or 11A"** were a reference to "section 10 or 10ZA of the Social Security Contributions and Benefits Act 1992, or section 10 or 10ZA of the Social Security Contributions and Benefits (Northern Ireland) Act 1992, as the case may be"; and

(b) in paragraph 29O(1) for "within the meaning given in paragraph 1(2)" there were substituted "within the meaning given in regulation 70(4)".

History – Reg. 83A inserted by SI 2012/821, reg. 17, with effect from 6 April 2012.

SPECIAL PROVISIONS RELATING TO PRIMARY CLASS 1 CONTRIBUTIONS

84(1) If in accordance with an arrangement authorised under regulation 68, notwithstanding paragraph 3(1) of Schedule 1 to the Act (method of paying Class 1 contributions), an earner is required to make direct payments in respect of primary Class 1 contributions in respect of earnings paid to him or for his benefit, the following provisions of this regulation apply.

84(2) In a case to which this regulation applies–

(a) the earner shall be liable for such of the primary Class 1 contributions as are specified in the arrangements authorised under regulation 68, and

(b) the secondary contributor shall be liable for any other Class 1 contributions,

in respect of earnings paid to the earner or for the earner's benefit from the employment in question.

84(3) The Board shall notify the secondary contributor in writing of–

(a) the arrangement,

(b) the contributions for which, notwithstanding the arrangement, he will remain accountable to the Board, and

(c) the period to which the arrangement relates (**"the relevant period"**).

84(4) During the relevant period, paragraph 3(1) of Schedule 1 to the Act (method of paying Class 1 contributions) shall not apply to the secondary contributor in respect of those contributions–

(a) to which the arrangement relates, and

(b) for which he would otherwise have been accountable to the Board,

unless and until the arrangement has been cancelled before the end of the period and the secondary contributor has been notified in writing of its cancellation.

History – Reg. 84 substituted by SI 2003/193, reg. 8 with effect from 6 April 2003.
Derivations – SI 1979/591 reg. 48.

EXCEPTION IN RELATION TO EARNINGS TO WHICH REGULATION 84 APPLIES

85 [Omitted by SI 2003/193, reg. 9.]

History – Reg. 85 omitted by SI 2003/193, reg. 9 with effect from 6 April 2003.
Derivations – SI 1979/591 reg. 49.

SPECIAL PROVISIONS RELATING TO CULPABLE EMPLOYED EARNERS AND TO SECONDARY CONTRIBUTORS OR EMPLOYERS EXEMPTED BY TREATY ETC., FROM ENFORCEMENT OF THE ACT OR LIABILITY UNDER IT

86(1) As respects any employed earner's employment

(a) where there has been a failure to pay any primary contribution which a secondary contributor is, or but for the provisions of this regulation would be, liable to pay on behalf of the earner and

(i) the failure was due to an act or default of the earner and not to any negligence on the part of the secondary contributor, or

(ii) it is shown to the satisfaction of an officer of the Board that the earner knows that the secondary contributor has wilfully failed to pay the primary contribution which the secondary contributor was liable to pay on behalf of the earner and has not recovered that primary contribution from the earner; or

(b) where the secondary contributor is a person against whom, by reason of any international treaty or convention as mentioned in paragraph 30 of Schedule 4, the provisions of the Act are not enforceable and who is not willing to pay on behalf of the earner any contribution due in respect of earnings paid to or for the benefit of the earner in respect of that employment,

the provisions of paragraph 3(1) of Schedule 1 to the Act (method of paying Class 1 contributions) shall not apply in relation to that contribution.

86(2) Where, as respects any employed earner's employment, the employer is a person who by reason of any such international treaty or convention is exempt from the provisions of the Act, he may, if he so wishes, pay contributions in respect of any earnings paid to or for the benefit of the earner in respect of the employment, or contributions under section 10 of the Act, in either case to the same extent to which he could have paid such contributions if he had not been so exempt.

86(3) In this regulation **"employer"** has the same meaning as it has in paragraph 30 of Schedule 4.

History – In reg. 86(1)(a) the reference to "(i)" inserted and the words ", or" and item (ii) inserted by SI 2004/770, reg. 22, with effect from 6 April 2004.
In reg. 86(2) words "in respect of any car made available to the earner or to a member of his family or household by reason of the employment." omitted by SI 2004/770, reg. 22 and Schedule, with effect from 6 April 2004.

Derivations – SI 1979/591 reg. 50

NOTIFICATION OF COMMENCEMENT OR CESSATION OF PAYMENT OF CLASS 2 OR CLASS 3 CONTRIBUTIONS ON OR BEFORE 5TH APRIL 2009

History – In the heading to reg. 87, the words "on or before 5th April 2009" inserted by SI 2009/600, reg. 5(a), with effect from 6 April 2009.

87(1) Every person to whom paragraph (2) applies shall immediately notify the relevant date to the Board in writing or by such means of electronic communications as may be approved.

87(2) This paragraph applies to a person who on or before 5th April 2009

(a) becomes, or ceases to be, liable to pay a Class 2 contribution;

(b) becomes, or ceases to be, entitled to pay a Class 2 contribution although not liable to do so; or

(c) is entitled to pay a Class 3 contribution and wishes either to do so or to cease doing so.

87(3) [Omitted by SI 2015/478, reg. 24(1)(h).]

87(4) [Omitted by SI 2015/478, reg. 24(1)(h).]

87(5) [Omitted by SI 2015/478, reg. 24(1)(h).]

87(6) [Omitted by SI 2015/478, reg. 24(1)(h).]

87(7) [Omitted by SI 2015/478, reg. 24(1)(h).]

87(8) [Omitted by SI 2015/478, reg. 24(1)(h).]

History – In reg. 87(2), the words "on or before 5th April 2009" inserted by SI 2009/600, reg. 5(b), with effect from 6 April 2009.
Reg. 87(3)–(8) omitted by SI 2015/478, reg. 24(1)(h), with effect from 6 April 2015.

Derivations – SI 1979/591 reg. 53A.

NOTIFICATION OF COMMENCEMENT OR CESSATION OF PAYMENT OF CLASS 2 OR CLASS 3 CONTRIBUTIONS ON OR AFTER 6TH APRIL 2009 BUT BEFORE 6TH APRIL 2015

History – In heading, the words "but before 6th April 2015" inserted by SI 2015/478, reg. 10, with effect from 6 April 2015.

87A(1) A person (P) to whom paragraph (2) applies shall immediately notify the relevant date to HMRC in writing or by such means of electronic communications as may be approved.

87A(2) This paragraph applies where P on or after but before 6th April 2015–

(a) becomes, or ceases to be, liable to pay a Class 2 contribution;

(b) becomes, or ceases to be, entitled to pay a Class 2 contribution although not liable to do so; or

(c) is entitled to pay a Class 3 contribution and wishes either to do so or to cease doing so.

87A(3) In paragraph (1) **"the relevant date"** means–

(a) in relation to a person to whom paragraph (2)(a) applies, the date on which P commences or ceases to be a self-employed earner;

(b) in relation to a person to whom paragraph (2)(b) or (c) applies, the date on which P wishes to commence or cease paying either Class 2 or Class 3 contributions, as the case may be.

87A(4) P is to be treated as having immediately notified HMRC in accordance with paragraph (1) if P has notified HMRC within such further time, if any, as HMRC may allow.

History – In reg. 87A(2), the words "but before 6th April 2015" inserted by SI 2015/478, reg. 10, with effect from 6 April 2015.
Reg. 87A inserted by SI 2009/600, reg. 6, with effect from 6 April 2009.

NOTIFICATION OF COMMENCEMENT OR CESSATION OF SELF-EMPLOYMENT OR CLASS 3 CONTRIBUTIONS ON OR AFTER 6TH APRIL 2015

87AA(1) A person (P) to whom paragraph (2) applies shall immediately notify the relevant date to HMRC in writing or by such means of electronic communication as may be approved.

87AA(2) *This paragraph applies* where P on or after 6th April 2015–

(a) commences or ceases to be a self-employed earner; or

(b) is entitled to pay a Class 3 contribution and either wishes to do so or cease doing so.

87AA(3) In paragraph (1) **"the relevant date"** means–

(a) in relation to a person to whom paragraph (2)(a) applies, the date on which P commences or ceases to be a self-employed earner;

(b) in relation to a person to whom paragraph (2)(b) applies, the date on which P wishes to commence or cease paying Class 3 contributions.

87AA(4) P is to be treated as having immediately notified HMRC in accordance with paragraph (1) if P has notified HMRC within such further time, if any, as HMRC may allow.

History – Reg. 87AA and heading immediately preceding it inserted by SI 2015/478, reg. 11, with effect from 6 April 2015.

PENALTY FOR FAILURE TO NOTIFY

87B [Omitted by SI 2015/478, reg. 24(1)(i).]

History – Reg. 87B omitted by SI 2015/478, reg. 24(1)(i), with effect from 6 April 2015.

DISCLOSURE

87C [Omitted by SI 2015/478, reg. 24(1)(i).]

History – Reg. 87C omitted by SI 2015/478, reg. 24(1)(i), with effect from 6 April 2015.

REDUCTION OF PENALTY FOR DISCLOSURE

87D [Omitted by SI 2015/478, reg. 24(1)(i).]

History – Reg. 87D omitted by SI 2015/478, reg. 24(1)(i), with effect from 6 April 2015.

SPECIAL REDUCTION

87E [Omitted by SI 2015/478, reg. 24(1)(i).]

History – Reg. 87E omitted by SI 2015/478, reg. 24(1)(i), with effect from 6 April 2015.

NOTICE OF DECISION ETC.

87F [Omitted by SI 2015/478, reg. 24(1)(i).]

History – Reg. 87F omitted by SI 2015/478, reg. 24(1)(i), with effect from 6 April 2015.

DOUBLE JEOPARDY

87G [Omitted by SI 2015/478, reg. 24(1)(i).]

History – Reg. 87G omitted by SI 2015/478, reg. 24(1)(i), with effect from 6 April 2015.

NOTIFICATION OF CHANGE OF ADDRESS

88 A person liable to pay Class 2 contributions, or paying Class 2 contributions (although not liable to do so) or Class 3 contributions, shall immediately notify the Board of any change of his address in writing or by such means of electronic communications as may be approved.

Derivations – SI 1979/591 reg. 53B.

METHOD OF, AND TIME FOR, PAYMENT OF CLASS 2 AND CLASS 3 CONTRIBUTIONS ETC.

89(1) Where Class 2 or Class 3 contributions are payable by a person other than in accordance with the Taxes Management Act 1970 (as modified by section 11A of the Act) or in accordance with, arrangements approved under regulation 90 or in accordance with regulation 90ZA or 148C, such contributions shall be paid in accordance with paragraph (2A), (3) or (4), as the case may be.

89(1A) [Omitted by SI 2015/478, reg. 12(3).]

89(2) [Omitted by SI 2015/478, reg. 12(3).]

89(2A) Where–

(a) a person who is entitled, although not liable, to pay a Class 2 contribution in any year has notified HMRC of his entitlement in accordance with the provisions of regulation 87, 87A or 87AA; and

(b) HMRC has, no later than the notification date, issued him with written notice of the amount he may pay in respect of his entitlement in that period;

that person may, if the person so wishes, pay to HMRC a sum not exceeding that amount.

89(3) Where

(a) a person who is entitled to pay a Class 3 contribution, in any year, has notified HMRC of his entitlement in accordance with regulation 87, 87A or 87AA; and

(b) HMRC, within 14 days after the end of a contribution quarter which commences in that year, have issued him with written notice of the amount he may pay in respect of his entitlement in that quarter;

that person may, if he so wishes, pay to HMRC a sum not exceeding that amount.

89(4) Where

(a) paragraph (5) applies to a person; and

(b) HMRC have then, in respect of that entitlement to pay Class 2 or Class 3 contributions, issued or re-issued him, as the case may be, with written notice of the amount of his entitlement;

that person may pay a sum not exceeding the amount of his entitlement, to HMRC.

89(5) This paragraph applies to a person who–

(a) has notified HMRC in accordance with the provisions of regulation 87, 87A or 87AA that–

(i) [omitted by SI 2015/478, reg. 12(7)(a)(ii),]

(ii) he is entitled although not liable to pay a Class 2 contribution in a tax year, or is entitled to pay a Class 3 contribution in a contribution quarter; and

(b) has–

(i) not, by the notification date, had written notice issued to him in respect of that week or weeks of the kind referred to in paragraph (2A);

(ii) not had written notice issued to him in respect of that week or weeks of a kind mentioned in paragraph (3) and more than 14 days have elapsed since the end of the contribution quarter in question; or

(iii) notified HMRC in accordance with regulation 87, 87A or 87AA that he has ceased to be entitled to pay Class 2 or Class 3 contributions.

89(6) [Omitted by SI 2015/478, reg. 12(8).]

89(7) In this regulation–

(a) [omitted by SI 2015/478, reg. 12(9)(a);]

(b) [omitted by SI 2015/478, reg. 12(9)(a);]

(c) [omitted by SI 2015/478, reg. 12(9)(a);]

(d) **"contribution quarter"** means one of the four periods of not less than 13 contribution weeks commencing on the first, fourteenth, twenty-seventh or fortieth contribution week, as the case may be, in any year;

(e) **"notification date"** means 31st October following the end of the tax year.

History – In reg. 89(1), the words "the Taxes Management Act 1970 (as modified by section 11A of the Act) or in accordance with," inserted by SI 2015/478, reg. 12(2)(a), with effect from 6 April 2015.

In reg. 89(1), the words "or in accordance with regulation 90ZA or 148C" inserted by SI 2015/478, reg. 12(2)(b), with effect from 6 April 2015.

In reg. 89(1), the word "(2)" (which appeared after the word "paragraph"), omitted by SI 2015/478, reg. 12(2)(c), with effect from 6 April 2015.

In reg. 89(1), "(2A)," inserted by SI 2011/797, reg. 6(a), with effect in relation to Class 2 contributions in respect of contribution weeks beginning on or after 10 April 2011.

Reg. 89(1A) omitted by SI 2015/478, reg. 12(3), with effect from 6 April 2015.

Former Reg. 89(1A) inserted by SI 2011/797, reg. 6(b), with effect in relation to Class 2 contributions in respect of contribution weeks beginning on or after 10 April 2011.

Reg. 89(2) omitted by SI 2015/478, reg. 12(3), with effect from 6 April 2015.

Reg. 89(2) substituted by SI 2011/797, reg. 6(c), with effect in relation to Class 2 contributions in respect of contribution weeks beginning on or after 10 April 2011.

In reg. 89(2A)(a), the words "or 87AA" inserted (and the "," after the words "regulation 87" substituted for the word "or") by SI 2015/478, reg. 12(4), with effect from 6 April 2015.

Reg. 89(2A) inserted by SI 2011/797, reg. 6(d), with effect in relation to Class 2 contributions in respect of contribution weeks beginning on or after 10 April 2011.

In reg. 89(3)(a), the words ", 87A or 87AA" substituted for "or 87A" by SI 2015/478, reg. 12(5), with effect from 6 April 2015.

In reg. 89(3)(a), the words "who is entitled although not liable to pay a Class 2 contribution, or", which appeared after the words "a person", omitted by SI 2011/797, reg. 6(e)(i), with effect in relation to Class 2 contributions in respect of contribution weeks beginning on or after 10 April 2011.

In reg. 89(3)(a), "or 87A" inserted by SI 2011/797, reg. 6(e)(ii), with effect in relation to Class 2 contributions in respect of contribution weeks beginning on or after 10 April 2011.

In reg. 89(3), "HMRC" substituted for "the Board", in each place it occurs, by SI 2011/797, reg. 6(e)(iii), with effect in relation to Class 2 contributions in respect of contribution weeks beginning on or after 10 April 2011.

In reg. 89(4)(a), the words "or (6)" (which appeared after the words "paragraph (5)") omitted by SI 2015/478, reg. 12(6)(a), with effect from 6 April 2015.

In reg. 89(4)(b), the words "person's liability for Class 2 contributions or" (which appeared after the words "in respect of that"), the words "the number of contribution weeks in respect of which the liability arises together with the weekly rate, and of the date specified asthe date of notification, or, where he is entitled to pay contributions, of" (which appeared after the words "written notice of" and the words "shall, if he is liable to pay a contribution, pay the amount of contributions for which he is liable not later than the date for payment specified in the notice and, if he is entitled to pay a contribution, he" (which appeared after the words "that person") omitted by SI 2015/478, reg. 12(6)(b) and (c), with effect from 6 April 2015.

In reg. 89(4), the words "the date for payment specified in the notice" substituted for the words "28 days after the specified date of notification" by SI 2011/797, reg. 6(f)(i), with effect in relation to Class 2 contributions in respect of contribution weeks beginning on or after 10 April 2011.

In reg. 89(4), "HMRC" substituted for "the Board", in each place it occurs, by SI 2011/797, reg. 6(f)(ii), with effect in relation to Class 2 contributions in respect of contribution weeks beginning on or after 10 April 2011.
In reg. 89(5)(a), the words ", 87A or 87AA" substituted for the words "or 87A" by SI 2015/478, reg. 12(7)(a)(i), with effect from 6 April 2015.
Reg. 89(5)(a)(i) omitted by SI 2015/478, reg. 12(7)(a)(ii), with effect from 6 April 2015.
In reg. 89(5)(a)(ii), the words "tax year" substituted for the words "biannual contribution period" by SI 2015/478, reg. 12(7)(a)(iii), with effect from 6 April 2015.
In reg. 89(5)(b)(iii), the words ", 87A or 87AA" substituted for the words "or 87A" by SI 2015/478, reg. 12(7)(b)(i), with effect from 6 April 2015.
In reg. 89(5)(b)(iii), the words "ceased to be liable to pay Class 2 contributions or" (which appeared after the words "that he has") omitted by SI 2015/478, reg. 12(7)(b)(ii), with effect from 6 April 2015.
In reg. 89(5)(b)(iii), the words "as the case may be" (which appeared after the words "Class 2 or Class 3 contributions") omitted by SI 2015/478, reg. 12(7)(b)(iii), with effect from 6 April 2015.
Reg. 89(6) omitted by SI 2015/478, reg. 12(8), with effect from 6 April 2015.
Reg. 89(7)(a)–(c) omitted by SI 2015/478, reg. 12(9)(a), with effect from 6 April 2015.
Reg. 89(7)(e) substituted by SI 2015/478, reg. 12(9)(b), with effect from 6 April 2015.
Reg. 89(5)–(7) substituted by SI 2011/797, reg. 6(g), with effect in relation to Class 2 contributions in respect of contribution weeks beginning on or after 10 April 2011.
Derivations – SI 1979/591 reg. 54.

CLASS 2 CONTRIBUTIONS FOR TAX YEARS UP TO 2014–15

89A(1) This regulation applies where a person (P) is liable to pay a Class 2 contribution in respect of any contribution week in a tax year up to and including the 2014–15 tax year.

89A(2) An officer of HMRC may issue P with written notice of the amount of Class 2 contributions for which P is liable in respect of any tax year up to and including the 2014–15 tax year.

89A(3) P shall pay the amount of contributions for which he is liable no later than the date specified in the notice. This paragraph is subject to paragraphs (4) and (5).

89A(4) Where P–

(a) is liable to pay a Class 2 contribution in respect of any contribution week falling within the period defined in paragraph (5) ("the specified contribution period"); and

(b) has notified HMRC of such liability in accordance with the provisions of regulation 87 or 87A,

HMRC shall issue P with written notice of the amount of Class 2 contributions for which P is liable to pay in respect of the specified contribution period no later than 1st June 2015 and P shall pay the amount set out in that notice to HMRC no later than 31st July 2015.

89A(5) For the purposes of paragraph (4), the specified contribution period is the period of not less than 26 contribution weeks falling within the 2014–15 tax year commencing with the first day of the twenty seventh contribution week in that year.

History – Reg. 89A and the heading immediately preceding it inserted by SI 2015/478, reg. 13, with effect from 6 April 2015.

ARRANGEMENTS APPROVED BY THE BOARD FOR METHOD OF, AND TIME FOR, PAYMENT OF CLASS 2 AND CLASS 3 CONTRIBUTIONS

90(1) The Board may from time to time approve arrangements under which contributions are paid at times or in a manner different from those prescribed by regulation 89.

This is subject to paragraphs (2) to (4).

90(2) When granting approval under paragraph (1), the Board may impose such conditions as they see fit.

90(3) The Board may, in particular, grant approval under paragraph (1) if, as respects any year in which a person is both an employed earner and a self-employed earner, the condition in paragraph (4) is satisfied.

90(4) The condition is that the Board are satisfied that the total amounts of primary Class 1 contributions and Class 2 contributions likely to be paid by or in respect of that person in respect of that year will exceed the amount equal to 53 primary Class 1 contributions payable on earnings at the upper earnings limit for that year at the main primary percentage.

90(5) The provisions of these Regulations shall, subject to the provisions of the arrangements, apply to the person affected by the arrangements.

90(6) Where in respect of an earner arrangements are approved under paragraph (1) for payment of contributions by way of direct debit of a bank, those arrangements shall be subject to the condition that any payment by way of direct debit on account of such contributions after the authority of the bank to make such payment has for any reason ceased to be effective, shall not be a payment of contributions for the purposes of the Act.

History – In reg. 90(4), the words "total amounts of primary Class 1 contributions and Class 2 contributions" and the words "the amount equal to 53 primary Class 1 contributions payable on earnings at the upper earnings limit for that year at the main primary percentage" substituted by SI 2003/193, reg. 10 with effect from 6 April 2003.
Derivations – SI 1979/591 reg. 54A.

CLASS 2 CONTRIBUTIONS – MATERNITY ALLOWANCE

90ZA(1) This regulation applies in connection with maternity allowance under section 35 or 35B of the Act.

90ZA(2) A person who is, or will be, either liable or entitled to pay a Class 2 contribution in respect of a week in a tax year may pay a Class 2 contribution in respect of that week at any time in the period–

(a) beginning with that week; and

(b) ending with 31st January next following the end of the relevant tax year.

90ZA(3) Where a person pays a Class 2 contribution in accordance with paragraph (2)–

(a) the contribution is to be treated, before the end of the tax year, as a Class 2 contribution under section 11(6) of the Act, and

(b) the contribution is to be treated after the end of the tax year–

(i) if the person is liable under section 11(2) of the Act to pay a Class 2 contribution in respect of that week, as a Class 2 contribution under section 11(2) of the Act; or

(ii) otherwise, as a Class 2 contribution under section 11(6) of the Act.

History – Reg. 90ZA and the heading immediately preceding it inserted by SI 2015/478, reg. 14, with effect from 6 April 2015.

PART 7A – ELECTRONIC COMMUNICATIONS

WHETHER INFORMATION HAS BEEN DELIVERED ELECTRONICALLY

History – Pt. 7A inserted by SI 2004/770, reg. 23, with effect from 6 April 2004.

90A(1) For the purposes of these Regulations, information is taken to have been delivered to an official computer system by an approved method of electronic communications only if it is accepted by that official computer system.

90A(2) References in these Regulations to information and to the delivery of information must be construed in accordance with section 135(8) of the Finance Act 2002 (mandatory e-filing).

History – Reg. 90A inserted by SI 2004/770, reg. 23, with effect from 6 April 2004.

PROOF OF CONTENT OF ELECTRONIC DELIVERY

90B(1) A document certified by the Board to be a printed-out version of any information delivered by an approved method of electronic communications is evidence, unless the contrary is proved, that the information–

(a) was delivered by an approved method of electronic communications on that occasion, and

(b) constitutes everything which was delivered on that occasion.

90B(2) A document which purports to be a certificate given in accordance with paragraph (1) is presumed to be such a certificate unless the contrary is proved.

History – Reg. 90B inserted by SI 2004/770, reg. 23, with effect from 6 April 2004.

PROOF OF IDENTITY OF PERSON SENDING OR RECEIVING ELECTRONIC DELIVERY

90C The identity of–

(a) the person sending any information delivered by an approved method of electronic communications to the Board,

(b) the person receiving any information delivered by an approved method of electronic communications by the Board,

is presumed, unless the contrary is proved, to be the person recorded as such on an official computer system.

History – Reg. 90C inserted by SI 2004/770, reg. 23, with effect from 6 April 2004.

INFORMATION SENT ELECTRONICALLY ON BEHALF OF A PERSON

90D(1) Any information delivered by an approved method of electronic communications–

(a) to the Board, or

(b) to an official computer system,

on behalf of a person is taken to have been delivered by that person.

90D(2) But this does not apply if the person proves that the information was delivered without the person's knowledge or connivance.

History – Reg. 90D inserted by SI 2004/770, reg. 23, with effect from 6 April 2004.

PROOF OF DELIVERY OF INFORMATION SENT ELECTRONICALLY

90E(1) The use of an approved method of electronic communications is presumed, unless the contrary is proved, to have resulted in the delivery of information–

(a) to the Board, if the delivery of the information has been recorded on an official computer system;

(b) by the Board, if the despatch of the information has been recorded on an official computer system.

90E(2) The use of an approved method of electronic communications is presumed, unless the contrary is proved, not to have resulted in the delivery of information–

(a) to the Board, if the delivery of the information has not been recorded on an official computer system;

(b) by the Board, if the despatch of the information has not been recorded on an official computer system.

90E(3) The time of receipt or despatch of any information delivered by an approved method of electronic communications is presumed, unless the contrary is proved, to be the time recorded on an official computer system.

History – Reg. 90E inserted by SI 2004/770, reg. 23, with effect from 6 April 2004.

PROOF OF PAYMENT SENT ELECTRONICALLY

90F(1) The use of a method of electronic communications is presumed, unless the contrary is proved, to have resulted in the making of a payment–

(a) to the Board, if the making of the payment has been recorded on an official computer system;

(b) by the Board, if the despatch of the payment has been recorded on an official computer system.

90F(2) The use of a method of electronic communications is presumed, unless the contrary is proved, not to have resulted in the making of a payment–

(a) to the Board, if the making of the payment has not been recorded on an official computer system;

(b) by the Board, if the despatch of the payment has not been recorded on an official computer system.

90F(3) The time of receipt or despatch of any payment sent by a method of electronic communications is presumed, unless the contrary is proved, to be the time recorded on an official computer system.

History – Reg. 90F inserted by SI 2004/770, reg. 23, with effect from 6 April 2004.

USE OF UNAUTHORISED METHOD OF ELECTRONIC COMMUNICATIONS

90G(1) This regulation applies to information which is required to be delivered to the Board or to an official computer system under a provision of these Regulations.

90G(2) The use of a method of electronic communications for the purpose of delivering such information is conclusively presumed not to have resulted in the delivery of that information, unless that method of electronic communications is for the time being approved for delivery of that kind under that provision.

History – Reg. 90G inserted by SI 2004/770, reg. 23, with effect from 6 April 2004.

MANDATORY ELECTRONIC PAYMENT

90H(1) An employer who is a large employer within the meaning of regulation 198A (large employers) of the PAYE Regulations must pay the specified payment using an approved method of electronic communications

90H(2) Paragraph (1) applies regardless of whether a payment of tax is due under regulation 67G or 68 of the PAYE Regulations (payment and recovery of tax by employer).

90H(3) If the Board have given a direction under regulation 199(3) of the PAYE Regulations requiring a particular method of electronic communications to be used in the case of an employer, he must use that method.

90H(4) This regulation does not apply to a payment of contributions, whether primary or secondary, in respect of retrospective earnings where those earnings relate to a tax year which is closed (see paragraph 1(2) of Schedule 4) at the time the relevant retrospective contributions regulations come into force.

90H(5) A specified payment is not treated as received in full by HMRC on or before the date by which that specified payment is required in accordance with paragraph 10 or paragraph 11 of Schedule 4 unless it is made in a manner which secures (in a case where the specified payment is made otherwise than in cash) that, on or before that date, all transactions can be completed which need to be completed before the whole amount of the specified payment becomes available to the Commissioners for Her Majesty's Revenue and Customs.

History – In reg. 90H(1) the words "198A (large employers)" substituted for the words "191 (large and medium sized employers)" by SI 2010/721, reg. 5(b), with effect from 6 April 2010 (but only in relation to 2011–12 and subsequent tax years).
Reg. 90H(1) substituted by SI 2010/721, reg. 5(a), with effect from 6 April 2010 (but only in relation to 2010–11 and subsequent tax years).

In reg. 90H(2), "67G or" inserted by SI 2012/821, reg. 4, with effect from 6 April 2012.
Reg. 90H(4) inserted by SI 2007/1056, reg. 6, with effect from 6 April 2007.
Reg. 90H(5) inserted by SI 2010/721, reg. 5(c), with effect from 6 April 2010 (but only in relation to 2010–11 and subsequent tax years).
Reg. 90H inserted by SI 2004/770, reg. 23, with effect from 6 April 2004.

Cross references – Direction of the Board, 5 April 2004: direction consolidating various directions in respect of the electronic delivery of information and specifying approved methods of electronic payments of sums due.

EMPLOYER IN DEFAULT IF SPECIFIED PAYMENT NOT RECEIVED BY APPLICABLE DUE DATE

90I [Omitted by SI 2010/721, reg. 6(a).]

History – Reg. 90I omitted by SI 2010/721, reg. 6(a), with effect from 6 April 2010 (but only in relation to 2010–11 and subsequent tax years).

DEFAULT NOTICE AND APPEAL

90J [Omitted by SI 2010/721, reg. 6(b).]

History – Reg. 90J omitted by SI 2010/721, reg. 6(b), with effect from 6 April 2010 (but only in relation to 2010–11 and subsequent tax years).

DEFAULT SURCHARGE

90K [Omitted by SI 2010/721, reg. 6(c).]

History – Reg. 90K omitted by SI 2010/721, reg. 6(c), with effect from 6 April 2010 (but only in relation to 2010–11 and subsequent tax years).

SURCHARGE NOTICE AND APPEAL

90L [Omitted by SI 2010/721, reg. 6(d).]

History – Reg. 90L omitted by SI 2010/721, reg. 6(d), with effect from 6 April 2010 (but only in relation to 2010–11 and subsequent tax years).

PARAGRAPH 22 RETURN AND SPECIFIED PAYMENTS

History – The heading to reg. 90M substituted by SI 2009/2028, reg. 4, with effect in relation to deferred payment agreements made on or after 13 August 2009. Former heading was "SPECIFIED INFORMATION AND SPECIFIED PAYMENTS".

90M In this Part–

"paragraph 22 return" means the return and accompanying information required by paragraph 22 of Schedule 4 (return by employer at the end of the year);

"specified payments" means payments of earnings-related contributions under paragraph 10 (payments made monthly by employer) or paragraph 11 (payments made quarterly by employer) of Schedule 4.

History – In reg. 90M the definition of specified payments substituted by SI 2010/721, reg. 7, with effect from 6 April 2010 (but only in relation to 2010–11 and subsequent tax years).
In reg. 90M, definition of "paragraph 22 return" substituted for definition of "specified information" by SI 2009/2028, reg. 5(a), with effect in relation to the tax year 2009–10 and subsequent tax years.
In reg. 90M, in the definition of "specified payments", the words "of Schedule 4" inserted by SI 2009/2028, reg. 5(b), with effect in relation to the tax year 2009–10 and subsequent tax years.
Reg. 90M inserted by SI 2004/770, reg. 23, with effect from 6 April 2004.

MANDATORY USE OF ELECTRONIC COMMUNICATIONS

90N(1) An employer (as to which see regulation 90NA) must deliver a paragraph 22 return to an official computer system using an approved method of electronic communications.

90N(2) If the Commissioners for Her Majesty's Revenue and Customs have made a direction under regulation 205(2) of the PAYE Regulations requiring a particular method of electronic communication to be used in the case of an employer, the employer must use that method.

90N(3) This regulation does not apply to a return in respect of retrospective earnings where those earnings relate to a tax year which is closed (see paragraph 1(2) of Schedule 4) at the time the relevant retrospective contributions regulations come into force.

History – In reg. 90N(2), "205(2)" substituted for "205B(1)" by SI 2010/721, reg. 8(2), with effect from 6 April 2010 (but only in relation to 2011–12 and subsequent tax years).
Reg. 90N and 90NA substituted for former reg. 90N by SI 2010/721, reg. 8(1), with effect from 6 April 2010 (but only in relation to *2010–11 and subsequent tax years*).

EMPLOYERS

90NA(1) For the purposes of regulation 90N, the following shall not be regarded as employers–

(a) an individual who is a practising member of a religious society or order whose beliefs are incompatible with the use of electronic communications,

(b) a partnership, if all the partners fall within sub-paragraph (a),

(c) a company, if all the directors and company secretary fall within sub-paragraph (a),

(d) [omitted by SI 2013/622, reg. 3,] and

(e) a care and support employer.

90NA(2) In paragraph (1)(c), **"company"** means a body corporate or unincorporated association but does not include a partnership.

90NA(3) In paragraph (1)(e), a **"care and support employer"** means an individual ("the employer") who employs a person to provide domestic or personal services at or from the employer's home where–

(a) the services are provided to the employer or a member of the employer's family,

(b) the recipient of the services has a physical or mental disability, or is elderly or infirm,

(c) the employer has not received an incentive payment in respect of the last 3 tax years, and

(d) it is the employer who delivers the paragraph 22 return (and not some other person on the employer's behalf).

90NA(4) In this regulation **"incentive payment"** means an incentive payment received under the Income Tax (Incentive Payments for Voluntary Electronic Communication of PAYE Returns) Regulations 2003.

History – Reg. 90NA(1)(d) (but not the "and" after it) omitted by SI 2013/622, reg. 3, with effect from 6 April 2014 in relation to the tax year 2014–15.

STANDARDS OF ACCURACY AND COMPLETENESS

90O(1) Any paragraph 22 return delivered by a method of electronic communications must meet the standards of accuracy or completeness set by specific or general directions given by the Board.

90O(2) Any paragraph 22 return which fails to meet those standards must be treated as not having been delivered.

History – In reg. 90O(1) and (2), the words "Any paragraph 22 return" substituted for the words "Specified information" by SI 2009/2028, reg. 7, with effect in relation to the tax year 2009–10 and subsequent tax years.
Reg. 90O inserted by SI 2004/770, reg. 23, with effect from 6 April 2004.

PENALTIES AND APPEALS

90P(1) An employer who fails to deliver a paragraph 22 return or any part of it in accordance with regulation 90N is liable to a penalty.

90P(2) Table 2 sets out the penalties for employers for the tax year ending 5th April 2010, depending on the number of employees for whom particulars should have been included with the paragraph 22 return.

TABLE 2 – PENALTIES: TAX YEAR ENDING 5TH APRIL 2010

1. Number of employees for whom particulars should have been included with the return	*2. Penalty*
1–5	Nil
6–49	£100
50–249	£600
250–399	£900
400–499	£1200
500–599	£1500
600–699	£1800
700–799	£2100
800–899	£2400
900–999	£2700
1000 or more	£3,000

90P(2A) Table 3 sets out the penalties for employers for the tax years ending 5th April 2011 and subsequent years, depending on the number of employees for whom particulars should have been included with the paragraph 22 return.

TABLE 3 – PENALTIES: TAX YEAR ENDING 5TH APRIL 2011 AND SUBSEQUENT YEARS

1. Number of employees for whom particulars should have been included with the return	*2. Penalty*
1–5	£100
6–49	£300
50–249	£600
250–399	£900
400–499	£1200
500–599	£1500
600–699	£1800
700–799	£2100
800–899	£2400
900–999	£2700
1000 or more	£3000

90P(3) An employer is not liable to a penalty if the employer had–

(a) a reasonable excuse for failing to comply with regulation 90N which had not ceased at the time the paragraph 22 return was delivered, or

(b) been subject to a penalty for failing to deliver the return and accompanying information required by regulation 73 of the PAYE Regulations (annual return of relevant payments liable to deduction of tax (Forms P35 and P14)) in accordance with regulation 205 (mandatory use of electronic communication) of those Regulations.

90P(4) A notice of appeal against a determination under section 100 of the Management Act of a penalty under this paragraph can only be on the grounds that–

(a) the employer did comply with regulation 90N,

(aa) the employer is not regarded as an employer for the purposes of regulation 90N,

(b) the amount of the penalty is incorrect, or

(c) paragraph (3) applies.

90P(5) Section 103A of the Management Act (interest on penalties) applies to penalties payable under this paragraph.

History – In reg. 90P(1), the words "a paragraph 22 return" substituted for the words "specified information" by SI 2009/2028, reg. 8(a), with effect in relation to the tax year 2009–10 and subsequent tax years.
Reg. 90P(2) and (2A) substituted for former reg. 90P(2) by SI 2009/2028, reg. 8(b), with effect in relation to the tax year 2009–10 and subsequent tax years.
Reg. 90P(3)(b) substituted by SI 2010/721, reg. 9(a), with effect from 6 April 2010 (but only in relation to 2011–12 and subsequent tax years).
In reg. 90P(3), the words "paragraph 22 return" in para. (a) substituted for the words "specified information", and para. (b) substituted, by SI 2009/2028, reg. 8(c), with effect in relation to the tax year 2009–10 and subsequent tax years.
Reg. 90P(4)(aa) inserted by SI 2010/721, reg. 9(b), with effect from 6 April 2010 (but only in relation to 2010–11 and subsequent tax years).
Reg. 90P inserted by SI 2004/770, reg. 23, with effect from 6 April 2004.

APPEALS: SUPPLEMENTARY PROVISIONS

90Q(1) Section 31A(5) of the Management Act applies to appeals under regulation 90J as it applies to an appeal under section 31 of that Act.

90Q(2) [Omitted by SI 2009/56, art. 3(2) and Sch. 2, para. 75(2).]

90Q(3) [Omitted by SI 2009/56, art. 3(2) and Sch. 2, para. 75(2).]

History – Reg. 90Q(1) substituted by SI 2009/56, art. 3(2) and Sch. 2, para. 75(1), operative from 1 April 2009 subject to transitional and saving provisions in SI 2009/56, Sch. 3.
Reg. 90Q(2) omitted by SI 2009/56, art. 3(2) and Sch. 2, para. 75(2), operative from 1 April 2009 subject to transitional and saving provisions in SI 2009/56, Sch. 3.
Reg. 90Q(3) omitted by SI 2009/56, art. 3(2) and Sch. 2, para. 75(2), operative from 1 April 2009 subject to transitional and saving provisions in SI 2009/56, Sch. 3.
Reg. 90Q inserted by SI 2004/770, reg. 23, with effect from 6 April 2004.

INTERPRETATION

90R In this Part **"the Management Act"** means the Taxes Management Act 1970.

History – Reg. 90R inserted by SI 2004/770, reg. 23, with effect from 6 April 2004.

PART 8 – CLASS 4 CONTRIBUTIONS

EXCEPTION FROM CLASS 4 LIABILITY OF PERSONS OVER PENSIONABLE AGE AND PERSONS NOT RESIDENT IN THE UNITED KINGDOM

91 Any earner who

(a) at the beginning of a year of assessment is over pensionable age; or

(b) for the purposes of income tax is not resident in the United Kingdom in the year of assessment;

shall be excepted from liability for contributions under section 15 of the Act (Class 4 contributions).

Derivations – SI 1979/591, reg. 58.

EXCEPTION OF DIVERS AND DIVING SUPERVISORS FROM LIABILITY FOR CLASS 4 CONTRIBUTIONS

92 A person who performs the duties of an employment to which section 314 of the Taxes Act applies (divers and diving supervisors) shall be excepted from liability for contributions under section 15 of the Act on so much of his profits or gains as are derived from that employment.

Derivations – SI 1979/591, reg. 59.

EXCEPTION OF PERSONS UNDER THE AGE OF 16 FROM LIABILITY FOR CLASS 4 CONTRIBUTIONS

93(1) Where, as respects any year of assessment, a person to whom this regulation applies wishes to be excepted from liability to pay contributions under section 15 of the Act for that year, the following provisions of this regulation shall apply, subject to the provisions of regulations 97 and 98.

93(2) Any such person shall make application to the Board for a certificate of exception for that year.

93(3) If it is shown to the satisfaction of the Board that the applicant is a person to whom this regulation applies and the application is made before the beginning of the year of assessment to which it relates, the Board shall issue in respect of the applicant such a certificate of exception for that year.

93(4) If the application is not made until after the beginning of the year of assessment to which it relates, but is made before contributions under that section 15 of the Act for that year become due and payable and it is shown to the satisfaction of the Board that the applicant is a person to whom this regulation applies, the Board may issue in respect of the applicant a certificate of exception for that year.

93(5) Where under paragraphs (1) to (4) a certificate of exception has been issued in respect of an applicant for any year of assessment, the Board shall not collect any contributions under section 15 of the Act from the applicant for that year.

93(6) This regulation applies to any person who at the beginning of the year of assessment is under the age of 16.

Derivations – SI 1979/591, reg. 60.

EXCEPTION FROM CLASS 4 LIABILITY IN RESPECT OF EARNINGS FROM EMPLOYED EARNER'S EMPLOYMENT CHARGEABLE TO INCOME TAX UNDER SCHEDULE D

History – Heading substituted by SI 2003/193, reg. 11(2) with effect from 6 April 2003.

94(1) If, for any year of assessment–

(a) an earner has earnings from employment which is employed earner's employment; and

(b) those earnings are chargeable to income tax under Schedule D;

the earner shall be excepted from liability to pay contributions under section 15 of the Act on those earnings.

This is subject to the following qualification.

94(2) It shall be a condition of exception from liability that the earner makes an application for such an exception to the Board before the beginning of the year of assessment to which the application relates, or before such later date as the Board may allow.

94(3) An application under paragraph (2) shall be made in such manner as the Board may direct and, for the purpose of enabling the Board to determine whether the earner is entitled to the exception, the earner shall furnish the Board with such information and evidence as the Board may require, whether the requirement is made at the time of the application or later.

94(4) Without prejudice to the earner's right to any such exception, nothing in paragraphs (1) to (3) shall affect the Board's powers under regulation 95 to defer, pending the determination of the application, the earner's liability under section 15 of the Act.

History – Reg. 94(1) substituted by SI 2003/193, reg. 11(3) with effect from 6 April 2003.

Derivations – SI 1979/591, reg. 61.

EXCEPTION FROM CLASS 4 LIABILITY IN RESPECT OF CERTAIN AMOUNTS CHARGEABLE TO INCOME TAX UNDER SCHEDULE D

94A Where–

(a) an earner has earnings from employment which is employed earner's employment; and

(b) an amount representing those earnings is included in the calculation of the profits chargeable to income tax under Schedule D,

the earner shall be excepted from liability to pay contributions under section 15 of the Act (Class 4 contributions) on that amount.

History – Reg. 94A inserted by SI 2003/2958, reg. 4, with effect from 10 December 2003, in relation to 2003–04 and subsequent tax years.

LIABILITY OF A PARTNER IN AN AIFM FIRM FOR CLASS 4 CONTRIBUTIONS

94B(1) This regulation applies if an AIFM firm makes an election under section 863H of ITTOIA 2005 (election for special provision for alternative investment fund managers to apply).

94B(2) Where a partner ("P") in an AIFM firm allocates a profit ("the allocated profit") to that firm as provided for in section 863I(2) of ITTOIA 2005 (allocation of profit to the AIFM firm), no Class 4 contributions are payable in respect of that allocated profit by virtue of the allocation.

94B(3) Paragraph (4) applies if all or part of the allocated profit vests in P at a time when P is carrying on the AIFM trade (whether as a partner in the AIFM firm or otherwise).

94B(4) The amount treated as a profit under section 863J(2) and (5) of ITTOIA 2005 (vesting of remuneration represented by the allocated profit) is to be treated for the purposes of the Act as if it were profits–

(a) to which section 15(1) of the Act (class 4 contributions recoverable under the Income Tax Acts) applies; and

(b) made by P in the tax year in which that profit is chargeable to income tax under Chapter 2 of Part 2 of ITTOIA 2005.

94B(5) In this regulation–

"AIFM firm" and **"AIFM trade"** have the meanings given in section 863H(3) and (4) of ITTOIA 2005; and

"ITTOIA 2005" means the Income Tax (Trading and Other Income) Act 2005.

History – Reg. 94B inserted by SI 2014/3196, reg. 2(2), with effect for the tax year 2014–15 and subsequent tax years.

DEFERMENT OF CLASS 4 LIABILITY WHERE SUCH LIABILITY IS IN DOUBT

95 Where, as respects any year of assessment before the tax year 2015–16, it appears to the Board that, by virtue of the provisions of this Part, there is doubt as to the extent, if any, of an earner's liability to pay contributions under section 15 of the Act (Class 4 contributions) for that year, or that at the date on which any application under regulation 96 is made, it is not possible to determine whether, having regard to the provisions of these Regulations, the earner is or will be liable to pay such contributions for that year, the Board may issue in respect of the earner a certificate of deferment deferring that earner's liability for such contributions and for such period as the Board may direct.

History – In reg. 95, the words "before the tax year 2015–16" inserted by SI 2015/478, reg. 15, with effect from 6 April 2015.
In reg. 95, the words "and for such period" substituted by SI 2003/193, reg. 12 with effect from 6 April 2003.

Derivations – SI 1979/591, reg. 62.

APPLICATION FOR DEFERMENT OF CLASS 4 LIABILITY

96(1) *If a person wishes his liability* to pay contributions under section 15 of the Act for any year of assessment to be deferred, he shall make an application for that purpose to the Board.

96(2) Any such application

(a) shall be made before the beginning of that year or before such later date as the Board may allow; and

(b) is subject to regulations 97 and 98.

Derivations – SI 1979/591, reg. 63.

GENERAL CONDITIONS FOR APPLICATION FOR, AND ISSUE OF, CERTIFICATES OF EXCEPTION AND DEFERMENT

97(1) Any application made under any of regulations 91 to 96, for a certificate of exception from, or deferment of, liability to pay contributions under section 15 of the Act for any particular year of assessment shall be made in such form and in such manner as the Board may approve.

97(2) Any person making such application shall furnish, or cause to be furnished, to the Board such information or evidence as they may require for the purpose of enabling them to determine whether such a certificate should be issued in respect of that person.

97(3) On the issue of such a certificate, the person in respect of whom the certificate is issued shall be excepted from liability to pay the contributions to which the certificate relates or his liability for such payment shall be deferred.

This is subject to paragraph (4).

97(4) If, for the purpose of obtaining a certificate of exception or deferment, the person making the application furnishes or causes to be furnished to the Board information which is erroneous, or fails to furnish or cause to be furnished to them information which is relevant, and but for such furnishing or failure the certificate would not have been issued for any particular year of assessment

(a) the Board may revoke the certificate in so far as it relates to that year; and

(b) the person who made the application shall be liable to pay contributions under section 15 of the Act for that year to the extent to which he would have been so liable if the certificate had not been issued.

Derivations – SI 1979/591, reg. 64.

REVOCATION OF CERTIFICATES OF EXCEPTION AND DEFERMENT

98 Where under regulation 97(4)(a) the Board revoke a certificate of exception or deferment

(a) they shall be responsible for calculating the contributions due under section 15 of the Act for the year specified in regulation 97(4)(b) (being the current or a past year) and for the collection of those contributions;

(b) the applicant shall

(i) furnish, or cause to be furnished, to the Board all such information or evidence as they may require for the purpose of calculating those contributions, and

(ii) within such period as the Board may direct, pay to them the contributions so calculated.

Derivations – SI 1979/591, reg. 65

CALCULATION OF LIABILITY FOR, AND RECOVERY OF, CLASS 4 CONTRIBUTIONS AFTER ISSUE OF CERTIFICATE OF DEFERMENT

99(1) Where a certificate of deferment has been issued in respect of any earner under regulations 91 to 98

(a) the profits or gains of that earner, in respect of which contributions would be payable under section 15 of the Act (Class 4 contributions), but for the issue of the certificate of deferment, shall be assessed under the Income Tax Acts for each year to which the certificate relates, in all respects as if no such certificate had been issued, provided that (without prejudice to the validity of the assessment of the amount of the earner's profits or gains and his right of appeal against that assessment) no figure representing contributions, the payment of which has been deferred, shall be shown in any such assessment or on any notice of such assessment nor shall any of the provisions of the Income Tax Acts (as applied or modified by section 16 of, and Schedule 2 to, the Act) as to collection, repayment or recovery apply to any such assessment; and

(b) the Board shall be responsible for the calculation, administration and recovery of Class 4 contributions ultimately payable in respect of the profits or gains so assessed for any year of assessment to which the certificate of deferment relates.

99(2) Any such calculation shall be subject to the provisions of regulations 94 and 100 and for the purpose of the calculation where the total amount of the profits or gains for any year of assessment to which the certificate relates includes a fraction of £1, that fraction shall be disregarded.

99(3) For the purpose of enabling the Board to make the calculation, they shall certify the amount of the earner's profits or gains, computed under Schedule 2 to the Act for each year of assessment.

This is subject to the following qualification.

99(4) Notwithstanding paragraph (3), the Board shall not be required to certify the amount referred to in that paragraph unless the assessment made under this regulation has become final and conclusive.

99(5) The Board, on making the calculation referred to in paragraph (3), shall give notice to the earner of the amount of the contributions due from him under section 15 of the Act for each year to which the certificate of deferment relates.

99(6) The earner shall pay to the Board those contributions within the period of 28 days from the receipt of the notice from them, unless before the expiry of that period the earner

(a) has appealed out of time or made a claim or appealed against the decision on a claim made under the Income Tax Acts on any matter concerning the amount of the profits or gains certified as mentioned in paragraph (3), and has notified the Board accordingly; or

(b) has appealed against a decision made under section 8 of the Transfer Act relating to those contributions.

99(7) If the amount of any assessment made under this regulation for any year is altered for any reason, or if a further assessment is made in respect of that year, subsequently to the certification by the Board of the amount of an earner's profits or gains computed in accordance with the provisions of this regulation and that alteration or further assessment affects the amount of the earner's profits or gains so computed they shall immediately, or in the case of a further assessment when that further assessment has become final and conclusive, certify to the earner the altered amount of the earner's profits or gains.

History – In reg. 99(1)(a), the words "contributions, the payment of which has been deferred," substituted by SI 2003/193, reg. 13(2) with effect from 6 April 2003.
In reg. 99(3), the words "This is subject to the following qualification." substituted by SI 2003/193, reg. 13(3) with effect from 6 April 2003.
In reg. 99(4), the words "final and conclusive" substituted by SI 2003/193, reg. 13(4) with effect from 6 April 2003.
Derivations – SI 1979/591, reg. 66.

ANNUAL MAXIMUM OF CLASS 4 CONTRIBUTIONS DUE UNDER SECTION 15 OF THE ACT

100(1) If, in respect of any year, there are payable by or in respect of an earner Class 4 contributions under section 15 of the Act and also–

(a) primary Class 1 contributions or Class 2 contributions; or

(b) primary Class 1 contributions and Class 2 contributions,

paragraph (2) applies.

100(2) If this paragraph applies, the earner's liability for Class 4 contributions shall not exceed the maximum found in accordance with paragraph (3).

100(3) The maximum is found as follows.

Step One

Subtract the lower profits limit from the upper profits limit for the year.

Step Two

Multiply the result of Step One by 9 per cent.

Step Three

Add to the result of Step Two 53 times the weekly amount of the appropriate Class 2 contribution.

Step Four

Subtract from the result of Step Three the aggregate amount of any Class 2 contributions and primary Class 1 contributions paid at the main primary percentage.

The application of the following steps is determined by reference to the following three Cases.

Case 1

If the result of this step is a positive value, and exceeds the aggregate of–

(a) primary Class 1 contributions payable at the main primary percentage,

(b) Class 2 contributions; and

(c) Class 4 contributions payable at the main Class 4 percentage,

in respect of the earner's earnings, profits and gains for the year, the result of this step is the maximum amount of Class 4 contributions payable.

Case 2

If the result of this step is a positive value, but does not exceed the aggregate mentioned in Case 1, the result of this step is the maximum amount of Class 4 contributions payable at the main Class 4 percentage.

Case 3

If the result of this step is a negative value, the maximum amount of a Class 4 contribution payable at the main Class 4 percentage is nil and the result of this step is treated as nil.

If Case 1 applies, Steps Five to Nine do not, but if Case 2 or Case 3 applies those Steps do apply.

Step Five
Multiply the result of Step Four by

$$\frac{100}{9}$$

Step Six
Subtract the lower profits limit from the lesser of the upper profits limit and the amount of profits for the year.
Step Seven
Subtract the result of Step Five from the result of Step Six.
If the result of this step is a negative value, it is treated as nil.
Step Eight
Multiply the result of Step Seven by 2 per cent.
Step Nine
Multiply the amount by which the profits and gains for the year exceed the upper profits limit for the year by 2 per cent.
The maximum amount of Class 4 contributions payable is–

(a) where Case 1 of Step Four applies, the result of that step, and
(b) where Case 2 or Case 3 of Step Four applies, the amount produced by adding together the results of Steps Four, Eight and Nine.

This is subject to the qualifications in paragraphs (4) to (6).
In this paragraph–

"lower profits limit" means the lesser of the two monetary sums specified in section 15(3)(a) of the Act; and

"upper profits limit" means the greater of those sums.

100(4) For the purpose only of determining the extent of the earner's liability for contributions under paragraph (3), the amount of a primary Class 1 contribution which would otherwise be payable at the main primary percentage but which is paid at a rate less than 12 per cent because the earner is a married woman who has made an election to pay contributions at the reduced rate as mentioned in regulation 127, shall be treated as equal to the amount of the primary Class 1 contribution payable at the main primary percentage, which would be so payable if the election had not been made.

100(5) Paragraph (2) is subject to the provisions of section 12 of the Act and to regulations 63 to 65.

100(6) Notwithstanding paragraphs (1) to (5), an earner shall be liable, in the first instance, for the full amount of the contributions which would have been payable but for this regulation.

History – In reg. 100(3), in Step Two, the words "9 per cent" substituted for the words "8 per cent" by SI 2012/573, reg. 3(a)(i), which came into force on 26 March 2012, with effect in relation to contributions paid in respect of the tax year 2011–12 and subsequent tax years.
In reg. 100(3), in Step Five, the fraction "100/9" substituted for the fraction "100/8" by SI 2012/573, reg. 3(a)(ii), which came into force on 26 March 2012, with effect in relation to contributions paid in respect of the tax year 2011–12 and subsequent tax years.
In reg. 100(3), in Step Eight, the words "2 per cent" substituted for the words "1 per cent" by SI 2012/573, reg. 3(a)(iii), which came into force on 26 March 2012, with effect in relation to contributions paid in respect of the tax year 2011–12 and subsequent tax years.
In reg. 100(3), in Step Nine, the words "12 per cent" substituted for the words "11 per cent" by SI 2012/573, reg. 3(a)(iv), which came into force on 26 March 2012, with effect in relation to contributions paid in respect of the tax year 2011–12 and subsequent tax years.
Reg. 100(4) substituted by SI 2016/352, reg. 15, with effect from 6 April 2016, subject to savings in relation to rights or obligations arising in connection with tax years beginning before 6 April 2016 (and for savings purposes, references to repealed provisions of the Pension Schemes Act 1993 are to be read as though such provisions were still in force). Former reg. 100(4) read as follows:
"**100(4)** For the purpose only of determining the extent of the earner's liability for contributions under paragraph (3), the amount of a primary Class 1 contribution which would otherwise be payable at the main primary percentage but which is paid at a rate less than 12 per cent. because the earner–
(a) is in contracted-out employment, or
(b) is a married woman who has made an election to pay contributions at the reduced rate as mentioned in regulation 127,
shall be treated as equal to the amount of the primary Class 1 contribution payable at the main primary percentage, which would be so payable if the employment were non-contracted-out employment or the election had not been made (as the case may be).".
In former reg. 100(4), the words "12 per cent" substituted for the words "11 per cent" by SI 2012/573, reg. 3(b), which came into force on 26 March 2012, with effect in relation to contributions paid in respect of the tax year 2011–12 and subsequent tax years.
Reg. 100 substituted by SI 2003/193, reg. 14 with effect from 6 April 2003.
Derivations – SI 1979/591, reg. 67.

DISPOSAL OF CLASS 4 CONTRIBUTIONS UNDER SECTION 15 OF THE ACT WHICH ARE NOT DUE

101 Where for any year of assessment any payment is made by an earner as on account of contributions under section 15 of the Act (Class 4 contributions) and

(a) a certificate of exception is issued for that year, or would have been so issued if application had been made for its issue before the beginning of that year;

(b) that payment is made in error;

(c) the payment is in excess of the amount which, subject to any exception under regulation 94, is due from that earner for that year or would have been so due if application for exception had been made under that regulation before the beginning of that year; or

(d) the payment is in excess of the amount calculated in accordance with regulation 100, the Board may treat that payment as made on account of other contributions properly payable by that person under the Act.

History – In reg. 101(b) words "in circumstances in which" to the end of the paragraph repealed by SI 2002/2366, reg. 14, with effect from 8 October 2002.

Derivations – SI 1979/591, reg. 101

REPAYMENT OF CLASS 4 CONTRIBUTIONS UNDER SECTION 15 OF THE ACT WHICH ARE NOT DUE

102(1) Subject to paragraph (2), any payment such as is specified in regulation 101 shall, except in so far as it is, under that regulation, treated by the Board as made on account of contributions under the Act, be repaid to the earner, unless the net amount of such repayment would not exceed in value 50 pence.

102(2) It is a condition of repayment under this regulation that the earner makes an application for the repayment–

(a) in such form and manner as the Board may determine; and

(b) in the case of contributions falling within paragraph (b) of regulation 101, within the time prescribed in paragraph (3).

102(3) The period referred to in paragraph (2) is one of–

(a) six years beginning with 6th April in the year of assessment next following that in respect of which the payment was made where the application is in respect of any year of assessment ending before 6th April 1996,

(b) five years beginning with 1st February in the year of assessment next following that in respect of which the payment was made where the application is in respect of any year of assessment beginning on or after 6th April 1996, or

(c) if later than sub-paragraph (a) or (b), two years beginning with 6th April in the year of assessment next following that in which the payment was made.

History – In reg. 102(1) words "to the earner" substituted by SI 2002/2366, reg. 15, with effect from 8 October 2002. Reg. 102(2) substituted by SI 2002/2366, reg. 15, with effect from 8 October 2002.

Derivations – SI 1979/591, reg. 69.

CLASS 4 LIABILITY OF EARNERS TREATED AS SELF-EMPLOYED EARNERS WHO WOULD OTHERWISE BE EMPLOYED EARNERS

103(1) Subject to regulation 108, where

(a) an earner, in respect of any one or more employments of his, is treated by regulations under section 2(2)(b) of the Act (treatment of a person in employment of any prescribed description as falling in one or other of the categories of earner) as being self-employed;

(b) in any year he has earnings from any such employment (one or more) which fall within section 11(3) of the Act (higher weekly rate of Class 2 contributions), but is not liable for a higher weekly rate of Class 2 contributions by virtue of regulations under that section;

(c) those earnings are chargeable to income tax as general earnings; and

(d) the total of those earnings exceeds the sum specified in section 18(1)(c) of the Act,

paragraph (2) applies.

103(2) If this paragraph applies, the earner shall be liable, in respect of the earnings mentioned in paragraph (1), to pay a Class 4 contribution (referred to in this Part as a **"special Class 4 contribution"**) of an amount equal to the aggregate of–

(a) the main Class 4 percentage of so much of the total of those earnings as exceeds the lower, but does not exceed the higher, of the money sums, and

(b) the additional Class 4 percentage of so much of the total of those earnings as exceeds the higher of the money sums,

for the time being specified in section 18(1A).

History – In reg. 103(1)(c) words "as general earnings" substituted by SI 2004/770, reg. 24, with effect from 6 April 2004. In reg. 103(2), the words from "of an amount equal to" to end, substituted by SI 2003/193, reg. 15 with effect from 6 April 2003.

Derivations – SI 1979/591, reg. 71.

NOTIFICATION OF NATIONAL INSURANCE NUMBER AND RECORDING OF CATEGORY LETTER ON DEDUCTIONS WORKING SHEET

104(1) Any earner to whom regulation 103 applies shall, on request, notify his national insurance number to the person who pays him the earnings referred to in that regulation.

104(2) The person who pays those earnings shall record on the earner's deductions working sheet the earner's national insurance number, and the appropriate category letter as indicated by the Board.

104(3) In this regulation **"deductions working sheet"** has the same meaning as in Schedule 4.

Derivations – SI 1979/591, reg. 72.

CALCULATION OF EARNINGS FOR THE PURPOSES OF SPECIAL CLASS 4 CONTRIBUTIONS

105 For the purpose of the calculation of an earner's liability for a special Class 4 contribution for any year

(a) the earnings of that earner for that year shall, subject to paragraph (b), be calculated by the Board on the basis that they are earnings to which regulations 24 and 25 and Schedules 2 and 3 apply;

(b) in the calculation of these earnings, if the total amount of the earnings for the year includes a fraction of a pound, that fraction shall be disregarded.

Derivations – SI 1979/591, reg. 73.

NOTIFICATION AND PAYMENT OF SPECIAL CLASS 4 CONTRIBUTIONS DUE

106 The Board shall, subject to any other arrangements notified by them to the earner specified in regulation 105, give notice to the earner of the special Class 4 contribution due from him for any year, and the earner shall pay that contribution to the Board within the period of 28 days from the receipt of the notice unless, before the expiry of that period, the earner has appealed against a decision made under section 8 of the Transfer Act relating to that contribution.

Derivations – SI 1979/591, reg. 74.

RECOVERY OF DEFERRED CLASS 4 AND SPECIAL CLASS 4 CONTRIBUTIONS AFTER APPEAL, CLAIM OR FURTHER ASSESSMENT UNDER THE INCOME TAX ACTS OR APPEAL UNDER SECTION 8 OF THE TRANSFER ACT

107(1) Where–

(a) the Board have been notified that there has been such a claim or appeal as is specified in regulation 99(6) or regulation 106; or

(b) the Board have certified in accordance with regulation 99(7) an altered amount of an earner's profits or gains, paragraph (2) applies.

107(2) If this paragraph applies, the Board shall, as soon as may be after the prescribed time, give to the earner notice or, as the case may be, revised notice of such contributions as might, having regard to the final decision on the claim or appeal or, the altered amount of profits or gains, be due from the earner

(a) under section 15 of the Act (Class 4 contributions) for the year or years to which the certificate referred to in regulation 99(7) relates; or

(b) by way of a special Class 4 contribution for the year to which the notice specified in regulation 106 relates,

and the earner shall within 28 days of receipt of that notice pay to the Board the contribution or contributions specified in that notice.

107(3) In this regulation **"prescribed time"** means

(a) except where sub-paragraph (c) applies

(i) in the case of an appeal out of time, the date of the determination of the appeal, and

(ii) in the case of a claim or appeal against a decision on a claim made under the Income Tax Acts, the date on which the time for appealing against the decision on the claim expires, or the date of the determination of the appeal, whichever is the later;

(b) in the case of an appeal under section 8 of the Transfer Act, the date on which the time for appealing against that decision expires or the date of the determination of the appeal, whichever is the later;

(c) in the case of an altered amount of profits or gains being certified by the Board, the date on which they are so certified.

Derivations – SI 1979/591, reg. 75.

ANNUAL MAXIMUM OF SPECIAL CLASS 4 CONTRIBUTION

108(1) Where for any year there are payable (or, but for this regulation, there would be payable) by or in respect of an earner a special Class 4 contribution and also any contribution under section 15 of the Act (in this regulation referred to as **"an ordinary Class 4 contribution"**) or any primary Class 1 contribution or any Class 2 contribution, or any combination of such contributions, the maximum amount of the special Class 4 contribution payable for that year shall not exceed the maximum specified in paragraph (2).

108(2) The maximum is–

(a) in the case of a special Class 4 contribution and an ordinary Class 4 contribution, the amount (if any) equal to the difference between the maximum amount of a special Class 4 contribution for which provision is made in section 18(1) of the Act and the amount of the ordinary Class 4 contributions ultimately payable for that year; or

(b) in any other case (whether or not a Class 4 contribution is also payable), the amount (if any) equal to the difference between the maximum amount prescribed in regulation 100 and the amount of such Class 4, primary Class 1 and Class 2 contributions as are ultimately payable for that year.

108(3) Paragraphs (1) and (2) are without prejudice to the earner's liability in the first instance for the full amount payable apart from those paragraphs.

Derivations – SI 1979/591, reg. 76.

DISPOSAL OF SPECIAL CLASS 4 CONTRIBUTIONS PAID IN EXCESS OR ERROR

109 Where any payment has been made by a person on account of a special Class 4 contribution and that payment has been made in excess of the amount prescribed under regulation 108 or has been made in error, the Board may treat that payment as made on account of other contributions properly payable by that person under the Act.

Derivations – SI 1979/591, reg. 77.

RETURN OF SPECIAL CLASS 4 CONTRIBUTIONS PAID IN EXCESS OR ERROR

110(1) Subject to regulation 109 and paragraphs (2) and (3), where any payment has been made by a person as on account of a special Class 4 contribution and that payment has been made in excess of the amount prescribed in regulation 108 or has been made in error, that payment shall be returned by the Board to that person, unless the net amount to be returned does not exceed 50 pence, if application is made to the Board, in writing or in such other form and manner as the Board may allow, within the time specified in paragraph (3).

110(2) In calculating the amount of any return of a special Class 4 contribution to be made under paragraph (1) there shall be deducted the amount (if any) treated under regulation 109 as paid on account of other contributions.

110(3) Any person desiring to apply for the return of a special Class 4 contribution (**"the applicant"**) shall make the application within the period of six years from the end of the year in which the contribution was due to be paid.

This is subject to the following qualification.

If the application is made after the end of that period, an officer of the Board shall admit it if satisfied that–

(a) the applicant had reasonable excuse for not making the application within that period; and

(b) the application was made without unreasonable delay after the excuse had ceased.

History – In reg. 110(3) words "("the applicant")" inserted by SI 2002/2366, reg. 16, with effect from 8 October 2002.
In reg. 110(3) words from "was due to be paid" to the end, substituted by SI 2002/2366, reg. 16, with effect from 8 October 2002.

Derivations – SI 1979/591, reg. 78.

PART 9 – SPECIAL CLASSES OF EARNERS

Case A – Airmen

INTERPRETATION

111 In this Case, unless the context otherwise requires

"airman" means a person who is, or has been, employed under a contract of service either as a pilot, commander, navigator or other member of the crew of any aircraft, or in any other capacity on board any aircraft where

(a) the employment in that other capacity is for the purposes of the aircraft or its crew or of any passengers or cargo or mails carried on that aircraft; and

(b) the contract is entered into in the United Kingdom with a view to its performance (in whole or in part) while the aircraft is in flight,

but does not include a person in so far as his employment is as a serving member of the forces;

"British aircraft" means any aircraft belonging to Her Majesty and any aircraft registered in the United Kingdom of which the owner (or managing owner if there is more than one owner) resides or has his principal place of business in the United Kingdom, and references to the owner of an aircraft shall, in relation to an aircraft which has been hired, be taken as referring to the person for the time being entitled as hirer to possession and control of the aircraft by virtue of the hiring or any subordinate hiring.

Derivations – SI 1979/591, reg. 81.

MODIFICATION OF EMPLOYED EARNER'S EMPLOYMENT

112(1) Subject to paragraphs (2) and (3), where an airman is employed as such on board any aircraft, and the employer of that airman or the person paying the airman his earnings in respect of the employment (whether or not the person making the payment is acting as agent for the employer) or the person under whose directions the terms of the airman's employment and the amount of the earnings to be paid in respect of that employment are determined has

(a) in the case of the aircraft being a British aircraft, a place of business in Great Britain or Northern Ireland; or

(b) in any other case, his principal place of business in Great Britain or Northern Ireland, then, notwithstanding that the airman does not fulfil the conditions of section 2(1)(a) of the Act (definition of employed earner), he shall be treated as employed in employed earner's employment and, for the purposes of regulation 145(1)(a), in respect of that employment, as present in Great Britain or Northern Ireland (as the case requires).

112(2) Subject to paragraph (3), notwithstanding that an airman is employed in an employment to which paragraph (1) applies, if that airman is neither domiciled nor has a place of residence in Great Britain or Northern Ireland (as the case requires) no contributions shall be payable by or in respect of him as an employed earner.

112(3) Paragraph (2) is subject to any Order in Council giving effect to any reciprocal agreement made under section 179 of the Administration Act (reciprocal agreements with countries outside the United Kingdom).

Derivations – SI 1979/591, reg. 82.

APPLICATION OF THE ACT AND REGULATIONS

113 Part I of the Act and so much of Part VI of the Act as relates to contributions and the regulations made under those provisions, so far as they are not inconsistent with this Case, apply to an airman with the modification that, where an airman is, on account of his being outside the United Kingdom by reason of his employment as an airman, unable to perform an act required to be done either immediately or upon the happening of a certain event or within a specified time, he shall be deemed to have complied with such requirement if he performs the act as soon as is reasonably practicable, although after the happening of the event or the expiration of the specified time.

Derivations – SI 1979/591, reg. 83.

Case B – Continental Shelf

APPLICATION TO EMPLOYMENT IN CONNECTION WITH CONTINENTAL SHELF OF PART I OF THE ACT AND SO MUCH OF PART VI OF THE ACT AS RELATES TO CONTRIBUTIONS

114(1) For the purposes of section 120 of the Act (employment at sea (continental shelf operations)), prescribed employment shall be any employment (whether under a contract of service or not) in any area which may from time to time be designated by Order in Council under section 1(7) of the Continental Shelf Act 1964, where the employment is in connection with any activity mentioned in section 11(2) of the Petroleum Act 1998 in the designated area.

114(2) Where a person is employed in any employment specified in paragraph (1), the provisions of Part I of the Act and so much of Part VI of the Act as relates to contributions shall, subject to the provisions of paragraph (3), apply as though the area so designated were in Great Britain, and notwithstanding that he does not satisfy the conditions as to residence or presence in Great Britain prescribed in regulation 145(1)(a).

114(3) Where a person employed in any employment specified in paragraph (1) is, on account of his being outside Great Britain by reason of that employment, unable to perform any act required to be done either immediately or on the happening of a certain event or within a specified time, he shall be deemed to have complied with the requirement if he performs the act as soon as reasonably practicable, although after the happening of the event or the expiration of the specified time.

114(4) Where a continental shelf worker is employed in any employment specified in paragraph (1) and that employment is on or in connection with an offshore installation the secondary contributor is–

(a) where the employer is present in Great Britain, the employer; or,

(b) where the employer is not present in Great Britain but has an associated company present in Great Britain, the associated company; or,

(c) where the employer is not present and does not have an associated company present in Great Britain, the oil field licensee.

Where the employer has more than one associated company present in Great Britain the associated company to which sub-paragraph (b) applies is the company which has the greatest taxable total profit within the meaning of section 4 of the Corporation Tax Act 2010 for the accounting period which precedes the tax year in which the contributions are due.

114(5) The modifications in paragraph (4) do not apply to a continental shelf worker–

(a) who is employed in a capacity described in Column (A) of Table 1,

(b) who holds a certificate of a description in Column (B) of that table, and

(c) whose presence on the ship is required in order to meet the requirement of regulation 46(1)(c) of the Merchant Shipping (Standards of Training, Certification and Watchkeeping) Regulations 2015.

Table 1

Column (A): capacity in which the continental shelf worker is employed	*Column (B): description of the certificate*
Master or chief mate on a ship of 3000 gross tonnage or more.	A certificate which complies with regulation 6 of the Merchant Shipping Regulations.
Master on a ship of between 500 gross tonnage and 2999 gross tonnage not engaged on near-coastal voyages.	A certificate which complies with regulation 6 of the Merchant Shipping Regulations.
Chief mate on a ship of between 500 gross tonnage and 2999 gross tonnage.	A certificate which complies with regulation 6 of the Merchant Shipping Regulations.
Officer in charge of an engineering watch in a manned engine-room, or designated duty engineer officer in a periodically unmanned engine-room, on a ship powered by main propulsion machinery of 750 kilowatts propulsion power or more.	A certificate which complies with regulation 6 of the Merchant Shipping Regulations.
Chief engineer officer and second engineer officer on a ship powered by main propulsion machinery of between 750 and 3000 kilowatts propulsion power.	A certificate which complies with regulation 6 of the Merchant Shipping Regulations.
Rating forming part of a navigational watch on a ship of 500 gross tonnage or more (who is not under training and whose duties are skilled in nature).	A certificate which complies with regulation 14 of the Merchant Shipping Regulations.
Rating forming part of an engine-room watch or designated to perform duties in a periodically unmanned engine-room on a ship powered by main propulsion machinery of 750 kilowatts propulsion power or more (who is not under training and whose duties are skilled in nature).	A certificate which complies with regulation 15 of the Merchant Shipping Regulations.

114(6) In Table 1 **"Merchant Shipping Regulations"** means the Merchant Shipping (Standards of Training, Certification and Watchkeeping) Regulations 2015;

114(7) To the extent that where this regulation and regulations 115 to 125 (case C Mariners) apply, this regulation takes precedence.

History – Reg. 114(4)–(7) inserted by SI 2014/572, reg. 2(2), with effect from 6 April 2014.

In reg. 114(5)(c), the words "regulation 46(1)(c) of the Merchant Shipping (Standards of Training, Certification and Watchkeeping) Regulations 2015" substituted for the words "regulation 5(1)(c) of the Merchant Shipping (Safe manning, Hours of Work and Watchkeeping) Regulations 1997" by SI 2016/1067, reg. 4(2)(a), with effect from 28 November 2016.

In reg. 114(5), table substituted by SI 2016/1067, reg. 4(2)(b), with effect from 28 November 2016. Former table read as follows:

Table 1

Column (A): capacity in which the continental shelf worker is employed	*Column (B): description of the certificate*
Master or chief mate on a ship of 3000 gross tons or more.	A certificate which complies with regulation 7 of the Merchant Shipping Regulations.
Master or chief mate on a ship of less than 3000 gross tons.	A certificate which complies with regulation 7 of the Merchant Shipping Regulations.
Officer in charge of an engineering watch in a manned engine-room, or a designated duty engineer officer in a periodically unmanned engine-room, on a ship powered by main propulsion machinery of 750kW propulsion power or more.	A certificate which complies with regulation 7 of the Merchant Shipping Regulations.
Chief engineer officer or second engineer officer on a ship powered by main propulsion machinery of between 750kW and 3000kW propulsion power.	A certificate which complies with regulation 7 of the Merchant Shipping Regulations.
Rating forming part of a navigational watch on a ship of 500 gross tons or more and whose duties are skilled in nature.	A certificate issued under regulation 8 of the Merchant Shipping Regulations.
Rating forming part of an engine-room watch or designated to perform duties in a periodically unmanned engine-room on a ship powered by main propulsion machinery of 750kW propulsion power or more.	A certificate issued under regulation 8 of the Merchant Shipping Regulations.

In reg. 114(6), the words "the Merchant Shipping (Standards of Training, Certification and Watchkeeping) Regulations 2015" substituted for the words "the Merchant Shipping (Training and Certification) Regulations 1997" by SI 2016/1067, reg. 4(2)(c), with effect from 28 November 2016.

Derivations – SI 1979/591, reg. 85.

Other material – Misc. 210: employing people on the UK continental shelf (UKCS).

CONTINENTAL SHELF WORKERS: PROVISIONS RELATING TO CERTIFICATES

Application for certificate

114A(1) An employer who meets the conditions in paragraph (2) may apply to HMRC for the issue of a UKCS continental shelf workers certificate.

114A(2) The conditions are that–

(a) the employer supplies or intends to supply a continental shelf worker for whom the secondary contributor, under regulation 114(4) (application of Part 1 and Part 6 of the Act to employment in connection with the continental shelf), is the oil field licensee;

(b) the employer has or intends to have a contractual relationship under which the employer acts, directly or indirectly, as an agent of the oil field licensee for the purposes of National Insurance; and

(c) the employer or an associated company has not had a certificate cancelled previously for a failure to comply with their obligations and responsibilities under regulation 114B.

114A(3) An application under this regulation must be made in writing and must include–

(a) the name and address of the employer and employer's PAYE reference;

(b) the name and address of a person in Great Britain who is authorised to accept service on behalf of the employer;

(c) confirmation that the employer understands and intends to discharge the obligations contained in regulation 114B; and

(d) the name, address, and employer's PAYE reference of any associated company which is a current or former holder of a UKCS continental shelf workers certificate.

114A(4) When the employer makes the first application under this regulation, the employer may also comply with the obligation under regulation 114B(e) by including those details (if known) in the application.

114A(5) An application made under this regulation may be combined with an application made under an equivalent PAYE provision.

114A(6) Upon receipt of an application under this regulation, an officer of Revenue and Customs may, if they are satisfied the conditions in paragraph (2) are met, issue a UKCS continental shelf workers certificate.

114A(7) A UKCS continental shelf workers certificate must include–

(a) the name of the UKCS continental shelf workers certificate holder;

(b) the employer's PAYE reference of the UKCS continental shelf workers certificate holder; and

(c) the date on which the certificate is issued.

114A(8) A UKCS continental shelf workers certificate may be issued to–

(a) the person authorised to accept service on behalf of the employer;

(b) the employer; or

(c) both the person authorised to accept service on behalf of the employer and the employer.

114A(9) A certificate may be combined with a certificate issued under an equivalent PAYE provision.

114A(10) Where an employer ceases to meet the conditions in paragraph (2) or to comply with its obligations under regulation 114B, or an equivalent PAYE provision, an officer of Revenue and Customs may, by notice in writing to the person authorised to accept service on behalf of the employer, cancel the UKCS continental shelf workers certificate from the date specified in the notice of cancellation.

114A(11) The date specified in paragraph (10) may not be earlier than 10 working days after the date of the notice.

114A(12) A notice under paragraph (10) may be combined with a notice under an equivalent PAYE provision.

History – Reg. 114A and the heading immediately preceding it inserted by SI 2014/572, reg. 2(3), with effect from 6 April 2014.

Other material – Misc. 210: employing people on the UK continental shelf (UKCS).

UKCS continental shelf workers certificate holder: obligations and responsibilities

114B A UKCS continental shelf workers certificate holder must–

(a) make such deductions, returns and repayments as are required of a secondary contributor;

(b) keep written records of–

(i) the name, date of birth, and national insurance number of the continental shelf workers supplied;

(ii) the name, registered office and oil field licence number of the oil field licensee to whom each of the workers were supplied;

(iii) the offshore installation to which each of the workers were supplied; and

(iv) the dates between which the workers worked on the offshore installation;

(c) keep the records required by sub-paragraph (b) for a period of 6 years from the end of the tax year to which they relate;

(d) where an officer of Revenue and Customs requires them in writing to do so, provide copies of the records required by sub-paragraph (b) to HMRC within 30 days of the date of the request; and

(e) before supplying the oil field licensee with continental shelf workers for the first time, inform HMRC in writing of the details of the oil field licensee including name, business address, and oil field licence number of the oil field licensee.

History – Reg. 114B and the heading immediately preceding it inserted by SI 2014/572, reg. 2(3), with effect from 6 April 2014.

Other material – Misc. 210: employing people on the UK continental shelf (UKCS).

UKCS oil field licensee certificate

114C(1) Where a UKCS continental shelf workers certificate holder has notified HMRC that the employer intends to supply continental shelf workers to an oil field licensee an officer of Revenue and Customs must issue a UKCS oil field licensee certificate to the oil field licensee.

114C(2) The UKCS oil field licensee certificate must include–

(a) the name of the oil field licensee;

(b) the registered office of that oil field licensee;

(c) the oil field licence number;

(d) the name of the UKCS continental shelf workers certificate holder;

(e) the date on which it is issued; and

(f) a description of the continental shelf workers to whom it applies.

114C(3) Where a UKCS oil field licensee certificate is in force the holder of that certificate is not liable to pay any contributions in respect of any continental shelf worker of a description set out in the certificate.

114C(4) If a UKCS continental shelf workers certificate is cancelled by an officer of Revenue and Customs that officer must also, by notice in writing, cancel the UKCS oil field licensee certificate.

114C(5) A notice under paragraph (4) must–

(a) be sent on the same day as the notice cancelling the UKCS continental shelf workers certificate;

(b) specify the date of cancellation of the UKCS oil field licensee certificate; and

(c) notify the oil field licensee that it is liable to meet its obligations as a secondary contributor.

114C(6) The date of cancellation of the UKCS oil field licensee certificate must be the same date as that specified in the UKCS continental shelf workers certificate cancellation notice.

History – Reg. 114C and the heading immediately preceding it inserted by SI 2014/572, reg. 2(3), with effect from 6 April 2014.

Other material – Misc. 210: employing people on the UK continental shelf (UKCS).

Interpretation of regulations 114 to 114C

114D In regulations 114 to 114C–

"associated company" means any company within the meaning of section 449 of the Corporation Tax Act 2010;

"an equivalent PAYE provision" means any provision in the PAYE Regulations which has an equivalent effect to the provisions in regulations 114A to 114C;

"employer's PAYE reference" has the meaning given in regulation 2(1) of the PAYE Regulations;

"offshore installation" means–

(a) a structure which is, is to be, or has been, put to a relevant use while in water;

(b) but a structure is not an offshore installation if–

(i) it has permanently ceased to be put to a relevant use,

(ii) it is not, and is not to be, put to any other relevant use, and

(iii) since permanently ceasing to be put to a relevant use, it has been put to a use which is not a relevant use;

(c) a use is a relevant use if it is–

(i) for the purposes of exploiting mineral resources,

(ii) for the purposes of exploration with a view to exploiting mineral resources,

(iii) for the storage of gas in or under the shore or the bed of any waters,

(iv) for the recovery of gas so stored,

(v) for the conveyance of things by means of a pipe,

(vi) mainly for the provision of accommodation for individuals who work on or from a structure which is, is to be, or has been put to any of the above uses while in the water,

(vii) for the purposes of decommissioning any structure which has been used for or in connection with any of the relevant uses above;

(d) a structure is put to use while in water if it is put to use while–

(i) standing in any waters,

(ii) stationed (by whatever means) in any waters, or

(iii) standing on the foreshore or other land intermittently covered with water;

(e) a **"structure"** includes a ship or other vessel except where it is used wholly or mainly–

(i) for the transport of supplies;

(ii) as a safety vessel;

(iii) for a combination of (i) and (ii); or

(iv) for the laying of cables;

"oil field licensee" means the holder of a licence under Part 1 of the Petroleum Act 1998 in respect of the area in which the duties of the continental shelf worker's employment are performed;

"UKCS continental shelf workers certificate" means a certificate issued under regulation 114A;

"UKCS oil field licensee certificate" means a certificate issued under regulation 114C(1).

History – Reg. 114D and the heading immediately preceding it inserted by SI 2014/572, reg. 2(3), with effect from 6 April 2014.

Other material – Misc. 210: employing people on the UK continental shelf (UKCS).

Case C – Mariners

INTERPRETATION

115 In this Case

"British ship" means

(a) any ship or vessel belonging to Her Majesty; or

(b) any ship or vessel whose port of registry is a port in the United Kingdom; or

(c) a hovercraft which is registered in the United Kingdom;

"foreign-going ship" means any ship or vessel which is not a home-trade ship;

"home-trade ship" includes

(a) every ship or vessel employed in trading or going within the following limits, that is to say, the United Kingdom (including for this purpose the Republic of Ireland), the Channel Islands, the Isle of Man, and the continent of Europe between the river Elbe and Brest inclusive;

(b) every fishing vessel not proceeding beyond the following limits

on the South, Latitude 48° 30'N.,

on the West, Longitude 12° W., and

on the North, Latitude 61° N.;

"managing owner" means the owner of any ship or vessel who, where there is more than one such owner, is responsible for the control and management of that ship or vessel;

"mariner" means a person who is or has been in employment under a contract of service either as a master or member of the crew of any ship or vessel, or in any other capacity on board any ship or vessel where

(a) the employment in that other capacity is for the purposes of that ship or vessel or her crew or any passengers or cargo or mails carried by the ship or vessel; and

(b) the contract is entered into in the United Kingdom with a view to its performance (in whole or in part) while the ship or vessel is on her voyage;

but does not include a person in so far as his employment is as a serving member of the forces;

"owner" in relation to any ship or vessel, means the person to whom the ship or vessel belongs and who, subject to the right of control of the captain or master of the ship or vessel (**"the master's rights"**), is entitled to control of that ship or vessel, and references to the owner of a ship or vessel shall, in relation to a ship or vessel which has been demised, be construed as referring to the person who for the time being is entitled as charterer to possession and, subject to the master's rights, to control of the ship or vessel by virtue of the demise or any sub-demise;

"passenger" means any person carried on a ship except

(a) a person employed or engaged in any capacity on board the ship on the business of the ship; and

(b) a person on board the ship either in pursuance of the obligation to carry shipwrecked, distressed or other persons, or by reason of any circumstance that neither the master nor the owner nor the charterer (if any) could have prevented or forestalled;

"pay period" in relation to any payment of a mariner's earnings means the period in respect of which the payment is made;

"radio officer" means a mariner employed in connection with the radio apparatus of any ship or vessel and holding a certificate of competence in radio telephony granted by the Secretary of State or by an authority empowered in that behalf by the legislature of some part of the Commonwealth or of the Republic of Ireland and recognised by the Secretary of State as equivalent to the like certificate granted by him;

"share fisherman" means any person who

(a) is ordinarily employed in the fishing industry, otherwise than under a contract of service, as the master or a member of the crew of any United Kingdom fishing vessel, within the meaning of section 1(3) of the Merchant Shipping Act 1995, manned by more than one person, and who is remunerated in respect of that employment in whole or in part by a share of the profits or gross earnings of the fishing vessel, or

(b) has ordinarily been so employed, but who by reason of age or infirmity permanently ceases to be so employed and becomes ordinarily engaged in employment ashore in the United Kingdom, otherwise than under a contract of service, making or mending any gear appurtenant to a United Kingdom fishing vessel or performing other services ancillary to or in connection with that vessel and is remunerated in respect of that employment in whole or in part by a share of the profits or gross earnings of that vessel and has not ceased to be ordinarily engaged in such employment;

"ship or vessel" for the purposes of this Case other than those of regulations 116 to 120 includes hovercraft;

"voyage period" means a pay period comprising an entire voyage or series of voyages (including any period of leave on pay which immediately follows the day on which the termination of that voyage or series of voyages occurs);

"week" means a period of 7 consecutive days and

"weekly" shall be construed accordingly.

Derivations – SI 1979/591, reg. 86.

MODIFICATION OF SECTION 162(5) OF THE ADMINISTRATION ACT

116 In section 162 of the Administration Act (destination of contributions), subsection (5) (which specifies the amount of the national health service allocation to be deducted from each class of contribution prior to their payment into the National Insurance Fund) shall be modified, in the case of contributions paid at the rate reduced in accordance with regulation 119(1), as if, instead of the percentage figure specified in paragraph (b) of that subsection, there were specified the percentage figure "0.6".

CONDITIONS OF DOMICILE OR RESIDENCE

117(1) As respects any employment of a person as a mariner and liability for payment of any contribution under the Act as an employed earner by or on behalf, or in respect, of that mariner in respect of that employment

(a) the provisions of Case F of these Regulations relating to conditions as to residence or presence in Great Britain or Northern Ireland (as the case requires) shall not apply; but

(b) it shall be a condition of liability to pay a contribution under the Act that the mariner is domiciled or resident in Great Britain or Northern Ireland (as the case requires); and

(c) it shall be a condition of liability to pay a secondary contribution under the Act that the secondary contributor is resident or has a place of business in Great Britain or Northern Ireland (as the case requires).

This is subject to the following qualification.

117(2) This regulation has effect subject to any Order in Council giving effect to any reciprocal agreement made under section 179 of the Administration Act (reciprocal agreements with countries outside the United Kingdom).

Derivations – SI 1979/591, reg. 87.

MODIFICATION OF EMPLOYED EARNER'S EMPLOYMENT

118 Where a mariner

(a) is employed as such and

(i) the employment is on board a British ship, or

(ii) the employment is on board a ship and the contract in respect of the employment is entered into in the United Kingdom with a view to its performance (in whole or in part) while the ship or vessel is on her voyage, and

(iii) in a case to which sub-paragraph (ii) applies, the person by whom the mariner's earnings are paid, or, in the case of employment as a master or member of the crew of a ship or vessel, either that person or the owner of the ship or vessel (or the managing owner if there is more than one owner) has a place of business in Great Britain or Northern Ireland (as the case requires); or

(b) is employed as a master, member of the crew or as a radio officer on board any ship or vessel, not being a mariner to whom paragraph (a) applies, and

(i) in the case of employment as a radio officer, if the contract under which the employment is performed is entered into in the United Kingdom, the employer or the person paying the radio officer his earnings for that employment has a place of business in Great Britain or Northern Ireland (as the case requires), or

(ii) in the case of the employment being a master, member of the crew or as a radio officer, if the contract is not entered into in the United Kingdom, the employer or the person paying the earnings has his principal place of business in Great Britain or Northern Ireland (as the case requires),

then, notwithstanding that he does not fulfil the conditions of section 2(1)(a) of the Act (definition of employed earner), the employment of the mariner as mentioned above shall be treated as employed earner's employment.

Derivations – SI 1979/591, reg. 88.

MODIFICATION OF SECTION 9(2) OF THE ACT

119(1) As respects earnings paid to or for the benefit of a mariner for employment as such in any employment specified in paragraph (2), being employment which by virtue of regulation 118 is treated as employed earner's employment, from the figure specified as the secondary percentage in section 9(2) of the Act there shall be subtracted 0.5 per cent and section 9 shall be modified accordingly.

119(2) The employment referred to in paragraph (1) is employment as a master or member of the crew of a ship where

(a) the employment is on a foreign-going ship and the payment of earnings is exclusively in respect of that employment; or

(b) the employment is partly on a foreign-going ship and partly otherwise than on such a ship and the payment of earnings in respect of that employment is made during the employment on the foreign-going ship.

119(3) In this regulation the word **"employment"** includes any period of leave, other than leave for the purpose of study, accruing from the employment.

Derivations – SI 1979/591, reg. 89.

EARNINGS PERIODS FOR MARINERS AND APPORTIONMENT OF EARNINGS

120(1) For the purposes of liability for and calculation of earnings-related contributions, paragraphs (2) to (9) apply where earnings are paid to or for the benefit of a mariner in respect of his employment as such for a voyage period.

120(2) In this regulation **"a relevant change"** means a change affecting the calculation of earnings-related contributions under the Act not being

(a) a change in the amount of the mariner's earnings; or

(b) a change in one or more of the following figures applicable in respect of the mariner's employment

(i) the main primary percentage or the additional primary percentage for a primary Class 1 contribution specified in section 8(2) of the Act or the percentage rate for a secondary Class 1 contribution specified in section 9(2) of the Act,

(ii) [omitted by SI 2016/352, reg. 16,]

(iii) the amount by which the percentage rate of a secondary Class 1 contribution is reduced in accordance with regulation 119(1),

(iv) the lower or upper earnings limit for primary Class 1 contributions specified in section 5(1) of the Act.

120(3) Where a voyage period falls wholly in one year, then

(a) if no relevant change occurs during the voyage period, the earnings period shall be the voyage period;

(b) if one or more than one relevant change occurs during the voyage period the earnings shall be apportioned to such periods as comprise

(i) the day on which the voyage period began and the day immediately before which the change occurred, and for any subsequent change, the day on which the immediately preceding change occurred and the day before which the next succeeding change occurred, and

(ii) so much of the voyage period as remains, according to the amounts earned in each period, and the earnings period in respect of each amount so apportioned shall be the length of the period to which it is apportioned.

120(4) Where a voyage period falls partly in one and partly in one or more other years, then if no relevant change occurs during the voyage period

(a) the earnings shall be apportioned to those years according to the amounts earned in each year; and

(b) the earnings period in respect of each amount shall be the length of the period to which that amount is apportioned.

120(5) Where a voyage period falls partly in one and partly in one or more other years and one or more than one relevant change occurs during the voyage period, then

(a) in respect of a year during which a relevant change or more than one relevant change occurs the earnings shall be apportioned to such periods as comprise

(i) the day on which the voyage period began, or where it began in another year, the beginning of the year in which the change occurred, and the day immediately before which the change occurred, and for any subsequent change, the day on which the immediately preceding change occurred and the day before which the next succeeding change occurred, and

(ii) so much of the voyage period as remains in the year, according to the amounts earned in each period, and the earnings period in respect of each amount so apportioned shall be the length of the period to which it is apportioned; and

(b) in respect of other years, the earnings shall be apportioned to those years according to the amounts earned in each year and the earnings period in respect of each amount so apportioned shall be the length of the period to which it is apportioned.

120(6) Where under paragraphs (3) to (5) an earnings period

(a) is less than a week, that period shall for the purposes of those paragraphs be treated as a week;

(b) exceeds a week or a whole multiple of a week by a part of a week,

(i) if that part of a week is a period in excess of 3 days, that part of a week shall be treated as a week for the purposes of paragraphs (3) to (5), and

(ii) if that part of a week is a period of 3 days or less, it shall be disregarded for those purposes.

120(7) For the purposes of paragraphs (3) to (5)

(a) where a period of leave on pay immediately follows the day on which the termination of an entire voyage or series of voyages occurs

(i) the earnings for that period of leave shall be treated as if they were earned during that period and shall be excluded from the earnings for any other period or periods, and

(ii) for the purpose of apportionment, the earnings for the period of leave shall be deemed to accrue from day to day by equal daily amounts; and

(b) **"earned"** includes treated as earned under this paragraph.

120(8) Where under paragraphs (1) to (7) earnings are apportioned to a period

(a) each amount so apportioned shall be treated as paid at the end of the period to which it is apportioned; and

(b) contributions paid in respect of the amount so apportioned shall be treated as paid in respect of the year in which the end of that period falls.

120(9) Notwithstanding paragraphs (3) to (5) and (8), where a voyage period extends beyond the date on which the earnings are paid, any amount of earnings which, by virtue of paragraphs (1) to (8), would be apportioned to a period in the year following that in which the earnings are paid

(a) shall be treated as paid at the end of the year in which the earnings are paid but shall not be aggregated with any other amount of earnings paid or treated as paid at the end of that year; and

(b) the earnings period in respect of that amount shall be a period of the same length as that to which it is apportioned.

History – In reg. 120(2)(b)(i), the words "the main primary percentage or the additional primary percentage" substituted by SI 2003/964, reg. 4 with effect from 6 April 2003.

Reg. 120(2)(b)(ii) omitted by SI 2016/352, reg. 16, with effect from 6 April 2016, subject to savings in relation to rights or obligations arising in connection with tax years beginning before 6 April 2016 (and for savings purposes, references to repealed provisions of the Pension Schemes Act 1993 are to be read as though such provisions were still in force). Former reg. 120(2)(b)(ii) read as follows:

"the contracted-out rate applying in the case of a primary or secondary Class 1 contribution in section 41(1) of the Pensions Act,".

Derivations – SI 1979/591, reg. 90.

CALCULATION OF EARNINGS-RELATED CONTRIBUTIONS FOR MARINERS

121(1) For the purpose of the calculation of earnings-related contributions payable in respect of earnings paid to or for the benefit of a person in respect of that person's employment as a mariner

(a) regulation 12(1) shall apply, save that in the case of a contribution payable on earnings above the upper earnings limit or the prescribed equivalent of that limit, the appropriate contributions calculator prepared by the Board may be applied;

(b) in the alternative, paragraphs (2), (3), (4) and (5) of that regulation shall, except in relation to secondary Class 1 contributions payable at a rate reduced in accordance with regulation 119, apply in respect of those earnings.

121(2) Subject to paragraphs (3), (4) and (5) of regulation 12 where the secondary Class 1 contribution is payable at a rate reduced in accordance with regulation 119, that contribution may be calculated in accordance with the scale prepared by the Board appropriate to that rate or, in the case of such a contribution payable on earnings above the upper earnings limit or the prescribed equivalent of that limit, a contributions calculator appropriate to that rate, prepared by the Board.

Derivations – SI 1979/591, reg. 91.

PRESCRIBED SECONDARY CONTRIBUTORS

122 In relation to any payment of earnings to or for the benefit of a mariner in respect of employment to which the provisions of regulation 118 apply, where the person employing the mariner does not satisfy the conditions specified in regulation 117(1)(c), but the person who pays the mariner those earnings does satisfy either of those conditions, that person shall be treated as the secondary contributor, whether or not he makes the payment as agent for the employer.

Derivations – SI 1979/591, reg. 93.

PAYMENTS TO BE DISREGARDED

123 [Omitted by SI 2012/817, reg. 7(2).]

History – Reg. 123 omitted by SI 2012/817, reg. 7(2), with effect from 6 April 2012.

Derivations – SI 1979/591, reg. 94.

APPLICATION OF THE ACT AND REGULATIONS

124(1) Part I of the Act and so much of Part VI of the Act as relates to contributions and the regulations made under those provisions shall, in so far as they are not inconsistent with the provisions of this Case, apply to mariners with the modification set out in paragraph (2).

124(2) The modification is that, where a mariner is, on account of his being at sea or outside Great Britain or Northern Ireland (as the case requires) by reason of his employment as a mariner, unable to perform an act required to be done either immediately or on the happening of a certain event or within a specified time, he shall be deemed to have complied with that requirement if he performs the act as soon as is reasonably practicable, although after the happening of the event or the expiration of the specified time.

Derivations – SI 1979/591, reg. 96.

MODIFICATION IN RELATION TO SHARE FISHERMEN OF PART I OF THE ACT AND SO MUCH OF PART VI OF THE ACT AS RELATES TO CONTRIBUTIONS

125 Part I of the Act and so much of Part VI of the Act as relates to contributions shall apply to share fishermen with the modification that

(a) employment as a share fisherman shall be employment as a self-employed earner notwithstanding that it is not employment in the United Kingdom;

(b) as respects liability of a share fisherman to pay Class 2 contributions in respect of his employment as a share fisherman, regulation 117(1)(a) and (b) and (2) shall apply as if the share fisherman were a mariner and as if the reference in regulation 117(1) to an employed earner were a reference to a self-employed earner and as if the words "or on behalf, or in respect, of" were omitted;

(c) for the purposes of entitlement to a contribution-based job-seeker's allowance, the weekly rate of any Class 2 contribution payable by a share fisherman for any contribution week while he is ordinarily employed as a share fisherman shall, notwithstanding the provisions of section 11(2) and (6) of the Act (Class 2 contributions), be £3.60;

(d) regulations 21, 100 and 108 shall apply to contributions payable at the weekly rate specified in paragraph (c) of this regulation as if references in those regulations to Class 2 contributions included, as may be appropriate, references to Class 2 contributions at that rate;

(e) regulation 43 shall apply to a share fisherman as if there were included at the end of paragraph (1)(a) of that regulation the words "or is entitled to a contribution-based jobseeker's allowance or, but for a failure to satisfy the contribution conditions for that benefit, would be so entitled";

(f) in so far as Class 4 contributions in respect of the profits or gains of a share fisherman in respect of his employment as such are not collected by the Board under section 16 of the Act (assessment and collection etc. of Class 4 contributions) regulations 103 to 110 shall apply as if the share fisherman were a person to whom section 18(1)(a) and (b) of the Act applied (Class 4 contributions for persons treated under section 2(2)(b) of the Act as self-employed earners); and

(g) for the purposes of section 12 of the Act and for the purposes of that section as modified by regulations 63 to 65, where an earner was a share fisherman when the earner became entitled to pay Class 2 contributions, any reference in section 12 to an ordinary contribution, and any reference in those regulations to the weekly applicable rate of a contribution, shall be a reference to the rate of Class 2 contributions prescribed for a share fisherman.

History – In reg. 125(c), the figure "£3.60" substituted for the figure "£3.50" by SI 2018/363, reg. 2, with effect from 6 April 2018 (immediately after the coming into force of SI 2018/337).

In reg. 125(c), the figure "£3.50" substituted for the figure "£3.45" by SI 2017/416, reg. 2, with effect from 6 April 2017 (immediately after the coming into force of SI 2017/415).

In reg. 125(c) the words "section 11(2) and (6) of the Act (Class 2 contributions), be £3.45" substituted for the words "section 11(1) of the Act (Class 2 contributions), be £3.40" by NICA 2015, s. 2 and Sch. 1, para. 33, with effect for the tax year 2015–16 and subsequent tax years.

In reg. 125(c), the figure "£3.40" substituted for the figure "£3.35" by SI 2014/634, reg. 2, with effect from 6 April 2014.

In reg. 125(c), the former figure "£3.35" substituted for the figure "£3.30" by SI 2013/619, reg. 2, with effect from 6 April 2013.

In reg. 125(c) the former figure "£3.30" substituted for "£3.15" by SI 2012/867, reg. 2, with effect from 6 April 2012.

In reg. 125(c) the former figure "£3.15" substituted for "£3.05" by SI 2011/1001, reg. 2, with effect from 6 April 2011.

In reg. 125(c) the former figure "£3.05" substituted for "£2.95" by SI 2009/696, reg. 2, with effect from 6 April 2009.

In reg. 125(c) the former figure "£2.95" substituted for "£2.85" by SI 2008/703, reg. 2, with effect from 6 April 2008.

In reg. 125(c) the former figure "£2.85" substituted for "£2.75" by SI 2007/1094, reg. 2, with effect from 6 April 2007.

In reg. 125(g), the words "the earner became entitled to pay Class 2 contributions" substituted for "liability for Class 2 contributions arose" by SI 2015/478, reg. 16, with effect from 6 April 2015.

Derivations – SI 1979/591, reg. 98.

Statutory instruments – SI 2007/1081: partly made under s. 175(1), (1A) and (3).

Case D – Married Women And Widows

INTERPRETATION

126(1) In this Case, unless the context otherwise requires

"personal death benefit" means any death benefit which, apart from any regulations made under section 73 of the Administration Act (overlapping benefits – general), is payable to a person otherwise than in respect of another person who is a child or an adult dependant;

"Personal Injuries Scheme" means any scheme made under the Personal Injuries (Emergency Provisions) Act 1939 or under the Pensions (Navy, Army, Air Force and Mercantile Marine) Act 1939;

"qualifying widow" has the meaning assigned to it in regulation 127(1);

"reduced rate" means the rate specified in regulation 131;

"regulation 91 of the 1975 Regulations" and**"regulation 94 of the 1975 Regulations"** mean respectively regulation 91 and regulation 94 of the Social Security (Contributions) Regulations 1975 before section 3(1) of the Social Security Pensions Act 1975 (married women and widows) came into force and sections 5(3) and 130(2) of the Social Security Act 1975 (Class 1 reduced rate and married women and widows) were repealed;

"Service Pensions Instrument" means those provisions and only those provisions of any Royal Warrant, Order in Council or other instrument (not being a 1914–1918 War Injuries Scheme) under which a death or a disablement pension (not including a pension calculated by reference to length of service) and allowances for dependants payable with either such pension may be paid out of public funds in respect of any death or disablement, wound, injury or disease due to service in the naval, military or air forces of the Crown or in any nursing service or other auxiliary service of any of those forces or in the Home Guard or in any other organisation established under the control of the Defence Council or formerly established under the control of the Admiralty, the Army Council or the Air Council;

"1914–1918 War Injuries Scheme" means any scheme made under the Injuries in War (Compensation) Act 1914 or under the Injuries in War Compensation Act 1914 (Session 2) or under any Government scheme for compensation in respect of persons injured in any merchant ship or fishing vessel as the result of hostilities during the 1914–1918 War.

126(2) Where, by any provision of this Case, notice is required to be or may be given in writing it shall be given on a form approved by the Board or in such other manner, being in writing, as they may accept as sufficient in any case.

Derivations – SI 1979/591, reg. 99.

ELECTIONS BY MARRIED WOMEN AND WIDOWS

127(1) A woman who on 6th April 1977 (the date on which section 3(1) of the Social Security Pensions Act 1975 (married women and widows) came into force) was married or was a widow who satisfied the conditions prescribed in paragraph (8) ("a qualifying widow") may

(a) elect that her liability in respect of primary Class 1 contributions shall be a liability to contribute at the reduced rate; and

(b) elect that she shall be under no liability to pay Class 2 contributions.

127(2) Any election made for the purpose of paragraph (1)(a) shall be treated as also made for the purpose of paragraph (1)(b) and any election made for the purpose of paragraph (1)(b) shall be treated as also made for the purpose of paragraph (1)(a) and any revocation of an election for the one purpose shall be treated also as a revocation of an election for the other purpose.

127(3) Where a woman has made an election to which this regulation applies–

(a) any primary Class 1 contributions which are–

  (i) attributable to section 8(1)(a) of the Act, and

  (ii) payable in respect of earnings paid to her or for her benefit in the period during which the election has effect under the following provisions of this Case,

shall be payable at the reduced rate; and

(b) she shall be under no liability to pay any Class 2 contribution, nor shall she be entitled to pay any such contribution, for any contribution week in that period.

127(4) Subject to regulation 134, no woman shall be entitled to make an election specified in paragraph (1) after 11th May 1977.

127(5) Every election shall be made by notice in writing to the Board and by notice in writing to the Board may be revoked by the woman who made the election.

127(6) Any revocation may be cancelled by notice in writing to the Board before the date upon which the notice of revocation is to have effect, and upon cancellation the revocation shall cease to have effect.

127(7) Every woman who makes an election under this regulation shall furnish such certificates, documents, information and other evidence for the purpose of enabling the Board to consider the validity of the election as the Board may require.

127(8) The conditions referred to in paragraph (1) are that the widow

(a) was entitled to

(i) widow's benefit under the Social Security Act 1975,

(ii) any personal death benefit which was payable to her as a widow under the provisions of Chapter IV of Part II of that Act at a weekly rate which was not less than the basic pension specified for the time being in section 6(1)(a) of the Social Security Pensions Act 1975 (rate of Category A retirement pension),

(iii) any personal death benefit by way of pension or allowance payable to her as a widow under any Personal Injuries Scheme or Service Pensions Instrument or any 1914–1918 War Injuries Scheme (not being a pension or allowance calculated by reference to the needs of the beneficiary), the rate of which is as set out in head (ii), or

(iv) benefit under section 39(4) of the Social Security Act 1975 (retirement benefits for the aged), other than a Category C retirement pension; and

(b) was not disentitled to payment of any such benefit by reason of her living with a man, to whom she was not married, as his wife.

History – In reg. 127(1), the words "Social Security Pensions Act 1975" substituted by SI 2003/964, reg. 5 with effect from 6 April 2003. Reg. 127(3) substituted by SI 2003/964, reg. 5 with effect from 6 April 2003.
In reg. 127(3)(b) the words ", nor shall she be entitled to pay any such contribution," inserted by NICA 2015, s. 2 and Sch. 1, para. 34, with effect for the tax year 2015–16 and subsequent tax years.

Derivations – SI 1979/591, reg. 100.

DURATION OF EFFECT OF ELECTION

128(1) Subject to paragraph (2), any election made under regulation 127 shall have effect from and including 6th April 1977 (the date on which section 3(1) of the Social Security Pensions Act 1975 (married women and widows) came into force) until whichever of the following events first occurs after the date of the election, namely

(a) the date on which the woman ceases to be married otherwise than by reason of the death of her husband;

(b) the end of the year in which she ceases to be a qualifying widow;

(c) the end of any two consecutive years which begin on or after 6th April 1978 and in which the woman who made the election has no earnings in respect of which any primary Class 1 contributions are payable in those years and in which that woman is not at any time a self-employed earner;

(d) in the case of a revocation which has not been cancelled in accordance with regulation 127(6), the end of the week in which the notice of revocation is given or, if the woman so wishes, the end of any subsequent week in the same year specified in the notice;

(e) where in any year after 5th April 1982 a payment ("an erroneous payment") is made by or on behalf of a woman on account of primary Class 1 contributions at the contracted-out rate and the woman wishes to pay contributions at the main primary percentage from the beginning of the year next following that year, the end of the year in respect of which the erroneous payment is made; or

(f) where

(i) in any year after 5th April 1982 a payment is made by or on behalf of a woman on account of primary Class 1 contributions at the non-contracted-out rate ("an erroneous payment"), or more that one such payment is made,

(ii) from the time of making that payment or, if these is more than one such payment, the first, to the time at which she notifies the Board in accordance with head (v), no contributions have been paid by her or on her behalf at the reduced rate and no contributions have been payable *by her or on her behalf* in respect of any contracted-out employment,

(iii) she has not procured a refund in respect of any erroneous payment,

(iv) she wishes to pay contributions at the main primary percentage from the date on which the only or first erroneous payment was made, and

(v) after 5th April 1983 and on or before the 31st December in the next complete calendar year following the end of the year in which any erroneous payment was made, she notifies the Board of her wish to pay contributions at the main primary percentage in accordance with head (iv),

the date on which the only or first erroneous payment was made.

128(2) Where a woman, to whom paragraph (1)(b) applies, remarries or again becomes a qualifying widow before the end of the year in which she ceases to be a qualifying widow, that woman's election shall, notwithstanding that sub-paragraph, but without prejudice to the application of paragraph (1)(c), (d), (e) or (f), continue to have effect from the end of that year.

History – In reg. 128(1)(e), (f)(iv), (v), the words "main primary percentage" substituted by SI 2003/964, reg. 9(2) with effect from 6 April 2003.

Derivations – SI 1979/591, reg. 101.

CONTINUATION OF ELECTIONS UNDER REGULATION 91 OF THE 1975 REGULATIONS

129 Where, but for regulation 91 of the 1975 Regulations ceasing to have effect on 6th April 1977 (the date on which section 130(2) of the Social Security Act 1975 was repealed) an election made under that regulation before that date would have continued to have effect on that date, that election shall be treated as made under regulation 127 and this Case shall apply accordingly.

Derivations – SI 1979/591, reg. 102.

CONTINUATION OF ELECTIONS ON WIDOWHOOD

130(1) If on 6th April 1977 (the date on which section 3(1) of the Social Security Pensions Act 1975 came into force) a woman –

(a) was married and subsequently becomes a widow; or

(b) was a widow and subsequently remarries and again becomes a widow,

paragraph (2) applies to her.

130(2) Where this paragraph applies to a woman any election

(a) which she had made under regulation 127 before the death of the husband which renders her a widow; or

(b) which she is, by virtue of regulation 129, treated as having made under regulation 127 before that death;

and which is still effective at the time of the husband's death, shall, subject to paragraphs (4) and (5) and notwithstanding regulation 128, continue to have effect until the end of the appropriate period.

130(3) For the purposes of this regulation the end of the appropriate period is

(a) the earliest of

(i) the end of the second year specified in regulation 128(1)(c),

(ii) the end of the period specified in regulation 128(1)(d) or (e), or

(iii) the date specified in regulation 128(1)(f); or

(b) subject to sub-paragraph (a) and paragraphs (4) and (5)

(i) where the husband's death occurs before 1st October in any year, the end of that year,

(ii) where the husband's death occurs after 30th September in any year, the end of the year next following that in which the death occurs.

130(4) Subject to regulation 128(1)(c), (d), (e) and (f) and to paragraph (5), if at the end of the year specified in head (i) or head (ii) of paragraph (3)(b) there is pending a claim or application made by or on behalf of the woman as a widow within 182 days (including Sundays) of her husband's death for any benefit specified in head (i) or (iv) or, irrespective of its rate, in head (ii) or (iii) of regulation 127(8)(a), the end of the appropriate period shall be the end of the year in which the claim or application is determined.

130(5) If at the end of the year specified in head (i) or (ii) of paragraph (3)(b) or, as the case may be, in paragraph (4) the woman is a qualifying widow or married, the election shall continue to have effect, unless she is then a person to whom regulation 128(1)(c), (d), (e) or (f) applies.

Derivations – SI 1979/591, reg. 103.

REDUCED RATE OF PRIMARY CLASS 1 CONTRIBUTIONS OTHERWISE PAYABLE AT THE MAIN PRIMARY PERCENTAGE

131 On and after 6th April 2011, the reduced rate of contribution for the purposes of section 19(4) of the Act (power to regulate liability in respect of certain married women and widows) in respect of so much of a married woman's liability for primary Class 1 contributions as is attributable to section 8(1)(a) of the Act shall be 5.85 per cent.

History – In reg. 131, the words "6th April 2011" substituted for the words "6th April 2003" by SI 2011/940, reg. 5(a), with effect from 6 April 2011.
In reg. 131, "5.85" substituted for "4.85" by SI 2011/940, reg. 5(b), with effect from 6 April 2011.
Reg. 131 substituted by SI 2003/964, reg. 6 with effect from 6 April 2003.
Derivations – SI 1979/591, reg. 104.

CLASS 3 CONTRIBUTIONS

132 A woman who has made, or is under regulations 126 to 131 treated as having made, an election under regulation 127, shall be precluded from paying Class 3 contributions for any year in respect of the whole of which that election has effect.
Derivations – SI 1979/591, reg. 105.

CERTIFICATES OF ELECTION

133(1) As respects any election made, or by virtue of regulation 129 as treated as made, under regulation 127

(a) where a woman makes an election under regulation 127, the Board shall issue, without charge, a certificate of election ("a certificate") to her;

(b) where a woman is treated as making such an election, the Board shall, on application and without charge, issue a certificate to her; and

(c) that certificate shall remain the property of the Board.

133(2) A woman to whom a certificate has been issued shall be responsible for its custody unless and until it is delivered to a secondary contributor or returned to the Board.

133(3) A woman in respect of whom an election has effect in accordance with regulations 126 to 132 shall, if any primary Class 1 contribution is payable by her or on her behalf, immediately deliver to the secondary contributor a certificate which is currently in force in respect of her and upon the delivery of the certificate, the secondary contributor shall become responsible for its custody unless and until it is delivered again to the woman or to the Board.

133(4) Where a certificate has ceased to be in force, the woman in respect of whom the certificate was issued shall immediately return it to the Board and for that purpose, if at the time when the certificate ceases to be in force it is in the custody of a secondary contributor, that contributor shall immediately return it to the woman.

133(5) The Board may at any time require the person for the time being responsible for the custody of a certificate to return it to the Board, and if at that time the election to which that certificate relates continues to have effect, the Board shall issue to that person a replacement certificate.

133(6) Where a woman in respect of whom an election has effect has more than one employed earner's employment the Board shall issue to her without charge, on her application, such number of certificates as will enable her to comply with the requirements of paragraph (3) in relation to each secondary contributor.

133(7) Where a certificate has been lost or destroyed the person responsible for its custody shall inform the Board of that loss or destruction.

133(8) When a woman gives notice in writing to the Board that she revokes an election she shall

(a) if the certificate is with a secondary contributor, recover it from him; and

(b) deliver the certificate to the Board.

133(9) Where a secondary contributor holds a certificate and

(a) is informed by the woman to whom it was issued that she intends to revoke her election and is requested to return the certificate to her so that she may return it to the Board; or

(b) the employment by him of the woman to whom the certificate was issued has terminated, he shall immediately return the certificate to her.

133(10) Where, under the preceding provisions of this Case, an election has been made by a woman to pay at the reduced rate in respect of so much of her liability for primary Class 1 contributions as is attributable to section 8(1)(a) of the Act and that election ceases to have effect, it shall be the duty of that woman to inform the secondary contributor accordingly.

133(11) Any certificate issued for the purpose of an election made or deemed to have been made under regulation 91 of the 1975 Regulations shall, if by virtue of regulation 129 the election is treated as made under regulation 127, continue in force for the purposes of that regulation.

History – In reg. 133(10), the words "to pay at the reduced rate in respect of so much of her liability for primary Class 1 contributions as is attributable to section 8(1)(a) of the Act" substituted by SI 2003/964, reg. 7 with effect from 6 April 2003.

Derivations – SI 1979/591, reg. 106.

SPECIAL TRANSITIONAL PROVISIONS CONSEQUENT UPON PASSING OF THE SOCIAL SECURITY PENSIONS ACT 1975

134(1) Any woman to whom this regulation applies

(a) shall, in respect of so much of her liability for primary Class 1 contributions as is attributable to section 8(1)(a) of the Act, be liable to pay those contributions at the reduced rate; and

(b) shall not be liable to pay any Class 2 contribution which, apart from the provisions of this paragraph, she would be liable to pay.

134(2) Subject to paragraphs (3) to (7), this regulation applies to any woman

(a) to whom, before 6th April 1977 (the date on which section 3(1) of the Social Security Pensions Act 1975 came into force and sections 5(3) and 130(2) of the Social Security Act 1975 were repealed), the provisions of section 5(3) of the Social Security Act 1975 or of regulation 94 of the 1975 Regulations (newly widowed women) applied and to whom those provisions would have continued to apply but for those provisions having been repealed or, as the case may be, having ceased to have effect on that date;

(b) who, not being a woman to whom regulation 130 applies

(i) on 6th April 1977 was a married woman and became a widow during the period from and including that date to 6th April 1978, or

(ii) on 6th April 1977 was a qualifying widow, remarried after that date and again became a widow during that period; or

(c) who on 6th April 1977 was married or a qualifying widow and had attained the age of 59.

134(3) In the case of a woman specified in paragraph (2)(a) or (b), the provisions of paragraph (1) shall, subject to the provisions of paragraphs (4) and (5), apply only during the period which

(a) in the case of a woman specified in paragraph (2)(a)

(i) began at the beginning of the year in which section 3(1) came into force, and

(ii) ended at the end of that year;

(b) in the case of a woman specified in paragraph (2)(b)

(i) began on the date on which that woman became or, as the case may be, again became a widow, and

(ii) ends at the end of whichever of the two periods specified in regulation 130(2)(b) is appropriate in her case in so far as that regulation relates to the date of the death of the husband.

134(4) In the case of a woman to whom paragraph (3)(a) or (b) applies, those sub-paragraphs shall be subject to regulation 130(4) and paragraph (5) below with the modification that

(a) in regulation 130(4), the reference to sub-paragraphs (d) and (e) of regulation 128(1) shall be omitted;

(b) in so far as regulation 128(1)(c) is incorporated in regulation 130(4) as modified for the purposes of this regulation, references in regulation 128(1)(c) to any election made under regulation 127 and to a woman who made the election shall respectively be construed as references to the application of paragraph (1) and to the woman to whom that paragraph applies.

134(5) Any woman

(a) who by virtue of paragraph (1)

(i) was, in respect of so much of her liability for primary Class 1 contributions as is attributable to section 8(1)(a) of the Act, liable to pay that contribution at the reduced rate, or

(ii) was not liable to pay any Class 2 contribution which apart from the provisions of that paragraph she would have been liable to pay; but

(b) to whom, by virtue of paragraphs (2) to (4), paragraph (1) ceases so to apply; and

(c) who has not, in relation to the application of paragraph (1), given the notice prescribed in paragraph (7),

may, subject to the conditions prescribed in paragraph (6), make an election under and in accordance with regulation 127, notwithstanding that she has not done so before the date prescribed in that regulation, and regulations 126 to 133 shall apply accordingly from the end of the year in which paragraph (1) ceases to apply to her.

134(6) The conditions referred to in paragraph (5) are that the woman

(a) shall make the election not later than 11th May next following the end of the year in which paragraph (1) ceases to apply to her; and

(b) is, at the beginning of the year next following the year in which paragraph (1) so ceases to apply, married or a qualifying widow.

134(7) Any woman to whom, by virtue of paragraph (2)(a) or (b), paragraph (1) applies may give notice in writing to the Board that she does not wish paragraph (1) to apply to her and upon the giving of such notice it shall accordingly cease to apply.

History – In reg. 134(1)(a), the words "so much of her liability for primary Class 1 contributions as is attributable to section 8(1)(a) of the Act" and the words "those contributions" substituted by SI 2003/964, reg. 8(2) with effect from 6 April 2003.
In reg. 134(5)(a)(i), the words "so much of her liability for primary Class 1 contributions as is attributable to section 8(1)(a) of the Act" substituted by SI 2003/964, reg. 8(3) with effect from 6 April 2003.

Derivations – SI 1979/591, reg. 107.

DEEMED ELECTION OF MARRIED WOMEN AND WIDOWS EXCEPTED FROM CONTRIBUTION LIABILITY UNDER THE NATIONAL INSURANCE ACT 1965

135 Where immediately before 6th April 1975 there was, or is deemed to have been, in issue a current certificate of exception under regulation 9(3) or (4A) of the National Insurance (Contributions) Regulations 1969 (exception for certain widows), or there was current an election under regulation 2(1)(a) of the National Insurance (Married Women) Regulations 1973 (married women who are employed persons), or a woman then was, or but for any exception under or by virtue of another provision of the National Insurance Act 1965 would have been, excepted under regulation 3(1)(a) of the 1973 Regulations (married women who are self-employed persons) from liability for contributions as a self-employed person under that Act and in any of these cases on that day the woman is a widow or, as the case may be, a married woman, that woman shall be deemed to have made an election under regulation 91 of the 1975 Regulations.

Derivations – SI 1979/591, reg. 108.

SPECIAL TRANSITIONAL PROVISIONS REGARDING DEEMED ELECTIONS

136(1) If, under regulation 135, a woman is deemed to have made an election under regulation 91 of the 1975 Regulations, this regulation applies.

136(2) Before the woman first becomes liable to pay a primary Class 1 contribution she may revoke any such election by notice in writing given to the Board and, if she so specified in that notice, the revocation shall have effect from and including the beginning of the year in which the notice is given.

136(3) If no notice of revocation is given and–

(a) in the first year (not being more than 2 years after 6th April 1978) in which the woman becomes liable to pay primary Class 1 contributions–

(i) she shall be entitled to choose whether with effect from the beginning of that year, to pay such contributions at the main primary percentage or at the reduced rate,

(ii) she shall notify any secondary contributor whether he is to pay such contributions on her behalf at the main primary percentage or the reduced rate, and

(iii) such secondary contributor shall pay those contributions in accordance with that notification until the woman notifies him to the contrary in accordance with the provisions of regulation 133(10);

(b) in that first year (not being more than 2 years after 6th April 1978) any primary Class 1 contribution at the standard rate is paid by or on behalf of the woman, unless it is shown to the satisfaction of the Board that the woman did not intend, by the making of that payment, to revoke the election she shall be deemed to have revoked the election.

History – In reg. 136(3)(a)(i), (ii), the words "main primary percentage" substituted by SI 2003/964, reg. 9 with effect from 6 April 2003.

Derivations – SI 1979/591, reg. 109.

APPLICATION OF REGULATIONS 126 TO 134 TO ELECTIONS AND REVOCATION OF ELECTIONS DEEMED MADE UNDER REGULATIONS 135 AND 136

137(1) Subject to paragraph (2), regulations 126 to 134, save only in so far as inconsistent with regulations 135 and 136, shall apply to any election deemed to have been made under regulation 91 of the 1975 Regulations by virtue of regulation 135 as if it had been made under, and in accordance with, regulation 127 except that the Board shall not be obliged to issue a certificate, and as if any revocation which is deemed to be made under regulation 136 were made under, and in accordance with, regulation 127(5).

137(2) Where a woman who, under regulation 135, is not liable for a primary Class 1 contribution otherwise than at the reduced rate and to whom no certificate of election under the Act has been issued becomes employed in employed earner's employment, she shall make application in writing to the Board for such a certificate and, notwithstanding paragraph (1), the Board shall issue such a certificate to her.

Derivations – SI 1979/591, reg. 110.

SAVINGS

138 For the purpose of facilitating the introduction of the scheme of social security contributions within the meaning of paragraph 9(1)(a)(i) of Schedule 3 to the Social Security (Consequential Provisions) Act 1975, regulations 2(2) (married women who are employed persons), 3(2) (married women who are self-employed persons), 4(2) (married women who are non-employed persons) and 16 (notice of marriage) of the National Insurance (Married Women) Regulations 1973 shall be saved.

Derivations – SI 1979/591, reg. 111.

MODIFICATION OF THE ACT

139 Part 1, Part 2 (except section 60), and Parts 3 and 4 of the Act shall have effect as respects married women and widows subject to the modifications contained in this Case.

History – The words "Part 1, Part 2 (except section 60(b)), and Parts 3 and 4 of the Act" substituted by SI 2003/964, reg. 10 with effect from 6 April 2003.

Derivations – SI 1979/591, reg. 112.

Case E – Members Of The Forces

ESTABLISHMENTS AND ORGANISATIONS OF WHICH HER MAJESTY'S FORCES ARE TAKEN TO CONSIST

140 Except in relation to the employment in any of the establishments or organisations specified in Part I of Schedule 6 of any person specified in Part II of that Schedule, Her Majesty's forces shall, for the purpose of the Act, be taken to consist of the establishments and organisations specified in Part I of that Schedule, and this Case shall be construed accordingly.

Derivations – SI 1979/591, reg. 113.

TREATMENT OF SERVING MEMBERS OF THE FORCES AS PRESENT IN GREAT BRITAIN

141 For the purposes of regulation 145(1)(a) a serving member of the forces shall, in respect of his employment as such, be treated as present in Great Britain.

Derivations – SI 1979/591, reg. 114.

TREATMENT OF CONTRIBUTIONS PAID AFTER DUE DATE

142 For the purpose of any entitlement to benefit, any earnings-related contribution paid after the due date, in respect of earnings paid to or for the benefit of a person in respect of his employment as a member of the forces, shall be treated as paid on that date.

Derivations – SI 1979/591, reg. 116.

SPECIAL PROVISIONS CONCERNING EARNINGS-RELATED CONTRIBUTIONS

143(1) For the purposes of earnings-related contributions, there shall be excluded from the computation of a person's earnings, as a serving member of the forces, any payment in so far as it is–

(a) a payment of or in respect of an Emergency Service grant;

(b) a payment of any sum referred to in sections 297 and 298 of ITEPA 2003 (armed forces' food, drink and mess allowances and reserve and auxiliary forces' training allowances); or

(c) a payment of liability bounty in recognition of liability for immediate call-up in times of emergency.

143(2) The earnings period for a person who is a serving member of the forces shall be as follows–

(a) in the case of a person serving in the regular naval, military or air forces of the Crown, whatever is the accounting period from time to time applying in his case under the Naval Pay Regulations or, as the case may be, the Army Pay Warrant, Queen's Regulations for the Army or for the Royal Air Force or the Air Council Instructions; or

(b) in the case of a person undergoing training in any of the establishments or organisations specified in paragraphs 2 to 9 of Part I of Schedule 6, a month.

History – In reg. 143(1)(b) words "sections 297 and 298 of ITEPA 2003 (armed forces' food, drink and mess allowances and reserve and auxiliary forces' training allowances)" substituted by SI 2004/770, reg. 25, with effect from 6 April 2004.

Derivations – SI 1979/591, reg. 117.

APPLICATION OF THE ACT AND REGULATIONS

144(1) Part I of the Act and so much of Part VI of the Act as relates to contributions and the regulations made under those provisions shall, in so far as they are not inconsistent with this Case, apply in relation to persons who are serving members of the forces with the modification prescribed in paragraph (2).

144(2) The modification is that where a person is, on account of his being at sea or outside the United Kingdom by reason of his employment as a serving member of the forces, unable to perform an act required to be done either immediately or on the happening of a certain event or within a specified time, he shall be deemed to have complied with that requirement if he performs the act as soon as is reasonably practicable, although after the happening of the event or the expiration of the specified time.

Derivations – SI 1979/591, reg. 118.

Case F – Residence And Persons Abroad

CONDITIONS AS TO RESIDENCE OR PRESENCE IN GREAT BRITAIN OR NORTHERN IRELAND

145(1) Subject to paragraph (2), for the purposes of section 1(6) of the Act (conditions as to residence or presence in Great Britain for liability or entitlement to pay Class 1 or Class 2 contributions, liability to pay Class 1A or Class 1B contributions or entitlement to pay Class 3 contributions) the conditions as to residence or presence in Great Britain or Northern Ireland (as the case requires) shall be–

(a) as respects liability of an employed earner to pay primary Class 1 contributions in respect of earnings for an employed earner's employment, that the employed earner is resident or present in Great Britain or Northern Ireland (or but for any temporary absence would be present in Great Britain or Northern Ireland) at the time of that employment or is then ordinarily resident in Great Britain or Northern Ireland (as the case may be);

(b) as respects liability to pay secondary Class 1 contributions, Class 1A contributions or Class 1B contributions that the person who, but for any conditions as to residence or presence in Great Britain or Northern Ireland (as the case may be and including the having of a place of business in Great Britain or Northern Ireland), would be the secondary contributor or the person liable for the payment of Class 1B contributions (in this Case referred to as "the employer") is resident or present in Great Britain or Northern Ireland when such contributions become payable or then has a place of business in Great Britain or Northern Ireland (as the case may be), so however that nothing in this paragraph shall prevent the employer paying those contributions if he so wishes;

(c) as respects entitlement of a self-employed earner to pay Class 2 contributions, that that earner is present in Great Britain or Northern Ireland (as the case may be) in the contribution week for which the contribution is to be paid;

(d) as respects liability of a self-employed earner to pay Class 2 contributions, that the self-employed earner is ordinarily resident in Great Britain or Northern Ireland (as the case may be), or, if he is not so ordinarily resident, that before the period in respect of which any such contributions are to be paid he has been resident in Great Britain or Northern Ireland (as the case may be) for a period of at least 26 out of the immediately preceding 52 contribution weeks under the Act, the Social Security Act 1975 or the National Insurance Act 1965 or under some or all of those Acts.

(e) as respects entitlement of a person to pay Class 3 contributions in respect of any year, either that–

(i) that person is resident in Great Britain or Northern Ireland (as the case may be) throughout the year,

(ii) that person has arrived in Great Britain or Northern Ireland (as the case may be) during that year and has been or is liable to pay Class 1 or Class 2 contributions in respect of an earlier period during that year,

(iii) that person has arrived in Great Britain or Northern Ireland (as the case may be) during that year and was either ordinarily resident in Great Britain or Northern Ireland (as the case may be) throughout the whole of that year or became ordinarily resident during the course of it, or

(iv) that person, not being ordinarily resident in Great Britain or Northern Ireland (as the case may be), has arrived in that year or the previous year and has been continuously present in Great Britain or Northern Ireland (as the case may be) for 26 complete contribution weeks, entitlement where the arrival has been in the previous year arising in respect only of the next year.

145(2) Where a person is ordinarily neither resident nor employed in the United Kingdom and, in pursuance of employment which is mainly employment outside the United Kingdom by an employer whose place of business is outside the United Kingdom (whether or not he also has a place of business in the United Kingdom) that person is employed for a time in Great Britain or Northern Ireland (as the case may be) as an employed earner and, but for the provisions of this paragraph, the provisions of sub-paragraph (a) of paragraph (1) would apply, the conditions prescribed in that sub-paragraph and in sub-paragraph (b) of that paragraph shall apply subject to the proviso that–

(a) no primary or secondary Class 1 contribution shall be payable in respect of the earnings of the employed earner for such employment;

(b) no Class 1A contribution shall be payable in respect of something which is made available to the employed earner or to a member of his family or household by reason of such employment; and

(c) no Class 1B contribution shall be payable in respect of any PAYE settlement agreement in connection with such employment,

after the date of the earner's last entry into Great Britain or Northern Ireland (as the case may be) and before he has been resident in Great Britain or Northern Ireland (as the case may be) for a continuous period of 52 contribution weeks from the beginning of the contribution week following that in which that date falls.

145(3) [Omitted by SI 2012/817, reg. 7(3)(b).]

History – In reg. 145(1), the words "paragraph (2)" substituted for the words "paragraphs (2) and (3)" by SI 2012/817, reg. 7(3)(a), with effect from 6 April 2012.
Reg. 145(3) omitted by SI 2012/817, reg. 7(3)(b), with effect from 6 April 2012.
Derivations – SI 1979/591, reg. 119.

PAYMENT OF CONTRIBUTIONS FOR PERIODS ABROAD

146(1) Where an earner is gainfully employed outside the United Kingdom, and that employment, if it had been in Great Britain or Northern Ireland, would have been employed earner's employment, that employment outside the United Kingdom shall be treated as employed earner's employment for the period for which under paragraph (2)(a) contributions are payable in respect of the earnings paid to the earner in respect of that employment provided that–

(a) the employer has a place of business in Great Britain or Northern Ireland (as the case may be);

(b) the earner is ordinarily resident in Great Britain or Northern Ireland (as the case may be); and

(c) immediately before the commencement of the employment the earner was resident in Great Britain or Northern Ireland (as the case may be).

146(2) Where, under paragraph (1), the employment outside the United Kingdom is treated as an employed earner's employment, the following provisions shall apply in respect of the payment of contributions–

(a) primary and secondary Class 1 contributions shall be payable in respect of any payment of earnings for the employment outside the United Kingdom during the period of 52 contribution weeks from the beginning of the contribution week in which that employment begins to the same extent as that to which such contributions would have been payable if the employment had been in Great Britain or Northern Ireland (as the case may be);

(b) subject to regulations 148 and regulations 148A, any earner by or in respect of whom contributions are or have been payable under sub-paragraph (a) shall be entitled to pay Class 3 contributions in respect of any year during which the earner is outside the United Kingdom from and including that in which the employment outside the United Kingdom begins until that in which he next returns to Great Britain or Northern Ireland (as the case may be);

(c) Class 1A contributions and Class 1B contributions shall be payable in respect of the period specified in sub-paragraph (a).

History – In reg. 146(2)(b) the words "regulations 148 and 148A" substituted by SI 2007/1838, reg. 4, with effect from 18 July 2007.
Derivations – SI 1979/591, reg. 120.

CLASS 2 AND CLASS 3 CONTRIBUTIONS FOR PERIODS ABROAD

147(1) Subject to regulation 148 and regulation 148A, a person (other than a person to whom regulation 146(2)(a) applies) may, notwithstanding the provisions of regulation 145(1)(c) and (e), if he so wishes and if he satisfies the conditions specified in paragraph (3) below pay contributions in respect of periods during which he is outside the United Kingdom as follows–

(a) in respect of any contribution week throughout which he is gainfully employed outside the United Kingdom in employment which is not employment in respect of earnings from which Class 1 contributions are payable, he may, if immediately before he last left Great Britain or Northern

Ireland (as the case may be) he was ordinarily an employed earner or a self-employed earner, pay a contribution as a self-employed earner;

(b) in respect of any year which includes a period during which he is outside the United Kingdom he may pay Class 3 contributions.

147(2) A person who is gainfully employed outside the United Kingdom and falls within the provisions of paragraph (1)(a) shall for the purposes of that paragraph be treated as being outside the United Kingdom for any period during which he is temporarily in the United Kingdom.

147(3) Subject to paragraph (4), the conditions referred to in paragraph (1) are that–

(a) the person has been resident in Great Britain or Northern Ireland (as the case may be) for a continuous period of not less than 3 years at any time before the period for which the contributions are to be paid;

(b) there have been paid by or on behalf of that person contributions of the appropriate amount–

(i) for each of 3 years ending at any time before the relevant period,

(ii) for each of 2 years ending at any time before the relevant period and, in addition, 52 contributions under either or both the Social Security Act 1975 or the National Insurance Act 1965, or

(iii) for any one year ending at any time before the relevant period and, in addition, 104 contributions under either or both the Social Security Act 1975 or the National Insurance Act 1965, or

(c) there have been paid by or on behalf of that person 156 contributions under either or both the Social Security Act 1975 or the National Insurance Act 1965.

147(4) In paragraph (3)–

"contributions of the appropriate amount" means contributions under the Act the earnings factor derived from which is not less than 52 times the lower earnings limit for the time being for primary Class 1 contributions;

"contributions under either or both the Social Security Act 1975 or the National Insurance Act 1965" means contributions of any class under section 4, 7 or 8 of the Social Security Act 1975 or section 3 of the National Insurance Act 1965 in respect of any period; and

"the relevant period" means the period for which it is desired to pay the Class 2 or Class 3 contributions specified in paragraph (1).

History – In reg. 147(1) the words "regulations 148 and 148A" substituted by SI 2007/1838, reg. 5, with effect from 18 July 2007.
Derivations – SI 1979/591, reg. 121.

CONDITIONS OF PAYMENT OF CLASS 2 OR CLASS 3 CONTRIBUTIONS FOR PERIODS ABROAD

148 Entitlement to pay Class 2 or Class 3 contributions under regulations 146 and 147 shall be subject to the following conditions–

(a) that the payment is made within the period specified in regulation 48(3)(b)(i); and

(b) that the payment is made only to the extent to which it could have been made if the contributor had been present in Great Britain or Northern Ireland (as the case may be) and otherwise entitled to make it.

Derivations – SI 1979/591, reg. 122.

CONDITIONS OF PAYMENT OF CLASS 3 CONTRIBUTIONS: TRANSFERS TO THE COMMUNITIES' PENSION SCHEME

148A(1) Entitlement to pay Class 3 contributions under regulations 146 and 147 is subject to the condition set out in paragraph (2).

148A(2) The condition is that a person may not pay a Class 3 contribution for any part of the period to which that person's Communities transfer relates.

148A(3) For the purposes of this regulation–

a **"Communities transfer"** means a transfer to the Communities pension scheme of rights to relevant benefits;

"the Communities' pension scheme" means the pension scheme provided for officials and other servants of Community institutions and bodies in accordance with regulations adopted by the Council of the European Communities;

"relevant benefits" means benefits under–

(a) Parts 2 to 5 and 10 of the Act,

(b) sections 36 and 37 of the National Insurance Act 1965 (graduated retirement benefit), and

(c) sections 1(2) and 2 of the Jobseekers Act 1995 (contribution-based jobseeker's allowance).

History – Reg. 148A inserted by SI 2007/1838, reg. 6, with effect from 18 July 2007.

148B(1) This regulation applies, in relation to a tax year, in respect of a person who is in that tax year–

(a) in employment as a self-employed earner; and

(b) a person to whom the Act applies by virtue of Regulation (EC) No 1408/71 or Regulation (EC) No 883/2004.

148B(2) Section 11 of the Act has effect in relation to the employment as if for subsection (3) there were substituted–

> "**11(3) "Relevant profits"** means profits from the employment in respect of which Class 4 contributions would be payable under section 15 for the relevant tax year if–
>
> (a) for the purposes of income tax, the earner were resident in the United Kingdom in that year;
>
> (b) the employment were carried on by the earner in Great Britain;
>
> (c) the amount of the profits were to exceed the amount specified in subsection (3)(a) of that section in excess of which the main Class 4 percentage is payable; and
>
> (d) any applicable arrangements having effect under section 2 of the Taxation (International and Other Provisions) Act 2010 (double taxation arrangements) were to be disregarded."

History – Reg. 148B inserted by SI 2015/478, reg. 17, with effect from 6 April 2015.

148C(1) This regulation applies in relation to a person (P)–

(a) who is liable under section 11(2) of the Act, or entitled under section 11(6) of the Act, to pay one or more Class 2 contributions in respect of a contribution week in a relevant tax year;

(b) who does not carry on a trade, profession or vocation the profits of which (if any) would be chargeable to income tax under Chapter 2 of Part 2 of the Income Tax (Trading and Other Income) Act 2005 for the relevant tax year; and

(c) in respect of whom regulation 148B applies in relation to the relevant tax year.

148C(2) Section 11(5) of the Act (Class 2 contributions payable in the same manner as Class 4 contributions) does not apply in relation to the Class 2 contributions (if it would otherwise do so).

148C(3) Section 12 of the Act (late paid Class 2 contributions) is to apply to the Class 2 contributions that P is liable to pay under section 11(2) of the Act as it applies to contributions paid under section 11(6) of the Act.

148C(4) If P is liable to pay the Class 2 contributions, P must, no later than 31st January next following the end of the relevant tax year–

(a) pay the Class 2 contributions for which P is liable in respect of any contribution weeks in that tax year; and

(b) make a return in such form as may be approved by HMRC.

148C(5) If P is entitled to pay a Class 2 contribution under section 11(6) of the Act, P may–

(a) make a return in such form as may be approved by HMRC; and

(b) pay the contribution.

148C(6) P must keep such records as may be necessary for the purposes of calculating P's–

(a) relevant profits from the employment for the purposes of section 11(2) of the Act; and

(b) liability or, as the case may be, entitlement to pay a Class 2 contribution,

for the relevant tax year and preserve such records until the sixth anniversary of the 31st January next following the end of the relevant tax year.

History – Reg. 148C inserted by SI 2015/478, reg. 18, with effect from 6 April 2015.

Case G – Volunteer Development Workers

INTERPRETATION

149(1) In this Case **"volunteer development worker"** means a person in respect of whom the Board has certified that it is consistent with the proper administration of the Act that, subject to the satisfaction of the conditions in paragraph (2), that person should be entitled to pay Class 2 contributions under regulation 151.

149(2) The conditions are–

(a) that that person is ordinarily resident in Great Britain or Northern Ireland (as the case may be); and

(b) that he is employed outside the United Kingdom.

History – In reg. 149(2)(b) words "outside the United Kingdom" substituted by SI 2002/2366, reg. 17, with effect from 8 October 2002.

Derivations – SI 1979/591, reg. 123A.

CERTAIN VOLUNTEER DEVELOPMENT WORKERS TO BE SELF-EMPLOYED EARNERS

150 Any employment as a volunteer development worker, which is not employment in respect of earnings from which Class 1 contributions are payable, or, where section 6A of the Act applies, are treated as having been paid, shall be employment as a self-employed earner notwithstanding that it is not employment in Great Britain or Northern Ireland.

Derivations – SI 1979/591, reg. 123B.

OPTION TO PAY CLASS 2 CONTRIBUTIONS

151 Notwithstanding section 11(1) of the Act and regulation 150, a volunteer development worker who by virtue of that regulation is a self-employer earner–

(a) [omitted by SI 2015/478, reg. 19(a);]

(b) shall be entitled to pay a Class 2 contribution if he so wishes at the rate prescribed in regulation 152(b).

History – Reg. 151(a) omitted by SI 2015/478, reg. 19(a), with effect from 6 April 2015.

In reg. 151(b), the words "a Class 2" substituted for the words "such a" by SI 2015/478, reg. 19(b), with effect from 6 April 2015.

Derivations – SI 1979/591, reg. 123C.

SPECIAL PROVISIONS AS TO RESIDENCE, RATE, ANNUAL MAXIMUM AND METHOD OF PAYMENT

152 In relation to the Class 2 contributions a volunteer development worker is entitled to pay by virtue of regulation 151–

(a) the provisions of Case F of these Regulations shall not apply;

(b) the weekly rate of any Class 2 contribution payable by a volunteer development worker for any contribution week while he is ordinarily employed as a volunteer development worker shall, notwithstanding section 11(2) of the Act (Class 2 contributions), be 5 per cent of the lower earnings limit for the year in which falls the week in respect of which the contribution is paid;

(c) for the purpose of determining the extent of an earner's liability for contributions under regulation 21 the amount prescribed in that regulation shall be reduced by the amount of any contributions paid in respect of the year in question by virtue of regulation 151; and

(d) regulation 89 shall not apply.

History – In reg. 152(b), "11(2)" substituted for "11(1)" by SI 2015/478, reg. 20, with effect from 6 April 2015.

Derivations – SI 1979/591, reg. 123D.

LATE PAID CONTRIBUTIONS

153(1) This regulation applies to any Class 2 contribution a volunteer development worker is entitled to pay by virtue of regulation 151, which is paid in respect of a week falling within a year ("the contribution year") earlier than the year in which it is paid.

153(2) Section 12 of the Act (late paid Class 2 contributions) shall not apply.

153(3) Subject to paragraph (4), the amount of a contribution to which this regulation applies shall be the amount which the volunteer development worker would have had to pay if he had paid the contribution in the contribution year.

153(4) In any case where–

(a) the volunteer development worker pays a contribution to which this regulation applies after the end of the year immediately following the contribution year; and

(b) the weekly rate of contributions applicable under regulation 152(b), for the week in respect of which the contribution is paid, differs from the weekly rate so applicable at the time of payment, the amount of the contributions shall be computed by reference to the highest weekly rate of contributions applicable in the period from the week in respect of which the contribution is paid to the day on which it is paid.

Derivations – SI 1979/591, reg. 123E.

MODIFICATIONS OF THE ACT AND THESE REGULATIONS

154 Part 1 of the Act and these Regulations shall have effect as respects volunteer development workers subject to the modification contained in this Case.

Derivations – SI 1979/591, reg. 123F.

CASE H

APPRENTICES: ZERO-RATE SECONDARY CLASS 1 CONTRIBUTIONS

154A(1) For the purposes of section 9B (zero-rate secondary Class 1 contributions for certain apprentices) of the Act, an apprentice is a person who falls within paragraphs (2) and (3).

154A(2) The person is employed under–

(a) an approved English apprenticeship agreement within the meaning of section A1 of the Apprenticeships, Skills, Children and Learning Act 2009 ("the 2009 Act"),

(b) an English apprenticeship agreement within the meaning of section 32 of the 2009 Act as saved by paragraph 2 of Part 2 of the Schedule to the Deregulation Act 2015 (Commencement No. 1 and Transitional and Saving Provisions) Order 2015,

(c) a Welsh apprenticeship agreement within the meaning of section 32 of the 2009 Act,

(d) arrangements made by the Secretary of State or the Scottish Ministers under section 2 of the Employment and Training Act 1973,

(e) arrangements made by the Secretary of State or the Scottish Ministers under section 2 of the Enterprise and New Towns (Scotland) Act 1990, or

(f) arrangements made by the Secretary of State or Northern Ireland Ministers under section 1 of the Employment and Training Act (Northern Ireland) 1950.

154A(3) The person is being trained pursuant to arrangements–

(a) in relation to which the Secretary of State has secured the provision of financial resources under section 100 of the 2009 Act, or

(b) which are set out in a written agreement made between that person, the employer and the training provider containing the following information–

(i) the type of apprenticeship framework or standard being followed,

(ii) the start date of the apprenticeship, and

(iii) the expected completion date of the apprenticeship.

History – Reg. 154A (and the headings before it) inserted by SI 2016/117, reg. 2(2), with effect from 6 April 2016.

PART 10 – MISCELLANEOUS PROVISIONS

TREATMENT OF CONTRIBUTION WEEK FALLING IN TWO YEARS

155 For the purposes of Class 2 contributions, where a contribution week falls partly in one year and partly in another, it shall be treated as falling wholly within the year in which it begins.

Derivations – SI 1979/591, reg. 131.

DECISIONS TAKEN BY OFFICERS OF THE INLAND REVENUE IN RESPECT OF CONTRIBUTIONS WHICH ARE PRESCRIBED FOR THE PURPOSES OF SECTION 8(1)(m) OF THE TRANSFER ACT

155A(1) For the purposes of section 8(1)(m) of the Transfer Act the decisions specified in paragraphs (2) to (5) are prescribed.

155A(2) The decisions specified in this paragraph are–

(a) whether a notice should be given under regulation 3(2B) and, if so, the terms of such a notice;

(b) whether a notice given under regulation 3(2B) should cease to have effect;

(c) whether a direction should be given under regulation 31 and, if so, the terms of the direction;

(d) whether the condition in regulation 50(2) is satisfied;

(e) whether a late application under regulation 52(8) for the refund of a contribution should be admitted;

(f) [omitted by SI 2016/352, reg. 17;]

(g) whether a late application under regulation 55(3) for the repayment of a Class 1A contribution should be admitted;

(h) whether, in a case where the secondary contributor has failed to pay a primary Class 1 contribution on behalf of the primary contributor, that failure was with the consent or connivance of the primary contributor or attributable to any negligence on the part of the primary contributor, as mentioned in regulation 60;

(i) whether the condition in regulation 61(2) is satisfied;

(j) whether, in the case of a Class 2 contribution remaining unpaid by the due date, the reason for the non-payment is the contributor's ignorance or error, and, if so, whether that ignorance or error was due to his failure to exercise due care and diligence, as mentioned in regulation 65(2);

(k) whether the reason for a contributor's failure to pay a Class 3 contribution within the period prescribed for its payment is his ignorance or error, and, if so, whether that ignorance or error was due to his failure to exercise due care and diligence, as mentioned in regulation 65(3);

(l) whether the reason for a contributor's failure to pay a Class 3 contribution falling to be computed under section 13(6) of the Act and which remains unpaid after the end of the second year following the contribution year, is his ignorance or error and if so whether that ignorance or error was due to his failure to exercise due care and diligence, as mentioned in regulation 65(4); and

(m) whether a late application under regulation 110(3) for the return of a special Class 4 contribution should be admitted.

155A(3) The decisions specified in this paragraph are–

(a) whether a contribution (other than a Class 4 contribution) has been paid in error as mentioned in regulation 52(1); and

(b) whether there has been a payment of contributions in excess of the amount specified in regulation 21, as mentioned in regulation 52A(1),

to the extent that they are not decisions falling within section 8(1)(c) or (d) (decisions as to liability and entitlement to pay contributions) of the Transfer Act.

155A(4) The decisions specified in this paragraph are–

(a) whether the delay in making payment of a contribution, payable by an employer on behalf of an insured person, was neither with the consent or connivance of the insured person nor attributable to any negligence on the part of the insured person, as mentioned in regulation 23 of the National Insurance (Contributions) Regulations 1969;

(b) whether, in the case of a contribution paid after the due date, the failure to pay the contribution before that time was attributable to ignorance or error on the part of the insured person, and, if so, whether that ignorance or error was due to the failure on the part of the insured person to exercise due care and diligence, as mentioned in regulation 24 of those Regulations; and

(c) whether the failure to pay a contribution to which regulation 32 of those Regulations applies within the prescribed period was attributable to ignorance or error on the part of the person entitled to pay it and, if so, whether that ignorance or error was due to the failure of the person entitled to pay the contribution to exercise due care and diligence.

155A(5) The decisions specified in this paragraph are–

(a) whether the delay in making payment of a primary Class 1 contribution which is payable on a primary contributor's behalf by a secondary contributor was neither with the consent or connivance of the primary contributor nor attributable to any negligence on the part of the primary contributor, as mentioned in regulation 5 of the Social Security (Crediting and Treatment of Contributions, and National Insurance Numbers) Regulations 2001 (treatment for the purpose of any contributory benefit of late paid primary Class 1 contributions where there was no consent, connivance or negligence by the primary contributor); and

(b) whether, in the case of a contribution paid by or in respect of a person after the due date, the failure to pay the contribution before that time was attributable to ignorance or error on the part of that person or the person making the payment and if so whether that ignorance or error was due to the failure on the part of such person to exercise due care and diligence, as mentioned in regulation 6 of the Social Security (Crediting and Treatment of Contributions, and National Insurance Numbers) Regulations 2001 (treatment for the purpose of any contributory benefit of contributions under the Act paid late through ignorance or error).

History – In reg. 155A(2)(e) words "regulation 52(8)" substituted by SI 2004/770, reg. 26, with effect from 6 April 2004, only in respect of contributions payable in respect of the year 2003–04 and subsequent years.

Reg. 155A(2)(f) omitted by SI 2016/352, reg. 17, with effect from 6 April 2016, subject to savings in relation to rights or obligations arising in connection with tax years beginning before 6 April 2016 (and for savings purposes, references to repealed provisions of the *Pension Schemes Act 1993* are to be read as though such provisions were still in force). Former reg. 155A(2)(f) read as follows:

"(f) whether a late application under regulation 54(3) for the return of a Class 1 contribution paid at the wrong rate should be admitted;".

In reg. 155A(3)(a) words "regulation 52(1)" substituted by SI 2004/770, reg. 26, with effect from 6 April 2004, only in respect of contributions payable in respect of the year 2003–04 and subsequent years.

In reg. 155A(3)(b) words "regulation 52A(1)" substituted by SI 2004/770, reg. 26, with effect from 6 April 2004, only in respect of contributions payable in respect of the year 2003–04 and subsequent years.

Reg. 155A inserted by SI 2002/2366, reg. 18, with effect from 8 October 2002.

NORTHERN IRELAND

156(1) Except where otherwise provided, the provisions of these Regulations shall apply to Northern Ireland as they apply to Great Britain.

156(2) Paragraph (1) does not apply to the provisions of Case B of Part 9 of these Regulations.

156(3) In the application of these Regulations to Northern Ireland other than this regulation, a reference to a provision of an enactment, which applies only to Great Britain, shall be construed so far as necessary as including a reference to the corresponding enactment applying in Northern Ireland.

156(4) Schedule 7 contains a Table showing, in column (1) details of enactments applying in Great Britain for which the enactment shown in column (2) is the corresponding enactment in Northern Ireland. Neither this paragraph nor Schedule 7 limits the operation of paragraph (3).

156(5) The reference –

(a) to an Order in Council under section 179 of the Administration Act shall be taken to include a reference to an order under section 155 of the Social Security Administration (Northern Ireland) Act 1992; and

(b) to the Secretary of State in regulation 59(3)(b) shall be taken to include a reference to the Department of Health and Social Services for Northern Ireland, but any other reference to the Secretary of State shall be taken to include a reference to the Department for Social Development.

156(6) The rate of interest prescribed for the purposes of regulations 75 and 76(1) and paragraphs 17(1) and 18(1) and (3) of Schedule 4, in their application to Northern Ireland, is the rate applicable under paragraph 6(3)(a) of Schedule 1 to the Social Security Contributions and Benefits (Northern Ireland) Act 1992 for the purpose of paragraph 6(3) of Schedule 1 to the Social Security Contributions and Benefits Act 1992.

History – In reg. 156(2), the words "or Case D" omitted by SI 2003/964, reg. 11 with effect from 6 April 2003.

REVOCATIONS

157(1) The Regulations specified in column (1) of Parts I and II of Schedule 8 are revoked to the extent mentioned in column (3) of that Schedule.

Part I of Schedule 8 contains revocations of provisions which extend either to Great Britain or to the whole of the United Kingdom, whilst Part II contains revocations of provisions which extend only to Northern Ireland.

157(2) Anything done, permitted to be done or required to be done, under any provision of the instruments revoked by these Regulations shall be treated as though it had been done or were permitted or required to be done (as the case may be) under the corresponding provision of these Regulations.

157(3) Without prejudice to the generality of paragraph (2), a person who would have been liable, immediately before the revocation of regulation 53A(4) of the Social Security (Contributions) Regulations 1979 by paragraph (1) to a penalty in respect of a failure which commenced before these Regulations come into force shall continue to be liable to that penalty.

157(4) The revocation by these Regulations of an instrument which itself revoked an earlier instrument subject to savings does not prevent the continued operation of those savings, insofar as they are capable of continuing to have effect.

157(5) In this regulation **"instrument"** includes a Statutory Rule of Northern Ireland.

SCHEDULES

SCHEDULE 1 – PROVISIONS CONFERRING POWERS EXERCISED IN MAKING THESE REGULATIONS

In this Schedule–

"the 1998 Act" means the Social Security Act 1998;

"the 1998 Order" means the Social Security (Northern Ireland) Order 1998;

"the 2000 Act" means the Child Support, Pensions and Social Security Act 2000;

"the Transfer Act" means the Social Security Contributions (Transfer of Functions, etc.) Act 1999;

"the Transfer Order" means the Social Security Contributions (Transfer of Functions, etc.) (Northern Ireland) Order 1999; and

"the Welfare Reform Act" means the Welfare Reform and Pensions Act 1999.

Part I – Powers Exercised by the Treasury

Column (1) *Enabling power*	*Column (2)* *Relevant amendment*
Social Security Contributions and Benefits Act 1992	
Section 1(6) and (7)	Paragraph 56(3) of Schedule 7 to the 1998 Act and paragraph 1(3) of Schedule 3 to the Transfer Act.
Section 3(2), (2A), (3) and (5)	Sections 48 and 49 of the 1998 Act and paragraph 3 of Schedule 3 to the Transfer Act.
Section 4(5), (6) and (7)	Section 50 of the 1998 Act, paragraph 4 of Schedule 3 to the Transfer Act and section 74(3) of the 2000 Act.
Section 5(1), (4) and (6)	Paragraph 1 of Schedule 9 to the Welfare Reform Act.
Section 6(3), (6) and (7)	Paragraph 2 of Schedule 9 to the Welfare Reform Act.
Section 6A(2) and (7)	Paragraph 3 of Schedule 9 to the Welfare Reform Act
Section 10(9)	
Section 10A(7)	Paragraph 11 of Schedule 3 to the Transfer Act.
Section 11(3), (4) and (5)	Paragraph 12 of Schedule 3 to the Transfer Act and article 3 of S.I.2001/477.
Section 12(6)	Paragraph 13 of Schedule 3 to the Transfer Act.
Section 13(1) and (7)	Paragraph 14(2) and (4) of Schedule 3 to the Transfer Act, and article 4 of S.I. 2001/477
Section 14(1), (2) and (5)	Paragraph 15 of Schedule 3 to the Transfer Act.
Section 19(1) to (5A)	Paragraph 19(2) of Schedule 3 to the Transfer Act.
Section 19A(2) and (3)	Paragraph 20 of Schedule 3, and paragraph 4 of Schedule 9, to the Transfer Act.
Section 116(2) and (3)	Paragraph 28 of Schedule 2 to the Jobseekers Act 1995, paragraph 67 of Schedule 7 to the 1998 Act and paragraph 22 of Schedule 3, and paragraph 5 of Schedule 7, to the Transfer Act.
Section 117	Paragraph 68 of Schedule 7 to the 1998 Act and paragraph 23 of Schedule 3 to, and paragraph 6 of Schedule 7 to, the Transfer Act.
Section 118	Paragraph 24 of Schedule 3 to the Transfer Act.
Section 119	Paragraph 69 of Schedule 7 to the 1998 Act and paragraph 25 of Schedule 3, and paragraph 7 of Schedule 7, to the Transfer Act.
Section 120	Paragraph 70 of Schedule 7 to the 1998 Act and paragraph 26 of Schedule 3, and paragraph 8 of Schedule 7, to the Transfer Act.
Section 122(1)	
Section 175(3), (4) and (5)	Paragraph 29(4) of Schedule 3 to the Transfer Act.
Schedule 1	
Paragraph 7A	Paragraph 37 of Schedule 3, and paragraph 6 Schedule 9, to the Transfer Act.
Paragraph 7B	Paragraph 38 of Schedule 3, and paragraph 7 of Schedule 9, and the relevant entry in Part I of Schedule 10, to the Transfer Act, and section 76(3) and (4) of the 2000 Act.

Column (1) *Enabling power*	*Column (2)* *Relevant amendment*
Paragraph 8(1)(a), (c), (ca), (e), (f), (g), (h), (ia), (j), (k), (l), (m) and (q) and (1A)	Paragraph 14 of Schedule 5 to the Pensions Act 1995, paragraph 77(15) and (16) of Schedule 7 to the 1998 Act, paragraph 39 of Schedule 3 to the Transfer Act and section 74(5) and 77(4)and (5) of the 2000 Act.
Paragraph 11	Paragraph 41 of Schedule 3 to the Transfer Act.
Social Security Contributions and Benefits (Northern Ireland) Act 1992	
Section 1(6) and (7)	Paragraph 38(3) of Schedule 6 to the 1998 Order and paragraph 2 of Schedule 3 to the Transfer Order.
Section 3(2), (2A), (3) and (5)	Articles 45 and 46 of the 1998 Order and paragraph 4 of Schedule 3 to the Transfer Order
Section 4(5), (6) and (7)	Paragraph 5 of Schedule 3 to the Transfer Order and section 78(3) of the 2000 Act.
Section 5(1), (4) and (6)	Paragraph 1 of Schedule 10 to the Welfare Reform Act.
Section 6(3), (6) and (7)	Paragraph 2 of Schedule 10 to the Welfare Reform Act.
Section 6A(2) and (7)	
Section 10(9)	
Section 10A(7)	Paragraph 12 of Schedule 3 to the Transfer Order.
Section 11(3), (4) and (5)	Paragraph 13 of Schedule 3 to the Transfer Order and article 3 of S.I. 2001/477.
Section 12(6)	Paragraph 14 of Schedule 3 to the Transfer Order.
Section 13(1) and (7)	Paragraph 15(2) and (4) of Schedule 3 to the Transfer Order and article 4 of S.I. 2001/477.
Section 14(1), (2) and (5)	Paragraph 16 of Schedule 3 to the Transfer Order.
Section 19(1) to (5A)	Paragraph 19(2) of Schedule 3 to the Transfer Order.
Section 116(2) and (3)	Paragraph 11 of Schedule 2 to the Jobseekers (Northern Ireland) Order 1995, paragraph 49 of Schedule 6 to the 1998 Order and paragraph 22 of Schedule 3, and paragraph 4 of Schedule 6 to the Transfer Order.
Section 117	Paragraph 50 of Schedule 6 to the 1998 Order and paragraph 23 of Schedule 3, and paragraph 5 of Schedule 6, to the Transfer Order.
Section 118	Paragraph 24 of Schedule 3 to the Transfer Order.
Section 119	Paragraph 51 of Schedule 6 to the 1998 Order and paragraph 25 of Schedule 3, and paragraph 6 of Schedule 6, to the Transfer Order.
Section 121(1)	
Section 171(3), (4), (5) and (10)	Paragraph 36 of Schedule 1 to the Social Security (Incapacity for Work) (Northern Ireland) Order 1994.
Schedule 1	
Paragraph 7A	Paragraph 36 of Schedule 3, and paragraph 4 of Schedule 8, to the Transfer Order.
Paragraph 7B	Paragraph 37 of Schedule 3, paragraph 5 of Schedule 8, and the relevant entry in Part I of Schedule 9 to the Transfer Order and section 80(3) and (4) of the 2000 Act.

Column (1) *Enabling power*	*Column (2)* *Relevant amendment*
Paragraph 8(1)(a), (c), (ca), (e), (f), (g), (h), (ia), (j), (k), (l), (m) and (q) and (1A)	Paragraph 11 of Schedule 3 to the Pensions (Northern Ireland) Order 1995, paragraph 58(15) and (16) of Schedule 6 to the 1998 Order, paragraph 38 of Schedule 3 to the Transfer Order and sections 78(5) and 81(4) and (5) of the 2000 Act.
Paragraph 10	Paragraph 19 of Schedule 21 to the Friendly Societies Act 1992 and paragraph 40 of Schedule 3 to the Transfer Order.

Part II – Powers Exercised by the Commissioners of Inland Revenue

Column (1) *Enabling power*	*Column (2)* *Relevant amendment*
Social Security Contributions and Benefits Act 1992	
Section 17(1), (2), (3) and (4)	Paragraph 6 of Schedule 1, paragraph 17 of Schedule 3, and the relevant entry in Part I of Schedule 10, to the Transfer Act.
Section 18	Paragraph 7 of Schedule 1, and paragraph 18 of Schedule 3, to the Transfer Act and article 5 of S.I. 2001/477.
Section 122(1)	
Schedule 1	
Paragraph 1	Section 148(2), (3) and (4) of the Pensions Act 1995, paragraph 77(2), (3) and (4) of Schedule 7 to the 1998 Act, paragraph 31 of Schedule 3 to the Transfer Act and paragraph 78(2) to (5) of Schedule 12, and Part VI of Schedule 13, to the Welfare Reform Act.
Paragraph 2	Paragraph 32 of Schedule 3 to the Transfer Act.
Paragraph 3	Section 55 of, and paragraph 77(5) of Schedule 7 to the 1998 Act, paragraph 33 of Schedule 3 to the Transfer Act and section 77(1) of and Part VIII of Schedule 9 to the 2000 Act.
Paragraph 3B(11)	
Paragraph 4	Paragraph 16 of Schedule 1, and paragraph 34 of Schedule 3 to the Transfer Act.
Paragraph 5	Paragraph 77(6) of Schedule 7 to the 1998 Act, paragraph 34 of Schedule 3 to the Transfer Act and section 74(4) of the 2000 Act.
Paragraph 5A	Paragraph 34 of Schedule 3 to the Transfer Act.
Paragraph 6	Paragraph 77(8), (9) and (11) of Schedule 7 to, and the relevant entry in Schedule 8 to the 1998 Act and paragraph 17 of Schedule 1, paragraph 35 of Schedule 3, paragraph 9 of Schedule 7, paragraph 5 of Schedule 9, and the relevant entry in Part I of Schedule 10, to the Transfer Act.
Paragraph 7BA	
Social Security Administration Act 1992	
Section 113	Section 60 of the 1998 Act, paragraph 5 of Schedule 5 to the Transfer Act and paragraph 7 of Schedule 6 to the 2000 Act.

Column (1) *Enabling power*	*Column (2)* *Relevant amendment*
Section 162(12)	Paragraph 52(11) of Schedule 3 to the Transfer Act.
Section 191	
Social Security Contributions and Benefits (Northern Ireland) Act 1992	
Section 17	Paragraph 7 of Schedule 1, paragraph 17 of Schedule 3, and the relevant entry in Part I of Schedule 9, to the Transfer Order.
Section 18	Paragraph 8 of Schedule 1, and paragraph 18 of Schedule 3 to the Transfer Order and article 5 of S.I. 2001/477.
Section 121(1)	
Schedule 1	
Paragraph 1	Article 145(2), (3) and (4) of the Pensions (Northern Ireland) Order 1995, paragraph 58(1) to (4) of Schedule 6 to the 1998 Order, paragraph 30 of Schedule 3 to the Transfer Order and paragraph 86(2) to (5) of Schedule 12, and the relevant entry in Part VI of Schedule 13, to the Welfare Reform Act.
Paragraph 2	Paragraph 31 of Schedule 3 to the Transfer Order.
Paragraph 3	Article 52 of, and paragraph 58(5) of Schedule 6 to, the 1998 Order, paragraph 32 of Schedule 3 to the Transfer Order, section 81(1) of, and the relevant entry in Part VIII of Schedule 9 to, the 2000 Act.
Paragraph 3B(11)	
Paragraph 4	Paragraph 16 of Schedule 1, and paragraph 33 of Schedule 3, to the Transfer Order.
Paragraph 5	Paragraph 58(6) of Schedule 7 to the 1998 Order, paragraph 34 of Schedule 3 to the Transfer Order and section 78(4) of the 2000 Act.
Paragraph 5A	Paragraph 33 of Schedule 3 to the Transfer Order.
Paragraph 6	Paragraph 58(8), (9) and (11) of Schedule 6, and the relevant entry in Schedule 7, to the 1998 Order, paragraph 20 of Schedule 1, paragraph 34 of Schedule 3, paragraph 7 of Schedule 6, paragraph 3 of Schedule 8, and the relevant entry in Part I of Schedule 9, to the Transfer Order.
Paragraph 7BA	
Social Security Administration (Northern Ireland) Act 1992	
Section 107	Article 56 of the 1998 Order, paragraph 5 of Schedule 4 to the Transfer Order and paragraph 7 of Schedule 6 to the Child Support, Pensions and Social Security Act (Northern Ireland) 2000.
Section 142(12)	Paragraph 45(12) of Schedule 3 to the Transfer Order.
Section 167(1)	
Finance Act 1999	
Section 133(1)	

SCHEDULE 2 – CALCULATION OF EARNINGS FOR THE PURPOSES OF EARNINGS-RELATED CONTRIBUTIONS IN PARTICULAR CASES

Regulation 24

CALCULATION OF EARNINGS

1 This Schedule contains rules for the calculation of earnings in the assessment of earnings-related contributions in particular cases.

Derivations – SI 1979/591, Sch. 1ZB, para. 1.

CALCULATION OF EARNINGS IN RESPECT OF BENEFICIAL INTEREST IN ASSETS WITHIN PART IV OF SCHEDULE 3

2(1) Except where paragraph 3, 4, 5 or 6 applies, the amount of earnings comprised in any payment by way of the conferment of any beneficial interest in any asset specified in Part IV of Schedule 3, and which falls to be taken into account in the calculation of a person's earnings shall be calculated or estimated at a price which that beneficial interest might reasonably be expected to fetch if sold in the open market on the day on which it is conferred.

2(2) For the purposes of sub-paragraph (1), where any asset is not quoted on a recognised stock exchange within the meaning of section 841 of the Taxes Act, it shall be assumed that, in the open market which is postulated, there is available to any prospective purchaser of the beneficial interest in the asset in question all the information which a prudent prospective purchaser might reasonably require if he were proposing to purchase it from a willing vendor by private treaty and at arm's length.

Derivations – SI 1979/591, Sch. 1ZB, para. 2.

VALUATION OF BENEFICIAL INTEREST IN UNITS IN A UNIT TRUST SCHEME

3 The amount of earnings which is comprised in any payment by way of the conferment of a beneficial interest in any units in a unit trust scheme (within the meaning of section 237 of the Financial Services and Markets Act 2000) having a published selling price and which falls to be taken into account in the calculation of a person's earnings shall be calculated or estimated by reference to the published selling price on the day in question.

Here **"published selling price"** means the lowest selling price published on the date on which the payment in question is made, and where no such price is published on that date, it means the lowest selling price published on the last previous date on which such a price was published.

History – In para. 3 the words "237 of the Financial Services and Markets Act 2000" substituted by SI 2001/3629, reg. 190 and 191 which came into force on 1 December 2001.

Derivations – SI 1979/591, Sch. 1ZB, para. 3.

CONFERMENT OF A BENEFICIAL INTEREST IN AN OPTION TO ACQUIRE AN ASSET FALLING WITHIN PART IV OF SCHEDULE 3

4 The amount of earnings which is comprised in a payment by way of the conferment of a beneficial interest in an option to acquire any asset falling within Part IV of Schedule 3 shall be calculated or estimated by reference to the amount which would be comprised in accordance with paragraph 2 or, if paragraph 3, 5 or 6 would apply in accordance with that paragraph, in a payment by way of the conferment of a beneficial interest–

(a) in the asset which may be acquired by the exercise of the option; or

(b) where that asset (the first asset) may be exchanged for another asset (the second asset) and the value of the beneficial interest in the second asset is greater than that in the first, in that second asset;

on the day on which the beneficial interest in the option is conferred.

The amount shall be reduced by the amount or value, or, if variable, the least amount or value, of the consideration for which the asset may be so acquired.

Derivations – SI 1979/591, Sch. 1ZB, para. 4.

READILY CONVERTIBLE ASSETS

5(1) The amount of earnings which is comprised in–

(a) any payment by way of the conferment of a beneficial interest in any asset falling within Part III of Schedule 3;

(b) any payment by way of the conferment of a beneficial interest in any asset falling within Part IV of Schedule 3 which is a readily convertible asset;

(c) any payment by way of–

(i) a voucher, stamp or similar document falling within paragraph 12 of Part IV of that Schedule where the asset for which it is capable of being converted is a readily convertible asset,

(ii) a non-cash voucher not falling within Part V (whether or not also falling within paragraph 12 of Part IV of that Schedule) which is capable of being exchanged for a readily convertible asset,

and which is to be taken into account in calculating a person's earnings, shall be calculated in accordance with sub-paragraphs (2) to (5).

5(2) In the case of an asset falling within paragraph 1 of Part III of Schedule 3, the amount is the best estimate that can reasonably be made of the amount of general earnings in respect of the provision of the asset.

5(3) In the case of an asset falling within paragraph 2of Part III of Schedule 3, the amount is the best estimate that can reasonably be made of the amount of general earnings in respect of the enhancement of its value.

5(4) In the case of a voucher, stamp or similar document falling within–

(a) sub-paragraph (1)(c); or

(b) paragraph 3 of Part III of Schedule 3,

the amount is the best estimate that can reasonably be made of the amount of general earnings in respect of the provision of any asset for which the voucher is capable of being exchanged.

5(5) In the case of an asset falling within sub-paragraph (1)(b), the amount is the best estimate that can reasonably be made of the amount of general earnings in respect of the provision of the asset.

History – In para. 5 the words "the amount of general earnings" substituted throughout by SI 2003/2085, reg. 7(2) with effect from 1 September 2003.

Derivations – SI 1979/591, Sch. 1ZB, para. 5.

ASSETS NOT READILY CONVERTIBLE: BENEFICIAL INTERESTS IN ALCOHOLIC LIQUOR ON WHICH DUTY HAS NOT BEEN PAID, GEMSTONES AND CERTAIN VOUCHERS AND NON-CASH VOUCHERS

6 The amount of earnings comprised in any payment by way of the conferment of a beneficial interest in–

(a) an asset which–

(i) falls within paragraph 9 or 10 of Part IV of Schedule 3 (payments by way of alcoholic liquor on which duty has not been paid or by way of gemstones not to be disregarded as payments in kind), and

(ii) is not a readily convertible asset;

(b) a voucher, stamp or similar document which falls within paragraph 12 of Part IV of that Schedule and which is not capable of being exchanged for a readily convertible asset; or

(c) a non-cash voucher not excluded by virtue of Part V of that Schedule and which falls within paragraph 12 of Part IV of that Schedule (assets not to be disregarded as payments in kind) which is not capable of being exchanged for a readily convertible asset;

shall be calculated or estimated on the basis of the cost of the asset in question.

Here **"the cost of the asset"** in relation to any voucher, stamp or similar document includes the cost of any asset for which that voucher, stamp or similar document is capable of being exchanged.

Derivations – SI 1979/591, Sch. 1ZB, para. 6.

CONVERTIBLE AND RESTRICTED INTERESTS IN SECURITIES AND CONVERTIBLE AND RESTRICTED SECURITIES

7(1) The amount of earnings comprised in any payment by way of the conferment of–

(a) a convertible interest in securities;

(b) a restricted interest in securities; or

(c) an interest in convertible or restricted securities,

falling to be taken into account in computing a person's earnings from employed earner's employment shall be computed in the same manner, and shall be taken into account at the same time, as applies under Chapters 1 to 5 of Part 7 of ITEPA 2003, for the purpose of computing his employment income.

This is subject to the following qualification.

7(2) For the purpose of sub-paragraph (1) no account shall be taken of any relief obtained under sections 428A or 442A of ITEPA 2003 (relief for secondary Class 1 contributions met by employee).

History – Para. 7 substituted by SI 2004/2096, reg. 5 with effect in relation to–

- agreements entered into after 1 September 2004 which are in respect of post-commencement employment income (presumably as defined in NICSPA 2004, s. 3(5)), and
- elections made after that date.

Former para. 7 substituted by SI 2003/2085, reg. 7(3) with effect from 1 September 2003.

Derivations – SI 1979/591, Sch. 1ZB, para. 7.

CONVERTIBLE INTEREST IN SHARES

8 [Omitted by SI 2003/2085, reg. 7(4).]

History – Para. 8 omitted by SI 2003/2085, reg. 7(4) with effect from 1 September 2003.

Derivations – SI 1979/591, Sch. 1ZB, para. 8.

ASSIGNMENT OR RELEASE OF RIGHT TO ACQUIRE SHARES WHERE NEITHER RIGHT NOR SHARES READILY CONVERTIBLE

9 [Omitted by SI 2003/2085, reg. 7(4).]

History – Para. 9 omitted by SI 2003/2085, reg. 7(4) with effect from 1 September 2003.

ASSIGNMENT OR RELEASE OF A RIGHT, ACQUIRED AS DIRECTOR OR EMPLOYEE BEFORE 6TH APRIL 1999, TO ACQUIRE SHARES WHERE NEITHER RIGHT NOR SHARES READILY CONVERTIBLE

10 [Omitted by SI 2003/2085, reg. 7(4).]

History – Para. 10 omitted by SI 2003/2085, reg. 7(4) with effect from 1 September 2003.

Derivations – SI 1979/591, Sch. 1ZB, para. 10.

EXERCISE OF A REPLACEMENT RIGHT TO ACQUIRE SHARES, OBTAINED AS AN EARNER BEFORE 6TH APRIL 1999

11(1) This paragraph applies if–

(a) an earner obtained, before 6th April 1999, a right to acquire shares in a body corporate;

(b) the earner subsequently obtained a replacement right (within the meaning given in paragraph 16A(3) of Part 9 of Schedule 3);

(c) the replacement right is exercised;

(d) paragraph 11A of this Schedule does not apply; and

(e) paragraph 16A of Part 9 of Schedule 3 does not apply because sub-paragraph (4) of that paragraph is not satisfied.

11(2) If this paragraph applies, the amount of earnings comprised in any payment realised by the exercise of the replacement right shall be calculated or estimated in accordance with sub-paragraph (3).

11(3) The basis for calculating the amount of a gain realised by the exercise of the replacement right shall be the best estimate that can reasonably be made of the amount found as follows.

Step One

Find the amount (if any) by which the sum of–

(a) the market value of the shares acquired by the exercise of the replacement right; and

(b) the market value of any other benefit in money or money's worth obtained by the exercise of the replacement right;

exceeds the amount required to be paid for the exercise of that right.

Step Two

Find the amount (if any) by which the market value of the shares, which were the subject of the right assigned or released on the first occasion in respect of which the condition in paragraph 16A(4) of Part 9 of Schedule 3 is not satisfied, exceeds the amount required to be paid for the exercise of that right immediately before that time.

Step Three

Subtract the amount found by Step Two from the amount found by Step One.

Step Four

Subtract from the result of Step Three–

(a) any amount taken into account in computing the earner's earnings for the purposes of Class 1 contributions at the time of the grant of the first right; and

(b) any amount given by or on behalf of the earner as consideration for the acquisition of the first right or any replacement right, but "consideration" does not include the value of any right assigned or released in exchange for the acquisition of a replacement right.

Subject to the following qualification, the result of this step is the amount of earnings referred to in sub-paragraph (2) above.

If the result of this step is a negative value, it is treated as nil for the purposes of computing the earner's earnings.

11(4) In this paragraph–

(a) **"market value"** means the price which the shares which are the subject of the right in question might reasonably be expected to fetch on a sale in the open market;

(b) neither the consideration given for the grant of any right to acquire shares, nor any entire consideration, shall be taken to include the performance of the duties in connection with the office or employment by reason of which the right was granted;

(c) no amount or value of the consideration given for the grant of a right to acquire shares shall be taken into account more than once;

(d) **"shares"** includes stock;

(e) **"body corporate"** includes–

(i) a body corporate constituted under the law of a country or territory outside the United Kingdom; and

(ii) an unincorporated association wherever constituted; and

(f) references to the release of a share option include agreeing to the restriction of the exercise of the option.

History – Para. 11 substituted by SI 2003/2085, reg. 7(5) with effect from 1 September 2003.
In former para. 11(1) the words "except where paragraph 11A applies" inserted by SI 2003/1059, reg. 3(2) with effect from 10 April 2003.

Derivations – SI 1979/591, Sch. 1ZB, para. 11.

EXERCISE, ASSIGNMENT OR RELEASE OF SHARE OPTION – MARKET VALUE OF OPTION OR RESULTING SHARES INCREASED BY THINGS DONE OTHERWISE THAN FOR GENUINE COMMERCIAL PURPOSES

11A(1) This paragraph applies for calculating or estimating the amount of earnings which is comprised in a payment which–

(a) would be disregarded in the computation of earnings for the purposes of earnings-related contributions by virtue of paragraph 16 of Part 9 of Schedule 3; but

(b) is not disregarded because paragraph 17 of that Part applies to it.

11A(2) If this paragraph applies, the amount of earnings to be taken into account for the purpose of earnings related contributions is the amount which would, but for paragraph 16 or 16A of Part 9 of Schedule 3, have been taken into account by virtue of section 4(4)(a) of the Act.

This is subject to the following qualification.

11A(3) If–

(a) the right to acquire shares in a body corporate is not capable of being exercised more than ten years after the date on which it was obtained,

(b) an amount of earnings was taken into account for the purpose of earnings-related contributions in respect of the earner's obtaining that right, at the time he obtained it (**"the deductible amount"**), and

(c) no exercise, assignment or release of the whole or any part of–

(i) that right,

(ii) any right replacing that right (**"a replacement right"**), or

(iii) any subsequent replacement right,

has occurred on or after 10th April 2003,

the deductible amount may be deducted from the amount otherwise to be taken into account by virtue of this paragraph.

History – In para. 11A(2) words "or 16A" inserted by SI 2003/2085, reg. 7(6) with effect from 1 September 2003.
Para. 11A inserted by SI 2003/1059, reg. 3(3) with effect from 10 April 2003.

INTERPRETATION OF PARAGRAPHS 9, 10 AND 11

12 [Omitted by SI 2003/2085, reg. 7(7).]

History – Para. 12 omitted by SI 2003/2085, reg. 7(7) with effect from 1 September 2003.

Derivations – SI 1979/591, Sch. 1ZB, para. 12.

APPORTIONMENT OF A PAYMENT TO A RETIREMENT BENEFITS SCHEME FOR BENEFIT OF TWO OR MORE PEOPLE

History – In the heading, "to" substituted by SI 2004/770, reg. 27, with effect from 6 April 2004.

13 [Omitted by SI 2006/576, reg. 7.]

History – Para. 13 omitted by SI 2006/576, reg. 7, with effect from 6 April 2006.
Derivations – SI 1979/591, Sch. 1ZB, para. 13.

VALUATION OF NON-CASH VOUCHERS

14(1) The amount of earnings comprised in any payment by way of a non-cash voucher which is not otherwise disregarded by these Regulations and which falls to be taken into account in calculating an employed earner's earnings shall be calculated or estimated on the basis set out in sub-paragraph (2).

14(1A) This paragraph is subject to paragraph 14A (valuation of non-cash vouchers provided under optional remuneration arrangements).

14(2) The basis referred to in sub-paragraph (1) is that of an amount equal to the expense incurred ("the chargeable expense")–

(a) by the person at whose cost the voucher and the money, goods or services, for which it is capable of being exchanged, are provided;

(b) in, or in connection with, that provision; and any money, goods or services obtained by the employed earner or any other person in exchange for the voucher shall be disregarded.

This is subject to the following qualifications.

14(3) For the purposes of sub-paragraph (2) the chargeable expense shall be reduced by any part of that which the employed earner makes good to the person incurring it.

14(4) The valuation of qualifying childcare vouchers is determined in accordance with paragraph 7 of Part 5 of Schedule 3.

History – Para. 14(1A) inserted by SI 2018/120, reg. 5(2), with effect from 6 April 2018.
In para. 14(2) the word "qualifications" substituted by SI 2005/778, reg. 8 with effect from 6 April 2005.
Para. 14(3) substituted by SI 2013/622, reg. 39, with effect from 6 April 2013 in relation to the tax year 2013–14 and subsequent tax years.
In para. 14(3)(b) the words "15 pence," substituted by SI 2001/2412, reg. 4, operative from 26 July 2001.
Para. 14(4) inserted by SI 2005/778, reg. 8 with effect from 6 April 2005.
Derivations – SI 1979/591, Sch. 1ZB, para. 14.

VALUATION OF NON-CASH VOUCHERS PROVIDED UNDER OPTIONAL REMUNERATION ARRANGEMENTS

14A(1) This paragraph applies for calculating the amount of earnings comprised in any payment by way of a non-cash voucher which falls to be taken into account in calculating an employed earner's earnings, if this is made pursuant to optional remuneration arrangements.

14A(2) The amount of earnings is the relevant amount.

14A(3) To find the relevant amount, first determine which (if any) is the greater of–

(a) the chargeable expense (without taking account of the qualification in paragraph 14(3)); or

(b) the amount foregone.

14A(4) If the amount in sub-paragraph (3)(a) is greater than or equal to the amount foregone, the **"relevant amount"** is the chargeable expense (taking account of the qualification in paragraph 14(3)).

14A(5) Otherwise, **"the relevant amount"** is the difference between–

(a) the amount foregone; and

(b) any part of the chargeable expense that the employed earner makes good to the person incurring it.

14A(6) For the purposes of sub-paragraphs (3) to (5), assume that the amount in sub-paragraph (3)(a) is zero if the condition in sub-paragraph (7) is met.

14A(7) The condition is that the payment would be exempt from income tax but for section 228A(1) of ITEPA 2003(1).

14A(8) In this paragraph–

(a) **"chargeable expense"** has the meaning given in paragraph 14; and

(b) ***"amount foregone"*** *means* the amount foregone with respect to the benefit of the non-cash voucher for the purposes of the benefits code as mentioned in section 69B of ITEPA 2003(2).

14A(9) Where a payment by way of a non-cash voucher is made partly pursuant to optional remuneration arrangements and partly otherwise than pursuant to such arrangements, these Regulations are to apply with any modifications (including provision for just and reasonable apportionments) that may be required for ensuring that it is treated–

(a) in accordance with this paragraph so far as it is made pursuant to optional remuneration arrangements; and

(b) in accordance with any other treatment that is applicable so far as it is made otherwise than pursuant to such arrangements.

History – Reg. 14A inserted by SI 2018/120, reg. 5(3), with effect from 6 April 2018.

APPORTIONMENT OF EARNINGS COMPRISED IN A CASH OR NON-CASH VOUCHER PROVIDED FOR BENEFIT OF TWO OR MORE EMPLOYED EARNERS

15(1) The amount of earnings comprised in any payment by way of a cash voucher or a non-cash voucher provided for the benefit of two or more employed earners and which falls to be taken into account in calculating the earnings of each of those earners shall be calculated or estimated on the basis set out in whichever of sub-paragraphs (2) or (3) applies.

15(2) If the respective proportion of the benefit of the voucher to which each of those earners is entitled is known at the time of the payment, the basis is that of a separate payment equal to that proportion.

15(3) In any case where the respective proportions are not known at the time of the payment, the basis is equal apportionment between all those earners.

15(4) In this paragraph–

(a) **"chargeable expense"** has the same meaning, and is calculated in the same way, as in paragraph 14; and

(b) if an employed earner makes good any part of the chargeable expense to the person incurring it, that chargeable expense in relation to that employed earner shall be reduced by that part.

Derivations – SI 1979/591, Sch. 1ZB, para. 15.

SCHEDULE 3 – PAYMENTS TO BE DISREGARDED IN THE CALCULATION OF EARNINGS FOR THE PURPOSES OF EARNINGS-RELATED CONTRIBUTIONS

Regulation 25

Part I – Introductory

INTRODUCTION

1(1) This Schedule contains provisions about payments which are to be disregarded in the calculation of earnings for the purposes of earnings-related contributions.

1(2) Part II contains provisions about the treatment of payments in kind.

1(3) Parts III and IV specify payments by way of assets which are not to be disregarded by virtue of paragraph 1 of Part II.

1(4) Part V specifies non-cash vouchers which are to be disregarded by virtue of paragraph 1 of Part II.

1(5) In calculating earnings there are also to be disregarded–

(a) the pensions and pension contributions specified in Part VI;

(b) the payments in respect of training and similar courses specified in Part VII;

(c) the travelling, relocation and overseas expenses specified in Part VIII;

(d) the incentives by way of securities specified in Part IX; and

(e) the miscellaneous payments specified in Part X.

History – In para. 1(5)(d) words "incentives by way of securities" substituted by SI 2003/2085, reg. 9 with effect from 1 September 2003.

Derivations – SI 1979/591, Sch. 1ZC, Pt. I, para. 1.

INTERPRETATION

2 In this Schedule, unless the context otherwise requires–

(a) a reference to a numbered Part is a reference to the Part of this Schedule which bears that number;

(b) a reference in a Part to a numbered paragraph is a reference to the paragraph of that Part which bears that number; and

(c) a reference in a paragraph to a lettered or numbered sub-paragraph is a reference to the sub-paragraph of that paragraph which bears that letter or number.

Derivations – SI 1979/591, Sch. 1ZC, Pt. I, para. 2.

Part II – Payments In Kind

CERTAIN PAYMENTS IN KIND TO BE DISREGARDED

1 A payment in kind, or by way of the provision of services, board and lodging or other facilities is to be disregarded in the calculation of earnings.

This is subject to paragraph 2 and to any provision about a payment in kind of a particular description or in particular circumstances in any other Part of this Schedule.

Derivations – SI 1979/591, Sch. 1ZC, Pt. II, para. 1.

PAYMENTS BY WAY OF ASSETS NOT TO BE DISREGARDED

2(1) Payments falling within paragraph 1 do not include any payment by way of–

(a) the conferment of any beneficial interest in–

(i) any asset mentioned in Part III or Part IV,

(ii) any contract of long-term insurance which falls within paragraph I, III or VI of Part II of Schedule 1 to the Financial Services and Markets Act 2000 (Regulated Activities) Order 2001;

(b) a non-cash voucher not of a description mentioned in Part V or to which paragraph 4 of Part X applies.

2(2) Sub-paragraph (1)(a)(i) is subject to the qualification that an asset, which falls within either Part III or Part IV, shall nevertheless be disregarded under paragraph 1 if no liability to income tax arises by virtue of section 323 of ITEPA 2003 (long service awards).

2(3) For the purposes of sub-paragraph (1)(a)(ii), if the contract–

(a) falls within Part II of Schedule 1 to the Financial Services and Markets Act 2000 (Regulated Activities) Order 2001 and Part I of that Schedule; or

(b) is treated for the purposes of that Order as falling within Part II of that Schedule by Article 3(3) of that Order,

that contract shall be treated as a contract of long-term insurance.

History – In Sch. 3, Pt. II, para. 2(2) words "if no liability to income tax arises by virtue of section 323 of ITEPA 2003 (long service awards)" substituted by SI 2004/770, reg. 28, with effect from 6 April 2004.

Sch. 3, Pt. II, para. 2(1)(a)(ii) substituted by SI 2001/3629, reg. 190 and 192 which came into force on 1 December 2001.

In Sch. 3, Pt. II, para. 2(3), the words from "contract" (where it occurs first) to the end of sub-para. (3) (i.e. including all of (3)(a) and (b)) substituted by SI 2001/3629, reg. 190 and 192 which came into force on 1 December 2001.

Derivations – SI 1979/591, Sch. 1ZC, Pt. II, para. 2.

Part III – Payments by Way of Readily Convertible Assets Not Disregarded As Payments In Kind

1 A readily convertible asset within the meaning of section 702 of ITEPA 2003.

History – Para. 1 substituted by SI 2003/2085, reg. 10(2) with effect from 1 September 2003.

Derivations – SI 1979/591, Sch. 1ZC, Pt. III, para. 1.

2 An asset which, in accordance with section 697 of ITEPA 2003 (PAYE: enhancing the value of an asset), would be treated, for the purposes of section 696 of that Act, as a readily convertible asset.

History – Para. 2 substituted by SI 2003/2085, reg. 10(2) with effect from 1 September 2003.

Derivations – SI 1979/591, Sch. 1ZC, Pt. III, para. 2.

3 Any voucher, stamp or similar document–

(a) whether used singularly or together with other such vouchers, stamps or documents; and

(b) which is capable of being exchanged for an asset falling within paragraph 1 or 2.

Derivations – SI 1979/591, Sch. 1ZC, Pt. III, para. 3.

Part IV – Payments by Way of Specific Assets Not Disregarded As Payments In Kind

SECURITIES

1 Securities.

History – Para. 1 and heading substituted by SI 2003/2085, reg. 11(a) with effect from 1 September 2003.

Derivations – SI 1979/591, Sch. 1ZC, Pt. IV, para. 1.

CERTAIN DEBENTURES AND OTHER SECURITIES FOR LOANS

2 [Omitted by SI 2003/2085, reg. 11(b).]

History – Para. 2 omitted by SI 2003/2085, reg. 11(b) with effect from 1 September 2003.

Derivations – SI 1979/591, Sch. 1ZC, Pt. IV, para. 2

LOAN STOCK OF PUBLIC AND LOCAL AUTHORITIES

3 [Omitted by SI 2003/2085, reg. 11(b).]

History – Para. 3 omitted by SI 2003/2085, reg. 11(b) with effect from 1 September 2003.

Derivations – SI 1979/591, Sch. 1ZC, Pt. IV, para. 3.

WARRANTS ETC. FOR SHARES, LOAN STOCK AND DEBENTURES

4 [Omitted by SI 2003/2085, reg. 11(b).]

History – Para. 4 omitted by SI 2003/2085, reg. 11(b) with effect from 1 September 2003.

Derivations – SI 1979/591, Sch. 1ZC, Pt. IV, para. 4.

UNITS IN COLLECTIVE INVESTMENT SCHEMES

5 [Omitted by SI 2003/2085, reg. 11(b).]

History – Para. 5 omitted by SI 2003/2085, reg. 11(b) with effect from 1 September 2003.

Derivations – SI 1979/591, Sch. 1ZC, Pt. IV, para. 5.

OPTIONS TO ACQUIRE ASSETS, CURRENCY, PRECIOUS METALS OR OTHER OPTIONS

6 Options to acquire, or dispose of–

(a) currency of the United Kingdom or any other country or territory;

(b) gold, silver, palladium or platinum;

(c) an asset falling within any other paragraph of this Part of this Schedule;

(d) an option to acquire, or dispose of, an asset falling within sub-paragraph (a), (b) or (c).

Derivations – SI 1979/591, Sch. 1ZC, Pt. IV, para. 6.

CONTRACTS FOR FUTURES

7 [Omitted by SI 2003/2085, reg. 11(c).]

History – Para. 7 omitted by SI 2003/2085, reg. 11(c) with effect from 1 September 2003.

Derivations – SI 1979/591, Sch. 1ZC, Pt. IV, para. 7.

CONTRACTS FOR DIFFERENCES OR TO SECURE PROFIT BY REFERENCE TO MOVEMENTS OF INDICES

8 [Omitted by SI 2003/2085, reg. 11(c).]

History – Para. 8 omitted by SI 2003/2085, reg. 11(c) with effect from 1 September 2003.

Derivations – SI 1979/591, Sch. 1ZC, Pt. IV, para. 8.

ALCOHOLIC LIQUOR ON WHICH DUTY HAS NOT BEEN PAID

9 Any alcoholic liquor, within the meaning of section 1 of the Alcoholic Liquor Duties Act 1979, in respect of which no duty has been paid under that Act.

Derivations – SI 1979/591, Sch. 1ZC, Pt. IV, para. 9.

GEMSTONES

10 Any gemstone, including stones such as diamond, emerald, ruby, sapphire, amethyst, jade, opal or topaz and organic gemstones such as amber or pearl, whether cut or uncut and whether or not having an industrial use.

Derivations – SI 1979/591, Sch. 1ZC, Pt. IV, para. 10.

CERTIFICATES ETC. CONFERRING RIGHTS IN RESPECT OF ASSETS

11 Certificates or other instruments which confer–

(a) property rights in respect of any asset falling within paragraphs 1, 9 or 10;

(b) any right to acquire, dispose of, underwrite or convert an asset, being a right to which the holder would be entitled if he held any such asset to which the certificate or instrument relates; or

(c) a contractual right, other than an option, to acquire any such asset otherwise than by subscription.

History – In para. 11(a) "1" substituted by SI 2003/2085, reg. 11(d) with effect from 1 September 2003.

Derivations – SI 1979/591, Sch. 1ZC, Pt. IV, para. 11.

VOUCHERS

12 Any voucher, stamp or similar document–

(a) whether used singularly or together with other such vouchers, stamps or documents; and

(b) which is capable of being exchanged for an asset falling within any other paragraph of this Part.

Derivations – SI 1979/591, Sch. 1ZC, Pt. IV, para. 12.

Part V – Certain Non-cash Vouchers to be Disregarded as Payments in Kind

1(1) Subject to sub-paragraph (2), a non-cash voucher provided, to or for the benefit of the employed earner, by the employer or any other person on his behalf is to be disregarded in the calculation of an employed earner's earnings by virtue of paragraph 1 of Part II only if it falls within any of paragraphs 2 to 9.

1(2) A non-cash voucher may also be disregarded–

(a) by virtue of paragraph 7D of Part VIII (car fuel);

(aa) by virtue of paragraph 7E of Part 8 (van fuel); or

(b) in the circumstances specified in paragraph 4 of Part X (payments by way of incidental overnight expenses).

History – In para. 1(1) "9" substituted for "8" by SI 2007/2091, reg. 2(2), with effect from 14 August 2007.
In para. 1(2)(b) words "incidental overnight expenses" substituted by SI 2004/770, reg. 28, with effect from 6 April 2004.
Para. 1(2)(aa) inserted by SI 2008/607, reg. 4(2)(b), with effect from 6 April 2008.
Para. 1(2) substituted by SI 2002/307, reg. 6, operative from 6 April 2002.

Derivations – SI 1979/591, Sch. 1ZC, Pt. V, para. 1.

2 A non-cash voucher which is not treated as an general earnings from employment for the purposes of section 86 of ITEPA 2003 (transport vouchers under pre-26th March arrangements).

This paragraph only applies in the case of an employee who is in lower paid employment, within the meaning of section 217 of ITEPA 2003.

History – In para. 2 words "general earnings" and "section 86 of ITEPA 2003 (transport vouchers under pre-26th March arrangements)." substituted by SI 2004/770, reg. 28, with effect from 6 April 2004.
In para. 2 words "This paragraph only applies in the case of an employee who is in lower paid employment, within the meaning of section 217 of ITEPA 2003" substituted by SI 2004/770, reg. 28, with effect from 6 April 2004.

Derivations – SI 1979/591, Sch. 1ZC, Pt. V, para. 2.

3 A non-cash voucher exempted from liability to income tax under Chapter 4 of Part 3 by virtue of sections 266(1)(a) or 269 of ITEPA 2003 (exemptions: non-cash vouchers and credit-tokens).

History – Para. 3 substituted for former para. 3 and 4 by SI 2004/770, reg. 28, with effect from 6 April 2004.

Derivations – SI 1979/591, Sch. 1ZC, Pt. V, para. 3.

4 [Sch. 3, Pt. V, para. 3 substituted for para. 3 and 4 by SI 2004/770, reg. 28.]

History – Para. 3 substituted for former para. 3 and 4 by SI 2004/770, reg. 28, with effect from 6 April 2004.

Derivations – SI 1979/591, Sch. 1ZC, Pt. V, para. 4.

5 A non-cash voucher in respect of which no liability to income tax arises by virtue of section 266(1) of ITEPA 2003 to the extent that the voucher is used to obtain anything the direct provision of which would fall within any of the following provisions of that Act–

(a) section 246 (transport between work and home for disabled employees: general);

(b) section 247 (provision of cars for disabled employees);

(c) section 248 (transport home: late night working and failure of car-sharing arrangements);

(d) section 320C (recommended medical treatment).

History – In para. (5)(c), at the end ";" substituted for "." and para. 5(d) inserted by SI 2014/3228, reg. 3, with effect from 1 January 2015.
Para. 5–6 substituted by SI 2003/2958, reg. 5(2), with effect from 10 December 2003.

Derivations – SI 1979/591, Sch. 1ZC, Pt. V, para. 5.

Cross references – ITEPA 2003, s. 266(3), 296: income tax exemption for non-cash vouchers relating to armed forces' leave travel facilities.

ITEPA 2003, s. 242, 266(2): income tax exemption for non-cash vouchers relating to works transport services.
ITEPA 2003, s. 244, 266(2): income tax exemption for non-cash vouchers relating to cycles and safety equipment.
ITEPA 2003, s. 261, 266(3): income tax exemption for non-cash vouchers relating to recreational benefits.

5A A non-cash voucher in respect of which no liability to income tax arises by virtue of section 266(2) of ITEPA 2003 if the voucher evidences entitlement to use anything the direct provision of which would fall within any of the following provisions of that Act–

(a) section 242 (works transport services);
(b) section 243 (support for public bus services);
(c) section 244 (cycles and cyclist's safety equipment);
(d) section 319 (mobile telephones).

History – Para. 5A(d) inserted by SI 2006/2003, reg. 2(2), with effect from 14 August 2006.
Para. 5–6 substituted by SI 2003/2958, reg. 5(2), with effect from 10 December 2003.

5B A non-cash voucher in respect of which no liability to income tax arises by virtue of section 266(3) of ITEPA 2003 if the voucher can be used only to obtain anything the direct provision of which would fall within any of the following provisions of that Act–

(a) section 245 (travelling and subsistence during public transport strikes);
(b) section 261 (recreational benefits);
(c) section 264 (annual parties and functions);
(d) section 296 (armed forces' leave travel facilities);
(e) section 317 (subsidised meals);
(f) section 320A (eye tests and special corrective appliances);

History – Para. 5B(f) inserted by SI 2006/2003, reg. 2(3), with effect from 14 August 2006.
Para. 5–6 substituted by SI 2003/2958, reg. 5(2), with effect from 10 December 2003.

6 A non-cash voucher to the extent that no liability to income tax arises by virtue of any of the following sections of ITEPA 2003–

(a) [omitted by SI 2001/2412, reg. 5;]
(b) section 305 (offshore oil and gas workers: mainland transfers);
(c) section 321 (suggestion awards);
(d) section 323 (long service awards);
(da) section 323A (trivial benefits provided by employers);
(e) section 324 (small gifts from third parties).

History – Para. 6(a) omitted by SI 2001/2412, reg. 5(2)(a), operative from 26 July 2001.
Para. 6(da) inserted by SI 2016/1067, reg. 5, with effect from 28 November 2016.
Para. 5–6 substituted by SI 2003/2958, reg. 5(2), with effect from 10 December 2003.
Derivations – SI 1979/591, Sch. 1ZC, Pt. V, para. 6.

6A [Omitted by SI 2013/622, reg. 40(a)(i).]

History – Para. 6A omitted by SI 2013/622, reg. 40(a)(i), with effect from 6 April 2013 in relation to the tax year 2013–14 and subsequent tax years.
Para. 6A inserted by SI 2001/2412, reg. 5(2)(b), operative from 26 July 2001.
Cross references – ITEPA 2003, s. 89: reduction in taxable benefit for meal vouchers.

INTERPRETATION – QUALIFYING CHILDCARE VOUCHERS

6B In paragraphs 7 and 7A–

(a) **"care"**, **"child"** and **"parental responsibility"** have the same meaning as in section 318B of ITEPA 2003;
(b) **"chargeable expense"** has the meaning given in paragraph 14 of Schedule 2;
(ba) **"eligible employee"** has the meaning given in section 270AA of ITEPA 2003;
(c) **"qualifying child care"** has the same meaning as in section 318C of ITEPA 2003;
(d) **"qualifying week"** means a tax week in respect of which a qualifying childcare voucher is received;
(e) **"relevant salary sacrifice arrangements"** means arrangements (whenever made) under which the employees for whom the vouchers are provided give up the right to receive an amount of general earnings or specific employment income in return for the provision of the vouchers;
(f) **"relevant flexible remuneration arrangements"** means arrangements (whenever made) under which the employees for whom the vouchers are provided agree with the employer that they are to be provided with the vouchers rather than receive some other description of employment income;
(g) **"relevant low-paid employees"** means any of the employer's employees who are remunerated by the employer at a rate such that, if the relevant salary sacrifice arrangements or relevant flexible remuneration arrangements applied to them, the rate at which they would then be so remunerated would be likely to be lower than the national minimum wage;

(h) **"scheme"** means the manner by which an employer provides qualifying childcare vouchers and an employee is taken to join a scheme or have joined a scheme when the employer has agreed that vouchers will be provided to the employee under the scheme and there is a child falling within Condition A of paragraph 7(7); and

(i) the administration costs for a voucher means the difference between the cost of provision of a voucher and its face value and the face value is the amount stated on or recorded in the voucher as the value of the provision of care for a child that may be obtained by using it.

History – Para. 6B(ba) inserted by SI 2018/120, reg. 7(2), with effect from 6 April 2018.
Para. 6B inserted by SI 2011/1000, reg. 3, with effect from 6 April 2011.

QUALIFYING CHILDCARE VOUCHERS FOR ELIGIBLE EMPLOYEES WHO JOINED A SCHEME BEFORE 6TH APRIL 2011

History – In the heading the word "ELIGIBLE" inserted by SI 2018/120, reg. 7(3)(a), with effect from 6 April 2018.
Heading before para. 7 substituted by SI 2011/1000, reg. 4(a), with effect from 6 April 2011 for employees who joined a scheme before 6 April 2011.

7(1) A qualifying childcare voucher, where an eligible employee joined a scheme–

(a) before 6th April 2011;

(b) before 6th April 2011 but ceased to be employed by the employer and was subsequently re-employed by the employer and re-joined the scheme before 6th April 2011; or

(c) before 6th April 2011 and there was a continuous period of 52 weeks ending before 6th April 2011 throughout which vouchers were not being provided for the employee under the scheme,

subject to the qualifications in sub-paragraphs (2) and (5).

7(1A) [Omitted by SI 2011/2700, reg. 4(b).]

7(2) Where the chargeable expense of the voucher exceeds the exempt amount, only that amount shall be disregarded by virtue of sub-paragraph (1).

7(3) The exempt amount is the amount found by the formula–

$$E \times QW.$$

Here–

E is the sum of–

(a) £55; and

(b) the administration costs for the qualifying childcare voucher;

QW is the number of qualifying weeks

(a) for which the earner has been employed by the secondary contributor during the tax year in which the qualifying childcare voucher is provided; and

(b) for which no other qualifying childcare voucher has been provided by the secondary contributor.

7(4) Where an earner has two or more employed earner's employments, the earnings from which fall to be aggregated in accordance with regulation 14 or 15, the reference to the secondary contributor in paragraph (b) of the definition of QW is a reference to the secondary contributor in respect any of those employments.

7(5) An earner is only entitled to one exempt amount even if childcare vouchers are provided in respect of more than one child.

7(6) In this paragraph **"qualifying childcare voucher"** means a non-cash voucher in relation to which Conditions A to C are met.

7(7) Condition A is that the voucher is provided to enable an employee to obtain care for a child who–

(a) is a child or stepchild of the employee and is maintained (wholly or partly) at the employee's expense; or

(b) is resident with the employee and is a person in respect of whom the employee has parental responsibility.

7(8) Condition B is that the voucher can only be used to obtain qualifying child care.

7(9) Condition C is that the vouchers are provided under a scheme that is open–

(a) *to the employer's eligible employees generally*; or

(b) generally to those at a particular location,

subject to sub-paragraph (10).

7(10) Where the scheme under which the vouchers are provided involves–

(a) relevant salary sacrifice arrangements; or

(b) relevant flexible remuneration arrangements,

Condition C is not prevented from being met by reason only that the scheme is not open to relevant low-paid employees.

History – In reg. 7(1) the word "eligible" inserted by SI 2018/120, reg. 7(3)(b), with effect from 6 April 2018.
Para. 7(1) substituted by SI 2011/2700, reg. 4(a), with effect from 6 December 2011.
Para. 7(1) substituted by SI 2011/1000, reg. 4(a), with effect from 6 April 2011 for employees who joined a scheme before 6 April 2011.
In former para. 7(1) words "Part 10 or 10A" substituted by SI 2004/770, reg. 28, with effect from 6 April 2004.
Para. 7(1A) omitted by SI 2011/2700, reg. 4(b), with effect from 6 December 2011.
Former para. 7(1A) inserted by SI 2011/1000, reg. 4(b), with effect from 6 April 2011 for employees who joined a scheme before 6 April 2011.
In para. 7(3) reference to "£55" substituted for "£50" by SI 2006/883, reg. 2, with effect from 6 April 2006.
Para. 7(6) substituted by SI 2011/1000, reg. 4(c), with effect from 6 April 2011 for employees who joined a scheme before 6 April 2011.
In reg. 7(9)(a) the word "eligible" inserted by SI 2018/120, reg. 7(3)(a), with effect from 6 April 2018.
Para. 7(7), (8), (9) and (10) inserted by SI 2011/1000, reg. 4(d), with effect from 6 April 2011 for employees who joined a scheme before 6 April 2011.
Para. 7 substituted by SI 2005/778, reg. 9(2) with effect from 6 April 2005.

Derivations – SI 1979/591, Sch. 1ZC, Pt. V, para. 7.

Cross references – ITEPA 2003, Pt. 3, Ch. 10: residual liability to charge under benefits code.
SI 2005/778, reg. 10 (transitional provision) (as substituted by SI 2005/1086, reg. 4 with effect from 5 April 2005): in relation to any earnings period ending on or before 6 October 2005, in para. 7(3) of Part 5, QW should be taken to be 26, regardless of the number of weeks for which the earner had actually been employed. This is subject to an overriding limit on the exemption of £1,300. The full text of reg. 10 (as substituted) is as follows:

"**10(1)** In relation to qualifying childcare vouchers provided during the period beginning on 6th April 2005 and ending on 5th October 2005 ("the transitional period"), paragraph 7(3) of Part 5 of Schedule 3 to the principal Regulations shall have effect as if, for the purposes of paragraph (a) of QW, the number of qualifying weeks were 26.

This is subject to the following qualification.

10(2) The sum of the exempt amounts which may be disregarded, in computing earnings during the transitional period, by virtue of paragraph 7(3) of Part 5 of Schedule 3 to the principal Regulations, as modified by paragraph (1) above, shall not exceed £1,300.".

QUALIFYING CHILDCARE VOUCHERS FOR ELIGIBLE EMPLOYEES WHO JOINED A SCHEME ON OR AFTER 6TH APRIL 2011, OR BEFORE 6TH APRIL 2011 WHERE THERE HAS BEEN A BREAK IN EMPLOYMENT OR A 52 WEEK BREAK IN RECEIVING VOUCHERS RECOMMENCING ON OR AFTER 6TH APRIL 2011

History – In the heading the word "ELIGIBLE" inserted by SI 2018/120, reg. 4(4)(a), with effect from 6 April 2018.
The heading to para. 7A substituted by SI 2011/2700, reg. 5(a) with effect from 6 December 2011.

7A(1) A qualifying childcare voucher, where an eligible employee joined a scheme

(a) on or after 6th April 2011;

(b) before 6th April 2011 but ceased to be employed by the employer and was subsequently re-employed by the employer and re-joined the scheme on or after 6th April 2011; or

(c) before 6th April 2011 and there was a continuous period of 52 weeks ending on or after 6th April 2011 throughout which vouchers were not being provided for the employee under the scheme,

subject to the qualifications in sub-paragraphs (3) and (6).

7A(2) In this paragraph a **"qualifying childcare voucher"** means a non-cash voucher in relation to which conditions A to D (see sub-paragraphs (7) to (11)) are met.

7A(3) Where the chargeable expense of the voucher exceeds the exempt amount, only that amount shall be disregarded by virtue of sub-paragraph (1).

7A(4) The exempt amount is the amount found by the formula–

$$E \times QW$$

Here–

E is, in the case of an employee the sum of–

(a) £25, if the relevant earnings amount for the tax year, as estimated in accordance with Condition D, exceeds the higher rate limit for the tax year;

(b) £28, if the relevant earnings amount for the tax year, as estimated in accordance with Condition D, exceeds the basic rate limit but does not exceed the higher rate limit for the tax year; or

(c) £55, in any other case; and

(d) the administration costs for the qualifying childcare voucher;

QW is the number of qualifying weeks–

(a) for which the earner has been employed by the secondary contributor during the tax year in which the qualifying childcare voucher is provided; and

(b) for which no other qualifying childcare voucher has been provided by the secondary contributor.

7A(5) Where an earner has two or more employed earner's employments, the earnings from which fall to be aggregated in accordance with regulation 14 or 15, the reference to the secondary contributor in paragraph (b) of the definition of QW is a reference to the secondary contributor in respect of any of those employments.

7A(6) An earner is only entitled to one exempt amount even if childcare vouchers are provided in respect of more than one child.

7A(7) Condition A is that the voucher is provided to enable an employee to obtain care for a child who–

(a) is a child or stepchild of the employee and is maintained (wholly or partly) at the employee's expense; or

(b) is resident with the employee and is a person in respect of whom the employee has parental responsibility.

7A(8) Condition B is that the voucher can only be used to obtain qualifying child care.

7A(9) Condition C is that the vouchers are provided under a scheme that is open–

(a) to the employer's eligible employees generally; or

(b) generally to those at a particular location,

subject to sub-paragraph (10).

7A(10) Where the scheme under which the vouchers are provided involves–

(a) relevant salary sacrifice arrangements; or

(b) relevant flexible remuneration arrangements,

Condition C is not prevented from being met by reason only that the scheme is not open to relevant low-paid employees.

7A(11) Condition D is that the employer has, at the required time, made an estimate of the employee's relevant earnings amount for the tax year in respect of which the voucher is provided.

7A(12) In sub-paragraph (11) **"the required time"**, in the case of an employee, means–

(a) if the employee joins the scheme under which the vouchers are provided at a time during the tax year, that time, and

(b) otherwise, the beginning of the tax year.

7A(13) In sub-paragraph (11) the **"relevant earnings amount"**, in the case of an employee provided with vouchers by an employer for any qualifying week in a tax year, and subject to sub-paragraph (14), means–

(a) the aggregate of–

(i) the amount of any relevant earnings (see sub-paragraph (15)) for the tax year from employment by the employer; and

(ii) any amounts to be treated under Chapters 2 to 12 of Part 3 of ITEPA 2003 as earnings from such employment; less

(b) the aggregate of any excluded amounts (see sub-paragraph (16)).

7A(14) But if the employee becomes employed by the employer during the tax year, what would otherwise be the amount of the aggregate mentioned in sub-paragraph (13)(a) is the relevant multiple of that amount; and the relevant multiple is–

$$\frac{365}{RD}$$

where–

RD is the number of days in the period beginning with the day on which the employee becomes employed by the employer and ending with the tax year.

7A(15) In sub-paragraph (13)(a) **"relevant earnings"** means–

(a) salary, wages or fees;

(b) guaranteed contractual bonuses;

(c) contractual commission;

(d) guaranteed overtime payments;

(e) location or cost of living allowances;

(f) shift allowances;

(g) skills allowances;

(h) retention and recruitment allowances; and

(i) market rate supplements.

7A(16) For the purposes of sub-paragraph (13)(b) the following are **"excluded amounts"**–

(za) contributions under a pension scheme if the employee has authorised the employer to make the deductions from relevant payments (as defined by regulation 4 of the PAYE Regulations) for which relief at source is given under section 192(1) of the Finance Act 2004 (relief at source);

(a) contributions under a pension scheme allowed under section 193(2) of Finance Act 2004 (relief under net pay arrangements) to be deducted by the employer from the employee's employment income for the tax year in accordance with the PAYE Regulations;

(b) donations for which a deduction is made under section 713 of ITEPA 2003 (payroll giving) in calculating the employee's net taxable earnings from employment by the employer for the tax year in accordance with the PAYE Regulations;

(c) expenses within Chapter 3 of Part 3 of ITEPA 2003 (expenses payments) which the employer is authorised to exclude from the employee's taxable earnings for the tax year in accordance with the PAYE Regulations;

(d) payments in respect of removal expenses to which section 271 of ITEPA 2003 applies (as defined in section 272) and which are taxable earnings of the employee from employment by the employer for the tax year;

(e) amounts equivalent to the amount of the personal allowance under section 35(1) of the Income Tax Act 2007, and in addition if applicable, the amount of the blind person's allowance under section 38 of that Act.

History – In reg. 7A(1) the word "eligible" inserted by SI 2018/120, reg. 4(4)(b), with effect from 6 April 2018.
Para. 7A(1) substituted by SI 2011/2700, reg. 5(a), with effect from 6 December 2011.
In para. 7A(4)(a), the figure "£25" substituted for "£22" by SI 2013/622, reg. 40(a)(ii), with effect from 6 April 2013 in relation to the tax year 2013–14 and subsequent tax years.
In reg. 7A(9)(a) the word "eligible" inserted by SI 2018/120, reg. 4(4)(a), with effect from 6 April 2018.
In para. 7A(15)(a) the word "and" omitted and para. 7A(15)(b)–(i) substituted for para. 7A(b) by SI 2011/2700, reg. 5(b), with effect from 6 December 2011.
Para. 7A(16)(za) inserted, in para. 7A(16)(a) the word "registered" omitted and the words "in accordance with the PAYE Regulations" inserted, in para. 7A(16)(b) the words "in accordance with the PAYE Regulations" inserted, in para. 7A(16)(c) the word "the" inserted and para. 7A(15)(e) substituted by SI 2011/2700, reg. 5(c), with effect from 6 December 2011.
Para. 7A inserted by SI 2011/1000, reg. 5, with effect from 6 April 2011 for employees who join a scheme on or after 6 April 2011.

8 A non-cash voucher provided to or for the benefit of an employed earner in respect of employed earner's employment by a person who is not the secondary contributor in respect of the provision of that voucher.

Derivations – SI 1979/591, Sch. 1ZC, Pt. V, para. 8.

Cross references – ITEPA 2003, s. 265, 266: income tax exemption for cash-vouchers relating to third party entertainment.

9 A non-cash voucher providing for health screening or medical check-ups to the extent that no liability to income tax arises in the provision of such health screening or medical check-ups by virtue of any provision of or under the Income Tax (Earnings and Pensions) Act 2003 which exempts from liability to income tax the provision by employers to employees of health screening and medical check-ups.

History – In para. 9, the words "by virtue of any provision of or under the Income Tax (Earnings and Pensions) Act 2003 which exempts from liability to income tax the provision by employers to employees of health screening and medical check-ups." substituted for the words "by virtue of the Income Tax (Exemption of Minor Benefits) Regulations 2002 regulation 7 (exemption in respect of the provision of health screening and medical checkups)." by SI 2009/600, reg. 7(1), with effect from 6 April 2009. But for the purposes of this amendment, there is to be disregarded any limitation of provision under ITEPA 2003 by virtue of which an exemption is conditional on the benefit being made available to the employer's employees generally on similar terms (SI 2009/600, reg. 7(2)).
Para. 9 inserted by SI 2007/2091, reg. 2(3), with effect from 14 August 2007.

Part VI – Pensions and Pension Contributions

PENSION PAYMENTS AND PENSION CONTRIBUTIONS TO BE DISREGARDED

1 The payments mentioned in this Part are disregarded in the calculation of earnings for the purposes of earnings-related contributions.

History – In para. 1, the words "this Part" substituted for "paragraphs 2 to 11" by SI 2015/543, reg. 3, with effect from 6 April 2015.
Para. 1 substituted by SI 2006/576, reg. 8(2), with effect from 6 April 2006.

Derivations – SI 1979/591, Sch. 1ZC, Pt. VI, para. 1.

CONTRIBUTIONS TO, AND BENEFITS FROM, REGISTERED PENSION SCHEMES

2 A payment–

(a) by way of employer's contribution towards a registered pension scheme to which section 308 of ITEPA 2003 (exemption of contributions to registered pension scheme) applies;

(b) by way of any benefit pursuant to a registered pension scheme to which–

(i) section 204(1) (authorised pensions and lump sums) of, and Schedule 31 (taxation of benefits under registered pension schemes) to, the Finance Act 2004 applies; or

(ii) section 208 or 209 of that Act (unauthorised payments) applies.

History – In para. 2(a), "(1)" after "section 308" omitted by SI 2012/817, reg. 6(a), with effect from 6 April 2012, subject to savings provisions in relation to obligations arising in connection with tax years beginning prior to 6 April 2012 (the operation of SI 2001/1004 is unaffected by the amendments made by SI 2012/817, reg. 3–6, and the reference to s. 9(3) of the Pensions Act in the former definition of "COMPS employment" in SI 2001/1004, reg. 1(2), is to be read as though that section were still in force).
Para. 2 substituted by SI 2006/576, reg. 8(3), with effect from 6 April 2006.
Former para. 2 substituted by SI 2004/770, reg. 28, with effect from 6 April 2004.

Derivations – SI 1979/591, Sch. 1ZC, Pt. VI, para. 2.

Cross references – ITEPA 2003, s. 308(1) rewrites ICTA 1988, s. 643(1).

MIGRANT MEMBER RELIEF AND CORRESPONDING RELIEFS ETC.

History – In the heading to para. 3, "etc." added by SI 2006/2829, reg. 3(2) with effect from 16 November 2006.

3(1) A payment by way of–

(a) an employer's contribution to which paragraph 2 of Schedule 33 of the Finance Act 2004 (relief for employers' contributions) applies and any benefit referable to that contribution;

(b) an employer's contribution to which article 15(2) of the Taxation of Pension Schemes (Transitional Provisions) Order 2006 (employers with precommencement entitlement to corresponding relief) applies and any benefit referable to that contribution;

(ba) an employer's contribution to a pension scheme established by a government outside the United Kingdom for the benefit of its employees or primarily for their benefit, and any benefit referable to such a contribution (whenever made);

(c) [omitted by SI 2006/2829, reg. 3(4)(d);]

(d) benefits from a pension scheme which are referable to contributions made before 6th April 2006, provided that section 386 of ITEPA 2003 did not apply to those contributions by virtue of section 390 of that Act; or

(e) benefits subject to the unauthorised payment charge imposed by section 208 of the Finance Act 2004 as applied to a relevant non-UK scheme by virtue of paragraph 1 of Schedule 34 to that Act.

3(2) Expressions defined in Schedule 34 to the Finance Act 2004 have the same meaning in this paragraph as they have there.

History – Para. 3 renumbered as sub-para. (1) by SI 2006/2829, reg. 3(3) with effect from 16 November 2006.
In para. 3(1)(a) and (b) the words "and any benefit referable to that contribution" added by SI 2006/2829, reg. 3(4)(a), (b) with effect from 16 November 2006.
Para. 3 substituted by SI 2006/576, reg. 8(3), with effect from 6 April 2006.
Former para. 3(a) substituted by SI 2004/770, reg. 28, with effect from 6 April 2004.
Para. 3(1)(ba) inserted and the word "or" at the end of cl. (b) omitted by SI 2006/2829, reg. 3(4)(c) with effect from 16 November 2006.
In former para. 3(b) "the Taxes Act" substituted by SI 2004/770, reg. 28, with effect from 6 April 2004.
Para. 3(1)(c) omitted by SI 2006/2829, reg. 3(4)(d) with effect from 16 November 2006.
In former para. 3(c) "or sections 590 (annuities) and 591 (taxable pension income) of ITEPA 2003 apply; or" substituted by SI 2004/770, reg. 28, with effect from 6 April 2004.
Para. 3(1)(d) inserted by SI 2006/2829, reg. 3(4)(e) with effect from 16 November 2006.
Para. 3(1)(e) inserted by SI 2006/2829, reg. 3(4)(e) with effect from 16 November 2006.
Para. 3(2) inserted by SI 2006/2829, reg. 3(5) with effect from 16 November 2006.

Derivations – SI 1979/591, Sch. 1ZC, Pt. VI, para. 3.

Cross references – ITEPA 2003, s. 386: charge on payments to non-approved retirement benefits schemes.
ITEPA 2003, s. 387(2) rewrites ICTA 1988, s. 596(1).
ITEPA 2003, s. 390 rewrites ICTA 1988, s. 596(2)(b).

FUNDED UNAPPROVED RETIREMENT BENEFITS SCHEMES

4 A payment by way of relevant benefits pursuant to a retirement benefits scheme which has not been approved by the Board for the purposes of Chapter I of Part XIV of the Taxes Act and attributable to payments prior to 6th April 1998.

Here **"relevant benefits"** has the meaning given in section 612 of the Taxes Act.

Derivations – SI 1979/591, Sch. 1ZC, Pt. VI, para. 4.

Cross references – ITEPA 2003, Pt. 6, Ch. 2: income tax charge on benefits from non-approved pension schemes.
ITEPA 2003, s. 586: approved schemes.

PAYMENTS TO PENSION PREVIOUSLY TAKEN INTO ACCOUNT IN CALCULATING EARNINGS

5 A payment by way of any benefit pursuant to a retirement benefits scheme which has not been approved by the Board for the purposes of Chapter I of Part XIV of the Taxes Act and attributable to payments on or after 6th April 1998 and before 6th April 2006 which have previously been included in a person's earnings for the purpose of the assessment of his liability for earnings-related contributions.

History – In para. 5 the words "and before 6th April 2006" inserted by SI 2006/576, reg. 8(4), with effect from 6 April 2006.

Derivations – SI 1979/591, Sch. 1ZC, Pt. VI, para. 5.

PAYMENTS IN GOOD FAITH TO SCHEME SOLELY FOR PROVIDING APPROVED BENEFITS

6 [Omitted by SI 2006/576, reg. 8(5).]

History – Para. 6 omitted by SI 2006/576, reg. 8(5), with effect from 6 April 2006.

Derivations – SI 1979/591, Sch. 1ZC, Pt. VI, para. 6.

PAYMENTS TO AND BENEFITS FROM PENSION SCHEMES EXEMPT FROM UK TAXATION UNDER DOUBLE TAXATION AGREEMENTS

History – In the heading to para. 7 the words "and benefits from" inserted by SI 2011/2700, reg. 6(a) with effect from 6 December 2011. Heading to para. 7 amended by SI 2005/778, reg. 9(3)(a) with effect from 6 April 2005.

7(1) A payment to a pension scheme which is afforded relief from taxation by virtue of any of the following provisions, and any benefit referable to that payment–

(a) Article 25(8) of the Convention set out in the Schedule to the Double Taxation Relief (Taxes on Income) (France) Order 1968;

(b) Article 17A of the Convention set out in the Schedule to the Double Taxation Relief (Taxes on Income) (Republic of Ireland) Order 1976;

(bb) Article 27(2) of the Convention set out in the Schedule to the Double Taxation Relief (Taxes on Income) (Canada) Order 1980;

(c) Article 28(3) of the Convention set out in the Schedule to the Double Taxation Relief (Taxes on Income) (Denmark) Order 1980.

(d) Article 18 of the Convention set out in the Schedule to the Double Taxation Relief (Taxes on Income) (The United States of America) Order 2002.

(e) Article 17(3) of the Convention set out in the Schedule to the Double Taxation Relief (Taxes on Income) (South Africa) Order 2002;

(f) Article 17(3) of the Convention set out in the Schedule to the Double Taxation Relief (Taxes on Income) (Chile) Order 2003.

7(2) [Omitted by SI 2006/576, reg. 8(6)(b).]

History – In para. 7(1) the words "any of the following provisions, and any benefit referable to that payment" inserted by SI 2011/2700, reg. 6(b), with effect from 6 December 2011.
Para. 7(1)(bb) inserted by SI 2006/576, reg. 8(6)(a), with effect from 6 April 2006.
Para. 7(1)(d) inserted by SI 2005/778, reg. 9(3)(b) (as amended by SI 2005/1086, reg. 3) with effect from 6 April 2005.
Para. 7(1)(e) inserted by SI 2006/576, reg. 8(6)(a), with effect from 6 April 2006.
Para. 7(1)(f) inserted by SI 2006/576, reg. 8(6)(a), with effect from 6 April 2006.
Para. 7(2) omitted by SI 2006/576, reg. 8(6)(b), with effect from 6 April 2006.

Derivations – SI 1979/591, Sch. 1ZC, Pt. VI, para. 7.

Notes – The original version of SI 2005/778 referred to the insertion of para. 7(d); SI 2005/1086 corrected this so that it effects the insertion of para. 7(1)(d).

CONTRIBUTIONS TO, AND BENEFITS FROM, EMPLOYER-FINANCED RETIREMENT BENEFIT SCHEMES

8 A payment by way of–

(a) an employer's contribution towards an employer-financed retirement benefits scheme; and

(b) benefits, pursuant to an employer-financed retirement benefits scheme, to which paragraph 10 applies.

Here and in paragraph 10 **"employer-financed retirement benefits scheme"** has the meaning given in section 393A of ITEPA 2003.

History – Para. 8 inserted by SI 2006/576, reg. 8(7), with effect from 6 April 2006.

CONTRIBUTIONS TO, AND PENSION PAYMENTS FROM, EMPLOYER-FINANCED PENSION ONLY SCHEMES

9(1) A payment by way of–

(a) an employer's contribution towards an employer-financed pension only scheme; and

(b) a pension, pursuant to an employer-financed pension only scheme, which is income charged to tax pursuant to Part 9 of ITEPA 2003 to which paragraph 10 applies.

9(2) In this paragraph **"employer-financed pension only scheme"** means a scheme–

(a) financed by payments made by or on behalf of the secondary contributor, and

(b) providing only a pension (and which is accordingly not an employer-financed retirement benefits scheme because it does not provide relevant benefits).

Here **"relevant benefits"** has the meaning given in section 393B of ITEPA 2003.

History – Para. 9 inserted by SI 2006/576, reg. 8(7), with effect from 6 April 2006.

PAYMENTS FROM EMPLOYER-FINANCED RETIREMENT BENEFITS SCHEMES AND EMPLOYER FINANCED PENSION ONLY SCHEMES

10(1) This paragraph applies to payments in paragraphs 8(b) and 9(1)(b) which–

(a) if the scheme had been a registered pension scheme–

(i) would have been authorised member payments under any of the provisions of section 164 of the Finance Act 2004 (authorised member payments) listed in sub-paragraph (4); and

(ii) would satisfy any of the conditions in sub-paragraph (5); and

(b) are made after the employment of the employed earner by–

(i) the secondary contributor,

(ii) a subsidiary of the secondary contributor, or

(iii) a person connected with the secondary contributor or a subsidiary of the secondary contributor,

has ceased.

For the purposes of this sub-paragraph–

"subsidiary" has the meaning given in section 838 of the Taxes Act 1988; and

an employer is connected with any of the persons with respect to whom he would be a connected person by virtue of section 839 of that Act.

10(2) In the following provisions of this paragraph–

(a) **"the Act"** means the Finance Act 2004;

(b) a reference to a numbered section or Schedule (without more) is a reference to the section or Schedule bearing that number in the Act; and

(c) any reference to a numbered pension rule is to the pension rule contained in section 165 bearing that number.

10(3) In applying any provision of the Act for the purposes of this paragraph, a reference to the scheme administrator is to be read as a reference to–

(a) the responsible person, within the meaning of section 399A of ITEPA 2003, in relation to the employer-financed retirement benefits scheme, or

(b) the person who would be the responsible person if the scheme were an employer-financed retirement benefits scheme.

10(4) The provisions referred to in sub-paragraph (1)(a)(i) are–

(a) section 164(1)(a) (pensions permitted by the pension rules (see section 165)),

(b) section 164(1)(b) (lump sums permitted by the lump sum rule (see section 166)),

(c) section 164(1)(e) (payments pursuant to a pension sharing order or provision), and

(d) section 164(1)(f) (payments of a description prescribed by regulations made by the Commissioners for Revenue and Customs).

10(5) The conditions referred to in sub-paragraph (1)(a)(ii) are that, if the scheme had been a registered pension scheme–

(a) any pension payable under its rules would have satisfied pension rules 1, 3 and 4;

(b) in relation to any lump sum payable under its rules, section 166(1)(a) (pension commencement lump sum) and paragraphs 1 to 3 of Schedule 29, as modified by sub-paragraph (6) below, would have been satisfied;

(c) in relation to any lump sum payable under its rules, section 166(1)(b) (serious illhealth lump sum) and paragraph 4 of Schedule 29, as modified by sub-paragraph (6) below, would have been satisfied; and

(d) any pension is payable until the member's death in instalments at least annually.

10(6) The amount to be disregarded shall be computed in accordance with Part 1 of Schedule 29 (lump sum rule) as if that Part were modified as follows–

(a) in paragraph 1 (pension commencement lump sum)–

(i) paragraphs (b) and (f) of sub-paragraph (1) were omitted,

(ii) for sub-paragraph (2) there were substituted–

"**1(2)** But if a lump sum falling within sub-paragraph (1) exceeds the permitted lump sum, no part of it shall be disregarded.";

(iii) sub-paragraph (4) were omitted; and

(iv) for sub-paragraph (5) there were substituted–

"**1(5)** Paragraph 2 defines the permitted lump sum.";

(b) for paragraph 2 there were substituted–

"2 The permitted lump sum is the higher of–

$$\frac{MVF}{4} \text{ and } \frac{LS + (MAP \times 20)}{4}$$

where–

MVF is the market value of the employee's employer-financed retirement benefits scheme fund at the time the benefit is paid to the individual,

LS is the amount of the lump sum, and

MAP is the maximum annual pension which could be paid to the member under the arrangement.";

(c) paragraph 3 were omitted;

(d) in paragraph 4, paragraphs (b) and (c) of sub-paragraph (1) and sub-paragraphs (2) and (3) were omitted.

10(7) No payment by way of benefits shall be disregarded by virtue of this paragraph if they are payable in respect of a period during which an earner is–

(a) engaged as a self-employed earner under a contract for services with, or

(b) re-employed as an employed earner by,

the secondary contributor from employment with whom the benefits were derived.

History – In para. 10(4)(a) the words "section 164(1)(a)" substituted for the words "section 164(a)" by SI 2011/2700, reg. 6(c), with effect from 6 December 2011.

In para. 10(4)(b) the words "section 164(1)(b)" substituted for the words "section 164(b)" by SI 2011/2700, reg. 6(c), with effect from 6 December 2011.

In para. 10(4)(c) the words "section 164(1)(e)" substituted for the words "section 164(e)" by SI 2011/2700, reg. 6(c), with effect from 6 December 2011.

In para. 10(4)(d) the words "section 164(1)(f)" substituted for the words "section 164(f)" by SI 2011/2700, reg. 6(c), with effect from 6 December 2011.

Para. 10(5)(a) substituted by SI 2012/817, reg. 6(b), with effect from 6 April 2012, subject to savings provisions in relation to obligations arising in connection with tax years beginning prior to 6 April 2012 (the operation of SI 2001/1004 is unaffected by the amendments made by SI 2012/817, reg. 3–6, and the reference to s. 9(3) of the Pensions Act in the former definition of "COMPS employment" in SI 2001/1004, reg. 1(2), is to be read as though that section were still in force). Former para. 10(5)(a) read as follows:

"(a) any pension payable under its rules would have satisfied pension rules 1, 3 and 4;any pension payable under its rules would have satisfied–

(i) pension rules 1 and 3,

(ii) pension rule 4 or pension rule 6, and

(iii) [omitted by SI 2011/2700, reg. 6(c)]".

Para. 10(5)(a)(iii) omitted by SI 2011/2700, reg. 6(c), with effect from 6 December 2011.

In para. 10(6)(d) the words "sub-paragraphs (2) and (3)" substituted for the words "sub-paragraph (2)" by SI 2011/2700, reg. 6(c), with effect from 6 December 2011.

Para. 10 inserted by SI 2006/576, reg. 8(7), with effect from 6 April 2006.

ARMED FORCES EARLY DEPARTURE SCHEME PAYMENTS

10A A payment under a scheme established by the Armed Forces Early Departure Payments Scheme Order 2005 (S.I. 2005/437) or by the Armed Forces Early Departure Payments Scheme Regulations 2014 (S.I. 2014/2328).

History – In para. 10A, the words "or by the Armed Forces Early Departure Payments Scheme Regulations 2014 (S.I. 2014/2328)" inserted by SI 2015/478, reg. 21(2), with effect from 1 April 2015.

Para. 10A inserted by SI 2013/622, reg. 40(b), with effect from 6 April 2013 in relation to the tax year 2013–14 and subsequent tax years.

Cross references – NICA 2014, s. 16: para. 10A also has effect for the tax years 2005–06 to 2012–13 inclusive.

SUPERANNUATION FUNDS TO WHICH SECTION 615(3) OF THE TAXES ACT APPLIES

11 A payment by way of employer's contribution to a superannuation fund to which section 615(3) of the Taxes Act applies, and a payment by way of a pension or an annuity paid by such a fund.

History – In para. 11 words "a pension or" inserted by SI 2006/2829, reg. 4(2) with effect from 16 November 2006.

In para. 11 words "from which income tax is not deducted" omitted from the end by SI 2006/2829, reg. 4(3) with effect from 16 November 2006.

Para. 11 inserted by SI 2006/576, reg. 8(7), with effect from 6 April 2006.

INDEPENDENT ADVICE IN RESPECT OF CONVERSIONS AND TRANSFERS OF PENSION SCHEME BENEFITS

12 A payment or reimbursement to which no liability to income tax arises by virtue of section 308B of ITEPA 2003 (independent advice in respect of conversions and transfers of pension scheme benefits).

History – Para. 12 inserted by SI 2015/543, reg. 4, with effect from 6 April 2015.

PAYMENTS AND REIMBURSEMENTS OF THE COST OF PENSIONS ADVICE

13(1) A payment or reimbursement of costs incurred, by or in respect of an employee or former or prospective employee, in obtaining relevant pensions advice, if Condition A or B is met.

13(2) This paragraph does not apply in relation to a person in a tax year so far as the total amount of any payments and reimbursements under sub-paragraph (1) in the person's case in that year exceeds £500.

13(3) If in a tax year there is in relation to an individual more than one person who is an employer or former employer, sub-paragraphs (1) and (2) apply in relation to the individual as employee or former or prospective employee of any one of those persons separately from their application in relation to the individual as employee or former or prospective employee of any other of those persons.

13(4) **"Relevant pensions advice"**, in relation to a person, means information or advice in connection with–

(a) the person's pension arrangements; or

(b) the use of the person's pension funds.

13(5) Condition A is that the payment or reimbursement is provided under a scheme that is open–

(a) to the employer's employees generally; or

(b) generally to the employer's employees at a particular location.

13(6) Condition B is that the payment or reimbursement is provided under a scheme that is open generally to the employer's employees, or generally to those of the employer's employees at a particular location, who–

(a) have reached the minimum qualifying age; or

(b) meet the ill-health condition.

13(7) The **"minimum qualifying age"**, in relation to an employee, means the employee's relevant pension age less 5 years.

13(8) **"Relevant pension age"**, in relation to an employee, means–

(a) where paragraph 22 or 23 of Schedule 36 to the Finance Act 2004 applies in relation to the employee and a registered pension scheme of which the employee is a member, the employee's protected pension age (see paragraphs 22(8) and 23(8) of Schedule 36 to the Finance Act 2004); or

(b) in any other case, the employee's normal minimum pension age, as defined by section 279(1) of the Finance Act 2004.

13(9) The **"ill-health condition"** is met by an employee if the employer is satisfied, on the basis of evidence provided by a registered medical practitioner, that the employee is (and will continue to be) incapable of carrying on his or her occupation because of physical or mental impairment.

History – Para. 13 inserted by SI 2017/307, reg. 4, with effect from 6 April 2017.

Part VII – Payments in Respect of Training and Similar Courses

PAYMENTS IN RESPECT OF TRAINING AND SIMILAR EXPENSES DISREGARDED

1 The training payments and vouchers mentioned in this Part are disregarded in the calculation of an employed earner's earnings.

Paragraphs 5 to 8 do not apply to Northern Ireland.

History – In para. 1 "Paragraphs 5 to 8" substituted by SI 2005/2422, reg. 2, with effect from 3 October 2005.
In para. 1 "Paragraphs 5 to 9" substituted by SI 2003/2340, reg. 2(1) with effect from 1 October 2003.

Derivations – SI 1979/591, Sch. 1ZC, Pt. VII, para. 1.

WORK-RELATED TRAINING

2 A payment of, or contribution towards, expenditure incurred in providing work-related training which, by virtue of sections 250 to 254 of ITEPA 2003 (exemption for work-related training), is not to be taken as general earnings of the office or employment in connection with which it is provided.

History – In Sch. 3, Pt. VII, para. 2 words "sections 250 to 254 of ITEPA 2003 (exemption for work-related training)" and "general earnings" substituted by SI 2004/770, reg. 28, with effect from 6 April 2004.

Derivations – SI 1979/591, Sch. 1ZC, Pt. VII, para. 2.

Cross references – ITEPA 2003, s. 250ff. rewrite ICTA 1988, s. 200Bff.

EDUCATION AND TRAINING FUNDED BY EMPLOYERS

3 A payment in respect of expenditure which, by virtue of section 255 of ITEPA 2003 (exemption for contributions to individual learning account training), is not to be taken as general earnings of the office or employment in connection with which it is provided.

History – In Sch. 3, Pt. VII, para. 3 words "section 255 of ITEPA 2003 (exemption for contributions to individual learning account training)" and "general earnings" substituted by SI 2004/770, reg. 28, with effect from 6 April 2004.

Derivations – SI 1979/591, Sch. 1ZC, Pt. VII, para. 3.

Cross references – ITEPA 2003, s. 255 rewrites ICTA 1988, s. 200E.

NEW DEAL 50PLUS: EMPLOYMENT GRANT AND TRAINING CREDIT

4 A payment to a person, as a participant in the scheme arranged under section 2(2) of the Employment and Training Act 1973 and known as New Deal 50plus, of an employment credit or a training grant under that scheme.

Derivations – SI 1979/591, Sch. 1ZC, Pt. VII, para. 4.

RETRAINING COURSES FOR CLAIMANTS FOR JOBSEEKER'S ALLOWANCE

5 A payment to a person as a participant in a scheme of the kind mentioned in section 60(1) of the Welfare Reform and Pensions Act 1999 (special schemes for claimants for jobseeker's allowances).

Derivations – SI 1979/591, Sch. 1ZC, Pt. VII, para. 5.

PAYMENTS TO JOBMATCH PARTICIPANTS

6 A payment made to a participant in a Jobmatch Scheme (including a pilot) arranged under section 2(1) of the Employment and Training Act 1973 in his capacity as such.

Derivations – SI 1979/591, Sch. 1ZC, Pt. VII, para. 6.

VOUCHERS PROVIDED TO JOBMATCH PARTICIPANTS

7 A payment by way of the discharge of any liability by the use of a voucher, given to a participant in a Jobmatch Scheme (including a pilot) arranged under section 2(1) of the Employment and Training Act 1973 in his capacity as such.

Derivations – SI 1979/591, Sch. 1ZC, Pt. VII, para. 7.

EMPLOYMENT RETENTION AND ADVANCEMENT PAYMENTS

8 A payment made to a participant in an Employment Retention and Advancement Scheme, arranged under section 2(1) of the Employment and Training Act 1973, in his capacity as such.

History – Para. 8 inserted by SI 2003/2340, reg. 2(2) with effect from 1 October 2003.

RETURN TO WORK CREDIT

9 A payment made to a participant in a Return to Work Credit Scheme, arranged under section 2(1) of the Employment and Training Act 1973 in his capacity as such.

History – Para. 9 substituted by SI 2003/2958, reg. 5(3), with effect from 10 December 2003.
Para. 9 previously inserted by SI 2003/2340, reg. 2(2) with effect from 1 October 2003.

WORKING NEIGHBOURHOODS PILOT

History – The heading "WORKING NEIGHBOURHOODS PILOT" inserted by SI 2004/770, reg. 28, with effect from 6 April 2004.

10 A payment made to a participant in a Working Neighbourhoods Pilot, arranged under section 2(1) of the Employment and Training Act 1973, in his capacity as such.

History – Para. 10 inserted by SI 2004/770, reg. 28, with effect from 6 April 2004.

IN-WORK CREDIT

History – The heading "IN-WORK CREDIT" inserted by SI 2004/770, reg. 28, with effect from 6 April 2004.

11 A payment made to a participant in an In-Work Credit scheme, arranged under section 2(1) of the Employment and Training Act 1973, in his capacity as such.

History – Para. 11 inserted by SI 2004/770, reg. 28, with effect from 6 April 2004.

PAYMENTS MADE BY EMPLOYERS TO EARNERS IN FULL-TIME ATTENDANCE AT UNIVERSITIES & C.

12(1) A payment to an employed earner receiving full-time instruction at a university, technical college or similar educational establishment (within the meaning of section 331 of the Taxes Act) if the conditions in sub-paragraphs (2) to (6) are satisfied, but subject to the exclusion in sub-paragraph (7).

12(2) The employed earner must have enrolled at the educational establishment for a course lasting at least one academic year at the time when payment is made.

12(3) The secondary contributor must require the employed earner to attend the course for an average of at least twenty weeks in an academic year.

12(4) The educational establishment–

(a) must be open to members of the public generally,

(b) must offer more than one course of practical or academic instruction.

12(5) The educational establishment must not be run by–

(a) the secondary contributor, or a person who would be treated by section 839 of the Taxes Act as connected with him; or

(b) a trade organisation of which the secondary contributor is a member.

12(6) The total amount of earnings payable to the earner in respect of his attendance, including lodging, travelling and subsistence allowances, but excluding any tuition fees, must not exceed £15,480 in respect of an academic year.

12(7) This paragraph does not apply to any payment made by the secondary contributor to the employed earner for, or in respect of, work done for the secondary contributor by the earner (whether during vacations or otherwise).

12(8) This paragraph has effect in respect of payments made in relation to the academic year beginning on 1st September 2005 and subsequent academic years.

12(9) In this paragraph–

"academic year" means the period beginning on 1st September of one calendar year and ending on 31st August of the following calendar year.

"trade organisation" means an organisation of secondary contributors (in their capacity as employers) the members of which carry on a particular profession or trade for the purposes of which the organisation exists.

History – In para. 12(6) "£15,480" substituted by SI 2007/2401, reg. 2, with effect in relation to payments of earnings made on or after 5 September 2007 in respect of the academic year beginning on 1 September 2007 and subsequent academic years.
Para. 12 inserted by SI 2005/728, reg. 4, with effect from 6 April 2005 in respect of the academic year beginning on 1 September 2005 and subsequent academic years.

Notes – ICTA 1988, s. 331 rewritten as ITTOIA 2005, s. 776.

Part VIII – Travelling, Relocation and Other Expenses and Allowances of the Employment

TRAVELLING, RELOCATION AND INCIDENTAL EXPENSES DISREGARDED

1 The travelling, relocation and other expenses and allowances mentioned in this Part are disregarded in the calculation of an employed earner's earnings.

Derivations – SI 1979/591, Sch. 1ZC, Pt. VIII, para. 1.

1A For the purposes of this paragraph none of the following amounts are to be disregarded in the calculation of an employed earner's earnings–

(a) any amount paid or reimbursed pursuant to relevant salary sacrifice arrangements as provided for in section 289A(5);

(b) any amount paid or reimbursed to an employed earner which falls within regulation 22(13); and

(c) any amount paid to an employed earner in respect of anticipated expenses that have yet to be incurred (whether or not such expenses are actually incurred after the payment is made).

History – Para. 1A inserted by SI 2016/352, reg. 5(2), with effect from 6 April 2016.

RELOCATION EXPENSES

2(1) A payment of, or contribution towards, expenses reasonably incurred by a person in relation to a change of residence in connection with the commencement of, or an alteration in, the duties of the person's employment or the place where those duties are normally to be performed is disregarded if the conditions *in sub-paragraphs* (2) to (6) are met.

2(2) The first condition is that–

(a) the payment or contribution–

(i) is not, by virtue of section 271 of ITEPA 2003 (limited exemption of removal benefits and expenses) liable to income tax as general earnings under that Act; or

(ii) would not have been so regarded, but is in fact disregarded by virtue of another provision of ITEPA 2003;

(b) [omitted by SI 2012/817, reg. 7(4)(a).]

2(3) The second condition is that the change of residence must result from–

(a) the employee becoming employed by an employer;

(b) an alteration of the duties of the employee's employment (where his employer remains the same); or

(c) an alteration of the place where the employee is normally to perform the duties of his employment (where both the employer and the duties which the employee is to perform remain the same).

2(4) The third condition is that the change of residence must be made wholly or mainly to allow the employee to have his residence within a reasonable daily travelling distance of–

(a) the place where he performs, or is to perform, the duties of his employment (in a case falling within paragraph (3)(a));

(b) the place where he performs, or is to perform, the new duties of his employment (in a case falling within paragraph (3)(b)); or

(c) the new place where he performs, or is to perform, the duties of his employment (in a case falling within paragraph (3)(c)).

References in this sub-paragraph and sub-paragraph (5) to the place where the employee performs, or is to perform, the duties of his employment are references to the place where he normally performs, or is normally to perform, the duties of the employment.

2(5) The fourth condition is that the employee's former residence must not be within a reasonable daily travelling distance of the place where the employee performs or is to perform the duties of the employment.

2(6) [Omitted by SI 2012/817, reg. 7(4)(b).]

2(7) For the purposes of this paragraph, Chapter 7 of Part 4 of ITEPA 2003 shall be read as if sections 272(1)(b), 272(3)(b), 274 and 287 were omitted.

History – Para. 2(2)(a)(i) substituted by SI 2004/770, reg. 28, with effect from 6 April 2004.
In para. 2(2)(a)(ii) "by virtue of another provision of ITEPA 2003; or" substituted by SI 2004/770, reg. 28, with effect from 6 April 2004.
Para. 2(2)(b) (and the "or" before it) omitted by SI 2012/817, reg. 7(4)(a), with effect from 6 April 2012.
Para. 2(6) omitted by SI 2012/817, reg. 7(4)(b), with effect from 6 April 2012.
Para. 2(7) substituted by SI 2004/770, reg. 28, with effect from 6 April 2004.

Derivations – SI 1979/591, Sch. 1ZC, Pt. VIII, para. 2.

Cross references – ITEPA 2003, Pt. 4, Ch. 7 rewrites ICTA 1988, Sch. 11A.
ITEPA 2003, s. 272(3)(b), 272(1)(b), 274, 287 rewrite ICTA 1988, Sch. 11A, para. 3(3), 4(3), 6 and 24 respectively.

TRAVELLING EXPENSES – GENERAL

3 A payment of, or a contribution towards, travel expenses which the holder of an office or employment is obliged to incur and pay as the holder of that office or employment but this paragraph is subject to paragraph 1A.

For the purposes of this paragraph–

(za) **"ordinary commuting"** means travel between–

(i) the employee's home and a permanent workplace; or

(ii) a place that is not a workplace and a permanent workplace;

(zb) **"private travel"** means travel between–

(i) the employee's home and a place that is not a workplace; or

(ii) two places neither of which is a workplace;

(a) **"travel expenses"** means amounts necessarily expended on travelling in the performance of the duties of the office or employment or other expenses of travelling which are attributable to the necessary attendance at any place of the holder of the office or employment in the performance of the duties of the office or employment and are not expenses of–

(i) ordinary commuting;

(ii) travel between any two places that is for practical purposes substantially ordinary commuting;

(iii) travel between any two places that is for practical purposes substantially private travel; or

(iv) private travel.

(b) [omitted by SI 2016/352, reg. 5(3)(d).]

(c) expenses of travel by the holder of an office or employment between two places at which he performs the duties of different offices or employments under or with companies in the same group are treated as necessarily expended in the performance of the duties which he is to perform at his destination; and

(d) for the purpose of sub-paragraph (c), companies are to be taken to be members of the same group if and only if–

(i) one is a 51 per cent. subsidiary of the other, or

(ii) both are 51 per cent. subsidiaries of a third company,

within the meaning of section 838(1)(a) of the Taxes Act (subsidiaries).

History – In para. 3, the words "but this paragraph is subject to paragraph 1A" inserted by SI 2016/352, reg. 5(3)(a), with effect from 6 April 2016.
In para. 3 "travel expenses" substituted in each place and the words "pay as the holder of that office or employment" substituted by SI 2004/770, reg. 28, with effect from 6 April 2004.
Para. 3(za) and (zb) inserted by SI 2016/352, reg. 5(3)(b), with effect from 6 April 2016.
Para. 3(a) substituted by SI 2016/352, reg. 5(3)(c), with effect from 6 April 2016.
In former para. 3(a)(ii) "section 338 of ITEPA 2003 (travel for necessary attendance)" substituted in each place by SI 2004/770, reg. 28, with effect from 6 April 2004.
Para. 3(b) omitted by SI 2016/352, reg. 5(3)(d), with effect from 6 April 2016.
Para. 3(b) substituted by SI 2004/770, reg. 28, with effect from 6 April 2004.

Derivations – SI 1979/591, Sch. 1ZC, Pt. VIII, para. 3.

Cross references – ITEPA 2003, s. 337ff.: income tax deduction for travel expenses.

MEANING OF "WORKPLACE" AND "PERMANENT WORKPLACE"

3ZA(1) For the purposes of paragraph 3–

(a) **"workplace"**, in relation to an employment, means a place at which the employee's attendance is necessary in the performance of the duties of the employment,

(b) **"permanent workplace"**, in relation to an employment, means a place which–

(i) the employee regularly attends in the performance of the duties of the employment, and

(ii) is not a temporary workplace.

This is subject to sub-paragraphs (3) to (7).

3ZA(2) In sub-paragraph (1)(b) **"temporary workplace"**, in relation to an employment, means a place which the employee attends in the performance of the duties of the employment–

(a) for the purpose of performing a task of limited duration, or

(b) for some other temporary purpose.

This is subject to sub-paragraphs (3) and (4).

3ZA(3) A place which the employee regularly attends in the performance of the duties of the employment is treated as a permanent workplace and not a temporary workplace if–

(a) it forms the base from which those duties are performed, or

(b) the tasks to be carried out in the performance of those duties are allocated there.

3ZA(4) A place is not regarded as a temporary workplace if the employee's attendance is–

(a) in the course of a period of continuous work at that place–

(i) lasting more than 24 months, or

(ii) comprising all or almost all of the period for which the employee is likely to hold the employment, or

(b) at a time when it is reasonable to assume that it will be in the course of such a period.

3ZA(5) For the purposes of sub-paragraph (4), a period is a period of continuous work at a place if over the period the duties of the employment are performed to a significant extent at the place.

3ZA(6) An actual or contemplated modification of the place at which duties are performed is to be disregarded for the purpose of sub-paragraphs (4) and (5) if it does not, or would not, have any substantial effect on the employee's journey, or expenses of travelling, to and from the place where they are performed.

3ZA(7) An employee is treated as having a permanent workplace consisting of an area if–

(a) the duties of the employment are defined by reference to an area (whether or not they also require attendance at places outside it),

(b) in the performance of those duties the employee attends different places within the area,

(c) none of the places the employee attends in the performance of those duties is a permanent workplace, and

(d) the area would be a permanent workplace if sub-paragraphs (1)(b), (2), (4), (5) and (6) referred to *the area where they refer* to a place.

History – Para. 3ZA inserted by SI 2016/352, reg. 5(4), with effect from 6 April 2016.

TRAVEL FOR NECESSARY ATTENDANCE: EMPLOYMENT INTERMEDIARIES

3ZB(1) This paragraph applies where an individual ("the worker")–

(a) personally provides services (which are not excluded services) to another person ("the client"), and

(b) the services are provided not under a contract directly between the client or a person connected with the client and the worker but under arrangements involving an employment intermediary.

This is subject to the following provisions of this paragraph.

3ZB(2) Where this paragraph applies, each engagement is for the purposes of paragraphs 3 and 3ZA to be regarded as a separate employment.

3ZB(3) This paragraph does not apply if it is shown that the manner in which the worker provides the services is not subject to (or to the right of) supervision, direction or control by any person.

3ZB(4) Sub-paragraph (3) does not apply in relation to an engagement if–

(a) Chapter 8 of Part 2 of ITEPA 2003 applies in relation to the engagement,

(b) the conditions in section 51, 52 or 53 of that Act are met in relation to the employment intermediary, and

(c) the employment intermediary is not a managed service company.

3ZB(5) This paragraph does not apply in relation to an engagement if–

(a) Chapter 8 of Part 2 of ITEPA 2003 does not apply in relation to the engagement merely because the circumstances in section 49(1)(c) of ITEPA 2003 are not met,

(b) assuming those circumstances were met, the conditions in section 51, 52 or 53 of that Act would be met in relation to the employment intermediary, and

(c) the employment intermediary is not a managed service company.

3ZB(6) In determining for the purposes of sub-paragraphs (4) to (5) whether the conditions in section 51, 52 or 53 of ITEPA 2003 are or would be met in relation to the employment intermediary–

(a) in section 51(1) of that Act–

(i) disregard "either" in the opening words, and

(ii) disregard paragraph (b) (and the preceding "or"), and

(b) read references to the intermediary as references to the employment intermediary.

3ZB(6A) Sub-paragraph (6B) applies if–

(a) the client or a relevant person provides the employment intermediary (whether before or after the worker begins to provide the services) with a fraudulent document which is intended to constitute evidence that, by virtue of sub-paragraph (3), this paragraph does not or will not apply in relation to the services,

(b) that paragraph is taken not to apply in relation to the services, and

(c) in consequence, the employment intermediary does not under these Regulations deduct and account for an amount that would have been deducted and accounted for if this paragraph had been taken to apply in relation to the services.

3ZB(6B) For the purpose of recovering the amount referred to in sub-paragraph (6A) ("the unpaid contributions")–

(a) the worker is to be treated as having an employment with the client or relevant person who provided the document, the duties of which consist of the services, and

(b) the client or relevant person is under these Regulations to account for the unpaid contributions as if they arose in respect of earnings from that employment.

3ZB(6C) In sub-paragraphs (6A) and (6B) **"relevant person"** means a person, other than the client, the worker or a person connected with the employment intermediary, who–

(a) is resident, or has a place of business, in the United Kingdom, and

(b) is party to a contract with the employment intermediary or a person connected with the employment intermediary under or in consequence of which–

(i) the services are provided, or

(ii) the employment intermediary, or a person connected with the employment intermediary makes payments in respect of the services.

3ZB(6D) Sub-paragraph (3) does not apply in relation to an engagement if–

(a) regulations 14 to 18 of the Social Security Contributions (Intermediaries) Regulations 2000 apply in relation to the engagement,

(b) one of conditions A to C in regulation 14 of those Regulations is met in relation to the employment intermediary, and

(c) the employment intermediary is not a managed service company.

3ZB(6E) This paragraph does not apply in relation to an engagement if–

(a) regulations 14 to 18 of the Social Security Contributions (Intermediaries) Regulations 2000 do not apply in relation to the engagement because the circumstances in regulation 13(1)(d) of those Regulations are not met,

(b) assuming those circumstances were met, one of conditions A to C in regulation 14 of those regulations would be met in relation to the employment intermediary, and

(c) the employment intermediary is not a managed service company.

3ZB(6F) In determining for the purposes of sub-paragraph (6D) or (6E) whether one of conditions A to C in regulation 14 is or would be met in relation to the employment intermediary, read references to the intermediary as references to the employment intermediary.

3ZB(7) In determining whether this paragraph applies, no regard is to be had to any arrangements the main purpose, or one of the main purposes, of which is to secure that this paragraph does not to any extent apply.

3ZB(8) In this paragraph–

"arrangements" includes any such scheme, transaction or series of transactions, agreement or understanding, whether or not enforceable, and any associated operations;

"employment intermediary" means a person, other than the worker or the client, who carries on a business (whether or not with a view to profit and whether or not in conjunction with any other business) of supplying labour;

"engagement" means any such provision of services as is mentioned in sub-paragraph (1)(a);

"excluded services" means services provided wholly in the client's home;

"managed service company" means a company which–

(a) is a managed service company within the meaning given by section 61B of ITEPA 2003, or

(b) would be such a company disregarding subsection (1)(c) of that section.

History – Para. 3ZB(6)(a) substituted by SI 2016/647, reg. 2, with effect from 6 July 2016. Former para. 3ZB(6)(a) read as follows: "in section 50(1)(b) of that Act, disregard the words "that is not employment income", and".
Para. 3ZB(6A)–(6C) inserted by SI 2016/1067, reg. 6, with effect from 28 November 2016.
Para. 3ZB(6D)–(6F) inserted by SI 2017/373, reg. 4(2), with effect from 6 April 2017.
Para. 3ZB inserted by SI 2016/352, reg. 5(4), with effect from 6 April 2016.

TRAVEL BY UNPAID DIRECTORS OF NOT-FOR-PROFIT COMPANIES

3A(1) A payment of, or contribution towards, the expenses of the earner's employment if or to the extent that payment or contribution is paid wholly and exclusively for the purposes of paying or reimbursing travel expenses in respect of which conditions A to C are met.

3A(2) Condition A is that–

(a) the earner is obliged to incur the expenses as holder of the employment, and

(b) the expenses are attributable to the earner's necessary attendance at any place in the performance of the duties of the employment.

3A(3) Condition B is that the employment is employment as a director of a not-for-profit company.

3A(4) Condition C is that the employment is one from which the earner receives no earnings other than sums–

(a) paid to the earner in respect of expenses, and

(b) which are so paid by reason of the employment.

3A(5) In this paragraph–

(a) **"director"** has the same meaning as in the benefits code (see section 67 of ITEPA 2003), and

(b) **"not-for-profit company"** means a company that does not carry on activities for the purpose of making profits for distribution to its members or others.

History – Para. 3A and the heading immediately preceding it inserted by SI 2014/608, reg. 4, with effect in relation to expenses incurred on or after 6 April 2014.

TRAVEL WHERE DIRECTORSHIP HELD AS PART OF A TRADE OR PROFESSION

3B *A payment of, or contribution towards, the expenses of the earner's employment to the extent that those expenses are travel expenses which are exempt from income tax in accordance with section 241B of ITEPA 2003 (travel where directorship held as part of a trade or profession).*

History – Para. 3B and the heading immediately preceding it inserted by SI 2014/608, reg. 4, with effect in relation to expenses incurred on or after 6 April 2014.

TRAVEL BETWEEN LINKED EMPLOYMENTS

3C A payment of, or contribution towards, the expenses of the earner's employment to the extent that those expenses are travel expenses deductible for income tax purposes in accordance with section 340A of ITEPA 2003 (travel between linked employments). This paragraph is subject to paragraph 1A.

History – In para. 3C, the words "This paragraph is subject to paragraph 1A." inserted by SI 2016/352, reg. 5(5), with effect from 6 April 2016.

Para. 3C and the heading immediately preceding it inserted by SI 2014/608, reg. 4, with effect in relation to expenses incurred on or after 6 April 2014.

TRAVEL AT START OR FINISH OF OVERSEAS EMPLOYMENT

4 A payment of, or a contribution towards, the expenses of the earner's employment to the extent that those expenses–

(a) are deductible for income tax purposes in accordance with section 341 of ITEPA 2003 (travel at start or finish of overseas employment); or

(b) would be so deductible if–

  (i) Conditions B and C were omitted from that section; and

  (ii) the earnings of the employment were subject to income tax as employment income under that Act.

This paragraph is subject to paragraph 1A.

History – In para. 4, the words "This paragraph is subject to paragraph 1A." inserted by SI 2016/352, reg. 5(5), with effect from 6 April 2016.

Para. 4, 4A, 4B, 4C, 4D and 5 substituted for para. 4 and 5 by SI 2004/770, reg. 28, with effect from 6 April 2004.

Derivations – SI 1979/591, Sch. 1ZC, Pt. VIII, para. 4.

Cross references – ITEPA 2003, s. 341, 376, 342 rewrite ICTA 1988, s. 193(3), (4), (6) respectively.

ITEPA 2003, s. 370 and 371 rewrite ICTA 1988, s. 194(1).

TRAVEL BETWEEN EMPLOYMENTS WHERE DUTIES PERFORMED ABROAD

4A A payment of, or a contribution towards, the expenses of the earner's employment to the extent that those expenses–

(a) are deductible for income tax purposes in accordance with section 342 of ITEPA 2003 (travel between employments where duties performed abroad), or

(b) would be so deductible if–

  (i) Conditions E and F were omitted from that section; and

  (ii) the earnings of the employment were subject to income tax as employment income under that Act.

This paragraph is subject to paragraph 1A.

History – In para. 4A, the words "This paragraph is subject to paragraph 1A." inserted by SI 2016/352, reg. 5(5), with effect from 6 April 2016.

Para. 4, 4A, 4B, 4C, 4D and 5 substituted for para. 4 and 5 by SI 2004/770, reg. 28, with effect from 6 April 2004.

TRAVEL COSTS AND EXPENSES WHERE DUTIES PERFORMED ABROAD: EARNER'S TRAVEL

4B(1) So much of an employed earner's earnings as equals the amount in sub-paragraph (2).

4B(2) The amount in this sub-paragraph is–

(a) the included amount within the meaning of section 370 of ITEPA 2003 (travel costs and expenses where duties performed abroad: employee's travel); or

(b) the amount which would be the included amount within the meaning of that section if the earner were resident and ordinarily resident in the United Kingdom.

This paragraph is subject to paragraph 1A.

History – In para. 4B, the words "This paragraph is subject to paragraph 1A." inserted by SI 2016/352, reg. 5(5), with effect from 6 April 2016.

Para. 4, 4A, 4B, 4C, 4D and 5 substituted for para. 4 and 5 by SI 2004/770, reg. 28, with effect from 6 April 2004.

TRAVEL COSTS AND EXPENSES WHERE DUTIES PERFORMED ABROAD: VISITING SPOUSE'S, CIVIL PARTNER'S OR CHILD'S TRAVEL

History – In the heading to para. 4C the words ", civil partner's" inserted by SI 2005/3130, reg. 5(2), with effect from 5 December 2005.

4C(1) So much of an employed earner's earnings as equals the amount in sub-paragraph (2).

4C(2) The amount in this sub-paragraph is–

(a) the included amount within the meaning of section 371 of ITEPA 2003 (travel costs and expenses where duties performed abroad: visiting spouse's, civil partner's or child's travel); or

(b) the amount which would be the included amount within the meaning of that section if the earner were resident and ordinarily resident in the United Kingdom.

This paragraph is subject to paragraph 1A.

History – In para. 4C, the words "This paragraph is subject to paragraph 1A." inserted by SI 2016/352, reg. 5(5), with effect from 6 April 2016.

In para. 4C(2)(a) the words ", civil partner's" inserted by SI 2005/3130, reg. 5(2), with effect from 5 December 2005.

Para. 4, 4A, 4B, 4C, 4D and 5 substituted for para. 4 and 5 by SI 2004/770, reg. 28, with effect from 6 April 2004.

FOREIGN ACCOMMODATION AND SUBSISTENCE COSTS AND EXPENSES (OVERSEAS EMPLOYMENTS)

4D So much of an employed earner's earnings as equals the amount of the deduction–

(a) permitted for income tax purposes under section 376 of ITEPA 2003 (foreign accommodation and subsistence costs and expenses (overseas employments)); or

(b) which would be so permitted if the earnings of the employment were subject to tax as employment income under ITEPA 2003.

This paragraph is subject to paragraph 1A.

History – In para. 4D, the words "This paragraph is subject to paragraph 1A." inserted by SI 2016/352, reg. 5(5), with effect from 6 April 2016.

Para. 4, 4A, 4B, 4C, 4D and 5 substituted for para. 4 and 5 by SI 2004/770, reg. 28, with effect from 6 April 2004.

TRAVEL COSTS AND EXPENSES OF NON-DOMICILED EMPLOYEE OR THE EMPLOYEE'S SPOUSE, CIVIL PARTNER OR CHILD WHERE DUTIES PERFORMED IN THE UNITED KINGDOM

History – The heading to para. 5 substituted by SI 2005/3130, reg. 5(3), with effect from 5 December 2005.

5 So much of an employed earner's earnings as equals the aggregate amount of the deductions–

(a) permitted for income tax purposes under sections 373 and 374 of ITEPA 2003 (travel costs and expenses of a non-domiciled employee or the employee's spouse, civil partner or child where duties are performed in the United Kingdom); or

(b) which would be so permitted if the earnings of the employment were subject to tax as employment income under ITEPA 2003.

This paragraph is subject to paragraph 1A.

History – In para. 5, the words "This paragraph is subject to paragraph 1A." inserted by SI 2016/352, reg. 5(5), with effect from 6 April 2016.

In para. 5(a) the words ", civil partner" inserted by SI 2005/3130, reg. 5(4), with effect from 5 December 2005.

Para. 4, 4A, 4B, 4C, 4D and 5 substituted for para. 4 and 5 by SI 2004/770, reg. 28, with effect from 6 April 2004.

Derivations – SI 1979/591, Sch. 1ZC, Pt. VIII, para. 5.

Cross references – ITEPA 2003, s. 373, 374 rewrite ICTA 1988, s. 195(7).

TRAVELLING EXPENSES OF WORKERS ON OFFSHORE GAS AND OIL RIGS

6 A payment of, or a contribution towards, expenses where that payment or contribution is disregarded for the purposes of calculating general earnings under section 305 of ITEPA 2003 (offshore oil and gas workers: mainland transfers).

History – In para. 6, the words "general earnings under section 305 of ITEPA 2003 (offshore oil and gas workers: mainland transfers)." substituted for the words "the emoluments of the employment which are charged to tax under Schedule E under Inland Revenue Extra-Statutory Concession A 65 (workers on offshore oil and gas rigs or platforms; free transfers to or from mainland)." by SI 2004/770, reg. 28, with effect from 6 April 2004.

Derivations – SI 1979/591, Sch. 1ZC, Pt. VIII, para. 6.

Cross references – ITEPA 2003, s. 305 gives statutory effect to ESC A65.

PAYMENTS CONNECTED WITH CARS AND VANS AND EXEMPT HEAVY GOODS VEHICLES PROVIDED FOR PRIVATE USE

History – The heading "PAYMENTS CONNECTED WITH CARS AND VANS AND EXEMPT HEAVY GOODS VEHICLES PROVIDED FOR PRIVATE USE" substituted for the heading "INCIDENTAL EXPENSES IN CONNECTION WITH CARS PROVIDED FOR PRIVATE USE" by SI 2004/770, reg. 28, with effect from 6 April 2004.

7(1) A payment–

(a) by way of the discharge of any liability, which by virtue of section 239(1) of ITEPA 2003 (payments and benefits connected with taxable cars and vans and exempt heavy goods vehicles); or

(b) of expenses, which by virtue of section 239(2) of that Act;

is not treated as general earnings of the employment chargeable to tax.

7(2) Sub-paragraph (1) does not apply so far as the payment is made pursuant to optional remuneration arrangements.

History – Reg. 7 renumbered as reg. 7(1) and reg. 7(2) inserted by SI 2018/120, reg. 6(2) and (3), with effect from 6 April 2018.
In para. 7(1)(a) "section 239(1) of ITEPA 2003 (payments and benefits connected with taxable cars and vans and exempt heavy goods vehicles)" substituted by SI 2004/770, reg. 28, with effect from 6 April 2004.
In para. 7(1)(b) "section 239(2)" and "general earnings" substituted and "under Schedule E" omitted by SI 2004/770, reg. 28, with effect from 6 April 2004.

Derivations – SI 1979/591, Sch. 1ZC, Pt. VIII, para. 7.

Cross references – ITEPA 2003, s. 239(1) and (2) rewrite ICTA 1988, s. 157(3)(a) and (c) respectively.

QUALIFYING AMOUNTS OF RELEVANT MOTORING EXPENDITURE

7A(1) To the extent that it would otherwise be earnings, the qualifying amount calculated in accordance with regulation 22A(4).

7A(2) Sub-paragraph (1) does not apply so far as the payment of relevant motoring expenditure within the meaning of regulation 22A(3) is made pursuant to optional remuneration arrangements.

History – Reg. 7A renumbered as reg. 7A(1) and reg. 7A(2) inserted by SI 2018/120, reg. 6(2) and (4), with effect from 6 April 2018.
Para. 7A inserted by SI 2002/307, reg. 7, operative from 6 April 2002.

QUALIFYING AMOUNTS OF MILEAGE ALLOWANCE PAYMENT IN RESPECT OF CYCLES

7B(1) To the extent that it would otherwise be earnings, the qualifying amount of a mileage allowance payment in respect of a cycle.

7B(2) The qualifying amount is that which would be produced by the formula in regulation 22A(4) if the value for R were the rate for the time being approved under section 230(2) of ITEPA 2003 in respect of a cycle.

7B(3) In this paragraph–

"cycle" has the meaning given in section 192(1) of the Road Traffic Act 1988; and

"mileage allowance payment" has the meaning given in section 229(2) of ITEPA 2003.

History – In para. 7B(2) "section 230(2) of ITEPA 2003" substituted by SI 2004/770, reg. 28, with effect from 6 April 2004.
In para. 7B(3) "section 229(2) of ITEPA 2003" substituted by SI 2004/770, reg. 28, with effect from 6 April 2004.
Para. 7B inserted by SI 2002/307, reg. 7, operative from 6 April 2002.

Cross references – ITEPA 2003, s. 230(2) rewrites ICTA 1988, Sch. 12AA, para. 4(2) (approved rate for cycles).
ITEPA 2003, s. 229(2) rewrites ICTA 1988, s. 197AD(2).

QUALIFYING AMOUNTS OF PASSENGER PAYMENT

7C(1) To the extent that it would otherwise be earnings, the qualifying amount of a passenger payment.

7C(2) The qualifying amount is that which would be produced by the formula in regulation 22A(4) if–

(a) references to business travel were to business travel for which the employee receives passenger payments within the meaning of section 233(3) of ITEPA 2003; and

(b) the value for R were the rate for the time being approved for a passenger payment under section 234 of ITEPA 2003.

7C(3) In this paragraph–

"passenger payment" has the meaning given in section 233(3) of ITEPA 2003; and

History – In para. 7C(2)(a) "receives passenger payments within the meaning of section 233(3) of ITEPA 2003" substituted by SI 2004/770, reg. 28, with effect from 6 April 2004.
In para. 7C(2)(b) "section 234 of ITEPA 2003" substituted by SI 2004/770, reg. 28, with effect from 6 April 2004.
In para. 7C(3) "section 233(3) of ITEPA 2003" substituted by SI 2004/770, reg. 28, with effect from 6 April 2004.
In para. 7C(3) the definition of "qualifying passenger" omitted by SI 2004/770, reg. 28, with effect from 6 April 2004.
Para. 7C inserted by SI 2002/307, reg. 7, operative from 6 April 2002.

Cross references – ITEPA 2003, s. 234 rewrites ICTA 1988, Sch. 12AA, para. 5.
ITEPA 2003, s. 233(3) rewrites ICTA 1988, s. 197AE(2).

CAR FUEL

7D A payment by way of the provision of car fuel which is chargeable to income tax under section 149 of ITEPA 2003.

History – Para. 7D substituted by SI 2004/770, reg. 28, with effect from 6 April 2004.
Para. 7D inserted by SI 2002/307, reg. 7, operative from 6 April 2002.

Cross references – ITEPA 2003, s. 149ff. rewrite ICTA 1988, s. 158.
ITEPA 2003, s. 149(3), 721(1) rewrite ICTA 1988, s. 158(3).

VAN FUEL

7E A payment by way of the provision of van fuel which is chargeable to income tax under section 160 of ITEPA 2003.

History – Para. 7E inserted by SI 2008/607, reg. 4(3)(a), with effect from 6 April 2008.

CAR PARKING FACILITIES

8 A payment of, or a contribution towards, the provision of car parking facilities at or near the earner's place of employment which, by virtue of section 237 of ITEPA 2003, is not regarded as general earnings of the earner's employment.

History – In para. 8 "section 237 of ITEPA 2003" substituted for "section 197A of the Taxes Act" and "general earnings" substituted for "an emolument" by SI 2004/770, reg. 28, with effect from 6 April 2004.

Derivations – SI 1979/591, Sch. 1ZC, Pt. VIII, para. 8.

Cross references – ITEPA 2003, s. 237 rewrites ICTA 1988, s. 197A.

AMOUNTS EXEMPTED FROM INCOME TAX UNDER SECTION 289A OF ITEPA 2003

8A Any amount which is exempted from income tax under section 289A of ITEPA 2003.

History – Para. 8A inserted by SI 2016/352, reg. 5(6), with effect from 6 April 2016.

SPECIFIC AND DISTINCT PAYMENTS OF, OR TOWARDS, EXPENSES ACTUALLY INCURRED

9(1) For the avoidance of doubt, there shall be disregarded any specific and distinct payment of, or contribution towards, expenses which an employed earner actually incurs in carrying out his employment. This is subject to the following qualifications.

9(2) Sub-paragraph (1) does not authorise the disregard of any amount by way of relevant motoring expenditure, within the meaning of paragraph (3) of regulation 22A–

(a) in excess of that permitted by the formula in paragraph (4) of that regulation; or

(b) so far as it is paid pursuant to optional remuneration arrangements.

9(3) Sub-paragraph (1) does not authorise the disregard of any amount which–

(a) falls within paragraphs (12) or (13) of regulation 22; or

(b) is paid to an employed earner in respect of anticipated expenses that have yet to be incurred (whether or not such expenses are actually incurred after the payment is made).

History – In para. 9(1), the word "there" substituted for the word "these" and the word "qualifications" substituted for the word "qualification" by SI 2016/352, reg. 5(7)(a), with effect from 6 April 2016.

Para. 9(1) so designated and proviso added, and para. 9(2) inserted by SI 2002/307, reg. 7, operative from 6 April 2002.

Para. 9(2) substituted by SI 2018/120, reg. 6(5), with effect from 6 April 2018. Former para. 9(2) read as follows:

"**9(2)** Sub-paragraph (1) does not authorise the disregard of any amount by way of relevant motoring expenditure, within the meaning of paragraph (3) of regulation 22A, in excess of that permitted by the formula in paragraph (4) of that regulation."

Para. 9(3) inserted by SI 2016/352, reg. 5(7)(b), with effect from 6 April 2016.

Derivations – SI 1979/591, Sch. 1ZC, Pt. VIII, para. 9.

COUNCIL TAX OR WATER OR SEWERAGE CHARGES ON ACCOMMODATION PROVIDED FOR EMPLOYEE'S USE

History – In the heading, the words "council tax or water or sewerage charges" substituted for the words "council tax" by SI 2004/770, reg. 28, with effect from 6 April 2004.

10 A payment of, or a contribution towards meeting, a person's liability for council tax or water or sewerage charges in respect of accommodation occupied by him and provided for him by reason of his employment if, by virtue of sections 99 or 100 of ITEPA 2003 (accommodation provided for performance of duties or as a result of a security threat), he is not liable to income tax in respect of the provision of that accommodation.

This paragraph does not apply to Northern Ireland.

History – In para. 10, the words "council tax or water or sewerage charges" substituted for the words "council tax", and the words "he is not liable to income tax" substituted, by SI 2004/770, reg. 28, with effect from 6 April 2004.

In para. 10, "sections 99 or 100 of ITEPA 2003 (accommodation provided for performance of duties or as a result of a security threat)" substituted, and "under Schedule E" omitted, by SI 2004/770, reg. 28, with effect from 6 April 2004.

Derivations – SI 1979/591, Sch. 1ZC, Pt. VIII, para. 10.

Cross references – ITEPA 2003, s. 99(1), (2), 100 rewrite ICTA 1988, s. 145(4) (exceptions from benefits charge on living accommodation).

ITEPA 2003, s. 314 rewrites ICTA 1988, s. 145(4) (exemption from council tax etc. paid for certain living accommodation).

RATES OR WATER OR SEWERAGE CHARGES ON ACCOMMODATION PROVIDED FOR EMPLOYEE'S USE

History – In the heading, the words "rates or water or sewerage charges" substituted for the word "rates" by SI 2004/770, reg. 28, with effect from 6 April 2004.

11 A payment of, or a contribution towards meeting, a person's liability for rates or water or sewerage charges in respect of accommodation occupied by him and provided for him by reason of his employment if, by virtue of sections 99 or 100 of ITEPA 2003 (accommodation provided for performance of duties or as a result of a security threat), he is not liable to tax in respect of the provision of that accommodation.

This paragraph applies only to Northern Ireland.

History – In para. 11, "sections 99 or 100 of ITEPA 2003 (accommodation provided for performance of duties or as a result of a security threat)" substituted, and "under Schedule E" omitted, by SI 2004/770, reg. 28, with effect from 6 April 2004.
In para. 11, the words "rates or water or sewerage charges" substituted by SI 2004/770, reg. 28, with effect from 6 April 2004.

Cross references – ITEPA 2003, s. 99(1), (2), 100 rewrite ICTA 1988, s. 145(4) (exceptions from benefits charge on living accommodation).
ITEPA 2003, s. 314 rewrites ICTA 1988, s. 145(4) (exemption from council tax etc. paid for certain living accommodation).

FOREIGN SERVICE ALLOWANCE

12 A payment by way of an allowance which is not regarded as income for any income tax purpose by virtue of section 299 of ITEPA 2003 (Crown employees' foreign service allowance).

History – In para. 12 "section 299 of ITEPA 2003 (Crown employees' foreign service allowance)" substituted by SI 2004/770, reg. 28, with effect from 6 April 2004.

Derivations – SI 1979/591, Sch. 1ZC, Pt. VIII, para. 11.

Cross references – ITEPA 2003, s. 299 rewrites ICTA 1988, s. 319.

HM FORCES' OPERATIONAL ALLOWANCE

12A(1) A payment of the Operational Allowance to members of the armed forces of the Crown.

12A(2) The Operational Allowance is an allowance designated as such under a Royal Warrant made under section 333 of the Armed Forces Act 2006.

History – Para. 12A substituted by SI 2012/817, reg. 9(a), with effect from 6 April 2012.
Para. 12A inserted by SI 2006/2924, reg. 2(2) with effect from 14 November 2006.

HM FORCES' COUNCIL TAX RELIEF

12B(1) A payment of Council Tax Relief to members of the armed forces of the Crown.

12B(2) Council Tax Relief is a payment designated as such under a Royal Warrant made under section 333 of the Armed Forces Act 2006.

History – Para. 12B substituted by SI 2012/817, reg. 9(b), with effect from 6 April 2012.
Para. 12B inserted by SI 2008/607, reg. 4(3)(b), with effect from 1 April 2008.

HM FORCES' CONTINUITY OF EDUCATION ALLOWANCE

12C(1) A payment of the Continuity of Education Allowance to or in respect of members of the armed forces of the Crown.

12C(1) The Continuity of Education Allowance is an allowance designated as such under a Royal Warrant made under section 333 of the Armed Forces Act 2006.

History – Para. 12C inserted by SI 2012/817, reg. 9(c), with effect from 6 April 2012.

COMMONWEALTH WAR GRAVES COMMISSION AND BRITISH COUNCIL: EXTRA COST OF LIVING ALLOWANCE

13 A payment by way of an allowance to a person in the service of the Commonwealth War Graves Commission or the British Council paid with a view to compensating him for the extra cost of living outside the United Kingdom in order to perform the duties of his employment.

Derivations – SI 1979/591, Sch. 1ZC, Pt. VIII, para. 12.

OVERSEAS MEDICAL TREATMENT

14 A payment of, or a contribution towards, expenses incurred in–

(a) providing an employee with medical treatment outside the United Kingdom (including providing for him to be an in-patient) in a case where the need for the treatment arises while the employee is outside the United Kingdom for the purposes of performing the duties of his employment; or

(b) providing insurance for the employee against the cost of such treatment in a case falling within sub-paragraph (a).

Here **"medical treatment"** includes all forms of treatment for, and all procedures for diagnosing, any physical or mental ailment, infirmity or defect.

Derivations – SI 1979/591, Sch. 1ZC, Pt. VIII, para. 13.

RECOMMENDED MEDICAL TREATMENT

14A A payment or reimbursement to which no liability to income tax arises by virtue of section 320C of ITEPA 2003 (recommended medical treatment).

History – Para. 14A inserted by SI 2014/3228, reg. 4, with effect from 1 January 2015.

EXPERTS SECONDED TO EUROPEAN COMMISSION

History – Heading inserted by SI 2004/770, reg. 28, with effect from 6 April 2004.

15 A payment in respect of daily subsistence allowances paid by the European Commission to persons whose services are made available to the Commission by their employers under the detached national experts scheme which is exempt from income tax by virtue of section 304 of ITEPA 2003 (experts seconded to European Commission).

History – Para. 15 inserted by SI 2004/770, reg. 28, with effect from 6 April 2004.

EXPERTS SECONDED TO A BODY OF THE EUROPEAN UNION

15A A payment in respect of subsistence allowances paid–

(a) by a body of the European Union that is located in the United Kingdom and listed in the table below;

(b) to persons who, because of their expertise in matters relating to the subject matter of the functions of the body, are seconded to the body by their employers.

Bodies of the European Union located in the United Kingdom

The European Medicines Agency

The European Police College

The European Banking Authority

History – Para. 15A inserted by SI 2011/797, reg. 7, with effect from 6 April 2011.

EXPENSES OF MPS AND OTHER REPRESENTATIVES

16 A payment to which no liability to income tax arises by virtue of any of the following provisions of ITEPA 2003–

(a) section 292 (accommodation expenses of MPs);

(b) section 293 (overnight expenses of other elected representatives);

(c) section 293A (UK travel and subsistence expenses of MPs);

(ca) section 293B (UK travel expenses of other elected representatives);

(d) section 294 (European travel expenses of MPs and other representatives).

History – Para. 16(ca) inserted by SI 2013/1907, reg. 4(a), with effect from 1 September 2013.
Para. 16 and the heading before it inserted by SI 2011/225, reg. 3, with effect from 28 February 2011.

TRAVEL EXPENSES OF MEMBERS OF LOCAL AUTHORITIES ETC

17 A payment to which no liability to income tax arises by virtue of section 295A of ITEPA 2003 (travel expenses of members of local authorities etc).

History – Para. 17 inserted by SI 2016/352, reg. 5(8), with effect from 6 April 2016.

Part IX – Incentives by way of Securities

History – Heading to Pt. IX substituted by SI 2003/2085, reg. 12(2) with effect from 1 September 2003.

CERTAIN PAYMENTS BY WAY OF SECURITIES, RESTRICTED SECURITIES AND RESTRICTED INTERESTS IN SECURITIES, AND GAINS ARISING FROM THEM, DISREGARDED

1 Payments by way of securities, restricted securities and restricted interests in securities, and gains arising from them, are disregarded in the calculation of an employed earner's earnings to the extent mentioned in this Part.

History – Para. 1 and heading substituted by SI 2003/2085, reg. 12(3) with effect from 1 September 2003.

Derivations – SI 1979/591, Sch. 1ZC, Pt. IX, para. 1.

SHARES IN SECONDARY CONTRIBUTOR OR ASSOCIATED BODY

2 [Omitted by SI 2003/2085, reg. 12(4).]

History – Para. 2 substituted by SI 2003/2085, reg. 12(3) with effect from 1 September 2003.

Derivations – SI 1979/591, Sch. 1ZC, Pt. IX, para. 2.

RIGHTS TO ACQUIRE SECURITIES

3 A payment by way of a right to acquire securities.

History – Para. 3 substituted by SI 2003/2085, reg. 12(5) with effect from 1 September 2003.

Derivations – SI 1979/591, Sch. 1ZC, Pt. IX, para. 3.

"SHORT" SHARE OPTIONS GRANTED ON OR AFTER 6TH APRIL 1999

3A [Omitted by SI 2003/2085, reg. 12(6).]

History – Para. 3A omitted by SI 2003/2085, reg. 12(6), with effect from 1 September 2003.
Para. 3A inserted by SI 2001/2412, reg. 5, operative from 26 July 2001.

ENTERPRISE MANAGEMENT INCENTIVES

4 [Omitted by SI 2003/2085, reg. 7(6).]

History – Para. 4 omitted by SI 2003/2085, reg. 12(6), with effect from 1 September 2003.

Derivations – SI 1979/591, Sch. 1ZC, Pt. IX, para. 4.

PRIORITY SHARE ALLOCATIONS

5 A payment by way of an allocation of shares in priority to members of the public in respect of which no liability to income tax arises by virtue of section 542 of ITEPA 2003.

History – Para. 5 substituted by SI 2003/2085, reg. 12(7) with effect from 1 September 2003.

Derivations – SI 1979/591, Sch. 1ZC, Pt. IX, para. 5.

PARTNERSHIP SHARE AGREEMENTS

6 A payment that is deducted from the earnings of the employment under a partnership share agreement.
Here **"partnership share agreement"** has the meaning given in paragraph 44 of Schedule 2 to ITEPA 2003.

History – In para. 6 words "paragraph 44 of Schedule 2 to ITEPA 2003" substituted by SI 2003/2085, reg. 12(8) with effect from 1 September 2003.

Derivations – SI 1979/591, Sch. 1ZC, Pt. IX, para. 6.

SHARES UNDER SHARE INCENTIVE PLANS

7 A payment by way of an award of shares under a share incentive plan within the meaning of Schedule 2 to ITEPA 2003.

History – Para. 7 and para. 7A substituted for para. 7 by SI 2003/2085, reg. 12(9) with effect from 1 September 2003.

Derivations – SI 1979/591, Sch. 1ZC, Pt. IX, para. 7.

SECURITIES AND INTERESTS IN SECURITIES WHICH ARE NOT READILY CONVERTIBLE ASSETS

7A A payment by way of the acquisition of securities, interests in securities or securities options in connection with employed earner's employment if, or to the extent that, what is acquired is not a readily convertible asset.
Here **"acquisition"** includes acquisition pursuant to an employment-related securities option within the meaning of section 471(5) of ITEPA 2003 as substituted by the Finance Act 2003.

History – Para. 7 and para. 7A substituted for para. 7 by SI 2003/2085, reg. 12(9) with effect from 1 September 2003.

SHARES UNDER APPROVED PROFIT SHARING SCHEMES

8 [Omitted by SI 2003/2085, reg. 12(10).]

History – Para. 8 omitted by SI 2003/2085, reg. 12(10) with effect from 1 September 2003.

Derivations – SI 1979/591, Sch. 1ZC, Pt. IX, para. 8.

RESTRICTED SECURITIES AND RESTRICTED INTERESTS IN SECURITIES

9(1) A payment by way of the acquisition of restricted securities, or a restricted interest in securities, where those securities are, or that interest is, employment-related, if no charge to income tax arises under section 425 of ITEPA 2003 other than by virtue of subsection (2) of that section.
This is subject to the following qualification.

9(2) This paragraph does not apply if an election has been made as mentioned in subsection (3) of section 425 of ITEPA 2003.

9(3) References in this paragraph to section 425 of ITEPA 2003 are to that section as substituted by paragraph 3(1) of Schedule 22 to the Finance Act 2003.

History – Para. 9 substituted by SI 2003/2085, reg. 12(11) with effect from 1 September 2003.

Derivations – SI 1979/591, Sch. 1ZC, Pt. IX, para. 9.

CONDITIONAL INTEREST IN SHARES: GAINS FROM EXERCISE ETC. OF SHARE OPTIONS

10 [Omitted by SI 2003/2085, reg. 12(12).]

History – Para. 10 omitted by SI 2003/2085, reg. 12(12) with effect from 1 September 2003.

Derivations – SI 1979/591, Sch. 1ZC, Pt. IX, para. 10.

CONVERTIBLE SHARES

11 [Omitted by SI 2003/2085, reg. 12(12).]

History – Para. 11 omitted by SI 2003/2085, reg. 12(12) with effect from 1 September 2003.

Derivations – SI 1979/591, Sch. 1ZC, Pt. IX, para. 11.

CONVERTIBLE SHARES: GAINS FROM THE EXERCISE ETC. OF SHARE OPTIONS

12 [Omitted by SI 2003/2085, reg. 12(12).]

History – Para. 12 omitted by SI 2003/2085, reg. 12(12) with effect from 1 September 2003.

Derivations – SI 1979/591, Sch. 1ZC, Pt. IX, para. 12.

SHARE OPTION GAINS BY DIRECTORS AND EMPLOYEES

13 [Omitted by SI 2003/2085, reg. 12(12).]

History – Para. 13 omitted by SI 2003/2085, reg. 12(12) with effect from 1 September 2003.

Derivations – SI 1979/591, Sch. 1ZC, Pt. IX, para. 13.

SHARES ACQUIRED UNDER OPTIONS GRANTED BEFORE 9TH APRIL 1998

14 [Omitted by SI 2003/2085, reg. 12(12).]

History – Para. 14 omitted by SI 2003/2085, reg. 12(12) with effect from 1 September 2003.

Derivations – SI 1979/591, Sch. 1ZC, Pt. IX, para. 14.

ASSIGNMENT OR RELEASE OF OPTION

15 [Omitted by SI 2003/2085, reg. 12(12).]

History – Para. 15 substituted by SI 2003/2085, reg. 12(12) with effect from 1 September 2003.

Derivations – SI 1979/591, Sch. 1ZC, Pt. IX, para. 15.

EXERCISE OF OPTIONS ACQUIRED BEFORE 6TH APRIL 1999

16(1) A gain realised by the exercise (in whole or in part) of a right, obtained before 6th April 1999, to acquire shares in a body corporate unless paragraph 17 applies, but only to the extent that the gain realised consists of the shares acquired.

16(2) In this paragraph and paragraphs 16A and 17–

"shares" includes stock; and

"body corporate" *includes*–

(a) a body corporate constituted under the law of a country or territory outside the United Kingdom; and

(b) an unincorporated association wherever constituted.

History – Para. 16 and para. 16A substituted for para. 16 by SI 2003/2085, reg. 12(13) with effect from 1 September 2003.
In former para. 16(1), the words from "chargeable to tax as employment income" to end previously substituted by SI 2003/1059, reg. 4(2)(a) with effect from 10 April 2003.

In former para. 16(4), the words "section 485 of the Income Tax (Earnings and Pensions) Act 2003" substituted by SI 2003/1059, reg. 4(2)(b) with effect from 10 April 2003.

Derivations – SI 1979/591, Sch. 1ZC, Pt. IX, para. 16.

EXERCISE OF REPLACEMENT SHARE OPTIONS WHERE ORIGINAL OPTION ACQUIRED BEFORE 6TH APRIL 1999

16A(1) A gain realised by the exercise of a replacement right to acquire shares in a body corporate where the original right was obtained before 6th April 1999 provided that–

(a) sub-paragraph (4) is satisfied, and

(b) paragraph 17 does not apply,

The disregard conferred by this paragraph is subject to the following limitation.

16A(2) Only the value of the shares acquired by the exercise of the replacement right shall be disregarded.

16A(3) In this paragraph and paragraph 17–

"the original right" means the right, acquired before 6th April 1999, to acquire shares in a body corporate; and

"replacement right" means a right to acquire shares, obtained, whether as the result of one transaction or a series of transactions, and whether directly or indirectly, in consequence of–

(a) the assignment or release of the original right; or

(b) the assignment or release of a right which was itself obtained in consequence of the assignment or release of that right.

16A(4) This sub-paragraph is satisfied in respect of a transaction through which the replacement right was obtained if **A** is not substantially greater than **R**.

Here–

A is the market value of the shares which may be obtained by the exercise of the right acquired on that occasion, less any consideration which would have to be given on that occasion by or on behalf of the earner if that right were to be exercised immediately after its acquisition (disregarding any restriction on its exercise); and

R is the market value of the shares subject to the right assigned or released on that occasion, immediately before that occasion, less any consideration which would have been required to be given by or on behalf of the earner for the exercise of that right, disregarding any restriction on its exercise, subject to the following qualification.

If a transaction involves only a partial replacement of an earlier right, the amount of the earlier consideration to be deducted in computing **R** shall be proportionately reduced.

History – Para. 16 and para. 16A substituted for para. 16 by SI 2003/2085, reg. 12(13) with effect from 1 September 2003.

PAYMENTS RESULTING FROM EXERCISE, ASSIGNMENT OR RELEASE OF OPTIONS WHICH ARE NOT DISREGARDED BY VIRTUE OF PARAGRAPH 16

17(1) This paragraph applies to a payment–

(a) made on or after 10th April 2003, and

(b) which would otherwise fall to be disregarded by virtue of paragraph 16 or 16A of this Part,

where the market value of the shares has been increased by more than 10% by things done, on or after 6th April 1999, otherwise than for genuine commercial purposes.

17(2) For the purposes of sub-paragraph (1) **"the shares"** includes–

(a) the shares subject to the right currently being exercised; and

(b) where the right to acquire shares held on 6th April 1999 has been replaced by a replacement right, includes the shares subject to a replacement right.

17(3) The following are among the things that are, for the purposes of this paragraph, done otherwise than for genuine commercial purposes–

(a) anything done as part of a scheme or arrangement the main purpose, or one of the main purposes, of which is the avoidance of tax or of contributions under the Act; and

(b) any transaction between companies which, at the time of the transaction, are members of the same group on terms which are not such as might be expected to be agreed between persons acting at arm's length.

17(4) But sub-paragraph (3)(b) does not apply to a payment for group relief within the meaning given in section 402(6) of the Taxes Act.

17(5) In sub-paragraph (3)(b) **"group"** means a body corporate and its 51% subsidiaries (within the meaning of section 838 of the Taxes Act), and other expressions used in this paragraph which are defined in, or for the purposes of, paragraph 16 have the same meaning here as they have in that paragraph.

History – In para. 17(1)(b) reference to para. 16A inserted, "replacement right", and in para. 17(2)(b) the words "a replacement right" substituted by SI 2003/2085, reg. 12(14) with effect from 1 September 2003.
Para. 17 inserted by SI 2003/1059, reg. 4(3) with effect from 10 April 2003.

PAYMENTS MADE TO INTERNATIONALLY MOBILE EMPLOYEES

18(1) So much of any payment as equals the amount in sub-paragraph (3).

18(2) For the purposes of calculating the amount in sub-paragraph (3) treat amounts which count as employment income under Chapters 2 to 5 of Part 7 of ITEPA 2003 as having been paid in equal instalments on each day of the "relevant period" as determined in accordance with section 41G of ITEPA 2003.

18(3) The amount in this sub-paragraph is calculated by adding together every instalment which would satisfy the condition in sub-paragraph (4), (5) or (6) on the day on which the instalment is treated as having been paid.

18(4) The condition in this sub-paragraph is that the instalment does not give rise to a liability to pay earnings-related contributions because the employed earner does not fulfil the prescribed conditions as to residence or presence in Great Britain or Northern Ireland (as the case requires) set out in paragraph (1) of regulation 145 or because the proviso in paragraph (2) of that regulation applies.

18(5) The condition in this sub-paragraph is that the instalment does not give rise to a liability to pay earnings-related contributions because the employed earner is determined in accordance with Title II of Regulation No (EC) 883/2004 and Title II of Regulation No (EC) 987/2009 to be subject only to the legislation of another EEA State or Switzerland.

18(6) The condition in this sub-paragraph is that the instalment does not give rise to a liability to pay earnings-related contributions because the employed earner is determined to be subject only to the legislation of a country outside the United Kingdom pursuant to an Order in Council having effect under section 179 of the Administration Act.

History – Para. 18 and the heading immediately preceding it inserted by SI 2015/478, reg. 21(3), with effect from 6 April 2015.

Part X – Miscellaneous and Supplemental

OTHER MISCELLANEOUS PAYMENTS TO BE DISREGARDED

1(1) The payments listed in this Part are disregarded in the calculation of earnings.

1(2) Paragraph 4 contains additional rules about the way in which the components of a payment by way of expenses incidental to a qualifying absence from home are to be treated for the purpose of earnings-related contributions if the permitted maximum is exceeded.

History – In para. 1(1) the words "this Part" substituted for the words "paragraphs 2 to 21" by SI 2011/225, reg. 4(a), with effect from 28 February 2011.
In para. 1(1) the former reference to "2 to 21" substituted by SI 2008/2624, reg. 2(2)(a), with effect from 27 October 2008.
In para. 1(1) the former reference to "2 to 20" substituted by SI 2008/1431, reg. 2(2)(a), with effect from 1 July 2008.
In para. 1, the former reference to para. 19 substituted for reference to para. 17 by SI 2008/607, reg. 4(4)(a), with effect from 6 April 2008. Formerly reference to para. 17 substituted for reference to para. 16 by SI 2003/2085, reg. 13(a) with effect from 1 September 2003, reference to para. 16 substituted for reference to para. 15 by SI 2001/2924, reg. 4, with effect from 17 December 2002 and reference to para. 15 substituted for reference to para. 14 by SI 2001/2412, reg. 5, operative from 26 July 2001.

Derivations – SI 1979/591, Sch. 1ZC, Pt. X, para. 1

PAYMENTS ON ACCOUNT OF SUMS ALREADY INCLUDED IN THE CALCULATION OF EARNINGS

2 A payment on account of a person's earnings in respect of his employment as an employed earner which comprises, or represents and does not exceed sums which have previously been included in his earnings for the purpose of his assessment of earnings-related contributions.

Derivations – SI 1979/591, Sch. 1ZC, Pt. X, para. 2.

PAYMENTS CONNECTED TO AMOUNTS WITHIN REGULATION 22B

2A(1) A payment ("A") the subject of which represents, or arises or derives (whether wholly or partly or directly or indirectly) from, an amount ("B") treated as remuneration under regulation 22B which has previously been included in an employed earner's earnings for the purposes of assessing earnings-related contributions.

2A(2) Paragraph (1) does not apply to the extent that A exceeds B.

2A(3) For the purposes of determining whether paragraph (1) applies, A is to be treated as including the value of any payment made before A which represents, or arises or derives (whether wholly or partly or directly or indirectly) from, B.

History – Para. 2A inserted by SI 2011/2700, reg. 7, with effect from 6 December 2011.

PAYMENTS DISCHARGING LIABILITY FOR SECONDARY CLASS 1 CONTRIBUTIONS FOLLOWING ELECTION UNDER PARAGRAPH 3B OF SCHEDULE 1 TO THE CONTRIBUTIONS AND BENEFITS ACT

3 A payment by way of the discharge of any liability for secondary Class 1 contributions which has been transferred from the secondary contributor to the employed earner by an election made jointly by them for the purposes of paragraph 3B(1) of Schedule 1 to the Contributions and Benefits Act (elections about contribution liability in respect of relevant employment income).

History – In para. 3, the words "relevant employment income" substituted by SI 2004/2096, reg. 6, with effect in relation to–

- agreements entered into after 1 September 2004 which are in respect of post-commencement employment income (presumably as defined in NICSPA 2004, s. 3(5)), and
- elections made after that date.

Derivations – SI 1979/591, Sch. 1ZC, Pt. X, para. 3.

PAYMENTS BY WAY OF INCIDENTAL OVERNIGHT EXPENSES

History – In the heading, the word "overnight" inserted by SI 2004/770, reg. 28, with effect from 6 April 2004.

4(1) A payment by way of incidental expenses, in whatever form, which by virtue of section 200A of the Taxes Act is not regarded as an emolument of the employment chargeable to tax under Schedule E.

4(2) If a payment is made by way of incidental expenses in connection with a qualifying absence from home, but the amount of that payment (calculated in accordance with section 200A of the Taxes Act) exceeds the authorised maximum, sub-paragraphs (3) to (6) apply.

4(3) So much of the payment as is made by way of cash shall be included in the calculation of earnings.

4(4) The amount of cash for which a cash voucher can be exchanged shall be included in the calculation of earnings.

4(5) The cost of provision of any non-cash voucher shall be included in the calculation of earnings and anything for which the voucher can be exchanged shall be disregarded in that calculation.

4(6) Any payment by way of a benefit in kind shall be disregarded in the calculation of earnings.

4(7) In this paragraph–

"the cost of provision" in relation to a non-cash voucher is the cost incurred by the person at whose expense the voucher is provided;

"the permitted amount" has the meaning given in section 241(3) of ITEPA 2003; and

"qualifying period" has the meaning given in section 240(1)(b) and (4) of ITEPA 2003.

History – Para. 4(1) and (2) substituted by SI 2004/770, reg. 28, with effect from 6 April 2004.
Para. 4(7) substituted by SI 2004/770, reg. 28, with effect from 6 April 2004.

Derivations – SI 1979/591, Sch. 1ZC, Pt. X, para. 4.

Cross references – ITEPA 2003, s. 240, 241 rewrite ICTA 1988, s. 200A.
"Authorised maximum": see ITEPA 2003, s. 241(3) (permitted amount).
"Qualifying absence from home": see ITEPA 2003, s. 240(4)ff (overnight stay conditions).

GRATUITIES AND OFFERINGS

5(1) A payment of, or in respect of, a gratuity or offering which–

(a) satisfies the condition in either sub-paragraph (2) or (3); and

(b) is not within sub-paragraph (4) or (5).

5(2) The condition in this sub-paragraph is that the payment–

(a) is not made, directly or indirectly, by the secondary contributor; and

(b) does not comprise or represent sums previously paid to the secondary contributor.

5(3) The condition in this sub-paragraph is that the secondary contributor does not allocate the payment, directly or indirectly, to the earner.

5(4) A payment made to the earner by a person who is connected with the secondary contributor is within this sub-paragraph unless–

(a) it is–

(i) made in recognition for personal services rendered to the connected person by the earner or by another earner employed by the same secondary contributor; and

(ii) similar in amount to that which might reasonably be expected to be paid by a person who is not so connected; or

(b) the person making the payment does so in his capacity as a tronc-master.

5(5) A payment made to the earner is within this sub-paragraph if it is made by a trustee holding property for any persons who include, or any class of persons which includes, the earner.

In this sub-paragraph **"trustee"** does not include a tronc-master.

5(6) A person is connected with the secondary contributor for the purposes of this paragraph if his relationship with the secondary contributor, or where the employer and secondary contributor are different, with either of them, is as described in subsection (2), (3), (4), (5), (6) or (7) of section 839of the Taxes Act (connected persons).

History – In para. 5(1) the words:
"which–
(a) satisfies the condition in either sub-paragraph (2) or (3); and
(b) is not within sub-paragraph (4) or (5)."
substituted for "which satisfies either of the conditions in this paragraph." by SI 2004/173, reg. 2(2), with effect from 23 February 2004.
In para. 5(2) the words "The condition in this sub-paragraph" substituted by SI 2004/173, reg. 2(3), with effect from 23 February 2004.
In para. 5(3) the words "The condition in this sub-paragraph" substituted by SI 2004/173, reg. 2(4), with effect from 23 February 2004.
Para. 5(4)–(6) inserted by SI 2004/173, reg. 2(5), with effect from 23 February 2004.

Derivations – SI 1979/591, Sch. 1ZC, Pt. X, para. 5.

REDUNDANCY PAYMENTS

6 For the avoidance of doubt, in calculating the earnings paid to or for the benefit of an earner in respect of an employed earner's employment, any payment by way of a redundancy payment shall be disregarded.

Derivations – SI 1979/591, Sch. 1ZC, Pt. X, para. 6.

SICKNESS PAYMENTS ATTRIBUTABLE TO CONTRIBUTIONS MADE BY EMPLOYED EARNER

7 If the funds for making a sickness payment under arrangements of the kind mentioned in section 4(1)(b) of the Contributions and Benefits Act are attributable in part to contributions to those funds made by the employed earner, for the purposes of section 4(1) of that Act the part of that payment which is attributable to those contributions shall be disregarded.

Derivations – SI 1979/591, Sch. 1ZC, Pt. X, para. 7.

EXPENSES AND OTHER PAYMENTS NOT CHARGED TO INCOME TAX UNDER MISCELLANEOUS EXEMPTIONS

8 A payment which is not charged to tax under any of the following provisions of ITEPA 2003–

(a) section 245 (travelling and subsistence during public transport strikes);

(b) section 246 (transport between work and home for disabled employees: general);

(c) section 248 (transport home: late night working and failure of car-sharing arrangements);

(d) section 290A (accommodation outgoings of ministers of religion);

(e) section 290B (allowances paid to ministers of religion in respect of accommodation outgoings);

(f) section 321 (suggestion awards).

History – Para. 8 and the previous heading substituted by SI 2010/188, reg. 2, with effect from 6 April 2010.

VAT ON THE SUPPLY OF GOODS AND SERVICES BY EMPLOYED EARNER

9 If–

(a) goods or services are supplied by an earner in employed earner's employment;

(b) earnings paid to or for the benefit of the earner in respect of that employment include the remuneration for the supply of those goods or services; and

(c) value added tax is chargeable on that supply;

an amount equal to the value added tax chargeable on that supply shall be excluded from the calculation of those earnings.

Derivations – SI 1979/591, Sch. 1ZC, Pt. X, para. 9.

EMPLOYEE'S LIABILITIES AND INDEMNITY INSURANCE

History – The heading of "EMPLOYEE'S LIABILITIES AND INDEMNITY INSURANCE" substituted for the heading of "EMPLOYEE'S INDEMNITY INSURANCE" by SI 2004/770, reg. 28, with effect from 6 April 2004.

10 A payment which by virtue of section 346 of ITEPA 2003 (deduction for employee liabilities) is deductible from the general earnings of the employment chargeable to tax under that Act. This paragraph is subject to paragraph 1A of Part 8 of this Schedule.

History – In para. 10, the words "This paragraph is subject to paragraph 1A of Part 8 of this Schedule." inserted by SI 2016/352, reg. 6(2), with effect from 6 April 2016.
Para. 10 substituted by SI 2004/770, reg. 28, with effect from 6 April 2004.

Derivations – SI 1979/591, Sch. 1ZC, Pt. X, para. 10.

Cross references – ITEPA 2003, s. 346 rewrites ICTA 1988, s. 201AA.

FEES AND SUBSCRIPTIONS TO PROFESSIONAL BODIES, LEARNED SOCIETIES ETC.

11 A payment of, or a contribution towards any fee, contribution or annual subscription which, under section 343 or 344 of ITEPA 2003 (deduction for professional membership fees or annual subscriptions) is deductible from the general earnings of any office or employment. This paragraph is subject to paragraph 1A of Part 8 of this Schedule.

History – In para. 11, the words "This paragraph is subject to paragraph 1A of Part 8 of this Schedule." inserted by SI 2016/352, reg. 6(3), with effect from 6 April 2016.
In para. 11 "section 343 or 344 of ITEPA 2003 (deduction for professional membership fees or annual subscriptions) is deductible from the general earnings of any office or employment" substituted by SI 2004/770, reg. 28, with effect from 6 April 2004.

Derivations – SI 1979/591, Sch. 1ZC, Pt. X, para. 11.

Cross references – ITEPA 2003, s. 343, 344 rewrite ICTA 1988, s. 201.

HOLIDAY PAY

12 [Revoked by SI 2007/2905, reg. 2(2) with effect from 30 October 2007, subject to saving provision in reg. 2(3).]

History – Para. 12 revoked by SI 2007/2905, reg. 2(2) with effect from 30 October 2007, subject to a saving provision in reg. 2(3) so that para. 12 continues to have effect until the fifth anniversary of the commencement date in the case of holiday pay derived from an employed earner's employment if the secondary contributor in relation to that employment is a person carrying on a business which includes construction operations; and the employed earner was personally engaged in such operations at the time that entitlement to that pay accrued. Para. 12 read as follows:

"12 A payment in respect of a period of holiday entitlement where–
(a) the sum paid is derived directly or indirectly from a fund–
(i) to which more than one secondary contributor contributes, and
(ii) the management and control of which are not vested in those secondary contributors; or
(b) the person making the payment is entitled to be reimbursed from such a fund.".

Derivations – SI 1979/591, Sch. 1ZC, Pt. X, para. 12.

PAYMENTS TO MINISTERS OF RELIGION

13 A payment of a fee in respect of employment as a minister of religion which does not form part of the stipend or salary paid in respect of that employment.

Derivations – SI 1979/591, Sch. 1ZC, Pt. X, para. 13.

PAYMENTS TO MINERS AND FORMER MINERS, ETC. IN LIEU OF COAL

History – The heading of "PAYMENTS TO MINERS AND FORMER MINERS, ETC. IN LIEU OF COAL" substituted for the heading of "PAYMENTS IN LIEU OF COAL" by SI 2004/770, reg. 28, with effect from 6 April 2004.

14(1) A payment in lieu of the provision of coal or smokeless fuel, if the employee is–

(a) a colliery worker;

(b) a former colliery worker;

and the condition in sub-paragraph (2) is met.

14(2) The condition is that the amount of coal or fuel in respect of which the payment is made does not substantially exceed the amount reasonably required for personal use.

14(3) That condition is assumed to be met unless the contrary is shown.

14(4) In this paragraph, **"colliery worker"** means a coal miner or any other person employed at or about a colliery otherwise than in clerical, administrative or technical work; and **"former colliery worker"** shall be construed accordingly.

14(5) This paragraph does not apply to Northern Ireland.

History – Para. 14 substituted by SI 2004/770, reg. 28, with effect from 6 April 2004.

Derivations – SI 1979/591, Sch. 1ZC, Pt. X, para. 14.

REWARDS FOR ASSISTANCE WITH LOST OR STOLEN CARDS

15(1) A payment made by an issuer of charge cards, cheque guarantee cards, credit cards or debit cards, as a reward to an individual who assists in identifying or recovering lost or stolen cards in the course of his or her employment as an employed earner (other than employment by the issuer), together with any income tax paid by the issuer for the purpose of discharging any liability of the individual to income tax on the payment.

15(2) In this paragraph–

"charge card" means a credit card, the terms of which include the obligations to settle the account in full at the end of a specified period;

"cheque guarantee card" means a card issued by a bank or building society for the purpose of guaranteeing a payment or supporting the encashment of a cheque up to a specified value;

"credit card" means a card which–

(a) may be used on its own to pay for goods or services or to withdraw cash, and

(b) enables the holder to make purchases and to draw cash up to a prearranged limit; and

"debit card" means a card linked to a bank or building society current account, used to pay for goods or services by debiting the holder's account.

History – Para. 15 and the heading before it inserted by SI 2001/2412, reg. 5, operative from 26 July 2001.

STUDENT LOANS

16(1) A payment made in accordance with Regulations made under section 186 of the Education Act 2002 in respect of the repayment, reduction or extinguishing of the amounts payable in respect of a loan.

16(2) A payment for the purpose of discharging any liability of the earner to income tax for any tax year where the income tax in question is tax chargeable in respect of–

(a) the payment referred to in paragraph (1), or

(b) the payment made for the purpose of discharging the income tax liability itself.

History – Para. 16 and the heading before it inserted by SI 2001/2924, reg. 4, with effect from 17 December 2002.

PAYMENT OF PAYE TAX IN RESPECT OF NOTIONAL PAYMENT

17 A payment by way of income tax for which the employer is required to account to the Board under section 710(1) of ITEPA 2003 (notional payments: accounting for tax).

History – Para. 17 and the heading before it inserted by SI 2003/2085, reg. 13(b) with effect from 1 September 2003.

PAYMENTS MADE FROM THE IN-WORK EMERGENCY DISCRETION FUND

18 Any In-Work Emergency Discretion Fund payment made to a person pursuant to arrangements made by the Secretary of State under section 2 of the Employment and Training Act 1973.

This paragraph does not apply in Northern Ireland.

History – Para. 18 and the heading before it inserted by SI 2008/607, reg. 4(4)(b), with effect from 6 April 2008.

PAYMENTS MADE FROM THE IN-WORK EMERGENCY FUND

19 Any In-Work Emergency Fund payment made to a person pursuant to arrangements made by the Department of Economic Development under section 1 of the Employment and Training Act (Northern Ireland) 1950.

This paragraph applies only in Northern Ireland.

History – Para. 19 and the heading before it inserted by SI 2008/607, reg. 4(4)(b), with effect from 6 April 2008.

UP-FRONT CHILDCARE FUND PAYMENTS

20 Any Up-Front Childcare Fund payment made pursuant to arrangements made by the Secretary of State under section 2 of the Employment and Training Act 1973.

This paragraph does not apply to Northern Ireland.

History – Para. 20 and the heading before it inserted by SI 2008/1431, reg. 2(2)(b), with effect from 1 July 2008.

BETTER OFF IN WORK CREDIT PAYMENTS

21 Any Better off in Work Credit payment made pursuant to arrangements made by the Secretary of State under section 2 of the Employment and Training Act 1973.

This paragraph does not apply to Northern Ireland.

History – Para. 21 and the heading before it inserted by SI 2008/2624, reg. 2(2)(b), with effect from 27 October 2008.

FEES RELATING TO THE PROTECTION OF VULNERABLE GROUPS (SCOTLAND) SCHEME

22 A payment of a fee in respect of an application to join the scheme administered under section 44 of the Protection of Vulnerable Groups (Scotland) Act 2007 (scheme to collate and disclose information about individuals working with vulnerable persons).

History – Para. 22 and the heading before it inserted by SI 2011/225, reg. 4(b), with effect from 28 February 2011.

FEES RELATING TO THE DISCLOSURE AND BARRING SERVICE

23(1) A fee paid by virtue of section 116A(4)(b) or (5)(b) of the Police Act 1997 ("the Police Act") (fee for up-dating certificates).

23(2) A fee paid under–

(a) section 113A(1)(b) of the Police Act (fee for criminal record certificates);

(b) section 113B(1)(b) of the Police Act (fee for enhanced criminal record certificates);

(c) section 114(1)(b) of the Police Act (fee for criminal record certificates: Crown employment); or

(d) section 116(1)(b) of the Police Act (fee for enhanced criminal record certificates: judicial appointments and Crown employment);

where the application is made at the same time as an application under section 116A(4) or (5) of the Police Act for the certificate to be subject to up-date arrangements.

History – Para. 23 inserted by SI 2013/1142, reg. 2, with effect from 10 June 2013.

ADVICE RELATING TO PROPOSED EMPLOYEE SHAREHOLDER AGREEMENTS

24(1) A payment, or reimbursement, in accordance with section 205A(7) of the Employment Rights Act 1996 (employee shareholder status), of any reasonable costs in obtaining relevant advice.

24(2) **"Relevant advice"** has the same meaning as section 326B(2) of ITEPA 2003 (advice relating to proposed employee shareholder agreements).

History – Para. 24 inserted by SI 2013/1907, reg. 4(b), with effect from 1 September 2013.

PAYMENTS ON WHICH CLASS 1 OR CLASS 1A CONTRIBUTIONS HAVE BEEN PAID PURSUANT TO THE SOCIAL SECURITY CONTRIBUTIONS (LIMITED LIABILITY PARTNERSHIP) REGULATIONS 2014

25 A payment made by an employer to an employed earner which represents an amount on which Class 1 or Class 1A contributions are payable by a limited liability partnership in respect of that earner by virtue of regulation 3 or 4 of the Social Security Contributions (Limited Liability Partnership) Regulations 2014.

History – Para. 25 inserted by SI 2014/3159, reg. 5(3), with effect for the tax year 2014–15 and subsequent tax years.

SCHEDULE 4 – PROVISIONS DERIVED FROM THE INCOME TAX ACTS AND THE INCOME TAX (PAY AS YOU EARN) REGULATIONS 2003

Regulation 67

Part I – General

History – Sch. 4 heading substituted by SI 2004/770, reg. 29, with effect from 6 April 2004.

INTERPRETATION

1(1) In this Schedule the **"PAYE Regulations"** means the Income Tax (Pay As You Earn) Regulations 2003

1(2) In this Schedule, except where the context otherwise requires–

"aggregated" means aggregated and treated as a single payment under paragraph 1(1) of Schedule 1 to the Act;

"allowable pension contributions" means any sum paid by an employee by way of contribution towards a pension fund or scheme which is withheld from the payment of PAYE income and for which a deduction must be allowed from employment income under section 592(7) or 594(1) of the Taxes Act (exempt approved schemes and exempt statutory schemes);

"closed tax year" means any year preceding the current year and cognate expressions shall be construed accordingly;

"Compensation of Employers Regulations" means the Statutory Maternity Pay (Compensation of Employers) and Miscellaneous Amendments Regulations 1994

"deductions working sheet" means any form of record on or in which are to be kept the matters required by this Schedule in connection with an employee's general earnings and earnings-related contributions;

"earnings-related contributions" means contributions payable under the Act by or in respect of an employed earner in respect of employed earner's employment;

"employed earner" and**"employed earner's employment"** have the same meaning as in the Act;

"employee" means any person in receipt of earnings;

"employer" means the secondary contributor determined–

(a) by section 7 of the Act;

(b) under regulation 5 of, and Schedule 3 to, the Social Security (Categorisation of Earners) Regulations 1978; or

(c) under regulation 122;

"Inland Revenue" means any officer of the Board of Inland Revenue;

"mariner" has the same meaning as in regulation 115;

"non-Real Time Information employer" means an employer other than one within sub-paragraph (4);

"Real Time Information employer" has the meaning given in sub-paragraph (4);

"tax month" means the period beginning on the 6th day of any calendar month and ending on the 5th day of the following calendar month;

"tax period" means a tax quarter where paragraph 11 has effect, but otherwise means a tax month;

"tax quarter" means the period beginning on 6th April and ending on 5th July, or beginning on 6th July and ending on 5th October, or beginning on 6th October and ending on 5th January, or beginning on 6th January and ending on 5th April;

"voyage period" has the same meaning as in regulation 115;

"year" means tax year; and other expressions have the same meaning as in the Income Tax Acts.

History – In para. 1, in the definition of "Compensation of Employers Regulations", the words "and the Statutory Sick Pay Percentage Threshold Order 1995" omitted by SI 2014/2397, reg. 3(2), with effect from 6 October 2014.

1(3) For the purposes of paragraphs 7(13), 9, 10, 11 and 22, **"primary Class 1 contributions"** and **"earnings-related contributions"** shall, unless the context otherwise requires, include any amount paid on account of earnings-related contributions in accordance with the provisions of regulation 8(6).

1(4) The following are Real Time Information employers for the purposes of this Schedule–

(a) an employer who has entered into an agreement with HMRC to comply with the provisions of this Schedule which are expressed as relating to Real Time Information employers;

(b) an employer within sub-paragraph (5);

(c) [omitted by SI 2013/622, reg. 6;] and

(d) on and after 6th October 2013, all employers.

1(5) An employer is within this paragraph if the employer has been given a general or specific direction by the Commissioners for Her Majesty's Revenue and Customs before 6th October 2013 to deliver to HMRC returns under paragraph 21A of this Schedule (real time returns of information about payments of earnings).

History – In para. 1(2), in the definition of "deductions working sheet", the words "or the form issued by the Inland Revenue under paragraph 31", which appeared after the word "contributions", omitted by SI 2014/608, reg. 6, with effect from 6 April 2014.
In para. 1(2), in the definition of "deductions working sheet", the words "or under regulation 35 of the PAYE Regulations (simplified deduction scheme)", which appeared after the words "paragraph 31", omitted by SI 2013/622, reg. 4(2), with effect from 6 April 2014 in relation to the tax year 2014–15.
In para. 1(2), in the definition of "employee", the word "general" (which appeared before the word "earnings") omitted by SI 2015/478, reg. 22(2)(a)(i), with effect from 6 April 2015.
In para. 1(2), definition of "general earnings" omitted by SI 2015/478, reg. 22(2)(a)(ii), with effect from 6 April 2015.
In para. 1(2), definition of "general earnings" substituted by SI 2012/821, reg. 20(a), with effect from 6 April 2012.
In para. 1(2), definitions of "non-Real Time Information employer" and "Real Time Information employer" inserted by SI 2012/821, reg. 5(a), with effect from 6 April 2012.
In para. 1(2), definition of "the Reimbursement Regulations" omitted by SI 2012/821, reg. 20(b), with effect from 6 April 2012.
In para. 1(2), definition of "HMRC" omitted by SI 2009/600, reg. 8(2), with effect from 1 April 2009.
In para. 1(2), definitions of "closed tax year" and "HMRC" inserted by SI 2007/1056, reg. 8(2), with effect from 6 April 2007.
Para. 1(1) and (2) substituted by SI 2004/770, reg. 30, with effect from 6 April 2004.
In former para. 1(2), definition of "employer" substituted by SI 2002/2929, reg. 4 (repealed by SI 2004/770, Sch. from 6 April 2004), with effect from 28 November 2002.
Para. 1(4)(c) (but not the "and" after it) omitted by SI 2013/622, reg. 6, with effect from 6 April 2013 in relation to the tax year 2013–14 and subsequent tax years.
In para. 1(5), the word "general" (which appeared before the word "earnings") omitted by SI 2015/478, reg. 22(2)(b), with effect from 6 April 2015.
Para. 1(4) and (5) inserted by SI 2012/821, reg. 5(b), with effect from 6 April 2012.

Derivations – SI 1979/591, Sch. 1, reg. 2(1).

Cross references – SI 2003/3682 rewrites the Income Tax Regulations.
SI 2003/3682, reg. 35(3) rewrites reg. 20 of the Income Tax Regulations (deductions working sheet).

MULTIPLE EMPLOYERS

2(1) If–

(a) an employer has made an election under regulation 98 of the PAYE Regulations to be treated as a different employer in respect of each group of employees specified in the election, and

(b) no improper purpose notice has been given, or if one has been given it has been withdrawn,

he shall be treated as having made an identical election for the purposes of this Schedule.

2(2) In this paragraph an **"improper purpose notice"** is a notice issued to the employer stating that it appears to the Inland Revenue that the election is made wholly or mainly for an improper purpose within the meaning of regulation 99(2) of the PAYE Regulations.

History – Para. 2 substituted by SI 2004/770, reg. 30, with effect from 6 April 2004.

Derivations – SI 1979/591, Sch. 1, reg. 2A.

Cross references – SI 2003/3682, reg. 98 rewrites reg. 3 of the Income Tax Regulations.

INTERMEDIATE EMPLOYERS

3(1) Where an employee works for a person who is not his immediate employer, that person shall be treated as the employer for the purpose of this Schedule, and the immediate employer shall furnish the principal employer with such particulars of the employee's earnings as may be necessary to enable the principal employer to comply with the provisions of this Schedule.

This is subject to the qualification in sub-paragraph (4).

3(2) In this paragraph–

"the principal employer" means the person specified as the relevant person in the direction referred to in sub-paragraph (4); and

"the immediate employer" means the person specified as the contractor in that direction.

3(3) If the employee's earnings are actually paid to him by the immediate employer–

(a) the immediate employer shall be notified by the principal employer of the amount of earnings-related contributions which may be deducted when those earnings are paid to the employee, and may deduct the amount so notified to him accordingly; and

(b) the principal employer may make a corresponding deduction on making to the immediate employer the payment out of which those earnings will be paid.

3(4) This paragraph only applies if a direction has been given by the Board under section 691 of ITEPA 2003 (PAYE: mobile UK workforce).

3(5) Where an employee is paid a sickness payment which by virtue of regulation 23 is not made through the secondary contributor in relation to the employment–

(a) the person making that payment shall furnish the secondary contributor with such particulars of that payment as may be necessary to enable the secondary contributor to comply with this Schedule; and

(b) for the purposes only of this Schedule the secondary contributor shall be treated as having made the sickness payment.

History – In para. 3(1), the word "general" (which appeared before the word "earnings") omitted by SI 2015/478, reg. 22(2)(c), with effect from 6 April 2015.

In para. 3(1) "general earnings" substituted by SI 2004/770, reg. 30, with effect from 6 April 2004.

In para. 3(3), the word "general" (which appeared before the word "earnings") omitted by SI 2015/478, reg. 22(2)(c), with effect from 6 April 2015.

In para. 3(3) "employee's general earnings" substituted by SI 2004/770, reg. 30, with effect from 6 April 2004.

In para. 3(3)(a) "those earnings" substituted by SI 2004/770, reg. 30, with effect from 6 April 2004.

In para. 3(3)(b) "those earnings" substituted by SI 2004/770, reg. 30, with effect from 6 April 2004.

In para. 3(4) "section 691 of ITEPA 2003" substituted by SI 2004/770, reg. 30, with effect from 6 April 2004.

Derivations – SI 1979/591, Sch. 1, reg. 3.

Cross references – ITEPA 2003, s. 691 rewrites ICTA 1988, s. 203E.

EMPLOYER'S EARNINGS-RELATED CONTRIBUTIONS

4 If, under this Schedule, a person pays any earnings-related contributions which, under section 6(4) of the Act, another person is liable to pay, his payment of those contributions shall be made as agent for that other person.

History – In para. 4, word "pays" substituted by SI 2002/2929, reg. 5, with effect from 28 November 2002.

Derivations – SI 1979/591, Sch. 1, reg. 3A.

INTERMEDIARIES

4A(1) Where any payment of earnings of an employee is made by an intermediary of the employer, the employer shall be treated, for the purposes of this Schedule other than–

(a) paragraph 7(1),

(b) paragraph 7(3)(a),

(c) the references to a subsequent payment of earnings or of monetary earnings in paragraph 7(3) and (8), and

(d) paragraph 7(11),

as making the payment of those earnings to the employee.

4A(2) For the purposes of this paragraph, a payment of earnings of an employee is made by an intermediary of the employer if it is made–

(a) either–

(i) by a person acting on behalf of the employer and at the expense of the employer, or

(ii) by a person connected with him, or

(b) by trustees holding property for any persons who include, or class of persons which includes, the employee.

4A(3) Section 839 of the Taxes Act (connected persons) applies for the purposes of this paragraph.

History – In para. 4A(1) and (2), the word "general" (which appeared before the word "earnings" in each place) omitted by SI 2015/478, reg. 22(2)(c), with effect from 6 April 2015.

In para. 4A "general earnings" substituted in each place by SI 2004/770, reg. 30, with effect from 6 April 2004.

Para. 4A inserted by SI 2002/2929, reg. 6, with effect from 28 November 2002.

CONTINUATION OF PROCEEDINGS ETC.

5 Any legal proceedings or administrative act authorised by or done for the purposes of this Schedule and begun by one Inland Revenue officer may be continued by another officer, and any officer may act for any division or other area.

History – Para. 5 substituted by SI 2004/770, reg. 31, with effect from 6 April 2004.

Derivations – SI 1979/591, Sch. 1, reg. 4A.

Part II – Deduction of Earnings-related Contributions

DEDUCTION OF EARNINGS-RELATED CONTRIBUTIONS

6(1) Every employer, on making during any year to any employee any payment of earnings in respect of which earnings-related contributions are payable, or are treated as payable–

(a) shall, if he has not already done so, prepare a deductions working sheet for that employee, and

(b) may deduct earnings-related contributions in accordance with this Schedule.

6(1A) Where a liability to pay retrospective contributions has arisen in respect of an employee, an employer shall amend the relevant deductions working sheet or where necessary prepare one in respect of that employee.

6(2) Subject to sub-paragraph (3), an employer shall not be entitled to recover any earnings-related contributions paid or to be paid by him on behalf of any employee otherwise than by deduction in accordance with this Schedule.

6(3) Sub-paragraph (2) does not apply to secondary Class 1 contributions in respect of which an election has been made jointly by the secondary contributor and the employed earner for the purposes of paragraph 3B(1) of Schedule 1 to the Act (election in respect of transfer of secondary contribution liability on relevant employment income) if the election provides for the collection of the amount in respect of which liability is transferred.

History – In para. 6(1), the word "general" (which appeared before the word "earnings") and the words ", or on making any payment of statutory maternity pay" (which appeared after the words "treated as payable") omitted by SI 2015/478, reg. 22(3)(a), with effect from 6 April 2015.

In para. 6(1) "general earnings" substituted by SI 2004/770, reg. 31, with effect from 6 April 2004.

In para. 6(1)(a), the words ", or in the case of an employee to whom regulation 35 of the PAYE Regulations (simplified deduction scheme) applies, maintain" omitted by SI 2013/622, reg. 4(3), with effect from 6 April 2014, in relation to the tax year 2014–15.

In para. 6(1)(a) "regulation 35 of the PAYE Regulations (simplified deduction scheme)" substituted by SI 2004/770, reg. 31, with effect from 6 April 2004.

Para. 6(1A) inserted by SI 2007/1056, reg. 8(3), with effect from 6 April 2007.

In para. 6(3), the words "relevant employment income" substituted by SI 2004/2096, reg. 7(a), with effect in relation to–

- agreements entered into after 1 September 2004 which are in respect of post-commencement employment income (presumably as defined in NICSPA 2004, s. 3(5)), and
- elections made after that date.

Derivations – SI 1979/591, Sch. 1, reg. 6.

Cross references – SI 2003/3682, reg. 35(3) rewrites reg. 20 of the Income Tax Regulations (deductions working sheet).

CALCULATION OF DEDUCTION

7(1) Subject to sub-paragraph (2), on making any payment of earnings to the employee, the employer may deduct from those earnings the amount of the earnings-related contributions based on those earnings which the employee is liable to pay under section 6(4) of the Act (the **"section 6(4)(a) amount"**).

7(1A) On making any chain payment the fee-payer may deduct the amount of earnings related contributions calculated by reference to the deemed direct earnings which the feepayer is liable to pay.

7(2) Where two of more payments of earnings fall to be aggregated, the employer may deduct the amount of the earnings-related contributions based on those earnings, which are payable by the employee, either wholly from one such payment or partly from one and partly from the other or any one or more of the others.

7(3) If the employer–

(a) on making any payment of earnings to an employee does not deduct from those earnings the full section 6(4)(a) amount, or

(b) is treated as making a payment of earnings by paragraph 4A,

he may recover, in a case falling within paragraph (a) the amount not so deducted or, in a case falling within paragraph (b) the section 6(4)(a) amount, by deduction from any subsequent payment of earnings made by the employer to that employee during the same year and, where the case falls within paragraph (b), or sub-paragraph 4(a) or (f) during the following year.

This sub-paragraph is subject to sub-paragraphs (4) and (5).

7(3A) Where an amount has been treated as retrospective earnings paid to or for the benefit of an employee, the employer may deduct the retrospective contributions based on those earnings from any payment of earnings made by him to that employee–

(a) after the relevant retrospective contributions regulations come into force, and

(b) during the same and the following year.

This sub-paragraph is subject to sub-paragraph (5).

7(4) Sub-paragraph (3) applies only where–

(a) the under-deduction occurred by reason of an error made by the employer in good faith;

(b) the earnings in respect of which the under-deduction occurred are treated as earnings by virtue of regulations made under section 112 of the Act (certain sums to be earnings);

(c) [omitted by SI 2016/352, reg. 18(a)(i);]

(d) the earnings in respect of which the under-deduction occurred are, by virtue of regulation 23, not paid through the secondary contributor in relation to the employment;

(e) the employer is treated as making a payment of earnings by paragraph 4A; or

(f) the payment in question is made to a person whose place of employment is outside the United Kingdom and on whose earnings Class 1 contributions are, but income tax is not, payable.

7(5) For the purposes of sub-paragraphs (3), (3A), (4), (8) and (11)–

(a) the amount which by virtue of those sub-paragraphs in a case falling within paragraph (a) of any of those sub-paragraphs may be deducted from any payment, or from any payments which fall to be aggregated, shall be an amount in addition to, but not in excess of, the amount deductible from those payments under the other provisions of this Schedule; and

(b) for the purposes of Part III of this Schedule an additional amount which may be deducted by virtue of those sub-paragraphs except sub-paragraph (3A) shall be treated as an amount deductible under this Schedule only in so far as the amount of the corresponding under-deduction has not been so treated.

This is subject to the following qualification

7(5A) Where a payment–

(a) falls within sub-paragraph (4)(e) or (f),

(b) comprises a beneficial interest in securities, or

(c) is treated as earnings within the meaning of Part 7 of the Income Tax (Earnings and Pensions) Act 2003,

sub-paragraph (5B) applies.

7(5B) If this sub-paragraph applies–

(a) sub-paragraph (5)(a) shall have effect as if ", but not in excess of," were omitted; and

(b) sub-paragraph (8) shall have effect as if at the end there were added "or the following year".

7(6) Sub-paragraph (8) applies where an employer makes a payment consisting either solely of non-monetary earnings, or a combination of monetary and non-monetary earnings, to–
(a) an employee;
(b) an ex-employee,
and at the time of the payment of those earnings there are no, or insufficient, monetary earnings from which the employer could deduct the section 6(4)(a) amount.

7(7) In sub-paragraph (6)(b) **"ex-employee"** means a person who–
(a) ceases to be employed by the employer in a particular year ("the cessation year"); and
(b) receives such earnings from the employer after the cessation of employment but in the cessation year.

7(8) Where, in the circumstances specified in sub-paragraph (6), the employer–
(a) does not deduct from the earnings referred to in that sub-paragraph the full section 6(4)(a) amount, or
(b) is treated as making a payment of earnings by paragraph 4A,
he may recover, in a case falling within paragraph (a) the amount not so deducted or, in a case falling within paragraph (b) the section 6(4)(a) amount, by deduction from any subsequent payment of monetary earnings to that employee, or ex-employee (as the case may be) during the same year.
This sub-paragraph is subject to sub-paragraph (5).

7(9) Sub-paragraph (11) applies where–
(a) an employee receives non-monetary earnings comprising, or derived from, relevant securities; or
(b) during the post-cessation period a former employee receives non-monetary earnings–
  (i) comprising, or derived from, relevant securities; and
  (ii) in connection with the former employment.
Here **"the post-cessation period"** means the period beginning with the day on which the employment ceased and ending with the last day of the next tax year.

7(10) [Para. 7(10) omitted by SI 2004/770, reg. 31.]

7(11) Where this sub-paragraph applies, the employer or former employer may–
(a) retain such of the relevant securities as is necessary to enable him to recover the whole or any part of the primary Class 1 contributions in respect of those securities; and
(b) sell those securities.
This sub-paragraph is subject to sub-paragraphs (12) and (12A).

7(11A) In sub-paragraphs (9), (11), (12) and (12A) **"relevant securities"** means securities in respect of which an amount is chargeable to income tax as employment income.

7(12) The employer or former employer shall not retain or sell relevant securities without the prior written consent of the employee or former employee.

7(12A) An employer or former employer who has retained relevant securities in accordance with sub-paragraph (11) shall account to the employee or former employee in respect of so much of the proceeds of sale as is not required to enable the employer or former employer to recover the primary Class 1 contributions in respect of those securities.

7(13) Subject to sub-paragraph (14), the employer shall record on the deductions working sheet for that employee the name and national insurance number of the employee, the year to which the working sheet relates, the appropriate category letter in relation to the employee (being the appropriate category letter indicated by the Board) and, in so far as relevant to that category letter, the following particulars regarding every payment of earnings which he makes to the employee namely–
(a) the date of payment;
(b) the amount of–
  (i) earnings up to and including the current lower earnings limit where earnings equal or exceed that figure,
  (ii) earnings which exceed the current lower earnings limit but do not exceed the current primary threshold,
  (iii) earnings which exceed the current primary threshold but do not exceed the current upper earnings limit,
  (iiia) earnings which exceed the upper accrual point but do not exceed the current upper earnings limit,
  (iv) the sum of the primary Class 1 contributions and secondary Class 1 contributions payable on all the employee's earnings, other than contributions recovered under sub-paragraph (3); and

(v) the primary Class 1 contributions and secondary Class 1 contributions payable on all the employee's earnings
(vi) any statutory maternity pay;
(vii) any statutory paternity pay;
(viii) [omitted by SI 2015/175, reg. 4(2)(b);]
(ix) any statutory adoption pay; and
(x) any statutory shared parental pay.

(c) [Omitted by SI 2003/193, reg. 16(2).]

7(14) Where 2 or more payments of earnings fall to be aggregated, the employer, instead of recording under heads (iv) and (v) of sub-paragraph (13)(b) separate amounts in respect of each such payment, shall under each head record a single amount, being the total of the contributions appropriate to the description specified in that head, in respect of the aggregated payments.

7(15) When an employer pays earnings he shall record under the name of the employee to whom he pays the earnings–

(a) the date of payment;

(b) the amount of the earnings, excluding any allowable pension contributions; and

(c) any allowable pension contributions;

and retain the record for a period of three years after the end of the year in which the earnings were paid.

History – In para. 7, the word "general" (which appeared before the word "earnings" in each place) omitted by SI 2015/478, reg. 22(3)(b), with effect from 6 April 2015.
In para. 7 "general earnings" substituted throughout by SI 2004/770, reg. 31, with effect from 6 April 2004.
In para. 7(1) the word "thereon" omitted and the words "(the "section 6(4)(a) amount")" inserted by SI 2002/2929, reg. 7(2), with effect from 28 November 2002.
Para. 7(1A) inserted by SI 2017/373, reg. 4(3), with effect from 6 April 2017.
In para. 7(3) "or sub-paragraph 4(a) or (f)" inserted before "during the following year" by SI 2004/770, reg. 31, with effect from 6 April 2004.
Sch. 4, para. 7(3) substituted by SI 2002/2929, reg. 7(3), with effect from 28 November 2002.
In para. 7(3), the words "the same year and, where the case falls within paragraph (b), during the following year" substituted for the words "the same year" by SI 2003/1337, reg. 2(2) with effect from 10 June 2003.
Para. 7(3A) inserted by SI 2007/1056, reg. 8(4)(a), with effect from 6 April 2007.
Para. 7(4)(c) (and the "or" following it) omitted by SI 2016/352, reg. 18(a)(i), with effect from 6 April 2016, subject to savings in relation to rights or obligations arising in connection with tax years beginning before 6 April 2016 (and for savings purposes, references to repealed provisions of the Pension Schemes Act 1993 are to be read as though such provisions were still in force). Former para. 7(4)(c) read as follows:
"(c) the under-deduction occurred as a result of the cancellation, variation or surrender of the contracting-out certificate issued in respect of the employment in respect of which the payment of earnings is made; or".
In para. 7(4) after (d) "or" omitted and after (e) "; or" and (f) inserted by SI 2004/770, reg. 31, with effect from 6 April 2004.
Para. 7(4)(e) inserted by SI 2002/2929, reg. 7(4), with effect from 28 November 2002.
In para. 7(5), the words "This is subject to the following qualification" inserted by SI 2003/1337, reg. 2 (3) with effect from 10 June 2003.
Para. 7(5) the reference to "(3A)" and the words "except sub-paragraph (3A)" inserted by SI 2007/1056, reg. 8(4)(b), with effect from 6 April 2007. It is assumed that the word "any", used to denote point of insertion for "except sub-paragraph (3A)", is included in SI 2007/1056, reg. 8(4)(b) in error.
In para. 7(5)(b) words "in a case … sub-paragraphs" inserted by SI 2002/2929, reg. 7(5), with effect from 28 November 2002.
In para. 7(5A)(a) "or (f)" inserted by SI 2004/770, reg. 31, with effect from 6 April 2004.
In Sch. 4, para. 7(5A)(b) "securities" substituted by SI 2003/2085, reg. 14(2) with effect from 1 September 2003.
Para. 7(5A), (5B) inserted by SI 2003/1337, reg. 2(4) with effect from 10 June 2003.
In Sch. 4, para. 7(6) words "section 6(4)(a) amount" substituted by SI 2002/2929, reg. 7(6), with effect from 28 November 2002.
Para. 7(9) substituted by SI 2004/2246, reg. 2(2) with effect from 22 September 2004.
In para. 7(9)(b) "securities" substituted throughout by SI 2004/770, reg. 31, with effect from 6 April 2004.
In para. 7(9)(b)(ii) "regulation 22(5), (6) or (7)" substituted by SI 2004/770, reg. 31, with effect from 6 April 2004.
In para. 7(9)(b)(iii) "section 4(4)(a) of the Act" substituted by SI 2004/770, reg. 31, with effect from 6 April 2004.
In Sch. 4, para. 7(9)(c) words "section 6(4)(a) amount" substituted to the end by SI 2002/2929, reg. 7(8), with effect from 28 November 2002.
Para. 7(10) omitted by SI 2004/770, reg. 31 and Schedule, with effect from 6 April 2004.
Para. 7(11), (11A), (12) and (12A) substituted for former para. 7(11) and (12) by SI 2004/2246, reg. 2(3) with effect from 22 September 2004.
In para. 7(11) "securities" substituted throughout by SI 2004/770, reg. 31, with effect from 6 April 2004.
In para. 7(12) "securities" substituted throughout by SI 2004/770, reg. 31, with effect from 6 April 2004.
In para. 7(13)(b), the words "or section 42A(1) to (2A)" omitted by SI 2012/817, reg. 5, with effect from 6 April 2012, subject to savings provisions in relation to obligations arising in connection with tax years beginning prior to 6 April 2012 (the operation of SI 2001/1004 is unaffectedby the amendments made by SI 2012/817, reg. 3–6, and the reference to s. 9(3) of the Pensions Act in the former definition of "COMPS employment" in SI 2001/1004, reg. 1(2), is to be read as though that section were still in force).
Para. 7(13)(b)(ii) substituted by SI 2012/821, reg. 21(a), with effect from 6 April 2012.
In para. 7(13)(b)(ii), the words "current upper earnings limit" substituted for the words "upper accrual point" by SI 2016/352, reg. 18(a)(ii)(aa), with effect from 6 April 2016, subject to savings in relation to rights or obligations arising in connection with tax years beginning before 6 April 2016 (and for savings purposes, references to repealed provisions of the Pension Schemes Act 1993 are to be read as though such provisions were still in force).
Para. 7(13)(b)(iii) substituted by SI 2012/821, reg. 21(b), with effect from 6 April 2012.
Para. 7(13)(b)(iiia) omitted by SI 2016/352, reg. 18(a)(ii)(bb), with effect from 6 April 2016, subject to savings in relation to rights or obligations arising in connection with tax years beginning before 6 April 2016 (and for savings purposes, references to repealed provisions of the Pension Schemes Act 1993 are to be read as though such provisions were still in force). Former para. 7(13)(b)(iiia) read as follows:
"(iiia) earnings which exceed the upper accrual point but do not exceed the current upper earnings limit,".

In para. 7(13)(b)(vii), the word "ordinary" omitted by SI 2015/175, reg. 4(2)(a), with effect from 5 April 2015, subject to the transitional provisions in SI 2015/175, reg. 9 (amendments do not have effect where they relate to additional statutory paternity pay or ordinary statutory paternity pay and payments of either on or after 5 April 2015).
Para. 7(13)(b)(viia) omitted by SI 2015/175, reg. 4(2)(b), with effect from 5 April 2015, subject to the transitional provisions in SI 2015/175, reg. 9 (amendments do not have effect where they relate to additional statutory paternity pay or ordinary statutory paternity pay and payments of either on or after 5 April 2015).
Para. 7(13)(b)(vii) and (viia) substituted for former para. 7(13)(b)(vii) by SI 2010/2450, reg. 4(2), with effect from 14 November 2010.
In para. 7(13)(b)(iii), the words "upper accrual point" substituted by SI 2009/111, reg. 4(2)(a), with effect from 6 April 2009.
Para. 7(13)(b)(iiia) inserted by SI 2009/111, reg. 4(2)(b), with effect from 6 April 2009.
In para. 7(13)(b), the words below (which appeared at the end) omitted by SI 2016/352, reg. 18(a)(ii)(cc), with effect from 6 April 2016, subject to savings in relation to rights or obligations arising in connection with tax years beginning before 6 April 2016 (and for savings purposes, references to repealed provisions of the Pension Schemes Act 1993 are to be read as though such provisions were still in force). Former words read as follows:
"The amounts to be recorded under sub-paragraphs (iv) and (v) are the amounts of contributions after deducting the amount of any reduction calculated in accordance with section 41(1) to (1B) of the Pensions Act (**"the reduction"**), subject to the following qualification.
If the amount of the reduction exceeds the amount of the contributions in respect of which it falls to be made, the amount to be entered under sub-paragraph (v) is nil.".
In para. 7(13), sub-para. (iv) and (v) substituted and sub-para. (vii) and (viii) and words following para. (viii) inserted, and para. (c) omitted by SI 2003/193, reg. 16(2) with effect from 6 April 2003.
Para. 7(13)(b)(ix) (and the word "; and" immediately preceding it) inserted (and the "and" at the end of (viia) omitted) by SI 2015/175, reg. 4(2), with effect from 5 March 2015.
In para. 7(15) "pension" substituted throughout by SI 2004/770, reg. 31, with effect from 6 April 2004.

Derivations – SI 1979/591, Sch. 1, reg. 13.

RECORDS WHERE LIABILITY TRANSFERRED FROM SECONDARY CONTRIBUTOR TO EMPLOYED EARNER: RELEVANT EMPLOYMENT INCOME

8 Where an election has been made for the purposes of paragraph 3B(1) of Schedule 1 to the Act (elections about transfer of liability for secondary contributions in respect of relevant employment income), the secondary contributor shall maintain records containing–

(a) a copy of any such election;

(b) a copy of the notice of approval issued by the Inland Revenue under paragraph 3B(1)(b) of that Schedule;

(c) the name and address of the secondary contributor who has entered into the election;

(d) the name of the employed earner; and

(e) the national insurance number allocated to the employed earner.

History – Para. 8 substituted by SI 2004/2096, reg. 7(b), with effect in relation to–

- agreements entered into after 1 September 2004 which are in respect of post-commencement employment income (presumably as defined in NICSPA 2004, s. 3(5)), and
- elections made after that date.

Former para. 8 substituted by SI 2002/2929, reg. 7(7), with effect from 28 November 2002.

Derivations – SI 1979/591, Sch. 1, reg. 13A.

CERTIFICATE OF CONTRIBUTIONS PAID

9(1) Where the employer is required to give the employee a certificate in accordance with regulation 67 of the PAYE Regulations (information to employees about payments and tax deducted (Form P 60)), the employer shall enter on the certificate, in respect of the year to which the certificate relates–

(a) the amount of any earnings up to and including the current lower earnings limit where earnings equal or exceed that figure;

(b) the amount of any earnings in respect of which primary Class 1 contributions were, by virtue of section 6A of the Act, treated as having been paid, which exceed the current lower earnings limit but do not exceed the current primary threshold;

(c) the amount of any earnings in respect of which primary Class 1 contributions were payable which exceed the current primary threshold but do not exceed the current upper earnings limit;

(ca) [omitted by SI 2016/352, reg. 18(b)(ii)(bb);]

(d) the amount of the earnings, if any, recorded under paragraphs (b) and (c), above the current lower earnings limit, in respect of which primary Class 1 contributions were payable or, where section 6A of the Act and regulation 127 applies, were treated as having been paid, at the reduced rate;

(e) the amount of primary Class 1 contributions paid by the employee;

(f) *the amount* of statutory maternity pay paid to the employee;

(g) the amount of statutory paternity pay paid to the employee;

(ga) [omitted by SI 2015/175, reg. 4(3);]

(h) the amount of statutory adoption pay paid to the employee; and

(i) the amount of statutory shared parental pay paid to the employee;

and shall enter the amounts under paragraph (e) under the appropriate category letter indicated by the Inland Revenue.

9(2) Where the employer is not required to give the employee a certificate in accordance with regulation 67 of the PAYE Regulations, because no tax has been deducted from the employee's relevant payments during the year concerned, but the employee–

(a) has paid, or

(b) is treated, by virtue of section 6A of the Act, as having paid,

primary Class 1 contributions in that year, the employer shall nevertheless give the employee such a certificate showing the information referred to in sub-paragraph (1).

9(3) In sub-paragraph (2), **"relevant payments"** has the meaning given in the PAYE Regulations.

History – In para. 9(1) "regulation 67 of the PAYE Regulations (information to employees about payments and tax deducted (Form P 60))" substituted for "regulation 39 of the Income Tax Regulations (certificate of tax deducted)" and "Inland Revenue" substituted for "Board" by SI 2004/770, reg. 31, with effect from 6 April 2004.

In para. 9(1)(b), the words ", other than earnings from non-contracted-out employment in respect of which primary Class 1 contributions were, by virtue of that section and regulation 127, treated as having been paid at the reduced rate" (which appeared after the words "current primary threshold" omitted by SI 2016/352, reg. 18(b)(i), with effect from 6 April 2016, subject to savings in relation to rights or obligations arising in connection with tax years beginning before 6 April 2016 (and for savings purposes, references to repealed provisions of the Pension Schemes Act 1993 are to be read as though such provisions were still in force).

In para. 9(1)(c), the words "upper accrual point" substituted by SI 2009/111, reg. 4(3)(a), with effect from 6 April 2009.

In para. 9(1)(c), the words "current upper earnings limit" substituted for the words "upper accrual point" by SI 2016/352, reg. 18(b)(ii)(aa), with effect from 6 April 2016, subject to savings in relation to rights or obligations arising in connection with tax years beginning before 6 April 2016 (and for savings purposes, references to repealed provisions of the Pension Schemes Act 1993 are to be read as though such provisions were still in force).

In para. 9(1)(c), the words", other than earnings from non-contracted-out employment in respect of which primary Class 1 contributions were payable at the reduced rate" (which appeared after the words "current upper earnings limit") omitted by SI 2016/352, reg. 18(b)(ii)(bb), with effect from 6 April 2016, subject to savings in relation to rights or obligations arising in connection with tax years beginning before 6 April 2016 (and for savings purposes, references to repealed provisions of the Pension Schemes Act 1993 are to be read as though such provisions were still in force).

Para. 9(1)(ca) omitted by SI 2016/352, reg. 18(b)(iii), with effect from 6 April 2016, subject to savings in relation to rights or obligations arising in connection with tax years beginning before 6 April 2016 (and for savings purposes, references to repealed provisions of the Pension Schemes Act 1993 are to be read as though such provisions were still in force). Former para. 9(1)(ca) read as follows:

"(ca) the amount of any earnings in respect of which primary Class 1 contributions were payable which exceed the upper accrual point but do not exceed the current upper earnings limit, other than earnings from non-contracted-out employment in respect of which primary Class 1 contributions were payable at the reduced rate;".

Former para. 9(1)(ca) inserted by SI 2009/111, reg. 4(3)(b), with effect from 6 April 2009.

In para. 9(1), cl. (f), (g) and (h) inserted and the words "paragraph (e)" substituted by SI 2003/193, reg. 16(3) with effect from 6 April 2003.

In para. 9(1)(g), the word "ordinary" omitted by SI 2015/175, reg. 4(3), with effect from 5 April 2015, subject to the transitional provisions in SI 2015/175, reg. 9 (amendments do not have effect where they relate to additional statutory paternity pay or ordinary statutory paternity pay and payments of either on or after 5 April 2015).

Para. 9(1)(ga) omitted by SI 2015/175, reg. 4(3), with effect from 5 April 2015, subject to the transitional provisions in SI 2015/175, reg. 9 (amendments do not have effect where they relate to additional statutory paternity pay or ordinary statutory paternity pay and payments of either on or after 5 April 2015).

Para. 9(1)(g) and (ga) substituted for former para. 9(1)(g) by SI 2010/2450, reg. 4(3), with effect from 14 November 2010.

Para. 9(1)(i) (and the word "; and" immediately preceding it) inserted (and the "and" at the end of (1)(ga) omitted) by SI 2015/175, reg. 4(3), with effect from 5 March 2015.

In para. 9(2) the words "relevant payments" substituted for the words "general earnings" by SI 2012/831, reg. 22(a), with effect from 6 April 2012.

In para. 9(2) the words "or the employee was not in the employer's employment on the last day of the tax year," omitted by SI 2010/721, reg. 10, with effect from 6 April 2010.

In para. 9(2) "regulation 67 of the PAYE Regulations" and "general earnings" substituted, by SI 2004/770, reg. 31, with effect from 6 April 2004.

In para. 9(2) words "or the employee was not in the employer's employment on the last day of the tax year," inserted by SI 2004/770, reg. 31, with effect from 6 April 2004.

In para. 9(2), the words from "but the employee" to the end substituted by SI 2003/1337, reg. 3 with effect from 10 June 2003.

Para. 9(3) inserted by SI 2012/821, reg. 22(b), with effect from 6 April 2012.

Derivations – SI 1979/591, Sch. 1, reg. 25.

Cross references – SI 2003/3682, reg. 67 rewrites reg. 39 of the Income Tax Regulations (form P60).

Part III – Payment and Recovery of Earnings-related Contributions, Class 1A Contributions and Class 1B Contributions, etc.

PAYMENT OF EARNINGS-RELATED CONTRIBUTIONS MONTHLY BY EMPLOYER

10(1) Subject to sub-paragraph (1A) and paragraph 11 and 15(8), the employer shall pay the amount specified in sub-paragraph (2) to the Inland Revenue within 14 days or, if payment is made by an approved method of electronic communications in respect of earnings paid after 5th April 2004, within 17 days of the end of every tax month.

10(1A) This paragraph does not apply in respect of amounts of retrospective earnings.

10(2) The amount specified in this sub-paragraph is the total amount of earnings-related contributions due in respect of earnings paid by the employer in that tax month (and, where required, reported under paragraph 21A or 21D), other than amounts deductible under paragraph 7(2) which he did not deduct and amounts which he deducted under the Compensation of Employers Regulations.

10(3) For the purposes of sub-paragraph (2), if two or more payments of earnings fall to be aggregated, the employer shall be treated as having deducted from the last of those payments the amount of any earnings-related contributions deductible from those payments which he did not deduct from the earlier payments.

10(3A) The amount specified in sub-paragraph (2) must be adjusted to take account of errors corrected under paragraph 21E(5), other than in cases where paragraph 21E(4) applies, or failures rectified under paragraph 21EA(2).

10(4) Where the amount specified in sub-paragraph (2) has been adjusted to take account of an error as provided for in sub-paragraph (3A) and the value of the adjustment is a negative amount, that amount is treated as having been paid to HMRC–

(a) 17 days after the end of the tax month in which the correction is made if payment is made using an approved method of electronic communications, and

(b) 14 days after the end of the tax month in which the correction is made, in any other case.

History – In para. 10(1) the words "sub-paragraph (1A) and" inserted by SI 2007/1056, reg. 8(5)(a), with effect from 6 April 2007.
In para. 10(1) "Inland Revenue" substituted, words "or, if payment is made by an approved method of electronic communications in respect of earnings paid after 5th April 2004, within 17 days" inserted, and "income" omitted by SI 2004/770, reg. 32, with effect from 6 April 2004.
Para. 10(1A) inserted by SI 2007/1056, reg. 8(5)(b), with effect from 6 April 2007.
In para. 10(2), the word "general" (which appeared before the word "earnings") omitted by SI 2015/478, reg. 22(4)(a), with effect from 6 April 2015.
In para. 10(2) the words "(and, where required, reported under paragraph 21A or 21D)" inserted by SI 2012/821, reg. 6(a), with effect from 6 April 2012.
In para. 10(2), the words "and the Reimbursement Regulations", which appeared at the end, omitted by SI 2012/821, reg. 23, with effect from 6 April 2012.
In para. 10(2) "general earnings" substituted, and "income" omitted by SI 2004/770, reg. 32, with effect from 6 April 2004.
In para. 10(3) "general earnings" substituted by SI 2004/770, reg. 32, with effect from 6 April 2004.
In para. 10(3A), the words ", or failures rectified under paragraph 21EA(2)" inserted by SI 2013/622, reg. 7, with effect from 6 April 2013 in relation to the tax year 2013–14 and subsequent tax years.
Para. 10(3A) inserted by SI 2012/821. reg. 6(b), with effect from 6 April 2012.
Para. 10(4) inserted by SI 2014/1016, reg. 2(a), with effect in relation to amounts which are due and payable for the tax year 2014–15 and subsequent tax years.

Derivations – SI 1979/591, Sch. 1, reg. 26.

Cross references – Direction of the Board, 5 April 2004: direction consolidating various directions in respect of the electronic delivery of information and specifying approved methods of electronic payments of sums due.

PAYMENT OF EARNINGS-RELATED CONTRIBUTIONS QUARTERLY BY EMPLOYER

11(1) Subject to sub-paragraph (1A) and paragraph 15(8), the employer shall pay the amount specified in sub-paragraph (2) to the Inland Revenue within 14 days of the end of every tax quarter or, if payment is made by an approved method of electronic communications in respect of earnings paid after 5th April 2004, within 17 days of the end of every tax quarter where–

(a) the employer has reasonable grounds for believing that the condition specified in sub-paragraph (4) applies and chooses to pay the amount specified in sub-paragraph (2) quarterly; or

(b) [omitted by SI 2004/770, reg. 32.]

11(1A) This paragraph does not apply in respect of amounts of retrospective earnings.

11(2) The amount specified in this sub-paragraph is the total amount of earnings-related contributions due in respect of earnings paid by the employer in that tax quarter (and, where required, reported under paragraph 21A or 21D), other than amounts deductible under paragraph 7(2) which he did not deduct and amounts which he deducted under the Compensation of Employers Regulations.

11(3) For the purposes of sub-paragraph (2), where two or more payments earnings fall to be aggregated, the employer shall be deemed to have deducted from the last of those payments the amount of any earnings-related contributions deductible from those payments which he did not deduct from the earlier payments.

11(3A) The amount specified in sub-paragraph (2) must be adjusted to take account of errors corrected under paragraph 21E(5), other than in cases where paragraph 21E(4) applies, or failures rectified under paragraph 21EA(2).

11(3B) Where the amount specified in sub-paragraph (2) has been adjusted to take account of an error as *provided for in sub*-paragraph (3A) and the value of the adjustment is a negative amount, that amount is treated as having been paid to HMRC–

(a) 17 days after the end of the tax quarter in which the correction is made if payment is made using an approved method of electronic communications, and

(b) 14 days after the end of the tax quarter in which the correction is made, in any other case.

11(4) The condition specified in this sub-paragraph is that for tax months falling within the current year, the average monthly amount found by the formula below will be less than £1500.
The formula is–

$$(N + P + L + S) - (SP + CD)$$

The expressions used in the formula have the following values.

N is the amount which would be payable to the Inland Revenue under the Social Security Contributions and Benefits Act 1992 and these Regulations but disregarding–

(a) any amount of secondary Class 1 contributions in respect of which liability has been transferred to the employed earner by an election made jointly by the employed earner and the secondary contributor for the purpose of paragraph 3B(1) of Schedule 1 to the Act (transfer of liability to be borne by the earner); and

(aa) any amount payable in respect of retrospective earnings;

(b) [omitted by SI 2006/576, reg. 9(2)(b);]

P is the amount which would be payable to HMRC under regulation 67G or 68 of the PAYE Regulations but disregarding any amount payable in respect of retrospective employment income (within the meaning of regulation 2 of those Regulations);

L is the amount which would be payable to the Inland Revenue under regulation 54(1) of the Education (Student Loans) (Repayment) Regulations 2009 (payment of repayments deducted to HMRC) if the reduction referred to in paragraph (3) of that regulation.

S is the sum of the amounts which the employer would be liable to deduct, under section 559 of the Taxes Act and the Income Tax (Sub-contractors in the Construction Industry) Regulations 1993, from payments made by him.

SP is the amount–

(a) recoverable by the employer from the Inland Revenue, or

(b) deductible from amounts for which the employer would otherwise be accountable to the Board,

in respect of payments to his employees by way of statutory maternity pay, statutory paternity pay, statutory shared parental pay and statutory adoption pay.

CD is the amount which would be deducted by others from sums due to the employer, in his position as a sub-contractor, under section 559 of the Taxes Act.

History – In para. 11(1) the words "sub-paragraph (1A) and" inserted by SI 2007/1056, reg. 8(6)(a), with effect from 6 April 2007.
In para. 11(1) "Inland Revenue" substituted, "income" omitted, and words "or, if payment is made by an approved method of electronic communications in respect of earnings paid after 5th April 2004, within 17 days of the end of every tax quarter" inserted, by SI 2004/770, reg. 32, with effect from 6 April 2004.
Para. 11(1)(b) omitted by SI 2004/770, reg. 32, with effect from 6 April 2004.
Para. 11(1A) inserted by SI 2007/1056, reg. 8(6)(b), with effect from 6 April 2007.
In para. 11(2) and (3), the word "general" (which appeared before the word "earnings") omitted by SI 2015/478, reg. 22(4)(a), with effect from 6 April 2015.
In para. 11(2) the words "(and, where required, reported under paragraph 21A or 21D)" inserted by SI 2012/821, reg. 7(a), with effect from 6 April 2012.
In para. 11(2) the words "and Reimbursement Regulations", which appeared at the end, omitted by SI 2012/821, reg. 24, with effect from 6 April 2012.
In para. 11(2) "general earnings" substituted, and "income" omitted by SI 2004/770, reg. 32, with effect from 6 April 2004.
In para. 11(3) "general earnings" substituted by SI 2004/770, reg. 32, with effect from 6 April 2004.
In para. 11(3A), the words ", or failures rectified under paragraph 21EA(2)" inserted by SI 2013/622, reg. 8, with effect from 6 April 2013 in relation to the tax year 2013–14 and subsequent tax years.
Para. 11(3A) inserted by SI 2012/821. reg. 7(b), with effect from 6 April 2012.
Para. 11(3B) inserted by SI 2014/1016, reg. 2(b), with effect in relation to amounts which are due and payable for the tax year 2014–15 and subsequent tax years.
In para. 11(4), the words "statutory paternity pay" substituted for "ordinary statutory paternity pay, additional statutory paternity pay" by SI 2015/175, reg. 4(4)(a), with effect from 5 April 2015, subject to the transitional provisions in SI 2015/175, reg. 9 (amendments do not have effect where they relate to additional statutory paternity pay or ordinary statutory paternity pay and payments of either on or after 5 April 2015).
In para. 11(4), the words ", statutory shared parental pay" inserted by SI 2015/175, reg. 4(4)(b), with effect from 5 March 2015.
In para. 11, in the definition of "P", "67G or" inserted by SI 2012/821, reg. 7(c), with effect from 6 April 2012.
In para. 11, in the definition of "L", the words "regulation 54(1) of the Education (Student Loans) (Repayment) Regulations 2009 (payment of repayments deducted to HMRC)" substituted for the words "regulation 39(1) of the Education (Student Loans) (Repayment) Regulations 2000 (payment of repayments deducted to the Inland Revenue)" by SI 2012/821, reg. 25, with effect from6 April 2012.
In para. 11(4), in the definition of "SP", the words "statutory sick pay," omitted by SI 2014/2397, reg. 3(3), with effect from 6 October 2014.
In para. 11(4), in the definition of "SP", the words "ordinary statutory paternity pay, additional statutory paternity pay" substituted for the words "statutory paternity pay" by SI 2010/2450, reg. 4(4), with effect from 14 November 2010.
In para. 11(4) the definition of "N" para. (aa) inserted by SI 2007/1056, reg. 8(6)(c)(i), with effect from 6 April 2007.
In para. 11(4) the definition of "P" substituted by SI 2007/1056, reg. 8(6)(c)(ii), with effect from 6 April 2007.
In para. 11(4) "tax months" and "Inland Revenue" substituted in each place by SI 2004/770, reg. 32, with effect from 6 April 2004.
In para. 11(4) the formula substituted by SI 2006/576, reg. 9(2)(a), with effect from 6 April 2006.
In para. 11(4), in the description of "N", para. (b) omitted by SI 2006/576, reg. 9(2)(b), with effect from 6 April 2006.

In para. 11(4), in the description of "P", the words "if any adjustment to that amount under regulation 7(2) of the Working Tax Credit (Payment by Employers) Regulations 2002 were disregarded" which appeared at the end omitted by SI 2006/576, reg. 9(2)(c), with effect from 6 April 2006.
In para. 11(4), in the description of "L", the words "and in regulation 7(2) of the Working Tax Credit (Payment by Employers) Regulations 2002 were disregarded" which appeared at the end omitted by SI 2006/576, reg. 9(2)(d), with effect from 6 April 2006.
In para. 11(4) the description of "T" omitted by SI 2006/576, reg. 9(2)(e), with effect from 6 April 2006.
In para. 11(4) "regulation 68 of the PAYE Regulations" and "the Inland Revenue" substituted by SI 2004/770, reg. 32, with effect from 6 April 2004.
Para. 11(4) substituted by SI 2003/193, reg. 16(4) with effect from 6 April 2003.

Derivations – SI 1979/591, Sch. 1, reg. 26A.

Cross references – Direction of the Board, 5 April 2004: direction consolidating various directions in respect of the electronic delivery of information and specifying approved methods of electronic payments of sums due.

PAYMENTS TO AND RECOVERIES FROM HMRC FOR EACH TAX PERIOD BY REAL TIME INFORMATION EMPLOYERS: RETURNS UNDER PARAGRAPH 21E(6) OR 21EA(3)

11ZA(1) This paragraph applies if, during any tax period, an employer makes a return under paragraph 21E(6) (returns under paragraph 21A and 21D: amendments) other than by virtue of paragraph 21E(4), or paragraph 21EA(3) (failure to make a return under paragraph 21A or 21D of Schedule 4.

11ZA(2) The amount specified in paragraph 10(2) or, as the case may be, 11(2) for the final tax period in the year covered by the return is to be adjusted to take account of the information in the return.

11ZA(3) If the value of the adjustment required by paragraph (2) is a negative amount, the employer may recover that amount–

(a) by setting it off against the amount the employer is liable to pay under paragraph 10(2) or, as the case may be, 11(2) for the tax period the return is made in; or

(b) from the Commissioners for Her Majesty's Revenue and Customs.

11ZA(3A) Where sub-paragraph (3) applies the negative amount is treated as having been paid to HMRC–

(a) 17 days after the end of the final tax period in the year covered by the return where payment is made using an approved method of electronic communication, and

(b) 14 days after the end of the final tax period in the year covered by the return in any other case.

11ZA(4) But paragraph (3) does not apply in relation to primary Class 1 contributions in a case where those contributions were deducted in error and the excess deduction has not been refunded to the employee.

History – In heading to para. 11ZA, the words "or 21EA(3)" inserted by SI 2013/622, reg. 9(2), with effect from 6 April 2013 in relation to the tax year 2013–14 and subsequent tax years.
In para. 11ZA(1), the words ", or paragraph 21EA(3) (failure to make a return under paragraph 21A or 21D of Schedule 4" inserted by SI 2013/622, reg. 9(1), with effect from 6 April 2013 in relation to the tax year 2013–14 and subsequent tax years.
Para. 11ZA(3A) inserted by SI 2014/1016, reg. 2(c), with effect in relation to amounts which are due and payable for the tax year 2014–15 and subsequent tax years.
Para. 11ZA inserted by SI 2012/821, reg. 8, with effect from 6 April 2012.

PAYMENTS OF EARNINGS-RELATED CONTRIBUTIONS IN RESPECT OF RETROSPECTIVE EARNINGS

11A(1) This paragraph applies where there are retrospective earnings in respect of which contributions (whether primary or secondary contributions) are payable.

11A(2) The employer shall pay the contributions referred to in sub-paragraph (1) to HMRC within 14 days or, if payment is made in respect of the current year by an approved method of electronic communications, 17 days of the end of the tax month immediately following the tax month in which the relevant retrospective contributions regulations came into force.

History – Para. 11A inserted by SI 2007/1056, reg. 8(7), with effect from 6 April 2007.

PAYMENT OF EARNINGS-RELATED CONTRIBUTIONS BY EMPLOYER (FURTHER PROVISIONS)

12(1) The Inland Revenue shall give a receipt to the employer for the total amount paid under paragraph 10, 11 or 11A if so requested, but if a receipt is given for the total amount of earnings-related contributions and any tax paid at the same time, a separate receipt need not be given for earnings-related contributions.

12(2) *Subject to sub-*paragraph (3), if the employer has paid to the Inland Revenue on account of earnings-related contributions under paragraph 10, 11 or 11A an amount which he was not liable to pay, or which has been refunded in accordance with regulation 2 of the Social Security (Refunds) (Repayment of Contractual Maternity Pay) Regulations 1990 (refunds of contributions), the amounts which he is liable to pay subsequently in respect of other payments of earnings made by him during the same year shall be reduced by the amount overpaid, so however that if there was a corresponding over-deduction from any payment of earnings to an employee, this paragraph shall apply only in so far as the employer has reimbursed the employee for that over-deduction.

12(3) Sub-paragraph (2) applies only if–

(a) the over-deduction occurred by reason of an error made by the employer in good faith;

(b) the over-deduction occurred as a result of the employment in respect of which the payment on account of earnings-related contributions is made being or, as the case may be, becoming contracted-out employment; or

(c) a refund has been made under regulation 2 of the Social Security (Refunds) (Repayment of Contractual Maternity Pay) Regulations 1990.

History – In para. 12 "10, 11 or 11A" substituted for "10 or 11" throughout by SI 2007/1056, reg. 8(8), with effect from 6 April 2007. Para. 12(1) substituted by SI 2004/770, reg. 32, with effect from 6 April 2004.

In para. 12(2), the word "general" (which appeared before the word "earnings") omitted by SI 2015/478, reg. 22(4)(a), with effect from 6 April 2015.

In para. 12(2), the words "Inland Revenue" substituted, and the words "general earnings" substituted for the word "emoluments" wherever that word occurs, by SI 2004/770, reg. 32, with effect from 6 April 2004.

Para. 12(3)(b) omitted by SI 2016/352, reg. 18(c), with effect from 6 April 2016, subject to savings in relation to rights or obligations arising in connection with tax years beginning before 6 April 2016 (and for savings purposes, references to repealed provisions of the Pension Schemes Act 1993 are to be read as though such provisions were still in force).

Derivations – SI 1979/591, Sch. 1, reg. 26B.

PAYMENT OF CLASS 1B CONTRIBUTIONS

13(1) A person who is liable to pay a Class 1B contribution (**"the employer"**), shall pay that Class 1B contribution to the Inland Revenue not later than 19th October or, if payment is made by an approved method of electronic communications in respect of earnings paid after 5th April 2004, not later than 22nd October in the year immediately following the end of the year in respect of which that contribution is payable.

13(2) If the employer has paid to the Inland Revenue under this paragraph an amount in respect of Class 1B contributions which he was not liable to pay, he shall be entitled to deduct the amount overpaid from any payment in respect of secondary earnings-related contributions which he is liable to pay subsequently to the Inland Revenue under paragraph 10 or 11 for any tax period in the same year.

History – In para. 13, the words "Inland Revenue" substituted wherever that word occurs by SI 2004/770, reg. 32, with effect from 6 April 2004.

In para. 13(1) "or, if payment is made by an approved method of electronic communications in respect of earnings paid after 5th April 2004, not later than 22nd October" inserted by SI 2004/770, reg. 32, with effect from 6 April 2004.

In para. 13(2) "income" omitted by SI 2004/770, reg. 32, with effect from 6 April 2004.

Derivations – SI 1979/591, Sch. 1, reg. 26C.

Cross references – Direction of the Board, 5 April 2004: direction consolidating various directions in respect of the electronic delivery of information and specifying approved methods of electronic payments of sums due.

EMPLOYER FAILING TO PAY EARNINGS-RELATED CONTRIBUTIONS

14(1) If within 17 days of the end of any tax period a non-Real Time Information employer has paid no amount of earnings-related contributions to the Inland Revenue under paragraph 10 or 11 for that tax period and the Inland Revenue is unaware of the amount, if any, which the employer is liable so to pay, the Inland Revenue may give notice to the employer requiring him to render, within 14 days, a return in the prescribed form showing the amount of earnings-related contributions which the employer is liable to pay to the Inland Revenue under that paragraph in respect of the tax period in question.

14(2) Where a notice given by the Inland Revenue under sub-paragraph (1) extends to two or more consecutive tax periods, the provisions of this Schedule shall have effect as if those tax periods were one tax period.

14(3) If the Inland Revenue is not satisfied that an amount of earnings-related contributions paid under paragraph 10 or 11 for any tax period is the full amount which the employer is liable to pay, the Inland Revenue may give a notice under sub-paragraph (1) despite the payment of that amount.

History – In para. 14(1), the words "a non-Real Time Information employer" substituted for the words "the employer" by SI 2012/821, reg. 9, with effect from 6 April 2012.

In para. 14 "Inland Revenue" substituted throughout, and "income" omitted throughout, by SI 2004/770, reg. 32, with effect from 6 April 2004.

In para. 14(1) "17 days" taken as substituted where those words first occur by SI 2004/770, reg. 32, with effect from 6 April 2004. Reg. 32 contains an anomaly in that it states: "in sub-paragraph (1) **after** for "14 days" where those words first occur, substitute "17 days"".

In para. 14(3) "to him" omitted throughout by SI 2004/770, reg. 32, with effect from 6 April 2004.

Derivations – SI 1979/591, Sch. 1, reg. 27.

SPECIFIED AMOUNT OF EARNINGS-RELATED CONTRIBUTIONS PAYABLE BY THE EMPLOYER

15(1) If after 17 days following the end of any tax period the employer has paid no amount of earnings-related contributions to HMRC under paragraph 10 or 11 for that tax period and there is reason to believe that the employer is liable to pay such contributions, HMRC, upon consideration of the employer's record of past payments, whether of earnings-related contributions or of combined amounts, may to the best of their judgement specify the amount of earnings-related contributions or of a combined amount which they consider the employer is liable to pay and give notice to him of that amount.

15(1A) For the purposes of this paragraph "combined amount" is an amount which includes earnings-related contributions due under these regulations and one or more of the following–

(a) tax due under the PAYE Regulations;

(b) amounts due under the Income Tax (Construction Industry Scheme) Regulations 2005;

(c) payments of repayments of student loans due under the Education (Student Loans) (Repayment) Regulations 2009.

15(1B) In arriving at an amount under paragraph (1), HMRC may also take into account any returns made by the employer under this Schedule in the tax period in question or earlier tax periods.

15(2) If, on the expiration of the period of 7 days allowed in the notice, the specified amount or any part of that amount is unpaid, the amount so unpaid–

(a) shall be treated for the purposes of this Schedule as an amount of earnings-related contributions or as including an amount of earnings-related contributions which the employer was liable to pay for that tax period in accordance with paragraph 10 or 11; and

(b) may be certified by HMRC.

15(3) The provisions of sub-paragraph (2) shall not apply if, during the period allowed in the notice, the employer pays to HMRC the full amount of earnings-related contributions which the employer is liable to pay under paragraph 10 or 11 for that tax period, or the employer satisfies HMRC that no amount of such contributions is due.

15(4) The production of a certificate such as is mentioned in sub-paragraph (2) shall, until the contrary is established, be sufficient evidence that the employer is liable to pay to HMRC the amount shown in it; and any document purporting to be such a certificate shall be treated as such a certificate until the contrary is proved.
Paragraph 16 shall apply, with any necessary modifications, to the amount shown in the certificate.

15(5) Where the employer has paid no amount of earnings-related contributions under paragraph 10 or 11 for any tax periods, a notice may be given by HMRC under sub-paragraph (1) which extends to two or more consecutive tax periods, and this Schedule shall have effect as if those tax periods were the latest tax period specified in the notice.

15(6) A notice may be given by HMRC under sub-paragraph (1) notwithstanding that an amount of earnings-related contributions has been paid by the employer under paragraph 10 or 11 for any tax period, if, after seeking the employer's explanation as to the amount of earnings-related contributions paid, HMRC is not satisfied that the amount so paid is the full amount which the employer is liable to pay for that period, and this paragraph shall have effect accordingly, except that sub-paragraph (2) shall not apply if, during the period allowed in the notice, the employer satisfies HMRC that no further amount of earnings-related contributions is due for the relevant tax period.

15(7) Where, during the period allowed in a notice given by HMRC under sub-paragraph (1), the employer claims, but does not satisfy HMRC, that the payment made in respect of any tax period specified in the notice is or includes the full amount of earnings-related contributions he is liable to pay to HMRC for that period, the employer may require HMRC to inspect the employer's documents and records as if HMRC had called upon the employer to produce those documents and records in accordance with Schedule 36 to the Finance Act 2008 (information and inspection powers) and the provisions of paragraph 26A shall apply in relation to that inspection, and the notice given by HMRC under sub-paragraph (1) shall be disregarded in relation to any subsequent time.

15(8) Notwithstanding anything in this paragraph, if the employer pays any amount of earnings-related contributions certified by HMRC under it whether separately or as part of a combined amount and that amount exceeds the amount which he would have been liable to pay in respect of that tax period apart from this paragraph, *he shall be entitled* to set off such excess against any amount which he is liable to pay to HMRC under paragraph 10 or 11 for any subsequent tax period.

15(9) If, after the end of the year, the employer renders the return required by paragraph 22(1) and the total earnings-related contributions he has paid in respect of that year in accordance with this Schedule exceeds the total amount of such contributions due for that year, any excess not otherwise recovered by set-off shall be repaid.

History – In para. 15, the word "HMRC" substituted throughout by SI 2008/636, reg. 4, with effect from 6 April 2008.
In para. 15 "Inland Revenue" previously substituted throughout, and "income" omitted throughout, by SI 2004/770, reg. 32, with effect from 6 April 2004.
In para. 15(1) the words "whether of earnings-related contributions or of combined amounts," and "or of a combined amount" inserted by SI 2008/636, reg. 4(1)(b) and 4(1)(c) respectively, with effect from 6 April 2008.
In para. 15(1) "17 days", "their judgment" and "they consider" substituted, by SI 2004/770, reg. 32, with effect from 6 April 2004.
In para. 15(1A)(c), the words "Education (Student Loans) (Repayment) Regulations 2009" substituted for the words "Education (Student Loans) (Repayment) Regulations 2000" by SI 2012/821, reg. 26(a), with effect from 6 April 2012.
Para. 15(1A) inserted by SI 2008/636, reg. 4(2), with effect from 6 April 2008.
Para. 15(1B) inserted by SI 2012/821, reg. 10, with effect from 6 April 2012.
In para. 15(2) the words "of earnings-related contributions", which followed the words "the specified amount", omitted by SI 2008/636, reg. 4(3)(a), with effect from 6 April 2008.
In para. 15(2)(a) the words "or as including an amount of earnings-related contributions" inserted by SI 2008/636, reg. 4(3)(b), with effect from 6 April 2008.
In para. 15(6) "to him" omitted throughout, by SI 2004/770, reg. 32, with effect from 6 April 2004.
In para. 15(7), the words "Schedule 36 to the Finance Act 2008 (information and inspection powers) and the provisions of paragraph 26A" substituted for the words "paragraph 26(1) and the provisions of paragraph 26" by SI 2009/600, reg. 8(3), with effect from 1 April 2009.
In para. 15(7) the words "of earnings-related contributions", which followed the words "satisfy HMRC, that the payment", omitted by SI 2008/636, reg. 4(8)(b) and the words "or includes" inserted by SI 2008/636, reg. 4(8)(c), with effect from 6 April 2008.
In para. 15(8) the words "whether separately or as part of a combined amount" inserted by SI 2008/636, reg. 4(9)(b), with effect from 6 April 2008.

Derivations – SI 1979/591, Sch. 1, reg. 27A.

RECOVERY OF EARNINGS-RELATED CONTRIBUTIONS OR CLASS 1B CONTRIBUTIONS

16(1) The Tax Acts and any regulations under section 684 of ITEPA 2003 (PAYE regulations) relating to the recovery of tax (**"the relevant provisions"**) shall apply to the recovery of–

(a) any amount of earnings-related contributions which an employer is liable to pay HMRC for any tax period in accordance with paragraph 10 or 11 or which he is treated as liable to HMRC whether separately or as part of a combined amount for any tax period under paragraph 15; or

(b) any amount of Class 1B contributions which an employer is liable to pay to HMRC in respect of any year in accordance with paragraph 13(1),

as if each of those amounts had been charged to tax by way of an assessment on the employer as employment income under ITEPA 2003.

16(2) Sub-paragraph (1) is subject to the qualification that, in the application to any proceedings taken, by virtue of this paragraph, of any of the relevant provisions limiting the amount which is recoverable in those proceedings, there shall be disregarded any other component of a combined amount which may, by virtue of sub-paragraphs (3) to (5), be included as part of the cause of action or matter of complaint in those proceedings.

16(3) Proceedings may be brought for the recovery of the total amount of–

(a) earnings-related contributions which the employer is liable to pay to HMRC for any tax period;

(b) Class 1B contributions which the employer is liable to pay to HMRC in respect of any year;

(c) a combination of those classes of contributions as specified in heads (a) and (b); or

(d) any of the contributions as specified in head (a), (b), or (c) in addition to any other component of a combined amount which the employer is liable to pay to HMRC for any tax period,

without specifying the respective amounts of those contributions and of other component of a combined amount, or distinguishing the amounts which the employer is liable to pay in respect of each employee and without specifying the employees in question.

16(4) For the purposes of–

(a) proceedings under section 66 of the Taxes Management Act 1970 (including proceedings under that section as applied by the provisions of this paragraph);

(b) *summary proceedings* (including in Scotland proceedings in the sheriff court or in the sheriff's small debt court),

the total amount of contributions, in addition to any other component of the combined amount which the employer is liable to pay to HMRC for any tax period, referred to in sub-paragraph (3) shall, subject to sub-paragraph (2), be one cause of action or one matter of complaint.

16(5) Nothing in sub-paragraph (3) or (4) shall prevent the bringing of separate proceedings for the recovery of each of the several amounts of–

(a) earnings-related contributions which the employer is liable to pay for any tax period in respect of each of his several employees;

(b) Class 1B contributions which the employer is liable to pay in respect of any year in respect of each of his several employees;

(c) tax which the employer is liable to pay for any tax period in respect of each of his several employees;

(d) amounts due under the Income Tax (Construction Industry Scheme) Regulations 2005; or

(e) payments of repayments of student loans due under the Education (Student Loans) (Repayment) Regulations 2009.

16(6) For the purposes of this paragraph "combined amount" has the meaning given in paragraph 15(1A).

History – In para. 16 the word "HMRC" substituted throughout by SI 2008/636, reg. 5, with effect from 6 April 2008.
In para. 16 "Inland Revenue" substituted throughout, and "income" omitted throughout (this has not been taken to apply to the inserted wording "as employment income under ITEPA 2003"), by SI 2004/770, reg. 32, with effect from 6 April 2004.
In para. 16(1) the words "whether separately or as part of a combined amount" inserted by SI 2008/636, reg. 5(1)(b), with effect from 6 April 2008.
In para. 16(1) "section 684 of ITEPA 2003 (PAYE regulations)" and "as employment income under ITEPA 2003" substituted by SI 2004/770, reg. 32, with effect from 6 April 2004.
In para. 16(2) the words "other component of a combined amount" substituted by SI 2008/636, reg. 5(2), with effect from 6 April 2008.
In para. 16(3) the words "other component of a combined amount" substituted, in both places where they appear, by SI 2008/636, reg. 5(3), with effect from 6 April 2008.
In para. 16(4) the words "other component of the combined amount" substituted by SI 2008/636, reg. 5(4)(a), with effect from 6 April 2008.
In para. 16(5)(e), the words "Education (Student Loans) (Repayment) Regulations 2009" substituted for the words "Education (Student Loans) (Repayment) Regulations 2000" by SI 2012/821, reg. 26(b), with effect from 6 April 2012.
Para. 16(5)(d) and (e) added by SI 2008/636, reg. 5(5)(b), with effect from 6 April 2008.
Para. 16(6) added by SI 2008/636, reg. 5(6), with effect from 6 April 2008.

Derivations – SI 1979/591, Sch. 1, reg. 28.

Cross references – ITEPA 2003, s. 684 rewrites ICTA 1988, s. 203.

INTEREST ON OVERDUE EARNINGS-RELATED CONTRIBUTIONS OR CLASS 1B CONTRIBUTIONS

17(1) Subject to sub-paragraph (4A) and paragraph 20[21], where, in relation to the year ended 5th April 1993 or any subsequent year, an employer has not–

(a) [omitted by SI 2014/992, art. 10(2);]

(b) paid a Class 1B contribution by 19th October or, if payment is made by an approved method of electronic communications in respect of earnings paid after 5th April 2004, not later than 22nd October next following the year in respect of which it was due,

any contribution not so paid shall carry interest at the rate applicable under paragraph 6(3) of Schedule 1 to the Act from the reckonable date until payment.

17(2) Interest payable under this paragraph shall be recoverable as if it were an earnings-related contribution or a Class 1B contribution, as the case may be, which an employer is liable under paragraph 10,11 or 13 to pay to HMRC.

17(3) For the purposes of this paragraph–

(a) **"employer"** means, in relation to a Class 1B contribution, the person liable to pay such a contribution in accordance with section 10A of the Act;

(b) **"the reckonable date"** means, in relation to–

(i) [omitted by SI 2014/992, art. 10(2);]

(ii) a Class 1B contribution, the 19th October or, if payment was made by an approved method of electronic communications in respect of earnings paid after 5th April 2004, the 22nd October next following the year in respect of which it was due.

(iii) a contribution payable in respect of retrospective earnings relating to a tax year which is closed at the time that the relevant retrospective contributions regulations come into force, the 14th day after the end of the tax month immediately following the tax month in which those regulations came into force.

17(4) A contribution to which sub-paragraph (1) applies shall carry interest from the reckonable date, even if that date is a non-business day within the meaning of section 92 of the Bills of Exchange Act 1882.

17(4A) Where an employer has not paid contributions in respect of retrospective earnings relating to a closed tax year by the date set out in paragraph 11A, any contribution not so paid shall carry interest at the rate applicable under paragraph 6(3) of Schedule 1 to the Act from the reckonable date until payment.

17(5) A certificate of HMRC that, to the best of their knowledge and belief, any amount of interest payable under this paragraph has not been paid by an employer or employee is sufficient evidence that the amount mentioned in the certificate is unpaid and due to be paid, and any document purporting to be such a certificate shall be presumed to be a certificate until the contrary is proved.

17(6) HMRC may prepare a certificate certifying the total amount of interest payable in respect of the whole or any component of a combined amount without specifying what component of the combined amount the interest relates to.

Sub-paragraph (5) shall apply, with any necessary modifications, to the certificate.

17(7) For the purposes of this paragraph "combined amount" has the meaning given in paragraph 15(1A).

History – In para. 17(1) the words "sub-paragraph (4A) and" inserted by SI 2007/1056, reg. 8(9)(a), with effect from 6 April 2007.
In para. 17(1) "Subject to paragraph 21" purported to be substituted by SI 2004/770, reg. 32(9)(a), with effect from 6 April 2004. Para. 21 is shown above in square brackets as the amendment is incorrect since the original wording it seeks to replace reads "Subject to paragraph 20".
Para. 17(1)(a) omitted by SI 2014/992, art. 10(2), with effect from 6 May 2014 in relation to payments which are due and payable in respect of the tax year 2014–15 and subsequent tax years.
In para. 17(1)(a) "or, if payment is made by an approved method of electronic communications in respect of earnings paid after 5th April 2004, 17 days" inserted by SI 2004/770, reg. 32, with effect from 6 April 2004.
In para. 17(1)(b) "or, if payment is made by an approved method of electronic communications in respect of earnings paid after 5th April 2004, not later than 22nd October" inserted by SI 2004/770, reg. 32, with effect from 6 April 2004.
In para. 17(2) the word "HMRC" substituted by SI 2008/636, reg. 6(1), with effect from 6 April 2008.
In para. 17(2) "Inland Revenue" substituted throughout by SI 2004/770, reg. 32, with effect from 6 April 2004.
Para. 17(3)(b)(i) omitted by SI 2014/992, art. 10(2), with effect from 6 May 2014 in relation to payments which are due and payable in respect of the tax year 2014–15 and subsequent tax years.
In para. 17(3)(b)(i) "or, if payment was made by an approved method of electronic communications in respect of earnings paid after 5th April 2004, the 17th day" inserted by SI 2004/770, reg. 32, with effect from 6 April 2004.
In para. 17(3)(b)(ii) "or, if payment was made by an approved method of electronic communications in respect of earnings paid after 5th April 2004, the 22nd October" inserted by SI 2004/770, reg. 32, with effect from 6 April 2004.
Para. 17(3)(b)(iii) inserted by SI 2007/1056, reg. 8(9)(b), with effect from 6 April 2007.
Para. 17(4A) inserted by SI 2007/1056, reg. 8(9)(c), with effect from 6 April 2007.
In para. 17(5) the word "HMRC" substituted by SI 2008/636, reg. 6(2), with effect from 6 April 2008.
Para. 17(5) substituted by SI 2004/770, reg. 32, with effect from 6 April 2004.
Para. 17(6) inserted by SI 2008/636, reg. 6(3), with effect from 6 April 2008.
Para. 17(7) inserted by SI 2008/636, reg. 6(4), with effect from 6 April 2008.

Derivations – SI 1979/591, Sch. 1, reg. 28A.

Cross references – Direction of the Board, 5 April 2004: direction consolidating various directions in respect of the electronic delivery of information and specifying approved methods of electronic payments of sums due.

17A(1) If regulation 86(1)(a) applies paragraphs 16 and 17, and section 101 of the Finance Act 2009, in respect of an earnings-related contribution, shall apply to the employed earner to the extent of the primary contribution which the secondary contributor wilfully failed to pay.

17A(2) For the purpose of sub-paragraph (1) any reference in paragraph 16 and 17 to an employer shall be construed as a reference to the employed earner.

History – In para. 17A(1), the words ", and section 101 of the Finance Act 2009, in respect of an earnings-related contribution" inserted by SI 2014/992, art. 10(3), with effect from 6 May 2014 in relation to payments which are due and payable in respect of the tax year 2014–15 and subsequent tax years.
Para. 17A inserted by SI 2004/770, reg. 32, with effect from 6 April 2004.

PAYMENT OF INTEREST ON REPAID EARNINGS-RELATED CONTRIBUTIONS OR CLASS 1B CONTRIBUTIONS

18(1) Where an earnings-related contribution paid by an employer in respect of the year ended 5th April 1993 or any subsequent year not later than the year ended 5th April 1999 is repaid to him and that repayment is made after the relevant date, any such repaid contribution shall carry interest at the rate applicable under paragraph 6(3) of Schedule 1 to the Act from the relevant date until the order for the repayment is issued.

18(2) For the purposes of sub-paragraph (1) **"the relevant date"** is–

(a) in the case of an earnings-related contribution overpaid more than 12 months after the end of the year in respect of which the payment was made, the last day of the year in which it was paid; and

(b) in any other case, the last day of the year after the year in respect of which the contribution in question was paid.

18(3) Where a Class 1B contribution paid by an employer in respect of the year ended 5th April 2000 or any subsequent year is repaid to him and that repayment is made after the relevant date, any such repaid contribution shall carry interest at the rate applicable under paragraph 6(3) of Schedule 1 to the Act from the relevant date until the order for the repayment is issued.

18(4) For the purposes of sub-paragraph (3) **"the relevant date"** is–

(a) in the case of–

(i) [omitted by SI 2014/992, art. 10(4);]

(ii) a Class 1B contribution, the 19th October next following the year in respect of which that contribution was paid; or

(b) the date on which the Class 1B contribution was paid if that date is later than the date referred to in paragraph (a).

History – In para. 18(3), the words "an earnings-related contribution or", which appeared after the word "Where", omitted by SI 2014/992, art. 10(4), with effect from 6 May 2014 in relation to payments which are due and payable in respect of the tax year 2014–15 and subsequent tax years.
Para. 18(4)(a)(ai) (and the "or" at the end of it) omitted by SI 2014/992, art. 10(4), with effect from 6 May 2014 in relation to payments which are due and payable in respect of the tax year 2014–15 and subsequent tax years.
In para. 18(4)(b), the words "earnings-related contribution or", which appeared before the words "Class 1B", omitted by SI 2014/992, art. 10(4), with effect from 6 May 2014 in relation to payments which are due and payable in respect of the tax year 2014–15 and subsequent tax years.

Derivations – SI 1979/591, Sch. 1, reg. 28B.

REPAYMENT OF INTEREST

19(1) Where a secondary contributor or a person liable to pay a Class 1B contribution has paid interest on an earnings-related contribution or a Class 1B contribution, that interest shall be repaid to him if–

(a) the interest paid is found not to have been due to be paid, although the contribution in respect of which it was paid was due to be paid;

(b) the earnings-related contribution or Class 1B contribution in respect of which interest was paid is returned or repaid to him in accordance with regulation 52, 52A or 55.

History – In para. 19 the word "if" inserted after "shall be repaid to him" by SI 2007/1056, reg. 8(10), with effect from 6 April 2007. In para. 19(1)(b) (referred to as "19(b)" in reg. 32(11)) "52, 52A or 55" substituted by SI 2004/770, reg. 32, with effect from 6 April 2004, in respect of contributions payable in respect of the year 2003–04 and subsequent years.

Derivations – SI 1979/591, Sch. 1, reg. 28C.

REMISSION OF INTEREST FOR OFFICIAL ERROR

20(1) Where interest is payable in accordance with paragraph 17, or section 101 of the Finance Act 2009 in relation to any earnings-related contribution, it shall be remitted for the period commencing on the first relevant date and ending on the second relevant date in the circumstances specified in sub-paragraph (2).

20(2) For the purposes of sub-paragraph (1), the circumstances are that the liability, or a greater liability, to pay interest in respect of an earnings-related contribution or a Class 1B contribution arises as the result of an official error being made.

20(3) In this paragraph–

(a) **"an official error"** means a mistake made, or something omitted to be done, by an officer of the Board, where the employer or any person acting on his behalf has not caused, or materially contributed to, that mistake or omission;

(b) **"the first relevant date"** means the reckonable date as defined in paragraph 17(3) or, if later, the date on which the official error occurs;

(c) **"the second relevant date"** means the date 14 days after the date on which the official error has been rectified and the employer is advised of its rectification.

History – In para. 20(1), the words ", or section 101 of the Finance Act 2009 in relation to any earnings-related contribution," inserted by SI 2014/992, art. 10(5), with effect from 6 May 2014 in relation to payments which are due and payable in respect of the tax year 2014–15 and subsequent tax years.

Derivations – SI 1979/591, Sch. 1, reg. 28D.

APPLICATION OF PARAGRAPHS 10, 12, 16, 17, 18, 19 AND 20

21(1) This paragraph applies where–

(a) secondary Class 1 contributions are payable in respect of relevant employment income; and

(b) an amount or proportion (as the case may be) of the liability of the secondary contributor to those contributions is transferred to the employed earner by an election made jointly by them for the purposes of paragraph 3B(1) of Schedule 1 to the Act.

21(2) Paragraphs 10, 12, 16, 17, 18 19 and 20 shall apply to the employed earner to the extent of the liability transferred by the election and, to that extent, those paragraphs shall not apply to the employer.

21(3) For the purposes of sub-paragraph (2)–

(a) any reference in paragraphs 10, 12, 16, 17, 18 and 20 to an employer; and

(b) the reference in paragraph 19 to a secondary contributor,

shall be construed as a reference to the employed earner to whom the liability is transferred by the election.

History – In para. 21(1)(a), the words "relevant employment income; and" substituted by SI 2004/2096, reg. 7(c), with effect in relation to–

- agreements entered into after 1 September 2004 which are in respect of post-commencement employment income (presumably as defined in NICSPA 2004, s. 3(5)), and
- elections made after that date.

Derivations – SI 1979/591, Sch. 1, reg. 28E.

REAL TIME RETURNS OF INFORMATION ABOUT PAYMENTS OF EARNINGS

History – In heading, the word "general" (which appeared before the word "earnings") omitted by SI 2015/478, reg. 22(4)(b), with effect from 6 April 2015.

21A(1) Subject to sub-paragraph (1A), on or before making any payment of earnings to an employee a Real Time Information employer must deliver to HMRC the information specified in Schedule 4A (real time returns) in accordance with this paragraph unless–

(a) the employer is not required to maintain a deductions working sheet for any employees, or

(b) an employee's earnings are below the lower earnings limit and the employer is required to make a return under regulation 67B(1), regulation 67D(3), regulation 67E(6) or regulation 67EA(3) of the PAYE Regulations.

21A(1A) But a Real Time Information employer–

(a) which for the tax year 2014–15 meets Conditions A and B, or

(b) which for the tax year 2015–16 meets Conditions A and C,

may instead for that tax year deliver to HMRC the information specified in Schedule 4A (real time returns) in respect of every payment of earnings made to an employee in a tax month on or before making the last payment of earnings in that month.

21A(1B) Condition A is that at 5th April 2014 the employer is one to whom HMRC has issued an employer's PAYE reference.

21A(1C) Condition B is that at 6th April 2014 the Real Time Information employer employs no more than 9 employees.

21A(1D) Condition C is that at 6th April 2015 the Real Time Information employer employs no more than 9 employees.

21A(1E) In this paragraph **"employer's PAYE reference"** means–

(a) the combination of letters, numbers, or both, used by HMRC to identify an employer for the purposes of the PAYE Regulations, and

(b) the number which identifies the employer's HMRC office.

21A(2) The information must be included in a return.

21A(3) Subject to paragraph (4), if payments of earnings are made to more than one employee at the same time, the return under sub-paragraph (2) must include the information required by Schedule 4A in respect of each employee to whom a payment of earnings is made at that time.

21A(4) If payments of earnings are made to more than one employee at the same time but the employer operates more than one payroll, the employer must make a return in respect of each payroll.

21A(5) The return is to be made using an approved method of electronic communications and regulation 90N(2) (mandatory use of electronic communications) applies as if the return was a paragraph 22 return within the meaning given by regulation 90M (paragraph 22 return and specified payments).

21A(6) [Omitted by SI 2013/622, reg. 10(3).]

21A(7) [Omitted by SI 2013/622, reg. 10(3).]

21A(8) Schedule 24 to the Finance Act 2007 (penalties for errors), as that Schedule applies to income tax returns, shall apply in relation to the requirement to make a return contained in sub-paragraph (2).

History – In para. 21A, the word "general" (which appeared before the word "earnings" in each place) omitted by SI 2015/478, reg. 22(4)(b), with effect from 6 April 2015.

In para. 21A(1), the words "sub-paragraph (1A)" substituted for "sub-paragraphs (1A) and (1B)" by SI 2014/608, reg. 7(a), with effect from 6 April 2014.

In para. 21A(1), the words "Subject to sub-paragraphs (1A) and (1B)," inserted by SI 2013/2301, reg. 3(a), with effect in relation to any payment of general earnings (as defined in Sch. 4, Pt. 1, para. 1(2)) made in the period beginning on 6 October 2013 and ending on 5 April 2014.

Para. 21A(1)(a) and (b) substituted by SI 2013/622, reg. 10(2), with effect from 6 April 2013 in relation to the tax year 2013–14 and subsequent tax years.

Para. 21A(1A)–(1E) substituted for former para. 21A(1A) and (1B) by SI 2014/608, reg. 7(b), with effect from 6 April 2014.

Para. 21A(1A) and (1B) inserted by SI 2013/2301, reg. 3(b), with effect in relation to any payment of general earnings (as defined in Sch. 4, Pt. 1, para. 1(2)) made in the period beginning on 6 October 2013 and ending on 5 April 2014.

Para. 21A(6) and (7) omitted by SI 2013/622, reg. 10(3), with effect from 6 April 2013 in relation to the tax year 2013–14 and subsequent tax years.

Para. 21A inserted by SI 2012/821, reg. 11, with effect from 6 April 2012.

EMPLOYEES IN RESPECT OF WHOM EMPLOYER IS NOT REQUIRED TO MAINTAIN A DEDUCTIONS WORKSHEET

21AA(1) This paragraph applies if an employer makes a payment of earnings to an employee in respect of whom the employer is not required to maintain a deductions working sheet.

21AA(2) The employer need not deliver the information required by paragraph 21A in respect of that employee on or before making the payment.

21AA(3) The employer must deliver that information no later than the end of the period of 7 days starting with the day following the day on which the payment is made.

History – In para. 21AA(1), the word "general" (which appeared before the word "earnings") omitted by SI 2015/478, reg. 22(4)(c), with effect from 6 April 2015.

Para. 21AA inserted by SI 2013/622, reg. 11, with effect from 6 April 2013 in relation to the tax year 2013–14 and subsequent tax years.

EMPLOYEES PAID IN SPECIFIED CIRCUMSTANCES

21AB(1) This paragraph applies if–

(a) an employer makes a payment of earnings to an employee, and

(b) all of the circumstances in sub-paragraph (2) apply.

21AB(2) The circumstances are that–

(a) the payment includes an amount of earnings which is for work undertaken by the employee on–

(i) the day the payment is made, or

(ii) provided that the payment is made before the employee leaves the place of work at the end of the employee's period of work, the day before the payment is made,

(b) in respect of the work mentioned in paragraph (a), it was not reasonably practicable for the employer to calculate the payment due before the completion of the work, and

(c) it is not reasonably practicable for the employer to deliver the information required by paragraph 21A on or before making the payment.

21AB(3) The employer need not deliver the information required by paragraph 21A on or before making the payment.

21AB(4) The employer must deliver that information no later than the end of the period of 7 days starting with the day following the day on which the payment is made.

History – In para. 21AB(1) and (2), the word "general" (which appeared before the word "earnings") omitted by SI 2015/478, reg. 22(4)(c), with effect from 6 April 2015.

Para. 21AB inserted by SI 2013/622, reg. 11, with effect from 6 April 2013 in relation to the tax year 2013–14 and subsequent tax years.

PARAGRAPHS 21AA AND 21AB: SUPPLEMENTARY

21AC Where paragraph 21AA or 21AB applies, the information required by paragraph 21A in respect of the payment of earnings may be included in a return with the information for any other payment of earnings.

History – In para. 21AC, the word "general" (which appeared before the word "earnings" in each place) omitted by SI 2015/478, reg. 22(4)(c), with effect from 6 April 2015.

Para. 21AC inserted by SI 2013/622, reg. 11, with effect from 6 April 2013 in relation to the tax year 2013–14 and subsequent tax years.

BENEFITS AND EXPENSES – RETURNS UNDER REGULATIONS 85 TO 87 OF THE PAYE REGULATIONS

21AD(1) his paragraph applies if an employer makes a payment of earnings to an employee which, for the purposes of tax, falls to be included in a return under–

(a) regulations 85 and 86 of the PAYE Regulations (employers: annual return of other earnings (Forms P11D and P9D) – information which must be provided for each employee), or

(b) regulations 85 and 87 of the PAYE Regulations (employers: annual return of other earnings (Forms P11D and P9D) – information which must also be provided for benefits code employees) or would fall to be so included if the employee's employment was subject to the benefits code for the purposes of regulation 85 of the PAYE Regulations.

21AD(2) If the employer is unable to comply with the requirement in paragraph 21A(1) to deliver the information required by that paragraph on or before making the payment, the employer must instead deliver the information as soon as reasonably practicable after the payment is made and in any event no later than 14 days after the end of the tax month in which the payment is made.

History – In para. 21AD(1), the word "general" (which appeared before the word "earnings") omitted by SI 2015/478, reg. 22(4)(c), with effect from 6 April 2015.

Para. 21AD inserted by SI 2013/622, reg. 11, with effect from 6 April 2013 in relation to the tax year 2013–14 and subsequent tax years.

*MODIFIC*ATION OF THE REQUIREMENTS OF PARAGRAPH 21A: NOTIONAL PAYMENTS

21B(1) This paragraph applies if an employer makes a payment of earnings to an employee which, for the purposes of tax, is a notional payment within the meaning given by section 710(2) of ITEPA 2003 (including a notional payment arising by virtue of a retrospective tax provision).

21B(2) If the employer is unable to comply with the requirement in paragraph 21A(1) to deliver the information required by that paragraph on or before making the payment, the employer must instead deliver the information as soon as reasonably practicable after the payment is made and in any event no later than–

(a) the time at which the employer delivers the information required by regulation 67B of the PAYE Regulations (real time returns of information about relevant payments) in respect of the payment;

(b) [omitted by SI 2013/622, reg. 12(3), or]

(c) 14 days after the end of the tax month the payment is made in,

whichever is earliest.

History – In para. 21B(1), the word "general" (which appeared before the word "earnings") omitted by SI 2015/478, reg. 22(4)(c), with effect from 6 April 2015.
In para. 21B(1), the word "paragraph" substituted for the word "regulation" by SI 2013/622, reg. 12(2), with effect from 6 April 2013 in relation to the tax year 2013–14 and subsequent tax years.
Para. 21B(2)(b) (but not the "or" after it) omitted by SI 2013/622, reg. 12(3), with effect from 6 April 2013 in relation to the tax year 2013–14 and subsequent tax years.
Para. 21B inserted by SI 2012/821, reg. 11, with effect from 6 April 2012.

RELATIONSHIP BETWEEN PARAGRAPH 21A AND AGGREGATION OF EARNINGS

21C(1) Where an employee's earnings are aggregated, a Real Time Information employer or, as the case may be, Real Time Information employers must make such arrangements as are necessary to ensure that the information specified in paragraph (2) in respect of all the aggregated earnings is included in the information given in respect of one of the employee's employments only.

21C(2) The information specified in this paragraph is the information specified in paragraphs 7 and 10(b) and (d) of Schedule 4A (real time returns).

History – Para. 21C inserted by SI 2012/821, reg. 11, with effect from 6 April 2012.

NOTIFICATIONS OF PAYMENTS OF EARNINGS TO AND BY PROVIDERS OF CERTAIN ELECTRONIC PAYMENT METHODS

History – In heading, the word "general" (which appeared before the word "earnings") omitted by SI 2015/478, reg. 22(4)(c), with effect from 6 April 2015.

21CA(1) A Real Time Information employer who makes a payment of earnings using an approved method of electronic communications which falls to be included in a return under paragraph 21A must–

(a) generate a reference and include it in that return,

(b) notify the service provider that the payment is a payment of earnings, and

(c) generate a sub-reference in respect of the payment of earnings and notify the service provider of that sub-reference.

21CA(2) A service provider who receives a notification under paragraph (1)(b) must notify HMRC of the information it holds that is required for generating a reference in relation to the payment of earnings.

21CA(3) In sub-paragraphs (1) and (2), **"service provider"** means the provider of the approved method of electronic communications by which the payment is made.

21CA(4) For the purposes of sub-paragraphs (1) and (3), an **"approved method of electronic communications"** is any method of electronic communications which has been approved for the purposes of regulation 90H (mandatory electronic payment).

21CA(5) Any direction given under regulation 67CA of the PAYE Regulations (notification of relevant payments to and by providers of certain electronic payment methods) applies for the purposes of the obligations in this paragraph as if it referred to payments of earnings.

History – In para. 21CA, the word "general" (which appeared before the word "earnings" in each place) omitted by SI 2015/478, reg. 22(4)(c), with effect from 6 April 2015.
Para. 21CA inserted by SI 2013/622, reg. 13, with effect from 6 April 2013 in relation to the tax year 2013–14 and subsequent tax years.

EXCEPTIONS TO PARAGRAPH 21A

21D(1) This paragraph applies to–

(a) an individual who is a practising member of a religious society or order whose beliefs are incompatible with the use of electronic communications;

(b) a partnership, if all the partners fall within sub-paragraph (a);

(c) a company, if all the directors and the company secretary fall within sub-paragraph (a);

(d) a care and support employer.

(e) an employer to whom a direction has been given under sub-paragraph (12).

But this is subject to sub-paragraph (2B).

21D(2) A Real Time Information employer to whom this paragraph applies may proceed in accordance with this paragraph instead of paragraph 21A.

21D(2A) Before 6th April 2014, a Real Time Information employer to whom this paragraph applies may proceed as if the employer were a non-Real Time Information employer and accordingly the provisions of this Schedule apply to such an employer.

21D(2B) This paragraph does not apply if a Real Time Information employer within sub-paragraph (1) makes a return using an approved method of electronic communications.

21D(3) On and after 6th April 2014, the Real Time Information employer must deliver to HMRC the information specified in Schedule 4A in respect of each employee to whom a payment of earnings is made in a tax quarter unless the employer is not required to maintain a deductions working sheet for any employees and, for the purposes of this paragraph, references in Schedule 4A to a payment of earnings shall be read as if they were references to all the payments made to the employee in the tax quarter.

21D(4) The information must be included in a return in such a form as HMRC may approve or prescribe.

21D(5) The return required under sub-paragraph (4) must be delivered within 14 days after the end of the tax quarter the return relates to.

21D(6) If payments of earnings have been made to more than one employee in the tax quarter, the return under sub-paragraph (4) must include the information required by Schedule 4A in respect of each employee to whom a payment of earnings has been made.

21D(7) [Omitted by SI 2013/622, reg. 14(5).]

21D(8) [Omitted by SI 2013/622, reg. 14(5).]

21D(9) Schedule 24 to the Finance Act 2007, as that Schedule applies to income tax returns, shall apply in relation to the requirement to make a return contained in sub-paragraph (4).

21D(10) In sub-paragraph (1)(c), **"company"** means a body corporate or unincorporated association but does not include a partnership.

21D(11) In sub-paragraph (1)(d), **"care and support employer"** means an individual ("the employer") who employs a person to provide domestic or personal services at or from the employer's home where–

(a) the services are provided to the employer or a member of the employer's family;

(b) the recipient of the services has a physical or mental disability, or is elderly or infirm; and

(c) it is the employer who delivers the return (and not some other person on the employer's behalf).

21D(12) Where the Commissioners for Her Majesty's Revenue and Customs are satisfied that–

(a) it is not reasonably practicable for an employer to make a return using an approved method of electronic communications, and

(b) it is the employer who delivers the return (and not some other person on the employer's behalf),

they may make a direction specifying that the employer is not required to make a return using an approved method of electronic communications.

History – In para. 21D(1), the words "But this is subject to sub-paragraph (2B)." inserted by SI 2014/608, reg. 8(a), with effect from 6 April 2014.

Para. 21D(1)(e) inserted by SI 2013/622, reg. 14(2), with effect from 6 April 2013 in relation to the tax year 2013–14 and subsequent tax years.

Para. 21D(2A) inserted by SI 2013/622, reg. 14(3), with effect from 6 April 2013 in relation to the tax year 2013–14 and subsequent tax years.

Para. 21D(2B) inserted by SI 2014/608, reg. 8(b), with effect from 6 April 2014.

In para. 21D(3), the word "general" (which appeared before the word "earnings" in each place) omitted by SI 2015/478, reg. 22(4)(c), with effect from 6 April 2015.

In para. 21D(3), the word "quarter" substituted for the word "month" by SI 2014/608, reg. 8(c), with effect from 6 April 2014.

In para. 21D(3), the words "On and after 6th April 2014, the" substituted for the word "A" by SI 2013/622, reg. 14(4), with effect from 6 April 2013 in relation to the tax year 2013–14 and subsequent tax years.

In para. 21D(5), the word "quarter" substituted for the word "month" by SI 2014/608, reg. 8(c), with effect from 6 April 2014.

In para. 21D(6), the word "general" (which appeared before the word "earnings" in each place) omitted by SI 2015/478, reg. 22(4)(c), with effect from 6 April 2015.

In para. 21D(6), the word "quarter" substituted for the word "month" by SI 2014/608, reg. 8(c), with effect from 6 April 2014.

Para. 21D(7) and (8) omitted by SI 2013/622, reg. 14(5), with effect from 6 April 2013 in relation to the tax year 2013–14 and subsequent tax years.

Para. 21D(12) inserted by SI 2013/622, reg. 14(6), with effect from 6 April 2013 in relation to the tax year 2013–14 and subsequent tax years.

Para. 21D inserted by SI 2012/821, reg. 11, with effect from 6 April 2012.

RETURNS UNDER PARAGRAPHS 21A AND 21D: AMENDMENTS

21E(1) This paragraph applies where there is an inaccuracy in a return, whether careless or deliberate, made under paragraph 21A (real time returns of information about payments of earnings) or 21D (exceptions to paragraph 21A) and sub-paragraph (2), (3) or (4) applies.

21E(2) This sub-paragraph applies where the inaccuracy relates to the information given in the return in respect of an employee under one or more of paragraphs 3A, 7, 10(b), 10(d), 13, 14, 15, 16 or 18 of Schedule 4A (real time returns).

21E(3) This sub-paragraph applies where the inaccuracy was the omission of details of a payment of earnings to an employee.

21E(4) This sub-paragraph applies where retrospective earnings increase the total amount of the earnings paid to the employee for any tax year in which the employer was a Real Time Information employer.

21E(5) When the employer becomes aware of an inaccuracy in a return under paragraph 21A or 21D, the employer must provide the correct information in the next return for the tax year in question.

21E(6) But if the information given has not been corrected before 20th April following the end of the tax year in question, the employer must make a return under this sub-paragraph.

21E(7) A return under sub-paragraph (6)–

(a) must include the following–

(i) the information specified in paragraphs 2 to 7 and 10 to 12 of Schedule 4A,

(ii) [omitted by SI 2013/622, reg. 15(3)(b),]

(iii) the value of the adjustment, if any, to the information given under each of the paragraphs of Schedule 4A referred to in sub-paragraph (2) in the final return under paragraph 21A or 21D containing information in respect of the employee in the tax year in question,

(iv) if an adjustment is made to the information given under paragraph 7 or 10(b) or (d) of Schedule 4A, the information specified in paragraph 6 of that Schedule,

(v) if an adjustment is made to the information given under paragraph 10(d) of Schedule 4A that decreases the amount reported under that paragraph, an indication of whether the employer has refunded the primary Class 1 contributions paid in error to the employee, and

(vi) if an adjustment is made to the information given under paragraph 16 of Schedule 4A, the information specified in paragraph 17 of that Schedule if it has not already been provided;

(b) must be made as soon as reasonably practicable after the employer becomes aware of the inaccuracy; and

(c) must be made using an approved method of electronic communications and regulation 90N(2) (mandatory use of electronic communications) applies as if the return was a paragraph 22 return within the meaning given by regulation 90M (paragraph 22 return and specified payments).

21E(8) In the application of sub-paragraphs (6) and (7) to cases within sub-paragraph (3), if no information was given in any returns under paragraph 21A or 21D in respect of the employee in the tax year, the value of any adjustments required must be calculated as if there was a final return containing information for the employee in the year and the figure requiring adjustment was zero.

21E(9) Sub-paragraph (7)(c) does not apply if the employer is one to whom paragraph 21D applies but in those circumstances the return must be in such a form as HMRC may approve or prescribe.

History – In para. 21E(1), the word "general" (which appeared before the word "earnings") omitted by SI 2015/478, reg. 22(4)(c), with effect from 6 April 2015.

In para. 21E(1), the words "there is an inaccuracy in a return, whether careless or deliberate," substituted for the words "an employer discovers an error in a return" by SI 2014/608, reg. 9(a), with effect from 6 April 2014.

In para. (21E)(2) and (3), the word "inaccuracy" substituted for "error" by SI 2014/608, reg. 9(b), with effect from 6 April 2014.

In para. 21E(2), the words "one or more of paragraphs 3A, 7" substituted for the words "paragraphs 7" by SI 2013/622, reg. 15(2), with effect from 6 April 2013 in relation to the tax year 2013–14 and subsequent tax years.

In para. 21E(3), the word "general" (which appeared before the word "earnings") omitted by SI 2015/478, reg. 22(4)(c), with effect from 6 April 2015.

In para. 21E(4), the word "general" (which appeared before the word "earnings") omitted by SI 2015/478, reg. 22(4)(c), with effect from 6 April 2015.

Para. 21E(5) substituted by SI 2014/608, reg. 9(c), with effect from 6 April 2014.

In para. 21E(7)(b), the words "employer becomes aware of the inaccuracy" substituted for "discovery of the error" by SI 2014/608, reg. 9(d), with effect from 6 April 2014.

In para. 21E(7)(a)(i), the words "2 to 7 and 10 to 12" substituted for the words "2 and 12" by SI 2013/622, reg. 15(3)(a), with effect from 6 April 2013 in relation to the tax year 2013–14 and subsequent tax years.

Para. 21E(7)(a)(ii) omitted by SI 2013/622, reg. 15(3)(b), with effect from 6 April 2013 in relation to the tax year 2013–14 and subsequent tax years.

In para. 21E(7)(c), the words "and regulation 90N(2) (mandatory use of electronic communications) applies as if the return was a paragraph 22 return within the meaning given by regulation 90M (paragraph 22 return and specified payments)" inserted by SI 2013/622, reg. 15(3)(c), with effect from 6 April 2013 in relation to the tax year 2013–14 and subsequent tax years.

Para. 21E inserted by SI 2012/821, reg. 11, with effect from 6 April 2012.

FAILURE TO MAKE A RETURN UNDER PARAGRAPH 21A OR 21D

21EA(1) This paragraph applies where an employer does not make a return required by paragraph 21A (real time returns of information about payments of earnings) or 21D (exceptions to paragraph 21A).

21EA(2) The employer must provide the information in the next return made under paragraph 21A or 21D for the tax year in question.

21EA(3) But if the information has not been provided before 20th April following the end of the tax year in question, the employer must submit a return under this sub-paragraph.

21EA(4) A return under sub-paragraph (3) must–

(a) include the information specified in Schedule 4A,

(b) be made as soon as reasonably practicable after the discovery of the failure to make the return, and

(c) be made using an approved method of electronic communications and regulation 90N(2) (mandatory use of electronic communications) applies as if the return were a paragraph 22 return within the meaning given by regulation 90M (paragraph 22 return and specified payments).

21EA(5) Sub-paragraph (4)(c) does not apply if the employer is one to whom paragraph 21D applies but in those circumstances the return must be in such a form as HMRC may approve or prescribe.

21EA(6) If a return under sub-paragraph (3) is not made before 20th May following the tax year in question Section 98A of TMA 1970 (special penalties in the case of certain returns) applies to that return, but this sub-paragraph does not apply to a return in respect of the tax year 2014–15 or a subsequent tax year.

History – In para. 21EA(1), the word "general" (which appeared before the word "earnings") omitted by SI 2015/478, reg. 22(4)(c), with effect from 6 April 2015.
In para. 21EA(3), the words "before 20th May following the tax year in question", which appeared after the words "a return under this sub-paragraph" omitted by SI 2013/2301, reg. 4(a), with effect from 6 October 2013.
In para. 21EA(6), the words ", but this sub-paragraph does not apply to a return in respect of the tax year 2014–15 or a subsequent tax year" inserted by SI 2014/2397, reg. 3(4), with effect in relation to a failure to deliver a return to HMRC in respect of any payment of general earnings (as defined at SI 2014/2397, reg. 1(3)) made on or after 6 October 2014.
In para. 21EA(6), the words "If a return under sub-paragraph (3) is not made before 20th May following the tax year in question" inserted and the words "that return" substituted for the words "a return under sub-paragraph (3)" by SI 2013/2301, reg. 4(b), with effect from 6 October 2013.
Para. 21EA inserted by SI 2013/622, reg. 16, with effect from 6 April 2013 in relation to the tax year 2013–14 and subsequent tax years.

ADDITIONAL INFORMATION ABOUT PAYMENTS

21F(1) A Real Time Information employer must inform HMRC of each of the amounts specified in Schedule 4B (additional information about payments) for each tax period unless sub-paragraph (4) or (5) applies.

21F(2) The information must be given in a return.

21F(3) The return must be delivered within 14 days after the end of the tax period.

21F(4) This sub-paragraph applies if–

(a) all of the amounts are zero; and

(b) the employer has not made a return under sub-paragraph (2) in the tax year.

21F(5) This paragraph applies if none of the amounts has changed in the tax period.

21F(6) If an employer makes an error in a return under this paragraph, the employer must provide the correct information in the first return made under sub-paragraph (2) after the discovery of the error.

21F(7) But if the information given has not been corrected before 20th April following the end of the year in question, the employer must provide the correct information for the year in question in a return under this sub-paragraph.

21F(7A) A Real Time Information employer may send to HMRC a notification (included within a return under this paragraph or otherwise) if–

(a) for a tax period, the employer was not required to make any returns in accordance with paragraph 21A or 21D because no payments of earnings were made during the tax periods, or

(b) the employer has sent the final return under paragraph 21A or 21D that the employer expects to make–

  (i) in the circumstances described in paragraph 5 of Schedule A1 to the PAYE Regulations (real time returns); or

  (ii) for the year.

21F(8) A return under sub-paragraph (2) or (7) and a notification under paragraph (7A)–

(a) must state–

  (i) the year to which the return relates,

  (ii) the employer's HMRC office number,

  (iii) the employer's PAYE reference,

  (iv) the employer's accounts office reference, and;

(v) if the notification is under sub-paragraph (7A)(b)(i), include the date of cessation;

(b) is to be made using an approved method of electronic communications.

21F(9) [Omitted by SI 2013/622, reg. 14(4).]

21F(10) For the purposes of sub-paragraph (8)(b), regulation 90N(2) (mandatory use of electronic communications) applies as if the return was a paragraph 22 return within the meaning given by regulation 90M (paragraph 22 return and specified payments).

21F(11) The requirement to use an approved method of electronic communications does not apply if the employer is one to whom paragraph 21D (exceptions to paragraph 21A) applies but in those circumstances the return must be in such a form as HMRC may approve or prescribe.

21F(12) Schedule 24 to the Finance Act 2007 (penalties for errors), as that Schedule applies to income tax returns, shall apply in relation to the requirement to make a return contained in sub-paragraph (2) or (7).

History – In para. 21F(7A)(a), the word "general" (which appeared before the word "earnings") omitted by SI 2015/478, reg. 22(4)(c), with effect from 6 April 2015.

Para. 21F(7A) inserted by SI 2013/622, reg. 17(2), with effect from 6 April 2013 in relation to the tax year 2013–14 and subsequent tax years.

In para. 21F(8), the words "and a notification under paragraph (7A)" inserted by SI 2013/622, reg. 17(3)(a), with effect from 6 April 2013 in relation to the tax year 2013–14 and subsequent tax years.

Para. 21F(8)(a)(v) (and the "and" before it) inserted (and the "and" after (iii) omitted) by SI 2013/622, reg. 17(3), with effect from 6 April 2013 in relation to the tax year 2013–14 and subsequent tax years.

Para. 21F(9) omitted by SI 2013/622, reg. 17(4), with effect from 6 April 2013 in relation to the 2013–14 tax year and subsequent tax years.

Para. 21F inserted by SI 2012/821, reg. 11, with effect from 6 April 2012.

PENALTY: FAILURE TO COMPLY WITH PARAGRAPH 21A OR 21D

21G(1) Where a Real Time Information employer fails to deliver a return in accordance with paragraph 21A (real time returns of information about payments of earnings) to paragraph 21AB (employees paid in specific circumstances), paragraph 21AD (benefits and expenses – returns under the PAYE Regulations), paragraph 21B (modification of the requirements of paragraph 21A: notional payments) or paragraph 21D (exceptions to paragraph 21A), Schedule 55 to the Finance Act 2009 (amount of penalty: real time information for PAYE) and regulations 67I to 67K of the PAYE Regulations (penalties) apply in relation that failure as if–

(a) the return under paragraph 21A (real time returns of information about payments of earnings) or paragraph 21D (exceptions to paragraph 21A), as the case may be, were a return falling within item 4 of the Table in paragraph 1 of Schedule 55, and

(b) references to the PAYE Regulations were references to these Regulations,

but this is subject to sub-paragraphs (2) and (2A).

21G(2) Where a Real Time Information employer (P) is liable to a penalty in consequence of a failure to deliver a return ("the tax return") under regulation 67B (real time returns of information about relevant payments) or regulation 67D (exceptions to regulation 67B) of the PAYE Regulations, P shall not also be liable to a penalty in respect of any failure in relation to an associated return under paragraph 21A (real time returns of information about payments of earnings) or 21D (exceptions to paragraph 21A).

21G(2A) Sub-paragraph (2) does not apply to a penalty imposed under paragraph 6D of Schedule 55 to the Finance Act 2009 (amount of penalty: real time information for PAYE).

21G(3) A tax return and a return under paragraph 21A or 21D are "associated" if the return under paragraph 21A or 21D is required to be delivered at the same time as the tax return.

History – In para. 21G(1) and (2), the word "general" (which appeared before the word "earnings" in each place) omitted by SI 2015/478, reg. 22(4)(c), with effect from 6 April 2015.

In para. 21G(1)(b), the words "sub-paragraphs (2) and (2A)" substituted for the words "sub-paragraph (2)" by SI 2016/352, reg. 7(2)(a), with effect from 6 April 2016.

Para. 21G(2A) inserted by SI 2016/352, reg. 7(2)(b), with effect from 6 April 2016.

Para. 21G and the heading immediately preceding it inserted by SI 2014/2397, reg. 3(5), with effect in relation to a failure to deliver a return to HMRC in respect of any payment of general earnings made–

(a) on or after 6th October 2014 where the employer is a large existing Real Time Information employer (as defined at SI 2014/2397, reg. 1(4)); and

(b) on or after 6th March 2015 where–

(i) the employer is a small existing Real Time Information employer (as defined at SI 2014/2397, reg. 1(4)); or

(ii) a person becomes a new Real Time Information employer after 6th October 2014 (as defined at SI 2014/2397, reg. 1(4)).

RETURN BY EMPLOYER AT END OF YEAR

22(A1) This paragraph applies to–

(a) non-Real Time Information employers;

(b) Real Time Information employers in relation to years in which they were, for the whole of the year, non-Real Time information employers; and

(c) Real Time Information employers to whom HMRC has given a notice requiring a return under regulation 73 of the PAYE Regulations (annual return of relevant payments liable to deduction of tax (Forms P35 and P14) in respect of a tax year.

22(1) Before 20th May following the end of the year the employer shall render to the Inland Revenue in such form as they may approve or prescribe, a return showing in respect of each employee, in respect of whom he was required at any time during the year to prepare or maintain a deductions working sheet in accordance with this Schedule–

(a) such particulars as the Inland Revenue may require for the identification of the employee;

(b) the year to which the return relates;

(c) in respect of each and under each of the category letters, the total amounts for the year shown under–

  (i) each of sub-paragraphs (i) to (v) severally of paragraph 7(13)(b) (such amounts being rounded down to the next whole pound if not already whole pounds in the case of paragraphs (i) to (iii)),

  (ii) [omitted by SI 2003/193, reg. 16(5)]

  (iii) [omitted by SI 2003/193, reg. 16(5)]

(d) the total amount of any statutory maternity pay paid during the year;

(da) the total amount of statutory paternity pay paid during the year;

(daa) [omitted by SI 2015/175, reg. 4(5)(a)(ii);]

(db) the total amount of statutory adoption pay paid during the year; and

(dc) the total amount of statutory shared parental pay paid during the year.

(e) [omitted by SI 2012/821, reg. 27.]

22(2) The return required by sub-paragraph (1) shall include a statement and declaration in the form approved or prescribed by HMRC containing a list of all deductions working sheets on which the employer was obliged to keep records in accordance with this Schedule in respect of that year, and shall also include a certificate showing–

(a) the total amount of earnings-related contributions payable by him in respect of each employee during that year;

(b) the total amount of earnings-related contributions payable in respect of all his employees during that year;

(c) [omitted by SI 2016/352, reg. 18(d)(ii);]

(d) in respect of statutory maternity pay paid during that year to all his employees, the total of amounts determined under regulation 3 of the Compensation of Employers Regulations and deducted by virtue of regulation 4 of those Regulations;

(da) in respect of statutory paternity pay paid during that year to all his employees the total of the amounts determined under regulation 5 of the Statutory Paternity Pay and Statutory Adoption Pay (Administration) Regulations 2002;

(daa) [omitted by SI 2015/175, reg. 4(5)(b)(ii);]

(db) in respect of statutory adoption pay paid during that year to all his employees the total of the amounts determined under regulation 5 of the Statutory Paternity Pay and Statutory Adoption Pay (Administration) Regulations 2002; and

(dc) in respect of statutory shared parental pay paid during the year to all his employees the total of the amounts determined under regulation 5 (deductions from payments to the Commissioners) of the Statutory Shared Parental Pay (Administration) Regulations 2014.

(e) [omitted by SI 2012/821, reg. 27.]

22(2A) Where a liability arises to pay contributions in respect of retrospective earnings relating to a closed tax year, the employer shall render a replacement return, or where necessary prepare one, in respect of the employee for that closed tax year before 20th May following the end of the year in which the relevant retrospective contributions regulations came into force, in accordance with paragraphs (a) to (c) of sub-paragraph (1), setting out the revised earnings and earnings-related contributions.

22(2B) The return required by sub-paragraph (2A) shall include a statement and declaration in a form *prescribed* by HMRC containing a list of all deductions working sheets in accordance with paragraph 6(1A) of this Schedule in respect of that year, and shall also include a certificate showing–

(a) the total amount of earnings-related contributions originally payable (in accordance with sub-paragraph (2)(a)) in respect of each employee to whom sub-paragraph (2A) applies;

(b) the total amount of earnings-related contributions originally payable (in accordance with sub-paragraph (2)(b)) in respect of all employees to whom sub-paragraph (2A) applies;

(c) the total amount of revised earnings-related contributions payable in respect of each of those employees;

(d) the total amount of revised earnings-related contributions payable in respect of all those employees,

(e) the difference between the amount certified in paragraph (b) and paragraph (d) of this sub-paragraph in respect of all of those employees.

(f) [omitted by SI 2016/352, reg. 18(d)(iii).]

22(3) [Omitted by SI 2014/2397, reg. 3(6).]

22(4) If the employer is a body corporate, the declarations and the certificates referred to in sub-paragraph (2) and (2B) shall be signed by the secretary or by a director of the body corporate.

22(5) If, within 14 days of the end of any year, an employer has failed to pay to HMRC the total amount of earnings-related contributions which he is liable so to pay, HMRC may prepare a certificate showing the amount of such contributions remaining unpaid for the year in question, excluding any amount deducted by the employer by virtue of the Compensation of Employers Regulations.

The provisions of paragraph 16 shall apply with any necessary modifications to the amount shown in that certificate.

22(6) Notwithstanding sub-paragraphs (2) to (5), the returns referred to in sub-paragraphs (1) and (2A) may be made in such other form as HMRC and the employer approve, and in that case–

(a) sub-paragraphs (2) to (5) shall not apply; and

(b) the making of the returns shall be subject to such conditions as HMRC may direct as to the method of making it.

22(7) Section 98A of the Taxes Management Act 1970 (special penalties in the case of certain returns) and Schedule 24 to the Finance Act 2007 (penalties for errors) as that Schedule applies to income tax returns as modified by the provisions of paragraph 7 of Schedule 1 to the Act shall apply in relation to the requirement to make a return contained in sub-paragraph (1) and (2A).

History – In para. 22 "HMRC" substituted throughout by SI 2007/1056, reg. 8(11), with effect from 6 April 2007.
In para. 22 "Inland Revenue" substituted throughout by SI 2004/770, reg. 32, with effect from 6 April 2004.
In para. 22(A1), the word "paragraph" substituted for the word "regulation" by SI 2013/622, reg. 18, with effect from 6 April 2013 in relation to the tax year 2013–14 and subsequent tax years.
Para. 22(A1) inserted by SI 2012/821, reg. 12, with effect from 6 April 2012.
In para. 22(1) "Before 20th May following the end of the year the employer shall render to the Inland Revenue in such form as they may approve or prescribe" substituted by SI 2004/770, reg. 32, with effect from 6 April 2004.
In para. 22(1)(c), the words "sub-paragraphs (i) to (v)" substituted by SI 2003/193, reg. 16(5) which came into force on 6 April 2003 and which has effect for the tax year 2003–04 and subsequent tax years.
In para. 22(1)(c)(i), the words "to (iii)" substituted for the words "to (iiia)" by SI 2016/352, reg. 18(d)(i), with effect from 6 April 2016, subject to savings in relation to rights or obligations arising in connection with tax years beginning before 6 April 2016 (and for savings purposes, references to repealed provisions of the Pension Schemes Act 1993 are to be read as though such provisions were still in force).
In para. 22(1)(c)(i), "(iiia)" substituted for "(iii)" by SI 2009/111, reg. 4(4), with effect from 6 April 2009.
In para. 22(1)(c), para. (ii) and (iii) omitted by SI 2003/193, reg. 16(5) which came into force on 6 April 2003 and which has effect for the tax year 2003–04 and subsequent tax years.
In para. 22(1)(d), the word "and" at the end omitted; para. (da) and (db) inserted by SI 2003/193, reg. 16(5) which came into force on 6 April 2003 and which has effect for the tax year 2003–04 and subsequent tax years.
In para. 22(1)(da), the word "ordinary" omitted by SI 2015/175, reg. 4(5)(a)(i), with effect from 5 April 2015, subject to the transitional provisions in SI 2015/175, reg. 9 (amendments do not have effect where they relate to additional statutory paternity pay or ordinary statutory paternity pay and payments of either on or after 5 April 2015).
In para. 22(1)(da), the words "ordinary statutory paternity pay" substituted for the words "statutory paternity pay" by SI 2010/2450, reg. 4(5)(a), with effect from 14 November 2010.
Para. 22(1)(daa) omitted by SI 2015/175, reg. 4(5)(a)(ii), with effect from 5 April 2015, subject to the transitional provisions in SI 2015/175, reg. 9 (amendments do not have effect where they relate to additional statutory paternity pay or ordinary statutory paternity pay and payments of either on or after 5 April 2015).
Former para. 22(1)(daa) inserted by SI 2010/2450, reg. 4(5)(b), with effect from 14 November 2010.
Para. 22(1)(dc) (and the word "; and" immediately preceding it) inserted (and the "and" at the end of (daa) omitted) by SI 2015/175, reg. 4(5)(a), with effect from 5 March 2015.
Para. 22(1)(e) omitted (and the "and" at the end of para. 22(1)(daa) inserted, and a full stop substituted for the "; and" at the end of para. 22(1)(db)) by SI 2012/821, reg. 27, with effect from 6 April 2012.
Para. 22(2)(c) omitted by SI 2016/352, reg. 18(d)(ii), with effect from 6 April 2016, subject to savings in relation to rights or obligations arising in connection with tax years beginning before 6 April 2016 (and for savings purposes, references to repealed provisions of the Pension Schemes Act 1993 are to be read as though such provisions were still in force). Former para. 22(2)(c) read as follows:
"(c) in relation to any contracted-out employment, the number notified by HMRC on the relevant contracting-out certificate as the employer's number;".
In para. 22(2)(da), the word "ordinary" omitted by SI 2015/175, reg. 4(5)(b)(i), with effect from 5 April 2015, subject to the transitional provisions in SI 2015/175, reg. 9 (amendments do not have effect where they relate to additional statutory paternity pay or ordinary statutory paternity pay and payments of either on or after 5 April 2015).
In para. 22(2)(da), the words "ordinary statutory paternity pay" substituted for the words "statutory paternity pay" by SI 2010/2450, reg. 4(5)(c), with effect from 14 November 2010.
Para. 22(2)(daa) omitted by SI 2015/175, reg. 4(5)(b)(ii), with effect from 5 April 2015, subject to the transitional provisions in SI 2015/175, reg. 9 (amendments do not have effect where they relate to additional statutory paternity pay or ordinary statutory paternity pay and payments of either on or after 5 April 2015).
Para. 22(2)(daa) inserted by SI 2010/2450, reg. 4(5)(b), with effect from 14 November 2010.
In para. 22(2), the word "and" at end of para. (d) omitted, and para. (da) and (db) inserted by SI 2003/193, reg. 16(5) which came into force on 6 April 2003 and which has effect for the tax year 2003–04 and subsequent tax years.
In para. 22(2)(daa), the word "Pay" inserted after "Paternity" by SI 2012/821, reg. 28, with effect from 6 April 2012.

Para. 22(2)(dc) (and the word "; and" immediately preceding it) inserted (and the "and" at the end of (daa) omitted) by SI 2015/175, reg. 4(5)(b), with effect from 5 March 2015.
Para. 22(2)(e) omitted (and the "and" at the end of para. 22(2)(daa) inserted, and a full stop substituted for the "; and" at the end of para. 22(2)(db)) by SI 2012/821, reg. 27, with effect from 6 April 2012.
Para. 22(2A) and (2B) inserted by SI 2007/1056, reg. 8(12), with effect from 6 April 2007.
Para. 22(2B)(f) omitted (and the "." at the end of (e) substituted for ";") by SI 2016/352, reg. 18(d)(iii), with effect from 6 April 2016, subject to savings in relation to rights or obligations arising in connection with tax years beginning before 6 April 2016 (and for savings purposes, references to repealed provisions of the Pension Schemes Act 1993 are to be read as though such provisions were still in force). Former para. 22(2B)(f) read as follows:
"(f) in relation to any contracted-out employment the number notified by HMRC on the relevant contracting-out certificate as the employer's number.".
Para. 22(3) omitted by SI 2014/2397, reg. 3(6), with effect from 6 October 2014.
In para. 22(4) the words "the declarations", "the certificates", and "sub-paragraphs (2) and (2B)" substituted by SI 2007/1056, reg. 8(13) with effect from 6 April 2007.
In para. 22(6) the words "the returns referred to in sub-paragraphs (1) and (2A)" substituted for "the return referred to in sub-paragraph (1)", and in (b) "the returns" substituted by SI 2007/1056, reg. 8(14) with effect from 6 April 2007.
In para. 22(7) the words "Section 98A of the Taxes Management Act 1970 (special penalties in the case of certain returns) and Schedule 24 to the Finance Act 2007 (penalties for errors) as that Schedule applies to income tax returns" substituted by SI 2008/636, reg. 7, with effect from 1 April 2008.
In para. 22(7) the words "and (2A)" inserted by SI 2007/1056, reg. 8(15) with effect from 6 April 2007.
Derivations – SI 1979/591, Sch. 1, reg. 30.

Cross references – Direction of the Board, 5 April 2004: direction consolidating various directions in respect of the electronic delivery of information and specifying approved methods of electronic payments of sums due.

NOTIFICATION BY EMPLOYER AT END OF YEAR THAT AN AGREEMENT DESCRIBED IN PARAGRAPH 3A(2) OR AN ELECTION UNDER PARAGRAPH 3B(1) OF SCHEDULE 1 TO THE ACT HAS BEEN OPERATED IN RELATION TO A SECONDARY CLASS 1 CONTRIBUTION

23(1) An employer must notify HMRC on or before 6th July if a relevant agreement or relevant election has been operated in relation to a Secondary Class 1 contribution payable in respect of the relevant employment income of a person ("the earner") in the year immediately preceding the year in which that day falls.

23(2) A relevant agreement has been operated in relation to the contribution described in sub-paragraph (1) if the employer has recovered the whole or any part of it pursuant to an agreement described in paragraph 3A(2) of Schedule 1 to the Act.

23(3) A relevant election has been operated in relation to the contribution described in sub-paragraph (1) if the liability for the whole or any part of it has been transferred to the earner pursuant to an election under paragraph 3B of that Schedule.

History – Para. 23 and the heading immediately preceding it substituted by SI 2015/478, reg. 22(5), with effect in relation to returns made by employers for the tax year 2014–15 and subsequent tax years.

SPECIAL RETURN BY EMPLOYER AT END OF VOYAGE PERIOD

24(1) This paragraph applies where earnings-related contributions are assessed in accordance with regulation 120(4) or (5) (earnings periods for mariners and apportionment of earnings).

24(2) Not later than 14 days after the end of the voyage period the employer shall render to the Inland Revenue in such form as the Inland Revenue may authorise a return in respect of each mariner showing–

(a) his name, discharge book number and national insurance number;

(b) the earnings periods and the amounts of earnings apportioned to each such period in the voyage period;

(c) the appropriate category letter for each apportionment of earnings;

(d) the amounts of all the earnings-related contributions payable on each apportionment of earnings otherwise than under paragraph 7(3);

(e) the amounts of primary Class 1 contributions included in the amounts shown under paragraph (d) for each apportionment of earnings; and

(f) the total amount of any earnings in respect of which primary Class 1 contributions were payable.

(g) [omitted by SI 2016/352, reg. 18(e).]

(h) [omitted by SI 2012/821, reg. 29.]

History – In para. 24 "Inland Revenue" and "general earnings" substituted throughout by SI 2004/770, reg. 32, with effect from 6 April 2004.
In para. 24(2), the word "general" (which appeared before the word "earnings" in each place) omitted by SI 2015/478, reg. 22(4)(d), with effect from 6 April 2015.
Para. 24(2)(f) substituted by SI 2016/352, reg. 18(e)(ii), with effect from 6 April 2016, subject to savings in relation to rights or obligations arising in connection with tax years beginning before 6 April 2016 (and for savings purposes, references to repealed provisions of the Pension Schemes Act 1993 are to be read as though such provisions were still in force). Former para. 24(2)(f) read as follows:

"(f) where the employment is contracted-out employment for any part of the voyage period–
(i) the amounts of that part of the contributions shown under paragraph (e) which were payable on earnings above the primary threshold, if primary Class 1 contributions were payable at the reduced rate, and
(ii) the number notified by the Inland Revenue on the relevant contracting-out certificate as the employer's number; and".

Para. 24(2)(g) omitted (and the "and" after (e) inserted) by SI 2016/352, reg. 18(e), with effect from 6 April 2016, subject to savings in relation to rights or obligations arising in connection with tax years beginning before 6 April 2016 (and for savings purposes, references to repealed provisions of the Pension Schemes Act 1993 are to be read as though such provisions were still in force). Former para. 24(2)(g) read as follows:

"(g) the total amount of any earnings in respect of which primary Class 1 contributions were payable, other than earnings from non-contracted-out employment in respect of which primary Class 1 contributions were payable at the reduced rate.".

Para. 24(2)(h) omitted (and the "and" at the end of para. 24(2)(f) inserted, and a full stop substituted for the "; and" at the end of para. 24(2)(g)) by SI 2012/821, reg. 29, with effect from 6 April 2012.

Derivations – SI 1979/591, Sch. 1, reg. 30A.

RETURN BY EMPLOYER OF RECOVERY UNDER THE STATUTORY SICK PAY PERCENTAGE THRESHOLD ORDER

25 [Omitted by SI 2014/2397, reg. 3(7).]

History – Para. 25 omitted by SI 2014/2397, reg. 3(7), with effect from 6 October 2014.

RETENTION BY EMPLOYER OF CONTRIBUTION AND ELECTION RECORDS

26(1) An employer must keep and preserve all contribution records which are not required to be sent to HMRC by other provisions in these Regulations for not less than–

(a) three years after the end of the tax year to which they relate; or

(b) for documents or records relating to information about the amounts of Class 1A and Class 1B contributions, three years after the end of the year in which a contribution became payable.

26(2) The duty under paragraph (1) may be discharged by preserving the contribution records in any form or by any means.

26(3) Where an election has been made jointly by the secondary contributor and the employed earner for the purposes of paragraph 3B(1) of Schedule 1 to the Act, the records which the secondary contributor is obliged by paragraph 8 to maintain shall be retained by the secondary contributor throughout the period for which the election is in force and for six years after the end of that period.

26(4) In this paragraph "contribution records" means wages sheets, deductions working sheets and other documents or records relating to–

(a) the calculation of payment of earnings to the employer's employees or the amount of the earnings-related contributions payable for those earnings;

(b) the amount of any Class 1A contributions or Class 1B contributions payable by the employer; and

(c) any information about the amounts of Class 1A and Class 1B contributions.

26(4A) Sub-paragraph (4B) applies in relation to an employer who makes deductions, or applies for a repayment, under section 4 of the National Insurance Contributions Act 2014 on account of an employment allowance for which the employer qualifies for a tax year (or who intends to do so).

26(4B) So far as they are not otherwise covered by sub-paragraph (4), **"contribution records"** includes any documents or records relating to–

(a) the employer's qualification for the employment allowance, or

(b) the calculation of any amount that has been, or could be, deducted or repaid under section 4 of the National Insurance Contributions Act 2014 on account of the employment allowance.

26(5) For the purposes of this paragraph **"employer"**–

(a) includes, in relation to a Class 1A contribution, the person liable to pay such a contribution in accordance with section 10ZA of the Act (liability of third party provider of benefits in kind); and

(b) means, in relation to a Class 1B contribution, the person liable to pay such a contribution in accordance with section 10A of the Act.

History – In para. 26(4), the words "(other than deductions working sheets issued under regulation 35 of the PAYE Regulations (simplified deduction schemes: records))" omitted by SI 2013/622, reg. 4(4), with effect from 6 April 2014 in relation to the tax year 2014–15.

Para. 26(4A) and (4B) inserted by NICA 2014, s. 7(3), with effect from 6 April 2014 subject to NICA 2014, s. 7(4).

Para. 26 and 26A substituted for former para. 26 by SI 2009/600, reg. 8(4), with effect from 1 April 2009.

Cross references – NICA 2011, s. 9(3) (regional secondary contributions holiday for new businesses): disapplication of para. 26(1) in respect of certain documents or records.

CERTIFICATE OF EMPLOYER'S LIABILITY TO PAY CONTRIBUTIONS AFTER INSPECTION OF DOCUMENTS

26A(1) An officer of Revenue and Customs may, by reference to the information obtained from an inspection of the documents and records produced under Schedule 36 to the Finance Act 2008 (information and inspection powers), and on the occasion of each inspection, prepare a certificate showing–

(a) the amount of earnings-related contributions which it appears that the employer is liable to pay to HMRC, excluding any amount deducted by the employer by virtue of the Compensation of Employers Regulations for the years or tax periods covered by the inspection; or

(b) the amount of any Class 1B contributions which it appears that the employer is liable to pay to HMRC for the years covered by the inspection, or such an amount in addition to an amount referred to in paragraph (a);

together with any amount of earnings-related contributions or Class 1B contributions or a combination of those classes of contributions, which has not been paid to HMRC or, to the best of the officer's knowledge and belief, to any other person to whom it might lawfully be paid.

26A(2) The production of a certificate mentioned in sub-paragraph (1) shall, unless the contrary is proved, be sufficient evidence that the employer is liable to pay to HMRC in respect of the years or, as the case may be, tax periods mentioned in the certificate, the amount shown in the certificate as unpaid; and any document purporting to be such a certificate shall be treated as such a certificate until the contrary is proved.

26A(3) The provisions of paragraph 16 shall apply with any necessary modifications to the amount shown in such a certificate.

26A(4) For the purposes of this paragraph **"employer"** has the meaning given by paragraph 26(5).

26A(5) In sub-paragraph (6)(a) of paragraph 29B (relevant contributions debts of managed service companies) for "paragraph 26 (inspection of employer's records)" substitute "paragraph 26A (certificate of employer's liability to pay contributions after inspection of documents)".

26A(6) In sub-paragraph (7) of paragraph 29D (time limits for issue of transfer notices) for "paragraph 26" substitute "Schedule 36 to the Finance Act 2008".

26A(7) After paragraph (4) of paragraph 29F insert–

> **"29F(5)** For the purposes of sub-paragraph (3) **"the reckonable date"** has the meaning given by paragraph 17(3)(b)(i).".

History – Para. 26 and 26A substituted for former para. 26 by SI 2009/600, reg. 8(4), with effect from 1 April 2009.

DEATH OF EMPLOYER

27 If an employer dies, anything which he would have been liable to do under this Schedule shall be done by his personal representatives, or, in the case of an employer who paid earnings on behalf of another person, by the person succeeding him or, if no person succeeds him, the person on whose behalf he paid general earnings.

History – In para. 27, the word "general" (which appeared before the word "earnings") omitted by SI 2015/478, reg. 22(4)(d), with effect from 6 April 2015.
In para. 27 "general earnings" substituted throughout by SI 2004/770, reg. 32, with effect from 6 April 2004.

Derivations – SI 1979/591, Sch. 1, reg. 33.

SUCCESSION TO A BUSINESS, ETC.

28(1) This paragraph applies where there has been a change in the employer from whom an employee receives emoluments in respect of his employment in any trade, business, concern or undertaking, or in connection with any property, or from whom an employee receives any annuity other than a pension.

28(2) Where this paragraph applies, in relation to any matter arising after the change, the employer after the change shall be liable to do anything which the employer before the change would have been liable to do under this Schedule if the change had not taken place.

28(3) Sub-paragraph (2) is subject to the qualification that the employee after the change shall not be liable for the payment of any earnings-related contributions which were deductible from earnings paid to the employee before, unless they are also deductible from general earnings paid to the employee after, the change took place, or of any corresponding employer's earnings-related contributions.

History – In para. 28 "general earnings" substituted throughout by SI 2004/770, reg. 32, with effect from 6 April 2004.
In para. 28(3), the word "general" (which appeared before the word "earnings") omitted by SI 2015/478, reg. 22(4)(d), with effect from 6 April 2015.
In para. 28(3) "the employee after" substituted throughout by SI 2004/770, reg. 32, with effect from 6 April 2004.

Derivations – SI 1979/591, Sch. 1, reg. 34.

PAYMENTS BY CHEQUE

29(1) Sub-paragraph (2) applies for the purposes of paragraphs 10, 11, 13, 15, 17 and 18.

29(2) If any payment to the Inland Revenue is made by cheque, and the cheque is paid on its first presentation to the banker on whom it is drawn, the payment shall be treated as made on the day on which the cheque was received by the Inland Revenue, and **"pay"**, **"paid"**, **"unpaid"** and **"overpaid"** shall be construed accordingly.

History – In para. 29 "Inland Revenue" substituted throughout by SI 2004/770, reg. 32, with effect from 6 April 2004.

Derivations – SI 1979/591, Sch. 1, reg. 34A.

Part 3A – Debts of Managed Service Companies

INTERPRETATION OF THIS PART

29A(1) In this Part of this Schedule–

"HM Revenue and Customs" means Her Majesty's Revenue and Customs;

"lower amount" means the amount mentioned in paragraph 29C(5);

"managed service company" has the meaning given by section 61B of ITEPA;

"paragraph (b) associate" means a person who–

(a) is within section 688A(2)(d)(b), and

(b) is within that provision by virtue of a connection with a person who is within section 688A(2)(b);

"paragraph (c) associate" means a person who–

(a) is within section 688A(2)(d), and

(b) is within that provision by virtue of a connection with a person who is within section 688A(2)(c);

"qualifying period" means a tax period beginning on or after 6th August 2007;

"relevant contributions debt" means a debt specified in paragraph 29B;

"specified amount" means the amount mentioned in paragraph 29C(1)(b);

"transfer notice" means the notice mentioned in paragraph 29C(4);

"transferee" means the person mentioned in paragraph 29C(4).

29A(2) In this Part of this Schedule references to section 688A, however expressed, are references to section 688A of ITEPA.

History – Pt. 3A inserted by SI 2007/2068, reg. 2, with effect from 6 August 2007.

RELEVANT CONTRIBUTIONS DEBTS OF MANAGED SERVICE COMPANIES

29B(1) A managed service company has a relevant contributions debt if–

(a) a managed service company must pay an amount of contributions for a qualifying period, and

(b) one of conditions A to E is met

29B(2) Condition A is met if–

(a) a decision has been made in accordance with section 8 of the Social Security Contributions (Transfer of Functions, etc.) Act 1999 that an amount of Class 1 National Insurance contributions is due in respect of a qualifying period, and

(b) any part of the amount has not been paid within 14 days from the date on which the decision became final and conclusive.

29B(3) Condition B is met if–

(a) an employer delivers a return under paragraph 22(1) (return by employer at end of year) for the tax year 2007–08, or any later tax year, showing an amount of total contributions deducted by the employer for that tax year,

(b) HM Revenue and Customs prepare a certificate under paragraph 22(5) (certificate that contributions specified in return under paragraph 22(1) remain unpaid) showing how much of that amount remains unpaid, and

(c) any part of that amount remains unpaid at the end of a period of 14 days beginning with the date on which the certificate is prepared.

29B(4) Condition C is met if–

(a) HM Revenue and Customs prepare a certificate under paragraph 14(1) (employer failing to pay earnings-related contributions) showing an amount of contributions which the employer is liable to pay for a qualifying period, and

(b) any part of that amount remains unpaid at the end of a period of 14 days beginning with the date on which the certificate is prepared.

29B(5) Condition D is met if–

(a) HM Revenue and Customs serve notice on an employer under paragraph 15(1) (specified amount of earnings-related contributions payable by the employer) requiring payment of the amount of Class 1 contributions which they consider the employer is liable to pay, and

(b) any part of that amount remains unpaid at the end of a period of 14 days beginning with the date on which the notice is prepared.

29B(6) Condition E is met if–

(a) HM Revenue and Customs prepare a certificate under paragraph 26A (certificate of employer's liability to pay contributions after inspection of documents) showing an amount of contributions which it appears that the employer is liable to pay for a qualifying period,

(b) HM Revenue and Customs make a written demand for payment of that amount of contributions, and

(c) any part of that amount remains unpaid at the end of a period of 14 days beginning with the date on which the written demand for payment is made.

History – In para. 29B(6)(a), the words "paragraph 26A (certificate of employer's liability to pay contributions after inspection of documents)" substituted for the words "paragraph 26 (inspection of employer's records)" by SI 2009/600, reg. 8(5), with effect from 1 April 2009.
Pt. 3A inserted by SI 2007/2068, reg. 2, with effect from 6 August 2007.

TRANSFER OF DEBT OF MANAGED SERVICE COMPANY

29C(1) This paragraph applies if–

(a) a managed service company has a relevant contributions debt, and

(b) an officer of Revenue and Customs is of the opinion that the relevant contributions debt or a part of the relevant contributions debt (the "specified amount") is irrecoverable from the managed service company within a reasonable period.

29C(2) HM Revenue and Customs may make a direction authorising the recovery of the specified amount from the persons specified in section 688A(2) (managed service companies: recovery from other persons).

29C(3) Upon the making of a direction under sub-paragraph (2), the persons specified in section 688A(2) become jointly and severally liable for the relevant contributions debt, but subject to what follows.

29C(4) HM Revenue and Customs may not recover the specified amount from any person in accordance with a direction made under sub-paragraph (2) until they have served a notice (a "transfer notice") on the person in question (the "transferee").

29C(5) If an officer of Revenue and Customs is of the opinion that it is appropriate to do so, HM Revenue and Customs may accept an amount less than the specified amount (the "lower amount") from a transferee; but this acceptance shall not prejudice the recovery of the specified amount from any other transferee.

29C(6) HM Revenue and Customs may not serve a transfer notice on a person mentioned in section 688A(2)(c), or on a paragraph (c) associate, if the relevant contributions debt is incurred before 6th January 2008.

29C(7) HM Revenue and Customs may not serve a transfer notice on a person mentioned in section 688A(2)(c), or on a paragraph (c) associate, unless an officer of Revenue and Customs certifies that, in his opinion, it is impracticable to recover the specified amount from persons mentioned in paragraphs (a) and (b) of section 688A(2) and from paragraph (b) associates.

29C(8) In determining, for the purposes of sub-paragraph (7), whether it is impracticable to recover the specified amount from the persons mentioned in paragraphs (a) and (b) of section 688A(2) and from paragraph (b) associates the officer of Revenue and Customs may have regard to all managed service companies in relation to which a person is a person mentioned in paragraph (a) or (b) of section 688A(2) or a paragraph (b) associate.

29C(9) In determining which of the persons mentioned in section 688A(2)(c) and which of the paragraph (c) associates are to be served with transfer notices and the amount of those notices, HM Revenue and Customs must have regard to the degree and extent to which those persons are persons who (directly or indirectly) have encouraged or been actively involved in the provision by the managed service company of the services of the individual mentioned in that provision.

History – Pt. 3A inserted by SI 2007/2068, reg. 2, with effect from 6 August 2007.

TIME LIMITS FOR ISSUE OF TRANSFER NOTICES

29D(1) A transfer notice must be served before the end of the period specified in this paragraph.

29D(2) Sub-paragraphs (3) to (7) apply if the transfer notice is served on a person mentioned in paragraph (a) or (b) of section 688A(2) or on a paragraph (b) associate.

29D(3) In a case in which condition A in paragraph 29B is met, the transfer notice must be served before the end of a period of 12 months beginning with the date on which the decision became final and conclusive.

29D(4) In a case in which condition B in paragraph 29B is met, the transfer notice must be served before the end of a period of 12 months beginning with the date on which HM Revenue and Customs received the return delivered under paragraph 22.

29D(5) In a case in which condition C in paragraph 29B is met, the transfer notice must be served before the end of a period of 12 months beginning with the date on which HM Revenue and Customs prepare the certificate under paragraph 14(1).

29D(6) In a case in which condition D in paragraph 29B is met, the transfer notice must be served before the end of a period of 12 months beginning with the date on which HM Revenue and Customs serve notice to the employer under paragraph 15(1).

29D(7) In a case in which condition E in paragraph 29B is met, the transfer notice must be served before the end of a period of 12 months beginning with the date on which HM Revenue and Customs carry out the inspection of the employer's contribution records under Schedule 36 to the Finance Act 2008.

29D(8) If the transfer notice is served on a person mentioned in paragraph (c) of section 688A(2), or on a paragraph (c) associate, the transfer notice must be served before the end of a period of there months beginning with the date on which the officer of Revenue and Customs certifies the matters specified in paragraph 29C(7).

History – In para. 29D(7), the words "Schedule 36 to the Finance Act 2008" substituted for the words "paragraph 26" by SI 2009/600, reg. 8(6), with effect from 1 April 2009.
Pt. 3A inserted by SI 2007/2068, reg. 2, with effect from 6 August 2007.

CONTENTS OF TRANSFER NOTICE

29E(1) A transfer notice must contain the following information–

(a) the name of the managed service company to which the relevant contributions debt relates;

(b) the address of the managed service company to which the relevant contributions debt relates;

(c) the amount of the relevant contributions debt;

(d) the tax periods to which the relevant contributions debt relates;

(e) if the tax periods to which the relevant contributions debt relates are comprised in more than one tax year, the apportionment of the relevant contributions debt among those tax years;

(f) which of the conditions A to E specified in paragraph 29B is met;

(g) the transferee's name;

(h) the transferee's address;

(j) whether the transferee is a person mentioned in paragraph (a), (b) or (c) of section 688A, a paragraph (b) associate or a paragraph (c) associate;

(k) if the transferee is a person mentioned in paragraph (c) of section 688A or a paragraph (c) associate–
   (i) the date on which the officer of Revenue and Customs certified the matters specified in paragraph 29C(7), and
   (ii) the names of the persons from whom it has been impracticable to recover the specified amount;

(l) the specified amount;

(m) the tax periods to which the specified amount relates;

(n) if the tax periods to which the specified amount relates are comprised in more than one tax year, the apportionment of the specified amount among those tax years;

(o) the address to which payment must be sent;

(p) the address to which an appeal must be sent.

29E(2) The transfer notice may specify the lower amount if HM Revenue and Customs are prepared to accept the lower amount from the transferee.

29E(3) The transfer notice must also contain a statement, made by the officer of Revenue and Customs serving the notice, that in his opinion the specified amount is irrecoverable from the managed service company within a reasonable period.

History – Pt. 3A inserted by SI 2007/2068, reg. 2, with effect from 6 August 2007.

PAYMENT OF THE SPECIFIED AMOUNT

29F(1) If a transfer notice is served, the transferee must pay the specified amount to HM Revenue and Customs at the address specified in the transfer notice.

29F(2) The transferee must pay the specified amount within 30 days beginning with the date on which the transfer notice is served (the "specified period").

29F(3) If a transfer notice is served on a person mentioned in paragraph (a) or (b) of section 688A(2), or on a paragraph (b) associate, the specified amount carries interest from the reckonable date until the date on which payment is made.

29F(4) If a transfer notice is served on a person mentioned in paragraph (c) of section 688A(2), or on a paragraph (c) associate, the specified amount carries interest from the day following the expiry of the specified period until the date on which payment is made.

29F(5) For the purposes of sub-paragraph (3) **"the reckonable date"** has the meaning given by paragraph 17(3)(b)(i).

History – Para. 29F(5) inserted by SI 2009/600, reg. 8(7), with effect from 1 April 2009.
Pt. 3A inserted by SI 2007/2068, reg. 2, with effect from 6 August 2007.

APPEALS

29G(1) A transferee may appeal against the transfer notice.

29G(2) A notice of appeal must–

(a) be given to HM Revenue and Customs at the address specified in the transfer notice within 30 days beginning with the date on which the transfer notice was served, and

(b) specify the grounds of the appeal.

29G(3) The grounds of appeal are any of the following–

(a) that the relevant contributions debt (or part of the relevant contributions debt) is not due from the managed service company to HM Revenue and Customs;

(b) that the specified amount does not relate to a company which is a managed service company;

(c) that the specified amount is not irrecoverable from the managed service company within a reasonable period;

(d) that the transferee is not a person mentioned in section 688A(2);

(e) that the transferee was not a person mentioned in section 688A(2) during the tax periods to which the specified amount relates;

(f) that the transferee was not a person mentioned in section 688A(2) during some part of the tax periods to which the specified amount relates;

(g) that the transfer notice was not served before the end of the period specified in paragraph 29D;

(h) that the transfer notice does not satisfy the requirements specified in paragraph 29E;

(j) in the case of a transferee mentioned in section 688A(2)(c) or of a paragraph (c) associate, that it is not impracticable to recover the specified amount from persons mentioned in paragraphs (a) and (b) of section 688A(2) or from paragraph (b) associates;

(k) in the case of a transferee mentioned in section 688A(2)(c) or of a paragraph (c) associate, that the amount specified in the transfer notice does not have regard to the degree and extent to which the transferee is a person who (directly or indirectly) has encouraged or been actively involved in the provision by the managed service company of the services of the individual mentioned in that provision.

29G(4) Sub-paragraph (3)(a) is subject to paragraph 29H(4).

29G(5) [Omitted by SI 2009/56, art. 3(2) and Sch. 2, para. 76(2).]

History – Para. 29G(5) omitted by SI 2009/56, art. 3(2) and Sch. 2, para. 76(2), operative from 1 April 2009 subject to transitional and saving provisions in SI 2009/56, Sch. 3. Former para. 29G(5) read as follows:
"**29G(5)** The appeal is to the Special Commissioners.".
Pt. 3A inserted by SI 2007/2068, reg. 2, with effect from 6 August 2007.

PROCEDURE ON APPEALS

29H(1) On an appeal that is notified to the tribunal, the tribunal shall uphold or quash the transfer notice.

29H(2) The general rule in sub-paragraph (1) is subject to the following qualifications.

29H(3) In the case of the ground of appeal specified in paragraph 29G(3)(a), the tribunal shall investigate the matter and shall–

(a) uphold the amount of the relevant contributions debt specified in the transfer notice, or

(b) reduce or increase the amount of the relevant contributions debt specified in the transfer notice to such amount as in the tribunal's opinion is just and reasonable.

29H(4) If the tribunal determines the amount of the relevant contributions debt of a managed service company under sub-paragraph (3), that amount is conclusive as to the amount of that relevant contributions debt in any later appeal relating to that debt.

29H(5) In the case of the ground of appeal specified in paragraph 29G(3)(f), the tribunal may reduce the amount specified in the transfer notice to an amount determined in accordance with the equation–

$$RA = \frac{P}{TP} \times AS$$

29H(6) In paragraph (5)–

RA means the reduced amount;

P means the number of days in the tax periods specified in the transfer notice during which the transferee was a person mentioned in section 688A(2);

TP means the number of days in the tax periods specified in the transfer notice;

AS means the amount specified in the transfer notice.

29H(7) In the case of the ground of appeal specified in paragraph 29G(3)(k), the tribunal may reduce the amount specified in the transfer notice to such amount as in the tribunal's opinion is just and reasonable.

History – In para. 29H(1), the words "that is notified to the tribunal, the tribunal" substituted for the words "the Special Commissioners" by SI 2009/56, art. 3(2) and Sch. 2, para. 76(3)(a), operative from 1 April 2009 subject to transitional and saving provisions in SI 2009/56, Sch. 3.
In para. 29H(3), the word "tribunal" substituted for the words "Special Commissioners" by SI 2009/56, art. 3(2) and Sch. 2, para. 76(3)(b)(i), operative from 1 April 2009 subject to transitional and saving provisions in SI 2009/56, Sch. 3.
In para. 29H(3)(b), the words "the tribunal's" substituted for the word "their" by SI 2009/56, art. 3(2) and Sch. 2, para. 76(3)(b)(ii), operative from 1 April 2009 subject to transitional and saving provisions in SI 2009/56, Sch. 3.
In para. 29H(4), the words "tribunal determines" substituted for the words "Special Commissioners determine" by SI 2009/56, art. 3(2) and Sch. 2, para. 76(3)(c), operative from 1 April 2009 subject to transitional and saving provisions in SI 2009/56, Sch. 3.
In para. 29H(5), the word "tribunal" substituted by SI 2009/56, art. 3(2) and Sch. 2, para. 76(d), operative from 1 April 2009 subject to transitional and saving provisions in SI 2009/56, Sch. 3.
In para. 29H(7), the word "tribunal" substituted by SI 2009/56, art. 3(2) and Sch. 2, para. 76(e)(i), operative from 1 April 2009 subject to transitional and saving provisions in SI 2009/56, Sch. 3.
In para. 29H(7), the words "the tribunal's" substituted by SI 2009/56, art. 3(2) and Sch. 2, para. 76(3)(e)(ii), operative from 1 April 2009 subject to transitional and saving provisions in SI 2009/56, Sch. 3.
Pt. 3A inserted by SI 2007/2068, reg. 2, with effect from 6 August 2007.

WITHDRAWAL OF TRANSFER NOTICES

29J(1) A transfer notice shall be withdrawn if the tribunal quashes it.

29J(2) A transfer notice may be withdrawn if, in the opinion of an officer of Revenue and Customs, it is appropriate to do so.

29J(3) If a transfer notice is withdrawn, HM Revenue and Customs must give written notice of that fact to the transferee.

History – In para. 29J(1), the words "tribunal quashes" substituted by SI 2009/56, art. 3(2) and Sch. 2, para. 76(4), operative from 1 April 2009 subject to transitional and saving provisions in SI 2009/56, Sch. 3.
Pt. 3A inserted by SI 2007/2068, reg. 2, with effect from 6 August 2007.

APPLICATION OF PART 6 OF THE TAXES MANAGEMENT ACT 1970

29K(1) For the purposes of this Chapter, Part 6 of the Taxes Management Act 1970 (collection and recovery) applies as if–

(a) the transfer notice were an assessment of tax on employment income, and

(b) the amount of earnings-related contributions specified in the transfer notice, and any interest payable on that amount under sub-paragraph (3) or (4) of paragraph 29F were income tax charged on the transferee;

and that Part of that Act applies with the modification specified in sub-paragraph (2) and any other necessary modifications.

29K(2) Summary proceedings for the recovery of the specified amount may be brought in England and Wales or Northern Ireland at any time before the end of a period of 12 months beginning immediately after the expiry of the period mentioned in paragraph 29F(2).

29K(3) The specified amount is one cause of action or one matter of complaint for the purposes of proceedings under sections 65, 66 and 67 of the Taxes Management Act 1970 (magistrates' courts, county courts and inferior courts in Scotland).

29K(4) But sub-paragraph (3) does not prevent the bringing of separate proceedings for the recovery of each of the amounts which the transferee is liable to pay for any tax period.

History – Pt. 3A inserted by SI 2007/2068, reg. 2, with effect from 6 August 2007.

REPAYMENT OF SURPLUS AMOUNTS

29L(1) This paragraph applies if the amounts paid to HM Revenue and Customs in respect of a relevant contributions debt exceed the specified amount.

29L(2) HM Revenue and Customs shall repay the difference on a just and equitable basis and without unreasonable delay.

29L(3) Interest on any sum repaid shall be paid in accordance with paragraph 18 (payment of interest on repaid earnings-related contributions).

History – Pt. 3A inserted by SI 2007/2068, reg. 2, with effect from 6 August 2007.

Part 3B – Security for the Payment of Class 1 Contributions

History – Pt. 3B inserted by SI 2012/821, reg. 18, with effect from 6 April 2012.

INTERPRETATION

29M In this Part–

"employer" has the meaning given in paragraph 29O(1);

"a further notice" has the meaning given in paragraph 29U(3);

"PGS" has the meaning given in paragraph 29S(1).

History – Pt. 3B inserted by SI 2012/821, reg. 18, with effect from 6 April 2012.

REQUIREMENT FOR SECURITY

29N In circumstances where an officer of Revenue and Customs considers it necessary for the protection of Class 1 contributions, the officer may require a person described in paragraph 29P(1) to give security or further security for the payment of amounts which an employer is or may be liable to pay to HMRC under paragraph 10, 11, 11ZA or 11A.

History – In para. 29N, ", 11ZA" inserted by SI 2013/622, reg. 19, with effect from 6 April 2013 in relation to the tax year 2013–14 and subsequent tax years.
Pt. 3B inserted by SI 2012/821, reg. 18, with effect from 6 April 2012.

EMPLOYERS

29O(1) An **"employer"** is any employer within the meaning given in paragraph 1(2) other than–

(a) the Crown;

(b) a person to whom sub-paragraph (2) applies;

(c) [omitted by SI 2013/622, reg. 4(5);] and

(d) a care and support employer within the meaning given in regulation 90NA(3) of these Regulations.

29O(2) This sub-paragraph applies to persons who at the relevant time could not be liable to a penalty under Schedule 56 to the Finance Act 2009 by virtue of paragraph 10 of that Schedule (suspension of penalty for failure to make payments on time during currency of agreement for deferred payment).

29O(3) In sub-paragraph (2), the relevant time is a time at which, but for sub-paragraph (1)(b), the officer would require security.

History – Para. 29O(1)(c) (but not the "and" after it) omitted by SI 2013/622, reg. 4(5), with effect from 6 April 2014 in relation to the tax year 2014–15.
Pt. 3B inserted by SI 2012/821, reg. 18, with effect from 6 April 2012.

PERSONS FROM WHOM SECURITY CAN BE REQUIRED

29P(1) The persons are–

(a) the employer;

(b) any of the following in relation to the employer–

(i) a director;

(ii) a company secretary;

(iii) any other similar officer; or

(iv) any person purporting to act in such a capacity; and

(c) in a case where the employer is a limited liability partnership, a member of the limited liability partnership.

29P(2) An officer of Revenue and Customs may require–

(a) a person to give security or further security of a specified value in respect of the employer; or

(b) more than one person to give security or further security of a specified value in respect of the employer, and where the officer does so those persons shall be jointly and severally liable to give that security or further security.

History – Pt. 3B inserted by SI 2012/821, reg. 18, with effect from 6 April 2012.

NOTICE OF REQUIREMENT

29Q(1) An officer of Revenue and Customs must give notice of a requirement for security to each person from whom security is required and the notice must specify–

(a) the value of security to be given;

(b) the manner in which security is to be given;

(c) the date on or before which security is to be given; and

(d) the period of time for which security is required.

29Q(2) The notice must include, or be accompanied by, an explanation of–

(a) the employer's right to make a request under paragraph 10(1) of Schedule 56 to the Finance Act 2009; and

(b) the effect of paragraph 29R(2) and (3).

29Q(3) In a case which falls within paragraph 29P(2)(b), the notice must include, or be accompanied by, the names of each other person from whom security is required.

29Q(4) The notice may contain such other information as the officer considers necessary.

29Q(5) A person shall not be treated as having been required to provide security unless HMRC comply with this paragraph and paragraph 29R(1).

29Q(6) Notwithstanding anything in regulation 1(4)(b), where the notice, or a further notice, ("contributions notice") is to be given with a notice or further notice mentioned in regulations 97Q(1) and 97U(3) of the PAYE Regulations ("PAYE notice") the contributions notice shall be taken to be given at the same time that the PAYE notice is given.

History – Pt. 3B inserted by SI 2012/821, reg. 18, with effect from 6 April 2012.

DATE ON WHICH SECURITY IS DUE

29R(1) The date specified under paragraph 29Q(1)(c) may not be earlier than the 30th day after the day on which the notice is given.

29R(2) If, before the date specified under paragraph 29Q(1)(c), the employer makes a request under paragraph 10(1) of Schedule 56 to the Finance Act 2009, the requirement to give security on or before that date does not apply.

29R(3) In a case which falls within sub-paragraph (2), if HMRC does not agree to the employer's request, security is to be given on or before the 30th day after the day on which HMRC notifies the employer of that decision.

History – Pt. 3B inserted by SI 2012/821, reg. 18, with effect from 6 April 2012.

APPLICATION FOR REDUCTION IN THE VALUE OF SECURITY HELD

29S(1) A person who has given security ("PGS") may apply to an officer of Revenue and Customs for a reduction in the value of security held by HMRC if–

(a) PGS' circumstances have changed since the day the security was given because–

(i) of hardship; or

(ii) PGS has ceased to be a person mentioned in paragraph 29P(1); or

(b) since the day the security was given there has been a significant reduction in the number of employed earners of the employer to whom the security relates or that employer has ceased to be an employer.

29S(2) Where paragraph 29P(2)(b) applies, a person who has not contributed to the value of the security given may not make an application under sub-paragraph (1).

History – Pt. 3B inserted by SI 2012/821, reg. 18, with effect from 6 April 2012.

OUTCOME OF APPLICATION UNDER PARAGRAPH 29S

29T(1) If an application under paragraph 29S(1) is successful, the officer must inform PGS of the reduced value of security that is still required or, where that value is nil, that the requirement for security has been cancelled.

29T(2) HMRC may make such arrangements as they think fit to ensure the necessary reduction in the value of security held.

History – Pt. 3B inserted by SI 2012/821, reg. 18, with effect from 6 April 2012.

OUTCOME OF APPLICATION UNDER PARAGRAPH 29S: FURTHER PROVISION

29U(1) This paragraph applies–

(a) in cases which fall within paragraph 29P(2)(b); and

(b) where PGS' application is made under paragraph 29S(1)(a).

29U(2) As a consequence of arrangements made under paragraph 29T(2), an officer of Revenue and Customs may require any other person who was given notice under paragraph 29Q in relation to the security ("the original security"), or any other person mentioned in paragraph 29P(1), to provide security in substitution for the original security.

29U(3) Where an officer of Revenue and Customs acts in reliance on sub-paragraph (2), the officer must give notice ("a further notice").

29U(4) Paragraph 29Q(1) to (5) and paragraph 29R apply in relation to a further notice.

29U(5) Subject to sub-paragraph (6), paragraph 29V(1) applies in relation to a further notice.

29U(6) A person who is given a further notice and who was also given notice under paragraph 29Q in relation to the original security may only appeal on the grounds that the person is not a person mentioned in paragraph 29P(1).

History – Pt. 3B inserted by SI 2012/821, reg. 18, with effect from 6 April 2012.

APPEALS

29V(1) A person who is given notice under paragraph 29Q may appeal against the notice or any requirement in it.

29V(2) PGS may appeal against–

(a) the rejection by an officer of Revenue and Customs of an application under paragraph 29S(1); and

(b) a smaller reduction in the value of security held than PGS applied for.

29V(3) Notice of an appeal under this paragraph must be given–

(a) before the end of the period of 30 days beginning with–

 (i) in the case of an appeal under sub-paragraph (1), the day after the day on which the notice was given; and

 (ii) in the case of an appeal under sub-paragraph (2), the day after the day on which PGS was notified of the outcome of the application; and

(b) to the officer of Revenue and Customs by whom the notice was given or the decision on the application was made, as the case may be.

29V(4) Notice of an appeal under this paragraph must state the grounds of appeal.

29V(5) On an appeal under sub-paragraph (1) that is notified to the tribunal, the tribunal may–

(a) confirm the requirements in the notice;

(b) vary the requirements in the notice; or

(c) set aside the notice.

29V(6) On an appeal under sub-paragraph (2) that is notified to the tribunal, the tribunal may–

(a) confirm the decision on the application; or

(b) vary the decision on the application.

29V(7) On the final determination of an appeal under this paragraph–

(a) subject to any alternative determination by a tribunal or court, any security to be given is due on the 30th day after the day on which the determination is made; or

(b) HMRC may make such arrangements as they think fit to ensure the necessary reduction in the value of the security held.

29V(8) Part 5 of the Taxes Management Act 1970 (appeals and other proceedings) applies in relation to an appeal under this paragraph as it applies in relation to an appeal under the Taxes Acts but as if–

(a) sections 46D, 47B, 50(6) to (9) and (11)(c) and 54A to 57 were omitted; and

(b) in section 48(1)–

(i) in paragraph (a) the reference to **"the Taxes Acts"** were a reference to "paragraph 29V of Schedule 4 to the Social Security (Contributions) Regulations 2001"; and

(ii) in paragraph (b) the reference to **"any provision of the Taxes Acts"** were a reference to "paragraph 29V of Schedule 4 to the Social Security (Contributions) Regulations 2001".

History – Pt. 3B inserted by SI 2012/821, reg. 18, with effect from 6 April 2012.

APPEALS: FURTHER PROVISION FOR CASES WHICH FALL WITHIN PARAGRAPH 29R(2)

29W In a case which falls within paragraph 29R(2), if the request mentioned in that provision is made before an appeal under paragraph 29V(1), paragraph 29V(3)(a)(i) applies as if the words "the day after the day on which the notice was given" were "the day after the day on which HMRC notifies the employer of its decision".

History – Pt. 3B inserted by SI 2012/821, reg. 18, with effect from 6 April 2012.

OFFENCE

29X(1) Section 684(4A) of the Income Tax (Earnings and Pensions) Act 2003 (PAYE regulations – security for payment of PAYE: offence) applies in relation to a requirement imposed under these Regulations as it applies in relation to a requirement imposed under the PAYE Regulations.

29X(2) For the purposes of section 684(4A) as it applies by virtue of sub-paragraph (1)–

(a) in relation to a requirement for security under a notice under paragraph 29Q the period specified is the period which starts with the day the notice is given and ends with–

(i) the first day after the date specified under paragraph 29Q(1)(c); or

(ii) in a case which falls within paragraph 29R(2), the first day after the date determined under paragraph 29R(3);

(b) in relation to a requirement for security under a further notice the period specified is the period which starts with the day the further notice is given and ends with–

(i) the first day after the date specified under paragraph 29Q(1)(c) as it applies in relation to the further notice; or

(ii) in a case which falls within paragraph 29R(2), the first day after the date determined under paragraph 29R(3) as it applies in relation to the further notice; and

(c) in relation to a requirement for security to which paragraph 29V(7)(a) applies the period specified is the period which starts with the day the determination is made and ends with the first day after–

(i) the day the tribunal or court determines to be the day that the security is to be given; or

(ii) the day determined in accordance with that paragraph,

as the case may be.

History – Pt. 3B inserted by SI 2012/821, reg. 18, with effect from 6 April 2012.

Part 3C – Certain Debts of Companies under Paragraph 3ZB of Part 8 of Schedule 3 (Travel Expenses of Workers Providing Services through Employment Intermediaries)

History – Pt. 3C inserted by SI 2016/1067, reg. 7, with effect from 28 November 2016.

INTERPRETATION OF PART 3C: "RELEVANT CONTRIBUTIONS DEBT" AND "RELEVANT DATE"

29Y(1) In this Part **"relevant contributions debt"**, in relation to a company means an amount within any of sub-paragraphs (2) to (5).

29Y(2) An amount within this sub-paragraph is an amount that the company is to account for in accordance with paragraph 3ZB(6A) to (6C) (persons providing fraudulent documents).

29Y(3) An amount within this sub-paragraph is an amount which a company is to deduct and pay by virtue of paragraph 3ZB in circumstances where–

(a) a company is an employment intermediary,

(b) on the basis that paragraph 3ZB does not apply by virtue of sub-paragraph (3) of that paragraph the company has not deducted and paid the amount, but

(c) the company has not been provided by any other person with evidence from which it would be reasonable in all the circumstances to conclude that sub-paragraph (3) of that paragraph applied (and the mere assertion by a person that the manner in which the worker provided the services was not subject to (or to the right of) supervision, direction or control by any person is not such evidence).

29Y(4) An amount within this sub-paragraph is an amount that the company is to deduct and pay in accordance with paragraph 3ZB in circumstances where sub-paragraph (4) of that paragraph applies (services provided under arrangements made by intermediaries).

29Y(5) An amount within this sub-paragraph is any interest or penalty in respect of an amount within any of sub-paragraphs (2) to (4) for which the company is liable.

29Y(6) In this paragraph, **"paragraph 3ZB"** means paragraph 3ZB of Part 8 of Schedule 3 to these Regulations.

29Y(7) In this Part, **"the relevant date"** in relation to a relevant contributions debt means the date on which the first payment is due on which contributions are not accounted for.

History – Pt. 3C inserted by SI 2016/1067, reg. 7, with effect from 28 November 2016.

INTERPRETATION OF PART 3C: GENERAL

29Z In this Part–

"company" includes a limited liability partnership;

"director" has the meaning given by section 67 of ITEPA 2003;

"personal liability notice" has the meaning given by paragraph 29Z1(2);

"the specified amount" has the meaning given by paragraph 29Z1(2).

History – Pt. 3C inserted by SI 2016/1067, reg. 7, with effect from 28 November 2016.

LIABILITY OF DIRECTORS FOR RELEVANT CONTRIBUTIONS DEBTS

29Z1(1) This paragraph applies in relation to an amount of relevant contributions debt of a company if the company does not deduct that amount by the time by which the company is required to do so.

29Z1(2) HMRC may serve a notice ("personal liability notice") on any person who was, on the relevant date, a director of the company–

(a) specifying the amount of relevant contributions debt in relation to which this paragraph applies ("the specified amount"), and

(b) requiring the director to pay HMRC–

(i) the specified amount, and

(ii) specified interest on that amount.

29Z1(3) The interest specified in the personal liability notice–

(a) is to be at the rate applicable under section 178 of the Finance Act 1989 for the purposes of section 86 of the Taxes Management Act 1970, and

(b) is to run from the date the notice is served.

29Z1(4) A director who is served with a personal liability notice is liable to pay to HMRC the specified amount and the interest specified in the notice within 30 days beginning with the day the notice is served.

29Z1(5) If HMRC serve personal liability notices on more than one director of the company in respect of the same amount of relevant contributions debt, the directors are jointly and severally liable to pay to HMRC the specified amount and the interest specified in the notices.

History – Pt. 3C inserted by SI 2016/1067, reg. 7, with effect from 28 November 2016.

APPEALS IN RELATION TO PERSONAL LIABILITY NOTICES

29Z2(1) A person who is served with a personal liability notice in relation to an amount of relevant contributions debt of a company may appeal against the notice.

29Z2(2) A notice of appeal must–

(a) be given to HMRC within 30 days beginning with the day the personal liability notice is served, and

(b) specify the grounds of the appeal.

29Z2(3) The grounds of appeal are–

(a) that all or part of the specified amount does not represent an amount of relevant contributions debt, of the company, to which paragraph 29Z1 applies, or

(b) that the person was not a director of the company on the relevant date.

29Z2(4) But a person may not appeal on the ground mentioned in sub-paragraph (3)(a) if it has already been determined, on an appeal by the company, that–

(a) the specified amount is a relevant contributions debt of the company, and

(b) the company did not deduct, account for, or (as the case may be) pay the debt by the time by which the company was required to do so.

29Z2(5) Subject to sub-paragraph (6), on an appeal that is notified to the tribunal, the tribunal is to uphold or quash the personal liability notice.

29Z2(6) In a case in which the ground of appeal mentioned in sub-paragraph (3)(a) is raised, the tribunal may also reduce or increase the specified amount so that it does represent an amount of relevant contributions debt, of the company, to which paragraph 29Z1 applies.

History – Pt. 3C inserted by SI 2016/1067, reg. 7, with effect from 28 November 2016.

WITHDRAWAL OF PERSONAL LIABILITY NOTICES

29Z3(1) A personal liability notice is withdrawn if the tribunal quashes it.

29Z3(2) An officer of Revenue and Customs may withdraw a personal liability notice if the officer considers it appropriate to do so.

29Z3(3) If a personal liability notice is withdrawn, HMRC must give notice of that fact to the person upon whom the notice was served.

History – Pt. 3C inserted by SI 2016/1067, reg. 7, with effect from 28 November 2016.

RECOVERY OF SUMS DUE UNDER PERSONAL LIABILITY NOTICE: APPLICATION OF PART 6 OF TAXES MANAGEMENT ACT 1970

29Z4(1) For the purposes of this Part, Part 6 of the Taxes Management Act 1970 (collection and recovery) applies as if–

(a) the personal liability notice were an assessment, and

(b) the specified amount and any interest on that amount under paragraph 29Z1(2)(b)(ii) were income tax charged on the director upon whom the notice is served, and that Part of that Act applies with the modification in paragraph (2) and any other necessary modifications.

29Z4(2) Summary proceedings for the recovery of the specified amount, and any interest on that amount under paragraph 29Z1(2)(b)(ii), may be brought in England and Wales or Northern Ireland at any time before the end of the period of 12 months beginning with the day after the day on which personal liability notice is served.

History – Pt. 3C inserted by SI 2016/1067, reg. 7, with effect from 28 November 2016.

REPAYMENT OF SURPLUS AMOUNTS

29Z5(1) This paragraph applies if–

(a) one or more personal liability notices are served in respect of an amount of relevant contributions debt of a company, and

(b) the amounts paid to HMRC (whether by directors upon whom notices are served or the company) exceed the aggregate of the specified amount and any interest on it under paragraph 29Z1(2)(b)(ii).

29Z5(2) HMRC is to repay the difference on a just and equitable basis and without unreasonable delay.

29Z5(3) HMRC is to pay interest on any sum repaid.

29Z5(4) The interest–

(a) is to be at the rate applicable under section 178 of the Finance Act 1989 for the purposes of section 824 of the Taxes Act, and

(b) is to run from the date the amounts paid to HMRC come to exceed the aggregate mentioned in sub-paragraph (1)(b).

History – Pt. 3C inserted by SI 2016/1067, reg. 7, with effect from 28 November 2016.

Part IV – Assessment and Direct Collection

PROVISIONS FOR DIRECT PAYMENT

30 In cases of employed earner's employment, where the employer does not fulfil the conditions prescribed in regulation 145(1)(b) as to residence or presence in Great Britain or Northern Ireland or is a person who, by reason of any international treaty to which the United Kingdom is a party or of any international convention binding on the United Kingdom, is exempt from the provisions of the Act or is a person against whom, for a similar reason, the provisions of the Act are not enforceable, the provisions of paragraph 31 shall apply to the employee, unless the employer, being a person entitled to pay the primary contributions due in respect of the earnings from that employment, is willing to pay those contributions.

Derivations – SI 1979/591, Sch. 1, reg. 50.

APPLICATION OF PARAGRAPHS 31 AND 31A

30A(1) Paragraph 31(4) to (7) does not apply on or after 6th April 2014.

30A(2) Paragraph 31(7A) and (7B) applies only in relation to closed tax years ending on or before 5th April 2014.

30A(3) Paragraph 31A applies on and after 6th April 2014.

History – Para. 30A inserted by SI 2013/622, reg. 20, with effect from 6 April 2013 in relation to the tax year 2013–14 and subsequent tax years.

DIRECT COLLECTION INVOLVING DEDUCTIONS WORKING SHEETS

31(1) In any case falling within paragraph 30, sub-paragraphs (2) to (8) shall apply.

31(2) The employee shall record on a working sheet his name, national insurance number and category letter indicated by HMRC, and whenever, in respect of an employment such as is specified in paragraph 30, the employee receives any earnings during the relevant tax year, he shall also record on that working sheet the amount of the earnings, the date on which he received them, and the earnings-related contributions payable by him in respect of those earnings.

31(3) Not later than the time for the payment of income tax, if any, the employee shall pay to HMRC the amount of the earnings-related contributions payable by the employee in respect of the earnings which have been received by him and for which the income tax is or would have been payable.

31(3A) Before 20 May 2014 the employee must deliver to HMRC a return in the prescribed form for the tax year 2013–14 showing the following information:

(a) the total amount of the earnings and earnings-related contributions payable during the tax year 2013–14,

(b) the appropriate category letter,

(c) the employee's name and address, and

(d) the employee's national insurance number, and

the provisions of paragraph 22(5) regarding the certification and recovery of earnings-related contributions remaining unpaid by an employer for any year shall apply in the case of any earnings-related contributions remaining unpaid by the employee.

31(4) If, by the time specified in sub-paragraph (3), the employee has paid no amount of earnings-related contributions to HMRC in respect of the earnings mentioned in that sub-paragraph, and HMRC is unaware of the amount, if any, which the employee is liable so to pay, or if an amount has been paid but HMRC is not satisfied that it is the full amount which the employee is liable to pay to him in respect of those earnings, sub-paragraph (5) applies.

31(5) If this sub-paragraph applies, HMRC may give notice to the employee requiring him to render, within the time limited in the notice, a return in the prescribed form containing particulars of all earnings received by him during the period specified in the notice and such other particulars affecting the calculations of the earnings-related contributions payable in respect of the earnings in question as may be specified in the notice, and in such a case the provisions of–

(a) paragraph 14 regarding the ascertaining and certifying by HMRC of earnings-related contributions payable by an employer; and

(b) paragraph 16 regarding the recovery of those contributions;

shall apply with the necessary modifications for the purposes of ascertaining, certifying and recovering the earnings-related contributions payable by the employee.

31(6) If the employee ceases to receive earnings falling within sub-paragraph (2), he shall immediately render to HMRC, in such form as they may prescribe, a return showing such particulars as they may require for the identification of the employee, the year to which the return relates, the appropriate category letter, the last date on which he received any such earnings, the total of those earnings and the earnings-related contributions payable from the beginning of the year to that date.

31(7) Before 20th May following the end of the year, the employee shall (unless sub-paragraph (6) has applied) render to HMRC, in such form as they may prescribe, a return showing such particulars as they may require for the identification of the employee, the year to which the return relates, the total of the earnings and earnings-related contributions payable during the year, together with the appropriate category letter, and the provisions of paragraph 22(5) regarding the certification and recovery of earnings-related contributions remaining unpaid by an employer for any year shall apply in the case of any earnings-related contributions remaining unpaid by the employee.

31(7A) Where a liability arises to pay contributions in respect of retrospective earnings relating to a closed tax year, the employee shall render a replacement return for the closed tax year before 20th May following the end of the year in which the relevant retrospective contributions regulations came into force in accordance with sub-paragraph (7), setting out the revised earnings and earnings-related contributions.

31(7B) Where sub-paragraph (7A) applies, the employee shall amend the relevant deductions working sheet or where necessary prepare one in accordance with sub-paragraph (2).

31(8) The employee shall retain deductions working sheets for not less than three years after the end of the year to which they relate.

31(9) Section 98A of the Taxes Management Act 1970 (special penalties in the case of certain returns) and Schedule 24 to the Finance Act 2007 (penalties for errors) as that Schedule applies to income tax returns as modified by the provisions of paragraph 7 of Schedule 1 to the Act, shall apply in relation to the requirement to make a return contained in sub-paragraphs (3A) and (7A).

History – In para. 31, in each place where it occurs, the word "general" omitted by SI 2015/478, reg. 22(6), with effect from 6 April 2015.

In para. 31 "HMRC" substituted throughout by SI 2007/1056, reg. 8(16)(a), with effect from 6 April 2007.

In para. 31 "Inland Revenue" substituted, "Collector", and "Board" throughout by SI 2004/770, reg. 32, with effect from 6 April 2004.

In para. 31(1), the words "HMRC may issue a deductions working sheet to the employee (and, if no such working sheet has been issued, the employee shall obtain one from HMRC), and, subject to paragraph 30A," omitted by SI 2014/608, reg. 10(a), with effect from 6 April 2014.

In para. 31(1), the words ", subject to paragraph 30A," inserted by SI 2013/622, reg. 21(2), with effect from 6 April 2013 in relation to the tax year 2013–14 and subsequent tax years.

In para. 31(2), the words "to whom a deductions working sheet has been issued under sub-paragraph (1)" omitted by SI 2014/608, reg. 10(b)(i), with effect from 6 April 2014.

In para. 31(2), the words "a working sheet" substituted for the words "that working sheet" by SI 2014/608, reg. 10(b)(ii), with effect from 6 April 2014.

In para. 31(2), the words "the relevant tax year" substituted for the words "the year for which the deductions working sheet was issued" by SI 2014/608, reg. 10(b)(iii), with effect from 6 April 2014.

In para. 31(2) "general earnings" substituted where it first occurs, and "earnings" substituted subsequently by SI 2004/770, reg. 32, with effect from 6 April 2004.

In para. 31(3) "general earnings" substituted by SI 2004/770, reg. 32, with effect from 6 April 2004.

Para. 31(3A) inserted by SI 2014/608, reg. 10(c), with effect from 6 April 2014.

In para. 31(4), (5), and (6) "general earnings" substituted where it first occurs, and "earnings" substituted subsequently by SI 2004/770, reg. 32, with effect from 6 April 2004.

In para. 31(6) "the Inland Revenue, in such form as they may prescribe" substituted by SI 2004/770, reg. 32, with effect from 6 April 2004.

In para. 31(7) "Before 20th May following", "the Inland Revenue, in such form as they may prescribe" substituted, and "general earnings" substituted by SI 2004/770, reg. 32, with effect from 6 April 2004.

In para. 31(7A) and (7B), the word "employee" substituted for the word "employer" by SI 2013/622, reg. 21(3), with effect from 6 April 2013 in relation to the tax year 2013–14 and subsequent tax years.

Para. 31(7A) and (7B) inserted by SI 2007/1056, reg. 8(16)(b), with effect from 6 April 2007.

In para. 31(8), the words "issued under sub-paragraph (1)" omitted by SI 2014/608, reg. 10(d), with effect from 6 April 2014.

In para. 31(9), the word "(3A)" substituted for "(6), (7)" by SI 2014/608, reg. 10(e), witheffect from 6 April 2014.

In para. 31(9) the words "Section 98A of the Taxes Management Act 1970 (special penalties in the case of certain returns) and Schedule 24 to the Finance Act 2007 (penalties for errors) as that Schedule applies to income tax returns" substituted by SI 2008/636, reg. 7, with effect from 1 April 2008.

In para. 31(9) "(6), (7) and (7A)" substituted by SI 2007/1056, reg. 8(16)(c), with effect from 6 April 2007. In making this amendment it is assumed that SI 2007/1056 contains a drafting error as reg. 8(16)(c) instructs the substitution to be made to para. 31(8) when the subsituted words appear in para. 31(9) rather than in para. 31(8).

Derivations – SI 1979/591, Sch. 1, reg. 51.

DIRECT COLLECTION INVOLVING DEDUCTIONS WORKING SHEETS ON AND AFTER 6TH APRIL 2014

31A(1) On receiving any earnings which fall to be recorded on a deductions working sheet under paragraph 31(2), subject to sub-paragraph (2), an employee must proceed in accordance with paragraph 21A(1), (2) and (5).

31A(2) If the employee falls within paragraph 21D(1)(a), the employee may instead proceed in accordance with paragraph 21D(3), (4) and (5).

31A(3) For the purposes of sub-paragraph (1), paragraph 21A(8) and paragraphs 21AB, 21AC, 21AD, 21B and 21C apply as if the employee were a Real Time Information employer.

31A(4) For the purposes of sub-paragraph (2), paragraph 21D(9) applies as if the employee were a Real Time Information employer.

31A(5) For the purposes of sub-paragraphs (1) and (2), paragraphs 15, 16, 21E, 21EA and 21F(7A) and (8) and Schedule 4A apply as if the employee were a Real Time Information employer, but the information required by paragraph 10(a) and (b) of that Schedule need not be provided.

History – In para. 31A(1), the word "general" omitted by SI 2015/478, reg. 22(6), with effect from 6 April 2015.
Para. 31A inserted by SI 2013/622, reg. 22, with effect from 6 April 2013 in relation to the tax year 2013–14 and subsequent tax years.

SCHEDULE 4A – REAL TIME RETURNS

Regulation 67(3)

History – Sch. 4A inserted by SI 2012/821, reg. 14 and Schedule, with effect from 6 April 2012.
Transitional – SI 2012/821, reg. 15, which refers to SI 2012/822, reg. 54, is relevant to Sch. 4A as inserted by SI 2012/821. SI 2012/821, reg. 15 reads as follows:
"**15** Regulation 54 of the 2012 Regulations (information about payments to employees) applies as if paragraph (2) of that regulation included a requirement to provide the information specified in paragraphs 6, 7 and 10 and, if applicable, paragraphs 5, 8 and 9 of Schedule 4A to the 2001 Regulations, as inserted by these Regulations.".

1 The information specified in this Schedule is as follows and terms used in this Schedule which are defined for the purposes of Schedule 4 bear the same meaning as in that Schedule.

INFORMATION ABOUT THE EMPLOYER AND THE EMPLOYEE

2 The information specified in paragraphs 2 to 6, 8 to 15 and 18 to 20 of Schedule A1 (real time returns) to the PAYE Regulations.

History – In para. 2, the words "6, 8 to 15 and 18 to 20" substituted for the words "4 and 18 to 14" by SI 2013/622, reg. 24, with effect from 6 April 2013 in relation to the tax year 2013–14 and subsequent tax years.

2A For the purposes of paragraph 2, the references in paragraphs 5 and 6 of Schedule A1 to the PAYE Regulations to regulation 67F of those Regulations shall be taken as references to paragraph 21F of Schedule 4 to these Regulations.

History – Para. 2A inserted by SI 2013/622, reg. 25, with effect from 6 April 2013 in relation to the tax year 2013–14 and subsequent tax years.

INFORMATION ABOUT PAYMENTS TO THE EMPLOYEE, ETC

3 The amount of the payment made that is included in the amount of the employee's earnings from the employment for the purposes of determining the amount of earnings-related contributions payable.

3A The total of the amounts referred to in paragraph 3 in the year to date.

History – Para. 3A inserted by SI 2013/622, reg. 26, with effect from 6 April 2013 in relation to the tax year 2013–14 and subsequent tax years.

4 For the purposes of assessing earnings-related contributions based on the payment, the number of earnings periods the payment relates to.

5 Where–

(a) the earner is concurrently employed in more than one employed earner's employment under the same employer but regulation 14 (aggregation of earnings paid in respect of separate employed earner's employments under the same employer) does not apply; or

(b) regulation 15 (aggregation of earnings paid in respect of different employed earner's employments by different persons and apportionment of contribution liability) applies in relation to the earner,

an indication of whether the return relates to earnings which have been or will be aggregated.

6 The appropriate category letter or, as the case may be, letters in relation to the employee (being the appropriate letter or letters indicated by HMRC).

7 For the category letter or, as the case may be, each category letter in relation to the employee (being the appropriate letter or letters indicated by HMRC), the total of the amounts required to be recorded by paragraph 7(13)(b)(i) to (iii) of Schedule 4 (calculation of deduction) for the year to date.

History – In para. 7, the words "to (iii)" substituted for the words "to (iiia)" by SI 2016/352, reg. 19(i), with effect from 6 April 2016, subject to savings in relation to rights or obligations arising in connection with tax years beginning before 6 April 2016 (and for savings purposes, references to repealed provisions of the Pension Schemes Act 1993 are to be read as though such provisions were still in force).

8 If the employee is a director, in so far as relevant to the relevant category letter (being the appropriate category letter indicated by HMRC) in relation to the employee–

(a) an indication of whether, for the purposes of assessing earnings-related contributions based on the payment, the employer has relied on regulation 8(2) or (3) (earnings periods for directors), or

(b) an indication of whether, for the purposes of assessing earnings-related contributions based on the payment, the employer has relied or, if the earnings fall to be aggregated, will rely on regulation 8(6).

9 Where regulation 8(2) applies and the appointment was in the current tax year, the week in which the appointment was made.

10 In so far as relevant to the relevant category letter or, as the case may be, letters (being the appropriate category letter or letters indicated by HMRC) in relation to the employee–

(a) the total amount of secondary Class 1 contributions payable on the employee's earnings in the earnings period in which the return is made,

(b) the total amount of secondary Class 1 contributions payable on the employee's earnings in the year to date,

(c) the total amount of primary Class 1 contributions payable on the employee's earnings in the earnings period in which the return is made, and

(d) the total amount of primary Class 1 contributions payable on the employee's earnings in the year to date.

11 In a case where the earnings the return relates to will fall to be aggregated with other earnings in the same earnings period, the information required by paragraphs 6, 7 and 10 need only be provided when the final payment of earnings in the earnings period is made.

History – In para. 11, the word "general" (which appeared before the word "earnings") omitted by SI 2015/478, reg. 23, with effect from 6 April 2015.

12 [Omitted by SI 2016/352, reg. 19(ii).]

History – Para. 12 omitted by SI 2016/352, reg. 19(ii), with effect from 6 April 2016, subject to savings in relation to rights or obligations arising in connection with tax years beginning before 6 April 2016 (and for savings purposes, references to repealed provisions of the Pension Schemes Act 1993 are to be read as though such provisions were still in force). Former para. 12 read as follows:

"**12** If the employee's employment is contracted-out or was contracted-out at any time during the year–

(a) the number notified by HMRC on the relevant contracting-out certificate as the employer's number, and

(b) the number notified by HMRC on the relevant contracting-out certificate as the registered pension scheme's number.".

Para. 12 substituted by SI 2013/622, reg. 27, with effect from 6 April 2013 in relation to the tax year 2013–14 and subsequent tax years.

12A Whether, during the period since the employer last made a return under paragraph 21A or 21D of Schedule 4 containing information about the employee–

(a) the employee has been absent from the employment because of a trade dispute at the employer's place of work, or

(b) the employee has been absent from the employment without pay for any other reason.

History – Para. 12A inserted by SI 2013/622, reg. 28, with effect from 6 April 2013 in relation to the tax year 2013–14 and subsequent tax years.

12B In cases–

(a) falling within paragraph 30 of Schedule 4, or

(b) where the employer has no obligation to deduct or repay tax in accordance with regulation 21 of the PAYE Regulations

the amount of the payment after statutory deductions, being the amount of the payment referred to in paragraph 3 minus the total amount of primary Class 1 contributions for the period (see paragraph 10(c)) minus the value of the deduction due under the Education (Student Loans) (Repayment) Regulations 2009 or the Education (Student Loans) (Repayment) Regulations (Northern Ireland) 2009.

History – Para. 12B inserted by SI 2013/622, reg. 28, with effect from 6 April 2013 in relation to the tax year 2013–14 and subsequent tax years.

12C The value of any amount which is not subject to tax or national insurance contributions paid to the employee at the same time as the payment.

History – Para. 12C inserted by SI 2013/622, reg. 28, with effect from 6 April 2013 in relation to the tax year 2013–14 and subsequent tax years.

12D The value of any deductions made from the payment which do not otherwise fall to be reported under Schedule 4.

History – Para. 12D inserted by SI 2013/622, reg. 28, with effect from 6 April 2013 in relation to the tax year 2013–14 and subsequent tax years.

INFORMATION ABOUT STATUTORY SICK PAY

13 [Omitted by SI 2014/2397, reg. 3(8).]

History – Para. 13 omitted by SI 2014/2397, reg. 3(8), with effect from 6 October 2014.

INFORMATION ABOUT STATUTORY MATERNITY PAY

14 If any, the total amount of statutory maternity pay paid during the year to date in this employment.

INFORMATION ABOUT ORDINARY STATUTORY PATERNITY PAY

15 If any, the total amount of statutory paternity pay paid during the year to date in this employment.

History – In para. 15, the word "ordinary" omitted by SI 2015/175, reg. 5(2), with effect from 5 April 2015, subject to the transitional provisions in SI 2015/175, reg. 9 (amendments do not have effect where they relate to additional statutory paternity pay or ordinary statutory paternity pay and payments of either on or after 5 April 2015).

INFORMATION ABOUT ADDITIONAL STATUTORY PATERNITY PAY

16 [Omitted by SI 2015/175, reg. 5(3).]

History – Para. 16 omitted by SI 2015/175, reg. 5(3), with effect from 5 April 2015, subject to the transitional provisions in SI 2015/175, reg. 9 (amendments do not have effect where they relate to additional statutory paternity pay or ordinary statutory paternity pay and payments of either on or after 5 April 2015).

17 [Omitted by SI 2015/175, reg. 5(3).]

History – Para. 17 omitted by SI 2015/175, reg. 5(3), with effect from 5 April 2015, subject to the transitional provisions in SI 2015/175, reg. 9 (amendments do not have effect where they relate to additional statutory paternity pay or ordinary statutory paternity pay and payments of either on or after 5 April 2015).

INFORMATION ABOUT STATUTORY SHARED PARENTAL PAY

17A If any, the total amount of statutory shared parental pay paid during the year to date in this employment.

History – Para. 17A inserted by SI 2015/175, reg. 5(4), with effect from 5 March 2015.

17B Where statutory shared parental pay has been paid during the year to date, the following information from the employee's application for the payment under, as the case may be, regulation 6, 7, 19, or 20 (notification and evidential requirements) of the Statutory Shared Parental Pay (General) Regulations 2014–

(a) the name of the employee's spouse or partner who has the main responsibility (apart from the employee) for the care of the child to which the application relates, and

(b) where there is such a number, the national insurance number of the employee's spouse or partner who has the main responsibility (apart from the employee) for the care of the child to whom the application relates.

For the purposes of this regulation **"partner"** has the meaning given in regulation 2(1) of the Statutory Shared Parental Pay (General) Regulations 2014.

History – Para. 17B inserted by SI 2015/175, reg. 5(4), with effect from 5 March 2015.

INFORMATION ABOUT STATUTORY ADOPTION PAY

18 If any, the total amount of statutory adoption pay paid in the year to date in this employment.

SCHEDULE 4B – ADDITIONAL INFORMATION ABOUT PAYMENTS

Regulation 67(3)

History – Sch. 4B inserted by SI 2012/821, reg. 14 and Schedule, with effect from 6 April 2012.

Transitional – SI 2012/821, reg. 16, which refers to SI 2012/822, reg. 56, is relevant to Sch. 4B as inserted by SI 2012/821. SI 2012/821, reg. 16 reads as follows:

"**16** A notification under regulation 56 of the 2012 Regulations (postponement of first return under regulation 67B or 67D of the 2003 Regulations) applies to returns under paragraphs 21A and 21D of Schedule 4 to the 2001 Regulations, as inserted by these Regulations, as if they were returns under regulations 67B (real time returns of information about relevant payments) and 67D (exceptions to regulation 67B) of the 2003 Regulations.".

1 The amounts specified in this Schedule are as follows and terms used in this Schedule which are defined for the purposes of Schedule 4 bear the same meaning as in that Schedule.

DEDUCTIONS IN RESPECT OF STATUTORY PAYMENTS

2 In respect of statutory maternity pay paid during the year to date to all employees the total of the amounts determined under regulation 3 (determination of the amount of additional payment to which a small employer shall be entitled) of the Statutory Maternity Pay (Compensation of Employers) and Miscellaneous Amendments Regulations 1994 and deducted by virtue of regulation 4 (right of employer to prescribed amount) of those Regulations.

3 In respect of statutory paternity pay paid during the year to date to all employees, the total of the amounts determined under regulation 5 (deductions from payments to HMRC) of the Statutory Paternity Pay and Statutory Adoption Pay (Administration) Regulations 2002.

History – In para. 3, the word "ordinary" omitted by SI 2015/175, reg. 6(2), with effect from 5 April 2015, subject to the transitional provisions in SI 2015/175, reg. 9 (amendments do not have effect where they relate to additional statutory paternity pay or ordinary statutory paternity pay and payments of either on or after 5 April 2015).

4 [Omitted by SI 2015/175, reg. 6(3).]

History – Para. 4 omitted by SI 2015/175, reg. 6(3), with effect from 5 April 2015, subject to the transitional provisions in SI 2015/175, reg. 9 (amendments do not have effect where they relate to additional statutory paternity pay or ordinary statutory paternity pay and payments of either on or after 5 April 2015).

4A In respect of statutory shared parental pay paid during the year to all employees, the total amounts determined under regulation 5 (deductions from payments to the Commissioners) of the Statutory Shared Parental Pay (Administration) Regulations 2014.

History – Para. 4A inserted by SI 2015/175, reg. 6(4), with effect from 5 March 2015.

5 In respect of statutory adoption pay paid during the year to date to all employees, the total of the amounts determined under regulation 5 of the Statutory Paternity Pay and Statutory Adoption Pay (Administration) Regulations 2002.

6 [Omitted by SI 2014/2397, reg. 3(9).]

History – Para. 6 omitted by SI 2014/2397, reg. 3(9), with effect from 6 October 2014.

REGIONAL SECONDARY CONTRIBUTIONS HOLIDAY FOR NEW BUSINESSES

7 The total of the appropriate amounts within the meaning given by section 7 of the National Insurance Contributions Act 2011 (regional secondary contributions holiday for new businesses) deducted by or refunded to the employer under section 4 of that Act in the year to date.

SCHEDULE 5 – ELECTIONS ABOUT SECURITIES OPTIONS, RESTRICTED SECURITIES AND CONVERTIBLE SECURITIES

Regulation 69

History – In Sch. 5, in the heading, the words "securities options, restricted securities and convertible securities" substituted for "share option gains" by SI 2004/2096, reg. 8(a), with effect in relation to–

- agreements entered into after 1 September 2004 which are in respect of post-commencement employment income (presumably as defined in NICSPA 2004, s. 3(5)), and
- elections made after that date.

1(1) An election for the purposes of paragraph 3B(1) of Schedule 1 to the Act shall contain–

(a) details of the securities options, restricted securities and convertible securities to which it relates, or of the period to which it relates, within which these are intended to be awarded or acquired;

(b) a statement that the election relates to relevant employment income arising from the securities or securities options referred to in sub-paragraph (1)(a) on which the employed earner is liable to pay secondary Class 1 contributions under–

(i) in the case of securities options, section 476 of ITEPA 2003 and section 4(4)(a) of the Act;
(ii) in the case of restricted securities, section 426 of ITEPA 2003 and regulation 22(7);
(iii) in the case of convertible securities, section 438 of ITEPA 2003 and regulation 22(7), and

an explanation of the effect of the relevant provision;

(c) the amount or proportion (as the case may be) of the liability for secondary Class 1 contributions to be transferred;

(d) a statement that its purpose is to transfer the liability for the secondary Class 1 contributions referred to in paragraph (c) from the secondary contributor to the employed earner;

(dd) a statement that it does not apply in relation to any liability, or any part of any liability, arising as a result of regulations being given retrospective effect by virtue of section 4B(2) of either the Social Security Contributions and Benefits Act 1992 or the Social Security Contributions and Benefits (Northern Ireland) Act 1992;

(e) a statement as to the method by which the secondary contributor will secure that the liability for amounts of contributions, transferred under the election, is met;

(f) a statement as to the circumstances in which it shall cease to have effect;

(g) a declaration by the employed earner that he agrees to be bound by its terms; and

(h) evidence sufficient to show that the secondary contributor agrees to be bound by its terms.

1(2) The declaration referred to in sub-paragraph (1)(g) shall either be signed by the employed earner or, if it is made by electronic communications, made by him in such electronic form and by such means of electronic communications as may be authorised by the Board.

History – Para. (1)(a) and (b) substituted by SI 2004/2096, reg. 8(b), with effect in relation to–

- agreements entered into after 1 September 2004 which are in respect of post-commencement employment income (presumably as defined in NICSPA 2004, s. 3(5)), and
- elections made after that date.

Para. 1(1)(dd) inserted by SI 2007/1175, reg. 2(2), with effect from 6 April 2007, but this amendment does not affect the continuing validity of any election made prior to the coming into force of SI 2007/1175, but subject to section 5(4) of NICA 2006

Derivations – SI 1979/591, Sch. 1ZA, para. 1.

2(1) An election to which this Schedule applies shall be made either in writing or in such electronic form and by such means of electronic communications as may be authorised by the Board.

2(2) An election to which this Schedule applies may be contained in two documents, one made by the employed earner and the other by the secondary contributor, in which case–

(a) the document made by the employed earner shall contain the matters listed in paragraph 1(1)(a) to (g); and

(b) the document made by the secondary contributor shall contain the matters listed in paragraph 1(1)(a) to (f) and (h).

Derivations – SI 1979/591, Sch. 1ZA, para. 2.

3(1) Where an election to which this Schedule applies has been made, the secondary contributor shall notify the employed earner to whom any of his liabilities are transferred by the election of–

(a) any transferred liability that arises;

(b) the amount of any transferred liability that arises; and

(c) the contents of any notice of withdrawal by the Board of any approval that relates to the election.

3(2) The secondary contributor shall notify the employed earner of the matters set out in sub-paragraph (1)(a) and (b) as soon as reasonably practicable.

3(3) The secondary contributor shall notify the employed earner of the matters set out in sub-paragraph (1)(c) within 14 days of receipt of the notice of withdrawal in question.

Derivations – SI 1979/591, Sch. 1ZA, para. 3.

SCHEDULE 6

Regulation 140

Part I – Prescribed Establishments and Organisations for the Purposes of Section 116(3) of the Act

Derivations – SI 1979/591, Sch. 3, Pt. I.

1 Any of the regular naval, military or air forces of the Crown.
2 Royal Fleet Reserve.
3 Royal Naval Reserve.
4 Royal Marines Reserve.
5 Army Reserve.

6 Territorial Army.

7 Royal Air Force Reserve.

8 Royal Auxiliary Air Force.

9 The Royal Irish Regiment, to the extent that its members are not members of any force falling within paragraph 1.

Part II – Establishments and Organisations of Which Her Majesty's Forces Shall Not Consist

Derivations – SI 1979/591, Sch. 3, Pt. II.

10 By virtue of regulation 140, Her Majesty's forces shall not be taken to consist of any of the establishments or organisations specified in Part I of this Schedule by virtue only of the employment in such establishment or organisation of the following persons

(a) any person who is serving as a member of any naval force of Her Majesty's forces and who (not having been an insured person under the National Insurance Act 1965 and not being a contributor under the Social Security Act 1975 or the Act) locally entered that force at an overseas base;

(b) any person who is serving as a member of any military force of Her Majesty's forces and who entered that force, or was recruited for that force outside the United Kingdom, and the depot of whose unit is situated outside the United Kingdom;

(c) any person who is serving as a member of any air force of Her Majesty's forces and who entered that force, or was recruited for that force, outside the United Kingdom, and is liable under the terms of his engagement to serve only in a specified part of the world outside the United Kingdom.

SCHEDULE 7 – CORRESPONDING NORTHERN IRELAND ENACTMENTS

Regulation 15

1 In this Schedule–

"the 1998 Order" means the Social Security (Northern Ireland) Order 1998

"the 2000 Act" means the Child Support, Pensions and Social Security Act 2000;

"the Transfer Order" means the Social Security Contributions (Transfer of Functions, etc.) (Northern Ireland) Order 1999;

"the Welfare Reform Act" means the Welfare Reform and Pensions Act 1999; and

"the Welfare Reform Order" means the Welfare Reform and Pensions (Northern Ireland) Order 1999.

Part I – Enactments Corresponding to Primary Legislation Applicable to Great Britain

Enactment applying in Great Britain	*Corresponding enactment applying in Northern Ireland*	*Relevant Northern Ireland amendment*
National Insurance Act 1965	National Insurance Act (Northern Ireland) 1966	
Section 3	Section 3	
Employment and Training Act 1973	Employment and Training Act (Northern Ireland) 1950	
Section 2(2)	Section 1	Article 3 of the Employment and Training (Amendment) (Northern Ireland) Order 1988 and Article 5 of the Industrial Training (Northern Ireland) Order 1990.
Social Security Act 1975	Social Security (Northern Ireland) Act 1975	
Section 4	Section 4	
Section 5(3)	Section 5(3)	
Section 7	Section 7	
Section 8	Section 8	
Section 39(4)	Section 39(4)	

Enactment applying in Great Britain	*Corresponding enactment applying in Northern Ireland*	*Relevant Northern Ireland amendment*
Section 130(2)	Section 130(2)	
Social Security Pensions Act 1975	Social Security Pensions (Northern Ireland) Order 1975	
Section 3(1)	Article 5(1)	
Section 6(1)(a)	Article 8(1)(a)	
Companies Act 1985	Companies (Northern Ireland) Order 1986	
Section 718	Article 667	Amended by paragraph 8 of Schedule 8 to S.R. 1997 No. 251.
Section 735 (definition of "company").	Article 3(1)	
Social Security Act 1986	Social Security (Northern Ireland) Order 1986	
Section 7	Article 9	
Children Act 1989	Children (Northern Ireland) Order 1995	
Part X	Part XI	
Section 71(13) (definition of "nanny")	Article 119(6)	
Section 105(1) (definition of "relative").	Article 2(2)	
Social Security Contributions and Benefits Act 1992	Social Security Contributions and Benefits (Northern Ireland) Act 1992	
Section 1(6)	Section 1(6)	Paragraph 38(3) of Schedule 6 to the 1998 Order and paragraph 2 of Schedule 3 to the Transfer Order
Section 2(1) and (2)	Section 2(1) and (2)	
Section 3	Section 3	Articles 45 and 46 of the 1998 Order and paragraph 4 of Schedule 3 to the Transfer Order.
Section 4(1) and (4)	Section 4(1) and (4)	Subsection (4) was substituted by Article 47(1) of the 1998 Order.
Section 5(1)	Section 5(1)	Substituted by paragraph 1 of Part I of Schedule 10 to the Welfare Reform Act.
Section 6	Section 6	Substituted by paragraph 2 of Part I of Schedule 10 to the Welfare Reform Act and amended by section 81(3) of the 2000 Act.
Section 6A	Section 6A	
Section 8(1) and (2)	Section 8(1) and (2)	Section 8 was substituted by paragraph 4 of Part I of Schedule 10 to the Welfare Reform Act.
Section 9	Section 9	Substituted by paragraph 5 of Part I of Schedule 10 to the Welfare Reform Act.
Section 10	Section 10	Substituted by section 78(2) of the 2000 Act.
Section 10ZA	Section 10ZA	

Enactment applying in Great Britain	*Corresponding enactment applying in Northern Ireland*	*Relevant Northern Ireland amendment*
Section 10A	Section 10A	Paragraph 12 of Schedule 3 to the Transfer Order and section 78 of the Welfare Reform Act.
Section 11	Section 11	Paragraph 13 of Schedule 3 to Transfer Order and article 3 of S.I. 2001/477.
Section 12	Section 12	Paragraph 14 of Schedule 3, and paragraph 1 of Schedule 8 to the Transfer Order.
Section 13	Section 13	Paragraph 15 of Schedule 3 to the Transfer Order and article 4 of S.I. 2001/477.
Section 14(1)	Section 14(1)	
Section 15	Section 15	Article 4 of S.I. 2000/755 and article 5 of S.I. 2001/477.
Section 16	Section 16	Paragraph 6 of Schedule 1 to the Transfer Order
Section 17	Section 17	Paragraph 7 of Schedule 1, paragraph 17 of Schedule 3 and Schedule 9 to the Transfer Order
Section 18	Section 18	Paragraph 8 of Schedule 1, paragraph 18 of Schedule 3 to the Transfer Order, article 4 of S.I. 2000/755 and article 5 of S.I. 2001/477.
Section 19(1), (2) and (4)	Section 19(1), (2) and (4) respectively.	
Section 19A	Section 19A	Paragraph 20 of Schedule 3 and paragraph 2 of Schedule 8 to the Transfer Order.
Section 20(1)	Section 20(1)	Paragraph 2(2) of Schedule 1 to the Social Security (Incapacity for Work) (Northern Ireland) Order 1994, Schedule 3 to the Jobseekers (Northern Ireland) Order 1995, paragraph 18(1) of Schedule 2 to the Pensions (Northern Ireland) Order 1995 and paragraph 2(2) of Schedule 8, paragraph 5(2) of Schedule 9 and Part V of Schedule 10 to the Welfare Reform Order.
Section 112	Section 112	Schedule 1 to the Employment Rights (Northern Ireland) Order 1996 and paragraph 21 of Schedule 3 to the Transfer Order.
Section 122(1) (definition of "pensionable age")	Section 121(1) (definition of "pensionable age")	Paragraph 9 of Schedule 2 to the Pensions (Northern Ireland) Order 1995.
Section 151(6)	Section 147(6)	Paragraph 10 of Schedule 1 to the Transfer Order
Section 164(9)(b)	Sections 160(9)(b)	Paragraph 14(2) of Schedule 1 to the Transfer Order.
Schedule 1	Schedule 1	
Paragraph 1(1)	Paragraph 1(1)	

Enactment applying in Great Britain	*Corresponding enactment applying in Northern Ireland*	*Relevant Northern Ireland amendment*
Paragraph 1(7)	Paragraph 1(7)	
Paragraph 1(8)	Paragraph 1(8)	
Paragraph 3(1)	Paragraph 3(1)	Paragraph 58(5) of Schedule 6 to the 1998 Order.
Paragraph 3B	Paragraph 3B	
Paragraph 6(3) and (4A)	Paragraph 6(3) and (4A)	Amended by paragraph 3 of Schedule 8 to the Transfer Order.
Schedule 2	Schedule 2	
Social Security Administration Act 1992	Social Security Administration (Northern Ireland) Act 1992	
Section 17	Section 15	
Section 18	Section 16	
Section 73	Section 71	Paragraph 32 of Schedule 2 to the Jobseekers (Northern Ireland) Order 1995.
Section 162(5)	Section 142(5)	Article 4(1) of the Social Security (Contributions) (Northern Ireland) Order 1994, Article 61(2) of the 1998 Order, paragraph 9(2) of Part III of Schedule 10 to the Welfare Reform Act and section 78(7) of the 2000 Act.
Section 179	Section 155.	Paragraph 48 of Schedule 2 to the Jobseekers (Northern Ireland) Order 1995, paragraph 84 of Schedule 6 to the 1998 Order and paragraph 5 of Schedule 1 to the Tax Credits Act 1999.
Trade Union and Labour Relations (Consolidation) Act 1992	Employment Rights (Northern Ireland) Order 1996	
Section 189	Article 217	Regulation 10 of S.R. 1999 No. 432.
Pension Schemes Act 1993	Pension Schemes (Northern Ireland) Act 1993	
Section 8(1)	Section 4(1)	Article 133(2) of, and paragraph 14 of Schedule 3 to the Pensions (Northern Ireland) Order 1995 and paragraph 37(a) of Schedule 1 to the Transfer Order.
Section 9(2)	Section 5(2)	Article 133(3) of the Pensions (Northern Ireland) Order 1995.
Section 9(3)	Section 5(3)	Article 133(4) of, and paragraph 17 of Schedule 3 to the Pensions (Northern Ireland) Order 1995, and paragraph 38(3) of Schedule 3 to the Transfer Order.
Section 41(1) to (1B)	Section 37(1) to (1B)	Subsection (1) was amended by paragraph 95 of Schedule 6 to the 1998 Order and further amended by paragraph 6(2), and subsections (1A) and (1B) were substituted by paragraph 6(3), of Part II of Schedule 10 to the Welfare Reform Act.

Enactment applying in Great Britain	*Corresponding enactment applying in Northern Ireland*	*Relevant Northern Ireland amendment*
Section 42A(1) to (2A)	Section 38A(1) to (2A).	Section 38A was inserted by Article 134(4) of the Pensions (Northern Ireland) Order 1995, subsections (1) to (2A) were substituted by paragraph 96 of Schedule 6 to the 1998 Order and subsections (2) and (2A) were further substituted by paragraph 7(3) of Part I of Schedule 10 to the Welfare Reform Act.
Section 43	Section 39	Paragraph 34 of Schedule 3 to the Pensions (Northern Ireland) Order 1995 and paragraph 54 of Schedule 1 to the Transfer Order.
Section 44(1)	Section 40(1)	Article 160(a) of the Pensions (Northern Ireland) Order 1995 and paragraph 55(2) and (3) of Schedule 1 to the Transfer Order.
Section 55(2)	Section 51(2)	Substituted by Article 138 of the Pensions (Northern Ireland) Order 1995 and amended by paragraph 7(2) of Schedule 2 to the Welfare Reform Act.
Jobseekers Act 1995	Jobseekers (Northern Ireland) Order 1995	
Section 2(1)(a)	Article 4(1)(a)	
Social Security Contributions (Transfer of Functions, etc.) Act 1999	The Transfer Order	
Section 8(1)(a) and (k)(ii)	Article 7(1)(a) and (k)(ii)	

Part 2 – Enactments Corresponding to Subordinate Legislation Applicable to Great Britain

Subordinate legislation applying in Great Britain	*Subordinate legislation applying in Northern Ireland*	*Relevant amendment to the Northern Ireland provision*
National Insurance (Contributions) Regulations 1969	National Insurance (Contributions) Regulations (Northern Ireland) 1962.	S.R.& O. (N.I.) 1963 No. 59 and 1970 No. 295
Regulation 9(3) and (4A)	Regulation 10(3) and (4A) respectively	
National Insurance (Married Women) Regulations 1973	National Insurance (Married Women) Regulations (Northern Ireland) 1973	
Regulation 2(1)(a)	Regulation 2(1)(a)	
Regulation 2(2)	Regulation 2(2)	
Regulation 3(1)(a)	Regulation 3(1)(a)	
Regulation 3(2)	Regulation 3(2)	
Regulation 4(2)	Regulation 4(2)	
Regulation 16	Regulation 16	
Social Security (Contributions) Regulations 1975	Social Security (Contributions) Regulations (Northern Ireland) 1975	

Subordinate legislation applying in Great Britain	*Subordinate legislation applying in Northern Ireland*	*Relevant amendment to the Northern Ireland provision*
Regulation 91	Regulation 89	
Regulation 94	Regulation 92	
Social Security (Categorisation of Earners) Regulations 1978	Social Security (Categorisation of Earners) Regulations (Northern Ireland) 1978	
Schedule 3	Schedule 3	Regulation 4 of S.R. 1984 No. 81, regulation 3 of S.R. 1990 No. 339, regulation 4 of S.R. 1994 No. 92 and regulation 4 of S.R. 1998 No. 250. See also S.R. 1999 No. 2.
Social Security (Payments on account, Overpayments and Recovery) Regulations 1988	Social Security (Payments on account, Overpayments and Recovery) Regulations (Northern Ireland) 1988	
Regulation 13	Regulation 13	Regulation 15(3) of S.R. 1996 No. 289 and regulation 11 of S.I. 1999/2573.
Social Security (Refunds) (Repayment of Contractual Maternity Pay) Regulations 1990	Social Security (Refunds) (Repayment of Contractual Maternity Pay) Regulations (Northern Ireland) 1990	
Regulation 2	Regulation 2	
Statutory Maternity Pay (Compensation of Employers) and Miscellaneous Amendments Regulations 1994	Statutory Maternity Pay (Compensation of Employers) and Miscellaneous Amendments Regulations (Northern Ireland) 1994	
Regulation 3	Regulation 3	
Regulation 4	Regulation 4	
Article 2	Article 2	
Social Security (Adjudication) Regulations 1995	Social Security (Adjudication) Regulations (Northern Ireland) 1995	
Regulation 13	Regulation 13	
Social Security (Additional Pension) (Contributions Paid in Error) Regulations 1996	Social Security (Additional Pension) (Contributions Paid in Error) Regulations (Northern Ireland) 1996	
Regulation 3	Regulation 3	
Employer's Contributions Re-imbursement Regulations 1996	Employer's Contributions Re-imbursement Regulations (Northern Ireland) 1996	
Regulations 5, 6 and 8	Regulations 5, 6 and 8 respectively.	
Education (Student Loans) (Repayment) Regulations 2009	Education (Student Loans) (Repayment) Regulations (Northern Ireland) 2009	
Regulation 39(1)	Regulation 39(1)	

Subordinate legislation applying in Great Britain	*Subordinate legislation applying in Northern Ireland*	*Relevant amendment to the Northern Ireland provision*
Social Security (Crediting and Treatment of Contributions, and National Insurance Numbers) Regulations 2001	Social Security (Crediting and Treatment of Contributions, and National Insurance Numbers) Regulations (Northern Ireland) 2001	
Regulation 4	Regulation 4	
Regulation 9	Regulation 9	

History – In the first column of the Table in Pt. 2, the words "Education (Student Loans) (Repayment) Regulations 2009" substituted for the words "Education (Student Loans) (Repayment) Regulations 2000" by SI 2012/821, reg. 26(c), with effect from 6 April 2012. In the first column of the Table in Pt. 2, the words "Education (Student Loans) (Repayment) Regulations (Northern Ireland) 2009" substituted for the words "Education (Student Loans) (Repayment) Regulations (Northern Ireland) 2000" by SI 2012/821, reg. 31, with effect from 6 April 2012.
Pt. 2, first column of table, the entry relating to "Statutory Sick Pay Percentage Threshold Order 1995" omitted by SI 2014/2397, reg. 3(10)(a), with effect from 6 October 2014.
Pt. 2, second column of table, the entry relating to "Statutory Sick Pay Percentage Threshold Order (Northern Ireland) 1995" omitted by SI 2014/2397, reg. 3(10)(b), with effect from 6 October 2014.

SCHEDULE 8 – REVOCATIONS

Regulation 15

Part I – Revocations Applicable to Great Britain or to the United Kingdom

Column (1) Regulations revoked	*Column (2) Reference*	*Column (3) Extent of revocation*
The Social Security (Contributions) Regulations 1979	S.I. 1979/591	The whole of the Regulations.
The Social Security (Contributions) Amendment Regulations 1980	S.I. 1980/1975	The whole of the Regulations.
The Social Security (Contributions) Amendment Regulations 1981	S.I. 1981/82	The whole of the Regulations.
The Social Security (Contributions) (Mariners) Amendment Regulations 1982	S.I. 1982/206	The whole of the Regulations.
The Contracting-out (Recovery of Class 1 Contributions) Regulations 1982	S.I. 1982/1033	The whole of the Regulations.
The Social Security (Contributions) Amendment Regulations 1982	S.I. 1982/1573	The whole of the Regulations.
The Social Security and Statutory Sick Pay (Oil and Gas (Enterprise) Act 1982) (Consequential) Regulations 1982	S.I. 1982/1738	Regulation 4.
The Social Security (Contributions) Amendment (No. 2) Regulations 1982	S.I. 1982/1739	The whole of the Regulations.
The Social Security (Contributions) Amendment Regulations 1983	S.I. 1983/10	The whole of the Regulations.
The Social Security (Contributions) Amendment (No. 2) Regulations 1983	S.I. 1983/53	The whole of the Regulations.
The Social Security (Contributions, Re-rating) Consequential Amendment Regulations 1983	S.I. 1983/73	The whole of the Regulations.
The Social Security (Contributions) Amendment (No. 4) Regulations 1983	S.I. 1983/395	The whole of the Regulations.
The Social Security (Contributions) Amendment (No. 3) Regulations 1983	S.I. 1983/496	The whole of the Regulations.
The Social Security (Contributions) Amendment (No. 5) Regulations 1983	S.I. 1983/1689	The whole of the Regulations.

Column (1) *Regulations revoked*	*Column (2)* *Reference*	*Column (3)* *Extent of revocation*
The Social Security (Contributions) Amendment Regulations 1984	S.I. 1984/77	The whole of the Regulations.
The Social Security (Contributions, Re-rating) Consequential Amendment Regulations 1984	S.I. 1984/146	The whole of the Regulations.
The Social Security (Contributions) Amendment (No. 2) Regulations 1984	S.I. 1984/1756	The whole of the Regulations.
The Social Security (Contributions, Re-rating) Consequential Amendment Regulations 1985	S.I. 1985/143	The whole of the Regulations.
The Social Security (Contributions) Amendment Regulations 1985	S.I. 1985/396	The whole of the Regulations.
The Social Security (Contributions) Amendment (No. 2) Regulations 1985	S.I. 1985/397	The whole of the Regulations.
The Social Security (Contributions) Amendment (No. 3) Regulations 1985	S.I. 1985/398	The whole of the Regulations.
The Social Security (Contributions) Amendment (No. 4) Regulations 1985	S.I. 1985/399	The whole of the Regulations.
The Social Security (Contributions) Amendment (No. 5) Regulations 1985	S.I. 1985/400	The whole of the Regulations.
The Social Security (Contributions and Credits) (Transitional and Consequential Provisions) Regulations 1985	S.I. 1985/1398	Regulations 2, 4, 5 and 6.
The Social Security (Contributions) Amendment (No. 6) Regulations 1985	S.I. 1985/1726	The whole of the Regulations.
The Social Security (Contributions, Re-rating) Consequential Amendment Regulations 1986	S.I. 1986/198	The whole of the Regulations.
The Social Security (Contributions) Amendment Regulations 1986	S.I. 1986/485	The whole of the Regulations.
The Social Security (Contributions) Amendment (No. 2) Regulations 1987	S.I. 1987/413	The whole of the Regulations.
The Social Security (Contributions) Amendment (No. 3) Regulations 1987	S.I. 1987/1590	The whole of the Regulations.
The Social Security (Contributions) Amendment (No. 4) Regulations 1987	S.I. 1987/2111	The whole of the Regulations.
The Social Security (Contributions) Amendment Regulations 1988	S.I. 1988/299	The whole of the Regulations.
The Social Security (Contributions) Amendment (No. 2) Regulations 1988	S.I. 1988/674	The whole of the Regulations.
The Social Security (Contributions) Amendment (No. 3) Regulations 1988	S.I. 1988/860	The whole of the Regulations.
The Social Security (Contributions) Amendment (No. 4) Regulations 1988	S.I. 1988/992	The whole of the Regulations.
The Social Security (Contributions) Amendment Regulations 1989	S.I. 1989/345	The whole of the Regulations.
The Social Security (Contributions) Amendment (No. 2) Regulations 1989	S.I. 1989/571	The whole of the Regulations.
The Social Security (Contributions) Amendment (No. 3) Regulations 1989	S.I. 1989/572	The whole of the Regulations.
The Social Security (Contributions) (Transitional and Consequential Provisions) Regulations 1989	S.I. 1989/1677	The whole of the Regulations.
The Social Security (Refunds) (Repayment of Contractual Maternity Pay) Regulations 1990	S.I. 1990/536	Regulation 4.

Column (1) *Regulations revoked*	*Column (2)* *Reference*	*Column (3)* *Extent of revocation*
The Social Security (Contributions) Amendment Regulations 1990	S.I. 1990/604	The whole of the Regulations.
The Social Security (Contributions) Amendment (No. 2) Regulations 1990	S.I. 1990/605	The whole of the Regulations.
The Social Security (Contributions) (Re-rating) Consequential Amendment Regulations 1990	S.I. 1990/906	The whole of the Regulations
The Social Security (Contributions) Amendment (No. 3) Regulations 1990	S.I. 1990/1779	The whole of the Regulations.
The Social Security (Contributions) Amendment (No. 4) Regulations 1990	S.I. 1990/1935	The whole of the Regulations.
The Social Security (Contributions) Amendment Regulations 1991	S.I. 1991/504	The whole of the Regulations.
The Social Security (Contributions) Amendment (No. 2) Regulations 1991	S.I. 1991/639	The whole of the Regulations.
The Social Security (Contributions) Amendment (No. 3) Regulations 1991	S.I. 1991/640	The whole of the Regulations.
The Social Security (Contributions) Amendment (No. 4) Regulations 1991	S.I. 1991/1632	The whole of the Regulations.
The Social Security (Contributions) Amendment (No. 5) Regulations 1991	S.I. 1991/1935	The whole of the Regulations.
The Social Security (Contributions) Amendment (No. 6) Regulations 1991	S.I. 1991/2505	The whole of the Regulations.
The Social Security (Contributions) Amendment Regulations 1992	S.I. 1992/97	The whole of the Regulations.
The Social Security (Contributions) Amendment (No. 2) Regulations 1992	S.I. 1992/318	The whole of the Regulations.
The Social Security (Contributions) Amendment (No. 3) Regulations 1992	S.I. 1992/667	The whole of the Regulations.
The Social Security (Contributions) Amendment (No. 4) Regulations 1992	S.I. 1992/668	The whole of the Regulations.
The Social Security (Contributions) Amendment (No. 5) Regulations 1992	S.I. 1992/669	The whole of the Regulations.
The Social Security (Contributions) Amendment (No. 6) Regulations 1992	S.I. 1992/1440	The whole of the Regulations.
The Social Security (Contributions) Amendment Regulations 1993	S.I. 1993/260	The whole of the Regulations.
The Social Security (Contributions) Amendment (No. 2) Regulations 1993	S.I. 1993/281	The whole of the Regulations.
The Social Security (Contributions) Amendment (No. 3) Regulations 1993	S.I. 1993/282	The whole of the Regulations.
The Social Security (Contributions) Amendment (No. 4) Regulations 1993	S.I. 1993/583	The whole of the Regulations.
The Social Security (Contributions) Amendment (No. 5) Regulations 1993	S.I. 1993/821	The whole of the Regulations.
The Social Security (Contributions) Amendment (No. 6) Regulations 1993	S.I. 1993/2094	The whole of the Regulations.
The Social Security (Miscellaneous Amendments) Regulations 1993	S.I. 1993/2736	The whole of the Regulations.
The Social Security (Contributions) Amendment (No. 7) Regulations 1993	S.I. 1993/2925	The whole of the Regulations.

Column (1) *Regulations revoked*	*Column (2)* *Reference*	*Column (3)* *Extent of revocation*
The Social Security (Contributions) Amendment Regulations 1994	S.I. 1994/563	The whole of the Regulations.
The Social Security (Contributions) (Miscellaneous Amendments) Regulations 1994	S.I. 1994/667	The whole of the Regulations.
The Social Security (Contributions) Amendment (No. 2) Regulations 1994	S.I. 1994/1553	The whole of the Regulations.
The Social Security (Contributions) Amendment (No. 3) Regulations 1994	S.I. 1994/2194	The whole of the Regulations.
The Social Security (Contributions) Amendment (No. 4) Regulations 1994	S.I. 1994/2299	The whole of the Regulations.
The Statutory Sick Pay Percentage Threshold Order 1995	S.I. 1995/512	Article 6(3).
The Social Security (Contributions) Amendment Regulations 1995	S.I. 1995/514	The whole of the Regulations.
The Social Security (Contributions) Amendment (No. 2) Regulations 1995	S.I. 1995/714	The whole of the Regulations.
The Social Security (Contributions) Amendment (No. 3) Regulations 1995	S.I. 1995/730	The whole of the Regulations.
The Social Security (Incapacity Benefit) (Consequential and Transitional Amendments and Savings) Regulations 1995	S.I. 1995/829	Regulation 13.
The Social Security (Contributions) Amendment (No. 4) Regulations 1995	S.I. 1995/1003	The whole of the Regulations.
The Social Security (Contributions) Amendment (No. 5) Regulations 1995	S.I. 1995/1570	The whole of the Regulations.
The Employer's Contributions Re-imbursement Regulations 1996	S.I. 1996/195	Regulation 13.
The Social Security (Contributions) Amendment Regulations 1996	S.I. 1996/486	The whole of the Regulations.
The Social Security (Contributions) Amendment (No. 2) Regulations 1996	S.I. 1996/663	The whole of the Regulations.
The Social Security (Contributions) Amendment (No. 3) Regulations 1996	S.I. 1996/700	The whole of the Regulations.
The Social Security Contributions, Statutory Maternity Pay and Statutory Sick Pay (Miscellaneous Amendments) Regulations 1996	S.I. 1996/777	Regulation 5.
The Social Security (Contributions) Amendment (No. 4) Regulations 1996	S.I. 1996/1047	The whole of the Regulations.
The Social Security (Additional Pension) (Contributions Paid in Error) Regulations 1996	S.I. 1996/1245	Regulation 4.
The Social Security (Credits and Contributions) (Jobseeker's Allowance Consequential and Miscellaneous Amendments) Regulations 1996	S.I. 1996/2367	Regulation 3.
The Social Security (Contributions) Amendment (No. 5) Regulations 1996	S.I. 1996/2407	The whole of the Regulations.
The Social Security (Contributions) Amendment (No. 6) Regulations 1996	S.I. 1996/3031	The whole of the Regulations.
The Social Security (Contributions) Amendment Regulations 1997	S.I. 1997/545	The whole of the Regulations.
The Social Security (Contributions) Amendment (No. 2) Regulations 1997	S.I. 1997/575	The whole of the Regulations.

Column (1) *Regulations revoked*	*Column (2)* *Reference*	*Column (3)* *Extent of revocation*
The Social Security (Contributions) Amendment (No. 3) Regulations 1997	S.I. 1997/820	The whole of the Regulations.
The Social Security (Contributions) Amendment (No. 4) Regulations 1997	S.I. 1997/1045	The whole of the Regulations.
The Social Security (Contributions) Amendment Regulations 1998	S.I. 1998/523	The whole of the Regulations.
The Social Security (Contributions) (Re-rating) Consequential Amendment Regulations 1998	S.I. 1998/524	The whole of the Regulations.
The Social Security (Contributions) Amendment (No. 2) Regulations 1998	S.I. 1998/680	The whole of the Regulations.
The Social Security (Contributions) Amendment (No. 3) Regulations 1998	S.I. 1998/2211	The whole of the Regulations.
The Social Security (Contributions) Amendment (No. 4) Regulations 1998	S.I. 1998/2320	The whole of the Regulations.
The Social Security (Contributions) Amendment (No. 5) Regulations 1998	S.I. 1998/2894	The whole of the Regulations.
The Social Security (Contributions) (Re-rating) Consequential Amendment Regulations 1999	S.I. 1999/361	The whole of the Regulations.
The Social Security (Contributions) Amendment Regulations 1999	S.I. 1999/561	The whole of the Regulations.
The Social Security Contributions, Statutory Maternity Pay and Statutory Sick Pay (Miscellaneous Amendments) Regulations 1999	S.I. 1999/567	Regulations 2 to 6 and 8 to 11.
The Social Security (Contributions and Credits) (Miscellaneous Amendments) Regulations 1999	S.I. 1999/568	Regulations 2 to 12 and 14 to 19.
The Social Security (Contributions) Amendment (No. 2) Regulations 1999	S.I. 1999/827	The whole of the Regulations.
The Social Security (Contributions) Amendment (No. 3) Regulations 1999	S.I. 1999/975	The whole of the Regulations.
The Social Security (Contributions) (Amendment No. 4) Regulations 1999	S.I. 1999/1965	The whole of the Regulations.
The Social Security (Contributions) (Amendment No. 5) Regulations 1999	S.I. 1999/2736	The whole of the Regulations.
The Social Security (Contributions) (Amendment) Regulations 2000	S.I. 2000/175	The whole of the Regulations.
The Social Security (Contributions) (Amendment No. 2) Regulations 2000	S.I. 2000/723	The whole of the Regulations.
The Social Security (Contributions) (Amendment No. 3) Regulations 2000	S.I. 2000/736	The whole of the Regulations.
The Social Security Contributions (Notional Payment of Primary Class 1 Contribution) Regulations 2000	S.I. 2000/747	Regulations 7 to 9.
The Social Security (Contributions) (Re-rating) Consequential Amendment Regulations 2000	S.I. 2000/760	The whole of the Regulations.
The Social Security (Contributions) (Amendment No. 4) Regulations 2000	S.I. 2000/761	The whole of the Regulations.
The Social Security (Contributions) (Amendment No. 5) Regulations 2000	S.I. 2000/1149	The whole of the Regulations.
The Social Security (Contributions) (Amendment No. 6) Regulations 2000	S.I. 2000/2084	The whole of the Regulations.

Column (1) *Regulations revoked*	*Column (2)* *Reference*	*Column (3)* *Extent of revocation*
The Social Security (Contributions) (Amendment No. 7) Regulations 2000	S.I. 2000/2077	The whole of the Regulations.
The Social Security (Contributions) (Amendment No. 8) Regulations 2000	S.I. 2000/2207	The whole of the Regulations.
The Social Security (Contributions) (Amendment No. 9) Regulations 2000	S.I. 2000/2343	The whole of the Regulations.
The Social Security (Contributions) (Amendment No. 10) Regulations 2000	S.I. 2000/2744	The whole of the Regulations.
The Social Security (Contributions) (Amendment) Regulations 2001	S.I. 2001/45	The whole of the Regulations.
The Social Security (Contributions) (Amendment No. 2) Regulations 2001	S.I. 2001/313	The whole of the Regulations.
The Social Security (Contributions) (Amendment No. 3) Regulations 2001	S.I. 2001/596	The whole of the Regulations.
The Social Security (Crediting and Treatment of National Insurance Contributions) Regulations 2001	S.I. 2001/769	Regulation 11.

Part II – Revocations Applicable to Northern Ireland

Column (1) *Regulations revoked*	*Column (2)* *Reference*	*Column (3)* *Extent of revocation*
The Social Security (Contributions) Regulations (Northern Ireland) 1979	S.R. 1979 No. 186	The whole of the Regulations.
The Social Security (Contributions, Re-rating) Consequential Amendment Regulations (Northern Ireland) 1980	S.R. 1980 No. 93	The whole of the Regulations.
The Social Security (Contributions) (Amendment) Regulations (Northern Ireland) 1980	S.R. 1980 No. 463	The whole of the Regulations.
The Social Security (Contributions) (Amendment) Regulations (Northern Ireland) 1981	S.R. 1981 No. 30	The whole of the Regulations.
The Social Security (Contributions) (Mariners) (Amendment) Regulations (Northern Ireland) 1982	S.R. 1982 No. 69	The whole of the Regulations.
The Social Security (Contributions) (Amendment) Regulations (Northern Ireland) 1982	S.R. 1982 No. 375	The whole of the Regulations.
The Social Security (Contributions) (Amendment No. 2) Regulations (Northern Ireland) 1982	S.R. 1982 No. 408	The whole of the Regulations.
The Social Security (Contributions) (Amendment) Regulations (Northern Ireland) 1983	S.R. 1983 No. 8	The whole of the Regulations.
The Social Security (Contributions, Re-rating) Consequential Amendment Regulations (Northern Ireland) 1983	S.R. 1983 No. 9	The whole of the Regulations.
The Social Security (Contributions) (Amendment No. 3) Regulations (Northern Ireland) 1983	S.R. 1983 No. 64	The whole of the Regulations.
The Social Security (Contributions) (Amendment No. 4) Regulations (Northern Ireland) 1983	S.R. 1983 No. 70	The whole of the Regulations.
The Social Security (Contributions) (Amendment No. 5) Regulations (Northern Ireland) 1983	S.R. 1983 No. 412	The whole of the Regulations.
The Social Security (Contributions) (Amendment) Regulations (Northern Ireland) 1984	S.R. 1984 No. 43	The whole of the Regulations.
The Social Security (Contributions, Re-rating) Consequential Amendment Regulations (Northern Ireland) 1984	S.R. 1984 No. 46	The whole of the Regulations.

Column (1) *Regulations revoked*	*Column (2)* *Reference*	*Column (3)* *Extent of revocation*
The Social Security (Contributions) (Amendment No. 2) Regulations (Northern Ireland) 1984	S.R. 1984 No. 403	The whole of the Regulations.
The Social Security (Contributions, Re-rating) Consequential Amendment Regulations (Northern Ireland) 1985	S.R. 1985 No. 25	The whole of the Regulations.
The Social Security (Contributions) (Amendment) Regulations (Northern Ireland) 1985	S.R. 1985 No. 59	The whole of the Regulations.
The Social Security (Contributions) (Amendment No. 2) Regulations (Northern Ireland) 1985	S.R. 1985 No. 61	The whole of the Regulations.
The Social Security (Contributions and Credits) (Transitional and Consequential Provisions) Regulations (Northern Ireland) 1985	S.R. 1985 No. 260	Regulations 2, 4, 5 and 6.
The Social Security (Contributions) (Amendment No. 3) Regulations (Northern Ireland) 1985	S.R. 1985 No. 334	The whole of the Regulations.
The Social Security (Contributions, Re-rating) Consequential Amendment Regulations (Northern Ireland) 1986	S.R. 1986 No. 45	The whole of the Regulations.
The Social Security (Contributions) (Amendment) Regulations (Northern Ireland) 1986	S.R. 1986 No. 71	The whole of the Regulations.
The Social Security (Contributions) (Amendment No. 2) Regulations (Northern Ireland) 1987	S.R. 1987 No. 143	The whole of the Regulations.
The Social Security (Contributions) (Amendment No. 3) Regulations (Northern Ireland) 1987	S.R. 1987 No. 348	The whole of the Regulations.
The Social Security (Contributions) (Amendment No. 4) Regulations (Northern Ireland) 1987	S.R. 1987 No. 468	The whole of the Regulations.
The Social Security (Contributions) (Amendment No. 2) Regulations (Northern Ireland) 1988	S.R. 1988 No. 121	The whole of the Regulations.
The Social Security (Contributions) (Amendment No. 4) Regulations (Northern Ireland) 1988	S.R. 1988 No. 204	The whole of the Regulations.
The Social Security (Contributions) (Amendment) Regulations (Northern Ireland) 1989	S.R. 1989 No. 70	The whole of the Regulations.
The Social Security (Contributions) (Amendment No. 2) Regulations (Northern Ireland) 1989	S.R. 1989 No. 104	The whole of the Regulations.
The Social Security (Contributions) (Transitional and Consequential Provisions) Regulations (Northern Ireland) 1989	S.R. 1989 No. 384	The whole of the Regulations.
The Social Security (Contributions) (Amendment) Regulations (Northern Ireland) 1990	S.R. 1990 No. 97	The whole of the Regulations.
The Social Security (Contributions) (Re-rating) Consequential Amendment Regulations) (Northern Ireland) 1990	S.R. 1990 No. 101	The whole of the Regulations.
The Social Security (Contributions) (Amendment No. 2) Regulations (Northern Ireland) 1990	S.R. 1990 No. 110	The whole of the Regulations.
The Social Security (Contributions) (Amendment No. 3) Regulations (Northern Ireland) 1990	S.R. 1990 No. 320	The whole of the Regulations.
The Social Security (Contributions) (Amendment No. 4) Regulations (Northern Ireland) 1990	S.R. 1990 No. 350	The whole of the Regulations.
The Social Security (Contributions) (Amendment) Regulations (Northern Ireland) 1991	S.R. 1991 No. 68	The whole of the Regulations.
The Social Security (Contributions) (Amendment No. 3) Regulations (Northern Ireland) 1991	S.R. 1991 No. 106	The whole of the Regulations.

Column (1) Regulations revoked	*Column (2) Reference*	*Column (3) Extent of revocation*
The Social Security (Contributions) (Amendment No. 4) Regulations (Northern Ireland) 1991	S.R. 1991 No. 310	The whole of the Regulations.
The Social Security (Contributions) (Amendment No. 5) Regulations (Northern Ireland) 1991	S.R. 1991 No. 404	The whole of the Regulations.
The Social Security (Contributions) (Amendment No. 6) Regulations (Northern Ireland) 1991	S.R. 1991 No. 490	The whole of the Regulations.
The Social Security (Contributions) (Amendment) Regulations (Northern Ireland) 1992	S.R. 1992 No. 41	The whole of the Regulations.
The Social Security (Contributions) (Amendment No. 3) Regulations (Northern Ireland) 1992	S.R. 1992 No. 126	The whole of the Regulations.
The Social Security (Contributions) (Amendment No. 4) Regulations (Northern Ireland) 1992	S.R. 1992 No. 127	The whole of the Regulations.
The Social Security (Contributions) (Amendment No. 5) Regulations (Northern Ireland) 1992	S.R. 1992 No. 138	The whole of the Regulations
The Social Security (Contributions) (Amendment) Regulations (Northern Ireland) 1993	S.R. 1993 No. 59	The whole of the Regulations.
The Social Security (Contributions) (Amendment No. 3) Regulations (Northern Ireland) 1993	S.R. 1993 No. 71	The whole of the Regulations.
The Social Security (Contributions) (Amendment No. 4) Regulations (Northern Ireland) 1993	S.R. 1993 No. 114	The whole of the Regulations.
The Social Security (Contributions) (Amendment No. 5) Regulations (Northern Ireland) 1993	S.R. 1993 No. 130	The whole of the Regulations.
The Social Security (Contributions) (Amendment No. 6) Regulations (Northern Ireland) 1993	S.R. 1993 No. 368	The whole of the Regulations
The Social Security (Contributions) (Miscellaneous Amendments) Regulations (Northern Ireland) 1993	S.R. 1993 No. 437	The whole of the Regulations.
The Social Security (Contributions) (Amendment No. 7) Regulations (Northern Ireland) 1993	S.R. 1993 No. 463	The whole of the Regulations.
The Social Security (Contributions) (Miscellaneous Amendments) Regulations (Northern Ireland) 1994	S.R. 1994 No. 94	The whole of the Regulations.
The Social Security (Contributions) (Amendment No. 2) Regulations (Northern Ireland) 1994	S.R. 1994 No. 219	The whole of the Regulations.
The Social Security (Contributions) (Amendment No. 3) Regulations (Northern Ireland) 1994	S.R. 1994 No. 328	The whole of the Regulations.
The Social Security (Contributions) (Amendment No. 4) Regulations (Northern Ireland) 1994	S.R. 1994 No. 343	The whole of the Regulations.
The Statutory Sick Pay Percentage Threshold Order (Northern Ireland) 1995	S.R. 1995 No. 69	Article 6(3).
The Social Security (Contributions) (Amendment) Regulations (Northern Ireland) 1995	S.R. 1995 No. 61	The whole of the Regulations.
The Social Security (Contributions) (Amendment No. 2) Regulations (Northern Ireland) 1995	S.R. 1995 No. 88	The whole of the Regulations.
The Social Security (Contributions) (Amendment No. 3) Regulations (Northern Ireland) 1995	S.R 1995 No. 91	The whole of the Regulations.
The Social Security (Incapacity Benefit) (Consequential and Transitional Amendments and Savings) Regulations (Northern Ireland) 1995	S.R. 1995 No. 150	Regulation 13.
The Social Security (Contributions) (Amendment No. 5) Regulations (Northern Ireland) 1995	S.R. 1995 No. 257	The whole of the Regulations.
The Employer's Contributions Re-imbursement Regulations (Northern Ireland) 1996	S.R. 1996 No. 30	Regulation 13.

Column (1) *Regulations revoked*	*Column (2)* *Reference*	*Column (3)* *Extent of revocation*
The Social Security (Contributions) (Amendment) Regulations (Northern Ireland) 1996	S.R. 1996 No. 58	The whole of the Regulations.
The Social Security (Contributions) (Amendment No. 2) Regulations (Northern Ireland) 1996	S.R. 1996 No. 79	The whole of the Regulations.
The Social Security (Contributions) (Amendment No. 3) Regulations (Northern Ireland) 1996	S.R 1996 No. 89	The whole of the Regulations.
The Social Security (Contributions) Statutory Maternity Pay and Statutory Sick Pay (Miscellaneous Amendments) Regulations (Northern Ireland) 1996	S.R. 1996 No. 108	Regulation 2.
The Social Security (Contributions) (Amendment No. 4) Regulations (Northern Ireland) 1996	S.R. 1996 No. 152	The whole of the Regulations.
The Social Security (Additional Pension) (Contributions Paid in Error) Regulations (Northern Ireland) 1996	S.R. 1996 No. 188	Regulation 4.
The Social Security (Credits and Contributions) (Jobseeker's Allowance Consequential and Miscellaneous Amendments) Regulations (Northern Ireland) 1996	S.R. 1996 No. 430	Regulation 3.
The Social Security (Contributions) (Amendment No. 5) Regulations (Northern Ireland) 1996	S.R. 1996 No. 433	The whole of the Regulations.
The Social Security (Contributions) (Amendment No. 6) Regulations (Northern Ireland) 1996	S.R. 1996 No. 566	The whole of the Regulations.
The Social Security (Contributions) (Amendment) Regulations (Northern Ireland) 1997	S.R. 1997 No. 100	The whole of the Regulations.
The Social Security (Contributions) (Amendment No. 3) Regulations (Northern Ireland) 1997	S.R. 1997 No. 163	The whole of the Regulations.
The Social Security (Contributions) (Amendment No. 4) Regulations (Northern Ireland) 1997	S.R. 1997 No. 180	The whole of the Regulations.
The Social Security (Contributions) (Re-rating) Consequential Amendment Regulations (Northern Ireland) 1998	S.R. 1998 No. 71	The whole of the Regulations.
The Social Security (Contributions) (Amendment No. 2) Regulations (Northern Ireland) 1998	S.R. 1998 No. 103	The whole of the Regulations.
The Social Security (Contributions) (Amendment No. 3) Regulations (Northern Ireland) 1998	S.R. 1998 No. 317	The whole of the Regulations.
The Social Security (Contributions) (Amendment No. 5) Regulations (Northern Ireland) 1998	S.R. 1998 No. 416	The whole of the Regulations.
The Social Security (Contributions) (Re-rating) Consequential Amendment Regulations (Northern Ireland) 1999	S.R. 1999 No. 64	The whole of the Regulations.
The Social Security (Contributions) Statutory Maternity Pay and Statutory Sick Pay (Miscellaneous Amendments) Regulations (Northern Ireland) 1999	S.R. 1999 No. 117	Regulations 2 to 10.
The Social Security (Contributions and Credits) (Miscellaneous Amendments) Regulations (Northern Ireland) 1999	S.R. 1999 No. 118	Regulations 3 to 13 and 15 to 21.
The Social Security (Contributions) (Amendment) Regulations (Northern Ireland) 1999	S.R. 1999 No. 119	The whole of the Regulations.
The Social Security (Contributions) (Amendment No. 2) Regulations (Northern Ireland) 1999	S.R. 1999 No. 151	The whole of the Regulations.

Column (1) *Regulations revoked*	*Column (2)* *Reference*	*Column (3)* *Extent of revocation*
The Social Security (Contributions) (Amendment No. 3) Regulations (Northern Ireland) 1999	S.R. 1999 No. 171	The whole of the Regulations.
The Social Security (Contributions) (Amendment No. 4) (Northern Ireland) Regulations 1999	S.I. 1999/1966	The whole of the Regulations.
The Social Security (Contributions) (Amendment) (Northern Ireland) Regulations 2000	S.I. 2000/176	The whole of the Regulations.
The Social Security (Contributions) (Amendment No. 2) (Northern Ireland) Regulations 2000	S.I. 2000/346	The whole of the Regulations.
The Social Security (Contributions) (Amendment No. 3) (Northern Ireland) Regulations 2000	S.I. 2000/737	The whole of the Regulations.
The Social Security Contributions (Notional Payment of Primary Class 1 Contribution) (Northern Ireland) Regulations 2000	S.I. 2000/748	Regulations 7 to 9.
The Social Security (Contributions) (Re-rating) Consequential Amendment (Northern Ireland) Regulations 2000	S.I. 2000/757	The whole of the Regulations.
The Social Security (Contributions) (Amendment No. 4) (Northern Ireland) Regulations 2000	S.I. 2000/758	The whole of the Regulations.
The Social Security (Contributions) (Amendment No. 5) (Northern Ireland) Regulations 2000	S.I. 2000/1150	The whole of the Regulations.
The Social Security (Contributions) (Amendment No. 6) (Northern Ireland) Regulations 2000	S.I. 2000/2086	The whole of the Regulations.
The Social Security (Contributions) (Amendment No. 7) (Northern Ireland) Regulations 2000	S.I. 2000/2078	The whole of the Regulations.
The Social Security (Contributions) (Amendment No. 8) (Northern Ireland) Regulations 2000	S.I. 2000/2208	The whole of the Regulations.
The Social Security (Contributions) (Amendment No. 9) (Northern Ireland) Regulations 2000	S.I. 2000/2344	The whole of the Regulations.
The Social Security (Contributions) (Amendment No. 10) (Northern Ireland) Regulations 2000	S.I. 2000/2743	The whole of the Regulations.
The Social Security (Contributions) (Amendment) (Northern Ireland) Regulations 2001	S.I. 2001/46	The whole of the Regulations.
The Social Security (Contributions) (Amendment No.2) (Northern Ireland) Regulations 2001	S.I. 2001/314	The whole of the Regulations.
The Social Security (Crediting and Treatment of National Insurance Contributions) Regulations (Northern Ireland) 2001	S.R. 2001 No. 102.	Regulation 10.

Column A	Column B	Column C	Column D
Age on last day of preceding tax year	*Earnings not exceeding LET*	*Earnings exceeding LET but not 3LET-2QEF*	*Earnings exceeding 3LET-2QEF*
54	21.0	5.25	10.5
55	21.0	5.25	10.5
56	21.0	5.25	10.5
57	21.0	5.25	10.5
58	21.0	5.25	10.5
59	21.0	5.25	10.5
60	21.0	5.25	10.5
61	21.0	5.25	10.5
62	21.0	5.25	10.5
63	21.0	5.25	10.5

SCHEDULE 2

Article 2(1)(b)

APPROPRIATE AGE-RELATED PERCENTAGES FOR THE TAX YEAR 2003–04

Column A	Column B	Column C	Column D
Age on last day of preceding tax year	*Earnings not exceeding LET*	*Earnings exceeding LET but not 3LET-2QEF*	*Earnings exceeding 3LET-2QEF*
15	8.4	2.10	4.2
16	8.4	2.10	4.2
17	8.4	2.10	4.2
18	8.6	2.15	4.3
19	8.6	2.15	4.3
20	8.8	2.20	4.4
21	8.8	2.20	4.4
22	9.0	2.25	4.5
23	9.0	2.25	4.5
24	9.0	2.25	4.5
25	9.2	2.30	4.6
26	9.2	2.30	4.6
27	9.4	2.35	4.7
28	9.4	2.35	4.7
29	9.6	2.40	4.8
30	9.6	2.40	4.8
31	9.8	2.45	4.9
32	9.8	2.45	4.9
33	10.0	2.50	5.0
34	10.0	2.50	5.0
35	10.0	2.50	5.0
36	10.2	2.55	5.1
37	10.2	2.55	5.1
38	10.4	2.60	5.2
39	10.4	2.60	5.2
40	10.6	2.65	5.3

Column A	*Column B*	*Column C*	*Column D*
Age on last day of preceding tax year	*Earnings not exceeding LET*	*Earnings exceeding LET but not 3LET-2QEF*	*Earnings exceeding 3LET-2QEF*
41	11.0	2.75	5.5
42	11.2	2.80	5.6
43	11.6	2.90	5.8
44	12.0	3.00	6.0
45	12.4	3.10	6.2
46	12.8	3.20	6.4
47	13.2	3.30	6.6
48	14.2	3.55	7.1
49	15.8	3.95	7.9
50	17.8	4.45	8.9
51	20.0	5.00	10.0
52	21.0	5.25	10.5
53	21.0	5.25	10.5
54	21.0	5.25	10.5
55	21.0	5.25	10.5
56	21.0	5.25	10.5
57	21.0	5.25	10.5
58	21.0	5.25	10.5
59	21.0	5.25	10.5
60	21.0	5.25	10.5
61	21.0	5.25	10.5
62	21.0	5.25	10.5
63	21.0	5.25	10.5

SCHEDULE 3

Article 2(1)(c)

APPROPRIATE AGE-RELATED PERCENTAGES FOR THE TAX YEAR 2004–05

Column A	*Column B*	*Column C*	*Column D*
Age on last day of preceding tax year	*Earnings not exceeding LET*	*Earnings exceeding LET but not 3LET-2QEF*	*Earnings exceeding 3LET-2QEF*
15	8.4	2.10	4.2
16	8.4	2.10	4.2
17	8.4	2.10	4.2
18	8.6	2.15	4.3
19	8.6	2.15	4.3
20	8.8	2.20	4.4
21	8.8	2.20	4.4
22	9.0	2.25	4.5
23	9.0	2.25	4.5
24	9.0	2.25	4.5
25	9.2	2.30	4.6
26	9.2	2.30	4.6
27	9.4	2.35	4.7

Column A	Column B	Column C	Column D
Age on last day of preceding tax year	*Earnings not exceeding LET*	*Earnings exceeding LET but not 3LET-2QEF*	*Earnings exceeding 3LET-2QEF*
28	9.4	2.35	4.7
29	9.6	2.40	4.8
30	9.6	2.40	4.8
31	9.8	2.45	4.9
32	9.8	2.45	4.9
33	10.0	2.50	5.0
34	10.0	2.50	5.0
35	10.2	2.55	5.1
36	10.2	2.55	5.1
37	10.2	2.55	5.1
38	10.4	2.60	5.2
39	10.4	2.60	5.2
40	10.6	2.65	5.3
41	10.6	2.65	5.3
42	11.0	2.75	5.5
43	11.4	2.85	5.7
44	11.8	2.95	5.9
45	12.0	3.00	6.0
46	12.4	3.10	6.2
47	12.8	3.20	6.4
48	13.2	3.30	6.6
49	14.4	3.60	7.2
50	16.0	4.00	8.0
51	18.0	4.50	9.0
52	20.2	5.05	10.1
53	21.0	5.25	10.5
54	21.0	5.25	10.5
55	21.0	5.25	10.5
56	21.0	5.25	10.5
57	21.0	5.25	10.5
58	21.0	5.25	10.5
59	21.0	5.25	10.5
60	21.0	5.25	10.5
61	21.0	5.25	10.5
62	21.0	5.25	10.5
63	21.0	5.25	10.5

SCHEDULE 4

Article 2(1)(d)

APPROPRIATE AGE-RELATED PERCENTAGES FOR THE TAX YEAR 2005–06

Column A	*Column B*	*Column C*	*Column D*
Age on last day of preceding tax year	*Earnings not exceeding LET*	*Earnings exceeding LET but not 3LET-2QEF*	*Earnings exceeding 3LET-2QEF*
15	8.4	2.10	4.2
16	8.4	2.10	4.2
17	8.4	2.10	4.2
18	8.6	2.15	4.3
19	8.6	2.15	4.3
20	8.8	2.20	4.4
21	8.8	2.20	4.4
22	9.0	2.25	4.5
23	9.0	2.25	4.5
24	9.0	2.25	4.5
25	9.2	2.30	4.6
26	9.2	2.30	4.6
27	9.4	2.35	4.7
28	9.4	2.35	4.7
29	9.6	2.40	4.8
30	9.6	2.40	4.8
31	9.8	2.45	4.9
32	9.8	2.45	4.9
33	10.0	2.50	5.0
34	10.0	2.50	5.0
35	10.2	2.55	5.1
36	10.2	2.55	5.1
37	10.4	2.60	5.2
38	10.4	2.60	5.2
39	10.4	2.60	5.2
40	10.6	2.65	5.3
41	10.6	2.65	5.3
42	10.8	2.70	5.4
43	11.2	2.80	5.6
44	11.4	2.85	5.7
45	11.8	2.95	5.9
46	12.2	3.05	6.1
47	12.6	3.15	6.3
48	13.0	3.25	6.5
49	13.4	3.35	6.7
50	14.6	3.65	7.3
51	16.0	4.00	8.0
52	18.0	4.50	9.0
53	20.4	5.10	10.2
54	21.0	5.25	10.5
55	21.0	5.25	10.5

Column A	Column B	Column C	Column D
Age on last day of preceding tax year	*Earnings not exceeding LET*	*Earnings exceeding LET but not 3LET-2QEF*	*Earnings exceeding 3LET-2QEF*
56	21.0	5.25	10.5
57	21.0	5.25	10.5
58	21.0	5.25	10.5
59	20.4	5.10	10.2
60	21.0	5.25	10.5
61	21.0	5.25	10.5
62	21.0	5.25	10.5
63	21.0	5.25	10.5

SCHEDULE 5

Article 2(1)(e)

APPROPRIATE AGE-RELATED PERCENTAGES FOR THE TAX YEAR 2006–07

Column A	Column B	Column C	Column D
Age on last day of preceding tax year	*Earnings not exceeding LET*	*Earnings exceeding LET but not 3LET-2QEF*	*Earnings exceeding 3LET-2QEF*
15	8.4	2.10	4.2
16	8.4	2.10	4.2
17	8.4	2.10	4.2
18	8.6	2.15	4.3
19	8.6	2.15	4.3
20	8.8	2.20	4.4
21	8.8	2.20	4.4
22	9.0	2.25	4.5
23	9.0	2.25	4.5
24	9.0	2.25	4.5
25	9.2	2.30	4.6
26	9.2	2.30	4.6
27	9.4	2.35	4.7
28	9.4	2.35	4.7
29	9.6	2.40	4.8
30	9.6	2.40	4.8
31	9.8	2.45	4.9
32	9.8	2.45	4.9
33	10.0	2.50	5.0
34	10.0	2.50	5.0
35	10.2	2.55	5.1
36	10.2	2.55	5.1
37	10.4	2.60	5.2
38	10.4	2.60	5.2
39	10.6	2.65	5.3
40	10.6	2.65	5.3
41	10.8	2.70	5.4
42	10.8	2.70	5.4

Column A	*Column B*	*Column C*	*Column D*
Age on last day of preceding tax year	*Earnings not exceeding LET*	*Earnings exceeding LET but not 3LET-2QEF*	*Earnings exceeding 3LET-2QEF*
43	11.0	2.75	5.5
44	11.2	2.80	5.6
45	11.6	2.90	5.8
46	12.0	3.00	6.0
47	12.4	3.10	6.2
48	12.8	3.20	6.4
49	13.2	3.30	6.6
50	13.6	3.40	6.8
51	14.6	3.65	7.3
52	16.2	4.05	8.1
53	18.2	4.55	9.1
54	20.6	5.15	10.3
55	21.0	5.25	10.5
56	21.0	5.25	10.5
57	21.0	5.25	10.5
58	21.0	5.25	10.5
59	19.6	4.90	9.8
60	20.6	5.15	10.3
61	21.0	5.25	10.5
62	21.0	5.25	10.5
63	21.0	5.25	10.5

SOCIAL SECURITY (REDUCED RATES OF CLASS 1 CONTRIBUTIONS, AND REBATES) (MONEY PURCHASE CONTRACTED-OUT SCHEMES) ORDER 2001

(SI 2001/1355)

Made on 3 April 2001. Operative from 6 April 2002.

Whereas the Secretary of State has, under s. 42B of the Pension Schemes Act 1993, laid before each House of Parliament a report, stating what, in view of the report of the Government Actuary under that section, he considers the appropriate flat-rate and age-related percentages should be for the purposes of s. 42A of that Act:

And whereas a draft of the following Order was, in accordance with s. 42B of the Pension Schemes Act 1993, laid before, and approved by a resolution of, each House of Parliament:

Now, therefore, the Secretary of State for Social Security, in exercise of powers conferred on him by s. 42B of the Pension Schemes Act 1993 and s. 38B and 181(9A) of the Pension Schemes (Northern Ireland) Act 1993, and of all other powers enabling him in that behalf, hereby makes the following Order:

CITATION AND COMMENCEMENT

1 This Order may be cited as the Social Security (Reduced Rates of Class 1 Contributions, and Rebates) (Money Purchase Contracted-out Schemes) Order 2001 and shall come into force on 6th April 2002.

REDUCED RATES OF CLASS 1 CONTRIBUTIONS, AND REBATES

2 For the purposes of section 42A of the Pension Schemes Act 1993 and section 38A of the Pension Schemes (Northern Ireland) Act 1993 (reduced rates of Class 1 contributions, and rebates)–

(a) the appropriate flat-rate percentage in respect of earners for the tax years 2002–2003 to 2006–2007–

  (i) in the case of a primary Class 1 contribution is 1.6 per cent, and

  (ii) in the case of a secondary Class 1 contribution is 1 per cent;

(b) the appropriate age-related percentages in respect of earners for each of the tax years 2002–2003 to 2006–2007 are the percentages specified in relation to that year in the Table set out in the Schedule to this Order, by reference to the earners' ages on the last day of the preceding tax year.

SCHEDULE

Article 2

TABLE – APPROPRIATE AGE-RELATED PERCENTAGES OF EARNINGS EXCEEDING THE LOWER EARNINGS LIMIT BUT NOT THE UPPER EARNINGS LIMIT

Age on last day of preceding tax year	*Appropriate age-related percentages for the tax year*				
	2002–03	*2003–04*	*2004–05*	*2005–06*	*2006–07*
15	2.6	2.6	2.6	2.6	2.6
16	2.6	2.6	2.6	2.6	2.6
17	2.7	2.7	2.7	2.7	2.7
18	2.7	2.7	2.7	2.7	2.7
19	2.8	2.8	2.8	2.8	2.8
20	2.8	2.8	2.8	2.8	2.8
21	2.9	2.9	2.9	2.9	2.9
22	2.9	2.9	2.9	2.9	3.0
23	3.0	3.0	3.0	3.0	3.0
24	3.1	3.1	3.1	3.1	3.1
25	3.1	3.1	3.1	3.1	3.1
26	3.2	3.2	3.2	3.2	3.2
27	3.2	3.2	3.2	3.2	3.2
28	3.3	3.3	3.3	3.3	3.3

Age on last day of preceding tax year	Appropriate age-related percentages for the tax year				
	2002–03	*2003–04*	*2004–05*	*2005–06*	*2006–07*
29	3.4	3.4	3.4	3.4	3.4
30	3.4	3.4	3.4	3.4	3.4
31	3.6	3.6	3.6	3.6	3.6
32	3.6	3.6	3.6	3.6	3.6
33	3.7	3.7	3.7	3.7	3.7
34	3.8	3.8	3.8	3.8	3.8
35	3.8	3.8	3.8	3.8	3.8
36	3.9	3.9	3.9	3.9	3.9
37	4.0	4.0	4.0	4.0	4.0
38	4.1	4.1	4.1	4.1	4.1
39	4.1	4.1	4.1	4.1	4.1
40	4.3	4.2	4.2	4.2	4.2
41	4.4	4.4	4.3	4.3	4.3
42	4.6	4.5	4.4	4.4	4.4
43	4.8	4.7	4.6	4.5	4.4
44	5.0	4.9	4.8	4.7	4.6
45	5.3	5.1	5.0	4.9	4.8
46	5.5	5.4	5.3	5.1	5.0
47	6.0	5.6	5.5	5.4	5.3
48	6.8	6.1	5.7	5.6	5.5
49	7.8	6.9	6.2	5.8	5.7
50	9.0	7.9	7.1	6.4	5.9
51	10.3	9.1	8.1	7.2	6.5
52	10.5	10.5	9.3	8.2	7.4
53	10.5	10.5	10.5	9.5	8.4
54	10.5	10.5	10.5	10.5	9.7
55	10.5	10.5	10.5	10.5	10.5
56	10.5	10.5	10.5	10.5	10.5
57	10.5	10.5	10.5	10.5	10.5
58	10.5	10.5	10.5	10.5	10.5
59	10.5	10.5	10.1	9.7	9.3
60	10.5	10.5	10.5	10.3	9.9
61	10.5	10.5	10.5	10.5	10.5
62	10.5	10.5	10.5	10.5	10.5
63	10.5	10.5	10.5	10.5	10.5

SOCIAL SECURITY CONTRIBUTIONS (SHARE OPTIONS) REGULATIONS 2001

(SI 2001/1817, as amended by SI 2003/2155)

Made on 11 May 2001 immediately after the passing of the Social Security Contributions (Share Options) Act 2001, by the Treasury, in exercise of the powers conferred upon them by s. 175(3) and (4) of, and para. 7B(1) and (2)(e), (f) and (g) and 8(1)(b) and (q) and (1A) of Sch. 1 to, the Social Security Contributions and Benefits Act 1992, s. 171(3) and (4) of, and para. 7B(1), (2)(e), (f) and (g) and (10) and 8(1)(b) and (q) and (1A) of Sch. 1 to, the Social Security Contributions and Benefits (Northern Ireland) Act 1992 and s. 5(3) of the Social Security Contributions (Share Options) Act 2001, and the Commissioners of Inland Revenue, in exercise of the powers conferred upon them by s. 175(3) and (4) of, and para. 6(1)(b) of Sch. 1 to, the Social Security Contributions and Benefits Act 1992, s. 171(3) and (4) of, and para. 6(1)(b) of Sch. 1 to, the Social Security Contributions and Benefits (Northern Ireland) Act 1992 and s. 1(5)(a) and (b) of the Social Security Contributions (Share Options) Act 2001. Operative from 12 May 2001.

CITATION AND COMMENCEMENT

1 These Regulations may be cited as the Social Security Contributions (Share Options) Regulations 2001 and shall come into force on 12th May 2001.

INTERPRETATION

2 In these Regulations–

"the Act" means the Social Security Contributions (Share Options) Act 2001 and references to a numbered section, without more, are references to the section bearing that number in the Act;

"the Contributions and Benefits Act" means–

(a) in the application of these Regulations to Great Britain, the Social Security Contributions and Benefits Act 1992; and

(b) in the application of these Regulations to Northern Ireland, the Social Security Contributions and Benefits (Northern Ireland) Act 1992;

"the day on which the Act is passed" means 11th May 2001;

"special contribution" means the contribution payable to the Inland Revenue under section 2.

MATTERS TO BE CONTAINED IN NOTICES UNDER SECTION 1

3(1) A notice under section 1 must contain the following–

(a) the name and address of the person giving the notice;

(b) the name and national insurance number of the person who has obtained a right to acquire shares in respect of which the notice is given;

(c) the date on which the right was granted;

(d) the amount that a person might reasonably have expected to have obtained from a sale in the open market on 7th November 2000 of each share to which the right relates together with a statement as to whether or not that amount has been agreed with Inland Revenue Shares Valuation;

(e) the price at which each share may be acquired by exercise of the right;

(f) any amount paid in consideration of the grant of the right, or, in cases where section 3 applies, the grant of the original right, by the person who has obtained it;

(g) the amount in respect of which Class 1 contributions would have been payable by virtue of section 4(4)(a) of the Contributions and Benefits Act if the right had been exercised in full on 7th November 2000 without the giving of any further consideration for the shares acquired by exercise of that right;

(h) the amounts of any Class 1 contributions that have already been paid to the Inland Revenue in respect of any liability to pay Class 1 contributions in respect of any gain realised on an exercise, assignment or release of the right after 7th November 2000 and before the day on which the Act is passed; and

(i) confirmation that the person giving the notice understands that the notice is irrevocable.

3(2) In cases where an election for the purposes of paragraph 3B(1) of Schedule 1 to the Contributions and Benefits Act which is in force on the day of the notice would relate to any gain realised on an exercise, assignment or release of the right on the day of the notice, the notice must also contain the following–

(a) a statement as to whether the person paying the special contribution is the person on whom (apart from the Act) any liability to pay secondary Class 1 contributions in respect of that gain would fall by virtue of the election;

(b) if different parts of that liability would fall (apart from the Act) on different persons by virtue of the election, a statement as to how much of the special contribution is being paid by the secondary contributor on whom (apart from the Act) that liability would fall if no election were in force; and

(c) if the notice is given–

(i) by the secondary contributor on whom (apart from the Act) any liability to pay secondary Class 1 contributions in respect of that gain would fall if no election were in force,

(ii) on behalf of the person on whom (apart from the Act) that liability would fall by virtue of the election,

a declaration that that person has consented to the notice being given by the secondary contributor.

3(3) In cases where section 3 applies, the notice must also contain confirmation that the person on whom any liability to pay Class 1 contributions in respect of any gain realised on the exercise, assignment or release of the replacement right referred to in that section or any subsequent replacement right would fall understands that section 2(1)(a) and (b) does not–

(a) prevent any such liability in respect of any such gain; or

(b) have the effect of deeming any such liability not to have arisen on any such gain.

FORM OF, AND MANNER OF GIVING, NOTICES UNDER SECTION 1

4(1) A notice under section 1 given in writing must be signed by the person giving it.

4(2) A notice under section 1 may also be given by electronic communication containing an electronic signature of the person giving the notice.

4(3) Where a notice under section 1 is to be given by a company, section 108(1) of the Taxes Management Act 1970 shall apply to that notice as it applies to a notice to be given by a company under the Taxes Acts.

4(4) In this regulation–

"electronic communication" includes any communication conveyed by means of an electronic communications network;

"electronic signature" has the meaning given by section 7(2) of the Electronic Communications Act 2000;

"the Taxes Acts" has the same meaning as is given by section 118(1) of the Taxes Management Act 1970.

History – In reg. 4(4) the definition of electronic communication substituted by SI 2003/2155, art. 3(1) and Schedule, para. 24(2), with effect from 17 September 2003.

PAYMENT OF SPECIAL CONTRIBUTIONS

5(1) Any special contribution must be paid to the Inland Revenue before the end of the period of ninety-two days beginning with the day on which the Act is passed or before the end of that period as extended by any such further period determined by the Inland Revenue under section 2(5).

5(2) For the purpose of this regulation and regulations 6 to 9 where–

(a) any payment to the Inland Revenue is made by cheque; and

(b) the cheque is paid on its first presentation to the banker on whom it is drawn,

the payment shall be treated as made on the day on which the cheque was received by the Inland Revenue and cognate expressions shall be construed accordingly.

INTEREST ON OVERDUE SPECIAL CONTRIBUTIONS

6(1) A special contribution which is not paid to the Inland Revenue before the end of the period of ninety-two days beginning with the day on which the Act is passed shall carry interest at the rate applicable under paragraph 6(3) of Schedule 1 to the Social Security Contributions and Benefits Act 1992 from the end of that period until payment.

6(2) Interest payable under this regulation shall be recoverable as if it were a Class 1A contribution.

6(3) A certificate of the Inland Revenue that any amount of interest payable under this regulation has not been paid to them, or, to the best of their knowledge and belief, to any person acting on their behalf, shall be sufficient evidence that a person is liable to pay to them the amount of interest shown on the certificate and that the sum is unpaid and due to be paid, and any document purporting to be such a certificate shall be deemed to be such a certificate until the contrary is proved.

PAYMENT OF INTEREST ON REPAID SPECIAL CONTRIBUTIONS

7 Where a special contribution is repaid to a person by the Inland Revenue, the repayment shall carry interest at the rate applicable under paragraph 6(3) of Schedule 1 to the Social Security Contributions and Benefits Act 1992 from the end of the period of ninety-two days beginning with the day on which the Act is passed, or, if later, from the date on which the special contribution was paid to the Inland Revenue, until the order for repayment is issued.

REPAYMENT OF INTEREST PAID ON SPECIAL CONTRIBUTIONS

8 Where a person has paid interest in respect of a special contribution, the Inland Revenue shall repay the interest to that person if–

(a) the interest is found not to have been due to be paid; or

(b) the special contribution is returned, or repaid, to that person.

REMISSION OF INTEREST ON SPECIAL CONTRIBUTIONS

9(1) Interest payable in respect of a special contribution shall be remitted for the period commencing on the first relevant date and ending on the second relevant date in the circumstances specified in paragraph (2).

9(2) The circumstances specified in this paragraph are that the liability, or a part of the liability, to pay the interest arises as the result of an official error being made.

9(3) In this regulation–

"official error" means a mistake made, or something omitted to be done, by an officer of, or person employed in relation to, the Inland Revenue acting as such, where the person by whom the interest was payable, or any person acting on his behalf, does not cause, or materially contribute to, that error or omission;

"the first relevant date" means the date after the end of the period of ninety-two days beginning with the day on which the Act is passed or, if later, the date on which the official error occurs;

"the second relevant date" means the date which is fourteen days after the date on which the official error is rectified and the person by whom the interest was payable is advised of its rectification.

RECORDS TO BE MAINTAINED

10(1) A person who has given a notice under section 1 must maintain the following records–

(a) a copy of the notice;

(b) evidence of the price at which each share may be acquired by exercise of the right in respect of which the notice is given;

(c) evidence of the amount that a person might reasonably have expected to have obtained from a sale in the open market on 7th November 2000 of each share to which the right relates;

(d) evidence that the special contribution was paid to the Inland Revenue before the end of the period of ninety-two days beginning with the day on which the Act is passed; and

(e) in cases where sub-paragraph (c) of regulation 3(2) applies, evidence of the consent referred to in that sub-paragraph.

10(2) Subject to paragraph (3), the records referred to in paragraph (1) must be retained by the person required to maintain them for a period of not less than three years beginning with 6th April following the date on which a gain is realised on the exercise, assignment or release of the right in respect of which the notice under section 1 is given.

10(3) In cases where–

(a) section 3 applies; and

(b) the notice under section 1 is given in respect of the original right,

the records referred to in paragraph (1) must be retained by the person required to maintain them for a period of not less than three years beginning with 6th April following the date on which a gain is realised on the exercise, assignment or release of the replacement right or any subsequent replacement right.

INSPECTION OF RECORDS

11(1) The following provisions of this regulation, which are a modified version of paragraphs (1) and (3) to (7) of regulation 55 of the Income Tax (Employments) Regulations 1993, shall apply in relation to every person required to maintain records under regulation 10 of these Regulations.

11(2) Every person required to maintain records under regulation 10, whenever called upon to do so by any authorised officer of the Inland Revenue, must produce those records to that officer for inspection, at such time as that officer may reasonably require, at the prescribed place.

11(3) **"The prescribed place"** mentioned in paragraph (2) means–

(a) such place in the United Kingdom as the person and the officer may agree upon;

(b) in default of such agreement, the place in the United Kingdom at which the records referred to in paragraph (2) are normally kept; or

(c) in default of such agreement and if there is no such place as is referred to in sub-paragraph (b), the person's principal place of business in the United Kingdom.

11(4) The authorised officer may–

(a) take copies of, or make extracts from, any document produced to him for inspection in accordance with paragraph (2); and

(b) remove any document so produced if it appears to him to be necessary to do so, at a reasonable time and for a reasonable period.

11(5) Where any document is removed in accordance with paragraph (4)(b), the authorised officer must provide–

(a) a receipt for any documents so removed; and

(b) a copy of the document, free of charge, within seven days, to the person by whom it was produced or caused to be produced where the document is reasonably required for the proper conduct of a business.

11(6) Where a lien is claimed on a document produced in accordance with paragraph (2), the removal of the document under paragraph (4)(b) shall not be regarded as breaking the lien.

11(7) Where records are maintained by computer, the person required to make them available for inspection shall provide the authorised officer with all facilities necessary for obtaining information from them.

SOCIAL SECURITY CONTRIBUTIONS (DEFERRED PAYMENTS AND INTEREST) REGULATIONS 2001

(SI 2001/1818)

Made on 11 May 2001 by the Commissioners of Inland Revenue, in exercise of the powers conferred upon them by para. 6(1)(b) of Sch. 1 to the Social Security Contributions and Benefits Act 1992 and para. 6(1)(b) of Sch. 1 to the Social Security Contributions and Benefits (Northern Ireland) Act 1992, after the signifying of Royal Assent to the Finance Act 2001. Operative from 12 May 2001.

CITATION AND COMMENCEMENT

1 These Regulations may be cited as the Social Security Contributions (Deferred Payments and Interest) Regulations 2001 and shall come into force on 12th May 2001.

APPLICATION OF SECTION 107 OF THE FINANCE ACT 2001FOR THE PURPOSES OF CLASS 1 CONTRIBUTIONS, CLASS 1A CONTRIBUTIONS AND CLASS 1B CONTRIBUTIONS

2(1) For the purposes of Class 1 contributions, Class 1A contributions and Class 1B contributions, section 107 of the Finance Act 2001 (interest on unpaid tax, etc.: foot-and-mouth disease) shall apply with the following modifications.

2(2) In subsection (1)–

(a) after "of tax", where it first occurs, add "or a relevant contribution"; and

(b) for the second paragraph substitute–

"For this purpose–

"relevant contribution" means a Class 1 contribution, a Class 1A contribution or a Class 1B contribution, within the meaning of section 1(2) of the Social Security Contributions and Benefits Act 1992, or, in the case of a contribution payable in Northern Ireland, section 1(2) of the Social Security Contributions and Benefits (Northern Ireland) Act 1992, in respect of which interest would apart from this section be chargeable; and

"tax" includes any amount chargeable by way of tax, or as a result of the non-payment of tax, in respect of which interest would apart from this section be chargeable.".

2(3) In subsection (2) for "31st January 2001" substitute "12th May 2001".

2(4) In subsection (6)(a) for "the passing of this Act" substitute "the coming into force of the Social Security Contributions (Deferred Payments and Interest) Regulations 2001".

SOCIAL SECURITY REVALUATION OF EARNINGS FACTORS ORDER 2002

(SI 2002/519)

Made on 7 March 2002 by the Secretary of State for Works and Pensions, in exercise of the powers conferred on him by s. 148(3) and (4) and 189(1), (3), (4) and (5) of the Social Security Administration Act 1992 and of all other powers enabling him in that behalf.

CITATION AND COMMENCEMENT

1 This Order may be cited as the Social Security Revaluation of Earnings Factors Order 2002 and shall come into force on 6th April 2002.

REVALUATION OF EARNINGS FACTORS

2 The earnings factors for tax years specified in the Schedule to this Order, in so far as they are relevant–

(a) to the calculation–

(i) of the additional pension in the rate of any long-term benefit; or

(ii) of any guaranteed minimum pension; or

(b) to any other calculation required under Part III of the Pension Schemes Act 1993 (including that Part as modified by or under any other enactment),

are directed to be increased for those tax years by the percentage of their amount shown opposite those tax years in that Schedule.

ROUNDING OF FRACTIONAL AMOUNTS

3 Where any earnings factor relevant to the calculation specified in article 2(a)(i) of this Order, as increased in accordance with this Order, would not but for this article be expressed as a whole number of pounds, it shall be so expressed by the rounding down of any fraction of a pound less than one half and the rounding up of any other fraction of a pound.

SCHEDULE

Article 2

Tax Year	Percentage
1978/79	500.7
1979/80	430.2
1980/81	342.9
1981/82	270.9
1982/83	236.9
1983/84	212.8
1984/85	189.7
1985/86	171.7
1986/87	149.5
1987/88	132.3
1988/89	113.7
1989/90	92.9
1990/91	79.8
1991/92	63.3
1992/93	53.3
1993/94	46.0
1994/95	41.6
1995/96	35.7
1996/97	32.0

Tax Year	Percentage
1997/98	25.7
1998/99	20.1
1999/2000	15.3
2000/2001	8.5
2001/2002	4.3

STATUTORY PAYMENT SCHEMES (ELECTRONIC COMMUNICATIONS) REGULATIONS 2002

(SI 2002/3047 as amended by SI 2010/2493)

Made on 11 December 2002 by the Commissioners of Inland Revenue in exercise of the powers conferred upon them by s. 132 and 133(2) of the Finance Act 1999. Operative from 1 January 2003.

PART 1 – INTRODUCTION

CITATION, COMMENCEMENT AND INTERPRETATION

1(1) These Regulations may be cited as the Statutory Payment Schemes (Electronic Communications) Regulations 2002 and shall come into force on 1st January 2003.

1(2) In these Regulations–

"the Board" means the Commissioners of Inland Revenue;

"official computer system" means a computer system maintained by or on behalf of the Board–

(a) to send or receive information or payments; or

(b) to process or store information; and

"the statutory payments" means statutory maternity pay, ordinary statutory paternity pay, additional statutory paternity pay and statutory adoption pay.

1(3) References in these Regulations to information and to the delivery of information shall be construed in accordance with section 132(8) of the Finance Act 1999.

History – In reg. 1(2), in the definition of "statutory payments", the words "ordinary statutory paternity pay, additional statutory paternity pay" substituted for the words "statutory paternity pay" by SI 2010/2493, reg. 3, with effect from 14 November 2010.

SCOPE OF THESE REGULATIONS

2 These Regulations apply to–

(a) the delivery of information to or by the Board, the delivery of which is required or authorised in connection with the statutory payments; and

(b) the making or recovery of any of the statutory payments or of any other sum in connection with those payments.

PART 2 – ELECTRONIC COMMUNICATIONS – GENERAL PROVISIONS

RESTRICTIONS ON THE USE OF ELECTRONIC COMMUNICATIONS

3(1) The Board may use electronic communications in connection with the matters referred to in regulation 2.

3(2) A person other than the Board may only use electronic communications in connection with the matters referred to in regulation 2 if the conditions specified in paragraphs (3) to (6) are satisfied.

3(3) The first condition is that the person is for the time being permitted to use electronic communications by an authorisation given by means of a direction of the Board.

3(4) The second condition is that the person uses–

(a) an approved method for authenticating the identity of the sender of the communication;

(b) an approved method of electronic communications; and

(c) an approved method for authenticating any information delivered by means of electronic communications.

3(5) The third condition is that any information or payment sent by means of electronic communications is in a form approved for the purposes of these Regulations.

3(6) The fourth condition is that the person maintains such records in written or electronic form as may be specified in a general or specific direction given by the Board.

3(7) In this regulation **"approved"** means approved for the purposes of these Regulations and for the time being by means of a general or specific direction of the Board.

USE OF INTERMEDIARIES

4 The Board may use intermediaries in connection with–

(a) the delivery of information about any statutory payment by means of electronic communications;

(b) the making or recovery of any statutory payment by those means; and

(c) the authentication or security of anything transmitted by any such means,

and may require other persons to use intermediaries in connection with those matters.

PART 3 – ELECTRONIC COMMUNICATIONS – EVIDENTIAL PROVISIONS

EFFECT OF DELIVERING INFORMATION BY MEANS OF ELECTRONIC COMMUNICATIONS

5(1) Information to which these Regulations apply, and which is delivered by means of electronic communications, shall be treated as having been delivered, in the manner or form required by or under any provision of the Social Security Acts, section 7 or 8 of the Employment Act 2002 or Article 8 or 9 of the Employment (Northern Ireland) Order 2002 if, but only if, all the conditions specified by–

(a) these Regulations, and

(b) any specific or general direction given by the Board,

are satisfied.

5(2) Information delivered by means of electronic communications shall be treated as having been delivered on the day on which the last of the conditions imposed as mentioned in paragraph (1) is satisfied. This is subject to the following qualification.

5(3) The Board may by a general or specific direction provide for information to be treated as delivered upon a different date (whether earlier or later) (than that given by paragraph (2).

5(4) In paragraph (1) **"the Social Security Acts"** means the Social Security Contributions and Benefits Act 1992, the Social Security Administration Act 1992, the Social Security Contributions and Benefits (Northern Ireland) Act 1992 and the Social Security Administration (Northern Ireland) Act 1992.

PROOF OF IDENTITY OF SENDER OR RECIPIENT OF INFORMATION

6 If it is necessary to prove, for any purpose, the identity of–

(a) the sender of any information delivered by means of electronic communications to an official computer system, or

(b) the recipient of any information delivered by means of electronic communications from an official computer system,

the sender or recipient (as the case may be) shall be presumed to be the person recorded as such on an official computer system unless the contrary is proved.

PROOF OF DELIVERY OF INFORMATION AND PAYMENTS

7(1) If it is necessary to prove, for any purpose, that the use of electronic communications has resulted in the making of any payment to or by the Board, or the delivery of any information to or by them, this shall be presumed, unless the contrary is proved–

(a) in the case of information delivered or a payment made to the Board, if the making of the payment, or the delivery of the information, has been recorded on an official computer system;

(b) in the case of information delivered, or payment made, by the Board, if the despatch of that payment or information has been recorded on an official computer system, and

(c) not to be the case if it has not been so recorded.

7(2) If it is necessary to prove, for any purpose, when any information or payment sent by electronic communications has been received, the time of receipt shall be presumed to be that recorded on an official computer system unless the contrary is proved.

PROOF OF CONTENT OF INFORMATION

8 If it is necessary to prove, for any purpose the content of any information sent by means of electronic communications, the content shall be presumed to be that recorded on an official computer system unless the contrary is proved.

CERTIFICATES AS TO OFFICIAL RECORDS

9 A document certified by an officer of the Board to be a printed-out version of any electronic communication recorded on an official computer system as at a particular date shall be presumed, unless the contrary is proved–

(a) to have been recorded on an official computer system at that date; and

(b) to constitute the entirety of the electronic communication so recorded.

PRESUMPTION AS TO CERTIFICATES

10 A document purporting to be a certificate issued by an officer of the Board under regulation 9 shall be presumed to be such a certificate unless the contrary is proved.

SOCIAL SECURITY CONTRIBUTIONS AND BENEFITS ACT 1992 (APPLICATION OF PARTS 12ZA, 12ZB AND 12ZC TO ADOPTIONS FROM OVERSEAS) REGULATIONS 2003

(SI 2003/499, as amended by SI 2004/488, SI 2010/751 and SI 2014/2857)

Made on 5 March 2003 by the Secretary of State, in exercise of the powers conferred on her by s. 171ZK and 171ZT of the Social Security Contributions and Benefits Act 1992 by this instrument, which contains only provision made by virtue of s. 2 and 4 of the Employment Act 2002 and is made before the end of the period of 6 months from the coming into force of those enactments. So far as applying enabling powers, operative from 10 March 2003. For all other purposes, operative from 6 April 2003.

History – In the title, the words ", 12ZB and 12ZC" substituted for "and 12ZB" by SI 2014/2857, reg. 3, with effect from 19 November 2014.

CITATION, COMMENCEMENT AND INTERPRETATION

1(1) These Regulations may be cited as the Social Security Contributions and Benefits Act 1992 (Application of Parts 12ZA, 12ZB and 12ZC to Adoptions from Overseas) Regulations 2003 and shall come into force, in so far as they apply powers to make regulations, on 10th March 2003, and for all other purposes on 6th April 2003.

1(2) In these Regulations–

"adoption from overseas" means the adoption of a child who enters Great Britain from outside the United Kingdom in connection with or for the purposes of adoption which does not involve the placement of the child for adoption under the law of any part of the United Kingdom;

"the Act" means the Social Security Contributions and Benefits Act 1992.

History – In reg. 1(1), the words ", 12ZB and 12ZC" substituted for "and 12ZB" by SI 2014/2857, reg. 4, with effect from 19 November 2014.

APPLICATION OF PART 12ZA OF THE ACT TO ADOPTIONS FROM OVERSEAS

2 Part 12ZA of the Act (as it concerns both ordinary statutory paternity pay and additional statutory paternity pay) shall apply in relation to adoptions from overseas, with the modifications of sections 171ZB, 171ZE, 171ZEB, 171ZEE and 171ZJ of the Act specified in the second column of Schedule 1.

History – In reg. 2 the words "(as it concerns both ordinary statutory paternity pay and additional statutory paternity pay)" and ", 171ZEB, 171ZEE" inserted by SI 2010/153, reg. 2(2), with effect from 6 April 2010.

APPLICATION OF PART 12ZB OF THE ACT TO ADOPTIONS FROM OVERSEAS

3 Part 12ZB of the Act shall apply in relation to adoptions from overseas, with the modifications of sections 171ZL and 171ZS of the Act specified in the second column of Schedule 2.

APPLICATION OF PART 12ZC OF THE ACT TO ADOPTIONS FROM OVERSEAS

4 Part 12ZC of the Act shall apply in relation to adoptions from overseas, with the modifications of section 171ZV of the Act specified in the second column of Schedule 3.

History – Reg. 4 inserted by SI 2014/2857, reg. 5, with effect from 19 November 2014.

SCHEDULES

SCHEDULE 1 – APPLICATION OF PART 12ZA OF THE ACT TO ADOPTIONS FROM OVERSEAS

Regulation 2

Provision	Modification
Section 171ZB(2)	In paragraph (a)(i), for "who is placed for adoption under the law of any part of the United Kingdom" substitute "who is adopted from overseas". In paragraph (a)(ii), for "a person with whom the child is so placed for adoption" substitute "an adopter of the child".

Provision	Modification
	In paragraph (b), "omit ending with the relevant week". In paragraph (d), for "the day on which the child is placed for adoption" substitute "the day on which the child enters Great Britain". In paragraph (e), for "a person with whom the child is placed for adoption" substitute "an adopter of the child".
Section 171ZB(3)	For subsection (3) substitute– "(3) The references in subsection (2)(c) and (d) to the relevant week are to–". (a) the week in which official notification is sent to the adopter, or (b) the week at the end of which the person satisfies the condition in subsection (2)(b), which ever is the later.
Section 171ZB(6)	For "the placement of adoption of more than one child as part of the same arrangement" substitute "the adoption from overseas of more than one child as part of the same arrangement".
Section 171ZB(7)	Omit subsection (7).
Section 171ZE(3)	In paragraph (b), for "with the date of the child's placement for adoption" substitute "with the date of the child's entry into Great Britain".
Section 171ZE(10)	For subsection (10) substitute– "(10) Where more than one child is the subject of adoption from overseas as part of the same arrangement, and the date of entry of each child is different, the reference in subsection (3)(b) to the date of the child's entry into Great Britain shall be interpreted as a reference to the date of the entry of the first child to enter Great Britain.".
Section 171ZEB(2)	In paragraph (a)(i), for "who has been placed for adoption under the law of any part of the United Kingdom" subsitute "who has been adopted from overseas". In paragraph (a)(ii), for "a person with whom the child is so placed for adoption" substitute "an adopter of the child". In paragraph (b), for "ending with a prescribed week" substitute "prior to the date of the child's entry into Great Britain". In paragraph (c), for "the placement of the child for adoption", substitute "the adoption of the child from overseas". In paragraph (g)(i) for "the placement of the child for adoption", substitute "the date of the child's entry into Great Britain".
Section 171ZEB(5)	For "the placement for adoption of more than one child as part of the same arrangement" substitute "the adoption from overseas of more than one child as part of the same arrangement".
Section 171ZEE(3)	For "the person with whom the child is placed for adoption", substitute "adopter".
Section 171ZEE(4)	In paragraph (c)(ii), for "person with whom the child is placed for adoption", substitute "adopter".
Section 171ZEE(5)	For paragraph (b), substitute– "(b) in the case of a person to whom the conditions in section 171ZEB(2) apply, the date of the child's entry into Great Britain (or, where more than one child is subject to adoption from overseas as part of the same arrangement, the date of the entry of the first child to enter Great Britain)."
Section 171ZJ(1)	In the appropriate places in the alphabetical order, insert– ""adopter", in relation to a child, means a person by whom the child has been or is to be adopted;"

Provision	Modification
	""adoption from overseas" means the adoption of a child who enters Great Britain from outside the United Kingdom in connection with or for the purposes of adoption which does not involve the placement of the child for adoption under the law of any part of the United Kingdom, and the references to a child adopted from overseas shall be construed accordingly;"
	""official notification" means written notification, issued by or on behalf of the relevant domestic authority, that it is prepared to issue a certificate to the overseas authority concerned with the adoption of the child, or has issued a certificate and sent it to that authority, confirming, in either case, that the adopter is eligible to adopt and has been assessed and approved as being a suitable adoptive parent;"
	""relevant domestic authority" means–
	(a) in the case of an adopter to whom the Intercountry Adoption (Hague Convention) Regulations 2003 apply and who is habitually resident in Wales, the National Assembly of Wales;
	(b) in the case of an adopter to whom the Intercountry Adoption (Hague Convention) (Scotland) Regulations 2003 apply and who is habitually resident in Scotland, the Scottish Ministers;
	(c) in any other case, the Secretary of State.".

History – In entry relating to "Section 171ZB(2)" words "For "the conditions are" substitute "subject to subsection (3A), the conditions are"." revoked by SI 2004/488, reg. 3(1) and (2)(a), with effect from 6 April 2004 (by virtue of SI 2004/488, reg. 1(1)).
In entry relating to "Section 171ZB(2)" words "In paragraph (b), omit "ending with the relevant week"." inserted by SI 2004/488, reg. 3(1) and (2)(b), with effect from 6 April 2004 (by virtue of SI 2004/488, reg. 1(1)).
The entry relating to "Section 171ZB(3)" substituted by SI 2004/488, reg. 3(1) and (2)(c), with effect from 6 April 2004 (by virtue of SI 2004/488, reg. 1(1)).
The entries relating to "Section 171ZEB(2)", "Section 171ZEB(5)", "Section 171ZEE(3)", "Section 171ZEE(4)" and "Section 171ZEE(5)" inserted by SI 2010/153, reg. 2(3), with effect from 6 April 2010.

SCHEDULE 2 – APPLICATION OF PART 12ZB OF THE ACT TO ADOPTIONS FROM OVERSEAS

Regulation 3

Provision	Modification
Section 171ZL(2)	For "The conditions are" substitute "Subject to subsection (3A), the conditions are".
	In paragraph (a), for "with whom a child is, or is expected to be, placed for adoption under the law of any part of the United Kingdom" substitute "who is, or is expected to be, an adopter of a child from overseas".
Section 171ZL(3)	
	For subsection (3) substitute–
	"(3) The references in subsection (2)(c) and (d) to the relevant week are to–".
	(a) the week in which official notification is sent to the adopter, or
	(b) the week at the end of which the person satisfies the condition in subsection (2)(b), which ever is the later.
Section 171ZL(4)	In paragraph (b), for "placed for adoption with him" substitute "adopted by him".
Section 171ZL(5)	For "the placement, or expected placement, for adoption of more than one child" substitute "the adoption, or expected adoption, from overseas of more than one child".
Section 171ZS(1)	In the appropriate places in the alphabetical order, insert–
	""adopter", in relation to a child, means a person by whom the child has been or is to be adopted;"

Provision	Modification
	""adoption from overseas" means the adoption of a child who enters Great Britain from outside the United Kingdom in connection with or for the purposes of adoption which does not involve the placement of the child for adoption under the law of any part of the United Kingdom, and the references to a child adopted from overseas shall be construed accordingly;"
	""official notification" means written notification, issued by or on behalf of the relevant domestic authority, that it is prepared to issue a certificate to the overseas authority concerned with the adoption of the child, or has issued a certificate and sent it to that authority, confirming, in either case, that the adopter is eligible to adopt and has been assessed and approved as being a suitable adoptive parent;"
	""relevant domestic authority" means–
	(a) in the case of an adopter to whom the Intercountry Adoption (Hague Convention) Regulations 2003 apply and who is habitually resident in Wales, the National Assembly of Wales;
	(b) in the case of an adopter to whom the Intercountry Adoption (Hague Convention) (Scotland) Regulations 2003 apply and who is habitually resident in Scotland, the Scottish Ministers;
	(c) in any other case, the Secretary of State."."

History – In entry relating to "Section 171ZL(2)" words "For "the conditions are" substitute "subject to subsection (3A), the conditions are"." revoked by SI 2004/488, reg. 3(1) and (3)(a), with effect from 6 April 2004 (by virtue of SI 2004/488, reg. 1(1)).
In entry relating to "Section 171ZL(2)" words "In paragraph (b), omit "ending with the relevant week"." inserted by SI 2004/488, reg. 3(1) and (3)(b), with effect from 6 April 2004 (by virtue of SI 2004/488, reg. 1(1)).
The entry relating to "Section 171ZL(3)" substituted by SI 2004/488, reg. 3(1) and (3)(c), with effect from 6 April 2004 (by virtue of SI 2004/488, reg. 1(1)).

SCHEDULE 3 – APPLICATION OF PART 12ZC OF THE ACT TO ADOPTIONS FROM OVERSEAS

Regulation 4

Provision	*Modification*
Section 171ZV	In subsection (1), for "with whom a child is, or is expected to be, placed for adoption under the law of any part of the United Kingdom" substitute "by whom a child is, or is expected to be, adopted from overseas".
	In paragraph (g) of subsection (2), for "placement for adoption of the child" substitute "adoption of the child from overseas".
	In paragraph (a) of subsection (4), for "with whom a child is, or is expected to be, placed for adoption under the law of any part of the United Kingdom" substitute "by whom a child is, or is expected to be, adopted from overseas".
	In paragraph (h) of subsection (4), for "placement for adoption of the child" substitute "adoption of the child from overseas".
	In subsection (16), for "placement for adoption" substitute "adoption from overseas".
	After subsection (16) insert–
	"(16A) For the purposes of this section, a person adopts a child from overseas if the person adopts a child who enters Great Britain from outside the United Kingdom in connection with or for the purposes of adoption which does not involve the placement of the child for adoption under the law of any part of the United Kingdom.".
	Omit subsection (17).
	Omit subsection (18).

History – Sch. 3 inserted by SI 2014/2857, reg. 6, with effect from 19 November 2014.

SOCIAL SECURITY REVALUATION OF EARNINGS FACTORS ORDER 2003

(SI 2003/517)

Made on 5 March 2003 by the Secretary of State for Work and Pensions, in exercise of the powers conferred upon him by s. 148(3) and (4) and 189(1), (4) and (5) of the Social Security Administration Act 1992 and of all other powers enabling him in that behalf, having on a review under the said s. 148 concluded, having had regard to earlier orders under that section, that earnings factors for the relevant previous tax years have not, during the period taken into account for that review, maintained their value in relation to the general level of earnings obtaining in Great Britain. Operative from 6 April 2003.

CITATION AND COMMENCEMENT

1 This Order may be cited as the Social Security Revaluation of Earnings Factors Order 2003 and shall come into force on 6th April 2003.

REVALUATION OF EARNINGS FACTORS

2 The earnings factors for tax years specified in the Schedule to this Order, in so far as they are relevant–

(a) to the calculation–

(i) of the additional pension in the rate of any long-term benefit; or

(ii) of any guaranteed minimum pension; or

(b) to any other calculation required under Part III of the *Pension Schemes Act* 1993 (including that Part as modified by or under any other enactment),

ROUNDING OF FRACTIONAL AMOUNTS

3 Where any earnings factor relevant to the calculation specified in article 2(a)(i) of this Order, as increased in accordance with this Order, would not but for this article be expressed as a whole number of pounds, it shall be so expressed by the rounding down of any fraction of a pound less than one half and the rounding up of any other fraction of a pound.

SCHEDULE

Article 2

Tax Year	*Percentage*
1978–79	522.3
1979–80	449.2
1980–81	358.8
1981–82	284.3
1982–83	249.0
1983–84	224.1
1984–85	200.1
1985–86	181.5
1986–87	158.5
1987–88	140.7
1988–89	121.4
1989–90	99.8
1990–91	86.2
1991–92	69.2
1992–93	58.8
1993–94	51.3
1994–95	46.7
1995–96	40.5
1996–97	36.7
1997–98	30.2

Tax Year	*Percentage*
1998–99	24.5
1999–2000	19.5
2000–2001	12.4
2001–2002	8.1
2002–2003	3.6

SOCIAL SECURITY CONTRIBUTIONS AND BENEFITS ACT 1992 (MODIFICATIONS FOR HER MAJESTY'S FORCES AND INCAPACITY BENEFIT) REGULATIONS 2003

(SI 2003/737)

Made on 14 March 2003 by the Treasury, with the concurrence of the Secretary of State, in exercise of the powers conferred on them by s. 116(2) and 175(3) and (5) of the Social Security Contributions and Benefits Act 1992, and of all other powers enabling them in that behalf. Operative from 6 April 2003 for the purposes of reg. 1 and 3, and from 5 May 2003 for all other purposes.

CITATION AND COMMENCEMENT

1 These Regulations may be cited as the Social Security Contributions and Benefits Act 1992 (Modifications for Her Majesty's Forces and Incapacity Benefit) Regulations 2003 and shall come into force for the purposes of this regulation and regulation 3 on 6th April 2003 and for all other purposes on 5th May 2003.

MODIFICATION OF SECTION 30A OF THE SOCIAL SECURITY CONTRIBUTIONS AND BENEFITS ACT 1992

2 Section 30A of the Social Security Contributions and Benefits Act 1992 (entitlement to incapacity benefit) shall be modified, in respect of persons who have been members of Her Majesty's forces, as if–

(a) at the beginning of subsection (3), there were inserted "Subject to subsection (3A),", and

(b) after subsection (3), there were inserted–

"**30A(3A)** Subsection (3) does not apply to a person–

(a) who is discharged from Her Majesty's forces, and

(b) for whom days of sickness absence from duty, which are recorded by the Secretary of State for Defence, are included in calculating the number of days for which the person has been entitled to short-term incapacity benefit.".

MODIFICATION OF SECTION 30D OF THE SOCIAL SECURITY CONTRIBUTIONS AND BENEFITS ACT 1992

3 Section 30D of the Social Security Contributions and Benefits Act 1992 (calculating days of entitlement to incapacity benefit) shall be modified, in respect of persons who have been members of Her Majesty's forces, as if, after subsection (3), there were inserted–

"**30D(3A)** In respect of a person who is discharged from Her Majesty's forces after 3rd May 2003, there shall also be included such days as may be prescribed.".

MODIFICATION OF PARAGRAPH 2(6) OF SCHEDULE 3 TO THE SOCIAL SECURITY CONTRIBUTIONS AND BENEFITS ACT 1992

4 Paragraph 2(6) of Schedule 3 to the Social Security Contributions and Benefits Act 1992 (contribution conditions for entitlement to incapacity benefit) shall be modified, in respect of persons who have been members of Her Majesty's forces, as if–

(a) after "is" in paragraph (b) (meaning of **"the relevant benefit year"**), there were inserted ", subject to paragraph (c),", and

(b) at the end, there were added–

"(c) in the case of a person who is discharged from Her Majesty's forces, and for whom days of sickness absence from duty recorded by the Secretary of State for Defence are included in calculating the number of days for which the person has been entitled to short-term incapacity benefit, "the relevant benefit year" is the benefit year in which there falls the beginning of the period to which the claim for incapacity benefit relates.".

STATUTORY PATERNITY PAY (ADOPTION) AND STATUTORY ADOPTION PAY (ADOPTIONS FROM OVERSEAS) (ADMINISTRATION) REGULATIONS 2003

(SI 2003/1192)

Made on 23 April 2003 by the Secretary of State, in exercise of the powers conferred on her by s. 7(1), (2)(a) and (b), (4)(a), (b) and (c) and (5), 8(1) and (2)(a), (b) and (c), 10(1) and (2) and 51(1) of the Employment Act 2002 and s. 8(1)(f) and 25 of the Social Security Contributions (Transfer of Functions, etc.) Act 1999 and with the concurrence of the Commissioners of Inland Revenue, hereby makes the following Regulations:

CITATION AND COMMENCEMENT

1 These Regulations may be cited as the Statutory Paternity Pay (Adoption) and Statutory Adoption Pay (Adoptions from Overseas) (Administration) Regulations 2003 and shall come into force on 23rd May 2003.

INTERPRETATION

2 In these Regulations, **"adoption from overseas"** means the adoption of a child who enters Great Britain from outside the United Kingdom in connection with or for the purposes of adoption which does not involve the placement of the child for adoption under the law of any part of the United Kingdom.

APPLICATION OF THE STATUTORY PATERNITY PAY AND STATUTORY ADOPTION PAY (ADMINISTRATION) REGULATIONS 2002 TO ADOPTIONS FROM OVERSEAS

3(1) The Statutory Paternity Pay and Statutory Adoption Pay (Administration) Regulations 2002 shall apply in the case of adoptions from overseas with the modifications set out in the following paragraphs of this regulation.

3(2) In regulation 2(1) (interpretation)–

(a) in the definition of "adopter", for the words "with whom the child is matched for adoption" substitute "by whom the child has been or is to be adopted";

(b) after the definition of "income tax quarter", insert–

""**official notification**" means written notification, issued by or on behalf of the relevant domestic authority, that it is prepared to issue a certificate to the overseas authority concerned with the adoption of the child, or has issued a certificate and sent it to that authority, confirming, in either case, that the adopter is eligible to adopt and has been assessed and approved as being a suitable adoptive parent;";

(c) in the definition of "paternity leave", insert at the end "as modified in its application to adoptions from overseas by the Employment Rights Act 1996 (Application of Section 80B to Adoptions from Overseas) Regulations 2003"; and

(d) after the definition of "paternity pay period" insert–

""**relevant domestic authority**" means–

(a) in the case of an adopter to whom the Intercountry Adoption (Hague Convention) Regulations 2003 apply and who is habitually resident in Wales, the National Assembly for Wales;

(b) in the case of an adopter to whom the Intercountry Adoption (Hague Convention) (Scotland) Regulations 2003 apply and who is habitually resident in Scotland, the Scottish Ministers; and

(c) in any other case, the Secretary of State;".

3(3) After regulation 2(2), insert–

"**2(3)** References in these Regulations to provisions of Parts 12ZA and 12ZB of the Contributions and Benefits Act are to be construed as references to those provisions as modified by the Social Security Contributions and Benefits Act 1992 (Application of Parts 12ZA and 12ZB to Adoptions from Overseas) Regulations 2003."

3(4) In regulation 11(3)(b)(ii) (time within which an employer is required to give decision that he has no liability to make payments), for "the end of the seven-day period that starts on the date on which the adopter is notified of having been matched with the child" substitute "the date on which the employee's evidence was provided, or, where not all of the evidence referred to in paragraph (1) was provided on one date, the date on which the last of the evidence was provided".

3(5) Omit regulation 11(4).

STATUTORY PATERNITY PAY (ADOPTION) AND STATUTORY ADOPTION PAY (ADOPTIONS FROM OVERSEAS) (NO. 2) REGULATION 2003

(SI 2003/1194, as amended by SI 2004/488 and SI 2005/2114)

Made on 29 April 2003, by the Secretary of State, in exercise of the powers conferred on her by s. 171ZB(2)(a), 171ZC(3)(a)–(d), (f) and (g), 171ZD(2) and (3), 171ZE(2)(a) and (b)(i), (3)(b), (7) and (8), 171ZG(3), 171ZJ(1), (3), (4), (7) and (8), 171ZL(8)(b)–(d), (f) and (g), 171ZM(2) and (3), 171ZN(2), (5) and (6), 171ZP(6), 171ZS(1), (3), (4), (7) and (8), and 175(4) of the Social Security Contributions and Benefits Act 1992, s. 5(1)(g), (i) and (p) of the Social Security Administration Act 1992 and with the concurrence of the Commissioners of Inland Revenue in so far as such concurrence is required, by this instrument, which contains only provision made by virtue of s. 2, 4 and 53 of and para. 8 and 11 of Sch. 7 to the Employment Act 2002 and is made before the end of the period of 6 months from the coming into force of these enactments, hereby makes the following Regulation. Operative from 30 May 2003

GENERAL

CITATION AND COMMENCEMENT

1 These Regulations may be cited as the Statutory Paternity Pay (Adoption) and Statutory Adoption Pay (Adoptions from Overseas) (No. 2) Regulations 2003 and shall come into force on 30th May 2003.

INTERPRETATION AND SCOPE

2(1) In these Regulations–

"the Act" means the Social Security Contributions and Benefits Act 1992;

"adopter", in relation to a child, means a person by whom the child has been or is to be adopted;

"adoption from overseas" means the adoption of a child who enters Great Britain from outside the United Kingdom in connection with or for the purposes of adoption which does not involve the placement of the child for adoption under the law of any part of the United Kingdom;

"the Application Regulations" means the Social Security Contributions and Benefits Act 1992 (Application of Parts 12ZA and 12ZB to Adoptions from Overseas) Regulations 2003;

"the Board" means the Commissioners of Inland Revenue;

"enter Great Britain" means enter Great Britain from outside the United Kingdom in connection with or for the purposes of adoption, and cognate expressions shall be construed accordingly;

"the General Regulations" means the Statutory Paternity Pay and Statutory Adoption Pay (General) Regulations 2002;

"official notification" means written notification, issued by or on behalf of the relevant domestic authority, that it is prepared to issue a certificate to the overseas authority concerned with the adoption of the child, or has issued a certificate and sent it to that authority, confirming, in either case, that the adopter is eligible to adopt, and has been assessed and approved as being a suitable adoptive parent;

"relevant domestic authority" means–

(a) in the case of an adopter to whom the Intercountry Adoption (Hague Convention) Regulations 2003 apply and who is habitually resident in Wales, the National Assembly for Wales;

(b) in the case of an adopter to whom the Intercountry Adoption (Hague Convention) (Scotland) Regulations apply and who is habitually resident in Scotland, the Scottish Ministers;

(c) in any other case, the Secretary of State;

"statutory paternity pay (adoption)" means statutory paternity pay payable in accordance with the provisions of Part 12ZA of the Act, as modified by the Application Regulations, where the conditions specified in section 171ZB(2) of the Act, as modified by the Application Regulations, are satisfied.

2(2) References in these Regulations to the provisions of Parts 12ZA and 12ZB of the Act are to be construed as references to those provisions as modified by the Application Regulations.

2(3) These Regulations apply to statutory paternity pay (adoption) and statutory adoption pay in respect of adoptions from overseas.

APPLICATION OF THE GENERAL REGULATIONS TO THESE REGULATIONS

3(1) Subject to paragraph (2), the provisions of the General Regulations mentioned in paragraph (3) shall, in so far as they apply to statutory paternity pay (adoption) and statutory adoption pay, apply to adoptions from overseas.

3(2) Any references to the provisions of Parts 12ZA or 12ZB of the Act in the regulations of the General Regulations mentioned in paragraph (3) shall be construed as references to those provisions as modified by the Application Regulations.

3(3) The provisions of the General Regulations referred to in paragraph (1) are regulations 17 to 19, 26 to 28, 31 to 39, 41 to 47 and, subject to paragraph (4), regulation 40.

3(4) In the General Regulations, the provisions of regulation 40 shall apply as if–

(a) in paragraph (2)(b), for "the week in which the adopter is notified of being matched with the child for the purposes of adoption" there were substituted–

"(b) the week in which–

(i) official notification is sent to the adopter or

(ii) the person satisfies the condition in section 171ZB(2)(b) or 171ZL(2)(b) of the Act (26 weeks' continuous employment),

whichever is the later";

(b) at the end of paragraph (2), there were added "**"official notification"** has the same meaning as in the Statutory Paternity Pay (Adoption) and Statutory Adoption Pay (Adoptions from Overseas) (No. 2) Regulations 2003".

History – Reg. 3(4)(a) substituted by SI 2004/488, reg. 4, with effect from 6 April 2004.

APPLICATION

4(1) Subject to the provisions of Part 12ZA of the Act (statutory paternity pay), the provisions of the General Regulations mentioned in paragraph (3) of regulation 3 and these Regulations, there is entitlement to statutory paternity pay (adoption) in respect of children who enter Great Britain on or after 6th April 2003.

4(2) Subject to the provisions of Part 12ZB of the Act (statutory adoption pay), the provisions of the General Regulations mentioned in paragraph (3) of regulation 3 and these Regulations, there is entitlement to statutory adoption pay in respect of children who enter Great Britain on or after 6th April 2003.

STATUTORY PATERNITY PAY (ADOPTION)

CONDITIONS OF ENTITLEMENT TO STATUTORY PATERNITY PAY (ADOPTION) IN RESPECT OF ADOPTIONS FROM OVERSEAS: RELATIONSHIP WITH CHILD AND WITH ADOPTER

5(1) The conditions prescribed under section 171ZB(2)(a) of the Act are that a person–

(a) is married to, the civil partner or the partner of a child's adopter (or in a case where there are two adopters, married to, the civil partner or the partner of the other adopter), and

(b) has, or expects to have, the main responsibility (apart from the responsibility of the child's adopter or, in a case where there are two adopters, together with the other adopter) for the upbringing of the child.

5(2) For the purposes of paragraph (1), **"partner"** means a person (whether of a different sex or the same sex) who lives with the adopter and the child in an enduring family relationship but is not a relative of the adopter of a kind specified in paragraph (3).

5(3) The relatives of a child's adopter referred to in the definition of "partner" in paragraph (2) are the adopter's parent, grandparent, sister, brother, aunt or uncle.

5(4) References to relationships in paragraph (3)–

(a) are to relationships of the full blood or half blood or, in the case of an adopted person, such of those relationships as would exist but for the adoption, and

(b) include the relationship of a child with his adoptive, or former adoptive parents but do not include any other adoptive relationships.

History – In reg. 5(1)(a) words ", the civil partner" inserted twice by SI 2005/2114, art. 2(17), Sch. 17, para. 6, with effect from 5 December 2005.

PERIOD OF PAYMENT OF STATUTORY PATERNITY PAY (ADOPTION) IN RESPECT OF ADOPTIONS FROM OVERSEAS

6(1) Subject to notice under section 171ZC(1) of the Act, paragraph (2) and regulation 8, a person entitled to statutory paternity pay (adoption) may choose the statutory paternity pay period to begin on–

(a) the date on which the child enters Great Britain or, where the person is at work on that day, the following day; or

(b) a predetermined date, specified by the person, which is later than the date on which the child enters Great Britain.

6(2) In a case where statutory paternity pay (adoption) is payable in respect of a child where the adopter has received official notification before 6th April 2003, the statutory paternity pay period shall begin on a predetermined date, later than the date of entry, specified by the person entitled to such pay in a notice under section 171ZC(1) of the Act, which is at least 28 days after the date on which that notice was given, unless the person liable to pay statutory paternity pay (adoption) agrees to the period beginning earlier.

6(3) A person may choose for statutory paternity pay (adoption) to be paid in respect of a period of a week.

6(4) A choice made in accordance with paragraph (1) is not irrevocable, but where a person subsequently makes a different choice in relation to the beginning of the statutory paternity pay period, section 171ZC(1) of the Act shall apply to it.

ADDITIONAL NOTICE REQUIREMENTS FOR STATUTORY PATERNITY PAY (ADOPTION) IN RESPECT OF ADOPTIONS FROM OVERSEAS

7(1) Where a person gives notice under section 171ZC(1) of the Act he shall give further notice of the following matters to the person liable to pay him statutory paternity pay (adoption)–

(a) the date on which official notification was received, within 28 days of that date, or within 28 days of his completion of 26 weeks of continuous employment with that person, whichever is the later;

(b) the date on which the child enters Great Britain, within 28 days of entry.

7(2) Where the child has not entered Great Britain on the expected date, the person shall, if he wishes to claim statutory paternity pay (adoption), give notice to the person liable to pay it, as soon as is reasonably practicable, that the period in respect of which statutory paternity pay is to be paid shall begin on a date different from that originally chosen by him.

7(3) That date may be any date chosen in accordance with paragraph (1) of regulation 6 or specified in accordance with paragraph (2) of that regulation.

7(4) Where it becomes known to that person that the child will not enter Great Britain, he shall notify the person who would have been liable to pay statutory pay (adoption), as soon as is reasonably practicable.

QUALIFYING PERIOD FOR STATUTORY PATERNITY PAY (ADOPTION) IN RESPECT OF ADOPTIONS FROM OVERSEAS

8 The qualifying period for the purposes of section 171ZE(2) of the Act (period within which the statutory pay period must occur) is a period of 56 days beginning with the date the child enters Great Britain.

EVIDENCE OF ENTITLEMENT FOR STATUTORY PATERNITY PAY (ADOPTION) IN RESPECT OF ADOPTIONS FROM OVERSEAS

9(1) A person shall produce evidence of his entitlement to statutory paternity pay (adoption) in respect of adoptions from overseas by providing in writing to the person who will be liable to pay him statutory paternity pay (adoption) the declarations specified in paragraph (2) and the information specified in paragraph (3).

9(2) The declarations referred to in paragraph (1) are as follows–

(a) that he meets the conditions prescribed under section 171ZB(2)(a) of the Act and that it is not the case that statutory paternity pay (adoption) is not payable to him by virtue of the provisions of section 171ZE(4) of the Act;

(b) that he has elected to receive statutory paternity pay (adoption), and not statutory adoption pay under Part 12ZB of the Act;

(c) that official notification has been received.

9(3) The information referred to in paragraph (1) is as follows–

(a) the name of the person claiming statutory paternity pay (adoption);

(b) the date on which it is expected that the child will enter Great Britain or, where the child has already entered Great Britain, that date;

(c) the date from which it is expected that the liability to pay statutory paternity pay (adoption) will begin;

(d) whether the period chosen in respect of which statutory paternity pay (adoption) is to be payable is a week.

9(4) The declarations mentioned in paragraph (2) and information mentioned in paragraph (3) shall be provided to the person liable to pay statutory paternity pay (adoption) at least 28 days before the date mentioned in sub-paragraph (c) of paragraph (3) or, if that is not reasonably practicable, as soon as is reasonably practicable thereafter.

ENTITLEMENT TO STATUTORY PATERNITY PAY (ADOPTION) WHERE THERE IS MORE THAN ONE EMPLOYER IN RESPECT OF ADOPTIONS FROM OVERSEAS

10 Statutory paternity pay (adoption) shall be payable to a person in respect of a statutory pay week during any part of which he works only for an employer–

(a) who is not liable to pay him statutory paternity pay (adoption); and

(b) for whom he has worked in the week in which the adopter receives official notification.

AVOIDANCE OF LIABILITY FOR STATUTORY PATERNITY PAY (ADOPTION) IN RESPECT OF ADOPTIONS FROM OVERSEAS

11(1) A former employer shall be liable to make payments of statutory paternity pay (adoption) to a former employee in any case where the employee has been employed for a continuous period of at least 8 weeks and his contract of service was brought to an end by the former employer solely, or mainly, for the purpose of avoiding liability for statutory paternity pay (adoption).

11(2) In a case falling within paragraph (1)–

(a) the employee shall be treated as if he had been employed for a continuous period ending with the day the child enters Great Britain;

(b) his normal weekly earnings shall be calculated by reference to his normal weekly earnings for the period of 8 weeks ending with the last day in respect of which he was paid under his former contract of service.

STATUTORY ADOPTION PAY

ADOPTION PAY PERIOD IN RESPECT OF ADOPTIONS FROM OVERSEAS

12(1) Subject to paragraph (2), a person entitled to statutory adoption pay may choose the adoption pay period to begin–

(a) on the date on which the child enters Great Britain or, where the person is at work on that day, on the following day;

(b) on the predetermined date, specified by him, which is no later than 28 days after the date the child enters Great Britain.

12(2) In a case where statutory adoption pay is payable in respect of a child where the adopter has received official notification before 6th April 2003, the statutory adoption pay period shall begin on a predetermined date, later than the date of entry, specified by the person entitled to such pay in a notice under section 171ZL(6) of the Act, which is at least 28 days after the date on which that notice was given, unless the person liable to pay statutory adoption pay agrees to the period commencing earlier.

12(3) Where the choice made is that mentioned in sub-paragraph (b) of paragraph (1) or in a case where paragraph (2) applies, the adoption pay period shall, unless the employer agrees to the adoption pay period beginning earlier, begin no earlier than 28 days after notice under section 171ZL(6) of the Act has been given.

12(4) Subject to regulation 13, the duration of any adoption pay period shall be a continuous period of 26 weeks.

12(5) A choice made under paragraph (1), or a date specified under paragraph (2), is not irrevocable, but where a person subsequently makes a different choice or specifies a different date in relation to the beginning of the statutory adoption pay period, section 171ZL(6) of the Act shall apply to it.

ADOPTION PAY PERIOD IN RESPECT OF ADOPTIONS FROM OVERSEAS WHERE ADOPTION IS DISRUPTED

13(1) Where after a child enters Great Britain the child–

(a) dies; or

(b) ceases to live with the adopter,

the adoption pay period shall terminate in accordance with the provisions of paragraph (2).

13(2) The adoption pay period shall, in a case falling within paragraph (1), terminate 8 weeks after the end of the week specified in paragraph (3).

13(3) The week referred to in paragraph (2) is–

(a) in a case falling within paragraph (1)(a), the week during which the child dies;

(b) in a case falling within paragraph (1)(b), the week during which the child ceases to live with the adopter.

13(4) For the purposes of paragraph (3), **"week"** means a period of seven days beginning with Sunday.

ADDITIONAL NOTICE REQUIREMENTS FOR STATUTORY ADOPTION PAY IN RESPECT OF ADOPTIONS FROM OVERSEAS

14(1) Where a person gives notice under section 171ZL(6) of the Act he shall give further notice of the following matters to the person liable to pay statutory adoption pay–

(a) the date on which official notification was received, within 28 days of that date, or within 28 days of his completion of 26 weeks of continuous employment, whichever is the later;

(b) the date on which the child enters Great Britain, within 28 days of entry.

14(2) Where the child has not entered Great Britain on the expected date, the person shall, if he wishes to claim statutory adoption pay, give notice to the person liable to pay it, as soon as is reasonably practicable, that the period in respect of which statutory adoption pay is to be paid shall begin on a date different from that originally chosen by him.

14(3) That date may be any date chosen in accordance with paragraph (1) of regulation 12 or specified in accordance with paragraph (2) of that regulation.

14(4) Where it becomes known to the adopter that the child will not enter Great Britain, he shall notify the person who would have been liable to pay statutory adoption pay as soon as is reasonably practicable.

EVIDENCE OF ENTITLEMENT TO STATUTORY ADOPTION PAY IN RESPECT OF ADOPTIONS FROM OVERSEAS

15(1) A person shall provide evidence of his entitlement to statutory adoption pay by providing, to the person who will be liable to pay it, a copy of the official notification and, in writing–

(a) the information specified in paragraph (2);

(b) a declaration that he has elected to receive statutory adoption pay, and not statutory paternity pay (adoption) under Part 12ZA of the Act;

(c) evidence, to be provided within 28 days of the child's entry into Great Britain, as to that date.

15(2) The information referred to in paragraph (1) is–

(a) the name and address of the person claiming statutory adoption pay;

(b) the date on which it is expected that the child will enter Great Britain or, where he has already done so, the date of entry.

15(3) The information and declaration referred to in paragraph (1) shall be provided to the person liable to pay statutory adoption pay at least 28 days before the date chosen as the beginning of the adoption pay period in accordance with paragraph (1) of regulation 12 or specified in accordance with paragraph (2) of that regulation or, if that is not reasonably practicable, as soon as is reasonably practicable thereafter.

ENTITLEMENT TO STATUTORY ADOPTION PAY IN RESPECT OF ADOPTIONS FROM OVERSEAS WHERE THERE IS MORE THAN ONE EMPLOYER

16 Statutory adoption pay shall be payable to a person in respect of a week during any part of which he works for an employer–

(a) who is not liable to pay him statutory adoption pay and

(b) for whom he has worked in the week in which he receives official notification.

TERMINATION OF EMPLOYMENT AND LIABILITY TO PAY STATUTORY ADOPTION PAY IN RESPECT OF ADOPTIONS FROM OVERSEAS

17(1) Where the employment of a person who satisfies the conditions of entitlement to statutory adoption pay in respect of adoptions from overseas terminates for whatever reason (including dismissal) before the adoption pay period chosen or specified by that person in accordance with regulation 12 has begun, the period shall begin on a date chosen by that person which is at least 28 days after notice has been given and within 28 days of the date of the child's entry into Great Britain.

17(2) Where the statutory adoption pay period has not commenced within a period of 6 months of the adopter's leaving his employer, liability to pay statutory adoption pay shall, notwithstanding section 171ZM(1) of the Act, pass to the Board.

17(3) Where liability to pay statutory adoption pay has passed to the Board in accordance with paragraph (2) and the adopter, having started employment as an employed earner, becomes entitled to statutory adoption pay by virtue of that employment, the liability of the Board shall cease and section 171ZM(1) of the Act shall apply.

AVOIDANCE OF LIABILITY FOR STATUTORY ADOPTION PAY IN RESPECT OF ADOPTIONS FROM OVERSEAS

18(1) A former employer shall be liable to make payments of statutory adoption pay to a former employee in any case where the employee had been employed for a continuous period of at least 8 weeks and his contract of service was brought to an end by the former employer solely, or mainly, for the purpose of avoiding liability for statutory adoption pay.

18(2) In a case falling within paragraph (1)–

(a) the employee shall be treated as if he had been employed for a continuous period ending with the week in which he received official notification; and

(b) his normal weekly earnings shall be calculated by reference to his normal weekly earnings for the period of 8 weeks ending with the last day in respect of which he was paid under his former contract of service.

REVOCATION

19 The Statutory Paternity Pay (Adoption) and Statutory Adoption Pay (Adoptions from Overseas) Regulations 2003 are hereby revoked.

SOCIAL SECURITY CONTRIBUTIONS AND BENEFITS ACT 1992 (MODIFICATION OF SECTION 4A) ORDER 2003

(SI 2003/1874)

Made on 17 July 2003 by the Treasury, with the concurrence of the Secretary of State, in exercise of the powers conferred upon them by s. 4A(9) of the Social Security Contributions and Benefits Act 1992. Operative from 8 August 2003.

CITATION AND COMMENCEMENT

1 This Order may be cited as the Social Security Contributions and Benefits Act 1992 (Modification of Section 4A) Order 2003 and shall come into force on 8th August 2003.

MODIFICATION OF THE SOCIAL SECURITY CONTRIBUTIONS AND BENEFITS ACT 1992

2 Section 4A of Part 1 of the Social Security Contributions and Benefits Act 1992 is modified as follows.

3 In subsection (1)(a) for "for the purposes of a business carried on by another person" substitute "for another person".

4 In consequence of the above modification omit the definition of "business" in subsection (6).

SOCIAL SECURITY CONTRIBUTIONS (INTERMEDIARIES) (AMENDMENT) REGULATIONS 2003

(SI 2003/2079)

Made on 11 August 2003 by the Treasury, with the concurrence of the Secretary of State, in exercise of the powers conferred upon them by s. 4A and 175(3) and (4) of the Social Security Contributions and Benefits Act 1992. Operative from 1 September 2003.

CITATION, COMMENCEMENT AND EFFECT

1(1) These Regulations may be cited as the Social Security Contributions (Intermediaries) (Amendment) Regulations 2003 and shall come into force on 1st September 2003.

1(2) These Regulations have effect for the tax year 2003–04 and subsequent years and apply in relation to services performed or due to be performed on or after 1st September 2003.

INTERPRETATION

2 In these Regulations–

"the principal Regulations" means the Social Security Contributions (Intermediaries) Regulations 2000;

"intermediary" has the meaning given in regulation 5 of the principal Regulations;

"worker" has the meaning given in regulation 6(1)(a) of the principal Regulations.

Notes – The principal Regulations are the Social Security Contributions (Intermediaries) Regulations 2000 (SI 2000/727).

AMENDMENT OF THE PRINCIPAL REGULATIONS

3 [Amends SI 2000/727 as follows.]

4 [Amends SI 2000/727, reg. 2(1).]

5 [Amends SI 2000/727, reg. 6(1)(a); "for another person".]

6(1) [Amends SI 2000/727, reg. 7 as follows.]

6(2) [Amends SI 2000/727, reg. 7(1).]

6(3) [Amends SI 2000/727, reg. 7(5).]

6(4) [Amends SI 2000/727, reg. 7(8)(b).]

6(5) [Amends SI 2000/727, reg. 7(10).]

TRANSITIONAL PROVISION

7(1) This regulation applies for the purposes of the tax year 2003–04 ("the relevant year") in the case of a worker to whom the principal Regulations apply only by virtue of the amendment made by regulation 5 of these Regulations.

7(2) For the purposes of the relevant year regulation 7(1) of the principal Regulations shall have effect as if–

(a) for "a tax year" there were substituted "the relevant period";

(b) for each of the references to "in that year" there were substituted "in that period";

(c) in Step Six for "for that year" there were substituted "for the relevant period"; and

(d) at the end there were added–

"In this paragraph **"the relevant period"** means the period beginning with 1st September 2003 and ending with 5th April 2004.".

7(3) Paragraph (4) applies for the purpose of the relevant year in the case of a worker who is not a director of the intermediary through which services are provided under the arrangements.

7(4) Where this paragraph applies, regulation 8(2) of the principal Regulations shall have effect as if–

(a) for "the year concerned" there were substituted "the relevant period";

(b) for "during that year" there were substituted "during that period"; and

(c) at the end there were added–

"In this paragraph "the relevant period" has the same meaning as in regulation 7(1).".

Notes – The principal Regulations are the Social Security Contributions (Intermediaries) Regulations 2000 (SI 2000/727).

SOCIAL SECURITY REVALUATION OF EARNINGS FACTORS ORDER 2006

(SI 2006/496)

Made on 27 February 2006 by the Secretary of State in exercise of the powers conferred upon him by s. 148(3) and (4) and 189(1), (4) and (5) of the Social Security Administration Act 1992. Operative from 6 April 2006.

CITATION AND COMMENCEMENT

1 This Order may be cited as the Social Security Revaluation of Earnings Factors Order 2006 and shall come into force on 6th April 2006.

REVALUATION OF EARNINGS FACTORS

2 The earnings factors for tax years specified in the Schedule to this Order in so far as they are relevant–

(a) to the calculation–

(i) of the additional pension in the rate of any long-term benefit; or

(ii) of any guaranteed minimum pension; or

(b) to any other calculation required under Part III of the Pension Schemes Act 1993 (including that Part as modified by or under any other enactment),

are directed to be increased for those tax years by the percentage of their amount shown opposite those tax years in that Schedule.

ROUNDING OF FRACTIONAL AMOUNTS

3 Where any earnings factor relevant to the calculation specified in article 2(a)(i) of this Order, as increased in accordance with this Order, would not but for this article be expressed as a whole number of pounds, it shall be so expressed by the rounding down of any fraction of a pound less than one half and the rounding up of any other fraction of a pound.

SCHEDULE

Article 2

Tax Year	*Percentage*
1978–79	595.3
1979–80	513.7
1980–81	412.7
1981–82	329.4
1982–83	290.0
1983–84	262.1
1984–85	235.3
1985–86	214.5
1986–87	188.8
1987–88	168.9
1988–89	147.4
1989–90	123.3
1990–91	108.1
1991–92	89.0
1992–93	77.5
1993–94	69.0
1994–95	63.9
1995–96	57.0
1996–97	52.7
1997–98	45.5
1998–99	39.1

Tax Year	*Percentage*
1999–2000	33.5
2000–2001	25.6
2001–2002	20.7
2002–2003	15.8
2003–2004	11.7
2004–2005	7.6
2005–2006	3.4

SOCIAL SECURITY (REDUCED RATES OF CLASS 1 CONTRIBUTIONS, REBATES AND MINIMUM CONTRIBUTIONS) ORDER 2006

(SI 2006/1009 as amended by SI 2009/3094)

Made on 30 March 2006 by the Secretary of State for Work and Pensions in exercise of the powers conferred by s. 42, 42B, 45A and 182(2) of the Pension Schemes Act 1993 and s. 38(1), 38B and 41A of the Pension Schemes (Northern Ireland) Act 1993. Operative from 6 April 2007.

CITATION, COMMENCEMENT, INTERPRETATION AND EXTENT

1(1) This Order may be cited as the Social Security (Reduced Rates of Class 1 Contributions, Rebates and Minimum Contributions) Order 2006 and shall come into force on 6th April 2007.

1(2) In this Order–

"the 1993 Act" means the Pension Schemes Act 1993;

"the Northern Ireland Act" means the Pension Schemes (Northern Ireland) Act 1993;

"the low earnings threshold", in relation to a tax year, means the low earnings threshold for that tax year as specified in–

(a) section 44A of the Social Security Contributions and Benefits Act 1992 (deemed earnings factors); or

(b) in relation to Northern Ireland, section 44A(5) of the Social Security Contributions and Benefits (Northern Ireland) Act 1992 (deemed earnings factors);

"qualifying earnings factor", in relation to a tax year, has the same meaning as in–

(a) section 122(1) of the Social Security Contributions and Benefits Act 1992 (interpretation); or

(b) in relation to Northern Ireland, section 121(1) of the Social Security Contributions and Benefits (Northern Ireland) Act 1992 (interpretation);

"the upper earnings threshold" means 3LET minus 2QEF, where–

(a) 3LET means the amount produced by multiplying the low earnings threshold by 3; and

(b) 2QEF means the amount produced by doubling the qualifying earnings factor and rounding the resulting figure to the nearest whole £100 (taking any amount of £50 as nearest to the previous whole £100);

"relevant tax year" means any of the following tax years–

(a) 2007–2008;

(b) 2008–2009;

(c) 2009–2010;

(d) 2010–2011;

(e) 2011–2012.

1(3) These provisions of this Order extend to England and Wales and Scotland–

(a) articles 2 to 4;

(b) this article, and the Schedules, so far as they relate to articles 2 to 4.

1(4) These provisions of this Order extend to Northern Ireland–

(a) articles 5 to 7;

(b) this article, and the Schedules, so far as they relate to articles 5 to 7.

ALTERATION OF REDUCED RATES OF SECONDARY CLASS 1 CONTRIBUTIONS FOR SALARY RELATED CONTRACTEDOUT SCHEMES

2 In section 41(1B) of the 1993 Act (reduced rates of secondary Class 1 contributions in contracted-out employment) for "3.5 per cent" substitute "3.7 per cent".

REDUCED RATES OF CLASS 1 CONTRIBUTIONS AND REBATES FOR MONEY PURCHASE CONTRACTED-OUT SCHEMES

3(1) This article applies for the purposes of section 42A of the 1993 Act (reduced rates of Class 1 contributions, and rebates).

3(2) For the purposes of section 42A(2) of the 1993 Act (reduction of primary Class 1 contributions), the appropriate flat-rate percentage for each of the relevant tax years is 1.6 per cent.

3(3) For the purposes of section 42A(2A) of the 1993 Act (reduction of secondary Class 1 contributions), the appropriate flat-rate percentage for each of the relevant tax years is 1.4 per cent.

3(4) For the purposes of section 42A(3) of the 1993 Act (appropriate age-related percentage), the appropriate age-related percentage in respect of an earner for a relevant tax year is the percentage given in the table in Schedule 1 by reference to–

(a) that tax year, and

(b) the age of the earner on the day immediately before the start of that tax year.

APPROPRIATE AGE-RELATED PERCENTAGES FOR APPROPRIATE PERSONAL PENSION SCHEMES

4(1) This article applies for the purposes of section 45(1) of the 1993 Act (amount of minimum contributions).

4(2) For the tax years 2007–2008, 2008–2009 and 2009–2010, the appropriate age-related percentage in respect of earnings of an earner is determined in accordance with paragraph (3), (4) or (5).

4(3) If the earnings do not exceed the low earnings threshold, the appropriate age-related percentage is the column B percentage.

4(4) If the earnings exceed the low earnings threshold, but do not exceed the upper earnings threshold, then–

(a) in respect of the part of the earnings that does not exceed the low earnings threshold, the appropriate age-related percentage is the column B percentage;

(b) in respect of the part of the earnings that exceeds the low earnings threshold, the appropriate age-related percentage is the column C percentage.

4(5) If the earnings exceed the low earnings threshold and the upper earnings threshold, then–

(a) in respect of the part of the earnings that does not exceed the low earnings threshold, the appropriate age-related percentage is the column B percentage;

(b) in respect of the part of the earnings that exceeds the low earnings threshold but does not exceed the upper earnings threshold, the appropriate age-related percentage is the column C percentage; and

(c) in respect of the part of the earnings that exceeds the upper earnings threshold, the appropriate age-related percentage is the column D percentage.

4(5A) For the tax years 2010–2011 and 2011–2012, the appropriate age-related percentage in respect of earnings of an earner is determined in accordance with paragraph (5B) or (5C).

4(5B) If the earnings do not exceed the low earnings threshold, the appropriate age-related percentage is the column B percentage.

4(5C) If the earnings exceed the low earnings threshold, then–

(a) in respect of the part of the earnings that does not exceed the low earnings threshold, the appropriate age-related percentage is the column B percentage; and

(b) in respect of the part of the earnings that exceeds the low earnings threshold, the appropriate age-related percentage is the column C percentage.

4(6) For a relevant tax year, in respect of earnings of an earner–

(a) the column B percentage is the percentage given in column B of the appropriate table by reference to the age of the earner on the day immediately before the start of that tax year;

(b) the column C percentage is the percentage given in column C of the appropriate table by reference to the age of the earner on the day immediately before the start of that tax year;

(c) [omitted by SI 2009/3094, art. 2(4).]

4(6A) For the tax years 2007–2008, 2008–2009 and 2009–2010, in respect of earnings of an earner, the column D percentage is the percentage given in column D of the appropriate table by reference to the age of the earner on the day immediately before the start of that tax year.

4(7) The appropriate table is the table in–

(a) Schedule 2, if the relevant tax year is 2007–2008;

(b) Schedule 3, if the relevant tax year is 2008–2009;

(c) Schedule 4, if the relevant tax year is 2009–2010;

(d) Schedule 5, if the relevant tax year is 2010–2011;

(e) Schedule 6, if the relevant tax year is 2011–2012.

History – In reg. 4(2) the words "the tax years 2007–2008, 2008–2009 and 2009–2010" substituted by SI 2009/3094, art. 2(2), with effect from 6 April 2010.

Reg. 4(5A) inserted by SI 2009/3094, art. 2(3), with effect from 6 April 2010.

Reg. 4(5B) inserted by SI 2009/3094, art. 2(3), with effect from 6 April 2010.

Reg. 4(5C) inserted by SI 2009/3094, art. 2(3), with effect from 6 April 2010.
Reg. 4(6)(c) omitted by SI 2009/3094, art. 2(4), with effect from 6 April 2010.
Reg. 4(6A) inserted by SI 2009/3094, art. 2(5), with effect from 6 April 2010.

ALTERATION OF REDUCED RATES OF SECONDARY CLASS 1 CONTRIBUTIONS FOR SALARY RELATED CONTRACTED-OUT SCHEMES

5 In section 37(1B) of the Northern Ireland Act (reduced rates of secondary Class 1 contributions) for "3.5 per cent" substitute "3.7 per cent".

REDUCED RATES OF CLASS 1 CONTRIBUTIONS AND REBATES FOR MONEY PURCHASE CONTRACTED-OUT SCHEMES

6(1) This article applies for the purposes of section 38A of the Northern Ireland Act (reduced rates of Class 1 contributions, and rebates in contracted-out employment).

6(2) For the purposes of section 38A(2) of the Northern Ireland Act (reduction of primary Class 1 contributions), the appropriate flat-rate percentage for each of the relevant tax years is 1.6 per cent.

6(3) For the purposes of section 38A(2A) of the Northern Ireland Act (reduction of secondary Class 1 contributions), the appropriate flat-rate percentage for each of the relevant tax years is 1.4 per cent.

6(4) For the purposes of section 38A(3) of the Northern Ireland Act (appropriate age-related percentage), the appropriate age-related percentage in respect of an earner for a relevant tax year is the percentage given in the table in Schedule 1 by reference to–

(a) that tax year, and

(b) the age of the earner on the day immediately before the start of that tax year.

APPROPRIATE AGE-RELATED PERCENTAGES FOR APPROPRIATE PERSONAL PENSION SCHEMES

7(1) This article applies for the purposes of section 41(1) of the Northern Ireland Act(c) (amount of minimum contributions).

7(2) For a relevant tax year, the appropriate age-related percentage in respect of earnings of an earner is determined in accordance with paragraph (3), (4) or (5).

7(3) If the earnings do not exceed the low earnings threshold, the appropriate age-related percentage is the column B percentage;

7(4) If the earnings exceed the low earnings threshold, but do not exceed the upper earnings threshold, then–

(a) in respect of the part of the earnings that does not exceed the low earnings threshold, the appropriate age-related percentage is the column B percentage;

(b) in respect of the part of the earnings that exceeds the low earnings threshold, the appropriate age-related percentage is the column C percentage.

7(5) If the earnings exceed the low earnings threshold and the upper earnings threshold, then–

(a) in respect of the part of the earnings that does not exceed the low earnings threshold, the appropriate age-related percentage is the column B percentage;

(b) in respect of the part of the earnings that exceeds the low earnings threshold but does not exceed the upper earnings threshold, the appropriate age-related percentage is the column C percentage; and

(c) in respect of the part of the earnings that exceeds the upper earnings threshold, the appropriate age-related percentage is the column D percentage.

7(6) For a relevant tax year, in respect of earnings of an earner–

(a) the column B percentage is the percentage given in column B of the appropriate table by reference to the age of the earner on the day immediately before the start of that tax year;

(b) the column C percentage is the percentage given in column C of the appropriate table by reference to the age of the earner on the day immediately before the start of that tax year;

(c) the column D percentage is the percentage given in column D of the appropriate table by reference to the age of the earner on the day immediately before the start of that tax year.

7(7) The appropriate table is the table in–

(a) Schedule 2, if the relevant tax year is 2007–2008;

(b) Schedule 3, if the relevant tax year is 2008–2009;

(c) Schedule 4, if the relevant tax year is 2009–2010;

(d) Schedule 5, if the relevant tax year is 2010–2011;

(e) Schedule 6, if the relevant tax year is 2011–2012.

SCHEDULE 1

Articles 3(4) and 6(4)

APPROPRIATE AGE-RELATED PERCENTAGES FOR MONEY PURCHASE CONTRACTED-OUT SCHEMES

Age on last day of preceding tax year	*Appropriate age-related percentages for the tax year*				
	2007–2008	2008–2009	2009–2010	2010–2011	2011–2012
15	3.0%	3.0%	3.0%	3.0%	3.0%
16	3.0%	3.0%	3.0%	3.0%	3.0%
17	3.1%	3.1%	3.1%	3.1%	3.1%
18	3.2%	3.2%	3.2%	3.2%	3.2%
19	3.3%	3.3%	3.3%	3.3%	3.3%
20	3.4%	3.4%	3.4%	3.4%	3.4%
21	3.4%	3.4%	3.4%	3.4%	3.4%
22	3.5%	3.5%	3.5%	3.5%	3.5%
23	3.6%	3.6%	3.6%	3.6%	3.6%
24	3.7%	3.7%	3.7%	3.7%	3.7%
25	3.8%	3.8%	3.8%	3.8%	3.8%
26	3.9%	3.9%	3.9%	3.9%	3.9%
27	4.0%	4.0%	4.0%	4.0%	4.0%
28	4.1%	4.1%	4.1%	4.1%	4.1%
29	4.1%	4.2%	4.2%	4.2%	4.2%
30	4.2%	4.3%	4.3%	4.3%	4.3%
31	4.3%	4.4%	4.4%	4.4%	4.4%
32	4.5%	4.5%	4.5%	4.5%	4.5%
33	4.6%	4.6%	4.6%	4.6%	4.6%
34	4.7%	4.7%	4.7%	4.7%	4.7%
35	4.8%	4.8%	4.8%	4.8%	4.8%
36	5.0%	5.0%	5.0%	5.0%	5.0%
37	5.1%	5.1%	5.1%	5.1%	5.2%
38	5.3%	5.3%	5.3%	5.3%	5.3%
39	5.5%	5.5%	5.5%	5.5%	5.5%
40	5.6%	5.6%	5.6%	5.6%	5.6%
41	5.8%	5.8%	5.8%	5.8%	5.8%
42	5.9%	5.9%	6.0%	6.0%	6.0%
43	6.1%	6.1%	6.1%	6.1%	6.1%
44	6.3%	6.3%	6.3%	6.3%	6.3%
45	6.6%	6.4%	6.4%	6.5%	6.5%
46	6.9%	6.7%	6.6%	6.6%	6.6%
47	7.2%	7.1%	6.9%	6.8%	6.8%
48	7.4%	7.4%	7.2%	7.1%	7.0%
49	7.4%	7.4%	7.4%	7.4%	7.3%
50	7.4%	7.4%	7.4%	7.4%	7.4%
51	7.4%	7.4%	7.4%	7.4%	7.4%
52	7.4%	7.4%	7.4%	7.4%	7.4%
53	7.4%	7.4%	7.4%	7.4%	7.4%
54	7.4%	7.4%	7.4%	7.4%	7.4%
55	7.4%	7.4%	7.4%	7.4%	7.4%

Age on last day of preceding tax year	*Appropriate age-related percentages for the tax year*				
	2007–2008	2008–2009	2009–2010	2010–2011	2011–2012
56	7.4%	7.4%	7.4%	7.4%	7.4%
57	7.4%	7.4%	7.4%	7.4%	7.4%
58	7.4%	7.4%	7.4%	7.4%	7.4%
59	7.4%	7.4%	7.4%	7.4%	7.4%
60	7.4%	7.4%	7.4%	7.4%	7.4%
61	7.4%	7.4%	7.4%	7.4%	7.4%
62	7.4%	7.4%	7.4%	7.4%	7.4%
63	7.4%	7.4%	7.4%	7.4%	7.4%

SCHEDULE 2

Articles 4 and 7

APPROPRIATE AGE-RELATED PERCENTAGES FOR APPROPRIATE PERSONAL PENSION SCHEMES FOR THE TAX YEAR 2007–2008

Column A	*Column B*	*Column C*	*Column D*
Age on last day of preceding tax year	*Earnings not exceeding low earnings threshold*	*Earnings exceeding low earnings threshold but not exceeding upper earnings threshold*	*Earnings exceeding upper earnings threshold*
15	9.4%	2.35%	4.7%
16	9.4%	2.35%	4.7%
17	9.6%	2.4%	4.8%
18	9.8%	2.45%	4.9%
19	9.8%	2.45%	4.9%
20	10.0%	2.5%	5.0%
21	10.2%	2.55%	5.1%
22	10.4%	2.6%	5.2%
23	10.4%	2.6%	5.2%
24	10.6%	2.65%	5.3%
25	10.8%	2.7%	5.4%
26	11.0%	2.75%	5.5%
27	11.0%	2.75%	5.5%
28	11.2%	2.8%	5.6%
29	11.4%	2.85%	5.7%
30	11.6%	2.9%	5.8%
31	11.8%	2.95%	5.9%
32	12.0%	3.0%	6.0%
33	12.0%	3.0%	6.0%
34	12.2%	3.05%	6.1%
35	12.6%	3.15%	6.3%
36	12.8%	3.2%	6.4%
37	13.0%	3.25%	6.5%
38	13.4%	3.35%	6.7%
39	13.6%	3.4%	6.8%
40	14.0%	3.5%	7.0%
41	14.2%	3.55%	7.1%

Column A Age on last day of preceding tax year	Column B Earnings not exceeding low earnings threshold	Column C Earnings exceeding low earnings threshold but not exceeding upper earnings threshold	Column D Earnings exceeding upper earnings threshold
42	14.4%	3.6%	7.2%
43	14.8%	3.7%	7.4%
44	14.8%	3.7%	7.4%
45	14.8%	3.7%	7.4%
46	14.8%	3.7%	7.4%
47	14.8%	3.7%	7.4%
48	14.8%	3.7%	7.4%
49	14.8%	3.7%	7.4%
50	14.8%	3.7%	7.4%
51	14.8%	3.7%	7.4%
52	14.8%	3.7%	7.4%
53	14.8%	3.7%	7.4%
54	14.8%	3.7%	7.4%
55	14.8%	3.7%	7.4%
56	14.8%	3.7%	7.4%
57	14.8%	3.7%	7.4%
58	14.8%	3.7%	7.4%
59	14.8%	3.7%	7.4%
60	14.8%	3.7%	7.4%
61	14.8%	3.7%	7.4%
62	14.8%	3.7%	7.4%
63	14.8%	3.7%	7.4%

SCHEDULE 3

Articles 4 and 7

APPROPRIATE AGE-RELATED PERCENTAGES FOR APPROPRIATE PERSONAL PENSION SCHEMES FOR THE TAX YEAR 2008–2009

Column A Age on last day of preceding tax year	Column B Earnings not exceeding low earnings threshold	Column C Earnings exceeding low earnings threshold but not exceeding upper earnings threshold	Column D Earnings exceeding upper earnings threshold
15	9.4%	2.35%	4.7%
16	9.4%	2.35%	4.7%
17	9.6%	2.4%	4.8%
18	9.8%	2.45%	4.9%
19	9.8%	2.45%	4.9%
20	10.0%	2.5%	5.0%
21	10.2%	2.55%	5.1%
22	10.4%	2.6%	5.2%
23	10.4%	2.6%	5.2%
24	10.6%	2.65%	5.3%
25	10.8%	2.7%	5.4%
26	11.0%	2.75%	5.5%

Column A Age on last day of preceding tax year	*Column B* Earnings not exceeding low earnings threshold	*Column C* Earnings exceeding low earnings threshold but not exceeding upper earnings threshold	*Column D* Earnings exceeding upper earnings threshold
27	11.0%	2.75%	5.5%
28	11.2%	2.8%	5.6%
29	11.4%	2.85%	5.7%
30	11.6%	2.9%	5.8%
31	11.8%	2.95%	5.9%
32	12.0%	3.0%	6.0%
33	12.0%	3.0%	6.0%
34	12.2%	3.05%	6.1%
35	12.6%	3.15%	6.3%
36	12.8%	3.2%	6.4%
37	13.2%	3.3%	6.6%
38	13.4%	3.35%	6.7%
39	13.6%	3.4%	6.8%
40	14.0%	3.5%	7.0%
41	14.2%	3.55%	7.1%
42	14.4%	3.6%	7.2%
43	14.8%	3.7%	7.4%
44	14.8%	3.7%	7.4%
45	14.8%	3.7%	7.4%
46	14.8%	3.7%	7.4%
47	14.8%	3.7%	7.4%
48	14.8%	3.7%	7.4%
49	14.8%	3.7%	7.4%
50	14.8%	3.7%	7.4%
51	14.8%	3.7%	7.4%
52	14.8%	3.7%	7.4%
53	14.8%	3.7%	7.4%
54	14.8%	3.7%	7.4%
55	14.8%	3.7%	7.4%
56	14.8%	3.7%	7.4%
57	14.8%	3.7%	7.4%
58	14.8%	3.7%	7.4%
59	14.8%	3.7%	7.4%
60	14.8%	3.7%	7.4%
61	14.8%	3.7%	7.4%
62	14.8%	3.7%	7.4%
63	14.8%	3.7%	7.4%

SCHEDULE 4

Articles 4 and 7

APPROPRIATE AGE-RELATED PERCENTAGES FOR APPROPRIATE PERSONAL PENSION SCHEMES FOR THE TAX YEAR 2009–2010

Column A *Age on last day of preceding tax year*	*Column B* *Earnings not exceeding low earnings threshold*	*Column C* *Earnings exceeding low earnings threshold but not exceeding upper earnings threshold*	*Column D* *Earnings exceeding upper earnings threshold*
15	9.4%	2.35%	4.7%
16	9.4%	2.35%	4.7%
17	9.6%	2.4%	4.8%
18	9.8%	2.45%	4.9%
19	9.8%	2.45%	4.9%
20	10.0%	2.5%	5.0%
21	10.2%	2.55%	5.1%
22	10.4%	2.6%	5.2%
23	10.4%	2.6%	5.2%
24	10.6%	2.65%	5.3%
25	10.8%	2.7%	5.4%
26	11.0%	2.75%	5.5%
27	11.2%	2.8%	5.6%
28	11.2%	2.8%	5.6%
29	11.4%	2.85%	5.7%
30	11.6%	2.9%	5.8%
31	11.8%	2.95%	5.9%
32	12.0%	3.0%	6.0%
33	12.0%	3.0%	6.0%
34	12.2%	3.05%	6.1%
35	12.6%	3.15%	6.3%
36	12.8%	3.2%	6.4%
37	13.2%	3.3%	6.6%
38	13.4%	3.35%	6.7%
39	13.6%	3.4%	6.8%
40	14.0%	3.5%	7.0%
41	14.2%	3.55%	7.1%
42	14.4%	3.6%	7.2%
43	14.8%	3.7%	7.4%
44	14.8%	3.7%	7.4%
45	14.8%	3.7%	7.4%
46	14.8%	3.7%	7.4%
47	14.8%	3.7%	7.4%
48	14.8%	3.7%	7.4%
49	14.8%	3.7%	7.4%
50	14.8%	3.7%	7.4%
51	14.8%	3.7%	7.4%
52	14.8%	3.7%	7.4%
53	14.8%	3.7%	7.4%
54	14.8%	3.7%	7.4%

Column A	*Column B*	*Column C*	*Column D*
Age on last day of preceding tax year	*Earnings not exceeding low earnings threshold*	*Earnings exceeding low earnings threshold but not exceeding upper earnings threshold*	*Earnings exceeding upper earnings threshold*
55	14.8%	3.7%	7.4%
56	14.8%	3.7%	7.4%
57	14.8%	3.7%	7.4%
58	14.8%	3.7%	7.4%
59	14.8%	3.7%	7.4%
60	14.8%	3.7%	7.4%
61	14.8%	3.7%	7.4%
62	14.8%	3.7%	7.4%
63	14.8%	3.7%	7.4%

SCHEDULE 5

Articles 4 and 7

APPROPRIATE AGE-RELATED PERCENTAGES FOR APPROPRIATE PERSONAL PENSION SCHEMES FOR THE TAX YEAR 2010–2011

Column A	*Column B*	*Column C*
Age on last day of preceding tax year	*Earnings not exceeding low earnings threshold*	*Earnings exceeding low earnings threshold*
15	9.4%	2.35%
16	9.4%	2.35%
17	9.6%	2.4%
18	9.8%	2.45%
19	9.8%	2.45%
20	10.0%	2.5%
21	10.2%	2.55%
22	10.4%	2.6%
23	10.4%	2.6%
24	10.6%	2.65%
25	10.8%	2.7%
26	11.0%	2.75%
27	11.2%	2.8%
28	11.4%	2.85%
29	11.4%	2.85%
30	11.6%	2.9%
31	11.8%	2.95%
32	12.0%	3.0%
33	12.2%	3.05%
34	12.2%	3.05%
35	12.6%	3.15%
36	12.8%	3.2%
37	13.2%	3.3%
38	13.4%	3.35%
39	13.6%	3.4%
40	14.0%	3.5%
41	14.2%	3.55%

Column A	*Column B*	*Column C*
Age on last day of preceding tax year	*Earnings not exceeding low earnings threshold*	*Earnings exceeding low earnings threshold*
42	14.4%	3.65%
43	14.8%	3.7%
44	14.8%	3.7%
45	14.8%	3.7%
46	14.8%	3.7%
47	14.8%	3.7%
48	14.8%	3.7%
49	14.8%	3.7%
50	14.8%	3.7%
51	14.8%	3.7%
52	14.8%	3.7%
53	14.8%	3.7%
54	14.8%	3.7%
55	14.8%	3.7%
56	14.8%	3.7%
57	14.8%	3.7%
58	14.8%	3.7%
59	14.8%	3.7%
60	14.8%	3.7%
61	14.8%	3.7%
62	14.8%	3.7%
63	14.8%	3.7%

History – In Sch. 5, Col. C the words "but not exceeding upper earnings threshold" omitted by SI 2009/3094, art. 3(2), with effect from 6 April 2010.
In Sch. 5, Col. D omitted by SI 2009/3094, art. 3(3), with effect from 6 April 2010.

SCHEDULE 6

Articles 4 and 7

APPROPRIATE AGE-RELATED PERCENTAGES FOR APPROPRIATE PERSONAL PENSION SCHEMES FOR THE TAX YEAR 2011–2012

Column A	*Column B*	*Column C*
Age on last day of preceding tax year	*Earnings not exceeding low earnings threshold*	*Earnings exceeding low earnings threshold*
15	9.4%	2.35%
16	9.4%	2.35%
17	9.6%	2.4%
18	9.8%	2.45%
19	10.0%	2.5%
20	10.0%	2.5%
21	10.2%	2.55%
22	10.4%	2.6%
23	10.4%	2.6%
24	10.6%	2.65%
25	10.8%	2.7%
26	11.0%	2.75%
27	11.2%	2.8%

Column A	*Column B*	*Column C*
Age on last day of preceding tax year	*Earnings not exceeding low earnings threshold*	*Earnings exceeding low earnings threshold*
28	11.2%	2.8%
29	11.4%	2.85%
30	11.6%	2.9%
31	11.8%	2.95%
32	12.0%	3.0%
33	12.2%	3.05%
34	12.2%	3.05%
35	12.6%	3.15%
36	12.8%	3.2%
37	13.2%	3.3%
38	13.4%	3.35%
39	13.8%	3.45%
40	14.0%	3.5%
41	14.2%	3.55%
42	14.6%	3.65%
43	14.8%	3.7%
44	14.8%	3.7%
45	14.8%	3.7%
46	14.8%	3.7%
47	14.8%	3.7%
48	14.8%	3.7%
49	14.8%	3.7%
50	14.8%	3.7%
51	14.8%	3.7%
52	14.8%	3.7%
53	14.8%	3.7%
54	14.8%	3.7%
55	14.8%	3.7%
56	14.8%	3.7%
57	14.8%	3.7%
58	14.8%	3.7%
59	14.8%	3.7%
60	14.8%	3.7%
61	14.8%	3.7%
62	14.8%	3.7%
63	14.8%	3.7%

History – In Sch. 6, Col. C the words "but not exceeding upper earnings threshold" omitted by SI 2009/3094, art. 3(2), with effect from 6 April 2010.
In Sch. 6, Col. D omitted by SI 2009/3094, art. 3(3), with effect from 6 April 2010.

SOCIAL SECURITY REVALUATION OF EARNINGS FACTORS ORDER 2007

(SI 2007/781)

Made on 8 March 2007 by the Secretary of State for Work and Pensions in accordance with s. 148(3) and (4) and s. 189(1), (4) and (5) of the Social Security Administration Act 1992. Operative from 6 April 2007.

CITATION AND COMMENCEMENT

1 This Order may be cited as the Social Security Revaluation of Earnings Factors Order 2007 and shall come into force on 6th April 2007.

REVALUATION OF EARNINGS FACTORS

2 The earnings factors for tax years specified in the Schedule to this Order in so far as they are relevant–

(a) to the calculation–

(i) of the additional pension in the rate of any long-term benefit; or

(ii) of any guaranteed minimum pension; or

(b) to any other calculation required under Part III of the Pension Schemes Act 1993 (including that Part as modified by or under any other enactment),

are directed to be increased for those tax years by the percentage of their amount shown opposite those tax years in that Schedule.

ROUNDING OF FRACTIONAL AMOUNTS

3 Where any earnings factor relevant to the calculation specified in article 2(a)(i) of this Order, as increased in accordance with this Order, would not but for this article be expressed as a whole number of pounds, it shall be so expressed by the rounding down of any fraction of a pound less than one half and the rounding up of any other fraction of a pound.

SCHEDULE

Article 2

Tax Year	*Percentage*
1978–79	623.8
1979–80	538.8
1980–81	433.7
1981–82	347.0
1982–83	306.0
1983–84	276.9
1984–85	249.0
1985–86	227.4
1986–87	200.7
1987–88	179.9
1988–89	157.5
1989–90	132.4
1990–91	116.6
1991–92	96.7
1992–93	84.7
1993–94	75.9
1994–95	70.7
1995–96	63.5
1996–97	59.0
1997–98	51.4
1998–99	44.8
1999–2000	38.9

Tax Year	*Percentage*
2000–2001	30.7
2001–2002	25.7
2002–2003	20.5
2003–2004	16.3
2004–2005	12.1
2005–2006	7.6
2006–2007	4.1

SOCIAL SECURITY CONTRIBUTIONS (MANAGED SERVICE COMPANIES) REGULATIONS 2007

(SI 2007/2070)

Made on 25 July 2007 by the Treasury under the powers conferred upon them by s. 4A, 122(1) and 175(1A) of the Social Security Contributions and Benefits Act 1992 and s. 4A, 121 and 171(1) of the Social Security Contributions and Benefits (Northern Ireland) Act 1992 and by the Commissioners for Her Majesty's Revenue and Customs by s. 8(1)(m) of the Social Security Contributions (Transfer of Functions, etc.) Act 1999 and art. 7(1)(m) of the Social Security Contributions (Transfer of Functions, etc.) (Northern Ireland) Order 1999. Operative from 6 August 2007.

Cross references – NICA 2011, s. 6(5)(b): disapplication of SI 2007/2070 for the purposes of NICA 2011, Pt. 2 (regional secondary contributions holiday for new businesses).

CITATION AND COMMENCEMENT

1 These Regulations may be cited as the Social Security Contributions (Managed Service Companies) Regulations 2007 and shall come into force on 6th August 2007.

INTERPRETATION

2(1) In these Regulations "ITEPA" means the Income Tax (Earnings and Pensions) Act 2003, and the following expressions have the same meaning as they have for the purposes of Chapter 9 of Part 2 of that Act–

"associate";

"managed service company";

"payment or benefit";

"worker"

2(2) In these Regulations–

"attributable earnings" has the meaning given by regulation 3(2);

"secondary Class 1 contributions" has the meaning given by section 6 of SSCBA;

"secondary contributor" has the meaning given by section 7 of SSCBA;

"SSCBA" means the Social Security Contributions and Benefits Act 1992;

"SSCR" means the Social Security (Contributions) Regulations 2001.

2(3) In the application of these Regulations to Northern Ireland a reference to an enactment applying to Great Britain is to be read as a reference to the corresponding enactment applying in Northern Ireland.

PAYMENTS AND BENEFITS RECEIVED BY WORKERS TREATED AS EARNINGS

3(1) This regulation applies if–

(a) the services of an individual ("the worker") are provided (directly or indirectly) by a managed service company ("the MSC"),

(b) the worker, or an associate of the worker, receives (from any person) a payment or benefit which can reasonably be taken to be in respect of the services, and

(c) the payment or benefit is not earnings derived from an employed earner's employment of the worker with the MSC.

3(2) Where this regulation applies, the MSC is treated as making to the worker, and the worker is treated as receiving, a payment or benefit which is to be treated as earnings from an employed earner's employment ("the worker's attributable earnings").

3(3) The amount of the worker's attributable earnings comprised in any payment or benefit is computed in accordance with section 61E of ITEPA.

3(4) The time at which a worker is treated as receiving that payment or benefit is determined in accordance with section 61F of ITEPA.

3(5) The worker's attributable earnings shall be aggregated with any other earnings paid to or for the benefit of the worker by the MSC in respect of the earnings period in which the payment or benefit mentioned in paragraph (1)(b) is received by the worker, and the amount of contributions shall be assessed in accordance with the appropriate earnings period determined in accordance with regulations 3 to 6 of SSCR.

3(6) Any issue whether the circumstances are such as are mentioned in paragraph (1) is an issue relating to contributions that is prescribed for the purposes of section 8(1)(m) of the Social Security Contributions (Transfer of Functions, etc.) Act 1999 (decision by officer of Revenue and Customs).

DEEMED EMPLOYED EARNER'S EMPLOYMENT

4 Where regulation 3 applies–

(a) the worker is treated, for the purposes of Parts 1 to 5 of SSCBA, and in relation to the worker's attributable earnings, as employed in employed earner's employment by the MSC, and

(b) the MSC, whether or not it fulfils the conditions prescribed under section 1(6)(a) of SSCBA for secondary contributors, is treated for those purposes as the secondary contributor in respect of the worker's attributable earnings,

and Parts 1 to 5 of SSCBA have effect accordingly.

AMENDMENT OF SSCR

5 In regulation 1(2) of SSCR (interpretation) in the definition of "secondary contributor" for "a second Class 1 contribution" substitute "a secondary Class 1 contribution".

SOCIAL SECURITY CONTRIBUTIONS AND BENEFITS ACT 1992 (MODIFICATION OF SECTION 4A) ORDER 2007

(SI 2007/2071)

Made on 23 July 2007 by the Treasury in exercise of the power conferred upon them by s. 4A(9) of the Social Security Contributions and Benefits Act 1992. Operative from 24 July 2007.

CITATION AND COMMENCEMENT

1 This Order may be cited as the Social Security Contributions and Benefits Act 1992 (Modification of Section 4A) Order 2007 and shall come into force on 24th July 2007.

MODIFICATION OF SECTION 4A OF THE SOCIAL SECURITY CONTRIBUTIONS AND BENEFITS ACT 1992

2(1) Section 4A of the Social Security Contributions and Benefits Act 1992 is modified as follows.

2(2) After subsection (2) insert–

"**4A(2A)** Regulations may also make provision for securing that, where the services of an individual ("the worker") are provided (directly or indirectly) by a managed service company ("the MSC") relevant payments or benefits are, to the specified extent, to be treated for the purposes of the applicable provisions of this Act as earnings paid to the worker in respect of an employed earner's employment of his.

4A(2B) In subsection (2A) "managed service company" has the same meaning as it has for the purposes of Chapter 9 of Part 2 of ITEPA 2003.".

2(3) In subsection (3)–

(a) in paragraph (a) after "by the intermediary" insert "or the MSC (as the case requires)";

(b) in paragraph (b) for "intermediary (whether or not he fulfils" substitute "intermediary or the MSC (whether or not fulfilling";

(c) in paragraph (g) after "the intermediary" insert "or the MSC".

2(4) In subsection (4)(b)–

(a) in sub-paragraph (i) after "intermediary" insert "or the MSC"; and

(b) in sub-paragraph (ii) for "him" substitute "that person".

2(5) In subsection (6) in the definition of "relevant payments or benefit" after "the intermediary" insert "or the MSC,".

FIRST-TIER TRIBUNAL AND UPPER TRIBUNAL (CHAMBERS) ORDER 2008

(SI 2008/2684, as amended by SI 2009/196, SI 2009/1021, SI 2009/1590 and SI 2010/40)

Made on 13 October 2008 by the Lord Chancellor, with the concurrence of the Senior President of Tribunals, in exercise of the power conferred by s. 7(1) and (9) of the Tribunals, Courts and Enforcement Act 2007. Operative from 3 November 2008.

CITATION AND COMMENCEMENT

1 This Order may be cited as the First-tier Tribunal and Upper Tribunal (Chambers) Order 2008 and shall come into force on 3rd November 2008.

FIRST-TIER TRIBUNAL CHAMBERS

2 The First-tier Tribunal shall be organised into the following chambers–

(a) the Social Entitlement Chamber;

(b) the War Pensions and Armed Forces Compensation Chamber;

(c) the Health, Education and Social Care Chamber.

(d) the Tax Chamber.

(e) the General Regulatory Chamber.

(f) the Immigration and Asylum Chamber.

History – In art. 2(b), the "and" at the end omitted by SI 2009/196, art. 3(a), with effect from 1 April 2009, subject to transitional rules in SI 2009/196, art. 9.
Art. 2(d) inserted by SI 2009/196, art. 3(b), with effect from 1 April 2009, subject to transitional rules in SI 2009/196, art. 9.
Art. 2(e) inserted by SI 2009/1590, art. 3, with effect from 1 September 2009.
Art. 2(f) inserted by SI 2010/40, art. 7, with effect from 15 February 2010.

FUNCTIONS OF THE SOCIAL ENTITLEMENT CHAMBER

3 To the Social Entitlement Chamber are assigned all functions relating to appeals–

(a) in cases regarding support for asylum seekers, failed asylum seekers, persons designated under section 130 of the Criminal Justice and Immigration Act 2008, or the dependants of any such persons;

(b) in criminal injuries compensation cases;

(c) regarding entitlement to, payments of, or recovery or recoupment of payments of, social security benefits, child support, vaccine damage payment, health in pregnancy grant, and tax credits, with the exception of–

(ai) appeals under section 11 of the Social Security Contributions (Transfer of Functions, etc.) Act 1999 (appeals against decisions of Her Majesty's Revenue and Customs);

(i) appeals in respect of employer penalties or employer information penalties (as defined in section 63(11) and (12) of the Tax Credits Act 2002);

(ii) appeals under regulation 28(3) of the Child Trust Funds Regulations 2004;

(ca) regarding saving gateway accounts with the exception of appeals against requirements to account for an amount under regulations made under section 14 of the Saving Gateway Accounts Act 2009;

(cb) regarding child trust funds with the exception of appeals against requirements to account for an amount under regulations made under section 22(4) Child Trust Funds Act 2004 in relation to section 13 of that Act;

(d) regarding payments in consequence of diffuse mesothelioma;

(e) regarding a certificate or waiver decision in relation to NHS charges;

(f) regarding entitlement to be credited with earnings or contributions;

(g) against a decision as to whether an accident was an industrial accident.

History – Art. 3(a) substituted by SI 2009/196, art. 4(a), with effect from 1 April 2009, subject to transitional rules in SI 2009/196, art. 9. Former art. 3(a) read as follows:
"(a) in asylum support cases;".
Art. 3(c)(ai) inserted by SI 2009/1590, art. 4, with effect from 1 September 2009.
In art. 3(c), the words "and child trust funds" omitted (and the word "and" inserted after "pregnancy grant,") by SI 2010/40, art. 8(a), with effect from 18 January 2010.

In art. 3(c), the words "health in pregnancy grant," inserted by SI 2009/1021, art. 3, with effect from 1 June 2009.
In art. 3(c), the words ", with the exception of–", and art, 3(c)(i) and (ii), inserted by SI 2009/196, art. 4(b), with effect from 1 April 2009, subject to transitional rules in SI 2009/196, art. 9.
Art. 3(ca) inserted by SI 2010/40, art. 8(b), with effect from 18 January 2010.
Art. 3(cb) inserted by SI 2010/40, art. 8(b), with effect from 18 January 2010.

FUNCTIONS OF THE TAX CHAMBER

5A To the Tax Chamber are assigned all functions, except those functions assigned to the Social Entitlement Chamber by article 3 or to the Tax and Chancery Chamber by article 8, relating to–

(a) an appeal, application, reference or other proceeding in respect of a function of the Commissioners for Her Majesty's Revenue and Customs or an officer of Revenue and Customs;

(b) an appeal in respect of the exercise by the Serious Organised Crime Agency of general Revenue functions or Revenue inheritance tax functions (as defined in section 323 of the Proceeds of Crime Act 2002).

History – In art. 5A, the words "Tax and Chancery" substituted for the words "Finance and Tax" by SI 2010/40, art. 10, with effect from 6 April 2010.
Art. 5A inserted by SI 2009/196, art. 5, with effect from 1 April 2009, subject to transitional rules in SI 2009/196, art. 9.

UPPER TRIBUNAL CHAMBERS

6 The Upper Tribunal shall be organised into the following chambers–

(a) the Administrative Appeals Chamber;

(b) the Tax and Chancery Chamber;

(c) the Lands Chamber.

(d) the Immigration and Asylum Chamber of the Upper Tribunal.

History – Art. 6(b) substituted by SI 2009/1590, art. 6, with effect from 1 September 2009.
Art. 6(c) inserted by SI 2009/1021, art. 4, with effect from 1 June 2009.
Art. 6(d) inserted by SI 2010/40, art. 12, with effect from 15 February 2010.
Art. 6 substituted by SI 2009/196, art. 6, with effect from 1 April 2009, subject to transitional rules in SI 2009/196, art. 9. Former art. 6 read as follows:

"UPPER TRIBUNAL CHAMBER

6 The Upper Tribunal shall be organised as the Administrative Appeals Chamber.".

FUNCTIONS OF THE ADMINISTRATIVE APPEALS CHAMBER

7 To the Administrative Appeals Chamber are assigned all functions relating to–

(a) an appeal–

(i) against a decision made by the First-tier Tribunal, except an appeal assigned to the Tax and Chancery Chamber by article 8(a) or the Immigration and Asylum Chamber of the Upper Tribunal by article 9A(a);

(ii) under section 5 of the Pensions Appeal Tribunals Act 1943 (assessment decision) against a decision of the Pensions Appeal Tribunal in Northern Ireland established under paragraph 1(2) of Schedule 1 to the Pensions Appeal Tribunals Act 1943;

(iii) against a decision of the Pensions Appeal Tribunal in Scotland established under paragraph 1(2) of Schedule 1 to the Pensions Appeal Tribunals Act 1943;

(iv) against a decision of the Mental Health Review Tribunal for Wales established under section 65 of the Mental Health Act 1983;

(v) against a decision of the Special Educational Needs Tribunal for Wales;

(vi) under section 4 of the Safeguarding Vulnerable Groups Act 2006 (appeals);

(vii) against a decision of the Information Commissioner transferred to the Upper Tribunal from the First-tier Tribunal under Tribunal Procedure Rules;

(viii) against a decision of a traffic commissioner.

(b) an application, except an application assigned to the Tax and Chancery Chamber by article 8(e), for the Upper Tribunal–

(i) to grant the relief mentioned in section 15(1) of the Tribunal, Courts and Enforcement Act 2007 (Upper Tribunal's "judicial review" jurisdiction);

(ii) to exercise the powers of review under section 21(2) of that Act (Upper Tribunal's "judicial *review" jurisdiction: Scotland*).

(c) a matter referred to the Upper Tribunal by the First-tier Tribunal under section 9(5)(b) of the Tribunals, Courts and Enforcement Act 2007, except where the reference is assigned to the Tax and Chancery Chamber by article 8(d) or the Immigration and Asylum Chamber of the Upper Tribunal by article 9A(b).

(d) a determination or decision under section 4 of the Forfeiture Act 1982.

History – In art. 7(a)(i), the words "or the Immigration and Asylum Chamber of the Upper Tribunal by article 9A(a)" inserted by SI 2010/40, art. 13(a), with effect from 15 February 2010.
In art. 7(a)(i) the words "an appeal assigned to the Tax and Chancery Chamber by article 8(a)" substituted for the words "decisions made in the Tax Chamber" and art. 7(a)(vii) and (viii) inserted by SI 2009/1590, art. 7(a) and (b), with effect from 1 September 2009.
In art. 7(a)(i), the words "the First-tier Tribunal, except decisions made in the Tax Chamber" substituted for the words "a chamber of the First-tier Tribunal" by SI 2009/196, art. 7(a), with effect from 1 April 2009, subject to transitional rules in SI 2009/196, art. 9.
In art. 7(b) the words ", except an application assigned to the Tax and Chancery Chamber by article 8(e), for the Upper Tribunal" inserted by SI 2009/1590, art. 7(c), with effect from 1 September 2009.
In art. 7(c), the words "or the Immigration and Asylum Chamber of the Upper Tribunal by article 9A(b)" inserted by SI 2010/40, art. 13(b), with effect from 15 February 2010.
In art. 7(c) the words "except where the reference is assigned to the Tax and Chancery Chamber by article 8(d)" substituted for the words "unless the reference is made by the Tax Chamber" by SI 2009/1590, art. 7(d), with effect from 1 September 2009.
Art. 7(c) inserted by SI 2009/196, art. 7(b), with effect from 1 April 2009, subject to transitional rules in SI 2009/196, art. 9.
Art. 7(d) inserted by SI 2009/1590, art. 7(e), with effect from 1 September 2009.

FUNCTIONS OF THE TAX AND CHANCERY CHAMBER

8(1) To the Tax and Chancery Chamber are assigned all functions relating to–

(a) an appeal against a decision of the First-tier Tribunal made–
  (i) in the Tax Chamber; or
  (ii) in a charities case;

(aa) a reference or appeal in respect of–
  (i) a decision of the Financial Services Authority;
  (ii) a decision of the Bank of England; or
  (iii) a decision of a person relating to the assessment of any compensation or consideration under the Banking (Special Provisions) Act 2008;

(ab) a reference in respect of a decision of the Pensions Regulator;

(b) an application under paragraph 50(1)(d) of Schedule 36 to the Finance Act 2008;

(c) proceedings transferred to the Upper Tribunal under Tribunal Procedure Rules–
  (i) from the Tax Chamber of the First-tier Tribunal; or
  (ii) from the First-tier Tribunal in a charities case;

(d) a matter referred to the Upper Tribunal under section 9(5)(b) of the Tribunals, Courts and Enforcement Act 2007–
  (i) by the Tax Chamber of the First-tier Tribunal; or
  (ii) by the First-tier Tribunal in a charities case;

(e) an application for the Upper Tribunal to grant the relief mentioned in section 15(1) of the Tribunals, Courts and Enforcement Act 2007 (Upper Tribunal's "judicial review" jurisdiction), or to exercise the powers of review under section 21(2) of that Act (Upper Tribunal's "judicial review" jurisdiction: Scotland), which relates to–
  (i) a decision of the First-tier Tribunal mentioned in paragraph (a)(i) or (ii);
  (ii) a function of the Commissioners for Her Majesty's Revenue and Customs or an officer of Revenue and Customs, with the exception of any function in respect of which an appeal would be allocated to the Social Entitlement Chamber by article 3;
  (iii) the exercise by the Serious Organised Crime Agency of general Revenue functions or Revenue inheritance tax functions (as defined in section 323 of the Proceeds of Crime Act 2002), with the exception of any function in relation to which an appeal would be allocated to the Social Entitlement Chamber by article 3;
  (iv) a function of the Charity Commission, or one of the bodies mentioned in paragraph (aa) or (ab).

8(2) In this article **"a charities case"** means an appeal or application in respect of a decision, order or direction of the Charity Commission, or a reference under Schedule 1D of the Charities Act 1993.

History – Art. 8(1)(aa) and (ab) inserted by SI 2010/40, art. 14(a), with effect from 6 April 2010.
In art. 8(1)(e)(iv), the words ", or one of the bodies mentioned in paragraph (aa) or (ab)" inserted by SI 2010/40, art. 14(b), with effect from 6 April 2010.
Art. 8 substituted by SI 2009/1590, art. 8, with effect from 1 September 2009.
Former art. 8 inserted by SI 2009/196, art. 8, with effect from 1 April 2009, subject to transitional rules in SI 2009/196, art. 9.

RESOLUTION OF DOUBT OR DISPUTE AS TO CHAMBER

10 If there is any doubt or dispute as to the chamber in which a particular matter is to be dealt with, the Senior President of Tribunals may allocate that matter to the chamber which appears to the Senior President of Tribunals to be most appropriate.

History – Art. 10 inserted by SI 2009/1021, art. 5, with effect from 1 June 2009.

RE-ALLOCATION OF A CASE TO ANOTHER CHAMBER

11(1) Subject to paragraph (2), the Chamber President of the chamber to which a case has been assigned or allocated by or under this Order may allocate that case to another chamber within the same tribunal, by giving a direction to that effect.

11(2) A Chamber President may give a direction under paragraph (1) only if the Chamber President of the chamber to which the case is to be allocated has first consented to the giving of the direction.

11(3) A direction under paragraph (1) may be given at any point in the proceedings.

History – Art. 11 inserted by SI 2010/40, art. 16, with effect from 18 January 2010.

TRIBUNAL PROCEDURE (FIRST-TIER TRIBUNAL) (SOCIAL ENTITLEMENT CHAMBER) RULES 2008

(SI 2008/2685, as amended by SI 2009/274, SI 2009/1975, SI 2010/43, SI 2010/2653, SI 2011/651, SI 2012/500, SI 2012/2007, SI 2013/477, SI 2013/2067, SI 2014/514, SI 2014/2128 and SI 2015/1510)

Made on 9 October 2008 by the Tribunal Procedure Committee in exercise of the powers conferred by s. 20(2) and (3) of the Social Security Act 1998 and s. 9(3), 22 and 29(3) of, and Sch. 5 to, the Tribunals, Courts and Enforcement Act 2007. Operative from 3 November 2008.

PART 1 – INTRODUCTION

CITATION, COMMENCEMENT, APPLICATION AND INTERPRETATION

1(1) These Rules may be cited as the Tribunal Procedure (First-tier Tribunal) (Social Entitlement Chamber) Rules 2008 and come into force on 3rd November 2008.

1(2) These Rules apply to proceedings before the Social Entitlement Chamber of the First-tier Tribunal.

1(3) In these Rules–

"the 2007 Act" means the Tribunals, Courts and Enforcement Act 2007;

"appeal" includes an application under section 19(9) of the Tax Credits Act 2002;

"appellant" means a person who makes an appeal to the Tribunal, or a person substituted as an appellant under rule 9(1) (substitution of parties);

"asylum support case" means proceedings concerning the provision of support for an asylum seeker, a failed asylum seeker or a person designated under section 130 of the Criminal Justice and Immigration Act 2008 (designation), or the dependants of any such person;

"criminal injuries compensation case" means proceedings concerning the payment of compensation under a scheme made under the Criminal Injuries Compensation Act 1995 or section 47 of the Crime and Security Act 2010;

"decision maker" means the maker of a decision against which an appeal has been brought;

"dispose of proceedings" includes, unless indicated otherwise, disposing of a part of the proceedings;

"document" means anything in which information is recorded in any form, and an obligation under these Rules to provide or allow access to a document or a copy of a document for any purpose means, unless the Tribunal directs otherwise, an obligation to provide or allow access to such document or copy in a legible form or in a form which can be readily made into a legible form;

"hearing" means an oral hearing and includes a hearing conducted in whole or in part by video link, telephone or other means of instantaneous two-way electronic communication;

"legal representative" means a person who, for the purposes of the Legal Services Act 2007, is an authorised person in relation to an activity which constitutes the exercise of a right of audience or the conduct of litigation within the meaning of that Act, an advocate or solicitor in Scotland or a barrister or solicitor in Northern Ireland;

"party" means–

(a) a person who is an appellant or respondent in proceedings before the Tribunal;

(b) a person who makes a reference to the Tribunal under section 28D of the Child Support Act 1991;

(c) a person who starts proceedings before the Tribunal under paragraph 3 of Schedule 2 to the Tax Credits Act 2002; or

(d) if the proceedings have been concluded, a person who was a party under paragraph (a), (b) or (c) when the Tribunal finally disposed of all issues in the proceedings;

"practice direction" means a direction given under section 23 of the 2007 Act;

"respondent" means–

(a) in an appeal against a decision, the decision maker and any person other than the appellant who had a right of appeal against the decision;

(b) in a reference under section 28D of the Child Support Act 1991–

(i) the absent parent or non-resident parent;
(ii) the person with care; and
(iii) in Scotland, the child if the child made the application for a departure direction or a variation;

(c) in proceedings under paragraph 3 of Schedule 2 to the Tax Credits Act 2002, a person on whom it is proposed that a penalty be imposed;

(d) an affected party within the meaning of section 61(5) of the Childcare Payments Act 2014, other than an appellant; or

(e) a person substituted or added as a respondent under rule 9 (substitution and addition of parties);

"social security and child support case" means any case allocated to the Social Entitlement Chamber of the First-tier Tribunal except an asylum support case or a criminal injuries compensation case;

"Tribunal" means the First-tier Tribunal.

History – R. 1(2) substituted by SI 2010/2653, r. 5(2), with effect from 29 November 2010.
In r. 1(3), in the definition of "asylum support case", the words ", a failed asylum seeker or a person designated under section 130 of the Criminal Justice and Immigration Act 2008 (designation), or the dependants of any such person" substituted for the words "or his or her dependants" by SI 2009/274, r. 2, with effect from 1 April 2009.
In r. 1(3), in the definition of "criminal injuries compensation case", the words "or section 47 of the Crime and Security Act 2010" inserted by SI 2013/477, r. 23, with effect from 8 April 2013.
In r. 1(3), in the definition of "legal representative", the words "a person who, for the purposes of the Legal Services Act 2007, is an authorised person in relation to an activity which constitutes the exercise of a right of audience or the conduct of litigation within the meaning of that Act" substituted for the words "an authorised advocate or authorised litigator as defined by section 119(1) of the Courts and Legal Services Act 1990" by SI 2010/43, r. 3, with effect from 18 January 2010.
In r. 1(3), in the definition of "respondent", para. (cc) inserted (and the "or" before it omitted) by SI 2015/1510, r. 12, with effect from 21 August 2015.
In r. 1(3), definition of "Social Entitlement Chamber" omitted by SI 2011/651, r. 4(2)(a), with effect from 1 April 2011.
In r. 1(3), in the definition of "social security and child support case", the words "of the First-tier Tribunal" inserted by SI 2011/651, r. 4(2)(b), with effect from 1 April 2011.

OVERRIDING OBJECTIVE AND PARTIES' OBLIGATION TO CO-OPERATE WITH THE TRIBUNAL

2(1) The overriding objective of these Rules is to enable the Tribunal to deal with cases fairly and justly.

2(2) Dealing with a case fairly and justly includes–

(a) dealing with the case in ways which are proportionate to the importance of the case, the complexity of the issues, the anticipated costs and the resources of the parties;

(b) avoiding unnecessary formality and seeking flexibility in the proceedings;

(c) ensuring, so far as practicable, that the parties are able to participate fully in the proceedings;

(d) using any special expertise of the Tribunal effectively; and

(e) avoiding delay, so far as compatible with proper consideration of the issues.

2(3) The Tribunal must seek to give effect to the overriding objective when it–

(a) exercises any power under these Rules; or

(b) interprets any rule or practice direction.

2(4) Parties must–

(a) help the Tribunal to further the overriding objective; and

(b) co-operate with the Tribunal generally.

ALTERNATIVE DISPUTE RESOLUTION AND ARBITRATION

3(1) The Tribunal should seek, where appropriate–

(a) to bring to the attention of the parties the availability of any appropriate alternative procedure for the resolution of the dispute; and

(b) if the parties wish and provided that it is compatible with the overriding objective, to facilitate the use of the procedure.

3(2) Part 1 of the Arbitration Act 1996 does not apply to proceedings before the Tribunal.

PART 2 – GENERAL POWERS AND PROVISIONS

DELEGATION TO STAFF

4(1) Staff appointed under section 40(1) of the 2007 Act (tribunal staff and services) may, with the approval of the Senior President of Tribunals, carry out functions of a judicial nature permitted or required to be done by the Tribunal.

4(2) The approval referred to at paragraph (1) may apply generally to the carrying out of specified functions by members of staff of a specified description in specified circumstances.

4(3) Within 14 days after the date on which the Tribunal sends notice of a decision made by a member of staff under paragraph (1) to a party, that party may apply in writing to the Tribunal for that decision to be considered afresh by a judge.

CASE MANAGEMENT POWERS

5(1) Subject to the provisions of the 2007 Act and any other enactment, the Tribunal may regulate its own procedure.

5(2) The Tribunal may give a direction in relation to the conduct or disposal of proceedings at any time, including a direction amending, suspending or setting aside an earlier direction.

5(3) In particular, and without restricting the general powers in paragraphs (1) and (2), the Tribunal may–

(a) extend or shorten the time for complying with any rule, practice direction or direction;

(aa) [omitted by SI 2015/1510, r. 13;]

(b) consolidate or hear together two or more sets of proceedings or parts of proceedings raising common issues, or treat a case as a lead case (whether in accordance with rule 18 (lead cases) or otherwise);

(c) permit or require a party to amend a document;

(d) permit or require a party or another person to provide documents, information, evidence or submissions to the Tribunal or a party;

(e) deal with an issue in the proceedings as a preliminary issue;

(f) hold a hearing to consider any matter, including a case management issue;

(g) decide the form of any hearing;

(h) adjourn or postpone a hearing;

(i) require a party to produce a bundle for a hearing;

(j) stay (or, in Scotland, sist) proceedings;

(k) transfer proceedings to another court or tribunal if that other court or tribunal has jurisdiction in relation to the proceedings and–

  (i) because of a change of circumstances since the proceedings were started, the Tribunal no longer has jurisdiction in relation to the proceedings; or

  (ii) the Tribunal considers that the other court or tribunal is a more appropriate forum for the determination of the case; or

(l) suspend the effect of its own decision pending the determination by the Tribunal or the Upper Tribunal of an application for permission to appeal against, and any appeal or review of, that decision.

History – R. 5(3)(aa) omitted by SI 2015/1510, r. 13, with effect from 21 August 2015. Former r. 5(3)(aa) read as follows:

"(aa) extend the time within which an appeal must be brought under regulation 28(1) of the Child Benefit and Guardian's Allowance (Decisions and Appeals) Regulations 2003".

R. 5(3)(aa) inserted by SI 2013/2067, r. 23, with effect from 1 November 2013.

PROCEDURE FOR APPLYING FOR AND GIVING DIRECTIONS

6(1) The Tribunal may give a direction on the application of one or more of the parties or on its own initiative.

6(2) An application for a direction may be made–

(a) by sending or delivering a written application to the Tribunal; or

(b) orally during the course of a hearing.

6(3) An application for a direction must include the reason for making that application.

6(4) Unless the Tribunal considers that there is good reason not to do so, the Tribunal must send written notice of any direction to every party and to any other person affected by the direction.

6(5) If a party or any other person sent notice of the direction under paragraph (4) wishes to challenge a direction which the Tribunal has given, they may do so by applying for another direction which amends, suspends or sets aside the first direction.

FAILURE TO COMPLY WITH RULES ETC.

7(1) An irregularity resulting from a failure to comply with any requirement in these Rules, a practice direction or a direction, does not of itself render void the proceedings or any step taken in the proceedings.

7(2) If a party has failed to comply with a requirement in these Rules, a practice direction or a direction, the Tribunal may take such action as it considers just, which may include–

(a) waiving the requirement;

(b) requiring the failure to be remedied;

(c) exercising its power under rule 8 (striking out a party's case); or

(d) exercising its power under paragraph (3).

7(3) The Tribunal may refer to the Upper Tribunal, and ask the Upper Tribunal to exercise its power under section 25 of the 2007 Act in relation to, any failure by a person to comply with a requirement imposed by the Tribunal–

(a) to attend at any place for the purpose of giving evidence;

(b) otherwise to make themselves available to give evidence;

(c) to swear an oath in connection with the giving of evidence;

(d) to give evidence as a witness;

(e) to produce a document; or

(f) to facilitate the inspection of a document or any other thing (including any premises).

STRIKING OUT A PARTY'S CASE

8(1) The proceedings, or the appropriate part of them, will automatically be struck out if the appellant has failed to comply with a direction that stated that failure by a party to comply with the direction would lead to the striking out of the proceedings or that part of them.

8(2) The Tribunal must strike out the whole or a part of the proceedings if the Tribunal–

(a) does not have jurisdiction in relation to the proceedings or that part of them; and

(b) does not exercise its power under rule 5(3)(k)(i) (transfer to another court or tribunal) in relation to the proceedings or that part of them.

8(3) The Tribunal may strike out the whole or a part of the proceedings if–

(a) the appellant has failed to comply with a direction which stated that failure by the appellant to comply with the direction could lead to the striking out of the proceedings or part of them;

(b) the appellant has failed to co-operate with the Tribunal to such an extent that the Tribunal cannot deal with the proceedings fairly and justly; or

(c) the Tribunal considers there is no reasonable prospect of the appellant's case, or part of it, succeeding.

8(4) The Tribunal may not strike out the whole or a part of the proceedings under paragraph (2) or (3)(b) or (c) without first giving the appellant an opportunity to make representations in relation to the proposed striking out.

8(5) If the proceedings, or part of them, have been struck out under paragraph (1) or (3)(a), the appellant may apply for the proceedings, or part of them, to be reinstated.

8(6) An application under paragraph (5) must be made in writing and received by the Tribunal within 1 month after the date on which the Tribunal sent notification of the striking out to the appellant.

8(7) This rule applies to a respondent as it applies to an appellant except that–

(a) a reference to the striking out of the proceedings is to be read as a reference to the barring of the respondent from taking further part in the proceedings; and

(b) a reference to an application for the reinstatement of proceedings which have been struck out is to be read as a reference to an application for the lifting of the bar on the respondent from taking further part in the proceedings.

8(8) If a respondent has been barred from taking further part in proceedings under this rule and that bar has not been lifted, the Tribunal need not consider any response or other submission made by that respondent and may summarily determine any or all issues against that respondent.

History – In r. 8(8), the words "and may summarily determine any or all issues against that respondent" inserted by SI 2010/2653, r. 5(3), with effect from 29 November 2010.

SUBSTITUTION AND ADDITION OF PARTIES

9(1) The Tribunal may give a direction substituting a party if–

(a) the wrong person has been named as a party; or

(b) the substitution has become necessary because of a change in circumstances since the start of proceedings.

9(2) The Tribunal may give a direction adding a person to the proceedings as a respondent.

9(3) If the Tribunal gives a direction under paragraph (1) or (2) it may give such consequential directions as it considers appropriate.

NO POWER TO AWARD COSTS

10 The Tribunal may not make any order in respect of costs (or, in Scotland, expenses).

REPRESENTATIVES

11(1) A party may appoint a representative (whether a legal representative or not) to represent that party in the proceedings.

11(2) Subject to paragraph (3), if a party appoints a representative, that party (or the representative if the representative is a legal representative) must send or deliver to the Tribunal written notice of the representative's name and address.

11(3) In a case to which rule 23 (cases in which the notice of appeal is to be sent to the decision maker) applies, if the appellant (or the appellant's representative if the representative is a legal representative) provides written notification of the appellant's representative's name and address to the decision maker before the decision maker provides its response to the Tribunal, the appellant need not take any further steps in order to comply with paragraph (2).

11(4) If the Tribunal receives notice that a party has appointed a representative under paragraph (2), it must send a copy of that notice to each other party.

11(5) Anything permitted or required to be done by a party under these Rules, a practice direction or a direction may be done by the representative of that party, except signing a witness statement.

11(6) A person who receives due notice of the appointment of a representative–

(a) must provide to the representative any document which is required to be provided to the represented party, and need not provide that document to the represented party; and

(b) may assume that the representative is and remains authorised as such until they receive written notification that this is not so from the representative or the represented party.

11(7) At a hearing a party may be accompanied by another person whose name and address has not been notified under paragraph (2) or (3) but who, with the permission of the Tribunal, may act as a representative or otherwise assist in presenting the party's case at the hearing.

11(8) Paragraphs (2) to (6) do not apply to a person who accompanies a party under paragraph (7).

CALCULATING TIME

12(1) Except in asylum support cases, an act required by these Rules, a practice direction or a direction to be done on or by a particular day must be done by 5pm on that day.

12(2) If the time specified by these Rules, a practice direction or a direction for doing any act ends on a day other than a working day, the act is done in time if it is done on the next working day.

12(3) In this rule **"working day"** means any day except a Saturday or Sunday, Christmas Day, Good Friday or a bank holiday under section 1 of the Banking and Financial Dealings Act 1971.

SENDING AND DELIVERY OF DOCUMENTS

13(1) *Any document* to be provided to the Tribunal under these Rules, a practice direction or a direction must be–

(a) sent by pre-paid post or delivered by hand to the address specified for the proceedings;

(b) sent by fax to the number specified for the proceedings; or

(c) sent or delivered by such other method as the Tribunal may permit or direct.

13(2) Subject to paragraph (3), if a party provides a fax number, email address or other details for the electronic transmission of documents to them, that party must accept delivery of documents by that method.

13(3) If a party informs the Tribunal and all other parties that a particular form of communication (other than pre-paid post or delivery by hand) should not be used to provide documents to that party, that form of communication must not be so used.

13(4) If the Tribunal or a party sends a document to a party or the Tribunal by email or any other electronic means of communication, the recipient may request that the sender provide a hard copy of the document to the recipient. The recipient must make such a request as soon as reasonably practicable after receiving the document electronically.

13(5) The Tribunal and each party may assume that the address provided by a party or its representative is and remains the address to which documents should be sent or delivered until receiving written notification to the contrary.

USE OF DOCUMENTS AND INFORMATION

14(1) The Tribunal may make an order prohibiting the disclosure or publication of–

(a) specified documents or information relating to the proceedings; or

(b) any matter likely to lead members of the public to identify any person whom the Tribunal considers should not be identified.

14(2) The Tribunal may give a direction prohibiting the disclosure of a document or information to a person if–

(a) the Tribunal is satisfied that such disclosure would be likely to cause that person or some other person serious harm; and

(b) the Tribunal is satisfied, having regard to the interests of justice, that it is proportionate to give such a direction.

14(3) If a party ("the first party") considers that the Tribunal should give a direction under paragraph (2) prohibiting the disclosure of a document or information to another party ("the second party"), the first party must–

(a) exclude the relevant document or information from any documents that will be provided to the second party; and

(b) provide to the Tribunal the excluded document or information, and the reason for its exclusion, so that the Tribunal may decide whether the document or information should be disclosed to the second party or should be the subject of a direction under paragraph (2).

14(4) The Tribunal must conduct proceedings as appropriate in order to give effect to a direction given under paragraph (2).

14(5) If the Tribunal gives a direction under paragraph (2) which prevents disclosure to a party who has appointed a representative, the Tribunal may give a direction that the documents or information be disclosed to that representative if the Tribunal is satisfied that–

(a) disclosure to the representative would be in the interests of the party; and

(b) the representative will act in accordance with paragraph (6).

14(6) Documents or information disclosed to a representative in accordance with a direction under paragraph (5) must not be disclosed either directly or indirectly to any other person without the Tribunal's consent.

EVIDENCE AND SUBMISSIONS

15(1) Without restriction on the general powers in rule 5(1) and (2) (case management powers), the Tribunal may give directions as to–

(a) issues on which it requires evidence or submissions;

(b) the nature of the evidence or submissions it requires;

(c) whether the parties are permitted or required to provide expert evidence;

(d) any limit on the number of witnesses whose evidence a party may put forward, whether in relation to a particular issue or generally;

(e) the manner in which any evidence or submissions are to be provided, which may include a direction for them to be given–

  (i) orally at a hearing; or

  (ii) by written submissions or witness statement; and

(f) the time at which any evidence or submissions are to be provided.

15(2) The Tribunal may–

(a) admit evidence whether or not–

(i) the evidence would be admissible in a civil trial in the United Kingdom; or

(ii) the evidence was available to a previous decision maker; or

(b) exclude evidence that would otherwise be admissible where–

(i) the evidence was not provided within the time allowed by a direction or a practice direction;

(ii) the evidence was otherwise provided in a manner that did not comply with a direction or a practice direction; or

(iii) it would otherwise be unfair to admit the evidence.

15(3) The Tribunal may consent to a witness giving, or require any witness to give, evidence on oath, and may administer an oath for that purpose.

SUMMONING OR CITATION OF WITNESSES AND ORDERS TO ANSWER QUESTIONS OR PRODUCE DOCUMENTS

16(1) On the application of a party or on its own initiative, the Tribunal may–

(a) by summons (or, in Scotland, citation) require any person to attend as a witness at a hearing at the time and place specified in the summons or citation; or

(b) order any person to answer any questions or produce any documents in that person's possession or control which relate to any issue in the proceedings.

16(2) A summons or citation under paragraph (1)(a) must–

(a) give the person required to attend 14 days' notice of the hearing or such shorter period as the Tribunal may direct; and

(b) where the person is not a party, make provision for the person's necessary expenses of attendance to be paid, and state who is to pay them.

16(3) No person may be compelled to give any evidence or produce any document that the person could not be compelled to give or produce on a trial of an action in a court of law in the part of the United Kingdom where the proceedings are due to be determined.

16(4) A summons, citation or order under this rule must–

(a) state that the person on whom the requirement is imposed may apply to the Tribunal to vary or set aside the summons, citation or order, if they have not had an opportunity to object to it; and

(b) state the consequences of failure to comply with the summons, citation or order.

WITHDRAWAL

17(1) Subject to paragraph (2), a party may give notice of the withdrawal of its case, or any part of it–

(a) by sending or delivering to the Tribunal a written notice of withdrawal; or

(b) orally at a hearing.

17(2) In the circumstances described in paragraph (3), a notice of withdrawal will not take effect unless the Tribunal consents to the withdrawal.

17(3) The circumstances referred to in paragraph (2) are where a party gives notice of withdrawal–

(a) in a criminal injuries compensation case; or

(b) in a social security and child support case where the Tribunal has directed that notice of withdrawal shall take effect only with the Tribunal's consent; or

(c) at a hearing.

17(4) An application for a withdrawn case to be reinstated may be made by–

(a) the party who withdrew the case;

(b) where an appeal in a social security and child support case has been withdrawn, a respondent.

17(5) An application under paragraph (4) must be made in writing and be received by the Tribunal within 1 month after the earlier of–

(a) the date on which the applicant was sent notice under paragraph (6) that the withdrawal had taken effect; or

(b) if the applicant was present at the hearing when the case was withdrawn orally under paragraph (1)(b), the date of that hearing.

17(6) The Tribunal must notify each party in writing that a withdrawal has taken effect under this rule.

History – In r. 17(1)(a), the words "at any time before a hearing to consider the disposal of the proceedings (or, if the Tribunal disposes of the proceedings without a hearing, before that disposal)," which appeared at the beginning omitted by SI 2013/477, r. 24(a), with effect from 8 April 2013.
In r. 17(3)(a), the words "under paragraph (1)(a)" which appeared at the beginning omitted and r. 17(b) and (c) substituted for former r. 17(3)(b) by SI 2013/477, r. 24(b) and (c), with effect from 8 April 2013.
R. 17(4) and (5) substituted by SI 2015/1510, r. 14, with effect from 21 August 2015. Former r. 17(4) and (5) read as follows:
"**17(4)** A party who has withdrawn their case may apply to the Tribunal for the case to be reinstated.
17(5) An application under paragraph (4) must be made in writing and be received by the Tribunal within 1 month after–
(a) the date on which the Tribunal received the notice under paragraph (1)(a); or
(b) the date of the hearing at which the case was withdrawn orally under paragraph (1)(b).".
In r. 17(6), the words "that a withdrawal has taken effect" substituted for the words "of an withdrawal" by SI 2013/477, r. 24(d), with effect from 8 April 2013.

LEAD CASES

18(1) This rule applies if–
(a) two or more cases have been started before the Tribunal;
(b) in each such case the Tribunal has not made a decision disposing of the proceedings; and
(c) the cases give rise to common or related issues of fact or law.

18(2) The Tribunal may give a direction–
(a) specifying one or more cases falling under paragraph (1) as a lead case or lead cases; and
(b) staying (or, in Scotland, sisting) the other cases falling under paragraph (1) ("the related cases").

18(3) When the Tribunal makes a decision in respect of the common or related issues–
(a) the Tribunal must send a copy of that decision to each party in each of the related cases; and
(b) subject to paragraph (4), that decision shall be binding on each of those parties.

18(4) Within 1 month after the date on which the Tribunal sent a copy of the decision to a party under paragraph (3)(a), that party may apply in writing for a direction that the decision does not apply to, and is not binding on the parties to, a particular related case.

18(5) The Tribunal must give directions in respect of cases which are stayed or sisted under paragraph (2)(b), providing for the disposal of or further directions in those cases.

18(6) If the lead case or cases lapse or are withdrawn before the Tribunal makes a decision in respect of the common or related issues, the Tribunal must give directions as to–
(a) whether another case or other cases are to be specified as a lead case or lead cases; and
(b) whether any direction affecting the related cases should be set aside or amended.

CONFIDENTIALITY IN SOCIAL SECURITY AND CHILD SUPPORT CASES

19(1) Paragraph (4) applies to–
(a) proceedings under the Child Support Act 1991 in the circumstances described in paragraph (2), other than an appeal against a reduced benefit decision (as defined in section 46(10)(b) of the Child Support Act 1991, as that section had effect prior to the commencement of section 15(b) of the Child Maintenance and Other Payments Act 2008);
(b) proceedings where the parties to the appeal include former joint claimants who are no longer living together in the circumstances described in paragraph (3).

19(2) The circumstances referred to in paragraph (1)(a) are that the absent parent, nonresident parent or person with care would like their address or the address of the child to be kept confidential and has given notice to that effect–
(a) in the notice of appeal or when notifying the Secretary of State or the Tribunal of any subsequent change of address; or
(b) within 14 days after an enquiry is made by the recipient of the notice of appeal or the notification referred to in sub-paragraph (a).

19(3) The circumstances referred to in paragraph (1)(b) are that one of the former joint claimants would like their address to be kept confidential and has given notice to that effect–
(a) in the notice of appeal or when notifying the decision maker or the tribunal of any subsequent change of address; or
(b) within 14 days after an enquiry is made by the recipient of the notice of appeal or the notification referred to in sub-paragraph (a).

19(4) Where this paragraph applies, the Secretary of State or other decision maker and the Tribunal must take appropriate steps to secure the confidentiality of the address and of any information which could reasonably be expected to enable a person to identify the address, to the extent that the address or that information is not already known to each other party.

19(5) In this rule–

"absent parent", **"non-resident parent"** and **"person with care"** have the meanings set out in section 3 of the Child Support Act 1991;

"joint claimants" means the persons who made a joint claim for a jobseeker's allowance under the Jobseekers Act 1995, a tax credit under the Tax Credits Act 2002 or in relation to whom an award of universal credit is made under Part 1 of the Welfare Reform Act 2012.

History – R. 19 and the heading preceding it substituted by SI 2014/2128, r. 35, with effect from 20 October 2014.

EXPENSES IN CRIMINAL INJURIES COMPENSATION CASES

20(1) This rule applies only to criminal injuries compensation cases.

20(2) The Tribunal may meet reasonable expenses–

(a) incurred by the appellant, or any person who attends a hearing to give evidence, in attending the hearing; or

(b) incurred by the appellant in connection with any arrangements made by the Tribunal for the inspection of the appellant's injury.

EXPENSES IN SOCIAL SECURITY AND CHILD SUPPORT CASES

21(1) This rule applies only to social security and child support cases.

21(2) The Secretary of State may pay such travelling and other allowances (including compensation for loss of remunerative time) as the Secretary of State may determine to any person required to attend a hearing in proceedings under section 20 of the Child Support Act 1991, section 12 of the Social Security Act 1998 or paragraph 6 of Schedule 7 to the Child Support, Pensions and Social Security Act 2000.

PART 3 – PROCEEDINGS BEFORE THE TRIBUNAL

Chapter 1 – Before the Hearing

CASES IN WHICH THE NOTICE OF APPEAL IS TO BE SENT TO THE TRIBUNAL

22(1) This rule applies to all cases except those to which–

(a) rule 23 (cases in which the notice of appeal is to be sent to the decision maker), or

(b) rule 26 (social security and child support cases started by reference or information in writing),

applies.

22(2) An appellant must start proceedings by sending or delivering a notice of appeal to the Tribunal so that it is received–

(a) in asylum support cases, within 3 days after the date on which the appellant received written notice of the decision being challenged;

(b) in criminal injuries compensation cases, within 90 days after the date of the decision being challenged.

(c) in appeals under the Vaccine Damage Payments Act 1979, at any time;

(d) in other cases–

(i) if mandatory reconsideration applies, within 1 month after the date on which the appellant was sent notice of the result of mandatory reconsideration;

(ii) if mandatory reconsideration does not apply, within the time specified in Schedule 1 to these Rules (time limits for providing notices of appeal in social security and child support cases where mandatory reconsideration does not apply).

22(3) The notice of appeal must be in English or Welsh, must be signed by the appellant and must state–

(a) the name and address of the appellant;

(b) the name and address of the appellant's representative (if any);

(c) an address where documents for the appellant may be sent or delivered;

(d) the name and address of any respondent other than the decision maker; and

(e) [omitted by SI 2013/477, r. 25(c);]

(f) the grounds on which the appellant relies.

22(4) The appellant must provide with the notice of appeal–

(a) a copy of–

(i) the notice of the result of mandatory reconsideration, in any social security and child support case to which mandatory reconsideration applies;

(ii) the decision being challenged, in any other case;

(b) any statement of reasons for that decision that the appellant has; and

(c) any documents in support of the appellant's case which have not been supplied to the respondent;

(d) [omitted by SI 2013/477, r. 25(d).]

22(5) In asylum support cases the notice of appeal must also–

(a) state whether the appellant will require an interpreter at any hearing, and if so for which language or dialect; and

(b) state whether the appellant intends to attend or be represented at any hearing.

22(6) If the appellant provides the notice of appeal to the Tribunal later than the time required by paragraph (2) or by an extension of time allowed under rule 5(3)(a) (power to extend time)–

(a) the notice of appeal must include a request for an extension of time and the reason why the notice of appeal was not provided in time; and

(b) subject to paragraph (8) unless the Tribunal extends time for the notice of appeal under rule 5(3)(a) (power to extend time) the Tribunal must not admit the notice of appeal.

22(7) The Tribunal must send a copy of the notice of appeal and any accompanying documents to each other party–

(a) in asylum support cases, on the day that the Tribunal receives the notice of appeal, or (if that is not reasonably practicable) as soon as reasonably practicable on the following day;

(b) in all other, as soon as reasonably practicable after the Tribunal receives the notice of appeal.

22(7A) Her Majesty's Revenue and Customs must, upon receipt of the notice of appeal from the Tribunal under the Childcare Payments Act 2014, inform the Tribunal whether there are any affected parties within the meaning of section 61(5) of that Act other than the appellant and, if so, provide their names and addresses.

22(8) Where an appeal in a social security and child support case is not made within the time specified in paragraph (2)–

(a) it will be treated as having been made in time, unless the Tribunal directs otherwise, if it is made within not more than 12 months of the time specified and neither the decision maker nor any other respondent objects;

(b) the time for bringing the appeal may not be extended under rule 5(3)(a) by more than 12 months.

22(9) For the purposes of this rule, mandatory reconsideration applies where–

(a) the notice of the decision being challenged includes a statement to the effect that there is a right of appeal in relation to the decision only if the decision-maker has considered an application for the revision, reversal, review or reconsideration (as the case may be) of the decision being challenged; or

(b) the appeal is brought against a decision made by Her Majesty's Revenue and Customs.

History – R. 22(1) substituted by SI 2013/477, r. 25(a), with effect from 8 April 2013.
R. 22(2)(c) and (d) inserted by SI 2013/477, r. 25(b), with effect from 8 April 2013.
In r. 22(2)(d)(ii), the words "(time limits for providing notices of appeal in social security and child support cases where mandatory reconsideration does not apply)" substituted for the words "(time specified for providing notice of appeal)" by SI 2015/1510, r. 15(a), with effect from 21 August 2015.
In r. 22(3)(d) the words "other than the decision maker" inserted and r. 22(3)(e) omitted by SI 2013/477, r. 25(c), with effect from 8 April 2013.
R. 22(4)(a) substituted, in r. 22(4)(b) the words "; and" substituted for the words "or can reasonably obtain" and r. 22(4)(d) and the word "; and" at the end of r. 22(4)(c) omitted by SI 2013/477, r. 25(d), with effect from 8 April 2013.
In r. 22(6), the words "or (aa)" omitted (in both places) by SI 2014/514, r. 22, with effect from 6 April 2014.
In r. 22(6), the former words "or (aa)" inserted (in both places) by SI 2013/2067, r. 25, with effect from 1 November 2013.
In r. 22(6)(b) the words "subject to paragraph (8)" inserted by SI 2013/477, r. 25(e), with effect from 8 April 2013.
In r. 22(7)(b) the words "all other" substituted for the words "criminal injuries compensation cases" by SI 2013/477, r. 25(f), with effect from 8 April 2013.
R. 22(7A) inserted by SI 2015/1510, r. 15(b), with effect from 21 August 2015.
R. 22(8) inserted by SI 2013/477, r. 25(g), with effect from 8 April 2013.
R. 22(9) substituted by SI 2015/1510, r. 15(c), with effect from 21 August 2015. Former r. 22(9) read as follows:

"**22(9)** For the purposes of this rule, mandatory reconsideration applies where the notice of the decision being challenged includes a statement to the effect that there is a right of appeal in relation to the decision only if the decision-maker has considered an application for the revision, reversal, review or reconsideration (as the case may be) of the decision being challenged.".

R. 22(9) inserted by SI 2013/477, r. 25(g), with effect from 8 April 2013.

CASES IN WHICH THE NOTICE OF APPEAL IS TO BE SENT TO THE DECISION MAKER

23(1) This rule applies to appeals under paragraph 6 of Schedule 7 to the Child Support, Pensions and Social Security Act 2000 (housing benefit and council tax benefit: revisions and appeals) or under section 22 of the Child Trust Funds Act 2004.

23(2) An appellant must start proceedings by sending or delivering a notice of appeal to the decision maker so that it is received no later than the latest of–

(a) in a housing benefit or council tax benefit case–

(i) one month after the date on which notice of the decision being challenged was sent to the appellant;

(ii) if a written statement of reasons for the decision was requested within that month, 14 days after the later of–

(aa) the end of that month; or

(ab) the date on which the written statement of reasons was provided; or

(iii) if the appellant made an application for revision of the decision under regulation 4(1)(a) of the Housing Benefit and Council Tax Benefit (Decisions and Appeals) Regulations 2001 and that application was unsuccessful, one month after the date on which notice that the decision would not be revised was sent to the appellant;

(b) in an appeal under section 22 of the Child Trust Funds Act 2004, the period of 30 days specified in section 23(1) of that Act.

23(3) If the appellant provides the notice of appeal to the decision maker later than the time required by paragraph (2)(a) the notice of appeal must include the reason why the notice of appeal was not provided in time.

23(4) Subject to paragraph (5), where an appeal is not made within the time specified in paragraph (2), it will be treated as having been made in time if neither the decision maker nor any other respondent objects.

23(5) No appeal may be made more than 12 months after the time specified in paragraph (2).

23(6) The notice of appeal must be in English or Welsh, must be signed by the appellant and must state–

(a) the name and address of the appellant;

(b) the name and address of the appellant's representative (if any);

(c) an address where documents for the appellant may be sent or delivered;

(d) details of the decision being appealed; and

(e) the grounds on which the appellant relies.

23(7) The decision maker must refer the case to the Tribunal immediately if–

(a) the appeal has been made after the time specified in paragraph (2) and the decision maker or any other respondent objects to it being treated as having been made in time; or

(b) the decision maker considers that the appeal has been made more than 12 months after the time specified in paragraph (2).

23(8) Notwithstanding rule 5(3)(a) (case management powers) and rule 7(2) (failure to comply with rules etc.), the Tribunal must not extend the time limit in paragraph (5).

History – In r. 23(1), the words "appeals under paragraph 6 of Schedule 7 to the Child Support, Pensions and Social Security Act 2000 (housing benefit and council tax benefit: revisions and appeals) or under section 22 of the Child Trust Funds Act 2004" substituted for the words "social security and child support cases in which the notice of decision being challenged informs the appellant that any appeal must be sent to the decision maker." by SI 2015/1510, r. 16(a), with effect from 21 August 2015, subject to savings provision in SI 2015/1510, r. 18 (amendments have no effect in relation to any appeal against a decision made before 6 April 2014 where the decision maker was HMRC).
R. 23(1) substituted by SI 2013/477, r. 26, with effect from 8 April 2013.
R. 23(2)(a) and (b) and the words "no later than the latest of–" before them substituted for the words "within the time specified in Schedule 1 to these Rules (time limits for providing notices of appeal to the decision maker)" by SI 2015/1510, r. 16(b), with effect from 21 August 2015, subject to savings provision in SI 2015/1510, r. 18 (amendments have no effect in relation to any appeal against a decision made before 6 April 2014 where the decision maker was HMRC).
In r. 23(3), the words "paragraph (2)(a)" substituted for the words "paragraph (2)" by SI 2015/1510, r. 16(c), with effect from 21 August 2015, subject to savings provision in SI 2015/1510, r. 18 (amendments have no effect in relation to any appeal against a decision made before 6 April 2014 where the decision maker was HMRC).
In r. 23(4), the words "if neither the decision maker nor any other respondent objects" substituted for the words "if the decision maker does not object" by SI 2012/500, r. 4(2), with effect from 6 April 2012.
In r. 23(4), (5), (7)(a) and (b), the words "paragraph (2)" substituted for the words "Schedule 1" by SI 2015/1510, r. 16(d), with effect from 21 August 2015, subject to savings provision in SI 2015/1510, r. 18 (amendments have no effect in relation to any appeal against a decision made before 6 April 2014 where the decision maker was HMRC).
In r. 23(7), the words "or any other respondent" inserted by SI 2012/500, r. 4(2), with effect from 6 April 2012.
In r. 23(8), the words "or (aa)" omitted by SI 2015/1510, r. 16(e), with effect from 21 August 2015, subject to savings provision in SI 2015/1510, r. 18 (amendments have no effect in relation to any appeal against a decision made before 6 April 2014 where the decision maker was HMRC).
In r. 23(8), the words "or (aa)" inserted by SI 2013/2067, r. 26, with effect from 1 November 2013.
R. 23(8) inserted by SI 2009/1975, r. 3, with effect from 1 September 2009.

RESPONSES AND REPLIES

24(1) When a decision maker receives a copy of a notice of appeal from the Tribunal under rule 22(7), the decision maker must send or deliver a response to the Tribunal–

(a) in asylum support cases, so that it is received within 3 days after the date on which the Tribunal received the notice of appeal;

(b) in–

(i) criminal injuries compensation cases, or

(ii) appeals under the Child Support Act 1991,

within 42 days after the date on which the decision maker received the copy of the notice of appeal; and

(c) in other cases, within 28 days after the date on which the decision maker received the copy of the notice of appeal.

24(1A) Where a decision maker receives a notice of appeal from an appellant under rule 23(2), the decision maker must send or deliver a response to the Tribunal so that it is received as soon as reasonably practicable after the decision maker received the notice of appeal.

24(2) The response must state–

(a) the name and address of the decision maker;

(b) the name and address of the decision maker's representative (if any);

(c) an address where documents for the decision maker may be sent or delivered;

(d) the names and addresses of any other respondents and their representatives (if any);

(e) whether the decision maker opposes the appellant's case and, if so, any grounds for such opposition which are not set out in any documents which are before the Tribunal; and

(f) any further information required by a practice direction or direction.

24(3) The response may include a submission as to whether it would be appropriate for the case to be disposed of without a hearing.

24(4) The decision maker must provide with the response–

(a) a copy of any written record of the decision under challenge, and any statement of reasons for that decision, if they were not sent with the notice of appeal;

(b) copies of all documents relevant to the case in the decision maker's possession, unless a practice direction or direction states otherwise; and

(c) in cases to which rule 23 (cases in which the notice of appeal is to be sent to the decision maker) applies, a copy of the notice of appeal, any documents provided by the appellant with the notice of appeal and (if they have not otherwise been provided to the Tribunal) the name and address of the appellant's representative (if any).

24(5) The decision maker must provide a copy of the response and any accompanying documents to each other party at the same time as it provides the response to the Tribunal.

24(6) The appellant and any other respondent may make a written submission and supply further documents in reply to the decision maker's response.

24(7) Any submission or further documents under paragraph (6) must be provided to the Tribunal within 1 month after the date on which the decision maker sent the response to the party providing the reply, and the Tribunal must send a copy to each other party.

History – R. 24(1)(b) substituted by SI 2014/2128, r. 37, with effect from 20 October 2014.
R. 24(1) and (1A) substituted for former r. 24(1) by SI 2013/477, r. 27, with effect from 1 October 2014.
R. 24(1)(aa) inserted (and the "and" at the end of r. 24(1)(a) omitted) by SI 2011/651, r. 4(3), with effect from 1 April 2011.
In r. 24(2)(f) the words "or documents", which appeared after the words "further information", omitted by SI 2013/477, r. 27, with effect from 1 October 2014.

MEDICAL AND PHYSICAL EXAMINATION IN APPEALS UNDER SECTION 12 OF THE SOCIAL SECURITY ACT 1998

25(1) This rule applies only to appeals under section 12 of the Social Security Act 1998.

25(2) At a hearing an appropriate member of the Tribunal may carry out a physical examination of a person if the case relates to–

(a) the extent of that person's disablement and its assessment in accordance with section 68(6) of and Schedule 6 to, or section 103 of, the Social Security Contributions and Benefits Act 1992; or

(b) diseases or injuries prescribed for the purpose of section 108 of that Act.

25(3) If an issue which falls within Schedule 2 to these Rules (issues in relation to which the Tribunal may refer a person for medical examination) is raised in an appeal, the Tribunal may exercise its power under section 20 of the Social Security Act 1998 to refer a person to a health care professional approved by the Secretary of State for–

(a) the examination of that person; and

(b) the production of a report on the condition of that person.

25(4) Neither paragraph (2) nor paragraph (3) entitles the Tribunal to require a person to undergo a physical test for the purpose of determining whether that person is unable to walk or virtually unable to do so.

SOCIAL SECURITY AND CHILD SUPPORT CASES STARTED BY REFERENCE OR INFORMATION IN WRITING

26(1) This rule applies to proceedings under section 28D of the Child Support Act 1991 and paragraph 3 of Schedule 2 to the Tax Credits Act 2002.

26(2) A person starting proceedings under section 28D of the Child Support Act 1991 must send or deliver a written reference to the Tribunal.

26(3) A person starting proceedings under paragraph 3 of Schedule 2 to the Tax Credits Act 2002 must send or deliver an information in writing to the Tribunal.

26(4) The reference or the information in writing must include–

(a) an address where documents for the person starting proceedings may be sent or delivered;

(b) the names and addresses of the respondents and their representatives (if any); and

(c) a submission on the issues that arise for determination by the Tribunal.

26(5) Unless a practice direction or direction states otherwise, the person starting proceedings must also provide a copy of each document in their possession which is relevant to the proceedings.

26(6) Subject to any obligation under rule 19(3) (confidentiality in child support cases), the person starting proceedings must provide a copy of the written reference or the information in writing and any accompanying documents to each respondent at the same time as they provide the written reference or the information in writing to the Tribunal.

26(7) Each respondent may send or deliver to the Tribunal a written submission and any further relevant documents within one month of the date on which the person starting proceedings sent a copy of the written reference or the information in writing to that respondent.

Chapter 2 – Hearings

DECISION WITH OR WITHOUT A HEARING

27(1) Subject to the following paragraphs, the Tribunal must hold a hearing before making a decision which disposes of proceedings unless–

(a) each party has consented to, or has not objected to, the matter being decided without a hearing; and

(b) the Tribunal considers that it is able to decide the matter without a hearing.

27(2) This rule does not apply to decisions under Part 4.

27(3) The Tribunal may in any event dispose of proceedings without a hearing under rule 8 (striking out a party's case).

27(4) In a criminal injuries compensation case–

(a) the Tribunal may make a decision which disposes of proceedings without a hearing; and

(b) subject to paragraph (5), if the Tribunal makes a decision which disposes of proceedings without a hearing, any party may make a written application to the Tribunal for the decision to be reconsidered at a hearing.

27(5) An application under paragraph (4)(b) may not be made in relation to a decision–

(a) not to extend a time limit;

(b) not to set aside a previous decision;

(c) not to allow an appeal against a decision not to extend a time limit; or

(d) not to allow an appeal against a decision not to reopen a case.

27(6) An application under paragraph (4)(b) must be received within 1 month after the date on which the Tribunal sent notice of the decision to the party making the application.

ENTITLEMENT TO ATTEND A HEARING

28 Subject to rule 30(5) (exclusion of a person from a hearing), each party to proceedings is entitled to attend a hearing.

NOTICE OF HEARINGS

29(1) The Tribunal must give each party entitled to attend a hearing reasonable notice of the time and place of the hearing (including any adjourned or postponed hearing) and any changes to the time and place of the hearing.

29(2) The period of notice under paragraph (1) must be at least 14 days except that–

(a) in an asylum support case the Tribunal must give at least 1 day's and not more than 5 days' notice; and

(b) the Tribunal may give shorter notice–

(i) with the parties' consent; or

(ii) in urgent or exceptional circumstances.

PUBLIC AND PRIVATE HEARINGS

30(1) Subject to the following paragraphs, all hearings must be held in public.

30(2) A hearing in a criminal injuries compensation case must be held in private unless–

(a) the appellant has consented to the hearing being held in public; and

(b) the Tribunal considers that it is in the interests of justice for the hearing to be held in public.

30(3) The Tribunal may give a direction that a hearing, or part of it, is to be held in private.

30(4) Where a hearing, or part of it, is to be held in private, the Tribunal may determine who is permitted to attend the hearing or part of it.

30(5) The Tribunal may give a direction excluding from any hearing, or part of it–

(a) any person whose conduct the Tribunal considers is disrupting or is likely to disrupt the hearing;

(b) any person whose presence the Tribunal considers is likely to prevent another person from giving evidence or making submissions freely;

(c) any person who the Tribunal considers should be excluded in order to give effect to a direction under rule 14(2) (withholding information likely to cause harm); or

(d) any person where the purpose of the hearing would be defeated by the attendance of that person.

30(6) The Tribunal may give a direction excluding a witness from a hearing until that witness gives evidence.

HEARINGS IN A PARTY'S ABSENCE

31 If a party fails to attend a hearing the Tribunal may proceed with the hearing if the Tribunal–

(a) is satisfied that the party has been notified of the hearing or that reasonable steps have been taken to notify the party of the hearing; and

(b) considers that it is in the interests of justice to proceed with the hearing.

Chapter 3 – Decisions

CONSENT ORDERS

32(1) The Tribunal may, at the request of the parties but only if it considers it appropriate, make a consent order disposing of the proceedings and making such other appropriate provision as the parties have agreed.

32(2) Notwithstanding any other provision of these Rules, the Tribunal need not hold a hearing before making an order under paragraph (1), or provide reasons for the order.

NOTICE OF DECISIONS

33(1) The Tribunal may give a decision orally at a hearing.

33(2) Subject to rule 14(2) (withholding information likely to cause harm), the Tribunal must provide to each party as soon as reasonably practicable after making a decision (other than a decision under Part 4) which finally disposes of all issues in the proceedings or of a preliminary issue dealt with following a direction under rule 5(3)(e)–

(a) a decision notice stating the Tribunal's decision;

(b) where appropriate, notification of the right to apply for a written statement of reasons under rule 34(3); and

(c) notification of any right of appeal against the decision and the time within which, and the manner in which, such right of appeal may be exercised.

33(3) In asylum support cases the notice and notifications required by paragraph (2) must be provided at the hearing or sent on the day that the decision is made.

History – In r. 33(2) the words "a decision (other than a decision under Part 4) which finally disposes of all issues in the proceedings or of a preliminary issue dealt with following a direction under rule 5(3)(e)" substituted for the words "a decision which finally disposes of all issues in the proceedings (except a decision under Part 4)" by SI 2013/477, r. 28, with effect from 8 April 2013.

REASONS FOR DECISIONS

34(1) In asylum support cases the Tribunal must send a written statement of reasons for a decision which disposes of proceedings (except a decision under Part 4) to each party–

(a) if the case is decided at a hearing, within 3 days after the hearing; or

(b) if the case is decided without a hearing, on the day that the decision is made.

34(2) In all other cases the Tribunal may give reasons for a decision which disposes of proceedings (except a decision under Part 4)–

(a) orally at a hearing; or

(b) in a written statement of reasons to each party.

34(3) Unless the Tribunal has already provided a written statement of reasons under paragraph (2)(b), a party may make a written application to the Tribunal for such statement following a decision which finally disposes of–

(a) all issues in the proceedings; or

(b) a preliminary issue dealt with following a direction under rule 5(3)(e).

34(4) An application under paragraph (3) must be received within 1 month of the date on which the Tribunal sent or otherwise provided to the party a decision notice relating to the decision.

34(5) If a party makes an application in accordance with paragraphs (3) and (4) the Tribunal must, subject to rule 14(2) (withholding information likely to cause harm), send a written statement of reasons to each party within 1 month of the date on which it received the application or as soon as reasonably practicable after the end of that period.

History – In r. 34(3) the words from "which finally disposes of–" to the end of para. (b) substituted for the words "which finally disposes of all issues in the proceedings" by SI 2013/477, r. 29(a), with effect from 8 April 2013.
In r. 34(4) the words "which finally disposes of all issues in the proceedings" omitted by SI 2013/477, r. 29(b), with effect from 8 April 2013.

PART 4 – CORRECTING, SETTING ASIDE, REVIEWING AND APPEALING TRIBUNAL DECISIONS

INTERPRETATION

35 In this Part–

"appeal" means the exercise of a right of appeal–

(a) under paragraph 2(2) or 4(1) of Schedule 2 to the Tax Credits Act 2002;

(b) under section 21(10) of the Child Trust Funds Act 2004; or

(c) on a point of law under section 11 of the 2007 Act; and

"review" means the review of a decision by the Tribunal under section 9 of the 2007 Act.

CLERICAL MISTAKES AND ACCIDENTAL SLIPS OR OMISSIONS

36 The Tribunal may at any time correct any clerical mistake or other accidental slip or omission in a decision, direction or any document produced by it, by–

(a) sending notification of the amended decision or direction, or a copy of the amended document, to all parties; and

(b) making any necessary amendment to any information published in relation to the decision, direction or document.

SETTING ASIDE A DECISION WHICH DISPOSES OF PROCEEDINGS

37(1) The Tribunal may set aside a decision which disposes of proceedings, or part of such a decision, and re-make the decision, or the relevant part of it, if–

(a) the Tribunal considers that it is in the interests of justice to do so; and

(b) one or more of the conditions in paragraph (2) are satisfied.

37(2) The conditions are–

(a) a document relating to the proceedings was not sent to, or was not received at an appropriate time by, a party or a party's representative;

(b) a document relating to the proceedings was not sent to the Tribunal at an appropriate time;

(c) a party, or a party's representative, was not present at a hearing related to the proceedings; or

(d) there has been some other procedural irregularity in the proceedings.

37(3) A party applying for a decision, or part of a decision, to be set aside under paragraph (1) must make a written application to the Tribunal so that it is received no later than 1 month after the date on which the Tribunal sent notice of the decision to the party.

APPLICATION FOR PERMISSION TO APPEAL

38(1) This rule does not apply to asylum support cases or criminal injuries compensation cases.

38(2) A person seeking permission to appeal must make a written application to the Tribunal for permission to appeal.

38(3) An application under paragraph (2) must be sent or delivered to the Tribunal so that it is received no later than 1 month after the latest of the dates that the Tribunal sends to the person making the application–

(za) the relevant decision notice;

(a) written reasons for the decision, if the decision disposes of–

(i) all issues in the proceedings; or

(ii) subject to paragraph (3A), a preliminary issue dealt with following a direction under rule 5(3)(e);

(b) notification of amended reasons for, or correction of, the decision following a review; or

(c) notification that an application for the decision to be set aside has been unsuccessful.

38(3A) The Tribunal may direct that the 1 month within which a party may send or deliver an application for permission to appeal against a decision that disposes of a preliminary issue shall run from the date of the decision that disposes of all issues in the proceedings.

38(4) The date in paragraph (3)(c) applies only if the application for the decision to be set aside was made within the time stipulated in rule 37 (setting aside a decision which disposes of proceedings) or any extension of that time granted by the Tribunal.

38(5) If the person seeking permission to appeal sends or delivers the application to the Tribunal later than the time required by paragraph (3) or by any extension of time under rule 5(3)(a) (power to extend time)–

(a) the application must include a request for an extension of time and the reason why the application was not provided in time; and

(b) unless the Tribunal extends time for the application under rule 5(3)(a) (power to extend time) the Tribunal must not admit the application.

38(6) An application under paragraph (2) must–

(a) identify the decision of the Tribunal to which it relates;

(b) identify the alleged error or errors of law in the decision; and

(c) state the result the party making the application is seeking.

38(7) If a person makes an application under paragraph (2) in respect of a decision that disposes of proceedings or of a preliminary issue dealt with following a direction under rule 5(3)(e) when the Tribunal has not given a written statement of reasons for its decision–

(a) if no application for a written statement of reasons has been made to the Tribunal, the application for permission must be treated as such an application;

(b) unless the Tribunal decides to give permission and directs that this sub-paragraph does not apply, the application is not to be treated as an application for permission to appeal; and

(c) if an application for a written statement of reasons has been, or is, refused because of a delay in making the application, the Tribunal must only admit the application for permission if the Tribunal considers that it is in the interests of justice to do so.

History – R. 38(3)(za) inserted by SI 2013/477, r. 30(a), with effect from 8 April 2013.
In r. 38(3)(a) the words from ", if the decision disposes of–" to the end inserted by SI 2013/477, r. 30(b), with effect from 8 April 2013.
R. 38(3A) inserted by SI 2013/477, r. 30(c), with effect from 8 April 2013.
In r. 38(7) the words "in respect of a decision that disposes of proceedings or of a preliminary issue dealt with following a direction under rule 5(3)(e)" inserted by SI 2013/477, r. 30(d), with effect from 8 April 2013.

TRIBUNAL'S CONSIDERATION OF APPLICATION FOR PERMISSION TO APPEAL

39(1) On receiving an application for permission to appeal the Tribunal must first consider, taking into account the overriding objective in rule 2, whether to review the decision in accordance with rule 40 (review of a decision).

39(2) If the Tribunal decides not to review the decision, or reviews the decision and decides to take no action in relation to the decision, or part of it, the Tribunal must consider whether to give permission to appeal in relation to the decision or that part of it.

39(3) The Tribunal must send a record of its decision to the parties as soon as practicable.

39(4) If the Tribunal refuses permission to appeal it must send with the record of its decision–

(a) a statement of its reasons for such refusal; and

(b) notification of the right to make an application to the Upper Tribunal for permission to appeal and the time within which, and the method by which, such application must be made.

39(5) The Tribunal may give permission to appeal on limited grounds, but must comply with paragraph (4) in relation to any grounds on which it has refused permission.

REVIEW OF A DECISION

40(1) This rule does not apply to asylum support cases or criminal injuries compensation cases.

40(2) The Tribunal may only undertake a review of a decision–

(a) pursuant to rule 39(1) (review on an application for permission to appeal); and

(b) if it is satisfied that there was an error of law in the decision.

40(3) The Tribunal must notify the parties in writing of the outcome of any review, and of any right of appeal in relation to the outcome.

40(4) If the Tribunal takes any action in relation to a decision following a review without first giving every party an opportunity to make representations, the notice under paragraph (3) must state that any party that did not have an opportunity to make representations may apply for such action to be set aside and for the decision to be reviewed again.

POWER TO TREAT AN APPLICATION AS A DIFFERENT TYPE OF APPLICATION

41 The Tribunal may treat an application for a decision to be corrected, set aside or reviewed, or for permission to appeal against a decision, as an application for any other one of those things.

SCHEDULE 1 – TIME LIMITS FOR PROVIDING NOTICES OF APPEAL IN SOCIAL SECURITY AND CHILD SUPPORT CASES WHERE MANDATORY RECONSIDERATION DOES NOT APPLY

Rule 22

Type of proceedings	*Time for providing notice of appeal*
1 Appeal against a certification of NHS charges under section 157(1) of the Health and Social Care (Community Health and Standards) Act 2003	(a) 3 months after the latest of– (i) the date on the certificate; (ii) the date on which the compensation payment was made; (iii) if the certificate has been reviewed, the date the certificate was confirmed or a fresh certificate was issued; or (iv) the date of any agreement to treat an earlier compensation payment as having been made in final discharge of a claim made by or in respect of an injured person and arising out of the injury or death; or

Type of proceedings	*Time for providing notice of appeal*
	(b) if the person to whom the certificate has been issued makes an application under section 157(4) of the Health and Social Care (Community Health and Standards) Act 2003, one month after– (i) the date of the decision on that application; or (ii) if the person appeals against that decision under section 157(6) of that Act, the date on which the appeal is decided or withdrawn.
2 Appeal against a waiver decision under section 157(6) of the Health and Social Care (Community Health and Standards) Act 2003	One month after the date of the decision.
3 Appeal against a certificate of NHS charges under section 7 of the Road Traffic (NHS Charges) Act 1999	3 months after the latest of– (a) the date on which the liability under section 1(2) of the Road Traffic (NHS Charges) Act 1999 was discharged; (b) if the certificate has been reviewed, the date the certificate was confirmed or a fresh certificate was issued; or (c) the date of any agreement to treat an earlier compensation payment as having been made in final discharge of a claim made by or in respect of a traffic casualty and arising out of the injury or death.
4 Appeal against a certificate of recoverable benefits under section 11 of the Social Security (Recovery of Benefits) Act 1997	One month after the latest of– (a) the date on which any payment to the Secretary of State required under section 6 of the Social Security (Recovery of Benefits) Act 1997 was made; (b) if the certificate has been reviewed, the date the certificate was confirmed or a fresh certificate was issued; (c) the date of any agreement to treat an earlier compensation payment as having been made in final discharge of a claim made by or in respect of an injured person and arising out of the accident, injury or disease.
5 Cases other than those listed above	The latest of– (a) one month after the date on which notice of the decision being challenged was sent to the appellant; (b) if a written statement of reasons for the decision was requested within that month, 14 days after the later of– (i) the end of that month; or (ii) the date on which the written statement of reasons was provided; (c) if the appellant made an application for the revision of the decision under– (i) regulation 17(1)(a) of the Child Support (Maintenance Assessment Procedure) Regulations 1992; (ii) regulation 3(1) or (3) or 3A(1)(a) of the Social Security and Child Support (Decisions and Appeals) Regulations 1999; (iii) regulation 14(1)(a) of the Child Support Maintenance Calculation Regulations 2012(c); or

Type of proceedings	*Time for providing notice of appeal*
	(iv) regulation 5 of the Universal Credit, Personal Independence Payment, Jobseeker's Allowance and Employment and Support Allowance (Decisions and Appeals) Regulations 2013, and the application was unsuccessful, one month after the date on which notice that the decision would not be revised was sent to the appellant.

History – Sch. 1 substituted by SI 2015/1510, r. 17, with effect from 21 August 2015, subject to savings provision in SI 2015/1510, r. 18 (amendments have no effect in relation to any appeal against a decision made before 6 April 2014 where the decision maker was HMRC). Former Sch. 1 read as follows:

"**SCHEDULE 1 – TIME LIMITS FOR PROVIDING NOTICES OF APPEAL**

Rule 23

History – In the heading the words "to the decision maker" omitted by SI 2013/477, r. 31(a), with effect from 8 April 2013.

Type of proceedings	Time for providing notice of appeal
cases other than those listed below	the latest of– (a) one month after the date on which notice of the decision being challenged was sent to the appellant; (b) if a written statement of reasons for the decision was requested within that month, 14 days after the later of– (i) the end of that month; or (ii) the date on which the written statement of reasons was provided; or (c) if the appellant made an application for revision of the decision under– (i) regulation 14 of the Child Support Maintenance Calculation Regulations 2012; (ii) regulation 3(1) or (3) of the Social Security and Child Support (Decision and Appeals) Regulations 1999; (iii) regulation 4 of the Housing Benefit and Council Tax Benefit (Decisions and Appeals) Regulations 2001; (iv) regulation 17(1)(a) of the Child Support (Maintenance Assessment Procedure) Regulations 1992 (where still applicable to the particular case); or (v) regulation 3A(1) of the Social Security and Child Support (Decisions and Appeals) Regulations 1999 (where still applicable to the particular case), and that application was unsuccessful, 1 month after the date on which notice that the decision would not be revised was sent to the appellant.
appeal against a certificate of NHS charges under section 157(1) of the Health and Social Care (Community Health and Standards) Act 2003	(a) 3 months after the latest of– (i) the date on the certificate; (ii) the date on which the compensation payment was made; (iii) if the certificate has been reviewed, the date the certificate was confirmed or a fresh certificate was issued; or (iv) the date of any agreement to treat an earlier compensation payment as having been made in final discharge of a claim made by or in respect of an injured person and arising out of the injury or death; or (b) if the person to whom the certificate has been issued makes an application under section 157(4) of the Health and Social Care (Community Health and Standards) Act 2003, one month after– (i) the date of the decision on that application; or (ii) if the person appeals against that decision under section 157(6) of that Act, the date on which the appeal is decided or withdrawn
appeal against a waiver decision under section 157(6) of the Health and Social Care (Community Health and Standards) Act 2003	one month after the date of the decision
appeal against a certificate of NHS charges under section 7 of the Road Traffic (NHS Charges) Act 1999	3 months after the latest of– (a) the date on which the liability under section 1(2) of the Road Traffic (NHS Charges) Act 1999 was discharged; (b) if the certificate has been reviewed, the date the certificate was confirmed or a fresh certificate was issued; or (c) the date of any agreement to treat an earlier compensation payment as having been made in final discharge of a claim made by or in respect of a traffic casualty and arising out of the injury or death
appeal against a certificate of recoverable benefits under section 11 of the Social Security (Recovery of Benefits) Act 1997	one month after the latest of– (a) the date on which any payment to the Secretary of State required under section 6 of the Social Security (Recovery of Benefits) Act 1997 was made; (b) if the certificate has been reviewed, the date the certificate was confirmed or a fresh certificate was issued; or (c) the date of any agreement to treat an earlier compensation payment as having been made in final discharge of a claim made by or in respect of an injured person and arising out of the accident, injury or disease
appeal under the Vaccine Damage Payments Act 1979	no time limit

Type of proceedings	Time for providing notice of appeal
appeal under the Tax Credits Act 2002	as set out in the Tax Credits Act 2002
appeal under the Child Trust Funds Act 2004	as set out in the Child Trust Funds Act 2004
appeal against a decision in respect of a claim for child benefit or guardian's allowance under section 12 of the Social Security Act 1998	as set out in regulation 28 of the Child Benefit and Guardian's Allowance (Decisions and Appeals) Regulations 2003

History – In the Table, in the former first entry, in the second column, para. (c) substituted by SI 2013/477, r. 31(b) with effect from 8 April 2013.
In the Table, the first entry substituted by SI 2010/2653, r. 5(4), with effect from 29 November 2010.
In the Table, in the former first entry, in the second column, para (c) substituted by SI 2009/1975, r. 4, with effect from 1 September 2009.".

SCHEDULE 2 – ISSUES IN RELATION TO WHICH THE TRIBUNAL MAY REFER A PERSON FOR MEDICAL EXAMINATION UNDER SECTION 20(2) OF THE SOCIAL SECURITY ACT 1998

Rule 25(3)

An issue falls within this Schedule if the issue–

(a) is whether the claimant satisfies the conditions for entitlement to–
  (i) an attendance allowance specified in section 64 and 65(1) of the Social Security Contributions and Benefits Act 1992;
  (ii) severe disablement allowance under section 68 of that Act;
  (iii) the care component of a disability living allowance specified in section 72(1) and (2) of that Act;
  (iv) the mobility component of a disability living allowance specified in section 73(1), (8) and (9) of that Act;
  (v) a disabled person's tax credit specified in section 129(1)(b) of that Act.
  (vi) the daily living component of personal independence payment specified in section 78 of the Welfare Reform Act 2012; or
  (vii) the mobility component of personal independence payment specified in section 79 of the Welfare Reform Act 2012.

(b) relates to the period throughout which the claimant is likely to satisfy the conditions for entitlement to an attendance allowance or a disability living allowance;

(c) is the rate at which an attendance allowance is payable;

(d) is the rate at which the care component or the mobility component of a disability living allowance is payable;

(e) is whether a person is incapable of work for the purposes of the Social Security Contributions and Benefits Act 1992;

(f) relates to the extent of a person's disablement and its assessment in accordance with Schedule 6 to the Social Security Contributions and Benefits Act 1992;

(g) is whether the claimant suffers a loss of physical or mental faculty as a result of the relevant accident for the purposes of section 103 of the Social Security Contributions and Benefits Act 1992;

(h) relates to any payment arising under, or by virtue of a scheme having effect under, section 111 of, and Schedule 8 to, the Social Security Contributions and Benefits Act 1992 (workmen's compensation);

(i) is whether a person has limited capability for work or work-related activity for the purposes of the Welfare Reform Act 2007.

(j) is the rate at which the daily living component or mobility component of personal independence payment is payable.

History – In para. (a) the word "or" at end of para. (a)(iv) omitted and para. (a)(vi) and (vii) inserted by SI 2013/477, r. 32(a) and (b), with effect from 8 April 2013.
Para. (j) *inserted by SI 2013/477, r. 32(c), with effect from 8 April 2013.*

TRANSFER OF TRIBUNAL FUNCTIONS ORDER 2008

(SI 2008/2833)

Made on 29 October 2008 by the Lord Chancellor in exercise of the powers conferred by s. 30(1) and (4), 31(1), (2) and (9), 32(3) and (5), 33(2) and (3), 34(2) and (3), 37(1), 38 and 145 of, and para. 30 of Sch. 5 to, the Tribunals, Courts and Enforcement Act 2007. Operative from 3 November 2008.

CITATION, COMMENCEMENT, INTERPRETATION AND EXTENT

1(1) This Order may be cited as the Transfer of Tribunal Functions Order 2008 and comes into force on 3rd November 2008.

1(2) A reference in this Order to a Schedule by a number alone is a reference to the Schedule so numbered in this Order.

1(3) Subject as follows, this Order extends to England and Wales, Scotland and Northern Ireland.

1(4) Except as provided by paragraph (5) or (6), an amendment, repeal or revocation of any enactment by any provision of Schedule 3 extends to the part or parts of the United Kingdom to which the enactment extends.

1(5) [Not relevant to NI contributions.]

1(6) [Not relevant to NI contributions.]

TRANSFER OF FUNCTIONS OF CERTAIN TRIBUNALS

3(1) Subject to paragraph (3), the functions of the tribunals listed in Table 1 of Schedule 1 are transferred to the First-tier Tribunal.

3(2) Subject to paragraph (3), the functions of the tribunals listed in Table 2 of Schedule 1 are transferred to the Upper Tribunal.

3(3) [Not relevant to NI contributions.]

ABOLITION OF TRIBUNALS TRANSFERRED UNDER SECTION 30(1)

4(1) The tribunals listed in Table 1 and Table 2 of Schedule 1 are abolished except for–

(a) [not relevant to NI contributions;]

(b) [not relevant to NI contributions.]

TRANSFER OF PERSONS INTO THE FIRST-TIER TRIBUNAL AND THE UPPER TRIBUNAL

5(1) A person holding an office listed in a table in Schedule 2 who was, was a member of, or was an authorised decision-maker for, a tribunal listed in the corresponding table in Schedule 1 immediately before the functions of that tribunal were transferred under article 3 shall hold the corresponding office or offices.

5(2) In paragraph (1) **"corresponding"** means appearing in the corresponding entry in the table below.

Table in Schedule 1	*Table in Schedule 2*	*Office or offices*
Table 1	Table 1	Transferred-in judge of the First-tier Tribunal
Table 1	Table 2	Transferred-in other member of the First-tier Tribunal
Table 1	Table 3	Transferred in judge of the First-tier Tribunal and deputy judge of the Upper Tribunal
Table 2	Table 4	Transferred-in judge of the Upper Tribunal
Table 1 or 2	Table 5	Transferred-in other member of the Upper Tribunal

MINOR, CONSEQUENTIAL AND TRANSITIONAL PROVISIONS

9(1) Schedule 3 contains minor, consequential and supplemental amendments, and repeals and revocations as a consequence of those amendments.

9(2) Schedule 4 contains transitional provisions.

SCHEDULE 1 – FUNCTIONS TRANSFERRED TO THE FIRST-TIER TRIBUNAL AND UPPER TRIBUNAL

Articles 3, 4 and 5

Table 1: Functions transferred to the First-tier Tribunal

Tribunal	*Enactment*
Adjudicator	Section 5 of the Criminal Injuries Compensation Act 1995 (c.53)
Appeal tribunal	Chapter 1 of Part 1 of the Social Security Act 1998 (c.14)
Asylum Support Adjudicators	Section 102 of the Immigration and Asylum Act 1999 (c.33)
Mental Health Review Tribunal for a region of England	Section 65(1) and (1A)(a) of the Mental Health Act 1983 (c.20)
Pensions Appeal Tribunal in England and Wales	Section 8(2) of the War Pensions (Administrative Provisions) Act 1919 (c.53) and paragraph 1(1) of the Schedule to the Pensions Appeal Tribunals Act 1943 (c.39)
Special Educational Needs and Disability Tribunal	Section 28H of the Disability Discrimination Act 1995 (c.50) and section 333 of the Education Act 1996 (c.56) and
Tribunal, except in respect of its functions under section 4 of the Safeguarding Vulnerable Groups Act 2006 (c.47)	Section 9 of the Protection of Children Act 1999 (c.14)

Table 2: Functions transferred to the Upper Tribunal

Tribunal	*Enactment*
Child Support Commissioner	Section 22 of the Child Support Act 1991 (c.48)
Social Security Commissioner	Schedule 4 to the Social Security Act 1998 (c.14)
Tribunal, in respect of its functions under section 4 of the Safeguarding Vulnerable Groups Act 2006 (c.47)	Section 9 of the Protection of Children Act 1999 (c.14)

SCHEDULE 2 – PERSONS TRANSFERRED AS JUDGES AND MEMBERS OF THE FIRST-TIER TRIBUNAL AND UPPER TRIBUNAL

Article 5

Table 1: Members becoming transferred-in judges of the First-tier Tribunal

Tribunal Member	*Enactment*
A legal member of the Criminal Injuries Compensation Appeals Panel	Section 5 of the Criminal Injuries Compensation Act 1995 (c.53) and the Criminal Injuries Compensation Schemes
A legally qualified panel member	Section 6 of the Social Security Act 1998 (c.14)
The Deputy Chief Asylum Support Adjudicator or an adjudicator	Section 102 of and paragraph 1(a) and (c) of Schedule 10 to the Immigration and Asylum Act 1999 (c.33)
A legal member	Paragraph 1(a) of Schedule 2 to the Mental Health Act 1983 (c.20)
The Deputy President of Pensions Appeal Tribunals or a legally qualified member	Paragraphs 2A(1)(a) and 2B(1) of the Schedule to the Pensions Appeal Tribunals Act 1943 (c.39)
A member of the chairmen's panel	Section 333(2)(b) of the Education Act 1996 (c.56)

Tribunal Member	*Enactment*
A member of the chairmen's panel	Paragraph 1(1)(a) of the Schedule to the Protection of Children Act 1999 (c.14)

Table 2: Members becoming transferred-in other members of the First-tier Tribunal

Tribunal Member	*Enactment*
A member of the Criminal Injuries Compensation Appeals Panel other than the Chairman or a legal member	Section 5 of the Criminal Injuries Compensation Act 1995 (c.53) and the Criminal Injuries Compensation Schemes
A financially qualified panel member, a medically qualified panel member or a panel member with a disability qualification	Section 6 of the Social Security Act 1998 (c.14)
A medical member or other member	Paragraph 1(b) or (c) of Schedule 2 to the Mental Health Act 1983 (c.20)
A medically qualified member, a member with knowledge or experience of service, or other member	Paragraph 2A(1)(b), (c) or (d) of the Schedule to the Pensions Appeal Tribunals Act 1943 (c.39)
A member of the lay panel	Section 333(2)(c) of the Education Act 1996 (c.56)
A member of the lay panel, other than a member in Table 5	Paragraph 1(1)(c) of the Schedule to the Protection of Children Act 1999 (c.14)

Table 3: Members becoming transferred-in judges of the First-tier Tribunal and deputy judges of the Upper Tribunal

Tribunal Member	*Enactment*
The Chairman	Section 5(3)(b) of the Criminal Injuries Compensation Act 1995 (c.53) and the Criminal Injuries Compensation Schemes
The President	Section 5 of the Social Security Act 1998 (c.14)
The Chief Asylum Support Adjudicator	Section 102 of and paragraph 1(b) of Schedule 10 to the Immigration and Asylum Act 1999 (c.33)
A chairman of a Mental Health Review Tribunal	Paragraph 3 of Schedule 2 to the Mental Health Act 1983 (c.20)
A President of Pensions Appeal Tribunals	Paragraph 2B(1) of the Schedule to the Pensions Appeal Tribunals Act 1943 (c.39)
A President	Section 333(2)(a) of the Education Act 1996 (c.56)
The President	Paragraph 1(1)(a) of the Schedule to the Protection of Children Act 1999 (c.14)
The Deputy President	Appointed as a member of the chairmen's panel under paragraph 1(1)(b) of the Schedule to the Protection of Children Act 1999 (c.14) and also appointed as deputy president of the Tribunal
A deputy Child Support Commissioner	Paragraph 4 of Schedule 4 to the Child Support Act 1991 (c.48)
A deputy Commissioner	Paragraph 1(2) of Schedule 4 to the Social Security Act 1998 (c.14)

Table 4: Members becoming transferred-in judges of the Upper Tribunal

Tribunal Member	*Enactment*
The Chief Child Support Commissioner or a Child Support Commissioner	Section 22 of the Child Support Act 1991 (c.48)
The Chief Social Security Commissioner or a Social Security Commissioner	Paragraph 1 of Schedule 4 to the Social Security Act 1998 (c.14)

SCHEDULE 3 – MINOR, CONSEQUENTIAL AND SUPPLEMENTAL PROVISIONS

Article 6

SOCIAL SECURITY ADMINISTRATION ACT 1992

101 The Social Security Administration Act 1992 is amended as follows.

102 [Not relevant to National Insurance contributions.].

103 [Not relevant to National Insurance contributions.]

104(1) Schedule 4 (persons employed in social security administration or adjudication) is amended as follows.

104(2) [Amends SSAA 1992, Sch. 4, Pt. 1 entry headed "Government departments".]

104(3) [Amends SSAA 1992, Sch. 4, Pt. 1 entry headed "Adjudicating bodies".]

104(4) [Amends SSAA 1992, Sch. 4, Pt. 1 entry headed "Former officers".]

104(5) [Amends SSAA 1992, Sch. 4, Pt. 2, para. 3.]

104(6) [Inserts SSAA 1992, Sch. 4, Pt. 2, para. 3A.]

PENSIONS SCHEMES ACT 1993

111 The Pensions Schemes Act 1993 is amended as follows.

112 [Amends PSA 1993, s. 170(6).]

113 [Amends PSA 1993, s. 171A(1).]

SOCIAL SECURITY ACT 1998

143 The Social Security Act 1998 is amended as follows.

144 [Omits SSA 1998, s. 4.]

145 [Omits SSA 1998, s. 5.]

146 [Omits SSA 1998, s. 6.]

147 [Omits SSA 1998, s. 7.]

148 [Amends SSA 1998, s. 10(1)(b).]

149 In section 12 (appeal to appeal tribunal)–

(a) [amends heading to SSA 1998, s. 12;]

(b) [amends SSA 1998, s. 12(2), (4), (5) and (8).]

150 In section 13 (redetermination etc of appeals by tribunal)–

(a) [amends SSA 1998, s. 13(1);]

(b) [omits SSA 1998, s. 13(2);]

(c) [amends SSA 1998, s. 13(3).]

151 In section 14 (appeal from tribunal to Commissioner)–

(a) [amends heading to SSA 1998, s. 14;]

(b) [omits SSA 1998, s. 14(1);]

(c) [amends SSA 1998, s. 14(3) and (4);]

(d) [omits SSA 1998, s. 14(7)–(12).]

152 In section 15 (appeal from Commissioner on point of law)–

(a) [substitutes heading to SSA 1998, s. 15;]

(b) [omits SSA 1998, s. 15(1);]
(c) [amends SSA 1998, s. 15(3);]
(d) [omits SSA 1998, s. 15(4) and (5).]

153 [Inserts SSA 1998, s. 15A.]

154 [Omits SSA 1998, s. 16(2), (3)(a), and (6)–(9).]

155 [Amends SSA 1998, s. 17(1).]

156 [Amends SSA 1998, s. 18(1)(a).]

157 [Not relevant to National Insurance contributions.]

158 [Not relevant to National Insurance contributions.]

159 [Not relevant to National Insurance contributions.]

160 In section 24A (appeals dependent on issues falling to be decided by Inland Revenue)–
(a) [amends SSA 1998, s. 24A(1);]
(b) [amends SSA 1998, s. 24A(2)(c)(iii).]

161 [Amends SSA 1998, s. 25(1)(b).]

162(1) Section 26 (appeals involving issues that arise on appeal in other cases) is amended as follows.

162(2) [Amends SSA 1998, s. 26(1).]

162(3) [Amends SSA 1998, s. 26(2).]

162(4) [Amends SSA 1998, s. 26(3).]

162(5) [Amends SSA 1998, s. 26(4).]

162(6) [Amends SSA 1998, s. 26(5).]

162(7) [Amends SSA 1998, s. 26(7)(a).]

163 In section 27 (restrictions on entitlement to benefit in certain cases of error)–
(a) [amends SSA 1998, s. 27(1)(a) and (10)(a) and (b);]
(b) [amends SSA 1998, s. 27(3).]

164 In section 28 (correction of errors and setting aside of decisions)–
(a) [amends SSA 1998, s. 28(1);]
(b) [amends SSA 1998, s. 28(1A);]
(c) [amends SSA 1998, s. 28(2).]

165 Amends SSA 1998, s. 29(3).

166 Inserts SSA 1998, s. 39ZA

167 Amends SSA 1998, s. 39(1).

168 In section 79 (regulations and orders)–
(a) [amends SSA 1998, s. 79(1);]
(b) [omits SSA 1998, s. 79(2) and (9).]

169 In section 80 (Parliamentary control of regulations)–
(a) [amends SSA 1998, s. 80(1)(a);]
(b) [amends SSA 1998, s. 80(1)(b);]
(c) [omits SSA 1998, s. 80(3) and (4).]

170 [Amends SSA 1998, s. 81(1).]

171 [Omits SSA 1998, Sch. 1.]

172 [Omits SSA 1998, Sch. 4.]

173 In Schedule 5 (regulations as to procedure: provision which may be made)–
(a) [amends SSA 1998, Sch. 5, para. 1(a) and (b);]
(b) [omits SSA 1998, Sch. 5, para. 2 and 5 to 8.]

REPEALS AND REVOCATIONS

228 In consequence of the amendments made by the above provisions of this Schedule, the following provisions are repealed or (as the case may be) revoked–
(a) [not relevant to National Insurance contributions;]
(b) [not relevant to National Insurance contributions;]
(c) [not relevant to National Insurance contributions;]

(d) paragraphs 3(1), 11, 29, 30, 36, 42, 47(a), 51, 52, 113(b), 152(1) and (3) and 153 of Schedule 7 to the Social Security Act 1998;
(e) [not relevant to National Insurance contributions;]
(f) [not relevant to National Insurance contributions;]
(g) [not relevant to National Insurance contributions;]
(h) [not relevant to National Insurance contributions;]
(i) [not relevant to National Insurance contributions;]
(j) [not relevant to National Insurance contributions;]
(k) [not relevant to National Insurance contributions;]
(l) [not relevant to National Insurance contributions;]
(m) [not relevant to National Insurance contributions;]
(n) [not relevant to National Insurance contributions;]
(o) [not relevant to National Insurance contributions;]
(p) [not relevant to National Insurance contributions;]
(q) [not relevant to National Insurance contributions;]
(r) [not relevant to National Insurance contributions;]
(s) [not relevant to National Insurance contributions;]
(t) [not relevant to National Insurance contributions;]
(u) [not relevant to National Insurance contributions;]
(v) [not relevant to National Insurance contributions;]
(w) [not relevant to National Insurance contributions;]
(x) [not relevant to National Insurance contributions;]
(y) [not relevant to National Insurance contributions.]

SCHEDULE 4 – TRANSITIONAL PROVISIONS

Article 6

TRANSITIONAL PROVISIONS

1 Subject to article 3(3)(a) any proceedings before a tribunal listed in Table 1 of Schedule 1 which are pending immediately before 3rd November 2008 shall continue on and after 3rd November 2008 as proceedings before the First-tier Tribunal.

2 Subject to article 3(3)(b) any proceedings before a tribunal listed in Table 2 of Schedule 1 which are pending immediately before 3rd November 2008 shall continue on and after 3rd November 2008 as proceedings before the Upper Tribunal.

3(1) The following sub-paragraphs apply where proceedings are continued in the First-tier Tribunal or Upper Tribunal by virtue of paragraph 1 or 2.

3(2) Where a hearing began before 3rd November 2008 but was not completed by that date, the First-tier Tribunal or the Upper Tribunal, as the case may be, must be comprised for the continuation of that hearing of the person or persons who began it.

3(3) The First-tier Tribunal or Upper Tribunal, as the case may be, may give any direction to ensure that proceedings are dealt with fairly and, in particular, may–

(a) apply any provision in procedural rules which applied to the proceedings before 3rd November 2008; or
(b) disapply provisions of Tribunal Procedure Rules.

3(4) In sub-paragraph (3) "procedural rules" means provision (whether called rules or not) regulating practice or procedure before a tribunal.

3(5) Any direction or order given or made in proceedings which is in force immediately before 3rd November 2008 remains in force on and after that date as if it were a direction or order of the First-tier Tribunal or Upper Tribunal, as the case may be.

3(6) A time period which has started to run before 3rd November 2008 and which has not expired shall continue to apply.

3(7) An order for costs may only be made if, and to the extent that, an order could have been made before 3rd November 2008.

4 Subject to article 3(3)(a) and (b) where an appeal lies to a Child Support or Social Security Commissioner from any decision made before 3rd November 2008 by a tribunal listed in Table 1 of Schedule 1, section 11 of the 2007 Act (right to appeal to Upper Tribunal) shall apply as if the decision were a decision made on or after 3rd November 2008 by the First-tier Tribunal.

5 Subject to article 3(3)(b) where an appeal lies to a court from any decision made before 3rd November 2008 by a Child Support or Social Security Commissioner, section 13 of the 2007 Act (right to appeal to Court of Appeal etc.) shall apply as if the decision were a decision made on or after 3rd November 2008 by the Upper Tribunal.

6 Subject to article 3(3)(a) and (b) any case to be remitted by a court on or after 3rd November 2008 in relation to a tribunal listed in Schedule 1 shall be remitted to the First-tier Tribunal or Upper Tribunal as the case may be.

SAVINGS PROVISIONS

7 [Not relevant to National Insurance contributions.]

TRANSFER OF TRIBUNAL FUNCTIONS AND REVENUE AND CUSTOMS APPEALS ORDER 2009

(SI 2009/56, as amended by SI 2009/777)

Made on 18 January 2009 by the Lord Chancellor and the Treasury in exercise of the powers conferred by s. 30(1) and (4), 31(1), (2) and (9) and 38 of, and para. 30 of Sch. 5 to, the Tribunals, Courts and Enforcement Act 2007 and s. 124(1)–(7) of the Finance Act 2008. Operative from 1 April 2009.

CITATION AND COMMENCEMENT

1(1) This Order may be cited as the Transfer of Tribunal Functions and Revenue and Customs Appeals Order 2009.

1(2) This Order comes into force on 1st April 2009.

THE EXISTING TRIBUNALS

2 In this Order **"existing tribunals"** means–

(a) the Commissioners for the general purposes of the income tax established under section 2 of the Taxes Management Act 1970;

(b) the Commissioners for the special purposes of the Income Tax Acts established under section 4 of the Taxes Management Act 1970;

(c) [not relevant to National Insurance contributions;]

(d) [not relevant to National Insurance contributions;]

(e) [not relevant to National Insurance contributions.]

TRANSFER OF FUNCTIONS, CONSEQUENTIAL AND OTHER AMENDMENTS

3(1) Schedule 1 contains amendments to primary legislation which–

(a) transfer functions of existing tribunals, and

(b) make consequential and other provision (including provision about reviews of decisions by Her Majesty's Revenue and Customs).

3(2) Schedule 2 contains amendments to secondary legislation which–

(a) transfer functions of existing tribunals, and

(b) make consequential and other provision (including provision about reviews of decisions by Her Majesty's Revenue and Customs).

ABOLITION OF EXISTING TRIBUNALS

4 The existing tribunals (apart from the Commissioners for the general purposes of the income tax) are abolished.

TRANSFER OF MEMBERS OF EXISTING TRIBUNALS

5 A person who, immediately before this Order comes into force, holds an office listed in column 1 of any of the following tables is to hold the office or offices listed in the corresponding entry in column 2 of that table–

THE SPECIAL COMMISSIONERS

1. Office held	2. Office or offices to be held
Commissioner for the special purposes of the Income Tax Acts appointed under section 4 of the Taxes Management Act 1970	Transferred-in judge of the Upper Tribunal
Deputy Commissioner for the special purposes of the Income Tax Acts appointed under section 4A of the Taxes Management Act 1970	Transferred-in judge of the First-tier Tribunal and deputy judge of the Upper Tribunal

TRANSITIONALS AND SAVINGS

6 Schedule 3 contains–

(a) transitional provision, and

(b) saving provision.

SCHEDULES

SCHEDULE 1 – CONSEQUENTIAL AMENDMENTS AND SUPPLEMENTAL PROVISIONS – PRIMARY LEGISLATION

Article 3

SOCIAL SECURITY CONTRIBUTIONS AND BENEFITS ACT 1992

169(1) The Social Security Contributions and Benefits Act 1992 is amended as follows.

169(2)–(5) [Amends SSCBA 1992, Sch. 1, para. 3B.]

SOCIAL SECURITY ADMINISTRATION ACT 1992

170 The Social Security Administration Act 1992 is amended as follows.

171(1)–(4) [Amends SSAA 1992, s. 121D.]

SOCIAL SECURITY ACT 1998

247 The Social Security Act 1998 is amended as follows.

248 [Amends SSA 1998, s. 10A(2)(d).]

249 [Amends SSA 1998, s. 24A(2)(c).]

250 [Amends SSA 1998, s. 39.]

SOCIAL SECURITY CONTRIBUTIONS (TRANSFER OF FUNCTIONS, ETC) ACT 1999

268 The Social Security Contributions (Transfer of Functions, etc) Act 1999 is amended as follows.

269 [Amends SSC(TF)A 1999, s. 10(1)(c).]

270 [Amends SSC(TF)A 1999, s. 11(2).]

271 [Amends SSC(TF)A 1999, s. 12.]

272 [Amends SSC(TF)A 1999, s. 13.]

273 [Amends SSC(TF)A 1999, s. 14.]

274 [Substitutes SSC(TF)A 1999, s. 19.]

275 [Omits SSC(TF)A 1999, Sch. 7, para. 2 and 3.]

EMPLOYMENT ACT 2002

321 Schedule 1 of the Employment Act 2002 is amended as follows.

322 [Amends EA 2002, Sch. 1, para. 3.]

323 [Amends EA 2002, Sch. 1, para. 4.]

324 [Amends EA 2002, Sch. 1, para. 7.]

325 [Amends EA 2002, Sch. 1, para. 9.]

SCHEDULE 2 – CONSEQUENTIAL AMENDMENTS AND SUPPLEMENTAL PROVISIONS – SECONDARY LEGISLATION

Article 3

SOCIAL SECURITY CONTRIBUTIONS (DECISIONS AND APPEALS) REGULATIONS 1999

59(1) The Social Security Contributions (Decisions and Appeals) Regulations 1999 are amended as follows.

60 [Amends SI 1999/1027, reg. 3(3).]

61 [Amends SI 1999/1027, reg. 5(4).]

62 [Substitutes SI 1999/1027, reg. 7.]

63 [Omits SI 1999/1027, reg. 8 and 8A.]

64 [Amends SI 1999/1027, reg. 9.]

65 [Amends SI 1999/1027, reg. 10.]

66 [Amends SI 1999/1027, reg. 11(1) and (5).]

67 [Omitted by SI 2009/777, art. 7, with effect from 1 April 2009.]

SOCIAL SECURITY (CONTRIBUTIONS) REGULATIONS 2001

74 The Social Security (Contributions) Regulations 2001 are amended as follows.

75 [Substitutes SI 2001/1004, reg. 90Q(1).]

76 [Amends SI 2001/1004, Sch. 4, Pt. 3A.]

REVOCATIONS

187 The following instruments are revoked–

(a)–(d) [Not relevant to National Insurance contributions.]

(e) The Special Commissioners (Jurisdiction and Procedure) Regulations 1994.

(f) The General Commissioners (Jurisdiction and Procedure) Regulations 1994.

(h) The Retirement Age of General Commissioners Order 1995.

(i) The Special Commissioners (Jurisdiction and Procedure) (Amendment) Regulations 1999.

(j) The General Commissioners (Jurisdiction and Procedure) (Amendment) Regulations 1999.

(k) The Special Commissioners (Amendment of the Taxes Management Act 1970) Regulations 1999.

(l) The Special Commissioners (Jurisdiction and Procedure) (Amendment) Regulations 2000.

(o) The Referrals to the Special Commissioners Regulations 2001.

(p) The General Commissioners and Special Commissioners (Jurisdiction and Procedure) (Amendment) Regulations 2002.

(q) The Special Commissioners (Jurisdiction and Procedure) (Amendment) Regulations 2003.

(s) The General Commissioners (Jurisdiction and Procedure) (Amendment) Regulations 2005.

(t) The Special Commissioners (Jurisdiction and Procedure) (Amendment) Regulations 2005.

(v) The General Commissioners and Special Commissioners (Jurisdiction and Procedure) (Amendment) Regulations 2007.

SCHEDULE 3 – TRANSITIONAL AND SAVING PROVISIONS

Article 6

GENERAL

1(1) In this Schedule–

"commencement date" means the date on which this Order comes into force;

"enactment" includes subordinate legislation (within the meaning of the Interpretation Act 1978);

"HMRC" means Her Majesty's Revenue and Customs;

"tribunal" means the First-tier Tribunal or, where determined by or under Tribunal Procedure Rules, the Upper Tribunal.

1(2) For the purposes of this Schedule there are "current proceedings" if, before the commencement date–

(a) any party has served notice on an existing tribunal for the purpose of beginning proceedings before the existing tribunal, and

(b) the existing tribunal has not concluded proceedings arising by virtue of that notice.

FORMER VAT AND DUTIES TRIBUNALS MATTERS (EXCEPT VAT)

2(1) This paragraph applies in relation to the following decisions–

(a) any relevant decision which HMRC notify before the commencement date, unless–

(i) the period to require a review of the decision has expired before that date, or

(ii) a review of the decision has been required before that date;

(b) any relevant review decision which HMRC notify before the commencement date unless–

(i) the period to serve notice of appeal against the decision on an existing tribunal has expired before that date, or

(ii) notice of appeal against the decision has been served on an existing tribunal before that date.

2(2) On and after the commencement date, the following enactments continue to apply (subject to sub-paragraphs (3) and (4)) as they applied immediately before that date–

(a) the review and appeal provisions,

(b) rule 4(2) of the Value Added Tax Tribunals Rules 1986, and

(c) any other enactments that apply in relation to relevant decisions or relevant review decisions.

2(3) Those enactments apply subject to Tribunal Procedure Rules.

2(4) Any reference to an existing tribunal is to be substituted with a reference to the tribunal.

2(5) Any time period which has started to run before the commencement date and has not expired will continue to apply.

2(6) In this paragraph–

"relevant decision" means a decision to which a review and appeal provision applies (apart from a relevant review decision);

"relevant review decision" means a decision–

(a) that is made on a review of a relevant decision, and

(b) to which a review and appeal provision applies,

and includes a relevant decision that is treated as having been confirmed under a review and appeal provision.

"review and appeal provisions" means–

(a) sections 14 to 16 of the Finance Act 1994,

(b) sections 59 and 60 of the Finance Act 1994,

(c) sections 54 to 56 of the Finance Act 1996,

(d) paragraphs 121 to 123 of Schedule 6 to the Finance Act 2000,

(e) sections 40 to 42 of the Finance Act 2001,

(f) sections 33 to 37 of the Finance Act 2003,

(g) regulations 9 to 13 of the Export (Penalty) Regulations 2003,

(h) regulations 4 to 7 of the Control of Cash (Penalties) Regulations 2007,

(i) regulations 43 and 44 of the Money Laundering Regulations 2007, and

(j) regulations 12 and 13 of the Transfer of Funds (Information on the Payer) Regulations 2007.

3(1) This paragraph applies in relation to a relevant decision if, before the commencement date–

(a) HMRC have notified the relevant decision, and

(b) a review of the decision has begun under a review and appeal provision (whether or not a relevant review decision has been notified).

3(2) On and after the commencement date the following enactments continue to apply (subject to sub-paragraphs (3) and (4)), as they applied immediately before that date–

(a) the review and appeal provisions,

(b) rule 4(2) of the VAT Tribunals Rules 1986, and

(c) any other enactments that apply in relation to relevant decisions or relevant review decisions.

3(3) Those enactments apply subject to Tribunal Procedure Rules.

3(4) Any reference to an existing tribunal is to be substituted with a reference to the tribunal.

3(5) Any time period which has started to run before the commencement date and has not expired will continue to apply.

3(6) On and after the commencement date, no notification offering or requiring a review may be given under any review and appeal provision or any other enactments that are applicable to the decision as they apply after that date.

3(7) In this paragraph **"review and appeal provision"**, **"relevant decision"** and **"relevant review decision"** have the same meaning as in paragraph 2.

FORMER VAT AND DUTIES TRIBUNALS MATTERS: VAT

4(1) This paragraph applies if, before the commencement date–

(a) HMRC have notified a decision relating to a matter to which section 83 of the Value Added Tax Act 1994 applies, and

(b) no party has served notice on a VAT and duties tribunal for the purpose of beginning proceedings before such a tribunal in relation to that decision.

4(2) On and after the commencement date, the following enactments continue to apply (subject to sub-paragraphs (3) and (4)) as they applied immediately before that date–

(a) the Value Added Tax Act 1994,

(b) rule 4(2) of the VAT Tribunals Rules 1986, and

(c) any other enactments that are applicable to the decision.

4(3) Those enactments apply subject to Tribunal Procedure Rules.

4(4) Any reference to an existing tribunal is to be substituted with a reference to the tribunal.

4(5) Any time period which has started to run before the commencement date and has not expired will continue to apply.

MATTERS FORMERLY HEARD BY EXISTING TRIBUNALS (EXCEPT VAT AND DUTIES TRIBUNALS)

5(1) This paragraph applies if, before the commencement date–

(a) a notice of appeal has been given to HMRC; but

(b) no party has served notice on an existing tribunal for the purpose of beginning proceedings before the existing tribunal in relation to that appeal.

5(2) Where the date on which a review is required or offered falls on or before 31 March 2010, the period for HMRC to give notice of their conclusions for the purposes of the relevant provision is to be 90 days (but without prejudice to any power to agree to a different period).

5(3) In this paragraph–

"review" means a review under–

(a) section 49B or 49C of the Taxes Management Act 1970, or

(b) any other enactment which, as amended by this Order, contains provisions corresponding to section 49B or 49C for review to be required or offered;

"relevant provision" means–

(a) in the case of a review under section 49B or 49C of the Taxes Management Act 1970, section 49E(6) of that Act, or

(b) in the case of a review under any other enactment amended by this Order, the provision that corresponds to section 49E(6) of the Taxes Management Act 1970 in relation to that review.

CURRENT PROCEEDINGS

6 Any current proceedings are to continue on and after the commencement date as proceedings before the tribunal.

7(1) This paragraph applies to current proceedings that are continued before the tribunal by virtue of paragraph 6.

7(2) Where a hearing before an existing tribunal (except for the Commissioners for the general purposes of the income tax) began before the commencement date but was not completed by that date, the tribunal must be comprised for the continuation of that hearing of the person or persons who began it.

7(3) The tribunal may give any direction to ensure that proceedings are dealt with fairly and justly and, in particular, may–

(a) apply any provision in procedural rules which applied to the proceedings before the commencement date; or

(b) disapply any provision of Tribunal Procedure Rules.

7(4) In sub-paragraph (3) **"procedural rules"** means any provision (whether called rules or not) regulating practice or procedure before an existing tribunal.

7(5) Any direction or order made or given in proceedings which is in force immediately before the commencement date remains in force on and after that date as if it were a direction or order of the tribunal relating to proceedings before that tribunal.

7(6) A time period which has started to run before the commencement date and which has not expired will continue to apply.

7(7) An order for costs may only be made if, and to the extent that, an order could have been made before the commencement date (on the assumption, in the case of costs actually incurred after that date, that they had been incurred before that date).

CASES TO BE REMITTED BY COURTS

8 Any case to be remitted by a court on or after the commencement date in relation to an existing tribunal shall be remitted to the tribunal.

DECISIONS OF VAT AND DUTIES TRIBUNALS AND COURTS: INTEREST AND PAYMENT

9(1) This paragraph applies in relation to any decision of a VAT and duties tribunal made before the commencement date.

9(2) On and after that date, the following provisions continue to apply as they applied immediately before that date–

(a) section 84(8) of the Value Added Tax Act 1994 (VAT),

(b) section 60(6) to (8) of the Finance Act 1994 (insurance premium tax),

(c) paragraphs 8 and 10 of Schedule 6 to the Finance Act 1994 (air passenger duty),

(d) section 56(3) to (5) of the Finance Act 1996 (landfill tax),

(e) paragraph 123(4) to (6) of Schedule 6 to the Finance Act 2000 (climate change levy),

(f) section 42(4) to (6) of the Finance Act 2001 (aggregates levy),

(g) paragraph 14(4) of Schedule 3 to the Finance Act 2001 (excise and customs).

10(1) This paragraph applies if an appeal from a decision of a VAT and duties tribunal, or from a court, is made before the commencement date.

10(2) Section 85B of the Value Added Tax Act 1994 does not apply in relation to that decision.

DECISIONS OF EXISTING TRIBUNALS: RIGHTS OF APPEAL, REVIEWS AND IRREGULARITIES

11(1) This paragraph applies to a decision of an existing tribunal if, immediately before the commencement date–

(a) an appeal lies to a court from that decision,

(b) an application may be or has been made to an existing tribunal seeking a review of that decision, or

(c) the existing tribunal wishes to correct an irregularity.

11(2) Except as provided for in sub-paragraph (3), on and after the commencement date such rights of appeal shall lie from the decision as would lie from a decision of the First-tier Tribunal made on or after that date.

11(3) Subject to the modifications specified in sub-paragraphs (4) and (5) the following enactments continue to apply for the purposes of a case to be stated, a review, or for correcting an irregularity in respect of any decision of the Commissioners for the general purposes of the income tax made before the commencement date, as if the amendments in this Order had not been made–

(a) sections 56 and 58 of the Taxes Management Act 1970,

(b) regulations 17 and 20 to 24 of the General Commissioners (Jurisdiction and Procedure) Regulations 1994, and

(c) the General Commissioners of Income Tax (Costs) Regulations 2001.

11(4) Section 56(6) of the Taxes Management Act 1970 is modified so that for "the Commissioners" there is substituted "the tribunal".

11(5) Section 58 of the Taxes Management Act 1970 is modified as follows–

(a) omit subsection (2B); and

(b) in subsection (2C) omit "or on an appeal under section 56A of this Act".

11(6) In article 4 of the Tribunals, Courts and Enforcement Act 2007 (Commencement No. 6 and Transitional Provisions) Order 2008–

(a) for "section 56 of the 1970 Act (statement of case for opinion of the High Court)" substitute "sections 56(3) and (11) and 58 of the 1970 Act (statement of case for opinion of the High Court) and regulations 17 and 20 to 24 of the General Commissioners (Jurisdiction and Procedure) Regulations 1994 (review of tribunal's final determination, stated case procedures and correction of irregularities)"; and

(b) after "commenced" insert ", and the amendments to the 1970 Act and the revocation of the General Commissioners (Jurisdiction and Procedure) Regulations 1994, the General Commissioners (Jurisdiction and Procedure) (Amendment) Regulations 1999, the General Commissioners (Jurisdiction and Procedure) (Amendment) Regulations 2005 and the General Commissioners and Special Commissioners (Jurisdiction and Procedure) (Amendment) Regulations 2007 (as they relate to the General Commissioners) in the Transfer of Tribunal Functions and Revenue and Customs Appeals Order 2009 had not been made".

EXISTING TRIBUNALS – STAFF

12 Staff appointed to the existing tribunals (except to the Commissioners for the general purposes of the income tax) before the commencement date are, on and after that date, to be treated, for the purpose of any enactment, as if they had been appointed by the Lord Chancellor under section 40(1) of the Tribunals, Courts and Enforcement Act 2007 (tribunal staff and services).

TRANSITIONAL: GENERAL

13(1) In so far as appropriate in consequence of this Order, a reference in an enactment, instrument or other document to an existing tribunal, or a member or official of an existing tribunal (however expressed) is to be taken to be a reference to the tribunal.

13(2) Sub-paragraph (1) does not apply to any reference that is amended by Schedule 1 or 2.

SOCIAL SECURITY REVALUATION OF EARNINGS FACTORS ORDER 2009

(SI 2009/608)

Made on 10 March 2009 by the Secretary of State, in exercise of the powers conferred upon him by s. 148(3) and (4) and s. 189(1), (4) and (5) of the Social Security Administration Act 1992. Operative from 6 April 2009.

CITATION AND COMMENCEMENT

1 This Order may be cited as the Social Security Revaluation of Earnings Factors Order 2009 and shall come into force on 6th April 2009.

REVALUATION OF EARNINGS FACTORS

2 The earnings factors for tax years specified in the Schedule to this Order in so far as they are relevant–

(a) to the calculation–

(i) of the additional pension in the rate of any long-term benefit; or

(ii) of any guaranteed minimum pension; or

(b) to any other calculation required under Part 3 of the Pension Schemes Act 1993 (including that Part as modified by or under any other enactment),

are directed to be increased for those tax years by the percentage of their amount shown opposite those tax years in that Schedule.

ROUNDING OF FRACTIONAL AMOUNTS

3 Where any earnings factor relevant to the calculation specified in article 2(a)(i) of this Order, as increased in accordance with this Order, would not but for this article be expressed as a whole number of pounds, it shall be so expressed by rounding down any fraction of a pound less than one half and rounding up any other fraction of a pound.

SCHEDULES

SCHEDULE – PERCENTAGE INCREASE OF EARNINGS FACTOR FOR SPECIFIED TAX YEARS

Article 2

Tax year	*Percentage increase*
1978–1979	677.6
1979–1980	586.3
1980–1981	473.3
1981–1982	380.2
1982–1983	336.1
1983–1984	305.0
1984–1985	275.0
1985–1986	251.7
1986–1987	223.0
1987–1988	200.7
1988–1989	176.7
1989–1990	149.7
1990–1991	132.7
1991–1992	111.4
1992–1993	98.5
1993–1994	89.0
1994–1995	83.3

Tax year	*Percentage increase*
1995–1996	75.6
1996–1997	70.8
1997–1998	62.7
1998–1999	55.5
1999–2000	49.3
2000–2001	40.4
2001–2002	35.0
2002–2003	29.5
2003–2004	25.0
2004–2005	20.4
2005–2006	15.6
2006–2007	11.8
2007–2008	7.4
2008–2009	3.1

NATIONAL INSURANCE CONTRIBUTION CREDITS (TRANSFER OF FUNCTIONS) ORDER 2009

(SI 2009/1377)

Made on 10 June 2009 by Her Majesty, The Queen, in pursuance of the powers conferred on Her by s. 23(1)(d), (3)(b) and (4)(d) of the Social Security Contributions (Transfer of Functions, etc.) Act 1999 and with the advice of Her Privy Council. Operative from 6 April 2010.

CITATION, COMMENCEMENT AND EXTENT

1(1) This Order may be cited as the National Insurance Contribution Credits (Transfer of Functions) Order 2009 and shall come into force on 6th April 2010.

1(2) This Order extends to England and Wales and to Scotland.

TRANSFER OF FUNCTIONS

2(1) The decisions to which this article applies are to be made by the Commissioners for Her Majesty's Revenue and Customs (rather than the Secretary of State).

2(2) This article applies to any decision which relates to the crediting of Class 3 contributions for a week falling after 6th April 2010 under section 23A(2) of the Social Security Contributions and Benefits Act 1992 (contributions credits for relevant carers) by virtue of the contributor concerned being a relevant carer in respect of that week under–

(a) section 23A(3)(a) (persons awarded child benefit in respect of a child under the age of 12);

(b) section 23A(3)(b) (foster parents, within the meaning of regulations); or

(c) regulations providing, for the purposes of section 23A(3)(c) (other persons engaged in caring, within the meaning given by regulations), that a person is engaged in caring in any week if that person is the partner of a person to whom section 23A(3)(a) applies.

DECISIONS AND APPEALS

3(1) The following provisions of Chapter 2 (social security decisions and appeals) of Part 1 (decisions and appeals) of the Social Security Act 1998 apply to a decision to which article 2 applies as they apply in relation to a decision of the Secretary of State mentioned in section 8(1) (decisions by the Secretary of State) of that Act.

3(2) The provisions are–

(a) section 9 (revision of decisions);

(b) section 10 (decisions superseding earlier decisions);

(c) section 11 (regulations with respect to decisions);

(d) section 12 (appeal to First-tier Tribunal), except for subsections (4) and (5);

(e) section 13 (redetermination etc of appeals by tribunal);

(f) section 14 (appeal from First-tier Tribunal to Upper Tribunal), except for subsections (3)(c) and (4) to (6);

(g) section 15 (applications for permission to appeal against a decision of the Upper Tribunal);

(h) section 15A (functions of Senior President of Tribunals);

(i) section 16 (procedure), except for subsections (4) and (5);

(j) section 17 (finality of decisions);

(k) section 18 (matters arising as respects decisions), except for subsection (2);

(l) section 21 (suspension in prescribed circumstances);

(m) section 22 (suspension for failure to furnish information etc.), except for subsection (4);

(n) section 23 (termination in cases of failure to furnish information);

(o) section 25 (decisions involving issues that arise on appeal in other cases);

(p) section 26 (appeals involving issues that arise on appeal in other cases);

(q) section 27 (restrictions on entitlement to benefit in certain cases of error);

(r) section 28 (correction of errors and setting aside of decisions), except for subsection (1A); and

(s) section 39ZA (certificates).

4(1) In the application of the provisions listed in article 3(2) to a decision to which article 2 applies, any reference to the Secretary of State (other than in a reference to a decision of the Secretary of State under section 8(1)) is to have effect as a reference to the Commissioners for Her Majesty's Revenue and Customs.

4(2) Paragraph (1) does not apply to references contained in sections 21 to 23.

AMENDMENT OF THE SOCIAL SECURITY CONTRIBUTIONS AND BENEFITS ACT 1992

5 In section 23A(4)(b) of the Social Security Contributions and Benefits Act 1992, after "the Secretary of State" insert "or to the Commissioners for Her Majesty's Revenue and Customs".

SOCIAL SECURITY (CONTRIBUTIONS CREDITS FOR PARENTS AND CARERS) REGULATIONS 2010

(SI 2010/19, as amended by SI 2010/385, SI 2011/709, SI 2013/388 and SI 2010/591)

Made on 5 January 2010 by the Secretary of State in exercise of the powers conferred by s. 23A(3)(c), (4) and (9) and s. 175(1), (4) and (5) of the Social Security Contributions and Benefits Act 1992. Operative from 6 April 2010.

ARRANGEMENT OF REGULATIONS

REGULATION

PART 1 – GENERAL PROVISIONS

CITATION AND COMMENCEMENT

1 These Regulations may be cited as the Social Security (Contributions Credits for Parents and Carers) Regulations 2010 and shall come into force on 6th April 2010.

INTERPRETATION

2(1) In these Regulations–

"partner" means the person with whom another person–

(a) resides; and

(b) shares responsibility for a child under the age of 12;

"relevant benefit" means–

(a) attendance allowance in accordance with section 64 (entitlement);

(b) the care component of disability living allowance in accordance with section 72 (the care component), at the middle or highest rate prescribed in accordance with subsection (3) of that section;

(c) an increase in the rate of disablement pension in accordance with section 104 (increase where constant attendance needed);

(d) any benefit by virtue of–

(i) the Pneumoconiosis, Byssinosis and Miscellaneous Diseases Benefit Scheme 1983; or

(ii) regulations made under paragraph 7(2) in Part 2 (regulations providing for benefit) of Schedule 8 (industrial injuries and diseases (old cases)),

which is payable as if the injury or disease were one in respect of which a disablement pension were for the time being payable in respect of an assessment of 100 per cent.;

(e) a constant attendance allowance payable by virtue of–
 (i) article 8 (constant attendance allowance) of the Naval, Military and Air Forces etc. (Disablement and Death) Service Pensions Order 2006; or
 (ii) article 14 (constant attendance allowance) of the Personal Injuries (Civilians) Scheme 1983.
(f) the daily living component of personal independence payment in accordance with section 78 of the Welfare Reform Act 2012.
(g) armed forces independence payment in accordance with the Armed Forces and Reserve Forces (Compensation Scheme) Order 2011.

2(2) In these Regulations, a reference to a section or Schedule by number alone is a reference to the section or Schedule so numbered in the Social Security Contributions and Benefits Act 1992.

History – Reg. 2(1)(f) inserted by SI 2013/388, art. 8 and Sch., para. 46, with effect from 8 April 2013.
Reg. 2(1)(g) inserted by SI 2013/591, art. 7 and Sch., para. 44(2), with effect from 8 April 2013.

TRANSITIONAL PROVISION

3 For the period of 12 weeks from the date on which these Regulations come into force, regulation 7(1)(a) has effect as if the reference in regulation 7(1) to 12 weeks were a reference to the number of complete weeks since these Regulations came into force.

PART 2 – MEANING OF "FOSTER PARENT" AND "ENGAGED IN CARING"

MEANING OF "FOSTER PARENT"

4(1) For the purposes of subsection (3)(b) of section 23A (contributions credits for relevant parents and carers), a foster parent is a person approved as–
(a) a foster parent in accordance with Part 4 (approval of foster parents) of the Fostering Services Regulations 2002;
(aa) a kinship carer in accordance with Part 5 (kinship care) of the Looked After Children (Scotland) Regulations 2009;
(b) a foster carer in accordance with Part 7 (fostering) of the Looked After Children (Scotland) Regulations 2009; or
(c) a foster parent in accordance with Part 2 (approvals and placements) of the Foster Placement (Children) Regulations (Northern Ireland) 1996.

4(2) Paragraph (1) is subject to regulation 8.

History – Reg. 4(1)(aa) inserted, and the "or" at the end of reg. 4(1)(a) omitted, by SI 2011/709, reg. 3(2)(b) and (a) respectively, with effect from 5 April 2011.
Reg. 4(1)(c) (and the "; or" at the end of reg. 4(1)(b)) inserted by SI 2011/709, reg. 3(2)(c), with effect from 5 April 2011.

MEANING OF "ENGAGED IN CARING"

5(1) For the purposes of subsection (3)(c) of section 23A, a person is engaged in caring in a week–
(a) if that person is the partner of a person who is awarded child benefit for any part of that week in respect of a child under the age of 12;
(b) if that person is caring for another person or persons for a total of 20 or more hours in that week and–
 (i) that other person is, or each of the persons cared for are, entitled to a relevant benefit for that week; or
 (ii) the Secretary of State considers that level of care to be appropriate;
(c) if that person is one to whom any of paragraphs 4 to 6 (persons caring for another person) of Schedule 1B (prescribed categories of person) to the Income Support (General) Regulations 1987 applies.

5(2) Paragraph (1) is subject to regulations 6 to 8.

LIMIT ON THE PERIOD IN RESPECT OF PARTNERS OF PERSONS AWARDED CHILD BENEFIT

6(1) Regulation 5(1)(a) does not apply to any week which falls within a tax year in respect of which the person awarded child benefit satisfies the following condition.

6(2) The condition is that that person's earnings factor for the purposes of section 45 (additional pension in a Category A retirement pension) does not exceed the qualifying earnings factor for that year.

6(3) In calculating a person's earnings factor for the purposes of paragraph (2), no account is to be taken of any earnings factor derived from contributions credited by virtue of that person being a relevant carer due to an award of child benefit.

ADDITIONAL PERIOD IN RESPECT OF ENTITLEMENT TO CARER'S ALLOWANCE AND RELEVANT BENEFITS

7(1) A person is engaged in caring for a period of 12 weeks–

(a) prior to the date on which that person becomes entitled to carer's allowance by virtue of subsection (1) of section 70 (carer's allowance);

(b) subject to paragraph (2), following the end of the week in which that person ceases to be entitled to carer's allowance by virtue of that subsection;

(c) following the end of a week in which regulation 5(1)(b) ceases to be satisfied.

7(2) For the purposes of paragraph (1)(b), a person is not engaged in caring in a week in respect of which that person is entitled, under regulations made under subsection (5) of section 22 (earnings factors), to be credited with contributions by virtue of being entitled to an allowance under section 70.

DISQUALIFICATION DUE TO RESIDENCE OR IMPRISONMENT

8 A person is not a foster parent or engaged in caring for the purposes of section 23A during any period in respect of which that person is–

(a) not ordinarily resident in Great Britain; or

(b) undergoing imprisonment or detention in legal custody.

PART 3 – APPLICATIONS

APPLICATIONS: FOSTER PARENTS AND PARTNERS OF PERSONS AWARDED CHILD BENEFIT

9 A person shall not be entitled to be credited with Class 3 contributions under–

(a) subsection (3)(b) (foster parent) of section 23A; or

(b) subsection (3)(c) (person engaged in caring) of section 23A by virtue of regulation 5(1)(a),

unless an application to be so credited is received by the Commissioners for Her Majesty's Revenue and Customs.

APPLICATIONS: CARERS FOR 20 OR MORE HOURS PER WEEK

10(1) A person shall not be entitled to be credited with Class 3 contributions under subsection (3)(c) of section 23A by virtue of regulation 5(1)(b) unless an application to be so credited is received by the Secretary of State.

10(2) Paragraph (1) does not apply where that person–

(a) [omitted by SI 2010/385, reg. 3;]

(b) is a married woman who is not entitled to be credited with contributions under paragraph (1) of regulation 7A (credits for carer's allowance) of the Social Security (Credits) Regulations 1975 by virtue of paragraph (2)(b) (reduced contribution rate election under regulations under section 19(4)) of that regulation.

History – Reg. 10(2)(a) omitted by SI 2010/385, reg. 3, with effect from 6 April 2010.

PROVISION OF INFORMATION: CARERS FOR 20 OR MORE HOURS PER WEEK

11(1) With respect to an application to which regulation 10(1) applies, the application must include–

(a) a declaration by the applicant that the applicant cares for a person or persons for 20 or more hours per week;

(b) the name and, where known, the national insurance number of each person cared for;

(c) where applicable, which relevant benefit each person cared for is entitled to; and

(d) where requested by the Secretary of State, a declaration signed by an appropriate person as to the level of care which is required for each person cared for.

11(2) For the purposes of paragraph (1)(d), an appropriate person is a person who is–

(a) involved in the health care or social care of the person cared for; and

(b) considered by the Secretary of State as appropriate to make a declaration as to the level of care required.

TIME LIMIT FOR APPLICATIONS

12 An application under regulation 9 or 10 must be received–

(a) before the end of the tax year following the tax year in which a week, which is the subject of the application, falls; or

(b) within such further time as the Secretary of State or the Commissioners for Her Majesty's Revenue and Customs, as the case may be, consider reasonable in the circumstances.

SOCIAL SECURITY REVALUATION OF EARNINGS FACTORS ORDER 2010

(SI 2010/470)

Made on 23 February 2010 by the Secretary of State in exercise of the powers conferred upon her by s. 148(3) and (4) and s. 189(1), (4) and (5) of the Social Security Administration Act 1992. Operative from 6 April 2010.

CITATION AND COMMENCEMENT

1 This Order may be cited as the Social Security Revaluation of Earnings Factors Order 2010 and shall come into force on 6th April 2010.

REVALUATION OF EARNINGS FACTORS

2 The earnings factors for tax years specified in the Schedule to this Order in so far as they are relevant–

(a) to the calculation–

(i) of the additional pension in the rate of any long-term benefit, or

(ii) of any guaranteed minimum pension; or

(b) to any other calculation required under Part 3 of the Pension Schemes Act 1993 (including that Part as modified by or under any other enactment),

are directed to be increased for those tax years by the percentage of their amount shown opposite those tax years in that Schedule.

ROUNDING OF FRACTIONAL AMOUNTS

3 Where any earnings factor relevant to the calculation specified in article 2(a)(i) of this Order, as increased in accordance with this Order, would not but for this article be expressed as a whole number of pounds, it shall be so expressed by rounding down any fraction of a pound less than one half and rounding up any other fraction of a pound.

SCHEDULES

SCHEDULE – PERCENTAGE INCREASE OF EARNINGS FACTOR FOR SPECIFIED TAX YEARS

Article 2

Tax year	*Percentage increase*
1978–1979	686.9
1979–1980	594.5
1980–1981	480.2
1981–1982	385.9
1982–1983	341.4
1983–1984	309.8
1984–1985	279.5
1985–1986	256.0
1986–1987	226.9
1987–1988	204.3
1988–1989	180.0
1989–1990	152.7
1990–1991	135.5
1991–1992	113.9
1992–1993	100.8
1993–1994	91.3
1994–1995	85.5

Tax year	*Percentage increase*
1995–1996	77.7
1996–1997	72.9
1997–1998	64.6
1998–1999	57.4
1999–2000	51.1
2000–2001	42.1
2001–2002	36.6
2002–2003	31.0
2003–2004	26.5
2004–2005	21.8
2005–2006	17.0
2006–2007	13.2
2007–2008	8.7
2008–2009	4.3
2009–2010	1.2

RECOVERY OF SOCIAL SECURITY CONTRIBUTIONS DUE IN OTHER MEMBER STATES REGULATIONS 2010

(SI 2010/926, as amended by SI 2011/701)

Made on 23 March 2010 by the Treasury in exercise of the powers conferred by s. 2(2) of the European Communities Act 1972. Operative from 1 May 2010.

CITATION AND COMMENCEMENT

1 These Regulations may be cited as the Recovery of Social Security Contributions Due in Other Member States Regulations 2010 and come into force on 1st May 2010.

INTERPRETATION

2 In these Regulations–

"applicant party" has the meaning assigned to it by Article 75 of Council Regulation (EC) No 987/2009;

"claim" has the meaning assigned to it by Article 75 of Council Regulation (EC) No 987/2009, except for the second and third times it occurs in regulation 4(1) of these Regulations;

"Commissioners" means the Commissioners for Her Majesty's Revenue and Customs;

"instrument permitting enforcement" means–

(i) any instrument issued by an applicant party in relation to a claim; or

(ii) a decision relating to a claim given in favour of an applicant party in any member State by a court or tribunal or other competent body in that State which permits recovery of that claim, or part thereof, in that State;

"officer" means an officer of Revenue and Customs.

ENFORCEMENT OF CLAIMS

3(1) An instrument permitting enforcement of a claim, recognised by the Commissioners as an instrument authorising enforcement of the claim in the United Kingdom, together with a certificate of an officer that payment of the claim has not been made to that officer, or, to the best of that officer's knowledge and belief, to any other person acting on behalf of the Commissioners, or to the applicant party, is sufficient evidence that the sum mentioned in the instrument is unpaid and is due to the applicant party.

3(2) A certificate of an officer that interest is payable under regulation 4(1) and that payment of the interest has not been made to that officer, or, to the best of that officer's knowledge and belief, to any other person acting on behalf of the Commissioners, or to the applicant party, is sufficient evidence that the sum mentioned in the instrument is unpaid and is due to the applicant party.

3(3) For the purposes of this regulation, any document purporting to be such a certificate as is mentioned in paragraph (1) or (2) is deemed to be such a certificate unless the contrary is proved.

INTEREST FOR LATE PAYMENT OF CLAIMS

4(1) A claim corresponding to a claim for outstanding Class 1, 1A, 1B or 4 national insurance contributions carries interest in respect of the principal amount and any penalty claimed at the rate applicable to the corresponding claim under–

(a) section 178 of the Finance Act 1989 for the purposes of Class 1, 1A and 1B national insurance contributions, or

(b) sections 101 and 103 of the Finance Act 2009 for the purposes of Class 4 national insurance contributions,

from the date of recognition until the date of payment inclusive.

4(2) In this Regulation **"the date of recognition"** means the earlier of–

(i) the date following the expiry of three months from the date of receipt by the Commissioners of the request for recovery of the claim; and

(ii) the date the instrument permitting enforcement of the claim is recognised by the Commissioners as an instrument authorising enforcement of the claim in the United Kingdom.

4(3) Interest is payable under this regulation without any deduction of income tax.

4(4) For the purposes of this regulation, where–

(a) any payment is made by cheque to–

(i) the Commissioners, or

(ii) the applicant party, and

(b) the cheque is paid on its first presentation to the banker on whom it is drawn;

the payment shall be treated as made on the date on which the cheque was received by the Commissioners or the applicant party.

4(5) Interest payable under this regulation shall be recoverable as if it were interest charged under a provision of the Taxes Management Act 1970.

History – In reg. 4(1) the words from "under–" to "inclusive" substituted for the words "under section 178 of the Finance Act 1989 from the date of recognition until the date of payment inclusive" by SI 2011/701, art. 11, with effect from 31 October 2011.

SOCIAL SECURITY REVALUATION OF EARNINGS FACTORS ORDER 2011

(SI 2011/475)

Made on 22 February 2011 by the Secretary of State in exercise of the powers conferred upon him by s. 148(3) and (4) and s. 189(1), (4) and (5) of the Social Security Administration Act 1992. Operative from 6 April 2011.

CITATION AND COMMENCEMENT

1 This Order may be cited as the Social Security Revaluation of Earnings Factors Order 2011 and shall come into force on 6th April 2011.

REVALUATION OF EARNINGS FACTORS

2 The earnings factors for tax years specified in the Schedule to this Order in so far as they are relevant–

(a) to the calculation–

(i) of the additional pension in the rate of any long-term benefit, or

(ii) of any guaranteed minimum pension; or

(b) to any other calculation required under Part 3 of the Pension Schemes Act 1993 (including that Part as modified by or under any other enactment),

are directed to be increased for those tax years by the percentage of their amount shown opposite those tax years in that Schedule.

ROUNDING OF FRACTIONAL AMOUNTS

3 Where any earnings factor relevant to the calculation specified in article 2(a)(i) of this Order, as increased in accordance with this Order, would not but for this article be expressed as a whole number of pounds, it shall be so expressed by rounding down any fraction of a pound less than one half and rounding up any other fraction of a pound.

SCHEDULE – PERCENTAGE INCREASE OF EARNINGS FACTOR FOR SPECIFIED TAX YEARS

Article 2

Tax year	*Percentage increase*
1978–1979	705.0
1979–1980	610.5
1980–1981	493.6
1981–1982	397.1
1982–1983	351.5
1983–1984	319.2
1984–1985	288.2
1985–1986	264.2
1986–1987	234.4
1987–1988	211.3
1988–1989	186.4
1989–1990	158.5
1990–1991	140.9
1991–1992	118.8
1992–1993	105.5
1993–1994	95.7
1994–1995	89.8
1995–1996	81.8
1996–1997	76.8
1997–1998	68.4

Tax year	*Percentage increase*
1998–1999	61.0
1999–2000	54.5
2000–2001	45.4
2001–2002	39.8
2002–2003	34.0
2003–2004	29.4
2004–2005	24.6
2005–2006	19.7
2006–2007	15.8
2007–2008	11.2
2008–2009	6.7
2009–2010	3.5
2010–2011	2.3

SOCIAL SECURITY (REDUCED RATES OF CLASS 1 CONTRIBUTIONS, REBATES AND MINIMUM CONTRIBUTIONS) ORDER 2011

(SI 2011/1036)

Made on 31 March 2011 by the Secretary of State for Work and Pensions. Operative from 6 April 2012.

CITATION, COMMENCEMENT, INTERPRETATION AND EXTENT

1(1) This Order may be cited as the Social Security (Reduced Rates of Class 1 Contributions, Rebates and Minimum Contributions) Order 2011 and shall come into force on 6th April 2012.

1(2) In this Order–

"the 1993 Act" means the Pension Schemes Act 1993;

"the low earnings threshold", in relation to a tax year, means the low earnings threshold for that tax year as specified in–

(a) section 44A of the Social Security Contributions and Benefits Act 1992 (deemed earnings factors); or

(b) in relation to Northern Ireland, section 44A of the Social Security Contributions and Benefits (Northern Ireland) Act 1992 (deemed earnings factors);

"the Northern Ireland Act" means the Pension Schemes (Northern Ireland) Act 1993.

1(3) These provisions of this Order extend to England and Wales and Scotland–

(a) articles 2 to 4;

(b) this article, and the Schedules, so far as they relate to articles 2 to 4.

1(4) These provisions of this Order extend to Northern Ireland–

(a) articles 5 to 7;

(b) this article, and the Schedules, so far as they relate to articles 5 to 7.

ALTERATION OF REDUCED RATES OF CLASS 1 CONTRIBUTIONS FOR SALARY RELATED CONTRACTED-OUT SCHEMES

2(1) This article applies for the purposes of section 41 of the 1993 Act (reduced rates of Class 1 contributions).

2(2) In section 41(1A) of the 1993 Act (reduced rates of primary Class 1 contributions in contracted-out employment) for "1.6 per cent" substitute "1.4 per cent".

2(3) In section 41(1B) of the 1993 Act (reduced rates of secondary Class 1 contributions in contracted-out employment) for "3.7 per cent" substitute "3.4 per cent".

REDUCED RATES OF CLASS 1 CONTRIBUTIONS AND REBATES FOR MONEY PURCHASE CONTRACTED-OUT SCHEMES

3(1) This article applies for the purposes of section 42A of the 1993 Act (reduced rates of Class 1 contributions, and rebates).

3(2) For the purposes of section 42A(2) of the 1993 Act (reduction of primary Class 1 contributions), the appropriate flat-rate percentage for the 2012–2013 tax year is 1.4 per cent.

3(3) For the purposes of section 42A(2A) of the 1993 Act (reduction of secondary Class 1 contributions), the appropriate flat-rate percentage for the 2012–2013 tax year is 1.0 per cent.

3(4) For the purposes of section 42A(3) of the 1993 Act (appropriate age-related percentage), the appropriate age-related percentage in respect of an earner for the 2012–2013 tax year is the percentage given in the table in Schedule 1 by reference to the age of the earner on the day immediately before the start of that tax year.

APPROPRIATE AGE-RELATED PERCENTAGES FOR APPROPRIATE PERSONAL PENSION SCHEMES

4(1) This article applies for the purposes of section 45(1) of the 1993 Act (amount of minimum contributions).

4(2) For the 2012–2013 tax year, the appropriate age-related percentage in respect of earnings of an earner is determined in accordance with paragraph (3) or (4).

4(3) If the earnings do not exceed the low earnings threshold, the appropriate age-related percentage is the column B percentage.

4(4) If the earnings exceed the low earnings threshold, then–

(a) in respect of the part of the earnings that does not exceed the low earnings threshold, the appropriate age-related percentage is the column B percentage; and

(b) in respect of the part of the earnings that exceeds the low earnings threshold, the appropriate age-related percentage is the column C percentage.

4(5) In respect of earnings of an earner–

(a) the column B percentage is the percentage given in column B of the table in Schedule 2 by reference to the age of the earner on the day immediately before the start of the 2012–2013 tax year; and

(b) the column C percentage is the percentage given in column C of the table in Schedule 2 by reference to the age of the earner on the day immediately before the start of the 2012–2013 tax year.

ALTERATION OF REDUCED RATES OF CLASS 1 CONTRIBUTIONS FOR SALARY RELATED CONTRACTED-OUT SCHEMES – NORTHERN IRELAND

5(1) This article applies for the purposes of section 37 of the Northern Ireland Act (reduced rates of Class 1 contributions).

5(2) In section 37(1A) of the Northern Ireland Act (reduced rates of primary Class 1 contributions) for "1.6 per cent" substitute "1.4 per cent".

5(3) In section 37(1B) of the Northern Ireland Act(a) (reduced rates of secondary Class 1 contributions) for "3.7 per cent" substitute "3.4 per cent".

REDUCED RATES OF CLASS 1 CONTRIBUTIONS AND REBATES FOR MONEY PURCHASE CONTRACTED-OUT SCHEMES – NORTHERN IRELAND

6(1) This article applies for the purposes of section 38A of the Northern Ireland Act (reduced rates of Class 1 contributions, and rebates).

6(2) For the purposes of section 38A(2) of the Northern Ireland Act (reduction of primary Class 1 contributions), the appropriate flat-rate percentage for the 2012–2013 tax year is 1.4 per cent.

6(3) For the purposes of section 38A(2A) of the Northern Ireland Act (reduction of secondary Class 1 contributions), the appropriate flat-rate percentage for the 2012–2013 tax year is 1.0 per cent.

6(4) For the purposes of section 38A(3) of the Northern Ireland Act (appropriate age-related percentage), the appropriate age-related percentage in respect of an earner for the 2012–2013 tax year is the percentage given in the table in Schedule 1 by reference to the age of the earner on the day immediately before the start of that tax year.

APPROPRIATE AGE-RELATED PERCENTAGES FOR APPROPRIATE PERSONAL PENSION SCHEMES – NORTHERN IRELAND

7(1) This article applies for the purposes of section 41(1) of the Northern Ireland Act (amount of minimum contributions).

7(2) For the 2012–2013 tax year, the appropriate age-related percentage in respect of earnings of an earner is determined in accordance with paragraph (3) or (4).

7(3) If the earnings do not exceed the low earnings threshold, the appropriate age-related percentage is the column B percentage.

7(4) If the earnings exceed the low earnings threshold, then–

(a) in respect of the part of the earnings that does not exceed the low earnings threshold, the appropriate age-related percentage is the column B percentage; and

(b) in respect of the part of the earnings that exceeds the low earnings threshold, the appropriate age-related percentage is the column C percentage.

7(5) In respect of earnings of an earner–

(a) the column B percentage is the percentage given in column B of the table in Schedule 2 by reference to the age of the earner on the day immediately before the start of the 2012–2013 tax year; and

(b) the column C percentage is the percentage given in column C of the table in Schedule 2 by reference to the age of the earner on the day immediately before the start of the 2012–2013 tax year.

SCHEDULES

SCHEDULE 1

Articles 3(4) and 6(4)

APPROPRIATE AGE-RELATED PERCENTAGES FOR MONEY PURCHASE CONTRACTED-OUT SCHEMES FOR THE 2012–2013 TAX YEAR

Age on last day of preceding tax year	Appropriate age-related percentage
15	2.4%
16	2.5%
17	2.5%
18	2.6%
19	2.7%
20	2.7%
21	2.8%
22	2.9%
23	2.9%
24	3.0%
25	3.1%
26	3.1%
27	3.2%
28	3.3%
29	3.4%
30	3.4%
31	3.5%
32	3.6%
33	3.7%
34	4.1%
35	4.2%
36	4.3%
37	4.4%
38	4.5%
39	4.7%
40	4.8%
41	5.0%
42	5.1%
43	5.7%
44	5.9%
45	6.0%
46	6.2%
47	6.3%
48	6.5%
49	6.6%
50	6.9%

Age on last day of preceding tax year	Appropriate age-related percentage
51	7.3%
52	7.4%
53	7.4%
Missing entry 54	XX%
55	7.4%
56	7.4%
57	7.4%
58	7.4%
59	7.4%
60	7.4%
61	7.4%
62	7.4%
63	7.4%

SCHEDULE 2

Articles 4 and 7

APPROPRIATE AGE-RELATED PERCENTAGES FOR APPROPRIATE PERSONAL PENSION SCHEMES FOR THE 2012–2013 TAX YEAR

Column A	Column B	Column C
Age on last day of preceding tax year	Earnings not exceeding low earnings threshold	Earnings exceeding low earnings threshold
15	7.6%	1.9%
16	7.8%	1.95%
17	8.0%	2.0%
18	8.0%	2.0%
19	8.2%	2.05%
20	8.2%	2.05%
21	8.4%	2.1%
22	8.6%	2.15%
23	8.6%	2.15%
24	8.8%	2.2%
25	9.0%	2.25%
26	9.0%	2.25%
27	9.2%	2.3%
28	9.2%	2.3%
29	9.4%	2.35%
30	9.6%	2.4%
31	9.6%	2.4%
32	9.8%	2.45%
33	10.0%	2.5%
34	10.8%	2.7%
35	11.0%	2.75%
36	11.2%	2.8%
37	11.4%	2.85%
38	11.6%	2.9%
39	11.8%	2.95%
40	12.2%	3.05%

Column A	Column B	Column C
Age on last day of preceding tax year	Earnings not exceeding low earnings threshold	Earnings exceeding low earnings threshold
41	12.4%	3.1%
42	12.6%	3.15%
43	13.8%	3.45%
44	14.0%	3.5%
45	14.2%	3.55%
46	14.6%	3.65%
47	14.8%	3.7%
48	14.8%	3.7%
49	14.8%	3.7%
50	14.8%	3.7%
51	14.8%	3.7%
52	14.8%	3.7%
53	14.8%	3.7%
[Missing entry 54	XX%	X.X%]
55	14.8%	3.7%
56	14.8%	3.7%
57	14.8%	3.7%
58	14.8%	3.7%
59	14.8%	3.7%
60	14.8%	3.7%
61	14.8%	3.7%
62	14.8%	3.7%
63	14.8%	3.7%

SOCIAL SECURITY REVALUATION OF EARNINGS FACTORS ORDER 2012

(SI 2012/187)

Made on 26 January 2012 by the Secretary of State in exercise of the powers conferred by s. 148(3) and (4) and 189(1), (4) and (5) of the Social Security Administration Act 1992. Operative from 6 April 2012.

CITATION AND COMMENCEMENT

1 This Order may be cited as the Social Security Revaluation of Earnings Factors Order 2012 and shall come into force on 6th April 2012.

REVALUATION OF EARNINGS FACTORS

2 The earnings factors for tax years specified in the Schedule to this Order in so far as they are relevant–

(a) to the calculation–

(i) of the additional pension in the rate of any long-term benefit, or

(ii) of any guaranteed minimum pension; or

(b) to any other calculation required under Part 3 of the Pension Schemes Act 1993 (including that Part as modified by or under any other enactment),

are directed to be increased for those tax years by the percentage of their amount shown opposite those tax years in that Schedule.

ROUNDING OF FRACTIONAL AMOUNTS

3 Where any earnings factor relevant to the calculation specified in article 2(a)(i) of this Order, as increased in accordance with this Order, would not but for this article be expressed as a whole number of pounds, it shall be so expressed by rounding down any fraction of a pound less than one half and rounding up any other fraction of a pound.

SCHEDULE – PERCENTAGE INCREASE OF EARNINGS FACTOR FOR SPECIFIED TAX YEARS

Article 2

Tax year	Percentage increase
1978–1979	719.5
1979–1980	623.3
1980–1981	504.3
1981–1982	406.1
1982–1983	359.6
1983–1984	326.8
1984–1985	295.2
1985–1986	270.7
1986–1987	240.4
1987–1988	217.0
1988–1989	191.6
1989–1990	163.2
1990–1991	145.3
1991–1992	122.8
1992–1993	109.2
1993–1994	99.2
1994–1995	93.2
1995–1996	85.1
1996–1997	80.0
1997–1998	71.5
1998–1999	63.9

Tax year	Percentage increase
1999–2000	57.3
2000–2001	48.0
2001–2002	42.3
2002–2003	36.4
2003–2004	31.7
2004–2005	26.9
2005–2006	21.9
2006–2007	17.9
2007–2008	13.2
2008–2009	8.7
2009–2010	5.4
2010–2011	4.1
2011–2012	1.8

NATIONAL INSURANCE CONTRIBUTIONS (APPLICATION OF PART 7 OF THE FINANCE ACT 2004) REGULATIONS 2012

(SI 2012/1868, as amended by SI 2013/2600, SI 2015/531 and SI 2017/1174)

Made on 16 July 2012 by the Treasury, in exercise of the powers conferred upon them by s. 132A(1) and 189(4) and (5) of the Social Security Administration Act 1992. Operative from 1 September 2012.

PART 1 – INTRODUCTION

CITATION AND COMMENCEMENT

1 These Regulations may be cited as the National Insurance Contributions (Application of Part 7 of the Finance Act 2004) Regulations 2012 and shall come into force on 1st September 2012.

INTERPRETATION

2 In these Regulations–

"the Descriptions Regulations" means the Tax Avoidance Schemes (Prescribed Descriptions of Arrangements) Regulations 2006 as modified by these Regulations.

"employer" means the secondary contributor determined under–

(a) section 7 of the Social Security Contributions and Benefits Act 1992;

(b) regulation 5 of, and Schedule 3 to, the Social Security (Categorisation of Earners) Regulations 1978; or

(c) regulation 122 of the Social Security (Contributions) Regulations 2001;

"the Information Regulations" means the Tax Avoidance (Information) Regulations 2012 as modified by these Regulations.

"introducer", in relation to a notifiable contribution proposal, has the meaning given by regulation 7(2);

"HMRC" means the Commissioners for Her Majesty's Revenue and Customs;

"notifiable arrangements" and **"notifiable proposal"** have the meaning given to them in section 306 of the Finance Act 2004;

"Part 7" means Part 7 of the Finance Act 2004 (disclosure of tax avoidance schemes) and a reference to a numbered section (without more) is a reference to a section of Part 7;

"prescribed" means prescribed by the Information Regulations, unless the context otherwise requires;

"promoter", in relation to notifiable contribution arrangements or a notifiable contribution proposal, has the meaning given by regulation 7;

"reference number" means the reference number allocated under regulation 12 or section 311 as the case may be;

"tribunal" means the First-tier Tribunal or, where determined by or under Tribunal Procedure Rules, the Upper Tribunal.

"working day" means a day which is not a Saturday or a Sunday, Christmas Day, Good Friday or a bank holiday under the Banking and Financial Dealings Act 1971 in any part of the United Kingdom.

History – In reg. 2 the definition of "employer" inserted by SI 2017/1174, reg. 3, with effect from 21 December 2017.
In reg. 2, definition of "working day" inserted by SI 2015/531, reg. 3, with effect in relation to prescribed information about notifiable contribution proposals or notifiable contribution arrangements provided by a person in compliance, or purported compliance, with reg. 8, 10 and 11 on or after 12 April 2015.

STRUCTURE OF THE REGULATIONS

3(1) Regulations 5 to 21D make provision corresponding to Part 7 (other than section 314 (legal professional privilege)) in so far as that Part applies to income tax.

3(2) Regulations 22 to 24 make provision corresponding to section 98C and section 118(2) of the Taxes Management Act 1970 (penalties for failure to comply with Part 7 of the Finance Act 2004) and other provisions of the Taxes Management Act 1970 in so far as they relate to a penalty under section 98C.

3(3) Regulations 25 to 28 modify regulations made under Part 7 in so far as they apply to income tax.

History – In reg. 3(1) "21D" substituted for "21" by SI 2017/1174, reg. 4, with effect from 21 December 2017.

REVOCATIONS

4(1) The regulations described in Regulation 29 are revoked.

4(2) Anything begun under or for the purpose of any regulations revoked by these Regulations shall be continued under or, as the case may be, for the purpose of the corresponding provision of these Regulations.

4(3) Where any document refers to a provision of a regulation revoked by these Regulations, such reference shall, unless the context otherwise requires, be construed as a reference to the corresponding provision of these Regulations.

History – In reg. 4(2) "continued" substituted for "construed" by correction slip dated 31 January 2013.

PART 2 – PROVISIONS CORRESPONDING TO PART 7 OF THE FINANCE ACT 2004

APPLICATION OF PART 2

5(1) This Part applies to–

(a) notifiable contribution arrangements; and

(b) notifiable contribution proposals

which fall within any description prescribed by the Descriptions Regulations.

5(2) The Table below shows which of the following regulations corresponds to which provision of Part 7.

Section within Part 7	*Corresponding provision of these Regulations*
Section 306 (meaning of "notifiable arrangements" and "notifiable proposal")	Regulation 5
Section 306A (doubt as to notifiability)	Regulation 6
Section 307 (meaning of promoter)	Regulation 7
Section 308 (duties of promoter)	Regulation 8
Section 308A (supplemental information)	Regulation 9
Section 309 (duty of person dealing with promoter outside the United Kingdom)	Regulation 10
Section 310 (duty of parties to notifiable arrangements not involving promoter)	Regulation 11
Section 310A (duty to provide further information requested by HMRC)	Regulation 11A
Section 310B (failure to provide information under section 310A: application to the Tribunal)	Regulation 11B
Section 310C (duty of promoters to provide updated information)	Regulation 11C
Section 311 (arrangements to be given reference number)	Regulation 12
Section 312 (duty of promoter to notify client of number)	Regulation 13
Section 312A (duty of client to notify parties of number)	Regulation 14
Section 312B (duty of client to provide information to promoter)	Regulation 14A
Section 313 (duty of parties to notifiable arrangements to notify Board of number etc)	Regulation 15
Section 313ZA (duty of promoter to provide details of clients)	Regulation 16
Section 313ZB (enquiry following disclosure of client details)	Regulation 16A
Section 313ZC (duty of employer to notify HMRC of details of employees etc)	Regulation 16B
Section 313A (pre-disclosure enquiry)	Regulation 17

Section within Part 7	*Corresponding provision of these Regulations*
Section 313B (reasons for non-disclosure: supporting information)	Regulation 18
Section 313C (information provided to introducers)	Regulation 19
Section 314A (order to disclose)	Regulation 20
Section 316 (information to be provided in form and manner specified by Board)	Regulation 21
Section 316A (duty to provide additional information)	Regulation 21A
Section 316B (confidentiality)	Regulation 21B
Section 316C (publication by HMRC)	Regulation 21C
Section 316D (section 316C: subsequent judicial rulings)	Regulation 21D

History – In reg. 5(2), in the Table, entry "Section 310C (duty of promoters to provide updated information)"inserted by SI 2017/1174, reg. 5(a), with effect from 21 December 2017.
In reg. 5(2), in the Table, entry "Section 313ZC (duty of employer to notify HMRC of details of employees etc)"inserted by SI 2017/1174, reg. 5(b), with effect from 21 December 2017.
In reg. 5(2), in the Table, entries "Section 316A (duty to provide additional information)", "Section 316B (confidentiality)", "Section 316C (publication by HMRC)" and "Section 316D (section 316C: subsequent judicial rulings)"inserted by SI 2017/1174, reg. 5(c), with effect from 21 December 2017.
In reg. 5(2), in the Table, entries "Section 310A (duty to provide further information requested by HMRC)" and "Section 310B (failure to provide information under section 310A: application to the Tribunal)" inserted by SI 2015/531, reg. 4, with effect in relation to prescribed information about notifiable contribution proposals or notifiable contribution arrangements provided by a person in compliance, or purported compliance, with reg. 8, 10 and 11 on or after 12 April 2015.
In reg. 5(2), in the Table, entries "Section 312B (duty of client to provide information to promoter)" and "Section 313ZB (enquiry following disclosure of client details)" inserted by SI 2013/2600, reg. 3, with effect from 4 November 2013 (but the amendments do not have effect for the purposes of reg. 8(1), if the relevant date (reg. 8(2)) falls before 4 November 2013 or for the purposes of reg. 8(3), if the date on which the promoter first becomes aware of any transaction forming part of notifiable contribution arrangements falls before 4 November 2013.

DOUBT AS TO NOTIFIABILITY

6(1) HMRC may apply to the tribunal for an order that–
(a) a proposal is to be treated as a notifiable contribution proposal; or
(b) arrangements are to be treated as notifiable contribution arrangements.

6(2) An application must specify–
(a) the proposal or arrangements in respect of which the order is sought; and
(b) the promoter.

6(3) On an application the tribunal may make the order only if satisfied that HMRC–
(a) have taken all reasonable steps to establish whether the proposal is a notifiable contribution proposal or the arrangements are notifiable contribution arrangements; and
(b) have reasonable grounds for suspecting that the proposal may be a notifiable contribution proposal or the arrangements may be notifiable contribution arrangements.

6(4) Reasonable steps under paragraph (3)(a) may (but need not) include taking action under regulation 17 or 18.

6(5) Grounds for suspicion under paragraph (3)(b) may include–
(a) the fact that the relevant arrangements fall within a description prescribed by the Descriptions Regulations;
(b) an attempt by the promoter to avoid or delay providing information or documents about the proposal or arrangements under or by virtue of regulation 17 or 18;
(c) the promoter's failure to comply with a requirement under or by virtue of regulation 17 or 18 or section 313A or 313B in relation to another proposal or other arrangements.

6(6) Where an order is made under this regulation in respect of a proposal or arrangements, the period for the purposes of paragraphs (1) and (3) of regulation 8 is that prescribed.

6(7) An order under this regulation in relation to a proposal or arrangements is without prejudice to the possible application of regulation 8, other than by virtue of this regulation, to the proposal or arrangements.

MEANING OF PROMOTER

7(1) For the purposes of this Part a person is a promoter–

(a) in relation to a notifiable contribution proposal if, in the course of a relevant business, the person ("P")–

(i) is to any extent responsible for the design of the proposed arrangements;

(ii) makes a firm approach to another person ("C") in relation to the proposal with a view to P making the proposal available for implementation by C or any other person; or

(iii) makes the notifiable contribution proposal available for implementation by other persons; and

(b) in relation to notifiable contribution arrangements, if the person ("P") is by virtue of sub-paragraph (a)(ii) or (iii) a promoter in relation to a notifiable contribution proposal which is implemented by those arrangements or if, in the course of a relevant business, P is to any extent responsible for–

(i) the design of the arrangements, or

(ii) the organisation or management of the arrangements.

7(2) For the purposes of this Part a person is an introducer in relation to a notifiable contribution proposal if the person makes a marketing contact with another person in relation to the proposal.

7(3) In this regulation **"relevant business"** means any trade, profession or business which–

(a) involves the provision to other persons of services relating to national insurance contributions, or

(b) is carried on by a bank, as defined by section 1120 of the Corporation Tax Act 2010, or by a securities house, as defined by section 1009(3) of that Act.

7(4) For the purposes of this regulation anything done by a company is to be taken to be done in the course of a relevant business if it is done for the purposes of a relevant business falling within paragraph (3)(b) carried on by another company which is a member of the same group.

7(5) Section 170 of the Taxation of Chargeable Gains Act 1992 has effect for determining for the purposes of paragraph (4) whether two companies are members of the same group, but as if in that section–

(a) for each of the references to a 75% subsidiary there were substituted a reference to a 51% subsidiary, and

(b) subsection (3)(b) and subsections (6) to (8) were omitted.

7(6) For the purposes of this Part a person makes a firm approach to another person in relation to a notifiable contribution proposal if the person makes a marketing contact with the other person in relation to the proposal at a time when the proposed arrangements have been substantially designed.

7(7) For the purposes of this Part a person makes a marketing contact with another person in relation to a notifiable contribution proposal if–

(a) the person communicates information about the proposal to the other person;

(b) the communication is made with a view to that other person, or any other person, entering into transactions forming part of the proposed arrangements; and

(c) the information communicated includes an explanation of the advantage in relation to any contribution that might be expected to be obtained from the proposed arrangements.

7(8) For the purposes of paragraph (6) proposed contribution arrangements have been substantially designed at any time if by that time the nature of the transactions to form part of them has been sufficiently developed for it to be reasonable to believe that a person who wished to obtain the advantage mentioned in paragraph (7)(c) might enter into–

(a) transactions of the nature developed; or

(b) transactions not substantially different from transactions of that nature.

7(9) A person is not to be treated as a promoter or introducer for the purposes of this Part by reason of anything done in circumstances prescribed by the Tax Avoidance Schemes (Promoters and Prescribed Circumstances) Regulations 2004 as modified by these Regulations.

7(10) In the application of this Part to a proposal which is not a notifiable contribution proposal or arrangements which are not notifiable contribution arrangements, a reference to a promoter or introducer is a reference to a person who would be a promoter or introducer under paragraphs (1) to (9) if the proposal were a notifiable contribution proposal or arrangements were notifiable contribution arrangements.

History – In reg. 7(5), "(4)" substituted for "(3)" by correction slip dated 31 January 2013.

DUTIES OF PROMOTER

8(1) A person who is a promoter in relation to a notifiable contribution proposal must, within the prescribed period after the relevant date, provide HMRC with the prescribed information relating to the notifiable contribution proposal.

8(2) In paragraph (1) **"the relevant date"** means the earliest of the following–

(a) the date on which the promoter first makes a firm approach to another person in relation to a notifiable contribution proposal;

(b) the date on which the promoter makes the notifiable contribution proposal available for implementation by any other person; or

(c) the date on which the promoter first becomes aware of any transaction forming part of notifiable contribution arrangements implementing the notifiable contribution proposal.

8(3) A person who is a promoter in relation to notifiable contribution arrangements must, within the prescribed period after the date on which the person first becomes aware of any transaction forming part of the notifiable contribution arrangements, provide HMRC with the prescribed information relating to those arrangements, unless those arrangements implement a proposal in respect of which notice has been given under paragraph (1).

8(4) Paragraph (5) applies where a person complies with paragraph (1) in relation to a notifiable contribution proposal for arrangements and another person is–

(a) also a promoter in relation to the notifiable contribution proposal or is a promoter in relation to a notifiable contribution proposal for arrangements which are substantially the same as the proposed arrangements (whether they relate to the same or different parties); or

(b) a promoter in relation to notifiable contribution arrangements implementing the notifiable contribution proposal or notifiable contribution arrangements which are substantially the same as notifiable contribution arrangements implementing the notifiable contribution proposal (whether they relate to the same or different parties).

8(5) Any duty of the other person under paragraph (1) or (3) in relation to the notifiable contribution proposal or notifiable contribution arrangements is discharged if–

(a) the person who complied with paragraph (1) has notified the identity and address of the other person to HMRC or the other person holds the reference number allocated to the proposed notifiable contribution arrangements under regulation 12; and

(b) the other person holds the information provided to HMRC in compliance with paragraph (1).

8(6) Paragraph (7) applies where a person complies with section 308(1) in relation to a notifiable proposal and another person is–

(a) a promoter in relation to a notifiable contribution proposal for arrangements which are substantially the same as the notifiable proposal (whether they relate to the same or different parties); or

(b) a promoter in relation to notifiable contribution arrangements which are substantially the same as notifiable arrangements implementing the notifiable proposal (whether they relate to the same or different parties).

8(7) Any duty of the other person under paragraph (1) or (3) in relation to the notifiable contribution proposal or notifiable contribution arrangements is discharged if–

(a) the person who complied with section 308(1) in relation to the notifiable proposal has notified the identity and address of the other person to HMRC or the other person holds the reference number allocated to the proposed notifiable arrangements under section 311; and

(b) the other person holds the information provided to HMRC in compliance with section 308(1).

8(8) Paragraph (9) applies where a person complies with paragraph (3) in relation to notifiable contribution arrangements and another person is–

(a) a promoter in relation to a notifiable contribution proposal for arrangements which are substantially the same as the notifiable contribution arrangements (whether they relate to the same or different parties); or

(b) also a promoter in relation to the notifiable contribution arrangements or notifiable contribution arrangements which are substantially the same (whether they relate to the same or different parties).

8(9) Any duty of the other person under paragraph (1) or (3) in relation to the notifiable contribution *proposal or notifiable contribution* arrangements is discharged if–

(a) the person who complied with paragraph (3) has notified the identity and address of the other person to HMRC or the other person holds the reference number allocated to the notifiable contribution arrangements under regulation 12; and

(b) the other person holds the information provided to HMRC in compliance with paragraph (3).

8(10) Paragraph (11) applies where a person complies with section 308(3) in relation to notifiable arrangements and another person is a promoter in relation to a notifiable contribution proposal for arrangements or notifiable contribution arrangements which are substantially the same as the notifiable arrangements (whether they relate to the same or different parties).

8(11) Any duty of the other person under paragraph (1) or (3) in relation to the notifiable contribution proposal or notifiable contribution arrangements is discharged if–

(a) the person who complied with section 308(3) in relation to the notifiable contribution arrangements has notified the identity and address of the other person to HMRC or the other person holds the reference number allocated to the notifiable contribution arrangements under section 311; and

(b) the other person holds the information provided to HMRC in compliance with section 308(3).

8(12) Where a person is a promoter in relation to two or more notifiable contribution proposals or sets of notifiable contribution arrangements which are substantially the same (whether they relate to the same parties or different parties), that person need not provide information under paragraph (1) or (3) if that person has already provided information under either of those paragraphs in relation to any of the other contribution proposals or contribution arrangements.

SUPPLEMENTAL INFORMATION

9(1) This regulation applies where–

(a) a promoter ("P") has provided information in purported compliance with paragraph (1) or (3) of regulation 8; but

(b) HMRC believe that P has not provided all the prescribed information.

9(2) HMRC may apply to the tribunal for an order requiring P to provide specified information about, or documents relating to, the notifiable contribution proposal or notifiable contribution arrangements.

9(3) The tribunal may make an order under paragraph (2) in respect of information or documents only if satisfied that HMRC have reasonable grounds for suspecting that the information or documents–

(a) form part of the prescribed information; or

(b) will support or explain the prescribed information.

9(4) A requirement by virtue of paragraph (2) shall be treated as part of P's duty under paragraph (1) or (3) of regulation 8.

9(5) In so far as P's duty under paragraph (1) or (3) of regulation 8 arises out of a requirement by virtue of paragraph (2) above, the period for the purposes of those paragraphs of regulation 8 and the date after which it begins are those prescribed.

9(6) In so far as P's duty under paragraph (1) or (3) of regulation 8 arises out of a requirement by virtue of paragraph (2) above, the prescribed period may be extended by HMRC by direction.

DUTY OF PERSON DEALING WITH PROMOTER OUTSIDE UNITED KINGDOM

10(1) Any person ("the client") who enters into any transaction forming part of any notifiable contribution arrangements in relation to which–

(a) a promoter is resident outside the United Kingdom, and

(b) no promoter is resident in the United Kingdom,

must provide HMRC with the prescribed information relating to the notifiable contribution arrangements within the prescribed period.

10(2) Compliance with regulation 8(1) by any promoter in relation to the notifiable contribution arrangements discharges the duty of the client under paragraph (1).

DUTY OF PARTIES TO NOTIFIABLE CONTRIBUTION ARRANGEMENTS NOT INVOLVING PROMOTER

11 Any person who enters into any transaction forming part of notifiable contribution arrangements as respects which neither that person nor any other person in the United Kingdom is liable to comply with regulation 8 or regulation 10 must at the prescribed time provide HMRC with the prescribed information relating to the notifiable contribution arrangements.

DUTY TO PROVIDE FURTHER INFORMATION REQUESTED BY HMRC

11A(1) This regulation applies where–

(a) a person has provided the prescribed information about notifiable contribution proposals or notifiable contribution arrangements in compliance with regulation 8, 10 or 11, or

(b) a person has provided information in purported compliance with regulation 10 or 11 but HMRC believe that the person has not provided all the prescribed information.

11A(2) HMRC may require the person to provide–

(a) further specified information about the notifiable contribution proposals or notifiable contribution arrangements (in addition to the prescribed information under regulation 8, 10 or 11);

(b) documents relating to the notifiable contribution proposals or notifiable contribution arrangements.

11A(3) Where HMRC impose a requirement on a person under this regulation, the person must comply with the requirement within–

(a) the period of 10 working days beginning with the day on which HMRC imposed the requirement, or

(b) such longer period as HMRC may direct.

History – Reg. 11A and the heading preceding it inserted by SI 2015/531, reg. 5, with effect in relation to prescribed information about notifiable contribution proposals or notifiable contribution arrangements provided by a person in compliance, or purported compliance, with reg. 8, 10 and 11 on or after 12 April 2015.

FAILURE TO PROVIDE INFORMATION UNDER REGULATION 11A: APPLICATION TO THE TRIBUNAL

11B(1) This regulation applies where HMRC–

(a) have required a person to provide information or documents under regulation 11A, but

(b) believe that the person has failed to provide the information or documents required.

11B(2) HMRC may apply to the tribunal for an order requiring the person to provide the information or documents required.

11B(3) The tribunal may make an order under paragraph (2) only if satisfied that HMRC have reasonable grounds for suspecting that the information or documents will assist HMRC in considering the notifiable contribution proposals or notifiable contribution arrangements.

11B(4) Where the tribunal makes an order under paragraph (2), the person must comply with it within–

(a) the period of 10 working days beginning with the day on which the tribunal made the order, or

(b) such longer period as HMRC may direct.

History – Reg. 11B and the heading preceding it inserted by SI 2015/531, reg. 5, with effect in relation to prescribed information about notifiable contribution proposals or notifiable contribution arrangements provided by a person in compliance, or purported compliance, with reg. 8, 10 and 11 on or after 12 April 2015.

DUTY OF PROMOTERS TO PROVIDE UPDATED INFORMATION

11C(1) This regulation applies where–

(a) information has been provided under regulation 8 about any notifiable contribution arrangements, or proposed notifiable contribution arrangements, to which a reference number is allocated under regulation 12, and

(b) after the provision of information, there is a change in relation to the arrangements of a kind mentioned in paragraph (2).

11C(2) The changes referred to in paragraph (1)(b) are–

(a) a change in the name by which the notifiable contribution arrangements or proposed notifiable contribution arrangements, are known;

(b) a change in the name or address of any person who is a promoter in relation to the notifiable contribution arrangements or, in the case of proposed notifiable contribution arrangements, the notifiable contribution proposal.

11C(3) A person who is a promoter in relation to the notifiable contribution arrangements or, in the case of proposed notifiable contribution arrangements, the notifiable contribution proposal must inform HMRC of the change mentioned in paragraph (1)(b) within 30 days after it is made.

11C(4) Paragraphs (5) and (6) apply for the purposes of paragraph (3) where there is more than one person who is a promoter in relation to the notifiable contribution arrangements or notifiable contribution proposal.

11C(5) If the change in question is a change in the name or address of a person who is a promoter in relation to the notifiable contribution arrangements or notifiable contribution proposal, it is the duty of that person to comply with paragraph (3).

11C(6) If a person provides information in compliance with paragraph (3), the duty imposed by that paragraph on any other person, so far as relating to the provision of that information, is discharged.

History – Reg. 11C inserted by SI 2017/1174, reg. 6, with effect from 6 April 2018.

ARRANGEMENTS TO BE GIVEN REFERENCE NUMBER

12(1) Where a person complies or purports to comply with regulation 8(1) or (3), regulation 10(1) or regulation 11 in relation to any notifiable contribution proposal or notifiable contribution arrangements, HMRC–

(a) may within 90 days allocate a reference number in relation to the notifiable contribution arrangements, or in the case of a notifiable contribution proposal, to the proposed notifiable contribution arrangements; and

(b) if they do so, must notify that number to the person and (where the person is one who has complied or purported to comply with paragraph (1) or (3) of regulation 8) to any other person–

(i) who is a promoter in relation to the notifiable contribution proposal (or arrangements implementing the notifiable contribution proposal) or the notifiable contribution arrangements (or proposal implemented by the notifiable contribution arrangements), and

(ii) whose identity and address has been notified to HMRC by the person,

except that where the arrangements or proposal concern both national insurance contributions and tax, HMRC shall allocate a single reference number in respect of both matters.

12(2) The allocation of a reference number to any notifiable contribution arrangements (or proposed notifiable contribution arrangements) is not to be regarded as constituting any indication by HMRC that the arrangements could as a matter of law result in the obtaining by any person of an advantage in relation to a contribution.

History – In reg. 12(1)(a) the words "90 days" substituted for the words "30 days" by SI 2017/1174, reg. 7, with effect from 21 December 2017.

DUTY OF PROMOTER TO NOTIFY CLIENT OF NUMBER

13(1) This regulation applies where a person who is a promoter in relation to notifiable contribution arrangements is providing (or has provided) services to any person ("the client") in connection with the notifiable contribution arrangements.

13(2) The promoter must, within 30 days after the relevant date, provide the client with the prescribed information relating to any reference number (or, if more than one, any one reference number) that has been notified to the promoter (whether by HMRC or any other person) in relation to–

(a) the notifiable contribution arrangements; or

(b) any arrangements, including notifiable arrangements, which are substantially the same as the notifiable contribution arrangements (whether involving the same or different parties).

13(3) In paragraph (2) **"the relevant date"** means the later of–

(a) the date on which the promoter becomes aware of any transaction which forms part of the notifiable contribution arrangements; and

(b) the date on which the reference number is notified to the promoter.

13(4) But where the conditions in paragraph (5) are met the duty imposed on the promoter under paragraph (2) to provide the client with information in relation to notifiable contribution arrangements is discharged.

13(5) Those conditions are that–

(a) the promoter is also a promoter in relation to a notifiable contribution proposal and provides services to the client in connection with them both;

(b) the notifiable contribution proposal and the notifiable contribution arrangements are substantially the same; and

(c) the promoter has provided to the client, in a form and manner specified by HMRC, prescribed information relating to the reference number that has been notified to the promoter in relation to the proposed notifiable contribution arrangements.

13(6) HMRC may give notice that, in relation to notifiable contribution arrangements specified in the notice, promoters are not under the duty under paragraph (2) after the date specified in the notice.

DUTY OF CLIENT TO NOTIFY PARTIES OF NUMBER

14(1) This regulation applies where a person (the "client") to whom a person who is a promoter in relation to notifiable contribution arrangements or a notifiable contribution proposal is providing (or has provided) services in connection with the notifiable contribution arrangements or notifiable contribution proposal receives prescribed information relating to the reference number allocated to–

(a) the notifiable contribution arrangements,

(b) the notifiable contribution proposal, or

(c) proposed notifiable arrangements, or notifiable arrangements, which are substantially the same as the notifiable contribution proposal or notifiable contribution arrangements.

14(2) The client must, within the prescribed period, provide the prescribed information relating to the reference number to any other person–

(a) who the client might reasonably be expected to know is or is likely to be a party to the arrangements or proposed arrangements, and

(b) who might reasonably be expected to gain an advantage by reason of the arrangements or proposed arrangements.

14(2A) Where the client–

(a) is an employer, and

(b) by reason of the contribution arrangements or proposed contribution arrangements, receives or might reasonably be expected to receive an advantage, in relation to the employment of one or more of the client's employees,

the client must, within the prescribed period, provide to each of the client's relevant employees prescribed information relating to the reference number.

14(3) HMRC may give notice that, in relation to notifiable contribution arrangements or a notifiable contribution proposal specified in the notice, persons are not under the duty under paragraph (2) or (2A) after the date specified in the notice.

14(3A) For the purposes of this regulation–

(a) "**relevant employee**" means an employee in relation to whose employment the client receives or might reasonably be expected to receive the advantage mentioned in paragraph (2A);

(b) "**employee**" includes former employee; and

(c) a reference to employment includes holding an office (and references to "**employee**" and "**employer**" are to be construed accordingly).

14(4) The duty under paragraph (2) or (2A) does not apply in the prescribed circumstances.

History – Reg. 14(2A) inserted by SI 2017/1174, reg. 8(1), with effect from 21 December 2017.
In reg. 14(3) the words "paragraph (2) or (2A)" substituted for the words "paragraph (2)" by SI 2017/1174, reg. 8(2), with effect from 21 December 2017.
In reg. 14(4) the words "paragraph (2) or (2A)" substituted for the words "paragraph (2)" by SI 2017/1174, reg. 8(2), with effect from 21 December 2017.
Reg. 14(3A) inserted by SI 2017/1174, reg. 8(3), with effect from 21 December 2017.

DUTY OF CLIENT TO PROVIDE INFORMATION TO PROMOTER

14A(1) This regulation applies where a person who is a promoter in relation to notifiable contribution arrangements has provided a person ("the client") with information under regulation 13(2) (duty of promoter to notify client of reference number).

14A(2) The client must, within the prescribed period, provide the promoter with the prescribed information relating to the client.

History – Reg. 14A (and the heading before it) inserted by SI 2013/2600, reg. 4, with effect from 4 November 2013 (but the amendments do not have effect for the purposes of reg. 8(1), if the relevant date (reg. 8(2)) falls before 4 November 2013 or for the purposes of reg. 8(3), if the date on which the promoter first becomes aware of any transaction forming part of notifiable contribution arrangements falls before 4 November 2013.

DUTY OF PARTIES TO NOTIFIABLE CONTRIBUTION ARRANGEMENTS TO NOTIFY HMRC OF NUMBER ETC

15(1) Any person who is a party to any notifiable contribution arrangements must, at the prescribed time or times, provide HMRC with the prescribed information relating to–

(a) any reference number notified to him, whether the reference number was allocated under regulation 12 or section 311, and

(b) the time when he obtains or expects to obtain by virtue of the arrangements an advantage in relation to any contribution.

15(2) HMRC may give notice that, in relation to notifiable contribution arrangements specified in the notice, persons are not under the duty under paragraph (1) after the date specified in the notice.

15(3) The duty under paragraph (1) does not apply in prescribed circumstances.

History – *Reg. 15(3) inserted by SI 2017/1174, reg. 9, with effect from 21 December 2017.*

DUTY TO PROVIDE DETAILS OF CLIENTS

16(1) This regulation applies where a person who is a promoter in relation to notifiable contribution arrangements is providing (or has provided) services to any person ("the client") in connection with the notifiable contribution arrangements and either–

(a) the promoter is subject to the reference number information requirement; or

(b) the promoter has failed to comply with regulation 8(1) or (3) in relation to the notifiable contributions arrangements (or the notifiable contribution proposal for them) but would be subject to the reference number information requirement if a reference number had been allocated to the notifiable contribution arrangements.

16(2) For the purposes of this regulation **"the reference number information requirement"** is the requirement under regulation 13(2) to provide to the client prescribed information relating to the reference number allocated to the notifiable contribution arrangements.

16(3) The promoter must, within the prescribed period after the end of the relevant period, provide HMRC with the prescribed information in relation to the client.

16(4) In paragraph (3) **"the relevant period"** means the prescribed period during which the promoter is or would be subject to the reference number information requirement.

16(5) The promoter need not comply with paragraph (3) in relation to any notifiable contribution arrangements at any time after HMRC have given notice under regulation 13(6) in relation to the arrangements.

ENQUIRY FOLLOWING DISCLOSURE OF CLIENT DETAILS

16A(1) This regulation applies where–

(a) a person who is a promoter in relation to notifiable contribution arrangements has provided HMRC with information in relation to a person ("the client") under regulation 16(3) (duty to provide details of clients); and

(b) HMRC suspect that a person other than the client is or is likely to be a party to the arrangements.

16A(2) HMRC may by written notice require the promoter to provide the prescribed information in relation to any person other than the client who the promoter might reasonably be expected to know is or is likely to be a party to the arrangements.

16A(3) The promoter must comply with a requirement under or by virtue of paragraph (2) within–

(a) the prescribed period; or

(b) such longer period as HMRC may direct.

History – Reg. 16A (and the heading before it) inserted by SI 2013/2600, reg. 5, with effect from 4 November 2013 (but the amendments do not have effect for the purposes of reg. 8(1), if the relevant date (reg. 8(2)) falls before 4 November 2013 or for the purposes of reg. 8(3), if the date on which the promoter first becomes aware of any transaction forming part of notifiable contribution arrangements falls before 4 November 2013.

DUTY OF EMPLOYER TO NOTIFY HMRC OF DETAILS OF EMPLOYEES ETC

16B(1) This regulation applies if conditions A, B and C are met.

16B(2) Condition A is that a person who is a promoter in relation to notifiable contribution arrangements or a notifiable contribution proposal is providing (or has provided) services in connection with the notifiable contribution arrangements or notifiable contribution proposal to a person ("the client").

16B(3) Condition B is that the client receives information under regulation 13(2) or as mentioned in regulation 13(5).

16B(4) Condition C is that the client is an employer in circumstances where, as a result of the notifiable contribution arrangements or proposed notifiable contribution arrangements–

(a) one or more of the client's employees receive, or might reasonably be expected to receive, in relation to their employment, an advantage, or

(b) the client receives or might reasonably be expected to receive an advantage in relation to the employment of one or more of the client's employees.

16B(5) Where an employee is within paragraph (4)(a), or is an employee mentioned in paragraph (4)(b), the client must provide HMRC with prescribed information relating to the employee at the prescribed time or times.

16B(6) The client need not comply with paragraph (5) in relation to any notifiable contribution arrangements at any time after HMRC has given notice under regulation 13(6) or 15(2) in relation to the notifiable contribution arrangements.

16B(7) The duty under paragraph (5) does not apply in prescribed circumstances.

16B(8) Regulation 14(3A) applies for the purposes of this regulation as it applies for the purpose of that regulation.

History – Reg. 16B inserted by SI 2017/1174, reg. 10, with effect from 21 December 2017.

PRE-DISCLOSURE ENQUIRY

17(1) Where HMRC suspect that a person ("P") is the promoter or introducer of a proposal or arrangements which may be a notifiable contribution proposal or notifiable contribution arrangements, HMRC may by written notice require P to state–

(a) whether in P's opinion the proposal or arrangements are notifiable by P, and

(b) if not, the reasons for P's opinion.

17(2) A notice must specify the proposal or arrangements to which it relates.

17(3) For the purpose of paragraph (1)(b)–

(a) it is not sufficient to refer to the fact that a lawyer or other professional has given an opinion,

(b) the reasons must show, by reference to this Part and the Descriptions Regulations why P thinks the proposal or arrangements are not notifiable by P, and

(c) in particular, if P asserts that the arrangements do not fall within any description prescribed by the Descriptions Regulations the reasons must provide sufficient information to enable HMRC to confirm the assertion.

17(4) P must comply with a requirement under or by virtue of paragraph (1) within–

(a) the prescribed period, or

(b) such longer period as HMRC may direct.

REASONS FOR NON-DISCLOSURE: SUPPORTING INFORMATION

18(1) Where HMRC receive from a person ("P") a statement of reasons why a proposal or arrangements are not notifiable by P, HMRC may apply to the tribunal for an order requiring P to provide specified information or documents in support of the reasons.

18(2) P must comply with a requirement under or by virtue of paragraph (1) within–

(a) the prescribed period, or

(b) such longer period as HMRC may direct.

18(3) The power under paragraph (1)–

(a) may be exercised more than once, and

(b) applies whether or not the statement of reasons was received under regulation 17(1)(b).

PROVISION OF INFORMATION TO HMRC BY INTRODUCERS

History – The heading substituted for the former heading "INFORMATION PROVIDED TO INTRODUCERS" by SI 2017/1174, reg. 11(a), with effect from 6 April 2018.

19(1) This regulation applies where HMRC suspect–

(a) that a person ("P") is an introducer in relation to a proposal; and

(b) that the proposal may be a notifiable contribution proposal.

19(1A) HMRC may by written notice require P to provide HMRC with one or both of the following–

(a) prescribed information in relation to each person who has provided P with any information relating to the proposal;

(b) prescribed information in relation to each person with whom P has made a marketing contact in relation to the proposal.

19(2) A notice must specify the proposal to which it relates.

19(3) P must comply with a requirement under paragraph (1A) within–

(a) the prescribed period; or

(b) such longer period as HMRC may direct.

History – Reg. 19(1) substituted by SI 2017/1174, reg. 11(b), with effect from 6 April 2018. Former reg. 19(1) read as follows:

"19(1) Where HMRC suspect–

(a) that a person ("P") is an introducer in relation to a proposal; and

(b) that the proposal may be a notifiable contribution proposal,

HMRC may by written notice require P to provide HMRC with the prescribed information in relation to each person who has provided P with any information relating to the proposal."

Reg. 19(1A) inserted by SI 2017/1174, reg. 11(c), with effect from 6 April 2018.

In reg. 19(3) the words "paragraph (1A)" substituted for the words "paragraph (1)" by SI 2017/1174, reg. 11(d), with effect from 6 April 2018.

ORDER TO DISCLOSE

20(1) HMRC may apply to the tribunal for an order that–

(a) a proposal is a notifiable contribution proposal, or

(b) arrangements are notifiable contribution arrangements.

20(2) An application must specify–

(a) the proposal or arrangements in respect of which the order is sought, and

(b) the promoter.

20(3) On an application the tribunal may make the order only if satisfied that section 132A(3) of the Social Security Administration Act 1992 applies to the relevant arrangements and that they are within a description prescribed by the Descriptions Regulations.

INFORMATION TO BE PROVIDED IN FORM AND MANNER SPECIFIED BY HMRC

21(1) HMRC may specify the form and manner in which information required to be provided by any of the information provisions must be provided if the provision is to be complied with.

21(2) The **"information provisions"** are regulations 8(1) and (3), 10(1), 11, 11A, 11C, 13(2), 14(2), 15(1), 16(3) and 16B(5)and the Information Regulations.

History – In reg. 21(2) "11C," inserted and the words ", 16(3) and 16B(5)"substituted for the words "and 16(3)" by SI 2017/1174, reg. 12(1), with effect from 21 December 2017.

In reg. 21(2), "11A," inserted by SI 2015/531, reg. 6, with effect in relation to prescribed information about notifiable contribution proposals or notifiable contribution arrangements provided by a person in compliance, or purported compliance, with reg. 8, 10 and 11 on or after 12 April 2015.

DUTY TO PROVIDE ADDITIONAL INFORMATION

21A(1) This regulation applies where a person is required to provide information under regulation 13(2) or 14(2) or (2A).

21A(2) HMRC may specify additional information which must be provided by that person to the recipients under regulation 13(2) or 14(2) or (2A) at the same time as the information referred to in paragraph (1).

21A(3) HMRC may specify the form and manner in which the additional information is to be provided.

21A(4) For the purposes of this regulation **"additional information"** means information supplied by HMRC which relates to notifiable contribution proposals or notifiable contribution arrangements in general.

History – Reg. 21A inserted by SI 2017/1174, reg. 12(2), with effect from 21 December 2017.

CONFIDENTIALITY

21B No duty of confidentiality or other restriction on disclosure (however imposed) prevents the voluntary disclosure by any person to HMRC of information or documents which the person has reasonable grounds for suspecting will assist HMRC in determining whether there has been a breach of any requirement imposed by or under these Regulations.

History – Reg. 21B inserted by SI 2017/1174, reg. 12(2), with effect from 21 December 2017.

PUBLICATION BY HMRC

21C(1) HMRC may publish information about–

(a) any notifiable contribution arrangements, or proposed notifiable contribution arrangements, to which a reference number is allocated under regulation 12;

(b) any person who is a promoter in relation to the notifiable contribution arrangements or, in the case of proposed notifiable contribution arrangements, the notifiable contribution proposal.

21C(2) The information that may be published is (subject to paragraph (4))–

(a) any information relating to arrangements within paragraph (1)(a), or a person within paragraph (1)(b), that is prescribed information for the purposes of regulation 8, 10 or 11;

(b) any ruling of a court or tribunal relating to any such arrangements or person (in that person's capacity as a promoter in relation to a notifiable contribution proposal or notifiable contribution arrangements);

(c) the number of persons in any period who enter into transactions forming part of notifiable contribution arrangements within paragraph (1)(a);

(d) whether notifiable contribution arrangements within paragraph (1)(a) are APN relevant;

(e) any other information that HMRC considers it appropriate to publish for the purpose of identifying arrangements within paragraph (1)(a) or a person within paragraph (1)(b).

21C(3) The information may be published in any manner that HMRC considers appropriate.

21C(4) No information may be published under this regulation that identifies a person who enters into a transaction forming part of notifiable contribution arrangements within paragraph (1)(a).

21C(5) But where a person who is a promoter within paragraph (1)(b) is also a person mentioned in paragraph (4), nothing in paragraph (4) is to be taken as preventing the publication under this regulation of information so far as relating to the person's activities as a promoter.

21C(6) Before publishing any information under this regulation that identifies a person as a promoter within paragraph (1)(b), HMRC must–

(a) inform the person that they are considering doing so, and

(b) give the person reasonable opportunity to make representations about whether it should be published.

21C(7) Arrangements are **"APN relevant"** for the purposes of paragraph (2)(d) if HMRC has indicated in a publication that it may exercise (or has exercised) its power under section 219 of the Finance Act 2014 (accelerated payment notices) by virtue of the arrangements being DOTAS arrangements within the meaning of that section.

History – Reg. 21C inserted by SI 2017/1174, reg. 12(2), with effect from 21 December 2017.

SUBSEQUENT JUDICIAL RULINGS

21D(1) This regulation applies if–

(a) information about notifiable contribution arrangements, or proposed notifiable contribution arrangements, is published under regulation 21C,

(b) at any time after the information is published, a ruling of a court or tribunal is made in relation to contribution arrangements, and

(c) HMRC is of the opinion that the ruling is relevant to the arrangements mentioned in sub-paragraph (a).

21D(2) A ruling is **"relevant"** to the arrangements if–

(a) the principles laid down, or reasoning given, in the ruling would, if applied to the arrangements, allow the purported advantage arising from the arrangements in relation to contributions, and

(b) the ruling is final.

21D(3) HMRC must publish information about the ruling.

21D(4) The information must be published in the same manner as HMRC published the information mentioned in sub-paragraph (1)(a) (and may also be published in any other manner that HMRC considers appropriate).

21D(5) A ruling is **"final"** if it is—

(a) a ruling of the Supreme Court, or

(b) a ruling of any other court or tribunal in circumstances where–

  (i) no appeal may be made against the ruling,

  (ii) if an appeal may be made against the ruling with permission, the time limit for applications has expired and either no application has been made or permission has been refused,

  (iii) if such permission to appeal against the ruling has been granted or is not required, no appeal has been made within the time limit for appeals, or

  (iv) if an appeal was made, it was abandoned or otherwise disposed of before it was determined by the court or tribunal to which it was addressed.

21D(6) Where a ruling is final by virtue of paragraph (5)(b)(ii), (iii) or (iv), the ruling is to be treated as made at the time when the paragraph in question is first satisfied.

21D(7) In this regulation, **"contribution arrangements"** means arrangements in respect of which it would be reasonable to conclude (having regard to all the circumstances) that the obtaining of an advantage in relation to contributions was the main purpose, or one of the main purposes.

History – Reg. 21D inserted by SI 2017/1174, reg. 12(2), with effect from 21 December 2017.

PART 3 – PROVISIONS CORRESPONDING TO SECTION 98C AND SECTION 118(2) OF THE TAXES MANAGEMENT ACT 1970AND MODIFICATIONS OF RELATED PROVISIONS

NOTIFICATION UNDER PART 2

22(1) A person who fails to comply with any of the provisions of Part 2 mentioned in paragraph (2) below shall be liable–

(a) to a penalty not exceeding–

(i) in the case of a provision mentioned in sub-paragraph (a), (b), (c) or (ca) of that paragraph, £600 for each day during the initial period (but see also paragraphs (5), (7) and (8) below); and

(ii) in any other case, £5,000; and

(b) if the failure continues after a penalty is imposed under sub-paragraph (a) above, to a further penalty or penalties not exceeding £600 for each day on which the failure continues after the day on which the penalty under sub-paragraph (a) was imposed (but excluding any day for which a penalty under this paragraph has already been imposed).

This is subject to paragraph (14).

22(2) Those provisions are–

(a) regulation 8(1) and (3) (duty of promoter in relation to notifiable contribution proposals and notifiable contribution arrangements),

(b) regulation 10(1) (duty of person dealing with promoter outside United Kingdom),

(c) regulation 11 (duty of parties to notifiable contribution arrangements not involving promoter),

(ca) regulation 11A (duty to provide further information requested by HMRC),

(cb) regulation 11C (duty of promoters to provide updated information),

(d) regulation 13(2) (duty of promoter to notify client of reference number),

(e) regulation 14(2) and 14(2A) (duty of client to notify parties of reference number),

(ea) regulation 14A(2) (duty of client to provide information to promoter),

(f) regulation 16 (duty of promoter to provide details of clients),

(fa) regulation 16A (duty of promoter to provide further information),

(fb) regulation 16B (duty of employer to notify HMRC of details of employees etc),

(g) regulations 17 and 18 (duty of promoter to respond to inquiry),

(h) regulation 19 (provision of information to HMRC by introducers), and

(i) regulation 21A (duty to provide additional information).

22(3) In this regulation **"the initial period"** means the period–

(a) beginning with the relevant day; and

(b) ending with the earlier of the day on which the penalty under paragraph (1)(a)(i) is determined and the last day before the failure ceases;

and for this purpose **"the relevant day"** is the day specified in relation to the failure in the following table.

TABLE

Failure	*Relevant day*
A failure to comply with paragraph (1) or (3) of regulation 8 in so far as the paragraph applies by virtue of an order under regulation 6	The first day of the prescribed period
A failure to comply with paragraph (1) or (3) of regulation 8 in so far as the paragraph applies by virtue of an order under regulation 9(2)	The first day after the end of the prescribed period (as it may have been extended by a direction under regulation 9(6))
Any other failure to comply with paragraph (1) of regulation 8	The first day after the end of the prescribed period
Any other failure to comply with paragraph (3) of regulation 8	The first day after the end of the prescribed period

Failure	*Relevant day*
A failure to comply with paragraph (1) of regulation 10	The first day after the end of the prescribed period
A failure to comply with regulation 11	The first day after the latest time by which regulation 11 must be complied with in the case concerned
A failure to comply with regulation 11A	The first day after the end of the period within which the person must comply with regulation 11A

22(4) The amount of a penalty under paragraph (1)(a)(i) is to be arrived at after taking account of all relevant considerations, including the desirability of its being set at a level which appears appropriate for deterring the person, or other persons, from similar failures to comply on future occasions having regard (in particular)–

(a) in the case of a penalty for a promoter's failure to comply with regulation 8(1) or (3) or regulation 11A, to the amount of any fees received, or likely to have been received, by the promoter in connection with the notifiable contribution proposal (or arrangements implementing the notifiable contribution proposal), or with the notifiable contribution arrangements;

(b) in the case of a penalty for the relevant person's failure to comply with regulation 10(1), 11 or 11A, to the amount of any advantage gained, or sought to be gained, by the relevant person in relation to any contribution.

22(4A) In paragraph 4–

(a) **"promoter"** has the same meaning as in regulation 7, and

(b) **"relevant person"** means a person who enters into any transaction forming part of notifiable contribution arrangements within the meaning of regulation 5.

22(5) If the maximum penalty under paragraph (1)(a)(i) above appears inappropriately low after taking account of those considerations, the penalty is to be of such amount not exceeding £1 million as appears appropriate having regard to those considerations.

22(6) Where it appears to an officer of Revenue and Customs that a penalty under paragraph (1)(a)(i) above has been determined on the basis that the initial period begins with a day later than that which the officer considers to be the relevant day, an officer of Revenue and Customs may commence proceedings for a re-determination of the penalty.

22(7) Where a failure to comply with a provision mentioned in paragraph (2) concerns a proposal or arrangements in respect of which an order has been made under regulation 6 (doubt as to notifiability), the amounts specified in paragraph (1)(a)(i) and (b) shall be increased to the sum prescribed by the Tax Avoidance Schemes (Penalty) Regulations 2007 (as modified by these Regulations).

22(8) Where a failure to comply with a provision mentioned in paragraph (2) concerns a proposal or arrangements in respect of which an order has been made under regulation 20 (order to disclose), the amounts specified in paragraph (1)(a)(i) and (b) shall be increased to the sum prescribed by the Tax Avoidance Schemes (Penalty) Regulations 2007 (as modified by these Regulations) in relation to the days falling after the prescribed period.

22(9) The making of an order under regulation 6 or 20 does not of itself mean that, for the purposes of regulation 23, a person either did or did not have a reasonable excuse for non-compliance before the order was made.

22(10) Where an order is made under regulation 6 or 20 then for the purposes of regulation 23–

(a) the person identified in the order as the promoter of the proposal or arrangements cannot, in respect of any time after the end of the period mentioned in paragraph (8), rely on doubt as to notifiability as an excuse for failure to comply with regulation 8, and

(b) any delay in compliance with that regulation after the end of that period is unreasonable unless attributable to something other than doubt as to notifiability.

22(10A) Where a person fails to comply with–

(a) regulation 10 and the promoter for the purposes of that regulation is a monitored promoter for the purposes of Part 5 of the Finance Act 2014, or

(b) regulation 11 and the notifiable contribution arrangements for the purposes of that regulation are arrangements of such a monitored promoter,

then for the purposes of regulation 23 (interpretation) legal advice which the person took into account is to be disregarded in determining whether the person had a reasonable excuse, if the advice was given or procured by that monitored promoter.

22(10B) In determining for the purpose of regulation 23 whether or not a person who is a monitored promoter within the meaning of Part 5 of the Finance Act 2014 had a reasonable excuse for a failure to do anything required to be done under a provision mentioned in paragraph (2), reliance on legal advice is to be taken automatically not to constitute a reasonable excuse if either–

(a) the advice was not based on a full and accurate description of the facts, or

(b) the conclusions in the advice that the person relied on were unreasonable.

22(11) A person who fails to comply with regulation 15(1) (duty of parties to notifiable contribution arrangements to notify HMRC of number, etc.) or regulation 10 of the Information Regulations shall be liable to a penalty not exceeding the relevant sum.

This is subject to paragraph (14).

22(12) In paragraph (11) **"the relevant sum"** means–

(a) in relation to a person not falling within sub-paragraph (b) or (c) below, £5,000 in respect of each scheme to which the failure relates,

(b) in relation to a person who has previously failed to comply with regulation 15(1) or regulation 10 of the Information Regulations on one (and only one) occasion during the period of 36 months ending with the date on which the current failure to comply with that provision began, £7,500 in respect of each scheme to which the current failure relates (whether or not the same as the scheme to which the previous failure relates), or

(c) in relation to a person who has previously failed to comply with regulation 15(1) or regulation 10 of the Information Regulations on two or more occasions during the period of 36 months ending with the date on which the current failure to comply with that provision began, £10,000 in respect of each scheme to which the current failure relates (whether or not the same as the schemes to which any of the previous failures relates).

22(13) In paragraph (12) above **"scheme"** means any notifiable contribution arrangements which fall within any description prescribed by the Descriptions Regulations.

22(14) Where the notifiable contribution arrangements or proposed notifiable contribution arrangements are, or are substantially the same as, a notifiable arrangements or proposed notifiable arrangements under Part 7 in relation to which a penalty has been imposed under section 98C of the Taxes Management Act 1970 in respect of a failure to comply with the provisions of Part 7, this regulation shall not apply to impose a penalty in respect of the failure to comply with the corresponding provision of these Regulations.

History – In reg. 22(1)(a)(i), the words ", (c) or (ca)" substituted for "or (c)" by SI 2015/531, reg. 7(a), with effect in relation to prescribed information about notifiable contribution proposals or notifiable contribution arrangements provided by a person in compliance, or purported compliance, with reg. 8, 10 and 11 on or after 12 April 2015.

Reg. 22(2)(cb) inserted by SI 2017/1174, reg. 13(2)(a), with effect from 21 December 2017.

In reg. 22(2)(e) the words "and 14(2A)" inserted by SI 2017/1174, reg. 13(2)(b), with effect from 21 December 2017.

Reg. 22(2)(fb) inserted by SI 2017/1174, reg. 13(2)(c), with effect from 21 December 2017 (though the commencement provisions of SI 2017/1174 set 6 April 2018 for amendments made by reg. 14(2)(c) but as that does not exist it is possible that they meant to say reg. 13(2)(c)).

In reg. 22(2)(g) the word "and" omitted and reg. 22(2)(h) substituted by SI 2017/1174, reg. 13(2)(d) and (e), with effect from 21 December 2017. Former reg. 22(2)(h) read as follows:

"(h) regulation 19 (duty of introducer to give details of persons who have provided information)."

In reg. 22(2)(i) inserted by SI 2017/1174, reg. 13(2)(f), with effect from 21 December 2017.

Reg. 22(2)(ca) inserted by SI 2015/531, reg. 7(b), with effect in relation to prescribed information about notifiable contribution proposals or notifiable contribution arrangements provided by a person in compliance, or purported compliance, with reg. 8, 10 and 11 on or after 12 April 2015.

Reg. 22(2)(ea) and (fa) inserted by SI 2013/2600, reg. 6, with effect from 4 November 2013 (but the amendments do not have effect for the purposes of reg. 8(1), if the relevant date (reg. 8(2)) falls before 4 November 2013 or for the purposes of reg. 8(3), if the date on which the promoter first becomes aware of any transaction forming part of notifiable contribution arrangements falls before 4 November 2013.

In reg. 22(3), in the table, the entry "A failure to comply with regulation 11A" inserted by SI 2015/531, reg. 7(c), with effect in relation to prescribed information about notifiable contribution proposals or notifiable contribution arrangements provided by a person in compliance, or purported compliance, with reg. 8, 10 and 11 on or after 12 April 2015.

In reg. 22(4)(a), the word "promoter's" substituted for "person's" by SI 2015/531, reg. 7(d)(i), with effect in relation to prescribed information about notifiable contribution proposals or notifiable contribution arrangements provided by a person in compliance, or purported compliance, with reg. 8, 10 and 11 on or after 12 April 2015.

In reg. 22(4)(a), the words "or regulation 11A" inserted by SI 2015/531, reg. 7(d)(ii), with effect in relation to prescribed information about notifiable contribution proposals or notifiable contribution arrangements provided by a person in compliance, or purported compliance, with reg. 8, 10 and 11 on or after 12 April 2015.

In reg. 22(4)(a), the word "promoter" substituted for "person" by SI 2015/531, reg. 7(d)(iii), with effect in relation to prescribed informationabout notifiable contribution proposals or notifiable contribution arrangements provided by a person in compliance, or purported compliance, with reg. 8, 10 and 11 on or after 12 April 2015.

In reg. 22(4)(b), the word "relevant" inserted by SI 2015/531, reg. 7(e)(i), with effect in relation to prescribed information about notifiable contribution proposals or notifiable contribution arrangements provided by a person in compliance, or purported compliance, with reg. 8, 10 and 11 on or after 12 April 2015.

In reg. 22(4)(b), the word ", 11 or 11A" substituted for "or 11" by SI 2015/531, reg. 7(e)(ii), with effect in relation to prescribed information about notifiable contribution proposals or notifiable contribution arrangements provided by a person in compliance, or purported compliance, with reg. 8, 10 and 11 on or after 12 April 2015.

In reg. 22(4)(b), the word "relevant" inserted by SI 2015/531, reg. 7(e)(iii), with effect in relation to prescribed information about notifiable contribution proposals or notifiable contribution arrangements provided by a person in compliance, or purported compliance, with reg. 8, 10 and 11 on or after 12 April 2015.

Reg. 22(4A) inserted by SI 2015/531, reg. 7(f), with effect in relation to prescribed information about notifiable contribution proposals or notifiable contribution arrangements provided by a person in compliance, or purported compliance, with reg. 8, 10 and 11 on or after 12 April 2015.
Reg. 22(10A) and (10B) inserted by SI 2015/531, reg. 7(g), with effect in relation to prescribed information about notifiable contribution proposals or notifiable contribution arrangements provided by a person in compliance, or purported compliance, with reg. 8, 10 and 11 on or after 12 April 2015.
In reg. 22(11) the words "penalty not exceeding the relevantsum" substituted for the words "penalty of the relevant sum" by SI 2017/1174, reg. 13(3), with effect from 21 December 2017.
In reg. 22(12) "£5,000" substituted for "£100", "£7,500" substituted for "£500" and "£10,000" substituted for "£1,000" by SI 2017/1174, reg. 13(4), with effect from 21 December 2017.

INTERPRETATION

23 For the purposes of this Part–

(a) a person shall be deemed not to have failed to do anything required to be done within a limited time if it was done within such further time, if any, as HMRC may have allowed; and

(b) where a person had a reasonable excuse for not doing anything required to be done–

(i) that person shall be deemed not to have failed to do it unless the excuse ceased; and

(ii) after the excuse ceased, that person shall be deemed not to have failed to do it if it was done without unreasonable delay after the excuse had ceased.

MODIFICATION OF PART 10 OF THE TAXES MANAGEMENT ACT 1970

24(1) Part 10 of the Taxes Management Act 1970 so far as it relates to a penalty under section 98C of that Act shall apply in relation to a penalty under regulation 22 with the following modifications.

24(2) In section 100 (determination of penalties by officer of Board) for subsection (2)(f) (penalties to which subsection (1) of the section does not apply) substitute–

"(f) regulation 22(1)(a) of the National Insurance Contributions (Application of Part 7 of the Finance Act 2004) Regulations 2012.".

PART 4 – MODIFICATION OF REGULATIONS UNDER PART 7

MODIFICATION OF THE DESCRIPTIONS REGULATIONS

25(1) The Descriptions Regulations apply to notifiable contribution arrangements and notifiable contribution proposals with the following modifications and any reference in those Regulations to sections 306 to 313C and section 314A shall be construed as a reference to the corresponding provision of these Regulations (see regulation 5(2)).

25(2) In regulation 1 (citation, commencement and effect) omit paragraphs (2) and (3).

25(3) In regulation 5 (prescribed descriptions of arrangements)–

(a) in paragraph (1) for "income tax, corporation tax and capital gains tax" substitute "national insurance contributions", and

(b) in paragraph (2) omit sub-paragraphs (f) to (g).

25(4) In Part 3–

(a) for "tax advantage" wherever it occurs substitute "advantage within the meaning given by section 132A(7) of the Social Security Administration Act 1992"; and

(b) for "a tax advantage" wherever it occurs substitute "an advantage within the meaning given by section 132A(7) of the Social Security Administration Act 1992".

25(5) In regulation 10 (Description 5: standardised tax products), in the heading and paragraphs (1) and (3) for "tax product" substitute "national insurance contributions product".

25(6) Omit regulations 12 to 17.

History – In reg. 25(3)(b), the words "sub-paragraphs (f) to (g)" substituted for the words "sub-paragraphs (f) to (h)" by SI 2013/2600, reg. 7(a), with effect from 4 November 2013 (but the amendments do not have effect for the purposes of reg. 8(1), if the relevant date (reg. 8(2)) falls before 4 November 2013 or for the purposes of reg. 8(3), if the date on which the promoter first becomes aware of any transaction forming part of notifiable contribution arrangements falls before 4 November 2013.
In reg. 25(6), the words "regulations 12 to 17" substituted for the words "regulations 12 to 17A" by SI 2013/2600, reg. 7(b), with effect from 4 November 2013 (but the amendments do not have effect for the purposes of reg. 8(1), if the relevant date (reg. 8(2)) falls before 4 November 2013 or for the purposes of reg. 8(3), if the date on which the promoter first becomes aware of any transaction forming part of notifiable contribution arrangements falls before 4 November 2013.

THE INFORMATION REGULATIONS

26(1) The Information Regulations apply to notifiable contribution arrangements and notifiable contribution proposals with the following modifications and–

(a) any reference in those Regulations to sections 306 to 313C and section 314A shall be construed as a reference to the corresponding provision of these Regulations (see regulation 5(2)); and

(b) any reference in those Regulations to section 98C of the Taxes Management Act 1970 shall be construed as a reference to regulation 22 of these Regulations.

26(2) In regulation 2 (interpretation)–

(a) insert the following definition immediately before the definition of "employment"–

""**contributions**" means national insurance contributions;";

(aa) in sub-paragraph (a) of the definition of **"the filing date"** omit "or in the case of inheritance tax the last day of the period mentioned in regulation 9(5)(b)".

(b) after the definition of "filing date" insert–

""**notifiable contribution arrangements**" has the meaning given by section 132A(3) of the Social Security Administration Act 1992;

"notifiable contribution proposal" has the meaning given by section 132A(3) of the Social Security Administration Act 1992;";

(c) omit the definition of "the prescribed taxes".

26(3) In regulation 4 (prescribed information in respect of notifiable proposals and arrangements)–

(a) wherever the words appear–

(i) for "any of the prescribed taxes" substitute "the contributions";

(ii) for "notifiable arrangements" substitute "notifiable contribution arrangements";

(iii) for "notifiable proposal" substitute "notifiable contribution proposal"; and

(iv) for "tax advantage" substitute "advantage";

(b) in paragraphs (1)(b), (2)(c) and (3)(b) omit ", the ATED Arrangements Regulations, the IHT Arrangements Regulations or the SDLT Arrangements Regulations"; and

(c) in paragraph (5) omit the definitions of **"the ATED Arrangements Regulations"**, **"the IHT Arrangements Regulations"** and **"the SDLT Arrangements Regulations"**.

26(4) In regulation 5 (time for providing information under section 308, 308A, 309 or 310)–

(a) in paragraph (2) for "proposal or arrangements" substitute "contribution proposal or contribution arrangements";

(b) in paragraph (3) for "notifiable proposal or arrangements" substitute "notifiable contribution proposal or notifiable contribution arrangements"; and

(c) in paragraphs (6), (7) and (8) for "notifiable arrangements" substitute "notifiable contribution arrangements".

26(5) In regulation 7 (time for providing information under section 312A) for "notifiable arrangements" substitute "notifiable contribution arrangements".

26(6) [Omitted by SI 2017/1174, reg. 14(a).]

26(6A) In regulation 8A (prescribed information under section 312B: information and timing) for "notifiable arrangements" wherever it occurs substitute "notifiable contribution arrangements".

26(7) Omit regulation 9.

26(8) For regulation 10 (prescribed cases under section 313(3)(b)) substitute–

"PRESCRIBED INFORMATION UNDER REGULATION 15 OF THE NATIONAL INSURANCE CONTRIBUTIONS (APPLICATION OF PART 7 OF THE FINANCE ACT 2004) REGULATIONS 2012: TIMING AND MANNER OF DELIVERY

10(1) For the purposes of regulation 15 of the National Insurance Contributions (Application of Part 7 of the Finance Act 2004) Regulations 2012 (duty of parties to notifiable contribution arrangements to notify HMRC of number, etc) the prescribed information is–

(a) the reference number allocated by HMRC under regulation 12 to the notifiable contribution arrangements or notifiable contribution proposal;

(b) the earnings period in which the person making the notification expects an advantage to be obtained; and

(c) the employer's name, address and Unique Taxpayer Reference (UTR).

10(2) The prescribed information shall be provided by the employer to HMRC in such form and manner as they may specify.

10(3) Unless paragraph (4) applies, the prescribed time at which a person who is a party to notifiable contribution arrangements must provide HMRC with information under regulation 15 is 14 days after the end of the final tax period of the tax year in respect of which any person first enters into a transaction forming part of the notifiable contribution arrangements and in respect of each subsequent year until an advantage ceases to apply to any person.

In this paragraph, "**tax period**" has the meaning given in paragraph 1(2) of Schedule 4 to the Social Security (Contribution) Regulations 2001 (interpretation).

10(4) Where the advantage which is expected to arise from the notifiable contribution arrangements relates to Class 1A contributions only, and the transactions which comprise the notifiable contribution arrangements do not give rise to an advantage in relation to tax, the prescribed time is any time before the date on which the return under regulation 80(1) of the Social Security (Contributions) Regulations 2001 (return by employer) is or would be due–

(a) for the year in which the employer first enters into a transaction forming part of the notifiable contribution arrangements; and

(b) for each subsequent year until the advantage ceases to apply to any person.

In this paragraph the term **"an advantage in relation to tax"** shall be construed in accordance with section 318(1).".

26(9) Omit regulations 11 and 12.

26(10) In regulation 13(1)(b)(i) (prescribed information under section 313ZA: information and timing) before "arrangements" insert "contribution".

26(10A) In regulation 13A(1)(b)(i) (prescribed information under section 313ZB: information and timing) for "a tax advantage" substitute "an advantage".

26(11) In regulation 15(1)(b) (prescribed information under section 313C: information and timing) before "proposal" insert "contribution".

26(12) In regulation 17 (electronic delivery of information)–

(a) in paragraph (2)–

(i) for sub-paragraph (a) substitute–

"(a) it is authorised by virtue of Part 7A of the Social Security (Contributions) Regulations 2001 (electronic communications); and";

(ii) in paragraph (b) for "section" substitute "Part".

(b) in paragraph (3)(a) for "regulations under section 132 of the Finance Act 1999" substitute "Part 7A of the Social Security (Contributions) Regulations 2001 (electronic communications)".

26(13) Omit regulation 18.

History – Reg. 26(2)(aa) inserted by SI 2013/2600, reg. 8, with effect from 4 November 2013 (but the amendments do not have effect for the purposes of reg. 8(1), if the relevant date (reg. 8(2)) falls before 4 November 2013 or for the purposes of reg. 8(3), if the date on which the promoter first becomes aware of any transaction forming part of notifiable contribution arrangements falls before 4 November 2013.

In reg. 26(3)(b), the words ", the ATED Arrangements Regulations, the IHT Arrangements Regulations or the SDLT Arrangements Regulations" substituted for the words ", the IHT Arrangements Regulations or the SDLT Arrangements Regulations" by SI 2013/2600, reg. 9, with effect from 4 November 2013 (but the amendments do not have effect for the purposes of reg. 8(1), if the relevant date (reg. 8(2)) falls before 4 November 2013 or for the purposes of reg. 8(3), if the date on which the promoter first becomes aware of any transaction forming part of notifiable contribution arrangements falls before 4 November 2013.

In reg. 26(3)(c), the words ""the ATED Arrangements Regulations"," inserted by SI 2013/2600, reg. 10, with effect from 4 November 2013 (but the amendments do not have effect for the purposes of reg. 8(1), if the relevant date (reg. 8(2)) falls before 4 November 2013 or for the purposes of reg. 8(3), if the date on which the promoter first becomes aware of any transaction forming part of notifiable contribution arrangements falls before 4 November 2013.

Reg. 26(6) omitted by SI 2017/1174, reg. 14(a), with effect from 21 December 2017.

Reg. 26(6A) inserted by SI 2013/2600, reg. 11, with effect from 4 November 2013 (but the amendments do not have effect for the purposes of reg. 8(1), if the relevant date (reg. 8(2)) falls before 4 November 2013 or for the purposes of reg. 8(3), if the date on which the promoter first becomes aware of any transaction forming part of notifiable contribution arrangements falls before 4 November 2013.

In reg. 26(8, the substituted reg. 10(3) substituted by SI 2017/1174, reg. 14(b), with effect from 21 December 2017.

Reg. 26(10A) inserted by SI 2013/2600, reg. 12, with effect from 4 November 2013 (but the amendments do not have effect for the purposes of reg. 8(1), if the relevant date (reg. 8(2)) falls before 4 November 2013 or for the purposes of reg. 8(3), if the date on which the promoter first becomes aware of any transaction forming part of notifiable contribution arrangements falls before 4 November 2013.

THE TAX AVOIDANCE SCHEMES (PROMOTERS AND PRESCRIBED CIRCUMSTANCES) REGULATIONS 2004

27(1) The Tax Avoidance Schemes (Promoters and Prescribed Circumstances) Regulations 2004 apply to notifiable contribution arrangements and notifiable contribution proposals as they apply to income tax with the following modifications and any reference in those Regulations to sections 306 to 313C and section 314A shall be construed as a reference to the corresponding provision of these Regulations (see regulation 5(2)).

27(2) In regulation 1 (citation, commencement and interpretation) for paragraph (2) substitute–

"**1(2)** In these Regulations–

"notifiable contribution arrangements" and **"notifiable contribution proposal"** have the meanings given by section 132A(3) of the Social Security Administration Act 1992.".

27(3) In regulation 4 (persons not to be treated as promoters under section 307(1)(a)(i) or (b)(i))–

(a) for "tax advice" wherever it occurs substitute "advice about national insurance contributions"; and

(b) for "tax advantage" wherever it occurs substitute "advantage".

27(4) In regulation 6 (legal professional privilege) for "section 314" substitute "section 132A(6) of the Social Security Administration Act 1992".

THE TAX AVOIDANCE SCHEMES (PENALTY) REGULATIONS 2007

28 The Tax Avoidance Schemes (Penalty) Regulations 2007 apply to notifiable contribution arrangements and notifiable contribution proposals as they apply to income tax and–

(a) any reference in those Regulations to sections 306 to 313C and section 314A shall be construed as a reference to the corresponding provision of these Regulations (see regulation 5(2)); and

(b) any reference in those Regulations to section 98C of the Taxes Management Act 1970 shall be construed as a reference to regulation 22 of these Regulations.

PART 5 – REVOCATIONS

29 [Revokes SI 2007/785.]

SOCIAL SECURITY REVALUATION OF EARNINGS FACTORS ORDER 2013

(SI 2013/527)

Made on 6 March 2013 by the Secretary of State, in exercise of the powers conferred by s. 148(3) and (4) and 189(1), (4) and (5) of the Social Security Administration Act 1992. Operative from 6 April 2013.

CITATION AND COMMENCEMENT

1 This Order may be cited as the Social Security Revaluation of Earnings Factors Order 2013 and shall come into force on 6th April 2013.

REVALUATION OF EARNINGS FACTORS

2 The earnings factors for tax years specified in the Schedule to this Order in so far as they are relevant–

(a) to the calculation–

(i) of the additional pension in the rate of any long-term benefit, or

(ii) of any guaranteed minimum pension; or

(b) to any other calculation required under Part 3 of the Pension Schemes Act 1993 (including that Part as modified by or under any other enactment),

are directed to be increased for those tax years by the percentage of their amount shown opposite those tax years in that Schedule.

ROUNDING OF FRACTIONAL AMOUNTS

3 Where any earnings factor relevant to the calculation specified in article 2(a)(i) of this Order, as increased in accordance with this Order, would not but for this article be expressed as a whole number of pounds, it shall be so expressed by rounding down any fraction of a pound less than one half and rounding up any other fraction of a pound.

SCHEDULE – PERCENTAGE INCREASE OF EARNINGS FACTOR FOR SPECIFIED TAX YEARS

Article 2

Tax year	Percentage increase
1978–1979	734.2
1979–1980	636.3
1980–1981	515.1
1981–1982	415.2
1982–1983	367.9
1983–1984	334.5
1984–1985	302.3
1985–1986	277.4
1986–1987	246.5
1987–1988	222.7
1988–1989	196.8
1989–1990	167.9
1990–1991	149.7
1991–1992	126.8
1992–1993	112.9
1993–1994	102.8
1994–1995	96.7
1995–1996	88.4
1996–1997	83.3
1997–1998	74.5
1998–1999	66.9

Tax year	Percentage increase
1999–2000	60.1
2000–2001	50.7
2001–2002	44.9
2002–2003	38.9
2003–2004	34.1
2004–2005	29.2
2005–2006	24.1
2006–2007	20.0
2007–2008	15.3
2008–2009	10.9
2009–2010	7.3
2010–2011	6.0
2011–2012	3.6
2012–2013	1.8

SOCIAL SECURITY PENSIONS (LOW EARNINGS THRESHOLD) ORDER 2013

(SI 2013/528)

Made on 6 March 2013 by the Secretary of State, in exercise of the powers conferred by s. 148A(3) and (4) of the Social Security Administration Act 1992. Operative from 6 April 2013.

CITATION AND COMMENCEMENT

1 This Order may be cited as the Social Security Pensions (Low Earnings Threshold) Order 2013 and shall come into force on 6th April 2013.

LOW EARNINGS THRESHOLD

2 For the purposes of the Social Security Contributions and Benefits Act 1992, it is directed that the low earnings threshold for the tax years following the tax year 2012–2013 shall be £15,000.

SOCIAL SECURITY PENSIONS (FLAT RATE ACCRUAL AMOUNT) ORDER 2013

(SI 2013/529)

Made on 6 March 2013 by the Secretary of State, in exercise of the powers conferred by s. 148AA(3)–(6) of the Social Security Administration Act 1992. Operative from 6 April 2013.

CITATION AND COMMENCEMENT

1 This Order may be cited as the Social Security Pensions (Flat Rate Accrual Amount) Order 2013 and shall come into force on 6th April 2013.

FLAT RATE ACCRUAL AMOUNT

2 For the purpose of paragraph 13(2) of Schedule 4B to the Social Security Contributions and Benefits Act 1992, the flat rate accrual amount for the tax year beginning 6th April 2013 and subsequent tax years shall be £91.00.

SOCIAL SECURITY (CONTRIBUTIONS) (AMENDMENT AND APPLICATION OF SCHEDULE 38 TO THE FINANCE ACT 2012) REGULATIONS 2013

(SI 2013/622)

Made on 14 March 2012 by the Treasury and the Commissioners for Her Majesty's Revenue and Customs in exercise of the powers conferred by s. 1(6),3(2) and (3), 10(9), 12(6), 13(1) and (7), 19(1) and (5A), and 175(3) and (4) of, and para. 7B(5A) of Sch. 1 to, the Social Security Contributions and Benefits Act 1992 and s. 1(6), 3(2) and (3), 10(9), 12(6), 13(1) and (7), 19(1) and (5A) and 171(3), (4) and (10) of, and para. 7B(5A) of Sch. 1 to, the Social Security Contributions and Benefits (Northern Ireland) Act 1992 and by s. 175(4) of, and para. 6(1) and (2) of Sch. 1 to, the Social Security Contributions and Benefits Act 1992 and s. 171(4) and (10) of, and para. 6(1) and (2) of Sch. 1 to, the Social Security Contributions and Benefits (Northern Ireland) Act 1992. Operative in accordance with reg. 1.

PART 1 – GENERAL

CITATION, COMMENCEMENT, EFFECT AND INTERPRETATION

1(1) These Regulations may be cited as the Social Security (Contributions) (Amendment and Application of Schedule 38 to the Finance Act 2012) Regulations 2013.

1(2) Regulations 1, 2 and 5 to 42 come into force on 6th April 2013 and apply in relation to the tax year 2013–14 and subsequent tax years.

1(3) Regulations 3 and 4 come into force on 6th April 2014 and apply in relation to the tax year 2014–15.

1(4) The amendments made by regulation 36 have effect in relation to contributions paid in respect of the tax year 2012–2013 and subsequent tax years.

1(5) In these Regulations **"the 2001 Regulations"** mean the Social Security (Contributions) Regulations 2001.

AMENDMENT OF THE 2001 REGULATIONS

2 The 2001 Regulations are amended as provided for in regulations 3 to 28 and 33 to 40.

PART 2 – CLOSURE OF THE SIMPLIFIED DEDUCTION SCHEME

AMENDMENT OF REGULATION 90NA

3 [Amending provisions not reproduced.]

AMENDMENT OF SCHEDULE 4

4 [Amending provisions not reproduced.]

PART 3 – REAL TIME INFORMATION

Chapter 1 – Real Time Information

AMENDMENT OF SCHEDULE 4 (PROVISIONS DERIVED FROM THE INCOME TAX ACTS AND THE INCOME TAX (PAY AS YOU EARN) REGULATIONS 2003

5 Schedule 4 (provisions derived from the Income Tax Acts and the Income Tax (Pay As You Earn) Regulations is amended as provided for in regulations 6 to 22.

INTERPRETATION

6 [Amending provisions not reproduced.]

PAYMENT OF EARNINGS-RELATED CONTRIBUTIONS MONTHLY BY EMPLOYER

7 [Amending provisions not reproduced.]

PAYMENT OF EARNINGS-RELATED CONTRIBUTIONS QUARTERLY BY EMPLOYER

8 [Amending provisions not reproduced.]

PAYMENTS TO AND RECOVERIES FROM HMRC FOR EACH TAX PERIOD BY REAL TIME INFORMATION EMPLOYERS: RETURN UNDER PARAGRAPH 21E(6) OR 21EA(3)

9 [Amending provisions not reproduced.]

REAL TIME RETURNS OF INFORMATION ABOUT PAYMENTS OF GENERAL EARNINGS

10 [Amending provisions not reproduced.]

EXCEPTIONS TO PARAGRAPH 21A

11 [Amending provisions not reproduced.]

MODIFICATION OF THE REQUIREMENTS OF PARAGRAPH 21A: NOTIONAL PAYMENTS

12 [Amending provisions not reproduced.]

NOTIFICATIONS OF PAYMENTS OF GENERAL EARNINGS TO AND BY PROVIDERS OF CERTAIN ELECTRONIC PAYMENT METHODS

13 [Amending provisions not reproduced.]

EXCEPTIONS TO PARAGRAPH 21A

14 [Amending provisions not reproduced.]

RETURNS UNDER PARAGRAPHS 21A AND 21D: AMENDMENTS

15 [Amending provisions not reproduced.]
16 [Amending provisions not reproduced.]

ADDITIONAL INFORMATION ABOUT PAYMENTS

17 [Amending provisions not reproduced.]

RETURN BY EMPLOYER AT END OF YEAR

18 [Amending provisions not reproduced.]

REQUIREMENT FOR SECURITY

19 [Amending provisions not reproduced.]

DIRECT COLLECTION INVOLVING DEDUCTIONS WORKING SHEETS

20 [Amending provisions not reproduced.]
21–22 [Amending provisions not reproduced.]

REAL TIME RETURNS

23–28 [Amending provisions not reproduced.]

Chapter 2 – Real Time Information: Transitional Provisions

INFORMATION ABOUT EMPLOYEES

29 On becoming a Real Time Information employer, an employer must provide to HMRC–

(a) the information specified in paragraphs 2 to 4 of Schedule A1 to the PAYE Regulations,

(b) the income tax year in which the employer became a Real Time Information employer,

(c) the following information about each of the employer's employees during the tax year in which the employer became a Real Time Information employer–

(i) the employee's name,

(ii) the employee's date of birth,

(iii) the employee's current gender,

(iv) if known, the employee's national insurance number,

(v) the employee's address, and

(vi) the number used by the employer to identify the employee, if any.

INFORMATION ABOUT PAYMENTS TO EMPLOYEES

30(1) Within one month of making the first return under paragraph 21A or 21D of Schedule 4 to the 2001 Regulations, a Real Time Information employer must provide to HMRC the information specified in paragraph (2) in respect of–

(a) each employee who has been employed in the tax year the return was made in but whose employment had ceased before the date on which the return was made, and

(b) each employee to whom the relevant payments are made on an irregular basis and–

(i) in respect of whom information was not included on that return, and

(ii) to whom the employer does not expect to make a relevant payment within one month of making the return.

30(2) The information specified in this paragraph is that specified in–

(a) paragraphs 3A, 6 to 9, 10(b), 10(d) and 12 of Schedule 4A to the 2001 Regulations, and

(b) paragraphs 2 to 4 of Schedule A1 to the PAYE Regulations.

PROVISION OF INFORMATION UNDER REGULATIONS 29 AND 30

31(1) If an employer is one to whom paragraph (3) applies, the information required by regulation 27 must be provided before the employer makes any returns under paragraph 21A or 21D of Schedule 4 to the 2001 Regulations.

31(2) Any other employer may provide the information required by regulation 27 as part of the first return the employer makes under paragraph 21A or 21D of Schedule 4 to the 2001 Regulations.

31(3) This paragraph applies to an employer who, on the day the employer becomes a Real Time Information employer, employs 250 or more employees.

31(4) The information required by regulations 29 and 30 must be provided using an approved method of electronic communications unless the employer is one to whom paragraph 21D of Schedule 4 to the 2001 Regulations applies in which case the information must be provided in the form specified by HMRC.

REGULATIONS 29 TO 31 INTERPRETATION

32 Terms used in regulations 29 to 31 have the same meaning as they have in the 2001 Regulations.

PART 4 – OTHER PROVISIONS RELATING TO CLASS 1, 1A, 2 AND 3 CONTRIBUTIONS

AMENDMENT OF THE SOCIAL SECURITY (CONTRIBUTIONS) REGULATIONS 2001

33–40 *[Amending provisions not reproduced.]*

PART 5 – TAX AGENTS: DISHONEST CONDUCT

APPLICATION OF SCHEDULE 38 TO THE FINANCE ACT 2012

41 The provisions of Schedule 38 to the Finance Act 2012 (tax agents: dishonest conduct) apply in relation to Class 1, Class 1A, Class 1B and Class 2 National Insurance contributions as in relation to tax to the extent that they do not already apply

PART 6 – REPEALS

AMENDMENT OF THE SOCIAL SECURITY (CONTRIBUTIONS) (AMENDMENT NO. 5) REGULATIONS 2001

42 [Amending provisions not reproduced.]

PUBLIC BODIES (ABOLITION OF ADMINISTRATIVE JUSTICE AND TRIBUNALS COUNCIL) ORDER 2013

(SI 2013/2042)

Made on 18 August 2013 by the Secretary of State, in exercise of the powers conferred by s. 1(1), 6(1) and (5) and 35(2) of the Public Bodies Act 2011. Operative in accordance with art. 1.

CITATION, COMMENCEMENT AND EXTENT

1(1) This Order may be cited as the Public Bodies (Abolition of Administrative Justice and Tribunals Council) Order 2013.

1(2) Subject to paragraph (3), this Order comes into force on the day after the date on which it is made.

1(3) Paragraph 41(a) of the Schedule comes into force on the day after that on which the other provisions of this Order come into force.

1(4) Amendments, repeals and revocations in this Order have the same extent as the provisions amended, repealed or revoked.

ABOLITION OF THE ADMINISTRATIVE JUSTICE AND TRIBUNALS COUNCIL

2(1) The Administrative Justice and Tribunals Council is abolished.

2(2) The Schedule (which makes consequential provision etc) has effect.

SCHEDULE – CONSEQUENTIAL PROVISION ETC

Article 2(2)

CHRONICALLY SICK AND DISABLED PERSONS ACT 1970

1 [Not relevant to National Insurance contributions.]

HEALTH AND SAFETY AT WORK ETC ACT 1974

2 [Not relevant to National Insurance contributions.]

HOUSE OF COMMONS DISQUALIFICATION ACT 1975

3–4 [Not relevant to National Insurance contributions.]

TOWN AND COUNTRY PLANNING ACT 1990

5 [Not relevant to National Insurance contributions.]

SOCIAL SECURITY ADMINISTRATION ACT 1992

6 The Social Security Administration Act 1992 is amended as follows.

7–8 [Amending provisions not reproduced.]

TRANSPORT AND WORKS ACT 1992

9 [Not relevant to National Insurance contributions.]

TRIBUNALS AND INQUIRIES ACT 1992

10–14 [Not relevant to National Insurance contributions.]

PENSION SCHEMES ACT 1993

15 [Amending provision not reproduced.]

LAW OF PROPERTY (MISCELLANEOUS PROVISIONS) ACT 1994

16 [Not relevant to National Insurance contributions.]

TOWN AND COUNTRY PLANNING (SCOTLAND) ACT 1997

17 [Not relevant to National Insurance contributions.]

SCHOOL STANDARDS AND FRAMEWORK ACT 1998

18 [Not relevant to National Insurance contributions.]

GREATER LONDON AUTHORITY ACT 1999

19 [Not relevant to National Insurance contributions.]

WELFARE REFORM AND PENSIONS ACT 1999

20 [Amending provision not reproduced.]

FREEDOM OF INFORMATION ACT 2000

21–22 [Not relevant to National Insurance contributions.]

EDUCATION ACT 2002

23 [Not relevant to National Insurance contributions.]

TITLE CONDITIONS (SCOTLAND) ACT 2003

24–26 [Not relevant to National Insurance contributions.]

GENDER RECOGNITION ACT 2004

27–28 [Not relevant to National Insurance contributions.]

CIVIL CONTINGENCIES ACT 2004

29 [Not relevant to National Insurance contributions.]

SERIOUS ORGANISED CRIME AND POLICE ACT 2005

30 [Not relevant to National Insurance contributions.]

TRIBUNALS, COURTS AND ENFORCEMENT ACT 2007

31–37 [Not relevant to National Insurance contributions.]

LEGAL SERVICES ACT 2007

38–39 [Not relevant to National Insurance contributions.]

PLANNING ACT 2008

40 [Not relevant to National Insurance contributions.]

PUBLIC BODIES ACT 2011

41 [Not relevant to National Insurance contributions.]

CHILDREN'S HEARINGS (SCOTLAND) ACT 2011

42 [Not relevant to National Insurance contributions.]

THE NATIONAL HEALTH SERVICE (SERVICE COMMITTEES AND TRIBUNAL) REGULATIONS 1992

43–46 [Not relevant to National Insurance contributions.]

THE DEREGULATION (MODEL APPEAL PROVISIONS) ORDER 1996

47 [Not relevant to National Insurance contributions.]

THE SCOTLAND ACT 1998(CROSS-BORDER PUBLIC AUTHORITIES) (SPECIFICATION) ORDER 1999

48–49 [Not relevant to National Insurance contributions.]

THE SCOTLAND ACT 1998(CROSS-BORDER PUBLIC AUTHORITIES) (ADAPTATION OF FUNCTIONS ETC.) ORDER 1999

50–51 [Not relevant to National Insurance contributions.]

THE SEEDS (NATIONAL LISTS OF VARIETIES) REGULATIONS 2001

52 [Not relevant to National Insurance contributions.]

THE PAROLE BOARD (SCOTLAND) RULES 2001

53 [Not relevant to National Insurance contributions.]

THE LEASEHOLD VALUATION TRIBUNALS (PROCEDURE) (ENGLAND) REGULATIONS 2003

54 [Not relevant to National Insurance contributions.]

THE ADJUDICATOR TO HER MAJESTY'S LAND REGISTRY (PRACTICE AND PROCEDURE) RULES 2003

55 [Not relevant to National Insurance contributions.]

THE EMPLOYMENT TRIBUNALS (CONSTITUTION AND RULES OF PROCEDURE) REGULATIONS 2004

56 [Not relevant to National Insurance contributions.]

THE NATIONAL HEALTH SERVICE (TRIBUNAL) (SCOTLAND) REGULATIONS 2004

57 [Not relevant to National Insurance contributions.]

THE PENSION PROTECTION FUND (REVIEW AND RECONSIDERATION OF REVIEWABLE MATTERS) REGULATIONS 2005

58 [Not relevant to National Insurance contributions.]

THE PENSION PROTECTION FUND (PPF OMBUDSMAN) ORDER 2005

59 [Not relevant to National Insurance contributions.]

THE PENSION PROTECTION FUND (REFERENCE OF REVIEWABLE MATTERS TO THE PPF OMBUDSMAN) REGULATIONS 2005

60 [Not relevant to National Insurance contributions.]

THE FINANCIAL ASSISTANCE SCHEME (APPEALS) REGULATIONS 2005

61 [Not relevant to National Insurance contributions.]

THE MENTAL HEALTH TRIBUNAL FOR SCOTLAND (PRACTICE AND PROCEDURE) (NO. 2) RULES 2005

62 [Not relevant to National Insurance contributions.]

THE RAILWAYS AND OTHER GUIDED TRANSPORT SYSTEMS (SAFETY) REGULATIONS 2006

63 [Not relevant to National Insurance contributions.]

THE ADDITIONAL SUPPORT NEEDS TRIBUNALS FOR SCOTLAND (PRACTICE AND PROCEDURE) RULES 2006

64 [Not relevant to National Insurance contributions.]

THE NATIONAL HEALTH SERVICE (DISCIPLINE COMMITTEES) (SCOTLAND) REGULATIONS 2006

65 [Not relevant to National Insurance contributions.]

THE ADMINISTRATIVE JUSTICE AND TRIBUNALS COUNCIL (LISTED TRIBUNALS) (WALES) ORDER 2007

66 [Not relevant to National Insurance contributions.]

THE ADMINISTRATIVE JUSTICE AND TRIBUNALS COUNCIL (LISTED TRIBUNALS) ORDER 2007

67 [Not relevant to National Insurance contributions.]

THE ADMINISTRATIVE JUSTICE AND TRIBUNALS COUNCIL (LISTED TRIBUNALS) (SCOTLAND) ORDER 2007

68 [Not relevant to National Insurance contributions.]

THE ADJUDICATOR TO HER MAJESTY'S LAND REGISTRY (PRACTICE AND PROCEDURE) (AMENDMENT) RULES 2008

69 [Not relevant to National Insurance contributions.]

THE COMPANY NAMES ADJUDICATOR RULES 2008

70 [Not relevant to National Insurance contributions.]

THE TRIBUNALS, COURTS AND ENFORCEMENT ACT 2007(TRANSITIONAL AND CONSEQUENTIAL PROVISIONS) ORDER 2008

71 [Not relevant to National Insurance contributions.]

THE TRANSFER OF TRIBUNAL FUNCTIONS ORDER 2008

72 [Not relevant to National Insurance contributions.]

THE MENTAL HEALTH TRIBUNAL FOR SCOTLAND (PRACTICE AND PROCEDURE) (NO. 2) AMENDMENT RULES 2008

73 [Not relevant to National Insurance contributions.]

THE TRANSFER OF TRIBUNAL FUNCTIONS AND REVENUE AND CUSTOMS APPEALS ORDER 2009

74 [Not relevant to National Insurance contributions.]

THE TRANSFER OF TRIBUNAL FUNCTIONS (LANDS TRIBUNAL AND MISCELLANEOUS AMENDMENTS) ORDER 2009

75 [Not relevant to National Insurance contributions.]

THE TRANSFER OF FUNCTIONS OF THE CHARITY TRIBUNAL ORDER 2009

76 [Not relevant to National Insurance contributions.]

THE TRANSFER OF FUNCTIONS OF THE CONSUMER CREDIT APPEALS TRIBUNAL ORDER 2009

77 [Not relevant to National Insurance contributions.]

THE ADMINISTRATIVE JUSTICE AND TRIBUNALS COUNCIL (LISTED TRIBUNALS) (AMENDMENT) ORDER 2009

78 [Not relevant to National Insurance contributions.]

THE NATIONAL HEALTH SERVICE (PHARMACEUTICAL SERVICES) (SCOTLAND) REGULATIONS 2009

79 [Not relevant to National Insurance contributions.]

THE TRANSFER OF FUNCTIONS OF THE ASYLUM AND IMMIGRATION TRIBUNAL ORDER 2010

80 [Not relevant to National Insurance contributions.]

THE TRANSFER OF TRIBUNAL FUNCTIONS ORDER 2010

81 [Not relevant to National Insurance contributions.]

THE ROAD TRAFFIC (PARKING ADJUDICATORS) (RENFREWSHIRE COUNCIL) REGULATIONS 2010

82 [Not relevant to National Insurance contributions.]

THE TRAIN DRIVING LICENCES AND CERTIFICATES REGULATIONS 2010

83 [Not relevant to National Insurance contributions.]

THE ADDITIONAL SUPPORT NEEDS TRIBUNALS FOR SCOTLAND (PRACTICE AND PROCEDURE) AMENDMENT RULES 2010

84 [Not relevant to National Insurance contributions.]

THE PAROLE BOARD (SCOTLAND) AMENDMENT RULES 2010

85 [Not relevant to National Insurance contributions.]

THE NATIONAL HEALTH SERVICE (DISCIPLINE COMMITTEES) (SCOTLAND) AMENDMENT REGULATIONS 2010

86 [Not relevant to National Insurance contributions.]

THE NATIONAL HEALTH SERVICE (TRIBUNAL) (SCOTLAND) AMENDMENT REGULATIONS 2010

87 [Not relevant to National Insurance contributions.]

THE RESIDENTIAL PROPERTY TRIBUNAL PROCEDURES AND FEES (ENGLAND) REGULATIONS 2011

88–90 [Not relevant to National Insurance contributions.]

THE RAILWAYS AND OTHER GUIDED TRANSPORT SYSTEMS (SAFETY) (AMENDMENT) REGULATIONS 2011

91 [Not relevant to National Insurance contributions.]

THE RAILWAYS (INTEROPERABILITY) REGULATIONS 2011

92 [Not relevant to National Insurance contributions.]

THE ADDITIONAL SUPPORT NEEDS TRIBUNALS FOR SCOTLAND (DISABILITY CLAIMS PROCEDURE) RULES 2011

93 [Not relevant to National Insurance contributions.]

THE ADMINISTRATIVE JUSTICE AND TRIBUNALS COUNCIL (LISTED TRIBUNALS) (SCOTLAND) AMENDMENT ORDER 2011

94 [Not relevant to National Insurance contributions.]

THE BUS LANE CONTRAVENTIONS (CHARGES, ADJUDICATION AND ENFORCEMENT) (SCOTLAND) REGULATIONS 2011

95 [Not relevant to National Insurance contributions.]

THE ROAD TRAFFIC (PARKING ADJUDICATORS) (EAST AYRSHIRE COUNCIL) REGULATIONS 2012

96 [Not relevant to National Insurance contributions.]

THE ROAD TRAFFIC (PARKING ADJUDICATORS) (SOUTH AYRSHIRE COUNCIL) REGULATIONS 2012

97 [Not relevant to National Insurance contributions.]

THE RESIDENTIAL PROPERTY TRIBUNAL PROCEDURES AND FEES (WALES) REGULATIONS 2012

98 [Not relevant to National Insurance contributions.]

SOCIAL SECURITY REVALUATION OF EARNINGS FACTORS ORDER 2014

(SI 2014/367)

Made on 19 February 2014 by the Secretary of State in exercise of the powers conferred upon them by s. 148(3) and (4) and 189(1), (4) and (5) of the Social Security Administration Act 1992. Operative from 6 April 2014.

CITATION AND COMMENCEMENT

1 This Order may be cited as the Social Security Revaluation of Earnings Factors Order 2014 and shall come into force on 6th April 2014.

REVALUATION OF EARNINGS FACTORS

2 The earnings factors for tax years specified in the Schedule to this Order in so far as they are relevant–

(a) to the calculation–

(i) of the additional pension in the rate of any long-term benefit, or

(ii) of any guaranteed minimum pension; or

(b) to any other calculation required under Part 3 of the Pension Schemes Act 1993 (including that Part as modified by or under any other enactment),

are directed to be increased for those tax years by the percentage of their amount shown opposite those tax years in that Schedule.

ROUNDING OF FRACTIONAL AMOUNTS

3 Where any earnings factor relevant to the calculation specified in article 2(a)(i) of this Order, as increased in accordance with this Order, would not but for this article be expressed as a whole number of pounds, it shall be so expressed by rounding down any fraction of a pound less than one half and rounding up any other fraction of a pound.

SCHEDULE

Article 2

PERCENTAGE INCREASE OF EARNINGS FACTOR FOR SPECIFIED TAX YEARS

Tax year	*Percentage increase*
1978–1979	741.7
1979–1980	642.9
1980–1981	520.7
1981–1982	419.8
1982–1983	372.1
1983–1984	338.4
1984–1985	305.9
1985–1986	280.8
1986–1987	249.7
1987–1988	225.6
1988–1989	199.5
1989–1990	170.3
1990–1991	151.9
1991–1992	128.8
1992–1993	114.8
1993–1994	104.6
1994–1995	98.5
1995–1996	90.1
1996–1997	84.9

Tax year	*Percentage increase*
1997–1998	76.1
1998–1999	68.4
1999–2000	61.6
2000–2001	52.0
2001–2002	46.2
2002–2003	40.1
2003–2004	35.3
2004–2005	30.3
2005–2006	25.2
2006–2007	21.1
2007–2008	16.3
2008–2009	11.6
2009–2010	8.3
2010–2011	7.0
2011–2012	4.6
2012–2013	2.7
2013–2014	0.9

SOCIAL SECURITY PENSIONS (LOW EARNINGS THRESHOLD) ORDER 2014

(SI 2014/368)

Made on 19 February 2014 by the Secretary of State in exercise of the powers conferred upon them by s. 148A(3)–(5) and 189(1), (4) and (5) of the Social Security Administration Act 1992. Operative from 6 April 2014.

CITATION AND COMMENCEMENT

1 This Order may be cited as the Social Security Pensions (Low Earnings Threshold) Order 2014 and shall come into force on 6th April 2014.

LOW EARNINGS THRESHOLD

2 For the purposes of the Social Security Contributions and Benefits Act 1992, it is directed that the low earnings threshold for the tax years following the tax year 2013–2014 shall be £15,100.

SOCIAL SECURITY PENSIONS (FLAT RATE ACCRUAL AMOUNT) ORDER 2014

(SI 2014/369)

Made on 19 February 2014 by the Secretary of State in exercise of the powers conferred upon them by s. 148AA(3)–(6) and 189(1), (4) and (5) of the Social Security Administration Act 1992. Operative from 6 April 2014.

CITATION AND COMMENCEMENT

1 This Order may be cited as the Social Security Pensions (Flat Rate Accrual Amount) Order 2014 and shall come into force on 6th April 2014.

FLAT RATE ACCRUAL AMOUNT

2 For the purpose of paragraph 13(2) of Schedule 4B to the Social Security Contributions and Benefits Act 1992, the flat rate accrual amount for the tax year beginning 6th April 2014 and subsequent tax years shall be £92.00.

SOCIAL SECURITY (CONTRIBUTIONS) (AMENDMENT NO. 4) REGULATIONS 2014

(SI 2014/2397)

Made on 11 September 2014 by the Commissioners for Her Majesty's Revenue and Customs in exercise of the powers conferred by s. 175(4)(a) of, and para. 6(1) and (2) of Sch. 1 to, the Social Security Contributions and Benefits Act 1992 and by s. 171(4)(c) of, and para. 6(1) and (2) of Sch. 1 to, the Social Security Contributions and Benefits (Northern Ireland) Act 1992. Operative from 6 October 2014.

CITATION, COMMENCEMENT, EFFECT AND INTERPRETATION

1(1) These Regulations may be cited as the Social Security (Contributions) (Amendment No. 4) Regulations 2014 and come into force on 6th October 2014.

1(2) Regulation 3(4) has effect in relation to a failure to deliver a return to Her Majesty's Revenue and Customs in respect of any payment of general earnings made on or after 6th October 2014.

1(3) Regulation 3(5) has effect in relation to a failure to deliver a return to Her Majesty's Revenue and Customs in respect of any payment of general earnings made–

(a) on or after 6th October 2014 where the employer is a large existing Real Time Information employer; and

(b) on or after 6th March 2015 where–

(i) the employer is a small existing Real Time Information employer; or

(ii) a person becomes a new Real Time Information employer after 6th October 2014.

1(4) In this regulation–

"general earnings" has the meaning given by paragraph 1(2) of Schedule 4 to the Social Security (Contributions) Regulations 2001 (interpretation);

"large existing Real Time Information employer" means a Real Time Information employer which as at 6th October 2014 employs at least 50 employees;

"new Real Time Information employer" means a Real Time Information employer to which HMRC issues an employer's PAYE reference after 6th October 2014;

"Real Time Information employer" has the meaning given by paragraph 1(4) of Schedule 4 to the Social Security (Contributions) Regulations 2001 (interpretation);

"small existing Real Time Information employer" means a Real Time Information employer which as at 6th October 2014 employs no more than 49 employees.

1(5) For the purposes of paragraph (4) **"employer's PAYE reference"** in relation to a Real Time Information employer means the combination of letters, numbers, or both, used by HMRC to identify a Real Time Information employer for the purposes of the Income Tax (Pay As You Earn) Regulations 2003 and the number which identifies that employer's HMRC office.

AMENDMENT OF THE SOCIAL SECURITY (CONTRIBUTIONS) REGULATIONS 2001

2 The Social Security (Contributions) Regulations 2001 are amended as provided for in regulation 3.

3(1) Schedule 4 to the Social Security (Contributions) Regulations 2001 (provisions derived from the Income Tax Acts etc) is amended as provided for in paragraphs (2) to (7).

3(2) [Amends SI 2001/1004, Sch. 4, para. 1.]

3(3) [Amends SI 2001/1004, Sch. 4, para. 11(4).]

3(4) [Amends SI 2001/1004, Sch. 4, para. 21EA(6).]

3(5) [Inserts SI 2001/1004, Sch. 4, para. 21G.]

3(6) [Omits SI 2001/1004, Sch. 4, para. 22(3).]

3(7) [Omits SI 2001/1004, Sch. 4, para. 25.]

3(8) [Omits SI 2001/1004, Sch. 4A, para. 13.]

3(9) [Omits SI 2001/1004, Sch. 4B, para. 6.]

3(10) [Amends SI 2001/1004, Sch. 7, Pt. 2.]

SOCIAL SECURITY CONTRIBUTIONS AND BENEFITS ACT 1992 (APPLICATION OF PARTS 12ZA, 12ZB AND 12ZC TO PARENTAL ORDER CASES) REGULATIONS 2014

(SI 2014/2866)

Made on 20 October 2014 by the Secretary of State in exercise by the powers conferred upon them by s. 171ZK(2), 171ZT(2) and 171ZZ5(2) of the Social Security Contributions and Benefits Act 1992. Operative in accordance with regulation 1.

CITATION, COMMENCEMENT AND APPLICATION

1(1) These Regulations may be cited as the Social Security Contributions and Benefits Act 1992 (Application of Parts 12ZA, 12ZB and 12ZC to Parental Order Cases) Regulations 2014.

1(2) Subject to paragraphs (3) and (4), these Regulations come into force on 19th November 2014.

1(3) The modification of section 171ZA of the Social Security Contributions and Benefits Act 1992 by the insertion of subsection (3C) as set out in Schedule 1 to these Regulations comes into force on the date that section 171ZA(2)(ba) comes into force.

1(4) The modification of section 171ZL of the Social Security Contributions and Benefits Act 1992 by the insertion of subsection (3B) as set out in Schedule 2 to these Regulations comes into force on the date that section 171ZL(2)(ba) comes into force.

1(5) Regulation 4 does not have effect in cases involving children whose expected week of birth ends on or before 4th April 2015.

INTERPRETATION

2 In these Regulations–

"the Act" means the Social Security Contributions and Benefits Act 1992;

"intended parent", in relation to a child, means a person who, on the day of the child's birth–

(a) applies, or intends to apply during the period of 6 months beginning with that day, with another person for a parental order in respect of the child, and

(b) expects the court to make a parental order on that application in respect of the child;

"parental order" means an order under section 54(1) of the Human Fertilisation and Embryology Act 2008; and

"parental order parent" means a person–

(a) on whose application the court has made a parental order in respect of a child, or

(b) who is an intended parent of a child.

APPLICATION OF PART 12ZA OF THE ACT TO PARENTAL ORDER PARENTS

3 Part 12ZA of the Act (statutory paternity pay) has effect in relation to parental order parents with the modifications of sections 171ZA, 171ZB and 171ZE of the Act specified in the second column of Schedule 1 to these Regulations.

APPLICATION OF PART 12ZB OF THE ACT TO PARENTAL ORDER PARENTS

4 Part 12ZB of the Act (statutory adoption pay) has effect in relation to parental order parents with the modifications of sections 171ZL and 171ZN of the Act specified in the second column of Schedule 2 to these Regulations.

APPLICATION OF PART 12ZC OF THE ACT TO PARENTAL ORDER PARENTS

5 Part 12ZC of the Act (statutory shared parental pay) has effect in relation to parental order parents with the modifications of section 171ZV of the Act specified in the second column of Schedule 3 to these Regulations.

SCHEDULES

SCHEDULE 1 – APPLICATION OF PART 12ZA OF THE ACT TO PARENTAL ORDER CASES

Regulation 3

Provision	*Modification*
Section 171ZA	After subsection (4) insert– "(4A) A person who satisfies the conditions in section 171ZB(2)(a) to (d) in relation to a child is not entitled to statutory paternity pay under this section in respect of that child.".
Section 171ZB	For paragraph (a) of subsection (2) substitute– "(a) that he satisfies prescribed conditions as to being a person– (i) on whose application the court has made a parental order in respect of a child, or (ii) who is an intended parent of a child; (ab) that he satisfies prescribed conditions as to relationship with the other person on whose application the parental order was made or who is an intended parent of the child;". In paragraph (d) of subsection (2), for "placed for adoption" substitute "born". In paragraph (e) of subsection (2), omit "where he is a person with whom the child is placed for adoption,". For subsection (3) substitute– "(3) The references in this section to the relevant week are to the week immediately preceding the 14th week before the expected week of the child's birth.". After subsection (3) insert– "(3B) In a case where a child is born earlier than the 14th week before the expected week of the child's birth– (a) subsection (2)(b) shall be treated as satisfied in relation to a person if, had the birth occurred after the end of the relevant week, the person would have been in employed earner's employment with an employer for a continuous period of at least 26 weeks ending with the relevant week; (b) subsection (2)(c) shall be treated as satisfied in relation to a person if the person's normal weekly earnings for the period of 8 weeks ending with the week immediately preceding the week in which the child is born are not less than the lower earnings limit in force under section 5(1)(a) immediately before the commencement of the week in which the child is born; and (c) subsection (2)(d) shall not apply. (3C) In a case where a child is born before the end of the relevant week, subsection (2)(ba) shall be treated as satisfied in relation to a person if, had the birth occurred after the end of the relevant week, the person would have been entitled to be in the relevant employment at the end of the relevant week. In this subsection **"the relevant employment"** means the employment by reference to which the person satisfies the condition in subsection (2)(b).". In subsection (6), for "placement for adoption of more than one child as part of the same arrangement" substitute "birth, or expected birth, of more than one child as a result of the same pregnancy". For subsection (7) substitute– "(7) In this section– **"intended parent"**, in relation to a child, means a person who, on the day of the child's birth–

Provision	Modification
	(a) applies, or intends to apply during the period of 6 months beginning with that day, with another person for a parental order in respect of the child, and (b) expects the court to make a parental order on that application in respect of the child; and **"parental order"** means an order under section 54(1) of the Human Fertilisation and Embryology Act 2008.". Omit subsection (8). Omit subsection (9).
Section 171ZE	In paragraph (b) of subsection (3), for "placement for adoption" substitute "birth". In subsection (4)– (a) in paragraph (a), for "sub-paragraph (i) of section 171ZA(2)(a)" substitute "section 171ZA(2)(a)(i)"; (b) in paragraph (b), for "sub-paragraph (ii) of that provision" substitute "section 171ZA(2)(a)(ii) or 171ZB(2)(ab)". In subsection (9), for "the reference in subsection (3)(a) to the date of the child's birth shall be read as a reference" substitute "the references in subsection (3)(a) and (b) to the date of the child's birth shall be read as references". Omit subsection (10). Omit subsection (12).

SCHEDULE 2 – APPLICATION OF PART 12ZB OF THE ACT TO PARENTAL ORDER CASES

Regulation 4

Provision	Modification
Section 171ZL	For paragraph (a) of subsection (2) substitute– "(a) that he is– (i) a person on whose application the court has made a parental order in respect of a child, or (ii) an intended parent of a child;". For subsection (3) substitute– "(3) The references in this section to the relevant week are to the week immediately preceding the 14th week before the expected week of the child's birth.". After subsection (3) insert– "(3A) In a case where a child is born earlier than the 14th week before the expected week of the child's birth– (a) subsection (2)(b) shall be treated as satisfied in relation to a person if, had the birth occurred after the end of the relevant week, the person would have been in employed earner's employment with an employer for a continuous period of at least 26 weeks ending with the relevant week; and (b) subsection (2)(d) shall be treated as satisfied in relation to a person if the person's normal weekly earnings for the period of 8 weeks ending with the week immediately preceding the week in which the child is born are not less than the lower earnings limit in force under section 5(1)(a) immediately before the commencement of the week in which the child is born. (3B) In a case where a child is born before the end of the relevant week, subsection (2)(ba) shall be treated as satisfied in relation to a person if, had the birth occurred after the end of the relevant week, the person would have been entitled to be in the relevant employment at the end of the relevant week.

Provision	Modification
	In this subsection **the relevant employment** means the employment by reference to which the person satisfies the condition in subsection (2)(b).".
	For paragraph (b) of subsection (4), substitute–
	"(b) the other person on whose application the court has made a parental order in respect of the child or who is an intended parent of the child–
	(i) is a person to whom the conditions in subsection (2) above apply, and
	(ii) has elected to receive statutory adoption pay.".
	Omit subsection (4A).
	Omit subsection (4B).
	In subsection (5), for "placement, or expected placement, for adoption of more than one child as part of the same arrangement" substitute "birth, or expected birth, of more than one child as a result of the same pregnancy".
	After subsection (8) insert–
	"(8A) In this section–
	"intended parent", in relation to a child, means a person who, on the day of the child's birth–
	(a) applies, or intends to apply during the period of 6 months beginning with that day, with another person for a parental order in respect of the child, and
	(b) expects the court to make a parental order on that application in respect of the child; and
	"parental order" means an order under section 54(1) of the Human Fertilisation and Embryology Act 2008.".
	Omit subsection (9).
	Omit subsection (10).
Section 171ZN	In subsection (2F), for "in which the person is notified that the person has been matched with a child for the purposes of adoption" substitute "immediately preceding the 14th week before the expected week of the child's birth".
	Omit subsection (9).

SCHEDULE 3 – APPLICATION OF PART 12ZC OF THE ACT TO PARENTAL ORDER CASES

Regulation 5

Provision	Modification
Section 171ZV	In subsection (1), for "with whom a child is, or is expected to be, placed for adoption under the law of any part of the United Kingdom" substitute "on whose application the court has made a parental order in respect of a child or who is an intended parent of a child".
	In paragraph (a) of subsection (2), for "another person" substitute "the other person on whose application the court has made a parental order in respect of the child or who is an intended parent of the child".
	In paragraph (g) of subsection (2), for "the placement for adoption of the child" substitute "being a person on whose application the court has made a parental order in respect of the child or being an intended parent of the child". In paragraph (a) of subsection (4), for "with whom a child is, or is expected to be, placed for adoption under the law of any part of the United Kingdom" substitute "on whose application the court has made a parental order in respect of a child or who is an intended parent of a child".

Provision	*Modification*
	In paragraph (h) of subsection (4), for "the placement for adoption of the child" substitute "being a person on whose application the court has made a parental order in respect of the child or being an intended parent of the child". In subsection (16), for "the placement for adoption of more than one child as part of the same arrangement" substitute "the birth of more than one child as a result of the same pregnancy".
	After subsection (16) insert–
	"(16A) In this section–
	"intended parent", in relation to a child, means a person who, on the day of the child's birth–
	(a) applies, or intends to apply during the period of 6 months beginning with that day, with another person for a parental order in respect of the child, and
	(b) expects the court to make a parental order on that application in respect of the child; and
	"parental order" means an order under section 54(1) of the Human Fertilisation and Embryology Act 2008.".
	Omit subsection (17).
	Omit subsection (18).

SOCIAL SECURITY CONTRIBUTIONS (LIMITED LIABILITY PARTNERSHIP) REGULATIONS 2014

(SI 2014/3159 as amended by SI 2015/607)

Made on 4 December 2014 by the Treasury in exercise of the powers conferred upon them by s. 4AA and 175(3) and (4) of the Social Security Contributions and Benefits Act 1992, 4AA and 171(3) and (4) of the Social Security Contributions and Benefits (Northern Ireland) Act 1992. Operative from 5 December 2014.

CITATION, COMMENCEMENT, EFFECT AND EXTENT

1(1) These Regulations may be cited as the Social Security Contributions (Limited Liability Partnership) Regulations 2014.

1(2) These Regulations come into force on the day after the day on which they are made, and have effect for the tax year 2014–15 and subsequent tax years.

1(2A) Regulations 2A, 2B and 2C have effect for the tax year 2015–16 and subsequent tax years.

1(3) Regulations 2B, 3 and 6 extend only to England and Wales and to Scotland and regulations 2C, 4 and 7 extend only to Northern Ireland.

History – Reg. 1(2A) inserted by SI 2015/607, reg. 3(a), with effect from 6 April 2015.
In reg. 1(3), "2B," and "2C," inserted by SI 2015/607, reg. 3(b), with effect from 6 April 2015.

INTERPRETATION

2 In these Regulations–

"employment income" has the meaning given by section 7 of ITEPA 2003;

"ITTOIA 2005" means the Income Tax (Trading and Other Income) Act 2005;

"LLP" means limited liability partnership;

"SSCBA 1992" means the Social Security Contributions and Benefits Act 1992; and

"SSCB(NI)A 1992" means the Social Security Contributions and Benefits (Northern Ireland) Act 1992.

MEMBERS OF LLPS: EMPLOYMENT

2A(1) The modification in paragraph (2) applies to–

(a) Part 1 and so much of Part 6 of SSCBA 1992 as relates to contributions, and

(b) Part 1 and so much of Part 6 of SSCB(NI)A 1992 as relates to contributions.

2A(2) The modification is that **"employment"** includes membership of an LLP which carries on a trade, profession or business with a view to profit.

History – Reg. 2A inserted by SI 2015/607, reg. 4, with effect from 6 April 2015.

MEMBERS OF LLPS: GREAT BRITAIN

2B A person in employment in Great Britain as a member of an LLP which carries on a trade, profession or business with a view to profit is, unless regulation 3 applies, to be treated as a self-employed earner for the purposes of SSCBA 1992.

History – Reg. 2B inserted by SI 2015/607, reg. 4, with effect from 6 April 2015.

MEMBERS OF LLPS: NORTHERN IRELAND

2C A person in employment in Northern Ireland as a member of an LLP which carries on a trade, profession or business with a view to profit is, unless regulation 4 applies, to be treated as a self-employed earner for the purposes of SSCB(NI)A 1992.

History – Reg. 2C inserted by SI 2015/607, reg. 4, with effect from 6 April 2015.

SALARIED MEMBERS OF LLPS: GREAT BRITAIN

3(1) This regulation applies where–

(a) for the purposes of the Income Tax Acts an individual is treated by section 863A of ITTOIA 2005 (limited liability partnerships: salaried members) as being employed by an LLP under a contract of service, including where that is the case by virtue of section 863G of ITTOIA 2005 (anti-avoidance), ("the deemed tax employment"); and

(b) if the services performed, or to be performed, by the individual as a member of the LLP in the relevant period (as defined in section 863B(3) of ITTOIA 2005) were actually performed (or to be performed) under a contract of service with the LLP, the employment under that contract of service would be employment in Great Britain.

3(2) For the purposes of SSCBA 1992–

(a) the individual ("the Salaried Member") is to be treated as employed in employed earner's employment by the LLP (being the deemed tax employment);

(b) any amount treated by virtue of section 863A or 863G(4) of ITTOIA 2005 as employment income from the deemed tax employment, other than employment income under Chapters 2 to 11 of Part 3 of ITEPA 2003 (the benefits code), is to be treated as an amount of earnings paid to or for the benefit of the Salaried Member in respect of the Salaried Member's employed earner's employment with the LLP;

(c) the secondary contributor in relation to those earnings is the LLP; and

(d) in the case of an amount of earnings which is an amount of employment income by virtue of section 863G(4) of ITTOIA 2005, the earnings are to be treated as being paid by the LLP to the Salaried Member when the amount mentioned in section 863G(2)(d) of that Act arises.

3(3) The reference in paragraph (1)(b) to services performed (or to be performed) by the individual as a member of the LLP includes services personally performed by the individual for the LLP under arrangements by virtue of which section 863G(4) of ITTOIA 2005 applies.

3(4) The definitions of "employer" and "employee" in–

(a) section 163 (interpretation of Part 11 and supplementary provisions);

(b) section 171 (interpretation of Part 12 and supplementary provisions);

(c) section 171ZJ (Part 12ZA: supplementary); and

(d) section 171ZS (Part 12ZB: supplementary)

of the SSCBA 1992 have effect as if the Salaried Member were gainfully employed in Great Britain by the LLP under a contract of service with the earnings mentioned in paragraph (2)(b).

SALARIED MEMBERS OF LLPS: NORTHERN IRELAND

4(1) This regulation applies where–

(a) for the purposes of the Income Tax Acts an individual is treated by section 863A of ITTOIA 2005 (limited liability partnerships: salaried members) as being employed by an LLP under a contract of service, including where that is the case by virtue of section 863G of ITTOIA 2005 (anti-avoidance), ("the deemed tax employment"); and

(b) if the services performed, or to be performed, by the individual as a member of the LLP in the relevant period (as defined in section 863B(3) of ITTOIA 2005) were actually performed (or to be performed) under a contract of service, the employment under that contract of service would be employment in Northern Ireland.

4(2) For the purposes of SSCB(NI)A 1992–

(a) the individual ("the Salaried Member") is to be treated as employed in employed earner's employment by the LLP (being the deemed tax employment);

(b) any amount treated as employment income by virtue of section 863A or section 863G(4) of ITTOIA 2005 as employment income from the deemed tax employment, other than employment income under Chapters 2 to 11 of Part 3 of ITEPA 2003 (the benefits code), is to be treated as an amount of earnings paid to or for the benefit of the Salaried Member in respect of the Salaried Member's employed earner's employment with the LLP;

(c) the secondary contributor in relation to those earnings is the LLP; and

(d) in the case of an amount of earnings which is an amount of employment income by virtue of section 863G(4) of ITTOIA 2005, the earnings are to be treated as being paid by the LLP to the Salaried Member when the amount mentioned in section 863G(2)(d) of that Act arises.

4(3) The reference in paragraph (1)(b) to services performed by the individual as a member of the LLP includes services personally performed by the individual for the LLP under arrangements by virtue of which section 863G(4) of ITTOIA 2005 applies.

4(4) The definitions of "employer" and "employee" in–

(a) section 159 (interpretation of Part 11 and supplementary provisions);

(b) section 167 (interpretation of Part 12, etc.);

(c) section 167ZJ (Part 12ZA: supplementary); and

(d) section 167ZS (Part 12ZB: supplementary)

of SSCB(NI)A 1992 have effect as if the Salaried Member were gainfully employed in Northern Ireland by the LLP under a contract of service with the earnings mentioned in sub- paragraph (2)(b).

CONSEQUENTIAL AMENDMENT TO THE SOCIAL SECURITY (CONTRIBUTIONS) REGULATIONS 2001

5(1) The Social Security (Contributions) Regulations 2001 are amended as follows.

5(2) [Inserts SI 2001/1004, reg. 40A.]

5(3) [Inserts SI 2001/1004, Sch. 3, Pt. X, para. 25.]

CONSEQUENTIAL AMENDMENTS TO THE SOCIAL SECURITY CONTRIBUTIONS (INTERMEDIARIES) REGULATIONS 2000

6 [Amends SI 2000/727, reg. 7(1).]

CONSEQUENTIAL AMENDMENTS TO THE SOCIAL SECURITY CONTRIBUTIONS (INTERMEDIARIES) (NORTHERN IRELAND) REGULATIONS 2000

7(1) The Social Security Contributions (Intermediaries) (Northern Ireland) Regulations 2000 are amended as follows.

7(2) In regulation 7(1) (worker's attributable earnings – calculation)–

(a) in "*Step One*" after "arrangements" insert "but excluding amounts on which Class 1 or Class 1A contributions are payable by virtue of regulation 3 or 4 of the Social Security Contributions (Limited Liability Partnership) Regulations 2014"; and

(b) in "*Step Seven*" in sub-paragraph (a) after "Three" insert "and payments within paragraph 25 of Part 10 of Schedule 3 to the Contributions Regulations".

SOCIAL SECURITY CLASS 3A CONTRIBUTIONS (UNITS OF ADDITIONAL PENSION) REGULATIONS 2014

(SI 2014/3240)

Made on 8 December 2014 by the Treasury in exercise of the powers conferred upon them by s. 14A(3) (the Treasury having consulted the Government Actuary) and 14A(6) of, and para. 8(1)(q) of Sch. 1 to, the Social Security Contributions and Benefits Act 1992 and s. 14A(3) (the Treasury having consulted the Government Actuary) and 14A(6) of, and para. 8(1)(q) of Sch. 1 to, the Social Security Contributions and Benefits (Northern Ireland) Act 1992 and by the Secretary of State in exercise of the powers conferred upon them by s. 45(2A) of the Social Security Contributions and Benefits Act 1992. Operative in accordance with reg. 1(2) and (3).

CITATION AND COMMENCEMENT

1(1) These Regulations may be cited as the Social Security Class 3A Contributions (Units of Additional Pension) Regulations 2014.

1(2) These Regulations come into force in Great Britain on 12th October 2015.

1(3) Regulations 1, 2 and 3 come into force in Northern Ireland on the same day as the coming into force for all purposes of paragraph 17 of Schedule 15 to the Pensions Act 2014.

DETERMINATION OF AMOUNT OF A CLASS 3A CONTRIBUTION NEEDED TO OBTAIN A UNIT OF ADDITIONAL PENSION

2(1) The amount of a Class 3A contribution needed by an eligible person to obtain a unit of additional pension is determined by the Table, subject to paragraph (2).

Age of person on the date of payment	*Amount of Class 3A contribution needed to obtain a unit of additional pension*
62 (women only)	£956
63 (women only)	£934
64 (women only)	£913
65	£890
66	£871
67	£847
68	£827
69	£801
70	£779
71	£761
72	£738
73	£719
74	£694
75	£674
76	£646
77	£625
78	£596
79	£574
80	£544
81	£514
82	£484
83	£454
84	£424
85	£394
86	£366
87	£339
88	£314

Age of person on the date of payment	*Amount of Class 3A contribution needed to obtain a unit of additional pension*
89	£291
90	£270
91	£251
92	£232
93	£216
94	£200
95	£185
96	£172
97	£159
98	£148
99	£137
100 and over	£127

2(2) If an eligible person pays a Class 3A contribution before reaching pensionable age the amount of contribution needed to obtain a unit of additional pension is the amount that that person would have needed to pay if on the date of payment the person had reached pensionable age.

2(3) The date of payment for a Class 3A contribution is the date the contribution is received by Her Majesty's Revenue and Customs.

MAXIMUM NUMBER OF UNITS OF ADDITIONAL PENSION

3 The maximum number of units of additional pension that a person may obtain is 25.

SPECIFIED AMOUNT FOR EACH UNIT OF ADDITIONAL PENSION

4 The specified amount for the purposes of section 45(1)(b) and (2)(e) of the Social Security Contributions and Benefits Act 1992 (the additional pension in a category A retirement pension) is £1.

OCCUPATIONAL PENSION SCHEMES (POWER TO AMEND SCHEMES TO REFLECT ABOLITION OF CONTRACTING-OUT) REGULATIONS 2015

(SI 2015/118)

Made on 25 February 2015 by the Secretary of State for Work and Pensions in exercise of the powers conferred upon them by s. 24(5) and 54(5) and (6), of and para. 2(3) and (4), 4, 6, 10(1), 12, 13, and 14(1) and (2) of Sch. 14 to, the Pensions Act 2014. Operative from 6 April 2015.

CITATION AND COMMENCEMENT

1(1) These Regulations may be cited as the Occupational Pension Schemes (Power to Amend Schemes to Reflect Abolition of Contracting-out) Regulations 2015.

1(2) These Regulations come into force on 6th April 2015.

INTERPRETATION

2 In these Regulations–

"the Act" means the Pensions Act 2014;

"the 2004 Act" means the Pensions Act 2004;

"actuarial valuation" has the meaning given by section 224(2)(a) of the 2004 Act (actuarial valuations and reports);

"the actuary" means the actuary appointed in accordance with regulation 10(2);

"the amendment date" means the date amendments made using the power take effect;

"the calculation date" means the date chosen in accordance with regulation 8(7);

"effective date" means the date referred to in section 224(2)(b) of the 2004 Act;

"the power" means the power under section 24(2) of the Act to amend an occupational pension scheme;

"principal employer" means, in relation to a multi-employer scheme–

(a) a person nominated by the employers, or by rules of the scheme, to act on behalf of the employers for the purposes of section 229 of the 2004 Act (matters requiring agreement of the employer), or

(b) where there is no such nominee, a person nominated by the employers to act on their behalf for the purposes of the use of the power;

"proposed amendments" means the amendments to be certified under paragraph 6(1) of Schedule 14 to the Act;

"segregated scheme" means a multi-employer scheme which is divided into two or more sections where–

(a) any contributions payable to the scheme by an employer in relation to the scheme, or by a member employed by that employer, are allocated to that employer's section, and if more than one section applies to an employer, to the section to which the employment relates, and

(b) a specified proportion of the assets of the scheme is attributable to each section of the scheme and cannot be used for the purposes of any other section; and

"technical provisions" has the meaning given by section 222(2) of the 2004 Act (the statutory funding objective).

PROTECTED PERSONS TO WHOM THE POWER DOES NOT APPLY

3(1) For the purposes of section 24(4)(a) of the Act (when the power may not be used) a person listed in this regulation is a "protected person in relation to a scheme".

3(2) A person who is a **"protected employee"** as defined by regulation 2(1) of the Electricity (Protected Persons) (England and Wales) Pension Regulations 1990 (interpretation) on or after the amendment date.

3(3) A person who is a **"protected employee"** as defined by regulation 2(1) of the Electricity (Protected Persons) (Scotland) Pension Regulations 1990 (interpretation) on or after the amendment date.

3(4) A person who is a **"protected employee"** as defined by article 1(2) of the Railway Pensions (Protection and Designation of Schemes) Order 1994 (citation, commencement and interpretation) to whom part II of that Order has effect in relation to relevant pension rights, within the meaning of paragraph 6(3) of Schedule 11 to the Railways Act 1993 (the powers of protection), accruing on or after the amendment date.

3(5) A person who is a **"protected employee"** as defined by regulation 2(1) of the Coal Industry (Protected Persons) Pensions Regulations 1994 (interpretation) on or after the amendment date.

3(6) A person who is a **"protected person"** as defined by article 1(3) of the London Transport Pension Arrangements Order 2000 (citation, commencement and interpretation) to whom that Order has effect on or after the amendment date.

3(7) A person who falls within paragraph 9(5) of Schedule 8 to the Energy Act 2004 (persons entitled to pension protection under paragraphs 10 and 11)(g) and to whom paragraph 9(2) of that Schedule applies.

TOTAL ANNUAL EMPLOYEE CONTRIBUTIONS OF THE RELEVANT MEMBERS

4(1) For the purposes of paragraph 2(3)(a) of Schedule 14 to the Act (what can the power be used to do?), the **"total annual employee contributions of the relevant members"** means the total annual amount of employee contributions for the relevant members calculated using the employee contribution rates shown in the schedule of contributions adopted in relation to the scheme for the purposes of Part 3 of the 2004 Act (scheme funding) as at the calculation date.

4(2) The actuary is to calculate the increase, due to the proposed amendments, in the total annual employee contributions of the relevant members–

(a) estimated to be payable over the period of one year beginning with the calculation date;

(b) using the earnings data specified in regulation 7; and

(c) in accordance with the requirements in regulation 8.

ANNUAL INCREASE IN AN EMPLOYER'S NATIONAL INSURANCE CONTRIBUTIONS IN RESPECT OF THE RELEVANT MEMBERS

5(1) For the purposes of paragraph 2(3)(b) of Schedule 14 to the Act, the **"annual increase in an employer's national insurance contributions in respect of the relevant members"** means the increase of 3.4% in the annual amount of national insurance contributions payable by the employer in respect of so much of the earnings of relevant members as exceeds the applicable lower earnings limit but not the upper accrual point (or the prescribed equivalents if the earner is paid otherwise than weekly).

5(2) The actuary is to calculate the annual increase in the employer's national insurance contributions in respect of the relevant members–

(a) estimated to be payable over the period of one year beginning with the calculation date;

(b) using the earnings data specified in regulation 7; and

(c) in accordance with the requirements in regulation 8.

5(3) In this regulation–

"the 1992 Act" means the Social Security Contributions and Benefits Act 1992;

"applicable" in relation to the lower earnings limit, means the limit or limits in force during the one year after the calculation date;

"lower earnings limit" is to be construed in accordance with section 5 of the 1992 Act (earnings limits and thresholds for class 1 contributions);

"the prescribed equivalents"–

(a) in the context of the lower earnings limit, means the equivalent prescribed under section 5(4) of the 1992 Act, and

(b) in the context of the upper accrual point, means the equivalent prescribed under section 122(6A) of that Act (interpretation); and

"the upper accrual point" has the meaning given by section 122(1) of the 1992 Act.

SCHEME LIABILITIES IN RESPECT OF THE BENEFITS THAT ACCRUE ANNUALLY FOR OR IN RESPECT OF THE RELEVANT MEMBERS

6(1) For the purposes of paragraph 2(3)(c) of Schedule 14 to the Act, a **"scheme's liabilities in respect of the benefits that accrue annually for or in respect of the relevant members"** means any liabilities which arise by virtue of any rights accruing to future benefits under the scheme rules for or in respect of the relevant members.

6(2) Where those rights include discretionary benefits, the discretionary benefits are to be taken into account in the same way as in the scheme's technical provisions–

(a) where the calculation date is the same date as the effective date of an actuarial valuation, calculated by reference to that date, or

(b) where the calculation date is not the same date as that date, calculated by reference to the date of the most recent actuarial valuation before the calculation date.

6(3) Where those rights include money purchase benefits, the money purchase benefits are not to be taken into account.

6(4) The actuary is to calculate the reduction, due to the proposed amendments, in the scheme's liabilities in respect of the benefits that accrue annually for or in respect of the relevant members–

(a) estimated for the period of one year beginning with the calculation date;

(b) using the earnings data specified in regulation 7; and

(c) in accordance with the requirements of regulation 8.

6(5) In this regulation, **"money purchase benefits"** have the meaning given by section 181 of the Pension Schemes Act 1993 (general interpretation).

EARNINGS DATA

7(1) The actuary must use earnings data which, except where paragraph (3) applies, is for the period of one year ending with the calculation date.

7(2) Where paragraph (3) applies, calculations may be made using earnings data which refers to the period of three years ending with the calculation date.

7(3) This paragraph applies where–

(a) the actuary is satisfied that the earnings data for some or all of the relevant members for the period of one year ending with the calculation date is significantly abnormal; and

(b) the–

(i) principal employer in a case falling within regulation 14 or 15, or

(ii) employer in any other case;

writes to the actuary stating that it is also so satisfied.

GENERAL CALCULATION REQUIREMENTS

8(1) The actuary must comply with the following requirements in carrying out the calculations under regulations 4(2), 5(2) and 6(4).

8(2) The calculations are to be carried out–

(a) as if the proposed amendments took effect on the calculation date;

(b) taking account only of the effect of the proposed amendments;

(c) at the present value at the calculation date; and

(d) where an assumption is used in more than one calculation, using the same assumption for each calculation in which it is used.

8(3) Any data used in the calculations, other than earnings data, must be data–

(a) the actuary considers is relevant; and

(b) which–

(i) is as at the calculation date, or

(ii) refers to the period of one year ending with the calculation date,

as the actuary considers appropriate.

8(4) Calculations must be made using–

(a) the methods and assumptions used to calculate the scheme's technical provisions–

(i) where the calculation date is the same date as the effective date of an actuarial valuation, calculated by reference to that date, or

(ii) where the calculation date is not the same date as that date, calculated by reference to the date of the most recent actuarial valuation before the calculation date, updated if necessary to reflect market conditions at the calculation date; and

(b) any other assumptions which the actuary considers necessary and which are consistent with the assumptions used to calculate the scheme's technical provisions, updated if necessary to reflect market conditions at the calculation date.

8(5) Where paragraph (6) applies, the actuary must adjust the requested assumptions to a best estimate basis by removing any margin for prudence provided the actuary is satisfied such adjustments are consistent with the principles that would be used by the trustees or managers of the scheme in calculating an initial cash equivalent under regulation 7B of the Occupational Pension Schemes (Transfer Values) Regulations 1996 (initial cash equivalents for salary related benefits other than cash balance benefits not calculated by reference to final salary) at the calculation date.

8(6) This paragraph applies where the–

(a) principal employer in a case falling within regulation 14 or 15; or

(b) employer in any other case,

writes to the actuary instructing the actuary to adjust any assumptions ("the requested assumptions") to remove any margin for prudence.

8(7) Subject to regulation 8(8), the–

(a) principal employer in a case falling within regulation 14 or 15; or

(b) employer in any other case,

must choose a calculation date which may be any date after 31st December 2011.

8(8) Where the power is used in relation to the same members in the same scheme on a second or subsequent occasion the calculation date must be the same date as on the first occasion the power was used.

8(9) In this regulation, **"any margin for prudence"** means any margin for adverse deviation allowed for in accordance with regulation 5(4)(a) of the Occupational Pension Schemes (Scheme Funding) Regulations 2005 (calculation of technical provisions).

FURTHER RESTRICTIONS ON THE USE OF THE POWER

9(1) The power may not be used to make amendments which would remove a power to determine any matter from the trustees or managers of a scheme.

ACTUARY

10(1) For the purposes of paragraph 6(2)(a) of Schedule 14 to the Act (requirement for actuary's certificate), **"actuary"** means a Fellow of the Institute and Faculty of Actuaries.

10(2) The–

(a) principal employer in a case falling within regulation 14 or 15; or

(b) employer in any other case,

must appoint an actuary.

REQUIREMENT FOR ACTUARY'S CERTIFICATE

11(1) Except in a case where regulation 8(8) applies, the actuary must certify whether, in the actuary's opinion–

(a) the proposed amendments comply with paragraph 2(2) of Schedule 14 to the Act; and

(b) the calculations have been made in accordance with the requirements of regulations 4(2), 5(2), 6(2) to (4), 7 and 8(2) to (6).

11(2) In a case where regulation 8(8) applies, the actuary must certify whether, in the actuary's opinion–

(a) all the amendments comply with the requirement in paragraph (1)(a) as if all the amendments are being made on this second or subsequent (as appropriate) occasion; and

(b) the calculations have been made in accordance with the requirements in paragraph (1)(b) and regulation 8(8).

11(3) For the purposes of this regulation, **"all the amendments"** means the proposed amendments and the amendments made by the previous use, or uses, of the power in relation to the same members in the same scheme as covered by the proposed amendments.

11(4) The actuary must provide a certificate under this regulation that includes the information specified in the Schedule.

11(5) The actuary must issue a certificate under this regulation to the trustees or managers of the scheme and–

(a) the principal employer in a case falling within regulation 14 or 15; or

(b) in any other case, the employer,

before any amendments are made.

INFORMATION

12(1) The trustees or managers of an occupational pension scheme must provide any information reasonably requested by–

(a) the principal employer in a case falling within regulation 14 or 15; or

(b) in any other case, the employer,

in connection with the use of the power.

12(2) The information must be provided in writing within such reasonable period as agreed with the principal employer or employer as applicable.

12(3) Where the trustees or managers of a scheme have failed to take all reasonable steps to comply with any requirement imposed on them by this regulation, section 10 of the Pensions Act 1995 (civil penalties) applies.

SEGREGATED SCHEMES WITH SINGLE EMPLOYER SECTIONS

13(1) This regulation applies to a section of a segregated scheme where there is one employer in relation to that section of the scheme.

13(2) Section 24 of the Act (abolition of contracting-out for salary related schemes etc) and Schedule 14 to the Act (power to amend schemes to reflect abolition of contracting-out) apply with the following modifications.

13(3) In section 24(2) the reference to–

(a) **"an employer"** is to be read as a reference to "an employer in relation to a section of an occupational pension scheme"; and

(b) **"an occupational pension scheme"** is to be read as a reference to "that section of an occupational pension scheme".

13(4) In Schedule 14 in paragraphs 2(2), 3(1), 9 and 15, references to a **"scheme"** are to be read as references to a "section of a scheme".

13(5) Where these Regulations (apart from this regulation) apply to a section of a segregated scheme where there is one employer in relation to that section of the scheme, they shall apply to that section as if the section were a separate scheme.

NON-SEGREGATED MULTI-EMPLOYER SCHEMES

14(1) This regulation applies to multi-employer schemes which are not segregated schemes.

14(2) Section 24 of the Act and Schedule 14 to the Act apply with the following modifications.

14(3) In section 24(2) the reference to–

(a) **"an employer"** is to be read as a reference to "the principal employer"; and

(b) **"the employer's national insurance contributions"** is to be read as a reference to "the employers' national insurance contributions".

14(4) In Schedule 14–

(a) in paragraph 2(2), references to **"the employer's national insurance contributions"** are to be read as references to "the employers' national insurance contributions"; and

(b) in paragraph 2(5), the reference to **"the employer is"** is to be read as a reference to "the employers are".

SEGREGATED SCHEMES WITH MULTI-EMPLOYER SECTIONS

15(1) This regulation applies to a section of a segregated scheme where there is more than one employer in relation to that section of the scheme.

15(2) Section 24 of the Act and Schedule 14 to the Act apply with the following modifications.

15(3) In section 24(2) the reference to–

(a) **"an employer"** is to be read as a reference to "the principal employer in relation to a section of an occupational pension scheme";

(b) **"an occupational pension scheme"** is to be read as a reference to "that section of an occupational pension scheme"; and

(c) **"the employer's national insurance contributions"** is to be read as a reference to "the employers' national insurance contributions".

15(4) In Schedule 14–

(a) in paragraph 2(2), references to **"the employer's national insurance contributions"** are to be read as references to "the employers' national insurance contributions"; and

(b) in paragraphs 2(2), 3(1), 9 and 15, references to a **"scheme"** are to be read as references to a "section of a scheme".

15(5) Where these Regulations (apart from this regulation) apply to a section of a segregated scheme where there is more than one employer in relation to that section of the scheme, they shall apply to that section as if the section were a separate scheme.

NOTIFICATION OF AMENDMENT DATE

16(1) Following the issue of a certificate by the actuary in accordance with regulation 11(5), the–

(a) principal employer in a case falling within regulation 14 or 15; or

(b) employer in any other case,

must consult the trustees or managers of the scheme about an appropriate amendment date.

16(2) The principal employer or employer as applicable, must, as soon as reasonably practicable after consultation, notify the trustees or managers of the scheme of the amendment date.

16(3) The notification required by paragraph (2) must be in writing.

16(4) Amendments may not have effect before 6th April 2016.

SCHEDULES

SCHEDULE – INFORMATION TO BE INCLUDED IN ACTUARY'S CERTIFICATE

Regulation 11

Name and address of employer/principal employer

Name and Scheme Contracted-out Number (SCON(s)) of scheme/section

The amendments proposed to be made.

Data and assumptions used

Calculation date

Date of scheme actuarial valuation

Any additional assumptions used

Any assumptions which the employer requested were adjusted to remove the margin for prudence

What earnings data used: 1 year to calculation date or 3 years to calculation date

Other data sources used

Estimates of values of scheme amendments

A statement that the Actuary's estimate of the following values is for the proposed amendments as set out in the certificate and on the basis of the data referred to, the methods and assumptions used to calculate the scheme's technical provisions and the additional assumptions set out in the certificate.

The values for–

the annual increase in the employer's national insurance contributions in respect of the earnings of relevant members as exceeds the lower earnings limit but not the upper accrual point

the increase in the total annual employee contributions of the relevant members (if applicable)

the reduction in the scheme's liabilities in respect of the benefits that accrue annually for or in respect of the relevant members (if applicable)

the sum of the increase in the total annual employee contributions and the reduction in the scheme's liabilities in respect of the benefits that accrue annually for or in respect of the relevant members (if applicable).

Note: In a case where the power is being used on a second or subsequent occasion, estimates should be for the changes due to all the amendments, those proposed and the amendments made by the previous use or uses of the power.

Certification

A statement that, in the actuary's opinion–

The proposed amendments to the scheme/section set out in this certificate comply with paragraph 2(2) of Schedule 14 to the Pensions Act 2014.

The calculations have been made in accordance with the requirements of regulations 4(2), 5(2), 6(2) to (4), 7 and 8(2) to (6) of the Occupational Pension Schemes (Power to Amend Schemes to Reflect Abolition of Contracting-out) Regulations 2015.

Alternative certification where the power is being used on a second or subsequent occasion

A statement that, in the actuary's opinion–

All the amendments to the scheme/section, those proposed and set out in this certificate and those made by the previous use or uses of the power and set out in resolutions (give dates) comply with paragraph 2(2) of Schedule 14 to the Pensions Act 2014.

The calculations have been made in accordance with the requirements of regulations 4(2), 5(2), 6(2) to (4), 7, 8(2) to (6) and 8(8) of the Occupational Pension Schemes (Power to Amend Schemes to Reflect Abolition of Contracting-out) Regulations 2015.

PROMOTERS OF TAX AVOIDANCE SCHEMES (PRESCRIBED CIRCUMSTANCES UNDER SECTION 235) REGULATIONS 2015

(SI 2015/130)

Made on 6 February 2015 by the Commissioners for Her Majesty's Revenue and Customs in exercise of the powers conferred upon them by s. 235(6) and (7) and 283(1) of the Finance Act 2014. Operative from 2 March 2015.

CITATION, COMMENCEMENT AND EFFECT

1(1) These Regulations may be cited as the Promoters of Tax Avoidance Schemes (Prescribed Circumstances under Section 235) Regulations 2015 and come into force on 2nd March 2015.

1(2) Regulations 2 and 3 have effect from 17th July 2014.

COMPANY IN SAME GROUP NOT PROMOTER

2(1) A company ("C") is not a promoter to the extent that–

(a) C carries on a business within the meaning of section 235(1);

(b) the other person (or each of the other persons) to whom C provides services in connection with the relevant proposal or relevant arrangements is a company in the same group as C; and

(c) C has not during the previous three years provided services of that kind to a person other than a company which is in the same group as C.

2(2) If C at any subsequent time provides services of that kind to a person other than a company which is in the same group as C, paragraph (1) will be deemed not to have applied during the previous three years.

2(3) A company cannot rely on paragraph (1) whilst a conduct notice or a monitoring notice has effect in relation to it.

2(4) For the purposes of this regulation companies are members of the same group if one is the 51% subsidiary of the other, or both are 51% subsidiaries of a third company.

2(5) In this regulation **"51% subsidiary"** has the same meaning as it does for the purposes of the Corporation Tax Acts.

PERSONS NOT PROMOTERS – SPECIAL CASES

3(1) A person ("P") is not a promoter on account of section 235(2)(a), or by virtue of being responsible to any extent for the design of arrangements within the meaning of section 235(3)(b), where any of the following conditions are met.

3(2) P does not provide any tax advice in connection with the respective proposed arrangements or arrangements.

3(3) P could not reasonably be expected to know that the proposed arrangements, or arrangements, are a relevant proposal or relevant arrangements respectively.

FINANCE ACT 2014 (SCHEDULE 34 PRESCRIBED MATTERS) REGULATIONS 2015

(SI 2015/131)

Made on 6 February 2015 by the Commissioners for Her Majesty's Revenue and Customs in exercise of the powers conferred upon them by s. 283(1) of, and para. 8(1), 8(3) and 9(2) of Sch. 34 to, the Finance Act 2014. Operative from 2 March 2015.

CITATION AND COMMENCEMENT

1 These Regulations may be cited as the Finance Act 2014 (Schedule 34 Prescribed Matters) Regulations 2015 and come into force on 2nd March 2015.

PRESCRIBED MISCONDUCT

2(1) Prescribed misconduct for the purposes of paragraph 8(1)(a) of Schedule 34 to the Finance Act 2014 means any conduct by a person–

(a) which a professional body describes as misconduct, or

(b) which is a breach of a rule or condition imposed by a professional body,

and is relevant to the provision of tax advice or tax related services.

PRESCRIBED ACTION

3 Prescribed action for the purposes of paragraph 8(1)(b) of Schedule 34 to the Finance Act 2014 means any action by a professional body which results in any claim of misconduct being referred to–

(a) a disciplinary process which determines–

  (i) the seriousness of the misconduct, and

  (ii) the level of any penalty to be imposed; or

(b) a conciliation, arbitration or similar settlement process (however described) which determines the seriousness of the misconduct and the level of any penalty to be imposed.

PRESCRIBED PENALTY

4 A penalty is prescribed for the purposes of paragraph 8(1)(c) of Schedule 34 to the Finance Act 2014 where it is imposed by a professional body and results in one or more of the following in relation to a person–

(a) a fine or financial penalty greater than £5,000;

(b) a condition or restriction on, or attached to, a certificate or licence required to practice under the professional body;

(c) suspension, withdrawal or non-renewal of a certificate or licence required to practice under the professional body;

(d) suspension, expulsion or exclusion from membership of the professional body, however described (including removal from a membership register, striking off), whether temporary or permanent.

PRESCRIBED PROFESSIONAL BODIES

5 The following are prescribed professional bodies for the purposes of paragraph 8(3)(l) of Schedule 34 to the Finance Act 2014–

(a) the Chartered Institute of Taxation;

(b) Chartered Accountants Ireland.

PRESCRIBED RELEVANT SANCTION

6(1) In paragraph 9 of Schedule 34 to the Finance Act 2014 a sanction is prescribed under sub-paragraph (2)(b) if a regulatory authority imposes one or more of the following in relation to a person–

(a) a fine or financial penalty;

(b) a suspension of an approval issued by the regulatory authority to perform any function to which the approval relates;

(c) the imposition of limitations or other restrictions in relation to the performance of any function to which any approval issued by the regulatory authority relates;

(d) the imposition of any conditions in relation to any approval issued by the regulatory authority.

6(2) A sanction is also prescribed in relation to a person if a regulatory authority publishes a statement of misconduct by that person.

SOCIAL SECURITY PENSIONS (FLAT RATE ACCRUAL AMOUNT) ORDER 2015

(SI 2015/185)

Made on 9 February 2015 by the Secretary of State in exercise of the powers conferred upon them by s. 148AA(3)–(6) and 189(1), (4) and (5) of the Social Security Administration Act 1992. Operative from 6 April 2015.

CITATION AND COMMENCEMENT

1 This Order may be cited as the Social Security Pensions (Flat Rate Accrual Amount) Order 2015 and comes into force on 6th April 2015.

FLAT RATE ACCRUAL AMOUNT

2 For the purpose of paragraph 13(2) of Schedule 4B to the Social Security Contributions and Benefits Act 1992, the flat rate accrual amount for the tax year beginning 6th April 2015 and subsequent tax years shall be £93.60.

SOCIAL SECURITY PENSIONS (LOW EARNINGS THRESHOLD) ORDER 2015

(SI 2015/186)

Made on 9 February 2015 by the Secretary of State in exercise of the powers conferred upon them by s. 148A(3)–(5) and 189(1), (4) and (5) of the Social Security Administration Act 1992. Operative from 6 April 2015.

CITATION AND COMMENCEMENT

1 This Order may be cited as the Social Security Pensions (Low Earnings Threshold) Order 2015 and comes into force on 6th April 2015.

LOW EARNINGS THRESHOLD

2 For the purposes of the Social Security Contributions and Benefits Act 1992, it is directed that the low earnings threshold for the tax years following the tax year 2014–2015 shall be £15,300.

SOCIAL SECURITY REVALUATION OF EARNINGS FACTORS ORDER 2015

(SI 2015/187)

Made on 9 February 2015 by the Secretary of State in exercise of the powers conferred upon them by s. 148(3) and (4) and 189(1), (4) and (5) of the Social Security Administration Act 1992. Operative from 6 April 2015.

CITATION AND COMMENCEMENT

1 This Order may be cited as the Social Security Revaluation of Earnings Factors Order 2015 and comes into force on 6th April 2015.

REVALUATION OF EARNINGS FACTORS

2 The earnings factors for tax years specified in the Schedule to this Order in so far as they are relevant–

(a) to the calculation–

(i) of the additional pension in the rate of any long-term benefit, or

(ii) of any guaranteed minimum pension; or

(b) to any other calculation required under Part 3 of the Pension Schemes Act 1993 (including that Part as modified by or under any other enactment),

are directed to be increased for those tax years by the percentage of their amount shown opposite those tax years in that Schedule.

ROUNDING OF FRACTIONAL AMOUNTS

3 Where any earnings factor relevant to the calculation specified in article 2(a)(i) of this Order, as increased in accordance with this Order, would not but for this article be expressed as a whole number of pounds, it shall be so expressed by rounding down any fraction of a pound less than one half and rounding up any other fraction of a pound.

SCHEDULE

Article 2

PERCENTAGE INCREASE OF EARNINGS FACTOR FOR SPECIFIED TAX YEARS

Tax year	*Percentage increase*
1978–1979	754.4
1979–1980	654.1
1980–1981	530.0
1981–1982	427.6
1982–1983	379.2
1983–1984	345.0
1984–1985	312.0
1985–1986	286.5
1986–1987	254.9
1987–1988	230.4
1988–1989	204.0
1989–1990	174.4
1990–1991	155.7
1991–1992	132.2
1992–1993	118.1
1993–1994	107.7
1994–1995	101.4
1995–1996	93.0
1996–1997	87.7

Tax year	*Percentage increase*
1997–1998	78.8
1998–1999	70.9
1999–2000	64.0
2000–2001	54.3
2001–2002	48.4
2002–2003	42.2
2003–2004	37.3
2004–2005	32.3
2005–2006	27.1
2006–2007	22.9
2007–2008	18.0
2008–2009	13.3
2009–2010	9.9
2010–2011	8.6
2011–2012	6.1
2012–2013	4.3
2013–2014	2.4
2014–2015	1.5

FINANCE ACT 2014 (HIGH RISK PROMOTERS PRESCRIBED INFORMATION) REGULATIONS 2015

(SI 2015/549)

Made on 5 March 2015 by the Commissioners for Her Majesty's Revenue and Customs in exercise of the powers conferred upon them by s. 249(3), (10) and (11), 253(2) and (4), 257(2), 259(9), 260(7), 261(2), 268(1), 282(4) and 283(1) of the Finance Act 2014. Operative from 27 March 2015.

CITATION, COMMENCEMENT AND INTERPRETATION

1(1) These Regulations may be cited as the Finance Act 2014 (High Risk Promoters Prescribed Information) Regulations 2015 and come into force on 27th March 2015.

1(2) In these Regulations–

"accounting period" for the purposes of corporation tax has the same meaning as that given in sections 9 to 12 of the Corporation Tax Act 2009 and **"beginning of accounting period"** and **"end of accounting period"** shall be construed accordingly;

"the Act" means the Finance Act 2014;

"audiovisual formats" means any method of presenting information that uses an audible and visible format including broadcasting by electronic means or transmission over, or publication on, the internet; **"chargeable period"** shall be construed–

(a) for the purposes of annual tax on enveloped dwellings, in accordance with section 94(8) of the Finance Act 2013;

(b) for the purposes of petroleum revenue tax, in accordance with section 1(3) of the Oil Taxation Act 1975;

"effective date" has the meaning given by section 119 of the Finance Act 2003;

"tax year" means a year beginning on 6th April and ending on the following 5th April;

PRESCRIBED PUBLICATION OR CORRESPONDENCE

2(1) The following publications and correspondence are prescribed for the purposes of subsection (10) of section 249 of the Act (publication by monitored promoter)–

(a) any publication or correspondence that–

(i) with the exception of correspondence with HMRC, contains information about any relevant arrangements or any relevant proposal offered or promoted by the monitored promoter;

(ii) is shown, given or sent to clients or prospective clients in relation to any relevant arrangements or any relevant proposal (whether or not the relevant arrangements or relevant proposal is provided by the monitored promoter);

(iii) is shown, given or sent to intermediaries or prospective intermediaries in relation to any relevant arrangements or any relevant proposal (whether or not the relevant arrangements or relevant proposal is provided by the monitored promoter);

(b) any correspondence with–

(i) a professional body referred to in paragraph 8(3) of Schedule 34 to the Act of which the monitored promoter is a member, prospective member or former member and which concerns any relevant arrangements or any relevant proposal;

(ii) a regulatory authority referred to in paragraph 9(3) of Schedule 34 to the Act which the monitored promoter is regulated by and which concerns the monitored promoter's conduct in respect of any relevant arrangements or any relevant proposal.

2(2) In paragraph (1)–

(a) **"correspondence"** includes correspondence in writing or by electronic means;

(b) **"publication"** means publication in any format (including audiovisual formats).

INFORMATION PUBLICISED BY A MONITORED PROMOTER

3(1) For the purposes of subsection (11) of section 249 of the Act (publication by monitored promoter), the prescribed form and manner is as set out in paragraphs (2), (3) and (4).

3(2) Notification given under subsection (1) of section 249 must–

(a) be in writing;

(b) set out clearly and precisely the information required to be stated under paragraphs (a) and (b) of section 249(1) of the Act so that–

(i) in respect of the information required by section 249(1)(a) of the Act, it is clear that the promoter is being monitored by HMRC because it breached a condition or conditions of a conduct notice identified under section 249(1)(b) of the Act, and

(ii) in respect of the information required by section 249(1)(b) of the Act, the specific details of each of the conditions which it has been determined that the person has failed to comply with.

3(3) In respect of subsection (3) of section 249 of the Act, the monitored promoter shall publish on the internet the information mentioned in paragraph (a) and (b) of section 249(1) of the Act. The published information must–

(a) appear in a prominent position on the monitored promoter's or other websites promoting, or providing information on, the activities of the promoter;

(b) if in writing, be legible;

(c) if in an audiovisual format, be clearly audible or visible;

(d) not in any way be concealed;

(e) be specifically referred to or included in any promotional material (of whatever kind or format);

(f) not be presented in a way that it promotes the activity of tax avoidance.

3(4) The information to be provided under subsection (10) of section 249 of the Act and regulation 2 to these Regulations (prescribed publication or correspondence) must–

(a) be prominent and not in any way be concealed;

(b) if in writing, be legible;

(c) if in an audiovisual format, be clearly audible or visible;

(d) not be presented in a way that promotes the activity of tax avoidance.

DUTY OF PERSONS TO NOTIFY THE COMMISSIONERS: PRESCRIBED INFORMATION

4(1) The following information is prescribed for the purposes of paragraphs 2(b) and 4(b) of section 253 of the Act (duty of persons to notify the Commissioners)–

(a) the full name and address (including postcode) of the person reporting the promoter reference number;

(b) the promoter reference number which is the subject of the report;

(c) the type of tax in respect of which the person expects to obtain a tax advantage;

(d) the unique identifier (as to the meaning of which see paragraph (3)(a));

(e) the relevant date of the transaction(s) (as to the meaning of which see paragraph (3)(b));

(f) a declaration that the information provided is correct and complete to the best of the knowledge and belief of the person making the report;

(g) the signature of the person making the report;

(h) the full name of the person signing the report;

(i) the date on which the report is made.

4(2) For relevant arrangements involving annual tax on enveloped dwellings, stamp duty land tax or stamp duty reserve tax transactions under regulation 4 of the Stamp Duty Reserve Tax Regulations 1986 (notice of charge and payment), the unique identifier in sub-paragraph (1)(d) is to be replaced by the following additional prescribed information–

(a) for annual tax on enveloped dwellings–

(i) title number or numbers of the dwelling associated with the relevant arrangements;

(ii) full address of the dwelling including the postcode sufficient to be able to identify it;

(b) for stamp duty land tax–

(i) the unique transaction reference number (if a land transaction return has been submitted to HMRC at the time the prescribed information is provided);

(ii) title number or numbers of the land associated with the relevant arrangements;

(iii) full address or situation of the land including (where available) the postcode, or information sufficient that the land can be uniquely identified;

(c) for stamp duty reserve tax transactions a full description of the shares or securities associated with the relevant arrangements, including the–

(i) number of shares or securities;

(ii) class or classes of the shares;
(iii) name of the company or other body to which the shares relate;
(iv) nominal value;
(v) consideration paid.

4(3) For the purposes of paragraph (1)–

(a) **"unique identifier"** is to be construed as follows–

(i) where the promoter reference number is not reported in a tax return for an individual, the national insurance number and unique tax reference number of the person making the report;

(ii) where the promoter reference number is not reported in a tax return for a trust or company, the unique tax reference number for the trust or company (as the case may be);

(iii) for inheritance tax purposes, the unique tax reference number and any inheritance tax reference previously allocated by HMRC to the person making the report;

(iv) for stamp duty reserve tax transactions authorised by different arrangements under regulation 4A of the Stamp Duty Reserve Tax Regulations 1986, the unique transaction reference provided by the reporting system under the authorised arrangements;

(b) **"relevant date of the transaction(s)"** means–

(i) in respect of capital gains tax or income tax, the date on which the tax year, in which the relevant arrangements enable or seek to enable a tax advantage to be obtained, ends;

(ii) in respect of corporation tax, with the exception of partnerships where one or more of the partners is a company, either the date on which the accounting period, in which the relevant arrangements enable or seek to enable a tax advantage to be obtained, ends, or, where the company does not have an accounting period, the date of the first transaction forming part of the relevant arrangements;

(iii) in respect of corporation tax in relation to partnerships, including where one or more of the partners is a company, the date on which the tax year in which the relevant arrangements enable or seek to enable a tax advantage to be obtained, ends;

(iv) in respect of annual tax on enveloped dwellings, the date on which the chargeable period, in which the relevant arrangements enable or seek to enable a tax advantage to be obtained, ends;

(v) in respect of inheritance tax, the date of the first transaction forming part of the relevant arrangements;

(vi) in respect of stamp duty land tax, the effective date of the land transaction that forms part of the relevant arrangements that enable a tax advantage to be obtained;

(vii) in respect of stamp duty reserve tax, the date of the transaction that forms part of the relevant arrangements that enable a tax advantage to be obtained;

(viii) in respect of petroleum revenue tax, the end of each chargeable period within which a tax advantage may arise.

REPORT OF PROMOTER REFERENCE NUMBER: PRESCRIBED FORM AND MANNER

5(1) The report made under paragraphs 2(b) and 4(b) of section 253 of the Act (duty of persons to notify the Commissioners) must be made in the form prescribed in Schedule 1 to these Regulations. A separate report must be made for each tax which the relevant arrangements enable or seek to enable an advantage to be obtained.

5(2) The completed report must be sent by post to one of the addresses listed in Schedule 2 to these Regulations.

REPORT OF PROMOTER REFERENCE NUMBER: PRESCRIBED TIME

6(1) A report under section 253 of the Act (duty of persons to notify the Commissioners) must be made by the deadlines set out in paragraphs (2), (3) and (4).

6(2) Where a tax return for an individual, partnership, trustee, company or a return for the purposes of the annual tax on enveloped dwellings is not submitted by the date in section 253(3)(a) or (b) of the Act in relation to the period within which a tax advantage may arise, the report must be made by the end of the fifth working day following the date on which the return was required to be submitted.

6(3) Where there is no tax return covering the period within which a tax advantage may arise, then the report must be made–

(a) in the case of an individual, partnership or trustee, by 31st January following the end of each tax year within which a tax advantage may arise;

(b) in the case of a company, not later than 12 months from the end of each accounting period within which a tax advantage may arise;

(c) in the case of an annual tax on enveloped dwellings return, not later than 30 days from the first day of the chargeable period in which the person is within the charge or would have been within the charge but for the relevant arrangements, for each period within which a tax advantage may arise.

6(4) For the purposes of inheritance tax, stamp duty land tax, stamp duty reserve tax, and petroleum revenue tax, the report must be made–

(a) for inheritance tax, not later than the sixth month after the end of the month which the first transaction under the relevant arrangements was entered into;

(b) for stamp duty land tax, not later than 30 days from the effective date of each land transaction which forms part of the relevant arrangements within which a tax advantage may arise;

(c) for stamp duty reserve tax–

(i) in respect of transactions under regulation 4 of the Stamp Duty Reserve Tax Regulations 1986, not later than the time that the notice of the charge to tax is due to be made to HMRC (the accountable date), or

(ii) where a transaction is authorised by different arrangements under regulation 4A of the Stamp Duty Reserve Tax Regulations 1986, not later than the seventh day of the month after the month in which the charge to tax occurred or would have occurred but for the relevant arrangements;

(d) for petroleum revenue tax, not later than 7 days from the end of each chargeable period within which a tax advantage may arise.

6(5) Where a company does not have an accounting period, the report must be made not later than 24 months from the date of the first transaction which forms part of the relevant arrangements and annually thereafter for any period within which a tax advantage arises.

6(6) For the purposes of paragraph (2), **"working day"** means a day that is not a Saturday or Sunday, Christmas Day, Good Friday or any day that is a bank holiday under the Banking and Finance Dealings Act 1971.

ONGOING DUTY TO PROVIDE INFORMATION: PRESCRIBED INFORMATION AND DOCUMENTS

7(1) The following information is prescribed for the purposes of section 257(2) of the Act (ongoing duty to provide information following HMRC notice)–

(a) the name or names by which the monitored promoter refers to the monitored arrangements or monitored proposal;

(b) a summary description of the monitored arrangements or monitored proposal and how they are intended to result in a tax advantage;

(c) a detailed description of each part of the monitored arrangements or monitored proposal and the details of how they are intended to result in a tax advantage;

(d) the legislative provisions (whether in primary legislation, secondary legislation or both) that the person identified in section 257(1) contends provide the basis for the intended tax advantage under the monitored arrangements or monitored proposal;

(e) any reference number allocated under section 311 of the Finance Act 2004 (arrangements to be given reference number);

(f) if the monitored arrangements or monitored proposal have not been disclosed under Part 7 of the Finance Act 2004 (disclosure of tax avoidance schemes), an explanation as to why the monitored arrangements or monitored proposal have not been disclosed;

(g) if the monitored arrangements or monitored proposal are funded by or will require funding from third parties, the names and addresses of the third parties, the level of funding required and the date on which the third parties agreed to provide funding;

(h) the name and address of any person (including any legal advisers) consulted in respect of the monitored arrangements or monitored proposal;

(i) the name and address of any person otherwise involved in planning, organising or operating the monitored arrangements and detailed information on the involvement and role of that person;

(j) a list of each and every fee paid or to be paid by clients to use or participate in the monitored arrangements with a description of what each fee is charged for or will be charged for;

(k) if not included in (b), (c) or (d) above, a list of all taxes in respect of which it is expected to obtain a tax advantage.

7(2) The following are prescribed documents for the purposes of section 257(2) of the Act–

(a) standard letters and templates of documents to be sent to clients regarding the monitored arrangements and monitored proposals;

(b) documentation which is designed or intended to be used in the operation of the monitored arrangements and monitored proposals;

(c) copies of all documents used to market, promote or advertise the monitored arrangements and monitored proposals;

(d) all correspondence which has been sent to, or received from, a client or prospective client or other person involved in the monitored arrangements and monitored proposals and which concerns the arrangements or the proposal;

(e) all correspondence which has been sent to, or received from, any other person which concerns the monitored arrangements and monitored proposals or matters related to the monitored arrangements and monitored proposals;

(f) any agreement signed or otherwise entered into by each client in respect of the monitored arrangements and monitored proposals.

7(3) **"Prescribed documents"** in paragraph (2) includes documents produced in writing or by electronic means.

MONITORED PROMOTERS: PRESCRIBED CLIENT INFORMATION

8 The following information is prescribed for the purposes of section 259(9)(b) of the Act (monitored promoters: duty to provide information about clients)–

(a) where C is an individual, the national insurance number and unique tax reference number identifying C;

(b) where C is a trust, partnership or company, the unique tax reference number identifying C;

(c) in compliance with subsection (3) of section 265 of the Act (duty to provide information to monitored promoter), where C has not provided the information in sub-paragraph (a) or (b), whether or not C has informed the monitored promoter that C has neither a national insurance number nor a unique tax reference number;

(d) the date on which C became a client of the monitored promoter within the meaning of section 259(5) of the Act;

(e) the date on which C entered into transactions referred to in subsection (7) of section 259 of the Act;

(f) the date on which C informed the monitored promoter of the information required by section 265(2) or 265(3) of the Act or, if provided to the monitored promoter earlier, the earlier date;

(g) whether C was a direct client of the monitored promoter, or was acting through an intermediary ("I") and the name and address of I;

(h) the fee or commission paid or payable by C to I in respect of the monitored arrangements or monitored proposals.

INTERMEDIARIES: PRESCRIBED CLIENT INFORMATION

9 The following information about the person ("C") is prescribed for the purposes of section 260(7)(b) of the Act (intermediaries: duty to provide information about clients)–

(a) where the intermediary knows the national insurance number, unique tax reference number or both which identify C, those numbers;

(b) the name, address and the promoter reference number of the monitored promoter in respect of the monitored proposals referred to in section 260(1);

(c) the name and address of any other intermediary from which, or to which, C has been referred in relation to the monitored proposals;

(d) the date on which the information referred to in section 260(5) was communicated;

(e) any fee or commission paid or payable to I in respect of the monitored proposals.

ENQUIRY FOLLOWING PROVISION OF CLIENT INFORMATION: PRESCRIBED INFORMATION

10(1) The information set out in paragraphs (2), (3) and (4) is prescribed for the purposes of section 261(2) of the Act (enquiry following provision of client information).

10(2) Where the authorised officer's suspicion referred to in section 261(1)(b) of the Act is that information has not been provided in respect of a person under section 259 of the Act, the prescribed information under section 261(2) of the Act is–

(i) the information prescribed by regulation 8;

(ii) the reason or reasons why the prescribed information in regulation 8 was not provided as required by section 259.

10(3) Where the authorised officer's suspicion referred to in section 261(1)(b) of the Act is that information has not been provided in respect of a person under section 260 of the Act, the prescribed information under section 261(2) of the Act is–

(a) the information prescribed by regulation 9;

(b) the date of any transaction under section 261(2) of the Act implementing the relevant arrangements or relevant proposal;

(c) the reason or reasons why the prescribed information in regulation 9 was not provided as required by section 260 of the Act.

COPY DOCUMENTS: PRESCRIBED CONDITIONS OR EXCEPTIONS

11(1) The following conditions are prescribed for the purposes of section 268(1) of the Act (production of documents: compliance)–

(a) the copy document must be an exact copy of the original document, without any amendments, corrections or deletions;

(b) the original document must be retained by the person as required;

(c) the person required to produce the document must not alter the original document or allow it to be altered.

11(2) Subject to other provisions in the Tax Acts on the retention of records and documents, the original document under paragraph (1)(b) shall be retained–

(i) for the purposes of sections 255 and 257 of the Act until such time as the monitoring notice or replacement monitoring is withdrawn under section 245 of the Act;

(ii) for the purposes of section 262 of the Act, until such time as the conduct notice or replacement conduct notice is withdrawn under section 240 of the Act or expires at the end of the period under section 241(2) of the Act.

11(3) Nothing in paragraph (1)(a) prevents a person from redacting information in a copy document which is privileged information within the meaning given in section 271 of the Act.

SCHEDULE 1 – REPORT OF PROMOTER REFERENCE NUMBERS

Regulation 5(1)

HM Revenue & Customs

Report of promoter reference number

When to use this form

Please fill in this form if you have been given a promoter reference number (PRN) and you expect to get a tax advantage from one of the promoter's tax avoidance schemes. It is important that you report the PRN to HM Revenue & Customs (HMRC). If you fail to report a PRN to HMRC we will ask you to pay a penalty.

Details about the promoter reference number

If you complete a personal, trust partnership, company or Annual Tax on Enveloped Dwellings (ATED) tax return, you usually have to report the PRN in your tax return.

If your tax return is late you will need to report the PRN on this form within 5 working days of the date the return was due.

If there is no return covering the period, you will need to make the report by:

- 31 January following the end of the tax year for which you expect to get a tax advantage
- 12 months after the end of the accounting period for which you expect to get a tax advantage
- 30 days of the first day in the chargeable period for which you expect to get a tax advantage on which you were within the charge to the ATED

If exceptionally, you are a company and do not have an accounting period, you will need to report the PRN within 24 months of the first transaction forming part of the tax avoidance scheme (and annually thereafter).

When to report the PRN

You will need to use this form to report the PRN if the tax advantage is expected to arise for:

- Inheritance Tax - within 6 months of the end of the month in which the first transaction forming part of the tax avoidance scheme took place
- Petroleum Revenue Tax - within 7 days of the end of the half-year chargeable period in which you expect to get a tax advantage
- Stamp Duty Land Tax - within 30 days of the transaction forming part of the tax avoidance scheme or for which you expect to get a tax advantage
- Stamp Duty Reserve Tax - where the transaction is not settled through CREST, with the notice of the charge to tax but no later than 7 days from the end of the month in which the transaction took place
- Stamp Duty Reserve Tax - within 7 days of the end of the month in which the transaction took place where the transaction is settled through CREST

For details on where to submit this form, please read 'Where to send this form' on page 3.

Your details

1 Full name use capital letters

2 Full address

Postcode

Your promoter reference number

3 Promoter reference number (PRN)

About the tax advantage

4 Which tax do you expect to get a tax advantage?
Please tick 1 box and provide the relevant details in box 5 below. Enter:

Annual Tax on Enveloped Dwellings	the title number or numbers and the full address of the property (if the property does not have a postcode you must provide sufficient detail to allow us to identify the property)
Capital Gains Tax	your Unique Taxpayer Reference (UTR) and National Insurance number (for trustees or partnerships, enter the UTR for the trust or partnership)
Corporation Tax	the UTR of the company (or if the form is being sent by a partnership the UTR of the partnership)
Income Tax	your UTR and National Insurance number (for trustees or partnerships, enter the UTR for the trust or partnership)
Inheritance Tax	your UTR and any Inheritance Tax reference previously allocated to you by HM Revenue & Customs
Petroleum Revenue Tax	the name of the oil field for which you expect to get a tax advantage and your participator's reference for that field
Stamp Duty Land Tax	the title number or numbers, full address of the property (if the property does not have a postcode you must provide sufficient detail to allow us to identify the property) and the Unique Transaction Reference number
Stamp Duty Reserve Tax	(if the transaction is not settled through CREST) a full description of the shares or securities, including number, class, nominal value, the name of the company to which the shares relate and consideration paid (if the transaction is settled through CREST) the CREST transaction reference ID

5 Unique identifier details – include reference number(s), names and addresses as explained in question 4 above

Details of transaction

Consider when you expect to get a tax advantage and enter the end of the accounting period or transaction date for:

- Annual Tax on Enveloped Dwellings - the end of the chargeable period
- Capital Gains Tax, Income Tax and trustees and partnerships - the end of the tax year
- Corporation Tax - the end of the accounting period unless exceptionally there is no accounting period - then enter the date of the first transaction
- Inheritance Tax - the date of the first transaction
- Petroleum Revenue Tax - the end of the half-year chargeable period
- Stamp Duty Land Tax or Stamp Duty Reserve Tax - the date of the transaction

6 Date of transaction DD MM YYYY or End of period DD MM YYYY

Declaration

The information I have given on this form is correct and complete to the best of my knowledge and belief.

Full name of signatory use capital letters

Signature

Date DD MM YYYY

Where to send this form

Please return your completed form to:

HM Revenue & Customs
Counter Avoidance Directorate
CA Intelligence S0528
PO Box 194
BOOTLE
L69 9AA

In the case of Stamp Duty Reserve Tax where the transaction is not settled through CREST, send this form to:

HM Revenue & Customs
SDRT Compliance Team
9th Floor, City Centre House
30 Union Street
BIRMINGHAM
B2 4AB

SCHEDULE 2 – ADDRESSES TO SEND THE PROMOTER REFERENCE NUMBER REPORTS

Regulation 5(2)

In respect of arrangements involving stamp duty reserve tax transactions under regulation 4 of the Stamp Duty Reserve Tax Regulations (1986), the completed report under section 253 must be sent to–

HM Revenue and Customs
SDRT Compliance Team
9th Floor, City Centre House
30 Union Street
BIRMINGHAM
B2 4AR

For all other reports made under section 253 (including those involving stamp duty reserve tax transactions under regulation 4A of the Stamp Duty Reserve Tax Regulations (1986)), the completed report must be sent to–

HM Revenue and Customs
Counter Avoidance Directorate
CA Intelligence S0528
PO Box 194
BOOTLE
L69 9AA

PENSIONS ACT 2014 (SAVINGS) ORDER 2015

(SI 2015/1502, as amended by SI 2015/2058 and SI 2016/252)

Made on 14 July 2015 by the Secretary of State for Work and Pensions in exercise of the powers conferred upon them by s. 56(8) of the Pensions Act 2014.

CITATION, COMMENCEMENT AND INTERPRETATION

1(1) This Order may be cited as the Pensions Act 2014 (Savings) Order 2015.

1(2) This Order comes into force on 6th April 2016.

1(3) Articles 2(1), (2), (3A) and (5A) cease to have effect on 6th April 2019.

1(4) In this Order–

"the Act" means the Pensions Act 2014;

"the 1993 Act" means the Pension Schemes Act 1993;

"contracted-out employment" and **"contributions equivalent premium"** have the meanings given in section 181(1) of the 1993 Act;

"earner" has the meaning given in section 181(1) of the 1993 Act;

"HMRC" means the Commissioners for Her Majesty's Revenue and Customs;

"PPF assessment period" means an assessment period in relation to the Board of the Pension Protection Fund within the meaning of section 132 of the Pensions Act 2004;

"reference scheme minimum benefit" means a salary related benefit which is defined by reference to section 12B of the 1993 Act (reference scheme) and which, under the provisions of the scheme, will be provided as a minimum pension payable to the member;

"salary related contracted-out scheme" and **"the second abolition date"** have the meanings given in section 181(1) of the 1993 Act.

History – In art. 1(3), the words "2(1), (2) and (3A)" substituted for the words "2(1) and (2)" by SI 2015/2058, art. 3(2)(a), with effect from 6 April 2016.
In art. 1(3), the words ", (3A) and (5A)" substituted for the words "and (3A)" by SI 2016/252, art. 5(2), with effect from 6 April 2016.
In art. 1(4), definition of "reference scheme minimum benefit" inserted by SI 2015/2058, art. 3(2)(b), with effect from 6 April 2016.

SAVINGS

2(1) The provisions of the 1993 Act specified in paragraph (2) and repealed by paragraphs 5, 8, 9 to 11, 22, 28, 29, 36 and 46(1), (2) and (4) of Schedule 13 to the Act (abolition of contracting-out for salary related schemes) continue to have effect, despite those repeals, for the purposes of allowing or requiring the trustees or managers of a scheme that was a salary related contracted-out scheme, and HMRC, to carry out any necessary activity relating to any period of contracted-out employment which occurred before the second abolition date.

2(2) The provisions are–

(a) section 7 (issue of contracting-out certificates);

(b) section 9 (requirements for certification of schemes: general);

(c) section 11 (elections as to employment covered by contracting-out certificates);

(d) sections 12A to 12D (requirements for certification of occupational pension schemes applying from 6th April 1997);

(e) sections 34 to 36 (cancellation, variation, surrender and refusal of certificates);

(f) section 41 (reduced rates of Class 1 contributions);

(g) [omitted by SI 2015/2058, art. 3(3)(b);]

(h) section 53(3) (supervision: former contracted-out schemes);

(i) [omitted by SI 2016/252, art. 5(3)(b);]

(j) Schedule 2, paragraphs 1 to 4 and 6 to 8 (certification regulations).

2(2A) Sections 12A to 12D of the 1993 Act (requirements for certification of occupational pension schemes applying from 6th April 1997) continue to have effect, as if the repeals made by paragraphs 10 and 11 of Schedule 13 to the Act had not been made, in relation to a scheme that was a salary related contracted-out scheme and which provides a reference scheme minimum benefit in order to meet the statutory standard in section 12A, and in relation to the period of a member's contracted-out employment which ended before or on the second abolition date.

2(3) Section 16(2) of the 1993 Act (revaluation of earnings factors for the purposes of section 14: early leavers etc) continues to have effect, as if that subsection had not been substituted by paragraph 16 of Schedule 13 to the Act, in relation to earners whose service in contracted-out employment ended before the second abolition date.

2(3A) Section 50 of the 1993 Act (powers of HMRC to approve arrangements for scheme ceasing to be certified) continues to have effect, as if that section had not been repealed by paragraph 33 of Schedule 13 to the Act, in relation to a salary related contracted-out scheme which ceased to be such a scheme before the second abolition date.

2(4) Sections 55 to 68 of the 1993 Act continue to have effect as if they had not been repealed by paragraph 37 of Schedule 13 to the Act, for the purposes of allowing or requiring the trustees or managers of a scheme described in paragraph (5) to elect to pay, and pay, a contributions equivalent premium in relation to members of the scheme whose contracted-out employment ended before the second abolition date.

2(5) A scheme referred to in paragraph (4) is–

(a) one which started to wind up before the second abolition date; or

(b) one–

(i) which had not started to wind up before the second abolition date;

(ii) which entered a PPF assessment period before 6th April 2016, and where the assessment period continues after 6th April 2019; and

(iii) where the trustees or managers of the scheme elected to pay a contributions equivalent premium after the start of the PPF assessment period but cannot make that payment during the assessment period due to the restriction in section 135(4)(b) of the Pensions Act 2004 (restrictions on winding up, discharge of liabilities etc).

2(5A) Sections 55 to 68 of the 1993 Act (state scheme premiums) continue to have effect as if they had not been repealed by paragraph 37 of Schedule 13 to the 2014 Act (abolition of contracting-out for salary related schemes) for the purposes of allowing action to be taken by HMRC and the trustees or managers of a scheme in relation to the payment of a contributions equivalent premium in respect of an earner to whom section 55(2)(a) to (c) applied before the second abolition date.

2(5B) Sections 56 to 68 of the 1993 Act additionally continue to have effect as if they had not been repealed by paragraph 37 of Schedule 13 to the 2014 Act insofar as necessary for the purposes of article 3 of the Pensions Act 2014 (Contributions Equivalent Premium) (Consequential Provision) and (Savings) (Amendment) Order 2016 with the modifications specified in paragraphs (5C) to (5F).

2(5C) In section 56 (provisions supplementary to s55)–

(a) omit subsection (2);

(b) in subsection (4) for the wording following paragraph (b) substitute–

"the earner's length of service in employment for the purposes of article 3(3)(b) of the Pensions Act 2014 (Contributions Equivalent Premium) (Consequential Provision) and (Savings) (Amendment) Order 2016 shall include any period of linked qualifying service which was contracted-out employment by reference to the other scheme.";

(c) in subsection (6) for "section 55(2A)" substitute "article 3(5) of the Pensions Act 2014 (Contributions Equivalent Premium) (Consequential Provision) and (Savings) (Amendment) Order 2016";

(d) in subsection (7)–

(i) for "section 55" substitute "article 3 of the Pensions Act 2014 (Contributions Equivalent Premium) (Consequential Provision) and (Savings) (Amendment) Order 2016"; and

(ii) for "sections 55 to 68" substitute "sections 56 to 68"; and

(e) in subsection (8) for "section 55" substitute "article 3 of the Pensions Act 2014 (Contributions Equivalent Premium) (Consequential Provision) and (Savings) (Amendment) Order 2016".

2(5D) In section 57 (elections to pay contributions equivalent premiums)–

(a) for subsection (1) substitute–

"57(1) Where the relevant person is required to make a contributions equivalent premium or elects to do so under article 3 of the Pensions Act 2014 (Contributions Equivalent Premium) (Consequential Provision) and (Savings) (Amendment) Order 2016, the relevant person must notify HMRC in writing in such form as HMRC may reasonably require for the purpose of identifying the earner to whom the election relates.

57(1A) Such notification must be given–

(a) where the circumstances specified in article 3(5)(d) of that Order apply, within the period of two years starting with the date the scheme began to be wound up; or

(b) where the circumstances specified in article 3(5)(a), (b) or (c) apply, within the period beginning one month before, and ending 6 months after, the date on which the earner's service in employment in relation to the scheme or membership of the scheme ceased.

57(1B) In this section the **"relevant person"** means–

(a) in a case where a transfer has been made in relation to the scheme under section 161 of the Pensions Act 2004 (effect of Board assuming responsibility for a scheme), the Board of the Pension Protection Fund (as defined in that Act); and

(b) in all other cases, the trustees or managers of the scheme.";

(b) in subsection (2) for "prescribed person" substitute "relevant person"; and

(c) omit subsection (4).

2(5E) In section 58 (amount of premiums payable under s. 55) for "section 55(2)" substitute "article 3 of the Pensions Act 2014 (Contributions Equivalent Premium) (Consequential Provision) and (Savings) (Amendment) Order 2016".

2(5F) In section 60 (effect of payment of premium on rights)–

(a) in subsection (4) for "section 55(2A)(a) and (b), (d) and (e)" substitute "article 3(5)(a), (b) and (d) of the Pensions Act 2014 (Contributions Equivalent Premium) (Consequential Provision) and (Savings) (Amendment) Order 2016"; and

(b) in subsection (5) for "section 55(2A)(c)" substitute "article 3(5)(c) of the Pensions Act 2014 (Contributions Equivalent Premium) (Consequential Provision) and (Savings) (Amendment) Order 2016".

2(6) Section 87(1)(a) of the 1993 Act (general protection principle) continues to have effect, as if sub-paragraph (i) had not been substituted by paragraph 38 of Schedule 13 to the Act, in relation to earners whose service in contracted-out employment ended before the second abolition date.

History – In art. 2(1), "33," (which appeared after "29, ") omitted by SI 2015/2058, art. 3(3)(a), with effect from 6 April 2016.
In art. 2(1), ", 37" (which appeared after "36 "omitted by SI 2016/252, art. 5(3)(a), with effect from 6 April 2016.
Art. 2(2)(g) omitted by SI 2015/2058, art. 3(3)(b), with effect from 6 April 2016.
Art. 2(2)(i) omitted by SI 2016/252, art. 5(3)(b), with effect from 6 April 2016.
Art. 2(2A) inserted by SI 2015/2058, art. 3(3)(c), with effect from 6 April 2016.
Art. 2(3A) inserted by SI 2015/2058, art. 3(3)(d), with effect from 6 April 2016.
In art. 2(4), the words "on or" (which appeared after the words "employment ended" omitted by SI 2016/252, art. 5(3)(c), with effect from 6 April 2016.
Art. 2(5A)–(5F) inserted by SI 2016/262, art. 5(3)(d), with effect from 6 April 2016.
Art. 2(6) inserted by SI 2015/2058, art. 3(3)(e), with effect from 6 April 2016.

ENFORCEMENT BY DEDUCTION FROM ACCOUNTS (PRESCRIBED INFORMATION) REGULATIONS 2015

(SI 2015/1986)

Made on 8 December 2015 by the Commissioners for Her Majesty's Revenue and Customs in exercise of the powers conferred upon them by para. 3(2), 8(2)(a), 8(2)(c), 8(2)(d), 8(4)(b) and 23(1) of Sch. 8 to the Finance (No.2) Act 2015. Operative from 25 January 2016.

CITATION, COMMENCEMENT AND EXTENT

1(1) These Regulations may be cited as the Enforcement by Deduction from Accounts (Prescribed Information) Regulations 2015 and come into force on 25th January 2016.

1(2) These Regulations extend to England and Wales and Northern Ireland only.

INTERPRETATION

2 In these Regulations–

"account details" in respect of an account held by P means–

(a) any account number;

(b) any roll number;

(c) any sort code;

(d) the type of account, including whether or not it is a joint account;

(e) the account balance (in the currency in which the account is held);

(f) whether interest is payable in respect of amounts standing to the credit of the account and, if so, the rate of interest payable;

(g) any minimum balance required to keep the account open;

(h) any contractual term by virtue of which an account holder or interested third party may suffer economic loss where a hold notice or deduction notice is, or has been, given;

(i) specified information about–

(i) any account holder other than P;

(ii) any person (not falling within paragraph (i)) who is an interested third party in relation to the account;

(iii) any person who, in respect of the account, has power of attorney;

"P" means the person in respect of whom HMRC has given an information notice or, as the case may be, hold notice;

"Schedule 8" means Schedule 8 to the Finance (No.2) Act 2015;

"specified information" in respect of a person means–

(a) name and address;

(b) national insurance number;

(c) all email addresses;

(d) all telephone numbers;

(e) in respect of an account which is a joint account, the proportion of the balance of that joint account to which the person is entitled.

INFORMATION

3(1) Information is only prescribed under these Regulations if it–

(a) is in the possession of, or immediately available to, a deposit-taker at the time the deposit-taker is given an information notice or, as the case may be, a hold notice, and

(b) describes the account, or, as the case may be, person, at the relevant time.

3(2) The relevant time for the purposes of regulation 3(1)(b) is–

(a) in the case of the information prescribed by regulations 5(1)(f) and 5(1)(g), immediately after the deposit-taker has complied with the hold notice, and

(b) in any other case, immediately before the deposit-taker complies with the information notice, or, as the case may be, hold notice.

PRESCRIBED INFORMATION IN RESPECT OF AN INFORMATION NOTICE

4 The following information is prescribed for the purposes of paragraph 3(2) of Schedule 8 (information notice)–

(a) account details for each account P holds with the deposit-taker;

(b) specified information in relation to P.

PRESCRIBED INFORMATION IN RESPECT OF A HOLD NOTICE WHERE AN ACCOUNT IS AN AFFECTED ACCOUNT

5(1) The following information is prescribed for the purposes of paragraph 8(2) of Schedule 8 (duty to notify HMRC and account-holders etc)–

(a) account details for each account P holds with the deposit-taker;

(b) specified information in relation to P;

(c) confirmation of which of the accounts that P holds with the deposit-taker is an affected account;

(d) the date on which the deposit-taker complied with paragraph 6(1) of Schedule 8 (effect of hold notice);

(e) confirmation that the deposit-taker understands the effect of paragraph 14(1)(g) of Schedule 8 (penalties);

(f) the total of all held amounts notified by the deposit-taker under paragraph 8(2)(b) of Schedule 8 in response to a hold notice;

(g) in respect of each account which P holds with the deposit-taker, the amount standing to the credit of the account which is not subject to action taken by the deposit-taker under paragraph 6(3) of Schedule 8;

(h) a description of any economic loss suffered by an account holder or interested third party as a result of any contractual term specified in the definition of **"account details"** in regulation 2 at sub-paragraph (h).

5(2) In this regulation **"held amounts"** is to be read in accordance with paragraph 7 of Schedule 8.

PRESCRIBED INFORMATION IN RESPECT OF A HOLD NOTICE WHERE AN ACCOUNT IS NOT AFFECTED ACCOUNT

6(1) The following information is prescribed for the purposes of paragraph 8(4)(b) of Schedule 8.

6(2) The information which the deposit-taker has taken into account to determine that there are no affected accounts.

ENFORCEMENT BY DEDUCTION FROM ACCOUNTS (IMPOSITION OF CHARGES BY DEPOSIT-TAKERS) REGULATIONS 2016

(SI 2016/44)

Made on 18 January 2016 by the Commissioners for Her Majesty's Revenue and Customs in exercise of the powers conferred upon them by para. 20(2)(e) of Sch. 8 to the Finance (No. 2) Act 2015. Operative from 10 February 2016.

CITATION, COMMENCEMENT AND EXTENT

1(1) These Regulations may be cited as the Enforcement by Deduction from Accounts (Imposition of Charges by Deposit-takers) Regulations 2016 and come into force on 10th February 2016.

1(2) These Regulations extend to England and Wales and Northern Ireland only.

INTERPRETATION

2 In these Regulations **"administrative costs"** means the administrative costs incurred by a deposit-taker in complying with an obligation under Schedule 8 to the Finance (No.2) Act 2015 to which a final payment required under paragraph 13(11)(b)(ii) of that Schedule relates.

IMPOSITION OF CHARGES

3 A deposit-taker may impose a charge upon an account holder in respect of administrative costs only where–

(a) there is an agreement between it and the account holder (or, as the case may be, account holders), which provides that the deposit-taker may charge a fee in respect of those costs,

(b) the deposit taker–

(i) has made the final payment required by paragraph 13(11)(b)(ii), and

(ii) has not previously imposed a charge in respect of those costs, and

(c) the amount of the charge imposed does not exceed the amount specified in regulation 4.

AMOUNT THAT CAN BE CHARGED FOR ADMINISTRATIVE COSTS

4 The amount specified in this regulation is the lesser of–

(a) the amount of those administrative costs reasonably incurred by the deposit-taker, and

(b) £55.

SOCIAL SECURITY REVALUATION OF EARNINGS FACTORS ORDER 2016

(SI 2016/205)

Made on 22 February 2016 by the Secretary of State in exercise of the powers conferred upon them by s. 148(3) and (4) and 189(1), (4) and (5) of the Social Security Administration Act 1992. Operative from 6 April 2016.

CITATION AND COMMENCEMENT

1 This Order may be cited as the Social Security Revaluation of Earnings Factors Order 2016 and shall come into force on 6th April 2016.

REVALUATION OF EARNINGS FACTORS

2 The earnings factors for tax years specified in the Schedule to this Order in so far as they are relevant–

(a) to the calculation–

(i) of the additional pension in the rate of any long-term benefit, or

(ii) of any guaranteed minimum pension; or

(b) to any other calculation required under Part 3 of the Pension Schemes Act 1993 (including that Part as modified by or under any other enactment),

are directed to be increased for those tax years by the percentage of their amount shown opposite those tax years in that Schedule.

ROUNDING OF FRACTIONAL AMOUNTS

3 Where any earnings factor relevant to the calculation specified in article 2(a)(i) of this Order, as increased in accordance with this Order, would not but for this article be expressed as a whole number of pounds, it shall be so expressed by rounding down any fraction of a pound less than one half and rounding up any other fraction of a pound.

SCHEDULE

Article 2

Percentage increase of earnings factor for specified tax years

Tax year	*Percentage increase*
1978–1979	771.5
1979–1980	669.2
1980–1981	542.6
1981–1982	438.2
1982–1983	388.8
1983–1984	353.9
1984–1985	320.2
1985–1986	294.2
1986–1987	262.0
1987–1988	237.1
1988–1989	210.1
1989–1990	179.9
1990–1991	160.8
1991–1992	136.9
1992–1993	122.4
1993–1994	111.8
1994–1995	105.5
1995–1996	96.8
1996–1997	91.4
1997–1998	82.3

Tax year	*Percentage increase*
1998–1999	74.3
1999–2000	67.3
2000–2001	57.4
2001–2002	51.3
2002–2003	45.1
2003–2004	40.0
2004–2005	34.9
2005–2006	29.6
2006–2007	25.3
2007–2008	20.4
2008–2009	15.5
2009–2010	12.1
2010–2011	10.7
2011–2012	8.3
2012–2013	6.3
2013–2014	4.5
2014–2015	3.5
2015–2016	2.0

STATE PENSION REVALUATION FOR TRANSITIONAL PENSIONS ORDER 2016

(SI 2016/1141)

Made on 23 November 2016 by the Secretary of State for Work and Pensions in exercise of the powers conferred upon them by s. 148AC(3) and 189(1) and (4) of the Social Security Administration Act 1992. Operative in accordance with art. 1(2).

CITATION, COMMENCEMENT AND INTERPRETATION

1(1) This Order may be cited as the State Pension Revaluation for Transitional Pensions Order 2016.

1(2) This Order comes into force on–

(a) 19th December 2016 for the purpose of making an award on a claim for a state pension under regulation 15(1) of the Social Security (Claims and Payments) Regulations 1987 to a person who reaches pensionable age on or after 10th April 2017; and

(b) 9th April 2017 for all other purposes.

1(3) In this article **"a state pension"** means a state pension under Part 1 of the Pensions Act 2014.

THE INCREASE IN THE GENERAL LEVEL OF PRICES

2 For the purposes of section 148AC(3) and (4) of the Social Security Administration Act 1992 (revaluation for transitional pensions under Pensions Act 2014), the increase in the general level of prices during the review period is 1.0 per cent.

SOCIAL SECURITY REVALUATION OF EARNINGS FACTORS ORDER 2017

(SI 2017/287)

Made on 7 March 2017 by the Secretary of State for Work and Pensions in exercise of the powers conferred upon them by s. 148(2) of the Social Security Administration Act 1992. Operative from 6 April 2017.

CITATION AND COMMENCEMENT

1 This Order may be cited as the Social Security Revaluation of Earnings Factors Order 2017 and shall come into force on 6th April 2017.

REVALUATION OF EARNINGS FACTORS

2 The earnings factors for tax years specified in the Schedule to this Order in so far as they are relevant–

(a) to the calculation–

(i) of the additional pension in the rate of any long-term benefit, or

(ii) of any guaranteed minimum pension; or

(b) to any other calculation required under Part 3 of the Pension Schemes Act 1993 (including that Part as modified by or under any other enactment),

are directed to be increased for those tax years by the percentage of their amount shown opposite those tax years in that Schedule.

ROUNDING OF FRACTIONAL AMOUNTS

3 Where any earnings factor relevant to the calculation specified in article 2(a)(i), as increased in accordance with this Order, would not but for this article be expressed as a whole number of pounds, it shall be so expressed by rounding down any fraction of a pound less than one half and rounding up any other fraction of a pound.

SCHEDULE

Article 2

Percentage increase of earnings factor for specified tax years

Tax year	*Percentage increase*
1978–1979	794.1
1979–1980	689.2
1980–1981	559.3
1981–1982	452.2
1982–1983	401.5
1983–1984	365.7
1984–1985	331.2
1985–1986	304.5
1986–1987	271.4
1987–1988	245.8
1988–1989	218.1
1989–1990	187.1
1990–1991	167.6
1991–1992	143.0
1992–1993	128.2
1993–1994	117.3
1994–1995	110.8
1995–1996	101.9
1996–1997	96.4
1997–1998	87.1

Tax year	*Percentage increase*
1998–1999	78.8
1999–2000	71.6
2000–2001	61.5
2001–2002	55.3
2002–2003	48.9
2003–2004	43.7
2004–2005	38.4
2005–2006	33.0
2006–2007	28.6
2007–2008	23.5
2008–2009	18.6
2009–2010	15.0
2010–2011	13.6
2011–2012	11.1
2012–2013	9.1
2013–2014	7.2
2014–2015	6.2
2015–2016	4.7
2016–2017	2.6

STATE PENSION REVALUATION FOR TRANSITIONAL PENSIONS ORDER 2017

(SI 2017/1151)

Made on 27 November 2017 by the Secretary of State in exercise of the powers conferred upon them by s. 148AC(3), 189(1), (4) of the Social Security Administration Act 1992. Operative in accordance with art. 1(2).

CITATION AND COMMENCEMENT

1(1) This Order may be cited as the State Pension Revaluation for Transitional Pensions Order 2017.

1(2) This Order comes into force on–

(a) the day which is 21 days after the date on which this Order is laid for the purpose of making an award on a claim for a state pension under regulation 15(1) of the Social Security (Claims and Payments) Regulations 1987 (advance notice of retirement and claim for and award of pension) to a person who reaches pensionable age on or after 10th April 2018; and

(b) 9th April 2018 for all other purposes.

1(3) In this article **"a state pension"** means a state pension under Part 1 of the Pensions Act 2014.

INCREASE IN THE GENERAL LEVEL OF PRICES

2 For the purposes of section 148AC(3) and (4) of the Social Security Administration Act 1992 (revaluation for transitional pensions under Pensions Act 2014), the increase in the general level of prices during the review period is 4 per cent.

PENALTIES FOR ENABLERS OF DEFEATED TAX AVOIDANCE (LEGALLY PRIVILEGED COMMUNICATIONS DECLARATIONS) REGULATIONS 2017

(SI 2017/1245)

Made on 11 December 2017 by the Treasury in exercise of the powers conferred upon them by para. 44(4) of Sch. 16 to the Finance (No. 2) Act 2017. Operative from 2 January 2018.

CITATION AND COMMENCEMENT

1 These Regulations may be cited as the Penalties for Enablers of Defeated Tax Avoidance (Legally Privileged Communications Declarations) Regulations 2017 and come into force on 2nd January 2018.

INTERPRETATION

2 In these Regulations a reference to a numbered paragraph is a reference to the paragraph in Schedule 16 to the Finance Act (No. 2) 2017 which is so numbered.

THE DECLARATION

3 A declaration under paragraph 44 must satisfy Conditions A, B and C.

CONDITION A

4 Condition A is that the declaration must contain sufficient information as might reasonably be expected to enable HMRC to identify–

(a) the person who would rely on the declaration for the purpose of establishing that that person is not liable to a penalty under paragraph 1;

(b) the relevant lawyer making the declaration;

(c) the relevant lawyers whose legally privileged communications would otherwise be relied upon to establish that the person referred to in paragraph (a) is not a person who enabled the arrangements for the purposes of paragraph 1; and

(d) the arrangements (and, where appropriate, the proposal which was implemented by the arrangements) to which the declaration relates.

CONDITION B

5 Condition B is that the declaration must contain the confirmations set out in regulations 6 to 10 which must be made by the relevant lawyer making the declaration.

DESIGNER OF ARRANGEMENTS (PARAGRAPH 8)

6 In relation to whether the person referred to in regulation 4(a) is a designer of arrangements falling within paragraph 8, the confirmation is that the person–

(a) was not, in the course of a business carried on by that person, responsible to any extent for the design of the arrangements or a proposal which was implemented by the arrangements; or

(b) was responsible to an extent for such design because of having provided advice but–

  (i) the advice provided is not relevant advice within the meaning of paragraph 8(3); or

  (ii) the knowledge condition in paragraph 8(4) is not met.

MANAGERS OF ARRANGEMENTS (PARAGRAPH 9)

7(1) In relation to whether the person referred to in regulation 4(a) is a manager of the arrangements falling within paragraph 9(1), the confirmation is that–

(a) the person was not, in the course of a business carried on by that person, to any extent responsible for the organisation or management of the arrangements; or

(b) if the person was so responsible for the organisation or management of the arrangements, the condition set out in paragraph 9(1)(b) is not met.

7(2) Where the person referred to in regulation 4(a) is not a manager of the arrangements because of paragraph 9(2), the confirmation is that the person referred to in regulation 4(a) meets the condition set out in paragraph 9(2)(b).

MARKETERS OF ARRANGEMENTS (PARAGRAPH 10)

8 In relation to whether the person referred to in regulation 4(a) marketed arrangements to T so as to fall within paragraph 10, the confirmation is that the person did not in the course of a business carried on by that person–

(a) make available for implementation by T a proposal which has since been implemented, in relation to T, by the arrangements; or

(b) communicate information to T or another person about a proposal which has since been implemented, in relation to T, by the arrangements with a view to T entering into the arrangements or transactions forming part of the arrangements.

ENABLING PARTICIPANTS (PARAGRAPH 11)

9 In relation to whether the person referred to in regulation 4(a) is an enabling participant falling within paragraph 11, the confirmation is that–

(a) the person is not a person (other than T) who entered into the arrangements or a transaction forming part of the arrangements; or

(b) if the person did enter into the arrangements or a transaction forming part of the arrangements, the condition set out in paragraph 11(c) is not met.

FINANCIAL ENABLERS (PARAGRAPH 12)

10 In relation to whether the person referred to in regulation 4(a) is a financial enabler falling within paragraph 12, the confirmation is that–

(a) the person did not in the course of a business carried on by that person, provide a financial product (directly or indirectly) to a relevant party within the meaning of paragraph 12; or

(b) to the extent that the person did provide a financial product, the condition set out in paragraph 12(1)(c) is not met.

CONDITION C

11 Condition C is that the declaration must contain–

(a) a certificate that the information provided by the relevant lawyer making the declaration is correct to the best of their knowledge and belief; and

(b) a statement that the relevant lawyer making the declaration understands that any of the persons referred to in regulation 4 may have to pay financial penalties as set out in paragraphs 1 and 45 and that any relevant lawyer named in the declaration may face prosecution for providing false information should that declaration prove to be incorrect.

MULTIPLE IMPLEMENTATIONS OF A PROPOSAL

12 Where a proposal for arrangements was implemented more than once by arrangements which are substantially similar, the declaration may contain a statement that this is the case and that the involvement of the person referred to in regulation 4(a) in relation to those arrangements was such that all the things stated in the declaration are equally true in relation to those arrangements.

SOCIAL SECURITY REVALUATION OF EARNINGS FACTORS ORDER 2018

(SI 2018/271)

Made on 27 February 2018 by the Secretary of State in exercise of the powers conferred upon them by s. 148(3) and (4) and 189(1), (4) and (5) of the Social Security Administration Act 1992. Operative from 6 April 2018.

CITATION AND COMMENCEMENT

1 This Order may be cited as the Social Security Revaluation of Earnings Factors Order 2018 and shall come into force on 6th April 2018.

REVALUATION OF EARNINGS FACTORS

2 The earnings factors for the tax years specified in the Schedule to this Order in so far as they are relevant–

(a) to the calculation of–

(i) the additional pension in the rate of any long-term benefit; or

(ii) any guaranteed minimum pension; or

(b) to any other calculation required under Part 3 of the Pension Schemes Act 1993 (including that Part as modified by or under any other enactment),

are directed to be increased by the percentage of their amount shown opposite those tax years in that Schedule.

ROUNDING OF FRACTIONAL AMOUNTS

3 Where any earnings factor relevant to the calculation specified in article 2(a)(i), as increased in accordance with this Order, would not but for this article be expressed as a whole number of pounds, it shall be so expressed by rounding down any fraction of a pound less than one half and rounding up any other fraction of a pound.

HMRC DIRECTIONS

Table of Contents

Entries in italics are those which have been classified by HM Revenue and Customs as obsolete and/or have been enacted in other legislation.

continued over

DIRECTIONS BY THE BOARD OF HM REVENUE AND CUSTOMS RELATING TO THE SUBMISSION OF RETURNS USING THE INTERNET

HMRC DIRECTIONS

DIRECTIONS UNDER REGULATION 189 AND 205B OF THE INCOME TAX (PAY AS YOU EARN) REGULATIONS 2003 (SI 2003/2682) AND REGULATION 1(2) OF THE SOCIAL SECURITY (CONTRIBUTIONS) REGULATIONS 2001 (SI 2001/1004) AND APPROVAL UNDER REGULATION 211(5) OF THE INCOME TAX (PAY AS YOU EARN) REGULATIONS 2003 (SI 2003/2682) OF THE MANNER OF AUTHENTICATION OF EMPLOYERS' ANNUAL RETURNS DELIVERED ELECTRONICALLY [HMRC, 13 August 2009]

Notes – Revoked by Direction of 4 April 2011.

DIRECTIONS UNDER REGULATIONS 189 AND 205(2) OF THE INCOME TAX (PAY AS YOU EARN) REGULATIONS 2003 (SI 2003/2682) AND REGULATION 1(2) OF THE SOCIAL SECURITY (CONTRIBUTIONS) REGULATIONS 2001 (SI 2001/1004) AND APPROVAL UNDER REGULATION 211(5) OF THE INCOME TAX (PAY AS YOU EARN) REGULATIONS 2003 (SI 2003/2682) [HMRC, 4 April 2011]

Interpretation

In these directions and this approval–

"EDI" means the Electronic Data Interchange;

"PAYE Regulations" means the Income Tax (Pay As You Earn) Regulations 2003 (S.I. 2003/2682);

"Contributions Regulations" means the Social Security (Contributions) Regulations 2001 (S.I. 2001/1004).

Directions

The Commissioners for Her Majesty's Revenue and Customs (HMRC) make the following directions about approved methods of electronic communications for the delivery of information and the making of payments and approve the manner of authentication of employers' annual returns delivered electronically. The directions and approval have effect from 6 April 2011.

Approved methods of electronic communications for delivery of information by employers or persons acting on behalf of employers to HMRC

1. The methods of electronic communications approved for the delivery of the information listed in column 1 of the table by an employer or a person acting on behalf of an employer are:
   a. the internet services provided through PAYE Online for Employers and PAYE Online for Agents, where indicated in column 2, and
   b. the EDI services provided through PAYE Online for Employers and PAYE Online for Agents, where indicated in column 3.

1	2	3
Description of the kind of information to be delivered	**Internet**	**EDI**
PAYE Regulations[(1)]		
Simplified deductions scheme: deductions working sheet. Form P12 (regulation 35).	Yes	No
Simplified deductions scheme: annual return of deductions working sheets. Form P37 (regulation 35).	Yes	No
Cessation of employment. Form P45, Part 1 (regulation 36).	Yes	Yes
Death of employee. Form P45, Part 1 (regulation 38).	Yes	Yes
Death of pensioner. Form P45, Part 1 (regulation 39).	Yes	Yes
Procedure if new employer receives Form P45. Form P45, Part 3 (regulation 42).	Yes	Yes

1	2	3
Description of the kind of information to be delivered	**Internet**	**EDI**
Information to be provided if code not known. Form P46 (regulations 47, 48 and 49).	Yes	Yes
Late presentation of Form P45. Form P45, Part 3 (regulation 52).	Yes	Yes
Information on retirement. Form P46 (Pen) (regulation 55).	Yes	Yes
Procedure if new pension payer receives Form P45. Form P45, Part 3 (regulation 56).	Yes	Yes
Information to be provided if code not known (non-UK resident pensioners). Form P46 (Pen) (regulation 57).	Yes	Yes
Information to be provided if code not known (UK resident pensioners). Form P46 (Pen) (regulation 58).	Yes	Yes
Late presentation of Form P45. Form P45, Part 3 (regulation 60).	Yes	Yes
Annual return of relevant payments liable to deduction of tax. Forms P35 and P14 (regulation 73).	Yes	Yes
Annual return of relevant payments not liable to deduction of tax. Form P38A (regulation 74).	Yes	Yes
Employers: annual return of other PAYE income: benefits code employee. Form P11D (regulation 85).	Yes	Yes
Employers: annual return of other PAYE income: declaration. Form P11D(b) (regulation 85).	Yes	Yes
Quarterly return of cars becoming available or unavailable. Form P46 (Car) (regulation 90).	Yes	Yes
	Yes	Yes
Contributions Regulations		
Return by employer of Class 1A National Insurance Contributions. Form P11D(b) (regulation 80).	Yes	Yes
Return by employer at end of year. Forms P35 and P14 (paragraph 22 of Schedule 4).	Yes	Yes

(1) Regulation 211 permits electronic delivery of certain information. This direction approves the methods of electronic communications for delivery of that information.

Approved methods of electronic communications for mandatory electronic filing of specified information

2. The methods of electronic communications approved for the delivery of specified information, by an employer or a person acting on behalf of an employer, in accordance with regulation 205 of the PAYE Regulations (and, in respect of paragraph 22 returns, in accordance with regulation 90N(1) of the Contributions Regulations) are the internet services and the EDI services provided through PAYE Online for Employers and PAYE Online for Agents.

Approved methods of electronic communications for delivery of information by HMRC to employers or persons acting on behalf of employers

3. The methods of electronic communications approved for delivery of the information listed in column 1 of the table by HMRC to an employer or a person acting on behalf of an employer are:
   a. the internet services provided through PAYE Online for Employers and PAYE Online for Agents, where indicated in column 2, and
   b. the EDI services provided through PAYE Online for Employers and PAYE Online for Agents, where indicated in column 3.

1 **Description of the kind of information to be delivered**	2 **Internet**	3 **EDI**
PAYE Regulations[(2)]		
Issue of code to employer or agent. Form P6 or P9 (regulations 8 and 20).	Yes	Yes
Notice to employer to amend codes. Form P7X or P9X (regulation 20).	Yes	Yes
Notice to employer of payments and total net tax deducted. Form P6 (regulation 53).	Yes	Yes
Notice to pension payer of payments and total net tax deducted. Form P6 (regulation 61).	Yes	Yes

[(2)] Regulation 213 permits electronic delivery of certain information. This direction approves the methods of electronic communications for delivery of that information.

Approved method of authentication of the return required by regulation 73 (annual return of relevant payments liable to deduction of tax, Forms P35 and P14) where the return is delivered electronically

4. The method approved for authenticating a return required by regulation 73 of the PAYE Regulations and delivered by a method of electronic communications is the completion of any certificate or declaration contained in the electronic return or form and, where the sender is acting on behalf of an employer, completion of the following procedure before the information is sent:
   a. the sender must make a copy of the information before it is sent, and
   b. the employer must confirm to the sender that the information is complete and accurate to the best of his knowledge and belief.

Approved methods of electronic communications for the making of a payment

5. The methods of electronic communications approved for the making of payments required by the PAYE Regulations and the Contributions Regulations are the services known as Direct Debit, BACS Direct Credit (including telephone and internet banking), CHAPS, debit and credit card over the internet ("BillPay"), Government Banking Service (formerly known as Paymaster), Bank Giro and payments made through the Post Office.

Revocations

6. The Directions under regulation 189 and 205B of the Income Tax (Pay As You Earn) Regulations 2003 (S.I. 2003/2682) and regulation 1(2) of the Social Security (Contributions) Regulations 2001 (S.I. 2001/1004) and Approval under regulation 211(5) of the Income Tax (Pay As You Earn) Regulations 2003 (S.I. 2003/2682) of the manner of authentication of employers' annual returns delivered electronically dated 13th August 2009 are revoked.

DIRECTIONS UNDER REGULATIONS 189 AND 205(2) OF THE INCOME TAX (PAY AS YOU EARN) REGULATIONS 2003 (S.I. 2003/2682) AND REGULATION 1(2) OF THE SOCIAL SECURITY (CONTRIBUTIONS) REGULATIONS 2001 (S.I. 2001/1004) AND APPROVAL UNDER REGULATION 211(5) OF THE INCOME TAX (PAY AS YOU EARN) REGULATIONS 2003 (S.I. 2003/2682) AND 80(3A) OF THE SOCIAL SECURITY (CONTRIBUTIONS) REGULATIONS 2001 (S.I. 2001/1004) [HMRC, 16 March 2012]

Interpretation

In these directions and this approval–

"EDI" means the Electronic Data Interchange;

"PAYE Regulations" means the Income Tax (Pay As You Earn) Regulations 2003 (S.I. 2003/2682);

"Contributions Regulations" means the Social Security (Contributions) Regulations 2001 (S.I. 2001/1004).

Directions

The Commissioners for Her Majesty's Revenue and Customs (HMRC) give the following directions about approved methods of electronic communications for the delivery of information and the making of payments and approve the specified manner of authentication of employers' annual returns delivered electronically. The directions and approval have effect from 6 April 2012.

Approved methods of electronic communications for delivery of information by employers or persons acting on behalf of employers to HMRC

1. The methods of electronic communications approved for the delivery of the information listed in column 1 of the table by an employer or a person acting on behalf of an employer are:
   a. the internet services provided through PAYE Online for Employers and PAYE Online for Agents, where indicated in column 2, and
   b. the EDI services provided through PAYE Online for Employers and PAYE Online for Agents, where indicated in column 3.

1	**2**	**3**
Description of the kind of information to be delivered	**Internet**	**EDI**
PAYE Regulations[(1)]		
Simplified deductions scheme: deductions working sheet. Form P12 (regulation 35).	Yes	No
Simplified deductions scheme: annual return of deductions working sheets. Form P37 (regulation 35).	Yes	No
Cessation of employment. Form P45, Part 1 (regulation 36).	Yes	Yes
Death of employee. Form P45, Part 1 (regulation 38).	Yes	Yes
Death of pensioner. Form P45, Part 1 (regulation 39).	Yes	Yes
Procedure if new employer receives Form P45. Form P45, Part 3 (regulation 42).	Yes	Yes
Information to be provided if code not known. Form P46 (regulations 47, 48 and 49).	Yes	Yes
Late presentation of Form P45. Form P45, Part 3 (regulation 52).	Yes	Yes
Information on retirement. Form P46 (Pen) (regulation 55).	Yes	Yes
Procedure if new pension payer receives Form P45. Form P45, Part 3 (regulation 56).	Yes	Yes
Information to be provided if code not known (non-UK resident pensioners). Form P46 (Pen) (regulation 57).	Yes	Yes
Late presentation of Form P45. Form P45, Part 3 (regulation 60).	Yes	Yes
Annual return of relevant payments liable to deduction of tax. Forms P35 and P14 (regulation 73).	Yes	Yes
Annual return of relevant payments not liable to deduction of tax. Form P38A (regulation 74).	Yes	Yes
Employers: annual return of other PAYE income: benefits code employee. Form P11D (regulation 85).	Yes	Yes
Quarterly return of cars becoming available or unavailable. Form P46 (Car) (regulation 90).	Yes	Yes
Contributions Regulations		
Return by employer of Class 1A National Insurance Contributions. Form P11D(b) (regulation 80(1)).	Yes	Yes
Return by employer at end of year. Forms P35 and P14 (paragraph 22 of Schedule 4).	Yes	Yes

(1) Regulation 211 permits electronic delivery of certain information. This direction approves the methods of electronic communications for delivery of that information.

Approved methods of electronic communications for mandatory electronic filing of specified information

2. The methods of electronic communications approved for the delivery of specified information, by an employer or a person acting on behalf of an employer, in accordance with regulation 205 of the PAYE Regulations (and, in accordance with paragraph 22 of Schedule 4 and regulation 90N(1) of the Contributions Regulations) are the internet services and the EDI services provided through PAYE Online for Employers and PAYE Online for Agents.

Approved methods of electronic communications for delivery of information by HMRC to employers or persons acting on behalf of employers

3. The methods of electronic communications approved for delivery of the information listed in column 1 of the table by HMRC to an employer or a person acting on behalf of an employer are:

(a) the internet services provided through PAYE Online for Employers and PAYE Online for Agents, where indicated in column 2, and

(b) the EDI services provided through PAYE Online for Employers and PAYE Online for Agents, where indicated in column 3.

1 **Description of the kind of information to be delivered**	2 **Internet**	3 **EDI**
PAYE Regulations(2)		
Issue of code to employer or agent. Form P6 or P9 (regulations 8 and 20).	Yes	Yes
Notice to employer to amend codes. Form P7X or P9X (regulation 20).	Yes	Yes
Notice to employer of payments and total net tax deducted. Form P6 (regulation 53).	Yes	Yes
Notice to pension payer of payments and total net tax deducted. Form P6 (regulation 61).	Yes	Yes

(2) Regulation 213 permits electronic delivery of certain information. This direction approves the methods of electronic communications for delivery of that information.

Approved method of authentication of the return required by regulation 73 (annual return of relevant payments liable to deduction of tax, Forms P35 and P14) of the PAYE Regulations and regulation 80 (Return by employer) of the Contributions Regulations where the return is delivered electronically

4. The method approved for authenticating a return required by regulation 73 of the PAYE Regulations or regulation 80 of the Contributions Regulations and delivered by a method of electronic communications is the completion of any certificate or declaration contained in the electronic return or form and, where the sender is acting on behalf of an employer, completion of the following procedure before the information is sent:

(a) the sender must make a copy of the information before it is sent, and

(b) the employer must confirm to the sender that the information is complete and accurate to the best of his knowledge and belief.

Approved methods of electronic communications for the making of a payment

5. The methods of electronic communications approved for the making of payments required by the PAYE Regulations and the Contributions Regulations are the services known as Direct Debit, BACS Direct Credit (including telephone and internet banking), CHAPS, debit and credit card over the internet ("BillPay"), Government Banking Service (formerly known as Paymaster), Bank Giro and payments made through the Post Office.

DIRECTION UNDER REGULATION 2A(1)(B) AND (2) OF THE INCOME TAX (PAY AS YOU EARN) REGULATIONS 2003 AND PARAGRAPH 1(4) AND (5) OF SCHEDULE 4 TO THE SOCIAL SECURITY (CONTRIBUTIONS) REGULATIONS 2001 – REAL TIME INFORMATION EMPLOYERS: MIGRATION DURING TAX YEAR 2012–13 [HMRC, 11 July 2012]

The Commissioners for Her Majesty's Revenue and Customs give the following direction under regulation 2A(1)(b) and (2) of the Income Tax (Pay As You Earn) Regulations 2003 (S.I. 2003/2682) and paragraph 1(4) and (5) of Schedule 4 to the Social Security (Contributions) Regulations 2001 (S.I. 2001/1004):

Real Time Information employers

1. An employer within paragraph 2 is required to deliver to HMRC returns under regulation 67B of the PAYE Regulations and paragraph 21A of Schedule 4 to the Contributions Regulations.
2. An employer is within this paragraph if:
   a. apart from this direction, the employer is not a Real Time Information employer for the purposes of the PAYE Regulations and the Contributions Regulations,
   b. the employer receives a notification, howsoever expressed, from HMRC requiring compliance with the provisions of the PAYE Regulations and the Contributions Regulations that are expressed as relating to Real Time Information employers,
   c. within the period specified in the notification, the employer does not object to the notification, and
   d. subject to sub-paragraph (c), the notification requires compliance with those provisions before the end of tax year 2012–13.
3. The employer is required to deliver to HMRC returns under regulation 67B of the PAYE Regulations and paragraph 21A of Schedule 4 to the Contributions Regulations with effect from the date specified in the notification.

Interpretation

4. In this direction:

"the Contributions Regulations" means the Social Security (Contributions) Regulations 2001 (S.I. 2001/1004);

"the PAYE Regulations" means the Income Tax (Pay As You Earn) Regulations 2003 (S.I. 2003/2682);

"employer":

(a) so far as this direction relates to the PAYE Regulations, has the meaning given in regulation 2(1) of those Regulations, and

(b) so far as this direction relates to the Contributions Regulations, has the meaning given in paragraph 1(2) of Schedule 4 to those Regulations; and

"HMRC" means Her Majesty's Revenue and Customs.

DIRECTION UNDER REGULATIONS 2A(1)(B) AND (2) AND 2B(1)(B) AND (2) OF THE INCOME TAX (PAY AS YOU EARN) REGULATIONS 2003 AND PARAGRAPH 1(4) AND (5) OF SCHEDULE 4 TO THE SOCIAL SECURITY (CONTRIBUTIONS) REGULATIONS 2001 – REAL TIME INFORMATION EMPLOYERS AND REAL TIME INFORMATION PENSION PAYERS: MIGRATION DURING TAX YEAR 2013–14 [HMRC, 3 October 2012]

The Commissioners for Her Majesty's Revenue and Customs give the following direction under regulation 2A(1)(b) and (2) and regulation 2B(1)(b) and (2) of the Income Tax (Pay As You Earn) Regulations 2003 (S.I. 2003/2682) and paragraph 1(4) and (5) of Schedule 4 to the Social Security (Contributions) Regulations 2001 (S.I. 2001/1004):

Real Time Information employers

1. Any employer who, apart from this direction, is not a Real Time Information employer for the purposes of the PAYE Regulations and the Contributions Regulations is required to deliver to HMRC returns under regulation 67B of the PAYE Regulations and paragraph 21A of Schedule 4 to the Contributions Regulations with effect from the date mentioned in paragraph 2.
2. The date is 6th April 2013 unless HMRC specifies a later date.

Real Time Information pension payers

3. Any pension payer who, apart from this direction, is not a Real Time Information pension payer for the purposes of the PAYE Regulations is required to deliver to HMRC returns under regulation 67B of the PAYE Regulations with effect from the date mentioned in paragraph 4.
4. The date is 6th April 2013 unless HMRC specifies a later date.

Interpretation

5. In this direction:

"the Contributions Regulations" means the Social Security (Contributions) Regulations 2001 (S.I. 2001/1004);

"the PAYE Regulations" means the Income Tax (Pay As You Earn) Regulations 2003 (S.I. 2003/2682);

"employer":

(a) so far as this direction relates to the PAYE Regulations, has the meaning given in regulation 2(1) of those Regulations, and

(b) so far as this direction relates to the Contributions Regulations, has the meaning given in paragraph 1(2) of Schedule 4 to those Regulations;

"HMRC" means Her Majesty's Revenue and Customs; and

"pension payer" has the meaning given in regulation 2(1) of the PAYE Regulations.

DIRECTION UNDER REGULATION 2A(1)(B) AND (2) AND REGULATION 2B(1) AND (2) OF THE INCOME TAX (PAY AS YOU EARN) REGULATIONS 2003 AND PARAGRAPH 1(4) AND (5) OF SCHEDULE 4 TO THE SOCIAL SECURITY (CONTRIBUTIONS) REGULATIONS 2001 – REAL TIME INFORMATION EMPLOYERS AND REAL TIME INFORMATION PENSION PAYERS: MIGRATION DURING TAX YEAR 2013–14 [HMRC, 20 March 2013]

On 24 September 2012 the Commissioners for Her Majesty's Revenue and Customs gave a direction under regulation 2A(1)(b) and (2) and regulation 2B(1)(b) and (2) of the Income Tax (Pay As You Earn) Regulations 2003 (S.I. 2003/2682) and paragraph 1(4) and (5) of Schedule 4 to the Social Security (Contributions) Regulations 2001 (S.I. 2001/1004).

The Commissioners for Her Majesty's Revenue and Customs now issue a revised direction under regulation 2A(1)(b) and (2) and regulation 2B(1)(b) and (2) of the Income Tax (Pay As You Earn) Regulations 2003 and paragraph 1(4) and (5) of Schedule 4 to the Social Security (Contributions) Regulations 2001:

Real Time Information employers

1. Any employer, except an excluded employer, who, apart from this direction or directions previously issued under regulation 2A(1)(b) and (2) of the PAYE Regulations and under paragraph 1(4) and (5) of Schedule 4 to the Contributions Regulations is not a Real Time Information employer for the purposes of the PAYE Regulations and the Contributions Regulations is required to deliver to HMRC returns under regulation 67B of the PAYE Regulations and paragraph 21A of Schedule 4 to the Contributions Regulations with effect from the date mentioned in paragraph 2.
2. The date is 6th April 2013 unless HMRC specifies or has already specified a later date.

Real Time Information pension payers

3. Any pension payer who, apart from this direction or directions previously issued under regulation 2B(1)(b) and (2) of the PAYE Regulations, is not a Real Time Information pension payer for the purposes of the PAYE Regulations is required to deliver to HMRC returns under regulation 67B of the PAYE Regulations with effect from the date mentioned in paragraph 4.
4. The date is 6th April 2013 unless HMRC specifies or has already specified a later date.

Interpretation

In this direction:

"the Contributions Regulations" means the Social Security (Contributions) Regulations 2001 (S.I. 2001/1004);

"the PAYE Regulations" means the Income Tax (Pay As You Earn) Regulations 2003 (S.I. 2003/2682);

"employer":

(a) so far as this direction relates to the PAYE Regulations, has the meaning given in regulation 2(1) of those Regulations, and

(b) so far as this direction relates to the Contributions Regulations, has the meaning given in paragraph 1(2) of Schedule 4 to those Regulations;

"excluded employer" means

(a) any employer who is an ex aminations board or authorised examiner which has made special arrangements with HMRC in accordance with regulation 141 of the PAYE Regulations; or

(b) any employer who has been appointed to act as a Returning Officer or an Acting Returning Officer under the Representation of the People Act 1983 or an employer who acts as deputy for such a Returning or Acting Returning Officer and who has made special arrangements with HMRC in accordance with regulation 141 of the PAYE Regulations;

"HMRC" means Her Majesty's Revenue and Customs;

"pension payer" has the meaning given in regulation 2(1) of the PAYE Regulations.

NIC EUROPEAN MATERIAL

Table of Contents

continued over

REGULATION 1408/71

On the application of social security schemes to employed persons, to self-employed persons and to members of their families moving within the [European] Community

(14 June 1971, OJ 1971(II), Eng. Spec. Ed., p. 416)

History – Regulation 1408/71 is repealed for most purposes from the date of application of Regulation 883/2004 (1 May 2010 – the date of entry into force of the *Implementing Regulation* (as provided for by Regulation 883/2004, art. 89)). Regulation 1408/71 continues to remain in force and shall continue to have legal effect for the purposes of:

(a) Regulation 859/2003 of 14 May 2003 which extends the provisions of Regulation 1408/71 and Regulation 574/72 to nationals of third countries who are not already covered by those provisions solely on the ground of their nationality, for as long as that Regulation has not been repealed or modified;

(b) Regulation 1661/85 of 13 June 1985 which lays down the technical adaptations to the Community rules on social security for migrant workers with regard to Greenland, for as long as that Regulation has not been repealed or modified;

(c) the Agreement on the European Economic Area and the Agreement between the European Community and its Member States, of the one part, and the Swiss Confederation, of the other part, on the free movement of persons and other agreements which contain a reference to Regulation (EEC) No 1408/71, for as long as those agreements have not been modified in the light of Regulation 883/2004.

The consolidated text of Regulation 1408/71 (OJ 1997 L28/4) is therefore reproduced below:

"TITLE I – GENERAL PROVISIONS

ART. 1 Definitions

1 For the purpose of this Regulation:

(a) **"employed person"** and **"self-employed person"** mean respectively:

(i) any person who is insured, compulsorily or on an optional continued basis, for one or more of the contingencies covered by the branches of a social security scheme for employed or self-employed persons or a special scheme for civil servants;

(ii) any person who is compulsorily insured for one or more of the contingencies covered by the branches of social security dealt with in this Regulation, under a social security scheme for all residents or for the whole working population, if such person:

– can be identified as an employed or self-employed person by virtue of the manner in which such scheme is administered or financed, or,

– failing such criteria, is insured for some other contingency specified in Annex I under a scheme for employed or self-employed persons, or under a scheme referred to in (iii), either compulsorily or on an optional continued basis, or, where no such scheme exists in the Member State concerned, complies with the definition given in Annex I;

(iii) any person who is compulsorily insured for several of the contingencies covered by the branches dealt with in this Regulation, under a standard social security scheme for the whole rural population in accordance with the criteria laid down in Annex I;

(iv) any person who is voluntarily insured for one or more of the contingencies covered by the branches dealt with in this Regulation, under a social security scheme of a Member State for employed or self-employed persons or for all residents or for certain categories of residents:

– if such person carries out an activity as an employed or self-employed person, or

– if such person has previously been compulsorily insured for the same contingency under a scheme for employed or self-employed persons of the same Member State;

(b) **"frontier worker"** means any employed or self-employed person who pursues his occupation in the territory of a Member State and resides in the territory of another Member State to which he returns as a rule daily or at least once a week; however, a frontier worker who is posted elsewhere in the territory of the same or another Member State by the undertaking to which he is normally attached, or who engages in the provision of services elsewhere in the territory of the same or another Member State, shall retain the status of frontier worker for a period not exceeding four month[s], even if he is prevented, during that period, from returning daily or at least once a week to the place where he resides;

(c) **"seasonal worker"** means any employed person who goes to the territory of a Member State other than the one in which he is resident to do work there of a seasonal nature for an undertaking or an employer of that state for a period which may on no account exceed eight month[s], and who stays in the territory of the said state for the duration of this work; **"work of a seasonal nature"** shall be taken to mean work which, being dependent on the succession of the seasons, automatically recurs each year;

(ca) **"student"** means any person other than an employed or self-employed person or a member of his family or survivor within the meaning of this Regulation who studies or receives vocational training leading to a qualification officially recognised by the authorities of a Member State, and is insured under a general social security scheme or a special social security scheme applicable to students;

(d) **"refugee"** shall have the meaning assigned to it in article 1 of the Convention of the Status of Refugees, signed at Geneva on 28 July 1951;

(e) **"stateless person"** shall have the meaning assigned to it in article 1 of the Convention on the Status of Stateless Persons, signed in New York on 28 September 1954;

(f), (g) [not relevant to NI contributions;]

(h) **"residence"** means habitual residence;

(i) **"stay"** means temporary residence;

(j) **"legislation"** means in respect of each Member State statutes, regulations and other provisions and all other implementing measures, present or future, relating to the branches and schemes of social security covered by article 4(1) and (2) or those special non-contributory benefits covered by article 4(2a).

The term excludes provisions of existing or future industrial agreements, whether or not they have been the subject of a decision by the authorities rendering them compulsory or extending their scope. However, in so far as such provisions

(i) serve to put into effect compulsory insurance imposed by the laws and regulations referred to in the preceding subparagraph; or

(ii) set up a scheme administered by the same institution as that which administers the schemes set up by the laws and regulations referred to in the preceding subparagraph,

the limitation on the term may at any time be lifted by a declaration of the Member State concerned specifying the schemes of such a kind to which this Regulation applies. Such a declaration shall be notified and published in accordance with the provisions of article 97.

The provisions of the preceding subparagraph shall not have effect of exempting from the application of this Regulation the schemes to which Regulation 3/58 applied.

The term **"legislation"** also excludes provisions governing special schemes for self-employed persons the creation of which is left to the initiatives of those concerned or which apply only to a part of the territory of the Member State concerned, irrespective of whether or not the authorities decided to make them compulsory or extend their scope. The special schemes in question are specified in Annex II;

(ja) **"special scheme for civil servants"** means any social security scheme which is different from the general social security scheme applicable to employed persons in the Member States concerned and to which all, or certain categories of, civil servants or persons treated as such are directly subject:

(k) **"social security convention"** means any bilateral or multilateral instrument which binds or will bind two or more Member States exclusively, and any other multilateral instrument which binds or will bind at least two Member States and one or more other states in the field of social security, for all or part of the branches and schemes set out in article 4(1) and (2), together with agreements, of whatever kind, concluded pursuant to the said instruments;

(l) **"competent authority"** means, in respect of each Member State, the Minister, Ministers or other equivalent authority responsible for social security schemes throughout or in any part of the territory of the state in question;

(m) **"Administrative Commission"** means the commission referred to in article 80;

(n) **"institution"** means, in respect of each Member State the body or authority responsible for administering all or part of the legislation;

(o) **"competent institution"** means:
  (i) the institution with which the person concerned is insured at the time of the application for benefit; or
  (ii) the institution from which the person concerned is entitled or would be entitled to benefits if he or a member or members of his family were resident in the territory of the Member State in which the institution is situated; or
  (iii) the institution designated by the competent authority of the Member State concerned; or
  (iv) in the case of a scheme relating to an employer's liability in respect of the benefits set out in article 4(1), either the employer or the insurer involved or, in default thereof, a body or authority designated by the competent authority of the Member State concerned;

(p) **"institution of the place of residence"** and **"institution of the place of stay"** mean respectively the institution which is competent to provide benefits in the place where the person concerned resides and the institution which is competent to provide benefits in the place where the person concerned is staying, under the legislation administered by that institution or, where no such institution exists, the institution designated by the competent authority of the Member State in question;

(q) **"competent state"** means the Member State in whose territory the competent institution is situated;

(r) **"periods of insurance"** means periods of contribution or period[s] of employment or self-employment as defined or recognised as periods of insurance by the legislation under which they were completed or considered as completed, and all periods treated as such, where they are regarded by the said legislation as equivalent to periods of insurance; periods completed under a special scheme for civil servants are also considered as periods of insurance

(s) **"periods of employment"** and **"periods of self-employment"** mean periods so defined or recognised by the legislation under which they were completed, and all periods treated as such, where they are regarded by the said legislation as equivalent to periods of employment or of self-employment; periods completed under a special scheme for civil servants are also considered as periods of insurance

(sa)–(v) [Not relevant to NI contributions.]

History – Art. 1(a)(i), the words "or, by a special scheme for civil servants", art. 1(ja) and the words " periods completed under a special scheme for civil servants are also considered as periods of insurance" in art. 1(r) and 1(s) inserted by Regulation 1606/98 (OJ 1998 L209).
Art. 1(ca) inserted by Regulation 307/99 (OJ 1999 L38).

ART. 2 Persons covered

2(1) This Regulation shall apply to employed or self-employed persons and to students who are or have been subject to the legislation of one or more Member States and who are nationals of one of the Member States, as well as to the members of their families and their survivors.

2(2) This Regulation shall apply to the survivors of employed or self-employed persons and of students who have been subject to the legislation of one or more Member States, irrespective of the nationality of such persons, where their survivors are nationals of one of the Member States, or stateless persons or refugees residing within the territory of one of the Member States.

History – Art. 2 was substituted by Regulation 307/99, art. 1(2) (OJ 1999 L38/3), with effect from 1 May 1999.

ART. 3 Equality of treatment

3(1) Subject to the special provisions of this Regulation, persons to whom this Regulation applies shall be subject to the same obligations and enjoy the same benefits under the legislation of any Member State as the nationals of that state.

3(2) [Not relevant to NI contributions.]

3(3) Save as provided in Annex III, the provisions of social security conventions which remain in force pursuant to article 7(2)(c), shall apply to all persons to whom this Regulation applies.

History – In art. 3(1) the words "resident in the territory of one of the Member States" which appeared after "persons" repealed by Regulation 647/2005, art. 1(1)(a) (OJ L 117).
In art. 3(3) the words "and the provisions of conventions concluded pursuant to article 8(1)" which appeared after "article 7(2)(c)" repealed by Regulation 647/2005, art. 1(1)(b) (OJ L 117).

ART. 4 Matters covered

4(1) This Regulation shall apply to all legislation concerning the following branches of social security:
(a) sickness and maternity benefits;
(b) invalidity benefits, including those intended for the maintenance or improvement of earning capacity;
(c) old-age benefits;
(d) survivor's benefits;
(e) benefits in respect of accidents at work and occupational diseases;
(f) death grants;
(g) unemployment benefits;
(h) family benefits.

4(2) This Regulation shall apply to all general and special social security schemes, whether contributory or non-contributory, and to schemes concerning the liability of an employer or shipowner in respect of the benefits referred to in paragraph 1.

4(2a)–(3) [Not relevant to NI contributions.]

4(4) This Regulation shall not apply to social and medical assistance, to benefit schemes for victims of war or its consequences, or to special schemes for civil servants and persons treated as such.

History – In art. 4(4) words ", or to special schemes for civil servants and persons treated as such" repealed by Regulation 1606/98 (OJ 1998 L209).

ART. 5 Declarations of Member States on the scope of this Regulation

5 The Member States shall specify the legislation and schemes referred to in article 4(1) and (2), the special non-contributory benefits referred to in article 4(2a), the minimum benefits referred to in article 50 and the benefits referred to in articles 77 and 78 in declarations to be notified and published in accordance with article 97.

Cross references – Art. 50 (not reproduced): minimum benefits.
Art. 77, 78 (not reproduced): benefits for dependent children of pensioners and for orphans.

Notes – Art. 50, 77 and 78 are not relevant to NI contributions.

ART. 6 Social security conventions replaced by this Regulation

6 Subject to the provisions of articles 7, 8 and 46(4), this Regulation shall, as regards persons and matters which it covers, replace the provisions of any social security convention binding either:

(a) two or more Member States exclusively; or

(b) at least two Member States and one or more other states, where settlement of the cases concerned does not involve any institution of one of the latter states.

Cross references – Art. 7 (not reproduced): international provisions not affected by this Regulation.
Art. 46(4) (not reproduced): total of benefits due from two Member States.

Notes – Art. 7 and 46 are not relevant to NI contributions.

ART. 8 Conclusion of conventions between Member States

8(1) Two or more Member States may, as need arises, conclude conventions with each other based on the principles and in the spirit of this Regulation.

8(2) Each Member State shall notify, in accordance with the provisions of article 97(1), any convention concluded with another Member State under the provisions of paragraph 1.

Cross references – Art. 97: notification pursuant to certain provisions.

ART. 9 Admission to voluntary or optional continued insurance

9(1) The provisions of the legislation of any Member State which make admission to voluntary or optional continued insurance conditional upon residence in the territory of that state shall not apply to persons resident in the territory of another Member State, provided that at some time in their past working life they were subject to the legislation of the first state as employed or as self-employed persons.

9(2) Where, under the legislation of a Member State, admission to voluntary or optional continued insurance is conditional upon completion of periods of insurance, the periods of insurance or residence completed under the legislation of another Member State shall be taken into account, to the extent required, as if they were completed under the legislation of the first state.

Cross references – Regulation 574/72, art. 6: implementation of art. 9.

TITLE II – DETERMINATION OF THE LEGISLATION APPLICABLE

ART. 13 General rules

13(1) Subject to article 14c and 14f, persons to whom this Regulation applies shall be subject to the legislation of a single Member State only. That legislation shall be determined in accordance with the provisions of this title.

13(2) Subject to articles 14 to 17:

(a) a person employed in the territory of one Member State shall be subject to the legislation of that state even if he resides in the territory of another Member State or if the registered office or place of business of the undertaking or individual employing him is situated in the territory of another Member State;

(b) a person who is self-employed in the territory of one Member State shall be subjected to the legislation of that state even if he resides in the territory of another Member State;

(c) a person employed on board a vessel flying the flag of a Member State shall be subject to the legislation of that state;

(d) civil servants and persons treated as such shall be subject to the legislation of the Member State to which the administration employing them is subject;

(e) a person called up or recalled for service in the armed forces, or for civilian service, of a Member State shall be subject to the legislation of that state. If entitlement under that legislation is subject to the completion of periods of insurance before entry into or after release from such military or civilian service, periods of insurance completed under the legislation of any other Member State shall be taken into account, to the extent necessary, as if they were periods of insurance completed under the legislation of the first state. The employed or self-employed person called up or recalled for service in the armed forces or for civilian service shall retain the status of employed or self-employed person;

(f) a person to whom the legislation of a Member State ceases to be applicable, without the legislation of another Member State becoming applicable to him in accordance with one of the rules laid down in the aforegoing subparagraphs or in accordance with one of the exceptions or special provisions laid down in articles 14 to 17 shall be subject to the legislation of the Member State in whose territory he resides in accordance with the provisions of that legislation alone.

History – In art. 13(1), the words "and 14f" inserted by Regulation 1606/98 (OJ 1998 L209).
Art. 13(2)(f) inserted by Regulation 2195/91 (OJ 1991 L206).

Cross references – Regulation 574/72, art. 11: implements art. 13.

ART. 14 Special rules applicable to persons, other than mariners, engaged in paid employment

Article 13(2)(a) shall apply subject to the following exceptions and circumstances:

14(1)

(a) A person employed in the territory of a Member State by an undertaking to which he is normally attached who is posted by that undertaking to the territory of another Member State to perform work there for that undertaking shall continue to be subject to the legislation of the first Member State, provided that the anticipated duration of that work does not exceed 12 months and that he is not sent to replace another person who has completed his term of posting.

(b) If the duration of the work to be done extends beyond the duration originally anticipated, owing to unforeseeable circumstances, and exceeds 12 months, the legislation of the first Member State shall continue to apply until the completion of such work, provided that the competent authority of the Member State in whose territory, the person concerned is posted or the body designated by that authority gives its consent; such consent must be requested before the end of the initial 12-month period. Such consent cannot, however, be given for a period exceeding 12 months.

14(2) A person normally employed in the territory of two or more Member States shall be subject to the legislation determined as follows:

(a) A person who is a member of the travelling or flying personnel of an undertaking which, for hire or reward or on its own account, operates international transport services for passengers or goods by rail, road, air or inland waterway and has its registered office or place of business in the territory of a Member State shall be subject to the legislation of the latter state, with the following restrictions:

(i) where the said undertaking has a branch or permanent representation in the territory of a Member State other than that in which it has its registered office or place of business, a person employed by such branch or permanent representation shall be subject to the legislation of the Member State in whose territory such branch or permanent representation is situated;

(ii) where a person is employed principally in the territory of the Member State in which he resides, he shall be subject to the legislation of that state, even if the undertaking which employs him has no registered office or place of business or branch or permanent representation in that territory.

(b) A person other than that referred to in (a) shall be subject:

(i) to the legislation of the Member State in whose territory he resides, if he pursues his activity partly in that territory or if he is attached to several undertakings or several employers who have their registered offices or places of business in the territory of different Member States;

(ii) to the legislation of the Member State in whose territory is situated the registered office or place of business of the undertaking or individual employing him, if he does not reside in the territory of any of the Member States where he is pursuing his activity.

14(3) A person who is employed in the territory of one Member State by an undertaking which has its registered office or place of business in the territory of another Member State and which straddles the common frontier of these states shall be subject to the legislation of the Member State in whose territory the undertaking has its registered office or place of business.

Cross references – Regulation 574/72, art. 11, 12, 12a: implement art. 14.

ART. 14a Special rules applicable to persons, other than mariners, who are self-employed

Article 13(2)(b) shall apply subject to the following exceptions and circumstances:

14a(1)

(a) A person normally self-employed in the territory of a Member State and who performs work in the territory of another Member State shall continue to be subject to the legislation of the first Member State, provided that the anticipated duration of the work does not exceed 12 months.

(b) If the duration of the work to be done extends beyond the duration originally anticipated, owing to unforeseeable circumstances, and exceeds 12 months, the legislation of the first Member State shall continue to apply until the completion of such work, provided that the competent authority of the Member State in whose territory the person concerned has entered to perform the work in question or the body appointed by that authority gives its consent; such consent must be requested before the end of the initial 12-month period. Such consent cannot, however, be given for a period exceeding 12 months.

14a(2) A person normally self-employed in the territory of two or more Member States shall be subject to the legislation of the Member State in whose territory he resides if he pursues any part of his activity in the territory of that Member State. If he does not pursue any activity in the territory of the Member State in which he resides, he shall be subject to the legislation of the Member State in whose territory he pursues his main activity. The criteria used to determine the principal activity are laid down in the Regulation referred to in article 98.

14a(3) A person who is self-employed in an undertaking which has its registered office or place of business in the territory of one Member State and which straddles the common frontier of two Member States shall be subject to the legislation of the Member State in whose territory the undertaking has its registered office or place of business.

14a(4) If the legislation to which a person should be subject in accordance with paragraph 2 or 3 does not enable that person, even on a voluntary basis, to join a pension scheme, the person concerned shall be subject to the legislation of the other Member State which would apply apart from these particular provisions, or should the legislations of two or more Member States apply in this way, he shall be subject to the legislation decided on by common agreement amongst the Member States concerned or their competent authorities.

Cross references – Regulation 574/72, art. 11, 11a, 12a: implement art. 14a.

ART. 14b Special rules applicable to mariners

Article 13(2)(c) shall apply subject to the following exceptions and circumstances:

14b(1) A person employed by an undertaking to which he is normally attached, either in the territory of a Member State or on board a vessel flying the flag of a Member State who is posted by that undertaking on board a vessel flying the flag of another Member State to perform work there for that undertaking shall, subject to the conditions provided in article 14(1), continue to be subject to the legislation of the first Member State.

14b(2) A person normally self-employed, either in the territory of a Member State or on board a vessel flying the flag of a Member State and who performs work on his own account on board a vessel flying the flag of another Member State shall, subject to the conditions provided in article 14a(1), continue to be subject to the legislation of the first Member State.

14b(3) A person who, while not being normally employed at sea, performs work in the territorial waters or in a port of a Member State on a vessel flying the flag of another Member State within those territorial waters or in that port, but is not a member of the crew of the vessel, shall be subject to the legislation of the first Member State.

14b(4) A person employed on board a vessel flying the flag of a Member State and remunerated for such employment by an undertaking or a person whose registered office or place of business is in the territory of another Member State shall be subject to the legislation of the latter state if he is resident in the territory of that state; the undertaking or person paying the remuneration shall be considered as the employer for the purposes of the said legislation.

Cross references – Regulation 574/72, art. 11, 11a, 12: implement art. 14b.

ART. 14c Special rules applicable to persons who are simultaneously employed in the territory of one Member State and self-employed in the territory of another Member State

14c A person who is simultaneously employed in the territory of one Member State and self-employed in the territory of another Member State shall be subject:

(a) save as otherwise provided in subparagraph (b) to the legislation of the Member State in the territory of which he is engaged in paid employment or, where he pursues such an activity in the territory of two or more Member States, to the legislation determined in accordance with article 14(2) or (3);

(b) in the cases mentioned in Annex VII:
   – to the legislation of the Member State in the territory of which he is engaged in paid employment, that legislation having been determined in accordance with the provisions of article 14(2) or (3), where he pursues such an activity in the territory of two or more Member States, and
   – to the legislation of the Member State in the territory of which he is self-employed, that legislation having been determined in accordance with article 14a(2), (3) or (4), where he pursues such an activity in the territory of two or more Member States.

History – Art. 14c substituted by Regulation 3811/86 (OJ 1986 L355).

Cross references – Annex VII: instances in which person shall be simultaneously subject to the legislation of two Member States. Regulation 574/72, art. 12a: implements art. 14c.

ART. 14d Miscellaneous provisions

14d(1) The person referred to in articles 14(2) and (3), 14a(2), (3) and (4) and 14c(a) and article 14e shall be treated, for the purposes of application of the legislation laid down in accordance with these provisions, as if he pursued all his professional activity or activities in the territory of the Member State concerned.

14d(2) The person referred to in article 14c(b) shall be treated, for the purposes of determining the rates of contributions to be charged to self-employed workers under the legislation of the Member State in whose territory he is self-employed, as if he pursued his paid employment in the territory of the Member State concerned.

14d(3) [Not relevant to NI contributions.]

History – In art. 14d(1), the words "and article 14e" inserted by Regulation 1606/98 (OJ 1998 L209). Art. 14d(2) substituted by Regulation 3811/86 (OJ 1986 L355).

ART. 14e Special rules applicable to persons insured in a special scheme for civil servants who are simultaneously employed and/or self-employed in the territory of one or more other Member States

14e A person who is simultaneously employed as a civil servant or a person treated as such and insured in a special scheme for civil servants in one or more Member State and how is employed and/or self-employed in the territory of one or more other Member States shall be subject to the legislation of the Member State in which he is insured in a special scheme for civil servants.

History – Art. 14e inserted by Regulation 1606/98 (OJ 1998 L209).

ART. 14f Special rules applicable to civil servant simultaneously employed in more than one Member State and insured in one of these states in a special scheme

14f A person who is simultaneously employed in two or more Member States as a civil servant or a person treated as such and insured in at least one of those Member States in a special scheme for civil servants shall be subject to the legislation of each of these Member States.

History – Art. 14f inserted by Regulation 1606/98 (OJ 1998 L209).

ART. 15 Rules concerning voluntary insurance or optional continued insurance

15(1) Articles 13 to 14d shall not apply to voluntary insurance or to optional insurance unless, in respect of one of the branches referred to in article 4, there exists in any Member State only a voluntary scheme of insurance.

15(2) Where application of the legislations of two or more Member States entails overlapping of insurance:

– under a compulsory insurance scheme and one or more voluntary or optional continued insurance schemes, the person concerned shall be subject exclusively to the compulsory insurance scheme,

– under two or more voluntary or optional continued insurance schemes, the person concerned may join only the voluntary or optional continued insurance scheme for which he has opted.

15(3) However, in respect of invalidity, old age and death (pensions), the person concerned may join the voluntary or optional continued insurance scheme of a Member State, even if he is compulsorily subject to the legislation of another Member State, to the extent that such overlapping is explicitly or implicitly admitted in the first Member State.

ART. 16 Special rules regarding persons employed by diplomatic missions and consular posts, and auxiliary staff of the European Communities

16(1) The provisions of article 13(2)(a) shall apply to persons employed by diplomatic missions and consular posts and to the private domestic staff of agents of such missions or posts.

16(2) However, employed persons covered by paragraph 1 who are nationals of the Member State which is the accrediting or sending state may opt to be subject to the legislation of that state. Such right of option may be renewed at the end of each calendar year and shall not have retrospective effect.

16(3) Auxiliary staff of the European Communities may opt to be subject to the legislation of the Member State in whose territory they are employed, to the legislation of the Member State to which they were last subject or to the legislation of the Member State whose nationals they are, in respect of provisions other than those relating to family allowances, the granting of which is governed by the conditions of employment applicable to such staff. This right of option, which may be exercised once only, shall take effect from the date of entry into employment.

Cross references – Administrative Commission of the EU on social security for migrant workers Decision 89 (OJ 1973 C86/7): art. 16(1) and (2) to apply to all workers (other than civil servants and those treated as such) employed in diplomatic missions and consular posts or who are in the service of officials in such missions or posts.
Regulation 574/72, art. 13: exercise of the right of option by persons employed by diplomatic missions and consular posts.
Regulation 574/72, art. 14: exercise of the right of option by auxiliary staff of the European Communities.

ART. 17 Exceptions to articles 13 to 16

17 Two or more Member States, the competent authorities of these states or the bodies designated by these authorities may by common agreement provide for exceptions to the provisions of articles 13 to 16 in the interest of certain categories of persons or of certain persons.

History – Art. 17 substituted by Regulation 2195/91 (OJ 1991 L206).

ART. 17a Special rules concerning recipients of pensions due under the legislation of one or more Member State

17a The recipient of a pension due under the legislation of a Member State or of pensions due under the legislation of several Member States who resides in the territory of another Member State may at his request be exempted from the legislation of the latter state provided that he is not subject to that legislation because of the pursuit of an occupation.

History – Art. 17a inserted by Regulation 2195/91 (OJ 1991 L206).

TITLE VI – MISCELLANEOUS PROVISIONS

ART. 84 Co-operation between competent authorities

84(1) The competent authorities of Member States shall communicate to each other all information regarding:

(a) measures taken to implement this Regulation;

(b) changes in their legislation which are likely to affect the implementation of this Regulation.

84(2) For the purposes of implementing this Regulation, the authorities and institutions of Member States shall lend their good offices and act as though implementing their own legislation. The administrative assistance furnished by the said authorities and institutions shall, as a rule, be free of charge. However, the competent authorities of the Member States may agree to certain expenses being reimbursed.

84(3) The authorities and institutions of Member States may, for the purpose of implementing this Regulation, communicate directly with one another and with the persons concerned or their representatives.

84(4) The authorities, institutions and tribunals of one Member State may not reject claims or other documents submitted to them on the grounds that they are written in an official language of another Member State. They shall have recourse where appropriate to the provisions of article 81(b).

84(5)

(a) Where, under this Regulation or under the implementing Regulation referred to in article 98, the authorities or institutions of a Member State communicate personal data to the authorities or institutions of another Member State, that communication shall be subject to the legal provisions governing protection of data laid down by the Member State providing the data.
Any subsequent transmission as well as the storage, alteration and destruction of the data shall be subject to the provisions of the legislation on data protection of the receiving Member State.

(b) The use of personal data for purposes other than those of social security shall be subject to the approval of the person concerned or in accordance with the other guarantees provided for by national legislation.

Cross references – Art. 81(b) (not reproduced): translation of documents by the Administrative Commission on Social Security for Migrant Workers
Art. 98: implementing Regulation 574/72 made by virtue of art. 98.

ART. 84a Relations between the institutions and the persons covered by this Regulation.

84a(1) The institutions and persons covered by this Regulation shall have a duty of mutual information and cooperation to ensure the correct implementation of this Regulation.

The institutions, in accordance with the principle of good administration, shall respond to all queries within a reasonable period of time and shall in this connection provide the persons concerned with any information required for exercising the rights conferred on them by this Regulation.

The persons concerned shall inform the institutions of the competent State and of the State of residence as soon as possible of any changes in their personal or family situation which affect their right to benefits under this Regulation.

84a(2) Failure to respect the obligation of information referred to in paragraph 1, third subparagraph, may result in the application of proportionate measures in accordance with national law. Nevertheless, these measures shall be equivalent to those applicable to similar situations under domestic law and shall not make it impossible or excessively difficult in practice for claimants to exercise the rights conferred on them by this Regulation.

84a(3) In the event of difficulties in the interpretation or application of this Regulation which could jeopardise the rights of a person covered by it, the institution of the competent State or of the State of residence of the person involved shall contact the institution(s) of the Member State(s) concerned. If a solution cannot be found within a reasonable period, the authorities concerned may call on the Administrative Commission to intervene.

History – Reg. 84a inserted by Regulation 631/2004, art. 1 (OJ 2004 L100), which entered into force on 1 June 2004.

ART. 91 Contributions chargeable to employers or undertakings not established in the competent state

91 An employer shall not be bound to pay increased contributions by reason of the fact that his place of business or the registered office or place of business of his undertaking is in the territory of a Member State other than the competent state.

ART. 92 Collection of contributions

92(1) Contributions payable to an institution of one Member State may be collected in the territory of another Member State in accordance with the administrative procedure and with the guarantees and privileges applicable to the collection of contributions payable to the corresponding institution of the latter state.

92(2) The procedure for the implementation of the provisions of paragraph 1 shall be governed, in so far as is necessary, by the implementing Regulation referred to in article 98 or by means of agreements between Member States. Such implementing procedure may also cover procedure for enforcing payment.

ART. 95d Transitional provisions applicable to students

95d(1) No rights shall be acquired under this Regulation by students, members of their families or their survivors for any period prior to 1 May 1999.

95d(2) Any period of insurance and, where appropriate, any period of employment, self-employment or residence completed under the legislation of a Member State before 1 May 1999 shall be taken into account for the determination of rights acquired in accordance with the provisions of this Regulation.

95d(3) Subject to the provisions of paragraph 1, a right shall be acquired under this Regulation even if it relates to a contingency arising prior to 1 May 1999.

95d(4) Any benefit that has not been awarded or that has been suspended on account of the nationality or the residence of the person concerned shall, at the latter's request, be awarded or resumed from 1 May 1999, provided that the rights for which benefits were previously awarded did not give rise to a lump-sum payment.

95d(5) If the request referred to in paragraph 4 is lodged within two years from 1 May 1999, rights deriving from this Regulation in favour of students, members of their families and their survivors shall be acquired from that date and the provisions of the legislation of any Member State on the forfeiture or lapse of rights may not be applied to the persons concerned.

95d(6) If the request referred to in paragraph 4 is lodged after expiry of the period of two years following 1 May 1999, rights not forfeited or lapsed shall be acquired from the date of such request, subject to any more favourable provisions of the legislation of any Member State.

History – Art. 95d inserted by Regulation 307/99, art. 1(11) (OJ 1999 L38/4), with effect from 1 May 1999.

TITLE VII – TRANSITIONAL AND FINAL PROVISIONS

ART. 97 Notification pursuant to certain provisions

97(1) The notifications referred to in articles 1(j), 5 and 8(2) shall be addressed to the President of the Council. They shall indicate the date of entry into force of the laws and schemes in question or, in the case of the notifications referred to in article 1(j), the date from which this Regulation shall apply to the schemes mentioned in the declarations of the Member States.

97(2) Notifications received in accordance with the provisions of paragraph 1 shall be published in the *Official Journal of the European Communities*.

ART. 98 Implementing regulation

98 A further regulation shall lay down the procedure for implementing this Regulation.

Notes – Regulation 574/72 implements Regulation 1408/71.

ANNEX I – PERSONS COVERED BY THE REGULATION

I. Employed persons and/or self-employed persons

(Article 1(a)(ii) and (iii) of the Regulation)

A. BELGIUM

Does not apply.

B. BULGARIA

Any person working without an employment contract within the meaning of points 5 and 6 of Article 4(3) of the Social Security Code shall be considered a self-employed person within the meaning of Article 1(a)(ii) of the Regulation.

C. CZECH REPUBLIC

Does not apply.

D. DENMARK

1. Any person who, from the fact of pursuing an activity as an employed person, is subject:

(a) to the legislation on accidents at work and occupational diseases for the period prior to 1 September 1977;

(b) to the legislation on supplementary pensions for employed persons (arbejdsmarkedets tillaegspension, ATP) for a period commencing on or after 1 September 1977, shall be considered as an employed person within the meaning of article 1(a)(ii) of the Regulation.

2. Any person who, pursuant to the law on daily cash benefits in the event of sickness or maternity, is entitled to such benefits on the basis of an earned income other than a wage or salary shall be considered a self-employed person within the meaning of article 1(a)(ii) of the Regulation.

E. GERMANY

If the competent institution for granting family benefits in accordance with Chapter 7 of Title III of the Regulation is a German institution, then within the meaning of article 1(a)(ii) of the Regulation:

(a) **"employed person"** means any person compulsorily insured against unemployment or any person who, as a result of such insurance, obtains cash benefits under sickness insurance or comparable benefits or any established civil servant in receipt of a salary in respect of his or her civil servant status which is at least equal to that which, in the case of an employed person, would result in compulsory insurance against unemployment;

(b) **"self-employed person"** means any person pursuing self-employment which is bound:

– to join, or pay contributions in respect of, an old-age insurance within a scheme for self-employed persons, or

– to join a scheme within the framework of compulsory pension insurance.

F. ESTONIA

Does not apply.

G. GREECE

1. Persons insured under the OGA scheme who pursue exclusively activities as employed persons or who are or have been subject to the legislation of another Member State and who consequently are or have been "employed persons" within the meaning of article 1(a) of the Regulation are considered as employed persons within the meaning of article 1(a)(iii) of the Regulation.

2. For the purposes of granting the national family allowances, persons referred to in article 1(a)(i) and (iii) of the Regulation are considered as employed persons within the meaning of article 1(a)(ii) of the Regulation.

H. SPAIN

Does not apply.

I. FRANCE

If a French institution is the competent institution for the grant of family benefits in accordance with Title III, Chapter 7 of the Regulation:

(1) **"employed person"** within the meaning of article 1(a)(ii) of the Regulation shall be deemed to mean any person who is compulsorily insured under the social security scheme in accordance with article L 311-2 of the Social Security Code and who fulfils the minimum conditions regarding work or remuneration provided for in article L 313-1 of the Social Security Code in order to benefit from cash benefits under sickness insurance, maternity and invalidity cover or the person who benefits from these cash benefits;

(2) **"self-employed person"** within the meaning of article 1(a)(ii) of the Regulation shall be deemed to mean any person who performs a self-employed activity and who is required to take out insurance and to pay old-age benefit contributions to a self-employed persons' scheme.

J. IRELAND

1. Any person who is compulsorily or voluntarily insured pursuant to the provisions of sections 12, 24 and 70 of the Social Welfare Consolidation Act 2005 shall be considered an employed person within the meaning of article 1(a)(ii) of the Regulation.

2. Any person who is compulsorily or voluntarily insured pursuant to the provisions of sections 20 and 24 of the Social Welfare Consolidation Act 2005 shall be considered a self-employed person within the meaning of article 1(a)(ii) of the Regulation.

K. ITALY

Does not apply.

L. CYPRUS

Does not apply.

M. LATVIA

Does not apply.

N. LITHUANIA

Does not apply.

O. LUXEMBOURG

Does not apply.

P. HUNGARY

Does not apply.

Q. MALTA

Any person who is a self-employed person or a self-occupied person within the meaning of the Social Security Act (Cap. 318) 1987 shall be considered as a self-employed person within the meaning of Article 1(a)(ii) of the Regulation.

R. NETHERLANDS

Any person pursuing an activity without a contract of employment shall be considered a self-employed person within the meaning of article 1(a)(ii) of the Regulation.

S. AUSTRIA

Does not apply.

T. POLAND

Does not apply.

U. PORTUGAL

Does not apply.

V. ROMANIA

Does not apply.

W. SLOVENIA

Does not apply.

X. SLOVAKIA

For the purpose of determining entitlement to benefits in kind pursuant to the provisions of Chapter 1 of title III of the Regulation, **"member of the family"** means a spouse and/or a dependent child as defined by the Act on Child Allowance.

Y. FINLAND

Any person who is an employed or self-employed person within the meaning of the legislation on the Employment Pensions Scheme shall be considered respectively as employed or self-employed within the meaning of article 1(a)(ii) of the Regulation.

Z. SWEDEN

Persons who are engaged in gainful activity and who pay their own contributions on this income pursuant to Chapter 3, paragraph 3, of the Social Insurance Contributions Act (2000:980) shall be considered as self-employed.

AA. UNITED KINGDOM

Any person who is an "employed earner" or a "self-employed earner" within the meaning of the legislation of Great Britain or of the legislation of Northern Ireland shall be regarded respectively as an employed person or a self-employed person within the meaning of article 1(a)(ii) of the Regulation. Any person in respect of whom contributions are payable as an "employed person" or a "self-employed person" in accordance with the legislation of Gibraltar shall be regarded respectively as an employed person or a self-employed person within the meaning of article 1(a)(ii) of the Regulation.

History – In entry for Ireland, references to the Social Welfare Consolidation Act 2005 amended by Regulation 592/2008 with effect from 7 July 2008.
Entries re-ordered as a result of insertion of entries for Bulgaria and Romania, by Regulation 1791/2006, art. 1, Annex, para. 2 (OJ L363).
Entries re-ordered as a result of insertion of entries for Czech Republic, Estonia, Cyprus, Latvia, Lithuania, Hungary, Poland, Slovenia and Slovakia by virtue of Annex II, being the list referred to in Article 20, of the Act of Accession of the Czech Republic, Estonia, Cyprus, Latvia, Lithuania, Hungary, Malta, Poland, Slovenia and the Slovak Republic (OJ 2003 L236) with effect from 1 May 2004.
Entries for Czech Republic, Estonia, Cyprus, Latvia, Lithuania, Hungary, Poland, Slovenia and Slovakia, with the words "Does not apply" under each of the aforementioned headings, inserted by Annex II, being the list referred to in Article 20, of the Act of Accession of the Czech Republic, Estonia, Cyprus, Latvia, Lithuania, Hungary, Malta, Poland, Slovenia and the Slovak Republic (OJ 2003 L236) with effect from 1 May 2004.
Entry for Bulgaria inserted by Regulation 1791/2006, art. 1, Annex, para. 2 (OJ L363).
In entry for Germany, in para. (a), "the words benefits or any established civil servant in receipt of a salary in respect of his or her civil servant status which is at least equal to that which, in the case of an employed person, would result in compulsory insurance against unemployment" inserted by Regulation 1399/99 (OJ 1999 L164) with effect from 1 September 1999.
Entry for France substituted by Regulation 3427/89 (OJ 1989 L331).
In entry for Ireland, references to the Social Welfare (Consolidation) Act 1993 amended by Regulation 1223/98 (OJ 1998 L168/1) with effect from 1 July 1998.
Entry for Malta, with the words of "Any person who is a self-employed person or a self-occupied person within the meaning of the Social Security Act (Cap. 318) 1987 shall be considered as a self-employed person within the meaning of Article 1(a)(ii) of the Regulation." were inserted by Annex II, being the list referred to in Article 20, of the Act of Accession of the Czech Republic, Estonia, Cyprus, Latvia, Lithuania, Hungary, Malta, Poland, Slovenia and the Slovak Republic (OJ 2003 L236) with effect from 1 May 2004.
Entry for Romania inserted by Regulation 1791/2006, art. 1, Annex, para. 2 (OJ L363).
Entry for Slovakia substituted by Regulation 629/2006, art. 1, Annex, para. 1 (OJ L114).
Entry for Sweden substituted by Regulation 1992/2006, art. 1, Annex, para. 1 (OJ L392). This entry, as substituted, was preceded by a letter "X". This appears to be an error as it ignores re-numbering by Regulation 1791/2006 so Croner-i has retained the letter "Z".

Cross references – EEA Agreement annex VI(1)(g): for the purposes of the EEA Agreement, annex I of Regulation 1408/71 is to be read subject to the following adaptations.

"Iceland

Any person who is an employed or self-employed person within the meaning of the provisions relating to the occupational injuries insurance in the Social Security Act shall be considered respectively as employed and self-employed within the meaning of article 1(a)(ii) of the Regulation.

…

Norway

Any person who is an employed or self-employed person within the meaning of the National Insurance Act shall be considered respectively as employed or self-employed within the meaning of article 1(a)(ii) of the Regulation."

ANNEX II

I. Special schemes for self-employed persons excluded from the scope of the Regulation pursuant to the fourth sub-paragraph of article 1(j)

(Article 1(j) and (u) of the Regulation)

A. BELGIUM

Does not apply.

B. BULGARIA

Does not apply.

C. CZECH REPUBLIC

Does not apply.

D. DENMARK

Does not apply.

E. GERMANY

Does not apply.

F. ESTONIA

Does not apply.

G. GREECE

Does not apply.

H. SPAIN

1. Self-employed persons as referred to in article 10(2)(c) of the Consolidated Text of the General Law on Social Security (Royal Legislative Decree No. 1/1994 of 20 June 1994) and in article 3 of Decree 2530/1970 of 20 August 1970 regulating the special scheme for self-employed persons who join a professional association and decide to become members of the mutual insurance society set up by the said association instead of joining the special social security scheme for self-employed persons.

2. Welfare system and/or with the character of social assistance or a charity, managed by institutions not subject to the General Law on Social Security or to the Law of 6 December 1941.

I. FRANCE

1. Supplementary benefit schemes for self-employed persons in craft-trade, industrial or commercial occupations or the liberal professions, supplementary old-age insurance schemes for self-employed persons in the liberal professions, supplementary insurance schemes for self-employed persons in the liberal professions covering invalidity or death, and supplementary old-age benefit schemes for contractual medical

practitioners and auxiliaries, as referred to respectively in articles L.615–20, L.644–1, L.644–2, L.645–1 and L.723–14 of the Social Security Code.

2. Supplementary sickness and maternity insurance schemes for self-employed workers in agriculture, as referred to in Article L.727–1 of the Rural Code

J. IRELAND

In order to determine the right to benefits in kind for sickness and maternity in application of the Regulation, the term **"member of the family"** shall mean any person considered as being a dependent of an employed person or of a self-employed person for the application of the Health Acts 1947 to 2004.

K. ITALY

Does not apply.

L. CYPRUS

1. Pension scheme for doctors in private practice set up under the Medical (Pensions and Allowances) Regulations of 1999 (P.I. 295/99) issued under the Medical (Associations, Discipline and Pension Fund) Law of 1967 (Law 16/67), as amended.

2. Advocates' pension scheme set up under the Advocates (Pensions and Allowances) Regulations of 1966 (P.I. 642/66), as amended, issued under the Advocates Law, Cap. 2, as amended.

M. LATVIA

Does not apply.

N. LITHUANIA

Does not apply.

O. LUXEMBOURG

Does not apply.

P. HUNGARY

For the purpose of determining entitlement to benefits in kind pursuant to the provisions of Chapter 1 of Title III of the Regulations, member of the family shall mean a spouse or dependent child as defined by Article 685(b) of the Civil Code.

Q. MALTA

Does not apply.

R. NETHERLANDS

For the purpose of determining entitlement to benefits pursuant to Chapters 1 and 4 of Title III of this Regulation, **"member of the family"** means a spouse, registered partner or child under the age of 18.

S. AUSTRIA

Does not apply.

T. POLAND

Does not apply.

U. PORTUGAL

Does not apply.

V. ROMANIA

For the purposes of determining entitlement to benefits in kind pursuant to the provisions of Chapter 1 of Title III of the Regulation, **"member of the family"** means a spouse, a dependent parent, a child under the age of 18 (or under the age of 26 and dependent).

W. SLOVENIA

Does not apply.

X. SLOVAKIA

Does not apply.

Y. FINLAND

Does not apply.

Z. SWEDEN

Does not apply.

AA. UNITED KINGDOM

Does not apply.

History – Entry for Hungary replaced by Regulation 592/2008 with effect from 7 July 2008.
Entry for Ireland replaced by Regulation 592/2008 with effect from 7 July 2008.
Entries re-ordered as a result of insertion of entries for Bulgaria and Romania, by Regulation 1791/2006, art. 1, Annex, para. 2 (OJ L363, 20.12.2006).
Entries re-ordered as a result of insertion of entries for Czech Republic, Estonia, Cyprus, Latvia, Lithuania, Hungary, Poland, Slovenia and Slovakia by virtue of Annex II, being the list referred to in Article 20, of the Act of Accession of the Czech Republic, Estonia, Cyprus, Latvia, Lithuania, Hungary, Malta, Poland, Slovenia and the Slovak Republic (OJ 2003 L236) with effect from 1 May 2004.
Entries for Czech Republic, Estonia, Cyprus, Latvia, Lithuania, Hungary, Poland, Slovenia and Slovakia, with the words of "Does not apply" under each of the aforementioned headings, were inserted by Annex II, being the list referred to in Article 20, of the Act of Accession of the Czech Republic, Estonia, Cyprus, Latvia, Lithuania, Hungary, Malta, Poland, Slovenia and the Slovak Republic (OJ 2003 L236) with effect from 1 May 2004.
Entries for Austria, Portugal, Finland, Sweden and United Kingdom inserted by Annex 1 of the Act of Accession of Austria, Finland and Sweden (as adjusted by Decision 95/1 (OJ 1995 L1/1) with effect from 1 January 1995.
Entry for Austria substituted by Regulation 647/2005, art. 10, Annex I, para. 1 (OJ L117).
Entry for Bulgaria inserted by Regulation 1791/2006, art. 1, Annex, para. 2 (OJ L363).
The entry for Cyprus, with the words of "1. Pension scheme for doctors in private practice set up under the Medical (Pensions and Allowances) Regulations of 1999 (P.I. 295/99) issued under the Medical (Associations, Discipline and Pension Fund) Law of 1967 (Law 16/67), as amended. 2. Advocates' pension scheme set up under the Advocates (Pensions and Allowances) Regulations of 1966 (P.I. 642/66), as amended, issued under the Advocates Law, Cap. 2, as amended.", inserted by Annex II, being the list referred to in Article 20, of the Act of Accession of the Czech Republic, Estonia, Cyprus, Latvia, Lithuania, Hungary, Malta, Poland, Slovenia and the Slovak Republic (OJ 2003 L236) with effect from 1 May 2004.
Entry for France substituted by Regulation 629/2006, art. 1, Annex, para. 2 (OJ L114).
Entry for Germany substituted by Regulation 647/2005, art. 10, Annex I, para. 1 (OJ L117).
Entry for the Netherlands substituted by Regulation 1992/2006, art. 1, Annex, para. 1 (OJ L392). This entry, as substituted, was preceded by a letter "Q". This appears to be an error as it ignores re-numbering by Regulation 1791/2006 so Croner-i has retained the letter "R".

Entry for Portugal substituted by Annex 1 of the Act of Accession of Austria, Finland and Sweden (as adjusted by Decision 95/1 (OJ 1995 L1/1) with effect from 1 January 1995.
Entryfor Romania inserted by Regulation 1791/2006, art. 1, Annex, para. 2 (OJ L363).
Entry for Spain substituted by Regulation 1290/97, art. 1(7) (OJ 1997 L176/1), with effect from 4 October 1997.
Former entry for Spain substituted by Annex 1 of the Act of Accession of Austria, Finland and Sweden (as adjusted by Decision 95/1 (OJ 1995 L1/1) with effect from 1 January 1995.

ANNEX III – PROVISIONS OF SOCIAL SECURITY CONVENTIONS REMAINING APPLICABLE NOTWITHSTANDING ARTICLE 6 OF THE REGULATION – PROVISIONS OF SOCIAL SECURITY CONVENTIONS WHICH DO NOT APPLY TO ALL PERSONS TO WHOM THE REGULATION APPLIES

(Articles 7(2)(c) and (3)(3) of the Regulation)

General comments

1. In so far as the provisions contained in this annex provide for references to the provisions of other conventions, those references shall be replaced by references to the corresponding provisions of this Regulation, unless the provisions of the conventions in question are themselves contained in this annex.

2. The termination clause provided for in a social security convention, some of whose provisions are contained in this annex, shall continue to apply as regards those provisions.

3. Account being taken of the provisions of Article 6 of this Regulation, it is to be noted that the provisions of bilateral Conventions which do not fall within the scope of this Regulation and which remain in force between Member States are not listed in this Annex, inter alia, provisions providing for aggregation of insurance periods fulfilled in a third country.

History – Para. 3 inserted by Regulation 647/2005, art. 10, Annex I, para. 3 (OJ L117).

A. Provisions of social security conventions remaining applicable notwithstanding article 6 of the Regulation

(Article 7(2)(c) of the Regulation)

…

23. GERMANY–UNITED KINGDOM

(a) Article 7(5) and (6) of the Convention on social security of 20 April 1960 (legislation applicable to civilians serving the military forces);

(b) Article 5(5) and (6) of the Convention on unemployment insurance of 20 April 1960 (legislation applicable to civilians serving the military forces)

24. BELGIUM–UNITED KINGDOM

[Repealed by Regulation 647/2005, art. 10, Annex I, para. 3 (OJ L117; 4.5.2005).]

…

25. IRELAND–UNITED KINGDOM

Article 8 of the Agreement of 14 September 1971 on social security (concerning the transfer and reckoning of certain disability credits)

…

30. PORTUGAL–UNITED KINGDOM

(a) Article 2(1) of the Protocol on medical treatment of 15 November 1978.

(b) As regards Portuguese employed persons, and for the period from 22 October 1987 to the end of the transitional period provided for in Article 220(1) of the Act relating to the conditions of accession of Spain and Portugal: Article 26 of the Social Security Convention of 15 November 1978, as amended by the Exchange of Letters of 28 September 1987.

…

47. CZECH REPUBLIC–UNITED KINGDOM

[Repealed by Regulation 629/2006, art. 1, Annex, para. 5 (OJ L114).]

69. DENMARK–UNITED KINGDOM

[Repealed by Regulation 647/2005, art. 10, Annex I, para. 3 (OJ L117).

…

110. ESTONIA–UNITED KINGDOM

[Repealed by Regulation 629/2006, art. 1, Annex, para. 5 (OJ L114).]

…

129. GREECE–UNITED KINGDOM

[Repealed by Regulation 647/2005, art. 10, Annex I, para. 3 (OJ L117).]

…

147. SPAIN–UNITED KINGDOM

[Repealed by Regulation 647/2005, art. 10, Annex I, para. 3 (OJ L117).]

…

164. FRANCE–UNITED KINGDOM

[Repealed by Regulation 647/2005, art. 10, Annex I, para. 3 (OJ L117).]

…

195. ITALY–UNITED KINGDOM

[Repealed by Regulation 647/2005, art. 10, Annex I, para. 3 (OJ L1175).]

…

209. CYPRUS–UNITED KINGDOM

[Repealed by Regulation 629/2006, art. 1, Annex, para. 5 (OJ L114).]

…

222. LATVIA–UNITED KINGDOM

[Repealed by Regulation 629/2006, art. 1, Annex, para. 5 (OJ L114).]

…

234. LITHUANIA–UNITED KINGDOM

[Repealed by Regulation 629/2006, art. 1, Annex, para. 5 (OJ L114).]

…

245. LUXEMBOURG–UNITED KINGDOM

[Repealed by Regulation 647/2005, art. 10, Annex I, para. 3 (OJ L117).]

…

255. HUNGARY–UNITED KINGDOM

[Repealed by Regulation 629/2006, art. 1, Annex, para. 5 (OJ L114).]

…

264. MALTA–UNITED KINGDOM

[Repealed by Regulation 629/2006, art. 1, Annex, para. 5 (OJ L114).]

…

272. NETHERLANDS–UNITED KINGDOM

[Repealed by Regulation 647/2005, art. 10, Annex I, para. 3 (OJ L117).]

…

279. AUSTRIA–UNITED KINGDOM

[Repealed by Regulation 647/2005, art. 10, Annex I, para. 3 (OJ L117).]

…

285. POLAND–UNITED KINGDOM

[Repealed by Regulation 629/2006, art. 1, Annex, para 5 (OJ L114).]

…

294. SLOVENIA–UNITED KINGDOM

[Repealed by Regulation 629/2006, art. 1, Annex, para. 5 (OJ L114).]

…

297. SLOVAKIA–UNITED KINGDOM

[Repealed by Regulation 629/2006, art. 1, Annex, para. 5 (OJ L114).]

…

299. FINLAND–UNITED KINGDOM

[Repealed by Regulation 647/2005, art. 10, Annex I, para. 3 (OJ L1175).]

300. SWEDEN–UNITED KINGDOM

[Repealed by Regulation 647/2005, art. 10, Annex I, para. 3 (OJ L117).]

B. Provisions of conventions which do not apply to all persons to whom the Regulation applies

(Article 3(3) of the Regulation)

…

24. BELGIUM–UNITED KINGDOM

[Repealed by Regulation 647/2005, art. 10, Annex I, para. 3 (OJ L117).]

…

47. CZECH REPUBLIC–UNITED KINGDOM

[Repealed by Regulation 629/2006, art. 1, Annex, para. 5 (OJ L114).]

…

69. DENMARK–UNITED KINGDOM

[Repealed by Regulation 647/2005, art. 10, Annex I, para. 3 (OJ L117).]

…

90. GERMANY–UNITED KINGDOM

[Repealed by Regulation 647/2005 art. 10, Annex I, para. 3 (OJ L117).]

…

110. ESTONIA–UNITED KINGDOM

[Repealed by Regulation 629/2006, art. 1, Annex, para. 5 (OJ L114).]

…

129. GREECE–UNITED KINGDOM

[Repealed by Regulation 647/2005, art. 10, Annex I, para. 3 (OJ L117).]

…

147. SPAIN–UNITED KINGDOM

[Repealed by Regulation 647/2005, art. 10, Annex I, para. 3 (OJ L117).]

…

164. FRANCE–UNITED KINGDOM

[Repealed by Regulation 647/2005, art. 10, Annex I, para. 3 (OJ L117).]

…

180. IRELAND–UNITED KINGDOM

[Repealed by Regulation 647/2005, art. 10, Annex I, para. 3 (OJ L117).]

…

195. ITALY–UNITED KINGDOM

[Repealed by Regulation 647/2005, art. 10, Annex I, para. 3 (OJ L117).]

…

209. CYPRUS–UNITED KINGDOM

[Repealed by Regulation 629/2006, art. 1, Annex, para. 5 (OJ L114).]

…

222. LATVIA–UNITED KINGDOM

[Repealed by Regulation 629/2006, art. 1, Annex, para. 5 (OJ L114).]

…

234. LITHUANIA–UNITED KINGDOM

[Repealed by Regulation 629/2006, art. 1, Annex, para. 5 (OJ L114).]

…

245. LUXEMBOURG–UNITED KINGDOM

[Repealed by Regulation 647/2005, art. 10, Annex I, para. 3 (OJ L117).]

…

255. HUNGARY–UNITED KINGDOM

[Repealed by Regulation 629/2006, art. 1, Annex, para. 5 (OJ L114).]

…

264. MALTA–UNITED KINGDOM

[Repealed by Regulation 629/2006, art. 1, Annex, para. 5 (OJ L114).]

…

272. NETHERLANDS–UNITED KINGDOM

[Repealed by Regulation 647/2005, art. 10, Annex I, para. 3 (OJ L117).]

…

279. AUSTRIA–UNITED KINGDOM

[Repealed by Regulation 647/2005, art. 10, Annex I, para. 3 (OJ L117).]

…

285. POLAND–UNITED KINGDOM

[Repealed by Regulation 629/2006, art. 1, Annex, para. 5 (OJ L114).]

…

290. PORTUGAL–UNITED KINGDOM

[Repealed by Regulation 647/2005, art. 10, Annex I, para. 3 (OJ L117).]

…

294. SLOVENIA–UNITED KINGDOM

[Repealed by Regulation 629/2006, art. 1, Annex, para. 5 (OJ L114).]

…

297. SLOVAKIA–UNITED KINGDOM

[Repealed by Regulation 629/2006, art. 1, Annex, para. 5 (OJ L114).]

…

299. FINLAND–UNITED KINGDOM

[Repealed by Regulation 647/2005, art. 10, Annex I, para. 3 (OJ L117).]

300. SWEDEN–UNITED KINGDOM

[Repealed by Regulation 647/2005, art. 10, Annex I, para. 3 (OJ L117).]

History – In Parts A and B, entries renumbered by virtue of Annex II, being the list referred to in Article 20, of the Act of Accession of the Czech Republic, Estonia, Cyprus, Latvia, Lithuania, Hungary, Malta, Poland, Slovenia and the Slovak Republic (OJ 2003 L236) with effect from 1 May 2004.

In Parts A and B, entries for Czech Republic–United Kingdom, Estonia–United Kingdom, Cyprus–United Kingdom, Latvia–United Kingdom, Lithuania–United Kingdom, Hungary–United Kingdom, Malta–United Kingdom, Poland–United Kingdom, Slovenia–United Kingdom and Slovakia–United Kingdom inserted by Annex II, being the list referred to in Article 20, of the Act of Accession of the Czech Republic, Estonia, Cyprus, Latvia, Lithuania, Hungary, Malta, Poland, Slovenia and the Slovak Republic (OJ 2003 L236) with effect from 1 May 2004.

Entry for Portugal (Part A) substituted by Regulation 2332/89/EEC (OJ L224).

In the entry for Germany (Part A), words substituted by Regulation 647/2005, art. 10, Annex I, para. 3 (OJ L117).

In the entry for Ireland (Part A), words substituted by Regulation 647/2005, art. 10, Annex I, para. 3 (OJ L117).

Cross references – Cross references – Title III, Ch. 1 (art. 18–36): sickness and maternity benefits.

SI 1961/1202, Sch. 1 (not reproduced): convention on social security (Germany–UK) of 20 April 1960.

SI 1961/1513, Sch. 1 (not reproduced): Convention on unemployment insurance (Germany–UK) of 20 April 1960.

EEA Agreement annex VI(1)(k): for the purposes of the EEA Agreement, annex III(A) of Regulation 1408/71 is to be read subject to the following adaptations.

"…

Iceland–United Kingdom

None.

…

Liechtenstein–United Kingdom

No convention.

…

Norway–United Kingdom

None."

EEA Agreement annex VI(1)(l): for the purposes of the EEA Agreement, annex III(B) of Regulation 1408/71 is to be read subject to the following adaptations.

"…

Iceland–United Kingdom

None.

…

Liechtenstein–United Kingdom
No convention.
…
Norway–United Kingdom
None."

ANNEX VII – INSTANCES IN WHICH A PERSON SHALL BE SIMULTANEOUSLY SUBJECT TO THE LEGISLATION OF TWO MEMBER STATES

(Article 14c(1)(b) of the Regulation)

1. Where he is self-employed in Belgium and gainfully employed in any other Member State..
2. Where a person is self-employed in Bulgaria and gainfully employed in any other Member State.
3. Where a person is self-employed in the Czech Republic and gainfully employed in any other Member State.
4. Where a person resident in Denmark is self-employed in Denmark and gainfully employed in any other Member State.
5. For the agricultural accident insurance scheme and the old-age insurance scheme for farmers: where he is self-employed in farming in Germany and gainfully employed in any other Member State.
6. Where a person resident in Estonia is self-employed in Estonia and gainfully employed in any other Member State.
7. For the pension insurance scheme for self-employed persons: where he is self-employed in Greece and gainfully employed in any other Member State.
8. Where a person resident in Spain is self-employed in Spain and gainfully employed in any other Member State.
9. Where he is self-employed in France and gainfully employed in any other Member State, except Luxembourg.
10. Where he is self-employed in farming in France and gainfully employed in Luxembourg.
11. Where he is self-employed in Italy and gainfully employed in any other Member State.
12. Where a person resident in Cyprus is self-employed in Cyprus and gainfully employed in any other Member State.
13. Where a person is self-employed in Malta and gainfully employed in any other Member State.
14. Where he is self-employed in Portugal and gainfully employed in any other Member State.
15. Where a person is self-employed in Romania and gainfully employed in any other Member State.
16. Where a person resident in Finland is self-employed in Finland and gainfully employed in any other Member State.
17. Where a person is self-employed in Slovakia and gainfully employed in any other Member State.
18. Where a person resident in Sweden is self-employed in Sweden and gainfully employed in any other Member State.

History – Annex substituted by Regulation 1791/2006, art. 1, Annex, para. 2 (OJ L 363).
Former Annex renumbered by Regulation 3096/95 (OJ 1995 L335) with effect from 1 January 1996.

Cross references – EEA Agreement annex VI(1)(o): for the purposes of the EEA Agreement, annex VI of Regulation 1408/71 is to be read subject to the following adaptations.

"…

Where a person resident in Iceland is self-employed in Iceland and gainfully employed in any other state to which this Regulation applies.

…

Where a person resident in Norway is self-employed in Norway and gainfully employed in any other state to which this Regulation applies.""

REGULATION 574/72

Laying down the procedure for implementing Regulation 1408/71 on the application of social security schemes to employed persons, to self-employed persons and to members of their families moving within the [European] Community.

(21 March 1972, OJ 1972(I), Eng. Spec. Ed., p. 159)

Notes – Regulation 1408/71 is repealed for most purposes from the date of application of Regulation 883/2004 (1 May 2010 – the date of entry into force of the *Implementing Regulation* (as provided for by Regulation 883/2004, art. 89)). Regulation 1408/71 continues to remain in force and shall continue to have legal effect for the purposes of:

(a) Regulation 859/2003 of 14 May 2003 which extends the provisions of Regulation 1408/71 and Regulation 574/72 to nationals of third countries who are not already covered by those provisions solely on the ground of their nationality, for as long as that Regulation has not been repealed or modified;

(b) Regulation 1661/85 of 13 June 1985 which lays down the technical adaptations to the Community rules on social security for migrant workers with regard to Greenland, for as long as that Regulation has not been repealed or modified;

(c) *the Agreement on the* European Economic Area and the Agreement between the European Community and its Member States, of the one part, and the Swiss Confederation, of the other part, on the free movement of persons and other agreements which contain a reference to Regulation (EEC) No 1408/71, for as long as those agreements have not been modified in the light of Regulation 883/2004.

The consolidated text of Regulation 574/72 (OJ 1997 L28/102) is therefore reproduced below:

"TITLE I – GENERAL PROVISIONS

ART. 1 Definitions

1 For the purposes of this regulation:

(a) **"regulation"** means Regulation 1408/71;

(b) **"implementing regulation"** means this regulation;

(c) the definitions in article 1 of the regulation have the meaning assigned to them in the said article.

ART. 2 Printed model forms – Information on legislations – Guides

2(1) Models of the documents necessary for application of the Regulation and of the implementing Regulation shall be drawn up by the Administrative Commission. These documents may be transferred between institutions either in paper or other form or by means of telematic services as standardised electronic messages in accordance with Title VIa. The exchange of information by means of telematic services shall be subject to agreement between the competent authorities or the bodies designated by the competent authorities of the sending Member State and those of the receiving Member State.

2(2) For the benefit of the competent authorities of each member state, the Administrative Commission may assemble information on the provisions of the regulation.

2(3) The Administrative Commission shall prepare guides for the purpose of advising persons concerned of their rights and of the administrative formalities to be completed for the exercise of those rights.

The Advisory Committee shall be consulted before such guides are drawn up.

History – Art. 2(1) substituted by Regulation 631/2004, art. 2 (OJ 2004 L100) which entered into force on 1 June 2004. The former art. 2(1) read:

"**2(1)** Models of certificates, certified statements, declarations, claims and other documents necessary for the application of the regulation and of the implementing regulation shall be drawn up by the Administrative Commission.

Two member states or their competent authorities may, by mutual agreement and having received the opinion of the Administrative Commission, adopt simplified models for use between them.

The certificates, certified statements, declarations, claims and other documents may be transferred between institutions either in paper form or by means of telematic services as standardised electronic messages in accordance with the provisions of Title Via. Exchanges of information by means of telematic services is subject to an agreement between the competent authorities of the sending and the receiving member states.".

Art. 2(1) substituted by Regulation 1290/97, art. 2(1) (OJ 1997 L176/1), with effect from 4 October 1997.

ART. 3 Liaison bodies – Communications between institutions and between beneficiaries and institutions

3(1) The competent authorities may designate liaison bodies which may communicate directly with each other.

3(2) Any institution of a member state, and any person residing or staying in the territory of a member state, may make application to the institution of another member state, either directly or through the liaison bodies.

3(3) Decisions and other documents emanating from an institution of a member state and intended for persons residing or staying in the territory of another member state may be communicated directly by registered letter with acknowledgement of receipt.

History – Reg. 3(3) added by Regulation 2332/89/EEC (OJ L224).

TITLE II – IMPLEMENTATION OF THE GENERAL PROVISIONS OF THE REGULATION

Implementation of articles 6 and 7 of the regulation

ART. 5 Replacement by the implementing regulation of arrangements for implementing conventions

5 The provisions of the implementing regulation shall replace those of the arrangements for implementing the conventions referred to in article 6 of the regulation; they shall also replace the provisions relating to the implementation of the provisions of the conventions referred to in article 7(2)(c) of the regulation in so far as they are not listed in Annex 5.

Implementation of article 9 of the regulation

ART. 6 Admission to voluntary or optional continued insurance

6(1) If by virtue of articles 9 and 15(3) of the regulation, a person satisfies the conditions for admission to a voluntary or optional continued insurance in respect of invalidity, old age and death (pensions) in several schemes under the legislation of one member state, and if he has not been subject to compulsory insurance under one of those schemes by virtue of his last employment or self-employment he may, under the said articles, join the voluntary or optional continued insurance scheme specified by the legislation of that member state or, failing that, the scheme of his choice.

6(2) In order to invoke the provisions of article 9(2) of the regulation, a person shall submit to the institution of the member state in question a certified statement relating to the insurance periods or periods of residence completed under the legislation of any other member state. Such certified statement shall be issued, at the request of the person concerned, by the institution or institutions who administer the legislation under which he has completed those periods.

TITLE III – IMPLEMENTATION OF THE PROVISIONS OF THE REGULATION FOR DETERMINING THE LEGISLATION APPLICABLE

Implementation of articles 13 to 17 of the regulation

ART. 10b Formalities pursuant to article 13(2)(f) of the regulation

10b The date and conditions on which the legislation of a member state ceases to be applicable to a person referred to in article 13(2)(f) of the regulation shall be determined in accordance with that legislation. The institution designated by the competent authority of the member state whose legislation becomes applicable to the person shall apply to the institution designated by the competent authority of the former member state with a request to specify this date.

ART. 11 Formalities in the case of the posting elsewhere of an employed person pursuant to articles 14(1) and 14b(1) of the regulation and in the case of agreements concluded under article 17 of the regulation

11(1) The institutions designated by the competent authority of the member states whose legislation is to remain applicable shall issue a certificate stating that an employed person shall remain subject to that legislation up to a specific date:

(a) at the request of the employed person or his employer in cases referred to in article 14(1) and 14b(1) of the regulation;

(b) in cases where article 17 of the regulation applies.

11(2) The consent provided for in cases referred to in article 14(1)(b) and 14b(1) of the regulation shall be requested by the employer.

ART. 11a Formalities pursuant to articles 14a(1) and 14b(2) of the regulation and in the case of agreements concluded under article 17 of the regulation in the case of work carried out in the territory of a member state other than that in which the person concerned is normally self-employed

11a(1) The institution designated by the competent authority of the member state whose legislation is to remain applicable shall issue a certificate stating that the self-employed person shall remain subject to that legislation up to a specified date:

(a) at the request of the self-employed person in cases referred to in articles 14a(1) and 14b(2) of the regulation;

(b) in cases where article 17 of the regulation applies.

11a(2) The consent provided for in cases referred to in articles 14a(1)(b) and 14b(2) of the regulation shall be requested by the self-employed person.

ART. 12 Special provisions concerning insurance of employed persons under the German social security scheme

12 Where, under the terms of articles 13(2)(a), 14(1) and (2) or 14b(1) of the regulation, or under an agreement concluded pursuant to article 17 of the regulation, German legislation applies to a person employed by an undertaking or employer whose registered office or place of business is not situated on German territory, and the person concerned has no fixed job on German territory, this legislation shall apply as if the person concerned were employed in his place of residence on German territory.

If the employed person has no residence on German territory, German legislation shall apply as if he were employed in a place for which the Allgemeine Ortskrankenkasse Bonn (Local General Sickness Fund of Bonn), Bonn, is competent.

ART. 12a Rules applicable in respect of the persons referred to in articles 14(2) and (3), 14a(2) to (4) and article 14c of the regulation who normally carry out an employed or self-employed activity in the territory of two or more member states

For the application of the provisions of article 14(2) and (3), article 14a(2) and (4) and article 14c of the regulation, the following rules shall apply:

History – The text of the heading and introductory sentence substituted by Reg 2005/647, with effect from 5 May 2005.

12a(1)

(a) A person who normally pursues his activity in the territory of two or more member states or in an undertaking which has its registered office or place of business in the territory of one member state and which straddles the common frontier of two member states, or who is employed simultaneously in the territory of one member state and self-employed in the territory of another member state shall notify this situation to the institution designated by the competent authority of the member state in the territory of which he resides.

(b) Where the legislation of the member state in the territory of which the person resides is not applicable to him, the institution designated by the competent authority of that member state shall in turn notify the situation to the institution designated by the competent authority of the member state whose legislation is applicable.

12a(1a) Where, in accordance with article 14(2)(a) of the regulation, a person who is a member of the travelling or flying personnel of an international transport undertaking is subject to the legislation of the member state in whose territory the registered office or place of business of the undertaking, or the branch or permanent establishment employing him, is located, or where he resides and is predominately employed, the institution designated by the competent authority of that member state shall issue to the person concerned a certificate stating that he is subject to its legislation.

12a(2)

(a) Where, in accordance with article 14(2)(b)(i) or the first sentence of paragraph 2 of article 14a of the regulation, a person who is normally employed or self-employed in the territory of two or more member states and who pursues part of his activity in the member state in whose territory he resides is subject to the legislation of that member state, the institution designated by the competent authority of that member state shall issue to the person concerned a certificate stating that he is subject to its legislation and shall send a copy thereof to the institution designated by the competent authority of any other member state:
   (i) in the territory of which the person concerned pursues a part of his activity, and/or
   (ii) if he is an employed person, in the territory of which an undertaking or an employer by whom he is employed has its registered office or place of business.

(b) The latter institution shall, where necessary, send to the institution designated by the competent authority of the member state whose legislation is applicable the information necessary to assess the contributions for which the employer or employers and/or the person concerned are liable by virtue of that legislation.

12a(3)

(a) Where, in accordance with article 14(3) or 14a(3) of the regulation, a person who is employed in the territory of one member state by an undertaking which has its registered office or place of business in the territory of another member state and which straddles the common frontier of those states, or who is self-employed in such an undertaking, is subject to the legislation of the member state in whose territory the undertaking has its registered office or place of business, the institution designated by the competent authority of the latter member state shall issue to the person concerned a certificate stating that he is subject to its legislation and shall send a copy thereof to the institution designated by the competent authority of any other member state:
   (i) in the territory of which the person concerned is employed or self-employed;
   (ii) in the territory of which the person concerned resides.

(b) Paragraph 2(b) above shall apply by analogy.

12a(4)

(a) Where, in accordance with article 14(2)(b)(ii) of the regulation, an employed person who does not reside in the territory of any of the member states in which he is pursuing his activity, is subject to the legislation of the member state in whose territory is situated the registered office or place of business of the undertaking or individual employing him, the institution designated by the competent authority of the latter member state shall issue to the employed person a certificate stating that he is subject to its legislation and shall send a copy thereof to the institution designated by the competent authority of any other member state:
   (i) in the territory of which the employed person pursues a part of his activity;
   (ii) in the territory of which the employed person resides.

(b) Paragraph 2(b) above shall apply by analogy.

12a(5)

(a) Where, in accordance with the provisions of the second sentence of paragraph 2 of article 14a of the regulation, a person who is normally self-employed in the territory of two or more member states but who does not pursue any part of his activity in the territory of the member state in which he resides, is subject to the legislation of the member state in whose territory he pursues his principal activity, the institution designated by the competent authority of the member state in the territory of which he resides shall forthwith inform the institution designated by the competent authorities of the other member states concerned.

(b) The competent authorities of the member states concerned or the institutions designated by those competent authorities shall by common agreement determine the legislation applicable to the person concerned, account being taken of the provisions of subparagraph (d) and, where appropriate, of the provisions of article 14a(4) of the regulation, within a period of not more than six months counting from the day on which the situation of the person concerned was notified to one of the institutions concerned.

(c) The institution administering the legislation that has been determined as being applicable to the person concerned shall issue a certificate to that person showing that he is subject to that legislation and shall send a copy thereof to the other institutions concerned.

(d) For the purpose of determining, in pursuance of the third sentence of article 14a(2) of the regulation, the principal activity of the person concerned, account shall be taken first and foremost of the locality in which the fixed and permanent premises from which the person concerned pursues his activities is situated. Failing this, account shall be taken of criteria such as the usual nature or the duration of the activities pursued, the number of services rendered and the income arising from those activities.

(e) The institution concerned shall exchange all information necessary to determine both the principal activity of the person concerned and the contributions payable under the legislation that has been determined as being applicable to him.

12a(6)
(a) Without prejudice to paragraph 5, and in particular to subparagraph (b) thereof, if the institution designated by the competent authority of the member state whose legislation would be applicable by virtue of article 14a(2) or (3) of the regulation establishes that the provisions of paragraph 4 of the said article apply in the case of the person concerned, it shall notify the competent authorities of the other member states concerned or the institutions designated by those authorities; where necessary, the legislation to be applicable to the person concerned shall be decided on by common agreement.
(b) The information referred to in paragraph 2(b) above shall be sent by the other institutions concerned to the institutions designated by the competent authority of the member state whose legislation is determined to be applicable.

12a(7)
(a) Where, in accordance with article 14c(a) of the regulation, a person who is employed simultaneously in the territory of one member state and is self-employed in the territory of another member state, is subject to the legislation of the member state in whose territory he is engaged in paid employment, the institution designated by the competent authority of the latter member state shall issue to the employed person a certificate stating that he is subject to its legislation and shall send a copy thereof to the institution designated by the competent authority of any other member state:
  (i) in the territory of which that person is self-employed;
  (ii) in the territory of which that person resides.
(b) Paragraph 2(b) above shall apply by analogy.

12a(8) Where, in accordance with the provisions of article 14c(b) of the regulation, a person who is simultaneously employed in the territory of one member state and self-employed in the territory of another member state is subject to the legislation of two member states, the provisions of points 1, 2, 3 and 4 shall be applicable in respect of paid employment, and the provisions of points 1, 2, 3, 5 and 6 shall be applicable mutatis mutandis in respect of self-employment.
The institutions designated by the competent authorities of the two Member States, whose legislation is determined to be applicable, shall inform each other accordingly.

History – Art. 12a(1a) inserted by Reg. 2005/647, with effect from 5 May 2005.

ART. 12b Rules applicable in respect of persons referred to in Articles 14e or 14f of the Regulation
12b The provisions of Article 12a(1), (2), (3) and (4) shall apply by analogy to those persons covered by Articles 14e or 14f of the Regulation. In cases covered by Article 14f of the Regulation, the institution designated by the competent authorities of the Member States whose legislation is determined to be applicable shall inform each other accordingly.

History – Art. 12b inserted by Reg. 1606/98, with effect from 25 October 1998.

ART. 13 Exercise of the right of option by persons employed by diplomatic missions and consular posts
13(1) The right of option provided for in article 16(2) of the regulation must be exercised in the first instance within the three months following the date on which the employed person was engaged by the diplomatic mission or consular post concerned, or on which he entered into the personal service of agents of such mission or post. The option shall take effect on the date of entry into employment.
When the person concerned renews his right of option at the end of a calendar year, the option shall take effect on the first day of the following calendar year.
13(2) The person concerned who exercises his right of option shall inform the institution designated by the competent authority of the member state for whose legislation he has opted, at the same time notifying his employer thereof. The said institution shall, where necessary, forward such information to all other institutions of the same member state, in accordance with directives issued by the competent authority of that member state.
13(3) The institution designated by the competent authority of the member state for whose legislation the person concerned has opted, shall issue to him a certificate testifying that he is subject to the legislation of that member state while he is employed by the diplomatic mission or consular post in question or in the personal service, of agents of such mission or post.
13(4) Where the person concerned has opted for German legislation to be applied, the provisions of that legislation shall be applied as though he were employed in the place where the German Government has its seat. The competent authority shall designate the competent sickness insurance institution.

ART. 14 Exercise of the right of option by auxiliary staff of the European Communities
14(1) The right of option provided for in article 16(3) of the regulation must be exercised at the time when the contract of employment is concluded. The authority empowered to conclude such contract shall inform the institution designated by the competent authority of the member state for whose legislation the auxiliary staff member has opted. The said institution shall, where necessary, forward such information to all other institutions of the same member state.
14(2) The institution designated by the competent authority of the member state for whose legislation the auxiliary staff member has opted shall issue to him a certificate testifying that he is subject to the legislation of that member state while he is employed by the European Communities as an auxiliary staff member.
14(3) The competent authorities of the member states shall, where necessary, designate the competent institutions in respect of members of the auxiliary staff of the European Communities.
14(4) Where an auxiliary staff member, employed in the territory of a member state other than Germany, has opted for German legislation to be applied, the provisions of that legislation shall be applied as though that auxiliary staff member were employed in the place where the German Government has its seat. The competent authority shall designate the competent sickness insurance institution.

TITLE VI – MISCELLANEOUS PROVISIONS

ART. 109 Arrangement for payment of contributions
109 The employer who has no place of business in the member state in whose territory the employed person is employed may agree with the latter that he shall assume the obligations of the employer with regard to the payment of contributions. The employer shall notify the competent institution or, where necessary, the institution designated by the competent authority of the said member state of any such arrangement.

ART. 116 Agreements relating to the recovery of contributions
116(1) Agreements concluded pursuant to article 92(2) of the regulation shall be entered in Annex 5 to the implementing regulation.
116(2) Agreements concluded for the implementation of article 51 of the regulation shall continue to apply provided they are included in Annex 5 to the implementing regulation.

Notes – The UK has concluded no agreements concerning the collection of contributions."

REGULATION 859/2003
Extending the provisions of Regulation (EEC) No 1408/71 and Regulation (EEC) No 574/72 to nationals of third countries who are not already covered by those provisions solely on the ground of their nationality

Notes – Regulation 1408/71 is repealed for most purposes from the date of application of Regulation 883/2004 (1 May 2010 – the date of entry into force of the *Implementing Regulation* (as provided for by Regulation 883/2004, art. 89)). Regulation 1408/71 continues to remain in force and shall continue to have legal effect for the purposes of:

(a) Regulation 859/2003 of 14 May 2003 which extends the provisions of Regulation 1408/71 and Regulation 574/72 to nationals of third countries who are not already covered by those provisions solely on the ground of their nationality, for as long as that Regulation has not been repealed or modified;

(b) Regulation 1661/85 of 13 June 1985 which lays down the technical adaptations to the Community rules on social security for migrant workers with regard to Greenland, for as long as that Regulation has not been repealed or modified;

(c) the Agreement on the European Economic Area and the Agreement between the European Community and its Member States, of the one part, and the Swiss Confederation, of the other part, on the free movement of persons and other agreements which contain a reference to Regulation (EEC) No 1408/71, for as long as those agreements have not been modified in the light of Regulation 883/2004.

The text of Regulation 859/2003 is therefore reproduced below:

"**1** Subject to the provisions of the Annex to this Regulation, the provisions of Regulation (EEC) No 1408/71 and Regulation (EEC) No 574/72 shall apply to nationals of third countries who are not already covered by those provisions solely on the ground of their nationality, as well as to members of their families and to their survivors, provided they are legally resident in the territory of a Member State and are in a situation which is not confined in all respects within a single Member State.

ART. 2

2(1) This Regulation shall not create any rights in respect of the period before 1 June 2003.

2(2) Any period of insurance and, where appropriate, any period of employment, self-employment or residence completed under the legislation of a Member State before 1 June 2003 shall be taken into account for the determination of rights acquired in accordance with the provisions of this Regulation.

2(3) Subject to the provisions of paragraph 1, a right shall be acquired under this Regulation even if it relates to a contingency arising prior to 1 June 2003.

2(4) Any benefit that has not been awarded or that has been suspended on account of the nationality or the residence of the person concerned shall, at the latter's request, be awarded or resumed from 1 June 2003, provided that the rights for which benefits were previously awarded did not give rise to a lumpsum payment.

2(5) The rights of persons who prior to 1 June 2003, obtained the award of a pension may be reviewed at their request, account being taken of the provisions of this Regulation.

2(6) If the request referred to in paragraph 4 or paragraph 5 is lodged within two years from 1 June 2003, rights deriving from this Regulation shall be acquired from that date and the provisions of the legislation of any Member State on the forfeiture or lapse of rights may not be applied to the persons concerned.

2(7) If the request referred to in paragraph 4 or paragraph 5 is lodged after expiry of the deadline referred to in paragraph 6, rights not forfeited or lapsed shall be acquired from the date of such request, subject to any more favourable provisions of the legislation of any Member State.

3 This Regulation shall enter into force on the first day of the month following its publication in the Official Journal of the European Union.

Notes – This Regulation entered into force on 1 June 2003 (it was published in the Official Journal on 20 May 2003 (OJ 2003 L124)).

ANNEX: SPECIAL PROVISIONS REFERRED TO IN ARTICLE 1

[Not relevant to NI contributions.]"

REGULATION 883/2004
On the coordination of social security systems

(29 April 2004, OJ 2004 L200/1)

Commencement Date – Regulation 883/2004 entered into force on 20 May 2004. However, its effective date is 1 May 2010 (the date of entry into force of the *Implementing Regulation* (as provided for by Regulation 883/2004, art. 89)).

Notes – Under Regulation 883/2004, art. 90, Regulation 1408/71 is repealed for most purposes when Regulation 883/2004 applies. In accordance with Regulation 883/2004, art. 91, the date of application of Regulation 883/2004 is the date of entry into force of the *Implementing Regulation*. By virtue of Regulation 883/2004, art. 89, the *Implementing Regulation* lays down the procedure for implementing Regulation 883/2004.

Regulation 1231/2010 extends this Regulation and Regulation 987/2009 to nationals of third countries who are not already covered by these Regulations solely on the ground of their nationality. However, as expressly provided by para. (18) of the Preamble of that Regulation, the UK is not bound by this Regulation or subject to its application. Therefore, Regulation 1231/2010 is not reproduced here. It should be noted that for those member states that are bound by it, it repeals Regulation 859/2003.

THE EUROPEAN PARLIAMENT AND THE COUNCIL OF THE EUROPEAN UNION,

Having regard to the Treaty establishing the European Community, and in particular Articles 42 [now TFEU, art. 42] and 308 [now TFEU, art. 352] thereof,

Having regard to the proposal from the Commission presented after consultation with the social partners and the Administrative Commission on Social Security for Migrant Workers,

Having regard to the Opinion of the European Economic and Social Committee,

Acting in accordance with the procedure laid down in Article 251 of the Treaty [now TFEU, art. 292],

Whereas:

(1) The rules for coordination of national social security systems fall within the framework of free movement of persons and should contribute towards improving their standard of living and conditions of employment.

(2) The Treaty does not provide powers other than those of Article 308 [now TFEU, art. 352] to take appropriate measures within the field of social security for persons other than employed persons.

(3) Council Regulation (EEC) No 1408/71 of 14 June 1971 on the application of social security schemes to employed persons, to self-employed persons and to members of their families moving within the Community has been amended and updated on numerous occasions in order to take into account not only developments at Community level, including judgments of the Court of Justice, but also changes in legislation at national level. Such factors have played their part in making the Community coordination rules complex and lengthy. Replacing, while modernising and simplifying, these rules is therefore essential to achieve the aim of the free movement of persons.

(4) It is necessary to respect the special characteristics of national social security legislation and to draw up only a system of coordination.

(5) It is necessary, within the framework of such coordination, to guarantee within the Community equality of treatment under the different national legislation for the persons concerned.

(6) The close link between social security legislation and those contractual provisions which complement or replace such legislation and which have been the subject of a decision by the public authorities rendering them compulsory or extending their scope may call for similar protection with regard to the application of those provisions to that afforded by this Regulation. As a first step, the experience of Member States who have notified such schemes might be evaluated.

(7) Due to the major differences existing between national legislation in terms of the persons covered, it is preferable to lay down the principle that this Regulation is to apply to nationals of a Member State, stateless persons and refugees resident in the territory of a Member State who are or have been subject to the social security legislation of one or more Member States, as well as to the members of their families and to their survivors.

(8) The general principle of equal treatment is of particular importance for workers who do not reside in the Member State of their employment, including frontier workers.

(9) The Court of Justice has on several occasions given an opinion on the possibility of equal treatment of benefits, income and facts; this principle should be adopted explicitly and developed, while observing the substance and spirit of legal rulings.

(10) However, the principle of treating certain facts or events occurring in the territory of another Member State as if they had taken place in the territory of the Member State whose legislation is applicable should not interfere with the principle of aggregating periods of insurance, employment, self-employment or residence completed under the legislation of another Member State with those completed under the legislation of the competent Member State. Periods completed under the legislation of another Member State should therefore be taken into account solely by applying the principle of aggregation of periods.

(11) The assimilation of facts or events occurring in a Member State can in no way render another Member State competent or its legislation applicable.

(12) In the light of proportionality, care should be taken to ensure that the principle of assimilation of facts or events does not lead to objectively unjustified results or to the overlapping of benefits of the same kind for the same period.

(13) The coordination rules must guarantee that persons moving within the Community and their dependants and survivors retain the rights and the advantages acquired and in the course of being acquired.

(14) These objectives must be attained in particular by aggregating all the periods taken into account under the various national legislation for the purpose of acquiring and retaining the right to benefits and of calculating the amount of benefits, and by providing benefits for the various categories of persons covered by this Regulation.

(15) It is necessary to subject persons moving within the Community to the social security scheme of only one single Member State in order to avoid overlapping of the applicable provisions of national legislation and the complications which could result therefrom.

(16) Within the Community there is in principle no justification for making social security rights dependent on the place of residence of the person concerned; nevertheless, in specific cases, in particular as regards special benefits linked to the economic and social context of the person involved, the place of residence could be taken into account.

(17) With a view to guaranteeing the equality of treatment of all persons occupied in the territory of a Member State as effectively as possible, it is appropriate to determine as the legislation applicable, as a general rule, that of the Member State in which the person concerned pursues his activity as an employed or self-employed person.

(17a) Once the legislation of a Member State becomes applicable to a person under Title II of this Regulation, the conditions for affiliation and entitlement to benefits should be defined by the legislation of the competent Member State while respecting Community law.

(18) In specific situations which justify other criteria of applicability, it is necessary to derogate from that general rule.

(18a) The principle of single applicable legislation is of great importance and should be enhanced. This should not mean, however, that the grant of a benefit alone, in accordance with this Regulation and comprising the payment of insurance contributions or insurance coverage for the beneficiary, renders the legislation of the Member State, whose institution has granted that benefit, the applicable legislation for that person.

(18b) In Annex III to Council Regulation (EEC) No 3922/91 of 16 December 1991 on the harmonization of technical requirements and administrative procedures in the field of civil aviation, the concept of "home base" for flight crew and cabin crew members is defined as the location nominated by the operator to the crew member from where the crew member normally starts and ends a duty period, or a series of duty periods, and where, under normal conditions, the operator is not responsible for the accommodation of the crew member concerned. In order to facilitate the application of Title II of this Regulation for flight crew and cabin crew members, it is justified to use the concept of "home base" as the criterion for determining the applicable legislation for flight crew and cabin crew members. However, the applicable legislation for flight crew and cabin crew members should remain stable and the home base principle should not result in frequent changes of applicable legislation due to the industry's work patterns or seasonal demands.

(19) In some cases, maternity and equivalent paternity benefits may be enjoyed by the mother or the father and since, for the latter, these benefits are different from parental benefits and can be assimilated to maternity benefits *strictu sensu* in that they are provided during the first months of a new-born child's life, it is appropriate that maternity and equivalent paternity benefits be regulated jointly.

(20) In the field of sickness, maternity and equivalent paternity benefits, insured persons, as well as the members of their families, living or staying in a Member State other than the competent Member State, should be afforded protection.

(21) Provisions on sickness, maternity and equivalent paternity benefits were drawn up in the light of Court of Justice case-law. Provisions on prior authorisation have been improved, taking into account the relevant decisions of the Court of Justice.

(22) The specific position of pension claimants and pensioners and the members of their families makes it necessary to have provisions governing sickness insurance adapted to this situation.

(23) In view of the differences between the various national systems, it is appropriate that Member States make provision, where possible, for medical treatment for family members of frontier workers in the Member State where the latter pursue their activity.

(24) It is necessary to establish specific provisions regulating the non-overlapping of sickness benefits in kind and sickness benefits in cash which are of the same nature as those which were the subject of the judgments of the Court of Justice in Case C-215/99 *Jauch* and C-160/96 *Molenaar*, provided that those benefits cover the same risk.

(25) In respect of benefits for accidents at work and occupational diseases, rules should be laid down, for the purpose of affording protection, covering the situation of persons residing or staying in a Member State other than the competent Member State.

(26) For invalidity benefits, a system of coordination should be drawn up which respects the specific characteristics of national legislation, in particular as regards recognition of invalidity and aggravation thereof.

(27) It is necessary to devise a system for the award of old-age benefits and survivors' benefits where the person concerned has been subject to the legislation of one or more Member States.

(28) There is a need to determine the amount of a pension calculated in accordance with the method used for aggregation and pro-rata calculation and guaranteed by Community law where the application of national legislation, including rules concerning reduction, suspension or withdrawal, is less favourable than the aforementioned method.

(29) To protect migrant workers and their survivors against excessively stringent application of the national rules concerning reduction, suspension or withdrawal, it is necessary to include provisions strictly governing the application of such rules.

(30) As has constantly been reaffirmed by the Court of Justice, the Council is not deemed competent to enact rules imposing a restriction on the overlapping of two or more pensions acquired in different Member States by a reduction of the amount of a pension acquired solely under national legislation.

(31) According to the Court of Justice, it is for the national legislature to enact such rules, bearing in mind that it is for the Community legislature to fix the limits within which the national provisions concerning reduction, suspension or withdrawal are to be applied.

(32) In order to foster mobility of workers, it is particularly appropriate to facilitate the search for employment in the various Member States; it is therefore necessary to ensure closer and more effective coordination between the unemployment insurance schemes and the employment services of all the Member States.

(33) It is necessary to include statutory pre-retirement schemes within the scope of this Regulation, thus guaranteeing both equal treatment and the possibility of exporting pre-retirement benefits as well as the award of family and health-care benefits to the person concerned, in accordance with the provisions of this Regulation; however, the rule on the aggregation of periods should not be included, as only a very limited number of Member States have statutory pre-retirement schemes.

(34) Since family benefits have a very broad scope, affording protection in situations which could be described as classic as well as in others which are specific in nature, with the latter type of benefit having been the subject of the judgments of the Court of Justice in Joined Cases C-245/94 and C-312/94 *Hoever and Zachow* and in Case C-275/96 *Kuusijärvi*, it is necessary to regulate all such benefits.

(35) In order to avoid unwarranted overlapping of benefits, there is a need to lay down rules of priority in the case of overlapping of rights to family benefits under the legislation of the competent Member State and under the legislation of the Member State of residence of the members of the family.

(36) Advances of maintenance allowances are recoverable advances intended to compensate for a parent's failure to fulfil his legal obligation of maintenance to his own child, which is an obligation derived from family law. Therefore, these advances should not be considered as a direct benefit from collective support in favour of families. Given these particularities, the coordinating rules should not be applied to such maintenance allowances.

(37) As the Court of Justice has repeatedly stated, provisions which derogate from the principle of the exportability of social security benefits must be interpreted strictly. This means that they can apply only to benefits which satisfy the specified conditions. It follows that Chapter 9 of Title III of this Regulation can apply only to benefits which are both special and non-contributory and listed in Annex X to this Regulation.

(38) It is necessary to establish an Administrative Commission consisting of a government representative from each Member State, charged in particular with dealing with all administrative questions or questions of interpretation arising from the provisions of this Regulation, and with promoting further cooperation between the Member States.

(39) The development and use of data-processing services for the exchange of information has been found to require the creation of a Technical Commission, under the aegis of the Administrative Commission, with specific responsibilities in the field of data-processing.

(40) The use of data-processing services for exchanging data between institutions requires provisions guaranteeing that the documents exchanged or issued by electronic means are accepted as equivalent to paper documents. Such exchanges are to be carried out in accordance with the Community provisions on the protection of natural persons with regard to the processing and free movement of personal data.

(41) It is necessary to lay down special provisions which correspond to the special characteristics of national legislation in order to facilitate the application of the rules of coordination.

(42) In line with the principle of proportionality, in accordance with the premise for the extension of this Regulation to all European Union citizens and in order to find a solution that takes account of any constraints which may be connected with the special characteristics of systems based on residence, a special derogation by means of an Annex XI – "DENMARK" entry, limited to social pension entitlement exclusively in respect of the new category of non-active persons, to whom this Regulation has been extended, was deemed appropriate due to the specific features of the Danish system and in the light of the fact that those pensions are exportable after a ten-year period of residence under the Danish legislation in force (Pension Act).

(43) *In line with the principle* of equality of treatment, a special derogation by means of an Annex XI – "FINLAND" entry, limited to residence-based national pensions, is deemed appropriate due to the specific characteristics of Finnish social security legislation, the objective of which is to ensure that the amount of the national pension cannot be less than the amount of the national pension calculated as if all insurance periods completed in any Member State were completed in Finland.

(44) It is necessary to introduce a new Regulation to repeal Regulation (EEC) No 1408/71. However, it is necessary that Regulation (EEC) No 1408/71 remain in force and continue to have legal effect for the purposes of certain Community acts and agreements to which the Community is a party, in order to secure legal certainty.

(45) Since the objective of the proposed action, namely the coordination measures to guarantee that the right to free movement of persons can be exercised effectively, cannot be sufficiently achieved by the Member States and can therefore, by reason of the scale and effects of that action, be better achieved at Community level, the Community may adopt measures in accordance with the principle of subsidiarity as set out in Article 5 of the Treaty. In accordance with the principle of proportionality as set out in that article, this Regulation does not go beyond what is necessary, in order to achieve that objective,

HAVE ADOPTED THIS REGULATION:

History – Recital (17a) inserted by Reg. 988/2009, art. 1(1), with effect from 1 May 2010.
Recital (18a) inserted by Reg. 988/2009, art. 1(2), with effect from 1 May 2010.
Recital (18b) inserted by Reg. 465/2012, art. 1(2), with effect from 28 June 2012.

TITLE I – GENERAL PROVISIONS

ART. 1 Definitions

1 For the purposes of this Regulation:

(a) **"activity as an employed person"** means any activity or equivalent situation treated as such for the purposes of the social security legislation of the Member State in which such activity or equivalent situation exists;

(b) **"activity as a self-employed person"** means any activity or equivalent situation treated as such for the purposes of the social security legislation of the Member State in which such activity or equivalent situation exists;

(c) **"insured person,"** in relation to the social security branches covered by Title III, Chapters 1 and 3, means any person satisfying the conditions required under the legislation of the Member State competent under Title II to have the right to benefits, taking into account the provisions of this Regulation;

(d) **"civil servant"** means a person considered to be such or treated as such by the Member State to which the administration employing him is subject;

(e) **"special scheme for civil servants"** means any social security scheme which is different from the general social security scheme applicable to employed persons in the Member State concerned and to which all, or certain categories of, civil servants are directly subject;

(f) **"frontier worker"** means any person pursuing an activity as an employed or self-employed person in a Member State and who resides in another Member State to which he returns as a rule daily or at least once a week;

(g) **"refugee"** shall have the meaning assigned to it in Article 1 of the Convention relating to the Status of Refugees, signed in Geneva on 28 July 1951;

(h) **"stateless person"** shall have the meaning assigned to it in Article 1 of the Convention relating to the Status of Stateless Persons, signed in New York on 28 September 1954;

(i) **"member of the family"** means

(1)

(i) any person defined or recognised as a member of the family or designated as a member of the household by the legislation under which benefits are provided;

(ii) with regard to benefits in kind pursuant to Title III, Chapter 1 on sickness, maternity and equivalent paternity benefits, any person defined or recognised as a member of the family or designated as a member of the household by the legislation of the Member State in which he resides;

(2) If the legislation of a Member State which is applicable under subparagraph (1) does not make a distinction between the members of the family and other persons to whom it is applicable, the spouse, minor children, and dependent children who have reached the age of majority shall be considered members of the family;

(3) If, under the legislation which is applicable under subparagraphs (1) and (2), a person is considered a member of the family or member of the household only if he lives in the same household as the insured person or pensioner, this condition shall be considered satisfied if the person in question is mainly dependent on the insured person or pensioner;

(j) **"residence"** means the place where a person habitually resides;

(k) **"stay"** means temporary residence;

(l) **"legislation"** means, in respect of each Member State, laws, regulations and other statutory provisions and all other implementing measures relating to the social security branches covered by Article 3(1);

This term excludes contractual provisions other than those which serve to implement an insurance obligation arising from the laws and regulations referred to in the preceding subparagraph or which have been the subject of a decision by the public authorities which makes them obligatory or extends their scope, provided that the Member State concerned makes a declaration to that effect, notified to the President of the European Parliament and the President of the Council of the European Union. Such declaration shall be published in the Official Journal of the European Union;

(m) **"competent authority"** means, in respect of each Member State, the Minister, Ministers or other equivalent authority responsible for social security schemes throughout or in any part of the Member State in question;

(n) **"Administrative Commission"** means the commission referred to in Article 71;

(o) **"Implementing Regulation"** means the Regulation referred to in Article 89;

(p) **"institution"** means, in respect of each Member State, the body or authority responsible for applying all or part of the legislation;

(q) **"competent institution"** means:

(i) the institution with which the person concerned is insured at the time of the application for benefit; or

(ii) the institution from which the person concerned is or would be entitled to benefits if he or a member or members of his family resided in the Member State in which the institution is situated; or

(iii) the institution designated by the competent authority of the Member State concerned; or

(iv) in the case of a scheme relating to an employer's obligations in respect of the benefits set out in Article 3(1), either the employer or the insurer involved or, in default thereof, the body or authority designated by the competent authority of the Member State concerned;

(r) **"institution of the place of residence"** and **"institution of the place of stay"** mean respectively the institution which is competent to provide benefits in the place where the person concerned resides and the institution which is competent to provide benefits in the place where the person concerned is staying, in accordance with the legislation administered by that institution or, where no such institution exists, the institution designated by the competent authority of the Member State concerned;

(s) **"competent Member State"** means the Member State in which the competent institution is situated;

(t) **"period of insurance"** means periods of contribution, employment or self-employment as defined or recognised as periods of insurance by the legislation under which they were completed or considered as completed, and all periods treated as such, where they are regarded by the said legislation as equivalent to periods of insurance;

(u) **"period of employment"** or **"period of self-employment"** mean periods so defined or recognised by the legislation under which they were completed, and all periods treated as such, where they are regarded by the said legislation as equivalent to periods of employment or to periods of self-employment;

(v) **"period of residence"** means periods so defined or recognised by the legislation under which they were completed or considered as completed;

(va) **"Benefits in kind"** means:

(i) for the purposes of Title III, Chapter 1 (sickness, maternity and equivalent paternity benefits), benefits in kind provided for under the legislation of a Member State which are intended to supply, make available, pay directly or reimburse the cost of medical care and products and services ancillary to that care. This includes long-term care benefits in kind.;

(ii) for the purposes of Title III, Chapter 2 (accidents at work and occupational diseases), all benefits in kind relating to accidents at work and occupational diseases as defined in point (i) above and provided for under the Member States' accidents at work and occupational diseases *schemes*.

(w) **"pension"** covers not only pensions but also lump-sum benefits which can be substituted for them and payments in the form of reimbursement of contributions and, subject to the provisions of Title III, revaluation increases or supplementary allowances;

(x) **"pre-retirement benefit"** means:

all cash benefits, other than an unemployment benefit or an early old-age benefit, provided from a specified age to workers who have reduced, ceased or suspended their remunerative activities until the age at which they qualify for an old-age pension or an early retirement pension, the receipt of which is not conditional upon the person concerned being available to the employment services of the competent State; "early old-age benefit" means a benefit provided before the normal pension entitlement age is reached and which either continues to be provided once the said age is reached or is replaced by another old-age benefit;

(y) **"death grant"** means any one-off payment in the event of death excluding the lump-sum benefits referred to in subparagraph (w);

(z) **"family benefit"** means all benefits in kind or in cash intended to meet family expenses, excluding advances of maintenance payments and special childbirth and adoption allowances mentioned in Annex I.

History – Art. 1(va) inserted by Reg. 988/2009, art. 1(3), with effect from 1 May 2010.

ART. 2 Persons covered

2(1) This Regulation shall apply to nationals of a Member State, stateless persons and refugees residing in a Member State who are or have been subject to the legislation of one or more Member States, as well as to the members of their families and to their survivors.

2(2) It shall also apply to the survivors of persons who have been subject to the legislation of one or more Member States, irrespective of the nationality of such persons, where their survivors are nationals of a Member State or stateless persons or refugees residing in one of the Member States.

ART. 3 Matters covered

3(1) This Regulation shall apply to all legislation concerning the following branches of social security:

(a) sickness benefits;

(b) maternity and equivalent paternity benefits;

(c) invalidity benefits;

(d) old-age benefits;

(e) survivors' benefits;

(f) benefits in respect of accidents at work and occupational diseases;

(g) death grants;

(h) unemployment benefits;

(i) pre-retirement benefits;

(j) family benefits.

3(2) Unless otherwise provided for in Annex XI, this Regulation shall apply to general and special social security schemes, whether contributory or non-contributory, and to schemes relating to the obligations of an employer or shipowner.

3(3) This Regulation shall also apply to the special non-contributory cash benefits covered by Article 70.

3(4) The provisions of Title III of this Regulation shall not, however, affect the legislative provisions of any Member State concerning a shipowner's obligations.

3(5) This Regulation shall not apply to:

(a) social and medical assistance or

(b) benefits in relation to which a Member State assumes the liability for damages to persons and provides for compensation, such as those for victims of war and military action or their consequences; victims of crime, assassination or terrorist acts; victims of damage occasioned by agents of the Member State in the course of their duties; or victims who have suffered a disadvantage for political or religious reasons or for reasons of descent.

History – Art. 3(5) replaced by Reg. 988/2009, art. 1(4), with effect from 1 May 2010.

ART. 4 Equality of treatment

4 Unless otherwise provided for by this Regulation, persons to whom this Regulation applies shall enjoy the same benefits and be subject to the same obligations under the legislation of any Member State as the nationals thereof.

ART. 5 Equal treatment of benefits, income, facts or events

5 Unless otherwise provided for by this Regulation and in the light of the special implementing provisions laid down, the following shall apply:

(a) where, under the legislation of the competent Member State, the receipt of social security benefits and other income has certain legal effects, the relevant provisions of that legislation shall also apply to the receipt of equivalent benefits acquired under the legislation of another Member State or to income acquired in another Member State;

(b) where, under the legislation of the competent Member State, legal effects are attributed to the occurrence of certain facts or events, that Member State shall take account of like facts or events occurring in any Member State as though they had taken place in its own territory.

ART. 6 Aggregation of periods

6 Unless otherwise provided for by this Regulation, the competent institution of a Member State whose legislation makes:

– the acquisition, retention, duration or recovery of the right to benefits,

– the coverage by legislation, or

– the access to or the exemption from compulsory, optional continued or voluntary insurance,

conditional upon the completion of periods of insurance, employment, self-employment or residence shall, to the extent necessary, take into account periods of insurance, employment, self-employment or residence completed under the legislation of any other Member State as though they were periods completed under the legislation which it applies.

ART. 7 Waiving of residence rules

7 Unless otherwise provided for by this Regulation, cash benefits payable under the legislation of one or more Member States or under this Regulation shall not be subject to any reduction, amendment, suspension, withdrawal or confiscation on account of the fact that the beneficiary or the members of his family reside in a Member State other than that in which the institution responsible for providing benefits is situated.

ART. 8 Relations between this Regulation and other coordination instruments

8(1) This Regulation shall replace any social security convention applicable between Member States falling under its scope. Certain provisions of social security conventions entered into by the Member States before the date of application of this Regulation shall, however, continue to apply provided that they are more favourable to the beneficiaries or if they arise from specific historical circumstances and their effect is limited in time. For these provisions to remain applicable, they shall be included in Annex II. If, on objective grounds, it is not possible to extend some of these provisions to all persons to whom the Regulation applies this shall be specified.

8(2) Two or more Member States may, as the need arises, conclude conventions with each other based on the principles of this Regulation and in keeping with the spirit thereof.

ART. 9 Declarations by the Member States on the scope of this Regulation

9(1) The Member States shall notify the European Commission in writing of the declarations made in accordance with point (l) of Article 1, the legislation and schemes referred to in Article 3, the conventions entered into as referred to in Article 8(2), the minimum benefits referred to in Article 58, and the lack of an insurance system as referred to in Article 65a(1), as well as substantive amendments. Such notifications shall indicate the date from which this Regulation will apply to the schemes specified by the Member States therein.

9(2) These notifications shall be submitted to the European Commission every year and shall be given the necessary publicity.

History – Art. 9 substituted by Reg. 465/2012, art. 1(3) with effect from 28 June 2012.

ART. 10 Prevention of overlapping of benefits

10 Unless otherwise specified, this Regulation shall neither confer nor maintain the right to several benefits of the same kind for one and the same period of compulsory insurance.

TITLE II – DETERMINATION OF THE LEGISLATION APPLICABLE

ART. 11 General rules

11(1) Persons to whom this Regulation applies shall be subject to the legislation of a single Member State only. Such legislation shall be determined in accordance with this Title.

11(2) For the purposes of this Title, persons receiving cash benefits because or as a consequence of their activity as an employed or self-employed person shall be considered to be pursuing the said activity. This shall not apply to invalidity, old-age or survivors' pensions or to pensions in respect of accidents at work or occupational diseases or to sickness benefits in cash covering treatment for an unlimited period.

11(3) Subject to Articles 12 to 16:

(a) a person pursuing an activity as an employed or self-employed person in a Member State shall be subject to the legislation of that Member State;

(b) a civil servant shall be subject to the legislation of the Member State to which the administration employing him is subject;

(c) a person receiving unemployment benefits in accordance with Article 65 under the legislation of the Member State of residence shall be subject to the legislation of that Member State;

(d) a person called up or recalled for service in the armed forces or for civilian service in a Member State shall be subject to the legislation of that Member State;

(e) any other person to whom subparagraphs (a) to (d) do not apply shall be subject to the legislation of the Member State of residence, without prejudice to other provisions of this Regulation guaranteeing him benefits under the legislation of one or more other Member States.

11(4) For the purposes of this Title, an activity as an employed or self-employed person normally pursued on board a vessel at sea flying the flag of a Member State shall be deemed to be an activity pursued in the said Member State. However, a person employed on board a vessel flying the flag of a Member State and remunerated for such activity by an undertaking or a person whose registered office or place of business is in another Member State shall be subject to the legislation of the latter Member State if he resides in that State. The undertaking or person paying the remuneration shall be considered as the employer for the purposes of the said legislation.

11(5) An activity as a flight crew or cabin crew member performing air passenger or freight services shall be deemed to be an activity pursued in the Member State where the home base, as defined in Annex III to Regulation (EEC) No 3922/91, is located.

History – Art. 11(5) inserted by Reg. 465/2012, art. 1(4) with effect from 28 June 2012.

ART. 12 Special rules

12(1) A person who pursues an activity as an employed person in a Member State on behalf of an employer which normally carries out its activities there and who is posted by that employer to another Member State to perform work on that employer's behalf shall continue to be subject to the legislation of the first Member State, provided that the anticipated duration of such work does not exceed 24 months and that he/she is not sent to replace another posted person.

12(2) A person who normally pursues an activity as a self-employed person in a Member State who goes to pursue a similar activity in another Member State shall continue to be subject to the legislation of the first Member State, provided that the anticipated duration of such activity does not exceed twenty-four months.

History – Art. 12(1) substituted by Reg. 465/2012, art. 1(5) with effect from 28 June 2012.

ART. 13 Pursuit of activities in two or more Member States

13(1) A person who normally pursues an activity as an employed person in two or more Member States shall be subject:

(a) to the legislation of the Member State of residence if he/she pursues a substantial part of his/her activity in that Member State; or

(b) if he/she does not pursue a substantial part of his/her activity in the Member State of residence:

(i) to the legislation of the Member State in which the registered office or place of business of the undertaking or employer is situated if he/she is employed by one undertaking or employer; or

(ii) to the legislation of the Member State in which the registered office or place of business of the undertakings or employers is situated if he/she is employed by two or more undertakings or employers which have their registered office or place of business in only one Member State; or

(iii) to the legislation of the Member State in which the registered office or place of business of the undertaking or employer is situated other than the Member State of residence if he/she is employed by two or more undertakings or employers, which have their registered office or place of business in two Member States, one of which is the Member State of residence; or

(iv) to the legislation of the Member State of residence if he/she is employed by two or more undertakings or employers, at least two of which have their registered office or place of business in different Member States other than the Member State of residence.

13(2) A person who normally pursues an activity as a self-employed person in two or more Member States shall be subject to:

(a) the legislation of the Member State of residence if he pursues a substantial part of his activity in that Member State; or

(b) the legislation of the Member State in which the centre of interest of his activities is situated, if he does not reside in one of the Member States in which he pursues a substantial part of his activity.

13(3) A person who normally pursues an activity as an employed person and an activity as a self-employed person in different Member States shall be subject to the legislation of the Member State in which he pursues an activity as an employed person or, if he pursues such an activity in two or more Member States, to the legislation determined in accordance with paragraph 1.

13(4) A person who is employed as a civil servant by one Member State and who pursues an activity as an employed person and/or as a self-employed person in one or more other Member States shall be subject to the legislation of the Member State to which the administration employing him is subject.

13(5) Persons referred to in paragraphs 1 to 4 shall be treated, for the purposes of the legislation determined in accordance with these provisions, as though they were pursuing all their activities as employed or self-employed persons and were receiving all their income in the Member State concerned.

History – Art. 13(1) substituted by Reg. 465/2012, art. 1(6) with effect from 28 June 2012.

ART. 14 Voluntary insurance or optional continued insurance

14(1) Articles 11 to 13 shall not apply to voluntary insurance or to optional continued insurance unless, in respect of one of the branches referred to in Article 3(1), only a voluntary scheme of insurance exists in a Member State.

14(2) Where, by virtue of the legislation of a Member State, the person concerned is subject to compulsory insurance in that Member State, he may not be subject to a voluntary insurance scheme or an optional continued insurance scheme in another Member State. In all other cases in which, for a given branch, there is a choice between several voluntary insurance schemes or optional continued insurance schemes, the person concerned shall join only the scheme of his choice.

14(3) However, in respect of invalidity, old age and survivors' benefits, the person concerned may join the voluntary or optional continued insurance scheme of a Member State, even if he is compulsorily subject to the legislation of another Member State, provided that he has been subject, at some stage in his career, to the legislation of the first Member State because or as a consequence of an activity as an employed or self-employed person and if such overlapping is explicitly or implicitly allowed under the legislation of the first Member State.

14(4) Where the legislation of a Member State makes admission to voluntary insurance or optional continued insurance conditional upon residence in that Member State or upon previous activity as an employed or self-employed person, Article 5(b) shall apply only to persons who have been subject, at some earlier stage, to the legislation of that Member State on the basis of an activity as an employed or self-employed person.

History – Art. 14(4) replaced by Reg. 988/2009, art. 1(5), with effect from 1 May 2010.

ART. 15 Auxiliary staff of the European Communities

15 Contract staff of the European Communities may opt to be subject to the legislation of the Member State in which they are employed, to the legislation of the Member State to which they were last subject or to the legislation of the Member State whose nationals they are, in respect of provisions other than those relating to family allowances, provided under the scheme applicable to such staff. This right of option, which may be exercised once only, shall take effect from the date of entry into employment.

History – In art. 15 the words "Contract staff" replaced the words "Auxiliary staff" by Reg. 988/2009, art. 1(6), with effect from 1 May 2010.

ART. 16 Exceptions to Articles 11 to 15

16(1) Two or more Member States, the competent authorities of these Member States or the bodies designated by these authorities may by common agreement provide for exceptions to Articles 11 to 15 in the interest of certain persons or categories of persons.

16(2) A person who receives a pension or pensions under the legislation of one or more Member States and who resides in another Member State may at his request be exempted from application of the legislation of the latter State provided that he is not subject to that legislation on account of pursuing an activity as an employed or self-employed person.

TITLE III – SPECIAL PROVISIONS CONCERNING THE VARIOUS CATEGORIES OF BENEFITS

Chapter 1 – Sickness, maternity and equivalent paternity benefits

Section 1 – Insured persons and members of their families, except pensioners and members of their families

ART. 17 Residence in a Member State other than the competent Member State

17 An insured person or members of his family who reside in a Member State other than the competent Member State shall receive in the Member State of residence benefits in kind provided, on behalf of the competent institution, by the institution of the place of residence, in accordance with the provisions of the legislation it applies, as though they were insured under the said legislation.

ART. 18 Stay in the competent Member State when residence is in another Member State – Special rules for the members of the families of frontier workers

18(1) Unless otherwise provided for by paragraph 2, the insured person and the members of his family referred to in Article 17 shall also be entitled to benefits in kind while staying in the competent Member State. The benefits in kind shall be provided by the competent institution and at its own expense, in accordance with the provisions of the legislation it applies, as though the persons concerned resided in that Member State.

18(2) The members of the family of a frontier worker shall be entitled to benefits in kind during their stay in the competent Member State.

Where the competent Member State is listed in Annex III however, the members of the family of a frontier worker who reside in the same Member State as the frontier worker shall be entitled to benefits in kind in the competent Member State only under the conditions laid down in Article 19(1).

History – Art. 18(2) replaced by Reg. 988/2009, art. 1(7), with effect from 1 May 2010.

ART. 19 Stay outside the competent Member State

19(1) Unless otherwise provided for by paragraph 2, an insured person and the members of his family staying in a Member State other than the competent Member State shall be entitled to the benefits in kind which become necessary on medical grounds during their stay, taking into account the nature of the benefits and the expected length of the stay. These benefits shall be provided on behalf of the competent institution by the institution of the place of stay, in accordance with the provisions of the legislation it applies, as though the persons concerned were insured under the said legislation.

19(2) The Administrative Commission shall establish a list of benefits in kind which, in order to be provided during a stay in another Member State, require for practical reasons a prior agreement between the person concerned and the institution providing the care.

ART. 20 Travel with the purpose of receiving benefits in kind – Authorisation to receive appropriate treatment outside the Member State of residence

20(1) Unless otherwise provided for by this Regulation, an insured person travelling to another Member State with the purpose of receiving benefits in kind during the stay shall seek authorisation from the competent institution.

20(2) An insured person who is authorised by the competent institution to go to another Member State with the purpose of receiving the treatment appropriate to his condition shall receive the benefits in kind provided, on behalf of the competent institution, by the institution of the place of stay, in accordance with the provisions of the legislation it applies, as though he were insured under the said legislation. The authorisation shall be accorded where the treatment in question is among the benefits provided for by the legislation in the Member State where the person concerned resides and where he cannot be given such treatment within a time-limit which is medically justifiable, taking into account his current state of health and the probable course of his illness.

20(3) Paragraphs 1 and 2 shall apply mutatis mutandis to the members of the family of an insured person.

20(4) If the members of the family of an insured person reside in a Member State other than the Member State in which the insured person resides, and this Member State has opted for reimbursement on the basis of fixed amounts, the cost of the benefits in kind referred to in paragraph 2 shall be borne by the institution of the place of residence of the members of the family. In this case, for the purposes of paragraph 1, the institution of the place of residence of the members of the family shall be considered to be the competent institution.

ART. 21 Cash benefits

21(1) An insured person and members of his family residing or staying in a Member State other than the competent Member State shall be entitled to cash benefits provided by the competent institution in accordance with the legislation it applies. By agreement between the competent institution and the institution of the place of residence or stay, such benefits may, however, be provided by the institution of the place of residence or stay at the expense of the competent institution in accordance with the legislation of the competent Member State.

21(2) The competent institution of a Member State whose legislation stipulates that the calculation of cash benefits shall be based on average income or on an average contribution basis shall determine such average income or average contribution basis exclusively by reference to the incomes confirmed as having been paid, or contribution bases applied, during the periods completed under the said legislation.

21(3) The competent institution of a Member State whose legislation provides that the calculation of cash benefits shall be based on standard income shall take into account exclusively the standard income or, where appropriate, the average of standard incomes for the periods completed under the said legislation.

21(4) Paragraphs 2 and 3 shall apply mutatis mutandis to cases where the legislation applied by the competent institution lays down a specific reference period which corresponds in the case in question either wholly or partly to the periods which the person concerned has completed under the legislation of one or more other Member States.

ART. 22 Pension claimants

22(1) An insured person who, on making a claim for a pension, or during the investigation thereof, ceases to be entitled to benefits in kind under the legislation of the Member State last competent, shall remain entitled to benefits in kind under the legislation of the Member State in which he resides, provided that the pension claimant satisfies the insurance conditions of the legislation of the Member State referred to in paragraph 2. The right to benefits in kind in the Member State of residence shall also apply to the members of the family of the pension claimant.

22(2) The benefits in kind shall be chargeable to the institution of the Member State which, in the event of a pension being awarded, would become competent under Articles 23 to 25.

Section 2 – Pensioners and members of their families

ART. 23 Right to benefits in kind under the legislation of the Member State of residence

23 A person who receives a pension or pensions under the legislation of two or more Member States, of which one is the Member State of residence, and who is entitled to benefits in kind under the legislation of that Member State, shall, with the members of his family, receive such benefits in kind from and at the expense of the institution of the place of residence, as though he were a pensioner whose pension was payable solely under the legislation of that Member State.

ART. 24 No right to benefits in kind under the legislation of the Member State of residence

24(1) A person who receives a pension or pensions under the legislation of one or more Member States and who is not entitled to benefits in kind under the legislation of the Member State of residence shall nevertheless receive such benefits for himself and the members of his family, insofar as he would be entitled thereto under the legislation of the Member State or of at least one of the Member States competent in respect of his pensions, if he resided in that Member State. The benefits in kind shall be provided at the expense of the institution referred to in paragraph 2 by the institution of the place of residence, as though the person concerned were entitled to a pension and benefits in kind under the legislation of that Member State.

24(2) In the cases covered by paragraph 1, the cost of benefits in kind shall be borne by the institution as determined in accordance with the following rules:

(a) where the pensioner is entitled to benefits in kind under the legislation of a single Member State, the cost shall be borne by the competent institution of that Member State;

(b) where the pensioner is entitled to benefits in kind under the legislation of two or more Member States, the cost thereof shall be borne by the competent institution of the Member State to whose legislation the person has been subject for the longest period of time; should the application of this rule result in several institutions being responsible for the cost of benefits, the cost shall be borne by the institution applying the legislation to which the pensioner was last subject.

ART. 25 Pensions under the legislation of one or more Member States other than the Member State of residence, where there is a right to benefits in kind in the latter Member State

25 Where the person receiving a pension or pensions under the legislation of one or more Member States resides in a Member State under whose legislation the right to receive benefits in kind is not subject to conditions of insurance, or of activity as an employed or self-employed person, and no pension is received from that Member State, the cost of benefits in kind provided to him and to members of his family shall be borne by the institution of one of the Member States competent in respect of his pensions determined in accordance with Article 24(2), to the extent that the pensioner and the members of his family would be entitled to such benefits if they resided in that Member State.

ART. 26 Residence of members of the family in a Member State other than the one in which the pensioner resides

26 Members of the family of a person receiving a pension or pensions under the legislation of one or more Member States who reside in a Member State other than the one in which the pensioner resides shall be entitled to receive benefits in kind from the institution of the place of their residence in accordance with the provisions of the legislation it applies, insofar as the pensioner is entitled to benefits in kind under the legislation of a Member State. The costs shall be borne by the competent institution responsible for the costs of the benefits in kind provided to the pensioner in his Member State of residence.

ART. 27 Stay of the pensioner or the members of his family in a Member State other than the Member State in which they reside – Stay in the competent Member State – Authorisation for appropriate treatment outside the Member State of residence

27(1) Article 19 shall apply *mutatis mutandis* to a person receiving a pension or pensions under the legislation of one or more Member States and entitled to benefits in kind under the legislation of one of the Member States which provide his pension(s) or to the members of his family who are staying in a Member State other than the one in which they reside.

27(2) Article 18(1) shall apply mutatis mutandis to the persons described in paragraph 1 when they stay in the Member State in which is situated the competent institution responsible for the cost of the benefits in kind provided to the pensioner in his Member State of residence and the said Member State has opted for this and is listed in Annex IV.

27(3) Article 20 shall apply *mutatis mutandis* to a pensioner and/or the members of his family who are staying in a Member State other than the one in which they reside with the purpose of receiving there the treatment appropriate to their condition.

27(4) Unless otherwise provided for by paragraph 5, the cost of the benefits in kind referred to in paragraphs 1 to 3 shall be borne by the competent institution responsible for the cost of benefits in kind provided to the pensioner in his Member State of residence.

27(5) The cost of the benefits in kind referred to in paragraph 3 shall be borne by the institution of the place of residence of the pensioner or of the members of his family, if these persons reside in a Member State which has opted for reimbursement on the basis of fixed amounts. In these cases, for the purposes of paragraph 3, the institution of the place of residence of the pensioner or of the members of his family shall be considered to be the competent institution.

ART. 28 Special rules for retired frontier workers

28(1) A frontier worker who has retired because of old-age or invalidity is entitled in the event of sickness to continue to receive benefits in kind in the Member State where he/she last pursued his/her activity as an employed or self-employed person, in so far as this is a continuation of treatment which began in that Member State. **"Continuation of treatment"** means the continued investigation, diagnosis and treatment of an illness for its entire duration.

The first subparagraph shall apply *mutatis mutandis* to the members of the family of the former frontier worker unless the Member State where the frontier worker last pursued his/her activity is listed in Annex III.

28(2) A pensioner who, in the five years preceding the effective date of an old-age or invalidity pension has been pursuing an activity as an employed or self-employed person for at least two years as a frontier worker shall be entitled to benefits in kind in the Member State in which he pursued such an activity as a frontier worker, if this Member State and the Member State in which the competent institution responsible for the costs of the benefits in kind provided to the pensioner in his Member State of residence is situated have opted for this and are both listed in Annex V.

28(3) Paragraph 2 shall apply mutatis mutandis to the members of the family of a former frontier worker or his survivors if, during the periods referred to in paragraph 2, they were entitled to benefits in kind under Article 18(2), even if the frontier worker died before his pension commenced, provided he had been pursuing an activity as an employed or self-employed person as a frontier worker for at least two years in the five years preceding his death.

28(4) Paragraphs 2 and 3 shall be applicable until the person concerned becomes subject to the legislation of a Member State on the basis of an activity as an employed or self-employed person.

28(5) The cost of the benefits in kind referred to in paragraphs 1 to 3 shall be borne by the competent institution responsible for the cost of benefits in kind provided to the pensioner or to his survivors in their respective Member States of residence.

History – Art. 28(1) replaced by Reg. 988/2009, art. 1(8), with effect from 1 May 2010.

ART. 29 Cash benefits for pensioners

29(1) Cash benefits shall be paid to a person receiving a pension or pensions under the legislation of one or more Member States by the competent institution of the Member State in which is situated the competent institution responsible for the cost of benefits in kind provided to the pensioner in his Member State of residence. Article 21 shall apply mutatis mutandis.

29(2) Paragraph 1 shall also apply to the members of a pensioner's family.

ART. 30 Contributions by pensioners

30(1) The institution of a Member State which is responsible under the legislation it applies for making deductions in respect of contributions for sickness, maternity and equivalent paternity benefits, may request and recover such deductions, calculated in accordance with the legislation it applies, only to the extent that the cost of the benefits under Articles 23 to 26 is to be borne by an institution of the said Member State.

30(2) Where, in the cases referred to in Article 25, the acquisition of sickness, maternity and equivalent paternity benefits is subject to the payment of contributions or similar payments under the legislation of a Member State in which the pensioner concerned resides, these contributions shall not be payable by virtue of such residence.

Section 3 – Common provisions

ART. 31 General provision

31 Articles 23 to 30 shall not apply to a pensioner or the members of his family who are entitled to benefits under the legislation of a Member State on the basis of an activity as an employed or self-employed person. In such a case, the person concerned shall be subject, for the purposes of this Chapter, to Articles 17 to 21.

ART. 32 Prioritising of the right to benefits in kind – Special rule for the right of members of the family to benefits in the Member State of residence

32(1) An independent right to benefits in kind based on the legislation of a Member State or on this Chapter shall take priority over a derivative right to benefits for members of a family. A derivative right to benefits in kind shall, however, take priority over independent rights, where the independent right in the Member State of residence exists directly and solely on the basis of the residence of the person concerned in that Member State.

32(2) Where the members of the family of an insured person reside in a Member State under whose legislation the right to benefits in kind is not subject to conditions of insurance or activity as an employed or self-employed person, benefits in kind shall be provided at the expense of the competent institution in the Member State in which they reside, if the spouse or the person caring for the children of the insured person pursues an activity as an employed or self-employed person in the said Member State or receives a pension from that Member State on the basis of an activity as an employed or self-employed person.

ART. 33 Substantial benefits in kind

33(1) An insured person or a member of his family who has had a right to a prosthesis, a major appliance or other substantial benefits in kind recognised by the institution of a Member State, before he became insured under the legislation applied by the institution of another Member State, shall receive such benefits at the expense of the first institution, even if they are awarded after the said person has already become insured under the legislation applied by the second institution.

33(2) The Administrative Commission shall draw up the list of benefits covered by paragraph 1.

ART. 34 Overlapping of long-term care benefits

34(1) If a recipient of long-term care benefits in cash, which have to be treated as sickness benefits and are therefore provided by the Member State competent for cash benefits under Articles 21 or 29, is, at the same time and under this Chapter, entitled to claim benefits in kind intended for the same purpose from the institution of the place of residence or stay in another Member State, and an institution in the first Member State is also required to reimburse the cost of these benefits in kind under Article 35, the general provision on prevention of overlapping of benefits laid down in Article 10 shall be applicable, with the following restriction only: if the person concerned claims and receives the benefit in kind, the amount of the benefit in cash shall be reduced by the amount of the benefit in kind which is or could be claimed from the institution of the first Member State required to reimburse the cost.

34(2) The Administrative Commission shall draw up the list of the cash benefits and benefits in kind covered by paragraph 1.

34(3) Two or more Member States, or their competent authorities, may agree on other or supplementary measures which shall not be less advantageous for the persons concerned than the principles laid down in paragraph 1.

ART. 35 Reimbursements between institutions

35(1) The benefits in kind provided by the institution of a Member State on behalf of the institution of another Member State under this Chapter shall give rise to full reimbursement.

35(2) The reimbursements referred to in paragraph 1 shall be determined and effected in accordance with the arrangements set out in the Implementing Regulation, either on production of proof of actual expenditure, or on the basis of fixed amounts for Member States the legal or administrative structures of which are such that the use of reimbursement on the basis of actual expenditure is not appropriate.

35(3) Two or more Member States, and their competent authorities, may provide for other methods of reimbursement or waive all reimbursement between the institutions coming under their jurisdiction.

Chapter 2 – Benefits in respect of accidents at work and occupational diseases

ART. 36 Right to benefits in kind and in cash

36(1) Without prejudice to any more favourable provisions in paragraphs 2 and 2a of this Article, Articles 17, 18(1), 19(1) and 20(1) shall also apply to benefits relating to accidents at work or occupational diseases.

36(2) A person who has sustained an accident at work or has contracted an occupational disease and who resides or stays in a Member State other than the competent Member State shall be entitled to the special benefits in kind of the scheme covering accidents at work and occupational diseases provided, on behalf of the competent institution, by the institution of the place of residence or stay in accordance with the legislation which it applies, as though he were insured under the said legislation.

36(2a) The competent institution may not refuse to grant the authorisation provided for in Article 20(1) to a person who has sustained an accident at work or who has contracted an occupational disease and who is entitled to benefits chargeable to that institution, where the treatment appropriate to his/her condition cannot be given in the Member State in which he/she resides within a time-limit which is medically justifiable, taking into account his/her current state of health and the probable course of the illness.

36(3) Article 21 shall also apply to benefits falling within this Chapter.

History – Art. 36(1) replaced by Reg. 988/2009, art. 1(9), with effect from 1 May 2010.
Art. 36(2a) substituted by Reg. 465/2012, art. 1(10), with effect from 28 June 2012.
Former art. 36(2a) inserted by Reg. 988/2009, art. 1(10), with effect from 1 May 2010.

ART. 37 Costs of transport

37(1) The competent institution of a Member State whose legislation provides for meeting the costs of transporting a person who has sustained an accident at work or is suffering from an occupational disease, either to his place of residence or to a hospital, shall meet such costs to the corresponding place in another Member State where the person resides, provided that that institution gives prior authorisation for such transport, duly taking into account the reasons justifying it. Such authorisation shall not be required in the case of a frontier worker.

37(2) The competent institution of a Member State whose legislation provides for meeting the costs of transporting the body of a person killed in an accident at work to the place of burial shall, in accordance with the legislation it applies, meet such costs to the corresponding place in another Member State where the person was residing at the time of the accident.

ART. 38 Benefits for an occupational disease where the person suffering from such a disease has been exposed to the same risk in several Member States

38 When a person who has contracted an occupational disease has, under the legislation of two or more Member States, pursued an activity which by its nature is likely to cause the said disease, the benefits that he or his survivors may claim shall be provided exclusively under the legislation of the last of those States whose conditions are satisfied.

ART. 39 Aggravation of an occupational disease

39 In the event of aggravation of an occupational disease for which a person suffering from such a disease has received or is receiving benefits under the legislation of a Member State, the following rules shall apply:

(a) if the person concerned, while in receipt of benefits, has not pursued, under the legislation of another Member State, an activity as an employed or self-employed person likely to cause or aggravate the disease in question, the competent institution of the first Member State shall bear the cost of the benefits under the provisions of the legislation which it applies, taking into account the aggravation;

(b) if the person concerned, while in receipt of benefits, has pursued such an activity under the legislation of another Member State, the competent institution of the first Member State shall bear the cost of the benefits under the legislation it applies without taking the aggravation into account. The competent institution of the second Member State shall grant a supplement to the person concerned, the amount of which shall be equal to the difference between the amount of benefits due after the aggravation and the amount which would have been due prior to the aggravation under the legislation it applies, if the disease in question had occurred under the legislation of that Member State;

(c) the rules concerning reduction, suspension or withdrawal laid down by the legislation of a Member State shall not be invoked against persons receiving benefits provided by institutions of two Member States in accordance with subparagraph (b).

ART. 40 Rules for taking into account the special features of certain legislation

40(1) If there is no insurance against accidents at work or occupational diseases in the Member State in which the person concerned resides or stays, or if such insurance exists but there is no institution responsible for providing benefits in kind, those benefits shall be provided by the institution of the place of residence or stay responsible for providing benefits in kind in the event of sickness.

40(2) If there is no insurance against accidents at work or occupational diseases in the competent Member State, the provisions of this Chapter concerning benefits in kind shall nevertheless be applied to a person who is entitled to those benefits in the event of sickness, maternity or equivalent paternity under the legislation of that Member State if that person sustains an accident at work or suffers from an occupational disease during a residence or stay in another Member State. Costs shall be borne by the institution which is competent for the benefits in kind under the legislation of the competent Member State.

40(3) Article 5 shall apply to the competent institution in a Member State as regards the equivalence of accidents at work and occupational diseases which either have occurred or have been confirmed subsequently under the legislation of another Member State when assessing the degree of incapacity, the right to benefits or the amount thereof, on condition that:

(a) no compensation is due in respect of an accident at work or an occupational disease which had occurred or had been confirmed previously under the legislation it applies; and

(b) no compensation is due in respect of an accident at work or an occupational disease which had occurred or had been confirmed subsequently, under the legislation of the other Member State under which the accident at work or the occupational disease had occurred or been confirmed.

ART. 41 Reimbursements between institutions

41(1) Article 35 shall also apply to benefits falling within this Chapter, and reimbursement shall be made on the basis of actual costs.

41(2) Two or more Member States, or their competent authorities, may provide for other methods of reimbursement or waive all reimbursement between the institutions under their jurisdiction.

Chapter 3 – Death grants

ART. 42 Right to grants where death occurs in, or where the person entitled resides in, a Member State other than the competent Member State

42(1) When an insured person or a member of his family dies in a Member State other than the competent Member State, the death shall be deemed to have occurred in the competent Member State.

42(2) The competent institution shall be obliged to provide death grants payable under the legislation it applies, even if the person entitled resides in a Member State other than the competent Member State.

42(3) Paragraphs 1 and 2 shall also apply when the death is the result of an accident at work or an occupational disease.

ART. 43 Provision of benefits in the event of the death of a pensioner

43(1) In the event of the death of a pensioner who was entitled to a pension under the legislation of one Member State, or to pensions under the legislations of two or more Member States, when that pensioner was residing in a Member State other than that of the institution responsible for the cost of benefits in kind provided under Articles 24 and 25, the death grants payable under the legislation administered by that institution shall be provided at its own expense as though the pensioner had been residing at the time of his death in the Member State in which that institution is situated.

43(2) Paragraph 1 shall apply *mutatis mutandis* to the members of the family of a pensioner.

Chapter 4 – Invalidity Benefits

ART. 44 Persons subject only to type A legislation

44(1) For the purposes of this Chapter, **"type A legislation"** means any legislation under which the amount of invalidity benefits is independent of the duration of the periods of insurance or residence and which is expressly included by the competent Member State in Annex VI, and **"type B legislation"** means any other legislation.

44(2) A person who has been successively or alternately subject to the legislation of two or more Member States and who has completed periods of insurance or residence exclusively under type A legislations shall be entitled to benefits only from the institution of the Member State whose legislation was applicable at the time when the incapacity for work followed by invalidity occurred, taking into account, where appropriate, Article 45, and shall receive such benefits in accordance with that legislation.

44(3) A person who is not entitled to benefits under paragraph 2 shall receive the benefits to which he is still entitled under the legislation of another Member State, taking into account, where appropriate, Article 45.

44(4) If the legislation referred to in paragraph 2 or 3 contains rules for the reduction, suspension or withdrawal of invalidity benefits in the case of overlapping with other income or with benefits of a different kind within the meaning of Article 53(2), Articles 53(3) and 55(3) shall apply mutatis mutandis.

ART. 45 Special provisions on aggregation of periods

45 The competent institution of a Member State whose legislation makes the acquisition, retention or recovery of the right to benefits conditional upon the completion of periods of insurance or residence shall, where necessary, apply Article 51(1) *mutatis mutandis*.

ART. 46 Persons subject either only to type B legislation or to type A and B legislation

46(1) A person who has been successively or alternately subject to the legislation of two or more Member States, of which at least one is not a type A legislation, shall be entitled to benefits under Chapter 5, which shall apply mutatis mutandis taking into account paragraph 3.

46(2) However, if the person concerned has been previously subject to a type B legislation and suffers incapacity for work leading to invalidity while subject to a type A legislation, he shall receive benefits in accordance with Article 44, provided that:

- he satisfies the conditions of that legislation exclusively or of others of the same type, taking into account, where appropriate, Article 45, but without having recourse to periods of insurance or residence completed under a type B legislation, and
- he does not assert any claims to old-age benefits, taking into account Article 50(1).

46(3) A decision taken by an institution of a Member State concerning the degree of invalidity of a claimant shall be binding on the institution of any other Member State concerned, provided that the concordance between the legislation of these Member States on conditions relating to the degree of invalidity is acknowledged in Annex VII.

ART. 47 Aggravation of invalidity

47(1) In the case of aggravation of an invalidity for which a person is receiving benefits under the legislation of one or more Member States, the following provisions shall apply, taking the aggravation into account:

(a) the benefits shall be provided in accordance with Chapter 5, applied mutatis mutandis;

(b) however, where the person concerned has been subject to two or more type A legislations and since receiving benefit has not been subject to the legislation of another Member State, the benefit shall be provided in accordance with Article 44(2).

47(2) If the total amount of the benefit or benefits payable under paragraph 1 is lower than the amount of the benefit which the person concerned was receiving at the expense of the institution previously competent for payment, that institution shall pay him a supplement equal to the difference between the two amounts.

47(3) If the person concerned is not entitled to benefits at the expense of an institution of another Member State, the competent institution of the Member State previously competent shall provide the benefits in accordance with the legislation it applies, taking into account the aggravation and, where appropriate, Article 45.

ART. 48 Conversion of invalidity benefits into old-age benefits

48(1) Invalidity benefits shall be converted into old-age benefits, where appropriate, under the conditions laid down by the legislation or legislations under which they are provided and in accordance with Chapter 5.

48(2) Where a person receiving invalidity benefits can establish a claim to old-age benefits under the legislation of one or more other Member States, in accordance with Article 50, any institution which is responsible for providing invalidity benefits under the legislation of a Member State shall continue to provide such a person with the invalidity benefits to which he is entitled under the legislation it applies until paragraph 1 becomes applicable in respect of that institution, or otherwise for as long as the person concerned satisfies the conditions for such benefits.

48(3) Where invalidity benefits provided under the legislation of a Member State, in accordance with Article 44, are converted into old-age benefits and where the person concerned does not yet satisfy the conditions laid down by the legislation of one or more of the other Member States for receiving those benefits, the person concerned shall receive, from that or those Member States, invalidity benefits from the date of the conversion.

Those invalidity benefits shall be provided in accordance with Chapter 5 as if that Chapter had been applicable at the time when the incapacity for work leading to invalidity occurred, until the person concerned satisfies the qualifying conditions for old-age benefit laid down by the national legislations concerned or, where such conversion is not provided for, for as long as he is entitled to invalidity benefits under the latter legislation or legislations.

48(4) The invalidity benefits provided under Article 44 shall be recalculated in accordance with Chapter 5 as soon as the beneficiary satisfies the qualifying conditions for invalidity benefits laid down by a type B legislation, or as soon as he receives old-age benefits under the legislation of another Member State.

ART. 49 Special provisions for civil servants

49 Articles 6, 44, 46, 47 and 48 and Article 60(2) and (3) shall apply *mutatis mutandis* to persons covered by a special scheme for civil servants.

Chapter 5 – Old-age and survivors' pensions

ART. 50 General provisions

50(1) All the competent institutions shall determine entitlement to benefit, under all the legislations of the Member States to which the person concerned has been subject, when a request for award has been submitted, unless the person concerned expressly requests deferment of the award of old-age benefits under the legislation of one or more Member States.

50(2) If at a given moment the person concerned does not satisfy, or no longer satisfies, the conditions laid down by all the legislations of the Member States to which he has been subject, the institutions applying legislation the conditions of which have been satisfied shall not take into account, when performing the calculation in accordance with Article 52(1)(a) or (b), the periods completed under the legislations the conditions of which have not been satisfied, or are no longer satisfied, where this gives rise to a lower amount of benefit.

50(3) Paragraph 2 shall apply mutatis mutandis when the person concerned has expressly requested deferment of the award of old-age benefits.

50(4) A new calculation shall be performed automatically as and when the conditions to be fulfilled under the other legislations are satisfied or when a person requests the award of an old-age benefit deferred in accordance with paragraph 1, unless the periods completed under the other legislations have already been taken into account by virtue of paragraph 2 or 3.

ART. 51 Special provisions on aggregation of periods

51(1) Where the legislation of a Member State makes the granting of certain benefits conditional upon the periods of insurance having been completed only in a specific activity as an employed or self-employed person or in an occupation which is subject to a special scheme for employed or self-employed persons, the competent institution of that Member State shall take into account periods completed under the legislation of other Member States only if completed under a corresponding scheme or, failing that, in the same occupation, or where appropriate, in the same activity as an employed or self-employed person.

If, account having been taken of the periods thus completed, the person concerned does not satisfy the conditions for receipt of the benefits of a special scheme, these periods shall be taken into account for the purposes of providing the benefits of the general scheme or, failing that, of the scheme applicable to manual or clerical workers, as the case may be, provided that the person concerned had been affiliated to one or other of those schemes.

51(2) The periods of insurance completed under a special scheme of a Member State shall be taken into account for the purposes of providing the benefits of the general scheme or, failing that, of the scheme applicable to manual or clerical workers, as the case may be, of another Member State, provided that the person concerned had been affiliated to one or other of those schemes, even if those periods have already been taken into account in the latter Member State under a special scheme.

51(3) Where the legislation or specific scheme of a Member State makes the acquisition, retention or recovery of the right to benefits conditional upon the person concerned being insured at the time of the materialisation of the risk, this condition shall be regarded as having been satisfied if that person has been previously insured under the legislation or specific scheme of that Member State and is, at the time of the materialisation of the risk, insured under the legislation of another Member State for the same risk or, failing that, if a benefit is due under the legislation of another Member State for the same risk. The latter condition shall, however, be deemed to be fulfilled in the cases referred to in Article 57.

History – Art. 51(3) replaced by Reg. 988/2009, art. 1(11), with effect from 1 May 2010.

ART. 52 Award of benefits

52(1) The competent institution shall calculate the amount of the benefit that would be due:

(a) under the legislation it applies, only where the conditions for entitlement to benefits have been satisfied exclusively under national law (independent benefit);

(b) by calculating a theoretical amount and subsequently an actual amount (pro-rata benefit), as follows:

(i) the theoretical amount of the benefit is equal to the benefit which the person concerned could claim if all the periods of insurance and/or of residence which have been completed under the legislations of the other Member States had been completed under the legislation it applies on the date of the award of the benefit. If, under this legislation, the amount does not depend on the duration of the periods completed, that amount shall be regarded as being the theoretical amount;

(ii) the competent institution shall then establish the actual amount of the pro-rata benefit by applying to the theoretical amount the ratio between the duration of the periods completed before materialisation of the risk under the legislation it applies and the total duration of the periods completed before materialisation of the risk under the legislations of all the Member States concerned.

52(2) Where appropriate, the competent institution shall apply, to the amount calculated in accordance with subparagraphs 1(a) and (b), all the rules relating to reduction, suspension or withdrawal, under the legislation it applies, within the limits provided for by Articles 53 to 55.

52(3) The person concerned shall be entitled to receive from the competent institution of each Member State the higher of the amounts calculated in accordance with subparagraphs 1(a) and (b).

52(4) Where the calculation pursuant to paragraph 1(a) in one Member State invariably results in the independent benefit being equal to or higher than the pro rata benefit, calculated in accordance with paragraph 1(b), the competent institution shall waive the pro rata calculation, provided that:

(i) such a situation is set out in Part 1 of Annex VIII;

(ii) no legislation containing rules against overlapping, as referred to in Articles 54 and 55, is applicable unless the conditions laid down in Article 55(2) are fulfilled; and

(iii) Article 57 is not applicable in relation to periods completed under the legislation of another Member State in the specific circumstances of the case.

52(5) Notwithstanding the provisions of paragraphs 1, 2 and 3, the pro rata calculation shall not apply to schemes providing benefits in respect of which periods of time are of no relevance to the calculation, subject to such schemes being listed in part 2 of Annex VIII. In such cases, the person concerned shall be entitled to the benefit calculated in accordance with the legislation of the Member State concerned.

History – Art. 52(4) replaced by Reg. 988/2009, art. 1(12), with effect from 1 May 2010.
Art. 52(5) inserted by Reg. 988/2009, art. 1(13), with effect from 1 May 2010.

ART. 53 Rules to prevent overlapping

53(1) Any overlapping of invalidity, old-age and survivors' benefits calculated or provided on the basis of periods of insurance and/or residence completed by the same person shall be considered to be overlapping of benefits of the same kind.

53(2) Overlapping of benefits which cannot be considered to be of the same kind within the meaning of paragraph 1 shall be considered to be overlapping of benefits of a different kind.

53(3) The following provisions shall be applicable for the purposes of rules to prevent overlapping laid down by the legislation of a Member State in the case of overlapping of a benefit in respect of invalidity, old age or survivors with a benefit of the same kind or a benefit of a different kind or with other income:

(a) the competent institution shall take into account the benefits or incomes acquired in another Member State only where the legislation it applies provides for benefits or income acquired abroad to be taken into account;

(b) the competent institution shall take into account the amount of benefits to be paid by another Member State before deduction of tax, social security contributions and other individual levies or deductions, unless the legislation it applies provides for the application of rules to prevent overlapping after such deductions, under the conditions and the procedures laid down in the Implementing Regulation;

(c) the competent institution shall not take into account the amount of benefits acquired under the legislation of another Member State on the basis of voluntary insurance or continued optional insurance;

(d) if a single Member State applies rules to prevent overlapping because the person concerned receives benefits of the same or of a different kind under the legislation of other Member States or income acquired in other Member States, the benefit due may be reduced solely by the amount of such benefits or such income.

ART. 54 Overlapping of benefits of the same kind

54(1) Where benefits of the same kind due under the legislation of two or more Member States overlap, the rules to prevent overlapping laid down by the legislation of a Member State shall not be applicable to a pro-rata benefit.

54(2) The rules to prevent overlapping shall apply to an independent benefit only if the benefit concerned is:

(a) a benefit the amount of which does not depend on the duration of periods of insurance or residence, or

(b) a benefit the amount of which is determined on the basis of a credited period deemed to have been completed between the date on which the risk materialised and a later date, overlapping with:

  (i) a benefit of the same type, except where an agreement has been concluded between two or more Member States to avoid the same credited period being taken into account more than once, or

  (ii) a benefit referred to in subparagraph (a).

The benefits and agreements referred to in subparagraphs (a) and (b) are listed in Annex IX.

ART. 55 Overlapping of benefits of a different kind

55(1) If the receipt of benefits of a different kind or other income requires the application of the rules to prevent overlapping provided for by the legislation of the Member States concerned regarding:

(a) two or more independent benefits, the competent institutions shall divide the amounts of the benefit or benefits or other income, as they have been taken into account, by the number of benefits subject to the said rules;

however, the application of this subparagraph cannot deprive the person concerned of his status as a pensioner for the purposes of the other Chapters of this Title under the conditions and the procedures laid down in the Implementing Regulation;

(b) one or more pro-rata benefits, the competent institutions shall take into account the benefit or benefits or other income and all the elements stipulated for applying the rules to prevent overlapping as a function of the ratio between the periods of insurance and/or residence established for the calculation referred to in Article 52(1)(b)(ii);

(c) one or more independent benefits and one or more pro-rata benefits, the competent institutions shall apply *mutatis mutandis* subparagraph (a) as regards independent benefits and subparagraph (b) as regards pro-rata benefits.

55(2) The competent institution shall not apply the division stipulated in respect of independent benefits, if the legislation it applies provides for account to be taken of benefits of a different kind and/or other income and all other elements for calculating part of their amount determined as a function of the ratio between periods of insurance and/or residence referred to in Article 52(1)(b)(ii).

55(3) Paragraphs 1 and 2 shall apply mutatis mutandis where the legislation of one or more Member States provides that a right to a benefit cannot be acquired in the case where the person concerned is in receipt of a benefit of a different kind, payable under the legislation of another Member State, or of other income.

ART. 56 Additional provisions for the calculation of benefits

56(1) For the calculation of the theoretical and pro-rata amounts referred to in Article 52(1)(b), the following rules shall apply:

(a) where the total length of the periods of insurance and/or residence completed before the risk materialised under the legislations of all the Member States concerned is longer than the maximum period required by the legislation of one of these Member States for receipt of full benefit, the competent institution of that Member State shall take into account this maximum period instead of the total length of the periods completed; this method of calculation shall not result in the imposition on that institution of the cost of a benefit greater than the full benefit provided for by the legislation it applies. This provision shall not apply to benefits the amount of which does not depend on the length of insurance;

(b) the procedure for taking into account overlapping periods is laid down in the Implementing Regulation;

(c) if the legislation of a Member State provides that the benefits are to be calculated on the basis of incomes, contributions, bases of contributions, increases, earnings, other amounts or a combination of more than one of them (average, proportional, fixed or credited), the competent institution shall:

  (i) determine the basis for calculation of the benefits in accordance only with periods of insurance completed under the legislation it applies;

  (ii) use, in order to determine the amount to be calculated in accordance with the periods of insurance and/or residence completed under the legislation of the other Member States, the same elements determined or recorded for the periods of insurance completed under the legislation it applies;

where necessary in accordance with the procedures laid down in Annex XI for the Member State concerned.

(d) In the event that point (c) is not applicable because the legislation of a Member State provides for the benefit to be calculated on the basis of elements other than periods of insurance or residence which are not linked to time, the competent institution shall take into account, in respect of each period of insurance or residence completed under the legislation of any other Member State, the amount of the capital accrued, the capital which is considered as having been accrued or any other element for the calculation under the legislation it administers divided by the corresponding units of periods in the pension scheme concerned.

56(2) The provisions of the legislation of a Member State concerning the revalorisation of the elements taken into account for the calculation of benefits shall apply, as appropriate, to the elements to be taken into account by the competent institution of that Member State, in accordance with paragraph 1, in respect of the periods of insurance or residence completed under the legislation of other Member States.

History – In art. 56(1)(c) the words "where necessary" inserted by Reg. 988/2009, art. 1(14), with effect from 1 May 2010. Art. 56(1)(d) inserted by Reg. 988/2009, art. 1(15), with effect from 1 May 2010.

ART. 57 Periods of insurance or residence of less than one year

57(1) Notwithstanding Article 52(1)(b), the institution of a Member State shall not be required to provide benefits in respect of periods completed under the legislation it applies which are taken into account when the risk materialises, if:

– the duration of the said periods is less than one year, and

– taking only these periods into account no right to benefit is acquired under that legislation.

For the purposes of this Article, "periods" shall mean all periods of insurance, employment, self-employment or residence which either qualify for, or directly increase, the benefit concerned.

57(2) The competent institution of each of the Member States concerned shall take into account the periods referred to in paragraph 1, for the purposes of Article 52(1)(b)(i).

57(3) If the effect of applying paragraph 1 would be to relieve all the institutions of the Member States concerned of their obligations, benefits shall be provided exclusively under the legislation of the last of those Member States whose conditions are satisfied, as if all the periods of insurance and residence completed and taken into account in accordance with Articles 6 and 51(1) and (2) had been completed under the legislation of that Member State.

57(4) This Article shall not apply to schemes listed in Part 2 of Annex VIII.

History – Art. 57(4) inserted by Reg. 988/2009, art. 1(16), with effect from 1 May 2010.

ART. 58 Award of a supplement

58(1) A recipient of benefits to whom this Chapter applies may not, in the Member State of residence and under whose legislation a benefit is payable to him, be provided with a benefit which is less than the minimum benefit fixed by that legislation for a period of insurance or residence equal to all the periods taken into account for the payment in accordance with this Chapter.

58(2) The competent institution of that Member State shall pay him throughout the period of his residence in its territory a supplement equal to the difference between the total of the benefits due under this Chapter and the amount of the minimum benefit.

ART. 59 Recalculation and revaluation of benefits

59(1) If the method for determining benefits or the rules for calculating benefits are altered under the legislation of a Member State, or if the personal situation of the person concerned undergoes a relevant change which, under that legislation, would lead to an adjustment of the amount of the benefit, a recalculation shall be carried out in accordance with Article 52.

59(2) On the other hand, if, by reason of an increase in the cost of living or changes in the level of income or other grounds for adjustment, the benefits of the Member State concerned are altered by a percentage or fixed amount, such percentage or fixed amount shall be applied directly to the benefits determined in accordance with Article 52, without the need for a recalculation.

ART. 60 Special provisions for civil servants

60(1) Articles 6, 50, 51(3) and 52 to 59 shall apply *mutatis mutandis* to persons covered by a special scheme for civil servants.

60(2) However, if the legislation of a competent Member State makes the acquisition, liquidation, retention or recovery of the right to benefits under a special scheme for civil servants subject to the condition that all periods of insurance be completed under one or more special schemes for civil servants in that Member State, or be regarded by the legislation of that Member State as equivalent to such periods, the competent institution of that State shall take into account only the periods which can be recognised under the legislation it applies.

If, account having been taken of the periods thus completed, the person concerned does not satisfy the conditions for the receipt of these benefits, these periods shall be taken into account for the award of benefits under the general scheme or, failing that, the scheme applicable to manual or clerical workers, as the case may be.

60(3) Where, under the legislation of a Member State, benefits under a special scheme for civil servants are calculated on the basis of the last salary or salaries received during a reference period, the competent institution of that State shall take into account, for the purposes of the calculation, only those salaries, duly revalued, which were received during the period or periods for which the person concerned was subject to that legislation.

Chapter 6 – Unemployment benefits

ART. 61 Special rules on aggregation of periods of insurance, employment or self-employment

61(1) The competent institution of a Member State whose legislation makes the acquisition, retention, recovery or duration of the right to benefits conditional upon the completion of either periods of insurance, employment or self-employment shall, to the extent necessary, take into account periods of insurance, employment or self-employment completed under the legislation of any other Member State as though they were completed under the legislation it applies.

However, when the applicable legislation makes the right to benefits conditional on the completion of periods of insurance, the periods of employment or self-employment completed under the legislation of another Member State shall not be taken into account unless such periods would have been considered to be periods of insurance had they been completed in accordance with the applicable legislation.

61(2) Except in the cases referred to in Article 65(5)(a), the application of paragraph 1 of this Article shall be conditional on the person concerned having the most recently completed, in accordance with the legislation under which the benefits are claimed:

– periods of insurance, if that legislation requires periods of insurance,
– periods of employment, if that legislation requires periods of employment, or
– periods of self-employment, if that legislation requires periods of self-employment.

ART. 62 Calculation of benefits

62(1) The competent institution of a Member State whose legislation provides for the calculation of benefits on the basis of the amount of the previous salary or professional income shall take into account exclusively the salary or professional income received by the person concerned in respect of his last activity as an employed or self-employed person under the said legislation.

62(2) Paragraph 1 shall also apply where the legislation administered by the competent institution provides for a specific reference period for the determination of the salary which serves as a basis for the calculation of benefits and where, for all or part of that period, the person concerned was subject to the legislation of another Member State.

62(3) By way of derogation from paragraphs (1) and (2), as far as the unemployed persons covered by Article 65(5)(a) are concerned, the institution of the place of residence shall take into account the salary or professional income received by the person concerned in the Member State to whose legislation he was subject during his last activity as an employed or self-employed person, in accordance with the Implementing Regulation.

History – In art. 62(3) the words "unemployed persons" replaced the words "frontier workers" by Reg. 988/2009, art. 1(17), with effect from 1 May 2010.

ART. 63 Special provisions for the waiving of residence rules

63 For the purpose of this Chapter, Article 7 shall apply only in the cases provided for by Articles 64, 65 and 65a and within the limits prescribed therein.

History – Art. 63 substituted by Reg. 465/2012, art. 1(8), with effect from 28 June 2012.

ART. 64 Unemployed persons going to another Member State

64(1) A wholly unemployed person who satisfies the conditions of the legislation of the competent Member State for entitlement to benefits, and who goes to another Member State in order to seek work there, shall retain his entitlement to unemployment benefits in cash under the following conditions and within the following limits:

(a) before his departure, the unemployed person must have been registered as a person seeking work and have remained available to the employment services of the competent Member State for at least four weeks after becoming unemployed. However, the competent services or institutions may authorise his departure before such time has expired;

(b) the unemployed person must register as a person seeking work with the employment services of the Member State to which he has gone, be subject to the control procedure organised there and adhere to the conditions laid down under the legislation of that Member State. This condition shall be considered satisfied for the period before registration if the person concerned registers within seven days of the date on which he ceased to be available to the employment services of the Member State which he left. In exceptional cases, the competent services or institutions may extend this period;

(c) entitlement to benefits shall be retained for a period of three months from the date when the unemployed person ceased to be available to the employment services of the Member State which he left, provided that the total duration for which the benefits are provided does not exceed the total duration of the period of his entitlement to benefits under the legislation of that Member State; the competent services or institutions may extend the period of three months up to a maximum of six months;

(d) the benefits shall be provided by the competent institution in accordance with the legislation it applies and at its own expense.

64(2) If the person concerned returns to the competent Member State on or before the expiry of the period during which he is entitled to benefits under paragraph 1(c), he shall continue to be entitled to benefits under the legislation of that Member State. He shall lose all entitlement to benefits under the legislation of the competent Member State if he does not return there on or before the expiry of the said period, unless the provisions of that legislation are more favourable. In exceptional cases the competent services or institutions may allow the person concerned to return at a later date without loss of his entitlement.

64(3) Unless the legislation of the competent Member State is more favourable, between two periods of employment the maximum total period for which entitlement to benefits shall be retained under paragraph 1 shall be three months; the competent services or institutions may extend that period up to a maximum of six months.

64(4) The arrangements for exchanges of information, cooperation and mutual assistance between the institutions and services of the competent Member State and the Member State to which the person goes in order to seek work shall be laid down in the Implementing Regulation.

ART. 65 Unemployed persons who resided in a Member State other than the competent State

65(1) A person who is partially or intermittently unemployed and who, during his last activity as an employed or self-employed person, resided in a Member State other than the competent Member State shall make himself available to his employer or to the employment services in the competent Member State. He shall receive benefits in accordance with the legislation of the competent Member State as if he were residing in that Member State. These benefits shall be provided by the institution of the competent Member State.

65(2) A wholly unemployed person who, during his last activity as an employed or self-employed person, resided in a Member State other than the competent Member State and who continues to reside in that Member State or returns to that Member State shall make himself available to the employment services in the Member State of residence. Without prejudice to Article 64, a wholly unemployed person may, as a supplementary step, make himself available to the employment services of the Member State in which he pursued his last activity as an employed or self-employed person.

An unemployed person, other than a frontier worker, who does not return to his Member State of residence, shall make himself available to the employment services in the Member State to whose legislation he was last subject.

65(3) The unemployed person referred to in the first sentence of paragraph 2 shall register as a person seeking work with the competent employment services of the Member State in which he resides, shall be subject to the control procedure organised there and shall adhere to the conditions laid down under the legislation of that Member State. If he chooses also to register as a person seeking work in the Member State in which he pursued his last activity as an employed or self-employed person, he shall comply with the obligations applicable in that State.

65(4) The implementation of the second sentence of paragraph 2 and of the second sentence of paragraph 3, as well as the arrangements for exchanges of information, cooperation and mutual assistance between the institutions and services of the Member State of residence and the Member State in which he pursued his last occupation, shall be laid down in the Implementing Regulation.

65(5)

(a) The unemployed person referred to in the first and second sentences of paragraph 2 shall receive benefits in accordance with the legislation of the Member State of residence as if he had been subject to that legislation during his last activity as an employed or self-employed person. Those benefits shall be provided by the institution of the place of residence.

(b) However, a worker other than a frontier worker who has been provided benefits at the expense of the competent institution of the Member State to whose legislation he was last subject shall firstly receive, on his return to the Member State of residence, benefits in accordance with Article 64, receipt of the benefits in accordance with (a) being suspended for the period during which he receives benefits under the legislation to which he was last subject.

65(6) The benefits provided by the institution of the place of residence under paragraph 5 shall continue to be at its own expense. However, subject to paragraph 7, the competent institution of the Member State to whose legislation he was last subject shall reimburse to the institution of the place of residence the full amount of the benefits provided by the latter institution during the first three months. The amount of the reimbursement during this period may not be higher than the amount payable, in the case of unemployment, under the legislation of the competent Member State. In the case referred to in paragraph 5(b), the period during which benefits are provided under Article 64 shall be deducted from the period referred to in the second sentence of this paragraph. The arrangements for reimbursement shall be laid down in the Implementing Regulation.

65(7) However, the period of reimbursement referred to in paragraph 6 shall be extended to five months when the person concerned has, during the preceding 24 months, completed periods of employment or self-employment of at least 12 months in the Member State to whose legislation he was last subject, where such periods would qualify for the purposes of establishing entitlement to unemployment benefits.

65(8) For the purposes of paragraphs 6 and 7, two or more Member States, or their competent authorities, may provide for other methods of reimbursement or waive all reimbursement between the institutions falling under their jurisdiction.

ART. 65a Special provisions for wholly unemployed self-employed frontier workers where no unemployment benefits system covering self-employed persons exists in the Member State of residence

65a(1) By way of derogation from Article 65, a wholly unemployed person who, as a frontier worker, has most recently completed periods of insurance as a self-employed person or periods of self-employment recognised for the purposes of granting unemployment benefits in a Member State other than his/her Member State of residence and whose Member State of residence has submitted notification that there is no possibility for any category of self-employed persons to be covered by an unemployment benefits system of that Member State, shall register with and make himself/herself available to the employment services in the Member State in which he/she pursued his/her last activity as a self-employed person and, when he/she applies for benefits, shall continuously adhere to the conditions laid down under the legislation of the latter Member State. The wholly unemployed person may, as a supplementary step, make himself/herself available to the employment services of the Member State of residence.

65a(2) Benefits shall be provided to the wholly unemployed person referred to in paragraph 1 by the Member State to whose legislation he/she was last subject in accordance with the legislation which that Member State applies.

65a(3) If the wholly unemployed person referred to in paragraph 1 does not wish to become or remain available to the employment services of the Member State of last activity after having been registered there, and wishes to seek work in the Member State of residence, Article 64 shall apply mutatis mutandis, except Article 64(1)(a). The competent institution may extend the period referred to in the first sentence of Article 64(1)(c) up to the end of the period of entitlement to benefits.

History – Art. 65a inserted by Reg. 465/2012, art. 1(9), with effect from 28 June 2012.

Chapter 7 – Pre-retirement benefits

ART. 66 Benefits

66 When the applicable legislation makes the right to pre-retirement benefits conditional on the completion of periods of insurance, of employment or of self-employment, Article 6 shall not apply.

Chapter 8 – Family benefits

ART. 67 Members of the family residing in another Member State

67 A person shall be entitled to family benefits in accordance with the legislation of the competent Member State, including for his family members residing in another Member State, as if they were residing in the former Member State. However, a pensioner shall be entitled to family benefits in accordance with the legislation of the Member State competent for his pension.

ART. 68 Priority rules in the event of overlapping

68(1) Where, during the same period and for the same family members, benefits are provided for under the legislation of more than one Member State the following priority rules shall apply:

(a) in the case of benefits payable by more than one Member State on different bases, the order of priority shall be as follows: firstly, rights available on the basis of an activity as an employed or self-employed person, secondly, rights available on the basis of receipt of a pension and finally, rights obtained on the basis of residence;

(b) in the case of benefits payable by more than one Member State on the same basis, the order of priority shall be established by referring to the following subsidiary criteria:

(i) in the case of rights available on the basis of an activity as an employed or self-employed person: the place of residence of the children, provided that there is such activity, and additionally, where appropriate, the highest amount of the benefits provided for by the conflicting legislations. In the latter case, the cost of benefits shall be shared in accordance with criteria laid down in the Implementing Regulation;

(ii) in the case of rights available on the basis of receipt of pensions: the place of residence of the children, provided that a pension is payable under its legislation, and additionally, where appropriate, the longest period of insurance or residence under the conflicting legislations;

(iii) in the case of rights available on the basis of residence: the place of residence of the children.

68(2) In the case of overlapping entitlements, family benefits shall be provided in accordance with the legislation designated as having priority in accordance with paragraph 1. Entitlements to family benefits by virtue of other conflicting legislation or legislations shall be suspended up to the amount provided for by the first legislation and a differential supplement shall be provided, if necessary, for the sum which exceeds this amount. However, such a differential supplement does not need to be provided for children residing in another Member State when entitlement to the benefit in question is based on residence only.

68(3) If, under Article 67, an application for family benefits is submitted to the competent institution of a Member State whose legislation is applicable, but not by priority right in accordance with paragraphs 1 and 2 of this Article:

(a) that institution shall forward the application without delay to the competent institution of the Member State whose legislation is applicable by priority, inform the person concerned and, without prejudice to the provisions of the Implementing Regulation concerning the provisional award of benefits, provide, if necessary, the differential supplement mentioned in paragraph 2;

(b) the competent institution of the Member State whose legislation is applicable by priority shall deal with this application as though it were submitted directly to itself, and the date on which such an application was submitted to the first institution shall be considered as the date of its claim to the institution with priority.

ART. 68a Provision of benefits

68a In the event that family benefits are not used by the person to whom they should be provided for the maintenance of the members of the family, the competent institution shall discharge its legal obligations by providing those benefits to the natural or legal person in fact maintaining the members of the family, at the request and through the agency of the institution in their Member State of residence or of the designated institution or body appointed for that purpose by the competent authority of their Member State of residence.

History – Art. 68a inserted by Reg. 988/2009, art. 1(18), with effect from 1 May 2010.

ART. 69 Additional provisions

69(1) If, under the legislation designated by virtue of Articles 67 and 68, no right is acquired to the payment of additional or special family benefits for orphans, such benefits shall be paid by default, and in addition to the other family benefits acquired in accordance with the abovementioned legislation, under the legislation of the Member State to which the deceased worker was subject for the longest period of time, insofar as the right was acquired under that legislation. If no right was acquired under that legislation, the conditions for the acquisition of such right under the legislations of the other Member States shall be examined and benefits provided in decreasing order of the length of periods of insurance or residence completed under the legislation of those Member States.

69(2) Benefits paid in the form of pensions or supplements to pensions shall be provided and calculated in accordance with Chapter 5.

Chapter 9 – Special non-contributory cash benefits

ART. 70 General provision

70(1) This Article shall apply to special non-contributory cash benefits which are provided under legislation which, because of its personal scope, objectives and/or conditions for entitlement, has characteristics both of the social security legislation referred to in Article 3(1) and of social assistance.

70(2) For the purposes of this Chapter, **"special non-contributory cash benefits"** means those which:

(a) are intended to provide either:

(i) supplementary, substitute or ancillary cover against the risks covered by the branches of social security referred to in Article 3(1), and which guarantee the persons concerned a minimum subsistence income having regard to the economic and social situation in the Member State concerned; or

(ii) solely specific protection for the disabled, closely linked to the said person's social environment in the Member State concerned,

and

(b) where the financing exclusively derives from compulsory taxation intended to cover general public expenditure and the conditions for providing and for calculating the benefits are not dependent on any contribution in respect of the beneficiary. However, benefits provided to supplement a contributory benefit shall not be considered to be contributory benefits for this reason alone, and

(c) are listed in Annex X.

70(3) Article 7 and the other Chapters of this Title shall not apply to the benefits referred to in paragraph 2 of this Article.

70(4) The benefits referred to in paragraph 2 shall be provided exclusively in the Member State in which the persons concerned reside, in accordance with its legislation. Such benefits shall be provided by and at the expense of the institution of the place of residence.

TITLE IV – ADMINISTRATIVE COMMISSION AND ADVISORY COMMITTEE

ART. 71 Composition and working methods of the Administrative Commission

71(1) The Administrative Commission for the Coordination of Social Security Systems (hereinafter called "the Administrative Commission") attached to the Commission of the European Communities shall be made up of a government representative from each of the Member States, assisted, where necessary, by expert advisers. A representative of the Commission of the European Communities shall attend the meetings of the Administrative Commission in an advisory capacity.

71(2) The Administrative Commission shall act by a qualified majority as defined by the Treaties, except when adopting its rules which shall be drawn up by mutual agreement among its members.

Decisions on questions of interpretation referred to in Article 72(a) shall be given the necessary publicity.

71(3) Secretarial services for the Administrative Commission shall be provided by the Commission of the European Communities.

History – Art. 71(2) substituted by Reg. 465/2012, art. 1(10), with effect from 28 June 2012.

ART. 72 Tasks of the Administrative Commission

72 The Administrative Commission shall:

(a) deal with all administrative questions and questions of interpretation arising from the provisions of this Regulation or those of the Implementing Regulation, or from any agreement concluded or arrangement made thereunder, without prejudice to the right of the authorities, institutions and persons concerned to have recourse to the procedures and tribunals provided for by the legislation of the Member States, by this Regulation or by the Treaty;

(b) facilitate the uniform application of Community law, especially by promoting exchange of experience and best administrative practices;

(c) foster and develop cooperation between Member States and their institutions in social security matters in order, inter alia, to take into account particular questions regarding certain categories of persons; facilitate realisation of actions of crossborder cooperation activities in the area of the coordination of social security systems;

(d) encourage as far as possible the use of new technologies in order to facilitate the free movement of persons, in particular by modernising procedures for exchanging information and adapting the information flow between institutions for the purposes of exchange by electronic means, taking account of the development of data processing in each Member State; the Administrative Commission shall adopt the common structural rules for data processing services, in particular on security and the use of standards, and shall lay down provisions for the operation of the common part of those services;

(e) undertake any other function falling within its competence under this Regulation and the Implementing Regulation or any agreement or arrangement concluded thereunder;

(f) make any relevant proposals to the Commission of the European Communities concerning the coordination of social security schemes, with a view to improving and modernising the Community "acquis" by drafting subsequent Regulations or by means of other instruments provided for by the Treaty;

(g) establish the factors to be taken into account for drawing up accounts relating to the costs to be borne by the institutions of the Member States under this Regulation and to adopt the annual accounts between those institutions, based on the report of the Audit Board referred to in Article 74.

ART. 73 Technical Commission for Data Processing

73(1) A Technical Commission for Data Processing (hereinafter called the "Technical Commission") shall be attached to the Administrative Commission. The Technical Commission shall propose to the Administrative Commission common architecture rules for the operation of data-processing services, in particular on security and the use of standards; it shall deliver reports and a reasoned opinion before decisions are taken by the Administrative Commission pursuant to Article 72(d). The composition and working methods of the Technical Commission shall be determined by the Administrative Commission.

73(2) To this end, the Technical Commission shall:

(a) gather together the relevant technical documents and undertake the studies and other work required to accomplish its tasks;

(b) submit to the Administrative Commission the reports and reasoned opinions referred to in paragraph 1;

(c) carry out all other tasks and studies on matters referred to it by the Administrative Commission;

(d) ensure the management of Community pilot projects using data-processing services and, for the Community part, operational systems using data-processing services.

ART. 74 Audit Board

74(1) An Audit Board shall be attached to the Administrative Commission. The composition and working methods of the Audit Board shall be determined by the Administrative Commission.

The Audit Board shall:

(a) verify the method of determining and calculating the annual average costs presented by Member States;

(b) collect the necessary data and carry out the calculations required for establishing the annual statement of claims of each Member State;

(c) give the Administrative Commission periodic accounts of the results of the implementation of this Regulation and of the Implementing Regulation, in particular as regards the financial aspect;

(d) provide the data and reports necessary for decisions to be taken by the Administrative Commission under Article 72(g);

(e) make any relevant suggestions it may have to the Administrative Commission, including those concerning this Regulation, in connection with subparagraphs (a), (b) and (c);

(f) carry out all work, studies or assignments on matters referred to it by the Administrative Commission.

ART. 75 Advisory Committee for the Coordination of Social Security Systems

75(1) An Advisory Committee for the Coordination of Social Security Systems (hereinafter referred to as "Advisory Committee") is hereby established, comprising, from each Member State:

(a) one government representative;

(b) one representative from the trade unions;

(c) one representative from the employers' organisations.

For each of the categories referred to above, an alternate member shall be appointed for each Member State.

The members and alternate members of the Advisory Committee shall be appointed by the Council. The Advisory Committee shall be chaired by a representative of the Commission of the European Communities. The Advisory Committee shall draw up its rules of procedure.

75(2) The Advisory Committee shall be empowered, at the request of the Commission of the European Communities, the Administrative Commission or on its own initiative:

(a) to examine general questions or questions of principle and problems arising from the implementation of the Community provisions on the coordination of social security systems, especially regarding certain categories of persons;

(b) to formulate opinions on such matters for the Administrative Commission and proposals for any revisions of the said provisions.

TITLE V – MISCELLANEOUS PROVISIONS

ART. 76 Cooperation

76(1) The competent authorities of the Member States shall communicate to each other all information regarding:

(a) measures taken to implement this Regulation;

(b) changes in their legislation which may affect the implementation of this Regulation.

76(2) For the purposes of this Regulation, the authorities and institutions of the Member States shall lend one another their good offices and act as though implementing their own legislation. The administrative assistance given by the said authorities and institutions shall, as a rule, be free of charge. However, the Administrative Commission shall establish the nature of reimbursable expenses and the limits above which their reimbursement is due.

76(3) The authorities and institutions of the Member States may, for the purposes of this Regulation, communicate directly with one another and with the persons involved or their representatives.

76(4) The institutions and persons covered by this Regulation shall have a duty of mutual information and cooperation to ensure the correct implementation of this Regulation.

The institutions, in accordance with the principle of good administration, shall respond to all queries within a reasonable period of time and shall in this connection provide the persons concerned with any information required for exercising the rights conferred on them by this Regulation.

The persons concerned must inform the institutions of the competent Member State and of the Member State of residence as soon as possible of any change in their personal or family situation which affects their right to benefits under this Regulation.

76(5) Failure to respect the obligation of information referred to in the third subparagraph of paragraph 4 may result in the application of proportionate measures in accordance with national law. Nevertheless, these measures shall be equivalent to those applicable to similar situations under domestic law and shall not make it impossible or excessively difficult in practice for claimants to exercise the rights conferred on them by this Regulation.

76(6) In the event of difficulties in the interpretation or application of this Regulation which could jeopardise the rights of a person covered by it, the institution of the competent Member State or of the Member State of residence of the person concerned shall contact the institution(s) of the Member State(s) concerned. If a solution cannot be found within a reasonable period, the authorities concerned may call on the Administrative Commission to intervene.

76(7) The authorities, institutions and tribunals of one Member State may not reject applications or other documents submitted to them on the grounds that they are written in an official language of another Member State, recognised as an official language of the Community institutions in accordance with Article 290 of the Treaty.

ART. 77 Protection of personal data

77(1) Where, under this Regulation or under the Implementing Regulation, the authorities or institutions of a Member State communicate personal data to the authorities or institutions of another Member State, such communication shall be subject to the data protection legislation of the Member State transmitting them. Any communication from the authority or institution of the receiving Member State as well as the storage, alteration and destruction of the data provided by that Member State shall be subject to the data protection legislation of the receiving Member State.

77(2) Data required for the application of this Regulation and the Implementing Regulation shall be transmitted by one Member State to another Member State in accordance with Community provisions on the protection of natural persons with regard to the processing and free movement of personal data.

ART. 78 Data processing

78(1) Member States *shall* progressively use new technologies for the exchange, access and processing of the data required to apply this Regulation and the Implementing Regulation. The Commission of the European Communities shall lend its support to activities of common interest as soon as the Member States have established such data-processing services.

78(2) Each Member State shall be responsible for managing its own part of the data-processing services in accordance with the Community provisions on the protection of natural persons with regard to the processing and the free movement of personal data.

78(3) An electronic document sent or issued by an institution in conformity with this Regulation and the Implementing Regulation may not be rejected by any authority or institution of another Member State on the grounds that it was received by electronic means, once the receiving institution has declared that it can receive electronic documents. Reproduction and recording of such documents shall be presumed to be a correct and accurate reproduction of the original document or representation of the information it relates to, unless there is proof to the contrary.

78(4) An electronic document shall be considered valid if the computer system on which the document is recorded contains the safeguards necessary in order to prevent any alteration, disclosure or unauthorised access to the recording. It shall at any time be possible to reproduce the recorded information in an immediately readable form. When an electronic document is transferred from one social security institution to another, appropriate security measures shall be taken in accordance with the Community provisions on the protection of natural persons with regard to the processing and the free movement of personal data.

ART. 79 Funding of activities in the social security field

79 In connection with this Regulation and the Implementing Regulation, the Commission of the European Communities may fund in full or in part:

(a) activities aimed at improving exchanges of information between the social security authorities and institutions of the Member States, particularly the electronic exchange of data;

(b) any other activity aimed at providing information to the persons covered by this Regulation and their representatives about the rights and obligations deriving from this Regulation, using the most appropriate means.

ART. 80 Exemptions

80(1) Any exemption from or reduction of taxes, stamp duty, notarial or registration fees provided for under the legislation of one Member State in respect of certificates or documents required to be produced in application of the legislation of that Member State shall be extended to similar certificates or documents required to be produced in application of the legislation of another Member State or of this Regulation.

80(2) All statements, documents and certificates of any kind whatsoever required to be produced in application of this Regulation shall be exempt from authentication by diplomatic or consular authorities.

ART. 81 Claims, declarations or appeals

81 Any claim, declaration or appeal which should have been submitted, in application of the legislation of one Member State, within a specified period to an authority, institution or tribunal of that Member State shall be admissible if it is submitted within the same period to a corresponding authority, institution or tribunal of another Member State. In such a case the authority, institution or tribunal receiving the claim, declaration or appeal shall forward it without delay to the competent authority, institution or tribunal of the former Member State either directly or through the competent authorities of the Member States concerned. The date on which such claims, declarations or appeals were submitted to the authority, institution or tribunal of the second Member State shall be considered as the date of their submission to the competent authority, institution or tribunal.

ART. 82 Medical examinations

82 Medical examinations provided for by the legislation of one Member State may be carried out at the request of the competent institution, in another Member State, by the institution of the place of residence or stay of the claimant or the person entitled to benefits, under the conditions laid down in the Implementing Regulation or agreed between the competent authorities of the Member States concerned.

ART. 83 Implementation of legislation

83 Special provisions for implementing the legislation of certain Member States are referred to in Annex XI.

ART. 84 Collection of contributions and recovery of benefits

84(1) Collection of contributions due to an institution of one Member State and recovery of benefits provided by the institution of one Member State but not due may be effected in another Member State in accordance with the procedures and with the guarantees and privileges applicable to the collection of contributions due to the corresponding institution of the latter Member State and the recovery of benefits provided by it but not due.

84(2) Enforceable decisions of the judicial and administrative authorities relating to the collection of contributions, interest and any other charges or to the recovery of benefits provided but not due under the legislation of one Member State shall be recognised and enforced at the request of the competent institution in another Member State within the limits and in accordance with the procedures laid down by the legislation and any other procedures applicable to similar decisions of the latter Member State. Such decisions shall be declared enforceable in that Member State insofar as the legislation and any other procedures of that Member State so require.

84(3) Claims of an institution of one Member State shall in enforcement, bankruptcy or settlement proceedings in another Member State enjoy the same privileges as the legislation of the latter Member State accords to claims of the same kind.

84(4) The procedure for implementing this Article, including costs reimbursement, shall be governed by the Implementing Regulation or, where necessary and as a complementary measure, by means of agreements between Member States.

ART. 85 Rights of institutions

85(1) If a person receives benefits under the legislation of one Member State in respect of an injury resulting from events occurring in another Member State, any rights of the institution responsible for providing benefits against a third party liable to provide compensation for the injury shall be governed by the following rules:

(a) where the institution responsible for providing benefits is, under the legislation it applies, subrogated to the rights which the beneficiary has against the third party, such subrogation shall be recognised by each Member State;

(b) where the institution responsible for providing benefits has a direct right against the third party, each Member State shall recognise such rights.

85(2) If a person receives benefits under the legislation of one Member State in respect of an injury resulting from events occurring in another Member State, the provisions of the said legislation which determine the cases in which the civil liability of employers or of their employees is to be excluded shall apply with regard to the said person or to the competent institution. Paragraph 1 shall also apply to any rights of the institution responsible for providing benefits against employers or their employees in cases where their liability is not excluded.

85(3) Where, in accordance with Article 35(3) and/or Article 41(2), two or more Member States or their competent authorities have concluded an agreement to waive reimbursement between institutions under their jurisdiction, or, where reimbursement does not depend on the amount of benefits actually provided, any rights arising against a liable third party shall be governed by the following rules:

(a) where the institution of the Member State of residence or stay accords benefits to a person in respect of an injury sustained in its territory, that institution, in accordance with the provisions of the legislation it applies, shall exercise the right to subrogation or direct action against the third party liable to provide compensation for the injury;

(b) for the application of (a):

(i) the person receiving benefits shall be deemed to be insured with the institution of the place of residence or stay, and

(ii) that institution shall be deemed to be the institution responsible for providing benefits;

(c) Paragraphs 1 and 2 shall remain applicable in respect of any benefits not covered by the waiver agreement or a reimbursement which does not depend on the amount of benefits actually provided.

ART. 86 Bilateral agreements

86 As far as relations between, on the one hand, Luxembourg and, on the other hand, France, Germany and Belgium are concerned, the application and the duration of the period referred to in Article 65(7) shall be subject to the conclusion of bilateral agreements.

TITLE VI – TRANSITIONAL AND FINAL PROVISIONS

ART. 87 Transitional provisions

87(1) No rights shall be acquired under this Regulation for the period before its date of application.

87(2) Any period of insurance and, where appropriate, any period of employment, self-employment or residence completed under the legislation of a Member State prior to the date of application of this Regulation in the Member State concerned shall be taken into consideration for the determination of rights acquired under this Regulation.

87(3) Subject to paragraph 1, a right shall be acquired under this Regulation even if it relates to a contingency arising before its date of application in the Member State concerned.

87(4) Any benefit which has not been awarded or which has been suspended by reason of the nationality or place of residence of the person concerned shall, at the request of that person, be provided or resumed with effect from the date of application of this Regulation in the Member State concerned, provided that the rights for which benefits were previously provided have not given rise to a lump-sum payment.

87(5) The rights of a person to whom a pension was provided prior to the date of application of this Regulation in a Member State may, at the request of the person concerned, be reviewed, taking into account this Regulation.

87(6) If a request referred to in paragraph 4 or 5 is submitted within two years from the date of application of this Regulation in a Member State, the rights acquired under this Regulation shall have effect from that date, and the legislation of any Member State concerning the forfeiture or limitation of rights may not be invoked against the persons concerned.

87(7) If a request referred to in paragraph 4 or 5 is submitted after the expiry of the two-year period following the date of application of this Regulation in the Member State concerned, rights not forfeited or not time-barred shall have effect from the date on which the request was submitted, subject to any more favourable provisions under the legislation of any Member State.

87(8) If, as a result of this Regulation, a person is subject to the legislation of a Member State other than that determined in accordance with Title II of Regulation (EEC) No 1408/71, that legislation shall continue to apply while the relevant situation remains unchanged and in any case for no longer than 10 years from the date of application of this Regulation unless the person concerned requests that he/she be subject to the legislation applicable under this Regulation. The request shall be submitted within 3 months after the date of application of this Regulation to the competent institution of the Member State whose legislation is applicable under this Regulation if the person concerned is to be subject to the legislation of that Member State as of the date of application of this Regulation. If the request is made after the time limit indicated, the change of applicable legislation shall take place on the first day of the following month.

87(9) Article 55 of this Regulation shall apply only to pensions not subject to Article 46c of Regulation (EEC) No 1408/71 on the date of application of this Regulation.

87(10) The provisions of the second sentences of Article 65(2) and (3) shall be applicable to Luxembourg at the latest two years after the date of application of this Regulation.

87(10a) The entries in Annex III corresponding to Estonia, Spain, Italy, Lithuania, Hungary and the Netherlands shall cease to have effect 4 years after the date of application of this Regulation.

87(10b) The list contained in Annex III shall be reviewed no later than 31 October 2014 on the basis of a report by the Administrative Commission. That report shall include an impact assessment of the significance, frequency, scale and costs, both in absolute and in relative terms, of the application of the provisions of Annex III. That report shall also include the possible effects of repealing those provisions for those Member States which continue to be listed in that Annex after the date referred to in paragraph 10a. In the light of that report, the Commission shall decide whether to submit a proposal concerning a review of the list, with the aim in principle of repealing the list unless the report of the Administrative Commission provides compelling reasons not to do so.

87(11) Member States shall ensure that appropriate information is provided regarding the changes in rights and obligations introduced by this Regulation and the Implementing Regulation.

History – Art. 87(8) replaced by Reg. 988/2009, art. 1(19)(a), with effect from 1 May 2010.
Art. 87(10a) inserted by Reg. 988/2009, art. 1(19)(b), with effect from 1 May 2010.
Art. 87(10b) inserted by Reg. 988/2009, art. 1(19)(b), with effect from 1 May 2010.

ART. 87a Transitional provision for application of Regulation (EU) No 465/2012

87a(1) If as a result of the entry into force of Regulation (EU) No 465/2012, a person is subject, in accordance with Title II of this Regulation, to the legislation of a different Member State than that to which he/she was subject before that entry into force, the legislation of the Member State applicable before that date shall continue to apply to him/her for a transitional period lasting for as long as the relevant situation remains unchanged and, in any case, for no longer than 10 years from the date of entry into force of Regulation (EU) No 465/2012. Such a person may request that the transitional period no longer applies to him/her. Such request shall be submitted to the institution designated by the competent authority of the Member State of residence. Requests submitted by 29 September 2012 shall be deemed to take effect on 28 June 2012. Requests submitted after 29 September 2012 shall take effect on the first day of the month following that of their submission.

87a(2) No later than 29 June 2014, the Administrative Commission shall evaluate the implementation of the provisions laid down in Article 65a of this Regulation and present a report on their application. On the basis of this report, the European Commission may, as appropriate, submit proposals to amend those provisions.

History – Art. 87a inserted by Reg. 465/2012, art. 1(11), with effect from 28 June 2012.

ART. 88 Updating of the Annexes

88 The Annexes of this Regulation shall be revised periodically.

ART. 89 Implementing Regulation

89 A further Regulation shall lay down the procedure for implementing this Regulation.

ART. 90 Repeal

90(1) Council Regulation (EEC) No 1408/71 shall be repealed from the date of application of this Regulation.

However, Regulation (EEC) No 1408/71 shall remain in force and shall continue to have legal effect for the purposes of:

(a) Council Regulation (EC) No 859/2003 of 14 May 2003 extending the provisions of Regulation (EEC) No 1408/71 and Regulation (EEC) No 574/72 to nationals of third countries who are not already covered by those provisions solely on the ground of their nationality, for as long as that Regulation has not been repealed or modified;

(b) Council Regulation (EEC) No 1661/85 of 13 June 1985 laying down the technical adaptations to the Community rules on social security for migrant workers with regard to Greenland, for as long as that Regulation has not been repealed or modified;

(c) the Agreement on the European Economic Area and the Agreement between the European Community and its Member States, of the one part, and the Swiss Confederation, of the other part, on the free movement of persons and other agreements which contain a reference to Regulation (EEC) No 1408/71, for as long as those agreements have not been modified in the light of this Regulation.

90(2) References to Regulation (EEC) No 1408/71 in Council Directive 98/49/EC of 29 June 1998 on safeguarding the supplementary pension rights of employed and self-employed persons moving within the Community are to be read as referring to this Regulation.

ART. 91 Entry into force

91 This Regulation shall enter into force on the twentieth day after its publication in the Official Journal of the European Union.

It shall apply from the date of entry into force of the Implementing Regulation.

This Regulation shall be binding in its entirety and directly applicable in all Member States.

ANNEX I – ADVANCES OF MAINTENANCE PAYMENTS AND SPECIAL CHILDBIRTH AND ADOPTION ALLOWANCES (ARTICLE 1(Z))

I. Advances of maintenance payments

BELGIUM

Advances of maintenance allowances under the law of 21 February 2003 creating a maintenance payments agency within the federal public service, Finance Department

BULGARIA

Maintenance payments made by the State under Article 92 of the Family Code.

DENMARK

Advance payment of child support laid down in the Act on Child Benefits

Advance payment of child support consolidated by Law No 765 of 11 September 2002

GERMANY

Advances of maintenance payments under the German law on advances of maintenance payments (Unterhaltsvorschussgesetz) of 23 July 1979

ESTONIA

Maintenance allowances under the Maintenance Allowance Act of 21 February 2007;

SPAIN

Advances of maintenance payments under the Royal Decree 1618/2007 of 7 December 2007.

FRANCE

Family support allowance paid to a child one of whose parents or both of whose parents are in default or are unable to meet their maintenance obligations or the payment of a maintenance allowance laid down by a court decision

CROATIA

Temporary advances paid by Centres for Social Welfare on the basis of the obligation to provide temporary maintenance pursuant to the Family Act (OG 116/03, as amended)

LITHUANIA

Payments from the Children's Maintenance Fund under the Law on the Children's Maintenance Fund.

LUXEMBOURG

Advances and recovery of maintenance payments within the meaning of the Act of 26 July 1980.

AUSTRIA

Advances of maintenance payments under the Federal Law on the grant of advances of child maintenance (Unterhaltsvorschussgesetz 1985 – UVG)

POLAND

Benefits from the Alimony Fund under the Act of Assistance to the Persons Entitled to Alimony

PORTUGAL

Advances of maintenance payments (Act No 75/98, 19 November, on the guarantee of maintenance for minors)

SLOVENIA

Maintenance replacement in accordance with the Act of Public Guarantee and Maintenance Fund of the Republic of Slovenia of 25 July 2006.

SLOVAKIA

Substitute alimony benefit (substitute maintenance payment) pursuant to the Act No 452/2004 Coll. on substitute alimony benefit as amended by later regulations.

FINLAND

Maintenance allowance under the Security of Child Maintenance Act (671/1998)

SWEDEN

Maintenance allowance under the Maintenance Support Act (1996:1030)

II. Special childbirth and adoption allowances

BELGIUM

Childbirth allowance and adoption grant

BULGARIA

Maternity lump sum allowance (Law on Family Allowances for Children).

CZECH REPUBLIC

Childbirth allowance.

ESTONIA

(a) Childbirth allowance;

(b) Adoption allowance.

SPAIN

Single payment birth and adoption grants

FRANCE

Birth or adoption grants as part of the "early childhood benefit", except when they are paid to a person who remains subject to French legislation pursuant to Article 12 or Article 16

CROATIA

One-off cash benefit for a newborn child under the Maternity and Parental Benefits Act (OG 85/08, as amended)

One-off cash benefit for an adopted child under the Maternity and Parental Benefits Act (OG 85/08, as amended)

One-off cash benefits for a newborn child or an adopted child provided by regulations on local and regional self- government pursuant to Article 59 of the Maternity and Parental Benefits Act (OG 85/08, as amended)

LATVIA

(a) Childbirth grant;

(b) Adoption allowance.

LITHUANIA

Child lump sum grant.

LUXEMBOURG

Antenatal allowances

Childbirth allowances

HUNGARY

Maternity grant.

POLAND

Single payment birth grant (Act on Family Benefits).

ROMANIA

(a) Childbirth allowance;

(b) Layette for newborn children.

SLOVENIA

Childbirth grant.

SLOVAKIA

(a) Childbirth allowance;

(b) Supplement to childbirth allowance.

FINLAND

Maternity package, maternity lump-sum grant and assistance in the form of a lump sum intended to offset the cost of international adoption pursuant to the Maternity Grant Act

History – In Pt. 1, the entry for Croatia inserted by Reg. 517/2013, art. 2 and Annex, Pt. 2(a), with effect from 1 July 2013.
In Pt. I, the prefix letters removed form the country headings and the entries for Bulgaria, Estonia, Spain, Lithuania, Luxembourg, Poland, Slovenia, Slovakia added and in Pt. II, the prefix letters removed and entries for Bulgaria, Czech Republic, Estonia, Latvia, Lithuania, Hungary, Poland, Romania, Slovenia and Slovakia added, the entry for Spain replaced and the entry for France amended by Reg. 988/2009, art. 2 and Annex, Pt. A, with effect from 1 May 2010.
In Pt. 2, the entry for Croatia inserted by Reg. 517/2013, art. 2 and Annex, Pt. 2(b), with effect from 1 July 2013.

ANNEX II – PROVISIONS OF CONVENTIONS WHICH REMAIN IN FORCE AND WHICH, WHERE APPLICABLE, ARE RESTRICTED TO THE PERSONS COVERED THEREBY (ARTICLE 8(1))

General comments

It is to be noted that the provisions of bilateral conventions which do not fall within the scope of this Regulation and which remain in force between Member States are not listed in this Annex. This includes obligations between Member States arising from conventions providing, for example, for provisions regarding aggregation of insurance periods fulfilled in a third country.

Provisions of social security conventions remaining applicable:

BELGIUM-GERMANY

Articles 3 and 4 of the Final Protocol of 7 December 1957 to the General Convention of that date, as set out in the Complementary Protocol of 10 November 1960 (reckoning of insurance periods completed in some border regions before, during and after the Second World War).

BELGIUM-LUXEMBOURG

Convention of 24 March 1994 on social security for frontier workers (relating to the complementary flat rate reimbursement).

BULGARIA-GERMANY

Article 28(1)(b) of the Convention on social security of 17 December 1997 (maintenance of conventions concluded between Bulgaria and the former German Democratic Republic for persons who already received a pension before 1996).

BULGARIA-CROATIA

Article 35(3) of the Convention on Social Security of 14 July 2003 (recognition of periods of insurance completed until 31 December 1957 at the expense of the contracting state in which the insured person resided on 31 December 1957).

BULGARIA-AUSTRIA

Article 38(3) of the Convention on social security of 14 April 2005 (reckoning of periods of insurance completed before 27 November 1961); the application of that provision remains restricted to the persons covered by that Convention.

BULGARIA-SLOVENIA

Article 32(2) of the Convention on Social Security of 18 December 1957 (reckoning of periods of insurance completed until 31 December 1957).

CZECH REPUBLIC-GERMANY

Article 39(1)(b) and (c) of the Convention on Social Security of 27 July 2001 (maintenance of the convention concluded between the former Czechoslovak Republic and the former German Democratic Republic for persons who already received a pension before 1996; reckoning of periods of insurance completed in one of the contracting States for persons who already received a pension for these periods on 1 September 2002 from the other contracting State, while residing in its territory).

CZECH REPUBLIC-CYPRUS

Article 32(4) of the Convention on Social Security of 19 January 1999 (determining competence for the calculation of periods of employment completed under the relevant Convention of 1976); the application of that provision remains restricted to the persons covered by it.

CZECH REPUBLIC-LUXEMBOURG

Article 52(8) of the Convention on Social Security of 17 November 2000 (reckoning of pension insurance periods for political refugees).

CZECH REPUBLIC-AUSTRIA

Article 32(3) of the Convention on social security of 20 July 1999 (reckoning of periods of insurance completed before 27 November 1961); the application of that provision remains restricted to the persons covered by it.

CZECH REPUBLIC-SLOVAKIA

Articles 12, 20 and 33 of the Convention on Social Security of 29 October 1992 (Article 12 determines competence for a grant of survivor's benefits; Article 20 determines competence for calculation of insurance periods completed until the day of dissolution of the Czech and Slovak Federal Republic; Article 33 determines competence for payment of pensions awarded before the day of the dissolution of the Czech and Slovak Federal Republic).

DENMARK-FINLAND

Article 7 of the Nordic Convention on social security of 18 August 2003 (concerning coverage of extra travel expenses in case of sickness during stay in another Nordic country increasing the cost of return travel to the country of residence).

DENMARK-SWEDEN

Article 7 of the Nordic Convention on social security of 18 August 2003 (concerning coverage of extra travel expenses in case of sickness during stay in another Nordic country increasing the cost of return travel to the country of residence).

GERMANY-SPAIN

Article 45(2) of the Social Security Convention of 4 December 1973 (representation by diplomatic and consular authorities).

GERMANY-FRANCE

(a) Complementary Agreement No 4 of 10 July 1950 to the General Convention of the same date, as set out in Supplementary Agreement No 2 of 18 June 1955 (reckoning of periods of insurance completed between 1 July 1940 and 30 June 1950);

(b) Title I of that Supplementary Agreement No 2 (reckoning of periods of insurance completed before 8 May 1945);

(c) points 6, 7 and 8 of the General Protocol of 10 July 1950 to the General Convention of the same date (administrative arrangements);

(d) Titles II, III and IV of the Agreement of 20 December 1963 (social security in the Saar).

GERMANY-CROATIA

Article 41 of the Convention on Social Security of 24 November 1997 (settlement of rights acquired before 1 January 1956 under the social security scheme of the other contracting state); the application of that provision remains restricted to the persons covered by it.

GERMANY-LUXEMBOURG

Articles 4, 5, 6 and 7 of the Convention of 11 July 1959 (reckoning of insurance periods completed between September 1940 and June 1946).

GERMANY-HUNGARY

Article 40(1)(b) of the Convention on social security of 2 May 1998 (maintenance of the convention concluded between the former German Democratic Republic and Hungary for persons who already received a pension before 1996).

GERMANY-NETHERLANDS

Articles 2 and 3 of Complementary Agreement No 4 of 21 December 1956 to the Convention of 29 March 1951 (settlement of rights acquired under the German social insurance scheme by Dutch workers between 13 May 1940 and 1 September 1945).

GERMANY-AUSTRIA

(a) Article 1(5) and Article 8 of the Convention on Unemployment Insurance of 19 July 1978 and Article 10 of the Final Protocol to this Convention (granting of unemployment allowances to frontier workers by the previous State of employment) shall continue to apply to persons who have exercised an activity as a frontier worker on or before 1 January 2005 and become unemployed before 1 January 2011;

(b) Article 14(2)(g), (h), (i) and (j) of the Convention on social security of 4 October 1995 (determination of competencies between both countries with regard to former insurance cases and acquired insurance periods); the application of that provision remains restricted to the persons covered by it.

GERMANY-POLAND

(a) Convention of 9 October 1975 on old-age and work injury provisions, under the conditions and the scope defined by Article 27(2) to (4) of the Convention on social security of 8 December 1990 (maintenance of legal status, on the basis of the Convention of 1975, of the persons who had established their residence in the territory of Germany or Poland before 1 January 1991 and who continue to reside there);

(b) Articles 27(5) and 28(2) of the Convention on social security of 8 December 1990 (maintenance of entitlement to a pension paid on the basis of the Convention of 1957 concluded between the former German Democratic Republic and Poland; reckoning of periods of insurance completed by Polish employees under the Convention of 1988 concluded between the former German Democratic Republic and Poland).

GERMANY-ROMANIA

Article 28(1)(b) of the Convention on social security of 8 April 2005 (maintenance of the Convention concluded between the former German Democratic Republic and Romania for persons who already received a pension before 1996).

GERMANY-SLOVENIA

Article 42 of the Convention on social security of 24 September 1997 (settlement of rights acquired before 1 January 1956 under the social security scheme of the other contracting state); the application of that provision remains restricted to the persons covered by it.

GERMANY-SLOVAKIA

Article 29(1), second and third subparagraphs of the Agreement of 12 September 2002 (maintenance of the Convention concluded between the former Czechoslovak Republic and the former German Democratic Republic for persons who already received a pension before 1996; reckoning of periods of insurance completed in one of the contracting States for persons who already received a pension for these periods on 1 December 2003 from the other contracting State, while residing in its territory).

GERMANY-UNITED KINGDOM

(a) Article 7(5) and (6) of the Convention on social security of 20 April 1960 (legislation applicable to civilians serving in the military forces);

(b) Article 5(5) and of the Convention on unemployment insurance of 20 April 1960 (legislation applicable to civilians serving in the military forces).

IRELAND-UNITED KINGDOM

Article 19(2) of the Agreement of 14 December, 2004 on social security (concerning the transfer and reckoning of certain disability credits).

SPAIN-PORTUGAL

Article 22 of the General Convention of 11 June 1969 (export of unemployment benefits). This entry will remain valid for 2 years from the date of application of this Regulation.

CROATIA-ITALY

(a) The Agreement between Yugoslavia and Italy on Regulation of Mutual Obligations in Social Insurance with Reference to Paragraph 7 of Annex XIV to the Peace Treaty, concluded by exchange of notes on 5 February 1959 (reckoning of periods of insurance completed before 18 December 1954); the application remains restricted to the persons covered by that Agreement;

(b) Article 44(3) of the Convention on Social Security between the Republic of Croatia and the Italian Republic of 27 June 1997, concerning ex Zone B of the Free Territory of Trieste (reckoning of periods of insurance completed before 5 October 1956); the application of that provision remains restricted to persons covered by that Convention.

CROATIA-HUNGARY

Article 43(6) of the Convention on Social Security of 8 February 2005 (recognition of periods of insurance completed until 29 May 1956 at the expense of the contracting state in which the insured person resided on 29 May 1956).

CROATIA-AUSTRIA

Article 35 of the Convention on Social Security of 16 January 1997 (reckoning of periods of insurance completed before 1 January 1956); the application of that provision remains restricted to the persons covered by it.

CROATIA-SLOVENIA

(a) Article 35(3) of the Agreement on Social Security of 28 April 1997 (recognition of periods with bonus under the legislation of the former common State);

(b) Articles 36 and 37 of the Agreement on Social Security of 28 April 1997 (benefits acquired before 8 October 1991 remain the obligation of the contracting state that granted them; pensions granted between 8 October 1991 and 1 February 1998, the date of entry into force of the said Agreement, in respect of the periods of insurance completed in the other contracting state until 31 January 1998, are subject to recalculation).

ITALY-SLOVENIA

(a) Agreement on regulation of mutual obligations in social insurance with reference to paragraph 7 of Annex XIV to the Peace Treaty, concluded by exchange of notes on 5 February 1959 (reckoning of periods of insurance completed before 18 December 1954); the application of that provision remains restricted to the persons covered by that Agreement;

(b) Article 45(3) of the Convention on social security of 7 July 1997 concerning ex-Zone B of the Free Territory of Trieste (reckoning of periods of insurance completed before 5 October 1956); the application of that provision remains restricted to the persons covered by that Convention.

LUXEMBOURG-PORTUGAL

Agreement of 10 March 1997 (on the recognition of decisions by institutions in one contracting party concerning the state of invalidity of applicants for pensions from institutions in the other contracting party).

LUXEMBOURG-SLOVAKIA

Article 50(5) of the Convention on Social Security of 23 May 2002 (reckoning of pension insurance periods for political refugees).

HUNGARY-AUSTRIA

Article 36(3) of the Convention on social security of 31 March 1999 (reckoning of periods of insurance completed before 27 November 1961); the application of that provision remains restricted to the persons covered by it.

HUNGARY-SLOVENIA

Article 31 of the Convention on social security of 7 October 1957 (reckoning of periods of insurance completed before 29 May 1956); the application of that provision remains restricted to the persons covered by it.

HUNGARY-SLOVAKIA

Article 34(1) of the Convention on social security of 30 January 1959 (Article 34(1) of that Convention provides that the insurance periods awarded before the day of signing that Convention are the insurance periods of the contracting State on which territory the entitled person had a residence); the application of that provision remains restricted to the persons covered by it.

AUSTRIA-POLAND

Article 33(3) of the Convention on social security of 7 September 1998 (reckoning of periods of insurance completed before 27 November 1961); the application of that provision remains restricted to the persons covered by it.

AUSTRIA-ROMANIA

Article 37(3) of the Agreement on social security of 28 October 2005 (reckoning of periods of insurance completed before 27 November 1961); the application of that provision remains restricted to the persons covered by it.

AUSTRIA-SLOVENIA

Article 37 of the Convention on social security of 10 March 1997 (reckoning of periods of insurance completed before 1 January 1956); the application of that provision remains restricted to the persons covered by it.

AUSTRIA-SLOVAKIA

Article 34(3) of the Convention of 21 December 2001 on Social Security (reckoning of periods of insurance completed before 27 November 1961); the application of that provision remains restricted to the persons covered by it.

FINLAND-SWEDEN

Article 7 of the Nordic Convention on social security of 18 August 2003 (concerning coverage of extra travel expenses in case of sickness during stay in another Nordic country increasing the cost of return travel to the country of residence).

History – The entries for "Bulgaria-Croatia", "Germany-Croatia", "Croatia-Italy", "Croatia-Hungary", "Croatia-Austria" and "Croatia-Slovenia" inserted by Reg. 517/2013, art. 2 and Annex, Pt. 2(c), with effect from 1 July 2013.
Annex II replaced by Reg. 988/2009, art. 2 and Annex, Pt. B, with effect from 1 May 2010.

ANNEX III – RESTRICTION OF RIGHTS TO BENEFITS IN KIND FOR MEMBERS OF THE FAMILY OF A FRONTIER WORKER (REFERRED TO IN ARTICLE 18(2))

DENMARK

ESTONIA (this entry will be valid during the period referred to in Article 87(10a))

IRELAND

SPAIN (this entry will be valid during the period referred to in Article 87(10a))

CROATIA

ITALY (this entry will be valid during the period referred to in Article 87(10a))

LITHUANIA (this entry will be valid during the period referred to in Article 87(10a))

HUNGARY (this entry will be valid during the period referred to in Article 87(10a))

NETHERLANDS (this entry will be valid during the period referred to in Article 87(10a))

FINLAND

SWEDEN

UNITED KINGDOM.

History – The entry for Croatia inserted by Reg. 517/2013, art. 2 and Annex, Pt. 2(d), with effect from 1 July 2013.
Annex III replaced by Reg. 988/2009, art. 2 and Annex, Pt. C, with effect from 1 May 2010.

ANNEX IV – MORE RIGHTS FOR PENSIONERS RETURNING TO THE COMPETENT MEMBER STATE (ARTICLE 27(2))

BELGIUM

BULGARIA

CZECH REPUBLIC

GERMANY

GREECE

SPAIN

FRANCE

CYPRUS

LUXEMBOURG

HUNGARY

THE NETHERLANDS

AUSTRIA

POLAND

SLOVENIA.

SWEDEN

History – The entries for Bulgaria, Czech Republic, Cyprus, Hungary, The Netherlands, Poland and Slovenia added and the entry for Italy deleted by Reg. 988/2009, art. 2 and Annex, Pt. D, with effect from 1 May 2010.

ANNEX V – MORE RIGHTS FOR FORMER FRONTIER WORKERS WHO RETURN TO THEIR PREVIOUS MEMBER STATE OF ACTIVITY AS AN EMPLOYED OR SELF-EMPLOYED PERSON (APPLICABLE ONLY IF THE MEMBER STATE IN WHICH THE COMPETENT INSTITUTION RESPONSIBLE FOR THE COSTS OF THE BENEFITS IN KIND PROVIDED TO THE PENSIONER IN HIS MEMBER STATE OF RESIDENCE IS SITUATED ALSO APPEARS ON THE LIST) (ARTICLE 28(2))

BELGIUM

GERMANY

SPAIN

FRANCE

LUXEMBOURG

AUSTRIA

PORTUGAL

ANNEX VI – IDENTIFICATION OF TYPE A LEGISLATION WHICH SHOULD BE SUBJECT TO SPECIAL COORDINATION (ARTICLE 44(1))

CZECH REPUBLIC

Full disability pension for persons whose total disability arose before reaching 18 years of age and who were not insured for the required period (Section 42 of the Pension Insurance Act No 155/1995 Coll.).

ESTONIA

(a) Invalidity pensions granted before 1 April 2000 under the State Allowances Act and which are retained under the State Pension Insurance Act.

(b) National pensions granted on the basis of invalidity according to the State Pension Insurance Act.

(c) Invalidity pensions granted according to the Defence Forces Service Act, Police Service Act, Prosecutor's Office Act, Status of Judges Act, Members of the Riigikogu Salaries, Pensions and Other Social Guarantees Act and President of the Republic Official Benefits Act.;

IRELAND

Part 2, Chapter 17 of the Social Welfare Consolidation Act 2005;

GREECE

Legislation relating to the agricultural insurance scheme (OGA), under Law No 4169/1961

CROATIA

(a) Invalidity pension due to occupational injury or disease according to Article 52(5) of the Pension Insurance Act (OG 102/98, as amended).

(b) Physical damage allowance according to Article 56 of the Pension Insurance Act (OG 102/98, as amended).

LATVIA

Invalidity pensions (third group) under Article 16(1)(2) of the Law on State Pensions of 1 January 1996.;

FINLAND

National Pensions to persons who are born disabled or become disabled at an early age (the National Pension Act, 568/2007);

Invalidity pensions determined according to transitional rules and awarded prior to 1 January 1994 (Act on Enforcement of the National Pensions Act, 569/2007).;

SWEDEN

Income-related sickness benefit and activity compensation (Act 1962:381 as amended by Act 2001:489)

UNITED KINGDOM

(a) Great Britain

Sections 30A(5), 40, 41 and 68 of the Contributions and Benefits Act 1992.

(b) Northern Ireland

Sections 30A(5), 40, 41 and 68 of the Contributions and Benefits (Northern Ireland) Act 1992.

History – The entry for Croatia inserted by Reg. 517/2013, art. 2 and Annex, Pt. 2(e), with effect from 1 July 2013.
The prefix letter for headings removed, the entries for Czech Republic, Estonia, Latvia added, the entry for Ireland moved and amended and the entries for Greece and Finland amended by Reg. 988/2009, art. 2 and Annex, Pt. E, with effect from 1 May 2010.

ANNEX VII – CONCORDANCE BETWEEN THE LEGISLATIONS OF MEMBER STATES ON CONDITIONS RELATING TO THE DEGREE OF INVALIDITY (ARTICLE 46(3) OF THE REGULATION)

BELGIUM

Member State	Schemes administered by institutions of Member States which have taken a decision recognising the degree of invalidity	Schemes administered by Belgian institutions on which the decision is binding in cases of concordance				
		General scheme	Miners' scheme		Mariners' scheme	Ossom
			General invalidity	Occupational invalidity		
FRANCE	1. General scheme:					
	– Group III (constant attendance)	Concordance	Concordance	Concordance	Concordance	No concordance
	– Group II	Concordance	Concordance	Concordance	Concordance	No concordance
	– Group I	Concordance	Concordance	Concordance	Concordance	No concordance
	2. Agricultural scheme					
– Total, general invalidity	Concordance	Concordance	Concordance	Concordance	No concordance	
	–Two-thirds general invalidity	Concordance	Concordance	Concordance	Concordance	No concordance
	– Constant attendance	Concordance	Concordance	Concordance	Concordance	No concordance
	3. Miners' scheme:					
	– Partial, general invalidity	Concordance	Concordance	Concordance	Concordance	No concordance
	– Constant attendance	Concordance	Concordance	Concordance	Concordance	No concordance
	– Occupational invalidity	No concordance	No concordance	No concordance	No concordance	No concordance

Member State	Schemes administered by institutions of Member States which have taken a decision recognising the degree of invalidity	Schemes administered by Belgian institutions on which the decision is binding in cases of concordance				
		General scheme	Miners' scheme		Mariners' scheme	Ossom
			General invalidity	Occupational invalidity		
	4. Mariners' scheme:					
	– General invalidity	Concordance	Concordance	Concordance	Concordance	No concordance
	– Constant attendance	Concordance	Concordance	Concordance	Concordance	No concordance
	– Occupational invalidity	No concordance	No concordance	No concordance	No concordance	No concordance
ITALY	1. General scheme:					
	– Invalidity – manual workers	No concordance	Concordance	Concordance	Concordance	No concordance
	– Invalidity – clerical staff	No concordance	Concordance	Concordance	Concordance	No concordance
	2. Mariners' scheme:					
	– Unfitness for seafaring	No concordance	No concordance	No concordance	No concordance	No concordance

FRANCE

Member State	Schemes administered by institutions of Member States which have taken a decision recognising the degree of invalidity	Schemes administered by French institutions on which the decision is binding in cases of concordances											
		General scheme			Agricultural scheme			Miners' scheme			Mariners' scheme		
		Group I	Group II	Group III Constant attendance	2/3 Invalidity	Total invalidity	Constant attendance	2/3 General invalidity	Constant attendance	Occupational invalidity	2/3 General invalidity	Total occupational invalidity	Constant attendance
BELGIUM	1. General scheme	Concordance	No concordance	No concordance	Concordance	No concordance	No concordance	Concordance	No concordance	No concordance	No concordance	No concordance	No concordance
	2. Miners' scheme												
	– partial general invalidity	Concordance	No concordance	No concordance	Concordance	No concordance	No concordance	Concordance	No concordance	No concordance	No concordance	No concordance	No concordance
	– occupational invalidity No concordance	No concordance	No concordance	No concordance	No concordance	No concordance	No concordance	No concordance	Concordance				
	3. Mariners' scheme	Concordance	No concordance	No concordance	Concordance	No concordance	No concordance	Concordance	No concordance	No concordance	No concordance	No concordance	No concordance
ITALY	1. General scheme												
	– invalidity – manual workers	Concordance	No concordance	No concordance	Concordance	No concordance	No concordance	Concordance	No concordance	No concordance	No concordance	No concordance	No concordance
	– invalidity – clerical staff	Concordance	No concordance	No concordance	Concordance	No concordance	No concordance	Concordance	No concordance	No concordance	No concordance	No concordance	No concordance
	2. Mariners' scheme												
	– unfitness for seafaring	No concordance	No concordance	No concordance	No concordance	No concordance	No concordance	No concordance	No concordance	No concordance	No concordance	No concordance	No concordance

ITALY

Member State	Schemes administered by institutions of Member States which have taken a decision recognising the degree of invalidity	Schemes administered by Italian institutions on which the decision is binding in cases of concordance		
		General scheme		Mariners Unfit for navigation
		Manual workers	Clerical staff	
BELGIUM	1. General scheme	No concordance	No concordance	No concordance
	2. Miners' scheme			
	– partial general invalidity	Concordance	Concordance	No concordance
	– occupational invalidity	No concordance	No concordance	No concordance
	3. Mariners' scheme	No concordance	No concordance	No concordance
FRANCE	1. General scheme			
	– Group III (constant attendance)	Concordance	Concordance	No concordance
	– Group II	Concordance	Concordance	No concordance
– Group I	Concordance	Concordance	No concordance	
	2. Agricultural scheme			
	– total general invalidity	Concordance	Concordance	No concordance
	– partial general invalidity	Concordance	Concordance	No concordance
	– constant attendance	Concordance	Concordance	No concordance
	3. Miners' scheme			
	– partial general invalidity	Concordance	Concordance	No concordance
	–constant attendance	Concordance	Concordance	No concordance
	–occupational invalidity	No concordance	No concordance	No concordance
	4. Mariners' scheme			
	– partial general invalidity	No concordance	No concordance	No concordance
	– constant attendance	No concordance	No concordance	No concordance
	– occupational invalidity			

History – All references to Luxembourg removed by Reg. 988/2009, art. 2 and Annex, Pt. F, with effect from 1 May 2010.

ANNEX VIII – CASES IN WHICH THE PRO RATA CALCULATION SHALL BE WAIVED OR SHALL NOT APPLY (ARTICLE 52(4) AND 52(5))

Part 1: Cases in which the pro rata calculation shall be waived pursuant to Article 52(4)

DENMARK

All applications for pensions referred to in the law on social pensions, except for pensions mentioned in Annex IX.

IRELAND

All applications for state pension (transition), state pension (contributory), widow's (contributory) pension and widower's (contributory) pension.

CYPRUS

All applications for old age, invalidity, widow's and widower's pensions.

LATVIA

(a) All applications for invalidity pensions (Law on State Pensions of 1 January 1996);

(b) All applications for survivor's pensions (Law on State Pensions of 1 January 1996; Law on State Funded Pensions of 1 July 2001).

LITHUANIA

All applications for State social insurance survivor's pensions calculated on the basis of the basic amount of survivor's pension (Law on State Social Insurance Pensions).

NETHERLANDS

All applications for old-age pensions under the law on general old-age insurance (AOW).

AUSTRIA

(a) All applications for benefits under the Federal Act of 9 September 1955 on General Social Insurance – ASVG, the Federal Act of 11 October 1978 on social insurance for self-employed persons engaged in trade and commerce – GSVG, the Federal Act of 11 October 1978 on social insurance for self-employed farmers – BSVG and the Federal Act of 30 November 1978 on social insurance for the self-employed in the liberal professions (FSVG);

(b) All applications for invalidity pensions based on a pension account pursuant to the General Pensions Act (APG) of 18 November 2004;

(c) All applications for survivors' pensions based on a pension account pursuant to the General Pensions Act (APG) of 18 November 2004, if no increase in benefits is to be applied in respect of additional months of insurance pursuant to Article 7(2) of the General Pensions Act (APG);

(d) All applications for invalidity and survivors' pensions of the Austrian Provincial Chambers of Physicians (Landesärztekammer) based on basic provision (basic and any supplementary benefit, or basic pension);

(e) All applications for permanent occupational invalidity support and survivors' support from the pension fund of the Austrian Chamber of Veterinary Surgeons;

(f) All applications for benefits from occupational invalidity, widows and orphans pensions according to the statutes of the welfare institutions of the Austrian bar associations, Part A.

POLAND

All applications for disability pensions, old-age pensions under the defined benefits scheme and survivors' pensions.

PORTUGAL

All applications for invalidity, old-age and survivors' pension claims, except for the cases where the totalised periods of insurance completed under the legislation of more than one Member State are equal to or longer than 21 calendar years but the national periods of insurance are equal or inferior to 20 years, and the calculation is made under Articles 32 and 33 of Decree-Law No 187/2007 of 10 May 2007.

SLOVAKIA

(a) All applications for survivors' pension (widow's pension, widower's and orphan's pension) calculated according to the legislation in force before 1 January 2004, the amount of which is derived from a pension formerly paid to the deceased;

(b) All applications for pensions calculated pursuant to Act No 461/2003 Coll. on social security as amended.

SWEDEN

All applications for guarantee pension in the form of old-age pension (Act 1998:702) and old-age pension in the form of supplementary pension (Act 1998:674).

UNITED KINGDOM

All applications for retirement pension, widows' and bereavement benefits, with the exception of those for which during a tax year beginning on or after 6 April 1975:

(i) the party concerned had completed periods of insurance, employment or residence under the legislation of the United Kingdom and another Member State; and one (or more) of the tax years was not considered a qualifying year within the meaning of the legislation of the United Kingdom;

(ii) the periods of insurance completed under the legislation in force in the United Kingdom for the periods prior to 5 July 1948 would be taken into account for the purposes of Article 52(1)(b) of the Regulation by application of the periods of insurance, employment or residence under the legislation of another Member State.

All applications for additional pension pursuant to the Social Security Contributions and Benefits Act 1992, section 44, and the Social Security Contributions and Benefits (Northern Ireland) Act 1992, section 44.

Part 2: Cases in which Article 52(5) applies

BULGARIA

Old age pensions from the Supplementary Compulsory Pension Insurance, under Part II, Title II, of the Social Insurance Code.

CZECH REPUBLIC

Pensions paid from the Second Pillar scheme established by Act No 426/2011 Coll., on pension savings.

ESTONIA

Mandatory funded old-age pension scheme.

FRANCE

Basic or supplementary schemes in which old-age benefits are calculated on the basis of retirement points.

CROATIA

Pensions from the compulsory insurance scheme based on the individual capitalised savings according to the Compulsory and Voluntary Pension Funds Act (OG 49/99, as amended) and the Act on Pension Insurance Companies and Payment of Pensions Based on Individual Capitalised Savings (OG 106/99, as amended), except in the cases provided by Articles 47 and 48 of the Compulsory and Voluntary Pension Funds Act (invalidity pension based on general incapacity to work and survivor's pension).

LATVIA

Old-age pensions (Law on State Pensions of 1 January 1996; Law on State Funded Pensions of 1 July 2001).

HUNGARY

Pension benefits based on membership of private pension funds.

AUSTRIA

(a) Old-age pensions and survivor's pensions derived thereof based on a pension account pursuant to the General Pensions Act (APG) of 18 November 2004;

(b) Compulsory allowances under Article 41 of the Federal Law of 28 December 2001, BGBl I Nr. 154 on the general salary fund of Austrian pharmacists (Pharmazeutische Gehaltskasse für Österreich);

(c) Retirement and early retirement pensions of the Austrian Provincial Chambers of Physicians based on basic provision (basic and any supplementary benefit, or basic pension), and all pension benefits of the Austrian Provincial Chambers of Physicians based on additional provision (additional or individual pension);

(d) Old-age support from the pension fund of the Austrian Chamber of Veterinary Surgeons;

(e) *Benefits according to the statutes* of the welfare institutions of the Austrian bar associations, Parts A and B, with the exception of applications for benefits from disability, widows' and orphans' pensions according to the statutes of the welfare institutions of the Austrian bar associations, Part A;

(f) Benefits by the welfare institutions of the Federal Chamber of Architects and Consulting Engineers under the Austrian Civil Engineers' Chamber Act (Ziviltechnikerkammergesetz) 1993 and the statutes of the welfare institutions, with the exception of benefits on grounds of occupational invalidity and survivors' benefits deriving from the last-named benefits;

(g) Benefits according to the statute of the welfare institution of the Federal Chamber of Professional Accountants and Tax Advisors under the Austrian Professional Accountants and Tax Advisors' Act (Wirtschaftstreuhand-berufsgesetz).

POLAND

Old-age pensions under the defined contribution scheme.

PORTUGAL

Supplementary pensions granted pursuant to Decree-Law No 26/2008 of 22 February 2008 (public capitalisation scheme).

SLOVENIA

Pension from compulsory supplementary pension insurance.

SLOVAKIA

Mandatory old-age pension saving.

SWEDEN

Income-based pension and premium pension (Act 1998:674).

UNITED KINGDOM

Graduated retirement benefits paid pursuant to the National Insurance Act 1965, sections 36 and 37, and the National Insurance Act (Northern Ireland) 1966, sections 35 and 36.;

History – In Pt. 2, the entry for Czech Republic inserted by Reg. 1372/2013, art. 1(1)(b), with effect from 1 January 2014.
In Pt. 2, in the entry for Austria, para. (a) replaced by Reg. 1372/2013, art. 1(1)(a), with effect from 1 January 2014.
In Pt. 2, the entry for Croatia inserted by Reg. 517/2013, art. 2 and Annex, Pt. 2(f), with effect from 1 July 2013.
Annex VIII replaced by Reg. 988/2009, art. 2 and Annex, Pt. G, with effect from 1 May 2010.
In Pt. 1, the entry for Portugal replaced by Reg. 1244/2010, art. 1(1)(a), with effect from 11 January 2011.
In Pt. 2, the entry for Portugal added by Reg. 1244/2010, art. 1(1)(b), with effect from 11 January 2011.

ANNEX IX – BENEFITS AND AGREEMENTS WHICH ALLOW THE APPLICATION OF ARTICLE 54

I. Benefits referred to in Article 54(2)(a) of the Regulation, the amount of which is independent of the length of periods of insurance or residence completed

BELGIUM

Benefits relating to the general invalidity scheme, the special invalidity scheme for miners and the special scheme for merchant navy mariners

Benefits on insurance for self-employed persons against incapacity to work

Benefits relating to invalidity in the overseas social insurance scheme and the invalidity scheme for former employees of the Belgian Congo and Ruanda-Urundi

DENMARK

The full Danish national old-age pension acquired after 10 years' residence by persons who will have been awarded a pension by 1 October 1989

IRELAND

Type A Invalidity Pension

GREECE

Benefits under Law No 4169/1961 relating to the agricultural insurance scheme (OGA)

SPAIN

Survivors' pensions granted under the general and special schemes, with the exception of the Special Scheme for Civil Servants

FRANCE

Invalidity pension under the general social security system or under the agricultural workers scheme

Widower's or widow's invalidity pension under the general social security system or under the agricultural workers scheme where it is calculated on the basis of the deceased spouse's invalidity pension settled in accordance with Article 52(1)(a)

LATVIA

Invalidity pensions (third group) under Article 16(1)(2) of the Law on State Pensions of 1 January 1996.

NETHERLANDS

The Work and Income according to Labour Capacity Act of 10 November 2005 (WIA).

Disability Insurance Act of 18 February 1966, as amended (WAO)

Self-employed Persons Disablement Benefits Act of 24 April 1997, as amended (WAZ)

General Surviving Relatives Act of 21 December 1995 (ANW)

FINLAND

National pensions to persons who are born disabled or become disabled at an early age (the National Pensions Act, 568/2007);

National pensions and spouse's pensions determined according to the transitional rules and awarded prior to the 1 of January 1994 (Act on Enforcement of the National Pensions Act, 569/2007);

The additional amount of child's pension when calculating independent benefit according to the National Pension Act (the National Pension Act, 568/2007).

SWEDEN

Swedish income-related sickness compensation and activity compensation (Act 1962:381).

Swedish guarantee pension and guaranteed compensation which replaced the full Swedish state pensions provided under the legislation on the state pension which applied before 1 January 1993, and the full state pension awarded under the transitional rules of the legislation applying from that date.

Earnings-related survivor's pension in the form of child's pension allowance and adjustment pension when the death occurred on 1 January 2003 or later when the deceased was born in 1938 or later (Act 2000:461)

II. Benefits referred to in Article 54(2)(b) of the Regulation, the amount of which is determined by reference to a credited period deemed to have been completed between the date on which the risk materialised and a later date

GERMANY

Invalidity and survivors' pensions, for which account is taken of a supplementary period

Old-age pensions, for which account is taken of a supplementary period already acquired

SPAIN

The pensions for retirement or retirement for permanent disability (invalidity) under the Special Scheme for Civil Servants due under Title I of the consolidated text of the Law on State Pensioners if at the time of materialisation of the risk the beneficiary was an active civil servant or treated as such; death and survivors' (widows'/widowers', orphans' and parents') pensions due under Title I of the consolidated text of the Law on State Pensioners if at the time of death the civil servant was active or treated as such

ITALY

Italian pensions for total incapacity for work (inabilità)

LATVIA

Survivors' pension calculated on the basis of assumed insurance periods (Article 23(8) of the Law on State Pensions of 1 January 1996).

LITHUANIA

(a) State social insurance work incapacity pensions, paid under the Law on State Social Insurance Pensions;

(b) State social insurance survivors' and orphans' pensions, calculated on the basis of the work incapacity pension of the deceased under the Law on State Social Insurance Pensions.

LUXEMBOURG

Invalidity and survivors' pensions

SLOVAKIA

(a) Slovak invalidity pension and survivors' pension derived therefrom;

(b) Invalidity pension for a person who became invalid as a dependent child and who is always deemed to have fulfilled the required period of insurance (Article 70(2), Article 72(3) and Article 73(3) and (4), of Act No 461/2003 on social insurance, as amended).

FINLAND

Employment pensions for which account is taken of future periods according to the national legislation

SWEDEN

Sickness benefit and activity compensation in the form of guarantee benefit (Act 1962:381)

Survivor's pension calculated on the basis of assumed insurance periods (Act 2000:461 and 2000:462)

Old-age pension in the form of guarantee pension calculated on the basis of assumed periods previously counted (Act 1998:702)

III. Agreements referred to in Article 54(2)(b)(i) of the Regulation intended to prevent the same credited period being taken into account two or more times:

The Social Security Agreement of 28 April 1997 between the Republic of Finland and the Federal Republic of Germany

The Social Security Agreement of 10 November 2000 between the Republic of Finland and the Grand Duchy of Luxembourg

Nordic Convention on social security of 18 August 2003.

History – In Pt. I, the prefix letters in headings removed, the entries for Latvia added, the entry for Ireland moved, the entry for The Netherlands amended and the entries for Finland and Sweden replaced and in Pt. II the prefix letters in headings removed, the entries for Latvia, Lithuania and Slovakia added and in Pt. III the words "Nordic Convention on social security of 18 August 2003" replaced by Reg. 988/2009, art. 2 and Annex, Pt. H, with effect from 1 May 2010.
In Pt. I, the entry for the Netherlands amended by Regulation 1244/2010, art. 2, with effect from 11 January 2011.

ANNEX X – SPECIAL NON-CONTRIBUTORY CASH BENEFITS (ARTICLE 70(2)(c))

BELGIUM

(a) Income replacement allowance (Law of 27 February 1987);

(b) Guaranteed income for elderly persons (Law of 22 March 2001).

BULGARIA

Social Pension for old age (Article 89 of the Social Insurance Code).

CZECH REPUBLIC

Social allowance (State Social Support Act No 117/1995 Sb.).

DENMARK

Accommodation expenses for pensioners (Law on individual accommodation assistance, consolidated by Law No 204 of 29 March 1995).

GERMANY

(a) Basic subsistence income for the elderly and for persons with reduced earning capacity under Chapter 4 of Book XII of the Social Code;

(b) Benefits to cover subsistence costs under the basic provision for jobseekers unless, with respect to these benefits, the eligibility requirements for a temporary supplement following receipt of unemployment benefit (Article 24(1) of Book II of the Social Code) are fulfilled.

ESTONIA

(a) Disabled adult allowance (Social Benefits for Disabled Persons Act of 27 January 1999);

(b) State unemployment allowance (Labour Market Services and Support Act of 29 September 2005).

IRELAND

(a) Jobseekers' allowance (Social Welfare Consolidation Act 2005, Part 3, Chapter 2);

(b) State pension (non-contributory) (Social Welfare Consolidation Act 2005, Part 3, Chapter 4);

(c) Widow's (non-contributory) pension and widower's (non-contributory) pension (Social Welfare Consolidation Act 2005, Part 3, Chapter 6);

(d) Disability allowance (Social Welfare Consolidation Act 2005, Part 3, Chapter 10);

(e) Mobility allowance (Health Act 1970, Section 61);

(f) Blind pension (Social Welfare Consolidation Act 2005, Part 3, Chapter 5).

GREECE

Special benefits for the elderly (Law 1296/82).

SPAIN

(a) Minimum income guarantee (Law No 13/82 of 7 April 1982);

(b) Cash benefits to assist the elderly and invalids unable to work (Royal Decree No 2620/81 of 24 July 1981);

(c)

(i) Non-contributory invalidity and retirement pensions as provided for in Article 38(1) of the Consolidated Text of the General Law on Social Security, approved by Royal Legislative Decree No 1/1994 of 20 June 1994; and

(ii) the benefits which supplement the above pensions, as provided for in the legislation of the Comunidades Autonómas, where such supplements guarantee a minimum subsistence income having regard to the economic and social situation in the Comunidades Autonómas concerned;

(d) Allowances to promote mobility and to compensate for transport costs (Law No 13/1982 of 7 April 1982).

FRANCE

(a) Supplementary allowances of:

(i) the Special Invalidity Fund; and

(ii) the Old Age Solidarity Fund in respect of acquired rights

(Law of 30 June 1956, codified in Book VIII of the Social Security Code);

(b) Disabled adults' allowance (Law of 30 June 1975, codified in Book VIII of the Social Security Code);

(c) Special allowance (Law of 10 July 1952, codified in Book VIII of the Social Security Code) in respect of acquired rights;

(d) Old-age solidarity allowance (ordinance of 24 June 2004, codified in Book VIII of the Social Security Code) as of 1 January 2006.

ITALY

(a) Social pensions for persons without means (Law No 153 of 30 April 1969);

(b) Pensions and allowances for the civilian disabled or invalids (Laws No 118 of 30 March 1971, No 18 of 11 February 1980 and No 508 of 23 November 1988);

(c) Pensions and allowances for the deaf and dumb (Laws No 381 of 26 May 1970 and No 508 of 23 November 1988);

(d) Pensions and allowances for the civilian blind (Laws No 382 of 27 May 1970 and No 508 of 23 November 1988);

(e) Benefits supplementing the minimum pensions (Laws No 218 of 4 April 1952, No 638 of 11 November 1983 and No 407 of 29 December 1990);

(f) Benefits supplementing disability allowances (Law No 222 of 12 June 1984);

(g) Social allowance (Law No 335 of 8 August 1995);

(h) Social increase (Article 1(1) and (12) of Law No 544 of 29 December 1988 and successive amendments).

CYPRUS

(a) Social Pension (Social Pension Law of 1995 (Law 25(I)/95), as amended);

(b) Severe motor disability allowance (Council of Ministers' Decisions Nos 38210 of 16 October 1992, 41370 of 1 August 1994, 46183 of 11 June 1997 and 53675 of 16 May 2001);

(c) Special grant to blind persons (Special Grants Law of 1996 (Law 77(I)/96), as amended).

LATVIA

(a) State Social Security Benefit (Law on State Social Benefits of 1 January 2003);

(b) Allowance for the compensation of transportation expenses for disabled persons with restricted mobility (Law on State Social Benefits of 1 January 2003).

LITHUANIA

(a) Social assistance pension (Law of 2005 on State Social Assistance Benefits, Article 5);

(b) Relief compensation (Law of 2005 on State Social Assistance Benefits, Article 15);

(c) Transport compensation for the disabled who have mobility problems (Law of 2000 on Transport Compensation, Article 7).

LUXEMBOURG

Income for the seriously disabled (Article 1(2), Law of 12 September 2003), with the exception of persons recognised as being disabled workers and employed on the mainstream labour market or in a sheltered environment.

HUNGARY

(a) Invalidity annuity (Decree No 83/1987 (XII 27) of the Council of Ministers on Invalidity Annuity);

(b) Non-contributory old age allowance (Act III of 1993 on Social Administration and Social Benefits);

(c) Transport allowance (Government Decree No 164/1995 (XII 27) on Transport Allowances for Persons with Severe Physical Handicap).

MALTA

(a) Supplementary allowance (Section 73 of the Social Security Act (Cap. 318) 1987);

(b) Age pension (Social Security Act (Cap. 318) 1987).

NETHERLANDS

(a) Work and Employment Support for Disabled Young Persons Act of 24 April 1997 (Wet Wajong)

(b) Supplementary Benefits Act of 6 November 1986 (TW).

AUSTRIA

Compensatory supplement (Federal Act of 9 September 1955 on General Social Insurance – ASVG, Federal Act of 11 October 1978 on Social insurance for persons engaged in trade and commerce – GSVG and Federal Act of 11 October 1978 on Social insurance for farmers – BSVG).

POLAND

Social pension (Act of 27 June 2003 on social pensions).

PORTUGAL

(a) Non-contributory State old-age and invalidity pension (Decree-Law No 464/80 of 13 October 1980);

(b) Non-contributory widowhood pension (Regulatory Decree No 52/81 of 11 November 1981);

(c) Solidarity supplement for the elderly (Decree – Law No 232/2005 of 29 December 2005, amended by Decree – Law No 236/2006 of 11 December 2006).

SLOVENIA

(a) State pension (Pension and Disability Insurance Act of 23 December 1999);

(b) Income support for pensioners (Pension and Disability Insurance Act of 23 December 1999);

(c) Maintenance allowance (Pension and Disability Insurance Act of 23 December 1999).

SLOVAKIA

(a) Adjustment awarded before 1 January 2004 to pensions constituting the sole source of income;

(b) Social pension which has been awarded before 1 January 2004.

FINLAND

(a) Housing allowance for pensioners (Act concerning the Housing Allowance for pensioners, 571/2007);

(b) Labour market support (Act on Unemployment Benefits 1290/2002);

(c) Special assistance for immigrants (Act on Special Assistance for Immigrants, 1192/2002).

SWEDEN

(a) Housing supplements for persons receiving a pension (Law 2001:761);

(b) Financial support for the elderly (Law 2001:853).

UNITED KINGDOM

(a) State Pension Credit (State Pension Credit Act 2002 and State Pension Credit Act (Northern Ireland) 2002);

(b) Income-based allowances for jobseekers (Jobseekers Act 1995 and Jobseekers (Northern Ireland) Order 1995);

(c) [Deleted by Reg. 465/2012, Annex.]

(d) Disability Living Allowance mobility component (Social Security Contributions and Benefits Act 1992 and Social Security Contributions and Benefits (Northern Ireland) Act 1992).

(e) Employment and Support Allowance Income-related (Welfare Reform Act 2007 and Welfare Reform Act (Northern Ireland) 2007).

History – Annex X replaced by Reg. 988/2009, art. 2 and Annex, Pt. I, with effect from 1 May 2010.
In entry for Netherlands, point (a) substituted by Reg. 465/2012, Annex with effect from 28 June 2012.
In entry for United Kingdom, point (c) deleted and point (e) inserted by Reg. 465/2012, Annex with effect from 28 June 2012.

ANNEX XI – SPECIAL PROVISIONS FOR THE APPLICATION OF THE LEGISLATION OF THE MEMBER STATES (ARTICLES 51(3), 56(1) and 83)

BULGARIA

Article 33(1) of the Bulgarian Health Insurance Act shall apply to all persons for whom Bulgaria is the competent Member State under Chapter 1 of Title III of this Regulation;

CZECH REPUBLIC

For the purposes of defining members of the family according to Article 1(i), "spouse" also includes registered partners as defined in the Czech act no. 115/2006 Coll., on registered partnership;

DENMARK

(1)

(a) For the purpose of calculating the pension under the "lov om social pension" (Social Pension Act), periods of activity as an employed or self-employed person completed under Danish legislation by a frontier worker or a worker who has gone to Denmark to do work of a seasonal nature are regarded as periods of residence completed in Denmark by the surviving spouse in so far as, during those periods, the surviving spouse was linked to the abovementioned worker by marriage without separation from bed and board or de facto separation on grounds of incompatibility, and provided that, during those periods, the spouse resided in the territory of another Member State. For the purposes of this point, "work of a seasonal nature" means work which, being dependent on the succession of the seasons, automatically recurs each year.

(b) For the purpose of calculating the pension under the "lov om social pension" (Social Pension Act), periods of activity as an employed or self-employed person completed under Danish legislation before 1 January 1984 by a person to whom point 1(a) does not apply shall be regarded as periods of residence completed in Denmark by the surviving spouse, in so far as, during those periods, the surviving spouse was linked to the person by marriage without separation from bed and board or de facto separation on grounds of incompatibility, and provided that, during those periods, the spouse resided in the territory of another Member State.

(c) Periods to be taken into account under points (a) and (b) shall not be taken into consideration if they coincide with the periods taken into account for the calculation of the pension due to the person concerned under the legislation on compulsory insurance of another Member State or with the periods during which the person concerned received a pension under such legislation. These periods shall, however, be taken into consideration if the annual amount of the said pension is less than half the basic amount of the social pension.

(2)

(a) Notwithstanding the provisions of Article 6 of this Regulation, persons who have not been gainfully employed in one or more Member States are entitled to a Danish social pension only if they have been, or have previously been, permanent residents of Denmark for at least 3 years, subject to the age limits prescribed by Danish legislation. Subject to Article 4 of this Regulation, Article 7 does not apply to a Danish social pension to which entitlement has been acquired by such persons.

(b) The abovementioned provisions do not apply to Danish social pension entitlement for the members of the family of persons who are or have been gainfully employed in Denmark, or for students or the members of their families.

(3) The temporary benefit for unemployed persons who have been admitted to the ledighedsydelse (flexible job scheme) (Law No 455 of 10 June 1997) is covered by Title III, Chapter 6 of this Regulation. As regards unemployed persons going to another Member State, Articles 64 and 65 will be applicable when this Member State has similar employment schemes for the same category of persons.

(4) Where the beneficiary of a Danish social pension is also entitled to a survivor's pension from another Member State, these pensions for the implementation of Danish legislation shall be regarded as benefits of the same kind within the meaning of Article 53(1) of this Regulation, subject to the condition, however, that the person whose periods of insurance or of residence serve as the basis for the calculation of the survivor's pension had also acquired a right to a Danish social pension.

GERMANY

(1) Notwithstanding Article 5(a) of this Regulation and Article 5(4) point 1 of the Sozialgesetzbuch VI (Volume VI of the Social Code), a person who receives a full old-age pension under the legislation of another Member State may request to be compulsorily insured under the German pension insurance scheme.

(2) Notwithstanding Article 5(a) of this Regulation and Article 7 of the Sozialgesetzbuch VI (Volume VI of the Social Code), a person who is compulsorily insured in another Member State or receives an old-age pension under the legislation of another Member State may join the voluntary insurance scheme in Germany.

(3) For the purpose of granting cash benefits under §47(1) of SGB V, §47(1) of SGB VII and §200(2) of the Reichsversicherungsordnung to insured persons who live in another Member State, German insurance schemes calculate net pay, which is used to assess benefits, as if the insured person lived in Germany, unless the insured person requests an assessment on the basis of the net pay which he actually receives.

(4) Nationals of other Member States whose place of residence or usual abode is outside Germany and who fulfil the general conditions of the German pension insurance scheme may pay voluntary contributions only if they had been voluntarily or compulsorily insured in the German pension insurance scheme at some time previously; this also applies to stateless persons and refugees whose place of residence or usual abode is in another Member State.

(5) The pauschale Anrechnungszeit (fixed credit period) pursuant to Article 253 of the Sozialgesetzbuch VI (Volume VI of the Social Code) shall be determined exclusively with reference to German periods.

(6) In cases where the German pension legislation, in force on 31 December 1991, is applicable for the recalculation of a pension, only the German legislation applies for the purposes of crediting German Ersatzzeiten (substitute periods).

(7) The German legislation on accidents at work and occupational diseases to be compensated for under the law governing foreign pensions and on benefits for insurance periods which can be credited under the law governing foreign pensions in the territories named in paragraph 1(2)(3) of the Act on affairs of displaced persons and refugees (Bundesvertriebenengesetz) continues to apply within the scope of application of this Regulation, notwithstanding the provisions of paragraph 2 of the Act on foreign pensions (Fremdrentengesetz).

(8) For the calculation of the theoretical amount referred to in Article 52(1)(b)(i) of this Regulation, in pension schemes for liberal professions, the competent institution shall take as a basis, in respect of each of the years of insurance completed under the legislation of any other Member State, the average annual pension entitlement acquired during the period of membership of the competent institution through the payment of contributions.

ESTONIA

For the purpose of calculating parental benefits, periods of employment in Member States other than Estonia shall be considered to be based on the same average amount of Social Tax as paid during the periods of employment in Estonia with which they are aggregated. If during the reference year the person has been employed only in other Member States, the calculation of the benefit shall be considered to be based on the average Social Tax paid in Estonia between the reference year and the maternity leave.

IRELAND

(1) Notwithstanding Articles 21(2) and 62 of this Regulation, for the purposes of calculating the prescribed reckonable weekly earnings of an insured person for the grant of sickness or unemployment benefit under Irish legislation, an amount equal to the average weekly wage of employed persons in the relevant prescribed year shall be credited to that insured person in respect of each week of activity as an employed person under the legislation of another Member State during that prescribed year.

(2) Where Article 46 of this Regulation applies, if the person concerned suffers incapacity for work leading to invalidity while subject to the legislation of another Member State, Ireland shall, for the purposes of Section 118(1)(a) of the Social Welfare Consolidation Act 2005, take account of any periods during which, in respect of the invalidity that followed that incapacity for work, he/she would have been regarded as being incapable of work under Irish legislation.

GREECE

(1) Law No 1469/84 concerning voluntary affiliation to the pension insurance scheme for Greek nationals and foreign nationals of Greek origin is applicable to nationals of other Member States, stateless persons and refugees, where the persons concerned, regardless of their place of residence or stay, have at some time in the past been compul-sorily or voluntarily affiliated to the Greek pension insurance scheme.

(2) Notwithstanding Article 5(a) of this Regulation and Article 34 of Law 1140/1981, a person who receives a pension in respect of accidents at work or occupational diseases under the legislation *of another Member* State may request to be compulsorily insured under the legislation applied by OGA, to the extent that he/she pursues an activity falling within the scope of that legislation.

SPAIN

(1) For the purposes of implementing Article 52(1)(b)(i) of this Regulation, the years which the worker lacks to reach the pensionable or compulsory retirement age as stipulated under Article 31(4) of the consolidated version of the Ley de Clases Pasivas del Estado (Law on State Pensioners) shall be taken into account as actual years of service to the State only if at the time of the event in respect of which invalidity or death pensions are due, the beneficiary was covered by Spain's special scheme for civil servants or was performing an activity assimilated under the scheme, or if, at the time of the event in respect of which the pensions are due, the beneficiary was performing an activity that would have required the person concerned to be included under the State's special scheme for civil servants, the armed forces or the judiciary, had the activity been performed in Spain.

(2)

(a) Under Article 56(1)(c) of this Regulation, the calculation of the theoretical Spanish benefit shall be carried out on the basis of the actual contributions of the person during the years immediately preceding payment of the last contribution to Spanish social security. Where, in the calculation of the basic amount for the pension, periods of insurance and/or residence under the legislation of other Member States have to be taken into account, the contribution basis in Spain which is closest in time to the reference periods shall be used for the aforementioned periods, taking into account the development of the retail price index.

(b) The amount of the pension obtained shall be increased by the amount of the increases and revaluations calculated for each subsequent year for pensions of the same nature.

(3) Periods completed in other Member States which must be calculated in the special scheme for civil servants, the armed forces and the judicial administration, will be treated in the same way, for the purposes of Article 56 of this Regulation, as the periods closest in time covered as a civil servant in Spain.

(4) The additional amounts based on age referred to in the Second Transitional Provision of the General Law on Social Security shall be applicable to all beneficiaries of the Regulation who have contributions to their name under the Spanish legislation prior to 1 January 1967; it shall not be possible, by application of Article 5 of this Regulation, to treat periods of insurance credited in another Member State prior to the aforementioned date as being the same as contributions paid in Spain, solely for the present purposes. The date corresponding to 1 January 1967 shall be 1 August 1970 for the Special Scheme for Seafarers and 1 April 1969 for the Special Social Security Scheme for Coal Mining.

FRANCE

(1) [Paragraph (1) deleted by Reg. 465/2012, Annex.]

(2) For persons receiving benefits in kind in France pursuant to Articles 17, 24 or 26 of this Regulation who are resident in the French departments of Haut-Rhin, Bas-Rhin or Moselle, benefits in kind provided on behalf of the institution of another Member State which is responsible for bearing their cost include benefits provided by both the general sickness insurance scheme and the obligatory supplementary local sickness insurance scheme of Alsace-Moselle.

(3) French legislation applicable to a person engaged, or formerly engaged, in an activity as an employed or self-employed person for the application of Chapter 5 of Title III of this Regulation includes both the basic old-age insurance scheme(s) and the supplementary retirement scheme(s) to which the person concerned was subject.

CYPRUS

For the purpose of applying the provisions of Articles 6, 51 and 61 of this Regulation, for any period commencing on or after 6 October 1980, a week of insurance under the legislation of the Republic of Cyprus is determined by dividing the total insurable earnings for the relevant period by the weekly amount of the basic insurable earnings applicable in the relevant contribution year, provided that the number of weeks so determined shall not exceed the number of calendar weeks in the relevant period.

MALTA

Special provisions for civil servants

(a) Solely for the purposes of the application of Articles 49 and 60 of this Regulation, persons employed under the Malta Armed Forces Act (Chapter 220 of the Laws of Malta), the Police Act (Chapter 164 of the Laws of Malta) and the Prisons Act (Chapter 260 of the Laws of Malta) shall be treated as civil servants.

(b) Pensions payable under the above Acts and under the Pensions Ordinance (Chapter 93 of the Laws of Malta) shall, solely for the purposes of Article 1(e) of the Regulation, be considered as "special schemes for civil servants".

NETHERLANDS

(1) Health care insurance

(a) As regards entitlement to benefits in kind under Dutch legislation, persons entitled to benefits in kind for the purpose of the implementation of Chapters 1 and 2 of Title III of this Regulation shall mean:

(i) persons who, under Article 2 of the Zorgverzekeringswet (Health Care Insurance Act), are obliged to take out insurance under a health care insurer; and

(ii) in so far as they are not already included under point (i), members of the family of active military personnel who are living in another Member State and persons who are resident in another Member State and who, under this Regulation are entitled to health care in their state of residence, the costs being borne by the Netherlands.

(b) The persons referred to in point 1(a)(i) must, in accordance with the provisions of the Zorgverzekeringswet (Health Care Insurance Act) take out insurance with a health care insurer, and the persons referred to in point 1(a)(ii) must register with the College voor zorgverzekeringen (Health Care Insurance Board).

(c) The provisions of the Zorgverzekeringswet (Health Care Insurance Act) and the Algemene Wet Bijzondere Ziek-tekosten (General Act on Exceptional Medical Expenses) concerning liability for the payment of contributions shall apply to the persons referred to in point (a) and the members of their families. In respect of members of the family, the contributions shall be levied on the person from whom the right to health care is derived with the exception of the members of the family of military personnel living in another Member State, who shall be levied directly.

(d) The provisions of the Zorgverzekeringswet (Health Care Insurance Act) concerning late insurance shall apply *mutatis mutandis* in the event of late registration with the College voor zorgverzekeringen (Health Care Insurance Board) in respect of the persons referred to in point 1(a)(ii).

(e) Persons entitled to benefits in kind by virtue of the legislation of a Member State other than the Netherlands who reside in the Netherlands or stay temporarily in the Netherlands shall be entitled to benefits in kind in accordance with the policy offered to insured persons in the Netherlands by the institution of the place of residence or the place of stay, taking into account Article 11(1), (2) and (3) and Article 19(1) of the Zorgverzekeringswet (Health Care Insurance Act), as well as to benefits in kind provided for by the Algemene Wet Bijzondere Ziektekosten (General Act on Exceptional Medical Expenses).

(f) For the purposes of Articles 23 to 30 of this Regulation, the following benefits (in addition to pensions covered by Title III, Chapters 4 and 5 of this Regulation) shall be treated as pensions due under Dutch legislation:

– pensions awarded under the Law of 6 January 1966 on pensions for civil servants and their survivors (Algemene burgerlijke pensioenwet) (Netherlands Civil Service Pensions Act),

– pensions awarded under the Law of 6 October 1966 on pensions for military personnel and their survivors (Algemene militaire pensioenwet) (Military Pensions Act),

– benefits for incapacity for work awarded under the Law of 7 June 1972 on benefits for incapacity for work for military personnel (Wetarbeidsongeschiktheidsvoorziening militairen) (Military Personnel Incapacity for Work Act),

– pensions awarded under the Law of 15 February 1967 on pensions for employees of the NV Nederlandse Spoorwegen (Dutch Railway Company) and their survivors (Spoorwegpensioenwet) (Railway Pensions Act),

– pensions awarded under the Reglement Dienstvoorwaarden Nederlandse Spoorwegen (Regulation governing conditions of employment of the Netherlands Railway Company),

– benefits awarded to retired persons before reaching the pensionable age of 65 years under a pension designed to provide income for former employed persons in their old age, or benefits provided in the event of premature exit from the labour market under a scheme set up by the state or by an industrial agreement for persons aged 55 or over,

– benefits awarded to military personnel and civil servants under a scheme applicable in the event of redundancy, superannuation and early retirement.

(g) *[Deleted by Reg. 465/2012, Annex.]*

(h) For the purposes of Article 18(1) of this Regulation, the persons referred to in point 1(a)(ii) of this Annex who stay temporarily in the Netherlands shall be entitled to benefits in kind in accordance with the policy offered to insured persons in the Netherlands by the institution of the place of stay, taking into account Article 11(1), (2) and (3) and Article 19(1) of the

Zorgverzekeringswet (Health Care Insurance Act), as well as to benefits in kind provided for by the Algemene Wet Bijzondere Ziektekosten (General Act on Exceptional Medical Expenses).

(2) Application of the Algemene Ouderdomswet (AOW) (General Old Age Pensions Act)

(a) The reduction referred to in Article 13(1) of the Algemene Ouderdomswet (AOW) (General Old Age Pensions Act) shall not be applied for calendar years before 1 January 1957 during which a recipient not satisfying the conditions for having such years treated as periods of insurance:

- resided in the Netherlands between the ages of 15 and 65, or
- while residing in another Member State, worked in the Netherlands for an employer established in the Netherlands, or
- worked in another Member State during periods regarded as periods of insurance under the Dutch social security system.

By way of derogation from Article 7 of the AOW, anyone who resided or worked in the Netherlands in accordance with the above conditions only prior to 1 January 1957 shall also be regarded as being entitled to a pension.

(b) The reduction referred to in Article 13(1) of the AOW shall not apply to calendar years prior to 2 August 1989 during which, between the ages of 15 and 65, a person who is or was married was not insured under the above legislation, while being resident in the territory of a Member State other than the Netherlands, if these calendar years coincide with periods of insurance completed by the person's spouse under the above legislation or with calendar years to be taken into account under point 2(a), provided that the couple's marriage subsisted during that time.

By way of derogation from Article 7 of the AOW, such a person shall be regarded as entitled to a pension.

(c) The reduction referred to in Article 13(2) of the AOW shall not apply to calendar years before 1 January 1957 during which a pensioner's spouse who fails to satisfy the conditions for having such years treated as periods of insurance:

- resided in the Netherlands between the ages of 15 and 65, or
- while residing in another Member State, worked in the Netherlands for an employer established in the Netherlands, or
- worked in another Member State during periods regarded as periods of insurance under the Netherlands social security system.

(d) The reduction referred to in Article 13(2) of the AOW shall not apply to calendar years prior to 2 August 1989 during which, between the ages of 15 and 65, a pensioner's spouse resident in a Member State other than the Netherlands was not insured under the above legislation, if those calendar years coincide with periods of insurance completed by the pensioner under that legislation or with calendar years to be taken into account under point 2(a), provided that the couple's marriage subsisted during that time.

(e) Points 2(a), 2(b), 2(c) and 2(d) shall not apply to periods which coincide with:

- periods which may be taken into account for calculating pension rights under the old-age insurance legislation of a Member State other than the Netherlands, or
- periods for which the person concerned has drawn an old-age pension under such legislation.

Periods of voluntary insurance under the system of another Member State shall not be taken into account for the purposes of this provision.

(f) Points 2(a), 2(b), 2(c) and 2(d) shall apply only if the person concerned has resided in one or more Member States for 6 years after the age of 59 and only for such time as that person is resident in one of those Member States.

(g) By way of derogation from Chapter IV of the AOW, anyone resident in a Member State other than the Netherlands whose spouse is covered by compulsory insurance under that legislation shall be authorised to take out voluntary insurance under that legislation for periods during which the spouse is compulsorily insured.

This authorisation shall not cease where the spouse's compulsory insurance is terminated as a result of his death and where the survivor receives only a pension under the Algemene nabestaandenwet (General Surviving Relatives Act).

In any event, the authorisation in respect of voluntary insurance ceases on the date on which the person reaches the age of 65.

The contribution to be paid for voluntary insurance shall be set in accordance with the provisions relating to the determination of the contribution for voluntary insurance under the AOW. However, if the voluntary insurance follows on from a period of insurance as referred to in point 2(b), the contribution shall be set in accordance with the provisions relating to the determination of the contribution for compulsory insurance under the AOW, with the income to be taken into account being deemed to have been received in the Netherlands.

(h) The authorisation referred to in point 2(g) shall not be granted to anyone insured under another Member State's legislation on pensions or survivors' benefits.

(i) Anyone wishing to take out voluntary insurance under point 2(g) shall be required to apply for it to the Social Insurance Bank (Sociale Verzekeringsbank) not later than 1 year after the date on which the conditions for participation are fulfilled.

(3) Application of the Algemene nabestaandenwet (ANW) (General Surviving Relatives Act)

(a) Where the surviving spouse is entitled to a survivor's pension under the Algemene Nabestaandenwet (ANW) (General Surviving Relatives Act) pursuant to Article 51(3) of this Regulation, that pension shall be calculated in accordance with Article 52(1)(b) of this Regulation.

For the application of these provisions, periods of insurance prior to 1 October 1959 shall also be regarded as periods of insurance completed under Dutch legislation if during those periods the insured person, after the age of 15:

– resided in the Netherlands, or
– while resident in another Member State, worked in the Netherlands for an employer established in the Netherlands, or
– worked in another Member State during periods regarded as periods of insurance under the Dutch social security system.

(b) Account shall not be taken of the periods to be taken into consideration under point 3(a) which coincide with periods of compulsory insurance completed under the legislation of another Member State in respect of survivor's pensions.

(c) For the purposes of Article 52(1)(b) of this Regulation, only periods of insurance completed under Dutch legislation after the age of 15 shall be taken into account as periods of insurance.

(d) By way of derogation from Article 63a(1) of the ANW, a person resident in a Member State other than the Netherlands whose spouse is compulsorily insured under the ANW shall be authorised to take out voluntary insurance under the above legislation, provided that such insurance has already begun by the date of application of this Regulation, but only for periods during which the spouse is compulsorily insured.

This authorisation shall cease as from the date of termination of the spouse's compulsory insurance under the ANW, unless the spouse's compulsory insurance is terminated as a result of his death and where the survivor only receives a pension under the ANW.

In any event, the authorisation in respect of voluntary insurance ceases on the date on which the person reaches the age of 65.

The contribution to be paid for voluntary insurance shall be set in accordance with the provisions relating to the determination of contributions for voluntary insurance under the ANW. However, if the voluntary insurance follows on from a period of insurance as referred to in point 2(b), the contribution shall be set in accordance with the provisions relating to the determination of contributions for compulsory insurance under the ANW, with the income to be taken into account being deemed to have been received in the Netherlands.

(4) Application of Dutch legislation relating to incapacity for work

(a) Where, pursuant to Article 51(3) of this Regulation, the person concerned is entitled to a Netherlands invalidity benefit, the amount referred to in Article 52(1)(b) of this Regulation for calculating that benefit shall be determined:

(i) where, prior to the occurrence of incapacity for work, the person last exercised an activity as an employed person within the meaning of Article 1(a) of this Regulation:

– in accordance with the provisions laid down in the Wet op arbeidsongeschiktheidsverzekering (WAO) (Disability Insurance Act) if the *incapacity* for work occurred before 1 January 2004, or
– in accordance with the provisions laid down in the Wet Werk en inkomen naar arbeidsvermogen (WIA) (Work and Income according to labour capacity Act) if the incapacity for work occurred on or after 1 January 2004;

(ii) where, prior to the occurrence of the incapacity for work, the person concerned last exercised an activity as a self-employed person within the meaning of Article 1(b) of this Regulation, in accordance with the provisions laid down in the Wet arbeidsongeschiktheidsverzekering zelfstandigen (WAZ) Self-employed Persons Disablement Benefits Act) if the incapacity for work occurred before 1 August 2004.

(b) In calculating benefits under either the WAO, WIA or the WAZ, the Netherlands institutions shall take account of:

- periods of paid employment, and periods treated as such, completed in the Netherlands before 1 July 1967,
- periods of insurance completed under the WAO,
- periods of insurance completed by the person concerned, after the age of 15, under the Algemene Arbeidsongeschiktheidswet (AAW) (General Act on Incapacity for Work), in so far as these do not coincide with the periods of insurance completed under the WAO,
- periods of insurance completed under the WAZ,
- periods of insurance completed under the WIA.

AUSTRIA

(1) For the purpose of acquiring periods in the pension insurance, attendance at a school or comparable educational establishment in another Member State shall be regarded as equivalent to attendance at a school or educational establishment pursuant to Articles 227(1)(1) and 228(1)(3) of the Allgemeines Sozialversicherungsgesetz (ASVG) (General Social Security Act), Article 116(7) of the Gewerbliches Sozialversicherungsgesetz (GSVG) (Federal Act on Social Insurance for Persons engaged in Trade and Commerce) and Article 107(7) of the Bauern-Sozialversicherungsgesetz (BSVG) (Social Security Act for Farmers), when the person concerned was subject at some time to Austrian legislation on the grounds that he pursued an activity as an employed or self-employed person, and the special contributions provided for under Article 227(3) of the ASVG, Article 116(9) of the GSVG and Article 107(9) of the BSGV for the purchase of such periods of education, are paid.

(2) For the calculation of the pro rata benefit referred to in Article 52(1)(b) of this Regulation, special increments for contributions for supplementary insurance and the miners' supplementary benefit under Austrian legislation shall be disregarded. In these cases the pro rata benefit calculated without those contributions shall, if appropriate, be increased by unreduced special increments for contributions for supplementary insurance and the miners' supplementary benefit.

(3) Where pursuant to Article 6 of this Regulation substitute periods under an Austrian pension insurance scheme have been completed, but these cannot form a basis for calculation pursuant to Articles 238 and 239 of the Allgemeines Sozialversicherungsgesetz (ASVG) (General Social Security Act), Articles 122 and 123 of the Gewerbliches Sozial-versicherungsgesetz (GSVG) (Federal Act on Social Insurance for Persons engaged in Trade and Commerce) and Articles 113 and 114 of the Bauern-Sozialversicherungsgesetz (BSVG) (Social Security Act for Farmers), the calculation basis for periods of childcare pursuant to Article 239 of the ASVG, Article 123 of the GSVG and Article 114 of the BSVG shall be used.

FINLAND

(1) For the purposes of determining entitlement and of calculating the amount of the Finnish national pension under Articles 52 to 54 of this Regulation, pensions acquired under the legislation of another Member State are treated in the same way as pensions acquired under Finnish legislation.

(2) When applying Article 52(1)(b)(i) of this Regulation for the purpose of calculating earnings for the credited period under Finnish legislation on earnings-related pensions, where an individual has pension insurance periods based on activity as an employed or self-employed person in another Member State for part of the reference period under Finnish legislation, the earnings for the credited period shall be equivalent to the sum of earnings obtained during the part of the reference period in Finland, divided by the number of months for which there were insurance periods in Finland during the reference period.

SWEDEN

(1) When parental leave allowance is paid under Article 67 of this Regulation to a member of the family who is not employed, the parental leave allowance is paid at a level corresponding to the basic or lowest level.

(2) For the purpose of calculating parental leave allowance in accordance with Chapter 4, paragraph 6 of the Lag (1962:381) om allmän försäkring (the National Insurance Act) for persons eligible for a work-based parental leave allowance, the following shall apply:

For a parent for whom sickness benefit generating income is calculated on the basis of income from gainful employment in Sweden, the requirement to have been insured for sickness benefit above the minimum level for at least 240 consecutive days preceding the child's birth shall be satisfied if, during the period mentioned, the parent had income from gainful employment in another Member State corresponding to insurance above the minimum level.

(3) The provisions of this Regulation on the aggregation of insurance periods and periods of residence shall not apply to the transitional provisions in the Swedish legislation on entitlement to guarantee pension for persons born in or before 1937 who have been resident in Sweden for a specified period before applying for a pension (Act 2000:798).

(4) For the purpose of calculating income for notional income-related sickness compensation and income-related activity compensation in accordance with Chapter 8 of the Lag (1962:381) om allmän försäkring (the National Insurance Act), the following shall apply:

(a) where the insured person, during the reference period, has also been subject to the legislation of one or more other Member States on account of activity as an employed or self-employed person, income in the Member State(s) concerned shall be deemed to be equivalent to the insured person's average gross income in Sweden during the part of the reference period in Sweden, calculated by dividing the earnings in Sweden by the number of years over which those earnings accrued;

(b) where the benefits are calculated pursuant to Article 46 of this Regulation and persons are not insured in Sweden, the reference period shall be determined in accordance with Chapter 8, paragraphs 2 and 8 of the above-mentioned Act as if the person concerned were insured in Sweden. If the person concerned has no pension-generating income during this period under the Act on income-based old-age pension (1998:674), the reference period shall be permitted to run from the earlier point in time when the insured person had income from gainful activity in Sweden.

(5)

(a) For the purpose of calculating notional pension assets for income-based survivor's pension (Act 2000:461), if the requirement in Swedish legislation for pension entitlement in respect of at least three out of the 5 calendar years immediately preceding the insured person's death (reference period) is not met, account shall also be taken of insurance periods completed in other Member States as if they had been completed in Sweden. Insurance periods in other Member States shall be regarded as based on the average Swedish pension base. If the person concerned has only 1 year in Sweden with a pension base, each insurance period in another Member State shall be regarded as constituting the same amount.

(b) For the purpose of calculating notional pension credits for widows' pensions relating to deaths on or after 1 January 2003, if the requirement in Swedish legislation for pension credits in respect of at least two out of the 4 years immediately preceding the insured person's death (reference period) is not met and insurance periods were completed in another Member State during the reference period, those years shall be regarded as being based on the same pension credits as the Swedish year.

UNITED KINGDOM

(1) Where, in accordance with United Kingdom legislation, a person may be entitled to a retirement pension if:

(a) the contributions of a former spouse are taken into account as if they were that person's own contributions; or

(b) the relevant contribution conditions are satisfied by that person's spouse or former spouse, then provided, in each case, that the spouse or former spouse is or had been exercising an activity as an employed or self-employed person, and had been subject to the legislation of two or more Member States, the provisions of Chapter 5 of Title III of this Regulation shall apply in order to determine entitlement under United Kingdom legislation. In this case, references in the said Chapter 5 to "periods of insurance" shall be construed as references to periods of insurance completed by:

(i) a spouse or former spouse where a claim is made by:

– a married woman, or

– a person whose marriage has terminated otherwise than by the death of the spouse; or

(ii) a former spouse, where a claim is made by:

– a widower who immediately before pensionable age is not entitled to widowed parent's allowance, or

– a widow who immediately before pensionable age is not entitled to widowed mother's allowance, widowed parent's allowance or widow's pension, or who is only entitled to an age-related widow's pension calculated pursuant to Article 52(1)(b) of this Regulation, and for this purpose "age-related widow's pension" means a widow's pension payable at a reduced rate in accordance with section 39(4) of the Social Security Contributions and Benefits Act 1992.

(2) For the purposes of applying Article 6 of this Regulation to the provisions governing entitlement to attendance allowance, carer's allowance and disability living allowance, a period of employment, self-employment or residence completed in the territory of a Member State other than the United Kingdom shall be taken into account in so far as is necessary to satisfy conditions as to required periods of presence in the United Kingdom, prior to the day on which entitlement to the benefit in question first arises.

(3) For the purposes of Article 7 of this Regulation, in the case of invalidity, old-age or survivors' cash benefits, pensions for accidents at work or occupational diseases and death grants, any beneficiary under United Kingdom legislation who is staying in the territory of another Member State shall, during that stay, be considered as if he resided in the territory of that other Member State.

(4) Where Article 46 of this Regulation applies, if the person concerned suffers incapacity for work leading to invalidity while subject to the legislation of another Member State, the United Kingdom shall, for the purposes of Section 30A(5) of the Social Security Contributions and Benefits Act 1992, take account of any periods during which the person concerned has received, in respect of that incapacity for work:

(i) cash sickness benefits or wages or salary in lieu thereof; or

(ii) benefits within the meaning of Chapters 4 and 5 of Title III of this Regulation granted in respect of the invalidity which followed that incapacity for work, under the legislation of the other Member State, as though they were periods of short-term incapacity benefit paid in accordance with Sections 30A(1)–(4) of the Social Security Contributions and Benefits Act 1992.

In applying this provision, account shall only be taken of periods during which the person would have been incapable of work within the meaning of United Kingdom legislation.

(5)

(1) For the purpose of calculating an earnings factor in order to determine entitlement to benefits under United Kingdom legislation, for each week of activity as an employed person under the legislation of another Member State, and which commenced during the relevant income tax year within the meaning of United Kingdom legislation, the person concerned shall be deemed to have paid contributions as an employed earner, or have earnings on which contributions have been paid, on the basis of earnings equivalent to two-thirds of that year's upper earnings limit.

(2) For the purposes of Article 52(1)(b)(ii) of this Regulation, where:

(a) in any income tax year starting on or after 6 April 1975, a person carrying out activity as an employed person has completed periods of insurance, employment or residence exclusively in a Member State other than the United Kingdom, and the application of point 5(1) above results in that year being counted as a qualifying year within the meaning of United Kingdom legislation for the purposes of Article 52(1)(b)(i) of this Regulation, he shall be deemed to have been insured for 52 weeks in that year in that other Member State;

(b) any income tax year starting on or after 6 April 1975 does not count as a qualifying year within the meaning of United Kingdom legislation for the purposes of Article 52(1)(b)(i) of this Regulation, any periods of insurance, employment or residence completed in that year shall be disregarded.

(3) For the purpose of converting an earnings factor into periods of insurance, the earnings factor achieved in the relevant income tax year within the meaning of United Kingdom legislation shall be divided by that year's lower earnings limit. The result shall be expressed as a whole number, any remaining fraction being ignored. The figure so calculated shall be treated as representing the number of weeks of insurance completed under United Kingdom legislation during that year, provided that such figure shall not exceed the number of weeks during which in that year the person was subject to that legislation.

History – In the entry for Germany, para. (2) substituted by Reg. 465/2012, with effect from 28 June 2012.
In the entry for France, para. (1) deleted by Reg. 465/2012, with effect from 28 June 2012.
The entry for the Netherlands amended by Reg. 465/2012, with effect from 28 June 2012.
Annex XI replaced by Reg. 988/2009, art. 2 and Annex, Pt. J, with effect from 1 May 2010.

Notes – In the entry for the Netherlands, para. 1(fa) was to be inserted by Reg. 1372/2013, art. 1(2), with effect from 1 January 2014, however, Reg. 1368/2014 retrospectively deleted Reg. 1372/2013, art. 1(2), with effect from 1 January 2014.

REGULATION 987/2009
Laying down the procedure for implementing Regulation (EC) No 883/2004 on the coordination of social security systems

(16 September 2009, as amended by Commission Regulation (EU) No. 1368/2014)

Notes – Regulation 1231/2010 extends this Regulation and Regulation 883/2204 to nationals of third countries who are not already covered by these Regulations solely on the grounds of their nationality. However, as expressly provided by para. (18) of the Preamble, the UK is not bound by the Regulation nor subject to its application. Therefore, Regulation 1231/2010 is not reproduced here. It should also be noted that for those member states that are bound by the Regulation, it repeals Regulation 859/2003.

THE EUROPEAN PARLIAMENT AND THE COUNCIL OF THE EUROPEAN UNION,

Having regard to the Treaty establishing the European Community, and in particular Articles 42 [now TFEU, art. 48] and 308 [now TFEU, art. 352] thereof,

Having regard to Regulation (EC) No 883/2004 of the European Parliament and of the Council of 29 April 2004 on the coordination of social security systems, and in particular Article 89 thereof,

Having regard to the proposal from the Commission,

Having regard to the Opinion of the European Economic and Social Committee,

Acting in accordance with the procedure laid down in Article 251 [now TFEU, art. 292] of the Treaty,

Whereas:

(1) Regulation (EC) No 883/2004 modernises the rules on the coordination of Member States' social security systems, specifying the measures and procedures for implementing them and simplifying them for all the players involved. Implementing rules should be laid down.

(2) Closer and more effective cooperation between social security institutions is a key factor in allowing the persons covered by Regulation (EC) No 883/2004 to access their rights as quickly as possible and under optimum conditions.

(3) Electronic communication is a suitable means of rapid and reliable data exchange between Member States' institutions. Processing data electronically should help speed up the procedures for everyone involved. The persons concerned should also benefit from all the guarantees provided for in the Community provisions on the protection of natural persons with regard to the processing and free movement of personal data.

(4) Availability of the details (including electronic details) of those national bodies likely to be involved in implementing Regulation (EC) No 883/2004, in a form which allows them to be updated in real time, should facilitate exchanges between Member States' institutions. This approach, which focuses on the relevance of purely factual information and its immediate accessibility to citizens, is a valuable simplification which should be introduced by this Regulation.

(5) Achieving the smoothest possible operation and the efficient management of the complex procedures implementing the rules on the coordination of social security systems requires a system for the immediate updating of Annex 4. The preparation and application of provisions to that effect calls for close cooperation between the Member States and the Commission, and their implementation should be carried out rapidly, in view of the consequences of delays for citizens and administrative authorities alike. The Commission should therefore be empowered to establish and manage a database and ensure that it is operational at least from the date of entry into force of this Regulation. The Commission should, in particular, take the necessary steps to integrate into that database the information listed in Annex 4.

(6) Strengthening certain procedures should ensure greater legal certainty and transparency for the users of Regulation (EC) No 883/2004. For example, setting common deadlines for fulfilling certain obligations or completing certain administrative tasks should assist in clarifying and structuring relations between insured persons and institutions.

(7) The persons covered by this Regulation should receive from the competent institution a timely response to their requests. The response should be provided at the latest within the time-limits prescribed by the social security legislation of the Member State in question, where such time-limits exist. It would be desirable for Member States whose social security legislation does not make provision for such time-limits to consider adopting them and making them available to the persons concerned as necessary.

(8) The Member States, their competent authorities and the social security institutions should have the option of agreeing among themselves on simplified procedures and administrative arrangements which they consider to be more effective and better suited to the circumstances of their respective social security systems. However, such arrangements should not affect the rights of the persons covered by Regulation (EC) No 883/2004.

(9) The inherent complexity of the field of social security requires all institutions of the Member States to make a particular effort to support insured persons in order to avoid penalising those who have not submitted their claim or certain information to the institution responsible for processing this application in accordance with the rules and procedures set out in Regulation (EC) No 883/2004 and in this Regulation.

(10) To determine the competent institution, namely the one whose legislation applies or which is liable for the payment of certain benefits, the circumstances of the insured person and those of the family members must be examined by the institutions of more than one Member State. To ensure that the person concerned is protected for the duration of the necessary communication between institutions, provision should be made for provisional membership of a social security system.

(11) Member States should cooperate in determining the place of residence of persons to whom this Regulation and Regulation (EC) No 883/2004 apply and, in the event of a dispute, should take into consideration all relevant criteria to resolve the matter. These may include criteria referred to in the appropriate Article of this Regulation.

(12) Many measures and procedures provided for in this Regulation are intended to ensure greater transparency concerning the criteria which the institutions of the Member States must apply under Regulation (EC) No 883/2004. Such measures and procedures are the result of the case-law of the Court of Justice of the European Communities, the decisions of the Administrative Commission and the experience of more than 30 years of application of the coordination of social security systems in the context of the fundamental freedoms enshrined in the Treaty.

(13) This Regulation provides for measures and procedures to promote the mobility of employees and unemployed persons. Frontier workers who have become wholly unemployed may make themselves available to the employment services in both their country of residence and the Member State where they were last employed. However, they should be entitled to benefits only from their Member State of residence.

(14) Certain specific rules and procedures are required in order to define the legislation applicable for taking account of periods during which an insured person has devoted time to bringing up children in the various Member States.

(15) Certain procedures should also reflect the need for a balanced sharing of costs between Member States. In particular in the area of sickness, such procedures should take account of the position of Member States which bear the costs of allowing insured persons access to their healthcare system and the position of Member States whose institutions bear the cost of benefits in kind received by their insured persons in a Member State other than that in which they are resident.

(16) In the specific context of Regulation (EC) No 883/2004, it is necessary to clarify the conditions for meeting the costs of sickness benefits in kind as part of scheduled treatments, namely treatments for which an insured person goes to a Member State other than that in which he is insured or resident. The obligations of the insured person with regard to the application for prior authorisation should be specified, as should the institution's obligations towards the patient with regard to the conditions of authorisation. The consequences for the chargeability of the costs of care received in another Member State on the basis of an authorisation should also be clarified.

(17) This Regulation, and especially the provisions concerning the stay outside the competent Member State and concerning scheduled treatment, should not prevent the application of more favourable national provisions, in particular with regard to the reimbursement of costs incurred in another Member State.

(18) More binding procedures to reduce the time needed for payment of these claims between Member States' institutions are essential in order to maintain confidence in the exchanges and meet the need for sound management of Member States' social security systems. Procedures for the processing of claims relating to sickness and unemployment benefits should therefore be strengthened.

(19) Procedures between institutions for mutual assistance in recovery of social security claims should be strengthened in order to ensure more effective recovery and smooth functioning of the coordination rules. Effective recovery is also a means of preventing and tackling abuses and fraud and a way of ensuring the sustainability of social security schemes. This involves the adoption of new procedures, taking as a basis a number of existing provisions in Council Directive 2008/55/EC of 26 May 2008 on mutual assistance for the recovery of claims relating to certain levies, duties, taxes and other measures. Such new recovery procedures should be reviewed in the light of the experience after five years of implementation and adjusted if necessary, in particular to ensure they are fully operable.

(20) For the purposes of provisions on mutual assistance regarding the recovery of benefits provided but not due, the recovery of provisional payments and contributions and the offsetting and assistance with recovery, the jurisdiction of the requested Member State is limited to actions regarding enforcement measures. Any other action falls under the jurisdiction of the applicant Member State.

(21) The enforcement measures taken in the requested Member State do not imply the recognition by that Member State of the substance or basis of the claim.

(22) Informing the persons concerned of their rights and obligations is a crucial component of a relationship of trust with the competent authorities and the Member States' institutions. Information should include guidance on administrative procedures. The persons concerned may include, depending on the situation, the insured persons, their family members and/or their survivors or other persons.

(23) Since the objective of this Regulation, namely the adoption of coordination measures in order to guarantee the effective exercise of the free movement of persons, cannot be sufficiently achieved by the Member States and can therefore, by reason of its scale and effects, be better achieved at Community level, the Community may adopt measures, in accordance with the principle of subsidiarity as set out in Article 5 of the Treaty. In accordance with the principle of proportionality, as set out in that Article, this Regulation does not go beyond what is necessary to achieve that objective.

(24) This Regulation should replace Council Regulation (EEC) No 574/72 of 21 March 1972 fixing the procedure for implementing Regulation (EEC) No 1408/71 on the application of social security schemes to employed persons and their families moving within the Community,

HAVE ADOPTED THIS REGULATION:

TITLE I – GENERAL PROVISIONS

Chapter I – Definitions

ART. 1 Definitions

1(1) For the purposes of this Regulation:

(a) **"basic Regulation"** means Regulation (EC) No 883/2004;

(b) **"implementing Regulation"** means this Regulation; and

(c) the definitions set out in the basic Regulation shall apply.

1(2) In addition to the definitions referred to in paragraph 1,

(a) **"access point"** means an entity providing:

(i) an electronic contact point;

(ii) automatic routing based on the address; and

(iii) intelligent routing based on software that enables automatic checking and routing (for example, an artificial intelligence application) and/or human intervention;

(b) **"liaison body"** means any body designated by the competent authority of a Member State for one or more of the branches of social security referred to in Article 3 of the basic Regulation to respond to requests for information and assistance for the purposes of the application of the basic Regulation and the implementing Regulation and which has to fulfil the tasks assigned to it under Title IV of the implementing Regulation;

(c) **"document"** means a set of data, irrespective of the medium used, structured in such a way that it can be exchanged electronically and which must be communicated in order to enable the operation of the basic Regulation and the implementing Regulation;

(d) **"Structured Electronic Document"** means any structured document in a format designed for the electronic exchange of information between Member States;

(e) **"transmission by electronic means"** means the transmission of data using electronic equipment for the processing (including digital compression) of data and employing wires, radio transmission, optical technologies or any other electromagnetic means;

(f) **"Audit Board"** means the body referred to in Article 74 of the basic Regulation.

Chapter II – Provisions concerning cooperation and exchanges of data

ART. 2 Scope and rules for exchanges between institutions

2(1) For the purposes of the implementing Regulation, exchanges between Member States' authorities and institutions and persons covered by the basic Regulation shall be based on the principles of public service, efficiency, active assistance, rapid delivery and accessibility, including e-accessibility, in particular for the disabled and the elderly.

2(2) The institutions shall without delay provide or exchange all data necessary for establishing and determining the rights and obligations of persons to whom the basic Regulation applies. Such data shall be transferred between Member States directly by the institutions themselves or indirectly via the liaison bodies.

2(3) Where a person has mistakenly submitted information, documents or claims to an institution in the territory of a Member State other than that in which the institution designated in accordance with the implementing Regulation is situated, the information, documents or claims shall be resubmitted without delay by the former institution to the institution designated in accordance with the implementing Regulation, indicating the date on which they were initially submitted. That date shall be binding on the latter institution. Member State institutions shall not, however, be held liable, or be deemed to have taken a decision by virtue of their failure to act as a result of the late transmission of information, documents or claims by other Member States' institutions.

2(4) Where data are transferred indirectly via the liaison body of the Member State of destination, time limits for responding to claims shall start from the date when that liaison body received the claim, as if it had been received by the institution in that Member State.

ART. 3 Scope and rules for exchanges between the persons concerned and institutions

3(1) Member States shall ensure that the necessary information is made available to the persons concerned in order to inform them of the changes introduced by the basic Regulation and by the implementing Regulation to enable them to assert their rights. They shall also provide for user friendly services.

3(2) Persons to whom the basic Regulation applies shall be required to forward to the relevant institution the information, documents or supporting evidence necessary to establish their situation or that of their families, to establish or maintain their rights and obligations and to determine the applicable legislation and their obligations under it.

3(3) When collecting, transmitting or processing personal data pursuant to their legislation for the purposes of implementing the basic Regulation, Member States shall ensure that the persons concerned are able to exercise fully their rights regarding personal data protection, in accordance with Community provisions on the protection of individuals with regard to the processing of personal data and the free movement of such data.

3(4) To the extent necessary for the application of the basic Regulation and the implementing Regulation, the relevant institutions shall forward the information and issue the documents to the persons concerned without delay and in all cases within any time limits specified under the legislation of the Member State in question.

The relevant institution shall notify the claimant residing or staying in another Member State of its decision directly or through the liaison body of the Member State of residence or stay. When refusing the benefits it shall also indicate the reasons for refusal, the remedies and periods allowed for appeals. A copy of this decision shall be sent to other involved institutions.

ART. 4 Format and method of exchanging data

4(1) The Administrative Commission shall lay down the structure, content, format and detailed arrangements for exchange of documents and structured electronic documents.

4(2) The transmission of data between the institutions or the liaison bodies shall be carried out by electronic means either directly or indirectly through the access points under a common secure framework that can guarantee the confidentiality and protection of exchanges of data.

4(3) In their communications with the persons concerned, the relevant institutions shall use the arrangements appropriate to each case, and favour the use of electronic means as far as possible. The Administrative Commission shall lay down the practical arrangements for sending information, documents or decisions by electronic means to the person concerned.

ART. 5 Legal value of documents and supporting evidence issued in another Member State

5(1) Documents issued by the institution of a Member State and showing the position of a person for the purposes of the application of the basic Regulation and of the implementing Regulation, and supporting evidence on the basis of which the documents have been issued, shall be accepted by the institutions of the other Member States for as long as they have not been withdrawn or declared to be invalid by the Member State in which they were issued.

5(2) Where there is doubt about the validity of a document or the accuracy of the facts on which the particulars contained therein are based, the institution of the Member State that receives the document shall ask the issuing institution for the necessary clarification and, where appropriate, the withdrawal of that document. The issuing institution shall reconsider the grounds for issuing the document and, if necessary, withdraw it.

5(3) Pursuant to paragraph 2, where there is doubt about the information provided by the persons concerned, the validity of a document or supporting evidence or the accuracy of the facts on which the particulars contained therein are based, the institution of the place of stay or residence shall, insofar as this is possible, at the request of the competent institution, proceed to the necessary verification of this information or document.

5(4) Where no agreement is reached between the institutions concerned, the matter may be brought before the Administrative Commission by the competent authorities no earlier than one month following the date on which the institution that received the document submitted its request. The Administrative Commission shall endeavour to reconcile the points of view within six months of the date on which the matter was brought before it.

ART. 6 Provisional application of legislation and provisional granting of benefits

6(1) Unless otherwise provided for in the implementing Regulation, where there is a difference of views between the institutions or authorities of two or more Member States concerning the determination of the applicable legislation, the person concerned shall be made provisionally subject to the legislation of one of those Member States, the order of priority being determined as follows:

(a) the legislation of the Member State where the person actually pursues his employment or self-employment, if the employment or self-employment is pursued in only one Member State;

(b) the legislation of the Member State of residence if the person concerned pursues employment or self-employment in two or more Member States and performs part of his/her activity or activities in the Member State of residence, or if the person concerned is neither employed nor self-employed;

(c) in all other cases, the legislation of the Member State, the application of which was first requested if the person pursues an activity, or activities, in two or more Member States.

6(2) Where there is a difference of views between the institutions or authorities of two or more Member States about which institution should provide the benefits in cash or in kind, the person concerned who could claim benefits if there was no dispute shall be entitled, on a provisional basis, to the benefits provided for by the legislation applied by the institution of his place of residence or, if that person does not reside on the territory of one of the Member States concerned, to the benefits provided for by the legislation applied by the institution to which the request was first submitted.

6(3) Where no agreement is reached between the institutions or authorities concerned, the matter may be brought before the Administrative Commission by the competent authorities no earlier than one month after the date on which the difference of views, as referred to in paragraph 1 or 2 arose. The Administrative Commission shall seek to reconcile the points of view within six months of the date on which the matter was brought before it.

6(4) Where it is established either that the applicable legislation is not that of the Member State of provisional membership, or the institution which granted the benefits on a provisional basis was not the competent institution, the institution identified as being competent shall be deemed retroactively to have been so, as if that difference of views had not existed, at the latest from either the date of provisional membership or of the first provisional granting of the benefits concerned.

6(5) If necessary, the institution identified as being competent and the institution which provisionally paid the cash benefits or provisionally received contributions shall settle the financial situation of the person concerned as regards contributions and cash benefits paid provisionally, where appropriate, in accordance with Title IV, Chapter III, of the implementing Regulation.

Benefits in kind granted provisionally by an institution in accordance with paragraph 2 shall be reimbursed by the competent institution in accordance with Title IV of the implementing Regulation.

History – Art. 6(1)(b) and (c) substituted by Reg. 465/2012, art. 2(1), with effect from 28 June 2012.

ART. 7 Provisional calculation of benefits and contributions

7(1) Unless otherwise provided for in the implementing Regulation, where a person is eligible for a benefit, or is liable to pay a contribution in accordance with the basic Regulation, and the competent institution does not have all the information concerning the situation in another Member State which is necessary to calculate definitively the amount of that benefit or contribution, that institution shall, on request of the person concerned, award this benefit or calculate this contribution on a provisional basis, if such a calculation is possible on the basis of the information at the disposal of that institution.

7(2) The benefit or the contribution concerned shall be recalculated once all the necessary supporting evidence or documents are provided to the institution concerned.

Chapter III – Other general provisions for the application of the basic Regulation

ART. 8 Administrative arrangements between two or more Member States

8(1) The provisions of the implementing Regulation shall replace those laid down in the arrangements for the application of the conventions referred to in Article 8(1) of the basic Regulation, except the provisions concerning the arrangements concerning the conventions referred to in Annex II to the basic Regulation, provided that the provisions of those arrangements are included in Annex 1 to the implementing Regulation.

8(2) Member States may conclude between themselves, if necessary, arrangements pertaining to the application of the conventions referred to in Article 8(2) of the basic Regulation provided that these arrangements do not adversely affect the rights and obligations of the persons concerned and are included in Annex 1 to the implementing Regulation.

ART. 9 Other procedures between authorities and institutions

9(1) Two or more Member States, or their competent authorities, may agree procedures other than those provided for by the implementing Regulation, provided that such procedures do not adversely affect the rights or obligations of the persons concerned.

9(2) Any agreements concluded to this end shall be notified to the Administrative Commission and listed in Annex 1 to the implementing Regulation.

9(3) Provisions contained in implementing agreements concluded between two or more Member States with the same purpose as, or which are similar to, those referred to in paragraph 2, which are in force on the day preceding the entry into force of the implementing Regulation and are included in Annex 5 to Regulation (EEC) No 574/72, shall continue to apply, for the purposes of relations between those Member States, provided they are also included in Annex 1 to the implementing Regulation.

ART. 10 Prevention of overlapping of benefits

10 Notwithstanding other provisions in the basic Regulation, when benefits due under the legislation of two or more Member States are mutually reduced, suspended or withdrawn, any amounts that would not be paid in the event of strict application of the rules concerning reduction, suspension or withdrawal laid down by the legislation of the Member States concerned shall be divided by the number of benefits subjected to reduction, suspension or withdrawal.

ART. 11 Elements for determining residence

11(1) Where there is a difference of views between the institutions of two or more Member States about the determination of the residence of a person to whom the basic Regulation applies, these institutions shall establish by common agreement the centre of interests of the person concerned, based on an overall assessment of all available information relating to relevant facts, which may include, as appropriate:

(a) the duration and continuity of presence on the territory of the Member States concerned;

(b) the person's situation, including:

- (i) the nature and the specific characteristics of any activity pursued, in particular the place where such activity is habitually pursued, the stability of the activity, and the duration of any work contract;
- (ii) his family status and family ties;
- (iii) the exercise of any non-remunerated activity;
- (iv) in the case of students, the source of their income;
- (v) his housing situation, in particular how permanent it is;
- (vi) the Member State in which the person is deemed to reside for taxation purposes.

11(2) Where the consideration of the various criteria based on relevant facts as set out in paragraph 1 does not lead to agreement between the institutions concerned, the person's intention, as it appears from such facts and circumstances, especially the reasons that led the person to move, shall be considered to be decisive for establishing that person's actual place of residence.

ART. 12 Aggregation of periods

12(1) For the purposes of applying Article 6 of the basic Regulation, the competent institution shall contact the institutions of the Member States to whose legislation the person concerned has also been subject in order to determine all the periods completed under their legislation.

12(2) The respective periods of insurance, employment, self-employment or residence completed under the legislation of a Member State shall be added to those completed under the legislation of any other

Member State, insofar as necessary for the purposes of applying Article 6 of the basic Regulation, provided that these periods do not overlap.

12(3) Where a period of insurance or residence which is completed in accordance with compulsory insurance under the legislation of a Member State coincides with a period of insurance completed on the basis of voluntary insurance or continued optional insurance under the legislation of another Member State, only the period completed on the basis of compulsory insurance shall be taken into account.

12(4) Where a period of insurance or residence other than an equivalent period completed under the legislation of a Member State coincides with an equivalent period on the basis of the legislation of another Member State, only the period other than an equivalent period shall be taken into account.

12(5) Any period regarded as equivalent under the legislation of two or more Member States shall be taken into account only by the institution of the Member State to whose legislation the person concerned was last compulsorily subject before that period. In the event that the person concerned was not compulsorily subject to the legislation of a Member State before that period, the latter shall be taken into account by the institution of the Member State to whose legislation the person concerned was compulso-rily subject for the first time after that period.

12(6) In the event that the time in which certain periods of insurance or residence were completed under the legislation of a Member State cannot be determined precisely, it shall be presumed that these periods do not overlap with periods of insurance or residence completed under the legislation of another Member State, and account shall be taken thereof, where advantageous to the person concerned, insofar as they can reasonably be taken into consideration.

ART. 13 Rules for conversion of periods

13(1) Where periods completed under the legislation of a Member State are expressed in units different from those provided for by the legislation of another Member State, the conversion needed for the purpose of aggregation under Article 6 of the basic Regulation shall be carried out under the following rules:

(a) the period to be used as the basis for the conversion shall be that communicated by the institution of the Member State under whose legislation the period was completed;

(b) in the case of schemes where the periods are expressed in days the conversion from days to other units, and vice versa, as well as between different schemes based on days shall be calculated according to the following table:

Scheme based on	1 day corresponds to	1 week corresponds to	1 month corresponds to	1 quarter corresponds to	Maximum of days in one calendar year
5 days	9 hours	5 days	22 days	66 days	264 days
6 days	8 hours	6 days	26 days	78 days	312 days
7 days	6 hours	7 days	30 days	90 days	360 days

(c) in the case of schemes where the periods are expressed in units other than days,

(i) three months or 13 weeks shall be equivalent to one quarter, and vice versa;

(ii) one year shall be equivalent to four quarters, 12 months or 52 weeks, and vice versa;

(iii) for the conversion of weeks into months, and vice versa, weeks and months shall be converted into days in accordance with the conversion rules for the schemes based on six days in the table in point (b);

(d) in the case of periods expressed in fractions, those figures shall be converted into the next smaller integer unit applying the rules laid down in points (b) and (c). Fractions of years shall be converted into months unless the scheme involved is based on quarters;

(e) if the conversion under this paragraph results in a fraction of a unit, the next higher integer unit shall be taken as the result of the conversion under this paragraph.

13(2) The application of paragraph 1 shall not have the effect of producing, for the total sum of the periods completed during one calendar year, a total exceeding the number of days indicated in the last column in the table in paragraph 1(b), 52 weeks, 12 months or four quarters.

If the periods to be converted correspond to the maximum annual amount of periods under the legislation of the Member State in which they have been completed, the application of paragraph 1 shall not result within one calendar year in periods that are shorter than the possible maximum annual amount of periods provided under the legislation concerned.

13(3) The conversion shall be carried out either in one single operation covering all those periods which were communicated as an aggregate, or for each year, if the periods were communicated on a year-by-year basis.

13(4) Where an institution communicates periods expressed in days, it shall at the same time indicate whether the scheme it administers is based on five days, six days or seven days.

TITLE II – DETERMINATION OF THE LEGISLATION APPLICABLE

ART. 14 Details relating to Articles 12 and 13 of the basic Regulation

14(1) For the purposes of the application of Article 12(1) of the basic Regulation, a "person who pursues an activity as an employed person in a Member State on behalf of an employer which normally carries out its activities there and who is posted by that employer to another Member State" shall include a person who is recruited with a view to being posted to another Member State, provided that, immediately before the start of his employment, the person concerned is already subject to the legislation of the Member State in which his employer is established.

14(2) For the purposes of the application of Article 12(1) of the basic Regulation, the words "which normally carries out its activities there" shall refer to an employer that ordinarily performs substantial activities, other than purely internal management activities, in the territory of the Member State in which it is established, taking account of all criteria characterising the activities carried out by the undertaking in question. The relevant criteria must be suited to the specific characteristics of each employer and the real nature of the activities carried out.

14(3) For the purposes of the application of Article 12(2) of the basic Regulation, the words "who normally pursues an activity as a self-employed person" shall refer to a person who habitually carries out substantial activities in the territory of the Member State in which he is established. In particular, that person must have already pursued his activity for some time before the date when he wishes to take advantage of the provisions of that Article and, during any period of temporary activity in another Member State, must continue to fulfil, in the Member State where he is established, the requirements for the pursuit of his activity in order to be able to pursue it on his return.

14(4) For the purposes of the application of Article 12(2) of the basic Regulation, the criterion for determining whether the activity that a self-employed person goes to pursue in another Member State is "similar" to the self-employed activity normally pursued shall be that of the actual nature of the activity, rather than of the designation of employed or self-employed activity that may be given to this activity by the other Member State.

14(5) For the purposes of the application of Article 13(1) of the basic Regulation, a person who "normally pursues an activity as an employed person in two or more Member States" shall refer to a person who simultaneously, or in alternation, for the same undertaking or employer or for various undertakings or employers, exercises one or more separate activities in two or more Member States.

14(5a) For the purposes of the application of Title II of the basic Regulation, **"registered office or place of business"** shall refer to the registered office or place of business where the essential decisions of the undertaking are adopted and where the functions of its central administration are carried out.

For the purposes of Article 13(1) of the basic Regulation, an employed flight crew or cabin crew member normally pursuing air passenger or freight services in two or more Member States shall be subject to the legislation of the Member State where the home base, as defined in Annex III to Council Regulation (EEC) No 3922/91 of 16 December 1991 on the harmonization of technical requirements and administrative procedures in the field of civil aviation, is located.

14(5b) Marginal activities shall be disregarded for the purposes of determining the applicable legislation under Article 13 of the basic Regulation. Article 16 of the implementing Regulation shall apply to all cases under this Article.

14(6) For the purposes of the application of Article 13(2) of the basic Regulation, a person who "normally pursues an activity as a self-employed person in two or more Member States" shall refer, in particular, to a person who simultaneously or in alternation pursues one or more separate self-employed activities, irrespective of the nature of those activities, in two or more Member States.

14(7) For the purpose of distinguishing the activities under paragraphs 5 and 6 from the situations described in Article 12(1) and (2) of the basic Regulation, the duration of the activity in one or more other Member States (whether it is permanent or of an ad hoc or temporary nature) shall be decisive. For these purposes, an overall assessment shall be made of all the relevant facts including, in particular, in the case of an employed person, the place of work as defined in the employment contract.

14(8) For the purposes of the application of Article 13(1) and (2) of the basic Regulation, a **"substantial part of employed or self-employed activity"** pursued in a Member State shall mean a quantitatively substantial part of all the activities of the employed or self-employed person pursued there, without this necessarily being the major part of those activities.

To determine whether a substantial part of the activities is pursued in a Member State, the following indicative criteria shall be taken into account:

(a) in the case of an employed activity, the working time and/or the remuneration; and

(b) in the case of a self-employed activity, the turnover, working time, number of services rendered and/or income.

In the framework of an overall assessment, a share of less than 25% in respect of the criteria mentioned above shall be an indicator that a substantial part of the activities is not being pursued in the relevant Member State.

14(9) For the purposes of the application of Article 13(2)(b) of the basic Regulation, the "centre of interest" of the activities of a self-employed person shall be determined by taking account of all the aspects of that person's occupational activities, notably the place where the person's fixed and permanent place of business is located, the habitual nature or the duration of the activities pur sued, the number of services rendered, and the intention of the person concerned as revealed by all the circumstances.

14(10) For the determination of the applicable legislation under paragraphs 8 and 9, the institutions concerned shall take into account the situation projected for the following 12 calendar months.

14(11) If a person pursues his activity as an employed person in two or more Member States on behalf of an employer established outside the territory of the Union, and if this person resides in a Member State without pursuing substantial activity there, he shall be subject to the legislation of the Member State of residence.

History – Art. 14(5) substituted by Reg. 564/2012, art. 2(2)(a), with effect from 28 June 2012.
Art. 14(5a) and 14(5b) inserted by Reg. 564/2012, art. 2(2)(b), with effect from 28 June 2012.

ART. 15 Procedures for the application of Article 11(3)(b) and (d), Article 11(4) and Article 12 of the basic Regulation (on the provision of information to the institutions concerned)

15(1) Unless otherwise provided for by Article 16 of the implementing Regulation, where a person pursues his activity in a Member State other than the Member State competent under Title II of the basic Regulation, the employer or, in the case of a person who does not pursue an activity as an employed person, the person concerned shall inform the competent institution of the Member State whose legislation is applicable thereof, whenever possible in advance. That institution shall issue the attestation referred to in Article 19(2) of the implementing Regulation to the person concerned and shall without delay make information concerning the legislation applicable to that person, pursuant to Article 11(3)(b) or Article 12 of the basic Regulation, available to the institution designated by the competent authority of the Member State in which the activity is pursued.

15(2) Paragraph 1 shall apply *mutatis mutandis* to persons covered by Article 11(3)(d) of the basic Regulation.

15(3) An employer within the meaning of Article 11(4) of the basic Regulation who has an employee on board a vessel flying the flag of another Member State shall inform the competent institution of the Member State whose legislation is applicable thereof whenever possible in advance. That institution shall, without delay, make information concerning the legislation applicable to the person concerned, pursuant to Article 11(4) of the basic Regulation, available to the institution designated by the competent authority of the Member State whose flag, the vessel on which the employee is to perform the activity, is flying.

History – In art. 15(1), second sentence substituted by Reg. 465/2012, art. 2(3), with effect from 28 June 2012.

ART. 16 Procedure for the application of Article 13 of the basic Regulation

16(1) A person who pursues activities in two or more Member States shall inform the institution designated by the competent authority of the Member State of residence thereof.

16(2) The designated institution of the place of residence shall without delay determine the legislation applicable to the person concerned, having regard to Article 13 of the basic Regulation and Article 14 of the implementing Regulation. That initial determination shall be provisional. The institution shall inform the designated institutions of each Member State in which an activity is pursued of its provisional determination.

16(3) The provisional determination of the applicable legislation, as provided for in paragraph 2, shall become definitive within two months of the institutions designated by the competent authorities of the Member States concerned being informed of it, in accordance with paragraph 2, unless the legislation has already been definitively determined on the basis of paragraph 4, or at least one of the institutions concerned informs the institution designated by the competent authority of the Member State of residence by the end of this two-month period that it cannot yet accept the determination or that it takes a different view on this.

16(4) Where uncertainty about the determination of the applicable legislation requires contacts between the institutions or authorities of two or more Member States, at the request of one or more of the institutions designated by the competent authorities of the Member States concerned or of the competent authorities themselves, the legislation applicable to the person concerned shall be determined by common agreement, having regard to Article 13 of the basic Regulation and the relevant provisions of Article 14 of the implementing Regulation.

Where there is a difference of views between the institutions or competent authorities concerned, those bodies shall seek agreement in accordance with the conditions set out above and Article 6 of the implementing Regulation shall apply.

16(5) The competent institution of the Member State whose legislation is determined to be applicable either provisionally or definitively shall without delay inform the person concerned.

16(6) If the person concerned fails to provide the information referred to in paragraph 1, this Article shall be applied at the initiative of the institution designated by the competent authority of the Member State of residence as soon as it is appraised of that person's situation, possibly via another institution concerned.

ART. 17 Procedure for the application of Article 15 of the basic Regulation

17 Contract staff of the European Communities shall exercise the right of option provided for in Article 15 of the basic Regulation when the employment contract is concluded. The authority empowered to conclude the contract shall inform the designated institution of the Member State for whose legislation the contract staff member of the European Communities has opted.

ART. 18 Procedure for the application of Article 16 of the basic Regulation

18 A request by the employer or the person concerned for exceptions to Articles 11 to 15 of the basic Regulation shall be submitted, whenever possible in advance, to the competent authority or the body designated by the authority of the Member State, whose legislation the employee or person concerned requests be applied.

ART. 19 Provision of information to persons concerned and employers

19(1) The competent institution of the Member State whose legislation becomes applicable pursuant to Title II of the basic Regulation shall inform the person concerned and, where appropriate, his employer(s) of the obligations laid down in that legislation. It shall provide them with the necessary assistance to complete the formalities required by that legislation.

19(2) At the request of the person concerned or of the employer, the competent institution of the Member State whose legislation is applicable pursuant to Title II of the basic Regulation shall provide an attestation that such legislation is applicable and shall indicate, where appropriate, until what date and under what conditions.

ART. 20 Cooperation between institutions

20(1) The relevant institutions shall communicate to the competent institution of the Member State whose legislation is applicable to a person pursuant to Title II of the basic Regulation the necessary information required to establish the date on which that legislation becomes applicable and the contributions which that person and his employer(s) are liable to pay under that legislation.

20(2) The competent institution of the Member State whose legislation becomes applicable to a person pursuant to Title II of the basic Regulation shall make the information indicating the date on which the application of that legislation takes effect available to the institution designated by the competent authority of the Member State to whose legislation that person was last subject.

ART. 21 Obligations of the employer

21(1) An employer who has his registered office or place of business outside the competent Member State shall fulfil all the obligations laid down by the legislation applicable to his employees, notably the obligation to pay the contributions provided for by that legislation, as if he had his registered office or place of business in the competent Member State.

21(2) An employer who does not have a place of business in the Member State whose legislation is applicable and the employee may agree that the latter may fulfil the employer's obligations on its behalf as regards the payment of contributions without prejudice to the employer's underlying obligations. The employer shall send notice of such an arrangement to the competent institution of that Member State.

TITLE III – SPECIAL PROVISIONS CONCERNING VARIOUS CATEGORIES OF BENEFITS

Chapter I – Sickness, maternity and equivalent paternity benefits

ART. 22 General implementing provisions

22(1) The competent authorities or institutions shall ensure that any necessary information is made available to insured persons regarding the procedures and conditions for the granting of benefits in kind where such benefits are received in the territory of a Member State other than that of the competent institution.

22(2) Notwithstanding Article 5(a) of the basic Regulation, a Member State may become responsible for the cost of benefits in accordance with Article 22 of the basic Regulation only if, either the insured person has made a claim for a pension under the legislation of that Member State, or in accordance with Articles 23 to 30 of the basic Regulation, he receives a pension under the legislation of that Member State.

ART. 23 Regime applicable in the event of the existence of more than one regime in the Member State of residence or stay

23 If the legislation of the Member State of residence or stay comprises more than one scheme of sickness, maternity and paternity insurance for more than one category of insured persons, the provisions applicable under Articles 17, 19(1), 20, 22, 24 and 26 of the basic Regulation shall be those of the legislation on the general scheme for employed persons.

ART. 24 Residence in a Member State other than the competent Member State

24(1) For the purposes of the application of Article 17 of the basic Regulation, the insured person and/or members of his family shall be obliged to register with the institution of the place of residence. Their right to benefits in kind in the Member State of residence shall be certified by a document issued by the competent institution upon request of the insured person or upon request of the institution of the place of residence.

24(2) The document referred to in paragraph 1 shall remain valid until the competent institution informs the institution of the place of residence of its cancellation.

The institution of the place of residence shall inform the competent institution of any registration under paragraph 1 and of any change or cancellation of that registration.

24(3) This Article shall apply *mutatis mutandis* to the persons referred to in Articles 22, 24, 25 and 26 of the basic Regulation.

ART. 25 Stay in a Member State other than the competent Member State

Procedure and scope of right

25(1) For the purposes of the application of Article 19 of the basic Regulation, the insured person shall present to the health care provider in the Member State of stay a document issued by the competent institution indicating his entitlement to benefits in kind. If the insured person does not have such a document, the institution of the place of stay, upon request or if otherwise necessary, shall contact the competent institution in order to obtain one.

25(2) That document shall indicate that the insured person is entitled to benefits in kind under the conditions laid down in Article 19 of the basic Regulation on the same terms as those applicable to persons insured under the legislation of the Member State of stay.

25(3) The benefits in kind referred to in Article 19(1) of the basic Regulation shall refer to the benefits in kind which are provided in the Member State of stay, in accordance with its legislation, and which become necessary on medical grounds with a view to preventing an insured person from being forced to return, before the end of the planned duration of stay, to the competent Member State to obtain the necessary treatment.

Procedure and arrangements for meeting the costs and providing reimbursement of benefits in kind

25(4) If the insured person has actually borne the costs of all or part of the benefits in kind provided within the framework of Article 19 of the basic Regulation and if the legislation applied by the institution of the place of stay enables reimbursement of those costs to an insured person, he may send an application for reimbursement to the institution of the place of stay. In that case, that institution shall reimburse directly to that person the amount of the costs corresponding to those benefits within the limits of and under the conditions of the reimbursement rates laid down in its legislation.

25(5) If the reimbursement of such costs has not been requested directly from the institution of the place of stay, the costs incurred shall be reimbursed to the person concerned by the competent institution in accordance with the reimbursement rates administered by the institution of the place of stay or the amounts which would have been subject to reimbursement to the institution of the place of stay, if Article 62 of the implementing Regulation had applied in the case concerned.

The institution of the place of stay shall provide the competent institution, upon request, with all necessary information about these rates or amounts.

25(6) By way of derogation from paragraph 5, the competent institution may undertake the reimbursement of the costs incurred within the limits of and under the conditions of the reimbursement rates laid down in its legislation, provided that the insured person has agreed to this provision being applied to him/her.

25(7) If the legislation of the Member State of stay does not provide for reimbursement pursuant to paragraphs 4 and 5 in the case concerned, the competent institution may reimburse the costs within the limits of and under the conditions of the reimbursement rates laid down in its legislation, without the agreement of the insured person.

25(8) The reimbursement to the insured person shall not, in any event, exceed the amount of costs actually incurred by him/her.

25(9) In the case of substantial expenditure, the competent institution may pay the insured person an appropriate advance as soon as that person submits the application for reimbursement to it.

Family Members

25(10) Paragraphs 1 to 9 shall apply *mutatis mutandis* to the members of the family of the insured person.

ART. 26 Scheduled treatment

Authorisation procedure

26(1) For the purposes of the application of Article 20(1) of the basic Regulation, the insured person shall present a document issued by the competent institution to the institution of the place of stay. For the purposes of this Article, the competent institution shall mean the institution which bears the cost of the scheduled treatment; in the cases referred to in Article 20(4) and 27(5) of the basic Regulation, in which the benefits in kind provided in the Member State of residence are reimbursed on the basis of fixed amounts, the competent institution shall mean the institution of the place of residence.

26(2) If an insured person does not reside in the competent Member State, he shall request authorisation from the institution of the place of residence, which shall forward it to the competent institution without delay.

In that event, the institution of the place of residence shall certify in a statement whether the conditions set out in the second sentence of Article 20(2) of the basic Regulation are met in the Member State of residence.

The competent institution may refuse to grant the requested authorisation only if, in accordance with the assessment of the institution of the place of residence, the conditions set out in the second sentence of Article 20(2) of the basic Regulation are not met in the Member State of residence of the insured person, or if the same treatment can be provided in the competent Member State itself, within a time-limit which is medically justifiable, taking into account the current state of health and the probable course of illness of the person concerned.

The competent institution shall inform the institution of the place of residence of its decision.

In the absence of a reply within the deadlines set by its national legislation, the authorisation shall be considered to have been granted by the competent institution.

26(3) If an insured person who does not reside in the competent Member State is in need of urgent vitally necessary treatment, and the authorisation cannot be refused in accordance with the second sentence of Article 20(2) of the basic Regulation, the authorisation shall be granted by the institution of the place of residence on behalf of the competent institution, which shall be immediately informed by the institution of the place of residence.

The competent institution shall accept the findings and the treatment options of the doctors approved by the institution of the place of residence that issues the authorisation, concerning the need for urgent vitally necessary treatment.

26(4) At any time during the procedure granting the authorisation, the competent institution shall retain the right to have the insured person examined by a doctor of its own choice in the Member State of stay or residence.

26(5) The institution of the place of stay shall, without prejudice to any decision regarding authorisation, inform the competent institution if it appears medically appropriate to supplement the treatment covered by the existing authorisation.

Meeting the cost of benefits in kind incurred by the insured person

26(6) Without prejudice to paragraph 7, Article 25(4) and (5) of the implementing Regulation shall apply *mutatis mutandis*.

26(7) If the insured person has actually borne all or part of the costs for the authorised medical treatment him or herself and the costs which the competent institution is obliged to reimburse to the institution of the place of stay or to the insured person according to paragraph 6 (actual cost) are lower than the costs which it would have had to assume for the same treatment in the competent Member State (notional cost), the competent institution shall reimburse, upon request, the cost of treatment incurred by the insured person up to the amount by which the notional cost exceeds the actual cost. The reimbursed sum may not, however, exceed the costs actually incurred by the insured person and may take account of the amount which the insured person would have had to pay if the treatment had been delivered in the competent Member State.

Meeting the costs of travel and stay as part of scheduled treatment

26(8) Where the national legislation of the competent institution provides for the reimbursement of the costs of travel and stay which are inseparable from the treatment of the insured person, such costs for the person concerned and, if necessary, for a person who must accompany him/her, shall be assumed by this institution when an authorisation is granted in the case of treatment in another Member State.

Family members

26(9) Paragraphs 1 to 8 shall apply *mutatis mutandis* to the members of the family of the insured persons.

ART. 27 Cash benefits relating to incapacity for work in the event of stay or residence in a Member State other than the competent Member State

Procedure to be followed by the insured person

27(1) If the legislation of the competent Member State requires that the insured person presents a certificate in order to be entitled to cash benefits relating to incapacity for work pursuant to Article 21(1) of the basic Regulation, the insured person shall ask the doctor of the Member State of residence who established his state of health to certify his incapacity for work and its probable duration.

27(2) The insured person shall send the certificate to the competent institution within the time limit laid down by the legislation of the competent Member State.

27(3) Where the doctors providing treatment in the Member State of residence do not issue certificates of incapacity for work, and where such certificates are required under the legislation of the competent Member State, the person concerned shall apply directly to the institution of the place of residence. That institution shall immediately arrange for a medical assessment of the person's incapacity for work and for the certificate referred to in paragraph 1 to be drawn up. The certificate shall be forwarded to the competent institution forthwith.

27(4) The forwarding of the document referred to in paragraphs 1, 2 and 3 shall not exempt the insured person from fulfilling the obligations provided for by the applicable legislation, in particular with regard to his employer. Where appropriate, the employer and/or the competent institution may call upon the employee to participate in activities designed to promote and assist his return to employment.

Procedure to be followed by the institution of the Member State of residence

27(5) At the request of the competent institution, the institution of the place of residence shall carry out any necessary administrative checks or medical examinations of the person concerned in accordance with the legislation applied by this latter institution. The report of the examining doctor concerning, in particular, the probable duration of the incapacity for work, shall be forwarded without delay by the institution of the place of residence to the competent institution.

Procedure to be followed by the competent institution

27(6) The competent institution shall reserve the right to have the insured person examined by a doctor of its choice.

27(7) Without prejudice to the second sentence of Article 21(1) of the basic Regulation, the competent institution shall pay the cash benefits directly to the person concerned and shall, where necessary, inform the institution of the place of residence thereof.

27(8) For the purposes of the application of Article 21(1) of the basic Regulation, the particulars of the certificate of incapacity for work of an insured person drawn up in another Member State on the basis of the medical findings of the examining doctor or institution shall have the same legal value as a certificate drawn up in the competent Member State.

27(9) If the competent institution refuses the cash benefits, it shall notify its decision to the insured person and at the same time to the institution of the place of residence.

Procedure in the event of a stay in a Member State other than the competent Member State

27(10) Paragraphs 1 to 9 shall apply *mutatis mutandis* when the insured person stays in a Member State other than the competent Member State.

ART. 28 Long-term care benefits in cash in the event of stay or residence in a Member State other than the competent Member State

Procedure to be followed by the insured person

28(1) In order to be entitled to long-term care benefits in cash pursuant to Article 21(1) of the basic Regulation, the insured person shall apply to the competent institution. The competent institution shall, where necessary, inform the institution of the place of residence thereof.

Procedure to be followed by the institution of the place of residence

28(2) At the request of the competent institution, the institution of the place of residence shall examine the condition of the insured person with respect to his need for long-term care. The competent institution shall give the institution of the place of residence all the information necessary for such an examination.

Procedure to be followed by the competent institution

28(3) In order to determine the degree of need for long-term care, the competent institution shall have the right to have the insured person examined by a doctor or any other expert of its choice.

28(4) Article 27(7) of the implementing Regulation shall apply *mutatis mutandis*.

Procedure in the event of a stay in a Member State other than the competent Member State

28(5) Paragraphs 1 to 4 shall apply *mutatis mutandis* when the insured person stays in a Member State other than the competent Member State.

Family members

28(6) Paragraphs 1 to 5 shall apply *mutatis mutandis* to the members of the family of the insured person.

ART. 29 Application of Article 28 of the basic Regulation

29 If the Member State where the former frontier worker last pursued his activity is no longer the competent Member State, and the former frontier worker or a member of his family travels there with the purpose of receiving benefits in kind pursuant to Article 28 of the basic Regulation, he shall submit to the institution of the place of stay a document issued by the competent institution.

ART. 30 Contributions by pensioners

30 If a person receives a pension from more than one Member State, the amount of contributions deducted from all the pensions paid shall under no circumstances be greater than the amount deducted in respect of a person who receives the same amount of pension from the competent Member State.

ART. 31 Application of Article 34 of the basic Regulation

Procedure to be followed by the competent institution

31(1) The competent institution shall inform the person concerned of the provision contained in Article 34 of the basic Regulation regarding the prevention of overlapping of benefits. The application of such rules shall ensure that the person not residing in the competent Member State is entitled to benefits of at least the same total amount or value as those to which he would be entitled if he resided in that Member State.

31(2) The competent institution shall also inform the institution of the place of residence or stay about the payment of long-term care cash benefits where the legislation applied by the latter institution provides for the long-term care benefits in kind included in the list referred to in Article 34(2) of the basic Regulation.

Procedure to be followed by the institution of the place of residence or stay

31(3) Having received the information provided for in paragraph 2, the institution of the place of residence or stay shall without delay inform the competent institution of any long-term care benefit in kind intended for the same purpose granted under its legislation to the person concerned and of the rate of reimbursement applicable thereto.

31(4) The Administrative Commission shall lay down implementing measures for this Article where necessary.

ART. 32 Special implementing measures

32(1) When a person or a group of persons are exempted upon request from compulsory sickness insurance and such persons are thus not covered by a sickness insurance scheme to which the basic Regulation applies, the institution of another Member State shall not, solely because of this exemption, become responsible for bearing the costs of benefits in kind or in cash provided to such persons or to a member of their family under Title III, Chapter I, of the basic Regulation.

32(2) For the Member States referred to in Annex 2, the provisions of Title III, Chapter I, of the basic Regulation relating to benefits in kind shall apply to persons entitled to benefits in kind solely on the basis of a special scheme for civil servants only to the extent specified therein.

The institution of another Member State shall not, on those grounds alone, become responsible for bearing the costs of benefits in kind or in cash provided to those persons or to members of their family.

32(3) When the persons referred to in paragraphs 1 and 2 and the members of their families reside in a Member State where the right to receive benefits in kind is not subject to conditions of insurance, or of activity as an employed or self-employed person, they shall be liable to pay the full costs of benefits in kind provided in their country of residence.

Chapter II – Benefits in respect of accidents at work and occupational diseases

ART. 33 Right to benefits in kind and in cash in the event of residence or stay in a Member State other than the competent Member State

33(1) For the purposes of the application of Article 36 of the basic Regulation, the procedures laid down in Articles 24 to 27 of the implementing Regulation shall apply *mutatis mutandis*.

33(2) When providing special benefits in kind in connection with accidents at work and occupational diseases under the national legislation of the Member State of stay or residence, the institution of that Member State shall without delay inform the competent institution.

ART. 34 Procedure in the event of an accident at work or occupational disease which occurs in a Member State other than the competent Member State

34(1) If an accident at work occurs or an occupational disease is diagnosed for the first time in a Member State other than the competent Member State, the declaration or notification of the accident at work or the occupational disease, where the declaration or notification exists under national legislation, shall be carried out in accordance with the legislation of the competent Member State, without prejudice, where appropriate, to any other applicable legal provisions in force in the Member State in which the accident at work occurred or in which the first medical diagnosis of the occupational disease was made, which remain applicable in such cases. The declaration or notification shall be addressed to the competent institution.

34(2) The institution of the Member State in the territory of which the accident at work occurred or in which the occupational disease was first diagnosed, shall notify the competent institution of medical certificates drawn up in the territory of that Member State.

34(3) Where, as a result of an accident while travelling to or from work which occurs in the territory of a Member State other than the competent Member State, an inquiry is necessary in the territory of the first Member State in order to determine any entitlement to relevant benefits, a person may be appointed for that purpose by the competent institution, which shall inform the authorities of that Member State. The institutions shall cooperate with each other in order to assess all relevant information and to consult the reports and any other documents relating to the accident.

34(4) Following treatment, a detailed report accompanied by medical certificates relating to the permanent consequences of the accident or disease, in particular the injured person's present state and the recovery or stabilisation of injuries, shall be sent upon request of the competent institution. The relevant fees shall be paid by the institution of the place of residence or of stay, where appropriate, at the rate applied by that institution to the charge of the competent institution.

34(5) At the request of the institution of the place of residence or stay, where appropriate, the competent institution shall notify it of the decision setting the date for the recovery or stabilisation of injuries and, where appropriate, the decision concerning the granting of a pension.

ART. 35 Disputes concerning the occupational nature of the accident or disease

35(1) Where the competent institution disputes the application of the legislation relating to accidents at work or occupational diseases under Article 36(2) of the basic Regulation, it shall without delay inform the institution of the place of residence or stay which provided the benefits in kind, which will then be considered as sickness insurance benefits.

35(2) When a *final decision has been taken* on that subject, the competent institution shall without delay inform the institution of the place of residence or stay which provided the benefits in kind.

Where an accident at work or occupational disease is not established, benefits in kind shall continue to be provided as sickness benefits if the person concerned is entitled to them.

Where an accident at work or occupational disease is established, sickness benefits in kind provided to the person concerned shall be considered as accident at work or occupational disease benefits from the date on which the accident at work occurred or the occupational disease was first medically diagnosed.

35(3) The second subparagraph of Article 6(5) of the implementing Regulation shall apply *mutatis mutandis*.

ART. 36 Procedure in the event of exposure to the risk of an occupational disease in more than one Member State

36(1) In the case referred to in Article 38 of the basic Regulation, the declaration or notification of the occupational disease shall be sent to the competent institution for occupational diseases of the last Member State under the legislation of which the person concerned pursued an activity likely to cause that disease. When the institution to which the declaration or notification was sent establishes that an activity likely to cause the occupational disease in question was last pursued under the legislation of another Member State, it shall send the declaration or notification and all accompanying certificates to the equivalent institution in that Member State.

36(2) Where the institution of the last Member State under the legislation of which the person concerned pursued an activity likely to cause the occupational disease in question establishes that the person concerned or his survivors do not meet the requirements of that legislation, inter alia, because the person concerned had never pursued in that Member State an activity which caused the occupational disease or because that Member State does not recognise the occupational nature of the disease, that institution shall forward without delay the declaration or notification and all accompanying certificates, including the findings and reports of medical examinations performed by the first institution to the institution of the previous Member State under the legislation of which the person concerned pursued an activity likely to cause the occupational disease in question.

36(3) Where appropriate, the institutions shall reiterate the procedure set out in paragraph 2 going back as far as the equivalent institution in the Member State under whose legislation the person concerned first pursued an activity likely to cause the occupational disease in question.

ART. 37 Exchange of information between institutions and advance payments in the event of an appeal against rejection

37(1) In the event of an appeal against a decision to refuse benefits taken by the institution of one of the Member States under the legislation of which the person concerned pursued an activity likely to cause the occupational disease in question, that institution shall inform the institution to which the declaration or notification was sent, in accordance with the procedure provided for in Article 36(2) of the implementing Regulation, and shall subsequently inform it when a final decision is reached.

37(2) Where a person is entitled to benefits under the legislation applied by the institution to which the declaration or notification was sent, that institution shall make the advance payments, the amount of which shall be determined, where appropriate, after consulting the institution which made the decision against which the appeal was lodged, and in such a way that overpayments are avoided. The latter institution shall reimburse the advance payments made if, as a result of the appeal, it is obliged to provide those benefits. That amount will then be deducted from the benefits due to the person concerned, in accordance with the procedure provided for in Articles 72 and 73 of the implementing Regulation.

37(3) The second subparagraph of Article 6(5) of the implementing Regulation shall apply *mutatis mutandis*.

ART. 38 Aggravation of an occupational disease

38 In the cases covered by Article 39 of the basic Regulation, the claimant must provide the institution in the Member State from which he is claiming entitlement to benefits with details concerning benefits previously granted for the occupational disease in question. That institution may contact any other previously competent institution in order to obtain the information it considers necessary.

ART. 39 Assessment of the degree of incapacity in the event of occupational accidents or diseases which occurred previously or subsequently

39 Where a previous or subsequent incapacity for work was caused by an accident which occurred when the person concerned was subject to the legislation of a Member State which makes no distinction according to the origin of the incapacity to work, the competent institution or the body designated by the competent authority of the Member State in question shall:

(a) upon request by the competent institution of another Member State, provide information concerning the degree of the previous or subsequent incapacity for work, and where possible, information making it possible to determine whether the incapacity is the result of an accident at work within the meaning of the legislation applied by the institution in the other Member State;

(b) take into account the degree of incapacity caused by these previous or subsequent cases when determining the right to benefits and the amount, in accordance with the applicable legislation.

ART. 40 Submission and investigation of claims for pensions or supplementary allowances

40 In order to receive a pension or supplementary allowance under the legislation of a Member State, the person concerned or his survivors residing in the territory of another Member State shall submit, where appropriate, a claim either to the competent institution or to the institution of the place of residence, which shall send it to the competent institution.

The claim shall contain the information required under the legislation applied by the competent institution.

ART. 41 Special implementing measures

41(1) In relation to the Member States referred to in Annex 2, the provisions of Title III, Chapter 2 of the basic Regulation relating to benefits in kind shall apply to persons entitled to benefits in kind solely on the basis of a special scheme for civil servants, and only to the extent specified therein.

41(2) Article 32(2) second subparagraph and Article 32(3) of the implementing Regulation shall apply *mutatis mutandis*.

Chapter III – Death grants

ART. 42 Claim for death grants

42 For the purposes of applying Articles 42 and 43 of the basic Regulation, the claim for death grants shall be sent either to the competent institution or to the institution of the claimant's place of residence, which shall send it to the competent institution.

The claim shall contain the information required under the legislation applied by the competent institution.

Chapter IV – Invalidity benefits and old-age and survivors' pensions

ART. 43 Additional provisions for the calculation of benefit

43(1) For the purposes of calculating the theoretical amount and the actual amount of the benefit in accordance with Article 52(1)(b) of the basic Regulation, the rules provided for in Article 12(3), (4), (5) and (6) of the implementing Regulation shall apply.

43(2) Where periods of voluntary or optional continued insurance have not been taken into account under Article 12(3) of the implementing Regulation, the institution of the Member State under whose legislation those periods were completed shall calculate the amount corresponding to those periods under the legislation it applies. The actual amount of the benefit, calculated in accordance with Article 52(1)(b) of the basic Regulation, shall be increased by the amount corresponding to periods of voluntary or optional continued insurance.

43(3) The institution of each Member State shall calculate, under the legislation it applies, the amount due corresponding to periods of voluntary or optional continued insurance which, under Article 53(3)(c) of the basic Regulation, shall not be subject to another Member State's rules relating to withdrawal, reduction or suspension.

Where the legislation applied by the competent institution does not allow it to determine this amount directly, on the grounds that that legislation allocates different values to insurance periods, a notional amount may be established. The Administrative Commission shall lay down the detailed arrangements for the determination of that notional amount.

ART. 44 Taking into account of child raising-periods

44(1) For the purposes of this Article, "child-raising period" refers to any period which is credited under the pension legislation of a Member State or which provides a supplement to a pension explicitly for the reason that a person has raised a child, irrespective of the method used to calculate those periods and whether they accrue during the time of child-raising or are acknowledged retroactively.

44(2) Where, under the legislation of the Member State which is competent under Title II of the basic Regulation, no child-raising period is taken into account, the institution of the Member State whose legislation, according to Title II of the basic Regulation, was applicable to the person concerned on the grounds that he or she was pursuing an activity as an employed or self-employed person at the date when, under that legislation, the child-raising period started to be taken into account for the child concerned, shall remain responsible for taking into account that period as a child-raising period under its own legislation, as if such child-raising took place in its own territory.

44(3) Paragraph 2 shall not apply if the person concerned is, or becomes, subject to the legislation of another Member State due to the pursuit of an employed or self-employed activity.

ART. 45 Claim for benefits

Submission of the claim for benefits under type A legislation under Article 44(2) of the basic Regulation

45(1) In order to receive benefits under type A legislation under Article 44(2) of the basic Regulation, the claimant shall submit a claim to the institution of the Member State, whose legislation was applicable at the time when the incapacity for work occurred followed by invalidity or the aggravation of such invalidity, or to the institution of the place of residence, which shall forward the claim to the first institution.

45(2) If sickness benefits in cash have been awarded, the expiry date of the period for awarding these benefits shall, where appropriate, be considered as the date of submission of the pension claim.

45(3) In the case referred to in Article 47(1) of the basic Regulation, the institution with which the person concerned was last insured shall inform the institution which initially paid the benefits of the amount and the date of commencement of the benefits under the applicable legislation. From that date benefits due before aggravation of the invalidity shall be withdrawn or reduced to the supplement referred to in Article 47(2) of the basic Regulation.

Submission of other claims for benefits

45(4) In situations other than those referred to in paragraph 1, the claimant shall submit a claim to the institution of his place of residence or to the institution of the last Member State whose legislation was applicable. If the person concerned was not, at any time, subject to the legislation applied by the institution of the place of residence, that institution shall forward the claim to the institution of the last Member State whose legislation was applicable.

45(5) The date of submission of the claim shall apply in all the institutions concerned.

45(6) By way of derogation from paragraph 5, if the claimant does not, despite having been asked to do so, notify the fact that he has been employed or has resided in other Member States, the date on which the claimant completes his initial claim or submits a new claim for his missing periods of employment or/and residence in a Member State shall be considered as the date of submission of the claim to the institution applying the legislation in question, subject to more favourable provisions of that legislation.

ART. 46 Certificates and information to be submitted with the claim by the claimant

46(1) The claim shall be submitted by the claimant in accordance with the provisions of the legislation applied by the institution referred to in Article 45(1) or (4) of the implementing Regulation and be accompanied by the supporting documents required by that legislation. In particular, the claimant shall supply all available relevant information and supporting documents relating to periods of insurance (institutions, identification numbers), employment (employers) or self-employment (nature and place of activity) and residence (addresses) which may have been completed under other legislation, as well as the length of those periods.

46(2) Where, in accordance with Article 50(1) of the basic Regulation, the claimant requests deferment of the award of old-age benefits under the legislation of one or more Member States, he shall state that in his claim and specify under which legislation the deferment is requested. In order to enable the claimant to exercise that right, the institutions concerned shall, upon the request of the claimant, notify him of all the information available to them so that he can assess the consequences of concurrent or successive awards of benefits which he might claim.

46(3) Should the claimant withdraw a claim for benefits provided for under the legislation of a particular Member State, that withdrawal shall not be considered as a concurrent withdrawal of claims for benefits under the legislation of other Member States.

ART. 47 Investigation of claims by the institutions concerned

Contact institution

47(1) The institution to which the claim for benefits is submitted or forwarded in accordance with Article 45(1) or (4) of the implementing Regulation shall be referred to hereinafter as the "contact institution". The institution of the place of residence shall not be referred to as the contact institution if the person concerned has not, at any time, been subject to the legislation which that institution applies.

In addition to investigating the claim for benefits under the legislation which it applies, this institution shall, in its capacity as contact institution, promote the exchange of data, the communication of decisions and the operations necessary for the investigation of the claim by the institutions concerned, and supply the claimant, upon request, with any information relevant to the Community aspects of the investigation and keep him/her informed of its progress.

Investigation of claims for benefits under type A legislation under Article 44 of the basic Regulation

47(2) In the case referred to in Article 44(3) of the basic Regulation, the contact institution shall send all the documents relating to the person concerned to the institution with which he was previously insured, which shall in turn examine the case.

47(3) Articles 48 to 52 of the implementing Regulation shall not be applicable to the investigation of claims referred to in Article 44 of the basic Regulation.

Investigation of other claims for benefits

47(4) In situations other than those referred to in paragraph 2, the contact institution shall, without delay, send claims for benefits and all the documents which it has available and, where appropriate, the relevant documents supplied by the claimant to all the institutions in question so that they can all start the investigation of the claim concurrently. The contact institution shall notify the other institutions of periods of insurance or residence subject to its legislation. It shall also indicate which documents shall be submitted at a later date and supplement the claim as soon as possible.

47(5) Each of the institutions in question shall notify the contact institution and the other institutions in question, as soon as possible, of the periods of insurance or residence subject to their legislation.

47(6) Each of the institutions in question shall calculate the amount of benefits in accordance with Article 52 of the basic Regulation and shall notify the contact institution and the other institutions concerned of its decision, of the amount of benefits due and of any information required for the purposes of Articles 53 to 55 of the basic Regulation.

47(7) Should an institution establish, on the basis of the information referred to in paragraphs 4 and 5 of this Article, that Article 46(2) or Article 57(2) or (3) of the basic Regulation is applicable, it shall inform the contact institution and the other institutions concerned.

ART. 48 Notification of decisions to the claimant

48(1) Each institution shall notify the claimant of the decision it has taken in accordance with the applicable legislation. Each decision shall specify the remedies and periods allowed for appeals. Once the contact institution has been notified of all decisions taken by each institution, it shall send the claimant and the other institutions concerned a summary of those decisions. A model summary shall be drawn up by the Administrative Commission. The summary shall be sent to the claimant in the language of the institution or, at the request of the claimant, in any language of his choice recognised as an official language of the Community institutions in accordance with Article 290 of the Treaty.

48(2) Where it appears to the claimant following receipt of the summary that his rights may have been adversely affected by the interaction of decisions taken by two or more institutions, the claimant shall have the right to a review of the decisions by the institutions concerned within the time limits laid down in the respective national legislation. The time limits shall commence on the date of receipt of the summary. The claimant shall be notified of the result of the review in writing.

ART. 49 Determination of the degree of invalidity

49(1) Where Article 46(3) of the basic Regulation is applicable, the only institution authorised to take a decision concerning the claimant's degree of invalidity shall be the contact institution, if the legislation applied by that institution is included in Annex VII to the basic Regulation, or failing that, the institution whose leg islation is included in that Annex and to whose legislation the claimant was last subject. It shall take that decision as soon as it can determine whether the conditions for eligibility laid down in the applicable legislation are met, taking into account, where appropriate, Articles 6 and 51 of the basic Regulation. It shall without delay notify the other institutions concerned of that decision.

Where the eligibility criteria, other than those relating to the degree of invalidity, laid down in the applicable legislation are not met, taking into account Articles 6 and 51 of the basic Regulation, the contact institution shall without delay inform the competent institution of the last Member State to whose legislation the claimant was subject. The latter institution shall be authorised to take the decision concerning the degree *of invalidity of* the claimant if the conditions for eligibility laid down in the applicable legislation are met. It shall without delay notify the other institutions concerned of that decision.

When determining eligibility, the matter may, if necessary have to be referred back, under the same conditions, to the competent institution in respect of invalidity of the Member State to whose legislation the claimant was first subject.

49(2) Where Article 46(3) of the basic Regulation is not applicable, each institution shall, in accordance with its legislation, have the possibility of having the claimant examined by a medical doctor or other expert of its choice to determine the degree of invalidity. However, the institution of a Member State shall take into consideration documents, medical reports and administrative information collected by the institution of any other Member State as if they had been drawn up in its own Member State.

ART. 50 Provisional instalments and advance payment of benefit

50(1) Notwithstanding Article 7 of the implementing Regulation, any institution which establishes, while investigating a claim for benefits, that the claimant is entitled to an independent benefit under the applicable legislation, in accordance with Article 52(1)(a) of the basic Regulation, shall pay that benefit without delay. That payment shall be considered provisional if the amount might be affected by the result of the claim investigation procedure.

50(2) Whenever it is evident from the information available that the claimant is entitled to a payment from an institution under Article 52(1)(b) of the basic Regulation, that institution shall make an advance payment, the amount of which shall be as close as possible to the amount which will probably be paid under Article 52(1)(b) of the basic Regulation.

50(3) Each institution which is obliged to pay the provisional benefits or advance payment under paragraphs 1 or 2 shall inform the claimant without delay, specifically drawing his attention to the provisional nature of the measure and any rights of appeal in accordance with its legislation.

ART. 51 New calculation of benefits

51(1) Where there is a new calculation of benefits in accordance with Articles 48(3) and (4), 50(4) and 59(1) of the basic Regulation, Article 50 of the implementing Regulation shall be applicable *mutatis mutandis*.

51(2) Where there is a new calculation, withdrawal or suspension of the benefit, the institution which took the decision shall inform the person concerned without delay and shall inform each of the institutions in respect of which the person concerned has an entitlement.

ART. 52 Measures intended to accelerate the pension calculation process

52(1) In order to facilitate and accelerate the investigation of claims and the payment of benefits, the institutions to whose legislation a person has been subject shall:

(a) exchange with or make available to institutions of other Member States the elements for identifying persons who change from one applicable national legislation to another, and together ensure that those identification elements are retained and correspond, or, failing that, provide those persons with the means to access their identification elements directly;

(b) sufficiently in advance of the minimum age for commencing pension rights or before an age to be determined by national legislation, exchange with or make available to the person concerned and to institutions of other Member States information (periods completed or other important elements) on the pension entitlements of persons who have changed from one applicable legislation to another or, failing that, inform those persons of, or provide them with, the means of familiarising themselves with their prospective benefit entitlement.

52(2) For the purposes of applying paragraph 1, the Administrative Commission shall determine the elements of information to be exchanged or made available and shall establish the appropriate procedures and mechanisms, taking account of the characteristics, administrative and technical organisation, and the technological means at the disposal of national pension schemes. The Administrative Commission shall ensure the implementation of those pension schemes by organising a follow-up to the measures taken and their application.

52(3) For the purposes of applying paragraph 1, the institution in the first Member State where a person is allocated a Personal Identification Number (PIN) for the purposes of social security administration should be provided with the information referred to in this Article.

ART. 53 Coordination measures in Member States

53(1) Without prejudice to Article 51 of the basic Regulation, where national legislation includes rules for determining the institution responsible or the scheme applicable or for designating periods of insurance to a specific scheme, those rules shall be applied, taking into account only periods of insurance completed under the legislation of the Member State concerned.

53(2) Where national legislation includes rules for the coordination of special schemes for civil servants and the general scheme for employed persons, those rules shall not be affected by the provisions of the basic Regulation and of the implementing Regulation.

Chapter V – Unemployment benefits

ART. 54 Aggregation of periods and calculation of benefits

54(1) Article 12(1) of the implementing Regulation shall apply *mutatis mutandis* to Article 61 of the basic Regulation. Without prejudice to the underlying obligations of the institutions involved, the person concerned may submit to the competent institution a document issued by the institution of the Member State to whose legislation he was subject in respect of his last activity as an employed or self-employed person specifying the periods completed under that legislation.

54(2) For the purposes of applying Article 62(3) of the basic Regulation, the competent institution of the Member State to whose legislation the person concerned was subject in respect of his/her last activity as an employed or self-employed person shall, without delay, at the request of the institution of the place of residence, provide it with all the information necessary to calculate unemployment benefits which can be obtained in the Member State where it is situated, in particular the salary or professional income received.

54(3) For the purposes of applying Article 62 of the basic Regulation and notwithstanding Article 63 thereof, the competent institution of a Member State whose legislation provides that the calculation of benefits varies with the number of members of the family shall also take into account the members of the family of the person concerned residing in another Member State as if they resided in the competent Member State. This provision shall not apply where, in the Member State of residence of members of the family, another person is entitled to unemployment benefits calculated on the basis of the number of members of the family.

History – Art. 54(2) substituted by Reg. 465/2012, art. 2(4), with effect from 28 June 2012.

ART. 55 Conditions and restrictions on the retention of the entitlement to benefits for unemployed persons going to another Member State

55(1) In order to be covered by Article 64 or Article 65a of the basic Regulation, the unemployed person going to another Member State shall inform the competent institution prior to his/her departure and request a document certifying that he/she retains his/her entitlement to benefits under the conditions laid down in Article 64(1)(b) of the basic Regulation.

That institution shall inform the person concerned of his obligations and shall provide the abovementioned document which shall include the following information:

(a) the date on which the unemployed person ceased to be available to the employment services of the competent State;

(b) the period granted in accordance with Article 64(1)(b) of the basic Regulation in order to register as a person seeking work in the Member State to which the unemployed person has gone;

(c) the maximum period during which the entitlement to benefits may be retained in accordance with Article 64(1)(c) of the basic Regulation;

(d) circumstances likely to affect the entitlement to benefits.

55(2) The unemployed person shall register as a person seeking work with the employment services of the Member State to which he goes in accordance with Article 64(1)(b) of the basic Regulation and shall provide the document referred to in paragraph 1 to the institution of that Member State. If he has informed the competent institution in accordance with paragraph 1 but fails to provide this document, the institution in the Member State to which the unemployed person has gone shall contact the competent institution in order to obtain the necessary information.

55(3) The employment services in the Member State to which the unemployed person has gone to seek employment shall inform the unemployed person of his obligations.

55(4) The institution in the Member State to which the unemployed person has gone shall immediately send a document to the competent institution containing the date on which the unemployed person registered with the employment services and his new address.

If, in the period during which the unemployed person retains entitlement to benefits, any circumstance likely to affect the entitlement to benefits arises, the institution in the Member State to which the unemployed person has gone shall send immediately to the competent institution and to the person concerned a document containing the relevant information.

At the request of the competent institution, the institution in the Member State to which the unemployed person has gone shall provide relevant information on a monthly basis concerning the follow-up of the unemployed person's situation, in particular whether the latter is still registered with the employment services and is complying with organised checking procedures.

55(5) The institution in the Member State to which the unemployed person has gone shall carry out or arrange for checks to be carried out, as if the person concerned were an unemployed person obtaining benefits under its own legislation. Where necessary, it shall immediately inform the competent institution if any circumstances referred to in paragraph 1(d) arise.

55(6) The competent authorities or competent institutions of two or more Member States may agree amongst themselves specific procedures and time-limits concerning the follow-up of the unemployed person's situation as well as other measures to facilitate the job-seeking activities of unemployed persons who go to one of those Member States under Article 64 of the basic Regulation.

55(7) Paragraphs 2 to 6 shall apply mutatis mutandis to the situation covered by Article 65a(3) of the basic Regulation.

History – Art. 55(1) substituted by Reg. 465/2012, art. 2(5)(a), with effect from 28 June 2012.
Art. 55(7) inserted by Reg. 465/2012, art. 2(5)(b), with effect from 28 June 2012.

ART. 56 Unemployed persons who resided in a Member State other than the competent Member State

56(1) Where the unemployed person decides, in accordance with Article 65(2) or Article 65a(1) of the basic Regulation, to make himself/herself also available to the employment services in the Member State not providing the benefits, by registering there as a person seeking work, he/she shall inform the institution and the employment services of the Member State providing the benefits.

At the request of the employment services of the Member State not providing the benefits, the employment services in the Member State that is providing the benefits shall send the relevant information concerning the unemployed person's registration and his/her search for employment.

56(2) Where the legislation applicable in the Member States concerned requires the fulfilment of certain obligations and/or job-seeking activities by the unemployed person, the obligations and/or job-seeking activities by the unemployed person in the Member State providing the benefits shall have priority.

The non-fulfilment by the unemployed person of all the obligations and/or job-seeking activities in the Member State which does not provide the benefits shall not affect the benefits awarded in the other Member State.

56(3) For the purposes of applying Article 65(5)(b) of the basic Regulation, the institution of the Member State to whose legislation the worker was last subject shall inform the institution of the place of residence, when requested to do so by the latter, whether the worker is entitled to benefits under Article 64 of the basic Regulation.

History – Art. 56(1) and (2) substituted by Reg. 465/2012, art. 2(6), with effect from 28 June 2012.

ART. 57 Provisions for the application of Articles 61, 62, 64 and 65 of the basic Regulation regarding persons covered by a special scheme for civil servants

57(1) Articles 54 and 55 of the implementing Regulation shall apply *mutatis mutandis* to persons covered by a special unemployment scheme for civil servants.

57(2) Article 56 of the implementing Regulation shall not apply to persons covered by a special unemployment scheme for civil servants. An unemployed person who is covered by a special unemployment scheme for civil servants, who is partially or wholly unemployed, and who, during his last employment, was residing in the territory of a Member State other than the competent State, shall receive the benefits under the special unemployment scheme for civil servants in accordance with the provisions of the legislation of the competent Member State as if he were residing in the territory of that Member State. Those benefits shall be provided by the competent institution, at its expense.

Chapter VI – Family benefits

ART. 58 Priority rules in the event of overlapping

58 For the purposes of applying Article 68(1)(b)(i) and (ii) of the basic Regulation, where the order of priority cannot be established on the basis of the children's place of residence, each Member State concerned shall calculate the amount of benefits including the children not resident within its own territory. In the event of applying Article 68(1)(b)(i), the competent institution of the Member State whose legislation provides for the highest level of benefits shall pay the full amount of such benefits and be reimbursed half this sum by the competent institution of the other Member State up to the limit of the amount provided for in the legislation of the latter Member State.

ART. 59 Rules applicable where the applicable legislation and/or the competence to grant family benefits changes

59(1) Where the applicable legislation and/or the competence to grant family benefits change between Member States during a calendar month, irrespective of the payment dates of family benefits under the legislation of those Member States, the institution which has paid the family benefits by virtue of the legislation under which the benefits have been granted at the beginning of that month shall continue to do so until the end of the month in progress.

59(2) It shall inform the institution of the other Member State or Member States concerned of the date on which it ceases to pay the family benefits in question. Payment of benefits from the other Member State or Member States concerned shall take effect from that date.

ART. 60 Procedure for applying Articles 67 and 68 of the basic Regulation

60(1) The application for family benefits shall be addressed to the competent institution. For the purposes of applying Articles 67 and 68 of the basic Regulation, the situation of the whole family shall be taken into account as if all the persons involved were subject to the legislation of the Member State concerned and residing there, in particular as regards a person's entitlement to claim such benefits. Where a person entitled to claim the benefits does not exercise his right, an application for family benefits submitted by the other parent, a person treated as a parent, or a person or institution acting as guardian of the child or children, shall be taken into account by the competent institution of the Member State whose legislation is applicable.

60(2) The institution to which an application is made in accordance with paragraph 1 shall examine the application on the basis of the detailed information supplied by the applicant, taking into account the overall factual and legal situation of the applicant's family.

If that institution concludes that its legislation is applicable by priority right in accordance with Article 68(1) and (2) of the basic Regulation, it shall provide the family benefits according to the legislation it applies.

If it appears to that institution that there may be an entitlement to a differential supplement by virtue of the legislation of another Member State in accordance with Article 68(2) of the basic Regulation, that institution shall forward the application, without delay, to the competent institution of the other Member State and inform the person concerned; moreover, it shall inform the institution of the other Member State of its decision on the application and the amount of family benefits paid.

60(3) Where the institution to which the application is made concludes that its legislation is applicable, but not by priority right in accordance with Article 68(1) and (2) of the basic Regulation, it shall take a provisional decision, without delay, on the priority rules to be applied and shall forward the application, in accordance with Article 68(3) of the basic Regulation, to the institution of the other Member State, and shall also inform the applicant thereof. That institution shall take a position on the provisional decision within two months.

If the institution to which the application was forwarded does not take a position within two months of the receipt of the application, the provisional decision referred to above shall apply and the institution shall pay the benefits provided for under its legislation and inform the institution to which the application was made of the amount of benefits paid.

60(4) Where there is a difference of views between the institutions concerned about which legislation is applicable by priority right, Article 6(2) to (5) of the implementing Regulation shall apply. For this purpose the institution of the place of residence referred to in Article 6(2) of the implementing Regulation shall be the institution of the child's or childrens' place of residence.

60(5) If the institution which has supplied benefits on a provisional basis has paid more than the amount for which it is ultimately responsible, it may claim reimbursement of the excess from the institution with primary responsibility in accordance with the procedure laid down in Article 73 of the implementing Regulation.

ART. 61 Procedure for applying Article 69 of the basic Regulation

61 For the purposes of applying Article 69 of the basic Regulation, the Administrative Commission shall draw up a list of the additional or special family benefits for orphans covered by that Article. If there is no provision for the institution competent to grant, by priority right, such additional or special family benefits for orphans under the legislation it applies, it shall without delay forward any application for family benefits, together with all relevant documents and information, to the institution of the Member State to whose legislation the person concerned has been subject, for the longest period of time and which provides such additional or special family benefits for orphans. In some cases, this may mean referring back, under the same conditions, to the institution of the Member State under whose legislation the person concerned has completed the shortest of his or her insurance or residence periods.

TITLE IV – FINANCIAL PROVISIONS

Chapter I – Reimbursement of the cost of benefits in application of Article 35 and Article 41 of the basic Regulation

Section 1 – Reimbursement on the basis of actual expenditure

ART. 62 Principles

62(1) For the purposes of applying Article 35 and Article 41 of the basic Regulation, the actual amount of the expenses for benefits in kind, as shown in the accounts of the institution that provided them, shall be reimbursed to that institution by the competent institution, except where Article 63 of the implementing Regulation is applicable.

62(2) If any or part of the actual amount of the expenses for benefits referred to in paragraph 1 is not shown in the accounts of the institution that provided them, the amount to be refunded shall be determined on the basis of a lump-sum payment calculated from all the appropriate references obtained from the data available. The Administrative Commission shall assess the bases to be used for calculation of the lump-sum payment and shall decide the amount thereof.

62(3) Higher rates than those applicable to the benefits in kind provided to insured persons subject to the legislation applied by the institution providing the benefits referred to in paragraph 1 may not be taken into account in the reimbursement.

Section 2 – Reimbursement on the basis of fixed amounts

ART. 63 Identification of the Member States concerned

63(1) The Member States referred to in Article 35(2) of the basic Regulation, whose legal or administrative structures are such that the use of reimbursement on the basis of actual expenditure is not appropriate, are listed in Annex 3 to the implementing Regulation.

63(2) In the case of the Member States listed in Annex 3 to the implementing Regulation, the amount of benefits in kind supplied to:

(a) family members who do not reside in the same Member State as the insured person, as provided for in Article 17 of the basic Regulation; and to

(b) pensioners and members of their family, as provided for in Article 24(1) and Articles 25 and 26 of the basic Regulation;

shall be reimbursed by the competent institutions to the institutions providing those benefits, on the basis of a fixed amount established for each calendar year. This fixed amount shall be as close as possible to actual expenditure.

ART. 64 Calculation method of the monthly fixed amounts and the total fixed amount

64(1) For each creditor Member State, the monthly fixed amount per person (Fi) for a calendar year shall be determined by dividing the annual average cost per person (Yi), broken down by age group (i), by 12 and by applying a reduction (X) to the result in accordance with the following formula:

$F_i = Y_i \times 1/12 \times (1 - X)$

where:

– the index (i = 1, 2 and 3) represents the three age groups used for calculating the fixed amounts:
  i = 1: persons aged under 20,
  i = 2: persons aged from 20 to 64,
  i = 3: persons aged 65 and over,

– Y_i represents the annual average cost per person in age group i, as defined in paragraph 2,

– the coefficient X (0,20 or 0,15) represents the reduction as defined in paragraph 3,

64(2) The annual average cost per person (Y_i) in age group i shall be obtained by dividing the annual expenditure on all benefits in kind provided by the institutions of the creditor Member State to all persons in the age group concerned subject to its legislation and residing within its territory by the average number of persons concerned in that age group in the calendar year in question. The calculation shall be based on the expenditure under the schemes referred to in Article 23 of the implementing Regulation.

64(3) The reduction to be applied to the monthly fixed amount shall, in principle, be equal to 20 % (X = 0,20). It shall be equal to 15 % (X = 0,15) for pensioners and members of their family where the competent Member State is not listed in Annex IV to the basic Regulation.

64(4) For each debtor Member State, the total fixed amount for a calendar year shall be the sum of the products obtained by multiplying, in each age group i, the determined monthly fixed amounts per person by the number of months completed by the persons concerned in the creditor Member State in that age group.

The number of months completed by the persons concerned in the creditor Member State shall be the sum of the calendar months in a calendar year during which the persons concerned were, because of their residence in the territory of the creditor Member State, eligible to receive benefits in kind in that territory at the expense of the debtor Member State. Those months shall be determined from an inventory kept for that purpose by the institution of the place of residence, based on documentary evidence of the entitlement of the beneficiaries supplied by the competent institution.

64(5) No later than 1 May 2015, the Administrative Commission shall present a specific report on the application of this Article and in particular on the reductions referred to in paragraph 3. On the basis of that report, the Administrative Commission may present a proposal containing any amendments which may prove necessary in order to ensure that the calculation of fixed amounts comes as close as possible to the actual expenditure incurred and the reductions referred to in paragraph 3 do not result in unbalanced payments or double payments for the Member States.

64(6) The Administrative Commission shall establish the methods for determining the elements for calculating the fixed amounts referred to in paragraphs 1 to 5.

64(7) Notwithstanding paragraphs 1 to 4, Member States may continue to apply Articles 94 and 95 of Regulation (EEC) No 574/72 for the calculation of the fixed amount until 1 May 2015, provided that the reduction set out in paragraph 3 is applied.

ART. 65 Notification of annual average costs

65(1) The annual average cost per person in each age group for a specific year shall be notified to the Audit Board at the latest by the end of the second year following the year in question. If the notification is not made by this deadline, the annual average cost per person which the Administrative Commission has last determined for a previous year will be taken.

65(2) The annual average costs determined in accordance with paragraph 1 shall be published each year in the *Official Journal of the European Union*.

Section 3 – Common provisions

ART. 66 Procedure for reimbursement between institutions

66(1) The reimbursements between the Member States concerned shall be made as promptly as possible. Every institution concerned shall be obliged to reimburse claims before the deadlines mentioned in this Section, as soon as it is in a position to do so. A dispute concerning a particular claim shall not hinder the reimbursement of another claim or other claims.

66(2) The reimbursements between the institutions of the Member States, provided for in Articles 35 and 41 of the basic Regulation, shall be made via the liaison body. There may be a separate liaison body for reimbursements under Article 35 and Article 41 of the basic Regulation.

ART. 67 Deadlines for the introduction and settlement of claims

67(1) Claims based on actual expenditure shall be introduced to the liaison body of the debtor Member State within 12 months of the end of the calendar half-year during which those claims were recorded in the accounts of the creditor institution.

67(2) Claims of fixed amounts for a calendar year shall be introduced to the liaison body of the debtor Member State within the 12-month period following the month during which the average costs for the year concerned were published in the *Official Journal of the European Union*. The inventories referred to Article 64(4) of the implementing Regulation shall be presented by the end of the year following the reference year.

67(3) In the case referred to in Article 6(5) second subparagraph of the implementing Regulation, the deadline set out in paragraphs 1 and 2 of this Article shall not start before the competent institution has been identified.

67(4) Claims introduced after the deadlines specified in paragraphs 1 and 2 shall not be considered.

67(5) The claims shall be paid to the liaison body of the creditor Member State referred to in Article 66 of the implementing Regulation by the debtor institution within 18 months of the end of the month during which they were introduced to the liaison body of the debtor Member State. This does not apply to the claims which the debtor institution has rejected for a relevant reason within that period.

67(6) Any disputes concerning a claim shall be settled, at the latest, within 36 months following the month in which the claim was introduced.

67(7) The Audit Board shall facilitate the final closing of accounts in cases where a settlement cannot be reached within the period set out in paragraph 6, and, upon a reasoned request by one of the parties, shall give its opinion on a dispute within six months following the month in which the matter was referred to it.

ART. 68 Interest on late payments and down payments

68(1) From the end of the 18-month period set out in Article 67(5) of the implementing Regulation, interest can be charged by the creditor institution on outstanding claims, unless the debtor institution has made, within six months of the end of the month during which the claim was introduced, a down payment of at least 90 % of the total claim introduced pursuant to Article 67(1) or (2) of the implementing Regulation. For those parts of the claim not covered by the down payment, interest may be charged only from the end of the 36-month period set out in Article 67(6) of the implementing Regulation.

68(2) The interest shall be calculated on the basis of the reference rate applied by the European Central Bank to its main refinancing operations. The reference rate applicable shall be that in force on the first day of the month on which the payment is due.

68(3) No liaison body shall be obliged to accept a down payment as provided for in paragraph 1. If however, a liaison body declines such an offer, the creditor institution shall no longer be entitled to charge interest on late payments related to the claims in question other than under the second sentence of paragraph 1.

ART. 69 Statement of annual accounts

69(1) The Administrative Commission shall establish the claims situation for each calendar year in accordance with Article 72(g) of the basic Regulation, on the basis of the Audit Board's report. To this end, the liaison bodies shall notify the Audit Board, by the deadlines and according to the procedures laid down by the latter, of the amount of the claims introduced, settled or contested (creditor position) and the amount of claims received, settled or contested (debtor position).

69(2) The Administrative Commission may perform any appropriate checks on the statistical and accounting data used as the basis for drawing up the annual statement of claims provided for in paragraph 1 in order, in particular, to ensure that they comply with the rules laid down under this Title.

Chapter II – Reimbursement of unemployment benefits pursuant to Article 65 of the basic Regulation

ART. 70 Reimbursement of unemployment benefits

70 If there is no agreement in accordance with Article 65(8) of the basic Regulation, the institution of the place of residence shall request reimbursement of unemployment benefits pursuant to Article 65(6) and (7) of the basic Regulation from the institution of the Member State to whose legislation the beneficiary was last subject. The request shall be made within six months of the end of the calendar half-year during which the last payment of unemployment benefit, for which reimbursement is requested, was made. The request shall indicate the amount of benefit paid during the three or five month-period referred to in Article 65(6) and (7) of the basic Regulation, the period for which the benefits were paid and the identification data of the unemployed person. The claims shall be introduced and paid via the liaison bodies of the Member States concerned.

There is no requirement to consider requests introduced after the time-limit referred to in the first paragraph. Articles 66(1) and 67(5) to (7) of the implementing Regulation shall apply *mutatis mutandis*.

From the end of the 18-month period referred to in Article 67(5) of the implementing Regulation, interest may be charged by the creditor institution on outstanding claims. The interest shall be calculated in accordance with Article 68(2) of the implementing Regulation.

The maximum amount of the reimbursement referred to in the third sentence of Article 65(6) of the basic Regulation is in each individual case the amount of the benefit to which a person concerned would be entitled according to the legislation of the Member State to which he was last subject if registered with the employment services of that Member State. However, in relations between the Member States listed in Annex 5 to the implementing Regulation, the competent institutions of one of those Member States to whose legislation the person concerned was last subject shall determine the maximum amount in each individual case on the basis of the average amount of unemployment benefits provided under the legislation of that Member State in the preceding calendar year.

Chapter III – Recovery of benefits provided but not due, recovery of provisional payments and contributions, offsetting and assistance with recovery

Section 1 – Principles

ART. 71 Common provisions

71 For the purposes of applying Article 84 of the basic Regulation and within the framework defined therein, the recovery of claims shall, wherever possible, be by way of offsetting either between the institutions of Member States concerned, or vis-à-vis the natural or legal person concerned in accordance with Articles 72 to 74 of the implementing Regulation. If it is not possible to recover all or any of the claim via this offsetting procedure, the remainder of the amount due shall be recovered in accordance with Articles 75 to 85 of the implementing Regulation.

Section 2 – Offsetting

ART. 72 Benefits received unduly

72(1) If the institution of a Member State has paid undue benefits to a person, that institution may, within the terms and limits laid down in the legislation it applies, request the institution of any other Member State responsible for paying benefits to the person concerned to deduct the undue amount from arrears or on-going payments owed to the person concerned regardless of the social security branch under which the benefit is paid. The institution of the latter Member State shall deduct the amount concerned subject to the conditions and limits applying to this kind of offsetting procedure in accordance with the legislation it applies in the same way as if it had made the overpayments itself, and shall transfer the amount deducted to the institution that has paid undue benefits.

72(2) By way of derogation from paragraph 1, if, when awarding or reviewing benefits in respect of invalidity benefits, old-age and survivors' pensions pursuant to Chapter 4 and 5 of Title III of the basic Regulation, the institution of a Member State has paid to a person benefits of undue sum, that institution may request the institution of any other Member State responsible for the payment of corresponding benefits to the person concerned to deduct the amount overpaid from the arrears payable to the person concerned. After the latter institution has informed the institution that has paid an undue sum of these arrears, the institution which has paid the undue sum shall within two months communicate the amount of the undue sum. If the institution which is due to pay arrears receives that communication within the deadline it shall transfer the amount deducted to the institution which has paid undue sums. If the deadline expires, that institution shall without delay pay out the arrears to the person concerned.

72(3) If a person has received social welfare assistance in one Member State during a period in which he was entitled to benefits under the legislation of another Member State, the body which provided the assistance may, if it is legally entitled to reclaim the benefits due to the person concerned, request the institution of any other Member State responsible for paying benefits in favour of the person concerned to deduct the amount of assistance paid from the amounts which that Member State pays to the person concerned.

This provision shall apply *mutatis mutandis* to any family member of a person concerned who has received assistance in the territory of a Member State during a period in which the insured person was entitled to benefits under the legislation of another Member State in respect of that family member.

The institution of a Member State which has paid an undue amount of assistance shall send a statement of the amount due to the institution of the other Member State, which shall then deduct the amount, subject to the conditions and limits laid down for this kind of offsetting procedure in accordance with the legislation it applies, and transfer the amount without delay to the institution that has paid the undue amount.

ART. 73 Provisionally paid benefits in cash or contributions

73(1) For the purposes of applying Article 6 of the implementing Regulation, at the latest three months after the applicable legislation has been determined or the institution responsible for paying the benefits has been identified, the institution which provisionally paid the cash benefits shall draw up a statement of the amount provisionally paid and shall send it to the institution identified as being competent.

The institution identified as being competent for paying the benefits shall deduct the amount due in respect of the provisional payment from the arrears of the corresponding benefits it owes to the person concerned and shall without delay transfer the amount deducted to the institution which provisionally paid the cash benefits.

If the amount of provisionally paid benefits exceeds the amount of arrears, or if arrears do not exist, the institution identified as being competent shall deduct this amount from ongoing payments subject to the conditions and limits applying to this kind of offsetting procedure under the legislation it applies, and without delay transfer the amount deducted to the institution which provisionally paid the cash benefits.

73(2) The institution which has provisionally received contributions from a legal and/or natural person shall not reimburse the amounts in question to the person who paid them until it has ascertained from the institution identified as being competent the sums due to it under Article 6(4) of the implementing Regulation.

Upon request of the institution identified as being competent, which shall be made at the latest three months after the applicable legislation has been determined, the institution that has provisionally received contributions shall transfer them to the institution identified as being competent for that period for the purpose of settling the situation concerning the contributions owed by the legal and/or natural person to it. The contributions transferred shall be retroactively deemed as having been paid to the institution identified as being competent.

If the amount of provisionally paid contributions exceeds the amount the legal and/or natural person owes to the institution identified as being competent, the institution which provisionally received contributions shall reimburse the amount in excess to the legal and/or natural person concerned.

ART. 74 Costs related to offsetting

74 No costs are payable where the debt is recovered via the offsetting procedure provided for in Articles 72 and 73 of the implementing Regulation.

Section 3 – Recovery

ART. 75 Definitions and common provisions

75(1) For the purposes of this Section:

- **"claim"** means all claims relating to contributions or to benefits paid or provided unduly, including interest, fines, administrative penalties and all other charges and costs connected with the claim in accordance with the legislation of the Member State making the claim;
- **"applicant party"** means, in respect of each Member State, any institution which makes a request for information, notification or recovery concerning a claim as defined above,
- **"requested party"** means, in respect of each Member State, any institution to which a request for information, notification or recovery can be made,

75(2) Requests and any related communications between the Member States shall, in general, be addressed via designated institutions.

75(3) Practical implementation measures, including, among others, those related to Article 4 of the implementing Regulation and to setting a minimum threshold for the amounts for which a request for recovery can be made, shall be taken by the Administrative Commission.

ART. 76 Requests for information

76(1) At the request of the applicant party, the requested party shall provide any information which would be useful to the applicant party in the recovery of its claim.

In order to obtain that information, the requested party shall make use of the powers provided for under the laws, regulations or administrative provisions applying to the recovery of similar claims arising in its own Member State.

76(2) The request for information shall indicate the name, last known address, and any other relevant information relating to the identification of the legal or natural person concerned to whom the information to be provided relates and the nature and amount of the claim in respect of which the request is made.

76(3) The requested party shall not be obliged to supply information:

(a) which it would not be able to obtain for the purpose of recovering similar claims arising in its own Member State;

(b) which would disclose any commercial, industrial or professional secrets; or

(c) the disclosure of which would be liable to prejudice the security of or be contrary to the public policy of the Member State.

76(4) The requested party shall inform the applicant party of the grounds for refusing a request for information.

ART. 77 Notification

77(1) The requested party shall, at the request of the applicant party, and in accordance with the rules in force for the notification of similar instruments or decisions in its own Member State, notify the addressee of all instruments and decisions, including those of a judicial nature, which come from the Member State of the applicant party and which relate to a claim and/or to its recovery.

77(2) The request for notification shall indicate the name, address and any other relevant information relating to the identification of the addressee concerned to which the applicant party normally has access, the nature and the subject of the instrument or decision to be notified and, if necessary the name, address and any other relevant information relating to the identification of the debtor and the claim to which the instrument or decision relates, and any other useful information.

77(3) The requested party shall without delay inform the applicant party of the action taken on its request for notification and, particularly, of the date on which the decision or instrument was forwarded to the addressee.

ART. 78 Request for recovery

78(1) The request for recovery of a claim, addressed by the applicant party to the requested party, shall be accompanied by an official or certified copy of the instrument permitting its enforcement, issued in the Member State of the applicant party and, if appropriate, by the original or a certified copy of other documents necessary for recovery.

78(2) The applicant party may only make a request for recovery if:

(a) the claim and/or the instrument permitting its enforcement are not contested in its own Member State, except in cases where the second subparagraph of Article 81(2) of the implementing Regulation is applied;

(b) it has, in its own Member State, applied appropriate recovery procedures available to it on the basis of the instrument referred to in paragraph 1, and the measures taken will not result in the payment in full of the claim;

(c) the period of limitation according to its own legislation has not expired.

78(3) The request for recovery shall indicate:

(a) the name, address and any other relevant information relating to the identification of the natural or legal person concerned and/or to the third party holding his or her assets;

(b) the name, address and any other relevant information relating to the identification of the applicant party;

(c) a reference to the instrument permitting its enforcement, issued in the Member State of the applicant party;

(d) the nature and amount of the claim, including the principal, the interest, fines, administrative penalties and all other charges and costs due indicated in the currencies of the Member States of the applicant and requested parties;

(e) the date of notification of the instrument to the addressee by the applicant party and/or by the requested party;

(f) the date from which and the period during which enforcement is possible under the laws in force in the Member State of the applicant party;

(g) any other relevant information.

78(4) The request for recovery shall also contain a declaration by the applicant party confirming that the conditions laid down in paragraph 2 have been fulfilled.

78(5) The applicant party shall forward to the requesting party any relevant information relating to the matter which gave rise to the request for recovery, as soon as this comes to its knowledge.

ART. 79 Instrument permitting enforcement of the recovery

79(1) In accordance with Article 84(2) of the basic Regulation, the instrument permitting enforcement of the claim shall be directly recognised and treated automatically as an instrument permitting the enforcement of a claim of the Member State of the requested party.

79(2) Notwithstanding paragraph 1, the instrument permitting enforcement of the claim may, where appropriate and in accordance with the provisions in force in the Member State of the requested party, be accepted as, recognised as, supplemented with, or replaced by an instrument authorising enforcement in the territory of that Member State.

Within three months of the date of receipt of the request for recovery, Member States shall endeavour to complete the acceptance, recognition, supplementing or replacement, except in cases where the third subparagraph of this paragraph applies. Member States may not refuse to complete these actions where the instrument permitting enforcement is properly drawn up. The requested party shall inform the applicant party of the grounds for exceeding the three-month period.

If any of these actions should give rise to a dispute in connection with the claim and/or the instrument permitting enforcement issued by the applicant party, Article 81 of the implementing Regulation shall apply.

ART. 80 Payment arrangements and deadlines

80(1) Claims shall be recovered in the currency of the Member State of the requested party. The entire amount of the claim that is recovered by the requested party shall be remitted by the requested party to the applicant party.

80(2) The requested party may, where the laws, regulations or administrative provisions in force in its own Member State so permit, and after consulting the applicant party, allow the debtor time to pay or authorise payment by instalment. Any interest charged by the requested party in respect of such extra time to pay shall also be remitted to the applicant party.

From the date on which the instrument permitting enforcement of the recovery of the claim has been directly recognised in accordance with Article 79(1) of the implementing Regulation, or accepted, recognised, supplemented or replaced in accordance with Article 79(2) of the implementing Regulation, interest shall be charged for late payment under the laws, regulations and administrative provisions in force in the Member State of the requested party and shall also be remitted to the applicant party.

ART. 81 Contestation concerning the claim or the instrument permitting enforcement of its recovery and contestation concerning enforcement measures

81(1) If, in the course of the recovery procedure, the claim and/or the instrument permitting its enforcement issued in the Member State of the applicant party are contested by an interested party, the action shall be brought by this party before the appropriate authorities of the Member State of the applicant party, in accordance with the laws in force in that Member State. The applicant party shall without delay notify the requested party of this action. The interested party may also inform the requested party of the action.

81(2) As soon as the requested party has received the notification or information referred to in paragraph 1 either from the applicant party or from the interested party, it shall suspend the enforcement procedure pending the decision of the appropriate authority in the matter, unless the applicant party requests other wise in accordance with the second subparagraph of this paragraph. Should the requested party deem it necessary, and without prejudice to Article 84 of the implementing Regulation, it may take precautionary measures to guarantee recovery insofar as the laws or regulations in force in its own Member State allow such action for similar claims.

Notwithstanding the first subparagraph, the applicant party may, in accordance with the laws, regulations and administrative practices in force in its own Member State, request the requested party to recover a contested claim, in so far as the relevant laws, regulations and administrative practices in force in the requested party's Member State allow such action. If the result of the contestation is subsequently favourable to the debtor, the applicant party shall be liable for the reimbursement of any sums recovered, together with any compensation due, in accordance with the legislation in force in the requested party's Member State.

81(3) Where the contestation concerns enforcement measures taken in the Member State of the requested party, the action shall be brought before the appropriate authority of that Member State in accordance with its laws and regulations.

81(4) Where the appropriate authority before which the action is brought in accordance with paragraph 1 is a judicial or administrative tribunal, the decision of that tribunal, insofar as it is favourable to the applicant party and permits recovery of the claim in the Member State of the applicant party, shall constitute the "instrument permitting enforcement" within the meaning of Articles 78 and 79 of the implementing Regulation and the recovery of the claim shall proceed on the basis of that decision.

ART. 82 Limits applying to assistance

82(1) The requested party shall not be obliged:

(a) to grant the assistance provided for in Articles 78 to 81 of the implementing Regulation if recovery of the claim would, because of the situation of the debtor, create serious economic or social difficulties in the Member State of the requested party, insofar as the laws, regulations or administrative practices in force in the Member State of the requested party allow such action for similar national claims;

(b) to grant the assistance provided for in Articles 76 to 81 of the implementing Regulation, if the initial request under Articles 76 to 78 of the implementing Regulation applies to claims more than five years old, dating from the moment the instrument permitting the recovery was established in accordance with the laws, regulations or administrative practices in force in the Member State of the applicant party at the date of the request. However, if the claim or instrument is contested, the time limit begins from the moment that the Member State of the applicant party establishes that the claim or the enforcement order permitting recovery may no longer be contested.

82(2) The requested party shall inform the applicant party of the grounds for refusing a request for assistance.

ART. 83 Periods of limitation

83(1) Questions concerning periods of limitation shall be governed as follows:

(a) by the laws in force in the Member State of the applicant party, insofar as they concern the claim and/or the instrument permitting its enforcement; and

(b) by the laws in force in the Member State of the requested party, insofar as they concern enforcement measures in the requested Member State.

Periods of limitation according to the laws in force in the Member State of the requested party shall start from the date of direct recognition or from the date of acceptance, recognition, supplementing or replacement in accordance with Article 79 of the implementing Regulation.

83(2) Steps taken in the recovery of claims by the requested party in pursuance of a request for assistance, which, if they had been carried out by the applicant party, would have had the effect of suspending or interrupting the period of limitation according to the laws in force in the Member State of the applicant party, shall be deemed to have been taken in the latter State, in so far as that effect is concerned.

ART. 84 Precautionary measures

84 Upon reasoned request by the applicant party, the requested party shall take precautionary measures to ensure recovery of a claim in so far as the laws and regulations in force in the Member State of the requested party so permit.

For the purposes of implementing the first paragraph, the provisions and procedures laid down in Articles 78, 79, 81 and 82 of the implementing Regulation shall apply *mutatis mutandis*.

ART. 85 Costs related to recovery

85(1) The requested party shall recover from the natural or legal person concerned and retain any costs linked to recovery which it incurs, in accordance with the laws and regulations of the Member State of the requested party that apply to similar claims.

85(2) Mutual assistance afforded under this Section shall, as a rule, be free of charge. However, where recovery poses a specific problem or concerns a very large amount in costs, the applicant and the requested parties may agree on reimbursement arrangements specific to the cases in question.

85(3) The Member State of the applicant party shall remain liable to the Member State of the requested party for any costs and any losses incurred as a result of actions held to be unfounded, as far as either the substance of the claim or the validity of the instrument issued by the applicant party is concerned.

Cross references – Decision No R1 of 20 June 2013: interpretation of art. 85.

ART. 86 Review clause

86(1) No later than the fourth full calendar year after the entry into force of the implementing Regulation, the Administrative Commission shall present a comparative report on the time limits set out in Article 67(2), (5) and (6) of the implementing Regulation.

On the basis of this report, the European Commission may, as appropriate, submit proposals to review these time limits with the aim of reducing them in a significant way.

86(2) No later than the date referred to in paragraph 1, the Administrative Commission shall also assess the rules for conversion of periods set out in Article 13 with a view to simplifying those rules, if possible.

86(3) No later than 1 May 2015, the Administrative Commission shall present a report specifically assessing the application of Chapters I and III of Title IV of the implementing Regulation, in particular with regard to the procedures and time limits referred to in Article 67(2), (5) and (6) of the implementing Regulation and to the recovery procedures referred to in Articles 75 to 85 of the implementing Regulation. In the light of this report, the European Commission may, if necessary, submit appropriate proposals to make these procedures more efficient and balanced.

TITLE V – MISCELLANEOUS, TRANSITIONAL AND FINAL PROVISIONS

ART. 87 Medical examination and administrative checks

87(1) Without prejudice to other provisions, where a recipient or a claimant of benefits, or a member of his family, is staying or residing within the territory of a Member State other than that in which the debtor institution is located, the medical examination shall be carried out, at the request of that institution, by the institution of the beneficiary's place of stay or residence in accordance with the procedures laid down by the legislation applied by that institution.

The debtor institution shall inform the institution of the place of stay or residence of any special requirements, if necessary, to be followed and points to be covered by the medical examination.

87(2) The institution of the place of stay or residence shall forward a report to the debtor institution that requested the medical examination. This institution shall be bound by the findings of the institution of the place of stay or residence.

The debtor institution shall reserve the right to have the beneficiary examined by a doctor of its choice. However, the beneficiary may be asked to return to the Member State of the debtor institution only if he or she is able to make the journey without prejudice to his health and the cost of travel and accommodation is paid for by the debtor institution.

87(3) Where a recipient or a claimant of benefits, or a member of his family, is staying or residing in the territory of a Member State other than that in which the debtor institution is located, the administrative check shall, at the request of the debtor institution, be performed by the institution of the beneficiary's place of stay or residence.

Paragraph 2 shall also apply in this case.

87(4) Paragraphs 2 and 3 shall also apply in determining or checking the state of dependence of a recipient or a claimant of the long-term care benefits mentioned in Article 34 of the basic Regulation.

87(5) The competent authorities or competent institutions of two or more Member States may agree specific provisions and procedures to improve fully or partly the labour-market readiness of claimants and recipients and their participation in any schemes or programmes available in the Member State of stay or residence for that purpose.

87(6) As an exception to the principle of free-of-charge mutual administrative cooperation in Article 76(2) of the basic Regulation, the effective amount of the expenses of the checks referred to in paragraphs 1 to 5 shall be refunded to the institution which was requested to carry them out by the debtor institution which requested them.

ART. 88 Notifications

88(1) The Member States shall notify the European Commission of the details of the bodies defined in Article 1(m), (q) and (r) of the basic Regulation and Article 1(2)(a) and (b) of the implementing Regulation, and of the institutions designated in accordance with the implementing Regulation.

88(2) The bodies specified in paragraph 1 shall be provided with an electronic identity in the form of an identification code and electronic address.

88(3) The Administrative Commission shall establish the structure, content and detailed arrangements, including the common format and model, for notification of the details specified in paragraph 1.

88(4) Annex 4 to the implementing Regulation gives details of the public database containing the information specified in paragraph 1. The database shall be established and managed by the European Commission. The Member States shall, however, be responsible for the input of their own national contact information into this database. Moreover, the Member States shall ensure the accuracy of the input of the national contact information required under paragraph 1.

88(5) The Member States shall be responsible for keeping the information specified in paragraph 1 up to date.

ART. 89 *Information*

89(1) The Administrative Commission shall prepare the information needed to ensure that the parties concerned are aware of their rights and the administrative formalities required in order to assert them. This information shall, where possible, be disseminated electronically via publication online on sites accessible to the public. The Administrative Commission shall ensure that the information is regularly updated and monitor the quality of services provided to customers.

89(2) The Advisory Committee referred to in Article 75 of the basic Regulation may issue opinions and recommendations on improving the information and its dissemination.

89(3) The competent authorities shall ensure that their institutions are aware of and apply all the Community provisions, legislative or otherwise, including the decisions of the Administrative Commission, in the areas covered by and within the terms of the basic Regulation and the implementing Regulation.

ART. 90 Currency conversion

90 For the purposes of applying the basic Regulation and the implementing Regulation, the exchange rate between two currencies shall be the reference rate published by the European Central Bank. The date to be taken into account for determining the exchange rate shall be fixed by the Administrative Commission.

ART. 91 Statistics

91 The competent authorities shall compile statistics on the application of the basic Regulation and the implementing Regulation and forward them to the secretariat of the Administrative Commission. Those data shall be collected and organised according to the plan and method defined by the Administrative Commission. The European Commission shall be responsible for disseminating the information.

ART. 92 Amendment of the Annexes

92 Annexes 1, 2, 3, 4 and 5 to the implementing Regulation and Annexes VI, VII, VIII and IX to the basic Regulation may be amended by Commission Regulation at the request of the Administrative Commission.

ART. 93 Transitional provisions

93 Article 87 of the basic Regulation shall apply to the situations covered by the implementing Regulation.

ART. 94 Transitional provisions relating to pensions

94(1) Where the contingency arises before the date of entry into force of the implementing Regulation in the territory of the Member State concerned and the claim for pension has not been awarded before that date, such claim shall give rise to a double award, in as much as benefits must be granted, pursuant to such contingency, for a period prior to that date:

(a) for the period prior to the date of entry into force of the implementing Regulation in the territory of the Member State concerned, in accordance with Regulation (EEC) No 1408/71, or with agreements in force between the Member States concerned;

(b) for the period commencing on the date of entry into force of the implementing Regulation in the territory of the Member State concerned, in accordance with the basic Regulation.

However, if the amount calculated pursuant to the provisions referred to under point (a) is greater than that calculated pursuant to the provisions referred to under point (b), the person concerned shall continue to be entitled to the amount calculated pursuant to the provisions referred to under point (a).

94(2) A claim for invalidity, old age or survivors' benefits submitted to an institution of a Member State from the date of entry into force of the implementing Regulation in the territory of the Member State concerned shall automatically necessitate the reassessment of the benefits which have been awarded for the same contingency prior to that date by the institution or institutions of one or more Member States, in accordance with the basic Regulation; such reassessment may not give rise to any reduction in the amount of the benefit awarded.

ART. 95 Transitional period for electronic data exchanges

95(1) Each Member State may benefit from a transitional period for exchanging data by electronic means as provided for by Article 4(2) of the implementing Regulation.

These transitional periods shall not exceed 24 months from the date of entry into force of the implementing Regulation.

However, if the delivery of the necessary Community infrastructure (Electronic Exchange of Social Security information – EESSI) is significantly delayed with regard to the entry into force of the implementing Regulation, the Administrative Commission may agree on any appropriate extension of these periods.

95(2) The practical arrangements for any necessary transitional periods referred to in paragraph 1 shall be laid down by the Administrative Commission with a view to ensuring the necessary data exchange for the application of the basic Regulation and the implementing Regulation.

ART. 96 Repeal

96(1) Regulation (EEC) No 574/72 is repealed with effect from 1 May 2010.

However, Regulation (EEC) No 574/72 shall remain in force and continue to have legal effect for the purposes of:

(a) Council Regulation (EC) No 859/2003 of 14 May 2003 extending the provisions of Regulation (EEC) No 1408/71 and Regulation (EEC) No 574/72 to nationals of third countries who are not already covered by those provisions solely on the grounds of their nationality, until such time as that Regulation is repealed or amended;

(b) Council Regulation (EEC) No 1661/85 of 13 June 1985 laying down the technical adaptations to the Community rules on social security for migrant workers with regard to Greenland, until such time as that Regulation is repealed or amended;

(c) the Agreement on the European Economic Area, the Agreement between the European Community and its Member States, of the one part, and the Swiss Confederation, of the other, on the free movement of persons and other agreements containing a reference to Regulation (EEC) No 574/72, until such time as those agreements are amended on the basis of the implementing Regulation.

96(2) In Council Directive 98/49/EC of 29 June 1998 on safeguarding the supplementary pension rights of employed and self-employed persons moving within the Community (1), and more generally in all other Community acts, the references to Regulation (EEC) No 574/72 shall be understood as referring to the implementing Regulation.

ART. 97 Publication and entry into force

97 This Regulation shall be published in the *Official Journal of the European Union*. It shall enter into force on 1 May 2010.

This Regulation shall be binding in its entirety and directly applicable in all Member States.

ANNEX 1 – IMPLEMENTING PROVISIONS FOR BILATERAL AGREEMENTS REMAINING IN FORCE AND NEW BILATERAL IMPLEMENTING AGREEMENTS (REFERRED TO IN ARTICLE 8(1) AND ARTICLE 9(2) OF THE IMPLEMENTING REGULATION)

BELGIUM – DENMARK

The Exchange of Letters of 8 May 2006 and 21 June 2006 on the Agreement of reimbursement with the actual amount of the benefit provided to members of the family of an employed or self-employed person insured in Belgium, where the family member resides in Denmark and to pensioners and/or members of their family insured in Belgium but residing in Denmark

BELGIUM – GERMANY

The Agreement of 29 January 1969 on the collection and recovery of social security contributions

BELGIUM – IRELAND

The Exchange of Letters of 19 May and 28 July 1981 concerning Articles 36(3) and 70(3) of Regulation (EEC) No 1408/71 (reciprocal waiving of reimbursement of the costs of benefits in kind and of unemployment benefits under Chapters 1 and 6 of Title III of Regulation (EEC) No 1408/71) and Article 105(2) of Regulation (EEC) No 574/72 (reciprocal waiving of reimbursement of the costs of administrative checks and medical examinations).

BELGIUM – SPAIN

The Agreement of 25 May 1999 on the reimbursement of benefits in kind according to the provisions of Regulations (EEC) No 1408/71 and No 574/72

BELGIUM – FRANCE

(a) The Agreement of 4 July 1984 relating to medical examinations of frontier workers resident in one country and working in another

(b) The Agreement of 14 May 1976 on the waiving of reimbursement of the costs of administrative checks and medical examinations, adopted pursuant to Article 105(2) of Regulation (EEC) No 574/72

(c) The Agreement of 3 October 1977 implementing Article 92 of Regulation (EEC) No 1408/71 (recovery of social security contributions)

(d) The Agreement of 29 June 1979 concerning the reciprocal waiving of reimbursement provided for in Article 70(3) of Regulation (EEC) No 1408/71 (costs of unemployment benefit)

(e) The Administrative Arrangement of 6 March 1979 on the procedures for the implementation of the Additional Convention of 12 October 1978 on social security between Belgium and France in respect of its provisions relating to self-employed persons

(f) The Exchange of Letters of 21 November 1994 and 8 February 1995 concerning the procedures for the settlement of reciprocal claims pursuant to Articles 93, 94, 95 and 96 of Regulation (EEC) No 574/72

BELGIUM – ITALY

(a) The Agreement of 12 January 1974 implementing Article 105(2) of Regulation (EEC) No 574/72

(b) The Agreement of 31 October 1979 implementing Article 18(9) of Regulation (EEC) No 574/72

(c) The Exchange of Letters of 10 December 1991 and 10 February 1992 concerning the reimbursement of reciprocal claims under Article 93 of Regulation (EEC) No 574/72

(d) The Agreement of 21.11.2003 on the terms for settling reciprocal claims under Articles 94 and 95 of Council Regulation (EEC) No 574/72

BELGIUM – LUXEMBOURG

(a) The Agreement of 28 January 1961 on the recovery of social security contributions

(b) The Agreement of 16 April 1976 on the waiving of reimbursement of the costs of administrative checks and medical examinations, as provided for in Article 105(2) of Regulation (EEC) No 574/72

BELGIUM – NETHERLANDS

(a) [Deleted by Regulation 1244/2010, art. 2(1).]

(b) The Agreement of 13 March 2006 on health care insurance

(c) The Agreement of 12 August 1982 on sickness, maternity and invalidity insurance

BELGIUM – UNITED KINGDOM

(a) The Exchange of Letters of 4 May and 14 June 1976 regarding Article 105(2) of Regulation (EEC) No 574/72 (waiving of reimbursement of the costs of administrative checks and medical examinations)

(b) The Exchange of Letters of 18 January and 14 March 1977 regarding Article 36(3) of Regulation (EEC) No 1408/71 (arrangement for reimbursement or waiving of reimbursement of the costs of benefits in kind provided under the terms of Chapter 1 of Title III of Regulation (EEC) No 1408/71) as amended by the Exchange of Letters of 4 May and 23 July 1982 (agreement for reimbursement of costs incurred under Article 22(1)(a) of Regulation (EEC) No 1408/71)

BULGARIA – CZECH REPUBLIC

Article 29(1) and (3) of the Agreement of 25 November 1998 and Article 5(4) of the Administrative Arrangement of 30 November 1999 on the waiving of reimbursement of the costs of administrative checks and medical examinations

BULGARIA – GERMANY

Articles 8 to 9 of the Administrative Agreement on implementing the Convention on social security of 17 December 1997 in the pension field

CZECH REPUBLIC – SLOVAKIA

Articles 15 and of the Administrative Arrangement of 8 January 1993 concerning the specification of a seat of the employer and the place of residence for the purposes of application of Article 20 of the Convention of 29 October 1992 on social security

DENMARK – IRELAND

The Exchange of Letters of 22 December 1980 and 11 February 1981 on the reciprocal waiving of reimbursement of the costs of benefits in kind granted under insurance for sickness, maternity, accidents at work and occupational diseases, and of unemployment benefits and of the costs of administrative checks and medical examinations (Articles 36(3), 63(3) of Regulation (EEC) No 1408/71 and Article 105(2) of Regulation (EEC) No 574/72)

DENMARK – GREECE

Agreement of 8 May 1986 on the partial reciprocal waiving of reimbursement in respect of benefits in kind for sickness, maternity, accidents at work and occupational diseases and waiving of reimbursement in respect of administrative checks and medical examinations

DENMARK – SPAIN

Agreement of 11 December 2006 of advance payment, time-limits and reimbursement with the actual amount of the benefit provided to members of the family of an employed or self-employed person insured in Spain, where the family member resides in Denmark and to pensioners and/or members of their family insured in Spain but residing in Denmark

DENMARK – PORTUGAL

The Agreement of 17 April 1998 on the partial waiving of reimbursement of costs of benefits in kind under insurance for sickness, maternity, accidents at work and occupational diseases and administrative checks and medical examinations

DENMARK – FINLAND

Article 15 of the Nordic Convention on Social Security of 18 August 2003: Agreement on the reciprocal waiver of refund pursuant to Articles 36, 63 and 70 of Regulation (EEC) No 1408/71 (cost of benefits in kind in respect of sickness and maternity, accidents at work and occupational diseases, and unemployment benefits) and Article 105 of Regulation (EEC) No 574/72 (costs of administrative checks and medical examinations)

DENMARK – SWEDEN

Article 15 of the Nordic Convention on Social Security of 18 August 2003: Agreement on the reciprocal waiver of refund pursuant to Articles 36, 63 and 70 of Regulation (EEC) No 1408/71 (cost of benefits in kind in respect of sickness and maternity, accidents at work and occupational diseases, and unemployment benefits) and Article 105 of Regulation (EEC) No 574/72 (costs of administrative checks and medical examinations)

DENMARK – UNITED KINGDOM

The Exchange of Letters of 30 March and 19 April 1977 as modified by an Exchange of Letters of 8 November 1989 and of 10 January 1990 on agreement of waiving of reimbursement of the costs of benefits in kind and administrative checks and medical examinations

GERMANY – FRANCE

The Agreement of 26 May 1981 implementing Article 92 of Regulation (EEC) No 1408/71 (collection and recovery of social security contributions)

GERMANY – ITALY

The Agreement of 3 April 2000 on the collection and recovery of social security contributions

GERMANY – LUXEMBOURG

(a) The Agreement of 14 October 1975 on the waiving of reimbursement of the costs of administrative checks and medical examinations, adopted pursuant to Article 105(2) of Regulation (EEC) No 574/72

(b) The Agreement of 14 October 1975 on the collection and recovery of social security contributions

(c) The Agreement of 25 January 1990 relating to the application of Articles 20 and 22(1)(b) and (c) of Regulation (EEC) No 1408/71

GERMANY – AUSTRIA

Section II, Number 1, and section III of the Agreement of 2 August 1979 on the implementation of the Convention on unemployment insurance of 19 July 1978 shall continue to apply to persons who have exercised an activity as a frontier worker on or before 1 January 2005 who become unemployed before 1 January 2011

GERMANY – POLAND

The Agreement of 11 January 1977 on the implementation of the Convention of 9 October 1975 on old-age pensions and benefits for accidents at work

ESTONIA – UNITED KINGDOM

The Arrangement finalised on 29 March 2006 between the Competent Authorities of the Republic of Estonia and of the United Kingdom under Articles 36(3) and 63(3) of Regulation (EEC) No 1408/71 establishing other methods of reimbursement of the costs of benefits in kind provided under this Regulation by both countries with effect from 1 May 2004

IRELAND – FRANCE

The Exchange of Letters of 30 July 1980 and 26 September 1980 concerning Articles 36(3) and 63(3) of Regulation (EEC) No 1408/71 (reciprocal waiving of reimbursement of the costs of benefits in kind) and Article 105(2) of Regulation (EEC) No 574/72 (reciprocal waiving of reimbursement of the costs of administrative checks and medical examinations)

IRELAND – LUXEMBOURG

The Exchange of Letters of 26 September 1975 and 5 August 1976 concerning Articles 36(3) and 63(3) of Regulation (EEC) No 1408/71 and Article 105(2) of Regulation (EEC) No 574/72 (waiving of reimbursement of the costs of benefits in kind provided pursuant to Chapter 1 or 4 of Title III of Regulation (EEC) No 1408/71, and of the costs of administrative checks and medical examinations referred to in Article 105 of Regulation (EEC) No 574/72)

IRELAND – NETHERLANDS

The Exchange of Letters of 22 April and 27 July 1987 concerning Article 70(3) of Regulation (EEC) No 1408/71 (waiving of costs of reimbursement in respect of benefits awarded in application of Article 69 of Regulation (EEC) No 1408/71) and Article 105(2) of Regulation (EEC) No 574/72 (waiving of the reimbursement of the costs of administrative checks and medical examinations referred to in Article 105 of Regulation (EEC) No 574/72)

IRELAND – SWEDEN

The Agreement of 8 November 2000 on the waiving of reimbursement of the costs of benefits in kind of sickness, maternity, accidents at work and occupational diseases, and the costs of administrative and medical controls

IRELAND – UNITED KINGDOM

The Exchange of Letters of 9 July 1975 regarding Articles 36(3) and 63(3) of Regulation (EEC) No 1408/71 (arrangement for reimbursement or waiving of reimbursement of the costs of benefits in kind provided under the terms of Chapter 1 or 4 of Title III of Regulation (EEC) No 1408/71) and Article 105(2) of Regulation (EEC) No 574/72 (waiving of reimbursement of the costs of administrative checks and medical examinations)

SPAIN – FRANCE

The Agreement of 17 May 2005 establishing the specific arrangements for the management and settlement of reciprocal claims in respect of health care benefits pursuant to Regulations (EEC) No 1408/71 and (EEC) No 574/72

SPAIN – ITALY

The Agreement on a new procedure for the improvement and simplification of reimbursements of costs for health care of 21 November 1997 concerning Article 36(3) of Regulation (EEC) No 1408/71 (reimbursement of sickness and maternity benefits in kind) and Articles 93, 94, 95, 100 and 102(5) of Regulation (EEC) No 574/72 (procedures for the refund and sickness and maternity insurance benefits and late claims)

SPAIN – PORTUGAL

(a) Articles 42, 43 and 44 of the Administrative Arrangement of 22 May 1970 (export of unemployment benefits). This entry will remain valid for two years from the date of application of Regulation (EC) No 883/2004

(b) The Agreement of 2 October 2002 laying down detailed arrangements for the management and settlement of reciprocal claims for health care with a view to facilitating and accelerating the settlement of these claims

SPAIN – SWEDEN

The Agreement of 1 December 2004 on the reimbursement of the costs of benefits in kind provided under Regulations (EEC) No 1408/71 and (EEC) No 574/72

SPAIN – UNITED KINGDOM

The Agreement of 18 June 1999 on the reimbursement of costs for benefits in kind granted pursuant to the provisions of Regulations (EEC) No 1408/71 and (EEC) No 574/72

FRANCE – ITALY

(a) The Exchange of Letters of 14 May and 2 August 1991 concerning the terms for settling reciprocal claims under Article 93 of Regulation (EEC) No 574/72

(b) The supplementary Exchange of Letters of 22 March and 15 April 1994 concerning the procedures for the settlement of reciprocal debts under the terms of Articles 93, 94, 95 and 96 of Regulation (EEC) No 574/72

(c) The Exchange of Letters of 2 April 1997 and 20 October 1998 modifying the Exchange of Letters mentioned under points (a) and (b) concerning the procedures for the settlement of reciprocal debts under the terms of Articles 93, 94, 95 and 96 of Regulation (EEC) No 574/72

(d) The Agreement of 28 June 2000 waiving reimbursement of the costs referred to in Article 105(1) of Regulation (EEC) No 574/72 for administrative checks and medical examinations requested under *Article 51 of the* abovementioned Regulation

FRANCE – LUXEMBOURG

(a) [Deleted by Reg. 1372/2013, art. 2(1).]

(b) [Deleted by Reg. 1372/2013, art. 2(1).]

(a) The Agreement of 2 July 1976 on the waiving of reimbursement of the costs of administrative checks and medical examinations provided for in Article 105(2) of Council Regulation (EEC) No 574/72 of 21 March 1972

(b) The Exchange of Letters of 17 July and 20 September 1995 concerning the terms for settling reciprocal claims under Articles 93, 95 and 96 of Regulation (EEC) No 574/72 and the Exchange of Letters dated 10 July and 30 August 2013

FRANCE – NETHERLANDS

(a) The Agreement of 28 April 1997 on the waiving of reimbursement of the costs of administrative checks and medical examinations pursuant to Article 105 of Regulation (EEC) No 574/72

(b) [Deleted by Reg. 1372/2013, art. 2(1).]

(c) [Deleted by Reg. 1372/2013, art. 2(1).]

FRANCE – PORTUGAL

The Agreement of 28 April 1999 laying down special detailed rules governing the administration and settlement of reciprocal claims for medical treatment pursuant to Regulations (EEC) No 1408/71 and EEC No 574/72

FRANCE – UNITED KINGDOM

(a) The Exchange of Letters of 25 March and 28 April 1997 regarding Article 105(2) of Regulation (EEC) No 574/72 (waiving of reimbursement of the costs of administrative checks and medical examinations)

(b) The Agreement of 8 December 1998 on the specific methods of determining the amounts to be reimbursed for benefits in kind pursuant to Regulations (EEC) No 1408/71 and (EEC) No 574/72

ITALY – LUXEMBOURG

Article 4(5) and (6) of the Administrative Arrangement of 19 January 1955 on the implementing provisions of the General Convention on Social Security (sickness insurance for agricultural workers)

ITALY – UNITED KINGDOM

The Arrangement signed on 15 December 2005 between the Competent Authorities of the Italian Republic and of the United Kingdom under Articles 36(3) and 63(3) of Regulation (EEC) No 1408/71 establishing other methods of reimbursement of the costs of benefits in kind provided under this Regulation by both countries with effect from 1 January 2005

LUXEMBOURG – NETHERLANDS

The Agreement of 1 November 1976 on the waiving of reimbursement of the costs of administrative checks and medical examinations adopted pursuant to Article 105(2) of Regulation (EEC) No 574/72

LUXEMBOURG – SWEDEN

The Arrangement of 27 November 1996 on the reimbursement of expenditure in the field of social security

LUXEMBOURG – UNITED KINGDOM

The Exchange of Letters of 18 December 1975 and 20 January 1976 regarding Article 105(2) of Regulation (EEC) No 574/72 (waiving of reimbursement of the costs entailed in administrative checks and medical examinations referred to in Article 105 of Regulation (EEC) No 574/72)

HUNGARY – UNITED KINGDOM

The Arrangement finalised on 1 November 2005 between the Competent Authorities of the Republic of Hungary and of the United Kingdom under Articles 35(3) and 41(2) of Regulation (EEC) No 883/2004 establishing other methods of reimbursement of the costs of benefits in kind provided under that Regulation by both countries with effect from 1 May 2004

MALTA – UNITED KINGDOM

The Arrangement finalised on 17 January 2007 between the Competent Authorities of Malta and of the United Kingdom under Articles 35(3) and 41(2) of Regulation (EEC) No 883/2004 establishing other methods of reimbursement of the costs of benefits in kind provided under that Regulation by both countries with effect from 1 May 2004

NETHERLANDS – UNITED KINGDOM

(a) The second sentence of Article 3 of the Administrative Arrangement of 12 June 1956 on the implementation of the Convention of 11 August 1954

(b) [Deleted by Reg. 1372/2013, art. 2(1).]

PORTUGAL – UNITED KINGDOM

The Arrangement of 8 June 2004 establishing other methods of reimbursement of the costs of benefits in kind provided by both countries with effect from 1 January 2003

FINLAND – SWEDEN

Article 15 of the Nordic Convention on Social Security of 18 August 2003: Agreement on the reciprocal waiver of refund pursuant to Articles 36, 63 and 70 of Regulation (EEC) No 1408/71 (cost of benefits in kind in respect of sickness and maternity, accidents at work and occupational diseases, and unemployment benefits) and Article 105 of Regulation (EEC) No 574/72 (costs of administrative checks and medical examinations)

FINLAND – UNITED KINGDOM

The Exchange of Letters 1 and 20 June 1995 concerning Articles 36(3) and 63(3) of Regulation (EEC) No 1408/71 (reimbursement or waiving of reimbursement of the cost of benefits in kind) and Article 105(2) of Regulation (EEC) 574/72 (waiving of reimbursement of the cost of administrative checks and medical examinations)

SWEDEN – UNITED KINGDOM

The Arrangement of 15 April 1997 concerning Article 36(3) and Article 63(3) of Regulation (EEC) No 1408/71 (reimbursement or waiving of reimbursement of the cost of benefits in kind) and Article 105(2) of Regulation (EEC) No 574/72 (waiving of refunds of the costs of administrative checks and medical examinations)

History – The entry for point (a) in Belgium–Netherlands deleted by Regulation 1244/2010, art. 2(1), with effect from 11 January 2011. The entries for Denmark–France, Denmark–Netherlands, Greece–Netherlands, Spain–Netherlands and Italy–Netherlands deleted by Reg. 1372/2013, art. 2(1)(a)–(d) and (g) respectively, with effect from 1 January 2014.
Entry for Denmark-Italy deleted by Reg. 1368/2014, art. 1(a), with effect from 1 January 2015.
The entries for Denmark–Luxembourg, Germany–Netherlands and Netherlands–Portugal deleted by Regulation 1244/2010, art. 2(1), with effect from 11 January 2011.
In the entry for France-Luxembourg, point (b) substituted by Reg. 1368/2014, art. 1(2), with effect from 1 January 2015.
In the entry for France–Luxembourg, points (a) and (b) deleted, and points (c) and (d) replaced with new points (a) and (b), by Reg. 1372/2013, art. 2(1)(e), with effect from 1 January 2014.
In the entry for France–Netherlands, points (b) and (c) deleted, and point (a) replaced, by Reg. 1372/2013, art. 2(1)(f), with effect from 1 January 2014.
In the entry for Netherlands–United Kingdom, point (b) deleted, and point (a) replaced, by Reg. 1372/2013, art. 2(1)(h), with effect from 1 January 2014.

ANNEX 2 – SPECIAL SCHEMES FOR CIVIL SERVANTS (REFERRED TO IN ARTICLES 32(2) AND 41(1) OF THE IMPLEMENTING REGULATION)

A. Special schemes for civil servants which are not covered by Title III, Chapter 1 of Regulation (EC) No 883/2004 concerning benefits in kind

Germany

Special sickness scheme for civil servants

B. Special schemes for civil servants which are not covered by Title III, Chapter 1 of Regulation (EC) No 883/2004, with the exception of Article 19, paragraph 1 of Article 27 and Article 35, concerning benefits in kind

Spain

Special scheme of social security for civil servants

Special scheme of social security for the armed forces

Special scheme of social security for the court officials and administrative staff

C. Special schemes for civil servants which are not covered by Title III, Chapter 2 of Regulation (EC) No 883/2004 concerning benefits in kind

Germany

Special accident scheme for civil servants

History – In the heading to Annex 2, the words "Articles 32(2) and 41(1)" substituted for the words "Articles 31 and 41" by Regulation 1244/2010, art. 2(2), with effect from 11 January 2011.

ANNEX 3 – MEMBER STATES CLAIMING THE REIMBURSEMENT OF THE COST OF BENEFITS IN KIND ON THE BASIS OF FIXED AMOUNTS (REFERRED TO IN ARTICLE 63(1) OF THE IMPLEMENTING REGULATION)

IRELAND

SPAIN

ITALY

MALTA

THE NETHERLANDS

PORTUGAL

FINLAND

SWEDEN

UNITED KINGDOM

ANNEX 4 – DETAILS OF THE DATABASE REFERRED TO IN ARTICLE 88(4) OF THE IMPLEMENTING REGULATION

1. Content of the database

An electronic directory (URL) of the bodies concerned shall indicate:

(a) the names of the bodies in the official language(s) of the Member State as well as in English

(b) the identification code and the EESSI electronic addressing

(c) their function in respect of the definitions in Article 1(m), (q) and (r) of the basic Regulation and Article 1(a) and (b) of the implementing Regulation

(d) their competence as regards the different risks, types of benefits, schemes and geographical coverage

(e) which part of the basic Regulation the bodies are applying

(f) the following contact details: postal address, telephone, telefax, e-mail address and the relevant URL address

(g) any other information necessary for the application of the basic Regulation or the implementing Regulation.

2. Administration of the database

(a) The electronic directory is hosted in EESSI at the level of the European Commission.

(b) Member States are responsible for collecting and checking the necessary information of bodies and for the timely submission to the European Commission of any entry or change of the entries falling under their responsibility.

3. Access

Information used for operational and administrative purposes is not accessible to the public.

4. Security

All modifications to the database (insert, update, delete) shall be logged. Prior to accessing the Directory for the purposes of modifying entries, users shall be identified and authenticated. Prior to any attempt of a modification of an entry, the user's authorisation to perform this action will be checked. Any unauthorised action shall be rejected and logged.

5. Language Regime

The general language regime of the database is English. The name of bodies and their contact details should also be inserted in the official language(s) of the Member State.

ANNEX 5 – MEMBER STATES DETERMINING, ON A RECIPROCAL BASIS, THE MAXIMUM AMOUNT OF REIMBURSEMENT REFERRED TO IN THE THIRD SENTENCE OF ARTICLE 65(6) OF THE BASIC REGULATION, ON THE BASIS OF THE AVERAGE AMOUNT OF UNEMPLOYMENT BENEFITS PROVIDED UNDER THEIR LEGISLATIONS IN THE PRECEDING CALENDAR YEAR (REFERRED TO IN ARTICLE 70 OF THE IMPLEMENTING REGULATION)

BELGIUM

CZECH REPUBLIC

GERMANY

NETHERLANDS

AUSTRIA

SLOVAKIA

FINLAND

History – The entry for Netherlands inserted by Reg. 1372/2013, art. 2(2), with effect from 1 January 2014.

REGULATION 988/2009

Amending Regulation (EC) No 883/2004 on the coordination of social security systems, and determining the content of its Annexes

(16 September 2009)

THE EUROPEAN PARLIAMENT AND THE COUNCIL OF THE EUROPEAN UNION,

Having regard to the Treaty establishing the European Community, and in particular Articles 42 and 308 thereof,

Having regard to the proposal from the Commission,

Having regard to the Opinion of the European Economic and Social Committee,

Acting in accordance with the procedure laid down in Article 251 of the Treaty,

Whereas:

(1) Regulation (EC) No 883/2004 of the European Parliament and of the Council of 29 April 2004 on the coordination of social security systems provides for the content of Annexes II, X and XI to that Regulation to be determined before its date of application.

(2) Annexes I, III, IV, VI, VII, VIII and IX to Regulation (EC) No 883/2004 should be adapted in order to take into account both the requirements of the Member States which have acceded to the European Union since that Regulation was adopted and recent developments in other Member States.

(3) Articles 56(1) and 83 of Regulation (EC) No 883/2004 provide for special provisions for the implementation of the legislation of certain Member States to be set out in Annex XI to that Regulation. Annex XI is intended to take account of the particularities of the various social security systems of Member States in order to facilitate the application of the rules on coordination. A number of Member States have asked for entries concerning the application of their social security legislation to be included in this Annex and have provided the Commission with legal and practical explanations of their legislation and systems.

(4) In accordance with the need for rationalisation and simplification, a common approach is needed in order to ensure that entries in respect of different Member States which are of a similar nature or pursue the same objective are in principle dealt with in a similar manner.

(5) As the aim of Regulation (EC) No 883/2004 is to coordinate social security legislation for which Member States are exclusively responsible, entries which are not compatible with its purpose or objectives, and entries seeking solely to clarify the interpretation of national legislation, should not be included in that Regulation.

(6) Some requests raised issues that were common to several Member States: it is therefore appropriate to deal with those issues at a more general level, either by clarification in the body of Regulation (EC) No 883/2004 or in another of its Annexes, which should therefore be amended accordingly, or through a provision in the implementing Regulation referred to in Article 89 of Regulation (EC) No 883/2004, rather than by inserting similar entries in Annex XI for several Member States.

(7) Article 28 of Regulation (EC) No 883/2004 should be amended in order to clarify and extend its scope and to ensure that the members of the family of former frontier workers may also benefit from the possibility of continuing medical treatment in the former country of employment of the insured person after his/her retirement, unless the Member State where the frontier worker last pursued his/her last activity is listed in Annex III.

(8) It is appropriate to assess the significance, frequency, scale and costs relating to the application of the restriction of rights to benefits in kind for members of the family of frontier workers under Annex III to Regulation (EC) No 883/2004 for those Member States still listed in that Annex 4 years after the date of application of that Regulation.

(9) It is also appropriate to deal with certain specific issues in other Annexes to Regulation (EC) No 883/2004, according to their purpose and content, rather than in Annex XI thereto, in order to ensure consistency in the Annexes to that Regulation.

(10) Some Member States' entries in Annex VI to Regulation (EEC) No 1408/71 of the Council are now covered by certain general provisions in Regulation (EC) No 883/2004. Consequently, a number of entries in Annex VI to Regulation (EEC) No 1408/71 have become superfluous.

(11) In order to facilitate the use of Regulation (EC) No 883/2004 by citizens when asking for information or making claims to the institutions of the Member States, references to the legislation of the Member States concerned should also be made in the original language wherever necessary in order to avoid any possible misunderstanding.

(12) Regulation (EC) No 883/2004 should therefore be amended accordingly.

(13) Regulation (EC) No 883/2004 provides that it is to apply from the date of entry into force of the implementing Regulation. This Regulation should therefore apply from the same date,

HAVE ADOPTED THIS REGULATION:

ART. 1 Article 1

1 Regulation (EC) No 883/2004 is hereby amended as follows:

1(1) [Inserts Reg. 883/2004, art. 17a.]
1(2) [Inserts Reg. 883/2004, art. 18a.]
1(3) [Inserts Reg. 883/2004, art. 1(va).]
1(4) [Replaces Reg. 883/2004, art. 3(5).]
1(5) [Replaces Reg. 883/2004, art. 14(4).]
1(6) [Amends Reg. 883/2004, art. 15.]
1(7) [Replaces Reg. 883/2004, art. 18(2).]
1(8) [Replaces Reg. 883/2004, art. 28(1).]
1(9) [Replaces Reg. 883/2004, art. 36(1).]
1(10) [Inserts Reg. 883/2004, art. 36(2a).]
1(11) [Replaces Reg. 883/2004, art. 51(3).]
1(12) [Replaces Reg. 883/2004, art. 52(4).]
1(13) [Inserts Reg. 883/2004, art. 52(5).]
1(14) [Amends Reg. 883/2004, art. 56(1)(c).]
1(15) [Inserts Reg. 883/2004, art. 56(1)(d).]
1(16) [Inserts Reg. 883/2004, art. 57(4).]
1(17) [Amends Reg. 883/2004, art. 62(3).]
1(18) [Inserts Reg. 883/2004, art. 68a.]
1(19) Article 87 shall be amended as follows:
(a) [replaces Reg. 883/2004, art. 87(8),]
(b) [inserts Reg. 883/2004, art. 87(10a) and (10b).]
1(20) the Annexes shall be amended in accordance with the Annex to this Regulation.

ART. 2 Article 2

2 This Regulation shall enter into force on the day following its publication in the *Official Journal of the European Union*.

It shall apply from the date of entry into force of the implementing Regulation referred to in Article 89 of Regulation (EC) No 883/2004.

This Regulation shall be binding in its entirety and directly applicable in all Member States.

ANNEX – AMENDMENTS TO THE ANNEXES TO REGULATION (EC) NO 883/2004

[Pt. A amends Reg. 883/2004, Annex I, Pt. B replaces Reg. 883/2004, Annex II, Pt. C replaces Reg. 883/2004, Annex III, Pt. D amends Reg. 883/2004, Annex IV, Pt. E amends Reg. 883/2004, Annex VI, Pt. F amends Reg. 883/2004, Annex VII, Pt. G replaces Reg. 883/2004, Annex VIII, Pt. H amends Reg. 883/2004, Annex IX, Pt. I replaces Reg. 883/2004, Annex X and Pt. J replaces Reg. 883/2004, Annex XI.]

REGULATION 1244/2010

Amending Regulation (EC) No 883/2004 on the coordination of social security systems and Regulation (EC) No 987/2009 laying down the procedure for implementing Regulation (EC) No 883/2004

(9 December 2010)

Notes – The text of this Regulation has relevance for the EEA and for Switzerland.

THE EUROPEAN COMMISSION,

Having regard to the Treaty on the Functioning of the European Union,

Having regard to Regulation (EC) No 883/2004 of the European Parliament and of the Council of 29 April 2004 on the coordination of social security systems,

Having regard to Regulation (EC) No 987/2009 of the European Parliament and of the Council of 16 September 2009 laying down the procedure for implementing Regulation (EC) No 883/2004 on the coordination of social security systems, and in particular Article 92 thereof,

Whereas:

(1) Two Member States or their competent authorities have requested amendments to Annexes VIII and IX to Regulation (EC) No 883/2004.

(2) Some Member States or their competent authorities have requested amendments to Annexes 1 and 2 to Regulation (EC) No 987/2009.

(3) Annexes VIII and IX to Regulation (EC) No 883/2004 and Annexes 1 and 2 to Regulation (EC) No 987/2009 need to be adapted in order to take into account recent developments in national legislation and to guarantee transparency and legal certainty for stakeholders.

(4) The Administrative Commission on Coordination of Social Security Systems has agreed to the amendments.

(5) Regulations (EC) No 883/2004 and (EC) No 987/2009 should therefore be amended accordingly,

HAS ADOPTED THIS REGULATION:

ART. 1 Article 1

1 Regulation (EC) No 883/2004 is amended as follows:

1(1) [Amends Annex VIII.]

1(2) [Amends Annex IX, Part 1.]

ART. 2 Article 2

2 Regulation (EC) No 987/2009 is amended as follows:

2(1) [Amends Annex 1.]

2(2) [Amends Annex 2.]

ART. 3 Article 3

3 This Regulation shall enter into force on the 20th day following its publication in the *Official Journal of the European Union*.

This Regulation shall be binding in its entirety and directly applicable in all Member States.

DECISION 20/06/2013
Decision No R1 of 20 June 2013 concerning the interpretation of Article 85 of Regulation (EC) No 987/2009

(20 June 2013, OJ 2013, C 279/11)

The Administrative Commission for the Coordination of Social Security Systems,

Having regard to Article 72(a) of Regulation (EC) No 883/2004, under which the Administrative Commission is responsible for dealing with all administrative questions or questions of interpretation arising from the provisions of Regulation (EC) No 883/2004 and Regulation (EC) No 987/2009,

Having regard to Article 84(2) and (4) of Regulation (EC) No 883/2004,

Having regard to Articles 80(1) and 85(1) and (2) of Regulation (EC) No 987/2009,

Acting in accordance with the conditions laid down in Article 71(2), first subparagraph, of Regulation (EC) No 883/2004,

Whereas:

[1] Chapter III of Title IV of Regulation (EC) No 987/2009 on recovery of benefits and contributions was originally based on the EU provisions relating to recovery applicable in the tax field, namely Directive 76/308/EEC, subsequently replaced by Directive 2008/55/EC.

[2] During the discussions in the Administrative Commission the question arose whether the costs related to recovery by the requested party, which could not be recovered from the person concerned, should be reimbursed by the applicant party.

[3] Pursuant to Article 84(2) of Regulation (EC) No 883/2004, enforceable decisions of the judicial and administrative authorities relating to the collection of contributions, interest and any other charges, or to the recovery of benefits provided but not due under the legislation of one Member State, shall be recognised and enforced at the request of the competent institution in another Member State within the limits and in accordance with the procedures laid down by the legislation and any other procedures applicable to similar decisions of the latter Member State.

[4] Following the recently adopted Directive 2010/24/EU (concerning mutual assistance for the recovery of claims relating to taxes, duties and other measures) which replaces the former Directive 2008/55/EC on that matter, the approach in the tax field concerning the recovery of requested party costs which cannot be recovered from the person concerned has been reassessed and clarified.

[5] In accordance with Article 85(1) of Regulation (EC) No 987/2009 the requested party shall recover from the natural or legal person concerned, and subsequently retain, any costs it incurs, linked to the recovery, in accordance with the laws and regulations of the Member State of the requested party that apply to similar claims.

[6] In accordance with Article 85(2) of Regulation (EC) No 987/2009 mutual assistance shall, as a rule, be free of charge, reconfirming the general rule laid down in Article 76(2) of Regulation (EC) No 883/2004. It is therefore necessary to determine the scope of mutual assistance for the purposes of cross-border recovery of claims.

[7] It is desirable, wherever possible, to align the interpretation of Chapter III of Title IV of Regulation (EC) No 987/2009 with the rules and principles concerning the mutual assistance for the recovery of claims relating to taxes and duties,

has decided as follows:

(1) Mutual assistance shall, as a rule, be free of charge. This means that institutions of the Member States shall provide administrative assistance to each other free of charge. This applies only to the costs of activities undertaken by the requested party itself.

(2) The costs related to recovery shall be charged in accordance with the laws and regulations of the requested party and, as a rule, be refunded by the debtor in addition to the amount of the claim.

(3) The costs related to recovery shall be settled first, and only after these costs are settled shall the claim of the applicant party be satisfied (priority rule for the costs).

(4) In cases where costs related to recovery cannot be recovered directly from the debtor by the requested party as a consequence of the national legislation of the requested party, or because the amount recovered from the debtor does not permit the satisfaction of the entire claim including costs related to recovery, such costs can be deducted from the recovered amount and only the balance shall be remitted by the requested party to the applicant party. Evidence that these costs were incurred by the requested party during the recovery procedure shall be provided by the requested party to the applicant party.

(5) In cases where recovery action does not result in the recovery of an amount which at least covers the costs related to recovery, or where recovery action was completely unsuccessful but costs related to recovery other than those referred to in paragraph 1 were incurred by the requested party, the applicant party shall reimburse these costs, unless the parties agree on a reimbursement arrangement specific to the case, or a waiver of reimbursement of such costs is concluded between the applicant party and the requested party.

(6) Where it is obvious that recovery poses a specific problem or concerns a very large amount in costs which are not likely to be recovered from the debtor, the applicant and requested parties may agree, preferably in advance, on reimbursement arrangements specific to the case in question.

(7) This decision shall be published in the *Official Journal of the European Union*. It shall apply from the date of its publication.

NIC EXTRA-STATUTORY MATERIAL

Table of Contents

EXTRA-STATUTORY CONCESSIONS

Concessions applicable to individuals (Income Tax and Interest on Tax)

HMRC BRIEFS

continued over

EXTRA-STATUTORY CONCESSIONS

HMRC's Extra-Statutory Concessions as published on 6 April 2015 contained the following caveat:

> "The concessions described within are of general application, but it must be borne in mind that in a particular case there may be special circumstances which will require to be taken into account in considering the application of the concession. A concession will not be given in any case where an attempt is made to use it for tax avoidance."

Every Extra-Statutory Concession is to be read as if this caveat is part of each Concession. This principle was confirmed in the case of *R v HMIT, ex parte Fulford-Dobson* [1987] BTC 158 where McNeill J stated that:

> "In my judgment, the [caveat] is effectively part of each concession. It loses none of its force by being given a special and early place in the booklet: indeed, perhaps, it gains force from that."

The House of Lords' decision in *R v IR Commrs, ex parte Wilkinson* made it clear that the scope of HMRC's administrative discretion to make concessions that depart from the strict application of the letter of the law is not as wide as had previously been supposed. In the light of that decision HMRC are reviewing their concessions. The indications are that most concessions will be able to continue in their current form as they are within the scope of HMRC's administrative discretion, although concessions will continue to be withdrawn where they appear to be obsolete. Where an existing concession exceeds the scope of HMRC's discretion and it is deemed appropriate to preserve its effect, this will be achieved by legislation if possible. If it is not possible put the effect of the concession on a legislative basis, the concession will join obsolete concessions and need to be withdrawn. HMRC have confirmed that no extra-statutory concession will be withdrawn retrospectively and that they will generally offer an appropriate period of notice before a concessionary treatment formally comes to an end.

A. CONCESSIONS APPLICABLE TO INDIVIDUALS (INCOME TAX AND INTEREST ON TAX)

A11 RESIDENCE IN THE UNITED KINGDOM: YEAR OF COMMENCEMENT OR CESSATION OF RESIDENCE

[Obsolete. Replaced by FA 2013, Sch. 45 from 6 April 2013.]

A37 TAX TREATMENT OF DIRECTORS' FEES RECEIVED BY PARTNERSHIPS AND OTHER COMPANIES

1. Where fees are received in respect of directorships held by members of a professional partnership they are in strictness assessable on the individual partners under employment income. It is however the practice of HM Revenue and Customs (HMRC) to accede to a request from the partnership for the inclusion of the fees as receipt of the profession provided that–

(a) the directorship is a normal incident of the profession and of the particular practice concerned;

(b) the fees are only a small part of the profits; and

(c) under the partnership agreement the fees are pooled for division among the partners.

Partnerships seeking such treatment are expected to provide HMRC with a written undertaking that directors' fees received in full will be included in the gross income or receipts of the basis period, whether or not the directorship is still held in the year of assessment and whether or not the partner concerned is still a partner.

2. It is also the practice of HMRC that, where a company has the right to appoint a director to the board of another company, by virtue of its shareholdings in, or a formal agreement with, the second company then, provided the director is required to hand over to the first company any fees or other earnings received in respect of his directorship with the second company and does so, and the first company is chargeable to *corporation tax and agrees to accept liability* on the fees, those fees are treated as income of the company and not of the director, and tax is not deducted from the fees under PAYE. Where the first company is chargeable not to corporation tax but to income tax (for example, if it is a non-resident company not trading through a branch or agency in the United Kingdom) and agrees to accept liability, tax is deducted at the basic rate of income tax from the fees.

3. With effect from 6 April 1980, the practice described in the previous paragraph will be extended to the case where the first company has no formal right to appoint the director to the board but the director is nevertheless required to (and does) hand over his fees to that company, provided it is:

(a) a company resident in the United Kingdom liable to United Kingdom corporation tax or, if non-resident, is trading through a branch or agency in the United Kingdom so that its income is chargeable to corporation tax under section 11, ICTA 1988 and the fees are included in that income; and

(b) not a company over which the director has control. (For this purpose "control" has the meaning given to it by section 840, ICTA 1988, but in determining whether the company is controlled by the director the rights and powers of his spouse or civil partner, his children and their spouses or civil partners and his parents will also be taken into account.)

Cross references – SI 2001/1004, reg. 40(7): ESC A37 applies to Class 1A NIC.

Notes – The text given above is as it appears in HMRC's Extra-Statutory Concessions as published on 6 April 2013.

A56 BENEFITS IN KIND: THE TAX TREATMENT OF ACCOMMODATION IN SCOTLAND PROVIDED FOR EMPLOYEES

1. Section 102 of (ITEPA) charges to tax in certain circumstances the benefit of living accommodation provided by reason of a person's employment. The charge is based either on the rent paid by the person providing the accommodation, or the property's "annual value" if greater, less any amount made good by the employee.

2. Annual value is defined in Section 110 ITEPA 2003 in terms similar to the definition of "gross value" for rating purposes in the General Rate Act 1967. In practice, therefore, a property's gross rateable value may be taken as its annual value for Sections 105 and 106 ITEPA purposes where the property is situated in the United Kingdom.

3. To avoid unfairness as between taxpayers in different parts of the United Kingdom, the Inland Revenue will not assess the benefit arising on property in Scotland in accordance with the 1985 Scottish rating revaluation figures.

4. Instead, the existing 1978 valuations will form the basis of assessment for existing properties for 1985/86 and 1986/87. For 1987/88 and subsequent years and for new properties the Inland Revenue will scale back the 1985 figures by the average increase in rateable values in Scotland between 1978 and 1985 (170 per cent); (e.g. a 1985 gross rateable value of £270 will be reduced to £100 for the purposes of section 33).

5. Additional yearly rent which is required for properties costing over £75,000 by Section 106(2) Step 2 of ITEPA is unaffected.

Cross references – SI 2001/1004, reg. 40: ESC A56 applies to Class 1A NIC.

HMRC Manuals – Employment Income Manual, EIM 11432.

Notes – See ESC A91 regarding accommodation provided by reason of employment.

A91 LIVING ACCOMMODATION PROVIDED BY REASON OF EMPLOYMENT

This concession applies to living accomodation treated as earnings under Part 3, Chapter 5 ITEPA 2003. Where section 106 ITEPA 2003 applies and the cash equivalent of the benefit of the accomodation is calculated by reference to the annual rent the property might fetch on the open market, the Inland Revenue will disregard "additional yearly rent". If "the additional yearly rent" is disregarded then the amount of "the excess rent" is deemed to be nil.

Cross references – SI 2001/1004, reg. 40: ESC A91 applies to Class 1A NIC.

Notes – The text given above is as it appears in HMRC's Extra-Statutory Concessions as published on 6 April 2013.

HMRC BRIEFS

BRIEFS

HMRCBrf 25/09 THE FIRST AID TRAINING SECTOR AND THE SOCIAL SECURITY (CATEGORISATION OF EARNERS) REGULATIONS 1978 [HMRC Brief 25/09, 1 April 2009] [Withdrawn on 6 October 2011.]

HMRCBrf 50/09 TEMPORARY WORKERS: THE APPLICATION OF TAX, NATIONAL INSURANCE AND NATIONAL MINIMUM WAGE LEGISLATION [HMRC Brief 50/09, 6 August 2009.]

Who should read this?

- Those involved directly or indirectly in the provision of temporary workers to end clients
- End user businesses provided with temporary workers
- Temporary workers

In the last two years HM Revenue and Customs (HMRC) have seen a growth in arrangements which are variously described as "Travel and Subsistence Schemes" or "Mobile Worker Schemes". These schemes are operated by many businesses involved in the supply of temporary workers to end users: Employment Businesses and umbrella companies. The labour supply businesses seek to obtain a tax and National Insurance advantage by the creation of a purported overarching employment contract which is intended to enable temporary workers who would not otherwise be entitled to tax relief on travel and subsistence expenses to gain such tax relief.

These schemes often involve the use of salary sacrifice arrangements and rely for their effectiveness on the fact that HMRC have issued a dispensation in accordance with section 65 Income Tax (Earnings and Pensions) Act 2003.

In many cases such schemes are marketed to workers as representing a tax and National Insurance saving for the worker. However, the major saving is not to the worker, rather to the party who would bear the higher employer's National Insurance contributions costs if it were not for the arrangement.

Following responses to the July 2008 consultation "Tax relief for travel expenses: temporary workers and overarching employment contracts", HMRC commenced compliance activity to identify and take action against those Employment Businesses and umbrella companies which are operating in contravention of tax, National Insurance or national minimum wage legislation.

Current compliance activity has identified a number of concerns that are the subject of more detailed, ongoing investigation. These include:

- Potentially ineffective overarching employment contracts
- Dispensations which are invalid, or which have been wrongly applied
- Not complying with the terms of the dispensation
- "Expense payments" made tax-free without that level of expense, or in many cases any expense, having been incurred
- Potential illegal deductions from workers' pay
- Ineffective and sometimes unlawful management processes; and
- Breaches of national minimum wage

HMRC are working with other Government Departments, including the Department for Business Innovation & Skills, and Authorities, particularly the Gangmasters Licensing Authority, to identify businesses acting in contravention of legislation and will penalise breaches of the law as they are identified. In addition, HMRC are also working with end users of temporary labour to raise their awareness of the consequences of sourcing their temporary workers from businesses which act in contravention of the law.

HMRC are concerned that many lower paid workers being paid through such schemes do not understand the arrangements and in many cases are given little choice as to whether or not they are paid through such schemes. There are also concerns about low paid workers in such schemes opting out of the Conduct of Employment Agencies and Employment Businesses Regulations 2003 without fully understanding the implications of what the opt-out means.

End user businesses which use temporary workers paid though Employment Businesses and/or umbrella companies which do not fully comply with their statutory obligations, clearly run a risk of damage to their reputation and their business if HMRC takes action.

HMRC will continue to investigate and challenge non-compliant Employment Businesses and umbrella companies and will report to ministers in due course on the outcome of that action and the extent of issues being discovered. Ministers will then be able to consider the extent to which compliance action is able to address the undesirable effects of these schemes and whether further measures are required.

Action you should take

Workers:

If you have concerns regarding the minimum wage, your rights as an agency worker or the working time directive, you can report these in confidence to the Pay and Work Rights Helpline Tel 0800 917 2368

If you are concerned about other employment rights, you should contact Acas Helpline Tel 08457 474747.

End user businesses:

HMRC produce a leaflet – Use of Labour Providers: Advice on due diligence [http://www.labourproviders.org.uk/files/HMRC_Leaflet_Due_Diligence_in_the_use_of_Labour _Providers_January_09.pdf], which you are recommended to read.

If you have concerns about how a business in your labour supply chain may be using these schemes, you can also provide details in confidence to HMRC by emailing Temporary workers* [http://www.hmrc.gov.uk/asplib/mailer/mailer_form.asp?dpt=TEMP_WORKERS]

Others operating in the temporary labour marker sector:

If you have concerns about how a business in the temporary labour market is operating, you can also provide details in confidence to HMRC by emailing Temporary workers*

*Please note that we cannot guarantee the security of emails you send to us or we send to you over the internet. Information sent by email over the internet is not secure and is at risk of being intercepted and read by people other than those it was intended for. Any information you send to us by email is at your own risk.

HMRCBrf 10/11 NATIONAL INSURANCE: ITV SERVICES LTD ("ITV") AND THE COMMISSIONERS FOR HM REVENUE & CUSTOMS ("HMRC") FIRST TIER TRIBUNAL – TAX CHAMBER DECISION OF 23 NOVEMBER 2010 (TC/2009/10166) [HMRC Brief 10/11, 2 March 2011]

This Brief outlines the salient facts and the National Insurance implications of the above decision for the entertainment industry. You can read the full text of the decision on the Tax Tribunals Service website [http://www.financeandtaxtribunals.gov.uk/Aspx/view.aspx?id=5205].

This case concerned the employment status for National Insurance contributions purposes of actors engaged by ITV under a variety of contract types. The legislation in point is the Social Security (Categorisation of Earners) Regulations 1978 (SI 1978/1689) [the "Entertainers Regulations" as amended in 2003.]

The Tribunal judges found that except for the ITV "All Rights Agreement", in all other contracts, including contracts for walk-ons, the actor's remuneration included "any payment by way of salary" as defined in the Entertainers Regulations. As such their contracts provide for remuneration which does include salary and there was a liability for Class 1 National Insurance contributions on all the remuneration payable under the contract.

The tribunal's decision confirms the HMRC technical view and Policy intention stated by Ministers at the time the regulations were first laid in 1998, that the majority of entertainers in the TV, film and theatre industries, engaged on Equity contracts, are to be treated as employed earners for National Insurance contributions purposes. The implications of the decision are that only actors who have entered into "All Rights Agreements" or are engaged for a specific production, programme or episode that does not involve payment to provide their services as and when required for a specified period of engagement will be excepted from the Entertainers Regulations.

Consequently, the Entertainers Regulations will also now apply to the minority of actors who had previously entered into Equity contracts on the common understanding that, as the production was dependent on them for box office success, they would remain outside of the ambit of the legislation. The tribunal has decided that there is an element of salary in the payments made under such contracts and confirmed that the essential quality of salary was to "purchase the individual's time for some definite or indefinite period, short or long, rather than to pay for specific services". The wider implication of this decision is that this test should be applied to contracts for all actors whatever their status within the profession and parties *cannot contract out of the liability* for Class 1 National Insurance Contributions if the nature of the contract is that it includes payment "by way of salary."

In the light of the First Tier Tax Tribunal decision there is a liability for Class 1 National Insurance contributions for all actors on existing Equity contracts. HMRC is also obliged to apply the law immediately to all Equity contracts that are either newly entered into, revised, renewed or extended from the date of this briefing and from 6 April 2011 in respect of all current Equity contracts that continue beyond the end of the 2010/11 tax year, which are of a type that has been previously accepted by HMRC as falling outside of the regulations. This means that engagers have until 5 April 2011 to make the necessary administrative arrangements to ensure that they start to pay Class 1 National Insurance contributions in respect of these existing contracts that now fall within the regulations as well as such contracts that might be agreed in the future.

HMRC's current published guidance on the National Insurance contributions liability for entertainers in the Employment Status Manual (ESM 4145 to 4147) and the document "Guidelines on the Special National Insurance contributions Rules for Entertainers" published in April 2005 on the HMRC website will be amended in due course to reflect this judgment.

HMRCBrf 19/12 NATIONAL INSURANCE CONTRIBUTIONS (NICS): HMRC'S POSITION FOLLOWING THE UPPER TRIBUNAL DECISION IN THE CASE OF ITV SERVICES LTD

[HMRC Brief 19/12, 14 June 2012]

This brief confirms Her Majesty's Revenue & Customs' ("HMRC") position following the decision in the case of ITV Services Ltd ("ITV") at the Upper Tribunal ("UT"). The case concerned the application of the Social Security (Categorisation of Earners) Regulations 1978 ("the Regulations") to payments made to actors engaged by ITV under specific contract types. The tribunal found against ITV and upheld the decision of the First Tier Tribunal ("FTT") (see R & C Brief 10/11 issued 2 March 2011) that the actors' contracts provided for remuneration by way of salary and there was liability for Class 1 National Insurance contributions ("NICs") under the Regulations on all the remuneration payable under the contract types.

You can read the full text of the UT decision on the Tax Tribunals Service website ITV Services_Ltd_v_HMRC (PDF 82K) (Opens new window).

Readership

Any individuals or businesses engaging entertainers as actors, singers or musicians; or in any similar performing capacity, and the representative bodies for any of these groups are advised to read this brief.

Action required by those engaging entertainers

The decisions of the FTT and UT in the case of ITV have clearly stated the law on the matter. HMRC now expects those in the industry engaging entertainers to comply with the Tribunals' decisions.

Background

The Regulations relating to entertainers were introduced to provide earnings-related contributory benefit protection to entertainers. At the time the Regulations were introduced it was accepted that a small number of highly-paid celebrity entertainers referred to by the entertainment industry as "Key Talent" or "Marquee Talent", would be excluded because they did not need earnings-related contributory benefit protection.

HMRC believed that the wording of the Regulations in 1998, as amended in 2003, excluded certain entertainers not paid by way of salary (as defined in the Regulations) and that one such group was those entertainers termed "Key Talent". However, it has now become clear that many entertainers termed "Key Talent" are engaged contractually under terms which bring them within the ambit of the Regulations.

HMRC also believed that the majority of musicians not engaged directly under employment contracts were excluded from the Regulations because they were not paid by way of salary. The decision of the UT in the ITV case now clarifies that musicians' contracts which HMRC previously believed to be outside the ambit of the Regulations, and where in some cases it had given a written opinion to that effect, are in fact within the Regulations.

The FTT in its decision of 23 November 2010 found that, except for the ITV "All Rights Contract", where the contract specifies a fee without any relation to time taken, all other actors' contracts including bespoke contracts (used extensively for engaging "Key Talent",) provided for remuneration which included salary. One of the grounds of ITV's appeal was that the FTT erred in concluding that the contractual payments computed by reference to the time services are to be rendered fell within the definition of salary in the Regulations.

The Upper Tribunal's decision

The UT rejected the "are to be rendered" argument and all other of ITV's arguments and decided that entertainers' contracts are forward looking and the wording of the legislation is consistent with the natural contract-based interpretation of the notion of "remuneration" and in the context of the NICs legislative regime. This means that the Regulations apply to any contract that provides for payment for the individual's time for some definite or indefinite period (as opposed to being for a specific performance). However, the judge also observed that contracts that include reference to hourly payments such as overtime or overage payments, if and when paid, that will be computed by reference to time, fall within the ambit of the Regulations irrespective of whether such additional payments are actually made to the entertainer.

The effect of the Upper Tribunal's decision

The UT decision has provoked comments from some observers from the entertainment sector as to the correct interpretation of the penultimate paragraph of Revenue & Customs Brief 10/11. In particular, a query has been raised as regards the category of entertainer to which the following statement was intended to apply:

> "HMRC is obliged to apply the law immediately to all Equity contracts that are newly entered into, revised, renewed or extended from the date of this briefing (2/3/11) and from 6 April 2011 in respect of all current Equity contracts that continue beyond the end of the 2010/11 tax year, which are of a type that had previously been accepted by HMRC as falling outside of the regulations."

That paragraph referred to the liability for Class 1 NICs for all actors on Equity contracts. The second part of that statement made no concession for any specific type of contract, it simply deferred compliance with the FTT decision to the beginning of the new tax year in the limited circumstances where HMRC had previously given a written opinion that a particular contract (or contracts in cases where more than one actor are engaged on precisely the same terms in the same production) fell outside of the Regulations.

It has also been suggested that the following extract from the Employment Status Manual 4147 shows that HMRC previously took the view that those entertainers referred to by the industry as "Key Talent" are excluded from the Regulations:

> "The last bullet ensures that Key talent artistes are excluded from the Regulations as they will be contracted to appear in productions for which their remuneration is not directly calculated according to the period of weeks or months they are assigned to the production."

HMRC is of the view that the above extract in respect of "Key Talent" artistes makes it clear that only those entertainers engaged without specific reference to time are intended to be excluded from the Regulations. Various HMRC guidance published since 2003 clearly articulates that those "Key Talent" entertainers whose remuneration does not include any element of "salary" – that is the remuneration payable under their contract of engagement does not include any payment computed by reference to the amount of time for which work is performed – are excluded from the Regulations. See particularly Tax Bulletin Issues 65 and 74.

In its published "Guidelines on the Special NIC Rules for Entertainers (PDF 194K)", HMRC clearly explains that the Regulations are to be applied to the exact terms of a particular entertainer's contract in order to determine whether the earnings from the contract are to be treated as employed earnings for NICs purposes.

HMRC's position going forward

"Actors" and "entertainers" were referred to specifically in Revenue & Customs Brief 10/11. To clarify, liability for Class 1 NICs arises in relation to all types of entertainers (for example, musicians, singers) engaged under contracts where the remuneration includes an element of salary (as defined in the Regulations).

HMRC has no plans to undertake concerted compliance activity in the media sector in respect of entertainers and the Regulations as a result of the ITV Services case. It will, however, continue to scrutinise those cases currently the subject of investigation and to apply its normal risk based approach to identifying cases which represent a high risk in terms of tax and/or NICs and it reserves the right to investigate such cases. Where HMRC is undertaking, or undertakes, an investigation into an entertainer or media company, it will apply the law in terms of the Regulations as enunciated by the UT.

Retrospective application of the Upper Tribunal's decision

The extent to which HMRC will seek to apply the UT decision retrospectively will be determined by a number of different factors.

Written opinion previously given

Where HMRC has previously issued a written opinion that Class 1 NICs are not due in respect of a particular contract because HMRC did not consider that it provided for payment by way of salary, it will *not seek from the party to* whom that written opinion was given retrospective recovery of the unpaid NICs that were due and payable prior to **6 April 2011** (unless HMRC has expressly advised an engager that NICs should be operated from an earlier date).

Extent of a written opinion

Where HMRC has previously provided a written opinion to an engager that Class 1 NICs are not due in respect of a particular contract, and that engager used an identical (other than for individual personal details) contract to engage other entertainers in the same production, HMRC will not seek arrears of Class 1 NICs due and payable prior to 6 April 2011.

No written opinion previously given

Where HMRC has not given a written opinion, then it reserves the right to seek retrospective recovery of any NICs arrears under its normal risk based approach, and subject to the provisions of the Limitation Act 1980.

ESM 4147 will be updated shortly to reflect the position following the UT decision.

Further information

Under the terms of its "Non-statutory clearance" service to businesses, should an engager have material uncertainty on the tax (or NICs) consequences of a particular contractual engagement, if appropriate, HMRC can provide its view of how the law applies to that contract.

Any such requests should be made by formal "Non-statutory clearance" application to Large Business Customer Relationship Managers, Film & Production or TV Broadcasting Units as appropriate enclosing details of the particular engagement and a copy of the relevant (signed) contract.

HMRCBrf 28/12 THE SOCIAL SECURITY (CATEGORISATION OF EARNERS) REGULATIONS 1978 IN RELATION TO LECTURERS, TEACHERS, INSTRUCTORS OR THOSE IN A SIMILAR CAPACITY [HMRC Brief 28/12, 17 October 2012]

Applications for refunds of National Insurance contributions paid in error or claims for financial redress

Who should read this?

Those who engage lecturers, teachers, instructors or trainers in a similar capacity, particularly, vocational and recreational training providers, including First Aid Training Providers.

Trainers particularly in the vocational and recreational fields who were engaged by their training provider under contracts for services (self-employment contracts) but who had Class 1 (employees') National Insurance contributions deducted.

Background

1. The Social Security (Categorisation of Earners) Regulations 1978 (the Regulations) made provision for treating lecturers, teachers, instructors or those in a similar capacity in traditional educational establishments, such as schools, colleges or universities etc, who were not employed under a contract of service (an employment contract) as employees for NICs purposes.

2. With effect from 6 April 2012 the relevant provisions of the Regulations were repealed so that the Regulations no longer apply to lecturers, teachers, instructors or those in a similar capacity.

3. However, prior to repeal, it is possible that earlier published HMRC guidance may have led some training providers particularly in the vocational or recreational sector to incorrectly apply the Regulations to payments made to trainers engaged under self-employment contracts. If the Regulations were incorrectly applied, Class 1 NICs may have been accounted for and paid to HMRC in error. HMRC will now consider claims for the refund of any incorrectly paid contributions. Such claims are limited by statute so that refunds may only be made in respect of the last two tax years or, where a decision was requested/challenged and this remains undetermined, the tax year in which the challenge was made and the preceding tax year.

Arrangements for claiming refunds of Class 1 National Insurance contributions paid in error

Who can claim refunds?

4. Refunds may be made by trainers or instructors, or those who engaged them, and where amounts of NICs were paid in error following HMRC's guidance. This is primarily going to affect those engaged in the provision of vocational or recreational training as set out in HMRC's guidance prior to repeal of the relevant provisions of the Regulations.

5. Refunds are not due where educational training providers applied the Regulations. This is because there is no dispute or doubt that the Regulations prior to 6 April 2012 applied to the providers of educational training. In this context educational training provider means a school, college, university or any such similar educational establishment.

6. Refunds are also not due where any trainer or instructor was engaged under an employment contract and Income Tax (PAYE) and Class 1 NICs were correctly accounted for.

7. Where a training provider owes HMRC any outstanding sums (including Income Tax, National Insurance contributions or VAT) any secondary Class 1 NICs refundable will, in the first instance, be set against those outstanding sums and only the balance repaid.

How do I know if I am entitled to apply for a refund?

Vocational and Recreational Training Providers

8. We believe there are likely to be three categories of training provider who may be eligible to apply for refunds:

- First Aid training providers who were subject to a compliance intervention by HMRC and Class 1 NICs were recovered under the Regulations where those amounts of NICs were paid in error following HMRC's guidance: HMRC is corresponding directly with these training providers. However, if you fall into this category and have not received a letter you should contact HMRC in writing at the address provided below.
- Other vocational and recreational training providers who were subject to a compliance intervention by HMRC, Class 1 NICs was recovered under the Regulations and where those amounts of NICs were paid in error following HMRC's guidance.
- Any other First Aid training or other vocational and recreational training providers not the subject of a compliance intervention but who wrote to HMRC requesting a decision as to the NICs category under which their trainers should be included.

Applications for refunds from Trainers and Engagers

9. Trainers who were engaged under self-employment contracts and who were subject to the Regulations by their training provider engager can choose not to have any primary contributions paid in error refunded to them but to let them count instead towards their contributory benefit entitlement as if they had been correctly paid. If a successful refund claim is received from a training provider which meets the statutory criteria, HMRC will write to the affected trainers asking them whether they wish the contributions refunded or not.

10. This does not prevent the engager from seeking a refund of the wrongly paid secondary contributions where one is due or the trainer notifying HMRC before they reach pension age that they now wish to apply for a refund. Any such claim in these circumstances would be subject to the statutory conditions for the claiming of refunds of erroneously paid contributions including those noted in paragraph 3 above.

11. Where trainers elect to have Class 1 contributions refunded, HMRC will offset the contributions refundable against the Class 2 and 4 National Insurance contributions correctly payable by virtue of the trainer's self-employed status. Additionally, where a trainer owes HMRC any outstanding sums (including Income Tax, NICs or VAT) any contributions refundable will be set against those outstanding sums and only the balance repaid.

How to apply for a refund

12. Training providers who engaged trainers under self-employment contracts and accounted for Class 1 NICs under the Social Security (Categorisation of Earners) Regulations 1978 and who think that they fall into any of the categories identified above should contact HMRC in writing. When writing they should provide the information detailed below. This will help us to check that their particular circumstances meet the statutory qualifying rules governing the refunding of Class 1 NICs.

Please write to:

The Employment Status Team
HM Revenue & Customs
PT (Product & Process)
Area 1E 09
100 Parliament Street
London
SW1A 2HQ

Please provide the following information:

- training provider's name
- whether a company, partnership or sole trader
- address

- PAYE reference
- Accounts Office reference
- precise nature of business
- the years for which a refund is claimed
- the amount of refund being claimed
- the name, NI number and address of the actual training provider's trainers in respect of whom a refund is being sought
- full details of any written request made by the provider or the trainer to an officer of HMRC (including the date of the request) asking for a decision, or a variation of a previous decision, as to the category of earner under which any of the training providers workers should be included – this should be accompanied by a copy of any decision received from HMRC

Financial Redress

HMRC can make Financial Redress payments under its complaints policy. Our guiding principle when making such payments is to ensure that the customer is not out of pocket as a direct result of our mistake. In the majority of cases, this will mean reimbursing the additional costs incurred as a direct result of our mistake, to the extent that they are reasonable. Common examples include the cost of telephone calls, postage, and any additional professional fees incurred, again to the extent that they are reasonable and proportionate. We will also consider payments for demonstrable financial loss, but not for any loss which is hypothetical, speculative or insubstantial, or the value of any refundable Class1 NICs paid in error.

Further information about our complaints processes can be found within the "Complaints" factsheet from the link below.

Complaints [http://www.hmrc.gov.uk/factsheets/complaints-factsheet.pdf]

HMRCBrf 29/13 NICS: HMRC'S POSITION FOLLOWING THE COURT OF APPEAL DECISION IN THE CASE OF ITV SERVICES LTD V COMMRS FOR HMRC [HMRC Brief 29/13, 2 October 2013]

Purpose of the Brief

This Brief sets out HM Revenue & Customs' (HMRC) position following the decision by the Court of Appeal (CoA) in the case of ITV Services Ltd (ITV). The case concerned the employment status for National Insurance contributions purposes of actors engaged by ITV under specific contract types. The Court handed down its judgment on 23 July 2013 and found against ITV unanimously upholding the decisions of the First Tier Tribunal (FTT) and Upper Tribunal (UT) that the actors' contracts provided for remuneration by way of salary and there was liability for Class 1 National Insurance contributions on all the remuneration payable under the contract. See also Revenue & Customs Brief 19/12 issued 14 June 2012.

You can read the full text of the decision on the British and Irish Legal Information Institute's website: ITV Services Ltd v Commissioners for HMRC [http://www.bailii.org/ew/cases/EWCA/Civ/2013/867.html].

Readership

All national broadcasters, film companies, theatre managers, independent production companies, their representative bodies and agents in the Film & TV Production Industries, Equity, individual entertainers and any other companies engaging entertainers to whom this judgement may also be relevant are encouraged to read this briefing.

Background

By a decision released on 23 November 2010, the FTT dismissed the appeals by ITV against three determinations made by HMRC. ITV appealed the FTT decision to the UT. By a decision released on 7 February 2012, the UT upheld the decision of the FTT and dismissed ITV's appeal. On 25 May 2012 ITV was given permission to appeal the decision of the UT to the CoA. This appeal was heard on 12 and 13 December 2012 and 18 March 2013.

ITV's appeal to the CoA again focused primarily on whether actors engaged by ITV were to be treated as "employed earners" for National Insurance purposes under the provisions of paragraph 5A of Part 1, Schedule 1 to the Social Security (Categorisation of Earners) Regulations 1978 (the Regulations) by virtue of the fact that the payments made to the actors by ITV were "by way of salary" within the meaning of "salary" as defined in that paragraph of the Regulations.

The CoA decision

By a decision handed down on 23 July 2013, the Court unanimously dismissed ITV's appeal and upheld the principal position maintained by HMRC throughout that whether or not the provisions of the Regulations apply is to be determined at the outset of an actor's engagement by reference to the terms of their specific contract.

In particular, the Court decided that where contracts between the engager and the entertainer incorporated the payment provisions of collective agreements (that is, national standard agreements negotiated between producers' representatives and Equity) the effect of such provisions would be to include payments "by way of salary" as defined. Save for what was described as an "All Rights Contract" (which HMRC had previously agreed was not within the Regulations), the two "All Inclusive Fees Equity Agreements", the "Weekly Equity Agreement" and the "Option Equity Agreement", the Court found that the remuneration agreed to be paid under all other contracts presented to it included payments provided for in the collective agreements (for example production day and attendance day payments) and, therefore, included a payment by way of salary. Furthermore, except for the All Rights Contract, in all other contracts where the terms entitled the entertainer to receive payment on a contingent basis (for example on account of overage/overtime), that payment was a "payment by way of salary".

HMRC does not consider that Lord Justice Rimer's views expressed at paragraphs 35, 36 and 37 of the judgment (and the conclusions that he reached on the contracts based on those paragraphs) alter the decision reached by both Tribunals below that, under the terms of their contract, where an actor is required to make himself/herself available for work as and when required by the engager for the period of the engagement they are performing work (as defined in the Regulations). Both the other CoA judges (Sir Stanley Burnton and the President of the Family Division, Sir James Munby,) expressed reservations on Rimer LJ's comments on this issue but reserved their position, since it was not necessary to determine the point to determine the appeal.

Future application of the Regulations following the judgment

Although the specific contracts cited in the CoA judgment only concerned actors engaged by ITV, HMRC considers that the principles established in this and the previous decisions in the Tribunals below cover all "entertainers" as statutorily defined in the Regulations – "a person employed as an actor, singer, or musician or in any similar performing capacity". HMRC now expects those in the industry engaging entertainers to comply with the Court's decision.

In particular all three judges agreed with the UT in its observation that hourly or daily payments such as overtime or overage payments, to which an entertainer is entitled under the contract, even though contingent and whether or not actually paid in practice, are computed by reference to the amount of time for which work is performed and are consequently payments by way of salary. This part of the judgment will have particular significance for those actors and musicians whose contracts are subject to the terms providing for payments under collective agreements with Equity and Musicians' Union respectively.

Given that HMRC now expects voluntary compliance with the Regulations, it does not intend to undertake concerted compliance activity in the media sector in respect of entertainers as a direct result of the ITV case. It will, however, continue to apply its normal risk-based approach to identifying individual cases which represent a high risk and reserves the right to investigate such cases. It will also continue to scrutinise those cases currently the subject of investigation.

Where HMRC is undertaking or undertakes an investigation into an entertainer or media company, it will apply the law in terms of the Regulations applying the decision and judgment of the UT and the CoA.

Retrospective application of the Court of Appeal decision

HMRC's position regarding retrospective liability is that set out in Revenue & Customs Brief 19/12 on 14 June 2012, following the UT decision. As such the extent to which HMRC will seek to apply the CoA decision retrospectively will be determined by a number of different factors.

Written opinion previously given

Where HMRC has previously issued a written opinion to a party that Class 1 National Insurance contributions are not due in respect of payments made under a particular contract because HMRC did not consider those payments to be "by way of salary", it will not seek recovery retrospectively of the unpaid National Insurance contributions that were due and payable prior to 6 April 2011 (unless HMRC has *expressly advised an engager that* National Insurance contributions should be operated from an earlier date).

Extent of written opinion

Where HMRC has previously provided a written opinion to an engager that Class 1 National Insurance contributions are not due in respect of a particular contract, and the engager used identical (other than for individual personal details) contract(s) to engage other entertainers, HMRC will not seek arrears of Class 1 National Insurance contributions due and payable prior to 6 April 2011 in respect of these other contracts.

No written opinion previously given

Where HMRC has not given such a written opinion, then it reserves the right to seek to recover any National Insurance contributions arrears under its normal compliance subject to the provisions of the Limitation Act 1980.

Consultation on National Insurance and self-employed entertainers

HMRC is mindful of the fact that it undertook a recent public consultation on options for amending the National Insurance treatment of entertainers at some point in the future and that its preferred option was to revoke those provisions of the Regulations that relate to entertainers with effect from 6 April 2014. If an amendment is made to the Regulations, such an amendment will only have prospective effect. The CoA judgment concerns the current and retrospective application of the relevant provisions in the Regulations and therefore will apply to any contracts entered into up until the point that any amendments to the current Regulations come into force. HMRC will be publishing a summary of the consultation responses and confirm the intended way forward later this year.

Further information

Under the terms of its Non-statutory clearance service to businesses, should an engager have material uncertainty on the National Insurance contributions consequences of a particular contractual engagement with an entertainer, if appropriate, HMRC can provide its view of how the law applies to that contract. Any such requests should be made by formal "Non-statutory clearance" application to Large Business Customer Relationship Managers, Film & Production or TV Broadcasting Units as appropriate enclosing details of the particular engagement and a copy of the relevant (signed) contract.

HMRCBrf 35/13 NICs: REPEAL OF THE SOCIAL SECURITY (CATEGORISATION OF EARNERS) REGULATIONS 1978 ("THE REGULATIONS") IN RESPECT OF ENTERTAINERS FROM 6 APRIL 2014 [HMRC Brief 35/13, 18 November 2013]

This Brief sets out HM Revenue & Customs (HMRC) position in relation to the liability of entertainers to pay National Insurance Contributions ("NICs") with effect from **6 April 2014** subject to the proposed changes in the Regulations being approved by Parliament.

Readership

All national broadcasters, film companies, theatre managers, independent production companies, their representative bodies and agents in the Film & TV Production Industries, Equity, individual entertainers, companies engaging entertainers, and any other interested parties.

Background

As a generality, entertainers (that is, those engaged as an actor, singer, or musician, or in any similar performing capacity) are engaged under self-employment terms and that their employment status, for both tax and NICs purposes, applying relevant case law criteria, is self-employment.

Since 1998 however, The Social Security (Categorisation of Earners) Regulations 1978 ("the Regulations") have deemed self-employed entertainers, in certain prescribed circumstances, to be employed earners for National Insurance purposes. The principal policy reason for this was to provide entertainers, through the payment of Class 1 NICs, with access to earnings-related contributory benefit entitlement when out of work.

In more recent years though, the manner in which entertainers have been and are being engaged and paid for their work has made it increasingly difficult for the Regulations to be applied and operated as intended, causing uncertainties and fundamental, problems for both entertainers and engagers in deciding whether Class 1 NICs should be deducted and accounted for on payments made to and by them.

Public consultation

Following 18 months of extensive engagement with representatives from all fields of the entertainment industry, HMRC published on 15 May 2013 a public consultation document: "National Insurance and Self-Employed Entertainers", which discussed the precise difficulties being caused by the current application of the Regulations. The consultation presented four possible options for simplifying the NICs treatment of entertainers going forwards.

The consultation ran for 12 weeks receiving 11,814 individual responses of which 99.1% supported the option of repealing the Social Security (Categorisation of Earners) Regulations in relation to the entertainers. On 23 October 2013 HMRC published a summary of the consultation responses which included the announcement of the Government's decision to repeal these Regulations insofar as they relate to entertainers from 6 April 2014 and a first draft of the legislation implementing this.

You can read the full consultation document and the summary of consultation responses on the central Government website.

HMRC consultation on NICs and entertainers [http://bit.ly/11E5Dbf].

The current NICs position for entertainers until 5 April 2014

The Regulations as articulated in the Upper Tribunal and Court of Appeal decision and judgement in the case of ITV Services Ltd v HMRC continue to apply up to and including 5 April 2014.

The Regulations are applied to entertainers on an engagement by engagement basis. This means each contract of engagement they enter into is looked at separately for the purposes of deciding whether the Regulations should apply to the payments to be made under its terms.

Where the Regulations currently apply to a particular contract of an entertainer, the earnings derived from that contract are presently subject to primary and secondary Class 1 NICs as defined in Section 6 of the Social Security Contributions and Benefits Act 1992 ("SSCBA 1992"). This includes any additional payments that derive from that engagement such as royalties or residuals payments that may continue to be paid to an entertainer for some time after their original performance/engagement has ended.

Under the current Regulations the primary Class 1 NICs contributor is the entertainer, and the secondary contributor is the producer of the entertainment from which the entertainer's earnings are derived. The secondary contributor (that is, the producer of the entertainment) is liable to deduct and account for the primary Class 1 NICs from the entertainer at time of payment and to pay both these and the secondary Class 1 NICs due to HMRC.

Further details of when the Regulations currently apply to an entertainer's contract can be found in HMRC's published guidance for entertainers, available on its website.

Entertainers – Guidelines on the Specials NIC Rules for Entertainers (select from on-screen guidance menu) [http://www.hmrc.gov.uk/menus/techmenu.htm]

Revenue and Customs Brief 19/12 [http://www.hmrc.gov.uk/briefs/national-insurance/brief1912.htm]

Revenue and Customs Brief 29/13 [http://www.hmrc.gov.uk/briefs/national-insurance/brief2913.htm]

HMRC expects engagers of entertainers to continue following this guidance and where the Regulations apply, operating primary and secondary Class 1 NICs on payments to entertainers up to and including 5 April 2014.

The future NICs position for entertainers from 6 April 2014

Subject to the proposed changes being approved by Parliament, from 6 April 2014, entertainers will no longer be included in the provisions of the Regulations. This in turn means that entertainers' earnings will no longer be brought within the ambit of Section 6 of SSCBA 1992 (which places a Class 1 NICs charge on them) from this date.

Where there is no Class 1 NICs charge under SSCBA 1992, the earnings will be self-employed earnings and subject to Class 2 NICs (subject to the existing Class 2 Small Earnings Exemption rules) and Class 4 NICs (subject to the existing the Class 4 Upper and Lower Earnings Limit rules).

As the point at which Class 1 NICs is charged is the time of payment (as opposed to the time of the engagement or the contract of engagement being entered into), the practical effect of repealing the Regulations for entertainers will be that from 6 April 2014 payments to entertainers paid under a contract for services (that, is self-employment) will be liable to Class 2 and Class 4 NICs under section 11 (Class 2) and sections 15 to 18 (Class 4) of SSCBA 1992 and subject to the existing Class 2 and Class 4 NICs rules.

The Regulations will not therefore apply to any payments made to entertainers after 6 April 2014.

These payments will not attract a Class 1 NICs liability from this date and will instead attract a Class 2 and (where applicable) Class 4 NICs liability as detailed above. This includes payments made to entertainers after 6 April 2014 but which derive from a contract for services entered into before this date.

What happens next?

If you are an entertainer

From 6 April 2014, producers engaging your performance services will not be required to deduct Class 1 NICs contributions from any payments they make to you. This includes additional use payments such as royalties. Your engager will make payments to you gross of tax and NICs and you must declare these earnings as part of your normal self-employed Self-Assessment return.

Please note that this guidance does not apply if you are on an employment contract, and receive a regular salary from your engager with tax and NICs deducted at source under the Pay As You Earn (PAYE) system.

If you engage the services of entertainers

From 6 April 2014, you will not be required to operate Class 1 NICs for the entertainers you engage. If you are currently deducting employees' Class 1 NICs from the payments you make to your entertainers (including additional use payments such as royalties), and paying the respective employers' Class 1 NICs on these payments, you should continue to do so up until 5 April 2014. From 6 April 2014 however you should cease to do this.

If you use an automated payroll system or an external payroll provider service you will need to ensure your systems or payroll arrangements are updated to ensure that Class 1 NICs continue to operate on payments you make to entertainers up to 5 April 2014, and cease to be operated from 6 April 2014.

If you provide advice to those in the entertainment industry

You should refer any parties you advise to the contents of this Revenue and Customs brief and to HMRC's other published guidance on this issue as listed earlier in this brief.

Retrospective recovery of Class 1 NICs

Revenue and Customs Brief 29/13 (hyperlink above) explains HMRC's position in respect of Class 1 NICs that are due for entertainers in respect of all periods up to 5 April 2014.

HMRC now expects voluntary compliance with the Regulations as detailed in Revenue and Customs brief 29/13 and therefore it does not intend to undertake concerted compliance activity in the media sector in respect of entertainers. It will, however, continue to apply its normal risk-based approach to identifying individual cases which represent a high risk and reserves the right to investigate such cases. HMRC will also continue to inspect those cases currently the subject of investigation.

Where HMRC is undertaking or undertakes an investigation into an entertainer or media company, it will apply the law in terms of the Regulations as they currently stand, applying the decision and judgement of the Upper Tribunal and the Court of Appeal in the case of ITV Services Ltd v HMRC for any relevant periods up to and including 5 April 2014.

HMRC will in due course publish separate guidance for entertainers with National Insurance records that may have been affected by this decision and judgement.

Further information

Under the terms of its Non-statutory clearance service to businesses, should an engager have material uncertainty on the NICs consequences of a particular contractual engagement with an entertainer, if appropriate, HMRC can provide its view of how the law applies to that contract.

Any such requests should be made by formal "Non-statutory clearance" application to Large Business Customer Relationship Managers, Film & Production or TV Broadcasting Units as appropriate enclosing details of the particular engagement and a copy of the relevant (signed) contract.

HMRCBrf11/14 THE SOCIAL SECURITY (CATEGORISATION OF EARNERS) REGULATIONS IN RELATION TO ENTERTAINERS [HMRC Brief 11/14, 31 March 2014]

Who should read this?

Any individual engaged as an entertainer (i.e. actor, singer, musician or in any similar performing capacity) under standard Equity or Musicians' Union contract(s) for any period(s) between 6 April 2003 and 5 April 2011.

Agents or accountants acting for any entertainer described above who potentially may fall into one of the categories further described.

Equity, Musicians Union officials or other representative bodies able to identify any individual or groups of entertainers who potentially satisfy the qualifying conditions described below. In these circumstances it would be appreciated if this briefing was brought to the attention of the entertainers concerned.

Background

The Social Security (Categorisation of Earners) Regulations 1978 made provision for treating entertainers who were not employed under a contract of service (an employee's contract) as employees for NIC purposes. The Regulations were revised in 2003 to their present format and it was announced in R & C Brief 35/13 that the regulations are to be revoked from 6 April 2014.

R & C Brief 19/12 issued on 14 June 2012 set out HMRC's position on the liability of entertainers following the decision of the Upper Tribunal (UT) to uphold the decision of the First Tier Tribunal (FTT) which dismissed an appeal in the case of ITV Services Ltd v Commissioners for HMRC. A further appeal by ITV Services Ltd to the Court of Appeal was also dismissed and the relevant details of this decision were reported in R & C Brief 29/13 on 2 October 2013. Both of these decisions effectively widened the scope of the legislation as it stood following the decision of the FTT on 23 November 2010 to the extent that some contracts previously considered not to fall within the legislation now did so. For that reason HMRC set out its position on the retrospective application of the UT and COA decisions in the above briefings as follows:

> "Where HMRC had previously issued a written opinion to a party that Class 1 NICs were not due in respect of a particular contract (or identical contracts) because HMRC did not consider the relevant payments to be "by way of salary," it would not seek recovery retrospectively of the unpaid NICs that were due and payable prior to 6 April 2011."

This could potentially leave the individual entertainer with a shortfall in their NIC record through no fault of their own which HMRC is obliged to redress.

Legislation

Where a liability to pay Class 1 NICs arises, those NICs should be paid and recorded to the individual's NI account. However, there are occasions, like those covered by this briefing, where despite their being a Class 1 liability, no NICs are recorded on an individual's account for that employment. Where this is the case it may be possible to record the missing NICs as "Treated as Paid".

Treating as paid is legislative and is provided for under the provisions of Regulation 60 of the Social Security (Contributions) Regulations 2001. This regulation allows for unpaid primary Class 1 NICs to be treated as paid, but only for the purpose of entitlement to contributory benefit.

Primary Class 1 NICs can be treated as paid provided the failure to pay was not:

- with the consent or connivance of the employee; or
- attributable to any negligence on the part of the employee

Treating NICs as paid under regulation 60 may only be considered when primary Class 1 NICs have not been paid to HMRC.

Regulation 60 therefore serves to protect the benefit entitlement of the individual where primary NICs have not been paid but the employee cannot be held responsible for that failure to pay.

Primary Class 1 NICs will therefore be treated as paid where we can establish that:

- there is a Class 1 NICs liability
- the primary Class 1 NICs have not been paid to HMRC
- the failure to pay was not due to the consent or connivance, or any negligence on the part of the employee

In the case of qualifying entertainers the above will apply and Primary NICs for those engagements can be treated as paid.

Arrangements for applying to have Class 1 employee's NI contributions treated as paid

Who can apply?

HMRC believes that the Regulation 60 provisions apply to a small number of entertainers who were engaged for periods between 6 April 2003 (when the current "entertainers" regulations were introduced) and 5 April 2011 and, for the period(s) of the engagement(s), their engager did not pay employers and employees Class 1 NIC because HMRC had given a written opinion to their engager that there was no liability for Class1 NICs.

How do I know if I am eligible to have Class 1 employee's NI contributions treated as paid?

Applications for treating Class 1 employee's NI contributions as paid

How to apply

Entertainers who were engaged to provide their services between 6 April 2003 and 5 April 2011 and were aware or have been made aware that a written opinion was given by HMRC between these dates that no Class 1 NICs were due for that engagement are invited to apply by downloading an application form CA9184 as soon as possible.

When applying all sections of the form must be completed to enable us to check that your particular circumstances meet the criteria for entitlement to have employees' Class 1 NICs treated as paid. The form will ask you to provide:

- the name of the party that engaged you (if this was not the producer)
- the start and end dates that work was undertaken for the engagement, the title of the entertainment production and the engager's name (producer of the entertainment)
- information relating to the frequency of payment i.e. whether monies were received weekly/monthly etc…
- the amount of payment you received gross of any agent's or other fees for each tax year whilst employed by this engager
- details of any self employment undertaken during t he same period that you were engaged

A copy of the original written opinion from HMRC should also be included with the application where this is available.

Please address applications to:

Film & Production Unit, Floor 2
HM Revenue & Customs
Weardale House
Washington
Tyne & Wear
NE37 1LW

The above location applies to ALL applications whether from entertainers in the TV industry, Film Industry or musicians. The special arrangements which HMRC is making in order to undertake action in these cases is expected to last no more than 2 years so it is important to apply as soon as possible.

If your application is accepted you will be notified once your NI record has been amended.

TAX BULLETIN

INTERPRETATIONS

IRInt. 3001 REVISED SPECIAL NIC RULES FOR ENTERTAINERS [HMRC Tax Bulletin 65, June 2003]

Background

The NIC treatment of entertainers is different from that which applies for tax.

Following the Special Commissioner's case for McCowen and West the Revenue accepted that most performers/artistes in the entertainment sector were engaged under contracts for services and would generally be assessable to tax under Schedule D. However, it was acknowledged that to follow this line for NIC purposes would mean that the majority of entertainers who had previously paid Class 1 NICs would only be liable for Class 2 and Class 4 NICs which would not provide them with universal title to contributory benefits.

DSS Ministers decided to introduce regulations in 1998 which would treat the majority of entertainers as employed earners for NIC purposes. This would enable entertainers to build up entitlement to contribution based Jobseeker's Allowance and ensure that, in a precarious industry, new talent could be encouraged to weather long periods without work whilst they established themselves.

Prior to 1998, the main category of performer in the entertainment industry not paying Class 1 contributions were certain "key talent" stars who were generally regarded as having been engaged on productions because of their celebrity status. To try and ensure this practice continued The Social Security (Categorisation of Earners) (Amendment) Regulations 1998 were introduced from 17 July 1998 which created a liability for Class 1 NICs for entertainers whose earnings consisted "wholly or mainly of salary". Those who negotiated a fee or received rights and additional use payments higher than the salary element were not liable to pay Class 1 NICs but were regarded as self-employed as such payments did not come within the accepted description of "salary".

However, in all but a few exceptional cases it has become the usual practice for the majority of entertainers to receive as part of their remuneration package pre-purchase payments as compensation for the loss of future repeat fees and rights and royalties worth many times the salary element. Very few actors were, therefore, paid "wholly or mainly" by salary and the regulations did not achieve the object of bringing most entertainers into Class 1.

The Revenue, therefore, accepted that the 1998 regulations were not sustainable and new regulations were introduced from 6 April 2003. These are the Social Security (Categorisation of Earners) (Amendment) Regulations 2003 [SI 2003 No. 736]. Equivalent regulations SI 2003 No 733 apply for Northern Ireland.

What do the new regulations mean?

The new regulations reflect the fact that instead of a "wholly or mainly" salary test, those entertainers whose remuneration includes any element of salary would be treated as employed earners. Once subject to the regulations there will be liability for Class 1NICs on all earnings from the engagement (including rights payments.)

Where the payment is a fee for the production, not a salary, and this would have to be made clear in the contract, the entertainer would remain self-employed and would be liable to Class 2 and Class 4 NICs.

The legislative definition of Salary requires that the remuneration satisfies the following four conditions:

- made for services rendered;
- paid under a contract for services;
- where there is more than one payment, payable at a specified period or interval; and computed by reference to the amount of time for which work has been performed.

The third bullet point includes those entertainers engaged on a single day or two day engagement. This means that the policy intention of ensuring that the regulations apply to film extras and walk-on parts is achieved. The last bullet point ensures that key talent artistes are excluded as they will be contracted to appear in productions for which their remuneration is not directly calculated according to the period of weeks or months they are assigned to the production.

What if the entertainer is engaged through an agency?

The legislation also includes provisions which amend paragraph 10 of Schedule 3 to the Social Security (Categorisation of Earners) Regulations 1978 to ensure that where an entertainer is engaged through a third party (an agency) the producer of the entertainment in respect of which the payments of salary are made is treated as the secondary contributor. However, this does not override the effect of the Intermediaries legislation (IR35) which provides that where an entertainer provides his services to a client through a personal service company it is the latter which is the secondary contributor.

Exceptions

In accordance with the Revenue's policy intention Session Musicians and Session Singers, who are generally engaged through Musicians Union approved contractors and whose earnings were not previously subject to Class 1NICs, are excepted from the new regulations.

Arrangements For Claiming Refunds Of Class 1 NICs Paid In Error

Who can claim refunds

The 1998 Regulations have led to some entertainers being wrongly categorised as employed earners because their remuneration did not consist "wholly or mainly of salary" and therefore any primary or secondary Class 1 contributions which have been paid in relation to entertainers on the footing that they were employed earners may have been incorrectly paid. There is provision under National Insurance legislation for the return of contributions which have been paid in error and refund claims will be invited for appropriate periods between 17 July 1998 and 5 April 2003.

The restriction of refund claims to 2 years provided for in section 19A of the Social Security Contributions and Benefits Act 1992 will be waived for the purposes of this exercise until a cut-off point is announced. However, individuals can choose not to have their primary contributions refunded, but to let them count instead towards their Additional Pension (AP) entitlement, as if they had been correctly paid. This does not prevent the engager from seeking a refund of the wrongly paid secondary contributions or the individual notifying the Revenue that they wish to claim a refund before they reach pension age, subject to the appropriate time limits.

Primary NICs refunded to entertainers will be reduced by the amount of any Class 2 and 4 contributions which were due from them as self-employed earners, and of any contributory benefits paid on the basis of the incorrect Class 1 contributions.

How to make a claim

An engager or entertainer who considers that Class 1 NI contributions may have been incorrectly paid between 17 July 1998 and 5 April 2003 can apply for a refund. Claims for all tax years should be submitted together. Anyone who wishes to do so in the belief that workers previously treated as employed earners should have been regarded as self-employed should write to:

Inland Revenue
National Insurance Contributions Office
Refunds Group (Erroneous 4)
Room BP1001
Benton Park View
Newcastle upon Tyne
NE98 1ZZ

Alternatively they should telephone Refunds Group on 084591 – 2254042 [calls will be charged at BT local rates]

Claim forms will be available on request from the end of June 2003 and Refunds Group will begin dealing with refund applications shortly after that. As an alternative to the written application form some engagers may find it more convenient to submit claims for refunds by CD-Rom or floppy disk and this facility will be available on request.

What information is needed?

Engagers will need to give as much information as possible when making a claim i.e. Full name of individual / Stage Name (where appropriate)/ NINO/ Date of Birth/ Correct address. They will also be required to declare:

i) All Basic and Rights Payments made in each tax year for which a claim is made.
ii) Total earnings on which NICs were deducted and total amount of NICs paid.
iii) Amounts of employers and employees contributions.
iv) The type of contract under which the individual has been engaged; If it is either of the standard BBC/EQUITY, ITVA/EQUITY or PACT/EQUITY contracts then no other proof of payment will be required. Contracts and/or invoices will be required in all other cases.

What happens when claims are received?

On receipt the claim will be registered and if sufficient information is supplied, all secondary Class 1 NICs confirmed as erroneously paid will be refunded. All claims will be dealt with in the order they are received and will be processed as soon as possible. Employees named on the claim form who, as a result of previous refund action, have already notified the Inland Revenue that they did not wish to claim a refund of primary NICs, will not be contacted but applications will be accepted from those individuals who choose not to allow their wrongly paid contributions to remain on their NI record.

How do applicants know if they are entitled to a refund?

If Class 1 NICs have been paid between 17 July 1998 and 5 April 2003 in respect of entertainers whose remuneration does not satisfy the "wholly or mainly of salary" criteria in the 1998 regulations then a refund of those contributions may be claimed. For example remuneration made up of 60% Rights Payments and 40% Salary would not be "wholly or mainly of salary" and there would have been no liability for Class 1 NICs. However, Class 1 NICs were properly payable in cases where, at the time of the engagement, it was known that the salary element of the remuneration exceeded any residuals. Therefore, any subsequent residual payments not quantifiable at the time of the original engagement will not change the nature of the original payment. The rule of thumb being that the status decision at the point of first contact is the deciding factor.

The following table indicates whether or not the various elements of remuneration under any of the standard BBC/Equity, ITVA/Equity or PACT/Equity contracts satisfy the case law definition of salary:

Type of Payment	Salary/Rights Payment
Engagement Fees	Salary or negotiable payment depending upon contract type
Attendance days	Salary
Standby days	Salary
Holiday pay	Salary
Overtime	Salary
Additional Use fee	Rights payment for pre-purchase
Retainer	Salary – to ensure services available when needed
Secondary Sales	Rights payment – "one off" for sale of programme
Repeat fees	Rights payment – either pre-purchase or at each repeat
Option fee	Rights payment – to ensure an engager has priority use of an entertainers services

What now?

If any entertainers, practitioners or engagers are in any doubt about the new regulations or whether they are entitled to a refund they should contact their nearest Inland Revenue office and ask to speak to a member of the Status team. Enquiries about entertainers engaged by TV Broadcasting Companies should be made to the TV Industry Unit on 0161 2613255.

Guidance notes on the new legislation and the arrangements for claiming refunds have been prepared for the entertainment industry and these will also be available at: [http://www.hmrc.gov.uk/guidance/nicrules-ents.pdf] from the end of June 2003.

IRInt. 3002 NATIONAL INSURANCE CONTRIBUTIONS LIABILITY ON PAYMENTS INTO FUNDED UNAPPROVED RETIREMENT BENEFITS SCHEMES [HMRC Tax Bulletin 65, June 2003]

Introduction

You may be aware that, as a result of the High Court decision in Tullett & Tokyo Forex International Ltd and Others v The Secretary of State for Social Security [2000] EWHC Admin 350, the Inland Revenue has been reconsidering its position on the National Insurance contributions (NICs) liability on payments into a Funded Unapproved Retirement Benefits Scheme (FURBS). This article sets out the conclusion of its deliberations. It confirms the Revenue's existing and published view that such payments are liable for Class 1 NICs.

All the legislative references mentioned in this article are those which apply in Great Britain. Northern Ireland has its own legislation which, in the main, is the same as that for Great Britain. But, for ease, we refer only to the latter in this article.

Background

In May 1998 the Secretary of State (SofS) for Social Security decided, under section 17 of the Social Security Administration Act 1992 (SSAA 1992), that bonuses made by way of additional payments in the form of short-dated gilts to life assurance policies were earnings and liable for Class 1 NICs.

The three employers involved appealed against the SofS's decisions. In May 2000, the High Court gave judgement, when it decided in favour of the companies and allowed the appeals. Under section 18(6) SSAA 1992, a decision of the High Court is final.

Legislation

Subject to certain conditions, section 6(1) Social Security Contributions and Benefits Act 1992 (CBA 1992) provides that a Class 1 NICs liability arises when "earnings are paid to or for the benefit of an earner [employee]". "Earnings" are defined in section 3(1) CBA 1992 as including "any remuneration or profit derived from an employment".

The High Court's decision

The court decided that payments by the employers of the short-dated gilts to life assurance policies held by their employees were not earnings "paid to or for the benefit of" the employees in question within the meaning of section 6(1) CBA 1992. Mr Justice Collins held that, in construing section 6(1), it was necessary to look at what the employee receives. As such, the "earnings paid to or for the benefit" of the employees was:

- the enhancement in the value of the life assurance policies held by the employees; and
- not the gilts paid into the assurance policies, which was merely the cost to the employers of making such payments.

The enhancement in the value of the policies was a payment in kind. As such, it fell to be disregarded, for the purposes of calculating the amount of the employees' gross earnings for Class 1 NICs purposes, by virtue of regulation 19(1)(d) of the Social Security (Contributions) Regulations 1979 (since 6th April 2001, paragraph 1 of Part II of Schedule 3 to the Social Security (Contributions) Regulations 2001 (SI No. 2001/1004; the 2001 Regulations)).

NICs liability on payments into a FURBS

Since November 1997, the view has been that employer's cash payments into a FURBS are earnings "paid to or for the benefit of" an employee within the meaning of section 6(1) CBA 1992. Where such a payment is made in respect of two or more employees, paragraph 13 of Schedule 2 to the 2001 Regulations sets out how the amount of earnings for each employee comprised in the payments into the FURBS must be calculated.

Implications of the Tullett & Tokyo decision on the NICs liability on payments into a FURBS

The Revenue has been considering the effect of the Tullett & Tokyo judgement on the NICs liability on payments into a FURBS. After full and careful consideration, the Revenue does not accept the High Court's reasoning as applying to a payment into a FURBS.

We consider that:

- in reaching his decision, Mr Justice Collins put too much emphasis on Schedule E tax case law when the three appeals concerned the interpretation of NICs legislation;
- the definition of "earnings" in section 3(1) CBA 1992 is much wider than "emoluments" in section 131(1) ICTA 1988 (from 6th April 2003, "earnings" within section 62 Income Tax (Earnings and Pensions) Act 2003);
- the wording of section 6(1) CBA 1992 – "…earnings…paid to or for the benefit of…" – further extends the meaning of "earnings"
- so in some circumstances, as in the case of employer payments into a FURBS, "earnings" includes payments made to a third party for the benefit of the employee.

All of which means that there is no change to the Revenue's stated position that a payment into a FURBS is liable for Class 1 NICs. This position is set out:

- in booklet CWG2 (2003) "Employer's Further Guide to PAYE and NICs":
- in paragraph 81 on page 57; and
- on page 76 under "retirement benefits schemes"
- on pages 02155 to 02163 of the Revenue's internal guidance, the "National Insurance Manual"

Unpaid Class 1 NICs on payments into a FURBS

Where due, the Revenue will seek payment of any Class 1 NICs which have not been paid on payments into a FURBS. It will also seek interest on the unpaid amount.

Requests for refunds of Class 1 NICs paid on payments into a FURBS

As a result of the Tullett & Tokyo judgement, the Revenue has received a number of requests for refunds of the Class 1 NICs which have been paid on payments into a FURBS. These requests have been refused.

A refund can only be made if the NICs have been paid in error (regulation 52(1)(a) of the 2001 Regulations). "Error" is defined in regulation 52(12) as meaning, and only meaning, an error which:

- is made at the time of payment; and
- relates to some present or past matter.

As explained above, the Revenue's view is that a payment into a FURBS is liable for Class 1 NICs. It follows that the NICs paid on a payment into a FURBS have not been paid in error within the meaning of regulation 52(12) of the 2001 Regulations. So the NICs cannot be refunded.

OTHER HMRC MATERIAL

HMRC SPOTLIGHTS

SPOTLIGHT 24 – EMPLOYMENT ALLOWANCE AVOIDANCE SCHEME – CONTRIVED ARRANGEMENTS CAUGHT BY EXISTING RULES [HMRC, June 2015]

Contents

The Employment Allowance entitles employers to save up to £2,000 of employer's National Insurance contributions (NICs), and since its launch in 2014 over a million employers have benefited. To ensure that the benefit of the allowance was felt where it was most needed, anti-avoidance arrangements were included in the allowance from launch. An attempted avoidance scheme designed to exploit the Employment Allowance has recently caught the attention of the media, including BBC's Today programme and BBC online on 29 May 2015.

HM Revenue and Customs (HMRC) view is that this scheme simply does not work. HMRC strongly advises anyone who has used such a scheme to withdraw. By withdrawing and notifying HMRC, people will avoid the costs of investigation and litigation and minimise interest on underpaid National Insurance and any penalties that might be applicable. HMRC is investigating cases where people have used this scheme and will challenge every case it sees. HMRC recommends that employers considering the use of such a scheme should think again. Users will find themselves out of pocket from the promoter's fees, and possible interest and penalties on the NICs liability.

Scheme promoters suggest that users of the scheme can save themselves their entire employer NICs bill. The proposition is that a payroll company takes on your staff and sets up underlying companies, each of which employs small numbers of your staff. You are invoiced for the services your ex staff provide – as you no longer employ them. Each company claims the full Employment Allowance to wipe out the employer NICs liability.

This scheme sounds too good to be true and it is. There is a targeted anti-avoidance rule in the Employment Allowance, so attempted avoidance schemes like this, which seek to use artificial and contrived arrangements to get an unintended advantage, do not work.

HMRC's firm view is that such schemes are notifiable under the Disclosure of Tax Avoidance Schemes (DOTAS) rules. Anyone who comes within the meaning of a promoter for such a scheme who has not notified it under the DOTAS rules could be liable for a fine of up to £1 million. The definition of "promoter" under the DOTAS rules (https://www.gov.uk/government/publications/disclosure-of-tax-avoidance-schemes-guidance) goes beyond those who devise the scheme itself.

It includes people who:

- make a firm approach to another person with a view to making a scheme available for implementation by that person or others
- make a scheme available for implementation by others
- organise or manage the implementation of a scheme

SPOTLIGHT 31: CHANGE OF DATE FOR WITHDRAWAL OF TRANSITIONAL RELIEF ON INVESTMENT GROWTH [HMRC, August 2016]

Change of date for withdrawal of transitional relief on investment growth

The government intends to extend the date for withdrawal of transitional relief on investment growth currently available under paragraph 59 of Schedule 2 to Finance Act 2011 (Para 59) from 30 November 2016 to 31 March 2017.

The withdrawal of the relief was announced at Budget [https://www.gov.uk/government/topical-events/budget-2016] on 16 March 2016, as part of the package of changes to tackle the use of disguised remuneration avoidance schemes (such as Employee Benefit Trusts (EBTs) and contractor loans) and ensure that those who have used these schemes pay their fair share of tax and National Insurance contributions. More information can be found in the Technical note [https://www.gov.uk/government/publications/tackling-disguised-remuneration-avoidance-schemes-overview-of-changes-and-technical-note/technical-note].

The transitional relief was intended to work alongside the EBT settlement opportunity, which closed on 31 March 2015.

Customers, their advisers and promoters should be aware that HM Revenue and Customs (HMRC) continues to believe that disguised remuneration schemes don't work, and will challenge these rigorously.

The government wants to ensure all users of disguised remuneration schemes have the opportunity to settle with HMRC before the transitional relief in Para 59 is withdrawn. Therefore an amendment to Finance Bill 2016 [https://www.gov.uk/government/collections/finance-bill-2016] has been tabled to extend the date for the withdrawal to 31 March 2017. The amendment, once agreed by Parliament, will mean that users who want to benefit from the transitional relief on investment growth in Para 59 must have settled on or before 31 March 2017.

If you or your clients have used or are using a disguised remuneration scheme you should seriously consider settling your tax affairs and talk to HMRC about how to do this. If you are already speaking to someone at HMRC about your use of a disguised remuneration scheme you should contact them in the first instance. If you don't have a contact, you should email: ca.admin@hmrc.gsi.gov.uk and someone will get back to you very quickly.

Related guidance

Disguised remuneration: transitional relief on investment growth (https://www.gov.uk/guidance/disguised-remuneration-transitional-relief-on-investment-growth)

Register to settle with HMRC by 31 October 2016 if you want to get transitional relief on your investment growth.

Employee Benefit Trust settlements after 31 July 2015 (https://www.gov.uk/government/publications/employee-benefit-trust-settlements-after-31-july-2015)

The general principles that HMRC will apply to settlements following the withdrawal of the Employee Benefit Trust Settlement Opportunity.

SPOTLIGHT 32: MANAGED SERVICE COMPANY LEGISLATION: UNPAID PAYE AND CLASS 1 NI CONTRIBUTIONS AVOIDANCE SCHEMES [HMRC, February 2018]

1. First-tier Tribunal and Upper Tribunal decisions

HM Revenue and Customs (HMRC) has won a case in the First-tier Tribunal (FTT) involving attempts to avoid PAYE Income Tax and Class 1 National Insurance Contributions (NICs) on employment income.

HMRC successfully argued that the managed service companies (MSC) legislation (Chapter 9 of Part 2 of the Income Tax (Earnings and Pensions) Act 2003 and equivalent National Insurance contributions legislation) applied to arrangements established and run by a third party – Costelloe Business Services Limited.

Following an appeal, the Upper Tribunal (UT) agreed with the original FTT decision that the appellant's companies were operating as MSCs.

In addition to the original decision, the UT considered 2 additional areas.

Firstly, the definition of a MSC provider as "a person who carries on a business of promoting or facilitating the use of companies to provide the services of individuals". This decision confirms HMRC's view that if the answer to both of the following questions is yes, a person is a MSC provider:

- does the person promote or facilitate the use of a company?
- does that company provide the services of individual?

Secondly, the UT decided that "influences" or "control" has a wider meaning than that expressed in the FTT decision. In this case, Costelloe Business Services Limited influenced how payments were made to workers through the use of a standard product, by causing the workers to receive wages and dividends instead of just wages.

When workers buy into such products, allowing the MSC provider to determine the amount to be paid as a dividend and to carry out the administrative steps to affect this, it amounts to "control".

2. Effect of the MSC legislation

Where a company is set up to provide a worker's services to an engager and the MSC legislation applies, amounts paid to an MSC for those services that are not already subject to PAYE Income Tax and Class 1 NICs (for example, share dividends), are treated as employment income.

HMRC's firm view, now supported by the tribunal decision, has always been that these types of arrangements do not work.

HMRC continues to open enquiries into users of similar arrangements that include the provision of workers in many different industry sectors, including road haulage, healthcare and education.

HMRC will investigate and challenge these arrangements through every route open to it (including litigation) and seek full settlement of the tax due, plus interest and penalties where appropriate.

The FTT recently granted the appellant's leave to appeal.

We expect those using these or similar arrangements to pay the tax and NICs they owe following this emphatic win for HMRC.

If any part of the tax and NICs are irrecoverable, HMRC will transfer unpaid debts to others, including the service company's directors, the MSC provider and the MSC provider's directors and associates. All are jointly and severally liable for the debts.

Promoters should carefully consider the Disclosure of Tax Avoidance Scheme (DOTAS) rules to determine if the arrangements they are marketing should be declared to HMRC.

HMRC's DOTAS taskforce will closely examine whether DOTAS should apply to individual cases.

HMRC is relentless in closing down avoidance schemes and encourages users of similar products operated to settle their outstanding tax or NICs enquiries now.

If you're ever tempted to enter an avoidance scheme, remember that you can end up significantly worse off. If the scheme looks too good to be true, it almost certainly is.

FTT decision: *Christianuyi Ltd & Ors v HM Revenue and Customs* UKFTT 272 (TC) (21 April 2016)

UT decision: *Christianuyi Ltd and Others v The Commissioners for HM Revenue and Customs* [2018] UKUT 10 (TCC)

SPOTLIGHT 36: DISGUISED REMUNERATION: SCHEMES CLAIMING TO AVOID THE NEW LOAN CHARGE [HMRC, December 2017]

Disguised remuneration avoidance schemes are used by employers and individuals to avoid Income Tax and National Insurance contributions. Although there are various types, they normally result in a loan from a third party on such terms that mean it's unlikely to ever be repaid.

At Budget 2016 the government announced a number of changes to tackle existing avoidance schemes and prevent their future use.

The changes will include a new "loan charge" on disguised remuneration loans which are outstanding on 5 April 2019. To prevent attempts to exploit the new loan charge, a targeted anti-avoidance rule will ensure further avoidance schemes don't work.

More details on these changes can be found in the consultation on tackling disguised remuneration (https://www.gov.uk/government/consultations/tackling-disguised-remuneration-technical-consultation).

Schemes claiming to avoid the loan charge

Some promoters claim to have come up with schemes that enable users to get out of the loan arrangements and avoid the loan charge, in return for a fee.

Spotlight 39 (https://www.gov.uk/guidance/disguised-remuneration-re-describing-loans-spotlight-39) sets out details of one of these schemes. Another example is that some promoters say that individuals should enter into a bet with the trust that granted them the loan. The terms of the **"bet"** mean the individual is almost certain to win, and then able to use the winnings to repay the loan. This scheme will not prevent the loan charge arising as the loan repayment is connected to a new tax avoidance arrangement.

These schemes don't work. The only way you can avoid the new loan charge is by making a genuine repayment of the loan balance or settling the tax liability with HM Revenue and Customs (HMRC) in advance. Any repayments connected to a new tax avoidance arrangement will be ignored and the loan charge will still apply.

Why you shouldn't use these schemes

Using such a scheme and paying further fees to a promoter won't prevent the loan charge from applying to disguised remuneration loans outstanding on 5 April 2019. HMRC will investigate any attempts to avoid the new loan charge.

For transactions taking place after 16 July 2013, HMRC will consider whether the General Anti-Abuse Rule (GAAR) (https://www.gov.uk/government/publications/tax-avoidance-general-anti-abuse-rules) may apply. After 14 September 2016, transactions where the GAAR applies will be subject to a 60% GAAR penalty.

What to do if you're using one of these schemes

Users of these schemes can pay back the outstanding loan in full by 5 April 2019 or settle with HMRC to avoid accruing interest.

If you're already speaking to someone at HMRC about your use of a disguised remuneration scheme, you should contact them.

If you're not already speaking to someone at HMRC, you should email: exitsteam.counteravoidance@hmrc.gsi.gov.uk

Find out more about how to identify tax avoidance schemes (https://www.gov.uk/guidance/tax-avoidance-an-introduction# how-to-identify-tax-avoidance-schemes).

Published 14 February 2017

Last updated 2 December 2017 + show all updates

(1) 2 December 2017 The section "Schemes claiming to avoid the loan charge" has been updated with more information and to clarify some points.

(2) 14 February 2017 First published.

Related content

Detailed guidance

- Disguised remuneration trust schemes: misleading advertising (Spotlight 40) (https://www.gov.uk/guidance/income-trust-schemes-misleading-advertising-spotlight-40)

Explore the topic

- PAYE (https://www.gov.uk/topic/business-tax/paye)
- Tax avoidance (https://www.gov.uk/topic/dealing-with-hmrc/tax-avoidance)
- Income Tax (https://www.gov.uk/topic/personal-tax/income-tax)

Collection

- Tax avoidance: disguised remuneration (https://www.gov.uk/government/collections/tax-avoidance-disguised-remuneration)
- Tax avoidance schemes currently in the spotlight (https://www.gov.uk/government/collections/tax-avoidance-schemes-currently-in-the-spotlight)

Is this page useful?

Yes this page is useful (https://www.gov.uk/contact/govuk) No this page is not useful (https://www.gov.uk/contact/govuk) Is there anything wrong with this page? (https://www.gov.uk/contact/govuk)

Thank you for your feedback

Close

Help us improve GOV.UK

Don't include personal or financial information like your National Insurance number or credit card details.

What were you doing?

What went wrong?

Send

Close

Help us improve GOV.UK

To help us improve GOV.UK, we'd like to know more about your visit today. We'll send you a link to a feedback form. It will take only 2 minutes to fill in. Don't worry we won't send you spam or share your email address with anyone.

Email address

Send me the survey

Don't have an email address?

(https://www.smartsurvey.co.uk/s/gov-uk-banner/?c=/guidance/disguised-remuneration-schemes-claiming-to-avoid-thenew-%20loan-charge-spotlight-36&gcl;=1627485790.1515403243)

MISCELLANEOUS

MISC. 201 HM REVENUE & CUSTOMS APPROVAL OF JOINT NATIONAL INSURANCE CONTRIBUTION ELECTIONS [HMRC, 10 November 2008.]

A *facility to allow an employee* to meet the employer's secondary Class 1 National Insurance contributions (NICs) liability arising on share option gains was introduced in the Child Support, Pensions and Social Security Act 2000 (CSPSSA) on 28 July 2000.[1]

[1] Subsequent changes to legislation increased the scope of NIC Joint Elections (& Agreements) so that they can include employment income arising from restricted securities (section 426 of ITEPA 2003) and convertible securities (section 438 of ITEPA 2003).

This can be achieved either by Agreement or Joint Election. However, unlike an agreement, a joint election constitutes the legal transfer of liability for payment from the employer to the employee and the law requires that any joint election must be approved by an officer of HM Revenue & Customs (HMRC). The Employee Shares and Securities Unit (ESSU) are responsible for the administration of the approval process and publish model forms of election to facilitate it.[2]

For various reasons the model elections may not always be suitable for a particular company's needs and practitioners may wish to customise them to suit a particular client. Whether or not the model election is used, HMRC still needs to approve whatever form of election is used by each company or group of companies. Before an election can be approved it must contain a number of elements to satisfy legislative requirements.

1) The parties to the election must be clearly identified. The Company (the "secondary contributor"), its registered office address and company registration number must be included in the draft election and provision made for the full name of the employee to be recorded along with their National Insurance number.

2) The purpose and scope of the joint election (see model document) needs to be set out and this should clearly specify the option grant or award of securities which is subject to the election, the relevant legislation and the relevant employment income. An election will not be approved if it does not clearly identify the option grant or award to which it is to apply. For example, an election that is said to apply to all options whenever they may be granted will not be approved. This section also needs to include declarations (see model document) concerning Chapter 3A of Part 7 and retrospection (section 4B(2) SSCBA 1992).

3) The election should also state what arrangements are in place as to how the employee will account for the secondary NICs liability and ensure that it is paid over to HMRC in good time. Where the relevant employment income will be received from a third party then the employee should authorise that party to withhold a sufficient amount of cash (or sell sufficient shares) to cover the liability, and this should be provided for in this section. A clear statement that the employee understands that they are personally liable for the secondary NICs covered by the election should also be included in this section.

4) A clear statement of the means for determining that the election is no longer in force (see model document).

5) A clear statement that the election will continue in full force regardless of whether the employee ceases to be an employee of the company. Similarly a statement may be included concerning residency.

6) A declaration by both the company and the employee that they agree to be bound by the terms of the election which may be by deed if so required.

Recently a number of draft elections submitted for approval include other elements that are not within the scope of the legislation and they do not require HMRC approval. Including those elements within the election means that HMRC is being asked to recognise terms or clauses that are not a requirement of the legislation. Examples of terms or clauses which are being included are:

1) Transfer of employment within the group whereby the secondary contributor changes and the employee undertakes to enter into a new election with the new employer. This is not necessary as the joint election remains in force even if employment ceases (see section 5).

2) An indemnity in favour of the company against any expense incurred if the employee fails to satisfy their liability for secondary NIC. This expands the scope of the joint election and cannot be approved. If the company requires such an indemnity then it should be included within the option agreement or other similar document which does not require HMRC approval.

3) A power of attorney in order to enable enforcement of either of the above or any other aspect of the election. This again expands the scope of the election and cannot be approved. If required then it should be included in the option agreement or other similar document and could also be used to implement the joint election if required.

From the 1 December 2008 where draft elections are presented for approval that include additional elements not required by the legislation nor essential for the implementation of the election then approval will not be given. Further guidance on NIC Elections can be found in the Employment Related Securities Manual (ERSM 170750 and 170760).

---

[2] Applications for approval should be sent to Charity Assets and Residence, Employee Shares & Securities Unit, Nottingham Team, 1st Floor, Ferrers House, Castle Meadow Road, Nottingham, NG2 1BB. The application should include draft joint election, supporting documentation for grant or award and if the model documents are being used then a statement to that effect.

Misc. 202 INFORMATION ABOUT CLASS 2 VOLUNTARY CONTRIBUTIONS FOR NON-RESIDENTS [HMRC, 25 November 2009]

The following information will be of interest to people who have previously applied to pay Class 2 voluntary contributions and had their application rejected due to not being employed/self-employed "immediately" before leaving the UK.

The relevant legislation has recently been revisited, and this has resulted in a change in the way applications to pay voluntary contributions are processed. Therefore, if you wish, you can resubmit your application so that the original decision can be reviewed. Please complete a CF83 (at the back of the NI38 (PDF 260K)) and submit this with a covering note explaining that you would like your case reviewed. We will then let you know whether we have been able to accept your application.

Misc. 203 PAYE/NATIONAL INSURANCE LATE PAYMENT PENALTIES [HMRC, 18 May 2010]

This guide tells you about the late payments penalties which apply for all employers and contractors from May 2010.

If you have 250 or more employees, please note that these penalties have replaced the Mandatory Electronic Payment surcharge which previously applied to you.

Penalties charged are in addition to any interest that may be due.

PAYE/NICs payment deadlines

For information on PAYE/NICs payment deadlines (including student loan deduction, CIS and PSA payments) – and the interest charges you will face if you miss them, follow the link at the end of this section.

To help you avoid missing a payment deadline you can create a calendar of key tax deadlines on the Business Link website. You can also sign up to have regular email alerts as each date approaches.

Create a tax deadlines calendar and sign up for email alerts on the Business Link website [http://www.businesslink.gov.uk/bdotg/action/keydates]

PAYE/National Insurance payments and deadlines [http://www.hmrc.gov.uk/paye/file-or-pay/payments/deadlines.htm]

Who and what late payment penalties apply to

The late payment penalties apply to all employers and contractors – whether you employ one or several hundred employees or subcontractors. They apply to monthly, quarterly and annual periods of PAYE starting on or after 6 April 2010.

HM Revenue & Customs (HMRC) charges late payment penalties on PAYE amounts due that are not paid in full on time, including:

- monthly, quarterly or annual PAYE (Pay As You Earn)
- student loan deductions
- Construction Industry Scheme (CIS) deductions
- Class 1 National Insurance contributions (NICs)
- annual payments of employers' Class 1A and Class 1B NICs
- determinations made by HMRC where it appears that there may be further tax payable – for example under Regulation 80 of the Income Tax (Pay As You Earn) Regulations 2003
- decisions under Section 8 of the Social Security Contributions (Transfer of Functions, Etc) Act 1999 – for example about a person's liability to pay NICs and the amount payable

Late payment penalty warning letters

HMRC may send you a warning letter if you do not pay on time. They may do this the first time in the tax year they think your PAYE payment is late. The letter is issued about two weeks after the payment date.

The letter is only to let you know that HMRC think you have made a PAYE payment late and that a penalty could be charged. It is not a penalty notice and you can't appeal against it.

It also:

- explains how to avoid a penalty in the future
- reminds you to pay – if you have not already paid by the time you receive the letter

Importantly, it does not mean a penalty will definitely be charged, and you may get a penalty even if you do not get a letter.

No PAYE/NICs to pay – how to avoid warning letters and payment reminders

If you have no PAYE/NICs payment to make for a month or quarter, you can avoid an unnecessary warning letter or payment reminder by simply telling HMRC on or before your normal payment date that no payment is due.

You can do this quickly and easily using HMRC's online notification service.

Notify HMRC that no PAYE/NICs payment is due [http://www.hmrc.gov.uk/payinghmrc/paye-nil.htm]

What to do if you get a warning letter

If you agree that you have made a late payment, you should make sure you pay on time and in full in future. The next time you pay late you may become liable to a penalty. HMRC will contact you before a penalty is charged. If they charge a penalty they will send you a penalty notice. The section "Notification of a late payment penalty" gives more information.

If you believe you have received a letter in error, perhaps because you have already paid, have a time to pay agreement or have a "reasonable excuse" you don't need to contact HMRC yet. But you may find it helpful make a note of why you don't think a penalty is chargeable in case HMRC contact you about penalty action in future.

To help you remember these important dates, you can create a calendar of key tax deadlines for the next 12 months on the Business Link website. It also allows you to sign up to receive email alerts as each date approaches.

Create a tax deadlines calendar and sign up for email alerts on the Business Link website [http://www.businesslink.gov.uk/bdotg/action/keydates]

What to do if you get a warning letter

If you agree that you have made a late payment, you should make sure you pay on time and in full in future. The next time you pay late you may become liable to a penalty. HMRC will contact you before a penalty is charged. If they charge a penalty they will send you a penalty notice. The section "Notification of a late payment penalty" gives more information.

If you believe you have received a letter in error, perhaps because you have already paid, have a time to pay agreement or have a "reasonable excuse" you don't need to contact HMRC yet. But you may find it helpful make a note of why you don't think a penalty is chargeable in case HMRC contact you about penalty action in future.

To help you remember these important dates, you can create a calendar of key tax deadlines for the next 12 months on the Business Link website. It also allows you to sign up to receive email alerts as each date approaches.

Create a tax deadlines calendar and sign up for email alerts on the Business Link website

Notification of a late payment penalty

If a penalty is due, HMRC will send you a late payment penalty letter telling you how much you owe and when you have to pay it by. It will also tell you what to do if you think the penalty is wrong, including how to appeal.

For penalties relating to late payments that occurred in the 2010–11 tax year, HMRC will send notifications of late payment penalty charges after the end of the year. HMRC has up to two years after the late payment occurred to issue a penalty letter.

It is your responsibility to make sure that you pay on time. HMRC does not issue reminder letters.

PAYE/National Insurance payments and deadlines [http://www.hmrc.gov.uk/paye/file-or-pay/payments/deadlines.htm]

Penalty rates and how they will apply

Penalties will be charged on each PAYE reference number (also called a "PAYE scheme") independently. Therefore, if you operate more than one PAYE scheme you need to make sure that amounts due for each individual PAYE scheme reference is paid in full on time.

The rest of this section explains how the penalties apply for different types of payment.

Monthly or quarterly PAYE payments

You will not be charged a penalty if only one PAYE amount is late in a tax year – unless that payment is over six months late.

The amount of the penalty will depend on how much is late and how many times your payments are late in a tax year. So if you pay part of what is due on time then any penalty will only be charged on the part that is late. The table below shows how the penalties are calculated.

Penalty charges for late monthly and quarterly PAYE payments

No. of times payments are late in a tax year	Penalty percentage	Amount to which penalty percentages apply
1	No penalty (as long as the payment is less than six months late)	
2–4	1%	Total amount that is late in the tax year (ignoring the first late payment in that tax year)
5–7	2%	"
8–10	3%	"
11 or more	4%	"

Additional penalties for monthly and quarterly payments over six months late

If you have still not paid a monthly or quarterly amount in full, after six months you may have to pay a penalty of 5 per cent. A further penalty of 5 per cent may be charged if you have not paid after 12 months. These penalties may be charged in addition to the penalties for monthly and quarterly payments described in the previous section and apply even where only one payment in the tax year is late.

End of year adjustments

You may be charged a late payment penalty if you pay less than is actually due. This applies even where you pay roughly the right amount each month and then make an end of year adjustment. You should therefore make sure you pay in full each month, rather than estimate the amounts you need to pay.

However if you pay an adjustment after the end of the year under a special arrangement such as applying the Intermediaries' rules (these are often referred to as IR35) or a formal modified PAYE arrangement known as Employment Procedures Appendix 6, HMRC will not charge late payment penalties providing the terms of the arrangement are kept.

To avoid receiving a penalty you must make certain that you pay the right amount on time each month.

Amounts due annually or occasionally

You may have to pay a penalty of 5 per cent of the amount that is late if you have not paid the full amount by the date known as the "penalty date". There's more information about the different "penalty dates" later in the section.

You may have to pay an additional 5 per cent penalty if you have still not paid the full amount within five months of the penalty date.

You may have to pay further 5 per cent penalty if you have still not paid the full amount within 11 months of the penalty date.

Penalty dates

The penalty date varies according to the type of payment.

For payments such as Class 1A and 1B NICs; HMRC determinations and assessments; and amendments or corrections to returns the "penalty date" is 30 days after the due date. This means that for these payments you may have to pay:

- a 5 per cent penalty if you have not paid the full amount within 30 days of the due date
- an additional 5 per cent penalty if you have not paid the full amount within six months of the due date
- a further 5 per cent penalty if you have not paid the full amount within 12 months of the due date

In most other cases, the penalty date is the day after the due date.

There's a link to the Compliance Handbook in "Technical Guidance" at the end of this guide for more detail on annual or occasional penalties

If there's a good reason for not paying in full on time

You won't have to pay a penalty if HMRC agrees that there is a reasonable excuse for it being late and you paid as soon as you reasonably could after the reason for lateness ended.

What is reasonable will be different from person to person depending on their individual circumstances. However, it is normally something exceptional that you could not have predicted and that is outside your control. It is not possible to give a precise list of what is reasonable.

Some excuses that may count as a reasonable excuse

These can include:

- The death of a close relative or domestic partner around the time that payment was due.
- The payment is lost or delayed because of an unforeseen event. For example, a fire or flood at the sorting office where the payment would be held.
- Serious illness of the person or of a close relative around the time the person should have made payment.

Some excuses HMRC would not usually accept as reasonable

These can include:

- pressure of work
- lack of information
- HMRC did not remind you to pay
- ignorance of basic law

In addition, the law says that HMRC cannot usually accept as reasonable:

- Lack of money. HMRC cannot treat lack of funds as reasonable unless the shortage is due to unforeseeable events outside your control. If you are having difficulty paying there's information in the next section "What to do if you can't pay".
- Relying on someone else. HMRC cannot normally accept that you have a reasonable excuse just because you asked someone else to make the payment and they did not. Exceptionally if you have done all you reasonably can to make sure the person does make the payment on time, you may have a reasonable excuse.

For example, you may have explained carefully to the person what they have to do, and by when. You may have checked on their progress and reminded them.

If you think you have a reasonable excuse

If you think you have a reasonable excuse you should contact the office that notifies you of the penalty.

If HMRC decides you do not have a reasonable excuse, and you do not agree, you can appeal.

What to do if you can't pay

HMRC expects payments to be made on time. However if you are experiencing any problems in paying what you owe you can find out what to do by following the link at the end of this section.

You should contact HMRC before any payment is due if you think you will have difficulty paying on time. If HMRC agrees to allow you time to pay and you contact them before the payment is due they will not charge penalties on those payments covered by that agreement, providing you stick to the agreement.

Business Payment Support Service [http://www.hmrc.gov.uk/payinghmrc/problems/bpps.htm]

What to do if you disagree with a penalty

If you disagree with the penalty, you have the right to appeal. You can appeal if:

- you don't think a penalty is due
- you disagree with the amount of the penalty

You can also appeal against HMRC's decision not to accept your reasonable excuse if you still think you have a reasonable excuse.

You can read more about how to appeal against a decision you disagree with in the guide "How to appeal against an HMRC decision – direct tax".

How to appeal against an HMRC decision – direct tax [http://www.hmrc.gov.uk/complaints-appeals/direct-tax-appeal.htm]

Late tax codes 2010–11

At the start of the tax year 2010–11 some tax code notifications, form P9, were sent out later than usual. If the tax code notification for any of your employees was not received by 6 April HMRC asked employers to use the same code they operated in March 2010. HMRC asked that all notifications, once received, be processed without unreasonable delay.

Employers who followed this guidance, and paid all PAYE monthly payments on time, have met their obligations.

In addition, there is no liability to a penalty if employers have a reasonable excuse. Whether an excuse is reasonable will depend on the merits of the case. Read the previous section "If there's good reason for not paying in full on time".

Technical guidance

Compliance Handbook [http://www.hmrc.gov.uk/manuals/chmanual/CH150000.htm]

Misc. 204 POTENTIAL OVERPAYMENTS OF CLASS 1A NATIONAL INSURANCE [HMRC, 25 February 2011]

Potential overpayments for the period 2003–2004 to 2005–2006

Mixed use benefits: partial deductions under sections 363 to 365 ITEPA 2003

Background

Where an employer provides a director or an employee with a benefit in kind that has mixed use – ie the director or employee uses the benefit for both private and business use – the Income Tax (Earnings and Pensions) Act 2003 (ITEPA) may allow a deduction from taxable earnings in respect of the business use. However, such deductions are disregarded when calculating the amount of general earnings on which Class 1A NICs are due. Class 1A NICs are therefore payable on the full cost of the benefit chargeable, before deduction, to income tax under ITEPA.

The exception to this is where the benefit is used solely for business purposes and ITEPA allows a deduction of the full cost of the benefit. Where this is the case, there is no liability to pay Class 1A NICs.

An appeal was heard last year by the First-tier Tribunal (Tax Chamber) in which the appellant claimed that partial deductions under section 365 of ITEPA were also deductible for Class 1A NICs for tax years from 2003–2004 to 2005–2006. The Tribunal judge found in favour of the appellant. HMRC consequently now accepts that partial deductions under sections 363 to 365 of ITEPA are not disregarded in the assessment of earnings liable to Class 1A NICs for the 2003–2004 to 2005–2006 tax years.

Legislative history and appeal against Class 1A NICs charge

Liability to pay Class 1A NICs arises under section 10 of the Social Security Contributions and Benefits Act 1992 (SSCBA). When Class 1A NICs were extended from 6 April 2000 to cover most benefits in kind a new section 10 was introduced.

Paragraph 7 of the new section 10, though allowing for no Class 1A NICs liability where there was a fully matching deduction, set out the specific deductions allowed under the Income and Corporation Taxes Act 1988 (ICTA) that were to be disregarded when assessing Class 1A NICs.

The introduction of ITEPA, which replaced ICTA, brought consequential amendments to paragraph 7 of section 10 of ITEPA, and the introduction of paragraphs 7A and 7B. Those amendments were intended to mirror the previous paragraph 7 so that all of the deductions that were previously disregarded continued to be disregarded for Class 1A NICs.

A query received by HMRC raised some doubt as to whether the new legislation did replicate the previous version. Specifically, it was suggested that deductions allowed under sections 363 to 365 of ITEPA were no longer to be disregarded when assessing liability to pay Class 1A NICs.

Although HMRC's position was that the overall application of the new legislation did achieve the intended policy, a further amendment was made to put beyond doubt the fact that the new legislation replicated the original provisions for mixed use benefits. This amended inserted, with effect from 6 April 2007, sections 363 to 365 of ITEPA into the excluded provisions listed in paragraph 7B of section 10 of SSCBA.

HMRC's position on the legislation in force from 6 April 2003 to 5 April 2006 was challenged and the case of Antique Buildings Limited and The Commissioners for HMRC (Appeal number: TC/2009/10182) was heard before the First-tier Tribunal (Tax Chamber).

Tribunal decision and current position

The appellant, Antique Buildings Limited, claimed that partial deductions allowed by section 365 of ITEPA for tax years from 2003–2004 to 2005–2006 were also deductible for Class 1A NICs. The Tribunal judge's *decision (decision number* [2010] TC 00408) found in favour of the appellant and allowed the appeal.

HMRC considered its position and decided not to seek permission to appeal against the decision. This means that HMRC now accepts that, for tax years from 2003–2004 to 2005–2006, partial deductions allowed by sections 363 to 365 of ITEPA are not to be disregarded when calculating liability to pay Class 1A NICs.

A refund can therefore be claimed in any case where Class 1A NICs have been calculated and paid without taking into account a deduction allowed by any of sections 363 to 365 of ITEPA.

It must be noted however, that this applies **only** to deductions under sections 363 to 365 of ITEPA and only to tax years from 2003–2004 to 2005–2006. The legislation prior to 6 April 2003 and from 6 April 2006 is clear in disregarding partial deductions for tax when calculating earnings for Class 1A NICs.

How to claim a Class 1A NICs refund

If you think that you have overpaid Class 1A NICs because you did not take into consideration deductions allowed by sections 363 to 365 of ITEPA you should write to:

HM Revenue and Customs
Customer Operations PAYE Employer Office
BP4009
Chillingham House
Benton Park View
Newcastle
NE98 1ZZ

Information to be provided:

- Why you think you have overpaid
- The tax year(s) for which you are claiming a refund
- Evidence of the amount paid
- The amount you are asking to be refunded
- Time limit for making a refund claim

Refund claims for the 2003–2004 year should generally be made to HMRC no later than 5 April 2011. HMRC can only consider claims made after that date if the applicant can show that he had a reasonable excuse for not making the application in time and that he applied without unreasonable delay after that excuse ceased.

Claims for 2004–2005 must generally be made by 5 April 2012 and claims for 2005–2006 by 5 April 2013.

Misc. 205 CHANGES TO PAYMENT DATES – CLASS 2 NATIONAL INSURANCE CONTRIBUTIONS [HMRC, 6 April 2011]

Through consultation with small businesses and self-employed customers measures were recommended to help reduce administrative burdens and simplify the tax system. This included the collection of National Insurance contributions for the self-employed.

Payment date changes

From April 2011 the payment of Class 2 National Insurance contributions will change and become due on the 31 July and 31 January each year, bringing payment dates in line with Self Assessment.

The link below takes you to the information you need about the change in payment dates and explains how you can pay, when you will receive a payment request and the dates you need to pay your National Insurance contributions by.

How to pay Class 2 National Insurance contributions [http://www.hmrc.gov.uk/payinghmrc/class2nics.htm]

Paying from an overseas bank account

Please note if you are abroad and paying or wish to pay voluntary Class 2 National Insurance contributions the dates and the payment conditions are fully explained in the link below and are the same as those of a UK based self-employed worker.

Paying from an overseas bank account

If you currently pay your voluntary Class 2 National Insurance or voluntary Class 3 National Insurance contributions annually whilst abroad, these changes will not impact you and your National Insurance contributions will be collected annually as normal. However, if you wish to start paying, or wish to change your method of payment you will need to read pages 11 to 15 of the leaflet NI38 and then complete and return the application form CF83 which can be found at the back of the leaflet.

Go to leaflet NI38 [http://www.hmrc.gov.uk/pdfs/nico/ni38.pdf]

Please note, unlike compulsory Class 2 National Insurance contributions, voluntary Class 2 National Insurance paid while overseas does **not** entitle you to Maternity Allowance should you make a claim on your return to the UK.

Misc. 206 REFUND APPLICATIONS INVITED FOR CLASS 1A NATIONAL INSURANCE CONTRIBUTIONS (NICS) PAID IN RESPECT OF CERTAIN OVERSEAS HOLIDAY HOMES PURCHASED THROUGH A COMPANY [HMRC, 14 April 2011]

Background

The Finance Act (FA) 2008 introduced new provisions to the Income Tax (Earnings and Pensions) Act 2003 (ITEPA): sections 100A and 100B. These provisions effectively provide an exemption from the living accommodation tax charge where living accommodation outside the UK is provided by a company for a director or other officer of the company (D) or a member of D's family or household where all of the following apply:

- the company is wholly owned by D or D and other individuals (and no interest in the company is partnership property),
- the company's main or only asset is a relevant interest in the property
- its only activities are ones that are incidental to its ownership of that interest

The new legislation was treated as having always had effect. In other words, the new legislation meant that since the coming into force of these provisions in the Finance Act 2008 a charge to Income Tax on the benefit provided through a qualifying overseas holiday home has never existed. As a consequence any liability to Class 1A National Insurance contributions, which was due on an amount equivalent to the general earnings charge in ITEPA, was also removed from 21 July 2008. At that time HM Revenue & Customs (HMRC) advised that refunds of tax could be claimed on the basis that the living accommodation tax charge was never intended to apply in these circumstances and the new legislation is treated as always having had effect.

However the same wasn't the case for Class 1A National Insurance contributions (employer only). In the case of overseas holiday homes, it remained the case that for the years prior to the enactment of Finance Act 2008, Class 1A National Insurance contributions remained due on the benefit in kind chargeable to Income Tax. HMRC published Regulations on 17 March 2011 that align the National Insurance contributions position with that for Income Tax – The Social Security (Contributions) (Amendment No. 3) Regulations 2011 (SI 2011/797). This means that it is now possible to claim a refund of Class 1A National Insurance contributions in the same way as it was possible for Income Tax. A refund of Class 1A National Insurance contributions can be claimed where contributions have been paid and an officer of HMRC is satisfied that the contribution was paid on the same amount treated as earnings that are now exempt under the relevant legislation in ITEPA.

Refunds

Any individual who can show that they have paid Class 1A National Insurance contributions for any year before 2008–09 on the benefit of living accommodation which qualifies for exemption in accordance with sections 100A and 100B of ITEPA should write giving the information listed below to:

HM Revenue & Customs
Customer Operations PAYE Employer Office
BP4009
Chillingham House
Benton Park View
Longbenton
Newcastle upon Tyne
NE98 1ZZ

Information to be provided:

1. name, address, National Insurance number and/or Unique Taxpayer's Reference
2. if agent acting – agent's name and address
3. details of the living accommodation outside the UK – address, type of property, uses made of the *property*
4. details of the company through which living accommodation outside the UK is provided including name, address, nature of company/entity, place of incorporation, ownership and activities
5. an explanation of why they consider that the exemption applies

6. the years for which Class 1A National Insurance contributions have been paid on the benefit of this accommodation
7. evidence that the benefit of the accommodation in question has been taxed – acceptable evidence would include for each year copies of one or more of the following documents which clearly show the benefit as taken into account as taxable income:
   – assessments/self-assessments
   – P11Ds and P11D(b)
   – correspondence with HMRC or the former Inland Revenue

Note that the above list is not intended to be exhaustive. HMRC will consider any other documentary evidence in the individual's possession that the individual believes can show that the benefit has been taxed as earnings and Class1A National Insurance contributions has been paid on the same amount treated as earnings.

Time limit for making a refund claim

Any application for a refund in these cases must be made in writing on or before 6 April 2015.

HMRC will take action to identify those customers who have previously claimed refunds of tax and Class 1A National Insurance contributions and arrange to refund the Class 1A National Insurance contributions already paid. However, if you wish to submit details of your original claim again please quote any reference number that you were given previously and send it to the above address.

Misc. 207 GUIDANCE: DISCLOSURE OF TAX AVOIDANCE SCHEMES – INCOME TAX, CORPORATION TAX, CAPITAL GAINS TAX, NATIONAL INSURANCE CONTRIBUTIONS, STAMP DUTY LAND TAX AND INHERITANCE TAX

[Reproduced in Vol 1F (income tax, corporation tax and capital gains tax) as M04/2014]

Misc. 208 EMPLOYMENT ALLOWANCE: UP TO £2,000 OFF YOUR CLASS 1 NICS [HMRC, 6 February 2014]

From 6 April 2014 employers can claim the Employment Allowance and reduce their employer Class 1 National Insurance contributions (NICs).

Key facts – who can claim

The Employment Allowance is available from 6 April 2014. If you are eligible you can reduce your employer Class 1 NICs by up to £2,000 each tax year.

You can claim the Employment Allowance if you are a business or charity (including Community Amateur Sports Clubs) that pays employer Class 1 NICs on your employees' or directors' earnings.

If your company belongs to a group of companies or your charity is part of a charities structure, only one company or charity can claim the allowance. It is up to you to decide which company or charity will claim the allowance.

You can only claim the £2,000 Employment Allowance against one PAYE scheme – even if your business runs multiple schemes (also see the further guidance on claiming the Employment Allowance).

Not all businesses can claim the Employment Allowance, see excluded employers for more information.

How to claim your Employment Allowance

You can use your own 2014 to 2015 payroll software (see your software provider's instructions), or HM Revenue and Customs' (HMRC's) Basic PAYE Tools for 2014 to 2015 to claim the Employment Allowance.

When you make your claim (using the software of your choice), you must reduce your employer Class 1 NICs payment by an amount of Employment Allowance equal to your employer Class 1 NICs due, but not more than £2,000 per year.

For example, if your employer Class 1 NICs are £1,200 each month, in April your Employment Allowance used will be £1,200 and in May £800, as the maximum is capped at £2,000.

Once made, HMRC will automatically carry your claim forward each tax year. So at the beginning of each year you should check your circumstances haven't changed.

You will be able to see how much of the Employment Allowance you have used in "View PAYE Liabilities and Payments" in HMRCs Online Service.

Exempt employers using HMRC paper returns

If you are exempt from filing, or unable to file online, you can claim the Employment Allowance, at the beginning of the tax year, using the paper Employer Payment Summary.

More information will be included in guidance provided to all exempt employers

Excluded employers

You cannot claim the Employment Allowance, for example if you:

- employ someone for personal, household or domestic work, such as a nanny, au pair, chauffeur, gardener, care support worker
- already claim the allowance through a connected company or charity
- are a public authority, this includes; local, district, town and parish councils
- carry out functions either wholly or mainly of a public nature (unless you have charitable status), for example:
  - NHS services
  - General Practitioner services
  - the managing of housing stock owned by or for a local council
  - providing a meals on wheels service for a local council
  - refuse collection for a local council
  - prison services
  - collecting debt for a government department

You do not carry out a function of a public nature, if you are:

- providing security and cleaning services for a public building, such as government or local council offices
- supplying IT services for a government department or local council

Personal and Managed Service Companies who pay contract fees instead of a wage or salary, may not be able to claim the Employment Allowance, as you cannot claim the allowance for any deemed payments of employment income.

Service companies can only claim the allowance, if you pay earnings and have an employer Class 1 NICs liability on these earnings.

The detailed guidance contains more about excluded business types.

Detailed guidance

You can find more information on eligibility, claiming, connected companies and connected charities in detailed guidance.

HMRC ARRANGEMENTS FOR PERSONS THAT QUALIFY FOR AN EMPLOYMENT ALLOWANCE

1. These arrangements are made by HM Revenue and Customs (HMRC) under section 4 of the National Insurance Contributions Act 2014 (c. 7) and set out how a person who qualifies for an employment allowance can receive it by making deductions from their qualifying payments.

2. Unless otherwise stated terms used in these arrangements have the same meaning as in, or as used in, the National Insurance Contributions Act 2014. References to paragraph numbers are to paragraphs in these arrangements.

3. A person may receive an employment allowance for a tax year in that tax year by making deductions against their qualifying payments on a single Pay As You Earn (PAYE) scheme in accordance with these arrangements.

4. A person with more than one PAYE scheme for a tax year may only deduct an employment allowance from one PAYE scheme in that year and must not deduct an employment allowance from any other PAYE scheme in that tax year.

5. Before making any deduction of an employment allowance a person must give notice to HMRC of the PAYE scheme from which deductions will be made in accordance with paragraph 7, 8 or 9.

6. Subject to paragraph 9, a person need only give notice in accordance with paragraph 5 once and the notice will apply for that tax year and subsequent tax years until such time as the person changes their notice in accordance with paragraphs 11 to 17, the notified PAYE scheme closes or these arrangements are amended to provide that the notice given is no longer effective or required.

7. A person submitting PAYE returns online whose payroll software supports the Employer Payment Summary (EPS) must give notice by indicating that they wish to claim an employment allowance within their payroll software, where this indication appears in the EPS submitted to HMRC.

8. A person submitting PAYE returns online whose payroll software does not support the EPS must give notice by selecting "yes" against the employment allowance indicator within the HMRC Basic PAYE Tools package.

9. A person submitting paper PAYE returns must, on each occasion they submit a return, give notice by selecting "yes" to the question relating to an employment allowance on the paper EPS known as the form RT5.

10. Once notice has been given deductions for an employment allowance must be made from qualifying payments as they occur in the tax year.

11. Once notice has been given a person may not change their notice for a tax year within that tax year except in accordance with paragraphs 12, 13, 16 or 17.

12. A person may change their notice for a second or subsequent tax year in which they claim an employment allowance in accordance with paragraphs 14 and 15.

13. Where in a tax year two or more companies or two or more charities become connected with one another, in the subsequent tax year the companies or charities must decide which PAYE scheme they want to make deductions from and notify HMRC in accordance with paragraphs 14 and 15.

14. A change of notice for the purposes of paragraphs 12 and 13 must be made before the first qualifying payment is made in the tax year to which the change of notice relates.

15. A person may change their notice for the purposes of paragraphs 12 and 13, either within their software or, if they submit paper PAYE returns, using form RT5, by–

(a) for the PAYE scheme from which they no longer want to make deductions, selecting "no" (or giving a negative indication) for the employment allowance indicator for which they had previously selected "yes" (or gave a positive indication) under paragraphs 7 to 9; and

(b) selecting "yes" (or giving a positive indication) for the employment allowance indicator for the PAYE scheme from which they want to make deductions in accordance with paragraphs 7 to 9.

16. Where a person has notified HMRC of the PAYE scheme from which deductions of an employment allowance will be made and in that tax year discovers that they do not qualify for an employment allowance they must cease making deductions from that scheme and notify HMRC as soon as possible in accordance with paragraph 15(a).

17. Where a person discovers that they have notified HMRC of more than one PAYE scheme from which deductions of an employment allowance will be made they must cease making deductions from all but one scheme and notify HMRC as soon as possible in accordance with paragraph 15(a).

Misc. 209 ELIGIBILITY FOR EMPLOYMENT ALLOWANCE: FURTHER EMPLOYER GUIDANCE [HMRC, Web]

If you are unsure of your eligibility you should read this further guidance to help you decide if your business or charity is able to claim the Employment Allowance.

Whilst not exhaustive, the principles outlined in this guidance may be applied to a wide range of business situations. Also where helpful we will add further examples.

Business functions and types:

- Functions either wholly or mainly of a public nature
- Public authorities
- Pharmacies
- Educational institutions
- Domestic staff
- Franchises
- Self employed
- Partnerships
- Community Amateur Sports Clubs
- Personal and Managed Service Companies
- Business takeovers
- Business demergers
- Connected businesses and charities

Functions either wholly or mainly of a public nature

Functions are either wholly or mainly of a public nature, if you are carrying out more than 50% of your work **in** or **for** the public sector. For example:

- NHS services
- General Practitioner services
- the managing of housing stock owned by or for a local council
- providing a meals on wheels service for a local council
- refuse collection for a local council
- prison services
- collecting debt for a government department

You do not carry out a function of a public nature, if you are:

- providing security and cleaning services for a public building, such as government or local council offices
- supplying IT services for a government department or local council

Registered charities can claim the Employment Allowance, even if they are wholly or mainly carrying out functions of a public nature. This is subject to the connected rules for charities.

Also, if less than 50% of a businesses work is of a public nature, it will be entitled to the Employment Allowance. When considering the proportion of the business which is of a public nature this could be based on the number of employees engaged in public nature duties or the percentage of time spent on public nature duties. Alternatively, a business can consider turnover derived from the public nature activities.

Examples of functions wholly or mainly of a public nature

The local surgery has 5 General Practitioners (GPs), 2 nurses, 3 receptionists and a cleaner. The GP's are all partners in the practice. NHS patients make up 90% of the GP's work. There is no entitlement to the Employment Allowance, because the majority of the work done, is wholly or mainly of a public nature.

A Council has set up a company limited by guarantee, which is an arms length management organisation (ALMO) whose sole responsibility is to look after the Council's housing stock. The ALMO is not eligible for the Employment Allowance as it is carrying out functions of a public nature (managing housing stock which used to be the responsibility of the local authority).

Example of functions that are not wholly or mainly of a public nature

Guarding prisoners on behalf of the government makes up 25% of Padlock Security Limited's business. The remaining 75% of the company's work is providing security to private businesses and individual clients. Padlock Security Limited is entitled to the Employment Allowance because the majority of their work is not of a public nature.

Public authorities

Public authorities (such as local authorities, town councils and parish councils) are not eligible for the Employment Allowance unless they have charitable status.

Pharmacies

Independent pharmacies conducting a business, including over the counter sales as well as dispensing NHS prescriptions, are entitled to claim the Employment Allowance.

Educational Institutions

Schools, academies, further education colleges and universities are entitled to claim the Employment Allowance if they are private businesses or charities. This includes local authority or central government funded institutions provided they have charitable status.

If your charity is connected to another charity, then there will be entitlement to just one allowance for all of the connected charities. So, an education trust which controls several academies with charitable status will be entitled to just one allowance and it will be up to them to decide which academy makes the claim.

Domestic staff

Employers of domestic staff will be unable to claim the Employment Allowance as the employees are all being employed in a personal capacity to support the running of a household.

Franchises

Where a person operates a franchise, the employer (franchise holder) will be entitled to the Employment Allowance. However, if the franchise holder controls more than one franchise of a business, there will only be entitlement to one Employment Allowance for all of the franchises of the business controlled by that franchise holder.

Self employed

Can the self-employed claim the Employment Allowance?

Yes, but only if you have employees and your business pays employer Class 1 NICs on your employees' earnings.

Partnerships

Can a partnership claim the Employment Allowance?

Yes, but only if your partnership pays employer Class 1 NICs on your employees' or directors' earnings.

Community Amateur Sports Clubs

Can a Community Amateur Sports Club (CASC) claim the Employment Allowance?

Yes, if your CASC pays employer Class 1 NICs on your employees' or directors' earnings.

Personal and Managed Service Companies

You cannot claim the allowance for any deemed payments of employment income. However, you can claim the Employment Allowance against the employers Class 1 NICs arising on the earnings paid to your employees. For more information about Service Companies and deemed payments go to http://www.hmrc.gov.uk/ir35

Business takeovers

If your business takes over another business during the tax year there will be no entitlement to any remaining balance of the Employment Allowance due from the employer's Class 1 NICs of the employees who worked for the business you have taken over or for employees who are carrying on the work of the business you have taken over. This also applies to employees moved as part of regulations relating to Transfer of Undertakings (Protection of Employment), known as "TUPE transfers".

Example of a business takeover and effect on entitlement to the Employment Allowance

A is self employed and owns a plumbing business and employs 2 employees. A claims the Employment Allowance in respect of the employers Class 1 NICs that are due on the earnings paid to the 2 employees. During the year, A decides to sell his business to B, who owns an electrical business and who wishes to diversify into other areas. B completes the takeover on 1 November. B retains the 2 employees as they have plumbing expertise. B is not entitled to any remaining unclaimed balance of the Employment Allowance on A's former employees or for A's former business irrespective of whether or not A's employees are retained. B is, however, entitled to the Employment Allowance for the full year on his electrical business. Any Employment Allowance already claimed by A prior to the business takeover does not become due to be repaid by A or B.

Business demergers

If your business splits during the tax year and creates new businesses there will be no entitlement to the Employment Allowance in that tax year for any of the new businesses.

Example of a business demerger and effect on entitlement to the Employment Allowance

A and his wife B run a hairdressing salon and are claiming the Employment Allowance on the employers Class 1 NICs arising on earnings paid to their employees. In October, they decide to split the business with A taking all of the male customers and B taking all of the female customers and create 2 new companies. The 2 new companies are not entitled to the Employment Allowance in the year that the business is split, nor are they entitled to any balance of the Employment Allowance that was unclaimed by the original business. In the next tax year, both businesses will be entitled to the Employment Allowance, provided they are not connected companies.

Connected businesses and charities

Can connected businesses and charities claim the Employment Allowance? If a company has control of another company, or both companies are under the control of the same person or persons for example, companies linked in a group, these companies are connected.

If the same person or connected persons control 2 or more charities and the charities share the same (or substantially similar) purpose and activities, or both charities belong to a group of charities, the charities for the purpose of the Employment Allowance are connected.

If a charity controls a trading business, they are also considered connected for the purposes of the Employment Allowance.

Where this is the case, you will only be entitled to **one Employment Allowance** to use against one **PAYE scheme** (regardless of how many PAYE schemes you operate). It is up to you to nominate which PAYE scheme to claim the allowance against.

If your business controls a charity, they are not connected and you can claim the Employment Allowance for both the company and the charity.

See guidance on connected companies and connected charities for more information.

Misc. 210 NATIONAL INSURANCE CONTRIBUTIONS (NICS) – EMPLOYING PEOPLE ON THE UK CONTINENTAL SHELF (UKCS) [HMRC, April 2014]

Introduction

On 6 April 2014 the Government changed the PAYE and National Insurance rules for employment intermediaries where the workers are employed on the UKCS.

Offshore Employment Intermediaries

This note is aimed at agents. It looks at the new legislation in more detail and covers practical issues.

Background

From 6 April 2014 new rules changed the treatment of offshore employers and agencies with workers on the UKCS. These rules tackle attempts to avoid secondary "employer" National Insurance by moving staff to contracts with foreign employers. The avoidance schemes then argued that an exemption from employer NICs for certain host employers of mariners could be applied to the UK business.

The new rules

Where a worker is employed on the UKCS, the new rules apply the obligation for secondary National Insurance on:

- the employer in the UK; or
- the associated company, where the employer is not in the UK but has an associated company in the UK; or
- the oil or gas field licensee, where the employer is not present in the UK and has no associated company in the UK.

Where there is more than one associated company present in the UK, the one with the largest profits in the preceding year becomes the secondary contributor.

There is a system of certification in place for foreign employers to comply by paying secondary Class 1 NICs and operating PAYE. They can apply to HMRC for a certificate that will discharge the Oil and Gas field licensee's filing and payment responsibilities.

Certificate Process

To obtain a certificate, a foreign employer must set up a Real Time Information (RTI) scheme with HMRC as if it were in the UK and should comply with all requirements to operate PAYE and Class 1 National Insurance, including secondary Class 1 National Insurance. In some cases, foreign employers will already have an existing scheme they have been operating on a voluntary basis. Where that is the case, they should start operating secondary Class 1 National Insurance too.

To apply to HMRC for a certificate, a foreign employer should write to:

Oil and Gas Certificates Unit
Grayfield House
Bankhead Avenue
Edinburgh
Lothian
EH11 4UY.

They should include:

- the name and address of the employer;
- the PAYE reference number;
- the name and address of a person in the UK who is authorised to accept service on their behalf;
- confirmation that the employer understands and intends to discharge the Oil and Gas field licensee's obligations;
- The name, address and PAYE reference number of any associated company which is a current or former holder of a UKCS worker certificate.

Where this is the first application being made, they should also include the name, business address and oil field licence number of the oil field licensees to whom they supply or intend to supply a UKCS worker.

Where HMRC is satisfied that certain conditions are met, a certificate will be issued to the foreign employer. A certificate is also issued to the relevant Oil and Gas field licensee who is exempt from their liabilities as the secondary contributor as long as the certificate is held.

Withdrawing certificates

HMRC checks the foreign employer is complying. Companies that fail to comply will be warned and have a chance to put matters right before HMRC withdraws a certificate. When a certificate is withdrawn, HMRC will give 10 days' notice in writing. No further certificates will be issued to this employer.

HMRC prefers to work with employers to help them comply. Minor errors or delays will not normally result in cancellation providing the employer works with HMRC to rectify the error.

Interaction between UKCS and mariner rules

Regulation 114 Social Security (Contributions) Regulations 2001 sets out the rules for workers on the UK Continental Shelf and treats a person employed there in connection with an activity mentioned in section 11(2) of the Petroleum Act 1998, as though employed in Great Britain and as meeting the conditions as to residence or presence for National Insurance liability.

This rule takes precedence over the National Insurance mariner rules, so that a person who might normally be a mariner but who is working on the UKCS, will be treated as being in the UK and liable to Class 1 National Insurance. The new rules will appoint a secondary contributor for them.

There is an exception from the new UKCS rules where the person is a mariner with a Safe Manning Certificate and falling within the following groups:

- Master or chief mate.
- Officer in charge of an engineering watch in a manned engine room, or a duty engineer officer in a periodically unmanned engine room, on a ship powered by main propulsion machinery of 750kW propulsion power or more.
- Chief engineer officer or second engineer officer on a ship powered by main propulsion machinery of 750kW to 3000kW propulsion power.
- Rating forming part of a navigational watch on a ship of 500 gross tons or more and whose duties are skilled in nature.
- Rating forming part of an engine-room watch or designated to perform duties in a periodically unmanned engine room on a ship powered by main propulsion machinery of 750kW propulsion power or more.

The new rules only apply in relation to persons employed on or in connection with an offshore installation.

Meaning of offshore installation

This is a structure put to relevant use while in water. It does not include structures

- that have permanently ceased to be put to relevant use;
- is not and is not to be put to relevant use;
- since ceasing to be put to a relevant use, it has been put to a use which is not a relevant use.

This is drawn so that for example, a vessel involved in drilling does not cease to be a structure in between drilling operations or each time it detaches from the well head.

The measure does not apply to vessels used wholly or mainly for the

- transport of supplies;
- as safety vessels;
- as cable laying vessels.

A use is a relevant use if it is:

- for the purposes of exploiting mineral resources;
- for the purposes of exploration with a view to exploiting mineral resources;
- for the storage of gas;
- for the recovery of gas;
- for the conveyance of things by means of a pipe;
- mainly for the provision of accommodation for people working on the structure;
- for de-commissioning.

It is important to remember that if a person or employer is not within the UKCS rules they may still be liable under the mariner rules. These can be found on our website.

When would I be liable to pay National Insurance contributions in the UK?

Foreign employees on UKCS

Although the UKCS rules treat a person as being employed in the UK when they work on the UKCS and liable to Class 1 National Insurance, there is an exception for the first 52 weeks of employment in the UK where the worker is coming from abroad to work temporarily on the UKCS and all the following conditions are met:

- not ordinarily resident in the UK;
- not ordinarily employed in the UK;
- employed by a foreign employer;
- their employment is one carried on mainly outside the UK.

Example

A Mexican employee, ordinarily resident there, who normally works for their employer in the Gulf of Mexico comes to work temporarily on the UKCS would benefit from this – as would the UK secondary contributor.

The exemption would not apply to a worker ordinarily resident in the UK or one who was hired to work on the UKCS and does not normally work for the foreign employer abroad.

UK/Norway agreement – Norwegians working temporarily on the UKCS

Some Norwegians working temporarily on the UK Continental shelf are exempt under the provisions of the bi-lateral social security agreement between the two countries. A person claiming to be exempt should be able to produce a certificate of continuing liability in Norway in case HMRC require it.

EU regulations 883/2004 and bi-lateral agreements

Special EU social security coordinating rules do not apply to the UKCS. If an employee is seconded to the UKCS by an employer in another Member state, the work lasts longer than the 52 week period and the person faces double charging of contributions it may be possible for HMRC to assist. Contact HMRC for further advice.

Employee works on UKCS and also outside the UKCS

National Insurance is calculated in relation to payments in a pay period (usually a month for monthly paid staff) rather than by looking at a tax year as a whole. An employee may be on the UKCS in one pay period and outside the next.

The employer or person treated as the secondary contributor under the new rules is required to operate Class 1 National Insurance in relation to earnings for work on the UKCS. If the employee works outside the UKCS and UK to a significant extent – not merely a temporary absence for a few days or weeks, then they need to consider whether:

- Mariner rules make the person liable when outside the UKCS and whether there is a secondary contributor; or
- if the person is working in another country, where UK National Insurance could apply and whether there is a secondary contributor. National Insurance for people going abroad

Difficulties letting payroll know where the employee is during the pay period

We know that when people are at sea and working both on UKCS and also elsewhere at sea that it can be hard for payroll operators to keep track of all employee movements in time to operate NICs accurately on or before the earnings are paid for the purposes of Real Time Information.

Providing errors or delays are corrected promptly – no later than the following month, HMRC would not seek to impose a penalty.

Personal Service Companies

If a personal service company is a foreign employer and the worker is on the UKCS then these new rules apply.

UK/Norway agreement – UK nationals working temporarily in Norway

Where an employer has workers on the UKCS and also working in Norway, it can simplify matters for the employer if the UK staff (and the employer) remain subject to UK Class 1 National Insurance and exempt Norwegian contributions. HMRC has had significant success (almost 100%) in securing special agreements for UK companies and workers to remain paying Class 1 National Insurance only for up to 5 years. You should apply in advance, see National Insurance contributions when you work outside the UK

Misc. 211 HOW AN EMPLOYER OPERATES A NATIONAL INSURANCE ONLY SCHEME [HMRC, September 2014]

Information about when an employer can operate a National Insurance contributions (NICs) only scheme and reporting the payroll.

NICs only employment schemes are set up by an employer when payment of Class 1 National Insurance only is due.

How to register

You should register by phone or post.

Contact HM Revenue and Customs – they'll arrange for someone to call you back to help you register.

What to report

When completing a Full Payment Summary (FPS), where earnings are subject to NICs only, you must:

- report the "Gross earnings for NICs in this period" and all appropriate NICs data
- enter zeros in the "Taxable pay" and associated tax fields
- enter code NT in the "Tax code" field on the FPS as this is a mandatory field

If you realise that you've made a mistake and you have included details in the taxable pay and tax fields you should correct the error by entering zeros in the taxable pay and associated tax fields on your next FPS.

Help and advice

Contact the Employer helpline or Customer Operations Employer Office

Misc. 212 SHARE FISHERMAN: INCOME TAX AND NATIONAL INSURANCE CONTRIBUTIONS [HMRC, September 2014]

Special Income Tax and National Insurance contributions rules for share fishermen

Overview

You're a share fisherman if you work in the fishing industry and you:

- aren't employed under a contract of service
- are a master or a crew-member of a British fishing boat manned by more than one person
- get all or part of your pay by sharing the profits or gross earnings of the fishing boat

You also count as a shared fisherman if you used to work on a British fishing boat, but now work ashore in Great Britain. This could be making and mending gear or any other work for a British fishing boat.

Fishermen employed under a contract of service aren't share fishermen.

Self Assessment

A share fisherman is classed as self-employed. You must register with HMRC as self-employed within 3 months of when you first started fishing.

Fill in a Self Assessment tax return

You must fill in a Self Assessment tax return each year. This is so that you can declare all of your income from any source (ie, self-employment, employment and Job Seeker's Allowance etc) and claim any business expenses. You must keep business records to support information you put in your tax return.

Don't record any tax that's been deducted by your settling agent on your tax return.

Pay Class 2 National Insurance

When you register as self-employed, you're also registering to pay Class 2 National Insurance contributions. The rate you pay in the tax year 2014 to 2015 is £3.40 a week. This contributes towards the basic State Pension, the normal range of benefits for self-employed people, and Jobseeker's Allowance.

Budget for your Income Tax and Class 4 National Insurance contributions

As a share fisherman, you can join a voluntary tax budgeting scheme to help you pay your Income Tax and National Insurance contributions.

Misc. 213 SHARE FISHERMAN: TAX BUDGETING SCHEME [HMRC, September 2014]

A voluntary scheme to help self-employed share fishermen budget for Income Tax and National Insurance contributions.

How the scheme works

Authorise your settling agent (payer) to deduct a minimum of 20% each time you're paid. They'll put this money into a dedicated, interest bearing bank account in your name (your fishing account). It will stay in that account until your tax and National Insurance become due.

Fill in a Direct Debit mandate, HM Revenue and Customs (HMRC) will take money from your fishing account, usually in January and July. They'll use the money to clear your outstanding Income Tax and Class 4 National Insurance contributions, settling the oldest liabilities first.

Join the scheme

Register with HMRC as self-employed within 3 months of when you first started fishing.

Contact HMRC to ask for a Tax Savings Scheme form and a Direct Debit mandate.

Fill in the Tax Savings Scheme form and the Direct Debit mandate. Ask your boat owner or settling agent (payer) to witness and sign the savings scheme form. They will send both forms to the HMRC Fishing Unit.

Your boat owner or settling agent will deduct the percentage you've agreed and pay it into your dedicated fishing account.

Deduction rates to use

The minimum deduction is 20%. But, if you've tax arrears or you earn more than £28,000 (gross) in a year, you must increase your percentage deduction. Do this in multiples of 5%.

To increase your percentage deduction you must fill in an additional Direct Debit mandate.

Claim sea kit expenses

If you join the scheme, you can claim an allowance for sea kit expenses. This is to cover things like:

- protective clothing
- oilskins
- boots
- gloves
- stones
- bedding

You won't normally be asked for proof of this expense as long as it falls below the agreed figure which is £700.

If you aren't fishing for a full year, you can only claim a proportion of this allowance. For example, if you've only been fishing for 6 months of the year, you can only claim a maximum of £350.

Get more help

If you need more help or want to speak to an adviser, please use the contact details below:

Fishing Units

HM Revenue & Customs
Caledonian House
Greenmarket
Dundee
DD1 4QX

HM Revenue & Customs
Longbrook House
New North Road
Exeter
EX4 4LD
Telephone: 03000 568 680
Telephone: 0845 0789 789

Self Assessment for the self-employed
Telephone: 0300 200 3310
Monday to Sunday, 8:00am to 8:00pm

National Insurance
Telephone: 0300 200 3505
Text phone: 0845 915 3296
Monday to Friday, 8:00am to 5:00pm
Find out about call charges

Misc. 214 FOLLOWER NOTICES AND ACCELERATED PAYMENTS [HMRC, 23 July 2015]

Introduction

This guidance relates to follower notices and accelerated payments. It supports the measures set out in the Finance Act (FA) 2014 (Part 4) and the National Insurance Contributions Act (NICA) 2015 (sections 4 and Schedule 2) (NICA 2015).

Where this guidance refers to an accelerated payment, it also means an accelerated partner payment, and where it refers to an accelerated payment notice, it also means a partner payment notice – except where specifically mentioned.

Finance Act 2015 extends the scope of Finance Act 2014 (Part 4) to situations involving a loss or other amount which has been claimed or surrendered as group relief.

Changing the economics of avoidance

The government set out in its consultations "Raising the Stakes on Tax Avoidance" (August 2013) and "Tackling Marketed Tax Avoidance" (January 2014) its aims to change the economics of entering into tax avoidance schemes, and to change the behaviours of people and promoters in relation to tax avoidance.

Following that consultation process, the measures on follower notices and accelerated payments were introduced by legislation enacted in FA 2014 and NICA 2015. The objective of the legislation is to ensure that tax in dispute in relation to the use of an avoidance scheme sits with the Exchequer during a dispute.

1 Follower notices (FA2014, Part 4, Chapter 2)

Follower notices

1.1 Background)

1.1.1 Little incentive to follow

When faced with a large number of very similar cases, it is often most efficient for HM Revenue and Customs (HMRC) to investigate "representative cases"; taking those cases to litigation, if necessary.

If HMRC is successful in that litigation, unpaid tax and/or National Insurance contributions (NICs) is recovered in those cases. However, there has been little incentive for others using the same or essentially similar arrangements (known as "followers") to accept the court's findings, and pay any underpaid tax and/or NICs toHMRC.

1.1.2 Drive to accelerate litigation

The follower notice rules are designed to improve the rate at which avoidance cases are resolved where the point at issue has, in HMRC's view, already been decided in another person's case.

When a judicial ruling is made by the court or tribunal that potentially resolves a large number of cases, many "followers" agree to settle, but some do not. They argue that small differences in the arrangements mean that the decision does not apply to them. This leads to further litigation, adding months or years to the time taken to resolve their dispute.

A person who is a "follower" will now be given a follower notice. If they do not settle their dispute (known as "taking corrective action"), they will be at risk of a penalty.

1.1.3 Tax and/or NICs in dispute to be paid to HMRC

Alongside the "follower" rules are the accelerated payment rules, which require recipients of an accelerated payment notice to pay the disputed tax and/or NICs to HMRC. So, if a person is given a follower notice and an accelerated payment notice and decides not to settle their dispute as requested by the follower notice, they will be required to pay the disputed tax and/or NICs to HMRC under the accelerated payment rules.

Accelerated payments will also apply to avoidance arrangements which are within the Disclosure of Tax Avoidance Schemes (DOTAS) rules or are given with a counteraction notice under the General Anti-Abuse Rule (GAAR). See Section 2 of this guidance "Accelerated payments".

1.1.4 Part 4 Finance Act 2014 and National Insurance Contributions Act 2015

The legislation introducing these rules was announced in the 2014 budget and enacted in Part 4 of the Finance Act 2014 (FA 2014). Part 4 was applied to NICs with effect from 12 April 2015 by the National Insurance Contributions Act 2015 (NICA 2015).

1.1.5 The National Insurance Contributions Act 2015 (NICA 2015)

Class 4 and Class 2 collected through Self Assessment (SA) Class 4

NICs are assessed and collected along with income tax via the SA regime. These contributions are also subject to the SA enquiry regime. Section 16 of the Social Security Contributions and Benefits Act 1992 (SSCBA) has been amended by NICA 2015 so that Part 4 FA 2014 applies to Class 4 NICs, with necessary modifications (section 4(3) and Part 3 of Schedule 2 to NICA 2015).

From the tax year 6 April 2015 to 5 April 2016, most Class 2 NICs will also be assessed and collected via SA, and subject to its enquiry regime. New section 11A of SSCBA (and equivalent legislation for Northern Ireland), introduced by NICA 2015, ensures that Part 4 FA 2014 applies to Class 2 NICs, with necessary modifications (section 2 and Schedule 1 NICA 2015).

Where this guidance deals with how Part 4 FA 2014 applies to tax, it includes Part 4 FA2014 as applied with necessary modifications to these classes of contributions collected through SA.

Class 1, 1A, 1B NICs and Class 2 NICs not collected through SA

For Class 1, 1A, 1B and Class 2 NICs that are not collectible through the SA system, NICA 2015 gives effect to part 4 of FA 2014 and makes modifications to that part so that it applies to both tax and NICs.

These classes of contributions are defined in NICA 2015 as "relevant contributions" (paragraph 22 of Schedule 2).

Where this guidance deals with how Part 4 FA 2014 is modified by Part 1 of Schedule 2 to NICA 2015, it applies to relevant contributions (see annex 1 of this guidance for definitions).

1.2 Follower notices

1.2.1 Overview

A follower notice can be given to a person (P) who has used an avoidance scheme that has been shown in another person's litigation to be ineffective. The follower notice tells P that they may be liable to a penalty of up to 50% of the tax and/or NICs in dispute if they do not amend their return or settle their dispute.

A "person" (P) is as defined in Schedule 1 to the Interpretation Act 1978, and includes "a body of persons corporate or unincorporated", as well as individuals.

1.3 When a follower notice may be given

HMRC may give a follower notice to a person (P) if all of the Conditions A to D are met.

1.3.1 Condition A

Condition A is met if:

- for tax, a tax enquiry is in progress into a return or a claim made by P in relation to a relevant tax; or P has made a tax appeal in relation to a relevant tax, but the appeal has not been determined by the tribunal or court, or abandoned or otherwise disposed of ("Tax" includes Class 4 NICs. It also includes Class 2 NICs for the tax year 6 April 2015 to 5 April 2016 and later years)
- for NICs, a relevant contribution dispute is in progress (see section 1.4 and annex 1 of this guidance); or P has made a NICs appeal in relation to a relevant contribution, but the appeal has not been determined by the tribunal or court, or abandoned or otherwise disposed of

This is an important step in the process. It means that HMRC cannot issue a follower notice unless:

- for tax, one of the following applies:
  - an enquiry has been opened into a return
  - an appeal has been made against a closure notice, assessment, or determination, (for example, a determination under regulation 80 of the Income Tax (Pay As You Earn) Regulations 2003)
- for NICs, one of the following applies:
  - a relevant contributions dispute is in progress (see section 1.4 and annex 1 of this guidance)
  - an appeal has been made against a NICs decision (see annex 1 of this guidance for definition of NICs decision and NICs appeal)

The person should, therefore, already be aware that their tax and/or NICs arrangements are being challenged.

1.3.2 Condition B (for tax)

Condition B is met for tax if the return, claim or appeal is made on the basis that a particular tax advantage ("asserted advantage") results from particular tax arrangements ("chosen arrangements"). ("Tax" includes Class 4 NICs. It also includes Class 2 NICs for the tax year 6 April 2015 to 5 April 2016 and later years.)

Note: The term "tax arrangements" is defined as arrangements where it is reasonable to conclude that the obtaining of a tax advantage is the main, or one of the main, purposes of the arrangements. For example a person has claimed a loss of £100,000, based on a set of transactions where one of the main purposes of the transactions was to generate that loss – rather than for them to participate in a commercial operation.

1.3.3 Condition B (for NICs)

Condition B is met for NICs if the appeal is made on the basis that a particular NICs advantage ("asserted advantage") results from particular NICs arrangements ("chosen arrangements"). Condition B is also met if, in a relevant contributions dispute (see section 1.4 and annex 1 of this guidance for definition), a person disputes liability for relevant contributions on that same basis, regardless of whether the person notified HMRC of the dispute on that basis.

Note: The modifications ensure that "tax arrangements" includes "NICs arrangements". That is, arrangements where it is reasonable to conclude that the obtaining of a NICs advantage is the main, or one of the main, purposes of the arrangements.

1.3.4 Condition C

Condition C is met if HMRC is of the opinion that there is a judicial ruling which is relevant to the chosen arrangements.

1.3.5 Condition D (for tax)

Condition D is met for tax if no previous follower notice has been given to the same person, by reference to the same tax advantage, tax arrangements, judicial ruling and tax period; unless the previous notice has been withdrawn.

1.3.6 Condition D (for NICs)

Condition D is met for NICs if no previous follower notice has been given to the same person, by reference to the same NICs advantage, NICs arrangements, judicial ruling and tax period; unless the previous notice has been withdrawn.

1.4 Relevant contributions dispute (Paragraph 6 of Schedule 2 to the NICA 2015)

1.4.1 Giving follower notices for NICs

For tax, follower notices can only be given where there is either an open tax enquiry or an open appeal. Whilst there is a NICs equivalent of an open appeal (against a NICs decision), there is no direct equivalent of a tax enquiry for NICs. Because of this, the NICA 2015 introduces the concept of a "relevant contributions dispute" (see annex 1 for definition). Creating this concept allows HMRC to give a follower notice in circumstances where there is a dispute about a NICs liability, but before an appealable NICs decision has been issued.

1.5 Giving follower notices for tax and NICs at different times

There are time limits for issuing tax assessments and determinations but not for issuing NICs decisions.

Because of this, HMRC may issue tax assessments or determinations sooner than they issue NICs decisions in relation to the same avoidance scheme used. This could mean that a tax appeal may be in place before there is a relevant contributions dispute or an appeal against a NICs decision.

Where there is an appeal against a tax assessment or determination and HMRC considers that NICs are also due, they may give the person a follower notice for tax before they give the follower notice for NICs. Once there is a relevant contributions dispute or NICs appeal, HMRC may then give the person a follower notice for NICs.

1.6 Judicial ruling

1.6.1 When a judicial ruling is relevant

A judicial ruling is a ruling of a court or tribunal.

It is "relevant" to the chosen arrangements if:

- it involves consideration of tax or NICs arrangements (see sections 1.3.2 and 1.3.3 or annex 1)
- the principles laid down or reasoning given in the ruling would, if applied to the chosen arrangements, deny the asserted advantage or part of that advantage
- it is a final ruling

1.6.2 When the judicial ruling is final

A judicial ruling is final if it is:

- a ruling of the Supreme Court
- a ruling of any other court or tribunal where:
  - no appeal may be made against the ruling
  - if any appeal may be made against the ruling, the time limit has expired and no application was made or permission was refused
  - if permission to appeal has been granted, or was not required, no appeal has been made within the time limits
  - if an appeal was made, it was subsequently abandoned or disposed of before the appeal was determined

1.6.3 Ruling does not set a precedent

It is important to note that a ruling can be final at any stage in the legal appeal process, including the First-tier Tribunal, if it is not appealed further. It does not, therefore, have to set a "precedent" in the strictly legal sense that a judgment of a senior court of record (Upper Tribunal/High Court and above) would.

1.7 What is a relevant ruling

1.7.1 Intention of legislation

The intention of the legislation is to tackle behaviour by those who use avoidance schemes; primarily schemes marketed to a large number of people. Those schemes can have small variations – for example, the avoidance may be based around a different type of asset in different variants, or may be set up slightly differently depending on whether an individual, company or partnership is involved.

This does not mean that follower notices will automatically be given to users of variants: each case will be considered by a senior HMRC panel (see section 1.19 of this guidance for more details about the governance process).

Example 1:

A tax avoidance scheme designed to generate losses in relation to a specific trading asset is defeated in the Tribunal on the basis that, by the nature of the scheme and structure, there is not a genuine trade. The decision is a final ruling. There are 25 other users of this scheme, who all implemented identical (but for the amount of the loss claimed) transactions. It is anticipated that all 25 of those users would be "followers" and could be given a follower notice if they chose not to settle in response to the Tribunal decision.

There are also 30 users of a very similar scheme, which differs only in the trading asset used. It is very likely that, subject to careful consideration of all the facts and circumstances, these 30 could also be given follower notices.

There are a further 20 users of a loss-generating scheme that uses a different structure; with different financing and a greater degree of participation and risk for the partners. HMRC's primary argument may still be that there is not a genuine trade, but it becomes a much more finely balanced decision whether the first judicial ruling above could be treated as "relevant" to this one, as the facts and context have now diverged to a greater extent.

1.7.2 Principles and reasoning

The legislation does not mean that a follower notice can, for example, be issued to any case involving a "trading or non-trading" argument, solely because there has been a judicial ruling on that point. The reasoning and principles behind that ruling must be scrutinised to consider whether or not they can be applied to the potential "follower cases". That is, the question that must be considered is: "the tribunal found that this person was not trading because……" The reasoning that follows "because" must then be examined in relation to the follower cases.

This will include considering carefully the context of the ruling and whether it is reasonable to apply the same reasoning to the context of the follower case(s). It is not about extracting a wide general principle from a case and then applying that to other cases where the context and facts are substantially different.

If a later case was to significantly change the effect of the relevant judicial ruling, HMRC will reconsider whether any follower notices that have been given (and any associated accelerated payment notices) should still be maintained, withdrawn or modified.

1.7.3 Marketed avoidance

Although the legislation does not exclusively apply to widely marketed schemes, the definition of "relevant" makes it much less likely that it will apply outside that context. Nonetheless, the legislation could apply to a judicial ruling which determines a case against one person, and there is only one or a small number of others that are potential followers. In these cases, facts would have been gathered about each potential follower to establish their similarity to the relevant judicial ruling, and whether the same principles or reasoning can apply to deny the tax and/or NICs advantage. Again, the important point is to consider critically the principles or reasoning in the ruling to see if it can reasonably apply to the follower case(s).

1.7.4 Application to other cases

To decide whether the principles or reasoning in a judicial ruling are applicable to other cases, it will be necessary to:

- ensure that the judicial ruling itself relates to tax and/or NICs arrangements, ie where there is a main tax and/or NICs purpose
- identify the principles and reasoning in the judicial ruling
- evaluate the facts of the other cases with reference to the evidence currently held by HMRC
- consider any additional information; eg other judicial rulings in the same area of tax and/or NICs
- apply the principles/reasoning in the judicial ruling to the facts of the other cases
- decide whether (and, if so, to what extent) the asserted tax and/or NICs advantage is denied as a consequence

1.8 What judicial rulings can be used to give follower notices

Judicial rulings must be final before they can be considered to set down principles and reasoning to be applied to follower cases. **"Final"** means that the case has either not been appealed further or has been decided by the Supreme Court. Thus a ruling can be final at First-tier Tribunal level if it is not appealed to the Upper Tribunal. See section 205(4) of FA 2014.

Before any follower notice is given in relation to a relevant judicial ruling, a senior HMRC governance panel will consider whether it is appropriate to apply the principles or reasoning established by the ruling. As explained below, the issue of a follower notice is also subject to time limits.

1.9 Normal time limits

1.9.1 Time limits (section 204(6) FA 2014)

A follower notice must be given within 12 months, beginning with the later of the day:

- on which the relevant judicial ruling is made (Condition C)
- that the return or claim, or notification of dispute in relation to a relevant contribution dispute, was received by HMRC
- that the tax and/or NICs appeal was made

See section 1.9.2 for the transitional time limits following enactment of FA 2014.

1.9.2 Transitional time limits for rulings prior to Royal Assent of FA 2014 (section 217 FA 2014)

Where a judicial ruling is made before this legislation was enacted, a follower notice must be given on or before the later of:

- 24 months following the date FA 2014 was passed
- 12 months beginning with the day the return or claim, or notification of dispute in relation to a relevant contribution dispute, was received by HMRC
- (if there is an appeal that has not yet been determined by the court) 12 months beginning with the day the tax and/or NICs appeal was made

Here's an example of how the transitional time limits operate.

Example 2:

Transitional time limits

A relevant judicial ruling was made on 1 February 2013.

Royal Assent to the FA 2014 was given on 17 July 2014. So 24 months after that is 16 July 2016.

HMRC received the person's 2013–2014 tax return on 1 June 2014.

The final date for HMRC to give a follower notice in this instance is 16 July 2016.

1.10 Content of a follower notice (section 206 FA 2014)

1.10.1 Identify the judicial ruling

The follower notice must identify the relevant judicial ruling and explain why it is relevant.

1.10.2 Other content

The follower notice must also explain how to make representations, the circumstances in which a penalty may be reduced for co-operation, and the maximum penalties thatHMRC may charge if corrective action is not taken. It must also explain that the penalty can be reduced by the quality of co-operation received by HMRC from the person.

1.10.3 Explain the consequences

The follower notice does not require corrective action to be taken, but explains that, if the necessary corrective action is not taken, the person may be charged a penalty under section 208 FA 2014. (See 1.12 and 1.15 below.)

1.11 Representations

1.11.1 Grounds for representations

The person can disagree with a follower notice by making representations to HMRC. Representations must be made in writing and can only be on the basis that one or more of 3 circumstances applies. The circumstances are that:

- Condition A, B or D was not met (see 1.3 of this guidance)
- the judicial ruling is not one which is relevant to the arrangements (i.e. that HMRC's opinion under Condition C is incorrect)
- the notice was not given within the time limit

To enable HMRC to fully consider the matter and come to a conclusion, any representations made should give as much information as possible about the grounds on which they are made.

There is no right of appeal to the Tribunal against a follower notice.

1.11.2 Time limit for representations

Representations must be made in writing to HMRC within 90 days of the date the notice was given.

1.11.3 HMRC response

HMRC must consider the representations and either confirm the follower notice (with or without amending it) or withdraw the notice. HMRC must notify the person of their decision.

The representations will be considered by an independent HMRC officer who is unconnected with the team that issued the follower notice, and with the governance panel that decided the judicial ruling relied upon was relevant. Section 1.19.2 contains more information on governance.

1.12 Corrective action

1.12.1 Where there is a tax enquiry or a tax and/or NICs appeal

After a follower notice is given, a person has 90 days to take corrective action in respect of the denied advantage by:

- (where there is a tax enquiry) amending their return or claim to counteract the denied advantage
- (where there is a tax and/or NICs appeal) taking all necessary action to enter into a written agreement with HMRC to relinquish the denied advantage

The person must also notify HMRC that they have taken corrective action, and tell them the amount of the denied advantage and, if different, the additional amount of tax and/or NICs due and payable.

1.12.2 Where there is a relevant contributions dispute in progress

Where a relevant contributions dispute is in progress (for a definition, see section 1.4 and annex 1 of this guidance), a person has 90 days to take corrective action in respect of the denied advantage by:

- (where the denied advantage can be counteracted by making a payment to HMRC) making a payment to HMRC and notifying them that they have done so
- (where the denied advantage cannot be counteracted by making a payment to HMRC) taking all necessary action to enter into a written agreement with HMRC for the purpose of counteracting the denied advantage

1.12.3 Confirmed notice

Where representations have been made and the notice is confirmed (with or without amendment) the time limit to take corrective action is the later of:

- the date for taking corrective action that was shown in the follower notice
- 30 days after the day on which the person is notified of HMRC's decision following representations

Section 208(8)(b)(ii) FA2014 allows 30 days beginning with the date that HMRC notifies the person of their decision. In practice, HMRC also allows additional time for postage.

> **Example 3:**
>
> A person was given a follower notice on 1 September 2014 and makes representations to HMRC on 1 November 2014.
>
> An independent HMRC officer considers the representations and confirms the follower notice on 10 December 2014.
>
> The date for taking corrective action is the later of:
>
> - 29 November 2014 (the date for taking corrective action that was shown in the follower notice)
> - 8 January 2015 (30 days after HMRC notifies their decision, plus extra time for postage)
>
> Therefore, the person has until 8 January 2015 to take the necessary corrective action.

1.12.4 The person can choose how to proceed

The person has a choice about how to proceed. The decision to settle or continue the dispute is entirely theirs, but they take that decision in the light of the penalty consequences if the dispute continues. The legislation does not in any way deny the person access to their full appeal rights to the courts and tribunals about the substantive liability (i.e. whether the tax and/or NICs arrangements give the result which the person believed they did).

1.13 Open appeal – written agreement

1.13.1 Appeal in progress

If the person chooses to settle or concede the dispute where there is an open appeal in progress, they are required to take all necessary steps to enter into a written agreement with HMRC to give up the advantage that their arrangements sought to obtain. A form will be issued for use in most cases and will include:

- acceptance that the judicial ruling is relevant to their arrangements
- agreement that the effect is that the tax and/or NICs advantage arising from the arrangements is denied
- agreement to withdraw the appeal in relation to the arrangements within 14 days of the agreement. If the appeal covers matters in addition to the tax and/or NICs arrangements, then it only has to be withdrawn to the extent it relates to those arrangements
- confirmation that any additional tax and/or NICs due as a result of giving up the tax and/or NICs advantage will be (or has been) paid by the required date
- signature by the person or properly authorised person who can sign on behalf of the person (for example, a director)

1.14 Penalty – calculating the denied advantage (the penalty base)

1.14.1 Basis of penalty

If corrective action is not taken by the deadline for taking it (which may have been extended if representations were made), the person will incur a penalty. The legislation sets out the basis for how the penalty will be calculated (sections 208 and 209 and Schedule 30 FA 2014).

The amount of the penalty is calculated by reference to the "denied advantage" (the penalty base). The denied advantage is defined as being the amount of the "asserted advantage" which is denied when the principles or reasoning laid down in the relevant ruling are applied to this person's circumstances. The "asserted advantage" is the tax and/or NICs advantage which would result from the use of the particular scheme used, if it achieved its aim.

Therefore, if the asserted advantage is £10,000, and the principles and reasoning in the relevant ruling mean that none of that advantage can be claimed by the person, then the denied advantage is £10,000. The penalty will be calculated by reference to £10,000.

It will not always be the case that the denied advantage and the asserted advantage are the same amount. The principles or reasoning laid down in the relevant ruling may only remove part of the asserted advantage; or it may be that parts of the advantage resulting from a scheme are not disputed as they rely on an accepted relief or allowance.

The "denied advantage" may be easy to calculate in some cases, and may apply to a single period or return. However, there will be cases which are more complicated to calculate – for example, deferred losses. This could mean that the penalty base may be a different amount to the amount of tax and/or NICs which is in dispute for a specific return.

1.14.2 Schedule 30

Schedule 30 to FA 2014 applies for calculating the value of the denied advantage for follower penalties.

1.14.3 Value of denied advantage

The value of the denied advantage is usually the additional amount due or payable in respect of the tax and/ or NICs that would be due following corrective action; ie the amount due if the avoidance scheme fails. However, this can be more complex where losses are involved, or where tax would have been deferred.

1.14.4 Amounts to include

The amount of the denied advantage includes any amount of tax and/or NICs that:

- the person has not yet paid
- has been repaid to the person by HMRC and is now no longer due to have been repaid
- was shown on the return or claim to be repayable and could have been repaid by HMRC, had the arrangements achieved the asserted advantage

1.14.5 Ignore group relief

When the value of the denied advantage is calculated, group relief should be ignored, and also any relief under section 458 CTA 2010 (loans to participators: relief in respect of repayment), which is deferred under section 458(5).

1.14.6 Losses

For direct tax, the value of the denied advantage involving losses is:

- the additional tax that would be chargeable following corrective action (as regards the part of the denied advantage used to reduce the amount of tax)
- 10% of the part of the loss not used (if any)

If the denied advantage creates or increases a loss for a group of companies, group relief may be taken into account.

> **Example 4:**
>
> *A singleton (non-group) company*
>
> Company A has profits of £20m and a created loss for the year of £30m.
>
> Losses to carry forward are £10m.
>
> The denied advantage is £5.2m ((losses used to reduce the amount of tax £20m × 21% = 4.2m) + (loss not used £10m × 10% = £1m))

Example 5:

A group company

	Group companies	
	Company A	Company B
	£m	£m
Profits	20	30
Created loss	(30)	nil
Group relief	nil	(10)
PCTCT	nil	20

The denied advantage is £6.3m (£30m × 21%).

This is comprised of £20m loss utilised in the year by Company A, plus £10m loss by group relief to Company B.

1.14.7 Denied advantage is a loss that will not be used

To the extent the denied advantage results in a loss, the value of the denied advantage is nil if there is no reasonable prospect of the loss being used to reduce a tax liability. "No reasonable prospect" will have to be assessed on a case by case basis, taking all the relevant circumstances of the person into account.

1.14.8 Denied advantage is a deferral of tax

To the extent the denied advantage is a deferral of tax, the value of the denied advantage is one of the following:

- 25% of the amount of the deferred tax for each year of the deferral
- 25% per year of the deferred tax for each separate period of deferral of less than a year
- if less, 100% of the amount of the deferred tax

Example 6

A person engages in a tax avoidance scheme which defers tax of £100,000 due in 2010, so that they pay it over the following 5 years.

25% of the amount of deferred tax, multiplied by 5 for the number of years of deferral, equals 125% of the deferred tax.

As the maximum penalty base is 100%, the penalty will be charged on £100,000.

1.15 Penalties

1.15.1 Corrective action not taken – general

If corrective action is not taken in respect of the denied advantage before the specified time, the person is liable to a penalty. However, it is important to note that the penalty is not due until it is assessed (section 211 FA 2014).

1.15.2 Corrective action not taken – open tax enquiry

Where the penalty has arisen in the course of an open tax enquiry, HMRC will normally assess the penalty after the conclusion of the enquiry. For example, after the issue of a closure notice in direct tax cases. At that stage the figure of understated tax that forms the basis of the penalty will have been calculated for the purpose of the closure notice.

1.15.3 Corrective action not taken – relevant contributions dispute in progress

Where the follower notice was issued while a relevant contributions dispute was in progress (for definitions, see section 1.4 and annex 1 of this guidance), but no corrective action has been taken, HMRC will normally assess the penalty after the relevant contributions dispute has been completed, in one of the following ways:

- HMRC issues a NICs decision(s) in relation to the person's liability for the disputed NICs
- the person accepts that NICs are due and pays the disputed contributions in full
- HMRC and the person reach an agreement in writing as to the person's liability for the disputed contribution and amounts of those agreements are paid

The figure that forms the basis of the penalty will have been calculated for the purpose of issuing the NICs decision(s) or will be based on the contributions paid when the dispute is either conceded or settled.

1.15.4 Corrective action not taken – open appeal

In cases where the penalty has arisen when the tax and/or NICs is under appeal, the penalty will normally be assessed when the amount of tax and/or NICs is finally determined.

1.15.5 Corrective action not taken – early assessment of penalty

None of the situations in 1.15.2, 1.15.3 or 1.15.4 prevents an earlier assessment of the penalty if the circumstances require, but the important requirement is that figures of tax and/or NICs are available to form the basis of the penalty and therefore earlier assessment is likely to happen only very exceptionally.

1.15.6 Rate of penalty

The maximum penalty is 50% of the value of the denied advantage. The minimum rate, taking into account the full availability of reduction for cooperation, is 10%. The penalty rates are different for partnerships (for more information see section 1.18.7).

1.15.7 Reduction of penalty for co-operation

Providing the penalty has not yet been assessed, and the person has co-operated with HMRC, then HMRC may reduce the penalty to reflect the quality of that co-operation.

1.15.8 Co-operation considered

A person is only considered to have co-operated with HMRC if they have co-operated in one or more of the following ways. By having:

- provided reasonable assistance to HMRC in quantifying the advantage
- counteracted the denied advantage (but at a time after the specified time for corrective action)
- provided HMRC with information enabling them to take corrective action
- provided HMRC with information enabling them to enter into an agreement with them (to counteract the denied advantage)
- allowed HMRC to access tax records to ensure the denied advantage is counteracted

The penalty must not be reduced to less than 10% of the value of the denied advantage

1.15.9 Part of advantage remaining

If, before the specified time for corrective action in the follower notice, the person does one or more of the following:

- amends a return or claim to counteract part of the denied advantage
- pays the tax and/or NICs that HMRC considers are due for payment, and notifies HMRC they have done so (where the denied advantage can be counteracted by making a payment to HMRC
- takes all necessary action to enter into an agreement with HMRC to relinquish part of the denied advantage

the penalty will only be calculated on the remainder of the denied advantage.

Example 7:

A person has been given a follower notice in relation to a complex scheme which depends on a number of transactions to produce a cumulative tax advantage.

Having reconsidered the scheme, the person accepts that a part of it does not achieve the intended tax advantage, so amends their return only to the extent of that part.

They continue to maintain the success of the remaining parts of the scheme.

The amendment to the return was before the due date of the notice.

Any penalty is only calculated on the tax advantage which is still being claimed as at the due date. Thus the penalty base will be reduced from the original amount for the scheme to the amended amount still on the return or in any appeal.

1.15.10 Assessment of the penalty

HMRC must notify the person who is liable for the penalty and state the tax period in respect of which the penalty is due.

1.15.11 Penalty due date

The penalty is due and payable 30 days after the person is notified of it.

1.15.12 Notification

The date by which HMRC must notify the penalty, is:

- (if the follower notice was issued whilst an enquiry was open or a relevant contributions dispute was in progress) no later than 90 days after the enquiry or relevant contributions dispute is completed (see paragraph 1.15.3)
- (if the follower notice was issued whilst an appeal is pending) no later than 90 days beginning with the earliest of the day on which:
  - the person takes corrective action
  - a final ruling is made on the tax and/or NICs appeal
  - the appeal, or any further appeal is abandoned or disposed of (to the extent it relates to the asserted tax and/or NICs advantage) before it is determined by the court or tribunal

Example 8a:

HMRC completes the compliance check into a person's use of an avoidance scheme and issues a closure notice.

If the person has been given a follower notice and not taken the corrective action by the due date, then they are liable to a penalty. Having now concluded the check and issued the closure notice, HMRC must issue any penalty assessment within 90 days.

Any such penalty assessment will take into account the degree of cooperation provided by the person.

Example 8b:

In a situation with an open appeal where a follower notice has been given, the person has not taken corrective action within the time limits; there are three potential time limits as shown below.

(1) the person decides to take the corrective action and withdraw the appeal and accept that the relevant ruling applies. HMRC must assess any penalty within 90 days of the date that corrective action is taken.

(2) the case has gone to the Court of Appeal, (for example), and the person loses and does not appeal further. HMRC must assess any penalty within 90 days of the date the ruling was made.

(3) the person decides to abandon their appeal and concede. HMRC has 90 days from the date that the case is formally acknowledged as abandoned by the court to assess any penalty.

1.15.13 Enforceable penalty – tax follower notice (section 211(4) FA 2014)

The penalty due for not complying with a follower notice relating to tax (not NICs) is treated in the same way as an assessment to tax and therefore will be enforced as if it were an assessment to tax. See section 1.16.2 of this guidance, which relates to interest charged on a penalty.

1.15.14 Enforceable penalty – NICs follower notice (paragraph 20 Schedule 2 NICA2015)

The penalty due for not complying with a NICs follower notice is recovered in the same way as unpaid relevant contributions (see annex 1 for definition). It is not treated in the same way as an assessment to tax. For the purposes of a Court determining whether civil proceedings can be adjourned; the penalty assessment is treated as if it were a NICs decision as to whether the person was liable for the penalty. The effect is that if there is an appeal against the penalty assessment, the Court must adjourn any civil proceedings taken to recover the penalty until the appeal is finally determined.

1.15.15 Supplementary penalty assessment (section 213 FA2014)

A supplementary penalty assessment may be issued if the value of the denied advantage was understated. In a case where the advantage was overstated, and a penalty has already been paid, the excess penalty will be repaid with interest.

1.16 Appeal against a penalty

1.16.1 Penalty appeals (section 214 FA 2014)

A person may appeal against a decision that a penalty is payable and against the amount of the penalty. The appeal:

- must be made within 30 days of the day the penalty was notified. The penalty is treated as notified when the penalty notice is delivered to the person

- is treated in the same way as an appeal against an assessment of the tax or NICs decision is concerned, whether the penalty was assessed on tax or NICs, but see section 1.15.14 about adjourning civil proceedings to recover the penalty where there is an appeal against a NICs decision

The grounds for an appeal can, in particular, include:

- the same grounds as for making representations
- that it was reasonable in all the circumstances for the person not to have taken the corrective action

If the tribunal upholds the appeal against the penalty on the grounds that Conditions A,B, C or D (see 1.3 of this guidance) were not satisfied, this would result in the follower notice being cancelled, together with any associated accelerated payment notice if that latter notice was only issued because of the follower notice. If required, HMRC will then, as appropriate, repay any amounts, plus interest, to the person.

If the tribunal upholds the appeal against the penalty solely on the grounds that it was reasonable for the person to proceed, this outcome does not overturn the follower notice itself.

1.16.2 Interest due on penalty

A person is not required to pay a penalty before an appeal against the assessment of the penalty is determined. However, interest, where appropriate, runs from the original due and payable date of the penalty.

1.16.3 Appeal against a penalty

The legislation gives the tribunal the power to affirm or cancel HMRC's decision, or to substitute an alternative decision.

This is fairly broadly drawn. Section 214 FA 2014 sets out some grounds on which the tribunal can consider and uphold an appeal, but these grounds are not intended to be exhaustive. It means that the tribunal could, for example, discharge the penalty because the tribunal does not agree that the decision cited by HMRC as the basis for a follower notice was "relevant", even though HMRC was ultimately successful in the substantive litigation. The relevance or otherwise may only have emerged during the tribunal's consideration of the substantive appeal.

1.16.4 Person is successful in substantive litigation

Where the person is successful in the substantive litigation, the penalty will be discharged as it is a tax-geared penalty and there will be no disputed tax to form the basis of the penalty. It should not normally be necessary for the penalty appeal to be heard by the tribunal in such instances.

Whilst the penalty does not have to be paid pending litigation, a person may pay it to prevent interest accruing on it. Any amount of penalty already paid will be repaid with interest in those circumstances. In addition, tax may be repayable, together with interest, to the person.

1.16.5 Aggregate Penalties (section 212 FA 2014)

The penalty for failure to take corrective action after receipt of a follower notice is based on the "denied advantage" (being the amount of the tax and/or NICs advantage that the person has tried to obtain that is actually denied by the application of the relevant judicial principle or reasoning). The person may also become liable to a penalty under other legislation, for example on the grounds that their return was incorrect because of deliberate action on their part. The follower notice penalties legislation is restricted so that the total penalties in relation to the same tax and/or NICs liability do not, in aggregate, exceed the maximum of certain of these other penalties.

If two or more penalties are determined by reference to the same amount of tax and/or NICs and:

- one is for failure to comply with a follower notice
- one or more are incurred under:
    - Schedule 24 FA 2007 – penalties for errors
    - Schedule 41 FA 2008 – penalties for failure to notify
    - Schedule 55 FA 2009 – penalties for failure to make returns

the aggregate amounts charged must not exceed the "relevant percentage".

The relevant percentage will usually be the maximum percentage chargeable under the other penalty if that exceeds 100%. In other cases, the maximum aggregated penalty will be 100%.

1.16.6 Aggregate penalties – NICs (section 212 FA 2014 and paragraphs 14 and 15 Schedule 2 NIC Act 2015)

The modifications made by NICA 2015 ensure that the penalties to be taken into account for the purposes of section 212 FA 2014 include those incurred for failure to make a Class 1 NICs return under:

- Schedule 55 FA 2009, as applied by paragraph 21G of Schedule 4 to the Social Security (Contributions) Regulations 2001 with effect from 6 October 2014
- section 98A TMA 1970, as applied by paragraph 22(7) of Schedule 4 to the Social Security (Contributions) Regulations 2001 for tax years up to and including 6 April 2013 to 5 April 2014

When considering the total of the aggregate penalties as described in section 1.16.5 of this guidance, if one or more of penalties are incurred under section 98A TMA 1970, the aggregate amounts charged must not exceed the "relevant percentage" described in section 1.16.5 of this guidance.

1.17 Late appeals against a final judicial ruling (section 216 FA2014)

1.17.1 Late appeals

It may be the case that HMRC has given follower notices based on a tribunal or court decision that had not initially been appealed within the time limit, and had therefore become "final" for this purpose. Where a person subsequently applied for and obtained leave to make a late appeal, (section 49 TMA 1970 and regulation 9 of the Social Security Contributions (Decisions and Appeals) Regulations 1999) the process for follower notices is suspended while the late appeal into that decision is heard.

1.17.2 Penalty not due

This means that any penalty assessed will not be due and payable during this time, and any accelerated payment will not be due for payment if the payment notice is based solely on the follower notice requirement of Condition C (see sections 1.3.4 and 2.2.6 of this guidance). If the late appeal is determined in favour of the person, any follower notice given on the basis of that decision will be discharged and any penalties paid or accelerated payments made as a result of that notice repaid with interest.

1.17.3 Leave to appeal out of time granted

This applies where the final judicial ruling is the subject of an appeal where the court or tribunal has granted leave to appeal out of time.

If a follower notice has been given identifying the original ruling (now subject to a late appeal), HMRC must notify the recipient of the notice as soon as practicable.

1.17.4 Follower notice suspended

If a follower notice has been given identifying the original ruling (now subject to a late appeal), HMRC must notify the person as soon as practicable.

The follower notice is suspended until HMRC notifies the person that either the appeal has:

- resulted in a judicial ruling which is a final ruling
- been abandoned or otherwise disposed of

If the new final ruling is not a judicial ruling which is relevant to the chosen arrangements then the follower notice ceases to have effect.

1.17.5 Notice remains effective

In any other case where leave to appeal is not granted, and HMRC are successful and the principles and reasoning previously identified are still relevant, the follower notice continues to have effect after the end of the period of suspension. It is treated as if it were in respect of the new final ruling resulting from the appeal.

1.18 Partnerships (Schedules 31 and 32 FA 2014)

1.18.1 Overview

Special rules for members of partnerships can be found in Schedules 31 and 32 to FA2014. These rules essentially reflect the general tax treatment of partnerships. In summary:

- a partnership follower notice for a partnership tax arrangement will be given to the representative partner, or their successor in that capacity, on behalf of the partnership as a whole
- that follower notice can then apply to generate a partner payment notice to each member of the partnership individually
- the members can also be given a follower notice and/or accelerated payment notice in respect of a scheme in their personal capacity, for example where a claim made personally relates to the tax affairs of the partnership but is not derived directly from the partnership return (for example, a personal loan interest claim)
- in those instances these will relate directly to their own tax return, which will include their share of the partnership profits and gains

1.18.2 Special rules for Stamp Duty Land Tax (SDLT) and Annual Tax on Enveloped Dwellings (ATED)

Specific partnership rules apply for SDLT and ATED to reflect the particular treatment of partnerships in relation to those taxes.

1.18.3 Partnership follower notice

The follower notice for a partnership is called a partnership follower notice. It is not materially different to a follower notice in content or purpose, but is given to the representative partner rather than to all the partners. There is provision in the law to give the partnership follower notice to a successor of the representative partner where necessary.

These rules only apply to partnerships required to deliver a partnership return under rules in section 12AA TMA 1970.

Rules applicable to SDLT and ATED are set out in sections 230 and 231 FA 2014 and guidance is at sections 3 and 4 of this guidance.

1.18.4 Representative partner

The representative partner is the person who is required to deliver the partnership return under section 12AA(2) or (3)TMA 1970. It is the responsibility of the representative partner to take the corrective action, if agreed to by the partners, in response to the partnership follower notice.

1.18.5 Partners are responsible for penalties

Whilst it is the representative partner's responsibility to take the corrective action on behalf of the partnership, any follower notice penalty which arises will be the responsibility of all the partners to pay.

1.18.6 Partnership denied advantage

The calculation of the penalty is based on the denied advantage, which will be calculated by reference to the amount by which the partnership return would be amended to negate the effects of the relevant judicial ruling. Therefore, the denied advantage for a partnership is a profit/loss figure rather than being the tax and/or NICsadvantage figure. This is why the corresponding penalty rates for partners are different to those for non-partners.

This gives the total penalty for the partnership as a whole, which needs to be apportioned across the partners by reference to their individual share in the partnership. Normally this would be by reference to their share in the profits or losses of the partnership.

1.18.7 Maximum penalty rate for partnerships

The rate of the penalty is modified by these rules from a maximum 50% to a maximum of 20% to be shared across the partners. Similarly the minimum amount of penalty, following any reduction for co-operation, is 4%.

1.18.8 Penalty aggregation applies

Penalty aggregation rules apply to partners as they would for nonpartners.

1.18.9 Representations

Representations can be made by the representative partner if they disagree with the partnership follower notice.

1.18.10 Partnership appeals

Only the representative partner can appeal against the calculation of the total penalty and the fact of the penalty. The representative partner cannot appeal against the calculation of the share of the penalty for an individual partner.

1.18.11 What if an individual partner wants to withdraw

Only the representative partner (often known as the "nominated" partner) can take the corrective action. Therefore, individual partners who would like to withdraw from the scheme transactions may still face a share of the follower penalty if the other partners do not agree to take the corrective action and instruct the representative partner to do so.

1.19 Governance

1.19.1 Selection of the follower cases

Decisions over the giving of follower notices will be taken by a senior HMRC panel. This panel will consider the principles and reasoning established by final judicial rulings and the context within which those principles arise.

The panel will be independent from the teams who investigate cases. It will consider both existing final cases which may be relevant, as well as new cases which will arise from time to time.

1.19.2 Review of representations

Representations made by a person about the giving of a notice will be considered by an independent Appeals and Reviews Team. This team will not be part of the investigating or case team, or connected to the governance panel.

2 Accelerated Payments

2.1 Overview

2.1.1 Remove cash flow advantage

There is no inherent presumption that tax and/or NICs in dispute should sit with the person, rather than the Exchequer. Under current rules, a person who can self assess the claimed tax and/or NICs advantage from an avoidance scheme can hold the money in dispute while the dispute is resolved. This can take a considerable time as these schemes are often highly complex and a considerable amount of information needs to be obtained from scheme users and advisers, and litigation may be required to resolve the dispute.

2.1.2 Repayments can already be retained

In certain circumstances, the disputed tax already rests with HMRC until the dispute is resolved. For example, where a person has to claim a repayment the Exchequer can retain the money while the dispute proceeds. The accelerated payment proposals bring the vast majority of remaining tax and/or NICs avoidance cases into line with this position.

2.1.3 Legislation

Legislation was announced in the Budget 2014 and enacted in Part 4 FA 2014. The legislation was extended to NICs with effect from 12 April 2015 by the National Insurance Contributions Act 2015.

2.2 Conditions for an accelerated payment (section 219 FA2014)

2.2.1 Certain conditions must be satisfied

Accelerated payment notices may be given to a person who has used an avoidance scheme and where one or more certain conditions are satisfied. Those conditions are that they:

- have been given a follower notice (see section 1 of this guidance)
- have used a DOTAS notifiable arrangement
- are subject to a GAAR counteraction notice

The accelerated payment notice tells the person that they must pay the specified amount which equates to the tax and/or NICs in dispute as a result of their use of the avoidance scheme.

2.2.2 When an accelerated payment notice may be given (section 219 FA 2014)

HMRC may give an accelerated payment notice to a person (P) if all three Conditions A to C are met

2.2.3 Condition A

For tax, a tax enquiry is in progress into a return or claim made by P in relation to a relevant tax; or P has made a tax appeal in relation to a relevant tax, but the appeal has not been determined by the tribunal or court, or abandoned/disposed of.

For relevant NICs, a relevant contributions dispute is in progress, (see section 2.3 and annex 1 of this guidance); or P has made a NICs appeal in relation to a relevant contribution, but the appeal has not been determined by the tribunal or court, or abandoned/disposed of.

This is an important step in the process. HMRC cannot give an accelerated payment notice unless:

- for tax:
  - an enquiry has been opened into a return
  - an appeal has been made against a closure notice, assessment, or determination, (for example, a determination under regulation 80 of the Income Tax (Pay As You Earn) Regulations 2003)
- for NICs:
  - a relevant contributions dispute is in progress (see section 2.3 and annex 1 of this guidance)
  - an appeal has been made against a NICs decision (see annex 1 for definition of NICs decision and NICs appeal)

The person should, therefore, already be aware that their tax and/or NICs arrangements are being challenged.

Once the:

- enquiry is opened (tax), or a relevant contributions dispute is in progress (NICs) (see section 2.3 and annex 1 of this guidance), and not closed
- appeal is made and not determined by the Tribunal or Court to which it is addressed, or otherwise settled

there is no time limit within which HMRC must give an accelerated payment notice.

Where an enquiry is open or a relevant contributions dispute is in progress and the amounts of unpaid tax and/or NICs have not already been established, HMRC will take necessary steps to obtain information from the person and/or their advisers to enable an accurate figure to be established.

The amount due in the accelerated payment notice will normally be the amount included in the closure notice, determination, assessment or NICs decision.

2.2.4 Condition B

The return, claim or appeal (including an appeal against a section 8 decision, (see Decisions and Appeals for National Insurance Contributions and Statutory Payments (DANSP) Manual) is made on the basis that a particular tax and/or NICs advantage (the asserted advantage) results from particular arrangements (the chosen arrangements).

Condition B is also met if, in a relevant contributions dispute, a person (see section 2.3 and annex 1 of this guidance) disputes liability for NICs on the basis that a particular NICs advantage (the asserted advantage) results from particular arrangements (the chosen arrangements), regardless of whether the person had originally notified the dispute as to the liability on that particular basis.

2.2.5 Condition C

There are three alternative requirements within Condition C, any one or more of which is sufficient to allow the giving of an accelerated payment notice, provided that Conditions A and B are also satisfied.

More than one of the following may be relevant and each must be specified in the accelerated payment notice if relevant:

2.2.6 Condition C, requirement 1: Follower notice

HMRC has given a follower notice (see section 1 of this guidance) in relation to the same return, claim or appeal and by reason of the same tax and/or NICs advantage and chosen arrangements.

2.2.7 Condition C, requirement 2: DOTAS

The chosen arrangements are DOTAS arrangements.

2.2.8 Condition C, requirement 3: GAAR

A GAAR counteraction notice has been given in relation to the same tax and/or NICs advantage (or part of), in a case where the stated opinion of at least two of the members of the sub-panel of the GAAR Advisory Panel concluded that entering into the arrangements was not a reasonable course of action.

2.2.9 The DOTAS requirement

The DOTAS requirement requires two conditions to be satisfied:

- the arrangements have been given a DOTAS Scheme Reference Number (SRN) under the DOTAS legislation (section 311 of FA 2004)
- the person has made a return asserting a tax and/or NICs advantage based on those arrangements

Note that the requirement for there to be an open enquiry, relevant contributions dispute in progress (see section 2.3 and annex 1 of this guidance) or appeal must be met. HMRC cannot give an accelerated payment notice on the basis of the DOTAS requirement when the disclosure is made, unless there is also an open enquiry, relevant contributions dispute in progress, or appeal at that point in time in relation to those disclosed arrangements.

It is also important to note that there must have been a disclosure that has given rise to an SRN. HMRC cannot give an accelerated payment notice unless there has been a disclosure or HMRC has successfully taken action under Part 7 FA 2004 or equivalent NICs legislation (See the National Insurance Manual) to enforce a disclosure.

Only those DOTAS SRNs which are published by HMRC on a list (to be updated from time to time) will be within the scope for receiving an accelerated payment notice. See section 2.2.13 of this guidance.

Example 9:

A person has gross income of £150,000 and claims a loss arising from an arrangement disclosed under DOTAS of £50,000. The person completes and submits a Self Assessment tax return on that basis, showing taxable income of £100,000 (subject to any other reliefs and allowances available). In this case, tax on £50,000 is the tax advantage referred to in the legislation.

If part of the relief claimed under the DOTAS disclosed arrangement is not considered to arise from an avoidance scheme, the tax advantage for these purposes will exclude that part of the total amount.

Example 10:

Of the £50,000 referred to in example 9, £30,000 is considered to arise from a claim to relief in line with the relevant legislation and £20,000 is considered to arise from tax avoidance. In this case, tax on £20,000 is the tax advantage.

2.2.10 Does a DOTAS SRN have to be notified by the person

Where a person is obliged by the law to notify HMRC of the SRN, but fails to do so, the legislation still applies providing the two criteria are satisfied (see section 2.2.9 of this guidance).

2.2.11 Not in possession of a DOTAS number

It is not open to a person to object to an accelerated payment notice simply on the grounds that they have not been given the SRN by whoever was required to do so by the DOTAS legislation. The legislation simply requires that the person's return has been made on the basis of a tax and/or NICs advantage arising from arrangements that have been given a DOTAS SRN.

2.2.12 Two or all three criteria: Condition C

It is possible for an accelerated payment notice to be given on the basis of two or all three of the criteria within Condition C. See sections 2.13 and 2.14 of this guidance for more details about what happens in these circumstances, and the particular rules that apply.

2.2.13 Publication of scheme reference numbers

HMRC has published a list of DOTAS SRNs. Users of schemes on that list may receive an accelerated payment notice from HMRC requiring an accelerated payment to be made.
HMRC updates the list at quarterly intervals.

2.2.14 DOTAS requirement met for tax – arrangements used to avoid tax and NICs

If the arrangement has been used to avoid tax and NICs, the DOTAS requirement will be met for both tax and NICs where the DOTAS requirement is met for tax (see section 2.2.9). This includes where the NICs element of the arrangements were not disclosable under the corresponding NICs equivalent disclosure provisions. However, where the asserted advantage relates to NICs only, the DOTAS requirement will only be met from the date that the DOTAS legislation took effect for NICs. For more information about DOTAS legislation for NICs see the National Insurance Manual.

2.2.15 Programme of work

The majority of accelerated payment notices based on current disclosed schemes will be given through a phased programme of work over the period from Royal Assent of the FA2014 through to the end of March 2016. This work will be ongoing and, as and when new schemes are disclosed, accelerated payment notices will be given as appropriate where the SRNs are on the published list. Those who are going to be given an accelerated payment notice will be contacted by HMRC before it is given. Where applicable, copies of correspondence will also be sent to the person's agent.

As noted above, an accelerated payment notice can only be given once an enquiry has been opened, a relevant contributions dispute is in progress (see section 2.3 and annex 1 of this guidance) or there is an open appeal, and, where it is based solely on the DOTAS requirement, the DOTAS SRN appears on the published list.

2.3 Relevant contributions dispute (paragraph 6 of Schedule 2 to the NICA 2015)

2.3.1 Giving accelerated payment notices for NICs

For tax, accelerated payment notices can only be given where there is either an open tax enquiry or an open appeal.

Whilst there is a NICs equivalent of an open appeal (against a NICs decision), there is no direct equivalent of a tax enquiry for NICs. Because of this, the National Insurance Contributions Act 2015 introduces the concept of a "relevant contributions dispute" (see annex 1 for definition). Creating this concept allows HMRC to give an accelerated payment notice in circumstances where there is a dispute about NICs but before a NICs decision has been made and can be appealed against.

2.4 Giving accelerated payment notices for tax and NICs at different times

There are time limits for issuing tax assessments and determinations but not for issuing NICs decisions. Because of this, HMRC may issue tax assessments or determinations sooner than they issue NICs decisions in relation to the same avoidance scheme used. This could mean that a tax appeal may be in place before there is a relevant contributions dispute or an appeal against a NICs decision.

Where there is an appeal against a tax assessment or determination and HMRC considers that NICs are also due, they may give a person an accelerated payment notice for tax before they give the accelerated payment notice for NICs.

2.5 Content of an accelerated payment notice where enquiry or relevant contributions dispute is in progress (section 220 FA 2014)

2.5.1 Notices

An accelerated payment notice must:

- specify the conditions that have been satisfied – including all applicable requirements under Condition C (see sections 2.2.5 to 2.2.8 of this guidance)
- tell the person the amount to pay
- (for tax) explain that the accelerated payment is to be treated as a payment on account of the tax in dispute
- (for NICs) explain that the AP is a payment of the NICs (paragraph 17(2) Schedule 2 NICA 2015)
- tell the person the deadline for paying the accelerated payment
- specify the late payment penalty terms, rates and structure
- (for tax) explain that any amounts subject to an accelerated payment notice cannot be postponed
- (for NICs) explain that, if HMRC has to take civil proceedings to recover the NICs included in the accelerated payment notice, those proceedings cannot be adjourned pending a NICs decision or appeal (paragraph 17(5) Schedule 2 NICA 2015) (see also paragraph 2.8.4 of this guidance)
- explain how representations may be made to HMRC about an accelerated payment notice – including the time limit and what HMRC must do in response
- tell the person that, in the event of their successful litigation, HMRC may apply to the court or tribunal for an order not to repay the tax and/or NICs in dispute, where HMRC pursues a further appeal, in order to protect the revenue

2.5.2 Designated officer

A designated officer – a senior official in HMRC – will determine the amount of the payment required in an accelerated payment notice. The payment required is the amount of the understated tax (see annex 1 for definition) calculated to the best of the officer's information and belief.

The information available will include that held by Customer Relationship Managers (CRM's) and case teams.

2.5.3 Understated tax and/or NICs

The understated tax and/or NICs is the additional amount that would be due and payable on the basis that the tax and/or NICs advantage has been denied.

In each case this will be determined by the designated HMRC officer. In follower notice and GAAR counteraction cases, the expected position would be as follows:

- follower notices: if HMRC has given a follower notice, the amount is the same as would be required if the person were to have taken the necessary corrective action to amend the return or claim, or otherwise settle the dispute
- GAAR counteraction notice: the amount will be the same as specified in the GAAR counteraction notice

2.5.4 Denied advantage

The legislation for the DOTAS criterion uses the term "so much of the asserted advantage as is not a tax advantage which results from the chosen arrangements, or otherwise". (The reference to "tax" includes NICs.)

That is, it is the amount which the person has asserted as a tax and/or NICs advantage but which HMRC considers will not ultimately be a tax and/or NICs advantage when the enquiry, relevant contributions dispute or appeal is finally resolved.

In example 9 (see section 2.2.9), this would be tax on the claimed loss of £50,000 (in the example where the whole amount arises from avoidance) or tax on £20,000 in example 10 (see section 2.2.9).

2.5.5 Requirements in Condition C (section 227 FA 2014)

In the event that more than one of the requirements in Condition C (see sections 2.2.5 to 2.2.8 of this guidance) is met, HMRC must specify in the accelerated payment notice which of them is being applied to determine the amount of the required accelerated payment. This may have further consequences if one or more of the original conditions changes; see sections 2.13 and 2.14 of this guidance.

2.5.6 Content of an accelerated payment notice given pending an appeal

Where an appeal is pending, an accelerated payment notice must:

- specify the conditions that have been satisfied (including which Condition C requirement(s) is met)
- specify the amount of the disputed tax and/or NICs
- (for tax) explain that any tax subject to an accelerated payment notice cannot be postponed
- (for a NICs decision) explain that, if HMRC has to take civil proceedings to recover the NICs included in the accelerated payment notice, those proceedings cannot be adjourned to await the outcome of an appeal against that NICs decision (paragraph 18(3) Schedule 2 NICA 2015). If such proceedings have already been adjourned, they cease to be adjourned (see section 2.8.4 of this guidance for details of the date from which they cease to be adjourned)
- tell the person the deadline for paying the accelerated payment
- explain how representations may be made to HMRC about an accelerated payment notice, including the time limit and what HMRC must do in response
- tell the person that in the event of their successful litigation, HMRC may apply to the court or tribunal for an order not to repay the tax and/or NICs in dispute, where HMRC pursues a further appeal, in order to protect the revenue

2.5.7 Disputed tax and/or NICs

The disputed tax and/or NICs is the amount HMRC is asking the person to pay. It will be determined by a designated officer and, in most cases, it is expected to be the amount which is under appeal in relation to the avoidance arrangements which have led to the accelerated payment notice. Care will be taken to distinguish what is the tax and/or NICs advantage arising from the chosen arrangements and any other amounts which may be in dispute.

2.5.8 Payment dates for accelerated payment notices

The time limits for making an accelerated payment depend on whether representations have been made (see section 2.6 of this guidance for information about representations). If:

- no representations have been made – payment is due no later than 90 days from the date the notice is given
- representations have been made – payment is due the later of:
  - 30 days from when HMRC issues its decision
  - 90 days from the date the original notice was given

2.6 Representations

2.6.1 Representations can be made

The person can object to an accelerated payment notice by making representations in writing to HMRC.

2.6.2 Time limit for representations

The person has 90 days from the date the notice is given to send written representations to HMRC.

2.6.3 Grounds for representations

Representations can only be made on one or more of the following grounds:

- Conditions A, B or C (see sections 2.2.3 to 2.2.8 of this guidance) are not met
- the amount specified in the accelerated payment notice does not accurately reflect the amount of tax and/or NICs in dispute in relation to the asserted advantage

2.6.4 How to make representations

Full information about where to send a representation and what it should contain will be included on the accelerated payment notice.

The normal timing rules that apply to determine, for example, the date of the submission of tax returns and the date of their receipt, will apply to accelerated payment notices and representations. Representations can be made by the person's authorised agent.

2.6.5 HMRC makes decision

The representations will be considered by an independent HMRC officer who is unconnected with the team which issued the accelerated payment notice.

If representations are made objecting to whether requirements A, B or C (see sections 2.2.3 to 2.2.8 of this guidance) are met, HMRC must decide whether to confirm the accelerated payment notice (with or without amendment), or to withdraw it.

Section 1.18 of this guidance contains more information on governance in relation to follower notices.

2.6.6 Changes to the amount specified

If representations are made objecting to the amount specified in the accelerated payment notice, HMRC must decide whether a different amount ought to have been specified, and either confirm the amount in the accelerated payment notice, or amend it to specify a different amount.

2.6.7 HMRC must notify outcome

HMRC must notify the person of the outcome of their representations.

2.6.8 Revised payment date

If an accelerated payment is still payable following notification of HMRC's decision, the person must pay the amount due by the later of:

- 30 days beginning with the date the decision was notified to them
- the deadline for payment that was shown in the accelerated payment notice

2.6.9 Accurate information essential

It is important for the person and their adviser to take all steps to give HMRC full information at the earliest opportunity, so that an accurate figure can be established for the accelerated payment. The accelerated payment is intended to represent only the additional amount that the person would have to pay for the period if their avoidance scheme fails. This may not necessarily be the total tax and/or NICs involved in the appeal or dispute as there may be other reliefs and allowances to take into account.

2.6.10 Potential impact on contributory social security benefits

The accelerated payment notice may be based on Classes 1 and 2 NICs that have not been paid. Such classes of NICs may affect entitlement to contributory social security benefits. Class 1 NICs paid only on earnings above the upper earnings limit do not count for contributory benefit.

2.6.11 Accelerated payment allocated to worker's National Insurance account (paragraphs 17(7) and 18(6) Schedule 2 NICA 2015)

If both:

- action was taken as set out in section 2.6.10 to amend the worker's National Insurance account
- HMRC accept that some or all of the NICs in the accelerated payment notice were not due, for example, because of a final judicial ruling

then, when the accelerated payment (either in part or full) is repaid, HMRC will amend the worker's National Insurance account to show the revised NICs due.

The worker will not be required to repay any benefit paid before the accelerated payment (in part or full) is repaid.

2.6.12 Consequential effects

Where denial of the disputed tax and/or NICs advantage would have a consequential effect on other areas of the person's returns, this will be taken into account. This could include consequential effects on other periods, for example where claims to capital allowances are involved.

2.6.13 More than one set of arrangements

It may be the case that a person has become involved with more than one set of arrangements that, in aggregate would, if successful, lead to their claiming more relief than their aggregate income and gains for the period. The total accelerated payment for the period would not be more than the tax and/or NICs on their total amount of income and gains for the same period, having regard to reliefs and allowances available (outside those claimed in relation to the arrangements).

2.6.14 Certificates of Tax Deposit

If a person has purchased a Certificate of Tax Deposit, they can redeem it against the accelerated payment in the normal way. A person in that position should contact HMRC as soon as possible to ensure that the amounts are allocated in the correct way.

2.6.15 Tax enquiry in progress (section 223(3) FA 2014 and paragraph 17(2) Schedule 2 NICA 2015)

An accelerated payment for understated tax is treated as if it were a payment on account of the understated tax for the period. This means that, once the final liability has been decided or agreed, the accelerated payment will be set against it.

An accelerated payment for understated NICs is treated as a payment of the understated NICs and not a payment on account of the NICs.

2.6.16 Inheritance Tax

If the accelerated payment relates to Inheritance Tax (IHT) and this tax is being paid by instalments, (as it is in special circumstances), then the due date for making an accelerated payment cannot be set before the due date for paying the instalment to which it relates.

2.6.17 Part of understated tax paid

If a person has paid any part of the understated tax before an accelerated payment notice is given, this amount will reduce the size of payment required by the accelerated payment notice.

Where amounts have been paid on account, but not yet allocated, or Certificates of Tax Deposit purchased, HMRC will discuss with the person how and if those may be used against the accelerated payment.

2.7 Interest

2.7.1 Accelerated payment does not attract late payment interest

Any late paid accelerated payment does not itself attract interest, but will normally be subject to a late payment penalty (see section 2.12 of this guidance). However, as it is paid in relation to the disputed tax and/or NICs, it will have an effect on the interest which is ultimately due and payable when the dispute is settled or agreed.

2.7.2 Alleviates interest on disputed tax

On receipt of the accelerated payment, interest will cease to accrue further on the disputed tax to the extent it is covered by the payment made.

Example 11:

A person submits a Self Assessment tax return for the year ended 5 April 2009, with any tax due on 31 January 2010. The person self assesses on the basis that an avoidance scheme will succeed. An accelerated payment notice is given on 1 September 2014, which the person pays on 31 October 2014.

If the person is ultimately unsuccessful and their self assessment is amended upwards to reflect the additional tax, then interest will be due on the extra amount from 31 January 2010 (the original payable date) to 31 October 2014 (the date when the accelerated payment was paid). If the final additional amount is more or less than the accelerated payment, the interest will be adjusted accordingly.

Example 12:

An employer uses an avoidance arrangement to pay earnings in the 2009–10 tax year. The employer considers that Class 1 NICs and PAYE Income Tax are not due.

An accelerated payment notice is given on 16 July 2015, which the employer pays on 5 September 2015.

If the outcome is that Class 1 NICs and PAYE Income Tax are due, interest will be due from 19 April 2010 (19 April following the end of the tax year in which the NICs and PAYE Income Tax were due) to 5 September 2015. If the amount due is more or less than the accelerated payment, the interest will be adjusted accordingly.

2.7.3 Accelerated payment attracts repayment interest

If an accelerated payment is received by HMRC and later has to be partly or wholly repaid, then repayment interest at the prevailing rates will be paid to the person.

2.8 Postponement

2.8.1 Restriction on postponement of tax (does not include NICs)

Tax under appeal can be subject to postponement under section 55 of TMA 1970, and the equivalents for other taxes. However, any amount that is under appeal and is also included in an accelerated payment notice cannot be postponed.

2.8.2 Accelerated payment notice cancels postponement of tax

If the payment of tax under appeal has already been postponed, then the accelerated payment notice has the effect of cancelling the postponement of that amount. The amount included in the accelerated payment notice that was previously postponed becomes due and payable under the normal rules for the specific tax involved. However, the 90 day time limit for payment under the accelerated payment rules applies, rather than any shorter payment period that might otherwise apply for the specific tax.

2.8.3 Tax not in an avoidance dispute

None of this affects the postponement of any amount of tax for which both of the following apply. Tax that:

- is under appeal in respect of the same tax return or claim
- is not included in an accelerated payment notice

Example 13:

A person has appealed in relation to a dispute over both:

- an avoidance scheme involving their Income Tax liability
- a liability to Capital Gains Tax

and applied for, and been given, postponement of the amounts under appeal.

They have been given an accelerated payment notice in respect of their use of the avoidance scheme. The liability to Capital Gains Tax can continue to be postponed under the existing rules, but the giving of the accelerated payment notice has the effect of cancelling the postponement of the amount relating to Income Tax.

2.8.4 Adjournment of civil proceedings to recover NICs accelerated payment (paragraph 17(5) and 18(3) Schedule 2 NICA 2015)

The postponement provisions legislation in section 55 TMA 1970 does not apply to NICs.

For NICs, HMRC is normally prevented from recovering NICs where it has not issued a NICs decision and/or where there is an ongoing appeal in respect of NICs by:

- section 117A of the Social Security Administration Act 1992 (which applies to Great Britain)
- section 111A of the Social Security Administration (Northern Ireland) Act 1992 (which applies to Northern Ireland)

This effectively postpones payment of NICs, as civil proceedings for their recovery would be suspended until a formal decision is made and any appeal is either settled by agreement or finally determined by a tribunal or courts.

However, the above provisions do not apply to the recovery of accelerated payment of understated NICs (where there is a relevant contributions dispute) or disputed NICs(where there is an open NICs appeal).

The effect of the modification made in Schedule 2 of NICA 2015 is that, if HMRC has to take civil proceedings to recover the unpaid NICs accelerated payment, the Court cannot adjourn the civil proceedings for either of the following:

- for HMRC to make a NICs decision
- to await the final outcome of any appeal against a NICs decision

If such proceedings have already been adjourned, they cease to be adjourned. The date from which they cease to be adjourned depends on whether representations have been made (see section 2.6 of this guidance for information about representations). If

- no representations have been made – that date is 90 days from the date the notice is given
- representations have been made – that date is the later of:
  - 30 days from when HMRC issues its decision about the representations
  - 90 days from the date the original notice was given

2.9 Civil proceedings for NICs

2.9.1 Evidence of unpaid NICs accelerated payment (Paragraph 17(6) and 18(5) Schedule 2 NICA 2015 and section 25A of CRCA 2005)

If it is necessary to take civil proceedings to recover any part of a NICs accelerated payment, HMRC will issue a certificate of debt. The court must accept this as conclusive evidence that the amount is unpaid. The civil recovery proceedings cannot be adjourned (see 2.8.4 above).

2.10 Protection of revenue pending further appeals

2.10.1 Additional power for accelerated payment

Section 56 of TMA 1970, and its equivalents for other taxes, directs that the unsuccessful party in a tribunal or court appeal must pay (in the case of the person) or repay (in the case of HMRC) the tax involved. The accelerated payments rules are not intended to override that position in the normal course of events. However, the new legislation does provide an additional, limited, power (see section 2.10.2 of this guidance).

Section 56 of TMA 1970 applies to NICs by regulation 12 of the Social Security Contributions (Decisions and Appeals) Regulations 1999 (SI 1999 No 1027).

2.10.2 No repayment cases

Where a person has been successful in litigation in a case where an accelerated payment notice has been given, the tax/NICs in dispute will normally be repaid to the person unless:

- HMRC applies to the tribunal or court in order to pursue a further appeal
- the relevant tribunal or court considers a risk to the Exchequer will develop if a repayment is made and gives a direction

In these cases the tribunal or court may:

- grant permission to withhold all or part of the repayment
- rule that the person must provide adequate security before being repaid

2.10.3 Genuine risk of non-payment

HMRC only expects to make application to the tribunal or court in cases where HMRC considers there is a genuine risk that tax due may not be paid on the outcome of the case.

2.11 Repayment of accelerated payments

2.11.1 General

The accelerated payment provisions in Part 4 FA 2014 do not make any express provision for the repayment of tax when the underlying liability dispute is determined in the persons favour, but rely on the existing administrative provisions that apply to final determinations or settled appeals, and the general binding nature of the courts decisions.

2.11.2 Authority for repayment of accelerated payments

Where the repayment of an accelerated payment of tax and NICs is due, there is no requirement for the person entitled to the repayment to make an application before any part of an accelerated payment is repaid.

2.12 Penalty or surcharge for failure to pay an accelerated payment

Much of Schedule 56 to FA 2009 (late payment penalties) applies to late payment of accelerated payments. This includes the rule that where an agreement for deferred payment is made, there will not be a late payment penalty provided the person keeps to the terms of the payment arrangement. (See section 2.12.7 of this guidance.)

2.12.1 Late payment penalties where a partner payment notice has been given (paragraph 7 of schedule 32, section 226 FA 2014 and Schedule 56 FA 2009)

Where a partner payment notice has been given and the accelerated partner payment remains unpaid at the end of the payment period, the person is liable to late payment penalties as follows:

- on the penalty day – an amount equal to 5% of the amount unpaid
- 5 months after the penalty day – an amount equal to 5% of any amount still unpaid at that date
- 11 months after the penalty day – an amount equal to 5% of any amount still unpaid at that date

The penalty day is the day immediately following the end of the payment period

2.12.2 Late payment penalties – tax enquiry or relevant contributions dispute in progress (section 226 FA 2014, paragraph 19 Schedule 2 NICA 2015 and Schedule 56 FA 2009) (does not include partner payment notices)

Where an accelerated payment notice has been given in a case where there is a tax enquiry or a relevant contributions dispute and the accelerated payment remains unpaid at the end of the payment period, the person is liable to late payment penalties as follows:

- on the penalty day – an amount equal to 5% of the amount unpaid
- 5 months after the penalty day – an amount equal to 5% of any amount still unpaid at that date
- 11 months after the penalty day – an amount equal to 5% of any amount still unpaid at that date

The penalty day is the day immediately following the end of the payment period.

Example 14:

An accelerated payment notice is given to the person in the amount of £100,000 on 1 October 2014. The payment is therefore due by 29 December 2014.

The person does not pay the accelerated payment.

A 5% penalty is due on 30 December 2014 (the penalty day) of £5,000.

The person pays the remaining £50,000 on 1 April 2015.

The person has now fully complied with the accelerated payment notice and no further penalties for late payment are due.

2.12.3 Late payment surcharges for open appeal cases – 2009 to 2010 and earlier years (section 59C TMA 1970) (does not include partner payment notices)

Where an accelerated payment notice has been given in a case where there is an open appeal for the tax year 2009 to 2010 or earlier and the accelerated payment remains unpaid at the end of the payment period, the person is liable to late payment surcharges as follows:

- 28 days after end of the payment period – an amount equal to 5% of the amount unpaid
- 6 months after the end of the payment period – an amount equal to 5% of any amount still unpaid at that date

These surcharges only apply to those taxes (including Class 4 NICs) which are already within the scope of section 59C Taxes Management Act 1970.

2.12.4 Late payment penalties for open appeal cases – 2010 to 2011 and later years (schedule 56 Finance Act 2009) (does not include partner payment notices)

Where an accelerated payment notice has been given in a case where there is an open appeal for the tax year 2010 to 2011 or later and the accelerated payment remains unpaid at the end of the payment period, the person is liable to late payment penalties as follows:

- on the penalty date – an amount equal to 5% of the amount unpaid
- 5 months after the penalty date – an amount equal to 5% of any amount still unpaid at that date
- 11 months after the penalty date – an amount equal to 5% of any amount still unpaid at that date

The penalty date will be 31 days after the due date in the accelerated payment notice.

These penalties only apply to those taxes (including Class 4 NICs) which are already within the scope of Schedule 56 FA 2009.

2.12.5 Appeals against late payment penalties and/or surcharges

A person has the right to appeal to the tribunal against late payment penalties and/or surcharges.

The rules set out in paragraph 13 schedule 56 to the FA 2009 apply to late payment penalties for accelerated payment notices.

2.12.6 Enforceable penalty – NICs accelerated payment notice (paragraph 20 Schedule 2 NICA 2015)

The penalty due for not complying with a NICs accelerated payment notice is recovered in the same way as unpaid relevant contributions (see annex 1 for definitions). It is not treated in the same way as an assessment to tax.

For the purposes of a court determining whether civil proceedings can be adjourned, the penalty assessment is treated as if it were a NICs decision as to whether the person was liable for the penalty. The effect is that if there is an appeal against the penalty assessment the court must adjourn any civil proceedings taken to recover the penalty until the appeal is finally determined.

2.12.7 Payment arrangements for accelerated payment notices

If a person asks to enter into a payment arrangement with HMRC for an amount of accelerated payment and HMRC agrees such an arrangement for a period (the deferral period), and the arrangement is fully adhered to, then:

- in respect of the amount included in the arrangement
- from the date on which the person asked to enter into the arrangement, until the end of the deferral period

the person will not become liable to the late payment penalties or surcharges that they would have become liable to if the arrangement was not in place.

This does not affect any late payment penalties or surcharges that the person had become liable to before they asked to enter into the payment arrangement. (paragraph 10 of schedule 56 to FA 2009, applied by section 226(7) of FA 2014).

2.13 Withdrawal, modification or suspension of accelerated payment notice (section 227 FA 2014 and paragraph 21 Schedule 2 NICA 2015)

2.13.1 Conditions

Where an accelerated payment notice has been issued, HMRC may, at any time:

- withdraw the notice
- reduce the amount of the accelerated payment when one of the requirements of Condition C (see sections 2.2.5 to 2.2.8 of this guidance) ceases to exist (this occurs when the notice remains effective as it is supported by another of the alternatives to Condition C)
- reduce the amount specified in the notice (this includes where there are multiple arrangements in the same tax year and one or more is successful in litigation)

2.13.2 Excess repaid

If the amount of an accelerated payment is reduced and a greater amount than this has already been paid, then HMRC will normally repay the excess with any applicable interest.

Similarly, if a late payment penalty or surcharge has been charged and paid, a replacement assessment for the correct penalty or surcharge will be issued and any excess repaid.

2.13.3 Accelerated payment notice withdrawn and specified amount repaid

If an accelerated payment notice is withdrawn, the specified amount paid plus any penalties or surcharges paid will normally be repaid with any applicable interest.

2.13.4 The person wants to settle

If, after receiving the accelerated payment notice, the person wants to settle the dispute with HMRC, there are a number of ways of dealing with this. For example, the person may:

- agree to amend their return or claim and pay the tax and/or NICs arising. They can choose to pay the tax and/or NICs either by the due date shown in the accelerated payment notice, or the normal due date(s) for paying the tax and/or NICs (if earlier)
- want to enter into a settlement agreement, accepting HMRC's view of the tax results of the scheme. And agree with HMRC a payment instalment plan because they cannot pay all the tax due at once

2.14 Modifications to an accelerated payment notice

2.14.1 Follower notice

If an accelerated payment notice is given because a follower notice has been given, and the follower notice is:

- withdrawn
- amended (when there has been a new relevant final judicial ruling after a late appeal)

then HMRC must amend or withdraw the accelerated payment notice.

2.14.2 DOTAS arrangements

If an accelerated payment notice has been given because of DOTAS arrangements and these arrangements are no longer notifiable or applicable, then HMRC must reduce the amount (as appropriate) of the accelerated payment to the extent to which it was based on this requirement. For example, HMRC has withdrawn the obligation to notify the scheme.

2.14.3 Condition C requirements

If at least one of the Condition C requirements (see sections 2.2.5 to 2.2.8 of this guidance) continues to be satisfied, then the accelerated payment notice will continue to have effect. Where more than one of the Condition C requirements was originally applicable and one or more no longer applies, HMRC must:

- withdraw the notice to the extent it is given by virtue of those requirements
- notify the modification of the accelerated payment notice to show one of the remaining Condition C requirements
- reduce the amount of the accelerated payment due if the disputed tax and/or NICs determined under the substituted requirement is less than the amount initially stated on the notice

2.14.4 Specify Condition C requirement

Sections 220(6) and 221(5) FA 2014 require HMRC to specify which Condition C requirement is used as the basis of an accelerated payment notice, where more than one of those requirements could apply. In the majority of cases it is likely that the resulting accelerated payment will be the same, but it might not be.

Any amount found to be overpaid as a result will be repaid with any applicable interest.

2.15 Suspension of an accelerated payment notice

2.15.1 Late appeal

If a follower notice is suspended because of a late appeal against the relevant judicial ruling, then an accelerated payment notice will also be suspended if it is based solely on the follower notice requirement of Condition C (see sections 2.2.5 to 2.2.8 of this guidance).

2.15.2 Accelerated payment notice remains effective despite late appeal against relevant judicial ruling

If another condition C (see sections 2.2.5 to 2.2.8 of this guidance) requirement is still met (either DOTAS arrangements or a GAAR counteraction notice) then the accelerated payment notice will not be suspended and will remain effective in relation to those conditions. In this circumstance HMRC must:

- withdraw the follower notice requirement
- notify the modification of the accelerated payment notice to show the remaining Condition C requirements
- reduce the amount of accelerated payment due if the disputed tax determined under the substituted requirement is less than the amount initially stated on the notice

2.15.3 Effect of suspension period (section 227(9) FA 2014 and paragraph 21 Schedule 2 NICA 2015)

If an accelerated payment notice is suspended, the period of suspension does not count towards the periods mentioned in the following provisions:

- section 223 FA 2014
- section 55(8D) of TMA 1970
- paragraph 39(11) of Schedule 10 to FA 2003
- paragraph 48(8C) of Schedule 33 to FA 2013

2.16 Partnerships – Summary

2.16.1 Special rules

Special rules for members of partnerships can be found in Schedules 31 and 32. These rules essentially reflect the general tax treatment of partnerships. In summary:

- a follower notice will be given to the representative partner, in that capacity, on behalf of the partnership as a whole
- that follower notice can then apply to generate an accelerated payment notice to the members of the partnership
- the members can also be given a follower notice or an accelerated payment notice in respect of a scheme in their personal capacity
- in those instances these will relate directly to their own tax return, which will of course include their share of the partnership profits and gains

These points are covered in more detail below.

2.16.2 Actions taken separately by partners

All actions taken in respect of accelerated payments, including representations, payment, late payment penalties etc., are undertaken separately by the individual partners. The representative partner has no role in that capacity, but may of course be involved in their own personal capacity as a partner.

2.16.3 Partners accelerated payments may vary

It is entirely possible for different partners to receive accelerated payment notices for different amounts, depending on other reliefs and allowances that they may have available personally.

2.16.4 SDLT and ATED rules

Specific partnership rules apply for SDLT and ATED to reflect the particular treatment of partnerships in relation to those heads of duty.

2.16.5 Partnership notices

Schedule 32 to FA 2014 sets out the additional special rules for partnerships. These rules apply to partnerships which are subject to TMA 1970 s12AA.

2.16.6 Partner payment notice

An accelerated payment notice for a partner is called a partner payment notice, and each partner of the partnership will be given an individual partner payment notice. The partner is responsible for paying the amount set out in their own notice, and will be liable for a late payment penalty if the amount is not paid by the due date (see section 2.12.1 of this guidance).

2.16.7 Giving a partner payment notice

The rules for giving a partner payment notice are adapted to refer to partnership returns as appropriate. Apart from this they are fundamentally the same as the rules for giving an accelerated payment notice.

2.16.8 Calculation of tax and/ or NICs advantage

The contents of a partner payment notice and the calculation of the payment are very similar to an accelerated payment, with modifications for partners. The denied advantage is calculated by reference to the amount of tax and/or NICs that becomes due and payable by counteracting the tax and/or NICs advantage in the relevant claim or return of the partner.

2.16.9 Partner representations

There is no direct right to appeal against a partner payment notice, but each partner has the right to make written representations to HMRC on the basis that either:

- any of the Conditions A to C (see sections 2.2.3 to 2.2.8 of this guidance) are not met
- the amount specified in the partner payment notice is not correct

2.16.10 Notification of decision

HMRC must consider the representations and notify the partner in writing of their decision – which will normally be to confirm, withdraw or modify the partner payment notice.

2.16.11 Time limits

Time limits for payment of the amount due on a partner payment notice are the same as for accelerated payment notices. Payment is due:

- if no representations have been made, 90 days from the date the partner payment notice was given
- if representations have been made, the later of the original 90 day payment period or the end of a 30 day period beginning on the date HMRC confirms their decision to issue the partner payment notice

2.16.12 Late-payment penalties

A late payment penalty applies to partners who do not pay by the due date. (See section 2.12.1 of this guidance).

2.16.13 Changes to partner payment notices

The rules for withdrawing, suspending and amending partner payment notices are the same as for accelerated payment notices.

3 Annual Tax on Enveloped Dwellings (ATED)

3.1 Amendments for ATED (section 231 FA 2014)

The guidance for follower notices and accelerated payments applies to ATED with the following amendments. They reflect the specific treatment of partnerships and other forms of joint ownership for ATED

3.2 Partners

Where the relevant tax is ATED, and the chargeable person is:

- a partnership
- two or more persons jointly and severally liable to pay the relevant tax, anything required or authorised (by the follower notice and accelerated payments legislation) to be done in relation to a person, must be done in relation to all the responsible partners and persons jointly and severally liable to pay the relevant tax

This in particular means that each person must be given a separate notice.

3.3 Liability

Any liability to:

- an accelerated payment
- a penalty for failure to pay an accelerated payment
- a penalty for failure to take corrective action in response to a follower notice

is the joint and several liability of all responsible partners, or all the persons jointly and severally liable to pay the relevant tax.

3.4 Responsible partners

The responsible partners are all persons who are members of the partnership on the first day of the period of ownership of the dwelling in the chargeable period.

3.5 Representations

Where a follower notice or an accelerated payment notice is given to more than one person, then representations against either may be made by each of those persons separately, or by two or more of them jointly.

4 Stamp Duty Land Tax (SDLT)

4.1 Amendments for SDLT (Section 230 FA 2014)

The guidance for follower notices and accelerated payments applies to SDLT with the following amendments. They reflect the specific treatment of partnerships and other forms of joint ownership for SDLT.

4.2 Partners

Where the relevant tax is SDLT, and:

- a partnership
- two or more persons acting jointly are the purchasers in respect of the land transaction

then anything required or authorised (by the follower notice and accelerated payments legislation) to be done in relation to P must be done in relation to all the responsible partners and persons acting jointly. This means, in particular, that each person involved must be given a separate notice.

4.3 Liability

Any liability to:

- an accelerated payment
- a penalty for failure to pay an accelerated payment
- a penalty for failure to take corrective action in response to a follower notice

is the joint and several liability of all responsible partners, or all persons acting jointly as purchasers in respect of the land transaction.

4.4 Effective date of transaction

Neither the accelerated payment nor the penalties can be recovered from a person who became a responsible partner after the effective date of the transaction in respect of which the accelerated payment relates.

4.5 Responsible partners

The responsible partners in relation to a transaction are the persons who are partners at the effective date of the transaction.

4.6 Trustees

Where the trustees of a settlement are liable to pay an accelerated payment or a penalty relating to SDLT, the payment or penalty may be recovered (but only once) from any one or more of the trustees.

However the penalty may not be recovered from any person who became a trustee after the time when the omission occurred that caused the penalty to become payable.

4.7 Representations

Where a follower notice or an accelerated payment notice is given to more than one person, representations may be made by each of those persons separately or by two or more of them jointly.

5 Accelerated payments and group relief

5.1 Amendments to FA 2014 for group relief

The Finance Act 2015 (section 118 and Schedule 18) (FA 2015) amends FA 2014 to include new provisions relating to the restriction of the surrender of losses and other amounts for the purposes of group relief.

Throughout this "group relief" section, the term **"P"** (meaning **"person"**) is used to refer to the company that has surrendered group relief.

5.2 Who the new provisions will affect

The new provisions will affect companies in groups who have either claimed or surrendered group relief where the loss or other amount arose from "chosen arrangements", and where the relevant conditions in FA14 for giving an accelerated payment notice (APN) have been met.

5.3 When the new provisions take effect

The new provisions for group relief cases in FA 2015 take effect from 26 March 2015, which was the date that FA 2015 received Royal Assent. It applies to APN issued on or after that date.

5.4 How the new provisions work

The new provisions apply if the "surrenderable loss" of a company (P) includes a loss that originates from a "denied advantage".

If the denied advantage consists, to any extent, of an "asserted surrenderable amount" HMRC may specify in an APN that some or all of that amount cannot be surrendered as group relief.

(See annex 1 of this guidance for definitions of the terms "surrenderable loss" and "asserted surrenderable amount").

5.5 The effect of giving an APN (section 225A(2) FA 2014)

Where an amount is specified in the APN, this prevents the company (P) (where the loss or other amount arose) from consenting to a claim for group relief in respect of that amount. If consent has already been given, P has 90 days to withdraw the consent. Any company that has already claimed the group relief must take the necessary action to amend its return to remove the relief.

Example 16:

A Ltd's "chosen arrangements" result in a £2,000,000 trading loss arising in its accounting period ended 31 December 2007. The conditions for giving an APN are satisfied and HMRC disputes that the £2,000,000 trading loss has arisen. A Ltd has no profits and no tax to pay, even if the loss is denied to it. A Ltd has no other losses available to surrender as group relief.

A Ltd agrees to surrender the £2,000,000 loss as group relief to B Ltd, which reduces B Ltd's taxable profits and tax payment as a result.

The surrenderable loss and asserted surrenderable amount are both £2,000,000 as this is the amount that HMRC considers would not be a surrenderable loss of A Ltd if the "chosen arrangements" fail to achieve their aim.

HMRC gives an APN to A Ltd, which has the effect that consent may not be given to B Ltd's £2,000,000 group relief claim. A Ltd has 90 days to make representations to HMRC, but if none are made (or if following representations, the APN is confirmed), then A Ltd must withdraw the consent and B Ltd must amend its return in accordance with paragraph 75(6) Schedule 18 FA 1998 and pay any additional tax that arises.

Example 17: Loss originates in different accounting periods

It is possible that the "chosen arrangements" could result in a loss that arises over more than one accounting period. In such a case each accounting period will have an asserted surrenderable amount, and separate APNs will need to be given for each accounting period.

Using the same basic facts in example 16, except that, instead of the £2,000,000 trading loss arising in a single accounting period, it arises over 2 accounting periods:

- £1,500,000 in the accounting period ended 31 December 2007
- £500,000 in the accounting period ended 31 December 2008

A Ltd surrenders these amounts in full to B Ltd in respect of each accounting period. Whilst the total trading loss arising by use of the "chosen arrangements" is still £2,000,000, APNs will need to be given for each of the accounting periods where the losses arose. In the accounting period ended:

- 31 December 2007 the surrenderable loss and asserted surrenderable amount are both £1,500,000
- 31 December 2008 the surrenderable loss and asserted surrenderable amount are both £500,000

The following APNs would need to be given to A Ltd, instructing that consent may not be given to B Ltd's group relief claims:

- £1,500,000 for the accounting period ended 31 December 2007
- £500,000 for the accounting period ended 31 December 2008

As in example 16, A Ltd has 90 days to make any representations to HMRC.

(See example 20 for details of what happens when a loss is carried forward and utilised in later accounting periods.)

Example 18:

X Ltd engages in a DOTAS notifiable arrangement that creates a non trading loan relationship (NTLR) debit of £12,000,000 which is in dispute with HMRC. The company has unrelated loan relationship credits of £10,000,000, so the net NTLR debit in the accounting period is £2,000,000 which is surrendered as group relief.

In the same accounting period X Ltd also has trading losses of £4,000,000 and management expenses of £3,000,000. These are not in dispute with HMRCand have also been surrendered as group relief: £3,000,000 to Y Ltd (relating to the management expenses) and £6,000,000 to Z Ltd (identified by X Ltd as relating to the NTLR deficit and trading loss).

The total surrenderable loss for the period is:

NTLR deficit	£2,000,000
Trading loss	£4,000,000
Management expenses	£3,000,000
Surrenderable loss/amount	£9,000,000

The "asserted surrenderable amount" is £5,000,000. This is the £2,000,000 net NTLR debit that is in dispute and the £3,000,000 management expenses that are no longer available to surrender as group relief by virtue of s105(2) CTA 2010.

The effect of this is that X Ltd profits chargeable to Corporation Tax are £7,000,000 (£10,000,000 minus £3,000,000 management expenses). The trading loss of £4,000,000 remains surrendered as group relief.

The conditions for giving an APN are satisfied so an APN can be given for the £12,000,000 which HMRC considers would not be a surrenderable loss of X Ltd if the "chosen arrangements" do not achieve their aim. The APN would both:

- show the payment due from X Ltd based on £7,000,000 at Corporation Tax rate
- instruct X Ltd not to consent to any claim for group relief in respect of the £5,000,000 asserted surrenderable amount

The result is that (subject to any representations that are made and upheld) the APN given to X Ltd produces the following effects:

- Y Ltd must amend its return and pay any additional amount that arises from the withdrawal of the £3,000,000 group relief
- Z Ltd must amend its return and pay any additional amount that arises from the withdrawal of the £2,000,000 group relief

5.6 Claimant company cannot or does not amend their return (section 225A(6) and (7) FA 2014)

Where there is a current tax enquiry into the tax return of the company that claimed the group relief (the **"claimant company"**), existing rules mean that, although the claimant company can amend its return to remove the group relief claimed (when the company (P) withdraws the consent for group relief), that amendment cannot take effect during the enquiry. This means that there is no immediate effect on the amount to pay.

So, where this is the case, the new provisions allow HMRC to also give an APN to the claimant company requiring it to pay the amount in relation to the withdrawn group relief.

If the claimant company return is not under enquiry and it does not take action to remove the group relief from its return, HMRC may send a tax assessment to the claimant company, requiring it to pay the amount in relation to the withdrawn group relief. Where such an assessment is sent, the claimant company cannot request postponement of the tax under section 55 of the Taxes Management Act 1970.

5.7 If the company disagrees with the amount specified in anAPN (section 222 FA 2014)

There is no right of appeal against an APN. However, if the company disagrees with the amount specified in the APN, it has 90 days beginning with the day on which the notice is given to make written representations to HMRC. The grounds on which the company can make representations are that:

- the conditions for issuing the APN have not been met
- the amount specified in the APN is incorrect

HMRC will consider any such representations and either confirm the APN (with or without amending it) or withdraw it.

5.8 If the asserted surrenderable amount has not yet been fully utilised

There may be instances where the asserted surrenderable amount hasn't been fully utilised against the company's (P's) own profits, or surrendered as group relief. In such instances, the APN given will instruct the company (P) not to consent to the group relief surrender. If the company (P) subsequently claims to utilise the losses against its own profits for a later accounting period before the dispute is resolved, a further APN will be given – requiring payment of the amount due.

Example 19:

A leasing company files its 2014 return on 31 December 2015. The return includes details of a DOTAS notifiable arrangement. Because the disclosure has been discussed before the return was filed, HMRC are in a position to open an enquiry and give an APN in January 2016.

The arrangement generates trade capital allowances of £10,000,000 which are disputed by HMRC. These reduce what would have been trading profits of £2,000,000 to a loss of £8,000,000. At the time the APN is given, there are no claims for group relief from other group companies.

The surrenderable loss is £8,000,000 – which is the unused balance of the £10,000,000 generated loss. The asserted surrenderable amount is also £8,000,000.

A single APN can be given to the company both:

- for the amount due in respect of the £2,000,000 trading profit that is now chargeable to Corporation Tax as a result of disputed £10,000,000 trade capital allowances
- instructing it not to consent to any claim for group relief in respect of the £8,000,000 balance

As there is no current claim to group relief there is nothing to pay in respect of the £8,000,000 asserted surrenderable amount at this time.

Where an APN is given, representations can be made within 90 days.

If a subsequent group relief claim is made in respect of the £8,000,000 before the dispute is resolved, this will be refused, as it is not a valid claim because an APN has already been given preventing the surrender. There is no need to give a further APN.

5.9 What happens following a final determination (section 227A FA 2014)

When a dispute involving potential group relief is finally determined, and the result is that there is group relief available to be surrendered, claimant companies can make a fresh claim for the group relief. The time limit for making a claim is 30 days after the amount is determined. Other time limits that would otherwise prevent this are relaxed by section 227A(2) and (3) FA 2014.

Even if all of the asserted surrenderable amount is then available for group relief, the original claim is not automatically reactivated. Instead revised group relief surrenders and claims would need to be made within 30 days.

5.10 Partnerships that include a corporate partner

Schedule 32 of FA 2014 contains provisions where a partner payment notice (PPN) is given to a partnership that includes a corporate partner.

Where the corporate partner's tax position includes relief for a disputed loss, HMRC can give a PPN to request payment for the amount due.

If a partnership generates a loss, whether consent for a group relief surrender can be given is a matter involving each individual company that is allocated the loss and there is no impact on the partnership as a whole, nor on any other member of the partnership. The extent to which a company that is a member of a partnership may surrender group relief is dependent solely on its own relationship to other companies in its group.

Paragraphs (4A) and (6A) of Schedule 32 to FA 2014 set this out by referring to the "surrenderable loss" of the partners and to the action that the partner must take. Section 2.16 of the main guidance contains further detail of how partnerships are affected by follower notices and accelerated payments.

Example 20:

K partnership LLP files its return for the tax year ended 5 April 2006 by the due date and declares a DOTAS notifiable arrangement that creates £10,000,000 trade losses in the year, which are disputed by HMRC. Each partner is allocated its share of the loss, £6,000,000 of which is given to corporate partner G Ltd for its accounting period ended 31 March 2006. G Ltd utilises its share of the loss as follows:

- £1,000,000 losses are set off against other profits of G Ltd in its accounting period ended 31 March 2006
- £3,000,000 losses are surrendered as group relief to a number of group companies
- £1,500,000 losses are carried forward and set off against profits of G Ltd in its accounting period ended 31 March 2007
- £500,000 losses are not yet been utilised and are still being carried forward

There is a tax enquiry into K partnership LLP but not into G Ltd.

The surrenderable loss is £6,000,000 which is G Ltd's share of the £10,000,000 disputed trade loss of K partnership LLP.

Based on the claims made in G Ltd's return, the asserted surrenderable amount is £3,500,000. This is the £3,000,000 surrendered as group relief and the £500,000 carried forward. Even though the £500,000 has not yet been utilised, it is not excluded from the provisions.

A PPN can be given to G Ltd in relation to the £6,000,000 allocated loss in dispute:

- showing the payment due in relation to the tax charge on the £1,000,000 loss utilised in its accounting period ended 31 March 2006
- showing the payment due in relation to the tax charge on the £1,500,000 losses carried forward and utilised against profits in its accounting period ended 31 March 2007
- instructing it not to consent to any claim for group relief in respect of the £3,500,000 asserted surrenderable amount

Annex 1: Definitions

Asserted advantage

The "asserted advantage" is the tax and/or NICs advantage which would result from the use of the particular scheme used, if it achieved its aim.

Asserted surrenderable amount

This is the amount of the surrenderable loss that a designated officer of HMRC determines, to the best of their information and belief, to not be available for surrender as group relief if P's "chosen arrangements" were not to achieve their aim, (less any amount of relief claimed by the company (P) against its own profits). (Section 220(4A) FA2014.)

Denied advantage

The denied advantage is defined as being the amount of the "asserted advantage" which is denied when the principles or reasoning laid down in the relevant ruling are applied to this person's circumstances.

DOTAS arrangements

DOTAS arrangements are notifiable arrangements to which HMRC has issued a Scheme Reference Number (SRN) under section 311 of FA 2004. In order to do so, HMRC must have received a disclosure of notifiable arrangements or a notifiable proposal under Part 7 of FA 2004, or must have successfully taken proceedings under Part 7 of FA 2004 to require such a disclosure.

"Enquiry in progress" for Inheritance Tax

For Inheritance Tax, an enquiry is deemed to be in progress during the period which:

- begins with the time the account is delivered or the statement, declaration, information or document is produced
- ends when the person is issued with a certificate or discharge under section 239 of that Act, or is discharged by virtue of section 256(1)(b) of that Act, in respect of the return (at which point the enquiry is to be treated as completed)

GAAR counteraction notice

A GAAR counteraction notice means a notice under paragraph 12 of Schedule 43 to FA2013. A GAAR counteraction notice is a written notice given if a designated officer considers that:

- a tax and/or NICs advantage has arisen to a person from arrangements that are abusive
- the advantage ought to be counteracted

Inheritance Tax returns

For Inheritance Tax, each of the following is treated as a return:

- an account delivered by a person under s216 or s217 of IHTA 1984 including an account delivered in accordance with regulations under section 256 of that Act
- a statement or declaration which amends or is otherwise connected with such an account produced by the person who delivered the account
- information or a document provided by a person in accordance with regulations under section 256 of that Act

And such a return is to be treated as made by the person in question.

NICs advantage

The term "NICs advantage" includes avoidance or reduction of a liability to pay relevant contributions.

NICs appeal

A NICs appeal is an appeal, under:

- section 11 of the Social Security Contributions (Transfer of Functions) Act 1999
- Article 10 of the Social Security Contributions (Transfer of Functions, etc) (Northern Ireland) Order 1999 (SI 1999 No 671), against a NICs decision relating to relevant contributions

Or an appeal against a determination of an appeal listed above.

NICs arrangements

Arrangements are NICs arrangements if, having regard to all the circumstances, it would be reasonable to conclude that the obtaining of a NICs advantage was the main purpose, or one of the main purposes of the arrangements.

NICs decision

A NICs decision is a decision under:

- section 8 of the Social Security Contributions (Transfer of Functions) Act 1999 (applies to Great Britain)
- Article 7 of the Social Security Contributions (Transfer of Functions, etc.) (Northern Ireland) Order 1999 (SI 1999 No 671) (applies to Northern Ireland)

Period for which an tax enquiry is in progress

Begins with the day on which the notice of compliance check or enquiry is given, and ends on the day on which the compliance check or enquiry is completed.

For Inheritance Tax, see above.

Person

A "person" (P) is as defined in Schedule 1 of the Interpretation Act 1978, and includes "a body of persons corporate or unincorporated", as well as individuals.

Relevant contributions

"Relevant contributions" means the following contributions under Part 1 of the Social Security Contributions and Benefits Act 1992 (applies to Great Britain) or Part 1 of the Social Security Contributions and Benefits (Northern Ireland) Act 1992 (applies to Northern Ireland):

- Class 1 contributions
- Class 1A contributions
- Class 1B contributions
- Class 2 contributions which a person is, or is alleged to be, liable to pay but which are not or would not be payable through the Self Assessment system

Relevant contributions dispute

A "relevant contributions dispute" arises if both:

- without making a NICs decision, HMRC notifies a person in writing that HMRC considers the person to be liable to pay an amount of relevant contributions
- the person notifies HMRC in writing (a "notification of dispute") that the person disputes liability for some or all of the contributions ("the disputed contributions")

Relevant contributions dispute in progress

A relevant contributions dispute is in progress in relation to the notification of dispute, during the period which:

- begins with the day on which the person gives the notification of dispute
- ends (at which point it is to be treated as completed) with the day on which one of the following occurs:
  - the disputed contributions are paid in full
  - HMRC and the person enter into an agreement in writing as to the person's liability for the disputed contributions and any amount of those contributions that the person is to pay under that agreement is paid
  - an officer of HMRC makes a NICs decision in relation to the person's liability for the disputed contributions
  - without making a NICs decision, HMRC notifies the person in writing that HMRC no longer considers the person to be liable to pay the disputed contributions

Relevant tax

The term **"relevant tax"** includes:

- Income Tax
- Capital Gains Tax

- Corporation Tax, including any amount chargeable or treated as if it were Corporation Tax
- Inheritance Tax
- Stamp Duty Land Tax
- Annual Tax on Enveloped Dwellings

References to relevant tax, other than references to particular taxes, include relevant contributions (see above).

Surrenderable loss

This is the total amount of loss or other amount that the company (P) could surrender as group relief – including any loss or other amount that would arise if P's "chosen arrangements" achieve their intended aim. (Section 220(4B) FA 2014.)

Tax advantage

The term **"tax advantage"** includes:

- relief or increased relief from tax
- repayment or increase in repayment of tax
- avoidance or reduction of a charge or assessment to tax
- avoidance of a possible assessment to tax
- deferral of a payment of tax or advancement of a repayment of tax
- avoidance of an obligation to deduct or account for tax

Tax appeal

A tax appeal means an appeal under:

- section 31 TMA 1970 (Income Tax appeals against amendments of Self Assessment, amendments made by closure notices under section 28A or 28B of that Act) including an appeal under that section by virtue of regulations under Part 11 of IEPA 2003 (PAYE)
- paragraph 9 of Schedule 1A to TMA 1970 (Income Tax: appeals against amendments made by closure notices under paragraph 7(2) of that Schedule etc)
- section 705 of ITA 2007 (Income Tax: appeals against counteraction notices)
- paragraph 34(3) or 48 of Schedule 18 to FA 1998 (corporation tax: appeals against amendment of a company's return made by closure notice, assessments other than Self Assessments etc)
- section 750 of CTA 2010 (Corporation Tax: appeals against counteraction notices)
- section 222 of IHTA 1984 (appeals against HMRC determinations) other than an appeal made by a person against a determination in respect of a transfer of value at a time when a tax enquiry is in progress in respect of a return made by that person in respect of that transfer
- paragraph 35 of Schedule 10 to FA 2003 (Stamp Duty Land Tax: appeals against amendment of Self Assessment, discovery assessments etc)
- paragraph 35 of Schedule 22 to FA 2013 (Annual Tax on Enveloped Dwellings: appeals against amendment of Self Assessment, discovery assessments etc)

Or an appeal against a determination of any appeal listed above.

Tax arrangements

Arrangements are tax arrangements if, having regard to all the circumstances, it would be reasonable to conclude that the obtaining of a tax advantage was the main purpose, or one of the main purposes of the arrangements.

Tax enquiry

The term **"tax enquiry"** includes a compliance check or an enquiry into a return or claim into:

- Self Assessment returns for Income Tax and Capital Gains Tax (section 9A or 12AC TMA 1970). This includes **"deemed"** checks or enquiries by virtue of section 12AC(6) TMA 1970
- a claim made otherwise than by being included in a return (paragraph 5 Schedule 1A TMA 1970)
- company tax returns for Corporation Tax (paragraph 24 of Schedule 18 to FA 1988). This includes **"deemed"** checks or enquiries by virtue of section 12 AC (6) TMA 1970
- SDLT returns (para 12 Schedule 10 FA 2003)
- Annual Tax on Enveloped Dwellings returns (para 8 Sch 22 FA 2013)
- Inheritance Tax returns (see above)

Tax period

Tax period means a tax year, accounting period or other period in respect of which tax is charged.

Misc. 215 TEN THINGS ABOUT ACCELERATED PAYMENT NOTICES (APNs)
[HMRC, September 2015]

Introduction

An accelerated payment notice (APN) is a requirement to pay an amount on account of tax or National Insurance Contributions (NICs). HMRC issues APNs to taxpayers involved in avoidance schemes disclosed under the Disclosure of Tax Avoidance Schemes (DOTAS) rules, or counter-acted under the General Anti Abuse Rule (GAAR).

They can also be issued to taxpayers who have received a Follower Notice in relation to the scheme. The effect of the notice is to ensure that disputed tax or NICs rests with the Exchequer in an avoidance case, so removing the cash flow advantage enjoyed by users of tax avoidance schemes and the benefit they currently have over the majority of taxpayers who pay their tax and NICs up front.

We will send out a letter some weeks in advance of the APN being issued, to let you know it is on its way, and to provide you with some information about APNs.

Here are **ten things** you need to know if you have received an APN:

1. You must pay within 90 days

You have 90 days to pay the amount shown on the APN, unless you make representations, in which case the period may be longer. The payment doesn't have to be made in one go as long as it is all paid by the due date.

2. Don't ignore it

Failure to pay an APN by the due date could lead to late payment penalties or surcharges becoming due and potential enforcement action being taken to recover the tax or NICs. So make sure that you take action and pay the APN promptly.

3. Problems paying

If you think you will have problems paying the APN you should contact the HMRC telephone number shown on the notice, or the earlier letter which tells you we are going to send out an APN. Please do this as soon as possible. We will talk to you about different payment options.

4. You may not get all your APNs at once

APNs are being issued on a scheme by scheme basis and so, if you are in a number of schemes, you may not get all of the APNs that HMRC plans to issue at the same time.

5. You can receive more than one APN

APNs are sent out for each year of the avoidance scheme you are in and for each type of tax involved. For example if you have used an employment scheme for two years and that scheme gives both a tax and national insurance advantage you may receive up to four APNs.

6. Paying the APN is not settling your tax affairs

The APN will only cover the tax or NICs advantage relating to the specific avoidance scheme covered by the APN. The amount shown may not be the final liability agreed, which may be larger or smaller than the amount of the APN. It will not include any interest, penalties or other tax that may be due in the year. Therefore when the enquiry or appeal is finalised, there may be additional amounts to pay.

7. Appeal rights

You have a right to make representations against the APN (see below). You also have a right to appeal against the underlying tax or NICs that are in dispute.

8. You can object to an APN under specific circumstances

If you feel the amount quoted is incorrect or the conditions have not been met, you may make a *representation* which HMRC will consider. Representations should be made in writing to the address shown on the notice, within the 90 days before payment becomes due – if you send this elsewhere it might not be processed in time. If you do make a representation, HMRC will write to you setting out the results of their review. The response to your representation will tell you what you need to do next.

9. The amount due on an APN may be different to a settlement opportunity calculation

If you receive an APN at the same time as a settlement opportunity is in place, the value of the APN will not necessarily be calculated on the same terms offered in the settlement opportunity. Settlement opportunity calculations may also include interest and penalties. The APN may therefore not be for the same amount as the figure requested in order to settle the matter in full with HMRC.

10. You can still settle your affairs after you've received an APN

If you want to settle your tax affairs and you've received an APN, you should contact us as soon as possible. You must still pay the APN by the due date to avoid late payment penalties, but any payment received will be treated as a payment on account of the final liability and will stop the interest accruing on the underlying debt from the date it was received.

Misc. 216 SHARE FISHERMAN: INCOME TAX AND NATIONAL INSURANCE CONTRIBUTIONS [HMRC, April 2016]

Overview

You're a share fisherman if you work in the fishing industry and you:

- aren't employed under a contract of service
- are a master or a crew-member of a British fishing boat manned by more than one person
- get all or part of your pay by sharing the profits or gross earnings of the fishing boat

You also count as a shared fisherman if you used to work on a British fishing boat, but now work ashore in Great Britain. This could be making and mending gear or any other work for a British fishing boat.

Fishermen employed under a contract of service aren't share fishermen.

Self Assessment

A share fisherman is classed as self-employed. You must register with HMRC as self-employed [https://www.gov.uk/register-for-self-assessment] within 3 months of when you first started fishing.

Fill in a Self Assessment tax return

You must fill in a Self Assessment tax return [https://www.gov.uk/self-assessment-tax-returns] each year. This is so that you can declare all of your income from any source (ie, self-employment, employment and Job Seeker's Allowance etc) and claim any business expenses. You must keep business records [https://www.gov.uk/self-employed-records] to support information you put in your tax return.

Don't record any tax that's been deducted by your settling agent on your tax return.

Pay Class 2 National Insurance

When you register as self-employed, you're also registering to pay Class 2 National Insurance contributions. The rate you pay in the tax year 2016 to 2017 is £3.45 a week. This contributes towards the basic State Pension, the normal range of benefits for self-employed people, and Jobseeker's Allowance.

Budget for your Income Tax and Class 4 National Insurance contributions

As a share fisherman, you can join a voluntary tax budgeting scheme (https://www.gov.uk/share-fisherman-tax-budgeting-scheme) to help you pay your Income Tax and National Insurance contributions.

TABLES OF DESTINATIONS

The tables, prepared by Croner-i editorial staff, relate the provisions of former legislation (in the left-hand column) to the corresponding provisions in the consolidated legislation (in the right-hand column).

The left-hand column sets out the provisions in the form which they took immediately before consolidation. Provisions which repealed, or partially repealed, earlier legislation are not included. Otherwise, all relevant substantive and amending provisions are included.

For additional information, former substantive provisions repealed prior to the consolidation are included in the left-hand column and designated as '(Previously repealed)'. Spent provisions are treated similarly, with '(Spent)' appearing by way of a description.

Those provisions which remain in force after consolidation are indicated to be '(Not repealed)'.

A list of the relevant consolidated provisions, and their abbreviation, is provided at the top of each table.

NATIONAL INSURANCE CONTRIBUTIONS

The consolidated provisions referred to in the destination column are:

- the *Social Security Contributions and Benefits Act* 1992 (SSCBA 1992);
- the *Social Security Administration Act* 1992 (SSAA 1992);
- the *Pension Schemes Act* 1993 (PSA 1993); and
- the *Social Security Administration (Northern Ireland) Act* 1992 (SSA(NI)A 1992).

Former Provision		**Destination**
	Social Security Act 1975	
s. 1(1)(a), (b)	Outline of contributory system	SSCBA 1992, s. 1(1)
s. 1(c)	(Previously repealed)	
s. 1(2), (3), (4)	Outline of contributory system	SSCBA 1992, s. 1(2), (3), (4)
s. 1(4A)		SSCBA 1992, s. 1(5)
s. 1(5), (5A)	(Previously repealed)	
s. 1(6)	Outline of contributory system	SSCBA 1992, s. 1(6)
s. 2	Categories of earners	SSCBA 1992, s. 2
s. 3(1)	"Earnings"	SSCBA 1992, s. 3(1)
s. 3(1A)		SSCBA 1992, s. 4(1)
s. 3(1B)		SSCBA 1992, s. 4(2)
s. 3(1C)(part)		SSCBA 1992, s. 4(3)
s. 3(1D)		SSCBA 1992, s. 4(4)
s. 3(2), (3)		SSCBA 1992, s. 3(2), (3)
s. 3(4)		SSCBA 1992, s. 4(5)
s. 4(1)	Class 1 contributions	SSCBA 1992, s. 5(1)
s. 4(2)		SSCBA 1992, s. 6(1)
s. 4(3)		SSCBA 1992, s. 6(3)
s. 4(4)		SSCBA 1992, s. 7(1)
s. 4(5)		SSCBA 1992, s. 7(2)
s. 4(6)		SSCBA 1992, s. 8(1)
s. 4(6A)		SSCBA 1992, s. 8(2)
s. 4(6B)		SSCBA 1992, s. 8(3)
s. 4(6C)		SSCBA 1992, s. 9(1)
s. 4(6D)		SSCBA 1992, s. 9(2)
s. 4(6E)		SSCBA 1992, s. 9(3)
s. 4(6F)		SSAA 1992, s. 146
s. 4(6G)		SSAA 1992, s. 147(1)
s. 4(6H)	(Not re-enacted)	
s. 4(6HH)	Class 1 contributions	SSAA 1992, s. 147(2)
s. 4(6J)		SSAA 1992, s. 147(3)
s. 4(6K)		SSAA 1992, s. 147(4), (5)
s. 4(7)		SSCBA 1992, s. 6(5)
s. 4A	Class 1A contributions	SSCBA 1992, s. 10
s. 5	(Previously repealed)	
s. 6	(Previously repealed)	
s. 7(1)	Class 2 contributions	SSBCA 1992, s. 11(1)
s. 7(2), (3)	(Previously repealed)	
s. 7(4), (5), (6)	Class 2 contributions	SSCBA 1992, s. 11(3), (4), (5)
s. 7A	Late paid Class 2 contributions	SSCBA 1992, s. 12
s. 8(1)	Class 3 contributions	SSCBA 1992, s. 13(1)
s. 8(2)(a)		SSCBA 1992, s. 13(2), (3)
s. 8(2)(b)	(Previously repealed)	
s. 8(2A)	*Class 3 contributions*	SSCBA 1992. s. 13(4)
s. 8(2B)		SSCBA 1992, s. 13(5)
s. 8(2C)		SSCBA 1992, s. 13(6)
s. 8(2D)		SSCBA 1992, s. 13(7)
s. 8(3)	(Previously repealed)	
s. 9(1)	Class 4 contributions recoverable under Tax Acts	SSCBA 1992, s. 15(1), (2), (5)
s. 9(2)		SSCBA 1992, s. 15(3)
s. 9(3)		SSCBA 1992, s. 16(1), (2)

Former Provision		Destination
Social Security Act 1975		
s. 9(4)		SSCBA 1992, s. 16(3)
s. 9(5)		SSCBA 1992, s. 16(4)
s. 9(6)		SSCBA 1992, s. 16(5)
s. 9(7)		SSCBA 1992, s. 17(1)
s. 9(8)		SSCBA 1992, s. 17(2)
s. 9(9)		SSCBA 1992, s. 17(3)–(6)
s. 10	Class 4 contributions recoverable under regulations	SSCBA 1992, s. 18
s. 11	General power to regulate liability for contributions	SSCBA 1992, s. 19
s. 13(1)	Contribution conditions and the earnings factor	SSCBA 1992, s. 21(1), (2)
s. 13(2) (part)		SSCBA 1992, s. 22(1)
s. 13(2)(a), (c)		SSCBA 1992, s. 22(2)
s. 13(2)(b)	(Previously repealed)	
s. 13(3)	Contribution conditions and the earnings factor	SSCBA 1992, s. 22(4)
s. 13(4)		SSCBA 1992, s. 22(5)
s. 13(5) (part)		SSCBA 1992, s. 23
s. 13(5)(i)–(iv)		SSCBA 1992, s. 22(3)
s. 13(5ZA)		SSCBA 1992, s. 23(2)
s. 13(5A)		SSCBA 1992, s. 23(4)
s. 13(5AA)		SSCBA 1992, s. 22(6)
s. 13(5B)		SSCBA 1992, s. 24(1)
s. 13(5C)		SSCBA 1992, s. 24(2)
s. 13(6) (part)		SSCBA 1992, s. 21(3)
s. 13(6)(a)–(d)		SSCBA 1992, s. 21(5)
s. 13(7)		SSCBA 1992, s. 21(6)
s. 13(8)		SSCBA 1992, s. 21(4)
s. 93(1)(a), (b)	Principal questions for Secretary of State	SSAA 1992, s. 17(1)(a), (b)
s. 93(1)(bb)		SSAA 1992, s. 17(1)(c)
s. 93(1)(c)	(Previously repealed)	
s. 93(1)(e)	Principal questions for Secretary of State	SSAA 1992, s. 17(1)(e)
s. 93(2)		SSAA 1992, s. 17(2)
s. 93(2A)		SSAA 1992, s. 17(3)
s. 93(3)		SSAA 1992, s. 17(4)
s. 94(1)–(5)	Appeal on question of law	SSAA 1992, s. 18(1)–(5)
s. 94(6)	(Previously repealed)	
s. 94(7), (8)	Appeal on question of law	SSAA 1992, s. 18(6), (7)
s. 96	Review of decisions under s. 93, 95	SSAA 1992, s. 19
s. 114(1)	Regulations as to determinations of questions	SSAA 1992, s. 58(1), (2)
s. 114(2)		SSAA 1992, s. 58(3)
s. 114(2B)		SSAA 1992, s. 58(5)
s. 114(3), (4)	(Previously repealed)	
s. 114(5)	Regulations as to determinations of questions	SSAA 1992, s. 58(8)
s. 115	Procedure	SSAA 1992, s. 59
s. 115A	Power of adjudicating authorities to refer matters to experts	SSAA 1992, s. 53
s. 115B	Assessors	SSAA 1992, s. 56
s. 117	Finality of decisions	SSAA 1992, s. 60
s. 119(1)–(2A)	(Previously repealed)	
s. 119(3)	Effect of adjudication on payment and recovery	SSAA 1992, s. 61(1)
s. 119(4)(a)		SSAA 1992, s. 61(4)
s. 119(4)(b)–(d), (5), (6)	(Previously repealed)	
s. 120(1)	(Not re-enacted)	
s. 120(2)–(7)	Annual review of contributions	SSAA 1992, s. 141(1)–(6)
s. 121	Orders under s. 120	SSAA 1992, s. 142
s. 122(1), (2)	Additional power to alter contributions	SSAA 1992, s. 143(1), (2)
s. 122(3)(a)		SSAA 1992, s. 143(3)
s. 122(3)(b), (4), (5)	(Previously repealed)	
s. 122(6)	Additional power to alter contributions	SSAA 1992, s. 143(4)
s. 123	Orders under s. 122	SSAA 1992, s. 144
s. *123A(1)–(4)*	*Further power to alter certain contributions*	SSAA 1992, s. 145
s. 123A(5)		SSAA 1992, s. 147(1)
s. 123A(6)	(Not re-enacted)	

Former Provision		Destination
Social Security Act 1975		
s. 123A(6A)	Further power to alter certain contributions	SSAA 1992, s. 147(2)
s. 123A(7)		SSAA 1992, s. 147(3)
s. 123A(8)		SSAA 1992, s. 147(4), (5)
s. 127	Crown employment	SSCBA 1992, s. 115(1)–(3)
s. 128(1)–(3)	Her Majesty's forces	SSCBA 1992, s. 116
s. 128(4)	(Not re-enacted)	
s. 129(1), (2)	Mariners, airmen etc.	SSCBA 1992, s. 117
s. 129(3)	(Previously repealed)	
s. 130(1)	Married women and widows	SSCBA 1992, s. 118
s. 130(2), (3)	(Previously repealed)	
s. 131	Persons outside Great Britain	SSCBA 1992, s. 119
s. 132	Employment at sea	SSCBA 1992, s. 120
s. 142(1)–(4)	Co-ordination with Northern Ireland	SSAA 1992, s. 177(1)–(5)
s. 142(5), (6)	(Not re-enacted)	
s. 143(1)	Reciprocity with other countries	SSAA 1992, s. 179(1)
s. 143(1A)		SSAA 1992, s. 179(2)
s. 143(2)		SSAA 1992, s. 179(3)
s. 144	(Previously repealed)	
s. 145	(Previously repealed)	
s. 146(1)	Offences and penalties	SSAA 1992, s. 114(1)
s. 146(2)		SSAA 1992, s. 114(3)
s. 146(3)(a), (b)		SSAA 1992, s. 114(4)
s. 146(3)(c)	(Previously repealed)	
s. 146(4)	Offences and penalties	SSAA 1992, s. 114(5), (6)
s. 146(6)	(Previously repealed)	
s. 147	(Previously repealed)	
s. 148	Questions arising in proceedings	SSAA 1992, s. 117
s. 149	Evidence of non-payment	SSAA 1992, s. 118
s. 150	Recovery on prosecution	SSAA 1992, s. 119
s. 151	Proof of previous offences	SSAA 1992, s. 120
s. 152(1) (part)	Provisions supplementary to s. 150, 151	SSAA 1992, s. 121(1)
s. 152(2), (3)		SSAA 1992, s. 121(2), (3)
s. 152(4)	(Previously repealed)	
s. 152(5)–(7)	Provisions supplementary to s. 150, 151	SSAA 1992, s. 121(4)–(6)
s. 153	(Previously repealed)	
s. 160(1)	Provisions relating to age, death and marriage	SSAA 1992, s. 124(1), (2)
s. 160(2)–(4)		SSAA 1992, s. 124(3)–(5)
s. 162	Treatment of certain marriages	SSCBA 1992, s. 121
s. 163	Exemption from stamp duty	SSAA 1992, s. 188
s. 164	(Previously repealed)	
s. 166(1)	Orders and regulations	SSCBA 1992, s. 175(2); SSAA 1992, s. 189(3)
s. 166(2)		SSCBA 1992, s. 175(3); SSAA 1992, s. 189(4)
s. 166(3)		SSCBA 1992, s. 175(4); SSAA 1992, s. 189(5)
s. 166(3A)		SSCBA 1992, s. 175(5); SSAA 1992, s. 189(6)
s. 166(4)	(Not re-enacted)	
s. 166(5)	Orders and regulations	SSCBA 1992, s. 175(7); SSAA 1992, s. 189(9)
s. 166(5A)		SSAA 1992, s. 189(10)
s. 166(6)		SSCBA 1992, s. 175(8)
s. 166(7)		SSCBA 1992, s. 175(9); SSAA 1992, s. 189(11)
s. 167(1)	Parliamentary control of orders and regulations	SSCBA 1992, s. 176(1); SSAA 1992, s. 190(1)
s. 167(2)		SSCBA 1992, s. 176(2)
s. 167(3)		SSCBA 1992, s. 176(3); SSAA 1992, s. 190(3)
s. 167(4)		SSAA 1992, s. 190(4)
s. 168(1)–(3)	(Unnecessary)	
s. 168(4)	Interpretation	SSCBA 1992, s. 175(10); SSAA 1992, s. 189(12)
s. 169	(Unnecessary)	
Sch. 1, para. 1(1)	Supplementary provisions relating to contributions of classes 1, 2 and 3	SSCBA 1992, Sch. 1, para. 1(1)
Sch. 1, para. 1(1A)		SSCBA 1992, Sch. 1, para. 1(2)
Sch. 1, para. 1(1B)		SSCBA 1992, Sch. 1, para. 1(3)

Former Provision		Destination
Social Security Act 1975		
Sch. 1, para. 1(1C)		SSCBA 1992, Sch. 1, para. 1(4)
Sch. 1, para. 1(1D)		SSCBA 1992, Sch. 1, para. 1(6)
Sch. 1, para. 1(2)		SSCBA 1992, Sch. 1, para. 1(7)
Sch. 1, para. 1(3)		SSCBA 1992, Sch. 1, para. 1(8)
Sch. 1, para. 2		SSCBA 1992, Sch. 1, para. 2
Sch. 1, para. 3		SSCBA 1992, Sch. 1, para. 3
Sch. 1, para. 4		SSCBA 1992, Sch. 1, para. 4
Sch. 1, para. 5(1)		SSCBA 1992, Sch. 1, para. 6(1)
Sch. 1, para. 5(1A)		SSCBA 1992, Sch. 1, para. 6(2)
Sch. 1, para. 5(1B)		SSCBA 1992, Sch. 1, para. 6(3)
Sch. 1, para. 5(1C)		SSCBA 1992, Sch. 1, para. 6(4)
Sch. 1, para. 5(2)		SSCBA 1992, Sch. 1, para. 6(7)
Sch. 1, para. 5(3)		SSCBA 1992, Sch. 1, para. 6(8)
Sch. 1, para. 5A		SSCBA 1992, Sch. 1, para. 7
Sch. 1, para. 6		SSCBA 1992, Sch. 1, para. 8
Sch. 1, para. 7		SSCBA 1992, Sch. 1, para. 9
Sch. 1, para. 8		SSCBA 1992, Sch. 1, para. 10
Sch. 1, para. 9		SSCBA 1992, Sch. 1, para. 11
Sch. 2, para. 1	Levy of class 4 contributions with income tax	SSCBA 1992, Sch. 2, para. 1
Sch. 2, para. 2		SSCBA 1992, Sch. 2, para. 2
Sch. 2, para. 3		SSCBA 1992, Sch. 2, para. 3
Sch. 2, para. 4	(Previously repealed)	
Sch. 2, para. 5	Levy of class 4 contributions with income tax	SSCBA 1992, Sch. 2, para. 4
Sch. 2, para. 6		SSCBA 1992, Sch. 2, para. 5
Sch. 2, para. 7		SSCBA 1992, Sch. 2, para. 6
Sch. 2, para. 8		SSCBA 1992, Sch. 2, para. 7
Sch. 2, para. 9		SSCBA 1992, Sch. 2, para. 8
Sch. 13, para. 1	Provision which may be made by procedure regulations	SSAA 1992, Sch. 3, para. 2
Sch. 13, para. 1A		SSAA 1992, Sch. 3, para. 3
Sch. 13, para. 2		SSAA 1992, Sch. 3, para. 4
Sch. 13, para. 3		SSAA 1992, Sch. 3, para. 5
Sch. 13, para. 4		SSAA 1992, Sch. 3, para. 6
Sch. 13, para. 5		SSAA 1992, Sch. 3, para. 7
Sch. 13, para. 11		SSAA 1992, Sch. 3, para. 12
Sch. 17	Constitution, etc., of Joint Authority for Great Britain and Northern Ireland	SSAA 1992, Sch. 8
Sch. 20	Glossary of expressions	
Sch. 20	"The 1973 Act" (unnecessary)	
Sch. 20	"Age"	SSCBA 1992, s. 173
Sch. 20	"Benefit"	SSCBA 1992, s. 122(1)
Sch. 20	"Benefit year"	SSCBA 1992, s. 21(6)
Sch. 20	"Claim"	SSCBA 1992, s. 122(1)
Sch. 20	"Claimant"	SSCBA 1992, s. 122(1)
Sch. 20	"Commissioner"	SSAA 1992, s. 191
Sch. 20	"Contract of service"	SSCBA 1992, s. 122(1)
Sch. 20	"Contribution card"	SSAA 1992, s. 114(6)
Sch. 20	"Current"	SSCBA 1992, s. 122(1)
Sch. 20	"Earner" and "earnings"	SSCBA 1992, s. 122
Sch. 20	"Earnings factor"	SSCBA 1992, s. 21(5)
Sch. 20	"Employed"	SSCBA 1992, s. 122(1)
Sch. 20	"Employed earner"	SSCBA 1992, s. 122(1)
Sch. 20	"Employment"	SSCBA 1992, s. 122(1)
Sch. 20	"Friendly society" (not re-enacted)	
Sch. 20	"The former Industrial Injuries Act" (unnecessary)	
Sch. 20	"The former principal Act" (unnecessary)	
Sch. 20	"Hovercraft" (not re-enacted)	
Sch. 20	"Industrial injuries benefit"	SSCBA 1992, s. 122(1); SSAA 1992, s. 191
Sch. 20	"Initial primary percentage"	SSCBA 1992, s. 122(1)
Sch. 20	"main primary percentage"	SSCBA 1992, s. 122(1)
Sch. 20	"primary percentage"	SSCBA 1992, s. 122(1)
Sch. 20	"The Inland Revenue"	SSCBA 1992, s. 122(1)

Former Provision		Destination
Social Security Act 1975		
Sch. 20	"Long-term benefit"	SSCBA 1992, s. 122(1)
Sch. 20	"Lower earnings limit"; "upper earnings limit"	SSCBA 1992, s. 122(1)
Sch. 20	"Main primary percentage"	SSCBA 1992, s. 122(1)
Sch. 20	"Medical practitioner"	SSAA 1992, s. 192
Sch. 20	"The Northern Ireland Department"	SSCBA 1992, s. 122(1); SSAA 1992, s. 191
Sch. 20	"The Old Cases Act"	SSAA 1992, s. 191
Sch. 20	"Pensionable age"	SSCBA 1992, s. 122(1)
Sch. 20	"The Pensions Act"	SSAA 1992 s. 191
Sch. 20	"Prescribe"	SSCBA 1992, s. 122(1); SSAA 1992, s. 191
Sch. 20	"Primary percentage"	SSCBA 1992, s. 122(1)
Sch. 20	"Procedure regulations"	SSAA 1992, s. 59(1)
Sch. 20	"Qualifying earnings factor"	SSCBA 1992, s. 122(1)
Sch. 20	"Regulations" (unnecessary)	
Sch. 20	"Self-employed earner"	SSCBA 1992, s. 122(1)
Sch. 20	"Short-term benefit"	SSCBA 1992, s. 122(1)
Sch. 20	"Tax week"	SSCBA 1992, s. 122(1)
Sch. 20	"Tax year"	SSCBA 1992, s. 122(1); SSAA 1992, s. 191
Sch. 20	"Trade or business"	SSCBA 1992, s. 122(1)
Sch. 20	"Trade union"	SSCBA 1992, s. 122(1)
Sch. 20	"Upper earnings limit"	SSCBA 1992, s. 122(1)
Sch. 20	"Week"	SSCBA 1992, s. 122(1)

Social Security Pensions Act 1975

s. 1	Earnings limits	SSCBA 1992, s. 5
s. 2	(Previously repealed)	
s. 3(1), (2)	Married women and widows	SSCBA 1992, s. 19(4)
s. 3(3), (4)		SSCBA 1992, s. 19(5), (6)
s. 4(1)	Persons over pensionable age	SSCBA 1992, s. 6(2)
s. 4(2)		SSCBA 1992, s. 11(2)
s. 4(3) (amending)	(Unnecessary)	
s. 5(1), (2)	Voluntary contributions	SSCBA 1992, s. 14(1), (2)
s. 5(3)	"qualifying earnings factor"	SSCBA 1992, s. 122(1)
s. 21(1), (2)	Revaluation of earnings factors	SSAA 1992, s. 148(1), (2)
s. 21(3)		SSAA 1992, s. 148(3), (4)
s. 21(4), (5)		SSAA 1992, s. 148(5), (6)
s. 21(6)	(Previously repealed)	
s. 21(7)	(Unnecessary)	
s. 26(1), (1A)	Contracting out of full contributions and benefits	PSA 1993, s. 40
s. 26(2)		PSA 1993, s. 8(2)
s. 27(1)–(3)	Contracted-out rates of class 1 contributions	PSA 1993, s. 41(1)
s. 27(4)		PSA 1993, s. 41(2)
s. 27(5)		PSA 1993, s. 41(3)
s. 27(6)	(Previously repealed)	
s. 28(1), (2)	Review and alteration of contracted-out rates of class 1 contributions	PSA 1993, s. 42(1)
s. 28(3)		PSA 1993, s. 42(2)
s. 28(4)		PSA 1993, s. 42(3)
s. 28(5)		PSA 1993, s. 42(4)
s. 28(6)		PSA 1993, s. 42(5)
s. 28(7)		PSA 1993, s. 42(6)
s. 30(1)	Contracted-out employment	PSA 1993, s. 7(1), 8(1)
s. 30(1A), (1B)		PSA 1993, s. 8(2)
s. 30(1C)		PSA 1993, s. 8(3)
s. 30(2)	(Previously repealed)	
s. 30(3)	Contracted-out employment	PSA 1993, s. 8(4)
s. 30(4)		PSA 1993, s. 8(5)
s. 30(5)	(Previously repealed)	
s. 31(1)	Contracting-out certificates	PSA 1993, s. 7(1), (2)
s. 31(2)		PSA 1993, s. 34(1)
s. 31(3)		PSA 1993, s. 11(1), (2)

Former Provision		Destination
Social Security Pensions Act 1975		
s. 31(4)		PSA 1993, s. 11(3), (4)
s. 31(5)		PSA 1993, s. 11(5)
s. 31(6)		PSA 1993, s. 34(2)
s. 31(7)		PSA 1993, s. 7(7), 34(8)
s. 31(8)		PSA 1993, s. 181(1)
s. 31(9)	(Previously repealed)	
s. 51A(1)	Refusal and cancellation of contracting-out certificates	PSA 1993, s. 35(1)
s. 51A(2)		PSA 1993, s. 36(1)
s. 51A(3)		PSA 1993, s. 35(2), 36(2)
s. 51A(4)		PSA 1993, s. 35(3)
s. 51A(5)		PSA 1993, s. 36(3)
s. 51A(6)		PSA 1993, s. 36(4)
s. 51A(7), (8)	(Unnecessary)	
s. 51A(9)	Refusal and cancellation of contracting-out certificates	PSA 1993, s. 35(4), 36(5)
s. 51A(10)		PSA 1993, s. 36(6)
s. 51A(11)		PSA 1993, s. 35(5), 36(7)
s. 51A(12)		PSA 1993, s. 35(6)
s. 51A(13)	(Previously repealed)	
s. 60(2), (3)	Determination of questions	PSA 1993, s. 170(3), (4)
s. 60(4)		PSA 1993, s. 173(1)
s. 61A(1)–(4)	(Not repealed)	
s. 61B(1)–(5)	(Not repealed)	
s. 62(1)	(Previously repealed)	
s. 62(2)	(Not repealed)	
s. 62(3)	(Previously repealed)	
s. 62(4)	(Unnecessary)	
s. 66	Interpretation	
s. 66(1)	"the Administration Act" (unnecessary)	
s. 66(1)	"the Contributions and Benefits Act" (unnecesary)	
s. 66(1)	"guaranteed minimum pension"	PSA 1993, s. 8(2)
s. 66(1)	"long-term benefit"	PSA 1993, s. 181(1), SSCBA 1992
s. 66(1)	"minimum payments"	PSA 1993, s. 8(2), "minimum payment"
s. 66(1)	"occupational pension scheme"	PSA 1993, s. 1
s. 66(1)	"the principal Act" (unnecessary)	
s. 66(1)	"qualifying earnings factor" (unnecessary)	
s. 66(6), (7)	(Not repealed)	
s. 67(1)–(4)	(Not repealed)	
s. 68(1), (2)	(Not repealed)	
s. 68(4) (part)	(Not re-enacted)	
s. 68(4) (part)	(Not repealed)	
Social Security (Miscellaneous Provisions) Act 1977		
s. 18(1)(a), (b)	Certain sums to be earnings for social security purposes	SSCBA 1992, s. 112(1)
s. 18(1)(c)	(Previously repealed)	
s. 18(2)(a), (b)	(Previously repealed)	
s. 18(2)(c)–(e)	Certain sums to be earnings for social security purposes	SSCBA 1992, s. 112(3)
s. 24(1)	(Not repealed)	
s. 24(2)	(Unnecessary)	
s. 24(3), (5), (6)	(Not repealed)	
s. 25	(Not repealed)	
Social Security Act 1980		
s. 9(1)	The Social Security Advisory Committee	SSAA 1992, s. 170(1)
s. 9(2)		SSAA 1992, s. 170(2)
s. 9(3) (part)		SSAA 1992, s. 170(3)
s. 9(3) (part)		SSA(NI)A 1992, s. 149(1)
s. 9(4) (part)		SSAA 1992, s. 170(4)
s. 9(4) (part)		SSA(NI)A 1992, s. 149(4)
s. 9(5)	(Unnecessary)	
s. 9(6)	(Not repealed)	

Former Provision		Destination
Social Security Act 1980		
s. 9(7)	The Social Security Advisory Committee	SSAA 1992, s. 170(5)
s. 10(1) (part)	Consultation with Committee on proposals for regulations	SSAA 1992, s. 172(1)
s. 10(1) (part)		SSA(NI)A 1992, s. 149(2)
s. 10(2) (part)		SSAA 1992, s. 172(3)
s. 10(2)(a), (b)	(Previously repealed)	
s. 10(3) (part)	Consultation with Committee on proposals for regulations	SSAA 1992, s. 174(1)
s. 10(3) (part)		SSA(NI)A 1992, s. 151
s. 10(4), (5)		SSAA 1992, s. 174(2), (3)
s. 10(6)		SSA(NI)A 1992, s. 151(2)
s. 10(7)	(Previously repealed)	
s. 10(8)	Consultation with Committee on proposals for regulations	SSA(NI)A 1992, s. 151(3)
s. 10(9) (part)		SSAA 1992, s. 172(5), 173(6), 174(4)
s. 10(9) (part)		SSA(NI)A 1992, s. 151(4)
s. 12	(Not repealed)	
s. 13(1)–(3)	Tenure of office of Commissioner	SSAA 1992, Sch. 2, para. 1(2)–(4)
s. 13(4)	(Not repealed)	
s. 13(5) (part)	Tenure of office of Commissioner	SSA(NI)A 1992, s. 50(2)
s. 13(5)(a)		SSAA 1992, Sch. 2, para. 1(6)
s. 13(5)(b)	(Not re-enacted)	
s. 13(6)	Tenure of office of Commissioner	SSAA 1992, Sch. 2, para. 1(5)
s. 13(7)	(Not re-enacted)	
s. 14(1)–(5)	Appeal from Commissioners etc. on point of law	SSAA 1992, s. 24(1)–(5)
s. 14(6)	(Previously repealed)	
s. 14(8) (part)	Appeal from Commissioners etc. on point of law	SSAA 1992, s. 24(6)
s. 14(8) (part)		SSAA 1992, s. 190(4)
s. 18	Computation of age in Scotland	SSCBA 1992, s. 173
s. 21	(Not repealed)	
Sch. 3, para. 1	Social Security Advisory Committee	SSAA 1992, Sch. 5, para. 1
Sch. 3, para. 2		SSAA 1992, Sch. 5, para. 2
Sch. 3, para. 3		SSAA 1992, Sch. 5, para. 3
Sch. 3, para. 4		SSAA 1992, Sch. 5, para. 4
Sch. 3, para. 5		SSAA 1992, Sch. 5, para. 5
Sch. 3, para. 6		SSAA 1992, Sch. 5, para. 6
Sch. 3, para. 7		SSAA 1992, Sch. 5, para. 7
Sch. 3, para. 8		SSAA 1992, Sch. 5, para. 8
Sch. 3, para. 9		SSAA 1992, Sch. 5, para. 9
Sch. 3, para. 10		SSAA 1992, Sch. 5, para. 10
Sch. 3, para. 12(2) (part)		SSAA 1992, Sch. 7, para. 3
Sch. 3, para. 13(1)		SSAA 1992, Sch. 7, para. 4
Sch. 3, para. 13(1A)		SSAA 1992, Sch. 7, para. 5
Sch. 3, para. 13(2)	(Not re-enacted)	
Sch. 3, para. 15A, 15AA	Social Security Advisory Committee	SSAA 1992, Sch. 7, para. 9
Sch. 3, para. 20		SSAA 1992, Sch. 7, para. 10
Sch. 3, para. 21		SSA(NI)A 1992, Sch. 5, para. 10

Social Security and Housing Benefits Act 1982

s. 9(1)	Recovery by employers of amounts paid by way of statutory sick pay	SSCBA 1992, s. 158(1)
s. 9(1A)	(Previously repealed)	
s. 9(1B)	Recovery by employers of amounts paid by way of statutory sick pay	SSCBA 1992, s. 158(2)
s. 9(1C)		SSCBA 1992, s. 159
s. 9(1D)		SSCBA 1992, s. 158(3)
s. 9(1E)	(Not re-enacted)	
s. 9(1F)	Recovery by employers of amounts paid by way of statutory sick pay	SSCBA 1992, s. 176(1) (part)
s. 9(3)(a)		SSAA 1992, s. 130(4)(c)

Former Provision		Destination
Social Security and Housing Benefits Act 1982		
s. 9(3)(b), (c)		SSCBA 1992, s. 158(5)
s. 9(4)		SSCBA 1992, Sch. 1, para. 6(5)
s. 9(5)		SSCBA 1992, Sch. 1, para. 6(6)
s. 9(6)		SSCBA 1992, s. 158(6)
s. 9(7)	(Not re-enacted)	
s. 9(8)–(10)	(Previously repealed)	
s. 23	Statutory sick pay to count as remuneration for principal Act	SSCBA 1992, s. 4(1) (part)
s. 26(1)	Interpretation	SSCBA 1992, s. 163(1)
s. 26(7)		SSCBA 1992, s. 172(a)
s. 27	Crown employment	SSCBA 1992, s. 161
s. 44(1)(b)	Application of social security legislation in relation to territorial waters	SSCBA 1992, s. 172
s. 44(2)(a), (b)		SSCBA 1992, s. 172
s. 45	(Not repealed)	
s. 48(1)	(Not repealed)	
s. 48(2)	(Not re-enacted)	
s. 48(3)	(Not repealed)	
s. 48(4)–(6)	(Unnecessary)	
s. 48(7)	(Not repealed)	
Social Security Act 1986		
s. 49(1)	Further provisions relating to statutory maternity pay etc.	SSCBA 1992, s. 1(4)
s. 50	Interpretation	SSCBA 1992, s. 171
s. 52(1)	(Unnecessary)	
s. 52(2)	Adjudication	PSA 1993, s. 170(1)
s. 52(3)–(8)	(Previously repealed)	
s. 54(1)	(Not repealed)	
s. 55	False representations for obtaining benefit etc.	SSAA 1992, s. 112
s. 56(1)–(3), (5)	(Not repealed)	
s. 57	(Not repealed)	
s. 58(1)–(7)	Inspection	SSAA 1992, s. 110(1)–(7)
s. 58(8), (9)		SSAA 1992, s. 111
s. 58(10)	(Not re-enacted)	
s. 59(1)	Disclosure of information	PSA 1993, s. 158(1)
s. 59(2)		PSA 1993, s. 158(4)
s. 59(3)		PSA 1993, s. 158(5), (6)
s. 60(1), (2)	Regulations as to notification of deaths	PSA 1993, s. 167(2), SSAA 1992, s. 125
s. 61(1)–(10)	Consultations on subordinate legislation	PSA 1993, s. 185(6), SSAA 1992, s. 173
s. 83(1)	(Not repealed)	
s. 83(3)(b)–(e)	(Not re-enacted)	
s. 83(4)–(6)	(Not repealed)	
s. 84	General interpretation	
s. 84(1) (part)	(Not repealed)	
s. 84(1)	"contract of service"	SSCBA 1992, s. 122(1)
s. 84(1)	"employed earner"	SSCBA 1992, s. 2
s. 84(1)	"employee"	PSA 1993, s. 181(1)
s. 84(1)	"employer"	PSA 1993, s. 181(1)
s. 84(1)	"prescribed"	SSCBA 1992, s. 137(1)
s. 84(1)	"regulations"	SSCBA 1992, s. 175(1)
s. 84(4)	(Not repealed)	
s. 87	(Not repealed)	
s. 88	(Not repealed)	
s. 90	(Not repealed)	
Sch. 4, para. 1	Statutory maternity pay etc.	SSCBA 1992, s. 167(1)
Sch. 4, para. 2		SSCBA 1992, s. 167(3)
Sch. 4, para. 3		SSCBA 1992, Sch. 1, para. 6(5)
Sch. 4, para. 4		SSCBA 1992, Sch. 1, para. 6(6)
Sch. 4, para. 5		SSCBA 1992, s. 167(4)
Sch. 4, para. 10		SSCBA 1992, s. 4(1) (part)

Former Provision		Destination
Social Security Act 1986		
Sch. 5, Pt. II, para. (a)	Adjudication	PSA 1993, s. 170(1)
Sch. 5, Pt. II, para. (b)(i)–(iv)		SSAA 1992, s. 17(1)(g)(i)–(iv)
Sch. 5, Pt. II, para. (b)(v)		SSAA 1992, s. 17(g)(vi)
Sch. 5, Pt. II, para. (b)(vi)		SSAA 1992, s. 17(g)(v)
Sch. 5, Pt. II, para. (c)		SSAA 1992, s. 17(h)

Social Security Act 1989

s. 3	(Not re-enacted)	
s. 19(1)–(10)	Unauthorised disclosure of information relating to particular persons	SSAA 1992, s. 123
s. 19(11)	(Not re-enacted)	
s. 29(1), (3)	(Not repealed)	
s. 29(4)	(Previously repealed)	
s. 29(6), (7)	(Not repealed)	
s. 30	(Not repealed)	
s. 31	(Not repealed)	
s. 32	(Not re-enacted)	
s. 33	(Not repealed)	
Sch. 2, Pt. I	Persons employed in social security administration or adjudication	SSAA 1992, Sch. 4, Pt. I
Sch. 2, Pt. II		SSAA 1992, Sch. 4, Pt. II

Social Security (Contributions) Regulations 1979 (SI 1979/591)

The consolidated table below relates the provisions of the former legislation (in the left-hand column) to the corresponding consolidated provisions in the right-hand column.

The consolidated provisions referred to in the destination column are: the *Social Security (Contributions) Regulations* 2001 (SI 2001/1004) and the *Social Security (Crediting and Treatment of Contributions and National Insurance Numbers) Regulations* 2001 (SI 2001/769).

Note: The left-hand column sets out the provisions in the form they took immediately before consolidation.

Social Security (Contributions) Regulations 1979

Former provision		Destination
	Part I – General	
Reg. 1(1)	Citation, commencement and interpretation	Spent
Reg. 1(2)	....	SI 2001/1004, reg. 1(2)
	Part II – Assessment of earnings-related contributions	
Reg. 2	Earnings periods	SI 2001/1004, reg. 2
Reg. 3	Earnings period for earnings normally paid or treated as paid at regular intervals	SI 2001/1004, reg. 3
Reg. 4	Earnings period for earnings normally paid otherwise than at regular intervals and not treated as paid at regular intervals	SI 2001/1004, reg. 4
Reg. 5	Earnings periods for sums deemed to be earnings by virtue of regulations made under section 18 of the Social Security (Miscellaneous Provisions) Act 1977 [SSCBA 1992, s. 112]	SI 2001/1004, reg. 5
Reg. 5A	Earnings periods for earnings to be aggregated where the earnings periods for those earnings otherwise would be of different lengths	SI 2001/1004, reg. 6
Reg. 6	Treatment of earnings paid otherwise than at regular intervals	SI 2001/1004, reg. 7
Reg. 6A	Earnings period for directors	SI 2001/1004, reg. 8
Reg. 6B	Earnings period for statutory maternity pay and statutory sick pay paid by the Secretary of State	SI 2001/1004, reg. 9
Reg. 7	Lower and upper earnings limits and primary and secondary thresholds	SI 2001/1004, reg. 10
Reg. 8	Prescribed equivalents	SI 2001/1004, reg. 11
Reg. 9	Calculation of earnings-related contributions	SI 2001/1004, reg. 12
Reg. 10	General provisions as to aggregation	SI 2001/1004, reg. 13
Reg. 11	Aggregation of earnings paid in respect of separate employed earner's employments under the same employer	SI 2001/1004, reg. 14
Reg. 12	Aggregation of earnings paid in respect of different employed earner's employments by different persons and apportionment of contribution liability	SI 2001/1004, reg. 15
Reg. 12A	Aggregation of earnings paid after pensionable age	SI 2001/1004, reg. 16
Reg. 13	Apportionment of single payment of earnings in respect of different employed earner's employments by different secondary contributors	SI 2001/1004, reg. 17
Reg. 14	Change of earnings period	SI 2001/1004, reg. 18
Reg. 15	Holiday payments	SI 2001/1004, reg. 19
Reg. 16	Joint employment of husband and wife	SI 2001/1004, reg. 20
Reg. 17	Annual maximum	SI 2001/1004, reg. 21

Social Security (Contributions) Regulations 1979

Former provision		Destination
Reg. 17A	Payments to be treated as earnings	SI 2001/1004, reg. 22
Reg. 17B	Manner of making sickness payments treated as remuneration	SI 2001/1004, reg. 23
Reg. 18	Calculation of earnings for the purpose of earnings-related contributions	SI 2001/1004, reg. 24
Reg. 19	Payments to be disregarded in the calculation of earnings for the purpose of earnings-related contributions	SI 2001/1004, reg. 25
Reg. 19A	Certain payments by trustees to be disregarded	SI 2001/1004, reg. 26
Reg. 19B	Payments to directors which are to be disregarded	SI 2001/1004, reg. 27
Reg. 20	Liability for Class 1 contributions in respect of earnings normally paid after pensionable age	SI 2001/1004, reg. 28
Reg. 20A	Liability for Class 1 contributions of persons over pensionable age	SI 2001/1004, reg. 29
Reg. 21	Abnormal pay practices	SI 2001/1004, reg. 30
Reg. 22	Practices avoiding or reducing liability	SI 2001/1004, reg. 31
	Part IIA – Exceptions from liability for Class 1A contributions and reduction of Class 1A contributions	
Reg. 22A	Interpretation for the purposes of this part	SI 2001/1004, reg. 32
Reg. 22B	Exception from liability to pay Class 1A contributions in respect of cars made available to members of an employed earner's family or household in certain circumstances	SI 2001/1004, reg. 33
Reg. 22C	Class 1A contributions payable where two or more cars are made available concurrently	SI 2001/1004, reg. 34
Reg. 22D	Reduction of certain Class 1A contributions in the case of a car made available by reason of two or more employments and of a car made available to two or more employed earners	SI 2001/1004, reg. 35
Reg. 22E	Reduction of certain Class 1A contributions on account of the number of employments in the cases of something provided or made available by reason of two or more employed earners	SI 2001/1004, reg. 36
Reg. 22F	Reduction of certain Class 1A contributions in respect of cars made available to employed earners who are disabled	SI 2001/1004, reg. 37
Reg. 22G	Exception from liability to pay Class 1A contributions in respect of cars made available to disabled employed earners for business and home to work travel only	SI 2001/1004, reg. 38
Reg. 22H	Calculation of Class 1A contributions	SI 2001/1004, reg. 39
Reg. 22HA	Prescribed emoluments in respect of which Class 1A contributions are not payable	SI 2001/1004, reg. 40
	Part IIB – Calculation of, an exception from, liability for Class 1B contributions	
Reg. 22I	Calculation of Class 1B contributions	SI 2001/1004, reg. 41
Reg. 22J	Exception from liability to pay Class 1B contributions	SI 2001/1004, reg. 42
	Part III – Exceptions from liability for Class 2 contributions and provisions relating to Class 3 contributions, appropriation, reallocation and refund of contributions (other than Class 4 contributions)	
Reg. 23	Exception from liability for Class 2 contributions	SI 2001/1004, reg. 43
Reg. 24	Application for, and duration and cancellation of, certificates of exception	SI 2001/1004, reg. 44

Social Security (Contributions) Regulations 1979

Former provision		Destination
Reg. 25	Earnings for the purposes of certificates of exception	SI 2001/1004, reg. 45
Reg. 26	Certificates of exception – exception from liability for, and entitlement to pay, Class 2 contributions	SI 2001/1004, reg. 46
Reg. 26A	Return of Class 2 contributions paid by low earners	SI 2001/1004, reg. 47
Reg. 27	Class 3 contributions	SI 2001/1004, reg. 48
Reg. 28	Precluded Class 3 contributions	SI 2001/1004, reg. 49
Reg. 29	Class 3 contributions not paid within prescribed periods	SI 2001/1004, reg. 50
Reg. 30	Appropriation of Class 3 contributions	SI 2001/769, reg. 2
Reg. 31	Disposal of contributions not properly paid	SI 2001/1004, reg. 51
Reg. 32	Return of contributions	SI 2001/1004, reg. 52
Reg. 32A	Return of contributions: further provisions	SI 2001/1004, reg. 53
Reg. 33	Return of Class 1 contributions paid at the non-contracted-out rate instead of the contracted-out rate	SI 2001/1004, reg. 54
Reg. 33A	Repayment of Class 1A contributions	SI 2001/1004, reg. 55
Reg. 34	Return of precluded Class 3 contributions	SI 2001/1004, reg. 56
Reg. 35	Calculation of return of contributions	SI 2001/1004, reg. 57
Reg. 36	Crediting of Class 3 contributions	SI 2001/769, reg. 3
Reg. 37	Reallocation of contributions for benefit purposes	SI 2001/1004, reg. 58
Reg. 37A	Circumstances in which two-year limit for refunds of Class 1, 1A or 1B not to apply	SI 2001/1004, reg. 59
	Part IV – Late paid and unpaid contributions	
Reg. 38	Treatment for purposes of contributory benefits of late paid contributions under the Act	SI 2001/769, reg. 4
Reg. 38A	Treatment for the purpose of contributory benefit of contribution paid by virtue of regulation 27(4)	SI 2001/769, reg. 4
Reg. 39	Treatment for the purpose of any contributory benefit of late paid or unpaid primary Class 1 contribution where there was no consent, connivance or negligence by the primary contributor	SI 2001/767, reg. 5; SI 2001/1004, reg. 60
Reg. 40	Voluntary Class 2 contributions not paid within permitted period	SI 2001/1004, reg. 61
Reg. 41	Treatment for the purpose of any contributory benefit of contributions under the Act paid late through ignorance or error	SI 2001/769, reg. 6
Reg. 41A	Treatment for the purpose of any contributory benefit of contributions paid under regulation 54	SI 2001/1004, reg. 7
Reg. 42	Treatment for the purpose of any contributory benefit of contributions paid under an arrangement	SI 2001/769, reg. 8
Reg. 43	Payment of contributions after death of contributor	SI 2001/1004, reg. 62
Reg. 43A	Class 2 and 3 contributions paid after 5 April 1985 in respect of a period before 6 April 1983	Spent
Reg. 43B	Class 2 contributions paid late in accordance with a payment undertaking	SI 2001/1004, reg. 63
Reg. 43C	Class 2 and Class 3 contributions paid within a month from notification of amount of arrears	SI 2001/1004, reg. 64

Social Security (Contributions) Regulations 1979

Former provision		Destination
Reg. 43D	Class 2 and Class 3 contributions paid late through error or ignorance	SI 2001/1004, reg. 65
	Part V – Collection of contributions (other than Class 4 contributions) and related matters	
Reg. 44	Application and allocation of National Insurance number	SI 2001/769, reg. 9
Reg. 45	Notification of National Insurance numbers to secondary contributors	SI 2001/1004, reg. 66
Reg. 46	Collection and recovery of earnings-related contributions, Class 1A contributions and Class 1B contributions	SI 2001/1004, reg. 67
Reg. 46A	Other methods of collection and recovery of earnings-related contributions	SI 2001/1004, reg. 68
Reg. 46B	Transfer of liability from secondary contributor to employed earner: share option gains	SI 2001/1004, reg. 69
Reg. 47	Payment of Class 1A contributions	SI 2001/1004, reg. 70
Reg. 47A	Due date for payment of a Class 1A contribution	SI 2001/1004, reg. 71
Reg. 47B	Provisions relating to a Class 1A contribution due on succession to business	SI 2001/1004, reg. 72
Reg. 47C	Provisions relating to a Class 1A contribution due on cessation of business	SI 2001/1004, reg. 73
Reg. 47D	Employer failing to pay a Class 1A contribution	SI 2001/1004, reg. 74
Reg. 47E	Specified amount of a Class 1A contribution	SI 2001/1004, reg. 75
Reg. 47F	Interest on an overdue Class 1A contribution	SI 2001/1004, reg. 76
Reg. 47G	Payment of interest on a repaid Class 1A contribution	SI 2001/1004, reg. 77
Reg. 47H	Repayment of interest on a Class 1A contribution	SI 2001/1004, reg. 78
Reg. 47I	Remission of interest on a Class 1A contribution	SI 2001/1004, reg. 79
Reg. 47J	Return by employer	SI 2001/1004, reg. 80
Reg. 47K	Penalties for failure to make a return and incorrect returns	SI 2001/1004, reg. 81
Reg. 47L	Application of the Management Act to penalties for failure to make a return and incorrect returns	SI 2001/1004, reg. 82
Reg. 47M	Set-off of Class 1A contributions falling to be repaid against earnings-related contributions	SI 2001/1004, reg. 83
Reg. 48	Special provisions relating to primary Class 1 contributions	SI 2001/1004, reg. 84
Reg. 49	Exception in relation to earnings to which regulation 48 applies	SI 2001/1004, reg. 85
Reg. 50	Special provisions relating to culpable contributors and to secondary contributors or, as the case may be, employers exempt by treaty etc. from enforcement of the Act or from liability under it	SI 2001/1004, reg. 86
Reg. 53A	Notification of commencement or cessation of payment of Class 2 or Class 3 contributions	SI 2001/1004, reg. 87
Reg. 53B	Notification of change of address	SI 2001/1004, reg. 88
Reg. 54	Method of, and time for, payment of Class 1 and Class 3 contributions etc.	SI 2001/1004, reg. 89

Social Security (Contributions) Regulations 1979

Former provision		**Destination**
Reg. 54A	Arrangements approved by the Inland Revenue for method of, and time for, payment of Class 2 and Class 3 contributions	SI 2001/1004, reg. 90
Reg. 55	Deduction of contributions from pensions etc. Prescribed enactment and instruments under which payable	SI 2001/769, reg. 10
Reg. 56	Contribution cars not to be assigned, defaced etc.	Spent
	Part VII – Class 4 contributions	
Reg. 58	Exception from Class 4 liability of persons over pensionable age and person not resident in the United Kingdom	SI 2001/1004, reg. 91
Reg. 59	Exception of divers and diving supervisors from liability for Class 4 contributions	SI 2001/1004, reg. 92
Reg. 60	Exception of person under the age of 16 from liability for Class 4 contributions	SI 2001/1004, reg. 93
Reg. 61	Exception from Class 4 liability by reference to Class 1 contributions paid on earnings chargeable to income tax under Schedule D	SI 2001/1004, reg. 94
Reg. 62	Deferment of Class 4 liability where such liability is in doubt	SI 2001/1004, reg. 95
Reg. 63	Application for deferment of Class 4 liability	SI 2001/1004, reg. 96
Reg. 64	General conditions for application for, and issue of, certificates of exception and deferment	SI 2001/1004, reg. 97
Reg. 65	Revocation of certificates of exception and deferment	SI 2001/1004, reg. 98
Reg. 66	Calculation of liability for, and recovery of, Class 4 contributions after issue of certificate of deferment	SI 2001/1004, reg. 99
Reg. 67	Annual maximum of Class 4 contributions due under section 9(1) of the Act [SSCBA 1992, s. 15] . . .	SI 2001/1004, reg. 100
Reg. 68	Disposal of Class 4 contributions under section 9(1) of the Act [SSCBA 1992, s. 15] which are not due	SI 2001/1004, reg. 101
Reg. 69	Repayment of Class 4 contributions under section 9(1) of the Act [SSCBA s. 15] which are not due	SI 2001/1004, reg. 103
Reg. 71	Class 4 liability of earners treated as self-employed who, but for such treatment, would be employed earners	SI 2001/1004, reg. 103
Reg. 72	Notification of National Insurance number and recording of category letter on deduction card	SI 2001/1004, reg. 104
Reg. 73	Calculation of earnings for the purposes of special Class 4 contributions	SI 2001/1004, reg. 105
Reg. 74	Notification and payment of special Class 4 contributions due	SI 2001/1004, reg. 106
Reg. 75	Recovery of deferred Class 4 and special Class 4 contributions after appeal, claim or further assessment under the income tax acts after the raising of a Secretary of State's question	SI 2001/1004, reg. 75
Reg. 76	Annual maximum of special Class 4 contributions	SI 2001/1004, reg. 76
Reg. 77	Disposal of special Class 4 contributions paid in error	SI 2001/1004, reg. 109

Social Security (Contributions) Regulations 1979

Former provision		Destination
Reg. 78	Return of special Class 4 contributions paid in excess or error	SI 2001/1004, reg. 110
Reg. 80	Service of notice by post	Spent
	Pt. VIII – Special classes of earner	
	Case A – Airmen	
Reg. 81	Interpretation	SI 2001/1004, reg. 111
Reg. 82	Modification of employed earner's employment	SI 2001/1004, reg. 112
Reg. 83	Application of the Act and regulations	SI 2001/1004, reg. 113
Reg. 84	Special transitional provisions	Spent
	Case B – Continental Shelf	
Reg. 85	Application to the employment in connection with Continental Shelf of Part I of the Act and so much of Part IV thereof as relates to contributions	SI 2001/1004, reg. 114
	Case C – Mariners	
Reg. 86	Interpretation	SI 2001/1004, reg. 115
Reg. 87	Conditions of domicile or residence	SI 2001/1004, reg. 117
Reg. 88	Modification of employed earner's employment	SI 2001/1004, reg. 118
Reg. 89	Modification of section 4 (6E) of the Act [SSCBA 1992, s. 9]	SI 2001/1004, reg. 119
Reg. 90	Earnings periods for mariners and apportionment of earnings	SI 2001/1004, reg. 120
Reg. 91	Calculation of earnings-related contributions for mariners	SI 2001/1004, reg. 121
Reg. 93	Prescribed secondary contributors	SI 2001/1004, reg. 122
Reg. 94	Payments to be disregarded	SI 2001/1004, reg. 123
Reg. 96	Application of the Act and Regulations	SI 2001/1004, reg. 124
Reg. 98	Modification in relation to share fishermen of Part I of the Act and so much of Part IV thereof as relates to contributions	SI 2001/1004, reg. 125
	Case D – Married women and widows	
Reg. 99	Interpretation	SI 2001/1004, reg. 126
Reg. 100	Elections by married women and widows	SI 2001/1004, reg. 127
Reg. 101	Duration of effect of election	SI 2001/1004, reg. 128
Reg. 102	Continuation of elections under the former regulation 91	SI 2001/1004, reg. 129
Reg. 103	Continuation of elections on widowhood	SI 2001/1004, reg. 130
Reg. 104	Reduced rate	SI 2001/1004, reg. 131
Reg. 105	Class 3 contributions	SI 2001/1004, reg. 132
Reg. 106	Certificates of election	SI 2001/1004, reg. 133
Reg. 107	Special transitional provisions consequent upon passing of Pensions Act	SI 2001/1004, reg. 134
Reg. 108	Deemed election for married women and widows excepted from contribution liability under former principal act	SI 2001/1004, reg. 135
Reg. 109	Special transitional provisions regarding deemed elections	SI 2001/1004, reg. 136
Reg. 110	Application of regulations 99 to 107 to elections and revocation of elections deemed made under regulations 108 and 109	SI 2001/1004, reg. 137
Reg. 111	Savings	SI 2001/1004, reg. 138
Reg. 112	Modifications of the Act	SI 2001/1004, reg. 139

Social Security (Contributions) Regulations 1979

Former provision		Destination
	Case E – Members of the Forces	
Reg. 113	Establishments and organisations of which Her Majesty's Forces are taken to consist	SI 2001/1004, reg. 140
Reg. 114	Treatment of serving members of the Forces as present in Great Britain	SI 2001/1004, reg. 141
Reg. 116	Treatment of contributions paid after due date	SI 2001/1004, reg. 142
Reg. 117	Special provisions concerning earnings-related contributions	SI 2001/1004, reg. 143
Reg. 118	Application of Act and Regulations	SI 2001/1004, reg. 144
	Case F – Residence and persons abroad	
Reg. 119	Conditions as to residence and presence in Great Britain	SI 2001/1004, reg. 145
Reg. 120	Payment on contributions for periods abroad	SI 2001/1004, reg. 146
Reg. 121	Class 2 and Class 3 contributions for periods abroad	SI 2001/1004, reg. 147
Reg. 122	Conditions of payment of Class 2 or Class 3 contributions for periods abroad	SI 2001/1004, reg. 148
Reg. 123	Persons outside Great Britain on the appointed day	Spent
	Case G – Volunteer Development Workers	
Reg. 123A	Interpretation	SI 2001/1004, reg. 149
Reg. 123B	Certain volunteer development workers to be self-employed earners	SI 2001/1004, reg. 150
Reg. 123C	Option to pay Class 2 contributions	SI 2001/1004, reg. 151
Reg. 123D	Special provision as to residence, rate, annual maximum and method of payment	SI 2001/1004, reg. 152
Reg. 123E	Late paid contributions	SI 2001/1004, reg. 153
Reg. 123F	Modifications of the Act and these regulations	SI 2001/1004, reg. 154
	Part IX – General (contributions) Transitional Provisions	
Reg. 124–130	Transitional provisions	Spent
	Part X – Miscellaneous provisions	
Reg. 131	Treatment of contribution week falling into 2 income tax years	SI 2001/1004, reg. 155
Reg. 132	Breach of regulations	Spent
Reg. 135	Northern Ireland	Spent
Reg. 136	Revocations and general savings	Spent
	Schedules	

Schedule 1 – Containing the provisions of the Income Tax (Employments) Regulations 1973 [Income Tax (Employments) Regulations 1993] as they apply to earnings related contributions, Class 1A contributions and Class 1B contributions under the Social Security Act 1975 [SSCBA 1992]

Former provision		Destination
	Part I – General	
Sch. 1		
Sch. 1, reg. 2	Interpretation	SI 2001/1004, Sch. 4, para. 1
Sch. 1, reg. 2A	Multiple employers	SI 2001/1004, Sch. 4, para. 2
Sch. 1, reg. 3	Intermediate employers	SI 2001/1004, Sch. 4, para. 3
Sch. 1, reg. 3A	Employer's earnings-related contributions	SI 2001/1004, Sch. 4, para. 4
Sch. 1, reg. 4A	Inspectors and collectors	SI 2001/1004, Sch. 4, para. 5
Sch. 1, reg. 5	Service by post	
Sch. 1, reg. 5A	Offences and penalties in relation to statutory sick pay	Spent
	Part II and III – Deduction of Earnings-Related Contributions	Spent

Social Security (Contributions) Regulations 1979

Former provision		Destination
Sch. 1, reg. 6	Deduction of earnings-related contributions	SI 2001/1004, Sch. 4, para. 6
Sch. 1, reg. 13	Calculation of deductions	SI 2001/1004, Sch. 4, para. 7
Sch. 1, reg. 13ZA	Records where liability transferred from secondary contributor to employed earner: share option gains	SI 2001/1004, Sch. 4, para. 8
	Part IV – Payment and recovery of earnings-related contributions, Class 1A contributions and Class 1B contributions etc.	
Sch. 1, reg. 25	Certificate of contributions paid	SI 2001/1004, Sch. 4, para. 9
Sch. 1, reg. 26	Payment of earnings-related contributions monthly by employer	SI 2001/1004, Sch. 4, para. 10
Sch. 1, reg. 26A	Payment of earnings-related contributions quarterly by employer	SI 2001/1004, Sch. 4, para. 11
Sch. 1, reg. 26B	Payment of earnings-related contributions by employer – further provisions	SI 2001/1004, Sch. 4, para. 12
Sch. 1, reg. 26C	Payment of Class 1B contributions	SI 2001/1004, Sch. 4, para. 13
Sch. 1, reg. 27	Employer failing to pay earnings-related contributions	SI 2001/1004, Sch. 4, para. 14
Sch. 1, reg. 27A	Specified amount of earnings-related contributions payable by the employer	SI 2001/1004, Sch. 4, para. 15
Sch. 1, reg. 28	Recovery of earnings-related contributions or Class 1B contributions	SI 2001/1004, Sch. 4, para. 16
Sch. 1, reg. 28A	Interest on overdue earnings-related contributions or Class 1B contributions	SI 2001/1004, Sch. 4, para. 17
Sch. 1, reg. 28B	Payment of interest on repaid earnings-related contributions or Class 1B contributions	SI 2001/1004, Sch. 4, para. 18
Sch. 1, reg. 28C	Repayment of interest	SI 2001/1004, Sch. 4, para. 19
Sch. 1, reg. 28D	Remission of interest for official error	SI 2001/1004, Sch. 4, para. 20
Sch. 1, reg. 28E	Application of regulations 26, 26B, 28, 28A, 28B, 28C and 28D where liability transferred from secondary contributor to employed earner: share option gains	SI 2001/1004, Sch. 4, para. 21
Sch. 1, reg. 30	Return by employer at end of year	SI 2001/1004, Sch. 4, para. 22
Sch. 1, reg. 30ZA	Additional return by employer at end of year where liability transferred to employed earner: share option gains	SI 2001/1004, Sch. 4, para. 23
Sch. 1, reg. 30A	Special return by employer at end of voyage period	SI 2001/1004, Sch. 4, para. 24
Sch. 1, reg. 30B	Return by employer of recovery under the statutory sick pay percentage threshold order	SI 2001/1004, Sch. 4, para. 25
Sch. 1, reg. 32	Inspection of employer's records	SI 2001/1004, Sch. 4, para. 26
Sch. 1, reg. 33	Death of employer	SI 2001/1004, Sch. 4, para. 27
Sch. 1, reg. 34	Succession to a business etc.	SI 2001/1004, Sch. 4, para. 28
Sch. 1, reg. 34A	Payments by cheque	SI 2001/1004, Sch. 4, para. 29
	Part VII – Assessment and direct collection	
Sch. 1, reg. 50, 51	Provision for direct payment	SI 2001/1004, Sch. 4, para. 30
	Schedule 1ZA – Elections about share option gains	
Sch. 1ZA, para. 1	. . . .	SI 2001/1004, Sch. 5, para. 1
Sch. 1ZA, para. 2	. . . .	SI 2001/1004, Sch. 5, para. 2
Sch. 1ZA, para. 3	. . . .	SI 2001/1004, Sch. 5, para. 3
Sch. 1ZA, para. 4	. . . .	Spent

Social Security (Contributions) Regulations 1979

Former provision		Destination
	Schedule 1ZB – Calculation of earnings for the purposes of earnings-related contributions in particular cases	
Sch. 1ZB, para. 1	Calculation of earnings	SI 2001/1004, Sch. 2, para. 1
Sch. 1ZB, para. 2	Calculation of earnings in respect of beneficial interest in assets within Part IV of Schedule 1ZC	SI 2001/1004, Sch. 2, para. 2
Sch. 1ZB, para. 3	Valuation of beneficial interest in units in a unit trust scheme	SI 2001/1004, Sch. 2, para. 3
Sch. 1ZB, para. 4	Conferment of a beneficial interest in an option to acquire an asset falling within Part IV of Schedule 1ZC	SI 2001/1004, Sch. 2, para. 4
Sch. 1ZB, para. 5	Readily convertible assets	SI 2001/1004, Sch. 2, para. 5
Sch. 1ZB, para. 6	Assets not readily convertible: beneficial interest in alcoholic liquor on which duty has not been paid, gemstones and certain vouchers and non-cash vouchers	SI 2001/1004, Sch. 2, para. 6
Sch. 1ZB, para. 7	Conditional interest in shares	SI 2001/1004, Sch. 2, para. 7
Sch. 1ZB, para. 8	Convertible interest in shares	SI 2001/1004, Sch. 2, para. 8
Sch. 1ZB, para. 9	Assignment or release of right to acquire shares where neither right nor shares readily convertible	SI 2001/1004, Sch. 2, para. 9
Sch. 1ZB, para. 10	Assignment or release of a right acquired as director or employee before 6 April 1999, to acquire shares where neither right nor shares readily convertible	SI 2001/1004, Sch. 2, para. 10
Sch. 1ZB, para. 11	Exercise of right to acquire shares gained as director or employee before 6 April 1999	SI 2001/1004, Sch. 2, para. 11
Sch. 1ZB, para. 12	Interpretation of paragraphs 9, 10 and 11	SI 2001/1004, Sch. 2, para. 12
Sch. 1ZB, para. 13	Apportionment of a payment from a retirement benefits scheme for benefit of two or more people	SI 2001/1004, Sch. 2, para. 13
Sch. 1ZB, para. 14	Valuation of non-cash assets	SI 2001/1004, Sch. 2, para. 14
Sch. 1ZB, para. 15	Apportionment of earnings comprised in cash or non-cash voucher provided for benefit of two or more employed earners	SI 2001/1004, Sch. 2, para. 15
	Schedule 1ZC – Payments to be disregarded in the calculation of earnings for the purposes of earnings-related contributions	
	Part 1 – Introductory	
Sch. 1ZC, Pt. I, para. 1	Introduction	SI 2001/1004, Sch. 3, Pt. I, para. 1
Sch. 1ZC, Pt. I, para. 2	Interpretation	SI 2001/1004, Sch. 3, Pt. I, para. 2
	Part II – Payments in kind	
Sch. 1ZC, Pt. II, para. 1	Certain payments in kind to be disregarded	SI 2001/1004, Sch. 3, Pt. II, para. 1
Sch. 1ZC, Pt. II, para. 2	Payments by way of assets not to be disregarded	SI 2001/1004, Sch. 3, Pt. II, para. 2
	Part III – Payments by way of readily convertible assets not disregarded as payments in kind	
Sch. 1ZC, Pt. III, para. 1		SI 2001/1004, Sch. 3, Pt. III, para. 1
Sch. 1ZC, Pt. III, para. 2		SI 2001/1004, Sch. 3, Pt. III, para. 2
Sch. 1ZC, Pt. III, para. 3		SI 2001/1004, Sch. 3, Pt. III, para. 3

Social Security (Contributions) Regulations 1979

Former provision		Destination
	Part IV – Payments by way of specific assets not disregarded as payments in kind	
Sch. 1ZC, Pt. IV, para. 1	Stocks and shares	SI 2001/1004, Sch. 3, Pt. IV, para. 1
Sch. 1ZC, Pt. IV, para. 2	Certain debentures and other securities for loans	SI 2001/1004, Sch. 3, Pt. IV, para. 2
Sch. 1ZC, Pt. IV, para. 3	Loan stock of public and local authorities	SI 2001/1004, Sch. 3, Pt. IV, para. 3
Sch. 1ZC, Pt. IV, para. 4	Warrants etc. for shares, loan stock and debentures	SI 2001/1004, Sch. 3, Pt. IV, para. 4
Sch. 1ZC, Pt. IV, para. 5	Units in collective investment schemes	SI 2001/1004, Sch. 3, Pt. IV, para. 5
Sch. 1ZC, Pt. IV, para. 6	Options to acquire assets, currency, precious metals or other options	SI 2001/1004, Sch. 3, Pt. IV, para. 6
Sch. 1ZC, Pt. IV, para. 7	Contracts for futures	SI 2001/1004, Sch. 3, Pt. IV, para. 7
Sch. 1ZC, Pt. IV, para. 8	Contract for differences or to secure profit by references to movement of indices	SI 2001/1004, Sch. 3, Pt. IV, para. 8
Sch. 1ZC, Pt. IV, para. 9	Alcoholic liquor on which duty has not been paid	SI 2001/1004, Sch. 3, Pt. IV, para. 9
Sch. 1ZC, Pt. IV, para. 10	Gemstones	SI 2001/1004, Sch. 3, Pt. IV, para. 10
Sch. 1ZC, Pt. IV, para. 11	Certificates etc. conferring rights in respect of assets	SI 2001/1004, Sch. 3, Pt. IV, para. 11
Sch. 1ZC, Pt. IV, para. 12	Vouchers	SI 2001/1004, Sch. 3, Pt. IV, para. 12
	Part V – Certain non-cash vouchers to be disregarded as payments in kind	
Sch. 1ZC, Pt. V, para. 1		SI 2001/1004, Sch. 3, Pt. V, para. 1
Sch. 1ZC, Pt. V, para. 2		SI 2001/1004, Sch. 3, Pt. V, para. 2
Sch. 1ZC, Pt. V, para. 3		SI 2001/1004, Sch. 3, Pt. V, para. 3
Sch. 1ZC, Pt. V, para. 4		SI 2001/1004, Sch. 3, Pt. V, para. 4
Sch. 1ZC, Pt. V, para. 5		SI 2001/1004, Sch. 3, Pt. V, para. 5
Sch. 1ZC, Pt. V, para. 6		SI 2001/1004, Sch. 3, Pt. V, para. 6
Sch. 1ZC, Pt. V, para. 7		SI 2001/1004, Sch. 3, Pt. V, para. 7
Sch. 1ZC, Pt. V, para. 8		SI 2001/1004, Sch. 3, Pt. V, para. 8
	Part VI – Pensions and pension contributions	
Sch. 1ZC, Pt. VI, para. 1	Pension payments and pension contributions to be disregarded	SI 2001/1004, Sch. 3, Pt. VI, para. 1
Sch. 1ZC, Pt. VI, para. 2	Personal pension contributions by employers	SI 2001/1004, Sch. 3, Pt. VI, para. 2
Sch. 1ZC, Pt. VI, para. 3	Approved schemes, relevant statutory schemes, pilots' benefit funds and schemes established by overseas governments	SI 2001/1004, Sch. 3, Pt. VI, para. 3
Sch. 1ZC, Pt. VI, para. 4	Funded unapproved retirement benefits schemes	SI 2001/1004, Sch. 3, Pt. VI, para. 4
Sch. 1ZC, Pt. VI, para. 5	Payments to pension previously taken into account in calculating earnings	SI 2001/1004, Sch. 3, Pt. VI, para. 5

Social Security (Contributions) Regulations 1979

Former provision		Destination
Sch. 1ZC, Pt. VI, para. 6	Payments in good faith to scheme solely for providing approved benefits	SI 2001/1004, Sch. 3, Pt. VI, para. 6
Sch. 1ZC, Pt. VI, para. 7	Pensions exempt from UK taxation under double agreements	SI 2001/1004, Sch. 3, Pt. VI, para. 7
	Part VII – Payments in respect of training and similar courses	
Sch. 1ZC, Pt. VII, para. 1	Payments in respect of training and similar expenses disregarded	SI 2001/1004, Sch. 3, Pt. VII, para. 1
Sch. 1ZC, Pt. VII, para. 2	Work-related training	SI 2001/1004, Sch. 3, Pt. VII, para. 2
Sch. 1ZC, Pt. VII, para. 3	Education and training funded by employers	SI 2001/1004, Sch. 3, Pt. VII, para. 3
Sch. 1ZC, Pt. VII, para. 4	New Deal 50plus: employment grant and training credit	SI 2001/1004, Sch. 3, Pt. VII, para. 4
Sch. 1ZC, Pt. VII, para. 5	Retraining courses for claimants for jobseekers allowance	SI 2001/1004, Sch. 3, Pt. VII, para. 5
Sch. 1ZC, Pt. VII, para. 6	Payments to jobmatch participants	SI 2001/1004, Sch. 3, Pt. VII, para. 6
Sch. 1ZC, Pt. VII, para. 7	Vouchers provided to jobmatch participants	SI 2001/1004, Sch. 3, Pt. VII, para. 7
	Part VIII – Travelling, relocation and other expenses and allowances of the employment	
Sch. 1ZC, Pt. VIII, para. 1	Travelling, relocation and incidental expenses disregarded	SI 2001/1004, Sch. 3, Pt. VIII, para. 1
Sch. 1ZC, Pt. VIII, para. 2	Relocation expenses	SI 2001/1004, Sch. 3, Pt. VIII, para. 2
Sch. 1ZC, Pt. VIII, para. 3	Travelling expenses – general	SI 2001/1004, Sch. 3, Pt. VIII, para. 3
Sch. 1ZC, Pt. VIII, para. 4	Travel and foreign travel expenses of overseas employment	SI 2001/1004, Sch. 3, Pt. VIII, para. 4
Sch. 1ZC, Pt. VIII, para. 5	Travel expenses of employees not domiciled in the United Kingdom	SI 2001/1004, Sch. 3, Pt. VIII, para. 5
Sch. 1ZC, Pt. VIII, para. 6	Travelling expenses of workers on offshore gas and oil rigs	SI 2001/1004, Sch. 3, Pt. VIII, para. 6
Sch. 1ZC, Pt. VIII, para. 7	Incidental expenses in connection with cars provided for private use	SI 2001/1004, Sch. 3, Pt. VIII, para. 7
Sch. 1ZC, Pt. VIII, para. 8	Car parking facilities	SI 2001/1004, Sch. 3, Pt. VIII, para. 8
Sch. 1ZC, Pt. VIII, para. 9	Specific and distinct payments of, or towards, expenses actually incurred	SI 2001/1004, Sch. 3, Pt. VIII, para. 9
Sch. 1ZC, Pt. VIII, para. 10	Council tax on accommodation provided for employee's use	SI 2001/1004, Sch. 3, Pt. VIII, para. 10
Sch. 1ZC, Pt. VIII, para. 11	Foreign service allowance	SI 2001/1004, Sch. 3, Pt. VIII, para. 12
Sch. 1ZC, Pt. VIII, para. 12	Commonwealth War Graves Commission and British Council: extra cost of living allowance	SI 2001/1004, Sch. 3, Pt. VIII, para. 13
Sch. 1ZC, Pt. VIII, para. 13	Overseas medical treatment	SI 2001/1004, Sch. 3, Pt. VIII, para. 14
	Part IX – Share incentives	
Sch. 1ZC, Pt. IX, para. 1	Certain payments by way of shares, interests in shares and gains arising from them disregarded	SI 2001/1004, Sch. 3, Pt. IX, para. 1
Sch. 1ZC, Pt. IX, para. 2	Shares in secondary contributor or associated body	SI 2001/1004, Sch. 3, Pt. IX, para. 2

Social Security (Contributions) Regulations 1979

Former provision		Destination
Sch. 1ZC, Pt. IX, para. 3	Rights to acquire shares	SI 2001/1004, Sch. 3, Pt. IX, para. 3
Sch. 1ZC, Pt. IX, para. 4	Enterprise management incentives	SI 2001/1004, Sch. 3, Pt. IX, para. 4
Sch. 1ZC, Pt. IX, para. 5	Priority share allocations	SI 2001/1004, Sch. 3, Pt. IX, para. 5
Sch. 1ZC, Pt. IX, para. 6	Partnership share allocations	SI 2001/1004, Sch. 3, Pt. IX, para. 6
Sch. 1ZC, Pt. IX, para. 7	Shares under employee share ownership plans	SI 2001/1004, Sch. 3, Pt. IX, para. 7
Sch. 1ZC, Pt. IX, para. 8	Shares under approved profit sharing schemes	SI 2001/1004, Sch. 3, Pt. IX, para. 8
Sch. 1ZC, Pt. IX, para. 9	Conditional interest in shares	SI 2001/1004, Sch. 3, Pt. IX, para. 9
Sch. 1ZC, Pt. IX, para. 10	Conditional interest in shares: gains from exercise etc. of share options	SI 2001/1004, Sch. 3, Pt. IX, para. 10
Sch. 1ZC, Pt. IX, para. 11	Convertible shares	SI 2001/1004, Sch. 3, Pt. IX, para. 11
Sch. 1ZC, Pt. IX, para. 12	Convertible shares; gains from the exercise etc. of share options	SI 2001/1004, Sch. 3, Pt. IX, para. 12
Sch. 1ZC, Pt. IX, para. 13	Share option gains by directors and employees	SI 2001/1004, Sch. 3, Pt. IX, para. 13
Sch. 1ZC, Pt. IX, para. 14	Shares acquired under options granted before 9 April 1998	SI 2001/1004, Sch. 3, Pt. IX, para. 14
Sch. 1ZC, Pt. IX, para. 15	Assignment or release of option	SI 2001/1004, Sch. 3, Pt. IX, para. 15
Sch. 1ZC, Pt. IX, para. 16	Exercise, assignment or release of options acquired before 6 April 1999	SI 2001/1004, Sch. 3, Pt. IX, para. 16
	Part X – Miscellaneous and supplemental	
Sch. 1ZC, Pt. X, para. 1	Other miscellaneous payments to be disregarded	SI 2001/1004, Sch. 3, Pt. X, para. 1
Sch. 1ZC, Pt. X, para. 2	Payments on account of sums already included in the calculation of earnings	SI 2001/1004, Sch. 3, Pt. X, para. 2
Sch. 1ZC, Pt. X, para. 3	Payments discharging liability for secondary Class 1 contributions following election under paragraph 3B of Schedule 1 to the Contributions and Benefits Act	SI 2001/1004, Sch. 3, Pt. X, para. 3
Sch. 1ZC, Pt. X, para. 4	Payments by way of incidental expenses	SI 2001/1004, Sch. 3, Pt. X, para. 4
Sch. 1ZC, Pt. X, para. 5	Gratuities and offerings	SI 2001/1004, Sch. 3, Pt. X, para. 5
Sch. 1ZC, Pt. X, para. 6	Redundancy payments	SI 2001/1004, Sch. 3, Pt. X, para. 6
Sch. 1ZC, Pt. X, para. 7	Sickness payments attributable to contributions made by employed earner	SI 2001/1004, Sch. 3, Pt. X, para. 7
Sch. 1ZC, Pt. X, para. 8	Expenses and other payments not charged to tax under extra-statutory concessions	SI 2001/1004, Sch. 3, Pt. X, para. 8
Sch. 1ZC, Pt. X, para. 9	VAT on the supply of goods and services by employed earner	SI 2001/1004, Sch. 3, Pt. X, para. 9
Sch. 1ZC, Pt. X, para. 10	Employees' indemnity insurance	SI 2001/1004, Sch. 3, Pt. X, para. 10
Sch. 1ZC, Pt. X, para. 11	Fees and subscriptions to professional bodies, learned societies, etc.	SI 2001/1004, Sch. 3, Pt. X, para. 11
Sch. 1ZC, Pt. X, para. 12	Holiday pay	SI 2001/1004, Sch. 3, Pt. X, para. 12

Social Security (Contributions) Regulations 1979

Former provision		Destination
Sch. 1ZC, Pt. X, para. 13	Payments to ministers of religion	SI 2001/1004, Sch. 3, Pt. X, para. 13
Sch. 1ZC, Pt. X, para. 14	Payments in lieu of coal	SI 2001/1004, Sch. 3, Pt. X, para. 14
	Schedule 2	
	Spent	
	Schedule 3	
Sch. 3, Pt. I	Part 1 – Prescribed Establishments and Organisations for purposes of Section 128(30) of the Act [SSCBA 1992, s. 116]	SI 2001/1004, Sch. 6, Pt. I
Sch. 3, Pt. II	Part II – Establishments and organisations of which Her Majesty's Forces shall not consist	SI 2001/1004, Sch. 6, Pt. II

INDEX TO NATIONAL INSURANCE CONTRIBUTIONS

For a list of abbreviations used in this Index see p. xi.

For a list of abbreviations used in this Index see p. xi.

For a list of abbreviations used in this Index see p. xi.

For a list of abbreviations used in this Index see p. xi.

NIC Indexes

For a list of abbreviations used in this Index see p. xi.

For a list of abbreviations used in this Index see p. xi.

For a list of abbreviations used in this Index see p. xi.

For a list of abbreviations used in this Index see p. xi.

NIC Indexes

For a list of abbreviations used in this Index see p. xi.

NIC Indexes

For a list of abbreviations used in this Index see p. xi.

For a list of abbreviations used in this Index see p. xi.

For a list of abbreviations used in this Index see p. xi.

For a list of abbreviations used in this Index see p. xi.

For a list of abbreviations used in this Index see p. xi.

For a list of abbreviations used in this Index see p. xi.

For a list of abbreviations used in this Index see p. xi.

For a list of abbreviations used in this Index see p. xi.

For a list of abbreviations used in this Index see p. xi.

For a list of abbreviations used in this Index see p. xi.

NIC Indexes

For a list of abbreviations used in this Index see p. xi.

NATIONAL INSURANCE CONTRIBUTIONS LIST OF DEFINITIONS AND MEANINGS

For a list of abbreviations used in this Index see p. xi.

NIC Indexes

TAX CREDITS

Table of Contents

TAX CREDITS STATUTES

Table of Contents

TAXES MANAGEMENT ACT 1970

(1970 Chapter 9)

[12th March 1970]

PART V – APPEALS AND OTHER PROCEEDINGS

Notes – The text of s. 54 below is shown as modified by SI 2002/2926, reg. 3.

PROCEEDINGS BEFORE COMMISSIONERS

54 Settling of appeals by agreement

54(1) Subject to the provisions of this section, where a person gives notice of appeal and, before the appeal is determined by the appeal tribunal or the First-tier Tribunal, the officer of the Board and the appellant come to an agreement, whether in writing or otherwise, that the decision under appeal should be treated as upheld without variation, or as varied in a particular manner or as discharged or cancelled, the like consequences shall ensue for all purposes as would have ensued if, at the time when the agreement was come to, the appeal tribunal or the First-tier Tribunal had determined the appeal and had upheld the decision without variation, had varied it in that manner or had discharged or cancelled it, as the case may be.

54(2) Subsection (1) of this section shall not apply where, within thirty days from the date when the agreement was come to, the appellant gives notice in writing to the officer of the Board that he desires to repudiate or resile from the agreement.

54(3) Where an agreement is not in writing–

(a) the preceding provisions of this section shall not apply unless the Board give notice, in such form and manner as they consider appropriate, to the appellant of the terms agreed between the officer of the Board and the appellant; and

(b) the references in those preceding provisions to the time when the agreement was come to shall be construed as references to the date of that notice.

54(4) Where–

(a) a person who has given a notice of appeal notifies the officer of the Board, whether orally or in writing, that he desires not to proceed with the appeal; and

(b) thirty days have elapsed since the giving of the notification without the officer of the Board giving to the appellant notice in writing indicating that he is unwilling that the appeal should be treated as withdrawn,

the preceding provisions of this section shall have effect as if, at the date of the appellant's notification, the appellant and the officer of the Board had come had come to an agreement, orally or in writing, as the case may be, that the decision under appeal should be upheld without variation.

54(5) The references in this section to an agreement being come to with an appellant and the giving of notice or notification to or by an appellant include references to an agreement being come to with, and the giving of notice or notification to or by, a person acting on behalf of the appellant in relation to the appeal.

54(6) In subsection (1) **"appeal tribunal"** means an appeal tribunal constituted in Northern Ireland, under Chapter 1 of Part 2 of the Social Security (Northern Ireland) Order 1998 (social security appeals: Northern Ireland).

FINANCE ACT 1989

(1989 Chapter 26)

[*27th July 1989*]

PART III – MISCELLANEOUS AND GENERAL

MISCELLANEOUS

182 Disclosure of information

182(1) A person who discloses any information which he holds or has held in the exercise of tax functions, tax credit functions or social security functions is guilty of an offence if it is information about any matter relevant, for the purposes of any of those functions–

(a) to tax or duty in the case of any identifiable person,

(aa) to a tax credit in respect of any identifiable person,

(ab) to a child trust fund of any identifiable person,

(b) to contributions payable by or in respect of any identifiable person, or

(c) to statutory sick pay, statutory maternity pay, statutory paternity pay, statutory adoption pay or statutory shared parental pay in respect of any identifiable person.

182(2) In this section **"tax functions"** means functions relating to tax or duty–

(a) of the Commissioners, the Board and their officers,

(b) of any person carrying out the administrative work of the First-tier Tribunal or Upper Tribunal, and

(c) of any other person providing, or employed in the provision of, services to any person mentioned in paragraph (a) or (b) above.

182(2ZA) In this section **"tax credit functions"** means the functions relating to tax credits–

(a) of the Board,

(b) of any person carrying out the administrative work of the First-tier Tribunal or Upper Tribunal, and

(c) of any other person providing, or employed in the provision of, services to the Board or to any person mentioned in paragraph (b) above.

182(2ZB) In this section **"child trust fund functions"** means the functions relating to child trust funds–

(a) of the Board and their officers,

(b) of any person carrying out the administrative work of the First-tier Tribunal or an appeal tribunal constituted under Chapter 1 of Part 2 of the Social Security (Northern Ireland) Order 1998, or

(c) of any person providing, or employed in the provision of, services to the Board or any person mentioned in paragraph (b) above.

182(2A) In this section **"social security functions"** means–

(a) the functions relating to contributions, child benefit, guardian's allowance, statutory sick pay, statutory maternity pay, statutory paternity pay, statutory adoption pay or statutory shared parental pay–

(i) of the Board and their officers,

(ii) of any person carrying out the administrative work of the First-tier Tribunal or Upper Tribunal, and

(iii) of any other person providing, or employed in the provision of, services to any person mentioned in sub-paragraph (i) or (ii) above, and

(b) the functions under Part III of the Pension Schemes Act 1993 or Part III of the Pension Schemes (Northern Ireland) Act 1993 of the Board and their officers and any other person providing, or employed in the provision of, services to the Board or their officers.

182(3) [Omitted by SI 2009/56, art. 3 and Sch. 1, para. 167(e).]

182(4) A person who discloses any information which–

(a) *he holds or has held in the* exercise of functions–

(i) of the Comptroller and Auditor General, the Comptroller and Auditor General for Northern Ireland and Auditor General, of the National Audit Office and any member or employee of that Office or any member of the staff of the National Audit Office that was established by section 3 of the National Audit Act 1983, (ia) of the Comptroller and Auditor General for Northern Ireland and any member of the staff of the Northern Ireland Audit Office,

(ii) of the Parliamentary Commissioner for Administration and his officers,

(iii) of the Auditor General for Wales and any member of his staff, or

(iiia) of the Wales Audit Office and any member or employee of that Office,

(iv) of the Public Services Ombudsman for Wales and any member of his staff, or

(b) is, or is derived from, information which was held by any person in the exercise of tax functions, tax credit functions, child trust fund functions or social security functions, and

(c) is information about any matter relevant, for the purposes of tax functions, tax credit functions, child trust fund functions or social security functions–

(i) to tax or duty in the case of any identifiable person,

(ia) to a tax credit in respect of any identifiable person,

(ib) to a child trust fund of any identifiable person,

(ii) to contributions payable by or in respect of any identifiable person, or

(iii) to child benefit, guardian's allowance, statutory sick pay, statutory maternity pay, statutory paternity pay, statutory adoption pay or statutory shared parental pay in respect of any identifiable person,

is guilty of an offence.

182(5) Subsections (1) and (4) above do not apply to any disclosure of information–

(a) with lawful authority,

(b) with the consent of any person in whose case the information is about a matter relevant to tax or duty to a tax credit or to a child trust fund or to contributions, statutory sick pay, statutory maternity pay, statutory paternity pay, statutory adoption pay or statutory shared parental pay, or

(c) which has been lawfully made available to the public before the disclosure is made.

182(6) For the purposes of this section a disclosure of any information is made with lawful authority if, and only if, it is made–

(a) by a Crown servant in accordance with his official duty,

(b) by any other person for the purposes of the function in the exercise of which he holds the information and without contravening any restriction duly imposed by the person responsible,

(c) to, or in accordance with an authorisation duly given by, the person responsible,

(d) in pursuance of any enactment or of any order of a court, or

(e) in connection with the institution of or otherwise for the purposes of any proceedings relating to any matter within the general responsibility of the Commissioners or, as the case requires, the Board,

and in this subsection **"the person responsible"** means the Commissioners, the Board, the Comptroller, the Parliamentary Commissioner, the Auditor General for Wales or the Public Services Ombudsman for Wales, as the case requires.

182(7) It is a defence for a person charged with an offence under this section to prove that at the time of the alleged offence–

(a) he believed that he had lawful authority to make the disclosure in question and had no reasonable cause to believe otherwise, or

(b) he believed that the information in question had been lawfully made available to the public before the disclosure was made and had no reasonable cause to believe otherwise.

182(8) A person guilty of an offence under this section is liable–

(a) on conviction on indictment, to imprisonment for a term not exceeding two years or a fine or both, and

(b) on summary conviction, to imprisonment for a term not exceeding six months or a fine not exceeding the statutory maximum or both.

182(9) No prosecution for an offence under this section shall be instituted in England and Wales or in Northern Ireland except–

(a) by the Commissioners or the Board, as the case requires, or

(b) by or with the consent of the Director of Public Prosecutions or, in Northern Ireland, the Director of Public Prosecutions for Northern Ireland.

182(10) In this section–

"the Board" means the Commissioners of Inland Revenue,

"child trust fund" has the same meaning as in the Child Trust Funds Act 2004,

"the Commissioners" means the Commissioners of Customs and Excise,

"contributions" means contributions under Part I of the Social Security Contributions and Benefits Act 1992 or Part I of the Social Security Contributions and Benefits (Northern Ireland) Act 1992;

"Crown servant" has the same meaning as in the Official Secrets Act 1989,

"tax credit" means a tax credit under the Tax Credits Act 2002, and

"tax or duty" means any tax or duty within the general responsibility of the Commissioners or the Board.

182(11) In this section–

(a) [omitted by the Budget Responsibility and National Audit Act 2011, s. 26 and Sch. 5, para. 14(4),]

(b) [omitted by the Budget Responsibility and National Audit Act 2011, s. 26 and Sch. 5, para. 14(4),]

(c) references to the Parliamentary Commissioner for Administration include the Health Service Commissioner for England, the Health Service Commissioner for Scotland, the Northern Ireland Parliamentary Commissioner for Administration and the Northern Ireland Commissioner for Complaints.

182(11A) In this section, references to statutory paternity pay, statutory adoption pay or statutory shared parental pay include statutory pay under Northern Ireland legislation corresponding to Part 12ZA, Part 12ZB or Part 12ZC of the Social Security Contributions and Benefits Act 1992 (c. 4).

182(12) This section shall come into force on the repeal of section 2 of the Official Secrets Act 1911.

History – In s. 182(1) the words ", child trust fund functions" inserted after "tax credit functions" and para. (ab) inserted by CTFA 2004, s. 18, with effect from 1 January 2005.

In s. 182(1), (4)(b) and (4)(c) the words ", tax credit functions" previously inserted by TCA 1999, s. 12(2)(a), (4)(a) and (4)(b) respectively, with effect from 5 October 1999 (TCA 1999, s. 20(2)), and continued by TCA 2002, s. 59 and Sch. 5, para. 11(2)(a) with effect for the purposes of TCA 2002 from 1 August 2002 by virtue of SI 2002/1727 (C. 52).

S. 182(1)(aa) substituted by TCA 2002, s. 59 and Sch. 5, para. 11(2)(b) with effect for the purposes of TCA 2002 from 1 August 2002 by virtue of SI 2002/1727 (C. 52).

Former s. 182(1)(aa) inserted by TCA 1999, s. 12(2)(b) and (4)(b) respectively, with effect from 5 October 1999 (TCA 1999, s. 20(2)).

In s. 182(1)(c), the words "statutory paternity pay," substituted for the words "ordinary statutory paternity pay, additional statutory paternity pay or" by Children and Families Act 2014, s. 126(1) and Sch. 7, para. 5(2)(a), with effect from 5 April 2015, subject to the transitional and saving provisions in SI 2014/1640, art. 16 (amendments do not have effect in relation to– (a) children whose expected week of birth ends on or before 4 April 2015; (b) children placed for adoption on or before 4 April 2015) and 17 (transitional and saving provisions applicable where Northern Ireland legislation contains provision on additional statutory paternity pay) (SI 2014/1640, art. 6 and 7).

In s. 182(1)(c), the words "or statutory shared parental pay" inserted (after the words "statutory adoption pay") by Children and Families Act 2014, s. 126(1) and Sch. 7, para. 5(2)(b), with effect from 1 December 2014 (SI 2014/1640, art. 5).

In s. 182(1)(c), the words "ordinary statutory paternity pay, additional statutory paternity pay" substituted for the words "statutory paternity pay" by the Work and Families Act 2006, s. 11 and Sch. 1, para. 2 with effect from 6 April 2010 (SI 2010/495).

In s. 182(1)(c) words ", statutory maternity pay, statutory paternity pay or statutory adoption pay" substituted by Employment Act 2002, s. 53 and Sch. 7, para. 1(2) with effect from 8 December 2002, by virtue of SI 2002/2866.

In s. 182(2A)(a), the words "statutory paternity pay," substituted for the words "ordinary statutory paternity pay, additional statutory paternity pay or" by Children and Families Act 2014, s. 126(1) and Sch. 7, para. 5(3)(a), with effect from 5 April 2015, subject to the transitional and saving provisions in SI 2014/1640, art. 16 (amendments do not have effect in relationto– (a) children whose expected week of birth ends on or before 4 April 2015; (b) children placed for adoption on or before 4 April 2015) and 17 (transitional and saving provisions applicable where Northern Ireland legislation contains provision on additional statutory paternity pay) (SI 2014/1640, art. 6 and 7).

In s. 182(2A)(a), the words "or statutory shared parental pay" inserted (after the words "statutory adoption pay") by Children and Families Act 2014, s. 126(1) and Sch. 7, para. 5(3)(b), with effect from 1 December 2014 (SI 2014/1640, art. 5).

In s. 182(2A)(a), the words "ordinary statutory paternity pay, additional statutory paternity pay" substituted for the words "statutory paternity pay" by the Work and Families Act 2006, s. 11 and Sch. 1, para. 2 with effect from 6 April 2010 (SI 2010/495).

In s. 182(2A)(a) words ", statutory maternity pay, statutory paternity pay or statutory adoption pay" substituted by Employment Act 2002, s. 53 and Sch. 7, para. 1(2) with effect from 8 December 2002, by virtue of SI 2002/2866.

In s. 182(1), the words "social security functions" were inserted, and the words from "any of those functions" to the end substituted, and s. 182(2A) inserted, by SSCTFA 1999, s. 6 and Sch. 6, para. 9(2), (3), with effect from 1 April 1999 by virtue of SI 1999/527 (C. 11), art. 2(b) and Sch. 2.

In s. 182(2)(b) the words "the First-tier Tribunal or Upper Tribunal" substituted by SI 2009/56, art. 3 and Sch. 1, para. 167(a), with effect from 1 April 2009, subject to transitional and saving provisions in SI 2009/56, Sch. 3.

In s. 182(2ZA)(b) the words "the First-tier Tribunal or Upper Tribunal" substituted for the words "General Commissioners or the Special Commissioners" by SI 2009/56, art. 3 and Sch. 1, para. 167(b), with effect from 1 April 2009, subject to transitional and saving provisions in SI 2009/56, Sch. 3.

S. 182(2ZA) substituted for s. 182(2AA) by TCA 2002, s. 59 and Sch. 5, para. 11(3), with effect for the purposes of TCA 2002 from 1 August 2002 by virtue of SI 2002/1727 (C. 52).

In s. 182(2ZB)(b) the words "First-tier Tribunal or an appeal tribunal constituted under Chapter 1 of Part 2 of the Social Security (Northern Ireland) Order 1998" substituted by SI 2009/56, art. 3 and Sch. 1, para. 167(c), with effect from 1 April 2009, subject to *transitional and saving provisions in SI 2009/56*, Sch. 3.

S. 182(2ZB) inserted by CTFA 2004, s. 18, (temporary modification contained in s. 24), with effect from 1 January 2005.

Former s. 182(2AA) inserted by TCA 1999, s. 12(3), with effect from 5 October 1999 (TCA 1999, s. 20(2)).

In s. 182(2A)(a)(ii) the words "the First-tier Tribunal or Upper Tribunal" substituted by SI 2009/56, art. 3 and Sch. 1, para. 167(d), with effect from 1 April 2009, subject to transitional and saving provisions in SI 2009/56, Sch. 3.

In s. 182(2A), words "child benefit, guardian's allowance," inserted by TCA 2002, s. 59 and Sch. 5, para. 11(4), with effect for the purposes of TCA 2002 from 1 August 2002 by virtue of SI 2002/1727 (C. 52).

S. 182(3) omitted by SI 2009/56, art. 3 and Sch. 1, para. 167(e), with effect from 1 April 2009, subject to transitional and saving provisions in SI 2009/56, Sch. 3.
In former s. 182(3) the words "or section 704 of the Income Tax Act 2007" inserted by ITA 2007, s. 1027 and Sch. 1, para. 282, with effect from 6 April 2007.
Former s. 182(3)(c) repealed by Statute Law (Repeals) Act 2004, s. 1(1) and Sch. 1, Pt. 5, Grp. 18, with effect from 22 July 2004.
In former s. 182(3)(c), the words "for the purposes of section 80(3) of the Taxes Management Act 1970 or" which followed the word "appointed" repealed by FA 1995, s. 162 and Sch. 29, Pt. VIII(16) for the purposes of income tax and capital gains tax in relation to 1996–97 and subsequent years of assessment and for the purposes of corporation tax, in relation to accounting periods beginning after 31 March 1996.
In s. 182(4)(a)(i), the words ", of the National Audit Office and any member or employee of that Office or any member of the staff of the National Audit Office that was established by section 3 of the National Audit Act 1983" substituted for the words "and any member of the staff of the National Audit Office" by the Budget Responsibility and National Audit Act 2011, s. 26 and Sch. 5, para. 14(2)(a), with effect from 1 April 2012 (SI 2011/2576, art. 5).
In s. 182(4)(a)(i), the words "and Auditor General, the Comptroller and Auditor General for Northern Ireland" inserted after the word "Comptroller" by the Budget Responsibility and National Audit Act 2011, s. 26 and Sch. 5, para. 14(3), with effect from 1 April 2012 (SI 2011/2576, art. 5).
S. 182(4)(a)(ia) inserted after s. 182(4)(a)(i) by the Budget Responsibility and National Audit Act 2011, s. 26 and Sch. 5, para. 14(2)(b), with effect from 1 April 2012 (SI 2011/2576, art. 5).
S. 182(4)(a)(iii), (iv) inserted by Government of Wales Act 1998, s. 125 and Sch. 12, para. 32, with effect from 1 February 1999 by virtue of SI 1999/118.
S. 182(4)(a)(iiia) inserted by Public Audit (Wales) Act 2013, s. 24 and Sch. 4, para. 2, with effect from 1 April 2014 (by virtue of Welsh SI 2013/1466, art. 3).
S. 182(4)(a)(iv) substituted by the Public Service Ombudsman Act 2005, s. 39 and Sch. 6, para. 22(a) with effect from1 April 2006 (by virtue of Welsh SI 2005/2008).
In s. 182(4)(b) and (c) the words ", child trust fund functions" inserted after "tax credit functions" by CTFA 2004, s. 18, with effect from 1 January 2005.
In s. 182(4)(b), words "social security functions" inserted, and in s. 182(4)(c), words "tax functions" to the end of para. (c) substituted by SSCTFA 1999, s. 6 and Sch. 6, para. 9(4), with effect from 1 April 1999 by virtue of SI 1999/527 (C. 11), art. 2(b) and Sch. 2.
In s. 182(4)(b) and (c), words ", tax credit functions" continued in force by TCA 2002, s. 59 and Sch. 5, para. 11(5)(a), (b), with effect for the purposes of TCA 2002 from 1 August 2002 by virtue of SI 2002/1727 (C. 52)
S. 182(4)(c)(ia) substituted by TCA 2002, s. 59 and Sch. 5, para. 11(5)(c), with effect for the purposes of TCA 2002 from 1 August 2002 by virtue of SI 2002/1727 (C. 52).
Former s. (4)(c)(ia) inserted by TCA 1999, s. 12(2)(b) and (4)(b) respectively, with effect from 5 October 1999 (TCA 1999, s. 20(2)).
S. 182(4)(c)(ib) inserted by CTFA 2004, s. 18, with effect from 1 January 2005.
In s. 182(4)(c), the words "statutory paternity pay," substituted for the words "ordinary statutory paternity pay, additional statutory paternity pay or" by Children and Families Act 2014, s. 126(1) and Sch. 7, para. 5(4)(a), with effect from 5 April 2015, subject to the transitional and saving provisions in SI 2014/1640, art. 16 (amendments do not have effect in relation to– (a) children whose expected week of birth ends on or before 4 April 2015; (b) children placed for adoption on or before 4 April 2015) and 17 (transitional and saving provisions applicable where Northern Ireland legislation contains provision on additional statutory paternity pay) (SI 2014/1640, art. 6 and 7).
In s. 182(4)(c)(iii), the words "or statutory shared parental pay" inserted (after the words "statutory adoption pay") by Children and Families Act 2014, s. 126(1) and Sch. 7, para. 5(4)(b), with effect from 1 December 2014 (SI 2014/1640, art. 5).
In s. 182(4)(c)(iii) words ", statutory maternity pay, statutory paternity pay or statutory adoption pay" substituted for "or statutory maternity pay", by Employment Act 2002, s. 53 and Sch. 7, para. 1(2) with effect from 8 December 2002, by virtue of SI 2002/2866.
In s. 182(4)(c)(iii), words "child benefit, guardian's allowance," inserted by TCA 2002, s. 59 and Sch. 5, para. 11(d), with effect for the purposes of TCA 2002 from 1 August 2002 by virtue of SI 2002/1727 (C. 52).
In s. 182(5)(b), the words "statutory paternity pay," substituted for the words "ordinary statutory paternity pay, additional statutorypaternity pay or" by Children and Families Act 2014, s. 126(1) and Sch. 7, para. 5(5)(a), with effect from 5 April 2015, subject to the transitional and saving provisions in SI 2014/1640, art. 16 (amendments do not have effect in relation to– (a) children whose expected week of birth ends on or before 4 April 2015; (b) children placed for adoption on or before 4 April 2015) and 17 (transitional and saving provisions applicable where Northern Ireland legislation contains provision on additional statutory paternity pay) (SI 2014/1640, art. 6 and 7).
In s. 182(5)(b), the words "or statutory shared parental pay" inserted (after the words "statutory adoption pay") by Children and Families Act 2014, s. 126(1) and Sch. 7, para. 5(5)(b), with effect from 1 December 2014 (SI 2014/1640, art. 5).
In s. 182(5)(b), the words "ordinary statutory paternity pay, additional statutory paternity pay" substituted for the words "statutory paternity pay" by the Work and Families Act 2006, s. 11 and Sch. 1, para. 2 with effect from 6 April 2010 (SI 2010/495).
In s. 182(5)(b) the words "to a tax credit or to a child trust fund" substituted by CTFA 2004, s. 18, with effect from 1 January 2005.
In s. 182(5)(b) words ", statutory maternity pay, statutory paternity pay or statutory adoption pay" substituted by Employment Act 2002, s. 53 and Sch. 7, para. 1(2) with effect from 8 December 2002, by virtue of SI 2002/2866.
In s. 182(5)(b), words "or to a tax credit" substituted for ", to working families' tax credit or disabled person's tax credit" by TCA 2002, s. 59 and Sch. 5, para. 11(6), with effect for the purposes of TCA 2002 from 1 August 2002 by virtue of SI 2002/1727 (C. 52).
In s. 182(5)(b) the former words ", to working families' tax credit or disabled person's tax credit" inserted by TCA 1999, s. 12(5), with effect from 5 October 1999 (TCA 1999, s. 20(2)).
In s. 182(5)(b), words "or to contributions, statutory sick pay or statutory maternity pay", and in s. 182(10) the definition of "contributions", inserted by SSCTFA 1999, s. 6 and Sch. 6, para. 9(5), (6), with effect from 1 April 1999 by virtue of SI 1999/527 (C. 11), art. 2(b) and Sch. 2.
In s. 182(6), the words "Public Services Ombudsman for Wales" substituted by the Public Services Ombudsman (Wales) Act 2005, s. 39 and Sch. 6, para. 22(b) with effect from 1 April 2006 (by virtue of Welsh SI 2005/2008).
In s. 182(6) words ", the Parliamentary Commissioner, the Auditor General for Wales or the Welsh Administration Ombudsman," substituted for "or the Parliamentary Commissioner" by Government of Wales Act 1998, s. 125 and Sch. 12, para. 31, with effect from 1 February 1999 by virtue of SI 1999/118.
In s. 182(10) the words ""childtrust fund" has the same meaning as in the Child Trust Funds Act 2004," inserted after the definition of "the Board" by CTFA 2004, s. 18, with effect from 1 January 2005.
In s. 182(10), definition of "tax credit" inserted by TCA 2002, s. 59 and Sch. 5, para. 11(7), with effect for the purposes of TCA 2002 from 1 August 2002 by virtue of SI 2002/1727 (C. 52).
S. 182(11)(a) and (b) omitted by the Budget Responsibility and National Audit Act 2011, s. 26 and Sch. 5, para. 14(4), with effect from 1 April 2012 (SI 2011/2576, art. 5).
In s. 182(11), the words ", the Health Service Commissioner for Wales" omitted by the Public Services Ombudsman (Wales) Act 2005, s. 39 and Sch. 6, para. 22(c) with effect from 1 April 2006 (by virtue of Welsh SI 2005/2008).
In s. 182(11A), the words "statutory paternity pay," substituted for the words "ordinary statutory paternity pay, additional statutory paternity pay or", the words "or statutory shared parental pay" inserted (after the words "statutory adoption pay") and the words ", Part 12ZB or Part 12ZC" substituted for the words "or Part 12ZB" by Children and Families Act 2014, s. 126(1) and Sch. 7, para. 5(6), with effect from 15 March 2015 (S.R. (N.I.) 2015/86, art. 3(e)), subject to the transitional and saving provisions in SI 2014/1640, art. 18 (amendments do not have effect in relation to– (a) children whose expected week of birth ends on or before 4 April 2015; (b) children placed for adoption on or before 4 April 2015) (SI 2014/1640, art. 8).

In s. 182(11A), the words "ordinary statutory paternity pay, additional statutory paternity pay" substituted for the words "statutory paternity pay" by the Work and Families Act 2006, s. 11 and Sch. 1, para. 2 with effect from 6 April 2010 (SI 2010/495).

S. 182(11A) inserted by Employment Act 2002, s. 53 and Sch. 7, para. 1(3), with effect from 8 December 2002, by virtue of SI 2002/2866.

Cross references – SI 1992/15, reg. 12: provision of information by banks and other payers of interest, disclosure of information under s. 182(5) not prevented by reg. 12.

TCA 2002, Sch. 5: use and disclosure of information relating to working tax credit and child tax credit.

TMA 1970, s. 80(3): disputes where profits of non-resident assessed with reference to percentage of turnover.

ICTA 1988, s. 706: tribunal in respect of disputes relating to application of ICTA 1988, s. 703 (cancellation of tax advantage from certain transactions in securities.

SSAA 1992, s. 122: disclosure of information by Inland Revenue.

SSAA 1992, s. 123: disclosure of information by DSS.

SI 1990/2231, reg. 16(2); SI 1990/2232, reg. 13(2): reg. 16(1) and 13(1) respectively (restrictions on use to which information supplied by building societies etc. may be put) are not to be construed as preventing any disclosure of information under s. 182(5).

SI 1992/12, reg. 12(2): para. 1 of the regulations shall not be construed as preventing any disclosure of information under s. 182(5).

SI 1994/2318, reg. 9(3): reg. 9(1) does not prevent disclosure of information within s. 182(5).

Notes – Official Secrets Act 1911, s. 2 (see s. 182(12)) is repealed by Official Secrets Act 1989, s. 16(4), (6) and Sch. 2, with effect from 1 March 1990 (SI 1990/199 (C. 8)).

FA 1969, s. 58: disclosure for statistical purposes of information regarding employment.

TMA 1970, s. 6: declarations by HMRC officials etc.

HMRC may also disclose personal information to other government departments under:

- Land Registration Act 1925, s. 129;
- Parliamentary Commissioner Act 1967, s. 8;
- FA 1972, s. 127;
- SSPA 1975, s. 59K(6) (from 18 July 1990, by virtue of SI 1990/1446);
- FA 1978, s. 77;
- Tenant's Rights etc. (Scotland) Act 1980, s. 1;
- SSHBA 1982, s. 25;
- National Audit Act 1983, s. 8;
- Data Protection Act 1984, s. 17;
- Housing Associations Act 1985, s. 62;
- SSA 1986, s. 59;
- ICTA 1988, s. 375(9), (10), 816;
- SSAA 1992, s. 122;
- Charities Act 1993, s. 10(2).

HMRC may also disclose personal information to the police under:

- Drug Trafficking Offences Act 1986, s. 30;
- Prevention of Terrorism (Temporary Provisions) Act 1989, s. 17 and Sch. 17.

SOCIAL SECURITY CONTRIBUTIONS AND BENEFITS ACT 1992

(1992 Chapter 4)

[*13th February 1992*]

ARRANGEMENT OF SECTIONS

Notes – In SSCBA 1992, in so far as it relates to working families' tax credit and disabled person's tax credit, the functions of the Secretary of State are generally transferred to HMRC; except for certain functions that are transferred to the Treasury etc. (TCA 1999, s. 2(1)(c); Sch. 2, para. 7); with effect from 5 October 1999 (TCA 1999, s. 20(2)). The Notes following relevant sections indicate where functions are transferred to the Treasury etc.

PART II – CONTRIBUTORY BENEFITS

45AA Effect of working families' tax credit and disabled person's tax credit on earnings factor

45AA(1) For the purposes of calculating additional pension under sections 44 and 45 where, in the case of any relevant year, working families' tax credit is paid in respect of any employed earner, or disabled person's tax credit is paid to any employed earner, section 44(6)(a)(i) shall have effect as if–

(a) where that person had earnings of not less than the qualifying earnings factor for that year, being earnings upon which primary class 1 contributions were paid or treated as paid (**"qualifying earnings"**) in respect of that year, the amount of those qualifying earnings were increased by the aggregate amount (**"AG"**) of working families' tax credit, or, as the case may be, disabled person's tax credit paid in respect of that year, and

(b) in any other case, that person had qualifying earnings in respect of that year and the amount of those qualifying earnings were equal to AG plus the qualifying earnings factor for that year.

45AA(2) The reference in subsection (1) to the person in respect of whom working families' tax credit is paid–

(a) where it is paid to one of a couple, is a reference to the prescribed member of the couple, and

(b) in any other case, is a reference to the person to whom it is paid.

45AA(3) A person's qualifying earnings in respect of any year cannot be treated by virtue of subsection (1) as exceeding the upper earnings limit for that year multiplied by 53.

45AA(4) Subsection (1) does not apply to any woman who has made, or is treated as having made, an election under regulations under section 19(4), which has not been revoked, that her liability in respect of primary Class 1 contributions shall be at a reduced rate.

45AA(5) In this section–

"couple" has the same meaning as in Part 7 (see section 137);

"relevant year" has the same meaning as in section 44.

History – S. 45AA inserted by PA 2008, s. 104 and Sch. 4, para. 5(1), with effect from 3 January 2012 (SI 2011/3033, art. 2).

45A Effect of working families' tax credit and disabled person's tax credit on earnings factor

45A [Repealed by TCA 2002, s. 60 and Sch. 6, with effect from 6 April 2003 (SI 2003/962, art. 2).]

PART VII – INCOME-RELATED BENEFITS

GENERAL

123 Income-related benefits

123(1) Prescribed schemes shall provide for the following benefits (in this Act referred to as **"income-related benefits"**)–

(a) income support;

(b) [repealed by TCA 2002, s. 60 and Sch. 6;]

(c) [repealed by TCA 2002, s. 60 and Sch. 6;]

(d) housing benefit; and

(e) council tax benefit.

123(2) The Secretary of State shall make copies of schemes prescribed under subsection (1)(a), (b) or (c) above available for public inspection at local offices of the Department of Social Security at all reasonable hours without payment.

123(3) [Not relevant to tax credits.]

123(4) [Not relevant to tax credits.]

History – S. 123(1)(b) and (c) (which referred to "working families' tax credit" and "disabled person's tax credit" respectively) repealed by TCA 2002, s. 60 and Sch. 6, with effect from 8 April 2003 (SI 2003/962, art. 2), subject to transitional provisions detailed in History notes to s. 128 and 129 respectively.

In former s. 123(1) the words "working families' tax credit" and the words "disabled person's tax credit" substituted by TCA 1999, s. 1(2) and Sch. 1, para. 2(f), with effect from 5 October 1999 (TCA 1999, s. 20(2)).

Cross references – TCA 1999, Sch. 2, para. 1(b): so far as they relate to working families' tax credit or disabled person's tax credit functions of the Secretary of State (or the Department) shall be functions of the Treasury.

TCA 1999, Sch. 2, para. 24: in relation to working families' tax credit the reference in s. 123(2) to local offices of the Department of Social Security is to be construed as a reference to offices of the Board of Inland Revenue.

Statutory instruments – SI 2001/1334: amendments consequential to introduction of "Intensive Activity Period" and "Intensive Activity Period for 50 plus" schemes.

WORKING FAMILIES' TAX CREDIT

Notes – The heading "WORKING FAMILIES' TAX CREDIT" amended by Croner-i to reflect the content of s. 128 (below) with effect from 5 October 1999.

128 Working families' tax credit

128 [Repealed by TCA 2002, s. 60 and Sch. 6.]

History – S. 128 repealed by TCA 2002, s. 60 and Sch. 6, with effect from 8 April 2003 (SI 2003/962), subject to the provisions of s. 128 applying where a claim has been made to working families' tax credit before 6 July 2003 in respect of a period ending on or before 7 April 2003.

DISABLED PERSON'S TAX CREDIT

Notes – The heading "DISABLED PERSON'S TAX CREDIT" amended by Croner-i to reflect the content of s. 129 (below) with effect from 5 October 1999.

129 Disabled person's tax credit

129 [Repealed by TCA 2002, s. 60 and Sch. 6.]

History – S. 129 repealed by TCA 2002, s. 60 and Sch. 6, with effect from 8 April 2003 (SI 2003/962), subject to the provisions of s. 129 applying where a claim has been made to disabled person's tax credit before 6 July 2003 in respect of a period ending on or before 7 April 2003.

GENERAL

134 Exclusions from benefit

134(1) No person shall be entitled to an income-related benefit if his capital or a prescribed part of it exceeds the prescribed amount.

134(2) Except in prescribed circumstances the entitlement of one member of a family to any one income-related benefit excludes entitlement to that benefit for any other member for the same period.

134(3) [...]

134(4) Where the amount of any income-related benefit would be less than a prescribed amount, it shall not be payable except in prescribed circumstances.

Cross references – TCA 1999, Sch. 2, para. 1(e): so far as they relate to working families' tax credit or disabled person's tax credit functions of the Secretary of State (or the Department) shall be functions of the Treasury.

135 The applicable amount

135(1) The applicable amount, in relation to any income-related benefit, shall be such amount or the aggregate of such amounts as may be prescribed in relation to that benefit.

135(2) The power to prescribe applicable amounts conferred by subsection (1) above includes power to prescribe nil as an applicable amount.

135(3) In prescribing, for the purposes of income support, amounts under subsection (1) above in respect of accommodation in any area for qualifying persons in cases where prescribed conditions are fulfilled, the Secretary of State shall take into account information provided by local authorities or other prescribed bodies or persons with respect to the amounts which they have agreed to pay for the provision of accommodation in relevant premises in that area.

135(4) In subsection (3) above–

"accommodation" includes any board or care;

"local authority"–

(a) in relation to areas in England and Wales, has the same meaning as it has in Part III of the National Assistance Act 1948; and

(b) (applies to Scotland only);

"qualifying person" means any person who falls within–

(a) subsection (l) of section 26A of the National Assistance Act 1948 (which is inserted by the National Health Service and Community Care Act 1990 and relates to persons ordinarily resident in residential care or nursing homes immediately before the commencement of that section); or

(b) (applies to Scotland only),

or who would fall within either of those subsections apart from any regulations under subsection (3) of the section in question;

"relevant premises"–

(a) in relation to areas in England and Wales, has the meaning given by section 26A(2) of the National Assistance Act 1948; and

(b) (applies to Scotland only).

135(5) The applicable amount for a severely disabled person shall include an amount in respect of his being a severely disabled person.

135(6) Regulations may specify circumstances in which persons are to be treated as being or as not being severely disabled.

History – In s. 135(5), words "In relation to income support, housing benefit and council tax benefit," (which appeared at the beginning of the subsection) repealed by TCA 2002, s. 60 and Sch. 6, with effect from 8 April 2003 (SI 2003/962).

Cross references – TCA 1999, Sch. 2, para. 1(f): so far as they relate to working families' tax credit or disabled person's tax credit functions of the Secretary of State (or the Department) shall be functions of the Treasury.

136 Income and capital

136(1) Where a person claiming an income-related benefit is a member of a family, the income and capital of any member of that family shall, except in prescribed circumstances, be treated as the income and capital of that person.

136(2) Regulations may provide that capital not exceeding the amount prescribed under section 134(1) above but exceeding a prescribed lower amount shall be treated, to a prescribed extent, as if it were income of a prescribed amount.

136(3) Income and capital shall be calculated or estimated in such manner as may be prescribed.

136(4) A person's income in respect of a week shall be calculated in accordance with prescribed rules; and the rules may provide for the calculation to be made by reference to an average over a period (which need not include the week concerned).

136(5) Circumstances may be prescribed in which–

(a) a person is treated as possessing capital or income which he does not possess;

(b) capital or income which a person does possess is to be disregarded;

(c) income is to be treated as capital;

(d) capital is to be treated as income.

Cross references – TCA 1999, Sch. 2, para. 1(g): so far as they relate to working families' tax credit or disabled person's tax credit functions of the Secretary of State (or the Department) shall be functions of the Treasury.

137 Interpretation of Part VII and supplementary provisions

137(1) In this Part of this Act, unless the context otherwise requires–

"billing authority" has the same meaning as in Part I of the Local Government Finance Act 1992;

"child" means a person under the age of 16;

"dwelling" means any residential accommodation, whether or not consisting of the whole or part of a building and whether or not comprising separate and self-contained premises;

"family" means–

(a) a couple;

(b) a couple and a member of the same household for whom one of them is or both are responsible and who is a child or a person of a prescribed description;

(c) except in prescribed circumstances, a person who is not a member of a couple and a member of the same household for whom that person is responsible and who is a child or a person of a prescribed description;

"local authority" in relation to Scotland means a council constituted under section 2 of the Local Government etc. (Scotland) Act 1994;

"prescribed" means specified in or determined in accordance with regulations;

"week", in relation to council tax benefit, means a period of 7 days beginning with a Monday.

137(1A) For the purposes of this Part, two people of the same sex are to be regarded as living together as if they were civil partners if, but only if, they would be regarded as living together as husband and wife were they instead two people of the opposite sex.

137(2) Regulations may make provision for the purposes of this Part of this Act–

(a) as to circumstances in which a person is to be treated as being or not being in Great Britain;

(b) continuing a person's entitlement to benefit during periods of temporary absence from Great Britain;

(c) as to what is or is not to be treated as remunerative work or as employment;

(d) as to circumstances in which a person is or is not to be treated as engaged or normally engaged in remunerative work.

(e) as to what is or is not to be treated as relevant education;

(f) as to circumstances in which a person is or is not to be treated as receiving relevant education;

(g) specifying the descriptions of pension increases under war pension schemes or industrial injuries schemes that are analogous to the benefits mentioned in section 129(2)(b)(i) to (iii) above;

(h) as to circumstances in which a person is or is not to be treated as occupying a dwelling as his home;

(i) for treating any person who is liable to make payments in respect of a dwelling as if he were not so liable;

(j) for treating any person who is not liable to make payments in respect of a dwelling as if he were so liable;

(k) for treating as included in a dwelling any land used for the purposes of the dwelling;

(l) as to circumstances in which persons are to be treated as being or not being members of the same household;

(m) as to circumstances in which one person is to be treated as responsible or not responsible for another.

Prospective amendments – S. 137 repealed by WRA 2012, s. 147 and Sch. 14, Pt. 1, with effect from a date to be set by order of the Secretary of State.

History – S. 137 repealed by WRA 2012, s. 147 and Sch. 14, Pt. 1, with effect from 1 April 2013 in so far as relating to the abolition of council tax benefit (SI 2013/358, art. 8(c)).

In s. 137(1) the definition of "local authority" inserted by Welfare Reform Act 2007, s. 40 and Sch. 5, para. 1(4), with effect from 3 July 2007.

In s. 137(1)(a), (b) and (c) of the definition of "family", the word "couple" substituted by Civil Partnership Act 2004, Sch. 24, para. 46(2), by virtue of SI 2005/3175, art. 2(1) and Sch. 1 with effect from 5 December 2005.

In s. 137(1) the definition of "couple" inserted by Civil Partnership Act 2004, Sch. 24, para. 46(3), with effect from a day to be appointed.

In s. 137(1) the definitions of "married couple" and "unmarried couple" omitted by Civil Partnership Act 2004, Sch. 24, para. 46(4), by virtue of SI 2005/3175, art. 2(1), (6) and Sch. 1 with effect from 5 December 2005.

S. 137(1A) inserted by Civil Partnership Act 2004, Sch. 24, para. 46(5), with effect from 5 December 2005 by virtue of SI 2005/3175, art. 2(1) and Sch. 1.

PART XIII – GENERAL

INTERPRETATION

172 Application of Act in relation to territorial waters

172 In this Act–

(a) any reference to **"Great Britain"** includes a reference to the territorial waters of the United Kingdom adjacent to Great Britain;

(b) any reference to **"the United Kingdom"** includes a reference to the territorial waters of the United Kingdom.

173 Age

173 For the purposes of this Act a person–

(a) is over or under a particular **"age"** if he has or, as the case may be, has not attained that age; and

(b) is between two particular ages if he has attained the first but not the second;

and in Scotland (as in England and Wales) the time at which a person attains a particular age expressed in years is the commencement of the relevant anniversary of the date of his birth.

174 References to Acts

174 In this Act–

"the 1975 Act" means the Social Security Act 1975;

"the 1986 Act" means the Social Security Act 1986;

"the Administration Act" means the Social Security Administration Act 1992;

"the Consequential Provisions Act" means the Social Security (Consequential Provisions) Act 1992;

"the Northern Ireland Contributions and Benefits Act" means the Social Security Contributions and Benefits (Northern Ireland) Act 1992;

"the Old Cases Act" means the Industrial Injuries and Diseases (Old Cases) Act 1975; and

"the Pensions Act" means the Pension Schemes Act 1993.

History – In s. 174, in the definition of "the Pensions Act", the words "Pension Schemes Act 1993" substituted by PSA 1993, s. 190 and Sch. 8, para. 41, with effect from 7 February 1994.

SUBORDINATE LEGISLATION

175 Regulations, orders and schemes

175(1) Subject to subsection (1A) below, regulations and orders under this Act shall be made by the Secretary of State.

175(1A) Subsection (1) above has effect subject to–

(a) any provision providing for regulations or an order to be made by the Treasury or by the Commissioners of Inland Revenue.

(b) [repealed by TCA 2002, s. 60 and Sch. 6;]

TC Statutes

175(2) Powers under this Act to make regulations, orders or schemes shall be exercisable by statutory instrument.

175(3) Except in the case of an order under section 145(3) above and in so far as this Act otherwise provides, any power under this Act to make regulations or an order may be exercised–

(a) either in relation to all cases to which the power extends, or in relation to those cases subject to specified exceptions, or in relation to any specified cases or classes of case;

(b) so as to make, as respects the cases in relation to which it is exercised–

(i) the full provision to which the power extends or any less provision (whether by way of exception or otherwise),

(ii) the same provision for all cases in relation to which the power is exercised, or different provision for different cases or different classes of case or different provision as respects the same case or class of case for different purposes of this Act,

(iii) any such provision either unconditionally or subject to any specified condition;

and where such a power is expressed to be exercisable for alternative purposes it may be exercised in relation to the same case for any or all of those purposes; and powers to make regulations or an order for the purposes of any one provision of this Act are without prejudice to powers to make regulations or an order for the purposes of any other provision.

175(4) Without prejudice to any specific provision in this Act, any power conferred by this Act to make regulations or an order (other than the power conferred in section 145(3) above) includes power to make thereby such incidental, supplementary, consequential or transitional provision as appears to the person making the regulations or order to be expedient for the purposes of the regulations or order.

175(5) Without prejudice to any specific provisions in this Act, a power conferred by any provision of this Act except–

(a) sections 30, 25B(2)(a), 47(6) and 145(3) above and paragraph 3(9) of Schedule 7 to this Act;

(b) section 122(1) above in relation to the definition of "payments by way of occupational or personal pension"; and

(c) Part XI,

to make regulations or an order includes power to provide for a person to exercise a discretion in dealing with any matter.

175(6) Any power conferred by this Act to make orders or regulations relating to housing benefit or council tax benefit shall include power to make different provisions for different areas.

175(7) Any power of the Secretary of State under any provision of this Act, except the provisions mentioned in subsection (5)(a) and (b) above and Part IX, to make any regulations or order, where the power is not expressed to be exercisable with the consent of the Treasury, shall if the Treasury so direct be exercisable only in conjunction with them.

175(8) Any power under any of sections 116 to 120 above to modify provisions of this Act or the Administration Act extends also to modifying so much of any other provision of this Act or that Act as re-enacts provisions of the 1975 Act which replaced provisions of the National Insurance (Industrial Injuries) Acts 1965 to 1974.

175(9) A power to make regulations under any of sections 116 to 120 above shall be exercisable in relation to any enactment passed after this Act which is directed to be construed as one with this Act; but this subsection applies only so far as a contrary intention is not expressed in the enactment so passed, and is without prejudice to the generality of any such direction.

175(10) Any reference in this section or section 176 below to an order or regulations under this Act includes a reference to an order or regulations made under any provision of an enactment passed after this Act and directed to be construed as one with this Act; but this subsection applies only so far as a contrary intention is not expressed in the enactment so passed, and without prejudice to the generality of any such direction.

Prospective amendments – S. 175(6) repealed by WRA 2012, s. 147 and Sch. 14, Pt. 1, with effect from a date to be set by order of the Secretary of State.

History – S. 175(6) repealed by WRA 2012, s. 147 and Sch. 14, Pt. 1, with effect from 1 April 2013 in so far as relating to the abolition of council tax benefit (SI 2013/358, art. 8(c)).

In s. 175, in relation to tax credit, references to the "Secretary of State" shall be construed, with effect from 5 October 1999, as if they were references to "the Treasury" or, as the case may be, "the Board" (TCA 1999, s. 20(2); s. 2 and Sch. 2, para. 20(a)).

In s. 175(1), reference to subs. (1A) substituted by SSC(TF)A 1999, s. 2 and Sch. 3, para. 29(2) with effect from 1 April 1999 (*SI 1999/527*).

In s. 175(1A)(a), words "of Part 1 or Part 6 of this Act" and para. (b) and the word "and" immediately preceding it repealed by TCA 2002, s. 60 and Sch. 6, with effect from 1 April 2003 (SI 2003/392, art. 2).

Former s. 175(1A) inserted by SSC(TF)A 1999, s. 2 and Sch. 3, para 29(3) with effect from 1 April 1999 (SI 1999/527).

In s. 175(4), reference to the "Secretary of State" removed by SSC(TF)A 1999, s. 2 and Sch. 3, para. 29(4) with effect from 1 April 1999 (SI 1999/527).

In s. 175(5)(a), "25B(2)(a)" substituted for "57(9)(a)" by the Social Security (Incapacity for Work) Act 1994, Sch. 1, para. 36, with effect from 13 April 1995 (SI 1994/2926).

Derivations – S. 175(1): SSA 1975, s. 168(1), Sch. 20 "regulations"; Child Benefit Act 1975, s. 22(1)(b); SS(MP)A 1977, s. 24(1) "regulations"; SS(No. 2)A 1980, s. 3(4), 5(3) "regulations"; SSHBA 1982, s. 47 "regulations"; SSA 1986, s. 84(1) "regulations"; SSA 1989, s. 30(1) "regulations".
S. 175(2): SSA 1975, s. 166(1); Industrial Injuries and Diseases (Old Cases) Act 1975, s. 4(8), 8(1); Child Benefit Act 1975, s. 22(3); SS(MP)A 1977, s. 24(3); SS(No. 2)A 1980, s. 7(3); SSHBA 1982, s. 45(2); SSA 1986, s. 83(1); SSA 1989, s. 29(1); SSA 1990, s. 21(1), Sch. 6, para. 8(7), 12.
S. 175(3): SSA 1975, s. 166(2); Child Benefit Act 1975, s. 22(6); SS(MP)A 1977, s. 24(3); SS(No. 2)A 1980, s. 7(3); SSHBA 1982, s. 45(1); SSA 1986, s. 83(1); SSA 1989, s. 29(1).
S. 175(4): SSA 1975, s. 166(3); Child Benefit Act 1975, s. 22(7); SS(MP)A 1977, s. 24(3); SS(No. 2)A 1980, s. 7(3); SSHBA 1982, s. 45(1); SSA 1986, s. 83(1); SSA 1989, s. 29(1), 31(1), Sch. 8, para. 10(1).
S. 175(5) (as originally enacted): SSA 1975, s. 166(3A); Child Benefit Act 1975, s. 22(7A); SS(MP)A 1977, s. 24(3); SSA 1986, s. 62(1), (2), 83(1); SSA 1989, s. 29(1).
S. 175(7): SSA 1975, s. 166(5); SS(MP)A 1977, s. 24(3); SSHBA 1982, s. 45(1); SSA 1986, s. 83(6); SSA 1989, s. 29(6).
S. 175(8): SSA 1975, s. 166(6).
S. 175(9): SSA 1975, s. 166(7).
S. 175(10): SSA 1975, s. 168(4).

Cross references – TCA 1999, Sch. 2, para. 20(a): so far as s. 175 relates to working families' tax credit or disabled person's tax credit references to the Secretary of State shall be construed as if they were references to the Treasury (or as the case may be, the Board of Inland Revenue).
TCA 1999, Sch. 2, para. 25: disapplication of s. 175(7) where regulations relating to tax credit are made by the Treasury under TCA 1999, s. 2(1) and Sch. 2, para. 20.
SSCBA 1992, s. 25B (not reproduced): Secretary of State's power to amend provisions as to days of entitlement.
SSCBA 1992, s. 30 (not reproduced): abatement of unemployment benefit on account of payments of occupational or personal pension.
SSCBA 1992, s. 47(6) (not reproduced): increases in Category A retirement pension for invalidity.
SSCBA 1992, s. 116: Her Majesty's forces.
SSCBA 1992, s. 117: mariners, airmen etc.
SSCBA 1992, s. 118: married women and widows.
SSCBA 1992, s. 119: persons outside Great Britain.
SSCBA 1992, s. 120: employment at sea (continental shelf operations).
SSCBA 1992, s. 122(1) (not reproduced): meaning of "payments by way of occupational or personal pension".
SSCBA 1992, s. 145 (not reproduced): rate of child benefit.
SSA 1989, s. 29: this section applies to powers to make regulations and orders under SSA 1989, s. 29.
SSPA 1994, s. 3(2): application of s. 175(2) to s. 2(1) of the 1994 Act.
Notes – Pt. XI: statutory sick pay.

176 Parliamentary control

176(1) Subject to the provisions of this section, a statutory instrument containing (whether alone or with other provisions)–

(za) regulations under section 5 specifying the lower earnings limit for the tax year following the designated tax year (see section 5(4) of the Pensions Act 2007) or any subsequent tax year;

(zb) regulations under section 5 specifying the upper earnings limit,

(a) regulations made by virtue of–

section 4B(2);
section 4C;
section 9A(7);
section 10ZC;
section 11(8) or (9);
section 14A;
section 18;
section 18A;
section 19(4) to (6);
section 28(3);
section 45(2A);
section 104(3);
section 117;
section 118;
section 145;
section 171ZE(1);
any of sections 171ZU to 171ZY

(aa) the first regulations made by virtue of section 23A(3)(c);

(b) regulations prescribing payments for the purposes of the definition of "payments by way of occupational or personal pension" in section 122(1) above;

TC Statutes

(c) an order under–
section 25B(1);
section 28(2);
section 148(3)(b);
section 157(2);
section 159A(1)

shall not be made unless a draft of the instrument has been laid before Parliament and been approved by a resolution of each House.

176(2) Subsection (1) above does not apply to a statutory instrument by reason only that it contains–

(a) regulations under section 117 which the instrument states are made for the purpose of making provision consequential on the making of an order under section 141, 143, 145, 146 or 162 of the Administration Act;

(b) regulations under powers conferred by any provision mentioned in paragraph (a) of that subsection which are to be made for the purpose of consolidating regulations to be revoked in the instrument;

(c) regulations which, in so far as they are made under powers conferred by any provision mentioned in paragraph (a) of that subsection (other than section 145), only replace provisions of previous regulations with new provisions to the same effect.

176(2A) In the case of a statutory instrument containing (whether alone or with other provisions) regulations made by virtue of section 4B(2) to which subsection (1) above applies, the draft of the instrument must be laid before Parliament before the end of the period of 12 months beginning with the appropriate date.

176(2B) For the purposes of subsection (2A), the **"appropriate date"** means–

(a) where the corresponding retrospective tax provision was passed or made before the day on which the National Insurance Contributions Act 2006 was passed, the date upon which that Act was passed, and

(b) in any other case, the date upon which the corresponding retrospective tax provision was passed or made.

176(2C) For the purposes of subsection (2B), **"the corresponding retrospective tax provision"** in relation to the regulations means–

(a) the retrospective tax provision mentioned in subsection (1) of section 4B in relation to which the regulations are to be made by virtue of subsection (2) of that section, or

(b) where there is more than one such tax provision, whichever of those provisions was the first to be passed or made.

176(3) A statutory instrument–

(a) which contains (whether alone or with other provisions) any order, regulations or scheme made under this Act by the Secretary of State, the Treasury or the Commissioners of Inland Revenue, other than an order under section 145(3) above; and

(b) which is not subject to any requirement that a draft of the instrument shall be laid before and approved by a resolution of each House of Parliament,

shall be subject to annulment in pursuance of a resolution of either House of Parliament.

176(4) Subsection (3) above does not apply to a statutory instrument by reason only that it contains an order appointing the first or second appointed year or designating the flat rate introduction year (within the meanings given by section 122(1) above).

Prospective amendments – In s. 176(1)(a), the words "section 9B(4), (8) or (10);" inserted after the words "section 9A(7);" by NICA 2015, s. 1(5), with effect from 6 April 2016 (except for the purposes of making regulations under s. 9B when it comes into effect from 11 April 2015).
In s. 176(1)(a), the words "section 30DD(5)(b) or (c);" repealed by the Welfare Reform Act 2007, s. 67 and Sch. 8, with effect from a date to be appointed (s. 70(2)).
S. 176(3A) inserted by PA 2011, s. 3 and Sch. 3, para. 5, with effect from a day to be appointed. New s. 176(3A) reads as follows:
"176(3A) Subsection (3) above does not apply to a statutory instrument by reason only that it contains an order under section 45(2)."
In s. 176(4) the words "or the additional pension consolidation year" inserted after the words "introduction year" by PA 2011, s. 3 and Sch. 3, para. 5, with effect from a day to be appointed.
In s. 176(1)(a), the words "or (2)(b)" inserted (after the words "section 171ZE(1)") by Children and Families Act 2014, s. 123(4), with effect from a day to be appointed by order of the Secretary of State.

History – S. 176(1)(za) inserted by PA 2007, s. 7(5), with effect from 26 September 2007 (s. 30).
S. 176(1)(zb) inserted by NICA 2008, s. 1(3), with effect in relation to regulations specifying the upper earnings limit for 2009–10 or any subsequent tax year.
In s. 176(1)(a), entry for "section 171ZN(1)" repealed by Children and Families Act 2014, s. 124(2), with effect from 5 April 2015 (SI 2014/1640, art. 6).
In s. 176(1)(a), entry for"171ZEA to 171ZEE" repealed by Children and Families Act, s. 126(1) and Sch. 7, para. 22, with effect from 5 April 2015, subject to the transitional and saving provisions in SI 2014/1640, art. 16 (amendments do not have effect in relation to– (a) children whose expected week of birth ends on or before 4 April 2015; (b) children placed for adoption on or before 4 April 2015) (SI 2014/1640, art. 6 and 7).

In s. 176(1)(a), the words "section 11(8) or (9)" substituted for the words "section 11(3)" by NICA 2015, s. 2 and Sch. 1, para. 8, with effect for the tax year 2015–16 and subsequent tax years.
In s. 176(1)(a), "section 14A" and "section 45(2A)" inserted by PA 2014, Sch. 15, para. 11, with effect from 13 October 2014.
In s. 176(1)(a), the words "any of sections 171ZU to 171ZY" inserted by Children and Families Act 2014, s. 119(2), with effect from 30 June 2014 (SI 2014/1640, art. 3).
In s. 176(1)(a) the words "section 9A(7)" inserted by NICA 2014, s. 9(5), with effect from 13 May 2014.
In s. 176(1)(a), the words "section 18A;" inserted by NICA 2014, s. 13(3), with effect from 13 May 2014.
In s. 176(1)(a) the former entry "sections 171ZEA to 171ZEE;" inserted by the Work and Families Act 2006, s. 11 and Sch. 1, para. 22, with effect from 3 March 2010 (SI 2010/495).
In s. 176(1)(a) references to s. 4B(2) and s. 4C inserted by NICA 2006, s. 1(2), with effect from 30 March 2006.
In s. 176(1)(a) references to s. 10ZC inserted by NICA 2006, s. 3(2), with effect from 30 March 2006.
In s. 176(1), (2), references to s. 158 and 159 omitted by SI 1995/512, with effect from 6 April 1995.
In s. 176(1)(a) the entry s. 171ZE(1) and former entry s. 171ZN(1) inserted by the Employment Act 2002, s. 53 and Sch. 7, para. 7, with effect from 8 December 2002, SI 2002/2866, art. 2(2), Sch. 1, Pt. 2.
In s. 176(1)(a), the words "section 32(2)" and the words "section 59(2)" repealed by the Social Security (Incapacity for Work) Act 1994, Sch. 1 and SI 1994/2926, with effect from 13 April 1995.
S. 176(1)(aa) inserted by PA 2007, Sch. 1, para. 10, and s. 3(3) with effect from 26 September 2007 (s. 30).
In s. 176(1)(c) the words "section 122(8)" repealed by NICA 2008, s. 4 and Sch. 2, with effect from 21 September 2008.
In s. 176(1)(c) the entry relating to s. 122(8) inserted by PA 2007, s. 12(4), and Sch. 1,para. 35(a), with effect from 26 September 2007 (s. 30).
In s. 176(1)(c), the words "section 159A(1)" inserted by SSPA 1994, s. 3(2) with effect from 10 February 1994.
In s. 176(1)(c), the words "section 57(8)" repealed, and the words "section 25B(1)" inserted, by the Social Security (Incapacity for Work) Act 1994, Sch. 1 and SI 1994/2926, with effect from 13 April 1995.
S. 176(2A)–(2C) inserted by NICA 2006, s. 1(2), with effect from 30 March 2006.
In s. 176(3), in relation to tax credit, references to the "Secretary of State" shall be construed, with effect from 5 October 1999, as if they were references to "the Treasury" or, as the case may be, "the Board" (TCA 1999, s. 20(2); s. 2 and Sch. 2, para. 20(b)).
In s. 176(3)(a), reference to the Treasury and the Commissioners of Inland Revenue inserted by SSC(TF)A 1999, s. 2; Sch. 3, para. 30 with effect from 1 April 1999 (SI 1999/527).
In s. 176(4) the words "or designating the flat rate introduction year" inserted by PA 2007, Sch. 1, para. 35(b), and s. 12(4), with effect from 26 September 2007 (s. 30).
S. 176(4) inserted by CSPSSA 2000, s. 35(1) with effect from 8 January 2001 for the purposes of making regulations and of making orders, SI 2000/2950, art. 6; with effect from 25 January 2001 for the purposes of making reports and orders under PSA 1993, s. 42, 42B and 45A, SI 2001/153, art. 2(a)(i) and with effect from 6 April 2002 for the remaining purposes, art. 2(a)(ii).

Derivations – S. 176(1) (as originally enacted): SSA 1975, s. 167(1); SSPA 1975, s. 62(1); Child Benefit Act 1975, s. 22(3); SS(No. 2)A 1980, s. 5(4); SSHBA 1982, s. 7(1B), 9(1F); SSA 1986, s. 43(3)(b), 62(3), 67(1), 83(3)(e), 86, Sch. 10, para. 65; SSA 1989, s. 9(1); SSA 1990, s. 21(1), Sch. 6, para. 8(2), (3), (5), 15(2); SSPA 1991, s. 2(1).
S. 176(2) (as originally enacted): SSA 1975, s. 167(2); Child Benefit Act 1975, s. 22(4); SSA 1990, s. 21(2), Sch. 6, para. 8(1), (3).
S. 176(3) (as originally enacted): SSA 1975, s. 167(3); Industrial Injuries and Diseases (Old Cases) Act 1975, s. 4(8), 8(1); Child Benefit Act 1975, s. 22(5); SS(MP)A 1977, s. 24(5); SS(No. 2)A, 1980, s. 7(4); SSHBA 1982, s. 45(2); SSA 1986, s. 83(4); SSA 1989, s. 29(3); SSA 1990, s. 21(1), Sch. 6, para. 8(1), (3), (4), (6), (7), (9), (12).

Cross references – S. 11(3): regulations may make provision for an earner to be liable for a higher rate of Class 2 contributions in certain cases.
S. 18: Class 4 contributions recoverable under regulations.
S. 19(4): election by women married or widowed before 6 April 1977 to pay reduced rate contributions.
S. 25B(1) (not reproduced): power to amend s. 25A (days of entitlement to unemployment benefit).
S. 28 (not reproduced): disqualifications from unemployment benefit.
S. 57 (not reproduced): determination of days for which child allowance payable.
S. 104 (not reproduced): increase in disablement pension where constant attendance needed.
S. 117: mariners, airmen etc.
S. 118: married women and widows.
S. 145 (not reproduced): rate of child benefit.
S. 148 (not reproduced): entitlement of pensioners to Christmas bonus.
S. 157 (not reproduced) rates of statutory sick pay.
S. 158: recovery by employers of amounts paid by way of statutory sick pay.
S. 159: power of Secretary of State to substitute provisions for s. 158(2).
S. 174: "the Administration Act" means SSAA 1992.
SSAA 1992, s. 141: annual review of contributions.
SSAA 1992, s. 143: power to alter contributions with a view to adjusting National Insurance Fund.
SSAA 1992, s. 145: power to alter primary and secondary contributions.
SSAA 1992, s. 146: power to alter number of secondary earnings brackets.
SSAA 1992, s. 162: destination of contributions.

SHORT TITLE, COMMENCEMENT AND EXTENT

177 Short title, commencement and extent

177(1) This Act may be cited as the Social Security Contributions and Benefits Act 1992.

177(2) This Act is to be read, where appropriate, with the Administration Act and the Consequential Provisions Act.

177(3) The enactments consolidated by this Act are repealed, in consequence of the consolidation, by the Consequential Provisions Act.

177(4) Except as provided in Schedule 4 to the Consequential Provisions Act, this Act shall come into force on 1st July 1992.

177(5) [Not relevant to working families' tax credit or disabled person's tax credit.]

177(6) Except as provided by this section, this Act does not extend to Northern Ireland.

EMPLOYMENT RIGHTS ACT 1996

(1996 Chapter 18) [*22nd May 1996*]

ARRANGEMENT OF SECTIONS

PART V – PROTECTION FROM SUFFERING DETRIMENT IN EMPLOYMENT

RIGHTS NOT TO SUFFER DETRIMENT

47D Tax credits

47D(1) An employee has the right not to be subjected to any detriment by any act, or any deliberate failure to act, by his employer, done on the ground that–

(a) any action was taken, or was proposed to be taken, by or on behalf of the employee with a view to enforcing, or otherwise securing the benefit of, a right conferred on the employee by regulations under section 25 of the Tax Credits Act 2002,

(b) a penalty was imposed on the employer, or proceedings for a penalty were brought against him, under that Act, as a result of action taken by or on behalf of the employee for the purpose of enforcing, or otherwise securing the benefit of, such a right, or

(c) the employee is entitled, or will or may be entitled, to working tax credit.

47D(2) It is immaterial for the purposes of subsection (1)(a) or (b)–

(a) whether or not the employee has the right, or

(b) whether or not the right has been infringed,

but, for those provisions to apply, the claim to the right and (if applicable) the claim that it has been infringed must be made in good faith.

47D(3) Subsections (1) and (2) apply to a person who is not an employee within the meaning of this Act but who is an employee within the meaning of section 25 of the Tax Credits Act 2002, with references to his employer in those subsections (and sections 48(2) and (4) and 49(1)) being construed in accordance with that section.

47D(4) Subsections (1) and (2) do not apply to an employee if the detriment in question amounts to dismissal (within the meaning of Part 10).

History – S. 47D inserted by TCA 2002, s. 27 and Sch. 1, para. 1(2) with effect 1 September 2002 by virtue of SI 2002/1727.

PART VIII

Chapter I – Maternity Leave

73 Additional maternity leave

73(1) An employee who satisfies prescribed conditions may be absent from work at any time during an additional maternity leave period.

73(2) An additional maternity leave period is a period calculated in accordance with regulations made by the Secretary of State.

73(3) Regulations under subsection (2)–

(a) may allow an employee to bring forward the date on which an additional maternity leave period ends, subject to prescribed restrictions and subject to satisfying prescribed conditions;

(aa) may allow an employee in prescribed circumstances to revoke, or to be treated as revoking, the bringing forward of that date;

(b) may specify circumstances in which an employee may work for her employer during an additional maternity leave period without bringing the period to an end.

73(3A) Provision under subsection (3)(a) is to secure that an employee may bring forward the date on which an additional maternity leave period ends only if the employee or another person has taken, or is taking, prescribed steps as regards leave under section 75E or statutory shared parental pay in respect of the child.

73(4) Subject to section 74, an employee who exercises her right under subsection (1)–

(a) is entitled, for such purposes and to such extent as may be prescribed, to the benefit of the terms and conditions of employment which would have applied if she had not been absent,

(b) is bound, for such purposes and to such extent as may be prescribed, by obligations arising under those terms and conditions (except in so far as they are inconsistent with subsection (1)), and

(c) is entitled to return from leave to a job of a prescribed kind.

73(5) In subsection (4)(a) **"terms and conditions of employment"**–

(a) includes matters connected with an employee's employment whether or not they arise under her contract of employment, but

(b) does not include terms and conditions about remuneration.

73(5A) In subsection (4)(c), the reference to return from leave includes, where appropriate, a reference to a continuous period of absence attributable partly to additional maternity leave and partly to ordinary maternity leave.

73(6) The Secretary of State may make regulations specifying matters which are, or are not, to be treated as remuneration for the purposes of this section.

73(7) The Secretary of State may make regulations making provision, in relation to the right to return under subsection (4)(c), about–

(a) seniority, pension rights and similar rights;

(b) terms and conditions of employment on return.

History – In s. 73(3)(a), the words "to bring forward the date on which an additional maternity leave period ends, subject to prescribed restrictions and subject to satisfying prescribed conditions;" substituted for the words "to choose, subject to prescribed restrictions, the date on which an additional maternity leave period ends;" by Children and Families Act 2014, s. 118(3), with effect from 30 June 2014 (SI 2014/1640, art. 3).
S. 73(3)(aa) inserted by Children and Families Act 2014, s. 118(3), with effect from 30 June 2014 (SI 2014/1640, art. 3).
S. 73(3) substituted by the Work and Families Act 2006, s. 11 and Sch. 1, para. 32, with effect for the purpose of the powers to prescribe matters by regulations from 27 June 2006 and for all other purposes from 1 October 2006 (SI 2006/1682).
S. 73(3A) inserted by Children and Families Act 2014, s. 118(3), with effect from 30 June 2014 (SI 2014/1640, art. 3).
S. 73(5A) inserted by the Employment Act 2002, s. 17(4), with effect in relation to employees whose expected week of childbirth begins on or after 6 April 2003 (SI 2002/2866).
S. 73 substituted by the Employment Relations Act 1999, s. 7 and Sch. 4, Pt. 1, with effect from 15 December 1999 in relation to employees whose expected week of childbirth begins on or after 30 April 2000 but in the case of a dismissal only where the dismissal falls on or after 15 December 1999 (SI 1999/2830).

PART X – UNFAIR DISMISSAL

Chapter I – Right not to be unfairly dismissed

FAIRNESS

104B Tax credits

104B(1) An employee who is dismissed shall be regarded for the purposes of this Part as unfairly dismissed if the reason (or, if more than one, the principal reason) for the dismissal is that–

(a) any action was taken, or was proposed to be taken, by or on behalf of the employee with a view to enforcing, or otherwise securing the benefit of, a right conferred on the employee by regulations under section 25 of the Tax Credits Act 2002,

(b) a penalty was imposed on the employer, or proceedings for a penalty were brought against him, under that Act, as a result of action taken by or on behalf of the employee for the purpose of enforcing, or otherwise securing the benefit of, such a right, or

(c) the employee is entitled, or will or may be entitled, to working tax credit.

104B(2) It is immaterial for the purposes of subsection (1)(a) or (b)–

(a) whether or not the employee has the right, or

(b) whether or not the right has been infringed,

but, for those provisions to apply, the claim to the right and (if applicable) the claim that it has been infringed must be made in good faith.

History – S. 104B substituted by TCA 2002, s. 27 and Sch. 1, para. 3(2) with effect 1 September 2002 by virtue of SI 2002/1727.

SOCIAL SECURITY ACT 1998

(1998 Chapter 14)

[*21st May 1998*]

ARRANGEMENT OF SECTIONS

PART I – DECISIONS AND APPEALS

CHAPTER II – SOCIAL SECURITY DECISIONS AND APPEALS

APPEALS

PROCEDURE ETC.

CASES OF ERROR

SUPPLEMENTAL

SCHEDULES

Notes – The text as set out below is shown as modified by SI 2002/2926.

PART I – DECISIONS AND APPEALS

Chapter II – Social Security Decisions and Appeals

APPEALS

12 Appeal to First-tier Tribunal

Notes – The text of s. 12 is shown here in its modified form (the modifications are applied by SI 2002/2926, reg. 4).

12(1) An appeal which is to the First-tier Tribunal by virtue of section 63 of the Tax Credits Act 2002, including an application for a direction under section 19(9) of that Act, (a **"tax credit appeal"**) may be brought by–

(a) a claimant whose claim for a tax credit is the subject of the appeal;

(b) the person on whom the penalty to which the appeal relates was imposed;

(c) the person applying for the direction under section 19(9) of that Act; or

(d) such other person as may be prescribed.

12(2) [S. 12(1) substituted for s. 12(1), (2) by SI 2002/2926, reg. 4(2): modified application of s. 12.]

12(3)–(6) [Omitted by SI 2002/2926, reg. 4(4): modified application of s. 12.]

12(7) Regulations may

(a) make provision as to the manner in which, and the time within which, appeals are to be brought and may in particular extend the time limit for giving notice of appeal specified in section 39(1) of the Tax Credits Act 2002

(b) provide that, where in accordance with regulations under subsection (3A) there is no right of appeal against a decision, any purported appeal may be treated as an application for revision under section 9.

12(8) In deciding a tax credit appeal, the First-tier Tribunal–

(a) [omitted by SI 2002/2926, reg. 4(8): modified application of s. 12;]

(b) shall not take into account any circumstances not obtaining at the time when the decision appealed against was made.

12(9) [Omitted by SI 2002/2926, reg. 4(8): modified application of s. 12.]

History – In the heading to s. 12, "First-tier Tribunal" substituted by SI 2008/2833, art. 9 and Sch. 3, para. 149(a), with effect from 3 November 2008.
In s. 12(5), "the First-tier Tribunal" substituted by SI 2008/2833, art. 9 and Sch. 3, para. 149(b), with effect from 3 November 2008.
S. 12(7)(b) inserted (and s. 12(7)(a) created from part of existing text of s. 12(7)) by WRA 2012, s. 102(4), with effect from 25 February 2013.
In s. 12(8), "the First-tier Tribunal" substituted by SI 2008/2833, art. 9 and Sch. 3, para. 149(b), with effect from 3 November 2008.

Cross references – SI 2002/2926, reg. 4: modified application of s. 12 in relation to a tax credit appeal to an appeal tribunal.
SI 2002/3196, reg. 3: other persons with a right of appeal where claimant is unable to exercise it.

Statutory instruments – SI 2002/3196.

13 Redetermination etc. of appeals by tribunal

Notes – The text of s. 13 is shown here in its modified form (the modifications are applied by SI 2002/2926, reg. 5).

13(1) This section applies where an application is made to the First-tier Tribunal for permission to appeal to the Upper Tribunal from any decision of the First-tier Tribunal under section 12 or this section.

13(2) [Omitted by SI 2008/2833, art. 9 and Sch. 3, para. 150(b).]

13(3) [Omitted by SI 2002/2969, reg. 5(2): modified application of s. 13.]

13(4) In section 14 below **"the principal parties"** means–

(a) the persons mentioned in subsection (3)(a) and (b) of that section,

(b) [omitted by SI 2002/2969, reg. 5(3)(b): modified application of s. 13.]

History – In s. 13(1), the words "to the First-tier Tribunal for permission to appeal to the Upper Tribunal from any decision of the First-tier Tribunal under section 12 or this section" substituted by SI 2008/2833, art. 9 and Sch. 3, para. 150(a), with effect from 3 November 2008.
S. 13(2) omitted by SI 2008/2833, art. 9 and Sch. 3, para. 150(b), with effect from 3 November 2008.
S. 13(4) substituted by SSC(TF)A 1999, s. 18 and Sch. 7, para. 26, from 1 April 1999 (SI 1999/527).

Cross references – SI 2002/2926, reg. 5: modified application of s. 13 in relation to a decision of an appeal tribunal on a tax credit appeal.

14 Appeal from First-tier Tribunal to Upper Tribunal

Notes – The text of s. 14 is shown here in its modified form (the modifications are applied by SI 2002/2926, reg. 5).

14(1) [Omitted by SI 2008/2833, art. 9 and Sch. 3, para. 151(b).]

14(2) [Omitted by SSC(TF)A 1999, s. 18 and Sch. 7 para. 27(a).]

14(3) An appeal to the Upper Tribunal under section 11 of the Tribunals, Courts and Enforcement Act 2007 from any decision of the First-Tier Tribunal under section 12 or 13 above lies at the instance of any of the following–

(a) the Board;

(b) the claimant and such other person as may be prescribed;

(c) in any of the cases mentioned in subsection (5) below, a trade union;

(d) [omitted by SI 2002/2969, reg. 6(2)(c): modified application of s. 14.]

14(4) [Omitted by SI 2002/2969, reg. 6(2)(c): modified application of s. 14.]

14(5) The following are the cases in which an appeal lies at the instance of a trade union–

(a) where the claimant is a member of the union at the time of the appeal and was so immediately before the matter in question arose;

(b) where that matter in any way relates to a deceased person who was a member of the union at the time of his death;

(c) [omitted by SI 2002/2969, reg. 6(2)(c): modified application of s. 14.]

14(6) Subsections (2), (3) and (5) above, as they apply to a trade union, apply also to any other association which exists to promote the interests and welfare of its members.

14(7) [Omitted by SI 2008/2833, art. 9 and Sch. 3, para. 151(d).]

14(8) [Omitted by SI 2008/2833, art. 9 and Sch. 3, para. 151(d).]

14(9) [Omitted by SI 2008/2833, art. 9 and Sch. 3, para. 151(d).]

14(10) *[Omitted by SI 2008/2833*, art. 9 and Sch. 3, para. 151(d).]

14(11) [Omitted by SI 2008/2833, art. 9 and Sch. 3, para. 151(d).]

14(12) [Omitted by SI 2008/2833, art. 9 and Sch. 3, para. 151(d).]

History – In the heading to s. 14, "First-tier Tribunal to Upper Tribunal" substituted by SI 2008/2833, art. 9 and Sch. 3, para. 151(a), with effect from 3 November 2008.

S. 14(1) omitted by SI 2008/2833, art. 9 and Sch. 3, para. 151(b), with effect from 3 November 2008.
S. 14(2) omitted (without entering into force) by SSC(TF)A 1999, s. 18 and Sch. 7, para. 27(a), with effect from 1 April 1999 (SI 1999/527).
In s. 14(3), the words "to the Upper Tribunal under section 11 of the Tribunals, Courts and Enforcement Act 2007 from any decision of the First-Tier Tribunal under section 12 or 13 above lies" substituted by SI 2008/2833, art. 9 and Sch. 3, para. 151(c), with effect from 3 November 2008.
In s. 14(3) the words "In any other case", at the beginning of the subsection, omitted with effect from 1 April 1999, by SSC(TF)A 1999, s. 18 and Sch. 7, para. 27(b).
S. 14(7)–(12) omitted by SI 2008/2833, art. 9 and Sch. 3, para. 151(d), with effect from 3 November 2008.
Cross references – SI 2002/2926, reg. 6: modified application of s. 14(1)–(10) in relation to a decision of an appeal tribunal on a tax credit appeal.
Statutory instruments – SI 2002/3196.
SI 2002/3237.

15 Applications for permission to appeal against a decision of the Upper Tribunal

15(1) [Omitted by SI 2008/2833, art. 9 and Sch. 3, para. 152(b).]

15(2) [Omitted by SI 2008/2833, art. 9 and Sch. 3, para. 152(b).]

15(3) An application for permission to appeal from a decision of the Upper Tribunal in respect of a decision of the First-tier Tribunal under section 12 or 13 may only be made by–

(a) a person who, before the proceedings before the Upper Tribunal were begun, was entitled to appeal to the Upper Tribunal from the decision to which the Upper Tribunal's decision relates;

(b) any other person who was a party to the proceedings in which the first decision mentioned in paragraph (a) above was given;

(c) any other person who is authorised by regulations to apply for permission.

15(4) [Omitted by SI 2008/2833, art. 9 and Sch. 3, para. 152(d).]

15(5) [Omitted by SI 2008/2833, art. 9 and Sch. 3, para. 152(b).]

History – Heading to s. 15 substituted by SI 2008/2833, art. 9 and Sch. 3, para. 152(a), with effect from 3 November 2008.
S. 15(1) and (2) omitted by SI 2008/2833, art. 9 and Sch. 3, para. 152(b), with effect from 3 November 2008.
In s. 15(3), the words "An application for permission to appeal from a decision of the Upper Tribunal in respect of a decision of the First-tier Tribunal under section 12 or 13" substituted by SI 2008/2833, art. 9 and Sch. 3, para. 152(c), with effect from 3 November 2008.
In s. 15(3)(a), "Upper Tribunal" substituted in both places, and "Upper Tribunal's" substituted for "Commissioner's", by SI 2008/2833, art. 9 and Sch. 3, para. 152(c), with effect from 3 November 2008.
In s. 15(3)(c), "permission" substituted by SI 2008/2833, art. 9 and Sch. 3, para. 152(c), with effect from 3 November 2008.
In s. 15(3), at the end, the words "and regulations may make provision with respect to the manner in which and the time within which applications must be made to a Commissioner for leave under this section and with respect to the procedure for dealing with such applications", omitted by SI 2008/2833, art. 9 and Sch. 3, para. 152(c), with effect from 3 November 2008.
S. 15(4) and (5) omitted by SI 2008/2833, art. 9 and Sch. 3, para. 152(d), with effect from 3 November 2008.
Cross references – SI 2002/2926, reg. 8: modified application of s. 15 in relation to a decision of a Social Security Commissioner on a tax credit appeal.
SI 2002/3237, reg. 27(3): a person who under SI 2002/2014 may act for another in making a claim for a tax credit is authorised for the purposes of s. 15 to apply for leave to appeal against the decision of a Social Security Commissioner.
Statutory instruments – SI 2002/3237.

15A Functions of Senior President of Tribunals

15A(1) The Senior President of Tribunals shall ensure that appropriate steps are taken by the First-tier Tribunal to secure the confidentiality, in such circumstances as may be prescribed, of any prescribed material, or any prescribed classes or categories of material.

15A(2) [Omitted by Deregulation Act 2015, s. 79.]

15A(3) [Omitted by Deregulation Act 2015, s. 79.]

History – S. 15A(2) and (3) omitted by Deregulation Act 2015, s. 79, with effect from the end of the period of 2 months beginning on 26 March 2015. Former s. 15A read as follows:
"**15A(2)** Each year the Senior President of Tribunals shall make to the Secretary of State a written report, based on the cases coming before the First-tier Tribunal, on the standards achieved by the Secretary of State in the making of decisions against which an appeal lies to the First-tier Tribunal.
15A(3) The Lord Chancellor shall publish the report.".
In former s. 15A(2), the words "and the Child Maintenance and Enforcement Commission" which appeared after the words "Secretary of State" (in both places) omitted by SI 2012/2007, art. 64(b), with effect from 31 July 2012.
S. 15A inserted by SI 2008/2833, art. 9 and Sch. 3, para. 153, with effect from 3 November 2008.

PROCEDURE ETC.

Notes – The text below reflects s. 16 as modified by SI 2002/2926 for tax credits purposes. The unmodified version of s. 16 is reproduced in the National Insurance contributions section of this work.

16 Procedure

16(1) Regulations ("procedure regulations") may make any such provision as is specified in Schedule 5 to this Act.

16(2) [Omitted by SI 2008/2833, art. 9 and Sch. 3, para. 154.]

16(3) [Omitted by SI 2002/2926, reg. 9(2): modified application of s. 16.]

16(4) [Omitted by SI 2002/2926, reg. 9(4): modified application of s. 16.]

16(5) [Omitted by SI 2002/2926, reg. 9(4): modified application of s. 16.]

16(6) [Omitted by SI 2008/2833, art. 9 and Sch. 3, para. 154.]

16(7) [Omitted by SI 2008/2833, art. 9 and Sch. 3, para. 154.]

16(8) [Omitted by SI 2008/2833, art. 9 and Sch. 3, para. 154.]

16(9) [Omitted by SI 2008/2833, art. 9 and Sch. 3, para. 154.]

History – S. 16(2) omitted by SI 2008/2833, art. 9 and Sch. 3, para. 154, with effect from 3 November 2008.
S. 16(6)–(9) omitted by SI 2008/2833, art. 9 and Sch. 3, para. 154, with effect from 3 November 2008.

Cross references – SI 2002/2926, reg. 9: modified application of s. 16 and Sch. 5 in relation to a tax credit appeal.

Statutory instruments – SI 2002/3196.
SI 2002/3237.

Notes – The above reflects s. 16 as modified by SI 2002/2926 for tax credits purposes. The unmodified version of s. 16 is reproduced in the National Insurance contributions section of this work.

17 Finality of decisions

17(1) Subject to the provisions of–

(a) sections 12 to 16 of this Act, and

(b) the Tax Credits Act 2002,

(c) any provision made by or under Chapter 2 of Part 1 of the Tribunals, Courts and Enforcement Act 2007,

any decision made in accordance with those provisions in respect of an appeal which, by virtue of section 63 of the Tax Credits Act 2002 (or of provisions of this Act applied by regulations made under that section), is to the First-tier Tribunal or lies to the Upper Tribunal, shall be final.

17(2) If and to the extent that regulations so provide, any finding of fact or other determination embodied in or necessary to such a decision, or on which such a decision is based, shall be conclusive for the purposes of–

(a) further such decisions;

(b) [omitted by SI 2002/2969, reg. 10(4): modified application of s. 17;]

(c) [omitted by SI 2002/2969, reg. 10(4): modified application of s. 17.]

Cross references – SI 2002/2926, reg. 10: modified application of s. 17 to a decision of an appeal tribunal or a Social Security Commissioner on a tax credit appeal.

CASES OF ERROR

28 Correction of errors and setting aside of decisions

28(1) Regulations may make provision with respect to–

(a) the correction of accidental errors in any decision of the Secretary of State or record of a decision of the Secretary of State made under any relevant enactment;

(b) [omitted by SI 2008/2833, art. 9 and Sch. 3, para. 164(a).]

28(1A) In subsection (1) **"decision"** does not include any decision of the First-tier Tribunal or any decision made by an officer of the Inland Revenue, other than a decision under or by virtue of Part III of the Pension Schemes Act 1993.

28(2) Nothing in subsection (1) above shall be construed as derogating from any power to correct errors which is exercisable apart from regulations made by virtue of that subsection.

28(3) In this section **"relevant enactment"** means any enactment contained in–

(a) this Chapter;

(b) the Contributions and Benefits Act;

(c) the Pension Schemes Act 1993;

(d) the Jobseekers Act;

(e) the Social Security (Recovery of Benefits) Act 1997;

(f) the State Pension Credit Act 2002;

(g) Part 1 of the Welfare Reform Act 2007;

(h) Part 1 of the Welfare Reform Act 2012;

(i) Part 4 of that Act or

(j) Part 1 of the Pensions Act 2014.

Prospective amendments – In s. 28(3)(j), the words "or section 30 of that Act" inserted after the words "Part 1 of the Pensions Act 2014" by PA 2014, s. 31 and Sch. 16, para. 42, with effect from a day to be appointed by order of the Secretary of State under PA 2014, s. 56(1).

History – In s. 28(1)(a), the words "of the Secretary of State" inserted in both places by SI 2008/2833, art. 9 and Sch. 3, para. 164(a), with effect from 3 November 2008.
S. 28(1)(b) (and the "and" immediately before it) omitted by SI 2008/2833, art. 9 and Sch. 3, para. 164(a), with effect from 3 November 2008.
In s. 28(1A), the words "any decision of the First-tier Tribunal or" inserted by SI 2008/2833, art. 9 and Sch. 3, para. 164(b), with effect from 3 November 2008.
S. 28(1A) inserted by SSC(TF)A 1999, s. 18 and Sch. 7, para. 34, with effect from 5 July 1999 (SI 1999/1662).
In s. 28(2), the words "or set aside decisions", which appeared after "correct errors", omitted by SI 2008/2833, art. 9 and Sch. 3, para. 164(c), with effect from 3 November 2008.
S. 28(3)(f) and word "or" immediately before it inserted by the State Pension Credit Act 2002, s. 11 and Sch. 1, para. 10 with effect from 2 July 2002 for the purpose only of making regulations and orders, by virtue of SI 2002/1691.
S. 28(3)(g) inserted by Welfare Reform act 2007, s. 28 and Sch. 3, para. 17(6), with effect from 18 March 2008 (for the purpose of making regulations) and 27 July 2008 (for other purposes) (SI 2008/787).
S. 28(3)(h) inserted (and the "or" at the end of s. 28(3)(f) repealed) by WRA 2012, s. 31 and Sch. 2, para. 48, with effect from 25 February 2013 (SI 2013/358, art. 2 and Sch. 2, para. 40).
S. 23(3)(i) inserted by WRA 2012, s. 91 and Sch. 9, para. 42, with effect from 25 February 2013 (SI 2013/358, art. 2 and Sch. 2, para. 43).
S. 28(3)(j) inserted (and the final "or" in s. 28(3)(h) omitted, and a final "or" inserted in s. 23(3)(i)) by PA 2014, s. 23 and Sch. 12, para. 36, with effect from 6 April 2016 (as not brought into force by any earlier order under PA 2014, s. 56(1)).

Cross references – SI 2002/2926, reg. 11: modified application of s. 28 to a decision of an appeal tribunal or a Social Security Commissioner on a tax credit appeal.

Statutory instruments – SI 2002/3196.
SI 2002/3237.

SUPPLEMENTAL

39ZA Certificates

39ZA A document bearing a certificate which–

(a) is signed by a person authorised in that behalf by the Secretary of State, and

(b) states that the document, apart from the certificate, is a record of a decision of an officer of the Secretary of State,

shall be conclusive evidence of the decision; and a certificate purporting to be so signed shall be deemed to be so signed unless the contrary is proved.

History – S. 39ZA inserted by SI 2008/2833, art. 9 and Sch. 3, para. 166, with effect from 3 November 2008.

39 Interpretation etc. of Chapter II

39(1) In this Chapter–

"claimant", in relation to a joint-claim couple claiming a joint-claim jobseeker's allowance (within the meaning of the Jobseekers Act 1995), means the couple or either member of the couple;

"claimant", in relation to a couple jointly claiming universal credit, means the couple or either member of the couple;

"relevant benefit" has the meaning given by section 8(3) above;

39(2) Expressions used in this Chapter to which a meaning is assigned by section 191 of the Administration Act have that meaning in this Chapter.

39(3) Part II of the Administration Act, which is superseded by the foregoing provisions of this Chapter, shall cease to have effect.

Commencement Date – In so far as it was not already in force s. 39 entered into force (except for the purposes of housing benefit, council tax benefit and decisions to which SI 1999/527, art. 4(6) applies; i.e. pre-1 April 1999 decisions under SSAA 1992, s. 17(1),s. 20(3) and PSA 1993, s. 170(1)) with effect from 29 November 1999 (SI 1999/3178 (C. 81), art. 2(1)(a); 2(2) and Sch. 1).
S. 39 entered into force; for the purposes of (i) decisions whether a person is entitled to be credited with earnings or contributions in accordance with regulations made under s. 22(5) of the Contributions and Benefits Act; and (ii) decisions whether a person was, within the meaning of regulations, precluded from regular employment by responsibilities at home; with effect from 18 October 1999 (SI 1999/2860 (C. 75), art. 2(c)(iv), (v) and Sch. 1).
S. 39 entered into force, for the purposes of any matter to which, by virtue of PSA 1993, s. 170, provisions of SSA 1998, Pt. I, Ch. II are to apply, with effect from 5 July 1999 (SI 1999/1958 (C. 51), art. 2(1)(b)(iv)).
S. 39 entered into force, for the purposes of benefits under SSCBA 1992, Pt. II except child's special allowance, with effect from 6 September 1999 (SI 1999/2422 (C. 61), art. 2(c)(i) and Sch. 1).
S. 39(3) entered into force on 18 October 1999 but only in so far as it provides for SSAA 1992, s. 63 (which is in Pt. II of the Administration Act) to cease to have effect (SI 1999/2860).

Prospective amendments – In s. 39(1), the definition of "claimant" repealed by WRA 2012, s. 147 and Sch. 14, Pt. 1, with effect from a date to be set by order of the Secretary of State.

History – In s. 39(1), second definition of "claimant" inserted by WRA 2012, s. 31 and Sch. 2, para. 49, with effect (for the purpose of making regulations) from 25 February 2013 (SI 2013/358, art. 2) and from 29 April 2013 for other purposes (SI 2013/983, art. 3(1)(b)).
In s. 39(1) the definition of "health care professional" inserted by WRA 2007, s. 62, with effect from 3 July 2007.
In s. 39(1), the definition of "tax appeal Commissioners" omitted by SI 2009/56, art. 3(1) and Sch. 1, para. 250, operative from 1 April 2009, subject to transitional and saving provisions in SI 2009/56, Sch. 3.
In s. 39(1) the definitions of "appeal tribunal" and "Commissioner" omitted by SI 2008/2833, art. 9 and Sch. 3, para. 167, with effect from 3 November 2008.

In s. 39(1) the words "(except in the expression "tax appeal Commissioners")" inserted in the meaning of "Commissioner" and the definition for "tax appeal Commissioners" added by SSC(TF)A 1999, s. 18 and Sch. 7, para. 35, with effect from 1 April 1999 (SI 1999/527).
In s. 39(1), the definition of "claimant" inserted by WRPA 1999, s. 59 and Sch. 7, para. 17, with effect from 19 March 2001 (by virtue of SI 2000/2958).

Cross references – TCA 2002, s. 51 and Sch. 4, para. 15: references in this Chapter to a decision of the Secretary of State are, where the context so requires in consequence of TCA 2002, s. 50 (functions transferred to the Board), to be construed as references to a decision of the Board, or, where the power to decide is exercised by an officer of the Board, an officer of the Board.
SI 2002/2926, reg. 12: modified application of s. 39 to a tax credit appeal.

Statutory instruments – 2002/3196.
2002/3237.

SCHEDULES

SCHEDULE 4 – SOCIAL SECURITY COMMISSIONERS

Section 14(12)

[Omitted by SI 2008/2833, art. 9 and Sch. 3, para. 172.]

History – Sch. 4 omitted by SI 2008/2833, art. 9 and Sch. 3, para. 172, with effect from 3 November 2008.

SCHEDULE 5 – REGULATIONS AS TO PROCEDURE: PROVISION WHICH MAY BE MADE

Section 16(1)

Cross references – SI 2002/2926, reg. 9: modified application of s. 16 and Sch. 5 in relation to a tax credit appeal.

Statutory instruments – SI 2002/3237: Social Security Commissioners (Procedure) (Tax Credits Appeals) Regulations 2002.

1 Provision prescribing the procedure to be followed in connection with–

(a) the making of decisions or determinations [by]; and

(b) the withdrawal of claims, applications, appeals or references falling to be decided or determined [by].

History – In para. 1(a) and 1(b), the words "an appeal tribunal or a Commissioner", which appeared after the word "by" in both places, omitted by SI 2008/2833, art. 9 and Sch. 3, para. 173(a), with effect from 3 November 2008. The text in both places now ends with the word "by", which is the (no doubt unintended) combined effect of the SI 2002/2926, reg. 9 modification and the SI 2008/2833 amendment.

2 [Omitted by SI 2008/2833, art. 9 and Sch. 3, para. 173(b).]

History – Para. 2 omitted by SI 2008/2833, art. 9 and Sch. 3, para. 173(b), with effect from 3 November 2008.

3 Provision as to the form which is to be used for any document, the evidence which is to be required and the circumstances in which any official record or certificate is to be sufficient or conclusive evidence.

4 Provision as to the time within which, or the manner in which–

(a) any evidence is to be produced; or

(b) any application, reference or appeal is to be made, including provision extending the time limit for giving notice of appeal specified in section 39(1) of the Tax Credits Act 2002.

5 [Omitted by SI 2008/2833, art. 9 and Sch. 3, para. 173(b).]

History – Para. 5 omitted by SI 2008/2833, art. 9 and Sch. 3, para. 173(b), with effect from 3 November 2008.

6 [Omitted by SI 2008/2833, art. 9 and Sch. 3, para. 173(b).]

History – Para. 6 omitted by SI 2008/2833, art. 9 and Sch. 3, para. 173(b), with effect from 3 November 2008.

7 [Omitted by SI 2008/2833, art. 9 and Sch. 3, para. 173(b).]

History – Para. 7 omitted by SI 2008/2833, art. 9 and Sch. 3, para. 173(b), with effect from 3 November 2008.

8 [Omitted by SI 2008/2833, art. 9 and Sch. 3, para. 173(b).]

History – Para. 8 omitted by SI 2008/2833, art. 9 and Sch. 3, para. 173(b), with effect from 3 November 2008.

9 Provision for the non-disclosure to a person of the particulars of any medical advice or medical evidence given or submitted for the purposes of a determination.

TAX CREDITS ACT 2002

(2002 Chapter 21)

[*8th July 2002*]

ARRANGEMENT OF SECTIONS

PART 1 – TAX CREDITS

PART 1 – TAX CREDITS

Prospective amendments – Pt. 1 (but not Sch. 1 or Sch. 3) repealed by WRA 2012, s. 147 and Sch. 14, Pt. 1, with effect from a date to be set by order of the Secretary of State.

Cross references – ITEPA 2003, s. 677(1): no liability to income tax arises on child tax credit and working tax credit.

GENERAL

1 Introductory

1(1) This Act makes provision for–

(a) a tax credit to be known as child tax credit, and

(b) a tax credit to be known as working tax credit.

1(2) In this Act references to a tax credit are to either of those tax credits and references to tax credits are to both of them.

1(3) The following (which are superseded by tax credits) are abolished–

(a) children's tax credit under section 257AA of the Income and Corporation Taxes Act 1988 (c. 1),

(b) working families' tax credit,

(c) disabled person's tax credit,

(d) the amounts which, in relation to income support and income-based jobseeker's allowance, are prescribed as part of the applicable amount in respect of a child or young person, the family premium, the enhanced disability premium in respect of a child or young person and the disabled child premium,

(e) increases in benefits in respect of children under sections 80 and 90 of the Social Security Contributions and Benefits Act 1992 (c. 4) and sections 80 and 90 of the Social Security Contributions and Benefits (Northern Ireland) Act 1992 (c. 7), and

(f) the employment credit under the schemes under section 2(2) of the Employment and Training Act 1973 (c. 50) and section 1 of the Employment and Training Act (Northern Ireland) 1950 (c. 29 (N.I.)) known as "New Deal 50plus".

Commencement Date – S. 1(1) and (2) entered into force on 9 July 2002 for all purposes of Pt. 1 and, as respects tax credits, Pt. 3 (SI 2002/1727 (C. 52)).
S. 1(3)(a) and (f) came into force on 6 April 2003 by virtue of SI 2003/962 (C. 51), art. 2(3)(a).
S. 1(3)(b) and (c) came into force on 8 April 2003 by virtue of SI 2003/962 (C. 51), art. 2(4)(a), subject to the savings contained in art. 3 of that Order.
S. 1(3)(d) will enter into force on 31 December 2014 by virtue of SI 2003/962, art. 2(5) as amended (most recently) by SI 2011/2910, art. 2. SI 2003/962 art. 2(5) originally specified a date of 6 April 2005.
S. 1(3)(e) entered into force on 6 April 2003 (SI 2003/938, art. 2), subject to the saving provision in SI 2003/938, art. 3 relating to certain child dependency increases to which a claimant is entitled before the commencement date.

Prospective amendments – Pt. 1 (but not Sch. 1 or Sch. 3) repealed by WRA 2012, s. 147 and Sch. 14, Pt. 1, with effect from a date to be set by order of the Secretary of State.

Cross references – ICTA 1988, s. 617A: payments of a tax credit are not treated as income for any purposes of the Income Tax Acts.
SI 2003/2170, contains transitional provisions in connection with the introduction of child tax credit.
SI 2005/773 and SI 2005/776: transitional provisions dealing with the migration to child tax credits of claimants previously receiving child premiums paid with Income Support and income-based Jobseekers Allowance, which are to be withdrawn with effect from 31 December 2006 by virtue of s. 1(3)(d).

2 Functions of Commissioners for Revenue and Customs

2 The Commissioners for Her Majesty's Revenue and Customs shall be responsible for the payment and management of tax credits.

Commencement Date – S. 2 entered into force on 9 July 2002 for all purposes of Pt. I and, as respects tax credits, Pt. 3 (SI 2002/1727 (C. 52)).

Prospective amendments – Pt. 1 (but not Sch. 1 or Sch. 3) repealed by WRA 2012, s. 147 and Sch. 14, Pt. 1, with effect from a date to be set by order of the Secretary of State.

History – S. 2 substituted for previous version and, in the heading, "Functions of Commissioners for Revenue and Customs" substituted, by CRCA 2005, s. 50 and Sch. 4, para. 88, with effect from 18 April, 2005 (SI 2005/1126, reg. 2(2)).

3 Claims

3(1) Entitlement to a tax credit for the whole or part of a tax year is dependent on the making of a claim for it.

3(2) Where the Board–

(a) decide under section 14 not to make an award of a tax credit on a claim, or

(b) decide under section 16 to terminate an award of a tax credit made on a claim,

(subject to any appeal) any entitlement, or subsequent entitlement, to the tax credit for any part of the same tax year is dependent on the making of a new claim.

3(3) A claim for a tax credit may be made–

(a) jointly by the members of a couple both of whom are aged at least sixteen and are in the United Kingdom, or

(b) by a person who is aged at least sixteen and is in the United Kingdom but is not entitled to make a claim under paragraph (a) (jointly with another).

3(4) Entitlement to a tax credit pursuant to a claim ceases–

(a) in the case of a joint claim, if the persons by whom it was made could no longer jointly make a joint claim, and

(b) in the case of a single claim, if the person by whom it was made could no longer make a single claim.

3(5A) In this Part **"couple"** means–

(a) a man and woman who are married to each other and are neither–

(i) separated under a court order, nor

(ii) separated in circumstances in which the separation is likely to be permanent,

(b) a man and woman who are not married to each other but are living together as husband and wife,

(c) two people of the same sex who are civil partners of each other and are neither–

(i) separated under a court order, nor

(ii) separated in circumstances in which the separation is likely to be permanent, or

(d) two people of the same sex who are not civil partners of each other but are living together as if they were civil partners.

3(7) Circumstances may be prescribed in which a person is to be treated for the purposes of this Part as being, or as not being, in the United Kingdom.

3(8) In this Part–

"joint claim" means a claim under paragraph (a) of subsection (3), and

"single claim" means a claim under paragraph (b) of that subsection.

Commencement Date – S. 3(1) and (3) entered into force by virtue of SI 2002/1727 (C. 52) on:

- 9 July 2002 for making regulations about claims;
- 1 August 2002 for making claims; and
- 1 January 2003 for making decisions on claims.

S. 3(1) and (3) entered into force by virtue of SI 2002/1727 (C. 52) on 6 April 2003 for all other purposes of Pt. I and, as respects tax credits, Pt. 3.

S. 3(2)(a) and (b) entered into force on 1 January 2003 for all purposes of Pt. I and, as respects tax credits, Pt. 3 (SI 2002/1727 (C. 52)).

S. 3(4) entered into force on 1 August 2002 for entitlement to make a claim (SI 2002/1727 (C. 52)).

S. 3(5)–(8) entered into force on 9 July 2002 for all purposes of Pt. I and, as respects tax credits, Pt. 3 (SI 2002/1727 (C. 52)).

Prospective amendments – Pt. 1 (but not Sch. 1 or Sch. 3) repealed by WRA 2012, s. 147 and Sch. 14, Pt. 1, with effect from a date to be set by order of the Secretary of State.

History – In s. 3(a) the word "couple" substituted by the Civil Partnership Act 2004, s. 254 and Sch. 24, para. 144(2), with effect from 5 December 2005 (by virtue of SI 2005/3175, art. 2(1)).

S. 3(5A) substituted for former s. 3(5) and (6) by the Civil Partnership Act 2004, s. 254 and Sch. 24, para. 144(3), with effect from 5 December 2005 (by virtue of SI 2005/3175, art. 2(1)).

Cross references – SI 2002/2014, reg. 21: requirement to notify Revenue where entitlement to tax credit ceases by virtue of s. 3(4).

SI 2003/742, reg. 4: modifications to s. 3 in relation to members of polygamous units.

Statutory instruments – SI 2003/654.

SI 2010/42 (not reproduced): working tax credit is qualifying benefit for purposes of determining exemption from fees payable when bringing appeal under Gambling Act 2005 to First-tier Tribunal.

SI 2003/742.

HMRC Manuals – TCTM02003: 'a person is ordinarily resident if they are normally residing in the United Kingdom (apart from temporary or occasional absences), and their residence here has been adopted voluntarily and for settled purposes as part of the regular order of their life for the time being.' Examples of 'relevant factors' in determining whether a person has come to live in the UK 'as part of the regular order of their life for the time being'.

Ibid.: a person who is in the UK as a result of their 'deportation, expulsion or some other legal form of compulsory removal from another country' may nevertheless be ordinary resident in the UK.

4 Claims: supplementary

4(1) Regulations may–

(a) require a claim for a tax credit to be made in a prescribed manner and within a prescribed time,

(b) provide for a claim for a tax credit made in prescribed circumstances to be treated as having been made on a prescribed date earlier or later than that on which it is made,

(c) *provide that, in prescribed circumstances*, a claim for a tax credit may be made for a period wholly or partly after the date on which it is made,

(d) provide that, in prescribed circumstances, an award on a claim for a tax credit may be made subject to the condition that the requirements for entitlement are satisfied at a prescribed time,

(e) provide for a claim for a tax credit to be made or proceeded with in the name of a person who has died,

(f) provide that, in prescribed circumstances, one person may act for another in making a claim for a tax credit,

(g) provide that, in prescribed circumstances, a claim for a tax credit made by one member of a couple is to be treated as also made by the other member of the couple, and

(h) provide that a claim for a tax credit is to be treated as made by a person or persons in such other circumstances as may be prescribed.

4(2) The Board may supply to a person who has made a claim for a tax credit (whether or not jointly with another)–

(a) any information relating to the claim, to an award made on the claim or to any change of circumstances relevant to the claim or such an award,

(b) any communication made or received relating to such an award or any such change of circumstances, and

(c) any other information which is relevant to any entitlement to tax credits pursuant to the claim or any such change of circumstances or which appeared to be so relevant at the time the information was supplied.

Commencement Date – S. 4(1) entered into force on 9 July 2002 for the purpose of making regulations (SI 2002/1727 (C. 52)).
S. 4(2) entered into force on 1 August 2002 for all purposes of the Act mentioned in that subsection (SI 2002/1727 (C. 52)).

Prospective amendments – Pt. 1 (but not Sch. 1 or Sch. 3) repealed by WRA 2012, s. 147 and Sch. 14, Pt. 1, with effect from a date to be set by order of the Secretary of State.

History – In s. 4(1)(g) the word "couple" substituted by the Civil Partnership Act 2004, s. 254 and Sch. 24, para. 145, with effect from 5 December 2005 (by virtue of SI 2005/3175, art. 2(1)).
In s. 4(1)(g) the words "the couple" substituted by the Civil Partnership Act 2004, s. 254 and Sch. 24, para. 146, with effect from 5 December 2005 (by virtue of SI 2005/3175, art. 2(1)).

Cross references – S. 58, and SI 2002/3036: providing of information or evidence to a relevant authority regarding a tax credit claim, giving of information or advice by relevant authorities, and recording, verification and holding, and forwarding, of claims received by relevant authorities.
SI 2002/2014:

- reg. 5–8: manner in which and time within which claim to be made (s. 4(1)(a), (b));
- reg. 9, 10: advance claims (s. 4(1)(b), (c));
- reg. 13: claims made by one member of a couple to be treated as also made by the other member of the couple (s. 4(1)(g));
- reg. 14: circumstances in which awards to be treated as conditional and claims treated as made (s. 4(1)(d));
- reg. 15, 16: persons who die after making a claim, or before making of a joint claim (s. 4(1)(e));
- reg. 17, 18: circumstances in which one person may act for another (s. 4(1)(f)).

SI 2003/742, reg. 5: modified application of s. 4(1)(g) to members of polygamous units.

Statutory instruments – SI 2002/2014.
SI 2003/742.

5 Period of awards

5(1) Where a tax credit is claimed for a tax year by making a claim before the tax year begins, any award of the tax credit on the claim is for the whole of the tax year.

5(2) An award on any other claim for a tax credit is for the period beginning with the date on which the claim is made and ending at the end of the tax year in which that date falls.

5(3) Subsections (1) and (2) are subject to any decision by the Board under section 16 to terminate an award.

Commencement Date – S. 5(1) and (3) entered into force on 1 January 2003 for the purposes of making decisions on claims before the end of the tax year (SI 2002/1727 (C. 52)).
S. 5(2) and (3) entered into force on 6 April 2002 for the purposes of making decisions on other claims (SI 2002/1727 (C. 52)).

Prospective amendments – Pt. 1 (but not Sch. 1 or Sch. 3) repealed by WRA 2012, s. 147 and Sch. 14, Pt. 1, with effect from a date to be set by order of the Secretary of State.

6 Notifications of changes of circumstances

6(1) Regulations may provide that any change of circumstances of a prescribed description which may increase the maximum rate at which a person or persons may be entitled to a tax credit is to do so only if notification of it has been given.

6(2) Regulations under subsection (1) may–

(a) provide for notification of a change of circumstances given in prescribed circumstances to be treated as having been given on a prescribed date earlier or later than that on which it is given,

(b) provide that, in prescribed circumstances, a notification of a change of circumstances may be given for a period wholly or partly after the date on which it is given, and

(c) provide that, in prescribed circumstances, an amendment of an award of a tax credit in consequence of a notification of a change of circumstances may be made subject to the condition that the requirements for entitlement to the amended amount of the tax credit are satisfied at a prescribed time.

6(3) Regulations may require that, where a person has or persons have claimed a tax credit, notification is to be given if there is a change of circumstances of a prescribed description which may decrease the rate at which he is or they are entitled to the tax credit or mean that he ceases or they cease to be entitled to the tax credit.

6(3A) For the purposes of this section, a change of circumstances shall be treated as having occurred where by virtue of the coming into force of Part 14 of Schedule 24 to the Civil Partnership Act 2004 (amendments of the Tax Credits Act 2002) two people of the same sex are treated as a couple.

6(3B) In subsection (3A), **"couple"** has the meaning given in paragraph 144(3) of Part 14 of Schedule 24 to the Civil Partnership Act 2004.

6(4) Regulations under this section may–

(a) require a notification to be given in a prescribed manner and within a prescribed time,

(b) specify the person or persons by whom a notification may be, or is to be, given, and

(c) provide that, in prescribed circumstances, one person may act for another in giving a notification.

Commencement Date – S. 6 entered into force on 9 July 2002 for the purposes of making regulations (SI 2002/1727 (C. 52)).

Prospective amendments – Pt. 1 (but not Sch. 1 or Sch. 3) repealed by WRA 2012, s. 147 and Sch. 14, Pt. 1, with effect from a date to be set by order of the Secretary of State.

History – S. 6(3A) and (3B) inserted by SI 2005/828, reg. 2(2) with effect from 8 April 2005.

Cross references – S. 58, and SI 2002/3036: providing of information or evidence to a relevant authority regarding a tax credit notification, giving of information or advice by relevant authorities, and recording, verification and holding, and forwarding, of notifications received by relevant authorities.
SI 2002/2014, reg. 20: changes of circumstances will result in increase of maximum rate of entitlement only if notified (s. 6(1)).
SI 2002/2014, reg. 21: requirement to notify changes of circumstances which may decrease rate of entitlement or mean that entitlement ceases (s. 6(3)).
SI 2002/2014, reg. 25: date of notification of changes of circumstances where change may increase maximum rate.

Statutory instruments – SI 2002/2014.
SI 2003/742.

7 Income test

7(1) The entitlement of a person or persons of any description to a tax credit is dependent on the relevant income–

(a) not exceeding the amount determined in the manner prescribed for the purposes of this paragraph in relation to the tax credit and a person or persons of that description (referred to in this Part as the income threshold), or

(b) exceeding the income threshold by only so much that a determination in accordance with regulations under section 13(2) provides a rate of the tax credit in his or their case.

7(2) Subsection (1) does not apply in relation to the entitlement of a person or persons to a tax credit for so long as the person, or either of the persons, is entitled to any social security benefit prescribed for the purposes of this subsection in relation to the tax credit.

7(3) In this Part **"the relevant income"** means–

(a) if an amount is prescribed for the purposes of this paragraph and the current year income exceeds the previous year income by not more than that amount, the previous year income,

(b) if an amount is prescribed for the purposes of this paragraph and the current year income exceeds the previous year income by more than that amount, the current year income reduced by that amount,

(c) if an amount is prescribed for the purposes of this paragraph and the previous year income exceeds the current year income by not more than that amount, the previous year income,

(d) if an amount is prescribed for the purposes of this paragraph and the previous year income exceeds the current year income by more than that amount, the current year income increased by that amount, and

(e) otherwise, the current year income.

7(4) In this Part **"the current year income"** means–

(a) in relation to persons by whom a joint claim for a tax credit is made, the aggregate income of the persons for the tax year to which the claim relates, and

(b) in relation to a person by whom a single claim for a tax credit is made, the income of the person for that tax year.

7(5) In this Part **"the previous year income"** means–

(a) in relation to persons by whom a joint claim for a tax credit is made, the aggregate income of the persons for the tax year preceding that to which the claim relates, and

(b) in relation to a person by whom a single claim for a tax credit is made, the income of the person for that preceding tax year.

7(6) Regulations may provide that, for the purposes of this Part, income of a prescribed description is to be treated as being, or as not being, income for a particular tax year.

7(7) In particular, regulations may provide that income of a prescribed description of a person for the tax year immediately before the preceding tax year referred to in subsection (5) is to be treated as being income of that preceding tax year (instead of any actual income of that description of the person for that preceding tax year).

7(8) Regulations may for the purposes of this Part make provision–

(a) as to what is, or is not, income, and

(b) as to the calculation of income.

7(9) Regulations may provide that, for the purposes of this Part, a person is to be treated–

(a) as having income which he does not in fact have, or

(b) as not having income which he does in fact have.

7(10) The Board may estimate the amount of the income of a person, or the aggregate income of persons, for any tax year for the purpose of making, amending or terminating an award of a tax credit; but such an estimate does not affect the rate at which he is, or they are, entitled to the tax credit for that or any other tax year.

Commencement Date – S. 7(1)–(5) entered into force by virtue of SI 2002/1727 (C. 52) on:
- 9 July 2002 for the purposes of making regulations;
- 1 August 2002 for the purposes of making claims; and
- 1 January 2003 for the purposes of making decisions on claims.

S. 7(1)–(5) entered into force by virtue of SI 2002/1727 (C. 52) on 6 April 2003 for entitlement to payment of award.
S. 7(6)–(9) entered into force on 9 July 2002 for the purposes of making regulations (SI 2002/1727 (C. 52)).
S. 7(10) entered into force on 1 August 2002 for estimating income for the purposes of making, amending or terminating awards (SI 2002/1727 (C. 52)).

Prospective amendments – Pt. 1 (but not Sch. 1 or Sch. 3) repealed by WRA 2012, s. 147 and Sch. 14, Pt. 1, with effect from a date to be set by order of the Secretary of State.

Cross references – Age-related Payments Act 2004: s. 6(c) (not reproduced) provides that age-related payments are disregarded in assessing a person's entitlement to tax credit.
SI 2002/1727, reg. 3 (as substituted by 2002/2158): for the purposes of s. 7(5), the previous year income, in relation to a claim for the year 2003–04, is income for the tax year 2001–02.
SI 2002/2008, reg. 3: prescribes manner in which amounts are to be determined for the purposes of s. 7(1)(a).
SI 2002/2008, reg. 4: social security benefits prescribed for the purposes of s. 7(2).
SI 2002/2008, reg. 5: amount prescribed for the purposes of s. 7(3)(a) and (b).
SI 2003/742, reg. 6: modified application of s. 7(2) to members of polygamous units.
SI 2014/1230, Sch., para. 2: modified application of s. 7(3) and (4) where SI 2014/1230, reg. 12A applies (claims for universal credit).

Statutory instruments – SI 2002/2006 (made under s. 7(8), (9)).
SI 2003/742.
SI 2006/963.
SI 2007/828.

CHILD TAX CREDIT

8 Entitlement

8(1) The entitlement of the person or persons by whom a claim for child tax credit has been made is dependent on him, or either or both of them, being responsible for one or more children or qualifying young persons.

8(2) Regulations may make provision for the purposes of child tax credit as to the circumstances in which a person is or is not responsible for a child or qualifying young person.

8(3) For the purposes of this Part a person is a child if he has not attained the age of sixteen; but regulations may make provision for a person who has attained that age to remain a child for the purposes of this Part after attaining that age for a prescribed period or until a prescribed date.

8(4) In this Part **"qualifying young person"** means a person, other than a child, who–

(a) has not attained such age (greater than sixteen) as is prescribed, and

(b) satisfies prescribed conditions.

8(5) Circumstances may be prescribed in which a person is to be entitled to child tax credit for a prescribed period in respect of a child or qualifying young person who has died.

Commencement Date – S. 8 entered into force by virtue of SI 2002/1727 (C. 52) on:
- 9 July 2002 for the purposes of making regulations;
- 1 August 2002 for the purposes of making claims;
- 1 January 2003 for the purposes of making decisions on claims.

S. 8 entered into force by virtue of SI 2002/1727 (C. 52) on 6 April 2003 for the purposes of entitlement to an award.

Prospective amendments – Pt. 1 (but not Sch. 1 or Sch. 3) repealed by WRA 2012, s. 147 and Sch. 14, Pt. 1, with effect from a date to be set by order of the Secretary of State.

Cross references – SI 2002/2007, reg. 3: circumstances in which a person is or is not responsible for a child or qualifying young person (s. 8(2)).
SI 2002/2007, reg. 4: period for which a person who attains the age of 16 remains a child (s. 8(3)).

SI 2002/2007, reg. 5: maximum age and prescribed conditions for a qualifying young person (s. 8(4)).
SI 2002/2007, reg. 6: entitlement to child tax credit after death of child or qualifying young person (s. 8(5)).
SI 2003/742, reg. 7: modified application of s. 8(1) to members of polygamous units.
SSCBA 1992, s. 30C(5), (5A), 42(1), (1A): entitlement to incapacity benefit where claimant entitled to any element of child tax credit other from family element.
Statutory instruments – SI 2002/2007.
SI 2002/2008.
SI 2003/742.

9 Maximum rate

9(1) The maximum rate at which a person or persons may be entitled to child tax credit is to be determined in the prescribed manner.

9(2) The prescribed manner of determination must involve the inclusion of–

(a) an element which is to be included in the case of every person or persons entitled to child tax credit who is, or either or both of whom is or are, responsible for a child or qualifying young person who was born before 6 April 2017,

(b) an element in respect of each child or qualifying young person for whom the person is, or either or both of them is or are, responsible.

(c) an element which is to be included in the case of a child or qualifying young person who is disabled or severely disabled.

9(3) The element specified in paragraph (a) of subsection (2) is to be known as the family element of child tax credit and that specified in paragraph (b) of that subsection is to be known as the individual element of child tax credit and that specified in paragraph (c) of that subsection is to be known as the disability element of child tax credit.

9(3A) Subsection (3B) applies in the case of a person or persons entitled to child tax credit where the person is, or either or both of them is or are, responsible for a child or qualifying young person born on or after 6 April 2017.

9(3B) The prescribed manner of determination in relation to the person or persons must not include an individual element of child tax credit in respect of the child or qualifying young person unless–

(a) he is (or they are) claiming the individual element of child tax credit for no more than one other child or qualifying young person, or

(b) a prescribed exception applies.

9(4) The prescribed manner of determination may involve the inclusion of such other elements as may be prescribed.

9(5) The prescribed manner of determination–

(a) may include provision for the amount of the family element of child tax credit to vary according to the age of any of the children or qualifying young persons or according to any such other factors as may be prescribed,

(b) may include provision for the amount of the individual element of child tax credit to vary according to the age of the child or qualifying young person or according to any such other factors as may be prescribed, and

(c) may include provision for the amount of the disability element of child tax credit to vary according to whether the child or qualifying young person is disabled or severely disabled.

9(6) A child or qualifying young person is disabled, or severely disabled, for the purposes of this section only if–

(a) he satisfies prescribed conditions, or

(b) prescribed conditions exist in relation to him.

9(7) If, in accordance with regulations under section 8(2), more than one claimant may be entitled to child tax credit in respect of the same child or qualifying young person, the prescribed manner of determination may include provision for the amount of any element of child tax credit included in the case of any one or more of them to be less than it would be if only one claimant were so entitled.

9(8) **"Claimant"** means–

(a) in the case of a single claim, the person who makes the claim, and

(b) in the case of a joint claim, the persons who make the claim.

Commencement Date – *S. 9 entered into force by virtue of SI 2002/1727 (C. 52) on:*

- 9 July 2002 for the purposes of making regulations;
- 1 August 2002 for the purposes of making claims; and
- 1 January 2003 for the purposes of making decisions on claims.

S. 9 entered into force by virtue of SI 2002/1727 (C. 52) on 6 April 2003 for the purposes of entitlement to payment of an award.

Prospective amendments – Pt. 1 (but not Sch. 1 or Sch. 3) repealed by WRA 2012, s. 147 and Sch. 14, Pt. 1, with effect from a date to be set by order of the Secretary of State.

History – In s. 9(2)(a), the words "every person or persons entitled to child tax credit who is, or either or both of whom is or are, responsible for a child or qualifying young person who was born before 6 April 2017," substituted for the words "all persons entitled to child tax credit, and" by Welfare Reform and Work Act 2016, s. 13(2)(a), with effect for the purposes of making regulations, on 16 March 2016 and for remaining purposes, on 6 April 2017.
S. 9(2)(c) inserted by Welfare Reform and Work Act 2016, s. 13(2)(b), with effect for the purposes of making regulations, on 16 March 2016 and for remaining purposes, on 6 April 2017.
In s. 9(3), the words "and that specified in paragraph (c) of that subsection is to be known as the disability element of child tax credit" inserted by Welfare Reform and Work Act 2016, s. 13(3), with effect for the purposes of making regulations, on 16 March 2016 and for remaining purposes, on 6 April 2017.
S. 9(3A) and (3B) inserted by Welfare Reform and Work Act 2016, s. 13(4), with effect for the purposes of making regulations, on 16 March 2016 and for remaining purposes, on 6 April 2017.
S. 9(5)(c) substituted by Welfare Reform and Work Act 2016, s. 13(5), with effect for the purposes of making regulations, on 16 March 2016 and for remaining purposes, on 6 April 2017.
Cross references – SI 2002/2007, reg. 7: determination of maximum rate at which a person may be entitled to child tax credit.
SI 2002/2007, reg. 8: prescribed conditions for a disabled or severely disabled child or qualifying young person (s. 9(6)).
SI 2003/742, reg. 8: modified application of s. 9(2)(b) to members of polygamous units.
Statutory instruments – SI 2002/2007.
SI 2006/963.
SI 2007/828.

WORKING TAX CREDIT

10 Entitlement

10(1) The entitlement of the person or persons by whom a claim for working tax credit has been made is dependent on him, or either or both of them, being engaged in qualifying remunerative work.

10(2) Regulations may for the purposes of this Part make provision–

(a) as to what is, or is not, qualifying remunerative work, and

(b) as to the circumstances in which a person is, or is not, engaged in it.

10(3) The circumstances prescribed under subsection (2)(b) may differ by reference to–

(a) the age of the person or either of the persons,

(b) whether the person, or either of the persons, is disabled,

(c) whether the person, or either of the persons, is responsible for one or more children or qualifying young persons, or

(d) any other factors.

10(4) Regulations may make provision for the purposes of working tax credit as to the circumstances in which a person is or is not responsible for a child or qualifying young person.

Commencement Date – S. 10 entered into force by virtue of SI 2002/1727 (C. 52) on:
- 9 July 2002 for the purposes of making regulations;
- 1 August 2002 for the purposes of making claims; and
- 1 January 2003 for the purposes of making decisions on claims.

S. 10 entered into force by virtue of SI 2002/1727 (C. 52) on 6 April 2003 for the purposes of entitlement to make an award.
Prospective amendments – Pt. 1 (but not Sch. 1 or Sch. 3) repealed by WRA 2012, s. 147 and Sch. 14, Pt. 1, with effect from a date to be set by order of the Secretary of State.
Cross references – SI 2002/2005, reg. 4–8: qualifying remunerative work.
SI 2002/2005, reg. 2(2), 14(7): circumstances in which a person is or is not responsible for a child or qualifying young person.
SI 2003/742, reg. 9: modified application of s. 10 to members of polygamous units.
SSCBA 1992, s. 30C(5), (5A), 42(1), (1A): entitlement to incapacity benefit where claimant entitled to any element of child tax credit other from family element.
SSCBA 1992, s. 30C(5), (5A), 42(1), (1A): entitlement to incapacity benefit where claimant entitled to disability element of working tax credit.
Statutory instruments – SI 2002/2005.
SI 2003/742.

11 Maximum rate

11(1) The maximum rate at which a person or persons may be entitled to working tax credit is to be determined in the prescribed manner.

11(2) The prescribed manner of determination must involve the inclusion of an element which is to be included in the case of all persons entitled to working tax credit.

11(3) The prescribed manner of determination must also involve the inclusion of an element in respect of the person, or either or both of the persons, engaged in qualifying remunerative work–

(a) having a physical or mental disability which puts him at a disadvantage in getting a job, and

(b) satisfying such other conditions as may be prescribed.

11(4) The element specified in subsection (2) is to be known as the basic element of working tax credit and the element specified in subsection (3) is to be known as the disability element of working tax credit.

11(5) The prescribed manner of determination may involve the inclusion of such other elements as may be prescribed.

TC Statutes

11(6) The other elements may (in particular) include–

(a) an element in respect of the person, or either of the persons or the two of them taken together, being engaged in qualifying remunerative work to an extent prescribed for the purposes of this paragraph,

(b) an element in respect of the persons being the members of a couple,

(c) an element in respect of the person not being a member of a married couple or an unmarried couple but being responsible for a child or qualifying young person,

(d) an element in respect of the person, or either or both of the persons, being severely disabled, and

(e) an element in respect of the person, or either or both of the persons, being over a prescribed age, satisfying prescribed conditions and having been engaged in qualifying remunerative work for not longer than a prescribed period.

11(7) A person has a physical or mental disability which puts him at a disadvantage in getting a job, or is severely disabled, for the purposes of this section only if–

(a) he satisfies prescribed conditions, or

(b) prescribed conditions exist in relation to him.

Commencement Date – S. 11 entered into force by virtue of SI 2002/1727 (C. 52) on:

- 9 July 2002 for the purposes of making regulations;
- 1 August 2002 for the purposes of making claims; and
- 1 January 2003 for the purposes of making decisions on claims.

S. 11 entered into force by virtue of SI 2002/1727 (C. 52) on 6 April 2003 for the purposes of entitlement to an award.

Prospective amendments – Pt. 1 (but not Sch. 1 or Sch. 3) repealed by WRA 2012, s. 147 and Sch. 14, Pt. 1, with effect from a date to be set by order of the Secretary of State.

History – In s. 11(6)(b) and (c) the word "couple" substituted for the words "married couple or unmarried couple" by the Civil Partnership Act 2004, s. 254 and Sch. 24, para. 145, with effect from 5 December 2005 (by virtue of SI 2005/3175, art. 2(1)).

Cross references – SI 2002/2005, reg. 3: prescribes elements for the purposes of s. 11(2) and (3).
SI 2002/2005, Pt. 2: conditions of entitlement to elements of working tax credit.
SI 2002/2005, Pt. 3: maximum rate of working tax credit.
SI 2003/742, reg. 10: modified application of s. 11 to members of polygamous units.

Statutory instruments – SI 2002/2005.
SI 2003/742.
SI 2006/963.
SI 2007/828.

12 Child care element

12(1) The prescribed manner of determination of the maximum rate at which a person or persons may be entitled to working tax credit may involve the inclusion, in prescribed circumstances, of a child care element.

12(2) A child care element is an element in respect of a prescribed proportion of so much of any relevant child care charges as does not exceed a prescribed amount.

12(3) **"Child care charges"** are charges of a prescribed description incurred in respect of child care by the person, or either or both of the persons, by whom a claim for working tax credit is made.

12(4) **"Child care"**, in relation to a person or persons, means care provided–

(a) for a child of a prescribed description for whom the person is responsible, or for whom either or both of the persons is or are responsible, and

(b) by a person of a prescribed description.

12(5) The descriptions of persons prescribed under subsection (4)(b) may include descriptions of persons approved in accordance with a scheme made by the appropriate national authority under this subsection.

12(6) **"The appropriate national authority"** means–

(a) in relation to care provided in England, the Secretary of State,

(b) in relation to care provided in Scotland, the Scottish Ministers,

(c) in relation to care provided in Wales, the National Assembly for Wales, and

(d) in relation to care provided in Northern Ireland, the Department of Health, Social Services and Public Safety.

12(7) The provision made by a scheme under subsection (5) must involve the giving of approvals, in accordance with criteria determined by or under the scheme, by such of the following as the scheme specifies–

(a) the appropriate national authority making the scheme,

(b) one or more specified persons or bodies or persons or bodies of a specified description, and

(c) persons or bodies accredited under the scheme in accordance with criteria determined by or under it.

12(8) A scheme under subsection (5) may authorise–

(a) the making of grants or loans to, and

(b) the charging of reasonable fees by,

persons and bodies giving approvals.

Commencement Date – S. 12(1)–(5) entered into force by virtue of SI 2002/1727 (C. 52) on:

- 9 July 2002 for the purposes of making regulations;
- 1 August 2002 for the purposes of making claims.

S. 12(1)–(5) entered into force by virtue of SI 2002/1727 (C. 52) on 6 April 2003 for the purposes of entitlement to payment of an award.

S. 12(5)–(8) entered into force on 9 July 2002 for the purposes of making schemes (SI 2002/1727 (C. 52)).

Prospective amendments – Pt. 1 (but not Sch. 1 or Sch. 3) repealed by WRA 2012, s. 147 and Sch. 14, Pt. 1, with effect from a date to be set by order of the Secretary of State.

Cross references – SI 2002/2005, reg. 13–16: regulations about childcare element.
SI 2003/742, reg. 11: modified application of s. 12(3), (4)(a) to members of polygamous units.

Statutory instruments – SI 2002/2005.
SI 2003/463, made by Secretary of State for Education and Skills under s. 12.
SI 2003/742.
SI 2007/226.
SI 2007/849.

Notes – See also The Tax Credit (New Category of Childcare Provider) Regulations, SI 1999/3110; The Tax Credit (New Category of Childcare Provider) Regulations, SI 2002/1417; The Domiciliary Care Agencies Regulations, SI 2002/3214.

RATE

13 Rate

13(1) Where, in the case of a person or persons entitled to a tax credit, the relevant income does not exceed the income threshold (or his or their entitlement arises by virtue of section 7(2)), the rate at which he is or they are entitled to the tax credit is the maximum rate for his or their case.

13(2) Regulations shall make provision as to the manner of determining the rate (if any) at which a person is, or persons are, entitled to a tax credit in any other case.

13(3) The manner of determination prescribed under subsection (2)–

(a) may involve the making of adjustments so as to avoid fractional amounts, and

(b) may include provision for securing that, where the rate at which a person or persons would be entitled to a tax credit would be less than a prescribed rate, there is no rate in his or their case.

Commencement Date – S. 13 entered into force by virtue of SI 2002/1727 (C. 52) on:

- 9 July 2002 for making regulations;
- 1 August 2002 for the purposes of making claims; and
- 1 January 2003 for the purposes of making decisions on claims.

S. 13 entered into force by virtue of SI 2002/1727 (C. 52) on 6 April 2003 for the purposes of entitlement to payment of award.

Prospective amendments – Pt. 1 (but not Sch. 1 or Sch. 3) repealed by WRA 2012, s. 147 and Sch. 14, Pt. 1, with effect from a date to be set by order of the Secretary of State.

Cross references – SI 2002/2008: manner of determining rate of tax credit under s. 13(2), (3).

Statutory instruments – SI 2002/2008.
SI 2006/963.
SI 2007/828.

DECISIONS

14 Initial decisions

14(1) On a claim for a tax credit the Board must decide–

(a) whether to make an award of the tax credit, and

(b) if so, the rate at which to award it.

14(2) Before making their decision the Board may by notice–

(a) require the person, or either or both of the persons, by whom the claim is made to provide any information or evidence which the Board consider they may need for making their decision, or

(b) require any person of a prescribed description to provide any information or evidence of a prescribed description which the Board consider they may need for that purpose,

by the date specified in the notice.

14(3) The Board's power to decide the rate at which to award a tax credit includes power to decide to award it at a nil rate.

Commencement Date – S. 14(1) and (3) entered into force on 1 January 2003 for the purposes of making decisions on claims (SI 2002/1727 (C. 52)).

S. 14(2) entered into force by virtue of SI 2002/1727 (C. 52) on:

- 9 July 2002 for the purposes of making regulations; and
- 1 August 2002 for the purposes of dealing with claims.

TC Statutes

Prospective amendments – Pt. 1 (but not Sch. 1 or Sch. 3) repealed by WRA 2012, s. 147 and Sch. 14, Pt. 1, with effect from a date to be set by order of the Secretary of State.

Cross references – SI 2002/2014, reg. 14: advance claims where Board give notice of their decision under s. 14(1) before 6 April 2003.
SI 2002/2014, reg. 15(1)(a): death of claimant before Board give decision under s. 14(1).
SI 2002/2014, reg. 30: notice to employers to provide information or evidence under s. 14(2)(b).
SI 2002/2014, reg. 31: notice to child care providers to provide information or evidence under s. 14(2)(b)).
SI 2002/2014, reg. 32: date which may be specified in a notice under s. 14(2).
SI 2003/653, reg. 4(3): omission of s. 14 for refugees whose asylum claims have been accepted.
SI 2003/692, reg. 3(1): a decision under s. 14(1) may be revised in favour of the person or persons to whom it relates if it is incorrect by reason of official error, as defined.
SI 2003/742, reg. 12: modified application of s. 14(2)(a) to members of polygamous units.

Statutory instruments – SI 2002/2014.

HMRC Manuals – CCM4000ff.: local office examinations.

Other material – COP23: local office examinations carried out under s. 14(2).

15 Revised decisions after notifications

15(1) Where notification of a change of circumstances increasing the maximum rate at which a person or persons may be entitled to a tax credit is given in accordance with regulations under section 6(1), the Board must decide whether (and, if so, how) to amend the award of the tax credit made to him or them.

15(2) Before making their decision the Board may by notice–

(a) require the person by whom the notification is given to provide any information or evidence which the Board consider they may need for making their decision, or

(b) require any person of a prescribed description to provide any information or evidence of a prescribed description which the Board consider they may need for that purpose,

by the date specified in the notice.

Commencement Date – S. 15(1) entered into force on 1 January 2003 for the purposes of making decisions on whether to amend awards (SI 2002/1727 (C. 52)).
S. 15(2) entered into force by virtue of SI 2002/1727 (C. 52) on:

- 9 July 2002 for the purposes of making regulations;
- 1 August 2002 for the purposes of dealing with notifications of change of circumstances.

Prospective amendments – Pt. 1 (but not Sch. 1 or Sch. 3) repealed by WRA 2012, s. 147 and Sch. 14, Pt. 1, with effect from a date to be set by order of the Secretary of State.

Cross references – SI 2002/2014, reg. 22: amendment of notification of change of circumstances before Board have made a decision under s. 15(1) in consequence of the notification.
SI 2002/2014, reg. 30: notice to employers to provide information or evidence under s. 15(2)(b).
SI 2002/2014, reg. 31: notice to child care providers to provide information or evidence under s. 15(2)(b)).
SI 2002/2014, reg. 32: date which may be specified in a notice under s. 15(2).
SI 2003/653: omission of s. 15(1) for refugees whose asylum claims have been accepted.
SI 2003/692, reg. 3(1): a decision under s. 15(1) may be revised in favour of the person or persons to whom it relates if it is incorrect by reason of official error, as defined.

Statutory instruments – SI 2002/2014.

HMRC Manuals – CCM4000ff.: local office examinations.

Other material – COP23: local office examinations carried out under s. 15(2).

16 Other revised decisions

16(1) Where, at any time during the period for which an award of a tax credit is made to a person or persons, the Board have reasonable grounds for believing–

(a) that the rate at which the tax credit has been awarded to him or them for the period differs from the rate at which he is, or they are, entitled to the tax credit for the period, or

(b) that he has, or they have, ceased to be, or never been, entitled to the tax credit for the period,

the Board may decide to amend or terminate the award.

16(2) Where, at any time during the period for which an award of a tax credit is made to a person or persons, the Board believe–

(a) that the rate at which a tax credit has been awarded to him or them for the period may differ from the rate at which he is, or they are, entitled to it for the period, or

(b) that he or they may have ceased to be, or never been, entitled to the tax credit for the period,

the Board may give a notice under subsection (3).

16(3) A notice under this subsection may–

(a) require the person, or either or both of the persons, to whom the tax credit was awarded to provide any information or evidence which the Board consider they may need for considering whether to amend or terminate the award under subsection (1), or

(b) require any person of a prescribed description to provide any information or evidence of a prescribed description which the Board consider they may need for that purpose,

by the date specified in the notice.

Commencement Date – S. 16(1) entered into force on 1 January 2003 for the purposes of making decisions on whether to amend or terminate awards (SI 2002/1727 (C. 52)).
S. 16(2) and (3) entered into force on 1 January 2003 for the purposes of giving notice under those subsections (SI 2002/1727 (C. 52)).
S. 16(3) entered into force on 9 July 2002 for the purposes of making regulations (SI 2002/1727 (C. 52)).

Prospective amendments – Pt. 1 (but not Sch. 1 or Sch. 3) repealed by WRA 2012, s. 147 and Sch. 14, Pt. 1, with effect from a date to be set by order of the Secretary of State.

Cross references – SI 2002/2014, reg. 22: amendment of notification of change of circumstances before Board have made a decision under s. 16(1) in consequence of the notification.
SI 2002/2014, reg. 30: notice to employers to provide information or evidence under s. 16(3)(b).
SI 2002/2014, reg. 31: notice to child care providers to provide information or evidence under s. 16(3)(b)).
SI 2002/2014, reg. 32: date which may be specified in a notice under s. 16(3).
SI 2003/653, reg. 4(3): omission of s. 16 for refugees whose asylum claims have been accepted.
SI 2003/692, reg. 3(1): a decision under s. 16(1) may be revised in favour of the person or persons to whom it relates if it is incorrect by reason of official error, as defined.
SI 2003/742, reg. 13: modified application of s. 16(3)(a) to members of polygamous units.

Statutory instruments – SI 2002/2014.

HMRC Manuals – CCM4000ff.: local office examinations.

17 Final notice

17(1) Where a tax credit has been awarded for the whole or part of a tax year–

(a) for awards made on single claims, the Board must give a notice relating to the tax year to the person to whom the tax credit was awarded, and

(b) for awards made on joint claims, the Board must give such a notice to the persons to whom the tax credit was awarded (with separate copies of the notice for each of them if the Board consider appropriate).

17(2) The notice must either–

(a) require that the person or persons must, by the date specified for the purposes of this subsection, declare that the relevant circumstances were as specified or state any respects in which they were not, or

(b) inform the person or persons that he or they will be treated as having declared in response to the notice that the relevant circumstances were as specified unless, by that date, he states or they state any respects in which they were not.

17(3) **"Relevant circumstances"** means circumstances (other than income) affecting–

(a) the entitlement of the person, or joint entitlement of the persons, to the tax credit, or

(b) the amount of the tax credit to which he was entitled, or they were jointly entitled,

for the tax year.

17(4) The notice must either–

(a) require that the person or persons must, by the date specified for the purposes of this subsection, declare that the amount of the current year income or estimated current year income (depending on which is specified) was the amount, or fell within the range, specified or comply with subsection (5), or

(b) inform the person or persons that he or they will be treated as having declared in response to the notice that the amount of the current year income or estimated current year income (depending on which is specified) was the amount, or fell within the range, specified unless, by that date, he complies or they comply with subsection (5).

17(5) To comply with this subsection the person or persons must either–

(a) state the current year income or his or their estimate of the current year income (making clear which), or

(b) declare that, throughout the period to which the award related, subsection (1) of section 7 did not apply to him or them by virtue of subsection (2) of that section.

17(6) The notice may–

(a) require that the person or persons must, by the date specified for the purposes of subsection (4), declare that the amount of the previous year income was the amount, or fell within the range, specified or comply with subsection (7), or

(b) inform the person or persons that he or they will be treated as having declared in response to the notice that the amount of the previous year income was the amount, or fell within the range, specified unless, by that date, he complies or they comply with subsection (7).

17(7) To comply with this subsection the person or persons must either–

(a) state the previous year income, or

(b) make the declaration specified in subsection (5)(b).

TC Statutes

17(8) The notice must inform the person or persons that if he or they–

(a) makes or make a declaration under paragraph (a) of subsection (4), or is or are treated as making a declaration under paragraph (b) of that subsection, in relation to estimated current year income (or the range within which estimated current year income fell), or

(b) states or state under subsection (5)(a) his or their estimate of the current year income,

he or they will be treated as having declared in response to the notice that the amount of the (actual) current year income was as estimated unless, by the date specified for the purposes of this subsection, he states or they state the current year income.

17(9) **"Specified"**, in relation to a notice, means specified in the notice.

17(10) Regulations may–

(a) provide that, in prescribed circumstances, one person may act for another in response to a notice under this section, and

(b) provide that, in prescribed circumstances, anything done by one member of a couple in response to a notice given under this section is to be treated as also done by the other member of the couple.

Prospective amendments – Pt. 1 (but not Sch. 1 or Sch. 3) repealed by WRA 2012, s. 147 and Sch. 14, Pt. 1, with effect from a date to be set by order of the Secretary of State.

History – In s. 17(10)(b) the word "couple" substituted by the Civil Partnership Act 2004, s. 254 and Sch. 24, para. 145, with effect from 5 December 2005 (by virtue of SI 2005/3175, art. 2(1)).
In s. 17(10)(b) the words "the couple" substituted by the Civil Partnership Act 2004, s. 254 and Sch. 24, para. 146, with effect from 5 December 2005 (by virtue of SI 2005/3175, art. 2(1)).

Cross references – SI 2002/2014, reg. 11: claims for tax credits treated as made where claimant(s) has(ve) made a declaration in response to a notice under s. 17(2)(a), (4)(a) or (6)(a) or any combination of those sections.
SI 2002/2014, reg. 12: claims for tax credits treated as made where claimant(s) is(are) treated as having made a declaration in response to a notice under s. 17(2)(b) or (4)(b) or any combination of those sections and s. 17(6)(b).
SI 2002/2014, reg. 33(a): date which may be specified for the purposes of s. 17(2), (4).
SI 2002/2014, reg. 33(b): date which may be specified for the purposes of s. 17(8).
SI 2002/2014, reg. 34: manner and form in which declaration or statement in response to a notice under s. 17 to be made.
SI 2002/2014, reg. 35, 36: circumstances where one person may act for another in response to a notice under s. 17.
SI 2003/653, reg. 4(3): omission of s. 17 for refugees whose asylum claims have been accepted.
SI 2003/742, reg. 14: modified application of s. 17(10)(b) to members of polygamous units.
SI 2014/1230, Sch., para. 3: modified application of s. 17(1), (3), (4), (5) and (8) where SI 2014/1230, reg. 12A applies (claims for universal credit).

Statutory instruments – SI 2002/2014.

18 Decisions after final notice

18(1) After giving a notice under section 17 the Board must decide–

(a) whether the person was entitled, or the persons were jointly entitled, to the tax credit, and

(b) if so, the amount of the tax credit to which he was entitled, or they were jointly entitled,

for the tax year.

18(2) But, subject to subsection (3), that decision must not be made before a declaration or statement has been made in response to the relevant provisions of the notice.

18(3) If a declaration or statement has not been made in response to the relevant provisions of the notice on or before the date specified for the purposes of section 17(4), that decision may be made after that date.

18(4) In subsections (2) and (3) **"the relevant provisions of the notice"** means–

(a) the provision included in the notice by virtue of subsection (2) of section 17,

(b) the provision included in the notice by virtue of subsection (4) of that section, and

(c) any provision included in the notice by virtue of subsection (6) of that section.

18(5) Where the Board make a decision under subsection (1) on or before the date referred to in subsection (3), they may revise it if a new declaration or statement is made on or before that date.

18(6) If the person or persons to whom a notice under section 17 is given is or are within paragraph (a) or (b) of subsection (8) of that section, the Board must decide again–

(a) whether the person was entitled, or the persons were jointly entitled, to the tax credit, and

(b) if so, the amount of the tax credit to which he was entitled, or they were jointly entitled,

for the tax year.

18(7) But, subject to subsection (8), that decision must not be made before a statement has been made in response to the provision included in the notice by virtue of subsection (8) of section 17.

18(8) If a statement has not been made in response to the provision included in the notice by virtue of that subsection on or before the date specified for the purposes of that subsection, that decision may be made after that date.

18(9) Where the Board make a decision under subsection (6) on or before the date referred to in subsection (8), they may revise it if a new statement is made on or before that date.

18(10) Before exercising a function imposed or conferred on them by subsection (1), (5), (6) or (9), the Board may by notice require the person, or either or both of the persons, to whom the notice under section 17 was given to provide any further information or evidence which the Board consider they may need for exercising the function by the date specified in the notice.

18(11) Subject to sections 19, 20, 21A and 21B and regulations under section 21 (and to any revision under subsection (5) or (9) and any appeal)–

(a) in a case in which a decision is made under subsection (6) in relation to a person or persons and a tax credit for a tax year, that decision, and

(b) in any other case, the decision under subsection (1) in relation to a person or persons and a tax credit for a tax year,

is conclusive as to the entitlement of the person, or the joint entitlement of the persons, to the tax credit for the tax year and the amount of the tax credit to which he was entitled, or they were jointly entitled, for the tax year.

Commencement Date – S. 18 entered into force on 6 April 2003 (SI 2002/1727 (C. 52)).

Prospective amendments – Pt. 1 (but not Sch. 1 or Sch. 3) repealed by WRA 2012, s. 147 and Sch. 14, Pt. 1, with effect from a date to be set by order of the Secretary of State.

History – In s. 18(11), the words "19, 20, 21A and 21B" substituted for "19 and 20" by SI 2014/886, art. 2(2), with effect from 6 April 2014.

Cross references – CTFA 2004, s. 9(5).
SI 2002/2014, reg. 15(1)(c): claimant who dies after end of tax year for which tax credit has been awarded, but before Board have made a decision under s. 18(1), (5), (6) or (9).
SI 2002/2014, reg. 32: date which may be specified in a notice under s. 18(10).
SI 2003/653, reg. 4(3): modified application of s. 18 for refugees whose asylum claims have been accepted.
SI 2003/692, reg. 3(1): a decision under s. 18(1), (5), (6) or (9) may be revised in favour of the person or persons to whom it relates if it is incorrect by reason of official error, as defined.
SI 2003/742, reg. 15: modified application of s. 18(10) to members of polygamous units.
SI 2014/1230, Sch., para. 4: modified application of s. 18(1), (6) to (9), (10) and (11) where SI 2014/1230, reg. 12A applies (claims for universal credit).

TC Statutes

19 Power to enquire into awards

19(1) The Board may enquire into–

(a) the entitlement of a person, or the joint entitlement of persons, to a tax credit for a tax year, and

(b) the amount of the tax credit to which he was entitled, or they were jointly entitled, for the tax year,

if they give notice to the person, or each of the persons, during the period allowed for the initiation of an enquiry.

19(2) As part of the enquiry the Board may by notice–

(a) require the person, or either or both of the persons, to provide any information or evidence which the Board consider they may need for the purposes of the enquiry, or

(b) require any person of a prescribed description to provide any information or evidence of a prescribed description which the Board consider they may need for those purposes,

by the date specified in the notice.

19(3) On an enquiry the Board must decide–

(a) whether the person was entitled, or the persons were jointly entitled, to the tax credit, and

(b) if so, the amount of the tax credit to which he was entitled, or they were jointly entitled,

for the tax year.

19(4) The period allowed for the initiation of an enquiry is the period beginning immediately after the relevant section 18 decision and ending–

(a) if the person, or either of the persons, to whom the enquiry relates is required by section 8 of the Taxes Management Act 1970 (c. 9) to make a return, with the day on which the return becomes final (or, if both of the persons are so required and their returns become final on different days, with the later of those days), or

(b) in any other case, one year after the beginning of the relevant section 17 date.

19(5) **"The relevant section 18 decision"** means–

(a) in a case in which a decision must be made under subsection (6) of section 18 in relation to the person or persons and the tax year to which the enquiry relates, that decision, and

(b) in any other case, the decision under subsection (1) of that section in relation to the person or persons and that tax year.

19(6) **"The relevant section 17 date"** means–

(a) in a case in which a statement may be made by the person or persons in response to provision included by virtue of subsection (8) of section 17 in the notice given to him or them under that section in relation to the tax year, the date specified in the notice for the purposes of that subsection, and

(b) in any other case, the date specified for the purposes of subsection (4) of that section in the notice given to him or them under that section in relation to the tax year.

19(7) A return becomes final–

(a) if it is enquired into under section 9A of the Taxes Management Act 1970 (c. 9), when the enquiries are completed (within the meaning of section 28A of that Act), or

(b) otherwise, at the end of the period specified in subsection (2) of that section in relation to the return.

19(8) An enquiry is completed at the time when the Board give notice to the person or persons of their decision under subsection (3); but if the Board give notice to the persons at different times the enquiry is completed at the later of those times.

19(9) The person, or either of the persons, to whom the enquiry relates may at any time before such notice is given apply for a direction that the Board must give such a notice.

19(10) Any such application is to be subject to the relevant provisions of Part 5 of the Taxes Management Act 1970 (see, in particular, section 48(2)(b) of that Act), and the tribunal must give the direction applied for unless satisfied that the Board have reasonable grounds for not making the decision or giving the notice.

19(11) Where the entitlement of a person, or the joint entitlement of persons, to a tax credit for a tax year has been enquired into under this section, it is not to be the subject of a further notice under subsection (1).

19(12) Subject to sections 20, 21A and 21B and regulations under section 21 (and to any appeal), a decision under subsection (3) in relation to a person or persons and a tax credit for a tax year is conclusive as to the entitlement of the person, or the joint entitlement of the persons, to the tax credit for the tax year and the amount of the tax credit to which he was entitled, or they were jointly entitled, for the tax year.

Commencement Date – S. 19 entered into force on 6 April 2003 for the purposes of enquiring into awards (SI 2002/1727 (C. 52)). S. 19(2) entered into force on 9 July 2002 for the purposes of making regulations (SI 2002/1727 (C. 52)).

Prospective amendments – In s. 19(4)(a) the words "to make a return under section 8 of the Taxes Management Act 1970" substituted for the words "by section 8 of the Taxes Management Act 1970 (c. 9) to make a return" by F(No. 2)A 2017, s. 61 and Sch. 14, para. 34, with effect from a day to be appointed under F(No. 2)A 2017, s. 61(6).
Pt. 1 (but not Sch. 1 or Sch. 3) repealed by WRA 2012, s. 147 and Sch. 14, Pt. 1, with effect from a date to be set by order of the Secretary of State.

History – S. 19(10) substituted by SI 2009/56, art. 3(1) and Sch. 1, para. 313, operative from 1 April 2009, subject to transitional and saving provisions in SI 2009/56, Sch. 3.
In s. 19(12), the words "sections 20, 21A and 21B" substituted for "section 20" by SI 2014/886, art. 2(3), with effect from 6 April 2014.

Cross references – S. 63(3): until a day to be appointed, the function of giving a direction under s. 19(10) is a function of an appeal tribunal rather than of the General Commissioners or the Special Commissioners.
CTFA 2004, s. 9(5).
SI 2002/2014, reg. 30: notice to employers to provide information or evidence under s. 19(2)(b).
SI 2002/2014, reg. 31 notice to child care providers to provide information or evidence under s. 19(2)(b)).
SI 2002/2014, reg. 32: date which may be specified in a notice under s. 19(2).
SI 2002/2926, reg. 4: provisions of SSA 1998, s. 12 and the Social Security (Northern Ireland) Order 1998, art. 13, applied with modifications in relation to an application for a direction under s. 19(9).
SI 2002/3196, reg. 3: other persons with a right to make an application for a direction where claimant is unable to exercise it.
SI 2003/653, reg. 4(3): modified application of s. 19 for refugees whose asylum claims have been accepted.
SI 2003/692, reg. 3(1): a decision under s. 19(3) may be revised in favour of the person or persons to whom it relates if it is incorrect by reason of official error, as defined.
SI 2003/742, reg. 16: modified application of s. 19 to members of polygamous units.
SI 2014/1230, Sch., para. 5: modified application of s. 19(1), (3), (5), (6), (11) and (12) where SI 2014/1230, reg. 12A applies (claims for universal credit).

Statutory instruments – SI 2002/2014.

HMRC Manuals – CCM12000ff.: local office examinations.

20 Decisions on discovery

20(1) Where in consequence of a person's income tax liability being revised the Board have reasonable grounds for believing that a conclusive decision relating to his entitlement to a tax credit for a tax year (whether or not jointly with another person) is not correct, the Board may decide to revise that decision.

20(2) A person's income tax liability is revised–

(a) on the taking effect of an amendment of a return of his under section 9ZA(1) of the Taxes Management Act 1970,

(b) on the issue of a notice of correction under section 9ZB of that Act amending a return of his (provided that he does not give a notice of rejection before the end of the period of thirty days beginning with the date of issue of the notice of correction),

(c) on the amendment of an assessment of his by notice under section 9C of that Act,

(d) on the amendment of a return of his under section 12ABA(3)(a) of that Act,

(e) on the amendment of a return of his under subsection (6)(a) of section 12ABB of that Act after the correction of a partnership return under that section (provided that the amendment does not cease to have effect by reason of the rejection of the correction under subsection (4) of that section),

(f) on the issue of a partial or final closure notice under section 28A of that Act making amendments of a return of his,
(g) on the amendment of a return of his under section 28B(4)(a) of that Act,
(h) on the making of an assessment as regards him under section 29(1) of that Act,
(i) on the vacation of the whole or part of an assessment of his under section 32 of that Act,
(j) on giving him relief under section 33 of that Act, or
(k) on the determination (or settlement) of an appeal against the making, amendment or vacation of an assessment or return, or a decision on a claim for relief, under any of the provisions mentioned in paragraphs (c), (f) and (h) to (j).

20(3) But no decision may be made under subsection (1)–
(a) unless it is too late to enquire into the person's entitlement under section 19, or
(b) after the period of one year beginning when the person's income tax liability is revised as specified in subsection (1).

20(4) Where the Board have reasonable grounds for believing that–
(a) a conclusive decision relating to the entitlement of a person, or the joint entitlement of persons, to a tax credit for a tax year is not correct, and
(b) that is attributable to fraud or neglect on the part of the person, or of either of the persons, or on the part of any person acting for him, or either of them,

the Board may decide to revise that decision.

20(5) But no decision may be made under subsection (4)–
(a) unless it is too late to enquire into the entitlement, or joint entitlement, under section 19, or
(b) after the period of five years beginning with the end of the tax year to which the conclusive decision relates.

20(6) **"Conclusive decision"**, in relation to the entitlement of a person, or joint entitlement of persons, to a tax credit for a tax year, means–
(a) a decision in relation to it under section 18(1), (5), (6) or (9) or 19(3) or a previous decision under this section, or
(b) a decision under regulations under section 21 relating to a decision within paragraph (a), or
(c) a decision within paragraph (a) or (b) as varied under section 21A(5)(b), or
(d) a decision on an appeal against a decision within paragraph (a), (b) or (c).

20(7) Subject to any subsequent decision under this section and to regulations under section 21 and to any review under section 21A (and to any appeal), a decision under subsection (1) or (4) in relation to a person or persons and a tax credit for a tax year is conclusive as to the entitlement of the person, or the joint entitlement of the persons, to the tax credit for the tax year and the amount of the tax credit to which he was entitled, or they were jointly entitled, for the tax year.

Commencement Date – S. 20 entered into force on 6 April 2003 (SI 2002/1727 (C. 52)).

Prospective amendments – Pt. 1 (but not Sch. 1 or Sch. 3) repealed by WRA 2012, s. 147 and Sch. 14, Pt. 1, with effect from a date to be set by order of the Secretary of State.

History – In s. 20(2)(f) the words "a partial or final closure notice" substituted for the words "a closure notice" by F(No. 2)A 2017, s. 61 and Sch. 15, para. 36(2) with effect in relation to an enquiry under TMA 1970, s. 9A, 12ZM or 12AC or FA 1998, Sch. 18, where notice of the enquiry is given on or after 16 November 2017 (Royal Assent) or the enquiry is in progress immediately before that day.
In s. 20(3)(b) the words "as specified in subsection (1)" inserted by F(No. 2)A 2017, s. 61 and Sch. 15, para. 36(3) with effect in relation to an enquiry under TMA 1970, s. 9A, 12ZM or 12AC or FA 1998, Sch. 18, where notice of the enquiry is given on or after 16 November 2017 (Royal Assent) or the enquiry is in progress immediately before that day.
In s. 20(6), the word "or" at the end of para. (b) inserted by SI 2014/886, art. 2(4)(a), with effect from 6 April 2014.
In s. 20(6), para. (c) and (d) substituted for the words "including a decision made on an appeal against such a decision." by SI 2014/886, art. 2(4)(b), with effect from 6 April 2014.
In s. 20(7), the words "and to any review under section 21A" inserted by SI 2014/886, art. 2(5), with effect from 6 April 2014.

Cross references – CTFA 2004, s. 9(5).
SI 2003/692, reg. 3(1): a decision under s. 20(1) or (4) may be revised in favour of the person or persons to whom it relates if it is incorrect by reason of official error, as defined.
SI 2003/742, reg. 17: *modified application of s. 20(4)(b) to members of polygamous units.*
SI 2014/1230, Sch., para. 6: modified application of s. 20(1), (4), (5), (6) and (7) where SI 2014/1230, reg. 12A applies (claims for universal credit).

21 Decisions subject to official error

21 Regulations may make provision for a decision under section 14(1), 15(1), 16(1), 18(1), (5), (6) or (9), 19(3) or 20(1) or (4) to be revised in favour of the person or persons to whom it relates if it is incorrect by reason of official error (as defined by the regulations).

Commencement Date – S. 21 entered into force on 9 July 2002 for the purposes of making regulations for the purposes of decisions under s. 14(1), 15(1), 16(1), 18(1), (5), (6) and (9), 19(3) and 20(1) and (4) (SI 2002/1727 (C. 52)).

TC Statutes

Prospective amendments – Pt. 1 (but not Sch. 1 or Sch. 3) repealed by WRA 2012, s. 147 and Sch. 14, Pt. 1, with effect from a date to be set by order of the Secretary of State.

Cross references – CTFA 2004, s. 9(5).

SI 2014/1230, Sch., para. 7: modified application of s. 21 where SI 2014/1230, reg. 12A applies (claims for universal credit).

Statutory instruments – SI 2003/692.

21A Review of decisions

21A(1) The Commissioners for Her Majesty's Revenue and Customs must review any decision within section 38(1) if they receive a written application to do so that identifies the applicant and decision in question, and–

(a) that application is received within 30 days of the date of the notification of the original decision or of the date the original decision was made if not notified because of section 23(3), or

(b) it is received within such longer period as may be allowed under section 21B.

21A(2) The Commissioners must carry out the review as soon as is reasonably practicable.

21A(3) When the review has been carried out, the Commissioners must give the applicant notice of their conclusion containing sufficient information to enable the applicant to know–

(a) the conclusion on the review,

(b) if the conclusion is that the decision is varied, details of the variation, and

(c) the reasons for the conclusion.

21A(4) The conclusion on the review must be one of the following–

(a) that the decision is upheld;

(b) that the decision is varied;

(c) that the decision is cancelled.

21A(5) Where–

(a) the Commissioners notify the applicant of further information or evidence that they may need for carrying out the review, and

(b) the information or evidence is not provided to them by the date specified in the notice,

the review may proceed without that information or evidence.

History – S. 21A inserted by SI 2014/886, art. 2(6), with effect from 6 April 2014.

21B Late application for a review

21B(1) The Commissioners for Her Majesty's Revenue and Customs may in a particular case extend the time limit specified in section 21A(1)(a) for making an application for a review if all of the following conditions are met.

21B(2) The first condition is that the person seeking a review has applied to the Commissioners for an extension of time.

21B(3) The second condition is that the application for the extension–

(a) explains why the extension is sought, and

(b) is made within 13 months of the notification of the original decision or of the date the original decision was made if not notified because of section 23(3).

21B(4) The third condition is that the Commissioners are satisfied that due to special circumstances it was not practicable for the application for a review to have been made within the time limit specified in section 21A(1)(a).

21B(5) The fourth condition is that the Commissioners are satisfied that it is reasonable in all the circumstances to grant the extension.

21B(6) In determining whether it is reasonable to grant an extension, the Commissioners must have regard to the principle that the greater the amount of time that has elapsed between the end of the time limit specified in section 21A(1)(a) and the date of the application, the more compelling should be the special circumstances on which the application is based.

21B(7) An application to extend the time limit specified in section 21A(1)(a) which has been refused may not be renewed.

History – S. 21B inserted by SI 2014/886, art. 2(6), with effect from 6 April 2014.

22 Information etc. requirements: supplementary

22(1) Regulations may make provision as to the manner and form in which–

(a) information or evidence is to be provided in compliance with a requirement imposed by a notice under section 14(2), 15(2), 16(3), 18(10) or 19(2), or

(b) a declaration or statement is to be made in response to a notice under section 17.

22(2) Regulations may make provision as to the dates which may be specified in a notice under section 14(2), 15(2), 16(3), 17, 18(10) or 19(2).

Commencement Date – S. 22 entered into force on 9 July 2002 for the purposes of making regulations (SI 2002/1727 (C. 52)).

Prospective amendments – Pt. 1 (but not Sch. 1 or Sch. 3) repealed by WRA 2012, s. 147 and Sch. 14, Pt. 1, with effect from a date to be set by order of the Secretary of State.

Statutory instruments – SI 2002/2014.

23 Notice of decisions

23(1) When a decision is made under section 14(1), 15(1), 16(1), 18(1), (5), (6) or (9), 19(3) or 20(1) or (4) or regulations under section 21, the Board must give notice of the decision to the person, or each of the persons, to whom it relates.

23(2) Notice of a decision must state the date on which it is given and include details of any right to a review under section 21A and of any subsequent right to appeal against the decision under section 38.

23(3) Notice need not be given of a decision made under section 14(1) or 18(1) or (6) on the basis of declarations made or treated as made by the person or persons in response to the notice given to him or them under section 17 if–

(a) that notice, or

(b) in the case of a decision under subsection (6) of section 18, that notice or the notice of the decision under subsection (1) of that section,

stated what the decision would be and the date on which it would be made.

Commencement Date – S. 23 entered into force by virtue of SI 2002/1727 on 1 January 2003 for the purposes of giving decisions under s. 14(1), 15(1) and 16(1) and revised decisions under those sections by virtue of regulations under s. 21.
S. 23 entered into force by virtue of SI 2002/1727 (C. 52) on 6 April 2003 for the purposes of giving decisions under s. 18(1), (5), (6) and (9), s. 19(3) and s. 20(1) and (4), and of revised decisions under those sections by virtue of regulations made under s. 21.

Prospective amendments – Pt. 1 (but not Sch. 1 or Sch. 3) repealed by WRA 2012, s. 147 and Sch. 14, Pt. 1, with effect from a date to be set by order of the Secretary of State.

History – In s. 23(2), the words "to a review under section 21A and of any subsequent right" inserted by SI 2014/886, art. 2(7), with effect from 6 April 2014.

Cross references – SI 2014/1230, Sch., para. 8: modified application of s. 23(1) and (3) where SI 2014/1230, reg. 12A applies (claims for universal credit).

PAYMENT

24 Payments

24(1) Where the Board have made an award of a tax credit, the amount of the tax credit awarded must be paid to the person to whom the award is made, subject to subsections (2) and (3).

24(2) Where an award of a tax credit is made to the members of a couple, payments of the tax credit, or of any element of the tax credit, are to be made to whichever of them is prescribed.

24(3) Where an award of a tax credit is made on a claim which was made by one person on behalf of another, payments of the tax credit, or of any element of the tax credit, are to be made to whichever of those persons is prescribed.

24(4) Where an award of a tax credit has been made to a person or persons for the whole or part of a tax year, payments may, in prescribed circumstances, continue to be made for any period, after the tax year, within which he is or they are entitled to make a claim for the tax credit for the next tax year.

24(5) Payments made under subsection (4) are to be treated for the purposes of this section and the following provisions of this Part as if they were payments of the tax credit for the next tax year.

24(6) Subject to section 25, payments of a tax credit must be made by the Board.

24(7) Regulations may make provision about the time when and the manner in which a tax credit, or any element of a tax credit, is to be paid by the Board.

24(8) If the regulations make provision for payments of a tax credit, or any element of a tax credit, to be made by the Board by way of a credit to a bank account or other account notified to the Board, the regulations may provide that entitlement to the tax credit or element is dependent on an account having been notified to the Board in accordance with the regulations.

Commencement Date – S. 24 entered into force by virtue of SI 2002/1727 (C. 52) on:

- 9 July 2002 for the purposes of making regulations;
- 1 August 2002 for the purposes of making claims; and
- 1 January 2003 for the purposes of making decisions on claims.

S. 24 entered into force by virtue of SI 2002/1727 (C. 52) on 6 April 2003 for the purposes of entitlement to payment of award.

Prospective amendments – Pt. 1 (but not Sch. 1 or Sch. 3) repealed by WRA 2012, s. 147 and Sch. 14, Pt. 1, with effect from a date to be set by order of the Secretary of State.

History – In s. 24(2) the word "couple" substituted by the Civil Partnership Act 2004, s. 254 and Sch. 24, para. 145, with effect from 5 December 2005 (by virtue of SI 2005/3175, art. 2(1)).

Cross references – SI 2002/2173, reg. 3: persons prescribed for the purposes of s. 24(2) in relation to payments of child tax credit and child care element of working tax credit.
SI 2002/2173, reg. 4: persons prescribed for the purposes of s. 24(2) in relation to payments of working tax credit other than any child care element.
SI 2002/2173, reg. 5: persons prescribed for the purposes of s. 24(2) where one member of a couple has died.
SI 2002/2173, reg. 6: persons prescribed for the purposes of s. 24(3).
SI 2002/2173, reg. 7: circumstances prescribed for the purposes of s. 24(4).
SI 2003/742, reg. 18: modified application of s. 24(2) to members of polygamous units.

Statutory instruments – SI 2002/2173.
SI 2003/742.

25 Payments of working tax credit by employers

25(1) Regulations may require employers, when making payments of, or on account of, PAYE income and in any such other circumstances as may be prescribed, to pay working tax credit, or prescribed elements of working tax credit, to employees.

25(2) The regulations may, in particular, include provision–

(a) requiring employers to make payments of working tax credit, or prescribed elements of working tax credit, in accordance with notices given to them by the Board,

(b) for the payment by the Board of working tax credit in cases where an employer does not make payments of working tax credit, or prescribed elements of working tax credit, in accordance with the regulations and with any notices given by the Board,

(c) prescribing circumstances in which employers are not required to make, or to continue making, payments of working tax credit, or prescribed elements of working tax credit,

(d) for the provision of information or evidence for the purpose of enabling the Board to be satisfied whether employers are complying with notices given by the Board and with the regulations,

(e) requiring employers to provide information to employees (in their itemised pay statements or otherwise),

(f) for the funding by the Board of working tax credit paid or to be paid by employers (whether by way of set off against income tax, national insurance contributions or student loan deductions for which they are accountable to the Board or otherwise),

(g) for the recovery by the Board from an employer of funding under paragraph (f) to the extent that it exceeds the amount of working tax credit paid by the employer,

(h) for the payment of interest at the prescribed rate on sums due from or to the Board, and for determining the date from which interest is to be calculated, and

(i) for appeals with respect to matters arising under the regulations which would otherwise not be the subject of an appeal.

25(3) [Omitted by FA 2008, s. 113 and Sch. 36, para. 90.]

25(4) [Omitted by FA 2008, s. 113 and Sch. 36, para. 90.]

25(5) In this Part–

"employee" means a person who receives any payment of, or on account of, PAYE income, and

"employer", in relation to an employee, means a person who makes any such payment to the employee.

25(6) [Omitted by ITEPA 2003, Sch. 6, para. 265(4) and repealed by ITEPA 2003, Sch. 8, Pt. 1.]

25(7) **"Student loan deductions"** means deductions in accordance with regulations under section 22(5) of the Teaching and Higher Education Act 1998 (c. 30), section 73B(3) of the Education (Scotland) Act 1980 (c. 44) or Article 3(5) of the Education (Student Support) (Northern Ireland) Order 1998 (S.I. 1998/1760 (N.I. 14)).

Commencement Date – S. 25(1), (2) and (5)–(7) entered into force on 9 July 2002 for the purposes of making regulations.
S. 25(3), (4) and (5) come into force on 6 April 2003 for the purposes of the power to call for documents etc. in relation to an employer's compliance with regulations under s. 25.

Prospective amendments – Pt. 1 (but not Sch. 1 or Sch. 3) repealed by WRA 2012, s. 147 and Sch. 14, Pt. 1, with effect from a date to be set by order of the Secretary of State.

History – In s. 25(1), the words "payments of, or on account of, PAYE income" substituted for the words "Schedule E payments" by ITEPA 2003, Sch. 6, para. 265(2) which has effect for the tax year 2003–04 and subsequent tax years.
S. 25(3) and (4) omitted by FA 2008, s. 113 and Sch. 36, para. 90, with effect from 1 April 2009 (SI 2009/404, art. 2, subject to savings at SI 2009/404, art. 3). Former s. 25(3) and (4) read as follows:

"**25(3)** Section 20 of the Taxes Management Act 1970 (c. 9) (power to call for documents etc.) applies (with sections 20B and 20BB) *in relation to an employer's* compliance with regulations under this section as in relation to a person's tax liability (but subject to the modifications provided by subsection (4)).

25(4) Those sections apply by virtue of subsection (3) as if–

(a) the references to the taxpayer, a taxpayer or a class of taxpayers were to the employer, an employer or a class of employers,

(b) the reference to any provision of the Taxes Acts were to regulations under this section,

(c) the references to the proper assessment or collection of tax were to the proper award or payment of working tax credit,

(d) the reference to an appeal relating to tax were to an appeal relating to compliance with regulations under this section, and

(e) the reference to believing that tax has been, or may have been, lost to the Crown were to believing that the Crown has, or may have, incurred a loss."

In s. 25(5), the words "payment of, or on account of, PAYE income" substituted for the words "Schedule E payment" by ITEPA 2003, Sch. 6, para. 265(3) which has effect for the tax year 2003–04 and subsequent tax years.
S. 25(6) omitted by ITEPA 2003, Sch. 6, para. 265(4) and repealed by ITEPA 2003, Sch. 8, Pt. 1 which have effect for the tax year 2003–04 and subsequent tax years.

Cross references – SI 2002/2173, reg. 9: time of payment to employee entitled to working tax credit where employer not required to make payment, or has failed to do so.
Employment Rights Act 1996, s. 47D (not reproduced); right of employee not to be subjected to any detriment by any act or omission by his employer done on certain grounds connected with the employee's entitlement, or possible entitlement, to working tax credit.
Employment Rights Act 1996, s. 104B (not reproduced): an employee is regarded as unfairly dismissed if the reason, or principal reason, for his dismissal was one connected with the employee's entitlement, or possible entitlement, to working tax credit.

Statutory instruments – SI 2002/2172.

Notes – S. 25(6) is unnecessary and so has not been rewritten into the provisions of ITEPA 2003.

26 Liability of officers for sums paid to employers

26(1) Regulations may provide that where–

(a) an employer which is a body corporate has failed to repay any funding to the Board in accordance with regulations made under section 25(2)(g), and

(b) the provision of the funding, or the failure by the employer to repay the funding, appears to the Board to be attributable to fraud or neglect on the part of one or more individuals who, at the time of the fraud or neglect, were officers of the body corporate ("culpable officers"),

the culpable officers are required to pay to the Board the amount of funding recoverable by the Board from the employer.

26(2) Regulations under this section must include provision–

(a) for any amount paid to the Board by a culpable officer in accordance with the regulations to be deducted from the amount of funding liable to be repaid by the employer,

(b) for the amount which a culpable officer is liable to pay under the regulations to be reduced where the amount of funding recoverable from the employer is reduced by payments made to the Board by the employer, and

(c) for the Board to repay to a culpable officer the amount (if any) by which the amount that he has paid to the Board pursuant to the regulations exceeds the reduced amount that he is liable to pay by virtue of paragraph (b).

26(3) Regulations under this section may include provision–

(a) requiring payments by culpable officers to be made in accordance with notices given to them by the Board,

(b) for determining, in cases of an employer in relation to which there is more than one culpable officer, the proportion of the amount of funding recoverable from the employer that is payable by each culpable officer,

(c) for the payment of interest at the prescribed rate on sums due to or from the Board, and for determining the date from which interest is to be calculated, and

(d) for appeals with respect to matters arising under the regulations.

26(4) **"Officer"**, in relation to a body corporate, means–

(a) any director, manager, secretary or other similar officer of the body corporate, or any person purporting to act as such, and

(b) in a case where the affairs of the body corporate are managed by its members, any member of the body corporate exercising functions of management with respect to it or purporting to do so.

Commencement Date – S. 26 entered into force on 1 January 2003 for the purposes of making regulations (SI 2002/1727 (C. 52)).

Prospective amendments – Pt. 1 (but not Sch. 1 or Sch. 3) repealed by WRA 2012, s. 147 and Sch. 14, Pt. 1, with effect from a date to be set by order of the Secretary of State.

27 Rights of employees

27 Schedule 1 (rights of employees not to suffer unfair dismissal or other detriment) has effect.

Commencement Date – S. 27 entered into force on 1 September 2002 in respect of rights conferred on employees by virtue of regulations under s. 25 (SI 2002/1727 (C. 52)).

Prospective amendments – Pt. 1 (but not Sch. 1 or Sch. 3) repealed by WRA 2012, s. 147 and Sch. 14, Pt. 1, with effect from a date to be set by order of the Secretary of State.

28 Overpayments

28(1) Where the amount of a tax credit paid for a tax year to a person or persons exceeds the amount of the tax credit to which he is entitled, or they are jointly entitled, for the tax year (as determined in accordance with the provision made by and by virtue of sections 18 to 21B), the Commissioners may decide that the excess, or any part of it, is to be–

(a) repaid to the Commissioners; or

(b) treated as if it were an amount recoverable by the Secretary of State under section 71ZB of the Administration Act or (as the case may be) by the relevant Northern Ireland Department under section 69ZB of the Administration (Northern Ireland) Act.

28(2) In this Part such an excess is referred to as an overpayment.

28(3) For overpayments made under awards on single claims, the person to whom the tax credit was awarded is liable to repay to the Commissioners, the Secretary of State or (as the case may be) the relevant Northern Ireland Department, the amount which the Commissioners decide is to be repaid or treated as recoverable under subsection (1)(b).

28(4) For overpayments made under awards on joint claims, the persons to whom the tax credit was awarded are jointly and severally liable to repay to the Commissioners, the Secretary of State or (as the case may be) the relevant Northern Ireland Department, the amount mentioned in subsection (3) unless the Commissioners decide that each is liable for a specified part of that amount.

28(5) Where it appears to the Commissioners that there is likely to be an overpayment of a tax credit for a tax year under an award made to a person or persons, the Commissioners may, with a view to reducing or eliminating the overpayment, amend the award or any other award of any tax credit made to the person or persons; but this subsection does not apply once a decision is taken in relation to the person or persons for the tax year under section 18(1).

28(6) Where the Commissioners decide under section 16 to terminate an award of a tax credit made to a person or persons on the ground that at no time during the period to which the award related did the person or persons satisfy–

(a) section 8(1) (if the award related to child tax credit), or

(b) section 10(1) (if it related to working tax credit),

the Commissioners may decide that the amount paid under the award, or any part of it, is to be treated for the purposes of this Part (apart from subsection (5)) as an overpayment.

28(7) In this section and in section 29–

"the Administration Act" means the Social Security Administration Act 1992;

"the Administration (Northern Ireland) Act" means the Social Security Administration (Northern Ireland) Act 1992;

"the relevant Northern Ireland Department" means the Department for Communities.

28(8) In this section,

"the Commissioners" means the Commissioners for Her Majesty's Revenue and Customs.

Commencement Date – S. 28 entered into force on 6 April 2003 as regards liability to repay overpayments or to be paid full entitlement where there is an underpayment (SI 2002/1727 (c. 52)).

Prospective amendments – Pt. 1 (but not Sch. 1 or Sch. 3) repealed by WRA 2012, s. 147 and Sch. 14, Pt. 1, with effect from a date to be set by order of the Secretary of State.

History – In s. 28(1), the words "Commissioners may" substituted for the words "Board may" by SI 2017/781, art. 6(2)(a), with effect from 25 September 2017.
S. 28(1)(a) and (b) (and the "–" before them) substituted for the words "repaid to the Board" by SI 2017/781, art. 6(2)(b), with effect from 25 September 2017.
In s. 28(1), the number "21B" substituted for "21" by SI 2014/886, art. 2(8), with effect from 6 April 2014.
In s. 28(3), the words "to the Commissioners, the Secretary of State or (as the case may be) the relevant Northern Ireland Department, the amount which the Commissioners decide is to be repaid or treated as recoverable under subsection (1)(b)" substituted for the words "the amount which the Board decide is to be repaid" by SI 2017/781, art. 6(2)(c), with effect from 25 September 2017.
In s. 28(4), the words "to the Commissioners, the Secretary of State or (as the case may be) the relevant Northern Ireland Department, the amount mentioned in subsection (3) unless the Commissioners decide that each is liable for" substituted for the words "the amount which the Board decide is to be repaid unless the Board decide that each is to repay" by SI 2017/781, art. 6(2)(d), with effect from 25 September 2017.
In s. 28(5) and (6), the word "Commissioners" substituted for the word "Board" by SI 2017/781, art. 6(2)(e), with effect from 25 September 2017.
S. 28(7) and (8) inserted by SI 2017/781, art. 6(2)(f), with effect from 25 September 2017.

Cross references – SI 2014/1230, reg. 12(3): modified application of s. 28 in relation to the introduction of Universal Credit.

29 Recovery of overpayments

29(1) Where an amount is liable to be repaid or paid by a person or persons under section 28, the Board must give him, or each of them, a notice specifying the amount.

29(2) The notice must state which of subsections (3) to (5) is to apply in relation to the amount or any specified part of the amount; and a notice may at any time be replaced by another notice containing a different statement.

29(3) Where a notice states that this subsection applies in relation to an amount (or part of an amount), it is to be treated for the purposes of Part 6 of the Taxes Management Act 1970 (c. 9) (collection and recovery) as if it were tax charged in an assessment and due and payable by the person or persons to whom the notice was given at the end of the period of thirty days beginning with the day on which the notice is given.

29(4) Where a notice states that this subsection applies in relation to an amount (or part of an amount), it may be recovered–

(a) subject to provision made by regulations, by deduction from payments of any tax credit under an award made for any period to the person, or either or both of the persons, to whom the notice was given;

(b) by the Secretary of State–

(i) by deductions under section 71ZC of the Administration Act (deduction from benefit);

(ii) by deductions under section 71ZD of that Act (deduction from earnings); or

(iii) as set out in section 71ZE of that Act (court action etc); or

(c) by the relevant Northern Ireland Department–

(i) by deductions under section 69ZC of the Administration (Northern Ireland) Act (deduction from benefit);

(ii) by deductions under section 69ZD of that Act (deduction from earnings); or

(iii) as set out in section 69ZE of that Act (court action etc).

29(5) Where a notice states that this subsection applies in relation to an amount (or part of an amount), PAYE regulations apply to it as if it were an underpayment of income tax for a previous year of assessment by the person or persons to whom the notice was given that is not a relevant debt (within the meaning of section 684 of the Income Tax (Earnings and Pensions) Act 2003).

Commencement Date – S. 29 in force on 6 April 2003 as regards liability to repay overpayments or to be paid full entitlement where there is an underpayment (SI 2002/1727 (C. 52)).

Prospective amendments – Pt. 1 (but not Sch. 1 or Sch. 3) repealed by WRA 2012, s. 147 and Sch. 14, Pt. 1, with effect from a date to be set by order of the Secretary of State.

History – In s. 29(1), the words "or paid" inserted by SI 2017/781, art. 6(3)(a), with effect from 25 September 2017.
S. 29(4) substituted by SI 2017/781, art. 6(3)(b), with effect from 25 September 2017. Former s. 29(4) read as follows:
"29(4) Where a notice states that this subsection applies in relation to an amount (or part of an amount), it may, subject to provision made by regulations, be recovered by deduction from payments of any tax credit under an award made for any period to the person, or either or both of the persons, to whom the notice was given.".
In s. 29(5), the words "income tax" substituted for "tax" and the words "that is not a relevant debt (within the meaning of section 684 of the Income Tax (Earnings and Pensions) Act 2003)" inserted by FA 2009, s. 109 and Sch. 58, para. 8 with effect from 21 July 2009.
In s. 29(5), the words "PAYE regulations" substituted by ITEPA 2003, Sch. 6, para. 266 which has effect for the tax year 2003–04 and subsequent tax years.

Cross references – SI 2014/1230, reg. 12(4): modified application of s. 29 in relation to the introduction of Universal Credit.
SI 2002/2173, reg. 12A: recovery of overpayments of tax credit from other payments of tax credit (see s. 29(4)).
SI 2003/742, reg. 19: modified application of s. 29(4) to members of polygamous units.

Statutory instruments – SI 2002/2173.

Other material – COP26: What happens when we pay you too much tax credit?: Revenue practice on overpayments.

30 Underpayments

30(1) Where it has been determined in accordance with the provision made by and by virtue of sections 18 to 21B that a person was entitled, or persons were jointly entitled, to a tax credit for a tax year and either–

(a) the amount of the tax credit paid to him or them for that tax year was less than the amount of the tax credit to which it was so determined that he is entitled or they are jointly entitled, or

(b) no payment of the tax credit was made to him or them for that tax year,

the amount of the difference, or of his entitlement or their joint entitlement, must be paid to him or to whichever of them is prescribed.

30(2) Where the claim for the tax credit was made by one person on behalf of another, the payment is to be made to whichever of those persons is prescribed.

Commencement Date – S. 30 in force on 6 April 2003 in respect of liability to repay overpayments or to be paid full entitlement where there is an underpayment (SI 2002/1727 (C. 52)).
S. 30 entered into force on 1 January 2003 as regards making regulations under that section (SI 2002/1727 (C. 52)).

Prospective amendments – Pt. 1 (but not Sch. 1 or Sch. 3) repealed by WRA 2012, s. 147 and Sch. 14, Pt. 1, with effect from a date to be set by order of the Secretary of State.

History – In s. 30(1), the number "21B" substituted for "21" by SI 2014/886, art. 2(8), with effect from 6 April 2014.

Cross references – *SI 2014/1230, Sch., para. 9: modified application of s. 30(1) where SI 2014/1230, reg. 12A applies (claims for universal credit).*

PENALTIES

31 Incorrect statements etc.

31(1) Where a person fraudulently or negligently–

(a) makes an incorrect statement or declaration in or in connection with a claim for a tax credit or a notification of a change of circumstances given in accordance with regulations under section 6 or in response to a notice under section 17, or

TC Statutes

(b) gives incorrect information or evidence in response to a requirement imposed on him by virtue of section 14(2), 15(2), 16(3), 18(10) or 19(2) or regulations under section 25 or in response to a notification under section 21A(5),

a penalty not exceeding £3,000 may be imposed on him.

31(2) Where a person liable to a penalty under subsection (1) is a person making, or who has made, a claim for a tax credit for a period jointly with another and the penalty is imposed–

(a) under paragraph (a) of that subsection in respect of the claim, a notification relating to the tax credit claimed or a notice relating to the tax credit awarded on the claim, or

(b) under paragraph (b) of that subsection in respect of a requirement imposed on him with respect to the tax credit for the period,

a penalty of an amount not exceeding £3,000 may be imposed on the other person unless subsection (3) applies.

31(3) This subsection applies if the other person was not, and could not reasonably have been expected to have been, aware that the person liable to the penalty under subsection (1) had fraudulently or negligently made the incorrect statement or declaration or given the incorrect information or evidence.

31(4) Where penalties are imposed under subsections (1) and (2) in respect of the same statement, declaration, information or evidence, their aggregate amount must not exceed £3,000.

31(5) Where a person acts for another–

(a) in or in connection with a claim or notification referred to in subsection (1), or

(b) in response to a notice so referred to,

subsection (1) applies to him (as well as to any person to whom it applies apart from this subsection).

Commencement Date – S. 31 entered into force by virtue of SI 2002/1727 (C. 52) on:

- 1 August 2002 as regards the imposition of penalties for incorrect statement or declaration in or in connection with a claim for a tax credit or a notification given in accordance with regulations under s. 6, or for incorrect information or evidence in response to a requirement imposed by virtue of regulations under s. 25; and
- 1 January 2003 as regards imposition of penalties for incorrect information or evidence in response to a requirement imposed by virtue of s. 14(2), 15(2) or 16(3).

S. 31 entered into force by virtue of SI 2002/1727 (C. 52) on 6 April 2003 as regards the imposition of penalties for incorrect information or evidence in response to a requirement imposed by virtue of s. 18(10) or 19(2) or for incorrect statement or declaration in response to a notice under s. 17.

Prospective amendments – Pt. 1 (but not Sch. 1 or Sch. 3) repealed by WRA 2012, s. 147 and Sch. 14, Pt. 1, with effect from a date to be set by order of the Secretary of State.

History – In s. 31(1)(b), the words "or in response to a notification under section 21A(5)" inserted by SI 2014/886, art. 2(9), with effect from 6 April 2014.

Cross references – SI 2003/742, reg. 20: modified application of s. 31(2) to members of polygamous units.

32 Failure to comply with requirements

32(1) Where a person fails–

(a) to provide any information or evidence which he is required to provide by virtue of section 14(2), 15(2), 16(3), 18(10) or 19(2) or regulations under section 25, or

(b) to comply with a requirement imposed on him by a notice under section 17 by virtue of subsection (2)(a), (4)(a) or (6)(a) of that section,

the penalties specified in subsection (2) may be imposed on him.

32(2) The penalties are–

(a) a penalty not exceeding £300, and

(b) if the failure continues after a penalty is imposed under paragraph (a), a further penalty or penalties not exceeding £60 for each day on which the failure continues after the day on which the penalty under that paragraph was imposed (but excluding any day for which a penalty under this paragraph has already been imposed).

32(3) Where a person fails to give a notification required by regulations under section 6(3), a penalty not exceeding £300 may be imposed on him.

32(4) No penalty under subsection (2) may be imposed on a person in respect of a failure after the failure has been remedied.

32(5) For the purposes of this section a person is to be taken not to have failed to provide information or evidence, comply with a requirement or give a notification which must be provided, complied with or given by a particular time –

(a) if he provided, complied with or gave it within such further time (if any) as the Board may have allowed,

(b) if he had a reasonable excuse for not providing, complying with or giving it by that time, or

(c) if, after having had such an excuse, he provided, complied with or gave it without unreasonable delay.

32(6) Where the members of a couple both fail as mentioned in subsection (1)(b), the aggregate amount of any penalties under subsection (2) imposed on them in relation to their failures must not exceed the amounts specified in that subsection; and where the members of a couple both fail as mentioned in subsection (3), the aggregate amount of any penalties imposed on them in relation to their failures must not exceed £300.

Commencement Date – S. 32 entered into force by virtue of SI 2002/1727 (C. 52) on 1 August 2002 as regards the imposition of a penalty for the failure to provide information or evidence required by regulations under s. 25 or for failure to give notification required by regulations under s. 6(3).

S. 32 entered into force by virtue of SI 2002/1727 (C. 52) on 6 April 2003 as regards the imposition of a penalty for failure to provide information or evidence under s. 18(10) or 19(2) or to comply with a requirement imposed by a notice under s. 17 by virtue of s. 17(2)(a), (4)(a) or (6)(a).

Prospective amendments – Pt. 1 (but not Sch. 1 or Sch. 3) repealed by WRA 2012, s. 147 and Sch. 14, Pt. 1, with effect from a date to be set by order of the Secretary of State.

History – In s. 32(6) the word "couple" substituted for the words "married couple or unmarried couple" by the Civil Partnership Act 2004, s. 254 and Sch. 24, para. 145, with effect from 5 December 2005 (by virtue of SI 2005/3175, art. 2(1)).

33 Failure by employers to make correct payments

33(1) Where an employer refuses or repeatedly fails to make to an employee payments of tax credits which he is required to make to him by regulations under section 25 and, as a result, the Board make payments to the employee in accordance with regulations under subsection (2)(b) of that section, a penalty not exceeding £3,000 may be imposed on the employer.

33(2) Where an employer has, by reason of his fraud or neglect, not paid to an employee for a tax year the correct amount of any tax credit which he is required by regulations under section 25 to pay to him for that tax year, a penalty not exceeding £3,000 may be imposed on the employer.

33(3) But no penalty may be imposed on an employer under subsection (2) in respect of payments which are incorrect only because of a refusal or failure in respect of which a penalty is imposed on him under subsection (1).

TC Statutes

Commencement Date – S. 33 entered into force on 6 April 2003 as regards the imposition of a penalty for failure by the employer to make a correct payment to the employee.

Prospective amendments – Pt. 1 (but not Sch. 1 or Sch. 3) repealed by WRA 2012, s. 147 and Sch. 14, Pt. 1, with effect from a date to be set by order of the Secretary of State.

34 Supplementary

34 Schedule 2 (penalties: supplementary) has effect.

Commencement Date – S. 34 and Sch. 2 entered into force, by virtue of SI 2002/1727 (C. 52), on:

- 1 August 2002 as regards the imposition of penalties under s. 31 for incorrect statement or declaration in or in connection with a claim for tax credit or a notification given in accordance with regulations under s. 6, or for incorrect information or evidence in response to a requirement imposed by regulations under s. 25; mitigation of such penalties, appeals against such penalties and recovery of such penalties;
- 1 January 2003 as regards imposition of penalties under s. 31 for incorrect information or evidence in response to a requirement imposed by virtue of s. 14(2), 15(2) or 16(3); mitigation of such penalties, appeals against such penalties and recovery of such penalties;
- 1 August 2002 as regards imposition of penalties under s. 32(2)(b) or (3) for failure to provide information or evidence required by regulations under s. 25, or for failure to give notification required by regulations under s. 6(3); bringing proceedings for penalties under s. 32(2)(a) before Commissioners for failure to provide information or evidence required by regulations under s. 25; mitigation of such penalties, appeals against such penalties and recovery of such penalties.
- 1 January 2003 as regards the imposition of penalties under s. 32(2)(b) for failure to provide information or evidence under s. 14(2), 15(2) or 16(3); bringing proceedings for such penalties under s. 32(2)(a) before Commissioners; mitigation of such penalties; appeals against such penalties and recovery of such penalties.

S. 34 and Sch. 2 come into force on 6 April 2003, by virtue of SI 2002/1727 (C. 52) as regards:

- imposition of penalties under s. 31 for incorrect information or evidence imposed by virtue of s. 18(10) or 19(2), or for incorrect statement or declaration in response to a notice under s. 17; mitigation of such penalties, appeals against such penalties and recovery of such penalties;
- the imposition of penalties under s. 32(2)(b) for failure to provide information or evidence under s. 18(10) or 19(2) or for failure to comply with the requirement imposed under s. 17 by virtue of s. 17(2)(a), (4)(a) or (6)(a); bringing proceedings for such penalties under s. 32(2)(a) before Commissioners; mitigation of such penalties; appeals against penalties and recovery of such penalties.
- the imposition of penalties under s. 33 for failure by the employer to make correct payment to the employee; mitigation of such penalties, appeals against such penalties and recovery of such penalties.

Prospective amendments – Pt. 1 (but not Sch. 1 or Sch. 3) repealed by WRA 2012, s. 147 and Sch. 14, Pt. 1, with effect from a date to be set by order of the Secretary of State.

FRAUD

35 Offence of fraud

35(1) A person commits an offence if he is knowingly concerned in any fraudulent activity undertaken with a view to obtaining payments of a tax credit by him or any other person.

35(2) A person who commits an offence under subsection (1) is liable—

(a) on summary conviction, to imprisonment for a term not exceeding six months, or a fine not exceeding the statutory maximum, or both, or

(b) on conviction on indictment, to imprisonment for a term not exceeding seven years, or a fine, or both.

Commencement Date – S. 35 entered into force on 1 August 2002 as regards instituting criminal proceedings for fraud in connection with obtaining payments of a tax credit (SI 2002/1727 (C. 52)).

Prospective amendments – S. 35(2)–(12) substituted for former s. 35(2) by WRA 2012, s. 124, with effect from a day to be appointed by order of the Secretary of State.

Prospective amendments – Pt. 1 (but not Sch. 1 or Sch. 3) repealed by WRA 2012, s. 147 and Sch. 14, Pt. 1, with effect from a date to be set by order of the Secretary of State.

36 Powers in relation to documents

36(1) Section 20BA of the Taxes Management Act 1970 (c. 9) (orders for delivery of documents) applies (with Schedule 1AA and section 20BB) in relation to offences involving fraud in connection with, or in relation to, tax credits as in relation to offences involving serious fraud in connection with, or in relation to, tax.

36(2) [Omitted by FA 2007, s. 84(4) and repealed by Sch. 22, para. 14, and FA 2007, s. 114 and Sch. 27, Pt. 5(1).]

36(3) [Omitted by FA 2007, s. 84(4) and repealed by Sch. 22, para. 14, and FA 2007, s. 114 and Sch. 27, Pt. 5(1).]

36(4) Any regulations under Schedule 1AA to the Taxes Management Act 1970 which are in force immediately before the commencement of subsection (1) apply, subject to any necessary modifications, for the purposes of that Schedule as they apply by virtue of that subsection (until amended or revoked).

Commencement Date – S. 36 entered into force on 1 August 2002 as regards the obtaining of documents in relation to offences involving fraud or serious fraud in connection with, or in relation to, tax credits (SI 2002/1727 (C. 52)).

Prospective amendments – Pt. 1 (but not Sch. 1 or Sch. 3) repealed by WRA 2012, s. 147 and Sch. 14, Pt. 1, with effect from a date to be set by order of the Secretary of State.

History – S. 36(2) and (3) omitted by FA 2007, s. 84(4) and repealed by Sch. 22, para. 14, and FA 2007, s. 114 and Sch. 27, Pt. 5(1) with effect from with effect from 1 December 2007 (by virtue of SI 2007/3166, art. 3(a)).

LOSS OF TAX CREDIT PROVISIONS

36A Loss of working tax credit in case of conviction etc for benefit offence

36A(1) Subsection (4) applies where a person ("the offender")–

(a) is convicted of one or more benefit offences in any proceedings, or

(b) after being given a notice under subsection (2) of the appropriate penalty provision by an appropriate authority, agrees in the manner specified by the appropriate authority to pay a penalty under the appropriate penalty provision to the appropriate authority, in a case where the offence to which the notice relates is a benefit offence, or

(c) is cautioned in respect of one or more benefit offences.

36A(2) In subsection (1)(b)–

(a) **"the appropriate penalty provision"** means section 115A of the Social Security Administration Act 1992 (penalty as alternative to prosecution) or section 109A of the Social Security Administration (Northern Ireland) Act 1992 (the corresponding provision for Northern Ireland);

(b) **"appropriate authority"** means–

(i) in relation to section 115A of the Social Security Administration Act 1992, the Secretary of State or an authority which administers housing benefit or council tax benefit, and

(ii) in relation to section 109A of the Social Security Administration (Northern Ireland) Act 1992, the Department (within the meaning of that Act) or the Northern Ireland Housing Executive.

36A(3) Subsection (4) does not apply by virtue of subsection (1)(a) if, because the proceedings in which the offender was convicted constitute the current set of proceedings for the purposes of section 36C, the restriction in subsection (3) of that section applies in the offender's case.

36A(4) If this subsection applies and the offender is a person who would, apart from this section, be entitled (whether pursuant to a single or joint claim) to working tax credit at any time within the disqualification period, then, despite that entitlement, working tax credit shall not be payable for any period comprised in the disqualification period–

(a) in the case of a single claim, to the offender, or

(b) in the case of a joint claim, to the offender or the other member of the couple.

36A(5) Regulations may provide in relation to cases to which subsection (4)(b) would otherwise apply that working tax credit shall be payable, for any period comprised in the disqualification period, as if the amount payable were reduced in such manner as may be prescribed.

36A(6) For the purposes of this section, the disqualification period, in relation to any disqualifying event, means the relevant period beginning with such date, falling after the date of the disqualifying event, as may be determined by or in accordance with regulations.

36A(7) For the purposes of subsection (6) the relevant period is–

(a) in a case falling within subsection (1)(a) where the benefit offence, or one of them, is a relevant offence, the period of three years,

(b) in a case falling within subsection (1)(a) (but not within paragraph (a) above)), the period of 13 weeks, or

(c) in a case falling within subsection (1)(b) or (c), the period of 4 weeks.

36A(8) The Treasury may by order amend subsection (7)(a), (b) or (c) to substitute a different period for that for the time being specified there.

36A(9) This section has effect subject to section 36B.

36A(10) In this section and section 36B–

"benefit offence" means any of the following offences committed on or after the day specified by order made by the Treasury–

(a) an offence in connection with a claim for a disqualifying benefit;

(b) an offence in connection with the receipt or payment of any amount by way of such a benefit;

(c) an offence committed for the purpose of facilitating the commission (whether or not by the same person) of a benefit offence;

(d) an offence consisting in an attempt or conspiracy to commit a benefit offence;

"disqualifying benefit" has the meaning given in section 6A(1) of the Social Security Fraud Act 2001;

"disqualifying event" means–

(a) the conviction falling within subsection (1)(a);

(b) the agreement falling within subsection (1)(b);

(c) the caution falling within subsection (1)(c);

"relevant offence" has the meaning given in section 6B of the Social Security Fraud Act 2001.

Commencement Date – The day specified under s. 36A(10) for the purposes of s. 36A–36D is 6 April 2013 (SI 2013/524).

Prospective amendments – Pt. 1 (but not Sch. 1 or Sch. 3) repealed by WRA 2012, s. 147 and Sch. 14, Pt. 1, with effect from a date to be set by order of the Secretary of State.

S. 36A(1)(c) repealed by WRA 2012, s. 121(2), with effect from a day to be appointed.

In s. 36A(7)(c) the words "or (c)" repealed by WRA 2012, s. 147 and Sch. 14, Pt. 12, with effect from a day to be appointed.

In s. 36A(10), in the definition of "disqualifying event" para. (c) repealed by WRA 2012, s. 147 and Sch. 14, Pt. 12, with effect from a day to be appointed.

History – S. 36A inserted by WRA 2012, s. 120(2), with effect from 6 April 2013 (SI 2013/524).

Cross references – SI 2013/715: for the purposes of s. 36A(6), the date on which the relevant period begins is the thirtieth day after the day on which the Commissioners for HMRC are notified of the disqualifying event mentioned in s. 36A(1).

Statutory instruments – SI 2013/715: partly made under s. 36A(5) and (6).

36B Section 36A: supplementary

36B(1) Where–

(a) the conviction of any person of any offence is taken in account for the purposes of the application of section 36A in relation to that person, and

(b) that conviction is subsequently quashed,

all such payments and other adjustments shall be made as would be necessary if no restriction had been imposed by or under section 36A that could not have been imposed if the conviction had not taken place.

36B(2) Where, after the agreement of any person ("P") to pay a penalty under the appropriate penalty provision is taken into account for the purposes of the application of section 36A in relation to that person–

(a) P's agreement to pay the penalty is withdrawn under subsection (5) of the appropriate penalty provision, or

(b) it is decided on an appeal or in accordance with regulations under the Social Security Act 1992 or the Social Security (Northern Ireland) Order 1998 (S.I. 1998/1506 (N.I. 10)) that the overpayment to which the agreement relates is not recoverable or due,

all such payments and other adjustments shall be made as would be necessary if no restriction had been imposed by or under section 36A that could not have been imposed if P had not agreed to pay the penalty.

36B(3) Where, after the agreement ("the old agreement") of any person ("P") to pay a penalty under the appropriate penalty provision is taken into account for the purposes of the application of section 36A in relation to P, the amount of any overpayment made to which the penalty relates is revised on an appeal

TC Statutes

or in accordance with regulations under the Social Security Act 1998 or the Social Security (Northern Ireland) Order 1998–

(a) section 36A shall cease to apply by virtue of the old agreement, and

(b) subsection (4) shall apply.

36B(4) Where this subsection applies–

(a) if there is a new disqualifying event consisting of–

(i) P's agreement to pay a penalty under the appropriate penalty regime in relation to the revised overpayment, or

(ii) P being cautioned in relation to the offence to which the old agreement relates,

the disqualification period relating to the new disqualifying event shall be reduced by the number of days in so much of the disqualification period relating to the old agreement as had expired when subsection 36A ceased to apply by virtue of the old agreement, and

(b) in any other case, all such payments and other adjustments shall be made as would be necessary if no restriction had been imposed by or under section 36A that could not have been imposed if P had not agreed to pay the penalty.

36B(5) For the purposes of section 36A–

(a) the date of a person's conviction in any proceedings of a benefit offence shall be taken to be the date on which the person was found guilty of that offence in those proceedings (whenever the person was sentenced) or in the case mentioned in paragraph (b)(ii) the date of the order for absolute discharge, and

(b) references to a conviction include references to–

(i) a conviction in relation to which the court makes an order for absolute or conditional discharge,

(ii) an order for absolute discharge made by a court of summary jurisdiction in Scotland under section 246(3) of the Criminal Procedure (Scotland) Act 1995 without proceeding to a conviction, and

(iii) a conviction in Northern Ireland.

36B(6) In this section **"the appropriate penalty provision"** has the meaning given by section 36A(2)(a).

Prospective amendments – Pt. 1 (but not Sch. 1 or Sch. 3) repealed by WRA 2012, s. 147 and Sch. 14, Pt. 1, with effect from a date to be set by order of the Secretary of State.

S. 36B(4)(a)(ii), and the word "or" preceding it repealed by WRA 2012, s. 147 and Sch. 14, Pt. 12, with effect from a day to be appointed.

History – S. 36B inserted by WRA 2012, s. 120(2), with effect from 6 April 2013 (SI 2013/524).

36C Loss of working tax credit for repeated benefit fraud

36C(1) If–

(a) a person ("the offender") is convicted of one or more benefit offences in a set of proceedings ("the current set of proceedings"),

(b) within the period of five years ending on the date on which the benefit offence was, or any of them were, committed, one or more disqualifying events occurred in relation to the offender (the event, or the most recent of them, being referred to in this section as "the earlier disqualifying event"),

(c) the current set of proceedings has not been taken into account for the purposes of any previous application of this section in relation to the offender,

(d) the earlier disqualifying event has not been taken into account as an earlier disqualifying event for the purposes of any previous application of this section in relation to the offender, and

(e) the offender is a person who would, apart from this section, be entitled (whether pursuant to a single or joint claim) to working tax credit at any time within the disqualification period,

then, despite that entitlement, the restriction in subsection (3) shall apply in relation to the payment of that benefit in the offender's case.

36C(2) The restriction in subsection (3) does not apply if the benefit offence referred to in subsection (1)(a), or any of them, is a relevant offence.

36C(3) Working tax credit shall not be payable for any period comprised in the disqualification period–

(a) *in the case of a single claim*, to the offender, or

(b) in the case of a joint claim, to the offender or the other member of the couple.

36C(4) Regulations may provide in relation to cases to which subsection (3)(b) would otherwise apply that working tax credit shall be payable, for any period comprised in the disqualification period, as if the amount payable were reduced in such manner as may be prescribed.

36C(5) For the purposes of this section the disqualification period, in an offender's case, means the relevant period beginning with a prescribed date falling after the date of the conviction in the current set of proceedings.

36C(6) For the purposes of subsection (5) the relevant period is–

(a) in a case where, within the period of five years ending on the date on which the earlier disqualifying event occurred, a previous disqualifying event occurred in relation to the offender, the period of three years;

(b) in any other case, 26 weeks.

36C(7) In this section and section 36D–

"appropriate penalty provision" has the meaning given in section 36A(2)(a);

"benefit offence" means any of the following offences committed on or after the day specified by order made by the Treasury–

(a) an offence in connection with a claim for a disqualifying benefit;

(b) an offence in connection with the receipt or payment of any amount by way of such a benefit;

(c) an offence committed for the purpose of facilitating the commission (whether or not by the same person) of a benefit offence;

(d) an offence consisting in an attempt or conspiracy to commit a benefit offence;

"disqualifying benefit" has the meaning given in section 6A(1) of the Social Security Fraud Act 2001;

"disqualifying event" has the meaning given in section 36A(10);

"relevant offence" has the meaning given in section 6B of the Social Security Fraud Act 2001.

36C(8) Where a person is convicted of more than one benefit offence in the same set of proceedings, there is to be only one disqualifying event in respect of that set of proceedings for the purposes of this section and–

(a) subsection (1)(b) is satisfied if any of the convictions take place in the five year period there;

(b) the event is taken into account for the purposes of subsection (1)(d) if any of the convictions have been taken into account as mentioned there;

(c) in the case of the earlier disqualifying event mentioned in subsection (6)(a), the reference there to the date on which the earlier disqualifying event occurred is a reference to the date on which any of the convictions take place;

(d) in the case of the previous disqualifying event mentioned in subsection (6)(a), that provision is satisfied if any of the convictions take place in the five year period mentioned there.

36C(9) The Treasury may by order amend subsection (6) to substitute different periods for those for the time being specified there.

36C(10) An order under subsection (9) may provide for different periods to apply according to the type of earlier disqualifying event or events occurring in any case.

36C(11) This section has effect subject to section 36D.

Commencement Date – The day specified under s. 36C(7) for the purposes of s. 36A–36D is 6 April 2013 (SI 2013/524).

Prospective amendments – Pt. 1 (but not Sch. 1 or Sch. 3) repealed by WRA 2012, s. 147 and Sch. 14, Pt. 1, with effect from a date to be set by order of the Secretary of State.

History – S. 36C inserted by WRA 2012, s. 120(2), with effect from 6 April 2013 (SI 2013/524).

Cross references – SI 2013/715: for the purposes of s. 36C(5), the prescribed date is the thirtieth day after the day on which the Commissioners for HMRC are notified of the offender's conviction mentioned in that section.

Statutory instruments – SI 2013/715: partly made under s. 36C(4) and (5).

36D Section 36C: supplementary

36D(1) Where–

(a) the conviction of any person of any offence is taken into account for the purposes of the application of section 36C in relation to that person, and

(b) that conviction is subsequently quashed,

all such payments and other adjustments shall be made as would be necessary if no restriction had been imposed by or under section 36C that could not have been imposed if the conviction had not taken place.

36D(2) Subsection (3) applies where, after the agreement of any person ("P") to pay a penalty under the appropriate penalty provision is taken into account for the purposes of the application of section 36C in relation to that person–

(a) P's agreement to pay the penalty is withdrawn under subsection (5) of the appropriate penalty provision,

(b) it is decided on an appeal or in accordance with regulations under the Social Security Act 1998 or the Social Security (Northern Ireland) Order 1998 (S.I. 1998/1506 (N.I. 10)) that any overpayment made to which the agreement relates is not recoverable or due, or

(c) the amount of any over payment to which the penalty relates is revised on an appeal or in accordance with regulations under the Social Security Act 1998 or the Social Security (Northern Ireland) Order 1998 and there is no new agreement by P to pay a penalty under the appropriate penalty provision in relation to the revised overpayment.

36D(3) In those circumstances, all such payments and other adjustments shall be made as would be necessary if no restriction had been imposed by or under section 36C that could not have been imposed if P had not agreed to pay the penalty.

36D(4) For the purposes of section 36C–

(a) the date of a person's conviction in any proceedings of a benefit offence shall be taken to be the date on which the person was found guilty of that offence in those proceedings (whenever the person was sentenced) or in the case mentioned in paragraph (b)(ii) the date of the order for absolute discharge, and

(b) references to a conviction include references to–

(i) a conviction in relation to which the court makes an order for absolute or conditional discharge,

(ii) an order for absolute discharge made by a court of summary jurisdiction in Scotland under section 246(3) of the Criminal Procedure (Scotland) Act 1995 without proceeding to a conviction, and

(iii) a conviction in Northern Ireland.

36D(5) In section 36C references to any previous application of that section–

(a) include references to any previous application of a provision having an effect in Northern Ireland corresponding to provision made by that section, but

(b) do not include references to any previous application of that section the effect of which was to impose a restriction for a period comprised in the same disqualification period.

Prospective amendments – Pt. 1 (but not Sch. 1 or Sch. 3) repealed by WRA 2012, s. 147 and Sch. 14, Pt. 1, with effect from a date to be set by order of the Secretary of State.

History – S. 36D inserted by WRA 2012, s. 120(2), with effect from 6 April 2013 (SI 2013/524).

INTEREST

37 Interest

37(1) If an overpayment of a tax credit for a period is attributable to fraud or neglect on the part of the person, or either or both of the persons, to whom the award of the tax credit was made (or a person acting for him, or for either or both of them, in making the claim for the tax credit), the Board may decide that the whole or any part of the overpayment is to carry interest.

37(2) Where the Board so decide the overpayment (or part of the overpayment) carries interest at a prescribed rate from the date thirty days after the appropriate date.

37(3) **"The appropriate date"** is–

(a) in the case of any amount treated as an overpayment by virtue of section 28(6), the date of the decision under section 16 to terminate the award, and

(b) in any other case, the date specified for the purposes of subsection (4) of section 17 in the notice given to the person or persons under that section in relation to the tax credit.

37(4) The Board must give notice of a decision under subsection (1) to the person, or each of the persons, to whom it relates; and the notice must state the date on which it is given and include details of the right to appeal against the decision under section 38.

37(5) A penalty under any of sections 31 to 33 carries interest at the prescribed rate from the date on which it becomes due and payable; but the Board may in their discretion mitigate any interest or entirely remit any interest which would otherwise be carried by a penalty.

37(6) Any interest carried under this section by an overpayment or penalty is to be regarded for the purposes of section 29(3) to (5) or paragraph 7 of Schedule 2 as if it were part of the overpayment or penalty.

Commencement Date – S. 37(1)–(4) and (6) come into force on 6 April 2003 in respect of interest on overpayment of a tax credit (SI 2002/1727 (C. 52)).

S. 37(2) and (5) entered into force on 9 July 2002 as regards making regulations to prescribe rates of interest (SI 2002/1727 (C. 52)).

S. 37(5) and (6) entered into force, by virtue of SI 2002/1727 (C. 52), on:

- 1 August 2002 as regards interest on penalties under s. 31 for incorrect statement or declaration in or in connection with a claim for a tax credit or a notification given in accordance with regulations under s. 6, or for incorrect information or evidence in response to a requirement imposed by virtue of s. 25;
- 1 August 2002 in respect of interest on penalties under s. 32 for failure to provide information or evidence required by regulations under s. 25 or for failure to give notification required by regulations under s. 6(3).
- 1 January 2003 as regards interest on penalties under s. 31 for incorrect information or evidence in response to a requirement imposed by virtue of s. 14(2), 15(2) or 16(3);
- 1 January 2003 as regards penalties under s. 32 for failure to provide information or evidence under s. 14(2), 15(2) or 16(3);

S. 37(5) and (6) come into force on 6 April 2003, by virtue of SI 2002/1727 (C. 52), as regards:

- interest on penalties under s. 31 for incorrect information or evidence in response to a requirement imposed by virtue of s. 18(10), 19(2) or for incorrect statement or declaration in response to a notice under s. 17;
- interest on penalties under s. 32 for failure to provide information or evidence under s. 18(10) or 19(2), or to comply with the requirement imposed by notice under s. 17 by virtue of s. 17(2)(a), (4)(a) or (6)(a); and
- interest on penalties under s. 33 for failure by the employer to make correct payment to the employee.

Prospective amendments – Pt. 1 (but not Sch. 1 or Sch. 3) repealed by WRA 2012, s. 147 and Sch. 14, Pt. 1, with effect from a date to be set by order of the Secretary of State.

Cross references – SI 2003/742, reg. 20: modifications to s. 37 in relation to members of polygamous units.

Statutory instruments – SI 2003/123.

APPEALS

38 Appeals

38(1) An appeal may, subject to subsection (1A), be brought against–

(a) a decision under section 14(1), 15(1), 16(1), 19(3) or 20(1) or (4) or regulations under section 21,

(b) the relevant section 18 decision in relation to a person or persons and a tax credit for a tax year and any revision of that decision under that section,

(c) a determination of a penalty under paragraph 1 of Schedule 2,

(ca) a decision under section 36A or 36C that working tax credit is not payable (or is not payable for a particular period), and

(d) a decision under section 37(1).

38(1A) An appeal may not be brought by virtue of subsection (1) against a decision unless a review of the decision has been carried out under section 21A and notice of the conclusion on the review has been given under section 21A(3).

38(1B) If in any case the conclusion of a review under section 21A is to uphold the decision reviewed, an appeal by virtue of subsection (1) in that case may be brought only against the original decision.

38(1C) If in any case the conclusion of a review under section 21A is to vary the decision reviewed, an appeal by virtue of subsection (1) in that case may be brought only against the decision as varied.

38(2) **"The relevant section 18 decision"** means–

(a) in a case in which a decision must be made under subsection (6) of section 18 in relation to the person or persons and the tax credit for the tax year, that decision, and

(b) in any other case, the decision under subsection (1) of that section in relation to the person or persons and the tax credit for the tax year.

Commencement Date – S. 38 entered into force, by virtue of SI 2002/1727 (C. 52), on:

- 1 September 2002 as regards appeals against determination of a penalty under Sch. 2, para. 1 where the penalty is imposed under s. 31 for incorrect statement or declaration in or in connection with a claim for a tax credit or a notification given in accordance with regulations under s. 6, or for incorrect information or evidence in response to a requirement imposed by virtue of regulations under s. 25;
- 1 September 2002 as regards an appeal against a determination of a penalty under Sch. 2, para. 1 where the penalty is imposed under s. 32(2)(b) or (3) for failure to provide evidence required by regulations under s. 25, or for failure to give notification required by regulations under s. 6(3).
- 1 January 2003 as regards appeals against determination of penalties under Sch. 2, para. 1 where the penalty is imposed under s. 31 for incorrect information or evidence in response to a requirement imposed by virtue of s. 14(2), 15(2) or 16(3);
- 1 January 2003 as regards an appeal against a determination of penalty under Sch. 2, para. 1 where the penalty is imposed under s. 32(2)(b) for failure to provide information or evidence under s. 14(2), 15(2) or 16(3);
- 1 January 2003 as regards an appeal against a determination of a penalty under s. 14(1), 15(1) or 16(1), or under regulations under s. 21; and

S. 38 entered into force, by virtue of SI 2002/1727 (C. 52), on:

- 6 April 2003 as regards an appeal against a determination of penalty under Sch. 2, para. 1 where the penalty is imposed under s. 31 for incorrect information or evidence in response to a requirement imposed by virtue of s. 18(10) or 19(2), or for failure to give notification required by regulations under s. 6(3);
- 6 April 2003 as regards an appeal against a determination of a penalty under Sch. 2, para. 1 where the penalty is imposed under s. 32(2)(b) for failure to provide information or evidence under s. 18(10) or 19(2) or to comply with the requirement imposed by a notice under s. 17 by virtue of s. 17(2)(a), (4)(A) or (6)(a);
- 6 April 2003 as regards an appeal against a determination of a penalty under Sch. 2, para. 1 where the penalty is imposed under s. 33 for failure by the employer to make correct payment to the employer;
- 6 April 2003 as regards an appeal against a decision under s. 18 (falling within s. 38(1)(b)); 19(3), 20(1)–(4) or 37(1).

Prospective amendments – Pt. 1 (but not Sch. 1 or Sch. 3) repealed by WRA 2012, s. 147 and Sch. 14, Pt. 1, with effect from a date to be set by order of the Secretary of State.

History – In s. 38(1), the words ", subject to subsection (1A)," inserted by SI 2014/886, art. 2(10), with effect from 6 April 2014.

S. 38(1)(ca) inserted (and the "and" at the end of s. 38(1)(c) repealed) by WRA 2012, s. 120(3), with effect from 6 April 2013 (SI 2013/178, art. 2).
S. 38(1A)–(1C) inserted by SI 2014/886, art. 2(11), with effect from 6 April 2014.

Cross references – S. 63(2): until a day to be appointed, an appeal under s. 38 (except an appeal against an employer penalty) is to an appeal tribunal rather than to the tax appeal commissioners.
SI 2003/1382, reg. 3–10: modified application of TMA 1970, Pt. 5 to an employer.
SI 2014/1230, Sch., para. 10: modified application of s. 38(1) and (2) where SI 2014/1230, reg. 12A applies (claims for universal credit).

39 Exercise of right of appeal

39(1) [Repealed by SI 2014/886, art. 2(12).]

39(2) [Repealed by SI 2014/886, art. 2(12).]

39(3) [Omitted by SI 2009/56, art. 3(1) and Sch. 1, para. 314(2).]

39(4) [Omitted by SI 2009/56, art. 3(1) and Sch. 1, para. 314(2).]

39(5) [Omitted by SI 2009/56, art. 3(1) and Sch. 1, para. 314(2).]

39(6) Part 5 of the Taxes Management Act 1970 (appeals and other proceedings) applies in relation to appeals under section 38 (as in relation to appeals under the Taxes Acts, within the meaning of that Act), but subject to such modifications as are prescribed.

39(7) [Omitted by SI 2009/56, art. 3(1) and Sch. 1, para. 314(4).]

Commencement Date – S. 39 entered into force, by virtue of SI 2002/1727 (C. 52), on:
- 1 September 2002 as regards appeals against determination of a penalty under Sch. 2, para. 1 where the penalty is imposed under s. 31 for incorrect statement or declaration in or in connection with a claim for a tax credit or a notification given in accordance with regulations under s. 6, or for incorrect information or evidence in response to a requirement imposed by virtue of regulations under s. 25;
- 1 September 2002 as regards an appeal against a determination of a penalty under Sch. 2, para. 1 where the penalty is imposed under s. 32(2)(b) or (3) for failure to provide evidence required by regulations under s. 25, or for failure to give notification required by regulations under s. 6(3).
- 1 January 2003 as regards appeals against determination of penalties under Sch. 2, para. 1 where the penalty is imposed under s. 31 for incorrect information or evidence in response to a requirement imposed by virtue of s. 14(2), 15(2) or 16(3);
- 1 January 2003 as regards an appeal against a determination of penalty under Sch. 2, para. 1 where the penalty is imposed under s. 32(2)(b) for failure to provide information or evidence under s. 14(2), 15(2) or 16(3);
- 1 January 2003 as regards an appeals against a determination of a penalty under s. 14(1), 15(1) or 16(1), or under regulations under s. 21; and

S. 39 entered into force, by virtue of SI 2002/1727 (C. 52), on:
- 6 April 2003 as regards an appeal against a determination of penalty under Sch. 2, para. 1 where the penalty is imposed under s. 31 for incorrect information or evidence in response to a requirement imposed by virtue of s. 18(10) or 19(2), or for failure to give notification required by regulations under s. 6(3);
- 6 April 2003 as regards an appeal against a determination of a penalty under Sch. 2, para. 1 where the penalty is imposed under s. 32(2)(b) for failure to provide information or evidence under s. 18(10) or 19(2) or to comply with the requirement imposed by a notice under s. 17 by virtue of s. 17(2)(a), (4)(a) or (6)(a);
- 6 April 2003 as regards an appeal against a determination of a penalty under Sch. 2, para. 1 where the penalty is imposed under s. 33 for failure by the employer to make correct payment to the employer;
- 6 April 2003 as regards an appeal against a decision under s. 18 (falling within s. 38(1)(b)), 19(3), 20(1)–(4) or 37(1).

Prospective amendments – Pt. 1 (but not Sch. 1 or Sch. 3) repealed by WRA 2012, s. 147 and Sch. 14, Pt. 1, with effect from a date to be set by order of the Secretary of State.

History – S. 39(1) and (2) repealed by SI 2014/886, art. 2(12), with effect from 6 April 2014.
S. 39(3)–(5) omitted by SI 2009/56, art. 3(1) and Sch. 1, para. 314(2), operative from 1 April 2009, subject to transitional and saving provisions in SI 2009/56, Sch. 3.
In s. 39(6), the words "(appeals and other proceedings)" substituted by SI 2009/56, art. 3(1) and Sch. 1, para. 314(3), operative from 1 April 2009, subject to transitional and saving provisions in SI 2009/56, Sch. 3.
S. 39(7) omitted by SI 2009/56, art. 3(1) and Sch. 1, para. 314(4), operative from 1 April 2009, subject to transitional and saving provisions in SI 2009/56, Sch. 3.

Cross references – S. 63(2): until a day to be appointed, an appeal under s. 38 (except an appeal against an employer penalty) is to an appeal tribunal rather than to the tax appeal commissioners, and reference in s. 39(5) to the General Commissioners or Special Commissioners is to the appeal tribunal.
S. 63(5)(b), (9): limited application of s. 39(3), (4), (6) and (7) until that appointed day.
SSA 1998, s. 12(7) and Sch. 5, para. 4(b) and Social Security (Northern Ireland) Order 1998, art. 13(7) and Sch. 4, para. 4(b), as modified by SI 2002/2926, reg. 4(5): vires for extension of time limit specified in s. 39(1).
SI 2002/3119, reg. 2: prescribed manner of giving notice of appeal under s. 39(1).
SI 2002/3196, reg. 4, 5: dispute arising as to whether appeal was brought within the time limit specified in s. 39(1), and late appeals.
SI 2003/742, reg. 21: modified application of s. 39(1) to members of polygamous units.

Statutory instruments – SI 2002/3119.
SI 2003/1382.

39A Late appeals

39A(1) The Commissioners for Her Majesty's Revenue and Customs may treat a late appeal under section 38 as made in time where the conditions specified in subsections (2) to (6) are satisfied, except that *the Commissioners may not do so in* the case of an appeal made more than one year after the expiration of the time (original or extended) for appealing.

39A(2) An appeal may be treated as made in time if the Commissioners are satisfied that it is in the interests of justice to do so.

39A(3) For the purposes of subsection (2) it is not in the interests of justice to treat an appeal as made in time unless–

(a) the special circumstances specified in subsection (4) are relevant; or

(b) some other special circumstances exist which are wholly exceptional and relevant,

and as a result of those special circumstances it was not practicable for the appeal to be made in time.

39A(4) The special circumstances mentioned in subsection (3)(a) are–

(a) the appellant or a partner or dependant of the appellant has died or suffered serious illness;

(b) the appellant is not resident in the United Kingdom; or

(c) normal postal services were disrupted.

39A(5) In determining whether it is in the interests of justice to treat an appeal as made in time, regard shall be had to the principle that the greater the amount of time that has elapsed between the expiration of the time for appealing and the submission of the notice of appeal, the more compelling should be the special circumstances.

39A(6) In determining whether it is in the interests of justice to treat an appeal as made in time, no account shall be taken of the following–

(a) that the appellant or any other person acting for the appellant was unaware of or misunderstood the law applicable to the appellant's case (including ignorance or misunderstanding of any time limit); or

(b) that the Upper Tribunal or a court has taken a different view of the law from that previously understood and applied.

39A(7) If in accordance with the preceding provisions of this section the Commissioners for Her Majesty's Revenue and Customs treat a late appeal under section 38 as made in time, it is to be treated as having been brought within any applicable time limit.

History – S. 39A inserted by SI 2014/885, art. 2(2), with effect from 1 April 2014, subject to SI 2014/885, art. 2(3):
"**2(3)** Where, in respect of a late appeal made on or after 1 April 2013 and before this Order comes into force, the Commissioners for Her Majesty's Revenue and Customs have before this Order comes into force notified the appellant that they consider the appeal should proceed even though it was not made within the period specified in section 39(1) of the Tax Credits Act 2002, that notification is to have effect after this Order comes into force as a decision under section 39A to treat the appeal as made in time."

SUPPLEMENTARY

40 Annual reports

40(1) The Board must make to the Treasury an annual report about–

(a) [ceased to have effect by CRCA 2005, s. 50 and Sch. 4, para. 89 and repealed by s. 52 and Sch. 5;]

(b) the number of awards of child tax credit and of working tax credit,

(c) the number of enquiries conducted under section 19,

(d) the number of penalties imposed under this Part, and

(e) the number of prosecutions and convictions for offences connected with tax credits.

40(2) The Treasury must publish each annual report made to it under subsection (1) and lay a copy before each House of Parliament.

Commencement Date – S. 40 entered into force on 6 April 2004 for the purposes of the making of an annual report by the Board to the Treasury (SI 2002/1727 (C. 52)).

Prospective amendments – Pt. 1 (but not Sch. 1 or Sch. 3) repealed by WRA 2012, s. 147 and Sch. 14, Pt. 1, with effect from a date to be set by order of the Secretary of State.

History – S. 40(1)(a) ceased to have effect by virtue of CRCA 2005, s. 50 and Sch. 4, para. 89 and repealed by s. 52 and Sch. 5, with effect from 18 April 2005 (SI 2005/1126, reg. 2(2)).

41 Annual review

41(1) The Treasury must, in each tax year, review the amounts specified in subsection (2) in order to determine whether they have retained their value in relation to the general level of prices in the United Kingdom as estimated by the Treasury in such manner as it considers appropriate.

41(2) The amounts are monetary amounts prescribed–

(a) under subsection (1)(a) of section 7,

(b) for the purposes of any of paragraphs (a) to (d) of subsection (3) of that section,

(c) under section 9,

(d) under section 11, otherwise than by virtue of section 12, or

(e) under subsection (2) of section 13, otherwise than by virtue of subsection (3) of that section.

41(3) The Treasury must prepare a report of each review.

TC Statutes

41(4) The report must include a statement of what each amount would be if it had fully retained its value.

41(5) The Treasury must publish the report and lay a copy of it before each House of Parliament.

Commencement Date – S. 41 entered into force on 6 April 2003 for the purposes of a review of prescribed monetary amounts (SI 2002/1727 (C. 52)).

Prospective amendments – Pt. 1 (but not Sch. 1 or Sch. 3) repealed by WRA 2012, s. 147 and Sch. 14, Pt. 1, with effect from a date to be set by order of the Secretary of State.

42 Persons subject to immigration control

42(1) Regulations may make provision in relation to persons subject to immigration control or in relation to prescribed descriptions of such persons–

(a) for excluding entitlement to, or to a prescribed element of, child tax credit or working tax credit (or both), or

(b) for this Part to apply subject to other prescribed modifications.

42(2) **"Person subject to immigration control"** has the same meaning as in section 115 of the Immigration and Asylum Act 1999 (c. 33).

Commencement Date – S. 42 entered into force on 9 July 2002 for the purposes of making regulations (SI 2002/1727 (C. 52)).

Prospective amendments – Pt. 1 (but not Sch. 1 or Sch. 3) repealed by WRA 2012, s. 147 and Sch. 14, Pt. 1, with effect from a date to be set by order of the Secretary of State.

Statutory instruments – SI 2003/653.
SI 2003/742.

43 Polygamous marriages

43(1) Regulations may make provision for this Part to apply in relation to persons who are parties to polygamous marriages subject to prescribed modifications.

43(2) A person is a party to a polygamous marriage if–

(a) he is a party to a marriage entered into under a law which permits polygamy, and

(b) either party to the marriage has a spouse additional to the other party.

Commencement Date – S. 43 entered into force on 9 July 2002 for the purposes of making regulations (SI 2002/1727 (C. 52)).

Prospective amendments – Pt. 1 (but not Sch. 1 or Sch. 3) repealed by WRA 2012, s. 147 and Sch. 14, Pt. 1, with effect from a date to be set by order of the Secretary of State.

Statutory instruments – SI 2003/742.

44 Crown employment

44 This Part applies in relation to persons employed by or under the Crown (as in relation to other employees).

Commencement Date – S. 44 entered into force on 9 July 2002 for the purposes of applyimg Pt. 1 to persons employed by or under the Crown (SI 2002/1727 (C. 52)).

Prospective amendments – Pt. 1 (but not Sch. 1 or Sch. 3) repealed by WRA 2012, s. 147 and Sch. 14, Pt. 1, with effect from a date to be set by order of the Secretary of State.

45 Inalienability

45(1) Every assignment of or charge on a tax credit, and every agreement to assign or charge a tax credit, is void; and, on the bankruptcy of a person entitled to a tax credit, the entitlement to the tax credit does not pass to any trustee or other person acting on behalf of his creditors.

45(2) In the application of subsection (1) to Scotland–

(a) the reference to assignment is to assignation ("assign" being construed accordingly), and

(b) the reference to the bankruptcy of a person is to the sequestration of his estate or the appointment on his estate of a judicial factor under section 41 of the Solicitors (Scotland) Act 1980 (c. 46).

Commencement Date – S. 45 entered into force on 1 January 2003 for all purposes of Pt. 1, and, as respects tax credits, Pt. 3 (SI 2002/1727 (C. 52)).

Prospective amendments – Pt. 1 (but not Sch. 1 or Sch. 3) repealed by WRA 2012, s. 147 and Sch. 14, Pt. 1, with effect from a date to be set by order of the Secretary of State.

46 Giving of notices by Board

46 The Board may give any notice which they are required or permitted to give under this Part in any manner and form which the Board consider appropriate in the circumstances.

Commencement Date – S. 46 entered into force on 1 August 2002 for all purposes of Pt. 1, and, as respects tax credits, Pt. 3 (SI 2002/1727 (C. 52)).

Prospective amendments – Pt. 1 (but not Sch. 1 or Sch. 3) repealed by WRA 2012, s. 147 and Sch. 14, Pt. 1, with effect from a date to be set by order of the Secretary of State.

47 Consequential amendments

47 Schedule 3 (consequential amendments) has effect.

Prospective amendments – Pt. 1 (but not Sch. 1 or Sch. 3) repealed by WRA 2012, s. 147 and Sch. 14, Pt. 1, with effect from a date to be set by order of the Secretary of State.

48 Interpretation

48(1) In this Part–

"child" has the meaning given by section 8(3),

"couple" has the meaning given by section 3(5A),

"the current year income" has the meaning given by section 7(4),

"employee" and **"employer"** have the meaning given by section 25(5),

"the income threshold" has the meaning given by section 7(1)(a),

"joint claim" has the meaning given by section 3(8),

"overpayment" has the meaning given by section 28(2) and (6),

"the previous year income" has the meaning given by section 7(5),

"qualifying remunerative work", and being engaged in it, have the meaning given by regulations under section 10(2),

"qualifying young person" has the meaning given by section 8(4),

"the relevant income" has the meaning given by section 7(3),

"responsible" in relation to a child or qualifying young person, has the meaning given by regulations under section 8(2) (for the purposes of child tax credit) or by regulations under section 10(4) (for the purposes of working tax credit),

"single claim" has the meaning given by section 3(8),

"tax year" means a period beginning with 6th April in one year and ending with 5th April in the next, and

48(2) For the purposes of this Part, two people of the same sex are to be regarded as living together as if they were civil partners if, but only if, they would be regarded as living together as husband and wife were they instead two people of the opposite sex.

Commencement Date – S. 48 entered into force on 9 July 2002 for all purposes of Pt. 1 (SI 2002/1727 (C. 52)).

Prospective amendments – Pt. 1 (but not Sch. 1 or Sch. 3) repealed by WRA 2012, s. 147 and Sch. 14, Pt. 1, with effect from a date to be set by order of the Secretary of State.

History – The definitions of "the General Commissioners" and "the Special Commissioners" omitted by SI 2009/56, art. 3(1) and Sch. 1, para. 315, operative from 1 April 2009, subject to transitional and saving provisions in SI 2009/56, Sch. 3.
S. 48 renumbered as s. 48(1), the definition of "couple" inserted, the definitions of "married couple" and "unmarried couple" omitted by the Civil Partnership Act 2004, s. 254 and Sch. 24, para. 147(1) and (2), with effect from 5 December 2005 (by virtue of SI 2005/3175, art. 2(1)).
S. 48(2) inserted by the Civil Partnership Act 2004, s. 254 and Sch. 24, para. 147(3), with effect from 5 December 2005 (by virtue of SI 2005/3175, art. 2(1)).

Cross references – SI 2014/1230, reg. 12(5): modified application of s. 48 in relation to the introduction of Universal Credit.

PART 3 – SUPPLEMENTARY

INFORMATION ETC.

58 Administrative arrangements

58(1) This section applies where regulations under–

(a) section 4 or 6 of this Act,

(b) section 5 of the Social Security Administration Act 1992 (c. 5), or

(c) section 5 of the Social Security Administration (Northern Ireland) Act 1992 (c. 8),

permit or require a claim or notification relating to a tax credit, child benefit or guardian's allowance to be made or given to a relevant authority.

58(2) Where this section applies, regulations may make provision–

(a) for information or evidence relating to tax credits, child benefit or guardian's allowance to be provided to the relevant authority (whether by persons by whom such claims and notifications are or have been made or given, by the Board or by other persons),

(b) for the giving of information or advice by a relevant authority to persons by whom such claims or notifications are or have been made or given, and

(c) for the recording, verification and holding, and the forwarding to the Board or a person providing services to the Board, of claims and notifications received by virtue of the regulations referred to in subsection (1) and information or evidence received by virtue of paragraph (a),

58(3) "Relevant authority" means–

(a) the Secretary of State,

(b) the Northern Ireland Department, or

(c) a person providing services to the Secretary of State or the Northern Ireland Department.

Commencement Date – S. 58 entered into force on 9 July 2002 for the purposes of making regulations in relation to tax credits only (SI 2002/1727 (C. 52)).

Statutory instruments – SI 2002/3036.

59 Use and disclosure of information

59 Schedule 5 (use and disclosure of information) has effect.

Commencement Date – S. 59 and Sch. 5 entered into force on 1 August 2002 for all purposes of Pt. 1, and, as respects tax credits, Pt. 3 (SI 2002/1727 (C. 52)).
S. 59 and Sch. 5 entered into force on 26 February 2003 for the purposes of child benefit and guardian's allowance (SI 2003/392, art. 2).

OTHER SUPPLEMENTARY PROVISIONS

60 Repeals

60 Schedule 6 (repeals) has effect.

Commencement Date – S. 60 and Sch. 6, in so far as it concerns TCA 1999, s. 6 entered into force on 27 August 2002 for the purposes of awards of working families' tax credit and disabled person's tax credit commencing on or after 27 August 2002 (SI 2002/1727 (C. 52)).
S. 60 and Sch. 6, in so far as it concerns TCA 1999, s. 6 and regulations made under that section entered into force the day immediately following the expiry of the period of 26 weeks from the date of the commencement of the award for the purposes of awards of working families' tax credit and disabled person's tax credit that commenced on or after 4 June 2002 but before 27 August 2002 and were existing on 27 August 2002 (SI 2002/1727 (C. 52)).
Other dates of entry into force of s. 60 and various provisions of Sch. 6 are as follows:

- on 1 April 2003 for various purposes connected with child benefit and guardian's allowance (SI 2003/392, art. 2);
- on 6 April 2003 for repeal of provisions relating to child dependency increases (SI 2003/938, art. 29(b) and Sch. 6);
- variously on 6 April and 8 April for other purposes (SI 2003/962 (C. 51), art. 2(3)(c), (e) and Sch. 1, art. 2(4)(c), (e) and Sch. 2, subject to savings in art. 3, 4).

61 Commencement

61 Apart from section 54(1) and (2), the preceding provisions of this Act come into force in accordance with orders made by the Treasury.

Statutory instruments – SI 2002/1727.
SI 2003/392.
SI 2003/938.
SI 2003/962.

62 Transitional provisions and savings

62(1) The Secretary of State may by order make as respects England and Wales and Scotland, and the Northern Ireland Department may by order make as respects Northern Ireland, any transitional provisions or savings which appear appropriate in connection with the commencement of the abolition of the increases referred to in section 1(3)(e).

62(2) Subject to any provision made by virtue of subsection (1), the Treasury may by order make any transitional provisions or savings which appear appropriate in connection with the commencement of any provision of this Act.

Statutory instruments – SI 2002/1727.
SI 2003/392.
SI 2003/938.
SI 2003/962.
SI 2003/2170.
SI 2008/3151.
SI 2010/644.

63 Tax credits appeals etc.: temporary modifications

63(1) Until such day as the Treasury may by order appoint, Part 1 of this Act has effect subject to the modifications specified in this section; and an order under this subsection may include any transitional provisions or savings which appear appropriate.

63(2) Except in the case of an appeal against an employer penalty, an appeal under section 38 is to–

(a) in Great Britain, the First-tier Tribunal; or

(b) in Northern Ireland, the appeal tribunal;

and in either case section 39(6) shall not apply.

63(3) The function of giving a direction under section 19(10) is a function of–

(a) in Great Britain, the First-tier Tribunal; or

(b) in Northern Ireland, the appeal tribunal; and in either case the relevant provisions of Part 5 of the Taxes Management Act 1970 shall not apply.

63(4) In Northern Ireland, except in the case of an employer information penalty, proceedings under paragraph 3 of Schedule 2 are by way of information in writing, made to the appeal tribunal (rather than to the tribunal), and upon summons issued by them to the defendant to appear before them at a time and place stated in the summons; and they must hear and decide each case in a summary way.

63(5) So far as is appropriate in consequence of subsections (2) to (4)–

(a) the references to the tribunal in section 19(10) and paragraphs 2 and 3(2) of Schedule 2 are to the First-tier Tribunal or the appeal tribunal,

(b) [omitted by SI 2009/56, art. 3(1) and Sch. 1, para. 316(5)(b).]

63(6) In Northern Ireland, an appeal under paragraph 2(2) or 4(1) of Schedule 2 from a decision of, or against the determination of a penalty by, the appeal tribunal lies to the Northern Ireland Social Security Commissioner (rather than to the Upper Tribunal).

63(7) So far as is appropriate in consequence of subsection (6), the references in paragraphs 2(2) and 4 of Schedule 2 to the Upper Tribunal are to the Northern Ireland Social Security Commissioner.

63(8) Regulations may apply any provision contained in–

(a) Chapter 2 of Part 1 of the Social Security Act 1998 (c. 14) (social security appeals: Great Britain),

(b) Chapter 2 of Part 2 of the Social Security (Northern Ireland) Order 1998 (S.I. 1998/1506 (N.I. 10)) (social security appeals: Northern Ireland), or

(c) section 54 of the Taxes Management Act 1970 (c. 9) (settling of appeals by agreement),

in relation to appeals which, by virtue of this section, are to the First-tier Tribunal or the appeal tribunal or lie to a Northern Ireland Social Security Commissioner, but subject to such modifications as are prescribed.

63(9) [Omitted by SI 2009/56, art. 3(1) and Sch. 1, para. 316(9).]

63(10) **"Appeal tribunal"** means an appeal tribunal constituted under Chapter 1 of Part 2 of the Social Security (Northern Ireland) Order 1998.

63(11) **"Employer penalty"** means–

(a) a penalty under section 31 or 32 relating to a requirement imposed by virtue of regulations under section 25, or

(b) a penalty under section 33.

63(12) **"Employer information penalty"** means a penalty under section 32(2)(a) relating to a requirement imposed by virtue of regulations under section 25.

63(13) **"Northern Ireland Social Security Commissioner"** means the Chief Social Security Commissioner or any other Social Security Commissioner appointed under the Social Security Administration (Northern Ireland) Act 1992 (c. 8) or a tribunal of two or more Commissioners constituted under Article 16(7) of the Social Security (Northern Ireland) Order 1998 (S.I. 1998/1506 (N.I. 10)).

63(14) **"tribunal"** (other than in the expression "appeal tribunal") shall have the meaning in section 47C of the Taxes Management Act 1970.

History – S. 63(2) substituted by SI 2009/56, art. 3(1) and Sch. 1, para. 316(2), operative from 1 April 2009, subject to transitional and saving provisions in SI 2009/56, Sch. 3.

In former s. 63(2), "the appropriate tribunal" substituted by SI 2008/2833, art. 9 and Sch. 3, para. 191(2), with effect from 3 November 2008.

S. 63(3) substituted by SI 2009/56, art. 3(1) and Sch. 1, para. 316(3), operative from 1 April 2009, subject to transitional and saving provisions in SI 2009/56, Sch. 3.

In former s. 63(3), "the appropriate tribunal" substituted by SI 2008/2833, art. 9 and Sch. 3, para. 191(2), with effect from 3 November 2008.

S. 63(4) substituted by SI 2009/56, art. 3(1) and Sch. 1, para. 316(4), operative from 1 April 2009, subject to transitional and saving provisions in SI 2009/56, Sch. 3.

In former s. 63(4), "the appropriate tribunal" substituted by SI 2008/2833, art. 9 and Sch. 3, para. 191(2), with effect from 3 November 2008.

In s. 63(5), the words "the First-tier Tribunal or" inserted by SI 2012/533, art. 2(2), with effect from 1 March 2012.

In s. 63(5)(a), the words "tribunal in section 19(10)" and the words "appeal tribunal" substituted and the word "and" at the end of s. 63(5)(a) and para. (b) omitted by SI 2009/56, art. 3(1) and Sch. 1, para. 316(5), operative from 1 April 2009, subject to transitional and saving provisions in SI 2009/56, Sch. 3.

In s. 63(5)(a), "appropriate tribunal" substituted by SI 2008/2833, art. 9 and Sch. 3, para. 191(3), with effect from 3 November 2008.

S. 63(6) substituted by SI 2009/56, art. 3(1) and Sch. 1, para. 316(6), operative from 1 April 2009, subject to transitional and saving provisions in SI 2009/56, Sch. 3.

In former s. 63(6), "the appropriate tribunal" substituted by SI 2008/2833, art. 9 and Sch. 3, para. 191(2), with effect from 3 November 2008.

In former s. 63(6), "the Upper Tribunal or a Northern Ireland Social Security Commissioner" substituted by SI 2008/2833, art. 9 and Sch. 3, para. 191(4), with effect from 3 November 2008.

In s. 63(7), the words "to the Upper Tribunal are to the Northern Ireland Social Security Commissioner" substituted by SI 2009/56, art. 3(1) and Sch. 1, para. 316(7), operative from 1 April 2009, subject to transitional and saving provisions in SI 2009/56, Sch. 3.
In s. 63(7), "the Upper Tribunal or the Northern Ireland Social Security Commissioner" substituted by SI 2008/2833, art. 9 and Sch. 3, para. 191(5), with effect from 3 November 2008.
In s. 63(8), the words "the First-tierTribunal or" inserted by SI 2012/533, art. 2(2), with effect from 1 March 2012.
In s. 63(8), the words "appeal tribunal or lie to" substituted by SI 2009/56, art. 3(1) and Sch. 1, para. 316(8), operative from 1 April 2009, subject to transitional and saving provisions in SI 2009/56, Sch. 3. It would appear that SI 2009/56 contains an error and should have instructed the new words to be substituted for the words "appropriate tribunal or lie to the Upper Tribunal or". This is the substitution that has been made above.
In s. 63(8), "the appropriate tribunal" substituted by SI 2008/2833, art. 9 and Sch. 3, para. 191(2), with effect from 3 November 2008.
In s. 63(8), "the Upper Tribunal or a Northern Ireland Social Security Commissioner" substituted by SI 2008/2833, art. 9 and Sch. 3, para. 191(6), with effect from 3 November 2008.
S. 63(9) omitted by SI 2009/56, art. 3(1) and Sch. 1, para. 316(9), operative from 1 April 2009, subject to transitional and saving provisions in SI 2009/56, Sch. 3.
S. 63(10) substituted by SI 2009/56, art. 3(1) and Sch. 1, para. 316(10), operative from 1 April 2009, subject to transitional and saving provisions in SI 2009/56, Sch. 3.
Former s. 63(10) substituted by SI 2008/2833, art. 9 and Sch. 3, para. 191(7), with effect from 3 November 2008.
In s. 63(13), the words ""**Northern Ireland Social Security Commissioner**" means" substituted by SI 2008/2833, art. 9 and Sch. 3, para. 191(8), with effect from 3 November 2008.
S. 63(14) inserted by SI 2009/56, art. 3(1) and Sch. 1, para. 316(11), operative from 1 April 2009, subject to transitional and saving provisions in SI 2009/56, Sch. 3.

Cross references – SI 2002/2926, reg. 1(2): those regulations cease to have effect on the day appointed for the purpose of s. 63(1).

Statutory instruments – SI 2014/1933: made under s. 63(8).
SI 2002/2926.

64 Northern Ireland

64(1) The Northern Ireland Act 1998 (c. 47) has effect subject to the amendments in subsections (2) and (3).

64(2) [Inserts NIA 1998, Sch. 2, para. 10A–10B.]

64(3) [Inserts NIA 1998, s. 87(6A).]

64(4) For the purposes of that Act, a provision of–

(a) an Act of the Northern Ireland Assembly, or

(b) a Bill for such an Act,

which amends or repeals any of the provisions of the Employment Rights (Northern Ireland) Order 1996 (S.I. 1996/1919 (N.I. 16)) dealt with in Schedule 1 shall not be treated as dealing with tax credits if the Act or Bill deals with employment rights conferred otherwise than by that Schedule in the same way.

65 Regulations, orders and schemes

65(1) Any power to make regulations under sections 3, 7 to 13, 42 and 43, and any power to make regulations under this Act prescribing a rate of interest, is exercisable by the Treasury.

65(2) Any other power to make regulations under this Act is exercisable by the Board.

65(3) Subject to subsection (4), any power to make regulations, orders or schemes under this Act is exercisable by statutory instrument.

65(4) The power–

(a) of the Department of Health, Social Services and Public Safety to make schemes under section 12(5), and

(b) of the Northern Ireland Department to make orders under section 62(1),

is exercisable by statutory rule for the purposes of the Statutory Rules (Northern Ireland) Order 1979 (S.I. 1979/1573 (N.I. 12)).

65(5) Regulations may not be made under section 25 or 26 in relation to appeals in Scotland without the consent of the Scottish Ministers.

65(6) Regulations may not be made under section 39(6) or 63(8) without the consent of the Lord Chancellor, the Department of Justice in Northern Ireland and the Scottish Ministers.

65(7) Any power to make regulations under this Act may be exercised–

(a) in relation to all cases to which it extends, to all those cases with prescribed exceptions or to prescribed cases or classes of case,

(b) so as to make as respects the cases in relation to which it is exercised the full provision to which it extends or any less provision (whether by way of exception or otherwise),

(c) so as to make the same provision for all cases in relation to which it is exercised or different provision for different cases or classes of case or different provision as respects the same case or class of case for different purposes,

(d) so as to make provision unconditionally or subject to any prescribed condition,

(e) so as to provide for a person to exercise a discretion in dealing with any matter.

65(8) Any regulations made under a power under this Act to prescribe a rate of interest may–

(a) either themselves specify a rate of interest or make provision for any such rate to be determined by reference to such rate or the average of such rates as may be referred to in the regulations,

(b) provide for rates to be reduced below, or increased above, what they otherwise would be by specified amounts or by reference to specified formulae,

(c) provide for rates arrived at by reference to averages to be rounded up or down,

(d) provide for circumstances in which alteration of a rate of interest is or is not to take place, and

(e) provide that alterations of rates are to have effect for periods beginning on or after a day determined in accordance with the regulations in relation to interest running from before that day as well as from or from after that day.

65(9) Any power to make regulations or a scheme under this Act includes power to make any incidental, supplementary, consequential or transitional provision which appears appropriate for the purposes of, or in connection with, the regulations or scheme.

History – In s. 65(6), the words ", the Department of Justice in Northern Ireland" inserted by SI 2010/976, art. 15 and Sch. 18, Pt. 1, with effect from 12 April 2010.

Statutory instruments – SI 2014/1933: made under s. 65(2) and (6).
SI 2002/2005: made under s. 65(1), (7).
SI 2002/2006: made under s. 65(1), (7), and (9), as amended by SI 2003/732, SI 2003/2815 and SI 2003/3240.
SI 2002/2007.
SI 2002/2008: made under s. 65(1) and (7).
SI 2002/2014: made under s. 65(1), (2) and (7).
SI 2002/2172.
SI 2002/3036: made under s. 65(1), (2), (7), (9).
SI 2003/653: made under s. 65(1).
SI 2003/731: made under s. 65(2).
SI 2003/742: made under s. 65(1), (2), (3), (7), (9).
SI 2003/1382: made under s. 65(2) and (6).
SI 2003/2041: partly made under s. 65(2).
SI 2004/1895: made under s. 65(2).
SI 2006/963.
SI 2007/828.
SI 2013/715: partly made under s. 65(2).

66 Parliamentary etc. control of instruments

66(1) No order or regulations to which this subsection applies may be made unless a draft of the instrument containing the order or regulations (whether or not together with other provisions) has been laid before, and approved by a resolution of, each House of Parliament.

66(2) Subsection (1) applies to–

(za) an order made by the Treasury under section 36A(8) or 36C(9),

(zb) regulations made under section 36A(5) or 36C(4),

(a) regulations prescribing monetary amounts that are required to be reviewed under section 41,

(b) regulations made by virtue of subsection (2) of section 12 prescribing the amount in excess of which charges are not taken into account for the purposes of that subsection, and

(c) the first regulations made under sections 7(8) and (9), 9, 11, 12 and 13(2).

66(3) A statutory instrument containing–

(a) an order or regulations under this Act,

(b) a scheme made by the Secretary of State under section 12(5), or

(c) an Order in Council under section 52(7),

is (unless a draft of the instrument has been laid before, and approved by a resolution of, each House of Parliament) subject to annulment in pursuance of a resolution of either House of Parliament.

66(4) A statutory instrument containing a scheme made by the Scottish Ministers under section 12(5) is subject to annulment in pursuance of a resolution of the Scottish Parliament.

66(5) A statutory rule containing a scheme made by the Department of Health, Social Services and Public Safety under section 12(5) is subject to negative resolution within the meaning of section 41(6) of the Interpretation Act (Northern Ireland) 1954 (c. 33 (N.I.)).

History – In s. 66(1), the words "order or" inserted by WRA 2012, s. 120(4)(a)(i), with effect from 1 February 2013 (SI 2013/178, art. 2).
In s. 66(1), the words "the order or regulations" substituted for the word "them" by WRA 2012, s. 120(4)(a)(ii), with effect from 1 February 2013 (SI 2013/178, art. 2).
S. 66(2)(za) and (zb) inserted by WRA 2012, s. 120(4)(b), with effect from 1 February 2013 (SI 2013/178, art. 2).
In s. 66(3)(a), the words "an order or" inserted by WRA 2012, s. 120(4)(c), with effect from 1 February 2013 (SI 2013/178, art. 2).

67 Interpretation

67 In this Act–

"the Board" means the Commissioners of Inland Revenue,

"cautioned", in relation to any person and any offence, means cautioned after the person concerned has admitted the offence; and **"caution"** is to be interpreted accordingly;

"modifications" includes alterations, additions and omissions, and **"modifies"** is to be construed accordingly,

"the Northern Ireland Department" means the Department for Social Development in Northern Ireland,

"prescribed" means prescribed by regulations, and

"tax credit" and **"tax credits"** have the meanings given by section 1(2).

Prospective amendments – In s. 67, definition of "cautioned" repealed by WRA 2012, s. 147 and Sch. 14, Pt. 12, with effect from a date to be appointed by order of the Secretary of State.

History – In s. 67, definition of "cautioned" inserted by WRA 2012, s. 120(5), with effect from 6 April 2013 (SI 2013/178, art. 2).

Statutory instruments – SI 2003/2041: made under s. 67.
SI 2004/1895: made under s. 67.
SI 2013/715: partly made under s. 67.

68 Financial provision

68(1) There is to be paid out of money provided by Parliament–

(a) any expenditure of a Minister of the Crown or government department under this Act, and

(b) any increase attributable to this Act in sums payable out of money provided by Parliament under any other Act.

68(2) There is to be paid into the Consolidated Fund any sums received by a government department by virtue of this Act (apart from any required by any other enactment to be paid into the National Insurance Fund).

69 Extent

69(1) The amendments, repeals and revocations made by this Act have the same extent as the enactments or instruments to which they relate.

69(2) Subject to that, this Act extends to Northern Ireland (as well as to England and Wales and Scotland).

70 Short title

70 This Act may be cited as the Tax Credits Act 2002.

SCHEDULES

SCHEDULE 1 – RIGHTS OF EMPLOYEES

Section 27

RIGHT NOT TO SUFFER DETRIMENT: GREAT BRITAIN

1(1) The Employment Rights Act 1996 (c. 18) has effect subject to the following amendments.

1(2) [Inserts ERA 1996, s. 47D.]

1(3) [Inserts ERA 1996, s. 48(1B).]

1(4) [Inserts ERA 1996, s. 49(7).]

1(5) [Amends ERA 1996, s. 192(2)(aa).]

1(6) [Amends ERA 1996, s. 194(2)(c) and ERA 1996, s. 195(2)(c).]

RIGHT NOT TO SUFFER DETRIMENT: NORTHERN IRELAND

2 [Amends Employment Rights (Northern Ireland) Order 1996 (SI 1996/1919 (NI 16)).]

RIGHT NOT TO BE UNFAIRLY DISMISSED: GREAT BRITAIN

3(1) The Employment Rights Act 1996 (c. 18) has effect subject to the following amendments.

3(2) [Substitutes ERA 1996, s. 104B.]

3(3) [Inserts ERA 1996, s. 105(7B).]
3(4) [Inserts ERA 1996, s. 108(3)(gh) and 109(2)(gh).]

RIGHT NOT TO BE UNFAIRLY DISMISSED: NORTHERN IRELAND

4 [Amends Employment Rights (Northern Ireland) Order 1996 (SI 1996/1919 (NI 16)).]

SCHEDULE 2 – PENALTIES: SUPPLEMENTARY

Section 34

Commencement Date – S. 34 and Sch. 2 entered into force, by virtue of SI 2002/1727 (C. 52), on:

- 1 August 2002 as regards the imposition of penalties under s. 31 for incorrect statement or declaration in or in connection with a claim for tax credit or a notification given in accordance with regulations under s. 6, or for incorrect information or evidence in response to a requirement imposed by regulations under s. 25; mitigation of such penalties, appeals against such penalties and recovery of such penalties;
- 1 August 2002 as regards imposition of penalties under s. 32(2)(b) or (3) for failure to provide information or evidence required by regulations under s. 25, or for failure to give notification required by regulations under s. 6(3); bringing proceedings for penalties under s. 32(2)(a) before Commissioners for failure to provide information or evidence required by regulations under s. 25; mitigation of penalties, appeals against such penalties and recovery of such penalties.
- 1 January 2003 as regards imposition of penalties under s. 31 for incorrect information or evidence in response to a requirement imposed by virtue of s. 14(2), 15(2) or 16(3); mitigation of such penalties, appeals against such penalties and recovery of such penalties;
- 1 January 2003 as regards the imposition of penalties under s. 32(2)(b) for failure to provide information or evidence under s. 14(2), 15(2) or 16(3); bringing proceedings for such penalties under s. 32(2)(a) before Commissioners; mitigation of such penalties; appeals against such penalties and recovery of such penalties.

S. 34 and Sch. 2 come into force, by virtue of SI 2002/1727 (C. 52), on:

- 6 April 2003 as regards imposition of penalties under s. 31 for incorrect information or evidence imposed by virtue of s. 18(10) or 19(2), or for incorrect statement or declaration in response to a notice under s. 17; mitigation of such penalties, appeals against such penalties and recovery of such penalties;
- 6 April 2003 as regards the imposition of penalties under s. 32(2)(b) for failure to provide information or evidence under s. 18(10) or 19(2) of for failure to comply with the requirement imposed under s. 17 by virtue of 17(2)(a), (4)(a) or (6)(a); bringing proceedings for such penalties under s. 32(2)(a) before Commissioners; mitigation of such penalties; appeals against penalties and recovery of such penalties.
- 6 April 2003 as regards the imposition of penalties under s. 33 for failure by the employer to make correct payment to the employee; mitigation of such penalties, appeals against such penalties and recovery of such penalties.

TC Statutes

DETERMINATION OF PENALTIES BY BOARD

1(1) The Board may make a determination–

(a) imposing a penalty under section 31, 32(2)(b) or (3) or 33, and

(b) setting it at such amount as, in their opinion, is appropriate.

1(2) The Board must give notice of a determination of a penalty under this paragraph to the person on whom the penalty is imposed.

1(3) The notice must state the date on which it is given and give details of the right to appeal against the determination under section 38.

1(4) After the notice of a determination under this paragraph has been given the determination must not be altered except on appeal.

1(5) A penalty determined under this paragraph becomes payable at the end of the period of thirty days beginning with the date on which the notice of determination is given.

2(1) On an appeal under section 38 against the determination of a penalty under paragraph 1 that is notified to the First-tier tribunal, the tribunal may–

(a) if it appears that no penalty has been incurred, set the determination aside,

(b) if the amount determined appears to be appropriate, confirm the determination,

(c) if the amount determined appears to be excessive, reduce it to such other amount (including nil) as the First-tier Tribunal considers appropriate, or

(d) if the amount determined appears to be insufficient, increase it to such amount not exceeding the permitted maximum as the First-tier Tribunal considers appropriate.

2(2) In addition to any right of appeal on a point of law under section 11(2) of the Tribunals, Courts and Enforcement Act 2007, the person liable to the penalty may appeal to the Upper Tribunal against the amount of the penalty which has been determined under sub-paragraph (1), but not against any decision which falls under section 11(5)(d) or (e) of that Act and was made in connection with the determination of the amount of the penalty.

2(2A) Section 11(3) and (4) of the Tribunals, Courts and Enforcement Act 2007 applies to the right of appeal under sub-paragraph (2) as it applies to the right of appeal under section 11(2) of that Act.

2(2B) On an appeal under this paragraph the Upper Tribunal has the same powers as are conferred on the First-tier Tribunal by virtue of this paragraph.

History – In para. 2(1), the words "to them" (which appeared after the words "On an appeal") omitted, the words "paragraph 1 that is notified to the First-tier tribunal, the tribunal" substituted and the words "the First-tier Tribunal considers" substituted (twice) by SI 2009/56, art. 3(1) and Sch. 1, para. 318(2), operative from 1 April 2009, subject to transitional and saving provisions in SI 2009/56, Sch. 3.
Para. 2(2) (along with para. 2(2A) and 2(2B)) substituted for former para. 2(2) by SI 2009/56, art. 3(1) and Sch. 1, para. 318(3), operative from 1 April 2009, subject to transitional and saving provisions in SI 2009/56, Sch. 3.
Para. 2(2A) (along with para. 2(2) and 2(2B)) substituted for former para. 2(2) by SI 2009/56, art. 3(1) and Sch. 1, para. 318(3), operative from 1 April 2009, subject to transitional and saving provisions in SI 2009/56, Sch. 3.
Para. 2(2B) (along with para. 2(2) and 2(2A)) substituted for former para. 2(2) by SI 2009/56, art. 3(1) and Sch. 1, para. 318(3), operative from 1 April 2009, subject to transitional and saving provisions in SI 2009/56, Sch. 3.

Cross references – S. 63(6), (7): until a day to be appointed, an appeal under para. 2(2) from a decision of, or against the determination of a penalty by, an appeal tribunal lies to a Social Security Commissioner rather than to the High Court or the Court of Session, and references in para. 2 to the General Commissioners or Special Commissioners are to the appeal tribunal.

PENALTY PROCEEDINGS BEFORE TRIBUNAL

History – In the heading to para. 3, the word "TRIBUNAL" substituted by SI 2009/56, art. 3(1) and Sch. 1, para. 319(2), operative from 1 April 2009, subject to transitional and saving provisions in SI 2009/56, Sch. 3.

3(1) The Board may commence proceedings for a penalty under section 32(2)(a) before the tribunal.

3(2) The person liable to the penalty shall be a party to the proceedings.

3(3) **"Tribunal"** is to be read in accordance with section 47C of the Taxes Management Act 1970.

History – In para. 3(1), the words "before the tribunal" inserted by SI 2009/56, art. 3(1) and Sch. 1, para. 319(3), operative from 1 April 2009, subject to transitional and saving provisions in SI 2009/56, Sch. 3.
Para. 3(2) substituted by SI 2009/56, art. 3(1) and Sch. 1, para. 319(4), operative from 1 April 2009, subject to transitional and saving provisions in SI 2009/56, Sch. 3.
Para. 3(3) inserted by SI 2009/56, art. 3(1) and Sch. 1, para. 319(5), operative from 1 April 2009, subject to transitional and saving provisions in SI 2009/56, Sch. 3.

Cross references – SI 2008/2685, Rule 23 and Rule 26: detailed requirements relating to proceedings under para. 3.
S. 63(4): until a day to be appointed, proceedings under para. 3 (except employer information penalty proceedings) are by way of information made to an appeal tribunal rather than to the General Commissioners or the Special Commissioners.

4(1) In addition to any right of appeal on a point of law under section 11(2) of the Tribunals, Courts and Enforcement Act 2007, the person liable to the penalty may appeal to the Upper Tribunal against the determination of a penalty in proceedings under paragraph 2(1), but not against any decision which falls under section 11(5)(d) or (e) of that Act and was made in connection with the determination of the amount of the penalty.

4(1A) Section 11(3) and (4) of the Tribunals, Courts and Enforcement Act 2007 applies to the right of appeal under sub-paragraph (1) as it applies to the right of appeal under section 11(2) of that Act.

4(2) On any such appeal the Upper Tribunal may–

(a) if it appears that no penalty has been incurred, set the determination aside,

(b) if the amount determined appears to be appropriate, confirm the determination,

(c) if the amount determined appears to be excessive, reduce it to such other amount (including nil) as the Upper Tribunal considers appropriate, or

(d) if the amount determined appears to be insufficient, increase it to such amount not exceeding the permitted maximum as the Upper Tribunal considers appropriate.

History – Para. 4(1) (along with para. 4(1A)) substituted for former para. 4(1) by SI 2009/56, art. 3(1) and Sch. 1, para. 320(2), operative from 1 April 2009, subject to transitional and saving provisions in SI 2009/56, Sch. 3.
Para. 4(1A) (along with para. 4(1)) substituted for former para. 4(1) by SI 2009/56, art. 3(1) and Sch. 1, para. 320(2), operative from 1 April 2009, subject to transitional and saving provisions in SI 2009/56, Sch. 3.
In para. 4(2), the words "Upper Tribunal" substituted (in three places) by SI 2009/56, art. 3(1) and Sch. 1, para. 320(3), operative from 1 April 2009, subject to transitional and saving provisions in SI 2009/56, Sch. 3.

Cross references – S. 63(6), (7): until a day to be appointed, an appeal under para. 4(1) from a decision of, or against the determination of a penalty by, an appeal tribunal lies to a Social Security Commissioner rather than to the High Court or the Court of Session.

MITIGATION OF PENALTIES

5 The Board may in their discretion mitigate any penalty under this Part or stay or compound any proceedings for any such penalty and may also, after judgment, further mitigate or entirely remit any such penalty.

TIME LIMITS FOR PENALTIES

6(1) In the case of a penalty under section 31 relating to a tax credit for a person or persons for the whole *or part of a* tax year (other than a penalty to which sub-paragraph (3) applies), the Board may determine the penalty at any time before the latest of–

(a) the end of the period of one year beginning with the expiry of the period for initiating an enquiry under section 19 into the entitlement of the person, or the joint entitlement of the persons, for the tax year,

(b) if such an enquiry is made, the end of the period of one year beginning with the day on which the enquiry is completed, and

(c) if a decision relating to the entitlement of the person, or the joint entitlement of the persons, for the tax year is made under section 20(1) or (4), the end of the period of one year beginning with the day on which the decision is made.

6(2) In the case of a penalty under section 32 relating to a tax credit for a person or persons for the whole or part of a tax year (other than a penalty to which sub-paragraph (3) applies), the Board may determine the penalty, or commence proceedings for it, at any time before–

(a) if an enquiry into the entitlement of the person, or the joint entitlement of the persons, for the tax year is made under section 19, the end of the period of one year beginning with the day on which the enquiry is completed, and

(b) otherwise, the end of the period of one year beginning with the expiry of the period for initiating such an enquiry.

6(3) In the case of–

(a) a penalty under section 31 or 32 relating to a requirement imposed by virtue of regulations under section 25, or

(b) a penalty under section 33,

the Board may determine the penalty, or commence proceedings for it, at any time before the end of the period of six years after the date on which the penalty was incurred or began to be incurred.

Cross references – SI 2014/1230, reg. 12(6): modified application of para. 6 in relation to the introduction of Universal Credit.

RECOVERY OF PENALTIES

7(1) A penalty payable under this Part is to be treated for the purposes of Part 6 of the Taxes Management Act 1970 (c. 9) (collection and recovery) as if it were tax charged in an assessment and due and payable.

7(2) Regulations under section 203(2)(a) of the Income and Corporation Taxes Act 1988 (c. 1) (PAYE) apply to a penalty payable under this Part as if it were an underpayment of tax for a previous year of assessment.

SCHEDULE 3 – TAX CREDITS: CONSEQUENTIAL AMENDMENTS

Section 47

ATTACHMENT OF EARNINGS ACT 1971 (c. 32)

1 [Inserts Attachment of Earnings Act 1971, s. 24(2)(ba).]

Commencement Date – Para. 1 came into force on 6 April 2003 by virtue of SI 2003/962 (C. 51), art. 2(3)(b) and (d)(i).

MAGISTRATES' COURTS ACT 1980 (c. 43)

2 [Repealed by Courts Act 2003, s. 109(3) and Sch. 10.]

Commencement Date – Para. 2 came into force on 6 April 2003 by virtue of SI 2003/962 (C. 51), art. 2(3)(b) and (d)(i).

History – Para. 2 repealed by Courts Act 2003, s. 109(3) and Sch. 10, with effect from 1 April 2005 (by virtue of SI 2005/547).

JUDGMENTS ENFORCEMENT (NORTHERN IRELAND) ORDER 1981 (S.I. 1981/226 (N.I. 6))

3 [Inserts Judgments Enforcement (Northern Ireland) Order 1991, art. 3(5)(ba).]

Commencement Date – Para. 3 came into force on 6 April 2003 by virtue of SI 2003/962 (C. 51), art. 2(3)(b) and (d)(i).

LEGAL AID, ADVICE AND ASSISTANCE (NORTHERN IRELAND) ORDER 1981 (S.I. 1981/228 (N.I. 8))

4 The Legal Aid, Advice and Assistance (Northern Ireland) Order 1981 has effect subject to the following amendments.

Commencement Date – Para. 4 came into force on 1 April 2003 by virtue of SI 2003/962 (C. 51), art. 2(2).

Prospective amendments – Para. 4 repealed by SI 2003/435, art. 49 and Sch. 5, with effect from a day to be appointed.

5 [Amends Legal Aid, Advice and Assistance (Northern Ireland) Order 1981, art. 3(1)(b).]

Commencement Date – Para. 5 came into force on 1 April 2003 by virtue of SI 2003/962 (C. 51), art. 2(2).

Prospective amendments – Para. 5 repealed by SI 2003/435, art. 49 and Sch. 5, with effect from a day to be appointed.

6 [Amends Legal Aid, Advice and Assistance (Northern Ireland) Order 1981, art. 7(2).]

Commencement Date – Para. 6 came into force on 1 April 2003 by virtue of SI 2003/962 (C. 51), art. 2(2).

Prospective amendments – Para. 6 repealed by SI 2003/435, art. 49 and Sch. 5, with effect from a day to be appointed.

7 [Amends Legal Aid, Advice and Assistance (Northern Ireland) Order 1981, art. 14(5).]

Commencement Date – Para. 7 came into force on 1 April 2003 by virtue of SI 2003/962 (C. 51), art. 2(2).

Prospective amendments – Para. 7 repealed by SI 2003/435, art. 49 and Sch. 5, with effect from a day to be appointed.

MAGISTRATES' COURTS (NORTHERN IRELAND) ORDER 1981 (S.I. 1981/1675 (N.I. 26))

8 [Amends Magistrates' Courts (Northern Ireland) Order 1981, art. 100(ba).]

Commencement Date – Para. 8 came into force on 6 April 2003 by virtue of SI 2003/962 (C. 51), art. 2(3)(b) and (d)(ii).

TRANSPORT ACT 1982 (c. 49)

9 [Amends Transport Act 1982, s. 70(2)(b).]

Commencement Date – Para. 9 came into force on 6 April 2003 by virtue of SI 2003/962 (C. 51), art. 2(3)(b) and (d)(ii).

LEGAL AID (SCOTLAND) ACT 1986 (c. 47)

10 The Legal Aid (Scotland) Act 1986 has effect subject to the following amendments.

Commencement Date – Para. 10 came into force on 8 April 2003 by virtue of SI 2003/962 (C. 51), art. 2(4)(b) and (d).

11 [Amends Legal Aid (Scotland) Act 1986, s. 8(b).]

Commencement Date – Para. 11 came into force on 8 April 2003 by virtue of SI 2003/962 (C. 51), art. 2(4)(b) and (d).

12 [Amends Legal Aid (Scotland) Act 1986, s. 11(2)(b).]

Commencement Date – Para. 12 came into force on 8 April 2003 by virtue of SI 2003/962 (C. 51), art. 2(4)(b) and (d).

DEBTORS (SCOTLAND) ACT 1987 (c. 18)

13 [Inserts Debtors (Scotland) Act 1987, s. 73(3)(da).]

Commencement Date – Para. 13 came into force on 6 April 2003 by virtue of SI 2003/962 (C. 51), art. 2(3)(b) and (d)(iii).

INCOME AND CORPORATION TAXES ACT 1988 (c. 1)

14 [Repealed by ITEPA 2003, Sch. 8, Pt. 1 which has effect for the tax year 2003–04 and subsequent tax years.]

CHILDREN ACT 1989 (c. 41)

15 The Children Act 1989 has effect subject to the following amendments.

Commencement Date – Para. 15 came into force on 6 April 2003 by virtue of SI 2003/962 (C. 51), art. 2(3)(b) and (d)(iii).

16(1) Section 17 (provision of services for children in need) is amended as follows.

16(2) [Amends Children Act 1989, s. 17(9).]

16(3) [Inserts Children Act 1989, s. 17(12).]

Commencement Date – Para. 16 came into force on 6 April 2003 by virtue of SI 2003/962 (C. 51), art. 2(3)(b) and (d)(iii).

Prospective amendments – Para. 16(2)(a) repealed by WRA 2009, s. 58 and Sch. 7, Pt. 1, with effect from a day to be appointed.

17 [Amends Children Act 1989, s. 17A(5)(b).]

Commencement Date – Para. 17 came into force on 6 April 2003 by virtue of SI 2003/962 (C. 51), art. 2(3)(b) and (d)(iii).

18 [Amends Children Act 1989, s. 29(3).]

Commencement Date – Para. 18 came into force on 6 April 2003 by virtue of SI 2003/962 (C. 51), art. 2(3)(b) and (d)(iii).

Prospective amendments – Para. 18(a) repealed by WRA 2009, s. 58 and Sch. 7, Pt. 1, with effect from a day to be appointed.

19 [Amends Children Act 1989, s. 104.]

Commencement Date – Para. 19 came into force on 6 April 2003 by virtue of SI 2003/962 (C. 51), art. 2(3)(b) and (d)(iii).

20 [Amends Children Act 1989, Sch. 2, para. 21(4).]

Commencement Date – Para. 20 came into force on 6 April 2003 by virtue of SI 2003/962 (C. 51), art. 2(3)(b) and (d)(iii).

Prospective amendments – Para. 20(a) repealed by WRA 2009, s. 58 and Sch. 7, Pt. 1, with effect from a day to be appointed.

EDUCATION REFORM (NORTHERN IRELAND) ORDER 1989 (S.I. 1989/2406 (N.I. 20))

21 [Amends Education Reform (Northern Ireland) Order 1989, art. 131(3)(b).]

Commencement Date – Para. 21 came into force on 6 April 2003 by virtue of SI 2003/962 (C. 51), art. 2(3)(b) and (d)(iii).

CHILD SUPPORT ACT 1991 (c. 48)

22 [Amends Child Support Act 1991, s. 47(3)(b).]

Commencement Date – Para. 22 came into force on 6 April 2003 by virtue of SI 2003/962 (C. 51), art. 2(3)(b) and (d)(iii).

CHILD SUPPORT (NORTHERN IRELAND) ORDER 1991 (S.I. 1991/2628 (N.I. 23))

23 [Amends Child Support (Northern Ireland) Order 1991, s. 44(2)(b).]

Commencement Date – Para. 23 came into force on 6 April 2003 by virtue of SI 2003/962 (C. 51), art. 2(3)(b) and (d)(iii).

SOCIAL SECURITY CONTRIBUTIONS AND BENEFITS ACT 1992 (c. 4)

24 The Social Security Contributions and Benefits Act 1992 has effect subject to the following amendments.

Commencement Date – Para. 24 came into force on 6 April 2003 by virtue of SI 2003/962 (C. 51), art. 2(3)(b) and (d)(iii).

25 [Substitutes SSCBA 1992, s. 30C(5)–(5A).]

Commencement Date – Para. 25 came into force on 6 April 2003 by virtue of SI 2003/962 (C. 51), art. 2(3)(b) and (d)(iii).

Prospective amendments – Para. 25 repealed by the Welfare Reform Act 2007, s. 67 and Sch. 8, with effect from a date to be appointed by virtue of s. 70(2).

26 [Repealed by the Welfare Reform Act 2007, s. 67 and Sch. 8.]

Commencement Date – Para. 26 came into force on 6 April 2003 by virtue of SI 2003/962 (C. 51), art. 2(3)(b) and (d)(iii).

History – Para. 26 repealed by the Welfare Reform Act 2007, s. 67 and Sch. 8, with effect from 7 October 2008 (by virtue of 2008/2101, art. 2(20(c).

27 [Amends SSCBA 1992, s. 39(1)–(3).]

Commencement Date – Para. 27 came into force on 6 April 2003 by virtue of SI 2003/962 (C. 51), art. 2(3)(b) and (d)(iii).

28 [Repealed by the Welfare Reform Act 2007, s. 67 and Sch. 8.]

Commencement Date – Para. 28 came into force on 6 April 2003 by virtue of SI 2003/962 (C. 51), art. 2(3)(b) and (d)(iii).

History – Para. 28 repealed by the Welfare Reform Act 2007, s. 67 and Sch. 8, with effect from 7 October 2008 (by virtue of SI 2008/2010, art. 2(2)(c).

29 [Amends SSCBA 1992, s. 39C(1), (3) and (4).]

Commencement Date – Para. 29 came into force on 6 April 2003 by virtue of SI 2003/962 (C. 51), art. 2(3)(b) and (d)(iii).

30 [Substitutes SSCBA 1992, s. 42(1).]

Commencement Date – Para. 30 came into force on 6 April 2003 by virtue of SI 2003/962 (C. 51), art. 2(3)(b) and (d)(iii).

Prospective amendments – Para. 30 repealed by the Welfare Reform Act 2007, s. 67 and Sch. 8, with effect from a date to be appointed by virtue of s. 70(2).

31 [Amends SSCBA 1992, s. 48BB(5) and (6).]

Commencement Date – Para. 31 came into force on 6 April 2003 by virtue of SI 2003/962 (C. 51), art. 2(3)(b) and (d)(iii).

32 [Amends SSCBA 1992, s. 51(2) and (3).]

Commencement Date – Para. 32 came into force on 6 April 2003 by virtue of SI 2003/962 (C. 51), art. 2(3)(b) and (d)(iii).

33 [Amends SSCBA 1992, s. 60(4) and (5).]

Commencement Date – Para. 33 came into force on 6 April 2003 by virtue of SI 2003/962 (C. 51), art. 2(3)(b) and (d)(iii).

34 [Amends SSCBA 1992, s. 114(4).]

Commencement Date – Para. 34 came into force on 6 April 2003 by virtue of SI 2003/962 (C. 51), art. 2(3)(b) and (d)(iii).

Prospective amendments – Para. 34 repealed by WRA 2009, s. 58 and Sch. 7, Pt. 2, with effect from a day to be appointed.

SOCIAL SECURITY ADMINISTRATION ACT 1992 (c. 5)

35 [Amends SSAA 1992, s. 150(1)(h).]

Commencement Date – Para. 35 came into force on 6 April 2003 by virtue of SI 2003/962 (C. 51), art. 2(3)(b) and (d)(iii).

SOCIAL SECURITY CONTRIBUTIONS AND BENEFITS (NORTHERN IRELAND) ACT 1992 (c. 7)

36–46 [Amends Social Security Contribution and Benefits (Northern Ireland) Act 1992.]

Commencement Date – Para. 36–46 came into force on 6 April 2003 by virtue of SI 2003/962 (C. 51), art. 2(3)(b) and (d)(iii).

VALUE ADDED TAX ACT 1994 (c. 23)

47 The Value Added Tax Act 1994 has effect subject to the following amendments.

Commencement Date – Para. 47 came into force on 6 April 2003 by virtue of SI 2003/962 (C. 51), art. 2(3)(b) and (d)(iii).

48 [Amends VATA 1994, Sch. 7A, para. 6(2)(c).]

Commencement Date – Para. 48 came into force on 6 April 2003 by virtue of SI 2003/962 (C. 51), art. 2(3)(b) and (d)(iii).

49 [Substitutes VATA 1994, Sch. 8, Group 15, note (1D)(e) and (f).]
Commencement Date – Para. 49 came into force on 6 April 2003 by virtue of SI 2003/962 (C. 51), art. 2(3)(b) and (d)(iii).

CHILDREN (SCOTLAND) ACT 1995 (c. 36)

50 [Inserts Children (Scotland) Act 1995, s. 22(4)(aa).]
Commencement Date – Para. 50 came into force on 6 April 2003 by virtue of SI 2003/962 (C. 51), art. 2(3)(b) and (d)(iii).

CHILDREN (NORTHERN IRELAND) ORDER 1995 (S.I. 1995/755 (N.I. 2))

51–56 [Amends Children (Northern Ireland) Order 1995.]
Commencement Date – Para. 51–56 came into force on 6 April 2003 by virtue of SI 2003/962 (C. 51), art. 2(3)(b) and (d)(iii).

ROAD TRAFFIC (NORTHERN IRELAND) ORDER 1995 (S.I. 1995/2994 (N.I. 18))

57 [Amends Road Traffic (Northern Ireland) Order 1995, art. 25(2)(b).]
Commencement Date – Para. 57 came into force on 6 April 2003 by virtue of SI 2003/962 (C. 51), art. 2(3)(b) and (d)(iii).

HOUSING GRANTS, CONSTRUCTION AND REGENERATION ACT 1996 (c. 53)

58 [Amends Housing Grants, Construction and Regeneration Act 1996, s. 77(1)(e).]
Commencement Date – Para. 58 came into force on 6 April 2003 by virtue of SI 2003/962 (C. 51), art. 2(3)(b) and (d)(iii).

FINANCE ACT 2000 (c. 17)

59 [Repealed by CTA 2009, s. 1326 and Sch. 3, Pt. 1.]
Commencement Date – Para. 59 came into force on 6 April 2003 by virtue of SI 2003/962 (C. 51), art. 2(3)(b) and (d)(iii).
History – Para. 59 repealed by CTA 2009, s. 1326 and Sch. 3, Pt. 1, with effect for corporation tax purposes for accounting periods ending on or after 1 April 2009, and for income tax and capital gains tax purposes for the tax year 2009–10 and subsequent tax years.

SCHEDULE 5 – USE AND DISCLOSURE OF INFORMATION

Section 59

Commencement Date – S. 59 and Sch. 5 entered into force on 1 August 2002 for all purposes of Pt. 1, and, as respects tax credits, Pt. 3 (SI 2002/1727 (C. 52)).

POWERS TO USE INFORMATION

1 Information which is held for the purposes of any functions relating to tax credits, child benefit or guardian's allowance–

(a) by the Board, or

(b) by a person providing services to the Board, in connection with the provision of those services,

may be used, or supplied to any person providing services to the Board, for the purposes of, or for any purposes connected with, the exercise of any such functions.

2 [Ceased to have effect by CRCA 2005, s. 52 and Sch. 5 and repealed by CRCA 2005, s. 52 and Sch. 5.]
History – Para. 2 ceased to have effect by virtue of CRCA 2005, s. 50 and Sch. 4, para. 91 and repealed by CRCA 2005, s. 52 and Sch. 5 with effect from 18 April 2005 (SI 2005/1126, art. 2(2)).

3(1) Information which is held for the purposes of any functions relating to social security (including child benefit and guardian's allowance) or tax credits–

(a) by the Secretary of State or the Northern Ireland Department, or

(b) by a person providing services to the Secretary of State or the Northern Ireland Department, in connection with the provision of those services,

may be used, or supplied to any person providing services to the Secretary of State or the Northern Ireland Department, for the purposes of, or for any purposes connected with, the exercise of any functions under relevant regulations.

3(2) In this paragraph **"relevant regulations"** are regulations made under–

(a) section 4, 6 or 58 of this Act,

(b) section 5 of the Social Security Administration Act 1992 (c. 5), or

(c) section 5 of the Social Security Administration (Northern Ireland) Act 1992 (c. 8).

EXCHANGE OF INFORMATION BETWEEN BOARD AND SECRETARY OF STATE OR NORTHERN IRELAND DEPARTMENTS

4(1) This paragraph applies to information which is held for the purposes of functions relating to tax credits, child benefit or guardian's allowance–

(a) by the Board, or

(b) by a person providing services to the Board, in connection with the provision of those services.

4(2) Information to which this paragraph applies may be supplied–

(a) to the Secretary of State, or

(b) to a person providing services to the Secretary of State,

for use for the purposes of functions relating to war pensions or for such purposes relating to evaluation or statistical studies as may be prescribed.

4(3) [Repealed by WRA 2012, s. 147 and Sch. 14, Pt. 13.]

4(3A) Information to which this paragraph applies may be supplied–

(a) to the Northern Ireland Department, or

(b) to a person providing services to the Northern Ireland Department,

for use for the purposes of functions relating to child support or war pensions or for such purposes relating to evaluation or statistical studies as may be prescribed.

4(3B) An authorised officer may require information to which this paragraph applies to be supplied–

(a) to the Northern Ireland Department, or

(b) to a person providing services to the Northern Ireland Department

for use for the purposes of functions relating to child support.

4(4) In sub-paragraph (3B) **"authorised officer"** means an officer of the Secretary of State or the Northern Ireland Department authorised for the purposes of this paragraph by the Secretary of State or the Northern Ireland Department.

4(5) In this paragraph **"war pension"** has the meaning given by section 25(4) of the Social Security Act 1989 (c. 24).

History – In para. 4(2), the words "social security or" repealed by WRA 2012, s. 147 and Sch. 14, Pt. 13, with effect from 8 May 2012.
Para. 4(2)–(3B) substituted for former para. (2) and (3) by Child Maintenance and Other Payments Act 2008, s. 57(1) and Sch. 7, para. 4(2), from 1 June 2009 (SI 2009/1314, art. 2(2)).
Para. 4(3) repealed by WRA 2012, s. 147 and Sch. 14, Pt. 13, with effect from 8 May 2012.
In para. 4(3A), the words "social security," repealed by WRA 2012, s. 147 and Sch. 14, Pt. 13, with effect from 8 May 2012.
In para. 4(3B), the words "social security or" repealed by WRA 2012, s. 147 and Sch. 14, Pt. 13, with effect from 8 May 2012.
In para. 4(4), the words "(3) and" repealed by WRA 2012, s. 147 and Sch. 14, Pt. 13, with effect from 8 May 2012.
In para. 4(4), the words "sub-paragraphs (3) and (3B)" substituted for the words "sub-paragraph (3)" by Child Maintenance and Other Payments Act 2008, s. 57(1) and Sch. 7, para. 4(3), from 1 June 2009 (SI 2009/1314, art. 2(2)).

Statutory instruments – SI 2003/3308: partly made under para. 4(2).

5(1) This paragraph applies to information which is held for the purposes of functions relating to tax credits, child benefit or guardian's allowance–

(a) by the Board, or

(b) by a person providing services to the Board, in connection with the provision of those services.

5(2) Information to which this paragraph applies may be supplied–

(a) to the Secretary of State or the Department for Employment and Learning in Northern Ireland, or

(b) to a person providing services to the Secretary of State or that Department,

for use for the purposes of such functions relating to employment or training as may be prescribed.

Statutory instruments – SI 2003/2041: partly made under para. 5(2).

6(1) This paragraph applies to information which is held for the purposes of functions relating to war pensions or employment or training–

(a) by the Secretary of State, or

(b) by a person providing services to the Secretary of State, in connection with the provision of those services.

6(1A) This paragraph also applies to information which is held for the purposes of functions relating to social security, child support, war pensions or employment or training–

(a) by the Northern Ireland Department or the Department for Employment and Learning in Northern Ireland, or

(b) by a person providing services to either of those Departments, in connection with the provision of those services.

TC Statutes

6(2) Information to which this paragraph applies may be supplied–

(a) to the Board, or

(b) to a person providing services to the Board,

for use for the purposes of functions relating to tax credits, child benefit or guardian's allowance.

6(3) The Board may require information to which this paragraph applies to be so supplied if the information is held for the purposes of functions relating to child support.

6(4) In this paragraph **"war pension"** has the meaning given by section 25(4) of the Social Security Act 1989 (c. 24).

History – In para. 6(1), the words "social security," repealed by WRA 2012, s. 147 and Sch. 14, Pt. 13, with effect from 8 May 2012. In para. 6(1A), the words "social security" repealed by WRA 2012, s. 147 and Sch. 14, Pt. 13, with effect from 8 May 2012. Para. 6(1) and (1A) substituted for former para. 6(1) by Child Maintenance and Other Payments Act 2008, s. 57(1) and Sch. 7, para. 4(4), from 1 June 2009 (SI 2009/1314, art. 2(2)).
In para. 6(3), the words "social security or" repealed by WRA 2012, s. 147 and Sch. 14, Pt. 13, with effect from 8 May 2012.

EXCHANGE OF INFORMATION BETWEEN BOARD AND AUTHORITIES ADMINISTERING CERTAIN BENEFITS

7(1) This paragraph applies to information which is held for the purposes of functions relating to tax credits, child benefit or guardian's allowance–

(a) by the Board, or

(b) by a person providing services to the Board, in connection with the provision of those services.

7(2) Information to which this paragraph applies may be supplied by or under the authority of the Board–

(a) to an authority administering housing benefit or council tax benefit, or

(b) to a person authorised to exercise any function of such an authority relating to such a benefit,

for use in the administration of such a benefit.

7(3) Information supplied under this paragraph is not to be supplied by the recipient to any other person or body unless it is supplied–

(a) to a person to whom the information could be supplied directly by or under the authority of the Board,

(b) for the purposes of any civil or criminal proceedings relating to the Social Security Contributions and Benefits Act 1992 (c. 4), the Social Security Administration Act 1992 (c. 5) or the Jobseekers Act 1995 (c. 18) or to any provision of Northern Ireland legislation corresponding to any of them, or

(c) under paragraph 8 below.

8(1) The Board may require–

(a) an authority administering housing benefit or council tax benefit, or

(b) a person authorised to exercise any function of such an authority relating to such a benefit,

to supply benefit administration information held by the authority or other person to, or to a person providing services to, the Board for use for any purpose relating to tax credits, child benefit or guardian's allowance.

8(2) In sub-paragraph (1) **"benefit administration information"** in relation to an authority or other person, means any information which is relevant to the exercise of any function relating to housing benefit or council tax benefit by the authority or other person.

PROVISION OF INFORMATION BY BOARD FOR HEALTH PURPOSES

Cross references – FA 1989, s. 182: sanctions for unauthorised disclosure of information.

9(1) This paragraph applies to information which is held for the purposes of functions relating to tax credits, child benefit or guardian's allowance–

(a) by the Board, or

(b) by a person providing services to the Board, in connection with the provision of those services.

9(2) Information to which this paragraph applies may be supplied –

(a) to the Secretary of State, the National Assembly for Wales, the Scottish Ministers or the Department of Health, Social Services and Public Safety in Northern Ireland, or

(b) to persons providing services to, or exercising functions on behalf of, the Secretary of State, the National Assembly for Wales, the Scottish Ministers or that Department,

for use for the purposes of such functions relating to health as may be prescribed.

9(3) Information supplied under this paragraph is not to be supplied by the recipient to any other person or body unless it is supplied–

(a) to a person to whom the information could be supplied directly by or under the authority of the Board, or

(b) for the purpose of civil or criminal proceedings,

and is not to be so supplied in those circumstances without the authority of the Board.

9(4) A person commits an offence if he discloses information supplied to him under this paragraph unless the disclosure is made–

(a) in accordance with sub-paragraph (3),

(b) in accordance with an enactment or an order of a court,

(c) with consent given by or on behalf of the person to whom the information relates, or

(d) in such a way as to prevent the identification of the person to whom it relates.

9(5) It is a defence for a person charged with an offence under sub-paragraph (4) to prove that he reasonably believed that his disclosure was lawful.

9(6) A person guilty of an offence under sub-paragraph (4) is liable–

(a) on conviction on indictment, to imprisonment for a term not exceeding two years, to a fine or to both, or

(b) on summary conviction, to imprisonment for a term not exceeding six months, to a fine not exceeding the statutory maximum or to both.

Cross references – SI 2003/731, reg. 3 and SI 2003/1650, reg. 2: prescribed functions for the purposes of Sch. 5, para 9.

Statutory instruments – SI 2003/731.
SI 2003/1650.
SI 2004/1895: made under para. 9.

PROVISION OF INFORMATION BY BOARD FOR EDUCATION PURPOSES

10 [Omitted by Education and Skills Act 2008, s. 169 and Sch. 1, para. 78.]

History – Para. 10 omitted by the Education and Skills Act 2008, s. 169 and Sch. 1, para. 78 with effect from 26 January 2009 (the date appointed by virtue of SI 2008/3077, art. 4).

PROVISION OF INFORMATION BY BOARD FOR PURPOSES RELATING TO WELFARE OF CHILDREN

10A(1) This paragraph applies to information, other than information relating to a person's income, which is held for the purposes of functions relating to tax credits, child benefit or guardian's allowance–

(a) by the Board, or

(b) by a person providing services to the Board, in connection with the provision of those services.

10A(2) Information to which this paragraph applies may be supplied to–

(a) a local authority in England and Wales for use for the purpose of any enquiry or investigation under Part 5 of the Children Act 1989 relating to the welfare of a child;

(b) a local authority in Scotland for use for the purpose of any enquiry or investigation under Chapter 3 of Part 2 of the Children (Scotland) Act 1995, or Part 5, 6, 13 or 14 of the Children's Hearings (Scotland) Act 2011, relating to the welfare of a child;

(c) an authority in Northern Ireland for use for the purpose of any enquiry or investigation under Part 6 of the Children (Northern Ireland) Order 1995 (S.I. 1995/755 (N.I.2)) relating to the welfare of a child.

10A(3) Information supplied under this paragraph is not to be supplied by the recipient to any other person or body unless it is supplied–

(a) for the purpose of any enquiry or investigation referred to in sub-paragraph (2) above,

(b) for the purpose of civil or criminal proceedings, or

(c) where paragraph (a) or (b) does not apply, to a person to whom the information could be supplied directly by or under the authority of the Board.

10A(4) Information may not be supplied under sub-paragraph (3)(b) or (c) without the authority of the Board.

10A(5) A person commits an offence if he discloses information supplied to him under this paragraph unless the disclosure is made–

(a) in accordance with sub-paragraph (3),

(b) in accordance with an enactment or an order of a court,

(c) with consent given by or on behalf of the person to whom the information relates, or

(d) in such a way as to prevent the identification of the person to whom it relates.

10A(6) It is a defence for a person charged with an offence under sub-paragraph (5) to prove that he reasonably believed that his disclosure was lawful.

10A(7) A person guilty of an offence under sub-paragraph (5) is liable–

(a) on conviction on indictment, to imprisonment for a term not exceeding two years, to a fine or to both;

(b) on summary conviction in England and Wales, to imprisonment for a term not exceeding twelve months, to a fine not exceeding the statutory maximum or to both;

(c) on summary conviction in Scotland or Northern Ireland, to imprisonment for a term not exceeding six months, to a fine not exceeding the statutory maximum or to both.

10A(8) In sub-paragraph (2) **"child"** means a person under the age of eighteen and–

(a) in paragraph (a), **"local authority"** has the meaning given by section 105(1) of the Children Act 1989;

(b) in paragraph (b), **"local authority"** has the meaning given by section 93(1) of the Children (Scotland) Act 1995; and

(c) in paragraph (c), **"authority"** has the meaning given by Article 2 of the Children (Northern Ireland) Order 1995 (S.I. 1995/755 (N.I.2)).

10A(9) The reference to an enactment in sub-paragraph (5)(b) includes a reference to an enactment comprised in, or in an instrument made under, an Act of the Scottish Parliament.

History – In para. 10(2)(b), the words ", or Part 5, 6, 13 or 14 of the Children's Hearings (Scotland) Act 2011," inserted by SI 2013/1465, art. 17 and Sch. 1, para. 8, with effect from 24 June 2013 (the day the Children's Hearings (Scotland) Act 2011, s. 7 comes into force by virtue of SSI 2013/195, art. 1(2)).
Para. 10A inserted by the Children Act 2004, s. 63, with effect from 15 November 2004.

UNAUTHORISED DISCLOSURE OF INFORMATION

11(1) Section 182 of the Finance Act 1989 (c. 26) (disclosure of information) is amended as follows.

11(2) [Amends FA 1989, s. 182(1).]

11(3) [Substitutes FA 1989, s. 182(2ZA).]

11(4) [Amends FA 1989, s. 182(2A).]

11(5) [Amends FA 1989, s. 182(4).]

11(6) [Amends FA 1989, s. 182(5)(b).]

11(7) [Amends FA 1989, s. 182(10).]

CONSEQUENTIAL AMENDMENTS

12 [Repealed by WRA 2012, s. 147 and Sch. 14, Pt. 13 and SI 2015/2006 (NI), art. 140 and Sch. 12, Pt. 12.]

History – Para. 12(a) repealed by WRA 2012, s. 147 and Sch. 14, Pt. 13, with effect from 8 May 2012.
Para. 12 repealed by SI 2015/2006 (NI), art. 140 and Sch. 12, Pt. 12, with effect from 17 February 2016 (S.R. 2016/46, art. 3(6)(c)). Former para. 12 amended SSAA 1992, s. 122(1)(a) and SSA(NI)A 1992, s. 116(1)(a).

13 [Amends FA 1997, s. 110(5A).]

COMMISSIONERS FOR REVENUE AND CUSTOMS ACT 2005

(2005 Chapter 11)

[*7th April 2005*]

Only those parts of CRCA 2005 which directly affect material in this division are reproduced here. The full text of CRCA 2005 is reproduced in the Income, Corporation and Capital Gains Taxes division (Vol. 1B).

SCHEDULES

SCHEDULE 4 – CONSEQUENTIAL AMENDMENTS, ETC.

TAX CREDITS ACT 2002 (C. 21)

88 [Substitutes TCA 2002, s. 2.]

89 [Ceases TCA 2002, s. 40(1)(a) to have effect.]

90 [Substitutes TCA 2002, s. 53.]

91 [Ceases TCA 2002, Sch. 5, para. 2 to have effect.]

92 To the extent that the Tax Credits Act 1999 (c. 10) is saved by the Tax Credits Act 2002 (Commencement No. 4, Transitional and Savings) Order 2003 (SI 2003/962), the modifications made by paragraphs 88 to 91 shall have effect in relation to the relevant provisions of that Act as they have effect in relation to the Tax Credits Act 2002 (c. 21).

FINANCE ACT 2007

(2007 Chapter 11)

[*19th July 2007*]

ARRANGEMENT OF SECTIONS

PART 6 – INVESTIGATION, ADMINISTRATION ETC

INVESTIGATION ETC

PART 8 – FINAL PROVISIONS

PART 6 – INVESTIGATION, ADMINISTRATION ETC

INVESTIGATION ETC

84 Sections 82 and 83: supplementary

84(1) [Amends CRCA 2005, Sch. 2.]

84(2) Nothing in section 6 or 7 of CRCA 2005 (initial functions) restricts the functions in connection with which officers of Revenue and Customs may exercise a power under–

(a) the Police and Criminal Evidence Act 1984 by virtue of section 114 of that Act (as amended by section 82 above), or

(b) the Police and Criminal Evidence (Northern Ireland) Order 1989 by virtue of Article 85 of that Order (as amended by section 83 above).

84(3) [Omitted by CFA 2017, s. 18(5).]

84(4) Schedule 22 contains amendments and repeals consequential on extension of police powers to Revenue and Customs.

84(5) Sections 82 and 83 and this section come into force in accordance with provision made by the Treasury by order.

84(6) The power to make an order under subsection (5) is exercisable by statutory instrument.

Commencement Date – S. 84 (other than s. 84(4) came into force on 8 November 2007. S. 84(4) came into force on 1 December 2007 (SI 2007/3166 (c. 129)).

History – S. 84(3) omitted by CFA 2017, s. 18(5), with effect from 17 June 2017 (being two months after 27 April 2017 (Royal Assent)). Former s. 84(3) read as follows:

"**84(3)** But neither an order under section 114 of the Police and Criminal Evidence Act 1984 nor an order under Article 85 of the Police and Criminal Evidence (Northern Ireland) Order 1989 has effect in relation to a matter specified in section 54(4)(b) or (f) of, or in paragraphs 3, 7, 10, 13 to 15, 19 or 24 to 29 of Schedule 1 to, CRCA 2005 (former Inland Revenue matters).".

PART 8 – FINAL PROVISIONS

114 Repeals

114 Schedule 27 contains repeals.

115 Short title

115 This Act may be cited as the Finance Act 2007.

PENSIONS ACT 2007

(2007 Chapter 22)

[26th July 2007]

ARRANGEMENT OF SECTIONS

PART 1 – STATE PENSION

CREDITS FOR BASIC STATE PENSION

3 Contributions credits for relevant parents and carers

3(1) [Not relevant to tax credits.]

3(2) [Not relevant to tax credits.]

3(3) Part 3 of Schedule 1 contains consequential amendments.

UP-RATING OF BASIC STATE PENSION AND OTHER BENEFITS

7 Removal of link between lower earnings limit and basic pension

7(1) Section 5 of the SSCBA (earnings limits and thresholds for Class 1 contributions) is amended as follows.

7(2)–(4) [Not relevant to tax credits.]

7(5) [Inserts SSCBA 1992, s. 176(1).]

ADDITIONAL PENSION: SIMPLIFICATION OF ACCRUAL RATES

12 Additional pension: upper accrual point

12(1)–(3) [Not relevant to tax credits.]

12(4) Part 7 of Schedule 1 contains consequential amendments.

12(5)–(10) *[Not relevant to tax credits.]*

PART 4 – GENERAL

30 Commencement

30(1) The following provisions of this Act come into force on the day on which it is passed–

(a) sections 5 and 6, and Part 5 of Schedule 1, so far as relating to the amounts mentioned in subsection (1)(d) of the new section 150A inserted into the Administration Act by section 5(1);

(b) sections 18(4) to (11) and 19;

(c) Part 3;

(d) this Part.

30(2) The following provisions of this Act come into force on such day as the Secretary of State may by order appoint–

(a) section 14;

(b) section 15(1), Part 2 of Schedule 4 and Part 7 of Schedule 7;

(c) section 17, Schedule 5 and Part 8 of Schedule 7;

(d) section 18(1) to (3).

30(3) The other provisions of this Act come into force at the end of the period of 2 months beginning with the day on which it is passed.

30(4) An order under subsection (2) may–

(a) appoint different days for different purposes;

(b) make such provision as the Secretary of State considers necessary or expedient for transitory, transitional or saving purposes in connection with the coming into force of any provision falling within subsection (2).

31 Short title

31 This Act may be cited as the Pensions Act 2007.

SCHEDULES

SCHEDULE 1 – STATE PENSION: CONSEQUENTIAL AND RELATED AMENDMENTS

Sections 1 to 5, 9, 12 and 13

Part 7 – Additional Pension: Simplified Accrual Rates

SOCIAL SECURITY CONTRIBUTIONS AND BENEFITS ACT 1992 (c. 4)

35 In section 176 of the SSCBA (parliamentary control)–

(a) [Amends SSCBA 1992, s. 176(1)(c).]

(b) [Amends SSCBA 1992, s. 176(4).]

PENSIONS ACT 2008

(2008 Chapter 30)

[*26th November 2008*]

ARRANGEMENT OF SECTIONS

PART 6 – GENERAL

SCHEDULES

PART 6 – GENERAL

149 Commencement

149(1) Subject to the following provisions, this Act comes into force in accordance with provision made by order by the Secretary of State.

149(2)–(5) [Not relevant to tax credits.]

149(6) An order under subsection (1) may appoint different days for different purposes.

150 Extent

150(1) Subject to the following provisions, this Act extends to England and Wales and Scotland.

150(2) [Relevant to Northern Ireland only.]

150(3) An amendment or repeal by this Act has the same extent as the enactment amended or repealed (subject to the provision made by section 63(3), section 64(2) and paragraph 9 of Schedule 10).

151 Short title

151 This Act may be cited as the Pensions Act 2008.

SCHEDULES

SCHEDULE 4 – ADDITIONAL PENSION ETC: MINOR AND CONSEQUENTIAL AMENDMENTS

Section 104

SOCIAL SECURITY CONTRIBUTIONS AND BENEFITS ACT 1992 (C. 4)

1–4 [Not relevant to tax credits.]

5 In paragraph 6 (application of Part 3 of Schedule)–

(a) after "if" insert "–

(a) ";

(b) after paragraph (a) (created by virtue of paragraph (a) above) insert "and

(b) *there would be a surplus in* the pensioner's earnings factor for the year if section 48A of the Pension Schemes Act 1993 did not apply in relation to any tax week falling in the year."

6–22 [Not relevant to tax credits.]

FINANCE ACT 2009

(2009 Chapter 10)

[*21st July 2009*]

ARRANGEMENT OF SECTIONS

PART 7 – ADMINISTRATION

PART 9 – FINAL PROVISIONS

SCHEDULES

PART 7 – ADMINISTRATION

INTEREST

103 Rates of interest

103(1) The late payment interest rate is the rate provided for in regulations made by the Treasury under this subsection.

103(2) The repayment interest rate is the rate provided for in regulations made by the Treasury under this subsection.

103(3) Regulations under subsection (1) or (2)–

(a) may make different provision for different purposes,

(b) may either themselves specify a rate of interest or make provision for such a rate to be determined (and to change from time to time) by reference to such rate, or the average of such rates, as may be referred to in the regulations,

(c) may provide for rates to be reduced below, or increased above, what they otherwise would be by specified amounts or by reference to specified formulae,

(d) may provide for rates arrived at by reference to averages to be rounded up or down,

(e) may provide for circumstances in which alteration of a rate of interest is or is not to be take place, and

(f) may provide that alterations of rates are to have effect for periods beginning on or after a day determined in accordance with the regulations in relation to interest running from before that day as well as from or from after that day.

Cross references – F(No. 2)A 2015, s. 52: rate of interest applicable to judgement debts etc in taxation matters in relation to interest for periods beginning on or after 8 July 2015 regardless of the date of the judgment or order in question, and whether interest begins to run on or after 8 July 2015, or began to run before that date.

Statutory instruments – SI 2011/2446: made under s. 103.

MISCELLANEOUS

110 Recovery of debts using PAYE regulations

110 Schedule 58 contains provision about the recovery of debts by means of deductions from PAYE income in accordance with PAYE regulations.

PART 9 – FINAL PROVISIONS

127 Short title

127 This Act may be cited as the Finance Act 2009.

SCHEDULES

SCHEDULE 58 – RECOVERY OF DEBTS UNDER PAYE REGULATIONS

Section 110

RECOVERY OF DEBTS UNDER PAYE REGULATIONS

1–7 [Not relevant to tax credits.]

CONSEQUENTIAL PROVISION

8 [Amends TCA 2002, s. 29(5).]

9, 10 [Not relevant to tax credits.]

WELFARE REFORM ACT 2012

(2012 Chapter 5)

[8th March 2012]

ARRANGEMENT OF SECTIONS

PART 1 – UNIVERSAL CREDIT

Chapter 3 – Supplementary and general

UNIVERSAL CREDIT AND OTHER BENEFITS

36 Migration to universal credit

36 Schedule 6 contains provision about the replacement of benefits by universal credit.

PART 3 – OTHER BENEFIT CHANGES

WORKING TAX CREDIT

76 Calculation of working tax credit

76(1) Step 5 in regulation 7(3) of the 2002 Regulations has effect in relation to awards of working tax credit for the whole or part of the relevant year as if from the beginning of the day on 6 April 2011 the percentage to be applied under step 5 in finding the amount of the reduction were 41% (instead of 39%).

76(2) Anything done by the Commissioners before the coming into force of this section in relation to awards of working tax credit for the whole or part of the relevant year is to be treated as having been duly done, if it would have been duly done but for being done on the basis that from the beginning of the day on 6 April 2011 the percentage to be applied under step 5 was 41%.

76(3) In this section–

"the 2002 Regulations" means the Tax Credits (Income Thresholds and Determination of Rates) Regulations 2002 (S.I. 2002/2008);

"the Commissioners" means the Commissioners for Her Majesty's Revenue and Customs;

"the relevant year" means the year beginning with 6 April 2011.

PART 5 – SOCIAL SECURITY: GENERAL

APPEALS

102 Power to require consideration of revision before appeal

102(1) The Social Security Act 1998 is amended as follows.

102(2) [Amends SSA 1998, s. 12(2).]

102(3) [Inserts SSA 1998, s. 12(3A)–(3C).]

102(4) [Amends SSA 1998, s. 12(7).]

102(5) [Amends SSA 1998, s. 80(1).]

102(6) Schedule 11 contains similar amendments to other Acts.

102(7) Subsection (8) applies where regulations under a provision mentioned in subsection (9) are made so as to have effect in relation to a limited area (by virtue of provision made under section 150(4)(b)).

102(8) Any power to make, in connection with those regulations, provision as respects decisions and appeals may be exercised so that that provision applies only in relation to the area mentioned in subsection (7).

102(9) The provisions referred to in subsection (7) are–

(a) section 12(3A) of the Social Security Act 1998;

(b) section 4(1B) of the Vaccine Damage Payments Act 1979;

(c) subsection (2A) of section 20 of the Child Support Act 1991 (as substituted by section 10 of the Child Support, Pensions and Social Security Act 2000);

(d) subsection (3A) of section 20 of the Child Support Act 1991 (as it has effect apart from section 10 of the Child Support, Pensions and Social Security Act 2000);

(e) section 11(2A) of the Social Security (Recovery of Benefits) Act 1997;

(f) paragraph 6(5A) of Schedule 7 to the Child Support, Pensions and Social Security Act 2000;

(g) section 50(1A) of the Child Maintenance and Other Payments Act 2008.

Commencement Date – 25 February 2013 is the day appointed for the coming into force of s. 102 for all purposes (SI 2013/358, art. 2(2) and Sch. 2, para. 37).

LOSS OF BENEFIT

120 Loss of tax credits

120(1) The Tax Credits Act 2002 is amended as follows.

120(2) [Inserts TCA 2002, s. 36A–36D.]

120(3) [Inserts TCA 2002, s. 38(1)(ca).]

120(4) [Amends TCA 2002, s. 66(1) and (3)(a) and inserts (2)(za) and (zb).]

120(5) [Amends TCA 2002, s. 67.]

Commencement Date – S. 120 comes into force on 6 April 2013 except s. 120(2) (and (1) in so far as it relates to it) which comes into force on 1 February 2013 only for the purpose of making regulations and orders, and s. 120(4) (and (1) in so far as it relates to it) which comes into force on 1 February 2013 (SI 2013/178, art. 2).

121 Cautions

121(1) [Not relevant to tax credits.]

121(2) In section 36A of the Tax Credits Act 2002 (loss of tax working tax credit in case of conviction, penalty or caution for benefit offence) subsection (1)(c) (cautions) is repealed.

ADMINISTRATION OF TAX CREDITS

122 Tax credit fraud: investigation

122 [Inserts SSAA 1992, s. 109A(9).]

Commencement Date – 6 June 2012 is the day appointed for the coming into force of s. 122 (SI 2012/1246, art. 2(2)).

123 Information-sharing for prevention etc of tax credit fraud

123(1) Section 122B of the Social Security Administration Act 1992 (supply of government information for fraud prevention etc) is amended as follows.

123(2) [Amends SSAA 1992, s. 122B(2)(a).]

123(3) [Amends SSAA 1992, s. 122B(3) and inserts (d).]

Commencement Date – 6 June 2012 is the day appointed for the coming into force of s. 123 (SI 2012/1246, art. 2(2)).

124 Tax credit fraud: prosecution and penalties

124 In section 35 of the Tax Credits Act 2002 (offence of fraud), for subsection (2) there is substituted–

"**35(2)** Where a person is alleged to have committed an offence under this section in relation to payments of a tax credit not exceeding £20,000, the offence is triable summarily only.

35(3) A person who commits an offence under this section is liable on summary conviction pursuant to subsection (2) to imprisonment for a term not exceeding the applicable term, or a fine not exceeding level 5 on the standard scale, or both.

35(4) In subsection (3) the applicable term is–

(a) for conviction in England and Wales, 51 weeks;

(b) for conviction in Scotland or Northern Ireland, 6 months.

35(5) Where a person is alleged to have committed an offence under this section in any other case, the offence is triable either on indictment or summarily.

35(6) A person who commits an offence under this section is liable–

(a) on summary conviction pursuant to subsection (5), to imprisonment for a term not exceeding the applicable term, or a fine not exceeding the statutory maximum, or both;

(b) on conviction on indictment pursuant to subsection (5) to imprisonment for a term not exceeding 7 years, or a fine, or both.

35(7) In subsection (6)(a) the applicable term is–

(a) for conviction in England and Wales or Scotland, 12 months;

(b) for conviction in Northern Ireland, 6 months.

35(8) In relation to an offence under this section committed in England and Wales before the commencement of section 281(5) of the Criminal Justice Act 2003, the reference in subsection (4)(a) to 51 weeks is to be read as a reference to 6 months.

35(9) In relation to an offence under this section committed in England and Wales before the commencement of section 154(1) of the Criminal Justice Act 2003, the reference in subsection (7)(a) to 12 months is to be read as a reference to 6 months.

35(10) In England and Wales–

(a) subsection (1) of section 116 of the Social Security Administration Act 1992 (legal proceedings) applies in relation to proceedings for an offence under this section;

(b) subsections (2)(a) and (3)(a) of that section apply in relation to proceedings for an offence under this section which is triable summarily only pursuant to subsection (2) above.

35(11) In Scotland, subsection (7)(a) and (b) of section 116 of the Social Security Administration Act 1992 (legal proceedings) apply in relation to proceedings for an offence under this section which is triable summarily only pursuant to subsection (2) above.

35(12) In Northern Ireland–

(a) subsection (1) of section 110 of the Social Security Administration (Northern Ireland) Act 1992 (legal proceedings) applies in relation to proceedings for an offence under this section;

(b) subsections (2)(a) and (3)(a) of that section apply in relation to proceedings for an offence under this section which is triable summarily only pursuant to subsection (2) above."

125 Unauthorised disclosure of information relating to tax credit offences

125 [Amends SSAA 1992, Sch. 4, Pt. 2, para. 1.]

Commencement Date – 6 June 2012 is the day appointed for the coming into force of s. 125 (SI 2012/1246, art. 2(2)).

126 Tax credits: transfer of functions etc

126(1) Her Majesty may by Order in Council–

(a) transfer to the Secretary of State any tax credit function of the Treasury or the Commissioners;

(b) direct that any tax credit function of the Treasury or the Commissioners is to be exercisable concurrently with the Secretary of State or is to cease to be so exercisable.

126(2) Provision within subsection (1) may be limited so as to apply only in relation to cases within a specified description.

126(3) Her Majesty may by Order in Council, as Her Majesty considers appropriate–

(a) make provision in connection with a transfer or direction under subsection (1);

(b) make other provision within one or more of the following sub-paragraphs–

(i) provision applying (with or without modifications) in relation to tax credits any provision of primary or secondary legislation relating to social security;

(ii) provision combining or linking any aspect of the payment and management of tax credits with any aspect of the administration of social security;

(iii) provision about the use or supply of information held for purposes connected with tax credits, including (in particular) provision authorising or requiring its use or supply for other purposes;

(iv) in relation to information held for purposes not connected with tax credits, provision authorising or requiring its use or supply for purposes connected with tax credits.

126(4) An Order may make provision under subsection (3)(b) only if–

(a) the Order also makes provision under subsection (1), or

(b) a previous Order has made provision under subsection (1).

126(5) Provision within subsection (3)–

(a) may confer functions on, or remove functions from, the Secretary of State, the Treasury, the Commissioners, a Northern Ireland department or any other person;

(b) may (in particular) authorise the Secretary of State and the Commissioners to enter into arrangements from time to time under which the Commissioners are to provide services to the Secretary of State in connection with tax credits.

126(6) Provision within subsection (3)–

(a) may expand the scope of the conduct which constitutes an offence under any primary or secondary legislation, but may not increase the scope of any punishment for which a person may be liable on conviction for the offence;

(b) may expand the scope of the conduct in respect of which a civil penalty may be imposed under any primary or secondary legislation, but may not increase the maximum amount of the penalty.

126(7) An Order under this section may include such consequential, supplementary, incidental or transitional provision as Her Majesty considers appropriate including (for example)—

(a) provision for transferring or apportioning property, rights or liabilities (whether or not they would otherwise be capable of being transferred or apportioned);

(b) provision for substituting any person for any other person in any instrument or other document or in any legal proceedings;

(c) provision with respect to the application in relation to the Crown of provision made by the Order.

126(8) A certificate issued by the Secretary of State that any property, rights or liabilities set out in the certificate have been transferred or apportioned by an Order under this section as set out in the certificate is conclusive evidence of the matters so set out.

126(9) An Order under this section may amend, repeal or revoke any primary or secondary legislation.

126(10) A statutory instrument containing an Order under this section is subject to annulment in pursuance of a resolution of either House of Parliament.

126(11) In this section references to tax credits are to child tax credit or working tax credit or both.

126(12) In this section references to primary or secondary legislation are to such legislation whenever passed or made.

126(13) In this section–

"the Commissioners" means the Commissioners for Her Majesty's Revenue and Customs;

"primary legislation" means an Act (including this Act) or Northern Ireland legislation;

"secondary legislation" means an instrument made under primary legislation (including an Order under this section);

"tax credit functions" means functions so far as relating to tax credits conferred by or under any primary or secondary legislation.

126(14) In section 5A(3) of the Ministers of the Crown Act 1975, for "section 5(1)" there is substituted "section 5(1)(a) or (b)".

Statutory instruments – SI 2014/3280: made under s. 126(1)–(3)(a) and (b)(i) and (9).

INFORMATION-SHARING: SECRETARY OF STATE AND HMRC

127 Information-sharing between Secretary of State and HMRC

127(1) This subsection applies to information which is held for the purposes of any HMRC functions–

(a) by the Commissioners for Her Majesty's Revenue and Customs, or

(b) by a person providing services to them.

127(2) Information to which subsection (1) applies may be supplied–

(a) to the Secretary of State, or to a person providing services to the Secretary of State, or

(b) to a Northern Ireland Department, or to a person providing services to a Northern Ireland Department,

for use for the purposes of departmental functions.

127(3) This subsection applies to information which is held for the purposes of any departmental functions–

(a) by the Secretary of State, or by a person providing services to the Secretary of State, or

(b) by a Northern Ireland Department, or by a person providing services to a Northern Ireland Department.

127(4) Information to which subsection (3) applies may be supplied–

(a) to the Commissioners for Her Majesty's Revenue and Customs, or

(b) to a person providing services to them,

for use for the purposes of HMRC functions.

127(5) Information supplied under this section must not be supplied by the recipient of the information to any other person or body without–

(a) the authority of the Commissioners for Her Majesty's Revenue and Customs, in the case of *information supplied under subsection* (2);

(b) the authority of the Secretary of State, in the case of information held as mentioned in subsection (3)(a) and supplied under subsection (4);

(c) the authority of the relevant Northern Ireland Department, in the case of information held as mentioned in subsection (3)(b) and supplied under subsection (4).

127(6) Where information supplied under this section has been used for the purposes for which it was supplied, it is lawful for it to be used for any purposes for which information held for those purposes could be used.

127(7) In this section–

"departmental functions" means functions relating to–

(a) social security,

(b) employment or training,

(c) the investigation or prosecution of offences relating to tax credits; or

(d) child support;

"HMRC function" means any function–

(a) for which the Commissioners for Her Majesty's Revenue and Customs are responsible by virtue of section 5 of the Commissioners for Revenue and Customs Act 2005,

(b) which relates to a matter listed in Schedule 1 to that Act, or

(c) which is conferred by or under the Childcare Payments Act 2014;

"Northern Ireland Department" means any of the following–

(a) the Department for Social Development;

(b) the Department of Finance and Personnel;

(c) the Department for Employment and Learning.

127(8) For the purposes of this section any reference to functions relating to social security includes a reference to functions relating to–

(a) statutory payments as defined in section 4C(11) of the Social Security Contributions and Benefits Act 1992;

(b) maternity allowance under section 35 of that Act;

(c) statutory payments as defined in section 4C(11) of the Social Security Contributions and Benefits (Northern Ireland) Act 1992;

(d) maternity allowance under section 35 of that Act.

127(9) This section does not limit the circumstances in which information may be supplied apart from this section.

127(10) In section 3 of the Social Security Act 1998 (use of information), in subsection (1A), after paragraph (d) there is inserted–

"(e) the investigation or prosecution of offences relating to tax credits."

History – In s. 127(7), in the definition of "HMRC function", para. (c) (and the ", or" before it) inserted (and the word "or" after (a) omitted) by CPA 2014, s. 27(6) with effect from 20 July 2016 (SI 2016/763, reg. 2(1)).
S. 127(7)(d) (and the "or" before it inserted (and the "or" after (b) omitted) by SI 2012/2007, art. 102, with effect from 31 July 2012.

PART 7 – FINAL

147 Repeals

147 Schedule 14 contains consequential repeals.

149 Extent

149(1) This Act extends to England and Wales and Scotland only, subject as follows.

149(2) The following provisions extend to England and Wales, Scotland and Northern Ireland–

(a) section 32 (power to make consequential and supplementary provision: universal credit);

(b) section 33 (abolition of benefits);

(c) section 76 (calculation of working tax credit);

(d) section 92 (power to make consequential and supplementary provision: personal independence payment);

(e) section 126(1) to (13) (tax credits: transfer of functions etc);

(f) section 127(1) to (9) (information-sharing between Secretary of State and HMRC);

(g) this Part, excluding Schedule 14 (repeals).

149(3) Sections 128 and 129 extend to England and Wales only.

149(4) Any amendment or repeal made by this Act has the same extent as the enactment to which it relates.

TC Statutes

150 Commencement

150(1) The following provisions of this Act come into force on the day on which it is passed–

(a) section 76 (calculation of working tax credit);

(b) section 103 and Schedule 12 (supersession of decisions of former appellate bodies) (but see section 103(2));

(c) section 108 (application of Limitation Act 1980) (but see section 108(4));

(d) section 109 (recovery of fines etc by deductions from employment and support allowance) (but see section 109(3));

(e) section 126 (tax credits: transfer of functions etc);

(f) this Part, excluding Schedule 14 (repeals).

150(2) The following provisions of this Act come into force at the end of the period of two months beginning with the day on which it is passed–

(a) section 50 (dual entitlement to employment and support allowance and jobseeker's allowance);

(b) section 60 and Part 6 of Schedule 14 (claimants dependent on drugs etc);

(c) sections 71 and 72 (social fund: purposes of discretionary payments and determination of amount or value of budgeting loan);

(d) section 107 (recovery of child benefit and guardian's allowance);

(e) section 111 (time limit for legal proceedings);

(f) section 127 and Part 13 of Schedule 14 (information-sharing between Secretary of State and HMRC);

(g) section 134 (information-sharing for social security or employment purposes etc);

(h) section 135 (functions of registration service);

(i) section 142 (exclusion of child support maintenance from individual voluntary arrangements);

(j) section 145 and Schedule 13 (Social Mobility and Child Poverty Commission);

(k) Part 2 of Schedule 14 (entitlement to jobseeker's allowance without seeking employment).

150(3) The remaining provisions of this Act come into force on such day as the Secretary of State may by order made by statutory instrument appoint.

150(4) An order under subsection (3) may–

(a) appoint different days for different purposes;

(b) appoint different days for different areas in relation to—

(i) any provision of Part 1 (universal credit) or of Part 1 of Schedule 14;

(ii) section 61 or 62 (entitlement to work: jobseeker's allowance and employment and support allowance);

(iii) any provision of Part 4 (personal independence payment) or of Part 9 of Schedule 14;

(iv) section 102 (consideration of revision before appeal);

(c) make such transitory or transitional provision, or savings, as the Secretary of State considers necessary or expedient.

151 Short title

151 This Act may be cited as the Welfare Reform Act 2012.

SCHEDULES

SCHEDULE 6 – MIGRATION TO UNIVERSAL CREDIT

Section 36

GENERAL

1(1) Regulations may make provision for the purposes of, or in connection with, replacing existing benefits with universal credit.

1(2) In this Schedule **"existing benefit"** means–

(a) a benefit abolished under section 33(1);

(b) any other prescribed benefit.

1(3) In this Schedule **"appointed day"** means the day appointed for the coming into force of section 1.

Commencement Date – 25 February 2013 is the day appointed for the coming into force of para. 1(1) and (2)(b) (and s. 36 in so far as it relates to those paragraphs) for all purposes (SI 2013/358, art. 2(2) and Sch. 2, para. 42).

CLAIMS BEFORE THE APPOINTED DAY

2(1) The provision referred to in paragraph 1(1) includes–

(a) provision for a claim for universal credit to be made before the appointed day for a period beginning on or after that day;

(b) provision for a claim for universal credit made before the appointed day to be treated to any extent as a claim for an existing benefit;

(c) provision for a claim for an existing benefit made before the appointed day to be treated to any extent as a claim for universal credit.

2(2) The provision referred to in paragraph 1(1) includes provision, where a claim for universal credit is made (or is treated as made) before the appointed day, for an award on the claim to be made in respect of a period before the appointed day (including provision as to the conditions of entitlement for, and amount of, such an award).

CLAIMS AFTER THE APPOINTED DAY

3(1) The provision referred to in paragraph 1(1) includes–

(a) provision permanently or temporarily excluding the making of a claim for universal credit after the appointed day by–

(i) a person to whom an existing benefit is awarded, or

(ii) a person who would be entitled to an existing benefit on making a claim for it;

(b) provision temporarily excluding the making of a claim for universal credit after the appointed day by any other person;

(c) provision excluding entitlement to universal credit temporarily or for a particular period;

(d) provision for a claim for universal credit made after the appointed day to be treated to any extent as a claim for an existing benefit;

(e) provision for a claim for an existing benefit made after the appointed day to be treated to any extent as a claim for universal credit.

3(2) The provision referred to in paragraph 1(1) includes provision, where a claim for universal credit is made (or is treated as made) after the appointed day, for an award on the claim to be made in respect of a period before the appointed day (including provision as to the conditions of entitlement for, and amount of, such an award).

Commencement Date – 25 February 2013 is the day appointed for the coming into force of para. 3(1)(a)–(c) (and s. 36 in so far as it relates to those paragraphs) for all purposes (SI 2013/358, art. 2(2) and Sch. 2, para. 42).

AWARDS

4(1) The provision referred to in paragraph 1(1) includes–

(a) provision for terminating an award of an existing benefit;

(b) provision for making an award of universal credit, with or without application, to a person whose award of existing benefit is terminated.

4(2) The provision referred to in sub-paragraph (1)(b) includes–

(a) provision imposing requirements as to the procedure to be followed, information to be supplied or assessments to be undergone in relation to an award by virtue of that sub-paragraph or an application for such an award;

(b) provision as to the consequences of failure to comply with any such requirement;

(c) provision as to the terms on which, and conditions subject to which, such an award is made, including–

(i) provision temporarily or permanently disapplying, or otherwise modifying, conditions of entitlement to universal credit in relation to the award;

(ii) provision temporarily or permanently disapplying, or otherwise modifying, any requirement under this Part for a person to be assessed in respect of capability for work or work-related activity;

(d) provision as to the amount of such an award;

TC Statutes

(e) provision that fulfilment of any condition relevant to entitlement to an award of an existing benefit, or relevant to the amount of such an award, is to be treated as fulfilment of an equivalent condition in relation to universal credit.

4(3) Provision under sub-paragraph (2)(d) may secure that where an award of universal credit is made by virtue of sub-paragraph (1)(b)–

(a) the amount of the award is not less than the amount to which the person would have been entitled under the terminated award, or is not less than that amount by more than a prescribed amount;

(b) if the person to whom it is made ceases to be entitled to universal credit for not more than a prescribed period, the gap in entitlement is disregarded in calculating the amount of any new award of universal credit.

Commencement Date – 25 February 2013 is the day appointed for the coming into force of para. 4(1)(a) (and s. 36 in so far as it relates to those paragraphs) for all purposes (SI 2013/358, art. 2(2) and Sch. 2, para. 42).

WORK-RELATED REQUIREMENTS AND SANCTIONS

5(1) The provision referred to in paragraph 1(1) includes–

(a) provision relating to the application of work-related requirements for relevant benefits;

(b) provision relating to the application of sanctions.

5(2) The provision referred to in sub-paragraph (1)(a) includes–

(a) provision that a claimant commitment for a relevant benefit is to be treated as a claimant commitment for universal credit;

(b) provision that a work-related requirement for a relevant benefit is treated as a work-related requirement for universal credit;

(c) provision for anything done which is relevant to compliance with a work-related requirement for a relevant benefit to be treated as done for the purposes of compliance with a work-related requirement for universal credit;

(d) provision temporarily disapplying any provision of this Part in relation to work-related requirements for universal credit.

5(3) The provision referred to in sub-paragraph (1)(b) includes–

(a) provision for a sanction relevant to an award of a relevant benefit to be applied to an award of universal credit;

(b) provision for anything done which is relevant to the application of a sanction for a relevant benefit to be treated as done for the purposes of the application of a sanction for universal credit;

(c) provision temporarily disapplying any provision of this Part in relation to the application of sanctions.

5(4) In this paragraph–

"relevant benefit" means–

(a) jobseeker's allowance,

(b) employment and support allowance, and

(c) income support;

"work-related requirement" means–

(a) for universal credit, a work-related requirement within the meaning of this Part;

(b) for jobseeker's allowance, a requirement imposed–

(i) by virtue of regulations under section 8 or 17A of the Jobseekers Act 1995,

(ii) by a jobseeker's direction (within the meaning of section 19A of that Act),

(iii) by virtue of regulations under section 2A, 2AA or 2D of the Social Security Administration Act 1992, or

(iv) by a direction under section 2F of that Act;

(c) for employment and support allowance, a requirement imposed–

(i) by virtue of regulations under section 8, 9, 11, 12 or 13 of the Welfare Reform Act 2007,

(ii) by a direction under section 15 of that Act,

(iii) by virtue of regulations under section 2A, 2AA or 2D of the Social Security Administration Act 1992, or

(iv) by a direction under section 2F of that Act;

(d) for income support, a requirement imposed–
   (i) by virtue of regulations under section 2A, 2AA or 2D of the Social Security Administration Act 1992, or
   (ii) by a direction under section 2F of that Act;

"sanction" means a reduction of benefit under–

(a) section 26 or 27 above,
(b) section 19, 19A or 19B of the Jobseekers Act 1995,
(c) section 11, 12 or 13 of the Welfare Reform Act 2007, or
(d) section 2A, 2AA or 2D of the Social Security Administration Act 1992.

Commencement Date – 25 February 2013 is the day appointed for the coming into force of para. 5(1), (2)(c) and (d) and (3)(a) (and s. 36 in so far as it relates to those paragraphs) for all purposes (SI 2013/358, art. 2(2) and Sch. 2, para. 42).

TAX CREDITS

6 In relation to the replacement of working tax credit and child tax credit with universal credit, the provision referred to in paragraph 1(1) includes–

(a) provision modifying the application of the Tax Credits Act 2002 (or of any provision made under it);
(b) provision for the purposes of recovery of overpayments of working tax credit or child tax credit (including in particular provision for treating overpayments of working tax credit or child tax credit as if they were overpayments of universal credit).

Commencement Date – 25 February 2013 is the day appointed for the coming into force of para. 6 (and s. 36 in so far as it relates to para. 6) for all purposes (SI 2013/358, art. 2(2) and Sch. 2, para. 42).

SUPPLEMENTARY

7 Regulations under paragraph 1(1) may secure the result that any gap in entitlement to an existing benefit (or what would, but for the provisions of this Part, be a gap in entitlement to an existing benefit) is to be disregarded for the purposes of provision under such regulations.

SCHEDULE 14 – REPEALS

Section 147

Part 1 – Abolition of benefits superseded by universal credit

Short title and chapter	*Extent of repeal*
Tax Credits Act 2002 (c. 21)	Part 1 (but not Schedule 1 or 3).

Part 12 – Loss of benefit: cautions

Short title and chapter	*Extent of repeal*
Tax Credits Act 2002 (c. 21).	In section 36A (as inserted by section 120 of this Act)– (a) in subsection (7)(c) "or (c)"; (b) in subsection (10), in the definition of "disqualifying event", paragraph (c). In section 36B (as so inserted), subsection (4)(a)(ii) and the preceding "or". In section 67, the definition of "cautioned".

Part 13 – Information-sharing between Secretary of State and HMRC

Short title and chapter	*Extent of repeal*
Tax Credits Act 2002 (c. 21).	In Schedule 5– (a) in paragraph 4(2) "social security or"; (b) paragraph 4(3) (c) in paragraph 4(3A) "social security,"; (d) in paragraph 4(3B), "social security or"; (e) in paragraph 4(4), "(3) and"; (f) in paragraph 6(1), "social security,"; (g) in paragraph 6(1A), "social security," (h) in paragraph 6(3) "social security or"; (i) paragraph 12(a).

PENSIONS ACT 2014

(2014 Chapter 19)

[*14th May 2014*]

ARRANGEMENT OF SECTIONS

PART 2 – OPTION TO BOOST OLD RETIREMENT PENSIONS

25 Option to boost old retirement pensions

25 In Schedule 15–

Part 1 contains amendments to allow certain people to pay additional contributions to boost their retirement pensions;

Part 2 contains amendments to allow corresponding legislation to be put in place for Northern Ireland.

Commencement Date – S. 25 comes into force on 12 October 2015 in so far as it relates to Sch. 15, para. 1–10 and 12–14 (SI 2015/1475, art. 3) and Sch. 15, para. 15–19, 21 and 22 (SI 2015/1670, art. 2).
S. 25 comes into effect on 1 October 2014 in so far as it relates to Sch. 15, para. 3 (SI 2014/2377).

PART 5 – BEREAVEMENT SUPPORT PAYMENT

31 Bereavement support payment: contribution condition and amendments

31(1) For the purposes of section 30(1)(d) the contribution condition is that, for at least one tax year during the deceased's working life–

(a) he or she actually paid Class 1 or Class 2 national insurance contributions, and

(b) those contributions give rise to an earnings factor (or total earnings factors) equal to or greater than 25 times the lower earnings limit for the tax year.

31(2) For earnings factors, see sections 22 and 23 of the Social Security Contributions and Benefits Act 1992.

31(3) For the purposes of section 30(1)(d) the contribution condition is to be treated as met if the deceased was an employed earner and died as a result of–

(a) a personal injury of the kind mentioned in section 94(1) of the Social Security Contributions and Benefits Act 1992, or

(b) a disease or personal injury of the kind mentioned in section 108(1) of that Act.

TC Statutes

31(4) In this section the following expressions have the meaning given by section 122(1) of the Social Security Contributions and Benefits Act 1992–

"employed earner",

"lower earnings limit",

"tax year", and

"working life".

31(5) Schedule 16 contains amendments to do with bereavement support payment.

PART 7 – FINAL PROVISIONS

53 Power to make consequential amendments etc

53(1) The Secretary of State or the Treasury may by order make consequential, incidental or supplementary provision in connection with any provision made by this Act.

53(2) An order under this section may amend, repeal, revoke or otherwise modify any enactment (whenever passed or made).

53(3) **"Enactment"** includes an enactment contained in subordinate legislation within the meaning of the Interpretation Act 1978.

54 Regulations and orders

54(1) Regulations and orders under this Act are to be made by statutory instrument.

54(2) A statutory instrument containing (whether alone or with other provisions)–

(a) regulations under section 3, 17, 18(3) or (5), 19, 20, 30, 32 or 34,

(b) the first regulations under section 10,

(c) an order under section 53 that amends or repeals a provision of an Act,

(d) regulations under Schedule 17,

(e) regulations under paragraph 2 of Schedule 18 or regulations under paragraph 7 of that Schedule that amend a provision of an Act, or

(e) the first regulations under paragraph 1 or 3 of that Schedule,

may not be made unless a draft of the instrument has been laid before and approved by a resolution of each House of Parliament.

54(3) Any other statutory instrument containing regulations or an order under this Act is subject to annulment in pursuance of a resolution of either House of Parliament.

54(4) Subsection (3) does not apply to a statutory instrument containing an order under section 56(1), (6) or (8) only.

54(5) A power to make regulations or an order under this Act may be used–

(a) to make different provision for different purposes;

(b) in relation to all or only some of the purposes for which it may be used.

54(6) Regulations or orders under this Act may include incidental, supplementary, consequential, transitional, transitory or saving provision.

55 Extent

55(1) This Act extends to England and Wales and Scotland only, subject to the following provisions of this section.

55(2) Any amendment or repeal made by this Act has the same extent as the enactment to which it relates.

55(3) This Part extends also to Northern Ireland.

56 Commencement

56(1) This Act comes into force on such day or days as the Secretary of State may by order appoint, subject as follows.

56(2) The following come into force on the day on which this Act is passed–

(a) section 29;

(b) section 51;

(c) this Part.

56(3) The following come into force at the end of the period of 2 months beginning with the day on which this Act is passed–

(a) Part 3;

(b) sections 34 and 35;

(c) section 41;

(d) sections 47 and 48;

(e) paragraph 30(2) of Schedule 13.

56(4) Part 1 comes into force on 6 April 2016, so far as not brought into force earlier by an order under subsection (1).

56(5) The Secretary of State may by order–

(a) amend subsection (4) so as to replace the reference to 6 April 2016 with a later date, and

(b) make corresponding amendments in Part 1 or any enactment amended by it.

56(6) Section 52 comes into force on such day or days as the Treasury may by order appoint.

56(7) An order under subsection (1) or (6) may appoint different days for different purposes.

56(8) The Secretary of State may by order make transitional, transitory or saving provision in connection with the coming into force of any provision of this Act.

57 Short title

57 This Act may be cited as the Pensions Act 2014.

SCHEDULES

SCHEDULE 15 – OPTION TO BOOST OLD RETIREMENT PENSIONS

Section 25

Commencement Date – Sch. 15, para. 1–10 and 12–14 came into force on 12 October 2015 (SI 2015/1475, art. 3). Para. 3 came into force on 1 October 2014 (SI 2014/2377, art. 2(3)(d)).

Part 1 – Great Britain

SOCIAL SECURITY CONTRIBUTIONS AND BENEFITS ACT 1992 (C. 4)

1 The Social Security Contributions and Benefits Act 1992 is amended as follows.

2(1) Section 1 (outline of contributory system) is amended as follows.

2(2) [Amends SSCBA 1992, s. 1(2).]

2(3) [Amends SSCBA 1992, s. 1(4)(a).]

3 [Inserts SSCBA 1992, s. 14A–14C.]

Commencement Date – Para. 3 came into force on 1 October 2014 (SI 2014/2377, art. 2(3)(d)).

4 If paragraph 3 comes into force before the day mentioned in section 56(4) of this Act, section 14A(2) as inserted by that paragraph has effect as if the reference to entitlement included the prospective entitlement of a person who–

(a) has not yet reached pensionable age, but

(b) will reach pensionable age before that day (assuming that the person lives until pensionable age).

10 [Amends SSCBA 1992, s. 122(1).]

11 [Amends SSCBA 1992, s. 176(1)(a).]

Commencement Date – *Para. 11 came into force* 13 October 2014 (SI 2014/2727, art. 2).

12 [Amends SSCBA 1992, Sch. 1, heading.]

SOCIAL SECURITY ADMINISTRATION ACT 1992 (C. 5)

13(1) Section 162 of the Social Security Administration Act 1992 (destination of contributions) is amended as follows.

13(2) [Inserts SSAA 1992, s. 162(5)(ea).]

13(3) [Amends SSAA 1992, s. 162(8)(c).]

TC Statutes

SCHEDULE 16 – BEREAVEMENT SUPPORT PAYMENT: AMENDMENTS

Section 31

FORFEITURE ACT 1982 (C. 34)

1 In section 4 of the Forfeiture Act 1982 (Upper Tribunal to decide whether forfeiture rule applies to social security benefits), in the definition of "relevant enactment" in subsection (5), after the entry relating to Part 1 of this Act (inserted by Schedule 12 to this Act) insert–

"section 30 of that Act,".

SOCIAL SECURITY CONTRIBUTIONS AND BENEFITS ACT 1992 (C. 4)

2 The Social Security Contributions and Benefits Act 1992 is amended as follows.

3(1) Section 20 (descriptions of contributory benefits) is amended as follows.

3(2) In subsection (1), for paragraph (ea) substitute–

"(ea) widowed parent's allowance;".

3(3) In subsection (2), in the definition of "long-term benefit" omit paragraph (bb).

4(1) Section 21 (contribution conditions) is amended as follows.

4(2) In the table in subsection (2) omit the entries for bereavement payment and bereavement allowance.

4(3) Omit subsection (4).

5 In section 22 (earnings factors), in subsection (2), after paragraph (c) (inserted by Schedule 12 to this Act) insert "and

"(d) establishing entitlement to bereavement support payment under section 30 of the Pensions Act 2014."

6(1) Section 23A (contributions credits for relevant parents and carers) is amended as follows.

6(2) In subsection (1) omit paragraph (e).

6(3) In subsection (6)(b) omit "or (e)".

SOCIAL SECURITY ADMINISTRATION ACT 1992 (C. 5)

20 The Social Security Administration Act 1992 is amended as follows.

26 In section 121DA (interpretation of Part 6), in subsection (1), after paragraph (hl) (inserted by Schedule 12 to this Act) insert–

"(hm) Part 5 of the Pensions Act 2014;".

27 In section 122B (supply of other government information for fraud prevention and verification), in subsection (3)(b), after ", Part 1 of the Pensions Act 2014" (inserted by Schedule 12 to this Act) insert ", section 30 of that Act".

28 In section 124 (age, death and marriage), in subsection (1), after paragraph (af) (inserted by Schedule 12 to this Act) insert–

"(ag) of section 30 of the Pensions Act 2014; and".

29 In section 125 (regulations as to notification of deaths), in subsection (1), after ", Part 1 of the Pensions Act 2014" (inserted by Schedule 12 to this Act) insert ", section 30 of that Act".

32 In section 170 (Social Security Advisory Committee), in subsection (5)–

(a) in the definition of "the relevant enactments", after paragraph (am) (inserted by Schedule 12 to this Act) insert–

"(an) section 30 of the Pensions Act 2014;";

(b) in the definition of "the relevant Northern Ireland enactments", after paragraph (am) (inserted by Schedule 12 to this Act) insert–

"(an) any provisions in Northern Ireland which correspond to section 30 of the Pensions Act 2014;".

33(1) Section 179 (reciprocal agreements) is amended as follows.

33(2) In subsection (3)(a), after "Pensions Act 2014" (inserted by Schedule 12 to this Act) insert ", Part 5 of that Act".

33(3) In subsection (4), after paragraph (ai) (inserted by Schedule 12 to this Act) insert–

"(aj) to Part 5 of the Pensions Act 2014;".

33(4) In subsection (5)–

(a) after "Pensions Act 2014" (inserted by Schedule 12 to this Act) insert "or section 30 of that Act";

(b) after paragraph (ad) (inserted by Schedule 12 to this Act) insert–

"(ae) bereavement support payment;".

35 In section 191 (interpretation), in the definition of "benefit", for "and personal independence payment" substitute ", personal independence payment and bereavement support payment under section 30 of the Pensions Act 2014".

SOCIAL SECURITY ACT 1998 (C. 14)

37 The Social Security Act 1998 is amended as follows.

38 In section 2 (use of computers), in subsection (2), after paragraph (m) (inserted by Schedule 12 to this Act) insert "or

"(n) section 30 of the Pensions Act 2014;".

39(1) Section 8 (decisions by Secretary of State) is amended as follows.

39(2) In subsection (3), after paragraph (ab) (inserted by Schedule 12 to this Act) insert–

"(ac) bereavement support payment under section 30 of the Pensions Act 2014;".

39(3) In subsection (4), after "Part 1 of the Pensions Act 2014" (inserted by Schedule 12 to this Act) insert "or section 30 of that Act".

40 In section 11 (regulations with respect to decisions), in subsection (3), in the definition of "the current legislation", after "Part 1 of the Pensions Act 2014" (inserted by Schedule 12 to this Act) insert "and section 30 of that Act".

41 In section 27 (restriction on entitlement in cases of error), in subsection (7), in the definition of "benefit"–

(a) after paragraph (df) insert–

"(dg) bereavement support payment under section 30 of the Pensions Act 2014;";

(b) in paragraph (e), for "to (df)" substitute "to (dg)".

42 In section 28 (correction of errors in decisions etc), in subsection (3)(j), after "Part 1 of the Pensions Act 2014" (inserted by Schedule 12 to this Act) insert "or section 30 of that Act".

FINANCE (NO. 2) ACT 2015

(2015 Chapter 33)

[*18th November 2015*]

ARRANGEMENT OF SECTIONS

PART 6 – ADMINISTRATION AND ENFORCEMENT

51 Enforcement by deduction from accounts

51(1) Schedule 8 contains provision about the enforcement of debts owed to the Commissioners for Her Majesty's Revenue and Customs by making deductions from accounts held with deposit-takers.

51(2) The Treasury may, by regulations made by statutory instrument, make consequential, incidental or supplementary provision in connection with any provision made by that Schedule.

51(3) Regulations under subsection (2) may amend, repeal or revoke any enactment (whenever passed or made).

51(4) **"Enactment"** includes an enactment contained in subordinate legislation within the meaning of the Interpretation Act 1978.

51(5) A statutory instrument containing (whether alone or with other provision) provision amending or repealing an Act may not be made unless a draft of the instrument has been laid before and approved by a resolution of the House of Commons.

51(6) Any other statutory instrument containing regulations under subsection (2) is subject to annulment in pursuance of a resolution of the House of Commons.

52 Rate of interest applicable to judgment debts etc in taxation matters

52(1) This section applies if a sum payable to or by the Commissioners under a judgment or order given or made in any court proceedings relating to a taxation matter (a "tax-related judgment debt") carries interest as a result of a relevant enactment.

52(2) The **"relevant enactments"** are–

(a) section 17 of the Judgments Act 1838 (judgment debts to carry interest), and

(b) any order under section 74 of the County Courts Act 1984 (interest on judgment debts etc).

52(3) The relevant enactment is to have effect in relation to the tax-related judgment debt as if for the rate specified in section 17(1) of the Judgments Act 1838 and any other rate specified in an order under section 74 of the County Courts Act 1984 there were substituted–

(a) in the case of a sum payable to the Commissioners, the late payment interest rate provided for in regulations made by the Treasury under section 103(1) of FA 2009, and

(b) in the case of a sum payable by the Commissioners, the special repayment rate.

52(4) Subsection (3) does not affect any power of the court under the relevant enactment to prevent any sum from carrying interest or to provide for a rate of interest which is lower than (and incapable of exceeding) that for which the subsection provides.

52(5) If section 44A of the Administration of Justice Act 1970 (interest on judgment debts expressed otherwise than in sterling), or any corresponding provision made under section 74 of the County Courts Act 1984 in relation to the county court, applies to a tax-related judgment debt–

(a) subsection (3) does not apply, but

(b) the court may not specify in an order under section 44A of the Administration of Justice Act 1970, or under any provision corresponding to that section which has effect under section 74 of the County Courts Act 1984, an interest rate which exceeds (or is capable of exceeding)–

(i) in the case of a sum payable to the Commissioners, the rate mentioned in subsection (3)(a), or

(ii) in the case of a sum payable by the Commissioners, the special repayment rate.

52(6) The **"special repayment rate"** is the percentage per annum given by the formula–

$$BR + 2$$

where BR is the official Bank rate determined by the Bank of England Monetary Policy Committee at the operative meeting.

52(7) **"The operative meeting"**, in relation to the special repayment rate applicable in respect of any day, means the most recent meeting of the Bank of England Monetary Policy Committee apart from any meeting later than the 13th working day before that day.

52(8) The Treasury may by regulations made by statutory instrument–

(a) repeal subsections (6) and (7), and

(b) provide that the **"special repayment rate"** for the purposes of this section is the rate provided for in the regulations.

52(9) Regulations under subsection (8)–

(a) may make different provision for different purposes,

(b) may either themselves specify a rate of interest or make provision for such a rate to be determined (and to change from time to time) by reference to such rate, or the average of such rates, as may be referred to in the regulations,

(c) may provide for rates to be reduced below, or increased above, what they would otherwise be by specified amounts or by reference to specified formulae,

(d) may provide for rates arrived at by reference to averages to be rounded up or down,

(e) may provide for circumstances in which the alteration of a rate of interest is or is not to take place, and

(f) may provide that alterations of rates are to have effect for periods beginning on or after a day determined in accordance with the regulations ("the effective date") regardless of–

(i) the date of the judgment or order in question, and

(ii) whether interest begins to run on or after the effective date, or began to run before that date.

52(10) A statutory instrument containing regulations under subsection (8) is subject to annulment in pursuance of a resolution of the House of Commons.

52(11) To the extent that a tax-related judgment debt consists of an award of costs to or against the Commissioners, the reference in section 24(2) of the Crown Proceedings Act 1947 (which relates to interest on costs awarded to or against the Crown) to the rate at which interest is payable upon judgment debts due from or to the Crown is to be read as a reference to the rate at which interest is payable upon tax-related judgment debts.

52(12) This section has effect in relation to interest for periods beginning on or after 8 July 2015, regardless of–

(a) the date of the judgment or order in question, and

(b) whether interest begins to run on or after 8 July 2015, or began to run before that date.

52(13) Subsection (14) applies where, at any time during the period beginning with 8 July 2015 and ending immediately before the day on which this Act is passed ("the relevant period")–

(a) a payment is made in satisfaction of a tax-related judgment debt, and

(b) the payment includes interest under a relevant enactment in respect of any part of the relevant period.

52(14) The court by which the judgment or order in question was given or made must, on an application made to it under this subsection by the person who made the payment, order the repayment of the amount by which the interest paid under the relevant enactment in respect of days falling within the relevant period exceeds the interest payable under the relevant enactment in respect of those days in accordance with the provisions of this section.

52(15) In this section–

"the Commissioners" means the Commissioners for Her Majesty's Revenue and Customs;

"taxation matter" means anything the collection and management of which is the responsibility of the Commissioners (or was the responsibility of the Commissioners of Inland Revenue or Commissioners of Customs and Excise);

"working day" means any day other than a non-business day as defined in section 92 of the Bills of Exchange Act 1882.

52(16) This section extends to England and Wales only.

History – In s. 52(15), in the definition of "taxation matter", the words ", other than national insurance contributions," (which appeared after the words "means anything") omitted by FA 2016, s. 172(1), with effect (in England and Wales only) in relation to interest for periods beginning on or after 15 September 2016, regardless of– (a) the date of the judgment or order in question, and (b) whether interest begins to run on or after 15 September 2016, or began to run before that date.

PART 7 – FINAL

53 Interpretation

53 In this Act–

"CAA 2001" means the Capital Allowances Act 2001,

"CTA 2009" means the Corporation Tax Act 2009,

"CTA 2010" means the Corporation Tax Act 2010,

"FA", followed by a year, means the Finance Act of that year,

"IHTA 1984" means the Inheritance Tax Act 1984,

"ITA 2007" means the Income Tax Act 2007,

"ITEPA 2003" means the Income Tax (Earnings and Pensions) Act 2003,

"ITTOIA 2005" means the Income Tax (Trading and Other Income) Act 2005,

"TCGA 1992" means the Taxation of Chargeable Gains Act 1992,

"TIOPA 2010" means the Taxation (International and Other Provisions) Act 2010,

"TMA 1970" means the Taxes Management Act 1970,

"VATA 1994" means the Value Added Tax Act 1994, and

"VERA 1994" means the Vehicle Excise and Registration Act 1994.

54 Short title

54 This Act may be cited as the Finance (No. 2) Act 2015.

SCHEDULES

SCHEDULE 8 – ENFORCEMENT BY DEDUCTION FROM ACCOUNTS

Section 51

Part 1 – Scheme for Enforcement by Deduction from Accounts

INTRODUCTION

1 This Part of this Schedule contains provision about the collection of amounts due and payable to the Commissioners by the making of deductions from accounts held with deposit-takers.

"RELEVANT SUM"

2(1) In this Part of this Schedule **"relevant sum"**, in relation to a person, means a sum that is due and payable by the person to the Commissioners–

(a) *under or by virtue of an enactment*, or

(b) under a contract settlement,

and in relation to which Conditions A to C are met.

2(2) Condition A is that the sum is at least £1,000.

2(3) Condition B is that the sum is–

(a) an established debt (see sub-paragraph (5)),

(b) due under section 223 of, or paragraph 6 of Schedule 32 to, FA 2014 (accelerated payment notice or partner payment notice), or

(c) the disputed tax specified in a notice under section 221(2)(b) of FA 2014 (accelerated payment of tax: notice given pending appeal).

2(4) Condition C is that HMRC is satisfied that the person is aware that the sum is due and payable by the person to the Commissioners.

2(5) A sum that is due and payable to the Commissioners is an **"established debt"** if there is no possibility that the sum, or any part of it, will cease to be due and payable to the Commissioners on appeal.

2(6) For the purposes of sub-paragraph (5) it does not matter whether the reason that there is no such possibility is–

(a) that there is no right of appeal in relation to the sum,

(b) that a period for bringing an appeal has expired without an appeal having been brought, or

(c) that an appeal which was brought has been finally determined or withdrawn;

and any power to grant permission to appeal out of time is to be disregarded.

INFORMATION NOTICE

3(1) This paragraph applies if it appears to HMRC that–

(a) a person has failed to pay a relevant sum, and

(b) that person holds one or more accounts with a deposit-taker.

3(2) HMRC may give the deposit-taker a notice under this paragraph (an "information notice") requiring the deposit-taker to provide HMRC with–

(a) prescribed information about accounts held by the person with the deposit-taker,

(b) in relation to any joint account held by the person with the deposit-taker, prescribed information about the other holder or holders of the account, and

(c) any other prescribed information.

3(3) HMRC may exercise the power under sub-paragraph (2) only for the purposes of determining whether to give a hold notice to the deposit-taker in respect of the person concerned (see paragraph 4).

3(4) Where a deposit-taker is given an information notice, it must comply with the notice as soon as reasonably practicable and, in any event, within the period of 10 working days beginning with the day on which the notice is given to it.

3(5) An information notice must explain the effect of–

(a) sub-paragraph (4), and

(b) paragraph 14 (penalties).

Statutory instruments – SI 2015/1986: partly made under para. 3(2).

HOLD NOTICE

4(1) If it appears to HMRC that–

(a) a person ("P") has failed to pay a relevant sum, and

(b) P holds one or more accounts with a deposit-taker,

HMRC may give the deposit-taker a notice under this paragraph (a "hold notice").

4(2) The hold notice must–

(a) specify P's name and last known address,

(b) specify as the "specified amount" an amount that meets the conditions in sub-paragraph (4),

(c) specify as the "safeguarded amount" an amount that meets the requirements set out in sub-paragraphs (6) to (8),

(d) set out any rules which are to apply for the purposes of paragraph 7(5)(b) (priority of accounts subject to a hold notice),

(e) explain the effect of–

(i) paragraphs 6 to 13 (effect of hold notice, duty to notify account holders etc),

(ii) paragraph 14 (penalties), and

(iii) any regulations under paragraph 20(2)(c) or (d) (powers to restrict the accounts or amounts in relation to which a hold notice may have effect, in addition to the powers to make provision in the hold notice under sub-paragraph (3)(b) and (c)), and

(f) contain a statement about HMRC's compliance with paragraph 5 in relation to the notice.

For provision about the particular relevant sums to which a hold notice relates see paragraph 8(6)(a)(ii) and (7) (notice to be given by HMRC to P).

4(3) The hold notice may–

(a) specify any other information which HMRC considers might assist the deposit-taker in identifying accounts which P holds with it;

(b) specify an account, or description of account, which is to be treated for the purposes of the hold notice and this Part of this Schedule as not being an account held by P with the deposit-taker;

(c) require that an amount specified in the notice is to be treated for the purposes of the hold notice and this Part of this Schedule as if it were not an amount standing to the credit of a specified account held by P.

4(4) The amount specified as the specified amount in the hold notice ("the current hold notice") must not exceed so much of the notified sum (see paragraph 8(6) to (8)) as remains after deducting–

(a) the amount specified as the **"specified amount"** in any hold notice which relates to the same debts as the current hold notice (see sub-paragraph (5)) and is given to another deposit-taker on the same day as that notice, and

(b) the amount specified as the **"specified amount"** in any hold notice which relates to the same debts as the current hold notice and is given to a deposit-taker on an earlier day, (unless HMRC has received a notification under paragraph 8(4) in relation to that earlier hold notice).

4(5) For the purposes of this paragraph, any two hold notices given in respect of the same person **"relate to the same debts"** if at least one relevant sum specified in relation to one of those notices by virtue of paragraph 8(7)(a) is the same debt as a relevant sum so specified in relation to the other notice.

4(6) The amount specified in the hold notice as the safeguarded amount must be at least £5,000; but this is qualified by sub-paragraphs (7) and (8).

4(7) The safeguarded amount must be nil if–

(a) HMRC has previously given a deposit-taker a hold notice ("the earlier hold notice") relating to the same debts as the hold notice mentioned in sub-paragraph (2) ("the new hold notice"), and

(b) within the period of 30 days ending with the day on which the new hold notice is given to the deposit-taker, HMRC has received a notice under paragraph 8 which states that there is a held amount as a result of the earlier hold notice.

4(8) HMRC may (in a case not falling within sub-paragraph (7)) determine that an amount less than £5,000 (which may be nil) is to be the safeguarded amount if HMRC considers it appropriate to do so having regard to the value (or aggregate value) in sterling at the relevant time of any amounts which at that time stand to the credit of a qualifying non-sterling account or accounts.

4(9) In sub-paragraph (8) **"qualifying non-sterling account"** means an account which, but for paragraph 6(6)(b) (account not denominated in sterling), would be a relevant account in relation to the hold notice.

4(10) For the purposes of sub-paragraph (8), the value in sterling of any amount is to be determined in the prescribed manner; and regulations for the purposes of this sub-paragraph may specify circumstances in which the exchange rate is to be determined in accordance with a notice published by the Commissioners.

4(11) In sub-paragraph (8) **"the relevant time"** means the time when the Commissioners determine the amount to be specified as the **"safeguarded amount"** under sub-paragraph (2)(c).

4(12) HMRC must not on any one day give to a single deposit-taker more than one hold notice relating to the same debts.

PERSONS AT A PARTICULAR DISADVANTAGE IN DEALING WITH REVENUE AND CUSTOMS AFFAIRS

5(1) Before deciding whether or not to exercise the power under paragraph 3(2) or 4(1) in relation to a person, HMRC must consider whether or not, to the best of HMRC's knowledge, there are any matters as a result of which the person is, or may be, at a particular disadvantage in dealing with the person's Revenue and Customs affairs.

5(2) If HMRC determines that there are any such matters, HMRC must take those matters into account in deciding whether or not to exercise the power concerned in relation to the person.

5(3) The Commissioners must publish guidance as to the factors which are relevant to determining whether or not a person is at a particular disadvantage in dealing with the person's Revenue and Customs affairs for the purposes of this Schedule.

5(4) In this paragraph **"Revenue and Customs affairs"**, in relation to a person by whom a relevant sum is payable, means any affairs of the person which relate to the relevant sum.

EFFECT OF HOLD NOTICE

6(1) A deposit-taker to whom a hold notice is given under paragraph 4 must, for each relevant account (see sub-paragraph (6))–

(a) determine whether or not there is a held amount (greater than nil) in relation to that account, and

(b) if there is such a held amount in relation to that account, take the first or second type of action (see sub-paragraph (3)) in respect of that account.

See paragraph 7 for how to determine the held amount in relation to any relevant account.

6(2) The deposit-taker must comply with sub-paragraph (1) as soon as is reasonably practicable and, in any event, within the period of 5 working days beginning with the day on which the hold notice is given.

6(3) In relation to each affected account (see sub-paragraph (7))–

(a) the first type of action is to put in place such arrangements as are necessary to ensure that the deposit-taker does not do anything, or permit anything to be done, that would reduce the amount standing to the credit of that account below the held amount in relation to that account;

(b) the second type of action is to–

(i) transfer an amount equal to the held amount from the affected account into an account created by the deposit-taker for the sole purpose of containing that transferred amount (a "suspense account"), and

(ii) put in place such arrangements as are necessary to ensure that the deposit-taker does not do anything, or permit anything to be done, that would reduce the amount standing to the credit of that suspense account below the amount that is the held amount in relation to the affected account.

6(4) The deposit-taker must maintain any arrangements made under sub-paragraph (3) until the hold notice ceases to be in force.

6(5) A hold notice ceases to be in force when–

(a) the deposit-taker is given a notice cancelling it under paragraph 9 or 11 or the hold notice is cancelled under paragraph 12, or

(b) the deposit-taker is given a deduction notice in relation to the hold notice (see paragraph 13).

6(6) In this Part of this Schedule **"relevant account"**, in relation to a hold notice, means an account held with the deposit-taker by P, but not including–

(a) an account excluded under paragraph 4(3)(b) or by regulations under paragraph 20(2)(c),

(b) an account not denominated in sterling, or

(c) any suspense account.

6(7) For the purposes of this Part of this Schedule, a relevant account is an **"affected account"** if, as a result of the hold notice, an amount is the held amount in relation to that account (see paragraph 7(1) and (2)).

DETERMINATION OF HELD AMOUNTS

7(1) If there is only one relevant account (see paragraph 6(6)) in existence at the time the deposit-taker complies with paragraph 6(1), **"the held amount"** in relation to that account is–

(a) if the available amount in respect of the account (see sub-paragraph (3)) exceeds the safeguarded amount, so much of the amount of the excess as does not exceed the specified amount, and

(b) if the available amount does not exceed the safeguarded amount, nil.

For the meaning of **"the safeguarded amount"** and **"the specified amount"** see paragraph 23(1).

7(2) If there is more than one relevant account in existence at the time the deposit-taker complies with paragraph 6(1), "the held amount" in relation to each relevant account is determined as follows–

Step 1

Determine the available amount in respect of each relevant account.

Step 2

Determine the total of the available amounts in respect of all of the relevant accounts.

If that total does not exceed the safeguarded amount, the held amount in relation to each relevant account is nil (and no further steps are to be taken). In any other case, go to Step 3.

Step 3
Match the safeguarded amount against the available amounts in respect of the relevant accounts, taking those accounts in reverse priority order (see sub-paragraph (6)).
Step 4
Match the specified amount against what remains of the available amounts in respect of the relevant accounts by taking each relevant account in priority order (see sub-paragraph (5)) and matching the specified amount (or, as the case may be, what remains of the specified amount) against the available amount for each account until either–

(a) the specified amount has been fully matched, or

(b) what remains of the available amounts is exhausted.

Where this sub-paragraph applies, **"the held amount"**, in relation to a relevant account–

(i) is so much of the amount standing to the credit of the account as is matched against the specified amount under Step 4, and

(ii) accordingly, is nil if no amount standing to the credit of the account is so matched against the specified amount.

7(3) In this paragraph **"the available amount"** means–

(a) in the case of an account other than a joint account, the amount standing to the credit of that account at the time the deposit-taker complies with paragraph 6(1), or

(b) in the case of a joint account, the appropriate fraction of the amount standing to the credit of that account at that time;

so, if no amount stands to the credit of an account at that time, **"the available amount"** is nil.

7(4) In this paragraph **"the appropriate fraction"**, in relation to a joint account, means–

$$\frac{1}{N}$$

where N is the number of persons who together hold the joint account.

7(5) In this paragraph **"priority order"** means such order as the deposit-taker considers appropriate, but the deposit-taker must ensure–

(a) that accounts other than joint accounts always have a higher priority than joint accounts, and

(b) subject to paragraph (a), that any rule set out in the hold notice under paragraph 4(2)(d) is adhered to.

7(6) In this paragraph **"reverse priority order"** means the reverse of the order determined under sub-paragraph (5).

7(7) In this paragraph references to an amount standing to the credit of an account are to be read subject to any regulations under paragraph 20(2)(d).

DUTY TO NOTIFY HMRC AND ACCOUNT HOLDERS ETC

8(1) This paragraph applies where a deposit-taker receives a hold notice.

8(2) If the deposit-taker determines that there are one or more affected accounts (see paragraph 5(7)) as a result of the hold notice, the deposit-taker must give HMRC a notice which sets out–

(a) prescribed information about each of the affected accounts held by P,

(b) the amount of the held amount in relation to each such account,

(c) if any of the affected accounts is a joint account held by P and one or more other persons, prescribed information about the other person or persons, and

(d) any other prescribed information.

8(3) The notice under sub-paragraph (2) must be given within the period of 5 working days beginning with the day on which the deposit-taker complies with paragraph 6(1).

8(4) If the deposit-taker determines that there are no affected accounts as a result of the hold notice, it must give HMRC a notice which–

(a) states that this is the case, and

(b) sets out any other prescribed information.

8(5) *The notice under sub-paragraph (4) must be given within the period of 5 working days beginning with the day on which the deposit-taker makes that determination.*

8(6) If HMRC receives a notice under sub-paragraph (2) it must as soon as reasonably practicable–

(a) give P–

(i) a copy of the hold notice, and

(ii) a notice under sub-paragraph (7), and

(b) in relation to each affected account, give a notice to each person within sub-paragraph (9) explaining that a hold notice has been given in respect of the account, the effect of the hold notice so far as it relates to the account and the effect of paragraphs 10 to 12.

8(7) A notice under this sub-paragraph must comply with the following requirements–

(a) the notice must specify the particular relevant sums (see paragraph 2) to which the hold notice relates;

(b) the details given for that purpose must include a statement, to the best of HMRC's knowledge, of the amount of each of those sums (that is, the unpaid amount) at the date of the notice;

(c) the notice must state the total of the amounts stated under paragraph (b) (if more than one), and

(d) the notice must state that the notified sum for the purposes of the hold notice (see paragraph 4(4)) is equal to–

(i) the total amount specified under paragraph (c) or,

(ii) if paragraph (c) is not applicable, the amount specified under paragraph (b) as the amount of the relevant sum to which the hold notice relates.

8(8) In this Part of this Schedule **"the notified sum"**, in relation to a hold notice, means the amount identified as such (or that is to be identified as such) in the notice under sub-paragraph (7).

8(9) The persons mentioned in sub-paragraph (6)(b) are–

(a) in the case of a joint account, any holder of the account other than P, and

(b) any person (not falling within paragraph (a)) who is an interested third party in relation to the affected account,

in respect of whom prescribed information has been provided under sub-paragraph (2)(c) or sufficient information has otherwise been given in the notice under sub-paragraph (2) to enable HMRC to give a notice.

8(10) After the deposit-taker has complied with paragraph 6(1), the deposit-taker may, in relation to any affected account, give a notice to–

(a) P,

(b) if the account is a joint account, any other holder of the account, and

(c) any person (not falling within paragraph (b)) who is an interested third party in relation to the account,

which states that a hold notice has been received by the deposit-taker in respect of the account and the effect of that notice so far as it relates to that account.

8(11) In this Part of this Schedule **"interested third party"**, in relation to a relevant account, means a person other than P who has a beneficial interest in–

(a) an amount standing to the credit of the account, or

(b) an amount which has been transferred from that account to a suspense account.

8(12) But, in relation to a hold notice, an interest which comes into existence after any arrangements under paragraph 6(3) have been put into place is treated as not being a beneficial interest for the purposes of sub-paragraph (11).

Statutory instruments – SI 2015/1986: partly made under para. 8(2)(a), (2)(c), (2)(d) and 8(4)(b).

CANCELLATION OR VARIATION OF EFFECTS OF HOLD NOTICE

9(1) Where a hold notice has been given to a deposit-taker HMRC may, by a notice given to the deposit-taker (a "notice of cancellation or variation")–

(a) cancel the hold notice,

(b) cancel the effect of the hold notice in relation to one or more accounts, or

(c) cancel the effect of the hold notice in relation to any part of the held amount standing to the credit of a particular account or accounts.

In this sub-paragraph references to the effect of a hold notice are to its effect by virtue of paragraph 6(4).

9(2) Where HMRC gives a notice under sub-paragraph (1) it must give a copy of that notice to–

(a) P, and

(b) any other person who HMRC considers is affected by the giving of the notice of cancellation or variation and is–

(i) a person who holds a relevant account of which P is also a holder and in respect of whom prescribed information is provided under paragraph 8(2)(c), or

(ii) an interested third party in relation to a relevant account in respect of whom sufficient information has been given in the notice under paragraph 8(2) to enable HMRC to give a notice.

9(3) Where the deposit-taker is given a notice under sub-paragraph (1), it must as soon as reasonably practicable and, in any event, within the period of 5 working days beginning with the day the notice is given–

(a) if the notice is given under sub-paragraph (1)(a), cancel the arrangements made under paragraph 6(3) as a result of the notice, and

(b) if the notice is given under sub-paragraph (1)(b) or (c), make such adjustments to those arrangements as are necessary to give effect to the notice.

MAKING OBJECTIONS TO HOLD NOTICE

10(1) Where a hold notice is given to a deposit-taker, a person within sub-paragraph (2) may by a notice given to HMRC (a "notice of objection") object against the hold notice.

10(2) The persons who may object are–

(a) P,

(b) any interested third party in relation to an affected account, and

(c) any person (not falling within paragraph (a) or (b)) who is a holder of an affected account which is a joint account,

but only P may object on the ground in sub-paragraph (3)(a).

10(3) An objection may only be made on one or more of the following grounds–

(a) that the debts to which the hold notice relates (see paragraph 8(7)(a)) have been wholly or partly paid,

(b) that at the time when the hold notice was given, either there was no sum that was a relevant sum in relation to P or P did not hold any account with the deposit-taker,

(c) that the hold notice is causing or will cause exceptional hardship to the person making the objection or another person, or

(d) that there is an interested third party in relation to one or more of the affected accounts.

10(4) A notice of objection must state the grounds of the objection.

10(5) Objections under this paragraph may only be made within the period of 30 days beginning with–

(a) in the case of–

(i) P, or

(ii) a person within sub-paragraph (2)(b) or (c) who has not been given a notice under paragraph 8(6)(b),

the day on which a copy of the hold notice is given to P under paragraph 8(6)(a), and

(b) in the case of a person given a notice under paragraph 8(6)(b), the day on which that notice is given.

10(6) Sub-paragraph (5) does not apply if HMRC agree to the notice of objection being given after the end of the period mentioned in that sub-paragraph.

10(7) HMRC must agree to a notice of objection being given after the end of that period if the following conditions are met–

(a) the person seeking to make the objection has made a request in writing to HMRC to agree to the notice of objection being given;

(b) HMRC is satisfied that there was reasonable excuse for not giving the notice before the relevant time limit, and

(c) HMRC is satisfied that the person complied with paragraph (a) without unreasonable delay after the reasonable excuse ceased.

10(8) If a request of the kind referred to in sub-paragraph (7)(a) is made, HMRC must by a notice inform the person making the request whether or not HMRC agrees to the request.

10(9) Nothing in Part 5 of TMA 1970 (appeals and other proceedings) applies to an objection under this paragraph.

CONSIDERATION OF OBJECTIONS

11(1) HMRC must consider any objections made under paragraph 10 within 30 working days of being given the notice of objection.

11(2) Having considered the objections, HMRC must decide whether–

(a) to cancel the hold notice,

(b) to cancel the effect of the hold notice in relation to the held amount, or any part of the held amount, in respect of a particular account or accounts, or

(c) to dismiss the objection.

11(3) HMRC must give a notice stating its decision to–

(a) P,

(b) each person other than P who objected, and

(c) any other person who HMRC considers is affected by the decision and is–

(i) a person who holds a relevant account of which P is also a holder and in respect of whom prescribed information is provided under paragraph 8(2)(c), or

(ii) an interested third party in relation to a relevant account in respect of whom sufficient information has been given in the notice under paragraph 8(2) to enable HMRC to give a notice.

11(4) HMRC must, by a notice to the deposit-taker–

(a) if it makes a decision under sub-paragraph (2)(a), cancel the hold notice;

(b) if it makes a decision under sub-paragraph (2)(b), cancel the effect of the hold notice in relation to the accounts or amounts in question.

11(5) HMRC must give each person to whom HMRC is required to give a notice under sub-paragraph (3) a copy of any notice given to the deposit-taker under sub-paragraph (4).

11(6) Where the deposit-taker is given a notice under sub-paragraph (4), it must as soon as reasonably practicable and, in any event, within the period of 5 working days beginning with the day the notice is given–

(a) if the notice is given under sub-paragraph (4)(a), cancel the arrangements mentioned in paragraph 6(3), or

(b) if the notice is given under sub-paragraph (4)(b), make such adjustments to those arrangements as are necessary to give effect to the notice.

11(7) In this paragraph references to the effect of a hold notice are to its effect by virtue of paragraph 6(4).

APPEALS

12(1) Where HMRC makes a decision under paragraph (b) or (c) of paragraph 11(2), a person within sub-paragraph (2) may appeal against the hold notice.

12(2) The persons who may appeal are–

(a) P,

(b) any interested third party in relation to an affected account, and

(c) any person not falling within paragraph (a) or (b) who is a holder of an affected account which is a joint account.

12(3) An appeal may only be made on one or more of the grounds set out in paragraph 10(3) (and for this purpose the reference in paragraph 10(3)(c) to **"the objection"** is to be read as a reference to the appeal).

12(4) An appeal under sub-paragraph (1) must be made–

(a) in England and Wales, to the county court, and

(b) in Northern Ireland, to a county court.

12(5) An appeal under this paragraph may only be made within the period of 30 days beginning–

(a) in the case of a person given a notice of HMRC's decision under paragraph 11(3), with the day on which that notice is given to that person, and

(b) in the case of any person within sub-paragraph (2)(b) or (c) to whom such a notice has not been given, the day on which P is given such a notice.

12(6) A notice of appeal must state the grounds of appeal.

12(7) On an appeal under this paragraph, the court may–

(a) cancel the hold notice,

(b) cancel the effect of the hold notice in relation to the held amount, or any part of the held amount, in respect of a particular account or accounts, or

(c) dismiss the appeal.

12(8) Where the deposit-taker is served with an order made by the court under sub-paragraph (7)(a) or (b), the deposit-taker must as soon as reasonably practicable and, in any event, within the period of 5 working days beginning with the day the notice is given take such steps as are necessary to give effect to the order.

12(9) Where an appeal on the ground that the hold notice is causing or will cause the person making the appeal or another person exceptional hardship (or a further appeal following such an appeal) is pending, the court to which the appeal is made may, on an application made by the person who made the appeal–

(a) suspend the effect of the hold notice if adequate security is provided in respect of so much of the notified sum as remains unpaid,

(b) suspend the effect of the hold notice in relation to a particular account if adequate security is provided in respect of the held amount in relation to that account, or

(c) suspend the effect of the hold notice in relation to any part of the held amount standing to the credit of a particular account, if adequate security is provided in respect of that part.

12(10) In this paragraph references to the effect of a hold notice are to its effect by virtue of paragraph 6(4).

12(11) Nothing in Part 5 of TMA 1970 (appeals and other proceedings) applies to an appeal under this paragraph.

DEDUCTION NOTICE

13(1) If it appears to HMRC that a person in respect of whom a hold notice given to a deposit-taker is in force–

(a) has failed to pay a relevant sum, and

(b) holds an account (or more than one account) with the deposit-taker in respect of which there is a held amount in relation to that sum,

HMRC may give the deposit-taker a deduction notice in respect of that person.

13(2) A **"deduction notice"** is a notice which–

(a) specifies the name of the person concerned,

(b) specifies one or more affected accounts held by that person with the deposit-taker, and

(c) in relation to each such specified account requires the deposit-taker to deduct and pay a qualifying amount (see sub-paragraph (6)) to the Commissioners by a day specified in the notice.

13(3) Where a deduction notice specifies a particular affected account–

(a) the deduction required to be made in relation to that account by virtue of sub-paragraph (2)(c) must be made from the appropriate account, that is to say–

(i) if the deposit-taker has by virtue of the hold notice transferred an amount from the specified account into a suspense account, that suspense account, or

(ii) otherwise, the specified account, and

(b) the deposit-taker must not during the period in which the deduction notice is in force do anything, or permit anything to be done (except in accordance with paragraph (a)) that would reduce the amount standing to the credit of the appropriate account below the balance required for the purpose of making that deduction.

13(4) A deduction notice must explain the effect of sub-paragraph (3)(b) and paragraph 14 (penalties).

13(5) A deduction notice may not be given in respect of an account unless–

(a) the period for making an objection under paragraph 10 has expired and either no objections were made or any objection made has been decided or withdrawn, and

(b) if objections were made and decided, the period for appealing under paragraph 12 has expired and any appeal or further appeal has been finally determined.

13(6) In this paragraph **"qualifying amount"**, in relation to an affected account, means an amount not exceeding the held amount in relation to that account (as modified, where applicable, under paragraph 9(3)(b), 11(6)(b) or 12(7)(b)).

13(7) The total of the qualifying amounts specified in the deduction notice must not exceed the unpaid amount of the notified sum (see paragraph 8(8)).

13(8) HMRC must–

(a) give a copy of the deduction notice to the person in respect of whom it is given, and

(b) in the case of each account in respect of which the notice is given, give a notice to each person within sub-paragraph (9) explaining that a deduction notice has been given in respect of that account and the effect of the deduction notice so far as it relates to that account.

13(9) The persons mentioned in sub-paragraph (8)(b) are–

(a) if the account is a joint account, each person other than P who is a holder of the account, and

(b) any person (not falling within paragraph (a))–

(i) who is an interested third party in relation to the account whom HMRC knows will be affected by the deduction notice, and

(ii) about whom HMRC has sufficient information to enable it to give the notice under sub-paragraph (8)(b).

13(10) HMRC may, by a notice given to the deposit-taker, amend or cancel the deduction notice, and where it does so it must–

(a) give a copy of the notice under this sub-paragraph to the person in respect of whom the deduction notice was given, and

(b) in the case of each account affected by the amendment or cancellation, give a notice to each person within sub-paragraph (9) explaining the effect of the amendment or cancellation so far as it relates to that account.

13(11) The deduction notice–

(a) comes into force at the time it is given to the deposit-taker, and

(b) ceases to be in force at the time–

(i) the deposit-taker is given a notice cancelling it under sub-paragraph (10), or

(ii) the deposit-taker makes the final payment required by virtue of sub-paragraph (2)(c).

PENALTIES

14(1) This paragraph applies to a deposit-taker who–

(a) fails to comply with an information notice,

(b) fails to comply with a hold notice or a deduction notice,

(c) fails to comply with an obligation under paragraph 8(2) in accordance with paragraph 8(3) (obligation to notify HMRC of effects of hold notice),

(d) fails to comply with an obligation under paragraph 8(4) in accordance with paragraph 8(5) (obligation to notify HMRC if no affected accounts),

(e) fails to comply with an obligation under paragraph 9(3) (obligation to cancel or modify effects of hold notice),

(f) fails to comply with an obligation under paragraph 11(6) (obligation to cancel or adjust arrangements to give effect to HMRC's decision of objection), or

(g) following receipt of an information notice or hold notice in relation to an account or accounts held with the deposit-taker by a person ("the affected person"), makes a disclosure of information to the affected person or any other person in circumstances where that disclosure is likely to prejudice HMRC's ability to use the provisions of this Part of this Schedule to recover a relevant sum owed by the affected person.

14(2) In sub-paragraph (1)(g), the reference to a disclosure of information does not include the giving of a notice in accordance with paragraph 8(10) to the affected person in respect of a hold notice.

14(3) The deposit-taker is liable to a penalty of £300.

14(4) If a failure within sub-paragraph (1)(a) to (f) continues after the day on which notice is given under paragraph 15(1) of a penalty in respect of the failure, the deposit-taker is liable to a further penalty or penalties not exceeding £60 for each subsequent day on which the failure continues.

14(5) A failure by a deposit-taker to do anything required to be done within a limited period of time does not give rise to liability to a penalty under this paragraph if the deposit-taker did it within such further time, if any, as HMRC may have allowed.

14(6) Liability to a penalty under this paragraph does not arise if the person satisfies HMRC or (on an appeal notified to the tribunal) the tribunal that there is a reasonable excuse for the failure or (as the case may be) disclosure.

14(7) For the purposes of this paragraph–

(a) where the deposit-taker relies on any other person to do anything, that is not a reasonable excuse unless the deposit-taker took reasonable care to avoid the failure or disclosure, and

(b) where the deposit-taker had a reasonable excuse for the failure but the excuse has ceased, the deposit-taker is to be treated as having continued to have the excuse if the failure is remedied without unreasonable delay after the excuse ceased.

ASSESSMENT OF PENALTY

15(1) Where a deposit-taker becomes liable to a penalty under paragraph 14–

(a) HMRC must assess the penalty, and

(b) if HMRC does so, it must notify the deposit-taker in writing.

15(2) An assessment of a penalty by virtue of paragraph (a) of paragraph 14(1) must be made within the period of 12 months beginning with the day on which the deposit-taker becomes liable to the penalty.

15(3) An assessment of a penalty under any of paragraphs (b) to (g) of paragraph 14(1) must be made within the period of 12 months beginning with the latest of the following–

(a) the day on which the deposit-taker became liable to the penalty,

(b) the end of the period in which notice of an appeal in respect of the hold notice could have been given, and

(c) if notice of such an appeal is given, the day on which the appeal is finally determined or withdrawn.

APPEAL AGAINST PENALTY

16(1) A deposit-taker may appeal against–

(a) a decision that a penalty is payable by the deposit-taker under paragraph 14, or

(b) a decision as to the amount of such a penalty.

16(2) Notice of an appeal must be given to HMRC before the end of the period of 30 days beginning with the day on which the notification under paragraph 15 was given.

16(3) Notice of an appeal must state the grounds of appeal.

16(4) On an appeal under sub-paragraph (1)(a) that is notified to the tribunal (in accordance with Part 5 of TMA 1970: see below) the tribunal may confirm or cancel the decision.

16(5) On an appeal under sub-paragraph (1)(b) that is notified to the tribunal, the tribunal may–

(a) confirm the decision, or

(b) substitute for the decision another decision that HMRC had power to make.

16(6) Subject to this paragraph and paragraph 17, the provisions of Part 5 of TMA 1970 relating to appeals have effect in relation to appeals under this paragraph as they have effect in relation to an appeal against an assessment to income tax.

ENFORCEMENT OF PENALTY

17(1) A penalty under paragraph 14 must be paid–

(a) before the end of the period of 30 days beginning with the day on which the notification under paragraph 15 was given, or

(b) if notice of an appeal against the penalty is given, before the end of the period of 30 days beginning with the day on which the appeal is finally determined or withdrawn.

17(2) A penalty under paragraph 14 may be enforced as if it were income tax charged in an assessment and due and payable.

PROTECTION OF DEPOSIT-TAKERS ACTING IN GOOD FAITH

18 A deposit-taker is not liable for damages in respect of anything done in good faith for the purposes of complying with a hold notice or a deduction notice.

POWER TO MODIFY AMOUNTS AND TIME LIMITS

19(1) The Commissioners may by regulations amend any of the following provisions by substituting a different amount for the amount for the time being specified there–

(a) paragraph 2(2) (requirement that relevant sum is a minimum amount);

(b) paragraph 4(6) and (8) (threshold for safeguarded amount);

(c) paragraph 14(3) or (4) (level of penalties).

19(2) The Commissioners may by regulations amend any of the following provisions by substituting a different period for the period for the time being specified there–

(a) paragraph 3(4) (time limit for complying with information notices);

(b) paragraph 6(2) (time limit for complying with hold notices);

(c) paragraph 8(3) or (5) (time limit for notifying HMRC of effects of hold notice);

(d) paragraph 9(3) (cancellation etc of hold notice: time limit for cancelling or adjusting arrangements);

(e) paragraph 10(5) (time limit for making objections);

(f) paragraph 11(1) (time limit for consideration of objections);

(g) paragraph 11(6) (consideration of objections: time limit for cancelling or adjusting arrangements);

(h) paragraph 12(8) (appeals: time limit for compliance with court order).

POWER TO MAKE FURTHER PROVISION

20(1) The Commissioners may by regulations make provision supplementing this Part of this Schedule.

20(2) The regulations may, in particular, make provision–

(a) about the manner in which a notice or a copy of a notice is to be given under this Part of this Schedule, or the circumstances in which a notice or a copy of a notice is to be treated as given, for the purposes of this Part of this Schedule;

(b) specifying circumstances in which a notice under this Part of this Schedule may not be given;

(c) specifying descriptions of account in respect of which a hold notice or deduction notice has no effect;

(d) specifying circumstances in which amounts standing to the credit of an account are to be treated as not standing to the credit of the account for the purposes of a hold notice or deduction notice;

(e) about fees a deposit-taker may charge a person in respect of whom a notice is given under this Part of this Schedule towards administrative costs in complying with that notice;

(f) with respect to priority as between a notice under this Part of this Schedule and–

(i) any other such notice, or

(ii) any notice or order under any other enactment.

Statutory instruments – SI 2016/44: made under para. 20(2)(e).

REGULATIONS

21(1) Regulations under this Part of this Schedule may–

(a) make different provision for different purposes,

(b) include supplementary, incidental and consequential provision, or

(c) make transitional provision and savings.

21(2) Regulations under this Part of this Schedule are to be made by statutory instrument.

21(3) A statutory instrument containing only regulations within sub-paragraph (4) is subject to annulment in pursuance of a resolution of the House of Commons.

21(4) The regulations within this sub-paragraph are–

(a) regulations which prescribe information for the purposes of paragraph 3(2) or any provision of paragraph 8,

(b) regulations under paragraph 4(10),

(c) regulations under paragraph (a), (b), (c), (d), (g) or (h) of paragraph 19(2), or

(d) regulations under paragraph 20(2).

21(5) Any other statutory instrument containing regulations under this Part of this Schedule may not be made unless a draft of the instrument has been laid before, and approved by a resolution of, the House of Commons.

JOINT ACCOUNTS

22 In this Part of this Schedule a reference to an account held by a person includes a reference to a joint account held by that person and one or more other persons.

DEFINED TERMS

23(1) In this Part of this Schedule–

"affected account" has the meaning given by paragraph 6(7);

"the Commissioners" means the Commissioners for Her Majesty's Revenue and Customs;

"contract settlement" means an agreement made in connection with any person's liability to make a payment to the Commissioners under or by virtue of an enactment;

"deduction notice" has the meaning given by paragraph 13;

"deposit-taker" means a person who may lawfully accept deposits in the United Kingdom in the course of a business (see sub-paragraph (2));

"HMRC" means Her Majesty's Revenue and Customs;

"hold notice" has the meaning given by paragraph 4;

"information notice" has the meaning given by paragraph 3;

"interested third party", in relation to a relevant account, has the meaning given by paragraph 8(11);

"joint account", in relation to a person, means an account held by the person and one or more other persons;

"notice" means notice in writing;

"notified sum", in relation to a hold notice, has the meaning given by paragraph 8(8);

"prescribed" means prescribed by regulations made by the Commissioners;

"relevant account" (in relation to a hold notice) has the meaning given by paragraph 6(6);

"relevant sum", in relation to a person, has the meaning given by paragraph 2(1);

"the safeguarded amount" (in relation to a hold notice) means the amount specified as the safeguarded amount in the notice (see paragraph 4(2)(c));

"the specified amount" (in relation to a hold notice) means the amount specified as such in the notice (see paragraph 4(2)(b));

"suspense account" has the meaning given by paragraph 6(3)(b)(i);

"the tribunal" means the First-tier Tribunal;

"working day" means a day other than–

(a) Saturday or Sunday,

(b) Christmas Eve, Christmas Day or Good Friday, or

(c) a day which is a bank holiday under the Banking and Financial Dealings Act 1971 in England and Wales or Northern Ireland.

23(2) The definition of **"deposit-taker"** in sub-paragraph (1) is to be read with–

(a) section 22 of the Financial Services and Markets Act 2000 (regulated activities),

(b) any relevant order under that section, and

(c) Schedule 2 to that Act.

Statutory instruments – SI 2015/1986: partly made under para. 23(1).

EXTENT

24 This Part of this Schedule extends to England and Wales and Northern Ireland.

FINANCE ACT 2016

(2016 Chapter 24)

[*15th September 2016*]

ARRANGEMENT OF SECTIONS

PART 11 – ADMINISTRATION, ENFORCEMENT AND SUPPLEMENTARY POWERS

JUDGMENT DEBTS

PART 13 – FINAL

PART 11 – ADMINISTRATION, ENFORCEMENT AND SUPPLEMENTARY POWERS

JUDGMENT DEBTS

170 Rate of interest applicable to judgment debts etc: Scotland

170(1) This section applies if–

(a) a sum is payable to or by the Commissioners under a decree or extract issued in any court proceedings relating to a taxation matter (a "tax-related judgment debt"), and

(b) interest in relation to the tax-related judgment debt is included in or payable under the decree or extract.

170(2) In a case where the rate of interest in relation to the tax-related judgment debt is stated in the decree or extract, the rate stated in relation to that debt may not exceed (and may not be capable of exceeding)–

(a) in the case of a sum payable to the Commissioners, the late payment interest rate, and

(b) in the case of a sum payable by the Commissioners, the special repayment rate.

170(3) In a case where the rate of interest in relation to the tax-related judgment debt is not stated in the decree or extract but provided for by an enactment or rule of court (whenever passed or made), that enactment or rule is to have effect in relation to the debt as if for the rate for which it provides there were substituted–

(a) in the case of a sum payable to the Commissioners, the late payment interest rate, and

(b) in the case of a sum payable by the Commissioners, the special repayment rate.

170(4) This section has effect in relation to interest for periods beginning on or after the day on which this Act is passed, regardless of–

(a) the date of the decree or extract in question, and

(b) whether interest begins to run on or after the day on which this Act is passed, or began to run before that date.

170(5) In this section–

"the Commissioners" means the Commissioners for Her Majesty's Revenue and Customs;

"enactment" includes an Act of the Scottish Parliament or an instrument made under such an Act;

"late payment interest rate" means the rate provided for in regulations made by the Treasury under section 103(1) of FA 2009;

"special repayment rate" has the same meaning as in section 52 of F(No. 2)A 2015 (and subsections (7) to (10) of that section apply for the purposes of this section as they apply for the purposes of that section);

"taxation matter" means anything the collection and management of which is the responsibility of the Commissioners (or was the responsibility of the Commissioners of Inland Revenue or Commissioners of Customs and Excise);

"working day" means any day other than a non-business day as defined in section 92 of the Bills of Exchange Act 1882.

170(6) This section extends to Scotland only.

171 Rate of interest applicable to judgment debts etc: Northern Ireland

171(1) This section applies if a sum payable to or by the Commissioners under a judgment or order given or made in any court proceedings relating to a taxation matter (a "tax-related judgment debt") carries interest.

171(2) In a case where the rate of interest is specified in the judgment (in the case of the High Court) or directed by the judge (in the case of a county court), the rate specified or directed in relation to that debt may not exceed (and may not be capable of exceeding)–

(a) in the case of a sum payable to the Commissioners, the late payment interest rate, and

(b) in the case of a sum payable by the Commissioners, the special repayment rate.

171(3) In a case where the rate of interest in relation to the tax-related judgment debt is not specified in the judgment or directed by the judge but provided for by an enactment or rule of court (whenever passed or made), that enactment or rule is to have effect in relation to the debt as if for the rate for which it provides there were substituted–

(a) in the case of a sum payable to the Commissioners, the late payment interest rate, and

(b) in the case of a sum payable by the Commissioners, the special repayment rate.

171(4) This section has effect in relation to interest for periods beginning on or after the day on which this Act is passed, regardless of–

(a) the date of the judgment or order in question, and

(b) whether interest begins to run on or after the day on which this Act is passed, or began to run before that date.

171(5) In this section–

"the Commissioners" means the Commissioners for Her Majesty's Revenue and Customs;

"enactment" includes Northern Ireland legislation or an instrument made under such legislation;

"late payment interest rate" means the rate provided for in regulations made by the Treasury under section 103(1) of FA 2009;

"special repayment rate" has the same meaning as in section 52 of F(No. 2)A 2015 (and subsections (7) to (10) of that section apply for the purposes of this section as they apply for the purposes of that section);

"taxation matter" means anything the collection and management of which is the responsibility of the Commissioners (or was the responsibility of the Commissioners of Inland Revenue or Commissioners of Customs and Excise);

"working day" means any day other than a non-business day as defined in section 92 of the Bills of Exchange Act 1882.

171(6) This section extends to Northern Ireland only.

172 Rate of interest applicable to judgment debts etc: England and Wales

172(1) [Amends F(No. 2)A 2015, s. 52(15).]

172(2) This section has effect in relation to interest for periods beginning on or after the day on which this Act is passed, regardless of–

(a) the date of the judgment or order in question, and

(b) whether interest begins to run on or after the day on which this Act is passed, or began to run before that date.

172(3) This section extends to England and Wales only.

PART 13 – FINAL

190 Interpretation

190 In this Act–

"ALDA 1979" means the Alcoholic Liquor Duties Act 1979;

"CAA 2001" means the Capital Allowances Act 2001;

"CEMA 1979" means the Customs and Excise Management Act 1979;

"CTA 2009" means the Corporation Tax Act 2009;

"CTA 2010" means the Corporation Tax Act 2010;

"FA", followed by a year, means the Finance Act of that year;

"F(No. 2)A", followed by a year means the Finance (No. 2) Act of that year;

"F(No. 3)A", followed by a year, means the Finance (No. 3) Act of that year;

"HODA 1979" means the Hydrocarbon Oil Duties Act 1979;

"ICTA" means the Income and Corporation Taxes Act 1988;

"IHTA 1984" means the Inheritance Tax Act 1984;

"ITA 2007" means the Income Tax Act 2007;

"ITEPA 2003" means the Income Tax (Earnings and Pensions) Act 2003;

"ITTOIA 2005" means the Income Tax (Trading and Other Income) Act 2005;

"OTA 1975" means the Oil Taxation Act 1975;

"TCGA 1992" means the Taxation of Chargeable Gains Act 1992;

"TIOPA 2010" means the Taxation (International and Other Provisions) Act 2010;

"TMA 1970" means the Taxes Management Act 1970;

"TPDA 1979" means the Tobacco Products Duty Act 1979;

"VATA 1994" means the Value Added Tax Act 1994;

"VERA 1994" means the Vehicle Excise and Registration Act 1994.

191 Short title

191 This Act may be cited as the Finance Act 2016.

FINANCE (NO. 2) ACT 2017

(2017 Chapter 32)

[*16th November 2017*]

ARRANGEMENT OF SECTIONS

PART 4 – ADMINISTRATION, AVOIDANCE AND ENFORCEMENT

PART 5 – FINAL

SCHEDULES

PART 4 – ADMINISTRATION, AVOIDANCE AND ENFORCEMENT

REPORTING AND RECORD-KEEPING

61 Digital reporting and record-keeping for income tax etc: further amendments

61(1) Schedule 14 contains provision amending TMA 1970 and other Acts.

61(2) The Commissioners for Her Majesty's Revenue and Customs may by regulations amend or modify any provision of the Taxes Acts in consequence of the provision made by section 60 or Schedule 14.

61(3) Regulations under subsection (2) may make transitional, transitory or saving provision.

61(4) Regulations under subsection (2) must be made by statutory instrument.

61(5) A statutory instrument containing regulations under subsection (2) may not be made unless a draft of the instrument has been laid before, and approved by a resolution of, the House of Commons.

61(6) Subsections (1) to (5) and Schedule 14 come into force on such day as the Treasury may by regulations made by statutory instrument appoint.

61(7) Regulations under subsection (6) may appoint different days for different purposes.

ENQUIRIES

63 Partial closure notices

63 Schedule 15 makes provision for partial closure notices in respect of enquiries under sections 9A, 12ZM and 12AC of TMA 1970 and Schedule 18 to FA 1998.

PART 5 – FINAL

71 *Interpretation*

71 In this Act the following abbreviations are references to the following Acts.

CAA 2001	Capital Allowances Act 2001
CEMA 1979	Customs and Excise Management Act 1979
CTA 2009	Corporation Tax Act 2009

CTA 2010	Corporation Tax Act 2010
CT(NI)A 2015	Corporation Tax (Northern Ireland) Act 2015
FA, followed by a year	Finance Act of that year
F(No. 2)A, followed by a year	Finance (No. 2) Act of that year
F(No. 3)A, followed by a year	Finance (No. 3) Act of that year
ICTA	Income and Corporation Taxes Act 1988
IHTA 1984	Inheritance Tax Act 1984
ITA 2007	Income Tax Act 2007
ITEPA 2003	Income Tax (Earnings and Pensions) Act 2003
ITTOIA 2005	Income Tax (Trading and Other Income) Act 2005
OTA 1975	Oil Taxation Act 1975
TCGA 1992	Taxation of Chargeable Gains Act 1992
TIOPA 2010	Taxation (International and Other Provisions) Act 2010
TMA 1970	Taxes Management Act 1970
TPDA 1979	Tobacco Products Duty Act 1979
VATA 1994	Value Added Tax Act 1994

72 Short title

72 This Act may be cited as the Finance (No. 2) Act 2017.

SCHEDULES

SCHEDULE 14 – DIGITAL REPORTING AND RECORD-KEEPING FOR INCOME TAX ETC: FURTHER AMENDMENTS

Section 61

Part 2 – Amendments of Other Acts

TAX CREDITS ACT 2002

34 In section 19(4)(a) of the Tax Credits Act 2002 (power to enquire) for "by section 8 of the Taxes Management Act 1970 (c. 9) to make a return" substitute "to make a return under section 8 of the Taxes Management Act 1970".

SCHEDULE 15 – PARTIAL CLOSURE NOTICES

Section 63

TAX CREDITS ACT 2002

35(1) Section 20 of the Tax Credits Act 2002 (decisions on discovery) is amended as follows.

35(2) In subsection (2)(f), for "a closure notice" substitute "a partial or final closure notice".

35(3) In subsection (3)(b), at the end insert "as specified in subsection (1)".

COMMENCEMENT

44 The amendments made by this Schedule have effect in relation to an enquiry under section 9A, 12ZM or 12AC of TMA 1970 or Schedule 18 to FA 1998 where–

(a) notice of the enquiry is given on or after the day on which this Act is passed, or

(b) the enquiry is in progress immediately before that day.

TAX CREDITS STATUTORY INSTRUMENTS

Table of Contents

Those statutory instruments listed below which contain substantive provisions are reproduced in the following pages. Statutory instruments which do no more than amend other instruments are not reproduced; the amendments made by them have been consolidated in the relevant amended regulations. They are, however, listed below for convenience.

STATUTORY INSTRUMENTS Page

CHRONOLOGICAL LISTING

continued over

continued over

continued over

continued over

continued over

		Page
2017/781	Tax Credits (Exercise of Functions in relation to Northern Ireland and Notices for Recovery of Tax Credit Overpayments) Order 2017 (amends TCA 2002, s. 28 and 29 and SI 2014/1230, reg. 12). Not reproduced.	
2018/65	Universal Credit (Miscellaneous Amendments, Saving and Transitional Provision) Regulations 2018 (amends SI 2014/1230). Not reproduced.	
2018/344	Tax Credits and Guardian's Allowance Up-rating etc Regulations 2018 (amends SI 2002/2005 and SI 2002/2007). Not reproduced.	
2018/365	Tax Credits and Childcare (Miscellaneous Amendments) Regulations 2018 (amends SI 2002//2005, SI 2002/2006 and SI 2002/2014). Not reproduced.	
2018/378	Secretaries of State for Health and Social Care and for Housing, Communities and Local Government and Transfer of Functions (Commonhold Land) Order 2018 (amends SI 2002/2006, reg. 19). Not reproduced.	

ALPHABETICAL LISTING

continued over

continued over

TC Statutory Instruments

continued over

continued over

continued over

TAX CREDIT (NEW CATEGORY OF CHILD CARE PROVIDER) REGULATIONS 1999

(SI 1999/3110 and partially revoked by SI 2007/2480)

Made on 18 November 1999. Operative from 2 December 1999. Whereas a draft of this instrument was laid before Parliament in accordance with s. 15(5) of the Tax Credits Act 1999 and approved by resolution of each House of Parliament; Now, therefore, the Secretary of State for Education and Employment, in exercise of the powers conferred by s. 15(1) and 15(4) of the Tax Credits Act 1999, hereby makes the following Regulations:

History – SI 1999/3110 revoked to the extent that they prescribe a description of persons by whom child care is provided, and whose charges fall to be taken into account in computing the child care element of a working tax credit by SI 2007/2480, reg. 2, with effect from 1 October 2007.

CITATION, EXTENT AND COMMENCEMENT

1(1) These Regulations may be cited as the Tax Credit (New Category of Child Care Provider) Regulations 1999 and shall come into force on the fourteenth day after the day on which they were made.

1(2) Paragraph (3) below applies if, before these Regulations come into force, the functions of the Secretary of State under section 15 of the Tax Credits Act 1999 in relation to the accreditation of organisations in accordance with criteria determined by or under a scheme made under that section have become vested in the National Assembly for Wales by virtue of an Order made under section 22 of the Government of Wales Act 1998.

1(3) Where this paragraph applies, references in these regulations to the Secretary of State shall be read in relation to Wales as references to the National Assembly for Wales.

INTERPRETATION

2(1) In these Regulations–

"accredited" in relation to an organisation means accredited by the Secretary of State in accordance with the criteria set out in these Regulations;

"child care provider" means a person who looks after one or more children over the age of seven and under the age of fifteen (under the age of sixteen if the child is disabled) for reward on domestic premises, or a person who provides day care for such children on premises (other than domestic premises) for a period, or for a total of the periods during which children are looked after in any day, exceeding two hours;

"disabled" in relation to a child under the age of sixteen means, a child–

(a) in respect of whom disability living allowance is payable, or has ceased to be payable solely because he is a patient within the meaning of regulation 10 of the Disability Working Allowance (General) Regulations 1991;

(b) who is registered as blind in a register compiled by a local authority under section 29 of the National Assistance Act 1948 (welfare services) or, in Scotland, has been certified as blind and in consequence he is registered as blind in a register maintained by or on behalf of a regional or islands council; or

(c) who ceased to be registered as blind in such a register within the 28 weeks immediately preceding the date of claim;

"disabled person's tax credit" shall be construed in accordance with section 1(1) of the Tax Credits Act 1999;

"system" means the quality assurance system operated by an accredited organisation for assessing the quality of child care provided and for approving such child care for the purposes of determining the amount of working families' tax credit or disabled person's tax credit available to users of such child care;

"working families' tax credit" shall be construed in accordance with section 1(1) of the Tax Credits Act 1999.

2(2) Except where the context otherwise requires, any reference in these Regulations to a regulation or Schedule is a reference to a regulation contained herein or to a Schedule hereto, any reference in a regulation or Schedule to a paragraph is a reference to a paragraph of the regulation or Schedule, and any reference in a paragraph to a sub-paragraph is a reference to a sub-paragraph thereof.

SCHEME FOR NEW CATEGORY OF CHILD CARE PROVIDERS

3 These Regulations establish a scheme for establishing a new category of persons whose charges for providing child care are to be taken into account for the purposes of determining the appropriate amount of working families' tax credit or disabled person's tax credit for the purposes of section 15 of the Tax Credits Act 1999.

REQUIREMENTS FOR THE SCHEME

4 No person shall fall within the new category unless he is approved by an accredited organisation.

CRITERIA FOR ACCREDITATION

5 The Secretary of State shall accredit an organisation for the purposes of the scheme if in his opinion it satisfies the following criteria–

(a) it operates a system for approving child care providers that meets the requirements set out in regulation 6 and is satisfactory to the Secretary of State;

(b) it has the ability to ensure the quality of child care provided by persons which it approves;

(c) it satisfies such other conditions relating to the system as the Secretary of State considers necessary and expedient; and

(d) it operates an equal opportunities policy for its employees, in relation to the services it provides, to the quality assurance scheme and to the training of assessors.

REQUIREMENTS OF THE SYSTEM

6 The system shall include the matters set out in the First Schedule.

APPLICATION FOR ACCREDITATION

7 An organisation seeking accreditation shall apply to the Secretary of State in a form substantially corresponding to that set out in Part I of the Second Schedule, containing the information therein specified and dated and authenticated by the signature of a duly authorised officer of the organisation.

GRANT OF ACCREDITATION

8(1) Subject to the following paragraphs of this regulation, where an organisation applies to the Secretary of State for accreditation he may–

(a) reject the application, or

(b) grant the accreditation on such conditions, if any, as he thinks necessary or expedient.

8(2) Before making a decision in accordance with paragraph (1), the Secretary of State may require further evidence from the organisation, and may consult any person as he thinks fit.

8(3) Before rejecting an application under paragraph (1), the Secretary of State shall advise the organisation in writing that he is minded not to accredit the organisation, giving his reasons, and inviting the organisation to make representations in support of its application within 28 days after the notification is issued.

8(4) The Secretary of State shall consider any representations made by the organisation before making his decision under paragraph (1).

8(5) Where the Secretary of State is minded to grant accreditation in principle under paragraph (1)(b), he shall notify the organisation in writing that he is minded to grant the accreditation on the conditions set out in the notification.

8(6) When the organisation receives a notice issued under paragraph (5) it shall within 28 days either

(a) advise the Secretary of State in writing that it accepts the conditions proposed; or

(b) make representations in support of its objections to the conditions proposed.

8(7) The Secretary of State shall consider any representation made by the organisation about the conditions, before he makes his decision under paragraph (1).

8(8) When the Secretary of State makes his decision under paragraph (1) he shall notify the organisation concerned in writing.

8(9) *When the Secretary of State* decides to accredit an organisation, the notice in writing issued under paragraph (8) shall specify the conditions of accreditation, and a copy of the notice of accreditation shall be sent to the Inland Revenue.

8(10) Accreditation shall be for a period of three years and shall be conditional upon the organisation continuing to meet the conditions and criteria for accreditation.

RENEWAL OF ACCREDITATION

9(1) If an accredited organisation wishes to renew its accreditation it must, during the period of two months prior to the expiry of its accreditation, make an application to renew in a form substantially corresponding to that set out in Parts I and II of the Second Schedule.

9(2) Where an organisation applies to the Secretary of State for renewal of an accreditation he may–

(a) reject the application, or

(b) grant the accreditation on such conditions, if any, as he thinks fit.

9(3) The Secretary of State shall follow the procedures set out in regulation 8(2) to (8) when making his decision, and may vary the conditions imposed on the accreditation.

9(4) Any renewed accreditation shall be for a period of three years from the expiry of the earlier accreditation, and shall be conditional upon the organisation continuing to meet the conditions and criteria for accreditation.

9(5) Until the determination of an application under paragraph (1), the accreditation shall continue in force, not withstanding that apart from this paragraph it would expire earlier.

WITHDRAWAL OF ACCREDITATION OR VARIATION OF CONDITIONS OF ACCREDITATION

10(1) Subject to the following paragraphs of this regulation, the Secretary of State may withdraw accreditation or vary the conditions of accreditation if he is satisfied that–

(a) the organisation no longer meets the criteria for accreditation set out in regulation 5; or

(b) the organisation has acted improperly.

10(2) The Secretary of State shall notify the organisation in writing if he is minded to withdraw the accreditation or vary the conditions of accreditation, giving his reasons and inviting the organisation to make representations within 28 days after the notice is issued.

10(3) The Secretary of State shall consider any representation before making his decision under paragraph (1).

10(4) When the Secretary of State makes his decision under paragraph (1), he shall notify the organisation concerned in writing.

10(5) If the decision is to withdraw the accreditation or vary the conditions of accreditation, such decision shall become effective 28 days after the date on which the organisation is informed of the decision, but otherwise the decision shall take effect when it is made.

10(6) If the Secretary of State is of the opinion that it is necessary to suspend the organisation's accreditation for the period during which he is considering withdrawing the accreditation or varying the conditions of accreditation, he may do so, provided that he has notified the organisation of this in the notice issued under paragraph (2).

10(7) If the accreditation is suspended in accordance with paragraph (6), the organisation shall not approve any child care providers during the period of the suspension, without prejudice to the validity of approvals already given.

REQUIREMENTS DURING THE PERIOD OF ACCREDITATION

11 During the period for which an organisation is accredited that organisation shall–

(a) provide, to the Inland Revenue or to the Secretary of State, such information as is requested about child care providers that it has approved under its system for the purposes of checking eligibility for child care tax credit or for insuring the effective operation of the system;

(b) maintain adequate records about the approval process it operates, including evidence supplied by child care providers seeking approval under the system, which shall be produced, on request, to the Secretary of State;

(c) allow the Secretary of State or his nominee to attend meetings of the panel awarding approval to child care providers, and to accompany assessors on visits to child care providers during the process of assessment and on any subsequent checks once the provider is approved under the system.

REQUIREMENTS DURING THE PERIOD OF APPROVAL

12 During the period for which he is approved by an accredited organisation a child care provider shall allow quality assessors and representatives of the accredited organisation, of the Secretary of State and of the Inland Revenue access at any reasonable time to the child care provider's premises and records.

CONSEQUENCES FOR CHILD CARE PROVIDERS APPROVED BY ORGANISATION WHEN ACCREDITATION IS WITHDRAWN OR EXPIRES

13(1) When an organisation's accreditation is withdrawn or expires without being renewed the Secretary of State may, by notice, substitute an alternative accredited organisation to replace the organisation which no longer has a valid accreditation.

13(2) The child care provider who has been approved by the organisation that no longer has a valid accreditation shall retain his approval for the remainder of the period of approval, unless the Secretary of State is of the opinion that such approval was improperly granted.

13(3) Where the Secretary of State is of such an opinion he shall serve a notice on the child care provider terminating the approval.

CRITERIA FOR APPROVAL OF CHILD CARE PROVIDER

14 An accredited organisation shall approve a child care provider who meets the criteria set out in the system, which criteria shall include those matters set out in the Third Schedule.

GRANT TO ACCREDITED ORGANISATION

15 The Secretary of State may make payments by way of grant or otherwise to an accredited organisation in respect of costs incurred by the organisation in carrying out its functions.

TAX CREDIT (NEW CATEGORY OF CHILD CARE PROVIDER) REGULATIONS 2002

(SI 2002/1417)

Made on 22 May 2002 by the Secretary of State for Defence, in exercise of the powers conferred by s. 15(1), (2) and (4) of the Tax Credits Act 1999.

CITATION AND COMMENCEMENT

1 These Regulations may be cited as the Tax Credit (New Category of Child Care Provider) Regulations 2002 and shall come into force on 20th June 2002.

INTERPRETATION

2 In these Regulations–

(a) where the doing of anything is required to be in writing and authenticated by a signature, the use of electronic communication is not permitted; and

(b) **"accredited"** in relation to an organisation means accredited by the Secretary of State in accordance with the criteria set out in these Regulations;

"child care provider" means a person who looks after one or more children under the age of 15 (under the age of 16 if the child is disabled) outside the United Kingdom for reward;

"disabled" in relation to a child under the age of 16 means a child–

(i) in respect of whom disability living allowance is payable, or has ceased to be payable solely because he is a patient within the meaning of regulation 10 of the Disability Working Allowance (General) Regulations 1991;

(ii) who is registered as blind in a register compiled by a local authority under section 29 of the National Assistance Act 1948 (welfare services) or, in Scotland, has been certified as blind and in consequence he is registered as blind in a register maintained by or on behalf of a regional or islands council; or

(iii) who ceased to be registered as blind in such a register within the 28 weeks immediately preceding the date of claim;

"electronic communication" means electronic communication as defined in section 15 of the Electronic Communications Act 2000;

"scheme" means the scheme made by these Regulations for establishing a new category of persons whose charges for providing child care are to be taken into account for the purposes set out in section 15(1) of the Tax Credits Act 1999;

"system" means the system operated by an accredited organisation for approving child care providers and assessing the quality of child care provided by them.

REQUIREMENTS OF THE SCHEME

3 A person shall only fall within the category of persons established by the scheme–

(a) if he is approved by an accredited organisation; and

(b) in relation to the provision by him of child care outside the United Kingdom.

CRITERIA FOR ACCREDITATION

4 The Secretary of State may accredit an organisation for the purposes of the scheme if in his opinion it satisfies the following criteria–

(a) it operates a system that includes the matters set out in Schedule 1 to these Regulations;

(b) it has the ability to ensure that the quality of child care provided by persons which it approves meets the criteria referred to in regulation 12 of and set out in Schedule 3 to these Regulations;

(c) it operates an equal opportunities policy for its employees in relation to the services it provides, to the system and to the training of assessors; and

(d) if it proposes to charge child care providers fees for its services, those fees are reasonable in the opinion of the Secretary of State.

APPLICATION FOR ACCREDITATION

5(1) An organisation seeking accreditation shall make an application to the Secretary of State which shall include the information specified in Part I of Schedule 2 to these Regulations.

5(2) An application for accreditation shall be in writing, dated and authenticated by the signature of a duly authorised officer of the organisation.

GRANT OF ACCREDITATION

6(1) Subject to the following paragraphs of this regulation, where an organisation applies to the Secretary of State for accreditation, he may–

(a) reject the application; or

(b) grant the accreditation on such conditions, if any, as he thinks necessary or expedient.

6(2) Before making a decision under paragraph (1), the Secretary of State may require further evidence from the organisation and may consult any person as he thinks fit.

6(3) Where the Secretary of State is minded to reject an application under paragraph (1)(a) he shall notify the organisation of this in writing, giving his reasons and inviting the organisation to make representations in support of its application within 28 days starting with the date of receipt of the notification.

6(4) The organisation may, within 28 days starting with the date of receipt of a notification under paragraph (3), make written representations to the Secretary of State in support of its application.

6(5) The Secretary of State shall consider any representations made by the organisation in accordance with paragraph (4) before making his decision under paragraph (1).

6(6) Where the Secretary of State is minded to grant accreditation on conditions under paragraph 1(b), he shall notify the organisation of this in writing, setting out the conditions he is minded to impose.

6(7) The organisation shall, within 28 days starting with the date of receipt of a notification under paragraph (6)–

(a) advise the Secretary of State in writing that it accepts the conditions proposed; or

(b) make written representations in support of its objections to the conditions proposed.

6(8) The Secretary of State shall consider any representations made by the organisation in accordance with paragraph (7)(b) before making his decision under paragraph (1).

6(9) When the Secretary of State has made his decision under paragraph (1) he shall notify the organisation concerned of his decision in writing. Where the decision is to grant the accreditation on conditions the notification shall specify those conditions.

6(10) Where the Secretary of State's decision is to accredit an organisation, a copy of the notice referred to in paragraph (9) shall be sent to the Inland Revenue.

6(11) Accreditation shall be for a period of three years and shall be conditional upon the organisation continuing to meet the criteria for accreditation set out in regulation 4 above and any conditions to which its accreditation is subject under paragraph 1(b) of this regulation.

RENEWAL OF ACCREDITATION

7(1) If an accredited organisation wishes to renew its accreditation it shall, during the period of two months prior to the expiry of its accreditation, make an application to the Secretary of State to renew its accreditation.

7(2) An application by an organisation to renew its accreditation shall include the information specified in Parts I and II of Schedule 2 to these Regulations.

7(3) An application by an organisation to renew its accreditation shall be in writing, dated and authenticated by the signature of a duly authorised officer of the organisation.

7(4) Subject to the following paragraphs of this regulation, where an organisation applies to the Secretary of State for renewal of its accreditation, he may –

(a) reject the application; or

(b) renew the accreditation on such conditions, if any, as he thinks necessary or expedient.

7(5) The Secretary of State may vary any conditions imposed on a previous accreditation.

7(6) The procedures set out in regulation 6(2) to (10) above shall apply to an application for renewal of accreditation as they apply to an application for the grant of accreditation, but for this purpose references in regulation 6 to a decision under paragraph (1) of that regulation shall be taken to be references to a decision under paragraph (4) of this regulation.

7(7) Any renewed accreditation shall be for a period of three years from the expiry of the earlier accreditation and shall be conditional upon the organisation continuing to meet the criteria for accreditation set out in regulation 4 above and any conditions to which its accreditation is subject under paragraph 4(b) of this regulation.

7(8) Where an organisation has made an application for renewal of its accreditation its accreditation shall remain in force until the Secretary of State has made a decision under paragraph 4 of this regulation, notwithstanding that apart from this paragraph it would expire earlier.

WITHDRAWAL OF ACCREDITATION OR VARIATION OF CONDITIONS OF ACCREDITATION

8(1) Subject to the following paragraphs of this regulation, the Secretary of State may withdraw an organisation's accreditation or vary the conditions of its accreditation if he is satisfied that–

(a) the organisation no longer meets the criteria for accreditation set out in regulation 4 above;

(b) the organisation has breached one or more of the conditions of its accreditation; or

(c) the organisation has acted improperly.

8(2) The Secretary of State shall notify the organisation in writing if he is minded to withdraw its accreditation or vary the conditions of its accreditation, giving his reasons for this and inviting the organisation to make representations in response to this notice within 28 days starting with the date of receipt of the notification.

8(3) The organisation may, within 28 days starting with the date of receipt of a notification under paragraph (2), make written representations to the Secretary of State in response to the notice.

8(4) The Secretary of State shall consider any representations made by the organisation in accordance with paragraph (3) before making a decision whether or not to withdraw its accreditation or vary the conditions of its accreditation.

8(5) When the Secretary of State has made a decision whether or not to withdraw an organisation's accreditation or vary the conditions of its accreditation he shall notify the organisation of his decision in writing.

8(6) Where the Secretary of State's decision is to withdraw an organisation's accreditation or vary the conditions of its accreditation, such decision shall take effect after 28 days starting with the date on which the organisation is notified of the decision.

8(7) The Secretary of State may by written notice suspend an organisation's accreditation for the period during which he is considering withdrawing its accreditation or varying the conditions of its accreditation if he considers this to be necessary. The suspension shall take effect from the date that the organisation receives this notification.

8(8) During the period in which an organisation's accreditation is suspended under paragraph (7) the organisation shall not approve any child care providers, but the suspension shall not affect the validity of approvals already given.

8(9) Where the Secretary of State decides to withdraw an organisation's accreditation or vary the conditions of its accreditation a copy of the notice referred to in paragraph 5 shall be sent to the Inland Revenue.

REQUIREMENTS DURING THE PERIOD OF ACCREDITATION

9 During the period for which an organisation is accredited that organisation shall–

(a) provide to the Inland Revenue such information as it may request about child care providers that the organisation has approved under its system for the purpose of checking eligibility for child care tax credit;

(b) provide to the Secretary of State such information as he may request about child care providers that the organisation has approved under its system for the purpose of ensuring the effective operation of the system;

(c) maintain adequate records about the approval process it operates, including evidence supplied by child care providers seeking approval under the system, which shall be produced to the Secretary of State on his request;

(d) allow the Secretary of State or his nominee to attend meetings of the panel awarding approval to child care providers, and to accompany assessors on visits to child care providers during the process of assessment and on any subsequent checks once the provider has been approved under the system.

REQUIREMENTS DURING THE PERIOD OF APPROVAL

10 During the period for which a child care provider is approved by an accredited organisation he shall allow quality assessors and representatives of the accredited organisation, the Secretary of State and the Inland Revenue access at any reasonable time to his premises and records.

CONSEQUENCES FOR CHILD CARE PROVIDERS APPROVED BY AN ORGANISATION WHOSE ACCREDITATION IS WITHDRAWN OR EXPIRES

11(1) When an organisation's accreditation is withdrawn or expires without being renewed the Secretary of State may, with effect from the date of that withdrawal or expiry, replace that organisation with an alternative accredited organisation by notice in writing to–

(a) the child care providers approved by the organisation whose accreditation is withdrawn or has expired; and

(b) the alternative accredited organisation.

11(2) A child care provider who has been approved by an organisation whose accreditation has been withdrawn or has expired without being renewed shall retain his approval for the remainder of the period of approval, unless the Secretary of State is of the opinion that such approval was improperly granted.

11(3) Where the Secretary of State is of such an opinion he shall serve a notice in writing on the child care provider terminating the approval, and the termination shall take effect from the date that the child care provider receives the notice.

CRITERIA FOR APPROVAL OF CHILD CARE PROVIDER

12 An accredited organisation shall approve a child care provider who meets the criteria set out in its system, which criteria shall include those matters set out in Schedule 3 to these Regulations.

GRANT TO ACCREDITED ORGANISATION

13 The Secretary of State may make payment by way of grant or otherwise to an accredited organisation in respect of costs incurred by the organisation in carrying out its functions.

SCHEDULES

SCHEDULE 1 – THE SYSTEM

Regulation 4

MATTERS THAT SHALL BE INCLUDED IN THE SYSTEM

The system shall–

1 establish an awarding panel, to include at least one individual with expertise in out of school child care provision, to approve child care providers;

2 set out the criteria, including those matters set out in Schedule 3, to be met by child care providers in order for them to be approved;

3 set out the procedures for applying for approval;

4 set out the documentary evidence a child care provider must produce to demonstrate that the criteria he is required to meet are met;

5 provide for a quality assessor to assess the extent to which the criteria are met by the child care provider including by visiting the premises and interviewing staff, parents and children as he sees fit;

6 ensure that any quality assessor has been properly trained in the requirements of the system

7 ensure that a quality assessor does not work and has not worked in any way with any child care provider he assesses (other than in assessing the quality of child care provided) and has not entered into any financial arrangement with the child care provider being assessed, other than any payment to cover the costs of the assessment;

8 provide for the awarding panel to approve or reject an application for approval after considering the evidence provided by the child care provider applying for approval, the report of the quality assessor and such other information as the panel thinks fit;

9 provide for a method of appeal against any refusal to approve a child care provider, involving independent arbitration;

10 fix a period of time (not exceeding two years) for which any approval will last;

11 provide for written confirmation to be given to the child care provider of any approval granted, the period for which approval lasts and the reference number allocated to that child care provider;

12 provide for a complaints procedure under which all complaints will be investigated and, if appropriate, approval of a child care provider will be withdrawn;

13 include a requirement that any complaints about approved child care providers are to be referred to the accredited organisation.

SCHEDULE 2 – THE APPLICATION

Regulations 5 and 7

Part I – Application for Accreditation

INFORMATION TO BE INCLUDED IN AN APPLICATION FOR ACCREDITATION

1 Background information about the organisation with evidence of its status and commitment to equality of opportunity.

2 A description of the organisation's system.

3 Details of the training of quality assessors.

4 Membership of the awarding panel.

5 Details of any charges to be levied on child care providers.

Part II – Renewal of Accreditation

INFORMATION TO BE INCLUDED IN AN APPLICATION FOR RENEWAL OF ACCREDITATION

1 Details of all child care providers who have been approved by the organisation during the previous period of its accreditation.

2 Details of any appeals against a refusal to grant approval of a child care provider.

3 Details of any complaints received about child care providers who the organisation has approved.

4 Identification of any changes proposed to the organisation's system.

SCHEDULE 3 – CRITERIA FOR APPROVAL OF CHILD CARE PROVIDERS

Regulation 12

The child care provider shall–

1 ensure the health, safety and welfare of all children cared for;

2 comply with all applicable health and safety legislation;

3 employ sufficient staff who are adequately trained and suitable to work with children;

4 offer a planned programme of supervised activities that reflect the developmental needs of the children being cared for;

5 operate an equal opportunities policy for parents, children and staff;

6 agree to allow quality assessors and representatives of the accredited organisation, the Secretary of State and the Inland Revenue access at any reasonable time to the child care provider's premises and records.

WORKING TAX CREDIT (ENTITLEMENT AND MAXIMUM RATE) REGULATIONS 2002

(SI 2002/2005, as amended by SI 2003/701, SI 2003/2815, SI 2004/762, SI 2004/941, SI 2004/1276, SI 2004/2663, SI 2005/681, SI 2005/769, SI 2005/2919, SI 2006/766, SI 2007/824, SI 2007/828, SI 2007/968, SI 2007/2479, SI 2008/604, SI 2008/796, SI 2008/1879, SI 2008/2169, SI 2009/697, SI 2009/800, SI 2009/1829, SI 2009/2887, SI 2010/751, SI 2010/918, SI 2010/981, SI 2010/986, SI 2010/2494, SI 2010/2914, SI 2011/721, SI 2011/1035, SI 2012/848, SI 2012/849, SI 2013/388, SI 2013/591, SI 2013/630, SI 2013/750, SI 2013/1736, SI 2014/384, SI 2014/658, SI 2014/845, SI 2014/2924, SI 2015/451, SI 2015/567, SI 2015/605, SI 2016/360, SI 2017/406, SI 2018/344 and SI 2018/365)

Made on 30 July 2002 by the Treasury, in exercise of the powers conferred on them by s. 10, 11, 12, 65(1) and (7) and 67 of the Tax Credits Act 2002. Coming into force in accordance with regulation 1.

PART 1 – GENERAL

CITATION AND COMMENCEMENT

1 These Regulations may be cited as the Working Tax Credit (Entitlement and Maximum Rate) Regulations 2002 and shall come into force–

(a) for the purpose of enabling claims to be made, on 1st August 2002;

(b) for the purpose of enabling decisions on claims to be made, on 1st January 2003; and

(c) for all other purposes, on 6th April 2003;

and shall have effect for the tax year beginning on 6th April 2003 and subsequent tax years.

INTERPRETATION

2(1) In these Regulations, except where the context otherwise requires–

"the Act" means the Tax Credits Act 2002, and a reference without more to a numbered section is a reference to the section of the Act bearing that number;

"armed forces independence payment" means armed forces independence payment under the Armed Forces and Reserve Forces (Compensation Scheme) Order 2011;

"the Board" means the Commissioners of Inland Revenue;

"the Contributions and Benefits Act" means the Social Security Contributions and Benefits Act 1992;

"child" has the same meaning as it has in the Child Tax Credit Regulations 2002;

"claim" means a claim for working tax credit and

"joint claim" and **"single claim"** have the meanings respectively assigned in section 3(8);

"claimant" means the person making a claim and, in the case of a joint claim, means either of the claimants;

"contributory employment and support allowance" means a contributory allowance under Part 1 of the Welfare Reform Act ("the 2007 Act") as amended by the provisions of Schedule 3, and Part 1 of Schedule 14, to the Welfare Reform Act 2012 that remove references to an income-related allowance, and a contributory allowance under Part 1 of the 2007 Act as that Part has effect apart from those provisions;

"couple" has the meaning given by section 3(5A) of the Act;

"the determination of the maximum rate" means the determination of the maximum rate of working tax credit;

"employed", except in the expression "self-employed", means employed under a contract of service or apprenticeship where the earnings under the contract are chargeable to income tax as employment income under Parts 2 to 7 of the Income Tax (Earnings and Pensions) Act 2003 otherwise than by reason of Chapter 8 of Part 2 of that Act (deemed employment in respect of arrangements made by intermediaries);

"employment zone" means an area within Great Britain–

(a) subject to a designation for the purposes of the Employment Zones Regulations 2003 by the Secretary of State, or

(b) listed in the Schedule to the Employment Zones (Allocation to Contractors) Pilot Regulations 2006,

pursuant to section 60 of the Welfare Reform and Pensions Act 1999;

"employment zone programme" means a programme which is–

(a) established for one or more employment zones, and

(b) designed to assist claimants for a jobseeker's allowance to obtain sustainable employment;

"initial claim" shall be construed in accordance with regulation 9A;

"limited capability for work credit" refers to a credit under regulation 8B(1) of the Social Security (Credits) Regulations 1975 where paragraph (2)(a)(iv) or (2)(a)(v) of that regulation applies, and which follows the cessation of the entitlement period of contributory employment and support allowance;

"local authority" means–

(a) in relation to England, the council of a county or district, a metropolitan district, a London Borough, the Common Council of the City of London or the Council of the Isles of Scilly;

(b) in relation to Wales, the council of a county or county borough; or,

(c) in relation to Scotland, a council constituted under section 2 of the Local Government, etc. (Scotland) Act 1994;

"partner" means a member of a couple making a joint claim;

"patient" means a person (other than a person who is serving a sentence, imposed by a court, in a prison or youth custody institution or, in Scotland, a young offenders' institution) who is regarded as receiving free in-patient treatment within the meaning of the Social Security (Hospital In-Patients) Regulations 2005;

"period of award" shall be construed in accordance with section 5;

"personal independence payment" means personal independence payment under Part 4 of the Welfare Reform Act 2012;

"qualifying young person" means a person who satisfies regulation 5 of the Child Tax Credit Regulations 2002;

"relevant child care charges" has the meaning given by regulation 14;

"self-employed" means engaged in carrying on a trade, profession or vocation on a commercial basis and with a view to the realisation of profits, either on one's own account or as a member of a business partnership and the trade, profession or vocation is organised and regular;

"sports award" means an award made by one of the Sports Councils named in 23(2) of the National Lottery etc. Act 1993 out of sums allocated to it for distribution under that section;

"surrogate child" means a child in respect of whom an order has been made under section 30 of the Human Fertilisation and Embryology Act 1990 (parental orders) or section 54 of the Human Fertilisation and Embryology Act 2008 (parental orders)

"training allowance" means an allowance (whether by way of periodical grants or otherwise) payable–

(a) out of public funds by a Government department or by or on behalf of the Secretary of State, Scottish Enterprise or Highlands and Islands Enterprise ("the relevant paying authority");

(b) to a person in respect of his maintenance or in respect of a member of his family; and

(c) for the period, or part of the period, during which he is following a course of training or instruction–

(i) provided by, or in pursuance of arrangements made with the relevant paying authority, or

(ii) approved by the relevant paying authority in relation to him,

but does not include an allowance, paid by a Government department or the Scottish Executive to or in respect of a person by reason of the fact that he is training as a teacher, or is following a course of full-time education, other than under arrangements made under section 2 of the Employment and Training Act 1973, section 2 or 3 of the Disabled Persons (Employment) Act (Northern Ireland) 1945, or section 1(1) of the Employment and Training Act (Northern Ireland) 1950

"training for work" shall be construed in accordance with regulation 9B;

"week" means a period of seven days beginning with midnight between Saturday and Sunday.

"the Welfare Reform Act" means the Welfare Reform Act 2007.

2(2) For the purposes of these Regulations a person is responsible for a child or qualifying young person if he is treated as being responsible for that child or qualifying young person in accordance with the rules contained in regulation 3 of the Child Tax Credit Regulations 2002.

2(3) A reference in these Regulations to an enactment applying to Great Britain but not to Northern Ireland shall, unless the context otherwise requires, include a reference to the corresponding enactment applying in Northern Ireland.

2(4) In these Regulations as they apply to an office a reference to being employed includes a reference to being the holder of an office.

2(5) For the purpose of these Regulations–

(a) two or more periods of entitlement to employment and support allowance are linked together if they satisfy the conditions in regulation 145 of the Employment and Support Allowance Regulations 2008 or regulation 86 of the Employment and Support Allowance Regulations 2013; and

(b) a period of entitlement to employment and support allowance is linked together with a period of entitlement to statutory sick pay if it follows that period within 12 weeks.

History – In reg. 2(1), definition of "armed forces independence payment" inserted by SI 2013/591, art. 7 and Sch., para. 24(2), with effect from 8 April 2013.
In reg. 2(1) in the definition of "claim" the words "section 3(8)" substituted by SI 2003/701, reg. 3 with effect from 6 April 2003.
In reg. 2(1), in the definition of "contributory employment and support allowance", the words "("the 2007 Act") as amended by the provisions of Schedule 3, and Part 1 of Schedule 14, to the Welfare Reform Act 2012 that remove references to an income-related allowance, and a contributory allowance under Part 1 of the 2007 Act as that Part has effect apart from those provisions" inserted by SI 2013/630, reg. 77(2)(a), with effect from 29 April 2013.
In reg. 2(1) definition of "contributory employment and support allowance" inserted by SI 2008/1879, reg. 20(2)(a)(i), with effect from 27 October 2008.
In reg. 2(1) the definition of "couple" substituted by SI 2005/2919, reg. 2(2), with effect from 5 December 2005.
In reg. 2(1) in the definition of "employed" the words "otherwise than" to the end inserted by SI 2003/2815, reg. 13 with effect from 26 November 2003.
In reg. 2(1) definitions of "employed" and "initial claim" substituted by SI 2003/701, reg. 3 with effect from 6 April 2003.
In reg. 2(1), in the definition of "employment zone", para. (b) substituted by SI 2007/824, reg. 3, with effect from 6 April 2007.
In reg. 2(1) definition of "employment zone" substituted by SI 2006/766, reg. 20, with effect from 6 April 2006.
In reg. 2(1) the definition of "limited capability for work credit" inserted by SI 2012/848, reg. 2(2)(a), with effect from 1 May 2012.
In reg. 2(1) definition of "patient", "2005" substituted for "1975" by SI 2012/848, reg. 2(2)(b), with effect from 6 April 2012.
In reg. 2(1) in the definition of "partner" the words "married or unmarried" which appeared before the word "couple" omitted by SI 2005/2919, reg. 2(2), with effect from 5 December 2005.
In reg. 2(1) definition of "partner" inserted by SI 2003/701, reg. 3 with effect from 6 April 2003.
In reg. 2(1) in the definition of "period of award" the words "section 5" substituted by SI 2003/701, reg. 3 with effect from 6 April 2003.
In reg. 2(1), definition of "personal independence payment" inserted by SI 2013/388, reg. 8 and Sch., para. 28(2), with effect from 8 April 2013.
In reg. 2(1) definitions of "Schedule E" and "the Taxes Act" omitted by SI 2003/701, reg. 3 with effect from 6 April 2003.
In reg. 2(1), the definition of "self-employed" substituted by SI 2015/605, reg. 3, with effect from 6 April 2015.
In reg. 2(1) in the definition of "surrogate child", the words "(parental orders) or section 54 of the Human Fertilisation and EmbryologyAct 2008 (parental orders)" inserted by SI 2010/986, art. 2 and Sch., para. 7, with effect from 6 April 2010.
In reg. 2(1) definition of "training for work" inserted by SI 2003/701, reg. 3 with effect from 6 April 2003.
In reg. 2(1) definition of "the Welfare Reform Act" inserted by SI 2008/1879, reg. 20(2)(a)(ii), with effect from 27 October 2008.
Reg. 2(4) inserted by SI 2003/701, reg. 3(9), with effect from 6 April 2003.
In reg. 2(5)(a), the words "or regulation 86 of the Employment and Support Allowance Regulations 2013" inserted by SI 2013/630, reg. 77(2)(b), with effect from 29 April 2013.
Reg. 2(5) inserted by SI 2008/1879, reg. 20(2)(b), with effect from 27 October 2008.

Cross references – SI 2003/742, reg. 27: modified application of reg. 2(1) to members of polygamous units.

OTHER ELEMENTS OF WORKING TAX CREDIT

3(1) For the purposes of determining the maximum rate of working tax credit, in addition to the basic element and the disability element, the following elements are prescribed–

(a) a 30 hour element;

(b) a second adult element;

(c) a lone parent element;

(d) a child care element and

(e) a severe disability element;

(f) [omitted by SI 2012/848, reg. 2(3)(a).]

3(2) It is a condition of entitlement to the other elements of working tax credit that the person making the claim for working tax credit is entitled to the basic element.

3(3) If the claim for working tax credit is a joint claim, and both members of the couple satisfy the conditions of entitlement for–

(a) the disability element or

(b) the severe disablement element;

(c) [omitted by SI 2012/848, reg. 2(3)(b),]

the award shall include two such elements.

3(4) In these Regulations as they apply to an office a reference to being employed includes a reference to being the holder of an office.

History – Reg. 3(1)(f) omitted (and the "and" before it omitted, and the "and" at the end of reg. 3(1)(d) inserted) by SI 2012/848, reg. 2(3)(a), with effect from 6 April 2012.
Reg. 3(3)(c) omitted (and the "or" before it omitted, and the "or" at the end of reg. 3(3)(a) inserted) by SI 2012/848, reg. 2(3)(b), with effect from 6 April 2012.
Reg. 3(4) inserted by SI 2003/701, reg. 3(9) with effect from 6 April 2003.

Cross references – SI 2003/742, reg. 28: modified application of reg. 3(3) to members of polygamous units.

PART 2 – CONDITIONS OF ENTITLEMENT

BASIC ELEMENT

Entitlement to basic element of Working Tax Credit: qualifying remunerative work

4(1) Subject to the qualification in paragraph (2), a person shall be treated as engaged in qualifying remunerative work if, and only if, he satisfies all of the following conditions (and in the case of the Second condition, one of the variations in that condition).

First condition

The person is employed or self-employed and–

(a) is working at the date of the claim; or

(b) has an offer of a job which he has accepted at the date of the claim and the work is expected to commence within 7 days of the making of the claim.

In relation to a case falling within sub-paragraph (b) of this condition, references in the second third and fourth conditions below to work which the person undertakes are to be construed as references to the work which the person will undertake when the job commences.

In such a case the person is only to be treated as being in qualifying remunerative work when he begins the work referred to in that sub-paragraph.

Second condition

First variation: In the case of a single claim, the person–

(a) is aged at least 16 and–

 (i) undertakes work for not less than 16 hours per week,

 (ii) is responsible for a child or qualifying young person, or he has a physical or mental disability which puts him at a disadvantage in getting a job and satisfies regulation 9(1)(c),

(b) [omitted by SI 2012/848, reg. 2(4)(b)(iii);]

(c) is aged at least 25 and undertakes not less than 30 hours work per week, or

(d) is aged at least 60 and undertakes not less than 16 hours work per week.

Second variation: In the case of a joint claim where neither person is responsible for a child or qualifying young person, the person–

(a) is aged at least 16 and undertakes work for not less than 16 hours per week and has a physical or mental disability which puts that person at a disadvantage in getting a job and satisfies regulation 9(1)(c);

(b) is aged at least 25 and undertakes work for not less than 30 hours per week; or

(c) is aged at least 60 and undertakes work for not less than 16 hours per week.

Third variation: In the case of a joint claim where a person or that person's partner is responsible for a child or qualifying young person, the person–

(a) is aged at least 16 and is a member of a couple where at least one partner undertakes work for not less than 16 hours per week and the aggregate number of hours for which the couple undertake work is not less than 24 hours per week;

(b) is aged at least 16 and undertakes work for not less than 16 hours per week and has a physical or mental disability which puts that person at a disadvantage in getting a job and satisfies regulation 9(1)(c);

(c) is aged at least 16 and undertakes work for not less than 16 hours per week and that person's partner is–

 (i) incapacitated and satisfies any of the circumstances in regulation 13(4) to (12); or

 (ii) an in-patient in hospital; or

(iii) in prison (whether serving a custodial sentence or remanded in custody awaiting trial or sentence); or

(iv) entitled to carer's allowance under section 70 of the Social Security Contributions and Benefits Act 1992;

(d) is aged at least 60 and undertakes work for not less than 16 hours per week.

Third condition

The work which the person undertakes is expected to continue for at least 4 weeks after the making of the claim or, in a case falling within sub-paragraph (b) of the first condition, after the work starts.

Fourth condition

The work is done for payment or in expectation of payment.

A social security benefit is not payment for the purposes of satisfying this condition.

4(1A) For the purposes of interpretation of paragraph (1)–

(a) paragraphs (3) and (4) provide the method of determining the number of hours of qualifying remunerative work that a person undertakes;

(b) regulations 5, 5A, 6 and 7A and 7B apply in relation to periods of absence from work connected with childbirth or adoption, sickness, strike periods or suspension from work;

(c) regulations 7 and 7C apply to term time and seasonal workers and where pay is received in lieu of notice;

(d) regulation 7D applies where a person or, in the case of a joint claim, one or both persons cease to work or reduce their hours to the extent that they no longer satisfy the Second condition in paragraph (1);

(e) regulation 8 applies where there is a gap between jobs;

(f) regulation 9 prescribes the conditions which must be satisfied by, or exist in relation to, a person so that he is to be treated as having a physical or mental disability which puts him at a disadvantage in getting a job.

4(2) A person who would otherwise satisfy the conditions in paragraph (1) shall not be regarded as engaged in qualifying remunerative work to the extent that he is–

(a) engaged by a charitable or voluntary organisation, or is a volunteer, if the only payment received by him or due to be paid to him is a payment by way of expenses which falls to be disregarded under item 1 in Table 7 in regulation 19 of the Tax Credits (Definition and Calculation of Income) Regulations 2002;

(b) engaged in caring for a person who is not a member of his household but is temporarily residing with him if the only payment made to him for providing that care is disregarded income by virtue of item 3 or 4 in Table 8 contained in regulation 19 of the Tax Credits (Definition and Calculation of Income) Regulations 2002;

(c) engaged on a scheme for which a training allowance is being paid;

(d) participating in the Intensive Activity Period specified in regulation 75(1)(a)(iv) of the Jobseeker's Allowance Regulations 1996 or the Preparation for Employment Programme specified in regulation 75(1)(a)(v) of the Jobseeker's Allowance Regulations (Northern Ireland) 1996;

(e) engaged in an activity in respect of which–

(i) a sports award has been made, or is to be made, to him, and

(ii) no other payment is made, or is expected to be made, to him; or

(f) participating in an employment zone programme, that is to say a programme established for one or more areas designated pursuant to section 60 of the Welfare Reform and Pensions Act 1999, and subject to the Employment Zones Regulations 2003 and the Employment Zones (Allocation to Contractors) Pilot Regulations 2005 if he receives no payments under that programme other than–

(i) discretionary payments disregarded in the calculation of a claimant's income under item (6)(b) in Table 6 in regulation 19 of the Tax Credits (Definition and Calculation of Income) Regulations 2002; or

(ii) training premiums.

(g) a person who–

(i) *is serving a custodial* sentence or has been remanded in custody awaiting trial or sentence, and

(ii) is engaged in work (whether inside or outside a prison) while he is serving the sentence or remanded in custody.

This is subject to the following qualification.

4(2A) Neither sub-paragraph (c) nor sub-paragraph (d) of paragraph (2) applies if–

(a) in a case falling within sub-paragraph (c), the training allowance, or

(b) in a case falling within sub-paragraph (d), any payment made by the Secretary of State, or, in Northern Ireland, by the Department for Social Development, in connection with the Intensive Activity Period,

is chargeable to income tax as the profits of a trade, profession or vocation.

4(3) The number of hours for which a person undertakes qualifying remunerative work is–

(a) in the case of an apprentice, employee or office-holder the number of hours of such work which he normally performs–

(i) under the contract of service or of apprenticeship under which he is employed; or

(ii) in the office in which he is employed;

(b) in the case of an agency worker, the number of hours in respect of which remuneration is normally paid to him by an employment agency with whom he has a contract of employment; or

(c) in the case of a person who is self-employed the number of hours he normally performs for payment or in expectation of payment.

This is subject to the following qualification.

4(4) In reckoning the number of hours of qualifying remunerative work which a person normally undertakes–

(a) any period of customary or paid holiday; and

(b) any time allowed for meals or refreshment, unless the person is, or expects to be paid earnings in respect of that time,

shall be disregarded.

4(5) In reckoning the number of hours of qualifying remunerative work which a person normally undertakes, any time allowed for visits to a hospital, clinic or other establishment for the purpose only of treating or monitoring the person's disability shall be included; but only if the person is, or expects to be, paid in respect of that time.

4(6) In this regulation **"work"** shall be construed as a reference to any work that the person undertakes whether as a person who is employed or self-employed or both.

History – In reg. 4(1), the words "is employed or self-employed and" inserted by SI 2015/605, reg. 4, with effect from 6 April 2015.
In reg. 4(1), the words "(and in the case of the Second condition, one of the variations in that condition)" inserted by SI 2012/848, reg. 2(4)(a), with effect from 6 April 2012.
In reg. 4(1), in the second condition, third variation, in para. (c)(i), the words "regulation 13(4) to (12)" substituted for the words "regulation 13(4) to (8)" by SI 2013/1736, reg. 2(2), with effect from 5 August 2013.
In reg. 4(1), in the second condition, the words "First variation: In the case of a single claim, the person–" substituted for the words "The person" by SI 2012/848, reg. 2(4)(b)(i), with effect from 6 April 2012.
In reg. 4(1), in the second condition, in para. (a)(ii), the words "either he or his partner", which appeared at the beginning, omitted by SI 2012/848, reg. 2(4)(b)(ii), with effect from 6 April 2012.
In reg. 4(1), in the second condition, para. (b) omitted by SI 2012/848, reg. 2(4)(b)(iii), with effect from 6 April 2012.
In reg. 4(1), in the second condition, the second variation and the third variation inserted by SI 2012/848, reg. 2(4)(b)(iv), with effect from 6 April 2012.
In reg. 4(1), the following wording, which appeared after the words "or in expectation of payment.", omitted by SI 2012/848, reg. 2(4)(c), with effect from 6 April 2012:
"Paragraphs (3) and (4) provide the method of determining the number of hours of qualifying remunerative work that a person undertakes.
Regulations 5 to 8 apply in relation to periods of absence from work connected with childbirth or adoption, sickness, seasonal absence from work in relation to which there is a recognised yearly cycle of employment and those who have a gap between periods of work.
Regulation 9 prescribes the conditions which must be satisfied by, or exist in relation to, a person so that he is to be treated as having a physical or mental disability which puts him at a disadvantage in getting a job.".
In reg. 4(1), in the second condition, the "or" immediately preceding para. (c) omitted by SI 2010/2914, reg. 11(a), with effect from 6 April 2011.
In reg. 4(1), in the second condition, in para. (c), the words "in any other case", which appeared at the end, omitted by SI 2010/2914, reg. 11(b), with effect from 6 April 2011.
In reg. 4(1), in the second condition, para. (d) (and the word ", or" at the end of para. (c)) inserted by SI 2010/2914, reg. 11(c), with effect from 6 April 2011.
In reg. 4(1), in the fourth condition, the words "A social security benefit is not payment for the purposes of satisfying this condition" inserted by SI 2009/697, reg. 3, with effect from 6 April 2009.
In reg. 4(1), in the wording relating to the second condition, para. (a) substituted by SI 2003/701, reg. 4(2), with effect from 6 April 2002.
Reg. 4(1A) inserted by SI 2012/848, reg. 2(5), with effect from 6 April 2012.
In reg. 4(2)(f) words "the Employment Zones Regulations 2003 and the Employment Zones (Allocation to Contractors) Pilot Regulations 2005" substituted for "the Employment Zones Regulations 2000" by SI 2006/766, reg. 20, with effect from 6 April 2006.
In reg. 4(2)(f)(i), the words "Table 6" substituted by SI 2003/701, reg. 4(3), with effect from 6 April 2002.
Reg. 4(2)(g) inserted by SI 2007/824, reg. 4, with effect from 6 April 2007.
In reg. 4(2) the words at the end "This is subject to the following qualification." inserted by SI 2004/762, reg. 5(2) with effect from 6 April 2004.
Reg. 4(2A) inserted by SI 2004/762, reg. 5(3), with effect from 6 April 2004.
Reg. 4(5) inserted by SI 2003/701, reg. 4(4), with effect from 6 April 2002.
Reg. 4(6) inserted by SI 2015/605, reg. 5, with effect from 6 April 2015.

Cross references – SI 2002/2014, reg. 10(2)(b): making of claim in case falling within reg. 4(1), First Condition, sub-para. (b).
SI 2003/742, reg. 29: modified application of reg. 4(1) to members of polygamous units.

HMRC Manuals – TCTM02401: examples and Revenue practice on the four conditions of qualifying remunerative work; meaning of expression "for payment or in expectation of payment".
TCTM02405: further Revenue guidance on "qualifying remunerative work", including in particular calculation of hours worked, holidays for term-time workers, recognised cycle of work, etc.

TIME OFF IN CONNECTION WITH CHILDBIRTH AND ADOPTION

History – In the heading the word "childbirth" substituted by SI 2004/762, reg. 6

5(1) This regulation applies for any period during which a person–

(a) is paid maternity allowance,

(b) is paid statutory maternity pay,

(c) is absent from work during an ordinary maternity leave period under section 71 of the Employment Rights Act 1996 or Article 103 of the Employment Rights (Northern Ireland) Order 1996,

(ca) is absent from work during the first 13 weeks of an additional maternity leave period under section 73 of the Employment Rights Act 1996 or article 105 of the Employment Rights (Northern Ireland) Order 1996,

(d) is paid ordinary statutory paternity pay,

(da) is paid additional statutory paternity pay,

(e) is absent from work during an ordinary paternity leave period under sections 80A or 80B of the Employment Rights Act 1996 or Articles 112A or 112B of the Employment Rights (Northern Ireland) Order 1996,

(ea) [omitted by SI 2016/360, reg. 2(2),]

(f) is paid statutory adoption pay,

(g) is absent from work during an ordinary adoption leave period under section 75A of the Employment Rights Act 1996 or Article 107A of the Employment Rights (Northern Ireland) Order 1996, or

(ga) is absent from work during the first 13 weeks of an additional adoption leave period under section 75B of the Employment Rights Act 1996 or article 107B of the Employment Rights (Northern Ireland) Order 1996.

5(2) For the purposes of the conditions of entitlement in this Part, the person is treated as being engaged in qualifying remunerative work during the period.

This is subject to paragraphs (3), (3A) and regulation 7D.

5(3) The person must have been engaged in qualifying remunerative work immediately before the beginning of the period.

5(3A) A person shall only be treated as being engaged in qualifying remunerative work by virtue of paragraph (1)(ea) for such period as that person would have been paid additional statutory paternity pay had the conditions of entitlement in Parts 2 or 3 of the Additional Statutory Paternity Pay (General) Regulations 2010 or Parts 2 or 3 of the Additional Statutory Paternity Pay (General) Regulations (Northern Ireland) 2010 been satisfied.

5(4) A person who is self-employed is treated as engaged in qualifying remunerative work for the requisite number of hours during any period for which paragraph (1) would have applied in his case but for the fact that the work he performed in the week immediately before the period began, although done for payment or in the expectation of payment, was not performed under a contract of service or apprenticeship.

History – Reg. 5(1)(ca) inserted by SI 2007/824, reg. 5(2), with effect from 6 April 2007.
In reg. 5(1)(d), the words "ordinary statutory paternity pay" substituted for the words "statutory paternity pay" by SI 2010/2494, reg. 3(2), with effect from 14 November 2010.
Reg. 5(1)(da) inserted by SI 2010/2494, reg. 3(3), with effect from 14 November 2010.
Reg. 5(1)(e) substituted by SI 2010/2494, reg. 3(4), with effect from 14 November 2010.
Reg. 5(1)(ea) omitted by SI 2016/360, reg. 2(2), with effect from 6 April 2016.
Former reg. 5(1)(ea) inserted by SI 2010/2494, reg. 3(5), with effect from 14 November 2010.
In reg. 5(1)(f) the word "and" omitted from the end by SI 2007/824, reg. 5(3), with effect from 6 April 2007.
Reg. 5(1)(ga) and the word "or," preceding it inserted by SI 2007/824, reg. 5(4), with effect from 6 April 2007.
In reg. 5(2), the words "paragraphs (3), (3A) and regulation 7D" substituted for the words "paragraphs (3) and (3A)" by SI 2012/848, reg. 2(6), with effect from 6 April 2012.
In reg. 5(2), "paragraphs (3) and (3A)" substituted for "paragraph (3)" by SI 2010/2494, reg. 3(6), with effect from 14 November 2010.
In reg. 5(2), the words "conditions of entitlement in this Part" substituted for the words "conditions in regulation 4(1)" by SI 2009/1829, reg. 3, with effect from 31 July 2009.
Reg. 5(3A) inserted by SI 2010/2494, reg. 3(7), with effect from 14 November 2010.
Reg. 5 substituted by SI 2003/701, reg. 5, with effect from 6 April 2003.

TIME OFF IN CONNECTION WITH CHILDBIRTH AND PLACEMENT FOR ADOPTION: FURTHER PROVISIONS

5A(1) This regulation applies to a person for any period–

(a) which falls within a period to which regulation 5 applies; and

(b) which follows the birth or the placement for adoption of the child in connection with whose birth or placement entitlement to the allowance, pay or leave mentioned in regulation 5(1) arises.

5A(2) A person who would have been treated as being engaged in qualifying remunerative work if they or, in the case of a joint claim, they or their partner had been responsible for a child or qualifying young person, immediately before the beginning of a period to which regulation 5 applies, shall be treated as being engaged in qualifying remunerative work for the purposes of the conditions of entitlement in this Part during the period mentioned in paragraph (1) above.

5A(3) Paragraph (4) of regulation 5 applies for the purpose of this regulation as it applies for the purpose of that regulation.

5A(4) This regulation is subject to regulation 7D.

History – In reg. 5A(2), the words "A person who would have been treated as being engaged in qualifying remunerative work if they or, in the case of a joint claim, they or their partner had been responsible for a child or qualifying young person" substituted for the words "A person who was undertaking qualifying remunerative work for at least 16 hours per week" by SI 2012/848, reg. 2(7)(a), with effect from 6 April 2012.

In reg. 5A(2), the words "being engaged in qualifying remunerative work for the purposes of the conditions of entitlement in this Part" substituted for the words "satisfying the requirements of regulation 4(1)" by SI 2009/1829, reg. 4, with effect from 31 July 2009.

Reg. 5A(4) inserted by SI 2012/848, reg. 2(7)(b), with effect from 6 April 2012.

Reg. 5A inserted by SI 2004/762, reg. 7 with effect from 6 April 2004.

PERIODS OF ILLNESS, INCAPACITY FOR WORK OR LIMITED CAPABILITY FOR WORK

History – In the heading to reg. 6, the words ", incapacity for work or limited capability for work" substituted for the words "or incapacity for work" by SI 2008/1879, reg. 20(3)(a), with effect from 27 October 2008.

6(1) This regulation applies for any period during which a person–

(a) is paid statutory sick pay,

(b) is paid short-term incapacity benefit at the lower rate under sections 30A to 30E of the Contributions and Benefits Act,

(c) is paid income support on the grounds of incapacity for work under paragraphs 7 and 14 of Schedule 1B to the Income Support (General) Regulations 1987,

(cc) is paid an employment and support allowance under Part 1 of the Welfare Reform Act, or

(d) receives national insurance credits on the grounds of incapacity for work or limited capability for work under regulation 8B of the Social Security (Credits) Regulations 1975.

6(2) For the purposes of the conditions of entitlement in this Part, the person is treated as being engaged in qualifying remunerative work during the period.

This is subject to paragraphs (3), (4) and regulation 7D.

6(3) The person must have been engaged in qualifying remunerative work immediately before the beginning of the period.

6(4) If the person is paid income support as specified in paragraph (1)(c) or employment and support allowance as specified in paragraph (1)(cc) or receives national insurance credits as specified in paragraph (1)(d) he is treated as being engaged in qualifying remunerative work for a period of 28 weeks only, beginning with the day on which he is first paid income support or employment and support allowance or receives national insurance credits (as the case may be).

6(5) A person who is self-employed is treated as engaged in qualifying remunerative work for the requisite number of hours during any period for which paragraph (1) would have applied in his case but for the fact that the work he performed in the week immediately before the period began, although done for payment or in the expectation of payment, was not performed under a contract of service or apprenticeship.

History – Reg. 6(1)(cc) inserted (and the "or" at the end of reg. 6(1)(c) omitted) by SI 2008/1879, reg. 20(3)(b)(i), with effect from 27 October 2008.

In reg. 6(1)(d), the words "or limited capability for work" inserted by SI 2008/1879, reg. 20(3)(b)(ii), with effect from 27 October 2008.

In reg. 6(2), the words "paragraphs (3), (4) and regulation 7D" substituted for the words "paragraphs (3) and (4)" by SI 2012/848, reg. 2(8), with effect from 6 April 2012.

In reg. 6(2), the words "conditions of entitlement in this Part" substituted for the words "conditions in regulation 4(1)" by SI 2009/1829, reg. 5, with effect from 31 July 2009.

In reg. 6(4), the words "or employment and support allowance as specified in paragraph (1)(cc)" and "or employment and support allowance" inserted by SI 2008/1879, reg. 20(3)(c), with effect from 27 October 2008.

Reg. 6 substituted by SI 2003/701, reg. 6, with effect from 6 April 2003.

TERM TIME AND OTHER SEASONAL WORKERS

7(1) For the purposes of the conditions of entitlement in this Part, paragraph (2) applies if a person–

(a) works at a school, other educational establishment or other place of employment,

(b) there is a recognisable cycle to his employment there; and

(c) the length of that recognisable cycle is one year and includes periods of school holidays or similar vacations during which he does not work.

7(2) If this paragraph applies, the periods mentioned in paragraph (1)(c) are disregarded in determining whether the conditions of entitlement in this Part are satisfied.

History – In reg. 7(1), the words "conditions of entitlement in this Part" substituted for the words "conditions in regulation 4(1)" by SI 2009/1829, reg. 6, with effect from 31 July 2009.

In reg. 7(2), the words "conditions of entitlement in this Part" substituted for the words "conditions in regulation 4(1)" by SI 2009/1829, reg. 5, with effect from 31 July 2009.

STRIKE PERIODS

7A(1) This regulation applies for any period during which a person is on strike.

7A(2) For the purposes of the conditions of entitlement in this Part, the person is treated as being engaged in qualifying remunerative work during the period.

This is subject to paragraph (3) and regulation 7D.

7A(3) The person–

(a) must have been engaged in qualifying remunerative work immediately before the beginning of the period, and

(b) must not be on strike for longer than a period of ten consecutive days on which he should have been working.

History – In reg. 7A(2), the words "paragraph (3) and regulation 7D" substituted for the words "paragraph (3)" by SI 2012/848, reg. 2(9), with effect from 6 April 2012.

In reg. 7A(2), the words "conditions of entitlement in this Part" substituted for the words "conditions in regulation 4(1)" by SI 2009/1829, reg. 7, with effect from 31 July 2009.

Reg. 7A inserted by SI 2003/701, reg. 7, with effect from 6 April 2003.

PERSONS SUSPENDED FROM WORK

7B(1) This regulation applies for any period during which a person is suspended from work while complaints or allegations against him are investigated.

7B(2) For the purposes of the conditions of entitlement in this Part, the person is treated as being engaged in qualifying remunerative work during the period.

This is subject to paragraph (3) and regulation 7D.

7B(3) The person must have been engaged in qualifying remunerative work immediately before the beginning of the period.

History – In reg. 7B(2), the words "paragraph (3) and regulation 7D" substituted for the words "paragraph (3)" by SI 2012/848, reg. 2(9), with effect from 6 April 2012.

In reg. 7B(2) the words "conditions of entitlement in this Part" substituted by SI 2009/1829, reg. 7, with effect from 31 July 2009.

Reg. 7B inserted by SI 2003/701, reg. 7, with effect from 6 April 2003.

PAY IN LIEU OF NOTICE

7C(1) This regulation applies if a person stops work and receives pay in lieu of notice.

7C(2) For the purposes of the conditions of entitlement in this Part, the person shall not be treated as being engaged in qualifying remunerative work during the period for which he receives the pay.

7C(3) This regulation is subject to regulation 7D.

History – In reg. 7C(2) the words "conditions of entitlement in this Part" substituted by SI 2009/1829, reg. 7, with effect from 31 July 2009.

Reg. 7C(3) inserted by SI 2007/968, reg. 2(2), with effect from 6 April 2007.

Reg. 7C inserted by SI 2003/701, reg. 7, with effect from 6 April 2003.

CEASING TO UNDERTAKE WORK OR WORKING LESS THAN 16, 24 OR 30 HOURS PER WEEK

7D(1) This regulation applies for the four-week period immediately after–

(a) a person, not being a member of a couple, who is engaged in qualifying remunerative work for not less than 16 hours per week, ceases to work or starts to work less than 16 hours per week,

(b) a person, being a member of a couple only one of whom is engaged in qualifying remunerative work for not less than 16 hours per week, ceases to work or starts to work less than 16 hours per week,

(c) both members of a couple, each of whom is engaged in qualifying remunerative work for not less than 16 hours per week, cease to work or start to work less than 16 hours per week,

(d) a person, being a member of a couple who is entitled to the childcare element of working tax credit each of whom is engaged in qualifying remunerative work for not less than 16 hours per week, ceases to work or start to work less than 16 hours per week, or

(e) a person who satisfies paragraph (c) of the first variation or paragraph (b) of the second variation of the second condition in regulation 4(1) and who is engaged in qualifying remunerative work for not less than 30 hours per week, ceases to work or starts to work less than 30 hours per week,

(f) one or both members of a couple who satisfy paragraph (a) of the third variation of the Second condition in regulation 4(1) and are engaged in qualifying remunerative work cease to work or reduce their hours to the extent that they cease to meet the condition that one member of the couple works not less than 16 hours per week and the aggregate number of hours for which the couple are engaged in qualifying remunerative work is not less than 24 hours per week.

7D(2) For the purposes of the conditions of entitlement in this Part, the person is treated as being engaged in qualifying remunerative work during that period.

History – In the heading to reg. 7D, ", 24" inserted by SI 2012/848, reg. 2(10)(a), with effect from 6 April 2012.

In reg. 7D(1)(e), the words "of the first variation or paragraph (b) of the second variation" inserted by SI 2012/848, reg. 2(10)(b), with effect from 6 April 2012.
Reg. 7D(1)(f) inserted by SI 2012/848, reg. 2(10)(c), with effect from 6 April 2012 (note that SI 2012/848, presumably in error, does not move the word "or" from the end of reg. 7D(1)(d) to the end of reg. 7D(1)(e)).
Reg. 7D substituted by SI 2009/1829, reg. 8, with effect from 31 July 2009.

GAPS BETWEEN JOBS

8 For the purposes of the conditions of entitlement in this Part a person shall be treated as being engaged in qualifying remunerative work for the requisite number of hours if he has been so engaged within the past 7 days.

History – In reg. 8, the words "conditions of entitlement in this Part" substituted for the words "conditions in regulation 4(1)" by SI 2009/1829, reg. 9, with effect from 31 July 2009.

DISABILITY ELEMENT

Disability element and workers who are to be treated as at a disadvantage in getting a job

9(1) The determination of the maximum rate must include the disability element if the claimant, or, in the case of a joint claim, one of the claimants–

(a) undertakes qualifying remunerative work for at least 16 hours per week;

(b) has any of the disabilities listed in Part 1 of Schedule 1, or in the case of an initial claim, satisfies the conditions in Part 2 of Schedule 1; and

(c) is a person who satisfies any of Cases A to G on a day for which the maximum rate is determined in accordance with these Regulations.

9(2) Case A is where the person has, for at least one day in the preceding 182 days ("the qualifying day"), been in receipt of–

(a) higher rate short-term incapacity benefit;

(b) long-term incapacity benefit;

(c) severe disablement allowance; or

(d) employment and support allowance or a limited capability for work credit, where entitlement to employment and support allowance or that credit or statutory sick pay or a benefit or allowance mentioned in sub-paragraphs (a) to (c) or the income support payable under paragraph (3)(a), has existed for a period of 28 weeks immediately preceding the qualifying day comprising one continuous period or two or more periods which are linked together.

9(3) Case B is where, for at least one day in the preceding 182 days, the person has been a person for whom at least one of the following benefits has been payable and for whom the applicable amount included a higher pensioner or disability premium in respect of him determined–

(a) in the case of income support, in accordance with paragraphs 10(1)(b) or (2)(b) or 11, and where applicable, 12, of Part III of Schedule 2 to the Income Support (General) Regulations 1987;

(b) in the case of income-based jobseeker's allowance, in accordance with paragraphs 12(1)(a), or (b)(ii), or (c), or 13, and where applicable 14 of Part 3 of Schedule 1 to the Jobseeker's Allowance Regulations 1996;

(c) in the case of housing benefit, in accordance with paragraphs 10(1)(b) or (2)(b) or 11, and where applicable, 12 of Part III of Schedule 2 to the Housing Benefit (General) Regulations 1987;

(d) [Revoked by SI 2014/658, reg. 2.]

For the purposes of this Case **"the applicable amount"** has the meaning given by section 135 of the Contributions and Benefits Act.

9(4) Case C is where the person is a person to whom at least one of the following is payable–

(a) a disability living allowance;

(b) an attendance allowance;

(c) a mobility supplement or a constant attendance allowance which is paid, in either case, in conjunction with a war pension or industrial injuries disablement benefit.

(d) personal independence payment.

(e) armed forces independence payment.

9(5) Case D is where the person has an invalid carriage or other vehicle provided under–

(a) section 5(2)(a) of, and Schedule 2 to, the National Health Service Act 1977,

(b) section 46 of the National Health Service (Scotland) Act 1978, or

(c) Article 30(1) of the Health and Personal Social Services (Northern Ireland) Order 1972.

9(6) Case E is where the person–

(a) has received–

(i) on account of his incapacity for work, statutory sick pay, occupational sick pay, short-term incapacity benefit payable at the lower rate or income support, for a period of 140 qualifying days, or has been credited with Class 1 or Class 2 contributions under the Contributions and Benefits Act for a period of 20 weeks on account of incapacity for work, and where the last of those days or weeks (as the case may be) fell within the preceding 56 days; or

(ii) on account of his incapacity for work or having limited capability for work, an employment and support allowance, or the pay or benefit mentioned in paragraph (i), for a period of 140 qualifying days, or has been credited with Class 1 or Class 2 contributions under the Contributions and Benefits Act for a period of 20 weeks on account of incapacity for work or having limited capability for work, and where the last of those days or weeks (as the case may be) fell within the preceding 56 days;

(b) has a disability which is likely to last for at least six months, or for the rest of his life if his death is expected within that time; and

(c) has gross earnings which are less than they were before the disability began by at least the greater of 20 per cent. and £15 per week.

For the purpose of this Case **"qualifying days"** are days which form part of a single period of incapacity for work within the meaning of Part 11 of the Contributions and Benefits Act or a period of limited capability for work within the meaning of regulation 2(1) of the Employment and Support Allowance Regulations 2008.

9(7) Case F is where the person–

(a) has undertaken training for work for at least one day in the preceding 56 days; and

(b) has, within 56 days before the first day of that period of training for work, received–

(i) higher rate short-term incapacity benefit;

(ii) long-term incapacity benefit;

(iii) severe disablement allowance; or

(iv) contributory employment and support allowance or a limited capability for work credit, where entitlement to that allowance or credit or statutory sick pay or a benefit or allowance mentioned in paragraphs (i) to (iii), has existed for a period of 28 weeks comprising one continuous period or two or more periods which are linked together provided that, if the person received statutory sick pay, the person satisfied the first and second contribution conditions set out in paragraphs 1 and 2 of Schedule 1 to the Welfare Reform Act.

Regulation 9B explains the meaning of **"training for work"** and of a period of training for work.

9(7A) In paragraph (7)(b)(iv), the reference to contributory employment and support allowance is a reference to an allowance under Part 1 of the Welfare Reform Act 2007 ("the 2007 Act") as amended by the provisions of Schedule 3, and Part 1 of Schedule 14, to the Welfare Reform Act 2012 that remove references to an income-based allowance, and a contributory allowance under Part 1 of the 2007 Act as that Part has effect apart from those provisions.

9(8) Case G is where the person was entitled, for at least one day in the preceding 56 days, to the disability element of working tax credit or to disabled person's tax credit by virtue of his having satisfied the requirements of Case A, B, E or F at some earlier time.

For the purposes of this Case a person is treated as having an entitlement to the disability element of working tax credit if that element is taken into account in determining the rate at which the person is entitled to a tax credit.

9(9) For the purposes of the Act, a person who satisfies paragraph (1)(b) is to be treated as having a physical or mental disability which puts him at a disadvantage in getting a job.

History – In reg. 9(2)(d), the words "or a limited capability for work credit," inserted by SI 2012/848, reg. 2(11)(a), with effect from 1 May 2012.

In reg. 9(2)(d), the words "or that credit" inserted by SI 2012/848, reg. 2(11)(b), with effect from 1 May 2012.

In reg. 9(2)(d), the words "or a benefit or allowance mentioned in sub-paragraphs (a) to (c) or the income support payable under paragraph (3)(a)," inserted by SI 2012/848, reg. 2(11)(c), with effect from 6 April 2012.

Reg. 9(2) substituted by SI 2008/1879, reg. 20(4)(a), with effect from 27 October 2008.

In reg. 9(3) the words "for whom at least one of the following benefits has been payable and for whom the applicable amount" substituted for the words "for whom the applicable amount" by SI 2003/2815, reg. 14 with effect from 26 November 2003.

In reg. 9(3) the words *"in respect of him"* inserted by SI 2003/2815, reg. 14 with effect from 26 November 2003.

In reg. 9(3)(a) the words "paragraphs 10(1)(b) or (2)(b) or 11, and where applicable, 12," substituted by SI 2003/2815, reg. 14 with effect from 26 November 2003.

In reg. 9(3)(b) the words "paragraphs 12(1)(a), or (b)(ii), or (c), or 13, and where applicable 14 of Part 3 of" substituted for "paragraph 12(1)(a), (b)(ii) or (c) or 13, and 14 of" by SI 2003/2815, reg. 14 with effect from 26 November 2003.

In reg. 9(3)(c) the words "paragraphs 10(1)(b) or (2)(b) or 11, and where applicable, 12" substituted by SI 2003/2815, reg. 14 with effect from 26 November 2003.
Reg. 9(3)(d) revoked by SI 2014/658, reg. 2, with effect from 6 April 2014.
In former reg. 9(3)(d) the words "paragraphs 11(1)(b) or (2)(b) or 12, and where applicable, 13" substituted by SI 2003/2815, reg. 14 with effect from 26 November 2003.
Reg. 9(4)(d) inserted by SI 2013/388, art. 8 and Sch., para. 28(3), with effect from 8 April 2013.
Reg. 9(4)(e) inserted by SI 2013/591, art. 7 and Sch., para. 24(3), with effect from 8 April 2013.
In reg. 9(6)(a)(ii), the first occurrence of the words "incapacity for work or" inserted by SI 2012/848, reg. 2(12)(a), with effect from 6 April 2012.
In reg. 9(6)(a)(ii), the words ", or the pay or benefit mentioned in paragraph (i)," inserted by SI 2012/848, reg. 2(12)(b), with effect from 6 April 2012.
In reg. 9(6)(a)(ii), the second occurrence of the words "incapacity for work or" inserted by SI 2012/848, reg. 2(12)(c), with effect from 6 April 2012.
Reg. 9(6)(a) substituted by SI 2008/1879, reg. 20(4)(b)(i), with effect from 27 October 2008.
In reg. 9(6), the words "or a period of limited capability for work within the meaning of regulation 2(1) of the Employment and Support Allowance Regulations 2008" inserted by SI 2008/1879, reg. 20(4)(b)(ii), with effect from 27 October 2008.
In reg. 9(7)(b)(iv), the words "or a limited capability for work credit," insertedby SI 2012/848, reg. 2(13)(a), with effect from 1 May 2012.
In reg. 9(7)(b)(iv), the words "or credit" inserted by SI 2012/848, reg. 2(13)(b), with effect from 1 May 2012.
In reg. 9(7)(b)(iv), the words "or a benefit or allowance mentioned in paragraphs (i) to (iii)," inserted by SI 2012/848, reg. 2(13)(c), with effect from 6 April 2012.
Reg. 9(7)(b) substituted by SI 2008/1879, reg. 20(4)(c), with effect from 27 October 2008.
Reg. 9(7A) inserted by SI 2013/630, reg. 77(3), with effect from 29 April 2013.
In reg. 9(8) the words "for at least one day in the preceding 56 days" substituted by SI 2003/2815, reg. 14(3) with effect from 26 November 2003.
Reg. 9, 9A, and 9B substituted by SI 2003/701, reg. 8, with effect from 6 April 2003.
Cross references – SI 2002/2014, reg. 26: date of notification of change of circumstances resulting in entitlement to disability element of working tax credit.

TC Statutory Instruments

Initial claims

9A(1) In regulation 9(1)(b) an **"initial claim"** means a claim which–

(a) is made for the disability element of working tax credit, and

(b) relates to a person who has not had an entitlement to that element or to disabled person's tax credit during the two years immediately preceding the making of the claim.

9A(2) In paragraph (1) any reference to the making of a claim includes the giving of notification, in accordance with regulation 20 of the Tax Credits (Claims and Notifications) Regulations 2002, of a change of circumstances falling within that regulation.

9A(3) For the purposes of paragraph (1)(b) a person is treated as having an entitlement to the disability element of working tax credit if, by virtue of the person being a person who satisfies regulation 9, that element is taken into account in determining the rate at which the person is entitled to a tax credit.

History – Reg. 9, 9A, and 9B substituted by SI 2003/701, reg. 8, with effect from 6 April 2003.

Training for work etc

9B(1) In regulation 9 **"training for work"** means training for work received–

(a) in pursuance of arrangements made under–

(i) section 2(1) of the Employment and Training Act 1973,

(ii) section 2(3) of the Enterprise and New Towns (Scotland) Act 1990, or

(iii) section 1(1) of the Employment and Training Act 1950, or

(b) on a course whose primary purpose is the teaching of occupational or vocational skills, and which the person attends for 16 hours or more a week.

9B(2) For the purposes of regulation 9(7) a period of training for work means a series of consecutive days of training for work, there being disregarded any day specified in paragraph (3).

9B(3) Those days are any day on which the claimant was–

(a) on holiday;

(b) attending court as a justice of the peace, a party to any proceedings, a witness or a juror;

(c) suffering from some disease or bodily or mental disablement as a result of which he was unable to attend training for work, or his attendance would have put at risk the health of other persons;

(d) unable to participate in training for work because–

(i) he was looking after a child because the person who usually looked after that child was unable to do so;

(ii) he was looking after a member of his family who was ill;

(iii) he was required to deal with some domestic emergency; or

(iv) he was arranging or attending the funeral of his partner or a relative; or

(e) authorised by the training provider to be absent from training for work.

9B(4) For the purposes of paragraph (3)(d)(iv) **"relative"** means close relative, grandparent, grandchild, uncle, aunt, nephew or niece; and in this paragraph **"close relative"** means parent, parent-in-law, son, son-in-law, daughter, daughter-in-law, step-parent, step-son, step-daughter, brother, sister, or the spouse of any of the preceding persons or, if that person is one of an unmarried couple, the other member of that couple.

History – Reg. 9, 9A, and 9B substituted by SI 2003/701, reg. 8, with effect from 6 April 2003.
In reg. 9B(1) the words "regulation 9" substituted by SI 2004/762, reg. 8 with effect from 6 April 2004.

30 HOUR ELEMENT

30-hour element

10(1) The determination of the maximum rate must include a 30 hour element if the claimant, or in the case of a joint claim, at least one of the claimants, is engaged in qualifying remunerative work for at least 30 hours per week.

10(2) The determination of the maximum must also include the 30 hour element if–

(a) the claim is a joint claim,

(b) at least one of the claimants is responsible for one or more children or qualifying young people,

(c) the aggregate number of hours which the couple engage in qualifying remunerative work is at least 30 hours per week, and

(d) at least one member of the couple engages in qualifying remunerative work for at least 16 hours per week.

10(3) [Omitted by SI 2012/848, reg. 2(14).]

History – Reg. 10(3) omitted by SI 2012/848, reg. 2(14), with effect from 6 April 2012.
Former reg. 10(3) inserted by SI 2003/701, reg. 9, with effect from 6 April 2003.

Cross references – SI 2003/742, reg. 30: modified application of reg. 10(2) to members of polygamous units.

SECOND ADULT ELEMENT

Second adult element

11(1) The determination of the maximum rate must include the second adult element if the claim is a joint claim.
This is subject to the following provisions of this regulation.

11(2) [Omitted by SI 2012/848, reg. 2(15)(a).]

11(3) [Omitted by SI 2012/848, reg. 2(15)(a).]

11(4) The determination of the maximum rate shall not include the second adult element if neither claimant has responsibility for a child or qualifying young person, and

(a) one claimant is serving a custodial sentence of more than twelve months, or

(b) one claimant is subject to immigration control within the meaning of section 115(9) of the Immigration and Asylum Act 1999.

11(5) Paragraph (4)(b) does not apply where the claimant subject to immigration control is a person to whom Case 4 of regulation 3(1) of the Tax Credits (Immigration) Regulations 2003 applies.

History – Reg. 11(2) omitted by SI 2012/848, reg. 2(15)(a), with effect from 6 April 2012.
Reg. 11(3) omitted by SI 2012/848, reg. 2(15)(a), with effect from 6 April 2012.
Former reg. 11(3)(c) inserted (and the "or" at the end of former reg. 11(3)(a) omitted, and the "or" at the end of former reg. 11(3)(b) inserted) by SI 2010/2914, reg. 12, with effect from 31 December 2011.
In reg. 11(4), the word "also", which appeared after the words "maximum rate shall", omitted by SI 2012/848, reg. 2(15)(b), with effect from 6 April 2012.
In reg. 11(4), "section 115(9)" substituted for "section 115(9)(a)" by SI 2009/2887, reg. 3(2), with effect from 6 April 2010.
Reg. 11(4) substituted by SI 2009/697, reg. 4, with effect from 6 April 2009.
Reg. 11(5) inserted by SI 2009/2887, reg. 3(3), with effect from 6 April 2010.
Reg. 11 substituted by SI 2003/701, reg. 10, with effect from 6 April 2003.

Cross references – SI 2003/742, reg. 31: modified application of reg. 11 to members of polygamous units.

LONE PARENT ELEMENT

Lone parent element

12 The determination of the maximum rate must include the lone parent element if–

(a) the claim is a single claim; and

(b) the claimant is responsible for a child or qualifying young person.

History – In reg. 12 words "a child or qualifying young person" substituted by SI 2003/701, reg. 11, with effect from 6 April 2003.

CHILD CARE ELEMENT

Entitlement to child care element of working tax credit

13(1) The determination of the maximum rate must include a child care element where that person, or in the case of a joint claim at least one of those persons, is incurring relevant child care charges and–

(a) is a person, not being a member of a couple, engaged in qualifying remunerative work;

(b) is a member or are members of a couple where both are engaged in qualifying remunerative work for not less than 16 hours per week; or

(c) is a member or are members of a couple where one is engaged in qualifying remunerative work for not less than 16 hours per week and the other–

(i) is incapacitated;

(ii) is an in-patient in hospital; or

(iii) is in prison (whether serving a custodial sentence or remanded in custody awaiting trial or sentence); or

(iv) is entitled to carer's allowance under section 70 of the Social Security Contributions and Benefits Act 1992.

13(2) For the purposes of paragraph (1) a person is not treated as incurring relevant child care charges where the average weekly charge calculated in accordance with regulation 15 is nil or where an agreement within regulation 15(4) has not yet commenced.

13(3) [Omitted by SI 2004/762, reg. 9.]

13(4) For the purposes of paragraph (1)(c)(i) the other member of a couple is incapacitated in any of the circumstances specified in paragraphs (5) to (12).

13(5) The circumstances specified in this paragraph are where housing benefit is payable under Part 7 of the Contributions and Benefits Act to the other member or the other member's partner and the applicable amount of the person entitled to the benefit includes a disability premium on account of the other member's incapacity or regulation 28(1)(c) of the Housing Benefit Regulations 2006 (treatment of child care charges) applies in that person's case.

13(6) The circumstances specified in this paragraph are where there is payable or – in the case of a credit – an entitlement in respect of him one or more of the following–

(a) short-term incapacity benefit payable at the higher rate under section 30A of the Contributions and Benefits Act;

(b) long term incapacity benefit under section 40 or 41 of the Contributions and Benefits Act;

(c) attendance allowance under section 64 of that Act;

(d) severe disablement allowance under section 68 of that Act;

(e) disability living allowance under section 71 of that Act;

(f) increase of disablement pension under section 104 of that Act;

(g) a pension increase under a war pension scheme or an industrial injuries scheme which is analogous to an allowance or increase of disablement pension under sub-paragraph (b), (d) or (e) above.

(h) contributory employment and support allowance or a limited capability for work credit, where entitlement to that allowance or credit or statutory sick pay or a benefit or allowance mentioned in sub-paragraph (a) or (b) or (d), has existed for a period of 28 weeks comprising one continuous period or two or more periods which are linked together provided that, if the person received statutory sick pay, the person satisfied the first and second contribution conditions set out in paragraphs 1 and 2 of Schedule 1 to the Welfare Reform Act;

(i) personal independence payment;

(j) armed forces independence payment;

(k) any benefit, allowance or credit of another EEA state or Switzerland which is substantially similar in character to the benefits, allowances and credits in subparagraphs (a) to (j).

13(6A) In paragraph (6)(h), the reference to contributory employment and support allowance is a reference to an allowance under Part 1 of the Welfare Reform Act 2007 ("the 2007 Act") as amended by the provisions of Schedule 3, and Part 1 of Schedule 14, to the Welfare Reform Act 2012 that remove references to an income-related allowance, and a contributory allowance under Part 1 of the 2007 Act as that Part has effect apart from those provisions.

13(7) The circumstances specified in this paragraph are where a pension or allowance to which sub-paragraph (c), (d), (e) or (f) of paragraph (6) refers, was payable on account of his incapacity but has ceased to be payable only in consequence of his becoming a patient.

13(8) The circumstances specified in this paragraph are where he has an invalid carriage or other vehicle provided to him under section 5(2)(a) of and Schedule 2 to the National Health Service Act 1977, section 46 of the National Health Service (Scotland) Act 1978; or Article 30(1) of the Health and Personal Social Services (Northern Ireland) Order 1972.

13(9) The circumstances specified in this paragraph are where, on 31st March 2013, council tax benefit was payable under Part 7 of the Contributions and Benefits Act (as then in force) to the other member or the other member's partner and the applicable amount of the person entitled to the benefit included a disability premium on account of the other member's incapacity.

13(10) Paragraph (9) is subject to paragraphs (11) and (12).

13(11) Paragraph (9) does not apply unless the other member of the couple was incapacitated (for the purposes of paragraph (1)(c)(i) and regulation 4(1) Second condition, Third variation (c)(i)) solely by virtue of that person or their partner having been in receipt, on 31st March 2013, of council tax benefit which included a disability premium on account of the other member's incapacity, and none of the other circumstances specified in paragraphs (5) to (8) applied on that date.

13(12) If–

(a) the other member of the couple is incapacitated in the circumstances specified in paragraph (9), and

(b) the couple ceases to be entitled to working tax credit (for any reason) on or after 1st April 2013,

that member of the couple shall not be treated as incapacitated in the circumstances specified in paragraph (9) in relation to any subsequent claim.

History – In reg. 13(1)(b), the words "for not less than 16 hours per week" inserted by SI 2012/848, reg. 2(16)(a), with effect from 6 April 2012.
In reg. 13(1)(c), the words "for not less than 16 hours per week" inserted by SI 2012/848, reg. 2(16)(a), with effect from 6 April 2012.
Reg. 13(1)(c)(iv) inserted (and "; or" substituted for "." in reg. 13(1)(c)(iii)) by SI 2012/848, reg. 2(16)(a), with effect from 6 April 2012.
In reg. 13(1) the words "married or unmarried" which appeared before the word "couple" omitted three times by SI 2005/2919, reg. 2(3), with effect from 5 December 2005.
In reg. 13(1)(a) words "qualifying remunerative work" substituted by SI 2003/701, reg. 12(2) with effect from 6 April 2003.
Reg. 13(1)(b), (c) substituted for reg. 13(1)(b) by SI 2003/701, reg. 12(3), with effect from 6 April 2003.
Reg. 13(3) omitted by SI 2004/762, reg. 9 (formerly substituted by SI 2003/701, reg. 12(4), with effect from 6 April 2003) with effect from 6 April 2004.
In reg. 13(4), the words "paragraphs (5) to (12)" substituted for the words "paragraphs (5) to (8)" by SI 2013/1736, reg. 3(2), with effect from 5 August 2013.
Reg. 13(4) substituted by SI 2003/701, reg. 12(4), with effect from 6 April 2003.
Reg. 13(5) substituted by SI 2013/1736, reg. 3(3), with effect from 5 August 2013.
In reg. 13(6), in the introductory words, the words "or – in the case of a credit – an entitlement" inserted by SI 2012/848, reg. 2(17)(a), with effect from 1 May 2012.
In reg. 13(6), in the introductory words, the words "pensions or allowances", which appeared after the words "of the following", omitted by SI 2012/848, reg. 2(17)(b), with effect from 1 May 2012.
In reg. 13(6)(a) words "payable at the higher rate" inserted by SI 2003/701, reg. 12(5), with effect from 6 April 2003.
In reg. 13(6)(h), the words "or a limited capability for work credit," inserted by SI 2012/848, reg. 2(17)(c)(i), with effect from 1 May 2012.
In reg. 13(6)(h), the words "or credit" inserted by SI 2012/848, reg. 2(17)(c)(ii), with effect from 1 May 2012.
In reg. 13(6)(h), the words "or a benefit or allowance mentioned in sub-paragraph (a) or (b) or (d)," inserted by SI 2012/848, reg. 2(17)(c)(iii), with effect from 6 April 2012.
Reg. 13(6)(h) inserted by SI 2008/1879, reg. 20(5), with effect from 27 October 2008.
Reg. 13(6)(i) inserted by SI 2013/388, art. 8 and Sch., para. 28(4), with effect from 8 April 2013.
Reg. 13(6)(j) inserted by SI 2013/591, art. 7 and Sch., para. 24(4), with effect from 8 April 2013.
Reg. 13(6)(k) inserted by SI 2018/365, reg. 4(2), with effect from 6 April 2018.
Reg. 13(6A) inserted by SI 2013/630, reg. 77(4), with effect from 29 April 2013.
In reg. 13(7) reference to "(c)" substituted by SI 2003/701, reg. 12(6), with effect from6 April 2003.
Reg. 13(9)–(12) inserted by SI 2013/1736, reg. 3(4), with effect from 5 August 2013.

Cross references – SI 2003/742, reg. 32: modified application of reg. 13 to members of polygamous units.

14(1) Subject to paragraph (1A), [f]or the purposes of section 12 of the Act charges incurred for child care are charges paid by the person, or in the case of a joint claim, by either or both of the persons, for child care provided for any child for whom the person, or at least one of the persons, is responsible within the meaning of regulation 3 of the Child Tax Credit Regulations 2002.

In these Regulations, such charges are called "relevant child care charges".

14(1A) Child care charges do not include charges in respect of care provided by–

(a) a relative of the child, wholly or mainly in the child's home, or

(b) [omitted by SI 2009/697, reg. 5(2)(a),]

(c) a provider mentioned in regulation 14(2)(c)(v), in circumstances where the care is excluded from being qualifying child care by Article 4(2)(c) of the Tax Credits (Approval of Home Child Care Providers) Scheme (Northern Ireland) 2006.

(d) a provider mentioned in regulation 14(2)(f)(vii), in circumstances where the care is excluded from being qualifying child care by Article 5(3)(d) of the Tax Credits (Approval of Child Care Providers) (Wales) Scheme 2007.

(e) a foster parent, a foster carer or a kinship carer in respect of a child whom that person is fostering or is looking after as the child's kinship carer.

14(1B) For the purposes of this regulation–

(a) **"relative"** means parent, grandparent, aunt, uncle, brother or sister whether by blood, half blood, marriage, civil partnership or affinity;

(b) **"the child's home"** means the home of the person, or in the case of a joint claim of either or both of the persons, responsible for the child.

(c) **"foster parent"** in relation to a child–

(i) in relation to England, means a person with whom the child is placed under the Fostering Services Regulations 2002;

(ii) in relation to Wales, means a person with whom the child is placed under the Fostering Services (Wales) Regulations 2003;

(iii) in relation to Northern Ireland, means a person with whom the child is placed under the Foster Placement (Children) Regulations (Northern Ireland) 1996; and

(d) **"foster carer"** and **"kinship carer"** have the meanings given in regulation 2 of the Looked After Children (Scotland) Regulations 2009.

14(2) **"Child care"** means care provided for a child–

(a) in England–

(i) [omitted by SI 2009/697, reg. 5(3)(a);]

(ii) [omitted by SI 2008/2169, reg. 2(2);]

(iia) by a person registered under Part 3 of the Childcare Act 2006;

(iii) in respect of any period on or before the last day the child is treated as a child for the purpose of this regulation by or under the direction of the proprietor of a school on the school premises (subject to paragraph (2B));

(iv) [omitted by SI 2007/2479, reg. 2(2);]

(v) [omitted by SI 2009/697, reg. 5(3)(c);]

(vi) [omitted by SI 2009/697, reg. 5(3)(d);]

(vii) by a carer provided by a person who is a service provider within the meaning of the Health and Social Care Act 2008 (Regulated Activities) Regulations 2014 in relation to the regulated activity of personal care within paragraph 1 of Schedule 1 to those Regulations;

(viii) [omitted by SI 2008/2169, reg. 2(2);]

(b) in Scotland–

(i) by a person in circumstances where the care service provided by him consists of child minding or of day care of children within the meaning of section 2 of the Regulation of Care (Scotland) Act 2001 and is registered under Part 1 of that Act;

(ia) by a child care agency where the service consists of or includes supplying, or introducing to persons who use the service, child carers within the meaning of sections 2(7) and (8) of the Regulation of Care (Scotland) Act 2001; or

(ii) by a local authority in circumstances where the care service provided by the local authority consists of child minding or of day care of children within the meaning of section 2 of the Regulation of Care (Scotland) Act 2001 and is registered under Part 2 of that Act.

(iii) [omitted by SI 2011/721, reg. 3(3).]

(c) in Northern Ireland–

(i) by persons registered under Part XI of the Children (Northern Ireland) Order 1995;

(ii) by institutions and establishments exempt from registration under that Part by virtue of Article 121 of that Order; or

(iii) in respect of any period ending on or before the day on which he ceases to be a child for the purposes of this regulation, where the care is provided out of school hours by a school on school premises or by an Education and Library Board or a Health and Social Services Trust; or

(iv) [omitted by SI 2011/721, reg. 3(4)(a);]

(v) by a child care provider approved in accordance with the Tax Credits (Approval of Home Child Care Providers) Scheme (Northern Ireland) 2006; or

(vi) by a foster parent in relation to a child (other than one whom the foster parent is fostering) in circumstances where, but for the fact that the child is too old, the care would fall within one of the descriptions in paragraph (2C);

(d) anywhere outside the United Kingdom–

(i) by a child care provider approved by an accredited organisation within the meaning given by regulation 4 of the Tax Credit (New Category of Child Care Provider) Regulations 2002; or

(e) [revoked by SI 2008/604, reg. 3(3), with effect from 6 April 2008;]

(f) in Wales–

(i) by persons registered under Part 2 of the Children and Families (Wales) Measure 2010;

(ii) by a person in circumstances where, but for article 11, 12 or 14 of the Child Minding and Day Care Exceptions (Wales) Order 2010, the care would be day care for the purposes of Part 2 of the Children and Families (Wales) Measure 2010;

(iii) in respect of any period on or before the last day he is treated as a child for the purposes of this regulation, where the care is provided out of school hours, by a school on school premises or by a local authority;

(iv) by a child care provider approved by an accredited organisation within the meaning given by regulation 4 of the Tax Credit (New Category of Child Care Provider) Regulations 1999;

(v) [omitted by SI 2011/721, reg. 3(5)(c);]

(vi) by a person who is employed or engaged under a contract for services to provide care and support by the provider of a domiciliary support service within the meaning of Part 1 of the Regulation and Inspection of Social Care (Wales) Act 2016;

(vii) by a child care provider approved under the Tax Credits (Approval of Child Care Providers) (Wales) Scheme 2007; or

(viii) by a foster parent in relation to a child (other than one whom the foster parent is fostering) in circumstances where, but for the fact that the child is too old, the care would fall within one of the descriptions in paragraph (2D).

14(2A) In paragraph (2)(a)(iii)–

"proprietor", in relation to a school, means–

(a) the governing body incorporated under section 19 of the Education Act 2002, or

(b) if there is no such body, the person or body of persons responsible for the management of the school;

"school" means a school that Her Majesty's Chief Inspector of Education, Children's Services and Skills (the "Chief Inspector") is or may be required to inspect;

"school premises" means premises that may be inspected as part of an inspection of the school by the Chief Inspector.

14(2B) Care provided for a child in England is not child care under paragraph (2)(a)(iii) if–

(a) it is provided during school hours for a child who has reached compulsory school age, or

(b) it is provided in breach of a requirement to register under Part 3 of the Childcare Act 2006.

14(2C) The descriptions referred to in paragraph (2)(c)(vi) are–

(a) child minding or day care for the purposes of Part 11 of the Children (Northern Ireland) Order 1995; and

(b) qualifying child care for the purposes of the Tax Credits (Approval of Home Child Care Providers) Scheme (Northern Ireland) 2006.

14(2D) The descriptions referred to in paragraph (2)(f)(viii) are–

(a) child minding, or day care, for the purposes of Part 2 of the Children and Families (Wales) Measure 2010; and

(b) qualifying child care for the purposes of the Tax Credits (Approval of Child Care Providers) (Wales) Scheme 2007.

14(3) For the purposes of this regulation a person is a child until the last day of the week in which falls the 1st September following that child's fifteenth birthday (or sixteenth birthday if the child is disabled).

14(4) For the purposes of paragraph (3) a child is disabled where–

(a) a disability living allowance is payable in respect of that child, or has ceased to be payable solely because he is a patient;

(b) the child is certified as severely sight impaired or blind by a consultant ophthalmologist;

(c) the child ceased to be certified as severely sight impaired or blind by a consultant ophthalmologist within the 28 weeks immediately preceding the date of claim;

(d) personal independence payment is payable in respect of that child, or would be payable but for regulations under section 86(1) (hospital in-patients) of the Welfare Reform Act 2012; or

(e) armed forces independence payment is payable in respect of that child.

14(5) Charges paid in respect of the child's compulsory education or charges paid by a person to a partner or by a partner to the person in respect of any child for whom either or any of them is responsible are not relevant child care charges.

14(6) Where regulation 15(4) (agreement for the provision of future child care) applies–

(a) the words "charges paid" in paragraph (1) include charges which will be incurred, and

(b) the words "child care provided" in paragraph (1) include care which will be provided.

14(7) [Omitted by SI 2004/762, reg. 10(b).]

14(8) Relevant child care charges are calculated on a weekly basis in accordance with regulation 15.

History – In reg. 14(1) words "Subject to paragraph (1A)," inserted by SI 2003/701, reg. 13(2), with effect from 6 April 2003 and the words "within the meaning of regulation 3 of the Child Tax Credit Regulations 2002" inserted by SI 2004/762, reg. 10(a), with effect from 6 April 2004.
Reg. 14(1A)(b) omitted by SI 2009/697, reg. 5(2)(a), with effect from 18 July 2009.
Reg. 14(1A)(c) inserted by SI 2006/766, reg. 20, with effect from 6 April 2006.
In reg. 14(1A)(d), "regulation 14(2)(f)(vii)" substituted for "regulation 14(2)(f)(ii)" by SI 2009/2887, reg. 4(2)(a), with effect from 21 November 2009.
In reg. 14(1A)(e), the words ", a foster carer or a kinship carer" inserted by SI 2009/2887, reg. 4(2)(b)(i), with effect from 21 November 2009.
In reg. 14(1A)(e), the words "that person is fostering or is looking after as the child's kinship carer" substituted for the words "that foster parent is fostering" by SI 2009/2887, reg. 4(2)(b)(ii), with effect from 21 November 2009.
Reg. 14(1A)(e) inserted by SI 2009/697, reg. 5(2)(b), with effect from 18 July 2009.
Reg. 14(1A) inserted by SI 2003/701, reg. 13(3), with effect from 6 April 2003.
Reg. 14(1A)(a) and (b) substituted for words "a relative of a child wholly or mainly in the child's home" by SI 2005/769, reg. 3, with effect from 6 April 2005.
Reg. 14(1A)(d) inserted by SI 2007/824, reg. 6(2), with effect from 6 April 2007.
Reg. 14(1A)(e) inserted by SI 2009/697, reg. 5(2)(b) with effect from 18 July 2009.
Reg. 14(1B)(c) inserted by SI 2009/2887, reg. 4(3), with effect from 21 November 2009.
Reg. 14(1B)(d) inserted by SI 2009/2887, reg. 4(3), with effect from 21 November 2009.
In reg. 14(1B) in the definition of "relative" the words ", civil partnership" inserted by SI 2005/2919, reg. 2(4), with effect from 5 December 2005.
Reg. 14(1B) inserted by SI 2003/701, reg. 13(3), with effect from 6 April 2003.
Reg. 14(2)(a)(i) omitted by SI 2009/697, reg. 5(3)(a), with effect from 6 April 2009.
Reg. 14(2)(a)(ii) omitted, reg. 14(2)(a)(iia) inserted, reg. 14(2)(a)(iii) substituted, the word "or" inserted at end of reg. 14(2)(a)(vi) and reg. 14(2)(a)(viii), and the word "or" preceding it, omitted by SI 2008/2169, reg. 2(2), with effect from 1 September 2008.
In reg. 14(2)(a), in the words before paragraph (i), the words "and Wales" omitted by SI 2008/604, reg. 3(2)(a), with effect from 6 April 2008.
In former reg. 14(2)(a)(iii) the words "on or before" substituted by SI 2004/1276, reg. 2(2)(a)(i), with effect from 1 June 2004 and the words "and the last day he is treated as a child for the purposes of this regulation," substituted by SI 2003/2815, reg. 15 with effect from 26 November 2003.
In reg. 14(2)(a)(iii), the words "(subject to paragraph (2B))" substituted by SI 2009/697, reg. 5(3)(b), with effectfrom 6 April 2009.
Reg. 14(2)(a)(iv) omitted by SI 2007/2479, reg. 2(2), with effect from 1 October 2007.
Reg. 14(2)(a)(v) omitted by SI 2009/697, reg. 5(3)(c), with effect from 18 July 2009.
In former reg. 14(2)(a)(v), the words "or the Fostering Services (Wales) Regulations 2003" omitted by SI 2008/604, reg. 3(2)(c), with effect from 6 April 2008.
Reg. 14(2)(a)(v) previously inserted by SI 2004/1276, reg. 2(2)(a)(iv), with effect from 1 June 2004.
Reg. 14(2)(a)(vi) omitted by SI 2009/697, reg. 5(3)(d), with effect from 18 July 2009.
Reg. 14(2)(a)(vi), (vii) and former (viii) inserted by SI 2008/604, reg. 3(2)(d), with effect from 6 April 2008.
Reg. 14(2)(a)(vii) substituted by SI 2016/360, reg. 2(3), with effect from 6 April 2016.
Reg. 14(2)(b)(ia) inserted by SI 2006/766, reg. 20, with effect from 6 April 2006.
Reg. 14(2)(b)(iii) (and the "or" at the end of reg. 14(2)(b)(ii)) omitted by SI 2011/721, reg. 3(3), with effect from 6 April 2011.
Reg. 14(2)(b)(iii) substituted by SI 2009/2887, reg. 4(4)(a), with effect from 21 November 2009.
Reg. 14(2)(b)(iii) inserted by SI 2004/1276, reg. 2(2)(b)(iii), with effect from 1 June 2004.
Reg. 14(2)(c)(iii) and (iv) inserted by SI 2004/1276, reg. 2(2)(c)(ii), with effect from 1 June 2004.
Reg. 14(2)(c)(iv) (and the "or" at the end of it) omitted by SI 2011/721, reg. 3(4)(a), with effect from 6 April 2011.
In former reg. 14(2)(c)(iv), the words "under the Foster Placement (Children) Regulations (Northern Ireland) 1996", which appeared after "foster parent", omitted by SI 2009/2887, reg. 4(4)(b), with effect from 21 November 2009.
Reg. 14(2)(c)(vi) (and the "; or" at the end of reg. 14(2)(c)(v)) inserted by SI 2011/721, reg. 3(4)(b), with effect from 6 April 2011.
Reg. 14(2)(c)(v) inserted by SI 2006/766, reg. 20, with effect from 6 April 2006.
In reg. 14(2)(d) words "anywhere outside the United Kingdom" substituted by SI 2003/701, reg. 13(4)(a), and para. (2)(d)(ii) omitted from 6 April 2003.
Reg. 14(2)(e) revoked by SI 2008/604, reg. 3(3), with effect from 6 April 2008.
Reg. 14(2)(e) inserted by SI 2003/701, reg. 13(5), with effect from 6 April 2003.
Reg. 14(2)(e)(i) omitted by SI 2005/769, reg. 4(a) with effect from 1 January 2006. Prior to its omission para (i) read "wholly or mainly in the child's home by a child care provider approved in accordance with the Tax Credits (Approval of Home Child Care Providers) Scheme 2003; or ".
In reg. 14(2)(e)(ia) the word "or" omitted at the end by SI 2007/824, reg. 6(3)(a), with effect from 6 April 2007.
Reg. 14(2)(e)(ia) inserted by SI 2005/769, reg. 4(b) with effect from 6 April 2005.
Reg. 14(2)(e)(ib) inserted by SI 2007/824, reg. 6(3)(b), with effect from 6 April 2007.
In reg. 14(2)(f)(i), the words "Part 2 of the Children and Families (Wales) Measure 2010" substitutedfor the words "Part 10A of the Children Act 1989" by SI 2011/721, reg. 3(5)(a), with effect from 6 April 2011.
Reg. 14(2)(f)(vi) substituted by SI 2018/365, reg. 4(3), with effect from 6 April 2018. Former reg. 14(2)(f)(vi) read as follows:
"(vi) by a domiciliary care worker under the Domiciliary Care Agencies (Wales) Regulations 2004;"
Reg. 14(2)(f)(ii) substituted by SI 2011/721, reg. 3(5)(b), with effect from 6 April 2011.
Reg. 14(2)(f)(v) omitted by SI 2011/721, reg. 3(5)(c), with effect from 6 April 2011.
Reg. 14(2)(f)(viii) and the "; or" at the end of reg. 14(2)(f)(vii) inserted, and the "or" at the end of reg. 14(2)(f)(vi) omitted, by SI 2011/721, reg. 3(5)(d) and (e), with effect from 6 April 2011.
Reg. 14(2)(f) substituted by SI 2008/604, reg. 3(4), with effect from 6 April 2008.
Reg. 14(2)(f)(ii) inserted by SI 2007/824, reg. 6(4), with effect from 6 April 2007. The original text has been designated as para. (i) in square brackets as it is assumed that this step was omitted in error.
Reg. 14(2)(f)(iii) inserted and the word "or" moved from end of reg. 14(2)(f)(i) to end of reg. 14(2)(f)(ii) by SI 2007/2479, reg. 2(3), with effect from 1 October 2007.

In reg. 14(2)(f)(v), the words "under the Fostering Services (Wales) Regulations 2003", which appeared after "foster parent", omitted by SI 2009/2887, reg. 4(4)(c), with effect from 21 November 2009.
Reg. 14(2)(f) inserted by SI 2004/2663, reg. 3(2), with effect from 3 November 2004.
Reg. 14(2A) inserted by SI 2008/2169, reg. 2(3), with effect from 1 September 2008.
In reg. 14(2B), "child care" substituted for "registered or approved care" by SI 2009/697, reg. 5(4), with effect from 6 April 2009.
Reg. 14(2B) inserted by SI 2008/2169, reg. 2(3), with effect from 1 September 2008.
Reg. 14(2C) and (2D) inserted by SI 2011/721, reg. 3(6), with effect from 6 April 2011.
Reg. 14(4)(b) substituted by SI 2014/2924, reg. 4(2)(a), with effect from 28 November 2014.
In reg. 14(4)(b) the words "a council constituted under section 2 of the Local Government etc. (Scotland) Act 1994" substituted for the words "a local authority in Scotland" by SI 2010/751, reg. 14, with effect from 6 April 2010.
In reg. 14(4)(c), the words "certified as severely sight impaired or blind by a consultant ophthalmologist" substituted for the words "registered as blind in such a register" by SI 2014/2924, reg. 4(2)(b), with effect from 28 November 2014.
Reg. 14(4)(d) (and the "; or" before it) inserted (and the "or" after (b) omitted) by SI 2013/388, art. 8 and Sch., para. 28(5), with effect from 8 April 2013.
Reg. 14(4)(e) (and the "; or" before it) inserted (and the "or" after (c) omitted) by SI 2013/591, art. 7 and Sch., para. 24(5), with effect from 8 April 2013.
Reg. 14(7) omitted by SI 2004/762, reg. 10(b), with effect from 6 April 2004.
Cross references – SI 2003/742, reg. 33: modified application of reg. 14 to members of polygamous units.

Calculation of relevant child care charges

15(1) Relevant child care charges are calculated by aggregating the average weekly charge paid for child care for each child in respect of whom charges are incurred and rounding up the total to the nearest whole pound.

This is subject to paragraphs (1A) and (2).

15(1A) In any case in which the charges in respect of child care are paid weekly, the average weekly charge for the purposes of paragraph (1) is established–

(a) where the charges are for a fixed weekly amount, by aggregating the average weekly charge paid for child care for each child in respect of whom charges are incurred in the most recent four complete weeks; or

(b) where the charges are for variable weekly amounts, by aggregating the charges for the previous 52 weeks and dividing the total by 52.

15(2) In any case in which the charges in respect of child care are paid monthly, the average weekly charge for the purposes of paragraph (1) is established–

(a) where the charges are for a fixed monthly amount, by multiplying that amount by 12 and dividing the product by 52; or

(b) where the charges are for variable monthly amounts, by aggregating the charges for the previous 12 months and dividing the total by 52.

15(3) In a case where there is insufficient information for establishing the average weekly charge paid for child care in accordance with paragraphs (1) and (2), an officer of the Board shall estimate the charge–

(a) in accordance with information provided by the person or persons incurring the charges; and

(b) by any method which in the officer's opinion is reasonable.

15(4) If a person–

(a) has entered into an agreement for the provision of child care; and

(b) will incur under that agreement relevant child care charges in respect of child care during the period of the award,

the average weekly charge for child care is based upon a written estimate of the future weekly charges provided by that person.

History – In reg. 15(1) words "and rounding up the total to the the[sic] nearest whole pound", and words "paragraphs (1A) and (2)" substituted by SI 2003/701, reg. 14(2), with effect from 6 April 2003.
Reg. 15(1A) inserted by SI 2003/701, reg. 14(3) with effect from 6 April 2003.

Change of circumstances

16(1) There is a relevant change in circumstances if–

(a) [omitted by SI 2003/701, reg. 15(2);]

(b) during the period of an award, the weekly relevant child care charges, rounded up to the nearest whole pound–

(i) exceed the average weekly charge calculated in accordance with regulation 15 by £10 a week or more;

(ii) are less than the average weekly charge calculated in accordance with regulation 15 by £10 a week or more; or

(iii) are nil.

If there is a relevant change in circumstances, the amount of the child care element of working tax credit shall be recalculated with effect from the specified date.

16(2) For the purposes of paragraph (1), the weekly relevant child care charge–

(a) where the child care charges are for a fixed weekly amount, is the aggregate of the weekly charge paid for child care for each child in respect of whom charges are incurred in each of the four consecutive weeks in which the change occurred; or

(b) where the child care charges are for variable weekly amounts, is established by aggregating the anticipated weekly charge paid for child care for each child in respect of whom charges will be incurred for the following 52 weeks and dividing the total by 52.

16(3) If in any case the charges in respect of child care are paid monthly, the weekly relevant child care charge for the purposes of paragraph (1) is established–

(a) where the charges are for a fixed monthly amount, by multiplying that amount by 12 and dividing the product by 52; or

(b) where the charges are for variable monthly amounts, by aggregating the anticipated charges for the next 12 months and dividing the total by 52.

16(4) In a case where there is insufficient information for establishing the weekly relevant child care charge paid for child care in accordance with paragraphs (2) and (3), an officer of the Board shall estimate the charge–

(a) in accordance with information provided by the person or persons incurring the charges; and

(b) by any method which in the officer's opinion is reasonable.

16(5) For the purpose of paragraph (1) the specified date is–

(a) where the child care charges are increased, the later of–

(i) the first day of the week in which the change occurred, and

(ii) the first day of the week in which falls the day which is one month prior to the date notification of the change is given;

(b) where the child care charges are decreased–

(i) in a case where an award of child care charges is a fixed period, the length of which is known when the award is first made, the first day of the week following the end of that fixed period, and

(ii) in all other cases, the first day of the week following the four consecutive weeks in which the change occurred.

History – Reg. 16(1)(a) omitted by SI 2003/701, reg. 15(2), with effect from 6 April 2003.
In reg. 16(1)(b) words "during the period of an award, the weekly relevant child care charges, rounded up to the nearest whole pound" substituted by SI 2003/701, reg. 15(3), with effect from 6 April 2003.
Reg. 16(2) substituted by SI 2003/701, reg. 15(4) with effect from 6 April 2003.
In reg. 16(3)(b) the word "anticipated" inserted and word "next" substituted by SI 2003/701, reg. 15(5), with effect from 6 April 2003.
In reg. 16(5)(a)(ii) the words "one month" substituted for the words "three months" by SI 2012/848, reg. 2(18), with effect from 6 April 2012.
Reg. 16(5)(b) substituted by SI 2010/918, reg. 3, with effect from 15 April 2010.

SEVERE DISABILITY ELEMENT

Severe disablement element

17(1) The determination of the maximum rate must include the severe disablement element if the claimant, or, in the case of a joint claim, one of the claimants satisfies paragraph (2) or (3) or (4).

17(2) A person satisfies this paragraph if a disability living allowance, attributable to the care component payable at the highest rate prescribed under section 72(3) of the Contributions and Benefits Act or an attendance allowance at the higher rate prescribed under section 65(3) of that Act–

(a) is payable in respect of him; or

(b) would be so payable but for a suspension of benefit by virtue of regulations under section 113(2) of the Contributions and Benefits Act (suspension during hospitalisation), or an abatement as a consequence of hospitalisation.

17(3) A person satisfies this paragraph if the enhanced rate of the daily living component of personal independence payment under section 78(2) of the Welfare Reform Act 2012–

(a) is payable in respect of that person; or

(b) would be so payable but for regulations made under section 86(1) (hospital in- patients) of that Act.

17(4) A person satisfies this paragraph if an armed forces independence payment is payable in respect of him.

History – In reg. 17(1), the words "or (3)" inserted by SI 2013/388, art. 8 and Sch., para. 28(6)(a), with effect from 8 April 2013.
In reg. 17(1), the words "or (4)" inserted by SI 2013/591, art. 7 and Sch., para. 24(6)(a), with effect from 8 April 2013.
Reg. 17(3) inserted by SI 2013/388, art. 8 and Sch., para. 28(6)(b), with effect from 8 April 2013.
Reg. 17(4) inserted by SI 2013/591, art. 7 and Sch., para. 24(6)(b), with effect from 8 April 2013.

Cross references – SI 2002/2014, reg. 26: date of notification of change of circumstances resulting in entitlement to severe disability element of working tax credit.

50 PLUS ELEMENT

50 plus element

18 [Omitted by SI 2012/848, reg. 2(19).]

History – Reg. 18 omitted by SI 2012/848, reg. 2(19), with effect from 6 April 2012.

DEATH OF A CHILD OR QUALIFYING YOUNG PERSON FOR WHOM THE CLAIMANT IS RESPONSIBLE

Entitlement after death of a child or qualifying young person for whom the claimant is responsible

19(1) Paragraph (2) applies if–

(a) the death occurs of a child or qualifying young person,

(b) working tax credit is payable to a person who was, or to a couple at least one of whom was, immediately before the death responsible for that child or qualifying young person;

(c) the prescribed conditions for an element of working tax credit were satisfied because the claimant, or at least one of the claimants, was responsible for that child or qualifying person, but would not have been satisfied but for that responsibility; and

(d) the prescribed conditions would have continued to be satisfied but for the death.

19(2) If this paragraph applies, working tax credit shall continue to be payable, as if the child or qualifying young person had not died, for the period for which child tax credit continues to be payable in accordance with regulation 6 of the Child Tax Regulation 2002.

PART 3 – MAXIMUM RATE

MAXIMUM RATES OF ELEMENTS OF WORKING TAX CREDIT

20(1) The maximum annual rate of working tax credit payable to a single claimant or to a couple making a joint claim is the sum of whichever of the following elements are applicable–

(a) the basic element specified in column (2) of the table in Schedule 2 at paragraph 1;

(b) in respect of a claimant who satisfies regulation 9(1), the disability element specified in column (2) of the table in Schedule 2 at paragraph 2;

(c) the 30 hour element specified in column (2) of the table in Schedule 2 at paragraph 3 in respect of–

(i) a single claimant who works for not less than 30 hours per week,

(ii) a couple either or both of whom work for not less than 30 hours per week; or

(iii) a couple, at least one of whom is responsible for a child or a qualifying young person and at least one of whom works for 16 hours per week if their hours of work when aggregated amount to at least 30 hours per week;

(d) the second adult element specified in column (2) of the table in Schedule 2 at paragraph 4 where regulation 11 so provides;

(e) the lone parent element specified in column (2) of the table in Schedule 2 at paragraph 5 where regulation 12 applies; and

(f) the severe disability element specified in column (2) of the table in Schedule 2 at paragraph 6–

(i) in respect of a single claimant who satisfies regulation 17; or

(ii) in respect of a member of a couple making a joint claim who satisfies regulation 17;

(g) [omitted by SI 2012/848, reg. 2(20).]

20(2) The maximum rate of the child care element of a working tax credit is 70 per cent. of the maxima specified in paragraph (3).

20(3) The maxima are–

(a) £175.00 per week, where the only one child in respect of whom relevant child care charges are paid; and

(b) £300.00 per week where the claimant or, in the case of a joint claim, at least one of the claimants, is responsible for more than one child in respect of whom relevant child care charges are paid.

History – Reg. 20(1)(g) omitted (and the "and" at the end of reg. 20(1)(f) omitted, and the "and" at the end of reg. 20(1)(e) inserted) by SI 2012/848, reg. 2(20), with effect from 6 April 2012.

In reg. 20(2), "70 per cent" substituted for "80 per cent" by SI 2011/1035, reg. 3(2), with effect in relation to awards of tax credits for the year beginning on 6 April 2011. By virtue of SI 2012/849, reg. 5(b), this substitution continues to have effect in relation to awards of tax credits for the year beginning on 6 April 2012 and subsequent tax years.

In reg. 20(2) the figure "80" substituted for "70" by SI 2006/963, reg. 3, with effect from 6 April 2006.
In reg. 20(3) the words "claimant or, in the case of a joint claim, at least one of the claimants, is responsible for" substituted for the words "claimant's family includes" by SI 2003/701, reg. 16, with effect from 6 April 2003 and the figures in sub-para. (a) and (b) substituted for the previous figures by SI 2005/681, reg. 3(1) in relation to awards of tax credits for the tax year beginning on 6 April 2005 and subsequent tax years.
Cross references – SI 2003/742, reg. 34: modified application of reg. 20 to members of polygamous units.

SCHEDULES

SCHEDULE 1 – DISABILITY WHICH PUTS A PERSON AT A DISADVANTAGE IN GETTING A JOB

Regulation 9(1)

PART 1

HMRC Manuals – TCTM 02505: HMRC explanation of words and phrases used in this Schedule.

1 When standing he cannot keep his balance unless he continually holds onto something.

2 Using any crutches, walking frame, walking stick, prosthesis or similar walking aid which he habitually uses, he cannot walk a continuous distance of 100 metres along level ground without stopping or without suffering severe pain.

3 He can use neither of his hands behind his back as in the process of putting on a jacket or of tucking a shirt into trousers.

4 He can extend neither of his arms in front of him so as to shake hands with another person without difficulty.

5 He can put neither of his hands up to his head without difficulty so as to put on a hat.

6 Due to lack of manual dexterity he cannot, with one hand, pick up a coin which is not more than 21/2 centimetres in diameter.

7 He is not able to use his hands or arms to pick up a full jug of 1 litre capacity and pour from it into a cup, without difficulty.

8 He can turn neither of his hands sideways through 180 degrees.

9 He is certified as severely sight impaired or blind by a consultant ophthalmologist.

History – Para. 9 substituted by SI 2014/2924, reg. 4(3), with effect from 28 November 2014.
In former para. 9(b), the words "section 2 of the Local Government etc. (Scotland) Act 1994" substituted for the words "the Local Government (Scotland) Act 1994" by SI 2010/751, reg. 15(2), with effect from 6 April 2010.
In former para. 9(c), the words "or partially sighted" inserted twice by SI 2010/751, reg. 15(3), with effect from 6 April 2010.

10 He cannot see to read 16 point print at a distance greater than 20 centimetres, if appropriate, wearing the glasses he normally uses.

11 He cannot hear a telephone ring when he is in the same room as the telephone, if appropriate, using a hearing aid he normally uses.

12 In a quiet room he has difficulty in hearing what someone talking in a loud voice at a distance of 2 metres says, if appropriate, using a hearing aid he normally uses.

13 People who know him well have difficulty in understanding what he says.

14 When a person he knows well speaks to him, he has difficulty in understanding what that person says.

15 At least once a year during waking hours he is in a coma or has a fit in which he loses consciousness.

16 He has a mental illness for which he receives regular treatment under the supervision of a medically qualified person.

17 Due to mental disability he is often confused or forgetful.

18 He cannot do the simplest addition and subtraction.

19 Due to mental disability he strikes people or damages property or is unable to form normal social relationships.

20 He cannot normally sustain an 8 hour working day or a 5 day working week due to a medical condition or intermittent or continuous severe pain.

PART 2

21 As a result of an illness or accident he is undergoing a period of habilitation or rehabilitation.

SCHEDULE 2 – MAXIMUM RATES OF THE ELEMENTS OF A WORKING TAX CREDIT

Regulation 20(1)

Relevant element of working tax credit	Maximum annual rate
1. Basic element	£1,960
2. Disability element	£3,090
3. 30 hour element	£810
4. Second adult element	£2,010
5. Lone Parent element	£2,010
6. Severe disability element	£1,330

History – In the table, figures in items 2 and 6 substituted for previous figures by SI 2018/344, reg. 2, with effect in relation to awards of tax credits for the tax year beginning on 6 April 2018 and subsequent tax years.
In the table, figures in items 2 and 6 substituted for previous figures by SI 2017/406, reg. 2, with effect in relation to awards of tax credits for the tax year beginning on 6 April 2017 and subsequent tax years.
In the table, figures in items 1, 3, 4 and 5 substituted for the previous figures by SI 2015/567, art. 4 with effect 6 April 2015.
In the table, figures in items 1, 3, 4 and 5 substituted for the previous figures by SI 2014/384, art. 4, with effect from 6 April 2014.
In the table, figures in items 2 and 6 substituted for the previous figures by SI 2015/451, reg. 3, with effect in relation to awards of tax credits for the tax year beginning on 6 April 2015 and subsequent years.
In the table, figures in items 2 and 6 substituted for the previous figures by SI 2014/845, reg. 3, with effect in relation to awards of tax credits for the tax year beginning 6 April 2014 and subsequent tax years.
Table substituted by SI 2013/750, reg. 3(2), with effect in relation to awards of tax credits for the tax year beginning on 6 April 2013 and subsequent tax years.
Table substituted by SI 2012/849, reg. 3(2), in relation to awards of tax credits for the tax year beginning on 6 April 2012 and subsequent years.
Table substituted by SI 2011/1035, reg. 3(2), in relation to awards of tax credits for the tax year beginning on 6 April 2011.
Table substituted by SI 2010/981, reg. 3, in relation to awards of tax credits for the tax year beginning on 6 April 2010.
Table substituted by SI 2009/800, reg. 3, in relation to awards of tax credits for the tax year beginning on 6 April 2009.
Table substituted by SI 2008/796, reg. 3, in relation to awards of tax credits for the tax year beginning on 6 April 2008 and subsequent tax years.
Table substituted by SI 2007/828, reg. 3, in relation to awards of tax credits for the tax year beginning on 6 April 2007 and subsequent years.
Table substituted by SI 2006/963, reg. 3(2), in relation to awards of tax credits for the tax year beginning on 6 April 2006 and subsequent years.

TAX CREDITS (DEFINITION AND CALCULATION OF INCOME) REGULATIONS 2002

(SI 2002/2006, as amended by SI 2003/732, SI 2003/2815, SI 2004/1748, SI 2004/2663, 2005/2919, 2006/745, SI 2006/766, SI 2007/824, SI 2007/1305, SI 2007/2538, SI 2008/604, SI 2008/1879, SI 2008/2169, SI 2009/697, SI 2009/2887, SI 2010/751, SI 2010/2494, SI 2010/2914, SI 2011/721, SI 2012/848, SI 2013/388, SI 2013/630, SI 2014/658, SI 2014/1230, SI 2014/2924, SI 2015/175, SI 2015/1985, SI 2016/360, SI 2016/978, SI 2017/396, SI 2017/422, SI 2018/365 and SI 2018/378)

Made on 30 July 2002 by the Treasury, in exercise of the powers conferred upon them by s. 7(8) and (9), 65(1), (7) and (9) and 67 of the Tax Credits Act 2002. Coming into force in accordance with reg. 1.

Cross references – Age-related Payments Act 2004: s. 6(c) provides that age-related payments are disregarded in assessing a person's entitlement to tax credit.

PART 1 – GENERAL PROVISIONS

CITATION, COMMENCEMENT AND EFFECT

1 These Regulations may be cited as the Tax Credits (Definition and Calculation of Income) Regulations 2002 and shall come into force–

(a) for the purpose of enabling claims to be made, on 1st August 2002;

(b) for the purpose of enabling awards to be made, on 1st January 2003; and

(c) for all other purposes, on 6th April 2003;

and shall have effect for the tax year beginning on 6th April 2003 and subsequent tax years.

INTERPRETATION

2(1) In these Regulations, unless the context otherwise requires–

"the Act" means the Tax Credits Act 2002;

"the Contributions and Benefits Act" means the Social Security Contributions and Benefits Act 1992;

"the Employment Act" means the Employment and Training Act 1973; and

"the Northern Ireland Contributions and Benefits Act" means the Social Security Contributions and Benefits (Northern Ireland) Act 1992.

2(2) In these Regulations except where the context otherwise requires–

"the 1992 Fund" means moneys made available from time to time by the Secretary of State for Social Security for the benefit of persons eligible for payment in accordance with the provisions of a scheme established by him on 24th April 1992 as respects England and Wales and Northern Ireland and on 10th April 1992 as respects Scotland;

"the Board" means the Commissioners for Her Majesty's Revenue and Customs;

"child" has the meaning given in the Child Tax Credit Regulations 2002;

"couple" has the meaning given by section 3(5A) of the Act;

"claim" means a claim for child tax credit or working tax credit and **"joint claim"** and **"single claim"** shall be construed in accordance with section 3(8) of the Act and **"claimant"** shall be construed accordingly;

"earnings" shall be construed in accordance with section 62 of the ITEPA;

"the Eileen Trust" means the charitable trust of that name established on 29th March 1993 out of funds provided by the Secretary of State for Social Security for the benefit of persons eligible in accordance with its provisions;

"employment zone" means an area within Great Britain–

(i) subject to a designation for the purposes of the Employment Zones Regulations 2003 by the Secretary of State, or

(ii) listed in the Schedule to the Employment Zones (Allocation to Contractors) Pilot Regulations 2006,

pursuant to section 60 of the Welfare Reform and Pensions Act 1999;

"employment zone programme" means a programme which is–

(a) established for one or more employment zones, and

(b) designed to assist claimants for a jobseeker's allowance to obtain sustainable employment;

"family" means–

(c) in the case of a joint claim, the couple by whom the claim is made and any child or qualifying young person for whom at least one of them is responsible, in accordance with regulation 3 of the Child Tax Credit Regulations 2002; and

(d) in the case of a single claim, the claimant and any child or qualifying young person for whom he is responsible in accordance with regulation 3 of the Child Tax Credit Regulations 2002;

"the Independent Living Fund" means the charitable trust of that name established out of funds provided by the Secretary of State for Social Services for the purpose of providing financial assistance to those persons incapacitated by or otherwise suffering from very severe disablement who are in need of such assistance to enable them to live independently;

"the Independent Living Fund (2006)" means the Trust of that name established by a deed dated 10th April 2006 and made between the Secretary of State for Work and Pensions of the one part and Margaret Rosemary Cooper, Michael Beresford Boyall and Marie Theresa Martin of the other part;

"the Independent Living Funds" means the Independent Living Fund, the Independent Living (Extension) Fund, the Independent Living (1993) Fund and the Independent Living Fund (2006);

"the Independent Living (Extension) Fund" means the trust of that name established on 25th February 1993 by the Secretary of State for Social Security and Robin Glover Wendt and John Fletcher Shepherd;

"the Independent Living (1993) Fund" means the trust of that name established on 25th February 1993 by the Secretary of State for Social Security and Robin Glover Wendt and John Fletcher Shepherd;

"ITA" means the Income Tax Act 2007;

"ITEPA" means the Income Tax (Earnings and Pensions) Act 2003;

"ITTOIA" means the Income Tax (Trading and Other Income) Act 2005;

"the Macfarlane (Special Payments) Trust" means the trust of that name established on 29th January 1990 partly out of funds provided by the Secretary of State for Health for the benefit of certain persons suffering from haemophilia;

"the Macfarlane (Special Payments) (No 2) Trust" means the trust of that name established on 3rd May 1991 partly out of funds provided by the Secretary of State for Health for the benefit of certain persons suffering from haemophilia and other beneficiaries;

"the Macfarlane Trust" means the charitable trust established partly out of funds provided by the Secretary of State for Health to the Haemophilia Society for the relief of poverty or distress among those suffering from haemophilia;

"the Macfarlane Trusts" means the Macfarlane Trust, the Macfarlane (Special Payments) Trust and the Macfarlane (Special Payments) (No.2) Trust;

"pensionable age" has the meaning given by the rules in paragraph 1 of Schedule 4 to the Pensions Act 1995;

"pension fund holder", in relation to a registered pension scheme means the trustees, managers or scheme administrators of the scheme;

"qualifying care receipts" has the meaning given to that expression by section 805 of the Income Tax (Trading and Other Income) Act 2005;

"qualifying young person" has the meaning given in the Child Tax Credit Regulations 2002;

"registered pension scheme" has the meaning given by section 150(2) of the Finance Act 2004;

"tax year" means a period beginning with the 6th April in one year and ending with 5th April in the next;

"the Taxes Act" means the Income and Corporation Taxes Act 1988;

"voluntary organisation" means a body, other than a public or local authority, the activities of which are carried on otherwise than for profit;

"war pension" has the meaning given in section 25(4) of the Social Security Act 1989.

2(3) For the purposes of these Regulations, whether a person is responsible for a child or a qualifying young person is determined in accordance with regulation 3 of the Child Tax Credits Regulations 2002.

2(4) In these Regulations–

(a) a reference to a claimant's partner is a reference to a claimant's spouse or civil partner or a person with whom the claimant lives as a spouse or civil partner; and

(b) a reference to a claimant's former partner is a reference to a claimant's former spouse or civil partner or a person with whom the claimant has lived as a spouse or civil partner; and

(c) a reference in these Regulations to an Extra Statutory Concession is a reference to that Concession as published by the Inland Revenue on 1st July 2002.

History – In reg. 2 the definition of "the Board" and "employment zone" substituted, the definition of "ITTOIA" inserted, and the definition of "Schedule D" omitted by SI 2006/766, reg. 7 with effect from 6 April 2006.
In reg. 2(1) the definition of "couple" inserted by SI 2005/2919, reg. 3(2), with effect from 5 December 2005.
In reg. 2(1) in the definition of "family" the words "married or unmarried" omitted by SI 2005/2919, reg. 3(2), with effect from 5 December 2005.
In reg. 2(1) definition of "the Northern Ireland Contributions and Benefits Act" inserted by SI 2004/762, reg. 13, with effect from 6 April 2004.
In reg. 2(2) in the definition of "claim" the words "section 3(8)" substituted by SI 2003/2815, reg. 3, with effect from 26 November 2003.
In reg. 2(2) definition of "earnings" and "ITEPA" inserted by SI 2003/732, reg. 4, with effect from 6 April 2003.
In reg. 2(2) definition of "emoluments" and "Schedule E" repealed by SI 2003/732, reg. 4, with effect from 6 April 2003.
In reg. 2(2) in the definition of "employment zone", para. (ii) substituted by SI 2007/824, reg. 8(2), with effect from 6 April 2007.
In reg. 2(2) the definition of "the Independent Living Fund (2006)" inserted and in the definition of "the Independent Living Funds" the words "the Independent Living (Extension) Fund, the Independent Living (1993) Fund and the Independent Living Fund (2006)" substituted by SI 2007/2538, art. 7, with effect from 1 October 2007.
In reg. 2(2) the definition of "ITA" inserted by SI 2007/1305, reg. 3 with effect from 16 May 2007.
In reg. 2(2) in the definition of "pension fund holder" the words "registered pension scheme" substituted and "or contract" omitted at the end by SI 2006/745, reg. 26 with effect from 6 April 2006.
In reg. 2(2) the definition of "personal pension scheme" omitted by SI 2006/745, reg. 26 with effect from 6 April 2006.
In reg. 2(2), the definition of "qualifying care receipts" inserted by SI 2011/721, reg. 2(2), with effect from 6 April 2011.
In reg. 2(2) the definition of "registered pension scheme" omitted by SI 2006/745, reg. 26 with effect from 6 April 2006.
In reg. 2(2) the definition of "retirement annuity contract" and "retirement benefits scheme" omitted by SI 2006/745, reg. 26 with effect from 6 April 2006.
In reg. 2(2) the definition of "Saving Gateway account" omitted by SI 2018/365, reg. 2(2), with effect from 6 April 2018. Definition previously read:
"**"Saving Gateway account"** has the meaning given by section 1 of the Saving Gateway Accounts Act 2009;"
In reg. 2(2) the definition of "Saving Gateway account" inserted by SI 2010/751, reg. 3, with effect from 6 April 2010.
In reg. 2(2) the definition of "the Service Pensions Order" omitted by SI 2010/2914, reg. 3, with effect from 31 December 2010.
In reg. 2(4)(a) and (b) the words "or civil partner" inserted four times by SI 2005/2919, reg. 3(2), with effect from 5 December 2005.

Cross references – SI 2003/742, reg. 36: modified application of reg. 2 to members of polygamous units.
SI 2013/386, reg. 17(2) and Schedule, para. 16: modified application of reg. 2 in relation to the introduction of Universal Credit.
SI 2014/1230, Sch., para. 12: modified application of reg. 2(2) where SI 2014/1230, reg. 12A applies (claims for universal credit).

TC Statutory Instruments

PART 2 – INCOME FOR THE PURPOSES OF TAX CREDITS

Chapter 1 – General

CALCULATION OF INCOME OF CLAIMANT

3(1) The manner in which income of a claimant or, in the case of a joint claim, the aggregate income of the claimants, is to be calculated for a tax year for the purposes of Part 1 of the Act is as follows.

Step one

Calculate and then add together–

(a) the pension income (as defined in regulation 5(1)),

(b) the investment income (as defined in regulation 10),

(c) the property income (as defined in regulation 11),

(d) the foreign income (as defined in regulation 12) and

(e) the notional income (as defined in regulation 13)

of the claimant, or, in the case of a joint claim, of the claimants.

If the result of this step is £300 or less, it is treated as nil.

If the result of this step is more than £300, only the excess is taken into account in the following steps.

Step Two

Calculate and then add together–

(a) the employment income (as defined in regulation 4),

(b) the social security income (as defined in regulation 7),

(c) the student income (as defined in regulation 8) and

(d) the miscellaneous income (as defined in regulation 18)

of the claimant, or in the case of a joint claim, of the claimants.

Step Three

Add together the results of Steps One and Two.

Step Four

Calculate the trading income (as defined in regulation 6) of the claimant, or in the case of a joint claim, of the claimants.

Add the result of this step to that produced by Step Three, in the year.

If there has been a trading loss in the year, subtract the amount of that loss from the result of Step Three. A loss shall not be available for tax credits purposes, unless the trade was being carried on upon a commercial basis and with a view to the realisation of profits in the trade or, where the carrying on of the trade formed part of a larger undertaking, in the undertaking as a whole.

Any trading loss in the year not set off as a result of the calculations in Steps One to Four above due to an insufficiency of income may be carried forward and set off against trading income (if any) of the same trade, profession or vocation in subsequent years (taking earlier years first) for the purposes of calculation of income under this regulation.

3(2) Subject to the qualifications in the following paragraphs of this regulation, and the provisions of Part 3, the result of Step Four in paragraph (1) is the income of the claimant, or, in the case of a joint claim, of the claimants, for the purposes of the Act.

3(3) Income which–

(a) arises in a territory outside the United Kingdom and

(b) is, for the time being, unremittable for the purposes of Chapter 4 of Part 8 of ITTOIA,

is disregarded in calculating the income of the claimant or, in the case of a joint claim, of the claimants.

3(4) Paragraph (5) applies in the case of a claimant who is, for income tax purposes–

(a) resident and domiciled in the United Kingdom,

(b) resident but not domiciled in the United Kingdom,

(c) [Omitted by SI 2014/658, reg. 4(3).]

3(5) In the case of a person to whom this paragraph applies–

(a) any income arising outside the United Kingdom is to be taken into account, subject to any specific provision of these Regulations, regardless of the domicile or residence of the claimant; and

(b) references to a sum being taken into account are to be construed as including a sum which would be taxable if he were resident and domiciled in the United Kingdom.

3(5A) Any income is to be taken into account, subject to any specific provision of these Regulations, notwithstanding the provision of any Order in Council under section 788 of the Taxes Act (double taxation agreements).

3(6) In the case of a claimant who would be chargeable to income tax but for some special exemption or immunity from income tax, income shall be calculated on the basis of the amounts which would be so chargeable but for that exemption or immunity.

3(6A) Income paid to a claimant in a currency other than sterling shall be converted into sterling at the average of the exchange rates applicable for the conversion of that currency into sterling in the period of 12 months ending on 31st March in the tax year in which the income arises.

3(7) In calculating income under this Part there shall be deducted–

(a) the amount of any banking charge or commission payable in converting to sterling a payment of income which is made in a currency other than sterling;

(b) the grossed-up amount of any qualifying donation (within the meaning of Chapter 2 of Part 8 of ITA (gift aid)), made by the claimant or, in the case of a joint claim, by either or both of the claimants; and

(c) the amount of any contribution made by the claimant, or in the case of a joint claim, by either or both of the claimants to a registered pension scheme together with the amount of any tax relief due on those contributions.

(d) [omitted by SI 2006/745, reg. 26.]

3(8) If–

(a) a claimant has sustained a loss in relation to a UK property business or an overseas property business; and

(b) the relief to which he is entitled in accordance with section 120 of ITA (deduction of property losses from general income) exceeds the amount of his property income or foreign income for tax credits purposes, for the year in question;

the amount of his total income for tax credit purposes, computed in accordance with the preceding provisions of this regulation, shall be reduced by the amount of the excess.

In this paragraph **"UK property business"** and **"overseas property business"** have the same meanings as they have in Chapter 2 of Part 3 of ITTOIA.

History – In reg. 3(1), in Step Four, the words from "A loss shall not" to "undertaking as a whole." inserted by SI 2006/766, reg. 7 with effect from 6 April 2006.
In reg. 3(1) the words from "Any trading loss " to the end inserted by SI 2003/2815, reg. 4, with effect from 26 November 2003.
In reg. 3(1), in step four, the words ", unless there has been a trading loss" repealed and "subtract" substituted by SI 2003/732, reg. 5, with effect from 6 April 2003.
In reg. 3(3)(b) words "Chapter 4 of Part 8 of ITTOIA," substituted for "section 584 of the Taxes Act," by SI 2006/766, reg. 8 with effect from 6 April 2006.
In reg. 3(4)(a), the words "but not ordinarily resident" omitted by SI 2014/658, reg. 4(2(a), with effect from 6 April 2014.
In reg. 3(4)(a) the word "or " omitted from the end by SI 2003/2815, reg. 4(3)(a), with effect from 26 November 2003.
In reg. 3(4) words ", for income tax purposes" inserted by SI 2003/732, reg. 5(3), with effect from 6 April 2003.
In reg. 3(4)(a) words "and domiciled but not ordinarily resident" substituted by SI 2003/732, reg. 5(3)(b), with effect from 6 April 2003.
In reg. 3(4)(b), the words "and ordinarily resident" omitted by SI 2014/658, reg. 4(2(b), with effect from 6 April 2014.
In reg. 3(4)(b) the word "or " inserted at the end by SI 2003/2815, reg. 4(3)(b), with effect from 26 November 2003.
Reg. 3(4)(c) omitted and the word "or" immediately preceding it omitted by SI 2014/658, reg. 4(3), with effect from 6 April 2014.
Reg. 3(4)(c) inserted by SI 2003/2815, reg. 4(3)(c), with effect from 26 November 2003.
Reg. 3(5)(a) substituted by SI 2003/732, reg. 5(4)(a), with effect from 6 April 2003.
In reg. 3(5)(b), the words ", ordinarily resident" omitted by SI 2014/658, reg. 4(4), with effect from 6 April 2014.
In reg. 3(5)(b) words "taken into account" substituted by SI 2003/732, reg. 5(4)(b), with effect from 6 April 2003.
Reg. 3(5A) inserted by SI 2003/732, reg. 5(5), with effect from 6 April 2003.
In reg. 3(6A) the words "ending on 31st March" substituted for "ending on 28th March" by SI 2007/824, reg. 9(2), with effect from 6 April 2007.
Reg. 3(6A) inserted by SI 2003/732, reg. 5(6), with effect from 6 April 2003.
In reg. 3(7)(c) the word "and" at end inserted by SI 2006/745, art. 26, with effect from 6 April 2006.
In reg. 3(7) words "the amount of" repealed by SI 2003/732, reg. 5(7)(a), with effect from 6 April 2003.
In reg. 3(7)(a) words "the amount of" inserted by SI 2003/732, reg. 5(7)(b), with effect from 6 April 2003.
In reg. 3(7)(b) the words "Chapter 2 of Part 8 of ITA (gift aid)" substituted by SI 2007/1305, reg. 4(2), with effect from 16 May 2007.
In reg. 3(7)(b) the word "and" inserted at the end by SI 2006/766, reg. 7 with effect from 6 April 2006.
In reg. 3(7)(b) the word "and " omitted from the end by SI 2003/2815, reg. 4(4)(a), with effect from 26 November 2003.
In reg. 3(7)(b) words "the grossed-up amount of" inserted by SI 2003/732, reg. 5(7)(c), with effect from 6 April 2003.
Reg. 3(7)(c) substituted by SI 2006/745, art. 26, with effect from 6 April 2006.
Former reg. 3(7)(c) substituted for para. (c) and (d) by SI 2006/766, reg. 7 with effect from 6 April 2006.
In former reg. 3(7)(c)(iii) the word "and " inserted at the end by SI 2003/2815, reg. 4(4)(b), with effect from 26 November 2003.
In former reg. 3(7)(c) words "the amount of" and "together with the amount of any tax relief due on those contributions" inserted by SI 2003/732, reg. 5(7)(d), with effect from 6 April 2003.
In former reg. 3(7)(c) words "Chapter 4 of Part 14 of that Act;" substituted for "Chapter 4 of that Part 14 of that Act;" by SI 2003/732, reg. 5(7)(d), with effect from 6 April 2003.
Reg. 3(7)(d) omitted by SI 2006/745, art. 26, with effect from 6 April 2006.
Former reg. 3(7)(d) inserted by SI 2003/2815, reg. 4(4)(c), with effect from 26 November 2003.
In reg. 3(8)(a) words "UK property business" substituted and words "In this paragraph "UK property business" and "overseas property business" have the same meanings as they have in Chapter 2 of Part 3 of ITTOIA." substituted by SI 2006/766, reg. 8 with effect from 6 April 2006.
Reg. 3(8) inserted by SI 2003/2815, reg. 4(5), with effect from 26 November 2003.
In reg. 3(8)(b) the words "section 120 of ITA (deduction of property losses from general income)" substituted by SI 2007/1305, reg. 4(3), with effect from 16 May 2007.

Cross references – SI 2003/742, reg. 37: modified application of reg. 3(7) to members of polygamous units.
SI 2013/386, reg. 17(2) and Schedule, para. 17: modified application of reg. 3 in relation to the introduction of Universal Credit.
SI 2014/1230, Sch., para. 13: modified application of reg. 3(1), (6A) and (8) where SI 2014/1230, reg. 12A applies (claims for universal credit).

Chapter 2 – Employment Income

EMPLOYMENT INCOME

4(1) In these regulations **"employment income"** means–

(a) any earnings from an office or employment received in the tax year;

(b) so much of any payment made to a claimant in that year in respect of expenses as is chargeable to income tax by virtue of section 62 or section 72 of ITEPA;

(c) the cash equivalent of any non-cash voucher received by the claimant in that year and chargeable to income tax under section 87 of ITEPA or, where there is an optional remuneration arrangement, the relevant amount;

(d) the cash equivalent of any credit-token received by the claimant in that year and chargeable to income tax under section 94 of ITEPA or, where such a credit-token is provided pursuant to an optional remuneration arrangement, the relevant amount;

(e) the cash equivalent of any cash voucher received by the claimant in that year and chargeable to income tax under section 81 of ITEPA or, where there is an optional remuneration arrangement, the relevant amount;

(f) any amount chargeable to tax under Chapter 3 of Part 6 of ITEPA;

(g) so much of a payment of statutory sick pay, received by the claimant during the year, as is subject to income tax by virtue of section 660 of ITEPA;

(h) the amount (if any) by which a payment of statutory maternity pay, statutory paternity pay, statutory shared parental pay or statutory adoption pay exceeds £100 per week;
(i) any amount charged to income tax for that year under section 120 or section 149 of ITEPA;
(j) the relevant amount in cases where a car is made available to the claimant or a member of the claimant's family pursuant to an optional remuneration arrangement where the car's CO_2 emissions figure exceeds 75 grams per kilometre;
(k) any sum to which section 225 of ITEPA applies;
(l) any amount paid in that year by way of strike pay to the claimant as a member of a trade union.
(m) any amount charged to income tax for that year under Part 7 of ITEPA.
(n) any amount paid to a person serving a custodial sentence or remanded in custody awaiting trial or sentence, for work done while serving the sentence or remanded in custody.

For the purposes of this paragraph, references to the receipt of a payment of any description are references to its receipt by or on behalf of the claimant, or in the case of a joint claim of either of the claimants, in any part of the world.

This paragraph is subject to the following qualifications.

4(2) Employment income does not include pension income.

4(2A) Paragraph (2B) applies if a claimant is a member of the Brigade of Gurkhas, to whom the voluntary settlement of tax liabilities of certain members of those units between the Ministry of Defence and the Board ("the voluntary settlement") applies.

4(2B) In the case of a claimant to whom this paragraph applies, the amount of his employment income from that employment for a particular tax year shall be the amount published by the Ministry of Defence as the UK equivalent rate in his case.

4(3) This paragraph applies if (apart from section 64 of ITEPA) the same benefit would give rise to two amounts ("A" and "B")–

(a) "A" being an amount of earnings from a claimant's employment as defined in section 62 of ITEPA, and
(b) "B" being an amount to be treated as earnings under any provision of Chapter 10 of Part 3 of ITEPA.

In such a case, the amount to be taken into account in computing the claimant's employment income is the greater of A and B, and the lesser amount shall be disregarded.

4(4) In calculating employment income, the payments and benefits listed in Table 1 shall be disregarded except where the payment or benefit is provided pursuant to optional remuneration arrangements and is neither a special case benefit nor an excluded benefit.

Table 1

Payments and benefits disregarded in the calculation of employment income

1.	Any payment in respect of qualifying removal expenses, or the provision of any qualifying removal benefit, within the meaning of Chapter 7 of Part 4 of ITEPA.
2A.	The payment or reimbursement of expenses incurred in the provision of transport to a disabled employee (as defined in section 246(4) of ITEPA) by his employer, if no liability to income tax arises in respect of that payment or reimbursement (as the case may be) by virtue of section 246 of ITEPA.
2B.	The provision to a disabled employee (as defined in section 246(4) of ITEPA) by his employer of a car, the provision of fuel for the car, or the reimbursement of expenses incurred in connection with the car, if no liability to income tax arises in respect of that provision or reimbursement (as the case may be) by virtue of section 247 of ITEPA.
2C.	The payment or reimbursement of expenses incurred on transport, if no liability to income tax arises in respect of that payment or reimbursement (as the case may be) by virtue of section 248 of ITEPA.
3.	Travel facilities provided for the claimant as a member of the naval, military or air forces of the Crown for the purpose of going on, or returning from, leave.
3A.	The payment under a Royal Warrant made under section 333 of the Armed Forces Act 2006 of an operational allowance to a member of Her Majesty's forces in respect of service in an operational area specified by the Secretary of State for Defence.
3B.	A payment designated under a Royal Warrant made under section 333 of the Armed Forces Act 2006 as Council Tax Relief and made by the Secretary of State for Defence to a member of Her Majesty's forces.

3C. The payment under a Royal Warrant made under section 333 of the Armed Forces Act 2006, of the Continuity of Education Allowance to or in respect of members of the armed forces of the Crown during their employment under the Crown or after their deaths.

3D. Any accommodation allowance which is payable out of public revenue for, or towards, the costs of accommodation to, or in respect of, a member of the armed forces of the Crown, providing that the payment meets any conditions which have been specified in regulations made by the Treasury.

4. Payment or reimbursement of expenses in connection with the provision for, or use by, the claimant as a person holding an office or employment of a car parking space at or near his place of work.

5. Any benefit or non-cash voucher provided to the claimant, or to any member of his family or household in respect of which no liability to income tax arises by virtue of Chapter 5 of Part 4 of ITEPA.

6. Any payment of incidental overnight expenses in respect of which no liability to income tax arises by virtue of section 240 of ITEPA.

7. Food, drink and mess allowances for the armed forces and training allowances payable to members of the reserve forces in respect of which no liability to income tax arises by virtue of section 297 or 298 of ITEPA.

8. The value of meal vouchers issued to the claimant as an employee, if section 89 of ITEPA applies to the vouchers.

9. Any cash payment received by the claimant as a miner in lieu of free coal, or the provision of the coal itself, in respect of which no liability to income tax arises by virtue of section 306 of ITEPA.

10. An award made to the claimant as a director or employee by way of a testimonial to mark long service, if, or to the extent that, no liability to income tax arises in respect of it by virtue of section 323 of ITEPA.

11. Payment of a daily subsistence allowance in respect of which no liability to income tax arises by virtue of section 304 of ITEPA.

11A. The payment or reimbursement of reasonable expenses incurred by an employee who has a permanent workplace at an offshore installation, on transfer transport, related accommodation and subsistence or local transport, if no liability to income tax arises in respect of that payment or reimbursement (as the case may be) by virtue of section 305 of ITEPA.
For the purposes of this item, expressions which are defined in section 305 of ITEPA have the same meaning here as they do there.

11B. Payment of an allowance to a person in employment under the Crown in respect of which no liability to income tax arises by virtue of section 299 of ITEPA.

11C. The payment or reimbursement to an employee of any sum in connection with work-related training, or individual learning account training (as respectively defined in sections 251 and 256 of ITEPA) if no liability to income tax arises in respect of that payment or reimbursement (as the case may be) by virtue of any provision of Chapter 4 of Part 4 of ITEPA.

11D. The provision for an employee of a non-cash voucher or a credit-token, to the extent that liability to income tax does not arise in respect of that voucher or credit-token (as the case may be), under Chapter 4 of Part 3 of ITEPA, by virtue of any provision of Chapter 6 of Part 4 of ITEPA.

11E. The provision for an employee of free or subsidised meal vouchers or tokens (within the meaning of section 317(5) of ITEPA), if no liability to income tax arises in respect of that provision by virtue of section 317 of ITEPA.

11F. The provision of one mobile telephone for an employee in respect of which no liability to income tax arises by virtue of section 319 of ITEPA.

12. An award made to the claimant under a Staff Suggestion Scheme, if the conditions specified in sections 321 and 322 of ITEPA are satisfied.

13. Travelling and subsistence allowances paid to or on behalf of the claimant by his employer in respect of which no liability to income tax arises by virtue of section 245 of ITEPA.

14. Any gift consisting of goods, or a voucher or token to obtain goods, in respect of which no liability to income tax arises by virtue of section 270 or 324 of ITEPA.

14A. Any payment or reimbursement of expenses incurred in connection with an employment-related asset transfer (as defined in section 326(2) of ITEPA), if no liability to income tax arises in respect of that payment or reimbursement (as the case may be) by virtue of section 326 of ITEPA.

14B. Any payment of expenses incurred by an employee in connection with a taxable car if no liability to income tax arises in respect of the payment by virtue of section 239(2) of ITEPA.

14C. The discharge of any liability of an employee in connection with a taxable car if no liability to income tax arises by virtue of section 239(1) of ITEPA.

14D. A benefit connected with a taxable car if no liability to income tax arises by virtue of section 239(4) of ITEPA.

15. A cash voucher, non-cash voucher or credit-token to the extent that it is used by the recipient for the provision of child care, the costs of which if borne by the recipient would be relevant child care charges within the meaning of regulation 14 of the Working Tax Credit (Entitlement and Maximum Rate) Regulations 2002.

16. A payment made by the Department for Work and Pensions under section 2 of the Employment Act–
(a) by way of In-Work Credit, Better Off In-Work Credit, Job Grant or Return to Work Credit,
(b) under the Employment Retention and Advancement Scheme or the Working Neighbourhoods Pilot
(c) under the City Strategy Pathfinder Pilots,
(d) by way of an In-Work Emergency Discretion Fund payment pursuant to arrangements made by the Secretary of State,
(e) by way of an Up-front Childcare Fund payment pursuant to arrangements made by the Secretary of State, or
(f) under the Future Capital pilot scheme.

16A. A payment made by the Department for Employment and Learning in Northern Ireland under section 1 of the Employment and Training Act (Northern Ireland) 1950 by way of Return to Work Credit.

16B. Any In-Work Emergency Fund payment made to a person pursuant to arrangements made by the Department of Economic Development under section 1 of the Employment and Training Act (Northern Ireland) 1950.

17. The payment or reimbursement of reasonable additional household expenses incurred by an employee who works from home, within the meaning of section 316A of ITEPA.

18. The payment or reimbursement of retraining course expenses within the meaning of section 311 of ITEPA.

19. Provision of computer equipment in respect of which no liability to income tax arises by virtue of section 320 of ITEPA

20. Pay As You Earn (PAYE) settlement agreements made under Part 6 of the Income Tax (PAYE) Regulations ("the PAYE Regulations") 2003.
For the purposes of this item the special arrangements under regulation 141 of the PAYE Regulations also apply.

21. The payment or reimbursement of a fee within section 326A(1) of ITEPA (fees relating to vulnerable persons' monitoring schemes).

22. The payment of a qualifying bonus within section 312A of ITEPA (limited exemption for qualifying bonus payments).

4(5) From the amount of employment income, calculated in accordance with the preceding provisions of this regulation, there shall be deducted the amount of any deduction permitted in calculating earnings by virtue of any provision of sections 231 to 232, 336 to 344, or section 346, 347, 351, 352, 362, 363, 367, 368, 370, 371, 373, 374, 376, 377 or 713 of ITEPA.

4(6) For the purposes of this regulation, a benefit is provided pursuant to optional remuneration arrangements *if it is provided* under either–

(a) arrangements under which, in return for the benefit, the claimant gives up the right (or a future right) to receive an amount of earnings within Chapter 1 of Part 3 of ITEPA ("Type A arrangements"), or

(b) arrangements (other than Type A arrangements) under which the claimant agrees to be provided with the benefit rather than an amount of earnings within Chapter 1 of Part 3 of ITEPA.

4(7) The relevant amount, in relation to a benefit provided pursuant to an optional remuneration arrangement, means the amount treated for income tax purposes as earnings from employment for the tax year by reason of the benefit being provided pursuant to optional remuneration arrangements.

4(8) A benefit is a special case benefit if it is exempted from a charge to income tax by any of the following provisions in ITEPA–

(a) section 289A (exemption for paid or reimbursed expenses),

(b) section 289D (exemption for other benefits),

(c) section 308B (independent advice in respect of conversions and transfers of pension scheme benefits),

(d) section 312A (limited exemption for qualifying bonus payments),

(e) section 317 (subsidised meals),

(f) section 320C (recommended medical treatment), and

(g) section 323A (trivial benefits provided by employers).

4(9) A benefit is an excluded benefit if–

(a) it is exempted from a charge to income tax by any of the following provisions in ITEPA–

(i) section 239 (payments and benefits connected with taxable cars and vans and exempt heavy goods vehicles),

(ii) section 244 (cycles and cyclist's safety equipment),

(iii) section 266(2)(c) (non-cash voucher regarding entitlement to exemption under section 244),

(iv) section 270A (limited exemption for qualifying childcare vouchers),

(v) section 308 (exemption of contribution to registered pension scheme),

(vi) section 308A (exemption of contribution to overseas pension scheme),

(vii) section 309 (limited exemptions for statutory redundancy payments),

(viii) section 310 (counselling and other outplacement services),

(ix) section 311 (retraining courses),

(x) section 318 (childcare: exemption for employer-provided care), or

(xi) section 318A (childcare: limited exemption for other care), or

(b) it is a payment, or reimbursement of costs incurred by the claimant, in respect of pension advice and that payment or reimbursement is exempt from a charge to income tax under Chapter 9 of Part 4 of ITEPA.

4(10) A car's CO_2 emissions figure is to be determined in accordance with sections 133 to 138 of ITEPA (cars: the appropriate percentage).

History – In Table 1, item 3A and 3B, the words "under a Royal Warrant made under section 333 of the Armed Forces Act 2006" substituted for "by the Secretary of State for Defence" by SI 2014/658, reg. 4(5), with effect from 6 April 2014.
In reg. 4(1)(a) "earnings" substituted for "emoluments" by SI 2003/732, reg. 6(2)(a) with effect from 6 April 2003.
In reg. 4(1)(b) "by virtue of section 62 or section 72 of ITEPA;" substituted for "under section 19(1) or 153 of the Taxes Act;" by SI 2003/732, reg. 6(2)(b) with effect from 6 April 2003.
In reg. 4(1)(c), the words "or, where there is an optional remuneration arrangement, the relevant amount," inserted by SI 2017/396, reg. 3(a)(i), with effect in relation to awards of tax credit for the tax year 2017-18 and subsequent tax years.
In reg. 4(1)(c) "section 87 of ITEPA" substituted for "section 141 of the Taxes Act" by SI 2003/732, reg. 6(2)(c)(ii) with effect from 6 April 2003.
In reg. 4(1)(d), the words "or, where such a credit-token is provided pursuant to an optional remuneration arrangement, the relevant amount" inserted by SI 2017/396, reg. 3(a)(ii), with effect in relation to awards of tax credit for the tax year 2017-18 and subsequent tax years.
In reg. 4(1)(d) "section 94 of ITEPA" substituted for "section 142 of the Taxes Act" by SI 2003/732, reg. 6(2)(c)(ii) with effect from 6 April 2003.
In reg. 4(1)(c), (d) and (e) words "the cash equivalent of" inserted by SI 2003/732, reg. 6(2) with effect from 6 April 2003.
In reg. 4(1)(e), the words "or, where there is an optional remuneration arrangement, the relevant amount," inserted by SI 2017/396, reg. 3(a)(i), with effect in relation to awards of tax credit for the tax year 2017-18 and subsequent tax years.
In reg. 4(1)(e) "section 81 of ITEPA" substituted for "section 143 of the Taxes Act" by SI 2003/732, reg. 6(2)(e)(ii) with effect from 6 April 2003.
Reg. 4(1)(f) substituted by SI 2003/732, reg. 6(2)(f) with effect from 6 April 2003.
In reg. 4(1)(g) "by virtue of section 660 of ITEPA" substituted for "under Schedule E by virtue of section 150(c) of the Taxes Act" by SI 2003/732, reg. 6(2)(g) with effect from 6 April 2003.
Reg. 4(1)(h) substituted by SI 2015/175, reg. 7, with effect from 5 April 2015, subject to the transitional provisions in SI 2015/175, reg. 9 (amendments do not have effect where they relate to additional statutory paternity pay or ordinary statutory paternity pay and payments of either on or after 5 April 2015).
In reg. 4(1)(h) the words "ordinary statutory paternity pay, additional statutory paternity pay" substituted for the words "statutory paternity pay" by SI 2010/2494, reg. 5, with effect from 14 November 2010.
In reg. 4(1)(h) "statutory maternity pay, statutory paternity pay or statutory adoption pay" substituted for "statutorymaternity pay" by SI 2003/732, reg. 6(2)(h) with effect from 6 April 2003.
In reg. 4(1)(i) "under section 120 or section 149 of ITEPA" substituted for "under section 157 of the Taxes Act (car made available for private use) or section 158 of that Act (car fuel)" by SI 2003/732, reg. 6(2)(i) with effect from 6 April 2003.
Reg. 4(1)(ia) inserted by SI 2017/396, reg. 3(a)(iii), with effect in relation to awards of tax credit for the tax year 2017–18 and subsequent tax years.
Reg. 4(1)(j) substituted by SI 2003/732, reg. 6(2)(j) with effect from 6 April 2003.
Reg. 4(1)(l) inserted by SI 2003/2815, reg. 5(2), with effect from 26 November 2003.

Reg. 4(1)(m) inserted by SI 2007/824, reg. 10(2), with effect from 6 April 2007.
Reg. 4(2A) and (2B) omitted by SI 2006/766, reg. 9 with effect from 6 April 2006.
Reg. 4(2A) and (2B) inserted by SI 2004/762, reg. 14(2), with effect from 6 April 2004.
Reg. 4(3) substituted by SI 2003/2815, reg. 5(3), with effect from 26 November 2003.
In reg. 4(4), the words "except where the payment or benefit is provided pursuant to optional remuneration arrangements and is neither a special case benefit nor an excluded benefit" inserted by SI 2017/396, reg. 3(b), with effect in relation to awards of tax credit for the tax year 2017–18 and subsequent tax years.
In Table 1, in the heading words "and benefits" inserted by SI 2003/732, reg. 6(4)(a) with effect from 6 April 2003.
In Table 1, item 1, the words "Chapter 7 of Part 4 of ITEPA" substituted for "Schedule 11A to the Taxes Act" by SI 2003/732, reg. 6(4) with effect from 6 April 2003.
In Table 1, items 2A–2C substituted for item 2 by SI 2003/732, reg. 6(4) with effect from 6 April 2003.
In Table 1, item 3A inserted by SI 2007/824, reg. 10(3)(a), with effect from 6 April 2007.
In Table 1, item 3B inserted by SI 2008/604, reg. 2(2), with effect from 1 April 2008.
In Table 1, item 3C inserted by SI 2012/848, reg. 3(1), with effect from 6 April 2012.
In Table 1, item 3D inserted by SI 2018/365, reg. 2(3), with effect from 6 April 2018.
In Table 1, item 5 the words "in respect of which no liability to income tax arises by virtue of Chapter 5 of Part 4 of ITEPA" substituted for the words "falling within section 197G of the Taxes Act (sporting and recreational faciliities)" by SI 2003/732, reg. 6(4) with effect from 6 April 2003.
In Table 1, item 6, the words "in respect of which no liability to income tax arises by virtue of section 240 of ITEPA" substituted for "falling within section 200A of the Taxes Act" by SI 2003/732, reg. 6(4) with effect from 6 April 2003.
In Table 1, item 7 substituted by SI 2003/732, reg. 6(4) with effect from 6 April 2003.
In Table 1, item 8, the words "if section 89 applies to the vouchers" substituted for the words "if the condition specified in Inland RevenueExtra Statutory Concession A2 are satisfied." by SI 2003/732, reg. 6(4) with effect from 6 April 2003.
In Table 1, item 9, the words "in respect of which no liability to income tax arises by virtue of section 306 of ITEPA" substituted for the words "in relation to which income tax is not charged under Inland Revenue Extra Statutory Concession A6" by SI 2003/732, reg. 6(4) with effect from 6 April 2003.
In Table 1, item 10, the words "if, or to the extent that, no liability to income tax arises by virtue of section 323 of ITEPA" substituted for the words "if the conditions specified in Inland Revenue Extra Statutory Concession A22 are satisfied." by SI 2003/732, reg. 6(4) with effect from 6 April 2003.
In Table 1, item 11, the words "in respect of which no liability to inocme tax arises by virtue of section 304 of ITEPA" substituted for the words "to which Extra Statutory Concession A84 applies " by SI 2003/732, reg. 6(4) with effect from 6 April 2003.
In Table 1, items 11A–11C inserted by SI 2003/732, reg. 6(4) with effect from 6 April 2003.
In Table 1, item 11D inserted by SI 2003/732, reg. 6(4) with effect from 6 April 2003, and the words, "Part 3 of ITEPA, by virtue of any provision of Chapter 6 of Part 4 of ITEPA" substituted for "Part 4 of ITEPA, by virtue of any provision of Chapter 6 of that Part." by SI 2003/2815, reg. 5(4)(a) with effect from 26 November 2003:
In Table 1, item 11E inserted by SI 2003/732, reg. 6(4) with effect from 6 April 2003.
In Table 1, item 11F inserted by SI 2007/824, reg. 10(3)(b), with effect from 6 April 2007.
In Table 1, item 12, the words "sections 321 and 322 of ITEPA" substituted for "Inland Revenue Extra Statutory Concession A57 are satisfied" by SI 2003/732, reg. 6(4) with effect from 6 April 2003 and the words "are satisfied" inserted by SI 2004/762, art.14(3)(a) with effect from 6 April 2004.
In Table 1, item 13, the words "in respect of which no liability to income tax arises by virtue of section 245 of ITEPA" substituted for "which fall within Inland Revenue Extra Statutory Concession A58 (public transport disruption)" by SI 2003/732, reg. 6(4) with effect from 6 April 2003.
In Table 1, item 14, the words "in respect of which no liability to income tax arises by virtue of section 270 or 324 of ITEPA" substituted for "if the conditions specified in Inland Revenue Extra Statutory Concession A70 are satisfied" by SI 2003/732, reg. 6(4) with effect from 6 April 2003.
In Table 1, items 14C and 14D inserted by SI 2003/2815, reg. 5(4)(b) with effect from 26 November 2003.
In Table 1, in item 16, in para. (a) the words ", Better Off In-Work Credit" inserted and the word "or" at the end omitted and para. (c), (d) and (e) inserted by SI 2008/2169, reg. 4(a), with effect from 1 September 2008.
In Table 1, item 16(f) inserted (and the "or" atthe end of item 16(d) omitted, and the "or" at the end of item 16(e) inserted) by SI 2009/2887, reg. 6, with effect from 21 November 2009.
In Table 1, item 16 inserted by SI 2003/732, reg. 6(4) with effect from 6 April 2003; the word "Scheme" substituted for "Project" by SI 2003/2815, reg. 5(4)(c) with effect from 26 November 2003 and substituted by SI 2004/762, reg. 14(3)(b).
In Table 1, item 16B inserted by SI 2008/2169, reg. 4(b), with effect from 1 September 2008.
In Table 1, item 16A inserted by SI 2006/766, reg. 9 with effect from 6 April 2006.
In Table 1, items 17 and 18 inserted by SI 2003/2815, reg. 5(4)(d) with effect from 26 November 2003.
In Table 1, item 19 inserted by SI 2004/2663, reg. 2(2) with effect from 3 November 2004.
In Table 1, item 20 inserted by SI 2008/2169, reg. 4(c), with effect from 1 September 2008.
In Table 1, item 21 inserted by SI 2012/848, reg. 3(2), with effect from 6 April 2012.
In Table 1, item 22 inserted by SI 2014/2924, reg. 5, with effect from 28 November 2014.
In reg. 4(5) words "231 to 232," inserted by SI 2003/2815, reg. 5(5) with effect from 26 November 2003, and the references to ITEPA 2003 substituted for references to corresponding sections of the Taxes Act by SI 2003/732, reg. 6(5) with effect from 6 April 2003.
Reg. 4(6)–(10) inserted by SI 2017/396, reg. 3(c), with effect in relation to awards of tax credit for the tax year 2017–18 and subsequent tax years.

Cross references – SI 2003/742, reg. 38: modified application of reg. 4(1) to members of polygamous units.
SI 2013/386, reg. 17(2) and Schedule, para. 18: modified application of reg. 4 in relation to the introduction of Universal Credit.
SI 2014/1230, Sch., para. 14: modified application of reg. 4(1), (4) and (5) where SI 2014/1230, reg. 12A applies (claims for universal credit).

Chapter 3 – Pension Income

PENSION INCOME

5(1) In these Regulations, except where the context otherwise require, **"pension income"** means–

(a) any pension to which section 577 or 629 of ITEPA applies;

(b) any pension to which section 569 of ITEPA applies;

(c) any voluntary annual payment to which section 633 of ITEPA applies;

(d) any pension, annuity or income withdrawal to which section 579A of ITEPA applies;

(e) any unauthorised member payments to which section 208(2)(a) or (b) of the Finance Act 2004 applies;
(f) any periodical payment to which section 619 of ITEPA applies;
(g) [omitted by SI 2006/745, reg. 26;]
(h) [omitted by SI 2006/745, reg. 26;]
(i) [omitted by SI 2006/745, reg. 26;]
(j) [omitted by SI 2006/745, reg. 26;]
(k) any annuity paid under a retirement annuity contract to which Chapter 9 of Part 9 of ITEPA applies;
(l) any annuity to which section 609, 610 or 611 of ITEPA applies;
(m) [omitted by SI 2008/604, reg. 2(3);]
(n) any social security pension lump sum to which section 7 of the Finance (No. 2) Act 2005 applies; and
(o) any lump sum payment to which section 636B or 636C of ITEPA applies.

5(2) In calculating the amount of a person's pension income there shall be disregarded any payment or benefit mentioned in Column 1 of Table 2 to the extent specified in the corresponding entry in Column 2.

Table 2

Pensions, other payments and benefits disregarded in the calculation of pension income

	1. Payment	*2. Extent of disregard*
1.	A wounds pension or disability pension to which section 641 of ITEPA applies.	So much of the payment as is disregarded by virtue of section 641 of ITEPA.
2.	An annuity or additional pension payable to a holder of the Victoria Cross, George Cross or any other decoration mentioned in section 638 of ITEPA.	The whole of the annuity or additional pension and, if both are payable, the whole of both such annuity and additional pension.
3.	A pension or allowance to which section 639 of ITEPA applies.	The amount of the pension or allowance.
4.	A pension or allowance by reason of payment of which a pension or allowance specified in section 639 of ITEPA is withheld or abated.	The amount treated as falling within section 639 of ITEPA by virtue of section 640(2) of that Act.
5.	[Omitted by SI 2010/2914, reg. 4(a).]	[Omitted by SI 2010/2914, reg. 4(a).]
6.	A mobility supplement, or a payment in respect of attendance, paid in conjunction with a war pension.	The amount of the supplement or payment.
7.	[Omitted by SI 2010/2914, reg. 4(b).]	[Omitted by SI 2010/2914, reg. 4(b).]
8.	A pension awarded at the supplementary rate under article 27(3) of the Personal Injuries (Civilians) Scheme 1983.	The amount for the time being specified in paragraph 1(c) of Schedule 4 to the Scheme.
9.	A pension awarded on retirement through disability caused by injury on duty or by a work-related illness.	The exempt amount of the pension calculated in accordance with section 644(3) of ITEPA.
10.	A lump sum on which no liability to income tax arises by virtue of section 636A of ITEPA.	The amount of the lump sum.
11.	Coal or smokeless fuel provided as mentioned in section 646(1) of ITEPA, or an allowance in lieu of such provision.	The amount on which no liability to income tax arises by virtue of that section.

5(3) From the amount of pension income, calculated in accordance with the preceding provisions of this regulation, there shall be deducted any amount deductible for income tax purposes in computing pension income (as defined in ITEPA) under section 713 of that Act.

History – Reg. 5(1)(d) and (e) substituted by SI 2006/745, reg. 26, with effect from 6 April 2006.
Reg. 5(1)(g)–(j) omitted by SI 2006/745, reg. 26, with effect from 6 April 2006.
Reg. 5(1)(k) substituted by SI 2006/745, reg. 26 with effect from 6 April 2006.
Reg. 5(1)(m) and the word "and" immediately preceding it omitted by SI 2008/604, reg. 2(3), with effect from 6 April 2008.
In reg. 5(1) para. (n) and (o) inserted by SI 2006/766, reg. 10 with effect from 6 April 2006.

Reg. 5(1) substituted by SI 2003/732, reg. 7(2), with effect from 6 April 2003.
In reg. 5(2) words "payment or benefit mentioned" substituted for "payment mentioned" by SI 2003/732, reg. 7(3), with effect from 6 April 2003.
In Table 2, in the heading words "Pensions, other payments and benefits" substituted for "Pensions and other payments" by SI 2003/732, reg. 7(4)(a) with effect from 6 April 2003.
In Table 2, item 1, the words "section 641 of ITEPA" substituted for "section 315 of the Taxes Act" in both places by SI 2003/732, reg. 7(4) with effect from 6 April 2003:
In Table 2, item 2, the words "section 638 of ITEPA" substituted for "section 317 of that Taxes Act" by SI 2003/732, reg. 7(4) with effect from 6 April 2003.
In Table 2, item 3, the words "section 639 of ITEPA" substituted for "section 318" and in column 2 the words "The amount of the pension or allowance" substituted for "The amount that is not to be treated as income for the purposes of the Income Tax Acts by virtue of s. 318(2)" by SI 2003/732, reg. 7(4) with effect from 6 April 2003.
In Table 2, item 4, the words "section 640(2) of ITEPA" substituted for "section 318(2)" and in column 2 the words "The amount treated as falling within section 639 of ITEPA by virtue of section 640(2) of that Act" substituted for "The amount treated as falling within section 318 by virtue of subsection (3) of that section" by SI 2003/732, reg. 7(4) with effect from 6 April 2003.
In Table 2, item 5 omitted by SI 2010/2914, reg. 4(a), with effect from 31 December 2010.
In Table 2, item 7 omitted by SI 2010/2914, reg. 4(b), with effect from 31 December 2010.
In Table 2, item 9, in the second column the words "The exempt amount of the pension calculated in accordance with sections 644(3) of ITEPA" substituted for "The amount by which the pension exceeds what would have been payable if the retirement had been on grounds of ill-health caused other than by an injury or illness of the kind mentioned in column 1" by SI 2003/732, reg. 7(4) with effect from 6 April 2003.
In Table 2, item 10 words "section 636A of ITEPA" substituted for "section 637 of ITEPA" by SI 2006/745, reg. 26 with effect from 6 April 2006.
In Table 2, items 10 and 11 inserted by SI 2003/732, reg. 7(4) with effect from 6 April 2003.

Cross references – SI 2013/386, reg. 17(2) and Schedule, para. 19: modified application of reg. 5 in relation to the introduction of Universal Credit.
SI 2014/1230, Sch., para. 15: modified application of reg. 5(1), (2), (3) where SI 2014/1230, reg. 12A applies (claims for universal credit).

Chapter 4 – Trading Income

TRADING INCOME

6 The claimant's trading income is–

(a) the amount of his taxable profits for the tax year from–

(i) any trade carried on in the United Kingdom or elsewhere;

(ii) any profession or vocation the income from which does not fall under any other provisions of these Regulations; or

(b) if the claimant is a partner in the trade, profession or vocation, his taxable profit for the year arising from his share of the partnership's trading or professional income.

Here **"taxable profits"** has the same meaning as it has in Part 2 of ITTOIA but disregarding Chapter 16 of that Part (averaging profits of farmers and creative artists).

History – In reg. 6 meaning of "taxable profits" substituted by SI 2006/766, reg. 11 with effect from 6 April 2006.

Cross references – SI 2013/386, reg. 17(2) and Schedule, para. 20 and 21: modified application of reg. 6, and deemed insertion of reg. 6A and 6B, in relation to the introduction of Universal Credit.
SI 2014/1230, Sch., para. 16: modified application of reg. 6 where SI 2014/1230, reg. 12A applies (claims for universal credit).

Chapter 5 – Social Security Income

SOCIAL SECURITY INCOME

7(1) The claimant's social security income is the total amount payable–

(a) under any provision of the Social Security Act 1988, the Contributions and Benefits Act, the Jobseekers Act 1995 or Part 1 of the Welfare Reform Act 2007 or under section 69 of the Child Support, Pensions and Social Security Act 2000;

(aa) under Part 3 of the Welfare Supplementary Payments Regulations (Northern Ireland) 2016(c) or Part 2 of the Welfare Supplementary Payment (Loss of Carer Payments) Regulations (Northern Ireland) 2016;

(b) [repealed by SI 2003/732, reg. 8(2);]

(c) by the Secretary of State in respect of the non-payment of a payment which ought to have been made under a provision mentioned in sub-paragraph (a); and

(d) by way of an ex gratia payment made by the Secretary of State, or in Northern Ireland by the *Department* for Communities, in connection with a benefit, pension or allowance under the Contributions and Benefits Act.

This is subject to the following provisions of this regulation.

7(2) Pensions under the Contributions and Benefits Act which are pension income by virtue of regulation 5(1)(a) are not social security income.

7(3) In calculating the claimant's social security income the payments in Table 3 shall be disregarded.

Table 3

Payments under, or in connection with, the Act, the Social Security Act 1988, the Contributions and Benefits Act, the Jobseekers Act 1995 or Part 1 of the Welfare Reform Act 2007 disregarded in calculation of social security income

1.	An attendance allowance under section 64 of the Contributions and Benefits Act.
2.	A back to work bonus under section 26 of the Jobseekers Act 1995.
3.	A bereavement supportpayment under section 30 of the Pensions Act 2014.
4.	Child benefit under Part 2 of the Act.
5.	A Christmas bonus under section 148 of the Contributions and Benefits Act.
6.	Council tax benefit under section 131 of the Contributions and Benefits Act.
7.	A disability living allowance under section 71 of the Contributions and Benefits Act.
8.	Disabled person's tax credit under section 129 of the Contributions and Benefits Act.
9.	Any discretionary housing payment pursuant to regulation 2(1) of the Discretionary Financial Assistance Regulations 2001.
10.	An ex-gratia payment by the Secretary of State or, in Northern Ireland, the Department for Communities, to a person over pensionable age by way of supplement to incapacity benefit.
11.	A guardian's allowance under section 77 of the Contributions and Benefits Act.
12.	Housing benefit under section 130 of the Contributions and Benefits Act.
13.	Income support under section 124 of the Contributions and Benefits Act, unless it is chargeable to tax under section 665 of ITEPA.
14.	Incapacity benefit which is– (a) short term incapacity benefit payable at the lower rate; or (b) payable to a person who had received invalidity benefit before 13th April 1995 if the period of incapacity for work is treated, by virtue of regulation 2 of the Social Security (Incapacity Benefit) (Transitional) Regulations 1995 (days to be treated as days of incapacity for work) as having begun before that date.
15.	Industrial injuries benefit (except industrial death benefit) under section 94 of the Contributions and Benefits Act.
16.	A contribution-based jobseeker's allowance under the Jobseekers Act 1995 as amended by the provisions of Part 1 of Schedule 14 to the Welfare Reform Act 2012 that remove references to an income-based allowance, and a contribution-based allowance under the Jobseekers Act 1995 as that Act has effect apart from those provisions, to the extent that it exceeds the maximum contained in section 674 of ITEPA.
17.	An income-based jobseeker's allowance under the Jobseekers Act 1995.
18.	A maternity allowance under section 35 or section 35B of the Contributions and Benefits Act.
19.	A severe disablement allowance under section 68 or 69 of the Contributions and Benefits Act.
20.	A social fund payment under Part 8 of the Contributions and Benefits Act.
20A.	Statutory adoption pay under Part 12ZB of the Contributions and Benefits Act.
21.	Statutory maternity pay under Part 12 of the Contributions and Benefits Act.
21A.	Ordinary statutory paternity pay additional statutory paternity pay under Part 12ZA of the Contributions and Benefits Act.
22.	Statutory sick pay under Part 11 of the Contributions and Benefits Act.
23.	Working families' tax credit under section 128 of the Contributions and Benefits Act.
24.	A payment by way of compensation for the non-payment of, or in respect of loss of entitlement (whether wholly or partly) of, income support, jobseeker's allowance, or housing benefit.
25.	A payment in lieu of milk tokens or the supply of vitamins under the Welfare Foods Regulations 1996.
26.	An income-related employment and support allowance payable under Part 1 of the Welfare Reform Act 2007.

27.	A payment by way of health in pregnancy grant made pursuant to Part 8A of the Contributions and Benefits Act.
28.	Personal independence payment under Part 4 of the Welfare Reform Act 2012.

7(4) If an increase in respect of a child dependant is payable with an allowance, benefit, pension or other payment ("the main payment") listed in Table 3, the increase shall also be wholly disregarded in calculating the income of the recipient of the main payment.

7(5) [Reg. 7(5) repealed by SI 2003/732, reg. 8(4).]

7(5A) From the amount of social security income, calculated in accordance with the preceding provisions of this regulation, there shall be deducted any amount deductible for income tax purposes in computing social security income (as defined in ITEPA) under section 713 of ITEPA.

7(6) A reference in this regulation to an enactment applying only in Great Britain includes a reference to a corresponding enactment applying in Northern Ireland.

History – In reg. 7(1)(a) the words ", the Jobseekers Act 1995 or Part 1 of the Welfare Reform Act 2007" substituted for the words "or the Jobseekers Act 1995" by SI 2008/1879, reg. 21(2(a), with effect from 27 October 2008.
Reg. 7(1)(aa) inserted by SI 2016/978, reg. 2(2)(a), with effect from 31 October 2016.
Reg. 7(1)(b) repealed by SI 2003/732, reg. 8(2) from 6 April 2003:
In reg. 7(1)(d), the words "Department for Communities" substituted for the words "Department for Social Development" by SI 2016/978, reg. 2(2)(b), with effect from 31 October 2016.
In Table 3, in the heading, the words ", the Jobseekers Act 1995 or Part 1 of the Welfare Reform Act 2007" substituted for the words "or the Jobseekers Act 1995" by SI 2008/1879, reg. 21(2)(b)(i), with effect from 27 October 2008.
In Table 3, item 3 substituted by SI 2017/422, art. 22, with effect from 6 April 2017 (the day on which PA 2014, s. 30 comes into force for all purposes (SI 2017/297, art. 3(b)), subject to SI 2017/422, art. 2 (later commencement for abolition of bereavement payment and bereavement allowance) and 3 (commencement for entitlement to bereavement payment and bereavement support payment).
In Table 3, in item 10, the words "Department for Communities" substituted for the words "Department for Social Development" by SI 2016/978, reg. 2(2)(c), with effect from 31 October 2016.
In Table 3, the following amendments made by SI 2003/732, reg. 8(3) with effect from 6 April 2003:

- in item 15 words "(except industrial death benefit)" inserted after "Industrial injuries benefit";
- in item 16 words "section 674 of ITEPA" substituted for "section 151A of the Taxes Act";
- items 20A and 21A inserted.

In Table 3, in item 16, the words "as amended by the provisions of Part 1 of Schedule 14 to the Welfare Reform Act 2012 that remove references to an income-based allowance, and a contribution-based allowance under the Jobseekers Act 1995 as that Act has effect apart from those provisions" inserted by SI 2013/630, reg. 78(2), with effect from 29 April 2013.
In Table 3, item 18, the words "or section 35B" inserted by SI 2014/658, reg. 4(6), with effect from 6 April 2014.
In Table 3, in item 21A, the word "and" (which appeared after the words "statutory paternity pay") omitted by SI 2016/360, reg. 3(2), with effect from 6 April 2016.
In Table 3, in item 21A, the words "Ordinary statutory paternity pay and additional statutory paternity pay" substituted for the words "Statutory paternity pay" by SI 2010/2494, reg. 6, with effect from 14 November 2010.
In Table 3, in item 24, the words "or housing benefit" substituted for the words "housing benefit" to the end by SI 2003/2815, reg. 6(2) with effect from 26 November 2003.
In Table 3, items 26 inserted by SI 2008/1879, reg. 21(2)(b)(ii), with effect from 27 October 2008.
In Table 3, item 27 inserted by SI 2009/697, reg. 7, with effect from 6 April 2009.
In Table 3, item 28 inserted by SI 2013/388, art. 8 and Sch., para. 29, with effect from 8 April 2013.
Reg. 7(5) repealed by SI 2003/732, reg. 8(4) from 6 April 2003.
Reg. 7(5A) inserted by SI 2003/732, reg. 8(5) from 6 April 2003.

Cross references – SI 2013/386, reg. 17(2) and Schedule, para. 22: modified application of reg. 7 in relation to the introduction of Universal Credit.
SI 2014/1230, Sch., para. 17: modified application of reg. 7(1) and (3) where SI 2014/1230, reg. 12A applies (claims for universal credit).

Chapter 6 – Student Income

STUDENT INCOME

8 "Student income" means, in relation to a student–

(a) in England, any adult dependant's grant payable pursuant to regulations under section 22 of the Teaching and Higher Education Act 1998;

(b) in Scotland, any dependant's grant payable under regulation 4(1)(c) of the Students' Allowances (Scotland) Regulations 2007;

(c) in Northern Ireland, any grant which corresponds to income treated as student income in England by virtue of paragraph (a); and

(d) in Wales, any adult dependant's grant payable pursuant to regulations under section 22 of the Teaching and Higher Education Act 1998.

History – In reg. 8(a), the words "pursuant to regulations under section 22 of the Teaching and Higher Education Act 1998;" substituted for the former wording by *SI 2012/848*, reg. 3(3)(a), with effect from 6 April 2012.
Reg. 8(a) substituted by SI 2008/2169, reg. 5(2), with effect from 1 September 2008.
In former reg. 8(a), para. (i) and (ii) substituted by SI 2007/824, reg. 11(2), with effect from 6 April 2007.
In former reg. 8, para. (a) substituted, word "and" omitted at end of para. (b), word "and" inserted at end of para. (c), and para. (d) inserted by SI 2006/766, reg. 12 with effect from 6 April 2006.
In reg. 8(b), "2007" substituted for "1999" by SI 2012/848, reg. 3(3)(b), with effect from 6 April 2012.

In reg. 8(c), the words "and Wales", which appeared after the word "England", omitted by SI 2012/848, reg. 3(3)(c), with effect from 6 April 2012.
In reg. 8(d), the words "pursuant to regulations under section 22 of the Teaching and Higher Education Act 1998." substituted for the former wording by SI 2012/848, reg. 3(3)(d), with effect from 6 April 2012.
Reg. 8(d) substituted by SI 2008/2169, reg. 5(3), with effect from 1 September 2008.
Former reg. 8(d)(i) and (ii) substituted by SI 2007/1305, reg. 5, with effect from 16 May 2007.
Reg. 8 substituted by SI 2003/2815, reg. 7 with effect from 26 November 2003.

Cross references – SI 2013/386, reg. 17(2) and Schedule, para. 23: modified application of reg. 8 in relation to the introduction of Universal Credit.
SI 2014/1230, Sch., para. 18: modified application of reg. 8 where SI 2014/1230, reg. 12A applies (claims for universal credit).

PAYMENTS OF INCOME IN CONNECTION WITH STUDENTS TO BE DISREGARDED FOR THE PURPOSES OF REGULATION 3

9 Income which is exempt from income tax by virtue of section 753 or 776 of ITTOIA (which deal respectively with interest on the repayment of student loans and scholarship income) is disregarded in calculating a claimant's income under regulation 3.

History – Reg. 9 substituted by SI 2006/766, reg. 13 with effect from 6 April 2006.

Chapter 7 – Investment Income

INVESTMENT INCOME

10(1) In these Regulations **"investment income"** means the gross amount of–

(a) any interest of money, whether yearly or otherwise, or any annuity or other annual payment, whether such payment is payable within or out of the United Kingdom, either as a charge on any property of the person paying it by virtue of any deed or will or otherwise, or as a reservation out of it, or as a personal debt or obligation by virtue of any contract, or whether the payment is received and payable half-yearly or at any shorter or longer periods, but not including property income;

(b) any discounts on securities;

(c) any income from securities payable out of the public revenues of the United Kingdom or Northern Ireland;

(d) dividends and other distributions of a company resident in the United Kingdom and any tax credit associated with that payment; and

(e) any amount treated as forming part of the individual's income for the year for income tax purposes by virtue of Chapter 9 of Part 4 of ITTOIA disregarding section 535 (top slicing relief).

This is subject to the following qualification.

10(2) In calculating investment income, there shall be disregarded–

(a) any amount listed in column 1 of Table 4 to the extent shown in the corresponding entry in column 2;

(b) any amount listed in column 1 of Table 5 during the period shown in the corresponding entry in column 2;

(c) any income arising from savings certificates, and interest on tax reserve certificates, exempted from tax by section 692, 693 or 750 of ITTOIA (savings certificates and tax reserve certificates);

(d) the first £70 in any tax year of interest on deposits with National Savings and Investments, exempted from income tax by section 691 of ITTOIA (National Savings Bank ordinary account interest).

(e) any payment to a claimant which does not form part of his income for the purposes of income tax by virtue of section 727 of ITTOIA (certain annual payments by individuals).

Table 4
Payments disregarded in the calculation of investment income

	1. Description of income to be disregarded	*2. Extent of disregard*
1.	Any interest, dividends, distributions, profits or gains in respect of investments under– (a) a Personal Equity Plan, or (b) an Individual Savings Account, in respect of which the claimant is entitled to relief from income tax under Chapter 3 of Part 6 of ITTOIA, or which is taxed only in accordance with regulation 23 of the Individual Savings Account Regulations 1998.	The whole amount, unless it is interest under a personal equity plan to which regulation 17A(2) of the Personal Equity Plan Regulations 1989 applies. Interest to which that paragraph applies is disregarded only to the extent that it does not exceed the annual limit of £180 mentioned in that regulation.

	1. Description of income to be disregarded	2. Extent of disregard
2.	[Omitted by SI 2006/766.]	
3.	Any interest payable under a certified SAYE savings arrangement for the purposes of Chapter 4 of Part 6 of ITTOIA.	The whole amount.
4.	Any winnings from betting, including pool betting, or lotteries or games with prizes.	The whole amount.
5.	Any interest on a payment of £10,000 made by the Secretary of State to a person who was held prisoner by the Japanese during the Second World War or to the spouse of such a person, if the payment is held in a distinct account and no payment (other than interest) has been added to the account.	The whole amount of the interest.
6.	Any interest on a payment made to the claimant by, or on behalf of a government of a country outside the United Kingdom, either from its own resources or with contributions from any other organisation, by way of compensation for a victim of National Socialism if the payment is held in a distinct account and no payment (other than interest) has been added to the account. Here a reference to a victim of National Socialism is a reference to a person who was required to work as a slave or a forced labourer for National Socialists or their sympathisers during the Second World War, or suffered property loss, or suffered injury or is the parent of a child who died, at the hands of National Socialists or their sympathisers during the Second World War.	The whole amount of the interest.
7.	Any monies paid to the claimant by a bank or building society as compensation in respect of an unclaimed account held by a Holocaust victim and which vested in the Custodian of Enemy Property under section 7 of the Trading with the Enemy Act 1939 and treated as exempt from income tax by section 756A of ITTOIA.	The amount of interest exempted from income tax under section 756A of ITTOIA.
8.	Any interest, or payment, which is disregarded for income tax purposes by virtue of– (a) section 751 of ITTOIA (interest on damages for personal injury), or (b) section 731 of ITTOIA (periodical payments of personal injury damages) (personal injury damages in the form of periodical payments).	The amount so disregarded.
9.	Annuity payments under an award of compensation made under the Criminal Injuries Compensation Scheme (within the meaning of section 732(3) of ITTOIA).	The amount of any payment which is treated as not being income of the claimant or his partner by virtue of section 731 of ITTOIA.
10.	A payment under a life annuity.	The amount of interest eligible for relief under section 353 of the Taxes Act by virtue of section 365 of that Act.
11.	Any interest, or payment in respect of interest, which is compensation to a person who is under the age of 18 years for the death of one or both of his parents.	The whole of the interest or payment.

	1. Description of income to be disregarded	2. Extent of disregard
12.	A purchased life annuity to which Chapter 7 of Part 4 of ITTOIA applies.	The amount exempted under section 717 of ITTOIA as calculated under section 719 of that Act.
13.	Any payments which are exempt from income tax by virtue of– (a) section 725 of ITTOIA (annual payments under immediate needs annuities), or (b) section 735 of ITTOIA (health and employment insurance payments).	The whole amount.
14.	[Omitted by SI 2018/365.]	[Omitted by SI 2018/365.]
15.	Any payment of, or in respect of, a government bonus under section 1 or 2 of the Savings (Government Contributions) Act 2017.	The whole amount.

Table 5

Payments in connection with very severe disablement, Creutzfeldt-Jakob disease and haemophilia

	1. Description of income to be disregarded	2. Applicable period
1.	A trust payment made to– (a) a diagnosed person; (b) the diagnosed person's partner; or (c) the person who was his partner at the date of his death.	The period beginning on the date on which the trust payment is made and ending with the death of the person to whom the payment is made.
2.	A trust payment made to a parent of a deceased diagnosed person, or a person acting in the place of his parent.	The period beginning on the date on which the trust payment is made and ending two years after that date.
3.	The amount of any payment out of the estate of a person to whom a trust payment has been made, which is made to the person who was the diagnosed person's partner at the date of his death.	The period beginning on the date on which the payment is made and ending on the date on which that person dies.
4.	The amount of any payment out of the estate of a person to whom a trust payment has been made, which is made to a parent of a deceased diagnosed person, or a person acting in the place of his parent.	The period beginning on the date on which the payment is made and ending two years after that date.

10(3) The amounts disregarded under items 3 and 4 in Table 5 shall not exceed the total amount of any trust payments made to the person to whom the trust payment had been made.

10(4) In this regulation **"diagnosed person"** means–

(a) a person who has been diagnosed as suffering from, or who after his death has been diagnosed as having suffered from, variant Creutzfeldt-Jakob disease;

(b) a person who is suffering or has suffered from haemophilia; or

(c) a person in respect of whom a payment has been made from the 1992 Fund, the Eileen Trust or the Independent Living Funds; and

a reference to a person being a member of the diagnosed person's household at the date of the diagnosed person's death includes a person who would have been a member of his household but for the diagnosed person being in residential accommodation, a residential care home or a nursing home on that date.

10(5) In this regulation–

"relevant trust" means–

(a) a trust established out of funds provided by the Secretary of State in respect of persons who suffered, or who are suffering, from variant Creutzfeldt-Jakob disease for the benefit of persons eligible for payments in accordance with its provisions;

(b) the Macfarlane Trusts, or

(c) the 1992 Fund, the Eileen Trust or the Independent Living Funds.

TC Statutory Instruments

"residential accommodation", **"residential care home"** and **"nursing home"** have the meanings given by regulation 2(1) of the Income Support (General) Regulations 1987; and

"trust payment" means a payment under a relevant trust.

History – In reg. 10(1)(e) words "Chapter 9 of Part 4 of ITTOIA disregarding section 535 (top slicing relief)." substituted by SI 2006/766, reg. 14 with effect from 6 April 2006.
In reg. 10(2)(c) words "section 692, 693 or 750 of ITTOIA" substituted by SI 2006/766, reg. 14 with effect from 6 April 2006.
In reg. 10(2)(d) words "section 691 of ITTOIA (National Savings Bank ordinary account interest)." substituted by SI 2006/766, reg. 14 with effect from 6 April 2006.
In reg. 10(2)(e) words "section 727 of ITTOIA (certain annual payments by individuals)." substituted by SI 2006/766, reg. 14 with effect from 6 April 2006.
In Table 4, in item 1, words "Chapter 3 of Part 6 of ITTOIA" substituted by SI 2006/766, reg. 14 with effect from 6 April 2006.
In Table 4, item 2 omitted by SI 2006/766, reg. 14 with effect from 6 April 2006.
In Table 4, item 3 substituted by SI 2006/766, reg. 14 with effect from 6 April 2006.
In Table 4, in item 7 the words "section 756A of ITTOIA" substituted for "Extra Statutory Concession A100" by SI 2007/824, reg. 12(2), with effect from 6 April 2007.
In Table 4, in item 7 the words "of interest exempted from income tax under section 756A of ITTOIA" substituted for "treated as exempt by the Extra Statutory Concession" by SI 2007/824, reg. 12(3), with effect from 6 April 2007.
In Table 4, in item 8, words "in respect of interest" omitted and para. (a) substituted and in para. (b) words "section 731 of ITTOIA (periodical payments of personal injury damages)" substituted for "section 329AA of the Taxes Act" by SI 2006/766, reg. 14 with effect from 6 April 2006.
In Table 4, in item 9, words "section 732(3) of ITTOIA" substituted, and in the entry in column 2 the words "section 731 of ITTOIA" substituted by SI 2006/766, reg. 14 with effect from 6 April 2006.
In Table 4, in item 12, words "Chapter 7 of Part 4 of ITTOIA" substituted for "section 656 of the Taxes Act", and entry in column 2 substituted by SI 2006/766, reg. 14, with effect from 6 April 2006.
In Table 4, item 12 inserted by SI 2003/2815, reg. 8(2) with effect from 26 November 2003.
Previously in Table 4 items 10, 11 and 12 respectively renumbered as items 9, 10 and 11, by SI 2003/732, reg. 9, with effect from 6 April 2003.
In Table 4, item 13 inserted by SI 2006/766, reg. 14, with effect from 6 April 2006.
In Table 4, item 14 omitted by SI 2018/365, reg. 2(4)(a), with effect from 6 April 2018. Former item 14 refereed to Saving Gateway account.
In Table 4, item 14 inserted by SI 2010/751, reg. 4, with effect from 6 April 2010.
In Table 4, item 15 the words "or (2)" inserted by SI 2018/365, reg. 2(4)(b), with effect from 6 April 2018.
In Table 4, item 15 inserted by SI 2017/396, reg. 4, with effect in relation to awards of tax credit for the tax year 2017–18 and subsequenttax years.

Cross references – SI 2011/1502, art. 6: Equitable Life "authorised payments" to be disregarded in calculating investment income in accordance with reg. 10.
SI 2013/386, reg. 17(2) and Schedule, para. 24: modified application of reg. 10 in relation to the introduction of Universal Credit.
SI 2014/1230, Sch., para. 19: modified application of reg. 10(1) and (2) where SI 2014/1230, reg. 12A applies (claims for universal credit).

Chapter 8 – Property Income

PROPERTY INCOME

11(1) In these Regulations **"property income"** means the annual taxable profits arising from a business carried on for the exploitation, as a source of rents or other receipts, of any estate, interest or rights in or over land in the United Kingdom.

Expressions which are used in this paragraph which are defined in Part 3 of ITTOIA for the purposes of that section bear the same meaning here as they bear in that section.

This paragraph is subject to the following qualifications.

11(2) In calculating property income there shall be disregarded any profits–

(a) treated as nil by section 791 to 794 of ITTOIA (full rent-a-room relief); or

(b) excluded from profits by section 795 to 798 of ITTOIA (alternative calculation of profits if amount exceeds limit).

11(2A) In calculating property income, the restrictions in section 272A of ITTOIA (restricting deductions for finance costs related to residential property) and section 399A of ITA (property partnerships: restriction of relief for investment loan interest) shall be disregarded.

11(3) Where a property business (as defined in Part 3 of ITTOIA) makes a loss to which the relief provisions contained in sections 118 (carry forward against subsequent property business profits) and 119 (how relief works) of ITA apply, then such relief as may arise under those sections shall be applied in calculating property income for the purposes of this regulation.

History – In reg. 11(1) words "Part 3 of ITTOIA" substituted by SI 2006/766, reg. 15, with effect from 6 April 2006.
In reg. 11(1) the word "qualifications" substituted by SI 2003/2815, reg. 9(2) with effect from 26 November 2003.
Reg. 11(2) substituted by SI 2006/766, reg. 15, with effect from 6 April 2006.
Reg. 11(2A) inserted by SI 2017/396, reg. 5, with effect in relation to awards of tax credit for the tax year 2017–18 and subsequent tax years.
In reg. 11(3) words "Where a property business (as defined in Part 3 of ITTOIA)" substituted by SI 2006/766, reg. 15, with effect from 6 April 2006.
Reg. 11(3) inserted by SI 2003/2815, reg. 9(3) with effect from 26 November 2003.
In reg. 11(3) the words "contained in sections 118 (carry forward against subsequent property business profits) and 119 (how relief works) of ITA" and the words "those sections" substituted by SI 2007/1305, reg. 6, with effect from 16 May 2007.

Cross references – SI 2013/386, reg. 17(2) and Schedule, para. 25: modified application of reg. 11 in relation to the introduction of Universal Credit.
SI 2014/1230, Sch., para. 20: modified application of reg. 11(1) where SI 2014/1230, reg. 12A applies (claims for universal credit).

Chapter 9 – Foreign Income

FOREIGN INCOME

12(1) In these Regulations **"foreign income"** means income arising, in the year in question, from a source outside the United Kingdom or from foreign holdings which is not–

(a) employment income;

(b) trading income; or

(c) investment income falling within regulation 10(1)(e).

This is subject to the following provisions of this regulation.

12(2) The reference in paragraph (1) to "foreign holdings" shall be construed in accordance with section 571 of ITTOIA.

12(3) In calculating the claimant's foreign income there shall be disregarded–

(a) any payment by way of an annuity or pension payable under any special provision for victims of National Socialist persecution which is made by the law of the Federal Republic of Germany, or any part of it, or of Austria;

(aa) any monies paid by a bank or building society which are exempted from income tax under section 756A of ITTOIA (interest on certain deposits of victims of National-Socialist persecution).

(bb) any pension, annuity, allowance or other payment provided in accordance with the provisions of the scheme established under the law of the Netherlands and known as *Wet uitkeringen vervolgingsslachtoffers 1940–1945* (Netherlands Benefit Act for Victims of Persecution 1940–1945).

(b) the amount authorised to be deducted by the relevant provision if the claimant's foreign income comprises or includes a pension to which the following provisions of ITEPA apply–

(i) section 567(5) and 617 (deduction allowed from taxable pension income);

(ii) section 575(2) (taxable pension income: foreign pensions);

(iii) section 613(3) (taxable pension income: foreign annuities); and

(iv) section 635(3) (taxable pension income: foreign voluntary annual payments); and

(c) any amount which would be disregarded for the purposes of income tax by virtue of–

(i) Extra Statutory Concession A 10 (lumps sums paid by overseas pension schemes);

(ii) section 681 of ITEPA;

(iii) section 751(1)(c) of ITTOIA (interest on damages for personal injuries awarded by a foreign court);

(iv) Extra Statutory Concession A 44 (education allowances payable to public officials of overseas territories) or

(v) section 730 of ITTOIA (foreign maintenance payments).

12(4) Where an overseas property business (within the meaning of Part 3 of ITTOIA) makes a loss to which the relief provisions contained in sections 118 (carry forward against subsequent property business profits) and 119 (how relief works) of ITA apply, then such relief as may arise under those sections shall be applied in calculating foreign income for the purposes of this regulation.

History – In reg. 12(1) words "a source outside the United Kingdom or from foreign holdings" substituted for "possessions or from securities out of the United Kingdom" by SI 2006/766, reg. 16, with effect from 6 April 2006.
Reg. 12(2) substituted by SI 2006/766, reg. 16, with effect from 6 April 2006.
Reg. 12(3)(aa) inserted by SI 2007/824, reg. 13(2), with effect from 6 April 2007.
Reg. 12(3)(bb) inserted by SI 2016/360, reg. 3(3), with effect from 6 April 2016.
Reg. 12(3)(b) substituted by SI 2006/766, reg. 16, with effect from 6 April 2006.
In former reg. 12(3)(b) words "or section 196" repealed by SI 2003/732, reg. 10(a)(i), with effect from 6 April 2003.
In former reg. 12(3)(b) words "or to which sections 567(5) and 617 of ITEPA apply" inserted after "the Taxes Act applies" by SI 2003/732, reg. 10(a)(ii), with effect from 6 April 2003.
In former reg. 12(3)(b) words "the relevant provision" substituted by SI 2003/732, reg. 10(a)(iii), with effect from 6 April 2003.
In reg. 12(3)(c)(ii) words "section 681 of ITEPA" substituted by SI 2003/732, reg. 10(b), with effect from 6 April 2003.
In reg. 12(3)(c)(iii) words "section 751(1)(c) of ITTOIA" substituted for "Extra Statutory Concession A30" and "or" omitted by SI 2006/766, reg. 16, with effect from 6 April 2006.
Reg. 12(3)(c)(v) inserted by SI 2006/766, reg. 16, with effect from 6 April 2006.
In reg. 12(4) words "(within the meaning of Part 3 of ITTOIA)" substituted by SI 2006/766, reg. 16, with effect from 6 April 2006.
Reg. 12(4) inserted by SI 2003/2815, reg. 10(1) with effect from 26 November 2003.
In reg. 12(4) the words "contained in sections 118 (carry forward against subsequent property business profits) and 119 (how relief works) of ITA apply" substituted and the words "those sections" substituted by SI 2007/1305, reg. 7, with effect from 16 May 2007.

Cross references – SI 2013/386, reg. 17(2) and Schedule, para. 26: modified application of reg. 12 in relation to the introduction of Universal Credit.

TC Statutory Instruments

SI 2014/1230, Sch., para. 21: modified application of reg. 12(1) where SI 2014/1230, reg. 12A applies (claims for universal credit).

Chapter 10 – Notional Income

INTRODUCTION

13 In these Regulations **"notional income"** means income which, by virtue of regulations 14 to 17 a claimant is treated as having, but which he does not in fact have.

Cross references – SI 2013/386, reg. 17(2) and Schedule, para. 27: modified application of reg. 13 in relation to the introduction of Universal Credit.
SI 2014/1230, Sch., para. 22: modified application of reg. 13 where SI 2014/1230, reg. 12A applies (claims for universal credit).

CLAIMANTS TREATED FOR ANY PURPOSE AS HAVING INCOME BY VIRTUE OF THE INCOME TAX ACTS

14(1) If an amount is treated for any purpose as the claimant's income under any provision mentioned in paragraph (2), he is to be treated as having that amount of income, but this is subject to paragraph (1A).

14(1A) Where paragraph (2)(b)(x) or (2)(b)(xi) applies, the amount of income that the claimant is to be treated as having is:

$$x - y$$

where

"x" is the amount of income under section 652, 654 or 655 of ITTOIA, and

"y" is the amount that would, but for section 272A of that Act, be deductible in calculating the profits for income tax purposes of a property business for the profits year.

14(2) The provisions mentioned in paragraph (1) are–

(a) the following provisions of the Taxes Act–

(i)–(viii) [omitted by SI 2006/766, reg. 17;]

(ix) section 714 (transfers of securities: treatment of deemed sums and reliefs) or 716 (transfer of unrealised interest);

(x) section 730 (transfers of income arising from securities);

(xi) [omitted by SI 2007/1305, reg. 8(2);]

(xii) [omitted by SI 2007/1305, reg. 8(2);]

(xiii) [omitted by SI 2007/1305, reg. 8(2);]

(xiv) section 761 (charge to income tax of offshore income gain); and

(xv) [omitted by SI 2007/1305, reg. 8(2); and]

(b) the following provisions of ITTOIA–

(i) sections 277 to 283 (amounts treated as receipts: leases);

(ii) Chapter 5 of Part 4 (stock dividends from UK resident companies);

(iii) Chapter 6 of Part 4 (release of loan to participator in close company);

(iv) section 427 (charge to tax on profits from deeply discounted securities);

(v) Chapter 11 of Part 4 (transactions in deposits);

(vi) sections 624 to 628 (income treated as income of settlor: retained interests);

(vii) sections 629 to 632 (income treated as income of settlor: unmarried children);

(viii) section 633 (capital sums paid to settlor by trustees of settlement);

(ix) section 641 (capital sums paid to settlor by body connected with settlement);

(x) section 652 (estate income: absolute interests in residue); and

(xi) sections 654 to 655 (estate income: interests in residue); and

(ba) the following provisions of ITA–

(i) Chapter 5 of Part 11 (price differences under repos);

(ii) Chapter 2 of Part 13 (transfer of assets abroad); and

(iii) Chapter 3 of Part 13 (transactions in land).

(c) section 84 and Schedule 15 to the Finance Act 2004 (charge to income tax by reference to enjoyment of property previously owned).

History – In reg. 14(1) the words ", but this is subject to paragraph (1A)" inserted by SI 2018/365, reg. 2(5)(a), with effect from 6 April 2018.
Reg. 14(1A) inserted by SI 2018/365, reg. 2(5)(b), with effect from 6 April 2018.
Reg. 14(2)(a)(i)–(viii) omitted by SI 2006/766, reg. 17, with effect from 6 April 2006.
Reg. 14(2)(b) and (c) substituted for para. (b) by SI 2006/766, reg. 17, with effect from 6 April 2006.

Reg. 14(2)(a)(xi)–(xiii) omitted by SI 2007/1305, reg. 8(2) with effect from 16 May 2007.
Reg. 14(2)(a)(xv) omitted by SI 2007/1305, reg. 8(2) with effect from 16 May 2007.
Reg. 14(2)(ba) inserted by SI 2007/1305, reg. 8(3) with effect from 16 May 2007.

CLAIMANTS DEPRIVING THEMSELVES OF INCOME IN ORDER TO SECURE ENTITLEMENT

15 If a claimant has deprived himself of income for the purpose of securing entitlement to, or increasing the amount of, a tax credit, he is treated as having that income.

HMRC Manuals – TCTM 04803: purpose of disposal of income – 'The claimant may have more than one reason for disposing of income, only one of which is to obtain tax credit or more tax credit. Securing or increasing entitlement to tax credit may not be a claimant's main motive but it must be a significant one.'

CLAIMANTS TO WHOM INCOME BECOMES AVAILABLE UPON THE MAKING OF A CLAIM

16(1) If income would become available to a claimant upon the making of an application for that income he is treated as having that income.

This is subject to the following qualification.

16(2) Paragraph (1) does not apply in relation to income–

(a) under a trust derived from a payment made in consequence of a personal injury;

(b) under a personal pension scheme or retirement annuity contract;

(c) consisting in a sum to which item 8 of Table 4 in regulation 10 refers (compensation for personal injuries which is administered by the Court); or

(d) consisting in a rehabilitation allowance made under section 2 of the Employment Act.

16(3) Paragraph (1) also does not apply to income by way of–

(a) a Category A or Category B retirement pension,

(aa) a state pension under Part 1 of the Pensions Act 2014 or Part 1 of the Pensions Act (Northern Ireland) 2015

(b) a graduated retirement benefit, or

(c) a shared additional pension, payment of which has been deferred.

Here–

"Category A retirement pension" means a pension to which a person is entitled by virtue of section 44 of the Contributions and Benefits Act or the Northern Ireland Contributions and Benefits Act;

"Category B retirement pension" means a pension to which a person is entitled by virtue of any of sections 48A to 48C of the Contributions and Benefits Act or sections 48A to 48C of the Northern Ireland Contributions and Benefits Act;

"graduated retirement benefit" means a pension payable under–

(a) sections 36 and 37 of the National Insurance Act 1965; or

(b) sections 35 and 36 of the National Insurance Act (Northern Ireland) 1966

and

"shared additional pension" means a pension to which a person is entitled by virtue of section 55A or 55AA of the Contributions and Benefits Act or section 55A or 55AA of the Northern Ireland Contributions and Benefits Act

History – Reg. 16(3) inserted by SI 2004/762 with effect from 6 April 2004.
Reg. 16(3)(aa) inserted by SI 2015/1985, art. 25(a), with effect from 6 April 2016 immediately after the State Pension Regulations 2015 (SI 2015/173).
In reg. 16(3)(c), in the definition of "shared additional pension", the words "or 55AA" inserted (in both places) by SI 2015/1985, art. 25(b), with effect from 6 April 2016 immediately after the State Pension Regulations 2015 (SI 2015/173).

CLAIMANTS PROVIDING SERVICES TO OTHER PERSONS FOR LESS THAN FULL EARNINGS

17(1) If a claimant provides a service for another person and–

(a) the other person makes no payment of earnings or pays less than those paid for a comparable employment (including self-employment) in the area; and

(b) the Board are satisfied that the means of the other person are sufficient for him to pay for, or to pay more for, the service,

the claimant is to be treated as having such an amount of employment income, or in the case of a service provided in the course of a trade or business, such an amount of trading income as is reasonable for the employment of the claimant to provide the service.

This is subject to the following qualification.

17(2) Paragraph (1) does not apply where–

(a) the claimant is a volunteer or is engaged to provide the service by a charitable or voluntary organisation and the Board are satisfied that it is reasonable for the claimant to provide the service free of charge; or

(b) the service is provided in connection with the claimant's participation in an employment or training programme–

(i) in Great Britain, which is approved by the Secretary of State;

(ii) in Northern Ireland in accordance with regulation 19(1)(p) of the Jobseeker's Allowance Regulations (Northern Ireland) 1996 other than where it is provided in connection with the claimant's participation in the Preparation for Employment Programme specified in regulation 75(1)(a)(v) of those Regulations.

History – Reg. 17(2)(b)(i) substituted by SI 2013/630, reg. 78(3), with effect from 29 April 2013.

Chapter 11 – Miscellaneous Income

MISCELLANEOUS INCOME

18 In these Regulations **"miscellaneous income"** means income which does not fall within any other provision of these Regulations and which is subject to income tax under Part 5 of ITTOIA.

History – In reg. 18 words "Part 5 of ITTOIA." substituted by SI 2006/766, reg. 18, with effect from 6 April 2006.

Cross references – SI 2013/386, reg. 17(2) and Schedule, para. 28: modified application of reg. 18 in relation to the introduction of Universal Credit.
SI 2014/1230, Sch., para. 23: modified application of reg. 18 where SI 2014/1230, reg. 12A applies (claims for universal credit).

PART 3 – SUMS DISREGARDED IN THE CALCULATION OF INCOME

GENERAL DISREGARDS IN THE CALCULATION OF INCOME

19(1) For the purposes of regulation 3–

(a) the sums specified in Table 6 are disregarded in the calculation of income;

(b) the sums specified in column 1 of Table 7 are disregarded in the calculation of income if the condition in the corresponding entry in column 2 of that Table is satisfied; and

(c) the sums specified in column 1 of Table 8 are disregarded in the calculation of income to the extent specified in the corresponding entry in column 2 of that Table.

19(2) In this regulation–

"the JSA Regulations" means the Jobseeker's Allowance Regulations 1996; and

"the JSA (NI) Regulations" means the Jobseeker's Allowance (Northern Ireland) Regulations 1996.

Table 6
Sums disregarded in the calculation of income

1.	Any payment of an employment credit under a scheme under section 2(2) of the Employment Act known as "New Deal 50 plus" or the corresponding scheme under section 1 of the Employment and Training Act (Northern Ireland) 1950.
2.	Any payment made– (a) under section 15 of the Disabled Persons (Employment Act) 1944 or section 15 of the Disabled Persons (Employment) Act (Northern Ireland) 1945; or (b) in accordance with arrangements made under section 2 of the Employment Act or section 1 of the Employment and Training Act (Northern Ireland) 1950 to assist disabled persons to obtain or retain employment despite their disability.
3.	Any mandatory top-up payment made pursuant to– (a) section 2 of the Employment Act or section 1 of the Employment and Training Act (Northern Ireland) 1950 in respect of the claimant's participation in– (i) an employment programme specified in regulation 75(1)(a)(ii)(bb) of the JSA Regulations or regulation 75(1)(a)– (ii) of the JSA(NI) Regulations (Voluntary Sector Option of the New Deal);

(ii) an employment programme specified in regulation 75(1)(a)(ii)(cc) of the JSA Regulations (Environmental Task Force Option of the New Deal) or regulation 75(1)(a)(iii) of the JSA(NI) Regulations;

(iia) an employment programme specified in regulation 75(1)(a)(ii)(dd) of the JSA Regulations (Community Task Force);

(iii) the Intensive Activity Period of the New Deal Pilots for 25 plus specified in regulation 75(1)(a)(iv) of the JSA Regulations or, in Northern Ireland, the Preparation for Employment Programme specified in regulation 75(1)(a)(v) of the JSA(NI) Regulations; or

(iv) the Backing Young Britain programme pursuant to arrangements made under section 2 of the Employment Act;

(b) a written arrangement entered into between–

(i) the Secretary of State and the person who has arranged for the claimant's participation in the Intensive Activity Period of the New Deal for 25 plus and which is made in respect of his participation in that Period; or

(ii) the Department for Employment and Learning and the person who has arranged for the claimant's participation in the Preparation

for Employment Programme and which is made in respect of the claimant's participation in the Programme; or

(c) the Steps to Work Programme specified in regulation 75(1)(a)(vi) of the Jobseeker's Allowance Regulations (Northern Ireland) 1996.

This item applies only to the extent that the payment is not taxable as a profit of a trade, profession or vocation.

4. Any discretionary payment pursuant to section 2 of the Employment Act, or, in Northern Ireland, section 1(1) of the Employment and Training Act (Northern Ireland) 1950 to meet, or help to meet, special needs in respect of the claimant's participation in the Full-Time Education and Training Option of the New Deal as specified in regulation 75(1)(b)(ii) of the JSA Regulations or of the JSA(NI) Regulations.

5. Any–

(a) education maintenance allowance in accordance with regulations made under section 518 of the Education Act 1996 (payment of school expenses; grant of scholarships etc.); or

(b) payment (not within sub-paragraph (a)) in respect of a course of study attended by a child or qualifying young person payable–

(i) in accordance with regulations made under section 518 of the Education (Scotland) Act 1980 (power to assist persons to take advantage of educational facilities) or section 12(2)(c) of the Further and Higher Education (Scotland) Act 1992 (provision of financial assistance to students); or

(ii) by virtue of regulations made Article 50, 51 or 55(1) of the Education and Libraries (Northern Ireland) Order 1986 (provisions to assist persons to take advantage of educational facilities).

6. Any payment made by an employment zone contractor payable in respect of the claimant's participation in the employment zone programme by way of–

(a) a training premium;

(b) a discretionary payment, being a fee, grant, loan or otherwise; or

(c) any arrears of subsistence allowance paid as a lump sum.

7. [Omitted by SI 2004/762, reg. 16(2)(b) with effect from 6 April 2004.]

8. An amount of income equal to any qualifying maintenance payment within section 347B of the Taxes Act.

9. Any payment by way of qualifying care receipts to the extent that those receipts qualify for relief under Chapter 2 of Part 7 of the Income Tax (Trading and Other Income) Act 2005.

10. Any payment of maintenance, whether under a court order or not, which is made or due to be made by–

(a) the claimant's former partner, or the claimant's partner's former partner; or

(b) the parent of a child or qualifying young person where that child or qualifying young person is a member of the claimant's household except where that parent is the claimant or the claimant's partner.

11. Any payment in respect of a child or qualifying young person who is a member of the claimant's household made–

(a) to adopters which is exempt from income tax by virtue of sections 744 to 746 of ITTOIA;

(b) by a local authority in pursuance of paragraph 15(1) of Schedule 1 to the Children Act 1989 (local authority contribution to child's maintenance);

(bb) by a local authority by way of special guardianship support services pursuant to regulations under section 14F(1)(b) of the Children Act 1989; or

(c) by an authority, as defined in Article 2 of the Children (Northern Ireland) Order 1995, in pursuance of Article 15 of, and paragraph 17 of Schedule 1 to, that Order (contribution by an authority to child's maintenance).

12. Any payment in respect of travelling expenses–

(a) in relation to England under regulation 5, 6 or 12 of the National Health Service (Travel Expenses and Remission of Charges) Regulations 2003;

(b) in relation to Wales under regulation 5, 6 or 11 of the National Health Service (Travelling Expenses and Remission of Charges) (Wales) Regulations 2007;

(c) in relation to Scotland, under regulation 3, 5, or 11 of the National Health Service (Travelling Expenses and Remission of Charges) (Scotland) (No. 2) Regulations 2003;

(d) in relation to Northern Ireland, under regulation 5, 6 or 11 of the Travelling Expenses and Remission of Charges Regulations (Northern Ireland) 2004; or

(e) made by the Secretary of State for Health and Social Care, the Scottish Ministers, the Welsh Ministers or the Department of Health, Social Services and Public Safety and which is analogous to a payment specified in paragraph (a), (b), (c) or (d).

13. Any payment made by the Secretary of State or the Scottish Ministers under a scheme established to assist relatives and other persons to visit persons in custody.

14. Any payment under the Community Care (Direct Payments) Act 1996, section 57 of the Health and Social Care Act 2001, section 12B of the Social Work (Scotland) Act 1968, Article 15A of the Health and Personal Social Services (Direct Payments) (Northern Ireland) Order 1996 or regulations made under section 57 of the Health and Social Care Act 2001 (direct payments), sections 50 to 53 of the Social Services and Well-being (Wales) Act 2014 or section 8 of the Carers and Direct Payments Act (Northern Ireland) 2002.

14A. Any payment made under the "Supporting People" programme–

(a) in England and Wales, under section 93 of the Local Government Act 2000;

(b) in Scotland, under section 91 of the Housing (Scotland) Act 2001; or

(c) in Northern Ireland, under Article 4 of the Housing Support Services (Northern Ireland) Order 2002.

15. Any payment or a voucher provided under section 95 or 98 of the Immigration and Asylum Act 1999 for any former asylum-seeker or his dependants.

16. Any payment of a provident benefit by a trade union.

Here–

"provident benefit" has the meaning given in section 467(2) of the Taxes Act; and

"trade union" has the meaning given in section 467(4) of the Taxes Act.

17. Armed forces independence payment under the Armed Forces and Reserve Forces (Compensation Scheme) Order 2011.

18. Any payment made under the Welfare Supplementary Payment (Loss of Disability Living Allowance) Regulations (Northern Ireland) 2016, the Welfare Supplementary Payment (Loss of Disability-Related Premiums) Regulations (Northern Ireland) 2016, Part 2 of the Welfare Supplementary Payments Regulations (Northern Ireland) 2016, or Parts 3 to 5 of the Welfare Supplementary Payment (Loss of Carer Payments) Regulations (Northern Ireland) 2016.

19.	Any payment made by the Scottish Ministers to a claimant who is, or who has been, in receipt of carer's allowance under section 70 of the Contributions and Benefits Act (carer's allowance) during the relevant tax year to supplement that allowance. In this item and in items 20 and 21 **"Scottish Ministers"** has the meaning given by section 44(2) of the Scotland Act 1998.
20.	Any payment in respect of funeral expense assistance which is made by the Scottish Ministers to a claimant who has accepted responsibility for the expenses of a funeral to meet, or help towards meeting, those expenses.
21.	Any payment made by the Scottish Ministers in respect of early years assistance, which is made for the purposes of meeting some of the costs associated with having, or expecting to have, a baby or child in the family.
22.	Any discretionary financial assistance payment which is made by a Scottish local authority to a claimant who is in receipt of housing benefit provided by virtue of a scheme under section 123 of the Contributions and Benefits Act (income-related benefits) to meet, or help towards meeting, a claimant's housing costs. In this item **"Scottish local authority"** means "a council constituted under section 2 of the Local Government etc. (Scotland) Act 1994".

Table 7
Sums disregarded in calculating income if conditions are satisfied

	1. Description of payment	*2. Conditions that must be satisfied*
1.	Any payment in respect of any expenses incurred by a claimant who is engaged by a charitable or voluntary organisation or is a volunteer.	The claimant does not receive remuneration or profit from the engagement and is not treated as possessing any employment income under regulation 17 in respect of that engagement.
2.	A payment by way of– (a) travelling expenses reimbursed to the claimant; (b) a living away from home allowance under section 2(2)(d) of the Employment Act, section 2(4)(c) of the Enterprise and New Towns (Scotland) Act 1990 or section 1 of the Employment and Training Act (Northern Ireland) 1950; (c) training grant; (d) child care expenses reimbursed to the claimant in respect of his participation in– (i) a New Deal option, (ii) the Intensive Activity Period of the New Deal Pilots for 25 plus, (iii) the Preparation for Employment Programme; (iv) the Flexible New Deal specified in regulation 75(1)(a)(v) of the JSA Regulations; or (v) the Community Task Force specified in regulation 75(1)(a)(ii)(dd) of the JSA Regulations; or (e) child care expenses under the Steps to Work Programme specified in regulation 75(1)(a)(vi) of the JSA (NI) Regulations.	The claimant– (a) participates in arrangements for training made under– (i) section 2 of the Employment Act; (ii) section 2 of the Enterprise and New Towns (Scotland) Act 1990; or (iii) section 1 of the Employment and Training Act (Northern Ireland) 1950; or (b) attends a course at an employment rehabilitation centre established under section 2 of the Employment Act. The payment is not taxable as a profit of a trade, profession or vocation.

TC Statutory Instruments

Table 8
Sums partly disregarded in the calculation of income

	Type of payment to be disregarded	*Limit on, or exception to, the extent of disregard*
1.	Any discretionary payment made pursuant to section 2 of the Employment Act, or, in Northern Ireland section 1(1) of the Employment and Training Act (Northern Ireland) 1950 to meet, or help meet, the claimant's special needs in undertaking a qualifying course within the meaning of regulation 17A(7) of the JSA Regulations or regulation 17A(7) of the JSA(NI) Regulations.	A payment is not within this item to the extent that it relates to travel expenses incurred as a result of the claimant's attendance on the course if an amount in respect of those expenses has already been disregarded pursuant to regulation 8.
2.	Any payment made in respect of a career development loan paid pursuant to section 2 of the Employment Act.	A payment is not within this item to the extent that the loan has been applied for or paid in respect of living expenses for the period of education and training supported by the loan.
3.	Any payment made to the claimant or his partner in respect of a person who is not normally a member of the claimant's household but is temporarily in his care, by– (a) a health authority; (b) a local authority; (c) a voluntary organisation; (d) that person pursuant to section 26(3A) of the National Assistance Act 1948; (dza) that person where the payment is for the provision of accommodation in respect of the meeting of that person's needs under section 18 or 19 of the Care Act 2014 (duty and power to meet needs for care and support) or section 35 or 36 of the Social Services and Well-being (Wales) Act 2014 (duty and power to meet care and supportneeds of an adult); (e) a primary care trust established under section 16A of the National Health Service Act 1977.	A payment is only to be disregarded by virtue of this item if (a) any profits arising from the payment mentioned in column 1 are treated as nil by section 791 to 794 of ITTOIA (full rent-a-room relief); or (b) excluded from profits by section 795 to 798 of ITTOIA (alternative calculation of profits if amount exceeds limit).
4.	Any payment made in Northern Ireland to the claimant or his partner in respect of a person who is not normally a member of the claimant's household but is temporarily in his care– (a) pursuant to Article 36(7) of the Health and Personal Social Services (Northern Ireland) Order 1972 by an authority; a voluntary organisation; or the person concerned, or (b) by a training school within the meaning of section 137 of the Children and Young Persons Act (Northern Ireland 1968. In this item **"an authority"** has the meaning given by *Article 2 of the Children* (Northern Ireland) Order 1995.	A payment is only to be disregarded by virtue of this item if (a) any profits or gains arising from the payment mentioned in column 1 are treated as nil by section 791 to 794 of ITTOIA (full rent-a-room relief); or (b) excluded from profits by section 795 to 798 of ITTOIA (alternative calculation of profits if amount exceeds limit).

	Type of payment to be disregarded	*Limit on, or exception to, the extent of disregard*
5.	Any payment under an insurance policy taken out to insure against the risk of being unable to maintain the repayments– (a) on a loan which is secured on the dwelling house which the claimant occupies as his home; or (b) under a regulated agreement or under a hire-purchase agreement or a conditional sale agreement. For the purposes of paragraph (b)– **"regulated agreement"** has the meaning given in the Consumer Credit Act 1974; and **"hire-purchase agreement"** and **"conditional sale agreement"** have the meanings given in Part 3 of the Hire-Purchase Act 1964.	A payment is only to be disregarded by virtue of this item to the extent that it is used to– (a) maintain the repayments referred to in column (1); and (b) meet any amount due by way of premiums on– (i) that policy; or (ii) in a case to which paragraph (a) of this item applies, an insurance policy taken out to insure against loss or damage to any building or part of a building which is occupied by the claimant as his home and which is required as a condition of the loan referred to in column (1).
6.	Any payment in respect of the claimant's attendance at court as a juror or witness.	This item applies only to the extent that the payment is not compensation for loss of earnings or for the loss of payment of social security income.
7.	Any payment of a sports award except to the extent that it has been made in respect of living expenses.	For the purposes of this item "living expenses'' does not include– (a) the cost of vitamins, minerals or other special dietary supplements intended to enhance the performance of the claimant in the sport in respect of which the award was made; or (b) accommodation costs incurred as a consequence of living away from home whilst training for, or competing in, the sport in respect of which the award was made.

History – In Table 6, item 3, the word "or" omitted before para. (a)(iii) and inserted after para. (a)(iii) and para. (a)(iia) and (a)(iv) inserted by SI 2010/751, reg. 5(2), with effect from 6 April 2010.
In Table 6, item 3(c) inserted (and the "or" at the end of item 3(a) omitted, and the "or" at the end of item 3(b) inserted) by SI 2009/2887, reg. 7(2), with effect from 21 November 2009.
In Table 6, item 3, the words "or section 1 of the Employment and Training Act (Northern Ireland) 1950" and "This item applies only to the extent that the payment is not taxable as a profit of a trade, profession or vocation" inserted by SI 2004/762, reg. 16(2)(a) with effect from 6 April 2004.
In Table 6, item 7 omitted by SI 2004/762, reg. 16(2)(b) with effect from 6 April 2004.
In Table 6, item 9 substituted by SI 2011/721, reg. 2(3), with effect from 6 April 2011.
In Table 6, item 9 substituted by SI 2003/2815, reg. 11(2) with effect from 26 November 2003.
In Table 6, item 9, words "Chapter 2 of Part 7 of ITTOIA." substituted for "Schedule 36 to the Finance Act 2003." by SI 2006/766, reg. 19 with effect from 6 April 2006.
In Table 6, item 11(a) substituted by SI 2003/2815 reg. 11(3) with effect from 26 November 2003 and item 11(bb) inserted by SI 2004/762, reg 16(2)(c) with effect from 6 April 2004.
In Table 6, item 11(a), words "sections 744 to 746 of ITTOIA;" substituted for "section 327A of the Taxes Act;" by SI 2006/766, reg. 19 with effect from 6 April 2006.
In Table 6, item 12(e), the words "and Social Care" inserted by SI 2018/378, art. 21(g), with effect from 11 April 2018.
In Table 6, item 12 substituted by SI 2010/2914, reg. 5, with effect from 31 December 2010.
In Table 6, in item 14, the words ", sections 50 to 53 of the Social Services and Well-being (Wales) Act 2014" inserted by SI 2016/360, reg. 3(4)(a), with effect from 6 April 2016.
In Table 6, item 14 words "or regulations made under section 57 of the Health and Social Care Act 2001 (direct payments)" inserted by SI 2004/1748, reg. 3, with effect from 1 November 2004.
In Table 6, item 14 substituted by SI 2003/2815, reg 11(4), with effect from 26 November 2003.
In Table 6, item 14A inserted by SI 2003/732, reg. 11(2) with effect from 6 April 2003.
In Table 6, item 15, the words "Any payment or a voucher " substituted for "Any payment of a voucher" by SI 2003/732, reg. 11(2) with effect from 6 April 2003.
In Table 6, item 17 inserted by SI 2013/591, art. 7 and Sch., para. 25(2), with effect from 8 April 2013.
In Table 6, item 18 inserted by SI 2016/978, reg. 2(3), with effect from 31 October 2016.
In Table 6, item 19 inserted by SI 2018/365, reg. 2(6), with effect from 6 April 2018.
In Table 6, item 20 inserted by SI 2018/365, reg. 2(6), with effect from 6 April 2018.
In Table 6, item 21 inserted by SI 2018/365, reg. 2(6), with effect from 6 April 2018.
In Table 6, item 22 inserted by SI 2018/365, reg. 2(6), with effect from 6 April 2018.
In Table 7, heading of second column the word "Conditions" substituted for "Condition" by SI 2004/762, reg. 16(3)(a) with effect from 6 April 2004.

In Table 7, item 2, the word "or" before para. (d)(iv) omitted, in para. (d)(iv) the words "JSA Regulations" substituted for the words "Jobseeker's Allowance Regulations 1996", para. (d)(v) inserted and in para. (e) the words "JSA (NI) Regulations" substituted for the words "Jobseeker's Allowance Regulations (Northern Ireland) 1996" by SI 2010/751, reg. 5(3), with effect from 6 April 2010.
In Table 7, in the first column, item 2(e) inserted (and the "or" at the end of item 2(c) omitted, and the "or" at the end of item 2(d) inserted) by SI 2009/2887, reg. 7(3), with effect from 21 November 2009.
In Table 7, after item 2(d), the word "or " in (ii) omitted, word "or" at end of (iii) and (iv) inserted by SI 2009/697, reg. 8 with effect from 5 October 2009.
In Table 7, the words "The payment is not taxable as a profit of a trade, profession or vocation" inserted by SI 2004/762, reg. 16(3)(b) with effect from 6 April 2004.
In Table 8, in item 3(dza), the words "or section 35 or 36 of the Social Services and Well-being (Wales) Act 2014 (duty and power to meet care and support needs of an adult)" inserted by SI 2016/360, reg. 3(4)(b), with effect from 6 April 2016.
In Table 8, item 3(dza) inserted by SI 2015/643, reg. 20, with effect from 1 April 2015 (SI 2015/993, art. 2(a)).
In Table 8, item 3 and 4 in column 2, para. (a) words "or gains" omitted and "section 791 to 794 of ITTOIA (full rent-a-room relief)" substituted for "paragraph 9 of Schedule 10 to the Finance (No. 2) Act 1992" by SI 2006/766, reg. 19 with effect from 6 April 2006.
In Table 8, item 3 and 4 in column 2, para. (b) words "by section 795 to 798 of ITTOIA (alternative calculation of profits if amount exceeds limit)" substituted for "or gains by paragraph 11 of that Schedule" by SI 2006/766, reg. 19 with effect from 6 April 2006.
In Table 8, item 3 and 4 in column 2, the words after "if" renumbered as para. (a) and para. (b) inserted by SI 2003/732, reg. 11(3) with effect from 6 April 2003.
In Table 8 there were originally two items numbered 5, the second item numbered 5 renumbered as item 6 and original item 6 renumbered as item 7 by SI 2003/732, reg. 11(3), with effect from 6 April 2003.

CHILD TAX CREDIT REGULATIONS 2002

(SI 2002/2007, amended by SI 2003/738, SI 2003/2815, SI 2004/762, SI 2004/941, SI 2005/681, SI 2005/2919, SI 2006/222, SI 2006/766, SI 2006/963, SI 2006/1163, SI 2007/828, SI 2007/2151, SI 2008/796, SI 2008/1879, SI 2008/2169, SI 2009/697, SI 2009/800, SI 2010/751, SI 2010/981, SI 2010/1172, SI 2010/2914, SI 2011/1035, SI 2011/1740, SI 2012/848, SI 2012/849, SI 2013/388, SI 2013/591, SI 2013/630, SI 2013/750, SI 2014/384, SI 2014/845, SI 2014/1231, SI 2014/2924, SI 2015/451, SI 2015/567, SI 2016/360, SI 2017/387, SI 2017/406 and SI 2018/344)

Made on 30 July 2002 by the Treasury, in exercise of the powers conferred on them by s. 8, 9, 65 and 67 of the Tax Credits Act 2002. Coming into force in accordance with reg. 1.

CITATION, COMMENCEMENT AND EFFECT

1 These Regulations may be cited as the Child Tax Credit Regulations 2002 and shall come into force–

(a) for the purpose of enabling claims to be made, on 1st August 2002;

(b) for the purpose of enabling awards to be made, on 1st January 2003; and

(c) for all other purposes on 6th April 2003;

and shall have effect for the tax year beginning on 6th April 2003 and subsequent tax years.

INTERPRETATION

2(1) In these Regulations, unless the context otherwise requires–

"A", as a noun, has the meaning given by regulation 7(2A);

"the Act" means the Tax Credits Act 2002;

"advanced education" means–

(a) a course in preparation for a degree, a diploma of higher education, a higher national diploma, a higher national diploma[sic] or higher national certificate of Edexcel or the Scottish Qualifications Authority, or a teaching qualification; or

(b) any other course which is of a standard above ordinary national diploma, a national diploma or national certificate of Edexcel, a general certificate of education (advanced level), or Scottish national qualifications at higher or advanced higher level;

"approved training" has the meaning given by regulation 1(3) of the Child Benefit (General) Regulations 2006.

"armed forces independence payment" means armed forces independence payment under the Armed Forces and Reserve Forces (Compensation Scheme) Order 2011;

"the Board" means the Commissioners for Her Majesty's Revenue and Customs;

"the Careers Service" means–

(a) in England and Wales, a person with whom the Secretary of State or the National Assembly of Wales has made arrangements under section 10(1) of the Employment Act, and a local authority to whom the Secretary of State or the National Assembly of Wales has given a direction under section 10(2) of that Act,

(b) in Scotland, a person with whom the Scottish Ministers have made arrangements under section 10(1) of the Employment Act and any education authority to which a direction has been given by the Scottish Ministers under section 10(2) of that Act, and

"child" means a person who has not attained the age of sixteen;

"claimant" has the meaning in section 9(8) of the Act, except in regulations 7 and 9 to 14 (for which see regulations 7(1) and 13(13) to (15));

"the Connexions Service" means a person of any description with whom the Secretary of State has made an arrangement under section 114(2)(a) of the Learning and Skills Act 2000 and section 10(1) of the Employment Act, and any person to whom he has given a direction under section 114(2)(b) of the former Act and section 10(2) of the latter Act;

"the Contributions and Benefits Act" means the Social Security Contributions and Benefits Act 1992;

"couple" has the meaning given by section 3(5A) of the Act;

"custodial sentence"–

(a) in England and Wales, has the meaning in section 76 of the Powers of Criminal Courts (Sentencing) Act 2000,

(b) in Scotland, means detention under a sentence imposed by a court under sections 44, 205, 207 or 208 of the Criminal Procedure (Scotland) Act 1995, and

(c) in Northern Ireland, means a custodial sentence under the Criminal Justice (Children) (Northern Ireland) Order 1998;

"disability living allowance" means a disability living allowance under section 71 of the Contributions and Benefits Act;

"the Employment Act" means the Employment and Training Act 1973;

"the family element of child tax credit" and **"the individual element of child tax credit"** shall be construed in accordance with section 9(3) of the Act;

"income support" means income support under section 124 of the Contributions and Benefits Act;

"joint claim" and **"single claim"** shall be construed in accordance with section 3(8) of the Act;

"looked after by a local authority" has the meaning in section 22 of the Children Act 1989, section 74 of the Social Services and Well-being (Wales) Act 2014, section 17(6) of the Children (Scotland) Act 1995 or (in Northern Ireland) Article 25 of the Children (Northern Ireland) Order 1995 (with the modification that for the reference to a local authority there is substituted a reference to an authority within the meaning in Article 2 of that Order), and (in Scotland) includes a child in respect of which a child assessment order within the meaning of section 35 of the Children's Hearings (Scotland) Act 2011 has been made or a child protection order within the meaning of section 37 of that Act has been made.

"the main responsibility test" has the meaning given in Rule 2.2. of regulation 3;

"the normally living with test" has the meaning given in Rule 1.1. of regulation 3;

"old style JSA" means a jobseeker's allowance under the Jobseekers Act 1995 as that Act has effect apart from the amendments made by Part 1 of Schedule 14 to the Welfare Reform Act 2012 that remove references to an income-based allowance;

"Part 1" means Part 1 of the Act;

"patient" means a person (other than a person who is serving a custodial sentence) who is regarded as receiving free in-patient treatment within the meaning of the Social Security (Hospital In-patients) Regulations 1975, or the Social Security (Hospital In-patients) Regulations (Northern Ireland) 1975;

"placing for adoption" means placing for adoption in accordance with–

(a) the Adoption Agencies Regulations 2005,

(b) the Adoption Agencies (Wales) Regulations 2005,

(c) the Adoption Agencies (Scotland) Regulations 2009, or

(d) the Adoption Agencies Regulations (Northern Ireland) 1989;

"personal independence payment" means personal independence payment under Part 4 of the Welfare Reform Act 2012;

"qualifying body" means–

(a) the Careers Service or Connexions Service;

(b) the Ministry of Defence;

(c) in Northern Ireland, the Department for Employment and Learning or an Education and Library Board established under Article 3 of the Education and Libraries (Northern Ireland) Order 1986; or

(d) for the purposes of applying Council Regulation (EEC) No. 1408/71 and Regulation (EC) No 883/2004 of the European Parliament and of the Council, any corresponding body in another member state;

"qualifying young person" means a person, other than a child, who–

(a) has not attained the age of twenty, and

(b) satisfies the conditions in regulation 5(3) and (4);

"remunerative work" means work which is–

(a) done for payment or in expectation of payment,

(b) undertaken for not less than 24 hours a week, calculated in accordance with regulation 4(3) of the Working Tax Credit (Entitlement and Maximum Rate) Regulations 2002, and

(c) not excluded from the meaning of engagement in remunerative work by regulation 4(2) of those Regulations;

and other expressions have the same meanings as defined in the Act.

"step-parent", in relation to A, means a person who is not A's parent but–

(a) is a member of a couple, the other member of which is a parent of A, where both are responsible for A; or

(b) was previously a member of–

(i) a couple, the other member of which was a parent of A, or

(ii) a polygamous unit (within the meaning of the Tax Credits (Polygamous Marriages) Regulations 2003), another member of which was a parent of A

if immediately prior to ceasing to be a member of that couple or that polygamous unit the person was, and has since remained, responsible for A;

2(2) In the application of these Regulations to Northern Ireland, a reference to a provision of an enactment which applies only to Great Britain or England and Wales, shall be construed, so far as necessary, as including a reference to the corresponding enactment applying to Northern Ireland.

History – In reg. 2(1), definition of "A" inserted by SI 2017/387, reg. 3(a), with effect from 6 April 2017.
In reg. 2(1), in the definition of "advanced education", the words "full-time education for the purposes of", following "means", omitted by SI 2014/1231, reg. 3(2)(a), with effect from 4 June 2014.
In reg. 2(1), in the definition of "advanced education", the words "or the Scottish Qualifications Authority", following "Edexcel", omitted by SI 2003/2815, reg. 17 with effect from 26 November 2003, and the words "or Scottish national qualifications at higher or advanced higher level" substituted by SI 2003/2815, reg. 17 with effect from 26 November 2003.
In reg. 2(1), the definition of "approved training" inserted by SI 2006/222, reg. 3(2), with effect from 6 April 2006.
In reg. 2(1), definition of "armed forces independence payment" inserted by SI 2013/591, art. 7 and Sch., para. 26, with effect from 8 April 2013.
In reg. 2(1), the definition of "the Board" inserted by SI 2003/738, reg. 3(a), with effect from 6 April 2003 and further amended by the substitution of the words "for Her Majesty's Revenue and Customs" by SI 2006/222, reg. 3(3) with effect from 6 April 2006.
In reg. 2(1), in the definition of "the Careers Service", in para. (a), the words "local authority" substituted for the words "local education authority" by SI 2010/1172, art. 4 and Sch. 3, para. 46, with effect from 5 May 2010.
In reg. 2(1), in the definition of "careers service" para. (c) omitted by SI 2003/738, reg. 3(b), with effect from 6 April 2003.
In reg. 2(1), in the definition of "child" the words" or who falls within the terms of regulation 4" at the end omitted by SI 2008/2169, reg. 7(2), with effect from 1 September 2008.
In reg. 2(1), in the definition of "claimant", the words "except in regulations 7 and 9 to 14 (for which see regulations 7(1) and 13(13) to (15))" substituted for the words "except in regulation 7, where that expression and joint claimants have the meanings given in regulation 7(1)" by SI 2017/387, reg. 3(b), with effect from 6 April 2017.
In reg. 2(1), the definition of "couple" inserted by SI 2005/2919, reg. 4(2), with effect from 5 December 2005.
In reg. 2(1), the definition of "full-time education" omitted by SI 2014/1231, reg. 3(2)(b), with effect from 4 June 2014.
In reg. 2(1), the former definition of "full-time education" inserted by SI 2008/2169, reg. 7(3), with effect from 1 September 2008.
In reg. 2(1), definition of "income support" inserted by SI 2017/387, reg. 3(c), with effect from 6 April 2017.
In reg. 2(1), in the definition of "looked after by a local authority", the words "section 74 of the Social Services and Well-being (Wales) Act 2014," inserted by SI 2016/360, reg. 4(2), with effect from 6 April 2016.
In reg. 2(1), in the definition of "looked after by a local authority", the words " and (in Scotland) includes a child in respect of which a child assessment order within the meaning of section 35 of the Children's Hearings (Scotland) Act 2011 has been made or a child protection order within the meaning of section 37 of that Act has been made." inserted by SI 2013/1465, art. 17 and Sch. 1, Pt. 2, para. 19(2), with effect from 24 June 2013 (SSI 2013195, art. 2).
In reg. 2(1), definition of "old style JSA" inserted by SI 2017/387, reg. 3(d), with effect from 6 April 2017.
In reg. 2(1), the definition of "placing for adoption" substituted by SI 2012/848, reg. 4(2), with effect from 6 April 2012.
In reg. 2(1), in former definition of "placing for adoption", the words "the Adoption Agencies (Scotland) Regulations 2009" substituted for the words "the Adoption Agencies (Scotland) Regulations 1984" by 2011/1740, art. 2 and Sch. 1, para. 29(2), with effect from 14 July 2011.
In reg. 2(1), definition of "personal independence payment" inserted by SI 2013/388, art. 8 and Sch., para. 30(2), with effect from 8 April 2013.
In reg. 2(1), in the definition of "qualifying body", in para. (d), the words "and Regulation (EC) No 883/2004 of the European Parliament and of the Council" inserted by SI 2010/2914, reg. 9, with effect from 31 December 2010.
In reg. 2(1), the definition of "qualifying body" inserted by SI 2008/2169, reg. 7(4), with effect from 1 September 2008.
In reg. 2(1), in the definition of "qualifying young person" the word "twenty" substituted by SI 2006/222, reg. 3(4) with effect from 6 April 2006. However, a person aged 19 or over on 6 April 2006 is not a qualifying young person regardless of this amendment (SI 2006/222, reg. 1(2)).
In reg. 2(1), the definition of "recognised educational establishment" omitted by SI 2008/2169, reg. 7(5), with effect from 1 September 2008.
In reg. 2(1), in the definition of "relevant training programme", para. (aa) inserted by SI 2003/738, reg. 3(c), with effect from 6 April 2003 and omitted by SI 2006/222, reg. 3(5), with effect from 6 April 2006.
In reg. 2(1), definition of "step-parent" inserted by SI 2017/387, reg. 3(e), with effect from 6 April 2017.

Cross references – SI 2003/742, reg. 23: modified application of reg. 2(1) to members of polygamous units.

HMRC Manuals – TCTM 02204: recognition of educational establishments; what constitutes 'advanced education'.

CIRCUMSTANCES IN WHICH A PERSON IS OR IS NOT RESPONSIBLE FOR A CHILD OR QUALIFYING YOUNG PERSON

3(1) For the purposes of child tax credit the circumstances in which a person is or is not responsible for a child or qualifying young person shall be determined in accordance with the following Rules.

Rule 1

1.1. A person shall be treated as responsible for a child or qualifying young person who is normally living with him (the "normally living with test").

TC Statutory Instruments

1.2. This Rule is subject to Rules 2 to 4.

Rule 2 (Competing claims)

2.1. This Rule applies where–

(a) a child or qualifying young person normally lives with two or more persons in–

(i) different households, or

(ii) the same household, where those persons are not limited to the members of a couple, or

(iii) a combination of (i) and (ii), and

(b) two or more of those persons make separate claims (that is, not a single joint claim made by a couple) for child tax credit in respect of the child or qualifying young person.

2.2. The child or qualifying young person shall be treated as the responsibility of–

(a) only one of those persons making such claims, and

(b) whichever of them has (comparing between them) the main responsibility for him (the "main responsibility test"),

subject to Rules 3 and 4.

Rule 3

3.1. The persons mentioned in Rule 2.2. (other than the child or qualifying young person) may jointly elect as to which of them satisfies the main responsibility test for the child or qualifying young person, and in default of agreement the Board may determine that question on the information available to them at the time of their determination.

Rule 4

4.1. A child or qualifying young person shall be treated as not being the responsibility of any person during any period in which any of the following Cases applies.

Case A

The child or qualifying young person is provided with, or placed in, accommodation under section 22C(10)(a) or Part III of the Children Act 1989, Parts 4 or 6 of the Social Services and Well-being (Wales) Act 2014, Part II of the Children (Scotland) Act 1995 by virtue of a requirement in a child assessment order within the meaning of section 35 of the Children's Hearings (Scotland) Act 2011, a child protection order within the meaning of section 37 of that Act, a compulsory supervision order within the meaning of section 83 of that Act or an interim compulsory supervision order within the meaning of section 86 of that Act, or Part IV of the Children (Northern Ireland) Order 1995, and the cost of that child's or qualifying young person's accommodation or maintenance is borne wholly or partly–

(i) out of local authority funds under section 22C(10) of the Children Act 1989 or section 81(13) of the Social Services and Well-being (Wales) Act 2014 or regulation 33 of the Looked After Children (Scotland) Regulations 2009,

(ii) in Northern Ireland, by an authority, within the meaning in Article 2, and under Article 27, of that Order, or

(iii) out of other public funds.

Case B

The child or qualifying young person–

(i) is being looked after by a local authority, and

(ii) has been placed for adoption by that authority in the home of a person proposing to adopt him,

and a local authority is making a payment in respect of the child's or qualifying young person's accommodation or maintenance, or both, under section 22C(10)(a) of the Children Act 1989, section 81(13) of the Social Services and Well-being (Wales) Act 2014, regulation 33 of the Looked After Children (Scotland) Regulations 2009 or Article 27 of the Children (Northern Ireland) Order 1995.

This Case applies in Northern Ireland with the modification that for references to a local authority there are substituted references to an authority (within the meaning in Article 2 of that Order).

Case C

A custodial sentence–

(a) for life,

(b) without limit of time,

(c) of detention during Her Majesty's pleasure,

(d) in Northern Ireland, of detention during the pleasure of the Secretary of State, or

(e) for a term or period of more than four months,

has been passed on the child or qualifying young person.

Case D

The qualifying young person claims and is awarded child tax credit in his or her own right, in respect of a child for whom he or she is responsible, for that period.

Case E

[T]he qualifying young person, claims incapacity benefit or contributory employment and support allowance payable under Part 1 of the Welfare Reform Act 2007 in his or her own right and that benefit is paid to or in respect of him or her for that period.

This Case does not apply at any time ("the later time") during a period of incapacity for work which began before 6th April 2004 in the case of a person in respect of whom, at a time–

(a) during that period of incapacity, and

(b) before that date,

both incapacity benefit and child tax credit were payable, if child tax credit has been payable in respect of him or her continuously since 5th April 2004 until that later time.

For the purposes of this Case **"period of incapacity"** shall be construed in accordance with section 30C of the 1992 Act (incapacity benefit: days and periods of incapacity for work) but disregarding subsections (5) and (5A) of that section.

Case F

[T]he qualifying young person claims and receives working tax credit in his or her own right (whether alone or on a joint claim).

Case G

The qualifying young person has a spouse, civil partner or partner with whom they are living and the spouse, civil partner or partner is not in full-time education or approved training as provided for under regulation 5(3).

Case H

The responsible person is the spouse, civil partner or partner of a qualifying young person with whom they are living.

Cases G and H do not apply to persons in receipt of child tax credit for a qualifying young person who is living with a partner on the day before 1st September 2008.

4.2. Where a child or qualifying young person is in residential accommodation referred to in regulation 9 of the Child Benefit (General) Regulations 2006 and in the circumstances prescribed in paragraphs (a) or (b) of that regulation, he shall be treated as being the responsibility of any person who was treated as being responsible for him immediately before he entered that accommodation.

3(2) Where–

(a) a claimant is treated as responsible for a child or qualifying young person by virtue of the preceding Rules, and

(b) the child or qualifying young person has a child of his or her own, normally living with him or her,

the claimant shall also be treated as responsible for, and as having made a claim for child tax credit in respect of, the child of the child or qualifying young person (but without prejudice to the facts as to which of them is mainly responsible for that child).

History – In reg. 3(1), Rule 2 in para. 2.1(a)(ii) and (b) the words "married couple or unmarried" omitted by SI 2005/2919, reg. 4(3), with effect from 5 December 2005.

In reg. 3(1), Rule 4, Case A, the words "This Case shall not apply in the circumstances prescribed in regulation 3 of the Child Benefit (General) Regulations 1976, or regulation 3 of the Child Benefit (General) Regulations (Northern Ireland) 1979." omitted by SI 2007/2151, reg. 3(a), with effect from 16 August 2007.

In reg. 3(1), Rule 4.1, Case A, the words "Parts 4 or 6 of the Social Services and Well-being (Wales) Act 2014," inserted by SI 2016/360, reg. 4(3)(a)(i), with effect from 6 April 2016.

In reg. 3(1), Rule 4.1, Case A, the words "by virtue of a requirement in a child assessment order within the meaning of section 35 of the Children's Hearings (Scotland) Act 2011, a child protection order within the meaning of section 37 of that Act, a compulsory supervision order within the meaning of section 83 of that Act or an interim compulsory supervision order within the meaning of section 86 of that Act," inserted by SI 2013/1465, art. 17 and Sch. 1, Pt. 2, para. 19(3), with effect from 24 June 2013 (SSI 2013/195, art. 2).

In reg. 3(1), Rule 4.1, Case A, sub-para. (i), the words "or section 23" (which appeared after the words "section 22C(10)(a)") omitted and the words "or section 81(13) of the Social Services and Well- being (Wales) Act 2014" inserted by SI 2016/360, reg. 4(3)(a)(ii)–(iii), with effect from 6 April 2016.

In reg. 3(1), Rule 4.1, Case A, sub-para. (i), the words "section 22C(10)(a) or" inserted by SI 2012/848, reg. 4(3)(a), with effect from 6 April 2012.

In reg. 3(1), Rule 4.1, Case A, sub-para. (i), the words "regulation 33 of the Looked After Children (Scotland) Regulations 2009" substituted for the words "section 26 of the Children (Scotland) Act 1995" by SI 2011/1740, art. 2 and Sch. 1, para. 29(3)(a), with effect from 14 July 2011.

In reg. 3(1), Rule 4.1, Case B, sub-para. (ii), the words "or section 23" (which appeared after the words "section 22C(10)(a)") omitted and the words "section 81(13) of the Social Services and Well-being (Wales) Act 2014" inserted by SI 2016/360, reg. 4(3)(b)(i)–(ii), with effect from 6 April 2016.

In reg. 3(1), Rule 4.1, Case B, sub-para. (ii), the words "section 22C(10)(a) or" inserted by SI 2012/848, reg. 4(3)(b), with effect from 6 April 2012.

In reg. 3(1), Rule 4.1, Case B, sub-para. (ii), the words "regulation 33 of the Looked After Children (Scotland) Regulations 2009" substituted for the words "section 26 of the Children (Scotland) Act 1995" by SI 2011/1740, art. 2 and Sch. 1, para. 29(3)(b), with effect from 14 July 2011.
In reg. 3(1), Rule 4, Case D the words "child (having attained the age of sixteen) or" omitted by SI 2008/2169, reg. 8(1)(a), with effectfrom 1 September 2008.
In reg. 3(1), Rule 4, Case E the words "or contributory employment and support allowance payable under Part 1 of the Welfare Reform Act 2007" inserted by SI 2008/1879, reg. 22(2), with effect from 27 October 2008.
In reg. 3(1), Rule 4, Case E the words "The child (having attained the age of sixteen) or" at start omitted by SI 2008/2169, reg. 8(1)(b), with effect from 1 September 2008.
In reg. 3(1), Rule 4, Case E inserted by SI 2004/762, reg. 2(2), with effect from 6 April 2004.
In reg. 3(1), Rule 4, Case F the words "The child (having attained the age of sixteen) or" at start and the second paragraph omitted by SI 2008/2169, reg. 8(1)(c), with effect from 1 September 2008.
In reg. 3(1), Rule 4, Case F inserted by SI 2006/1163, reg. 2(2), with effect from 24 May 2006.
In reg. 3(1), Rule 4, Case G inserted by SI 2008/2169, reg. 8(1)(d), with effect from 1 September 2008.
In reg. 3(1), Rule 4, Case H inserted by SI 2008/2169, reg. 8(1)(d), with effect from 1 September 2008.
In reg. 3(1), Rule 4, Case H, the words "Cases G and H do" substituted for the words "This case does" by SI 2009/697, reg. 10, with effect from 6 April 2009.
In reg. 3(1), Rule 4.1 inserted by SI 2007/2151, reg. 3(b), with effect from 16 August 2007.

Cross references – SI 2003/742, reg. 24: modified application of reg. 3(1) to members of polygamous units.

HMRC Manuals – TCTM 02201: Revenue interpretation of requirement that child or young person must 'normally live' with the claimant; factors determining 'main responsibility' and 'shared responsibility'.

PERIOD FOR WHICH A PERSON WHO ATTAINS THE AGE OF SIXTEEN IS A QUALIFYING YOUNG PERSON

4(1) Subject to paragraph (1A), a person who attains the age of sixteen is a qualifying young person from the date on which that person attained that age until 31st August which next follows that date.

4(1A) A person who attains the age of sixteen on 31st August is a qualifying young person from the date on which that person attained that age.

4(2) Paragraph (1) is subject to regulation 5 but as if there were no requirement to satisfy the first condition specified in paragraph (3) of that regulation.

4(2A) Paragraph (1A) is subject to regulation 5.

History – In reg. 4(1), the words "Subject to paragraph (1A), a" substituted for "A" by SI 2012/848, reg. 4(4)(a), with effect from 6 April 2012.
Reg. 4(1A) inserted by SI 2012/848, reg. 4(4)(b), with effect from 6 April 2012.
Reg. 4(2A) inserted by SI 2012/848, reg. 4(4)(c), with effect from 6 April 2012.
Reg. 4 substituted by SI 2008/2169, reg. 9(1), with effect from 1 September 2008.

MAXIMUM AGE AND PRESCRIBED CONDITIONS FOR A QUALIFYING YOUNG PERSON

5(1) For the purposes of Part 1 a person ceases to be a qualifying young person (unless disqualified earlier under the following paragraphs) on the date on which he attains the age of twenty.

5(2) A person who is not a child, but has not attained the age of twenty years, is a qualifying young person for any period during which the following conditions are satisfied with regard to him (and once a person falls within the terms of paragraph (3)(b), he shall be treated as having satisfied the first condition from the relevant leaving date mentioned in that paragraph).

5(3) The first condition is that he is–

(a) receiving full-time education, not being–

(i) advanced education,

(ii) education received by that person by virtue of his employment or of any office held by him; or

(ab) undertaking approved training, is enrolled or has been accepted to undertake such training, which is not provided by means of a contract of employment; or

(b) under the age of eighteen years and–

(i) he ceased to receive full-time education or to undertake approved training (the date of that event being referred to as "the leaving date");

(ii) within 3 months of the relevant leaving date, he has notified the Board (in the manner prescribed by regulation 22 of the Tax Credits (Claims and Notifications) Regulations 2002) that he is registered for work or training with a qualifying body, and

(iii) not more than 20 weeks has elapsed since the relevant leaving date.

5(3A) A person who has obtained the age of nineteen years satisfies paragraph (3)(a) or (ab) only where the course of education or training began before he attained that age, or he enrolled or was accepted to undertake that course before he attained that age.

5(4) The second condition is that the period in question is not (and does not include)–

(a) a week in which he (having ceased to receive full-time education or approved training) becomes engaged in remunerative work or;

(b) [omitted by SI 2006/222, reg. 4(6)(b), with effect from 6 April 2006;]

(c) a period in respect of which that person receives income support, income-related employment and support allowance payable under Part 1 of the Welfare Reform Act 2007, income-based jobseeker's allowance within the meaning of section 1(4) of the Jobseekers Act 1995 or universal credit under Part 1 of the Welfare Reform Act 2012.

5(5) For the purposes of paragraphs (3) and (4) a person shall be treated as being in full-time education if full-time education is received by that person by undertaking a course–

(a) at a school or college, or

(b) where that person has been receiving that education prior to attaining the age of sixteen, elsewhere, if approved by the Board,

where in pursuit of that course, the time spent receiving instruction or tuition, undertaking supervised study, examination or practical work or taking part in any exercise, experiment or project for which provision is made in the curriculum of the course, exceeds or exceeds on average 12 hours a week in normal term-time and shall include gaps between the ending of one course and the commencement of another, where the person enrols on and commences the latter course.

5(5A) If paragraph (5) does not apply, then for the purposes of paragraphs (3) and (4) a person shall be treated as being in full-time education if that person is being provided with "appropriate full-time education" in England within section 4 (appropriate full-time education or training) of the Education and Skills Act 2008.

5(6) In calculating the time spent in pursuit of the course, no account shall be taken of time occupied by meal breaks or spent on unsupervised study.

5(7) In determining whether a person is undertaking a course of full-time education or approved training, there shall be disregarded any interruption–

(a) for a period of up to 6 months, whether beginning before or after the person attains age 16, to the extent that it is reasonable in the opinion of the Board to do so; and

(b) for any period due to illness or disability of the mind or body of the person concerned provided it is reasonable in the opinion of the Board to do so.

History – In reg. 5(1), the word "twenty" substituted by SI 2006/222, reg. 4(2) with effect from 6 April 2006. However, a person aged 19 or over on 6 April 2006 is not a qualifying young person regardless of this amendment (SI 2006/222, reg. 1(2)).
In reg. 5(2) words "relevant leaving date" substituted by SI 2006/766, reg. 3, with effect from 6 April 2006.
In reg. 5(2) words "(and once ... in that paragraph" inserted by SI 2003/738, reg. 4, with effect from 6 April 2003 and the word "twenty" substituted by SI 2006/222, reg. 4(3) with effect from 6 April 2006. However, a person aged 19 or over on 6 April 2006 is not a qualifying young person regardless of this amendment (SI 2006/222, reg. 1(2)).
In reg. 5(3), the word "either" immediately before sub-para. (a), omitted by SI 2006/222, reg. 4(4)(a) with effect from 6 April 2006.
In reg. 5(3)(a), the word "or" at the end of the sub-paragraph omitted by SI 2006/222, reg. 4(4)(b) with effect from 6 April 2006.
In reg. 5(3)(ab) the words "by means of a contract of employment" substituted by SI 2008/2169, reg. 10(2)(a), with effect from 1 September 2008.
In reg. 5(3)(ab), the words ", is enrolled or has been accepted to undertake such training," inserted by SI 2007/2151, reg. 4(a), with effect from 16 August 2007.
Reg. 5(3)(ab) inserted by SI 2006/222, reg. 4(4)(c) with effect from 6 April 2006.
Reg. 5(3)(b)(i)–(iii) substituted by SI 2003/738, reg. 5, with effect from 6 April 2003.
Reg. 5(3)(b)(i) substituted for previous sub-para. by SI 2006/222, reg. 4(4)(d)(i) with effect from 6 April 2006.
In reg. 5(3)(b)(ii) and (iii), the words "relevant leaving date" substituted by SI 2006/222, reg. 4(4)(d)(ii) and (iii) with effect from 6 April 2006.
In reg. 5(3)(b)(ii) the words "a qualifying body" substituted by SI 2008/2169, reg. 10(2)(b), with effect from 1 September 2008.
In reg. 5(3A), the words ", or he enrolled or was accepted to undertake that course before he attained that age" inserted by SI 2007/2151, reg. 4(b), with effect from 16 August 2007.
Reg. 5(3A) inserted by SI 2006/222, reg 4(5), with effect from 6 April 2006.
In reg. 5(4)(a), the words "approved training" inserted and the word "or" inserted at the end by SI 2006/222, reg. 4(6)(a) with effect from 6 April 2006.
Reg. 5(4)(b) omitted by SI 2006/222, reg. 4(6)(b) with effect from 6 April 2006.
In reg. 5(4)(c), "," substituted for the word "or" (after Welfare Reform Act 2007) and the words "or universal credit under Part 1 of the Welfare Reform Act 2012" inserted by SI 2013/630, reg. 79, with effect from 29 April 2013.
In reg. 5(4)(c), the words ", income-related employment and support allowance payable under Part 1 of the Welfare Reform Act 2007" inserted by SI 2008/1879, reg. 22(3) with effect from 27 October 2008.
In reg. 5(5), the words "andshall include gaps between the ending of one course and the commencement of another, where the person enrols on and commences the latter course" inserted by SI 2014/2924, reg. 3(2), with effect from 28 November 2014.
In reg. 5(5) effectively substituted by SI 2008/2169, reg. 10(3), with effect from 1 September 2008.
In reg. 5(5), the words ", and shall include normal gaps between the ending of one course and the commencement of another, where the person is enrolled on and commences the latter course" omitted by SI 2007/2151, reg. 4(c), with effect from 16 August 2007.
In reg. 5(5)(b) words "the Board" inserted by SI 2003/738, reg. 6, with effect from 6 April 2003.
Reg. 5(5A) inserted by SI 2014/1231, reg. 3(3), with effect from 4 June 2014.
Reg. 5(7) inserted by SI 2006/2002, reg. 4(7), with effect from 6 April 2006.

ENTITLEMENT TO CHILD TAX CREDIT AFTER DEATH OF CHILD OR QUALIFYING YOUNG PERSON

6 If–

(a) a child or qualifying young person dies, and

(b) a person is (or would, if a claim had been made, have been) entitled to child tax credit in respect of the child or qualifying young person immediately before the death,

that person shall be entitled to child tax credit in respect of the child or qualifying young person for the period of eight weeks immediately following the death or, in the case of a qualifying young person, until the date on which he or she would have attained the age of twenty, if earlier.

History – In reg. 6, the word "twenty" substituted by SI 2006/222, reg. 5, with effect from 6 April 2006. However, a person aged 19 or over on 6 April 2006 is not a qualifying young person regardless of this amendment (SI 2006/222, reg. 1(2)).

DETERMINATION OF THE MAXIMUM RATE AT WHICH A PERSON OR PERSONS MAY BE ENTITLED TO CHILD TAX CREDIT

7(1) In the following paragraphs and in regulations 9 to 12 and 14–

(a) in the case of a single claim (but not a joint claim), the person making the claim is referred to as the "claimant"; and

(b) in the case of a joint claim, the members of the couple making the claim are referred to as the "joint claimants".

7(2) The maximum rate at which a claimant or joint claimants may be entitled to child tax credit shall be the aggregate of–

(a) the family element of child tax credit if the claimant is, or either or both the joint claimants are, responsible for a child or qualifying young person who was born before 6th April 2017, and

(b) an individual element of child tax credit, in respect of each child or qualifying young person for whom–

(i) the claimant, or

(ii) either or both of the joint claimants,

as the case may be, is or are responsible, but subject to paragraph (2A); and

(c) a disability element of child tax credit in the case of each child or qualifying young person who is disabled or severely disabled.

7(2A) Where the claimant, or either or both of the joint claimants, is or are responsible for a child or qualifying young person born on or after 6th April 2017 ("A"), the maximum rate referred to in paragraph (2) shall not include an individual element of child tax credit in respect of A unless–

(a) the claimant is, or the joint claimants are, claiming the individual element of child tax credit for no more than one other child or qualifying young person; or

(b) an exception applies in relation to A in accordance with regulation 9.

7(3) The family element of child tax credit is £545.

7(4) The individual element of child tax credit for any child or qualifying young person referred to in paragraph (2)(b) above–

(a) [omitted by SI 2017/387, reg. 4(f);]

(b) [omitted by SI 2017/387, reg. 4(f);]

(c) in the case of a child, is £2,780;

(d) [omitted by SI 2017/387, reg. 4(f);]

(e) [omitted by SI 2017/387, reg. 4(f);]

(f) in the case of a qualifying young person, is £2,780.

7(5) The disability element of child tax credit–

(a) where the child or qualifying young person is disabled, is £3,275;

(b) where the child or qualifying young person is severely disabled, is £4,600.

History – In reg. 7(1), the words "and in regulations 9 to 12 and 14" inserted by SI 2017/387, reg. 4(a), with effect from 6 April 2017.
In reg. 7(1)(b) the words "married couple or unmarried" omitted by SI 2005/2919, reg. 4(4), with effect from 5 December 2005.
In reg. 7(2)(a), the words "if the claimant is, or either or both the joint claimants are, responsible for a child or qualifying young person who was born before *6th April 2017*" inserted by SI 2017/387, reg. 4(b), with effect from 6 April 2017.
In reg. 7(2)(b), the words "responsible, but subject to paragraph (2A); and" substituted for the word "responsible." by SI 2017/387, reg. 4(c), with effect from 6 April 2017.
Reg. 7(2)(c) inserted by SI 2017/387, reg. 4(d), with effect from 6 April 2017.

Reg. 7(3) substituted by SI 2011/1035, reg. 2(2), with effect in relation to awards of tax credits for the year beginning on 6 April 2011. By virtue of SI 2012/849, reg. 5(a), this substitution continues to have effect in relation to awards of tax credits for the year beginning on 6 April 2012 and subsequent tax years.
Reg. 7(4)(a), (b), (d) and (e) omitted by SI 2017/387, reg. 4(f), with effect from 6 April 2017.
In reg. 7(4), the figures in para. (a), (b), (d) and (e) substituted for the previous figures by SI 2015/451, reg. 2(2), with effect in relation to awards of tax credits for the tax year beginning on 6 April 2015 and subsequent years.
In reg. 7(4), the figures in para. (a), (b), (d) and (e) substituted for the previous figures by SI 2014/845, reg. 2(2), with effect in relation to awards of tax credits for the tax year beginning on 6 April 2014 and subsequent tax years
In reg. 7(4), the figures in para. (c) and (f) substituted for the previous figures by SI 2015/567, art. 3(2), with effect from 6 April 2015.
In reg. 7(4), the figures in para. (c) and (f) substituted for the previous figures by SI 2014/384, art. 3(2)(a), with effect from 6 April 2014.
In reg. 7(4), the figures in para. (a)–(f) substituted for the previous figures by SI 2013/750, reg. 2(2), with effect in relation to awards of tax credits for the tax year beginning on 6 April 2013 and subsequent tax years.
In reg. 7(4), the figures in para. (a)–(f) substituted for the previous figures by SI 2012/849, reg. 2(2) in relation to awards of tax credits for the year beginning on 6 April 2012 and subsequent tax years.
In reg. 7(4), the figures in para. (a)–(f) substituted for the previous figures by SI 2011/1035, reg. 2(3) in relation to awards of tax credits for the year beginning on 6 April 2011.
In reg. 7(4), the figures in para. (a)–(f) substituted for the previous figures by SI 2010/981, reg. 2(2) in relation to awards of tax credits for the year beginning on 6 April 2010.
In reg. 7(4), the figures in para. (a)–(f) substituted for the previous figures by SI 2009/800, reg. 2(2) in relation to awards of tax credits for the year beginning on 6 April 2009.
In reg. 7(4), the figures in para. (a)–(f) substituted for the previous figures by SI 2008/796, reg. 2(2) in relation to awards of tax credits for the year beginning on 6 April 2008 and subsequent years.
In reg. 7(4), the figures in para. (a)–(f) substituted for the previous figures by SI 2007/828, reg. 2(2) in relation to awards of tax credits for the year beginning on 6 April 2007 and subsequent years.
In reg. 7(4), the figures in para. (a)–(f) substituted for the previous figures by SI 2006/963, reg. 2(2) in relation to awards of tax credits for the year beginning on 6 April 2006 and subsequent years.
In reg. 7(4), the figures in para. (a)–(f) substituted for the previous figures by SI 2005/681, reg. 2(2) in relation to awards of tax credits for the year beginning on 6 April 2005 and subsequent years.
In reg. 7(5), the figures in para. (a) and (b) substituted for the previous figures by SI 2018/344, reg. 3 in relation to awards of tax credits for the year beginning on 6 April 2018 and subsequent years.
Reg. 7(5) inserted by SI 2017/406, reg. 3, with effect in relationto awards of tax credits for the tax year beginning on 6 April 2017 and subsequent tax years.

Cross references – SI 2003/742, reg. 25: modified application of reg. 7 to members of polygamous units.

PRESCRIBED CONDITIONS FOR A DISABLED OR SEVERELY DISABLED CHILD OR QUALIFYING YOUNG PERSON

8(1) For the purposes of section 9 of the Act a child or qualifying young person–

(a) is disabled if he satisfies the requirements of paragraph (2); and

(b) is severely disabled if he satisfies the requirements of paragraph (3) or (4) or (5).

8(2) A person satisfies the requirements of this paragraph if–

(a) disability living allowance is payable in respect of him, or has ceased to be so payable solely because he is a patient; or

(b) he is certified as severely sight impaired or blind by a consultant ophthalmologist;

(c) he ceased to be so certified as severely sight impaired or blind within the 28 weeks immediately preceding the date of claim; or

(d) personal independence payment is payable in respect of that person, or would be so payable but for regulations made under section 86(1) (hospital in-patients) of the Welfare Reform Act 2012.

8(3) A person satisfies the requirements of this paragraph if the care component of disability living allowance–

(a) is payable in respect of him, or

(b) would be so payable but for either a suspension of benefit in accordance with regulations under section 113(2) of the Contributions and Benefits Act or an abatement as a consequence of hospitalisation,

at the highest rate prescribed under section 72(3) of that Act.

8(4) A person satisfies the requirements of this paragraph if the daily living component of personal independence payment–

(a) is payable in respect of that person, or

(b) would be so payable but for regulations made under section 86(1) (hospital in-patients) of the Welfare Reform Act 2012,

at the enhanced rate under section 78(2) of that Act.

8(5) A person satisfies the requirements of this paragraph if an armed forces independence payment is payable in respect of him.

History – In reg. 8(1)(b), the words "or (4)" inserted by SI 2013/388, art. 8 and Sch., para. 30(3)(a), with effect from 8 April 2013.
In reg. 8(1), the words "or (5)" inserted by SI 2013/591, art. 7 and Sch., para. 26(3)(a), with effect from 8 April 2013.
Reg. 8(2)(b) substituted by SI 2014/2924, reg. 3(3)(a), with effect from 28 November 2014.

In reg. 8(2)(b)(ii), the words "and in consequence is registered as blind" inserted and the words "a council constituted under section 2 of the Local Government etc. (Scotland) Act 1994" substituted for the words "a local government area (as defined in the Local Government etc (Scotland) Act 1994)" by SI 2010/751, reg. 19, with effect from 6 April 2010.
In reg. 8(2)(c), the words "registered or" omitted and the words "severely sight impaired or" inserted by SI 2014/2924, reg. 3(3)(b), with effect from 28 November 2014.
Reg. 8(2)(d) (and the "; or" before it) inserted by SI 2013/388, art. 8 and Sch., para. 30(3)(b), with effect from 8 April 2013.
Reg. 8(4) inserted by SI 2013/388, art. 8 and Sch., para. 30(3)(c), with effect from 8 April 2013.
Reg. 8(5) inserted by SI 2013/591, art. 7 and Sch., para. 26(3)(b), with effect from 8 April 2013.

Cross references – SI 2002/2014, reg. 26A: date of notification of change of circumstances resulting in entitlement to disabled child element or severely disabled child element of child tax credit.

INDIVIDUAL ELEMENT: EXCEPTIONS TO THE RESTRICTION ON NUMBERS

Exceptions for the purposes of regulation 7(2A)(b)

9(1) For the purposes of regulation 7(2A)(b), an exception applies in relation to A if–

(a) A is (in accordance with paragraphs (5) and (6)) the third or subsequent child or qualifying young person for whom the claimant, or either or both of the joint claimants, is or are responsible and any of regulations 10 to 14 applies in relation to A; or

(b) A is (in accordance with paragraphs (5) and (6)) the first or second child or qualifying young person for whom the claimant, or either or both of the joint claimants, is or are responsible and the condition in paragraph (2) is met.

9(2) The condition in this paragraph is met–

(a) where A is the second child or qualifying young person, if–

(i) there is another child or qualifying young person for whom the claimant, or either or both of the joint claimants, is or are responsible;

(ii) that other child or qualifying young person was born before 6th April 2017;

(iii) the claimant, or either or both of the joint claimants, was or were already responsible for A before the date on which the claimant, or either or both of the joint claimants, became responsible for that other child or qualifying young person; and

(iv) regulation 11 or 12 would have applied in relation to that other child or qualifying young person if references in those regulations to A were references to that other child or qualifying young person;

(b) where A is the first child or qualifying young person, if there is more than one child or qualifying young person who fulfils the description set out in paragraphs (i) to (iv) of sub-paragraph (a).

9(3) Where an exception applies in relation to A by virtue of paragraph (1), an exception applies also in relation to any other child or qualifying young person who was born on or after 6th April 2017 and for whom the claimant, or either or both of the joint claimants, is or are responsible, if–

(a) regulation 7(2A) would (apart from this paragraph) prevent the inclusion of an individual element of child tax credit in respect of that other child or qualifying young person, but would not do so if A were disregarded; and

(b) the claimant, or either or both of the joint claimants, was or were already responsible for that other child or qualifying young person before the date on which the claimant, or either or both of the joint claimants, became responsible for A.

9(4) Where any of regulations 10 to 14 applies in relation to more than one child or qualifying young person, or different ones apply in relation to different children or qualifying young persons–

(a) the reference to A in paragraph (3)(a) is a reference to all the children or qualifying young persons in respect of whom at least one of those regulations applies; and

(b) the date referred to in paragraph (3)(b) is the date on which the claimant, or either or both of the joint claimants, became responsible for the first such child or qualifying young person for whom the claimant, or either or both of the joint claimants, became responsible.

9(5) For the purposes of paragraphs (1) and (2), whether A is the first, second, third or subsequent child or qualifying young person is determined by treating children and qualifying persons as forming a single class and, subject to paragraph (6), the order of the members within that class is determined by the following date in relation to each member, taking the earliest date first:–

(a) where the claimant, or at least one of the joint claimants, is the member's parent or step-parent (in either case, other than by adoption), the member's date of birth; or

(b) in any other case, the date on which the claimant, or either or both of the joint claimants, became responsible for the member.

9(6) In a case where–

(a) the date determined under paragraph (5) is the same in respect of two or more members, or

(b) the claimant, or either of the joint claimants, gave birth to a member less than 10 months after becoming responsible for a member in relation to whom regulation 12 applies,

their order (as between themselves only) is to be such as the Board determines to be appropriate to ensure that the individual element of child tax credit is included in respect of the greatest number of members.

9(7) Where joint claimants became responsible for a child or qualifying young person on different dates, any reference in this regulation to the date on which either or both of the joint claimants became responsible for that child or qualifying young person is a reference to the earliest of those dates.

9(8) In paragraph (2)(a)(iv), the reference to regulation 11 includes a reference to regulation 14, but only where regulation 14 would have applied because–

(a) the reference to regulation 11 in regulation 14(2)(b) is the reason why the criterion in regulation 14(2)(b) or (5)(b) would have been satisfied; or

(b) the reference to regulation 11 in regulation 14(4)(b) is the reason why the criterion in that sub-paragraph would have been satisfied.

History – Reg. 9 inserted by SI 2017/387, reg. 5, with effect from 6 April 2017.

Multiple births

10 This regulation applies in relation to A if–

(a) the claimant, or at least one of the joint claimants, is a parent (other than an adoptive parent) of A;

(b) A was one of two or more children born as a result of the same pregnancy;

(c) the claimant, or either or both of the joint claimants, is or are responsible for at least two of the children or qualifying young persons born as a result of that pregnancy; and

(d) A is not the first in the order of those children or qualifying young persons as determined in accordance with regulation 9.

History – Reg. 10 inserted by SI 2017/387, reg. 5, with effect from 6 April 2017.

Adoption

11(1) This regulation applies in relation to A if A has been–

(a) placed for adoption with the claimant or either or both of the joint claimants; or

(b) adopted by the claimant, or either or both of the joint claimants, in accordance with–

(i) the Adoption and Children Act 2002 ("the 2002 Act");

(ii) the Adoption and Children (Scotland) Act 2007 ("the 2007 Act"); or

(iii) the Adoption (Northern Ireland) Order 1987 ("the 1987 Order").

11(2) But this regulation does not apply in relation to A if–

(a) the claimant or at least one of the joint claimants–

(i) was a step-parent of A immediately prior to the adoption; or

(ii) has been a parent of A (other than by adoption) at any time;

(b) the adoption order was made as a Convention adoption order within the meaning of–

(i) section 144 of the 2002 Act;

(ii) section 119(1) of the 2007 Act; or

(iii) article 2(2) of the 1987 Order; or

(c) prior to the adoption, A was adopted by the claimant, or either or both of the joint claimants, under the law of any country or territory outside the British Islands.

History – Reg. 11 inserted by SI 2017/387, reg. 5, with effect from 6 April 2017.

Non-parental caring arrangements

12(1) This regulation applies in relation to A if the claimant or at least one of the joint claimants–

(a) is a friend or family carer in relation to A; or

(b) is responsible for a child or qualifying young person who is a parent of A.

12(2) But this regulation does not apply in relation to A if the claimant, or at least one of the joint claimants, is–

(a) a parent of A; or

(b) a step-parent of A.

12(3) In this regulation, **"friend or family carer"** means a person who is responsible for A and–

(a) is named, in–

(i) a child arrangements order under section 8 of the Children Act 1989, or

(ii) a residence order under article 8 of the Children (Northern Ireland) Order 1995,

as a person with whom A is to live;

(b) is a guardian of A appointed under–

(i) section 5 of the Children Act 1989;

(ii) section 7 of the Children (Scotland) Act 1995; or

(iii) article 159 or 160 of the Children (Northern Ireland) Order 1995;

(c) is a special guardian of A appointed under section 14A of the Children Act 1989;

(d) is entitled to a guardian's allowance under section 77 of the Contributions and Benefits Act or section 77 of the Contributions and Benefits (Northern Ireland) Act 1992 in respect of A;

(e) is a person in whose favour a kinship care order, as defined in section 72(1) of the Children and Young People (Scotland) Act 2014, subsists in relation to A;

(f) is a person in whom one or more of the parental responsibilities or parental rights described in section 1 or 2 of that Act are vested by a permanence order made in respect of A under section 80 of the Adoption and Children (Scotland) Act 2007;

(g) fell within any of paragraphs (a) to (f) immediately prior to A's 16th birthday and has since continued to be responsible for A; or

(h) has undertaken the care of A in circumstances in which it is likely that A would otherwise be looked after by a local authority.

History – Reg. 12 inserted by SI 2017/387, reg. 5, with effect from 6 April 2017.

Non-consensual conception

13(1) This regulation applies in relation to A if–

(a) the claimant is A's parent; and

(b) the Board determines that–

(i) A is likely to have been conceived as a result of sexual intercourse to which the claimant did not agree by choice, or did not have the freedom and capacity to agree by choice; and

(ii) the claimant is not living at the same address as the other party to that intercourse ("B").

Control or coercion

13(2) For the purposes of paragraph (1)(b)(i), the circumstances in which the claimant is to be treated as not having the freedom or capacity to agree by choice are to include (but are not limited to) circumstances in which, at or around the time A was conceived–

(a) B was–

(i) personally connected to the claimant; and

(ii) repeatedly and continuously engaging in behaviour towards the claimant that was controlling or coercive; and

(b) that behaviour had a serious effect on the claimant.

13(3) For the purposes of paragraph (2)(a)(i), B is personally connected to the claimant if–

(a) B is in an intimate personal relationship with the claimant; or

(b) B and the claimant live together and–

(i) are members of the same family; or

(ii) have previously been in an intimate personal relationship with each other.

13(4) For the purposes of paragraph (2)(b), behaviour has a serious effect on the claimant if–

(a) it causes the claimant to fear, on at least two occasions, that violence will be used against the claimant; or

(b) it causes the claimant serious alarm or distress which has a substantial adverse effect on the complainant's day-to-day activities.

13(5) For the purposes of paragraph (3)(b)(i), B and the claimant are members of the same family if–

(a) they are, or have been, married to each other;

(b) they are, or have been, civil partners of each other;

(c) they are relatives (within the meaning of section 63(1) of the Family Law Act 1996);

(d) they have agreed to marry each other (whether or not the agreement has been terminated);
(e) they have entered into a civil partnership agreement (within the meaning of section 73 or 197 of the Civil Partnership Act 2004), whether or not the agreement has been terminated;
(f) they are both parents of the same child;
(g) they have, or have had, parental responsibility (within the meaning of section 3 of the Children Act 1989 or article 6 of the Children (Northern Ireland) Order 1995) for the same child; or
(h) they have, or have had, in respect of the same child, one or more of the parental responsibilities or parental rights described in section 1 or 2 of the Children (Scotland) Act 2007.

Determinations

13(6) The Board may make a determination under paragraph (1)(b)(i) if, and only if–
(a) the claimant provides evidence from an approved person which demonstrates that–
(i) the claimant has had contact with that person or another approved person; and
(ii) the claimant's circumstances are consistent with those of a person to whom paragraph (1)(a) and (b)(i) apply; or
(b) there has been–
(i) a conviction for–
(aa) an offence of rape under section 1 of the Sexual Offences Act 2003, section 1 of the Sexual Offences (Scotland) Act 2009 or article 5 of the Sexual Offences (Northern Ireland) Order 2008,
(bb) an offence of controlling or coercive behaviour in an intimate or family relationship under section 76 of the Serious Crime Act 2015, or
(cc) any offence under the law of any jurisdiction outside the United Kingdom that the Board considers to be analogous to an offence mentioned in paragraph (aa) or (bb), or
(ii) an award under the Criminal Injuries Compensation Scheme in respect of a relevant criminal injury sustained by the claimant,

and it appears to the Board to be likely (disregarding the matters mentioned in paragraph (7)) that the offence was committed, or the relevant criminal injury was caused, by B and either resulted in the conception of A or diminished the claimant's freedom or capacity to agree by choice to the sexual intercourse which resulted in that conception.

13(7) In considering, for the purposes of paragraph (6)(b), the likelihood that the offence or injury resulted in the conception of A the matters to be disregarded are any possibilities that the conception of A may have resulted from another such offence or injury, regardless of whether any conviction or award has occurred in respect of that other offence or injury.

13(8) In paragraph (6)(a), **"approved person"** means a person of a description specified on a list approved by the Board for the purposes of this regulation and acting in the capacity referred to in the description.

13(9) In paragraph (6)(b)(ii), **"relevant criminal injury"** means–
(a) a sexual offence (including a pregnancy sustained as a direct result of being the victim of a sexual offence),
(b) physical abuse of an adult, including domestic abuse, or
(c) mental injury,

as described in the tariff of injuries in the Criminal Injuries Compensation Scheme.

13(10) In paragraphs (6)(b)(ii) and (9), **"Criminal Injuries Compensation Scheme"** means the Criminal Injuries Compensation Scheme or the Northern Ireland Criminal Injuries Compensation Scheme as established from time to time under the Criminal Injuries Compensation Act 1995 or the Criminal Injuries Compensation (Northern Ireland) Order 2002 respectively.

13(11) *The Board may treat the condition in paragraph* (6)(a) as met if the Board are satisfied that the claimant has provided the evidence to the Secretary of State for corresponding purposes in relation to universal credit, income support or old style JSA.

13(12) The Board may make a determination under paragraph (1)(b)(ii) if the claimant confirms that the criterion in paragraph (1)(b)(ii) is met.

Application to single and joint claims

13(13) In this regulation, **"claimant"**, in relation to a single claim, means the person who makes the claim.

13(14) In relation to a joint claim–

(a) paragraph (1)(b)(i) applies if it applies to either of the joint claimants; and

(b) references in the other provisions of this regulation to **"the claimant"** mean the joint claimant to whom paragraph (1)(b)(i) applies (and, in paragraphs (6) and (11) include a joint claimant who purports to meet that criterion).

13(15) In paragraph (14), **"joint claimant"** means a member of the couple making the claim.

History – Reg. 13 inserted by SI 2017/387, reg. 5, with effect from 6 April 2017.

Continuation of certain exceptions

14(1) This regulation applies in relation to A if–

(a) no other exception applies in relation to A under these Regulations;

(b) the claimant, or at least one of the joint claimants, is A's step-parent (and, in this Regulation, **"C"** means the claimant or a joint claimant who is A's step-parent); and

(c) paragraph (2), (4) or (5) applies.

14(2) This paragraph applies if–

(a) C has previously been entitled to child tax credit jointly with a parent of A;

(b) immediately before that joint entitlement ceased, an exception applied under regulation 9(1) by virtue of regulation 10, 11 or 13 applying in relation to A;

(c) since that joint entitlement ceased, C has continuously been entitled to child tax credit (whether or not jointly with another person); and

(d) where the criterion in sub-paragraph (b) is met by virtue of its reference to regulation 10, the condition in paragraph (3) is met.

14(3) The condition in this paragraph is that–

(a) the claimant, or either or both of the joint claimants, is or are responsible for one or more other children or qualifying young persons born as a result of the same pregnancy as A; and

(b) A is not the first in the order of those children as determined in accordance with regulation 9.

Where a corresponding exception previously applied for the purposes of another benefit

14(4) This paragraph applies if–

(a) within the 6 months immediately preceding the day on which a relevant CTC entitlement began–

(i) C was entitled to an award of universal credit as a member of a couple jointly with a parent of A; or

(ii) C and a parent of A were a couple and either of them was entitled to an award of income support or old style JSA;

(b) immediately before the entitlement mentioned in sub-paragraph (a)(i) or (ii) ceased, the amount of that entitlement included an amount in respect of A by virtue of any exception corresponding, for the purposes of that entitlement, to an exception under regulation 9(1) by virtue of regulation 10, 11 or 13 applying in relation to A;

(c) C has continuously been entitled to child tax credit (whether or not jointly with another person) since the relevant CTC entitlement mentioned in sub-paragraph (a); and

(d) where the criterion in sub-paragraph (b) is met by virtue of its reference to regulation 10, the condition in paragraph (3) is met.

14(5) This paragraph applies if–

(a) within the 6 months immediately preceding the day on which a relevant CTC entitlement began–

(i) C was entitled to an award of universal credit (whether or not as a member of a couple jointly with another person); or

(ii) C was entitled to an award of income support or old style JSA (whether or not C was in a couple with another person);

(b) immediately before the entitlement mentioned in sub-paragraph (a)(i) or (ii) ceased, the amount of that entitlement included an amount in respect of A by virtue of any exception corresponding, for the purposes of that entitlement, to the exception that, under regulation 9(1), applies where this regulation applies;

(c) C has continuously been entitled to child tax credit (whether or not jointly with another person) since the relevant CTC entitlement mentioned in sub-paragraph (a); and

(d) where the criterion in sub-paragraph (b) is met by virtue of the reference to regulation 10 in paragraph (2), the condition in paragraph (3) is met.

Interpretation

14(6) In this regulation–

"couple" has the same meaning as in Part 1 of the Welfare Reform Act 2012; and

"relevant CTC entitlement" means an entitlement of C (whether or not jointly with another person) to child tax credit.

14(7) For the purposes of this regulation, an entitlement of C to child tax credit is to be regarded as continuous despite any interruption of less than 6 months in such an entitlement.

History – Reg. 14 inserted by SI 2017/387, reg. 5, with effect from 6 April 2017.

TAX CREDITS (INCOME THRESHOLDS AND DETERMINATION OF RATES) REGULATIONS 2002

(SI 2002/2008 as amended by SI 2003/2815, SI 2005/681, SI 2006/963, SI 2007/828, SI 2008/796, SI 2008/1879, SI 2009/800, SI 2010/751, SI 2010/981, SI 2011/1035, SI 2012/849, SI 2013/750, SI 2014/845, SI 2014/1230, SI 2015/451 and SI 2016/393)

Made on 30 July 2002 by the Treasury in exercise of the powers conferred on them by s. 8(1)–(3), 13(2) and (3), 65(1) and (7) and 67 of the Tax Credits Act 2002. Coming into force in accordance with reg. 1.

CITATION, COMMENCEMENT AND EFFECT

1(1) These Regulations may be cited as the Tax Credits (Income Thresholds and Determination of Rates) Regulations 2002 and shall come into force–

(a) for the purpose of enabling claims to be made, on 1st August 2002;

(b) for the purpose of enabling decisions on claims to be made, on 1st January 2003; and

(c) for all other purposes, on 6th April 2003.

1(2) These Regulations shall have effect for the tax year beginning with 6th April 2003 and subsequent tax years.

INTERPRETATION

2 In these Regulations–

"the Act" means the Tax Credits Act 2002;

"the income threshold" has the meaning given by section 7(1)(a) of the Act;

"period of award" shall be construed in accordance with section 5 of the Act;

"the relevant income" has the meaning given by section 7(3) of the Act;

"tax year" means a period beginning with 6th April in one year and ending with 5th April in the next.

Cross references – SI 2013/386, reg. 17(2) and Schedule, para. 30: modified application of reg. 2 in relation to the introduction of Universal Credit.
SI 2014/1230, Sch., para. 25: modified application of reg. 2 where SI 2014/1230, reg. 12A applies (claims for universal credit).

MANNER IN WHICH AMOUNTS TO BE DETERMINED FOR THE PURPOSES OF SECTION 7(1)(A) OF THE ACT

3(1) This regulation prescribes the manner in which amounts are to be determined for the purposes of section 7(1)(a) of the Act.

3(2) In the case of a person or persons entitled to working tax credit, the amount in relation to that tax credit is £6,420.

3(3) In the case of a person or persons entitled to child tax credit, the amount in relation to that tax credit is £16,105.

History – The figure in reg. 3(2) substituted for the previous figure by SI 2008/796, reg. 4(2) in relation to awards of tax credits for the tax year beginning on 6 April 2008 and subsequent tax years.
The figure in reg. 3(2) substituted for the previous figure by SI 2005/681, reg. 4(1) in relation to awards of tax credits for the tax year beginning on 6 April 2005 and subsequent tax years.
In reg. 3(3), the figure "£16,105" substituted for the figure "£16,010" by SI 2015/451, reg. 4(2), with effect in relation to awards of tax credits for the tax year beginning on 6 April 2015 and subsequent years.
In reg. 3(3), the figure "£16,010" substituted for the figure "£15,910" by SI 2014/845, reg. 4(2), with effect in relation to awards of tax credits for the tax year beginning on 6 April 2014 and subsequent tax years.
In reg. 3(3), the figure "£15,910" substituted for the figure "£15,860" by SI 2013/750, reg. 4(2), with effect in relation to awards of tax credits for the tax year beginning on 6 April 2013 and subsequent tax years.
The figure in reg. 3(3) substituted for the previous figure by SI 2011/1035, reg. 4(2), with effect in relation to awards of tax credits for the year beginning on 6 April 2011. By virtue of SI 2012/849, reg. 5(c), this substitution continues to have effect in relation to awards of tax credits for the year beginning on 6 April 2012 and subsequent tax years.
The figure in reg. 3(3) substituted for the previous figure by SI 2010/981, reg. 4(2) in relation to awards of tax credits for the tax year beginning on 6 April 2010.
The figure in reg. 3(3) substituted for the previous figure by SI 2009/800, reg. 4(2) in relation to awards of tax credits for the tax year beginning on 6 April 2009.
The figure in reg. 3(3) substituted for the previous figure by SI 2008/796, reg. 4(3) in relation to awards of tax credits for the tax year beginning on 6 April 2008 and subsequent tax years.
The figure in reg. 3(3) substituted for the previous figure by SI 2007/828, reg. 4(1) in relation to awards of tax credits for the tax year beginning on 6 April 2007 and subsequent tax years.
The figure in reg. 3(3) substituted for the previous figure by SI 2006/963, reg. 4(1) in relation to awards of tax credits for the tax year beginning on 6 April 2006 and subsequent tax years.

Cross references – WRA 2012, s. 76: modification of Step 5 in reg. 7(3) for working tax credit from 6 April 2011.

SOCIAL SECURITY BENEFITS PRESCRIBED FOR THE PURPOSES OF SECTION 7(2) OF THE ACT

4(1) Subject to paragraph (2), the following are social security benefits prescribed for the purposes of section 7(2) of the Act in relation to child tax credit and working tax credit–

(a) income support under Part 7 of the Social Security Contributions and Benefit Act 1992 other than income support to which a person is entitled only by virtue of regulation 6(2) and (3) of the Income Support (General) Regulations 1987;

(b) income support under Part 7 of the Social Security Contributions and Benefit (Northern Ireland) Act 1992 other than income support to which a person is entitled only by virtue of regulation 6(2) and (3) of the Income Support (General) Regulations (Northern Ireland) 1987;

(c) an income-based jobseeker's allowance within the meaning of the Jobseekers Act 1995 or the Jobseekers (Northern Ireland) Order 1995;

(d) state pension credit within the meaning of the State Pension Credit Act 2002 or the State Pension Credit Act (Northern Ireland) 2002.

(e) an income-related employment and support allowance payable under Part 1 of the Welfare Reform Act 2007.

4(2) Paragraph (1) shall not apply in relation to working tax credit during the four-week period described in regulation 7D of the Working Tax Credit (Entitlement and Maximum Rate) Regulations 2002 (ceasing to undertake work or working for less than 16 or 30 hours per week).

History – Reg. 4(1) created from existing text with words "Subject to paragraph (2)," inserted by SI 2010/751, reg. 17(1), with effect from 6 April 2010.
Reg. 4(1)(e) inserted by SI 2008/1879, reg. 23, with effect from 27 October 2008.
Reg. 4(1)(d) inserted by SI 2003/2815, reg. 18 with effect from 26 November 2003.
Reg. 4(2) inserted by SI 2010/751, reg. 17(2), with effect from 6 April 2010.

AMOUNTS PRESCRIBED FOR THE PURPOSES OF SECTION 7(3) OF THE ACT

History – In the heading before reg. 5, the words "Amounts prescribed for the purposes of section 7(3) of the Act" substituted for the words "Amounts prescribed for the purposes of section 7(3)(a) and (b) of the Act" by SI 2012/849, reg. 4(2), with effect in relation to awards of tax credits for the tax year beginning on 6 April 2012 and subsequent tax years.

5 The amount prescribed–

(a) for the purposes of section 7(3)(a) and (b) of the Act is £2,500; and

(b) for the purposes of section 7(3)(c) and (d) of the Act is £2,500.

History – In reg. 5(a), the figure "£2,500" substituted for the figure "£5,000" by SI 2016/393, reg. 2(2), with effect in relation to awards of tax credits for the tax year beginning on 6 April 2016 and subsequent tax years.
In reg. 5(a), the figure "£5,000" substituted for the figure "£10,000" by SI 2013/750, reg. 4(3), with effect in relation to awards of tax credits for the tax year beginning on 6 April 2013 and subsequent tax years.
Reg. 5 substituted by SI 2012/849, reg. 4(3), with effect in relation to awards of tax credits for the tax year beginning on 6 April 2012 and subsequent tax years.
The figure in former reg. 5 substituted for the previous figure by SI 2011/1035, reg. 4(3), with effect in relation to awards of tax credits for the year beginning on 6 April 2011.
The figure in former reg. 5 substituted for the previous figure by SI 2006/963, reg. 4(2) in relation to awards of tax credits for the tax year beginning on 6 April 2006 and subsequent tax years.

MANNER OF DETERMINING THE RATE AT WHICH A PERSON IS, OR PERSONS ARE, ENTITLED TO A TAX CREDIT

6 Regulations 7, 8 and 9 make provision as to the manner of determining the rate (if any) at which a person is, or persons are, entitled to a tax credit in any case where–

(a) the relevant income exceeds the income threshold; and

(b) his or their entitlement does not arise by virtue of section 7(2) of the Act.

DETERMINATION OF RATE OF WORKING TAX CREDIT

7(1) In relation to a person or persons entitled to working tax credit, the rate shall be determined by finding the rate for each relevant period and, where necessary, adding together those rates.

7(2) **"Relevant period"** means any part of the period of award throughout which–

(a) the elements of working tax credit (other than the child care element) to which the person or persons may be entitled, remain the same; and

(b) there is no relevant change of circumstances for the purposes of the child care element of working tax credit, within the meaning of regulation 16(1) of the Working Tax Credit (Entitlement and Maximum Rate) Regulations 2002 (change of circumstances for the purposes of child care element).

TC Statutory Instruments

7(3) The rate for each relevant period shall be found in accordance with the following steps–

Step 1 – finding the daily maximum rate for each element other than the child care element

For each element of the tax credit (other than the child care element) to be included in the case of the person or persons entitled to the tax credit, find the daily maximum rate using the following formula–

$$\frac{MR}{N1}$$

where–

"MR" is the maximum rate in relation to that element for the tax year to which the claim for the tax credit relates;

"N1" is the number of days in that tax year.

Step 2 – finding the maximum rate for the relevant period for each element other than the child care element

For each element of the tax credit to be so included, find the amount produced by multiplying the daily maximum rate (found under Step 1 and rounded up to the nearest penny) by the number of days in the relevant period.

Step 3 – finding the income for the relevant period

Find the income for the relevant period by using the following formula–

$$\frac{I}{N1} \times N2$$

where–

"I" is the relevant income for the tax year to which the claim for the tax credit relates;

"N1" is the number of days in that tax year;

"N2" is the number of days in the relevant period.

Step 4 – finding the threshold for the relevant period

Find the threshold for the relevant period using the following formula–

$$\frac{£6,420}{N1} \times N2$$

where–

"N1" is the number of days in that tax year;

"N2" is the number of days in the relevant period.

Step 5 – finding the amount of the reduction

Find the amount which is 41% of the amount by which the income for the relevant period (found under Step 3 and rounded down to the nearest penny) exceeds the threshold for the relevant period (found under Step 4 and rounded up to the nearest penny).

Step 6 – reducing the elements of the tax credit (other than any child care element)

If the amount found under Step 5 (rounded down to the nearest penny) is less than or equal to the total of the amounts found under Step 2 for the elements of the tax credit, deduct the amount found under Step 5 (rounded down to the nearest penny) from the total of those amounts found under Step 2.

Step 7 – finding the actual weekly child care costs for the relevant period

Find the relevant child care charges for the relevant period in accordance with regulation 15 of the Working Tax Credit (Entitlement and Maximum Rate) Regulations 2002.

Step 8 – finding the actual child care costs for the relevant period

Multiply the result of Step 7 by

$$\frac{52}{N1} \times N2$$

Here N1 and N2 have the same meanings as in Step 3.

The result of this step is the amount of actual child care costs for the relevant period.

Step 9 – finding the prescribed maximum child care costs for the relevant period

Divide whichever of the maxima in regulation 20(3) of the Working Tax Credit (Entitlement and Maximum Rate) Regulations 2002 is applicable by 7, round the result up to the nearest penny and multiply the resulting figure by the number of days in the relevant period.

The result of this is the prescribed maximum child care costs for the relevant period.

Step 10 – finding the child care element for the period

Take the lesser of the results of Steps 8 and 9.

Multiply that figure by 70% and round the result up to the nearest penny.

The result of this step is the maximum rate of the child care element for the relevant period.

Step 11 – reducing the elements of the tax credit (including any child care element)

If the amount found under Step 5 (rounded down to the nearest penny) exceeds the total of the amounts found under Step 2 for the elements of the tax credit–

(a) deduct the excess from the amount found under Step 10 for any child care element; and

(b) reduce the total of the amounts found under Step 2 for the other elements of the tax credit to nil.

Step 12 – finding the rate for the relevant period

Add together–

(a) the total of the amounts found under Step 2 for the elements of the tax credit (other than any child care element) after reduction in accordance with Step 6 or Step 11; and

(b) the amount found under Step 10 for any child care element after any reduction in accordance with Step 11.

This is the rate for the relevant period.

7(4) "Child care element" has the meaning given by section 12(2) of the Act.

History – The figure in reg. 7(3), Step 4, substituted for the previous figure by SI 2008/796, reg. 4(4)(a) in relation to awards of tax credits for the tax year beginning on 6 April 2008 and subsequent tax years.

The figure in reg. 7(3), Step 4, substituted for the previous figure by SI 2005/681, reg. 4(3) in relation to awards of tax credits for the tax year beginning on 6 April 2005 and subsequent tax years.

The percentage in reg. 7(3), Step 5, substituted for the previous percentage by SI 2012/849, reg. 4(4) in relation to awards of tax credits for the tax year beginning on 6 April 2012 and subsequent tax years.

The percentage in reg. 7(3), Step 5, substituted for the previous percentage by SI 2008/796, reg. 4(4)(b) in relation to awards of tax credits for the tax year beginning on 6 April 2008 and subsequent tax years.

In reg. 7(3), Step 10, "70%" substituted for "80%" by SI 2011/1035, reg. 4(4), with effect in relation to awards of tax credits for the year beginning on 6 April 2011. By virtue of SI 2012/849, reg. 5(c), this substitution continues to have effect in relation to awards of tax credits for the year beginning on 6 April 2012 and subsequent tax years.

In reg. 7(3), Step 10, "80%" substituted for "70%" by SI 2010/751, reg. 17(3), with effect from 6 April 2010.

Cross references – SI 2013/386, reg. 17(2) and Schedule, para. 31: modified application of reg. 7 in relation to the introduction of Universal Credit.

SI 2014/1230, Sch., para. 26: modified application of reg. 7(3) where SI 2014/1230, reg. 12A applies (claims for universal credit).

HMRC Manuals – TCTM 07030ff: explanation of steps in calculation of award with worked examples.

DETERMINATION OF RATE OF CHILD TAX CREDIT

8(1) In relation to a person or persons entitled to child tax credit, the rate shall be determined by finding the rate for each relevant period and, where necessary, adding together those rates.

8(2) "Relevant period" means–

(a) in the case of a person or persons entitled to child tax credit only, any part of the period of award throughout which the maximum rate at which he or they may be entitled to the tax credit remains the same;

(b) in the case of a person or persons entitled to both child tax credit and working tax credit, any part of the period of award throughout which the maximum rate of child tax credit to which he or they may be entitled remains the same and both sub-paragraphs (a) and (b) of regulation 7(2) are met.

8(3) The rate for each relevant period shall be found in accordance with the following steps–

Step 1 – finding the daily maximum rate for each element

For each element of the tax credit to be included in the case of the person or persons entitled to the tax credit, find the daily maximum rate using the following formula–

$$\frac{MR}{N1}$$

where–

"MR" is the maximum rate in relation to that element for the tax year to which the claim for the tax credit relates;

"N1" is the number of days in that tax year.

TC Statutory Instruments

Step 2 – finding the maximum rate for the relevant period for each element

For each element of the tax credit to be so included, find the amount produced by multiplying the maximum rate (found under Step 1 and rounded up to the nearest penny) by the number of days in the relevant period.

Step 3 – finding income for the relevant period

Find the income for the relevant period by using the following formula–

$$\frac{I}{N1} \times N2$$

where–

"I" is the relevant income for the tax year to which the claim for the tax credit relates;

"N1" is the number of days in that tax year;

"N2" is the number of days in the relevant period.

Step 4 – finding the threshold for the relevant period

Find the amount produced by the following formula–

$$\frac{£16{,}105}{N1} \times N2$$

where–

"N1" is the number of days in that tax year;

"N2" is the number of days in the relevant period.

The threshold for the relevant period is–

(a) in the case of a person or persons entitled to child tax credit only, that amount;

(b) in the case of a person or persons entitled to both child tax credit and working tax credit–

(i) that amount; or

(ii) if greater, the lowest amount of income for the relevant period (found under Step 3) which, disregarding regulation 9, would result in a determination in accordance with regulation 7 providing for no rate of working tax credit in his or their case for that period.

Step 5 – finding the amount of the reduction of the elements of the tax credit

Find the amount (if any) which is 41% of the amount by which the income for the relevant period (found under Step 3 and rounded down to the nearest penny) exceeds the threshold for the relevant period (found under Step 4 and rounded up to the nearest penny).

Step 6 – reducing the elements of the tax credit

If the amount found under Step 5 (rounded down to the nearest penny) is less than the total of the amounts found under Step 2 for the elements of the tax credit, deduct the amount found under Step 5 (rounded down to the nearest penny) from the total of those amounts.

Step 7 – reducing the elements of the tax credit to nil

If the amount found under Step 5 (rounded down to the nearest penny) is equal to or exceeds the total of the amounts found under Step 2 for the elements of the tax credit, reduce the total of those amounts to nil.

Step 8 – finding the rate for the relevant period

The rate for the relevant period is the total of the amounts found under Step 2 for the elements of the tax credit after any reduction in accordance with Step 6 or Step 7.

8(4) **"The family element"** means the family element of child tax credit within the meaning given by section 9(3) of the Act.

History – In reg. 8(3), in step 4, the figure "£16,105" substituted for the figure "£16,010" by SI 2015/451, reg. 4(3), with effect in relation to awards of tax credits for the tax year beginning on 6 April 2015 and subsequent years.

In reg. 8(3), in step 4, the figure "£16,010" substituted for the figure "£15,910" by SI 2014/845, reg. 4(3), with effect in relation to awards of tax credits for the tax year beginning on 6 April 2014 and subsequent tax years.

In reg. 8(3), in step 4, the figure "£15,910" substituted for the figure "£15,860" by SI 2013/750, reg. 4(4), with effect in relation to awards of tax credits for the tax year beginning on 6 April 2013 and subsequent tax years.

The figure in reg. 8(3), Step 4, substituted for the previous figure by SI 2011/1035, reg. 4(5)(a) in relation to awards of tax credits for the tax year beginning on 6 April 2011. By virtue of SI 2012/849, reg. 5(c), this substitution continues to have effect in relation to awards of tax credits for the year beginning on 6 April 2012 and subsequent tax years.

The figure in reg. 8(3), Step 4, substituted for the previous figure by SI 2010/981, reg. 4(3) in relation to awards of tax credits for the tax year beginning on 6 April 2010.

The figure in reg. 8(3), Step 4, substituted for the previous figure by SI 2009/800, reg. 4(3) in relation to awards of tax credits for the tax year beginning on 6 April 2009.

The figure in reg. 8(3), Step 4, substituted for the previous figure by SI 2008/796, reg. 4(5)(a) in relation to awards of tax credits for the tax year beginning on 6 April 2008 and subsequent tax years.

The figure in reg. 8(3), Step 4, substituted for the previous figure by SI 2007/828, reg. 4(2) in relation to awards of tax credits for the tax year beginning on 6 April 2007 and subsequent tax years.

The figure in reg. 8(3), Step 4, substituted for the previous figure by SI 2006/963, reg. 4(3) in relation to awards of tax credits for the tax year beginning on 6 April 2006 and subsequent tax years.
The previous figure in reg. 8(3), Step 4, substituted for the previous figure by SI 2005/681, reg. 4(4) in relation to awards of tax credits for the tax year beginning on 6 April 2005 and subsequent tax years.
In reg. 8(3), in the headings before Steps 5, 6 and 7, and in Steps 6 and 7, the words "(other than the family element)", which appeared after the words "tax credit", omitted by SI 2012/849, reg. 5(4)(a), with effect in relation to awards of tax credits for the tax year beginning on 6 April 2012 and subsequent tax years.
The percentage in reg. 8(3), Step 5, substituted for the previous percentage by SI 2011/1035, reg. 4(5)(b) in relation to awards of tax credits for the tax year beginning on 6 April 2011. By virtue of SI 2012/849, reg. 5(c), this substitution continues to have effect in relation to awards of tax credits forthe year beginning on 6 April 2012 and subsequent tax years.
The percentage in reg. 8(3), Step 5, substituted for the previous percentage by SI 2008/796, reg. 4(5)(b) in relation to awards of tax credits for the tax year beginning on 6 April 2008 and subsequent tax years.
The percentage in reg. 8(3), Step 8, substituted for the previous percentage by SI 2011/1035, reg. 4(5)(c)(i) in relation to awards of tax credits for the tax year beginning on 6 April 2011.
In reg. 8(3), former Step 11 renamed Step 8 and the wording of the Step substituted by SI 2012/849, reg. 4(5)(b), with effect in relation to awards of tax credits for the tax year beginning on 6 April 2012 and subsequent tax years.
In reg. 8(3) Steps 8, 9 and 10 omitted by SI 2012/849, reg. 4(5)(b), with effect in relation to awards of tax credits for the tax year beginning on 6 April 2012 and subsequent tax years.
The figure in reg. 8(3), former Step 8, substituted for the previous figure by SI 2011/1035, reg. 4(5)(c)(ii) in relation to awards of tax credits for the tax year beginning on 6 April 2011.
The figure in reg. 8(3), former Step 9, substituted for the previous figure by SI 2011/1035, reg. 4(5)(d) in relation to awards of tax credits for the tax year beginning on 6 April 2011.

Cross references – SI 2013/386, reg. 17(2) and Schedule, para. 32: modified application of reg. 8 in relation to the introduction of Universal Credit.
SI 2014/1230, Sch., para. 27: modified application of reg. 8(3) where SI 2014/1230, reg. 12A applies (claims for universal credit).

CASES IN WHICH THERE IS NO RATE OF TAX CREDIT

9(1) In the case of a person or persons entitled to working tax credit only or child tax credit only, where the rate at which the person or persons would be entitled to the tax credit (as determined in accordance with regulation 7 or 8) would be less than £26.00, there is no rate in his or their case.

9(2) In the case of a person or persons entitled to both working tax credit and child tax credit, where the total of the rates at which the person or persons would be entitled to the tax credits (as determined in accordance with regulations 7 and 8) would be less than £26.00, there are no rates in his or their case.

TAX CREDITS (CLAIMS AND NOTIFICATIONS) REGULATIONS 2002

(SI 2002/2014, as amended by SI 2003/723, SI 2003/3240, SI 2004/762, SI 2004/1241, SI 2005/2919, SI 2006/766, SI 2006/2689, SI 2007/824, SI 2008/604, SI 2008/2169, SI 2009/697, SI 2009/2887, SI 2010/751, SI 2010/2914, SI 2012/848, SI 2013/388, SI 2013/591, SI 2014/1230, SI 2015/669, SI 2017/597 and SI 2018/365)

Made on 31 July 2002 by the Commissioners of Inland Revenue, in exercise of the powers conferred upon them by s. 4(1), 6, 14(2), 15(2), 16(3), 17(10), 19(2), 22(1)(b) and (2), 65(1), (2) and (7) and 67 of the Tax Credits Act 2002. Coming into force from 12 August 2002.

PART 1 – GENERAL

CITATION, COMMENCEMENT AND EFFECT

1(1) These Regulations may be cited as the Tax Credits (Claims and Notifications) Regulations 2002 and shall come into force on 12th August 2002.

1(2) These Regulations have effect in relation to claims for a tax credit for periods of award beginning on or after 6th April 2003.

INTERPRETATION

2 In these Regulations–

"the Act" means the Tax Credits Act 2002;

"appropriate office" means any office specified in writing by the Board.

"armed forces independence payment" means armed forces independence payment under the Armed Forces and Reserve Forces (Compensation Scheme) Order 2011;

"the Board" means the Commissioners of Inland Revenue;

"couple" has the meaning given by section 3(5A) of the Act;

"disability element" shall be construed in accordance with section 11(4) of the Act;

"joint claim" has the meaning given by section 3(8) of the Act;

"personal independence payment" means personal independence payment under Part 4 of the Welfare Reform Act 2012;

"relevant authority" means–

(a) the Board;

(b) the Secretary of State or the Department for Social Development in Northern Ireland; or

(c) a person providing services to the Board, the Secretary of State or that Department in connection with tax credits;

"severe disability element" has the meaning in regulation 17 of the Working Tax Credit Regulations;

"single claim" has the meaning given by section 3(8) of the Act;

"tax year" means a period beginning on 6th April in one year and ending with 5th April in the next;

"the Working Tax Credit Regulations" means the Working Tax Credit (Entitlement and Maximum Rate) Regulations 2002.

History – In reg. 2, in the definition of "appropriate office" the word "any" substituted for the words "Comben House, Farriers Way, Netherton, Merseyside or any other" by SI 2018/365, reg. 3, with effect from 6 April 2018.
In reg. 2, the definition of "appropriate office" substituted by SI 2009/697, reg. 12, with effect from 6 April 2009.
In reg. 2, definition of "armed forces independence payment" inserted by SI 2013/591, art. 7 and Sch., para. 27(2), with effect from 8 April 2013.
In reg. 2 the definition of "couple" inserted by SI 2005/2919, reg. 5(2), with effect from 5 December 2005.
In reg. 2 the definitions of "married couple" and "unmarried couple" omitted by SI 2005/2919, reg. 5(2), with effect from 5 December 2005.
In reg. 2, definition of "personal independence payment" inserted by SI 2013/388, art. 8 and Sch., para. 31(2), with effect from 8 April 2013.
In reg. 2 definition of "relevant authority" inserted by SI 2003/723, reg. 3(1), with effect from 6 April 2003.
Cross references – SI 2003/742, reg. 40: modified application of reg. 2 to members of polygamous units.

USE OF ELECTRONIC COMMUNICATIONS TO MAKE CLAIMS OR TO GIVE NOTICES OR NOTIFICATIONS

3(1) In these Regulations **"writing"** includes writing produced by electronic communications that are approved by directions issued by or on behalf of the Board.

3(2) If a claim which is required by these Regulations to be made to a relevant authority at an appropriate office is made in writing produced by electronic communications, it shall be treated for the purposes of these Regulations as having been made to, and received by, a relevant authority at an appropriate office on the date on which it is recorded on an official computer system.

3(3) If a notice or notification which is required by these Regulations to be given to a relevant authority at an appropriate office is given in writing produced by electronic communications, it shall be treated for the purposes of these Regulations as having been given to, and received by, a relevant authority at an appropriate office on the date on which it is recorded on an official computer system.

3(4) In this regulation–

(a) **"electronic communications"** has the meaning given by section 132(10) of the Finance Act 1999;

"official computer system" means a computer system maintained by or on behalf of the Board to–

(i) send or receive information, or

(ii) process or store information.

History – In reg. 3(2), (3) words "a relevant authority at an appropriate office" substituted for words "an appropriate office" by SI 2003/723, reg. 3(2), with effect from 6 April 2003.

PART 2 – CLAIMS

INTERPRETATION OF THIS PART

4 In this Part (and Part 3) **"the relevant date"**, in relation to a claim for a tax credit, means–

(a) in cases where regulation 6 applies, the date on which the claim would be treated as being made by that regulation disregarding regulations 7, 7A and 8;

(b) in cases where sub-paragraph (d) of regulation 11(3) applies, the date on which the claim would be treated as being made by that sub-paragraph disregarding regulations 7, 7A and 8;

(c) in any other case, the date on which the claim is received by a relevant authority at an appropriate office.

History – In reg. 4(a) and (b), the words "regulations 7, 7A and 8" substituted for "regulations 7 and 8" by SI 2015/669, reg. 3, with effect from 6 April 2015.
In reg. 4(b), "(d)" substituted by SI 2009/697, reg. 13, with effect from 6 April 2009.
In reg. 4(c) words "a relevant authority at an appropriate office" substituted by SI 2003/723, reg. 3(2), with effect from 6 April 2003.

Cross references – SI 2013/386, reg. 17(2) and Schedule, para. 34: modified application of reg. 7 in relation to the introduction of Universal Credit.
SI 2014/1230, Sch., para. 29: modified application of reg. 4 where SI 2014/1230, reg. 12A applies (claims for universal credit).

HMRC Manuals – TCTM 06101: paper claims sent via the Rapid Data Capture (RDC) process will be stamped at the RDC processing centre on the day they are received; the day of receipt will be the date of claim.
TCTM 06102: practice where claims contain insufficient information.

MANNER IN WHICH CLAIMS TO BE MADE

5(1) This regulation prescribes the manner in which a claim for a tax credit is to be made.

5(2) A claim must be made to a relevant authority at an appropriate office–

(a) in writing on a form approved or authorised by the Board for the purpose of the claim, or

(b) in such other manner as the Board may decide having regard to all the circumstances.

5(3) A claim must contain the information requested on the form (or such of that information as the Board may accept as sufficient in the circumstances of the particular case).

5(4) In particular, a *claim must include* in respect of every person by whom the claim is made–

(a) a statement of the person's national insurance number and information or evidence establishing that that number has been allocated to the person; or

(b) information or evidence enabling the national insurance number that has been allocated to the person to be ascertained; or

(c) an application for a national insurance number to be allocated to the person which is accompanied by information or evidence enabling such a number to be so allocated.

This paragraph is subject to paragraphs (6) and (8).

5(5) **"National insurance number"** means the national insurance number allocated within the meaning of regulation 9 of the Social Security (Crediting and Treatment of Contributions, and National Insurance Numbers) Regulations 2001.

5(6) Paragraph (4) does not apply if the Board are satisfied that the person or persons by whom the claim was made had a reasonable excuse for making a claim which did not comply with the requirements of that paragraph.

5(7) At any time after a claim has been made but before the Board have given notice of their decision under section 14(1) of the Act in relation to the claim, the person or persons by whom the claim was made may amend the claim by giving notice orally or in writing to a relevant authority at an appropriate office.

5(8) Paragraph (4) does not apply to any person who is subject to immigration control within the meaning set out in section 115(9)(a) of the Immigration and Asylum Act 1999 and to whom a national insurance number has not been allocated.

History – Reg. 5(2)(b) substituted by SI 2008/2169, reg. 12, with effect from 1 September 2008.
In reg. 5(2), (7) words "a relevant authority at an appropriate office" substituted by SI 2003/723, reg. 3(2), with effect from 6 April 2003.
In reg. 5(4), "paragraphs (6) and (8)" substituted by SI 2009/697, reg. 14(1), with effect from 6 April 2009.
Reg. 5(8) inserted by SI 2009/697, reg. 14(2), with effect from 6 April 2009.

AMENDED CLAIMS

6(1) In the circumstances prescribed by paragraph (2) a claim for a tax credit which has been amended shall be treated as having been made as amended and, subject to regulations 7, 7A and 8, as having been made on the date prescribed by paragraph (3).

6(2) The circumstances prescribed by this paragraph are where a person has amended or persons have amended the claim in accordance with regulation 5(7).

6(3) The date prescribed by this paragraph is the date on which the claim being amended was received by a relevant authority at an appropriate office.

History – In reg. 6(1), the words "regulations 7, 7A and 8" substituted for "regulations 7 and 8" by SI 2015/669, reg. 3, with effect from 6 April 2015.
In reg. 6(3) words "a relevant authority at an appropriate office" substituted for words "an appropriate office" by SI 2003/723, reg. 3(2), with effect from 6 April 2003.

TIME LIMIT FOR CLAIMS (IF OTHERWISE ENTITLED TO TAX CREDIT UP TO 31 DAYS EARLIER)

History – In the heading to reg. 7, "31" substituted for "97" by SI 2012/848, reg. 5(2)(a), with effect from 6 April 2012.
In the heading to reg. 7, "93 days" substituted for "three months" by SI 2009/2887, reg. 8(2)(a), with effect from 21 November 2009.

7(1) In the circumstances prescribed by paragraph (2) a claim for a tax credit received by a relevant authority at an appropriate office shall be treated as having been made on the date prescribed by paragraph (3).

7(2) The circumstances prescribed by this paragraph are those where the person or persons by whom the claim is made would (if a claim had been made) have been entitled to the tax credit either–

(a) on the date falling 31 days before the relevant date (or on 6th April 2003, if later); or

(b) at any later time in the period beginning on the date in sub-paragraph (a) and ending on the relevant date.

7(3) The date prescribed by this paragraph is the earliest date falling within the terms of paragraph (2)(a) or (b) when the person or the persons by whom the claim is made would (if a claim had been made) have become entitled to the tax credit.

History – In reg. 7(1) words "a relevant authority at an appropriate office" substituted by SI 2003/723, reg. 3(2), with effect from 6 April 2003.
In reg. 7(2)(a), "31" substituted for "97" by SI 2012/848, reg. 5(2)(b), with effect from 6 April 2012.
In reg. 7(2)(a), "93 days" substituted for "3 months" by SI 2009/2887, reg. 8(2)(b), with effect from 21 November 2009.

TIME LIMIT FOR CLAIMS – THE CHILDCARE PAYMENTS ACT 2014

7A(1) Subject to paragraphs (2A) to (4), regulation 7 does not apply where the claim for a tax credit made by a person or persons is received by a relevant authority at an appropriate office during an entitlement period where the person making the claim, or in the case of joint claimants either person, has for that entitlement period made a valid declaration of eligibility under section 4(2) of the Childcare Payments Act 2014 (declarations of eligibility).

7A(2) Subject to paragraphs (2A) to (4), where a claim for tax credits is received by a relevant authority at an appropriate office during the period of 31 days beginning with the last day of the entitlement period for which the person making the claim or, in the case of joint claimants either person, has made a valid declaration of eligibility under section 4(2) of the Childcare Payments Act 2014, regulation 7 shall apply but the date prescribed by paragraph (3) of regulation 7 may be no earlier than the day following the last day of that entitlement period

7A(2A) Where–

(a) a claim for a tax credit is received by a relevant authority at an appropriate office and the person making the claim, or in the case of joint claimants either person, has made a valid declaration of eligibility under section 4(2) of the Childcare Payments Act 2014,

(b) no payments under section 20(1)(a) of the Childcare Payments Act 2014 have been made out of any childcare account held by the person making the claim, or in the case of joint claimants either person, and

(c) all the childcare accounts held by the person making the claim for tax credits, or in the case of joint claimants both persons, have been closed,

regulation 7 shall apply.

7A(3) For the purposes of this regulation, the **"appropriate date"** is the date on which–

(a) Her Majesty's Revenue and Customs makes an account restriction order in accordance with section 24 of the Childcare Payments Act 2014 (imposing restrictions on childcare accounts) for the purposes of giving effect to a determination made under section 18(2) of that Act (cases where there is more than one eligible person) and regulations made thereunder,

(b) a childcare account is closed in accordance with regulations made under section 25 of the Childcare Payments Act 2014 (closure of childcare accounts), or

(c) a child ceases to be a **"qualifying child"** for the purposes of the Childcare Payments Act 2014 as defined in regulation 5 of the Childcare Payments (Eligibility) Regulations 2015 except in the case where they cease to be a **"disabled child"** as defined in regulation 5(5) of those Regulations.

7A(4) Where a claim for tax credits is received by a relevant authority at an appropriate office–

(a) during an entitlement period relating to a childcare account where the person making the claim, or in the case of joint claimants either person, has for that entitlement period made a valid declaration of eligibility under section 4(2) of the Childcare Payments Act 2014, or

(b) during the period of 31 days beginning with the day following the last day of that entitlement period,

regulation 7 shall apply but the date prescribed in paragraph (3) of regulation 7 may be no earlier than the appropriate date.

7A(5) For the purposes of this regulation, the terms **"childcare account"** and **"entitlement period"** have the same meanings as they have for the purposes of the Childcare Payments Act 2014 and regulations made thereunder.

History – In reg. 7A(1) and (2), the words "paragraphs (2A) to (4)" substituted for the words "paragraphs (3) and (4)" by SI 2017/597, reg. 2(2), with effect from 17 May 2017.
Reg. 7A(2A) inserted by SI 2017/597, reg. 2(3), with effect from 17 May 2017.
Reg. 7A and the heading preceding it inserted by SI 2015/669, reg. 2, with effect from 6 April 2015.

DATE OF CLAIMS – DISABILITY ELEMENT OF WORKING TAX CREDIT

8(1) In the circumstances prescribed by paragraph (2), the claim referred to in paragraph (2)(a) shall be treated as having been made on the date prescribed by paragraph (3).

8(2) The circumstances prescribed by this paragraph are where–

(a) a claim for working tax credit including the disability element ("the tax credits claim") is made by a person or persons ("the claimants") which results in the Board making an award of working tax credit including the disability element;

(b) the claim is made within 31 days of the date that a claim for any of the benefits referred to in regulation 9(2) to (8) of the Working Tax Credit Regulations ("the benefits claim") is determined in favour of the claimants (or one of them); and

(c) the claimants would (subject to making a claim) have been entitled to working tax credit if (and only if) they had satisfied the requirements of regulation 9(1)(c) of the Working Tax Credit Regulations, on any day in the period–

(i) beginning on the date of the benefits claim, and

(ii) ending on the date of the tax credits claim.

8(3) The date prescribed by this paragraph is–

(a) the first date in respect of which the benefit claimed is payable; or

(b) if later, the date falling 31 days before the claim for the benefit is made; or

(c) if later, the first day identified under paragraph (2)(c).

History – In reg. 8(2)(b), "31" substituted for "97" by SI 2012/848, reg. 5(2)(c), with effect from 6 April 2012.
In reg. 8(2)(b), "93 days" substituted for "3 months" by SI 2009/2887, reg. 8(2)(c), with effect from 21 November 2009.

In reg. 8(3)(b), "31" substituted for "97" by SI 2012/848, reg. 5(2)(d), with effect from 6 April 2012.
In reg. 8(3)(b), "93 days" substituted for "3 months" by SI 2009/2887, reg. 8(2)(d), with effect from 21 November 2009.
Reg. 8 substituted by SI 2009/697, reg. 15, with effect from 6 April 2009.

ADVANCE CLAIMS BEFORE THE YEAR BEGINS

9(1) In the circumstances prescribed by paragraph (2) a claim for a tax credit may be made for a period after the relevant date.

9(2) The circumstances prescribed by this paragraph are where a tax credit is claimed for a tax year by making a claim before the tax year begins.

9(3) This regulation shall cease to have effect in relation to the tax year beginning on 6th April 2004 and subsequent tax years.

ADVANCE CLAIMS – WORKING TAX CREDIT

10(1) In the circumstances prescribed by paragraph (2) a claim for a tax credit may be made for a period after the relevant date.

10(2) The circumstances prescribed by this paragraph are where–

(a) the tax credit in question is working tax credit; and

(b) the case falls within sub-paragraph (b) of the First Condition in regulation 4(1) of the Working Tax Credit Regulations (person who has accepted an offer of work which is expected to commence within 7 days).

10(3) In the circumstances prescribed by paragraph (2)–

(a) an award on a claim for tax credit may be made subject to the condition that the requirements for entitlement are satisfied no later than the date prescribed by paragraph (4); and

(b) if those requirements are satisfied no later than that date, the claim shall be treated as being made on the date on which they are satisfied.

10(4) The date prescribed by this paragraph is the date falling 7 days after the relevant date.

Cross references – SI 2013/386, reg. 17(2) and Schedule, para. 35: deemed omission of reg. 10 in relation to the introduction of Universal Credit.

CIRCUMSTANCES IN WHICH CLAIMS TO BE TREATED AS MADE – NOTICES CONTAINING PROVISION UNDER SECTION 17(2)(a), (4)(a) OR (6)(a) OF THE ACT

11(1) In the circumstances prescribed by paragraph (2) a claim for a tax credit is to be treated as made.

11(2) The circumstances prescribed by this paragraph are where (in the case where there has been a previous single claim) a person has or (in the case where there has been a previous joint claim) either person or both persons have made a declaration in response to provision included in a notice under section 17 of the Act by virtue of–

(a) subsection (2)(a) of that section;

(b) subsection (4)(a) of that section;

(c) subsection (6)(a) of that section; or

(d) any combination of those subsections.

The declaration made shall (subject to regulation 5(3)) be treated as a claim for tax credit by that person or persons for the tax year following that to which the notice relates.

11(3) The claim shall be treated as made–

(a) in a case where the declaration is made by the date specified on the section 17 notice, on 6th April following the period to which the section 17 notice relates;

(aa) [deleted by SI 2010/751, reg. 7(3)(b);]

(b) in a case where the declaration, not having been made by the date specified on the section 17 notice, is made within 30 days following the date on the notice to the claimant that payments of tax credit under section 24(4) of the Act have ceased due to the claimant's failure to make the declaration, on 6th April following the period to which the section 17 notice relates;

(c) in a case where the declaration, not having been made by the date specified on the section 17 notice or within the 30 days specified in sub-paragraph (b), is made before 31st January in the tax year following the period to which the section 17 notice relates, and, in the opinion of the Board, the claimant had good cause for not making the declaration as mentioned in sub-paragraphs (a) or (b), on 6th April following the period to which the section 17 notice relates; or

(d) in any other case, on the latest date on which the declaration is received by a relevant authority at an appropriate office (subject to the application of regulations 7 and 7A).

11(4) Paragraph (3) does not apply–

(a) in the case where there has been a previous single claim (to which the notice referred to in paragraph (2) relates) if the person by whom it was made could no longer make a single claim;

(b) in the case where there has been a previous joint claim (to which the notice referred to in paragraph (2) relates) if the persons by whom it was made could no longer make a joint claim; or

(c) in the case where the response to the notice referred to in paragraph (2) specifies that such response is not to be treated as a new claim for the tax year beginning 6th April following the period to which the section 17 notice relates.

History – In reg. 11(2) the words "either person or" inserted by SI 2010/751, reg. 7(2), with effect from 6 April 2010.
In reg. 11(3)(a) the words "the date specified on the section 17 notice" substituted for the words "31st July next following the end of the tax year to which the claim relates" and the words "following the period to which the section 17 notice relates" substituted for the words "preceding that date" by SI 2010/751, reg. 7(3)(a), with effect from 6 April 2010.
Reg. 11(3)(aa) deleted by SI 2010/751, reg. 7(3)(b), with effect from 6 April 2010.
Former reg. 11(3)(aa) inserted by SI 2009/697, reg. 16(2), with effect from 6 April 2009.
In reg. 11(3)(b) the words "the date specified on the section 17 notice" substituted for the words "31st July next following the end of the tax year to which the claim relates", the word "next" omitted and the words "the period to which the section 17 notice relates" substituted for the words "the end of the tax year to which the claim relates" by SI 2010/751, reg. 7(3)(c), with effect from 6 April 2010.
In reg. 11(3)(b), the words "on 6th April next following the end of the tax year to which the claim relates" substituted for the words "on 6th April preceding the date on which the declaration is made" by SI 2009/697, reg. 16(3), with effect from 6 April 2009.
In reg. 11(3)(c) the words "the date specified on the section 17 notice" substituted for the words "31st July next following the end of the tax year to which the claim relates", the words "31st January in the tax year following the period to which the section 17 notice relates" substituted for the words "31st January next following the end of the tax year to which the claim relates" and the words "on 6th April following the period to which the section 17 notice relates" substituted for the words "on 6th April preceding the date on which the declaration is made" by SI 2010/751, reg. 7(3)(d), with effect from 6 April 2010.
In reg. 11(3)(d), the words "regulations 7 and 7A" substituted for "regulation 7" by SI 2015/669, reg. 4, with effect from 6 April 2015.
Reg. 11(3) substituted by SI 2008/604, with effect from 6 April 2008.
In former reg. 11(3)(a) the words "31st July" substituted by SI 2007/824, reg. 14(2), with effect from 6 April 2007.
In former reg. 11(3)(a) words "31st August" substituted by SI 2006/766, reg. 2(2) with effect from 6 April 2006.
In former reg. 11(3)(a), the words "in a case where the declaration is made by 30th September next following the end of the tax year to which the claim relates, on 6th April preceding that date;" substituted by SI 2004/762 reg. 3(2)(a) with effect from 6 April 2004.
Former reg. 11(3)(aa) inserted by SI 2004/762 reg. 3(2)(a) with effect from 6 April 2004.
In former reg. 11(3)(b) words "a relevantauthority at an appropriate office" substituted by SI 2003/723, reg. 3(2), with effect from 6 April 2003.
In reg. 11(4) the word "or" preceding sub-para. (b) omitted and inserted after sub-para. (b) and sub-para (c) inserted by SI 2010/751, reg. 7(4), with effect from 6 April 2010.
Reg. 11(4) inserted by SI 2004/762, reg. 3(2)(b), with effect from 6 April 2004.

Cross references – SI 2003/742, reg. 41: modified application of reg. 11(2) to members of polygamous units.
SI 2013/386, reg. 17(2) and Schedule, para. 36: deemed omission of reg. 11 in relation to the introduction of Universal Credit.
SI 2014/1230, Sch., para. 30: modified application of reg. 11 where SI 2014/1230, reg. 12A applies (claims for universal credit).

CIRCUMSTANCES IN WHICH CLAIMS TO BE TREATED AS MADE – NOTICES CONTAINING PROVISION UNDER SECTION 17(2)(b), (4)(b) AND (6)(b) OF THE ACT

12(1) In either of the circumstances prescribed by paragraphs (2) and (4) a claim for a tax credit is to be treated as made.

12(2) The circumstances prescribed by this paragraph are where a person is or persons are treated as having made a declaration in response to provision included in a notice under section 17 of the Act by virtue of–

(a) subsection (2)(b) of that section, and

(b) subsection (4)(b) of that section,

or a combination of those subsections and subsection (6)(b) of that section.

12(3) The declaration referred to in paragraph (2) shall (subject to regulation 5(3)) be treated as a claim by that person or persons for tax credit for the tax year following that to which the notice relates.

12(4) The circumstances prescribed by this paragraph are where a person or any of the persons has–

(a) made a statement under paragraph (b) of subsection (2) of section 17 of the Act in response to such a notice by the date specified for the purposes of that subsection, or

(b) made a statement under paragraph (b) of subsection (4) of that section in response to such a notice by the date specified for the purposes of that subsection,

or a combination of any of those subsections and subsection (6)(b) of that section.

12(5) The notice referred to in paragraph (4), together with (and as corrected by) the statement or statements there referred to, shall (subject to regulation 5(3)) be treated as a claim for tax credit by that person or persons for the tax year following that to which the notice relates.

12(6) The claim shall be treated as made on the 6th April preceding the dates specified in the notice for the purposes of subsections (2) or (4) of section 17 of the Act.

12(7) Paragraphs (3) and (5) shall not apply–

(a) in the case where there has been a previous single claim (to which the notice relates), the person by whom it was made could no longer make a single claim;

(b) in the case where there has been a previous joint claim (to which the notice relates), the persons by whom it was made could no longer jointly make a joint claim;

(c) in the case where, before the specified date, the person or persons to whom a notice under section 17 of the Act is given advise the Board that the person or persons do not wish to be treated as making a claim for tax credit for the tax year following that to which the notice relates; or

(d) in the case where there has been a previous single claim to which a notice under section 17 of the Act relates–

(i) a relevant notification is given to the person by whom the claim was made; and

(ii) the person fails to make a relevant request; and

(e) in the case where there has been a previous joint claim to which a notice under section 17 of the Act relates–

(i) a relevant notification is given to the persons by whom the claim was made; and

(ii) they fail to make a relevant request.

12(8) In this regulation–

(a) **"relevant notification"** means a written notification to a person or persons by whom a claim for tax credit was made which–

(i) is given by the Board at least 35 days before the Board gives notice under section 17 of the Act to the person or persons;

(ii) states the date on which it is given;

(iii) advises that the Board intends to give such a notice to the person or persons; and

(iv) advises that this regulation will not have effect to treat the person or persons as making a claim for tax credit for the tax year following that to which the notice relates unless a relevant request is made;

(b) **"relevant request"** means a request made to the Board by a person or persons to whom a relevant notification is given that–

(i) is made in response to the relevant notification within 30 days of the date on which it is given; and

(ii) requests that the person or persons will be treated by virtue of this regulation as making a claim for tax credit for the tax year following that to which the notice relates;

(c) **"specified date"** means the date specified for the purposes of section 17(2) and (4) of the Act or, where different dates are specified, the later of them.

History – In reg. 12(7), the words "Paragraphs (3) and (5) shall not apply" substituted for the words "Paragraph (5) shall not apply" by SI 2010/2914, reg. 14(a), with effect from 31 December 2010.
In reg. 12(7)(b), the "or" at the end omitted by SI 2010/2914, reg. 14(b), with effect from 31 December 2010.
In reg. 12(7) the word "or" preceding sub-para. (b) omitted and inserted after sub-para. (b) and sub-para (c) inserted by SI 2010/751, reg. 8, with effect from 6 April 2010.
Reg. 12(7)(c) substituted by SI 2010/2914, reg. 14(c), with effect from 31 December 2010.
Reg. 12(7)(d) inserted by SI 2010/2914, reg. 14(d), with effect from 31 December 2010.
Reg. 12(7)(e) inserted by SI 2010/2914, reg. 14(d), with effect from 31 December 2010.
Reg. 12(8) inserted by SI 2010/2914, reg. 15, with effect from 31 December 2010.

Cross references – SI 2013/386, reg. 17(2) and Schedule, para. 37: deemed omission of reg. 12 in relation to the introduction of Universal Credit.
SI 2014/1230, Sch., para. 31: modified application of reg. 12 where SI 2014/1230, reg. 12A applies (claims for universal credit).

CIRCUMSTANCES IN WHICH CLAIMS MADE BY ONE MEMBER OF A COUPLE TO BE TREATED AS ALSO MADE BY THE OTHER MEMBER OF THE COUPLE

13(1) In the circumstances prescribed by paragraph (2) or (3) a claim for a tax credit made by one member of a couple is to be treated as also made by the other member of the couple.

13(2) The circumstances prescribed by this paragraph are those where one member of a couple is treated by regulation 11 or regulation 12 as having made a claim for a tax credit in response to a notice under section 17 of the Act given to both members of the couple.

13(3) A claim for a tax credit made by one member of a couple is to be treated as also made by the other member of the couple in such manner and in such circumstances as the Board may decide.

History – In reg. 13(1) the words "or (3)" inserted by SI 2008/2169, reg. 13(2), with effect from 1 September 2008.
In reg. 13(2) the words "regulation 11 or" inserted by SI 2010/751, reg. 9, with effect from 6 April 2010.
Reg. 13(3) inserted by SI 2008/2169, reg. 13(3), with effect from 1 September 2008.
In reg. 13 the words "married couple or an unmarried" omitted twice and "married couple or unmarried" omitted once by SI 2005/2919, reg. 5(3), with effect from 5 December 2005.

Cross references – SI 2003/742, reg. 42: modified application of reg. 13 to members of polygamous units.
SI 2013/386, reg. 17(2) and Schedule, para. 38: modified application of reg. 13 in relation to the introduction of Universal Credit.
SI 2014/1230, Sch., para. 32: modified application of reg. 13(1) and (2) where SI 2014/1230, reg. 12A applies (claims for universal credit).

CIRCUMSTANCES IN WHICH AWARDS TO BE CONDITIONAL AND CLAIMS TREATED AS MADE – DECISIONS UNDER SECTION 14(1) OF THE ACT MADE BEFORE 6TH APRIL 2003

14(1) In the circumstances prescribed by paragraph (2) an award on a claim for a tax credit may be made subject to the condition that the requirements for entitlement are satisfied on 6th April 2003.

14(2) The circumstances prescribed by this paragraph are those where–

(a) an advance claim (under regulation 9) for a tax credit has been made for the tax year beginning on 6th April 2003; and

(b) the Board give notice of their decision under section 14(1) of the Act before that date.

14(3) Where, in a case falling within the terms of paragraph (2)–

(a) notification is given before 6th April 2003 of a change of circumstances (other than one increasing the maximum rate at which a person or persons may be entitled to a tax credit) which is expected to continue at that date, or

(b) the Board have reasonable grounds before that date for believing that the requirements for entitlement are otherwise expected to differ on that date from those in the claim,

the person or persons making the claim shall be treated as making a new claim (on the basis of the altered requirements for entitlement, together with so much of those requirements stated in the original claim as remain unchanged) in the place of the original claim.

PERSONS WHO DIE AFTER MAKING A CLAIM

15(1) This regulation applies where any person who has made a claim for a tax credit dies–

(a) before the Board have made a decision in relation to that claim under section 14(1) of the Act;

(b) having given a notification of a change of circumstances increasing the maximum rate at which a person or persons may be entitled to the tax credit, before the Board have made a decision whether (and, if so, how) to amend the award of tax credit made to him or them; or

(c) where the tax credit has been awarded for the whole or part of a tax year, after the end of that tax year but before the Board have made a decision in relation to the award under section 18(1), (5), (6) or (9) of the Act.

15(2) In the case of a single claim, the personal representatives of the person who has died may proceed with the claim in the name of that person.

15(3) In the case of a joint claim where only one of the persons by whom the claim was made has died, the other person with whom the claim was made may proceed with the claim in the name of the person who has died as well as in his own name.

15(4) In the case of a joint claim where both the persons by whom the claim was made have died, the personal representatives of the last of them to die may proceed with the claim in the name of both persons who have died.

15(5) For the purposes of paragraph (4), where persons have died in circumstances rendering it uncertain which of them survived the other–

(a) their deaths shall be presumed to have occurred in order of seniority; and

(b) the younger shall be treated as having survived the elder.

Cross references – SI 2003/742, reg. 43: modified application of reg. 15 to members of polygamous units.
SI 2013/386, reg. 17(2) and Schedule, para. 39: modified application of reg. 15 in relation to the introduction of Universal Credit.
SI 2014/1230, Sch., para. 33: modified application of reg. 15(1) where SI 2014/1230, reg. 12A applies (claims for universal credit).

PERSONS WHO DIE BEFORE MAKING JOINT CLAIMS

16(1) This regulation applies where one member of a couple dies and the other member of the couple wishes to make a joint claim for a tax credit.

16(2) The member who wishes to make the claim may make and proceed with the claim in the name of the member who has died as well as in his own name.

16(3) Any claim made in accordance with this regulation shall be for a tax credit for a period ending with–

(a) the date of the death of the member of the couple who has died; or

(b) if earlier, 5th April in the tax year to which the claim relates.

History – In reg. 16(1) the words "married couple or an unmarried" and "married couple or the unmarried" omitted by SI 2005/2919, reg. 5(4), with effect from 5 December 2005.
In reg. 16(3)(a) the words "married couple or unmarried" omitted by SI 2005/2919, reg. 5(4), with effect from 5 December 2005.

Cross references – SI 2003/742, reg. 44: modified application of reg. 16 to members of polygamous units.

CIRCUMSTANCES WHERE ONE PERSON MAY ACT FOR ANOTHER IN MAKING A CLAIM – RECEIVERS ETC.

17(1) In the circumstances prescribed by paragraph (2) any receiver or other person mentioned in sub-paragraph (b) of that paragraph may act for the person mentioned in sub-paragraph (a) of that paragraph in making a claim for a tax credit.

17(2) The circumstances prescribed by this paragraph are where–

(a) a person is, or is alleged to be, entitled to a tax credit but is unable for the time being to make a claim for a tax credit; and

(b) there are any of the following–

(i) a receiver appointed by the Court of Protection with power to make a claim for a tax credit on behalf of the person;

(ii) in Scotland, a tutor, curator or other guardian acting or appointed in terms of law who is administering the estate of the person; and

(iii) in Northern Ireland, a controller appointed by the High Court, with power to make a claim for a tax credit on behalf of the person.

CIRCUMSTANCES WHERE ONE PERSON MAY ACT FOR ANOTHER IN MAKING A CLAIM – OTHER APPOINTED PERSONS

18(1) In the circumstances prescribed by paragraph (2) any person mentioned in sub-paragraph (b) of that paragraph may act for the person mentioned in sub-paragraph (a) of that paragraph in making a claim for a tax credit.

18(2) The circumstances prescribed by this paragraph are where–

(a) a person is, or is alleged to be, entitled to a tax credit but is unable for the time being to make a claim for a tax credit; and

(b) in relation to that person, there is a person appointed under–

(i) regulation 33(1) of the Social Security (Claims and Payments) Regulations 1987;

(ii) regulation 33(1) of the Social Security (Claims and Payments) Regulations (Northern Ireland) 1987; or

(iii) paragraph (3)

18(3) Where there is no person mentioned in regulation 17(2)(b) in relation to the person who is unable to act, the Board may appoint under this paragraph a person who–

(a) has applied in writing to the Board to be appointed to act on behalf of the person who is unable to act; and

(b) if a natural person, is aged 18 years or more.

18(4) An appointment under paragraph (3) shall end if–

(a) the Board terminate it;

(b) the person appointed has resigned from the appointment having given one month's notice in writing to the Board of his resignation; or

(c) the Board are notified that a receiver or other person mentioned in regulation 17(2)(b) has been appointed in relation to the person who is unable to make a claim.

PART 3 – NOTIFICATIONS OF CHANGES OF CIRCUMSTANCES

INTERPRETATION OF THIS PART

19 In this Part **"the notification date"**, in relation to a notification, means–

(a) the date on which the notification is given to a relevant authority at an appropriate office; or

(b) in cases where regulation 24 applies, the date on which the notification would be treated by that regulation as being given disregarding regulations 25 and 26.

History – In reg. 19(a) words "a relevant authority at an appropriate office" substituted by SI 2003/723, reg. 3(2), with effect from 6 April 2003.

INCREASES OF MAXIMUM RATE OF ENTITLEMENT TO A TAX CREDIT AS A RESULT OF CHANGES OF CIRCUMSTANCES TO BE DEPENDENT ON NOTIFICATION

20(1) Any change of circumstances of a description prescribed by paragraph (2) which may increase the maximum rate at which a person or persons may be entitled to tax credit is to do so only if notification of it has been given in accordance with this Part.

20(2) The description of changes of circumstances prescribed by this paragraph are changes of circumstances other than those in consequence of which the Board have given notice of a decision under section 16(1) of the Act in accordance with section 23 of the Act.

REQUIREMENT TO NOTIFY CHANGES OF CIRCUMSTANCES WHICH MAY DECREASE THE RATE AT WHICH A PERSON OR PERSONS IS OR ARE ENTITLED TO TAX CREDIT OR MEAN THAT ENTITLEMENT CEASES

21(1) Subject to paragraph (1A), [w]here a person has or persons have claimed a tax credit, notification is to be given within the time prescribed by paragraph (3) if there is a change of circumstances of the description prescribed by paragraph (2) which may decrease the rate at which he is or they are entitled to the tax credit or mean that he ceases or they cease to be entitled to the tax credit.

21(1A) Paragraph (1) does not apply where advance notification has been given under regulation 27(2), (2A) or (3).

21(2) The changes of circumstances described by this paragraph are those where–

(a) entitlement to the tax credit ceases by virtue of section 3(4), or regulations made under section 3(7), of the Act;

(b) there is a change in the relevant child care charges which falls within regulation 16(1)(b) (omitting paragraph (i)) of the Working Tax Credit Regulations;

(c) a person ceases to undertake work for at least 16 hours per week for the purposes of–

(i) the Second Condition in regulation 4(1) (read with regulations 4(3) to (5) and 5 to 8) except where that person falls within paragraph (a) of the third variation of the Second Condition, or

(ii) regulation 13(1),

of the Working Tax Credit Regulations;

(d) a person ceases to undertake work for at least 30 hours per week for the purposes of the first or second variation of the Second Condition in regulation 4(1) of the Working Tax Credit Regulations (read with regulations 4(3) to (5) and 5 to 8), except in a case where that person still falls within the terms of paragraph (a) or (d) of the first variation or paragraph (a) or (c) of the second variation of that Condition;

(e) a person ceases to undertake, or engage in, qualifying remunerative work for at least 16 hours per week for the purposes of–

(i) regulation 9(1)(a) (disability element), or

(ii) regulation 10(2)(d) (30 hour element),

(iii) [omitted by SI 2012/848, reg. 5(3)(d),]

of the Working Tax Credit Regulations;

(f) a person ceases to engage in qualifying remunerative work for at least 30 hours per week, for the purposes of–

(i) regulation 10(1) (30 hour element), or

(ii) regulation 11(2)(c) (second adult element), in a case where the other claimant mentioned in that provision is not so engaged for at least 30 hours per week,

of the Working Tax Credit Regulations;

(g) a couple cease to engage in qualifying remunerative work for at least 30 hours per week, for the purposes of regulation 10(2)(c) (30 hour element) of the Working Tax Credit Regulations;

(h) a person ceases to be treated as responsible for a child or qualifying young person, for the purposes of child tax credit or of the Working Tax Credit Regulations;

(i) in a case where a person has given advance notification under regulation 27(2B) that a child is expected to become a qualifying young person, the child does not become a qualifying young person for the purposes of Part 1 of the Act;

(j) a person ceases to be a qualifying young person for the purposes of Part 1 of the Act, other than by attaining the age of twenty; or

(k) a child or qualifying young person dies

TC Statutory Instruments

(l) one or both members of a couple who satisfy paragraph (a) of the third variation of the Second Condition in regulation 4(1) of the Working Tax Credit Regulations (read with regulations 4(3) to (5) and 5 to 8) and are engaged in qualifying remunerative work cease to meet the condition that one member of the couple works not less than 16 hours per week and the aggregate number of hours for which the couple are engaged in qualifying remunerative work is not less than 24 hours per week, except in a case where the person or their partner still falls within the terms of paragraph (b), (c) or (d) of the third variation of that Condition.

21(3) The time prescribed by this paragraph is the period of 1 month[s] beginning on the date on which the change of circumstances occurs or (except in the case of paragraph (2)(j)), if later, the period of 1 month[s] beginning on the date on which the person first becomes aware of the change in circumstances.

History – In reg. 21(1A) "27(2), (2A) or (3)" substituted by SI 2006/2689, reg. 3, with effect from 1 November 2006.
In reg. 21(1) words "Subject to paragraph (1A)," and para. (1A) inserted by SI 2003/723, reg. 4(2) and (3) respectively, with effect from 6 April 2003.
In reg. 21(2)(c)(i), the words "except where that person falls within paragraph (a) of the third variation of the Second Condition" inserted by SI 2012/848, reg. 5(3)(a), with effect from 6 April 2012.
Reg. 21(2)(d) substituted by SI 2012/848, reg. 5(3)(b), with effect from 6 April 2012.
Reg. 21(2)(e)(iii) omitted (and the "or" at the end of reg. 21(2)(e)(ii) omitted, and the "or" at the end of reg. 21(2)(e)(i) inserted) by SI 2012/848, reg. 5(3)(c) and (d), with effect from 6 April 2012.
Reg. 21(2)(l) inserted by SI 2012/848, reg. 5(3)(e), with effect from 6 April 2012 (note that SI 2012/848, presumably in error, does not move the "or" from the end of reg. 21(2)(j) to the end of reg. 21(2)(k)).
Reg. 21(2) substituted by SI 2006/2689, reg. 4, with effect from 1 November 2006.
In former reg. 21(2)(a) the words "or 3(7)" inserted by SI 2004/1241, reg. 3, with effect from 1 May 2004.
In reg. 21(3) words from "(except" to "(j))" inserted after "or" by SI 2006/2689, reg. 5(a), with effect from 1 November 2006.
In reg. 21(3) "one" substituted in both places by SI 2006/2689, reg. 6, with effect from 6 April 2007. It is assumed this change refers to the number "3" in both places.
In reg. 21(3) words from "the date on which" to "circumstances" substituted by SI 2006/2689, reg. 5(b), with effect from 1 November 2006.

Cross references – SI 2013/386, reg. 17(2) and Schedule, para. 40: modified application of reg. 21 in relation to the introduction of Universal Credit.

MANNER IN WHICH NOTIFICATIONS TO BE GIVEN

22(1) This regulation prescribes the manner in which a notification is to be given.

22(2) A notification must be given to a relevant authority at an appropriate office.

22(3) A notification may be given orally or in writing.

22(4) At any time after a notification has been given but before the Board have made a decision under section 15(1) or 16(1) of the Act in consequence of the notification, the person or persons by whom the notification was given may amend the notification by giving notice orally or in writing to a relevant authority at an appropriate office.

History – In reg. 22(2), (4) words "a relevant authority at an appropriate office" substituted for words "an appropriate office" by SI 2003/723, reg. 3(2), with effect from 6 April 2003.

PERSON BY WHOM NOTIFICATION MAY BE, OR IS TO BE, GIVEN

23(1) In the case of a single claim, notification is to be given by the person by whom the claim for a tax credit was made.

23(2) In the case of a joint claim, notification may be given by either member of the couple by whom the claim for a tax credit was made.

History – In reg. 23(2) the words "married couple or unmarried" omitted by SI 2005/2919, reg. 5(5), with effect from 5 December 2005.

Cross references – SI 2003/742, reg. 45: modified application of reg. 23(2) to members of polygamous units.

AMENDED NOTIFICATIONS

24(1) In the circumstances prescribed by paragraph (2) a notification which has been amended shall be treated as having been given as amended and, subject to regulations 25, 26 and 26A as having been given on the date prescribed by paragraph (3).

24(2) The circumstances prescribed by this paragraph are where the person or persons by whom the notification is given amends or amend the notification in accordance with regulation 22(4).

24(3) The date prescribed by this paragraph is the date on which the notification being amended was given to a relevant authority at an appropriate office.

History – In reg. 24(1) the words "25, 26 and 26A" substituted for "25 and 26" by SI 2004/762 with effect from 6 April 2004.
In reg. 24(3) words "a relevant authority at an appropriate office" substituted for words "an appropriate office" by SI 2003/723, reg. 3(2), with effect from 6 April 2003.

DATE OF NOTIFICATION – CASES WHERE CHANGE OF CIRCUMSTANCES WHICH MAY INCREASE THE MAXIMUM RATE

25(1) Where a notification of a change of circumstances which may increase the maximum rate at which a person or persons may be entitled to tax credit is given in the circumstances prescribed by paragraph (2), that notification is to be treated as having been given on the date specified by paragraph (3).

25(2) The circumstances prescribed by this paragraph are where notification is given to a relevant authority at an appropriate office of a change of circumstances which has occurred other than in the circumstances prescribed by regulations 26(2) and 26A(2).

25(3) The date specified by this paragraph is–

(a) the date falling one month before the notification date; or

(b) if later, the date of the change of circumstances.

History – In reg. 25(2) "regulations" substituted, and "and 26A(2)" inserted, by SI 2009/697, reg. 17, with effect from 6 April 2009.
In reg. 25(2) words "a relevant authority at an appropriate office" substituted for words "an appropriate office" by SI 2003/723, reg. 3(2), with effect from 6 April 2003.
In reg. 25(3)(a), the words "one month" substituted for "3 months" by SI 2012/848, reg. 5(4)(a), with effect from 6 April 2012.

DATE OF NOTIFICATION – DISABILITY ELEMENT AND SEVERE DISABILITY ELEMENT OF WORKING TAX CREDIT

26(1) In the circumstances prescribed by paragraph (2), the notification of a change in circumstances is to be treated as having been given on the date prescribed by paragraph (3).

26(2) The circumstances prescribed by this paragraph are where–

(a) a notification is given of a change of circumstances in respect of a claim to working tax credit, which results in the Board making an award of the disability element or the severe disability element of working tax credit (or both of them) in favour of a person or persons; and

(b) the notification date is within one month of the date that a claim for any of the benefits referred to in regulation 9(2) to (8) or 17(2) of the Working Tax Credit Regulations is determined in favour of those persons (or one of them).

26(3) The date prescribed by this paragraph is the latest of the following:

(a) the first date in respect of which the benefit claimed was payable;

(b) the date falling one month before the claim for the benefit was made;

(c) the date the claim for working tax credit was made (or treated as made under regulations 7 and 7A);

(d) (for the purposes of the disability element only), the first date that the person or persons satisfied the conditions of entitlement for the disability element.

History – In reg. 26(2)(b), the words "one month" substituted for "3 months" by SI 2012/848, reg. 5(4)(b), with effect from 6 April 2012.
In reg. 26(3)(b), the words "one month" substituted for "3 months" by SI 2012/848, reg. 5(4)(c), with effect from 6 April 2012.
In reg. 26(3)(c), the words "regulations 7 and 7A" substituted for "regulation 7" by SI 2015/669, reg. 4, with effect from 6 April 2015.
Reg. 26 substituted by SI 2009/697, reg. 18, with effect from 6 April 2009.

DATE OF NOTIFICATION – DISABILITY ELEMENT AND SEVERE DISABILITY ELEMENT OF CHILD TAX CREDIT

26A(1) In the circumstances prescribed by paragraph (2), the notification of a change in circumstances is to be treated as having been given on the date prescribed by paragraph (3).

26A(2) The circumstances prescribed by this paragraph are where–

(a) a notification is given of a change of circumstances in respect of a claim to child tax credit which results in the Board making an award of the disability element or the severe disability element of child tax credit (or both of those elements) in favour of a person or persons, in respect of a child; and

(b) the notification date is within one month of the date that a claim for a disability living allowance or personal independence payment or armed forces independence payment in respect of the child is determined in favour of those persons (or one of them).

26A(3) The date prescribed by this paragraph is the latest of the following:

(a) the first date in respect of which the disability living allowance or personal independence payment or armed forces independence payment was payable;

(b) the date falling one month before the claim for the disability living allowance or personal independence payment or armed forces independence payment was made;

(c) the date the claim for child tax credit was made (or treated as made under regulations 7 and 7A).

History – In reg. 26A(2) and (3), the words "or personal independence payment" inserted (in each place) by SI 2013/388, art. 8 and Schedule, para. 31(3), with effect from 8 April 2013.
In reg. 26A(2) and (3), the words "or armed forces independence payment" inserted by SI 2013/591, art. 7 and Schedule, para. 27(3), with effect from 8 April 2013.

In reg. 26A(2)(b), the words "one month" substituted for "3 months" by SI 2012/848, reg. 5(4)(d), with effect from 6 April 2012.
In reg. 26A(3)(b), the words "one month" substituted for "3 months" by SI 2012/848, reg. 5(4)(e), with effect from 6 April 2012.
In reg. 26A(3)(c), the words "regulations 7 and 7A" substituted for "regulation 7" by SI 2015/669, reg. 4, with effect from 6 April 2015.
Reg. 26A substituted by SI 2009/697, reg. 19, with effect from 6 April 2009.

ADVANCE NOTIFICATION

27(1) In any of the circumstances prescribed by paragraphs (2) to (3) a notification of a change of circumstances may be given for a period after the date on which it is given.

27(2) The circumstances prescribed by this paragraph are those prescribed by regulation 10(2) (working tax credit: person who has accepted an offer of work expected to commence within 7 days), the reference to "the claim" being read as a reference to the notification.

27(2A) The circumstances prescribed by this paragraph are where either regulation 15(4) (agreement for the provision of future child care) or regulation 16(1) (relevant change in circumstances) of the Working Tax Credit Regulations applies.

27(2B) The circumstances prescribed by this paragraph are those where a child is expected to become a qualifying young person for the purposes of Part 1 of the Act.

27(3) The circumstances prescribed by this paragraph are where a tax credit has been claimed for the tax year beginning on 6th April 2003 by making a claim before that tax year begins, and the notification relates to that tax year and is given before that date.

27(4) In the circumstances prescribed by paragraph (2), an amendment of an award of a tax credit in consequence of a notification of a change of circumstances may be made subject to the condition that the requirements for entitlement to the amended amount of the tax credit are satisfied at the time prescribed by paragraph (5).

27(5) The time prescribed by this paragraph is the latest date which–

(a) is not more than 7 days after the date on which the notification is given; and

(b) falls within the period of award in which the notification is given.

27(5A) In the circumstances prescribed by paragraph (2A), an amendment of an award of tax credit in consequence of a notification of a change of circumstances may be made subject to the condition that the requirements for entitlement to the amended amount of the tax credit are satisfied at the time prescribed by paragraph (5B).

27(5B) The time prescribed by this paragraph is the first day of the week–

(a) in which the agreement within regulation 15(4) of the Working Tax Credit Regulations commences or the relevant change of circumstances occurs; and

(b) which is not more than 7 days after the date on which notification is given and falls within the period of award in which the notification is given.

27(5C) For the purposes of paragraph (5B), **"week"** means a period of 7 days beginning with midnight between Saturday and Sunday.

27(6) **"Period of award"** shall be construed in accordance with section 5 of the Act.

History – In reg. 27(1) word "to" substituted by SI 2006/2689, reg. 7(a), with effect from 1 November 2006.
In reg. 27(1) word "any" substituted and reference to para. (2A) inserted by SI 2003/723, reg. 5(2), with effect from 6 April 2003.
Reg. 27(2A) inserted by SI 2003/723, reg. 5(3), with effect from 6 April 2003.
Reg. 27(2B) inserted by SI 2006/2689, reg. 7(b) with effect from 1 November 2006.
Reg. 27(5A)–(5B) inserted by SI 2003/723, reg. 5(4), with effect from 6 April 2003.

Cross references – SI 2013/386, reg. 17(2) and Schedule, para. 41: modified application of reg. 27 in relation to the introduction of Universal Credit.

CIRCUMSTANCES WHERE ONE PERSON MAY ACT FOR ANOTHER IN GIVING A NOTIFICATION – RECEIVERS ETC.

28(1) In the circumstances prescribed by paragraph (2) any receiver or other person mentioned in sub-paragraph (b) of that paragraph may act for the person mentioned in sub-paragraph (a) of that paragraph in giving a notification.

28(2) The circumstances prescribed by this paragraph are where–

(a) a person is unable for the time being to give a notification; and

(b) there are any of the following–

(i) a receiver appointed by the Court of Protection with power to proceed with a claim for a tax credit on behalf of the person;

(ii) in Scotland, a tutor, curator or other guardian acting or appointed in terms of law who is administering the estate of the person; and

(iii) in Northern Ireland, a controller appointed by the High Court, with power to proceed with a claim for a tax credit on behalf of the person.

CIRCUMSTANCES WHERE ONE PERSON MAY ACT FOR ANOTHER IN GIVING A NOTIFICATION – OTHER APPOINTED PERSONS

29(1) In the circumstances prescribed by paragraph (2) any person mentioned in sub-paragraph (b) of that paragraph may act for the person mentioned in sub-paragraph (a) of that paragraph in giving a notification.

29(2) The circumstances prescribed by this paragraph are where–

(a) a person is unable for the time being to give a notification; and

(b) in relation to that person, there is a person appointed under–

(i) regulation 33(1) of the Social Security (Claims and Payments) Regulations 1987;

(ii) regulation 33(1) of the Social Security (Claims and Payments) Regulations (Northern Ireland) 1987; or

(iii) regulation 18(3);

and the provisions of regulation 18(3) shall apply to notifications and (under regulation 36) responses to notices under section 17 of the Act, as they apply to claims.

PART 4 – NOTICES TO PROVIDE INFORMATION OR EVIDENCE

FORM IN WHICH EVIDENCE OF BIRTH OR ADOPTION TO BE PROVIDED

29A If the Board require the person, or either or both of the persons, by whom a claim is made to provide a certificate of a child's birth or adoption, the certificate so produced must be either an original certificate or a copy authenticated in such manner as would render it admissible in proceedings in any court in the jurisdiction in which the copy was made.

History – Reg. 29A inserted by SI 2004/1241, reg. 4, with effect from 1 May 2004.

EMPLOYERS

30(1) For the purposes of sections 14(2)(b), 15(2)(b), 16(3)(b) and 19(2)(b) of the Act the persons specified in paragraph (2) are prescribed, and, in relation to those persons, the information or evidence specified in paragraph (4) is prescribed.

30(2) The persons specified in this paragraph are–

(a) any person named by a person or either of the persons by whom a claim for a tax credit is made as his employer or the employer of either of them; and

(b) any person whom the Board have reasonable grounds for believing to be an employer of a person or either of the persons by whom such a claim is made.

30(3) **"Employer"** has the meaning given by section 25(5) of the Act.

30(4) The information or evidence specified in this paragraph is information or evidence, including any documents or certificates, which relates to–

(a) the claim for the tax credit in question;

(b) the award of the tax credit in question; or

(c) any question arising out of, or under, that claim or award.

Cross references – SI 2003/742, reg. 46: modified application of reg. 30(2) to members of polygamous units.

PERSONS BY WHOM CHILD CARE IS PROVIDED

31(1) For the purposes of sections 14(2)(b), 15(2)(b), 16(3)(b) and 19(2)(b) of the Act the persons specified in paragraph (2) are prescribed, and, in relation to those persons, the information or evidence specified in paragraph (3) is prescribed.

31(2) The persons specified in this paragraph are–

(a) any person named by a person or persons by whom a claim for the child care element of working tax credit is made as being, in relation to him or either of them, a person by whom child care is provided; and

(b) any person whom the Board have reasonable grounds for believing to be, in relation to a person or persons by whom such a claim is made, a person by whom child care is provided.

31(3) The information or evidence specified in this paragraph is information or evidence, including any documents or certificates, which relates to–

(a) the claim for the tax credit in question;

(b) the award of the tax credit in question; or

(c) any question arising out of, or under, that claim or award.

31(4) **"Child care"** has the meaning given by regulation 14(2) of the Working Tax Credit Regulations.

Cross references – SI 2003/742, reg. 47: modified application of reg. 31(2)(a) to members of polygamous units.

DATES TO BE SPECIFIED IN NOTICES UNDER SECTION 14(2), 15(2), 16(3), 18(10) OR 19(2) OF THE ACT

32 In a notice under section 14(2), 15(2), 16(3), 18(10) or 19(2) of the Act, the date which may be specified shall not be less than 30 days after the date of the notice.

PART 5 – FINAL DECISIONS

DATES TO BE SPECIFIED IN NOTICES UNDER SECTION 17 OF THE ACT

33 In a notice under section 17 of the Act–

(a) the date which may be specified for the purposes of subsection (2) or subsection (4) shall be not later than 31st July following the end of the tax year to which the notice relates, or 30 days after the date on which the notice is given, if later; and

(b) the date which may be specified for the purposes of subsection (8) shall be not later than 31st January following the end of the tax year to which the notice relates, or 30 days after the date on which the notice is given, if later.

History – In reg. 33(a) the words "31st July" substituted for "31st August" by SI 2007/824, reg. 14(3), with effect from 6 April 2007. In reg. 33(a) words "31st August" substituted for "30th September" by SI 2006/766, reg. 2(3) with effect from 6 April 2006. Reg. 33 substituted by SI 2004/762, reg. 5 with effect from 6 April 2004.

Cross references – SI 2013/386, reg. 17(2) and Schedule, para. 42: modified application of reg. 33 in relation to the introduction of Universal Credit.
SI 2014/1230, Sch., para. 34: modified application of reg. 33 where SI 2014/1230, reg. 12A applies (claims for universal credit).

Notes – SI 2003/2815, reg. 22 purported to amend this regulation, in exercise of the Treasury's powers, by inserting the words "or 30 days after the date of the notice, if later" after "relates" in both places, with effect from 26 November 2003, but was invalid as the power to do so lay with the Board of Inland Revenue.

MANNER IN WHICH DECLARATION OR STATEMENT IN RESPONSE TO A NOTICE UNDER SECTION 17 OF THE ACT TO BE MADE

34(1) This regulation prescribes the manner in which a declaration or statement in response to a notice under section 17 of the Act must be made.

34(2) A declaration or statement must be made–

(a) in writing in a form approved by the Board for that purpose;

(b) orally to an officer of the Board; or

(c) in such other manner as the Board may accept as sufficient in the circumstances of any particular case.

34(3) In a case falling within paragraph (2)(b) one of two joint claimants may act for both of them in response to a notice under section 17 if, at the time the declaration or statement is made, a joint claim could be made by both of them.

History – Reg. 34 substituted by SI 2004/762, reg. 5 with effect from 6 April 2004.

Cross references – SI 2003/742, reg. 47A: modified application of reg. 34 for members of polygamous units.

CIRCUMSTANCES WHERE ONE PERSON MAY ACT FOR ANOTHER IN RESPONSE TO A NOTICE UNDER SECTION 17 OF THE ACT – RECEIVERS ETC.

35(1) *In the* circumstances prescribed by paragraph (2) any receiver or other person mentioned in sub-paragraph (b) of that paragraph may act for the person mentioned in sub paragraph (a) of that paragraph in response to a notice under section 17 of the Act.

35(2) The circumstances prescribed by this paragraph are where–

(a) a person is unable for the time being to act in response to a notice under section 17 of the Act; and

(b) there are any of the following–

(i) a receiver appointed by the Court of Protection with power to proceed with a claim for a tax credit on behalf of the person;

(ii) in Scotland, a tutor, curator or other guardian acting or appointed in terms of law who is administering the estate of the person; and

(iii) in Northern Ireland, a controller appointed by the High Court, with power to proceed with a claim for a tax credit and proceed with the claim on behalf of the person.

CIRCUMSTANCES WHERE ONE PERSON MAY ACT FOR ANOTHER IN RESPONSE TO A NOTICE UNDER SECTION 17 OF THE ACT

36(1) In the circumstances prescribed by paragraph (2) any person mentioned in sub-paragraph (b) of that paragraph may act for the person mentioned in sub-paragraph (a) of that paragraph in response to a notice under section 17 of the Act.

36(2) The circumstances prescribed by this paragraph are where–

(a) a person is unable for the time being to act in response to a notice under section 17 of the Act; and

(b) in relation to that person, there is a person appointed under–

(i) regulation 33(1) of the Social Security (Claims and Payments) Regulations 1987;

(ii) regulation 33(1) of the Social Security (Claims and Payments) Regulations (Northern Ireland) 1987; or

(iii) regulation 18(3).

TAX CREDITS (PAYMENTS BY THE COMMISSIONERS) REGULATIONS 2002

(SI 2002/2173, as amended by SI 2003/723, SI 2004/762, SI 2004/1241, SI 2005/2200, SI 2005/2919, SI 2007/824, SI 2008/604, SI 2008/2683, SI 2009/56, SI 2010/751, SI 2010/2914, SI 2012/848, SI 2014/1230 and SI 2016/360)

Made on 20 August 2002 by the Commissioners of Inland Revenue, in exercise of the powers conferred upon them by s. 24(2), (3), (4), (7) and (8), 65(1), (2) and (7) and 67 of the Tax Credits Act 2002. Operative from 6 April 2003.

History – In the heading, the words "the Commissioners" substituted for the words "the Board" by SI 2005/2200, reg. 7(2), with effect from 29 August 2005.

CITATION, COMMENCEMENT AND EFFECT

1(1) These Regulations may be cited as the Tax Credits (Payments by the Commissioners) Regulations 2002 and shall come into force on 6th April 2003.

1(2) These Regulations have effect in relation to payments of a tax credit, or any element of a tax credit, which must be made in relation to the tax year beginning with 6th April 2003 and subsequent tax years.

1(3) Regulations 8 to 14 have effect only in relation to such payments as must be made by the Board.

History – In reg. 1(1), the words "the Commissioners" substituted by SI 2005/2200, reg. 7(2), with effect from 29 August 2005.
In reg. 1(2) words "by the Board" repealed by SI 2003/723, reg. 7(2), with effect from 6 April 2003.
Reg. 1(3) inserted by SI 2003/723, reg. 7(3), with effect from 6 April 2003.

INTERPRETATION

2 In these Regulations–

"the Act" means the Tax Credits Act 2002;

"employee" and **"employer"** have the meaning given by section 25(5) of the Act;

"period of award" shall be construed in accordance with section 5 of the Act;

"the Commissioners" means Commissioners for Her Majesty's Revenue and Customs (see section 1 of the Commissioners for Revenue and Customs Act 2005);

"couple" has the meaning given by section 3(5A) of the Act;

"the relevant tax year" means the whole or part of the tax year for which an award of a tax credit has been made to a person or persons (referred to in section 24(4) of the Act);

"tax year" means a period beginning with 6th April in one year and ending with 5th April in the next;

History – In reg. 2, the definition of "couple" inserted by SI 2005/2919, reg. 6(2), with effect from 5 December 2005.
In reg. 2, the definitions of "married couple" and "unmarried couple" omitted by SI 2005/2919, reg. 6(2), with effect from 5 December 2005.
In reg. 2, the definition of "the Board" omitted by SI 2005/2200, reg. 7(3)(a), with effect from 29 August 2005.
In reg. 2, the definition of "the Commissioners" inserted by SI 2005/2200, reg. 7(3)(b), with effect from 29 August 2005.

Cross references – SI 2003/742, reg. 49: modified application of reg. 2 to members of polygamous units.

HMRC Manuals – TCTM 02207: 'main carer' is given its normal everyday meaning of 'someone who is normally answerable for, or called to account for, the child or young person'.

CHILD TAX CREDIT AND CHILD CARE ELEMENT – MEMBER OF A COUPLE PRESCRIBED FOR THE PURPOSES OF SECTION 24(2) OF THE ACT

3(1) This regulation has effect in relation to payments of–

(a) child tax credit; and

(b) any child care element of working tax credit.

3(2) Subject to regulation 5, the member of a couple prescribed by paragraph (3) is prescribed for the purposes of section 24(2) of the Act.

3(3) The member of a couple prescribed by this paragraph is–

(a) where the couple are for the time being resident at the same address–

(i) the member who is identified by both members of the couple as the main carer;

(ii) in default of a member being so identified, the member who appears to the Commissioners to be the main carer; and

(b) where–

(i) the members of the couple are for the time being resident at different addresses, or

(ii) one member of the couple is temporarily absent from the address at which they live together,

the member who appears to the Commissioners to be the main carer.

Here **"main carer"** means the member of the couple who is the main carer for the children and qualifying young persons for whom either or both of the members is or are responsible.

3(4) **"Children"** means persons who have not attained the age of sixteen or who fall within the terms of regulation 4 of the Child Tax Credit Regulations 2002.

3(5) **"Qualifying young persons"** means persons, other than children, who–

(a) have not attained the age of nineteen, and

(b) satisfy the conditions in regulation 5(3) and (4) of the Child Tax Credit Regulations 2002.

3(6) Where payments are being made to the member of a couple prescribed by virtue of paragraph (3) and the members of the couple jointly give notice to the Commissioners that, as a result of a change of circumstances, the payments should be made to the other member as the main carer, the other member shall, except where the notice appears to the Commissioners to be unreasonable, be treated as prescribed by virtue of paragraph (3).

3(7) For the purposes of this regulation, a person is responsible for a child or qualifying young person if he is treated as being responsible for that child or qualifying young person in accordance with the rules contained in regulation 3 of the Child Tax Credit Regulations 2002.

History – In reg. 3(2), (3) and (6) the word "couple" substituted for references to a married couple or an unmarried couple (however expressed) by SI 2005/2919, reg. 6(3), with effect from 5 December 2005.
In reg. 3 the words "the Commissioners" substituted wherever they occurred by SI 2005/2200, reg. 7(4), with effect from 29 August 2005.
In reg. 3(3) wording in sub-para. (a) and (b) substituted by SI 2004/1241, reg. 5(a), with effect from 1 May 2004.
In reg. 3(6) the words ", except where the notice appears to the Board to be unreasonable," inserted by SI 2004/1241, reg. 5(b), with effect from 1 May 2004.
Reg. 3(7) inserted by SI 2003/723, reg. 8, with effect from 6 April 2003.

Cross references – SI 2003/742, reg. 50: modified application of reg. 3 to members of polygamous units.

WORKING TAX CREDIT (EXCLUDING ANY CHILD CARE ELEMENT) – MEMBER OF A COUPLE PRESCRIBED FOR THE PURPOSES OF SECTION 24(2) OF THE ACT

4(1) This regulation has effect in relation to payments of working tax credit other than payments of any child care element.

4(2) Subject to regulation 5, the member of a couple prescribed by paragraph (3) is prescribed for the purposes of section 24(2) of the Act.

4(3) The member of a couple prescribed by this paragraph is–

(a) if only one member of the couple is engaged in remunerative work, that member;

(b) if both members of the couple are engaged in remunerative work–

(i) the member elected jointly by them; or

(ii) in default of any election, such of them as appears to the Commissioners to be appropriate.

4(4) Where payments are being made to the member of a couple prescribed by virtue of paragraph (3)(b) and the members of the couple jointly give notice to the Commissioners that, as a result of a change of circumstances, they wish payments to be made to the other member, the other member shall be treated as prescribed by virtue of paragraph (3)(b).

4(5) For the purposes of paragraph (3), a member of a couple is engaged in remunerative work if–

(a) he is engaged in qualifying remunerative work; or

(b) he works not less than 16 hours per week and the other member of the couple is engaged in qualifying remunerative work.

4(6) **"Qualifying remunerative work"**, and being engaged in it, have the meaning given by regulation 4 of the Working Tax Credit (Entitlement and Maximum Rate) Regulations 2002.

History – In reg. 4(2), (3), (4) and (5) the word "couple" substituted for references to a married couple or an unmarried couple (however expressed) by SI 2005/2919, reg. 6(3), with effect from 5 December 2005.
In reg. 4 the words "the Commissioners" substituted wherever they occurred by SI 2005/2200, reg. 7(4), with effect from 29 August 2005.

MEMBER OF A COUPLE PRESCRIBED FOR THE PURPOSES OF SECTION 24(2) OF THE ACT WHERE ONE OF THE MEMBERS OF THE COUPLE HAS DIED

5(1) This regulation applies where one of the members of a couple has died.

5(2) The member of the couple prescribed by paragraph (3) is prescribed for the purposes of section 24(2) of the Act.

5(3) The member of the couple prescribed by this paragraph is the member who survives.

5(4) For the purposes of this regulation, where persons have died in circumstances rendering it uncertain which of them survived the other–

(a) their deaths shall be presumed to have occurred in order of seniority; and

(b) the younger shall be treated as having survived the elder.

History – In reg. 5(1), (2) and (3) the word "couple" substituted for references to a married couple or an unmarried couple (however expressed) by SI 2005/2919, reg. 6(3), with effect from 5 December 2005.

PERSON PRESCRIBED FOR THE PURPOSES OF SECTION 24(3) OF THE ACT WHERE AN AWARD OF A TAX CREDIT IS MADE ON A CLAIM WHICH IS MADE BY ONE PERSON ON BEHALF OF ANOTHER

6 For the purposes of section 24(3) of the Act, the person prescribed is–

(a) the person by whom the claim on behalf of another was made; or

(b) if at any time the Commissioners do not consider it appropriate for payments of the tax credit to be made to that person, the person on behalf of whom the claim was made.

History – In reg. 6 the words "the Commissioners" substituted wherever they occurred by SI 2005/2200, reg. 7(4), with effect from 29 August 2005.

PRESCRIBED CIRCUMSTANCES FOR THE PURPOSES OF SECTION 24(4) OF THE ACT

7(1) Either of the circumstances prescribed by paragraphs (2) and (3) are prescribed circumstances for the purposes of section 24(4) of the Act.

7(2) The circumstances prescribed by this paragraph are where–

(a) a claim for a tax credit for the next tax year has been made or treated as made by the person or persons by the date specified for the purposes of subsection (4) of section 17 of the Act in the notice given to him or them under that section in relation to the relevant tax year; and

(b) the Commissioners have not made a decision under section 14(1) of the Act in relation to that claim.

7(3) The circumstances prescribed by this paragraph are where–

(a) a claim for a tax credit for the next tax year has not been made or treated as made by the person or persons; and

(b) the Commissioners have not made a decision under section 18(1) of the Act in relation to the person and persons for the relevant tax year.

History – In reg. 7 the words "the Commissioners" substituted for the words "the Board" wherever they occurred by SI 2005/2200, reg. 7(4), with effect from 29 August 2005.

Cross references – SI 2013/386, reg. 17(2) and Schedule, para. 44: deemed omission of reg. 7 in relation to the introduction of Universal Credit.
SI 2014/1230, Sch., para. 36: modified application of reg. 7 where SI 2014/1230, reg. 12A applies (claims for universal credit).

TIME OF PAYMENT BY WAY OF A CREDIT TO A BANK ACCOUNT OR OTHER ACCOUNT

8(1) This regulation applies where the tax credit or element is to be paid by way of a credit to a bank account or other account notified to the Commissioners.

8(2) Subject to paragraphs (2A) and (2B), the tax credit or element shall be paid–

(a) each week; or

(b) every four weeks,

in accordance with any election given by the person to whom payment is to be made.

8(2A) If a person makes elections under paragraph (2) for child tax credit and any child care element of working tax credit to be paid at differing intervals, the elections shall have no effect and the Commissioners may pay the child tax credit and any child care element together either each week or every four weeks as appears to them to be appropriate.

8(2B) Notwithstanding the terms of any election under paragraph (2), the Commissioners may pay the tax credit or element either each week or every four weeks as appears to them to be appropriate.

8(3) [Revoked by SI 2005/2200, reg. 9(2)(b).]

8(4) This regulation is subject to regulations 10 and 11.

History – In reg. 8 the words "the Commissioners" substituted wherever they occurred by SI 2005/2200, reg. 7(4), with effect from 29 August 2005.
In reg. 8(1) the words "Subject to paragraph (3)," which appeared at the beginning revoked by SI 2005/2200, reg. 9(2)(c), with effect from 1 April 2006.
In reg. 8(2), words "Subject to paragraph (2A)" inserted by SI 2003/723, reg. 9(2), with effect from 6 April 2003.
In reg. 8(2), the words "Subject to paragraphs (2A) and (2B)" substituted for the words "Subject to paragraph (2A)" by SI 2010/2914, reg. 7(a), with effect from 31 December 2010.
Reg. 8(2A) inserted by SI 2003/723, reg. 9(3), with effect from 6 April 2003.
Reg. 8(2B) inserted by SI 2010/2914, reg. 7(b), with effect from 31 December 2010.
Reg. 8(3) revoked by SI 2005/2200, reg. 9(2)(b), with effect from 1 April 2006.

TIME OF PAYMENT OTHER THAN BY WAY OF A CREDIT TO A BANK ACCOUNT OR OTHER ACCOUNT ETC.

9(1) This regulation applies where–

(a) the tax credit or element is to be paid other than by way of a credit to a bank account or other account notified to the Commissioners; or

(b) [revoked by SI 2005/2200, reg. 992)(b).]

9(2) The tax credit or element shall be paid at such times as appear to the Commissioners to be appropriate.

History – In reg. 9 the words "the Commissioners" substituted wherever they occurred by SI 2005/2200, reg. 7(4), with effect from 29 August 2005.
Reg. 9(1)(b) revoked by SI 2005/2200, reg. 9(2)(b), with effect from 1 April 2006.

SINGLE PAYMENT OF SMALL SUMS OF TAX CREDIT

10 The tax credit or element may be paid by way of a single payment, and at such time, and in such manner, as appear to the Commissioners to be appropriate, in any of the following cases–

(a) where the Commissioners are paying only child tax credit to a person and the weekly rate at which it is payable is less than £2.00;

(b) where the Commissioners are paying both any child care element (but no other element) of working tax credit and child tax credit to a person and the total weekly rate at which they are payable is less than £2.00;

(c) where the Commissioners are paying only working tax credit (apart from any child care element) to a person and the weekly rate at which it is payable (excluding any such child care element) is less than £2.00;

(d) where the Commissioners are paying both working tax credit (including elements other than, or in addition to, any child care element) and child tax credit to a person who has elected under regulation 8(2) to have them paid at the same intervals and the total weekly rate at which they are payable is less than £2.00;

(e) where the Commissioners are paying both working tax credit (apart from any child care element) and child tax credit to a person who has elected under regulation 8(2) to have them paid at differing intervals and–

(i) the total weekly rate at which any such child care element and the child tax credit are payable is less than £2.00; or

(ii) the weekly rate at which the working tax credit is payable (excluding any such child care element) is less than £2.00.

History – In reg. 10 the words "the Commissioners" substituted wherever they occurred by SI 2005/2200, reg. 7(4), with effect from 29 August 2005.
Reg. 10 substituted by SI 2003/723, reg. 10, with effect from 6 April 2003.

POSTPONEMENT OF PAYMENT

11(1) *The Commissioners* may postpone payment of the tax credit or element in any of the circumstances specified in paragraphs (2), (2A), (3) and (3A).

11(2) The circumstances specified in this paragraph are where there is a pending determination of an appeal against a decision of the First-tier Tribunal, the appeal tribunal, the Upper Tribunal, the Northern Ireland Social Security Commissioner or a court relating to–

(a) the case in question; or

(b) another case where it appears to the Commissioners that, if the appeal were to be determined in a particular way, an issue would arise as to whether the award in the case in question should be amended or terminated under section 16(1) of the Act.

11(2A) The circumstances specified in this paragraph are where–

(a) a notice in writing has been given by the Commissioners to a person to notify a bank account or other account to which the Commissioners may make payment of a tax credit or element to which the person is entitled;

(b) a period of four weeks has elapsed since the day on which the Commissioners gave their notice; and

(c) no bank account or other account has been notified to the Commissioners pursuant to their notice.

11(3) The circumstances specified in this paragraph are where confirmation is pending of–

(a) the details of a bank account or other account by way of a credit to which payment is to be made; or

(b) the address of the person to whom payment is to be made,

where it appears to the Commissioners that such details or address as were previously notified to them are incorrect.

11(3A) The circumstances specified in this paragraph are where–

(a) a notice under section 16(3) of the Tax Credits Act 2002 has been issued to the person, or either or both of the persons, to whom the tax credit or element was awarded, and

(b) such person or persons have not provided the information or evidence requested in that notice by the date specified in such notice

11(4) For the purposes of paragraph (2), the circumstances where a determination of an appeal is pending include circumstances where a decision of the First-tier Tribunal, the appeal tribunal, the Upper Tribunal, the Northern Ireland Social Security Commissioner or a court has been made and the Commissioners–

(a) are awaiting receipt of the decision;

(b) in the case of a decision by the First-tier Tribunal or the appeal tribunal, are considering whether to apply for a statement of reasons or have applied for, and are awaiting receipt of, a statement of reasons; or

(c) have received the decision or statement of reasons and are considering–

(i) whether to apply for permission to appeal; or

(ii) where permission is not needed or has been given, whether to appeal.

11(5) **"Appeal tribunal"** has the meaning given by section 63(10) of the Act.

11(6) **"Northern Ireland Social Security Commissioner"** has the meaning given by section 63(13) of the Act.

11(7) The postponement of payment pursuant to the circumstances specified in paragraph (2A) shall cease at the earlier of the time when–

(a) a bank account or other account is notified to the Commissioners; or

(b) the entitlement to the tax credit or element ceases in accordance with regulation 14.

History – In reg. 11(1) the words "paragraphs (2), (2A), (3) and (3A)" substituted for the words "paragraphs (2) and (3)" by SI 2010/751, reg. 10(2), with effect from 6 April 2010.

In reg. 11(2), the words "the First-tier Tribunal, the appeal tribunal, the" substituted by SI 2009/56, art. 3(2) and Sch. 2, para. 78(2), operative from 1 April 2009 subject to transitional and saving provisions in SI 2009/56, Sch. 3.

In reg. 11(2), the words "the appropriate tribunal, the Upper Tribunal, the Northern Ireland" substituted by SI 2008/2683, art. 6 and Sch. 1, para. 190(a), with effect from 3 November 2008.

Reg. 11(2A) inserted by SI 2010/751, reg. 10(3), with effect from 6 April 2010.

In reg. 11(2A)(b), the word "four" substituted for the word "eight" by SI 2012/848, reg. 6(2), with effect in relation to a notice given on or after 6 April 2012 under reg. 11(2A)(a).

Reg. 11(3A) inserted by SI 2010/751, reg. 10(4), with effect from 6 April 2010.

In reg. 11(4), the words "the First-tier Tribunal, the appeal tribunal, the" substituted by SI 2009/56, art. 3(2) and Sch. 2, para. 78(3)(a), operative from 1 April 2009 subject to transitional and saving provisions in SI 2009/56, Sch. 3.

In reg. 11(4), the words "the appropriate tribunal, the Upper Tribunal, the Northern Ireland" substituted by SI 2008/2683, art. 6 and Sch. 1, para. 190(a), with effect from 3 November 2008.

In reg. 11(4)(b), the words "First-tier Tribunal or the appeal tribunal" substituted by SI 2009/56, art. 3(2) and Sch. 2, para. 78(3)(b), operative from 1 April 2009 subject to transitional and saving provisions in SI 2009/56, Sch. 3.

In reg. 11(4)(b), the words "the appropriate tribunal" substituted by SI 2008/2683, art. 6 and Sch. 1, para. 190(b), with effect from 3 November 2008.

In reg. 11(5), the words "Appeal tribunal" substituted by SI 2009/56, art. 3(2) and Sch. 2, para. 78(4), operative from 1 April 2009 subject to transitional and saving provisions in SI 2009/56, Sch. 3.

In reg. 11(5), the words "Appropriate tribunal" substituted by SI 2008/2683, art. 6 and Sch. 1, para. 190(c), with effect from 3 November 2008.

In reg. 11(6), the words "Northern Ireland Social" substituted by SI 2008/2683, art. 6 and Sch. 1, para. 190(d), with effect from 3 November 2008.

Reg. 11(7) inserted by SI 2010/751, reg. 10(5), with effect from 6 April 2010.

In reg. 11, the words "the Commissioners" substituted wherever they occurred by SI 2005/2200, reg. 7(4), with effect from *29 August 2005*.

AMOUNTS OF PAYMENTS

12(1) The tax credit or element shall be paid in accordance with the most recent decision by the Commissioners under section 14(1), 15(1) or 16(1) of the Act.

12(2) Where the tax credit or element is to be paid other than by way of a single payment, it shall be paid so far as possible in such amounts as will result in the person to whom payment is to be made receiving regular payments of similar amounts over the entire period of award.

12(3) Where an award of tax credit is amended, the total amount paid prior to the award being amended may be taken into account by the Commissioners in determining the amount of any further payments for the remainder of the period of award.

12(4) Where payments under section 24(4) of the Act are to be made the Commissioners may take any or both of the following factors into account in determining the amount of those payments–

(a) the rate at which the person or persons were entitled to the tax credit for the relevant tax year;

(b) the estimated amount of income the person or persons referred to above may receive in the current tax year.

History – In reg. 12 the words "the Commissioners" substituted wherever they occurred by SI 2005/2200, reg. 7(4), with effect from 29 August 2005.
In reg. 12(3) the word "may" substituted by SI 2007/824, reg. 15, with effect from 6 April 2007.
Reg. 12(4) substituted by SI 2008/604, reg. 5(2), with effect from 6 April 2008.

RECOVERY OF OVERPAYMENTS OF TAX CREDIT FROM OTHER PAYMENTS OF TAX CREDIT

12A(1) This regulation applies where notice is given to a person or persons under subsection (4) of section 29 of the Act (deduction of overpayments from payments of tax credit).

12A(2) The maximum rate at which an overpayment may be recovered from payments of tax credit is–

(a) where the only amount of tax credit to which the person is, or, in the case of a joint claim, the persons are, entitled, is the family element of child tax credit, 100% of that tax credit;

(b) where the total amount of tax credit to which the person is, or, in the case of a joint claim, the persons are, entitled is not subject to reduction–

(i) by virtue of section 7(2) of the Act; or

(ii) because their income for the relevant year does not exceed the relevant income threshold prescribed in his or their case in regulation 3 of the Tax Credits (Income Thresholds and Determination of Rates) Regulations 2002;

10% of that tax credit; and

(c) in any other case, the income-related percentage of the tax credit to which the person is, or in the case of a joint claim, the persons are, entitled.

12A(2A) In paragraph (2)(c), "the income-related percentage" means–

(a) 50% if annual income exceeds £20,000; and

(b) 25% in any other case.

12A(2B) For the purposes of paragraph (2A)(a), "annual income"–

(a) means the annual income of the person or, in the case of a joint claim, the aggregate annual income of the persons, mentioned in paragraph (2)(c); and

(b) is to be taken to be the amount that the Commissioners are for the time being treating that income to be for the purposes of Part 1 of the Act, regardless of whether that amount is also "the relevant income" (as defined by section 7(3) of the Act) on which the entitlement to the tax credit mentioned in paragraph (2)(c) is dependent.

12A(3) In paragraph (2) a reference to the amount to which a person is, or persons are, entitled is a reference to the amount to which they would be entitled but for the operation of that paragraph.

History – In reg. 12A(2)(c), the words "the income-related percentage" substituted for "25%" by SI 2016/360, reg. 5(2)(a), with effect from 6 April 2016.
Reg. 12(2A) and (2B) inserted by SI 2016/360, reg. 5(2)(b), with effect from 6 April 2016.
Reg. 12A inserted by SI 2004/762, reg.18, with effect from 6 April 2004.

MANNER OF PAYMENT

13(1) Subject to paragraph (2), the tax credit or element shall be paid by way of a credit to a bank account or other account notified to the Commissioners by the person to whom payment is to be made.

13(2) Where it does not appear to the Commissioners to be appropriate for the tax credit or element to be paid by way of a credit to a bank account or other account notified to the Commissioners by the person to whom payment is to be made, the tax credit or element may be paid in such manner as appears to the Commissioners to be appropriate.

13(3) Subject to regulation 14, if no bank account or other account has been notified to the Commissioners, the tax credit or element shall be paid in such manner as appears to the Commissioners to be appropriate.

History – In reg. 13 the words "the Commissioners" substituted wherever they occurred by SI 2005/2200, reg. 7(4), with effect from 29 August 2005.
In reg. 13(2) the words "it does not appear to the Board to be appropriate" substituted by SI 2003/723, reg. 11, with effect from 6 April 2003.

ENTITLEMENT TO TAX CREDIT OR ELEMENT DEPENDENT ON A BANK ACCOUNT OR OTHER ACCOUNT HAVING BEEN NOTIFIED TO THE COMMISSIONERS

14(1) Subject to paragraph (3), where–

(a) payment of a tax credit or element is postponed pursuant to the circumstances specified in regulation 11(2A), and

(b) before the relevant time determined in accordance with this regulation, no bank account or other account is notified to the Commissioners by the person to whom a tax credit or element would have been paid if payment of it had not been postponed,

that person shall cease to be entitled to the tax credit or element for the remainder of the period of the award beginning on the day from which the Commissioners decide to postpone payment.

14(2) [Omitted by SI 2010/751, reg. 10(7).]

14(3) Where there are exceptional circumstances which are expected to result in a person not being able to obtain a bank account or other account throughout the period of award, paragraph (1) shall not have effect in relation to that person's entitlement to a tax credit or element for the period of award.

14(4) [Omitted by SI 2010/751, reg. 10(7).]

14(4A) Subject to paragraphs (4C) and (4E), the relevant time is the earlier of–

(a) three months after the time when the Commissioners decide to postpone payment of a tax credit or element; or

(b) immediately after the end of the relevant tax year.

14(4B) This paragraph applies where, before the time determined in accordance with paragraph (4A), the person entitled to payment of the tax credit or element–

(a) requests from the Commissioners authority to open an account for which such authority is required; and

(b) provides sufficient information from which the Commissioners can give that authority.

14(4C) Subject to paragraph (4E), where paragraph (4B) applies, the relevant time is the later of–

(a) the time determined in accordance with paragraph (4A); and

(b) the expiry of the period of 3 weeks from the day on which the Commissioners give their authority following a request described in paragraph (4B)(a).

14(4D) This paragraph applies where a person to whom a notice described in regulation 11(2A)(a) has been given has a reasonable excuse–

(a) for not being able to take all necessary steps to obtain a bank account or other account before a time determined in accordance with paragraphs (4A) or (4C), or

(b) for not being able to notify to the Commissioners the bank account or other account before a time determined in accordance with paragraphs (4A) or (4C).

14(4E) Where paragraph (4D) applies, the relevant time is the later of–

(a) the time determined in accordance with paragraph (4A);

(b) where paragraph (4B) applies, the time determined in accordance with paragraph (4C); and

(c) the date by which the account can reasonably be expected to be notified to the Commissioners.

14(5) **"Writing"** includes writing produced by electronic communications that are approved by the Commissioners.

History – Reg. 14(1) substituted by SI 2010/751, reg. 10(6), with effect from 6 April 2010.
Reg. 14(2) omitted by SI 2010/751, reg. 10(7), with effect from 6 April 2010.
Reg. 14(4) omitted by SI 2010/751, reg. 10(7), with effect from 6 April 2010.
In former reg. 14(4)(a), (b) the word "give" substituted by SI 2003/723, reg. 12, with effect from 6 April 2003.
Reg. 14(4A)–(4E) inserted by SI 2010/751, reg. 10(8), with effect from 6 April 2010.
In reg. 14 and the heading which precedes it the words "the Commissioners" substituted wherever they occurred by SI 2005/2200, reg. 7(4), with effect from 29 August 2005.

TAX CREDITS (APPEALS) REGULATIONS 2002

(SI 2002/2926, as amended by SI 2004/372, SI 2008/2683 and SI 2009/56)

Made on 26 November 2002 by the Commissioners of Inland Revenue, in exercise of the powers conferred upon them by s. 63(8) and 65(2) and (6) of the Tax Credits Act 2002. Operative from 17 December 2002.

CITATION, COMMENCEMENT AND DURATION

1(1) These Regulations may be cited as the Tax Credits (Appeals) Regulations 2002 and shall come into force on 17th December 2002.

1(2) These Regulations shall cease to have effect on such day as is appointed by order made under section 63(1) of the Tax Credits Act 2002 (tax credits appeals etc.: temporary modifications).

INTERPRETATION

2 In these Regulations–

"appeal tribunal" means an appeal tribunal constituted in Northern Ireland, under Chapter 1 of Part 2 of the Social Security (Northern Ireland) Order 1998 (social security appeals: Northern Ireland);

"tax credit appeal" means an appeal which, by virtue of section 63 of the Tax Credits Act 2002 or of provisions applied by these Regulations, is to an appeal tribunal or lies to a Social Security Commissioner;

"Social Security Commissioner" means the Chief Social Security Commissioner or any other Social Security Commissioner appointed under the Social Security Administration (Northern Ireland) Act 1992 or a tribunal of two or more Commissioners constituted under Article 16(7) of the Social Security (Northern Ireland) Order 1998;

"the 1998 Act" means the Social Security Act 1998;

"the 1998 Order" means the Social Security (Northern Ireland) Order 1998.

History – In reg. 2, in the definition of "appeal tribunal", sub-para. (a) (and the following "or" and "(b)") omitted by SI 2008/2683, art. 6 and Sch. 1, para. 192(a), with effect from 3 November 2008.

TC Statutory Instruments

APPLICATION OF SECTION 54 OF THE TAXES MANAGEMENT ACT 1970

3(1) Section 54 of the Taxes Management Act 1970 (settling of appeals by agreement) shall apply to a tax credit appeal to an appeal tribunal or the First-tier Tribunal with the modifications prescribed by paragraphs (2) to (8).

3(2) In subsection (1) for "tribunal", in both places where that word occurs, substitute the words "appeal tribunal or the First-tier Tribunal".

3(3) In subsections (1) and (4) omit the words "assessment or", in each place where they occur.

3(4) In subsections (1), (2) and (4)(a) for "inspector or other proper officer of the Crown" substitute the words "officer of the Board".

3(5) For subsection (3) substitute the following subsection–

"**54(3)** Where an agreement is not in writing–

(a) the preceding provisions of this section shall not apply unless the Board give notice, in such form and manner as they consider appropriate, to the appellant of the terms agreed between the officer of the Board and the appellant; and

(b) the references in those preceding provisions to the time when the agreement was come to shall be construed as references to the date of that notice."

3(6) In subsection (4)(b) for "inspector or other proper officer giving" substitute the words "officer of the Board giving".

3(7) In subsection (4) for "inspector or other proper officer had come" substitute the words "officer of the Board had come".

3(8) After subsection (5) add the following subsection–

"**54(6)** In subsection (1) **"appeal tribunal"** means an appeal tribunal constituted in Northern Ireland, under Chapter 1 of Part 2 of the Social Security (Northern Ireland) Order 1998 (social security appeals: Northern Ireland)."

History – In reg. 3(1), the words "or the First-tier Tribunal" inserted by SI 2008/2683, art. 6 and Sch. 1, para. 193(a), with effect from 3 November 2008.

In reg. 3(2), ""tribunal"" substituted by SI 2009/56, art. 3(2) and Sch. 2, para. 81, operative from 1 April 2009 subject to transitional and saving provisions in SI 2009/56, Sch. 3.

In reg. 3(2), the words "or the First-tier Tribunal" inserted by SI 2008/2683, art. 6 and Sch. 1, para. 193(a), with effect from 3 November 2008.

In reg. 3(8), in the inserted TMA 1970, s. 54(6), sub-para. (a) (and the following "and" and "(b)") omitted by SI 2008/2683, art. 6 and Sch. 1, para. 193(b), with effect from 3 November 2008.

APPLICATION OF SECTION 12 OF THE 1998 ACT AND ARTICLE 13 OF THE 1998 ORDER

4(1) Section 12 of the 1998 Act and Article 13 of the 1998 Order (appeals to an appeal tribunal or the First-tier Tribunal) shall apply to a tax credit appeal to an appeal tribunal or the First-tier Tribunal with the modifications prescribed by paragraphs (2) to (8).

4(2) For subsections (1) and (2) of that section substitute the following subsections–

"**12(1)** An appeal which is to the First-tier Tribunal by virtue of section 63 of the Tax Credits Act 2002, including an application for a direction under section 19(9) of that Act, (a **"tax credit appeal"**) may be brought by–

(a) a claimant whose claim for a tax credit is the subject of the appeal;

(b) the person on whom the penalty to which the appeal relates was imposed;

(c) the person applying for the direction under section 19(9) of that Act; or

(d) such other person as may be prescribed.".

4(3) For paragraphs (1) and (2) of that Article substitute the following paragraph–

"**13(1)** An appeal which is to an appeal tribunal by virtue of section 63 of the Tax Credits Act 2002, including an application for a direction under section 19(9) of that Act, (a **"tax credit appeal"**) may be brought by–

(a) a claimant whose claim for a tax credit is the subject of the appeal;

(b) the person on whom the penalty to which the appeal relates was imposed;

(c) the person applying for a direction under section 19(9) of that Act; or

(d) such other person as may be prescribed.".

4(4) Omit subsections (3) to (6) of that section and paragraphs (3) to (6) of that Article.

4(5) In subsection (7) of that section and paragraph (7) of that Article add at the end ", and may in particular extend the time limit for giving notice of appeal specified in section 39(1) of the Tax Credits Act 2002".

4(6) In subsection (8) of that section for "an appeal under this section" substitute "a tax credit appeal".

4(7) In paragraph (8) of that Article for "an appeal under this Article" substitute "a tax credit appeal".

4(8) Omit subsections (8)(a) and (9) of that section and paragraphs (8)(a) and (9) of that Article.

History – In reg. 4(1), the words "or the First-tier Tribunal" inserted in both places by SI 2008/2683, art. 6 and Sch. 1, para. 194(a), with effect from 3 November 2008.

In reg. 4(2), in the substituted SSA 1998, s. 12(1), the words "the First-tier Tribunal" substituted by SI 2008/2683, art. 6 and Sch. 1, para. 194(a), with effect from 3 November 2008.

APPLICATION OF SECTION 13 OF THE 1998 ACT AND ARTICLE 14 OF THE 1998 ORDER

5(1) Section 13 of the 1998 Act and Article 14 of the 1998 Order (redetermination etc. of appeals by tribunal) shall apply to a decision of an appeal tribunal or the First-tier Tribunal on a tax credit appeal (other than a decision on a tax credit appeal under Schedule 2 to the Tax Credits Act 2002) with the modifications prescribed by paragraphs (2) to (4).

5(2) Omit subsection (3) of that section and paragraph (3) of that Article.

5(3) In subsection (4) of that section–

(a) omit the words "this section and";

(b) omit paragraph (b) and the word "and" immediately preceding it.

5(4) In paragraph (4) of that Article–

(a) omit the words "this Article and";

(b) omit sub-paragraph (a);

(c) for sub-paragraph (b) substitute the following sub-paragraph–

"(b) the Board and the persons mentioned in paragraph (3)(b) of that Article.".

History – In reg. 5(1), the words "or the First-tier Tribunal" inserted by SI 2008/2683, art. 6 and Sch. 1, para. 195, with effect from 3 November 2008.

APPLICATION OF SECTION 14 OF THE 1998 ACT AND ARTICLE 15 OF THE 1998 ORDER

6(1) Section 14(2) to (6) of the 1998 Act and Article 15(1) to (10) of the 1998 Order (appeal from tribunal to Commissioner) shall apply to a decision of an appeal tribunal or the First-tier Tribunal on a tax credit appeal (other than a decision on a tax credit appeal under Schedule 2 to the Tax Credits Act 2002) with the modifications prescribed by paragraphs (2) and (3).

6(2) In that section–

(a) [omitted by SI 2008/2683, art. 6 and Sch. 1, para. 196(b).]

(b) in subsection (3)(a) for "Secretary of State" substitute "Board";

(c) omit subsections (3)(d), (4) and (5)(c).

6(3) In that Article–

(a) in paragraph (1) omit the words "under Article 13 or 14";

(b) in paragraph (3)(a) for "Department" substitute "Board";

(c) omit paragraphs (3)(d), (4) and (5)(c).

History – In reg. 6(1), "14(2) to (6)" substituted by SI 2008/2683, art. 6 and Sch. 1, para. 196(a)(i), with effect from 3 November 2008. In reg. 6(1), the words "or the First-tier Tribunal" inserted by SI 2008/2683, art. 6 and Sch. 1, para. 196(a)(ii), with effect from 3 November 2008.
Reg. 6(2)(a) omitted by SI 2008/2683, art. 6 and Sch. 1, para. 196(a)(ii), with effect from 3 November 2008.

7(1) Article 15(11) to (13) of the 1998 Order (appeals and procedure before Commissioner) shall apply to a decision of an appeal tribunal on a tax credit appeal (including a decision on a tax credit appeal under Schedule 2 to the Tax Credits Act 2002) with the modifications prescribed by paragraphs (2) and (3).

7(2) So far as concerns decisions on tax credit appeals under Schedule 2 to the Tax Credits Act 2002, paragraph (11) of that Article omit the words "and applications made for leave to appeal".

7(3) [Omitted by SI 2004/372, reg. 2(2) with effect from 16 March 2004.]

History – In reg. 7(1), at the beginning, the words "Section 14(11) and (12) of, and Schedule 4 to, the 1998 Act and" omitted by SI 2008/2683, art. 6 and Sch. 1, para. 197(a), with effect from 3 November 2008.
In reg. 7(2), the words "in subsection (11) of that section and", which appeared before "paragraph (11)", omitted by SI 2008/2683, art. 6 and Sch. 1, para. 197(b), with effect from 3 November 2008.
Reg. 7(3) omitted by SI 2004/372, reg. 2(2), with effect from 16 March 2004.

APPLICATION OF SECTION 15 OF THE SOCIAL SECURITY ACT 1998

8 Section 15 of the 1998 Act (applications for permission to appeal against a decision of the Upper Tribunal) shall apply to a decision of the Upper Tribunal on a tax credit appeal.

History – In reg. 8, the words "applications for permission to appeal against a decision of the Upper Tribunal" substituted for the words "appeal from Commissioner on a point of law", and the words "the Upper Tribunal" substituted for the words "a Social Security Commissioner", by SI 2008/2683, art. 6 and Sch. 1, para. 198, with effect from 3 November 2008.

APPLICATION OF SECTION 16 OF THE 1998 ACT AND ARTICLE 16 OF THE 1998 ORDER

9(1) Section 16 of, and Schedule 5 to, the 1998 Act and Article 16 of, and Schedule 4 to, the 1998 Order (procedure) shall apply for the purposes of a tax credit appeal with the modifications prescribed by paragraphs (2) to (6).

9(2) Omit subsection (3) of Section 16.

9(3) Omit paragraph (3)(b) of that Article and the word "and" immediately preceding it.

9(4) Omit subsections (4) and (5) of that section and paragraphs (4) and (5) of that Article.

9(5) In Schedule 5 to the 1998 Act–

(a) in paragraph 1, omit the words "the Secretary of State,", in both places where they occur;

(b) in paragraph 4(b), add at the end ", including provision extending the time limit for giving notice of appeal specified in section 39(1) of the Tax Credits Act 2002".

9(6) In Schedule 4 to the 1998 Order–

(a) in paragraph 1, omit the words "the Department", in both places where they occur;

(b) in paragraph 4(b), add at the end ", including provision for extending the time limit for giving notice of appeal specified in section 39(1) of the Tax Credits Act 2002".

History – Reg. 9(2) substituted by SI 2008/2683, art. 6 and Sch. 1, para. 199, with effect from 3 November 2008.

APPLICATION OF SECTION 17 OF THE 1998 ACT AND ARTICLE 17 OF THE 1998 ORDER

10(1) Section 17 of the 1998 Act and Article 17 of the 1998 Order (finality of decisions) shall apply to a decision of an appeal tribunal the First-tier Tribunal, the Upper Tribunal or a Social Security Commissioner on a tax credit appeal with the modifications prescribed by paragraphs (2) to (4).

10(2) For subsection (1) of that section substitute the following subsection–

"17(1) Subject to the provisions of–

(a) sections 12 to 16 of this Act, and

(b) the Tax Credits Act 2002,

(c) any provision made by or under Chapter 2 of Part 1 of the Tribunals, Courts and Enforcement Act 2007,

any decision made in accordance with those provisions in respect of an appeal which, by virtue of section 63 of the Tax Credits Act 2002 (or of provisions of this Act applied by regulations made under that section), is to the First-tier Tribunal or lies to the Upper Tribunal, shall be final.".

10(2) For paragraph (1) of that Article substitute the following paragraph–

"**17(1)** Subject to the provisions of–

(a) Articles 13 to 16 of this Order, and

(b) the Tax Credits Act 2002,

any decision made in accordance with those provisions in respect of an appeal which, by virtue of section 63 of the Tax Credits Act 2002 (or of provisions of this Order applied by regulations made under that section), is to an appeal tribunal or lies to a Commissioner, shall be final.".

10(4) Omit subsection (2)(b) and (c) of that section and paragraph (2)(b) and (c) of that Article.

History – In reg. 10(1), the words "the First-tier Tribunal, the Upper Tribunal" inserted by SI 2008/2683, art. 6 and Sch. 1, para. 200(a), with effect from 3 November 2008.

In reg. 10(2), in the substituted SSA 1998, s. 17(1), para. (c) inserted by SI 2008/2683, art. 6 and Sch. 1, para. 200(b)(i), with effect from 3 November 2008.

In reg. 10(2), in the substituted SSA 1998, s. 17(1), the words "the First-tier Tribunal or lies to the Upper Tribunal" substituted by SI 2008/2683, art. 6 and Sch. 1, para. 200(b)(ii), with effect from 3 November 2008.

APPLICATION OF ARTICLE 28 OF THE 1998 ORDER

History – In the heading to reg. 11, the words "section 28 of the 1998 Act and", which appeared before "article 28", omitted by SI 2008/2683, art. 6 and Sch. 1, para. 201(a), with effect from 3 November 2008.

11(1) Article 28 of the 1998 Order (correction of errors and setting aside of decisions) shall apply to a decision by an appeal tribunal or a Social Security Commissioner on a tax credit appeal with the modifications prescribed by paragraphs (2) to (4).

11(2) [Omitted by SI 2008/2683, art. 6 and Sch. 1, para. 201(c).]

11(3) For paragraph (3) of that Article substitute the following paragraph–

"**28(3)** In this Article **"relevant statutory provision"** means–

(a) any of Articles 13 to 17 above, and

(b) any statutory provision contained or referred to in section 19(10), 38 or 39 of, or Schedule 2 to, the Tax Credits Act 2002.".

11(4) Omit paragraph (1A) of that Article.

History – In reg. 11(1), at the beginning, the words "Section 28 of the 1998 Act and" omitted by SI 2008/2683, art. 6 and Sch. 1, para. 201(b), with effect from 3 November 2008.

Reg. 11(2) omitted by SI 2008/2683, art. 6 and Sch. 1, para. 201(c), with effect from 3 November 2008.

In reg. 11(4), the words "subsection (1A) of that section and", which appeared after "Omit", omitted by SI 2008/2683, art. 6 and Sch. 1, para. 201(d), with effect from 3 November 2008.

APPLICATION OF SECTION 39 OF THE 1998 ACT AND ARTICLE 39 OF THE 1998 ORDER

12(1) Section 39 of the 1998 Act and Article 39 of the 1998 Order (interpretation etc. of Chapter 2) shall apply for the purposes of a tax credit appeal with the modifications prescribed by paragraphs (2) to (4).

12(2) In subsection (1) of that section–

(a) in the appropriate place

""**the Board"** means the Commissioners of Inland Revenue;";

(b) for the definition of "claimant" substitute–

""**claimant"** means a person who makes (whether or not jointly with another) a claim for a tax credit in accordance with sections 3 and 4 of the Tax Credits Act 2002, and includes a person entitled to make such a claim on behalf of another person by virtue of regulation 17 or 18 of the Tax Credits (Claims and Notifications) Regulations 2002;";

(c) omit the definition of **"relevant benefit"**.

12(3) In paragraph (1) of that Article–

(a) for the definition of "Inland Revenue" substitute–

""**the Board"** means the Commissioners of Inland Revenue;

"claimant" means a person who makes (whether or not jointly with another) a claim for a tax credit in accordance with sections 3 and 4 of the Tax Credits Act 2002, and includes a person entitled to make such a claim on behalf of another person by virtue of regulation 17 or 18 of the Tax Credits (Claims and Notifications) Regulations 2002;";

(b) omit the definition of **"relevant benefit"**.

12(4) Omit subsections (2) and (3) of that section and paragraphs (2) and (3) of that Article.

History – In reg. 12(2)(a), the words "in the appropriate place" substituted by SI 2008/2683, art. 6 and Sch. 1, para. 202, with effect from 3 November 2008.

Reg. 12(2)(c) substituted by SI 2009/56, art. 3(2) and Sch. 2, para. 82(2), operative from 1 April 2009 subject to transitional and saving provisions in SI 2009/56, Sch. 3.

Reg. 12(3)(b) substituted by SI 2009/56, art. 3(2) and Sch. 2, para. 82(3), operative from 1 April 2009 subject to transitional and saving provisions in SI 2009/56, Sch. 3.

TAX CREDITS (ADMINISTRATIVE ARRANGEMENTS) REGULATIONS 2002

(SI 2002/3036, as amended by SI 2013/630 and S.R. 2016/236 (NI))

Made on 9 December 2002 by the Commissioners of Inland Revenue, in exercise of the powers conferred upon them by s. 58 and 65(1), (2), (7) and (9) of the Tax Credits Act 2002. Operative from 1 January 2003.

CITATION AND COMMENCEMENT

1 These Regulations may be cited as the Tax Credits (Administrative Arrangements) Regulations 2002 and shall come into force on 1st January 2003.

INTERPRETATION

2 In these Regulations–

"the Board" means the Commissioners of Inland Revenue;

"the principal Regulations" means the Tax Credits (Claims and Notifications) Regulations 2002;

"relevant authority" means–

(a) the Secretary of State;

(b) the Department for Social Development in Northern Ireland; or

(c) a person providing services to the Secretary of State or that Department.

PROVISION OF INFORMATION OR EVIDENCE TO RELEVANT AUTHORITIES

3(1) Information or evidence relating to tax credits which is held–

(a) by the Board; or

(b) by a person providing services to the Board, in connection with the provision of those services,

may be provided to a relevant authority for the purposes of, or for any purposes connected with, the exercise of that relevant authority's functions under the principal Regulations.

3(2) Information or evidence relating to tax credits may be provided to a relevant authority by persons other than the Board (whether or not persons by whom claims or notifications relating to tax credits are or have been made or given).

GIVING OF INFORMATION OR ADVICE BY RELEVANT AUTHORITIES

4 A relevant authority to which a claim or notification is or has been made or given by a person in accordance with the principal Regulations may give information or advice relating to tax credits to that person.

RECORDING, VERIFICATION AND HOLDING, AND FORWARDING, OF CLAIMS ETC. RECEIVED BY RELEVANT AUTHORITIES

5(1) A relevant authority may record and hold claims and notifications received by virtue of the principal Regulations and information or evidence received by virtue of regulation 3(2).

5(2) Subject to paragraphs (3) and (4), a relevant authority must forward to the Board or a person providing services to the Board such a claim or notification, or such information or evidence, as soon as reasonably practicable after being satisfied that it is complete.

5(3) Before forwarding a claim in accordance with paragraph (2), a relevant authority must verify–

(a) that any national insurance number provided in respect of the person by whom the claim is made exists and has been allocated to that person;

(b) that the matters verified in accordance with sub-paragraph (a) accord with–

(i) its own records; or

(ii) in the case of a person providing services to the Secretary of State or the Department for Social Development in Northern Ireland, records held by the Secretary of State or that Department; and

(c) whether the details of any relevant claim for benefit that have been provided are consistent with those held by it.

5(4) If a relevant authority cannot locate any national insurance number in respect of a person by whom such a claim is made, it must forward to the Board or a person providing services to the Board the claim (notwithstanding that it is not complete).

(b) any notice or other document is required to be given or sent to any person other than the Board, that notice or document shall, if sent to that person's last known address, be treated as having been given or sent on the day that it was posted.

History – In reg. 2(a), the words "to the clerk to the appeal tribunal or" and "by the clerk of the appeal tribunal or", which appeared before the "to the Board" and "by the Board" respectively, omitted by SI 2008/2683, art. 6 and Sch. 1, para. 206(a), with effect from 3 November 2008.
In reg. 2(b), the words "the clerk to the appeal tribunal or", which appeared before "the Board", omitted by SI 2008/2683, art. 6 and Sch. 1, para. 206(b), with effect from 3 November 2008.

PART 2 – GENERAL APPEAL MATTERS

OTHER PERSONS WITH A RIGHT OF APPEAL OR A RIGHT TO MAKE AN APPLICATION FOR A DIRECTION

3 For the purposes of section 12(2) of the Act (as applied and modified by the Appeals Regulations), where–

(a) a person has made a claim for a tax credit but is unable for the time being to make an appeal against a decision in respect of that tax credit; or

(b) a person is the person in respect of whom an enquiry has been initiated under section 19(1) of the 2002 Act, but is unable for the time being to make an application for a direction,

the following other persons have a right of appeal to the First-tier Tribunal or a right to make an application for a direction–

(i) a receiver appointed by the Court of Protection with power to make a claim for a tax credit on behalf of the person;

(ii) in Scotland, judicial factor, or guardian acting or appointed under the Adults with Incapacity (Scotland) Act 2000 who has power to claim, or as the case may be, receive a tax credit on his behalf who is administering the estate of the person;

(iii) a person appointed under regulation 33(1) of the Social Security (Claims and Payments) Regulations 1987 (persons unable to act);

(iv) where there is no person mentioned in sub-paragraph (iii) in relation to the person who is unable to act, a person who has applied in writing to the Board to be appointed to act on behalf of the person who is unable to act and, if a natural person, is aged 18 years or more and who has been so appointed by the Board for the purposes of this sub-paragraph.

History – In reg. 3, "the First-tier Tribunal" substituted by SI 2008/2683, art. 6 and Sch. 1, para. 207, with effect from 3 November 2008.
In reg. 3(b)(ii), the words "judicial factor, or guardian acting or appointed under the Adults with Incapacity (Scotland) Act 2000 who has power to claim, or as the case may be, receive a tax credit on his behalf" substituted by SI 2005/337, reg. 4(2), with effect from 18 March 2005.

TIME WITHIN WHICH AN APPEAL IS TO BE BROUGHT

4(1) Where a dispute arises as to whether an appeal was brought within the time limit specified in section 39(1) of the 2002 Act, the dispute shall be referred to, and be determined by, the First-tier Tribunal.

4(2) The time limit specified in section 39(1) of the 2002 Act may be extended in accordance with regulation 5.

History – In reg. 4, "the First-tier Tribunal" substituted by SI 2008/2683, art. 6 and Sch. 1, para. 208, with effect from 3 November 2008.

LATE APPEALS

5(1) The Board may treat a late appeal as made in time where the conditions specified in paragraphs (4) to (8) are satisfied, but no appeal shall in any event be brought more than one year after the expiration of the last day for appealing under section 39(1) of the 2002 Act.

5(2) [Omitted by SI 2008/2683, art. 6 and Sch. 1, para. 209(b).]

5(3) [*Omitted by SI* 2008/2683, art. 6 and Sch. 1, para. 209(b).]

5(4) An appeal may be treated as made in time if the Board is satisfied that it is in the interests of justice.

5(5) For the purposes of paragraph (4) it is not in the interests of justice to treat the appeal as made in time unless the Board are satisfied that–

(a) the special circumstances specified in paragraph (6) are relevant; or

(b) some other special circumstances exist which are wholly exceptional and relevant,

and as a result of those special circumstances, it was not practicable for the appeal to be made within the time limit specified in section 39(1) of the 2002 Act.

5(6) For the purposes of paragraph (5)(a), the special circumstances are that–

(a) the appellant or a partner or dependant of the appellant has died or suffered serious illness;

(b) the appellant is not resident in the United Kingdom; or

(c) normal postal services were disrupted.

5(7) In determining whether it is in the interests of justice to treat the appeal as made in time, regard shall be had to the principle that the greater the amount of time that has elapsed between the expiration of the time within which the appeal is to be brought under section 39(1) of the 2002 Act and the submission of the notice of appeal, the more compelling should be the special circumstances.

5(8) In determining whether it is in the interests of justice to treat the appeal as made in time, no account shall be taken of the following–

(a) that the applicant or any person acting for him was unaware of or misunderstood the law applicable to his case (including ignorance or misunderstanding of the time limit imposed by section 39(1) of the 2002 Act); or

(b) that the Upper Tribunal or a court has taken a different view of the law from that previously understood and applied.

5(9) An application under this regulation for an extension of time which has been refused may not be renewed.

5(10) The panel member who determines an application under this regulation shall record a summary of his decision in such written form as has been approved by the President.

5(11) As soon as practicable after the decision is made a copy of the decision shall be sent or given to every party to the proceedings.

History – In reg. 5(1), the words "The Board may treat a late appeal as made in time" substituted for the words "The time within which an appeal must be brought may be extended", and "(4)" substituted by SI 2008/2683, art. 6 and Sch. 1, para. 209(a), with effect from 3 November 2008.
Reg. 5(2) omitted by SI 2008/2683, art. 6 and Sch. 1, para. 209(b), with effect from 3 November 2008.
Reg. 5(3) omitted by SI 2008/2683, art. 6 and Sch. 1, para. 209(b), with effect from 3 November 2008.
Reg. 5(4) substituted by SI 2008/2683, art. 6 and Sch. 1, para. 209(c), with effect from 3 November 2008.
In reg. 5(5), the words "treat the appeal as made in time unless the Board are" substituted for the words "grant the application unless the panel member is, or the Board are, as the case may be," by SI 2008/2683, art. 6 and Sch. 1, para. 209(d)(i), with effect from 3 November 2008.
In reg. 5(5)(a), at the end, the words "to the application" omitted by SI 2008/2683, art. 6 and Sch. 1, para. 209(d)(ii), with effect from 3 November 2008.
In reg. 5(5)(b), at the end, the words "to the application" omitted by SI 2008/2683, art. 6 and Sch. 1, para. 209(d)(ii), with effect from 3 November 2008.
In reg. 5(6), "appellant" substituted by SI 2008/2683, art. 6 and Sch. 1, para. 209(e), with effect from 3 November 2008.
In reg. 5(7), the words "treat the appeal as made in time" substituted by SI 2008/2683, art. 6 and Sch. 1, para. 209(f)(i), with effect from 3 November 2008.
In reg. 5(7), the words "submission of the notice of appeal, the more compelling should be the special circumstances." substituted by SI 2008/2683, art. 6 and Sch. 1, para. 209(f)(ii), with effect from 3 November 2008.
In reg. 5(8), the words "treat the appeal as made in time" substituted by SI 2008/2683, art. 6 and Sch. 1, para. 209(g)(i), with effect from 3 November 2008.
In reg. 5(8)(b), "the Upper Tribunal" substituted by SI 2008/2683, art. 6 and Sch. 1, para. 209(g)(ii), with effect from 3 November 2008.

MAKING OF AN APPLICATION FOR AN EXTENSION OF TIME

6 [Omitted by SI 2008/2683, art. 6 and Sch. 1, para. 210.]

History – Reg. 6 omitted by SI 2008/2683, art. 6 and Sch. 1, para. 210, with effect from 3 November 2008.

MAKING AN APPLICATION FOR A DIRECTION

7 [Omitted by SI 2008/2683, art. 6 and Sch. 1, para. 210.]

History – Reg. 7 omitted by SI 2008/2683, art. 6 and Sch. 1, para. 210, with effect from 3 November 2008.

DEATH OF A PARTY TO AN APPEAL OR AN APPLICATION FOR A DIRECTION

8(1) In any proceedings relating to an appeal or an application for a direction, on the death of a party to those proceedings (other than the Board) the following persons may proceed with the appeal or application for a direction in the place of such deceased party–

(a) where the proceedings are in relation to a single claim, the personal representatives of the person who has died;

(b) where the proceedings are in relation to a joint claim, where only one of the persons by whom the claim was made has died, the other person with whom the claim was made;

(c) where the proceedings are in relation to a joint claim where both the persons by whom the claim was made have died, the personal representatives of the last of them to die;

(d) for the purposes of paragraph (c), where persons have died in circumstances rendering it uncertain which of them survived the other–
  (i) their deaths shall be presumed to have occurred in order of seniority; and
  (ii) the younger shall be treated as having survived the elder.

8(2) Where there is no person mentioned in paragraphs (1)(a) to (1)(c) to proceed with the appeal or application for a direction, the Board may appoint such person as they think fit to proceed with that appeal or that application in the place of such deceased party referred to in paragraph (1).

8(3) A grant of probate, confirmation or letters of administration to the estate of the deceased party, whenever taken out, shall have no effect on an appointment made under paragraph (2).

8(4) Where a person appointed under paragraph (2) has, prior to the date of such appointment, taken any action in relation to the appeal or application for a direction on behalf of the deceased party, the effective date of appointment by the Board shall be the day immediately prior to the first day on which such action was taken.

PART 3 – APPEAL TRIBUNALS FOR TAX CREDITS

Chapter 1 – Appeal Tribunals

COMPOSITION OF APPEAL TRIBUNALS

9 [Omitted by SI 2008/2683, art. 6 and Sch. 1, para. 210.]

History – Reg. 9 omitted by SI 2008/2683, art. 6 and Sch. 1, para. 210, with effect from 3 November 2008.

ASSIGNMENT OF CLERKS TO APPEAL TRIBUNALS: FUNCTION OF CLERKS

10 [Omitted by SI 2008/2683, art. 6 and Sch. 1, para. 210.]

History – Reg. 10 omitted by SI 2008/2683, art. 6 and Sch. 1, para. 210, with effect from 3 November 2008.

Chapter 2 – Procedure in Connection with Determination of Appeals, Applications for Directions and Penalty Proceedings

CONSIDERATION AND DETERMINATION OF APPEALS, APPLICATIONS FOR A DIRECTION AND PENALTY PROCEEDINGS

11 [Omitted by SI 2008/2683, art. 6 and Sch. 1, para. 210.]

History – Reg. 11 omitted by SI 2008/2683, art. 6 and Sch. 1, para. 210, with effect from 3 November 2008.

CHOICE OF HEARING

History – Heading amended by SI 2004/3368, reg. 6(2) with effect from 21 December 2004.

12 [Omitted by SI 2008/2683, art. 6 and Sch. 1, para. 210.]

History – Reg. 12 omitted by SI 2008/2683, art. 6 and Sch. 1, para. 210, with effect from 3 November 2008.

WITHDRAWAL OF APPLICATION FOR A DIRECTION OR PENALTY PROCEEDINGS

13 [Omitted by SI 2008/2683, art. 6 and Sch. 1, para. 210.]

History – Reg. 13 omitted by SI 2008/2683, art. 6 and Sch. 1, para. 210, with effect from 3 November 2008.

NON-DISCLOSURE OF MEDICAL ADVICE OR EVIDENCE

14 [Omitted by SI 2008/2683, art. 6 and Sch. 1, para. 210.]

History – Reg. 14 omitted by SI 2008/2683, art. 6 and Sch. 1, para. 210, with effect from 3 November 2008.

SUMMONING OF WITNESSES AND ADMINISTRATION OF OATHS

15 [Omitted by SI 2008/2683, art. 6 and Sch. 1, para. 210.]

History – Reg. 15 omitted by SI 2008/2683, art. 6 and Sch. 1, para. 210, with effect from 3 November 2008.

Chapter 3 – Striking Out Appeals and Applications for a Direction

CASES WHICH MAY BE STRUCK OUT

16 [Omitted by SI 2008/2683, art. 6 and Sch. 1, para. 210.]

History – Reg. 16 omitted by SI 2008/2683, art. 6 and Sch. 1, para. 210, with effect from 3 November 2008.

REINSTATEMENT OF STRUCK OUT CASES

17 [Omitted by SI 2008/2683, art. 6 and Sch. 1, para. 210.]

History – Reg. 17 omitted by SI 2008/2683, art. 6 and Sch. 1, para. 210, with effect from 3 November 2008.

Chapter 4 – Oral Hearings

PROCEDURE AT ORAL HEARINGS

18 [Omitted by SI 2008/2683, art. 6 and Sch. 1, para. 210.]

History – Reg. 18 omitted by SI 2008/2683, art. 6 and Sch. 1, para. 210, with effect from 3 November 2008.

MANNER OF PROVIDING EXPERT ASSISTANCE

19 [Omitted by SI 2008/2683, art. 6 and Sch. 1, para. 210.]

History – Reg. 19 omitted by SI 2008/2683, art. 6 and Sch. 1, para. 210, with effect from 3 November 2008.

POSTPONEMENT AND ADJOURNMENT

20 [Omitted by SI 2008/2683, art. 6 and Sch. 1, para. 210.]

History – Reg. 20 omitted by SI 2008/2683, art. 6 and Sch. 1, para. 210, with effect from 3 November 2008.

Chapter 5 – Decisions of Appeal Tribunals and Related Matters

DECISIONS OF APPEAL TRIBUNALS

21 [Omitted by SI 2008/2683, art. 6 and Sch. 1, para. 210.]

History – Reg. 21 omitted by SI 2008/2683, art. 6 and Sch. 1, para. 210, with effect from 3 November 2008.

LATE APPLICATIONS FOR A STATEMENT OF REASONS OF TRIBUNAL DECISION

22 [Omitted by SI 2008/2683, art. 6 and Sch. 1, para. 210.]

History – Reg. 22 omitted by SI 2008/2683, art. 6 and Sch. 1, para. 210, with effect from 3 November 2008.

RECORD OF TRIBUNAL PROCEEDINGS

23 [Omitted by SI 2008/2683, art. 6 and Sch. 1, para. 210.]

History – Reg. 23 omitted by SI 2008/2683, art. 6 and Sch. 1, para. 210, with effect from 3 November 2008.

CORRECTION OF ACCIDENTAL ERRORS

24 [Omitted by SI 2008/2683, art. 6 and Sch. 1, para. 210.]

History – Reg. 24 omitted by SI 2008/2683, art. 6 and Sch. 1, para. 210, with effect from 3 November 2008.

SETTING ASIDE DECISIONS ON CERTAIN GROUNDS

25 [Omitted by SI 2008/2683, art. 6 and Sch. 1, para. 210.]

History – Reg. 25 omitted by SI 2008/2683, art. 6 and Sch. 1, para. 210, with effect from 3 November 2008.

PROVISIONS COMMON TO REGULATIONS 24 AND 25

26 [Omitted by SI 2008/2683, art. 6 and Sch. 1, para. 210.]

History – Reg. 26 omitted by SI 2008/2683, art. 6 and Sch. 1, para. 210, with effect from 3 November 2008.

SERVICE OF DECISION NOTICE BY ELECTRONIC MAIL

26A [Omitted by SI 2008/2683, art. 6 and Sch. 1, para. 210.]

History – Reg. 26A omitted by SI 2008/2683, art. 6 and Sch. 1, para. 210, with effect from 3 November 2008.

APPLICATION FOR LEAVE TO APPEAL TO A COMMISSIONER FROM A DECISION OF AN APPEAL TRIBUNAL

27 [Omitted by SI 2008/2683, art. 6 and Sch. 1, para. 210.]

History – Reg. 27 omitted by SI 2008/2683, art. 6 and Sch. 1, para. 210, with effect from 3 November 2008.

TAX CREDITS (INTEREST RATE) REGULATIONS 2003

(SI 2003/123)

Made on 28 January 2003 by the Treasury, in exercise of the powers conferred upon them by s. 37(2) and (5), 65(1) and (8) and 67 of the Tax Credits Act 2002. Operative from 18 February 2003.

CITATION AND COMMENCEMENT

1 These Regulations may be cited as the Tax Credits (Interest Rate) Regulations 2003 and shall come into force on 18th February 2003.

INTERPRETATION

2(1) In these Regulations–

"the Board" means the Commissioners of Inland Revenue;

"established rate" means–

(a) on the coming into force of these Regulations, 6.5 per cent. per annum;

(b) in relation to any date after the first reference date after the coming into force of these Regulations, the reference rate found on the immediately preceding reference date;

"operative date" means the sixth day of each month;

"reference date" means the day of each month which is the twelfth working day before the sixth day of the following month;

"tax credit" means child tax credit or, as the case may be, working tax credit, provision for which is made by the Tax Credits Act 2002;

"working day" means any day other than a non-business day within the meaning of section 92 of the Bills of Exchange Act 1882.

2(2) For the purposes of regulation 4(2) the reference rate found on a reference date is the percentage per annum found by averaging the base lending rates at close of business on that date of–

(a) Bank of Scotland;

(b) Barclays Bank plc;

(c) Lloyds Bank plc;

(d) HSBC Bank plc;

(e) National Westminster Bank plc;

(f) The Royal Bank of Scotland plc,

and, if the result is not a whole number, rounding the result to the nearest such number, with any result midway between two whole numbers rounded down.

INTEREST ON OVERPAYMENTS OF TAX CREDIT AND PENALTIES

3(1) Where the Board decide in accordance with section 37(1) of the Tax Credits Act 2002 that the whole or part of an overpayment of a tax credit which is attributable to fraud or neglect is to carry interest, the rate of interest for the purposes of section 37(2) of that Act is that prescribed by regulation 4.

3(2) The rate of interest for the purposes of section 37(5) of the Tax Credits Act 2002 (interest on a penalty under any of sections 31 to 33 of that Act) is that prescribed by regulation 4.

PRESCRIBED RATE OF INTEREST

4(1) The rate of interest which is prescribed is, subject to paragraph (2), 6.5 per cent. per annum.

4(2) Where, on a reference date after the coming into force of these Regulations, the reference rate found on that date ("RR") differs from the established rate, the rate of interest which is prescribed shall, on and after the next operative date, be the percentage per annum found by applying the formula–

$$RR + 2.5.$$

TAX CREDITS ACT 2002 (COMMENCEMENT NO. 2) ORDER 2003

(SI 2003/392)

Made on 24 February 2003 by the Treasury, in exercise of the powers conferred upon them by s. 61 and 62(2) of the Tax Credits Act 2002.

SAVINGS

3(1) Notwithstanding the commencement of section 56 of the Act (presence in the United Kingdom) by virtue of article 2 on 26th February 2003 for the purposes of making subordinate legislation relating to child benefit, the Child Benefit (Residence and Persons Abroad) Regulations 1976 and the Child Benefit (Residence and Persons Abroad) Regulations (Northern Ireland) 1976 shall continue to have effect as follows.

3(2) Except as provided in paragraphs (3) and (4), both those Regulations shall continue to have effect up to and including 6th April 2003.

3(3) Regulation 7 of both those Regulations shall continue to apply to persons referred to in sub-paragraph (c) of regulation 6(1) of both those Regulations and, to the extent applicable to that sub-paragraph, persons referred to in sub-paragraphs (d) and (e) of that regulation, whose absence begins before 7th April 2003 and continues on and after that date until–

(a) the absence ceases, or

(b) 2nd April 2006,

whichever first occurs.

3(4) Regulation 9 of, and the Schedule to, both those Regulations (modification of the Child Benefit Act 1975 and the Child Benefit (Northern Ireland) Order 1975 to take account of reciprocal agreements relating to family allowances) shall continue to have effect indefinitely.

TAX CREDITS (IMMIGRATION) REGULATIONS 2003

(SI 2003/653, as amended by SI 2005/2919, SI 2012/848, SI 2014/658 and SI 2015/669)

Made on 11 March 2003 by the Treasury, in exercise of the powers conferred upon them by s. 42 and 65(1), (3), (7) and (9) of the Tax Credits Act 2002. Operative from 6 April 2003.

CITATION AND COMMENCEMENT

1 These Regulations may be cited as the Tax Credits (Immigration) Regulations 2003 and shall come into force on 6th April 2003.

INTERPRETATION

2 In these Regulations–

"the Act" means the Tax Credits Act 2002;

"the Child Tax Credit Regulations" means the Child Tax Credit Regulations 2002;

"couple" has the meaning given by section 3(5A) of the Act;

"immigration rules" has the meaning given by section 33 of the Immigration Act 1971;

"joint claim" has the meaning given by section 3(8) of the Act;

"limited leave" has the meaning given by section 33 of the Immigration Act 1971;

"person subject to immigration control" has the meaning in section 115(9) of the Immigration and Asylum Act 1999;

"refugee" means a person who has been recorded by the Secretary of State as a refugee within the definition in Article 1 of the Convention relating to the Status of Refugees done at Geneva on 28th July 1951 as extended by Article 1(2) of the Protocol relating to the Status of Refugees done at New York on 31st January 1967;

"tax credit" refers to either child tax credit or working tax credit and references to tax credits are to both of them;

"the Working Tax Credit Regulations" means the Working Tax Credit (Entitlement and Maximum Rate) Regulations 2002.

History – In reg. 2, the definition of "couple" inserted by SI 2005/2919, reg. 7(2), with effect from 5 December 2005.
In reg. 2, the definitions of "married couple" and "unmarried couple" omitted by SI 2005/2919, reg. 7(2), with effect from 5 December 2005.

Cross references – SI 2003/742, reg. 54: modified application of reg. 2 to members of polygamous units.

EXCLUSION OF PERSONS SUBJECT TO IMMIGRATION CONTROL FROM ENTITLEMENT TO TAX CREDITS

3(1) No person is entitled to child tax credit or working tax credit while he is a person subject to immigration control, except in the following Cases, and subject to paragraphs (2) to (9).

Case 1

He is a person who–

(a) has been given leave to enter, or remain in, the United Kingdom by the Secretary of State upon the undertaking of another person or persons, pursuant to the immigration rules, to be responsible for his maintenance and accommodation, and

(b) has been resident in the United Kingdom for a period of at least 5 years commencing on or after the date of his entry into the United Kingdom, or the date on which the undertaking was given in respect of him, whichever is the later.

Case 2

He is a person who–

(a) falls within the terms of paragraph (a) of Case 1, and

(b) has been resident in the United Kingdom for less than the 5 years mentioned in paragraph (b) of Case 1,

but the person giving the undertaking has died or, where the undertaking was given by more than one person, they have all died.

Case 3

[Omitted by SI 2014/658, reg. 3.]

Case 4

Where the claim is for working tax credit, he is–

(a) a national of a state which has ratified the European Convention on Social and Medical Assistance (done in Paris on 11th December 1953) or of a state which has ratified the Council of Europe Social Charter (signed in Turin on 18th October 1961), and

(b) lawfully present in the United Kingdom.

The Case so described also applies where–

(a) the claim is for child tax credit,

(b) the award of child tax credit would be made on or after 6th April 2004, and

(c) immediately before the award is made (and as part of the transition of claimants entitled to elements of income support and income-based jobseeker's allowance, to child tax credit) the person is, or will on the making of a claim be, entitled to any of the amounts in relation to income support or income-based jobseeker's allowance which are described in section 1(3)(d) of the Act.

Case 5

Where the claim is for child tax credit, he is–

(a) a person who is lawfully working in the United Kingdom, and

(b) a national of a State with which the Community has concluded an Agreement under Article 310 of the Treaty of Amsterdam amending the Treaty on European Union, the Treaties establishing the European Communities and certain related Acts providing, in the field of social security, for the equal treatment of workers who are nationals of the signatory State and their families.

3(2) Where one member of a couple is a person subject to immigration control, and the other member is not or is within any of Cases 1 to 5 or regulation 5–

(a) the calculation of the amount of tax credit under the Act, the Child Tax Credit Regulations and the Working Tax Credit Regulations (including any second adult element or other element in respect of, or determined by reference to, that person),

(b) the method of making (or proceeding with) a joint claim by the couple, and

(c) the method of payment of the tax credit,

shall, subject to paragraph (3), be determined in the same way as if that person were not subject to such control.

3(3) Where the other member is within Case 4 or 5 or regulation 5, paragraph (2) shall only apply to the tax credit to which he (in accordance with those provisions) is entitled.

3(4) Where a person has submitted a claim for asylum as a refugee and in consequence is a person subject to immigration control, in the first instance he is not entitled to tax credits, subject to paragraphs (5) to (9).

3(5) If that person–

(a) is notified that he has been recorded by the Secretary of State as a refugee, and

(b) claims tax credit within one month of receiving that notification,

paragraphs (6) to (9) and regulation 4 shall apply to him.

3(6) He shall be treated as having claimed tax credits–

(a) on the date when he submitted his claim for asylum, and

(b) on every 6th April (if any) intervening between the date in sub-paragraph (a) and the date of the claim referred to in paragraph (5)(b),

rather than on the date on which he makes the claim referred to in paragraph (5)(b).

3(7) Regulations 7, 7A and 8 of the Tax Credits (Claims and Notifications) Regulations 2002 shall not apply to claims treated as made by virtue of paragraph (6).

3(8) He shall have his claims for tax credits determined as if he had been recorded as a refugee on the date when he submitted his claim for asylum.

3(9) The amount of support provided under–

(a) section 95 or 98 of the Immigration and Asylum Act 1999,

(b) regulations made under Schedule 9 to that Act, by the Secretary of State in respect of essential living needs of the claimant and his dependants (if any), or

(c) regulations made under paragraph 3 of Schedule 8 to that Act,

(after allowing for any deduction for that amount under regulation 21ZB(3) of the Income Support (General) Regulations 1987) shall be deducted from any award of tax credits due to the claimant by virtue of paragraphs (6) and (8).

History – In reg. 3(1), the entry "Case 3" omitted by SI 2014/658, reg. 3, with effect from 6 April 2014.
In reg. 3(2), the words "married couple or unmarried" omitted by SI 2005/2919, reg. 7(3), with effect from 5 December 2005.
In reg. 3(5)(b), the words "one month" substituted for "3 months" by SI 2012/848, reg. 7, with effect from 6 April 2012.
In reg. 3(7), the words "Regulations 7, 7A and 8" substituted for "Regulations 7 and 8" by SI 2015/699, reg. 5, with effect from 6 April 2015.

Cross references – SI 2003/742, reg. 55: modified application of reg. 3 to members of polygamous units.

HMRC Manuals – TCTM 02104: lists countries which have ratified the agreements referred to in Cases 4 and 5 of reg. 3(1).

MODIFICATIONS OF PART 1 OF THE ACT FOR REFUGEES WHOSE ASYLUM CLAIMS HAVE BEEN ACCEPTED

4(1) For the purposes of claims falling within paragraph (2), Part 1 of the Act shall apply subject to the modifications set out in paragraphs (3) to (5).

4(2) A claim falls within this paragraph if it is a claim for tax credits which a person is treated as having made by virtue of regulation 3(6), other than a claim which he is treated as having made in the tax year in which he made his claim under regulation 3(5).

4(3) Omit sections 14 to 17 (initial decisions, revised decisions and final notices).

4(4) In section 18 (decisions after final notices)–

(a) in subsection (1) for "After giving a notice under section 17" substitute "In relation to each claim for a tax credit made by a person or persons for the whole or part of a tax year";

(b) omit subsections (2) to (9);

(c) for subsection (10) substitute–

"**18(10)** Before making their decision the Board may by notice–

(a) require the person, or either or both of the persons, by whom the claim is made to provide any information or evidence which the Board consider they may need for making their decision, or

(b) require any person of a prescribed description to provide any information or evidence of a prescribed description which the Board consider they may need for that purpose,

by the date specified in the notice.";

(d) in subsection (11) omit–

(i) "any revision under subsection (5) or (9) and";

(ii) paragraph (a);

(iii) in paragraph (b), "in any other case,".

4(5) In section 19 (enquiries)–

(a) in subsection (4), for paragraphs (a) and (b) substitute

"one year after that decision or, if–

(a) the person, or either of the persons, to whom the enquiry relates is required by section 8 of the Taxes Management Act 1970 to make a return, and

(b) the return becomes final on a day more than one year after that decision,

with that day (or, if both of the persons are so required and their returns become final on different days, with the later of those days).";

(b) in subsection (5) omit paragraph (a) and, in paragraph (b) "in any other case,";

(c) omit subsection (6).

Cross references – SI 2003/742, reg. 56: modified application of reg. 4 to members of polygamous units.

TRANSITIONAL RELIEF – CLAIMANTS MOVING FROM INCOME SUPPORT AND INCOME-BASED JOBSEEKER'S ALLOWANCE TO CHILD TAX CREDIT

5 In relation to child tax credit, a person is not treated for the purposes of these Regulations as subject to immigration control where–

(a) the award of child tax credit would be made on or after 6th April 2004;

(b) immediately before the award of child tax credit is made, he is, or will on the making of a claim be, entitled to any of the amounts in relation to income support or income-based jobseeker's allowance which are described in section 1(3)(d) of the Act; and

(c) he is a person who, immediately before the award of child tax credit is made–

(i) was receiving or entitled to income support by virtue of regulation 12(1) of the Social Security (Persons From Abroad) Miscellaneous Amendments Regulations 1996, and his claim for asylum has not been recorded by the Secretary of State as having been decided (other than on appeal) or abandoned; or

(ii) was receiving or entitled to income support or income-based jobseeker's allowance by virtue of regulation 12(3) of the Social Security (Immigration and Asylum) Consequential Amendments Regulations 2000, and his claim for asylum has not been so recorded as having been decided (other than on appeal) or abandoned.

TAX CREDITS (RESIDENCE) REGULATIONS 2003

(SI 2003/654 as amended by SI 2004/1243, SI 2005/2919, SI 2006/766, SI 2012/848, SI 2012/2612, SI 2014/1230 and SI 2014/1511)

Made on 11 March 2003 by the Treasury, in exercise of the powers conferred upon them by s. 3(7) and 65(1), (7) and (9) of the Tax Credits Act 2002. Operative from 6 April 2003.

HMRC Manuals – TCTM 02003: 'a person is ordinarily resident if they are normally residing in the United Kingdom (apart from temporary or occasional absences), and their residence here has been adopted voluntarily and for settled purposes as part of the regular order of their life for the time being.' Examples of 'relevant factors' in determining whether a person has come to live in the UK 'as part of the regular order of their life for the time being'.

Ibid.: a person who is in the UK as a result of their 'deportation, expulsion or some other legal form of compulsory removal from another country' may nevertheless be ordinary resident in the UK.

CITATION AND COMMENCEMENT

1 These Regulations may be cited as the Tax Credits (Residence) Regulations 2003 and shall come into force on 6th April 2003.

INTERPRETATION

2(1) In these Regulations–

"the Act" means the Tax Credits Act 2002;

"child" has the same meaning as it has in the Child Tax Credit Regulations 2002;

"couple" has the meaning given by section 3(5A) of the Act;

"Crown servant posted overseas" has the meaning given in regulation 5(2);

"partner" means where a person is a member of a couple, the other member of that couple;

"qualifying young person" has the meaning given in regulation 2, read with regulation 5, of the Child Tax Credit Regulations 2002;

"relative" means brother, sister, ancestor or lineal descendant.

2(2) In these Regulations a person is responsible for a child or qualifying young person if he is treated as being responsible for that child or qualifying young person in accordance with the rules contained in regulation 3 of the Child Tax Credit Regulations 2002.

History – In reg. 2(1) the definition of "couple" inserted by SI 2005/2919, reg. 8(2), with effect from 5 December 2005.

In reg. 2(1) in the definition of "partner" the words "married or unmarried" omitted by SI 2005/2919, reg. 8(2), with effect from 5 December 2005.

Cross references – SI 2003/742, reg. 52: modified application of reg. 2 to members of polygamous units.

CIRCUMSTANCES IN WHICH A PERSON IS TREATED AS NOT BEING IN THE UNITED KINGDOM

3(1) A person shall be treated as not being in the United Kingdom for the purposes of Part 1 of the Act if he is not ordinarily resident in the United Kingdom.

3(2) Paragraphs (1) and (6) do not apply to a Crown servant posted overseas or his partner.

3(3) A person who is in the United Kingdom as a result of his deportation, expulsion or other removal by compulsion of law from another country to the United Kingdom shall be treated as being ordinarily resident in the United Kingdom and paragraph (6) shall not apply.

3(4) For the purposes of working tax credit, a person shall be treated as being ordinarily resident if he is exercising in the United Kingdom his rights as a worker pursuant to Parliament and Council Regulation (EU) No 492/2011 or he is a person with a right to reside in the United Kingdom pursuant to Council Directive No 2004/38/EC.

3(5) A person shall be treated as not being in the United Kingdom for the purposes of Part 1 of the Act where he–

(a) makes a claim for child tax credit (other than being treated as making a claim, under regulation 11 or 12 of the Tax Credits (Claims and Notifications) Regulations 2002 or otherwise), on or after 1st May 2004; and

(i) does not have a right to reside in the United Kingdom; or

(ii) has a right to reside in the United Kingdom under:

– regulation 15A(1) of the Immigration (European Economic Area) Regulations 2006, but only in a case where the right exists under that regulation because the person satisfies the criteria in regulation 15A(4A) of those Regulations; or

– Article 20 of the Treaty on the Functioning of the European Union (in a case where the right to reside arises because a British citizen would otherwise be deprived of the genuine enjoyment of the substance of their rights as a European Union citizen).

3(6) Subject to paragraph (7), a person is to be treated as being in the United Kingdom for the purposes of Part 1 of the Act where he makes a claim for child tax credit only if that person has been living in the United Kingdom for 3 months before that claim plus any time taken into account by regulation 7 of the Tax Credits (Claims and Notifications) Regulations 2002 for determining for the purpose of that regulation when the claim is treated as having been made.

3(7) Paragraph (6) shall not apply where the person–

(a) most recently entered the United Kingdom before 1st July 2014;

(b) is a worker or a self-employed person in the United Kingdom for the purposes of Council Directive 2004/38/EC (rights of citizens of the European Union and their family members to move and reside freely within the territory of the Member States);

(c) retains the status of a worker or self-employed person in the United Kingdom pursuant to Article 7(3) of Council Directive 2004/38/EC;

(d) is treated as a worker in the United Kingdom pursuant to regulation 5 of the Accession of Croatia (Immigration and Worker Authorisation) Regulations 2013 (right of residence of a Croatian who is an "accession State national subject to worker authorisation");

(e) is a family member of a person referred to in sub-paragraphs (b), (c), (d) or (i);

(f) is a person to whom regulation 4 applies (persons temporarily absent from the United Kingdom) and who returns to the United Kingdom within 52 weeks starting from the first day of the temporary absence;

(g) returns to the United Kingdom after a period abroad of less than 52 weeks where immediately before departing from the United Kingdom that person had been ordinarily resident in the United Kingdom for a continuous period of 3 months;

(h) returns to the United Kingdom otherwise as a worker or self-employed person after a period abroad and where, otherwise than for a period of up to 3 months ending on the day of returning, that person has paid either Class 1 or Class 2 contributions pursuant to regulation 114, 118, 146 or 147 of the Social Security (Contributions) Regulations 2001 or pursuant to an Order in Council having effect under section 179 of the Social Security Administration Act 1992;

(i) is not a national of an EEA State and would be a worker or self-employed person in the United Kingdom for the purposes of Council Directive 2004/38/EC if that person were a national of an EEA State;

(j) is a refugee as defined in Article 1 of the Convention relating to the Status of Refugees done at Geneva on 28th July 1951, as extended by Article 1(2) of the Protocol relating to the Status of Refugees done at New York on 31st January 1967;

(k) has been granted leave, or is deemed to have been granted leave, outside the rules made under section 3(2) of the Immigration Act 1971 where that leave is–

(i) granted by the Secretary of State with recourse to public funds, or

(ii) deemed to have been granted by virtue of regulation 3 of the Displaced Persons (Temporary Protection) Regulations 2005;

(l) has been granted leave to remain in the United Kingdom by the Secretary of State pending an application for indefinite leave to remain as a victim of domestic violence;

(m) has been granted humanitarian protection by the Secretary of State under Rule 339C of Part 11 of the rules made under section 3(2) of the Immigration Act 1971.

3(8) In this regulation, a **"family member"** means a person who is defined as a family member of another person in Article 2 of Council Directive 2004/38/EC.

3(9) In this regulation, **"EEA State"**, in relation to any time, means a state which at that time is a member State, or any other state which at that time is a party to the agreement on the European Economic Area signed at Oporto on 2nd May, together with the Protocol adjusting that Agreement signed at Brussels on 17th March 1993, as modified or supplemented from time to time.

History – In reg. 3(2) the words "Paragraphs (1) and (6) do" substituted for the words "Paragraph (1) does" by SI 2014/1511, reg. 6(2), with effect from 1 July 2014.

In reg. 3(3) the words "and paragraph (6) shall not apply" inserted by SI 2014/1511, reg. 6(2), with effect from 1 July 2014.

In reg. 3(4), the words "Parliament and Council Regulation (EU) No 492/2011" substituted for the words "Council Regulation (EEC) No. 1612/68 as amended by Council Directive No 2004/38/EC, or Commission Regulation (EEC) No. 1251/70" by SI 2012/848, reg. 8, with effect from 6 April 2012.

In reg. 3(4) words "as amended by Council Directive No 2004/38/EC," inserted and words "Council Directive No 2004/38/EC." substituted for "Council Directive No. 68/360/EEC or No. 73/148/EEC." by SI 2006/766, reg. 4 with effect from 6 April 2006.

Reg. 3(5)(b) substituted by SI 2012/2612, reg. 6, with effect from 8 November 2012.

Reg. 3(5) added by SI 2004/1243, reg. 2, with effect from 1 May 2004. It will cease to have effect on 1 May 2006, unless revoked from an earlier date.
Reg. 3(6)–(9) inserted by SI 2014/1511, reg. 6(4), with effect from 1 July 2014.

Cross references – SI 2013/386, reg. 17(2) and Schedule, para. 46: modified application of reg. 3 in relation to the introduction of Universal Credit.
SI 2014/1230, Sch., para. 38: modified application of reg. 3(5)(a) where SI 2014/1230, reg. 12A applies (claims for universal credit).

PERSONS TEMPORARILY ABSENT FROM THE UNITED KINGDOM

4(1) A person who is ordinarily resident in the United Kingdom and is temporarily absent from the United Kingdom shall be treated as being in the United Kingdom during the first–

(a) 8 weeks of any period of absence; or

(b) 12 weeks of any period of absence where that period of absence, or any extension to that period of absence, is in connection with–

(i) the treatment of his illness or physical or mental disability;

(ii) the treatment of his partner's illness or physical or mental disability;

(iii) the death of a person who, immediately prior to the date of death, was his partner;

(iv) the death, or the treatment of the illness or physical or mental disability, of a child or qualifying young person for whom either he or his partner is, or both of them are, responsible; or

(v) the death, or the treatment of the illness or physical or mental disability, of his or his partner's relative.

4(2) A person is temporarily absent from the United Kingdom if at the beginning of the period of absence his absence is unlikely to exceed 52 weeks.

HMRC Manuals – TCTM 02004: Revenue interpretation of requirement that absence, or its extension, must be "in connection with" the death or treatment – i.e. "it is not enough for the two things simply to coincide" – although "where the extended absence coincides with the death of someone's child, partner or relative . . . it should normally be accepted that the two are connected".

CROWN SERVANTS POSTED OVERSEAS

5(1) A Crown servant posted overseas shall be treated as being in the United Kingdom.

5(2) A Crown servant posted overseas is a person performing overseas the duties of any office or employment under the Crown in right of the United Kingdom–

(a) who is, or was, immediately prior to his posting or his first of consecutive postings, ordinarily resident in the United Kingdom; or

(b) who, immediately prior to his posting or his first of consecutive postings, was in the United Kingdom in connection with that posting.

PARTNERS OF CROWN SERVANTS POSTED OVERSEAS

6(1) The partner of a Crown servant posted overseas who is accompanying the Crown servant posted overseas shall be treated as being in the United Kingdom when he is either–

(a) in the country where the Crown servant is posted, or

(b) absent from that country in accordance with regulation 4 as modified by paragraphs (3) and (4).

6(2) Regulation 4 applies to the partner of a Crown servant posted overseas with the modifications set out in paragraphs (3) and (4).

6(3) Omit the words "ordinarily resident in the United Kingdom and is".

6(4) In relation to a partner who is accompanying the Crown servant posted overseas the references to **"United Kingdom"** in the phrase "temporarily absent from the United Kingdom", in both places where it occurs, shall be construed as references to the country where the Crown servant is posted.

TRANSITIONAL PROVISION – INCOME SUPPORT AND INCOME-BASED JOBSEEKER'S ALLOWANCE

7 A person is exempt from the requirement to be ordinarily resident in the United Kingdom (which is set out in regulation 3(1)) in respect of child tax credit on and for three years after the date on which the award of child tax credit is made where–

(a) the award of child tax credit would be made on or after 6th April 2004;

(b) immediately before the award of child tax credit is made, he is, or will be on the making of a claim, entitled to any of the amounts in relation to income support and income-based jobseeker's allowance which are described in section 1(3)(d) of the Act; and

(c) he is a person to which one or more of the following provisions applies–

(i) paragraph (b) or (c) in the definition of "person from abroad" in regulation 21(3) of the Income Support (General) Regulations 1987;

(ii) paragraph (b) or (c) in the definition of "person from abroad" in regulation 85(4) of the Jobseeker's Allowance Regulations 1996;

(iii) paragraph (b) or (c) in the definition of "person from abroad" in regulation 21(3) of the Income Support (General) (Northern Ireland) Regulations 1987;

(iv) paragraph (b) or (c) in the definition of "person from abroad" in regulation 85(4) of the Jobseeker's Allowance Regulations (Northern Ireland) 1996.

TAX CREDITS (OFFICIAL ERROR) REGULATIONS 2003

(SI 2003/692, as amended by SI 2010/751)

Made on 13 March 2003 by the Commissioners of Inland Revenue, in exercise of the powers conferred upon them by s. 21 and 65(2), (3), (7) and (9) of the Tax Credits Act 2002. Operative from 6 April 2003.

CITATION AND COMMENCEMENT

1 These Regulations may be cited as the Tax Credits (Official Error) Regulations 2003 and shall come into force on 6th April 2003.

INTERPRETATION

2(1) In these Regulations–

"the Board" means the Commissioners of Inland Revenue;

"official error" means an error relating to a tax credit made by–

(a) an officer of the Board,

(b) an officer of the Department for Work and Pensions,

(c) an officer of the Department for Social Development in Northern Ireland, or

(d) a person providing services to the Board or to an authority mentioned in paragraph (b) or (c) of this definition, in connection with a tax credit or credits,

to which the claimant, or any of the claimants, or any person acting for him, or any of them, did not materially contribute, excluding any error of law which is shown to have been an error by virtue of a subsequent decision by a Social Security Commissioner or by a court;

"Social Security Commissioner" has the meaning given by section 63(13);

2(2) In these Regulations references to a section are to that section of the Tax Credits Act 2002.

History – In reg. 2(1) the definition of "tax year" omitted by SI 2010/751, reg. 12(1), with effect from 6 April 2010.

3(1) A decision under section 14(1), 15(1), 16(1), 18(1), (5), (6) or (9), 19(3) or 20(1) or (4) may be revised in favour of the person or persons to whom it relates if it is incorrect by reason of official error, subject to the following paragraphs.

3(2) In revising a decision, the officer or person in question need not consider any issue that is not raised by the application for revision by the claimant or claimants or, as the case may be, did not cause him to act on his own initiative.

3(3) A decision mentioned in paragraph (1) may be revised at any time not later than five years after the date of the decision.

History – In reg. 3(3) the words "the date of the decision" substituted for the words "the end of the tax year to which the decision relates" by SI 2010/751, reg. 12(2), with effect from 6 April 2010.

TAX CREDITS (PROVISION OF INFORMATION) (FUNCTIONS RELATING TO HEALTH) REGULATIONS 2003

(SI 2003/731, as amended by SI 2005/2919 and SI 2011/721)

Made on 14 March 2003 by the Commissioners of Inland Revenue, in exercise of the powers conferred upon them by s. 65(2) and 67 of, and para. 9(2) of Sch. 5 to, the Tax Credits Act 2002. Operative from 6 April 2003.

CITATION AND COMMENCEMENT

1 These Regulations may be cited as the Tax Credits (Provision of Information) (Functions Relating to Health) Regulations 2003 and shall come into force on 6th April 2003.

INTERPRETATION

2 In these Regulations–

"child tax credit" shall be construed in accordance with section 8 of the Tax Credits Act 2002;

"couple" has the meaning given by section 3(5A) of the Tax Credits Act 2002;

"disability element" means the disability element of working tax credit as specified in section 11(3) of the Tax Credits Act 2002;

"family" means–

(a) in the case of a joint claim for a tax credit under the Tax Credits Act 2002, the couple by whom the claim is made and any child or qualifying young person for whom at least one of them is responsible, in accordance with regulation 3 of the Child Tax Credit Regulations 2002;

(b) in the case of a single claim for a tax credit under the Tax Credits Act 2002, the claimant and any child or qualifying young person for whom he is responsible in accordance with regulation 3 of the Child Tax Credit Regulations 2002;

"qualifying family" means a family–

(a) that has a relevant income of £16,190 or less, and

(b) one member of which is a person who–

(i) is receiving child tax credit, and

(ii) is not eligible for working tax credit;

"qualifying young person" has the meaning given by regulation 2(1), read with regulation 5(3) and (4), of the Child Tax Credit Regulations 2002;

"relevant income" has the same meaning as in section 7(3) of the Tax Credits Act 2002;

"working tax credit" shall be construed in accordance with section 10 of the Tax Credits Act 2002.

History – In reg. 2 the definition of "couple" inserted by SI 2005/2919, reg. 9(2), with effect from 5 December 2005.
In reg. 2 in the definition of "family" the words "married or unmarried" omitted by SI 2005/2919, reg. 9(2), with effect from 5 December 2005.
In reg. 2, in the definition of "qualifying family" subpara. (a) and (b) substituted by SI 2011/721, reg. 4(2), with effect from 6 April 2011.

PRESCRIBED FUNCTIONS RELATING TO HEALTH

3 The following functions are prescribed for the purposes of paragraph 9 of Schedule 5 to the Tax Credits Act 2002 (provision of information by the Board of Inland Revenue for health purposes)–

(a) the issue by or on behalf of the Secretary of State, the National Assembly for Wales, the Scottish Ministers or the Department of Health, Social Services, and Public Safety in Northern Ireland of a certificate confirming that the family is a qualifying family;

(b) verification by or on behalf of the Secretary of State, the National Assembly for Wales, the Scottish Ministers or that Department at any time that a family is a qualifying family at that time;

(ba) the provision of benefits by or on behalf of the Secretary of State or the Department of Health, Social Services and Public Safety under a scheme established pursuant to section 13 of the Social Security Act 1988 or article 13 of the Social Security (Northern Ireland) Order 1988 in so far as such a scheme relates to the health of pregnant women, mothers or children.

(c) [omitted by SI 2011/721, reg. 4(2)(a);]

(d) [omitted by SI 2011/721, reg. 4(2)(a);]

(e) [omitted by SI 2011/721, reg. 4(2)(a).]

History – Reg. 3(ba) inserted by SI 2011/721, reg. 4(2)(b), with effect from 6 April 2011.
Reg. 3(c), (d) and (e) omitted by SI 2011/721, reg. 4(2)(a), with effect from 6 April 2011.

TC Statutory Instruments

TAX CREDITS (POLYGAMOUS MARRIAGES) REGULATIONS 2003

(SI 2003/742, as amended by SI 2004/762, SI 2012/848 and SI 2017/387)

Made on 14 March 2003 by the Treasury, in exercise of the powers conferred upon them by s. 3(7), 7(8) and (9), 8, 10 to 12, 42, 43 and 65(1), (3), (7) and (9) of the Tax Credits Act 2002, and the Commissioners of Inland Revenue, in exercise of the powers conferred on them by s. 4(1), 6, 24 and 65(2), (3), (7) and (9) of that Act, and of all other powers enabling them in that behalf. Operative from 6 April 2003.

CITATION, COMMENCEMENT AND EFFECT

1(1) These Regulations may be cited as the Tax Credits (Polygamous Marriages) Regulations 2003 and shall come into force on 6th April 2003, immediately after the coming into force of the Child Tax Credit (Amendment) Regulations 2003.

1(2) Regulations 22 to 56 only have effect in relation to members of polygamous units (and in the case of regulations 35 to 38, former members of such units).

INTERPRETATION

2 In these Regulations–

"the Act" means the Tax Credits Act 2002;

"polygamous couple" means a man and a woman who are married under a law which permits polygamy where–

(a) they are not separated under a court order or in circumstances in which the separation is likely to be permanent, and

(b) either of them has an additional spouse;

"polygamous unit" means–

(a) a polygamous couple, and

(b) any person who is married to either member of the polygamous couple and who is not separated from that member under a court order or in circumstances in which the separation is likely to be permanent.

MODIFICATIONS TO PART 1 OF THE ACT FOR MEMBERS OF POLYGAMOUS UNITS

3 Regulations 4 to 21 prescribe modifications to Part 1 of the Act so far as it applies to members of polygamous units.

4 In section 3–

(a) in subsection (3)(a) after "United Kingdom" insert "(and neither of whom are members of a polygamous unit)";

(b) after subsection (3)(a) insert–

"(aa) jointly by the members of a polygamous unit all of whom are aged at least sixteen and are in the United Kingdom, or";

(c) in subsection (3)(b) after "paragraph (a)" insert "or (aa)";

(d) after subsection (4)(a) insert–

"(aa) in the case of a joint claim under subsection (3)(a), if a member of the married or unmarried couple becomes a member of a polygamous unit, and

(ab) in the case of a joint claim under subsection (3)(aa), if there is any change in the persons who comprise the polygamous unit, and";

(e) after subsection (6) insert–

"**3(6A)** In this Part **"polygamous unit"** has the meaning given by regulation 2 of the Tax Credits (Polygamous Marriages) Regulations 2003.";

(f) in subsection (8), in the definition of "joint claim", after "paragraph (a)" insert "or paragraph (aa)".

5 In section 4(1)(g)–

(a) *for "member of a* married couple or an unmarried couple" substitute "or more members of a polygamous unit";

(b) for "of the married couple or unmarried couple" substitute "or members".

6 In section 7(2) for "either" substitute "any".

7 In section 8(1) for "either or both" substitute "any or all".

8 In both section 9(2)(b) and (3A) for "either or both" substitute "any or all".

History – In reg. 8, the words "both section 9(2)(b) and (3A)" substituted for the words "section 9(2)(b)" by SI 2017/387, reg. 7, with effect from 6 April 2017.

9 In section 10–

(a) in subsection (1) for "either or both" substitute "any or all".

(b) in subsection (3) for "either" wherever it appears substitute "any".

10 In section 11–

(a) in subsection (3) for "either or both" substitute "any or all";

(b) in subsection (6)(a) for "either of the persons or the two" substitute "any of the persons or all";

(c) in subsection (6)(b) for "married couple or unmarried couple" substitute "polygamous unit";

(d) omit subsection (6)(c);

(e) in both subsection (6)(d) and (e) for "either or both" substitute "any or all".

11 In both section 12(3) and (4)(a) for "either or both" substitute "any or all".

12 In section 14(2)(a) for "either or both" substitute "any or all".

13 In section 16(3)(a) for "either or both" substitute "any or all".

14 In section 17(10)(b)–

(a) for "member of a married couple or an unmarried couple" substitute "or more members of a polygamous unit";

(b) for "married couple or unmarried couple" substitute "or members".

15 In section 18(10) for "either or both" substitute "any or all".

16 In section 19–

(a) in subsection (2)(a) for "either or both" substitute "any or all";

(b) in subsection (4)(a) for "either" substitute "any" and for "both" substitute "more than one";

(c) in subsection (9) for "either" substitute "any".

17 In section 20(4)(b) for "either" (wherever it appears) substitute "any".

18 In section 24(2)–

(a) for "married couple or an unmarried couple" substitute "polygamous unit";

(b) for "whichever of them" substitute "one or more of those persons as".

19 In section 29(4) for "either or both" substitute "any or all".

20 In section 31(2)–

(a) after "another" insert "or others";

(b) for "unless subsection (3) applies" substitute "or each of them unless subsection (3) applies to the person in question".

21 In section 37(1) for "either or both" (in each place they appear) substitute "any or all".

AMENDMENTS TO THE CHILD TAX CREDIT REGULATIONS 2002

22 Amend the Child Tax Credit Regulations 2002 (for members of polygamous units only) as follows.

23 In regulation 2(1)–

(a) for the definition of "joint claim" substitute the following definition–
""**joint claim**" means a claim under section 3(3)(aa) of the Act, as inserted by regulation 4(b) of the Tax Credits (Polygamous Marriages) Regulations 2003;";

(b) insert at the appropriate place the following definition–
""**polygamous unit**" has the meaning in the Tax Credits (Polygamous Marriages) Regulations 2003;".

(c) in the definition of "step-parent", in paragraph (a) only, for "couple, the other" substitute "*polygamous unit, another*";

History – Reg. 23(c) inserted by SI 2017/387, reg. 8, with effect from 6 April 2017.

24 In regulation 3(1), in Rule 2.1., for "married couple or unmarried couple" in each place it appears substitute "polygamous unit".

25 In regulation 7–

(a) in paragraph (1)(b) for "married couple or unmarried couple" substitute "polygamous unit";

(b) in both paragraph (2)(a) and (b)(ii) for "either or both" substitute "any or all".

(c) in paragraph (2A) for "either or both" substitute "any or all".

History – In reg. 25, the words "both paragraph (2)(a) and (b)(ii)" substituted for the words "paragraph (2)(b)(ii)" by SI 2017/387, reg. 9(a), with effect from 6 April 2017.
Reg. 25(c) inserted by SI 2017/387, reg. 9(b), with effect from 6 April 2017.

25A In regulation 9–

(a) in paragraphs (1) to (5) for "either or both" (in each place they appear) substitute "any or all";

(b) in paragraph (6)(b) for "either" substitute "any";

(c) in paragraph (7) for "either or both" substitute "any or all".

History – Reg. 25A inserted by SI 2017/387, reg. 10, with effect from 6 April 2017.

25B In regulation 10(c) for "either or both" substitute "any or all".

History – Reg. 25B inserted by SI 2017/387, reg. 10, with effect from 6 April 2017.

25C In regulation 11 for "either or both" (in each place they appear) substitute "any or all";

History – Reg. 25C inserted by SI 2017/387, reg. 10, with effect from 6 April 2017.

25D In regulation 13–

(a) in paragraph (14)(a) for "either" substitute "any";

(b) in paragraph (15) for "couple" substitute "polygamous unit".

History – Reg. 25D inserted by SI 2017/387, reg. 10, with effect from 6 April 2017.

25E In regulation 14(3)(a) for "either or both" substitute "any or all".

History – Reg. 25E inserted by SI 2017/387, reg. 10, with effect from 6 April 2017.

AMENDMENTS TO THE WORKING TAX CREDIT (ENTITLEMENT AND MAXIMUM RATE) REGULATIONS 2002

26 Amend the Working Tax Credit (Entitlement and Maximum Rate) Regulations 2002 (for members of polygamous units only) as follows.

27 In regulation 2(1)–

(a) for the definition of "joint claim" substitute the following definition–
""**joint claim**" means a claim under section 3(3)(aa) of the Act (as inserted by regulation 4(b) of the Tax Credits (Polygamous Marriages) Regulations 2003);";

(b) insert at the appropriate place the following definition–
""**polygamous unit**" has the meaning in the Tax Credits (Polygamous Marriages) Regulations 2003;".

28 In regulation 3(3)–

(a) for "both members of the couple satisfy" substitute "more than one member of the polygamous unit satisfies"; and

(b) for "two such elements" substitute "one such element for each of them that satisfies those conditions".

29 In regulation 4(1) in the third variation of the Second Condition–

(a) in the introduction, for "that person's partner" substitute: "any other member of the polygamous unit"; and

(b) in paragraph (a)–

(i) for "couple" (in both places) substitute: "polygamous unit"; and

(ii) for "partner" substitute: "member of the unit".

History – Reg. 29 substituted by SI 2012/848, reg. 9, with effect from 6 April 2012.

30 In regulation 10(2)–

(a) in sub-paragraph (c) for "couple" substitute "members of the polygamous unit";

(b) in sub-paragraph (d) for "couple" substitute "unit".

31 In regulation 11–

(a) in paragraph (1) after "element" insert "(and an additional such element for each member of the polygamous unit exceeding two in number)";

(b) in paragraph (2)(c) for "neither of the claimants" substitute "no claimant";

(c) in paragraph (4) in the words preceding sub-paragraph (a) after "adult element" insert "for any claimant";

(d) in paragraph (4)(a) for "neither claimant" substitute "none of the claimants"; and

(e) in paragraph (4)(b) for "one claimant" substitute "the claimant in question".

32 In regulation 13–

(a) omit paragraph (1)(a);

(b) in paragraph (1)(b) for "married or unmarried couple where both" substitute "polygamous unit where at least two of them";

(c) in paragraph (1)(c) for the words preceding paragraph (i) substitute "is a member or are members of a polygamous unit where at least one member is engaged in qualifying remunerative work and at least one other".

(d) in paragraph (4) for "the other member of a couple" substitute "another member of the polygamous unit";

(e) in paragraph (5) for "the other member or his partner" substitute "him or another member of the polygamous unit".

33 In regulation 14–

(a) in paragraph (1) for "either or both" substitute "any or all";

(b) in paragraph (1B) for "either or both" substitute "any or all";

(c) in paragraph (5) for "a partner or by a partner" substitute "another member of the same polygamous unit or".

34 In regulation 20–

(a) in paragraph (1) for "single claimant or to a couple" substitute "polygamous unit";

(b) omit paragraph (1)(c)(i);

(c) in paragraph (1)(c)(ii) for "a couple either or both" substitute "the members of a polygamous unit, any or all of whom";

(d) in paragraph (1)(c)(iii) for "a couple" substitute "the members of a polygamous unit";

(e) omit paragraph (1)(e);

(f) omit paragraph (1)(f)(i);

(g) in paragraph (1)(f)(ii) for "couple" substitute "polygamous unit".

AMENDMENTS TO THE TAX CREDITS (DEFINITION AND CALCULATION OF INCOME) REGULATIONS 2002

35 Amend the Tax Credits (Definition and Calculation of Income) Regulations 2002 (for members or former members of polygamous units only) as follows.

36 In regulation 2 (interpretation)–

(a) in paragraph (2) in the definition of "family" for "married or unmarried couple" substitute "members of the polygamous unit";

(b) in paragraph (2) insert at the appropriate places the following definitions–
""**joint claim**" means a claim under section 3(3)(aa) of the Act, as inserted by regulation 4(b) of the Tax Credits (Polygamous Marriages) Regulations 2003;"**polygamous unit**" has the meaning in the Tax Credits (Polygamous Marriages) Regulations 2003;";

(c) in paragraph (4)(a) for the words from "a claimant's spouse" to the end substitute "another member of the same polygamous unit";

(d) in paragraph (4)(b) for the words from "claimant's former spouse" to the end substitute "person who was formerly a member with the claimant of the same polygamous unit".

37 In regulation 3(7) (calculation of income of claimant)–

(a) in sub-paragraph (b) for "either or both" substitute "any or all";

(b) in sub-paragraph (c) for "either or both" substitute "any or all".

38 In regulation 4(1) (employment income), in the words succeeding sub-paragraph (k) for "either" substitute "any".

AMENDMENTS TO THE TAX CREDITS (CLAIMS AND NOTIFICATIONS) REGULATIONS 2002

39 Amend the Tax Credits (Claims and Notifications) Regulations 2002 (for members of polygamous units only) as follows.

40 In regulation 2 (interpretation)–

(a) for the definition of "joint claim" substitute the following definition–
""**joint claim**" means a claim under section 3(3)(aa) of the Act, as inserted by regulation 4(b) of the Tax Credits (Polygamous Marriages) Regulations 2003;";

(b) insert at the appropriate place the following definition–
""**polygamous unit**" has the meaning in the Tax Credits (Polygamous Marriages) Regulations 2003;".

41 In regulation 11(2) for "both" substitute "all of the".

42 In regulation 13–

(a) in paragraph (1) for the words from "one member" to the end substitute "one or more members of a polygamous unit is to be treated as also made by the other member or members of that unit";

(b) in paragraph (2)–

(i) for "member of a married couple or an unmarried couple" substitute "or more members of a polygamous unit";

(ii) for "both members of the couple" substitute "all the members of the unit".

43 In regulation 15–

(a) in paragraph (3) for the words from "only one" to the end substitute "one or more members of a polygamous unit die, the other member or members of the unit may proceed with the claim in the name or names of the person or persons who have died, as well as in their own name or names";

(b) in paragraph (4) for "both" (in each place it appears) substitute "all of".

44 In regulation 16–

(a) in paragraph (1) for the words from "member of a" to the end substitute "or more members of a polygamous unit die and the other member or members of the unit wish to make a joint claim for a tax credit";

(b) for paragraph (2) substitute–

"**16(2)** The survivor or survivors may make and proceed with the claim in the name of the member or members who have died as well as in his or their own names.";

(c) in paragraph (3)(a)–

(i) for "married couple or unmarried couple" substitute "polygamous unit";

(ii) add at the end "(or the earliest such date if more than one)".

45 In regulation 23(2) for "either member of the married couple or unmarried couple" substitute "any member of the polygamous unit".

46 In regulation 30(2) for "either" (in each place it appears) substitute "any".

47 In regulation 31(2)(a) for "either" substitute "any".

47A In regulation 34(3)–

(a) for "one of two joint claimants" substitute "any member of a polygamous unit"; and

(b) for "both" (in each place where it occurs) substitute "all"

History – Reg. 47A inserted by SI 2004/762, reg. 19, with effect from 6 April 2004.

AMENDMENTS TO THE TAX CREDITS (PAYMENT BY THE BOARD) REGULATIONS 2002

48 Amend the Tax Credits (Payments by the Board) Regulations 2002 (for members of polygamous units only) as follows.

49 In regulation 2 (interpretation)–

(a) omit the definitions of "married couple" and "unmarried couple";

(b) insert at the appropriate place the following definition–

"**"polygamous unit"** has the meaning in the Tax Credits (Polygamous Marriages) Regulations 2003;".

50 In regulation 3–

(a) in the heading, for "couple" substitute "polygamous unit";

(b) for paragraphs (2) to (6) substitute–

"**3(2)** There shall be established, for each particular child or qualifying young person for whom any or all of the members of the polygamous unit is or are responsible–

(a) the member of that unit who is (for the time being) identified by all the members of the unit as the main carer for that child or qualifying young person; or

(b) in default of such a member, the member of that unit who appears to the Board to be the main carer for that child or qualifying young person.

3(3) The individual element, and any disability element, of child tax credit for any child or qualifying young person shall be paid to the main carer of that child or qualifying young person.

3(4) The family element of child tax credit for any polygamous unit shall be divided (pro rata) by the number of children and qualifying young persons for whom any or all of the members of that unit is or are responsible, and the proportion so attributable to each such child or qualifying young person shall be paid to the main carer of that child or qualifying young person.

3(5) Any child care element of working tax credit shall be divided (pro rata) by the number of children referred to in paragraph (2) in respect of whom relevant child care charges are paid, and the proportion so attributable to each such child shall be paid to the main carer of that child.

3(6) In this regulation–

"child" has the meaning given by the Child Tax Credit Regulations 2002;

"qualifying young person" has the meaning given by those Regulations; and

"relevant child care charges" has the meaning given by regulation 14(1) of the Working Tax Credit (Entitlement and Maximum Rate) Regulations 2002."

History – In reg. 50(3), the words ", and any disability element," inserted by SI 2017/387, reg. 11, with effect from 6 April 2017.

AMENDMENTS TO THE TAX CREDITS (RESIDENCE) REGULATIONS 2003

51 Amend the Tax Credits (Residence) Regulations 2003 (for members of polygamous units only) as follows.

52 In regulation 2 (Interpretation)–

(a) in the definition of "partner" for the words from "married" to the end substitute "polygamous unit, any other member of that unit";

(b) insert at the appropriate place the following definition–
""**polygamous unit"** has the meaning in the Tax Credits (Polygamous Marriages) Regulations 2003;".

AMENDMENTS TO THE TAX CREDITS (IMMIGRATION) REGULATIONS 2003

53 Amend the Tax Credits (Immigration) Regulations 2003 (for members of polygamous units only) as follows.

54 In regulation 2 (Interpretation)–

(a) for the definition of "joint claim" substitute the following definition–
""**joint claim"** means a claim under section 3(3)(aa) of the Act, as inserted by regulation 4(b) of the Tax Credits (Polygamous Marriages) Regulations 2003;";

(b) insert at the appropriate place the following definition–
""**polygamous unit"** has the meaning in the Tax Credits (Polygamous Marriages) Regulations 2003;".

55 In regulation 3(2)–

(a) for the words from "married couple" to "and the other" substitute "polygamous unit is a person subject to immigration control and any other";

(b) in sub-paragraph (b) for "couple" substitute "unit".

56 In regulation 4(1) (modifications to the Tax Credits Act 2002) add at the end "(which, in the case of a claim by the members of a polygamous unit, are subject to the modifications made by regulations 4 to 21 of the Tax Credits (Polygamous Marriages) Regulations 2003)".

TAX CREDITS ACT 2002 (COMMENCEMENT NO. 4, TRANSITIONAL PROVISIONS AND SAVINGS) ORDER 2003

(SI 2003/962, as amended by SI 2005/1106, SI 2006/3369, SI 2008/3151, SI 2010/644, SI 2011/2910 and SI 2014/1848)

Made on 31 March 2003 by the Treasury, in exercise of the powers conferred upon them by s. 61 and 62(2) of the Tax Credits Act 2002.

CITATION AND INTERPRETATION

1(1) This Order may be cited as the Tax Credits Act 2002 (Commencement No. 4, Transitional Provisions and Savings) Order 2003.

1(2) In this Order–

"the Act" means the Tax Credits Act 2002;

"the 1999 Act" means the Tax Credits Act 1999; and

"the superseded tax credits" means working families' tax credit and disabled person's tax credit.

COMMENCEMENT OF PROVISIONS OF THE ACT

2(1) Subject to the provisions of articles 3 and 4 (savings and transitional provisions), the provisions of the Act specified in this article shall come into force in accordance with the following paragraphs of this article.

2(2) Section 47 (consequential amendments), so far as it relates to paragraphs 4 to 7 of Schedule 3, shall come into force on 1st April 2003.

2(3) The following provisions of the Act shall come into force on 6th April 2003–

(a) section 1(3)(a) and (f) (abolition of children's tax credit under section 257AA of the Income and Corporation Taxes Act 1988 and employment credit);

(b) section 47, so far as it relates to the provisions of Schedule 3 specified in sub-paragraph (d);

(c) section 60 (repeals), so far as it relates to the provisions of Schedule 6 specified in sub-paragraph (e);

(d) in Schedule 3 (consequential amendments)–

(i) paragraphs 1 to 3,

(ii) paragraphs 8 and 9, and

(iii) paragraphs 13 to 59; and

(b) in Schedule 6, the entries relating to the enactments specified in column 1 of Schedule 1 to this Order to the extent shown in column 2 of that Schedule.

2(4) The following provisions of the Act shall come into force on 8th April 2003–

(a) section 1(3)(b) and (c) (abolition of working families' tax credit and disabled person's tax credit);

(b) section 47 so far as concerns the provisions of Schedule 3 mentioned in this paragraph;

(c) section 60 so far as concerns the entries in Schedule 6 referred to in sub-paragraph (e);

(d) paragraphs 10 to 12 of Schedule 3 to the Act; and

(e) in Schedule 6 to the Act, the entries relating to the enactments specified in column 1 of Schedule 2 to this Order to the extent shown in column 2 of that Schedule.

2(5) [Revoked by SI 2014/1848, art. 2.]

History – Art. 2(5) revoked by SI 2014/1848, art. 2, with effect from 14 July 2014.

SAVINGS

3(1) This article applies to any claim for either of the superseded tax credits made–

(a) on or before 6th July 2003; and

(b) in respect of a period ending on or before 7th April 2003.

Such a claim is referred to in the following provisions of this article as **"a relevant claim"**.

3(2) Notwithstanding the commencement of the repeals specified in paragraph (6)–

(a) a relevant claim may be made, inquired into by an officer of the Board, or decided by an officer of the Board; and

(b) a decision of an officer of the Board on a relevant claim may be–
(i) revised,
(ii) superseded, or
(iii) the subject of an appeal,
in accordance with the provisions specified in paragraph (3) as if the repeals specified in paragraph (6) had not taken place.

3(3) The provisions specified are–
(a) Chapter 2 of Part 1 of the Social Security Act 1998;
(b) in Northern Ireland, Chapter II of Part II of the Social Security (Northern Ireland) Order 1998; and
(c) regulations under the provisions mentioned in sub-paragraphs (a) and (b), as applied for the purposes of the superseded tax credits by section 21 or 23 of the 1999 Act (as the case may be).

3(4) Notwithstanding the commencement of the repeals specified in paragraph (6), payment of a superseded tax credit may be made on or after 8th April 2003 in pursuance of a decision of an officer of the Board on a relevant claim (including such a decision as revised, superseded or varied on appeal).

3(5) Notwithstanding the commencement of the repeals specified in paragraph (6)–
(a) an officer of the Board may make any decision in respect of an overpayment of a superseded tax credit, the recovery of such an overpayment, or the imposition of any penalty in respect of a superseded tax credit which he might have made but for the repeal in question, and
(b) the like consequences shall flow from the decision mentioned in sub-paragraph (a), including any right of appeal, as would have flowed but for the repeal in question.

3(6) The repeals specified in this paragraph are those contained in Schedule 6 to the Act relating to–
(a) the 1999 Act, other than section 6;
(b) sections 122(1), 123(1), 128, 129 and 135(5) of the Social Security Contributions and Benefits Act 1992;
(c) sections 5(2), 11, 71(11), 121DA(1), 124(2), 154(2), 163(2), 179(5), and 191 of the Social Security Administration Act;
(d) sections 121(1), 122(1), 127, 128 and 131(5) of the Social Security Contributions and Benefits (Northern Ireland) Act 1992; and
(e) sections 5(2), 9, 69(11), 115CA(1), 134(2), 155(5) and 167(1) of the Social Security Administration (Northern Ireland) Act 1992.

4 Notwithstanding the repeal in Schedule 6 of words in section 84 of the Finance Act 2000, section 84 of that Act shall apply to a payment of an employment credit made on or after 6th April 2003 as if the repeal had not occurred.

TRANSITIONAL PROVISIONS

5(1) If a claim has been made for a tax credit under the Act by two (or more) persons, at least one of whom was in receipt of either or both of the superseded tax credits immediately before the repeal of the 1999 Act, the Board may make any payment of a tax credit, due to them under the Act on or before 5th October 2003, to either or any of them, notwithstanding any provision of the Tax Credits (Payment by Employers) Regulations 2002 or the Working Tax Credit (Payment by the Board) Regulations 2002.

5(2) In respect of a person who claims the higher rate of short-term incapacity benefit, or long term incapacity benefit on or before 6th April 2005 section 30C of the Social Security Contributions and Benefits Act 1992 and section 30C of the Social Security Contributions and Benefits (Northern Ireland) Act 1992 shall have effect as if, after subsection (5A) there were inserted–

> "**30C(5B)** A person also satisfies the relevant tax credit conditions on any day before 7th April 2003 if that day falls within a week for which he is entitled to a disabled person's tax credit.".

5(3) *In respect of a person who claims incapacity benefit on or before 6th April 2005 under section 40 or 41 of either the Social Security Contributions and Benefits Act 1992 or the Social Security Contributions and Benefits (Northern Ireland) Act 1992, section 42 of the respective Act shall have effect as if, after subsection (1A), there were inserted–*

> "**42(1B)** A person also satisfies the relevant tax credit conditions on any day before 7th April 2003 if that day falls within a week for which he is entitled to a disabled person's tax credit.".

5(4) [Revoked by SI 2010/644, art. 5.]

History – Art. 5(4) revoked by SI 2010/644, art. 5, with effect from 1 April 2010.

SCHEDULE 1 – PROVISIONS OF SCHEDULE 6 TO THE ACT COMING INTO FORCE ON 6TH APRIL 2003

Article 2(3)(e)

Enactment	Extent of repeal or revocation commenced
Taxes Management Act 1970	The whole entry in Schedule 6.
Income and Corporation Taxes Act 1988	The whole entry in Schedule 6.
Children Act 1989	The whole entry in Schedule 6.
Education Reform (Northern Ireland) Order 1989	The whole entry in Schedule 6.
Disability Living Allowance and Disability Working Allowance Act 1991	The whole entry in Schedule 6.
Child Support Act 1991	The whole entry in Schedule 6.
Disability Living Allowance and Disability Working Allowance (Northern Ireland) Order 1991	The whole entry in Schedule 6.
Child Support (Northern Ireland) Order 1991	The whole entry in Schedule 6.
Social Security Contributions and Benefits Act 1992	So much of the entry in Schedule 6 as concerns sections 21(5A)(b) and 45A.
Social Security Administration Act 1992	So much of the entry in Schedule 6 as concerns sections 3(3) and 189(1)
Social Security Contributions and Benefits (Northern Ireland) Act 1992	So much of the entry in Schedule 6 as concerns sections 20(1), 21(5A)(b), 30B(3), 45A, 56(1), 60(6), 61(1) and (2), 63(c) and (f)(i), 77(1), 78(4)(d), 80, 81, 89(1), 90, 91(1)(b) and Schedules 4 and 5.
Social Security Administration (Northern Ireland) Act 1992	So much of the entry in Schedule 6 as concerns section 3(3).
Local Government Finance Act 1992	The whole entry in Schedule 6.
Finance Act 1994	The whole entry in Schedule 6.
Social Security (Incapacity for Work) Act 1994	The whole entry in Schedule 6.
Social Security (Incapacity for Work) (Northern Ireland) Order 1994	The whole entry in Schedule 6.
Pensions Act 1995	The whole entry in Schedule 6.
Pensions (Northern Ireland) Order 1995	The whole entry in Schedule 6.
Employment Tribunals Act 1996	The whole entry in Schedule 6.
Employment Rights (Northern Ireland) Order 1996	The whole entry in Schedule 6.
Finance Act 1999	The whole entry in Schedule 6.
Access to Justice Act 1999	The whole entry in Schedule 6.
Welfare Reform and Pensions Act 1999	The whole entry in Schedule 6.
Welfare Reform and Pensions (Northern Ireland) Order 1999	The whole entry in Schedule 6.
Finance Act 2000	The whole entry in Schedule 6.
Finance Act 2001	The whole entry in Schedule 6.

SCHEDULE 2 – PROVISIONS OF SCHEDULE 6 TO THE ACT COMING INTO FORCE ON 8TH APRIL 2003

Article 2(4)(e)

Enactment	Extent of repeal or revocation commenced
Social Security Contributions and Benefits Act 1992	So much of the entry in Schedule 6 as relates to sections 122(1), 123(1), 128, 129 and 135(5).
Social Security Administration Act 1992	So much of the entry in Schedule 6 as relates to sections 5(2), 11, 71(11), 121DA(1), 124(2), 163(2), 179(5) and 191.

Enactment	Extent of repeal or revocation commenced
Social Security Contributions and Benefits (Northern Ireland) Act 1992	So much of the entry in Schedule 6 as relates to sections 121(1), 122(1), 127, 128 and 131(5).
Social Security Administration (Northern Ireland) Act 1992	So much of the entry in Schedule 6 as relates to sections 5(2), 9, 69(11), 115CA(1), 134(2), 155(5) and 167(1).
Jobseekers Act 1995	The whole entry in Schedule 6.
Jobseekers (Northern Ireland) Order 1995	The whole entry in Schedule 6.
Finance Act 1997	The whole entry in Schedule 6.
Social Security Act 1998	The whole entry in Schedule 6.
Tax Credits (Initial Expenditure) Act 1998	The whole entry in Schedule 6.
Social Security (Northern Ireland) Order 1998	The whole entry in Schedule 6.
Tax Credits Act 1999	The whole entry in Schedule 6, insofar as it has not already been commenced.
Employment Relations Act 1999	The whole entry in Schedule 6.
Immigration and Asylum Act 1999	The whole entry in Schedule 6.
Employment Relations (Northern Ireland) Order 1999	The whole entry in Schedule 6.
Government Resources and Accounts Act 2000	The whole entry in Schedule 6.
Social Security Fraud Act 2001	The whole entry in Schedule 6.
Social Security Fraud Act (Northern Ireland) 2001	The whole entry in Schedule 6.
Employment Act 2002	The whole entry in Schedule 6.
Criminal Injuries Compensation (Northern Ireland) Order 2002	The whole entry in Schedule 6.

TAX CREDITS (EMPLOYER PENALTY APPEALS) REGULATIONS 2003

(SI 2003/1382, as amended by SI 2009/56)

Made on 23 May 2003 by the Commissioners of Inland Revenue, in exercise of the powers conferred upon them by s. 39(6), 65(2) and (6) and 67 of the Tax Credits Act 2002, with the consent of the Lord Chancellor and the Scottish Ministers. Operative from 18 June 2003.

CITATION AND COMMENCEMENT

1 These Regulations may be cited as the Tax Credits (Employer Penalty Appeals) Regulations 2003 and shall come into force on 18th June 2003.

INTERPRETATION

2 In these Regulations–

"the Act" means the Taxes Management Act 1970; and

"employer penalty" has the meaning given in section 63(11) of the Tax Credits Act 2002.

PART 5 OF THE TAXES MANAGEMENT ACT

3 Part 5 of the Act (appeals) applies to an appeal under section 38 of the Tax Credits Act 2002 against an employer penalty subject to the modifications set out in these Regulations.

History – In reg. 3, the word "(appeals)" substituted by SI 2009/56, art. 3(2) and Sch. 2, para. 85, operative from 1 April 2009 subject to transitional and saving provisions in SI 2009/56, Sch. 3.

4 [Omitted by SI 2009/56, art. 3(2) and Sch. 2, para. 86.]

History – Reg. 4 omitted by SI 2009/56, art. 3(2) and Sch. 2, para. 86, operative from 1 April 2009 subject to transitional and saving provisions in SI 2009/56, Sch. 3. Former reg. 4 read as follows:

"**4** In section 44 of the Act (General Commissioners)–

(a) for subsection (1) substitute–

"**44(1)** Proceedings before the General Commissioners in relation to an appeal against an employer penalty (as defined in section 63(11) of the Tax Credits Act 2002) shall, subject to the provisions of this section, be brought before the General Commissioners for the division in which the employer's place of business is situated.

44(1A) In this section **"employer's place of business"** means–

(a) the place where the trade, profession, vocation or business of the employer is carried on, or

(b) if the trade, profession, vocation or business of the employer is carried on at more than one place, the head office or the place where it is mainly carried on.";

(b) for the words "under the Taxes Acts" in each place where they occur, substitute "in relation to an appeal against an employer penalty (as defined in section 63(11) of the Tax Credits Act 2002)";

(c) in subsection (4) omit ", whether by a case stated under section 56 of this Act or otherwise,"; and

(d) in subsection (5) omit "by the Taxes Acts or".".

5 [Omitted by SI 2009/56, art. 3(2) and Sch. 2, para. 86.]

History – Reg. 5 omitted by SI 2009/56, art. 3(2) and Sch. 2, para. 86, operative from 1 April 2009 subject to transitional and saving provisions in SI 2009/56, Sch. 3. Former reg. 5 read as follows:

"**5** In section 46 of the Act (General and Special Commissioners)–

(a) in subsection (1) for "or other proceedings under the Taxes Act or Part II of the Social Security Contributions (Transfer of Functions, etc) Act 1999 or by Part III of the Social Security Contributions (Transfer of Functions, etc) (Northern Ireland) Order 1999" substitute "against an employer penalty (as defined in section 63(11) of the Tax Credits Act 2002)"; and

(b) in subsection (2)–

(i) omit "in the Taxes Acts or"; and

(ii) for the words "under the Taxes Acts" substitute "in relation to an appeal against an employer penalty (as defined in section 63(11) of the Tax Credits Act 2002)".".

6 [Omitted by SI 2009/56, art. 3(2) and Sch. 2, para. 86.]

History – Reg. 6 omitted by SI 2009/56, art. 3(2) and Sch. 2, para. 86, operative from 1 April 2009 subject to transitional and saving provisions in SI 2009/56, Sch. 3.

7 In section 48 of the Act–

(a) in subsection (1) for the definition of appeal substitute–

""**appeal"** means an appeal against an employer penalty (as defined in section 63(11) of the Tax Credits Act 2002) to the tribunal;"; and

(b) omit subsection (2).

History – In reg. 7, the word "tribunal" substituted by SI 2009/56, art. 3(2) and Sch. 2, para. 87, operative from 1 April 2009 subject to transitional and saving provisions in SI 2009/56, Sch. 3.

8 [Omitted by SI 2009/56, art. 3(2) and Sch. 2, para. 88.]

History – Reg. 8 omitted by SI 2009/56, art. 3(2) and Sch. 2, para. 88, operative from 1 April 2009 subject to transitional and saving provisions in SI 2009/56, Sch. 3.

9 In section 54 of the Act–

(a) in subsection (1) for the words "discharged or cancelled" substitute "set aside" and for the words "had discharged or cancelled it" substitute "had set it aside";

(b) for the words "the inspector or other proper officer of the Crown" and the words "the inspector or other proper officer", in each place where they occur, substitute "the officer of the Board"; and

(c) omit the words "assessment or" in each place where they occur.

10 Omit section 56 of the Act.

History – Reg. 10 substituted by SI 2009/56, art. 3(2) and Sch. 2, para. 89, operative from 1 April 2009 subject to transitional and saving provisions in SI 2009/56, Sch. 3.

TAX CREDITS (PROVISION OF INFORMATION) (FUNCTIONS RELATING TO HEALTH) (NO. 2) REGULATIONS 2003

(SI 2003/1650)

Made on 25 June 2003 by the Commissioners of Inland Revenue, in exercise of the powers conferred on them by s. 65(2) and s. 67 of Tax Credits Act 2002 (footnote 1).

CITATION AND COMMENCEMENT

1(1) These Regulations may be cited as the Tax Credits (Provision of Information) (Functions Relating to Health) (No. 2) Regulations 2003 and shall come into force on 17th July 2003.

1(2) These Regulations do not extend to Northern Ireland.

PRESCRIBED FUNCTIONS RELATING TO HEALTH

2(1) The function specified in paragraph (2) is prescribed for the purposes of paragraph 9 of Schedule 6 to the Tax Credits Act 2002 (provision of information by the Board of Inland Revenue for health purposes).

2(2) The function specified in this paragraph is the conduct, by a person providing services to the Secretary of State and the Scottish Ministers, of a survey of the mental health of persons in Great Britain who are under the age of 17 on 1st September 2003.

2(3) Nothing in these Regulations limits the operation of the Tax Credits (Provision of Information Relating to Health) Regulations 2003.

TAX CREDITS (PROVISION OF INFORMATION) (FUNCTION RELATING TO EMPLOYMENT AND TRAINING) REGULATIONS 2003

(SI 2003/2041)

Made on 6 August 2003 by the Commissioners of Inland Revenue, in exercise of the powers conferred upon them by s. 65(2) and 67 of, and para. 5(2) of Sch. 5 to, the Tax Credits Act 2002. Operative from 29 August 2003.

CITATION, COMMENCEMENT AND EXTENT

1(1) These Regulations may be cited as the Tax Credits (Provision of Information) (Function Relating to Employment and Training) Regulations 2003 and shall come into force on 29th August 2003.

1(2) These Regulations do not extend to Northern Ireland.

PRESCRIBED FUNCTION RELATING TO EMPLOYMENT AND TRAINING

2(1) The function specified in paragraph (2) is prescribed for the purposes of paragraph 5 of Schedule 5 to the Tax Credits Act 2002 (provision of information by the Board of Inland Revenue for employment and training purposes).

2(2) The function specified in this paragraph is the operation of the Employment Retention and Advancement Scheme, that is to say the scheme for assisting persons to improve their job retention or career advancement, established by the Secretary of State under section 2 of the Employment and Training Act 1973.

CHILDREN ACT 1989, SECTION 17(12) REGULATIONS 2003

(SI 2003/2077)

Made on 11 August 2003 by the Treasury, in exercise of the powers conferred upon them by s. 17(12) and 104 of the Children Act 1989. Operative from 1 September 2003.

CITATION AND COMMENCEMENT

1 These Regulations may be cited as the Children Act 1989, Section 17(12) Regulations 2003 and shall come into force on 1st September 2003.

INTERPRETATION

2 In these Regulations–

"child care" has the meaning in the Working Tax Credit (Entitlement and Maximum Rate) Regulations 2002;

"relevant child care charges" has the meaning given in regulation 14(1) of those Regulations.

TREATING A PERSON AS IN RECEIPT OF WORKING TAX CREDIT OR OF ANY ELEMENT OF CHILD TAX CREDIT OTHER THAN THE FAMILY ELEMENT

3 A person shall be treated, for the purposes of Part 3 of the Children Act 1989, as in receipt of working tax credit, or of any element of child tax credit other than the family element, where–

(a) the person is in receipt of assistance under section 17 of that Act, or of a direct payment or voucher under section 17A or 17B of that Act; and

(b) that assistance consists in the provision (or a direct payment or voucher to secure the provision) of child care, the cost of which (if paid for by the person out of his own resources) would–

(i) be relevant child care charges in relation to that person, and

(ii) cause that person (in circumstances where, but for that cost, he would otherwise not be) to be entitled to working tax credit, or to any element of child tax credit other than the family element.

TAX CREDITS ACT 2002 (CHILD TAX CREDIT) (TRANSITIONAL PROVISIONS) ORDER 2003

(SI 2003/2170)

Made on 21 August 2003 by the Treasury, in exercise of the powers conferred upon them by s. 62(2) of the Tax Credits Act 2002. Operative from 22 August 2003.

CITATION AND COMMENCEMENT

1 This Order may be cited as the Tax Credits Act 2002 (Child Tax Credit) (Transitional Provisions) Order 2003 and shall come into force on 22nd August 2003.

TRANSITIONAL PROVISION

2(1) This article applies in the case of a person who throughout the period beginning on 22nd August 2003 and ending on 28th September 2003 is–

(a) in receipt of income support;

(b) aged not less than 60; and

(c) responsible for a child (within the meaning of regulation 3 of the Child Tax Credit Regulations 2002).

2(2) Where this article applies to a person, he shall be treated as having made a claim for child tax credit in respect of the child for whom he is responsible as mentioned in paragraph (1)(c) of this article–

(a) on 22nd August 2003 for the purposes of enabling the Board to make an initial decision on the claim; and

(b) on the first day of the first benefit week in relation to income support beginning on or after 29th September 2003 for all other purposes.

2(3) In paragraph (2) **"benefit week"** has the same meaning–

(a) in relation to a person in Great Britain, as it bears in regulation 2(1) of the Income Support (General) Regulations 1987; and

(b) in relation to a person in Northern Ireland, as it bears in regulation 2(1) of the Income Support (General) Regulations (Northern Ireland) 1987.

TAX CREDITS (PROVISION OF INFORMATION) (EVALUATION AND STATISTICAL STUDIES) REGULATIONS 2003

(SI 2003/3308)

Made on 18 December 2003 by the Commissioners of Inland Revenue, in exercise of the powers conferred upon them by s. 65(2) and 67 of, and para. 4(2) of Sch. 5 to, the Tax Credits Act 2002. Operative from 9 January 2004.

CITATION, COMMENCEMENT AND EXTENT

1(1) These Regulations may be cited as the Tax Credits (Provision of Information) (Evaluation and Statistical Studies) Regulations 2003 and shall come into force on 9th January 2004.

1(2) These Regulations do not extend to Northern Ireland.

PURPOSES FOR WHICH INFORMATION MAY BE PROVIDED

2 The purposes of conducting evaluation and statistical studies in relation to–

(a) the education of children and young people under the age of 17; and

(b) the provision and use of child care,

are prescribed under paragraph 4 of Schedule 5 to the Tax Credits Act 2002 (provision of information by the Board of Inland Revenue for evaluation and statistical studies).

Here **"child care"** means any care provided for a child whether or not of a description prescribed for any purpose under the Act.

TAX CREDITS (PROVISION OF INFORMATION) (FUNCTIONS RELATING TO HEALTH) (SCOTLAND) REGULATIONS 2004

(SI 2004/1895)

Made on 20 July 2004 by the Commissioners of Inland Revenue, in exercise of the powers conferred upon them by s. 65(2) and 67 of, and para. 9 of Sch. 5 to, the Tax Credits Act 2002. Operative from 11 August 2004.

CITATION, COMMENCEMENT AND INTERPRETATION

1 These Regulations may be cited as the Tax Credits (Provision of Information) (Functions Relating to Health) (Scotland) Regulations 2004, shall come into force on 11th August 2004 and extend only to Scotland.

PURPOSE FOR WHICH INFORMATION MAY BE PROVIDED

2(1) The purpose of conducting surveys of the health of children and young people under the age of 17 and their families, by the Scottish Ministers or persons providing services to them, or exercising functions on behalf of them, is prescribed under paragraph 9 of Schedule 5 to the Tax Credits Act 2002 (provision of information by the Board of Inland Revenue for health purposes).

2(2) Nothing in these Regulations affects the operation of the Tax Credits (Provision of Information) (Functions Relating to Health) Regulations 2003 or the Tax Credits (Provision of Information) (Functions Relating to Health) (No. 2) Regulations 2003.

TAX CREDITS (PROVISION OF INFORMATION) (FUNCTION RELATING TO EMPLOYMENT AND TRAINING) REGULATIONS 2005

(SI 2005/66)

Made on 17 January 2005 by the Commissioners of Inland Revenue, in exercise of the powers conferred upon them by s. 65(2) and 67 of, and para. 5(2) of Sch. 5 to, the Tax Credits Act 2002. Operative from 8 February 2005.

CITATION AND COMMENCEMENT

1 These Regulations may be cited as the Tax Credits (Provision of Information) (Function Relating to Employment and Training) Regulations 2005 and shall come into force on 8th February 2005.

PRESCRIBED FUNCTION RELATING TO EMPLOYMENT AND TRAINING

2(1) The function specified in paragraph (2) is prescribed for the purposes of paragraph 5 of Schedule 5 to the Tax Credits Act 2002 (provision of information by the Board of Inland Revenue for employment and training purposes).

2(2) The function specified in this paragraph is evaluation of, and research in relation to, the employment and training programmes administered–

(a) in Great Britain, by the Department for Work and Pensions; or

(b) in Northern Ireland, the Department for Employment and Learning.

TAX CREDITS (APPROVAL OF CHILD CARE PROVIDERS) SCHEME 2005

(SI 2005/93 amended and partially revoked by SI 2007/2481)

Made on 24 January 2005 by the Secretary of State for Education and Skills, being the appropriate national authority under s. 12(6) of the Tax Credits Act 2002 and in exercise of the powers conferred on the Secretary of State by s. 12(5), (7) and (8) and 65(9) of that Act, and after consultation with the Council of Tribunals in accordance with s. 8(1) of the Tribunals and Inquiries Act 1992. Operative from 6 April 2005.

History – SI 2005/93 revoked by SI 2007/2481, with effect from 1 October 2007 except in relation to:

- any approval granted to a child care provider under that Scheme which is valid immediately before 1st October 2007; and
- any application for approval under that Scheme which has not been granted before 1st October 2007.

CITATION, COMMENCEMENT AND APPLICATION

1(1) This Scheme shall be known as the Tax Credits (Approval of Child Care Providers) Scheme 2005 and shall come into force on 6th April 2005.

1(2) This Scheme applies in relation to England.

DEFINITIONS

2 In this Scheme–

"the 1989 Act" means the Children Act 1989;

"approval body" means the body referred to in article 3;

"approval criteria" has the meaning given to it in article 7;

"child" has the meaning attributed to it by the Child Tax Credit Regulations 2002;

"domestic premises" means any premises which are wholly or mainly used as a private dwelling and **"premises"** includes any area and any vehicle;

"parent" includes a person who–

(a) has parental responsibility for a child;

(b) is a local authority foster parent in relation to a child;

(c) is a foster parent with whom a child has been placed by voluntary organisation; or

(d) fosters a child privately;

"parental responsibility" and **"fosters a child privately"** have the meanings attributed to those respective expressions by sections 3 and 66 of the 1989 Act;

"qualifying child care" has the meaning ascribed to it in article 5;

"relative" in relation to a child means a grand-parent, brother, sister, uncle or aunt (whether of the full blood or half blood or by affinity) or a step-parent;

"relevant first-aid certificate" means a certificate in respect of a course of first-aid training–

(a) which is suitable to the care of babies and children;

(b) which includes training in the following areas: dealing with emergencies; resuscitation; shock; choking; anaphylactic shock; and

(c) which has been undertaken by the applicant not more than three years before the date upon which the application for approval is made;

History – In reg. 2, the definitions of "the Tribunal" and "the Tribunal Regulations" omitted by SI 2007/2481, reg. 4(3)(a), with effect from 1 October 2007.

SPECIFIED BODY

3 The body specified for the purpose of giving approvals under this Scheme is Nestor Primecare Services Limited.

REQUIREMENTS OF THE SCHEME

4 For the purposes of regulations made under section 12 of the Tax Credits Act 2002, a person shall be a child care provider approved in accordance with this Scheme only–

(a) if he is for the time being approved by the approval body; and

(b) in respect of the provision by him of qualifying child care.

QUALIFYING CHILD CARE

5(1) Qualifying child care means care for a child provided by an individual on domestic premises for reward but does not include care referred to in paragraph (2).

5(2) Qualifying child care does not include–

(a) childminding which is subject to registration pursuant to Part 10A of the 1989 Act;

(b) child care provided wholly or mainly in the child's own home in respect of a child to whom the provider is a parent or relative; or

(c) child care provided wholly or mainly in the home of a relative of the child where such care is usually provided solely in respect of one or more child to whom the provider is a parent or relative.

APPROVED PERSON

6(1) A person shall be given approval as a child care provider under this Scheme if the approval body is satisfied that the approval criteria are met in relation to that person.

6(2) A person who has been given approval under paragraph (1) shall cease to be so approved if that approval is withdrawn by the approval body.

6(3) The approval body may withdraw an approval if satisfied that the approval criteria are no longer met in relation to that person.

APPROVAL CRITERIA

7 In relation to an application for approval as a child care provider the approval criteria are–

(a) that the applicant is 18 years of age or over;

(b) that the applicant–

(i) has obtained one of the qualifications from time to time specified in a list maintained by the Department for Education and Skills for the purpose of this article; or

(ii) has attended a basic course of training in the care of children being one specified in a list maintained by the Department for Education and Skills for the purpose of this article;

(c) that the applicant has obtained a relevant first-aid certificate; and

(d) that the applicant is not considered unsuitable to work with or have unsupervised access to children.

APPROVAL SYSTEM

8(1) The approval body shall operate a system for the determination of applications for approval made to it under this Scheme and shall make adequate arrangements to publicise the details of that system.

8(2) Without prejudice to the generality of paragraph (1), the approval system referred to in that paragraph shall in particular–

(a) provide for a procedure by which an applicant may apply for approval;

(b) set out requirements relating to the provision by an applicant of documentary or other evidence necessary to demonstrate that the approval criteria are met;

(c) provide for a procedure whereby approvals may be withdrawn;

(d) provide for the applicant to be given notice in writing in respect of a determination to grant, refuse or withdraw an approval;

(e) provide for a procedure whereby it may be ascertained whether an individual is for the time being approved under the Scheme; and

(f) provide for the keeping of appropriate records relating to applications for approvals and to the grant, refusal or withdrawal of such approvals.

8(3) The approval body shall maintain a record of those persons to whom an approval is granted for the time being under this Scheme.

8(4) The records referred to in paragraphs (2) and (3) may be kept by means of a computer.

PROVISION OF INFORMATION BY APPROVAL BODY

9 The approval body shall supply to the Commissioners of Inland Revenue such information as they may require for the discharge of any of their functions relating to working tax credit and which is information relating to the approval, or the refusal or withdrawal of approval, of persons under this Scheme.

PERIOD OF APPROVAL

10(1) An approval given under this Scheme shall state the period of its validity which shall not exceed a period of 12 months.

10(2) Nothing in this article shall prejudice the application of article 6(2).

APPEALS

11(1) Where the approval body refuses an application for the grant of an approval or withdraws an approval previously granted, an appeal shall lie to the First-tier Tribunal against that decision.

11(2) Tribunal Procedure Rules shall apply to an appeal under paragraph (1) as they apply to an appeal under section 79M of the 1989 Act.

11(3) [Omitted by SI 2007/2481, reg. 4(3)(c).]

11(4) [Omitted by SI 2007/2481, reg. 4(3)(c).]

11(5) On an appeal, the First-tier Tribunal may–

(a) confirm the refusal to grant the approval or the withdrawal of the approval;

(b) direct that the said refusal or withdrawal shall not have, or shall cease to have, effect; or

(c) direct the approval body to reconsider any decision which is the subject of the appeal.

History – In reg. 11(1) and (5), the words "First-tier Tribunal" substituted for the words "Tribunal" by SI 2007/2481, reg. 4(3)(b)(i), with effect from 1 October 2007.
Reg. 11(2) substituted by SI 2007/2481, reg. 4(3)(b)(i), with effect from 1 October 2007.
Reg. 11(3) omitted by SI 2007/2481, reg. 4(3)(c), with effect from 1 October 2007.
Reg. 11(4) omitted by SI 2007/2481, reg. 4(3)(c), with effect from 1 October 2007.

FEES

12 The approval body may charge any person seeking approval under this Scheme such reasonable fee as it shall, subject to the approval of the Secretary of State, determine.

REVOCATION AND SAVING

13(1) Subject to paragraph (2), the Tax Credit (Approval of Home Child Care Providers) Scheme 2003 (hereinafter referred to as "the 2003 Scheme") is hereby revoked.

13(2) The provisions of the 2003 Scheme shall continue to have effect to the extent necessary to give full effect to paragraph (3).

13(3) Any approval granted to any child care provider under the 2003 Scheme and which is in force on 6th April 2005 shall continue to have effect in respect of that provider under that Scheme until whichever is the earliest of–

(a) the date on which the approval is withdrawn or suspended in accordance with the 2003 Scheme;

(b) the date on which the child care provider concerned is given an approval by the approval body pursuant to article 6 of this Scheme; or

(c) 31st December 2005.

TAX CREDITS NOTIFICATION OF CHANGES OF CIRCUMSTANCES (CIVIL PARTNERSHIP) (TRANSITIONAL PROVISIONS) ORDER 2005

(SI 2005/828)

Made on 17 March 2005 by the Treasury, in exercise of the powers conferred upon them by s. 259(1) and (11) of the Civil Partnership Act 2004. Operative from 8 April 2005.

CITATION AND COMMENCEMENT

1 This Order may be cited as the Tax Credits Notification of Changes of Circumstances (Civil Partnership) (Transitional Provisions) Order 2005 and shall come into force on 8th April 2005.

MODIFICATION OF SECTION 6 OF THE TAX CREDITS ACT 2002

2(1) For the tax year 2005/06, section 6 of the Tax Credits Act 2002 (notification of changes of circumstances) shall be modified as follows.

2(2) After subsection (3) insert–

"**6(3A)** For the purposes of this section, a change of circumstances shall be treated as having occurred where by virtue of the coming into force of Part 14 of Schedule 24 to the Civil Partnership Act 2004 (amendments of the Tax Credits Act 2002) two people of the same sex are treated as a couple.

6(3B) In subsection (3A), **"couple"** has the meaning given in paragraph 144(3) of Part 14 of Schedule 24 to the Civil Partnership Act 2004.".

FIRST-TIER TRIBUNAL AND UPPER TRIBUNAL (CHAMBERS) ORDER 2008

(SI 2008/2684, as amended by SI 2009/196, SI 2009/1021, SI 2009/1590 and SI 2010/40)

Made on 13 October 2008 by the Lord Chancellor, with the concurrence of the Senior President of Tribunals, in exercise of the power conferred by s. 7(1) and (9) of the Tribunals, Courts and Enforcement Act 2007. Operative from 3 November 2008.

CITATION AND COMMENCEMENT

1 This Order may be cited as the First-tier Tribunal and Upper Tribunal (Chambers) Order 2008 and shall come into force on 3rd November 2008.

FIRST-TIER TRIBUNAL CHAMBERS

2 The First-tier Tribunal shall be organised into the following chambers–

(a) the Social Entitlement Chamber;

(b) the War Pensions and Armed Forces Compensation Chamber;

(c) the Health, Education and Social Care Chamber.

(d) the Tax Chamber.

(e) the General Regulatory Chamber.

(f) the Immigration and Asylum Chamber.

History – In art. 2(b), the "and" at the end omitted by SI 2009/196, art. 3(a), with effect from 1 April 2009, subject to transitional rules in SI 2009/196, art. 9.
Art. 2(d) inserted by SI 2009/196, art. 3(b), with effect from 1 April 2009, subject to transitional rules in SI 2009/196, art. 9.
Art. 2(e) inserted by SI 2009/1590, art. 3, with effect from 1 September 2009.
Art. 2(f) inserted by SI 2010/40, art. 7, with effect from 15 February 2010.

FUNCTIONS OF THE SOCIAL ENTITLEMENT CHAMBER

3 To the Social Entitlement Chamber are assigned all functions relating to appeals–

(a) in cases regarding support for asylum seekers, failed asylum seekers, persons designated under section 130 of the Criminal Justice and Immigration Act 2008, or the dependants of any such persons;

(b) in criminal injuries compensation cases;

(c) regarding entitlement to, payments of, or recovery or recoupment of payments of, social security benefits, child support, vaccine damage payment, health in pregnancy grant, and tax credits, with the exception of–

(ai) appeals under section 11 of the Social Security Contributions (Transfer of Functions, etc.) Act 1999 (appeals against decisions of Her Majesty's Revenue and Customs);

(i) appeals in respect of employer penalties or employer information penalties (as defined in section 63(11) and (12) of the Tax Credits Act 2002);

(ii) appeals under regulation 28(3) of the Child Trust Funds Regulations 2004;

(ca) regarding saving gateway accounts with the exception of appeals against requirements to account for an amount under regulations made under section 14 of the Saving Gateway Accounts Act 2009;

(cb) regarding child trust funds with the exception of appeals against requirements to account for an amount under regulations made under section 22(4) Child Trust Funds Act 2004 in relation to section 13 of that Act;

(d) regarding payments in consequence of diffuse mesothelioma;

(e) regarding a certificate or waiver decision in relation to NHS charges;

(f) regarding entitlement to be credited with earnings or contributions;

(g) against a decision as to whether an accident was an industrial accident.

History – Art. 3(a) substituted by SI 2009/196, art. 4(a), with effect from 1 April 2009, subject to transitional rules in SI 2009/196, art. 9. Former art. 3(a) read as follows:
"(a) in asylum support cases;".
Art. 3(c)(ai) inserted by SI 2009/1590, art. 4, with effect from 1 September 2009.
In art. 3(c), the words "and child trust funds" omitted (and the word "and" inserted after "pregnancy grant,") by SI 2010/40, art. 8(a), with effect from 18 January 2010.
In art. 3(c), the words "health in pregnancy grant," inserted by SI 2009/1021, art. 3, with effect from 1 June 2009.
In art. 3(c), the words ", with the exception of–", and art, 3(c)(i) and (ii), inserted by SI 2009/196, art. 4(b), with effect from 1 April 2009, subject to transitional rules in SI 2009/196, art. 9.
Art. 3(ca) inserted by SI 2010/40, art. 8(b), with effect from 18 January 2010.
Art. 3(cb) inserted by SI 2010/40, art. 8(b), with effect from 18 January 2010.

FUNCTIONS OF THE TAX CHAMBER

5A To the Tax Chamber are assigned all functions, except those functions assigned to the Social Entitlement Chamber by article 3 or to the Tax and Chancery Chamber by article 8, relating to–

(a) an appeal, application, reference or other proceeding in respect of a function of the Commissioners for Her Majesty's Revenue and Customs or an officer of Revenue and Customs;

(b) an appeal in respect of the exercise by the Serious Organised Crime Agency of general Revenue functions or Revenue inheritance tax functions (as defined in section 323 of the Proceeds of Crime Act 2002).

History – In art. 5A, the words "Tax and Chancery" substituted for the words "Finance and Tax" by SI 2010/40, art. 10, with effect from 6 April 2010.
Art. 5A inserted by SI 2009/196, art. 5, with effect from 1 April 2009, subject to transitional rules in SI 2009/196, art. 9.

UPPER TRIBUNAL CHAMBERS

6 The Upper Tribunal shall be organised into the following chambers–

(a) the Administrative Appeals Chamber;

(b) the Tax and Chancery Chamber;

(c) the Lands Chamber.

(d) the Immigration and Asylum Chamber of the Upper Tribunal.

History – Art. 6(b) substituted by SI 2009/1590, art. 6, with effect from 1 September 2009.
Art. 6(c) inserted by SI 2009/1021, art. 4, with effect from 1 June 2009.
Art. 6(d) inserted by SI 2010/40, art. 12, with effect from 15 February 2010.
Art. 6 substituted by SI 2009/196, art. 6, with effect from 1 April 2009, subject to transitional rules in SI 2009/196, art. 9. Former art. 6 read as follows:

"UPPER TRIBUNAL CHAMBER

6 The Upper Tribunal shall be organised as the Administrative Appeals Chamber.".

FUNCTIONS OF THE ADMINISTRATIVE APPEALS CHAMBER

7 To the Administrative Appeals Chamber are assigned all functions relating to–

(a) an appeal–

(i) against a decision made by the First-tier Tribunal, except an appeal assigned to the Tax and Chancery Chamber by article 8(a) or the Immigration and Asylum Chamber of the Upper Tribunal by article 9A(a);

(ii) under section 5 of the Pensions Appeal Tribunals Act 1943 (assessment decision) against a decision of the Pensions Appeal Tribunal in Northern Ireland established under paragraph 1(2) of Schedule 1 to the Pensions Appeal Tribunals Act 1943;

(iii) against a decision of the Pensions Appeal Tribunal in Scotland established under paragraph 1(2) of Schedule 1 to the Pensions Appeal Tribunals Act 1943;

(iv) against a decision of the Mental Health Review Tribunal for Wales established under section 65 of the Mental Health Act 1983;

(v) against a decision of the Special Educational Needs Tribunal for Wales;

(vi) under section 4 of the Safeguarding Vulnerable Groups Act 2006 (appeals);

(vii) against a decision of the Information Commissioner transferred to the Upper Tribunal from the First-tier Tribunal under Tribunal Procedure Rules;

(viii) against a decision of a traffic commissioner.

(b) an application, except an application assigned to the Tax and Chancery Chamber by article 8(e), for the Upper Tribunal–

(i) to grant the relief mentioned in section 15(1) of the Tribunal, Courts and Enforcement Act 2007 (Upper Tribunal's "judicial review" jurisdiction);

(ii) to exercise the powers of review under section 21(2) of that Act (Upper Tribunal's "judicial review" jurisdiction: Scotland).

(c) a matter referred to the Upper Tribunal by the First-tier Tribunal under section 9(5)(b) of the Tribunals, Courts and Enforcement Act 2007, except where the reference is assigned to the Tax and Chancery Chamber by article 8(d) or the Immigration and Asylum Chamber of the Upper Tribunal by article 9A(b).

(d) a determination or decision under section 4 of the Forfeiture Act 1982.

History – In art. 7(a)(i), the words "or the Immigration and Asylum Chamber of the Upper Tribunal by article 9A(a)" inserted by SI 2010/40, art. 13(a), with effect from 15 February 2010.
In art. 7(a)(i) the words "an appeal assigned to the Tax and Chancery Chamber by article 8(a)" substituted for the words "decisions made in the Tax Chamber" and art. 7(a)(vii) and (viii) inserted by SI 2009/1590, art. 7(a) and (b), with effect from 1 September 2009.

In art. 7(a)(i), the words "the First-tier Tribunal, except decisions made in the Tax Chamber" substituted for the words "a chamber of the First-tier Tribunal" by SI 2009/196, art. 7(a), with effect from 1 April 2009, subject to transitional rules in SI 2009/196, art. 9.
In art. 7(b) the words ", except an application assigned to the Tax and Chancery Chamber by article 8(e), for the Upper Tribunal" inserted by SI 2009/1590, art. 7(c), with effect from 1 September 2009.
In art. 7(c), the words "or the Immigration and Asylum Chamber of the Upper Tribunal by article 9A(b)" inserted by SI 2010/40, art. 13(b), with effect from 15 February 2010.
In art. 7(c) the words "except where the reference is assigned to the Tax and Chancery Chamber by article 8(d)" substituted for the words "unless the reference is made by the Tax Chamber" by SI 2009/1590, art. 7(d), with effect from 1 September 2009.
Art. 7(c) inserted by SI 2009/196, art. 7(b), with effect from 1 April 2009, subject to transitional rules in SI 2009/196, art. 9.
Art. 7(d) inserted by SI 2009/1590, art. 7(e), with effect from 1 September 2009.

FUNCTIONS OF THE TAX AND CHANCERY CHAMBER

8(1) To the Tax and Chancery Chamber are assigned all functions relating to–

(a) an appeal against a decision of the First-tier Tribunal made–
 (i) in the Tax Chamber; or
 (ii) in a charities case;

(aa) a reference or appeal in respect of–
 (i) a decision of the Financial Services Authority;
 (ii) a decision of the Bank of England; or
 (iii) a decision of a person relating to the assessment of any compensation or consideration under the Banking (Special Provisions) Act 2008;

(ab) a reference in respect of a decision of the Pensions Regulator;

(b) an application under paragraph 50(1)(d) of Schedule 36 to the Finance Act 2008;

(c) proceedings transferred to the Upper Tribunal under Tribunal Procedure Rules–
 (i) from the Tax Chamber of the First-tier Tribunal; or
 (ii) from the First-tier Tribunal in a charities case;

(d) a matter referred to the Upper Tribunal under section 9(5)(b) of the Tribunals, Courts and Enforcement Act 2007–
 (i) by the Tax Chamber of the First-tier Tribunal; or
 (ii) by the First-tier Tribunal in a charities case;

(e) an application for the Upper Tribunal to grant the relief mentioned in section 15(1) of the Tribunals, Courts and Enforcement Act 2007 (Upper Tribunal's "judicial review" jurisdiction), or to exercise the powers of review under section 21(2) of that Act (Upper Tribunal's "judicial review" jurisdiction: Scotland), which relates to–
 (i) a decision of the First-tier Tribunal mentioned in paragraph (a)(i) or (ii);
 (ii) a function of the Commissioners for Her Majesty's Revenue and Customs or an officer of Revenue and Customs, with the exception of any function in respect of which an appeal would be allocated to the Social Entitlement Chamber by article 3;
 (iii) the exercise by the Serious Organised Crime Agency of general Revenue functions or Revenue inheritance tax functions (as defined in section 323 of the Proceeds of Crime Act 2002), with the exception of any function in relation to which an appeal would be allocated to the Social Entitlement Chamber by article 3;
 (iv) a function of the Charity Commission, or one of the bodies mentioned in paragraph (aa) or (ab).

8(2) In this article **"a charities case"** means an appeal or application in respect of a decision, order or direction of the Charity Commission, or a reference under Schedule 1D of the Charities Act 1993.

History – Art. 8(1)(aa) and (ab) inserted by SI 2010/40, art. 14(a), with effect from 6 April 2010.
In art. 8(1)(e)(iv), the words ", or one of the bodies mentioned in paragraph (aa) or (ab)" inserted by SI 2010/40, art. 14(b), with effect from 6 April 2010.
Art. 8 substituted by SI 2009/1590, art. 8, with effect from 1 September 2009.
Former art. 8 inserted by SI 2009/196, art. 8, with effect from 1 April 2009, subject to transitional rules in SI 2009/196, art. 9.

RESOLUTION OF DOUBT OR DISPUTE AS TO CHAMBER

10 If there is any doubt or dispute as to the chamber in which a particular matter is to be dealt with, the Senior President of Tribunals may allocate that matter to the chamber which appears to the Senior President of Tribunals to be most appropriate.

History – Art. 10 inserted by SI 2009/1021, art. 5, with effect from 1 June 2009.

RE-ALLOCATION OF A CASE TO ANOTHER CHAMBER

11(1) Subject to paragraph (2), the Chamber President of the chamber to which a case has been assigned or allocated by or under this Order may allocate that case to another chamber within the same tribunal, by giving a direction to that effect.

11(2) A Chamber President may give a direction under paragraph (1) only if the Chamber President of the chamber to which the case is to be allocated has first consented to the giving of the direction.

11(3) A direction under paragraph (1) may be given at any point in the proceedings.

History – Art. 11 inserted by SI 2010/40, art. 16, with effect from 18 January 2010.

TRIBUNAL PROCEDURE (FIRST-TIER TRIBUNAL) (SOCIAL ENTITLEMENT CHAMBER) RULES 2008

(SI 2008/2685, as amended by SI 2009/274, SI 2009/1975, SI 2010/43, SI 2010/2653, SI 2011/651, SI 2012/500, SI 2012/2007, SI 2013/477, SI 2013/2067, SI 2014/514, SI 2014/2128 and SI 2015/1510)

Made on 9 October 2008 by the Tribunal Procedure Committee in exercise of the powers conferred by s. 20(2) and (3) of the Social Security Act 1998 and s. 9(3), 22 and 29(3) of, and Sch. 5 to, the Tribunals, Courts and Enforcement Act 2007. Operative from 3 November 2008.

PART 1 – INTRODUCTION

CITATION, COMMENCEMENT, APPLICATION AND INTERPRETATION

1(1) These Rules may be cited as the Tribunal Procedure (First-tier Tribunal) (Social Entitlement Chamber) Rules 2008 and come into force on 3rd November 2008.

1(2) These Rules apply to proceedings before the Social Entitlement Chamber of the First-tier Tribunal.

1(3) In these Rules–

"the 2007 Act" means the Tribunals, Courts and Enforcement Act 2007;

"appeal" includes an application under section 19(9) of the Tax Credits Act 2002;

"appellant" means a person who makes an appeal to the Tribunal, or a person substituted as an appellant under rule 9(1) (substitution of parties);

"asylum support case" means proceedings concerning the provision of support for an asylum seeker, a failed asylum seeker or a person designated under section 130 of the Criminal Justice and Immigration Act 2008 (designation), or the dependants of any such person;

"criminal injuries compensation case" means proceedings concerning the payment of compensation under a scheme made under the Criminal Injuries Compensation Act 1995 or section 47 of the Crime and Security Act 2010;

"decision maker" means the maker of a decision against which an appeal has been brought;

"dispose of proceedings" includes, unless indicated otherwise, disposing of a part of the proceedings;

"document" means anything in which information is recorded in any form, and an obligation under these Rules to provide or allow access to a document or a copy of a document for any purpose means, unless the Tribunal directs otherwise, an obligation to provide or allow access to such document or copy in a legible form or in a form which can be readily made into a legible form;

"hearing" means an oral hearing and includes a hearing conducted in whole or in part by video link, telephone or other means of instantaneous two-way electronic communication;

"legal representative" means a person who, for the purposes of the Legal Services Act 2007, is an authorised person in relation to an activity which constitutes the exercise of a right of audience or the conduct of litigation within the meaning of that Act, an advocate or solicitor in Scotland or a barrister or solicitor in Northern Ireland;

"party" means–

(a) a person who is an appellant or respondent in proceedings before the Tribunal;

(b) a person who makes a reference to the Tribunal under section 28D of the Child Support Act 1991;

(c) a person who starts proceedings before the Tribunal under paragraph 3 of Schedule 2 to the Tax Credits Act 2002; or

(d) if the proceedings have been concluded, a person who was a party under paragraph (a), (b) or (c) when the Tribunal finally disposed of all issues in the proceedings;

"practice direction" means a direction given under section 23 of the 2007 Act;

"respondent" means–

(a) in an appeal against a decision, the decision maker and any person other than the appellant who had a right of appeal against the decision;

(b) in a reference under section 28D of the Child Support Act 1991–
(i) the absent parent or non-resident parent;
(ii) the person with care; and
(iii) in Scotland, the child if the child made the application for a departure direction or a variation;
(c) in proceedings under paragraph 3 of Schedule 2 to the Tax Credits Act 2002, a person on whom it is proposed that a penalty be imposed;
(d) an affected party within the meaning of section 61(5) of the Childcare Payments Act 2014, other than an appellant; or
(e) a person substituted or added as a respondent under rule 9 (substitution and addition of parties);

"social security and child support case" means any case allocated to the Social Entitlement Chamber of the First-tier Tribunal except an asylum support case or a criminal injuries compensation case;

"Tribunal" means the First-tier Tribunal.

History – R. 1(2) substituted by SI 2010/2653, r. 5(2), with effect from 29 November 2010.
In r. 1(3), in the definition of "asylum support case", the words ", a failed asylum seeker or a person designated under section 130 of the Criminal Justice and Immigration Act 2008 (designation), or the dependants of any such person" substituted for the words "or his or her dependants" by SI 2009/274, r. 2, with effect from 1 April 2009.
In r. 1(3), in the definition of "criminal injuries compensation case", the words "or section 47 of the Crime and Security Act 2010" inserted by SI 2013/477, r. 23, with effect from 8 April 2013.
In r. 1(3), in the definition of "legal representative", the words "a person who, for the purposes of the Legal Services Act 2007, is an authorised person in relation to an activity which constitutes the exercise of a right of audience or the conduct of litigation within the meaning of that Act" substituted for the words "an authorised advocate or authorised litigator as defined by section 119(1) of the Courts and Legal Services Act 1990" by SI 2010/43, r. 3, with effect from 18 January 2010.
In r. 1(3), in the definition of "respondent", para. (cc) inserted (and the "or" before it omitted) by SI 2015/1510, r. 12, with effect from 21 August 2015.
In r. 1(3), definition of "Social Entitlement Chamber" omitted by SI 2011/651, r. 4(2)(a), with effect from 1 April 2011.
In r. 1(3), in the definition of "social security and child support case", the words "of the First-tier Tribunal" inserted by SI 2011/651, r. 4(2)(b), with effect from 1 April 2011.

OVERRIDING OBJECTIVE AND PARTIES' OBLIGATION TO CO-OPERATE WITH THE TRIBUNAL

2(1) The overriding objective of these Rules is to enable the Tribunal to deal with cases fairly and justly.

2(2) Dealing with a case fairly and justly includes–
(a) dealing with the case in ways which are proportionate to the importance of the case, the complexity of the issues, the anticipated costs and the resources of the parties;
(b) avoiding unnecessary formality and seeking flexibility in the proceedings;
(c) ensuring, so far as practicable, that the parties are able to participate fully in the proceedings;
(d) using any special expertise of the Tribunal effectively; and
(e) avoiding delay, so far as compatible with proper consideration of the issues.

2(3) The Tribunal must seek to give effect to the overriding objective when it–
(a) exercises any power under these Rules; or
(b) interprets any rule or practice direction.

2(4) Parties must–
(a) help the Tribunal to further the overriding objective; and
(b) co-operate with the Tribunal generally.

ALTERNATIVE DISPUTE RESOLUTION AND ARBITRATION

3(1) The Tribunal should seek, where appropriate–
(a) to bring to the attention of the parties the availability of any appropriate alternative procedure for the resolution of the dispute; and
(b) if the parties wish and provided that it is compatible with the overriding objective, to facilitate the use of the procedure.

3(2) Part 1 of the Arbitration Act 1996 does not apply to proceedings before the Tribunal.

PART 2 – GENERAL POWERS AND PROVISIONS

DELEGATION TO STAFF

4(1) Staff appointed under section 40(1) of the 2007 Act (tribunal staff and services) may, with the approval of the Senior President of Tribunals, carry out functions of a judicial nature permitted or required to be done by the Tribunal.

4(2) The approval referred to at paragraph (1) may apply generally to the carrying out of specified functions by members of staff of a specified description in specified circumstances.

4(3) Within 14 days after the date on which the Tribunal sends notice of a decision made by a member of staff under paragraph (1) to a party, that party may apply in writing to the Tribunal for that decision to be considered afresh by a judge.

CASE MANAGEMENT POWERS

5(1) Subject to the provisions of the 2007 Act and any other enactment, the Tribunal may regulate its own procedure.

5(2) The Tribunal may give a direction in relation to the conduct or disposal of proceedings at any time, including a direction amending, suspending or setting aside an earlier direction.

5(3) In particular, and without restricting the general powers in paragraphs (1) and (2), the Tribunal may–

(a) extend or shorten the time for complying with any rule, practice direction or direction;

(aa) [omitted by SI 2015/1510, r. 13;]

(b) consolidate or hear together two or more sets of proceedings or parts of proceedings raising common issues, or treat a case as a lead case (whether in accordance with rule 18 (lead cases) or otherwise);

(c) permit or require a party to amend a document;

(d) permit or require a party or another person to provide documents, information, evidence or submissions to the Tribunal or a party;

(e) deal with an issue in the proceedings as a preliminary issue;

(f) hold a hearing to consider any matter, including a case management issue;

(g) decide the form of any hearing;

(h) adjourn or postpone a hearing;

(i) require a party to produce a bundle for a hearing;

(j) stay (or, in Scotland, sist) proceedings;

(k) transfer proceedings to another court or tribunal if that other court or tribunal has jurisdiction in relation to the proceedings and–

(i) because of a change of circumstances since the proceedings were started, the Tribunal no longer has jurisdiction in relation to the proceedings; or

(ii) the Tribunal considers that the other court or tribunal is a more appropriate forum for the determination of the case; or

(l) suspend the effect of its own decision pending the determination by the Tribunal or the Upper Tribunal of an application for permission to appeal against, and any appeal or review of, that decision.

History – R. 5(3)(aa) omitted by SI 2015/1510, r. 13, with effect from 21 August 2015. Former r. 5(3)(aa) read as follows:
"(aa) extend the time within which an appeal must be brought under regulation 28(1) of the Child Benefit and Guardian's Allowance (Decisions and Appeals) Regulations 2003".
R. 5(3)(aa) inserted by SI 2013/2067, r. 23, with effect from 1 November 2013.

PROCEDURE FOR APPLYING FOR AND GIVING DIRECTIONS

6(1) The Tribunal may give a direction on the application of one or more of the parties or on its own initiative.

6(2) An application for a direction may be made–

(a) by sending or delivering a written application to the Tribunal; or

(b) orally during the course of a hearing.

6(3) An application for a direction must include the reason for making that application.

6(4) Unless the Tribunal considers that there is good reason not to do so, the Tribunal must send written notice of any direction to every party and to any other person affected by the direction.

6(5) If a party or any other person sent notice of the direction under paragraph (4) wishes to challenge a direction which the Tribunal has given, they may do so by applying for another direction which amends, suspends or sets aside the first direction.

FAILURE TO COMPLY WITH RULES ETC.

7(1) An irregularity resulting from a failure to comply with any requirement in these Rules, a practice direction or a direction, does not of itself render void the proceedings or any step taken in the proceedings.

7(2) If a party has failed to comply with a requirement in these Rules, a practice direction or a direction, the Tribunal may take such action as it considers just, which may include–

(a) waiving the requirement;

(b) requiring the failure to be remedied;

(c) exercising its power under rule 8 (striking out a party's case); or

(d) exercising its power under paragraph (3).

7(3) The Tribunal may refer to the Upper Tribunal, and ask the Upper Tribunal to exercise its power under section 25 of the 2007 Act in relation to, any failure by a person to comply with a requirement imposed by the Tribunal–

(a) to attend at any place for the purpose of giving evidence;

(b) otherwise to make themselves available to give evidence;

(c) to swear an oath in connection with the giving of evidence;

(d) to give evidence as a witness;

(e) to produce a document; or

(f) to facilitate the inspection of a document or any other thing (including any premises).

STRIKING OUT A PARTY'S CASE

8(1) The proceedings, or the appropriate part of them, will automatically be struck out if the appellant has failed to comply with a direction that stated that failure by a party to comply with the direction would lead to the striking out of the proceedings or that part of them.

8(2) The Tribunal must strike out the whole or a part of the proceedings if the Tribunal–

(a) does not have jurisdiction in relation to the proceedings or that part of them; and

(b) does not exercise its power under rule 5(3)(k)(i) (transfer to another court or tribunal) in relation to the proceedings or that part of them.

8(3) The Tribunal may strike out the whole or a part of the proceedings if–

(a) the appellant has failed to comply with a direction which stated that failure by the appellant to comply with the direction could lead to the striking out of the proceedings or part of them;

(b) the appellant has failed to co-operate with the Tribunal to such an extent that the Tribunal cannot deal with the proceedings fairly and justly; or

(c) the Tribunal considers there is no reasonable prospect of the appellant's case, or part of it, succeeding.

8(4) The Tribunal may not strike out the whole or a part of the proceedings under paragraph (2) or (3)(b) or (c) without first giving the appellant an opportunity to make representations in relation to the proposed striking out.

8(5) If the proceedings, or part of them, have been struck out under paragraph (1) or (3)(a), the appellant may apply for the proceedings, or part of them, to be reinstated.

8(6) An application under paragraph (5) must be made in writing and received by the Tribunal within 1 month after the date on which the Tribunal sent notification of the striking out to the appellant.

8(7) This rule applies to a respondent as it applies to an appellant except that–

(a) a reference to the striking out of the proceedings is to be read as a reference to the barring of the respondent from taking further part in the proceedings; and

(b) a reference to an application for the reinstatement of proceedings which have been struck out is to be read as a reference to an application for the lifting of the bar on the respondent from taking further part in the proceedings.

8(8) *If a respondent has been barred from* taking further part in proceedings under this rule and that bar has not been lifted, the Tribunal need not consider any response or other submission made by that respondent and may summarily determine any or all issues against that respondent.

History – In r. 8(8), the words "and may summarily determine any or all issues against that respondent" inserted by SI 2010/2653, r. 5(3), with effect from 29 November 2010.

SUBSTITUTION AND ADDITION OF PARTIES

9(1) The Tribunal may give a direction substituting a party if–

(a) the wrong person has been named as a party; or

(b) the substitution has become necessary because of a change in circumstances since the start of proceedings.

9(2) The Tribunal may give a direction adding a person to the proceedings as a respondent.

9(3) If the Tribunal gives a direction under paragraph (1) or (2) it may give such consequential directions as it considers appropriate.

NO POWER TO AWARD COSTS

10 The Tribunal may not make any order in respect of costs (or, in Scotland, expenses).

REPRESENTATIVES

11(1) A party may appoint a representative (whether a legal representative or not) to represent that party in the proceedings.

11(2) Subject to paragraph (3), if a party appoints a representative, that party (or the representative if the representative is a legal representative) must send or deliver to the Tribunal written notice of the representative's name and address.

11(3) In a case to which rule 23 (cases in which the notice of appeal is to be sent to the decision maker) applies, if the appellant (or the appellant's representative if the representative is a legal representative) provides written notification of the appellant's representative's name and address to the decision maker before the decision maker provides its response to the Tribunal, the appellant need not take any further steps in order to comply with paragraph (2).

11(4) If the Tribunal receives notice that a party has appointed a representative under paragraph (2), it must send a copy of that notice to each other party.

11(5) Anything permitted or required to be done by a party under these Rules, a practice direction or a direction may be done by the representative of that party, except signing a witness statement.

11(6) A person who receives due notice of the appointment of a representative–

(a) must provide to the representative any document which is required to be provided to the represented party, and need not provide that document to the represented party; and

(b) may assume that the representative is and remains authorised as such until they receive written notification that this is not so from the representative or the represented party.

11(7) At a hearing a party may be accompanied by another person whose name and address has not been notified under paragraph (2) or (3) but who, with the permission of the Tribunal, may act as a representative or otherwise assist in presenting the party's case at the hearing.

11(8) Paragraphs (2) to (6) do not apply to a person who accompanies a party under paragraph (7).

CALCULATING TIME

12(1) Except in asylum support cases, an act required by these Rules, a practice direction or a direction to be done on or by a particular day must be done by 5pm on that day.

12(2) If the time specified by these Rules, a practice direction or a direction for doing any act ends on a day other than a working day, the act is done in time if it is done on the next working day.

12(3) In this rule **"working day"** means any day except a Saturday or Sunday, Christmas Day, Good Friday or a bank holiday under section 1 of the Banking and Financial Dealings Act 1971.

SENDING AND DELIVERY OF DOCUMENTS

13(1) Any document to be provided to the Tribunal under these Rules, a practice direction or a direction must be–

(a) sent by pre-paid post or delivered by hand to the address specified for the proceedings;

(b) sent by fax to the number specified for the proceedings; or

(c) sent or delivered by such other method as the Tribunal may permit or direct.

13(2) Subject to paragraph (3), if a party provides a fax number, email address or other details for the electronic transmission of documents to them, that party must accept delivery of documents by that method.

13(3) If a party informs the Tribunal and all other parties that a particular form of communication (other than pre-paid post or delivery by hand) should not be used to provide documents to that party, that form of communication must not be so used.

13(4) If the Tribunal or a party sends a document to a party or the Tribunal by email or any other electronic means of communication, the recipient may request that the sender provide a hard copy of the document to the recipient. The recipient must make such a request as soon as reasonably practicable after receiving the document electronically.

13(5) The Tribunal and each party may assume that the address provided by a party or its representative is and remains the address to which documents should be sent or delivered until receiving written notification to the contrary.

USE OF DOCUMENTS AND INFORMATION

14(1) The Tribunal may make an order prohibiting the disclosure or publication of–

(a) specified documents or information relating to the proceedings; or

(b) any matter likely to lead members of the public to identify any person whom the Tribunal considers should not be identified.

14(2) The Tribunal may give a direction prohibiting the disclosure of a document or information to a person if–

(a) the Tribunal is satisfied that such disclosure would be likely to cause that person or some other person serious harm; and

(b) the Tribunal is satisfied, having regard to the interests of justice, that it is proportionate to give such a direction.

14(3) If a party ("the first party") considers that the Tribunal should give a direction under paragraph (2) prohibiting the disclosure of a document or information to another party ("the second party"), the first party must–

(a) exclude the relevant document or information from any documents that will be provided to the second party; and

(b) provide to the Tribunal the excluded document or information, and the reason for its exclusion, so that the Tribunal may decide whether the document or information should be disclosed to the second party or should be the subject of a direction under paragraph (2).

14(4) The Tribunal must conduct proceedings as appropriate in order to give effect to a direction given under paragraph (2).

14(5) If the Tribunal gives a direction under paragraph (2) which prevents disclosure to a party who has appointed a representative, the Tribunal may give a direction that the documents or information be disclosed to that representative if the Tribunal is satisfied that–

(a) disclosure to the representative would be in the interests of the party; and

(b) the representative will act in accordance with paragraph (6).

14(6) Documents or information disclosed to a representative in accordance with a direction under paragraph (5) must not be disclosed either directly or indirectly to any other person without the Tribunal's consent.

EVIDENCE AND SUBMISSIONS

15(1) Without restriction on the general powers in rule 5(1) and (2) (case management powers), the Tribunal may give directions as to–

(a) issues on which it requires evidence or submissions;

(b) the nature of the evidence or submissions it requires;

(c) whether the parties are permitted or required to provide expert evidence;

(d) any limit on the number of witnesses whose evidence a party may put forward, whether in relation to a particular issue or generally;

(e) the manner in which any evidence or submissions are to be provided, which may include a direction for them to be given–

(i) *orally at a hearing; or*

(ii) by written submissions or witness statement; and

(f) the time at which any evidence or submissions are to be provided.

15(2) The Tribunal may–
(a) admit evidence whether or not–
(i) the evidence would be admissible in a civil trial in the United Kingdom; or
(ii) the evidence was available to a previous decision maker; or
(b) exclude evidence that would otherwise be admissible where–
(i) the evidence was not provided within the time allowed by a direction or a practice direction;
(ii) the evidence was otherwise provided in a manner that did not comply with a direction or a practice direction; or
(iii) it would otherwise be unfair to admit the evidence.

15(3) The Tribunal may consent to a witness giving, or require any witness to give, evidence on oath, and may administer an oath for that purpose.

SUMMONING OR CITATION OF WITNESSES AND ORDERS TO ANSWER QUESTIONS OR PRODUCE DOCUMENTS

16(1) On the application of a party or on its own initiative, the Tribunal may–
(a) by summons (or, in Scotland, citation) require any person to attend as a witness at a hearing at the time and place specified in the summons or citation; or
(b) order any person to answer any questions or produce any documents in that person's possession or control which relate to any issue in the proceedings.

16(2) A summons or citation under paragraph (1)(a) must–
(a) give the person required to attend 14 days' notice of the hearing or such shorter period as the Tribunal may direct; and
(b) where the person is not a party, make provision for the person's necessary expenses of attendance to be paid, and state who is to pay them.

16(3) No person may be compelled to give any evidence or produce any document that the person could not be compelled to give or produce on a trial of an action in a court of law in the part of the United Kingdom where the proceedings are due to be determined.

16(4) A summons, citation or order under this rule must–
(a) state that the person on whom the requirement is imposed may apply to the Tribunal to vary or set aside the summons, citation or order, if they have not had an opportunity to object to it; and
(b) state the consequences of failure to comply with the summons, citation or order.

WITHDRAWAL

17(1) Subject to paragraph (2), a party may give notice of the withdrawal of its case, or any part of it–
(a) by sending or delivering to the Tribunal a written notice of withdrawal; or
(b) orally at a hearing.

17(2) In the circumstances described in paragraph (3), a notice of withdrawal will not take effect unless the Tribunal consents to the withdrawal.

17(3) The circumstances referred to in paragraph (2) are where a party gives notice of withdrawal–
(a) in a criminal injuries compensation case; or
(b) in a social security and child support case where the Tribunal has directed that notice of withdrawal shall take effect only with the Tribunal's consent; or
(c) at a hearing.

17(4) An application for a withdrawn case to be reinstated may be made by–
(a) the party who withdrew the case;
(b) where an appeal in a social security and child support case has been withdrawn, a respondent.

17(5) An application under paragraph (4) must be made in writing and be received by the Tribunal within 1 month after the earlier of–
(a) the date on which the applicant was sent notice under paragraph (6) that the withdrawal had taken effect; or
(b) if the applicant was present at the hearing when the case was withdrawn orally under paragraph (1)(b), the date of that hearing.

17(6) The Tribunal must notify each party in writing that a withdrawal has taken effect under this rule.

History – In r. 17(1)(a), the words "at any time before a hearing to consider the disposal of the proceedings (or, if the Tribunal disposes of the proceedings without a hearing, before that disposal)," wich appeared at the beginning omitted by SI 2013/477, r. 24(a), with effect from 8 April 2013.
In r. 17(3)(a), the words "under paragraph (1)(a)" at the beginning omitted and r. 17(b) and (c) substituted for former r. 17(3)(b) by SI 2013/477, r. 24(b) and (c), with effect from 8 April 2013.
R. 17(4) and (5) substituted by SI 2015/1510, r. 14, with effect from 21 August 2015. Former r. 17(4) and (5) read as follows:
"**17(4)** A party who has withdrawn their case may apply to the Tribunal for the case to be reinstated.
17(5) An application under paragraph (4) must be made in writing and be received by the Tribunal within 1 month after–
(a) the date on which the Tribunal received the notice under paragraph (1)(a); or
(b) the date of the hearing at which the case was withdrawn orally under paragraph (1)(b).".
In r. 17(6), the words "that a withdrawal has taken effect" substituted for the words "of an withdrawal" by SI 2013/477, r. 24(d), with effect from 8 April 2013.

LEAD CASES

18(1) This rule applies if–
(a) two or more cases have been started before the Tribunal;
(b) in each such case the Tribunal has not made a decision disposing of the proceedings; and
(c) the cases give rise to common or related issues of fact or law.
18(2) The Tribunal may give a direction–
(a) specifying one or more cases falling under paragraph (1) as a lead case or lead cases; and
(b) staying (or, in Scotland, sisting) the other cases falling under paragraph (1) ("the related cases").
18(3) When the Tribunal makes a decision in respect of the common or related issues–
(a) the Tribunal must send a copy of that decision to each party in each of the related cases; and
(b) subject to paragraph (4), that decision shall be binding on each of those parties.
18(4) Within 1 month after the date on which the Tribunal sent a copy of the decision to a party under paragraph (3)(a), that party may apply in writing for a direction that the decision does not apply to, and is not binding on the parties to, a particular related case.
18(5) The Tribunal must give directions in respect of cases which are stayed or sisted under paragraph (2)(b), providing for the disposal of or further directions in those cases.
18(6) If the lead case or cases lapse or are withdrawn before the Tribunal makes a decision in respect of the common or related issues, the Tribunal must give directions as to–
(a) whether another case or other cases are to be specified as a lead case or lead cases; and
(b) whether any direction affecting the related cases should be set aside or amended.

CONFIDENTIALITY IN SOCIAL SECURITY AND CHILD SUPPORT CASES

19(1) Paragraph (4) applies to–
(a) proceedings under the Child Support Act 1991 in the circumstances described in paragraph (2), other than an appeal against a reduced benefit decision (as defined in section 46(10)(b) of the Child Support Act 1991, as that section had effect prior to the commencement of section 15(b) of the Child Maintenance and Other Payments Act 2008);
(b) proceedings where the parties to the appeal include former joint claimants who are no longer living together in the circumstances described in paragraph (3).
19(2) The circumstances referred to in paragraph (1)(a) are that the absent parent, nonresident parent or person with care would like their address or the address of the child to be kept confidential and has given notice to that effect–
(a) in the notice of appeal or when notifying the Secretary of State or the Tribunal of any subsequent change of address; or
(b) within 14 days after an enquiry is made by the recipient of the notice of appeal or the notification referred to in sub-paragraph (a).
19(3) The circumstances referred to in paragraph (1)(b) are that one of the former joint claimants would like their address to be kept confidential and has given notice to that effect–
(a) in the notice of appeal or when notifying the decision maker or the tribunal of any subsequent change of address; or
(b) within 14 days after an enquiry is made by the recipient of the notice of appeal or the notification *referred to in sub-paragraph (a).*
19(4) Where this paragraph applies, the Secretary of State or other decision maker and the Tribunal must take appropriate steps to secure the confidentiality of the address and of any information which could reasonably be expected to enable a person to identify the address, to the extent that the address or that information is not already known to each other party.

19(5) In this rule–

"absent parent", **"non-resident parent"** and **"person with care"** have the meanings set out in section 3 of the Child Support Act 1991;

"joint claimants" means the persons who made a joint claim for a jobseeker's allowance under the Jobseekers Act 1995, a tax credit under the Tax Credits Act 2002 or in relation to whom an award of universal credit is made under Part 1 of the Welfare Reform Act 2012.

History – R. 19 and the heading preceding it substituted by SI 2014/2128, r. 35, with effect from 20 October 2014.

EXPENSES IN CRIMINAL INJURIES COMPENSATION CASES

20(1) This rule applies only to criminal injuries compensation cases.

20(2) The Tribunal may meet reasonable expenses–

(a) incurred by the appellant, or any person who attends a hearing to give evidence, in attending the hearing; or

(b) incurred by the appellant in connection with any arrangements made by the Tribunal for the inspection of the appellant's injury.

EXPENSES IN SOCIAL SECURITY AND CHILD SUPPORT CASES

21(1) This rule applies only to social security and child support cases.

21(2) The Secretary of State may pay such travelling and other allowances (including compensation for loss of remunerative time) as the Secretary of State may determine to any person required to attend a hearing in proceedings under section 20 of the Child Support Act 1991, section 12 of the Social Security Act 1998 or paragraph 6 of Schedule 7 to the Child Support, Pensions and Social Security Act 2000.

PART 3 – PROCEEDINGS BEFORE THE TRIBUNAL

Chapter 1 – Before the Hearing

CASES IN WHICH THE NOTICE OF APPEAL IS TO BE SENT TO THE TRIBUNAL

22(1) This rule applies to all cases except those to which–

(a) rule 23 (cases in which the notice of appeal is to be sent to the decision maker), or

(b) rule 26 (social security and child support cases started by reference or information in writing),

applies.

22(2) An appellant must start proceedings by sending or delivering a notice of appeal to the Tribunal so that it is received–

(a) in asylum support cases, within 3 days after the date on which the appellant received written notice of the decision being challenged;

(b) in criminal injuries compensation cases, within 90 days after the date of the decision being challenged.

(c) in appeals under the Vaccine Damage Payments Act 1979, at any time;

(d) in other cases–

(i) if mandatory reconsideration applies, within 1 month after the date on which the appellant was sent notice of the result of mandatory reconsideration;

(ii) if mandatory reconsideration does not apply, within the time specified in Schedule 1 to these Rules (time limits for providing notices of appeal in social security and child support cases where mandatory reconsideration does not apply).

22(3) The notice of appeal must be in English or Welsh, must be signed by the appellant and must state–

(a) the name and address of the appellant;

(b) the name and address of the appellant's representative (if any);

(c) an address where documents for the appellant may be sent or delivered;

(d) the name and address of any respondent other than the decision maker; and

(e) [omitted by SI 2013/477, r. 25(c);]

(f) the grounds on which the appellant relies.

TC Statutory Instruments

22(4) The appellant must provide with the notice of appeal–

(a) a copy of–

(i) the notice of the result of mandatory reconsideration, in any social security and child support case to which mandatory reconsideration applies;

(ii) the decision being challenged, in any other case;

(b) any statement of reasons for that decision that the appellant has; and

(c) any documents in support of the appellant's case which have not been supplied to the respondent;

(d) [omitted by SI 2013/477, r. 25(d).]

22(5) In asylum support cases the notice of appeal must also–

(a) state whether the appellant will require an interpreter at any hearing, and if so for which language or dialect; and

(b) state whether the appellant intends to attend or be represented at any hearing.

22(6) If the appellant provides the notice of appeal to the Tribunal later than the time required by paragraph (2) or by an extension of time allowed under rule 5(3)(a) (power to extend time)–

(a) the notice of appeal must include a request for an extension of time and the reason why the notice of appeal was not provided in time; and

(b) subject to paragraph (8) unless the Tribunal extends time for the notice of appeal under rule 5(3)(a) (power to extend time) the Tribunal must not admit the notice of appeal.

22(7) The Tribunal must send a copy of the notice of appeal and any accompanying documents to each other party–

(a) in asylum support cases, on the day that the Tribunal receives the notice of appeal, or (if that is not reasonably practicable) as soon as reasonably practicable on the following day;

(b) in all other, as soon as reasonably practicable after the Tribunal receives the notice of appeal.

22(7A) Her Majesty's Revenue and Customs must, upon receipt of the notice of appeal from the Tribunal under the Childcare Payments Act 2014, inform the Tribunal whether there are any affected parties within the meaning of section 61(5) of that Act other than the appellant and, if so, provide their names and addresses.

22(8) Where an appeal in a social security and child support case is not made within the time specified in paragraph (2)–

(a) it will be treated as having been made in time, unless the Tribunal directs otherwise, if it is made within not more than 12 months of the time specified and neither the decision maker nor any other respondent objects;

(b) the time for bringing the appeal may not be extended under rule 5(3)(a) by more than 12 months.

22(9) For the purposes of this rule, mandatory reconsideration applies where–

(a) the notice of the decision being challenged includes a statement to the effect that there is a right of appeal in relation to the decision only if the decision-maker has considered an application for the revision, reversal, review or reconsideration (as the case may be) of the decision being challenged; or

(b) the appeal is brought against a decision made by Her Majesty's Revenue and Customs.

History – R. 22(1) substituted by SI 2013/477, r. 25(a), with effect from 8 April 2013.
R. 22(2)(c) and (d) inserted by SI 2013/477, r. 25(b), with effect from 8 April 2013.
In r. 22(2)(d)(ii), the words "(time limits for providing notices of appeal in social security and child support cases where mandatory reconsideration does not apply)" substituted for the words "(time specified for providing notice of appeal)" by SI 2015/1510, r. 15(a), with effect from 21 August 2015.
In r. 22(3)(d) the words "other than the decision-maker" inserted and r. 22(3)(e) omitted by SI 2013/477, r. 25(c), with effect from 8 April 2013.
R. 22(4)(a) substituted, in r. 22(4)(b) the words "; and" substituted for the words "or can reasonably obtain" and r. 22(4)(d) and the word "; and" at the end of r. 22(4)(c) omitted by SI 2013/477, r. 25(d), with effect from 8 April 2013.
In r. 22(6), the words "or (aa)" omitted (in both places) by SI 2014/514, r. 22, with effect from 6 April 2014.
In r. 22(6), the former words "or (aa)" inserted (in both places) by SI 2013/2067, r. 25, with effect from 1 November 2013.
In r. 22(6)(b) the words "subject to paragraph (8)" inserted by SI 2013/477, r. 25(e), with effect from 8 April 2013.
In r. 22(7)(b) the words "all other" substituted for the words "criminal injuries compensation cases" by SI 2013/477, r. 25(f), with effect from 8 April 2013.
R. 22(7A) inserted by SI 2015/1510, r. 15(b), with effect from 21 August 2015.
R. 22(8) inserted by SI 2013/477, r. 25(g), with effect from 8 April 2013.
R. 22(9) substituted by SI 2015/1510, r. 15(c), with effect from 21 August 2015. Former r. 22(9) read as follows:
"*22(9) For the purposes of this rule, mandatory reconsideration* applies where the notice of the decision being challenged includes a statement to the effect that there is a right of appeal in relation to the decision only if the decision-maker has considered an application for the revision, reversal, review or reconsideration (as the case may be) of the decision being challenged.".
R. 22(9) inserted by SI 2013/477, r. 25(g), with effect from 8 April 2013.

CASES IN WHICH THE NOTICE OF APPEAL IS TO BE SENT TO THE DECISION MAKER

23(1) This rule applies to appeals under paragraph 6 of Schedule 7 to the Child Support, Pensions and Social Security Act 2000 (housing benefit and council tax benefit: revisions and appeals) or under section 22 of the Child Trust Funds Act 2004.

23(2) An appellant must start proceedings by sending or delivering a notice of appeal to the decision maker so that it is received no later than the latest of–

(a) in a housing benefit or council tax benefit case–

(i) one month after the date on which notice of the decision being challenged was sent to the appellant;

(ii) if a written statement of reasons for the decision was requested within that month, 14 days after the later of–

(aa) the end of that month; or

(ab) the date on which the written statement of reasons was provided; or

(iii) if the appellant made an application for revision of the decision under regulation 4(1)(a) of the Housing Benefit and Council Tax Benefit (Decisions and Appeals) Regulations 2001 and that application was unsuccessful, one month after the date on which notice that the decision would not be revised was sent to the appellant;

(b) in an appeal under section 22 of the Child Trust Funds Act 2004, the period of 30 days specified in section 23(1) of that Act.

23(3) If the appellant provides the notice of appeal to the decision maker later than the time required by paragraph (2)(a) the notice of appeal must include the reason why the notice of appeal was not provided in time.

23(4) Subject to paragraph (5), where an appeal is not made within the time specified in paragraph (2), it will be treated as having been made in time if neither the decision maker nor any other respondent objects.

23(5) No appeal may be made more than 12 months after the time specified in paragraph (2).

23(6) The notice of appeal must be in English or Welsh, must be signed by the appellant and must state–

(a) the name and address of the appellant;

(b) the name and address of the appellant's representative (if any);

(c) an address where documents for the appellant may be sent or delivered;

(d) details of the decision being appealed; and

(e) the grounds on which the appellant relies.

23(7) The decision maker must refer the case to the Tribunal immediately if–

(a) the appeal has been made after the time specified in paragraph (2) and the decision maker or any other respondent objects to it being treated as having been made in time; or

(b) the decision maker considers that the appeal has been made more than 12 months after the time specified in paragraph (2).

23(8) Notwithstanding rule 5(3)(a) (case management powers) and rule 7(2) (failure to comply with rules etc.), the Tribunal must not extend the time limit in paragraph (5).

History – In r. 23(1), the words "appeals under paragraph 6 of Schedule 7 to the Child Support, Pensions and Social Security Act 2000 (housing benefit and council tax benefit: revisions and appeals) or under section 22 of the Child Trust Funds Act 2004" substituted for the words "social security and child support cases in which the notice of decision being challenged informs the appellant that any appeal must be sent to the decision maker." by SI 2015/1510, r. 16(a), with effect from 21 August 2015, subject to savings provision in SI 2015/1510, r. 18 (amendments have no effect in relation to any appeal against a decision made before 6 April 2014 where the decision maker was HMRC).
R. 23(1) substituted by SI 2013/477, r. 26, with effect from 8 April 2013.
R. 23(2)(a) and (b) and the words "no later than the latest of–" before them substituted for the words "within the time specified in Schedule 1 to these Rules (time limits for providing notices of appeal to the decision maker)" by SI 2015/1510, r. 16(b), with effect from 21 August 2015, subject to savings provision in SI 2015/1510, r. 18 (amendments have no effect in relation to any appeal against a decision made before 6 April 2014 where the decision maker was HMRC).
In r. 23(3), the words "paragraph (2)(a)" substituted for the words "paragraph (2)" by SI 2015/1510, r. 16(c), with effect from 21 August 2015, subject to savings provision in SI 2015/1510, r. 18 (amendments have no effect in relation to any appeal against a decision made before 6 April 2014 where the decision maker was HMRC).
In r. 23(4), the words "if neither the decision maker nor any other respondent objects" substituted for the words "if the decision maker does not object" by SI 2012/500, r. 4(2), with effect from 6 April 2012.
In r. 23(4), (5), (7)(a) and (b), the words "paragraph (2)" substituted for the words "Schedule 1" by SI 2015/1510, r. 16(d), with effect from 21 August 2015, subject to savings provision in SI 2015/1510, r. 18 (amendments have no effect in relation to any appeal against a decision made before 6 April 2014 where the decision maker was HMRC).
In r. 23(7), the words "or any other respondent" inserted by SI 2012/500, r. 4(2), with effect from 6 April 2012.
In r. 23(8), the words "or (aa)" omitted by SI 2015/1510, r. 16(e), with effect from 21 August 2015, subject to savings provision in SI 2015/1510, r. 18 (amendments have no effect in relation to any appeal against a decision made before 6 April 2014 where the decision maker was HMRC).
In r. 23(8), the words "or (aa)" inserted by SI 2013/2067, r. 26, with effect from 1 November 2013.
R. 23(8) inserted by SI 2009/1975, r. 3, with effect from 1 September 2009.

RESPONSES AND REPLIES

24(1) When a decision maker receives a copy of a notice of appeal from the Tribunal under rule 22(7), the decision maker must send or deliver a response to the Tribunal–

(a) in asylum support cases, so that it is received within 3 days after the date on which the Tribunal received the notice of appeal;

(b) in–

(i) criminal injuries compensation cases, or

(ii) appeals under the Child Support Act 1991,

within 42 days after the date on which the decision maker received the copy of the notice of appeal; and

(c) in other cases, within 28 days after the date on which the decision maker received the copy of the notice of appeal.

24(1A) Where a decision maker receives a notice of appeal from an appellant under rule 23(2), the decision maker must send or deliver a response to the Tribunal so that it is received as soon as reasonably practicable after the decision maker received the notice of appeal.

24(2) The response must state–

(a) the name and address of the decision maker;

(b) the name and address of the decision maker's representative (if any);

(c) an address where documents for the decision maker may be sent or delivered;

(d) the names and addresses of any other respondents and their representatives (if any);

(e) whether the decision maker opposes the appellant's case and, if so, any grounds for such opposition which are not set out in any documents which are before the Tribunal; and

(f) any further information required by a practice direction or direction.

24(3) The response may include a submission as to whether it would be appropriate for the case to be disposed of without a hearing.

24(4) The decision maker must provide with the response–

(a) a copy of any written record of the decision under challenge, and any statement of reasons for that decision, if they were not sent with the notice of appeal;

(b) copies of all documents relevant to the case in the decision maker's possession, unless a practice direction or direction states otherwise; and

(c) in cases to which rule 23 (cases in which the notice of appeal is to be sent to the decision maker) applies, a copy of the notice of appeal, any documents provided by the appellant with the notice of appeal and (if they have not otherwise been provided to the Tribunal) the name and address of the appellant's representative (if any).

24(5) The decision maker must provide a copy of the response and any accompanying documents to each other party at the same time as it provides the response to the Tribunal.

24(6) The appellant and any other respondent may make a written submission and supply further documents in reply to the decision maker's response.

24(7) Any submission or further documents under paragraph (6) must be provided to the Tribunal within 1 month after the date on which the decision maker sent the response to the party providing the reply, and the Tribunal must send a copy to each other party.

History – R. 24(1)(b) substituted by SI 2014/2128, r. 37, with effect from 20 October 2014.
R. 24(1) and (1A) substituted for former r. 24(1) by SI 2013/477, r. 27, with effect from 1 October 2014.
R. 24(1)(aa) inserted (and the "and" at the end of r. 24(1)(a) omitted) by SI 2011/651, r. 4(3), with effect from 1 April 2011.
In r. 24(2)(f) the words "or documents", which appeared after the words "further information", omitted by SI 2013/477, r. 27, with effect from 1 October 2014.

MEDICAL AND PHYSICAL EXAMINATION IN APPEALS UNDER SECTION 12 OF THE SOCIAL SECURITY ACT 1998

25(1) This rule applies only to appeals under section 12 of the Social Security Act 1998.

25(2) At a hearing an appropriate member of the Tribunal may carry out a physical examination of a person if the case relates to–

(a) the extent of that person's disablement and its assessment in accordance with section 68(6) of and Schedule 6 to, or section 103 of, the Social Security Contributions and Benefits Act 1992; or

(b) diseases or injuries prescribed for the purpose of section 108 of that Act.

25(3) If an issue which falls within Schedule 2 to these Rules (issues in relation to which the Tribunal may refer a person for medical examination) is raised in an appeal, the Tribunal may exercise its power under section 20 of the Social Security Act 1998 to refer a person to a health care professional approved by the Secretary of State for–

(a) the examination of that person; and

(b) the production of a report on the condition of that person.

25(4) Neither paragraph (2) nor paragraph (3) entitles the Tribunal to require a person to undergo a physical test for the purpose of determining whether that person is unable to walk or virtually unable to do so.

SOCIAL SECURITY AND CHILD SUPPORT CASES STARTED BY REFERENCE OR INFORMATION IN WRITING

26(1) This rule applies to proceedings under section 28D of the Child Support Act 1991 and paragraph 3 of Schedule 2 to the Tax Credits Act 2002.

26(2) A person starting proceedings under section 28D of the Child Support Act 1991 must send or deliver a written reference to the Tribunal.

26(3) A person starting proceedings under paragraph 3 of Schedule 2 to the Tax Credits Act 2002 must send or deliver an information in writing to the Tribunal.

26(4) The reference or the information in writing must include–

(a) an address where documents for the person starting proceedings may be sent or delivered;

(b) the names and addresses of the respondents and their representatives (if any); and

(c) a submission on the issues that arise for determination by the Tribunal.

26(5) Unless a practice direction or direction states otherwise, the person starting proceedings must also provide a copy of each document in their possession which is relevant to the proceedings.

26(6) Subject to any obligation under rule 19(3) (confidentiality in child support cases), the person starting proceedings must provide a copy of the written reference or the information in writing and any accompanying documents to each respondent at the same time as they provide the written reference or the information in writing to the Tribunal.

26(7) Each respondent may send or deliver to the Tribunal a written submission and any further relevant documents within one month of the date on which the person starting proceedings sent a copy of the written reference or the information in writing to that respondent.

Chapter 2 – Hearings

DECISION WITH OR WITHOUT A HEARING

27(1) Subject to the following paragraphs, the Tribunal must hold a hearing before making a decision which disposes of proceedings unless–

(a) each party has consented to, or has not objected to, the matter being decided without a hearing; and

(b) the Tribunal considers that it is able to decide the matter without a hearing.

27(2) This rule does not apply to decisions under Part 4.

27(3) The Tribunal may in any event dispose of proceedings without a hearing under rule 8 (striking out a party's case).

27(4) In a criminal injuries compensation case–

(a) the Tribunal may make a decision which disposes of proceedings without a hearing; and

(b) subject to paragraph (5), if the Tribunal makes a decision which disposes of proceedings without a hearing, any party may make a written application to the Tribunal for the decision to be reconsidered at a hearing.

27(5) An application under paragraph (4)(b) may not be made in relation to a decision–

(a) not to extend a time limit;

(b) not to set aside a previous decision;

(c) not to allow an appeal against a decision not to extend a time limit; or

(d) not to allow an appeal against a decision not to reopen a case.

27(6) An application under paragraph (4)(b) must be received within 1 month after the date on which the Tribunal sent notice of the decision to the party making the application.

SETTING ASIDE A DECISION WHICH DISPOSES OF PROCEEDINGS

37(1) The Tribunal may set aside a decision which disposes of proceedings, or part of such a decision, and re-make the decision, or the relevant part of it, if–

(a) the Tribunal considers that it is in the interests of justice to do so; and

(b) one or more of the conditions in paragraph (2) are satisfied.

37(2) The conditions are–

(a) a document relating to the proceedings was not sent to, or was not received at an appropriate time by, a party or a party's representative;

(b) a document relating to the proceedings was not sent to the Tribunal at an appropriate time;

(c) a party, or a party's representative, was not present at a hearing related to the proceedings; or

(d) there has been some other procedural irregularity in the proceedings.

37(3) A party applying for a decision, or part of a decision, to be set aside under paragraph (1) must make a written application to the Tribunal so that it is received no later than 1 month after the date on which the Tribunal sent notice of the decision to the party.

APPLICATION FOR PERMISSION TO APPEAL

38(1) This rule does not apply to asylum support cases or criminal injuries compensation cases.

38(2) A person seeking permission to appeal must make a written application to the Tribunal for permission to appeal.

38(3) An application under paragraph (2) must be sent or delivered to the Tribunal so that it is received no later than 1 month after the latest of the dates that the Tribunal sends to the person making the application–

(za) the relevant decision notice;

(a) written reasons for the decision, if the decision disposes of–

(i) all issues in the proceedings; or

(ii) subject to paragraph (3A), a preliminary issue dealt with following a direction under rule 5(3)(e);

(b) notification of amended reasons for, or correction of, the decision following a review; or

(c) notification that an application for the decision to be set aside has been unsuccessful.

38(3A) The Tribunal may direct that the 1 month within which a party may send or deliver an application for permission to appeal against a decision that disposes of a preliminary issue shall run from the date of the decision that disposes of all issues in the proceedings.

38(4) The date in paragraph (3)(c) applies only if the application for the decision to be set aside was made within the time stipulated in rule 37 (setting aside a decision which disposes of proceedings) or any extension of that time granted by the Tribunal.

38(5) If the person seeking permission to appeal sends or delivers the application to the Tribunal later than the time required by paragraph (3) or by any extension of time under rule 5(3)(a) (power to extend time)–

(a) the application must include a request for an extension of time and the reason why the application was not provided in time; and

(b) unless the Tribunal extends time for the application under rule 5(3)(a) (power to extend time) the Tribunal must not admit the application.

38(6) An application under paragraph (2) must–

(a) identify the decision of the Tribunal to which it relates;

(b) identify the alleged error or errors of law in the decision; and

(c) state the result the party making the application is seeking.

38(7) If a person makes an application under paragraph (2) in respect of a decision that disposes of proceedings or of a preliminary issue dealt with following a direction under rule 5(3)(e) when the Tribunal has not given a written statement of reasons for its decision–

(a) if no application for a written statement of reasons has been made to the Tribunal, the application for permission must be treated as such an application;

(b) unless the Tribunal decides to give permission and directs that this sub-paragraph does not apply, the application is not to be treated as an application for permission to appeal; and

(c) if an application for a written statement of reasons has been, or is, refused because of a delay in making the application, the Tribunal must only admit the application for permission if the Tribunal considers that it is in the interests of justice to do so.

SCHEDULE 1 – FUNCTIONS TRANSFERRED TO THE FIRST-TIER TRIBUNAL AND UPPER TRIBUNAL

Articles 3, 4 and 5

Table 2: Functions transferred to the Upper Tribunal

Tribunal	*Enactment*
Child Support Commissioner	Section 22 of the Child Support Act 1991 (c. 48)
Social Security Commissioner	Schedule 4 to the Social Security Act 1998 (c. 14)
Tribunal, in respect of its functions under section 4 of the Safeguarding Vulnerable Groups Act 2006 (c. 47)	Section 9 of the Protection of Children Act 1999 (c. 14)

SCHEDULE 2 – PERSONS TRANSFERRED AS JUDGES AND MEMBERS OF THE FIRST-TIER TRIBUNAL AND UPPER TRIBUNAL

Article 5

Table 3: Members becoming transferred-in judges of the First-tier Tribunal and deputy judges of the Upper Tribunal

Tribunal Member	*Enactment*
The Chairman	Section 5(3)(b) of the Criminal Injuries Compensation Act 1995 (c. 53) and the Criminal Injuries Compensation Schemes
The President	Section 5 of the Social Security Act 1998 (c. 14)
The Chief Asylum Support Adjudicator	Section 102 of and paragraph 1(b) of Schedule 10 to the Immigration and Asylum Act 1999 (c. 33)
A chairman of a Mental Health Review Tribunal	Paragraph 3 of Schedule 2 to the Mental Health Act 1983 (c. 20)
A President of Pensions Appeal Tribunals	Paragraph 2B(1) of the Schedule to the Pensions Appeal Tribunals Act 1943 (c. 39)
A President	Section 333(2)(a) of the Education Act 1996 (c. 56)
The President	Paragraph 1(1)(a) of the Schedule to the Protection of Children Act 1999 (c. 14)
The Deputy President	Appointed as a member of the chairmen's panel under paragraph 1(1)(b) of the Schedule to the Protection of Children Act 1999 (c. 14) and also appointed as deputy president of the Tribunal
A deputy Child Support Commissioner	Paragraph 4 of Schedule 4 to the Child Support Act 1991 (c. 48)
A deputy Commissioner	Paragraph 1(2) of Schedule 4 to the Social Security Act 1998 (c. 14)

Table 4: Members becoming transferred-in judges of the Upper Tribunal

Tribunal Member	*Enactment*
The Chief Child Support Commissioner or a Child Support Commissioner	Section 22 of the Child Support Act 1991 (c .48)
The Chief Social Security Commissioner or a Social Security Commissioner	Paragraph 1 of Schedule 4 to the Social Security Act 1998 (c. 14)

SCHEDULE 3 – MINOR, CONSEQUENTIAL AND SUPPLEMENTAL PROVISIONS

Article 6

SOCIAL SECURITY ACT 1998

143 The Social Security Act 1998 is amended as follows.

144 [Not relevant to tax credits.]

145 [Not relevant to tax credits.]

146 [Not relevant to tax credits.]

147 [Not relevant to tax credits.]

148 [Not relevant to tax credits.]

149 In section 12 (appeal to appeal tribunal)–

(a) [amends heading to SSA 1998, s. 12;]

(b) [amends SSA 1998, s. 12(2), (4), (5) and (8).]

150 In section 13 (redetermination etc of appeals by tribunal)–

(a) [amends SSA 1998, s. 13(1);]

(b) [omits SSA 1998, s. 13(2);]

(c) [amends SSA 1998, s. 13(3).]

151 In section 14 (appeal from tribunal to Commissioner)–

(a) [amends heading to SSA 1998, s. 14;]

(b) [omits SSA 1998, s. 14(1);]

(c) [amends SSA 1998, s. 14(3) and (4);]

(d) [omits SSA 1998, s. 14(7) to (12).]

152 In section 15 (appeal from Commissioner on point of law)–

(a) [substitutes heading to SSA 1998, s. 15;]

(b) [omits SSA 1998, s. 15(1);]

(c) [amends SSA 1998, s. 15(3);]

(d) [omits SSA 1998, s. 15(4) and (5).]

153 [Inserts SSA 1998, s. 15A.]

154 [Omits SSA 1998, s. 16(2), (3)(a), and (6)–(9).]

155 [Amends SSA 1998, s. 17(1).]

156 [Not relevant to tax credits.]

157 [Not relevant to tax credits.]

158 [Not relevant to tax credits.]

159 [Not relevant to tax credits.]

160 [Not relevant to tax credits.]

161 [Not relevant to tax credits.]

162(1) [Not relevant to tax credits.]

162(2) [Not relevant to tax credits.]

162(3) [Not relevant to tax credits.]

162(4) [Not relevant to tax credits.]

162(5) [Not relevant to tax credits.]

162(6) [Not relevant to tax credits.]

162(7) [Not relevant to tax credits.]

163 [Not relevant to tax credits.]

164 In section 28 (correction of errors and setting aside of decisions)–

(a) [amends SSA *1998*, s. *28(1);]*

(b) [amends SSA 1998, s. 28(1A);]

(c) [amends SSA 1998, s. 28(2).]

165 [Not relevant to tax credits.]

166 [Inserts SSA 1998, s. 39ZA.]

167 [Amends SSA 1998, s. 39(1).]

168 [Not relevant to tax credits.]

169 [Not relevant to tax credits.]

170 [Not relevant to tax credits.]

171 [Not relevant to tax credits.]

172 [Omits SSA 1998, Sch. 4.]

173 In Schedule 5 (regulations as to procedure: provision which may be made)–

(a) [amends SSA 1998, Sch. 5, para. 1(a) and (b);]

(b) [omits SSA 1998, Sch. 5, para. 2 and 5 to 8.]

TAX CREDITS ACT 2002

191(1) Section 63 of the Tax Credits Act 2002 (tax credits appeals etc: temporary modifications) is amended as follows.

191(2)–(7) [Omitted by SI 2009/56, art. 3(2) and Sch. 2, para. 186.]

191(8) [Amends TCA 2002, s. 63(13).]

History – Para. 191(2)–(7) omitted by SI 2009/56, art. 3(2) and Sch. 2, para. 186, operative from 1 April 2009 subject to transitional and saving provisions in SI 2009/56, Sch. 3.

SCHEDULE 4 – TRANSITIONAL PROVISIONS

Article 6

TRANSITIONAL PROVISIONS

1 Subject to article 3(3)(a) any proceedings before a tribunal listed in Table 1 of Schedule 1 which are pending immediately before 3rd November 2008 shall continue on and after 3rd November 2008 as proceedings before the First-tier Tribunal.

2 Subject to article 3(3)(b) any proceedings before a tribunal listed in Table 2 of Schedule 1 which are pending immediately before 3rd November 2008 shall continue on and after 3rd November 2008 as proceedings before the Upper Tribunal.

3(1) The following sub-paragraphs apply where proceedings are continued in the First-tier Tribunal or Upper Tribunal by virtue of paragraph 1 or 2.

3(2) Where a hearing began before 3rd November 2008 but was not completed by that date, the First-tier Tribunal or the Upper Tribunal, as the case may be, must be comprised for the continuation of that hearing of the person or persons who began it.

3(3) The First-tier Tribunal or Upper Tribunal, as the case may be, may give any direction to ensure that proceedings are dealt with fairly and, in particular, may–

(a) apply any provision in procedural rules which applied to the proceedings before 3rd November 2008; or

(b) disapply provisions of Tribunal Procedure Rules.

3(4) In sub-paragraph (3) "procedural rules" means provision (whether called rules or not) regulating practice or procedure before a tribunal.

3(5) Any direction or order given or made in proceedings which is in force immediately before 3rd November 2008 remains in force on and after that date as if it were a direction or order of the First-tier Tribunal or Upper Tribunal, as the case may be.

3(6) A time period which has started to run before 3rd November 2008 and which has not expired shall continue to apply.

3(7) An order for costs may only be made if, and to the extent that, an order could have been made before 3rd November 2008.

4 Subject to article 3(3)(a) and (b) where an appeal lies to a Child Support or Social Security Commissioner from any decision made before 3rd November 2008 by a tribunal listed in Table 1 of Schedule 1, section 11 of the 2007 Act (right to appeal to Upper Tribunal) shall apply as if the decision were a decision made on or after 3rd November 2008 by the First-tier Tribunal.

5 Subject to article 3(3)(b) where an appeal lies to a court from any decision made before 3rd November 2008 by a Child Support or Social Security Commissioner, section 13 of the 2007 Act (right to appeal to Court of Appeal etc.) shall apply as if the decision were a decision made on or after 3rd November 2008 by the Upper Tribunal.

6 Subject to article 3(3)(a) and (b) any case to be remitted by a court on or after 3rd November 2008 in relation to a tribunal listed in Schedule 1 shall be remitted to the First-tier Tribunal or Upper Tribunal as the case may be.

SAVINGS PROVISIONS

7 [Not relevant to tax credits.]

TAX CREDITS ACT 2002 (TRANSITIONAL PROVISIONS) ORDER 2008

(SI 2008/3151 as amended by SI 2010/644 and SI 2014/1848)

Made on 9 December 2008 by the Treasury, in exercise of the powers conferred by s. 62(2) of the Tax Credits Act 2002.

CITATION

1 This Order may be cited as the Tax Credits Act 2002 (Transitional Provisions) Order 2008.

DEEMED CLAIMS FOR TAX CREDITS

2 [Revoked by SI 2010/644, art. 5.]

History – Art. 2 revoked by SI 2010/644, art. 5, with effect from 1 April 2010.

AMENDMENTS TO THE TAX CREDITS ACT 2002 (COMMENCEMENT NO. 4, TRANSITIONAL PROVISIONS AND SAVINGS) ORDER 2003

3(1) The Tax Credits Act 2002 (Commencement No. 4, Transitional Provisions and Savings) Order 2003 shall be amended as follows:

3(2) [Revoked by SI 2014/1848, art. 4.]

3(3) [Revoked by SI 2010/644, art. 5.]

History – Art. 3(2) revoked by SI 2014/1848, art. 4, with effect from 14 July 2014.
Art. 3(3) revoked by SI 2010/644, art. 5, with effect from 1 April 2010.

TRANSFER OF TRIBUNAL FUNCTIONS AND REVENUE AND CUSTOMS APPEALS ORDER 2009

(SI 2009/56, as amended by SI 2009/777)

Made on 18 January 2009 by the Lord Chancellor and the Treasury in exercise of the powers conferred by s. 30(1) and (4), 31(1), (2) and (9) and 38 of, and para. 30 of Sch. 5 to, the Tribunals, Courts and Enforcement Act 2007 and s. 124(1)–(7) of the Finance Act 2008. Operative from 1 April 2009.

CITATION AND COMMENCEMENT

1(1) This Order may be cited as the Transfer of Tribunal Functions and Revenue and Customs Appeals Order 2009.

1(2) This Order comes into force on 1st April 2009.

THE EXISTING TRIBUNALS

2 In this Order **"existing tribunals"** means–

(a) the Commissioners for the general purposes of the income tax established under section 2 of the Taxes Management Act 1970;

(b) the Commissioners for the special purposes of the Income Tax Acts established under section 4 of the Taxes Management Act 1970;

(c) [not relevant to tax credits;]

(d) [not relevant to tax credits;]

(e) [not relevant to tax credits.]

TRANSFER OF FUNCTIONS, CONSEQUENTIAL AND OTHER AMENDMENTS

3(1) Schedule 1 contains amendments to primary legislation which–

(a) transfer functions of existing tribunals, and

(b) make consequential and other provision (including provision about reviews of decisions by Her Majesty's Revenue and Customs).

3(2) Schedule 2 contains amendments to secondary legislation which–

(a) transfer functions of existing tribunals, and

(b) make consequential and other provision (including provision about reviews of decisions by Her Majesty's Revenue and Customs).

ABOLITION OF EXISTING TRIBUNALS

4 The existing tribunals (apart from the Commissioners for the general purposes of the income tax) are abolished.

TRANSFER OF MEMBERS OF EXISTING TRIBUNALS

5 A person who, immediately before this Order comes into force, holds an office listed in column 1 of any of the following tables is to hold the office or offices listed in the corresponding entry in column 2 of that table–

THE SPECIAL COMMISSIONERS

1. Office held	**2. Office or offices to be held**
Commissioner for the special purposes of the Income Tax Acts appointed under section 4 of the Taxes Management Act 1970	Transferred-in judge of the Upper Tribunal
Deputy Commissioner for the special purposes of the Income Tax Acts appointed under section 4A of the Taxes Management Act 1970	Transferred-in judge of the First-tier Tribunal and deputy judge of the Upper Tribunal

TRANSITIONALS AND SAVINGS

6 Schedule 3 contains–

(a) transitional provision, and

(b) saving provision.

SCHEDULES

SCHEDULE 1 – CONSEQUENTIAL AMENDMENTS AND SUPPLEMENTAL PROVISIONS – PRIMARY LEGISLATION

Article 3

TAX CREDITS ACT 2002

312 The Tax Credits Act 2002 is amended as follows.
313 [Substitutes TCA 2002, s. 19(10).]
314 [Amends TCA 2002, s. 39.]
315 [Amends TCA 2002, s. 48(1).]
316 [Amends TCA 2002, s. 63.]
317 Schedule 2 (penalties: supplementary) is amended as follows.
318 [Amends TCA 2002, Sch. 2, para. 2.]
319 [Amends TCA 2002, Sch. 2, para. 3.]
320 [Amends TCA 2002, Sch. 2, para. 4.]

SCHEDULE 2 – CONSEQUENTIAL AMENDMENTS AND SUPPLEMENTAL PROVISIONS – SECONDARY LEGISLATION

Article 3

TAX CREDITS (PAYMENTS BY THE COMMISSIONERS) REGULATIONS 2002

78 [Amends SI 2002/2173, reg. 11.]

TAX CREDITS (APPEALS) REGULATIONS 2002

80 The Tax Credits (Appeals) Regulations 2002 are amended as follows.
81 [Amends SI 2002/2926, reg. 3(2).]
82 [Amends SI 2002/2926, reg. 12.]

TAX CREDITS (EMPLOYER PENALTY APPEALS) REGULATIONS 2003

84 The Tax Credits (Employer Penalty Appeals) Regulations 2003 are amended as follows.
85 [Amends SI 2003/1382, reg. 3.]
86 [Amends SI 2003/1382, reg. 4–6.]
87 [Amends SI 2003/1382, reg. 7.]
88 [Amends SI 2003/1382, reg. 8.]
89 [Amends SI 2003/1382, reg. 10.]

REVOCATIONS

187 The following instruments are revoked–
(e) The Special Commissioners (Jurisdiction and Procedure) Regulations 1994.
(f) The General Commissioners (Jurisdiction and Procedure) Regulations 1994.
(h) The Retirement Age of General Commissioners Order 1995.
(i) The Special Commissioners (Jurisdiction and Procedure) (Amendment) Regulations 1999.
(j) The General Commissioners (Jurisdiction and Procedure) (Amendment) Regulations 1999.
(k) The Special Commissioners (Amendment of the Taxes Management Act 1970) Regulations 1999.
(l) The Special Commissioners (Jurisdiction and Procedure) (Amendment) Regulations 2000.

(o) The Referrals to the Special Commissioners Regulations 2001.

(p) The General Commissioners and Special Commissioners (Jurisdiction and Procedure) (Amendment) Regulations 2002.

(q) The Special Commissioners (Jurisdiction and Procedure) (Amendment) Regulations 2003.

(s) The General Commissioners (Jurisdiction and Procedure) (Amendment) Regulations 2005.

(t) The Special Commissioners (Jurisdiction and Procedure) (Amendment) Regulations 2005.

(v) The General Commissioners and Special Commissioners (Jurisdiction and Procedure) (Amendment) Regulations 2007.

SCHEDULE 3 – TRANSITIONAL AND SAVING PROVISIONS

Article 6

GENERAL

1(1) In this Schedule–

"commencement date" means the date on which this Order comes into force;

"enactment" includes subordinate legislation (within the meaning of the Interpretation Act 1978);

"HMRC" means Her Majesty's Revenue and Customs;

"tribunal" means the First-tier Tribunal or, where determined by or under Tribunal Procedure Rules, the Upper Tribunal.

1(2) For the purposes of this Schedule there are "current proceedings" if, before the commencement date–

(a) any party has served notice on an existing tribunal for the purpose of beginning proceedings before the existing tribunal, and

(b) the existing tribunal has not concluded proceedings arising by virtue of that notice.

MATTERS FORMERLY HEARD BY EXISTING TRIBUNALS (EXCEPT VAT AND DUTIES TRIBUNALS)

5(1) This paragraph applies if, before the commencement date–

(a) a notice of appeal has been given to HMRC; but

(b) no party has served notice on an existing tribunal for the purpose of beginning proceedings before the existing tribunal in relation to that appeal.

5(2) Where the date on which a review is required or offered falls on or before 31 March 2010, the period for HMRC to give notice of their conclusions for the purposes of the relevant provision is to be 90 days (but without prejudice to any power to agree to a different period).

5(3) In this paragraph–

"review" means a review under–

(a) section 49B or 49C of the Taxes Management Act 1970, or

(b) any other enactment which, as amended by this Order, contains provisions corresponding to section 49B or 49C for review to be required or offered;

"relevant provision" means–

(a) in the case of a review under section 49B or 49C of the Taxes Management Act 1970, section 49E(6) of that Act, or

(b) in the case of a review under any other enactment amended by this Order, the provision that corresponds to section 49E(6) of the Taxes Management Act 1970 in relation to that review.

CURRENT PROCEEDINGS

6 Any current proceedings are to continue on and after the commencement date as proceedings before *the tribunal*.

7(1) This paragraph applies to current proceedings that are continued before the tribunal by virtue of paragraph 6.

7(2) Where a hearing before an existing tribunal (except for the Commissioners for the general purposes of the income tax) began before the commencement date but was not completed by that date, the tribunal must be comprised for the continuation of that hearing of the person or persons who began it.

7(3) The tribunal may give any direction to ensure that proceedings are dealt with fairly and justly and, in particular, may–

(a) apply any provision in procedural rules which applied to the proceedings before the commencement date; or

(b) disapply any provision of Tribunal Procedure Rules.

7(4) In sub-paragraph (3) **"procedural rules"** means any provision (whether called rules or not) regulating practice or procedure before an existing tribunal.

7(5) Any direction or order made or given in proceedings which is in force immediately before the commencement date remains in force on and after that date as if it were a direction or order of the tribunal relating to proceedings before that tribunal.

7(6) A time period which has started to run before the commencement date and which has not expired will continue to apply.

7(7) An order for costs may only be made if, and to the extent that, an order could have been made before the commencement date (on the assumption, in the case of costs actually incurred after that date, that they had been incurred before that date).

CASES TO BE REMITTED BY COURTS

8 Any case to be remitted by a court on or after the commencement date in relation to an existing tribunal shall be remitted to the tribunal.

DECISIONS OF VAT AND DUTIES TRIBUNALS AND COURTS: INTEREST AND PAYMENT

9(1) This paragraph applies in relation to any decision of a VAT and duties tribunal made before the commencement date.

9(2) On and after that date, the following provisions continue to apply as they applied immediately before that date–

(a) section 84(8) of the Value Added Tax Act 1994 (VAT),

(b) section 60(6) to (8) of the Finance Act 1994 (insurance premium tax),

(c) paragraphs 8 and 10 of Schedule 6 to the Finance Act 1994 (air passenger duty),

(d) section 56(3) to (5) of the Finance Act 1996 (landfill tax),

(e) paragraph 123(4) to (6) of Schedule 6 to the Finance Act 2000 (climate change levy),

(f) section 42(4) to (6) of the Finance Act 2001 (aggregates levy),

(g) paragraph 14(4) of Schedule 3 to the Finance Act 2001 (excise and customs).

10(1) This paragraph applies if an appeal from a decision of a VAT and duties tribunal, or from a court, is made before the commencement date.

10(2) Section 85B of the Value Added Tax Act 1994 does not apply in relation to that decision.

DECISIONS OF EXISTING TRIBUNALS: RIGHTS OF APPEAL, REVIEWS AND IRREGULARITIES

11(1) This paragraph applies to a decision of an existing tribunal if, immediately before the commencement date–

(a) an appeal lies to a court from that decision,

(b) an application may be or has been made to an existing tribunal seeking a review of that decision, or

(c) the existing tribunal wishes to correct an irregularity.

11(2) Except as provided for in sub-paragraph (3), on and after the commencement date such rights of appeal shall lie from the decision as would lie from a decision of the First-tier Tribunal made on or after that date.

11(3) Subject to the modifications specified in sub-paragraphs (4) and (5) the following enactments continue to apply for the purposes of a case to be stated, a review, or for correcting an irregularity in respect of any decision of the Commissioners for the general purposes of the income tax made before the commencement date, as if the amendments in this Order had not been made–

(a) sections 56 and 58 of the Taxes Management Act 1970,

(b) regulations 17 and 20 to 24 of the General Commissioners (Jurisdiction and Procedure) Regulations 1994, and

(c) the General Commissioners of Income Tax (Costs) Regulations 2001.

11(4) Section 56(6) of the Taxes Management Act 1970 is modified so that for "the Commissioners" there is substituted "the tribunal".

11(5) Section 58 of the Taxes Management Act 1970 is modified as follows–

(a) omit subsection (2B); and

(b) in subsection (2C) omit "or on an appeal under section 56A of this Act".

11(6) In article 4 of the Tribunals, Courts and Enforcement Act 2007 (Commencement No. 6 and Transitional Provisions) Order 2008–

(a) for "section 56 of the 1970 Act (statement of case for opinion of the High Court)" substitute "sections 56(3) and (11) and 58 of the 1970 Act (statement of case for opinion of the High Court) and regulations 17 and 20 to 24 of the General Commissioners (Jurisdiction and Procedure) Regulations 1994 (review of tribunal's final determination, stated case procedures and correction of irregularities)"; and

(b) after "commenced" insert ", and the amendments to the 1970 Act and the revocation of the General Commissioners (Jurisdiction and Procedure) Regulations 1994, the General Commissioners (Jurisdiction and Procedure) (Amendment) Regulations 1999, the General Commissioners (Jurisdiction and Procedure) (Amendment) Regulations 2005 and the General Commissioners and Special Commissioners (Jurisdiction and Procedure) (Amendment) Regulations 2007 (as they relate to the General Commissioners) in the Transfer of Tribunal Functions and Revenue and Customs Appeals Order 2009 had not been made".

EXISTING TRIBUNALS – STAFF

12 Staff appointed to the existing tribunals (except to the Commissioners for the general purposes of the income tax) before the commencement date are, on and after that date, to be treated, for the purpose of any enactment, as if they had been appointed by the Lord Chancellor under section 40(1) of the Tribunals, Courts and Enforcement Act 2007 (tribunal staff and services).

TRANSITIONAL: GENERAL

13(1) In so far as appropriate in consequence of this Order, a reference in an enactment, instrument or other document to an existing tribunal, or a member or official of an existing tribunal (however expressed) is to be taken to be a reference to the tribunal.

13(2) Sub-paragraph (1) does not apply to any reference that is amended by Schedule 1 or 2.

TAX CREDITS ACT 2002 (TRANSITIONAL PROVISIONS) ORDER 2010

(SI 2010/644, as amended by SI 2011/2910 and SI 2014/1848)

Made on 8 March 2010 by the Treasury in exercise of the powers conferred by s. 62(2) of the Tax Credits Act 2002. Operative from 1 April 2010.

INTERPRETATION

2(1) In this Order–

"benefit week" has the meaning given in–

(a) regulation 2(1) of the Income Support Regulations 1987 in relation to income support, and

(b) regulation 1(3) of the Jobseeker's Allowance Regulations 1996 in relation to income-based jobseeker's allowance;

"child premia" means the amounts in respect of income support or income-based jobseeker's allowance referred to in section 1(3)(d) of the Tax Credits Act 2002;

"polygamous unit" has the meaning given in regulation 2 of the Tax Credits (Polygamous Marriages) Regulations 2003;

"specified date" has the meaning given by paragraph (2);

"specified person" has the meaning given by paragraph (3).

2(2) For the purposes of this Order the **"specified date"** is the day following the date notified to an officer of Revenue and Customs as the final day of the last benefit week for which the child premia is to be paid to the specified person–

(a) by the Department for Work and Pensions, if the specified person is claiming in Great Britain, or

(b) by the Department for Social Development, if the specified person is claiming in Northern Ireland.

2(3) For the purposes of this Order a **"specified person"** is a person who–

(a) until the specified date was receiving the child premia, and

(b) has not made a claim for child tax credit.

TC Statutory Instruments

TRANSITIONAL PROVISIONS

3(1) Notwithstanding section 5(2) of the Tax Credits Act 2002, an award on a claim for child tax credit made by a person who until the specified date was receiving the child premia is for the period specified in paragraph (2).

3(2) The period is a period beginning with the specified date and ending at the end of the tax year in which that date falls.

3(3) Notwithstanding regulation 7 of the Tax Credits (Claims and Notifications) Regulations 2002, a person shall not be entitled to child tax credit in respect of any day prior to the day on which that person makes a claim for it ("the earlier day") if–

(a) [revoked by SI 2014/1848, art. 3,]

(b) the claimant is entitled, or in the case of a joint claim, either of the claimants is entitled, to the child premia on the earlier day.

History – Art. 3(3)(a) revoked by SI 2014/1848, art. 3, with effect from 14 July 2014.
Art. 3(3)(a) substituted by SI 2011/2910, art. 3, with effect from 5 December 2011.

DEEMED CLAIMS FOR TAX CREDITS

4(1) A claim shall be deemed to be made under section 3(1) of the Tax Credits Act 2002 if Her Majesty's Revenue and Customs receive a claim for child tax credit from the Department of Work and Pensions or the Department for Social Development and the claim–

(a) is in respect of a specified person,

(b) complies with regulation 5(2) of the Tax Credits (Claims and Notifications) Regulations 2002, and

(c) contains the information required in paragraphs (3) to (5) of regulation 3 of those Regulations.

4(2) The claim shall be deemed to be made by the person in respect of whom it is made.

4(3) If the specified person is a member of a married couple or an unmarried couple or a polygamous unit, the specified person and the other member of the couple or member or members of the polygamous unit are treated as making a joint claim.

4(4) The specified person is treated as being responsible for the child or children or qualifying young person or persons to whom that person's entitlement to the child premia relates.

4(5) The claim shall be deemed to be made on the specified date.

4(6) This article is subject to article 3.

REVOCATION OF PREVIOUS COMMENCEMENT AND TRANSITIONAL PROVISIONS ORDERS

5 [Revokes SI 2003/962, art. 5(4), SI 2005/773, SI 2006/3369 and SI 2008/3151, art. 2 and 3(3).]

TAXATION OF EQUITABLE LIFE (PAYMENTS) ORDER 2011

(SI 2011/1502)

Made on 15 June 2011 by the Treasury in exercise of the powers conferred by s. 1(3) and (4) of the Equitable Life (Payments) Act 2010. Operative from 16 June 2011.

Other material – HMRC Brief 26/11: The Equitable Life Payment Scheme: tax and tax credit implications (reproduced in Vol. 1F).

Notes – This is an edited version of SI 2011/1502, containing only provisions relevant to tax credits.

CITATION, COMMENCEMENT, EFFECT AND INTERPRETATION

1(1) This Order may be cited as the Taxation of Equitable Life (Payments) Order 2011 and shall come into force on the day after the day on which it is made.

1(2) This Order has effect in relation to authorised payments made after the day on which this Order is made.

1(3) In this Order **"authorised payment"** means a payment to which section 1 of the Equitable Life (Payments) Act 2010 applies.

TAX CREDITS

6 In calculating investment income in accordance with regulation 10 of the Tax Credits (Definition and Calculation of Income) Regulations 2002, an authorised payment shall be disregarded.

UNIVERSAL CREDIT (TRANSITIONAL PROVISIONS) REGULATIONS 2013

(SI 2013/386)

Made on 25 February 2013 by the Secretary of State for Work and Pensions in exercise of the powers conferred upon them by s. 42(2) and (3) of and para. 1(1) and (2)(b), 3(1)(a), (b) and (c), 4(1)(a), 5(1), (2)(c) and (d) and (3)(a) and 6 of Sch. 6 to the Welfare Reform Act 2012. Operative from 29 April 2013.

[Note: this SI is revoked by SI 2014/1230, reg. 3(1), with effect from 16 June 2014, subject to savings provisions in SI 2014/1230, reg. 3(2).]

[Note: the text of this SI is reproduced only in so far as it related to tax credits.]

PART 1 – INTRODUCTION AND INTERPRETATION

CITATION AND COMMENCEMENT

1 [Revoked by SI 2014/1230, reg. 3(1).]

History – Reg. 1 revoked by SI 2014/1230, reg. 3(1), with effect from 16 June 2014, subject to savings provisions in SI 2014/1230, reg. 3(2). Former reg. 1 read as follows:

"**1(1)** These Regulations may be cited as the Universal Credit (Transitional Provisions) Regulations 2013.

1(2) These Regulations come into force on 29th April 2013.".

INTERPRETATION

2 [Revoked by SI 2014/1230, reg. 3(1).]

History – Reg. 2 revoked by SI 2014/1230, reg. 3(1), with effect from 16 June 2014, subject to savings provisions in SI 2014/1230, reg. 3(2). Former reg. 2 read as follows:

"**2(1)** In these Regulations–

"the Act" means the Welfare Reform Act 2012;

"the 2007 Act" means the Welfare Reform Act 2007;

"First-tier Tribunal" has the same meaning as in the Social Security Act 1998;

"new claimant partner" has the meaning given in regulation 16;

"tax credit", **"tax credits"** and **"tax year"** have the same meanings as in the Tax Credits Act 2002;

"Upper Tribunal" has the same meaning as in the Social Security Act 1998.

2(2) For the purposes of these Regulations, the date on which a claim for universal credit is made is to be determined in accordance with the Claims and Payments Regulations.".

PART 2 – FIRST STAGE OF TRANSITION TO UNIVERSAL CREDIT

The Pathfinder Group

THE PATHFINDER GROUP

4 [Revoked by SI 2014/1230, reg. 3(1).]

History – Reg. 4 revoked by SI 2014/1230, reg. 3(1), with effect from 16 June 2014, subject to savings provisions in SI 2014/1230, reg. 3(2). Former reg. 4 read as follows:

"**4(1)** A person falls within the Pathfinder Group if they meet the requirements of regulations 5 to 12.

4(2) Any declaration which is required by regulation 6(3)(c), 9(1), or 12(a) or (b) is to be made by such method as may be required by the Secretary of State in relation to the person.".

EXISTING BENEFITS

7 [Revoked by SI 2014/1230, reg. 3(1).]

History – Reg. 7 revoked by SI 2014/1230, reg. 3(1), with effect from 16 June 2014, subject to savings provisions in SI 2014/1230, reg. 3(2). Former reg. 7 read as follows:

"**7(1)** [Not relevant to tax credits.]

7(2) The person must not be treated by regulation 8 as being entitled to a tax credit.

7(3) [Not relevant to tax credits.]

7(4) [Not relevant to tax credits.]

7(5) [Not relevant to tax credits.]

7(6) [Not relevant to tax credits.]".

EXISTING BENEFITS: ONGOING AWARDS OF TAX CREDITS

8 [Revoked by SI 2014/1230, reg. 3(1).]

History – Reg. 8 revoked by SI 2014/1230, reg. 3(1), with effect from 16 June 2014, subject to savings provisions in SI 2014/1230, reg. 3(2). Former reg. 8 read as follows:

"**8(1)** For the purposes of regulations 7(2) and 16(4)–

(a) a person is to be treated as being entitled to working tax credit with effect from the start of the current tax year even though a decision has not been made under section 14 of the Tax Credits Act 2002 ("the 2002 Act") in respect of a claim for that tax credit for that tax year, if the person was entitled to working tax credit for the previous tax year and any of the cases specified in paragraph (2) applies; and

(b) a person is to be treated as being entitled to child tax credit with effect from the start of the current tax year even though a decision has not been made under section 14 of the 2002 Act in respect of a claim for that tax credit for that tax year, if the person was entitled to child tax credit for the previous tax year and any of the cases specified in paragraph (2) applies.

8(2) The cases are–

(a) a final notice has not been given to the person under section 17 of the 2002 Act in respect of the previous tax year;

(b) a final notice has been given, which includes provision by virtue of subsection (2) or (4) of section 17, or a combination of those subsections and subsection (6) and–

(i) the date specified in the notice for the purposes of section 17(2) and (4) or, where different dates are specified, the later of them, has not yet passed and no claim for a tax credit for the current year has been made, or treated as made; or

(ii) a claim for a tax credit has been made, or treated as made, on or before the date mentioned in paragraph (i), but no decision has been made in relation to that claim under section 14(1) of the 2002 Act;

(c) a final notice has been given, no claim for a tax credit for the current year has been made, or treated as made, and no decision has been made under section 18(1) of the 2002 Act in respect of entitlement to a tax credit for the previous tax year; or

(d) a final notice has been given and–

(i) the person did not make a declaration in response to provision included in that notice by virtue of section 17(2)(a), (4)(a) or (6)(a), or any combination of those provisions, by the date specified in the notice;

(ii) they were given notice that payments of tax credit under section 24(4) of the 2002 Act had ceased due to their failure to make the declaration; and

(iii) their claim for universal credit is made during the period of 30 days starting with the date on the notice referred to in paragraph (ii) or, where the person is a new claimant partner, notification of formation of a couple with a person who is entitled to universal credit is given to the Secretary of State during that period.".

PART 3 – EFFECT OF TRANSITION TO UNIVERSAL CREDIT

Entitlement to Existing Benefits

TERMINATION OF AWARDS OF EXISTING BENEFITS

16 [Revoked by SI 2014/1230, reg. 3(1).]

History – Reg. 16 revoked by SI 2014/1230, reg. 3(1), with effect from 16 June 2014, subject to savings provisions in SI 2014/1230, reg. 3(2). Former reg. 16 read as follows:

"**16(1)** This regulation applies where–

(a) a person ("A") to whom an award of universal credit was made as a single claimant ceases to be entitled as such by becoming a member of a couple;

(b) the other member of the couple ("B") was not entitled to universal credit as a single claimant immediately before formation of the couple; and

(c) an award of universal credit is made to the members of the couple jointly.

16(2) In these Regulations, B is referred to as **"the new claimant partner"**.

16(3) Where this regulation applies, all awards of an existing benefit to which the new claimant partner is entitled which did not terminate on formation of the couple are to terminate, by virtue of this regulation, on the day before the first date on which the joint claimants are entitled to universal credit.

16(4) Where the new claimant partner was, immediately before forming a couple with A, treated by regulation 8 as being entitled to a tax credit, the new claimant partner is to be treated, for the purposes of the Tax Credits Act 2002, as having made a claim for the tax credit in question for the current tax year.

16(5) Any award of a tax credit which is made in respect of a claim which is treated as having been made by virtue of paragraph (4) is to terminate, by virtue of this regulation, on the day before the first date on which the joint claimants are entitled to universal credit.".

FINALISATION OF TAX CREDITS AND MODIFICATION OF TAX CREDITS LEGISLATION

17 [Revoked by SI 2014/1230, reg. 3(1).]

History – Reg. 17 revoked by SI 2014/1230, reg. 3(1), with effect from 16 June 2014, subject to savings provisions in SI 2014/1230, reg. 3(2). Former reg. 17 read as follows:

"**17(1)** This regulation applies where an award of universal credit is made to a person who was previously entitled to a tax credit and the award of that tax credit terminated at any time during the tax year in which the award of universal credit is made.

17(2) Where this regulation applies–

(a) the Tax Credits Act 2002 ("the 2002 Act") is to apply in relation to the person with the modifications made by paragraphs 9, 10, 13 and 14 of the Schedule to these Regulations; and

(b) subject to paragraph (3), the amount of the tax credit to which the person is entitled is to be calculated in accordance with the 2002 Act and regulations made under that Act, as modified by the other provisions of that Schedule ("the legislation as further modified").

17(3) Where, in the opinion of the Commissioners of Her Majesty's Revenue and Customs, it is not reasonably practicable to apply the legislation as further modified in relation to any case or category of cases, the 2002 Act is to apply without further modification, and regulations made under that Act are to apply without modification, in that case or category of cases.".

31 In regulation 7(3)–
(a) in Step 1, in the definition of "MR", after "maximum rate" insert "(determined in the manner prescribed at the date on which the award of the tax credit terminated)";
(b) in Step 3–
(i) in the definition of "I", before "tax year" insert "part";
(ii) in the definition of "N1", before "tax year" insert "part".
32 In regulation 8(3)–
(a) in Step 1, in the definition of "MR", after "maximum rate" insert "(determined in the manner prescribed at the date on which the award of the tax credit terminated)";
(b) in Step 3–
(i) in the definition of "I", before "tax year" insert "part";
(ii) in the definition of "N1", before "tax year" insert "part".

MODIFICATIONS TO THE TAX CREDITS (CLAIMS AND NOTIFICATIONS) REGULATIONS 2002

33 Paragraphs 34 to 42 prescribe modifications to the application of the Tax Credits (Claims and Notifications) Regulations 2002 where regulation 17 applies.
34 In regulation 4, omit paragraph (b).
35 Omit regulation 10.
36 Omit regulation 11.
37 Omit regulation 12.
38 In regulation 13–
(a) in paragraph (1), after "prescribed by paragraph" omit "(2) or";
(b) omit paragraph (2).
39 In regulation 15(1)(c), for "section 18(1), (5), (6) or (9)" substitute "section 18(1) or (5)".
40 In regulation 21(1A), for "regulation 27(2), (2A) or (3)" substitute "regulation 27(2A) or (3)".
41 In regulation 27–
(a) in paragraph (1), after "prescribed by paragraphs" omit "(2),";
(b) omit paragraph (2).
42 In regulation 33–
(a) in paragraph (a), for the words from "not later than 31st July" to "if later", substitute "not less than 28 days after the date on which the notice is given";
(b) omit paragraph (b) and the "and" which precedes it.

MODIFICATION TO THE TAX CREDITS (PAYMENT BY THE COMMISSIONERS) REGULATIONS 2002

43 Paragraph 44 prescribes a modification to the application of the Tax Credits (Payment by the Commissioners) Regulations 2002 where regulation 17 applies.
44 Omit regulation 7.

MODIFICATION TO THE TAX CREDITS (RESIDENCE) REGULATIONS 2003

45 Paragraph 46 prescribes a modification to the application of the Tax Credits (Residence) Regulations 2003 where regulation 17 applies.
46 In regulation 3(5)(a), omit the words in brackets after "child tax credit".".

LOSS OF TAX CREDITS REGULATIONS 2013

(SI 2013/715)

Made on 26 March 2013 by the Commissioners for Her Majesty's Revenue and Customs, in the exercise of the powers conferred by s. 36A(5) and (6), 36C(4) and (5), 65(2) and 67 of the Tax Credits Act 2002. Operative from 6 April 2013.

CITATION, COMMENCEMENT AND INTERPRETATION

1(1) These Regulations may be cited as the Loss of Tax Credits Regulations 2013 and come into force on 6th April 2013.

1(2) In these Regulations, references to sections of the Act are to sections of the Tax Credits Act 2002.

LOSS OF WORKING TAX CREDIT FOR BENEFIT OFFENCE AND REPEATED BENEFIT FRAUD: BEGINNING OF DISQUALIFICATION PERIODS

2(1) For the purposes of section 36A(6) of the Act, the date on which the relevant period begins is the thirtieth day after the day on which the Commissioners for Her Majesty's Revenue and Customs ("the Commissioners") are notified of the disqualifying event mentioned in section 36A(1)–

(a) in relation to England and Wales and Scotland, by the Secretary of State or by an authority which administers housing benefit or council tax benefit,

(b) in relation to Northern Ireland, by the Department for Social Development, the Department of Finance and Personnel or the Northern Ireland Housing Executive.

2(2) For the purposes of section 36C(5) of the Act, the prescribed date is the thirtieth day after the day on which the Commissioners are notified of the offender's conviction mentioned in that section, by the prosecuting authority responsible for bringing the current set of proceedings in which the offender was convicted.

LOSS OF WORKING TAX CREDIT FOR BENEFIT OFFENCE AND REPEATED BENEFIT FRAUD

3 For the duration of any period–

(a) comprised in the offender's disqualification period for the purposes of section 36A(4)(b) or 36C(3)(b) of the Act, and

(b) not comprising any such disqualification period of the other member of the couple mentioned in either section,

the working tax credit in question shall be payable, but as if the amount payable were reduced by 50%.

TC Statutory Instruments

UNIVERSAL CREDIT (TRANSITIONAL PROVISIONS) REGULATIONS 2014

(SI 2014/1230, as amended by SI 2014/1626, 2016/232, SI 2017/781 and SI 2018/65)

Made on 12 May 2014 by the Secretary of State for Work and Pensions in exercise of the powers conferred upon them by s. 42(2) and (3) of and para. 1(1) and (2)(b), 3(1)(a) to (c), 4(1)(a), 5(1), (2)(c) and (d) and (3)(a) and 6 of Sch. 6 to the Welfare Reform Act 2012. Operative from 16 June 2014.

PART 1 – INTRODUCTORY

CITATION AND COMMENCEMENT

1(1) These Regulations may be cited as the Universal Credit (Transitional Provisions) Regulations 2014.

1(2) These Regulations come into force on 16th June 2014.

INTERPRETATION

2(1) In these Regulations–

"the 2002 Act" means the Tax Credits Act 2002;

"the 2007 Act" means the Welfare Reform Act 2007;

"the Act" means the Welfare Reform Act 2012;

"assessment period" has the same meaning as in the Universal Credit Regulations;

"the Claims and Payments Regulations" means the Universal Credit, Personal Independence Payment, Jobseeker's Allowance and Employment and Support Allowance (Claims and Payments) Regulations 2013;

"contributory employment and support allowance" means a contributory allowance under Part 1 of the 2007 Act as that Part has effect apart from the amendments made by Schedule 3, and Part 1 of Schedule 14, to the Act that remove references to an income-related allowance;

"existing benefit" means income-based jobseeker's allowance, income-related employment and support allowance, income support, housing benefit and child tax credit and working tax credit under the 2002 Act, but see also regulation 25(2);

"First-tier Tribunal" has the same meaning as in the Social Security Act 1998;

"housing benefit" means housing benefit under section 130 of the Social Security Contributions and Benefits Act 1992;

"income-based jobseeker's allowance" has the same meaning as in the Jobseekers Act 1995;

"income-related employment and support allowance" means an income-related allowance under Part 1 of the 2007 Act;

"income support" means income support under section 124 of the Social Security Contributions and Benefits Act 1992;

"joint-claim jobseeker's allowance" means old style JSA, entitlement to which arises by virtue of section 1(2B) of the Jobseekers Act 1995;

"new claimant partner" has the meaning given in regulation 7;

"new style ESA" means an allowance under Part 1 of the 2007 Act as amended by the amendments made by Schedule 3, and Part 1 of Schedule 14, to the Act that remove references to an income-related allowance;

"new style JSA" means an allowance under the Jobseekers Act 1995 as amended by the amendments made by Part 1 of Schedule 14 to the Act that remove references to an income-based allowance;

"old style ESA" means an employment and support allowance under Part 1 of the 2007 Act as that Part has effect apart from the amendments made by Schedule 3, and Part 1 of Schedule 14, to the Act that remove references to an income-related allowance;

"old style JSA" means a jobseeker's allowance under the Jobseekers Act 1995 as that Act has effect apart from the amendments made by Part 1 of Schedule 14 to the Act that remove references to an income-based allowance;

"specified accommodation" means accommodation to which one or more of sub-paragraphs (2) to (5) of paragraph 3A of Schedule 1 to the Universal Credit Regulations applies;

"temporary accommodation" means accommodation which falls within Case 1 or Case 2 under paragraph 3B of Schedule 1 to the Universal Credit Regulations;

"partner" in relation to a person ("A") means a person who forms part of a couple with A;

"tax credit" (including "child tax credit" and "working tax credit"), **"tax credits"** and **"tax year"** have the same meanings as in the 2002 Act;

"the Universal Credit Regulations" means the Universal Credit Regulations 2013;

"Upper Tribunal" has the same meaning as in the Social Security Act 1998.

2(2) For the purposes of these Regulations–

(a) the date on which a claim for universal credit is made is to be determined in accordance with the Claims and Payments Regulations;

(b) where a couple is treated, in accordance with regulation 9(8) of the Claims and Payments Regulations, as having made a claim for universal credit, references to the date on which the claim is treated as made are to the date of formation of the couple;

(c) where a regulation refers to entitlement to an existing benefit on the date on which a claim for universal credit is made or treated as made, such entitlement is to be taken into account notwithstanding the effect of regulations 5, 7 and 8 or termination of an award of the benefit before that date by virtue of an order made under section 150(3) of the Act.

History – In reg. 2(1), definition of "exempt accommodation" omitted by SI 2014/1626, reg. 3(a), with effect from 3 November 2014. In reg. 2(1), definition of "specified accommodation" inserted by SI 2014/1626, reg. 3(b), with effect from 3 November 2014. In reg. 2(1), definition of "temporary accommodation" inserted by SI 2018/65, reg. 6(3), with effect from 11 April 2018.

REVOCATION AND SAVING OF THE UNIVERSAL CREDIT (TRANSITIONAL PROVISIONS) REGULATIONS 2013

3(1) The Universal Credit (Transitional Provisions) Regulations 2013 ("the 2013 Regulations") are revoked, subject to the savings in paragraphs (2) to (4).

3(2) Chapters 2 and 3 of Part 2 (Pathfinder Group and treatment of invalid claims) of the 2013 Regulations continue to have effect in relation to a claim for universal credit–

(a) which was made before the date on which these Regulations come into force ("the commencement date"); and

(b) in respect of which no payment has been made to the claimant before the commencement date.

3(3) Regulation 19 of the 2013 Regulations (advance payments of universal credit) continues to have effect in relation to an advance payment which was made in accordance with that regulation before the commencement date and regulation 17 of these Regulations does not apply to such a payment.

3(4) Any other provision of the 2013 Regulations continues to have effect in so far as is necessary to give full effect to paragraphs (2) and (3).

PART 2 – TRANSITION TO UNIVERSAL CREDIT

Chapter 2 – Entitlement to Other Benefits

EXCLUSION OF ENTITLEMENT TO CERTAIN BENEFITS

5(1) Except as provided in paragraph (2), a claimant is not entitled to–

(a) [not relevant to tax credits;]

(b) [not relevant to tax credits;]

(c) a tax credit; or

(d) [not relevant to tax credits.]

in respect of any period when the claimant is entitled to universal credit.

5(2) Entitlement to universal credit does not preclude the claimant from entitlement–

(a) [not relevant to tax credits;]

(b) during the first assessment period for universal credit, where the claimant is a new claimant partner, to–

(i) [not relevant to tax credits;]

(ii) [not relevant to tax credits;]

(iii) a tax credit, where an award to which the new claimant partner is entitled terminates, in accordance with the 2002 Act, after the first date of entitlement to universal credit.

ENTITLEMENT TO UNIVERSAL CREDIT AND HOUSING BENEFIT: UNIVERSAL CREDIT WORK ALLOWANCE

5A [Not relevant to tax credits.]

History – Reg. 5A inserted by SI 2018/65, reg. 6(5), with effect from 11 April 2018.

TERMINATION OF AWARDS OF CERTAIN EXISTING BENEFITS: NEW CLAIMANT PARTNERS

7(1) This regulation applies where–

(a) a person ("A") who was previously entitled to universal credit as a single person ceases to be so entitled on becoming a member of a couple;

(b) the other member of the couple ("the new claimant partner") was not entitled to universal credit as a single person immediately before formation of the couple;

(c) the couple is treated, in accordance with regulation 9(8) of the Claims and Payments Regulations, as having made a claim for universal credit; and

(d) the Secretary of State is satisfied that the claimants meet the basic conditions specified in section 4(1)(a) to (d) of the Act (other than any of those conditions which they are not required to meet by virtue of regulations under section 4(2) of the Act).

7(2) [Not relevant to tax credits.]

7(3) [Not relevant to tax credits.]

7(4) [Not relevant to tax credits.]

7(5) [Not relevant to tax credits.]

7(6) [Not relevant to tax credits.]

7(7) Where the new claimant partner was, immediately before forming a couple with A, treated by regulation 11 as being entitled to a tax credit, the new claimant partner is to be treated, for the purposes of the 2002 Act, as having made a claim for the tax credit in question for the current tax year.

TERMINATION OF AWARDS OF CERTAIN EXISTING BENEFITS: OTHER CLAIMANTS

8(1) This regulation applies where–

(a) a claim for universal credit (other than a claim which is treated, in accordance with regulation 9(8) of the Claims and Payments Regulations, as having been made) is made; and

(b) the Secretary of State is satisfied that the claimant meets the basic conditions specified in section 4(1)(a) to (d) of the Act (other than any of those conditions which the claimant is not required to meet by virtue of regulations under section 4(2) of the Act).

8(2) [Not relevant to tax credits.]

8(2A) [Not relevant to tax credits.]

8(3) [Not relevant to tax credits.]

8(4) Where this regulation applies and the claimant (or, in the case of joint claimants, either of them) is treated by regulation 11 as being entitled to a tax credit–

(a) the claimant (or, as the case may be, the relevant claimant) is to be treated, for the purposes of the 2002 Act and this regulation, as having made a claim for the tax credit in question for the current tax year; and

(b) if the claimant (or the relevant claimant) is entitled on the date on which the claim for universal credit was made to an award of a tax credit which is made in respect of a claim which is treated as having been made by virtue of sub-paragraph (a), that award is to terminate, by virtue of this regulation–

   (i) on the day before the first date on which the claimant is entitled to universal credit; or

   (ii) if the claimant is not entitled to universal credit, on the day before the first date on which he or she would have been so entitled, if all of the basic and financial conditions applicable to the claimant had been met.

8(5) Where an award terminates by virtue of this regulation, any legislative provision under which the award terminates on a later date does not apply.

History – Reg. 8(2A) inserted by SI 2018/65, reg. 6(7)(b), with effect from 11 April 2018.

TRANSITIONAL HOUSING PAYMENT

8A [Not relevant to tax credits.]

History – Reg. 8A inserted by SI 2018/65, reg. 6(8), with effect from 11 April 2018.

ONGOING AWARDS OF TAX CREDITS

11(1) For the purposes of regulations 7(7) and 8(4)–

(a) a person is to be treated as being entitled to working tax credit with effect from the start of the current tax year even though a decision has not been made under section 14 of the 2002 Act in respect of a claim for that tax credit for that tax year, if the person was entitled to working tax credit for the previous tax year and any of the cases specified in paragraph (2) applies; and

(b) a person is to be treated as being entitled to child tax credit with effect from the start of the current tax year even though a decision has not been made under section 14 of the 2002 Act in respect of a claim for that tax credit for that tax year, if the person was entitled to child tax credit for the previous tax year and any of the cases specified in paragraph (2) applies.

11(2) The cases are–

(a) a final notice has not been given to the person under section 17 of the 2002 Act in respect of the previous tax year;

(b) a final notice has been given, which includes provision by virtue of subsection (2) or (4) of section 17, or a combination of those subsections and subsection (6) and–

(i) the date specified in the notice for the purposes of section 17(2) and (4) or, where different dates are specified, the later of them, has not yet passed and no claim for a tax credit for the current tax year has been made, or treated as made; or

(ii) a claim for a tax credit has been made, or treated as made, on or before the date mentioned in paragraph (i), but no decision has been made in relation to that claim under section 14(1) of the 2002 Act;

(c) a final notice has been given, no claim for a tax credit for the current year has been made, or treated as made, and no decision has been made under section 18(1) of the 2002 Act in respect of entitlement to a tax credit for the previous tax year;

(ca) a final notice has been given and the person made a declaration in response to a requirement included in that notice by virtue of section 17(2)(a), (4)(a) or (6)(a), or any combination of those provisions–

(i) by the date specified on the final notice;

(ii) if not in accordance with paragraph (i), within 30 days following the date on the notice to the person that payments of tax credit under section 24(4) of the 2002 Act have ceased due to the person's failure to make the declaration by the date specified in the final notice; or

(iii) if not in accordance with paragraph (i) or (ii), before 31 January in the tax year following the period to which the final notice relates and, in the opinion of Her Majesty's Revenue and Customs, the person had good reason for not making the declaration in accordance with paragraph (i) or (ii); or

(d) a final notice has been given and–

(i) the person did not make a declaration in response to provision included in that notice by virtue of section 17(2)(a), (4)(a) or (6)(a), or any combination of those provisions, by the date specified in the notice;

(ii) the person was given due notice that payments of tax credit under section 24(4) of the 2002 Act had ceased due to his or her failure to make the declaration; and

(iii) the person's claim for universal credit is made during the period of 30 days starting with the date on the notice referred to in paragraph (ii) or, where the person is a new claimant partner, notification of formation of a couple with a person entitled to universal credit is given to the Secretary of State during that period.

History – Reg. 11(2)(ca) inserted (and the word "or" at the end of reg. 11(2)(c) omitted) by SI 2018/65, reg. 6(9), with effect from 14 February 2018.

MODIFICATION OF TAX CREDITS LEGISLATION: OVERPAYMENTS AND PENALTIES

12(1) This regulation applies where–

(a) a claim for universal credit is made, or is treated as having been made;

(b) the claimant is, or was at any time during the tax year in which the claim is made or treated as made, entitled to a tax credit; and

(c) the Secretary of State is satisfied that the claimant meets the basic conditions specified in section 4(1)(a) to (d) of the Act (other than any of those conditions which the claimant is not required to meet by virtue of regulations under section 4(2) of the Act).

12(2) Where this regulation applies, the 2002 Act applies in relation to the claimant with the following modifications.

12(3) In section 28–

(a) in subsection (1)–

(i) after "tax year" in both places where it occurs, insert "or part tax year";

(ii) in paragraph (b), for the words from "as if it were" to the end substitute ""as an overpayment of universal credit";

(b) [omitted by SI 2017/781, art. 7(2)(b);]

(c) omit subsection (5);

(d) in subsection (6) omit "(apart from subsection (5))".

12(4) [Omitted by SI 2017/781, art. 7(3).]

12(5) In section 48 after the definition of "overpayment" insert–

""**part tax year**" means a period of less than a year beginning with 6th April and ending with the date on which the award of a tax credit terminated,".

12(6) In Schedule 2, in paragraph 6(1)(a) and (c) and (2)(a), after "for the tax year" insert "or part tax year".

History – Reg. 12(3)(a)(ii) substituted by SI 2017/781, art. 7(2)(a), with effect from 25 September 2017. Former reg. 12(3)(a)(ii) read as follows:

"(ii) at the end insert "or treated as an overpayment of universal credit";".

Reg. 12(3)(b) omitted by SI 2017/781, art. 7(2)(b), with effect from 25 September 2017. Former reg. 12(3)(b) read as follows:

"(b) in subsections (3) and (4), after "repaid" insert "to the Board or, as the case may be, to the Secretary of State";".

Reg. 12(4) omitted by SI 2017/781, art. 7(3), with effect from 25 September 2017. Former reg. 12(4) read as follows:

"**12(4)** For section 29(4) substitute–

"**29(4)** Where a notice states that this subsection applies in relation to an amount (or part of an amount), it may be recovered–

(a) subject to provision made by regulations, by deduction from payments of any tax credit under an award made for any period to the person, or either or both of the persons, to whom the notice was given; or

(b) subject to regulations made by the Secretary of State under the Social Security Administration Act 1992–

(i) by deductions under section 71ZC of that Act (Deduction from benefit–including universal credit);

(ii) by deductions under section 71ZD of that Act (Deduction from earnings); or

(iii) as set out in section 71ZE of that Act (Court action etc).""".

Former reg. 12(4) substituted by SI 2016/232, reg. 2, with effect from 1 April 2016.

MODIFICATION OF TAX CREDITS LEGISLATION: FINALISATION OF TAX CREDITS

12A(1) This regulation applies where–

(a) a claim for universal credit is made, or is treated as having been made;

(b) the claimant is, or was at any time during the tax year in which the claim is made or treated as made, entitled to a tax credit; and

(c) the Secretary of State is satisfied that the claimant meets the basic conditions specified in section 4(1)(a) to (d) of the Act (other than any of those conditions which the claimant is not required to meet by virtue of regulations under section 4(2) of the Act).

12A(2) Subject to paragraph (3), where this regulation applies, the amount of the tax credit to which the person is entitled is to be calculated in accordance with the 2002 Act and regulations made under that Act, as modified by the Schedule to these Regulations ("the modified legislation").

12A(3) Where, in the opinion of the Commissioners for Her Majesty's Revenue and Customs, it is not reasonably practicable to apply the modified legislation in relation to any case or category of cases, the 2002 Act and regulations made under that Act are to apply without modification in that case or category of cases.

History – Reg. 12A inserted by SI 2014/1626, reg. 4(a), with effect from 13 October 2014.

APPEALS ETC RELATING TO CERTAIN EXISTING BENEFITS

13(1) This regulation applies where, after an award of universal credit has been made to a claimant–

(a) an appeal against a decision relating to the entitlement of the claimant to income support, housing benefit or a tax credit (a "relevant benefit") is finally determined;

(b) [not relevant to tax credits;]

(c) [not relevant to tax credits;]

(d) a decision relating to the claimant's entitlement to a tax credit is revised under section 19 or 20 of the 2002 Act, or regulations made under section 21 of that Act, or is varied or cancelled under section 21A of that Act.

13(2) Where the claimant is a new claimant partner and, as a result of determination of the appeal or, as the case may be, revision or supersession of the decision the claimant would (were it not for the effect of these Regulations) be entitled to income support or housing benefit during the relevant period mentioned in regulation 7(3), awards of those benefits are to terminate in accordance with regulation 7.

13(3) Where the claimant is not a new claimant partner and, as a result of determination of the appeal or, as the case may be, revision, supersession, variation or cancellation of the decision, the claimant would (were it not for the effect of these Regulations) be entitled to a relevant benefit on the date on which the claim for universal credit was made, awards of relevant benefits are to terminate in accordance with regulation 8.

13(4) The Secretary of State is to consider whether it is appropriate to revise under section 9 of the 1998 Act the decision in relation to entitlement to universal credit or, if that decision has been superseded under section 10 of that Act, the decision as so superseded (in either case, "the UC decision").

13(5) Where it appears to the Secretary of State to be appropriate to revise the UC decision, it is to be revised in such manner as appears to the Secretary of State to be necessary to take account of–

(a) the decision of the First-tier Tribunal, Upper Tribunal or court, or, as the case may be, the decision relating to entitlement to a relevant benefit, as revised, superseded, varied or cancelled; and

(b) any finding of fact by the First-tier Tribunal, Upper Tribunal or court.

APPEALS ETC RELATING TO UNIVERSAL CREDIT

14(1) This regulation applies where–

(a) a decision is made that a claimant is not entitled to universal credit ("the UC decision");

(b) the claimant becomes entitled to income support, housing benefit or a tax credit (a "relevant benefit");

(c) an appeal against the UC decision is finally determined, or the decision is revised under section 9 of the Social Security Act 1998;

(d) an award of universal credit is made to the claimant in consequence of entitlement arising from the appeal, or from the decision as revised; and

(e) the claimant would (were it not for the effect of regulation 5 and this regulation) be entitled to both universal credit and a relevant benefit in respect of the same period.

14(2) Subject to paragraph (3), where this regulation applies–

(a) all awards of a relevant benefit to which the claimant would (were it not for the effect of these Regulations) be entitled are to terminate, by virtue of this regulation, at the beginning of the first day of entitlement to that award; and

(b) any legislative provision except regulation 8(2A) under which an award would otherwise terminate on a later date does not apply.

14(3) [Not relevant to tax credits.]

History – In reg. 14(2)(b) the words "except regulation 8(2A)" inserted by SI 2018/65, reg. 6(10)(a), with effect from 11 April 2018.

SCHEDULES

SCHEDULE – MODIFICATION OF TAX CREDITS LEGISLATION (FINALISATION OF TAX CREDITS)

Regulation 12A

History – Schedule inserted by SI 2014/1626, reg. 4(2), with effect from 13 October 2014.

MODIFICATIONS TO THE TAX CREDITS ACT 2002

1 Paragraphs 2 to 10 prescribe modifications to the application of the 2002 Act where regulation 12A of these Regulations applies.

2 In section 7 (income test)–

(a) in subsection (3), before "current year income" in each place where it occurs, insert "notional";

(b) in subsection (4)–

(i) for "current year" substitute "current part year";

(ii) in paragraphs (a) and (b), before "tax year" insert "part";

(c) after subsection (4), insert–

"**7(4A)** In this section **"the notional current year income"** means–

(a) in relation to persons by whom a joint claim for a tax credit is made, the aggregate income of the persons for the part tax year to which the claim relates, divided by the number of days in that part tax year, multiplied by the number of days in the tax year in which the part tax year is included and rounded down to the next whole number of pence; and

(b) in relation to a person by whom a single claim for a tax credit is made, the income of the person for that part tax year, divided by the number of days in that part tax year, multiplied by the number of days in the tax year in which the part tax year is included and rounded down to the next whole number of pence.".

3 In section 17 (final notice)–

(a) in subsection (1)–

(i) omit "the whole or"; and

(ii) in sub-paragraph (a), before "tax year" insert "part";

(b) in subsection (3), before "tax year" insert "part";

(c) in subsections (4)(a) and (4)(b), for "current year" in both places where it occurs, substitute "current part year";

(d) in subsection (5)(a) for "current year" in both places where it occurs, substitute "current part year";

(e) omit subsection (8).

4 In section 18 (decisions after final notice)–

(a) in subsection (1), before "tax year" insert "part";

(b) omit subsections (6) to (9);

(c) in subsection (10), for "subsection (1), (5), (6) or (9)" substitute "subsection (1) or (5)";

(d) in subsection (11)–

(i) after "subsection (5)" omit "or (9)";

(ii) omit paragraph (a);

(iii) in paragraph (b) omit "in any other case,";

(iv) before "tax year" in each place where it occurs, insert "part".

5 In section 19 (power to enquire)–

(a) in subsection (1)(a) and (b), before "tax year" insert "part";

(b) in subsection (3), before "tax year" insert "part";

(c) for subsection (5) substitute–

"**19(5)** ***"The relevant section 18 decision"*** means the decision under subsection (1) of section 18 in relation to the person or persons and the part tax year.";

(d) for subsection (6) substitute–

"19(6) **"The relevant section 17 date"** means the date specified for the purposes of subsection (4) of section 17 in the notice given to a person or persons under that section in relation to the part tax year.";

(e) in subsection (11), before "tax year" insert "part";

(f) in subsection (12), before "tax year" in each place where it occurs, insert "part".

6 In section 20 (decisions on discovery)–

(a) in subsection (1), before "tax year" insert "part";

(b) in subsection (4)(a), before "tax year" insert "part";

(c) in subsection (5)(b), before "tax year" insert "part";

(d) in subsection (6)–

(i) before "tax year" insert "part";

(ii) in paragraph (a), for "section 18(1), (5), (6) or (9)" substitute "section 18(1) or (5)";

(e) in subsection (7), before "tax year" in each place where it occurs, insert "part".

7 In section 21 (decisions subject to official error), for "18(1), (5), (6) or (9)" substitute "18(1) or (5)".

8 In section 23 (notice of decisions)–

(a) in subsection (1), for "18(1), (5), (6) or (9)" substitute "18(1) or (5)";

(b) in subsection (3)–

(i) after "18(1)" omit "or (6)";

(ii) for paragraph (b) substitute–

"(b) the notice of the decision under subsection (1) of section 18,".

9 In section 30(1) (underpayments), before "tax year" in each place where it occurs, insert "part".

10 In section 38 (appeals)–

(a) in subsection (1)(b), before "tax year" insert "part";

(b) for subsection (2), substitute–

""**The relevant section 18 decision"** means the decision under subsection (1) of section 18 in relation to the person or persons and the tax credit for the part tax year.".

MODIFICATIONS TO THE TAX CREDITS (DEFINITION AND CALCULATION OF INCOME) REGULATIONS 2002

11 Paragraphs 12 to 23 prescribe modifications to the application of the Tax Credits (Definition and Calculation of Income) Regulations 2002 where regulation 12A of these Regulations applies.

12 In regulation 2(2) (interpretation), after the definition of "the Macfarlane Trusts" insert–

""**part tax year"** means a period of less than a year beginning with 6th April and ending with the date on which the award of a tax credit terminated;".

13 In regulation 3 (calculation of income of claimant)–

(a) in paragraph (1)–

(i) before "tax year" insert "part";

(ii) in Steps 1 and 2, after "of the claimant, or, in the case of a joint claim, of the claimants" insert "received in or relating to the part tax year";

(iii) in the second and third sentences of Step 4, before "year" insert "part";

(b) in paragraph (6A)(c), for the words from "ending on 31st March" to the end, substitute "ending on the last day of the month in which the claimant's award of a tax credit terminated";

(c) in paragraph (8)(b), before "year" insert "part".

14 In regulation 4 (employment income)–

(a) in paragraph (1)(a), before "tax year" insert "part";

(b) in paragraph (1)(b), (c), (d), (e), (g) and (k), before "year" insert "part";

(c) in paragraph (1)(f), after "ITEPA" insert "which is treated as received in the part tax year and in respect of which the charge arises in the part tax year";

(d) in paragraph (1)(h), after "week" insert "in the part tax year";

(e) in paragraph (1)(i), for "that year" substitute "the tax year" and after "ITEPA" insert "which is treated as received in the part tax year";

(f) in paragraph (1)(j), after "applies" insert "which is received in the part tax year";

(g) in paragraph (1)(l), for "that year" substitute "the tax year" and after "ITEPA" insert "in respect of which the charge arises in the part tax year";

(h) in paragraph (1)(m), after "paid" insert "in the part tax year";

(i) in paragraph (4), in the first sentence and in the title of Table 1, after "employment income" insert "received in the part tax year";

(j) in paragraph (5), after "calculating earnings" insert "received in the part tax year".

15 In regulation 5 (pension income)–

(a) in paragraph (1), after "**"pension income"** means" insert "any of the following received in or relating to the part tax year";

(b) in paragraph (2), in the first sentence and in the title of Table 2, after "pension income" insert "received in or relating to the part tax year";

(c) in paragraph (3), after "income tax purposes", insert "in relation to the part tax year".

16 In regulation 6 (trading income)–

(a) re-number the existing regulation as paragraph (1);

(b) in paragraph (1) (as so re-numbered)–

(i) in sub-paragraph (a), for "taxable profits for the tax year" substitute "actual or estimated taxable profits attributable to the part tax year";

(ii) in sub-paragraph (b), for "taxable profit for the" substitute "actual or estimated taxable profit attributable to the part tax";

(c) after paragraph (1) insert–

"**6(2)** Actual or estimated taxable profits attributable to the part tax year ("the relevant trading income") is to be calculated by reference to the basis period (determined by reference to the rules in Chapter 15 of Part 2 of ITTOIA) ending during the tax year in which the claimant made, or was treated as making, a claim for universal credit.

6(3) The relevant trading income is to be calculated by–

(a) taking the figure for the actual or estimated taxable income earned in the basis period;

(b) dividing that figure by the number of days in the basis period to give the daily figure; and

(c) multiplying the daily figure by the number of days in the part tax year on which the trade, profession or vocation was carried on.".

17 In regulation 7 (social security income)–

(a) in paragraph (1), after "social security income" insert "received in the part tax year";

(b) in paragraph (3), in the opening words and in the title of Table 3, after "social security income" insert "received in the part tax year".

18 In regulation 8 (student income), after "in relation to a student" insert ", any of the following which is received in the part tax year".

19 In regulation 10 (investment income)–

(a) in paragraph (1), after "gross amount" insert "received in the part tax year";

(b) in paragraph (1)(e), before "year" insert "part tax";

(c) in paragraph (2), in the opening words and in the title of Table 4, after "investment income" insert "received in the part tax year".

20 In regulation 11(1) (property income)–

(a) omit "annual";

(b) after "taxable profits" insert "for the part tax year".

21 In regulation 12(1) (foreign income), before "year" insert "part tax".

22 In regulation 13 (notional income), after "means income" insert "received in the part tax year".

23 In regulation 18 (miscellaneous income), after "means income" insert "received in the part tax year".

MODIFICATIONS TO THE TAX CREDITS (INCOME THRESHOLDS AND DETERMINATION OF RATES) REGULATIONS 2002

24 *Paragraphs 25 to 27 prescribe modifications* to the application of the Tax Credits (Income Thresholds and Determination of Rates) Regulations 2002 where regulation 12A of these Regulations applies.

25 In regulation 2 (interpretation)–

(a) after the definition of "the income threshold" insert–

""**part tax year**" means a period of less than a year beginning with 6th April and ending with the date on which the award of a tax credit terminated;";

(b) in the definition of "the relevant income" insert "as modified by the Universal Credit (Transitional Provisions) Regulations 2014" at the end.

26 In regulation 7(3) (determination of rate of working tax credit)–

(a) in Step 1, in the definition of "MR", after "maximum rate" insert "(determined in the manner prescribed at the date on which the award of the tax credit terminated)";

(b) in Step 3–

(i) in the definition of "I", before "tax year" insert "part";

(ii) in the definition of "N1", before "tax year" insert "part".

27 In regulation 8(3) (determination of rate of child tax credit)–

(a) in Step 1, in the definition of "MR", after "maximum rate" insert "(determined in the manner prescribed at the date on which the award of the tax credit terminated)";

(b) in Step 3–

(i) in the definition of "I", before "tax year" insert "part";

(ii) in the definition of "N1", before "tax year" insert "part".

MODIFICATIONS TO THE TAX CREDITS (CLAIMS AND NOTIFICATIONS) REGULATIONS 2002

28 Paragraphs 29 to 34 prescribe modifications to the application of the Tax Credits (Claims and Notifications) Regulations 2002 where regulation 12A of these Regulations applies.

29 In regulation 4 (interpretation), omit paragraph (b).

30 Omit regulation 11 (circumstances in which claims to be treated as made).

31 Omit regulation 12 (further circumstances in which claims to be treated as made).

32 In regulation 13 (circumstances in which claims made by one member of a couple to be treated as also made by the other)–

(a) in paragraph (1)(h), after "prescribed by paragraph" omit "(2) or";

(b) omit paragraph (2).

33 In regulation 15(1)(c) (persons who die after making a claim)–

(a) omit "the whole or" and "after the end of that tax year but"; and

(b) for "section 18(1), (5), (6) or (9)" substitute "section 18(1) or (5)".

34 In regulation 33 (dates to be specified in notices)–

(a) in paragraph (a), for the words from "not later than 31st July" to "if later", substitute "not less than 30 days after the date on which the notice is given";

(b) omit paragraph (b) and the "and" which precedes it.

MODIFICATION TO THE TAX CREDITS (PAYMENT BY THE COMMISSIONERS) REGULATIONS 2002

35 Paragraph 36 prescribes a modification to the application of the Tax Credits (Payment by the Commissioners) Regulations 2002 where regulation 12A of these Regulations applies.

36 Omit regulation 7 (prescribed circumstances for certain purposes).

MODIFICATION TO THE TAX CREDITS (RESIDENCE) REGULATIONS 2003

37 Paragraph 38 prescribes a modification to the application of the Tax Credits (Residence) Regulations 2003 where regulation 12A of these Regulations applies.

38 In regulation 3(5)(a) (circumstances in which a person is treated as not being in the United Kingdom), omit "under regulation 11 or 12 of the Tax Credits (Claims and Notifications) Regulations 2002 or otherwise".

TAX CREDITS (SETTLEMENT OF APPEALS) REGULATIONS 2014

(SI 2014/1933)

Made on 21 July 2014 by the Commissioners for Her Majesty's Revenue and Customs in exercise of the powers conferred upon them by s. 63(8) and 65(2) and (6) of the Tax Credits Act 2002. Operative from 12 August 2014.

CITATION, COMMENCEMENT AND EXTENT

1(1) These Regulations may be cited as the Tax Credits (Settlement of Appeals) Regulations 2014 and come into force on 12th August 2014

1(2) These Regulations extend to England and Wales and Scotland only.

INTERPRETATION

2 In these Regulations–

"tax credits appeal" means an appeal which, by virtue of section 63 of the Tax Credits Act 2002 (tax credits appeals etc: temporary modifications), is to the First-tier Tribunal.

APPLICATION OF SECTION 54 OF THE TAXES MANAGEMENT ACT 1970

3(1) Section 54 of the Taxes Management Act 1970 (settling of appeals by agreement) shall apply to a tax credits appeal, with the modifications prescribed by paragraphs (2) to (7).

3(2) In subsection (1) for "tribunal" (in both places) substitute "First-tier Tribunal".

3(3) In subsections (1) and (4) for "assessment" (in each place) substitute "determination".

3(4) In subsections (1), (2) and (4)(a) for "the inspector or other proper officer of the Crown" substitute "an officer of Revenue and Customs".

3(5) For subsection (3) substitute–

"54(3) Where an agreement is not in writing–

(a) the preceding provisions of this section shall not apply unless the Board give notice, in such form and manner as they consider appropriate, to the appellant of the terms agreed between the officer of Revenue and Customs and the appellant; and

(b) the references in those preceding provisions to the time when the agreement was come to shall be construed as references to the date of that notice.".

3(6) In subsection (4)(b) for "the inspector or other proper officer" substitute "an officer of Revenue and Customs".

3(7) In subsection (4), in the words after paragraph (b), for "the inspector or other proper officer" substitute "an officer of Revenue and Customs".

TAX CREDITS (EXERCISE OF FUNCTIONS) ORDER 2014

(SI 2014/3280)

Made on 10 December 2014 by the Treasury in exercise of the powers conferred upon them by s. 126(1)–(3)(a) and (b)(i) and (9) of the Welfare Reform Act 2012. Operative from 1 April 2015.

CITATION AND COMMENCEMENT

1 This Order may be cited as the Tax Credits (Exercise of Functions) Order 2014 and comes into force on 1st April 2015.

INTERPRETATION

2(1) In this Order–

"the 2002 Act" means the Tax Credits Act 2002;

"the Administration Act" means the Social Security Administration Act 1992;

"the 2013 Regulations" means the Social Security (Overpayments and Recovery) Regulations 2013;

"notice" means a notice given under section 29 of the 2002 Act (recovery of overpayments of tax credits);

"penalty" means a penalty imposed under section 31 (incorrect statements etc.) or 32 (failure to comply with requirements) of the 2002 Act.

2(2) Any interest carried under section 37 of the 2002 Act on an amount specified in a notice or on a penalty is to be regarded for the purpose of this Order as if it were specified in the notice or formed part of the penalty respectively.

FUNCTIONS EXERCISABLE BY THE SECRETARY OF STATE

3(1) The functions of the Commissioners under section 2 of the 2002 Act specified in paragraph (2) are to be exercisable concurrently with the Secretary of State.

3(2) The functions are those that relate to–

(a) the recovery from a person to whom a notice has been given of the amount specified in a notice;

(b) the recovery from a person on whom a penalty has been imposed of the amount of the penalty.

APPLICATION OF THE ADMINISTRATION ACT

4(1) Subject to paragraph (2), the amount specified in a notice or, as the case may be, the amount of a penalty is, for the purposes of the Administration Act, to be treated as if it were an amount recoverable under section 71ZB of that Act.

4(2) Section 71ZB of the Administration Act has effect in relation to the amount specified in a notice or, as the case may be, the amount of a penalty, as if subsection (3) were omitted.

APPLICATION OF THE 2013 REGULATIONS

5(1) The amount specified in a notice is, for the purposes of the 2013 Regulations, to be treated as if it were an overpayment as defined in regulation 2 of those Regulations.

5(2) The amount of a penalty is, for the purposes of the 2013 Regulations, to be treated as if it were an amount recoverable under a provision of the Administration Act specified in regulation 3(2) of those Regulations.

AMENDMENT OF THE 2013 REGULATIONS

6 In the definition of **"overpayment"** in regulation 2 of the 2013 Regulations (interpretation) omit paragraph (b).

ENFORCEMENT BY DEDUCTION FROM ACCOUNTS (PRESCRIBED INFORMATION) REGULATIONS 2015

(SI 2015/1986)

Made on 8 December 2015 by the Commissioners for Her Majesty's Revenue and Customs in exercise of the powers conferred upon them by para. 3(2), 8(2)(a), 8(2)(c), 8(2)(d), 8(4)(b) and 23(1) of Sch. 8 to the Finance (No.2) Act 2015. Operative from 25 January 2016.

CITATION, COMMENCEMENT AND EXTENT

1(1) These Regulations may be cited as the Enforcement by Deduction from Accounts (Prescribed Information) Regulations 2015 and come into force on 25th January 2016.

1(2) These Regulations extend to England and Wales and Northern Ireland only.

INTERPRETATION

2 In these Regulations–

"account details" in respect of an account held by P means–

(a) any account number;

(b) any roll number;

(c) any sort code;

(d) the type of account, including whether or not it is a joint account;

(e) the account balance (in the currency in which the account is held);

(f) whether interest is payable in respect of amounts standing to the credit of the account and, if so, the rate of interest payable;

(g) any minimum balance required to keep the account open;

(h) any contractual term by virtue of which an account holder or interested third party may suffer economic loss where a hold notice or deduction notice is, or has been, given;

(i) specified information about–

(i) any account holder other than P;

(ii) any person (not falling within paragraph (i)) who is an interested third party in relation to the account;

(iii) any person who, in respect of the account, has power of attorney;

"P" means the person in respect of whom HMRC has given an information notice or, as the case may be, hold notice;

"Schedule 8" means Schedule 8 to the Finance (No. 2) Act 2015;

"specified information" in respect of a person means–

(a) name and address;

(b) national insurance number;

(c) all email addresses;

(d) all telephone numbers;

(e) in respect of an account which is a joint account, the proportion of the balance of that joint account to which the person is entitled.

INFORMATION

3(1) Information is only prescribed under these Regulations if it–

(a) is in the possession of, or immediately available to, a deposit-taker at the time the deposit-taker is given an information notice or, as the case may be, a hold notice, and

(b) describes the account, or, as the case may be, person, at the relevant time.

3(2) The relevant time for the purposes of regulation 3(1)(b) is–

(a) in the case of the information prescribed by regulations 5(1)(f) and 5(1)(g), immediately after the deposit-taker has complied with the hold notice, and

(b) in any other case, immediately before the deposit-taker complies with the information notice, or, as the case may be, hold notice.

PRESCRIBED INFORMATION IN RESPECT OF AN INFORMATION NOTICE

4 The following information is prescribed for the purposes of paragraph 3(2) of Schedule 8 (information notice)–

(a) account details for each account P holds with the deposit-taker;

(b) specified information in relation to P.

PRESCRIBED INFORMATION IN RESPECT OF A HOLD NOTICE WHERE AN ACCOUNT IS AN AFFECTED ACCOUNT

5(1) The following information is prescribed for the purposes of paragraph 8(2) of Schedule 8 (duty to notify HMRC and account-holders etc)–

(a) account details for each account P holds with the deposit-taker;

(b) specified information in relation to P;

(c) confirmation of which of the accounts that P holds with the deposit-taker is an affected account;

(d) the date on which the deposit-taker complied with paragraph 6(1) of Schedule 8 (effect of hold notice);

(e) confirmation that the deposit-taker understands the effect of paragraph 14(1)(g) of Schedule 8 (penalties);

(f) the total of all held amounts notified by the deposit-taker under paragraph 8(2)(b) of Schedule 8 in response to a hold notice;

(g) in respect of each account which P holds with the deposit-taker, the amount standing to the credit of the account which is not subject to action taken by the deposit-taker under paragraph 6(3) of Schedule 8;

(h) a description of any economic loss suffered by an account holder or interested third party as a result of any contractual term specified in the definition of **"account details"** in regulation 2 at sub-paragraph (h).

5(2) In this regulation **"held amounts"** is to be read in accordance with paragraph 7 of Schedule 8.

PRESCRIBED INFORMATION IN RESPECT OF A HOLD NOTICE WHERE AN ACCOUNT IS NOT AFFECTED ACCOUNT

6(1) The following information is prescribed for the purposes of paragraph 8(4)(b) of Schedule 8.

6(2) The information which the deposit-taker has taken into account to determine that there are no affected accounts.

ENFORCEMENT BY DEDUCTION FROM ACCOUNTS (IMPOSITION OF CHARGES BY DEPOSIT-TAKERS) REGULATIONS 2016

(SI 2016/44)

Made on 18 January 2016 by the Commissioners for Her Majesty's Revenue and Customs in exercise of the powers conferred upon them by para. 20(2)(e) of Sch. 8 to the Finance (No. 2) Act 2015. Operative from 10 February 2016.

CITATION, COMMENCEMENT AND EXTENT

1(1) These Regulations may be cited as the Enforcement by Deduction from Accounts (Imposition of Charges by Deposit-takers) Regulations 2016 and come into force on 10th February 2016.

1(2) These Regulations extend to England and Wales and Northern Ireland only.

INTERPRETATION

2 In these Regulations **"administrative costs"** means the administrative costs incurred by a deposit-taker in complying with an obligation under Schedule 8 to the Finance (No. 2) Act 2015 to which a final payment required under paragraph 13(11)(b)(ii) of that Schedule relates.

IMPOSITION OF CHARGES

3 A deposit-taker may impose a charge upon an account holder in respect of administrative costs only where–

(a) there is an agreement between it and the account holder (or, as the case may be, account holders), which provides that the deposit-taker may charge a fee in respect of those costs,

(b) the deposit taker–

(i) has made the final payment required by paragraph 13(11)(b)(ii), and

(ii) has not previously imposed a charge in respect of those costs, and

(c) the amount of the charge imposed does not exceed the amount specified in regulation 4.

AMOUNT THAT CAN BE CHARGED FOR ADMINISTRATIVE COSTS

4 The amount specified in this regulation is the lesser of–

(a) the amount of those administrative costs reasonably incurred by the deposit-taker, and

(b) £55.

TAX CREDITS EXTRA-STATUTORY MATERIAL

Table of Contents

OTHER HMRC MATERIAL

HMRC Codes of Practice

Tax Credit Factsheets

HMRC Leaflets

HMRC BRIEFS

HMRC CODES OF PRACTICE

COP 26: WHAT HAPPENS IF WE'VE PAID YOU TOO MUCH TAX CREDITS [HMRC, April 2018]

We've a range of services for disabled people. These include guidance in Braille, audio and large print. Most of our forms are also available in large print. Contact our helplines for more information.

This leaflet explains why overpayments happen and how to pay them back. It also tells you when you don't have to pay them back and how to dispute an overpayment.

Introduction

An overpayment means we've paid you more money than you're entitled to.

Mandatory reconsideration

If you think the amount of tax credits is wrong, you can ask us to look at the decision again. This is called mandatory reconsideration and you must normally contact us within 30 days of the date shown on your decision notice. You can also ask us to look at any penalty we've imposed in connection with your tax credits claim or if we decided to charge interest on your overpayment.

When we've looked at the decision again we'll send you a Mandatory Reconsideration Notice explaining what we've done. This will include all the information you need to appeal to HM Courts and Tribunals Service in England, Scotland and Wales or The Appeals Service in Northern Ireland, if you're still unhappy with our decision.

Appeals to the Tribunals or Appeals Service must be made in writing and within one month (30 days in Northern Ireland) of the date of the Mandatory Reconsideration Notice.

We'll put any recovery action on hold while we carry out there consideration or while your appeal is being considered.

For more information see our factsheet WTC/AP, "What to do if you think your Child Tax Credit or Working Tax Credit is wrong".

Go to GOV.UK and search for WTC/AP or phone the Tax Credit Helpline on 0345 300 3900 for a copy.

When you should dispute an overpayment

If you think our decision is right, but you don't agree that you should repay the overpayment, read pages 8 to 12 of this leaflet for more information about whether you should dispute our decision to recover the overpayment.

Contact us (read page 17) if you don't:

- agree that you've been overpaid
- know if you should ask us to look at the decision that generated the overpayment again under mandatory reconsideration
- know if you should ask us to dispute the decision to recover an overpayment

How we work out the amount of your tax credits

Tax credits depend on your income and your family circumstances. When your income or family circumstances change then your entitlement or the amount we pay you may change.

We pay you tax credits for a tax year – from 6 April one year to 5 April the next. When we first work out what to pay you, we look at your family's circumstances now and your income for the last tax year. If you think your income for the current tax year is going to be different than in the last year you can give us an estimate of what it will be. If we use this estimated figure it's important you tell us as straightaway if you think your income is going to be lower or higher than the estimate you provided. If you don't, we may not be paying you enough tax credits or you maybe overpaid.

After 5 April each year, we send you a renewal pack asking you to:

- check the information we hold about you is up to date
- tell us how much income you had in the last tax year

If your tax credits award is renewed automatically and you're in PAYE employment, we may have used income figures given to us by your employer. It's important that you check these figures are correct for tax credits. Your renewal notes will help you do this. Contact us if you think they're not and tell us why.

You should fill in and return your renewal form straightaway. We'll then work out the actual amount due to you for the year that has just ended and also the amount for the year that started on 6 April.

If you claim Universal Credit, we may end your tax credits during the year rather than wait until the end of the year. We'll write to you to tell you what you need to do.

How an overpayment happens

An overpayment can happen if:

- you don't give us the right information either when you claim or when you renew your claim at the end of the year
- you're late telling us about a change in your circumstances
- your income in 2017 to 2018 is more than £2,500 higher than it was in 2016 to 2017
- you gave us an estimated current year income which turns out to be too low
- you give us wrong information when you tell us about a change in your circumstances or income
- we make a mistake when we record the information you give us
- we don't act on information you give us

Changes in your circumstances or income

You should keep us up to date with any changes in your income and your family circumstances. The law says that you must tell us about certain changes within one month of them happening.

Sometimes it might not be clear exactly when there has been a change so you must tell us within one month of the date when you realised a change has happened.

You should use the checklist TC602(SN) "Check your tax credits award notice now" that we sent with your award notice to check what changes you need to tell us about. If you need to tell us about a change, you may find it helpful to keep a note of the date you contacted us, the name of the person you spoke to and details of the change.

After you tell us about a change we'll work out the new amount of tax credits payments you're due and send you a new award notice.

Where a change of circumstances means you have already received more than we estimate for your full year award, tax credits payments will normally stop. If this leaves you without enough to live on, tell us and we may consider making further payments. Each case is assessed on an individual basis. Where the change of circumstances means you haven't received more than we estimated for your full year award, your tax credits payments will continue at a reduced rate (read page 15, "Financial hardship")

If you start living with a partner, you separate from your partner or your partner dies

You must let us know **within one month** if

- you marry or enter into a civil partnership or start living with someone as though you're married or in a civil partnership
- you're married, or in a civil partnership, and you separate legally or in circumstances likely to be permanent
- you stop living with someone as though you're married or in a civil partnership
- your partner dies

Your claim will legally end in these circumstances. If you can still claim tax credits, you'll need to make a new claim. If you do make a new claim, it may be backdated up to one month.

The longer you delay telling us about this type of change, the bigger any overpayment may be. If you've started a new claim we may consider reducing the amount that you have to pay back. We'll work out how much you would have been paid in your new claim if you'd told us about the change on time and take that amount off your overpayment.

Our responsibilities and yours

To help get your award right and to help avoid building up an overpayment, it's important that we meet our responsibilities and you meet yours.

Our responsibilities

When you contact us we should:

- give you correct advice based on the information you give us when you contact us for information
- accurately record and use the information you give us when you make or renew your claim, to work out your tax credits and pay you the correct amount

- include information you've given us about your family and your income when we send you an award notice – if you tell us that there's a mistake or something missing on your award notice, we should put it right and send you a corrected award notice
- accurately record what you've told us and send you anew award notice within 30 days when you tell us about a change of circumstance – the 30 days doesn't start until we get all of the information we need from you to make the change so it's important you give us all of the information about a change

Your responsibilities

You should:

- give us accurate, complete and up-to-date information
- tell us about any changes of circumstance throughout the year so we've accurate and up-to-date information, the law says you must tell us about certain changes within one month of them happening (you should use the checklist TC602(SN) we sent with your award notice to check what these changes are) – to reduce the chance of building up an overpayment, we recommend that you tell us about any changes in income as soon as possible
- use the checklist TC602(SN) we send with each award notice to check all the items listed and tell us straightaway if anything is wrong, missing or incomplete.

You must tell us about some changes **within one month** of them happening – these are listed on the back of the checklist.

The main details we expect you to check are:

- if it's a joint award (for you and your partner) ora single award (based on your individual circumstances)
- the hours you work
- if you get Income Support, income-based Jobseeker's Allowance, income-related Employment and Support Allowance or Pension Credit
- that a disability element is shown if you, or anyone in the household, is entitled to it
- the number and age of any children in your household
- any childcare costs
- your total household income for the period shown on the award notice

We'll send you a corrected award notice if you tell us anything is wrong, missing or incomplete. If you don't get an award notice within 30 days of telling us about a change in circumstance, let us know as soon as possible.

You should check that the payments you get match what we said they should be on your award notice. Tell us if you get any payments that don't match what is shown on your award notice.

If anything is wrong, missing or incomplete you must tell us straightaway. Make a note of when you got your award notice and when you told us about the mistake. We may ask you for this information to show that you acted within 30 days.

If you had difficult personal circumstances that meant you couldn't check your award notice or bank payments, for example, a member of your family has been seriously ill, let us know as soon as possible.

If you don't understand your award notice, phone our helpline (read page 17).

If we fail to meet our responsibilities

If we fail to meet our responsibilities, but you meet all of yours, we won't ask you to pay back all of an overpayment caused by our failure.

However – you must tell us about any mistakes on your award notice within 30 days of the date on your award notice. If you do, then you won't be responsible for an overpayment caused by our mistake. If you tell us about a mistake more than 30 days after the date on your award notice we may ask you to pay back an overpayment up to the date you contacted us.

Example 1

On 1 September you tell us about a change in your circumstances but we don't change your award until 16 October. We won't collect back any overpayment that arises after 30 September.

Example 2

On 12 August you tell us about a change in your income. We send you a new award notice which you get on 19 August, but we haven't correctly recorded the information you gave us. If you spot this and tell us about the mistake by 18 September (30 days from 19 August) we won't collect any overpayment caused by our mistake.

Example 3

On 12 August you tell us about a change in your income. We send you a new award notice which you get on 19 August, but we haven't correctly recorded the information you gave us. If you spot this and don't tell us about the mistake until 27 September (39 days from 19 August) you may be responsible for the overpayment up to the date you contacted us.

Whenever you tell us about a mistake we won't collect an overpayment that may build up if we don't correct our mistake from this time.

If you fail to meet your responsibilities

If you fail to meet your responsibilities, but we meet all of ours, we'll normally ask you to pay back all of an overpayment. For example, if you tell us about a mistake on your award notice more than 30 days after the date on your award notice, then you may have to pay back an overpayment which has built up until the time you contacted us. But also read "Exceptional circumstances" below.

If we both fail to meet our responsibilities

If we both fail to meet one or more of our responsibilities, we'll look at the circumstances of your case and may write off parts of an overpayment.

If we both meet our responsibilities

If we both meet our responsibilities, we'll usually ask you to pay back the overpayment.

Example 4

On 12 August you told us your income increased from 15 July. We updated your tax credit record on 11 September. We'll still ask you to pay back any overpayments made during the period 15 July to 11 September.

If it takes you some time to tell us we didn't meet our responsibilities

We ask you to tell us about any mistakes we've made within 30 days of the date on your award notice. If you don't tell us within 30 days, we'll ask you to pay back an overpayment up to the date you told us. We won't ask you to pay back an overpayment, which is caused by our mistake, after the date you told us.

Exceptional circumstances

We understand that exceptional circumstances may prevent you from meeting your responsibilities on time. For example, you or a close family member may have been seriously ill so you couldn't report a change, check your award notice or tell us about our mistake within 30 days of the date on your award notice. Let us know, as soon as it becomes possible, if you think this applies to you, or if you're not sure whether we've made a mistake.

If you don't understand why there's an overpayment, contact us. We can give you an explanation over the phone or in writing. Our leaflet WTC8, "Why overpayments happen" gives more information about things that can cause overpayments. You can get a copy:

- online, go to GOV.UK and search for WTC8
- by phoning our helpline (read page 17) if you don't have access to the internet

We know that some customers may not be able to manage their own affairs, handle money or understand or complete forms. In such circumstances another person may act on their behalf. These people are called appointees.

Appointees

Appointees can sometimes be appointed by:

- a court or government department, for example the Department for Work and Pensions
- an individual who decides that they need help in dealing with their affairs
- a carer, a voluntary sector organisation or a mental health or social care professional who would be able to act in all dealings with us

For more information, go to www.gov.uk/getting-help-with-your-tax-credits-claim/appointees

Challenging the recovery of an overpayment

How to dispute an overpayment

If you don't agree that we should ask you to pay back an overpayment you can ask us to look at this again. We call this disputing an overpayment. To do this, complete and return form TC846, "Tax credits overpayment". You can get a copy:

- online, go to GOV.UK and search for TC846
- by phoning our helpline (read page 17) if you don't have access to the internet

You can write to us instead, but you must make sure you give us full details including:

- in what tax year the overpayment being disputed happened
- if and when you contacted us
- why you think the overpayment happened
- why you think you shouldn't have to pay back the overpayment

Usually you have to dispute recovery of an overpayment within 3 months from the date of:

- your final decision notice
- the decision on your Annual Review notice (if your award is renewed automatically)
- your Statement of Account
- the decision on your Award Review notice (if your award is ended automatically due to a claim for Universal Credit)
- the letter which gives you our decision on your mandatory reconsideration
- the letter from the Tribunals or Appeals Service which gives you their decision on your appeal

You can only dispute recovery of an overpayment that happened in the tax year the notice or letter relates to. You won't normally be able to dispute overpayments from earlier tax years. We'll only accept a late dispute in exceptional circumstances, for example, if you were in hospital for that 3-month period. If you do send usa dispute, we'll continue to seek recovery of the overpayment while we're considering your dispute.

If we later change our decision and you receive another decision notice for the same year, you have 3 months from the date of that notice to dispute recovery of an overpayment.

Example 5

Mary and Alan have overpayments from 2012 to 2013 and 2013 to 2014 tax years. They're paying the overpayments back from their tax credits award in 2016 to 2017. They were late reporting a change of circumstances in 2016 to 2017 and there's a new overpayment show non their final 2016 to 2017 award notice. Their final award notice also shows the overpayments from the earlier tax years.

Mary and Alan have 3 months from the date of their 2016 to 2017 decision notice to dispute the new overpayment only. But they'll not be able to dispute the overpayments from 2012 to 2013 and 2013 to 2014 tax years.

Historic debt

If you no longer get tax credits, you'll have been informed on past notices that, if you want to dispute an overpayment, you should do so as quickly as possible. If you didn't do this, you can't dispute overpayments from previous awards where it's been more than 3 months since you received your final decision notice. However, if you can show there are exceptional circumstances why you didn't previously dispute the overpayment, such as being in hospital, we'll consider the dispute.

If you no longer get tax credits, but have received a final decision notice from us in the last 3 months you'll only be able to dispute the overpayment occurring in the tax year the notice relates to.

If you reclaim tax credits and receive payments, we'll tell you if we're recovering historic debts from your ongoing award. You'll only be able to dispute the overpayment in the 3 months after you received the final decision notice relating to your previous award. Read page 13 "Paying back an overpayment"

Example 6

You receive your tax credits renewal pack on 21 May 2017 which requires you to confirm family circumstances and income for the previous 12 months ending 5 April 2017. You check your household details and decide you've no changes to report. We then send out a final decision notice on 15 August 2017. This shows you have been overpaid tax credits because your eldest child left school in September 2016 though your award was only changed in January 2017.

You don't notice the information about the overpayment until December 2017 when you realise your monthly tax credits payments are being reduced to pay it back. You agree there's been an overpayment but believe you shouldn't have to pay it back because you told HMRC about your daughter leaving school in September 2016 and we didn't change your award until January 2017. You had 3 months to dispute the overpayment from 15 August 2017, when we sent the final decision notice. This means that you needed to dispute the overpayment by 15 November 2017.

As you're now out of time you can't dispute the overpayment unless you can show there are exceptional circumstances for missing the deadline, such as being in hospital.

Where we got a decision wrong

In some cases we may revise the decision which caused the overpayment. We can only do this where the decision is incorrect as a result of an error by us and we find that you didn't materially contribute to the error. We call this type of error an "official error". However, we won't revise a decision which is incorrect due to official error if more than 5 years have passed from the date of the decision, or if the revised decision wouldn't be in your favour.

Where a dispute is found in your favour, we'll refund the amount already recovered.

Example 7

You have received Working Tax Credit since 2012. You became entitled to Disability Living Allowance in 2013 and asked us whether you were entitled to the disability element of Working Tax Credit.

We incorrectly advised you and said you were not entitled to the disability element. In 2015 you visited Citizens Advice with a query about your tax credits award. The adviser noticed that you qualified for the disability element but it wasn't included on your award. You contacted us and asked about our original advice. Since our decision was wrong, solely because of our error, your awards would be revised all the way back to 2013.

How we decide if you should pay back some or all of an overpayment

When we're deciding if you should pay back an overpayment we'll check:

- that we accurately recorded and acted on any information you gave us within 30 days of you telling us about a change of circumstance
- that we accurately worked out and paid you your correct entitlement
- that the information we included on your award notice was accurate at the date of the notice
- what you told us if you contacted us, and whether the advice we gave you based on that information was correct
- whether you contacted us to discuss any queries on your award notice, and whether we answered them correctly
- that you gave us accurate and up-to-date information when you claimed tax credits
- that you told us about any changes of circumstance at the right time
- that you checked your award notice within 30 days of the date on your award notice and if and when you told us about any mistakes
- that you checked the payments you got matched the amounts on your award notice and if not, that you told us within 30 days of the date on your award notice
- if you told us of any exceptional circumstances that meant you couldn't tell us about a change of circumstance or about our mistake within 30 days

Once we've checked whether we've met our responsibilities and you've met yours, we'll decide if:

- an overpayment should be paid back
- you must pay back all or only part of an overpayment

We'll normally give you our decision, along with our reasons, in writing. However, we won't stop collecting an overpayment while we do this.

We may not ask you to pay back an overpayment if you contacted us to tell us that your exceptional personal circumstances meant you couldn't check your award notice or bank payments. For example, a member of your family may have been seriously ill. If this is the case let us know as soon as possible.

If you still think you shouldn't pay back an overpayment

If you're still unhappy that we've decided to continue collecting an overpayment you can ask us to look at the decision again if you give us new and relevant information. You can only ask us to review the decision once and you'll have to do this within 30 days of receiving your dispute decision letter. Your overpayment will continue to be collected while we do this. We'll only accept a late request for a review in exceptional circumstances, for example, if you were in hospital for that 30 day period.

If you don't have any new information to give us, but you're still unhappy with our decision, you can contact a professional adviser or organisation, for example, Citizens Advice. You can consider what options are open to you, including any through the courts.

If you're not happy with our service, read "Customer service" on page 17.

Paying back an overpayment

We may collect back an overpayment from you in a number of ways including:

- reducing your payments from an ongoing tax credits award
- asking you to make direct payments to us
- adjusting your tax code

If you claim Universal Credit we may ask the Department for Work and Pensions or the Department for Communities (in Northern Ireland) to recover your tax credits overpayment.

In exceptional circumstances we may recover the overpayment directly from your bank account.

In some exceptional cases we may ask you to do more than one of the above.

From an ongoing tax credits award

If you're still getting tax credits payments we'll automatically reduce these payments to recover an overpayment from your ongoing tax credits. Overpayments we'll recover may be from awards you:

- or your partner have had as single people
- and your partner have had together either now or previously

We won't recover from your ongoing tax credits, any overpayments from awards you or your partner have had with other partners.

Recovery from an on-going tax credits award only takes place where an overpayment is established at the end of the year and that overpayment falls for cross year recovery.

If an overpayment still exists at the end of the year we'll recover from the award starting at 6 April of the following year.

How much we reduce your payments by will depend on how much you're getting. We reduce awards at different levels, read the table on page 14 to see the different rates used to recover overpayment.

If you want help understanding which recovery rate applies to you,contact us (read page 17).

Type of award	The most we'll take back from your award
If you're entitled to the maximum tax credits with no reduction due to income	10%
If you're getting Child Tax Credit or Working Tax Credit below the maximum and your total household income is £20,000 or less	25%
If your total household income exceeds £20,000	50%
If you're only getting the family element of Child Tax Credit	100%

By direct payment

If you're no longer entitled to tax credits, we'll ask you to make a direct payment to us. We'll also ask you to make a direct payment to us if your tax credits award has ended (this might happen if there's a change in your household, for example, you were in a couple and now you're single).

From an ongoing tax credits award and by direct payment

This may happen if you have an overpayment from an old award which ended and you also have an overpayment from a current award. For example, you and your partner separated and you then made another claim asa single person or in a new couple. We could ask you to pay back an overpayment from your current award as well as a direct payment from your previous award. If this happens to you, you can ask for the direct payment to be put on hold until you have paid back the overpayment from your ongoing tax credits payments.

If you do have an outstanding overpayment from an old claim, in some circumstances we may recover this from your ongoing award, instead of asking you to pay this overpayment back directly.

Asking for more time to pay back a direct payment

If we've asked you to pay back an overpayment from a previous award directly, but you need more time to pay it back, phone our Payment Helpline on 0345 302 1429 as soon as possible. We may be able to arrange for you to pay it back in equal instalments. If you'd like more details on different direct payment options, tell us when you phone.

By an adjustment to your tax code

If you're in PAYE employment or getting pension income and have a tax credits overpayment we may be able to adjust your tax code to collect your overpayment. We'll write to you and let you know if we can collect your overpayment this way. If we do write to you and you would prefer not to have your tax

TC Extra-statutory Material

code adjusted, you can contact us to pay in full or agree an instalment arrangement. The amount that is recovered depends on your income.

If you claim Universal Credit

If you claim Universal Credit we may transfer your tax credits debt(s) to the Department for Work and Pensions or the Department for Communities (in Northern Ireland) for them to recover. This includes where we've previously agreed a payment plan with you. If this is going to happen we'll write to you with more details. For more information go to www.gov.uk/tax-credits-overpayments

If you no longer claim tax credits and have an outstanding debt

If you're no longer claiming tax credits and have an outstanding overpayment or penalty, we may transfer these to the Department for Work and Pensions or the Department for Communities (in Northern Ireland) for them to recover.

Financial hardship

If you need to discuss financial hardship with us, phone us to explain this.

When you phone we may ask you about any family circumstances that may lead to extra living costs. For example, if you're looking after someone who is chronically ill or disabled. In some exceptional circumstances, we may cancel an overpayment altogether

If you can't pay for your essential living expenses

If you can't pay for your essential living expenses such as your rent, gas or electricity and:

- you're paying back an overpayment directly
- we've asked you to pay back an overpayment

phone the Payment Helpline on 0345 302 1429. We'll ask you about your circumstances in more detail.

If we've reduced your ongoing payments so you can pay back an overpayment you can find more information at www.gov.uk/tax-credits-overpayments or you can phone us on 0345 300 3900. You may be asked for more information regarding your income and living costs. Once we have this information we aim to make a decision within two working days.

Whether you're repaying your overpayment through a reduction in your tax credits payments or through a direct payment, we may offer you an option for extending the period of time over which you payback the overpayment. We can do this by reducing the amount being recovered each month. If we do reduce the monthly amount of your repayment, it'll take you longer to pay off the overpayment

If you can't pay for your essential living expenses and you're getting Universal Credit, you should contact the Department for Work and Pensions or the Department for Communities (in Northern Ireland).

If you and your partner separate

If you and your partner separate and your joint claim ends, we'll work out if you've been overpaid. If you have, we'll write to you both, usually at the end of the tax year to:

- tell you how much we've overpaid you by
- ask you to contact us to arrange to pay back the money

You and your ex-partner are both responsible for paying back an overpayment from your joint claim. The letter sent to each of you will show the total overpayment that you both owe.

You should try to agree with your ex-partner how much each of you should pay. The options are that:

- each of you pays half
- each of you pays a different amount
- one of you pays the full amount

When you've reached an agreement with your ex-partner, you should phone the Payment Helpline on 0345 302 1429 to arrange repaying the overpayment. You'll then get a letter confirming what you have to pay back.

You might not be able to talk it over with your ex-partner, either because you don't want to contact them or you don't know where they are. Even if you do speak to them, you might not be able to agree on what each of you should pay back. If this happens, you should speak to the Payment Helpline as quickly as possible. You'll then be asked to pay back half of the overpayment, with your partner being asked to pay back the rest. You won't be asked to pay back more than half of the overpayment.

If you and your partner separate, you may decide to make a new claim as a single person or with a new partner.

We can't reduce your payments from your new claim to collect back an overpayment that you had with your previous partner.

You must pay this overpayment back directly by ringing the Payment Helpline.

However, if you get back together with your ex-partner and claim again, we can reduce your payments to recover the overpayment.

Contact us

When you contact us tell us:

- your full name
- your National Insurance number
- a daytime phone number

By phone

Tax Credits Helpline	0345 300 3900
Payment Helpline	0345 302 1429
Textphone	0345 300 3909
If you prefer to speak in Welsh, phone	0300 200 1900
If you're abroad and can't get through on the helpline, phone	+44 2890 538 192

In writing

You can write to the address shown on your award notice, or to the address below.

Tax Credits Office
HM Revenue and Customs

Customer service

For information about our complaints procedure, go to www.gov.uk/complain-to-hm-revenue-and-customs

Your rights and obligations

"Your Charter" explains what you can expect from us and what we expect from you. For more information, go to www.gov.uk/hmrc/your-charter

TAX CREDIT FACTSHEETS

WTC/FS1: TAX CREDITS ENQUIRY [HMRC, April 2018]

The check

Every year we check thousands of tax credits awards to make sure that we:

- have awarded the right amount of tax credits based on customers' income and circumstances
- are running the tax credits system fairly and efficiently

If we check your previous tax credits award, it's known as an "enquiry"

You can ask an independent tribunal at any time for a direction that we stop our check into your previous tax credits award. If we think we should continue with the check we'll ask the tribunal to decide what should happen

About your check

To help us get a picture of your household, we may ask you for things like bank statements, payslips, household bills and details of your income and circumstances.

We can also ask employers and childcare providers for information.

We can't accept photocopies if we ask you for any original documents.

If we can't confirm that the documents are genuine or belong to you we'll keep them for further checks. Once we've confirmed the documents are genuine we'll return them to you.

Important

If you give false information or don't tell us about any of your income, we may charge you a penalty and/or we may prosecute you.

If we don't hear from you

You must tell us if you can't give us the information or explain why there's a delay. If you don't send us the information by the date on our letter, you may be charged a penalty.

Mistakes

We won't charge you a penalty if you:

- tell us about a relevant change in circumstances in time, see opposite
- take reasonable care to give us correct information on your claim
- took care with your claim, but still made a mistake

Asking someone to help you

If you'd like independent help, you can ask a friend, a professional adviser or an organisation like Citizens Advice to help you. You can also ask them to talk to us on your behalf, but we can't talk to anyone without your permission.

If you do ask someone to act for you either:

complete and return form TC689 "Authority for an intermediary to act on your behalf" – go to GOV.UK and search for TC689, fill in the online form and return to us

- write to us at

Tax Credit Office
PRESTON
PR1 4AT

to request a TC689 form

About our decision

You have the right to ask us to reconsider our decision if we:

- change your award
- ask you to pay a penalty
- charge interest on any overpayment

We call this mandatory reconsideration. We'll tell you how to ask us to reconsider our decision in the letter we send telling you what we've done.

Our leaflet WTC/AP, "What to do if you think our decision is wrong" gives more information about how to ask for a reconsideration.

Go to GOV.UK and search for WTC/AP.

If you're still unhappy after the reconsideration, you can appeal to an independent tribunal. Our Mandatory Reconsideration Notice will tell you how to do this.

Child Benefit

If you're claiming Child Benefit, changes to your family circumstances may affect the amount you receive.

Your rights and obligations

"Your Charter" explains what you can expect from us and what we expect from you.

For more information, go to www.gov.uk/hmrc/your-charter

Help

If you have any questions or would like more details, contact the HMRC office shown on the covering letter.

Change of circumstances

You must tell us within one month if you:

- get married, become a civil partner or part of a couple living together as if you're married or in a civil partnership
- stop being part of a married couple, civil partnership ora couple living together as if you're married *or in a civil partnership*
- or your partner (if you have one)
  - leave the UK permanently
  - go abroad for a temporary absence lasting more than 8 weeks (or more than 12 weeks if you go abroad because you're ill, or because a member of your family is ill or has died)

Getting advice

You can get advice from a professional adviser or organisation. You can also ask Citizens Advice.

Go to **www.citizensadvice.org.uk** or you can find them in "The Phone Book".

Open government

The Claimant Compliance Manual contains more details about our work in this area.

Go to GOV.UK and search for the Claimant Compliance Manual.

Complaints

For more information about our complaints procedures go to **www.gov.uk/complain-to-hm-revenue-and-customs**

Yr laith Gymraeg

Ffoniwch 0300 200 1900 i dderbyn fersiynau Cymraeg o ffurflenni a chanllawiau.

We've a range of services for disabled people. These include guidance in Braille, audio and large print. Most of our forms are also available in large print. Contact our helplines for more information.

WTC/FS4: TAX CREDITS MEETINGS [HMRC, January 2015]

About tax credits meetings

We hope that you will be able to meet us to talk about your tax credits claim.

You do not have to meet us, but meetings give us both an opportunity to talk about your claim in more detail. It will give you the chance to ask us questions. You may find it easier to talk about your claim with someone face-to-face rather than over the phone or by letter.

We will tell you why we want to meet you. If anything is not clear, ask us to explain.

Arranging the meeting

Meetings normally take place in office hours, let us know if this is a problem. We can arrange to meet you at another time. Meetings normally last between 1 and 2 hours.

We can hold the meeting at:

- our offices
- your adviser's office
- your home

We will try to agree the:

- date
- place
- list of things we need to talk about with you in advance.

If you cannot come to the meeting, you must tell us straightaway and we will try to arrange another meeting.

Asking someone to help you

You can ask someone to help you prepare for the meeting or come to the meeting with you. For example, you can ask:

- a friend
- a relative
- a professional adviser
- an interpreter

What you need to bring to the meeting

Please make sure that you, or the person who is helping you, bring any papers or documents that we have asked for.

Taking notes

We will take notes in the meeting and let you have a copy. We will ask you to check the notes and confirm we have included everything we have talked about. If you agree with the notes, we will ask you to sign them, but you do not have to.

You, or the person helping you, can also take notes in the meeting. This will help you to remember what we talked about. It might also help you when you check the notes we have made.

Couples

If it would be difficult for you both to attend, we will still be able to hold the meeting but we might need to:

- speak to your partner at a later date
- confirm the details that you gave us

We will always let you both know the outcome of any meeting.

Answering our questions

If you do not want to answer our questions during the meeting, or there is anything you do not understand or cannot answer, tell us. We will try to arrange another meeting or agree how best you can answer the questions.

If you do not give us the information we need we may make a decision on your claim based on the information that we have already.

Home visits

We may need to visit you at your home without your agreement. We will only do this if we have repeatedly tried, and failed, to contact you in writing and by phone. If we do call on you unannounced you can refuse to let us in or answer our questions. If this happens we will try to rearrange another time to see you.

If we visit you at home, we will always show you official identification.

We will never visit you at work without agreeing the time and date with you in advance.

Your rights and obligations

"Your Charter" explains what you can expect from us and what we expect from you. For more information, go to **www.gov.uk/hmrc/your-charter**

WTC/FS5: TAX CREDITS – COMING TO THE UNITED KINGDOM (UK) [HMRC, October 2017]

This factsheet tells you what tax credits are and what you need to know about them if you are coming to the UK from abroad. The UK is England, Scotland, Wales and Northern Ireland (but not the Channel Islands or the Isle of Man). There are 2 types of tax credit – Child Tax Credit and Working Tax Credit. You can't receive both tax credits and Universal Credit payments at the same time.

Universal Credit

Universal Credit supports people who are on a low income or out of work. It's being introduced in stages and will eventually replace tax credits. Whether you can claim depends on where you live and your personal circumstances.

For more information about Universal Credit, go to www.gov.uk/universal-credit

Who can claim tax credits

If you're aged 16 or over you may qualify for tax credits.

Your right to get one or both tax credits may be affected by rules on:

- immigration control
- presence in the UK
- whether you're ordinarily resident in the UK
- right to reside in the UK

Child Tax Credit

You can claim Child Tax Credit if you're responsible for at least one qualifying child or young person. You don't have to be working to claim.

Child Tax Credit helps to support a:

- child until 31 August after their 16th birthday
- *young person aged 16, 17, 18 or 19* who is in full-time non-advanced education at a school or college, or somewhere other than at a school or college, if the child received that education before their 16th birthday
- young person who is in approved training

- young person aged 16 or 17 who is registered with a Careers Service, Ministry of Defence, Connexions or local authority support service (in Northern Ireland, the Department for Communities) or any corresponding body in another member state after leaving full-time non-advanced education or approved training

Working Tax Credit

You can claim Working Tax Credit if you're employed or self-employed. There are extra amounts given for the costs of qualifying childcare and for working households where someone has a disability.

If you have children

To get Working Tax Credit you need to be aged at least 16, responsible for children and work the following hours. If you're:

- single, you need to do paid work of at least 16 hours a week
- a couple, your joint paid working hours need to be at least 24 a week, with one of you working at least 16 hours a week
- a couple and only one of you is working, that person will need to work at least 24 hours a week

If your joint working hours are less than 24 a week, you can still get Working Tax Credit if one of you:

- is aged 60 or over and working at least 16 hours a week
- is aged 16 or over, has a physical or mental disability that puts you at a disadvantage of getting a job, receives a qualifying disability benefit and works at least 16 hours per week
- works at least 16 hours a week, and the other is entitled to Carer's Allowance even if they don't get any payments because they receive other benefits instead
- works at least 16 hours a week, and the other is "incapacitated", an inpatient in hospital, or in prison (serving a custodial sentence, or remanded in custody awaiting trial or sentence)

If you don't have children

If you're not responsible for children, you can get Working Tax Credit if you or your partner are aged:

- 16 or over, work at least 16 hours a week and qualify for the disability element of Working Tax Credit
- 25 or over and work at least 30 hours a week
- 60 or over and work at least 16 hours a week

The detailed rules for people with disabilities are in the claim form notes.

Income

The amount of tax credits you get depends on your annual income. For tax credits claims, your annual income is your income for a tax year (your joint income if you are a couple). A tax year runs from 6 April one year to 5 April the next.

Income includes any money you were paid from working outside the UK, or any profit from trading outside the UK. For example, income from investments or property overseas and social security payments from overseas governments.

You need to work out how much income you have in British pounds, not foreign currency.

To convert your income, use the annual average exchange rate for the 12 months to 31 March in the tax year your income is due.

For more information, go to www.gov.uk/government/collections/exchange-rates-for-customs-and-vat

Immigration control and tax credits

You may not be able to get tax credits if you're subject to immigration control.

You're subject to immigration control if:

- the Home Office says you have permission to stay in the UK (known as "leave to enter or remain") but this permission is given to you on the grounds that you don't claim benefits, tax credits or housing help paid by the UK government (known as "recourse to public funds")
- you need permission to stay in the UK – again known as "leave to enter or remain" – but you don't have it
- you've been refused permission to stay in the UK, but you've appealed against that decision, and your appeal hasn't been decided yet

TC Extra-statutory Material

- you've been given permission to stay in the UK, but on the condition that someone else, like a friend or relative, pays for your upkeep and provides you with somewhere to live

You're not subject to immigration control if you:

- are a national of the UK, another European Economic Area (EEA) country or Switzerland
- have been given leave to enter the UK, without restriction on your access to public funds
- have been given leave to stay in the UK – for a limited period (unless it's on the condition that you don't have recourse to public funds)
- have been given leave to stay in the UK – for an indefinite period
- have claimed asylum and been told by the Home Office that you can stay in the UK as a refugee

If you're not sure if you're subject to immigration control, contact us.

If you're subject to immigration control you may still be able to get:

- both tax credits if you're:
  - claiming as a couple and only one of you is subject to immigration control
  - a sponsored immigrant under the Home Office rules and you've been here for at least 5 years, or your sponsor has died
- Child Tax Credit if you:
  - (or your partner) are lawfully working in the UK and are nationals of Algeria, Morocco, San Marino, Tunisia or Turkey
  - claimed asylum before April 2000 and were getting financial support for your children through Income Support or income-based Jobseeker's Allowance
- Working Tax Credit if you're:
  - lawfully present in the UK
  - a national of Turkey or the former Yugoslav Republic of Macedonia

The European Economic Area, Switzerland and tax credits

If you're in the UK, you may be able to get Child Tax Credit even if your family live in another EEA country or Switzerland.

For more information, go to www.gov.uk/tax-credits-if-moving-country-or-travelling

Presence, living in the UK for 3 months, ordinarily resident and right to reside

To get Working Tax Credit you must be working. You must generally also be present, and ordinarily resident in the UK.

To get Child Tax Credit you must be responsible for a child and:

- be present in the UK
- be ordinarily resident in the UK
- have a right to reside in the UK
- have been living in the UK for at least 3 months

Presence

Normally, you have to be physically present in the UK every day during the period of a tax credits award. There are rules, however, that allow tax credits awards to continue during short temporary absences.

For more information go to GOV.UK and search for "WTC/FS6".

Living in the UK for 3 months

If you've entered the UK on or after 1 July 2014, you'll generally need to live in the UK for 3 months before you can claim Child Tax Credit.

This rule doesn't apply if you:

- are a worker or self-employed person
- are a family member of a worker or self-employed person
- were working in the UK (or are a family member of such a person), but you were made redundant *and you're registered* as a jobseeker with the relevant employment office
- were made redundant and you've started a vocational training course
- are temporarily unable to work as a result of illness or accident

- are a Croatian national who has an accession worker authorisation document (or a family member of such a person) – read "Special rules for nationals of Croatia who want to work in the UK" on page 5
- are normally ordinarily resident in the UK, receiving Child Tax Credit and return to the UK after a temporary absence of less than 52 weeks - read "Ordinarily resident examples" in the right hand column on this page
- were ordinarily resident in the UK for a continuous period of 3 months immediately before you left and returned to the UK after a temporary absence of less than 52 weeks
- paid Class 1 or Class 2 National Insurance contributions while working abroad – and paid these within 3 months of returning
- are a non-EEA national who is working or self-employed in the UK and isn't restricted from receiving Child Tax Credit because of your immigration status (or are a family member of such a person)
- are a refugee (under defined circumstances)
- are a person who has been granted
  - discretionary leave to enter or remain in the UK with recourse to public funds
  - leave to remain pending an application for leave to remain as a victim of domestic violence
  - leave to remain under the Displaced Persons (Temporary Protection) Regulations
  - humanitarian protection

Right to reside

You may have a right to reside in the UK if you're:

- a UK national or have a right to reside in the Common Travel Area, this covers the UK, the Republic of Ireland, the Channel Islands and the Isle of Man
- an EEA or Swiss national who
  - is in work that is genuine and effective – if you can prove you have or will be earning £157 (gross) a week or more, you'll automatically be considered to be in genuine and effective work – if you can't, you'll be asked to prove that the work is genuine and effective
  - is a jobseeker, seeking employment, have a genuine chance of being employed and your right to reside as a jobseeker will generally last for 91 days
  - has a permanent right of residence
  - is self-sufficient, but only if you've enough money to stay above the level of Income Support and have comprehensive sickness insurance for yourself and any family members in the UK
  - is a student, but only if you've enough money to stay above the level of Income Support and have comprehensive sickness insurance
- a non-EEA national who has permission to enter or remain in the UK
- a family member of someone who has a right to reside, this means
  - spouse or civil partner and descendants who are dependent on them or are under 21
  - dependent relatives of the claimant or civil partner in the ascending line (for example, parents or grandparents)
  - for students, a spouse or civil partner and dependent children

If none of these apply to you, you may not have a right to reside. If your circumstances change and none of these apply to you any more, you may lose your right to reside.

Special rules for nationals of Croatia who want to work in the UK

If you want the right to reside in the UK as an employed person you'll need an accession worker authorisation document before you start work. The document can be:

- a passport or other travel document (designed to serve the same purpose as a passport) endorsed before 1st July 2013 to show that you have leave to enter or remain in the UK under the Immigration Act 1971, subject to a condition restricting your employment in the UK to a particular employer or category of employment – but this shall cease to be a valid accession worker authorisation document
  - at the end of the period for which leave to enter or remain was given
  - when you cease working for the employer, or in the employment, specified in the document for a period of time that exceeds 30 days in total
- a worker authorisation registration certificate issued in accordance with the "Accession of Croatia (Immigration and Worker Authorisation) Regulations 2013" and endorsed with a condition restricting your employment to a particular employer and authorised category of employment but this shall cease to be a valid accession worker authorisation document

TC Extra-statutory Material

– at the end of any time limit placed on the validity of the document
– when you cease working for the employer, or in the authorised category of employment, specified in the document for a period of time that exceeds 30 days in total
– when the document is revoked

There are a number of exceptions to this rule. If you're not sure if this rule applies to you, tell us about your circumstances and we'll let you know.

Who should make the claim for tax credits

Your tax credits claim must be made either as a single person or as a couple. It's very important to get this right.

You must claim as a couple if you're:

- married or in a civil partnership unless you're separated under a court order or your separation is likely to be permanent
- living with someone as if you're married or in a civil partnership
- living apart temporarily, for example, one of you is working away

If you don't have a partner you should make a single claim based on your individual circumstances.

Help with tax credits

For more information, go to www.gov.uk/topic/benefits-credits/tax-credits

If you want to order a claim pack, you can:

go online at www.gov.uk/qualify-tax-credits

- phone our helpline on 0345 300 3900
- textphone our helpline (for people with hearing or speech difficulties) on 0345 300 3909
- write to us at

Tax Credit Office
Preston
PR1 4AT
United Kingdom

If you live abroad and can't get through on our helpline number, phone +44 28 9053 8192.

For our opening hours, go to www.gov.uk/contact-hmrc

When you get in touch with us tell us your:

- full name
- National Insurance number
- daytime phone number

Getting help

If English isn't your first language you may use family, friends or a local support service to interpret for you.

If this isn't possible, we offer an interpretation service.

Interpretation service

If you'd like to use this service, tell us straightaway when you contact us.

Getting advice

You can get help and advice from independent organisations. You can ask them to talk to us on your behalf, but we can't talk to anyone without your permission. If you do ask someone to act for you either:

complete and return form TC689 "Authority for an intermediary to act on your behalf" – go to GOV.UK and search for TC689, fill in the online form and return to us, or

- write to us at the address on page 1 to request a TC689 form

Independent organisations

Citizens Advice

For:

- England
- Wales

- Northern Ireland go to
  www.citizensadvice.org.uk
- Scotland go to
  www.cas.org.uk

Civil Legal Advice in England and Wales

For advice:

go to www.gov.uk/civil-legal-advice

- phone 0345 345 4345

Scottish Legal Aid Board in Scotland

For advice:

- go to www.slab.org.uk
- phone 0131 226 7061

The Legal Services Commission in Northern Ireland

For advice:

- go to https://www.justice-ni.gov.uk/
- phone 0289 076 3000

Local offices of all these organisations are also listed:

- in the business section of "The Phone Book"
- in Yellow Pages
- at any public library

The European Economic Area

The European Economic Area (EEA) is made up of the following countries: Austria, Belgium, Bulgaria, Croatia, Cyprus, Czech Republic, Denmark, Estonia, Finland, France, Germany, Greece, Hungary, Iceland, Italy, Ireland, Latvia, Liechtenstein, Lithuania, Luxembourg, Malta, Netherlands, Norway, Poland, Portugal, Romania, Slovakia, Slovenia, Spain, Sweden and the UK.

Ordinarily resident examples

Here are some examples to help show whether you're ordinarily resident in the UK or not. None of these examples on their own will usually show that a person is, or is not, ordinarily resident.

You're ordinarily resident if:

- your partner and your children have also come to live in the UK – this may show that you and your family plan to stay in the UK
- your visit to the UK is part of a regular pattern of visits over a number of years or it is the start of such a pattern
- you've already lived here for a number of years – we may accept that you're ordinarily resident

You're not considered ordinarily resident if:

- you're just here for a holiday
- you plan to leave the UK in the near future – this may show you haven't settled here

Living in the UK

If you recently arrived in the UK but had to go abroad for a short period of time, we'll make a judgement on whether you ceased to be living in the UK during this absence. We'll apply a common sense approach to the normal everyday meaning of "living in" and we'll look at all the facts and circumstances of your case, including the reason you left and the length of time you were absent from the UK.

UK Visas and Immigration

For more information, go to www.gov.uk/government/organisations/uk-visas-and-immigration

Complaints

For more information about complaints procedures, go to www.gov.uk/complain-to-hm-revenue-and-customs

Your rights and obligations

"Your Charter" explains what you can expect from us and what we expect from you.

For more information, go to www.gov.uk/hmrc/your-charter

We've a range of services for disabled people. These include guidance in Braille, audio and large print. Most of our forms are also available in large print. Contact our helplines for more information.

WTC/FS6: TAX CREDITS – FOR PEOPLE LEAVING THE UNITED KINGDOM (UK)
[HMRC, April 2017]

This factsheet tells you what you need to do if you leave the UK and how it affects tax credits. The UK is England, Scotland, Wales, Northern Ireland and adjacent islands. However, it doesn't include the Isle of Man or the Channel Islands.

You must tell us straightaway if you, your partner (if you have one), your child or children or all of you leave the UK permanently.

> If you delay telling us and we pay you too much tax credits, you'll have to pay it back. You might also have to pay a penalty.

If you're going abroad permanently but your partner and child or children are staying in the UK, your partner should contact us straightaway.

If you, your partner, your child or children or all of you go abroad temporarily (by temporarily we mean an absence that's unlikely to last for more than 52 weeks from the date of leaving the UK), you can continue to get tax credits for a short period of time. For up to:

- 8 weeks, whatever the reason for your absence
- 12 weeks, if
  - you go or stay abroad because you, or a member of your family is, receiving treatment for an illness or disability
  - a member of your family has died

When you contact us, you'll need to tell us:

- the name or names of the person or persons going abroad
- the date they're leaving the UK
- how long they plan to be abroad
- the reason for going abroad
- the address abroad

You have a child who lives abroad

You may be entitled to Child Tax Credit if you're responsible for a child who lives in a country in the European Economic Area (EEA) or Switzerland. You can't usually claim Child Tax Credit for a child who lives outside the EEA or Switzerland. There's an exception if you or your partner are a Crown Servant posted abroad. Details of the countries in the EEA are on page 2.

Crown Servants posted overseas

Special rules apply if you or your partner are posted abroad as a Crown Servant. For example, as a UK civil servant or a member of HM Armed Forces.

If you have to work abroad you may be able to claim tax credits, just as if you were living in the UK. We'll treat you as being in the UK if you were:

- living in the UK, and it was your main home, just before you were posted abroad
- in the UK in connection with your posting, not just visiting the UK, before your posting began

You can get tax credits while you're working abroad whether your child goes abroad with you or stays in the UK.

While you're serving abroad, we'll normally pay tax credits into an account in the UK.

If your partner is a Crown Servant and their employer has posted them abroad, you should continue to make a joint claim to tax credits. For example, they're in the armed forces.

Help with tax credits

If you'd like more help:

- go to www.gov.uk/taxcredits
- phone our helpline on 0345 300 3900
- textphone our helpline (for people with hearing or speech difficulties) on 0345 300 3909

Getting advice

You can get advice from a professional adviser or organisation. You can also ask Citizens Advice. You can find them in "The Phone Book".

You can ask them to talk to us on your behalf, but we can't talk to anyone without your permission.

If you'd like to give someone permission, you can either:

- complete online and return form TC689, "Tax credits and Child Benefit – Authority for an intermediary to act on your behalf". Go to GOV.UK and search for TC689
- write and tell us the name and address of the person or the address and contact details of the organisation and send to:

Tax Credit Office
HM Revenue and Customs
BX9 1ER

Getting help

If English isn't your first language you can use family, friends or a local support service to interpret for you. If this isn't possible, we offer an interpretation service.

Interpretation service

If you'd like to use this service, tell us straightaway when you contact us.

Yr laith Gymraeg

Ffoniwch 0300 200 1900 i dderbyn fersiynau Cymraeg o ffurflenni a chanllawiau.

We've a range of services for disabled people. These include guidance in Braille, audio and large print. Most of our forms are also available in large print. Contact our helplines for more information.

The European Economic Area

The European Economic Area (EEA) is made up of:

- Austria
- Belgium
- Bulgaria
- Croatia
- Cyprus
- Czech Republic
- Denmark
- Estonia
- Finland
- France
- Germany
- Greece
- Hungary
- Iceland
- Ireland
- Italy
- Latvia
- Liechtenstein
- Lithuania
- Luxembourg
- Malta

- Netherlands
- Norway
- Poland
- Portugal
- Romania
- Slovakia
- Slovenia
- Spain
- Sweden
- UK

Open government

The Claimant Compliance Manual contains more details about our work in this area.

Go to GOV.UK and search for the Claimant Compliance Manual.

Your rights and obligations

"Your Charter" explains what you can expect from us and what we expect from you.

For more information, go to www.gov.uk/hmrc/your-charter

WTC/FS9: TAX CREDITS – SUSPENSION OF PAYMENTS [HMRC, April 2018]

What will happen if you don't contact us

It's very important you give us the information we've asked for or tell us about any difficulties you have providing it. If you don't give us this information we may suspend your tax credits payments.

If we suspend your payments and you still don't give us this information, we may stop or reduce your tax credits. You may then have to pay back any tax credits that we've already paid you. It's very important that you contact us.

If you're not sure what to do we suggest you take independent advice before you decide.

Difficulties in giving us the information

If you have a good reason for not giving us the information, let us know. We'll listen to what you say and, if you can't provide the information, or if it doesn't exist, we'll work with you to find alternatives.

A good reason for not providing information might be that:

- your documents have been lost through fire, flood or theft and you can't replace them in time
- you have a serious illness or other personal circumstances that prevents you from sending the information

What isn't a good reason is that you have been too busy to send us the information.

About our decision

If you feel your payments shouldn't be suspended, you have the right to contact us to discuss whether or not they can be reinstated. If your payments have been suspended and you have sent us the required information, we will make a decision based on the information we hold within 4 weeks. You do have the right to ask us to reconsider if we decide to reduce or stop your award.

Our leaflet WTC/AP, "What to do if you think your Child Tax Creditor Working Tax Credit is wrong" gives more information about how to ask for a reconsideration.

Go to GOV.UK and search for WTC/AP.

Complaints

For information about our complaints procedures,

go to www.gov.uk/complain-to-hm-revenue-and-customs

Your rights and obligations

Your Charter explains what you can expect from us and what we expect from you.

For more information, go to www.gov.uk/hmrc/your-charter

Help

If you have any questions or you would like more details, contact the HMRC office shown in the covering letter.

Getting advice

You can get advice from a professional adviser or organisation, for example, Citizens Advice.

Go to www.citizens-advice.org.uk or you can find them in "The Phone Book".

Open government

The Claimant Compliance Manual contains more details about our work in this area.

Go to GOV.UK and search the HMRC manuals for the Claimant Compliance Manual.

Yr laith Gymraeg

Ffoniwch 0300 200 1900 i dderbyn fersiynau Cymraeg o ffurflennia chanllawiau.

We've a range of services for disabled people. These include guidance in Braille, audio and large print. Most of our forms are also available in large print. Contact our helplines for more information.

WTC/FS10: TAX CREDITS CHECKS [HMRC, April 2018]

The check

Every year we check thousands of tax credits awards to make sure that we:

- have awarded the right amount of tax credits based on customers' income and circumstances
- are running the tax credits system fairly and efficiently

If we check your current tax credits award, we call this an "examination".

If we check your previous tax credits award, we call this an "enquiry".

You can ask an independent tribunal at any time for a direction that we stop our enquiry. If we think we should continue with the check we'll ask the tribunal to decide what should happen.

About your check

To help us get a picture of your household, we may ask you for things like bank statements, payslips, household bills and details of your income and circumstances. If we ask you for any original documents then we can't accept photocopies.

We may also ask your employers and childcare providers for information.

If we can't confirm that the documents are genuine or belong to you, we'll need to keep them for further checks. Once we've confirmed that the documents are genuine, we'll return them to you.

What will happen if you don't contact us

It's very important you give us the information we need, or tell us about any difficulties you have providing it. If you don't send us this information by the date we gave you, we may suspend your tax credits payments. We can also ask an independent tribunal to charge you a penalty of up to £300.

If we suspend your payments and you still don't give us this information, we may stop or reduce your tax credits. You may then have to pay back any tax credits that we've already paid you. It's very important that you contact us.

Mistakes

We won't charge you a penalty if you:

- tell us about a change in circumstances within one month of the change, see opposite
- take reasonable care to give us correct information on your claim
- took care with your claim, but still made a mistake.

Difficulties supplying information

If you have a good reason for not giving us the information, tell us. We'll listen to what you say and, if you can't provide the information or it doesn't exist, we'll work with you to find alternatives.

A good reason for not providing information might be that:

- your documents have been lost through fire, flood or theft and you can't replace them in time
- you have a serious illness or other personal circumstances that prevents you from sending the information

What isn't a good reason is that you have been too busy to send us the information.

Asking someone to help you

If you'd like independent help, you can ask a friend, relative, professional adviser or an organisation like Citizens Advice to help you. You can also ask them to talk to us on your behalf, but we can't talk to anyone without your permission.

If you do ask someone to act for you, either:

Complete and return form TC869 "Authority for an intermediary to act on your behalf" – go to GOV.UK and search for TC689, fill in the online form and return to us

• write to us at

Tax Credit Office
PRESTON
PR1 4AT

to request a TC689 form

Co-operation

The extent to which you co-operate and give us information is entirely up to you.

If you're not sure whether to give us the information, we suggest you get independent advice before deciding what to do. We may decide to reduce or stop your tax credits payments based on the information we hold.

About our decision

If you feel your payments shouldn't be suspended, you have the right to contact us to discuss whether or not they can be reinstated.

You have the right to ask us to reconsider if we:

- change your award
- ask you to pay a penalty
- charge you interest on any overpayment

We call this mandatory reconsideration and we'll tell you how to ask us to reconsider our decision in the letter we'll send telling you what we've done.

Our leaflet WTC/AP, "What to do if you think your Child Tax Creditor Working Tax Credit decision is wrong" gives more information about how to ask for a reconsideration. If you want to get a copy,

go to GOV.UK and search for WTC/AP.

If you're still unhappy after the reconsideration, you can appeal to an independent tribunal. Our Mandatory Reconsideration Notice will tell you how to do this.

Child Benefit

If you're claiming Child Benefit, any changes to your family circumstances may affect the amount you receive.

Your rights and obligations

"Your Charter" explains what you can expect from us and what we expect from you.

For more information, go to www.gov.uk/hmrc/your-charter

Help

If you have any questions or would like more details, contact the HMRC office shown on the covering letter.

Changes in circumstances

You must tell us within one month if:

- you get married, become a civil partner or part of a couple living together as if you're married
- you stop being part of a married couple, civil partnership or a couple living together as if you're married
- your childcare costs go down by an average of £10 a week or more
- your childcare costs stop or you stop paying for childcare costs
- you (or your partner)
  - leave the UK permanently
  - go abroad for a temporary absence lasting more than 8 weeks (or more than 12 weeks if you go abroad because you're ill, or because a member of your family is ill or has died)
  - lose your right to reside in the UK

- you're a couple responsible for a child and you work at least 16 hours but you or your partner are no longer
  - incapacitated
  - an inpatient in hospital
  - in prison or custody awaiting trial or sentence
  - entitled to Carers Allowance
- you start working, either in employment or self-employment
- your working hours drop below 16 a week
- you're a couple responsible for a child and your joint working hours drop below 24 a week (to qualify one of you must work at least 16 hours)
- you're working 30 hours or more a week and your hours drop below 30 (joint hours count for couples with children)
- you're laid off or stop work
- you have been on strike for more than 10 days
- a child or young person you're responsible for leaves the family to live with someone else or dies
- a child or young person you're responsible for stops qualifying for support, for example, they
  - leave full-time non-advanced education or approved training before the age of 20
  - start to have their training provided under a contract of employment
  - start paid work for 24 hours or more a week and they're not in full-time non-advanced education
  - stop being registered with a careers service, Connexions, local authority support service, Ministry of Defence or similar organisation within the EU
  - start to claim Income Support, income-based Jobseeker's Allowance, Employment and Support Allowance, Child Tax Credit, Working Tax Credit or Universal Credit in their own right

You should also tell us about any other changes which you think might affect your entitlement.

For more information go to www.gov.uk/changes-affect-tax-credits

Open government

The Claimant Compliance Manual contains more details about our work in this area. To read the manual,

Go to GOV.UK and search for the the Claimant Compliance Manual

Yr Iaith Gymraeg

Ffoniwch 0300 200 1900 i dderbyn fersiynau Cymraeg o ffurflennia chanllawiau

We've a range of services for disabled people. These include guidance in Braille, audio and large print. Most of our forms are also available in large print. Contact our helplines for more information.

WTC/AP: TAX CREDITS: IF YOU THINK A DECISION IS WRONG (WTC/AP)
[HMRC, 6 April 2018]

Use the online form service [https://www.tax.service.gov.uk/gg/sign-in?continue=%2Fforms%2Fform%2Ftax-credits-if-you-think-a-decision-is-wrong%2Fnew&accountType=individual] to ask for a Child Tax Credit or Working Tax Credit decision to be looked at again.

Details

If you think a Child Tax Credit or Working Tax Credit decision or penalty is wrong, you can ask the Tax Credit Office to look at it again.

You usually need to make your request within 30 days of the original decision.

To fill in the form you'll need:

- the date of the decision you want us to look at
- details of why you want us to look at it
- if you've also asked us to reconsider a decision about Child Benefit or Guardian's Allowance, the date you asked us to reconsider it

If you've a representative helping you with your request you'll also need their name and address.

If you use the online form, you'll get a reference number that you can use to track the progress of your form.

Send a postal form

You can ask the Tax Credit Office to reconsider a decision by printing one of the postal forms [https://assets.publishing.service.gov.uk/government/uploads/system/uploads/attachment_data/file/692187/WTC_AP_02_18.pdf] or [https://assets.publishing.service.gov.uk/government/uploads/system/uploads/attachment_data/file/539741/WTCAP_HMRC07-13.pdf], filling it in by hand and posting it to HM Revenue and Customs.

You need to send the postal form to:

Tax Credit Office
Preston
BX9 1ER

WTC1: CHILD TAX CREDIT AND WORKING TAX CREDIT [HMRC, April 2017]

An introduction

We've a range of services for disabled people. These include guidance in Braille, audio and large print. Most of our forms are also available in large print. Contact our helplines for more information.

This leaflet explains what Child Tax Credit and Working Tax Credit are, who can get them and how to make a claim.

Introduction

Child Tax Credit supports families with children (this can include children until their 16th birthday and young persons aged from 16 but under 20 years old). You can claim whether or not you're in work.

The amount you get is based on your income. As a rough guide, you may get an award of tax credits if you have:

- one child and a household income up to £26,200
- 2 children and a household income up to £32,900

It's important to know that these figures are a guide only.

Depending on your circumstances you may still qualify if your household income is higher. For example, if you pay for registered or approved childcare, are claiming for more than 2 children or have a child with a disability. See the table on page 6.

From 6 April 2017, the following changes apply:

- the individual child element of Child Tax Credit will no longer be awarded for third and subsequent children or qualifying young persons in a household, born on or after 6 April 2017, there are exceptions, for more information go to www.gov.uk/hmrc/ctc-exceptions
- the family element of Child Tax Credit will only be payable if you're responsible for a child or qualifying young person born before 6 April 2017

The 2 child limit doesn't apply to the childcare element of Working Tax Credit or the disability element of Child Tax Credit. You can claim these 2 elements for all children who meet the conditions.

For more information, go to GOV.UK and search for WTC5 (childcare element) or TC956 (child disability element).

To ensure you don't miss out on what you're entitled to, you should still report the birth of a child and any changes involving your children or young people, even if you won't get the child or family elements for them.

Working Tax Credit supports working people on low incomes, whether employed or self-employed, by topping up earnings.

Child Tax Credit and Working Tax Credit don't affect Child Benefit payments, which we pay separately.

To qualify for tax credits, you have to be aged 16 or over and usually live in the UK – that is, England, Scotland, Wales or Northern Ireland. The UK doesn't include the Channel Islands or the Isle of Man.

Phone our helpline on 0345 300 3900 for more information if you don't live in the UK but you (or your partner if you have one) are a national of a country in the European Economic Area (EEA*) or of Switzerland and you:

- work in the UK
- are a Crown servant posted overseas or their accompanying partner
- live in the EEA or Switzerland and are getting
  - UK State Pension
  - contribution-based Employment and Support Allowance
  - Industrial Injuries Disablement Benefit
  - Widow's Benefit or Bereavement Benefit

– Incapacity Benefit
– Severe Disablement Allowance

You may not be able to get tax credits if you're subject to "immigration control". Immigration control means:

- the Home Office gives you permission to stay in the UK – known as "leave to enter or remain" – but this permission is given to you on the grounds that you don't claim certain benefits, tax credits or housing assistance paid by the UK government – known as "recourse to public funds"
- you need permission to stay in the UK – again known as "leave to enter or remain" – but you don't have it
- you have been refused permission to stay in the UK, but you have appealed against that decision and your appeal hasn't been decided yet
- you have been given permission to stay in the UK, but on the condition that somebody else, like a friend or relative, pays for your upkeep and provides you with somewhere to live

Sometimes if you're subject to immigration control you might still be able to claim tax credits, for example, if you're part of a couple and only one of you is subject to immigration control.

For more information read our factsheet WTC/FS5, "Tax credits – coming to the UK".

Go to GOV.UK and search for WTC/FS5

- phone our helpline on 0345 300 3900 if you don't have internet access

You can also get our factsheet WTC/FS6, "Tax credits – for people leaving the UK".

Go to GOV.UK and search for WTC/FS6

- phone our helpline on 0345 300 3900 if you don't have internet access

You must make a joint claim as a couple if you're:

- married or in a civil partnership – unless you are separated under a court order or your separation is likely to be permanent
- living with somebody you're in a relationship with as if you're married or in a civil partnership – for example,
  - sometimes live in the same household
  - share costs and have joint financial arrangements
  - have dependent children, which you jointly care for in your household

You should still make a joint claim as a couple even if you're apart for short periods, for example, your partner is working away from home, on holiday or in hospital.

If you don't have a partner you should make a claim as a single person based on your individual circumstances.

Child Tax Credit

From 6 April 2017, the following changes apply:

- the individual child element of Child Tax Credit will no longer be awarded for third and subsequent children or qualifying young persons in a household, born on or after 6 April 2017, there are exceptions, for more information go to www.gov.uk/hmrc/ctc-exceptions
- the family element of Child Tax Credit will only be payable if you're responsible for a child or qualifying young person born before 6 April 2017

The 2 child limit doesn't apply to the childcare element of Working Tax Credit or the disability element of Child Tax Credit. You can claim these 2 elements for all children who meet the conditions.

For more information, go to GOV.UK and search for WTC5 (childcare element) or TC956 (child disability element).

To ensure you don't miss out on what you're entitled to, you should still report the birth of a child and any changes involving your children or young people, even if you won't get the child or family elements for them.

Child Tax Credit supports families with children.

About Child Tax Credit

You can claim Child Tax Credit if you're responsible for at least one child or young person. You don't have to be working to claim.

* The EEA consists of all EU member states plus Norway, Iceland and Liechtenstein.

TC Extra-statutory Material

You can usually claim Child Tax Credit for a child who lives with you until the 31 August after their 16th birthday. After this, you can still claim for them as long as they're under 20 and in full-time non-advanced education or approved training.

Full-time nonadvanced education

Full-time non-advanced education will usually be in a school or college but may also include education provided at home, if the child was receiving this education before their 16th birthday and the home schooling had previously been approved.

By full-time, in this situation, we mean an average of more than 12 hours supervised study a week, during term time, not counting breaks for meals and homework.

In England full-time non-advanced education could also take place other than at a school. Here full-time would include a study programme that is delivered to a person in at least 540 hours in any 12 month period. It could also include traineeship, a condensed study programme in England which could last between 6 weeks and 6 months.

We don't mean courses or education provided by an employer or as part of a job contract.

Examples of full-time non-advanced education are:

- GCSEs, A levels and other general academic qualifications of a similar standard, for example, iGCSEs, Pre-U and the International Baccalaureate
- NVQ level 1, 2 or 3
- BTEC National Diploma, National Certificate and First Diploma
- Traineeships (England)
- National 4 and 5 (Scotland)
- SVQ level 1, 2 or 3
- Scottish Group Awards

Approved training

Training is approved if it's provided under one of the following programmes.

In Scotland – The Employability Fund

In Wales – Foundation Apprenticeships or Traineeships

In Northern Ireland:

- United Youth Pilot
- Training for Success (including Programme Led Apprenticeships)
- Pathways for Success (Pathways for Young People element) or The Collaboration and Innovation Programme

Training provided by an employer as part of a contract of employment doesn't count as approved.

If your child is 16 or 17 and has left full-time non-advanced education or approved training, you may be able to get Child Tax Credit for them for up to 20 weeks after they left. To qualify for these extra weeks, your child needs to have registered for work or training with a qualifying body, such as the:

- careers service, Connexions, local authority support service or similar organisation within the European Union
- Ministry of Defence, if they're waiting to join the armed forces

To get these extra weeks, you must claim within 3 months of your child leaving education or training.

You can't claim Child Tax Credit for a young person aged 16 to 19 who:

- leaves full-time non-advanced education or approved training and is in paid work for 24 hours or more a week
- gets benefits or tax credits in their own right
- is serving a custodial sentence (imposed by a court) of more than 4 months

We pay Child Tax Credit on top of Child Benefit and any Working Tax Credit you may be able to get.

How much you can claim

The table below shows how much money you could get for the tax year 6 April 2017 to 5 April 2018 if you can't get Working Tax Credit. You could get more if you're in work.

The first figure in each column shows the maximum amount available and goes down as your income (or joint income, if you're part of a couple) goes up.

In general, taxable income such as:

- earnings from employment or profits from self-employment
- some social security benefits
- income from savings

counts as income in both Child Tax Credit and Working Tax Credit claims.

The claim form notes explain in more detail what counts as income.

For more information, go to GOV.UK and search for TC600 Notes

Child Tax Credit only (£)			
Annual income (£)	1 child/young person	2 children/young persons	3 children/young persons
No income	3,330	6,110	8,890
5,000	3,330	6,110	8,890
8,000	3,330	6,110	8,890
10,000	3,330	6,110	8,890
15,000	3,330	6,110	8,890
20,000	1,730	4,515	7,295
7,295	0	2,465	5,245
30,000	0	415	3,195
35,000	0	0	1,145
40,000	0	0	0

Using this table, if your income is £15,000 a year and you have 2 children but are not eligible for Working Tax Credit, you could get an annual Child Tax Credit award of £6,110 equivalent to £117.50 a week.

Note: If you have a child with a disability, you may be entitled to more.

For more information go www.gov.uk/child-tax-credit/what-youll-get

How Child Tax Credit is paid

We pay Child Tax Credit directly to the bank, building society or Post Office® card account of the main carer for all the children in the family. You can choose who is the main carer and whether to get payments weekly or every 4 weeks.

If you're getting another benefit

You're entitled to the maximum amount of Child Tax Credit for your children if you get:

- Income Support
- income-based Jobseeker's Allowance
- income-related Employment and Support Allowance
- Pension Credit

Working Tax Credit

About Working Tax Credit

Working Tax Credit is for working people (employed or self-employed) on low incomes, including those who don't have children. There are extra amounts for:

- working households in which someone has a disability
- the costs of qualifying childcare

If you're responsible for a child or young person and you're not part of a couple you can claim Working Tax Credit if you're aged 16 or over and you work at least 16 hours a week.

If you're responsible for a child or young person and you're part of a couple you can claim Working Tax Credit if you're both aged 16 or over and:

- you work at least 24 hours a week between you with one partner working at least 16 hours a week
- one partner works at least 16 hours a week and that partner qualifies for the disability element of Working Tax Credit or is aged 60 or over

TC Extra-statutory Material

- one partner works at least 16 hours a week and the other partner can't work because they're
  - incapacitated (getting certain benefits because of disability or ill health)
  - an inpatient in hospital
  - in prison serving a custodial sentence or remanded in custody awaiting trial or sentence
  - entitled to Carer's Allowance

If you're not responsible for a child or young person you can claim Working Tax Credit if you or your partner are aged:

- 25 or over and work at least 30 hours a week
- 16 or over, work at least 16 hours a week and qualify for the disability element of Working Tax Credit
- 60 or over and work at least 16 hours a week

The detailed rules for people with disabilities are in the claim form notes.

For more information, go to GOV.UK and search for TC600 Notes

How much you can claim

The amount of Working Tax Credit you get is based on your circumstances, for example, how many hours you normally work, and your income (or joint income, if you're part of a couple).

The table below shows how much money you could get for the tax year 6 April 2017 to 5 April 2018 if you're in work and responsible for at least one child or young person.

Working Tax Credit and Child Tax Credit (£)			
Annual income (£)	1 child/young person	2 children/young persons	3 children/young persons[3]
6,240[1]	7,300	10,080	12,865
11,700[2]	5,945	8,725	11,510
15,000	4,595	7,375	10,155
20,000	2,545	5,325	8,105
25,000	495	3,275	6,055
30,000	0	1,225	4,005
35,000	0	0	1,955
40,000	0	0	0

[1] Those with incomes of £6,240 a year are assumed to work part-time (working between 16 and 29 hours a week).

[2] In families with an income of £11,700 or more a year, at least one adult is assumed to be working 30 hours or more a week (consistent with the national living wage of £7.50 based on April 2017 rates for those aged 25 and over).

[3] For more information on child eligibility see Child Tax Credit section on page 4

Note: If you have a child with a disability, you may be entitled to more.

For more information go www.gov.uk/child-tax-credit/what-youll-get

The table below shows how much money you could get if you're in work but not responsible for any children or young persons.

Working Tax Credit, for those without children (£)		
Annual income (£)	Single person aged 25 or over working 30 hours or more a week	Couple, working adults aged 25 or over, working 30 hours or more a week
11,700[1]	605	2,615
13,000	75	2,085
14,000	0	1,675
15,000	0	1,265
16,000	0	855
17,000	0	445
18,000	0	35
19,000	0	0

[1] Someone aged 25 or over, working 30 hours a week on national living wage (based on April 2017 rates) would earn £11,700 a year.

You can get a higher rate of Working Tax Credit if you (or your partner, if you have one):

- are a working person who qualifies for a disability element
- have a severe disability

You may be able to get extra help with the costs of registered or approved childcare. We call this the childcare element of Working Tax Credit. The claim form notes tell you what "registered" or "approved" childcare is.

Help with the costs of childcare if you're working

You can only get the childcare element if you're working at least 16 hours a week. If you're part of a couple, generally both you and your partner must work at least 16 hours a week to qualify. Only one of you must work at least 16 hours if the other can't work because they're:

- incapacitated (getting certain benefits because of ill health or disability)
- an inpatient in hospital
- in prison serving a custodial sentence or remanded in custody awaiting trial or sentence
- entitled to Carer's Allowance

The childcare element is worth up to 70 pence in tax credits for every £1 a week you spend on approved childcare. This is limited to a childcare cost of £175 a week if you have one child and £300 a week for 2 or more children. The maximum childcare element you can get is either:

- £122.50 a week (70% of £175) for one child
- £210 a week (70% of £300) for 2 or more children

For example, if you spend £100 a week, the childcare element is worth up to £70 in tax credits. If you spend £40 a week, the childcare element is worth up to £28.

The childcare element is in addition to the amount of Working Tax Credit you can get, but is paid with Child Tax Credit to the main carer in the family. The final amount you get will depend on your income (or joint income, if you're part of a couple).

ⓘ You may get extra help with the costs of registered or approved childcare for a child, even if you don't receive the child element for them.

How Working Tax Credit is paid

We pay Working Tax Credit directly to your bank, building society or Post Office® card account.

How you can claim or get more information

For more information about tax credits, to check if you can claim and to order a claim form, go to www.gov.uk/taxcredits

For an estimate of how much you may get, go to www.gov.uk/tax-credits-calculator

If you want any more advice about tax credits, you can:

- phone the Tax Credit Helpline on 0345 300 3900
- textphone the Tax Credit Helpline (for people with hearing or speech difficulties) on 0345 300 3909

For our opening hours,

go to www.gov.uk/contact-hmrc

Help and advice

If you phone for a claim pack it will help us if you can tell us your :

- income details (and those of your partner if you have one) for the tax year from 6 April 2016 to 5 April 2017
- National Insurance number

Backdating your claim

We can normally only backdate your tax credits for up to one month from the date we get your claim. So, to avoid losing money make sure you claim straightaway.

You'll need to ask for backdating if any of the following apply, you're:

- receiving Income Support, income-based Jobseeker's Allowance, income-related Employment and Support Allowance, or Pension Credit
- only claiming Working Tax Credit and haven't received Income Support, income-based Jobseeker's Allowance, income-related Employment and Support Allowance, or Pension Credit in the last 31 days

- claiming either Working Tax Credit or Child Tax Credit or both, and have come off Income Support, income-based Jobseeker's Allowance, income-related Employment and Support Allowance, or Pension Credit in the last 31 days

To ask for backdating, send us a separate sheet of paper with your claim form telling us:

- your name, address and National Insurance number
- the date you started work or the date you started getting one of the benefits listed above

Tax credit claims can sometimes be backdated more than a month if you apply within one month of the decision awarding you certain qualifying sickness or disability benefits, for example, Disability Living Allowance or Personal Independence Payment. Tell us the date your benefit was awarded from, if this applies to you.

For more information about backdating a claim, go to www.gov.uk/claim-tax-credits/backdate-a-claim

Universal Credit and tax credits

Universal Credit supports people who are on a low income or out of work. It's being introduced in stages and will eventually replace Working Tax Credit and Child Tax Credit.

It will affect people at different times depending on where they live, their circumstances and what benefits they claim. To see the list of areas where you can claim Universal Credit instead of tax credits, go to

www.gov.uk/guidance/jobcentres-where-you-can-claim-universal-credit

If you're already getting tax credits, you don't need to do anything yet. You should continue to report changes in your circumstances that could affect your tax credits straightaway.

If your change of circumstances means you become entitled to Universal Credit, for example, if you lose your job or start living with a partner who already gets Universal Credit, your tax credits payments will stop and you'll make a Universal Credit claim instead.

You can't claim Universal Credit and tax credits at the same time.

For more information about Universal Credit, go to www.gov.uk/universal-credit

Your rights and obligations

"Your Charter" explains what you can expect from us and what we expect from you. For more information, go to

www.gov.uk/hmrc/your-charter

If you give us incorrect information, we may charge you a penalty up to £3,000 or we may prosecute you. Our leaflet WTC7, "Tax credits penalties" gives more information about penalties.

Go to GOV.UK and search for WTC7

- phone our helpline on 0345 300 3900 if you don't have access to the internet

WTC2: A GUIDE TO CHILD TAX CREDIT AND WORKING TAX CREDIT [HMRC, April 2018]

1 Introduction

There are 2 tax credits, Child Tax Credit and Working Tax Credit.

This guide explains in detail what they are, who is eligible and how to claim.

More information about Child Tax Credit is on page 5 and Working Tax Credit on page 8.

If you're responsible for children or are working as an employee or a self-employed person, you should find out more about tax credits.

The claim form includes comprehensive guidance notes.

Child Tax Credit and Working Tax Credit don't affect Child Benefit payments, which we pay separately.

Child Tax Credit supports families with children. This can include children until their 16th birthday and young persons aged from 16 but under 20 years old. You can claim whether or not you're in work.

The amount you get is based on your income. As a rough guide, you may get an award of Child Tax Credit if you have:

- *one child and a* household income of up to about £26,200
- 2 children and a household income of up to about £32,900

It's important to know that these figures are a guide only. Depending on your circumstances you may still qualify if your household income is higher. For example, if you're claiming for more than 2 children or have a child with a disability – read the information in the table on page 7.

Working Tax Credit is for working people on a low income and is based on the hours you work and get paid for, or expect to get paid for. You can claim whether you're an employee or a self-employed person. Unpaid work doesn't count for Working Tax Credit. You may also be able to get help with childcare costs.

From 6 April 2017, the following changes apply:

- the individual child element of Child Tax Credit will no longer be awarded for third and subsequent children or qualifying young persons in a household, born on or after 6 April 2017, there are exceptions, for more information go to www.gov.uk/hmrc/ctc-exceptions
- the family element of Child Tax Credit will only be payable if you're responsible for a child or qualifying young person born before 6 April 2017

The 2 child limit doesn't apply to the childcare element of Working Tax Credit or the disability element of Child Tax Credit. You can claim these 2 elements for all children who meet the conditions.

For more information, go to GOV.UK and search for WTC5 (childcare element) or TC956 (child disability element)

To ensure you don't miss out on what you're entitled to, you should still report the birth of a child and any changes involving your children or young people, even if you won't get the child or family elements for them.

Phone the Tax Credit Helpline on 0345 300 3900 if you need any more help.

For more information for people arriving to live or work in the UK and the exceptions, go to www.gov.uk/tax-credits-if-moving-country-or-travelling

Or, phone the Tax Credit Helpline on 0345 300 3900.

Who is eligible

To qualify for tax credits, you must be aged 16 or over and usually live in the United Kingdom (UK), that is, England, Scotland, Wales and Northern Ireland. The UK doesn't include the Channel Islands or the Isle of Man. Short absences of up to 8 weeks, or in some cases 12 weeks, won't affect your eligibility.

For Child Tax Credit you must have the right to reside in the UK.

Some people may be eligible even if they don't live in the UK. For example, if you live outside the UK but you, or your partner if you have one, are a national of another country in the European Economic Area (EEA), or of Switzerland and you:

- work in the UK
- are a Crown servant posted overseas or their accompanying partner
- live in the EEA or Switzerland, and get
  - UK State Pension
  - contribution-based Employment and Support Allowance
  - Industrial Injuries Disablement Benefit
  - Widow's Benefit or Bereavement Benefit
  - Incapacity Benefit
  - Severe Disablement Allowance

Countries in the European Economic Area are:

Austria	Greece	Norway
Belgium	Hungary	Poland
Bulgaria	Iceland	Portugal
Croatia	Ireland	Romania
Cyprus	Italy	Slovakia
Czech Republic	Latvia	Slovenia
Denmark	Liechtenstein	Spain
Estonia	Lithuania	Sweden
Finland	Luxembourg	United Kingdom
France	Malta	
Germany	Netherlands	

Element	Annual amount for 2018 to 2019 (£)
Family element (one per family)	545
Child element (paid for each child or qualifying young person)	2,780
Disability element of Child Tax Credit, where the child or qualifying young person is disabled (paid in addition to the child element)	3,275
Disability element of Child Tax Credit, where the child or qualifying young person is severely disabled[1] (paid in addition to the child element)	4,600

[1] Shown as 2 separate elements on your Award Notice – Disability element of £3,275 and Severe Disability element of £1,325 totalling £4,600.

You may get a disability element of £3,275 for each child or qualifying young person you're responsible for if:

- Disability Living Allowance (DLA) or Personal Independence Payment (PIP) is being paid for him or her or would be so payable but for hospitalisation of the child or qualifying young person
- the child or qualifying young person is certified as severely sight impaired or blind by a consultant ophthalmologist
- the child ceased to be certified as severely sight impaired or blind by a consultant ophthalmologist in the 28 weeks before the date of your claim

You may get a disability element of £4,600 for each child or qualifying young person you're responsible for if they're paid either:

- DLA (highest rate care component) or would be so payable but for suspension of the benefit or hospitalisation of the child or qualifying young person
- enhanced daily living component of PIP or would be so payable but for hospitalisation of the child or qualifying young person
- Armed Forces Independence Payment

From 6 April 2017, the following changes apply:

- the individual child element of Child Tax Credit will no longer be awarded for third and subsequent children or qualifying young persons in a household, born on or after 6 April 2017, there are exceptions, for more information go to www.gov.uk/hmrc/ctc-exceptions
- the family element of Child Tax Credit will only be payable if you're responsible for a child or qualifying young person born before 6 April 2017

The 2 child limit doesn't apply to the childcare element of Working Tax Credit or the disability element of Child Tax Credit. You can claim these 2 elements for all children who meet the conditions.

For more information, go to GOV.UK and search for WTC5 (childcare element) or TC956 (child disability element)

To ensure you don't miss out on what you're entitled to, you should still report the birth of a child and any changes involving your children or young people, even if you won't get the child or family elements for them.

How much you can get

The table [below] shows how much money you could get for the tax year 6 April 2018 to 5 April 2019 if you can't get Working Tax Credit. You could get more if you're in work. The first figure in each column shows the maximum amount available and goes down as your income (or joint income, if you're part of a couple) goes up.

If your child has a disability, the amount you can get will be higher.

Child Tax Credit is paid in addition to Child Benefit. The amounts of Child Tax Credit are shown below in pounds.

Annual income (£)	One child/ qualifying young person	2 children/ qualifying young persons	3 children/ qualifying young persons
No income	3,330	6,110	8,890
5,000	3,330	6,110	8,890
8,000	3,330	6,110	8,890
10,000	3,330	6,110	8,890
15,000	3,330	6,110	8,890
20,000	1,730	4,515	7,295

Annual income (£)	One child/ qualifying young person	2 children/ qualifying young persons	3 children/ qualifying young persons
25,000	0	2,465	5,245
30,000	0	415	3,195
35,000	0	0	1,145
40,000+	0	0	0

Using this table, if your income is £15,000 a year and you have 2 children but aren't eligible for Working Tax Credit, you could get an annual Child Tax Credit award of £6,110, equivalent to £117.50 a week.

Child Tax Credit will be paid directly to the main carer for all the children in the family. If you're part of a couple, you'll need to tell us which of you is the main carer for the children. If you're a single parent, this will be paid direct to you. You can choose whether to get payments weekly or every 4 weeks.

Payments will normally be made into a bank, building society or Post Office® card account.

If you're getting another benefit

You're entitled to the maximum amount of Child Tax Credit for your children if you get:

- Income Support
- income-based Jobseeker's Allowance
- income-related Employment and Support Allowance
- Pension Credit

3 Working Tax Credit

Working Tax Credit

Working Tax Credit is for working people on a low income. You can be employed or self-employed, and you don't have to have children to claim. In all cases you have to be either:

- working (whether in employment or self-employment) when you make your claim
- starting paid work within 7 days of making your claim

You may get more if you have a disability or are responsible for children and have childcare costs.

Working Tax Credit is paid directly to the person who is working.

The childcare element of Working Tax Credit is paid directly to the main carer of the child or children along with Child Tax Credit.

How Working Tax Credit is made up

Working Tax Credit contains several elements, including additional amounts for:

- working people with a disability
- people with a severe disability
- the costs of registered or approved childcare

The maximum value of each element is listed below, but the amount you get depends on your income.

Element	Annual amount for 2018 to 2019 (£)
Basic element (one per single person or couple)	1,960
Couple element[2] (paid in addition to basic element but only one couple element allowed per couple)	2,010
Lone parent element (paid in addition to basic element for single customers who are responsible for a child or qualifying young person)	2,010
30-hour element[3] (paid in addition to other elements but only one 30-hour element allowed per couple)	810
Disability worker element[1] (paid in addition to other elements)	3,090
Severe disability element[1] (paid in addition to other elements)	1,330
Childcare element, maximum eligible cost for families with childcare for one child	£175 a week
Childcare element, maximum eligible cost for families with childcare for 2 or more children	£300 a week
Percentage of eligible childcare costs covered	70%

Notes

[1] If the claim is a joint claim and you're both entitled to any of these elements, the award will include 2 elements per couple.

[2] If you're in a couple and one of you is subject to immigration control, and you're not claiming for any children, you won't normally be able to get the couple element. But you still need to make a joint claim.

[3] The 30-hour element is available to those working 30 hours or more per week.

Working hours

You usually need to be working a minimum number of hours a week to claim Working Tax Credit.

If you're responsible for a child or qualifying young person and you're not part of a couple, you can claim Working Tax Credit if you:

- are aged 16 or over
- work at least 16 hours a week

If you're responsible for a child or qualifying young person and you're part of a couple, you can claim Working Tax Credit if you're both aged 16 or over and:

- you work at least 24 hours a week between you, with one partner working at least 16 hours a week
- one partner works at least 16 hours a week and qualifies for the disability element of Working Tax Credit
- one partner works at least 16 hours a week and is aged 60 or over
- one partner works at least 16 hours a week and the other partner can't work because they're
  - incapacitated (getting certain benefits because of a disability or ill health)
  - an inpatient in hospital
  - in prison either on remand or serving a custodial sentence
  - entitled to Carer's Allowance

Also see pages 13 to 15 about the disability elements.

If you're not responsible for a child or qualifying young person you can claim Working Tax Credit if you or your partner, if you have one, are aged:

- 25 or over and work at least 30 hours a week
- 16 or over, work at least 16 hours a week and qualify for the disability element of Working Tax Credit
- over 60 and work at least 16 hours a week

If you're part of a couple with children, you're eligible for the 30-hour element if you jointly work at least 30 hours a week. This is providing one of you works at least 16 hours. Couples without children can't add their hours together to qualify for the 30-hour element.

You must expect the work to:

- continue for at least 4 weeks after you've made the claim
- be paid, so for example, working as a volunteer where you're not paid doesn't normally count

You can still claim Working Tax Credit if you work at a school or college and don't work during school or college holidays.

For more information on how to work out your hours, go to www.gov.uk/claim-tax-credits/working-hours

For self-employed customers, go to www.gov.uk/hmrc-internal-manuals/claimant-compliance-manual and search for CCM6755

If you're a foster carer the hours you work as a foster carer may count for tax credits if you're paid by your local authority. If foster caring is your main source of income or your main job you may get Working Tax Credit.

Limitations to entitlement

Entitlement to Working Tax Credit is deliberately wide ranging but some restrictions apply. Working Tax Credit may not be available to you, if you are:

- engaged by a charitable organisation, or a volunteer, and get only expenses payments
- working for a local authority, health authority, charitable or voluntary organisation caring for someone *who isn't a member* of your household and where the only payment you get is covered by the Rent-a-Room scheme
- engaged on a scheme for which a training allowance is being paid unless the training allowance is taxable as part of your employed or self-employed income

- participating in the Intensive Activity Period or Preparation for Employment Programme, unless the payments you get are taxable as part of your employed or self-employed income
- engaged in an activity where a sports award has been made
- participating in an Employment Zone programme unless you only get disregarded discretionary payments or a training premium
- serving a custodial sentence or remanded in custody and are engaged in work while serving the sentence or remanded in custody
- a student only doing work as part of your course, as any grant or loan that you receive is for maintenance and doesn't count as payment for work
- a student nurse, as the NHS Bursary and other grants or loans you receive don't count as payment for work

Maternity leave

Most women get Statutory Maternity Pay (SMP) or Maternity Allowance (MA) for the first:

- 26 weeks of ordinary maternity leave
- 13 weeks of any additional maternity leave

This can be followed by up to 13 weeks of unpaid leave.

For the 26 weeks of ordinary maternity leave, and for the first 13 weeks of additional maternity leave, that is, for a total of 39 weeks, whether or not you're getting SMP or MA, you're still treated as being in work and able to claim Working Tax Credit. This is providing you and your partner, if you have one, worked the required number of hours applicable to your circumstances immediately before going on maternity leave. This also applies if you're self-employed.

If you're a first-time mother, you can claim Working Tax Credit from the date of birth of your first child. This is providing you and your partner, if you have one, usually worked the required number of hours applicable to your circumstances, as a person responsible for a child, immediately before going on maternity leave (read Working hours on page 9).

When the 39 weeks (this includes 26 weeks of ordinary maternity leave and 13 weeks additional maternity leave) are over, you continue to be eligible for Working Tax Credit if you begin work again at that point. Any further additional maternity leave doesn't count as being in work. You must tell us within one month if you don't go back to work after the 39 weeks.

Adoption leave or paternity leave

If you adopt a child you may be eligible for Statutory Adoption Pay (SAP) for the first:

- 26 weeks of ordinary adoption leave
- 13 weeks of any additional adoption leave

New parents may be eligible for 2 weeks ordinary paternity leave and be paid Ordinary Statutory Paternity Pay (OSPP) for those 2 weeks. New parents may be eligible for up to 26 weeks additional paternity leave and be paid Additional Statutory Paternity Pay (ASPP) if your partner has returned to work.

If you're on ordinary adoption leave, ordinary or additional paternity leave, or on the first 13 weeks of any additional adoption leave, whether or not you're getting SAP, OSPP or ASPP, you'll still count as being in work and able to claim Working Tax Credit. This is providing you and your partner, if you have one, worked the required number of hours applicable to your circumstances immediately before going on adoption or paternity leave. This also applies if you're self-employed (read Working hours on page 9).

If you're a first-time parent, you can claim Working Tax Credit from the date of placement for adoption or birth of your first child. This is providing you and your partner, if you have one, worked the required number of hours applicable to your circumstances as a person responsible for a child immediately before your adoption or paternity leave began.

When your time on:

- ordinary adoption leave
- ordinary or additional paternity leave
- the first 13 weeks of additional adoption leave

is over, you continue to be eligible for Working Tax Credit if you begin working again at that point. Any further leave doesn't count as being in work. You must tell us within one month if you don't go back to work after this time.

Shared Parental Leave

You may be entitled to Shared Parental Leave (SPL) and Statutory Shared Parental Pay (ShPP) if:

- your baby was born on or after 5 April 2015
- you adopted a child on or after 5 April 2015

You can start SPL if you're eligible and you or your partner end their maternity or adoption leave or pay early. The remaining leave will be available as SPL. The remaining pay may be available as ShPP.

You can take SPL in up to 3 separate blocks. You can also share the leave with your partner if they're also eligible. Parents can choose how much of the SPL each of them will take.

SPL and ShPP must be taken between the baby's birth and first birthday (or within one year of adoption). SPL and ShPP are only available in England, Scotland and Wales.

If you're eligible and you or your partner end maternity or adoption leave and pay (or Maternity Allowance) early, then you can take the rest of the:

- 52 weeks of leave (up to a maximum of 50 weeks) as Shared Parental Leave (SPL)
- 39 weeks of pay (up to a maximum of 37 weeks) as Statutory Shared Parental Pay (ShPP)

A mother must take a minimum of 2 weeks maternity leave following the birth (4 if she works in a factory).

For any period you or your partner are receiving Statutory Shared Parental Pay you're still treated as being in work and able to claim Working Tax Credit. This is providing you and your partner, if you have one, worked the required number of hours applicable to your circumstances immediately before going on Shared Parental Leave (SPL). This also applies if you're self-employed.

When your time on SPL is over, you continue to be eligible for Working Tax Credit if you begin working again at that point. Any further leave doesn't count as being in work. You must tell us within one month if you don't go back to work after this time.

Sick leave

If you're off work for up to 28 weeks because of illness and are getting either:

- Statutory Sick Pay (SSP)
- short-term Incapacity Benefit at the lower rate
- Employment and Support Allowance
- Income Support paid on the grounds of incapacity for work
- National Insurance credits on the grounds of incapacity for work or limited capability for work

then you'll still count as being in work and be able to claim Working Tax Credit. This is providing you and your partner, if you have one, worked the required number of hours applicable to your circumstances immediately before you started getting any of these benefits. This also applies if you're self-employed (read Working hours on page 9).

When the 28 weeks of sick leave are over you continue to be eligible for Working Tax Credit if you begin work again at that point. Any further sick leave doesn't count as being in work. You must tell us within one month if you don't go back to work after the 28 weeks.

The disability element

If you meet all of the following 3 conditions, you may be able to get the disability element of Working Tax Credit. If you're claiming as a couple and your partner also meets all 3 conditions, you may be able to get 2 disability elements.

Condition 1: You usually work 16 hours or more a week.

Condition 2: You have a disability which puts you at a disadvantage in getting a job.

Details of the disabilities which count to meet this condition are set out in the notes that go with the tax credits claim form. They relate to a wide range of things, for example:

- seeing
- hearing
- communicating with people
- getting around
- using your hands
- reaching with your arms
- mental disabilities
- exhaustion and pain

We may ask you to give us the name of a healthcare professional who can confirm how your disability affects you. For example, a doctor, a district or community nurse, or an occupational therapist.

Condition 3: You currently get, or have been getting, a qualifying sickness or disability benefit.

You'll meet this condition if at least one of the following 4 descriptions applies to you, or if you:

- were entitled to the disability element of Working Tax Credit within the last 8 weeks
- had this entitlement because you satisfied one of the descriptions in 2, 3 or 4 on the following pages

1 You're getting one of the following qualifying benefits:

- Attendance Allowance
- Disability Living Allowance, Personal Independence Payment or Armed Forces Independence Payment
- Industrial Injuries Disablement Benefit (with Constant Attendance Allowance for you)
- a vehicle provided under the Invalid Vehicle Scheme
- War Pension (with Constant Attendance Allowance or Mobility Supplement for you)

2 You have received a sickness or disability benefit for at least one day in the last 6 months. The benefits that count are:

- Employment and Support Allowance (ESA), where you have received this allowance for 28 weeks or more or you received Statutory Sick Pay (SSP) followed by ESA for a combined period of 28 weeks or more (see Note 1 below)
- Incapacity Benefit at the short-term higher rate or the long-term rate
- income-based Jobseeker's Allowance*
- Income Support*
- Housing Benefit*
- Severe Disablement Allowance

Note 1: The 28 weeks doesn't need to be a single continuous period. You can add together any periods that you got:

- Employment and Support Allowance (ESA), as long as they were no more than 12 weeks apart
- Statutory Sick Pay (SSP), as long as they were no more than 8 weeks apart
- SSP with periods that you got ESA, as long as they were no more than 12 weeks apart

3 You have been "training for work" for at least one day in the last 8 weeks.

"Training for work" means attending government-run training such as that provided by the Work Programme in the UK, Work Based Learning for Adults in Wales, Training for Work in Scotland or a course that you attended for 16 hours or more a week to learn an occupational or vocational skill.

In the 8 weeks before you started training for work you must have been getting:

- Incapacity Benefit paid at the short-term higher rate or long-term rate
- Severe Disablement Allowance
- contribution-based ESA for 28 weeks or more
- Statutory Sick Pay (SSP) followed by contribution-based ESA for a combined period of 28 weeks or more (see Note 2)

Note 2: The 28 weeks doesn't need to be a single continuous period. You can add together any periods that you got:

- contribution-based ESA, as long as they were no more than 12 weeks apart
- any periods that you got SSP, as long as they were no more than 8 weeks apart
- SSP with periods that you got contribution-based ESA, this is providing they were no more than 12 weeks apart and you met the contribution conditions for contribution-based ESA on the days that you got SSP

4 All of the following 4 points (4.1 to 4.4) apply to you.

4.1 You've been getting at least one of the benefits in box A or box B for 20 weeks or more (read Note 3 overleaf), and you got this benefit within the last 8 weeks.

A

- Statutory Sick Pay
- Occupational Sick Pay
- Incapacity Benefit at the short-term lower rate
- Income Support paid because of incapacity for work
- National Insurance credits awarded because of incapacity for work

---

* This must include a Disability Premium or a Higher Pensioner Premium for you.

- an approved foster carer registered with Ofsted –but the childcare must be for a child who isn't the carer's foster child
- a care worker or a nurse from a registered domiciliary care agency, looking after your child in your own home

For more information about childcare in England, go to www.gov.uk/childcare-tax-credits

In Scotland

To get help with childcare costs in Scotland, your childcare provider must be:

- registered with Social Care and Social Work Improvement Scotland
- a childcare club registered with Social Care and Social Work Improvement Scotland to provide childcare outside of school hours
- a person from a registered childcare agency, sitter service or nanny agency providing childcare in your child's home

You can also claim help with your childcare costs in Scotland if you use:

- an approved foster carer
- a kinship carer

but the childcare must be for a child who isn't the carer's foster or kinship child. The foster carer or kinship carer must be registered with Social Care and Social Work Improvement Scotland as a childminder or a day care provider.

For more information about childcare in Scotland, go to www.scottishfamilies.gov.uk

In Wales

To get help with childcare costs in Wales, your childcare provider must be:

- registered by the National Assembly for Wales through the Care and Social Services Inspectorate for Wales (CSSIW)
- a person who is employed or engaged under a contract for services to provide care and support by the provider of domiciliary care support service within the meaning of Part 1 of the Regulation and Inspection of Social Care (Wales) Act 2016
- a school that provides childcare outside of school hours and on the school premises
- a local authority that provides childcare outside of school hours
- someone approved by the Approval of Childcare Providers (Wales) Scheme 2007 who provides childcare in the child's home, or if several children are being looked after, in one of the children's homes
- an approved foster carer but the childcare must be for a child who isn't the carer's foster child and the foster carer must be
  - registered with the Care and Social Services Inspectorate Wales if your child is under age 8
  - approved under the Approval of Child Care Providers (Wales) Scheme if the care is in your child's home and your child is under age 16

For more information about childcare in Wales, go to www.wales.gov.uk and search for childcare

In Northern Ireland

To get help with childcare costs in Northern Ireland, your childcare provider must be:

- registered with a Health and Social Care Trust
- a school that provides childcare outside of school hours, on the school premises
- a person approved under the Approval of Home Child Care Providers (Northern Ireland) 2006 Scheme providing childcare in the child's home
- an Education and Library Board that provides childcare outside of school hours
- an approved foster carer, but the childcare must be for a child who isn't the carer's foster child, and the foster carer must be
  - registered with a Health and Social Care Trust if your child is under age 12
  - approved under the Approval of Home Child Care Providers (Northern Ireland) 2006 Scheme if the care is in your child's home and your child is under age 16

For more information about childcare in Northern Ireland contact the Early Years Team in your local Health and Social Care Trust.

Go to www.nidirect.gov.uk/early-years-teams

Crown servants working abroad

If you're a civil servant or a member of the armed forces posted overseas, and your child has gone with you, you may get help with childcare costs if your childcare provider is approved by a Ministry of Defence accreditation scheme abroad.

Childcare provided by a relative

A relative could be your child's:

- parent
- grandparent
- aunt or uncle
- brother or sister
- step-parent

A person who has entered into a civil partnership is recognised as being able to provide childcare as a parent, grandparent, aunt or uncle, or step-parent.

If you have any questions about the meaning of "relative", phone the Tax Credit Helpline on 0345300 3900.

You can't get the childcare element of Working Tax Credit if your childcare is provided by a relative even if they're registered or approved.

The exception to this is when your child is cared for by a relative who's a:

- registered childminder who cares for your child, away from your child's own home
- childcare provider approved under a Home Child Care Providers Scheme in Wales or Northern Ireland, who cares for your child away from your child's own home. They must also care for at least one other child who's not related to them

The relationship can be by blood, half-blood, marriage, civil partnership or affinity. **"Affinity"** means a person with a strong relationship to the child, for example, someone in a parental position regarding their partner's children, and this could include step-parents.

You can't claim the costs of childcare if it isn't registered or approved. Your provider should be able to tell you whether or not they're registered or approved. Some providers have to renew their registration each year. Ask to see their registration or approval certificate to check that it's still valid.

In order to claim the childcare element you must work out your average weekly childcare costs. For more information about how to do this, read our leaflet WTC5, "Working Tax Credit: help with the costs of childcare".

Go to GOV.UK and search for WTC5.

If you don't have internet access, phone the Tax Credit Helpline on 0345 300 3900 for a copy.

How much Working Tax Credit you can get

Working Tax Credit is paid in addition to any Child Tax Credit you may be entitled to. Some people will be paid both Child Tax Credit and Working Tax Credit.

The amount of your Working Tax Credit award is based on your circumstances (for example, how many hours you work or whether you're disabled) and your income. The table below provides a guide to how much (in pounds) you could get for the tax year 6 April 2018 to 5 April 2019.

The table below shows how much money you could get if you are in work and not responsible for any children or young persons.

Annual income (£)	Single person aged 25 or over, working 30 hours or more a week	Couple (working adults aged 25 or over) working 30 hours or more a week
12,215[1]	395	2,405
13,000	75	2,085
14,000	0	1,675
15,000	0	1,265
16,000	0	855
17,000	0	445
18,000	0	35
19,000+	0	0

[1] Someone aged 25 or over, working 30 hours a week on National Living Wage (based on April 2018 rates) would earn £12,215 a year.

TC Extra-statutory Material

The table below shows how much money you could get for the tax year 6 April 2018 to 5 April 2019 if you're in work and responsible for at least one child or young person.

Annual income (£)	One child/ qualifying young person	2 children/ qualifying young persons	3 children/ qualifying young persons
6,240[1]	7,300	10,080	12,865
12,215[2]	5,735	8,515	11,295
15,000	4,595	7,375	10,155
20,000	2,545	5,325	8,105
25,000	495	3,275	6,055
30,000	0	1,225	4,005
35,000	0	0	1,955
40,000+	0	0	0

[1] Those with incomes of £6,240 a year are assumed to work part-time (working between 16 and 29 hours a week).

[2] In families with an income of £12,215 a year or more, at least one adult is assumed to be working 30 or more hours a week (consistent with National Living Wage of £7.83 based on April 2018 rates for those aged 25 and over).

Note: If you have a child with a disability you may be entitled to more.

Using these tables, for example, if you are claiming as a lone parent or a couple with 2 children and working 30 hours or more a week, with an income of £12,215 a year, you could get an annual tax credits award of £8,515.

The maximum amounts may be higher if you're entitled to the disability or childcare elements of Working Tax Credit.

4 Income and capital

For more information about what types of income count for tax credits purposes, phone the Tax Credit Helpline on 0345 300 3900.

The amount of tax credits you'll get depends on your circumstances, for example:

- how many children or qualifying young persons you're responsible for
- how many hours you work each week
- whether you're disabled
- how much you pay for registered or approved childcare

It also depends on the level of your income. If you're part of a couple, it depends on your joint income.

As Child Tax Credit and Working Tax Credit are annual tax credits, we'll look at your income for a tax year to work out your award, usually the last complete tax year before the year of the tax credits claim.

What income you have to report

For tax credits, we generally take into account your gross earnings figure (this is before Income Tax and National Insurance deductions). There are exceptions, some of which are outlined on the next page.

If you make contributions from your earnings to buy shares in your employers company under Share Incentive Plan, then those contributions must be added back to your gross pay.

Contributions to any HM Revenue and Customs registered pension scheme (such as a personal pension plan or retirement annuity) and payments under the Gift Aid scheme should be deducted when you workout your income for a tax credits claim. If you made personal pension or retirement annuity contributions, Gift Aid payments or a trading loss, read TC825, "Working sheet for tax credits relief for Gift Aid donations, pension contributions and trading losses".

Go to GOV.UK and search for TC825

If you don't have internet access phone the Tax Credit Helpline on 0345 300 3900 for a copy. This will help you to work out the income to enter on your tax credits claim.

You shouldn't normally deduct any contributions to an occupational pension scheme or payments under a payroll giving or Give As You Earn scheme. This is because your employer will have already deducted these payments from your gross pay.

We take the full amount of salary and wages into account when we work out how much tax credits to pay, this includes:

- commission
- bonuses

- tips
- gratuities
- profit-related pay
- holiday pay
- statutory Sick Pay (SSP)
- some benefits in kind which may be provided by your employer (for example, car and car fuel, allowances for the use of your own car on business, vouchers and credit tokens)

Although Statutory Maternity Pay (SMP), Statutory Paternity Pay (SPP) and Statutory Adoption Pay (SAP) are taxable, you should deduct the actual amount paid up to a maximum of £100 for each week of payment from your income for tax credits purposes.

You should include any earnings from employment outside the UK, for example:

- taxable profits from self-employment, including any from outside the UK
- the following taxable social security benefits
  - Carer's Allowance
  - Bereavement Allowance
  - contribution-based Jobseeker's Allowance
  - contribution-based Employment and Support Allowance
  - Income Support paid to a couple and the person getting it was on strike
  - Incapacity Benefit paid after the first 28 weeks of incapacity (at the short-term higher and long-term rates, including any child dependency increases paid with these benefits)

  But not, non-taxable benefits such as
  - Child Benefit
  - Attendance Allowance
  - Disability Living Allowance or Personal Independence Payment
  - Council Tax Reduction (sometimes called Council Tax Support) or Housing Benefit
  - income-related Employment and Support Allowance
- income-based Jobseeker's Allowance is taxable but isn't included as income for tax credits
- an Adult Dependants' Grant paid to students with a spouse, unmarried partner or a dependent adult and in Scotland, any Childs Dependant's Grant
- miscellaneous income that's taxable such as copyright royalties paid to someone who isn't a professional author or composer, which is taxable under Part 5 of the Income Tax (Trading and Other Income) Act 2005

We also take into account:

- State Retirement Pensions (including Widowed Parent's Allowance, Widowed Mother's Allowance, Widow's Pension and Industrial Death Benefit) and occupational or personal pensions –but not war pensions, whether paid on grounds of wounds or disability or paid to widows
- most income from savings and investments (for instance, interest from bank and building society accounts, dividends from UK companies, payments from trusts or the estate of a deceased person in administration)
  - but not income from certain tax exempt investments, such as, Individual Savings Accounts (ISAs), Personal Equity Plans (PEPs) or non-taxable National Savings products
- rental income from property – but not income which is exempt from Income Tax under the Rent a Room scheme (briefly, if you let furnished accommodation in your own home for up to £7,500 a year)
- foreign income, for example, from investments or property overseas and social security payments from overseas governments, before any overseas tax was taken off but deducting any bank charges or commission when converting foreign currency to pounds – we want to know about all foreign income, whether or not it was received and taxed in the UK, unless you were unable to send the income to the UK because of exchange controls in the country of origin

But you should deduct the first £300 from the combined total apart from:

- income from employment
- self employment
- taxable social security benefits
- student dependant's grant
- miscellaneous income

You only need to report other income if it's more than £300 a year in total. If it is, you only need to enter the amount over £300 on the tax credits claim form. If you make a claim as a couple, the £300 limit applies to your joint income, not to each of you separately.

For help on how to work out your income if you're employed or self-employed, go to www.gov.uk/tax-credits-working-out-income

About capital

We'll not normally take capital (that is, deposits in current and savings accounts at banks and building societies, most lump sum payments and the value of property, shares and other investments) into account when we work out your entitlement to tax credits.

However, in some cases where the Income Tax rules treat capital as income, and tax it as such, you'll be expected to include the taxable amount as income in your tax credits claim. This can happen if, for example, you hold shares in a UK company and the company gives you a stock dividend (new shares) instead of a cash dividend. This is part of what we call "notional income".

What "notional income" means

Besides capital that's treated as income under the Income Tax rules, notional income also includes income that you can be treated as having which you may not in fact have, such as:

- trust income payable to one person but which the Income Tax rules treat as the income of another person – the tax credits rules also treat the income as belonging to that other person (for example, investment income of a child where trust funds have been provided by a parent and the amount exceeds £100)
- income you may have deprived yourself of for the purpose of getting tax credits or more tax credits
- income that would be available to you if you applied for it, for example, a social security benefit. There are some exceptions, for example,
  - a deferred state or personal pension or retirement annuity
  - compensation for personal injury
- if you work or provide a service for free or less than the going rate, you're treated as getting the going rate for the job if the person you're working for or to whom you're providing the service has the means to pay – this doesn't apply if you're working as a volunteer (for example, helping out in a charity shop or a Citizens Advice Bureau) or you're on an employment or training programme

Tax credits and maintenance payments

We don't take maintenance payments, such as child support or payments under a divorce settlement into account when calculating your tax credits award. You'll be able to have full use of any maintenance that you get in addition to your tax credits.

Child Tax Credit and student loans or grants

We don't take student loans or grants to meet the cost of tuition fees, childcare or the Parent's Learning Allowance into account when calculating your tax credits award. But you should tell us if you get an Adult Dependant's Grant for a spouse, unmarried partner or a dependant adult and in Scotland, any Childs Dependant's Grant.

If you're a student nurse or a health profession trainee and you get a bursary under the NHS Bursary Scheme, you don't need to tell us about these payments in your claim.

When you've finished your studies and start work, repayments of student loans aren't deductible from income in tax credits claims.

Where you can find details of your income

For more information, or if you haven't sent us a tax return, see the notes that come with the claim form.

If you were employed in the tax year 2017 to 2018, details of your earnings will be shown on your:

- P60 tax certificate given to you by your employer after the end of that tax year, or a P45 if you left before 5 April 2018
- pay slips
- P11D certificate (if you got relevant benefits in kind) given to you by your employer

If you were self-employed in the tax year 2017 to 2018, details of your earnings will be shown on your Self Assessment tax return.

If your tax credits award is renewed automatically and you're in PAYE employment, we'll have used income figures provided to us by your employer. It's important that you check these figures are correct for tax credits. Contact us if you think they're not. Your renewal notes will help.

Benefits in kind from your employer

Your employer will give you the details you need on a form P11D. The notes with the tax credits claim form will tell you exactly which benefits to tell us about. If your employer has "payrolled" these benefits you'll need to deduct the total cash equivalent from the total of your P60 and P45 income.

If you're self-employed, you should tell us the taxable profit calculated in your Self Assessment tax return for 2017 to 2018. However, if you're a farmer, market gardener or a creator of literary or artistic works, averaging relief for fluctuating profits isn't allowed in tax credits claims; further details are provided in the notes (page 15) that go with the tax credits claim form (TC600). If you haven't yet sent us your Self Assessment tax return for 2017 to 2018, you must estimate your profits for that year

If your business made a loss in that tax year, for tax credits purposes you can offset that loss against:

- other income you may have for that year
- any income of your spouse or civil partner for that year
- any income of your personal partner (but not your business partner) for that year

If this doesn't use up the entire loss, the balance (that is, the unused part of the loss after deducting the amounts set against other income of that year) must be carried forward to offset against the profits of the same business in a future tax year. For example, if your business made a loss in 2016 to 2017 and there is some loss remaining after the deduction from other income of 2016 to 2017, the unused part of the 2016 to 2017 loss must be brought forward and deducted from the profits of the same business in the tax year 2017 to 2018.

If you made a trading loss, read TC825, "Working sheet for tax credits relief for Gift Aid donations, pension contributions and trading losses".

Go to GOV.UK and search for TC825.

If you don't have internet access, phone the Tax Credit Helpline on 0345 300 3900 for a copy.

If you got taxable social security benefits in 2017 to 2018, the Department for Work and Pensions (in Northern Ireland, the Department for Communities) should have sent you a record of the taxable amount of benefit.

If you got other types of income, you should refer to the statements, passbooks or to tax deduction certificates provided by the payer of the income and which you should be keeping for tax purposes.

5 How your award is worked out

You can see some examples of how we calculate tax credits awards on pages 36 to 45.

The amount of tax credits that you and your partner, if you have one, will get is worked out by dividing each of the elements of Child Tax Credit and Working Tax Credit which your family is entitled to by the number of days in the tax year and rounding up to the nearest penny to give a daily rate. These daily rates are then multiplied by the number of days in the relevant period and added together to give your family's maximum entitlement.

We then look at your income, and your partner's if you have one, to work out whether you'll get tax credits in full or at a reduced rate. We'll send you an award notice which tells you how much tax credits you'll get and when payments will start.

If you or your partner, if you have one, get Income Support, income-based Jobseeker's Allowance, income-related Employment and Support Allowance or Pension Credit you'll automatically get the full amount of tax credits that you qualify for.

If you're entitled to Child Tax Credit only, you'll get the full amount until your annual income reaches £16,105.

If you're entitled to Working Tax Credit, whether on its own or in addition to Child Tax Credit, and your family's annual income is below the threshold of £6,420, you'll get the maximum amount of all the elements that you qualify for. If your income is over £6,420, the maximum amount is reduced by 41 pence for every pound of income (41%) over the £6,420 (rounded down to the nearest penny).

If your income is over £6,420, your tax credits will be reduced in the following order:

- Working Tax Credit apart from the childcare element
- the childcare element of Working Tax Credit
- the child elements of Child Tax Credit
- the family element of Child Tax Credit

What happens once you're getting tax credits

Your tax credits award will initially be based on your current circumstances and your income for the previous tax year.

If your circumstances don't change and there are no significant changes in your income during the year, the initial award will run until the end of the tax year (5 April).

At the end of the tax year, we'll send you a renewal notice that tells you the information we hold about your claim, in particular the circumstances and income we based the award and the amount of tax credits paid to you over the year. You should check this notice carefully and:

- confirm that the details are correct, if we've asked you to
- correct the details if there are changes that you haven't previously told us about

You also need to tell us about your income for the year just ended. You can do this by:

- going online at www.gov.uk/manage-your-tax-credits
- phoning the Tax Credit Helpline on 0345 300 3900
- completing the notice and returning it in the envelope provided

Once we've all the details, we'll:

- check whether the amount we paid you was right
- work out your award for the following year, as the renewal notice will also act as your claim for the following year

If your circumstances and income stayed the same throughout the year that has just ended, or if your income in that year wasn't more than £2,500 higher than the year before that, you should have got the right amount of tax credits for that year.

If your income goes down by £2,500 or less throughout the year, the amounts of tax credits you get won't be affected.

As your current year payments are provisional and based on your previous years income, you should let us know of any changes to your income as they happen. Waiting until you make your renewal declaration at the end of the year will lead to an overpayment in some cases which you may be asked to repay.

If you only get the family element of Child Tax Credit, or have been getting the full amount of Child Tax Credit you qualify for because you've been getting Income Support, income-based Jobseeker's Allowance, income-related Employment and Support Allowance or Pension Credit for the whole of the period of your award, you don't have to do anything if your income remains within the range specified in the end-of-year notice, provided your circumstances haven't changed. This notice will tell you whether you need to return it or not.

If you don't have to return the notice, you'll be treated as having automatically made a new claim for the next award.

What happens if your circumstances or income change

You can tell us about any of these changes by:

going online at www.gov.uk/manage-tax-credits

Or if you don't have internet access by

phoning the Tax Credit Helplineon 0345 300 3900

writing to us at HM Revenue and Customs Tax Credit Office (Change of circumstances) BX9 1ER United Kingdom

There are some changes that could affect the amount of your tax credits award. They include:

- changes to the number of adults in the household, for example, if you and your partner stop living together or if you've been living on your own and you begin living with someone as a couple
- changes affecting the elements of tax credits you're eligible to, such as
  - the birth or death of a child
  - a child or qualifying young person leaving the household or stopping full-time non-advanced education or approved training
  - stopping using registered or approved childcare
  - changing your usual weekly working hours
  - moving abroad
- you or your partner begin to qualify for a disability element of Working Tax Credit
- you or your partner no longer have a disability which puts you at a disadvantage in getting a job
- a child you're responsible for is certified as severely sight impaired or blind by a consultant ophthalmologist

- Disability Living Allowance or Personal Independence Payment starts or stops being paid for a child you're responsible for
- the highest rate care component of Disability Living Allowance or the enhanced daily living component of Personal Independence Payment starts or stops being paid for you, your partner, or a child you're responsible for
- the higher rate of Attendance Allowance starts or stops being paid for you or your partner
- changes in income between the previous year and the current year

You should keep:

- a record of any changes in circumstances you've told us about
- your new award notice after you've told us about a change of circumstances

Changes in circumstances

You need to tell us about any changes in your circumstances. If you don't, you may be overpaid tax credits or you may not get the full amount you're entitled to. You may also have to pay a penalty of up to £300.

If a change increases the amount of tax credits you receive, it can only be backdated by up to one month. For example, if you had a baby on 12 June but you didn't report this until 12 October, your tax credits would only increase from 12 September.

The child element for a young person aged 16, 18 or 19 will automatically stop each year unless you tell us that they're staying in full-time non-advanced education or approved training.

The child element for a young person aged 17 staying in full-time non-advanced education or approved training will automatically continue.

You must tell us within one month if you made a:

- single claim but you're now married, in a civil partnership, or living with someone as if you're married or in a civil partnership
- joint claim (as part of a couple) but are now separated, or one of you dies

If any of these changes happen you'll need to make a new claim.

You must also tell us within one month if you:

- or your partner stop working
- or your partner stop working more than the relevant minimum of 16 or 30 hours a week (for couples with children 24 hours a week is the combined minimum and one of you must work at least 16 hours a week)
- are laid off
- have been on strike for more than 10 days
- or your partner leave the UK permanently or go abroad for more than 8 weeks (12 weeks if you go or remain abroad because you're ill or because a member of your family is ill or has died)
- and your partner lose the right to reside in the UK

For more information, go to www.gov.uk/tax-credits-if-moving-country-or-travelling

You must also tell us within one month if:

- a child or qualifying young person leaves the family and moves to live with someone else – this includes a child or qualifying young person who has been
  - taken into care or fostered to another family
  - sentenced to custody or detention for a period of more than 4 months
- a child or qualifying young person dies
- a qualifying young person leaves full-time non-advanced education or approved training before age 20 years or stops being registered with a careers service, Connexions, local authority support service, Ministry of Defence or similar organisation
- a qualifying young person starts to have their training provided under a contract of employment
- a qualifying young person starts to get Income Support, income-based Jobseeker's Allowance, Employment and Support Allowance, Child Tax Credit, Working Tax Credit or Universal Credit in their own right
- you told us that your child was continuing in full-time non-advanced education or approved training after 31 August following their 16th birthday, but didn't then do so

If you claimed childcare costs you must tell us if:

- your average weekly costs go down by £10 or more
- your costs go down to zero

- your childcare provider stops being registered or approved
- you start getting help with your childcare from a local authority or any government department – such as early years education grant for 3 to 4 year olds
- you start getting help with your childcare costs through your employer, such as childcare vouchers or childcare vouchers in return for a reduction in your salary (known as salary sacrifice)
- you no longer qualify for childcare costs as a couple because one of you is now working less than 16 hours a week

You should tell us if you change to a different registered or approved childcare provider. We'll need to know your new provider's registration or approval number. The amount of tax credits you get won't usually be affected if all your other circumstances stay the same. We may need to contact your childcare provider from time to time to make checks. If we are unable to contact your provider, we may stop paying you the extra Working Tax Credit for your childcare.

Changes to your working hours

You must tell us within one month if:

- you stop working 16 or 30 hours a week (for couples with children, 24 hours a week between you, with at least one of you working 16 hours a week)
- you work at least 30 hours a week and your hours drop to less than 30 (for couples with children, your joint working hours count towards the 30 hours)
- you stop work
- your employer lays you off

You may get Working Tax Credit for 4 weeks from the change if:

- your working hours drop to less than 16 or 30 hours a week (for couples with children 24 hours between you and one of you must work at least 16 hours a week)
- you stop work completely

If your employer lays you off and tells you it's temporary, you're treated as though you're still working for up to 4 weeks from the date your employer lays you off. If there's no work for you after that, you're treated as not working. You'll be entitled to a "run on" payment of Working Tax Credit for a further 4 weeks before your Working Tax Credit stops.

You can only get Working Tax Credit for up to 8 weeks after your employer lays you off.

Example 1

John Smith is laid off for 4 weeks on 8 January. His employer tells him that he can expect to go back to work on 5 February. John phones the Tax Credit Helpline to tell them about this. He also tells them when he expects to go back to work.

On 5 February he goes into work. His employer has no work for John and doesn't know if he will in the future. John phones the Tax Credit Helpline to tell them the layoff is now indefinite. He'll continue to get Working Tax Credit up to 5 March.

If your employer lays you off but can't tell you if you'll go back to work or you'll lose your job

If during the first 4 weeks you're laid off your employer says you:

- are now laid off indefinitely
- have lost your job

you'll be treated as if you've stopped work from the day they told you. You'll still get Working Tax Credit for 4 more weeks from that date.

Example 2

Anne Jones is laid off on 8 January. Her employer tells her she can expect to go back to work on 1 February. Anne phones the Tax Credit Helpline and tells them the layoff is temporary. On 26 January her employer tells her that they don't know if she'll be able to go back to work at all. Anne phones the Tax Credit Helpline to tell them the layoff is now indefinite. Anne is treated as though she has stopped work. She'll get Working Tax Credit up to 23 February (4 weeks from 26 January).

Example 3

On 8 January Anita Roberts is told that her employer has to lay her off indefinitely. Her employer doesn't know if she'll be able to go back to work at all. Anita phones the Tax Credit Helpline to tell them she's been laid off indefinitely. Anita will get Working Tax Credit up to 5 February.

You need to tell us straightaway about any changes that may increase your tax credits award such as:

- a new child in the family
- starting to use registered or approved childcare
- your average weekly childcare costs increase by £10 a week or more
- an increase in your working hours (or those of your partner) so you meet the working hours conditions for Working Tax Credit, read page 9

To get any increase backdated from the date your circumstances change, you must tell us within one month.

Changes in income

Your award will initially be based on your income for the previous tax year.

If your income throughout the current tax year rises by less than £2,500, it won't affect your award and we'll still base it on your income for the previous year. So for the current year, you'll get the benefit of a rise in income up to £2,500 without it reducing your tax credits award.

The increased level of your income isn't taken into account until the next year, but you should tell us about the increase on or before 6 April to avoid an overpayment of your provisional payments.

If your income goes down by £2,500 or less throughout the year, the amount of tax credits you get won't be affected.

If your income in the current year is lower than last year's income by more than £2,500, we'll disregard the first £2,500. For example, if your income last year was £20,000 and this year you expect it to be £15,000 we'll calculate your tax credits award on an income of £17,500. In this case, you may be due more tax credits. You can:

- tell us about this drop during the year – we'll then adjust your payments to make sure you get the right amount in-year
- wait until we finalise your award and we'll pay you any extra tax credits you're due in a lump sum

We'll check at the end of the year what your income was. If you tell us during the year about a fall in your income and it's less than you expected, you'll have to pay back any tax credits you've been overpaid.

If your income increases by more than £2,500, then we'll calculate your final award on your current year's income after disregarding the first £2,500 of the increase. We will, however, use the full amount of income when calculating your award for the following year.

What happens if there are changes in your tax credits award

You should tell us immediately if you think that your income will increase by more than £2,500 in the current tax year. This will help you to avoid building up an overpayment of tax credits which you'll have to pay back after we finalise your award at the end of the year.

If your tax credits award goes up because of a change in circumstances which increases your entitlement, and if you've told us about this during the year, we'll:

- pay any extra tax credits for up to one month before the adjustment was made in a lump sum
- increase your award for the rest of the year

If your income has reduced by more than £2,500 and you tell us about it during the year, we'll pay you any extra tax credits due from the date you tell us about it. If, at the end of the tax year, we find that you were due more tax credits than you were in fact paid because of a change in circumstances or income, we'll pay the extra amount as a lump sum. You should tell us immediately if you think that your income will go down in the current tax year. Your award may not go up this year, but you may get more next year.

If your tax credits award goes down because of a change in circumstances which reduces your entitlement, or an increase of more than £2,500 in your income that you've told us about during the year, we'll reduce your tax credits award for the whole period so that we pay you the right amount for the year overall.

Alternatively, if we've paid you too much in this tax year (or a previous one) we'll automatically reduce your ongoing payments until you pay back the overpaid money.

The amount we reduce your payments by depends on the amount of tax credits you receive. We make our decision based on the information you gave us about your income. The higher your income, the more your tax credits payments are reduced.

Check your award notice to find out if you get tax credits at a reduced rate.

If you do, it's shown as "reduction due to your income" in part 2 of your award notice – "How we work out your tax credits".

For those entitled to the maximum tax credits with no reduction due to income, the most we'll take back is 10% of your ongoing payments.

If you're getting Child Tax Credit or Working Tax Credit below the maximum and your total household income is £20,000 or less, the most we'll take back is 25% of your ongoing payments.

If your total household income exceeds £20,000, the most we'll take back is 50% of your ongoing payments.

If you're only getting the family element of Child Tax Credit, we'll take back up to 100% of your ongoing payments.

If you disagree with the level of your tax credits award or with having to pay a penalty

If you think that something on your notice is wrong or missing then contact us straightaway and we'll try to put it right.

If we can't resolve your tax credits or penalty problem and you're not satisfied, you can ask us to look at the decision again. We call this "mandatory reconsideration". Normally you have to do this within 30 days of the date of your award notice.

To find out more, see our leaflet WTC/AP, "What to do if you think your Child Tax Credit or Working Tax Credit is wrong".

Go to GOV.UK and search for WTC/AP.

If you don't have internet access, phone the Tax Credit Helpline on 0345 300 3900 for a copy.

When we've looked at the decision again we'll send you a Mandatory Reconsideration Notice to tell you what we've done. If you're still unhappy with the decision, the Mandatory Reconsideration Notice will include all the information you need to make an appeal to HM Courts and Tribunals Service (HMCTS) in England, Scotland and Wales or The Appeals Service in Northern Ireland.

6 Help and advice

How to claim or get more information about tax credits

You can make a claim by filling in and returning the claim form TC600.

To get a claim form or for more advice about Child Tax Credit or Working Tax Credit you can:

- online, go to www.gov.uk/claim-tax-credit
- phone the Tax Credit Helpline on 0345 300 3900
- textphone the Tax Credit Helpline on 0345 300 3909

For our opening hours, go to www.gov.uk/contact-hmrc

Backdating your claim

We can normally only backdate your tax credits for up to 31 days from the date we get your claim. So, to avoid losing money make sure you claim straightaway.

You'll need to ask for backdating if any of the following apply. You're:

- receiving Income Support, income-based Jobseeker's Allowance, income-related Employment and Support Allowance, or Pension Credit
- only claiming Working Tax Credit and haven't received Income Support, income-based Jobseeker's Allowance, income-related Employment and Support Allowance, or Pension Credit in the last 31 days
- claiming both Working Tax Credit and Child Tax Credit, and have come off Income Support, income-based Jobseeker's Allowance,income-related Employment and Support Allowance, or Pension Credit in the last 31 days

To ask for backdating, send us a separate sheet of paper with your claim form telling us:

- your name, address and National Insurance number
- the date you started work or the date you started getting one of the benefits listed above

Tax credits claims can sometimes be backdated more than 31 days if you apply within one month of being granted asylum or of the decision awarding you certain qualifying sickness or disability benefits, for example, Disability Living Allowance or Personal Independence Payment. Tell us the date your benefit was awarded from, if this applies to you.

Note: We can't backdate your claim into a period where you received Universal Credit.

For more information on backdating your claim, go to www.gov.uk/claim-tax-credits/backdate-a-claim

Leaving the tax credits system

There are 3 reasons your tax credits may stop.

You can phone the Tax Credit Helpline on 0345 300 3900 or write to us to tell us that you don't want to claim.

If you do this before 31 July, your claim for the current year won't be renewed.

You may have already got provisional payments for the current year which we'll ask you to pay back.

If you contact us after 31 July, your claim will continue until the end of the tax year but will not be renewed for the next tax year.

You may get a letter from us telling you that we'll not renew your claim for the next year because the level of your income means that you don't currently get or won't get tax credits payments for the next year.

If you want to renew your claim, you should contact us by the date shown in the letter.

Even though you may not get any payments, you can still renew and continue your claim – if you do, this will protect your claim if your income later reduces and you then become eligible you'll not need to make a new claim, or if you currently qualify for the disability element of Working Tax Credit you may continue to qualify.

You claim Universal Credit (you can't claim tax credits and Universal Credit at the same time).

Whether you've asked us to stop your claim or we've written to you to tell you that we'll not renew your claim, we'll still send you an end of year notice. You should still provide us with any information requested on the notice so that we can finalise your claim for the year just ended. If your claim is not renewed for the next tax year and your circumstances change, you'll need to make a new claim. If you do make a new claim:

- we'll only usually backdate your new claim up to 31 days
- you may not qualify for the disability element of Working Tax Credit (if claimed previously)

In some cases we may have paid you too much tax credits, this is called an overpayment. This may happen if you tell us that you no longer want to claim tax credits for the new tax year. How we deal with tax credits overpayments is set out in our Code of Practice 26.

Go to GOV.UK and search for COP26.

For more information on other help that might be available, go to www.gov.uk/browse/benefits/families

For help with health costs, go to www.nhsbsa.nhs.uk and select "Help with Health Costs".

What other help you can get

If your income is below a certain level you may be entitled to benefits and services, such as help with the costs of health services, provided by other government departments, agencies or local authorities. You may need to use your tax credits award notice as proof of your income for these benefits and services.

For information about these benefits and services, you'll need to contact the organisation that provides them.

If you get Housing Benefit, Council Tax Reduction (sometimes called Council Tax Support), your tax credits award may affect the amount of benefits you're entitled to. When you get your award or renewal notice, you should contact your local authority's Housing Benefit, Council Tax Reduction (sometimes called Council Tax Support) office so that they can reassess your case.

For more information about Child Benefit, go to www.gov.uk/child-benefit

Child Benefit

If you're claiming Child Tax Credit because you're responsible for a child or qualifying young person, you may also be entitled to Child Benefit. If you've not already done so, you should make a claim for Child Benefit.

Write to us at:
Child Benefit Office
PO Box 1
NEWCASTLE UPON TYNE
NE88 1AA

Child Benefit

If you're claiming Child Tax Credit because you're responsible for a child or qualifying young person, you may also be entitled to Child Benefit. If you've not already done so, you should make a claim for Child Benefit

About Child Benefit

Child Benefit can be claimed by anyone bringing up a child or qualifying young person. It's paid for each child or young person that qualifies.

You don't need to be the parent of the child or young person to qualify, but you must be responsible for them.

The child or young person doesn't need to live with you, but if they live with someone else you can only get Child Benefit if:

- you pay money to bring up the child
- the amount you pay is the same as, or more than, the weekly rate of Child Benefit you get for them
- the person the child lives with is not getting Child Benefit for them

Additional qualifying conditions apply once a child reaches age 16.

When and how to claim Child Benefit

Child Benefit can only be backdated for up to 3 months from the date your claim is received in the Child Benefit Office. To avoid losing money make your claim straightaway.

You should claim Child Benefit as soon as:

- your child is born
- a child or young person that you're responsible for comes to live with you
- you adopt a child who is living with you
- you start to contribute to the cost of looking after a child that you're responsible for, unless the person the child lives with is already getting Child Benefit for them and the amount you contribute is the same as, or more than, the weekly amount of Child Benefit they get for that child

If you have a baby, the bounty pack you may get from the hospital when your baby is born has a Child Benefit claim pack inside. Alternatively, or if another child comes to live with you, fill in a claim form online.

Go to www.gov.uk/child-benefit

You can also:

- phone the Child Benefit Helpline on 0300 200 3100 or if your preferred language is Welsh, phone 0300 200 1900
- textphone the Child Benefit Helpline on 0300 200 3103

National Insurance credits for social security benefits

For advice on National Insurance, including National Insurance credits and Small Earnings Exception, go to www.gov.uk/personal-tax

7 Examples of tax credits calculations

The following examples explain how tax credits will help people in differing circumstances. Other than example 11, for easy reference, these calculations don't take account of the rounding procedures and the weekly amounts are calculated assuming a 52-week year.

Example 1 – single parent, working less than 30 hours a week, with one child.

Patricia Taylor is a single parent with one child aged 12 and works less than 30 hours a week. Patricia's gross earnings last tax year were £8,000 (rising to £8,400 in the current year) and apart from Child Benefit (which is disregarded for tax credits purposes) she has no other income. She doesn't use registered or approved childcare.

Patricia's maximum tax credits entitlement will be a combination of:

- Child Tax Credit – family element (£545) and child element (£2,780), giving £3,325 a year
- Working Tax Credit – basic element (£1,960) and lone parent's element (£2,010), giving £3,970 a year

A total of £7,295.

As her income in the current year is expected to rise by less than £2,500, her tax credits award for the year will be based on last year's income. The income threshold is £6,420. Patricia's award is worked out as follows:

Annual income	£8,000.00	
Less threshold	–£6,420.00	
Excess income	£1,580.00	
Maximum tax credits		£7,295.00
Less 41% of excess income		–£647.80
Award		**£6,647.20 (£127.83 a week)**

Example 2 – single parent, working more than 30 hours a week, with one child and uses a registered childminder.

Rebecca Dobson is a single parent with one child aged 4 and works more than 30 hours a week. She uses a registered childminder, which costs her £100 a week. Her gross earnings last tax year were £15,000 (rising to £15,750 in the current year). She gets Child Benefit and maintenance from the child's father of £1,200 each year. She also has £5,000 in her building society account which in the previous tax year paid gross interest (that is, before tax) of £150 and she expects the same amount this current year. Her total gross income last tax year was therefore £16,350 (not including Child Benefit, which is disregarded). For the purposes of tax credits we also disregard the:

- maintenance payments
- gross interest, because it is below the £300 limit for reporting in the tax credits claim form

Therefore, her income for tax credits purposes is only her earnings of £15,000 last year and £15,750 this year.

Rebecca's maximum tax credits entitlement will be a combination of:

- Child Tax Credit – family element (£545) and a child element (£2,780), giving £3,325
- Working Tax Credit – basic element (£1,960), a lone parent element (£2,010), a 30-hour element (£810) and 70% of the eligible childcare costs of £100 a week (£5,200 a year), which is £3,640 a year, giving £8,420

A total of £11,745.

As her income in the current year is expected to rise by less than £2,500, her tax credits award for the year will be based on last year's income. The income threshold is £6,420. Rebecca's award is worked out as follows:

Annual income	£15,000.00	
Less threshold	–£6,420.00	
Excess income	£8,580.00	
Maximum tax credits		£11,745.00
Less 41% of excess income		–£3,517.80
Award		**£8,227.20 (£158.22 a week)**

Example 3 – couple, working less than 30 hours a week, with one child.

Jenny and Mike Smith have one child aged 5. Mike works 16 hours a week while Jenny works 8 hours a week. Mike had gross earnings last tax year of £15,000. Jenny's gross earnings were £5,000 and apart from Child Benefit (which is disregarded for tax credits purposes) they have no other income. They don't use registered or approved childcare.

Mike and Jenny's maximum tax credits entitlement will be a combination of:

- Child Tax Credit – family element (£545) and a child element (£2,780), giving £3,325
- Working Tax Credit – basic element (£1,960) and couple element (£2,010) giving £3,970

A total of £7,295.

As Mike and Jenny's income in the current year is expected to rise by less than £2,500, their tax credits award for the year will be based on last year's income. The income threshold is £6,420. Mike and Jenny's award is worked out as follows:

Annual income	£20,000.00	
Less threshold	–£6,420.00	
Excess income	£13,580.00	
Maximum tax credits		£7,295.00
Less 41% of excess income		£5,567.80
Award		**£1,727.20 (£33.22 a week)**

However, if Mike's hours dropped to below 16 hours a week, Mike and Jenny wouldn't be entitled to Working Tax Credit because as a couple with children they have to work 24 hours a week between them with at least one of them working 16 hours a week.

Example 4 – couple, both work more than 30 hours a week, with 3 children all of school age

Rashid and Yasmin Ali both work more than 30 hours a week and have 3 children, all of school age. They don't use registered or approved childcare. Last tax year, Rashid earned £15,000 (rising to £15,750 in the current year) and Yasmin earned £11,700 (rising to £12,000 in the current year). She also got Child Benefit for the children. The couple also have £12,000 in a joint building society account, which last tax year paid gross interest of £360 and they expect the same amount this current year.

Their total gross income last tax year was therefore £26,760 (not including Child Benefit).

Their maximum tax credits entitlement will be a combination of:

- Child Tax Credit – family element (£545) and a child element (£2,780 per child), giving £8,885
- Working Tax Credit – basic element (£1,960), couple element (£2,010) and a 30-hour element (£810), giving £4,780

A total of £13,665.

As Rashid and Yasmin's income in the current year is expected to rise by less than £2,500, their tax credits award for the year will be based on last year's income, with £300 of the gross interest being disregarded. This gives last year's income of £26,760. The income threshold is £6,420. Their award is worked out as follows:

Annual income	£26,760.00	
Less threshold	–£6,420.00	
Excess income	£20,340.00	
Maximum tax credits		£13,665.00
Less 41% of excess income		–£8,339.40
Award		**£5,325.60 (£102.42 a week)**

Example 5 – couple, one who works more than 30 hours a week, with a disabled child.

Mike and Claire Jones have one child, aged 10, who is disabled. Mike works more than 30 hours a week while Claire stays at home to look after their child. Mike had gross earnings last tax year of £20,000 (rising to £21,000 in the current year). Claire gets Child Benefit and Personal Independence Payment (PIP) on behalf of the child, both of which are disregarded for tax credits purposes. The couple also have £12,000 in their joint building society account, which last tax year paid gross interest of £360 and they expect the same amount this current year. Their total gross income last tax year was therefore £20,360 (not including Child Benefit and or PIP).

Their maximum tax credits entitlement will be a combination of:

- Child Tax Credit – family element (£545), a child element (£2,780) and a disabled child element (£3,275), giving £6,600
- Working Tax Credit – basic element (£1,960), couple element (£2,010) and a 30-hour element (£810), giving £4,780

A total of £11,380.

As Mike and Claire's income in the current year is expected to rise by less than £2,500, their tax credits award for the year will be based on last year's income, with £300 of the gross interest being disregarded. This gives last year's income of £20,060. The income threshold is £6,420. Their award is worked out as follows:

Annual income	£20,060.00	
Less threshold	–£6,420.00	
Excess income	£13,640.00	
Maximum tax credits		£11,380.00
Less 41% of excess income		–£5,592.40
Award		**£5,787.60 (£111.30 a week)**

Example 6 – single person, working more than 30 hours a week

Nick Sinclair is single, aged 25, works more than 30 hours a week and has no children. His gross earnings last tax year were £12,700 (rising to £13,000 in the current year) and he's no other income.

Nick's maximum tax credits entitlement will be a combination of Working Tax Credit – basic element (£1,960) and a 30-hour element (£810), giving £2,770.

As his income in the current year is expected to rise by less than £2,500, his tax credits award for the year will be based on last year's income. The income threshold is £6,420. Nick's award is worked out as follows:

Annual income	£12,700.00	
Less threshold	–£6,420.00	
Excess income	£6,280.00	
Maximum tax credits		£2,770.00
Less 41% of excess income		–£2,574.80
Award		**£195.20 (£3.75 a week)**

Example 7 – couple, one who works more than 30 hours a week, with one child

Vicky and Simon Graham have one child aged 12. Vicky works more than 30 hours a week and Simon is unemployed. They don't use registered or approved childcare. Last tax year their gross earnings were £12,000. They've no other income (apart from Child Benefit, which is disregarded).

Their maximum tax credits entitlement will be a combination of:

- Child Tax Credit – family element (£545) and a child element (£2,780), giving £3,325
- Working Tax Credit – basic element (£1,960), couple element (£2,010) and a 30-hour element (£810), giving £4,780

A total of £8,105.

The income threshold is £6,420. Based on last year's income, Vicky and Simon's tax credits award would be as follows:

Annual income	£12,000.00	
Less threshold	–£6,420.00	
Excess income	£5,580.00	
Maximum tax credits		£8,105.00
Less 41% of excess income		–£2,287.80
Award		**£5,817.20 (£111.87 a week)**

However, at the start of the new tax year, Vicky takes a better paid job and expects to earn £13,500 gross a year. Simon also gets a job and expects to earn £21,000. This joint rise in income of £22,500 (£1,500 plus £21,000) is £20,000 higher than the £2,500 limit for reporting increases in income. They contact us immediately to have their tax credits award reassessed on the basis of their current year's income.

Their maximum tax credits entitlement based on their circumstances remains the same but the increase in income will reduce their tax credits award. The first £2,500 of the increase in earnings is disregarded, so the revised award will be based on income of £32,000 (that is, £34,500 less £2,500). We'll therefore amend Vicky and Simon's award as follows:

Annual income	£32,000.00	
Less threshold	–£6,420.00	
Excess income	£25,580.00	
Maximum tax credits		£8,105.00
Less 41% of excess income		–£10,487.80
Award		**£0**

Example 8 – single person, works more than 30 hours a week, with a disability

Mark Joyce is single, aged 30, works more than 30 hours a week and has no children. He's deaf and gets Personal Independence Payment (PIP). Mark's gross earnings last tax year were £12,700 (rising to £13,000 in the current year) and, apart from PIP (which is disregarded for tax credits purposes), he's no other income.

His maximum tax credits entitlement will be a combination of Working Tax Credit - basic element (£1,960), a 30-hour element (£810) and disability element (£3,090), giving £5,860.

As his income in the current year is expected to rise by less than £2,500, his tax credits award for the year will be based on last year's income. The income threshold is £6,420. Mark's award is worked out as follows:

Annual income	£12,700.00	
Less threshold	–£6,420.00	
Excess income	£6,280.00	
Maximum tax credits		£5,860.00
Less 41% of excess income		–£2,574.80
Award		**£3,285.20 (£63.18 a week)**

Example 9 – couple, one who starts working more than 30 hours a week

John Smith, aged 51, starts work at the beginning of the new tax year, having spent the previous year on contribution-based Jobseeker's Allowance (JSA). His new job means that he works more than 30 hours a week and he expects to earn £29,000 gross a year. He and his wife Margaret, have £5,000 in their joint building society account, which currently pays £150 a year gross interest (this is disregarded as it's below the £300 limit for reporting on the tax credits claim form). Margaret stays at home and the couple have no children or qualifying young persons living with them.

John and Margaret's maximum tax credits entitlement will bea combination of Working Tax Credit – basic element (£1,960), couple element (£2,010) and a 30-hour element (£810), giving £4,780.

Their tax credits award will initially be based on their previous years income and then revised when they tell us their current year's income. The first £2,500 of the increased income is disregarded. So the award will be based on income of £26,500 (that's £29,000 less £2,500). The income threshold is £6,420. John and Margaret's award is worked out as follows:

Annual income	£26,500.00	
Less threshold	–£6,420.00	
Excess income	£20,080.00	
Maximum tax credits		£4,780.00
Less 41% of excess income		–£8,232.80
Award		**£0**

Example 10 – couple, both working with a child born after 6 April 2017

Reece and Scarlett Jones both work more than 30 hours a week and each get a salary of £12,000 a year and have 2 children of school age. On 8 October 2017, their third child is born who is disabled. Scarlett gets Child Benefit, and Personal Independence Payment (PIP) on behalf of the disabled child, both of which are disregarded for tax credits purposes. They use a registered childminder for the child born on 8 October 2017, which costs £100 a week

Their maximum tax credits entitlement will be a combination of:

- Child Tax Credit:
  - family element (£545) – payable as they have 2 children born before 6 April 2017, and the child element totalling £5,560 (£2,780 for each child born before 6 April 2017), a disabled child element (3,275) payable for the relevant period (in this example of 180 days) of £1,615 for the child born on 8 October 2017

Giving a Child Tax Credit entitlement of £7,720.

- Working Tax Credit

– basic element (£1,960), the couple element (£2,010) and the 30-hour element (£810), 70% of the eligible Childcare costs which is £3,640 a year payable for the relevant period (in this example of 180 days) of £1,795.07

Giving a Working Tax Credit entitlement of £6,575.07.

Annual income	£24,000.00	
Less threshold	–£6,420.00	
Excess income	£17,580.00	
Maximum tax credits		£14,295.07
Less 41% of excess income		–£7,207.80
Award		**£7,087.27**

The following example takes account of the rounding process.

Example 11– couple, who both work and their first child is born after 6 April 2017.

Colin and Mary Owen are in their early twenties. They both work more than 30 hours a week and each get a salary of £12,000 a year. On 8 October 2018, their first child is born and Mary gives up work permanently to look after the child. Colin continues to work at the same level of salary. Mary gets Child Benefit but this is disregarded for tax credits purposes. Their tax credits entitlement for the tax year 2018 to 2019 will be based on Colin's salary of £12,000 and Mary's salary for the first 6 months of the tax year of £6,000, giving a total gross income of £18,000.

Colin and Mary can't claim tax credits for the first 6 months of 2018 to 2019 because they're both under 25, neither have a disability and at that stage, have no children. For the next 6 months, 8 October 2018 to 5 April 2019, they can claim both Child Tax Credit and Working Tax Credit – as they're now responsible for a child.

Their maximum tax credits entitlement will be a combination of:

- Child Tax Credit – they're not entitled to the family element (£545) as the child was born after 6 April 2017, child element (£2,780) which is divided by the number of days in the tax year (365 days in 2018 to 2019) and rounded up to the nearest penny to give a daily rate – these daily rates are then multiplied by the number of days in the relevant period (in this example 180 days) and added together, giving a Child Tax Credit total of £1,371.60
- Working Tax Credit – basic element (£1,960), couple element (£2,010), 30-hour element (£810) which are divided by the number of days in the tax year and rounded up to the nearest penny to give a daily rate – these daily rates are then multiplied by the number of days in the relevant period and added together, giving a Working Tax Credit total of £2,358.00

Total tax credits of £3,729.60

As the fall in their income was over £2,500, their tax credits award will be based on the current year's income (£18,000) plus £2,500 (disregard) giving an income of £20,500. This figure is then divided by 365 (the number of days in the tax year) and multiplied by 180 (the number of days in the relevant period). This gives an income of £10,109.59. The income threshold is £6,420 divided by 365 and multiplied by 180 giving £3,166.03. Colin and Mary's award is worked out as follows:

Annual income	£10,109.59	
Less threshold	–£3,166.03	
Excess income	£6,943.56	
Maximum tax credits		£3,729.60
Less 41% of excess income		–£2,846.86
Award		**£882.74 (£16.98 a week from 8 October 2018 to 5 April 2019)**

8 Universal Credit and tax credits

Universal Credit supports people who are on a low income or out of work and is gradually replacing a range of existing benefits, including Working Tax Credit and Child Tax Credit. Eligibility to claim Universal Credit depends on where you live and your personal circumstances. You can't receive Universal Credit and tax credits payments at the same time.

If you claim Universal Credit your tax credits award will end. If you're already getting tax credits, you don't need to do anything yet. You should continue to report changes in your circumstances that could affect your tax credits straightaway. If your change of circumstances means you claim Universal Credit, for example, if you lose your job or start living with a partner who already gets Universal Credit, your tax credits payments will stop.

For more information about Universal Credit, go to www.gov.uk/universal-credit

9 Your rights and obligations

"Your Charter" explains what you can expect from us and what we expect from you.

For more information, go to www.gov.uk/hmrc/your-charter

If you give us incorrect information, we may charge you a penalty up to £3,000 or we may prosecute you.

Our leaflet WTC7, "Tax credit penalties" gives more information about penalties.

For a copy:

- go to GOV.UK and search for WTC7
- phone the Tax Credit Helpline on 0345 300 3900 if you don't have internet access

WTC5 – WORKING TAX CREDIT: HELP WITH THE COSTS OF CHILDCARE
[HMRC, April 2018]

If you receive tax credits you could claim extra help with costs if all of the following apply to you:

- you're responsible for a child
- you work at least 16 hours a week (see page 3)
- your childcare provider is registered or approved

Read this leaflet for more information and help to work out what you can claim

If you need a tax credit claim pack, you can:

- phone the Tax Credit Helpline on 0345 300 3900
- textphone the Tax Credit Helpline on 0345 300 3909

For our opening hours, go to www.gov.uk/contact-hmrc

Who can claim

You can claim for help with childcare costs if:

- you're responsible for a child
- you work at least 16 hours a week
- your childcare provider is registered or approved

You can only claim help with childcare costs for a child up to the Saturday:

- following 1 September after their 15th birthday
- following 1 September after their 16th birthday if:
  - they're certified as severely sight impaired or blind by a consultant ophthalmologist
  - you receive Disability Living Allowance or Personal Independence Payment for that child

If you're claiming childcare costs for more than one child, and the oldest child reaches the cut-off age, work out your new childcare costs for any younger children staying in childcare. If your average weekly costs stop or go down by £10.00 or more you must tell us straightaway and within one month from the date of the change.

Responsibility for a child

You're responsible for a child if they usually live with you. If you share responsibility for a child with someone who isn't your partner, decide who has the main responsibility. That person should then claim Child Tax Credit for the child.

You're not responsible for a child if they:

- get tax credits, Employment and Support Allowance, Universal Credit, Income Support or income-based Jobseeker's Allowance in their own right
- are looked after by a local authority that's paying towards the cost of their accommodation or maintenance

- have been sentenced to more than 4 months in custody or detention
- have ceased full-time non-advanced education or approved training and have started work for 24 hours or more a week

Working hours

If you're part of a couple and responsible for a child you can claim if:

- you both usually work at least 16 hours a week each
- one of you usually works at least 16 hours a week and the other is:
  - incapacitated and getting a benefit for disability or illness
  - an inpatient in hospital
  - in prison (whether serving a custodial sentence or remanded in custody awaiting trial or sentence)
  - entitled to Carer's Allowance

From 6 April 2017, the following changes apply:

- the individual child element of Child Tax Credit will no longer be awarded for third and subsequent children or qualifying young persons in a household, born on or after 6 April 2017, there are exceptions – for more information go to www.gov.uk/hmrc/ctc-exceptions
- the family element of Child Tax Credit will only be payable if you're responsible for a child or qualifying young person born before 6 April 2017

The 2 child limit doesn't apply to the childcare element of Working Tax Credit or the disability element of Child Tax Credit. You can claim these 2 elements for all children who meet the conditions.

For more information about child disability element, go to GOV.UK and search for TC956.

To ensure you don't miss out on what you're entitled to you should still report the birth of a child and any changes involving your children or young people, even if you won't get the child or family elements for them.

Who we treat as incapacitated

You're treated as incapacitated if you receive:

- Disability Living Allowance, Personal Independence Payment or Armed Forces Independence Payment
- Attendance Allowance
- Severe Disablement Allowance
- Incapacity Benefit at the short-term higher rate or long-term rate
- Industrial Injuries Disablement Benefit (with Constant Attendance Allowance for you)
- War Disablement Pension (with Constant Attendance Allowance or Mobility Supplement for you)
- Council Tax Benefit or Housing Benefit with a Disability Premium or Higher Pensioner Premium for you
- contribution-based Employment and Support Allowance (ESA) if you've had
  - this allowance for 28 weeks or more
  - Statutory Sick Pay (SSP) followed by contribution-based ESA for a combined period of 28 weeks or more

The 28 weeks doesn't need to be a single continuous period. You can add together any periods that you were paid:

- contribution-based ESA, as long as they were no more than 12 weeks apart
- SSP, as long as they were no more than 8 weeks apart
- SSP, with periods that you got contribution-based ESA, as long as they were no more than 12 weeks apart and you met the contribution conditions for contribution-based ESA on the days that you got SSP

If you're temporarily absent from work

You may still get help with childcare costs when you're on:

- sick leave
- maternity leave
- paternity leave
- adoption leave

- shared parental leave

But usually you'll still need to have worked a certain number of hours immediately before you went on leave.

If you're off sick

If all of the following apply, we'll treat you as working if:

- you're off sick for 28 weeks or less
- you were working 16 hours or more a week immediately before going off sick

We'll also treat you as working if you were:

- on maternity, paternity or adoption leave
- on the first 10 days of strike leave
- suspended from work

  (These conditions apply as long as you were working at least 16 hours a week before taking leave or being suspended)
- getting one of a number of state benefits, for example Employment and Support Allowance, Statutory Sick Pay or National Insurance Credits because you have limited capability for work (that is, your illness or disability affects the amount and type of work you can do or would do but you don't qualify because you're self-employed)

If you're on maternity, paternity, adoption or shared parental leave

We treat you as working if, immediately before you went on leave, you were working the required number of hours applicable to your circumstances and you are:

- getting Maternity Allowance
- on ordinary maternity or adoption leave
- in the first 13 weeks of additional maternity or adoption leave
- on your 2 weeks ordinary paternity leave
- on shared parental leave

If you don't return to work after 39 weeks you may not qualify anymore. Phone our helpline if this happens.

Registered or approved childcare providers

Your responsibility when claiming childcare costs

You can only claim help with your childcare costs if your childcare provider is registered or approved. You're responsible for making sure that the childcare provider you use is registered or approved. You should:

- check your childcare provider's documents to confirm that they're registered or approved
- keep a record of the date their registration or approval is due to expire and
  - close to the expiry date check to make sure that your provider is renewing their registration or approval
  - ask to see their new evidence of registration or approval

What is registered or approved childcare

England – read pages 5 and 6.

Scotland – read page 7.

Wales – read pages 7 and 8.

Northern Ireland – read page 8.

Crown servants working abroad – read page 8.

Registered or approved childcare: England

To get help with childcare costs in England, your childcare provider must be registered or approved. You won't be able to claim tax credits if they're not.

If you use a childminder, playscheme, childcare clubor nursery

Your childcare provider needs to be registered in one of the following ways. They need to be registered on the:

- Early Years Register (EYR) with either Ofsted or an Ofsted registered childminder agency if your child is under 5 years of age

- compulsory part of the General Childcare Register (GCR) with either Ofsted or an Ofsted registered childminder agency if your child is aged 5 to 7
- voluntary part of the GCR with either Ofsted or an Ofsted registered childminder agency if your child is aged 8 or over

Before claiming help with your childcare costs, check with your provider that they're on the correct register. Some providers,such as nannies who provide care in the child's own home, don't need to register on the EYR or the compulsory part of the GCR. If you use this type of provider and you want to get help with your childcare costs, your provider must register on the voluntary part of the GCR.

If an approved foster carer looks after your child

You can claim help with your childcare costs if you use an approved foster carer, but they must be registered with Ofsted on the Early Years Register or General Childcare Register. You can't claim for childcare costs for looking after your own foster child.

If a care worker or nurse looks after your child

You can claim help with your childcare costs if you use a domiciliary care worker or nurse to look after your child at home. However, they must be from an agency that's registered under the Domiciliary Care Agencies Regulations 2002.

Early education for 2, 3 and 4-year-olds

Some eligible 2-year-olds (including some from families receiving Working Tax Credit) and all 3 and 4-year-olds are entitled to 570 hours a year of free early education with a registered provider. This is normally taken as 15 hours per week during term time, but can betaken as fewer hours per week over more weeks if available.

There's no obligation to take the full number of hours and you may be able to take fewer hours to begin with and increase them later as your child settles in. You don't need to pay for a child's free early education place and don't have to take up additional services to access their free place. However, you can claim for any additional childcare you pay for outside of the free entitlement.

For more information about free early education, go to www.gov.uk/freechildcare

If you use childcare provided by a school

If your child is 3 or 4 years old, both the following must apply for this type of care to count as approved for tax credits, the childcare:

- is provided under the direction of the school's governing body or the person responsible for managing the school
- takes place on school premises or on other premises that may be inspected as part of an inspection of the whole school by Ofsted or an equivalent inspection body appointed to inspect certain independent schools, for example, the Independent Schools Inspectorate, Bridge Schools Inspectorate or the Schools Inspection Service

If your child is between 5 and 15 years old (or 16 years old if your child is disabled), all of the following must apply for this type of care to count as approved for tax credits. The childcare must be provided:

- out of school hours
- under the direction of the school's governing body or under the direction of the person responsible for managing the school
- takes place on school premises, or on other premises that may be inspected by Ofsted or by an equivalent inspection body appointed to inspect certain independent schools, for example, the Independent Schools Inspectorate, Bridge Schools Inspectorate or the School Inspection Service – an example of other premises could be a village hall used by the school for its out of school hours childcare activities

How to check if your childcare provider is registered or approved in England

All childcare providers who are registered by Ofsted or an Ofsted registered childminder agency in England are given a letter or certificateas evidence of their registration or approval.

Some childcare providers must regularly (for example, each year) reapply for registration or approval. If this applies to your childcare provider, the letter or certificate issued to them will clearly show when their registration or approval expires. To check if their registration is still valid you can contact Ofsted:

go to www.gov.uk/government/organisations/ofsted

- phone 0300 123 1231

Where a provider is registered with a childminder agency, you'll need to check with the relevant agency to see if the provider's registration is valid. The provider will be able to give you contact details for the childminder agency and these will also be available on the Ofsted website.

Registered or approved childcare: Scotland

To get help with your childcare costs in Scotland only one of the following must apply, your childcare provider must either be:

- registered with the Social Care and Social Work Improvement Scotland (SCSWIS) – also known as the Care Inspectorate
- a childcare club that is registered with SCSWIS to provide childcare out of school hours
- a person from a registered childcare agency, sitter service or nanny agency providing childcare in the child's home

You can also claim help with your childcare costs if you use:

- an approved foster carer
- a kinship carer

A kinship carer is like a foster carer but they already know the child they're looking after because they're either related or a family friend.

If you use a foster carer or kinship carer for your childcare they must be registered with SCSWIS as a childminder or a daycare provider.

You can't claim for childcare costs for looking after:

- your own foster child
- a child as part of a kinship care arrangement

How to check if your childcare provider is registered or approved in Scotland

ⓘ All childcare providers who are registered by SCSWIS are given a letter or certificate as evidence of their registration or approval.

Some childcare providers must regularly (for example, each year) reapply for registration or approval. If this applies to your childcare provider, the letter or certificate issued to them will clearly show when their registration or approval expires.

For more information on childcare, go to www.scottishfamilies.gov.uk

For more information on registered childcare, go to www.scswis.com

Registered or approved childcare: Wales

To get help with your childcare costs in Wales your childcare provider must be one of the following:

- registered with the Care and Social Services Inspectorate Wales (CSSIW)
- a school that provides childcare out of school hours and on school premises
- a local authority that provides childcare out of school hours
- a domiciliary care worker or nurse providing care to your child at home – however, they must be from an agency that's registered under the Domiciliary Care Agencies Regulations 2002
- someone approved by the Approval of Child Care Providers (Wales) Scheme 2007 providing childcare in the child's home, or if several children are being looked after, in one of the children's homes

If a foster carer cares for your child

You can claim help with your childcare costs if you use a foster carer for your childcare and your child is under:

- 8, the foster carer must be registered with the CSSIW
- 16, and the care is in your child's home, the foster carer must be approved by the Childcare at Home Approval Scheme

You can't claim for childcare costs for looking after your own foster child.

How to check if your childcare provider is registered or approved in Wales

ⓘ Childcare providers are given a letter or certificate as evidence of their registration or approval if they're:

- registered by the CSSIW
- approved under a home childcare providers scheme

For more information on childcare, go to www.wales.gov.uk andsearch for childcare.

Registered or approved: Northern Ireland and Crown servants working abroad

Northern Ireland

To get help with your childcare costs in Northern Ireland only one of the following must apply, your childcare provider must be:

- registered with a Health and Social Services Trust
- a school that provides out of school hours childcare on the school premises
- an Education and Library Board that provides out of school hours childcare
- a person approved by the Approval of Home Child Care Providers (Northern Ireland) 2006 Scheme, providing childcare in the child's home

If a foster carer cares for your child

You can claim help with your childcare costs in Northern Ireland if you use a foster carer for the childcare. If your child is under:

- 12, the foster carer must be registered with a Health and Social Services Trust
- 16, and the care is in your child's home, the foster carer must be approved under the Home Childcare Approval Scheme

You can't claim for childcare costs for looking after your own foster child.

How to check if your childcare provider is registered or approved in Northern Ireland

Childcare providers are given a letter or certificate as evidence of their registration if they're:

- registered by a Health and Social Services Trust
- approved under the Home Child Care Providers Scheme

To check their registration is still valid contact the Early Years Team in your local Health and Social Care Trust.

Go to www.nidirect.gov.uk andsearch for Early Years Teams.

Crown servants working abroad

If you're a civil servant or a member of the Armed Forces posted overseas and your child has gone with you, you can get help with your childcare costs if your childcare provider is approved under a Ministry of Defence accreditation scheme abroad.

Changing your childcare provider

If your provider stops being registered or approved, and you want to carry on getting help with your childcare costs, you'll need to make alternative arrangements for registered or approved childcare.

Tell us straightaway, and within one month, if you stop using registered or approved childcare. The help with childcare costs will stop the day after the registration or approval ends. If you don't tell us on time, we might pay you too much tax credits which you'll have to pay back. You might also have to pay a penalty of up to £300.

You should tell us if you change your childcare provider, even if you're still paying the same amount to the new provider, giving:

- their name
- their address, including the post code
- their phone number
- the name of the registration or approval body and registration number, if one was given to them as part of the registration process
- the date of the change
- the amount you're paying to them for childcare

Childcare costs paid by someone else

You can't claim for:

- any childcare costs you pay using childcare vouchers, this is the amount you get from your employer towards your childcare costs (either in cash or in vouchers) and includes vouchers in return fora reduction in your pay (known as a "salary sacrifice")

- childcare costs met by your local authority (or your local education authority) for early learning or nursery education for your child – for example, where your local authority in England meets the cost of 15 hours a week free early years education for children aged 3 and 4
- payments you get from the government towards your childcare costs because you're a student or you're starting work

You can still claim for any childcare costs that you actually pay for.

However, if your employer pays only some of your childcare cost in vouchers, and you pay for the rest, you can make a claim for what you pay.

Childcare vouchers

If your employer offers you childcare vouchers, including vouchers in return for a reduction in your pay through salary sacrifice, it will affect how much tax credits you can get.

If you want to know if you'd be better off taking the childcare vouchers, go to www.gov.uk/childcare-vouchers-better-off-calculator

Childcare provided by a relative

You can't usually claim help with childcare provided by relatives, even if they're registered or approved.

You can claim if the relative is a:

- registered childminder who cares for your child outside of your child's own home
- childcare provider approved under a Home Child Care Providers Scheme in Wales or Northern Ireland, who cares for your child outside of your child's own home – but they must also care for at least one other child that isn't related to them

What we mean by relative

A relative could be:

- your child's parent, grandparent, aunt, uncle, brother, sister or step-parent
- a person with a strong relationship to the child, for example, someone in a parental position regarding their partner's children

What childcare costs you can claim

You can only claim for the actual amounts you pay for any childcare you use. If your costs include an amount paid as a retainer, phone our helpline for more information. See page 19 for contact details.

How much help you can get

You can get help with up to 70% of your childcare costs – subject to a maximum weekly limit. If you pay childcare for:

- one child, the maximum childcare costs you can claim is £175 a week
- 2 or more children, the maximum childcare costs you can claim is £300 a week

This means that the maximum help you can get for your childcare through tax credits is:

- £122.50 a week for one child
- £210 a week for 2 or more children

Number of children	Weekly limit on costs	Percentage of costs you can get help with	Maximum tax credits for childcare
One child	£175	70%	£175 × 70% = £122.50
2 or more children	£300	70%	£300 × 70% = £210

The actual amount you get will also depend on your income.

If you employ someone as a registered or approved home childcare provider, for example a nanny, you can get help for up to 70% of the gross costs of employing them – within the limits above. You can include the costs of any:

- employer's National Insurance contributions you pay
- benefits in kind you give
- *other costs linked* with employing that person

We may need more information

We may write to you and ask for information to make sure you're getting the right help with your childcare costs.

We may ask you to:

- tell us how you worked out your average weekly childcare costs
- tell us whether your childcare costs have changed
- send us evidence to show how much you pay for childcare costs,such as invoices, bank statements or receipts

It's important to keep these documents safe so you can send them to us if we ask for them. We can't accept photocopies so please send original documents. We'll return them to you.

It's also important that you give us the information we need, or tell us about any difficulties you have providing it. If you don't send us this information we may reduce or stop your tax credits.

When to claim

You can claim help with your childcare costs:

- as soon as you start paying for childcare
- up to 7 days before your childcare starts
- even if you need the childcare for only a short time –read page 14

You need to claim help with childcare costs within one month of when you start to pay them – we can't pay you for any costs you've paid before then.

What information we'll need from you

As part of your claim, whether you're filling in the tax credits claim form or phoning our helpline, we'll need you to give us:

- the contact details for your childcare provider, including
  - name
  - address, including postcode
  - phone number
  - name of registering or approving body
  - registration or approval number
- your average weekly childcare costs – read pages 12 to 14

We may check information with your provider, so we need the correct details for them.

If you use more than one childcare provider, or you use a different provider at different times of the year (for example, in school holidays), you need to give us the details of all your providers. Tell us straightaway if you:

- change your provider(s)
- stop using the childcare – to avoid building up too much tax credits which you'll have to pay back

Claiming childcare costs for the first time

ⓘ To claim help with your ongoing childcare costs

Fill in Part 3 of the claim form when claiming tax credits.

To claim help for a short fixed period of childcare

(1) Leave out the details of your childcare when claiming tax credits.

(2) Send your claim form to us.

(3) Phone our helpline once your award has gone into payment and tell us you want to claim for a short fixed period of childcare– but don't phone earlier than 7 days before your childcare starts.

Read page 14 for more information about claiming for short periods of childcare.

We use your average weekly childcare costs to work out how much help you can get. On your claim form only state your average weekly costs. The way you work out your average weekly costs depends on the way you pay for childcare – *read pages 12 to 14*. Always round your average up to the nearest pound.

Already getting tax credits

If you're already getting tax credits but start paying for registered or approved childcare and want to claim help with your costs, phone our helpline.

You pay childcare for more than one child or to more than one provider

Use the total amount you pay each week to work out your average weekly costs – read page 15.

What to include in your childcare costs

Only include what you actually pay when working out your average weekly costs.

Don't include costs covered by childcare:

- payments from your employer – either in money or childcare vouchers
- vouchers in return for a reduction in your pay – this is called a "salary sacrifice"
- payments or grants from a government scheme, for example, to help you start work or included in your student grant
- costs met by your educational or local authority for your child's nursery childcare

Also tell us straightaway if you stop using the childcare to avoid building up an overpayment of tax credits, which you'll have to pay back.

How to work out your average weekly childcare costs

If you've been using childcare for less thana year

Use this table or the online calculator to help you work out your average weekly childcare costs.

Go to www.gov.uk/childcare-costs-for-tax-credits

You always pay the same weekly amount	Use the total amount you pay each week – this is your average weekly childcare costs.
You pay different weekly amounts	(1) Work out what you expect to spend in total on childcare over the next 52 weeks – start from the date you're working out your costs (2) Divide the total by 52 – this is your average weekly childcare costs.
You always pay the same monthly amount	(1) Take the total amount you pay each month. (2) Multiply that amount by 12. (3) Divide the total by 52 – this is your average weekly childcare costs.
You pay different monthly amounts, or you pay by	(1) Work out the total amount you expect to spend on childcare over the next 12 months. (2) Divide the total by 52 – this is your average weekly childcare costs.

If you've arranged childcare that's due to start in the next 7 days

Ask your childcare provider for a written estimate of how much they will charge you and use that amount to work out your average weekly costs.

Example: your childcare is due to start in the next 7 days

Sinead has just arranged to pay a nursery £100 a week to look after her daughter. She'll pay the same amount every week. The arrangement doesn't start until next week. Sinead's average weekly costs are £100.

If you've been using childcare for a year or more and always pay the same amount

Use this table to help you work out your average weekly childcare costs.

Always round your average up to the nearest pound.

You pay weekly	Use the total amount you pay each week – this is your average weekly childcare costs.
You pay monthly	(1) Take the total amount you pay each month. (2) Multiply that amount by 12. (3) Divide the total by 52 – this is your average weekly childcare costs.
You pay fortnightly (every 2 weeks)	(1) Take the total amount you pay each fortnight. (2) Divide that amount by 2 – this is your average weekly childcare costs.

You pay every 4 weeks	(1) Take the total amount you pay every 4 weeks. (2) Divide that amount by 4 – this is your average weekly childcare costs.
You pay yearly	(1) Take the total amount you pay every year. (2) Divide that amount by 52 – this is your average weekly childcare costs.
You pay each term	Phone the Tax Credit Helpline on 0345 300 3900 for help in working out your average weekly childcare costs.

If you've been using childcare for a year or more and pay different amounts

Sometimes you may pay, or expect to pay, different amounts for childcare. For example, you regularly use childcare, but may pay more, or less, during school holidays than you do in term-time.

Work out your average costs as follows:

(1) Work out the total amount you've paid for childcare in the last 52 weeks (or 12 months if you pay monthly or any other frequency) – start backwards from the date you're working out your costs.

(2) Divide the total by 52 – this is your average weekly childcare costs.

Example 1 – You pay monthly, but different amounts

Irene pays for childcare monthly but the amount she pays changes from month to month. In the last 12 months Irene's costs were:

1 month at £240	1 x £240 = £240
3 months at £200	3 x £200 = £600
2 months at £320	2 x £320 = £640
6 months at £160	6 x £160 = £960
Total for year	£2,440

To work out the average, the total amount is divided by 52 (because there are 52 weeks in a year).

So Irene's average weekly costs are £2,440 ÷52 = £46.92. Round this up to £47.

Example 2 – You pay weekly but different amounts

Ahmed normally pays £60 a week for registered childcare during term-time.

In the school holidays he pays for 10 weeks at £100 a week.

His total costs for 52 weeks are:

39 weeks at £60	39 x £60 = £2,340
10 weeks at £100	10 x £100 = £1,000
Total for year	£3,340

To work out the average, the total amount is divided by 52 (because there are 52 weeks in a year).

So Ahmed's average weekly costs are £3,340 ÷52 = £64.23. Round this up to £65.

Note: Ahmed has correctly only included costs for the weeks that he has actually paid for.

If you only use childcare for short periods once in a while

Even if you don't normally use childcare, you might need it once in a while for short fixed periods. For example this could be during school holidays, or to cover an emergency. You may be able to claim help with your costs just for the short time you need the childcare. This means the help for your childcare is worked out and paid over the short time you use the care.

For this to happen:

- you must only use childcare once in a while – for example only during the summer holidays or in an emergency
- your childcare must be for a fixed period – this means you know when it will start and end

Otherwise, the help for your childcare will be worked out and paid over 52 weeks.

If you'd prefer to claim help averaged and paid over the year, work out your average weekly costs by following the guidance –read pages 12 and 13.

If you're already getting tax credits, phone the helpline to claim help for a short period of childcare. Do this as soon as your childcare starts, or up to 7 days before.

You'll need to tell us:

- the start and end dates of the childcare
- your actual childcare costs for the short period
- your childcare provider's details – their name, address (including post code), phone number and childcare registration or approval number

If you're not already getting tax credits, you'll need to fill in a claim form – read the information box on page 11.

Changes you must tell us about straightaway

You must tell us if:

- your childcare provider stops being registered or approved
- you stop using a registered or approved childcare provider
- your average weekly childcare costs go down by £10 or more
- your childcare costs fall to zero
- you start getting other help towards your childcare costs

You must tell us straightaway and within one month if you have any of these changes.

ⓘ If you delay telling us and we pay you too much tax credits, you'll have to pay it back. You may also have to pay a penalty of up to £300 if you don't report the change to us within one month.

If you give wrong childcare costs you may have to pay a penalty up to £3,000 or be prosecuted.

How to work out if your average weekly childcare costs have changed

Your childcare costs might go up or down

How you work out changes in your average weekly childcare costs will depend on how you worked out your average weekly childcare costs in the first place.

If you always pay the same amount

You pay weekly

Work out your new average weekly costs – read page 12 for help on how to do this.

Compare your new average weekly costs with the old average you gave us. If it's different by £10 a week or more in each week for 4 weeks in a row and your new average weekly costs are at least £10 lower or higher than your old average weekly costs, you need to tell us about it.

You pay monthly or any other frequency

Work out your new average weekly costs – read page 12 for help on how to do this.

Compare your new average weekly costs with the old average you gave us. If it's different by £10 a week or more, you need to tell us about it.

If you don't always pay the same amount

To work out your new average weekly costs:

(1) Add up what you expect to pay in total over the next 52 weeks (or 12 months if you pay monthly or any other frequency).

(2) Divide the total by 52 – this is your new average weekly childcare costs

(3) Compare your new average weekly costs with the old average you gave us. If it's different by £10 a week or more, you need to tell us about it.

If you pay childcare for more than one child or to more than one provider

It's the change in the total you pay each week that we're interested in:

(1) Add together all the average weekly costs you pay for your children – this is your new average weekly childcare costs.

(2) Compare your new weekly average costs with the old average you gave us. If it's different by £10 a week or more, you need to tell us about it.

Changes you can tell us about

Phone our Childcare Provider's Helpline on 0345 300 3941 if you think a parent hasn't:

- reported a change in their childcare costs to us when they should have
- told us that they stopped using you for their childcare

However, we can't discuss any other details of a parent's claim with you.

When we get in touch with a parent to check the details of their tax credits award, we may give them details of the information that you gave to us.

You provide childcare and you're a relative of the child or parent making the claim

Parents claiming tax credits can't usually claim help for childcare provided by relatives. However, they can if you're a:

- registered childminder who cares for the child outside of the child's own home
- childcare provider approved under an Approval of Child Care Providers (Wales) Scheme or a Home Child Care Provider's Scheme in Northern Ireland and you care for the child outside of the child's own home – but you must also care for at least one other child that isn't related to you

Can childcare providers claim tax credits

If you're responsible for your own children you can claim Child Tax Credit. You may also be able to claim Working Tax Credit.

To claim Working Tax Credit, you can:

- count any hours you work as a childminder or in a nursery or playscheme
- claim if you're employed or self-employed as long as you work enough hours
- add together the hours you work in different jobs

The amount of Child Tax Credit and Working Tax Credit you get will depend on your income (or joint income, if you're part of a couple).

Looking after your own child as a childminder or working in the nursery your child attends

If you're a childminder, you can't claim for the costs of looking after your own children even if you look after them at the same time as you provide childcare for other children.

If you work for a registered or approved nursery or playscheme that your child attends, and you pay for your child to attend, then you can claim for those costs.

To get a tax credits claim form, phone the Tax Credit Helpline.

Making a claim

To work out your tax credits, we need your:

- income details (and those of your partner, if you have one) for the previous tax year (a tax year runs from 6 April one year to 5 April the next)
- National Insurance number (and that of your partner) – it looks like this: QQ123456A

To help you claim, you (and your partner, if you have one) need to keep any information you have about your income for the relevant tax year, including:

- the P60, "End of Year Certificate" your employer gave you, and your form P11D (if you get one)
- any bank and building society statements showing any taxable interest you received in that year
- details of your taxable profits or losses, if you were self-employed

If you're a self-employed childminder, you need to give us details of your taxable profits from childminding, even if you didn't earn enough to pay any tax.

Taxable profits are the amount you received in fees, less any expenses you paid for running your childminding business. For example, you should take off the costs of:

- any business phone calls
- providing meals for the children
- maintaining and heating the part of your house that you use for childminding

Help

For more information on tax credits:

go to www.gov.uk/taxcredits

- phone our Childcare Provider's Helpline on 0345 300 3941
- textphone the Tax Credit Helpline (for people with hearing or speech difficulties) on 0345 300 3909

- write to us at:

Tax Credit Office
HM Revenue and Customs
BX9 1ER

For all other tax credits enquiries, phone the Tax Credit Helpline on 0345 300 3900.

For our opening hours, go to www.gov.uk/contact-hmrc

Yr laith Gymraeg

Ffonwich 0300 200 1900 i dderbyn fersiynau Cymraeg o ffurflenni a chanllawiau.

Your rights and obligations

"Your Charter" explains what you can expect from us and what we expect from you.

For more information, go to www.gov.uk/hmrc/your-charter

We've a range of services for disabled people. These include guidance in Braille, audio and large print. Most of our forms are also available in large print. Contact our helplines for more information.

Our guide "Help with the costs of childcare"

To get a copy of our guide WTC5, "Help with the costs of childcare", you can:

go to GOV.UK and search for "WTC5"

- if you don't have access to the internet, phone the Tax Credit Helpline on 0345 300 3900

What we mean by relative

A relative can be a:

- child's parent
- child's grandparent
- child's aunt or uncle
- child's brother or sister
- child's step-parent
- person with a strong relationship to the child, for example someone in a parental role regarding their partner's children

Find out if you can claim tax credits

To find out more about tax credits and to see if you can claim, you can:

go to www.gov.uk/taxcredits

go to GOV.UK and search for WTC2, "A guide to Child Tax Credit and Working Tax Credit"

- if you don't have access to the internet, phone the Tax Credit Helpline on 0345 300 3900

Help to work out your taxable profits

If you need help working out your taxable profits:

- phone the Self Assessment Helpline on 0300 200 3310
- get a copy of our helpsheet HS222, "How to calculate your taxable profits"

go to GOV.UK and search for HS222

– phone the Self Assessment Orderline on 0300 200 3610

WTC6: TAX CREDITS – OTHER TYPES OF HELP YOU COULD GET [HMRC, December 2014]

If you get tax credits, you may also be able to get other help with day-to-day costs. The help you could get may depend on where you live in the UK and the type and amount of tax credits you get.

This factsheet gives you some examples of the type of help that may be available if you claim or receive tax credits.

Help with health costs

If you meet the criteria, you will be able to get help with the cost of:

- prescriptions, wigs and fabric supports if they are not already free where you live
- dental treatment
- eyesight tests
- glasses or contact lenses
- travel for treatment after referral by a doctor, dentist or optician

If you qualify, you will automatically be sent an NHS Tax Credit Exemption Certificate in the post, normally within 8 weeks of your tax credits being awarded.

If you meet the criteria and you don't get your certificate before you need treatment, you can use your award or renewal notice as proof you're entitled to tax credits. If you haven't received your award or renewal notice, you will need to:

- pay for your treatment and get a receipt
- ask about claiming a refund afterwards

For more information and details of the criteria:

- for England, go to **www.nhs.uk/healthcosts**
- for Wales, go to **www.healthcosts.wales.nhs.uk**
- for Scotland, go to **www.scotland.gov.uk** and search for "Help with health costs"
- for Northern Ireland, go to **www.nidirect.gov.uk/help-with-health-costs**

Or phone:

- for England, Scotland and Wales **0300 330 1343**
- for Northern Ireland **0800 587 8982**

For information about NHS Tax Credit Exemption Certificates, phone **0300 330 1347**.

Help with a baby or child under the age of 4

Healthy Start

If you are expecting a baby, or have a child under 4, you may be able to get help from Healthy Start. You could get:

- free vitamins
- vouchers to buy fresh or frozen fruit and vegetables, milk and infant formula milk

For more information or an application form, go to:

- **www.healthystart.nhs.uk**
- phone **0845 607 6823**

Sure Start Maternity Grant

This is a lump sum of £500 for your baby (or each of your babies in a multiple birth), which you don't have to pay back. **Please note**, if you already have children, you won't get a grant unless you're expecting a multiple birth. You can qualify even if you're not the mother or expectant mother of the baby, for example, you're adopting a baby.

For more information:

- for England, Scotland and Wales, go to **www.gov.uk/sure-start-maternity-grant**
- for Northern Ireland, go to **www.nidirect.gov.uk/sure-start-maternity-grant**
- visit your Jobcentre Plus office (Social Security or Jobs and Benefits office in Northern Ireland)

Help with school costs

If you get tax credits, you may be able to get:

- free school meals
- free transport to and from school
- help with the cost of uniforms, or activities such as school trips

Get in touch with your school, local authority or Education and Library Board in Northern Ireland to find out what help you could get.

To find contact details:

- in England, Scotland and Wales, go to **www.gov.uk/find-your-local-council**
- in Northern Ireland, go to **www.nidirect.gov.uk/education-and-library-boards**
- look in "The Phone Book" under "local authority" or "Education and Library Boards"

Other help you may be able to get

If you get tax credits, you can also sometimes get help with other costs. Examples include:

- some home improvements, including help towards heating and insulation costs – for more information, phone the Energy Saving Advice Service Helpline on **0300 123 1234**
- court and tribunal costs
- funeral costs
- help towards prison visits

For details and advice on what help may be available:

- for England, Scotland and Wales, go to **www.gov.uk**
- for Northern Ireland, go to **www.nidirect.gov.uk** or mention that you claim tax credits to see if there's any help available to you with costs.

WTC7: TAX CREDITS PENALTIES [HMRC, April 2017]

What happens at the end of a tax credits check

This factsheet tells you about the penalties we may impose if you have failed to comply with requirements or acted fraudulently or negligently in connection with your claim. It also explains how to ask for a reconsideration if you disagree with those penalties.

Introduction

When you claim Child Tax Credit or Working Tax Credit you're responsible for making sure that the information on your claim is right.

This factsheet is for anyone who may be charged a penalty after we've made a check on their tax credits claim. It doesn't tell you everything about penalties, but it does tell you what's likely to happen and what you can do if we charge you a penalty.

Information about how and why we carry out tax credits checks is in factsheets WTC/FS1, "Tax credits enquiry" and WTC/FS2, "Tax credits examinations". We normally give these to customers when we start a check.

You can also get a copy online, go to GOV.UK and search for WTC/FS1 or WTC/FS2.

Why we charge penalties

We charge penalties to:

- encourage people to be careful and make sure their claims are right in the future
- stop customers from giving us wrong information in the future
- penalise people who try to defraud the system

Your penalty

We can charge you a penalty of up to £3,000 if you deliberately or negligently gave the wrong information:

- on your claim
- when telling us about a change of circumstances
- when providing information to us as part of our checks

We can also charge you a penalty of up to £300 if you have failed to give us information or tell us about certain changes of circumstances within one month.

We'll explain why we believe you have failed to tell us of a change of circumstances within one month or why we believe you have deliberately declared the wrong information. If you don't accept our explanation, you can ask an independent tribunal to decide.

If we believe you may have committed a criminal offence, we may carry out an investigation and prosecute you. If this happens, we'll not charge you a penalty.

What is deliberate error

Deliberate error is where you deliberately gave the wrong information. This includes claiming for an element of tax credits you're not entitled to or to increase an element by making a false statement about your circumstances. This can include:

- claiming for a fictitious child or children, or the wrong number of children
- claiming for childcare costs when none are paid for
- claiming for childcare costs in excess of what is actually paid where there's clearly no basis for the amount claimed
- claiming for a young person as being in education/training that counts for tax credits when they aren't
- giving us wrong working hours information such as
  - claiming to be working when you're not
  - claiming to be working over 16 or 30 hours when you don't
  - for couples with children, claiming to be working a combined total of 24 hours when you don't work those hours, haven't done so recently and have no intention of doing so

- claiming to be in prison, an inpatient in hospital or incapacitated when you're not
- claiming to be entitled to Carer's Allowance when you're not
- claiming for the disability element with no basis to support such a claim
- understating your income where there was no basis for the amount of income declared
- failing to tell us about a source of income
- claiming as a single person when a partner is present and it's clear a joint claim should have been made
- making any other wrong declarations where the information concerns your own circumstances which you can be reasonably expected to know

Couples

If you have made a joint claim with your partner, you're both responsible for the information you provide in your claim.

We may charge you a penalty as a couple where either of you could have:

- told us about any change in circumstances
- given us new information

If the information relates to one member of a couple and their partner couldn't reasonably have known it was wrong, we'll only charge a penalty to the partner who knew it wasn't right.

The maximum penalty for a joint claim is no more than the maximum penalty for an individual claim.

The amount of your penalty

The maximum penalty for failing to notify a change of circumstance within one month is £300.

The maximum penalty for failing to declare circumstances or income when requested to do so in an annual review or failing to comply with a request for information is £300, but we have to ask an independent tribunal to impose this penalty. If this failure continues, we may charge a penalty not exceeding £60 per day.

For deliberate and wrong new claims the penalty levels are:

- £600 for a first wrong new claim
- £1,000 for a second wrong new claim
- £1,500 for a third and subsequent wrong new claim

For a deliberate and wrong declaration when reporting any other information, the penalty levels are for a:

- first wrong declaration, 30% of the over-claimed tax credits up to a maximum of £3,000
- second wrong declaration, 50% of the over-claimed tax credits up to a maximum of £3,000
- third or subsequent wrong declaration, 100% of the over-claimed tax credits up to a maximum of £3,000

If you don't understand our explanation of the penalty, you can ask us to put it in writing so that you can seek independent advice.

Interest

We may charge you interest if you pay a penalty late.

We'll contact you if we think that you have become liable to a penalty. We can do this:

- by phone
- in a meeting
- in writing

We'll explain why we're charging you a penalty and tell you both the maximum amount we can charge and the amount of the penalty we propose to charge. We're always willing to discuss with you the amount of the penalty and the reasons for it.

Paying your penalty

We'll discuss the arrangements for payment covering:

- any overpaid tax credits
- the penalty
- any interest due

You can pay by debit card, credit card or Direct Debit using the internet and telephone banking.

For more information on how to pay, go to **www.gov.uk/dealing-with-hmrc/paying-hmrc**

TC Extra-statutory Material

Co-operation

The extent to which you co-operate and give us information is entirely up to you. If you're not sure whether to give us the information or if you're reluctant to co-operate, we suggest you get independent advice before deciding what to do.

We may decide to reduce or stop your current tax credits payments based on the information we hold.

A number of independent organisations offer help with tax credits, such as Citizens Advice.

Go to **www.citizensadvice.org.uk** or you can find them in "The Phone Book".

About our decision

You have the right to ask us to reconsider our decision if we:

- ask you to pay penalties or interest on an overpayment
- change your award

We call this mandatory reconsideration. Our decision notice will tell you how to ask us to reconsider our decision.

Our leaflet WTC/AP, "What to do if you think your Child Tax Credit or Working Tax Credit is wrong" gives more information about how to ask for a reconsideration.

Go to GOV.UK and search for WTC/AP. If we charge you a penalty, you'll get a copy of this leaflet with our decision notice.

We won't treat your request to reconsider as non co-operation.

Independent tribunals

If we can't change our decision, you can appeal to an independent tribunal. Details of what you need to do will be given in our Mandatory Reconsideration notice.

Help with tax credits

For more information:

go to **www.gov.uk/taxcredits**

- telephone the Tax Credit Helpline on 0345 300 3900
- textphone the Tax Credit Helpline (for people with hearing or speech difficulties) on 0345 300 3909
- write to us at

Tax Credit Office
PRESTON
PR1 4AT

When you contact us, tell us your:

- full name
- National Insurance number
- daytime phone number

Yr Iaith Gymraeg

Ffoniwch 0300 200 1900 i dderbyn fersiynau Cymraeg o ffurflenni a chanllawiau.

Your rights and obligations

"Your Charter" explains what you can expect from us and what we expect from you.

For more information, go to **www.gov.uk/hmrc/your-charter**

Complaints

For more information about our complaints procedures, go to **www.gov.uk/complain-to-hmrevenue-and-customs**

We've a range of services for disabled people. These include guidance in Braille, audio and large print. Most of our forms are also available in large print. Contact our helplines for more information.

WTC8 – CHILD TAX CREDIT AND WORKING TAX CREDIT [HMRC, April 2018]

Why overpayments happen

We've a range of services for disabled people. These include guidance in Braille, audio and large print. Most of our forms are also available in large print. Contact our helplines for more information.

Yr Iaith Gymraeg

Ffoniwch 0300 200 1900 I dderbyn fersiynau Cymraeg o ffurflenni a chanllawiau.

Your rights and obligations.

"Your Charter" explains what you can expect from us and what we expect from you.

For more information, go to www.gov.uk/hmrc/your-charter

Tax credits are flexible and change when your life changes. If you don't tell us straightaway when things change, you may be overpaid.

Introduction

We tell you which changes you need to tell us about in the checklist TC602(SN), "Check your tax credits award notice now" that we send with every award notice.

Here are some of the most common reasons why people end up with an overpayment.

Your income changes

Tax credits are based on your income as well as your family circumstances.

When we first work out what to pay you, we look at your income for the last tax year – a tax year runs from 6 April one year to 5 April the next. If we don't have this information, we may use your income from the year before the last tax year.

Your income goes down

If your annual income for the current tax year is lower than last year, you may get extra tax credits for the current year. The lower your income, the more tax credits you may get. But when your income goes down it might not affect your payments until the following year.

You should always tell us your new lower income, to help make sure you get the correct amount of tax credits.

However, if your income goes down by £2,500 or less and all of your other circumstances stay the same, your payments won't be affected until the following year. We'll use your new income figure to work out what to pay you for the following year.

If your income goes down by more than £2,500, we'll revise your tax credits but will ignore the first £2,500 of the reduction.

If you tell us your income for this tax year is going to go down, we can use an estimate of what your income for this year will be.

If we use this lower figure it's important you tell us straightaway if your income is going to be higher than you estimated, as this may cause an overpayment.

Your income goes up

It's also important for you to tell us if your income for this tax year is going to be higher than it was in the last tax year. This may not make any difference to the money that you get this tax year, because we'll ignore the first £2,500 of any increase. However, if you don't tell us straightaway when you know your income will be higher, you may be paid too much when we work out what to pay you in the next tax year.

What happens after the end of the tax year

After 5 April each year your payments will continue, but they're provisional and may be based on out of date information. So we'll ask you to:

- check that the information we hold about you is up to date
- tell us how much income you had in the last tax year

We can then work out:

- the actual amount of money due to you for the tax year that has just ended
- your payments for the current tax year

If you don't keep us up to date with your income changes you:

- may not be getting all the money you're entitled to
- could be building up an overpayment that you have to pay back

Example

Karl's income for the last tax year was £22,000. He phoned us on 6 August to tell us he had started a new job.

He estimated his income for this tax year would be £18,500. As his income reduced by £3,500, we ignored the first £2,500 and used the income of £21,000 to calculate his new tax credits payments. He then started working overtime and didn't tell us that his estimated income would be more than he originally told us in August. He waited until he got his renewal pack the following May and then told us his income for the year was £20,000. As his actual income had reduced by less than £2,500 his final tax credits entitlement was based on his previous year's income of £22,000.

As we worked out Karl's tax credits based on income of £21,000, rather than £22,000, this caused an overpayment. If Karl had told us during the year that his original estimate was going to increase because of his overtime, he might not have had this overpayment.

You split up with your partner, or you start living with a partner.

If you're a couple, you must make a joint claim based on your joint circumstances. If you're single, you must make a single claim based on your individual circumstances. If your partner leaves or a new partner moves in and you don't tell us straightaway you may be overpaid.

For more information on when to make a joint or single tax credits claim,

go to www.gov.uk/claim-tax-credits/joint-claims

Example

Robyn's relationship with John ends on 13 January. The children stayed with Robyn after John left. Neither Robyn nor John tell us of the change. Robyn and John's entitlement to tax credits as a couple ends on 13 January.

When Robyn returns their annual declaration on 27 July she tells us about the change. Because their joint claim ended on 13 January, there's an overpayment from:

- 14 January to 5 April (the end of the last tax year)
- 6 April (the start of this tax year) to 27 July

If Robyn or John had contacted us at the time John left, we could have helped them claim separately from 14 January. And, the overpayment on their joint claim would have been smaller.

You don't renew your tax credits on time

We ask you to renew your tax credits claim each year. We send you a renewal pack, which includes your annual declaration. The pack tells you what you need to do, and by when. If we ask you to reply and you don't do this on time, you may end up with an overpayment.

Example

Abdul gets his renewal pack on 3 May. The pack tells him he has until 31 July to renew his claim. He puts the pack to one side meaning to do it later. But he forgets.

As Abdul hasn't renewed his claim, his payments stop on 6 August. We ask him to pay back the money he has had from 6 April.

If Abdul had replied on time, any overpayment he had would have been smaller, or he may not have been overpaid at all.

Abdul will get a letter telling him about his overpayment. If he returns his annual declaration or phones us to give us the details within 30 days of the letter, his tax credits will be reinstated and he may not have an overpayment.

A change in your childcare costs

You may be overpaid tax credits if you don't tell us when you stop paying for childcare, or the amount goes down by an average of £10 a week or more. For example, if you start getting:

- childcare vouchers from your employer
- early learning or nursery education support (for example, where your local authority in England meets the cost of 15 hours a week *free* early years education for children aged 3 and 4 and for some *children* aged 2)
- help with your costs from anywhere else

You also need to tell us if your childcare provider stops being approved or registered, or if you change to a different registered or approved childcare provider and the amount goes down by an average of £10 a week or more.

Example

Marie's 2 children go to nursery 5 days a week and she pays childcare costs of £300 a week. In September, her eldest child, Annie, starts school and she no longer pays for a nursery place for her. Her childcare costs go down to £150 a week. Marie doesn't tell us about this change until December. The first 4 weeks after Marie's childcare costs change don't affect the money we pay her, but she'll have to pay back any overpayment from 4 weeks after her childcare costs went down, to December.

Your child leaves full-time non-advanced education or approved training

You must tell us straightaway if your child leaves full-time non-advanced education or approved training. You must tell the Child Benefit Office too. If you delay you may get too much tax credits and Child Benefit.

Example

Olga's eldest son Victor starts A levels at college in September. By October, he decides to leave college and gets a full-time job instead.

Olga doesn't tell us this until the following March. All the tax credits she had for Victor from October to March is an overpayment.

Including children on your claim

If you include a child on your claim who isn't living with you, or you're getting tax credits for a child and they go to live with someone else, you may be overpaid. This is the same for Child Benefit too.

Example

Raj's children live with him and he gets tax credits for them. Then they go to live with their mum Vimla.

Raj didn't tell us that his children were no longer living with him. He's not entitled to the money he got when the children weren't living with him. He'll now have to pay back the overpaid amount.

You stop work or reduce your hours

If you stop work or reduce your hours and don't tell us, you could end up with an overpayment.

Example

Sandra claims Working Tax Credit (WTC) only, as she doesn't have any children. On 3 May, she reduces her working hours from 32 to 14 hours a week, but she doesn't tell us until 12 July.

In these circumstances, we continue to treat a person as working their old number of hours for the first 4 weeks, unless they claim Universal Credit during that period. So, Sandra continues to be treated as working for 32 hours a week for the first 4 weeks after she reduced her hours. This means that she's not entitled to WTC from 31 May. We ask her to pay back the money she had from 31 May to 12 July.

You get contribution-based benefits

Contribution-based Jobseeker's Allowance and contribution-based Employment and Support Allowance count as part of your income for tax credits. Contribution-based benefits are paid where you've paid or been credited Class 1 or Class 2 National Insurance contributions in the relevant tax years. Your benefit notice tells you if you're getting a contribution-based benefit. If you don't tell us that you're getting contribution-based benefits, you may be overpaid and will have to pay back any tax credits you've had.

You get income-based benefits

Income-based Jobseeker's Allowance or income-related Employment and Support Allowance are paid where you haven't paid or been credited enough National Insurance contributions. If you're getting these income-based benefits, we'll automatically pay you the maximum entitlement to any tax credits you can claim. If you tell us that you're getting an income-based benefit, when you're getting a contribution-based benefit, you may be overpaid and will have to pay back any tax credits you've had.

Example

Ben and Claire are getting tax credits. Claire earned £16,000 last year and works full-time. Ben earned £10,000 last year and works part-time. In June, Ben loses his job and claims Jobseeker's Allowance. As he's paid enough contributions during the relevant period, he qualifies for contribution-based Jobseeker's Allowance. Ben and Claire incorrectly tell us that Ben is getting income-based Jobseeker's Allowance. Because of this, we pay them the maximum entitlement.

Ben phones us in October to tell us about his new job and earnings. He also tells us that he had in fact received contribution-based, not income-based, Jobseeker's Allowance.

We paid Ben and Claire maximum tax credits for the period when we thought he was getting income-based Jobseeker's Allowance. This meant they got too much money, and now have an overpayment.

Tax credits are often paid in advance

You should tell us about changes straightaway to avoid building up an overpayment. But, even though you've told us on time about a change in your life, you may still have an overpayment. This is because we often pay you tax credits in advance.

Example

Melissa moves in with Sam on 15 February and tells us on the same day. She is told her claim as a single person will end. So she asks for a new claim form to make a joint claim.

Melissa had received a 4-weekly payment on 12 February, but this covered her tax credits up to 28 February.

Melissa is asked to pay back the money paid for 15 February to 28 February because her single claim ended on 14 February. As long as she makes her joint claim with Sam within 1 month of moving in with him, their joint claim will be treated as if made on 15 February.

You don't check your award notice and tell us if it's wrong

Sometimes we do get things wrong. You should check your award notice and tell us straightaway if there's anything wrong, missing or incomplete. Use the checklist sent with the award notice to help you do this.

If you don't do this within 30 days, you may have to pay back any overpayment.

Example

Michael is sent an award notice on 10 June which incorrectly says that he is disabled. He doesn't check his award notice properly, using the checklist. So he doesn't see this mistake until he gets a renewal pack the following April. When he phones to renew his claim, he tells us his award notice was wrong.

All the extra money that Michael had for disability is an overpayment. He'll have to pay it back.

You claim Universal Credit

Universal Credit supports people who are on a low income or out of work and replaces a range of existing benefits, including tax credits. Eligibility to claim Universal Credit depends on where you live and your personal circumstances. You cannot receive both tax credits and Universal Credit payments at the same time.

If you claim Universal Credit you'll continue to receive tax credits until we've been told that your Universal Credit claim has been assessed. This means you're not left without money while your claim is dealt with, but may mean you've received some tax credits that you'll have to pay back.

To make sure you've been paid the right money for the period of your award, we'll ask you to finalise your tax credits award and will send you an Award Review. If we ask you to reply to the Award Review, do this on-time, otherwise this may increase any overpayment.

Example

Sandra claims Working Tax Credit (WTC) only, as she doesn't have any children. On 3 May, she reduces her working hours from 32 to 14 hours a week, and she tells us on 5 May.

In these circumstances, we continue to treat a person as working their old number of hours for the first 4 weeks. So, Sandra continues to be treated as working for 32 hours a week for the first 4 weeks after she reduced her hours. This means that she's not entitled to WTC from 31 May.

On 12 May Universal Credit tell us they accepted a claim Sandra made on the 6 May, so her entitlement to tax credits now ends on 5 May. We ask her to pay back any money she had from 6 May onwards.

If we make a mistake

To help us get your award right and avoid building up an overpayment it's important that we meet our responsibilities and you meet yours.

If we fail to meet our responsibilities, but you meet all yours, we won't ask you to pay back all of an overpayment caused by our failure.

Usually you have to dispute recovery of an overpayment within 3 months from the date of:

- your final decision notice
- the decision on your Annual Review notice (if your award is renewed automatically)
- your Statement of Account
- the decision on your Award Review notice (if your award ended automatically due to a claim for Universal Credit)
- the notice which gives you our decision on your mandatory reconsideration
- the letter from the Tribunal or Appeals Service which gives you their decision on your appeal

You can only dispute having to pay back an overpayment that happened in the tax year the notice or letter relates to. You can't normally dispute overpayments that occurred in earlier tax years. We'll only accept a late dispute in exceptional circumstances, for example, if you were in hospital for that 3 month period and no one else could deal with your affairs.

If you do send us a dispute, we'll continue to seek recovery of the overpayment while we're considering your dispute.

You can find more detailed guidance in our leaflet COP26, "What happens if we've paid you too much tax credits". For a copy of this leaflet,

go to GOV.UK and search for COP26 or you can phone our helpline if you don't have internet access.

> **Example**
>
> Barbara has 2 children and gets tax credits. In March her eldest child, Julie, leaves school and starts work. Barbara contacts us straightaway to tell us about the change. We don't note the change until June and show Julie's leaving date as June.
>
> Barbara phones us to let us know of the mistake as soon as she gets her revised award notice, but we don't correct it until September. We would correct the decision so that it removes Julie from the award from March. Because Barbara has met her responsibilities, but we didn't meet ours, we don't ask Barbara to pay back all of the overpayment that occurred from March to September.

More information

If this leaflet doesn't answer all your questions, and you still don't know why you have an overpayment, get in touch with us. You can:

- phone the Tax Credit Helpline on 0345 300 3900
- textphone the Tax Credit Helpline (for people with hearing or speech difficulties) on 0345 300 3909

for our opening hours, go to www.gov.uk/contact-hmrc

- write to us at
  Tax Credit Office
  HM Revenue and Customs
  BX9 1ER

When you contact us, tell us:

- your full name
- your National Insurance number
- a daytime phone number

If, after receiving an explanation, you still don't agree that we should ask you to pay back an overpayment, you can ask us to look at this again. We call this disputing an overpayment. To do this, complete and return form TC846, "Tax credits overpayment". You can get a copy:

online, go to GOV.UK and search for TC846

- by phoning our helpline if you don't have internet access

You can write to us instead, but you must make sure you give us full details including:

- in what tax year the overpayment being disputed happened
- if and when you contacted us
- why you think the overpayment happened
- why you think you shouldn't have to pay back the overpayment

TCAR: TAX CREDITS ANNUAL REVIEW HELP SHEETS [HMRC, April 2013]

These notes are to help you understand the Annual Review process and help your clients take the right action at the right time.

When and how Annual Review packs will be issued

From April following the year in which a customer receives tax credits, they will receive an annual review pack. If a customer has received tax credits during the 2012–13 tax year, they will receive an annual review pack between mid April and the end of June 2013.

Annual review packs will be issued in priority order as follows:

(1) customers who have been in receipt of Income Support (IS), Job Seeker's Allowance (JSA), Employment and Support Allowance (ESA) or Pension Credit (PC).

(2) customers on the maximum tax credits award (reply required)

(3) customers in receipt of tapered amounts of WTC and/or CTC (reply required)

(4) customers on the family element only (auto renewals), ceased awards or withdrawn claims.

Packs that include an annual declaration and annual review form will be sent out in white A4 size envelopes and those that include an annual review form only, will be sent out in brown A5 size envelopes.

Types of Annual Review packs

Depending on the type of review pack received, different action needs to be taken.

Reply required consisting of an annual review and annual declaration form. These are generally cases still in payment where we need the customer to confirm their income and circumstances for the previous year

Automatic renewals consisting of an annual review form only. In these cases a reply is not normally required because, for example, the customer receives the family element only. Customers in receipt of IS, income-based JSA, income-related ESA or PC for all of the 2012–13 tax year will be included in the auto renewals process. However, customers are asked to check their annual review notice and report changes if they will impact on their award, for example, change of income

Ceased cases consisting of an annual review form only. These cases will be automatically finalised by the tax credits system, using the latest information held. Customers are asked to check their annual review form and report any changes

Withdrawn cases consisting of an annual review form only. Customers are asked to check their annual review form and report any changes. Some customers will have received a separate letter (TC1015) telling them that their claim will not be renewed for the next year because the level of their income means that they do not currently receive or will not receive tax credits payments for the next year. Customers will be given the option to renew and continue with their claim by contacting Tax Credit Office within 30 days of the date on the letter. They may choose to do this because:

- they will not need to make a new claim if their income later falls or their circumstances change
- they will continue to qualify for the disability element of WTC if they currently qualify

Multiple awards

A customer with more than one award during the year should expect a separate review pack in respect of each award period. For example a person may have:

- claimed as both an individual and as a member of a couple
- been a member of more than one couple
- had more than one claim during a year due to stopping and restarting work.

All notices that request a response should be responded to even if the customer is not currently receiving tax credits. Failure to respond may lead to an overpayment.

Couples

Where one member of a couple with continuing entitlement provides full, signed declaration/review details for a notice given to both members of the couple, they are both treated as having made a declaration for the previous year and a claim for tax credits for the new tax year.

In cases where a couple have separated during the renewals period (that is from the 6 April and before they respond to the renewals notice) and only one of the couple responds to the notice, we treat that response as a new joint claim for the short period in the new tax year. However, both members of a separated couple are required to make signed declarations for the year passed. If only one of the couple makes a signed declaration, the year will be finalised for the other partner on the information held by Tax Credit Office. Both partners will be jointly liable for any overpayment due to non return of their declaration however HMRC will not normally seek to recover more than 50% from each member of a joint household, where that couple have separated.

How to make a declaration and deadlines

1. If your client has been sent an Annual Declaration form and an Annual Review notice

They can make their declaration by either:

- completing the Annual Declaration form and returning it in the envelope provided
- calling the Tax Credit Helpline on Tel 0345 300 3900

Due to the increased level of calls during the renewals period, your client may wish to call at the quieter times, usually before 9.30am or between 2.30pm and 4.00pm

The campaign of reducing error & fraud and encouraging customers to renew accurately will be continued into 2013. We will ask a number of customers who we believe are at risk of making a mistake on their form to contact operations staff on a direct dial telephone number for assistance. We will not finalise their award until we are satisfied it is correct.

Deadlines

- They should return the Annual Declaration form or give the Helpline the information asked for by **31 July** (1st specified date). The Annual Review notice and Declaration will tell them if they have a different deadline. If they can't provide details of actual income for the last tax year before the deadline, because for example they are self employed, they should still make a declaration by **31 July** by providing us with an estimate of their income. They should show that the income is an estimate by either ticking the "estimate" box on their declaration form or by advising the helpline that the income they are declaring is an estimate.
- If they have given details of estimated income by their deadline, a reminder will be issued to your client asking them to provide actual income details by **31 January** (2 specified date). Step C of their Annual Review notice will advise them if they've been given a different date however they should be encouraged to provide this information as soon as it is available. If the actual income at 31 January matches the estimate originally provided, they do not need to do anything as HMRC will finalise their claim based on the information already provided.

If your client misses the deadline for making a declaration

If no further action is taken by your client, the Tax Credit Office will finalise the previous year's award on the information they hold and will stop your client's current payments. Tax Credit Office will send a statement showing whether your client has been paid too much or not enough tax credit in the previous year. The payments made from 6 April of the current year to the date payments were stopped will become overpaid.

Don't panic. There are things you or your client can do:

- Your client will be allowed a further 30 days from the date on the notice telling them that their payments have stopped (TC607), to provide the information asked for. If your client provides this information within the 30 days, their current year claim will be reinstated. If this information is not provided by this date then your client will usually have to make a new tax credits claim. The claim will be automatically backdated up to a maximum of 31 days if they still meet the eligibility criteria for the full 31 days. If the eligibility criteria have not been met for the full 31 days, your client should include a letter with their claim form advising the correct date for backdating.
- If your client does not renew within 30 days after the deadline and before 31 January, we will consider accepting a late response in this period if they had good cause for not renewing on time. Good cause could include the customer not being able to complete the form earlier due to exceptional circumstances or the customer not being able to make arrangements for someone to handle their affairs. Each case will be reviewed on its own merits and if good cause is accepted, the claim will be reinstated from 6 April.

2. If your client received an Annual Review notice only

They need to check the information provided on the Annual Review notice. They only need to contact us if any of the following applies. They should either write to us or call the Tax Credit Helpline on Tel 0345 300 3900 if:

- they have had any change in their circumstances – further information can be found on our website at **www.hmrc.gov.uk/taxcreditschanges**
- their income is above or below the limits shown in the notice
- there are mistakes or missing details in the notice
- they have received a TC1015 letter but would like to continue and renew their claim

If none of these apply, they don't need to do anything – their tax credits will be automatically renewed and their payments will continue unless their claim has ceased or they have been told their claim will not be renewed.

If they don't know what their income will be and can't be sure if it will fall outside the income range, they should provide an estimate anyway. This will ensure that they have until 31 January (unless the notice specifies differently) to submit actual earnings.

Deadlines

The deadline is usually 31 July. The first page of their Annual Review notice will tell them if they have a different deadline.

Note: The deadline only applies in these cases if they need to tell the Tax Credit Office of any information that has changed, is wrong, missing or incomplete.

If your client misses the deadline or if the deadline doesn't apply

The Tax Credit Office will:

- treat the information on the Annual Review notice as correct for the whole of the period shown
- make a final decision on the award for the period covered by the Annual Review notice by checking the payments received against the information shown about the customers circumstances
- renew your client's claim for the current tax year if your client still qualifies for tax credits.

If it is later discovered that your client knew the information was not right or incomplete, they may be asked to pay back tax credits overpaid and may also be asked to pay a penalty.

3. If your client has not received an Annual Declaration or Review notice and believes they should have

- HMRC will have generally issued all Annual Declarations and Review notices by the end of June. If your client has not received theirs and they believe they should have, they should contact the tax credits helpline for further guidance
- Has your client moved address? It is extremely important customers keep HMRC updated with any change of address. If they do not, HMRC could send the annual declaration to the wrong address and this could lead to an overpayment of tax credits that they may have to pay back.

Further guidance on renewing and deadlines

www.hmrc.gov.uk/taxcreditsrenewals

4. If your client wants to leave Tax Credits

If your client wishes to stop claiming tax credits, they must **still** confirm their income and circumstances for the previous year by providing their declaration details to Tax Credit Office. They should also tell us that they don't want to continue their claim. If your client does this before 31 July, their claim for the current year will not be renewed and your client will be asked to pay back any provisional payments they may have received for the current year. If your client does this after 31 July, their claim will continue until the end of the tax year but will not be renewed for the next tax year.

Your client should be made aware that if their claim is not renewed for the next tax year and their circumstances change, they will need to make a new claim. If they make a new claim:

- and their income has dropped, we will only calculate their income for part of the year (the income for the whole year will be calculated if they continue to renew their claim)
- *we will only usually* backdate the new claim up to 31 days
- they may not qualify for the disability element of WTC (if claimed previously)

Check the Annual Review and complete the Annual Declaration

Please refer to the guidance notes *Renewing your tax credits – Getting it right* in the renewal pack and/or at **www.***hmrc.gov.uk*

Note:

- If your client is subject to a compliance examination or enquiry which is still open over the renewal period, they will receive a letter from the compliance team inviting them to make their declaration direct with their compliance officer. The officer will be responsible for processing the declaration, in conjunction with any compliance amendments, when a decision on the award is made.
- If resources allow, you may wish to consider proactively contacting vulnerable customers to check if they require assistance with their renewal.
- If your client returns their declaration by post, they should be advised to tick Box 3.2 only if they had a relevant change of circumstances in the year that the Annual Review notice relates. They should attach a note advising us of the change/s and when they took place. They should not tick Box 3.2 if the change took place in the current year (after 5 April). They should contact us separately by phone or in writing and let us know of this change.
- If there were no change in circumstances in the year to which the notice relates, Box 3.1 should be ticked. If boxes 3.1 or 3.2 are not ticked, we will treat as "no changes reported".

What happens next

Once the Tax Credit Office have complete information, either by the helpline or by post, the previous year will be finalised. Where the declaration is to be treated as a claim for the current tax year, the payments for the current year will be recalculated and adjusted accordingly.

Your client will receive a finalised decision notice for the previous year and an award notice for the current year, where applicable. Due to the increased volume around renewal time, the award notices may take longer than normal to be issued. If your client has not received new notices within 30 days, then you or your client should contact the tax credits helpline.

If you think a decision is wrong

- If your client believes that the finalised decision is incorrect, they can ask for the decision to be revised, as long as the final decision and the request to revise it is made on or before the 1st specified date (usually 31 July)
- After this date, the decision may only be amended:
  - following a successful appeal or settlement
  - following a compliance enquiry
  - following an amendment to your client's income tax liability
  - where we have reasonable grounds for believing that the decision was wrong and this was due to fraud or neglect on the part of your client or any person acting for them.
  - where the decision is wrong due to our or another government department's error and, your client did not contribute to the error and, the revised decision is in your clients favour.
- If your client believes that the finalised decision is incorrect and it is after the 1st specified date, they usually have 30 days from the date the award notice was issued to appeal against the notice.
- If your client wishes to appeal, they can do this by writing to us or by completing a form (available as part of fact sheet WTC/AP) which provides comprehensive guidance on the appeals process. This is available on our website **www.hmrc.gov.uk/leaflets/wtc_ap/pdf**
- Their correspondence should tell us that they want to appeal; the reason for appealing, their name and National Insurance number and the date of the award notice they wish to appeal against. The appeal must reach HMRC within 30 days from the date on the award notice. An appeal outside of the 30 days will be considered if the customer can provide an acceptable reason for the delay. Acceptable reasons may include:
  - the appellant, or a partner or a dependant of the appellant, has died or suffered severe illness
  - the appellant is not resident in the United Kingdom
  - normal postal services were disrupted
- The appeal will be considered and if we agree, the decision may be amended under section 54 of the Taxes Management Act. If we do not agree, we will send the appeal to be heard by an independent tribunal.

Please note:

- A current award can be adjusted at any point during the year so it's always worth trying to contact us before making a formal appeal. This way, if we agree the award is wrong, we can make sure it's changed for your client.
- An appeal must be against a notice of decision and not against the overpayment generated by a decision, for example, an appeal may be accepted where childcare costs were amended incorrectly but an appeal would not be accepted where the customer disagrees with an overpayment resulting from a change in circumstances advised after the date the change occurred. If the overpayment is at issue, the customer should dispute the overpayment by either writing to us and explaining why they consider that we should not recover the overpayment or by completing form TC846 *"Tax credit overpayment"* available on our website. For more detailed information about how we deal with tax credits overpayments, you should refer to COP26 – *What happens if we have paid you too much tax credit?* **http://www.hmrc.gov.uk/leaflets/cop26.pdf**

TC956: HOW TO QUALIFY FOR THE DISABILITY ELEMENTS OF TAX CREDITS [HMRC, October 2017]

Working Tax Credit

To qualify for the disability element of Working Tax Credit you must meet all 3 conditions below.

Condition 1

You usually work for 16 hours or more a week.

Condition 2

You have a disability that puts you at a disadvantage in getting a job. Details of the disabilities which count to meet this condition are on pages 1 to 3.

They relate to a wide range of things, for example:

- physical disability
- visual impairment
- hearing impairment
- other disability
- illness or accident

Condition 3

You currently get, or have been getting, a qualifying sickness or disability benefit. You need to satisfy one of the qualifying benefit conditions shown on pages 3 to 7.

If you don't meet all 3 conditions you won't be entitled to the disability element of Working Tax Credit.

Condition 2: Disability that puts you at a disadvantage in getting a job

We may ask for the name of someone involved in your care, like an occupational therapist, community nurse, district nurse or doctor, who can confirm how your disability affects you.

At least one of the following descriptions must apply to you.

Physical disability

(1) When standing you can't keep your balance unless you continuously hold on to something.

(2) You can't walk a continuous distance of 100 metres along level ground without stopping or without suffering severe pain. This is even when you use your usual walking aid, such as crutches, walking frame, walking stick, prosthesis or similar.

(3) You can't use either of your hands behind your back, as if you were putting on a jacket or tucking a shirt into trousers.

(4) You can't extend either of your arms in front of you, as if you were shaking hands with someone, without difficulty.

(5) You can't put either of your hands up to your head, as if putting on a hat, without difficulty.

(6) Due to a lack of ability in using your hands, you can't pick up a coin that is 2.5 centimetres or less in diameter, such as a 10 pence coin, with one hand.

(7) You find it difficult to use your hands or arms to pick up a full, one litre jug and pour from it into a cup.

(8) You can't turn either of your hands sideways through 180 degrees.

Visual impairment

(1) You've been certified as severely sight impaired or blind by a consultant ophthalmologist.

(2) You can't see to read 16 point print at a distance greater than 20 centimetres, even if you're wearing your usual glasses.

Hearing impairment

(1) You can't hear a phone ring when you are in the same room as the phone, even if you are using your usual hearing aid.

(2) You have difficulty hearing what someone 2 metres away is saying, even when they're talking loudly in a quiet room, and you're using your usual hearing aid.

Other disability

(1) You have a mental illness that you receive regular treatment for under supervision of a medically qualified person.

(2) Due to mental disability, you're often confused or forgetful.

(3) You can't do the simplest addition and subtraction.

(4) Due to mental disability, you strike people or damage property, or are unable to form normal social relationships.

(5) People who know you well have difficulty in understanding what you say.

(6) When a person that you know well speaks to you, you have difficulty in understanding what that person says.

(7) At least once a year, during waking hours, you're in a coma or have a fit where you lose consciousness.

(8) You can't normally sustain an 8 hour working day or a 5 day working week, due to a medical condition or, to intermittent or continuous severe pain.

Illness or accident

As a result of an illness or accident, you're undergoing a period of habilitation or rehabilitation. This doesn't apply to you if you've been getting a disability element of Working Tax Credit in the past 2 years.

Condition 3: Qualifying benefit conditions

You'll meet this condition if you're getting, or have been getting, one of the following sickness or disability-related benefits at the specified rate and can satisfy the qualifying conditions.

Employment & Support Allowance (ESA)

To meet this condition you need to have been getting:

- ESA or Statutory Sick Pay for at least one of the 182 days before you claimed the disability element and entitlement has existed for a period of 28 weeks immediately preceding that day (see Note 1 on page 7)
- ESA for a period of 140 qualifying days, with the last day of receipt falling within the 56 days before you claimed the disability element (see Note 2 on page 8) and the following apply, where your:
  - disability is likely to last for at least 6 months or the rest of your life
  - gross earnings are at least 20% less than they were before the disability began, with a minimum reduction of £15 (gross) a week

Employment & Support Allowance (ESA)

You get contributory ESA. To meet this condition, you need to have been training for work for at least one day in the 56 days before you claimed the disability element of Working Tax Credit. It also needs to be within 56 days before the first day of that period of training for work where you got contributory ESA for a period of 28 weeks (see Note 1 on page 7).

Housing Benefit

You get Housing Benefit which includes a Disability Premium or Higher Pensioner Premium because of your own disability. To meet this condition you need to receive this benefit for at least one of the 182 days before you claimed the disability element of Working Tax Credit.

Incapacity Benefit

You get Incapacity Benefit at the lower rate short-term. You meet this condition if all the following apply:

- you've been getting this benefit for 140 days or more, with the last day of receipt falling within the 56 days before you claimed the disability element of Working Tax Credit (see Note 2 on page 8)
- your disability is likely to last for at least 6 months or the rest of your life
- your gross earnings are at least 20% less than they were before the disability began, with a minimum reduction of £15 (gross) a week

You get Incapacity Benefit at the higher rate short-term or long-term rate. To meet this condition you need to have been:

- getting this benefit for at least one of the 182 days before you claimed the disability element of Working Tax Credit
- training for work for at least one day in the 56 days before you claimed the disability element of Working Tax Credit and within 56 days before the first day of that period of training for work, you got this benefit

Income Support

You get Income Support which includes a Disability Premium or Higher Pensioner Premium because of your own disability. To meet this condition you need to have been getting this benefit for at least one of the 182 days before you claimed the disability element of Working Tax Credit.

You get Income Support on account of incapacity for work. You meet this condition if all the following apply:

- you've been getting Income Support for a period of 140 qualifying days and the last of those fell within 56 days before you claimed the disability element of Working Tax Credit (see Note 2 on page 8)
- your disability is likely to last for at least 6 months or the rest of your life
- your gross earnings are at least 20% less than they were before the disability began, with a minimum reduction of £15 (gross) a week

Income-based Jobseeker's Allowance

You get income-based Jobseeker's Allowance which includes a Disability Premium or Higher Pensioner Premium. To meet this condition you need to get this benefit for at least one of the preceding 182 days.

National Insurance Credits

You get these credits on account of having a limited capability for work or on account of incapacity for work. You meet this condition if all the following apply:

- you've been getting these credits for a period of 20 weeks, and the last of those fell within the 56 days before you claimed the disability element of Working Tax Credit (see Note 2 on page 8)
- your disability is likely to last for at least 6 months or the rest of your life
- your gross earnings are at least 20% less than they were before the disability began, with a minimum reduction of £15 (gross) a week

You get these credits because you've a limited capability for work credit awarded, as your 12 month entitlement to contribution-based Employment and Support Allowance has run out. To meet this condition you need to have been either:

- getting these credits for at least one of the 182 days before you claimed the disability element of Working Tax Credit
- training for work for at least one day in the 56 days before you claimed the disability element of Working Tax Credit and within 56 days before the first day of that period of training for work, you got these credits

Occupational Sick Pay (OSP)

You get Occupational Sick Pay. You meet this condition if all the following apply:

- you've been getting this benefit for 140 days or more, with the last day of receipt falling within the 56 days before you claimed the disability element of Working Tax Credit (see Note 2 on page 8)
- your disability is likely to last for at least 6 months or the rest of your life
- your gross earnings are at least 20% less than they were before the disability began, with a minimum *reduction of £15* (gross) a week

Severe Disablement Allowance

To meet this condition you need to either have been:

- getting this benefit for at least one of the 182 days before you claimed the disability element of Working Tax Credit
- training for work for at least one day in the 56 days before you claimed the disability element of Working Tax Credit and within 56 days before the first day of that period of training for work, you got Severe Disablement Allowance

Statutory Sick Pay (SSP)

To meet this condition you need to either have been getting:

- this benefit for 140 days or more, with the last day of receipt falling within the 56 days before you claimed the disability element of Working Tax Credit (see Note 2 on page 8) and the following apply
  - your disability is likely to last for at least 6 months or the rest of your life
  - your gross earnings are at least 20% less than they were before the disability began, with a minimum reduction of £15 (gross) a week
- SSP followed by contribution-based Employment and Support Allowance for a combined period of 28 weeks or more and have been training for work for at least one day in the 56 days before you claimed the disability element

Working Tax Credit

You qualify if you've been entitled to the disability element of Working Tax Credit in the 56 days before your claim for the disability element by satisfying the qualifying conditions under one of the sickness or disability-related benefits listed on pages 3 to 7, or by getting Disabled Person's Tax Credit, at some earlier time*.

* The period "some earlier time" can allow continuing entitlement to the disability element long after the qualifying sickness or disability-related benefit stopped being paid.

Other benefits

You meet the qualifying condition if you're currently getting one of the following benefits:

- Attendance Allowance
- Disability Living Allowance, Personal Independence Payment or Armed Forces Independence Payment
- Industrial Injuries Disablement Benefit with a mobility supplement or a constant attendance allowance
- War Pension with a mobility supplement or a constant attendance allowance
- Invalid carriage scheme and you've an invalid carriage or other vehicle provided under the Invalid Vehicle Scheme

Notes

Note 1

The 28 weeks doesn't need to be a single continuous period. You can add together any periods that you got:

- Employment and Support Allowance (ESA)
- limited capability for work credit
- Statutory Sick Pay (SSP)
- Incapacity Benefit (short term or long term rate)
- Severe Disablement Allowance
- Income Support with a disability premium or higher pensioner premium
- SSP, as long as they were no more than 8 weeks apart
- SSP with periods that you got
  - contribution-based ESA
  - limited capability for work credit
  - Incapacity Benefit (short term or long term rate)
  - Severe Disablement Allowance

as long as they were no more than 12 weeks apart and they met the contribution conditions for contribution-based ESA on the days that you got SSP.

Note 2

The 140 days (20 weeks) doesn't need to be a single continuous period. It can be made up of any periods where you are/were in receipt of:

- Employment and Support Allowance
- Statutory Sick Pay
- Occupational Sick Pay
- Incapacity Benefit (short term or long term rate)
- Income Support awarded due to incapacity for work

which are separated by 8 weeks or less. Any such periods can be linked together to satisfy the 140 days (20 weeks) condition.

The severe disability element of Working Tax Credit

If you or your partner (if you're claiming as a couple) get:

- Disability Living Allowance (DLA) (highest rate care component)
- enhanced daily living component of Personal Independence Payment
- Armed Forces Independence Payment
- Attendance Allowance (higher rate)

you can get the severe disability element.

You don't have to be working to qualify for the severe disability element as long as your partner does. If you both qualify, you'll get 2 severe disability elements.

Child Tax Credit: The disability element of Child Tax Credit for a disabled or severely disabled child or qualifying young person

Disabled child element for a disabled child or qualifying young person

You may get a disabled child element for each child or qualifying young person you're responsible for if:

- DLA or Personal Independence Payment is being paid for him or her (or would be so payable but for hospitalisation of the child or young person)
- the child or qualifying young person is certified as severely sight impaired or blind by a consultant ophthalmologist
- the child ceased to be certified as severely sight impaired or blind by a consultant ophthalmologist in the 28 weeks before the date of claim

For a severely disabled child or qualifying young person you may get the disabled child element paid at a higher rate for each child or qualifying young person you're responsible for if any of the following is being paid for them:

- highest rate care component of DLA (or would be so payable but for suspension of the benefit or hospitalisation of the child or qualifying young person)
- enhanced daily living component of Personal Independence Payment (or would be so payable but for hospitalisation of the child or qualifying young person)
- Armed Forces Independence Payment

Disability Helpsheet

Helpline

For our opening hours. go to www.gov.uk/contact-hmrc

Phone

0345 300 3900

Textphone

0345 300 3909

Your rights and obligations

Your Charter explains what *you can expect* from us and what we expect from you.

For more information, go to www.gov.uk/hmrc/your-charter

We've a range of services for disabled people. These include guidance in Braille, audio and large print. Most of our forms are also available in large print. Contact our helplines for more information.

HMRC LEAFLETS

TC1: HOW HM REVENUE & CUSTOMS HANDLE TAX CREDITS OVERPAYMENTS [HMRC, April 2012]

Introduction

This is a guide aimed at advisers and intermediaries who provide support and guidance to tax credits customers.

HM Revenue & Customs (HMRC) will ask customers who have been paid too much tax credits to pay back the extra money. A customer can challenge the overpayment by appealing or disputing. More information is available at Section 1.

HMRC can recover an overpayment from its customers in two ways.

Section 1 – overview of overpayment recovery

If the customer is still getting tax credits under their original claim

If the customer's original claim is continuing, HMRC will take 25 per cent from their four weekly or weekly payments of tax credits until the overpayment is recovered.

If the customer's original claim is continuing and the customer is getting maximum tax credits HMRC will take 10 per cent.

If the customer's original claim is continuing and the customer is getting only the family element of Child Tax Credit HMRC will take 100 per cent, so the customer will receive nothing until the overpayment is repaid.

HMRC call this "ongoing recovery".

If the customer is no longer entitled to tax credits or has made a new claim

If a customer is no longer entitled to tax credits or gets tax credits because they have made a new claim and have an overpayment from an old claim, HMRC ask them to repay the overpayment direct. This is known as "direct recovery".

If a customer is currently paying back one tax credits overpayment by direct payment, and paying back another from an ongoing award at either 10 per cent or 25 per cent, they can contact the **Payment Helpline (0845 302 1429)** and ask for the overpayment being recovered by direct payment to be suspended until the overpayment being recovered from the ongoing award is completed.

The earlier a customer contacts HMRC, the easier it is to resolve any issues the customer has with the repayment. If the customer doesn't make a payment or doesn't contact HMRC it will seek to recover the debt.

Challenging an overpayment

Appeal

Customers may appeal if they think that the decision HMRC made, which created the overpayment, was incorrect. More detail about how to do this can be found in leaflet "WTC/AP – Child Tax Credit and Working Tax Credit: how to appeal against a tax credit decision or award". You can get a copy of this leaflet:

- by phoning the Tax Credits Helpline on 0345 300 3900
- by downloading a copy from the HMRC website at WTC/AP – Child Tax Credit and Working Tax Credit: how to appeal against a tax credit decision or award

Example:

Daisha claims tax credits for her three children. Her eldest child finished her GCSEs but decided to stay on at school to do her A levels. Daisha told HMRC and continued to receive tax credits for three children. When HMRC worked out Daisha's final tax credits for the year, they included only two children. Because Daisha received money for three children, HMRC thought that it had overpaid her. Daisha appealed the decision and asked HMRC to change her award as she should have received tax credits for three children. If she is successful, the overpayment will disappear.

If a customer appeals a decision, which created the overpayment, then any recovery action will be suspended until the outcome of the appeal is known. Benefits and Credits will write to the customer explaining the outcome of the appeal.

Dispute

Customers who accept that they have received more than they were due may still dispute recovery of the overpayment if they believe the overpayment was caused by HMRC failing to meet its responsibilities. Customers should contact the Helpline (0345 300 3900) as soon as possible. More detailed advice can be found in leaflet "COP26 – What happens if we've paid you too much tax credit?" You can get a copy of this leaflet:

- By phoning the Tax Credits Helpline on 0345 300 3900
- By downloading a copy from the HMRC website at COP26 – What happens if we've paid you too much tax credit?

Example:

Eric and his wife were paid tax credits for three children when they only have two. When Eric received his award notice, he phoned HMRC to say the number of children was wrong. HMRC did not correct the mistake and kept on paying Eric too much tax credit. After the end of the year, Eric had received more tax credits than he should have and so had an overpayment. Eric used the dispute process because he doesn't think he should have to pay it back because he told HMRC of the mistake as soon as he saw his award notice.

If a customer disputes recovery of an overpayment, then Benefits and Credits will arrange for suspension of any recovery action while HMRC reconsider. If HMRC decide that the customer should repay the overpayment then action to recover it will continue. Benefits and Credits will write to the customer explaining the outcome of the dispute.

Code of Practice 26 (COP26)

Customers who contact HMRC because they do not understand why they have an overpayment or to dispute the overpayment, will get a written explanation from Benefits and Credits and be advised to go to the website or contact the Helpline to get a copy of Code of Practice COP26 which explains the principles behind HMRC's approach.

Section 2 – the "ongoing recovery"process

Process

Where a customer has an overpayment in an ongoing award, recovery of the overpayment is automatic. The automatic rates of recovery are set at 10 per cent, 25 per cent or 100 per cent and applied as set out in section 1. These rates are designed to avoid the reduction in payments causing financial difficulty to the customer.

Automatic Recovery Rate Causing Hardship

If a customer cannot afford the reduction in the payments they receive, they should contact the **Tax Credits Helpline on 0345 300 3900**. The Helpline will arrange for Benefits and Credits to check if the rate of recovery can be adjusted.

An adjustment to increase the amount of tax credits paid will not normally be made if the award is only made up of the Family or Baby elements of Child Tax Credit or if the customer's payments have reduced following an investigation that established deliberate error or fraud.

Where a decision on hardship is required Benefits and Credits will arrange to contact the customer to check what is affordable. Benefits and Credits will consider the financial and personal circumstances to determine whether a relaxation of the recovery rates, or if a full or partial remission of the overpayment is appropriate. The decision on hardship will be in line with considerations applied to direct recovery cases so in some circumstances income and expenditure detail may be required from the customer to inform the decision. Benefits and Credits will also review the customer's employment status, whether on sickness or incapacity benefits, and prospects for any improvement.

Benefits and Credits will inform the customer of the outcome in writing.

If an intermediary has all the relevant information, and decides to write, they should address the letter to Benefits and Credits at: **Tax Credits Office, Preston, PR1 0SB**.

Section 3 – the "direct recovery"process (customer no longer receives tax credits or has made a new claim)

Notifying the customer of an overpayment – TC610

When, following the end of an award, a tax credits overpayment has been established a Notice to Pay form (TC610) is automatically issued to the customer. The TC610 advises the customer of the amount due to be repaid to HMRC, within 42 days, and advises them that they can opt to spread the repayment over a period of 12 months. The TC610 also notifies the customer of the Payment Helpline telephone number (0845 302 1429), which they can contact to discuss paying back their overpayment. The Payment Helpline is part of Personal Tax Operations An example of the TC610 can be found at Section 5.

- If the customer pays in full HMRC will take no further action.
- If the customer contacts HMRC for help HMRC can discuss their affordability to repay and agree a Time to Pay arrangement appropriate to the customer's financial circumstances. Where there is low affordability due to unemployment, or the customer is on sickness or incapacity benefits, HMRC may consider putting on hold or remitting the debt – depending on individual circumstances. Further information is available at Section 4.
- If the customer contacts the Tax Credit Helpline to dispute their overpayment HMRC can send forms TC846 and COP26 or the customer can download these from the HMRC website. Suspension of the overpayment will be automatically applied on receipt of the completed TC846. If HMRC receive correspondence, disputing the overpayment, it will suspend recovery until a decision has been reached.

Written reminders

If an overpayment has not been fully repaid 42 days following the issue of the TC610 notice to pay, and the customer has not contacted HMRC, details of the overpayment will be automatically sent to DMB. A reminder letter asking for payment will be sent automatically by DMB's computer system:

- if the customer pays in full following this letter, HMRC will take no further action
- if the customer disputes the recovery of the overpayment, HMRC will suspend action to recover the overpayment while it reconsiders
- if the customer contacts HMRC for help, HMRC can agree a payment arrangement or consider putting on hold or remitting the debt due to low affordability
- if the customer does not pay in full, or contact HMRC to agree a payment arrangement, HMRC will issue a further (stronger worded) warning letter

Collecting tax credits debts through PAYE

DMB will identify tax credits direct recovery overpayment cases that may be suitable for collection by an adjustment to a customer's PAYE code. Customers in PAYE employment, or receiving pension income, with a tax credits overpayment not exceeding £3,000.00 may be able to have their tax code adjusted to collect the outstanding amount.

Recovery of a tax credits overpayment through PAYE is on a voluntary basis and the customer may choose to repay by an alternative method.

DMB will issue a letter, to the selected customers, which explains that HMRC are considering collecting the tax credit overpayment by adjusting their tax code and increasing the amount of tax they will pay in the next tax year. The letter asks the customer to call DMB on 0845 302 1421 within 30 days, from the date of the letter, if they do not want HMRC to take this action.

The customer can contact DMB to discuss an alternative method of repaying the overpayment. DMB will not be aware of other financial commitments the customer has and it may be that in some circumstances agreeing a time to pay for the tax credits overpayment is more appropriate.

If the customer does not contact DMB then checks will be made to ensure a code adjustment can be made. Existing safeguards that limit the amount that can be collected through PAYE will be preserved.

In a joint household award, two people will be named in the letter. DMB will attempt to adjust the tax code of the first named person. However, if this cannot be done DMB will then attempt to adjust the tax code of the second named person.

Where the code can be adjusted a form P2 Coding Notice will be sent to the customer around January / February.

If the code cannot be adjusted DMB will write to the customer and request an alternative method of repaying; normally by direct debit.

Where a couple are no longer together (Household Breakdown) DMB will not attempt to collect the overpayment by adjustment to either of their tax codes. In these circumstances DMB will expect each former partner to pay 50% of the overpayment. (But please refer to the guidance below if one former partner wants to pay more than 50%).

Telephone contact

Following the issue of the reminder letters, if the customer has not contacted HMRC, the Debt Management Telephone Centre (DMTC) will call them. The DMTC will discuss the customer's ability to repay (as detailed previously) and payment options, including an instalment arrangement:

- If the customer pays in full HMRC will take no further action.
- If the customer disputes the recovery of the overpayment, HMRC will refer the customer to the Tax Credit Helpline. DMB will withhold recovery action, allowing the customer time to do this.
- If the customer sets up a time to pay arrangement then recovery action will stop providing payments are kept up to date.

If DMTC establish that the customer cannot currently make an arrangement to repay the overpayment, and meet their living expenses at the same time, they will explain to the customer that the case will be put on hold for 12 months. Following this period the Debt Technical Office (DTO) will review the case and decide on the most appropriate action. In some cases HMRC will remit the overpayment immediately, depending on the customer's circumstances. In these cases DMTC will refer details to the DTO to deal with.

Personal contact

If the customer still fails to pay in full, or has not been in contact, the overpayment will be transferred to the DTO to follow up. The DTO will check that the customer is due to repay the overpayment. The case will be reviewed for Household Breakdown, Dual Recovery and to ensure that the customer has been notified of the overpayment. Where HMRC have confirmed that the customer is due to repay, it will try to contact the customer by phone or letter to set up an arrangement to pay wherever possible. Any letter sent by the DTO will provide the customer with a telephone number to contact them on.

If the DTO cannot make contact with the customer they may refer the case to the Field Force staff for a visit. This is normally at the customer's home but it can be arranged elsewhere if it is more convenient for the customer. At this stage HMRC will consider the customer's ability to repay and can still agree a payment arrangement. Every effort is made to contact the customer before HMRC start enforcement action.

Household breakdown cases

When a couple split up, and an overpayment arises from their joint claim, HMRC will ask each former partner for 50 per cent of the overpayment.

If one of the former partners wishes to pay more than 50 per cent, this can be accepted without the need of agreement with the ex-partner. Former partners may agree, between themselves, to vary the percentage that they each repay. However, if no offer is made, or a payment arrangement is not adhered to, HMRC reserve the right to seek 50 per cent from each former partner.

Enforcement

If the customer still does not pay or HMRC have, despite all efforts, been unable to establish any contact with them, HMRC will decide the most appropriate next action. This may be to arrange a visit to the customer's home. If the customer can afford to repay but chooses not to do so HMRC will consider distraint action. This may include the removal of goods from the home to sell at public auction. For more information on distraint please visit **www.hmrc.gov.uk/payinghmrc** and under *Payment problems and getting help* select *What could happen if you don't pay HMRC*.

HMRC may also decide to refer the overpayment to a Debt Collection Agency (DCA) to collect on their behalf.

Although distraint or referral to a DCA will be the normal process HMRC may go to court to obtain judgment to enable it to enforce payment of an outstanding debt.

Charging Orders

Charging Orders on the customer's primary residence will not be considered for a stand alone tax credits debt. However, where an order is appropriate for other HMRC debts, HMRC can include the amount of any tax credits overpayment.

Section 4 – how HMRC decide what's affordable (direct recovery)

Time to Pay – introduction

When a customer contacts HMRC about repaying a tax credit overpayment HMRC will discuss their ability to repay. HMRC will make an informed decision using the new tax credits Time to Pay Negotiating Framework or, where appropriate, the information obtained relating to income and expenditure (more details of this follows in the sections below). In all cases special circumstances, such as employment status and receipt of benefits, are taken into account. Where there is low affordability due to unemployment or the customer is in receipt of sickness or incapacity benefits HMRC will arrange to either put recovery on hold or remit the overpayment depending on the individual circumstances.

Time to Pay – up to ten years

If the customer cannot or does not wish to repay the overpayment immediately then up to 12 months Time to Pay is offered as standard. The Payment Helpline will agree a Time to Pay arrangement up to three years for customers who can afford to repay within this period. If a customer requires an arrangement in excess of three years, or is unable to repay due to low affordability, the Payment Helpline will transfer the call to DMTC. If a customer asks for a repayment period of more than 12 months, and up to ten years, then HMRC will consider the request. HMRC will make an informed decision based on the responses to a short series of questions, laid out on the tax credits Time to Pay Negotiating Framework. A copy of the Negotiating Framework can be found at Section 5. Income and expenditure details are not required for agreements up to ten years.

Time to Pay – more than ten years

If a customer requests a period longer than ten years they will have to give HMRC full details of their income and outgoings to help HMRC see what is affordable and sustainable for the customer. HMRC do not wish to enter into agreements with an unrealistic repayment plan as this will cause stress for the customer and be less effective in recovering the overpayment. When HMRC consider these cases it will take into account any exceptional circumstances the customer advise of that may lead to extra living costs, for example, if the customer is looking after someone who is chronically ill or disabled.

Payment arrangements set up for periods of ten years or more are reviewed periodically. If, after ten years, the customer has consistently adhered to their payment plan HMRC will remit any outstanding balance.

Offers of less than £10 per month

Time to Pay arrangements will not be set up for amounts of less than £10 per month, unless the arrangement will clear the total overpayment within three years. If the customer cannot afford to pay £10 per month HMRC will withhold recovery action for 12 months. If the customer can still not afford to pay this minimum amount, and there is little or no prospect for improvement, HMRC will consider remitting the overpayment.

Low affordability

In assessing a customer's ability to repay an overpayment, HMRC compare their actual expenditure with figures provided by research carried out by the Office for National Statistics. HMRC will ask customers for an explanation if they say they have to spend more.

HMRC understand that customers have less discretion or control over existing commitments and fixed costs as listed in the following chart, and HMRC will take these fully into account unless they appear excessive.

Rent	Pension payments
Mortgage	Life assurance
Secured loans	HP or conditional sale
Council Tax	TV licence
Court fines	Maintenance or child support

The Income and Expenditure form shows, in more detail, the information HMRC ask customers to provide if they want to spread their instalment payments over more than ten years. HMRC prefer to collect information on this form but it will accept others detailing what's coming in and what's being paid out. An example of the Income and Expenditure form can be found at Section 5.

Customer is unemployed and has no savings or assets

Where the customer advises they are unemployed, and have no savings or realisable assets, the case will be reviewed in 12 months and consideration given to remit the outstanding overpayment. After this period, the DTO will contact the customer to establish if their circumstances have improved. Where the circumstances have improved sufficiently HMRC will seek to negotiate a suitable Time to Pay arrangement. If circumstances have not improved the DTO will remit the overpayment and notify the customer in writing.

Customer is on Sickness/Incapacity benefits

Where a customer is in receipt of Sickness or Incapacity Benefit or Employment and Support Allowance, and has little prospect of ever gaining paid employment, HMRC will remit the outstanding overpayment

TC Extra-statutory Material

and write to the customer. If, however, there is some prospect of the customer re-gaining paid employment HMRC will withhold any recovery action for a suitable period of time and then review the customer's financial circumstances and their ability to pay. HMRC will inform its decision by asking appropriate questions.

Customer is unable to meet living expenses

As explained in the introduction, HMRC can recover overpayments from customers in two ways:

- recovery from an ongoing tax credits award
- direct recovery

Benefits and Credits manage the process for recovery from an ongoing award. The customer should call the Tax Credits Helpline (0345 300 3900) for any queries about recovery from an ongoing award.

DMB manage the direct recovery process including cases where a customer cannot afford to repay an overpayment.

If the DMTC establish that a customer cannot currently make an arrangement to repay an overpayment and meet their living expenses at the same time they will refer the case to the DTO.

The DTO will look at each case on its own merits and at the ability of the customer to make repayments. COP 26 underpins this activity.

The DTO may need to phone the customer to obtain documentary evidence of income and expenditure details. If the DTO cannot contact the customer by phone it will write and ask the customer to get in touch. The letter will have the phone number of the DTO. If the customer gets in touch, the DTO will discuss the current income and expenditure to establish whether anything has changed since initial contact with the customer.

In some cases the DTO will set a date for a further review, usually 12 months but shorter if appropriate, if the customer's circumstances are expected to change (for example by returning to employment or self-employment).

If the customer still does not have the means to clear the overpayment, and there is little prospect of the position changing then the DTO will consider remitting the overpayment. The customer will be informed, by letter, of the outcome.

Special circumstances

Mental health cases

HMRC will deal with mental health cases carefully and sympathetically to avoid distress to the customer. HMRC will need a letter from a health care professional or mental health social worker explaining the mental health problem to enable it to deal with these cases. The evidence should include the nature of the illness and as far as possible, whether the illness is likely to be long-term (for example, schizophrenia) or where the prospects for recovery are expected to be good.

If the information has not been provided HMRC will need to write to the claimant or third party asking for the documentary evidence.

If the mental health problems existed at the time the overpayment occurred then Benefits and Credits can consider whether exceptional circumstances are such that writing off the overpayment is appropriate. If the mental health problems exist at the time the overpayment is being recovered then DMB will review the circumstances. The DMB office to write to is DMB, Ryscar House, Faraday Way, Blackpool, FY2 OJJ.

- For sole debts HMRC will write to the third party and the customer to let them know that it will not continue with recovery of the overpayment.
- For joint debts HMRC will continue with recovery from the other partner in line with the section above.
- For Household Breakdown cases HMRC will write to the customer to advise them that it will not continue with recovery of their share of the debt. However, HMRC will pursue the ex-partner for their share of the debt (more information is available at section 3).

For more information on how HMRC deal with customers with mental health issues please go to **www.hmrc.gov.uk/manuals/dmbmanual/DMBM585185.htm**

Exceptional circumstances

In exceptional circumstances, for example if a customer or family member of the customer is seriously ill HMRC may be able to put direct recovery of an overpayment on hold until the customer is able to fully discuss their financial situation. DMB may write off the overpayment altogether. Customers/advisors should phone the Payment Helpline to explain the exceptional circumstances.

Section 5 – useful information

Useful Tax Credits Helpline numbers

Tax Credits Helpline				
name	**opening hours**	**contact number**		**description**
customer Helpline	8.00 am to 8.00 pm seven days a week	telephone	0345 300 3900	for information about tax credits, including Working Tax Credits and Child Tax Credits also for customers wishing to give information about possible tax credit fraud or abuse
		textphone	0345 300 3909	
		overseas	+44 28 9053 8192	for customers living abroad who are not able to contact HMRC using the 0845 number
intermediaries priority line	8.00 am to 8.00 pm seven days a week	telephone	0845 300 3946	for information about tax credits, including Working Tax Credits and Child Tax Credits
tax credit overpayment Helpline	8.00 am to 8.00 pm seven days a week	telephone	0845 302 1429	all customer enquiries regarding the recovery of an overpayment of tax credits

Business process flowchart

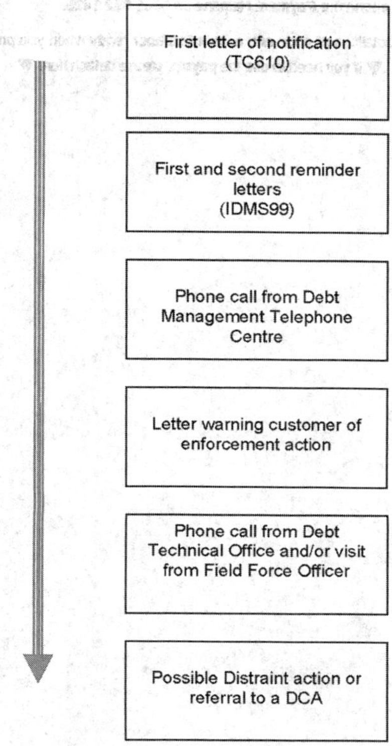

An example of the initial letter TC610 asking for repayment

HM Revenue & Customs

Helpline 08:00 to 20:00 0845 300 3900
Minicom/Textphone 0845 300 3909

Reprint ref 999999999

Date 99 X<---------- 9999

RECIPIENTNAMEto35CHARACTERS
RECIPIENTNAMEto35CHARACTERS
ADDRESS LINE 1 MAX 35 CHARACTERSXX
ADDRESS LINE 2 MAX 35 CHARACTERSXX
ADDRESS LINE 3 MAX 35 CHARACTERSXX
ADDRESS LINE 4 MAX 35 CHARACTERSXX
ADDRESS LINE 5 MAX 35 CHARACTERSXX
POSTCODE

HM Revenue & Customs
Accounts Office Cumbernauld
Glasgow
G67 1YZ

[As Appointee for:]
[Claimant 1 Name xxxxxxxxxxxx] National Insurance Number AANNNNNNA
[Claimant 2 Name xxxxxxxxxxxx] National Insurance Number AANNNNNNA

NOTICE TO PAY
Section 29 (3) of Tax Credits Act 2002

We have sent you a notice showing an overpayment of tax credits for the period ending[DD/MM/CCYY].

The total amount you have to pay back is shown below and is due by[DD/MM/CCYY].

The total amount of Working Tax Credit overpaid to you is	£[9999999.99]
The total amount of Child Tax Credit overpaid to you is	£[9999999.99]
The total amount of tax credits overpaid is	£[9999999.99]

[The total in Euros is €[9999999.99]
This conversion has been made under European Commission rules using a rate of @ x 0.000000 = £1]

Information on how to pay is shown on the back of this form.

You may spread your repayment over the next 12 months if you wish. To arrange this, or discuss other payment options please phone the Payment Helpline on 0845 302 1429.

Please have your bank details, sort code and account number ready when you phone us.

TC610 ▼ If you need to use the payslip, please detach here ▼ HMRC 09/08

Tax Credits

Time To Pay Negotiating Framework

For use in TTP requests for tax credits debts where the customer requires above a year and up to 10 years to repay the debt

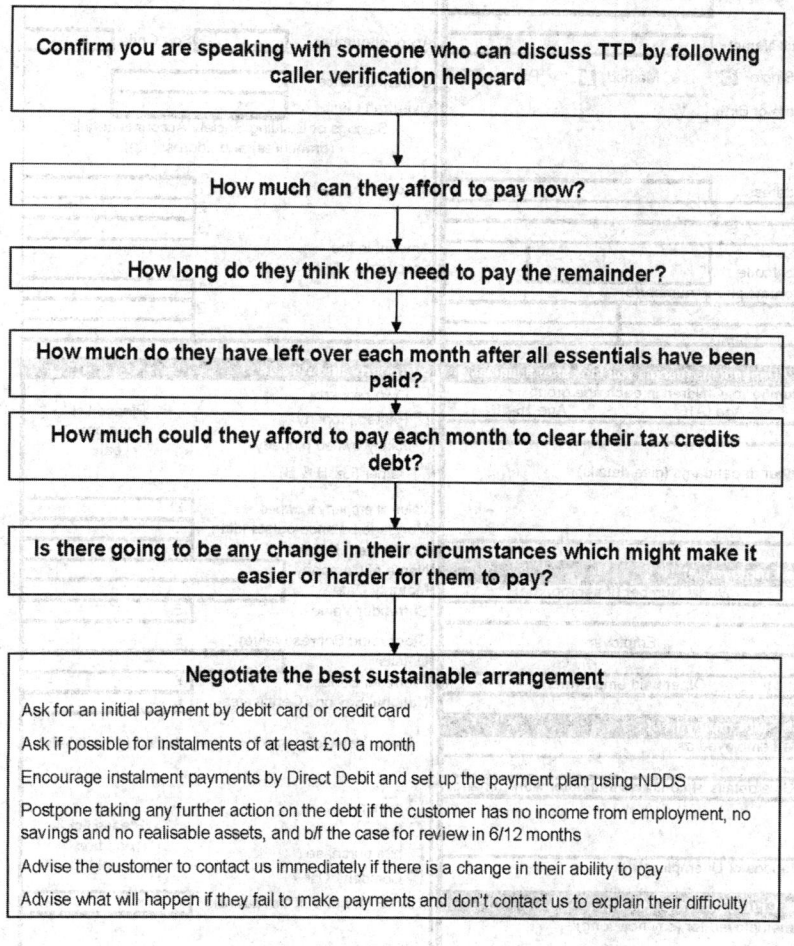

Confirm you are speaking with someone who can discuss TTP by following caller verification helpcard

↓

How much can they afford to pay now?

↓

How long do they think they need to pay the remainder?

↓

How much do they have left over each month after all essentials have been paid?

↓

How much could they afford to pay each month to clear their tax credits debt?

↓

Is there going to be any change in their circumstances which might make it easier or harder for them to pay?

↓

Negotiate the best sustainable arrangement

Ask for an initial payment by debit card or credit card

Ask if possible for instalments of at least £10 a month

Encourage instalment payments by Direct Debit and set up the payment plan using NDDS

Postpone taking any further action on the debt if the customer has no income from employment, no savings and no realisable assets, and b/f the case for review in 6/12 months

Advise the customer to contact us immediately if there is a change in their ability to pay

Advise what will happen if they fail to make payments and don't contact us to explain their difficulty

An example of the income and expenditure form used by HMRC

Reference: | Nino:

1 Personal Details

If Other Please state

Full Name:

Single ☐ Married ☐ Partner ☐

Date of Birth:

Address

Postcode

Contact phone number(s)

2 Dependants (people you look after financially)

Number of Children in each age group

Age 0-15 Age 16-18

Other dependants (give details)

3a Employment

Works Number (if appropriate)

Employer

Other paid employment

3b Self Employment

Self employed as:

Give details of contracts and other work in hand:

Periods of Unemployment

3c Current unemployment

Unemployed for (say how long):

Address of office where registered as unemployed

4 Bank and Savings account

Current account details

Account number Sort Code

Current balance

Overdraft Limit

Savings or Building Society Accounts details (branch(es) and address(es))

Account Number(s) 1 2 3

Amount in the accounts 1 2 3

5 Property and Assets

☐ Own property

☐ Rented property

☐ Jointly owned property

☐ Other (i.e. B & B)

Please tick one box only

Value of property if owned £ -

Mortgage balance outstanding £ -

Endowment Policies £ -

Name of Company

Maturity Date

Surrender Value £ -

Stocks and Shares (value) £ -

Details

Premium Bonds £ -

National Savings Certificates £ -

Motor Vehicle(s) make and registration (give details)

☐ owned

☐ lease

☐ hire purchase

☐ Company Car

Please tick one box only

If on HP give date of final payment

Any sums due for work done

6 Income (either per week (w), month (m) or year (y))

	amount	per
Net take home pay Including reg overtime, commission, bonuses etc)		
Self Employed Income/drawings		
Tax Credits		
Child benefit		
Income Support/Job Seekers Allowance		
Other social security benefits		
Spouse/ Partners/others contribution		
Pension income		
Other income		

Total Income weekly	£	-
Monthly	£	-
Yearly	£	-

7 Expenses (state whether per week, month or year)

Expenses. Do NOT include any payment made by other members of your household out of any income not included in Income section

	amount	per
Mortgage(s)/Rent		
Council Tax/Rates		
Utilities (water/electric/gas etc)		
HP payments		
Mail order payments		
Maintenance Payments		
Court Order payments		
Credit/store card minimum repayments		
Loan repayments payments		
Pension Contributions		
Media (internet/SKY/cable etc)		
Household expenses (food etc)		
Health (prescirptions etc)		
Child related costs (clothing/child care etc)		
Insurance payments (life/buildings/contents etc)		
Telephone (including mobile)		
(fuel/insurance/road tax etc)		
Other (including pets, repairs etc)		

Totals

Weekly	Monthly	Yearly
0.00	0.00	0.00

8 Liabilities (amount owed)

	Amounts owed	Last payment due
Loans		
Repayments of Social fund payment		
HP		
Court Orders		
Credit/store Cards		
Mortgage/rent arrears		
Council Tax arrears		
Utilities arrears		
Maintenance arrears		
Mail Orders		
Other Debts		

9

	Weekly	Monthly	Yearly
Total Income	0.00	0.00	0.00
Less			
Total Expenses	0.00	0.00	0.00
Disposable	0.00	0.00	0.00

INDEX TO TAX CREDITS

For a list of abbreviations used in this Index see p. xi.

For a list of abbreviations used in this Index see p. xi.

For a list of abbreviations used in this Index see p. xi.

TC Indexes

For a list of abbreviations used in this Index see p. xi.

For a list of abbreviations used in this Index see p. xi.

For a list of abbreviations used in this Index see p. xi.

TC Indexes

For a list of abbreviations used in this Index see p. xi.

TAX CREDITS LIST OF DEFINITIONS AND MEANINGS

For a list of abbreviations used in this Index see p. xi.

	Provision
Determination of the maximum rate	SI 2002/2005 reg. 2(1)
Diagnosed person	SI 2002/2006 reg. 10(4)
Direct service provider	SI 2002/3214 reg. 2(1)
Disability element	SI 2002/2014 reg. 2; SI 2003/731 reg. 2
Disability living allowance	SI 2002/2007 reg. 2(1)
Disabled	SI 1999/3110 reg. 2(1); SI 2002/1417 reg. 2
Domiciliary care worker	SI 2002/3214 reg. 2(1)
E	
Earnings	SI 2002/2006 reg. 2(2)
Eileen Trust	SI 2002/2006 reg. 2(2)
Electronic communication	SI 2002/1417 reg. 2
Electronic communications	SI 2002/2014 reg. 3(4)
Emolument	SI 2002/2172 reg. 2(1)
Emoluments	SI 2002/2006 reg. 2(2)
Employed	SI 2002/2005 reg. 2(1)
Employee	TCA2002 s. 25(6), 48; SI 2002/2172 reg. 2(1); SI 2002/2173 reg. 2
Employer	TCA2002 s. 25(6), 48; SI 2002/2172 reg. 2(1); SI 2002/2014 reg. 30(3); SI 2002/2173 reg. 2
Employer information penalty	TCA2002 s. 63(10)
Employer penalty	TCA2002 s. 63(11); SI 2003/1382 reg. 2
Employer's place of business	SI 2002/2172 reg. 2(1)
Employment Act	SI 2002/2006 reg. 2(1); SI 2002/2007 reg. 2(1)
Employment income	SI 2002/2006 reg. 4(1)
Employment-related benefit	SI 2002/2006 reg. 2(2)
Employments Regulations	SI 2002/2172 reg. 2(1)
Employment zone	SI 2002/2005 reg. 2(1); SI 2002/2006 reg. 2(2)
Employment zone programme	SI 2002/2005 reg. 2(1); SI 2002/2006 reg. 2(2)
Established rate	SI 2003/123 reg. 2(1)
Exempt accommodation	SI 2014/1230 reg. 2(1)
Existing benefit	SI 2014/1230 reg. 2(1)
Expert	SSA98 s. 16(6)
F	
Family	SI 2002/2006 reg. 2(2); SI 2003/731 reg. 2
Family element of child tax credit	SI 2002/2007 reg. 2(1)
Financially qualified panel member	SI 2002/3196 reg. 1(3)
First-tier Tribunal	SI 2014/1230 reg. 2(1)
Foreign income	SI 2002/2006 reg. 12(1)
Fosters a child privately	SI 2003/463 reg. 2

	Provision
G	
General Commissioners	TCA2002 s. 48
H	
Housing benefit	SI 2014/1230 reg. 2(1)
I	
Immigration rules	SI 2003/653 reg. 2
Income-based jobseeker's allowance	SI 2014/1230 reg. 2(1)
Income-related employment and support allowance	SI 2014/1230 reg. 2(1)
Income support	SI 2014/1230 reg. 2(1)
Income tax month	SI 2002/2172 reg. 2(1)
Income tax quarter	SI 2002/2172 reg. 2(1)
Income tax year	SI 2002/2172 reg. 2(1)
Income threshold	TCA2002 s. 48; SI 2002/2008 reg. 2
Independent Living (Extension) Fund	SI 2002/2006 reg. 2(2)
Independent Living Fund	SI 2002/2006 reg. 2(2)
Independent Living Funds	SI 2002/2006 reg. 2(2)
Independent Living (1993) Fund	SI 2002/2006 reg. 2(2)
Individual element of child tax credit	SI 2002/2007 reg. 2(1)
Initial claim	SI 2002/2005 reg. 2(1), 9A(1)
ITEPA	SI 2002/2006 reg. 2(2)
ITTOIA	SI 2002/2006 reg. 2(2)
J	
Joint claim	TCA2002 s. 48, 3(8); SI 2002/2005 reg. 2(1); SI 2002/2007 reg. 2(1); SI 2002/2014 reg. 2; SI 2002/3196 reg. 1(3); SI 2003/653 reg. 2
Joint claimant	SI 2002/3237 reg. 2
Joint-claim jobseeker's allowance	SI 2014/1230 reg. 2(1)
JSA Regulations	SI 2002/2006 reg. 19(2)
JSA (NI) Regulations	SI 2002/2006 reg. 19(2)
L	
Legally qualified	SI 2002/3237 reg. 2
Legally qualified panel member	SI 2002/3196 reg. 1(3)
Limited leave	SI 2003/653 reg. 2
Live television link	SI 2002/3196 reg. 18(14)
Local authority	SI 2002/2005 reg. 2(1)
Looked after by a local authority	SI 2002/2007 reg. 2(1)
M	
Macfarlane (Special Payments) Trust	SI 2002/2006 reg. 2(2)

	Provision
Relevant tax year	SI 2002/2173 reg. 2
Relevant training programme	SI 2002/2007 reg. 2(1)
Relevant trust	SI 2002/2006 reg. 10(5)
Remunerative work	SI 2002/2007 reg. 2(1)
Residential accommodation	SI 2002/2006 reg. 10(5)
Residential care home	SI 2002/2006 reg. 10(5)
Respondent	SI 2002/3237 reg. 2
Responsible	TCA2002 s. 48
Responsible individual	SI 2002/3214 reg. 2(1)
Retirement annuity contract	SI 2002/2006 reg. 2(2)
Retirement benefits scheme	SI 2002/2006 reg. 2(2)
S	
Schedule D	SI 2002/2006 reg. 2(2)
Self-employed	SI 2002/2005 reg. 2(1)
Severe disability element	SI 2002/2014 reg. 2
Service Pensions Order	SI 2002/2006 reg. 2(2)
Service user	SI 2002/3214 reg. 2(1)
Service user's guide	SI 2002/3214 reg. 2(1)
Single claim	TCA2002 s. 3(8); SI 2002/2005 reg. 2(1); SI 2002/2007 reg. 2(1); SI 2002/2014 reg. 2; SI 2002/3196 reg. 1(3)
Social Security Commissioner	TCA2002 s. 63(13); SI 2002/2173 reg. 11(6); SI 2002/2926 reg. 2; SI 2003/692 reg. 2(1)
Social security functions	FA89 s. 182(2A)
Special Commissioners	TCA2002 s. 48
Sports award	SI 2002/2005 reg. 2(1)
Start notice	SI 2002/2172 reg. 2(1)
Statement of purpose	SI 2002/3214 reg. 2(1)
Stop notice	SI 2002/2172 reg. 2(1)
Student loan deductions	TCA2002 s. 25(7)
Summons	SI 2002/3237 reg. 2
Surrogate child	SI 2002/2005 reg. 2(1)
Suspension Regulations	SI 2003/463 reg. 2
System	SI 1999/3110 reg. 2(1); SI 2002/1417 reg. 2
T	
Tax credit	TCA2002 s. 67; SI 2002/3196 reg. 1(3); SI 2002/3237 reg. 2; SI 2003/123 reg. 2(1); SI 2003/653 reg. 2; SI 2014/1230 reg. 2(1)
Tax credit appeal	SSA98 s. 12(1); SI 2002/2926 reg. 2
Tax credit functions	FA89 s. 182(2AA)
Tax credits	SI 2014/1230 reg. 2(1)
Taxes Act	SI 2002/2006 reg. 2(2); SI 2002/2172 reg. 2(1)
Tax or duty	FA89 s. 182(10)
Tax year	TCA2002 s. 48; SI 2002/2006 reg. 2(2); SI 2002/2008 reg. 2; SI 2002/2014 reg. 2; SI 2002/2173 reg. 2; SI 2003/692 reg. 2(1); SI 2014/1230 reg. 2(1)
10 year general qualification	SSA98 Sch. 4, para. 1(3)
The 1989 Act	SI 2003/463 reg. 2
The 1998 Act	SI 2002/2926 reg. 2; SI 2002/3237 reg. 2
The 1998 Order	SI 2002/2926 reg. 2
The 1992 Fund	SI 2002/2006 reg. 2(2)
The 2002 Act	SI 2002/3196 reg. 1(3); SI 2002/3237 reg. 2; SI 2014/1230 reg. 2(1)
The 2007 Act	SI 2014/1230 reg. 2(1)
Training allowance	SI 2002/2005 reg. 2(1)
Training for work	SI 2002/2005 reg. 2(1), 9B(1)
Tribunal	SI 2003/463 reg. 2
Tribunal Regulations	SI 2003/463 reg. 2
Trust payment	SI 2002/2006 reg. 10(5)
U	
Universal Credit Regulations	SI 2014/1230 reg. 2(1)
Unmarried couple	SI 2002/2014 reg. 2; SI 2003/653 reg. 2
Upper Tribunal	SI 2014/1230 reg. 2(1)
V	
Voluntary organisation	SI 2002/2006 reg. 2(2)
W	
War pension	TCA2002 Sch. 5, para. 4(5), 6(4); SI 2002/2006 reg. 2(2)
Week	SI 2002/2005 reg. 2(1)
Working day	SI 2003/123 reg. 2(1)
Working tax credit	SI 2002/3196 reg. 1(3); SI 2003/731 reg. 2
Working Tax Credit Regulations	SI 2002/2014 reg. 2; SI 2003/653 reg. 2
Writing	SI 2002/2172 reg. 8(2); SI 2002/2173 reg. 14(5)

INHERITANCE TAX
CAPITAL TRANSFER TAX

Table of Contents

INHERITANCE TAX STATUTES

Table of Contents

continued over

PROBATE AND LEGACY DUTIES ACT 1808

(48 Geo. 3, Chapter 149)

[*2nd July 1808*]

42 Confirmations of testaments not to be granted for effects not included in such inventory. Executors not to recover effects unless so included

42(1) Subject to subsection (2) below, it shall not be lawful for any commissary court in Scotland, to grant confirmation of any testament, testamentary or dative, or eik thereto, of or for any estate or effects whatever, of any person dying after the tenth day of October one thousand eight hundred and eight, unless the same shall be mentioned and included in some such inventory, exhibited and recorded as aforesaid nor unless that inventory shows by means of such receipt or certification as may be prescribed by the Commissioners of Inland Revenue either that the capital transfer tax payable on the delivery of the inventory has been paid or that no capital transfer tax is so payable; and it shall not be competent to any executor or executors, or other person or persons, to recover any debt or other effects, in Scotland, of or belonging to any person dying after the said tenth day of October, unless the same shall have been previously included in some such inventory, exhibited and recorded as aforesaid; except the same respectively were vested in the deceased as a trustee for any other person or persons, and not beneficially; but these provisions are not, in other respects, to prejudice the law of Scotland, regarding total or partial confirmations, or the rules of succession there established.

Provided that arrangements may be made between the Court of Session and the said Commissioners providing for the purposes of this section in such cases as may be specified that the said inventory shall be effective without such receipt or certification as aforesaid, or that some other document may be substituted for the inventory.

42(2) In a case to which regulations under section 256(1)(aa) of the Inheritance Tax Act 1984 (c. 51) apply (excepted estates), it shall not be lawful to grant confirmation such as is mentioned in subsection (1) above except on the production of information or documents in accordance with those regulations.

History – The whole of former s. 42 became s. 42(1) by FA 2004, s. 294(2)(a), with effect from 1 November 2004 (SI 2004/2571).
In s. 42(1), the words "Subject to subsection (2) below," at the beginning substituted for the word "And" by FA 2004, s. 294(2)(b), with effect from 1 November 2004 (SI 2004/2571).
S. 42(2) inserted by FA 2004, s. 294(2)(c), with effect from 1 November 2004 (SI 2004/2571).
The words "nor unless … is so payable" and the proviso were added by FA 1975, s. 19(2) and Sch. 4, para. 38(2), (4).

Notes – FA 1986, s. 100(1)(b): any reference to capital transfer tax (except where it relates to a liability to tax arising before 25 July 1986) has effect as a reference to inheritance tax.

ADMINISTRATION OF ESTATES ACT 1925

(15 & 16 Geo. 5, Chapter 23) [*9th April 1925*]

PART IV – DISTRIBUTION OF RESIDUARY ESTATE

46 Succession to real and personal estate on intestacy

46(1) The residuary estate of an intestate shall be distributed in the manner or be held on the trusts mentioned in this section, namely–

(i) If the intestate leaves a spouse or civil partner, then in accordance with the following table:

TABLE

(1) If the intestate leaves no issue:	the residuary estate shall be held in trust for the surviving spouse or civil partner absolutely.
(2) If the intestate leaves issue:	(A) the surviving spouse or civil partner shall take the personal chattels absolutely; (B) the residuary estate of the intestate (other than the personal chattels) shall stand charged with the payment of a fixed net sum, free of death duties and costs, to the surviving spouse or civil partner, together with simple interest on it from the date of the death at the rate provided for by subsection (1A) until paid or appropriated; and (C) subject to providing for the sum and interest referred to in paragraph (B), the residuary estate (other than the personal chattels) shall be held– (a) as to one half, in trust for the surviving spouse or civil partner absolutely, and (b) as to the other half, on the statutory trusts for the issue of the intestate.

The fixed net sums referred to in paragraphs (2) and (3) of this Table shall be of the amounts provided by or under section 1 of the Family Provision Act 1966.

(ii) If the intestate leaves issue but no spouse or civil partner, the residuary estate of the intestate shall be held on the statutory trusts for the issue of the intestate;

(iii) If the intestate leaves no spouse or civil partner and no issue but both parents, then the residuary estate of the intestate shall be held in trust for the father and mother in equal shares absolutely;

(iv) If the intestate leaves no spouse or civil partner and no issue but one parent, then the residuary estate of the intestate shall be held in trust for the surviving father or mother absolutely;

(v) If the intestate leaves no spouse or civil partner and no issue and no parent, then the residuary estate of the intestate shall be held in trust for the following persons living at the death of the intestate, and in the following order and manner, namely–

First, on the statutory trusts for the brothers and sisters of the whole blood of the intestate; but if no person takes an absolutely vested interest under such trusts, then

Secondly, on the statutory trusts for the brothers and sisters of the half blood of the intestate; but if no person takes an absolutely vested interest under such trusts; then

Thirdly, for the grandparents of the intestate and, if more than one survive the intestate, in equal shares; but if there is no member of this class; then

Fourthly, on the statutory trusts for the uncles and aunts of the intestate (being brothers or sisters of the whole blood of a parent of the intestate); but if no person takes an absolutely vested interest under such trusts; then

Fifthly, on the statutory trusts for the uncles and aunts of the intestate (being brothers or sisters of the half blood of a parent of the intestate);

(vi) In default of any person taking an absolute interest under the foregoing provisions, the residuary estate of the intestate shall belong to the Crown or to the Duchy of Lancaster or to the Duke of

Cornwall for the time being, as the case may be, as bona vacantia, and in lieu of any right to escheat.

The Crown or the said Duchy or the said Duke may (without prejudice to the powers reserved by section nine of the Civil List Act, 1910, or any other powers), out of the whole or any part of the property devolving on them respectively, provide, in accordance with the existing practice, for dependants, whether kindred or not, of the intestate, and other persons for whom the intestate might reasonably have been expected to make provision.

46(1A) The interest rate referred to in paragraph (B) of case (2) of the Table in subsection (1)(i) is the Bank of England rate that had effect at the end of the day on which the intestate died.

46(2) A spouse or civil partner shall for all purposes of distribution or division under the foregoing provisions of this section be treated as two persons.

46(2A) Where the intestate's spouse or civil partner survived the intestate but died before the end of the period of 28 days beginning with the day on which the intestate died, this section shall have effect as respects the intestate as if the spouse or civil partner had not survived the intestate.

46(3) [Omitted by IHTPA 2014, s. 11 and Sch. 4, para. 1(2).]

46(4) The interest payable on the fixed net sum payable to a surviving spouse or civil partner shall be primarily payable out of income.

46(5) In subsection (1A) **"Bank of England rate"** means–

(a) the rate announced by the Monetary Policy Committee of the Bank of England as the official bank rate, or

(b) where an order under section 19 of the Bank of England Act 1998 (reserve powers) is in force, any equivalent rate determined by the Treasury under that section.

46(6) The Lord Chancellor may by order made by statutory instrument amend the definition of **"Bank of England rate"** in subsection (5) (but this subsection does not affect the generality of subsection (7)(b)).

46(7) The Lord Chancellor may by order made by statutory instrument–

(a) amend subsection (1A) so as to substitute a different interest rate (however specified or identified) for the interest rate for the time being provided for by that subsection;

(b) make any amendments of, or repeals in, this section that may be consequential on or incidental to any amendment made by virtue of paragraph (a).

46(8) A statutory instrument containing an order under subsection (6) is subject to annulment pursuant to a resolution of either House of Parliament.

46(9) A statutory instrument containing an order under subsection (7) may not be made unless a draft of the instrument has been laid before and approved by a resolution of each House of Parliament.

History – In s. 46 words "spouse or civil partner" substituted for words "husband or wife" in each place by Civil Partnership Act 2004, Sch. 4, para. 7, with effect from 5 December 2005 (by virtue of SI 2005/3175).

In s. 46(1)(i), the Table substituted by IHTPA 2014, s. 1(2), with effect in relation to deaths occurring after 1 October 2014 (IHTPA 2014, s. 12(4) and SI 2014/2039, art. 2). Former Table read as follows:

TABLE

If the intestate–	
(1) leaves– (a) no issue, and (b) no parent, or brother or sister of the whole blood, or issue of a brother or sister of the whole blood.	the residiary estate shall be held in trust for the surviving spouse or civil partner absolutely.
(2) leaves issue (whether or not persons mentioned in sub-paragraph (b) above also survive)	the surviving spouse or civil partner shall take the personal chattels absolutely and, in addition, the residuary estate of the intestate (other than the personal chattels) shall stand charged with the payment of a fixed net sum, free of death duties and costs, to the surviving spouse or civil partner with interest thereon from the date of the death at such rate as the Lord Chancellor may specify by order until paid or appropriated, and, subject to providing for that sum and the interest thereon, the residuary estate (other than the personal chattels) shall be held– (a) as to one half upon trust for the surviving spouse or civil partner during his or her life, and, subject to such life interest, on the statutory trusts for the issue of the intestate, and (b) as to the other half, on the statutory trusts for the issue of the intestate.

(3) leaves one or more of the following, that is to say, a parent, a brother or sister of the whole blood, or issue of a brother or sister of the whole blood, but leaves no issue

the surviving spouse or civil partner shall take the personal chattels absolutely and, in addition, the residuary estate of the intestate (other than the personal chattels) shall stand charged with the payment of a fixed net sum, free of death duties and costs, to the surviving spouse or civil partner with interest thereon from the date of the death at the rate of four pounds per cent per annum until paid or appropriated, and, subject to providing for that sum and the interest thereon, the residuary estate (other than the personal chattels) shall be held–

(a) as to one half in trust for the surviving spouse or civil partner absolutely, and

(b) as to the other half–
(i) where the intestate leaves one parent or both parents (whether or not brothers or sisters of the intestate or their issue also survive) in trust for the parent absolutely or, as the case may be, for the two parents in equal shares absolutely,
(ii) where the intestate leaves no parent, on the statutory trusts for the brothers and sisters of the whole blood of the intestate.

S. 46(1)(i)) substituted by the Intestates' Estates Act 1952, s. 1.
In para. 2 of the Table the words "at such rate … specify by order" substituted by the Administration of Justice Act 1977, s. 28(1).
In para. 2 and 3 of the Table, the words "fixed net sum" were substituted by the Family Provision Act 1966, s. 1(2)(a), as were the words from "The fixed net sums" to the end of s. 46(1)(i).
In s. 46(1)(iii) and (iv), the words "no husband or wife and" were inserted by, and the words "subject to the interests of a surviving husband or wife" were repealed by, the Intestates' Estates Act 1952, s. 1(3)(a).
In s. 46(1)(v), the words "husband or wife and no issue and no" were substituted for the words "issue or" by the Intestates' Estates Act 1952, s. 1(3)(b)(i).
In s. 46(1)(v), the words "subject to the interests of a surviving husband or wife", and the words "but if no person takes an absolutely vested interest under such trusts; then Sixthly for the surviving husband or wife of the intestate absolutely" (which occurred at the end of s. 46(1)(v)) were repealed by the Intestates' Estates Act 1952, s. 1(3)(b)(ii).
S. 46(1A) substituted by IHTPA 2014, s. 1(3), with effect in relation to deaths occurring after 1 October 2014 (IHTPA 2014, s. 12(4) and SI 2014/2039, art. 2). Former s. 46(1A) read as follows:
"**46(1A)** The power to make orders under subsection (1) above shall be exercisable by statutory instrument subject to annulment in pursuance of a resolution of either House of Parliament; and any such order may be varied or revoked by a subsequent order made under the power.".
Former s. 46(1A) was inserted by the Administration of Justice Act 1977, s. 28(1), and has effect in relation to deaths occurring both before 1953 and after 1952.
S. 46(2A) was inserted by the Law Reform (Succession) Act 1995, s. 1(1), (3) with effect from 8 November 1995.
S. 46(3) omitted by IHTPA 2014, s. 11 and Sch. 4, para. 1(2), with effect in relation to deaths occurring after 1 October 2014 (IHTPA 2014, s. 12(4) and SI 2014/2039). Former s. 46(3) read as follows:
"**46(3)** Where the intestate and the intestate's spouse or civil partner have died in circumstances rendering it uncertain which of them survived the other and the intestate's spouse or civil partner is by virtue of section one hundred and eighty-four of the Law of Property Act, 1925, deemed to have survived the intestate, this section shall, nevertheless, have effect as respects the intestate as if the spouse or civil partner had not survived the intestate.".
S. 46(3), (4) were inserted by the Intestates' Estates Act 1952, s. 1(4), and in s. 46(4) the words "fixed net sum" were substituted by the Family Provision Act 1966, s. 1(2)(b).
S. 46(5)–(9) inserted by IHTPA 2014, s. 1(4), with effect in relation to deaths occurring after 1 October 2014 (IHTPA 2014, s. 12(4) and SI 2014/2039).

Cross references – SI 1993/2906: the fixed net sums referred to in para. 2 and 3 of the Table were fixed, respectively, at £125,000 and £200,000, in the case of persons dying on or after 1 December 1993. The previous figures were, respectively, £75,000 and £125,000, and these applied in the case of persons dying between 1 June 1987 and 30 November 1993.
SI 2009/135: the fixed net sums referred to in para. 2 and 3 of the Table are fixed, respectively, at £250,000 and £450,000 in the case of persons dying on or after 1 February 2009.

46A Disclaimer or forfeiture on intestacy

46A(1) This section applies where a person–

(a) is entitled in accordance with section 46 to an interest in the residuary estate of an intestate but disclaims it, or

(b) would have been so entitled had the person not been precluded by the forfeiture rule from acquiring it.

46A(2) The person is to be treated for the purposes of this Part as having died immediately before the intestate.

46A(3) But in a case within subsection (1)(b), subsection (2) does not affect the power conferred by section 2 of the Forfeiture Act 1982 (power of court to modify the forfeiture rule).

46A(4) In this section **"forfeiture rule"** has the same meaning as in the Forfeiture Act 1982.

History – S. 46A inserted by Estates of Deceased Persons (Forfeiture Rule and Law of Succession) Act 2011, s. 1(2), with effect from 1 February 2012 (SI 2011/2913, art. 2).

47 Statutory trusts in favour of issue and other classes of relatives of intestate

47(1) Where under this Part of this Act the residuary estate of an intestate, or any part thereof, is directed to be held on the statutory trusts for the issue of the intestate, the same shall be held upon the following trusts, namely:–

(i) in trust, in equal shares if more than one, for all or any the children or child of the intestate, living at the death of the intestate, who attain the age of eighteen years or marry under that age or form a civil partnership under that age, and for all or any of the issue living at the death of the intestate who attain the age of eighteen years or marry, or form a civil partnership, under that age of any child of the intestate who predeceases the intestate, such issue to take through all degrees, according to their stocks, in equal shares if more than one, the share which their parent would have taken if living at the death of the intestate, and so that (subject to section 46A) no issue shall take whose parent is living at the death of the intestate and so capable of taking;

(ii) The statutory power of advancement, and the statutory provisions which relate to maintenance and accumulation of surplus income, shall apply, but when an infant marries, or forms a civil partnership, such infant shall be entitled to give valid receipts for the income of the infant's share or interest;

(iii) [repealed by Law Reform (Succession) Act 1995, s. 1(2)(a) and Schedule;]

(iv) The personal representatives may permit any infant contingently interested to have the use and enjoyment of any personal chattels in such manner and subject to such conditions (if any) as the personal representatives may consider reasonable, and without being liable to account for any consequential loss.

47(2) If the trusts in favour of the issue of the intestate fail by reason of no child or other issue attaining an absolutely vested interest–

(a) the residuary estate of the intestate and the income thereof and all statutory accumulations, if any, of the income thereof, or so much thereof as may not have been paid or applied under any power affecting the same, shall go, devolve and be held under the provisions of this Part of this Act as if the intestate has died without leaving issue living at the death of the intestate;

(b) references in this Part of this Act to the intestate ***"leaving no issue"*** shall be construed as "leaving no issue who attain an absolutely vested interest";

(c) references in this Part of this Act to the intestate **"leaving issue"** or **"leaving a child or other issue"** shall be construed as "leaving issue who attain an absolutely vested interest".

47(3) Where under this Part of this Act the residuary estate of an intestate or any part thereof is directed to be held on the statutory trusts for any class of relatives of the intestate, other than issue of the intestate, the same shall be held on trusts corresponding to the statutory trusts for the issue of the intestate (other than the provision for bringing any money or property into account) as if such trusts (other than as aforesaid) were repeated with the substitution of references to the members of member of that class for references to the children or child of the intestate.

47(4) References in paragraph (i) of subsection (1) of the last foregoing section to the intestate leaving, or not leaving, a member of the class consisting of brothers or sisters of the whole blood of the intestate and issue of brothers or sisters of the whole blood of the intestate shall be construed as references to the intestate leaving, or not leaving, a member of that class who attains an absolutely vested interest.

47(4A) Subsections (2) and (4) are subject to section 46A.

47(4B) Subsections (4C) and (4D) apply if a beneficiary under the statutory trusts–

(a) fails to attain an absolutely vested interest because the beneficiary dies without having reached 18 and without having married or formed a civil partnership, and

(b) dies leaving issue.

47(4C) The beneficiary is to be treated for the purposes of this Part as having died immediately before the intestate.

47(4D) The residuary estate (together with the income from it and any statutory accumulations of income from it) or so much of it as has not been paid or applied under a power affecting it is to devolve accordingly.

47(5) [Repealed by Family Provision Act 1966, s. 9 and Sch. 2.]

History – In s. 47(1)(i), the words "(subject to section 46A)" inserted by Estates of Deceased Persons (Forfeiture Rule and Law of Succession) Act 2011, s. 1(3), with effect from 1 February 2012 (SI 2011/2913, art. 2).

In s. 47(1)(i), the words "or form a civil partnership under that age" substituted for the words "or marry under that age" and the words ", or form a civil partnership," substituted for the words "or marry" by Civil Partnership Act 2004, s. 71 and Sch. 4, para. 8, with effect from 5 December 2005 (SI 2005/3175, art. 2).

In s. 47(1)(i), the words "eighteen years" substituted for the words "twenty-one years" by Family Law Reform Act 1969, s. 3(2), with effect from 1 January 1970 (SI 1969/1140, art. 2).

In s. 47(1)(ii), the words ", or forms a civil partnership," inserted by Civil Partnership Act 2004, s. 71 and Sch. 4, para. 8, with effect from 5 December 2005 (SI 2005/3175, art. 2).

S. 47(1)(iii) repealed by Law Reform (Succession) Act 1995, s. 1(2)(a) and Schedule, with effect as respects an intestate dying on or after 1 January 1996.

S. 47(4) inserted by Intestates' Estates Act 1952, s. 1(3)(c), with effect from 1 January 1953.

S. 47(4A) inserted by Estates of Deceased Persons (Forfeiture Rule and Law of Succession) Act 2011, s. 1(3), with effect from 1 February 2012 (SI 2011/2913, art. 2).

S. 47(4B), (4C) and (4D) inserted by Estates of Deceased Persons (Forfeiture Rule and Law of Succession) Act 2011, s. 3, with effect from 1 February 2012 (SI 2011/2913, art. 2).

S. 47(5) repealed by Family Provision Act 1966, s. 9 and Sch. 2, with effect from 1 January 1967 (SI 1966/1453, art. 1).

47A Right of surviving spouse to have own life interest redeemed

47A [Omitted by IHTPA 2014, s. 11 and Sch. 4, para. 1(3).]

History – S. 47A omitted by IHTPA 2014, s. 11 and Sch. 4, para. 1(3), with effect in relation to deaths occurring after 1 October 2014 (IHTPA 2014, s. 12(4) and SI 2014/2039, art. 2). Former s. 47A read as follows:

"47A Right of surviving spouse to have own life interest redeemed

47A(1) Where a surviving spouse or civil partner is entitled to a life interest in part of the residuary estate, and so elects, the personal representative shall purchase or redeem the life interest by paying the capital value thereof to the tenant for life, or the persons deriving title under the tenant for life, and the costs of the transaction: and thereupon the residuary estate of the intestate may be dealt with and distributed free from the life interest.

47A(2) [Repealed by Administration of Justice Act 1977, s. 28 and Sch. 5, Pt. VI.]

47A(3) An election under this section shall only be exercisable if at the time of the election the whole of the said part of the residuary estate consists of property in possession, but, for the purposes of this section, a life interest in property partly in possession and partly not in possession may be treated as consisting of two separate life interests in those respective parts of the property.

47A(3A) The capital value shall be reckoned in such manner as the Lord Chancellor may by order direct, and an order under this subsection may include transitional provisions.

47A(3B) The power to make orders under subsection (3A) above shall be exercisable by statutory instrument subject to annulment in pursuance of a resolution of either House of Parliament; and any such order may be varied or revoked by a subsequent order made under the power.

47A(4) [Repealed by Administration of Justice Act 1977, s. 28 and Sch. 5, Pt. VI.]

47A(5) An election under this section shall be exercisable only within the period of twelve months from the date on which representation with respect to the estate of the intestate is first taken out.

Provided that if the surviving spouse or civil partner satisfies the court that the limitation to the said period of twelve months will operate unfairly–

(a) in consequence of the representation first taken out being probate of a will subsequently revoked on the ground that the will was invalid or,

(b) in consequence of a question whether a person had an interest in the estate, or as to the nature of an interest in the estate, not having been determined at the time when representation was first taken out, or

(c) in consequence of some other circumstances affecting the administration or distribution of the estate,

the court may extend the said period.

47A(6) An election under this section shall be exercisable, except where the tenant for life is the sole personal representative, by notifying the personal representative (or, where there are two or more personal representatives of whom one is the tenant for life all of them except the tenant for life) in writing; and a notification in writing under this subsection shall not be revocable except with the consent of the personal representative.

47A(7) Where the tenant for life is the sole personal representative an election under this section shall not be effective unless written notice thereof is given to the Senior Registrar of the Family Division of the High Court within the period within which it must be made; and provision may be made by probate rules for keeping a record of such notices and making that record available to the public. In this subsection the expression **"probate rules"** means rules of court made under section 127 of the Supreme Court Act 1981.

47A(8) An election under this section by a tenant for life who is an infant shall be as valid and binding as it would be if the tenant for life were of age; but the personal representative shall, instead of paying the capital value of the life interest to the tenant for life, deal with it in the same manner as with any other part of the residuary estate to which the tenant for life is absolutely entitled.

47A(9) In considering for the purposes of the foregoing provisions of this section the question when representation was first taken out, a grant limited to settled land or to trust property shall be left out of account and a grant limited to real estate or to personal estate shall be left out of account unless a grant limited to the remainder of the estate has previously been made or is made at the same time.".

In former s. 47A(1), the words "spouse or civil partner" substituted for the words "husband or wife" by Civil Partnership Act 2004, s. 71 and Sch. 4, para. 9, with effect from 5 December 2005 (SI 2005/3175, art. 5(1)).

Former s. 47A(2) repealed by Administration of Justice Act 1977, s. 28(2) and Sch. 5, Pt. VI, with effect from 15 September 1977 (SI 1977/1490, art. 2).

Former s. 47A(3A) and (3B) inserted by Administration of Justice Act 1977, s. 28(3), with effect from 15 September 1977 (SI 1977/1490, art. 2).

Former s. 47A(4) repealed by Administration of Justice Act 1977, s. 28(2) and Sch. 5, Pt. VI, with effect from 15 September 1977 (SI 1977/1490, art. 2).

In former s. 47(5), the words "spouse or civil partner" substituted for the words "husband or wife" by Civil Partnership Act 2004, s. 71 and Sch. 4, para. 9, with effect from 5 December 2005 (SI 2005/3175, art. 5(1)).

In former s. 47A(7), the words "Senior Registrar" substituted for the words "principal registrar" by Supreme Court Act 1981, s. 152(1) and Sch. 5, with effect from 28 July 1981.

In former s. 47A(7), the words "of court made under section 127 of the Supreme Court Act 1981" substituted for the words "made under section one hundred of the Supreme Court of Judicature (Consolidation) Act, 1925" by Supreme Court Act 1981, s. 152(1) and Sch. 5, with effect from 28 July 1981.

In former s. 47A(7), the words "principal registrar of the Family Division of the High Court" substituted for the words "principal probate registrar" by Administration of Justice Act 1970, s. 1 and Sch. 2, para. 4, with effect from 1 October 1971.

Former s. 47A inserted by Intestates' Estates Act 1952, s. 2(b), with effect from 1 January 1953.

FINANCE (NO. 2) ACT 1931

(21 & 22 Geo. 5, Chapter 49)

[*5th October 1931*]

22 Provisions in cases where Treasury has power to borrow money

22(1) Any securities issued by the Treasury under any Act may be issued with the condition that–

(a) so long as the securities are in the beneficial ownership of persons who are not resident in the United Kingdom, the interest thereon shall be exempt from income tax; and

(b) so long as the securities are in the beneficial ownership of persons who are neither domiciled nor resident in the United Kingdom, neither the capital thereof nor the interest thereon shall be liable to any taxation present or future.

History – In s. 22(1)(a) and (b), the word "ordinarily" omitted by FA 2013, s. 219 and Sch. 46, para. 114(1), with effect from 17 July 2013 (Royal Assent) (subject to the provisions of para. 114(2)–(6)).

Cross references – IHTA 1984, s. 6(2): securities which are excluded property.
FA 1940, s. 60(1): extension of s. 22(1).

FINANCE ACT 1940

(3 & 4 Geo. 6, Chapter 29)

[*27th June 1940*]

60 Extension of power of Treasury to attach exemption from taxation to securities

60(1) The power of the Treasury under section twenty-two of the Finance (No. 2) Act, 1931, to issue securities with the condition as to exemption from taxation specified in that section shall extend to the issuing of securities with that condition so modified, whether as to the extent of the exemption or the cases in which the exemption is to operate, as the Treasury may specify in the terms of the issue.

History – S. 60(2) repealed by Income Tax Act 1952, s. 527 and Sch. 25, Pt. I.

CROWN PROCEEDINGS ACT 1947

(10 & 11 Geo. 6, Chapter 44)

[*31st July 1947*]

PART II – JURISDICTION AND PROCEDURE

14 Summary applications to High Court in certain revenue matters

14(1) Subject to and in accordance with rules of court, the Crown may apply in a summary manner to the High Court–

(a) for the furnishing of information required to be furnished by any person under the enactments relating to inheritance tax;

(b) for the delivery of accounts and payment of inheritance tax under the Inheritance Tax Act 1984.

History – In s. 14(1)(a) the words "inheritance tax" and in s. 14(1)(b) the words "payment of inheritance tax under the Inheritance Tax Act 1984" substituted by IHTA 1984, s. 274, 276 and Sch. 8, para. 2.

The words "capital transfer tax" in para. (a) were substituted by FA 1975, s. 52 and Sch. 12, para. 8(a).

The words "payment of capital transfer tax under the Capital Transfer Tax Act 1984" were substituted by IHTA 1984, s. 276 and Sch. 8, para. 2, with effect from 1 January 1985.

Notes – S. 42: s. 14 does not apply to Scotland.

FA 1986, s. 100(1)(b): any reference to capital transfer tax (except where it relates to a liability to tax arising before 25 July 1986) has effect as a reference to inheritance tax. See also FA 1986, s. 100(1)(a) for citation of the Capital Transfer Tax Act 1984 as the Inheritance Tax Act 1984.

In its application to Northern Ireland, with effect from 19 March 1981, s. 14 reads as follows (SI 1981/233, art. 1(1), (5), 31):

"14 Summary applications to High Court in certain matters concerning Northern Ireland revenue

14(1) Subject to and in accordance with rules of court, the Crown in right of His Majesty's Government in Northern Ireland may apply in a summary manner to the High Court–

(a) for payment of any tax (being a tax to which paragraph 8 of Schedule 2 to the Northern Ireland Constitution Act 1973 does not apply) levied under any enactment such as is mentioned in section 38(7) of this Act;

(b) for the delivery of any account required to be delivered, or the furnishing of any information required to be furnished, in connection with such a tax by any such enactment or by any instrument made thereunder."

IHT Statutes

SUCCESSION (SCOTLAND) ACT 1964

(1964 Chapter 41)

[*10th June 1964*]

ARRANGEMENT OF SECTIONS

PART II – LEGAL AND OTHER PRIOR RIGHTS IN ESTATES OF DECEASED PERSONS

PART II – LEGAL AND OTHER PRIOR RIGHTS IN ESTATES OF DECEASED PERSONS

8 Prior rights of surviving spouse, on intestacy, in dwelling house and furniture

8(1) Where a person dies intestate leaving a spouse or civil partner, and the intestate estate includes a relevant interest in a dwelling house to which this section applies, the surviving spouse or civil partner shall be entitled to receive out of the intestate estate–

(a) where the value of the relevant interest does not exceed £110,000 or such larger amount as may from time to time be fixed by order of the Secretary of State–

(i) if subsection (2) of this section does not apply, the relevant interest;

(ii) if the said subsection (2) applies, a sum equal to the value of the relevant interest;

(b) in any other case, the sum of £110,000 or such larger amount as may from time to time be fixed by order of the Secretary of State:

Provided that, if the intestate estate comprises a relevant interest in two or more dwelling houses to which this section applies, this subsection shall have effect only in relation to such one of them as the surviving spouse or civil partner may elect for the purposes of this subsection within six months of the date of death of the intestate.

8(2) This subsection shall apply for the purposes of paragraph (a) of the foregoing subsection if–

(a) the dwelling house forms part only of the subjects comprised in one tenancy or lease under which the intestate was the tenant; or

(b) the dwelling house forms the whole or part of subjects an interest in which is comprised in the intestate estate and which were used by the intestate for carrying on a trade, profession or occupation, and the value of the estate as a whole would be likely to be substantially diminished if the dwelling house were disposed of otherwise than with the assets of the trade, profession or occupation.

8(3) Where a person dies intestate leaving a spouse or civil partner, and the intestate estate includes the furniture and plenishings of a dwelling house to which this section applies (whether or not the dwelling house is comprised in the intestate estate), the surviving spouse or civil partner shall be entitled to receive out of the intestate estate–

(a) where the value of the furniture and plenishings does not exceed £20,000 or such larger amount as may from time to time be fixed by order of the Secretary of State, the whole thereof;

(b) in any other case, such part of the furniture and plenishings, to a value not exceeding £20,000 or such larger amount as may from time to time be fixed by order of the Secretary of State, as may be chosen by the surviving spouse:

Provided that, if the intestate estate comprises the furniture and plenishings of two or more such dwelling houses, this subsection shall have effect only in relation to the furniture and plenishings of such one of them as the surviving spouse or civil partner may elect for the purposes of this subsection within *six months of the date of death* of the intestate.

8(4) This section applies, in the case of any intestate, to any dwelling house in which the surviving spouse or civil partner of the intestate was ordinarily resident at the date of death of the intestate.

8(5) Where any question arises as to the value of any furniture or plenishings, or of any interest in a dwelling house, for the purposes of any provision of this section the question shall be determined by arbitration by a single arbiter appointed, in default of agreement, by the sheriff of the sheriffdom in which the intestate was domiciled at the date of his death or, if that sheriffdom is uncertain or the intestate was domiciled furth of Scotland, the sheriff of Lothian and Peebles at Edinburgh.

8(6) In this section–

(a) **"dwelling house"** includes a part of a building occupied (at the date of death of the intestate) as a separate dwelling; and any reference to a dwelling house shall be construed as including any garden or portion of ground attached to, and usually occupied with, the dwelling house or otherwise required for the amenity or convenience of the dwelling house;

(b) **"furniture and plenishings"** includes garden effects, domestic animals, plate, plated articles, linen, china, glass, books, pictures, prints, articles of household use and consumable stores; but does not include any article or animal used at the date of death of the intestate for business purposes, or money or securities for money, or any heirloom;

(c) **"heirloom"**, in relation to an intestate estate, means any article which has associations with the intestate's family of such nature and extent that it ought to pass to some member of that family other than the surviving spouse of the intestate;

(d) **"relevant interest"**, in relation to a dwelling house, means the interest therein of an owner, or the interest therein of a tenant, subject in either case to any heritable debt secured over the interest; and for the purposes of this definition **"tenant"** means a tenant under a tenancy or lease (whether of the dwelling house alone or of the dwelling house together with other subjects) which is not a tenancy to which the Rent Acts 1971–1974 apply.

History – In s. 8(1), (3) and (4), after "spouse" (in each place) the words "or civil partner" inserted by Civil Partnership Act 2004, Sch. 28, para. 4, with effect from 5 December 2005 (SSI 2005/604).
In s. 8(1)(a) and 8(1)(b), the words "£110,000" substituted by SI 1993/2690 in the case of a person dying on or after 26 November 1993. For deaths occurring between 1 May 1988 and 25 November 1993 the figure was £60,000.
In s. 8(3)(a) and 8(3)(b), the words "£20,000" substituted by SI 1993/2690 in the case of a person dying on or after 26 November 1993. For deaths occurring between 1 May 1988 and 25 November 1993 the figure was £12,000.

9 Prior right of surviving spouse to financial provision on intestacy

9(1) Where a person dies intestate and is survived by a husband, wife or civil partner the survivor shall be entitled to receive out of the intestate estate–

(a) if the intestate is survived by issue, the sum of £30,000 or such larger amount as may from time to time be fixed by order of the Secretary of State, or

(b) if the intestate is not survived by issue, the sum of £50,000 or such larger amount as may from time to time be fixed by order of the Secretary of State,

together with, in either case, interest at the rate of 7 per cent per annum or at such rate as may from time to time be fixed by order of the Secretary of State on such sum from the date of the intestate's death until payment.

Provided that where the surviving spouse is entitled to receive a legacy out of the estate of the intestate (other than a legacy of any dwelling house to which the last foregoing section applies or of any furniture and plenishings of any such dwelling house), he or she shall, unless he or she renounces the legacy, be entitled under this subsection to receive only such sum, if any, as remains after deducting from the sum fixed by virtue of paragraph (a) of this subsection or the sum fixed by virtue of paragraph (b) of this subsection, as the case may be, the amount or value of the legacy.

9(2) Where the intestate estate is less than the amount which the surviving spouse or civil partner is entitled to receive by virtue of subsection (1) of this section the right conferred by the said subsection on the surviving spouse or civil partner shall be satisfied by the transfer to him or her of the whole of the intestate estate.

9(3) The amount which the surviving spouse or civil partner is entitled to receive by virtue of subsection (1) of this section shall be borne by, and paid out of, the parts of the intestate estate consisting of heritable and moveable property respectively in proportion to the respective amounts of those parts.

9(4) Where by virtue of subsection (2) of this section a surviving spouse or civil partner has right to the whole of the intestate estate, he or she shall have the right to be appointed executor.

9(5) The rights conferred by the Intestate Husband's Estate (Scotland) Acts 1911 to 1959 on a surviving spouse in his or her deceased spouse's estate shall not be exigible out of the estate of any person dying after the commencement of this Act.

9(6) For the purposes of this section–

(a) the expression **"intestate estate"** means so much of the net intestate estate as remains after the satisfaction of any claims under the last foregoing section; and

(b) the expression **"legacy"** includes any payment or benefit to which a surviving spouse or civil partner becomes entitled by virtue of any testamentary disposition; and the amount or value of any legacy shall be ascertained as at the date of the intestate's death.

History – In s. 9(1) the words ", wife or civil partner the survivor" substituted for the words "or wife, the surviving spouse" by Civil Partnership Act 2004, Sch. 28, para. 5(a), with effect from 5 December 2005 (SSI 2005/604).
In s. 9(1)(a), the word "£30,000" substituted by SI 1993/2690 in the case of a person dying on or after 26 November 1993. For deaths occurring between 1 May 1988 and 25 November 1993, the figure was £21,000.
In s. 9(1)(b), the words "£50,000" substituted by SI 1993/2690 in the case of a person dying on or after 26 November 1993. For deaths occurring between 1 May 1988 and 25 November 1993, the figure was £35,000.
In s. 9(1) the words "7 per cent" substituted by SI 1981/805 with effect from 1 August 1981. Prior to this date the rate was 4 per cent.
In s. 9(2), (3), (4) and (6), after "spouse" (in each place) the words "or civil partner" inserted by Civil Partnership Act 2004, Sch. 28, para. 5(b), with effect from 5 December 2005 (SSI 2005/604).

9A Provisions supplementary to sections 8 and 9

9A Any order of the Secretary of State, under section 8 or 9 of this Act, fixing an amount or rate–

(a) shall be made by statutory instrument which shall be subject to annulment in pursuance of a resolution of either House of Parliament; and

(b) shall have effect in relation to the estate of any person dying after the coming into force of the order.

History – S. 9A inserted by Law Reform (Miscellaneous Provisions) (Scotland) Act 1980, s. 4.

FINANCE ACT 1975

(1975 Chapter 7)

[*13th March 1975*]

ARRANGEMENT OF SECTIONS

PART III – CAPITAL TRANSFER TAX

PART III – CAPITAL TRANSFER TAX

Notes – The following provisions of FA 1975 are of transitional interest.

35 Relief in certain circumstances for agricultural property

35 [Repealed by FA 1981, s. 96 and 139, Sch. 14, and Sch. 19, Pt. IX, and ceased to have effect in relation to transfers of value, distribution payments and capital distributions made from 10 March 1981.]

History – S. 35 and Sch. 8, Pt. I are still of transitional relevance by virtue of IHTA 1984, s. 116. Those provisions formerly read as follows:

"**35** Part I of Schedule 8 to this Act shall have effect for giving relief where the value transferred by a chargeable transfer is determined by reference to the value of agricultural property and the conditions mentioned in that Part are satisfied.

SCHEDULE 8 – RELIEF FOR AGRICULTURAL PROPERTY

Sections 35 and 49(2)

Part I – Capital Transfer Tax

NATURE OF RELIEF

1(1) Where the value transferred by a chargeable transfer is determined by reference to the value of agricultural property in the United Kingdom and the conditions stated in paragraph 3 below are satisfied, then, if–

(a) [Repealed by FA 1976, s. 74(2).]

(b) a person liable to pay the whole or part of the tax on the value transferred makes a claim in that behalf to the Board within two years of the transfer or such longer time as the Board may allow;

the value transferred shall be computed in accordance with paragraph 2 below and tax shall be chargeable accordingly, but subject to the limit imposed by paragraph 5 below.

1(2) The conditions stated in paragraph 3 below shall be deemed to be satisfied with respect to a transfer of value (in this sub-paragraph referred to as the current transfer) if–

(a) not more than two years before the current transfer there was (or would have been had this Act then been in force) a transfer of value and either that transfer or the current transfer was or would have been a transfer made on death; and

(b) the value transferred by the earlier transfer was or would have been determined by reference to the value of the same agricultural property as in the case of the current transfer; and

(c) the conditions stated in paragraph 3 below were or would have been satisfied with respect to the earlier transfer; and

(d) the agricultural property was, at the time of the current transfer, occupied for the purposes of agriculture by the transferor or by the personal representatives of the person who was or would have been the transferor in relation to the earlier transfer; and

(e) the agricultural property became, through the earlier transfer, the property of the person or of the spouse of the person who is the transferor in relation to the current transfer.

1(2A) Where, by virtue of sub-paragraph (2) above, the conditions stated in paragraph 3 below are deemed to be satisfied but, under the earlier transfer mentioned in that sub-paragraph, the amount of the value transferred which was attributable to the agricultural property was part only of the value of that property, a like part of its agricultural value shall be substituted for the agricultural value of the property in ascertaining the part eligible for relief under paragraph 2 below.

1(3) In the following provisions of this Part of this Schedule **"the unreduced value"**, in relation to a chargeable transfer, means the value transferred, calculated before the reduction and as if no tax were chargeable on it.

2 Where the value transferred is to be computed in accordance with this paragraph there shall first be ascertained such part of the unreduced value as is attributable to the agricultural value of the agricultural property (in this Part of this Schedule referred to as the part eligible for relief) and the value transferred shall then be computed as if the part eligible for relief were reduced by one-half.

CONDITIONS FOR RELIEF

3(1) The conditions referred to in paragraph 1(1) above are–

(a) that the transferor was, in not less than five of the seven years ending with 5th April immediately preceding the transfer, wholly or mainly engaged in the United Kingdom in any of the capacities mentioned in sub-paragraph (2) below (or partly in one of them and partly in another or others); and

(b) subject to paragraph 4 below, that the agricultural property was at the time of the transfer occupied by him for the purposes of agriculture and either was so occupied by him throughout the two years immediately preceding the transfer or replaced other agricultural property and was so occupied by him for a period which, when added to any period during which he so occupied the replaced property, comprised at least two years in the five years immediately preceding the transfer.

3(2) The capacities referred to in sub-paragraph (1) above are those of–

(a) a person who carries on farming as a trade either alone or in partnership;

(b) a person employed in farming carried on as a trade by another person;

(c) a director of a company carrying on farming in the United Kingdom as its main activity; or

(d) a person undergoing full-time education,

3(3) Where not less than 75 per cent of the transferor's relevant income was immediately derived by him from his engagement in agriculture in the United Kingdom, the condition in sub-paragraph (1)(a) above shall be taken to be satisfied; and for this purpose–

(a) **"relevant income"** is the aggregate of income in any five of the last seven years of assessment immediately preceding the transfer which is earned income for the purposes of income tax other than income from a pension, superannuation or other allowance, deferred pay or compensation for loss of office; and

(b) the question what was **the transferor's income** shall be determined without regard to section 37 of the Taxes Act (aggregation of wife's income).

3(4) Where the agricultural property had, at some time before the transfer, been occupied by the transferor for the purposes of agriculture and was, throughout the period between that time and the transfer, so occupied by a member of his family, the conditions in sub-paragraph (1) above shall be treated as satisfied if they would have been satisfied had the transfer occurred at that time.

3(5) Where the condition in sub-paragraph (1)(b) above is satisfied but the agricultural property which was occupied by the transferor at the time of the transfer was not occupied by him for the purposes of agriculture throughout the two years immediately preceding the transfer, then if the agricultural property which it replaced had, at the time when it ceased to be so occupied, a lower agricultural value than the first-mentioned property had at the time when it was first so occupied, the part eligible for relief shall be ascertained as if the agricultural value of the first-mentioned property were reduced by applying to it the fraction of which–

(a) the numerator is that lower agricultural value; and

(b) the denominator is the agricultural value which the first-mentioned property then had.

3(6) For the purposes of sub-paragraph 1 above, where the transferor became entitled to the agricultural property on the death of another person–

(a) his occupation of the agricultural property shall be deemed to have begun on the death of that person; and

(b) if that other person was the transferor's spouse and the condition stated in sub-paragraph (1)(a) above was at the time of the death satisfied with respect to the spouse, it shall be treated as having then been satisfied with respect to the transferor.

3(7) For the purposes of sub-paragraph (1) above occupation by a company which is controlled by the transferor shall be treated as occupation by the transferor; and for this purpose the question whether any company is controlled by the transferor shall be determined as for the purposes of paragraph 13 of Schedule 4 to this Act.

3(8) For the purposes of this paragraph, occupation of any property by a Scottish partnership shall, notwithstanding section 4(2) of the Partnership Act 1890, be treated as occupation of it by the partners.

3(9) For the purposes of sub-paragraph (4) above, a person is a member of the transferor's family if he is the transferor's spouse or a relative of the transferor or of the transferor's spouse or is the spouse of such a relative; and **"relative"** means ancestor, lineal descendant, brother, sister, uncle, aunt, nephew or niece, **"spouse"** includes former spouse, and an adopted person shall be treated as the child of the person or persons by whom he was adopted and an illegitimate person as the child of his mother and reputed father.

COMPANIES

4 So far as the value transferred is determined by reference to the value of shares in or debentures of a company it shall be taken for the purposes of this Schedule to be determined by reference to the value of any agricultural property if and only if–

(a) the agricultural property forms part of the company's assets and part of the value of the shares or debentures can be attributed to the agricultural value of the agricultural property; and

(b) the shares or debentures gave the transferor control of the company immediately before the transfer (the question whether they did so being determined as for the purposes of paragraph 13 of Schedule 4 to this Act); and

(bb) where the value of the shares or debentures is taken, by virtue of paragraph 9A of Schedule 10 to this Act to be less than their value as previously determined, they would have been sufficient, without any other property to give the transferor control as mentioned in sub-paragraph (b) above; and

(c) the main activity of the company is, and has been throughout the two years immediately preceding the transfer, farming in the United Kingdom; and

(d) the agricultural property was at the time of the transfer occupied by the company for the purposes of farming and either was so occupied by it throughout the two years immediately preceding the transfer or replaced other agricultural property and was so occupied by it for a period which, when added to any period during which it so occupied the replaced property, comprised at least two years in the five years immediately preceding the transfer;

and the condition stated in paragraph (d) above shall replace that stated in paragraph 3(1)(b) above, and the references to that paragraph and to the transferor in paragraph 3(5) above shall be construed accordingly.

LIMITATION OF RELIEF

5(1) Relief under this Part of this Schedule shall be given only to the extent that either–

(a) the part eligible for relief, when added to the part eligible for relief under any previous chargeable transfer made by the same transferor, does not exceed £250,000; or

(b) the area of the agricultural property by reference to which the relief is given, together with that of any agricultural property by reference to which relief was given under previous chargeable transfers made by the same transferor, does not exceed one thousand acres.

5(2) For the purposes of sub-paragraph (1)(b) above–

(a) where the transferor and some other person were together beneficially entitled to the agricultural property by reference to which the relief is given, the area of the property shall be taken to be such part thereof as corresponds to the transferor's share; and

(b) where the agricultural property by reference to which the relief is given forms part of the assets of a company, the area of the property shall be taken to be such part thereof as corresponds to the proportion which the value of the shares and debentures first mentioned in paragraph 4 above bears to the value of all the shares in and debentures of the company; and

(c) the area of any rough grazing land shall be counted as one-sixth of its actual area.

5(2A) The Board may consult the Minister of Agriculture, Fisheries and Food or, as the case may require, the Secretary of State or the Department of Agriculture for Northern Ireland on any question arising under this paragraph whether any land is rough grazing land; and paragraph 7(4) of Schedule 4 to this Act shall apply in relation to any such question as if it were a question as to the value of the land.

5(3) For the purposes of this paragraph chargeable transfers made by the same person on the same day shall be treated as one; and where the relief that could otherwise be given in respect of a chargeable transfer exceeds the limit imposed by this paragraph the excess shall be attributed to the agricultural properties concerned in proportion to their respective agricultural values or areas.

FARMING

6 In this Schedule **"farming"** has the meaning which it would have in the Tax Acts if in those Acts 'farm land' included market garden land; and for the purposes of this Schedule the question whether a person carries on farming as a trade shall be determined as for the purposes of income tax or, as the case may be, corporation tax.

AGRICULTURAL PROPERTY

7 In this Schedule **"agricultural property"** means agricultural land or pasture and includes woodland if occupied with agricultural land or pasture and the occupation is ancillary to that of the agricultural land or pasture; and also includes such cottages, farm buildings and farm-houses, together with the land occupied with them, as are of a character appropriate to the property.

AGRICULTURAL VALUE

8 For the purposes of this Schedule the **agricultural value** of any agricultural property shall be taken to be the value which would be the value of the property if the property were subject to a perpetual covenant prohibiting its use otherwise than as agricultural property.

MULTIPLIED RENTAL VALUE

9 [Repealed by FA 1976, s. 132 and Sch. 15, Pt. V.]

CHANNEL ISLANDS AND ISLE OF MAN

10 This Part of this Schedule applies in relation to land or activities carried on in the Channel Islands or the Isle of Man as if the land were situated or the activities were carried on in the United Kingdom.

SAVING

11 Nothing in this Part of this Schedule shall be taken to apply to the value included under section 22(5) of this Act in the value of a person's estate immediately before his death."

49 Abolition of estate duty and transitional provisions

49(1), (2) [Not reproduced.]

49(3) [Repealed by CTTA 1984, Sch. 9 with effect from 1 January 1985.]

49(4) Where estate duty is under section 61(5) of the Finance (1909–10) Act 1910 payable on the net moneys received from the sale of timber, trees or wood when felled or cut during the period referred to therein and that period has not ended before the passing of this Act, that period shall end immediately after the first transfer of value made after the passing of this Act in which the value transferred is, or is determined by reference to, the value of the land concerned, other than a transfer exempt by virtue of paragraph 1 of Schedule 6 to this Act or section 18 of the Capital Transfer Tax Act 1984.

49(5) [Repealed by CTTA 1984, Sch. 9 with effect from 1 January 1985.]

History – In s. 49(4), the words from "or section 18" to the end inserted by IHTA 1984, s. 276 and Sch. 8 para. 4, with effect from 1 January 1985.

Notes – F(1909–1910)A 1910, s. 61(5) read as follows:

"61(5) Where an estate, in respect of which estate duty is payable on the death of a person dying on or after the thirtieth day of April nineteen hundred and nine, comprises land on which timber, trees, wood, or underwood are growing, the value of such timber, trees, wood or underwood shall not be taken into account in estimating the principal value of the estate, or the amount of estate duty, and estate duty shall not be payable thereon, but shall be payable at the estate rate on the net moneys (if any), after deducting all necessary outgoings since the death of the deceased, which may from time to time be received from the sale of timber, trees or wood when felled or cut during the period which may elapse until the land, on the death of some other person, again becomes liable or would, but for this subsection, have become liable to estate duty, and the owners or trustees of such land shall account for and pay the same accordingly, as and when such moneys are received, with interest at the rate of three per cent per annum from the date when such moneys are received.

Provided that if at any time the timber, trees or wood are sold, either with or apart from the land on which they are growing, the amount of estate duty on the principal value thereof which, but for this subsection, would have been payable on the death of the deceased, after deducting the amount (if any) of estate duty paid in respect of the timber, trees or wood under this subsection since that date, shall become payable."

FINANCE ACT 1976

(1976 Chapter 40)

[*29th July 1976*]

PART V – MISCELLANEOUS AND SUPPLEMENTARY

131 Inter-American Development Bank

131(1) The following provisions of this section shall have effect on the United Kingdom's becoming a member of the Inter-American Development Bank (**"the Bank"**).

131(2) A security issued by the Inter-American Development Bank shall be taken for the purposes of capital transfer tax to be situated outside the United Kingdom.

History – In s. 131(2), the words "and capital gains tax" which followed the words "capital transfer tax" repealed by TCGA 1992, s. 290(3) and Sch 12.

In s. 131(2), the words "A security issued by the Inter-American Development Bank" were substituted by ICTA 1988, s. 844 and Sch. 29, para. 32, in relation to tax for 1988–89 and later years of assessment.

Notes – FA 1986, s. 100(1)(b): any reference to capital transfer tax (except where it relates to a liability to tax arising before 25 July 1986) has effect as a reference to inheritance tax.

NATIONAL HERITAGE ACT 1980

(1980 Chapter 17)

[*31st March 1980*]

ARRANGEMENT OF SECTIONS

PART II – PROPERTY ACCEPTED IN SATISFACTION OF TAX

9 Disposal of property accepted by Commissioners

9(1) Any property accepted in satisfaction of tax shall be disposed of in such manner as the Secretary of State may direct.

9(2) [Not reproduced.]

9(2A) [Not reproduced.]

9(3) Where the Secretary of State has determined that any property accepted in satisfaction of tax is to be disposed of under this section to any such institution or body as is mentioned in subsection (2) above or to any other person who is willing to accept it, he may direct that the disposal shall be effected by means of a transfer direct to that institution or body or direct to that other person instead of being transferred to the Commissioners.

9(4) The Secretary of State may in any case direct that any property accepted in satisfaction of tax shall, instead of being transferred to the Commissioners, be transferred to a person nominated by the Secretary of State; and where property is so transferred the person to whom it is transferred shall, subject to any directions subsequently given under subsection (1) or (2) above, hold the property and manage it in accordance with such directions as may be given by the Secretary of State.

9(5), (6) [Not reproduced.]

9(7) References in this section to the **"disposal or transfer of any property"** include references to leasing, sub-leasing or lending it for any period and on any terms.

9(8) The functions of the Ministers under this section in relation to the disposal or transfer of property in which there is a Scottish interest may be exercised separately.

9(9) For the purposes of subsection (8) a Scottish interest in the property exists where–

(a) the property is located in Scotland;

(b) the person liable to pay the tax has imposed a condition on his offer of the property in satisfaction of tax that it be displayed in Scotland or disposed of or transferred to a body or institution in Scotland; or

(c) only a body or institution. in Scotland has expressed an interest in acquiring the property; or

(d) a body or institution in Scotland and another body or institution have expressed an interest in acquiring the property.

History – In s. 9(1), (3), (4) the references to the Secretary of State were substituted by SI 1992/1311, art. 12(2), Sch. 2, para. 5(1), (2)(a)–(d), (4).
S. 9(8) inserted by SI 1999/1756, art. 2 and Sch., para. 7(1) with effect from immediately before the principal appointed day which is 1 July 1999 (by virtue of SI 1998/3178, art. 3).
S. 9(9) inserted by SI 1999/1756, art. 2 and Sch., para. 7(1) with effect from immediately before the principal appointed day which is 1 July 1999 (by virtue of SI 1998/3178, art. 3).

Notes – IHTA 1984, s. 230: acceptance of heritage property in satisfaction of tax.
Scotland Act 1998, Sch. 5, Pt. II, Head K, Section K4: property accepted in satisfaction of tax is a reserved matter for the purposes of the Scotland Act.

PART III – MISCELLANEOUS AND SUPPLEMENTARY

18 Short title, interpretation, repeals and extent

18(1) This Act may be cited as the National Heritage Act 1980.

18(2) In this Act **"financial year"** means the twelve months ending with 31st March.

18(3) [Repealed by SI 1981/207, Sch. 2.]

18(4) References in this Act to the **making of a grant or loan** or the **transfer or conveyance of any property** to any institution or body include references to the making of a grant or loan or to the transfer or conveyance of property to trustees for that institution or body.

18(5) [Not reproduced.]

18(6) This Act extends to Northern Ireland.

History – In s. 18(2), former definition of "the ministers" repealed by SI 1992/1311, art. 12(2) and Sch. 2, para. 5(1), (2).
S. 18(3) repealed by SI 1981/207, Sch. 2, operative from 1 April 1981.

SENIOR COURTS ACT 1981

(1981 Chapter 54)

[*28th July 1981*]

[This Act renamed (previously "Supreme Court Act 1981" by the Constitutional Reform Act 2005, s. 59 and Sch. 11, Pt. 1, with effect from 1 October 2009 (SI 2009/1604).]

109 Refusal of grant where capital transfer tax unpaid

109(1) No grant shall be made, and no grant made outside the United Kingdom shall be resealed, except–

(a) on the production of information or documents under regulations under section 256(1)(aa) of the Inheritance Tax Act 1984 (excepted estates); or

(b) on the production of an account prepared in pursuance of that Act showing by means of such receipt or certification as may be prescribed by the Commissioners either–

(i) that the inheritance tax payable on the delivery of the account has been paid; or

(ii) that no such tax is so payable.

109(2) Arrangements may be made between the President of the Family Division and the Commissioners providing for the purposes of subsection (1)(b) in such cases as may be specified in the arrangements that the receipt or certification of any account may be dispensed with or that some other document may be substituted for the account required by the Inheritance Tax Act 1984.

109(2A) In this section and the following section, **"the Commissioners"** means the Commissioners of Inland Revenue.

109(3) [Repealed by FA 2004, s. 294(1)(d) and Sch. 42, Pt. 4(1).]

History – S. 109(1) substituted by FA 2004, s. 294(1)(a), with effect from 1 November 2004 (SI 2004/2571).

Cross references – IHTA 1984, s. 256(1): regulations may be made by the Board dispensing with the delivery of accounts under IHTA 1984, s. 216 in such cases as specified in the regulations.

Notes – FA 1986, s. 100(1)(b): any reference to capital transfer tax (except where it relates to a liability to tax arising before 25 July 1986) has effect as a reference to inheritance tax; see also FA 1986, s. 100(1)(a) for citation of the Capital Transfer Tax Act 1984 as the Inheritance Tax Act 1984.

FINANCE ACT 1984

(1984 Chapter 43)

[*26th July 1984*]

PART VI – MISCELLANEOUS AND SUPPLEMENTARY

MISCELLANEOUS

126 Tax exemptions in relation to designated international organisations

126(1) Where–

(a) the United Kingdom or any of the Communities is a member of an international organisation; and

(b) the agreement under which it became a member provides for exemption from tax, in relation to the organisation, of the kind for which provision is made by this section;

the Treasury may, by order made by statutory instrument, designate that organisation for the purposes of this section.

126(2) Where an organisation has been so designated, the provisions mentioned in subsection (3) below shall, with the exception of any which may be excluded by the designation order, apply in relation to that organisation.

126(3) The provisions are–

(a) [repealed by ICTA 1988, s. 844 and Sch. 31.]

(b) any security issued by the organisation shall be taken, for the purposes of capital transfer tax to be situated outside the United Kingdom; and

(c), (d) [provisions dealing with stamp duty and stamp duty reserve tax.]

126(4) The Treasury may, by order made by statutory instrument, designate any of the Communities or the European Investment Bank for the purposes of this section, and references in subsections (2) and (3) above to an organisation designated for the purposes of this section include references to a body so designated by virtue of this subsection.

126(5) [Stamp duty provision.]

History – S. 126(3)(a) repealed by ICTA 1988, s. 844 and Sch. 31, with effect in relation to tax for 1988–89 and later years of assessment.

In s. 126(3)(b), reference to capital gains tax repealed by TCGA 1992, s. 290 and Sch. 12, with effect in relation to tax for 1992–93 and subsequent years of assessment.

S. 126(3)(d) inserted by FA 1990, s. 114 applicable, where an organisation or body is designated under s. 126(1) or (4) before 26 July 1990, in relation to the issue of securities on or after 26 July 1990, and, where an organisation or body is so designated on or after 26 July 1990, in relation to the issue of securities after the designation.

S. 126(4), (5) inserted by FA 1985, s. 96(1).

Cross references – FA 1985, s. 96(2) (not reproduced): orders under s. 126(4) may revoke or vary the European Communities (Loan Stock) (Stamp Duties) Order 1972 (SI 1972/1589).

ICTA 1988, s. 324: exemption from income and corporation taxes.

TCGA 1992, s. 265: exemption from capital gains tax.

Statutory instruments – SI 1984/1215, SI 1984/1634; SI 1985/1172; SI 1991/1202: designated bodies are The Asian Development Bank, The African Development Bank, The European Economic Community, The European Coal and Steel Community, The European Atomic Energy Community, The European Investment Bank and the European Bank for Reconstruction and Development.

INHERITANCE TAX ACT 1984
(CAPITAL TRANSFER TAX ACT 1984)

(1984 Chapter 51)

[*31st July 1984*]

ARRANGEMENT OF SECTIONS

PART I – GENERAL

MAIN CHARGES AND DEFINITIONS

RATES

DISPOSITIONS THAT ARE NOT TRANSFERS OF VALUE
(AND OMISSIONS THAT DO NOT GIVE RISE TO DEEMED DISPOSITIONS)

PART II – EXEMPT TRANSFERS

CHAPTER I – GENERAL

CHAPTER II – CONDITIONAL EXEMPTION

CHAPTER III – ALLOCATION OF EXEMPTIONS

PART III – SETTLED PROPERTY

CHAPTER I – PRELIMINARY

CHAPTER II – INTERESTS IN POSSESSION, REVERSIONARY INTERESTS AND SETTLEMENT POWERS

CHAPTER III – SETTLEMENTS WITHOUT INTERESTS IN POSSESSION, AND CERTAIN SETTLEMENTS IN WHICH INTERESTS IN POSSESSION SUBSIST

INTERPRETATION

PRINCIPAL CHARGE TO TAX

RATES OF PRINCIPAL CHARGE

SPECIAL CASES – CHARGES TO TAX

PART V – MISCELLANEOUS RELIEFS

CHAPTER I – BUSINESS PROPERTY

CHAPTER II – AGRICULTURAL PROPERTY

CHAPTER III – WOODLANDS

CHAPTER IV – TRANSFERS WITHIN SEVEN YEARS BEFORE DEATH

CHAPTER V – MISCELLANEOUS

PART VI – VALUATION

CHAPTER I – GENERAL

CHAPTER II – ESTATE ON DEATH

CHAPTER III – SALE OF SHARES ETC. FROM DECEASED'S ESTATE

CHAPTER IV – SALE OF LAND FROM DECEASED'S ESTATE

PART VII – LIABILITY

GENERAL RULES

INTEREST

INLAND REVENUE CHARGE FOR UNPAID TAX

CERTIFICATES OF DISCHARGE

ADJUSTMENTS

RECOVERY OF TAX

PENALTIES

MISCELLANEOUS

PART IX – MISCELLANEOUS AND SUPPLEMENTARY

MISCELLANEOUS

INTERPRETATION

IHT Statutes

Notes – See FA 1986, s. 100(1)(a) for citation of the Capital Transfer Tax Act 1984 as the Inheritance Tax Act 1984.

PART I – GENERAL

MAIN CHARGES AND DEFINITIONS

1 Charge on transfers

1 Capital transfer tax shall be charged on the value transferred by a chargeable transfer.

Notes – FA 1986, s. 100(1)(b): any reference to capital transfer tax (except where it relates to a liability to tax arising before 25 July 1986) has effect as a reference to inheritance tax.

2 Chargeable transfers and exempt transfers

2(1) A **chargeable transfer** is a transfer of value which is made by an individual but is not (by virtue of Part II of this Act or any other enactment) an exempt transfer.

2(2) A transfer of value made by an individual and exempt only to a limited extent–

(a) is, if all the value transferred by it is within the limit, an exempt transfer, and

(b) is, if that value is partly within and partly outside the limit, a chargeable transfer of so much of that value as is outside the limit as well as an exempt transfer of so much of that value as is within the limit.

2(3) Except where the context otherwise requires, references in this Act to **chargeable transfers**, to their making or to the values transferred by them shall be construed as including references to occasions on which tax is chargeable under Chapter III of Part III of this Act (apart from section 79), to their occurrence or to the amounts on which tax is then chargeable.

Cross references – Pt. III, Ch. III: charge on settlements without interests in possession, subject to exemption from ten-yearly charge in certain cases (s. 79).

3 Transfers of value

3(1) Subject to the following provisions of this Part of this Act, a **transfer of value** is a disposition made by a person (the transferor) as a result of which the value of his estate immediately after the disposition is less than it would be but for the disposition; and the amount by which it is less is the value transferred by the transfer.

3(2) For the purposes of subsection (1) above no account shall be taken of the value of excluded property which ceases to form part of a person's estate as a result of a disposition.

3(3) Where the value of a person's estate is diminished, and the value–

(a) of another person's estate, or

(b) of any settled property, other than settled property treated by section 49(1) below as property to which a person is beneficially entitled,

is increased by the first-mentioned person's omission to exercise a right, he shall be treated for the purposes of this section as having made a disposition at the time (or latest time) when he could have exercised the right, unless it is shown that the omission was not deliberate.

3(4) Except as otherwise provided, references in this Act to a **transfer of value made**, or made by any person, include references to events on the happening of which tax is chargeable as if a transfer of value had been made, or, as the case may be, had been made by that person; and **transferor** shall be construed accordingly.

History – In s. 3(3) the words from the beginning to "is increased" substituted for the words "Where the value of a person's estate is diminished and that of another person's estate, or of settled property in which no interest in possession subsists, is increased" by FA 2006, s. 156 and Sch. 20, para. 8, with effect from 22 March 2006.

Cross references – S. 19(5), 20(3), 21(5), 22(6): disapplication of s. 3(4) for purposes of s. 19–22 (annual exemption, small gifts, normal expenditure out of income, gifts in consideration of marriage).
S. 199: liability for tax on a disposition, including one by omission under s. 3(3).

Statements of practice – SP 5/92: failure to exercise right under TCGA 1992, Sch. 5, para. 6 (settlor's right of recovery of tax from trustee in certain cases) may fall under s. 3(3).

Other material – Tax Bulletin, TB02/92-3: retirement benefits under private pension contracts: circumstances in which CTO will regard failure to take up retirement benefit before death as giving rise to a charge to IHT under s. 3(3).
ICAEW Technical Release TR 825 (not reproduced): ICAEW state Capital Taxes Office view that where a retirement annuity contract is placed under trust, s. 3(3) may apply in respect of:

- the lump sum which the member could have received on exercise of an option to commute his annuity; and
- the open market value of the right to receive an annuity of any guarantee term.

Revenue letter dated 5 June 1991 to Association of British Insurers (see ICAEW Technical Release TR 854: HMRC policy on s. 3(3) claims in respect of retirement annuities, personal pensions, etc.).
Taxline 2000/2 (not reproduced): circumstances where a charge under s. 3(3) will not arise.

3A Potentially exempt transfers

3A(1) Any reference in this Act to a **potentially exempt transfer** is a reference to a transfer of value–

(a) which is made by an individual on or after 18th March 1986 but before 22nd March 2006; and

(b) which, apart from this section, would be a chargeable transfer (or to the extent to which, apart from this section, it would be such a transfer); and

(c) to the extent that it constitutes either a gift to another individual or a gift into an accumulation and maintenance trust or a disabled trust.

3A(1A) Any reference in this Act to a potentially exempt transfer is also a reference to a transfer of value–

(a) which is made by an individual on or after 22nd March 2006,

(b) which, apart from this section, would be a chargeable transfer (or to the extent to which, apart from this section, it would be such a transfer), and

(c) to the extent that it constitutes–

(i) a gift to another individual,

(ii) a gift into a disabled trust, or

(iii) a gift into a bereaved minor's trust on the coming to an end of an immediate post-death interest.

3A(1B) Subsections (1) and (1A) above have effect subject to any provision of this Act which provides that a disposition (or transfer of value) of a particular description is not a potentially exempt transfer.

3A(2) Subject to subsection (6) below, a transfer of value falls within subsection (1)(c) or (1A)(c)(i) above, as a gift to another individual,–

(a) to the extent that the value transferred is attributable to property which, by virtue of the transfer, becomes comprised in the estate of that other individual, or

(b) so far as that value is not attributable to property which becomes comprised in the estate of another person, to the extent that, by virtue of the transfer, the estate of that other individual is increased.

3A(3) Subject to subsection (6) below, a transfer of value falls within subsection (1)(c) above, as a gift into an accumulation and maintenance trust or a disabled trust, to the extent that the value transferred is attributable to property which, by virtue of the transfer, becomes settled property to which section 71 or 89 of this Act applies.

3A(3A) Subject to subsection (6) below, a transfer of value falls within subsection (1A)(c)(ii) above to the extent that the value transferred is attributable to property which, by virtue of the transfer, becomes settled property to which section 89 below applies.

3A(3B) A transfer of value falls within subsection (1A)(c)(iii) above to the extent that the value transferred is attributable to settled property (whenever settled) that becomes property to which section 71A below applies in the following circumstances–

(a) under the settlement, a person ("L") is beneficially entitled to an interest in possession in the settled property,

(b) the interest in possession is an immediate post-death interest,

(c) on or after 22nd March 2006, but during L's life, the interest in possession comes to an end,

(d) L is beneficially entitled to the interest in possession immediately before it comes to an end, and

(e) on the interest in possession coming to an end, the property–

(i) continues to be held on the trusts of the settlement, and

(ii) becomes property to which section 71A below applies.

3A(4) A potentially exempt transfer which is made seven years or more before the death of the transferor is an exempt transfer and any other potentially exempt transfer is a chargeable transfer.

3A(5) During the period beginning on the date of a potentially exempt transfer and ending immediately before–

(a) the seventh anniversary of that date, or

(b) if it is earlier, the death of the transferor,

it shall be assumed for the purposes of this Act that the transfer will prove to be an exempt transfer.

3A(6) Where, under any provision of this Act, tax is in any circumstances to be charged as if a transfer of value had been made, that transfer shall be taken to be a transfer which is not a potentially exempt transfer.

3A(6A) The reference in subsection (6) above to any provision of this Act does not include section 52 below except where the transfer of value treated as made by that section is one treated as made on the coming to an end of an interest which falls within section 5(1B) below.

3A(7) In the application of this section to an event on the happening of which tax is chargeable under section 52 below, the reference in subsection (1)(a) or (1A)(a) above to the individual by whom the transfer of value is made is a reference to the person who, by virtue of section 3(4) above, is treated as the transferor.

History – In s. 3A(1)(a) the words "but before 22nd March 2006" inserted by FA 2006, s. 156 and Sch. 20, para. 9(2), with effect from 22 March 2006.
In s. 3A(1) the words "but this subsection has effect subject to any provision of this Act which provides that a disposition (or transfer of value) of a particular description is not a potentially exempt transfer." which followed para. (c) repealed by FA 2006, s. 178 and Sch. 26, Pt. 6, with effect from 22 March 2006.
S. 3A(1A) inserted by FA 2006, s. 156 and Sch. 20, para. 9(3), with effect from 22 March 2006.
S. 3A(1B) inserted by FA 2006, s. 156 and Sch. 20, para. 9(3), with effect from 22 March 2006.
In s. 3A(2) the words "or (1A)(c)(i)" inserted by FA 2006, s. 156 and Sch. 20, para. 9(4), with effect from 22 March 2006.
S. 3A(2)(a), (b) partially repealed by F(No. 2)A 1987, s. 96(2) and Sch. 9, Pt. III, and s. 3A(6) amended by s. 96(2) by adding reference to s. 52, with respect to transfers of value made, and other events occurring, on or after 17 March 1987.
S. 3A(3A) inserted by FA 2006, s. 156 and Sch. 20, para. 9(5), with effect from 22 March 2006.
S. 3A(3B) inserted by FA 2006, s. 156 and Sch. 20, para. 9(5), with effect from 22 March 2006.
In s. 3A(6) the words "other than section 52", which appeared after the words "this Act", omitted by FA 2010, s. 53(2)(a), with effect in relation to an interest in possession to which a person is beneficially entitled if the person becomes beneficially entitled to it on or after 9 December 2009.
In s. 3A(6), the words "other than section 52" inserted by F(No. 2)A 1987, s. 96(1), (2)(c), with effect in relation to transfers of value made after 16 March 1987.
S. 3A(6A) inserted by FA 2010, s. 53(2)(b), with effect in relation to an interest in possession to which a person is beneficially entitled if the person becomes beneficially entitled to it on or after 9 December 2009.
In s. 3A(7) the words "or (1A)(a)" inserted by FA 2006, s. 156 and Sch. 20, para. 9(6), with effect from 22 March 2006.
S. 3A(7) inserted by F(No. 2)A 1987, s. 96(3), with respect to transfers of value made, and other events occurring, on or after 17 March 1987.
S. 3A inserted by FA 1986, s. 101 and Sch. 19, para. 1, with respect to transfers of value made, and other events occurring, on or after 18 March 1986.

Cross references – S. 30(3A): PETs and conditionally exempt transfers – interaction.
S. 52: charge on termination of interest in possession.
S. 71: special treatment for certain trusts, commonly termed "accumulation and maintenance" trusts.
S. 89: special treatment for certain trusts, commonly termed "disabled" trusts.
FA 1986, Sch. 19, para. 46: a transfer of value on or after 1 July 1986, which brings to an end an estate duty deferment period in respect of timber, is not a PET.
TCGA 1992, s. 165, 260: capital gains tax hold-over relief for gifts of certain business or agricultural assets, or where there is an immediate charge to inheritance tax.

Other material – Law Society's Gazette, 2 November 1988 (p. 45) and 14 December 1988 (p. 40) (not reproduced): not necessary to submit an account of a PET when made.

Notes – S. 226(3A): due date for payment of tax on PET which proves to be chargeable.
FA 1986, Sch. 19, para. 40(1): transitional – transfer of value occurring before, and death or other event occurring after, 18 March 1986.

4 Transfers on death

4(1) On the death of any person tax shall be charged as if, immediately before his death, he had made a transfer of value and the value transferred by it had been equal to the value of his estate immediately before his death.

4(2) For the purposes of this section, where it cannot be known which of two or more persons who have died survived the other or others they shall be assumed to have died at the same instant.

Cross references – S. 47A: settlement power.
S. 116(5D): agricultural property relief.
S. 154: exemption for death on active service etc.
S. 200: liability for tax on value transferred by chargeable transfer made on death.
S. 272: definitions of "property" and "settlement power".

Extra-statutory concessions – F2: property of Roman Catholic religious communities – tax not claimed on death of nominal owner.
F6: delayed remittances of foreign assets owing to restrictions imposed by foreign government.
F7: foreign-owned works of art situated in UK at owner's death.

Other material – Taxline 2004/12 (not reproduced): death in service awards caught under all of these sections if the employee may nominate a beneficiary for the proceeds.

Notes – S. 227: payment of tax by instalments.

5 Meaning of estate

5(1) For the purposes of this Act **"a person's estate"** is the aggregate of all the property to which he is beneficially entitled, except that–

(a) the estate of a person–

(i) does not include an interest in possession in settled property to which section 71A or 71D below applies, and

(ii) does not include an interest in possession that falls within subsection (1A) below unless it falls within subsection (1B) below, and

(b) the estate of a person immediately before his death does not include excluded property or a foreign-owned work of art which is situated in the United Kingdom for one or more of the purposes of public display, cleaning and restoration (and for no other purpose).

5(1A) An interest in possession falls within this subsection if–

(a) it is an interest in possession in settled property,

(b) the settled property is not property to which section 71A or 71D below applies,

(c) the person is beneficially entitled to the interest in possession,

(d) the person became beneficially entitled to the interest in possession on or after 22nd March 2006, and

(e) the interest in possession is–

(i) not an immediate post-death interest,

(ii) not a disabled person's interest, and

(iii) not a transitional serial interest.

5(1B) An interest in possession falls within this subsection if the person–

(a) was domiciled in the United Kingdom on becoming beneficially entitled to it, and

(b) became beneficially entitled to it by virtue of a disposition which was prevented from being a transfer of value by section 10 below.

5(2) A person who has a general power which enables him, or would if he were sui juris enable him, to dispose of any property other than settled property, or to charge money on any property other than settled property, shall be treated as beneficially entitled to the property or money; and for this purpose **"general power"** means a power or authority enabling the person by whom it is exercisable to appoint or dispose of property as he thinks fit.

5(3) In determining the value of a person's estate at any time his liabilities at that time shall be taken into account, except as otherwise provided by this Act.

5(4) The liabilities to be taken into account in determining the value of the transferor's estate immediately after a transfer of value include his liability for capital transfer tax on the value transferred but not his liability (if any) for any other tax or duty resulting from the transfer.

5(5) Except in the case of a liability imposed by law, a liability incurred by a transferor shall be taken into account only to the extent that it was incurred for a consideration in money or money's worth.

History – In s. 5(1)(a)(ii), the words "unless it falls within subsection (1B) below" inserted by FA 2010, s. 53(3)(a), with effect in relation to an interest in possession to which a person is beneficially entitled if the person becomes beneficially entitled to it on or after 9 December 2009.
In s. 5(1) the words "except that–" and para. (a) and (b) substituted for the words "except that the" by FA 2006, s. 156 and Sch. 20, para. 10(2), with effect from 22 March 2006.

In s. 5(1)(b), the words "or a foreign-owned work of art which is situated in the United Kingdom for one or more of the purposes of public display, cleaning and restoration (and for no other purpose)." inserted by SI 2009/730, art. 13(2), with effect in relation to deaths and ten-year anniversaries occurring on or after 6 April 2009.
S. 5(1A) inserted by FA 2006, s. 156 and Sch. 20, para. 10(3), with effect from 22 March 2006.
S. 5(1B) inserted by FA 2010, s. 53(3)(b), with effect in relation to an interest in possession to which a person is beneficially entitled if the person becomes beneficially entitled to it on or after 9 December 2009.

Cross references – S. 55(1): reversionary interest acquired by beneficiary does not form part of his estate.
S. 151(4): modification of s. 5(2) in relation to a pension or annuity fund or scheme.
FA 1986, s. 103(7): disallowance of certain liabilities arising in connection with policies of life insurance made on or after 1 July 1986.
SI 2011/1502, art. 5: Equitable Life "authorised payments" to be disregarded in determining value of estate.

Extra-statutory concessions – F18: deduction allowed under s. 5(3) for Canadian income tax charge on gains arising on a deemed disposal on death.
F19: a decoration awarded for valour is treated for IHT as "excluded property", if it is shown never to have been transferred for consideration in money or money's worth.
F20: the cash value of claims paid by schemes which provide compensation for wrongs suffered during World War II may be excluded from IHT where compensation is paid in modest round-sum, or otherwise cash-limited amounts; details of the schemes recognised for the ESC.

HMRC interpretations – IRInt. 202: HMRC view that where a bookmaker's pitch has been acquired by inheritance after the October 1998 changes to the allocation rules, it constitutes property to which the deceased was beneficially entitled.

Other material – Taxline 2004/12 (not reproduced): death in service awards caught under all of these sections if the employee may nominate a beneficiary for the proceeds.

Notes – FA 1986, s. 100(1)(b): any reference to capital transfer tax (except where it relates to a liability to tax arising before 25 July 1986) has effect as a reference to inheritance tax.

6 Excluded property

6(1) Property situated outside the United Kingdom is **"excluded property"** if the person beneficially entitled to it is an individual domiciled outside the United Kingdom.

6(1A) A holding in an authorised unit trust and a share in an open-ended investment company is excluded property if the person beneficially entitled to it is an individual domiciled outside the United Kingdom.

6(1B) A relevant decoration or award is excluded property if it has never been the subject of a disposition for a consideration in money or money's worth.

6(1BA) In subsection (1B) **"relevant decoration or award"** means a decoration or other similar award–

(a) that is designed to be worn to denote membership of–

  (i) an Order that is, or has been, specified in the Order of Wear published in the London Gazette (**"the Order of Wear"**), or

  (ii) an Order of a country or territory outside the United Kingdom,

(b) that is, or has been, specified in the Order of Wear,

(c) that was awarded for valour or gallant conduct,

(d) that was awarded for, or in connection with, a person being, or having been, a member of, or employed or engaged in connection with, the armed forces of any country or territory,

(e) that was awarded for, or in connection with, a person being, or having been, an emergency responder within the meaning of section 153A (death of emergency service personnel etc), or

(f) that was awarded by the Crown or a country or territory outside the United Kingdom for, or in connection with, public service or achievement in public life.

6(1C) In subsection (1B) the reference to a disposition of the decoration or other award includes–

(a) a reference to a disposition of part of it, and

(b) a reference to a disposition of an interest in it (or in part of it).

6(2) Where securities have been issued by the Treasury subject to a condition authorised by section 22 of the Finance (No. 2) Act 1931 (or section 47 of the Finance (No. 2) Act 1915) for exemption from taxation so long as the securities are in the beneficial ownership of persons of a description specified in the condition, the securities are excluded property if they are in the beneficial ownership of such a person.

6(3) Where the person beneficially entitled to the rights conferred by any of the following, namely–

(a) war savings certificates;

(b) national savings certificates (including Ulster savings certificates);

(c) premium savings bonds;

(d) deposits with the National Savings Bank or with a trustee savings bank;

(e) a certified SAYE savings arrangement within the meaning of section 703(1) of the Income Tax *(Trading and Other Income)* Act 2005;

is domiciled in the Channel Islands or the Isle of Man, the rights are excluded property.

6(4) Property to which this subsection applies by virtue of section 155(1) or (5A) below is excluded property.

6(5) This section is subject to Schedule A1 (non-excluded overseas property).

History – S. 6(1A) inserted by FA 2003, s. 186(2), with effect in relation to transfers of value or other events occurring on or after 16 October 2002.
S. 6(1B) and (1BA) substituted for former s. 6(1B) by FA 2015, s. 74(1), with effect in relation to transfers of value made, or treated as made, on or after 31 December 2014. Former s. 6(1B) read as follows:
"**6(1B)** A decoration or other award is excluded property if–
(a) it was awarded for valour or gallant conduct, and
(b) it has never been the subject of a disposition for a consideration in money or money's worth."
Former s. 6(1B) inserted by SI 2009/730, art. 14(1), with effect in relation to transfers of value or other events occurring on or after 6 April 2009.
S. 6(1C) inserted by SI 2009/730, art. 14(1), with effect in relation to transfers of value or other events occurring on or after 6 April 2009.
In s. 6(2), the words "of a description specified in the condition" substituted for the previous words "neither domiciled nor ordinarily resident in the United Kingdom" by FA 1996, s. 154 and Sch. 28, para. 7, with effect in accordance with FA 1996, s. 154(9).
In s. 6(3)(e), the words "certified SAYE savings arrangement" substituted for "certified contractual savings scheme" by ITTOIA 2005, s. 882(2) and Sch. 1, para. 394(a), with effect from 6 April 2005.
In s. 6(3)(e), the words "section 703(1) of the Income Tax (Trading and Other Income) Act 2005" substituted for "section 326 of the Taxes Act 1988" by ITTOIA 2005, s. 882(2) and Sch. 1, para. 394(b), with effect from 6 April 2005.
In s. 6(3)(e), reference to ICTA 1988 substituted by ICTA 1988, Sch. 29, para. 32.
In s. 6(4), the words "or (5A)" inserted by FA 2012, s. 220 and Sch. 37, para. 2, with effect from 17 July 2012.
S. 6(5) inserted by F(No. 2)A 2017, s. 33 and Sch. 10, para. 3, with effect in relation to times after 5 April 2017 subject to Sch. 10, para. 9 and 10.
Cross references – S. 48: settled property which is excluded property.
S. 155(1): emoluments and tangible moveable property of members of overseas forces visiting the UK.
S. 267(2); disapplication of deemed domicile provision in respect of s. 6(2), (3).
F(No. 2)A 1931, s. 22: power of Treasury to issue tax exempt securities to non-residents.
FA 1998, s. 161(2)(c): treatment of gilt-edged securities issued on non-FOTRA terms before 6 April 1998 as FOTRA securities: to be treated as excluded property for IHTA 1984 purposes, but only as regards any time on or after that date.

RATES

7 Rates

7(1) Subject to subsections (2), (4) and (5) below and to section 8D and Schedule 1A the tax charged on the value transferred by a chargeable transfer made by any transferor shall be charged at the following rate or rates, that is to say–

(a) if the transfer is the first chargeable transfer made by that transferor in the period of seven years ending with the date of the transfer, at the rate or rates applicable to that value under the Table in Schedule 1 to this Act;

(b) in any other case, at the rate or rates applicable under that Table to such part of the aggregate of–

(i) that value, and

(ii) the values transferred by previous chargeable transfers made by him in that period,

as is the highest part of that aggregate and is equal to that value.

7(2) Except as provided by subsection (4) below, the tax charged on the value transferred by a chargeable transfer made before the death of the transferor shall be charged at one-half of the rate or rates referred to in subsection (1) above.

7(3) In the Table in Schedule 1 to this Act any rate shown in the third column is that applicable to such portion of the value concerned as exceeds the lower limit shown in the first column but does not exceed the upper limit (if any) shown in the second column.

7(4) Subject to subsection (5) below, subsection (2) above does not apply in the case of a chargeable transfer made at any time within the period of seven years ending with the death of the transferor but, in the case of a chargeable transfer made within that period but more than three years before the death, the tax charged on the value transferred shall be charged at the following percentage of the rate or rates referred to in subsection (1) above–

(a) where the transfer is made more than three but not more than four years before the death, 80 per cent;

(b) where the transfer is made more than four but not more than five years before the death, 60 per cent;

(c) where the transfer is made more than five but not more than six years before the death, 40 per cent; and

(d) where the transfer is made more than six but not more than seven years before the death, 20 per cent.

7(5) If, in the case of a chargeable transfer made before the death of the transferor, the tax which would fall to be charged in accordance with subsection (4) above is less than the tax which would have been chargeable (in accordance with subsection (2) above) if the transferor had not died within the period of seven years beginning with the date of the transfer, subsection (4) above shall not apply in the case of that transfer.

History – In s. 7(1), the words "section 8D and" inserted by F(No. 2)A 2015, s. 9(2), with effect from 18 November 2015 (Royal Assent).
In s. 7(1), the words "and to Schedule 1A" inserted after "(4) and (5) below" by FA 2012, s. 209 and Sch. 33, para. 3, with effect in cases where D's death occurs on or after 6 April 2012.

IHT Statutes

In s. 7(1), the words "Subject to subsections (2), (4) and (5) below" inserted, "seven years" in para. (a) substituted, and "appropriate" between "the" and "Table" in para. (a) repealed, by FA 1986, s. 101 and Sch. 19, para. 2(1), with effect, with respect to transfers of value made, and other events occurring, on or after 18 March 1986.
S. 7(2) was substituted by FA 1986, Sch. 19, para. 2(2), with effect, with respect to transfers of value made, and other events occurring, on or after 18 March 1986.
In s. 7(3) the words "the Table" substituted by FA 1986, Sch. 19, para. 2(3), with effect, with respect to transfers of value made, and other events occurring, on or after 18 March 1986.
S. 7(4), (5) inserted by FA 1986, Sch. 19, para. 2(4), with effect, with respect to transfers of value made, and other events occurring, on or after 18 March 1986.

Cross references – S. 131: relief for transfers within seven years of death.
Sch. 4, para. 14: rates of tax in respect of property leaving maintenance funds.
FA 1986, Sch. 19, para. 40(1): transitional – transfer of value occurring before, and death or other event occurring after, 18 March 1986.
FA 1986, Sch. 19, para. 41: rates applicable to chargeable transfers made before 18 March 1986 when the transferor dies on or after that date.

8 Indexation of rate bands

8(1) If the consumer prices index for the month of September in any year is higher than it was for the previous September, then, unless Parliament otherwise determines, section 7 above and Schedule 1 to this Act shall apply to chargeable transfers made on or after 6th April in the following year with the substitution of a new Table for the Table applying (whether by virtue of this section or otherwise) to earlier chargeable transfers.

8(1A) [Repealed by FA 1988, s. 136(3) and Sch. 14, Pt. X.]

8(2) The new Table shall differ from the Table it replaces in that for each of the amounts specified in the first and second columns there shall be substituted amounts arrived at by increasing the previous amounts by the same percentage as the percentage increase in the consumer prices index and, if the result is not a multiple of £1,000, rounding it up to the nearest amount which is such a multiple.

8(3) In this section, **"consumer prices index"** means the all items consumer prices index published by the Statistics Board.

8(4) The Treasury shall before 6th April 1994 and each subsequent 6th April make an order specifying the amounts which by virtue of this section will be treated, in relation to chargeable transfers on or after that date, as specified in the Table in Schedule 1 to this Act; and any such order shall be made by statutory instrument.

History – In s. 8(1), the words "consumer prices index for the month of September in any year" substituted for "retail prices index for the month of September in 1993 or any later year" by FA 2012, s. 208(2), with effect for the purposes of chargeable transfers made on or after 6 April 2015.
In s. 8(1), the words "September in 1993" and "previous September" substituted by FA 1993, s. 197(1)(a), in relation to chargeable transfers made on or after 6 April 1994.
In s. 8(1), the words "a new Table for the Table" substituted by FA 1986, s. 101 and Sch. 19, para. 3(1), in respect of transfers of value made, and other events occurring, on or after 18 March 1986.
S. 8(1A) repealed by FA 1988, s. 136(3) and Sch. 14, Pt. X, with effect in relation to transfers of value made on or after 15 March 1988.
In s. 8(2), the words "consumer prices index" substituted for "retail prices index" by FA 2012, s. 208(3), with effect for the purposes of chargeable transfers made on or after 6 April 2015.
In s. 8(2), the words "Table" and "it replaces" substituted by FA 1986, Sch. 19, para. 3(3), in respect of transfers of value made, and other events occurring on or after 18 March 1986.
S. 8(3) substituted by FA 2012, s. 208(4), with effect for the purposes of chargeable transfers made on or after 6 April 2015. Former s. 8(3) to read as follows:
"8(3) The references in this section to the **"retail prices index"** are references to the general index of retail prices (for all items) published by the Statistics Board; and if that index is not published for a month of September those references shall be construed as references to any substituted index or index figures published by the Board."
In former s. 8(3), words "Statistics Board" substituted for the words "Office for National Statistics" and the words "the Board" substituted for the words "that Office" by Statistics and Registration Service Act 2007, s. 60 and Sch. 3, para. 3, with effect from 1 April 1998.
In former s. 8(3), reference to the Office for National Statistics substituted by SI 1996/273, with effect from 6 April 1996.
In former s. 8(3), the word "September" substituted by FA 1993, s. 197(1)(b) in relation to chargeable transfers made on or after 6 April 1994.
In s. 8(4), the word "Table" substituted by FA 1986, Sch. 19, para. 3(4), in respect of transfers of value made, and other events occurring, on or after 18 March 1986.
In s. 8(4), "1994" substituted by FA 1993, s. 197(1)(c), in relation to chargeable transfers made on or after 6 April 1994.

Cross references – FA 1986, Sch. 19, para. 40(1): transitional – transfer of value occurring before, and death or other event occurring after, 18 March 1986.
FA 1997, s. 93: s. 8 disapplied as respects any difference between the retail prices index for September 1995 and that for September 1996.
FA 2002, s. 118(2): s. 8(1) disapplied as respects any difference between the retail prices index for September 2000 and that for September 2001.
FA 2005, s. 98(6): s. 8(1) disapplied as respects any difference between the retail prices index for September 2003 and that for September 2004; for September 2004 and that for September 2005; and for September 2005 and that for September 2006.
FA 2010, s. 8(3): s. 8 disapplied as regards any difference between the retail prices index for the month of September in 2010, 2011, 2012 or 2013 and the previous September.
FA 2014, Sch. 25, para. 2: s. 8 disapplied as regards any difference between the consumer prices index for the month of September in 2014, 2015 or 2016 and the previous September.
F(No. 2)A 2015, s. 10: s. 8 disapplied as regards any difference between the consumer prices index for the month of September in 2017, 2018 or 2019 and the previous September.

8A Transfer of unused nil-rate band between spouses and civil partners

8A(1) This section applies where–

(a) immediately before the death of a person (a "deceased person"), the deceased person had a spouse or civil partner ("the survivor"), and

(b) the deceased person had unused nil-rate band on death.

8A(2) A person has unused nil-rate band on death if–

$$M > VT$$

where–

M is the maximum amount that could be transferred by a chargeable transfer made (under section 4 above) on the person's death if it were to be wholly chargeable to tax at the rate of nil per cent. (assuming, if necessary, that the value of the person's estate were sufficient but that the maximum amount chargeable at nil per cent. under section 8D(2) is equal to the person's residence nil-rate amount and otherwise having regard to the circumstances of the person); and

VT is the value actually transferred by the chargeable transfer so made (or nil if no chargeable transfer is so made).

8A(3) Where a claim is made under this section, the nil-rate band maximum at the time of the survivor's death is to be treated for the purposes of the charge to tax on the death of the survivor as increased by the percentage specified in subsection (4) below (but subject to subsection (5) and section 8C below).

8A(4) That percentage is–

$$\frac{E}{NRBMD} \times 100$$

where–

E is the amount by which M is greater than VT in the case of the deceased person; and

NRBMD is the nil-rate band maximum at the time of the deceased person's death.

8A(5) If (apart from this subsection) the amount of the increase in the nil-rate band maximum at the time of the survivor's death effected by this section would exceed the amount of that nil-rate band maximum, the amount of the increase is limited to the amount of that nil-rate band maximum.

8A(6) Subsection (5) above may apply either–

(a) because the percentage mentioned in subsection (4) above (as reduced under section 8C below where that section applies) is more than 100 because of the amount by which M is greater than VT in the case of one deceased person, or

(b) because this section applies in relation to the survivor by reference to the death of more than one person who had unused nil-rate band on death.

8A(7) In this Act **"nil-rate band maximum"** means the amount shown in the second column in the first row of the Table in Schedule 1 to this Act (upper limit of portion of value charged at rate of nil per cent.) and in the first column in the second row of that Table (lower limit of portion charged at next rate).

History – In s. 8A(2), in the definition of "M", the words "that the maximum amount chargeable at nil per cent. under section 8D(2) is equal to the person's residence nil-rate amount and" inserted by F(No. 2)A 2015, s. 9(3), with effect from 18 November 2015 (Royal Assent).

S. 8A inserted by FA 2008, s. 10 and Sch. 4, para. 2, with effect in relation to cases where the survivor's death occurs on or after 9 October 2007.

Cross references – FA 2008, Sch. 4, para. 10: modification of s. 8A where the deceased person died before 25 July 1986.

8B Claims under section 8A

8B(1) A claim under section 8A above may be made–

(a) by the personal representatives of the survivor within the permitted period, or

(b) (if no claim is so made) by any other person liable to the tax chargeable on the survivor's death within such later period as an officer of Revenue and Customs may in the particular case allow.

8B(2) If no claim under section 8A above has been made in relation to a person (P) by reference to whose death that section applies in relation to the survivor, the claim under that section in relation to the survivor may include a claim under that section in relation to P if that does not affect the tax chargeable on the value transferred by the chargeable transfer of value made on P's death.

8B(3) In subsection (1)(a) above **"the permitted period"** means–

(a) the period of two years from the end of the month in which the survivor dies or (if it ends later) the period of three months beginning with the date on which the personal representatives first act as such, or

(b) such longer period as an officer of Revenue and Customs may in the particular case allow.

8B(4) A claim made within either of the periods mentioned in subsection (3)(a) above may be withdrawn no later than one month after the end of the period concerned.

History – S. 8B inserted by FA 2008, s. 10 and Sch. 4, para. 2, with effect in relation to cases where the survivor's death occurs on or after 9 October 2007.

8C Section 8A and subsequent charges

8C(1) This section applies where–

(a) the conditions in subsection (1)(a) and (b) of section 8A above are met, and

(b) after the death of the deceased person, tax is charged on an amount under any of sections 32, 32A and 126 below by reference to the rate or rates that would have been applicable to the amount if it were included in the value transferred by the chargeable transfer made (under section 4 above) on the deceased person's death.

8C(2) If the tax is charged before the death of the survivor, the percentage referred to in subsection (3) of section 8A above is (instead of that specified in subsection (4) of that section)–

$$\left(\frac{E}{NRBMD} - \frac{TA}{NRBME}\right) \times 100$$

where–

E and NRBMD have the same meaning as in subsection (4) of that section;

TA is the amount on which tax is charged; and

NRBME is the nil-rate band maximum at the time of the event occasioning the charge.

8C(3) If this section has applied by reason of a previous event or events, the reference in subsection (2) to the fraction

$$\frac{TA}{NRBME}$$

is to the aggregate of that fraction in respect of the current event and the previous event (or each of the previous events).

8C(4) If the tax is charged after the death of the survivor, it is charged as if the personal nil-rate band maximum of the deceased person were appropriately reduced.

8C(5) In subsection (4) above–

"the personal nil-rate band maximum of the deceased person" is the nil rate band maximum which is treated by Schedule 2 to this Act as applying in relation to the deceased person's death, increased in accordance with section 8A above where that section effected an increase in that nil-rate band maximum in the case of the deceased person (as survivor of another deceased person), and

"appropriately reduced" means reduced by the amount (if any) by which the amount on which tax was charged at the rate of nil per cent. on the death of the survivor was increased by reason of the operation of section 8A above by virtue of the position of the deceased person.

History – S. 8C inserted by FA 2008, s. 10 and Sch. 4, para. 2, with effect in relation to cases where the survivor's death occurs on or after 9 October 2007.

Cross references – FA 2008, Sch. 4, para. 11: modification of s. 8C where the deceased person died before 25 July 1986.

8D Extra nil-rate band on death if interest in home goes to descendants etc

8D(1) Subsections (2) and (3) apply for the purpose of calculating the amount of the charge to tax under section 4 on a person's death if the person dies on or after 6 April 2017.

8D(2) If the person's residence nil-rate amount is greater than nil, the portion of VT that does not exceed the person's residence nil-rate amount is charged at the rate of 0%.

8D(3) References in section 7(1) to the value transferred by the chargeable transfer under section 4 on the person's death are to be read as references to the remainder (if any) of VT.

8D(4) The person's residence *nil-rate amount* is calculated in accordance with sections 8E to 8G (and see also section 8M).

8D(5) For the purposes of those sections and this section–

(a) the **"residential enhancement"** is–

(i) £100,000 for the tax year 2017–18,

(ii) £125,000 for the tax year 2018–19,
(iii) £150,000 for the tax year 2019–20, and
(iv) £175,000 for the tax year 2020–21 and subsequent tax years,
but this is subject to subsections (6) and (7),

(b) the **"taper threshold"** is £2,000,000 for the tax year 2017–18 and subsequent tax years, but this is subject to subsections (6) and (7),
(c) TT is the taper threshold at the person's death,
(d) E is the value of the person's estate immediately before the person's death,
(e) VT is the value transferred by the chargeable transfer under section 4 on the person's death,
(f) the person's **"default allowance"** is the total of–
(i) the residential enhancement at the person's death, and
(ii) the person's brought-forward allowance (see section 8G), and
(g) the person's **"adjusted allowance"** is–
(i) the person's default allowance, less
(ii) the amount given by–

$$\frac{E - TT}{2}$$

but is nil if that amount is greater than the person's default allowance.

8D(6) Subsection (7) applies if–
(a) the consumer prices index for the month of September in any tax year ("the prior tax year") is higher than it was for the previous September, and
(b) the prior tax year is the tax year 2020–21 or a later tax year.

8D(7) Unless Parliament otherwise determines, the amount of each of–
(a) the residential enhancement for the tax year following the prior tax year, and
(b) the taper threshold for that following tax year,

is its amount for the prior tax year increased by the same percentage as the percentage increase in the index and, if the result is not a multiple of £1,000, rounded up to the nearest amount which is such a multiple.

8D(8) The Treasury must before 6 April 2021 and each subsequent 6 April make an order specifying the amounts that in accordance with subsections (6) and (7) are the residential enhancement and taper threshold for the tax year beginning on that date; and any such order is to be made by statutory instrument.

8D(9) In this section–

"consumer prices index" means the all items consumer prices index published by the Statistics Board,

"tax year" means a year beginning on 6 April and ending on the following 5 April, and

"the tax year 2017–18" means the tax year beginning on 6 April 2017 (and any corresponding expression in which two years are similarly mentioned is to be read in the same way).

History – In s. 8D(4), the words "(and see also section 8M)" inserted by FA 2016, s. 93 and Sch. 15, para. 2(2), with effect from 15 September 2016 (Royal Assent).
In s. 8D(9), definition of "consumer prices index" inserted by FA 2016, s. 93 and Sch. 15, para. 2(3), with effect from 15 September 2016 (Royal Assent).
S. 8D inserted by F(No. 2)A 2015, s. 9(4), with effect from 18 November 2015 (Royal Assent).

8E Residence nil-rate amount: interest in home goes to descendants etc

8E(1) Subsections (2) to (7) apply if–
(a) the person's estate immediately before the person's death includes a qualifying residential interest, and
(b) N% of the interest is closely inherited, where N is a number–
(i) greater than 0, and
(ii) less than or equal to 100,

and in those subsections **"NV/100"** means N% of so much (if any) of the value transferred by the transfer of value under section 4 as is attributable to the interest.

8E(2) Where–
(a) E is less than or equal to TT, and
(b) NV/100 is less than the person's default allowance,

the person's residence nil-rate amount is equal to NV/100 and an amount, equal to the difference between NV/100 and the person's default allowance, is available for carry-forward.

8E(3) Where–

(a) E is less than or equal to TT, and

(b) NV/100 is greater than or equal to the person's default allowance,

the person's residence nil-rate amount is equal to the person's default allowance (and no amount is available for carry-forward).

8E(4) Where–

(a) E is greater than TT, and

(b) NV/100 is less than the person's adjusted allowance,

the person's residence nil-rate amount is equal to NV/100 and an amount, equal to the difference between NV/100 and the person's adjusted allowance, is available for carry-forward.

8E(5) Where–

(a) E is greater than TT, and

(b) NV/100 is greater than or equal to the person's adjusted allowance,

the person's residence nil-rate amount is equal to the person's adjusted allowance (and no amount is available for carry-forward).

8E(6) Subsections (2) to (5) have effect subject to subsection (7) and sections 8FC and 8M(2B) to (2E).

8E(7) Where the person's residence nil-rate amount as calculated under subsections (2) to (5) without applying this subsection is greater than VT–

(a) the person's residence nil-rate amount is equal to VT,

(b) where E is less than or equal to TT, an amount, equal to the difference between VT and the person's default allowance, is available for carry-forward, and

(c) where E is greater than TT, an amount, equal to the difference between VT and the person's adjusted allowance, is available for carry-forward.

8E(8) See also–

section 8FC (modifications of this section where there is entitlement to a downsizing addition),

section 8H (meaning of "qualifying residential interest", "qualifying former residential interest" and "residential property interest"),

section 8J (meaning of "inherit"),

section 8K (meaning of "closely inherited"), and

section 8M (cases involving conditional exemption).

History – In s. 8E(6), the words "and sections 8FC and 8M(2B) to (2E)" inserted by FA 2016, s. 93 and Sch. 15, para. 3(2), with effect from 15 September 2016 (Royal Assent).

S. 8E(7)(a)–(c) substituted for (a) and (b) by FA 2016, s. 93 and Sch. 15, para. 3(3), with effect from 15 September 2016 (Royal Assent). Former s. 8E(7)(a) and (b) read as follows:

"(a) subsections (2) to (5) have effect as if each reference in them to NV/100 were a reference to VT,

(b) each of subsections (3) and (5) has effect as if it provided that the person's residence nil-rate amount were equal to VT (rather than the person's default allowance or, as the case may be, the person's adjusted allowance)."

In s. 8E(8), entry for "section 8FC" inserted by FA 2016, s. 93 and Sch. 15, para. 3(4)(a), with effect from 15 September 2016 (Royal Assent).

In s. 8E(8), in the entry for "section 8H", the words ", "qualifying former residential interest" and "residential property interest"" inserted by FA 2016, s. 93 and Sch. 15, para. 3(4)(b), with effect from 15 September 2016 (Royal Assent).

S. 8E inserted by F(No. 2)A 2015, s. 9(4), with effect from 18 November 2015 (Royal Assent).

8F Residence nil-rate amount: no interest in home goes to descendants etc

8F(1) Subsections (2) and (3) apply if the person's estate immediately before the person's death–

(a) does not include a qualifying residential interest, or

(b) includes a qualifying residential interest but none of the interest is closely inherited.

8F(2) The person's residence nil-rate amount is nil.

8F(3) An amount–

(a) equal to the person's default allowance, or

(b) if E is greater than TT, equal to the person's adjusted allowance,

is available for carry-forward.

8F(4) See also–

section 8FD (which applies instead of this section where there is entitlement to a downsizing addition), section 8H (meaning of "qualifying residential interest", "qualifying former residential interest" and "residential property interest"),

section 8J (meaning of "inherit"),

section 8K (meaning of "closely inherited"), and

section 8M (cases involving conditional exemption).

History – In s. 8F(4), entry for "section 8FD" inserted by FA 2016, s. 93 and Sch. 15, para. 4(a), with effect from 15 September 2016 (Royal Assent).
In s. 8F(4), in the entry for "section 8H", the words ", "qualifying former residential interest" and "residential property interest"" inserted by FA 2016, s. 93 and Sch. 15, para. 4(b), with effect from 15 September 2016 (Royal Assent).
S. 8F inserted by F(No. 2)A 2015, s. 9(4), with effect from 18 November 2015 (Royal Assent).

8FA Downsizing addition: entitlement: low-value death interest in home

8FA(1) There is entitlement to a downsizing addition in calculating the person's residence nil-rate amount if each of conditions A to F is met (see subsection (8) for the amount of the addition).

8FA(2) Condition A is that–

(a) the person's residence nil-rate amount is given by section 8E(2) or (4), or

(b) the person's estate immediately before the person's death includes a qualifying residential interest but none of the interest is closely inherited, and–

(i) where E is less than or equal to TT, so much of VT as is attributable to the person's qualifying residential interest is less than the person's default allowance, or

(ii) where E is greater than TT, so much of VT as is attributable to the person's qualifying residential interest is less than the person's adjusted allowance.

Section 8E(6) and (7) do not apply, and any entitlement to a downsizing addition is to be ignored, when deciding whether paragraph (a) of condition A is met.

8FA(3) Condition B is that not all of VT is attributable to the person's qualifying residential interest.

8FA(4) Condition C is that there is a qualifying former residential interest in relation to the person (see sections 8H(4A) to (4F) and 8HA).

8FA(5) Condition D is that the value of the qualifying former residential interest exceeds so much of VT as is attributable to the person's qualifying residential interest.

Section 8FE(2) explains what is meant by the value of the qualifying former residential interest.

8FA(6) Condition E is that at least some of the remainder is closely inherited, where **"the remainder"** means everything included in the person's estate immediately before the person's death other than the person's qualifying residential interest.

8FA(7) Condition F is that a claim is made for the addition in accordance with section 8L(1) to (3).

8FA(8) Where there is entitlement as a result of this section, the addition–

(a) is equal to the lost relievable amount (see section 8FE) if that amount is less than so much of VT as is attributable to so much of the remainder as is closely inherited, and

(b) otherwise is equal to so much of VT as is attributable to so much of the remainder as is closely inherited.

8FA(9) Subsection (8) has effect subject to section 8M(2G) (reduction of downsizing addition in certain cases involving conditional exemption).

8FA(10) See also–

section 8FC (effect of an addition: section 8E case),

section 8FD (effect of an addition: section 8F case),

section 8H (meaning of "qualifying residential interest", "qualifying former residential interest" and "residential property interest"),

section 8J (meaning of "inherit"),

section 8K (meaning of "closely inherited"), and

section 8M (cases involving conditional exemption).

History – S. 8FA inserted by FA 2016, s. 93 and Sch. 15, para. 5, with effect from 15 September 2016 (Royal Assent).

8FB Downsizing addition: entitlement: no residential interest at death

8FB(1) There is also entitlement to a downsizing addition in calculating the person's residence nil-rate amount if each of conditions G to K is met (see subsection (7) for the amount of the addition).

8FB(2) Condition G is that the person's estate immediately before the person's death ("the estate") does not include a residential property interest.

8FB(3) Condition H is that VT is greater than nil.

8FB(4) Condition I is that there is a qualifying former residential interest in relation to the person (see sections 8H(4A) to (4F) and 8HA).

8FB(5) Condition J is that at least some of the estate is closely inherited.

8FB(6) Condition K is that a claim is made for the addition in accordance with section 8L(1) to (3).

8FB(7) Where there is entitlement as a result of this section, the addition–

(a) is equal to the lost relievable amount (see section 8FE) if that amount is less than so much of VT as is attributable to so much of the estate as is closely inherited, and

(b) otherwise is equal to so much of VT as is attributable to so much of the estate as is closely inherited.

8FB(8) Subsection (7) has effect subject to section 8M(2G) (reduction of downsizing addition in certain cases involving conditional exemption).

8FB(9) See also–

section 8FD (effect of an addition: section 8F case),

section 8H (meaning of "qualifying residential interest", "qualifying former residential interest" and "residential property interest"),

section 8J (meaning of "inherit"),

section 8K (meaning of "closely inherited"), and

section 8M (cases involving conditional exemption).

History – S. 8FB inserted by FA 2016, s. 93 and Sch. 15, para. 5, with effect from 15 September 2016 (Royal Assent).

8FC Downsizing addition: effect: section 8E case

8FC(1) Subsection (2) applies if–

(a) as a result of section 8FA, there is entitlement to a downsizing addition in calculating the person's residence nil-rate amount, and

(b) the person's residence nil-rate amount is given by section 8E.

8FC(2) Section 8E has effect as if, in subsections (2) to (5) of that section, each reference to NV/100 were a reference to the total of–

(a) NV/100, and

(b) the downsizing addition.

History – S. 8FC inserted by FA 2016, s. 93 and Sch. 15, para. 5, with effect from 15 September 2016 (Royal Assent).

8FD Downsizing addition: effect: section 8F case

8FD(1) This section applies if–

(a) as a result of section 8FA or 8FB, there is entitlement to a downsizing addition in calculating the person's residence nil-rate amount, and

(b) apart from this section, the person's residence nil-rate amount is given by section 8F.

8FD(2) Subsections (3) to (6) apply instead of section 8F.

8FD(3) The person's residence nil-rate amount is equal to the downsizing addition.

8FD(4) Where–

(a) E is less than or equal to TT, and the downsizing addition is equal to the person's default allowance, or

(b) E is greater than TT, and the downsizing addition is equal to the person's adjusted allowance,

no amount is available for carry-forward.

8FD(5) Where–

(a) E is less than or equal to TT, and

(b) the downsizing addition is less than the person's default allowance,

an amount, equal to the difference between the downsizing addition and the person's default allowance, is available for carry-forward.

8FD(6) Where–

(a) E is greater than TT, and

(b) the downsizing addition is less than the person's adjusted allowance,

an amount, equal to the difference between the downsizing addition and the person's adjusted allowance, is available for carry-forward.

History – S. 8FD inserted by FA 2016, s. 93 and Sch. 15, para. 5, with effect from 15 September 2016 (Royal Assent).

8FE Calculation of lost relievable amount

8FE(1) This section is about how to calculate the person's lost relievable amount for the purposes of sections 8FA(8) and 8FB(7).

8FE(2) For the purposes of this section and section 8FA(5), the value of the person's qualifying former residential interest is the value of the interest at the time of completion of the disposal of the interest.

8FE(3) In this section, the person's **"former allowance"** is the total of–

(a) the residential enhancement at the time of completion of the disposal of the qualifying former residential interest,

(b) any brought-forward allowance that the person would have had if the person had died at that time, having regard to the circumstances of the person at that time (see section 8G as applied by subsection (4)), and

(c) if the person's allowance on death includes an amount of brought-forward allowance which is greater than the amount of brought-forward allowance given by paragraph (b), the difference between those two amounts.

8FE(4) For the purposes of calculating any brought-forward allowance that the person ("P") would have had as mentioned in subsection (3)(b)–

(a) section 8G (brought-forward allowance) applies, but as if references to the residential enhancement at P's death were references to the residential enhancement at the time of completion of the disposal of the qualifying former residential interest, and

(b) assume that a claim for brought-forward allowance was made in relation to an amount available for carry-forward from a related person's death if, on P's death, a claim was in fact made in relation to the amount.

8FE(5) For the purposes of subsection (3)(c), where the person's allowance on death is equal to the person's adjusted allowance, the amount of brought-forward allowance included in the person's allowance on death is calculated as follows.

Step 1

Express the person's brought-forward allowance as a percentage of the person's default allowance.

Step 2

Multiply–

$$\frac{E - TT}{2}$$

by the percentage given by step 1.

Step 3

Reduce the person's brought-forward allowance by the amount given by step 2.

The result is the amount of brought-forward allowance included in the person's allowance on death.

8FE(6) If completion of the disposal of the qualifying former residential interest occurs before 6 April 2017–

(a) for the purposes of subsection (3)(a), the residential enhancement at the time of completion of the disposal is treated as being £100,000, and

(b) for the purposes of subsection (3)(b), the amount of brought-forward allowance that the person would have had at that time is treated as being nil.

8FE(7) In this section, the person's **"allowance on death"** means–

(a) where E is less than or equal to TT, the person's default allowance, or

(b) where E is greater than TT, the person's adjusted allowance.

8FE(8) For the purposes of this section, **"completion"** of the disposal of a residential property interest occurs at the time of the disposal or, if the disposal is under a contract which is completed by a conveyance, at the time when the interest is conveyed.

8FE(9) Where, as a result of section 8FA, there is entitlement to a downsizing addition in calculating the person's residence nil-rate amount, take the following steps to calculate the person's lost relievable amount.

Step 1

Express the value of the person's qualifying former residential interest as a percentage of the person's former allowance, but take that percentage to be 100% if it would otherwise be higher.

Step 2

Express QRI as a percentage of the person's allowance on death, where QRI is so much of VT as is attributable to the person's qualifying residential interest, but take that percentage to be 100% if it would otherwise be higher.

Step 3

Subtract the percentage given by step 2 from the percentage given by step 1, but take the result to be 0% if it would otherwise be negative. The result is P%.

Step 4

The person's lost relievable amount is equal to P% of the person's allowance on death.

8FE(10) Where, as a result of section 8FB, there is entitlement to a downsizing addition in calculating the person's residence nil-rate amount, take the following steps to calculate the person's lost relievable amount.

Step 1

Express the value of the person's qualifying former residential interest as a percentage of the person's former allowance, but take that percentage to be 100% if it would otherwise be higher.

Step 2

Calculate that percentage of the person's allowance on death.

The result is the person's lost relievable amount.

History – S. 8FE inserted by FA 2016, s. 93 and Sch. 15, para. 5, with effect from 15 September 2016 (Royal Assent).

8G Meaning of "brought-forward allowance"

8G(1) This section is about the amount of the brought-forward allowance (see section 8D(5)(f)) for a person ("P") who dies on or after 6 April 2017.

8G(2) In this section **"related person"** means a person other than P where–

(a) the other person dies before P, and

(b) immediately before the other person dies, P is the other person's spouse or civil partner.

8G(3) P's brought-forward allowance is calculated as follows–

(a) identify each amount available for carry-forward from the death of a related person (see sections 8E, 8F and 8FD, and subsections (4) and (5)),

(b) express each such amount as a percentage of the residential enhancement at the death of the related person concerned,

(c) calculate the percentage that is the total of those percentages, and

(d) the amount that is that total percentage of the residential enhancement at P's death is P's brought-forward allowance or, if that total percentage is greater than 100%, P's brought-forward allowance is the amount of the residential enhancement at P's death,

but P's brought-forward allowance is nil if no claim for it is made under section 8L.

8G(4) Where the death of a related person occurs before 6 April 2017–

(a) an amount equal to £100,000 is treated for the purposes of subsection (3) as being the amount available for carry-forward from the related person's death, but this is subject to subsection (5), and

(b) the residential enhancement at the related person's death is treated for those purposes as being £100,000.

8G(5) If the value ("RPE") of the related person's estate immediately before the related person's death is greater than £2,000,000, the amount treated under subsection (4)(a) as available for carry-forward is reduced (but not below nil) by–

$$\frac{RPE - £2{,}000{,}000}{2}$$

History – In s. 8G(3)(a), the words ", 8F and 8FD" substituted for the words "and 8F" by FA 2016, s. 93 and Sch. 15, para. 6, with effect from 15 September 2016 (Royal Assent).

S. 8G inserted by F(No. 2)A 2015, s. 9(4), with effect from 18 November 2015 (Royal Assent).

8H Meaning of "qualifying residential interest", "qualifying former residential interest" and "residential property interest"

History – In heading to s. 8H, the words ", "qualifying former residential interest" and "residential property interest"" inserted by FA 2016, s. 93 and Sch. 15, para. 7(2), with effect from 15 September 2016 (Royal Assent).

8H(1) This section applies for the purposes of sections 8E to 8FE and section 8M.

8H(2) A **"residential property interest"**, in relation to a person, means an interest in a dwelling-house which has been the person's residence at a time when the person's estate included that, or any other, interest in the dwelling-house.

8H(3) Where a person's estate immediately before the person's death includes residential property interests in just one dwelling-house, the person's interests in that dwelling-house are a qualifying residential interest in relation to the person.

8H(4) Where–

(a) a person's estate immediately before the person's death includes residential property interests in each of two or more dwelling-houses, and

(b) the person's personal representatives nominate one (and only one) of those dwelling-houses,

the person's interests in the nominated dwelling-house are a qualifying residential interest in relation to the person.

8H(4A) Subsection (4B) or (4C) applies where–

(a) a person disposes of a residential property interest in a dwelling-house on or after 8 July 2015 (and before the person dies), and

(b) the person's personal representatives nominate–

(i) where there is only one such dwelling-house, that dwelling-house, or

(ii) where there are two or more such dwelling-houses, one (and only one) of those dwelling-houses.

8H(4B) Where–

(a) the person–

(i) disposes of a residential property interest in the nominated dwelling-house at a post-occupation time, or

(ii) disposes of two or more residential property interests in the nominated dwelling-house at the same post-occupation time or at post-occupation times on the same day, and

(b) the person does not otherwise dispose of residential property interests in the nominated dwelling-house at post-occupation times,

the interest disposed of is, or the interests disposed of are, a qualifying former residential interest in relation to the person.

8H(4C) Where–

(a) the person disposes of residential property interests in the nominated dwelling-house at post-occupation times on two or more days, and

(b) the person's personal representatives nominate one (and only one) of those days,

the interest or interests disposed of at post-occupation times on the nominated day is or are a qualifying former residential interest in relation to the person.

8H(4D) For the purposes of subsections (4A) to (4C)–

(a) a person is to be treated as not disposing of a residential property interest in a dwelling-house where the person disposes of an interest in the dwelling-house by way of gift and the interest is, in relation to the gift and the donor, property subject to a reservation within the meaning of section 102 of the Finance Act 1986 (gifts with reservation), and

(b) a person is to be treated as disposing of a residential property interest in a dwelling-house if the person is treated as making a potentially exempt transfer of the interest as a result of the operation of section 102(4) of that Act (property ceasing to be subject to a reservation).

8H(4E) Where–

(a) a transfer of value by a person is a conditionally exempt transfer of a residential property interest, and

(b) at the time of the person's death, no chargeable event has occurred with respect to that interest,

that interest may not be, or be included in, a qualifying former residential interest in relation to the person.

8H(4F) In subsections (4B) and (4C) **"post-occupation time"** means a time–

(a) on or after 8 July 2015, and

(b) after the nominated dwelling-house first became the person's residence.

(c) before the person dies.

8H(4G) For the purposes of subsections (4A) to (4C), if the disposal is under a contract which is completed by a conveyance, the disposal occurs at the time when the interest is conveyed.

8H(5) A reference in this section to a dwelling-house–

(a) includes any land occupied and enjoyed with it as its garden or grounds, but

(b) does not include, in the case of any particular person, any trees or underwood in relation to which an election is made under section 125 as it applies in relation to that person's death.

8H(6) If at any time when a person's estate includes an interest in a dwelling-house, the person–

(a) resides in living accommodation which for the person is job-related, and

(b) intends in due course to occupy the dwelling-house as the person's residence,

this section applies as if the dwelling-house were at that time occupied by the person as a residence.

8H(7) Section 222(8A) to (8D) of the 1992 Act (meaning of "job-related"), but not section 222(9) of that Act, apply for the purposes of subsection (6).

History – In s. 8H(1), the words "to 8FE and section 8M" substituted for the words "and 8F" by FA 2016, s. 93 and Sch. 15, para. 7(3), with effect from 15 September 2016 (Royal Assent).

In s. 8H(2), the word "A" substituted for the words "In this section" by FA 2016, s. 93 and Sch. 15, para. 7(4), with effect from 15 September 2016 (Royal Assent).

S. 8H(4A)–(4G) inserted by FA 2016, s. 93 and Sch. 15, para. 7(5), with effect from 15 September 2016 (Royal Assent).

S. 8H inserted by F(No. 2)A 2015, s. 9(4), with effect from 18 November 2015 (Royal Assent).

8HA "Qualifying former residential interest": interests in possession

8HA(1) This section applies for the purposes of determining whether certain interests may be, or be included in, a qualifying former residential interest in relation to a person (see section 8H(4A) to (4C)).

8HA(2) This section applies where–

(a) a person ("P") is beneficially entitled to an interest in possession in settled property, and

(b) the settled property consists of, or includes, an interest in a dwelling-house.

8HA(3) Subsection (4) applies where–

(a) the trustees of the settlement dispose of the interest in the dwelling-house to a person other than P,

(b) P's interest in possession in the settled property subsists immediately before the disposal, and

(c) P's interest in possession–

(i) falls within subsection (7) throughout the period beginning with P becoming beneficially entitled to it and ending with the disposal, or

(ii) falls within subsection (8).

8HA(4) The disposal is to be treated as a disposal by P of the interest in the dwelling-house to which P is beneficially entitled as a result of the operation of section 49(1).

8HA(5) Subsection (6) applies where–

(a) P disposes of the interest in possession in the settled property, or P's interest in possession in the settled property comes to an end in P's lifetime,

(b) the interest in the dwelling-house is, or is part of, the settled property immediately before the time when that happens, and

(c) P's interest in possession–

(i) falls within subsection (7) throughout the period beginning with P becoming beneficially entitled to it and ending with the time mentioned in paragraph (b), or

(ii) falls within subsection (8).

8HA(6) The disposal, or (as the case may be) the coming to an end of P's interest in possession, is to be treated as a disposal by P of the interest in the dwelling-house to which P is beneficially entitled as a result of the operation of section 49(1).

8HA(7) An interest in possession falls within this subsection if–

(a) P became beneficially entitled to it before 22 March 2006 and section 71A does not apply to the settled property; or

(b) P becomes beneficially entitled to it on or after 22 March 2006 and the interest is–

(i) an immediate post-death interest,

(ii) a disabled person's interest, or

(iii) a transitional serial interest.

8HA(8) An interest in possession falls within this subsection if P becomes beneficially entitled to it on or after 22 March 2006 and it falls within section 5(1B).

History – S. 8HA inserted by FA 2016, s. 93 and Sch. 15, para. 8, with effect from 15 September 2016 (Royal Assent).

8J Meaning of "inherited"

8J(1) This section explains for the purposes of sections 8E, 8F, 8FA, 8FB and 8M whether a person ("B") inherits, from a person who has died ("D"), property which forms part of D's estate immediately before D's death.

8J(2) B inherits the property if there is a disposition of it (whether effected by will, under the law relating to intestacy or otherwise) to B.

8J(3) Subsection (2) does not apply if–

(a) the property becomes comprised in a settlement on D's death, or

(b) immediately before D's death, the property was settled property in which D was beneficially entitled to an interest in possession.

8J(4) Where the property becomes comprised in a settlement on D's death, B inherits the property if–

(a) B becomes beneficially entitled on D's death to an interest in possession in the property, and that interest in possession is an immediate post-death interest or a disabled person's interest, or

(b) the property becomes, on D's death, settled property–

(i) to which section 71A or 71D applies, and

(ii) held on trusts for the benefit of B.

8J(5) Where, immediately before D's death, the property was settled property in which D was beneficially entitled to in an interest in possession, B inherits the property if B becomes beneficially entitled to it on D's death.

8J(6) Where the property forms part of D's estate immediately before D's death as a result of the operation of section 102(3) of the Finance Act 1986 (gifts with reservation) in relation to a disposal of the property made by D by way of gift, B inherits the property if B is the person to whom the disposal was made.

History – In s. 8J(1), the words ", 8F, 8FA, 8FB and 8M" substituted for the words "and 8F" by FA 2016, s. 93 and Sch. 15, para. 9, with effect from 15 September 2016 (Royal Assent).
S. 8J inserted by F(No. 2)A 2015, s. 9(4), with effect from 18 November 2015 (Royal Assent).

8K Meaning of "closely inherited"

8K(1) In relation to the death of a person ("D"), something is **"closely inherited"** for the purposes of sections 8E, 8F, 8FA, 8FB and 8M if it is inherited for those purposes (see section 8J) by–

(a) a lineal descendant of D,

(b) a person who, at the time of D's death, is the spouse or civil partner of a lineal descendant of D, or

(c) a person who–

(i) at the time of the death of a lineal descendant of D who died no later than D, was the spouse or civil partner of the lineal descendant, and

(ii) has not, in the period beginning with the lineal descendant's death and ending with D's death, become anyone's spouse or civil partner.

8K(2) The rules in subsections (3) to (8) apply for the interpretation of subsection (1).

8K(3) A person who is at any time a step-child of another person is to be treated, at that and all subsequent times, as if the person was that other person's child.

8K(4) Any rule of law, so far as it requires an adopted person to be treated as not being the child of a natural parent of the person, is to be disregarded (but this is without prejudice to any rule of law requiring an adopted person to be treated as the child of an adopter of the person).

8K(5) A person who is at any time fostered by a foster parent is to be treated, at that and all subsequent times, as if the person was the foster parent's child.

8K(6) Where–

(a) an individual ("G") is appointed (or is treated by law as having been appointed) under section 5 of the Children Act 1989, or under corresponding law having effect in Scotland or Northern Ireland or any country or territory outside the United Kingdom, as guardian (however styled) of another person, and

(b) the appointment takes effect at a time when the other person ("C") is under the age of 18 years,

C is to be treated, at all times after the appointment takes effect, as if C was G's child.

8K(7) Where–

(a) an individual ("SG") is appointed as a special guardian (however styled) of another person ("C") by an order of a court–

(i) that is a special guardianship order as defined by section 14A of the Children Act 1989, or

IHT Statutes

(ii) that is a corresponding order under legislation having effect in Scotland or Northern Ireland or any country or territory outside the United Kingdom, and

(b) the appointment takes effect at a time when C is under the age of 18 years,

C is to be treated, at all times after the appointment takes effect, as if C was SG's child.

8K(8) In particular, where under any of subsections (3) to (7) one person is to be treated at any time as the child of another person, that first person's lineal descendants (even if born before that time) are accordingly to be treated at that time (and all subsequent times) as lineal descendants of that other person.

8K(9) In subsection (4) **"adopted person"** means–

(a) an adopted person within the meaning of Chapter 4 of Part 1 of the Adoption and Children Act 2002, or

(b) a person who would be an adopted person within the meaning of that Chapter if, in section 66(1)(e) of that Act and section 38(1)(e) of the Adoption Act 1976, the reference to the law of England and Wales were a reference to the law of any part of the United Kingdom.

8K(10) In subsection (5) **"foster parent"** means–

(a) someone who is approved as a local authority foster parent in accordance with regulations made by virtue of paragraph 12F of Schedule 2 to the Children Act 1989,

(b) a foster parent with whom the person is placed by a voluntary organisation under section 59(1)(a) of that Act,

(c) someone who looks after the person in circumstances in which the person is a privately fostered child as defined by section 66 of that Act, or

(d) someone who, under legislation having effect in Scotland or Northern Ireland or any country or territory outside the United Kingdom, is a foster parent (however styled) corresponding to a foster parent within paragraph (a) or (b).

History – In s. 8K(1), the words ", 8F, 8FA, 8FB and 8M" substituted for the words "and 8F" by FA 2016, s. 93 and Sch. 15, para. 10, with effect from 15 September 2016 (Royal Assent).
S. 8K inserted by F(No. 2)A 2015, s. 9(4), with effect from 18 November 2015 (Royal Assent).

8L Claims for brought-forward allowance and downsizing addition

History – In heading to s. 8L, the words "and downsizing addition" inserted by FA 2016, s. 93 and Sch. 15, para. 11(a), with effect from 15 September 2016 (Royal Assent).

8L(1) A claim for brought-forward allowance for a person (see section 8G) or for a downsizing addition for a person (see sections 8FA to 8FD) may be made–

(a) by the person's personal representatives within the permitted period, or

(b) (if no claim is so made) by any other person liable to the tax chargeable on the person's death within such later period as an officer of Revenue and Customs may in the particular case allow.

8L(2) In subsection (1)(a) **"the permitted period"** means–

(a) the period of 2 years from the end of the month in which the person dies or (if it ends later) the period of 3 months beginning with the date on which the personal representatives first act as such, or

(b) such longer period as an officer of Revenue and Customs may in the particular case allow.

8L(3) A claim under subsection (1) made within either of the periods mentioned in subsection (2)(a) may be withdrawn no later than one month after the end of the period concerned.

8L(4) Subsection (5) applies if–

(a) no claim under this section has been made for brought-forward allowance for a person ("P"),

(b) the amount of the charge to tax under section 4 on the death of another person ("A") would be different if a claim under subsection (1) had been made for brought-forward allowance for P, and

(c) the amount of the charge to tax under section 4 on the death of P, and the amount of the charge to tax under section 4 on the death of any person who is neither P nor A, would not have been different if a claim under subsection (1) had been made for brought-forward allowance for P.

8L(5) A claim for brought-forward allowance for P may be made–

(a) by A's personal representatives within the allowed period, or

(b) (if no claim is so made) by any other person liable to the tax chargeable on A's death within such later period as an officer of Revenue and Customs may in the particular case allow.

8L(6) In subsection (5)(a) **"the allowed period"** means–

(a) the period of 2 years from the end of the month in which A dies or (if it ends later) the period of 3 months beginning with the date on which the personal representatives first act as such, or

(b) such longer period as an officer of Revenue and Customs may in the particular case allow.

8L(7) A claim under subsection (5) made within either of the periods mentioned in subsection (6)(a) may be withdrawn no later than one month after the end of the period concerned.

History – In s. 8L(1), the words "or for a downsizing addition for a person (see sections 8FA to 8FD)" inserted by FA 2016, s. 93 and Sch. 15, para. 11(b), with effect from 15 September 2016 (Royal Assent).
S. 8L inserted by F(No. 2)A 2015, s. 9(4), with effect from 18 November 2015 (Royal Assent).

8M Residence nil-rate amount: cases involving conditional exemption

8M(1) This section applies where–

(a) a person ("D") dies on or after 6 April 2017,

(b) ignoring the application of this section, D's residence nil-rate amount is greater than nil, and

(c) some or all of the transfer of value under section 4 on D's death is a conditionally exempt transfer of property consisting of, or including, any of the following–

(i) some or all of a qualifying residential interest;

(ii) some or all of a residential property interest, at least some portion of which is closely inherited, and which is not, and is not included in, a qualifying residential interest;

(iii) one or more closely inherited assets that are not residential property interests.

8M(2) Subsections (2B) to (2E) apply for the purposes of sections 8E to 8FD if–

(a) ignoring the application of this section, D's residence nil-rate amount is given by section 8E, and

(b) some or all of the transfer of value under section 4 is a conditionally exempt transfer of property mentioned in subsection (1)(c)(i).

8M(2A) In subsections (2B) to (2E), but subject to subsection (3)(a), **"the exempt percentage of the QRI"** is given by–

$$\frac{X}{QRI} \times 100$$

where–

X is the attributable portion of the value transferred by the conditionally exempt transfer,

QRI is the attributable portion of the value transferred by the transfer of value under section 4, and

"the attributable portion" means the portion (which may be the whole) attributable to the qualifying residential interest.

8M(2B) If–

(a) the exempt percentage of the QRI is 100%, and

(b) D has no entitlement to a downsizing addition,

D's residence nil-rate amount and amount available for carry-forward are given by section 8F(2) and (3) (instead of section 8E).

8M(2C) If–

(a) the exempt percentage of the QRI is 100%, and

(b) D has an entitlement to a downsizing addition,

D's residence nil-rate amount and amount available for carry-forward are given by section 8FD(3) to (6) (instead of section 8E as modified by section 8FC(2)).

See also subsection (2G).

8M(2D) If–

(a) the exempt percentage of the QRI is less than 100%, and

(b) D has no entitlement to a downsizing addition,

D's residence nil-rate amount and amount available for carry-forward are given by section 8E but as if, in subsections (2) to (5) of that section, each reference to NV/100 were a reference to NV/100 multiplied by the percentage that is the difference between 100% and the exempt percentage of the QRI.

8M(2E) If–

(a) the exempt percentage of the QRI is less than 100%, and

(b) D has an entitlement to a downsizing addition,

D's residence nil-rate amount and amount available for carry-forward are given by section 8E as modified by section 8FC(2), but as if the reference to NV/100 in section 8FC(2)(a) were a reference to NV/100 multiplied by the percentage that is the difference between 100% and the exempt percentage of the QRI.

See also subsection (2G).

8M(2F) Subsection (2G) applies for the purposes of sections 8FA to 8FD if–

(a) some or all of the transfer of value under section 4 is a conditionally exempt transfer of property mentioned in subsection (1)(c)(ii) or (iii) (or both),

(b) D has an entitlement to a downsizing addition, and

(c) DA exceeds Y (see subsection (2H)).

8M(2G) Subject to subsection (3)(aa) and (ab), the amount of the downsizing addition is treated as reduced by whichever is the smaller of–

(a) the difference between DA and Y, and

(b) Z.

8M(2H) In subsections (2F) and (2G)–

DA is the amount of the downsizing addition to which D has an entitlement (ignoring the application of subsection (2G));

Y is so much (if any) of the value transferred by the transfer of value under section 4 as–

(a) is not transferred by a conditionally exempt transfer, and

(b) is attributable to–

(i) the closely inherited portion (which may be the whole) of any residential property interests that are not, and are not included in, a qualifying residential interest, or

(ii) closely inherited assets that are not residential property interests;

Z is the total of–

(a) the closely inherited conditionally exempt values of all residential property interests mentioned in subsection (1)(c)(ii), and

(b) so much of the value transferred by the conditionally exempt transfer as is attributable to property mentioned in subsection (1)(c)(iii).

8M(2I) For the purposes of the definition of "Z", **"the closely inherited conditionally exempt value"** of a residential property interest means–

(a) so much of the value transferred by the conditionally exempt transfer as is attributable to the interest, multiplied by

(b) the percentage of the interest which is closely inherited.

8M(3) For the purposes of calculating tax chargeable under section 32 or 32A by reference to a chargeable event related to property forming the subject-matter of the conditionally exempt transfer where D is the relevant person for the purposes of section 33–

(a) where subsections (2B) to (2E) apply and the chargeable event relates to property mentioned in subsection (1)(c)(i), in calculating the exempt percentage of the QRI, X is calculated as if the attributable portion of the value transferred by the conditionally exempt transfer had not included the portion (which may be the whole) of the qualifying residential interest on which the tax is chargeable,

(aa) where subsection (2G) applies and the chargeable event relates to property mentioned in subsection (1)(c)(ii), Z is calculated as if it had not included the portion (which may be the whole) of the closely inherited conditionally exempt value of the residential property interest on which the tax is chargeable,

(ab) where subsection (2G) applies and the chargeable event relates to an asset mentioned in subsection (1)(c)(iii) ("the taxable asset"), Z is calculated as if it had not included so much of the value transferred by the conditionally exempt transfer as is attributable to the taxable asset,

(b) in the cases mentioned in paragraphs (a), (aa) and (ab), section 33 has effect as if for subsection (1)(b)(ii) there were substituted–

"(ii) if the relevant person is dead, the rate or rates that would have applied to that amount in accordance with section 8D(2) and (3) above and the appropriate provision of section 7 above if–

(a) that amount had been added to the value transferred on the relevant person's death, and

(b) the unrelieved portion of that amount had formed the highest part of that value."

(c) for the purposes of that substituted section 33(1)(b)(ii) **"the unrelieved portion"** of the amount on which tax is chargeable is that amount itself reduced (but not below nil) by the amount (if any) by which–

(i) D's residence nil-rate amount for the purposes of the particular calculation under section 33, exceeds

(ii) D's residence nil-rate amount for the purposes of the charge to tax under section 4 on D's death, and

(d) where the chargeable event relates to property mentioned in subsection (1)(c)(i) and subsections (2B) to (2E) do not apply, section 33 has effect as if in subsection (1)(b)(ii) after "in accordance with" there were inserted "section 8D(2) and (3) above and".

8M(4) The following provisions of this section apply if immediately before D's death there is a person ("P") who is D's spouse or civil partner.

8M(5) For the purposes of calculating tax chargeable under section 32 or 32A by reference to a chargeable event related to property which forms the subject-matter of the conditionally exempt transfer where the chargeable event occurs after P's death, the amount that would otherwise be D's residence nil-rate amount for those purposes is reduced by the amount (if any) by which P's residence nil-rate amount, or the residence nil-rate amount of any person who dies after P but before the chargeable event occurs, was increased by reason of an amount being available for carry-forward from D's death.

8M(6) Where tax is chargeable under section 32 or 32A by reference to a chargeable event related to property which forms the subject-matter of the conditionally exempt transfer and the chargeable event occurs before P's death, section 8G(3) has effect for the purpose of calculating P's brought-forward allowance as if–

(a) before the "and" at the end of paragraph (c) there were inserted–

"(ca) reduce that total (but not below nil) by deducting from it the recapture percentage,",

(b) in paragraph (d), before "total", in both places, there were inserted "reduced", and

(c) the reference to the recapture percentage were to the percentage given by–

$$\frac{TA}{REE} \times 100$$

where–

REE is the residential enhancement at the time of the chargeable event, and

TA is the amount on which tax is chargeable under section 32 or 32A.

8M(7) If subsection (6) has applied by reason of a previous event or events related to property which forms the subject-matter of the conditionally exempt transfer, the reference in subsection (6)(c) to the fraction–

$$\frac{TA}{REE}$$

is to the aggregate of that fraction in respect of the current event and the previous event (or each of the previous events).

History – S. 8M(1)–(2I) substituted for s. 8M(1) and (2) by FA 2016, s. 93 and Sch. 15, para. 12(2), with effect from 15 September 2016 (Royal Assent). Former s. 8M(1) and (2) read as follows:

"**8M(1)** This section applies where–

(a) the estate of a person ("D") immediately before D's death includes a qualifying residential interest,

(b) D dies on or after 6 April 2017, and

(c) some or all of the transfer of value under section 4 on D's death is a conditionally exempt transfer of property consisting of, or including, some or all of the qualifying residential interest.

8M(2) For the purposes of sections 8E and 8F, but subject to subsection (3), the exempt percentage of the qualifying residential interest is treated as being not closely inherited; and for this purpose **"the exempt percentage"** is given by–

$$\frac{X}{QRI} \times 100$$

where–

X is the attributable portion of the value transferred by the conditionally exempt transfer,

QRI is the attributable portion of the value transferred by the transfer under section 4, and

"the attributable portion" means the portion (which may be the whole) attributable to the qualifying residential interest."

S. 8M(3)(a)–(ab) and words before (a) substituted for para. (a) (and words before para. (a)) by FA 2016, s. 93 and Sch. 15, para. 12(3), with effect from 15 September 2016 (Royal Assent). The former para. (a) and the words before it read as follows:

"For the purposes of calculating tax chargeable under section 32 or 32A by reference to a chargeable event related to the qualifying residential interest where D is the relevant person for the purposes of section 33–

(a) in subsection (2), X is calculated as if the property forming the subject-matter of the conditionally exempt transfer had not included the property on which the tax is chargeable,"

In s. 8M(3)(b), the words "in the cases mentioned in paragraphs (a), (aa) and (ab)," inserted by FA 2016, s. 93 and Sch. 15, para. 12(4)(a), with effect from 15 September 2016 (Royal Assent).

In s. 8M(3)(c), the words "reduced (but not below nil) by" substituted for the word "less" by FA 2016, s. 93 and Sch. 15, para. 12(4)(c), with effect from 15 September 2016 (Royal Assent).

S. 8M(3)(c) (and the ", and" before it) inserted (and the "and" after (b) omitted) by FA 2016, s. 93 and Sch. 15, para. 12(4), with effect from 15 September 2016 (Royal Assent).

In s. 8M(5), the words "property which forms the subject-matter of the conditionally exempt transfer where the chargeable event" substituted for the words "the qualifying residential interest which" by FA 2016, s. 93 and Sch. 15, para. 12(5), with effect from 15 September 2016 (Royal Assent).

In s. 8M(6), the words "property which forms the subject-matter of the conditionally exempt transfer and the chargeable event" substituted for the words "the qualifying residential interest which" by FA 2016, s. 93 and Sch. 15, para. 12(6), with effect from 15 September 2016 (Royal Assent).

In s. 8M(7), the words "property which forms the subject-matter of the conditionally exempt transfer" substituted for the words "the qualifying residential interest" by FA 2016, s. 93 and Sch. 15, para. 12(7), with effect from 15 September 2016 (Royal Assent).

S. 8M inserted by F(No. 2)A 2015, s. 9(4), with effect from 18 November 2015 (Royal Assent).

9 Transitional provisions on reduction of tax

9 The transitional provisions in Schedule 2 to this Act shall have effect in relation to any enactment by virtue of which tax is reduced by the substitution of a new Table in Schedule 1.

History – The words "a new Table" were substituted by FA 1986, s. 101 and Sch. 19, para. 4, with respect to transfers of value made, and other events occurring, on or after 18 March 1986.

Cross references – FA 1986, Sch. 19, para. 40(1): transitional – transfer of value occurring before, and death or other event occurring after, 18 March 1986.

DISPOSITIONS THAT ARE NOT TRANSFERS OF VALUE (AND OMISSIONS THAT DO NOT GIVE RISE TO DEEMED DISPOSITIONS)

History – In heading before s. 10, the words "(and omissions that do not give rise to deemed dispositions)" inserted by FA 2016, s. 94(2), with effect from 15 September 2016 (Royal Assent).

10 Dispositions not intended to confer gratuitous benefit

10(1) A disposition is not a transfer of value if it is shown that it was not intended, and was not made in a transaction intended, to confer any gratuitous benefit on any person and either–

(a) that it was made in a transaction at arm's length between persons not connected with each other, or

(b) that it was such as might be expected to be made in a transaction at arm's length between persons not connected with each other.

10(2) Subsection (1) above shall not apply to a sale of unquoted shares or unquoted debentures unless it is shown that the sale was at a price freely negotiated at the time of the sale or at a price such as might be expected to have been freely negotiated at the time of the sale.

10(3) In this section–

"disposition" includes anything treated as a disposition by virtue of section 3(3) above;

"transaction" includes a series of transactions and any associated operations.

History – In s. 10(2), the words "unquoted shares or unquoted debentures" substituted by FA 1987, Sch. 8, para. 1, in relation to transfers of value made, and other events occurring, on or after 17 March 1987.

Cross references – S. 55(2): s. 10(1) does not apply when a reversionary interest in settled property is acquired by a person with an interest in possession in that property.

S. 55A(1): s. 10(1) does not apply where a person makes a disposition as a result of which that person acquires a settlement power for consideration in money or money's worth.

S. 65(6): application of s. 10 where discretionary trustees make a disposition as a result of which the value of settled property is reduced.

S. 70(4): application of s. 10 to property leaving temporary charitable trusts.

Extra-statutory concessions – F10: partnership assurance policies.

Statements of practice – E14: pools etc. syndicates.

E15: close companies – dividends paid by subsidiary to parent; group transfers.

Other material – HMRC Brief 18/11: HMRC view on IHT position in relation to contributions to Employee Benefit Trusts: meeting the tests in s. 10.

IR press release, 6 January 1976 (not reproduced): payments to employees under accident insurance schemes do not constitute a transfer of value if employer and employee are at arm's length and not connected with each other and there is no intention to confer a gratuitous benefit.

11 Dispositions for maintenance of family

11(1) A disposition is not a transfer of value if it is made by one party to a marriage or civil partnership in favour of the other party or of a child of either party and is–

(a) for the maintenance of the other party, or

(b) for the maintenance, education or training of the child for a period ending not later than the year in which he attains the age of eighteen or, after attaining that age, ceases to undergo full-time education or training.

11(2) A disposition is not a transfer of value if it is made in favour of a child who is not in the care of a parent of his and is for his maintenance, education or training for a period ending not later than the year in which–

(a) he attains the age of eighteen, or

(b) after attaining that age he ceases to undergo full-time education or training;

but paragraph (b) above applies only if before attaining that age the child has for substantial periods been *in the care of the person making* the disposition.

11(3) A disposition is not a transfer of value if it is made in favour of a dependent relative of the person making the disposition and is a reasonable provision for his care or maintenance.

11(4) A disposition is not a transfer of value if it is made in favour of an illegitimate child of the person making the disposition and is for the maintenance, education or training of the child for a period ending not later than the year in which he attains the age of eighteen or, after attaining that age, ceases to undergo full-time education or training.

11(5) Where a disposition satisfies the conditions of the preceding provisions of this section to a limited extent only, so much of it as satisfies them and so much of it as does not satisfy them shall be treated as separate dispositions.

11(6) In this section–

"child" includes a step-child and an adopted child and **"parent"** shall be construed accordingly;

"civil partnership", in relation to a disposition made on the occasion of the dissolution or annulment of a civil partnership, and in relation to a disposition varying a disposition so made, includes a former civil partnership;

"dependent relative" means, in relation to any person–

(a) a relative of his, or of his spouse or civil partner, who is incapacitated by old age or infirmity from maintaining himself, or

(b) his mother or father or his spouse's or civil partner's mother or father;

"marriage", in relation to a disposition made on the occasion of the dissolution or annulment of a marriage, and in relation to a disposition varying a disposition so made, includes a former marriage;

"year" means period of twelve months ending with 5th April.

History – In s. 11(1) the words "or civil partnership" inserted by SI 2005/3229, reg. 4(2), with effect from 5 December 2005.

In s. 11(6), in the definition of "dependent relative", the words "or civil partner" inserted by SI 2005/3229, reg. 4(3)(a)(i), with effect from 5 December 2005.

In s. 11(6), in the definition of "dependent relative", para. (b) substituted by SI 2005/3229, reg. 4(3)(a)(ii), with effect in relation to dispositions made on or after 5 December 2005. Former s. 11(6)(b) read as follows

"(b) his mother or his spouse's mother, if she is widowed, or living apart from her husband, or a single woman in consequence of dissolution or annulment of marriage;"

In s. 11(6) the definition of "civil partnership" inserted by SI 2005/3229, reg. 4(3)(b), with effect from 5 December 2005.

Cross references – Civil Partnership Act 2004, Sch. 21, para. 54: references to an individual's stepchildren to include references to children of that individual's civil partner; in force from 5 December 2005.

FA 2004, Sch. 15, para. 10(1)(d), (2)(d): charge to income tax on benefits received by former owner of property, for 2005–06 onwards.

Extra-statutory concessions – F12 (to be withdrawn with effect from April 2015): disposition by a child in favour of his unmarried mother (s. 11(3)).

Other material – Taxline 2005/1 (not reproduced): these sections can now work together to the effect that dispositions onto a disabled trust are not transfers of value provided they fulfil the requirements of both sections and subject to the condition that provisions are "reasonable" (it was held that a transfer of £100,000 was reasonable).

12 Dispositions allowable for income tax or conferring retirement benefits

12(1) A disposition made by any person is not a transfer of value if it is allowable in computing that person's profits or gains for the purposes of income tax or corporation tax or would be so allowable if those profits or gains were sufficient and fell to be so computed.

12(2) Without prejudice to subsection (1) above, a disposition made by any person is not a transfer of value if it is a contribution under a registered pension scheme, a qualifying non-UK pension scheme or a section 615(3) scheme in respect of an employee of the person making the disposition.

12(2ZA) Where a person who is a member of a registered pension scheme, a qualifying non-UK pension scheme or a section 615(3) scheme omits to exercise pension rights under the pension scheme, section 3(3) above does not apply in relation to the omission.

12(2A) [Omitted by FA 2011, s. 65 and Sch. 16, para. 47(3).]

12(2B) [Omitted by FA 2011, s. 65 and Sch. 16, para. 47(3).]

12(2C) [Omitted by FA 2011, s. 65 and Sch. 16, para. 47(3).]

12(2D) [Omitted by FA 2011, s. 65 and Sch. 16, para. 47(3).]

12(2E) [Omitted by FA 2011, s. 65 and Sch. 16, para. 47(3).]

12(2F) For the purposes of this section–

(a) a person omits to exercise pension rights under a pension scheme if he does not become entitled to the whole or any part of a pension or lump sum (or both) under the pension scheme at a time when he was eligible to become so entitled (whether or not he does become entitled to any other benefits under the pension scheme);

(b) [omitted by FA 2011, s. 65 and Sch. 16, para. 50(2).]

12(2G) In this section–

"entitled" in relation to a pension or lump sum shall be construed in accordance with section 165(3) or 167(1A), or section 166(2), of the Finance Act 2004;

"pension" has the same meaning as in Part 4 of that Act (see section 165(2) of that Act);

and, in the sidenote, for "retirement benefits" substitute "benefits under pension scheme"

12(3) [Omitted by FA 2004, s. 203(2)(b) and repealed by FA 2004, s. 326 and Sch. 42, Pt. 3.]

12(4) [Omitted by FA 2004, s. 203(2)(b) and repealed by FA 2004, s. 326 and Sch. 42, Pt. 3.]

12(5) Where a disposition satisfies the conditions of the preceding provisions of this section to a limited extent only, so much of it as satisfies them and so much of it as does not satisfy them shall be treated as separate dispositions.

History – In s. 12(2) the words ", a qualifying non-UK pension scheme or a" substituted for the word "or" by FA 2008, s. 92 and Sch. 29, para. 18(2), with effect from 6 April 2006.

In s. 12(2) the words "it is a contribution under a registered pension scheme or section 615(3) scheme in respect of an employee of the person making the disposition." substituted by FA 2004, s. 203(2)(a) with effect from 6 April 2006 (FA 2004, s. 284(1)).

In former s. 12(2)(b)(ii) the words "or surviving civil partner" inserted by SI 2005/3229, reg. 5, with effect from 5 December 2005.

Former s. 12(2)(c) inserted by F(No. 2)A 1987, s. 98(2); and see ICTA 1988, Sch. 29, para. 32 for substitution of references to that Act.

S. 12(2ZA) inserted by FA 2011, s. 65 and Sch. 16, para. 47(2), with effect in relation to dispositions made (or treated as made) on or after 6 April 2011.

S. 12(2A)–(2E) omitted by FA 2011, s. 65 and Sch. 16, para. 47(3), with effect in relation to dispositions made (or treated as made) on or after 6 April 2011.

S. 12(2F)(b), and the "and" before it, omitted by FA 2011, s. 65 and Sch. 16, para. 50(2), with effect in relation to dispositions made (or treated as made) on or after 6 April 2011.

In s. 12(2G), in the definition of "entitled", the words "167(1A), or section 166(2)," substituted for "166(2)" by FA 2016, s. 94(3), with effect from 15 September 2016 (Royal Assent).

In s. 12(2G), the definitions of "lump sum death benefit", "pension death benefit" and "relevant dependant" omitted by FA 2011, s. 65 and Sch. 16, para. 50(3)(a), with effect in relation to dispositions made (or treated as made) on or after 6 April 2011.

In s. 12(2G), in the definition of "pension", the words "Part 4" substituted for the words "that Part" by FA 2011, s. 65 and Sch. 16, para. 50(3)(b), with effect in relation to dispositions made (or treated as made) on or after 6 April 2011.

S. 12(2A)–(2G) inserted by FA 2006, s. 160 and Sch. 22, para. 2, with effect from 6 April 2006, subject to the transitional provision at FA 2006, Sch. 22), para. 12.

S. 12(3) omitted by FA 2004, s. 203(2)(b) and repealed by FA 2004, s. 326 and Sch. 42, Pt. 3 with effect from 6 April 2006 (FA 2004, s. 284(1)).

Other material – HMRC Brief 18/11: HMRC view on IHT position in relation to contributions to Employee Benefit Trusts: meeting the tests in s. 12.

12A Pension drawdown fund not used up: no deemed disposition

12A(1) Where a person has a drawdown fund, section 3(3) above does not apply in relation to any omission that results in the fund not being used up in the person's lifetime.

12A(2) For the purposes of subsection (1) above, a person has a drawdown fund if the person has–

(a) a member's drawdown pension fund,

(b) a member's flexi-access drawdown fund,

(c) a dependant's drawdown pension fund,

(d) a dependant's flexi-access drawdown fund,

(e) a nominee's flexi-access drawdown fund, or

(f) a successor's flexi-access drawdown fund, and

in respect of a money purchase arrangement under a registered pension scheme.

12A(3) For the purposes of subsection (1) above, a person also has a drawdown fund if sums or assets held for the purposes of a money purchase arrangement under a corresponding scheme would, if that scheme were a registered pension scheme, be the person's–

(a) member's drawdown pension fund,

(b) member's flexi-access drawdown fund,

(c) dependant's drawdown pension fund,

(d) dependant's flexi-access drawdown fund,

(e) nominee's flexi-access drawdown fund, or

(f) successor's flexi-access drawdown fund,

in respect of the arrangement.

12A(4) In this section–

"corresponding scheme" *means*–

(a) a qualifying non-UK pension scheme (see section 271A below), or

(b) a section 615(3) scheme that is not a registered pension scheme;

"money purchase arrangement" has the same meaning as in Part 4 of the Finance Act 2004 (see section 152 of that Act);

"member's drawdown pension fund", **"member's flexi-access drawdown fund"**, **"dependant's drawdown pension fund"**, **"dependant's flexi-access drawdown fund"**, **"nominee's flexi-access drawdown fund"** and **"successor's flexi-access drawdown fund"** have the meaning given, respectively, by paragraphs 8, 8A, 22, 22A, 27E and 27K of Schedule 28 to that Act.

History – S. 12A inserted by FA 2016, s. 94(4), with effect: (a) in relation to funds within s. 12A(2)(a) or (c), or a fund within 12A(3) that corresponds to such a fund, as having come into force on 6 April 2011, where the person who has the fund dies on or after 6 April 2011; and (b) in relation to funds within s. 12A(2)(b), (d), (e) or (f), or a fund within 12A(3) that corresponds to such a fund, as having come into force on 6 April 2015, where the person who has the fund dies on or after 6 April 2015.

Cross references – FA 2016, s. 94(6): where a repayment of inheritance tax or interest on inheritance tax arises as a result of the insertion of s. 12A, IHTA 1984, s. 241(1) applies as if the last date for making a claim for repayment of the amount were 5 April 2020 if that is later than what would otherwise be the last date for that purpose.

13 Dispositions by close companies for benefit of employees

13(1) A disposition of property made to trustees by a close company whereby the property is to be held on trusts of the description specified in section 86(1) below is not a transfer of value if the persons for whose benefit the trusts permit the property to be applied include all or most of either–

(a) the persons employed by or holding office with the company, or

(b) the persons employed by or holding office with the company or any one or more subsidiaries of the company.

13(2) Subsection (1) above shall not apply if the trusts permit any of the property to be applied at any time (whether during any such period as is referred to in section 86(1) below or later) for the benefit of–

(a) a person who is a participator in the company making the disposition, or

(b) any other person who is a participator in any close company that has made a disposition whereby property became comprised in the same settlement, being a disposition which but for this section would have been a transfer of value, or

(c) any other person who has been a participator in any such company as is mentioned in paragraph (a) or (b) above at any time after, or during the ten years before, the disposition made by that company, or

(d) any person who is connected with any person within paragraph (a), (b) or (c) above.

13(3) The participators in a company who are referred to in subsection (2) above do not include any participator who–

(a) is not beneficially entitled to, or to rights entitling him to acquire, 5 per cent or more of, or of any class of the shares comprised in, its issued share capital, and

(b) on a winding-up of the company would not be entitled to 5 per cent or more of its assets.

13(4) In determining whether the trusts permit property to be applied as mentioned in subsection (2) above, no account shall be taken–

(a) of any power to make a payment which is the income of any person for any of the purposes of income tax, or would be the income for any of those purposes of a person not resident in the United Kingdom if he were so resident, or

(b) if the trusts are those of a profit sharing scheme approved under Schedule 9 to the Taxes Act 1988, of any power to appropriate shares in pursuance of the scheme, or

(c) if the trusts are those of a share incentive plan approved under Schedule 2 to the Income Tax (Earnings and Pensions) Act 2003, of any power to appropriate shares to, or acquire shares on behalf of, individuals under the plan.

13(5) In this section–

"close company" and **"participator"** have the same meanings as in Part IV of this Act;

"ordinary shares" means shares which carry either–

(a) a right to dividends not restricted to dividends at a fixed rate, or

(b) a right to conversion into shares carrying such a right as is mentioned in paragraph (a) above;

"subsidiary" has the meaning given by section 1159 of and Schedule 6 to the Companies Act 2006;

and references in subsections (2) and (3) above to a **participator in a company** shall, in the case of a company which is not a close company, be construed as references to a person who would be a participator in the company if it were a close company.

History – In s. 13(4)(c), the words "a share incentive plan approved under Schedule 2 to the Income Tax (Earnings and Pensions) Act 2003" substituted for the words "an employee share ownership plan approved under Schedule 8 to the Finance Act 2000" by ITEPA 2003, Sch. 6, para. 151(1)(a) and para. 151(2) which have effect for the tax year 2003–04 and subsequent tax years.

S. 13(4)(c) inserted by FA 2000, s. 138(2).

In s. 13(4), reference to ICTA 1988 substituted by Sch. 29, para. 32 of that Act.

In s. 13(5), in the definition of "subsidiary", the words "1159 of and Schedule 6 to" substituted for the words "736 of", and "2006" substituted for "1985", by SI 2009/1890, art. 4(1)(f), with effect from 1 October 2009.

In s. 13(5), the words "the meaning given by section 736 of" were substituted for the former words "the same meaning as in" by Companies Act 1989, s. 144(4) and Sch. 18, para. 30(1), (2), with effect from 1 November 1990. The reference to Companies Act 1985 substituted by Companies Consolidation (Consequential Provisions) Act 1985.

Cross references – S. 86(1): certain employee benefit trusts.

TCGA 1992, s. 239: deemed no gain, no loss for the purposes of tax on chargeable gains on certain disposals within s. 13.

Statements of practice – E11: application of s. 13(1) where employees of a subsidiary company are included in the trust.

Other material – HMRC Brief 18/11: HMRC view on IHT position in relation to contributions to Employee Benefit Trusts made by close companies.

13A Dispositions by close companies to employee-ownership trusts

13A(1) A disposition of property made to trustees by a close company ("C") whereby the property is to be held on trusts of the description specified in section 86(1) is not a transfer of value if–

(a) C meets the trading requirement,

(b) the trusts are of a settlement which meets the all-employee benefit requirement, and

(c) the settlement does not meet the controlling interest requirement immediately before the beginning of the tax year in which the disposition of property occurs but does meet it at the end of that year.

13A(2) Sections 236I, 236J, 236K, 236M and 236T (but not 236L) of the 1992 Act apply to determine whether–

(a) C meets the trading requirement;

(b) the settlement meets the all-employee benefit requirement;

(c) the settlement meets the controlling interest requirement;

with references in those sections to "C" being read accordingly.

13A(3) In this section–

"close company" has the same meaning as in Part 4 of this Act;

"tax year" means a year beginning on 6 April and ending on the following 5 April.

History – S. 13A inserted by FA 2014, s. 290 and Sch. 37, para. 10(1), with effect in relation to dispositions of property made on or after 6 April 2014.

14 Waiver of remuneration

14(1) Subject to subsection (2) below, the waiver or repayment of an amount of remuneration is not a transfer of value if, apart from the waiver or repayment, that amount would be earnings, or would be treated as earnings, and would constitute employment income (see section 7(2)(a) or (b) of the Income Tax (Earnings and Pensions) Act 2003).

14(2) Where, apart from the waiver or repayment, the amount of the remuneration would be allowable as a deduction in computing for the purposes of income tax or corporation tax the profits or gains or losses of the person by whom it is payable or paid, this section shall apply only if, by reason of the waiver or repayment, it is not so allowed or is otherwise brought into charge in computing those profits or gains or losses.

History – In s. 14(1), the words "would be earnings, or would be treated as earnings, and would constitute employment income (see section 7(2)(a) or (b) of the Income Tax (Earnings and Pensions) Act 2003)" substituted for the words "would be assessable to income tax under Schedule E" by ITEPA 2003, Sch. 6, para. 152 which has effect for the tax year 2003–04 and subsequent tax years.

15 Waiver of dividends

15 A person who waives any dividend on shares of a company within twelve months before any right to the dividend has accrued does not by reason of the waiver make a transfer of value.

16 Grant of tenancies of agricultural property

16(1) The grant of a tenancy of agricultural property in the United Kingdom, the Channel Islands or the Isle of Man for use for agricultural purposes is not a transfer of value by the grantor if he makes it for full consideration in money or money's worth.

16(2) Expressions used in subsection (1) above and in Chapter II of Part V of this Act have the same meaning in that subsection as in that Chapter.

Cross references – S. 65(6): application of s. 16 where discretionary trustees make a disposition as a result of which the value of settled property is reduced.

S. 70(4): application of s. 16 to property leaving temporary charitable trusts.

Other material – *Law Society's Gazette, 5 September 1984* (not reproduced): note on grants of agricultural tenancies – extraneous matters to be considered when determining whether tenancy granted at "full consideration".

17 Changes in distribution of deceased's estate, etc.

17 None of the following is a transfer of value–

(a) a variation or disclaimer to which section 142(1) below applies;

(b) a transfer to which section 143 below applies;

(c) [omitted by IHTPA 2014, s. 11 and Sch. 4, para. 4(a);]

(d) the renunciation of a claim to legitim or rights under section 131 of the Civil Partnership Act 2004 within the period mentioned in section 147(6) below.

History – S. 17(c) omitted by IHTPA 2014, s. 11 and Sch. 4, para. 4(a), with effect in relation to deaths occurring after 1 October 2014 (IHTPA 2014, s. 12(4) and SI 2014/2039, art. 2). Former s. 17(c) read as follows:
"(c) an election by a surviving spouse or civil partner under section 47A of the Administration of Estates Act 1925;".
In former s. 17(c) the words "or civil partner" inserted by SI 2005/3229, reg. 6(a), with effect from 5 December 2005.
In s. 17(d) the words "or rights under section 131 of the Civil Partnership Act 2004" inserted by SI 2005/3229, reg. 6(b), with effect from 5 December 2005.

Cross references – FA 2004, Sch. 15, para. 16: charge to income tax on benefits received by former owner of property, effective for 2005–06 onwards.
S. 142(1): variation or disclaimer within two years of dispositions taking effect on death.
S. 143: transfers within two years of death in accordance with testator's wishes.
S. 147(6): renunciation of claim to legitim within two years of attaining 18 (Scotland).
Civil Partnership Act 2004, s. 131: reproduced in the annotations to IHTA 1984, s. 147.
Administration of Estates Act 1925, s. 47A: right of surviving spouse of intestate to have own life interest redeemed.

PART II – EXEMPT TRANSFERS

Chapter I – General

18 Transfers between spouses or civil partners

History – In the heading to s. 18 the words "or civil partners" inserted by SI 2005/3229, reg. 7(5), with effect from 5 December 2005.

18(1) A transfer of value is an exempt transfer to the extent that the value transferred is attributable to property which becomes comprised in the estate of the transferor's spouse or civil partner or, so far as the value transferred is not so attributable, to the extent that that estate is increased.

18(2) If, immediately before the transfer, the transferor but not the transferor's spouse or civil partner is domiciled in the United Kingdom the value in respect of which the transfer is exempt (calculated as a value on which no tax is chargeable) shall not exceed the exemption limit at the time of the transfer, less any amount previously taken into account for the purposes of the exemption conferred by this section.

18(2A) For the purposes of subsection (2), the exemption limit is the amount shown in the second column of the first row of the Table in Schedule 1 (upper limit of portion of value charged at rate of nil per cent).

18(3) Subsection (1) above shall not apply in relation to property if the testamentary or other disposition by which it is given–

(a) takes effect on the termination after the transfer of value of any interest or period, or

(b) depends on a condition which is not satisfied within twelve months after the transfer;

but paragraph (a) above shall not have effect by reason only that the property is given to a spouse or civil partner only if he survives the other spouse or civil partner for a specified period.

18(4) For the purposes of this section, property is given to a person if it becomes his property or is held on trust for him.

History – In s. 18(1) the words "or civil partner" inserted by SI 2005/3229, reg. 7(2), with effect from 5 December 2005.
In s. 18(2), the words "the exemption limit at the time of the transfer," substituted for the figure "£55,000" by FA 2013, s. 178(2), with effect in relation to transfers of value made on or after 6 April 2013.
In s. 18(2) the words "or civil partner" inserted by SI 2005/3229, reg. 7(3), with effect from 5 December 2005.
S. 18(2A) inserted by FA 2013, s. 178(3), with effect in relation to transfers of value made on or after 6 April 2013.
In s. 18(3) the words "or civil partner" inserted twice by SI 2005/3229, reg. 7(4), with effect from 5 December 2005.

Cross references – S. 30(1) (conditionally exempt transfers) does not apply to an exempt transfer under s. 18.
S. 36–41: allocation of exemptions and burden of tax where a transfer of value is partly, but not wholly, exempt.
S. 55A(1)(d) (purchased settlement powers): s. 18 does not apply in relation to a transfer of value which arises where a person makes a disposition as a result of which that person acquires a settlement power for consideration in money or money's worth.
S. 56(1), (2): transfers involving reversionary interests – exclusion of exemptions in certain cases.
S. 268(3): associated operations.
FA 1986, s. 102(5): s. 102 (gifts with reservation) does not apply to gifts which are exempt transfers by virtue of s. 18.

19 Annual exemption

19(1) Transfers of value made by a transferor in any one year are exempt to the extent that the values transferred by them (calculated as values on which no tax is chargeable) do not exceed £3,000.

19(2) Where those values fall short of £3,000, the amount by which they fall short shall, in relation to the next following year, be added to the £3,000 mentioned in subsection (1) above.

19(3) Where those values exceed £3,000, the excess–

(a) shall, as between transfers made on different days, be attributed so far as possible to a later rather than an earlier transfer, and

(b) shall, as between transfers made on the same day, be attributed to them in proportion to the values transferred by them.

19(3A) A transfer of value which is a potentially exempt transfer–

(a) shall in the first instance be left out of account for the purposes of subsections (1) to (3) above; and

(b) if it proves to be a chargeable transfer, shall for the purposes of those subsections be taken into account as if, in the year in which it was made, it was made later than any transfer of value which was not a potentially exempt transfer.

19(4) In this section **"year"** means period of twelve months ending with 5th April.

19(5) Section 3(4) above shall not apply for the purposes of this section (but without prejudice to sections 57 and 94(5) below).

History – S. 19(3A) inserted by FA 1986, Sch. 19, para. 5, with respect to transfers of value made, and other events occurring, on or after 18 March 1986.

Cross references – FA 2004, Sch. 15 para. 10(1)(e), (2)(e): charge to income tax on benefits received by former owner of property, effective for 2005–06 onwards.
S. 3(4): "transfer of value" generally includes events on the happening of which tax is chargeable as if there had been such a transfer.
S. 57: "transfer of value" includes events triggering a charge under s. 52 (termination of interest in possession).
S. 94(5): "transfers of value by a transferor" and "the values transferred by them" include apportionments under s. 94 to participators in close companies.
FA 1986, Sch. 19, para. 40(1): transitional – transfer of value occurring before, and death or other event occurring after, 18 March 1986.

HMRC interpretations – IRInt. 1001: where a PET arises by the release of a reservation in the donor's lifetime, the Revenue take the view that the annual exemption is not available to reduce the value of the PET.

20 Small gifts

20(1) Transfers of value made by a transferor in any one year by outright gifts to any one person are exempt if the values transferred by them (calculated as values on which no tax is chargeable) do not exceed £250.

20(2) In this section **"year"** means period of twelve months ending with 5th April.

20(3) Section 3(4) above shall not apply for the purposes of this section.

Cross references – S. 3(4): "transfer of value" generally includes events on the happening of which tax is chargeable as if there had been such a transfer.
FA 1986, s. 102(5): s. 102 does not apply to gifts which are exempt transfers by virtue of s. 20.
FA 2004, Sch. 15, para. 10(1)(e), (2)(e): charge to income tax on benefits received by former owner of property, effective for 2005–06 onwards.

21 Normal expenditure out of income

Notes – ITTOIA 2005 amends s. 21(3), with effect from 6 April 2005: see the History notes for details.

21(1) A transfer of value is an exempt transfer if, or to the extent that, it is shown–

(a) that it was made as part of the normal expenditure of the transferor, and

(b) that (taking one year with another) it was made out of his income, and

(c) that, after allowing for all transfers of value forming part of his normal expenditure, the transferor was left with sufficient income to maintain his usual standard of living.

21(2) A payment of a premium on a policy of insurance on the transferor's life, or a gift of money or money's worth applied, directly or indirectly, in payment of such a premium, shall not for the purposes of this section be regarded as part of his normal expenditure if, when the insurance was made or at any earlier or later time, an annuity was purchased on his life, unless it is shown that–

(a) the purchase of the annuity, and

(b) the making or any variation of the insurance or of any prior insurance for which the first-mentioned insurance was directly or indirectly substituted,

were not associated operations.

21(3) So much of a purchased life annuity (within the meaning of section 423 of the Income Tax (Trading and Other Income) Act 2005) as is exempt from income tax under section 717 of that Act, shall not be regarded as part of the transferor's income for the purposes of this section.

21(4) Subsection (3) above shall not apply to annuities purchased before 13th November 1974.

21(5) Section 3(4) above shall not apply for the purposes of this section.

History – In s. 21(3), the words "section 423 of the Income Tax (Trading and Other Income) Act 2005 " substituted for "section 657 of the Taxes Act" by ITTOIA 2005, s. 882(2) and Sch. 1, para. 395(a), with effect from 6 April 2005.
In s. 21(3), the words "exempt from income tax under section 717 of that Act" substituted by ITTOIA 2005, s. 882(2) and Sch. 1, *para. 395(b), with effect from 6 April 2005.*

Cross references – S. 3(4): "transfer of value" generally includes events on the happening of which tax is chargeable as if there had been such a transfer.

Other material – Revenue letter, Law Society's Gazette, 9 June 1976 (not reproduced): "income" to be interpreted in accordance with "normal accountancy rules" which implies taking income net of tax.

22 Gifts in consideration of marriage or civil partnership

History – In the heading to s. 22 the words "or civil partnership" inserted by SI 2005/3229, reg. 8(8), with effect from 5 December 2005.

22(1) Transfers of value made by gifts in consideration of marriage or civil partnership are exempt to the extent that the values transferred by such transfers made by any one transferor in respect of any one marriage or civil partnership (calculated as values on which no tax is chargeable) do not exceed–

(a) in the case of gifts within subsection (2) below by a parent of a party to the marriage or civil partnership, £5,000,

(b) in the case of other gifts within subsection (2) below, £2,500, and

(c) in any other case £1,000;

any excess being attributed to the transfers in proportion to the values transferred.

22(2) A gift is within this subsection if–

(a) it is an outright gift to a child or remoter descendant of the transferor, or

(b) the transferor is a parent or remoter ancestor of either party to the marriage or civil partnership, and either the gift is an outright gift to the other party to the marriage or civil partnership or the property comprised in the gift is settled by the gift, or

(c) the transferor is a party to the marriage or civil partnership, and either the gift is an outright gift to the other party to the marriage or civil partnership or the property comprised in the gift is settled by the gift;

and in this section **"child"** includes an illegitimate child, an adopted child and a step-child and **"parent"**, **"descendant"** and **"ancestor"** shall be construed accordingly.

22(3) A disposition which is an outright gift shall not be treated for the purposes of this section as a gift made in consideration of marriage or civil partnership if, or in so far as, it is a gift to a person other than a party to the marriage or civil partnership.

22(4) A disposition which is not an outright gift shall not be treated for the purposes of this section as a gift made in consideration of marriage or civil partnership if the persons who are or may become entitled to any benefit under the disposition include any person other than–

(a) the parties to the marriage or civil partnership, any child of the family of the parties to the marriage or civil partnership, or a spouse or civil partner of any such child;

(b) persons becoming entitled on the failure of trusts for any such child under which trust property would (subject only to any power of appointment to a person falling within paragraph (a) or (c) of this subsection) vest indefeasibly on the attainment of a specified age or either on the attainment of such an age or on some earlier event, or persons becoming entitled (subject as aforesaid) on the failure of any limitation in tail;

(c) a subsequent spouse or civil partner of a party to the marriage or civil partnership, any child of the family of the parties to any such subsequent marriage or civil partnership, or a spouse or civil partner of any such child;

(d) persons becoming entitled under such trusts, subsisting under the law of England and Wales or of Northern Ireland, as are specified in section 33(1) of the Trustee Act 1925 or section 34(1) of the Trustee Act (Northern Ireland) 1958 (protective trusts), the principal beneficiary being a person falling within paragraph (a) or (c) of the subsection, or under such trusts, modified by the enlargement, as respects any period during which there is no such child as aforesaid in existence, of the class of potential beneficiaries specified in paragraph (ii) of the said section 33(1) or paragraph (b) of the said section 34(1);

(e) persons becoming entitled under trusts subsisting under the law of Scotland and corresponding with such trusts as are mentioned in paragraph (d) above;

(f) as respects a reasonable amount of remuneration, the trustees of the settlement.

22(4A) In subsection (4) child of the family, in relation to parties to a marriage or civil partnership, means a child of one or both of them.

22(5) [Omitted by SI 2005/3229, reg. 8(7).]

22(6) Section 3(4) above shall not apply for the purposes of this section (but without prejudice to section 57 below).

History – In s. 22(1) the words "or civil partnership" inserted three times by SI 2005/3229, reg. 8(2), with effect from 5 December 2005.
In s. 22(2) the words "or civil partnership" inserted four times by SI 2005/3229, reg. 8(3), with effect from 5 December 2005.
In s. 22(3) the words "or civil partnership" inserted twice by SI 2005/3229, reg. 8(4), with effect from 5 December 2005.
In s. 22(4) the words "or civil partnership" inserted, para. (a) and (c) substituted and in para. (b) and (d) the word "child" substituted for the word "issue" by SI 2005/3229, reg. 8(5), with effect in relation to dispositions made on or after 5 December 2005. The former s. 22(4)(a) and (c) read as follows:

"(a) the parties to the marriage, issue of the marriage, or wife or husband of any such issue;

(c) a subsequent wife or husband of a party to the marriage, or any issue, or the wife or husband of any issue, of a subsequent marriage of either party;"

S. 22(4A) inserted by SI 2005/3229, reg. 8(6), with effect in relation to dispositions made on or after 5 December 2005.
S. 22(5) omitted by SI 2005/3229, reg. 8(7), with effect in relation to dispositions made on or after 5 December 2005. Former s. 22(5) read as follows:
"**22(5)** References in subsection (4) above to issue shall apply as if any person legitimated by a marriage, or adopted by the husband and wife jointly, were included among the issue of that marriage."
Cross references – S. 3(4): "transfer of value" generally includes events on the happening of which tax is chargeable as if there had been such a transfer.
S. 57: "transfer of value" includes events triggering a charge under s. 52 (termination of interest in possession).
Civil Partnership Act 2004, Sch. 21, para. 54 (not reproduced): references to an individual's stepchildren to include references to children of that individual's civil partner; in force from 5 December 2005.
FA 1986, s. 102(5): s. 102 (gifts with reservation) does not apply to gifts which are exempt transfers by virtue of s. 22.
Trustee Act 1925, s. 33(1) (not reproduced): protective trusts.

23 Gifts to charities or registered clubs

History – In the heading to s. 23, the words "or registered clubs" inserted by CTA 2010, s. 1177 and Sch. 1, para. 189(6), with effect for corporation tax purposes for accounting periods ending on or after 1 April 2010, and for income tax and capital gains tax purposes for the tax year 2010–11 and subsequent tax years.

23(1) Transfers of value are exempt to the extent that the values transferred by them are attributable to property which is given to charities or registered clubs.

23(2) Subsection (1) above shall not apply in relation to property if the testamentary or other disposition by which it is given–

(a) takes effect on the termination after the transfer of value of any interest or period, or

(b) depends on a condition which is not satisfied within twelve months after the transfer, or

(c) is defeasible;

and for this purpose any disposition which has not been defeated at a time twelve months after the transfer of value and is not defeasible after that time shall be treated as not being defeasible (whether or not it was capable of being defeated before that time).

23(3) Subsection (1) above shall not apply in relation to property which is an interest in other property if–

(a) that interest is less than the donor's, or

(b) the property is given for a limited period;

and for this purpose any question whether an interest is less than the donor's shall be decided as at a time twelve months after the transfer of value.

23(4) Subsection (1) above shall not apply in relation to any property if–

(a) the property is land or a building and is given subject to an interest reserved or created by the donor which entitles him, his spouse or civil partner or a person connected with him to possession of, or to occupy, the whole or any part of the land or building rent-free or at a rent less than might be expected to be obtained in a transaction at arm's length between persons not connected with each other, or

(b) the property is not land or a building and is given subject to an interest reserved or created by the donor other than–

(i) an interest created by him for full consideration in money or money's worth, or

(ii) an interest which does not substantially affect the enjoyment of the property by the person or body to whom it is given;

and for this purpose any question whether property is given subject to an interest shall be decided as at a time twelve months after the transfer of value.

23(5) In the case of any property which is given to charities, subsection (1) above shall not apply in relation to the property if it or any part of it may become applicable for purposes other than charitable purposes or those of a body mentioned in section 24 or 25 below or, where it is land, of a body mentioned in section 24A below.

23(5A) In the case of any property which is given to a registered club, subsection (1) above shall not apply in relation to the property if it or any part of it may become applicable for purposes other than–

(a) the purposes of the club in question;

(b) the purposes of another registered club;

(c) the purposes of the governing body of an eligible sport for the purposes of which the club in question exists; or

(d) charitable purposes.

23(6) For the purposes of this section–

(a) property is given to charities if it becomes the property of charities or is held on trust for charitable purposes only; and

(b) property is given to registered clubs if it becomes the property of registered clubs or is held on trust for purposes of registered clubs only;

and **"donor"** shall be construed accordingly.

23(7) For the purposes of this section **"registered club"** and **"eligible sport"** have the same meaning as in Chapter 9 of Part 13 of the Corporation Tax Act 2010.

History – In s. 23(1) the words "or registered clubs" inserted by CTA 2010, s. 1177 and Sch. 1, para. 189(2), with effect for corporation tax purposes for accounting periods ending on or after 1 April 2010, and for income tax and capital gains tax purposes for the tax year 2010–11 and subsequent tax years.
In s. 23(4)(a) the words "or civil partner" inserted three times by SI 2005/3229, reg. 9, with effect from 5 December 2005.
In s. 23(5) the words "In the case of any property which is given to charities," and "the" after "in relation to" inserted by CTA 2010, s. 1177 and Sch. 1, para. 189(3), with effect for corporation tax purposes for accounting periods ending on or after 1 April 2010, and for income tax and capital gains tax purposes for the tax year 2010–11 and subsequent tax years.
In s. 23(5), words "or 25" substituted for former words "25 or 26" by FA 1998, s. 143(2)(a), in respect of any transfer of value made on or after 17 March 1998.
S. 23(5) amended by FA 1989, s. 171(2), inserting the reference to bodies within s. 24A, in relation to transfers of value made after 13 March 1989.
S. 23(5A) inserted by CTA 2010, s. 1177 and Sch. 1, para. 189(4), with effect for corporation tax purposes for accounting periods ending on or after 1 April 2010, and for income tax and capital gains tax purposes for the tax year 2010–11 and subsequent tax years.
S. 23(6) substituted by CTA 2010, s. 1177 and Sch. 1, para. 189(5), with effect for corporation tax purposes for accounting periods ending on or after 1 April 2010, and for income tax and capital gains tax purposes for the tax year 2010–11 and subsequent tax years.
S. 23(7) effectively inserted by CTA 2010, s. 1177 and Sch. 1, para. 189(5), with effect for corporation tax purposes for accounting periods ending on or after 1 April 2010, and for income tax and capital gains tax purposes for the tax year 2010–11 and subsequent tax years.

Cross references – S. 30(1) (conditionally exempt transfers) does not apply to an exempt transfer under s. 23.
S. 36–41: allocation of exemptions and burden of tax where a transfer of value is partly, but not wholly, exempt.
S. 55A(1) (purchased settlement powers): s. 23 does not apply in relation to a transfer of value which arises where a person makes a disposition as a result of which that person acquires a settlement power for consideration in money or money's worth.
S. 56: exclusion of exemptions in some cases when interests in settled property are transferred to exempt bodies.
S. 161(2)(b)(i): when property given to charity is related to estate of transferor (or spouse).
FA 1986, s. 102(5): s. 102 (gifts with reservation) does not apply to gifts which are exempt transfers by virtue of s. 23.

Statements of practice – E13: exemption extends to whole value transferred.

24 Gifts to political parties

24(1) Transfers of value are exempt to the extent that the values transferred by them–

(a) are attributable to property which becomes the property of a political party qualifying for exemption under this section.

(b) [Repealed by FA 1988, s. 137 and Sch. 14, Pt. X.]

24(2) A political party qualifies for exemption under this section if, at the last general election preceding the transfer of value,–

(a) two members of that party were elected to the House of Commons, or

(b) one member of that party was elected to the House of Commons and not less than 150,000 votes were given to candidates who were members of that party.

24(3) Subsection (2) to (5) of section 23 above shall apply in relation to subsection (1) above as they apply in relation to section 23(1).

24(4) For the purposes of section 23(2) to (5) as they apply by virtue of subsection (3) above property is given to any person or body if it becomes the property of or is held on trust for that person or body, and **"donor"** shall be construed accordingly.

History – S. 24(1)(b) repealed by FA 1988, s. 137 and Sch. 14, Pt. X, with effect in relation to transfers of value made on or after 15 March 1988.

Cross references – S. 36–41: allocation of exemptions and burden of tax where a transfer of value is partly, but not wholly exempt.
S. 55A (purchased settlement powers): s. 24 does not apply in relation to a transfer of value which arises where a person makes a disposition as a result of which that person acquires a settlement power for consideration in money or money's worth.
S. 56: exclusion of exemptions in some cases when interests in settled property are transferred to exempt bodies.
S. 76: exemption for property ceasing to be relevant property within Pt. III, Ch. III on becoming the property of a political party qualifying for exemption under s. 24.
S. 161(2)(b)(ii): when property given to a political party is related to estate of transferor (or spouse).
FA 1986, s. 102(5): s. 102 (gifts with reservation) does not apply to gifts which are exempt transfers by virtue of s. 24.
TCGA 1992, s. 260: capital gains tax hold-over relief in respect of transfers within s. 24.

Statements of practice – E13: exemption extends to whole value transferred.

24A Gifts to housing associations

24A(1) A transfer of value is exempt to the extent that the value transferred by it is attributable to land in the United Kingdom given to a body falling within subsection (2) below.

24A(2) A body falls within this subsection if it is–

(za) a non-profit registered provider of social housing;

(a) a registered social landlord within the meaning of Part I of the Housing Act 1996;

(b) a registered housing association within the meaning of the Housing Associations Act 1985; or

IHT Statutes

(c) a registered housing association within the meaning of Part II of the Housing (Northern Ireland) Order 1992.

24A(3) Subsections (2) to (5) of section 23 and subsection (4) of section 24 above shall apply in relation to subsection (1) above as they apply in relation to section 24(1).

History – In s. 24A(1) the words "body falling within subsection (2) below" substituted by SI 1996/2325, art. 5(1), Sch. 2, para. 12(2) with effect from 1 October 1996.
S. 24A(2)(za) inserted by the Housing and Regeneration Act 2008, s. 277 and Sch. 9, para. 7, with effect from 1 April 2010 (SI 2010/862).
S. 24A(2) substituted by SI 1996/2325, art. 5(1), Sch. 2, para. 12(3) with effect from 1 October 1996.
S. 24A inserted by FA 1989, s. 171(1) in respect of transfers of value made after 13 March 1989.

Cross references – S. 36–41: allocation of exemptions and burden of tax where a transfer of value is partly, but not wholly exempt.
S. 55A (purchased settlement powers): s. 24A does not apply in relation to a transfer of value which arises where a person makes a disposition as a result of which that person acquires a settlement power for consideration in money or money's worth.
S. 56: exclusion of exemptions in some cases where interests in settled property are transferred to exempt bodies.
S. 161(2)(b)(ii): when property given to a housing association is related to estate of transferor (or spouse).
FA 1986, s. 102(5): s. 102 (gifts with reservation) does not apply to gifts which are exempt by virtue of s. 24A.
Housing Associations Act 1985, s. 1(1); Housing (Northern Ireland) Order 1981, art. 114: a housing association is a non-profit-making body established for the provision or encouragement of housing; in Ulster it may take the form of a public utility society, housing trust or company.

25 Gifts for national purposes, etc.

25(1) A transfer of value is an exempt transfer to the extent that the value transferred by it is attributable to property which becomes the property of a body within Schedule 3 to this Act.

25(2) Subsections (2) to (5) of section 23 and subsection (4) of section 24 above shall apply in relation to subsection (1) above as they apply in relation to section 24(1), except that section 23(3) shall not prevent subsection (1) above from applying in relation to property consisting of the benefit of an agreement restricting the use of land.

25(3) A transfer of value is an exempt transfer to the extent that the value transferred by it is attributable to property that is being transferred in the circumstances described in paragraph 1 of Schedule 14 to the Finance Act 2012 (gifts to the nation).

History – S. 25(3) inserted by FA 2012, s. 49 and Sch. 14. para. 27, with effect from 17 July 2012.

Cross references – S. 36–41: allocation of exemptions and burden of tax where a transfer of value is partly, but not wholly, exempt.
S. 55A (purchased settlement powers): s. 25 does not apply in relation to a transfer of value which arises where a person makes a disposition as a result of which that person acquires a settlement power for consideration in money or money's worth.
S. 56: exclusion of exemptions in some cases when interests in settled property are transferred to exempt bodies.
S. 161(2)(b)(ii): when property given to heritage body is related to estate of transferor (or spouse).
FA 1986, s. 102(5): s. 102 (gifts with reservation) does not apply to gifts which are exempt transfers by virtue of s. 25.

Statements of practice – E13: exemption extends to whole value transferred.

26 Gifts for public benefit

26 [Repealed by FA 1998, s. 143(1) and 165 and Sch. 27, Pt. IV, with effect in relation to any transfer of value made on or after 17 March 1998.]

26A Potentially exempt transfer of property subsequently held for national purposes etc.

26A A potentially exempt transfer which would (apart from this section) have proved to be a chargeable transfer shall be an exempt transfer to the extent that the value transferred by it is attributable to property which has been or could be designated under section 31(1) below and which, during the period beginning with the date of the transfer and ending with the death of the transferor,–

(a) has been disposed of by sale by private treaty to a body mentioned in Schedule 3 to this Act or has been disposed of to such a body otherwise than by sale, or

(b) has been disposed of in pursuance of section 230 below or in the circumstances described in paragraph 1 of Schedule 14 to the Finance Act 2012 (gifts to the nation).

History – In s. 26A(b), the words "or in the circumstances described in paragraph 1 of Schedule 14 to the Finance Act 2012 (gifts to the nation)" inserted by FA 2012, s. 49 and Sch. 14. para. 28 with effect from 17 July 2012.
S. 26A inserted by FA 1986, Sch. 19, para. 6, with respect to transfers of value and other events occurring on or after 18 March 1986.

Cross references – S. 36–41: allocation of exemptions and burden of tax where a transfer of value is partly, but not wholly, exempt.
S. 55A (purchased settlement powers): s. 26A does not apply in relation to a transfer of value which arises where a person makes a disposition as a result of which that person acquires a settlement power for consideration in money or money's worth.
S. 56: exclusion of exemptions in some cases when interests in settled property are transferred to exempt bodies.
S. 230: acceptance of property in satisfaction of tax.

27 Maintenance funds for historic buildings, etc.

27(1) Subject to subsection 1A below, a transfer of value is an exempt transfer to the extent that the value transferred by it is attributable to property which by virtue of the transfer becomes comprised in a settlement and in respect of which–

(a) a direction under paragraph 1 of Schedule 4 to this Act has effect at the time of the transfer, or
(b) such a direction is given after the time of the transfer.

27(1A) Subsection (1) above does not apply in the case of a direction given after the time of the transfer unless the claim for the direction (if it is not made before that time) is made no more than two years after the date of that transfer, or within such longer period as the Board may allow.

27(2) Subsections (2) and (3) of section 23 and subsection (4) of section 24 above shall apply in relation to subsection (1) above as they apply in relation to section 24(1).

History – S. 27(1A) and words in s. 27(1) "Subject to subsection (1A) below," inserted by FA 1998, s. 144(1), with effect in relation to transfers of value made on or after 17 March 1998.

Cross references – S. 36–41: allocation of exemptions and burden of tax where a transfer of value is partly, but not wholly, exempt.
S. 55A (purchased settlement powers): s. 27 does not apply in relation to a transfer of value which arises where a person makes a disposition as a result of which that person acquires a settlement power for consideration in money or money's worth.
S. 56: exclusion of exemptions in some cases when interests in settled property are transferred to exempt bodies.
S. 57(5): property remaining comprised in a settlement immediately after a transfer of value.
FA 1985, s. 95(1): treasury functions under Pt. II transferred to the Commissioners of Inland Revenue ("the Board") from 25 July 1985.
FA 1986, s. 102(5): s. 102 (gifts with reservation) does not apply to gifts which are exempt transfers by virtue of s. 27.
TCGA 1992, s. 260: capital gains tax hold-over relief in respect of transfer within s. 27. See also TCGA 1992, s. 258 (works of art).

28 Employee trusts

28(1) A transfer of value made by an individual who is beneficially entitled to shares in a company is an exempt transfer to the extent that the value transferred is attributable to shares in or securities of the company which become comprised in a settlement if–
(a) the trusts of the settlement are of the description specified in section 86(1) below, and
(b) the persons for whose benefit the trusts permit the settled property to be applied include all or most of the persons employed by or holding office with the company.

28(2) Subsection (1) above shall not apply unless at the date of the transfer, or at a subsequent date not more than one year thereafter, both the following conditions are satisfied, that is to say–
(a) the trustees–
  (i) hold more than one half of the ordinary shares in the company, and
  (ii) have powers of voting on all questions affecting the company as a whole which if exercised would yield a majority of the votes capable of being exercised on them; and
(b) there are no provisions in any agreement or instrument affecting the company's constitution or management or its shares or securities whereby the condition in paragraph (a) above can cease to be satisfied without the consent of the trustees.

28(3) Where the company has shares or securities of any class giving powers of voting limited to either or both of the following–
(a) the question of winding up the company, and
(b) any question primarily affecting shares or securities of that class,

the reference in subsection (2)(a)(ii) above to all questions affecting the company as a whole shall be read as a reference to all such questions except any in relation to which those powers are capable of being exercised.

28(4) Subsection (1) above shall not apply if the trusts permit any of the settled property to be applied at any time (whether during any such period as is referred to in section 86(1) below or later) for the benefit of–
(a) a person who is a participator in the company mentioned in subsection (1) above; or
(b) any other person who is a participator in any close company that has made a disposition whereby property became comprised in the same settlement, being a disposition which but for section 13 above would have been a transfer of value; or
(c) any other person who has been a participator in the company mentioned in subsection (1) above or in any such company as is mentioned in paragraph (b) above at any time after, or during the ten years before, the transfer of value mentioned in subsection (1) above; or
(d) any person who is connected with any person within paragraph (a), (b) or (c) above.

28(5) The participators in a company who are referred to in subsection (4) above do not include any participator who–
(a) is not beneficially entitled to, or to rights entitling him to acquire, 5 per cent or more of, or of any class of the shares comprised in, its issued share capital, and
(b) on a winding-up of the company would not be entitled to 5 per cent or more of its assets.

28(6) In determining whether the trusts permit property to be applied as mentioned in subsection (4) above, no account shall be taken of any power to make a payment which is the income of any person for any of the purposes of income tax, or would be the income for any of those purposes of a person not resident in the United Kingdom if he were so resident.

28(7) Subsection (5) of section 13 above shall have effect in relation to this section as it has effect in relation to that section.

Cross references – S. 75: exemption for property ceasing to be relevant property within Pt. III, Ch. III on becoming held on employee trusts.
S. 86(1): special provisions relating to employee benefit trusts.
FA 1986, s. 102(5): s. 102 (gifts with reservation) does not apply to gifts which are exempt transfers by virtue of s. 28.
TCGA 1992, s. 239: deemed no gain, no loss for the purposes of tax on chargeable gains on certain disposals within s. 28.

28A Employee-ownership trusts

28A(1) A transfer of value made by an individual who is beneficially entitled to shares in a company ("C") is an exempt transfer to the extent that the value transferred is attributable to shares in or securities of C which become comprised in a settlement if–

(a) C meets the trading requirement,

(b) the settlement meets the all-employee benefit requirement, and

(c) the settlement does not meet the controlling interest requirement immediately before the beginning of the tax year in which the transfer of value is made but does meet it at the end of that year.

28A(2) Sections 236I, 236J, 236K, 236M and 236T (but not 236L) of the 1992 Act apply to determine whether–

(a) C meets the trading requirement;

(b) the settlement meets the all-employee benefit requirement;

(c) the settlement meets the controlling interest requirement;

with references in those sections to "C" being read accordingly.

28A(3) In this section **"tax year"** means a year beginning on 6 April and ending on the following 5 April.

History – S. 28A inserted by FA 2014, s. 290 and Sch. 37, para. 11(1), with effect in relation to transfers of value made on or after 6 April 2014.

29 Loans – modifications of exemptions

29(1) If or to the extent that a transfer of value is a disposition whereby the use of money or other property is allowed by one person to another (**"the borrower"**), the preceding provisions of this Chapter shall apply to it with the following modifications.

29(2) For the purposes of section 18 the borrower's estate shall be treated as increased by an amount equal to the value transferred; and section 18(3) shall not apply.

29(3) For the purposes of sections 20 and 22 the transfer of value shall be treated as made by outright gift.

29(4) Section 21(1) shall apply as if for the conditions stated in paragraphs (a) and (b) there were substituted the condition that the transfer was a normal one on the part of the transferor.

29(5) For the purposes of sections 23 to 25–

(a) the value transferred shall be treated as attributable to the property of which the borrower is allowed the use, and

(b) that property shall be treated as given to, or as becoming the property of, the borrower unless the use allowed includes use for purposes other than charitable purposes or those of a body mentioned in section 24 or 25 or, where it is land, of a body mentioned in section 24A;

and sections 23(2) to (6), 24(3) and (4), 24A(3), and 25(2) shall not apply.

History – S. 29(5) amended by FA 1998, s. 143(2)(b) so as to remove references to provisions of IHTA 1984, s. 26, in relation to any transfer of value made on or after 17 March 1998.
S. 29(5) amended by inserting references to s. 24A in relation to transfers of value made after 13 March 1989, by FA 1989, s. 171(3).
In s. 29(5), the words "(1)(b)," which followed "24" in the second place, were repealed by FA 1988, s. 148 and Sch. 14, Pt. X, in relation to transfers of value made on or after 15 March 1988.

29A Abatement of exemption where claim settled out of beneficiary's own resources

29A(1) *This section applies where–*

(a) apart from this section the transfer of value made on the death of any person is an exempt transfer to the extent that the value transferred by it is attributable to an exempt gift, and

(b) the exempt beneficiary, in settlement of the whole or part of any claim against the deceased's estate, effects a disposition of property not derived from the transfer.

29A(2) The provisions of this Act shall have effect in relation to the transfer as if–

(a) so much of the relevant value as is equal to the following amount, namely the amount by which the value of the exempt beneficiary's estate immediately after the disposition is less than it would be but for the disposition, or

(b) where that amount exceeds the relevant value, the whole of the relevant value,

were attributable to such a gift to the exempt beneficiary as is mentioned in subsection (3) below (instead of being attributable to a gift with respect to which the transfer is exempt).

29A(3) The gift referred to in subsection (2) above is a specific gift with respect to which the transfer is chargeable, being a gift which satisfies the conditions set out in paragraphs (a) and (b) of section 38(1) below.

29A(4) In determining the value of the exempt beneficiary's estate for the purposes of subsection (2) above–

(a) no deduction shall be made in respect of the claim referred to in subsection (1)(b) above, and

(b) where the disposition referred to in that provision constitutes a transfer of value–

(i) no account shall be taken of any liability of the beneficiary for any tax on the value transferred, and

(ii) sections 104 and 116 below shall be disregarded.

29A(5) Subsection (1)(b) above does not apply in relation to any claim against the deceased's estate in respect of so much of any liability as is, in accordance with this Act, to be taken into account in determining the value of the estate.

29A(6) In this section–

"exempt gift", in relation to a transfer of value falling within subsection (1)(a) above, means–

(a) a gift with respect to which the transfer is (apart from this section) exempt by virtue of the provisions of any one or more of sections 18 and 23 to 28A, or

(b) where (apart from this section) the transfer is so exempt with respect to a gift up to a limit, so much of the gift as is within that limit;

"the exempt beneficiary", in relation to an exempt gift, means any of the following, namely–

(a) where the gift is exempt by virtue of section 18 above, the deceased's spouse or civil partner,

(b) where the gift is exempt by virtue of section 23 above, any person or body–

(i) whose property the property falling within subsection (1) of that section becomes, or

(ii) by whom that property is held on trust for charitable purposes,

(c) where the gift is exempt by virtue of section 24 or 25 above, any body whose property the property falling within subsection (1) of that section becomes,

(d) where the gift is exempt by virtue of section 24A above, any body to whom the land falling within subsection (1) of that section is given, and

(e) where the gift is exempt by virtue of section 27, 28 or 28A above, the trustees of any settlement in which the property falling within subsection (1) of that section becomes comprised;

"gift" and **"specific gift"** have the same meaning as in Chapter III of this Part; and

"the relevant value", in relation to a transfer of value falling within subsection (1)(a) above, means so much of the value transferred by the transfer as is attributable to the gift referred to in that provision.

History – In s. 29A(6), "to 28A" substituted for "to 28" by FA 2014, s. 290 and Sch. 27, para. 12(1)(a), with effect in relation to transfers of value made on or after 6 April 2014.

In s. 29A(6), ", 28 or 28A" substituted for "or 28" by FA 2014, s. 290 and Sch. 37, para. 12(1)(b), with effect in relation to transfers of value made on or after 6 April 2014.

In s. 29A(6), in para. (a) of the definition of the exempt beneficiary, the words "or civil partner" inserted by SI 2005/3229, reg. 10, with effect from 5 December 2005.

In s. 29A(6), words "or 25" substituted for former words "25 or 26" by FA 1998, s. 143(2)(a), in relation to transfers of value made on or after 17 March 1998.

S. 29A inserted by FA 1989, s. 172, in relation to deaths occurring on or after 27 July 1989.

Cross references – S. 38(1)(a), (b): gifts which are not exempt (or wholly exempt) and which do not bear their own tax.

S. 104: business property relief.

S. 116: agricultural property relief.

Chapter II – Conditional Exemption

30 Conditionally exempt transfers

30(1) A transfer of value is an exempt transfer to the extent that the value transferred by it is attributable to property–

(a) which, on a claim made for the purpose, is designated by the Treasury under section 31 below, and

(b) with respect to which the requisite undertaking described in that section is given by such person as the Treasury think appropriate in the circumstances of the case or (where the property is an area of land within subsection (1)(d) of that section) with respect to which the requisite undertakings described in that section are given by such person or persons as the Treasury think appropriate in the circumstances of the case.

30(2) A transfer of value exempt with respect to any property under this section or under section 76 of the Finance Act 1976 is referred to in this Act as a **conditionally exempt transfer** of that property.

30(3) Subsection (1) above shall not apply to a transfer of value other than one which under section 4 above a person makes on his death unless–

(a) the transferor or his spouse or civil partner, or the transferor and his spouse or civil partner between them, have been beneficially entitled to the property throughout the six years ending with the transfer, or

(b) the transferor acquired the property on a death on the occasion of which there was a transfer of value under section 4 above which was itself a conditionally exempt transfer of the property.

30(3A) The provisions of this section shall be disregarded in determining under section 3A above whether a transfer of value is a potentially exempt transfer.

30(3B) No claim may be made under subsection (1) above with respect to a potentially exempt transfer until the transferor has died.

30(3BA) A claim under subsection (1) above must be made no more than two years after the date of the transfer of value to which it relates or, in the case of a claim with respect to a potentially exempt transfer, the date of the death, or (in either case) within such longer period as the Board may allow.

30(3C) Subsection (1) above shall not apply to a potentially exempt transfer to the extent that the value transferred by it is attributable to property which has been disposed of by sale during the period beginning with the date of the transfer and ending with the death of the transferor.

30(4) Subsection (1) above does not apply to a transfer of value to the extent to which it is an exempt transfer under section 18 or 23 above.

History – In s. 30(1), the words from "or (where the property" to the end were inserted by FA 1985, s. 94(1) and Sch. 26, para. 1, in relation to events on or after 19 March 1985.
In s. 30(3)(a) the words "or civil partner" inserted twice by SI 2005/3229, reg. 11, with effect from 5 December 2005.
S. 30(3A) and (3B) inserted by FA 1986, s. 101 and Sch. 19, para. 7, with respect to transfers of value made, and other events occurring, on or after 18 March 1986.
S. 30(3BA) inserted by FA 1998, s. 142 and Sch. 25, para. 2, with effect in relation to any transfer of value or death on or after 17 March 1998.
S. 30(3C) inserted by FA 1986, s. 101 and Sch. 19, para. 7, with respect to transfers of value made, and other events occurring, on or after 18 March 1986.

Cross references – S. 3A: potentially exempt transfers.
S. 18: transfers between spouses.
S. 23: gifts to charities.
S. 36–41: allocation of exemptions and burden of tax where a transfer of value is partly, but not wholly, exempt.
S. 78: conditionally exempt occasions in relation to property comprised in discretionary trusts.
S. 79(3): designated property comprised in discretionary trusts – disapplication of ten-year charge.
FA 1986, Sch. 19, para. 40(1): transitional – transfer of value occurring before, and death or other event occurring after, 18 March 1986.
TCGA 1992, s. 260: capital gains tax hold-over relief in respect of transfers within s. 30. See also TCGA 1992, s. 258 (works of art).
FA 1998, Sch. 25, para. 10(5)(a) and (6)(b): variation of undertakings given under s. 30 with respect to any property before 31 July 1998.

Other material – Tax Bulletin, TB12/95-7: Capital Taxes Office no longer requires to see, at the pre-grant stage, HMRC accounts in which a claim for conditional exemption is made.

31 Designation and undertakings

31(1) The Treasury may designate under this section–

(a) any relevant object which appears to the Board to be pre-eminent for its national, scientific, historic or artistic interest;

(aa) any collection or group of relevant objects which, taken as a whole, appears to the Board to be pre-eminent for its national, scientific, historic or artistic interest;

(b) any land which in the opinion of the Treasury is of outstanding scenic or historic or scientific interest;

(c) any building for the preservation of which special steps should in the opinion of the Treasury be taken by reason of its outstanding historic or architectural interest;

(d) any area of land which in the opinion of the Treasury is essential for the protection of the character and amenities of such a building as is mentioned in paragraph (c) above;

(e) any object which in the opinion of the Treasury is historically associated with such a building as is mentioned in paragraph (c) above.

31(1A) Where the transfer of value in relation to which the claim for designation is made is a potentially exempt transfer which (apart from section 30 above) has proved to be a chargeable transfer, the question whether any property is appropriate for designation under this section shall be determined by reference to circumstances existing after the death of the transferor.

31(2) In the case of property within subsection (1)(a) or (aa) above, the requisite undertaking is that, until the person beneficially entitled to the property dies or the property is disposed of, whether by sale or gift or otherwise–

(a) the property will be kept permanently in the United Kingdom and will not leave it temporarily except for a purpose and a period approved by the Treasury, and

(b) such steps as are agreed between the Treasury and the person giving the undertaking, and are set out in it, will be taken for the preservation of the property and for securing reasonable access to the public.

31(3) If it appears to the Treasury, on a claim made for the purpose, that any documents which are designated or to be designated under subsection (1)(a) or (aa) above contain information which for personal or other reasons ought to be treated as confidential, they may exclude those documents, either altogether or to such extent as they think fit, from so much of an undertaking given or to be given under subsection (2)(b) above as relates to public access.

31(4) In the case of other property within subsection (1) above, the requisite undertaking is that, until the person beneficially entitled to the property dies or the property is disposed of, whether by sale or gift or otherwise, such steps as are agreed between the Treasury and the person giving the undertaking, and are set out in it, will be taken–

(a) in the case of land falling within subsection (1)(b) above, for the maintenance of the land and the preservation of its character, and

(b) in the case of any other property, for the maintenance, repair and preservation of the property and, if it is an object falling within subsection (1)(e) above, for keeping it associated with the building concerned;

and for securing reasonable access to the public.

31(4A) In the case of an area of land within subsection (1)(d) above (relevant land) there is an additional requisite undertaking, which is that, until the person beneficially entitled to property falling within subsection (4C) below dies, or it is disposed of, whether by sale or gift or otherwise, specified steps will be taken for its maintenance, repair and preservation and for securing reasonable access to the public; and **"specified steps"** means such steps as are agreed between the Treasury and the person giving the undertaking, and are set out in it.

31(4B) Where different persons are entitled (either beneficially or otherwise) to different properties falling within subsection (4C) below, subsection (4A) above shall have effect to require separate undertakings as to the maintenance, repair, preservation and access of each of the properties to be given by such persons as the Treasury think appropriate in the circumstances of the case.

31(4C) The following property falls within this subsection–

(a) the building for the protection of whose character and amenities the relevant land is in the opinion of the Treasury essential;

(b) any other area (or areas) of land which, in relation to the building, falls (or fall) within subsection (1)(d) above and which either lies (or lie) between the relevant land and the building or is (or are) in the opinion of the Treasury physically closely connected with the relevant land or the building.

31(4D) Where subsection (4A) above requires an undertaking for the maintenance, repair, preservation and access of property, such an undertaking is required notwithstanding that some other undertaking for its maintenance, repair, preservation and access is effective.

31(4E) Any undertaking given in pursuance of subsection (4A) above is for the purposes of this Act given with respect to the relevant land.

31(4F) It is for the person seeking the designation of relevant land to secure that any undertaking required under subsection (4A) above is given.

31(4FA) For the purposes of this section, the steps agreed for securing reasonable access to the public must ensure that the access that is secured is not confined to access only where a prior appointment has been made.

31(4FB) Subject to subsection (3) above, where the steps that may be set out in any undertaking include steps for securing reasonable access to the public to any property, the steps that may be agreed and set out in that undertaking may also include steps involving the publication of–

IHT Statutes

(a) the terms of any undertaking given or to be given for any of the purposes of this Act with respect to the property; or

(b) any other information relating to the property which (apart from this subsection) would fall to be treated as confidential;

and references in this Act to an **"undertaking for access"** to any property shall be construed as including references to so much of any undertaking as provides for the taking of steps involving any such publication.

31(4G) In a case where–

(a) the transfer of value in question is a potentially exempt transfer which (apart from section 30 above) has proved to be a chargeable transfer, and

(b) at the time of the transferor's death an undertaking by such a person as is mentioned in section 30(1)(b) above given under paragraph 3(3) of Schedule 4 to this Act or under section 258 of the 1992 Act is in force with respect to any property to which the value transferred by the transfer is attributable,

that undertaking shall be treated for the purposes of this Chapter as an undertaking given under section 30 above.

31(5) In this section

"national interest" includes interest within any part of the United Kingdom; and

"relevant object" means

(a) a picture, print, book, manuscript, work of art or scientific object, or

(b) anything not falling within paragraph (a) above that does not yield income;

and in determining under subsection (1)(a) or (aa) above whether an object or a collection or group of objects is pre-eminent, regard shall be had to any significant association of the object, collection or group with a particular place.

History – S. 31(1)(a) and (aa) substituted for former s. 31(1)(a) by FA 1998, s. 142 and Sch. 25, para. 4(1), with effect in relation to any designation on a claim made on or after 31 July 1998.

S. 31(1)(d) substituted by FA 1985, s. 94(1) and Sch. 26, para. 2(2), in relation to events on or after 19 March 1985.

S. 31(1A) inserted by FA 1986, Sch. 19, para. 8(1), with respect to transfers of value made, and other events occurring on or after 18 March 1986.

In s. 31(2), (3), references to subs. (1)(a) or (aa) substituted for former references to subs. (1)(a) by FA 1998, s. 142 and Sch. 25, para. 4(2), with effect in relation to the making of any designation on a claim made on or after 31 July 1998.

In s. 31(2)(b) and (4), the words "such steps…set out in" substituted by FA 1985, s. 94(1) and Sch. 26, para. 2(3), in relation to events on or after 19 March 1985.

S. 31(4A)–(4F) inserted, in relation to events on or after 19 March 1985, by FA 1985, s. 94(1) and Sch. 26, para. 2(4).

S. 31(4FA) inserted by FA 1998, s. 142 and Sch. 25, para. 5(1), with effect in relation to the giving of any undertaking on or after 31 July 1998.

S. 31(4FB) inserted by FA 1998, s. 140 and Sch. 25, para. 6(1), with respect to the giving of any undertaking on or after 31 July 1998.

In s. 31(4G)(b) reference to "258 of the 1992 Act" substituted by TCGA 1992, s. 290 and Sch. 10, para. 8(2).

S. 31(4G) inserted by FA 1986, s. 101 and Sch. 19, para. 8(2), with respect to transfers of value made, and other events occurring, on or after 18 March 1986.

S. 31(5) substituted by FA 1998, s. 142 and Sch. 25, para. 4(3), with effect in relation to the making of any designation on a claim made on or after 31 July 1998.

Cross references – S. 78: conditionally exempt occasions in relation to property comprised in discretionary trusts.

S. 79(3): designated property comprised in discretionary trusts – exemption from ten-yearly charge.

Sch. 5, para. 5(2) (conditional exemption on deaths before 7 April 1976): s. 31(3) applies in relation to documents which are designated as objects to which FA 1975, s. 31 applies as it applies to documents designated under s. 31(1)(a) above.

FA 1986, Sch. 19, para. 40(1): transitional – transfer of value occurring before, and death or other event occurring after, 18 March 1986.

TCGA 1992, s. 258(3), (4): capital gains tax treatment of property designable under s. 31 where undertaking given.

Hansard – HC Written Answer, Hansard, 9 February 1987, col. 35: details of what is considered to be appropriate publicity regarding public access.

Other material – IR 67 (not reproduced): National Heritage booklet, "Capital Taxation and the National Heritage". See particularly para. 11.12: guidelines for expert advisers on what would satisfy the "pre-eminent" test in s. 31:

(i) does the object have an especially close association with our history and national life?

(ii) is the object of especial artistic or art-historical interest?

(iii) is the object of especial importance for the study of some particular form of art, learning or history?

(iv) does the object have an especially close association with a particular historic setting?

32 Chargeable events

32(1) Where there has been a conditionally exempt transfer of any property, tax shall be charged under this section on the first occurrence after the transfer (or, if the transfer was a potentially exempt transfer, after the death of the transferor) of an event which under this section is a chargeable event with respect to the property.

32(2) *If the Treasury are satisfied* that at any time an undertaking given with respect to the property under section 30 above or subsection (5AA) below has not been observed in a material respect, the failure to observe the undertaking is a chargeable event with respect to the property.

32(3) If–

(a) the person beneficially entitled to the property dies, or

(b) the property is disposed of, whether by sale or gift or otherwise,

the death or disposal is, subject to subsections (4), (4A) and (5) below, a chargeable event with respect to the property.

32(4) A death or disposal is not a chargeable event with respect to any property if the personal representatives of the deceased (or, in the case of settled property, the trustees or the person next entitled) within three years of the death make or, as the case may be, the disposal is–

(a) a disposal of the property by sale by private treaty to a body mentioned in Schedule 3 to this Act, or a disposal of it to such a body otherwise than by sale, or

(b) a disposal in pursuance of section 230 below,

and a death or disposal of the property after such a disposal as is mentioned in paragraph (a) or (b) above is not a chargeable event with respect to the property unless there has again been a conditionally exempt transfer of it after that disposal.

32(4A) A death or disposal is not a chargeable event with respect to any property if–

(a) in the case of a death, a person who became beneficially entitled to the property on the death disposes of it in the circumstances described in paragraph 1 of Schedule 14 to the Finance Act 2012 (gifts to the nation) within 3 years of the death, or

(b) in the case of a disposal, the disposal is made in the circumstances described in paragraph 1 of that Schedule,

and a death or disposal of the property after such a disposal as is mentioned in paragraph (a) or (b) is not a chargeable event with respect to the property unless there has again been a conditionally exempt transfer of it after that disposal.

32(5) A death or disposal otherwise than by sale is not a chargeable event with respect to any property if–

(a) the transfer of value made on the death or the disposal is itself a conditionally exempt transfer of the property, or

(b) the condition specified in subsection (5AA) below is satisfied with respect to the property.

32(5AA) The condition referred to in subsection (5)(b) above is satisfied if–

(a) the requisite undertaking described in section 31 above is given with respect to the property by such person as the Board think appropriate in the circumstances of the case, or

(b) (where the property is an area of land within section 31(1)(d) above) the requisite undertakings described in that section are given with respect to the property by such person or persons as the Board think appropriate in the circumstances of the case.

32(5A) This section does not apply where section 32A below applies.

32(6), (7) [Repealed by FA 1985, s. 94(1) and Sch. 26, para. 3(3).]

History – In s. 32(1), reference to s. 32(5AA) substituted for former reference to s. 32(5)(b) by FA 1998, s. 142 and Sch. 25, para. 7(1), with effect in relation to the giving of any undertaking on or after 31 July 1998.

In s. 32(1), the words "(or, if the transfer…death of the transferor)" were inserted by FA 1986, s. 101 and Sch. 19, para. 9, with respect to transfers of value made, and other events occurring, on or after 18 March 1986.

In s. 32(3), the words "subsections (4), (4A) and (5)" substituted for "subsections (4) and (5)" by FA 2012, s. 49 and Sch. 14, para. 29(2), with effect from 17 July 2012.

S. 32(4A) inserted by FA 2012, s. 49 and Sch. 14, para. 29(3), with effect from 17 July 2012.

S. 32(5)(b) substituted by FA 1998, s. 142 and Sch. 25, para. 7(1), with effect in relation to the giving of any undertaking on or after 31 July 1998.

S. 32(5AA) inserted by FA 1998, s. 142 and Sch. 25, para. 7(3), with effect in relation to the giving of any undertaking on or after 31 July 1998.

S. 32(5A) inserted by FA 1985, s. 94(1) and Sch. 26, para. 3(3), in relation to events on or after 19 March 1985.

S. 32(6), (7) repealed with effect in relation to events on or after 19 March 1985.

Cross references – S. 78(3): designated property comprised in discretionary trusts – conditionally exempt occasions.

S. 207(1), (2): liability for tax on chargeable events by virtue of s. 32(2), (3).

S. 216(7): time within which a person liable under s. 32 must deliver an account.

S. 221: notices of determination.

S. 226(4): due date for payment of tax on a chargeable event under s. 32.

S. 230: acceptance of property in satisfaction of tax.

S. 233(1)(c): interest on unpaid tax chargeable under s. 32.

Sch. 6: interaction with estate duty.

FA 1986, Sch. 19, para. 40(1): transitional – transfer of value occurring before, and death or other event occurring after, 18 March 1986.

FA 1986, Sch. 19, para. 41: chargeable events on or after 18 March 1986 – transitional provisions where rate to be determined by reference to a death which occurred before that date.

TCGA 1992, s. 258(5): capital gains tax treatment of asset sold where tax chargeable under s. 32.

FA 1998, Sch. 25, para. 10(5)(a) and 6(a): variation of undertakings given under s. 32 with respect to any property before 31 July 1998.

Statements of practice – SP 11/84: estate duty calculation of clawback charge on heritage objects previously granted conditional exemption.

32A Associated properties

32A(1) For the purposes of this section the following properties are **associated** with each other, namely, a building falling within section 31(1)(c) above and (to the extent that any of the following exists) an area or areas of land falling within section 31(1)(d) above in relation to the building and an object or objects falling within section 31(1)(e) above in relation to the building; and this section applies where there are such properties, which are referred to as associated properties.

32A(2) Where there has been a conditionally exempt transfer of any property (or part), tax shall be charged under this section in respect of that property (or part) on the first occurrence after the transfer (or, if the transfer was a potentially exempt transfer, after the death of the transferor) of an event which under this section is a chargeable event with respect to that property (or part).

32A(3) If the Treasury are satisfied that at any time an undertaking given under section 30 above or this section for the maintenance, repair, preservation, access or keeping of any of the associated properties has not been observed in a material respect, then (subject to subsection (10) below) the failure to observe the undertaking is a chargeable event with respect to the whole of each of the associated properties of which there has been a conditionally exempt transfer.

32A(4) If–

(a) the person beneficially entitled to property dies, or

(b) property (or part of it) is disposed of, whether by sale or gift or otherwise,

then, if the property is one of the associated properties and an undertaking for its maintenance, repair, preservation, access or keeping has been given under section 30 above or this section, the death or disposal is (subject to subsections (5) to (10) below) a chargeable event with respect to the whole of each of the associated properties of which there has been a conditionally exempt transfer.

32A(5) Subject to subsection (6) below, the death of a person beneficially entitled to property, or the disposal of property (or part), is not a chargeable event if the personal representatives of the deceased (or, in the case of settled property, the trustees or the person next entitled) within three years of the death make or, as the case may be, the disposal is–

(a) a disposal of the property (or part) concerned by sale by private treaty to a body mentioned in Schedule 3 to this Act, or to such a body otherwise than by sale, or

(b) a disposal of the property (or part) concerned in pursuance of section 230 below.

32A(5A) The death of a person beneficially entitled to property, or the disposal of property, is not a chargeable event if–

(a) in the case of a death, a person who became beneficially entitled to the property on the death disposes of it in the circumstances described in paragraph 1 of Schedule 14 to the Finance Act 2012 (gifts to the nation) within 3 years of the death, or

(b) in the case of a disposal, the disposal is made in the circumstances described in paragraph 1 of that Schedule.

32A(6) Where a disposal mentioned in subsection (5)(a) or (b) above is a part disposal, that subsection does not make the event non-chargeable with respect to property other than that disposed of unless–

(a) the requisite undertaking described in section 31 above is given with respect to the property (or part) not disposed of by such person as the Board think appropriate in the circumstances of the case, or

(b) (where any of the property or part not disposed of is an area of land within section 31(1)(d) above) the requisite undertakings described in that section are given with respect to that property (or that part) by such person or persons as the Board think appropriate in the circumstances of the case;

and in this subsection **"part disposal"** means a disposal of property which does not consist of or include the whole of each property which is one of the associated properties and of which there has been a conditionally exempt transfer.

32A(7) Where, after a relevant disposal (that is, a disposal mentioned in subsection (5)(a) or (b) or (5A)(a) or (b) above made in circumstances where that subsection applies), a person beneficially entitled to the property (or part) concerned dies or the property (or part) concerned is disposed of, the death or disposal is not a chargeable event with respect to the property (or part) concerned unless there has again been a conditionally exempt transfer of the property (or part) concerned after the relevant disposal.

32A(8) The death of a person beneficially entitled to property, or the disposal of property (or part) otherwise than by sale, is not a chargeable event if–

(a) the transfer of value made on the death or the disposal is itself a conditionally exempt transfer of the property (or part) concerned, or

(b) the condition specified in subsection (8A) below is satisfied with respect to the property (or part) concerned.

32A(8A) The condition referred to in subsection (8)(b) above is satisfied if–

(a) the requisite undertaking described in section 31 above is given with respect to the property (or part) by such person as the Board think appropriate in the circumstances of the case, or

(b) (where any of the property or part is an area of land within section 31(1)(d) above) the requisite undertakings described in that section are given with respect to the property (or part) by such person or persons as the Board think appropriate in the circumstances of the case.

32A(9) If the whole or part of any property is disposed of by sale and–

(a) the requisite undertaking described in section 31 above is given with respect to the property (or part) by such person as the Board think appropriate in the circumstances of the case, or

(b) (where any of the property or part is an area of land within section 31(1)(d) above) the requisite undertakings described in that section are given with respect to the property (or part) by such person or persons as the Board think appropriate in the circumstances of the case,

the disposal is a chargeable event only with respect to the whole or part actually disposed of (if it is a chargeable event with respect to such whole or part apart from this subsection).

32A(10) If–

(a) the Treasury are satisfied that there has been a failure to observe, as to one of the associated properties or part of it, an undertaking for the property's maintenance, repair preservation, access or keeping, or

(b) there is a disposal of one of the associated properties or part of it,

and it appears to the Treasury that the entity consisting of the associated properties has not been materially affected by the failure or disposal, they may direct that it shall be a chargeable event only with respect to the property or part as to which there has been a failure or disposal (if it is a chargeable event with respect to that property or part apart from this subsection).

History – In s. 32A(2), the words "(or, if the transfer … death of the transferor)" were inserted by FA 1986, s. 101(3) and Sch. 19 para. 10 with respect to transfers of value made, and other events occurring, on or after 18 March 1986.
S. 32A(5A) inserted by FA 2012, s. 49 and Sch. 14, para. 30(2), with effect from 17 July 2012.
In s. 32A(6), words from "unless–" before para. (a) to "and" following para. (b) substituted by FA 1998, s. 142 and Sch. 25, para. 7(4), with effect in relation to the giving of any undertaking on or after 31 July 1998.
In s. 32A(7), the words "or (5A)(a) or (b)" inserted after "(5)(a) or (b)" by FA 2012, s. 49 and Sch. 14, para. 30(3), with effect from 17 July 2012.
S. 32A(8)(b) substituted by FA 1998, s. 142 and Sch. 25, para. 7(5), with effect in relation to the giving of any undertaking on or after 31 July 1998.
S. 32A(8A) inserted by FA 1998, s. 142 and Sch. 25, para. 7(6), with effect in relation to the giving of any undertaking on or after 31 July 1998.
S. 32A(9) substituted by FA 1998, s. 142 and Sch. 25 para. 7(7), with effect in relation to the giving of any undertaking on or after 31 July 1998.
S. 32A inserted by FA 1985, Sch. 26, para. 4, in relation to events on or after 19 March 1985.

Cross references – S. 78(3): designated property comprised in discretionary trusts – conditionally exempt occasions.
S. 207(2A), (2B): liability for tax on chargeable events by virtue of s. 32A(3), (4).
S. 216(7): time within which a person liable under s. 32A must deliver an account.
S. 221: notices of determination.
S. 226(4): due date for payment of tax on a chargeable event under s. 32A.
S. 230: acceptance of property in satisfaction of tax.
S. 233(1)(c): interest on unpaid tax chargeable under s. 32A.
Sch. 6: interaction with estate duty.
FA 1986, Sch. 19, para. 40(1): transitional – transfer of value occurring before, and death or other event occurring after, 18 March 1986.
FA 1986, Sch. 19, para. 41: chargeable events occurring on or after 18 March 1986 – transitional provisions where rate to be determined by reference to a death which occurred before that date.
FA 1998, Sch. 25, para. 10(5)(a): variation of undertakings given under s. 32A with respect to any property before 31 July 1998.

33 Amount of charge under section 32 or 32A

Notes – Section heading altered by Croner-i to include "or 32A" so as to reflect altered content in relation to events on or after 19 March 1985.

33(1) Tax chargeable in respect of any property under section 32 or 32A above by reference to a chargeable event shall be charged–

(a) on an amount equal to the value of the property at the time of the chargeable event; and

(b) at the following rate or rates–

   (i) if the relevant person is alive, the rate or rates that would be applicable to that amount in accordance with section 7(2) above if it were the value transferred by a chargeable transfer made by the relevant person at that time;

   (ii) if the relevant person is dead, the rate or rates that would have applied to that amount in accordance with the appropriate provision of section 7 above if it had been added to the value transferred on his death and had formed the highest part of that value.

33(2) For the purposes of subsection (1)(b)(ii) above the appropriate provision of section 7 above is–

(a) if the conditionally exempt transfer by the relevant person was made on death (but the property was not treated as forming part of his estate immediately before his death only by virtue of section 102(3) of the Finance Act 1986), subsection (1) of section 7; and

(b) in any other case, subsection (2) of section 7.

33(2ZA) In determining for the purposes of subsection (1)(b)(ii) the rate or rates that would have applied in accordance with subsection (1) of section 7, the effect of Schedule 1A (if it would have applied) is to be disregarded.

33(2A) The rate or rates of tax determined under subsection (1)(b)(i) above in respect of any chargeable event shall not be affected by the death of the relevant person after that event.

33(3) Where the chargeable event is a disposal on sale and the sale–

(a) was not intended to confer any gratuitous benefit on any person, and

(b) was either a transaction at arm's length between persons not connected with each other or a transaction such as might be expected to be made at arm's length between persons not connected with each other,

the value of the property at the time of the chargeable event shall be taken for the purposes of subsection (1)(a) above to be equal to the proceeds of the sale.

33(4) Where by virtue of section 30(4) above the conditionally exempt transfer extended only to part of the property, the amount mentioned in subsection (1)(a) above shall be proportionately reduced.

33(5) The **relevant person** in relation to a chargeable event in respect of any property is–

(a) if there has been only one conditionally exempt transfer of the property before the event, the person who made that transfer;

(b) if there have been two or more such transfers and the last was before, or only one of them was within, the period of thirty years ending with the event, the person who made the last of those transfers;

(c) if there have been two or more such transfers within that period, the person who made whichever of those transfers the Board may select.

33(6) The conditionally exempt transfers to be taken into account for the purpose of subsection (5) above in relation to a chargeable event do not include transfers made before any previous chargeable event in respect of the same property or before any event which apart from section 32(4) or (4A) above would have been such a chargeable event or, where the property has been disposed of as mentioned in section 32A(5) or (5A) above, before any event which apart from section 32A(5) or (5A) would have been such a chargeable event.

33(7) Subject to subsection (8) below where after a conditionally exempt transfer of any property there is a chargeable transfer the value transferred by which is wholly or partly attributable to that property, any tax charged on that value so far as attributable to that property shall be allowed as a credit–

(a) if the chargeable transfer is a chargeable event with respect to the property, against the tax chargeable in accordance with this section by reference to that event;

(b) if the chargeable transfer is not such a chargeable event, against the tax chargeable in accordance with this section by reference to the next chargeable event with respect to the property.

33(8) Where after a conditionally exempt transfer of any property there is a potentially exempt transfer the value transferred by which is wholly or partly attributable to that property and either–

(a) the potentially exempt transfer is a chargeable event with respect to the property, or

(b) after the potentially exempt transfer, but before the death of the person who is the transferor in relation to the potentially exempt transfer, a chargeable event occurs with respect to the property,

the tax charged in accordance with this section by reference to that chargeable event shall be allowed as a credit against any tax which may become chargeable, by reason of the potentially exempt transfer proving to be a chargeable transfer, on so much of the value transferred by that transfer as is attributable to the property; and subsection (7) above shall not apply with respect to any tax so becoming chargeable.

History – In s. 33(1) the words "in accordance with section 7(2) above" in sub-para. (b)(i) and "in accordance with the appropriate provision of section 7 above" in sub-para. (b)(ii) were substituted by FA 1986, s. 94(1) and Sch. 19, para. 11(1), with respect to transfers of value made, and other events occurring, on or after 18 March 1986, and the words "or 32A" were inserted by FA 1985, s. 94(1) and Sch. 26, para. 5, in relation to events on or after 19 March 1985.

S. 33(2ZA) inserted by FA 2012, s. 209 and Sch. 33, para. 4, with effect in cases where D's death occurs on or after 6 April 2012.

S. 33(2) and (2A) substituted by FA 1986, s. 101 and Sch. 19, para. 11(2), with respect to transfers of value made, and other events occurring, on or after 18 March 1986.

In s. 33(6), the words "section 32(4) or (4A)" substituted for "section 32(4)" by FA 2012, s. 49 and Sch. 14, para. 31(a), with effect from 17 July 2012.

In s. 33(6), the words "section 32A(5) or (5A)" substituted for "section 32A(5)" in both places by FA 2012, s. 49 and Sch. 14, para. 31(b), with effect from 17 July 2012.

In s. 33(6), the words "or, where…such a chargeable event" were inserted by FA 1985, s. 94(1) and Sch. 26, para. 6, in relation to events on or after 19 March 1985.

In s. 33(7), the words "Subject to subsection (8) below" were inserted by FA 1986, s. 94(1) and Sch. 19, para. 11(3), with respect to transfers of value made, and other events occurring, on or after 18 March 1986.
S. 33(8) inserted by FA 1986, s. 101 and Sch. 19, para. 11(4), with respect to transfers of value made, and other events occurring, on or after 18 March 1986.

Cross references – S. 78(3)–(5): designated property comprised in discretionary trusts – conditionally exempt occasions.
Sch. 2, para. 5: rate to be determined under s. 33(1)(b)(ii) where there has been a reduction in the rate chargeable under Sch. 1 between death of relevant person and chargeable event.
Sch. 6, para. 4(3): interaction with estate duty.
FA 1986, Sch. 19, para. 40(1): transitional – transfer of value occurring before, and death or other event occurring after, 18 March 1986.
TCGA 1992, s. 258: interaction with capital gains tax.
Notes – FA 1986, s. 102(3): gifts with reservation.

34 Reinstatement of transferor's cumulative total

34(1) Where tax has become chargeable under section 32 or 32A above by reference to a chargeable event in respect of any property (**"the relevant event"**) the rate or rates of tax applicable to any subsequent chargeable transfer made by the person who made the last conditionally exempt transfer of the property before the relevant event shall be determined as if the amount on which tax has become chargeable as aforesaid were value transferred by a chargeable transfer made by him at the time of the relevant event.

34(2) Where the person who made the last conditionally exempt transfer of the property before the relevant event–

(a) is dead, and

(b) is for the purposes of section 33 above the relevant person in relation to a subsequent chargeable event,

section 33(1)(b)(ii) shall have effect as if the value transferred on his death were increased by the amount on which tax has become chargeable on the occasion of the relevant event.

34(3) If–

(a) the person who made the last conditionally exempt transfer of the property before the relevant event is not the relevant person for the purposes of section 33 above in relation to that event, and

(b) at the time of that event or within the previous five years the property is or has been comprised in a settlement made not more than thirty years before that event, and

(c) a person who is the settlor in relation to the settlement has made a conditionally exempt transfer of the property within those thirty years,

subsections (1) and (2) above shall have effect with the substitution for references to the person who made the last conditionally exempt transfer before the relevant event of a reference to any such person as is mentioned in paragraph (c) above.

34(4) The conditionally exempt transfers to be taken into account for the purposes of subsection (3)(c) above in relation to the relevant event do not include transfers made before any previous chargeable event in respect of the same property or before any event which apart from section 32(4) or (4A) above would have been such a chargeable event or, where the property has been disposed of as mentioned in section 32A(5) or (5A) above, before any event which apart from section 32A(5) or (5A) would have been such a chargeable event.

History – In s. 34(1), the words "or 32A", and in s. 34(4) the words "or, where … such a chargeable event" were inserted by FA 1985, s. 94(1) and Sch. 26, para. 5, 6, in relation to events on or after 19 March 1985.
In s. 34(4), the words "section 32(4) or (4A)" substituted for "section 32(4)" by FA 2012, s. 49 and Sch. 14, para. 32(a), with effect from 17 July 2012.
In s. 34(4), the words "section 32A(5) or (5A)" substituted for "section 32A(5)" in both places by FA 2012, s. 49 and Sch. 14, para. 32(b), with effect from 17 July 2012.

Cross references – S. 78(6): disapplication of s. 34 where conditionally exempt transfer of property is followed by a conditionally exempt occasion (within s. 78) in respect of it.
TCGA 1992, s. 258: interaction with capital gains tax.

35 Conditional exemption on death before 7 April 1976

35(1) Schedule 5 to this Act shall have effect with respect to certain cases where, by virtue of sections 31 to 34 of the *Finance Act 1975*, the value of any property was left out of account in determining the value transferred on a death before 7th April 1976.

35(2) Where there has been a transfer of value in relation to which the value of any property has been left out of account under the provisions of sections 31 to 34 of the Finance Act 1975 and, before any tax has become chargeable in respect of that property under those provisions, there is a conditionally exempt transfer of that property, then, on the occurrence of a chargeable event in respect of that property–

(a) tax shall be chargeable under section 32 or 32A (as the case may be), or

(b) tax shall be chargeable under Schedule 5,

as the Board may elect,

35(3) In section 33(7) and (8) above, references to a **conditionally exempt transfer of any property** include references to a transfer of value in relation to which the value of any property has been left out of account under the provisions of sections 31 to 34 of the Finance Act 1975 and, in relation to such property, references to a **chargeable event** or to the **tax chargeable** in accordance with section 33 above by reference to a chargeable event include references to an event on the occurrence of which tax becomes chargeable under Schedule 5 to this Act, or to the tax so chargeable.

History – S. 35(2)(a) and (b) (and words following para. (b)) substituted by FA 2016, s. 97(6), with effect in relation to a chargeable event where the conditionally exempt transfer referred to in IHTA 1984, s. 35(2) or Sch. 6, para. 4(2) occurred after 16 March 2016. Former para. (a) and (b) read as follows:

"(a) if there has been no conditionally exempt transfer of the property on death, tax shall be chargeable either–
- (i) under section 32 or 32A above (as the case may be), or
- (ii) under Schedule 5 to this Act,

as the Board may elect;

(b) if there has been such a conditionally exempt transfer, tax shall be chargeable under section 32 or 32A above (as the case may be) and not under that Schedule."

Former s. 35(2)(a) and (b), substituted by FA 1985, s. 94(1) and Sch. 26, para. 7, in relation to events on or after 19 March 1985.

In s. 35(3), the words "section 33(7) and (8) above, references" and "include references" were substituted by FA 1986, s. 101 and Sch. 19, para. 12, with respect to transfers of value made, and other events occurring, on or after 18 March 1986.

Cross references – S. 78(3): designated property comprised in discretionary trusts – conditionally exempt occasions.
FA 1986, Sch. 19, para. 40(1): transitional – transfer of value occurring before, and death or other event occurring after, 18 March 1986.
TCGA 1992, s. 258: interaction with capital gains tax.

35A Variation of undertakings

35A(1) An undertaking given under section 30, 32 or 32A above or paragraph 5 of Schedule 5 to this Act may be varied from time to time by agreement between the Board and the person bound by the undertaking.

35A(2) Where the tribunal is satisfied that–

(a) the Board have made a proposal for the variation of such an undertaking to the person bound by the undertaking,

(b) that person has failed to agree to the proposed variation within six months after the date on which the proposal was made, and

(c) it is just and reasonable, in all the circumstances, to require the proposed variation to be made,

the tribunal may direct that the undertaking is to have effect from a specified date as if the proposed variation had been agreed to by the person bound by the undertaking.

35A(3) The date specified by the tribunal must not be less than sixty days after the date of the tribunal's direction.

35A(4) A direction under this section shall not take effect if, before the date specified by the tribunal, a variation different from that to which the direction relates is agreed between the Board and the person bound by the undertaking.

History – In s. 35A(2) the words "the tribunal" substituted for the words "a Special Commissioner" and the words "the tribunal may direct that the undertaking is to have effect from a specified date" substituted for the words "the Commissioner may direct that the undertaking is to have effect from a date specified by him" by SI 2009/56, art. 3 and Sch. 1, para. 109(2), with effect from 1 April 2009, subject to transitional and saving provisions in SI 2009/56, Sch. 3.

In s. 35A(3) the word "tribunal" substituted for the words "Special Commissioner" and the words "the tribunal's direction" substituted for the words "his direction" by SI 2009/56, art. 3 and Sch. 1, para. 109(3), with effect from 1 April 2009, subject to transitional and saving provisions in SI 2009/56, Sch. 3.

In s. 35A(4) the word "tribunal" substituted for the words "Special Commissioner" by SI 2009/56, art. 3 and Sch. 1, para. 109(4), with effect from 1 April 2009, subject to transitional and saving provisions in SI 2009/56, Sch. 3.

S. 35A inserted by FA 1998, s. 142 and Sch. 25, para. 8(1), with effect in relation to undertakings given on or after 31 July 1998, and as modified by FA 1998, Sch. 25, para. 10 in relation to undertakings given before that day.

Cross references – SI 2009/275, art. 3(b): any decision under s. 35A(2) is an excluded decision for the purposes of TCEA 2007, s. 11(1) and 13(1).
Sch. 4, para. 3(3A): s. 35A applies to an undertaking given under Sch. 4, para. 3(3) (designation of maintenance funds for historic buildings etc.) as it applies to an undertaking given under s. 30.
TCGA 1992, s. 258(8A): s. 35A applies to an undertaking given under TCGA 1992, s. 258 (gain accruing on disposal of a work of art etc.) as it applies to an undertaking given under s. 30.
FA 1998, Sch. 25, para. 10: modifications of s. 35A as it applies in relation to undertakings given before 17 March 1998.

Chapter III – Allocation of Exemptions

36 Preliminary

36 Where any one or more of sections 18, 23 to 27 and 30 above apply in relation to a transfer of value *but the transfer is not wholly exempt*–

(a) any question as to the extent to which it is exempt or, where it is exempt up to a limit, how an excess over the limit is to be attributed to the gifts concerned shall be determined in accordance with sections 37 to 40 below; and

(b) section 41 below shall have effect as respects the burden of tax.

Cross references – S. 18: transfers between spouses.
S. 23–27 gifts to charities, political parties, housing associations etc.
S. 30: conditionally exempt transfers.

37 Abatement of gifts

37(1) Where a gift would be abated owing to an insufficiency of assets and without regard to any tax chargeable, the gift shall be treated for the purposes of the following provisions of this Chapter as so abated.

37(2) Where the value attributable, in accordance with section 38 below, to specific gifts exceeds the value transferred the gifts shall be treated as reduced to the extent necessary to reduce their value to that of the value transferred; and the reduction shall be made in the order in which, under the terms of the relevant disposition or any rule of law, it would fall to be made on a distribution of assets.

38 Attribution of value to specific gifts

38(1) Such part of the value transferred shall be attributable to specific gifts as corresponds to the value of the gifts; but if or to the extent that the gifts–

(a) are not gifts with respect to which the transfer is exempt or are outside the limit up to which the transfer is exempt, and

(b) do not bear their own tax,

the amount corresponding to the value of the gifts shall be taken to be the amount arrived at in accordance with subsections (3) to (5) below.

38(2) Where any question arises as to which of two or more specific gifts are outside the limit up to which a transfer is exempt or as to the extent to which a specific gift is outside that limit–

(a) the excess shall be attributed to gifts not bearing their own tax before being attributed to gifts bearing their own tax, and

(b) subject to paragraph (a) above, the excess shall be attributed to gifts in proportion to their values.

38(3) Where the only gifts with respect to which the transfer is or might be chargeable are specific gifts which do not bear their own tax, the amount referred to in subsection (1) above is the aggregate of–

(a) the sum of the value of those gifts; and

(b) the amount of tax which would be chargeable if the value transferred equalled that aggregate.

38(4) Where the specific gifts not bearing their own tax are not the only gifts with respect to which the transfer is or might be chargeable, the amount referred to in subsection (1) above is such amount as, after deduction of tax at the assumed rate specified in subsection (5) below, would be equal to the sum of the value of those gifts.

38(5) For the purposes of subsection (4) above–

(a) the **assumed rate** is the rate found by dividing the assumed amount of tax by that part of the value transferred with respect to which the transfer would be chargeable on the hypothesis that–

(i) the amount corresponding to the value of specific gifts not bearing their own tax is equal to the aggregate referred to in subsection (3) above, and

(ii) the parts of the value transferred attributable to specific gifts and to gifts of residue or shares in residue are determined accordingly; and

(b) the **assumed amount of tax** is the amount that would be charged on the value transferred on the hypothesis mentioned in paragraph (a) above.

38(6) For the purposes of this section, any liability of the transferor which is not to be taken into account under section 5(5) above or by virtue of section 103 of the Finance Act 1986 shall be treated as a specific gift and, to the extent that any liability of the transferor is abated under the said section 103, that liability shall be treated as a specific gift.

History – In s. 38(6), the words "or by virtue of section 103 of the Finance Act 1986", and "and to the extent that" to the end, were inserted by FA 1986, s. 101 and Sch. 19, para. 13, with respect to transfers of value made, and other events occurring, on or after 18 March 1986.

Cross references – S. 5(5): liabilities to be taken into account only if incurred for full consideration.
FA 1986, s. 103: treatment of certain debts and incumbrances.
FA 1986, Sch. 19, para. 40(1): transitional – transfer of value occurring before, and death or other event occurring after, 18 March 1986.

39 Attribution of value to residuary gifts

39 Such part only of the value transferred shall be attributed to gifts of residue or shares in residue as is not attributed under section 38 above to specific gifts.

39A Operation of sections 38 and 39 in cases of business or agricultural relief

39A(1) Where any part of the value transferred by a transfer of value is attributable to–

(a) the value of relevant business property, or

(b) the agricultural value of agricultural property,

then, for the purpose of attributing the value transferred (as reduced in accordance with section 104 or 116 below), to specific gifts and gifts of residue or shares of residue, sections 38 and 39 above shall have effect subject to the following provisions of this section.

39A(2) The value of any specific gifts of relevant business property or agricultural property shall be taken to be their value as reduced in accordance with section 104 or 116 below.

39A(3) The value of any specific gifts not falling within subsection (2) above shall be taken to be the appropriate fraction of their value.

39A(4) In subsection (3) above **"the appropriate fraction"** means a fraction of which–

(a) the numerator is the difference between the value transferred and the value, reduced as mentioned in subsection (2) above, of any gifts falling within that subsection, and

(b) the denominator is the difference between the unreduced value transferred and the value, before the reduction mentioned in subsection (2) above, of any gifts falling within that subsection;

and in paragraph (b) above **"the unreduced value transferred"** means the amount which would be the value transferred by the transfer but for the reduction required by sections 104 and 116 below.

39A(5) If or to the extent that specific gifts fall within paragraphs (a) and (b) of subsection (1) of section 38 above, the amount corresponding to the value of the gifts shall be arrived at in accordance with subsections (3) to (5) of that section by reference to their value reduced as mentioned in subsection (2) or, as the case may be, subsection (3) of this section.

39A(6) For the purposes of this section the value of a specific gift of relevant business property or agricultural property does not include the value of any other gift payable out of that property; and that other gift shall not itself be treated as a specific gift of relevant business property or agricultural property.

39A(7) In this section–

"agricultural property" and **"the agricultural value of agricultural property"** have the same meaning as in Chapter II of Part V of this Act; and

"relevant business property" has the same meaning as in Chapter I of that Part.

History – S. 39A inserted by FA 1986, s. 105, with respect to transfers of value made on or after 18 March 1986.

Cross references – S. 104: business property relief.
S. 116: agricultural property relief.

40 Gifts made separately out of different funds

40 Where gifts taking effect on a transfer of value take effect separately out of different funds the preceding provisions of this Chapter shall be applied separately to the gifts taking effect out of each of those funds, with the necessary adjustments of the values and amounts referred to in those provisions.

Other material – Law Society's Gazette, 9 May 1990 (not reproduced): where gifts are made out of different funds, the rate of tax to be used for grossing up should be found by looking at each fund in isolation.

41 Burden of tax

41 Notwithstanding the terms of any disposition–

(a) none of the tax on the value transferred shall fall on any specific gift if or to the extent that the transfer is exempt with respect to the gift, and

(b) none of the tax attributable to the value of the property comprised in residue shall fall on any gift of a share of residue if or to the extent that the transfer is exempt with respect to the gift.

42 Supplementary

42(1) In this Chapter–

"gift", in relation to any transfer of value, means the benefit of any disposition or rule of law by which, on the making of the transfer, any property becomes (or would but for any abatement become) the property of any person or applicable for any purpose;

"given", shall be construed accordingly;

"specific gift" means any gift other than a gift of residue or of a share in residue.

42(2) For the purposes of this Chapter a gift bears its own tax if the tax attributable to it falls on the person who becomes entitled to the property given or (as the case may be) is payable out of property applicable for the purposes for which the property given becomes applicable.

42(3) Where–

(a) the whole or part of the value transferred by a transfer of value is attributable to property which is the subject of two or more gifts, and

(b) the aggregate of the values of the property given by each of those gifts is less than the value transferred or, as the case may be, that part of it, then for the purposes of this Chapter (and notwithstanding the definition of a gift in subsection (1) above) the value of each gift shall be taken to be the relevant proportion of the value transferred or, as the case may be, that part of it; and the relevant proportion in relation to any gift is the proportion which the value of the property given by it bears to the said aggregate.

42(4) Where on the death of a person legal rights under the law of Scotland are claimed by a person entitled to claim them, they shall be treated for the purposes of this Chapter as a specific gift which bears its own tax; and in determining the value of such legal rights, any tax payable on the estate of the deceased shall be left out of account.

PART III – SETTLED PROPERTY

Cross references – S. 201: persons liable for tax on chargeable transfers made under Pt. III.
S. 227: payment of tax by instalments.

Chapter I – Preliminary

43 Settlement and related expressions

43(1) The following provisions of this section apply for determining what is to be taken for the purposes of this Act to be a settlement, and what property is, accordingly, referred to as property comprised in a settlement or as settled property.

43(2) **"Settlement"** means any disposition or dispositions of property, whether effected by instrument, by parol or by operation of law, or partly in one way and partly in another, whereby the property is for the time being–

(a) held in trust for persons in succession or for any person subject to a contingency, or

(b) held by trustees on trust to accumulate the whole or part of any income of the property or with power to make payments out of that income at the discretion of the trustees or some other person, with or without power to accumulate surplus income, or

(c) charged or burdened (otherwise than for full consideration in money or money's worth paid for his own use or benefit to the person making the disposition) with the payment of any annuity or other periodical payment payable for a life or any other limited or terminable period,

or would be so held or charged or burdened if the disposition or dispositions were regulated by the law of any part of the United Kingdom; or whereby, under the law of any other country, the administration of the property is for the time being governed by provisions equivalent in effect to those which would apply if the property were so held, charged or burdened.

43(3) A lease of property which is for life or lives, or for a period ascertainable only by reference to a death, or which is terminable on, or at a date ascertainable only by reference to, a death, shall be treated as a settlement and the property as settled property, unless the lease was granted for full consideration in money or money's worth; and where a lease not granted as a lease at a rack rent is at any time to become a lease at an increased rent it shall be treated as terminable at that time.

43(4) In relation to Scotland **"settlement"** also includes–

(a) an entail,

(b) any deed by virtue of which an annuity is charged on, or on the rents of, any property (the property being treated as the property comprised in the settlement), and

(c) any deed creating or reserving a proper liferent of any property whether heritable or moveable (the property from time to time subject to the proper liferent being treated as the property comprised in the settlement);

and for the purposes of this subsection **"deed"** includes any disposition, arrangement, contract, resolution, instrument or writing.

43(5) In the application of this Act to Northern Ireland this section shall have effect as if references to property held in trust for persons included references to property standing limited to persons and as if the lease referred to in subsection (3) did not include a lease in perpetuity within the meaning of section 1 of the Renewable Leasehold Conversion Act 1849 or a lease to which section 37 of that Act applies.

Cross references – S. 50(6): amount of lessee's interest.
S. 170: valuation of lessor's interest where a lease of property is to be treated as a settlement under s. 43(3).
FA 2004, Sch. 15, para. 12(3): charge to income tax on benefits received by former owner of property, effective for 2005–06 onwards.

Extra-statutory concessions – F10: partnership assurance schemes, under which each partner effects a policy on his own life in trust for the other partners, not regarded as a settlement for IHT purposes if certain conditions fulfilled.
F11 (to be withdrawn with effect from April 2015): where an annuity is charged on real or leasehold property and the annuitant under a settlement dies or disposes of the interest; relief will be due where the current valuation anticipates an increase in rents obtainable after the date the charge arises.

Statements of practice – SP 10/79: trustees of discretionary trust granting lease for life for less than full consideration.

HMRC interpretations – IR Int. 1007: HMRC view that assets added to a settlor's own settlement, made at an earlier time when the settlor was domiciled abroad, are not "excluded", wherever situated, if settlor has UK domicile at time of making the addition.

44 Settlor

44(1) In this Act **"settlor"**, in relation to a settlement, includes any person by whom the settlement was made directly or indirectly, and in particular (but without prejudice to the generality of the preceding words) includes any person who has provided funds directly or indirectly for the purpose of or in connection with the settlement or has made with any other person a reciprocal arrangement for that other person to make the settlement.

44(2) Where more than one person is a settlor in relation to a settlement and the circumstances so require, this Part of this Act (except section 48(4) to (6)) shall have effect in relation to it as if the settled property were comprised in separate settlements.

HMRC interpretations – IR Int. 1007: HMRC views on extent to which assets in a settlement can be "excluded property" where there is more than one settlor; when domicile of settlor is a "relevant required circumstance" under s. 43(2).

45 Trustee

45 In this Act **"trustee"**, in relation to a settlement in relation to which there would be no trustees apart from this section, means any person in whom the settled property or its management is for the time being vested.

46 Interest in possession: Scotland

46 In the application of this Act to Scotland, any reference to **an interest in possession in settled property** is a reference to an interest of any kind under a settlement by virtue of which the person in right of that interest is entitled to the enjoyment of the property or would be so entitled if the property were capable of enjoyment, including an interest of an assignee under an assignation of an interest of any kind (other than a reversionary interest) in property subject to a proper liferent; and the person in right of such an interest at any time shall be deemed to be entitled to a corresponding interest in the whole or any part of the property comprised in the settlement.

46A Contract of life insurance entered into before 22nd March 2006 which on that day is settled property in which interest in possession subsists

46A(1) Subsections (2) and (4) below apply where–

(a) a settlement commenced before 22nd March 2006,

(b) a contract of life insurance was entered into before that day,

(c) a premium payable under the contract is paid, or an allowed variation is made to the contract, at a particular time on or after that day,

(d) immediately before that day, and at all subsequent times up to the particular time, there were rights under the contract that–

  (i) were comprised in the settlement, and

  (ii) were settled property in which a transitionally-protected interest (whether or not the same such interest throughout that period) subsisted,

(e) rights under the contract become, by reference to payment of the premium or as a result of the variation,–

  (i) comprised in the settlement, and

  (ii) part of the settled property in which the then-current transitionally-protected interest subsists, and

(f) any variation of the contract on or after 22nd March 2006 but before the particular time, so far as it is a variation that–

(i) increased the benefits secured by the contract, or

(ii) extended the term of the insurance provided by the contract,

was an allowed variation.

46A(2) For the purposes of the provisions mentioned in subsection (3) below–

(a) the rights mentioned in subsection (1)(e) above shall be taken to have become comprised in the settlement, and

(b) the person beneficially entitled to the then-current transitionally-protected interest shall be taken to have become beneficially entitled to his interest in possession so far as it subsists in those rights,

before 22nd March 2006.

46A(3) Those provisions are–

section 3A(2) above;

section 5(1A) above;

section 49(1A) and (1B) below;

section 51(1A) and (1B) below;

section 52(2A) and (3A) below;

section 53(1A) and (2A) below;

section 54(2A) and (2B) below;

section 54A(1A) below;

section 57A(1A) below;

section 58(1B) and (1C) below;

section 59(1) and (2) below;

section 80(4) below;

section 100(1A) below;

section 101(1A) below;

section 102ZA(1) of the Finance Act 1986 (gifts with reservation); and

sections 72(1A) and (2A) and 73(2A) of the 1992 Act.

46A(4) If payment of the premium is a transfer of value made by an individual, that transfer of value is a potentially exempt transfer.

46A(5) In this section–

"allowed variation", in relation to a contract, means a variation that takes place by operation of, or as a result of exercise of rights conferred by, provisions forming part of the contract immediately before 22nd March 2006;

"transitionally-protected interest" means–

(a) an interest in possession to which a person was beneficially entitled immediately before, and on, 22nd March 2006, or

(b) a transitional serial interest.

History – S. 46A inserted by FA 2006, s. 156 and Sch. 20, para. 11(1), with effect from 22 March 2006.

46B Contract of life insurance entered into before 22nd March 2006 which immediately before that day is property to which section 71 applies

46B(1) Subsections (2) and (5) below apply where–

(a) a settlement commenced before 22nd March 2006,

(b) a contract of life insurance was entered into before that day,

(c) a premium payable under the contract is paid, or an allowed variation is made to the contract, at a particular time on or after that day,

(d) immediately before that day, and at all subsequent times up to the particular time, there were rights under the contract that–

(i) were comprised in the settlement, and

(ii) were settled property to which section 71 below applied,

(e) rights under the contract become, by reference to payment of the premium or as a result of the variation, comprised in the settlement, and

(f) any variation of the contract on or after 22nd March 2006 but before the particular time, so far as it was a variation that–

(i) increased the benefits secured by the contract, or

(ii) extended the term of the insurance provided by the contract,

was an allowed variation.

46B(2) If the rights mentioned in subsection (1)(e) above would, but for subsection (1A) of section 71 below, become property to which that section applies, those rights shall become settled property to which that section applies when they become comprised in the settlement.

46B(3) Subsection (5) below also applies where–

(a) a settlement commenced before 22nd March 2006,

(b) a contract of life insurance was entered into before that day,

(c) a premium payable under the contract is paid, or an allowed variation is made to the contract, at a particular time on or after that day when there are rights under the contract–

(i) that are comprised in the settlement and are settled property to which section 71A or 71D below applies,

(ii) that immediately before that day were settled property to which section 71 below applied, and

(iii) that on or after that day, but before the particular time, became property to which section 71A or 71D below applies in circumstances falling within subsection (4) below,

(d) rights under the contract become, by reference to payment of the premium or as a result of the variation, comprised in the settlement, and

(e) any variation of the contract on or after 22nd March 2006 but before the particular time, so far as it was a variation that–

(i) increased the benefits secured by the contract, or

(ii) extended the term of the insurance provided by the contract,

was an allowed variation.

46B(4) The circumstances referred to in subsection (3)(c)(iii) above are–

(a) in the case of property to which section 71D below applies, that the property on becoming property to which section 71D below applies ceased to be property to which section 71 below applied without ceasing to be settled property;

(b) in the case of property to which section 71A below applies–

(i) that the property on becoming property to which section 71A below applies ceased, by the operation of section 71(1B) below, to be property to which section 71 below applied, or

(ii) that the property, having become property to which section 71D below applied in circumstances falling within paragraph (a) above, on becoming property to which 71A below applies ceased, by the operation of section 71D(5)(a) below, to be property to which section 71D below applied.

46B(5) If payment of the premium is a transfer of value made by an individual, that transfer of value is a potentially exempt transfer.

46B(6) In this section **"allowed variation"**, in relation to a contract, means a variation that takes place by operation of, or as a result of exercise of rights conferred by, provisions forming part of the contract immediately before 22nd March 2006.

History – S. 46B inserted by FA 2006, s. 156 and Sch. 20, para. 11(1), with effect from 22 March 2006.

47 Reversionary interest

47 In this Act **"reversionary interest"** means a future interest under a settlement, whether it is vested or contingent (including an interest expectant on the termination of an interest in possession which, by virtue of section 50 below, is treated as subsisting in part of any property) and in relation to Scotland includes an interest in the fee of property subject to a proper liferent.

47A Settlement power

47A In this Act **"settlement power"** means any power over, or exercisable (whether directly or indirectly) in relation to, settled property or a settlement.

History – Section 47A inserted by FA 2002, s. 119(2). FA 2002, s. 119 has effect in relation to transfers of value on or after 17 April 2002. However, by virtue of FA 2002, s. 119(7), FA 2002, s. 119(2) is deemed always to have had effect (subject to and in accordance with the other provisions of IHTA 1984) for the purpose of determining the value of the estate of a person who has died before 17 April 2002 with regard to the transfer of value deemed to occur immediately before that person died.

48 Excluded property

48(1) A reversionary interest is excluded property unless–

(a) it has at any time been acquired (whether by the person entitled to it or by a person previously entitled to it) for a consideration in money or money's worth, or

(b) it is one to which either the settlor or his spouse or civil partner is or has been beneficially entitled, or

(c) it is the interest expectant on the determination of a lease treated as a settlement by virtue of section 43(3) above or,

(d) in a case where paragraphs (a), (b) and (d) of section 74A(1) are satisfied–

(i) it is a reversionary interest, in the relevant settled property, to which the individual is beneficially entitled, and

(ii) the individual has or is able to acquire (directly or indirectly) another interest in that relevant settled property.

Terms used in paragraph (d) have the same meaning as in section 74A.

48(2) In relation to a reversionary interest under a settlement made before 16th April 1976, subsection (1) above shall have effect with the omission of paragraph (b); and, if the person entitled to a reversionary interest under a settlement made on or after 16th April 1976 acquired the interest before 10th March 1981, that subsection shall have effect with the omission of the words "or has been" in paragraph (b).

48(3) Where property comprised in a settlement is situated outside the United Kingdom–

(a) the property (but not a reversionary interest in the property) is excluded property unless the settlor was domiciled in the United Kingdom at the time the settlement was made, and

(b) section 6(1) above applies to a reversionary interest in the property but does not otherwise apply in relation to the property;

but this subsection is subject to subsections (3B) to (3E) below and to Schedule A1.

48(3A) Where property comprised in a settlement is a holding in an authorised unit trust or a share in an open-ended investment company–

(a) the property (but not a reversionary interest in the property) is excluded property unless the settlor was domiciled in the United Kingdom at the time the settlement was made, and

(b) section 6(1A) above applies to a reversionary interest in the property but does not otherwise apply in relation to the property;

but this subsection is subject to subsections (3B) and (3E) below and to Schedule A1.

48(3B) Property is not excluded property by virtue of subsection (3) or (3A) above if–

(a) a person is, or has been, beneficially entitled to an interest in possession in the property at any time,

(b) the person is, or was, at that time an individual domiciled in the United Kingdom, and

(c) the entitlement arose directly or indirectly as a result of a disposition made on or after 5th December 2005 for a consideration in money or money's worth.

48(3C) For the purposes of subsection (3B) above–

(a) it is immaterial whether the consideration was given by the person or by anyone else, and

(b) the cases in which an entitlement arose indirectly as a result of a disposition include any case where the entitlement arose under a will or the law relating to intestacy.

48(3D) Where paragraphs (a) to (d) of section 74A(1) are satisfied, subsection (3)(a) above does not apply at the time they are first satisfied or any later time to make the relevant settled property (within the meaning of section 74A) excluded property.

48(3E) In a case where the settlor of property comprised in a settlement is not domiciled in the United Kingdom at the time the settlement is made, the property is not excluded property by virtue of subsection (3) or (3A) above at any time in a tax year if the settlor was a formerly domiciled resident for that tax year.

48(4) Where securities issued by the Treasury subject to a condition of the kind mentioned in subsection (2) of section 6 above are comprised in a settlement, that subsection shall not apply to them; but the securities are excluded property if–

(a) a person of a description specified in the condition in question is entitled to a qualifying interest in possession in them, or

(b) no qualifying interest in possession subsists in them but it is shown that all known persons for whose benefit the settled property or income from it has been or might be applied, or who are or might become beneficially entitled to an interest in possession in it, are persons of a description specified in the condition in question.

This subsection is subject to Schedule A1.

48(5) Where–

(a) property ceased to be comprised in one settlement before 10th December 1981 and after 19th April 1978 and, by the same disposition, became comprised in another settlement, or

(b) property ceased to be comprised in one settlement after 9th December 1981 and became comprised in another without any person having in the meantime become beneficially entitled to the property (and not merely to an interest in possession in the property),

subsection (4)(b) above shall, in its application to the second settlement, be construed as requiring the matters there stated to be shown both in relation to the property comprised in that settlement and in relation to the property that was comprised in the first settlement.

48(6) Subsection (5) above shall not apply where a reversionary interest in the property expectant on the termination a qualifying interest in possession subsisting under the first settlement was settled on the trusts of the second settlement before 10th December 1981.

48(7) In this section **"qualifying interest in possession"** has the same meaning as in Chapter III of this Part of this Act.

History – In s. 48(1)(b) the words "or civil partner" inserted by SI 2005/3229, reg. 12, with effect from 5 December 2005.
S. 48(1)(d), and the word "or," before it, inserted by FA 2012, s. 210(2)(a), with effect in relation to arrangements entered into on or after 20 June 2012.
In s. 48(3) the words "and to Schedule A1" inserted by F(No. 2)A 2017, s. 33 and Sch. 10, para. 4(a), with effect in relation to times after 5 April 2017 subject to Sch. 10, para. 9 and 10.
In s. 48(3)(b) the words "to (3E)" substituted for the words "and (3D)" by F(No. 2)A 2017, s. 30(4)(a), with effect in relation to times after 5 April 2017 subject to s. 30(10)–(17).
In s. 48(3), the words "subsections (3B) and (3D)" substituted for "subsection (3B)" by FA 2012, s. 210(2)(b), with effect in relation to arrangements entered into on or after 20 June 2012.
In s. 48(3) the words after para. (b) inserted by FA 2006, s. 157(2), with effect from 5 December 2005, subject to the provisions of FA 2006, s. 157(5).
In s. 48(3A) the words "and to Schedule A1" inserted by F(No. 2)A 2017, s. 33 and Sch. 10, para. 4(a), with effect in relation to times after 5 April 2017 subject to Sch. 10, para. 9 and 10.
In s. 48(3A)(b) the words "subsections (3B) and (3E)" substituted for the words "subsection (3B)" by F(No. 2)A 2017, s. 30(4)(b), with effect in relation to times after 5 April 2017 subject to s. 30(10)–(17).
In s. 48(3A) the words after para. (b) inserted by FA 2006, s. 157(3), with effect from 5 December 2005, subject to the provisions of FA 2006, s. 157(5).
S. 48(3A) inserted by FA 2003, s. 186(3), with effect in relation to transfers of value or other events occurring on or after 16 October 2002.
S. 48(3B) inserted by FA 2006, s. 157(4), with effect from 5 December 2005, subject to the provisions of FA 2006, s. 157(5).
S. 48(3C) inserted by FA 2006, s. 157(4), with effect from 5 December 2005, subject to the provisions of FA 2006, s. 157(5).
S. 48(3D) inserted by FA 2012, s. 210(2)(c), with effect in relation to arrangements entered into on or after 20 June 2012.
S. 48(3E) inserted by F(No. 2)A 2017, s. 30(4)(c), with effect in relation to times after 5 April 2017 subject to s. 30(10)–(17).
In s. 48(4) the words "This subsection is subject to Schedule A1." inserted by F(No. 2)A 2017, s. 33 and Sch. 10, para. 4(b), with effect in relation to times after 5 April 2017 subject to Sch. 10, para. 9 and 10.
In each of s. 48(4)(a) and (b) the words "of a description … condition in question" substituted by FA 1996, s. 154 and Sch. 28, para. 7, with effect for the year 1996–97 and subsequent years of assessment.

Cross references – S. 6: excluded property generally.
S. 65(7): discretionary trust property becoming excluded property by virtue of s. 48(3)(a) by ceasing to be situated in the UK.
S. 65(8): discretionary trust property becoming excluded property by virtue of s. 48(4)(b) by being invested in certain Treasury securities.
S. 82: additional condition to be satisfied for s. 48(3)(a) to apply when settlor or spouse of settlor has an initial interest in settled property, or where property moves between settlements.
S. 267(2): disapplication of deemed domicile provision in relation to s. 48(4).

HMRC interpretations – IR Int. 1007: application of excluded property rules where settlor domiciled overseas when settlement made but not when chargeable event occurs; and where several persons contribute to a single settlement.

Chapter II – Interests in Possession, Reversionary Interests and Settlement Powers

History – The title of Chapter II was changed from "Interests in possession and reversionary interests" to "Interests in possession, reversionary interests and settlement powers" by FA 2002, s. 119(5) which has effect in relation to transfers of value made on or after 17 April 2002.

49 Treatment of interests in possession

49(1) A person beneficially entitled to an interest in possession in settled property shall be treated for the purposes of this Act as beneficially entitled to the property in which the interest subsists.

49(1A) Where the interest in possession mentioned in subsection (1) above is one to which the person becomes beneficially entitled on or after 22nd March 2006, subsection (1) above applies in relation to that *interest only if, and for so long as, it is–*

(a) an immediate post-death interest,

(b) a disabled person's interest, or

(c) a transitional serial interest

or falls within section 5(1B) above.

49(1B) Where the interest in possession mentioned in subsection (1) above is one to which the person became beneficially entitled before 22nd March, subsection (1) above does not apply in relation to that interest at any time when section 71A below applies to the property in which the interest subsists.

49(2) Where a person becomes entitled to an interest in possession in settled property as a result of a disposition for a consideration in money or money's worth, any question whether and to what extent the giving of the consideration is a transfer of value or chargeable transfer shall be determined without regard to subsection (1) above.

49(3) [Repealed by F(No. 2)A 1987, s. 96(4) and Sch. 9, Pt. III.]

History – In s. 49(1A), the words "or falls within section 5(1B) above." inserted by FA 2010, s. 53(4)(a), with effect in relation to an interest in possession to which a person is beneficially entitled if the person becomes beneficially entitled to it on or after 9 December 2009.
S. 49(1A) inserted by FA 2006, s. 156 and Sch. 20, para. 4, with effect from 22 March 2006.
S. 49(1B) inserted by FA 2006, s. 156 and Sch. 20, para. 4, with effect from 22 March 2006.
S. 49(3) repealed by F(No. 2)A 1987, s. 96(4) and Sch. 9, Pt. III with effect with respect to transfers of value made, and other events occurring, on or after 17 March 1987.
Former s. 49(3) inserted by FA 1986, s. 101(1) and (3) and Sch. 19, Pt. I, para. 14)

Cross references – S. 142(5): property to which a person is treated as beneficially entitled under s. 49(1) is not property comprised in a person's estate for the purposes of disclaiming dispositions within two years of death.
S. 151(3): disapplication of s. 49–53 to pension and annuity rights etc.

Extra-statutory concessions – F11 (to be withdrawn with effect from April 2015): property chargeable on the ceasing of an annuity.
F13: seamen, marines and soldiers dying in the service of the Crown before 12 March 1952 – termination of limited interest in estate.

Statements of practice – E6: position where trustees augment beneficiary's income out of capital.

49A Immediate post-death interest

49A(1) Where a person ("L") is beneficially entitled to an interest in possession in settled property, for the purposes of this Chapter that interest is an "immediate post-death interest" only if the following conditions are satisfied.

49A(2) Condition 1 is that the settlement was effected by will or under the law relating to intestacy.

49A(3) Condition 2 is that L became beneficially entitled to the interest in possession on the death of the testator or intestate.

49A(4) Condition 3 is that–

(a) section 71A below does not apply to the property in which the interest subsists, and

(b) the interest is not a disabled person's interest.

49A(5) Condition 4 is that Condition 3 has been satisfied at all times since L became beneficially entitled to the interest in possession.

History – S. 49A inserted by FA 2006, s. 156 and Sch. 20, para. 5, with effect from 22 March 2006.

49B Transitional serial interests

49B Where a person is beneficially entitled to an interest in possession in settled property, for the purposes of this Chapter that interest is a **"transitional serial interest"** only–

(a) if section 49C or 49D below so provides, or

(b) if, and to the extent that, section 49E below so provides.

History – S. 49B inserted by FA 2006, s. 156 and Sch. 20, para. 5, with effect from 22 March 2006.

49C Transitional serial interest: interest to which person becomes entitled during period 22nd March 2006 to 5th October 2008

History – In the heading to s. 49C the word "October" substituted for the word "April" by FA 2008, s. 141(1)(a), with effect from 6 April 2008.

49C(1) Where a person ("B") is beneficially entitled to an interest in possession in settled property ("the current interest"), that interest is a transitional serial interest for the purposes of this Chapter if the following conditions are met.

49C(2) Condition 1 is that–

(a) the settlement commenced before 22nd March 2006, and

(b) immediately before 22nd March 2006, the property then comprised in the settlement was property in which B, or some other person, was beneficially entitled to an interest in possession ("the prior interest").

49C(3) Condition 2 is that the prior interest came to an end at a time on or after 22nd March 2006 but before 6th October 2008.

49C(4) Condition 3 is that B became beneficially entitled to the current interest at that time.

49C(5) Condition 4 is that–

(a) section 71A below does not apply to the property in which the interest subsists, and

(b) the interest is not a disabled person's interest.

History – In s. 49C(3) the word "October" substituted for the word "April" by FA 2008, s. 141(1)(a), with effect from 6 April 2008. S. 49C inserted by FA 2006, s. 156 and Sch. 20, para. 5, with effect from 22 March 2006.

49D Transitional serial interest: interest to which person becomes entitled on death of spouse or civil partner on or after 6th October 2008

History – In the heading to s. 49D the word "October" substituted for the word "April" by FA 2008, s. 141(1)(b), with effect from 6 April 2008.

49D(1) Where a person ("E") is beneficially entitled to an interest in possession in settled property ("the successor interest"), that interest is a transitional serial interest for the purposes of this Chapter if the following conditions are met.

49D(2) Condition 1 is that–

(a) the settlement commenced before 22nd March 2006, and

(b) immediately before 22nd March 2006, the property then comprised in the settlement was property in which a person other than E was beneficially entitled to an interest in possession ("the previous interest").

49D(3) Condition 2 is that the previous interest came to an end on or after 6th October 2008 on the death of that other person ("F").

49D(4) Condition 3 is that, immediately before F died, F was the spouse or civil partner of E.

49D(5) Condition 4 is that E became beneficially entitled to the successor interest on F's death.

49D(6) Condition 5 is that–

(a) section 71A below does not apply to the property in which the successor interest subsists, and

(b) the successor interest is not a disabled person's interest.

History – In s. 49D(3) the word "October" substituted for the word "April" by FA 2008, s. 141(1)(b), with effect from 6 April 2008. S. 49D inserted by FA 2006, s. 156 and Sch. 20, para. 5, with effect from 22 March 2006.

49E Transitional serial interest: contracts of life insurance

49E(1) Where–

(a) a person ("C") is beneficially entitled to an interest in possession in settled property ("the present interest"), and

(b) on C's becoming beneficially entitled to the present interest, the settled property consisted of, or included, rights under a contract of life insurance entered into before 22nd March 2006,

the present interest so far as subsisting in rights under the contract, or in property comprised in the settlement that directly or indirectly represents rights under the contract, is a **"transitional serial interest"** for the purposes of this Chapter if the following conditions are met.

49E(2) Condition 1 is that–

(a) the settlement commenced before 22nd March 2006, and

(b) immediately before 22nd March 2006–

 (i) the property then comprised in the settlement consisted of, or included, rights under the contract, and

 (ii) those rights were property in which C, or some other person, was beneficially entitled to an interest in possession ("the earlier interest").

49E(3) Condition 2 is that–

(a) the earlier interest came to an end at a time on or after 6th October 2008 ("the earlier-interest end-time") on the death of the person beneficially entitled to it and C became beneficially entitled to the present interest–

 (i) at the earlier-interest end-time, or

 (ii) on the coming to an end, on the death of the person beneficially entitled to it, of an interest in possession to which that person became beneficially entitled at the earlier-interest end-time, or

 (iii) on the coming to an end of the second or last in an unbroken sequence of two or more consecutive interests in possession to the first of which a person became beneficially entitled at the earlier-interest end-time and each of which ended on the death of the person beneficially entitled to it, or

(b) C became beneficially entitled to the present interest–

(i) on the coming to an end, on the death of the person entitled to it, of an interest in possession that is a transitional serial interest under section 49C above, or

(ii) on the coming to an end of the second or last in an unbroken sequence of two or more consecutive interests in possession the first of which was a transitional serial interest under section 49C above and each of which ended on the death of the person beneficially entitled to it.

49E(4) Condition 3 is that rights under the contract were comprised in the settlement throughout the period beginning with 22nd March 2006 and ending with C's becoming beneficially entitled to the present interest.

49E(5) Condition 4 is that–

(a) section 71A below does not apply to the property in which the present interest subsists, and

(b) the present interest is not a disabled person's interest.

History – In s. 49E(3) the word "October" substituted for the word "April" by FA 2008, s. 141(1)(c), with effect from 6 April 2008. S. 49D inserted by FA 2006, s. 156 and Sch. 20, para. 5, with effect from 22 March 2006.

50 Interests in part, etc.

50(1) Where the person referred to in section 49(1) above is entitled to part only of the income (if any) of the property, the interest shall be taken to subsist in such part only of the property as bears to the whole the same proportion as the part of the income to which he is entitled bears to the whole of the income.

50(2) Where the part of the income of any property to which a person is entitled is a specified amount (or the whole less a specified amount) in any period, his interest in the property shall be taken, subject to subsection (3) below, to subsist in such part (or in the whole less such part) of the property as produces that amount in that period.

50(3) The Treasury may from time to time by order prescribe a higher and a lower rate for the purposes of this section; and where tax is chargeable in accordance with subsection (2) above by reference to the value of the part of a property which produces a specified amount or by reference to the value of the remainder (but not where chargeable transfers are made simultaneously and tax is chargeable by reference to the value of that part as well as by reference to the value of the remainder) the value of the part producing that specified amount–

(a) shall, if tax is chargeable by reference to the value of that part, be taken to be not less than it would be if the property produced income at the higher rate so prescribed, and

(b) shall, if tax is chargeable by reference to the value of the remainder, be taken to be not more than it would be if the property produced income at the lower rate so prescribed;

but the value to be taken by virtue of paragraph (a) above as the value of part of a property shall not exceed the value of the whole of the property.

50(4) The power to make orders under subsection (3) above shall be exercisable by statutory instrument, which shall be subject to annulment in pursuance of a resolution of the House of Commons.

50(5) Where the person referred to in section 49(1) above is not entitled to any income of the property but is entitled, jointly or in common with one or more other persons, to the use and enjoyment of the property, his interest shall be taken to subsist in such part of the property as corresponds to the proportion which the annual value of his interest bears to the aggregate of the annual values of his interest and that or those of the other or others.

50(6) Where, under section 43(3) above, a lease of property is to be treated as a settlement, the lessee's interest in the property shall be taken to subsist in the whole of the property less such part of it as corresponds to the proportion which the value of the lessor's interest (as determined under Part VI of this Act) bears to the value of the property.

Cross references – S. 43(3): lease for life, lives or period referable to a death shall be treated as a settlement.
S. 151(3): disapplication of s. 49–53 to pension and annuity rights etc.
S. 200(3): a person entitled to part only of the income of any property is deemed to be entitled to an interest in the whole of the property for the purposes of liability to tax on death.

Statutory instruments – SI 2000/174: made under s. 50.

51 Disposal of interest in possession

51(1) Where a person beneficially entitled to an interest in possession in settled property disposes of his interest the disposal–

(a) is not a transfer of value, but

(b) shall be treated for the purposes of this Chapter as the coming to an end of his interest;

and tax shall be charged accordingly under section 52 below.

51(1A) Where the interest disposed of is one to which the person became beneficially entitled on or after 22nd March 2006, subsection (1) above applies in relation to the disposal only if the interest is–

(a) an immediate post-death interest,

(b) a disabled person's interest within section 89B(1)(c) or (d) below, or

(c) a transitional serial interest

or falls within section 5(1B) above.

51(1B) Where the interest disposed of is one to which the person became beneficially entitled before 22nd March 2006, subsection (1) above does not apply in relation to the disposal if, immediately before the disposal, section 71A or 71D below applies to the property in which the interest subsists.

51(2) Where a disposition satisfying the conditions of section 11 above is a disposal of an interest in possession in settled property, the interest shall not by virtue of subsection (1) above be treated as coming to an end.

51(3) References in this section to any property or to an interest in any property include references to part of any property or interest.

History – In s. 51(1A), the words "or falls within section 5(1B) above." inserted by FA 2010, s. 53(4)(b), with effect in relation to an interest in possession to which a person is beneficially entitled if the person becomes beneficially entitled to it on or after 9 December 2009.

S. 51(1A) inserted by FA 2006, s. 156 and Sch. 20, para. 12, with effect from 22 March 2006.

S. 51(1B) inserted by FA 2006, s. 156 and Sch. 20, para. 12, with effect from 22 March 2006.

Cross references – S. 11: dispositions for maintenance of family.

S. 151(3): disapplication of s. 49–53 to pension and annuity rights etc.

52 Charge on termination of interest in possession

52(1) Where at any time during the life of a person beneficially entitled to an interest in possession in settled property his interest comes to an end, tax shall be charged, subject to section 53 below, as if at that time he had made a transfer of value and the value transferred had been equal to the value of the property in which his interest subsisted.

52(2) If the interest comes to an end by being disposed of by the person beneficially entitled to it and the disposal is for a consideration in money or money's worth, tax shall be chargeable under this section as if the value of the property in which the interest subsisted were reduced by the amount of the consideration; but in determining that amount the value of a reversionary interest in the property or of any interest in other property comprised in the same settlement shall be left out of account.

52(2A) Where the interest mentioned in subsection (1) or (2) above is one to which the person became beneficially entitled on or after 22nd March 2006, that subsection applies in relation to the coming to an end of the interest only if the interest is–

(a) an immediate post-death interest,

(b) a disabled person's interest, or

(c) a transitional serial interest

or falls within section 5(1B) above.

52(3) Where a transaction is made between the trustees of the settlement and a person who is, or is connected with,–

(a) the person beneficially entitled to an interest in the property, or

(b) a person beneficially entitled to any other interest in that property or to any interest in any other property comprised in the settlement, or

(c) a person for whose benefit any of the settled property may be applied,

and, as a result of the transaction, the value of the first-mentioned property is less than it would be but for the transaction, a corresponding part of the interest shall be deemed for the purposes of this section to come to an end, unless the transaction is such that, were the trustees beneficially entitled to the settled property, it would not be a transfer of value.

52(3A) Where the interest mentioned in paragraph (a) of subsection (3) above is one to which the person mentioned in that paragraph became beneficially entitled on or after 22nd March 2006, that subsection applies in relation to the transaction only if the interest is–

(a) an immediate post-death interest,

(b) a *disabled person's interest*, or

(c) a transitional serial interest

or falls within section 5(1B) above.

52(4) References in this section or section 53 below to any property or to an interest in any property include references to part of any property or interest; and–

(a) the tax chargeable under this section on the coming to an end of part of an interest shall be charged as if the value of the property (or part) in which the interest subsisted were a corresponding part of the whole; and

(b) if the value of the property (or part) to which or to an interest in which a person becomes entitled as mentioned in subsection (2) of section 53 below is less than the value on which tax would be chargeable apart from that subsection, tax shall be chargeable on a value equal to the difference.

History – In s. 52(2A), the words "or falls within section 5(1B) above." inserted by FA 2010, s. 53(4)(c), with effect in relation to an interest in possession to which a person is beneficially entitled if the person becomes beneficially entitled to it on or after 9 December 2009.
S. 52(2A) inserted by FA 2006, s. 156 and Sch. 20, para. 13(2), with effect from 22 March 2006.
In s. 52(3A), the words "or falls within section 5(1B) above." inserted by FA 2010, s. 53(4)(c), with effect in relation to an interest in possession to which a person is beneficially entitled if the person becomes beneficially entitled to it on or after 9 December 2009.
S. 52(3A) inserted by FA 2006, s. 156 and Sch. 20, para. 13(3), with effect from 22 March 2006.

Cross references – S. 3A(6), (7): possible treatment as a potentially exempt transfer by reference to the person treated as the transferor.
S. 90: exemption for trustees' remuneration.
S. 146(6): disapplication of s. 52(1) in certain cases where the court orders property to be settled or a settlement to be varied under Inheritance (Provision for Family and Dependants) Act 1975.
S. 151(3): disapplication of s. 49–53 to pension and annuity rights etc.
S. 216(1), (6): delivery of account.
Sch. 6, para. 2: tax not chargeable under this section if spouse of person beneficially entitled died before 13 November 1974 and the value of the property in which the interest subsists would, by virtue of Sch. 6, para. 2 have been left out of account in determining value of survivor's estate, had he died immediately before the interest came to an end.

Statements of practice – E5: extension of relief under s. 52(2) to close companies.
E6: position where trustees augment beneficiary's income out of capital.

Other material – Law Society's Gazette, 9 May 1990 (not reproduced): when an interest in possession in settled property comes to an end during the lifetime of the person entitled to it, the settled property in which the interest subsisted should be valued in isolation for the purposes of s. 52(1) without reference to any similar property.

53 Exceptions from charge under section 52

53(1) Tax shall not be chargeable under section 52 above if the settled property is excluded property.

53(1A) Tax shall not be chargeable under section 52 above if–

(a) the person whose interest comes to an end became beneficially entitled to the interest before 22nd March 2006,

(b) the interest comes to an end on or after that day, and

(c) immediately before the interest comes to an end, section 71A or 71D below applies to the property in which the interest subsists.

53(2) Tax shall not be chargeable under section 52 above (except in the case mentioned in subsection (4)(b) of that section) if the person whose interest in the property comes to an end becomes on the same occasion beneficially entitled to the property or to another interest in possession in the property.

53(2A) Subsection (2) above applies by virtue of the person becoming beneficially entitled on or after 12 March 2008 to another interest in possession in the property only if that other interest is–

(a) a disabled person's interest, or

(b) a transitional serial interest;

and that is the case irrespective of whether the person's beneficial entitlement to the interest in possession in the property which comes to an end is one which began before, or on or after, 22 March 2006.

53(3) Tax shall not be chargeable under section 52 above if the interest comes to an end during the settlor's life and on the same occasion the property in which the interest subsisted reverts to the settlor.

53(4) Tax shall not be chargeable under section 52 above if on the occasion when the interest comes to an end–

(a) the settlor's spouse or civil partner, or

(b) where the settlor has died less than two years earlier, the settlor's widow or widower or surviving civil partner,

becomes beneficially entitled to the settled property and is domiciled in the United Kingdom.

53(5) Subsections (3) and (4) above shall not apply in any case where–

(a) the settlor or the spouse or civil partner (or in a case within subsection (4)(b), the widow or widower or surviving civil partner) of the settlor had acquired a reversionary interest in the property for a consideration in money or money's worth, or

(b) their application depends upon a reversionary interest having been transferred into a settlement on or after 10th March 1981.

53(6) For the purposes of subsection (5) above a person shall be treated as acquiring an interest for a consideration in money or money's worth if he becomes entitled to it as a result of transactions which include a disposition for such consideration (whether to him or another) of that interest or of other property.

IHT Statutes

53(7) Where the acquisition of the interest was before 12th April 1978, subsection (5)(a) above shall have effect, so far as it relates to subsection (3) above, with the omission of the reference to the spouse or civil partner of the settlor.

53(8) Subsection (6) above shall not apply where the person concerned became entitled to the interest before 12th April 1978.

History – S. 53(1A) inserted by FA 2006, s. 156 and Sch. 20, para. 14(2), with effect from 22 March 2006.
S. 53(2A) inserted by FA 2008, s. 140(1), with effect from 22 March 2006. The s. 53(2A) previously inserted by FA 2006, s. 156 and Sch. 20, para. 14(3) is treated as never having had effect.
In s. 53(4)(a) the words "or civil partner" inserted by SI 2005/3229, reg. 13(2)(a), with effect from 5 December 2005.
In s. 53(4)(b) the words "or surviving civil partner" inserted by SI 2005/3229, reg. 13(2)(b), with effect from 5 December 2005.
In s. 53(5)(a) the words "or civil partner" and "or surviving civil partner" inserted by SI 2005/3229, reg. 13(3), with effect from 5 December 2005.
In s. 53(7) the words "or civil partner" inserted by SI 2005/3229, reg. 13(4), with effect from 5 December 2005.

Cross references – S. 151(3): disapplication of s. 49–53 to pension and annuity rights etc.

Statements of practice – E5: extension of relief under s. 53(2) to close companies.
E6: position where trustees augment beneficiary's income out of capital.

54 Exceptions from charge on death

54(1) Where a person is entitled to an interest in possession in settled property which on his death, but during the settlor's life, reverts to the settlor, the value of the settled property shall be left out of account in determining for the purposes of this Act the value of the deceased's estate immediately before his death.

54(2) Where on the death of a person entitled to an interest in possession in settled property–

(a) the settlor's spouse or civil partner, or

(b) if the settlor has died less than two years earlier, the settlor's widow or widower or surviving civil partner,

becomes beneficially entitled to the settled property and is domiciled in the United Kingdom, the value of the settled property shall be left out of account in determining for the purposes of this Act the value of the deceased's estate immediately before his death.

54(2A) Where a person becomes beneficially entitled on or after 22nd March 2006 to an interest in possession in settled property, subsections (1) and (2) above apply in relation to the interest only if it is–

(a) a disabled person's interest, or

(b) a transitional serial interest.

54(2B) Where–

(a) a person ("B") becomes beneficially entitled on or after 22nd March 2006 to an interest in possession in settled property,

(b) B dies,

(c) the interest in possession, throughout the period beginning with when B becomes beneficially entitled to it and ending with B's death, is an immediate post-death interest,

(d) the settlor died before B's death but less than two years earlier, and

(e) on B's death, the settlor's widow or widower, or surviving civil partner, becomes beneficially entitled to the settled property and is domiciled in the United Kingdom,

the value of the settled property shall be left out of account in determining for the purposes of this Act the value of B's estate immediately before his death.

54(3) Subsections (5) and (6) of section 53 above shall apply in relation to subsections (1), (2) and (2B) above as they apply in relation to section 53(3) and (4), but as if the reference in section 53(5)(a) above to section 53(4)(b) above were to subsection (2)(b) or (2B) above.

54(4) For the purposes of this section, where it cannot be known which of two or more persons who have died survived the other or others they shall be assumed to have died at the same instant.

History – In s. 54(2)(a) the words "or civil partner" inserted by SI 2005/3229, reg. 14, with effect from 5 December 2005.
In s. 54(2)(b) the words "or surviving civil partner" inserted by SI 2005/3229, reg. 14, with effect from 5 December 2005.
S. 54(2A) inserted by FA 2006, s. 156 and Sch. 20, para. 15(2), with effect from 22 March 2006.
S. 54(2B) inserted by FA 2006, s. 156 and Sch. 20, para. 15(2), with effect from 22 March 2006.
In s. 54(3) the words "(1), (2) and (2B)" substituted for the words "(1) and (2)" and the words ", but as if the reference in section 53(5)(a) above to section 53(4)(b) above were to subsection (2)(b) or (2B) above." inserted by FA 2006, s. 156 and Sch. 20, para. 15(3), with effect from 22 March 2006.

54A Special rate of charge where settled property affected by potentially *exempt transfer*

54A(1) If the circumstances fall within subsection (2) below, this section applies to any chargeable transfer made–

(a) under section 52 above, on the coming to an end of an interest in possession in settled property during the life of the person beneficially entitled to it, or

(b) on the death of a person beneficially entitled to an interest in possession in settled property;

and in the following provisions of this section the interest in possession mentioned in paragraph (a) or paragraph (b) above is referred to as **"the relevant interest"**.

54A(1A) Where a person becomes beneficially entitled on or after 22nd March 2006 to an interest in possession in settled property, subsection (1)(b) above applies in relation to the person's death only if the interest is–

(a) a disabled person's interest, or

(b) a transitional serial interest.

54A(2) The circumstances referred to in subsection (1) above are–

(a) that the whole or part of the value transferred by the transfer is attributable to property in which the relevant interest subsisted and which became settled property in which there subsisted an interest in possession (whether the relevant interest or any previous interest) on the making by the settlor of a potentially exempt transfer at any time on or after 17th March 1987 and within the period of seven years ending with the date of the chargeable transfer; and

(b) that the settlor is alive at the time when the relevant interest comes to an end; and

(c) that, on the coming to an end of the relevant interest, any of the property in which that interest subsisted becomes settled property in which no qualifying interest in possession (as defined in section 59 below) subsists; and

(d) that, within six months of the coming to an end of the relevant interest, any of the property in which that interest subsisted has neither–

(i) become settled property in which a qualifying interest in possession subsists, nor

(ii) become property to which an individual is beneficially entitled.

54A(3) In the following provisions of this section **"the special rate property"**, in relation to a chargeable transfer to which this section applies, means the property in which the relevant interest subsisted or, in a case where–

(a) any part of that property does not fall within subsection (2)(a) above, or

(b) any part of that property does not become settled property of the kind mentioned in subsection (2)(c) above,

so much of that property as appears to the Board or, on appeal, to the tribunal to be just and reasonable.

54A(4) Where this section applies to a chargeable transfer (in this section referred to as **"the relevant transfer"**), the tax chargeable on the value transferred by the transfer shall be whichever is the greater of the tax that would have been chargeable apart from this section and the tax determined in accordance with subsection (5) below.

54A(5) The tax determined in accordance with this subsection is the aggregate of–

(a) the tax that would be chargeable on a chargeable transfer of the description specified in subsection (6) below, and

(b) so much (if any) of the tax that would, apart from this section, have been chargeable on the value transferred by the relevant transfer as is attributable to the value of property other than the special rate property.

54A(6) The chargeable transfer postulated in subsection (5)(a) above is one–

(a) the value transferred by which is equal to the value transferred by the relevant transfer or, where only part of that value is attributable to the special rate property, that part of that value;

(b) which is made at the time of the relevant transfer by a transferor who has in the preceding seven years made chargeable transfers having an aggregate value equal to the aggregate of the values transferred by any chargeable transfers made by the settlor in the period of seven years ending with the date of the potentially exempt transfer; and

(c) for which the applicable rate or rates are one-half of the rate or rates referred to in section 7(1) above.

54A(7) This section has effect subject to section 54B below.

History – S. 54A(1A) inserted by FA 2006, s. 156 and Sch. 20, para. 16(2), with effect from 22 March 2006.

In s. 54A(2)(c) the words ", other than property to which section 71 below applies" and in s. 54A(2)(d)(i) the words "or to which section 71 below applies" which in each case followed the word "subsists" omitted by FA 2006, s. 156 and Sch. 20, para. 16(3) and repealed by FA 2006, s. 178 and Sch. 26, Pt. 6, with effect from 22 March 2006, subject to the provisions of FA 2006, Sch. 20, para. 16(4).

In s. 54A(3) the word "tribunal" substituted for the words "Special Commissioners" by SI 2009/56, art. 3 and Sch. 1, para. 110, with effect from 1 April 2009, subject to transitional and saving provisions in SI 2009/56, Sch. 3.

S. 54A inserted by F(No. 2)A 1987, s. 96 and Sch. 7, para. 1, with respect to transfers of value made, and other events occurring, on or after 17 March 1987.

Cross references – S. 7(1): tax rates.

S. 71: accumulation and maintenance trusts.

54B Provisions supplementary to section 54A

54B(1) The death of the settlor, at any time after a chargeable transfer to which section 54A above applies, shall not increase the tax chargeable on the value transferred by the transfer unless, at the time of the transfer, the tax determined in accordance with subsection (5) of that section is greater than the tax that would be chargeable apart from that section.

54B(2) The death of the person who was beneficially entitled to the relevant interest, at any time after a chargeable transfer to which section 54A above applies, shall not increase the tax chargeable on the value transferred by the transfer unless, at the time of the transfer, the tax that would be chargeable apart from that section is greater than the tax determined in accordance with subsection (5) of that section.

54B(3) Where the tax chargeable on the value transferred by a chargeable transfer to which section 54A above applies falls to be determined in accordance with subsection (5) of that section, the amount referred to in paragraph (a) of that subsection shall be treated for the purposes of this Act as tax attributable to the value of the property in which the relevant interest subsisted.

54B(4) Subsection (5) below shall apply if–

(a) during the period of seven years preceding the date on which a chargeable transfer to which section 54A above applies (**"the current transfer"**) is made, there has been another chargeable transfer to which that section applied, and

(b) the person who is for the purposes of the current transfer the settlor mentioned in subsection (2)(a) of that section is the settlor for the purposes of the other transfer (whether or not the settlements are the same);

and in subsections (5) and (6) below the other transfer is referred to as the **"previous transfer"**.

54B(5) Where this subsection applies, the appropriate amount in relation to the previous transfer (or, if there has been more than one previous transfer, the aggregate of the appropriate amounts in relation to each) shall, for the purposes of calculating the tax chargeable on the current transfer, be taken to be the value transferred by a chargeable transfer made by the settlor immediately before the potentially exempt transfer was made.

54B(6) In subsection (5) above **"the appropriate amount"**, in relation to a previous transfer, means so much of the value transferred by the previous transfer as was attributable to the value of property which was the special rate property in relation to that transfer.

54B(7) In this section–

"the relevant interest" has the meaning given by subsection (1) of section 54A above; and

"the special rate property" has the meaning given by subsection (3) of that section.

History – S. 54B inserted by F(No. 2)A 1987, Sch. 7, para. 1, with respect to transfers of value made, and other events occurring, on or after 17 March 1987.

55 Reversionary interest acquired by beneficiary

55(1) Notwithstanding section 5(1) above, where a person entitled to an interest (whether in possession or not) in any settled property acquires a reversionary interest expectant (whether immediately or not) on that interest, the reversionary interest is not part of his estate for the purposes of this Act.

55(2) Section 10(1) above shall not apply to a disposition by which a reversionary interest is acquired in the circumstances mentioned in subsection (1) above.

History – S. 55(2), the words at the end "and such a disposition is not a potentially exempt transfer" were repealed by F(No. 2)A 1987, s. 96(5) and Sch. 9, Pt. III.

Cross references – S. 5(1): person's estate is the aggregate of all property to which he is beneficially entitled.
S. 10(1): dispositions not intended to confer gratuitous benefit are not generally transfers of value.

55A Purchased settlement powers

55A(1) Where a person makes a disposition by which he acquires a settlement power for consideration in money or money's worth–

(a) section 10(1) above shall not apply to the disposition;

(b) the person shall be taken for the purposes of this Act to make a transfer of value;

(c) the value transferred shall be determined without bringing into account the value of anything which the person acquires by the disposition; and

(d) sections 18 and 23 to 27 above shall not apply in relation to that transfer of value.

55A(2) For the purposes of this section, a person acquires a settlement power if he becomes entitled–

(a) to a settlement power,

(b) to exercise, or to secure or prevent the exercise of, a settlement power (whether directly or indirectly), or

(c) to restrict, or secure a restriction on, the exercise of a settlement power (whether directly or indirectly),

as a result of transactions which include a disposition (whether to him or another) of a settlement power or of any power of a kind described in paragraph (b) or (c) above which is exercisable in relation to a settlement power.

History – S. 55A inserted by FA 2002, s. 119(3) which has effect in relation to transfers of value on or after 17 April 2002.

56 Exclusion of certain exemptions

56(1) Sections 18 and 23 to 27 above shall not apply in relation to property which is given in consideration of the transfer of a reversionary interest if, by virtue of section 55(1) above, that interest does not form part of the estate of the person acquiring it.

56(2) Where a person acquires a reversionary interest in any settled property for a consideration in money or money's worth, section 18 above shall not apply in relation to the property when it becomes the property of that person on the termination of the interest on which the reversionary interest is expectant.

56(3) Sections 23 to 27 above shall not apply in relation to any property if–

(a) the property is an interest in possession in settled property and the settlement does not come to an end in relation to that settled property on the making of the transfer of value, or

(b) immediately before the time when it becomes the property of the exempt body it is comprised in a settlement and, at or before that time, an interest under the settlement is or has been acquired for a consideration in money or money's worth by that or another exempt body.

56(4) In subsection (3)(b) above **"exempt body"** means a charity, political party or other body within sections 23 to 25 above or the trustees of a settlement in relation to which a direction under paragraph 1 of Schedule 4 to this Act has effect; and for the purposes of subsection (3)(b) there shall be disregarded any acquisition from a charity, political party or body within sections 23 to 25.

56(5) For the purposes of subsections (2) and (3) above, a person shall be treated as acquiring an interest for a consideration in money or money's worth if he becomes entitled to it as a result of transactions which include a disposition for such consideration (whether to him or another) of that interest or of other property.

56(6) Nothing in this section shall apply to a transfer of value if or to the extent that it is a disposition whereby the use of money or other property is allowed by one person to another.

56(7) Subsection (2) above shall not apply where the acquisition of the reversionary interest was before 16th April 1976; and where the acquisition was on or after that date but before 12th April 1978 that subsection shall have effect–

(a) with the substitution for the words "section 18 above" of the words "sections 18 and 23 to 25 above", and

(b) with the insertion after the word "person" in both places where it occurs of the words "or body".

56(8) Subsection (3)(b) above shall not apply where the acquisition of the interest was before 12th April 1978; and subsection (5) above shall not apply where the person concerned became entitled to the interest before that date.

History – In s. 56(4), (7), words "to 25" substituted for former words "to 26" by FA 1998, s. 143(3), with effect in relation to any property becoming the property of any person on or after 17 March 1998.
In s. 56(5), the words "for such consideration" were inserted by F(No. 2)A 1987, Sch. 7, para. 2.

Cross references – S. 18: transfers between spouses.
S. 23–27: gifts to charities, political parties, housing associations etc.
Sch. 4, para. 1: maintenance funds for historic buildings etc.

57 Application of certain exemptions

57(1) Subject to subsection (3) below, references to transfers of value in sections 19 and 22 above shall be construed as including references to events on the happening of which tax is chargeable under section 52 above, and references to the transferor and (in section 22(3) and (4)) to a disposition shall be construed accordingly.

57(2) For the purposes of its application, by virtue of subsection (1) above, to the termination of interests in possession in settled property, section 22 above shall have effect as if–

(a) references to transfers of value made by gifts in consideration of marriage or civil partnership were references to the termination of such interests in consideration of marriage or civil partnership;

(b) references to outright gifts were references to cases where the property ceases on the termination to be settled property; and

(c) references to cases where the property is settled by the gift were references to cases where it remains settled property after the termination.

57(3) Subsection (1) above shall not apply to a transfer of value–

(a) unless the transferor has in accordance with subsection (4) below given to the trustees of the settlement a notice informing them of the availability of an exemption, and

(b) except to the extent specified in that notice.

57(4) A notice under subsection (3) above shall be in such form as may be prescribed by the Board and shall be given before the end of the period of six months beginning with the date of the transfer of value.

57(5) Section 27 above shall apply where the value transferred by a transfer of value is attributable to property which immediately after the transfer remains comprised in a settlement as it applies where property becomes comprised in a settlement by virtue of the transfer.

History – In s. 57(2)(a) the words "or civil partnership" inserted twice by SI 2005/3229, reg. 15, with effect from 5 December 2005.

Cross references – S. 19: annual exemption.
S. 22: gifts in consideration of marriage.
S. 27: maintenance funds for historic buildings etc.

57A Relief where property enters maintenance fund

57A(1) Subject to the following provisions, subsection (2) below applies where–

(a) a person dies who immediately before his death was beneficially entitled to an interest in possession in property comprised in a settlement, and

(b) within two years after his death the property becomes held on trusts (whether of that or another settlement) by virtue of which a direction under paragraph 1 of Schedule 4 to this Act is given in respect of the property.

57A(1A) Where the interest mentioned in subsection (1)(a) above is one to which the person became beneficially entitled on or after 22nd March 2006, subsection (2) below does not apply unless, immediately before the person's death, the interest was–

(a) an immediate post-death interest,

(b) a disabled person's interest, or

(c) a transitional serial interest

or fell within section 5(1B) above.

57A(2) Where this subsection applies, this Act shall have effect as if the property had on the death of the deceased become subject to the trust referred to in subsection (1)(b) above; and accordingly no disposition or other event occurring between the date of the death and the date on which the property becomes subject to those trusts shall, so far as it relates to the property, be a transfer of value or otherwise constitute an occasion for a charge to tax.

57A(3) Where property becomes held on trusts of the kind specified in paragraph (b) of subsection (1) above as the result of proceedings before a court and could not have become so held without such proceedings, that paragraph shall have effect as if it referred to three years instead of two.

57A(4) Subsection (2) above shall not apply if–

(a) the disposition by which the property becomes held on the trusts referred to in subsection (1)(b) above depends on a condition or is defeasible; or

(b) the property which becomes held on those trusts is itself an interest in settled property; or

(c) the trustees who hold the property on those trusts have, for a consideration in money or money's worth, acquired an interest under a settlement in which the property was comprised immediately before the death of the person referred to in subsection (1)(a) above or at any time thereafter; or

(d) the property which becomes held on those trusts does so for a consideration in money or money's worth, or is acquired by the trustees for such a consideration, or has at any time since the death of the person referred to in subsection (1)(a) above been acquired by any other person for such consideration.

57A(5) If the value of the property when it becomes held on the trusts referred to in subsection (1)(b) above is lower than so much of the value transferred on the death of the person referred to in subsection (1)(a) as is attributable to the property, subsection (2) above shall apply to the property only to the extent of the lower value.

57A(6) For the purposes of this section, a person shall be treated as acquiring property for a consideration in money or money's worth if he becomes entitled to it as a result of transactions which include a disposition for such consideration (whether to him or another) of that or other property.

History – In s. 57A(1A), the words "or fell within section 5(1B) above." inserted by FA 2010, s. 53(5), with effect in relation to an interest in possession to which a person is beneficially entitled if the person becomes beneficially entitled to it on or after 9 December 2009.
S. 57A(1A) inserted by FA 2006, s. 156 and Sch. 20, para. 17, with effect from 22 March 2006.
S. 57A inserted by FA 1987, s. 59 and Sch. 9, para. 1, in relation to deaths occurring on or after 17 March 1987.

Cross references – Sch. 4, para. 1: maintenance funds for historic buildings etc.
TCGA 1992, s. 260(1)(c), (2)(c): capital gains tax in respect of dispositions to which s. 57A applies.

Chapter III – Settlements Without Interests in Possession, and Certain Settlements in which Interests in Possession Subsist

History – In the heading to Ch. III, the words "and Certain Settlements in which Interests in Possession Subsist" inserted by FA 2006, s. 156 and Sch. 20, para. 20(5), with effect from 22 March 2006.

Cross references – FA 2004, Sch. 36, para. 57(1): transitional provisions for pension schemes; the protected proportion of the assets of a fund or scheme are not regarded as "relevant property" under Pt. III, Ch. III.

S. 226(3B): due date for payment of additional tax due on death of transferor within seven years of chargeable transfer under Pt. III, Ch. III.

S. 266(4): more than one chargeable transfer on the same day.

FA 1990, s. 126(5): pools payments for football ground improvements not relevant property for Pt. III, Ch. III. A corresponding exclusion applies under FA 1991 for pools payments to trustees established mainly for the support of athletic sports or games but with the power to support the arts.

FA 1994, s. 248(1): no property forming part of a premiums trust fund or an ancillary trust fund of a corporate member is to be relevant property for the purposes of Pt. III, Ch. III.

INTERPRETATION

58 Relevant property

58(1) In this Chapter **"relevant property"** means settled property in which no qualifying interest in possession subsists, other than–

(a) property held for charitable purposes only, whether for a limited time or otherwise;

(b) property to which section 71, 71A, 71D, 73, 74 or 86 below applies (but see subsection (1A) below);

(c) property held on trusts which comply with the requirements mentioned in paragraph 3(1) of Schedule 4 to this Act, and in respect of which a direction given under paragraph 1 of that Schedule has effect;

(d) property which is held for the purposes of a registered pension scheme, a qualifying non-UK pension scheme or a section 615(3) scheme;

(e) property comprised in a trade or professional compensation fund;

(ea) property comprised in an asbestos compensation settlement,

(eb) property comprised in a decommissioning security settlement; and

(f) excluded property.

58(1A) Settled property to which section 86 below applies is "relevant property" for the purposes of this Chapter if–

(a) an interest in possession subsists in that property, and

(b) that interest falls within subsection (1B) or (1C) below.

58(1B) An interest in possession falls within this subsection if–

(a) an individual is beneficially entitled to the interest in possession,

(b) the individual became beneficially entitled to the interest in possession on or after 22nd March 2006, and

(c) the interest in possession is–

(i) not an immediate post-death interest,

(ii) not a disabled person's interest, and

(iii) not a transitional serial interest.

58(1C) An interest in possession falls within this subsection if–

(a) a company is beneficially entitled to the interest in possession,

(b) the business of the company consists wholly or mainly in the acquisition of interests in settled property,

(c) the company has acquired the interest in possession for full consideration in money or money's worth from an individual who was beneficially entitled to it,

(d) the individual became beneficially entitled to the interest in possession on or after 22nd March 2006, and

(e) immediately before the company acquired the interest in possession, the interest in possession was neither an immediate post-death interest nor a transitional serial interest.

58(2) The reference in subsection (1)(d) above to property which is held for the purposes of a scheme does not include a reference to a benefit which, having become payable under the scheme becomes comprised in a settlement.

58(2A) For the purposes of subsection (1)(d) above–

(a) property applied to pay lump sum death benefits within section 168(1) of the Finance Act 2004 in respect of a member of a registered pension scheme is to be taken to be held for the purposes of the scheme from the time of the member's death until the payment is made, and

(b) property applied to pay lump sum death benefits in respect of a member of a qualifying non-UK pension scheme or a section 615(3) scheme is to be taken to be so held if the benefits are paid within the period of two years beginning with the earlier of the day on which the member's death was first known to the trustees or other persons having the control of the fund and the day on which they could first reasonably be expected to have known of it.

58(3) In subsection (1)(e) above **"trade or professional compensation fund"** means a fund which is maintained or administered by a representative association of persons carrying on a trade or profession and the only or main objects of which are compensation for or relief of losses or hardship that, through the default or alleged default of persons carrying on the trade or profession or of their agents or servants, are incurred or likely to be incurred by others.

58(4) In subsection (1)(ea) above **"asbestos compensation settlement"** means a settlement–

(a) the sole or main purpose of which is making compensation payments to or in respect of individuals who have, or had before their death, an asbestos-related condition, and

(b) which is made before 24 March 2010 in pursuance of an arrangement within subsection (5) below.

58(5) An arrangement is within this subsection if it is–

(a) a voluntary arrangement that has taken effect under Part 1 of the Insolvency Act 1986 or Part 2 of the Insolvency (Northern Ireland) Order 1989,

(b) a compromise or arrangement that has taken effect under section 425 of the Companies Act 1985, Article 418 of the Companies (Northern Ireland) Order 1986 or Part 26 of the Companies Act 2006, or

(c) an arrangement or compromise of a kind corresponding to any of those mentioned in paragraph (a) or (b) above that has taken effect under, or as a result of, the law of a country or territory outside the United Kingdom.

58(6) For the purposes of subsection (1)(eb) above a settlement is a **"decommissioning security settlement"** if the sole or main purpose of the settlement is to provide security for the performance of obligations under an abandonment programme.

58(7) In subsection (6)–

"abandonment programme" means an abandonment programme approved under Part 4 of the Petroleum Act 1998 (including such a programme as revised);

"security" has the same meaning as in section 38A of that Act.

History – In s. 58(1)(b) the words "71A, 71D," inserted by FA 2006, s. 156 and Sch. 20, para. 18, with effect from 22 March 2006.
In s. 58(1)(b) the words "(but see subsection (1A) below)" inserted by FA 2006, s. 156 and Sch. 20, para. 19(2), with effect from 22 March 2006.
In s. 58(1)(d) the words ", a qualifying non-UK pension scheme or a" substituted for the word "or" by FA 2008, s. 92 and Sch. 29, para. 18(3)(a), with effect from 6 April 2006.
S. 58(1)(d) substituted by FA 2004, s. 203(3) with effect from 6 April 2006 (FA 2004, s. 284(1)).
S. 58(1)(ea) substituted for the word "and" at the end of s. 58(1)(e) by F(No. 3)A 2010, s. 31 and Sch. 14, para. 1(2), and treated as having come into force on 6 April 2006.
S. 58(1)(eb) inserted (and the "and" after (ea) omitted) by FA 2013, s. 86(2), with effect from 17 July 2013 (Royal Assent) but treated as having come into force on 20 March 1993.
S. 58(1A) inserted by FA 2006, s. 156 and Sch. 20, para. 19(3), with effect from 22 March 2006.
S. 58(1B) inserted by FA 2006, s. 156 and Sch. 20, para. 19(3), with effect from 22 March 2006.
S. 58(1C) inserted by FA 2006, s. 156 and Sch. 20, para. 19(3), with effect from 22 March 2006.
In s. 58(2) the words "part of or" following the words "which is" and the words "fund or" preceding the word "scheme" in both places, repealed by FA 2004, s. 326 and Sch. 42, Pt. 3, with effect from 6 April 2006 (subject to the transitional provisions in FA 2004, Sch. 36).
In s. 58(2A)(b) the words "a qualifying non-UK pension scheme or" inserted by FA 2008, s. 92 and Sch. 29, para. 18(3)(a), with effect from 6 April 2006.
S. 58(2A) inserted by FA 2007, s. 70 and Sch. 20, para. 20, with effect in relation to lump sum death benefits paid on or after 6 April 2006.
S. 58(4) inserted by F(No. 3)A 2010, s. 31 and Sch. 14, para. 1(3), and treated as having come into force on 6 April 2006.
S. 58(5) inserted by F(No. 3)A 2010, s. 31 and Sch. 14, para. 1(3), and treated as having come into force on 6 April 2006.
S. 58(6) and (7) inserted by FA 2013, s. 86(3), with effect from 17 July 2013 (Royal Assent) but treated as having come into force on 20 March 1993.

Cross references – S. 86: trust for employees' benefit.
S. 151: certain pension scheme funds.
Sch. 4, para. 3(1): maintenance funds for historic buildings etc.
SI 2006/575, reg. 33: application of s. 58 to the Pension Protection Fund.
FA 2013, s. 86(5): references in s. 58 to Petroleum Act 1998, Pt. 4 have effect in relation to any period before the coming into force of that Part as a reference to Petroleum Act 1987, Pt. 1, and Petroleum Act 1998, s. 38A is treated as having come into force at the same time as s. 58.

Statements of practice – SP 8/86: accumulated income becomes relevant property when accumulation made.

59 Qualifying interest in possession

59(1) In this Chapter **"qualifying interest in possession"** means–

(a) an interest in possession–

(i) to which an individual is beneficially entitled, and

(ii) which, if the individual became beneficially entitled to the interest in possession on or after 22nd March 2006, is an immediate post-death interest, a disabled person's interest or a transitional serial interest, or

(b) an interest in possession to which, where subsection (2) below applies, a company is beneficially entitled.

59(2) This subsection applies where–

(a) the business of the company consists wholly or mainly in the acquisition of interests in settled property, and

(b) the company has acquired the interest for full consideration in money or money's worth from an individual who was beneficially entitled to it, and

(c) if the individual became beneficially entitled to the interest in possession on or after 22nd March 2006, the interest is an immediate post-death interest, or a disabled person's interest within section 89B(1)(c) or (d) below or a transitional serial interest, immediately before the company acquires it.

59(3) Where the acquisition mentioned in paragraph (b) of subsection (2) above was before 14th March 1975–

(a) the condition set out in paragraph (a) of that subsection shall be treated as satisfied if the business of the company was at the time of the acquisition such as is described in that paragraph, and

(b) that condition need not be satisfied if the company is an insurance company (within the meaning of Part 2 of the Finance Act 2012) and has permission–

(i) under Part 4A of the Financial Services and Markets Act 2000, or

(ii) under paragraph 15 of Schedule 3 to that Act (as a result of qualifying for authorisation under paragraph 12(1) of that Schedule),

to effect or carry out contracts of long-term insurance.

59(4) In subsection (3)(b) above **"contracts of long-term insurance"** means contracts which fall within Part II of Schedule 1 to the Financial Services and Markets Act 2000 (Regulated Activities) Order 2001 (SI 2001/544).

History – S. 59(1) substituted by FA 2006, s. 156 and Sch. 20, para. 20(2), with effect from 22 March 2006, subject to the provisions of FA 2006, Sch. 20, para. 20(4). Former s. 59(1) read as follows:

"59(1) In this Chapter **"qualifying interest in possession"** means an interest in possession to which an individual, or where subsection (2) below applies a company, is beneficially entitled.".

S. 59(2)(c), and the word "and" which precedes it, inserted by FA 2006, s. 156 and Sch. 20, para. 20(3), with effect from 22 March 2006, subject to the provisions of FA 2006, Sch. 20, para. 20(4).

In s. 59(3)(b), the words "Part 2 of the Finance Act 2012" substituted for "Chapter I of Part XII of the Taxes Act 1988" by FA 2012, s. 146 and Sch. 16, para. 69, with effect in relation to accounting periods of companies beginning on or after 1 January 2013, subject to the transitional provisions in FA 2012, Sch. 17.

In s. 59(3)(b), the substitution by the words from "has permission" to the words "long-term insurance" was made by SI 2001/3629, art. 5(2) which has effect in relation to the making, on an anniversary or other occasion on or after 1 December 2001, of any charge to tax under section 64 or 65 of the Inheritance Tax Act 1984.

In s. 59(3)(b), words from "if the company" to the end substituted by FA 1995, s. 52(4), with effect for the purposes of the making, on an anniversary or other occasion after 30 June 1994, of any charge to tax under s. 64 or 65.

In s. 59(3)(b)(i), the words "Part 4A" substituted for the words "Part 4" by Financial Services Act 2012, s. 114(1) and Sch. 18, para. 44, with effect from 1 April 2013 (SI 2013/423).

S. 59(4) inserted by SI 2001/3629, art. 5(3) which has effect in relation to the making, on an anniversary or other occasion on or after 1 December 2001, of any charge to tax under section 64 or 65 of the Inheritance Tax Act 1984.

Cross references – S. 271: for s. 59 purposes property to which person "beneficially entitled" may include property to which a person is entitled as corporation sole.

Insurance Companies Act 1982, s. 3, 4 (not reproduced): authorisation by Secretary of State to carry out certain classes of long-term business and general business.

Statements of practice – SP 10/79: power for trustees to allow beneficiary to occupy dwelling-house.

Other material – IR press release, 12 February 1976: Revenue view of meaning of "interest in possession".

60 Commencement of settlement

60 In this Chapter references to the **commencement of a settlement** are references to the time when property first becomes comprised in it.

61 Ten-year anniversary

61(1) In this Chapter **"ten-year anniversary"** in relation to a settlement means the tenth anniversary of the date on which the settlement commenced and subsequent anniversaries at ten-yearly intervals, but subject to subsections (2) to (4) below.

61(2) The ten-year anniversaries of a settlement treated as made under section 80 below shall be the dates that are (or would but for that section be) the ten-year anniversaries of the settlement first mentioned in that section.

61(3) No date falling before 1st April 1983 shall be a ten-year anniversary.

61(4) Where–

(a) the first ten-year anniversary of a settlement would apart from this subsection fall during the year ending with 31st March 1984, and

(b) during that year an event occurs in respect of the settlement which could not have occurred except as the result of some proceedings before a court, and

(c) the event is one on which tax was chargeable under Chapter II of Part IV of the Finance Act 1982 (or, apart from Part II of Schedule 15 to that Act, would have been so chargeable),

the first ten-year anniversary shall be taken to be 1st April 1984 (but without affecting the dates of later anniversaries).

Cross references – FA 1982, Pt. IV, Ch. II: capital transfer tax regime for discretionary trusts applying in relation to events after 8 March 1982.
FA 1982, Sch. 15, Pt. II: election to apply new rules from 1 April 1983 in respect of settlements which commenced before 27 March 1974.

62 Related settlements

62(1) For the purposes of this Chapter two settlements are **related** if and only if–

(a) the settlor is the same in each case, and

(b) they commenced on the same day,

but subject to subsection (2) below.

62(2) Two settlements are not related for the purposes of this Chapter if all the property comprised in one or both of them was immediately after the settlement commenced held for charitable purposes only without limit of time (defined by a date or otherwise).

Cross references – S. 80: deferral of tax when property treated as comprised in a settlement where settlor or spouse is beneficially entitled to interest in possession.

62A Same-day additions

62A(1) For the purposes of this Chapter, there is a **"same-day addition"**, in relation to a settlement ("settlement A"), if–

(a) there is a transfer of value by a person as a result of which the value immediately afterwards of the property comprised in settlement A is greater than the value immediately before,

(b) as a result of the same transfer of value, or as a result of another transfer of value made by that person on the same day, the value immediately afterwards of the property comprised in another settlement ("settlement B") is greater than the value immediately before,

(c) that person is the settlor of settlement A and settlement B,

(d) at any point in the relevant period, all or any part of the property comprised in settlement A was relevant property, and

(e) at that point, or at any other point in the relevant period, all or any part of the property comprised in settlement B was relevant property.

For exceptions, see section 62B.

62A(2) Where there is a same-day addition, references in this Chapter to its value are to the difference between the two values mentioned in subsection (1)(b).

62A(3) **"The relevant period"** means–

(a) in the case of settlement A, the period beginning with the commencement of settlement A and ending immediately after the transfer of value mentioned in subsection (1)(a), and

(b) in the case of settlement B, the period beginning with the commencement of settlement B and ending immediately after the transfer of value mentioned in subsection (1)(b)).

62A(4) The transfer or transfers of value mentioned in subsection (1) include a transfer or transfers of value as a result of which property first becomes comprised in settlement A or settlement B; but not if settlements A and B are related settlements.

62A(5) For the purposes of subsection (1) above, it is immaterial whether the amount of the property comprised in settlement A or settlement B (or neither) was increased as a result of the transfer or transfers of value mentioned in that subsection.

History – S. 62A inserted by F(No. 2)A 2015, s. 11 and Sch. 1, para. 2, with effect in relation to occasions on which tax falls to be charged under IHTA 1984, Pt. 3, Ch. 3 on or after 18 November 2015 (Royal Assent).

62B Same day additions: exceptions

62B(1) There is not a same-day addition for the purposes of this Chapter if any of the following conditions is met–

(a) immediately after the transfer of value mentioned in section 62A(1)(a) all the property comprised in settlement A was held for charitable purposes only without limit of time (defined by a date or otherwise),

(b) immediately after the transfer of value mentioned in section 62A(1)(b) all the property comprised in settlement B was so held,

(c) either or each of settlement A and settlement B is a protected settlement (see section 62C), and

(d) the transfer of value, or either or each of the transfers of value, mentioned in section 62A(1)(a) and (b)–

(i) results from the payment of a premium under a contract of life insurance the terms of which provide for premiums to be due at regular intervals of one year or less throughout the contract term, or

(ii) is made to fund such a payment.

62B(2) If the transfer of value, or each of the transfers of value, mentioned in section 62A(1) is not the transfer of value under section 4 on the settlor's death, there is a same-day addition for the purposes of this Chapter only if conditions A and B are met.

62B(3) Condition A is that–

(a) the difference between the two values mentioned in section 62A(1)(a) exceeds £5,000, or

(b) in a case where there has been more than one transfer of value within section 62A(1)(a) on the same day, the difference between–

(i) the value of the property comprised in settlement A immediately before the first of those transfers, and

(ii) the value of the property comprised in settlement A immediately after the last of those transfers,

exceeds £5,000.

62B(4) Condition B is that–

(a) the difference between the two values mentioned in section 62A(1)(b) exceeds £5,000, or

(b) in a case where there has been more than one transfer of value within section 62A(1)(b), the difference between–

(i) the value of the property comprised in settlement B immediately before the first of those transfers, and

(ii) the value of the property comprised in settlement B immediately after the last of those transfers,

exceeds £5,000.

History – S. 62B inserted by F(No. 2)A 2015, s. 11 and Sch. 1, para. 2, with effect in relation to occasions on which tax falls to be charged under IHTA 1984, Pt. 3, Ch. 3 on or after 18 November 2015 (Royal Assent).

62C Protected settlements

62C(1) For the purposes of this Chapter, a settlement is a **"protected settlement"** if it commenced before 10 December 2014 and either condition A or condition B is met.

62C(2) Condition A is met if there have been no transfers of value by the settlor on or after 10 December 2014 as a result of which the value of the property comprised in the settlement was increased.

62C(3) Condition B is met if–

(a) there has been a transfer of value by the settlor on or after 10 December 2014 as a result of which the value of the property comprised in the settlement was increased, and

(b) that transfer of value was the transfer of value under section 4 on the settlor's death before 6 April 2017 and it had the result mentioned by reason of a protected testamentary disposition.

62C(4) In subsection (3)(b) **"protected testamentary disposition"** means a disposition effected by provisions of the settlor's will that at the settlor's death are, in substance, the same as they were immediately before 10 December 2014.

History – S. 62C inserted by F(No. 2)A 2015, s. 11 and Sch. 1, para. 2, with effect in relation to occasions on which tax falls to be charged under IHTA 1984, Pt. 3, Ch. 3 on or after 18 November 2015 (Royal Assent).

63 Minor interpretative provisions

63 **In this Chapter, unless the context otherwise requires–**

"payment" includes a transfer of assets other than money;

"quarter" means period of three months.

PRINCIPAL CHARGE TO TAX

64 Charge at ten-year anniversary

64(1) Where immediately before a ten-year anniversary all or any part of the property comprised in a settlement is relevant property, tax shall be charged at the rate applicable under sections 66 and 67 below on the value of the property or part at that time.

64(1A) For the purposes of subsection (1) above, property held by the trustees of a settlement immediately before a ten-year anniversary is to be regarded as relevant property comprised in the settlement at that time if–

(a) it is income of the settlement,

(b) the income arose before the start of the five years ending immediately before the ten-year anniversary,

(c) the income arose (directly or indirectly) from property comprised in the settlement that, when the income arose, was relevant property, and

(d) when the income arose, no person was beneficially entitled to an interest in possession in the property from which the income arose.

64(1B) Where the settlor of a settlement was not domiciled in the United Kingdom at the time the settlement was made and is not a formerly domiciled resident for the tax year in which the ten-year anniversary falls, income of the settlement is not to be regarded as relevant property comprised in the settlement as a result of subsection (1A) above so far as the income–

(a) is situated outside the United Kingdom, or

(b) is represented by a holding in an authorised unit trust or a share in an open-ended investment company.

64(1C) Income of the settlement is not to be regarded as relevant property comprised in the settlement as a result of subsection (1A) above so far as the income–

(a) is represented by securities issued by the Treasury subject to a condition of the kind mentioned in subsection (2) of section 6 above, and

(b) it is shown that all known persons for whose benefit the settled property or income from it has been or might be applied, or who are or might become beneficially entitled to an interest in possession in it, are persons of a description specified in the condition in question.

64(2) For the purposes of subsection (1) above, a foreign-owned work of art which is situated in the United Kingdom for one or more of the purposes of public display, cleaning and restoration (and for no other purpose) is not to be regarded as relevant property.

History – In s. 64(1B) the words "and is not a formerly domiciled resident for the tax year in which the ten-year anniversary falls" inserted by F(No. 2)A 2017, s. 30(5), with effect in relation to times after 5 April 2017 subject to s. 30(10)–(17).

S. 64(1A), (1B) and (1C) inserted by FA 2014, s. 117 and Sch. 25, para. 4(1), with effect in relation to occasions on which tax falls to be charged under s. 64 on or after 6 April 2014.

S. 64(2) inserted (and former text of s. 64 redesignated as s. 64(1)) by SI 2009/730, art. 13(3), with effect in relation to deaths and ten-year anniversaries occurring on or after 6 April 2009.

Cross references – Sch. 2, para. 3: effect of a reduction in the tax rate determined by Sch. 1, where tax is charged between ten-yearly anniversaries.

SI 2011/1502, art. 5: Equitable Life "authorised payments" to be disregarded in determining value of relevant property immediately before ten-year anniversary.

Other material – HMRC Brief 22/13: discounted gift schemes: ten year anniversary values for inheritance tax and updated guidance on the calculation of transfer values when discounted gift schemes are effected.

65 Charge at other times

65(1) There shall be a charge to tax under this section–

(a) where the property comprised in a settlement or any part of that property ceases to be relevant property (whether because it ceases to be comprised in the settlement or otherwise); and

(b) in a case in which paragraph (a) above does not apply, where the trustees of the settlement make a disposition as a result of which the value of relevant property comprised in the settlement is less than it would be but for the disposition.

65(2) The amount on which tax is charged under this section shall be–

(a) the amount by which the value of relevant property comprised in the settlement is less immediately after the event in question than it would be but for the event, or

(b) where the tax payable is paid out of relevant property comprised in the settlement immediately after the event, the amount which, after deducting the tax, is equal to the amount on which tax would be charged by virtue of paragraph (a) above.

65(3) The rate at which tax is charged under this section shall be the rate applicable under section 68 or 69 below.

65(4) Subsection (1) above does not apply if the event in question occurs in a quarter beginning with the day on which the settlement commenced or with a ten-year anniversary.

65(5) Tax shall not be charged under this section in respect of–

(a) a payment of costs or expenses (so far as they are fairly attributable to relevant property), or

(b) a payment which is (or will be) income of any person for any of the purposes of income tax or would for any of those purposes be income of a person not resident in the United Kingdom if he were so resident,

or in respect of a liability to make such a payment.

65(6) Tax shall not be charged under this section by virtue of subsection (1)(b) above if the disposition is such that, were the trustees beneficially entitled to the settled property, section 10 or section 16 above would prevent the disposition from being a transfer of value.

65(7) Tax shall not be charged under this section by reason only that property comprised in a settlement ceases to be situated in the United Kingdom and thereby becomes excluded property by virtue of section 48(3)(a) above.

65(7A) Tax shall not be charged under this section by reason only that property comprised in a settlement becomes excluded property by virtue of section 48(3A)(a) (holding in an authorised unit trust or a share in an open-ended investment company is excluded property unless settlor domiciled in UK when settlement made).

65(7B) Tax shall not be charged under this section by reason only that property comprised in a settlement becomes excluded property by virtue of section 48(3E) ceasing to apply in relation to it.

65(7C) Tax shall not be charged under this section by reason only that property comprised in a settlement ceases to any extent to be property to which paragraph 2 or 3 of Schedule A1 applies and thereby becomes excluded property by virtue of section 48(3)(a) above.

65(7D) Tax shall not be charged under this section where property comprised in a settlement or any part of that property–

(a) is, by virtue of paragraph 5(2)(a) of Schedule A1, not excluded property for the two year period referred to in that paragraph, but

(b) becomes excluded property at the end of that period.

65(8) If the settlor of a settlement was not domiciled in the United Kingdom when the settlement was made, tax shall not be charged under this section by reason only that property comprised in the settlement is invested in securities issued by the Treasury subject to a condition of the kind mentioned in section 6(2) above and thereby becomes excluded property by virtue of section 48(4)(b) above.

65(9) For the purposes of this section trustees shall be treated as making a disposition if they omit to exercise a right (unless it is shown that the omission was not deliberate) and the disposition shall be treated as made at the time or latest time when they could have exercised the right.

History – S. 65(7A) inserted by FA 2013, s. 175(1), with effect from 17 July 2013 (Royal Assent) but treated as having come into force on 16 October 2002.

S. 65(7B) inserted by F(No. 2)A 2017, s. 30(6), with effect in relation to times after 5 April 2017 subject to s. 30(10)–(17).

S. 65(7C) inserted by F(No. 2)A 2017, s. 33 and Sch. 10, para. 5, with effect in relation to times after 5 April 2017 subject to Sch. 10, para. 9 and 10.

S. 65(7D) inserted by F(No. 2)A 2017, s. 33 and Sch. 10, para. 5, with effect in relation to times after 5 April 2017 subject to Sch. 10, para. 9 and 10.

Cross references – S. 6(2): excluded property generally – securities.

S. 10: disposition not intended to confer gratuitous benefit may not be transfer of value.

S. 16: grant of tenancy of UK agricultural property for money/money's worth is not a transfer of value.

S. 48(3)(a), (4)(b): settled property being excluded property.

S. 82: additional condition to be satisfied for s. 65(8) to apply when settlor or spouse of settlor has an initial interest in settled property, or where property moves between settlements.

S. 267(3): disapplication of deemed domicile provisions in relation to s. 65(8) in determining whether conditions in s. 82(3) satisfied.

Sch. 2, para. 3: effect of a reduction in the tax rate determined by Sch. 1, where tax is charged between ten-yearly anniversaries.

Sch. 4, para. 16, 17: property becoming comprised in a maintenance fund on ceasing to be relevant property.

FA 1986, Sch. 19, para. 43: transitional provisions where tax charged under s. 65 on an occasion falling on or after 18 March 1986 and the rate is to be determined with reference to the rate at which tax was charged on a ten-year anniversary falling before that date.

FA 1998, s. 161(3): charge to tax is not treated as arising under s. 65 by reason only of the coming into force of that section (gilt-edged securities issued on non-FOTRA terms before 6 April 1998 treated as issued with post-1996 conditions).

FA 2013, s. 86(6): no charge to tax under s. 65 if the only reason for such a charge would be that property ceases to be relevant property by virtue of the coming into force of FA 2013, s. 86.

Statements of practice – SP 10/79: effect, for purposes of s. 65(1)(b), of granting a lease for a term or periodic tenancy for less than full consideration.

RATES OF PRINCIPAL CHARGE

66 Rate of ten-yearly charge

66(1) Subject to subsection (2) below, the rate at which tax is charged under section 64 above at any time shall be three tenths of the effective rate (that is to say the rate found by expressing the tax chargeable as a percentage of the amount on which it is charged) at which tax would be charged on the value transferred by a chargeable transfer of the description specified in subsection (3) below.

66(2) Where the whole or part of the value mentioned in section 64 above is attributable to property which was not relevant property, or was not comprised in the settlement, throughout the period of ten years ending immediately before the ten-year anniversary concerned, the rate at which tax is charged on that value or part shall be reduced by one-fortieth for each of the successive quarters in that period which expired before the property became, or last became, relevant property comprised in the settlement.

66(2A) Subsection (2) above does not apply to property which is regarded as relevant property as a result of section 64(1A) (and accordingly that property is charged to tax at the rate given by subsection (1) above).

66(3) The chargeable transfer postulated in subsection (1) above is one–

(a) the value transferred by which is equal to an amount determined in accordance with subsection (4) below;

(b) which is made immediately before the ten-year anniversary concerned by a transferor who has in the preceding seven years made chargeable transfers having an aggregate value determined in accordance with subsection (5) below; and

(c) on which tax is charged in accordance with section 7(2) of this Act.

66(4) The amount referred to in subsection (3)(a) above is equal to the aggregate of–

(a) the value on which tax is charged under section 64 above;

(b) [omitted by F(No. 2)A 2015, s. 11 and Sch. 1, para. 3(2)(a);]

(c) the value, immediately after a related settlement commenced, of the relevant property then comprised in it;

(d) the value of any same-day addition; and

(e) where–

(i) an increase in the value of the property comprised in another settlement is represented by the value of a same-day addition aggregated under paragraph (d) above, and

(ii) that other settlement is not a related settlement,

the value immediately after that other settlement commenced of the relevant property then comprised in that other settlement;

but subject to subsection (6) below.

66(5) The aggregate value referred to in subsection (3)(b) above is equal to the aggregate of–

(a) the values transferred by any chargeable transfers made by the settlor in the period of seven years ending with the day on which the settlement commenced, disregarding transfers made on that day or before 27th March 1974, and

(b) the amounts on which any charges to tax were imposed under section 65 above in respect of the settlement in the ten years before the anniversary concerned;

but subject to subsection (6) and section 67 below.

66(6) In relation to a settlement which commenced before 27th March 1974–

(a) subsection (4) above shall have effect with the omission of paragraphs (c) to (e); and

(b) subsection (5) above shall have effect with the omission of paragraph (a);

and where tax is chargeable under section 64 above by reference to the first ten-year anniversary of a settlement which commenced before 9th March 1982, the aggregate mentioned in subsection (5) above shall be increased by the amounts of any distribution payments (determined in accordance with the rules applicable under paragraph 11 of Schedule 5 to the Finance Act 1975) made out of the settled property before 9th March 1982 (or, where paragraph 6, 7 or 8 of Schedule 15 to the Finance Act 1982 applied, 1st April 1983, or, as the case may be, 1st April 1984) and within the period of ten years before the anniversary concerned.

History – S. 66(2A) inserted by FA 2014, s. 117 and Sch. 25, para. 4(2), with effect in relation to occasions on which tax falls to be charged under s. 64 on or after 6 April 2014.

In s. 66(3), the words in para. (b) "preceding seven years", and para. (c), were substituted, and in s. 66(5) the word "seven" was substituted, by FA 1986, s. 101 and Sch. 19, para. 16(1)–(3), with respect to transfers of value made, and other events occurring on or after 18 March 1986.

S. 66(4)(b), and the word "and" following it, omitted, in s. 66(4)(c) the word "relevant" inserted and s. 66(4)(d) and (e) inserted by F(No. 2)A 2015, s. 11 and Sch. 1, para. 3(2), with effect in relation to occasions on which tax falls to be charged under IHTA 1984, Pt. 3, Ch. 3 on or after 18 November 2015 (Royal Assent). Former s. 66(4)(b) read as follows:

"(b) the value immediately after it became comprised in the settlement of any property which was not then relevant property and has not subsequently become relevant property while remaining comprised in the settlement; and"

In s. 66(6)(a), the words "paragraphs (c) to (e)" substituted for the words "paragraphs (b) and (c)" by F(No. 2)A 2015, s. 11 and Sch. 1, para. 3(3), with effect in relation to occasions on which tax falls to be charged under IHTA 1984, Pt. 3, Ch. 3 on or after 18 November 2015 (Royal Assent).

Cross references – S. 7(2): lifetime rates.

FA 1986, Sch. 19, para. 40(1): transitional – transfer of value occurring before, and death or other event occurring after, 18 March 1986.

Other material – ICAEW Technical Release TR 772: Subject to terms of trust, trustees have "reasonable time" after receipt of trust income to exercise their discretion whether to distribute or accumulate it. Also, suggested method of calculating accumulations over ten-year period.

67 Added property, etc.

67(1) This subsection applies where, after the settlement commenced and after 8th March 1982, but before the anniversary concerned, the settlor made a chargeable transfer as a result of which the value of the property comprised in the settlement was increased.

67(2) For the purposes of subsection (1) above, it is immaterial whether the amount of the property so comprised was increased as a result of the transfer, but a transfer as a result of which the value increased but the amount did not shall be disregarded if it is shown that the transfer–

(a) was not primarily intended to increase the value, and

(b) did not result in the value being greater immediately after the transfer by an amount exceeding five per cent of the value immediately before the transfer.

67(3) Where subsection (1) above applies in relation to a settlement which commenced after 26th March 1974, section 66(5)(a) above shall have effect as if it referred to the greater of–

(a) the aggregate of the values there specified, and

(b) the aggregate of the values transferred by any chargeable transfers made by the settlor in the period of seven years ending with the day on which the chargeable transfer falling within subsection (1) above was made–

 (i) disregarding transfers made on that day or before 27th March 1974, and

 (ii) excluding the values mentioned in subsection (5) below;

and where the settlor made two or more chargeable transfers falling with subsection (1) above, paragraph (b) above shall be taken to refer to the transfer in relation to which the aggregate there mentioned is the greatest.

67(4) Where subsection (1) above applies in relation to a settlement which commenced before 27th March 1974, the aggregate mentioned in section 66(5) above shall be increased (or further increased) by the aggregate of the values transferred by any chargeable transfers made by the settlor in the period of seven years ending with the day on which the chargeable transfer falling within subsection (1) above was made–

(a) disregarding transfers made on that day or before 27th March 1974, and

(b) excluding the values mentioned in subsection (5) below;

and where the settlor made two or more chargeable transfers falling within subsection (1) above, this subsection shall be taken to refer to the transfer in relation to which the aggregate to be added is the greatest.

67(5) The values excluded by subsections (3)(b)(ii) and (4)(b) above are–

(a) any value attributable to property whose value is taken into account in determining the amount mentioned in section 66(4) above; and

(b) any value attributable to property in respect of which a charge to tax has been made under section 65 above and by reference to which an amount mentioned in section 66(5)(b) above is determined.

67(6) Where the property comprised in a settlement immediately before the ten-year anniversary concerned, or any part of that property, had on any occasion within the preceding ten years ceased to be relevant property then, if on that occasion tax was charged in respect of the settlement under section 65 above, the aggregate mentioned in section 66(5) above shall be reduced by an amount equal to the lesser of–

(a) the amount on which tax was charged under section 65 (or so much of that amount as is attributable to the part in question), and

(b) the value on which tax is charged under section 64 above (or so much of that value as is attributable to the part in question);

and if there were two or more such occasions relating to the property or the same part of it, this subsection shall have effect in relation to each of them.

67(7) References in subsection (6) above to the property comprised in a settlement immediately before an anniversary shall, if part only of the settled property was then relevant property, be construed as references to that part.

History – In s. 67(3)(b) and (4), the word "seven" was substituted by FA 1986, s. 101 and Sch. 19, para. 17, with respect to transfers of value made, and other events occurring on or after 18 March 1986.

Cross references – FA 1986, Sch. 19, para. 40(1): transitional – transfer of value occurring before, and death or other event occurring after, 18 March 1986.

68 Rate before first ten-year anniversary

68(1) The rate at which tax is charged under section 65 above on an occasion preceding the first ten-year anniversary after the settlement's commencement shall be the appropriate fraction of the effective rate at which tax would be charged on the value transferred by a chargeable transfer of the description specified in subsection (4) below (but subject to subsection (6) below).

68(2) For the purposes of this section **the appropriate fraction** is three tenths multiplied by so many fortieths as there are complete successive quarters in the period beginning with the day on which the settlement commenced and ending with the day before the occasion of the charge, but subject to subsection (3) below.

68(3) Where the whole or part of the amount on which tax is charged is attributable to property which was not relevant property, or was not comprised in the settlement, throughout the period referred to in subsection (2) above, then in determining the appropriate fraction in relation to that amount or part–

(a) no quarter which expired before the day on which the property became, or last became, relevant property comprised in the settlement shall be counted, but

(b) if that day fell in the same quarter as that in which the period ends, that quarter shall be counted whether complete or not.

68(4) The chargeable transfer postulated in subsection (1) above is one–

(a) the value transferred by which is equal to an amount determined in accordance with subsection (5) below;

(b) which is made at the time of the charge to tax under section 65 by a transferor who has in the period of seven years ending with the day of the occasion of the charge made chargeable transfers having an aggregate value equal to that of any chargeable transfers made by the settlor in the period of seven years ending with the day on which the settlement commenced, disregarding transfers made on that day or before 27th March 1974; and

(c) on which tax is charged in accordance with section 7(2) of this Act.

68(5) The amount referred to in subsection (4)(a) above is equal to the aggregate of–

(a) the value, immediately after the settlement commenced, of the relevant property then comprised in it;

(b) the value, immediately after a related settlement commenced, of the relevant property then comprised in it;

(c) the value, immediately after it became comprised in the settlement, of property which–

(i) became comprised in the settlement after the settlement commenced and before the occasion of the charge under section 65 above, and

(ii) was relevant property immediately after it became so comprised,

whether or not the property has remained relevant property comprised in the settlement;

(d) the value, at the time it became (or last became) relevant property, of property which–

(i) was comprised in the settlement immediately after the settlement commenced and was not then relevant property but became relevant property before the occasion of the charge under section 65 above, or

(ii) became comprised in the settlement after the settlement commenced and before the occasion of the charge under section 65 above, and was not relevant property immediately after it became comprised in the settlement, but became relevant property before the occasion of the charge under that section,

whether or not the property has remained relevant property comprised in the settlement;

(e) the value of any same-day addition; and

(f) where–

(i) an increase in the value of the property comprised in another settlement is represented by the value of a same-day addition aggregated under paragraph (e) above, and

(ii) that other settlement is not a related settlement,

the value immediately after that other settlement commenced of the relevant property then comprised in that other settlement.

68(6) *Where the settlement* commenced before 27th March 1974, subsection (1) above shall have effect with the substitution of a reference to three tenths for the reference to the appropriate fraction; and in relation to such a settlement the chargeable transfer postulated in that subsection is one–

(a) the value transferred by which is equal to the amount on which tax is charged under section 65 above;

(b) which is made at the time of that charge to tax by a transferor who has in the period of seven years ending with the day of the occasion of the charge made chargeable transfers having an aggregate value equal to the aggregate of–

(i) any amounts on which any charges to tax have been imposed under section 65 above in respect of the settlement in the period of ten years ending with that day; and

(ii) the amounts of any distribution payments (determined in accordance with the rules applicable under paragraph 11 of Schedule 5 to the Finance Act 1975) made out of the settled property before 9th March 1982 (or, where paragraph 6, 7 or 8 of Schedule 15 to the Finance Act 1982 applied, 1st April 1983, or, as the case may be, 1st April 1984) and within the said period of ten years; and

(c) on which tax is charged in accordance with section 7(2) of this Act.

History – In s. 68(4)(b) the word "seven" (in both places), and in s. 68(6) the word "seven" in para. (b), the words "the period of ten years ending with that day" and para. (c), were substituted by FA 1986, s. 101 and Sch. 19, para. 18(1)–(3), with respect to transfers of value made, and other events occurring, on or after 18 March 1986.

In s. 68(5)(a) and (b) the word "relevant" inserted, the word "and" at the end of s. 68(5)(b) omitted and s. 68(c), (d), (e) and (f) substituted for former s. 68(5)(c) by F(No. 2)A 2015, s. 11 and Sch. 1, para. 4, with effect in relation to occasions on which tax falls to be charged under IHTA 1984, Pt. 3, Ch. 3 on or after 18 November 2015 (Royal Assent). Former s. 68(5)(c) read as follows:

"(c) the value, immediately after it became comprised in the settlement, of any property which became so comprised after the settlement commenced and before the occasion of the charge under section 65 (whether or not it has remained so comprised)."

Cross references – S. 7(2): lifetime rates.

FA 1986, Sch. 19, para. 40(1): transitional – transfer of value occurring before, and death or other event occurring after, 18 March 1986.

Other material – ICAEW Technical Release TR 772: Subject to terms of trust, trustees have a "reasonable time", after receipt of trust income, to exercise their discretion whether to distribute or accumulate it. Revenue will allow trustees to choose their own method of tracing capital paid out to accumulations or initial capital (or capital at previous ten-year charge) provided that trustees follow their choice consistently.

Taxline, 1991/12 (not reproduced): Capital Taxes Office confirmation that in calculating the effective rate of tax payable where property leaves a discretionary trust before the first ten-year anniversary, no business or agricultural property relief is taken into account; but these reliefs do apply to reduce the value of the property to which the effective rate is applied in calculating the liability.

Letter to Chartered Institute of Taxation, 27 September 1995 from Revenue's Capital Taxes Office (not reproduced): accumulated income and calculation of exit charge from discretionary trusts.

69 Rate between ten-year anniversaries

69(1) Subject to subsection (2A) below, the rate at which tax is charged under section 65 above on an occasion following one or more ten-year anniversaries after the settlement's commencement shall be the appropriate fraction of the rate at which it was last charged under section 64 (or would have been charged apart from section 66(2)).

69(2) Subsection (2A) below applies–

(a) if, at any time in the period beginning with the most recent ten-year anniversary and ending immediately before the occasion of the charge under section 65 above (the **"relevant period"**), property has become comprised in the settlement which was relevant property immediately after it became so comprised, or

(b) if–

(i) at any time in the relevant period, property has become comprised in the settlement which was not relevant property immediately after it became so comprised, and

(ii) at a later time in the relevant period, that property has become relevant property, or

(c) if property which was comprised in the settlement immediately before the relevant period, but was not then relevant property, has at any time during the relevant period become relevant property.

69(2A) Whether or not all of the property within any of paragraphs (a) to (c) of subsection (2) above has remained relevant property comprised in the settlement, the rate at which tax is charged under section 65 is to be the appropriate fraction of the rate at which it would last have been charged under section 64 above (apart from section 66(2) above) if–

(a) immediately before the most recent ten-year anniversary, all of that property had been relevant property comprised in the settlement with a value determined in accordance with subsection (3) below, and

(b) any same-day addition made on or after the most recent ten-year anniversary had been made immediately before that anniversary.

69(3) In the case of property within subsection (2)(a) above the value to be attributed to it for the purposes of subsection (2A) above is its value immediately after it became comprised in the settlement; and in any other case the value to be so attributed is the value of the property when it became (or last became) relevant property.

69(4) For the purposes of this section the appropriate fraction is so many fortieths as there are complete successive quarters in the period beginning with the most recent ten-year anniversary and ending with the day before the occasion of the charge; but subsection (3) of section 68 above shall have effect for the purposes of this subsection as it has effect for the purposes of subsection (2) of that section.

History – In s. 69(1) the words "subsection (2A)" substituted for the words "subsection (2)" by F(No. 2)A 2015, s. 11 and Sch. 1, para. 5(2), with effect in relation to occasions on which tax falls to be charged under IHTA 1984, Pt. 3, Ch. 3 on or after 18 November 2015 (Royal Assent).

S. 69(2) and (2A) substituted for former s. 69(2) by F(No. 2)A 2015, s. 11 and Sch. 1, para. 5(3), with effect in relation to occasions on which tax falls to be charged under IHTA 1984, Pt. 3, Ch. 3 on or after 18 November 2015 (Royal Assent). Former s. 69(2) read as follows:

"**69(2)** If at any time before the occasion of the charge under section 65 and on or after the most recent ten-year anniversary–

(a) property has become comprised in the settlement, or

(b) property which was comprised in the settlement immediately before the anniversary, but was not then relevant property, has become relevant property,

then, whether or not the property has remained comprised in the settlement or has remained relevant property, the rate at which tax is charged under section 65 shall be the appropriate fraction of the rate at which it would last have been charged under section 64 (apart from section 66(2)) if immediately before that anniversary the property had been relevant property comprised in the settlement with a value determined in accordance with subsection (3) below."

In s. 69(3)(b) the words below omitted and the words "purposes of subsection (2A)" substituted for the words "purposes of subsection (2)" by F(No. 2)A 2015, s. 11 and Sch. 1, para. 5(4), with effect in relation to occasions on which tax falls to be charged under IHTA 1984, Pt. 3, Ch. 3 on or after 18 November 2015 (Royal Assent). The omitted words read as follows:

"which either–

(a) property has become comprised in the settlement, or

(b) property which was comprised in the settlement immediately before the anniversary, but was not then relevant property, has become relevant property,"

Cross references – Sch. 2, para. 3: rate of tax between ten-year anniversaries where there has been a reduction in the rate determined by Sch. 1 since the last ten-year anniversary.

Other material – ICAEW Technical Release TR 772: Subject to terms of trust, trustees have a "reasonable time", after receipt of trust income, to exercise their discretion whether to distribute or accumulate it. HMRC will allow trustees to choose their own method of tracing capital paid out to accumulations or initial capital (or capital at previous ten-year charge) provided that they follow their choice consistently.

SPECIAL CASES – CHARGES TO TAX

70 Property leaving temporary charitable trusts

70(1) This section applies to settled property held for charitable purposes only until the end of a period (whether defined by a date or in some other way).

70(2) Subject to subsections (3) and (4) below, there shall be a charge to tax under this section–

(a) where settled property ceases to be property to which this section applies, otherwise than by virtue of an application for charitable purposes, and

(b) in a case in which paragraph (a) above does not apply, where the trustees make a disposition (otherwise than by an application of property for charitable purposes) as a result of which the value of settled property to which this section applies is less than it would be but for the disposition.

70(3) Tax shall not be charged under this section in respect of–

(a) a payment of costs or expenses (so far as they are fairly attributable to property to which this section applies), or

(b) a payment which is (or will be) income of any person for any of the purposes of income tax or would for any of those purposes be income of a person not resident in the United Kingdom if he were so resident,

or in respect of a liability to make such a payment.

70(4) Tax shall not be charged under this section by virtue of subsection (2)(b) above if the disposition is such that, were the trustees beneficially entitled to the settled property, section 10 or section 16 above would prevent the disposition from being a transfer of value.

70(5) The amount on which tax is charged under this section shall be–

(a) the amount by which the value of property which is comprised in the settlement and to which this section applies is less immediately after the event giving rise to the charge than it would be but for the event, or

(b) where the tax payable is paid out of settled property to which this section applies immediately after the event, the amount which after deducting the tax is equal to the amount on which tax would be charged by virtue of paragraph (a) above.

70(6) The rate at which tax is charged under this section shall be the aggregate of the following percentages–

(a) 0.25 per cent for each of the first forty complete successive quarters in the relevant period,

(b) 0.20 per cent for each of the next forty,

(c) 0.15 per cent for each of the next forty,

(d) 0.10 per cent for each of the next forty, and

(e) 0.05 per cent for each of the next forty.

70(7) Where the whole or part of the amount on which tax is charged under this section is attributable to property which was excluded property at any time during the relevant period then, in determining the rate at which tax is charged under this section in respect of that amount or part, no quarter throughout which that property was excluded property shall be counted.

70(8) In subsections (6) and (7) above **"the relevant period"** means the period beginning with the later of–

(a) the day on which the property in respect of which tax is chargeable became (or last became) property to which this section applies, and

(b) 13th March 1975,

and ending with the day before the event giving rise to the charge.

70(9) Where the property in respect of which tax is chargeable–

(a) was relevant property immediately before 10th December 1981, and

(b) became (or last became) property to which this section applies on or after that day and before 9th March 1982 (or, where paragraph 6, 7 or 8 of Schedule 15 to the Finance Act 1982 applied, 1st April 1983 or, as the case may be, 1st April 1984),

subsection (8) above shall have effect as if the day referred to in paragraph (a) of that subsection were the day on which the property became (or last became) relevant property before 10th December 1981.

70(10) For the purposes of this section trustees shall be treated as making a disposition if they omit to exercise a right (unless it is shown that the omission was not deliberate) and the disposition shall be treated as made at the time or latest time when they could have exercised the right.

Cross references – S. 10: dispositions not intended to confer gratuitous benefit.
S. 16: grant of tenancies of agricultural property.
Sch. 4, para. 8: application of s. 70 to property leaving maintenance funds.

71 Accumulation and maintenance trusts

71(1) Subject to subsections (1A) to (2) below, this section applies to settled property if–

(a) one or more persons (in this section referred to as beneficiaries) will, on or before attaining a specified age not exceeding eighteen, become beneficially entitled to it, and

(b) no interest in possession subsists in it and the income from it is to be accumulated so far as not applied for the maintenance, education or benefit of a beneficiary.

71(1A) This section does not apply to settled property at any particular time on or after 22nd March 2006 unless this section–

(a) applied to the settled property immediately before 22nd March 2006, and

(b) has applied to the settled property at all subsequent times up to the particular time.

71(1B) This section does not apply to settled property at any particular time on or after 22nd March 2006 if, at that time, section 71A below applies to the settled property.

71(2) This section does not apply to settled property unless either–

(a) not more than twenty-five years have elapsed since the commencement of the settlement or, if it was later, since the time (or latest time) when the conditions stated in paragraphs (a) and (b) of subsection (1) above became satisfied with respect to the property, or

(b) all the persons who are or have been beneficiaries are or were either–

(i) grandchildren of a common grandparent, or

(ii) children, widows or widowers or surviving civil partners of such grandchildren who were themselves beneficiaries but died before the time when, had they survived, they would have become entitled as mentioned in subsection (1)(a) above.

71(3) Subject to subsections (4) and (5) below, there shall be a charge to tax under this section–

(a) where settled property ceases to be property to which this section applies, and

(b) in a case in which paragraph (a) above does not apply, where the trustees make a disposition as a result of which the value of settled property to which this section applies is less than it would be but for the disposition.

71(4) Tax shall not be charged under this section–

(a) on a beneficiary's becoming beneficially entitled to, or to an interest in possession in, settled property on or before attaining the specified age, or

(b) on the death of a beneficiary before attaining the specified age.

71(5) Subsections (3) to (8) and (10) of section 70 above shall apply for the purposes of this section as they apply for the purposes of that section (with the substitution of a reference to subsection (3)(b) above for the reference in section 70(4) to section 70(2)(b)).

71(6) Where the conditions stated in paragraphs (a) and (b) of subsection (1) above were satisfied on 15th April 1976 with respect to property comprised in a settlement which commenced before that day, subsection (2)(a) above shall have effect with the substitution of a reference to that day for the reference to the commencement of the settlement, and the condition stated in subsection (2)(b) above shall be treated as satisfied if–

(a) it is satisfied in respect of the period beginning with 15th April 1976, or

(b) it is satisfied in respect of the period beginning with 1st April 1977 and either there was no beneficiary living on 15th April 1976 or the beneficiaries on 1st April 1977 included a living beneficiary, or

(c) there is no power under the terms of the settlement whereby it could have become satisfied in respect of the period beginning with 1st April 1977, and the trusts of the settlement have not been varied at any time after 15th April 1976.

71(7) In subsection (1) above **"persons"** includes unborn persons; but the conditions stated in that subsection shall be treated as not satisfied unless there is or has been a living beneficiary.

71(8) For the purposes of this section **a person's children** shall be taken to include his illegitimate children, his adopted children and his stepchildren.

History – In s. 71(1)(a) the word "eighteen" substituted for "twenty-five" by FA 2006, s. 156 and Sch. 20, para. 3(1)(a), with effect from 6 April 2008 (FA 2006, Sch. 20, para. 3(2) and (3)).
In s. 71(1)(a) the words "or to an interest in possession in it" omitted by FA 2006, s. 156 and Sch. 20, para. 3(1)(b) and repealed by FA 2006, s. 178 and Sch. 26, Pt. 6, with effect from 6 April 2008 (FA 2006, Sch. 20, para. 3(2) and (3)).
In s. 71(1) the words "subsections (1A) to" substituted for the words "subsection" by FA 2006, s. 156 and Sch. 20, para. 2(2), with effect from 22 March 2006, subject to the provisions of FA 2006, Sch. 20, para. 2(4).
S. 71(1A) inserted by FA 2006, s. 156 and Sch. 20, para. 2(3), with effect from 22 March 2006, subject to the provisions of FA 2006, Sch. 20, para. (4).
S. 71(1B) inserted by FA 2006, s. 156) and Sch. 20, para. 2(3), with effect from 22 March 2006, subject to the provisions of FA 2006, Sch. 20, para. 2(4) and para. 2(5).
In s. 71(2)(b)(ii) the words "or surviving civil partners" inserted by SI 2005/3229, reg. 16, with effect from 5 December 2005.

Cross references – S. 3A(3): a gift by an individual into an accumulation and maintenance trust is a potentially exempt transfer.
S. 54A: rate of charge where settled property affected by potentially exempt transfer.
Civil Partnership Act 2004, Sch. 21, para. 54 (not reproduced): references to an individual's stepchildren to include references to children of that individual's civil partner; in force from 5 December 2005.
TCGA 1992, s. 260: capital gains tax treatment of transfers to which s. 71 applies.

Extra-statutory concessions – F8 (to be withdrawn with effect from April 2015): no age specified in trust instrument for purposes of s. 71(1)(a).

Statements of practice – E1: powers of appointment.

Other material – IR press release, 24 September 1975 (not reproduced): beneficiary's entitlement to income on attaining his majority under Trustee Act 1925, s. 31(1)(ii) is regarded as an interest in possession on attaining a specified age not exceeding 25.
IR press release, 30 September 1996 (withdrawing SP E8): following *Begg-McBrearty (HMIT) v Stilwell* [1996] BTC 269, where Trustee Act 1925, s. 31 applies to property appointed after the commencement date of the Family Reform Act 1969 (1 January 1970) out of a settlement created before that date, the beneficiary's interest in possession is regarded as arising at age 18.
Letter to Chartered Institute of Taxation, 27 September 1995 from Revenue's Capital Taxes Office (not reproduced): school fees paid direct to the school by accumulation and maintenance trusts out of capital do not breach s. 71(1)(a).
Tax Bulletin, TB10/01-3: mere existence (as opposed to the actual exercise) of a power to appoint in favour of beneficiaries who are not grandchildren of a common grandparent will not take a settlement outside the common grandparent category.

71A Trusts for bereaved minors

71A(1) This section applies to settled property (including property settled before 22nd March 2006) if–

(a) it is held on statutory trusts for the benefit of a bereaved minor under sections 46 and 47(1) of the Administration of Estates Act 1925 (succession on intestacy and statutory trusts in favour of issue of intestate), or

(b) it is held on trusts for the benefit of a bereaved minor and subsection (2) below applies to the trusts,

but this section does not apply to property in which a disabled person's interest subsists.

71A(2) This subsection applies to trusts–

(a) established under the will of a deceased parent of the bereaved minor, or

(b) established under the Criminal Injuries Compensation Scheme,

(c) established under the Victims of Overseas Terrorism Compensation Scheme,

which secure that the conditions in subsection (3) below are met.

71A(3) Those conditions are–

(a) that the bereaved minor, if he has not done so before attaining the age of 18, will on attaining that age become absolutely entitled to–

(i) the settled property,

(ii) any income arising from it, and

(iii) any income that has arisen from the property held on the trusts for his benefit and been accumulated before that time,

(b) that, for so long as the bereaved minor is living and under the age of 18, if any of the settled property is applied for the benefit of a beneficiary, it is applied for the benefit of the bereaved minor, and

(c) that, for so long as the bereaved minor is living and under the age of 18, either–

(i) the bereaved minor is entitled to all of the income (if there is any) arising from any of the settled property, or

(ii) if any of the income arising from any of the settled property is applied for the benefit of a beneficiary, it is applied for the benefit of the bereaved minor.

71A(4) Trusts such as are mentioned in paragraph (a), (b) or (c) of subsection (2) above are not to be treated as failing to secure that the conditions in subsection (3) above are met by reason only of–

(za) the trustees' having powers that enable them to apply otherwise than for the benefit of the bereaved minor amounts (whether consisting of income or capital, or both) not exceeding the annual limit,

(a) the trustees' having the powers conferred by section 32 of the Trustee Act 1925 (powers of advancement),

(b) the trustees' having those powers but free from, or subject to a less restrictive limitation than, the limitation imposed by proviso (a) of subsection (1) of that section,

(c) the trustees' having the powers conferred by section 33 of the Trustee Act (Northern Ireland) 1958 (corresponding provision for Northern Ireland),

(d) the trustees' having those powers but free from, or subject to a less restrictive limitation than, the limitation imposed by subsection (1)(a) of that section, or

(e) the trustees' having powers to the like effect as the powers mentioned in any of paragraphs (a) to (d) above.

71A(4A) For the purposes of this section and section 71B, the **"annual limit"** is whichever is the lower of the following amounts–

(a) £3,000, and

(b) 3% of the amount that is the maximum value of the settled property during the period in question.

71A(4B) For those purposes the annual limit applies in relation to each period of 12 months that begins on 6 April.

71A(4C) The Treasury may by order made by statutory instrument–

(a) specify circumstances in which subsection (4)(za) is, or is not, to apply in relation to a trust, and

(b) amend the definition of **"the annual limit"** in subsection (4A).

71A(4D) An order under subsection (4C) may–

(a) make different provision for different cases, and

(b) contain transitional and saving provision.

71A(4E) A statutory instrument containing an order under subsection (4C) may not be made unless a draft of the instrument has been laid before, and approved by a resolution of, the House of Commons.

71A(5) In this section **"the Criminal Injuries Compensation Scheme"** means–

(a) the schemes established by arrangements made under the Criminal Injuries Compensation Act 1995,

(b) arrangements made by the Secretary of State for compensation for criminal injuries in operation before the commencement of those schemes, and

(c) the scheme established under the Criminal Injuries Compensation (Northern Ireland) Order 2002.

71A(6) The preceding provisions of this section apply in relation to Scotland as if, in subsection (2) above, before "which" there were inserted "the purposes of".

History – S. 71A(2)(c) inserted by the Crime and Security Act 2010, s. 48 and Sch. 2, para. 2(a), with effect from 8 April 2010.
S. 71A(3)(c)(ii) substituted by FA 2013, s. 216 and Sch. 44, para. 2(2), with effect in relation to property transferred into a settlement on or after 8 April 2013. Former s. 71A(3)(c)(ii) read as follows:
"(ii) no such income may be applied for the benefit of any other person.".
In s. 71A(4), ", (b) or (c)" substituted for ", or (b)" by the Crime and Security Act 2010, s. 48 and Sch. 2, para. 2(b), with effect from 8 April 2010.
S. 71A(4)(za) inserted by FA 2013, s. 216 and Sch. 44, para. 2(3), with effect in relation to property transferred into a settlement on or after 8 April 2013.
S. 71A(4A)–(4E) inserted by FA 2013, s. 216 and Sch. 44, para. 2(4), with effect in relation to property transferred into a settlement on or after 8 April 2013.
S. 71A inserted by FA 2006, s. 156 and Sch. 20, para. 1(1), with effect from 22 March 2006.

71B Charge to tax on property to which section 71A applies

71B(1) Subject to subsections (2), (2B) and (3) below, there shall be a charge to tax under this section–

(a) where settled property ceases to be property to which section 71A above applies, and

(b) in a case where paragraph (a) above does not apply, where the trustees make a disposition as a result of which the value of settled property to which section 71A above applies is less than it would be but for the disposition.

71B(2) Tax is not charged under this section where settled property ceases to be property to which section 71A applies as a result of–

(a) the bereaved minor attaining the age of 18 or becoming, under that age, absolutely entitled as mentioned in section 71A(3)(a) above, or

(b) the death under that age of the bereaved minor, or

(c) being paid or applied for the advancement or benefit of the bereaved minor.

71B(2A) Subsection (2B) applies in a case in which–

(a) an amount is paid or applied otherwise than for the benefit of the bereaved minor, and

(b) the exemptions provided by subsection (2) of this section and subsections (3) and (4) of section 70 do not apply.

71B(2B) In such a case, tax is not charged under this section in respect of whichever is the lower of the following amounts–

(a) the amount paid or applied, and

(b) the annual limit.

71B(3) Subsections (3) to (8) and (10) of section 70 above apply for the purposes of this section as they apply for the purposes of that section, but–

(a) with the substitution of a reference to subsection (1)(b) above for the reference in subsection (4) of section 70 above to subsection (2)(b) of that section,

(b) with the substitution of a reference to property to which section 71A above applies for each of the references in subsections (3), (5) and (8) of section 70 above to property to which that section applies,

(c) as if, for the purposes of section 70(8) above as applied by this subsection, property–

(i) which is property to which section 71A above applies,

(ii) which, immediately before it became property to which section 71A above applies, was property to which section 71 above applied, and

(iii) which, by the operation of section 71(1B) above, ceased on that occasion to be property to which section 71 above applied,

had become property to which section 71A above applies not on that occasion but on the occasion (or last occasion) before then when it became property to which section 71 above applied, and

(d) as if, for the purposes of section 70(8) above as applied by this subsection, property–

(i) which is property to which section 71A above applies,

(ii) which, immediately before it became property to which section 71A above applies, was property to which section 71D below applied, and

(iii) which, by the operation of section 71D(5)(a) below, ceased on that occasion ("the 71D-to-71A occasion") to be property to which section 71D below applied,

had become property to which section 71A above applies not on the 71D-to-71A occasion but on the relevant earlier occasion.

71B(4) In subsection (3)(d) above–

(a) **"the relevant earlier occasion"** means the occasion (or last occasion) before the 71D-to-71A occasion when the property became property to which section 71D below applied, but

(b) if the property, when it became property to which section 71D below applied, ceased at the same time to be property to which section 71 above applied without ceasing to be settled property, **"the relevant earlier occasion"** means the occasion (or last occasion) when the property became property to which section 71 above applied.

History – In s. 71B(1), ", (2B)" inserted by FA 2013, s. 216 and Sch. 44, para. 3(2), with effect in relation to property transferred into a settlement on or after 8 April 2013.

S. 71B(2A) and (2B) inserted by FA 2013, s. 216 and Sch. 44, para. 3(3), with effect in relation to property transferred into a settlement on or after 8 April 2013.

S. 71B inserted by FA 2006, s. 156 and Sch. 20, para. 1(1), with effect from 22 March 2006.

71C Sections 71A and 71B: meaning of "bereaved minor"

71C In sections 71A and 71B above **"bereaved minor"** means a person–

(a) who has not yet attained the age of 18, and

(b) at least one of whose parents has died.

History – S. 71C inserted by FA 2006, s. 156 and Sch. 20, para. 1(1), with effect from 22 March 2006

71D Age 18-to-25 trusts

71D(1) This section applies to settled property (including property settled before 22nd March 2006), but subject to subsection (5) below, if–

(a) the property is held on trusts for the benefit of a person who has not yet attained the age of 25,

(b) at least one of the person's parents has died, and

(c) subsection (2) below applies to the trusts.

71D(2) This subsection applies to trusts–

(a) established under the will of a deceased parent of the person mentioned in subsection (1)(a) above, or

(b) established under the Criminal Injuries Compensation Scheme,

(c) established under the Victims of Overseas Terrorism Compensation Scheme,

which secure that the conditions in subsection (6) below are met.

71D(3) Subsection (4) has effect where–

(a) at any time on or after 22nd March 2006 but before 6th April 2008, or on the coming into force of paragraph 3(1) of Schedule 20 to the Finance Act 2006, any property ceases to be property to which section 71 above applies without ceasing to be settled property, and

(b) immediately after the property ceases to be property to which section 71 above applies–

(i) it is held on trusts for the benefit of a person who has not yet attained the age of 25, and

(ii) the trusts secure that the conditions in subsection (6) below are met.

71D(4) From the time when the property ceases to be property to which section 71 above applies, but subject to subsection (5) below, this section applies to the property (if it would not apply to the property by virtue of subsection (1) above) for so long as–

(a) the property continues to be settled property held on trusts such as are mentioned in subsection (3)(b)(i) above, and

(b) the trusts continue to secure that the conditions in subsection (6) below are met.

71D(5) This section does not apply–

(a) to property to which section 71A above applies,

(b) to property to which section 71 above, or section 89 below, applies, or

(c) to settled property if a person is beneficially entitled to an interest in possession in the settled property and–

(i) the person became beneficially entitled to the interest in possession before 22nd March 2006, or

(ii) the interest in possession is an immediate post-death interest, or a transitional serial interest, and the person became beneficially entitled to it on or after 22nd March 2006.

71D(6) Those conditions are–

(a) that the person mentioned in subsection (1)(a) or (3)(b)(i) above ("B"), if he has not done so before attaining the age of 25, will on attaining that age become absolutely entitled to–

(i) the settled property,

(ii) any income arising from it, and

(iii) any income that has arisen from the property held on the trusts for his benefit and been accumulated before that time,

(b) that, for so long as B is living and under the age of 25, if any of the settled property is applied for the benefit of a beneficiary, it is applied for the benefit of B, and

(c) that, for so long as B is living and under the age of 25, either–

(i) B is entitled to all of the income (if there is any) arising from any of the settled property, or

(ii) if any of the income arising from any of the settled property is applied for the benefit of a beneficiary, it is applied for the benefit of B.

71D(6A) Where the income arising from the settled property is held on trusts of the kind described in section 33 of the Trustee Act 1925 (protective trusts), paragraphs (b) and (c) of subsection (6) have effect as if for "living and under the age of 25," there were substituted "under the age of 25 and the income arising from the settled property is held on trust for B,"

71D(7) For the purposes of this section, trusts are not to be treated as failing to secure that the conditions in subsection (6) above are met by reason only of–

(za) the trustees' having powers that enable them to apply otherwise than for the benefit of B amounts (whether consisting of income or capital, or both) not exceeding the annual limit,

(a) the trustees' having the powers conferred by section 32 of the Trustee Act 1925 (powers of advancement),

(b) the trustees' having those powers but free from, or subject to a less restrictive limitation than, the limitation imposed by proviso (a) of subsection (1) of that section,

(c) the trustees' having the powers conferred by section 33 of the Trustee Act (Northern Ireland) 1958 (corresponding provision for Northern Ireland),

(d) the trustees' having those powers but free from, or subject to a less restrictive limitation than, the limitation imposed by subsection (1)(a) of that section, or

(e) the trustees' having powers to the like effect as the powers mentioned in any of paragraphs (a) to (d) above.

71D(7A) For the purposes of this section and section 71E, the **"annual limit"** is whichever is the lower of the following amounts–

(a) £3,000, and

(b) 3% of the amount that is the maximum value of the settled property during the period in question.

71D(7B) For those purposes the annual limit applies in relation to each period of 12 months that begins on 6 April.

71D(7C) The Treasury may by order made by statutory instrument–

(a) specify circumstances in which subsection (7)(za) is, or is not, to apply in relation to a trust, and

(b) amend the definition of "the annual limit" in subsection (7A).

71D(7D) An order under subsection (7C) may–

(a) make different provision for different cases, and

(b) contain transitional and saving provision.

71D(7E) A statutory instrument containing an order under subsection (7C) may not be made unless a draft of the instrument has been laid before, and approved by a resolution of, the House of Commons.

71D(8) In this section **"the Criminal Injuries Compensation Scheme"** means–

(a) the schemes established by arrangements made under the Criminal Injuries Compensation Act 1995,

(b) arrangements made by the Secretary of State for compensation for criminal injuries in operation before the commencement of those schemes, and

(c) the scheme established under the Criminal Injuries Compensation (Northern Ireland) Order 2002.

71D(9) The preceding provisions of this section apply in relation to Scotland–

(a) as if, in subsection (2) above, before "which" there were inserted "the purposes of", and

(b) as if, in subsections (3)(b)(ii) and (4)(b) above, before "trusts" there were inserted "purposes of the".

History – S. 71D(2)(c) inserted by the Crime and Security Act 2010, s. 48 and Sch. 2, para. 2(c), with effect from 8 April 2010.
S. 71D(6)(c)(ii) substituted by FA 2013, s. 216 and Sch. 44, para. 4(2), with effect in relation to property transferred into a settlement on or after 8 April 2013. Former s. 71D(6)(c)(ii) read as follows:
"(ii) no such income may be applied for the benefit of any other person.".
S. 71D(6A) inserted by FA 2013, s. 216 and Sch. 44, para. 4(3), with effect in relation to property transferred into a settlement on or after 8 April 2013.
S. 71D(7)(za) inserted by FA 2013, s. 216 and Sch. 44, para. 4(4), with effect in relation to property transferred into a settlement on or after 8 April 2013.
S. 71D(7A)–(7E) inserted by FA 2013, s. 216 and Sch. 44, para. 4(5), with effect in relation to property transferred into a settlement on or after 8 April 2013.
S. 71D inserted by FA 2006, s. 156 and Sch. 20, para. 1(1), with effect from 22 March 2006.

71E Charge to tax on property to which section 71D applies

71E(1) Subject to subsections (2) to (4A) below, there shall be a charge to tax under this section–

(a) where settled property ceases to be property to which section 71D above applies, or

(b) in a case where paragraph (a) above does not apply, where the trustees make a disposition as a result of which the value of the settled property to which section 71D above applies is less than it would be but for the disposition.

71E(2) Tax is not charged under this section where settled property ceases to be property to which *section 71D above* applies as a result of–

(a) B becoming, at or under the age of 18, absolutely entitled as mentioned in section 71D(6)(a) above,

(b) the death, under the age of 18, of B,

(c) becoming, at a time when B is living and under the age of 18, property to which section 71A above applies, or

(d) being paid or applied for the advancement or benefit of B–

(i) at a time when B is living and under the age of 18, or

(ii) on B's attaining the age of 18.

71E(3) Tax is not charged under this section in respect of–

(a) a payment of costs or expenses (so far as they are fairly attributable to property to which section 71D above applies), or

(b) a payment which is (or will be) income of any person for any of the purposes of income tax or would for any of those purposes be income of a person not resident in the United Kingdom if he were so resident,

or in respect of a liability to make such a payment.

71E(4) Tax is not charged under this section by virtue of subsection (1)(b) above if the disposition is such that, were the trustees beneficially entitled to the settled property, section 10 or section 16 above would prevent the disposition from being a transfer of value.

71E(4A) If an amount is paid or applied otherwise than for the benefit of B and the exemptions provided by subsections (2) to (4) do not apply, tax is not charged under this section in respect of whichever is the lower of the following amounts–

(a) the amount paid or applied, and

(b) the annual limit.

71E(5) For the purposes of this section the trustees shall be treated as making a disposition if they omit to exercise a right (unless it is shown that the omission was not deliberate) and the disposition shall be treated as made at the time or latest time when they could have exercised the right.

History – In s. 71E(1), "(4A)" substituted for "(4)" by FA 2013, s. 216 and Sch. 44, para. 5(2), with effect in relation to property transferred into a settlement on or after 8 April 2013.

S. 71E(4A) inserted by FA 2013, s. 216 and Sch. 44, para. 5(3), with effect in relation to property transferred into a settlement on or after 8 April 2013.

S. 71E inserted by FA 2006, s. 156 and Sch. 20, para. 1(1), with effect from 22 March 2006.

71F Calculation of tax charged under section 71E in certain cases

71F(1) Where–

(a) tax is charged under section 71E above by reason of the happening of an event within subsection (2) below, and

(b) that event happens after B has attained the age of 18,

the tax is calculated in accordance with this section.

71F(2) Those events are–

(a) B becoming absolutely entitled as mentioned in section 71D(6)(a) above,

(b) the death of B, and

(c) property being paid or applied for the advancement or benefit of B.

71F(3) The amount of the tax is given by–

Chargeable amount × Relevant fraction × Settlement rate

71F(4) For the purposes of subsection (3) above, the **"Chargeable amount"** is–

(a) the amount by which the value of property which is comprised in the settlement and to which section 71D above applies is less immediately after the event giving rise to the charge than it would be but for the event, or

(b) where the tax is payable out of settled property to which section 71D above applies immediately after the event, the amount which, after deducting the tax, is equal to the amount on which tax would be charged by virtue of paragraph (a) above.

71F(5) For the purposes of subsection (3) above, the **"Relevant fraction"** is three tenths multiplied by so many fortieths as there are complete successive quarters in the period–

(a) beginning with the day on which B attained the age of 18 or, if later, the day on which the property became property to which section 71D above applies, and

(b) ending with the day before the occasion of the charge.

71F(6) Where the whole or part of the Chargeable amount is attributable to property that was excluded property at any time during the period mentioned in subsection (5) above then, in determining the "Relevant fraction" in relation to that amount or part, no quarter throughout which that property was excluded property shall be counted.

71F(7) For the purposes of subsection (3) above, the **"Settlement rate"** is the effective rate (that is to say, the rate found by expressing the tax chargeable as a percentage of the amount on which it is charged) at which tax would be charged on the value transferred by a chargeable transfer of the description specified in subsection (8) below.

71F(8) The chargeable transfer postulated in subsection (7) above is one–

(a) the value transferred by which is equal to an amount determined in accordance with subsection (9) below,

(b) which is made at the time of the charge to tax under section 71E above by a transferor who has in the period of seven years ending with the day of the occasion of the charge made chargeable transfers having an aggregate value equal to that of any chargeable transfers made by the settlor in the period of seven years ending with the day on which the settlement commenced, disregarding transfers made on that day, and

(c) on which tax is charged in accordance with section 7(2) above.

71F(9) The amount referred to in subsection (8)(a) above is equal to the aggregate of–

(a) the value, immediately after the settlement commenced, of the property then comprised in it,

(b) the value, immediately after a related settlement commenced, of the property then comprised in it which was property to which section 71D above applied, and

(c) the value, immediately after it became comprised in the settlement, of any property which became so comprised after the settlement commenced and before the occasion of the charge under section 71E above (whether or not it has remained so comprised).

History – In s. 71F(9)(b) the words "which was property to which section 71D above applied" inserted by F(No. 2)A 2015, s. 11 and Sch. 1, para. 6, with effect in relation to occasions on which tax falls to be charged under IHTA 1984, Pt. 3, Ch. 3 on or after 18 November 2015 (Royal Assent).
S. 71F inserted by FA 2006, s. 156 and Sch. 20, para. 1(1), with effect from 22 March 2006.

71G Calculation of tax charged under section 71E in all other cases

71G(1) Where–

(a) tax is charged under section 71E above, and

(b) the tax does not fall to be calculated in accordance with section 71F above,

the tax is calculated in accordance with this section.

71G(2) The amount on which the tax is charged is–

(a) the amount by which the value of property which is comprised in the settlement and to which section 71D above applies is less immediately after the event giving rise to the charge than it would be but for the event, or

(b) where the tax is payable out of settled property to which section 71D above applies immediately after the event, the amount which, after deducting the tax, is equal to the amount on which tax would be charged by virtue of paragraph (a) above.

71G(3) The rate at which the tax is charged is the rate that would be given by subsections (6) to (8) of section 70 above–

(a) if the reference to section 70 above in subsection (8)(a) of that section were a reference to section 71D above,

(b) if the other references in those subsections to section 70 above were references to section 71E above, and

(c) if, for the purposes of section 70(8) above, property–

(i) which is property to which section 71D above applies,

(ii) which, immediately before it became property to which section 71D above applies, was property to which section 71 applied, and

(iii) which ceased on that occasion to be property to which section 71 above applied without ceasing to be settled property,

had become property to which section 71D above applies not on that occasion but on the occasion (or last occasion) before then when it became property to which section 71 above applied.

History – S. 71G inserted by FA 2006, s. 156 and Sch. 20, para. 1(1), with effect from 22 March 2006.

71H Sections 71A to 71G: meaning of "parent"

71H(1) In sections 71A to 71G above "parent" includes step-parent.

71H(2) For the purposes of sections 71A to 71G above, a deceased individual ("D") shall be taken to have been a parent of another individual ("Y") if, immediately before D died, D had–

(a) parental responsibility for Y under the law of England and Wales,

(b) parental responsibilities in relation to Y under the law of Scotland, or

(c) parental responsibility for Y under the law of Northern Ireland.

71H(3) In subsection (2)(a) above **"parental responsibility"** has the same meaning as in the Children Act 1989.

71H(4) In subsection (2)(b) above **"parental responsibilities"** has the meaning given by section 1(3) of the Children (Scotland) Act 1995.

71H(5) In subsection (2)(c) above **"parental responsibility"** has the same meaning as in the Children (Northern Ireland) Order 1995.

History – S. 71H inserted by FA 2006, s. 156 and Sch. 20, para. 1(1), with effect from 22 March 2006.

72 Property leaving employee trusts and newspaper trusts

72(1) This section applies to settled property to which section 86 below applies if–

(a) no interest in possession subsists in it to which an individual is beneficially entitled, and

(b) no company-purchased interest in possession subsists in it.

72(1A) For the purposes of subsection (1)(b) above, an interest in possession is **"company-purchased"** if–

(a) a company is beneficially entitled to the interest in possession,

(b) the business of the company consists wholly or mainly in the acquisition of interests in settled property, and

(c) the company has acquired the interest in possession for full consideration in money or money's worth from an individual who was beneficially entitled to it.

72(1B) Section 59(3) and (4) above apply for the purposes of subsection (1A)(c) above as for those of section 59(2)(b) above, but as if the references to the condition set out in section 59(2)(a) above were to the condition set out in subsection (1A)(b) above.

72(2) Subject to subsections (3A), (4), (4A) and (5) below, there shall be a charge to tax under this section–

(a) where settled property ceases to be property to which this section applies, otherwise than by virtue of a payment out of the settled property, and

(b) where a payment is made out of settled property to which this section applies for the benefit of a person within subsection (3) below, or a person connected with such a person, and

(c) in a case in which paragraphs (a) and (b) above do not apply, where the trustees make a disposition (otherwise than by way of a payment out of the settled property) as a result of which the value of settled property to which this section applies is less than it would be but for the disposition.

72(3) A person is within this subsection if–

(a) he has directly or indirectly provided any of the settled property otherwise than by additions not exceeding in value £1,000 in any one year; or

(b) in a case where the employment in question is employment by a close company, he is a participator in relation to that company and either–

  (i) is beneficially entitled to, or to rights entitling him to acquire, not less than 5 per cent of, or of any class of the shares comprised in, its issued share capital, or

  (ii) would, on a winding-up of the company, be entitled to not less than 5 per cent of its assets; or

(c) he has acquired an interest in the settled property for a consideration in money or money's worth.

72(3A) Where settled property ceases to be property to which this section applies because paragraph (d) of section 86(3) no longer applies, tax is not chargeable under this section by virtue of subsection (2)(a) if the only reason that paragraph no longer applies is that one or both of the trading requirement and the controlling interest requirement mentioned in that paragraph are no longer met with respect to the company so mentioned.

72(4) If the trusts are those of a profit sharing scheme approved in accordance with Schedule 9 to the Taxes Act 1988, tax shall not be chargeable under this section by virtue of subsection (3)(b) above on an appropriation of shares in pursuance of the scheme.

72(4A) If the trusts are those of a share incentive plan approved under Schedule 2 to the Income Tax (Earnings and Pensions) Act 2003, tax shall not be chargeable under this section by virtue of subsection (3)(b) above on an appropriation of shares to, or acquisition of shares on behalf of, an individual under the plan.

72(5) Subsections (3) to (10) of section 70 above shall apply for the purposes of this section as they apply for the purposes of that section (with the substitution of a reference to subsection (2)(c) above for the reference in section 70(4) to section 70(2)(b)).

72(6) In this section–

(a) **"close company"** and **"participator"** have the same meanings as in Part IV of this Act; and

(b) **"year"** means the period beginning with 26th March 1974 and ending with 5th April 1974, and any subsequent period of twelve months ending with 5th April;

and a person shall be treated for the purposes of this section as acquiring an interest for a consideration in money or money's worth if he becomes entitled to it as a result of transactions which include a disposition for such consideration (whether to him or another) of that interest or of other property.

History – In s. 72(1) the word "if–" and para. (a) and (b) substituted for the words "if no qualifying interest in possession subsists in it" by FA 2006, s. 156 and Sch. 20, para. 21(2), with effect from 22 March 2006.
S. 72(1A) inserted by FA 2006, s. 156 and Sch. 20, para. 21(3), with effect from 22 March 2006.
S. 72(1B) inserted by FA 2006, s. 156 and Sch. 20, para. 21(3), with effect from 22 March 2006.
In s. 72(2), "(3A)," inserted by FA 2014, s. 290 and Sch. 37, para. 13(2). This amendment is treated as having come into force on 6 April 2014.
In s. 72(2), reference to (4A) inserted by FA 2000, s. 138(3)(a).
S. 72(3A) inserted by FA 2014, s. 290 and Sch. 37, para. 13(3). This amendment is treated as having come into force on 6 April 2014.
In s. 72(4A), the words "a share incentive plan approved under Schedule 2 to the Income Tax (Earnings and Pensions) Act 2003" substituted for the words "an employee share ownership plan approved under Schedule 8 to the Finance Act 2000" by ITEPA 2003, Sch. 6, para. 151(1)(b) and para. 151(2) which have effect for the tax year 2003–04 and subsequent tax years.
S. 72(4A) inserted by FA 2000, s. 138(3)(b)).
See ICTA 1988, Sch. 29, para. 32 for substitution of reference to that Act in s. 72(4).
Cross references – S. 86: trusts for employees' benefit.
ICTA 1988, Sch. 9: approved share option and profit sharing schemes.
Other material – HMRC Brief 18/11: HMRC view on IHT position in relation to property leaving Employee Benefit Trusts.

73 Pre-1978 protective trusts

73(1) This section applies to settled property which is held on trusts to the like effect as those specified in section 33(1)(ii) of the Trustee Act 1925 and which became held on those trusts on the failure or determination before 12th April 1978 of trusts to the like effect as those specified in section 33(1)(i).

73(2) Subject to subsection (3) below, there shall be a charge to tax under this section–

(a) where settled property ceases to be property to which this section applies, otherwise than by virtue of a payment out of the settled property for the benefit of the principal beneficiary within the meaning of section 33 of the Trustee Act 1925, and

(b) in a case in which paragraph (a) above does not apply, where the trustees make a disposition (otherwise than by way of such a payment) as a result of which the value of settled property to which this section applies is less than it would be but for the disposition.

73(3) Subsections (3) to (10) of section 70 above shall apply for the purposes of this section as they apply for the purposes of that section.

Cross references – S. 88: post-1978 protective trusts.
Trustee Act 1925, s. 33(1)(i) (not reproduced): protective trust in favour of beneficiary for trust period or until he forfeits his interest.
Trustee Act 1925, s. 33(1)(ii) (not reproduced): trusts following failure or determination of protective trusts under para. (i).
Statements of practice – E7: interpretation of "to the like effect" in s. 73(1).

74 Pre-1981 trusts for disabled persons

74(1) This section applies to settled property transferred into settlement before 10th March 1981 and held on trusts under which, during the life of a disabled person, no interest in possession in the settled property subsists, and which secure that any of the settled property which is applied during his life is applied only or mainly for his benefit.

74(2) Subject to subsection (3) below, there shall be a charge to tax under this section–

(a) where settled property ceases to be property to which this section applies, otherwise than by virtue of a payment out of the settled property for the benefit of the person mentioned in subsection (1) above, and

(b) in a case in which paragraph (a) above does not apply, where the trustees makes a disposition (otherwise than by way of such a payment) as a result of which the value of settled property to which this section applies is less than it would be but for the disposition.

74(3) Subsections (3) to (10) of section 70 above shall apply for the purposes of this section as they apply for the purposes of that section.

74(4) In this section **"disabled person"** means a person who–

(a) is by reason of mental disorder (within the meaning of the Mental Health Act 1983) incapable of administering his property or managing his affairs, or

(b) is in receipt of an attendance allowance under section 64 of the Social Security Contributions and Benefits Act 1992 or section 64 of the Social Security Contributions and Benefits (Northern Ireland) Act 1992, or

(c) is in receipt of a disability living allowance under section 71 of the Social Security Contributions and Benefits Act 1992 by virtue of entitlement to the care component at the highest or middle rate.

History – References to SSCBA 1992 and its Northern Ireland equivalent substituted by SS(CP)A 1992, s. 4 and Sch. 2, para. 66, and Social Security (Consequential Provisions) (Northern Ireland) Act 1992, s. 4 and Sch. 2, para. 29, respectively.
S. 74(4)(c) inserted by Disability Living Allowance and Disability Working Allowance Act 1991, Sch. 2, para. 14(1), with effect from 6 April 1992 by virtue of SI 1991/2617.

Cross references – S. 89: post-1981 trusts for disabled persons.

74A Arrangements involving acquisition of interest in settled property etc

74A(1) This section applies where–

(a) one or more persons enter into arrangements,

(b) in the course of the arrangements–

(i) an individual ("the individual") domiciled in the United Kingdom acquires or becomes able to acquire (directly or indirectly) an interest in property comprised in a settlement ("the relevant settled property"), and

(ii) consideration in money or money's worth is given by one or more of the persons mentioned in paragraph (a) (whether or not in connection with the acquisition of that interest or the individual becoming able to acquire it),

(c) there is a relevant reduction in the value of the individual's estate, and

(d) condition A or condition B is met.

74A(2) Condition A is that–

(a) the settlor was not domiciled in the United Kingdom at the time the settlement was made, and

(b) the relevant settled property is situated outside the United Kingdom at any time during the course of the arrangements.

74A(3) Condition B is that–

(a) the settlor was not an individual or a close company at the time the settlement was made, and

(b) condition A is not met.

74A(4) Subsection (6) applies if all or a part of a relevant reduction ("amount A") is attributable to the value of the individual's section 49(1) property being less than it would have been in the absence of the arrangements.

74A(5) **"The individual's section 49(1) property"** means settled property to which the individual is treated as beneficially entitled under section 49(1) by reason of the individual being beneficially entitled to an interest in possession in the property.

74A(6) Where this subsection applies–

(a) a part of that interest in possession is deemed, for the purposes of section 52, to come to an end at the relevant time, and

(b) that section applies in relation to the coming to an end of that part as if the reference in subsection (4)(a) of that section to a corresponding part of the whole value of the property in which the interest in possession subsists were a reference to amount A.

74A(7) Subsection (8) applies to so much (if any) of a relevant reduction as is not amount A ("amount B").

74A(8) Tax is to be charged as if the individual had made a transfer of value at the relevant time and the value transferred by it had been equal to amount B.

History – S. 74A inserted by FA 2012, s. 210(3), with effect in relation to arrangements entered into on or after 20 June 2012.

74B Section 74A: supplementary provision

74B(1) A transfer of value arising by virtue of section 74A is to be taken to be a transfer which is not a potentially exempt transfer.

74B(2) For the purposes of section 74A–

(a) when determining the value transferred by a transfer of value arising by virtue of that section, no account is to be taken of section 3(2),

(b) nothing in section 10(1) applies to prevent such a transfer, and

(c) nothing in sections 102 to 102C of the Finance Act 1986 applies in relation to such a transfer.

74B(3) Where, ignoring this subsection, a transfer of value would arise by virtue of section 74A ("the current transfer"), the value transferred by a relevant related transfer is to be treated as reducing the value transferred by the current transfer.

But this subsection does not apply if and to the extent that the relevant related transfer has already been applied to reduce another transfer of value arising by virtue of that section.

74B(4) **"Relevant related transfer"** means–

(a) where the arrangements consist of a series of operations, any transfer of value constituted by one or more of those operations which occur before or at the same time as the current transfer, other than a transfer of value arising by virtue of section 74A, and

(b) where the arrangements consist of a single operation, any transfer of value which arises from that operation, other than a transfer of value arising by virtue of section 74A.

74B(5) Section 268(3) does not apply to a transfer of value arising by virtue of section 74A.

74B(6) Where–

(a) a transfer of value has arisen by virtue of section 74A,

(b) in the course of the arrangements the individual acquires an interest in possession in settled property, and

(c) section 5(1B) applies to the interest in possession so that it forms part of the individual's estate,

this Act has effect as if that transfer of value had never arisen.

History – S. 74B inserted by FA 2012, s. 210(3), with effect in relation to arrangements entered into on or after 20 June 2012.

74C Interpretation of sections 74A and 74B

74C(1) Subsections (2) to (4) have effect for the purposes of sections 74A and 74B.

74C(2) An individual has an interest in property comprised in a settlement if–

(a) the property, or any derived property, is or will or may become payable to, or applicable for the benefit of–

(i) the individual,

(ii) the individual's spouse or civil partner, or

(iii) a close company in relation to which the individual or the individual's spouse or civil partner is a participator or a company which is a 51% subsidiary of such a close company,

in any circumstances whatsoever, or

(b) a person within sub-paragraph (i), (ii) or (iii) of paragraph (a) enjoys a benefit deriving (directly or indirectly) from the property or any derived property.

74C(3) A **"relevant reduction"** in the value of the individual's estate occurs–

(a) if and when the value of the individual's estate first becomes less than it would have been in the absence of the arrangements, and

(b) on each subsequent occasion when the value of that estate becomes less than it would have been in the absence of the arrangements and that difference in value is greater than the sum of any previous relevant reductions.

74C(4) The amount of a relevant reduction is–

(a) in the case of a reduction within subsection (3)(a), the difference between the value of the estate and its value in the absence of the arrangements, and

(b) in the case of a reduction within subsection (3)(b), the amount by which the difference in value mentioned in that provision exceeds the sum of any previous relevant reductions.

74C(5) In sections 74A and 74B and this section–

"arrangements" includes any scheme, transaction or series of transactions, agreement or understanding, whether or not legally enforceable, and any associated operations;

"close company" has the meaning given in section 102;

"derived property", in relation to any property, means–

(a) income from that property,

(b) property directly or indirectly representing–

(i) proceeds of that property, or

(ii) proceeds of income from that property, or

(c) income from property which is derived property by virtue of paragraph (b);

"operation" includes an omission;

"participator" has the meaning given in section 102;

"the relevant time" means–

(a) the time the relevant reduction occurs, or

(b) if later, the time section 74A first applied;

"51% subsidiary" has the same meaning as in the Corporation Tax Acts (see Chapter 3 of Part 24 of the Corporation Tax Act 2010).

History – S. 74C inserted by FA 2012, s. 210(3), with effect in relation to arrangements entered into on or after 20 June 2012.

SPECIAL CASES – RELIEFS

75 Property becoming subject to employee trusts

75(1) Tax shall not be charged under section 65 above in respect of shares in or securities of a company which cease to be relevant property on becoming held on trusts of the description specified in section 86(1) below if the conditions in subsection (2) below are satisfied.

75(2) The conditions referred to in subsection (1) above are–

(a) that the persons for whose benefit the trusts permit the settled property to be applied include all or most of the persons employed by or holding office with the company;

(b) that, at the date when the shares or securities cease to be relevant property or at a subsequent date not more than one year thereafter, both the conditions mentioned in subsection (2) of section 28 above (read with subsections (3) and (7)) are satisfied, without taking account of shares or securities held on other trusts; and

(c) that the trusts do not permit any of the property to be applied at any time (whether during any such period as is referred to in section 86(1) below or later) for the benefit of any of the persons mentioned in subsection (4) of section 28 above (read with subsections (5) to (7)) or for the benefit of the settlor or of any person connected with him.

75(3) In its application for the purposes of subsection (2)(c) above, section 28(4) shall be construed as if–

(a) references to section 28(1) were references to subsection (2) above, and

(b) references to the time of the transfer of value were references to the time when the property ceases to be relevant property.

Cross references – S. 28: conditions for transfer of shares/securities comprised in employee trusts, to be exempt.
S. 86(1): conditions for special treatment of certain employee benefit trusts.

75A Property becoming subject to employee-ownership trust

75A(1) Tax is not charged under section 65 in respect of shares in or securities of a company ("C") which cease to be relevant property on becoming held on trusts of the description specified in section 86(1) if the conditions in subsection (2) are satisfied.

75A(2) The conditions referred to in subsection (1) are–

(a) that C meets the trading requirement,

(b) that the trusts are of a settlement which meets the all-employee benefit requirement, and

(c) that the settlement does not meet the controlling interest requirement immediately before the beginning of the tax year in which the shares or securities cease to be relevant property but does meet it at the end of that year.

75A(3) Sections 236I, 236J, 236K, 236M and 236T (but not 236L) of the 1992 Act apply to determine whether–

(a) C meets the trading requirement;

(b) the settlement meets the all-employee benefit requirement;

(c) the settlement meets the controlling interest requirement;

with references in those sections to "C" being read accordingly.

75A(4) In this section **"tax year"** means a year beginning on 6 April and ending on the following 5 April.

History – S. 75A inserted by FA 2014, s. 290 and Sch. 37, para. 14(1), and treated as having come into force on 6 April 2014.

76 Property becoming held for charitable purposes, etc.

76(1) Tax shall not be charged under this Chapter (apart from section 79 below) in respect of property which ceases to be relevant property, or ceases to be property to which section 70, 71, 71A, 71D, 72, 73 or 74 above or paragraph 8 of Schedule 4 to this Act applies, on becoming–

(a) property held for charitable purposes only without limit of time (defined by a date or otherwise);

(b) the property of a political party qualifying for exemption under section 24 above; or

(c) the property of a body within Schedule 3 to this Act;

(d) [repealed by FA 1998, s. 143(4)(a) and 165 and Sch. 27, Pt. IV.]

76(2) [Repealed by FA 1998, s. 143(4)(a) and s. 165 and Sch. 27, Pt. IV.]

76(3) If the amount on which tax would be charged apart from this section in respect of any property exceeds the value of the property immediately after it becomes property of a description specified in paragraphs (a) to (c) of subsection (1) above (less the amount of any consideration for its transfer received by the trustees), that subsection shall not apply but the amount on which tax is charged shall be equal to the excess.

76(4) The reference in subsection (3) above to the amount on which tax would be charged is a reference to the amount on which it would be charged–

(a) assuming (if it is not in fact so) that the tax is not paid out of settled property, and

(b) apart from Chapters I and II of Part V of this Act;

and the reference in that subsection to the amount on which tax is charged is a reference to the amount on which it would be charged on that assumption and apart from those Chapters.

76(5) Subsection (1) above shall not apply in relation to any property if the disposition by which it becomes property of the relevant description is defeasible; but for this purpose a disposition which has not been defeated at a time twelve months after the property concerned becomes property of the relevant description and is not defeasible after that time shall be treated as not being defeasible, whether or not it was capable of being defeated before that time.

76(6) Subsection (1) above shall not apply in relation to any property if it or any part of it may become applicable for purposes other than charitable purposes or purposes of a body mentioned in subsection (1)(b) or (c) above.

76(7) Subsection (1) shall not apply in relation to any property if, at or before the time when it becomes property of the relevant description, an interest under the settlement is or has been acquired for a consideration in money or money's worth by an exempt body otherwise than from a charity or a body mentioned in subsection (1)(b) or (c) above.

76(8) In subsection (7) above **"exempt body"** means a charity or a body mentioned in subsection (1)(b) or (c) above; and for the purposes of subsection (7) above a body shall be treated as acquiring an interest for a consideration in money or money's worth if it becomes entitled to the interest as a result of transactions which include a disposition for such consideration (whether to that body or to another person) of that interest or of other property.

History – In s. 76(1) the words "71A, 71D," inserted by FA 2006, s. 156 and Sch. 20, para. 22, with effect from 22 March 2006.
In s. 76(1)(c) the word "or" at the end and s. 76(1)(d) and (2), repealed by FA 1998, s. 143(4)(a) and s. 165 and Sch. 27, Pt. IV, with effect with respect to property which ceases to be relevant property, or to be property to which any of sections 70 to 74 or Sch. 4, para. 8 apply, on or after 17 March 1998.
In s. 76(3), words "to (c)" substituted for former words "to (d)", and in s. 76(6), (8) words "or (c)" substituted for former words "(c) or (d)", by FA 1998, s. 143(4)(b), (c), consequential on repeal of s. 76(1)(d) (see note above).

Cross references – S. 24: gifts to political parties.
Sch. 3: national bodies in connection with gifts for national purposes.
Sch. 4, para. 8: charge on property leaving maintenance funds.
FA 1985, s. 95(1): Treasury functions under s. 76 transferred to the Commissioners of Inland Revenue ("the Board") from 25 July 1985.

WORKS OF ART, HISTORIC BUILDINGS, ETC.

77 Maintenance funds for historic buildings, etc.

77 Schedule 4 to this Act shall have effect.

78 Conditionally exempt occasions

78(1) A transfer of property or other event shall not constitute an occasion on which tax is chargeable *under any provision of this Chapter* other than section 64 if the property in respect of which the charge would have been made has been comprised in the settlement throughout the six years ending with the transfer or event, and–

(a) the property is, on a claim made for the purpose, designated by the Treasury under section 31, above, and

(b) the requisite undertaking described in that section is given with respect to the property by such person as the Treasury think appropriate in the circumstances of the case or (where the property is an area of land within subsection (1)(d) of that section) the requisite undertakings described in that section are given with respect to the property by such person or persons as the Treasury think appropriate in the circumstances of the case.

78(1A) A claim under subsection (1) above must be made no more than two years after the date of the transfer or other event in question or within such longer period as the Board may allow.

78(2) References in this Chapter to a **conditionally exempt occasion** are to–

(a) a transfer or event which by virtue of subsection (1) above does not constitute an occasion on which tax is chargeable under this Chapter;

(b) a transfer or event which, by virtue of section 81(1) of the Finance Act 1976, did not constitute an occasion on which tax was chargeable under Chapter II of Part IV of the Finance Act 1982;

(c) a conditionally exempt distribution within the meaning given by section 81(2) of the Finance Act 1976 as it had effect in relation to events before 9th March 1982.

78(3) Where there has been a conditionally exempt occasion in respect of any property, sections 32, 32A, 33(1), 33(2ZA) to (7) and 35(2) above shall have effect (and tax shall accordingly be chargeable under section 32 or 32A) as if–

(a) references to a **conditionally exempt transfer** and to such a transfer of property included references respectively to a conditionally exempt occasion and to such an occasion in respect of property;

(b) references to a **disposal otherwise than by sale** included references to any occasion on which tax is chargeable under any provision of this Chapter other than section 64;

(c) references to an **undertaking** given under section 30 above included references to an undertaking given under this section;

and the references in section 33(5) above to the **person who made a conditionally exempt transfer** shall have effect in relation to a conditionally exempt occasion as references to the person who is the settlor of the settlement in respect of which the occasion occurred (or if there is more than one such person, whichever of them the Board may select).

78(4) Where by virtue of subsection (3) above the relevant person for the purposes of section 33 above is the settlor of a settlement, the rate (or each of the rates) mentioned in section 33(1)(b)(i) or (ii)–

(a) shall, if the occasion occurred before the first ten-year anniversary to fall after the property became comprised in the settlement concerned, be 30 per cent of what it would be apart from this subsection, and

(b) shall, if the occasion occurred after the first and before the second ten-year anniversary to fall after the property became so comprised, be 60 per cent of what it would be apart from this subsection;

and the appropriate provision of section 7 for the purposes of section 33(1)(b)(ii) is, if the settlement was created on his death, subsection (1) and, if not, subsection (2).

78(5) Where by virtue of subsection (3) above the relevant person for the purposes of section 33 above is the settlor of a settlement and that settlor died before 13th March 1975, section 33(1)(b) above shall have effect (subject to subsection (4) above) with the substitution for sub-paragraph (ii) of the following subparagraph–

"(ii) the rate or rates that would have applied to that amount (**"the chargeable amount"**) in accordance with the appropriate provision of section 7 above if the relevant person had died when the chargeable event occurred, the value transferred on his death had been equal to the amount on which estate duty was chargeable when he in fact died, and the chargeable amount had been added to that value and had formed the highest part of it."

78(6) Section 34 above shall not apply to a chargeable event in respect of property if the last conditionally exempt transfer of the property has been followed by a conditionally exempt occasion in respect of it.

History – In s. 78(1)(b), the words "or (where … of the case" were added by FA 1985, Sch. 26, para. 8(a), in relation to events on or after 19 March 1985.

S. 78(1A) inserted by FA 1998, s. 142 and Sch. 25, para. 3(1), with effect in relation to transfers of property made, and other events occurring, on or after 17 March 1998.

In s. 78(3), the words "33(2ZA)" substituted for "33(3)" by FA 2012, s. 209 and Sch. 33, para. 5, with effect in cases where D's death occurs on or after 6 April 2012.

In s. 78(3), the references to s. 32A were inserted by FA 1985, Sch. 26, para. 8(b), in relation to events on or after 19 March 1985.

In s. 78(4), the words "and the appropriate provision" to the end were substituted by FA 1986, Sch. 19, para. 19(1), with respect to transfers of value made, and other events occurring, on or after 18 March 1986.

In s. 78(5), the words "in accordance with the appropriate provision of section 7 above" were substituted by FA 1986, Sch. 19, para. 19(2), with respect to transfers of value made, and other events occurring, on or after 18 March 1986.

Cross references – S. 30: conditionally exempt transfers – general.

S. 31: designation and undertakings in respect of conditionally exempt transfers.

S. 32, 32A, 33(1), (3)–(7), 35(2): charge on certain events with respect to property (or associated property) following conditionally exempt transfer of it.

S. 34: reinstatement of transferor's cumulative total where tax chargeable under s. 32 or 32A.
TCGA 1992, s. 260(1), (2)(e): capital gains tax in respect of occasions where inheritance tax is not chargeable by virtue of s. 78(1).
FA 1986, Sch. 19, para. 40(1): transitional – transfer of value occurring before, and death or other event occurring after, 18 March 1986.
FA 1998, Sch. 25, para. 10(5)(a): variation of undertakings given under s. 78 with respect to any property before 31 July 1998.

79 Exemption from ten-yearly charge

79(1) Where property is comprised in a settlement and there has been a conditionally exempt transfer of the property on or before the occasion on which it became comprised in the settlement, section 64 above shall not have effect in relation to the property on any ten-year anniversary falling before the first occurrence after the transfer of a chargeable event with respect to the property.

79(2) Where property is comprised in a settlement and there has been, on or before the occasion on which it became comprised in the settlement, a disposal of the property in relation to which subsection (4) of section 258 of the 1992 Act (capital gains tax relief for works of art etc.) had effect, section 64 above shall not have effect in relation to the property on any ten-year anniversary falling before the first occurrence after the disposal of an event on the happening of which the property is treated as sold under subsection (5) of the said section 258.

79(3) Where property is comprised in a settlement and there has been no such transfer or disposal of the property as is mentioned in subsection (1) or (2) above on or before the occasion on which it became comprised in the settlement, subsection (3A) below applies if–

(a) the property is, on a claim made for the purpose, designated by the Treasury under section 31 above,

(aa) that claim is made during the period beginning with the date of a ten-year anniversary of the settlement (**"the relevant ten-year anniversary"**) and ending–

(i) two years after that date, or

(ii) on such later date as the Board may allow,

(b) the requisite undertaking described in section 31 is given with respect to the property by such person as the Treasury think appropriate in the circumstances of the case or (where the property is an area of land within subsection (1)(d) of that section) the requisite undertakings described in that section are given with respect to the property by such person or persons as the Treasury think appropriate in the circumstances of the case, and

(c) the property is relevant property.

79(3A) Tax is not chargeable under section 64 above in relation to the property by reference to the relevant ten-year anniversary concerned or any subsequent ten-year anniversaries; but on the first occurrence of an event which, if there had been a conditionally exempt transfer of the property immediately before that relevant ten-year anniversary, would be a chargeable event with respect to the property–

(a) there is a charge to tax under this subsection, and

(b) on any ten-year anniversary falling after that event, tax is chargeable under section 64 above in relation to the property.

79(4) Tax shall not be charged under subsection (3A) above in respect of property if, after the occasion mentioned in subsection (3) above and before the occurrence mentioned in subsection (3A), there has been a conditionally exempt occasion in respect of the property.

79(5) The amount on which tax is charged under subsection (3A) above shall be an amount equal to the value of the property at the time of the event.

79(5A) Where the event giving rise to a charge to tax under subsection (3A) above is a disposal on sale, and the sale–

(a) was not intended to confer any gratuitous benefit on any person, and

(b) was either a transaction at arm's length between persons not connected with each other or a transaction such as might be expected to be made at arm's length between persons not connected with each other,

the value of the property at the time of that event shall be taken for the purposes of subsection (5) above to be equal to the proceeds of the sale.

79(6) The rate at which tax is charged under subsection (3A) above shall be the aggregate of the following percentages–

(a) 0.25 per cent for each of the first forty complete successive quarters in the relevant period,

(b) *0.20 per cent for each of the next forty,*

(c) 0.15 per cent for each of the next forty,

(d) 0.10 per cent for each of the next forty, and

(e) 0.05 per cent for each of the next forty.

79(7) In subsection (6) above **"the relevant period"** means the period given by subsection (7A) below or, if shorter, the period given by subsection (7B) below.

79(7A) The period given by this subsection is the period beginning with the latest of–

(a) the day on which the settlement commenced,

(b) the date of the last ten-year anniversary of the settlement to fall before the day on which the property became comprised in the settlement,

(c) the date of the last ten-year anniversary of the settlement to fall before the relevant ten-year anniversary, and

(d) 13th March 1975,

and ending with the day before the event giving rise to the charge.

79(7B) The period given by this subsection is the period equal in length to the number of relevant-property days in the period–

(a) beginning with the day that is the latest of those referred to in paragraphs (a) to (d) of subsection (7A) above, and

(b) ending with the day before the event giving rise to the charge.

79(7C) For the purposes of subsection (7B) above, a day is a **"relevant-property day"** if at any time on that day the property was relevant property.

79(8) Subsection (9) below shall have effect where–

(a) by virtue of subsection (3A) above, section 64 does not have effect in relation to property by reference to the relevant ten-year anniversary of the settlement,

(b) on that anniversary a charge to tax falls to be made in respect of the settlement under section 64, and

(c) the property became comprised in the settlement within the period of ten years ending with that anniversary.

79(9) In calculating the rate at which tax is charged under section 64 above, the value of the consideration given for the property on its becoming comprised in the settlement shall be treated for the purposes of section 66(5)(b) above as if it were an amount on which a charge to tax was imposed in respect of the settlement under section 65 above at the time of the property becoming so comprised.

79(9A) Subsection (9B) below applies where the same event gives rise–

(a) to a charge under subsection (3A) above in relation to any property, and

(b) to a charge under section 32 or 32A above in relation to that property.

79(9B) If the amount of each of the charges is the same, each charge shall have effect as a charge for one half of the amount that would be charged apart from this subsection; otherwise, whichever of the charges is lower in amount shall have effect as if it were a charge the amount of which is nil.

79(10) In subsection (1) above, the reference to a conditionally exempt transfer of any property includes a reference to a transfer of value in relation to which the value of any property has been left out of account under the provisions of sections 31 to 34 of the Finance Act 1975 and, in relation to such property, the reference to a chargeable event includes a reference to an event on the occurrence of which tax becomes chargeable under Schedule 5 to this Act.

History – In s. 79(3) the words "subsection (3A) below applies if" substituted for the words "then, if", in s. 79(3)(a) the words "is, on a claim made for the purpose," substituted for the words "has, on a claim made for the purpose, been", s. 79(3)(aa) inserted and in s. 79(3)(b) the words "section 31 is given" substituted for the words "that section has been given" and the words "are given" substituted for the words "have been given" and the words "section 64 above shall not have effect in relation to the property; but there shall be a charge to tax under this subsection on the first occurrence of an event which, if there had been a conditionally exempt transfer of the property when the claim was made and the undertaking had been given under section 30 above, would be a chargeable event with respect to the property." (which appeared at the end) omitted by F(No. 2)A 2015, s. 12(2), with effect in relation to occasions on which tax would (ignoring the effect of the amendments) fall to be charged under IHTA 1984, s. 64 on or after 18 November 2015 (Royal Assent).

In s. 79(3)(b), the words "with respect to the property" where first mentioned and "or (where … of the case" were inserted by FA 1985, s. 94(1) and Sch. 26, para. 9, in relation to events on or after 19 March 1985.

S. 79(3A) inserted by F(No. 2)A 2015, s. 12(3), with effect in relation to occasions on which tax would (ignoring the effect of the amendments) fall to be charged under IHTA 1984, s. 64 on or after 18 November 2015 (Royal Assent).

In s. 79(4) the words "subsection (3A) above in respect of property if, after the occasion mentioned in subsection (3) above and before the occurrence mentioned in subsection (3A)" substituted for the words "subsection (3) above in respect of property if, after the occasion and before the occurrence there mentioned" by F(No. 2)A 2015, s. 12(4), with effect in relation to occasions on which tax would (ignoring the effect of the amendments) fall to be charged under IHTA 1984, s. 64 on or after 18 November 2015 (Royal Assent).

In s. 79(5) the words "subsection (3A)" substituted for the words "subsection (3)" by F(No. 2)A 2015, s. 12(5), with effect in relation to occasions on which tax would (ignoring the effect of the amendments) fall to be charged under IHTA 1984, s. 64 on or after 18 November 2015 (Royal Assent).

In s. 79(5A) the words "subsection (3A)" substituted for the words "subsection (3)" by F(No. 2)A 2015, s. 12(5), with effect in relation to occasions on which tax would (ignoring the effect of the amendments) fall to be charged under IHTA 1984,s. 64 on or after 18 November 2015 (Royal Assent).

S. 79(5A) inserted by FA 2006, s. 156 and Sch. 20, para. 34(2), with effect from 19 July 2006 (Royal Assent).

In s. 79(6) the words "subsection (3A)" substituted for the words "subsection (3)" by F(No. 2)A 2015, s. 12(5), with effect in relation to occasions on which tax would (ignoring the effect of the amendments) fall to be charged under IHTA 1984, s. 64 on or after 18 November 2015 (Royal Assent).
In s. 79(7A) the words "relevant ten-year anniversary" substituted for the words "day on which the property was designated under section 31 above on a claim under this section" by F(No. 2)A 2015, s., 12(6), with effect in relation to occasions on which tax would (ignoring the effect of the amendments) fall to be charged under IHTA 1984, s. 64 on or after 18 November 2015 (Royal Assent).
S. 79(7)–(7C) substituted for former s. 79(7) by FA 2006, s. 156 and Sch. 20, para. 34(3), with effect from 19 July 2006 (Royal Assent).
In s. 79(8)(a) the words "by reference to the relevant ten-year anniversary of the settlement" substituted for the words "on the first ten-year anniversary of the settlement to fall after the making of the claim and the giving of the undertaking" and in s. 79(8)(c) the words ", and the claim was made and the undertaking was given," omitted by F(No. 2)A 2015, s. 12(7), with effect in relation to occasions on which tax would (ignoring the effect of the amendments) fall to be charged under IHTA 1984, s. 64 on or after 18 November 2015 (Royal Assent).
In s. 79(8)(a) the words "subsection (3A)" substituted for the words "subsection (3)" by F(No. 2)A 2015, s. 12(5), with effect in relation to occasions on which tax would (ignoring the effect of the amendments) fall to be charged under IHTA 1984, s. 64 on or after 18 November 2015 (Royal Assent).
In s. 79(9A)(a) the words "subsection (3A)" substituted for the words "subsection (3)" by F(No. 2)A 2015, s. 12(5), with effect in relation to occasions on which tax would (ignoring the effect of the amendments) fall to be charged under IHTA 1984, s. 64 on or after 18 November 2015 (Royal Assent).
S. 79(9A) inserted by FA 2006, s. 156 and Sch. 20, para. 34(4), with effect from 19 July 2006 (Royal Assent).
S. 79(9B) inserted by FA 2006, s. 156 and Sch. 20, para. 34(4), with effect from 19 July 2006 (Royal Assent).
References to "258 of the 1992 Act" substituted by TCGA 1992, s. 290 and Sch. 10, para. 8(3).

Cross references – S. 30: conditionally exempt transfers – general.
S. 31: designation and undertakings in respect of conditionally exempt transfers.
S. 207(3): liability for tax charged under s. 79(3).
S. 216(7): time within which a person liable under s. 79 must deliver an account.
S. 226(4): due date for payment of tax on a chargeable event under s. 79.
S. 233(1)(c): interest on unpaid tax chargeable under s. 79(3).
Sch. 5: conditional exemption in relation to deaths before 7 April 1976.
Sch. 6, para. 4(3): interaction with estate duty.
TCGA 1992, s. 258(2): exemption from tax on chargeable gains for disposal of asset with respect to which certain inheritance tax undertakings etc. given to a museum or similar body or to the Board in lieu of tax.
FA 1998, Sch. 25, para. 10(5): variation of undertakings given under s. 79 with respect to any property before 31 July 1998.

79A Variation of undertakings

79A(1) An undertaking given under section 78 or 79 above may be varied from time to time by agreement between the Board and the person bound by the undertaking.

79A(2) Where the tribunal is satisfied that–

(a) the Board have made a proposal for the variation of such an undertaking to the person bound by the undertaking,

(b) that person has failed to agree to the proposed variation within six months after the date on which the proposal was made, and

(c) it is just and reasonable, in all the circumstances, to require the proposed variation to be made,

the tribunal may direct that the undertaking is to have effect from a specified date as if the proposed variation had been agreed to by the person bound by the undertaking.

79A(3) The date specified by the tribunal must not be less than sixty days after the date of the tribunal's direction.

79A(4) A direction under this section shall not take effect if, before the date specified by the tribunal, a variation different from that to which the direction relates is agreed between the Board and the person bound by the undertaking.

History – In s. 79A(2) the words "the tribunal" substituted for the words "a Special Commissioner" and the words "the tribunal may direct that the undertaking is to have effect from a specified date" substituted for the words "the Commissioner may direct that the undertaking is to have effect from a date specified by him" by SI 2009/56, art. 3 and Sch. 1, para. 111(2), with effect from 1 April 2009, subject to transitional and saving provisions in SI 2009/56, Sch. 3.
In s. 79A(3) the word "tribunal" substituted for the words "Special Commissioner" and the words "the tribunal's direction" substituted for the words "his direction" by SI 2009/56, art. 3 and Sch. 1, para. 111(3), with effect from 1 April 2009, subject to transitional and saving provisions in SI 2009/56, Sch. 3.
In s. 79A(4) the word "tribunal" substituted for the words "Special Commissioner" by SI 2009/56, art. 3 and Sch. 1, para. 111(4), with effect from 1 April 2009, subject to transitional and saving provisions in SI 2009/56, Sch. 3.
S. 79A inserted by FA 1998, s. 142 and Sch. 25, para. 8(2), with effect in relation to undertakings given on or after 31 July 1998.

Cross references – SI 2009/275, art. 3(b): any decision under s. 79A(2) is an excluded decision for the purposes of TCEA 2007, s. 11(1) and 13(1).

MISCELLANEOUS

80 Initial interest of settlor or spouse or civil partner

History – In the heading to s. 80 the words "or civil partner" inserted by SI 2005/3229, reg. 17(4), with effect from 5 December 2005.

80(1) Where a settlor or his spouse or civil partner is beneficially entitled to a qualifying interest in possession in property immediately after it becomes comprised in the settlement, the property shall for the purposes of this Chapter be treated as not having become comprised in the settlement on that occasion; but when the property or any part of it becomes held on trusts under which neither of those persons is beneficially entitled to a qualifying interest in possession, the property or part shall for those purposes be treated as becoming comprised in a separate settlement made by that one of them who ceased (or last ceased) to be beneficially entitled to a qualifying interest in possession in it.

80(2) References in subsection (1) above to the **spouse or civil partner** of a settlor include references to the widow or widower or surviving civil partner of a settlor.

80(3) This section shall not apply if the occasion first referred to in subsection (1) above occurred before 27th March 1974.

80(4) Where the occasion first referred to in subsection (1) above occurs on or after 22nd March 2006, this section applies–

(a) as though for "a qualifying interest in possession" in each place where that appears in subsection (1) above there were substituted "a postponing interest", and

(b) as though, for the purposes of that subsection, each of the following were a "postponing interest"–

(i) an immediate post-death interest;

(ii) a disabled person's interest.

History – In s. 80(1), the words "a qualifying interest in possession" substituted (three times) for the words "an interest in possession" by F(No. 2)A 2015, s. 13(1), with effect from 18 November 2015 (Royal Assent) subject to the saving provisions at F(No. 2)A 2015, s. 13(3)–(7).

In s. 80(1) the words "or civil partner" inserted by SI 2005/3229, reg. 17(2), with effect from 5 December 2005.

In s. 80(2) the words "or civil partner" and "or surviving civil partner" inserted by SI 2005/3229, reg. 17(3), with effect from 5 December 2005.

In s. 80(4)(a), the words "a qualifying interest in possession" substituted for the words "an interest in possession" by F(No. 2)A 2015, s. 13(1), with effect from 18 November 2015 (Royal Assent) subject to the saving provisions at F(No. 2)A 2015, s. 13(3)–(7).

S. 80(4) inserted by FA 2006, s. 156 and Sch. 20, para. 23, with effect from 22 March 2006.

Notes – S. 62: related settlements.

81 Property moving between settlements

81(1) Where property which ceases to be comprised in one settlement becomes comprised in another then, unless in the meantime any person becomes beneficially entitled to the property (and not merely to an interest in possession in the property), it shall for the purposes of this Chapter be treated as remaining comprised in the first settlement.

81(2) Subsection (1) above shall not apply where the property ceased to be comprised in the first settlement before 10th December 1981; but where property ceased to be comprised in one settlement before 10th December 1981 and after 26th March 1974 and, by the same disposition, became comprised in another settlement, it shall for the purposes of this Chapter be treated as remaining comprised in the first settlement.

81(3) Subsection (1) above shall not apply where a reversionary interest in the property expectant on the termination of a qualifying interest in possession subsisting under the first settlement was settled on the trusts of the other settlement before 10th December 1981.

81A Reversionary interests in relevant property

81A(1) Where a reversionary interest in relevant property to which–

(a) a person who acquired it for a consideration in money or money's worth, or

(b) the settlor or the spouse or civil partner of the settlor,

(a "relevant reversioner") is beneficially entitled comes to an end by reason of the relevant reversioner becoming entitled to an interest in possession in the relevant property, the relevant reversioner is to be treated as having made a disposition of the reversionary interest at that time.

81A(2) A transfer of value of a reversionary interest in relevant property to which a relevant reversioner is beneficially entitled is to be taken to be a transfer which is not a potentially exempt transfer.

History – S. 81A inserted by FA 2010, s. 52, with effect in relation to reversionary interests to which a relevant reversioner becomes beneficially entitled on or after 9 December 2009.

82 Excluded property

82(1) In a case where, apart from this section, property to which section 80 or 81 applies would be excluded property by virtue of section 48(3)(a) above, that property shall not be taken to be excluded property at any time ("the relevant time") for the purposes of this Chapter (except sections 78 and 79) unless Conditions A and B are satisfied.

82(2) Section 65(8) above shall not have effect in relation to property to which section 80 or 81 above applies unless Condition A below is satisfied (in addition to the condition in section 65(8) that the settlor was not domiciled in the United Kingdom when the settlement was made).

82(3) Condition A referred to in subsections (1) and (2) above is–

(a) in the case of property to which section 80 above applies, that the person who is the settlor in relation to the settlement first mentioned in that section, and

(b) in the case of property to which subsection (1) or (2) of section 81 above applies, that the person who is the settlor in relation to the second of the settlements mentioned in the subsection concerned,

was not domiciled in the United Kingdom when that settlement was made.

82(4) Condition B referred to in subsection (1) above is–

(a) in the case of property to which section 80 above applies, that the person who is the settlor in relation to the settlement first mentioned in that section, and

(b) in the case of property to which subsection (1) or (2) of section 81 above applies, that the person who is the settlor in relation to the first or second of the settlements mentioned in that subsection,

was not a formerly domiciled resident for the tax year in which the relevant time falls.

History – S. 82(1) substituted by F(No. 2)A 2017, s. 30(7)(a), with effect in relation to times after 5 April 2017 subject to s. 30(10)–(17). Former s. 82(1) read as follows:

"**82(1)** For the purposes of this Chapter (except sections 78 and 79) property to which section 80 or 81 above applies shall not be taken to be excluded property by virtue of section 48(3)(a) above unless the condition in subsection (3) below is satisfied (in addition to the conditions in section 48(3) that the property is situated outside the United Kingdom and that the settlor was not domiciled there when the settlement was made)."

In s. 82(2) the words "Condition A" substituted for the words "the condition in subsection (3) below" by F(No. 2)A 2017, s. 30(7)(b), with effect in relation to times after 5 April 2017 subject to s. 30(10)–(17).

In s. 82(3) the words "Condition A" substituted for the words "The condition" by F(No. 2)A 2017, s. 30(7)(c), with effect in relation to times after 5 April 2017 subject to s. 30(10)–(17).

S. 82(4) inserted by F(No. 2)A 2017, s. 30(7)(d), with effect in relation to times after 5 April 2017 subject to s. 30(10)–(17).

Cross references – S. 48(3)(a): conditions to be satisfied for settled property situated outside the UK to be excluded property.

83 Property becoming settled on a death

83 Property which becomes comprised in a settlement in pursuance of a will or intestacy shall for the purposes of this Chapter be taken to have become comprised in it on the death of the testator or intestate (whether it occurred before or after the passing of this Act).

84 Income applied for charitable purposes

84 For the purposes of this Chapter (except sections 78 and 79) where the trusts on which settled property is held require part of the income of the property to be applied for charitable purposes, a corresponding part of the settled property shall be regarded as held for charitable purposes.

85 Credit for annual charges under Finance Act 1975

85 Any tax charged under paragraph 12(2) of Schedule 5 to the Finance Act 1975 and not already allowed as a credit under paragraph 12(3) of that Schedule or under section 125 of the Finance Act 1982 or under this section shall be allowed as a credit against tax chargeable under this Chapter (apart from section 79) in respect of the settled property or part concerned.

Cross references – FA 1975, Sch. 5, para. 12(2): pre-1982 regime for discretionary trusts – deemed yearly capital distribution where trustees were not UK-resident.

FA 1975, Sch. 5, para. 12(3) and FA 1982, s. 125: credit for annual charge against ten-yearly periodic charge.

Chapter IV – Miscellaneous

86 Trusts for benefit of employees

86(1) Where settled property is held on trusts which, either indefinitely or until the end of a period (whether defined by a date or in some other way) do not permit any of the settled property to be applied otherwise than for the benefit of–

(a) persons of a class defined by reference to employment in a particular trade or profession, or employment by, or office with, a body carrying on a trade, profession or undertaking, or

(b) persons of a class defined by reference to marriage to or civil partnership with, or relationship to, or dependence on, persons of a class defined as mentioned in paragraph (a) above,

then, subject to subsection (3) below, this section applies to that settled property or, as the case may be, applies to it during that period.

86(2) *Where settled property is held* on trusts permitting the property to be applied for the benefit of persons within paragraph (a) or (b) of subsection (1) above, those trusts shall not be regarded as outside the description specified in that subsection by reason only that they also permit the settled property to be applied for charitable purposes.

86(3) Where any class mentioned in subsection (1) above is defined by reference to employment by or office with a particular body, this section applies to the settled property only if–

(a) the class comprises all or most of the persons employed by or holding office with the body concerned, or

(b) the trusts on which the settled property is held are those of a profit sharing scheme approved in accordance with Schedule 9 to the Taxes Act 1988, or

(c) the trusts on which the settled property is held are those of a share incentive plan approved under Schedule 2 to the Income Tax (Earnings and Pensions) Act 2003, or

(d) the settled property consists of or includes ordinary share capital of a company which meets the trading requirement and the trusts on which the settled property is held are those of a settlement which–

(i) meets the controlling interest requirement with respect to the company, and

(ii) meets the all-employee benefit requirement with respect to the company.

86(3A) For the purpose of determining whether subsection (3)(d) is satisfied in relation to settled property which consists of or includes ordinary share capital of a company–

(a) section 236I of the 1992 Act applies to determine whether the company meets the trading requirement (with references to "C" being read as references to that company),

(b) sections 236J, 236K, 236M and 236T (but not 236L) of the 1992 Act apply to determine whether the settlement meets the all-employee benefit requirement and the controlling interest requirement (with references in those sections to "C" being read as references to that company), and

(c) **"ordinary share capital"** has the meaning given by section 1119 of the Corporation Tax Act 2010.

86(4) Where this section applies to any settled property–

(a) the property shall be treated as comprised in one settlement, whether or not it would fall to be so treated apart from this section, and

(b) an interest in possession in any part of the settled property shall be disregarded for the purposes of this Act (except section 55) if that part is less than 5 per cent of the whole.

86(5) Where any property to which this section applies ceases to be comprised in a settlement and, either immediately or not more than one month later, the whole of it becomes comprised in another settlement, then, if this section again applies to it when it becomes comprised in the second settlement, it shall be treated for all the purposes of this Act as if it had remained comprised in the first settlement.

History – In s. 86(1)(b) the words "to or civil partnership with," inserted by SI 2005/3229, reg. 18, with effect from 5 December 2005. In s. 86(3)(c), the words "a share incentive plan approved under Schedule 2 to the Income Tax (Earnings and Pensions) Act 2003" substituted for the words "an employee share ownership plan approved under Schedule 8 to the Finance Act 2000" by ITEPA 2003, Sch. 6, para. 151(1)(c) and para. 151(2) which have effect for the tax year 2003–04 and subsequent tax years.
S. 86(3)(c) inserted by FA 2000, s. 138(4).
S. 86(3)(d) (and the ", or" before it) inserted by FA 2014, s. 290 and Sch. 37, para. 15(2). This amendment is treated as having come into force on 6 April 2014.
S. 86(3A) inserted by FA 2014, s. 290 and Sch. 37, para. 15(3). This amendment is treated as having come into force on 6 April 2014.
See ICTA 1988, Sch. 29, para. 32 for substitution of reference to that Act in s. 86(3).

Cross references – S. 13(1): transfer to employee trust by a close company not a transfer of value (subject to conditions).
S. 28: a transfer of value made by an individual of shares etc. in a company into an employee trust within s. 86(1) is an exempt transfer (subject to conditions).
S. 55: reversionary interest acquired by beneficiary does not form part of his estate.
S. 58(1)(b): property to which s. 86 applies is not "relevant property" for the purposes of Ch. III.
S. 72: property leaving employee trusts and newspaper trusts.
S. 75(1): exemption for property ceasing to be relevant property within Pt. III, Ch. III on becoming held on employee trusts.
ICTA 1988, Sch. 9: approved share option and profit sharing schemes.
TCGA 1992, s. 239: deemed no gain, no loss for the purposes of tax on chargeable gains on certain disposals to employee trusts within s. 86(1).

Extra-statutory concessions – D35: when trustees of employee trust within s. 86 transfer assets to employees who pay income tax on the benefit, the trustees are not charged to CGT.

Other material – HMRC Brief 18/11: HMRC view on IHT position in relation to contributions to Employee Benefit Trusts.

87 Newspaper trusts

87(1) In relation to property comprised in a settlement to which this section applies, section 86 above shall have effect as if newspaper publishing companies were included among the persons within paragraphs (a) and (b) of subsection (1) of that section.

87(2) This section applies to a settlement if shares in a newspaper publishing company or a newspaper holding company are the only or principal property comprised in the settlement.

87(3) In this section–

"newspaper publishing company" means a company whose business consists wholly or mainly in the publication of newspapers in the United Kingdom;

"newspaper holding company" means a company which–

(a) has as its only or principal asset shares in a newspaper publishing company, and

(b) has powers of voting on all or most questions affecting the publishing company as a whole which if exercised would yield a majority of the votes capable of being exercised on them;

and for the purposes of this section shares shall be treated as the principal property comprised in a settlement or the principal asset of a company if the remaining property comprised in the settlement or the remaining assets of the company are such as may be reasonably required to enable the trustees or the company to secure the operation of the newspaper publishing company concerned.

88 Protective trusts

88(1) This section applies to settled property (other than property to which section 73 above applies) which is held on trusts to the like effect as those specified in section 33(1) of the Trustee Act 1925; and in this section **"the principal beneficiary"** and **"the trust period"** have the same meanings as in that section.

88(2) For the purposes of this Act–

(a) there shall be disregarded the failure or determination, before the end of the trust period, of trusts to the like effect as those specified in paragraph (i) of the said section 33(1), and

(b) the principal beneficiary shall be treated as beneficially entitled to an interest in possession in any property which is for the time being held on trusts to the like effect as those specified in paragraph (ii) of the said section 33(1).

88(3) Where–

(a) settled property became held before 22nd March 2006 on trusts to the like effect as those specified in section 33(1)(i) of the Trustee Act 1925, and

(b) as a result of the failure or determination of those trusts on or after 22nd March 2006, the principal beneficiary is treated by subsection (2)(b) above as beneficially entitled to an interest in possession,

this Act shall apply in relation to that interest in possession as if the principal beneficiary became beneficially entitled to that interest in possession before 22nd March 2006.

88(4) Subsection (5) below applies where–

(a) settled property becomes held on or after 22nd March 2006 on trusts to the like effect as those specified in section 33(1)(i) of the Trustee Act 1925,

(b) the interest of the principal beneficiary under those trusts is–

(i) an immediate post-death interest, or

(ii) a disabled person's interest within section 89B(1)(c) or (d) below, or

(iii) a transitional serial interest, and

(c) as a result of the failure or determination of those trusts, the principal beneficiary is treated by subsection (2)(b) above as beneficially entitled to an interest in possession.

88(5) This Act shall apply–

(a) as if that interest in possession were a continuation of the immediate post-death interest, disabled person's interest or transitional serial interest, and

(b) as if the immediate post-death interest, or transitional serial interest, had not come to an end on the failure or disabled person's interest or determination of the trusts.

88(6) Subsection (2) above does not apply in a case where–

(a) settled property becomes held on or after 22nd March 2006 on trusts to the like effect as those specified in section 33(1)(i) of the Trustee Act 1925, and

(b) the interest of the principal beneficiary under those trusts is–

(i) not an immediate post-death interest

(ii) not a disabled person's interest within section 89B(1)(c) or (d) below, and

(iii) not a transitional serial interest.

History – S. 88(3) inserted by FA 2006, s. 156 and Sch. 20, para. 24, with effect from 22 March 2006.
S. 88(4) inserted by FA 2006, s. 156 and Sch. 20, para. 24, with effect from 22 March 2006.
S. 88(5) inserted by FA 2006, s. 156 and Sch. 20, para. 24, with effect from 22 March 2006.
S. 88(6) inserted by FA 2006, s. 156 and Sch. 20, para. 24, with effect from 22 March 2006.

Cross references – Trustee Act 1925, s. 73: pre-1978 protective trusts.
Trustee Act 1925, s. 33(1)(i) (not reproduced): protective trusts for principal beneficiary for life or until deprivation of right to receive income.
Trustee Act 1925, s. 33(1)(ii): discretionary trusts following failure or determination of trust for principal beneficiary.

Statements of practice – E7: interpretation of "to the like effect" in s. 88(1).

89 Trusts for disabled persons

89(1) This section applies to settled property transferred into settlement after 9th March 1981 and held on trusts–

(a) under which, during the life of a disabled person, no interest in possession in the settled property subsists, and

(b) which secure that, if any of the settled property or income arising from it is applied during the disabled person's life for the benefit of a beneficiary, it is applied for the benefit of the disabled person.

89(2) For the purposes of this Act the person mentioned in subsection (1) above shall be treated as beneficially entitled to an interest in possession in the settled property.

89(3) The trusts on which the settled property is held are not to be treated as falling outside subsection (1) by reason only of–

(a) the trustees' having powers that enable them to apply otherwise than for the benefit of the disabled person amounts (whether consisting of income or capital, or both) not exceeding the annual limit,

(b) the trustees' having the powers conferred by section 32 of the Trustee Act 1925 (powers of advancement),

(c) the trustees' having those powers but free from, or subject to a less restrictive limitation than, the limitation imposed by proviso (a) of subsection (1) of that section,

(d) the trustees' having the powers conferred by section 33 of the Trustee Act (Northern Ireland) 1958 (corresponding provision for Northern Ireland),

(e) the trustees' having those powers but free from, or subject to a less restrictive limitation than, the limitation imposed by subsection (1)(a) of that section, or

(f) the trustees' having powers to the like effect as the powers mentioned in any of paragraphs (b) to (e).

89(3A) For the purposes of this section, the **"annual limit"** is whichever is the lower of the following amounts–

(a) £3,000, and

(b) 3% of the amount that is the maximum value of the settled property during the period in question.

89(3B) For those purposes the annual limit applies in relation to each period of 12 months that begins on 6 April.

89(3C) The Treasury may by order made by statutory instrument–

(a) specify circumstances in which subsection (3)(a) is, or is not, to apply in relation to a trust, and

(b) amend the definition of "the annual limit" in subsection (3A).

89(3D) An order under subsection (3C) may–

(a) make different provision for different cases, and

(b) contain transitional and saving provision.

89(3E) A statutory instrument containing an order under subsection (3C) may not be made unless a draft of the instrument has been laid before, and approved by a resolution of, the House of Commons.

89(4) The reference in subsection (1) above to **a disabled person** is, in relation to any settled property, a reference to a person who, when the property was transferred into settlement, was a disabled person.

89(4A) In this section **"disabled person"** has the meaning given by Schedule 1A to the Finance Act 2005.

History – References to SSCBA 1992 and its Northern Ireland equivalent substituted by SS(CP)A 1992, s. 4 and Sch. 2, para. 66, and Social Security (Consequential Provisions) (Northern Ireland) Act 1992, s. 4 and Sch. 2, para. 29, respectively.

S. 89(1)(b) substituted by FA 2013, s. 216 and Sch. 44, para. 6(2), with effect in relation to property transferred into a settlement on or after 8 April 2013 (subject to the provisions of Sch. 44, para. 9(2)). Former s. 89(1)(b) read as follows:

"(b) which secure that not less than half of the settled property which is applied during his life is applied for his benefit.".

S. 89(3)–(3E) substituted for s. 89(3) by FA 2013, s. 216 and Sch. 44, para. 6(3), with effect in relation to property transferred into a settlement on or after 8 April 2013 (subject to the provisions of Sch. 44, para. 9(2)). Former s. 89(3) read as follows:

"**89(3)** The trusts on which settled property is held shall not be treated as falling outside subsection (1) above by reason only of the powers conferred on the trustees by section 32 of the Trustee Act 1925 or section 33 of the Trustee Act (Northern Ireland) 1958 (powers of advancement).".

In s. 89(4), the words "was a disabled person" substituted for words following "into settlement," by FA 2013, s. 216 and Sch. 44, para. 6(4), with effect in relation to property transferred into a settlement on or after 8 April 2013 (subject to the provisions of Sch. 44, para. 9(2)). Former words following "into settlement," read as follows:

"was–

(a) incapable, by reason of mental disorder within the meaning of the Mental Health Act 1983, of administering his property or managing his affairs, or

(b) in receipt of an attendance allowance under section 64 of the Social Security Contributions and Benefits Act 1992 or section 64 of the Social Security Contributions and Benefits (Northern Ireland) Act 1992; or

IHT Statutes

(c) in receipt of or disability living allowance under section 71 of the Social Security Contributions and Benefits Act 1992 by virtue of entitlement to the care component at the highest or middle rate.".

S. 89(4)(c) inserted by Disability Living Allowance and Disability Working Allowance Act 1991, Sch. 2, para. 14(2), with effect from 6 April 1992 by virtue of SI 1991/2617.

S. 89(4A) substituted for (5) and (6) by FA 2013, s. 216 and Sch. 44, para. 6(5), with effect in relation to property transferred into a settlement on or after 8 April 2013 (subject to the provisions of Sch. 44, para. 9(2)). Former s. 89(5) and (6) read as follows:

"**89(5)** The reference in subsection (1) above to a disabled person includes, in relation to any settled property, a reference to a person who, when the property was transferred into settlement,–

(a) would have been in receipt of attendance allowance under section 64 of either of the Acts mentioned in subsection (4)(b) above had provision made by regulations under section 67(1) or (2) of that Act (non-satisfaction of conditions for attendance allowance where person is undergoing treatment for renal failure in a hospital or is provided with certain accommodation) been ignored, or

(b) would have been in receipt of disability living allowance by virtue of entitlement to the care component at the highest or middle rate had provision made by regulations under section 72(8) of either of the Acts mentioned in subsection (4)(c) above (no payment of disability living allowance for persons for whom certain accommodation is provided) been ignored.

89(6) The reference in subsection (1) above to a disabled person also includes, in relation to any settled property, a reference to a person who satisfies the Commissioners for Her Majesty's Revenue and Customs–

(a) that he would, when the property was transferred into settlement, have been in receipt of attendance allowance under section 64 of either of the Acts mentioned in subsection (4)(b) above–
  (i) had he met the conditions as to residence under section 64(1) of that Act, and
  (ii) had provision made by regulations under section 67(1) or (2) of that Act been ignored, or

(b) that he would, when the property was transferred into settlement, have been in receipt of a disability living allowance by virtue of entitlement to the care component at the highest or middle rate–
  (i) had he met the prescribed conditions as to residence under section 71(6) of either of the Acts mentioned in subsection (4)(c) above, and
  (ii) had provision made by regulations under section 72(8) of that Act been ignored.".

S. 89(5) inserted by FA 2006, s. 156 and Sch. 20, para. 6(2), with effect from 22 March 2006, but only in respect of property transferred into settlement on or after that day.

S. 89(6) inserted by FA 2006, s. 156 and Sch. 20, para. 6(2), with effect from 22 March 2006, but only in respect of property transferred into settlement on or after that day.

Cross references – S. 3A(3): a gift by an individual into a trust for a disabled person is a potentially exempt transfer. S. 74: pre-1981 trusts for disabled persons.

Other material – Taxline 2005/1 (not reproduced): these sections can now work together to the effect that dispositions onto a disabled trust are not transfers of value provided they fulfil the requirements of both sections and subject to the condition that provisions are "reasonable" (it was held that a transfer of £100,000 was reasonable).

89A Self-settlement by person expected to fall within the definition of "disabled person"

History – In the heading to s. 89A the words "expected to fall within the definition of "disabled person"" substituted for the words "with condition expected to lead to disability" substituted by FA 2013, s. 216 and Sch. 44, para. 7(7), with effect in relation to property transferred into a settlement on or after 8 April 2013 (subject to the provisions of Sch. 44, para. 9(2)).

89A(1) This section applies to property transferred by a person ("A") into settlement on or after 22nd March 2006 if–

(a) A was beneficially entitled to the property immediately before transferring it into settlement,

(b) A satisfies the Commissioners for Her Majesty's Revenue and Customs that, when the property was transferred into settlement, A had a condition that it was at that time reasonable to expect would have such effects on A as to lead to A becoming a person falling within any paragraph of the definition of "disabled person" in paragraph 1 of Schedule 1A to the Finance Act 2005

(c) the property is held on trusts–
  (i) under which, during the life of A, no interest in possession in the settled property subsists, and
  (ii) which secure that Conditions 1 and 2 are met.

89A(2) Condition 1 is that if any of the settled property or income arising from it is applied during A's life for the benefit of a beneficiary, it is applied for the benefit of A.

89A(3) Condition 2 is that any power to bring the trusts mentioned in subsection (1)(c) above to an end during A's life is such that, in the event of the power being exercised during A's life, either–

(a) A or another person will, on the trusts being brought to an end, be absolutely entitled to the settled property, or

(b) on the trusts being brought to an end, a disabled person's interest within section 89B(1)(a) or (c) below will subsist in the settled property.

89A(4) If this section applies to settled property transferred into settlement by a person, the person shall be treated as beneficially entitled to an interest in possession in the settled property.

89A(5) For the purposes of subsection (1)(b), assume–

(a) that A will meet any conditions as to residence or presence that are required to establish entitlement to the allowance, payment or increased pension in question,

(b) that there will be no provision made by regulations under any of the following–
  (i) sections 67(1) and (2), 72(8), 104(3) and 113(2) of SSCBA 1992,
  (ii) sections 67(1) and (2), 72(8), 104(3) and 113(2) of SSCB(NI)A 1992, and

(iii) sections 85 and 86 of WRA 2012 and the corresponding provision having effect in Northern Ireland, and

(c) that A will not be prevented from receiving the allowance, payment or increased pension in question by any of the following–

(i) section 113(1) of SSCBA 1992,

(ii) section 113(1) of SSCB(NI)A 1992,

(iii) section 87 of WRA 2012 and the corresponding provision having effect in Northern Ireland,

(iv) articles 61 and 64 of the Personal Injuries (Civilians) Scheme 1983 (SI 1983/686),

(v) article 53 of the Naval, Military and Air Forces etc (Disablement and Death) Service Pensions Order 2006 (SI 2006/606), and

(vi) article 42 of the Armed Forces and Reserve Forces (Compensation Scheme) Order 2011 (SI 2011/517).

89A(6A) The trusts on which the settled property is held are not to be treated as falling outside subsection (2) by reason only of–

(a) the trustees' having powers that enable them to apply otherwise than for the benefit of the disabled person amounts (whether consisting of income or capital, or both) not exceeding the annual limit,

(b) the trustees' having the powers conferred by section 32 of the Trustee Act 1925 (powers of advancement),

(c) the trustees' having those powers but free from, or subject to a less restrictive limitation than, the limitation imposed by proviso (a) of subsection (1) of that section,

(d) the trustees' having the powers conferred by section 33 of the Trustee Act (Northern Ireland) 1958 (corresponding provision for Northern Ireland),

(e) the trustees' having those powers but free from, or subject to a less restrictive limitation than, the limitation imposed by subsection (1)(a) of that section, or

(f) the trustees' having powers to the like effect as the powers mentioned in any of paragraphs (b) to (e).

89A(6B) For the purposes of this section, the **"annual limit"** is whichever is the lower of the following amounts–

(a) £3,000, and

(b) 3% of the amount that is the maximum value of the settled property during the period in question.

89A(6C) For those purposes the annual limit applies in relation to each period of 12 months that begins on 6 April.

89A(6D) The Treasury may by order made by statutory instrument–

(a) specify circumstances in which subsection (6A)(a) is, or is not, to apply in relation to a trust, and

(b) amend the definition of "the annual limit" in subsection (6B).

89A(6E) An order under subsection (6D) may–

(a) make different provision for different cases, and

(b) contain transitional and saving provision.

89A(6F) A statutory instrument containing an order under subsection (6D) may not be made unless a draft of the instrument has been laid before, and approved by a resolution of, the House of Commons.

89A(7) For the purposes of subsection (3) above, ignore–

(a) power to give directions as to the settled property that is exercisable jointly by the persons who between them are entitled to the entire beneficial interest in the property, and

(b) anything that could occur as a result of exercise of any such power.

89A(8) In this section–

"SSCBA 1992" means the Social Security Contributions and Benefits Act 1992,

"SSCB(NI)A 1992" means the Social Security Contributions and Benefits (Northern Ireland) Act 1992, and

"WRA 2012" means the Welfare Reform Act 2012.

History – In s. 89A(1)(b), the words "a person falling within any paragraph of the definition of "disabled person" in paragraph 1 of Schedule 1A to the Finance Act 2005" substituted for the words below by FA 2013, s. 216 and Sch. 44, para. 7(2), with effect in relation to property transferred into a settlement on or after 8 April 2013 (subject to the provisions of Sch. 44, para. 9(2)). The former words were as follows: "–

(i) a person falling within section 89(4)(a) above,

(ii) in receipt of an attendance allowance mentioned in section 89(4)(b) above, or

(iii) in receipt of a disability living allowance mentioned in section 89(4)(c) above by virtue of entitlement to the care component at the highest or middle rate, and".

In s. 89A(2), the words "or income arising from it" inserted by FA 2013, s. 216 and Sch. 44, para. 7(3), with effect in relation to property transferred into a settlement on or after 8 April 2013 (subject to the provisions of Sch. 44, para. 9(2)).
S. 89A(5) substituted for s. 89A(5) and (6) by FA 2013, s. 216 and Sch. 44, para. 7(4), with effect in relation to property transferred into a settlement on or after 8 April 2013 (subject to the provisions of Sch. 44, para. 9(2)). Former s. 89A(5) and (6) read as follows:
"**89A(5)** For the purposes of subsection (1)(b)(ii) above, assume–
(a) that A will meet the conditions as to residence under section 64(1) of whichever of the 1992 Acts is applicable, and
(b) that there will be no provision made by regulations under section 67(1) and (2) of that Act.
89A(6) For the purposes of subsection (1)(b)(iii) above, assume–
(a) that A will meet the prescribed conditions as to residence under section 71(6) of whichever of the 1992 Acts is applicable, and
(b) that there will be no provision made by regulations under section 72(8) of that Act.".
S. 89A(6A)–(6F) inserted by FA 2013, s. 216 and Sch. 44, para. 7(5), with effect in relation to property transferred into a settlement on or after 8 April 2013 (subject to the provisions of Sch. 44, para. 9(2)).
S. 89A(8) substituted by FA 2013, s. 216 and Sch. 44, para. 7(6), with effect in relation to property transferred into a settlement on or after 8 April 2013 (subject to the provisions of Sch. 44, para. 9(2)). Former s. 89A(8) read as follows:
"**89A(8)** In this section **"the 1992 Acts"** means–
the Social Security Contributions and Benefits Act 1992, and
the Social Security Contributions and Benefits (Northern Ireland) Act 1992.".
S. 89A inserted by FA 2006, s. 156 and Sch. 20, para. 6(1), with effect from 22 March 2006.

89B Meaning of "disabled person's interest"

89B(1) In this Act **"disabled person's interest"** means–

(a) an interest in possession to which a person is under section 89(2) above treated as beneficially entitled,

(b) an interest in possession to which a person is under section 89A(4) above treated as beneficially entitled,

(c) an interest in possession in settled property (other than an interest within paragraph (a) or (b) above) to which a disabled person becomes beneficially entitled on or after 22nd March 2006 if the trusts on which the settled property is held secure that, if any of the settled property is applied during the disabled person's life for the benefit of a beneficiary, it is applied for the benefit of the disabled person, or

(d) an interest in possession in settled property (other than an interest within paragraph (a) or (b) above) to which a person ("A") is beneficially entitled if–
   (i) A is the settlor,
   (ii) A was beneficially entitled to the property immediately before transferring it into settlement,
   (iii) A satisfies Her Majesty's Commissioners for Revenue and Customs as mentioned in section 89A(1)(b) above,
   (iv) the settled property was transferred into settlement on or after 22nd March 2006, and
   (v) the trusts on which the settled property is held secure that, if any of the settled property is applied during A's life for the benefit of a beneficiary, it is applied for the benefit of A.

89B(2) In subsection (1)(c) **"disabled person"** has the meaning given by Schedule 1A to the Finance Act 2005.

89B(2A) Where the income arising from the settled property is held on trusts of the kind described in section 33 of the Trustee Act 1925 (protective trusts), subsection (1)(d)(v) has effect as if for "A's life" there were substituted "the period during which the income from the property is held on trust for A".

89B(3) Section 71D above does not apply to property in which there subsists a disabled person's interest within subsection (1)(c) above (but see also section 71D(5) above).

History – In s. 89B(1)(c) the words "if the trusts on which the settled property is held secure that, if any of the settled property is applied during the disabled person's life for the benefit of a beneficiary, it is applied for the benefit of the disabled person" inserted by FA 2013, s. 216 and Sch. 44, para. 10(1), with effect in relation to property transferred into settlement on or after 17 July 2013 (Royal Assent) – subject to FA 2013, Sch. 44, para. 10(4) and (5).
S. 89B(2) substituted by FA 2013, s. 216 and Sch. 44, para. 8(2), with effect in relation to property transferred into a settlement on or after 8 April 2013 (subject to the provisions of Sch. 44, para. 9(2)). Former s. 89B(2) read as follows:
"**89B(2)** Subsections (4–6) of section 89 above (meaning of "disabled person" in subsection (1) of that section) have effect for the purposes of subsection (1)(c) above as they have effect for the purposes of subsection (1) of that section.".
S. 89B(2A) inserted by FA 2013, s. 216 and Sch. 44, para. 8(3), with effect in relation to property transferred into a settlement on or after 8 April 2013 (subject to the provisions of Sch. 44, para. 9(2)).
S. 89B inserted by FA 2006, s. 156 and Sch. 20, para. 6(1), with effect from 22 March 2006.

89C Disabled person's interest: powers of advancement etc

89C(1) The trusts on which settled property is held are not to be treated for the purposes of section 89B(1)(c) or (d) (meaning of "disabled person's interest": cases involving an interest in possession) as failing to secure that the settled property is applied for the benefit of a beneficiary by reason only of–

(a) the trustees' having powers that enable them to apply otherwise than for the benefit of the beneficiary amounts (whether consisting of income or capital, or both) not exceeding the annual limit,

(b) the trustees' having the powers conferred by section 32 of the Trustee Act 1925 (powers of advancement),

(c) the trustees' having those powers but free from, or subject to a less restrictive limitation than, the limitation imposed by proviso (a) of subsection (1) of that section,

(d) the trustees' having the powers conferred by section 33 of the Trustee Act (Northern Ireland) 1958 (corresponding provision for Northern Ireland),

(e) the trustees' having those powers but free from, or subject to a less restrictive limitation than, the limitation imposed by subsection (1)(a) of that section, or

(f) the trustees' having powers to the like effect as the powers mentioned in any of paragraphs (b) to (e).

89C(2) For the purposes of this section, the **"annual limit"** is whichever is the lower of the following amounts–

(a) £3,000, and,

(b) 3% of the amount that is the maximum value of the settled property during the period in question.

89C(3) For those purposes the annual limit applies in relation to each period of 12 months that begins on 6 April.

89C(4) The Treasury may by order made by statutory instrument–

(a) specify circumstances in which subsection (1)(a) is, or is not, to apply in relation to a trust, and

(b) amend the definition of "the annual limit" in subsection (2).

89C(5) An order under subsection (4) may–

(a) make different provision for different cases, and

(b) contain transitional and saving provision.

89C(6) A statutory instrument containing an order under subsection (4) may not be made unless a draft of the instrument has been laid before, and approved by a resolution of, the House of Commons.

History – S. 89C inserted by FA 2013, s. 216 and Sch. 44, para. 10(2), with effect in relation to property transferred into settlement on or after 17 July 2013 (Royal Assent) – subject to FA 2013, Sch. 44, para. 10(4) and (5).

90 Trustees' annuities, etc.

90 Where under the terms of a settlement a person is entitled by way of remuneration for his services as trustee to an interest in possession in property comprised in the settlement, then, except to the extent that the interest represents more than a reasonable amount of remuneration,–

(a) the interest shall be left out of account in determining for the purposes of this Act the value of his estate immediately before his death, and

(b) tax shall not be charged under section 52 above when the interest comes to an end.

Cross references – S. 52: charge on termination of interest in possession.

91 Administration period

91(1) Where a person would have been entitled to an interest in possession in the whole or part of the residue of the estate of a deceased person had the administration of that estate been completed, the same consequences shall follow under this Act as if he had become entitled to an interest in possession in the unadministered estate and in the property (if any) representing ascertained residue, or in a corresponding part of it, on the date as from which the whole or part of the income of the residue would have been attributable to his interest had the residue been ascertained immediately after the death of the deceased person.

91(2) In this section–

(a) **"unadministered estate"** means all the property for the time being held by personal representatives as such, excluding property devolving on them otherwise than as assets for the payment of debts and excluding property that is the subject of a specific disposition, and making due allowance for outstanding charges on residue and for any adjustments between capital and income remaining to be made in due course of administration;

(b) **"ascertained residue"** means property which, having ceased to be held by the personal representatives as such, is held as part of the residue;

(c) subject to subsection (3) below, **"charges on residue"** means, in relation to the estate of a deceased person, the following liabilities properly payable out of the estate and interest payable in respect of those liabilities–

(i) funeral, testamentary and administration expenses and debts,

(ii) general legacies, demonstrative legacies, annuities and any sum payable out of the residue of the estate to which a person is entitled under the law of intestacy of any part of the United Kingdom or any other country, and

(iii) any other liabilities of the deceased person's personal representatives as such,

(d) **"specific disposition"** has the meaning given in section 947(6) of the Corporation Tax Act 2009, and

(e) the reference to the completion of the administration of the estate shall be construed as if it were in Chapter 3 of Part 10 of that Act.

91(3) If, as between–

(a) persons interested under a specific disposition or in a general or demonstrative legacy or in an annuity, and

(b) persons interested in the residue of an estate,

any such liabilities as are mentioned in paragraph (c) of subsection (2) above fall exclusively or primarily on the property that is the subject of the specific disposition or on the legacy or annuity, only such part (if any) of those liabilities as falls ultimately on the residue shall be treated as charges on residue.

91(4) In the application of this section to Scotland, "charges on residue" shall include, in addition to the liabilities specified in subsection (2)(c), any sums required to meet–

(a) claims in respect of prior rights or legal rights by a surviving spouse or civil partner, or

(b) claims in respect of legal rights by children.

History – S. 91(2)(c)–(e) substituted for former s. 91(2)(c) by CTA 2009, s. 1322 and Sch. 1, para. 316(2), with effect, for corporation tax purposes, for accounting periods ending on or after 1 April 2009 and, for income tax and capital gains tax purposes, for the tax year 2009–10 and subsequent years.
S. 91(3) inserted by CTA 2009, s. 1322 and Sch. 1, para. 316(3), with effect, for corporation tax purposes, for accounting periods ending on or after 1 April 2009 and, for income tax and capital gains tax purposes, for the tax year 2009–10 and subsequent years.
S. 91(4) inserted by CTA 2009, s. 1322 and Sch. 1, para. 316(3), with effect, for corporation tax purposes, for accounting periods ending on or after 1 April 2009 and, for income tax and capital gains tax purposes, for the tax year 2009–10 and subsequent years.
See ICTA 1988, Sch. 29, para. 32, for substitution of former reference to that Act in s. 91(2)(c).

Cross references – ICTA 1988, s. 701(5): definition of specific disposition.
S. 701(6): definition of charges on residue (for application to Scotland see ICTA 1988, s. 702).

92 Survivorship clauses

92(1) Where under the terms of a will or otherwise property is held for any person on condition that he survives another for a specified period of not more than six months, this Act shall apply as if the dispositions taking effect at the end of the period or, if he does not survive until then, on his death (including any such disposition which has effect by operation of law or is a separate disposition of the income from the property) had had effect from the beginning of the period.

92(2) Subsection (1) above does not affect the application of this Act in relation to any distribution or application of property occurring before the dispositions there mentioned take effect.

93 Disclaimers

93 Where a person becomes entitled to an interest in settled property but disclaims the interest, then, if the disclaimer is not made for a consideration in money or money's worth, this Act shall apply as if he had not become entitled to the interest.

Cross references – S. 239(4): certificate of discharge does not affect tax under s. 93.

PART IV – CLOSE COMPANIES

TRANSFERS BY CLOSE COMPANIES

94 Charge on participators

94(1) Subject to the following provisions of this Part of this Act, where a close company makes a transfer of value, tax shall be charged as if each individual to whom an amount is apportioned under this section had made a transfer of value of such amount as after deduction of tax (if any) would be equal to the amount so apportioned, less the amount (if any) by which the value of his estate is more than it would be but for the company's transfer; but for this purpose his estate shall be treated as not including any rights or interests *in the company*.

94(2) For the purposes of subsection (1) above the value transferred by the company's transfer of value shall be apportioned among the participators according to their respective rights and interests in the company immediately before the transfer, and any amount so apportioned to a close company shall be further apportioned among its participators, and so on; but–

(a) so much of that value as is attributable to any payment or transfer of assets to any person which falls to be taken into account in computing that person's profits or gains or losses for the purposes of income tax or corporation tax (or would fall to be so taken into account but for section 1285 of the Corporation Tax Act 2009 (exemption for UK company distributions) shall not be apportioned, and

(b) if any amount which would otherwise be apportioned to an individual who is domiciled outside the United Kingdom is attributable to the value of any property outside the United Kingdom, that amount shall not be apportioned.

94(3) In determining for the purposes of this section whether a disposition made by a close company is a transfer of value or what value is transferred by such a transfer no account shall be taken of the surrender by the company, in pursuance of section 240 or 402 of the Taxes Act 1988, of any relief or of the benefit of any amount of advance corporation tax paid by it.

94(4) Where the amount apportioned to a person under this section is 5 per cent or less of the value transferred by the company's transfer of value then, notwithstanding section 3(4) above, tax chargeable under subsection (1) above shall be left out of account in determining, with respect to any time after the company's transfer, what previous transfers of value he has made.

94(5) References in section 19 above to transfers of value made by a transferor and to the values transferred by them (calculated as there mentioned) shall be treated as including references to apportionments made to a person under this section and to the amounts for the tax on which (if charged) he would be liable.

History – In s. 94(2)(a) the words "section 1285 of the Corporation Tax Act 2009 (exemption for UK company distributions)" substituted for the words "section 208 of the Taxes Act 1988" by CTA 2009, s. 1322 and Sch. 1, para. 317, with effect, for corporation tax purposes, for accounting periods ending on or after 1 April 2009 and, for income tax and capital gains tax purposes, for the tax year 2009–10 and subsequent years.
See ICTA 1988, Sch. 29, para. 32, for substitution of references to that Act.

Cross references – S. 3(4): definition of "transfer of value made".
S. 19: annual exemption.
S. 202: persons liable for tax under s. 94(1).
ICTA 1988, s. 208: UK company distributions not generally chargeable to corporation tax.
ICTA 1988, s. 240: surrender of surplus ACT to subsidiary.
ICTA 1988, s. 402: surrender of group relief between members of groups and consortia.

Statements of practice – E15: close companies: dividends paid by subsidiary to parent; group transfers.

Other material – HMRC Brief 18/11: HMRC view on IHT position in relation to contributions to Employee Benefit Trusts made by close companies.
Taxline 2005/8 (not reproduced): details how transfers to an EBT will be treated.

95 Participator in two companies

95(1) Where–

(a) the value of the estate of a company (**"the transferee company"**) is increased as the result of a transfer of value made by a close company (**"the transferor company"**), and

(b) an individual to whom part of the value transferred is apportioned under section 94 above has an interest in the transferee company (or in a company which is a participator of the transferee company or any of its participators, and so on),

subsection (2) below shall apply to the computation, for the purposes of section 94 above, of the amount to be offset, that is to say, the amount by which the value of his estate is more than it would be but for the transfer.

95(2) Where this subsection applies–

(a) the increase in the value of the transferee company's estate shall be taken to be such part of the value transferred as accounts for the increase, and

(b) the increase so computed shall be apportioned among the transferee company's participators according to their respective rights and interests in the company immediately before the transfer (and, where necessary, further apportioned among their participators, and so on),

and the amount so apportioned to the individual shall be taken to be the amount to be offset.

96 Preference shares disregarded

96 Where part of a close company's share capital consists of preference shares (within the meaning of section 1023(5) of the Corporation Tax Act 2010) and a transfer of value made by that or any other close company has only a small effect on the value of those shares, compared with its effect on the value of other parts of the company's share capital, the preference shares shall be left out of account in determining the respective rights and interests of the participators for the purposes of sections 94 and 95 above.

History – In s. 96 the words "section 1023(5) of the Corporation Tax Act 2010" substituted for the words "section 210(4) of the Taxes Act 1988" by CTA 2010, s. 1177 and Sch. 1, para. 190, with effect for corporation tax purposes for accounting periods ending on or after 1 April 2010, and for income tax and capital gains tax purposes for the tax year 2010–11 and subsequent tax years.

See ICTA 1988, Sch. 29, para. 32 for substitution of former reference to that Act.

97 Transfers within group, etc.

97(1) Where a close company (**"the transferor company"**) is a member, but not the principal company, of a group and–

(a) there is–

(i) a disposal of an asset by the transferor company, which is a disposal to which section 171(1) of the 1992 Act applies, or

(ii) by virtue of an election under section 171A(2) of that Act, a deemed transfer by the transferor company to another member of the group, or

(iii) [repealed by FA 2011, s. 45 and Sch. 10, para. 8(a),]

(aa) the disposal is also, or the election gives rise to, a transfer of value, and

(b) the transfer of value has only a small effect on the value of the minority participators' rights and interests in that company compared with its effect on the value of the other participators' rights and interests in the company,

the rights and interests of the minority participators shall be left out of account in determining the respective rights and interests of the transferor company's participators for the purpose of apportioning the value transferred under section 94 above.

97(2) For the purposes of subsection (1) above–

(a) section 170 of the 1992 Act (groups of companies: definitions) applies as for the purposes of sections 171 to 181 of that Act, and

(b) a **minority participator** is a participator of the transferor company who is not, and is not a person connected with, a participator of the principal company of the group or of any of the principal company's participators.

History – S. 97(1)(a)(iii) and the "or" before it repealed by FA 2011, s. 45 and Sch. 10, para. 8(a), with effect in relation to the disposal of an asset by one company in relation to any disposal of an asset by one company ("company B") to another company ("company A") made at a time when company B is a member of a group, if company A ceases to be a member of the group on or after 19 July 2011, subject to the provisions of FA 2011, Sch. 10, para. 9 which vary the commencement rules in certain circumstances. Former s. 97(1)(a)(iii) read as follows:

"(iii) an election under section 179A of that Act as a result of which a chargeable gain is treated as accruing to the transferor company instead of to another member of the group, or an allowable loss is treated as accruing to another member of the group instead of to the transferor company,".

S. 97(1)(a) and (aa) substituted for former s. 97(1)(a) by FA 2001, s. 106(2) which has effect, and shall be taken always to have had effect, in relation to disposals made, or transfers deemed to have been made, on or after 1 April 2000.

In s. 97(1)(a)(ii), the word "or" at the end and s. 97(1)(a)(iii) inserted by FA 2002, s. 42(3), with effect in relation to a case where a company is treated by virtue of TCGA 1992, s. 179(3) as having sold and immediately reacquired an asset, where the company's ceasing to be a member of the group in question happens after 31 March 2002; and in relation to a case where a company is so treated by virtue of TCGA 1992 s 179(6), where the relevant time (within the meaning of that subsection) is after that date.

In s. 97(1)(aa) the words "the election" substituted for the words "the deemed transfer" by FA 2002, s. 42(3), with effect in relation to a case where a company is treated by virtue of TCGA 1992, s. 179(3) as having sold and immediately reacquired an asset, where the company's ceasing to be a member of the group in question happens after 31 March 2002; and in relation to a case where a company is so treated by virtue of TCGA 1992 s 179(6), where the relevant time (within the meaning of that subsection) is after that date.

References to the "1992 Act" substituted by TCGA 1992, s. 290 and Sch. 10, para. 8(4)(b).

S. 97 amended by FA 1989, s. 138(6), 187 and Sch. 17, Pt. VII, with effect from 14 March 1989. The amendments continue to have effect even though FA 1989, s. 138 repealed by TCGA 1992 (see TCGA 1992, Sch. 10, para. 8(4)(a)).

Cross references – TCGA 1992, s. 171(1): deemed no gain, no loss on transfers of capital assets within a group, as defined (s. 170) by reference to 75 per cent subsidiary relationships.

By virtue of FA 2000, Sch. 29, para. 14, in relation to disposals on or after 1 April 2000, s. 97 is affected by the removal of TCGA 1992, s. 170(2)(a) and by the removal of the words "(although resident in the United Kingdom)" within TCGA 1992, s. 170(9)(b); both removals result from FA 2000, Sch. 29, para. 1.

ALTERATIONS OF CAPITAL, ETC.

98 Effect of alterations of capital, etc.

98(1) Where there is at any time–

(a) an alteration in so much of a close company's share or loan capital as does not consist of quoted shares or quoted securities, or

(b) an alteration in any rights attaching to unquoted shares in or unquoted debentures of a close company,

the alteration shall be treated as having been made by a disposition made at that time by the participators, whether or not it would fall to be so treated apart from this section, and shall not be taken to have affected the value immediately before that time of the unquoted shares or unquoted debentures.

98(2) In this section **"alteration"** includes extinguishment.

98(3) The disposition referred to in subsection (1) above shall be taken to be one which is not a potentially exempt transfer.

History – In s. 98(1) the words "quoted shares or quoted securities" in para. (a), and "unquoted shares in or unquoted debentures of a close company" and "unquoted shares or unquoted debentures" in para. (b), were substituted by FA 1987, s. 58 and Sch. 8, para. 2, in relation to transfers of value made, and other events occurring on or after 17 March 1987.
S. 98(3) inserted by FA 1986, s. 101 and Sch. 19, para. 20, with respect to transfers of value made, and other events occurring on or after 18 March 1986.

Cross references – S. 171: alteration under s. 98 does not constitute change in value by reason of death, for purposes of valuing an estate.
FA 1986, Sch. 19, para. 40(1): transitional – transfer of value occurring before, and death or other event occurring after, 18 March 1986.

Other material – Inland Revenue letter, 25 July 1991 (not reproduced): deferred shares coming to rank equally with shares of another class is regarded as an alteration of rights within s. 98(1)(b), and assessments will be raised accordingly where this occurs in respect of deferred shares issued after 5 August 1991.

SETTLED PROPERTY

99 Transfers where participators are trustees

99(1) Subsection (1) of section 94 above shall not apply in relation to a person who is a participator in his capacity as trustee of a settlement, but–

(a) the reference in subsection (2) of that section to subsection (1) shall have effect as including a reference to subsection (2) of this section, and

(b) in relation to tax chargeable by virtue of subsection (2) of this section, sections 94(4) and 95 above shall apply with the necessary modifications.

99(2) Where any part of the value transferred by a close company's transfer of value is apportioned to a trustee of a settlement under section 94 above, then–

(a) if a qualifying interest in possession subsists in the settled property, a part of that interest corresponding to such part of the property as is of a value equal to the part so apportioned less the amount specified in subsection (3) below shall be treated for the purposes of Chapter II of Part III of this Act as having come to an end on the making of the transfer, and

(b) if no qualifying interest in possession subsists in the settled property, Chapter III of Part III of this Act shall have effect as if on the making of the transfer the trustee had made a disposition as a result of which the value of the settled property had been reduced by an amount equal to the part so apportioned less the amount specified in subsection (3) below;

and where a qualifying interest in possession subsists in part only of the settled property paragraphs (a) and (b) above shall apply with the necessary adjustments of the values and amounts referred to there.

99(3) The amount referred to in paragraphs (a) and (b) of subsection (2) above is the amount (if any) by which the value of the settled property is more than it would be apart from the company's transfer, leaving out of account the value of any rights or interests in the company.

Cross references – S. 202: persons liable for tax under s. 99(2).

100 Alterations of capital, etc. where participators are trustees

100(1) This section applies where, by virtue of section 98 above, an alteration in a close company's share or loan capital or of any rights attaching to shares in or debentures of a close company is treated as a disposition made by the participators, and–

(a) a person is a participator in his capacity as trustee of a settlement, and

(b) the disposition would, if the trustee were beneficially entitled to the settled property, be a transfer of value made by him, and

(c) at the time of the alteration an individual is beneficially entitled to an interest in possession in the whole or part of so much of the settled property as consists of unquoted shares in or unquoted securities of the close company.

100(1A) Where the interest in possession is one to which the individual became beneficially entitled on or after 22nd March 2006, this section applies only if the interest in possession is–

(a) an immediate post-death interest,

(b) a disabled person's interest, or

(c) a transitional serial interest

or falls within section 5(1B) above.

100(2) Where this section applies, such part of the individual's interest shall be treated for the purposes of Chapter II of Part III of this Act as having come to an end at the time of the alteration as corresponds to the relevant decrease of the value of the property in which the interest subsists, that is to say the decrease caused by the alteration.

History – In s. 100(1)(c), the words "unquoted shares in or unquoted securities of the close company" were substituted by FA 1987, s. 58 and Sch. 8, para. 3, in relation to transfers of value made, and other events occurring, on or after 17 March 1987.

In s. 100(1A), the words "or falls within section 5(1B) above." inserted by FA 2010, s. 53(6), with effect in relation to an interest in possession to which a person is beneficially entitled if the person becomes beneficially entitled to it on or after 9 December 2009.
S. 100(1A) inserted by FA 2006, s. 156 and Sch. 20, para. 25, with effect from 22 March 2006.

101 Companies' interests in settled property

101(1) Where a close company is entitled to an interest in possession in settled property the persons who are participators in relation to the company shall be treated for the purposes of this Act (except section 55) as being the persons entitled to that interest according to their respective rights and interests in the company.

101(1A) Where the interest in possession mentioned in subsection (1) above is one to which the company became entitled on or after 22nd March 2006 (whether or not the company was a close company when it became entitled to the interest), subsection (1) above applies in relation to the interest only if it is–

(a) an immediate post-death interest, or

(b) a transitional serial interest

or falls within section 5(1B) above.

101(1B) Subsection (1C) below applies where any of the participators mentioned in subsection (1) above ("the prior participator") disposes of rights and interests of his in the company to another person ("the later participator").

101(1C) If and so far as the later participator is a participator in the company by virtue of having any of the rights and interests disposed of, subsection (1) above is to be applied to him only as a participator in his own right (in particular, he is not to be treated by virtue of that subsection as having entitlement to the interest in possession as a result of disposal to him of entitlement that the prior participator was treated as having by virtue of that subsection, but this is without prejudice to the application of this Act in relation to the prior participator as the person making the disposal).

101(2) Where–

(a) the participators mentioned in subsection (1) above include the trustees of a settlement, and

(b) a person is beneficially entitled to an interest in possession in the whole or part of the settled property by virtue of which the trustees are participators,

that person shall be treated for the said purposes as beneficially entitled to the whole or a corresponding part of the interest to which the trustees would otherwise be treated as entitled under that subsection.

History – In s. 101(1A), the words "or falls within section 5(1B) above." inserted by FA 2010, s. 53(7), with effect in relation to an interest in possession to which a person is beneficially entitled if the person becomes beneficially entitled to it on or after 9 December 2009.
S. 101(1A) inserted by FA 2006, s. 156 and Sch. 20, para. 26, with effect from 22 March 2006.
S. 101(1B) inserted by FA 2006, s. 156 and Sch. 20, para. 26, with effect from 22 March 2006.
S. 101(1C) inserted by FA 2006, s. 156 and Sch. 20, para. 26, with effect from 22 March 2006.

Cross references – S. 55: reversionary interest acquired by beneficiary.

Statements of practice – E5: extension of reliefs under s. 52(2) (reduction where interest in possession disposed of for consideration) and s. 53(2) (no charge on termination of interest in possession if beneficiary acquires further interest) to close companies.

GENERAL

102 Interpretation

102(1) In this Part of this Act–

"close company" means a company within the meaning of the Corporation Tax Acts which is (or would be if resident in the United Kingdom) a close company for the purposes of those Acts;

"participator", in relation to any company, means any person who is (or would be if the company were resident in the United Kingdom) a participator in relation to that company within the meaning given by section 454 of the Corporation Tax Act 2010, other than a person who would be such a participator by reason only of being a loan creditor;

"qualifying interest in possession" has the meaning given by section 59 above.

102(2) References in this Part of this Act to a **person's rights and interests in a company** include references to rights and interests in the assets of the company available for distribution among the participators in the event of a winding up or in any other circumstances.

History – In s. 102(1), in the definition of "participator", the words "within the meaning given by section 454 of the Corporation Tax Act 2010" substituted for the words "for the purposes of Chapter I of Part XI of the Taxes Act 1988" by CTA 2010, s. 1177 and Sch. 1, para. 191, with effect for corporation tax *purposes* for accounting periods ending on or after 1 April 2010, and for income tax and *capital gains tax purposes for the tax year* 2010–11 and subsequent tax years.

PART V – MISCELLANEOUS RELIEFS

Chapter I – Business Property

HMRC interpretations – IRInt. 1002: availability of relief on replacement of agricultural property with business property (or vice versa).

103 Preliminary

103(1) In this Chapter references to a **transfer of value** include references to an occasion on which tax is chargeable under Chapter III of Part III of this Act (apart from section 79), and

(a) references to the **value transferred by a transfer of value** include references to the amount on which tax is then chargeable, and

(b) references to the **transferor** include references to the trustees of the settlement concerned.

103(2) For the purposes of this Chapter a company and all its subsidiaries are members of a group, and **"holding company"** and **"subsidiary"** have the meanings given by section 1159 of and Schedule 6 to the Companies Act 2006.

103(3) In this Chapter **"business"** includes a business carried on in the exercise of a profession or vocation, but does not include a business carried on otherwise than for gain.

History – In s. 103(2), the words "1159 of and Schedule 6 to" substituted for the words "736 of", and "2006" substituted for "1985", by SI 2009/1890, art. 4(1)(f), with effect from 1 October 2009.

In s. 103(2), the words "the meanings given by section 736 of" were substituted for the former words "the same meaning as in" by Companies Act 1989, s. 144(4) and Sch. 18, para. 30(1), (3), with effect from 1 November 1990.

Former reference to Companies Act 1985 substituted by Companies Consolidation (Consequential Provisions) Act 1985.

Cross references – Pt. III, Ch. III: charge on settlements without interest in possession, subject to exemption from ten-yearly charge in certain cases (s. 79).

104 The relief

104(1) Where the whole or part of the value transferred by a transfer of value is attributable to the value of any relevant business property, the whole or that part of the value transferred shall be treated as reduced–

(a) in the case of property falling within section 105(1)(a)(b) or (bb) below, by 100 per cent;

(b) in the case of other relevant business property, by 50 per cent;

but subject to the following provisions of this Chapter.

104(2) For the purposes of this section, the value transferred by a transfer of value shall be calculated as a value on which no tax is chargeable.

History – In s. 104(1), the words "(b) or (bb)" were substituted by FA 1987, s. 58 and Sch. 8, para. 4, in relation to transfers of value made, and other events occurring, on or after 17 March 1987.

In s. 104(1)(a), (b), "100 per cent" and "50 per cent" substituted for "50 per cent" and "30 per cent" respectively by F(No. 2)A 1992, s. 73 and Sch. 14, para. 1, in relation to transfers of value made, and other events occurring, on or after 10 March 1992, subject to the transitional provisions in F(No. 2)A 1992, Sch. 14, para. 9.

Cross references – S. 29A(4): s. 104 to be disregarded in determining the value of an exempt beneficiary's estate for the purposes of s. 29A(2).

S. 39A: attribution of value transferred to specific gifts and gifts of residue where value transferred attributable to relevant business property.

105 Relevant business property

105(1) Subject to the following provisions of this section and to sections 106, 108, 112(3) and 113 below, in this Chapter **"relevant business property"** means, in relation to any transfer of value,–

(a) property consisting of a business or interest in a business;

(b) securities of a company which are unquoted and which (either by themselves or together with other such securities owned by the transferor and any unquoted shares so owned) gave the transferor control of the company immediately before the transfer;

(bb) any unquoted shares in a company;

(c) [repealed by FA 1996, s. 184(2)(c), s. 205 and Sch. 41, Pt. VI;]

(cc) shares in or securities of a company which are quoted and which (either by themselves or together with other such shares or securities owned by the transferor) gave the transferor control of the company immediately before the transfer;

(d) any land or building, machinery or plant which, immediately before the transfer, was used wholly or mainly for the purposes of a business carried on by a company of which the transferor then had control or by a partnership of which he then was a partner; and

(e) any land or building, machinery or plant which, immediately before the transfer, was used wholly or mainly for the purposes of a business carried on by the transferor and was settled property in which he was then beneficially entitled to an interest in possession.

105(1ZA) In subsection (1) above **"quoted"**, in relation to any shares or securities, means listed on a recognised stock exchange and **"unquoted"**, in relation to any shares or securities, means not so listed.

105(1A), (1B) [Repealed by FA 1996, s. 205 and Sch. 41, Pt. VI.]

105(2) Shares in or securities of a company do not fall within subsection (1)(cc) above if–

(a) they would not have been sufficient, without other property, to give the transferor control of the company immediately before the transfer, and

(b) their value is taken by virtue of section 176 below to be less than the value previously determined.

105(2A) [Repealed by FA 1996, s. 205 and Sch. 41, Pt. VI.]

105(3) A business or interest in a business, or shares in or securities of a company, are not relevant business property if the business or, as the case may be, the business carried on by the company consists wholly or mainly of one or more of the following, that is to say, dealing in securities, stocks or shares, land or buildings or making or holding investments.

105(4) Subsection (3) above–

(a) does not apply to any property if the business concerned is wholly that of a market maker or is that of a discount house and (in either case) is carried on in the United Kingdom, and

(b) does not apply to shares in or securities of a company if the business of the company consists wholly or mainly in being a holding company of one or more companies whose business does not fall within that subsection.

105(4A) Subsection (3) above also does not apply to any property if the business concerned is of a description set out in regulations under section 106(5) of the Finance Act 1986.

105(5) Shares in or securities of a company are not relevant business property in relation to a transfer of value if at the time of the transfer a winding-up order has been made in respect of the company or the company has passed a resolution for voluntary winding-up or is otherwise in process of liquidation, unless the business of the company is to continue to be carried on after a reconstruction or amalgamation and the reconstruction or amalgamation either is the purpose of the winding-up or liquidation or takes place not later than one year after the transfer of value.

105(6) Land, a building, machinery or plant owned by the transferor and used wholly or mainly for the purposes of a business carried on as mentioned in subsection (1)(d) or (e) above is not relevant business property in relation to a transfer of value, unless the business or the transferor's interest in it is, or shares or securities of the company carrying on the business immediately before the transfer are, relevant business property in relation to the transfer.

105(7) In this section **"market maker"** means a person who–

(a) holds himself out at all normal times in compliance with the rules of The Stock Exchange as willing to buy and sell securities, stocks or shares at a price specified by him, and

(b) is recognised as doing so by the Council of The Stock Exchange.

History – In the opening words to s. 105(1), reference to s. 109A repealed by FA 1996, s. 205 and Sch. 41, Pt. VI, with effect in relation to any transfer of value on or after 6 April 1996, and, for the purposes of any charge to tax by reason of an event occurring on or after 6 April 1996, with effect in relation to transfers of value before that date.

In s. 105(1), former reference to s. 109A inserted and para. (bb) and (c) substituted by FA 1987, s. 58 and Sch. 8, para. 5(1), (2), with effect in relation to transfers of value made, and other events occurring, on or after 17 March 1987.

In s. 105(1)(b), opening words "shares in or" omitted, and the words "securities owned by … shares so owned" substituted by FA 1996, s. 184(2)(a), 205 and Sch. 41, Pt. VI, with effect in relation to any transfer of value on or after 6 April 1996, and, for the purposes of any charge to tax by reason of an event occurring on or after 6 April 1996, with effect in relation to transfers of value before that date.

In s. 105(1)(b) the words "are unquoted and which", s. 105(1)(cc), s. 105(1ZA), and the reference to subsection (1)(cc) in s. 105(2), inserted by F(No. 2)A 1992, s. 73 and Sch. 14, para. 2, in relation to transfers of value made, and other events occurring, on or after 10 March 1992, but subject to the transitional provisions in Sch. 14, para. 9.

S. 105(1)(bb) substituted by FA 1996, s. 184(2)(b), with effect in relation to any transfer of value on or after 6 April 1996, and, for the purposes of any charge to tax by reason of an event occurring on or after 6 April 1996, with effect in relation to transfers of value before that date.

S. 105(1)(c) repealed by FA 1996, s. 184(2)(c), 205 and Sch. 41, Pt. VI, with effect in relation to any transfer of value on or after 6 April 1996, and, for the purposes of any charge to tax by reason of an event occurring on or after 6 April 1996, with effect in relation to transfers of value before that date.

In s. 105(1ZA), the word "listed" substituted in each place by FA 1996, s. 199 and Sch. 38, para. 2, with effect in relation to transfers of value on or after 1 April 1996 and, for the purposes of any charge to tax by reason of an event occurring on or after 1 April 1996, with effect in relation to transfers of value before that date.

S. 105(1A), (1B) and (2A) repealed by FA 1996, s. 205 and Sch. 41, Pt. VI, with effect in relation to any transfer of value on or after 6 April 1996, and, for the purposes of any charge to tax by reason of an event occurring on or after 6 April 1996, with effect in relation to transfers of value before that date.

S. 105(1A), (1B) inserted by FA 1987, s. 58 and Sch. 8, para. 5(3).

In s. 105(2) reference to s. 105(1)(b) repealed by FA 1996, s. 205 and Sch. 41, Pt. VI, with effect in relation to any transfer of value on or after6 April 1996, and, for the purposes of any charge to tax by reason of an event occurring on or after 6 April 1996, with effect in relation to transfers of value before that date.

S. 105(2A) inserted by FA 1987, s. 58 and Sch. 8, para. 5(4), with effect in relation to transfers of value made, and other events occurring, on or after 17 March 1987.

S. 105(4)(a) substituted, and s. 105(7) inserted, by FA 1986, s. 106(1), (2), in relation to transfers of value made, and other events occurring, on or after 27 October 1986 (the day of the Stock Exchange reforms).

S. 105(4A) inserted by SI 2012/2903, reg. 4, with effect from 31 December 2012.

Cross references – S. 176: sales of related property etc.

S. 269: interpretation of "control".
FA 1986, s. 106(4) (as amended by SI 2001/3629, art. 11 which came into force on 1 December 2001), (5): power of Board to make regulations on interpretation, and amending s. 105 in certain respects.
FA 1986, Sch. 20, para. 8(1A)(a): gift subject to a reservation including shares which qualify for 100 per cent relief.
SI 1992/3181: applicable from 23 March 1992, s. 105(7) is extended to include recognised business traders on LIFFE.
SI 2012/2903, reg. 6: description of a business for the purposes of s. 105(4A).

HMRC interpretations – IRInt. 202: HMRC view that where a bookmaker's pitch has been acquired by inheritance after the October 1998 changes to the allocation rules, it forms part of the deceased's estate and as such qualifies for business property relief if the statutory conditions are satisfied.

Other material – Taxline 1996/112 (not reproduced): Revenue confirmation that for the purposes of inheritance tax "recognised stock exchange" includes all those defined as such in ICTA 1988, s. 841 and additionally those in India, Israel, Kenya, Malaysia, Pakistan and Zimbabwe. Recognition for IHT purposes depends on whether the law of the country where it is situated recognises the exchange or market in question and whether it provides an adequate trading floor (although this requirement is likely to be replaced as trading floors are almost obsolete).
Taxline 1995/69 (not reproduced): relief available where there are intermediate holding companies.
Taxline 1994/134 (not reproduced): s. 105(3), (4)(b) do not operate to extend relief to dual holding company structure (e.g. where A owns B which owns trading company C).

106 Minimum period of ownership

106 Property is not relevant business property in relation to a transfer of value unless it was owned by the transferor throughout the two years immediately preceding the transfer.

Cross references – FA 1986, Sch. 20, para. 8(2): qualifying period of ownership where gift is subject to a reservation.

Hansard – Official Report Standing Committee E, 24 June 1976, col. 1,275–1,276 (not reproduced): Treasury statement indicates "ownership" in the context of s. 103–114 may be either legal or beneficial, so that either is sufficient on its own.

107 Replacements

107(1) Property shall be treated as satisfying the condition in section 106 above if–

(a) it replaced other property and it, that other property and any property directly or indirectly replaced by that other property were owned by the transferor for periods which together comprised at least two years falling within the five years immediately preceding the transfer of value, and

(b) any other property concerned was such that, had the transfer of value been made immediately before it was replaced, it would (apart from section 106) have been relevant business property in relation to the transfer.

107(2) In a case falling within subsection (1) above relief under this Chapter shall not exceed what it would have been had the replacement or any one or more of the replacements not been made.

107(3) For the purposes of subsection (2) above changes resulting from the formation, alteration or dissolution of a partnership, or from the acquisition of a business by a company controlled by the former owner of the business, shall be disregarded.

107(4) Without prejudice to subsection (1) above, where any shares falling within section 105(1)(bb) above which are owned by the transferor immediately before the transfer would under any of the provisions of sections 126 to 136 of the 1992 Act be identified with other shares previously owned by him his period of ownership of the first-mentioned shares shall be treated for the purposes of section 106 above as including his period of ownership of the other shares.

History – In s. 107(4) the words "Without prejudice … section 105(1)(bb) above which are" substituted for the previous words "Subsection (1) above does not apply to shares falling within section 105(1) or (c) above; but where such shares", by FA 1996, s. 184(3), and the words "and section 109A below" repealed by FA 1996, s. 205 and Sch. 41, Pt. VI, with effect in relation to any transfer of value on or after 6 April 1996 and, for the purposes of any charge to tax by reason of an event occurring on or after 6 April 1996, in relation to transfers of value before that date.
S. 107(4) previously amended by FA 1987, s. 58 and Sch. 8, para. 6, in relation to transfers of value made, and other events occurring, on or after 17 March 1987.
Reference to the 1992 Act substituted by TCGA 1992, s. 290 and Sch. 10, para. 8(5).

Cross references – TCGA 1992, s. 126–136: reorganisation of share capital, conversion of securities, exchange of securities and reconstruction involving the issue of securities etc.

108 Successions

108 For the purposes of sections 106 and 107 above, where the transferor became entitled to any property on the death of another person–

(a) he shall be deemed to have owned it from the date of the death, and

(b) if that other person was his spouse or civil partner he shall also be deemed to have owned it for any period during which the spouse or civil partner owned it.

History – In s. 108(b) the words "or civil partner" inserted twice by SI 2005/3229, reg. 19, with effect from 5 December 2005.

109 Successive transfers

109(1) Where–

IHT Statutes

(a) the whole or part of the value transferred by a transfer of value (in this section referred to as the earlier transfer) was eligible for relief under this Chapter (or would have been so eligible if such relief had been capable of being given in respect of transfers of value made at that time), and

(b) the whole or part of the property which, in relation to the earlier transfer, was relevant business property became, through the earlier transfer, the property of the person or of the spouse or civil partner of the person who is the transferor in relation to a subsequent transfer of value, and

(c) that property or part, or any property directly or indirectly replacing it, would (apart from section 106 above) have been relevant business property in relation to the subsequent transfer of value, and

(d) either the earlier transfer was, or the subsequent transfer of value is, a transfer made on the death of the transferor,

the property which would have been relevant business property but for section 106 above shall be relevant business property notwithstanding that section.

109(2) Where the property which, by virtue of subsection (1) above, is relevant business property replaced the property or part referred to in paragraph (c) of that subsection, relief under this Chapter shall not exceed what it would have been had the replacement or any one or more of the replacements not been made, but section 107(3) above shall apply with the necessary modifications for the purposes of this subsection.

109(3) Where, under the earlier transfer, the amount of the value transferred which was attributable to the property or part referred to in subsection (1)(c) above was part only of its value, a like part only of the value which (apart from this subsection) would fall to be reduced under this Chapter by virtue of this section shall be so reduced.

History – In s. 109(1)(b) the words "or civil partner" inserted by SI 2005/3229, reg. 20, with effect from 5 December 2005.

109A Additional requirement in case of minority shareholdings

109A [Repealed by FA 1996, s. 205 and Sch. 41, Pt. VI.]

History – S. 109A repealed by FA 1996, s. 205 and Sch. 41, Pt. VI, with effect in relation to any transfer of value on or after 6 April 1996 and, for the purposes of any charge to tax by reason of an event occurring on or after 6 April 1996, in relation to transfers of value before that date.

110 Value of business

110 For the purposes of this Chapter–

(a) the value of a business or of an interest in a business shall be taken to be its net value;

(b) the net value of a business is the value of the assets used in the business (including goodwill) reduced by the aggregate amount of any liabilities incurred for the purposes of the business;

(c) in ascertaining the net value of an interest in a business, no regard shall be had to assets or liabilities other than those by reference to which the net value of the entire business would fall to be ascertained.

111 Value of certain shares and securities

111 Where a company is a member of a group and the business of any other company which is a member of the group falls within section 105(3) above, then, unless either–

(a) that business also falls within section 105(4), or

(b) that business consists wholly or mainly in the holding of land or buildings wholly or mainly occupied by members of the group whose business either does not fall within section 105(3) or falls within both section 105(3) and section 105(4),

the value of shares in or securities of the company shall be taken for the purposes of this Chapter to be what it would be if that other company were not a member of the group.

112 Exclusion of value of excepted assets

112(1) In determining for the purposes of this Chapter what part of the value transferred by a transfer of value is attributable to the value of any relevant business property so much of the last-mentioned value as is attributable to any excepted assets within the meaning of subsection (2) below shall be left out of account.

112(2) An asset is an **excepted asset** in relation to any relevant business property if it was neither–

(a) used wholly or mainly for the purposes of the business concerned throughout the whole or the last two years of the relevant period defined in subsection (5) below, nor

(b) required at the time of the transfer for future use for those purposes;

but where the business concerned is carried on by a company which is a member of a group, the use of an asset for the purposes of a business carried on by another company which at the time of the use and immediately before the transfer was also a member of that group shall be treated as use for the purposes of the business concerned, unless that other company's membership of the group falls to be disregarded under section 111 above.

112(3) Subsection (2) above does not apply in relation to an asset which is relevant business property by virtue only of section 105(1)(d) above, and an asset is not relevant business property by virtue only of that provision unless either–

(a) it was used as mentioned in that provision throughout the two years immediately preceding the transfer of value, or

(b) it replaced another asset so used and it and the other asset and any asset directly or indirectly replaced by that other asset were so used for periods which together comprised at least two years falling within the five years immediately preceding the transfer of value;

but in a case where section 109 above applies this condition shall be treated as satisfied if the asset (or it and the asset or assets replaced by it) was or were so used throughout the period between the earlier and the subsequent transfer mentioned in that section (or throughout the part of that period during which it or they were owned by the transferor or the transferor's spouse or civil partner).

112(4) Where part but not the whole of any land or building is used exclusively for the purposes of any business and the land or building would, but for this subsection, be an excepted asset, or, as the case may be, prevented by subsection (3) above from being relevant business property, the part so used and the remainder shall for the purposes of this section be treated as separate assets, and the value of the part so used shall (if it would otherwise be less) be taken to be such proportion of the value of the whole as may be just.

112(5) For the purposes of this section **the relevant period**, in relation to any asset, is the period immediately preceding the transfer of value during which the asset (or, if the relevant business property is an interest in a business, a corresponding interest in the asset) was owned by the transferor or, if the business concerned is that of a company, was owned by that company or any other company which immediately before the transfer of value was a member of the same group.

112(6) For the purposes of this section an asset shall be deemed not to have been used wholly or mainly for the purposes of the business concerned at any time when it was used wholly or mainly for the personal benefit of the transferor or of a person connected with him.

History – In s. 112(3) the words "or civil partner" inserted by SI 2005/3229, reg. 21, with effect from 5 December 2005.

Other material – Taxline 1995/71 (not reproduced): companies and partnerships carrying on both trading and investment activities. Taxline 1993/45 (not reproduced): deathbed planning opportunities that can arise through transferring cash or assets to a company or including them in business assets of a business so as to qualify for business property relief.

113 Contracts for sale

113 Where any property would be relevant business property in relation to a transfer of value but a binding contract for its sale has been entered into at the time of the transfer, it is not relevant business property in relation to the transfer unless–

(a) the property is a business or interest in a business and the sale is to a company which is to carry on the business and is made in consideration wholly or mainly of shares in or securities of that company, or

(b) the property is shares in or securities of a company and the sale is made for the purpose of reconstruction or amalgamation.

Statements of practice – SP 12/80: effect of partnership etc. "buy and sell" agreements.

Other material – Revenue letter to Institute of Taxation, 11 May 1994: existence of accruer arrangement on partnership agreement does not necessarily jeopardise business property relief by amounting to a binding contract, but much will depend on the construction of the particular document. See also Law Society's *Gazette*, 4 September 1996 (also considers options to purchase share of deceased partner).

113A Transfers within seven years before death of transferor

113A(1) Where any part of the value transferred by a potentially exempt transfer which proves to be a chargeable transfer would (apart from this section) be reduced in accordance with the preceding provisions of this Chapter, it shall not be so reduced unless the conditions in subsection (3) below are satisfied.

113A(2) Where–

(a) any part of the value transferred by any chargeable transfer, other than a potentially exempt transfer, is reduced in accordance with the preceding provisions of this Chapter, and

(b) the transfer is made within seven years of the death of the transferor,

then, unless the conditions in subsection (3) below are satisfied, the additional tax chargeable by reason of the death shall be calculated as if the value transferred had not been so reduced.

IHT Statutes

113A(3) The conditions referred to in subsections (1) and (2) above are–

(a) that the original property was owned by the transferee throughout the period beginning with the date of the chargeable transfer and ending with the death of the transferor; and

(b) except to the extent that the original property consists of shares or securities to which subsection (3A) below applies, that, in relation to a notional transfer of value made by the transferee immediately before the death, the original property would (apart from section 106 above) be relevant business property.

113A(3A) This subsection applies to shares or securities–

(a) which were quoted at the time of the chargeable transfer referred to in subsection (1) or subsection (2) above; or

(b) which fell within paragraph (b) or (bb) of section 105(1) above in relation to that transfer and were unquoted throughout the period referred to in subsection (3)(a) above.

113A(3B) In subsection (3A) above **"quoted"**, in relation to any shares or securities, means listed on a recognised stock exchange and **"unquoted"**, in relation to any shares or securities, means not so listed.

113A(4) If the transferee has died before the transferor, the reference in subsection (3) above to the death of the transferor shall have effect as a reference to the death of the transferee.

113A(5) If the conditions in subsection (3) above are satisfied only with respect to part of the original property, then,–

(a) in a case falling within subsection (1) above, only a proportionate part of so much of the value transferred as is attributable to the original property shall be reduced in accordance with the preceding provisions of this Chapter, and

(b) in a case falling within subsection (2) above, the additional tax shall be calculated as if only a proportionate part of so much of the value transferred as was attributable to the original property had been so reduced.

113A(6) Where any shares owned by the transferee immediately before the death in question–

(a) would under any of the provisions of sections 126 to 136 of the 1992 Act be identified with the original property (or part of it), or

(b) were issued to him in consideration of the transfer of a business or interest in a business consisting of the original property (or part of it),

they shall be treated for the purposes of this section as if they were the original property (or that part of it).

113A(7) This section has effect subject to section 113B below.

113A(7A) The provisions of this Chapter for the reduction of value transferred shall be disregarded in any determination for the purposes of this section of whether there is a potentially exempt or chargeable transfer in any case.

113A(8) In this section–

"the original property" means the property which was relevant business property in relation to the chargeable transfer referred to in subsection (1) or subsection (2) above; and

"the transferee" means the person whose property the original property became on that chargeable transfer or, where on the transfer the original property became or remained settled property in which no qualifying interest in possession (within the meaning of Chapter III of Part III of this Act) subsists, the trustees of the settlement.

History – In s. 113A(3), the words "except … applies" in para. (b) were inserted by FA 1987, s. 58 and Sch. 8, para. 8(1), in relation to transfers of value made, and other events occurring, on or after 17 March 1987.

In s. 113A(3A) reference to s. 105(1)(bb) inserted by FA 1996, s. 184(4), with effect in relation to any transfer of value on or after 6 April 1996 and, for the purposes of any charge to tax by reason of an event occurring on or after 6 April 1996, in relation to transfers of value before that date.

S. 113A(3A) inserted by FA 1987, s. 58 and Sch. 8, para. 8(2), in relation to transfers of value made, and other events occurring, on or after 17 March 1987.

In s. 113A(3B), the word "listed" substituted in both places for the previous word "quoted", by FA 1996, s. 199 and Sch. 38, para. 2, with effect in relation to transfers of value on or after 1 April 1996 and, for the purposes of any charge to tax by reason of an event occurring on or after 1 April 1996, in relation to transfers of value before that date.

S. 113A(3B) inserted by F(No. 2)A 1992, s. 73 and Sch. 14, para. 3, in relation to transfers of value made, and other events occurring, on or after 10 March 1992, but subject to the transitional provisions in Sch. 14, para. 9.

In s. 113A(6), reference to the 1992 Act substituted by TCGA 1992, s. 290 and Sch. 10, para. 8(5).

S. 113A(7A) inserted by FA 1996, s. 184(5), with effect in relation to any transfer of value on or after 28 November 1995.

S. 113A inserted by FA 1986, s. 101 and Sch. 19, para. 21, with respect to transfers of value made, and other events occurring, on or after 18 March 1986.

Cross references – *FA 1986, Sch. 19*, para. 40(1): transitional – transfer of value occurring before, and death or other events occurring after, 18 March 1986.

FA 1987, s. 58(3): determination of relevant business property under s. 113A(3) when PET pre-dates, and death of transferor post-dates, 17 March 1987.

TCGA 1992, s. 126–136: reorganisation of share capital, conversion of securities, exchange of securities and reconstruction involving the issue of securities etc.

HMRC interpretations – IRInt. 1002: Revenue view that where donee of a PET of a non-agricultural business sells it and replaces it with a farming business, the latter may qualify as relevant business property.

Other material – ICAEW Technical Release TR 772 (not reproduced): Revenue do not consider it an anomaly that under s. 113A relief would be lost where beneficiaries under an accumulation and maintenance trust obtain an interest in possession, or where, for example, an interest in possession is given them at age 25 in the expectation that the trustees will appoint capital to them later on.
Taxline 1993/68 (not reproduced): prospective donor may be able to retain full business property relief even if the property is likely to be sold in the near future or the donor fails to survive seven years from date of gift, through transferring assets qualifying for relief into a discretionary trust (with hold-over relief claimed if necessary).

113B Application of section 113A to replacement property

113B(1) Subject to subsection (2) below, this section applies where–

(a) the transferee has disposed of all or part of the original property before the death of the transferor; and

(b) the whole of the consideration received by him for the disposal has been applied by him in acquiring other property (in this section referred to as **"the replacement property"**).

113B(2) This section does not apply unless–

(a) the replacement property is acquired, or a binding contract for its acquisition is entered into, within the allowed period after the disposal of the original property (or, as the case may be, the part concerned); and

(b) the disposal and acquisition are both made in transactions at arm's length or on terms such as might be expected to be included in a transaction at arm's length.

113B(3) Where this section applies, the conditions in section 113A(3) above shall be taken to be satisfied in relation to the original property (or, as the case may be, the part concerned) if–

(a) the replacement property is owned by the transferee immediately before the death of the transferor; and

(b) throughout the period beginning with the date of the chargeable transfer and ending with the death (disregarding any period between the disposal and acquisition) either the original property or the replacement property was owned by the transferee; and

(c) in relation to a notional transfer of value made by the transferee immediately before the death, the replacement property would (apart from section 106 above) be relevant business property.

113B(4) If the transferee has died before the transferor, any reference in subsections (1) to (3) above to the death of the transferor shall have effect as a reference to the death of the transferee.

113B(5) In any case where–

(a) all or part of the original property has been disposed of before the death of the transferor or is excluded by section 113 above from being relevant business property in relation to the notional transfer of value referred to in section 113A(3)(b) above, and

(b) the replacement property is acquired, or a binding contract for its acquisition is entered into, after the death of the transferor but within the allowed period after the disposal of the original property or part, and

(c) the transferor dies before the transferee,

subsection (3) above shall have effect with the omission of paragraph (a), and as if any reference to a time immediately before the death of the transferor or to the death were a reference to the time when the replacement property is acquired.

113B(6) Section 113A(6) above shall have effect in relation to the replacement property as it has effect in relation to the original property.

113B(7) Where a binding contract for the disposal of any property is entered into at any time before the disposal of the property, the disposal shall be regarded for the purposes of subsections (2)(a) and (5)(b) above as taking place at that time.

113B(8) In this section **"the original property"** and **"the transferee"** have the same meaning as in section 113A above and **"allowed period"** means the period of three years or such longer period as the Board may allow.

History – In s. 113B(2)(a) and (5)(b), the words "the allowed period" substituted for "twelve months" by FA 1994, 247(1)(a) in relation to transfers of value made, and other events occurring on or after 30 November 1993.
In s. 113B(8), the words "and "allowed period" … Board may allow" inserted by FA 1994, 247(1)(b), in relation to transfers of value made, and other events occurring, on or after 30 November 1993.
S. 113B inserted by FA 1986, s. 101 and Sch. 19, para. 21 with respect to transfers of value made, and other events occurring, on or after 18 March 1986.

Cross references – S. 227: payment of tax by instalments.
FA 1986, Sch. 19, para. 40(1): transitional – transfer of value occurring before, and death or other event occurring after, 18 March 1986.
FA 1987, s. 58(3): determination of relevant business property under s. 113B(3) when PET pre-dates, and death of transferor post-dates, 17 March 1987.

HMRC interpretations – IRInt. 1002: where donee of a PET of a non-agricultural business sells it and replaces it with a farming business, the latter can be "relevant business property" for the purposes of s. 113B(3)(c) if the appropriate requirements are met.

Other material – ICAEW Technical Release TR 772: HMRC regard fallow land as agricultural property.

114 Avoidance of double relief

114(1) Where any part of the value transferred by a transfer of value is reduced under Chapter II of this Part of this Act by reference to the agricultural value of any property, or would be so reduced but for section 121(3), such part of the value transferred as is or would be so reduced under that Chapter shall not be reduced under this Chapter.

114(2) Where the value transferred by a transfer of value is reduced under section 129 below by reference to the tax chargeable on the disposal of any trees or underwood, the value to be reduced under section 104 above shall be the value as reduced under section 129 (but subject to section 104(2) above).

Cross references – S. 121(3): reduction for agricultural property relief restricted to part of value transferred where there are successive transfers and subsequent transfer reflects part of the earlier value.
S. 129: credit for tax charged in calculating value transferred in respect of certain trees or underwood.

HMRC interpretations – IRInt. 1002: replacement of relevant business property with agricultural property, or vice versa, following a PET.

Hansard – See s. 105.

Chapter II – Agricultural Property

Cross references – FA 1995, s. 154: for the purposes of IHTA 1984, short rotation coppice is regarded as agriculture in relation to transfers of value and other events occurring on or after 6 April 1995.

HMRC interpretations – IRInt. 1002: availability of relief (1) where agricultural property is replaced with business property (or vice versa) and (2) on donor death where donee of PET of agricultural property has sold it and reinvested proceeds in non-agricultural property (or vice versa).

115 Preliminary

115(1) In this Chapter references to a **transfer of value** include references to an occasion on which tax is chargeable under Chapter III of Part III of this Act (apart from section 79) and–

(a) references to **the value transferred** by a transfer of value include references to the amount on which tax is then chargeable, and

(b) references to **the transferor** include references to the trustees of the settlement concerned.

115(2) In this Chapter **"agricultural property"** means agricultural land or pasture and includes woodland and any building used in connection with the intensive rearing of livestock or fish if the woodland or building is occupied with agricultural land or pasture and the occupation is ancillary to that of the agricultural land or pasture; and also includes such cottages, farm buildings and farmhouses, together with the land occupied with them, as are of a character appropriate to the property.

115(3) For the purposes of this Chapter the **agricultural value** of any agricultural property shall be taken to be the value which would be the value of the property if the property were subject to a perpetual covenant prohibiting its use otherwise than as agricultural property (or, in the case of property outside the United Kingdom, the Channel Islands and the Isle of Man, if it were subject to provisions equivalent in effect to such a covenant).

115(4) For the purposes of this Chapter the breeding and rearing of horses on a stud farm and the grazing of horses in connection with those activities shall be taken to be agriculture and any buildings used in connection with those activities to be farm buildings.

115(5) This Chapter applies to agricultural property only if it is in–

(a) the United Kingdom, the Channel Islands or the Isle of Man, or

(b) a state, other than the United Kingdom, which is an EEA state (within the meaning given by Schedule 1 to the Interpretation Act 1978) at the time of the transfer of value in question.

History – In s. 115(3) the words "(or, in the case of property outside the United Kingdom, the Channel Islands and the Isle of Man, if it were subject to provisions equivalent in effect to such a covenant)." inserted by FA 2009, s. 122(2), with effect in relation to transfers of value where the tax payable but for s. 122 (or, in the case of tax payable by instalments, the last instalment of the tax) would have been due on or after 22 April 2009 or was paid or due on or after 23 April 2003 (but see also FA 2009, s. 122(8) and (9)).
S. 115(5) substituted by FA 2009, s. 122(3), with effect in relation to transfers of value where the tax payable but for s. 122 (or, in the case of tax payable by instalments, the last instalment of the tax) would have been due on or after 22 April 2009 or was paid or due on or after 23 April 2003 (but see also FA 2009, s. 122(8) and (9)). Former s. 115(5) read as follows:
"115(5) This Chapter applies to agricultural property only if it is in the United Kingdom, the Channel Islands or the Isle of Man."

Cross references – Pt. III, Ch. III: charge as settlements without interest in possession, subject to exemption from ten-yearly charge *in certain cases (s. 79).*
TCGA 1992, s. 165 and Sch. 7, para. 1, 3, 5, 6: relief from tax on chargeable gains for gifts of agricultural property.

Notes – FA 1995, s. 154(2), (5): land used for short rotation coppice treated as agricultural land, and related buildings regarded as farm buildings, in relation to transfers of value or other events occurring on or after 6 April 1995.

116 The relief

116(1) Where the whole or part of the value transferred by a transfer of value is attributable to the agricultural value of agricultural property, the whole or that part of the value transferred shall be treated as reduced by the appropriate percentage, but subject to the following provisions of this Chapter.

116(2) The **appropriate percentage** is 100 per cent if–

(a) the interest of the transferor in the property immediately before the transfer carries the right to vacant possession or the right to obtain it within the next twelve months, or

(b) the transferor has been beneficially entitled to that interest since before 10th March 1981 and the conditions set out in subsection (3) below are satisfied; or

(c) the interest of the transferor in the property immediately before the transfer does not carry either of the rights mentioned in paragraph (a) above because the property is let on a tenancy beginning on or after 1st September 1995;

and, subject to subsection (4) below, it is 50 per cent in any other case.

116(2A) [Repealed by FA 1996, s. 185(3), 205 and Sch. 41, Pt. VI.]

116(3) The conditions referred to in subsection (2)(b) above are–

(a) that if the transferor had disposed of his interest by a transfer of value immediately before 10th March 1981 and duly made a claim under paragraph 1 of Schedule 8 to the Finance Act 1975, the value transferred would have been computed in accordance with paragraph 2 of that Schedule and relief would not have been limited by paragraph 5 of that Schedule (restriction to £250,000 or one thousand acres); and

(b) that the transferor's interest did not at any time during the period beginning with 10th March 1981 and ending with the date of the transfer carry a right mentioned in subsection (2)(a) above, and did not fail to do so by reason of any act or deliberate omission of the transferor during that period.

116(4) Where the appropriate percentage would be 100 per cent but for a limitation on relief that would have been imposed (as mentioned in subsection (3)(a) above) by paragraph 5 of Schedule 8 to the Finance Act 1975, the appropriate percentage shall be 100 per cent in relation to a part of the value transferred equal to the amount which would have attracted relief under that Schedule and 50 per cent in relation to the remainder.

116(5) In determining for the purposes of subsections (3)(a) and (4) above whether or to what extent relief under Schedule 8 to the Finance Act 1975 would have been limited by paragraph 5 of that Schedule, that paragraph shall be construed as if references to relief given under that Schedule in respect of previous chargeable transfers included references to–

(a) relief given under this Chapter by virtue of subsection (2)(b) or (4) above, and

(b) relief given under Schedule 14 to the Finance Act 1981 by virtue of paragraph 2(2)(b) or (4) of that Schedule,

in respect of previous chargeable transfers made on or after 10th March 1981.

116(5A) Where, in consequence of the death on or after 1st September 1995 of the tenant or, as the case may be, the last surviving tenant of any property, the tenancy–

(a) becomes vested in a person, as a result of his being a person beneficially entitled under the deceased tenant's will or other testamentary writing or on his intestacy, and

(b) is or becomes binding on the landlord and that person as landlord and tenant respectively,

subsection (2)(c) above shall have effect as if the tenancy so vested had been a tenancy beginning on the date of the death.

116(5B) Where in consequence of the death on or after 1st September 1995 of the tenant or, as the case may be, the last surviving tenant of any property, a tenancy of the property or of any property comprising the whole or part of it–

(a) is obtained by a person under or by virtue of an enactment, or

(b) is granted to a person in circumstances such that he is already entitled under or by virtue of an enactment to obtain such a tenancy, but one which takes effect on a later date, or

(c) is granted to a person who is or has become the only or only remaining applicant, or the only or only remaining person eligible to apply, under a particular enactment for such a tenancy in the particular case,

subsection (2)(c) above shall have effect as if the tenancy so obtained or granted had been a tenancy beginning on the date of the death.

116(5C) Subsection (5B) above does not apply in relation to property situate in Scotland.

116(5D) If, in a case where the transferor dies on or after 1st September 1995,–

(a) the tenant of any property has, before the death, given notice of intention to retire in favour of a new tenant, and

(b) the tenant's retirement in favour of the new tenant takes place after the death but not more than thirty months after the giving of the notice,

subsection (2)(c) above shall have effect as if the tenancy granted or assigned to the new tenant had been a tenancy beginning immediately before the transfer of value which the transferor is treated by section 4(1) above as making immediately before his death.

116(5E) In subsection (5D) above and this subsection–

"the new tenant" means–

(a) the person or persons identified in a notice of intention to retire in favour of a new tenant as the person or persons who it is desired should become the tenant of the property to which that notice relates; or

(b) the survivor or survivors of the persons so identified, whether alone or with any other person or persons;

"notice of intention to retire in favour of a new tenant" means, in the case of any property, a notice or other written intimation given to the landlord by the tenant, or (in the case of a joint tenancy or tenancy in common) all of the tenants, of the property indicating, in whatever terms, his or their wish that one or more persons identified in the notice or intimation should become the tenant of the property;

"the retiring tenant's tenancy" means the tenancy of the person or persons giving the notice of intention to retire in favour of a new tenant;

"the tenant's retirement in favour of the new tenant" means–

(a) the assignment, or (in Scotland) assignation, of the retiring tenant's tenancy to the new tenant in circumstances such that the tenancy is or becomes binding on the landlord and the new tenant as landlord and tenant respectively; or

(b) the grant of a tenancy of the property which is the subject of the retiring tenant's tenancy, or of any property comprising the whole or part of that property, to the new tenant and the acceptance of that tenancy by him;

and, except in Scotland, **"grant"** and **"acceptance"** in paragraph (b) above respectively include the deemed grant, and the deemed acceptance, of a tenancy under or by virtue of any enactment.

116(6) For the purposes of this Chapter the interest of one of two or more joint tenants or tenants in common (or, in Scotland, joint owners or owners in common) shall be taken to carry a right referred to in subsection (2)(a) above if the interests of all of them together carry that right.

116(7) For the purposes of this section, the value transferred by a transfer of value shall be calculated as a value on which no tax is chargeable.

116(8) In its application to property outside the United Kingdom, the Channel Islands and the Isle of Man, this section has effect as if any reference to a right or obligation under the law of any part of the United Kingdom were a reference to an equivalent right or obligation under the law governing dispositions of that property.

History – In s. 116(2), (4), "100 per cent" and "50 per cent" substituted for "50 per cent" and "30 per cent" respectively in each place by F(No. 2)A 1992, s. 73 and Sch. 14, para. 4, in relation to transfers of value made, and other events occurring, on or after 10 March 1992, but subject to the transitional provisions in Sch. 14, para. 9.

In s. 116(2) the word "either", which appeared after "100 per cent," omitted by FA 1995, s. 155(1), 162 and Sch. 29, Pt. XI, and the word "or" at the end of para. (b), and para. (c), inserted, by FA 1995, s. 155(1), in relation to transfers of value made, and other events occurring, on or after 1 September 1995.

S. 116(2A) repealed by FA 1996, s. 185(3), 205 and Sch. 41, Pt. VI, with effect in any case where the death of the tenant or, as the case may be, the sole surviving tenant, occurs on or after 1 September 1995. S. 116(2A) read as follows:

"**116(2A)** In the application of this section as respects property in Scotland, the reference in subsection (2)(c) above to a tenancy beginning on or after 1st September 1995 includes a reference to its being acquired on or after that date by right of succession (the date of acquisition being taken to be the date on which the successor gives relevant notice under section 12 of the Agricultural Holdings (Scotland) Act 1991)."

S. 116(2A) inserted by FA 1995, s. 155(2), in relation to transfers of value made, and other events occurring, on or after 1 September 1995.

S. 116(5A)–(5E) inserted by FA 1996, s. 185(2), with effect (s. 116(5A)–(5C)) in any case where the death of the tenant or, as the case may be, the sole surviving tenant, occurs on or after 1 September 1995, and (s. 116(5D), (5E)) in any case where the death of the transferor occurs on or after 1 September 1995.

S. 116(8) inserted by FA 2009, s. 122(4), with effect in relation to transfers of value where the tax payable but for s. 122 (or, in the case of tax payable by instalments, the last instalment of the tax) would have been due on or after 22 April 2009 or was paid or due on or after 23 April 2003 (but see also *FA 2009, s. 122(8) and (9)*).

Cross references – S. 29A(4): s. 116 to be disregarded in determining the value of an exempt beneficiary's estate for the purposes of s. 29A(2).

S. 39A: attribution of value transferred to specific gifts and gifts of residue where value transferred attributable to relevant business property.

S. 114(1): interaction with business property relief.

FA 1975, Sch. 8: pre-1981 scheme of agricultural property relief for capital transfer tax.

FA 1981, Sch. 14, para. 2(2)(b), (4) were the precursors to s. 116(2)(b), (4).

FA 1986, Sch. 20, para. 8: gift of agricultural property, to which s. 116 applies, and which is subject to a reservation.

Extra-statutory concessions – F17: 100 per cent relief given where transferor's interest carries a right to vacant possession within 24 months of the date of the transfer, or is, notwithstanding the terms of the tenancy, valued at an amount broadly equivalent to the vacant possession value of the property.

HMRC interpretations – IRInt. 1005: subject to the normal conditions, 100 per cent relief applies to all agricultural tenancies, throughout the UK starting on or after 1 September 1995 including a statutory succession to an existing tenancy and whether or not the tenancy is within the Agricultural Tenancies Act 1995.

Other material – ICAEW Technical Release TR 772: HMRC confirm they regard fallow land as agricultural property.

117 Minimum period of occupation or ownership

117 Subject to the following provisions of this Chapter, section 116 above does not apply to any agricultural property unless–

(a) it was occupied by the transferor for the purposes of agriculture throughout the period of two years ending with the date of the transfer, or

(b) it was owned by him throughout the period of seven years ending with that date and was throughout that period occupied (by him or another) for the purposes of agriculture.

Cross references – FA 1986, Sch. 20, para. 8(2): qualifying period of ownership where gift is subject to a reservation.

Extra-statutory concessions – F16: minimum period of ownership/occupation regarded as satisfied in respect of agricultural tied cottage occupied by retired farm employee or widow(er).

Hansard – Official Report Standing Committee E, 24 June 1976, col. 1,275–1,276 (not reproduced): Treasury statement in connection with "ownership" in the context of s. 103–114, indicates "ownership" for purposes of s. 117(b) may be either legal or beneficial.

118 Replacement

118(1) Where the agricultural property occupied by the transferor on the date of the transfer replaced other agricultural property, the condition stated in section 117(a) above shall be treated as satisfied if it, the other property and any agricultural property directly or indirectly replaced by the other property were occupied by the transferor for the purposes of agriculture for periods which together comprised at least two years falling within the five years ending with that date.

118(2) Where the agricultural property owned by the transferor on the date of the transfer replaced other agricultural property, the condition stated in section 117(b) above shall be treated as satisfied if it, the other property and any agricultural property directly or indirectly replaced by the other property were, for periods which together comprised at least seven years falling within the ten years ending with that date, both owned by the transferor and occupied (by him or another) for the purposes of agriculture.

118(3) In a case falling within subsection (1) or (2) above relief under this Chapter shall not exceed what it would have been had the replacement or any one or more of the replacements not been made.

118(4) For the purposes of subsection (3) above changes resulting from the formation, alteration or dissolution of a partnership shall be disregarded.

119 Occupation by company or partnership

119(1) For the purposes of sections 117 and 118 above, occupation by a company which is controlled by the transferor shall be treated as occupation by the transferor.

119(2) For the purposes of sections 117 and 118 above, occupation of any property by a Scottish partnership shall, notwithstanding section 4(2) of the Partnership Act 1890, be treated as occupation of it by the partners.

120 Successions

120(1) For the purposes of section 117 above, where the transferor became entitled to any property on the death of another person–

(a) he shall be deemed to have owned it (and, if he subsequently occupies it, to have occupied it) from the date of the death, and

(b) *if that other person was his spouse or civil partner* he shall also be deemed to have occupied it for the purposes of agriculture for any period for which it was so occupied by his spouse or civil partner, and to have owned it for any period for which his spouse or civil partner owned it.

120(2) Where the transferor became entitled to his interest on the death of his spouse or civil partner on or after 10th March 1981–

(a) he shall for the purposes of section 116(2)(b) above be deemed to have been beneficially entitled to it for any period for which his spouse or civil partner was beneficially entitled to it;

(b) the condition set out in section 116(3)(a) shall be taken to be satisfied if and only if it is satisfied in relation to his spouse or civil partner; and

IHT Statutes

(c) the condition set out in section 116(3)(b) shall be taken to be satisfied only if it is satisfied both in relation to him and in relation to his spouse or civil partner.

History – In s. 120(1)(b) and (2) the words "or civil partner" inserted seven times by SI 2005/3229, reg. 22, with effect from 5 December 2005.

121 Successive transfers

121(1) Where–

(a) the whole or part of the value transferred by a transfer of value (in this section referred to as the earlier transfer) was eligible for relief under this Chapter (or would have been so eligible if such relief had been capable of being given in respect of transfers of value made at that time), and

(b) the whole or part of the property which, in relation to the earlier transfer, was or would have been eligible for relief became, through the earlier transfer, the property of the person (or of the spouse or civil partner of the person) who is the transferor in relation to a subsequent transfer of value and is at the time of the subsequent transfer occupied for the purposes of agriculture either by that person or by the personal representative of the transferor in relation to the earlier transfer, and

(c) that property or part or any property directly or indirectly replacing it would (apart from section 117 above) have been eligible for relief in relation to the subsequent transfer of value, and

(d) either the earlier transfer was, or the subsequent transfer of value is, a transfer made on the death of the transferor,

the property which would have been eligible for relief but for section 117 above shall be eligible for relief notwithstanding that section.

121(2) Where the property which, by virtue of subsection (1) above, is eligible for relief replaced the property or part referred to in paragraph (c) of that subsection, relief under this Chapter shall not exceed what it would have been had the replacement or any one or more of the replacements not been made, but section 118(4) above shall apply for the purposes of this subsection as it applies for the purposes of section 118(3).

121(3) Where, under the earlier transfer, the amount of the value transferred which was attributable to the property or part referred to in subsection (1)(c) above was part only of its value, a like part only of the value which (apart from this subsection) would fall to be reduced under this Chapter by virtue of this section shall be so reduced.

History – In s. 121(1)(b) the words "or civil partner" inserted by SI 2005/3229, reg. 23, with effect from 5 December 2005.

Cross references – S. 114(1) interaction of s. 121(3) with business property relief.

122 Agricultural property of companies

122(1) Where the whole or part of the value transferred is attributable to the value of shares in or securities of a company it shall be taken for the purposes of this Chapter to be attributable (so far as appropriate) to the agricultural value of agricultural property if and only if–

(a) the agricultural property forms part of the company's assets and part of the value of the shares or securities can be attributed to the agricultural value of the agricultural property, and

(b) the shares or securities gave the transferor control of the company immediately before the transfer.

122(2) Shares or securities shall not be regarded for the purposes of subsection (1)(b) above as giving the transferor control of a company if–

(a) they would not have been sufficient, without other property, to give him control of the company immediately before the transfer, and

(b) their value is taken by virtue of section 176 below to be less than the value previously determined.

122(3) Where subsection (1) above applies–

(a) the references in section 116(2)(a) and (3)(b) above to the **transferor's interest** shall be construed as references to the company's interest, and

(b) section 123(1) below shall apply instead of section 117 above.

Cross references – S. 176: sales of related property etc.

FA 1986, Sch. 20, para. 8: gift of shares or securities, to which s. 122(1) applies, and which is subject to a reservation.

Other material – ICAEW Technical Release TR 854: where the value of shares is attributed to the agricultural value of agricultural property, CGT hold-over relief (TCGA 1992, s. 165(5) and Sch. 7, Pt. I) is available on a transfer of the underlying property, but not of the shares themselves.

123 Provisions supplementary to section 122

123(1) Section 116 above shall not apply by virtue of section 122(1) above unless–

(a) the agricultural property–
  (i) was occupied by the company for the purposes of agriculture throughout the period of two years ending with the date of the transfer, or
  (ii) was owned by the company throughout the period of seven years ending with that date and was throughout that period occupied (by the company or another) for the purposes of agriculture, and
(b) the shares or securities were owned by the transferor–
  (i) in a case within paragraph (a)(i) above, throughout the period there mentioned, or
  (ii) in a case within paragraph (a)(ii) above, throughout the period there mentioned.

123(2) Subsections (1) and (2) of section 118 above shall apply in relation to the conditions stated in subsection (1)(a) above as they apply in relation to the conditions stated in section 117 taking references to the transferor as references to the company.

123(3) Where the shares or securities owned by the transferor on the date of the transfer replaced other eligible property (that is to say, agricultural property or shares or securities the value of which is wholly or partly attributable to the value of such property) the condition stated in subsection (1)(b) above shall be treated as satisfied if the shares or securities, the other eligible property which they replaced and any eligible property directly or indirectly replaced by the other eligible property were owned by the transferor for periods which together comprised–

(a) in a case within subsection (1)(a)(i) above, at least two years falling within the five years ending with that date, or

(b) in a case within subsection (1)(a)(ii) above, at least seven years falling within the ten years ending with that date.

123(4) Subsections (3) and (4) of section 118 above shall have effect in relation to a case falling within subsections (2) and (3) above as they have effect in relation to a case falling within subsections (1) and (2) of that section.

123(5) For the purposes of subsection (1) above, a company shall be treated as having occupied the agricultural property at any time when it was occupied by a person who subsequently controls the company.

Cross references – FA 1986, Sch. 20, para. 8(3): period of ownership requirement (s. 123(1)) where gift is subject to a reservation.

124 Contracts for sale

124(1) Section 116 above shall not apply to agricultural property if at the time of the transfer the transferor has entered into a binding contract for its sale, except where the sale is to a company and is made wholly or mainly in consideration of shares in or securities of the company which will give the transferor control of the company.

124(2) Section 116 above shall not apply by virtue of section 122(1) above if at the time of the transfer the transferor has entered into a binding contract for the sale of the shares or securities concerned, except where the sale is made for the purpose of reconstruction or amalgamation.

Other material – Revenue letter to Institute of Taxation, 11 May 1994: existence of accruer arrangement in partnership agreement does not necessarily jeopardise agricultural property relief by amounting to a binding contract for sale, but much will depend upon the construction of the particular document. See also Law Society's *Gazette*, 4 September 1996 (also considers options to purchase share of deceased partner).

124A Transfers within seven years before death of transferor

124A(1) Where any part of the value transferred by a potentially exempt transfer which proves to be a chargeable transfer would (apart from this section) be reduced in accordance with the preceding provisions of this Chapter, it shall not be so reduced unless the conditions in subsection (3) below are satisfied.

124A(2) Where–

(a) any part of the value transferred by any chargeable transfer, other than a potentially exempt transfer, is reduced in accordance with the preceding provisions of this Chapter, and

(b) the transfer is made within seven years of the death of the transferor,

then, unless the conditions in subsection (3) below are satisfied, the additional tax chargeable by reason of the death shall be calculated as if the value transferred had not been so reduced.

124A(3) The conditions referred to in subsections (1) and (2) above are–

(a) that the original property was owned by the transferee throughout the period beginning with the date of the chargeable transfer and ending with the death of the transferor (in this subsection referred to as **"the relevant period"**) and is not at the time of the death subject to a binding contract for sale; and

IHT Statutes

(b) except in a case falling within paragraph (c) below, that the original property is agricultural property immediately before the death and has been occupied (by the transferee or another) for the purposes of agriculture throughout the relevant period; and

(c) where the original property consists of shares in or securities of a company, that throughout the relevant period the agricultural property to which section 116 above applied by virtue of section 122(1) above on the chargeable transfer was owned by the company and occupied (by the company or another) for the purposes of agriculture.

124A(4) If the transferee has died before the transferor, the reference in subsection (3) above to the death of the transferor shall have effect as a reference to the death of the transferee.

124A(5) If the conditions in subsection (3) above are satisfied only with respect to part of the original property, then,–

(a) in a case falling within subsection (1) above, only a proportionate part of so much of the value transferred as is attributable to the original property shall be reduced in accordance with the preceding provisions of this Chapter, and

(b) in a case falling within subsection (2) above, the additional tax shall be calculated as if only a proportionate part of so much of the value transferred as was attributable to the original property had been so reduced.

124A(6) Where any shares owned by the transferee immediately before the death in question–

(a) would under any of the provisions of sections 126 to 136 of the 1992 Act be identified with the original property (or part of it), or

(b) were issued to him in consideration of the transfer of agricultural property consisting of the original property (or part of it),

his period of ownership of the original property shall be treated as including his period of ownership of the shares.

124A(7) This section has effect subject to section 124B below.

124A(7A) The provisions of this Chapter for the reduction of value transferred shall be disregarded in any determination for the purposes of this section of whether there is a potentially exempt or chargeable transfer in any case.

124A(8) In this section–

"the original property" means the property which, in relation to the chargeable transfer referred to in subsection (1) or subsection (2) above, was either agricultural property to which section 116 above applied or shares or securities of a company owning agricultural property to which that section applied by virtue of section 122(1) above; and

"the transferee" means the person whose property the original property became on that chargeable transfer or, where on the transfer the original property became or remained settled property in which no qualifying interest in possession (within the meaning of Chapter III of Part III of this Act) subsists, the trustees of the settlement.

History – In s. 124A(6), the words "his period … of the shares" were substituted by FA 1987, s. 58 and Sch. 8, para. 9, in relation to transfers of value made, and other events occurring, on or after 17 March 1987.
S. 124A(7A) inserted by FA 1996, s. 185(4), with effect in relation to any transfer of value on or after 28 November 1995.
Reference to the 1992 Act in subsection (6) substituted by TCGA 1992, s. 290 and Sch. 10, para. 8(5).
S. 124A inserted by FA 1986, s. 101 and Sch. 19, para. 22, with respect to transfers of value made, and other events occurring, on or after 18 March 1986.

Cross references – FA 1986, Sch. 19, para. 40(1): transitional – transfer of value occurring before, and death or other event occurring after, 18 March 1986.
TCGA 1992, s. 126–136: reorganisation of share capital, conversion of securities, exchange of securities and reconstruction involving the issue of securities etc.
TCGA 1992, s. 165 and Sch. 7, para. 1, 3, 5, 6: relief from tax on chargeable gains for gifts of agricultural property.

HMRC interpretations – IRInt. 1002: where a donee of a PET of a farming business sells it and replaces it with a non-agricultural business, s. 124A(1) denies agricultural property relief on the PET, but s. 114(1) need not exclude business property relief.

Other material – ICAEW Technical Release TR 772: HMRC do not consider it an anomaly that, under s. 124A, relief could be lost where beneficiaries under a maintenance trust obtain an interest in possession, or where, for example, an interest in possession is given them at age 25 in the expectation that the trustees will appoint capital to them later on.

124B Application of section 124A to replacement property

124B(1) Subject to subsection (2) below, this section applies where–

(a) the transferee has disposed of all or part of the original property before the death of the transferor; and

(b) the whole of the consideration received by him for the disposal has been applied by him in acquiring other property (in this section referred to as **"the replacement property"**).

124B(2) This section does not apply unless–

(a) the replacement property is acquired, or a binding contract for its acquisition is entered into, within the allowed period after the disposal of the original property (or, as the case may be, the part concerned); and

(b) the disposal and acquisition are both made in transactions at arm's length or on terms such as might be expected to be included in a transaction at arm's length.

124B(3) Where this section applies, the conditions in section 124A(3) above shall be taken to be satisfied in relation to the original property (or, as the case may be, the part concerned) if–

(a) the replacement property is owned by the transferee immediately before the death of the transferor and is not at that time subject to a binding contract for sale; and

(b) throughout the period beginning with the date of the chargeable transfer and ending with the disposal, the original property was owned by the transferee and occupied (by the transferee or another) for the purposes of agriculture; and

(c) throughout the period beginning with the date when the transferee acquired the replacement property and ending with the death, the replacement property was owned by the transferee and occupied (by the transferee or another) for the purposes of agriculture; and

(d) the replacement property is agricultural property immediately before the death.

124B(4) If the transferee has died before the transferor, any reference in subsections (1) to (3) above to the death of the transferor shall have effect as a reference to the death of the transferee.

124B(5) In any case where–

(a) all or part of the original property has been disposed of before the death of the transferor or is subject to a binding contract for sale at the time of the death, and

(b) the replacement property is acquired, or a binding contract for its acquisition is entered into, after the death of the transferor but within the allowed period after the disposal of the original property or part, and

(c) the transferor dies before the transferee,

subsection (3) above shall have effect with the omission of paragraphs (a) and (c), and as if any reference to a time immediately before the death of the transferor were a reference to the time when the replacement property is acquired.

124B(6) Section 124A(6) above shall have effect in relation to the replacement property as it has effect in relation to the original property.

124B(7) Where a binding contract for the disposal of any property is entered into at any time before the disposal of the property, the disposal shall be regarded for the purposes of subsections (2)(a) and (5)(b) above as taking place at that time.

124B(8) In this section **"the original property"** and **"the transferee"** have the same meaning as in section 124A above and **"allowed period"** means the period of three years or such longer period as the Board may allow.

History – In s. 124B(2)(a) and (5)(b), the words "the allowed period" substituted for "twelve months" by FA 1994, s. 247(2)(a) in relation to transfers of value made, and other events occurring, on or after 30 November 1993.

In s. 124B(8), the words "and "allowed period" … Board may allow" inserted by FA 1994, s. 247(2)(b) in relation to transfers of value made, and other events occurring, on or after 30 November 1993.

S. 124B inserted by FA 1986, Sch. 19, para. 22, with respect to transfers of value made, and other events occurring, on or after 18 March 1986.

Cross references – S. 227: payment of tax by instalments.

FA 1986, Sch. 19, para. 40(1): transitional – transfer of value occurring before, and death or other event occurring after, 18 March 1986.

HMRC interpretations – IRInt. 1002: where a donee of a PET of a farming business sells it and replaces it with a non-agricultural business, s. 124A(1) denies agricultural property relief on the PET, but s. 114(1) need not exclude business property relief.

Other material – ICAEW Technical Release TR 772 : HMRC confirm they regard fallow land as agricultural property.

124C Land in habitat schemes

124C(1) For the purposes of this Chapter, where any land is in a habitat scheme–

(a) the land shall be regarded as agricultural land;

(b) the management of the land in accordance with the requirements of the scheme shall be regarded as agriculture; and

(c) buildings used in connection with such management shall be regarded as farm buildings.

124C(2) For the purposes of this section land is in a habitat scheme at any time if–

(a) an application for aid under one of the enactments listed in subsection (3) below has been accepted in respect of the land; and

(b) the undertakings to which the acceptance relates have neither been terminated by the expiry of the period to which they relate nor been treated as terminated.

124C(3) Those enactments are–

(a) regulation 3(1) of the Habitat (Water Fringe) Regulations 1994;

(b) the Habitat (Former Set-Aside Land) Regulations 1994;

(c) the Habitat (Salt-Marsh) Regulations 1994;

(d) the Habitats (Scotland) Regulations 1994, if undertakings in respect of the land have been given under regulation 3(2)(a) of those Regulations;

(e) the Habitat Improvement Regulations (Northern Ireland) 1995, if an undertaking in respect of the land has been given under regulation 3(1)(a) of those Regulations.

124C(4) The Treasury may by order made by statutory instrument amend the list of enactments in subsection (3) above.

124C(5) The power to make an order under subsection (4) above shall be exercisable by statutory instrument subject to annulment in pursuance of a resolution of the House of Commons.

124C(6) This section has effect–

(a) in relation to any transfer of value made on or after 26th November 1996; and

(b) in relation to transfers of value made before that date, for the purposes of any charge to tax, or to extra tax, which arises by reason of an event occurring on or after 26th November 1996.

History – S. 124C inserted by FA 1997, s. 94.

Chapter III – Woodlands

125 The relief

125(1) This section applies where–

(a) part of the value of a person's estate immediately before his death is attributable to the value of land on which trees or underwood are growing but which is not agricultural property within the meaning of Chapter II of this Part of this Act, and

(b) either he was beneficially entitled to the land throughout the five years immediately preceding his death, or he became beneficially entitled to it otherwise than for a consideration in money or money's worth.

125(1A) But this section applies only if the land is in the United Kingdom or another state which is an EEA state (within the meaning given by Schedule 1 to the Interpretation Act 1978) at the time of the person's death.

125(2) Where this section applies and the person liable for the whole or part of the tax so elects–

(a) the value of the trees or underwood shall be left out of account in determining the value transferred on the death, but

(b) tax shall be charged in the circumstances mentioned in section 126 below.

125(3) An election under this section must be made by notice in writing to the Board within two years of the death or such longer time as the Board may allow.

History – In s. 125(1)(a) the words "in the United Kingdom" omitted by FA 2009, s. 122(5), with effect in relation to transfers of value where the tax payable but for s. 122 (or, in the case of tax payable by instalments, the last instalment of the tax) would have been due on or after 22 April 2009 or was paid or due on or after 23 April 2003 (but see also FA 2009, s. 122(8) and (9)).

S. 125(1A) inserted by FA 2009, s. 122(6), with effect in relation to transfers of value where the tax payable but for s. 122 (or, in the case of tax payable by instalments, the last instalment of the tax) would have been due on or after 22 April 2009 or was paid or due on or after 23 April 2003 (but see also FA 2009, s. 122(8) and (9)).

126 Charge to tax on disposal of trees or underwood

126(1) Where under section 125 above the value of any trees or underwood has been left out of account in determining the value transferred on the death of any person, and the whole or any part of the trees or underwood is disposed of (whether together with or apart from the land on which they were growing) then, if the disposal occurs before any part of the value transferred on the death of any other person is attributable to the value of that land, tax shall be charged in accordance with sections 127 and 128 below.

126(2) Subsection (1) above shall not apply to a disposal made by any person to his spouse or civil partner.

126(3) Where tax has been charged under this section on the disposal of any trees or underwood tax shall not again be charged in relation to the same death on a further disposal of the same trees or underwood.

History – In s. 126(2) the words "or civil partner" inserted by SI 2005/3229, reg. 24, with effect from 5 December 2005.

Cross references – S. 208: liability for tax under s. 126.

S. 216(7): time within which a person liable under s. 126 must deliver an account.
S. 221: notices of determination.
S. 226(4): due date for payment of tax on a chargeable event under s. 126.
S. 233(1)(c): interest on unpaid tax chargeable under s. 126.

127 Amount subject to charge

127(1) The amount on which tax is charged under section 126 above on a disposal of trees or underwood shall be–

(a) if the disposal is a sale for full consideration in money or money's worth, an amount equal to the net proceeds of the sale, and

(b) in any other case, an amount equal to the net value of the trees or underwood at the time of the disposal.

127(2) Where, if the value of the trees or underwood had not been left out of account in determining the value transferred on the death of the person in question–

(a) it would have been taken into account in determining the value of any relevant business property for the purposes of relief under Chapter I of this Part of this Act in relation to the transfer of value made on his death, or

(b) it would have been so taken into account if this Act had then been in force,

the amount on which tax is charged under section 126 above shall be reduced by 50 per cent.

128 Rate of charge

128(1) Tax charged under section 126 above on an amount determined under section 127 above shall be charged at the rate or rates at which it would have been charged on the death first mentioned in section 126 if–

(a) that amount, and any amount on which tax was previously charged under section 126 in relation to that death, had been included in the value transferred on death, and

(b) the amount on which the tax is charged had formed the highest part of that value.

128(2) In determining for the purposes of subsection (1) the rate or rates at which tax would have been charged on the amount determined under section 127, the effect of Schedule 1A (if it would have applied) is to be disregarded.

History – S. 128(1) created from former text of s. 128 by FA 2012, s. 209 and Sch. 33, para. 6(a), with effect in cases where D's death occurs on or after 6 April 2012.
S. 128(2) inserted by FA 2012, s. 209 and Sch. 33, para. 6(b), with effect in cases where D's death occurs on or after 6 April 2012.

Cross references – Sch. 2, para. 4: determination of rate of tax where there has been a reduction in the rate chargeable under Sch. 1 between the death and the disposal.

129 Credit for tax charged

129 Where a disposal on which tax is chargeable under section 126 above is a chargeable transfer, the value transferred by it shall be calculated as if the value of the trees or underwood had been reduced by the tax chargeable under that section.

Cross references – S. 114(2): interaction with business property relief.
S. 229: payment of tax by instalments.

130 Interpretation

130(1) In this Chapter–

(a) references to the **value transferred on a death** are references to the value transferred by the chargeable transfer made on that death;

(b) references to the **net proceeds of sale** or the **net value** of any trees or underwood are references to the proceeds of sale or value after deduction of any expenses allowable under this Chapter so far as those expenses are not allowable for the purposes of income tax; and

(c) references to the **disposal** of any trees or underwood include references to the disposal of any interest in the trees or underwood (and references to a disposal of the same trees or underwood shall, where the case so requires, be construed as referring to a disposal of the same interest).

130(2) The expenses allowable under this Chapter are, in relation to any trees or underwood the value of which has been left out of account on any death,–

(a) the expenses incurred in disposing of the trees or underwood; and

(b) the expenses incurred in replanting within three years of a disposal (or such longer time as the Board may allow) to replace the trees or underwood disposed of; and

(c) the expenses incurred in replanting to replace trees or underwood previously disposed of, so far as not allowable on the previous disposal.

Chapter IV – Transfers Within Seven Years Before Death

Notes – Heading, altered by Croner-i to reflect amended content, originally read "Transfers Within Three Years Before Death".

131 The relief

131(1) Subject to section 132 below, this section applies where because of the transferor's death within seven years of the transfer, tax becomes chargeable in respect of the value transferred by a potentially exempt transfer or (by virtue of section 7(4) above) additional tax becomes chargeable in respect of the value transferred by any other chargeable transfer and (in either case) all or part of the value transferred is attributable to the value of property (**"the transferred property"**) which–

(a) is, at the date of the death, the property of the person (**"the transferee"**) whose property it became on the transfer or of his spouse or civil partner, or

(b) has, before that date, been sold by the transferee or his spouse or civil partner by a qualifying sale;

and in the following provisions of this section **"the relevant date"** means, in a case within paragraph (a) above, the date of the death, and in a case within paragraph (b), the date of the qualifying sale.

131(2) If–

(a) the market value of the transferred property at the time of the chargeable transfer exceeds its market value on the relevant date, and

(b) a claim is made by a person liable to pay the whole or part of the tax or, as the case may be, additional tax,

the tax or, as the case may be, the additional tax shall be calculated as if the value transferred were reduced by the amount of the excess.

131(2ZA) A claim under subsection (2)(b) must be made not more than 4 years after the transferor's death.

131(2A) Where so much of the value transferred as is attributable to the value, or agricultural value, of the transferred property is reduced by any percentage (in this subsection referred to as **"the appropriate percentage"**), in accordance with Chapter I or Chapter II of this Part of this Act, references in subsection (2) above to the **market value** of the transferred property at any time shall have effect–

(a) in a case within Chapter I, as references to that market value reduced by the appropriate percentage; and

(b) in a case within Chapter II, as references to that market value less the appropriate percentage of the agricultural value of the transferred property at that time.

131(3) A sale is a **qualifying sale** for the purposes of this section if–

(a) it is at arm's length for a price freely negotiated at the time of the sale, and

(b) no person concerned as vendor (or as having an interest in the proceeds of the sale) is the same as or connected with any person concerned as purchaser (or as having an interest in the purchase), and

(c) no provision is made, in or in connection with the agreement for the sale, that the vendor (or any person having an interest in the proceeds of sale) is to have any right to acquire some or all of the property sold or some interest in or created out of it.

History – In s. 131(1) the words "or civil partner" inserted twice by SI 2005/3229, reg. 25, with effect from 5 December 2005.
In s. 131(1), the words "because of the transferor's death … and (in either case)" were substituted by FA 1986, s. 101 and Sch. 19, para. 23(1), effective with respect to transfers of value made, and other events occurring, on or after 18 March 1986.
In s. 131(2), the words "the tax or, as the case may be, the additional tax" were substituted by FA 1986, s. 101 and Sch. 19, para. 23(2), effective with respect to transfers of value made, and other events occurring, on or after 18 March 1986.
S. 131(2ZA) inserted by FA 2009, s. 99 and Sch. 51, para. 6, with effect from 1 April 2011 (SI 2010/867, art. 2(2)).
S. 131(2A) was inserted by FA 1986, s. 101 and Sch. 19, para. 23(3), effective with respect to transfers of value made, and other events occurring, on or after 18 March 1986.

Cross references – S. 7(4): rates of tax on chargeable transfers within seven years of death.
FA 1986, Sch. 19, para. 40(1): transitional – transfer of value occurring before, and death or other events occurring after, 18 March 1986.

132 Wasting assets

132(1) Section 131 above shall not apply if the transferred property is tangible movable property that is a wasting asset.

132(2) The transferred property is a **wasting asset** for the purposes of this section if, immediately before the chargeable transfer, it had a predictable useful life not exceeding fifty years, having regard to the purpose for which it was held by the transferor; and plant and machinery shall in every case be regarded as having a predictable useful life of less than fifty years.

133 Shares – capital receipts

133(1) If the transferred property consists of shares and at any time before the relevant date the transferee or his spouse or civil partner becomes entitled to a capital payment in respect of them, then for the purposes of section 131 above the market value of the transferred property on the relevant date shall (except where apart from this section it reflects a right to the payment) be taken to be increased by an amount equal to the payment.

133(2) If at any time before the relevant date the transferee or his spouse or civil partner receives or becomes entitled to receive in respect of the transferred property a provisional allotment of shares and disposes of the rights, the amount of the consideration for the disposal shall be treated for the purposes of this section as a capital payment in respect of the transferred property.

133(3) In this section **"capital payment"** means any money or money's worth which does not constitute income for the purposes of income tax.

History – In s. 133(1) and (2) the words "or civil partner" inserted by SI 2005/3229, reg. 26, with effect from 5 December 2005.

Cross references – S. 203: liability of transferor's spouse for tax on chargeable transfer by transferor – qualifying sale by spouse.

134 Payments of calls

134 If the transferred property consists of shares and at any time before the relevant date the transferee or his spouse or civil partner becomes liable to make a payment in pursuance of a call in respect of them, then for the purposes of section 131 above the market value of the transferred property on the relevant date shall (except where apart from this section it reflects the liability) be taken to be reduced by an amount equal to the payment.

History – In s. 134 the words "or civil partner" inserted by SI 2005/3229, reg. 27, with effect from 5 December 2005.

Cross references – S. 203: liability of transferor's spouse for tax on chargeable transfer by transferor – qualifying sale by spouse.

135 Reorganisation of share capital, etc.

135(1) This section has effect where the transferred property consists of shares in relation to which there occurs before the relevant date a transaction to which section 127 of the 1992 Act applies or would apply but for section 134 of that Act, that is to say–

(a) a reorganisation within the meaning of section 126(1) of that Act,

(b) the conversion of securities within the meaning of section 132 of that Act,

(c) the issue by a company of shares in exchange for shares in another company in such circumstances that section 135 of that Act applies, or

(d) the issue by a company of shares under such an arrangement as is referred to in section 136 of that Act,

or any transaction relating to a unit trust scheme which corresponds to any of the transactions referred to in paragraphs (a) to (d) above and to which section 127 of that Act applies by virtue of section 99 of that Act.

135(2) In the following provisions of this section **"the original shares"** and **"the new holding"** shall be construed in accordance with section 126(1).

135(3) Where this section has effect the original shares and the new holding shall be treated as the same property for the purposes of this Chapter.

135(4) Where this section has effect and, as part of or in connection with the transaction concerned, the transferee or his spouse or civil partner becomes liable to give any consideration for the new holding or any part of it, then for the purposes of section 131 above the market value of the transferred property on the relevant date shall (except where apart from this section it reflects the liability) be taken to be reduced by an amount equal to that consideration.

135(5) For the purposes of subsection (4) above, there shall not be treated as consideration given for the new holding or any part of it–

(a) any surrender, cancellation or other alteration of any of the original shares or of the rights attached thereto, or

(b) any consideration consisting of any application, in paying up the new holding or any part of it, of assets of the company concerned or of any dividend or other distribution declared out of those assets but not made.

History – In s. 135(4) the words "or civil partner" inserted by SI 2005/3229, reg. 28, with effect from 5 December 2005.
References to provisions of the "1992 Act" (which includes the reference in s. 135(2) to s. 126(1) of the 1992 Act) substituted by TCGA 1992, s. 290 and Sch. 10, para. 8(6).

Cross references – S. 203: liability of transferor's spouse for tax on chargeable transfer by transferor – qualifying sale by spouse.
TCGA 1992, s. 126(1), 127, 132, 135, 136: equation of original and new holdings on a reorganisation, conversion of securities (excluding compensation for compulsory purchase: s. 134), exchange of securities and reconstruction involving the issue of securities.

136 Transactions of close companies

136(1) This section applies where the transferred property consists of shares in a close company and at any time after the chargeable transfer and before the relevant date there is a relevant transaction in relation to the shares; and for this purpose **"relevant transaction"** means a transaction which is–

(a) the making of a transfer of value by the company, or

(b) an alteration in so much of the company's share or loan capital as does not consist of quoted shares or an alteration in any rights attaching to unquoted shares in or unquoted debentures of the company,

but which does not give rise to an adjustment, under any of the preceding sections of this Chapter, in the market value of the transferred property on the relevant date.

136(2) Subject to subsections (3) and (4) below, where this section applies the market value of the transferred property on the relevant date shall for the purposes of section 131 above be taken to be increased by an amount equal to the difference between–

(a) the market value of the transferred property at the time of the chargeable transfer, and

(b) what that value would have been if the relevant transaction had occurred before rather than after that time.

136(3) Where the relevant transaction is the making by the company of a transfer of value by which the value of the estate of the person who made the chargeable transfer or, if his spouse or civil partner is domiciled in the United Kingdom, his spouse or civil partner is increased by any amount, the increase provided for by subsection (2) above shall be reduced by that amount.

136(4) Where the market value of the transferred property at the time of the chargeable transfer is less than it would have been as mentioned in subsection (2) above, that subsection shall apply as if, instead of providing for an increase, it provided for the market value on the relevant date to be reduced to what it would have been if the relevant transaction had not occurred.

History – In s. 136(1)(b), the words "quoted shares" and "unquoted shares … of the company" were substituted by FA 1987, s. 58 and Sch. 8, para. 10, in relation to transfers of value made, and other events occurring, on or after 17 March 1987.
In s. 136(3) the words "or civil partner" inserted twice by SI 2005/3229, reg. 29, with effect from 5 December 2005.

Cross references – S. 203: liability of transferor's spouse for tax on chargeable transfer by transferor – qualifying sale by spouse.

137 Interests in land

137(1) Where the transferred property is an interest in land in relation to which the conditions mentioned in subsection (2) below are not satisfied, then, subject to subsections (3) and (4) below, the market value of the transferred property on the relevant date shall for the purposes of section 131 above be taken to be increased by an amount equal to the difference between–

(a) the market value of the interest at the time of the chargeable transfer, and

(b) what that market value would have been if the circumstances prevailing on the relevant date and by reason of which the conditions are not satisfied had prevailed at the time of the chargeable transfer.

137(2) The conditions referred to in subsection (1) above are–

(a) that the interest was the same in all respects and with the same incidents at the time of the chargeable transfer and on the relevant date, and

(b) that the land in which the interest subsists was in the same state and with the same incidents at the time of the chargeable transfer and on the relevant date.

137(3) If after the date of the chargeable transfer but before the relevant date compensation becomes payable under any enactment to the transferee or his spouse or civil partner–

(a) because of the imposition of a restriction on the use or development of the land in which the interest subsists, or

(b) because the value of the interest is reduced for any other reason,

the imposition of the restriction or the other cause of the reduction in value shall be ignored for the purposes of subsections (1) and (2) above, but the market value of the interest on the relevant date shall be taken to be increased by an amount equal to the amount of the compensation.

137(4) Where the market value of the interest at the time of the chargeable transfer is less than it would have been as mentioned in subsection (1) above, that subsection shall apply as if, instead of providing for an increase, it provided for the market value on the relevant date to be reduced to what it would have been if the change in circumstances by reason of which the conditions mentioned in subsection (2) above are not satisfied had not occurred.

History – In s. 137(3) the words "or civil partner" inserted by SI 2005/3229, reg. 30, with effect from 5 December 2005.

Cross references – S. 203: liability of transferor's spouse for tax on chargeable transfer by transferor – qualifying sale by spouse.

138 Leases

138(1) Where the transferred property is the interest of a lessee under a lease the duration of which at the time of the chargeable transfer does not exceed fifty years, then for the purposes of section 131 above the market value of the interest on the relevant date shall be taken to be increased by an amount equal to the appropriate fraction of the market value of the interest at the time of the chargeable transfer.

138(2) In subsection (1) above, **"the appropriate fraction"** means the fraction–

$$\frac{P(1) - P(2)}{P(1)}$$

where

P(1) is the percentage that would be derived from the Table in paragraph 1 of Schedule 8 to the 1992 Act for the duration of the lease at the time of the chargeable transfer, and

P(2) is the percentage that would be so derived for the duration of the lease on the relevant date.

History – Reference to "the 1992 Act" substituted by TCGA 1992, s. 290 and Sch. 10, para. 8(7).

Cross references – S. 203: liability of transferor's spouse for tax on chargeable transfer by transferor – qualifying sale by spouse. TCGA 1992, Sch. 8, para. 1(6): table for calculating the curved line write-off of expenditure on leases.

139 Other property

139(1) Where the transferred property is neither shares nor an interest in land and the condition mentioned in subsection (2) below is not satisfied in relation to it, then, subject to subsections (3) and (4) below, the market value of the property on the relevant date shall for the purposes of section 131 above be taken to be increased by an amount equal to the difference between–

(a) the market value of the property at the time of the chargeable transfer, and

(b) what that value would have been if the circumstances prevailing at the relevant date and by reason of which the condition is not satisfied had prevailed at the time of the chargeable transfer.

139(2) The condition referred to in subsection (1) above is that the transferred property was the same in all respects at the time of the chargeable transfer and on the relevant date.

139(3) Where the market value of the transferred property at the time of the chargeable transfer is less than it would have been as mentioned in subsection (1) above, that subsection shall apply as if, instead of providing for an increase, it provided for the market value on the relevant date to be reduced to what it would have been if the property had remained the same in all respects as it was at the time of the chargeable transfer.

139(4) Where the transferred property is neither shares nor an interest in land and during the period between the time of the chargeable transfer and the relevant date benefits in money or money's worth are derived from it which exceed a reasonable return on its market value at the time of the chargeable transfer, then–

(a) any effect of the benefits on the transferred property shall be ignored for the purposes of the preceding provisions of this section, but

(b) the market value of the transferred property on the relevant date shall be taken for the purposes of section 131 above to be increased by an amount equal to the said excess.

Cross references – S. 203: liability of transferor's spouse for tax on chargeable transfer by transferor – qualifying sale by spouse.

140 Interpretation

140(1) In this Chapter–

"close company" has the same meaning as in Part IV of this Act;

"interest in land" does not include any estate, interest or right by way of mortgage or other security;

"shares" includes securities;and

"the relevant date", **"the transferee"** and **"the transferred property"** shall be construed in accordance with section 131(1) above.

140(2) For the purposes of this Chapter the market value at any time of any property is the price which the property might reasonably be expected to fetch if sold in the open market at that time; but–

(a) that price shall not be assumed to be reduced on the ground that the whole property is on the market at one and the same time, and

(b) in the case of unquoted shares, it shall be assumed that in that market there is available to any prospective purchaser of the shares all the information which a prudent prospective purchaser

IHT Statutes

might reasonably require if he were proposing to purchase them from a willing vendor by private treaty and at arm's length.

History – In s. 140(2)(b), the words "unquoted shares" substituted by FA 1987, s. 58 and Sch. 8, para. 11, in relation to transfers of value made, and other events occurring, on or after 17 March 1987.

Cross references – S. 203: liability of transferor's spouse for tax on chargeable transfer by transferor – qualifying sale by spouse.

Other material – Law Society/Inland Revenue meeting notes, 7 February 1978 (not reproduced): property valued with respect to the open market even if only a lower price could be obtained in an actual sale – the premium value of a tenancy is included even if it could not be realised where the Rent Acts would entitle the assignee to a refund.

Chapter V – Miscellaneous

SUCCESSIVE CHARGES

141 Two or more transfers within five years

141(1) Where the value of a person's estate was increased by a chargeable transfer (**"the first transfer"**) made not more than five years before–

(a) his death, or

(b) a chargeable transfer which is made by him otherwise than on his death and as to which the conditions specified in subsection (2) below are satisfied,

the tax chargeable on the value transferred by the transfer made on his death or, as the case may be, referred to in paragraph (b) above (**"the later transfer"**) shall be reduced by an amount calculated in accordance with subsection (3) below.

141(2) The conditions referred to in subsection (1)(b) above are–

(a) that the value transferred by the later transfer falls to be determined by reference to the value of settled property in which there subsists an interest in possession to which the transferor is entitled;

(b) that the value transferred by the first transfer also fell to be determined by reference to the value of that property; and

(c) that the first transfer either was or included the making of the settlement or was made after the making of the settlement.

141(3) The amount referred to in subsection (1) above is a percentage of the tax charged on so much of the value transferred by the first transfer as is attributable to the increase mentioned in that subsection; and the percentage is–

(a) 100 per cent if the period beginning with the date of the first transfer and ending with the date of the later does not exceed one year;

(b) 80 per cent if it exceeds one year but does not exceed two years;

(c) 60 per cent if it exceeds two years but does not exceed three years;

(d) 40 per cent if it exceeds three years but does not exceed four years; and

(e) 20 per cent if it exceeds four years.

141(4) Where in relation to the first transfer there is more than one later transfer, the reduction provided for by this section shall be given only in respect of the earliest of them, unless the reduction represents less than the whole of the tax charged as mentioned in subsection (3) above; and in that case a reduction may be made in respect of subsequent transfers (in chronological order) until reductions representing the whole of that tax have been made.

141(5) For the purposes of subsection (4) above, a reduction made in accordance with paragraph (a) of subsection (3) above represents an equivalent amount of tax, a reduction made in accordance with paragraph (b) represents the amount of tax of which it is 80 per cent, and so on.

141(6) In determining for the purposes of this section whether or to what extent the value of the transferor's estate was increased by a chargeable transfer, there shall be disregarded any excluded property consisting of a reversionary interest to which he became entitled on the occasion of or before the chargeable transfer.

141(7) Where–

(a) the value of the transferor's estate was increased in consequence of–

(i) a gift inter vivos, or

(ii) a disposition or determination of a beneficial interest in possession in property comprised in a settlement, and

(b) tax under section 22(5) of the Finance Act 1975 was by reason of the gift or interest payable on a subsequent death, this section shall apply as if the increase had been by the chargeable transfer made on the occasion of the death.

141A Apportionment of relief under section 141

141A(1) This section applies if any part of the value transferred by the later transfer qualifies for the lower rate of tax in accordance with Schedule 1A.

141A(2) The amount of the reduction made under section 141(1) is to be apportioned in accordance with this section.

141A(3) For each qualifying component, the tax chargeable on so much of the value transferred by the later transfer as is attributable to property in that component ("the relevant part of the tax") is to be reduced by the appropriate proportion of the amount calculated in accordance with section 141(3).

141A(4) **"The appropriate proportion"** is a proportion equal to the proportion that–

(a) the relevant part of the tax, bears to

(b) the tax chargeable on the value transferred by the later transfer as a whole.

141A(5) If parts of an estate are treated under Schedule 1A as a single component, subsection (3) applies to the single component (and not to individual components forming part of the deemed single component).

141A(6) If, after making the reductions required by subsection (3), there remains any part of the tax chargeable on the value transferred by the later transfer that has not been reduced, the remaining part of the tax is to be reduced by so much of the amount calculated in accordance with section 141(3) as has not been used up for the purposes of making the reductions required by subsection (3).

141A(7) In this section–

"component" means a component of the estate, as defined in paragraph 3 of Schedule 1A;

"the later transfer" has the meaning given in section 141(1);

"qualifying component" means a component (or deemed single component) for which the donated amount is at least 10% of the baseline amount, as determined in accordance with Schedule 1A.

History – S. 141A inserted by FA 2012, s. 209 and Sch. 33, para. 7, with effect in cases where D's death occurs on or after 6 April 2012.

CHANGES IN DISTRIBUTION OF DECEASED'S ESTATE, ETC.

142 Alteration of dispositions taking effect on death

142(1) Where within the period of two years after a person's death–

(a) any of the dispositions (whether effected by will, under the law relating to intestacy or otherwise) of the property comprised in his estate immediately before his death are varied, or

(b) the benefit conferred by any of those dispositions is disclaimed,

by an instrument in writing made by the persons or any of the persons who benefit or would benefit under the dispositions, this Act shall apply as if the variation had been effected by the deceased or, as the case may be, the disclaimed benefit had never been conferred.

142(2) Subsection (1) above shall not apply to a variation unless the instrument contains a statement, made by all the relevant persons, to the effect that they intend the subsection to apply to the variation.

142(2A) For the purposes of subsection (2) above the relevant persons are–

(a) the person or persons making the instrument, and

(b) where the variation results in additional tax being payable, the personal representatives.

Personal representatives may decline to make a statement under subsection (2) above only if no, or no sufficient, assets are held by them in that capacity for discharging the additional tax.

142(3) Subsection (1) above shall not apply to a variation or disclaimer made for any consideration in money or money's worth other than consideration consisting of the making, in respect of another of the dispositions, of a variation or disclaimer to which that subsection applies.

142(3A) Subsection (1) does not apply to a variation by virtue of which any property comprised in the estate immediately before the person's death becomes property in relation to which section 23(1) applies unless it is shown that the appropriate person has been notified of the existence of the instrument of variation.

142(3B) For the purposes of subsection (3A) **"the appropriate person"** is–

(a) the charity or registered club to which the property is given, or

(b) if the property is to be held on trust for charitable purposes or for the purposes of registered clubs, the trustees in question.

IHT Statutes

142(4) Where a variation to which subsection (1) above applies results in property being held in trust for a person for a period which ends not more than two years after the death, this Act shall apply as if the disposition of the property that takes effect at the end of the period had had effect from the beginning of the period; but this subsection shall not affect the application of this Act in relation to any distribution or application of property occurring before that disposition takes effect.

142(5) For the purposes of subsection (1) above the property comprised in a person's estate includes any excluded property but not any property to which he is treated as entitled by virtue of section 49(1) above or section 102 of the Finance Act 1986.

142(6) Subsection (1) above applies whether or not the administration of the estate is complete or the property concerned has been distributed in accordance with the original dispositions.

142(7) In the application of subsection (4) above to Scotland, property which is subject to a proper liferent shall be deemed to be held in trust for the liferenter.

History – S. 142(2) and s. 142(2A) substituted for former s. 142(2) by FA 2002, s. 120(1) which applies in relation to instruments made on or after 1 August 2002. The former s. 142(2), which applies in relation to instruments made before 1 August 2002, read as follows:
"**142(2)** Subsection (1) above shall not apply to a variation unless an election to that effect is made by written notice given to the Board within six months after the date of the instrument, or such longer time as the Board may allow, by–
(a) the person or persons making the instrument, and
(b) where the variation results in additional tax being payable, the personal representatives;
but personal representatives may decline to join in an election only if no, or no sufficient, assets are held by them in that capacity for discharging the additional tax."
S. 142(3A) inserted by FA 2012, s. 209 and Sch. 33, para. 9, with effect in cases where the person's death occurs on or after 6 April 2012.
S. 142(3B) inserted by FA 2012, s. 209 and Sch. 33, para. 9, with effect in cases where the person's death occurs on or after 6 April 2012.
In s. 142(5) the words "or section 102 of the Finance Act 1986" were inserted by FA 1986, s. 101 and Sch. 19, para. 24, with respect to transfers of value made, and other events occurring, on or after 18 March 1986.

Cross references – S. 17(a): a variation or disclaimer to which s. 142(1) applies is not a transfer of value.
S. 49(1): person treated as beneficially entitled to property in which he has an interest in possession.
S. 218A: instruments varying dispositions taking effect on death.
S. 239(4): certificate of discharge does not affect tax payable under s. 142.
FA 1986, s. 102: gifts with reservation.
FA 1986, Sch. 19, para. 40(1): transitional – transfer of value occurring before, and death or other event occurring after, 18 March 1986.

Statements of practice – E18: partial disclaimers competent under Scots law.

HMRC interpretations – IRInt. 1003: variation of inheritances following the death of an original beneficiary within the two year statutory period. Extent of statutory fiction following *Marshall (HMIT) v Kerr* [1994] BTC 258.
IRInt. 1006: variation of a deceased's interest in jointly held assets.

Hansard – Written Answer, 25 June 1975, vol. 894, col. 179–180 (not reproduced): predecessor applied to election not to claim legal rights; renunciation of rights should be under the words "… or otherwise".

Other material – Law Society's Gazette, 18 December 1991: while s. 142 does not require execution of a deed, but simply "an instrument in writing", in practice a deed is normally used as a "prudent precaution".
Taxline 1993/46 (not reproduced): use of a deed of variation to redirect business or agricultural property to the deceased's spouse to take advantage of the increased agricultural and business property relief percentages where taxpayer died before 10 March 1992.
Tax Bulletin, TB08/02-5: procedures for dealing with instruments of variation following changes in FA 2002.

143 Compliance with testator's request

143 Where a testator expresses a wish that property bequeathed by his will should be transferred by the legatee to other persons, and the legatee transfers any of the property in accordance with that wish within the period of two years after the death of the testator, this Act shall have effect as if the property transferred had been bequeathed by the will to the transferee.

Cross references – S. 17(b): a transfer to which s. 143 applies is not a transfer of value.
S. 239(4): certificate of discharge does not affect tax payable under s. 143.

144 Distribution etc. from property settled by will

144(1) Subsection (2) below applies where property comprised in a person's estate immediately before his death is settled by his will and, within the period of two years after his death and before any interest in possession has subsisted in the property, there occurs–

(a) an event on which tax would (apart from subsection (2) below) be chargeable under any provision, other than section 64 or 79, of Chapter III of Part III of this Act, or

(b) an event on which tax would be so chargeable but for section 65(4), 75, 75A or 76 above or paragraph 16(1) of Schedule 4 to this Act.

144(1A) Where the testator dies on or after 22nd March 2006, subsection (1) above shall have effect as if the reference to any interest in possession were a reference to any interest in possession that is–

(a) an immediate post-death interest, or

(b) a disabled person's interest.

144(2) Where this subsection applies by virtue of an event within paragraph (a) of subsection (1) above, tax shall not be charged under the provision in question on that event; and in every case in which this subsection applies in relation to an event, this Act shall have effect as if the will had provided that on the testator's death the property should be held as it is held after the event.

144(3) Subsection (4) below applies where–

(a) a person dies on or after 22nd March 2006,

(b) property comprised in the person's estate immediately before his death is settled by his will, and

(c) within the period of two years after his death, but before an immediate post-death interest or a disabled person's interest has subsisted in the property, there occurs an event that involves causing the property to be held on trusts that would, if they had in fact been established by the testator's will, have resulted in–

(i) an immediate post-death interest subsisting in the property, or

(ii) section 71A or 71D above applying to the property.

144(4) Where this subsection applies by virtue of an event–

(a) this Act shall have effect as if the will had provided that on the testator's death the property should be held as it is held after the event, but

(b) tax shall not be charged on that event under any provision of Chapter 3 of Part 3 of this Act.

144(5) Subsection (4) above also applies where–

(a) a person dies before 22nd March 2006,

(b) property comprised in the person's estate immediately before his death is settled by his will,

(c) an event occurs–

(i) on or after 22nd March 2006, and

(ii) within the period of two years after the testator's death,

that involves causing the property to be held on trusts within subsection (6) below,

(d) no immediate post-death interest, and no disabled person's interest, subsisted in the property at any time in the period beginning with the testator's death and ending immediately before the event, and

(e) no other interest in possession subsisted in the property at any time in the period beginning with the testator's death and ending immediately before 22nd March 2006.

144(6) Trusts are within this subsection if they would, had they in fact been established by the testator's will and had the testator died at the time of the event mentioned in subsection (5)(c) above, have resulted in–

(a) an immediate post-death interest subsisting in the property, or

(b) section 71A or 71D above applying to the property.

History – In s. 144(1)(b), "65(4)," inserted by F(No. 2)A 2015, s. 14, with effect in cases where the testator's death occurs on or after 10 December 2014.
In s. 144(1)(b), ", 75A" inserted by FA 2014, s. 290 and Sch. 37, para. 16(1). This amendment is treated as having come into force on 6 April 2014.
In s. 144(1) the words "Subsection (2) below applies" substituted for the words "This section applies" and in s. 144(1)(a) the words "(apart from subsection (2) below)" substituted for the words "(apart from this section)" by FA 2006, s. 156 and Sch. 20, para. 27(2), with effect from 22 March 2006.
In s. 144(1A) inserted by FA 2006, s. 156 and Sch. 20, para. 27(3), with effect from 22 March 2006.
In s. 144(2) the words "this subsection" substituted for the words "this section" twice by FA 2006, s. 156 and Sch. 20, para. 27(4), with effect from 22 March 2006.
S. 144(3) inserted by FA 2006, s. 156 and Sch. 20, para. 27(5), with effect from 22 March 2006.
S. 144(4) inserted by FA 2006, s. 156 and Sch. 20, para. 27(5), with effect from 22 March 2006.
S. 144(5) inserted by FA 2006, s. 156 and Sch. 20, para. 27(5), with effect from 22 March 2006.
S. 144(6) inserted by FA 2006, s. 156 and Sch. 20, para. 27(5), with effect from 22 March 2006.

Cross references – S. 64: ten yearly charge on settlements without interest in possession.
S. 75: property becoming subject to employee trusts.
S. 76: property becoming held for charitable purposes etc.
S. 79: exemption from ten-yearly charge in certain cases.
S. 239(4): certificate of discharge does not affect tax under s. 144.
Sch. 4, para. 16: property becoming comprised in maintenance fund for historic buildings etc.

145 Redemption of surviving spouse's or civil partner's life interest

145 [Omitted by IHTPA 2014, s. 11 and Sch. 4, para. 4(b).]

History – S. 145 omitted by IHTPA 2014, s. 11 and Sch. 4, para. 4(b), with effect in relation to deaths occurring after 1 October 2014 (IHTPA 2014, s. 12(4) and SI 2014/2039). Former s. 145 read as follows:

"145 Redemption of surviving spouse's or civil partner's life interest

History – In the heading to s. 145 the words "or civil partner's" inserted by SI 2005/3229, reg. 31(3), with effect from 5 December 2005.
Where an election is made by a surviving spouse or civil partner under section 47A of the Administration of Estates Act 1925, this Act shall have effect as if the surviving spouse or civil partner, instead of being entitled to the life interest, had been entitled to a sum equal to the capital value mentioned in that section.".
In former s. 145 the words "or civil partner" inserted twice by SI 2005/3229, reg. 31(2), with effect from 5 December 2005.

Cross references – S. 239(4): certificate of discharge does not affect tax under s. 145.

Administration of Estates Act 1925, s. 47A: right of surviving spouse under intestacy rules to redeem his/her life interest.

146 Inheritance (Provision for Family and Dependants) Act 1975

146(1) Where an order is made under section 2 of the Inheritance (Provision for Family and Dependants) Act 1975 (**"the 1975 Act"**) in relation to any property forming part of the net estate of a deceased person, then, without prejudice to section 19(1) of that Act, the property shall for the purposes of this Act be treated as if it had on his death devolved subject to the provisions of the order.

146(2) Where an order is made under section 10 of the 1975 Act requiring a person to provide any money or other property by reason of a disposition made by the deceased, then–

(a) if that disposition was a chargeable transfer and the personal representatives of the deceased make a claim for the purpose not more than 4 years after the date on which the order is made–

  (i) tax paid or payable on the value transferred by that chargeable transfer (whether or not by the claimants) shall be repaid to them by the Board or, as the case may be, shall not be payable, and

  (ii) the rate or rates of tax applicable to the transfer of value made by the deceased on his death shall be determined as if the values previously transferred by chargeable transfers made by him were reduced by that value;

(b) the money or property shall be included in the deceased's estate for the purpose of the transfer of value made by him on his death.

146(3) Where the money or other property ordered to be provided under section 10 of the 1975 Act is less than the maximum permitted by that section, subsection (2)(a) above shall have effect in relation to such part of the value there mentioned as is appropriate.

146(4) The adjustment in consequence of the provisions of this section or of section 19(1) of the 1975 Act of the tax payable in respect of the transfer of value made by the deceased on his death shall not affect–

(a) the amount of any deduction to be made under section 8 of that Act in respect of tax borne by the person mentioned in subsection (3) of that section, or

(b) the amount of tax to which regard is to be had under section 9(2) of that Act;

and where a person is ordered under that Act to make a payment or transfer property by reason of his holding property treated as part of the deceased's net estate under section 8 or 9 and tax borne by him is taken into account for the purposes of the order, any repayment of that tax shall be made to the personal representatives of the deceased and not to that person.

146(5) Tax repaid under paragraph (a)(i) of subsection (2) above shall be included in the deceased's estate for the purposes of the transfer of value made by him on his death; and tax repaid under that paragraph or under subsection (4) above shall form part of the deceased's net estate for the purposes of the 1975 Act.

146(6) Anything which is done in compliance with an order under the 1975 Act or occurs on the coming into force of such an order, and which would (apart from this subsection) constitute an occasion on which tax is chargeable under any provision, other than section 79, of Chapter III of Part III of this Act, shall not constitute such an occasion; and where an order under the 1975 Act provides for property to be settled or for the variation of a settlement, and (apart from this subsection) tax would be charged under section 52(1) above on the coming into force of the order, section 52(1) shall not apply.

146(7) In subsections (2)(a) and (5) above references to **tax** include references to interest on tax.

146(8) Where an order is made staying or dismissing proceedings under the 1975 Act on terms set out in or scheduled to the order, this section shall have effect as if any of those terms which could have been included in an order under section 2 or 10 of that Act were provisions of such an order.

146(9) In this section any reference to, or to any provision of, the 1975 Act includes a reference to, or to the corresponding provision of, the Inheritance (Provision for Family and Dependants) (Northern Ireland) Order 1979.

History – In s. 146(2)(a), the words "not more than 4 years after the date on which the order is made" inserted by FA 2009, s. 99 and Sch. 51, para. 7, with effect from 1 April 2011 (SI 2010/867, art. 2(2)).

Cross references – S. 52: charge on termination of interest in possession.
S. 236(2), (3): interest on tax overpaid or underpaid in consequence of s. 146(1), and on tax repayable on a claim under s. 146(2).
Inheritance (Provision for Family and Dependants) Act 1975, s. 2 (not reproduced): power of court to make order if it is satisfied that the disposition of the deceased's estate is not such as to make reasonable financial provision for the applicant; s. 8: power to treat property nominated by the deceased, or the subject of a donatio mortis causa, as part of the net estate of the deceased; s. 9: power to treat deceased's severable share of joint tenancy as part of the net estate of the deceased; s. 10: power of court to order recovery of property disposed of by the deceased with the intention of defeating an application for financial provision under the Act.
FA 2009, Sch. 53, para. 8: late payment interest start dates.
FA 2009, Sch. 54, para. 10: repayment interest start dates.

147 Scotland: legitim etc

History – In the heading to s. 147 "etc" inserted by SI 2005/3229, reg. 32(7), with effect from 5 December 2005.

147(1) Where a testator dies leaving a surviving spouse or civil partner and a person under the age of 18 entitled to claim legitim or rights under section 131 of the Civil Partnership Act 2004 ("section 131 rights"), and provision is made in his will or other testamentary document for a disposition to his spouse or civil partner which, if it could take effect, would leave insufficient property in the estate to satisfy the entitlement of that person in respect of legitim or to section 131 rights, the following provisions of this section shall apply.

147(2) Subject to subsections (3) and (4) below, tax shall be charged at the testator's death as if the disposition to the spouse or civil partner did not include any amount in respect of legitim or section 131 rights, but if within the period mentioned in subsection (6) below the person or persons concerned renounce their claim to legitim or section 131 rights, tax shall be repaid to the estate calculated on the basis that the disposition to the spouse or civil partner did include the amount renounced.

147(3) The executors or judicial factor of the testator may, in accordance with the provisions of this section, elect that subsection (2) above shall not apply but that subsection (4) below shall apply.

147(4) Tax shall be charged at the testator's death as if the disposition to the spouse or civil partner had taken effect, but where the person or persons concerned claim legitim or section 131 rights within the period mentioned in subsection (6) below, tax shall be charged on the amount so claimed calculated on the basis that the legitim fund had been paid out in full at the testator's death (excluding any part of the fund renounced before any claim has been made) or on the basis that all section 131 rights had been claimed in full at the testator's death (excluding any rights renounced before any claim has been made) and the tax chargeable thereon had been apportioned rateably among the persons entitled to claim legitim or section 131 rights (excluding any who have renounced as aforesaid).

147(5) Where the executors or judicial factor of the testator decide to make an election under subsection (3) above they shall give notice in writing of that election to the Board within two years from the date of death of the testator or such longer period as the Board may permit.

147(6) For the purposes of subsections (2) and (4) above, a person shall be treated as having claimed legitim or section 131 rights unless he has renounced his claim before attaining the age of 18 or he renounces his claim within two years of his attaining that age or such longer period as the Board may permit.

147(7) Where a person dies before attaining the age of 18 or before making a renunciation under subsection (6) above the provisions of this section shall apply in relation to that person's executors or judicial factor as they would have applied in relation to that person if that person had attained the age of 18 with the substitution of the date of death of that person for the date on which a person attained that age; but where the executors or factor renounce a claim to legitim or section 131 rights in respect of a person the amount renounced shall not be treated as part of that person's estate.

147(8) Where subsection (2) above applies in relation to any estate, then notwithstanding anything in section 241 below the Board may repay tax under that subsection without limit of time.

147(9) Where subsection (4) above applies in relation to any estate, then notwithstanding anything in section 239 below a certificate of discharge may be given under that section in respect of the whole estate, and notwithstanding anything in section 240 below the giving of the certificate shall not preclude the Board from claiming tax under subsection (4) above without limit of time.

147(10) Where the application of subsection (4) in relation to the estate of a person means that too great an increase has been made under subsection (3) of section 8A above in the case of another person, the claim under that section in that case may be amended accordingly by the Commissioners for Her Majesty's Revenue and Customs.

History – In s. 147(1) the words "or civil partner" inserted twice and the words "or rights under section 131 of the Civil Partnership Act 2004 ("section 131 rights")" and "or to section 131 rights" inserted by SI 2005/3229, reg. 32(2), with effect from 5 December 2005.
In s. 147(2) the words "or civil partner" and the words "or section 131 rights" inserted twice by SI 2005/3229, reg. 32(3), with effect from 5 December 2005.
In s. 147(4) the words "or civil partner" and "or on the basis that all section 131 rights had been claimed in full at the testator's death (excluding any rights renounced before any claim has been made)" inserted and the words "or section 131 rights" inserted twice by SI 2005/3229, reg. 32(4), with effect from 5 December 2005.
In s. 147(6) the words "or section 131 rights" inserted by SI 2005/3229, reg. 32(5), with effect from 5 December 2005.
In s. 147(7) the words "or section 131 rights" inserted by SI 2005/3229, reg. 32(6), with effect from 5 December 2005.
S. 147(10) inserted by FA 2008, s. 10 and Sch. 4, para. 3, with effect in relation to cases where the survivor's death occurs on or after 9 October 2007.

Cross references – S. 17(c): the renunciation of a claim to legitim within the period mentioned in s. 147(6) is not a transfer of value.
S. 209(2), (3): liability for tax chargeable under s. 147(4).
S. 236(4): interest on tax repayable under s. 147(2), and charged by virtue of s. 147(4).
S. 239: certificates of discharge.
S. 240: adjustments where tax underpaid.
S. 241: repayments of tax overpaid.
FA 2009, Sch. 53, para. 9: late payment interest start dates.

Notes – Section 131 of the Civil Partnership Act 2004 reads as follows:

"131 Succession: legal rights arising by virtue of civil partnership

131(1) Where a person dies survived by a civil partner then, unless the circumstance is as mentioned in subsection (2), the civil partner has right to half of the moveable net estate belonging to the deceased at the time of death.

131(2) That circumstance is that the person is also survived by issue, in which case the civil partner has right to a third of that moveable net estate and those issue have right to another third of it.

131(3) In this section–

"issue" means issue however remote, and

"net estate" has the meaning given by section 36(1) (interpretation) of the Succession (Scotland) Act 1964 (c. 41).

131(4) Every testamentary disposition executed after the commencement of this section by which provision is made in favour of the civil partner of the testator and which does not contain a declaration to the effect that the provision so made is in full and final satisfaction of the right to any share in the testator's estate to which the civil partner is entitled by virtue of subsection (1) or (2), has effect (unless the disposition contains an express provision to the contrary) as if it contained such a declaration.

131(5) In section 36(1) of the Succession (Scotland) Act 1964 (c. 41), in the definition of "legal rights", for "and legitim" substitute "legitim and rights under section 131 of the Civil Partnership Act 2004"."

MUTUAL AND VOIDABLE TRANSFERS

148 Mutual transfers: exemption for donee's gift

148 [Repealed by FA 1986, s. 101 and Sch. 19, para. 25 and s. 114 and Sch. 23, Pt. X, where the donee's transfer is made on or after 18 March 1986.]

149 Mutual transfers: relief for donor's gift

149 [Repealed by FA 1986, s. 101 and Sch. 19, para. 25 and s. 114 and Sch. 23, Pt. X, where the donee's transfer (defined in s. 148) is made on or after 18 March 1986.]

150 Voidable transfers

150(1) Where on a claim made for the purpose it is shown that the whole or any part of a chargeable transfer (**"the relevant transfer"**) has by virtue of any enactment or rule of law been set aside as voidable or otherwise defeasible–

(a) tax paid or payable by the claimant (in respect of the relevant transfer or any other chargeable transfer made before the claim) that would not have been payable if the relevant transfer had been void ab initio shall be repaid to him by the Board, or as the case may be shall not be payable, and

(b) the rate or rates of tax applicable to any chargeable transfer made after the claim by the person who made the relevant transfer shall be determined as if that transfer or that part of it had been void as aforesaid.

150(2) In subsection (1)(a) above the reference to tax includes a reference to interest on tax.

150(3) A claim under this section must be made not more than 4 years after the claimant knew, or ought reasonably to have known, that the relevant transfer has been set aside.

History – S. 150(3) inserted by FA 2009, s. 99 and Sch. 51, para. 8, with effect from 1 April 2011 (SI 2010/867, art. 2(2)).

Cross references – S. 236(3): interest on tax repayable on a claim under s. 150.

PENSION SCHEMES, ETC.

151 Treatment of pension rights, etc.

151(1) [Omitted by FA 2004, s. 203(4)(a); and repealed by FA 2004, s. 326 and Sch 42, Pt. 3.]

151(1A) [Omitted by FA 2004, s. 203(4)(a); and repealed by FA 2004, s. 326 and Sch 42, Pt. 3.]

151(2) An interest in or under a registered pension scheme, a qualifying non-UK pension scheme or a section 615(3) scheme which comes to an end on the death of the person entitled to it shall be left out of account in determining for the purposes of this Act the value of his estate immediately before his death, if the interest–

(a) is, or is a right to, a pension or annuity, and

(b) is not an interest resulting (whether by virtue of the instrument establishing the scheme or otherwise) from the application of any benefit provided under the scheme otherwise than by way of a pension or annuity.

151(3) Sections 49 to 53 above shall not apply in relation to an interest satisfying the conditions of paragraphs (a) and (b) of subsection (2) above.

151(4) In relation to an interest in or under a registered pension scheme, a qualifying non-UK pension *scheme or a section 615(3)* scheme, section 5(2) above shall apply as if the words "other than settled property" were omitted (in both places).

151(5) Where a benefit has become payable under a registered pension scheme, a qualifying non-UK pension scheme or a section 615(3) scheme, and the benefit becomes comprised in a settlement made by a person other than the person entitled to the benefit, the settlement shall for the purposes of this Act be treated as made by the person so entitled.

History – S. 151(1) and (1A) omitted by FA 2004, s. 203(4)(a); and repealed by FA 2004, s. 326 and Sch. 42, Pt. 3, with effect from 6 April 2006 (FA 2004, s. 284(1)).
Former s. 151(1A) inserted by F(No. 2)A 1987, s. 98(4).
In s. 151(2), the words "An interest" substituted for the words "Subject to sections 151A and 151C below, an interest" by FA 2011, s. 65 and Sch. 16, para. 51, with effect in relation to deaths occurring on or after 6 April 2011.
In s. 151(2), the words ", a qualifying non-UK pension scheme or a section" substituted for the words "or section" by FA 2008, s. 92 and Sch. 29, para. 18(4), with effect from 6 April 2006.
In s. 151(2) the words "Subject to sections 151A and 151C below," inserted by FA 2006, s. 160 and Sch. 22, para. 3, with effect from 6 April 2006.
In s. 151(2) the words "registered pension scheme or section 615(3) scheme" substituted for the words "fund or scheme to which this section applies" by FA 2004, s. 203(4)(b); with effect from 6 April 2006 (FA 2004, s. 284(1)).
In s. 151(2)(b) the word "scheme" substituted for the words "fund or scheme", in both places, by FA 2004, s. 203(4)(c); with effect from 6 April 2006 (FA 2004, s. 284(1)).
In s. 151(4), the words ", a qualifying non-UK pension scheme or a section" substituted for the words "or section" by FA 2008, s. 92 and Sch. 29, para. 18(4), with effect from 6 April 2006.
In s. 151(4) the words "registered pension scheme or section 615(3) scheme" substituted for the words "fund or scheme to which this section applies" by FA 2004, s. 203(4)(b); with effect from 6 April 2006 (FA 2004, s. 284(1)).
In s. 151(5), the words ", a qualifying non-UK pension scheme or a section" substituted for the words "or section" by FA 2008, s. 92 and Sch. 29, para. 18(4), with effect from 6 April 2006.
In s. 151(5) the words "registered pension scheme or section 615(3) scheme" substituted for the words "fund or scheme to which this section applies" by FA 2004, s. 203(4)(b); with effect from 6 April 2006 (FA 2004, s. 284(1)).
See ICTA 1988, Sch. 29, para. 32 for substitution of references to that Act.

Cross references – S. 5: a person's estate is the aggregate of all the property to which he is beneficially entitled.
S. 49–53: treatment of interests in possession.
S. 58(1)(d): property which is part of a scheme etc. to which s. 151 applies is not "relevant property" for the purposes of Pt. III, Ch. III.
S. 210: liability for tax on chargeable transfer which includes an interest satisfying the conditions of s. 151(2)(a), (b).
ICTA 1988, s. 615(3): overseas superannuation funds.
ICTA 1988, s. 620, 621: qualifying retirement annuity premiums and other approved contracts.
FA 2004, Sch. 36 para. 56: transitional provisions for pension schemes; the assets of specified non-registered funds or schemes continue to be within s. 151 in certain circumstances, after 6 April 2006.
FA 2004, Sch. 36 para. 58: transitional provisions for pension schemes; the assets of specified funds or schemes continue to be within s. 151 in certain circumstances, after 6 April 2006.
SI 2006/575, reg. 34: application of s. 151 to the Pension Protection Fund.

Statements of practice – E3: payments by trustees of a superannuation scheme to a member's dependants.
SP 10/86: exemption afforded by E3 not affected by gift with reservation rules.

Other material – Revenue notes (1988): inheritance tax on benefits under superannuation schemes.
Tax Bulletin, TB02/92-3: retirement benefits under private pension contracts: circumstances in which CTO will regard failure to take up retirement benefit before death as giving rise to a charge to IHT under s. 3(3).

151A Person dying with alternatively secured pension fund

151A [Omitted by FA 2011, s. 65 and Sch. 16, para. 48(a).]

History – S. 151A omitted by FA 2011, s. 65 and Sch. 16, para. 48(a), with effect in relation to deaths occurring on or after 6 April 2011.

151B Relevant dependant with pension fund inherited from member over 75

151B [Omitted by FA 2011, s. 65 and Sch. 16, para. 48(b).]

History – S. 151B omitted by FA 2011, s. 65 and Sch. 16, para. 48(b), with effect in relation to deaths occurring on or after 6 April 2011.

151BA Rate or rates of charge under section 151B

151BA [Omitted by FA 2011, s. 65 and Sch. 16, para. 48(c).]

History – S. 151BA omitted by FA 2011, s. 65 and Sch. 16, para. 48(c), with effect in relation to deaths occurring on or after 6 April 2011.

151C Dependant dying with other pension fund

151C [Omitted by FA 2011, s. 65 and Sch. 16, para. 48(d).]

History – S. 151C omitted by FA 2011, s. 65 and Sch. 16, para. 48(d), with effect in relation to deaths occurring on or after 6 April 2011.

151D Unauthorised payment where person dies over 75 with pension or annuity

151D [Omitted by FA 2011, s. 65 and Sch. 16, para. 48(e).]

History – S. 151D omitted by FA 2011, s. 65 and Sch. 16, para. 48(e), with effect in relation to deaths occurring on or after 6 April 2011.

151E Rate or rates of charge under section 151D

151E [Omitted by FA 2011, s. 65 and Sch. 16, para. 48(f).]

History – S. 151E omitted by FA 2011, s. 65 and Sch. 16, para. 48(f), with effect in relation to deaths occurring on or after 6 April 2011.

152 Cash options

152 Where on a person's death an annuity becomes payable under a registered pension scheme, a qualifying non-UK pension scheme or a section 615(3) scheme to a widow, widower, dependant or nominee of that person and under the terms of the scheme a sum of money might at his option have become payable instead to his personal representatives, he shall not, by virtue of section 5(2) above, be treated as having been beneficially entitled to that sum.

History – In s. 152, the words ", dependant or nominee" substituted for the words "or dependant" by FA 2016, s. 22 and Sch. 5, para. 11(1), with effect as having come into force from 6 April 2015 where the person on whose death an annuity is payable dies on or after that date.

In s. 152, the words ", a qualifying non-UK pension scheme or a section" substituted for the words "or section" by FA 2008, s. 92 and Sch. 29, para. 18(5), with effect from 6 April 2006.

In s. 152 the words "Where on a person's death an annuity becomes payable under a registered pension scheme or section 615(3) scheme to a widow, widower or dependant of that person and under the terms of the scheme" substituted for the words below by FA 2004, s. 203(5); with effect from 6 April 2006 (FA 2004, s. 284(1)). The substituted words read as follows:

"Where–

(a) under approved personal pension arrangements within the meaning of Chapter IV of Part XIV of the Taxes Act 1988, or

(b) under a contract or trust scheme approved by the Board under section 620 or 621 of the Taxes Act 1988 or (before 6th April 1970) under section 22 of the Finance Act 1956,

an annuity becomes payable on a person's death to a widow, widower, surviving civil partner or dependant of that person, and under the terms of the contract or scheme".

In s. 152 the words ", surviving civil partner" inserted by SI 2005/3229, reg. 33, with effect from 5 December 2005.

S. 152(a) and (b) substituted by F(No. 2)A 1987, s. 98(5).

References to ICTA 1988, and the words "6th April 1970", substituted by ICTA 1988, s. 844 and Sch. 29, para. 32, in relation to tax for 1988–89 and later years of assessment.

Cross references – ICTA 1988, s. 620, 621: qualifying retirement annuity premiums and other approved contracts.

153 Overseas pensions

153(1) In determining for the purposes of this Act the value of a person's estate immediately before his death there shall be left out of account any pension payable under the regulations or rules relating to any fund vested in Commissioners under section 273 of the Government of India Act 1935 or to any fund administered under a scheme made under section 2 of the Overseas Pensions Act 1973 which is certified by the Secretary of State for the purpose of this section to correspond to an Order in Council under subsection (1) of the said section 273.

153(2) For the purposes of this Act–

(a) a pension paid under the authority of a scheme made under section 2 of the Overseas Pensions Act 1973 which is constituted by the Pensions (India, Pakistan and Burma) Act 1955 or is certified by the Secretary of State for the purposes of this section to correspond to the said Act of 1955 shall be treated as if it had been paid by the Government of India or the Government of Pakistan (according as the arrangements in pursuance of which the pension was first paid under the said Act of 1955 were made with the one or the other Government);

(b) a pension paid out of any fund established in the United Kingdom by the Government of any country which, at the time when the fund was established, was, or formed part of, a colony, protectorate, protected state or United Kingdom trust territory shall, if the fund was established for the sole purpose of providing pensions, whether contributory or not, payable in respect of service under the Government be treated as if it had been paid by the Government by which the fund was established;

(c) a pension paid out of the Central African Pension Fund established by section 24 of the Federation of Rhodesia and Nyasaland (Dissolution) Order in Council 1963 shall be treated as if it had been paid by the Government of a territory outside the United Kingdom; and

(d) so much of any pension paid to or in respect of any person under–

  (i) the scheme which by virtue of subsection (3) of section 2 of the Overseas Pensions Act 1973 is constituted under that section by section 2 or subsection (2) of section 4 of the Overseas Service Act 1958, or

  (ii) such other scheme made under section 2 of the Overseas Pensions Act 1973 as is certified by the Secretary of State for the purposes of the Taxes Act to correspond to section 2 or subsection (2) of section 4 of the Overseas Service Act 1958,

as is certified by the Secretary of State to be attributable to service under the Government of an overseas territory shall be treated as if it had been paid by the Government of that territory.

153(3) Subsection (1) above shall be construed as if contained in section 273 of the Government of India Act 1935; and for the purposes of subsection (2) above–

(a) **"pension"** includes a gratuity and any sum payable on or in respect of death, and a return of contributions with or without interest thereon or any other addition thereto;

(b) **"United Kingdom trust territory"** means a territory administered by the Government of the United Kingdom under the trusteeship system of the United Nations;

(c) **"overseas territory"** means any country or territory outside the United Kingdom;

(d) references to the Government of any such country or territory as is mentioned in paragraph (b) or (d) of that subsection include a Government constituted for two or more such countries or territories and any authority established for the purpose of providing or administering services which are common to, or relate to matters of common interest to, two or more such countries or territories.

153(4) If, by reason of Her Majesty's Government in the United Kingdom having assumed responsibility for a pension, allowance or gratuity within the meaning of section 1 of the Overseas Pensions Act 1973, payments in respect of it are made under that section, this section shall apply in relation to the pension, allowance or gratuity, exclusive of so much (if any) of it as is paid by virtue of the application to it of any provisions of the Pensions (Increase) Act 1971 or any enactment repealed by that Act, as if it continued to be paid by the Government or other body or fund which had responsibility for it before that responsibility was assumed by Her Majesty's Government in the United Kingdom.

Cross references – Overseas Service Act 1958, s. 2, 4; Overseas Pensions Act 1973, s. 2 (not reproduced): schemes established by the Secretary of State providing pensions for persons formerly engaged in overseas civilian or police service.
Federation of Rhodesia and Nyasaland (Dissolution) Order 1963 (SI 1963/2085), art. 24 (not reproduced): pensions payable to persons by reason of former employment in the public service of the Federation of Rhodesia and Nyasaland.
Overseas Pensions Act 1973, s. 1 (not reproduced): pensions payable in the UK by the UK Government under agreements with overseas governments.
Pensions (India, Pakistan and Burma) Act 1985; Overseas Pensions Act 1973, s. 2 (not reproduced): schemes established by the Secretary of State providing pensions for persons including those entitled under pension arrangements in respect of sub-continental naval, military and civilian service taken over from the government of India by the UK.

PAYMENTS TO VICTIMS OF PERSECUTION DURING SECOND WORLD WAR ERA

History – Heading before s. 153ZA inserted by FA 2016, s. 95(1), with effect in relation to deaths occurring on or after 1 January 2015.

153ZA Qualifying payments

153ZA(1) This section applies where a qualifying payment has at any time been received by a person ("P"), or by the personal representatives of P.

153ZA(2) The tax chargeable on the value transferred by the transfer made on P's death (the "value transferred") is to be reduced by an amount equal to–

(a) the relevant percentage of the amount of the qualifying payment, or

(b) if lower, the amount of tax that would, apart from this section, be chargeable on the value transferred.

153ZA(3) In subsection (2) **"relevant percentage"** means the percentage specified in the last row of the third column of the Table in Schedule 1.

153ZA(4) For the purposes of this section, a **"qualifying payment"** is a payment that meets Condition A, B or C.

153ZA(5) Condition A is that the payment–

(a) is of a kind specified in Part 1 of Schedule 5A, and

(b) is made to a person, or the personal representatives of a person, who was–

 (i) a victim of National-Socialist persecution, or

 (ii) the spouse or civil partner of a person within sub-paragraph (i).

153ZA(6) Condition B is that the payment is of a kind listed in Part 2 of Schedule 5A.

153ZA(7) Condition C is that the payment–

(a) is of a kind specified in regulations made by the Treasury, and

(b) is made to a person, or the personal representatives of a person, who was–

 (i) held as a prisoner of war, or a civilian internee, during the Second World War, or

 (ii) the spouse or civil partner of a person within sub-paragraph (i).

153ZA(8) The Treasury may by regulations add a payment of a specified kind to the list in Part 1 of Schedule 5A.

153ZA(9) Regulations under this section are to be made by statutory instrument.

153ZA(10) A statutory instrument containing regulations under this section is subject to annulment in pursuance of a resolution of the House of Commons.

History – S. 153ZA inserted by FA 2016, s. 95(1), with effect in relation to deaths occurring on or after 1 January 2015.

EMERGENCY SERVICES

153A Death of emergency service personnel etc

153A(1) The reliefs in subsection (2) apply where a person–

(a) dies from an injury sustained, accident occurring or disease contracted at a time when that person was responding to emergency circumstances in that person's capacity as an emergency responder, or

(b) dies from a disease contracted at some previous time, the death being due to, or hastened by, the aggravation of the disease during a period when that person was responding to emergency circumstances in that person's capacity as an emergency responder.

153A(2) The reliefs are–

(a) that no potentially exempt transfer made by the person becomes a chargeable transfer under section 3A(4) because of the death,

(b) that section 4 (transfers on death) does not apply in relation to the death, and

(c) that no additional tax becomes due under section 7(4) because of a transfer made by the person within 7 years of the death.

153A(3) **"Emergency circumstances"** means circumstances which are present or imminent and are causing or likely to cause–

(a) the death of a person,

(b) serious injury to, or the serious illness of, a person,

(c) the death of an animal,

(d) serious injury to, or the serious illness of, an animal,

(e) serious harm to the environment (including the life and health of plants and animals),

(f) serious harm to any building or other property, or

(g) a worsening of any such injury, illness or harm.

153A(4) A person is **"responding to emergency circumstances"** if the person–

(a) is going anywhere for the purpose of dealing with emergency circumstances occurring there, or

(b) is dealing with emergency circumstances, preparing to do so imminently or dealing with the immediate aftermath of emergency circumstances.

153A(5) For the purposes of this section, circumstances to which a person is responding are to be taken to be emergency circumstances if the person believes and has reasonable grounds for believing they are or may be emergency circumstances.

153A(6) **"Emergency responder"** means–

(a) a person employed, or engaged, in connection with the provision of fire services or fire and rescue services,

(b) a person employed for the purposes of providing, or engaged to provide, search services or rescue services (or both),

(c) a person employed for the purposes of providing, or engaged to provide, medical, ambulance or paramedic services,

(d) a constable or a person employed for police purposes or engaged to provide services for police purposes,

(e) a person employed for the purposes of providing, or engaged to provide, services for the transportation of organs, blood, medical equipment or medical personnel, or

(f) a person employed, or engaged, by the government of a state or territory, an international organisation or a charity in connection with the provision of humanitarian assistance.

153A(7) For the purposes of subsection (6)–

(a) it is immaterial whether the employment or engagement is paid or unpaid, and

(b) **"international organisation"** means an organisation of which–

(i) two or more sovereign powers are members, or

(ii) the governments of two or more sovereign powers are members.

153A(8) The Treasury may, by regulations made by statutory instrument, extend the definition of **"emergency responder"** in subsection (6).

153A(9) Regulations under this section are subject to annulment in pursuance of a resolution of the House of Commons.

History – S. 153A inserted by FA 2015, s. 75(2), with effect in relation to deaths occurring on or after 19 March 2014.

ARMED FORCES

154 Death on active service, etc.

154(1) The reliefs in subsection (1A) apply in relation to the death of a person in whose case it is certified by the Defence Council or the Secretary of State–

(a) that he died from a wound inflicted, accident occurring or disease contracted at a time when the conditions specified in subsection (2) below were satisfied, or

(b) that he died from a disease contracted at some previous time, the death being due to or hastened by the aggravation of the disease during a period when those conditions were satisfied.

154(1A) The reliefs are–

(a) that no potentially exempt transfer made by the deceased becomes a chargeable transfer under section 3A(4) because of the death,

(b) that section 4 (transfers on death) does not apply in relation to the death, and

(c) that no additional tax becomes due under section 7(4) because of a transfer made by the deceased within 7 years of the death.

154(2) The conditions referred to in subsection (1) above are that the deceased was a member of any of the armed forces of the Crown or a civilian subject to service discipline within the meaning of the Armed Forces Act 2006 was subject to the law governing any of those forces by reason of association with or accompanying any body of those forces and (in any case) wasr–

(a) on active service against an enemy, or

(b) on other service of a warlike nature or which in the opinion of the Treasury involved the same risks as service of a warlike nature or

(c) responding to emergency circumstances in the course of the person's duties as a member of any of those armed forces or as a civilian subject to service discipline.

154(2A) Section 153A(3) to (5) applies for the purposes of this section.

154(3) In relation to any time before 28th July 1981 (the date of the passing of the Armed Forces Act 1981), the reference in subsection (2) above to membership of the armed forces of the Crown shall include a reference to employment as a person of any of the descriptions specified in paragraph 1(3) of Schedule 7 to the Finance Act 1975 (women's services).

History – In s. 154A(1) the words "The reliefs in subsection (1A) apply" substituted for the words "Section 4 shall not apply" by FA 2015, s. 75(3)(a), with effect in relation to deaths occurring on or after 19 March 2014.

S. 154A(1A) inserted by FA 2015, s. 75(3)(b), with effect in relation to deaths occurring on or after 19 March 2014.

S. 154A(2)(c) (and the word "or" preceding it) inserted and the word "either" and the end of the introductory words omitted by FA 2015, s. 75(3)(c), with effect in relation to deaths occurring on or after 19 March 2014.

In s. 154(2), the words "a civilian subject to service discipline within the meaning of the Armed Forces Act 2006" substituted for the words "(not being a member of any of those forces) was subject to the law governing any of those forces by reason of association with or accompanying any body of those forces)" by Armed Forces Act 2006, s. 378 and Sch. 16, para. 99, from 28 March 2009 for purposes under SI 2009/812, art. 3(a) and (b) – which read as follows:

"(a) the whole Act … so far as is necessary for the purpose of enabling–
(i) the Defence Council to make regulations,
(ii) the Secretary of State to make orders, regulations and rules
(iii) Royal Warrants to be made, and
(iv) Orders in Council to be made,
under the Act or under any other Act modified or amended by the Act;
(b) the whole Act so far as is necessary for the purpose of enabling the Defence Council to make appointments under the Act;"

S. 154A(2A) inserted by FA 2015, s. 75(3)(b2), with effect in relation to deaths occurring on or after 19 March 2014.

Cross references – S. 4: charge to tax for transfers on death.

Non-contentious Probate Fees Order 1999 (SI 1999/688), fee for grant of exemption (£50, and an additional £80 for a personal application); amended by SI 2003/1239 (which provides for a reduced fee of £8 where deceased is certified to be a member of the armed forces of the Crown killed on active service), with effect for deaths occurring on or after 20 March 2003).

Extra-statutory concessions – F5: deaths of members of the Royal Ulster Constabulary.

Hansard – HC Written Answers, vol. 974, col. 501–502, 26 November 1979 (not reproduced): test in determining whether a wound is the cause of death.

155 Visiting forces, etc.

155(1) Section 6(4) above applies to–

(a) the emoluments paid by the Government of any designated country to a member of a visiting force of that country, not being a British citizen, a British overseas territories citizen, a British National (Overseas) or a British Overseas citizen, and

(b) any tangible movable property the presence of which in the United Kingdom is due solely to the presence in the United Kingdom of such a person while serving as a member of the force.

155(2) A period during which any such member of a visiting force as is referred to in subsection (1) above is in the United Kingdom by reason solely of his being such a member shall not be treated for the purposes of this Act as a period of residence in the United Kingdom or as creating a change of his residence or domicile.

155(3) References in subsections (1) and (2) above to a visiting force shall apply to a civilian component of a visiting force as they apply to the force itself, and those subsections shall be construed as one with Part I of the Visiting Forces Act 1952, but so that for the purposes of this section references to a designated country shall be substituted in that Act for references to a country to which a provision of that Act applies.

155(4) For the purpose of conferring on persons attached to any designated international military headquarters the like benefits as are conferred by subsections (1) and (2) above on members of a visiting force or civilian component, any members of the armed forces of a designated country shall, while attached to any such headquarters, be deemed to constitute a visiting force of that country, and there shall be a corresponding extension of the class of persons who may be treated as members of a civilian component of such a visiting force.

155(5) In the case of persons of any category for the time being agreed between Her Majesty's Government in the United Kingdom and the other members of the North Atlantic Council, employment by a designated allied headquarters shall be treated for the purposes of subsections (1)(b) and (2) above as if it were service as a member of a visiting force of a designated country.

155(5A) Section 6(4) also applies to–

(a) the emoluments paid by the Government of any designated country to a person belonging to the EU civilian staff, not being a British citizen, a British overseas territories citizen, a British National (Overseas) or a British Overseas citizen, and

(b) any tangible movable property the presence of which in the United Kingdom is due solely to the presence in the United Kingdom of such a person serving as part of that staff.

155(5B) A period during which any such person belonging to the EU civilian staff as is referred to in subsection (5A) is in the United Kingdom by reason solely of that person belonging to that staff is not to be treated for the purposes of this Act as a period of residence in the United Kingdom or as creating a change of that person's residence or domicile.

155(6) For the purposes of this section–

"allied headquarters" means any international military headquarters established under the North Atlantic Council;

"designated" means designated for the purpose in question by or under any Order in Council made for giving effect to any international agreement.

"the EU civilian staff" means–

(a) civilian personnel seconded by a member State to an EU institution for the purposes of activities (including exercises) relating to the preparation for, and execution of, tasks mentioned in Article 43(1) of the Treaty on European Union (tasks relating to a common security and defence policy), as amended from time to time, and

(b) civilian personnel (other than locally hired personnel)–

(i) made available to the EU by a member State to work with designated international military headquarters or a force of a designated country, or

(ii) otherwise made available to the EU by a member State for the purposes of activities of the kind referred to in paragraph (a).

155(7) Any Order in Council made under section 73 of the Finance Act 1960 which is in force immediately before the passing of this Act shall have effect for the purposes of this section as if it had also been made under this section, and may be varied or revoked accordingly.

History – In s. 155(1)(a), words "a British overseas territories citizen" substituted for words "a British Dependent Territories citizen" by British Overseas Territories Act 2002, s. 2(3), with effect from 26 February 2002 (Royal Assent).
In s. 155(1)(a), the words ", a British National (overseas)" inserted by SI 1986/948, art. 4 and Schedule.
In s. 155(4), the words "international military" substituted for "allied" by FA 2012, s. 220 and Sch. 37, para. 3(2), with effect from 17 July 2012.
S. 155(5A) inserted by FA 2012, s. 220 and Sch. 37, para. 3(3), with effect from 17 July 2012.
S. 155(5B) inserted by FA 2012, s. 220 and Sch. 37, para. 3(3), with effect from 17 July 2012.
In s. 155(6), the definition of "the EU civilian staff" inserted by FA 2012, s. 220 and Sch. 37, para. 3(4), with effect from 17 July 2012.

Cross references – S. 6(4): excluded property generally.

Statutory instruments – SI 1998/1515: designation of countries and allied headquarters for the purposes of s. 155. Designated countries are Albania, Belgium, Bulgaria, Canada, the Czech Republic, Denmark, Estonia, the Federal Republic of Germany, France, Greece, Hungary, Italy, Latvia, Lithuania, Luxembourg, the Netherlands, Norway, Poland, Portugal, Romania, the Slovak Republic, Slovenia, Spain, Sweden, Turkey, the United States of America. *Designated allied* headquarters are Channel Committee, Channel Command, *Eastern Atlantic Area Command*, Supreme Headquarters Allied Powers Europe, Allied Command Atlantic Headquarters, Headquarters of the Supreme Allied Commander Atlantic (SACLANT), Headquarters Eastern Atlantic (EASTLANT), Headquarters Maritime Air Eastern Atlantic (MARAIREASTLANT), Headquarters Submarine Forces Eastern Atlantic (SUBEASTLANT), Headquarters Allied Forces North Western Europe (AFNORTHWEST), Headquarters Allied Naval Forces North Western Europe (NAVNORTHWEST), Headquarters Allied Air Forces North Western Europe (AIRNORTHWEST), NATO Airborne Early Warning Force Headquarters and NATO E-3A Component.

SI 1998/1516: designation of certain countries for the purpose of s. 155 on their becoming parties to the Agreement among the States parties to the North Atlantic Treaty and the Other States Participating in the Partnership for Peace regarding the Status of their Forces dated 19 June 1995. Designated countries are Armenia, Austria, Azerbaijan, Belarus, Finland, Georgia, Kazakhstan, Kyrgyzstan, the Former Yugoslav Republic of Macedonia, Moldova, Russia, Switzerland, Turkmenistan, Ukraine, and Uzbekistan.
SI 2012/3070 (partly made under s. 155): designation of countries and international military headquarters for the purposes of s. 155, with effect from immediately after the coming into force of the EU SOFA in respect of the United Kingdom.
SI 2012/3071 (partly made under s. 155): designation of NATO countries, PFP countries and headquarters for the purposes of s. 155, with effect from 13 December 2012.

CONSTABLES AND SERVICE PERSONNEL

155A Death of constables and service personnel targeted because of their status

155A(1) The reliefs in subsection (3) apply where a person–

(a) dies from an injury sustained or disease contracted in circumstances where the person was deliberately targeted by reason of his or her status as a constable or former constable, or

(b) dies from a disease contracted at some previous time, the death being due to, or hastened by, the aggravation of the disease by an injury sustained or disease contracted in circumstances mentioned in paragraph (a).

155A(2) The reliefs in subsection (3) apply where it is certified by the Defence Council or the Secretary of State that a person–

(a) died from an injury sustained or disease contracted in circumstances where the person was deliberately targeted by reason of his or her status as a service person or former service person, or

(b) died from a disease contracted at some previous time, the death being due to, or hastened by, the aggravation of the disease by an injury sustained or disease contracted in circumstances mentioned in paragraph (a).

155A(3) The reliefs are–

(a) that no potentially exempt transfer made by the person becomes a chargeable transfer under section 3A(4) because of the death,

(b) that section 4 (transfers on death) does not apply in relation to the death, and

(c) that no additional tax becomes due under section 7(4) because of a transfer made by the person within 7 years of the death.

155A(4) For the purposes of this section, it is immaterial whether a person who was a constable or service person at the time the injury was sustained or the disease was contracted was acting in the course of his or her duties as such at that time (and for this purpose ignore the references in subsections (1)(b) and (2)(b) to a disease contracted at some previous time).

155A(5) **"Service person"** means a person who is a member of the armed forces of the Crown or a civilian subject to service discipline (within the meaning of the Armed Forces Act 2006).

155A(6) This section does not apply where section 153A or 154 applies in relation to a person's death.

History – S. 155A inserted by FA 2015, s. 75(4), with effect in relation to deaths occurring on or after 19 March 2014.

APSLEY HOUSE AND CHEVENING ESTATE

156 Apsley House and Chevening Estate

156 This Act shall not apply in respect of–

(a) the rights conferred by section 3 of the Wellington Museum Act 1947, or

(b) property held on the trusts of the trust instrument set out in the Schedule to the Chevening Estate Act 1959.

NON-RESIDENTS' BANK ACCOUNTS

157 Non-residents' bank accounts

157(1) In determining for the purposes of this Act the value of the estate immediately before his death of a person to whom this section applies there shall be left out of account the balance on–

(a) any qualifying foreign currency account of his, and

(b) subject to subsection (3) below, any qualifying foreign currency account of the trustees of settled property in which he is beneficially entitled to an interest in possession.

157(2) This section applies to a person who is not domiciled and not resident in the United Kingdom immediately before his death.

157(3) Subsection (1)(b) above does not apply in relation to settled property if the settlor was domiciled in the United Kingdom when he made the settlement, or if the trustees are domiciled or resident in the United Kingdom immediately before the beneficiary's death.

157(3A) This section is subject to paragraph 5 of Schedule A1 (non-excluded overseas property).

157(4) For the purposes of this section–

(a) the question whether a person is resident in the United Kingdom shall, subject to paragraph (b) below, be determined as for the purposes of income tax; but

(b) the trustees of a settlement shall be regarded as not resident in the United Kingdom unless the general administration of the settlement is ordinarily carried on in the United Kingdom and the trustees or a majority of them (and, where there is more than one class of trustees, a majority of each class) are resident there.

157(5) In this section **"qualifying foreign currency account"** means a foreign currency account with a bank; and for this purpose–

(a) **"foreign currency account"** means any account other than one denominated in sterling,

(b) [repealed by FA 1996, s. 205 and Sch. 41, Pt. VIII(2).]

157(6) In this section **"bank"** has the meaning given by section 991 of the Income Tax Act 2007.

History – S. 157(2) substituted by FA 2013, s. 219 and Sch. 46, para. 118(2), with effect in relation to deaths on or after 6 April 2013. Former s. 157(2) read as follows:

"157(2) This section applies to a person who is not domiciled in the United Kingdom immediately before his death, and is neither resident nor ordinarily resident there at that time.".

In s. 157(3), the words "or resident" substituted for the words ", resident or ordinarily resident" by FA 2013, s. 219 and Sch. 46, para. 118(3), with effect in relation to deaths on or after 6 April 2013.

S. 157(3A) inserted by F(No. 2)A 2017, s. 33 and Sch. 10, para. 6, with effect in relation to times after 5 April 2017 subject to Sch. 10, para. 9 and 10.

In s. 157(4)(a), the words "or ordinarily resident" omitted by FA 2013, s. 219 and Sch. 46, para. 118(4)(a), with effect in relation to deaths on or after 6 April 2013.

In s. 157(4)(b), the words "or ordinarily resident" and "and ordinarily resident" omitted by FA 2013, s. 219 and Sch. 46, para. 118(4)(b), with effect in relation to deaths on or after 6 April 2013.

In s. 157(5), the words "or the Post Office" repealed by SI 2001/1149, art. 3(2) and Sch. 2, with effect from 26 March 2001.

In s. 157(5) the words "a bank or the Post Office" substituted for the previous words "the Bank of England, the Post Office or an authorised institution" by FA 1996, s. 198 and Sch. 37, para. 12, with effect in relation to deaths occurring on or after 29 April 1996.

S. 157(5) previously amended by the Banking Act 1987, s. 108(1) and Sch. 6, para. 17, with effect from 1 October 1987 (SI 1987/1664).

S. 157(5)(b) (which defined the term "authorised institution"), and the word "and" immediately preceding it, repealed by FA 1996, s. 205 and Sch. 41, Pt. VIII(2), with effect in relation to deaths occurring on or after 29 April 1996.

In s. 157(6) the words "section 991 of the Income Tax Act 2007" substituted for the words "section 840A of the Taxes Act 1988" by ITA 2007, s. 1027 and Sch. 1, para. 269 with effect from 6 April 2007.

S. 157(6) inserted by FA 1996, s. 198 and Sch. 37, para. 12, with effect in relation to deaths occurring on or after 29 April 1996.

DOUBLE TAXATION RELIEF

158 Double taxation conventions

158(1) If Her Majesty by Order in Council declares–

(a) that arrangements specified in the Order have been made with the government of any territory outside the United Kingdom with a view to affording relief from double taxation in relation to capital transfer tax payable under the laws of the United Kingdom and any tax imposed under the laws of that territory which is of a similar character or is chargeable on or by reference to death or gifts inter vivos, and

(b) that it is expedient that those arrangements should have effect,

the arrangements shall, notwithstanding anything in this Act, have effect so far as they provide for relief from capital transfer tax, or for determining the place where any property is to be treated as situated for the purposes of the tax.

158(1ZA) For the purposes of this section, arrangements made with a view to affording relief from double taxation include any arrangements which modify the effect of arrangements so made.

158(1ZB) Arrangements to which effect is given under this section may include provision conferring (with or without other functions) functions relating to the determination of matters arising under the arrangements on a public authority in the United Kingdom or in a territory outside the United Kingdom.

158(1A) [Repealed by FA 2006, s. 178 and Sch. 26, Pt. 8(2).]

158(2) Any arrangements to which effect is given under this section may include provision for relief in cases occurring before the making of the arrangements and provisions as to property which is not itself subject to double taxation.

158(3) *Any Order in Council under this section which revokes an earlier Order may contain such transitional provisions as appear to Her Majesty to be necessary or expedient.*

158(4) An Order under this section shall not be submitted to Her Majesty in Council unless a draft of it has been laid before, and approved by resolution of, the House of Commons.

158(5) Where any arrangements have effect by virtue of this section, no obligation as to secrecy shall prevent the Board or an authorised officer of the Board from disclosing to any authorised officer of the government with which the arrangements are made such information as is required to be disclosed under the arrangements.

158(6) Where arrangements with the government of any territory outside the United Kingdom are specified under any Order in Council which–

(a) was made, or has effect as made, under section 54 of the Finance (No. 2) Act 1945 or section 2 of the Finance Act (Northern Ireland) 1946, and

(b) had effect immediately before the passing of this Act,

the Order shall, notwithstanding the repeal of that section by the Finance Act 1975, remain in force and have effect as if any provision made by those arrangements in relation to estate duty extended to capital transfer tax chargeable by virtue of section 4 above; but the Order may be amended or revoked by an Order in Council made under this section.

History – S. 158(1ZA) inserted by FA 2018, s. 32(3), and is to be regarded as always having had effect and the provision made by s. 158(1ZA) in relation to Orders under s. 158 applies, and is to be regarded as always having applied, in relation to Orders in Council under any provision which that section replaces (directly or indirectly).
S. 158(1ZB) inserted by FA 2018, s. 32(3), and is to be regarded as always having had effect and the provision made by s. 158(1ZB) in relation to Orders under s. 158 applies, and is to be regarded as always having applied, in relation to Orders in Council under any provision which that section replaces (directly or indirectly).
S. 158(1A) repealed by FA 2006, s. 178 and Sch. 26, Pt. 8(2), with effect from with effect from 19 July 2006 (Royal Assent).
In former s. 158(1A), the words "foreseeably relevant to the administration or enforcement of" substituted for the words "necessary for carrying out" by FA 2003, s. 198, with effect from 10 July 2003.
Former s. 158(1A) inserted by FA 1987, s. 70(2).

Cross references – S. 267(2): disapplication of deemed domicile provisions in relation to provisions referred to in s. 158(6).

Notes – FA 1986, s. 100(1)(b): any reference to capital transfer tax (except where it relates to a liability to tax arising before 25 July 1986) to have effect as a reference to inheritance tax.

159 Unilateral relief

159(1) Where the Board are satisfied that in any territory outside the United Kingdom (an **"overseas territory"**) any amount of tax imposed by reason of any disposition or other event is attributable to the value of any property, then, if–

(a) that tax is of a character similar to that of capital transfer tax or is chargeable on or by reference to death or gifts inter vivos, and

(b) any capital transfer tax chargeable by reference to the same disposition or other event is also attributable to the value of that property,

they shall allow a credit in respect of that amount (**"the overseas tax"**) against that capital transfer tax in accordance with the following provisions.

159(2) Where the property is situated in the overseas territory and not in the United Kingdom, the credit shall be of an amount equal to the overseas tax.

159(3) Where the property–

(a) is situated neither in the United Kingdom nor in the overseas territory, or

(b) is situated both in the United Kingdom and in the overseas territory,

the credit shall be of an amount calculated in accordance with the following formula–

$$\frac{A}{A+B} \times C$$

where A is the amount of the capital transfer tax, B is the overseas tax and C is whichever of A and B is the smaller.

159(4) Where tax is imposed in two or more overseas territories in respect of property which–

(a) is situated neither in the United Kingdom nor in any of those territories, or

(b) is situated both in the United Kingdom and in each of those territories,

subsection (3) above shall apply as if, in the formula there set out, B were the aggregate of the overseas tax imposed in each of those territories and C were the aggregate of all, except the largest, of A and the overseas tax imposed in each of them.

159(5) Where credit is allowed under subsection (2) above or section 158 above in respect of overseas tax imposed in one overseas territory, any credit under subsection (3) above in respect of overseas tax imposed in another shall be calculated as if the capital transfer tax were reduced by the credit allowed under subsection (2) or section 158; and where, in the case of any overseas territory mentioned in subsection (3) or (4) above, credit is allowed against the overseas tax for tax charged in a territory in which the property is situated, the overseas tax shall be treated for the purposes of those provisions as reduced by the credit.

159(6) In this section references to tax imposed in an overseas territory are references to tax chargeable under the law of that territory and paid by the person liable to pay it.

159(7) Where relief can be given both under this section and under section 158 above, relief shall be given under whichever section provides the greater relief.

Cross references – FA 1986, s. 100(1)(b): any reference to capital transfer tax (except where it relates to a liability to tax arising before 25 July 1986) to have effect as a reference to inheritance tax.

PART VI – VALUATION

Chapter I – General

160 Market value

160 Except as otherwise provided by this Act, the value at any time of any property shall for the purposes of this Act be the price which the property might reasonably be expected to fetch if sold in the open market at that time; but that price shall not be assumed to be reduced on the ground that the whole property is to be placed on the market at one and the same time.

Cross references – TCGA 1992, s. 274: value determined for inheritance tax taken to be the market value at the date of death for capital gains tax.

Other material – HMRC Brief 23/08: inheritance tax and valuation of gifts involving a Discounted Gift Scheme.
HMRC Brief 22/13: discounted gift schemes: ten year anniversary values for inheritance tax and updated guidance on the calculation of transfer values when discounted gift schemes are effected.

161 Related property

161(1) Where the value of any property comprised in a person's estate would be less than the appropriate portion of the value of the aggregate of that and any related property, it shall be the appropriate portion of the value of that aggregate.

161(2) For the purposes of this section, **property is related** to the property comprised in a person's estate if–

(a) it is comprised in the estate of his spouse or civil partner; or

(b) it is or has within the preceding five years been–

(i) the property of a charity, or held on trust for charitable purposes only, or

(ii) the property of a body mentioned in section 24, 24A or 25 above,

and became so on a transfer of value which was made by him or his spouse or civil partner after 15th April 1976 and was exempt to the extent that the value transferred was attributable to the property.

161(3) The **appropriate portion** of the value of the aggregate mentioned in subsection (1) above is such portion thereof as would be attributable to the value of the first-mentioned property if the value of that aggregate were equal to the sums of the values of that and any related property, the value of each property being determined as if it did not form part of that aggregate.

161(4) For the purposes of subsection (3) above the proportion which the value of a smaller number of shares of any class bears to the value of a greater number shall be taken to be that which the smaller number bears to the greater; and similarly with stock, debentures and units of any other description of property.

161(5) Shares shall not be treated for the purposes of subsection (4) above as being of the same class unless they are so treated by the practice of a recognised stock exchange or would be so treated if dealt with on such a stock exchange.

History – In s. 161(2) the words "or civil partner" inserted twice by SI 2005/3229, reg. 34, with effect from 5 December 2005.
In s. 161(2)(b)(ii), words "or 25" substituted for former words "25 or 26" by FA 1998, s. 143(6), with effect in relation to any property becoming the property of a body on a transfer of value made on or after 17 March 1998.
S. 161(2)(b)(ii) amended by FA 1989, s. 171(4), inserting the references to s. 24A.

Cross references – S. 23, 24, 24A, 25: gifts to charities, political parties, housing associations or for national purposes.
S. 105(1A): application to business property relief.
S. 176: sale of related property within three years after death.

Other material – HMRC Brief 71/07: IHT and the valuation of property owned jointly by spouses or civil partners.

162 Liabilities

162(1) A liability in respect of which there is a right to reimbursement shall be taken into account only to the extent (if any) that reimbursement cannot reasonably be expected to be obtained.

162(2) Subject to subsection (3) below, where a liability falls to be discharged after the time at which it is to be taken into account it shall be valued as at the time at which it is to be taken into account.

162(3) In determining the value of a transferor's estate immediately after a transfer of value, his liability *for capital transfer tax shall* be computed–

(a) without making any allowance for the fact that the tax will not be due immediately, and

(b) as if any tax recovered otherwise than from the transferor (or a person liable for it under section 203(1) below) were paid in discharge of a liability in respect of which the transferor had a right to reimbursement.

162(4) A liability which is an incumbrance on any property shall, so far as possible and to the extent that it is not taken to reduce value in accordance with section 162B, be taken to reduce the value of that property.

162(5) Where a liability taken into account is a liability to a person resident outside the United Kingdom which neither–

(a) falls to be discharged in the United Kingdom, nor

(b) is an incumbrance on property in the United Kingdom,

it shall, so far as possible and to the extent that it is not taken to reduce value in accordance with section 162B, be taken to reduce the value of property outside the United Kingdom.

History – In s. 162(4), the words "and to the extent that it is not taken to reduce value in accordance with section 162B" inserted by FA 2013, s. 176 and Sch. 36, para. 2(2), with effect in relation to transfers of value made, or treated as made, on or after 17 July 2013 (Royal Assent).

In s. 162(5), the words "and to the extent that it is not taken to reduce value in accordance with section 162B" inserted by FA 2013, s. 176 and Sch. 36, para. 2(3), with effect in relation to transfers of value made, or treated as made, on or after 17 July 2013 (Royal Assent).

Cross references – S. 203(1): liability of spouse in respect of transfer of property where subsequent chargeable transfer.

FA 1986, s. 100(1)(b): any reference to capital transfer tax (except where it relates to a liability to tax arising before 25 July 1986) to have effect as a reference to inheritance tax.

162A Liabilities attributable to financing excluded property

162A(1) To the extent that a liability is attributable to financing (directly or indirectly)–

(a) the acquisition of any excluded property, or

(b) the maintenance, or an enhancement, of the value of any such property,

it may only be taken into account so far as permitted by subsection (2) to (4).

162A(2) Where the property mentioned in subsection (1) has been disposed of, in whole or in part, for full consideration in money or money's worth, the liability may be taken into account up to an amount equal to so much of that consideration as–

(a) is not excluded property, and

(b) has not been used–

(i) to finance (directly or indirectly) the acquisition of excluded property or the maintenance, or an enhancement, of the value of such property, or

(ii) to discharge (directly or indirectly) any other liability that, by virtue of this section, would not be taken into account.

162A(3) The liability may be taken into account up to an amount equal to the value of such of the property mentioned in subsection (1) as–

(a) has not been disposed of, and

(b) is no longer excluded property.

162A(4) To the extent that any remaining liability is greater than the value of such of the property mentioned in subsection (1) as–

(a) has not been disposed of, and

(b) is still excluded property,

it may be taken into account, but only so far as the remaining liability is not greater than that value for any of the reasons mentioned in subsection (7).

162A(5) Subsection (6) applies where–

(a) a liability or any part of a liability is attributable to financing (directly or indirectly)–

(i) the acquisition of property that was not excluded property, or

(ii) the maintenance, or an enhancement, of the value of such property, and

(b) the property or part of the property–

(i) has not been disposed of, and

(ii) has become excluded property.

162A(6) The liability or (as the case may be) the part may only be taken into account to the extent that it exceeds the value of the property, or the part of the property, that has become excluded property, but only so far as it does not exceed that value for any of the reasons mentioned in subsection (7).

162A(7) The reasons are–

(a) arrangements the main purpose, or one of the main purposes, of which is to secure a tax advantage,

IHT Statutes

(b) an increase in the amount of the liability (whether due to the accrual of interest or otherwise), or

(c) a disposal, in whole or in part, of the property.

162A(8) In this section–

"arrangements" includes any scheme, transaction or series of transactions, agreement or understanding, whether or not legally enforceable, and any associated operations;

"remaining liability" means the liability mentioned in subsection (1) so far as subsections (2) and (3) do not permit it to be taken into account;

"tax advantage" means–

(a) the avoidance or reduction of a charge to tax, or

(b) the avoidance of a possible determination in respect of tax.

History – S. 162A inserted by FA 2013, s. 176 and Sch. 36, para. 3, with effect in relation to transfers of value made, or treated as made, on or after 17 July 2013 (Royal Assent).

162AA Liabilities attributable to financing non-residents' foreign currency accounts

162AA(1) This section applies if–

(a) in determining the value of a person's estate immediately before death, a balance on any qualifying foreign currency account ("the relevant balance") is to be left out of account under section 157 (non-residents' bank accounts), and

(b) the person has a liability which is attributable, in whole or in part, to financing (directly or indirectly) the relevant balance.

162AA(2) To the extent that the liability is attributable as mentioned in subsection (1)(b), it may only be taken into account in determining the value of the person's estate immediately before death so far as permitted by subsection (3).

162AA(3) If the amount of the liability that is attributable as mentioned in subsection (1)(b) exceeds the value of the relevant balance, the excess may be taken into account, but only so far as the excess does not arise for either of the reasons mentioned in subsection (4).

162AA(4) The reasons are–

(a) arrangements the main purpose, or one of the main purposes, of which is to secure a tax advantage, or

(b) an increase in the amount of the liability (whether due to the accrual of interest or otherwise).

162AA(5) In subsection (4)(a)–

"arrangements" includes any scheme, transaction or series of transactions, agreement or understanding, whether or not legally enforceable, and any associated operations;

"tax advantage" means–

(a) the avoidance or reduction of a charge to tax, or

(b) the avoidance of a possible determination in respect of tax.

History – S. 162AA inserted by FA 2014, s. 117 and Sch. 25, para. 3(1), with effect in relation to transfers of value made, or treated as made, on or after 17 July 2014.

162B Liabilities attributable to financing certain relievable property

162B(1) Subsection (2) applies if–

(a) the whole or part of any value transferred by a transfer of value is to be treated as reduced, under section 104, by virtue of it being attributable to the value of relevant business property, and

(b) the transferor has a liability which is attributable, in whole or in part, to financing (directly or indirectly)–

(i) the acquisition of that property, or

(ii) the maintenance, or an enhancement, of its value.

162B(2) The liability is, so far as possible, to be taken to reduce the value attributable to the value of the relevant business property, before it is treated as reduced under section 104, but only to the extent that the liability–

(a) is attributable as *mentioned in* subsection (1)(b), and

(b) does not reduce the value of the relevant business property by virtue of section 110(b).

162B(3) Subsection (4) applies if–

(a) the whole or part of any value transferred by a transfer of value is to be treated as reduced, under section 116, by virtue of it being attributable to the agricultural value of agricultural property, and

(b) the transferor has a liability which is attributable, in whole or in part, to financing (directly or indirectly)–
  (i) the acquisition of that property, or
  (ii) the maintenance, or an enhancement, of its agricultural value.

162B(4) To the extent that the liability is attributable as mentioned in subsection (3)(b), it is, so far as possible, to be taken to reduce the value attributable to the agricultural value of the agricultural property, before it is treated as reduced under section 116.

162B(5) Subsection (6) applies if–

(a) part of the value of a person's estate immediately before death is attributable to the value of land on which trees or underwood are growing,

(b) the value of the trees or underwood is to be left out of account, under section 125(2)(a), in determining the value transferred by the chargeable transfer made on the person's death, and

(c) the person has a liability which is attributable, in whole or in part, to financing (directly or indirectly)–
  (i) the acquisition of the land or trees or underwood,
  (ii) planting the trees or underwood, or
  (iii) the maintenance, or an enhancement, of the value of the trees or underwood.

162B(6) To the extent that the liability is attributable as mentioned in subsection (5)(c), it is, so far as possible, to be taken to reduce the value of the trees or underwood, before their value is left out of account.

162B(7) Subject to subsection (8), to the extent that a liability is, in accordance with this section, taken to reduce value in determining the value transferred by a chargeable transfer, that liability is not then to be taken into account in determining the value transferred by any subsequent transfer of value by the same transferor.

162B(8) Subsection (7) does not prevent a liability from being taken into account by reason only that the liability has previously been taken into account in determining the amount on which tax is chargeable under section 64.

162B(9) For the purposes of subsections (1) to (4) and (7), references to a transfer of value or chargeable transfer include references to an occasion on which tax is chargeable under Chapter 3 of Part 3 (apart from section 79) and–

(a) references to the value transferred by a transfer of value or chargeable transfer include references to the amount on which tax is then chargeable, and

(b) references to the transferor include references to the trustees of the settlement concerned.

162B(10) In this section–

"agricultural property" and **"agricultural value"** have the same meaning as in Chapter 2 of Part 5;

"relevant business property" has the same meaning as in Chapter 1 of Part 5.

History – S. 162B inserted by FA 2013, s. 176 and Sch. 36, para. 3, with effect in relation to transfers of value made, or treated as made, on or after 17 July 2013 (Royal Assent) but only in relation to liabilities incurred (FA 2013, Sch. 36, para. 5(3)) on or after 6 April 2013.

162C Sections 162A, 162AA and 162B: supplementary provision

162C(1) This section applies for the purposes of determining the extent to which a liability is attributable as mentioned in section 162A(1) or (5), 162AA(1) or 162B(1)(b), (3)(b) or (5)(c).

162C(1A) In a case in which the value of a person's estate immediately before death is to be determined, where a liability was discharged in part before that time–

(a) any part of the liability that, at the time of discharge, was not attributable as mentioned in subsection (1) is, so far as possible, to be taken to have been discharged first,

(b) any part of the liability that, at the time of discharge, was attributable as mentioned in section 162B(1)(b), (3)(b) or (5)(c) is, so far as possible, only to be taken to have been discharged after any part of the liability within paragraph (a) was discharged,

(c) any part of the liability that, at the time of discharge, was attributable as mentioned in section 162AA(1) is, so far as possible, only to be taken to have been discharged after any parts of the liability within paragraph (a) or (b) were discharged, and

(d) any part of the liability that, at the time of discharge, was attributable as mentioned in section 162A(1) or (5) is, so far as possible, only to be taken to have been discharged after any parts of the liability within paragraphs (a) to (c) were discharged.

162C(2) In any other case, where a liability was discharged in part before the time in relation to which the question as to whether or how to take it into account arises–

(a) any part of the liability that, at the time of discharge, was not attributable as mentioned in section 162A(1) or (5) or 162B(1)(b), (3)(b) or (5)(c) is, so far as possible, to be taken to have been discharged first,

(b) any part of the liability that, at the time of discharge, was attributable as mentioned in section 162B(1)(b), (3)(b) or (5)(c) is, so far as possible, only to be taken to have been discharged after any part of the liability within paragraph (a) was discharged, and

(c) any part of the liability that, at the time of discharge, was attributable as mentioned in section 162A(1) or (5) is, so far as possible, only to be taken to have been discharged after any parts of the liability within paragraph (a) or (b) were discharged.

History – In the heading to s. 162C, ", 162AA" inserted by FA 2014, s. 117 and Sch. 25, para. 3(3), with effect in relation to transfers of value made, or treated as made, on or after 17 July 2014.
In s. 162C(1), ", 162AA(1)" inserted by FA 2014, s. 117 and Sch. 25, para. 3(4), with effect in relation to transfers of value made, or treated as made, on or after 17 July 2014.
S. 162C(1A) inserted by FA 2014, s. 117 and Sch. 25, para. 3(5), with effect in relation to transfers of value made, or treated as made, on or after 17 July 2014.
In s. 162C(2), the words "In any other case, where" substituted for the word "Where" by FA 2014, s. 117 and Sch. 25, para. 3(6)(a), with effect in relation to transfers of value made, or treated as made, on or after 17 July 2014.
In s. 162C(2)(a), the words "section 162A(1) or (5) or 162B(1)(b), (3)(b) or (5)(c)" substituted for "subsection (1)" by FA 2014, s. 117 and Sch. 25, para. 3(6)(b), with effect in relation to transfers of value made, or treated as made, on or after 17 July 2014.
S. 162C inserted by FA 2013, s. 176 and Sch. 36, para. 3, with effect in relation to transfers of value made, or treated as made, on or after 17 July 2013 (Royal Assent).

163 Restriction on freedom to dispose

163(1) Where, by a contract made at any time, the right to dispose of any property has been excluded or restricted, then, in determining the value of the property for the purpose of the first relevant event happening after that time,–

(a) the exclusion or restriction shall be taken into account only to the extent (if any) that consideration in money or money's worth was given for it, but

(b) if the contract was a chargeable transfer or was part of associated operations which together were a chargeable transfer, an allowance shall be made for the value transferred thereby (calculated as if no tax had been chargeable on it) or for so much of the value transferred as is attributable to the exclusion or restriction.

163(2) Where the contract was made before 27th March 1974 subsection (1) above applies only if the first relevant event is a transfer made on death.

163(3) In this section **"relevant event"**, in relation to any property, means–

(a) a chargeable transfer in the case of which the whole or part of the value transferred is attributable to the value of the property; and

(b) anything which would be such a chargeable transfer but for this section.

164 Transferor's expenses

164 In determining the value transferred by a transfer of value, expenses incurred by the transferor in making the transfer (but not his liability for capital transfer tax)–

(a) shall, if borne by him, be left out of account;

(b) shall, if borne by a person benefiting from the transfer, be treated as reducing the value transferred.

Cross references – FA 1986, s. 100(1)(b): any reference to capital transfer tax (except where it relates to a liability to tax arising before 25 July 1986) to have effect as a reference to inheritance tax.

165 Tax on capital gains

165(1) Where a chargeable transfer is or includes a disposal of an asset and on the disposal a gain accrues to the transferor for the purposes of the 1992 Act, then if–

(a) the whole or part of the gain is a chargeable gain or a development gain, and

(b) the whole or part of any capital gains tax or income tax chargeable on the gain is borne by the donee (within the meaning of section 282 of that Act),

the amount of the tax so borne shall be treated as reducing the value transferred by the chargeable transfer.

165(2) *Subsection (1) above shall* not apply where the chargeable transfer is made under Part III of this Act and the gain accrues to the trustees of the settlement; but if in such a case any capital gains tax chargeable on the gain is borne by a person who becomes absolutely entitled to the settled property concerned, the amount of the tax so borne shall be treated as reducing the value transferred by the chargeable transfer.

165(3) In any case where–

(a) payment of an amount of capital gains tax is postponed by virtue of Schedule 14 to the Finance Act 1984, and

(b) any of that capital gains tax becomes payable in accordance with paragraph 11 of that Schedule by reason of the receipt of a capital payment by a close relative of the beneficiary, as mentioned in sub-paragraph (3) of that paragraph, and

(c) all or part of the capital gains tax becoming so payable is paid by the close relative,

the payment by the close relative shall be treated for the purposes of this Act as made in satisfaction of a liability of his.

History – References to the 1992 Act substituted by TCGA 1992, s. 290 and Sch. 10, para. 8(8).

Cross references – FA 1984, Sch. 14 (beneficiary's liability for tax on gains of non-resident trustees) repealed by TCGA 1992, s. 290 and Sch. 12, in relation to tax for 1992–93 and subsequent years of assessment, but subject to saving in relation to amounts of tax postponed under that Schedule (see TCGA 1992, Sch. 11, para. 18(b)).
TCGA 1992, s. 282: donee includes case where a transaction is otherwise than at arm's length so far as money or money's worth passes without full consideration in money or money's worth.

166 Creditors' rights

166 In determining the value of a right to receive a sum due under any obligation it shall be assumed that the obligation will be duly discharged, except if or to the extent that recovery of the sum is impossible or not reasonably practicable and has not become so by any act or omission of the person to whom the sum is due.

167 Life policies, etc.

167(1) In determining in connection with a transfer of value the value of a policy of insurance on a person's life or of a contract for an annuity payable on a person's death, that value shall be taken to be not less than–

(a) the total of the premiums or other consideration which, at any time before the transfer of value, has been paid under the policy or contract or any policy or contract for which it was directly or indirectly substituted, less

(b) any sum which, at any time before the transfer of value, has been paid under, or in consideration for the surrender of any right conferred by, the policy or contract or a policy or contract for which it was directly or indirectly substituted.

167(2) Subsection (1) above shall not apply in the case of–

(a) the transfer of value which a person makes on his death, or

(b) any other transfer of value which does not result in the policy or contract ceasing to be part of the transferor's estate.

167(3) Subsection (1) above shall not apply where the policy is one–

(a) under which the sum assured becomes payable only if the person whose life is insured dies before the expiry of a specified term or both before the expiry of a specified term and during the life of a specified person, and

(b) which, if that specified term ends, or can, under the policy, be extended so as to end, more than three years after the making of the insurance, satisfies the condition that, if neither the person whose life is insured nor the specified person dies before the expiry of the specified term–

  (i) the premiums are payable during at least two-thirds of that term and at yearly or shorter intervals, and

  (ii) the premiums payable in any one period of twelve months are not more than twice the premiums payable in any other such period.

167(4) Where the policy is one under which–

(a) the benefit secured is expressed in units the value of which is published and subject to fluctuation, and

(b) the payment of each premium secures the allocation to the policy of a specified number of such units,

then, if the value, at the time of the transfer of value, of the units allocated to the policy on the payment of premiums is less than the aggregate of what the respective values of those units were at the time of allocation, the value to be taken under subsection (1) above as a minimum shall be reduced by the amount of the difference.

167(5) References in subsections (1) and (4) above to a transfer of value shall be construed as including references to an event on which there is a charge to tax under Chapter III of Part III of this Act (apart from section 79), other than an event on which tax is chargeable in respect of the policy or contract by reason only that its value (apart from this section) is reduced.

History – In s. 167(2), the words "and shall not apply in determining the amounts mentioned in sections 148(2)(a) and 149(5)(a)(ii) above" at the end were repealed by FA 1986, s. 114 and Sch. 23, Pt. X, where the donee's transfer within s. 148 was made on or after 18 March 1986.

Cross references – Pt. III, Ch. III: charge on settlements without interest in possession, subject to exemption from ten-yearly charge in certain cases (s. 79).

168 Unquoted shares and securities

168(1) In determining the price which unquoted shares or unquoted securities might reasonably be expected to fetch if sold in the open market it shall be assumed that in that market there is available to any prospective purchaser of the shares or securities all the information which a prudent prospective purchaser might reasonably require if he were proposing to purchase them from a willing vendor by private treaty and at arm's length.

168(2) [Repealed by FA 1987, s. 58 and Sch. 8, para. 12(2) and s. 72 and Sch. 16, Pt. IX.]

History – In s. 168(1), the word "unquoted" before "securities" where it first occurs was inserted by FA 1987, s. 58 and Sch. 8, para. 12(1), with effect in relation to transfers of value made, and other events occurring, on or after 17 March 1987.
S. 168(2) repealed by FA 1987, s. 58 and Sch. 8, para. 12(2) and s. 72 and Sch. 16, Pt. IX with effect in relation to transfers of value made, and other events occurring, on or after 17 March 1987.

169 Farm cottages

169(1) In determining the value of agricultural property which includes cottages occupied by persons employed solely for agricultural purposes in connection with the property, no account shall be taken of any value attributable to the fact that the cottages are suitable for the residential purposes of persons not so employed.

169(2) Expressions used in subsection (1) above and in Chapter II of Part V of this Act have the same meaning in that subsection as in that Chapter.

Extra-statutory concessions – F16: agricultural tied cottage occupied by retired farm worker or widow(er) regarded as satisfying occupation condition in s. 169.

170 Leases for life, etc.

170 Where under section 43(3) above a lease of property is to be treated as a settlement, the value of the lessor's interest in the property shall be taken to be such part of the value of the property as bears to it the same proportion as the value of the consideration, at the time the lease was granted, bore to what would then have been the value of a full consideration in money or money's worth.

Cross references – S. 43: settlement and related expressions.

Chapter II – Estate on Death

171 Changes occurring on death

171(1) In determining the value of a person's estate immediately before his death changes in the value of his estate which have occurred by reason of the death and fall within subsection (2) below shall be taken into account as if they had occurred before the death.

171(2) A change falls within this subsection if it is an addition to the property comprised in the estate or an increase or decrease of the value of any property so comprised, other than a decrease resulting from such an alteration as is mentioned in section 98(1) above; but the termination on the death of any interest or the passing of any interest by survivorship does not fall within this subsection.

Cross references – S. 98(1): alterations in close company's unquoted shares or securities or in rights attaching thereto.

172 Funeral expenses

172 In determining the value of a person's estate immediately before his death, allowance shall be made for reasonable funeral expenses.

Extra-statutory concessions – F1: reasonable mourning expenses.
Statements of practice – SP 7/87: "funeral expenses" includes cost of a tombstone or gravestone.

173 Expenses incurred abroad

173 In determining the value of a person's estate immediately before his death, an allowance against the value of property situated outside the United Kingdom shall be made for any expense incurred in administering or realising the property which is shown to be attributable to the situation of the property, but the allowance shall not exceed 5 per cent of the value of the property.

174 Income tax and unpaid capital transfer tax

174(1) In determining the value of a person's estate immediately before his death, allowance shall be made for–

(a) any liability for income tax in respect of an offshore income gain, within the meaning of regulations under section 354(1) of the Taxation (International and Other Provisions) Act 2010, arising on a disposal which is deemed, under such regulations (see regulation 34 of the Offshore Funds (Tax) Regulations 2009 (S.I. 2009/3001)), to occur on the death; and

(b) any liability to income tax arising under Chapter 8 of Part 4 of the Income Tax (Trading and Other Income) Act 2005 (deeply discounted securities) on a transfer which is treated as taking place by virtue of section 437(2) of that Act.

174(2) Where in determining the value of a person's estate immediately before his death a liability for capital transfer tax is taken into account, then, if that tax or any part of it is not in the event paid out of the estate, the value of the estate immediately before his death shall be treated as increased by an amount equal to that tax or so much of it as is not so paid.

History – In s. 174(1)(a) the words "under section 354(1) of the Taxation (International and Other Provisions) Act 2010" substituted for the words "made under section 41(1) of the Finance Act 2008" by TIOPA 2010, s. 374 and Sch. 8, para. 162, with effect for corporation tax purposes for accounting periods ending on or after 1 April 2010, for income tax and capital gains tax purposes for the tax year 2010–11 and subsequent tax years, and for petroleum revenue tax purposes for chargeable periods beginning on or after 1 July 2010.
In s. 174(1)(a), the words "regulations made under section 41(1) of the Finance Act 2008, arising on a disposal which is deemed, under such regulations (see regulation 34 of the Offshore Funds (Tax) Regulations 2009 (S.I. 2009/3001)), to occur on the death" substituted for the words "Chapter V of Part XVII of the Taxes Act 1988, arising on a disposal which is deemed to occur on the death by virtue of section 757(3) of that Act" by SI 2009/3001, reg. 125, with effect from 1 December 2009, in accordance with SI 2009/3001, reg. 1, subject to transitional and savings provisions in SI 2009/3001, Sch. 1.
In s. 174(1)(b), the words "Chapter 8 of Part 4 of the Income Tax (Trading and Other Income) Act 2005 (deeply discounted securities)" substituted for "Schedule 13 to the Finance Act 1996 (discounted securities)" by ITTOIA 2005, s. 882(2) and Sch. 1, para. 396(a).
In s. 174(1)(b), the words "section 437(2) of that Act" substituted for "paragraph 4(2) of that Schedule" by ITTOIA 2005, s. 882(2) and Sch. 1, para. 396(b).
In s. 174(1)(b), the words from "Schedule 13" to the end of that paragraph substituted for the previous words "paragraph 4 of Schedule 4 to that Act (deep discount securities) on a disposal which is deemed to occur by virtue of paragraph 7(2) of that Schedule.", by FA 1996, s. 104 and Sch. 14, para. 2, with respect to deaths on or after 6 April 1996.
See ICTA 1988, Sch. 29, para. 32, for substitution of reference to that Act.

Cross references – FA 1986, s. 100(1)(b): any reference to capital transfer tax (except where it relates to a liability arising before 25 July 1986) to have effect as a reference to inheritance tax.
ICTA 1988, s. 757(3): disposal of material interests in non-qualifying offshore funds.

175 Liability to make future payments, etc.

175 Where in determining the value of a person's estate immediately before his death a liability to make payments or transfer assets under such a disposition as is mentioned in section 262 below is taken into account, the liability shall be computed as if the amount or value of the payments or assets were reduced by the chargeable portion (as defined in that section).

Cross references – S. 262: dispositions where the transfer of assets etc. actually takes place more than one year later.

175A Discharge of liabilities after death

175A(1) In determining the value of a person's estate immediately before death, a liability may be taken into account to the extent that–

(a) it is discharged on or after death, out of the estate or from excluded property owned by the person immediately before death, in money or money's worth, and

(b) it is not otherwise prevented, under any provision of this Act, from being taken into account.

175A(2) Where the whole or any part of a liability is not discharged in accordance with paragraph (a) of subsection (1), the liability or (as the case may be) the part may only be taken into account for the purpose mentioned in that subsection to the extent that–

(a) there is a real commercial reason for the liability or the part not being discharged,

(b) securing a tax advantage is not the main purpose, or one of the main purposes, of leaving the liability or part undischarged, and

(c) the liability or the part is not otherwise prevented, under any provision of this Act, from being taken into account.

175A(3) For the purposes of subsection (2)(a) there is a real commercial reason for a liability, or part of a liability, not being discharged where it is shown that–

(a) the liability is to a person dealing at arm's length, or

(b) if the liability were to a person dealing at arm's length, that person would not require the liability to be discharged.

IHT Statutes

175A(4) Where, by virtue of this section, a liability is not taken into account in determining the value of a person's estate immediately before death, the liability is also not to be taken into account in determining the extent to which the estate of any spouse or civil partner of the person is increased for the purposes of section 18.

175A(5) In subsection (2)(b) **"tax advantage"** means–

(a) a relief from tax or increased relief from tax,

(b) a repayment of tax or increased repayment of tax,

(c) the avoidance, reduction or delay of a charge to tax or an assessment to tax, or

(d) the avoidance of a possible assessment to tax or determination in respect of tax.

175A(6) In subsection (5) **"tax"** includes income tax and capital gains tax.

175A(7) Where the liability is discharged as mentioned in subsection (1)(a) only in part–

(a) any part of the liability that is attributable as mentioned in section 162A(1) or (5) is, so far possible, taken to be discharged first,

(aa) any part of the liability that is attributable as mentioned in section 162AA(1) is, so far as possible, taken to be discharged only after any part of the liability within paragraph (a) is discharged,

(b) any part of the liability that is attributable as mentioned in section 162B(1)(b), (3)(b) or (5)(c) is, so far as possible, taken to be discharged only after any parts of the liability within paragraph (a) or (aa) are discharged, and

(c) the liability so far as it is not attributable as mentioned in any of paragraphs (a) to (b) is, so far as possible, taken to be discharged only after any parts of the liability within any of those paragraphs are discharged.

History – S. 175A(7)(aa) inserted by FA 2014, s. 117 and Sch. 25, para. 3(7)(a), with effect in relation to transfers of value made, or treated as made, on or after 17 July 2014.

In s. 175A(7)(b), the word "parts" substituted for the word "part" by FA 2014, s. 117 and Sch. 25, para. 3(7)(b)(i), with effect in relation to transfers of value made, or treated as made, on or after 17 July 2014.

In s. 175A(7)(b), "(a) or (aa) are" substituted for "(a) is" by FA 2014, s. 117 and Sch. 25, para. 3(7)(b)(ii), with effect in relation to transfers of value made, or treated as made, on or after 17 July 2014.

In s. 175A(7)(c), the words "any of paragraphs (a) to (b)" substituted for the words "paragraph (a) or (b)" by FA 2014, s. 117 and Sch. 25, para. 3(7)(c)(i), with effect in relation to transfers of value made, or treated as made, on or after 17 July 2014.

In s. 175A(7)(c), the word "any" substituted for the word "either" by FA 2014, s. 117 and Sch. 25, para. 3(7)(c)(ii), with effect in relation to transfers of value made, or treated as made, on or after 17 July 2014.

S. 175A inserted by FA 2013, s. 176 and Sch. 36, para. 4, with effect in relation to transfers of value made, or treated as made, on or after 17 July 2013 (Royal Assent).

176 Related property etc. – sales

176(1) This section has effect where, within three years after the death of any person, there is a qualifying sale of any property (**"the property concerned"**) comprised in his estate immediately before his death and valued for the purposes of this Act–

(a) in accordance with section 161 above, or

(b) in conjunction with property which was also comprised in the estate but has not at any time since the death been vested in the vendors.

176(2) If a claim is made for relief under this section the value of the property concerned immediately before the death shall be taken to be what it would have been if it had not been determined as mentioned in subsection (1) above.

176(3) For the purposes of subsection (1) above a sale is a **qualifying sale** if–

(a) the vendors are the persons in whom the property concerned vested immediately after the death or the deceased's personal representatives; and

(b) it is at arm's length for a price freely negotiated at the time of the sale and is not made in conjunction with a sale of any of the related property taken into account as mentioned in subsection (1)(a) above or any of the property mentioned in subsection (1)(b) above; and

(c) no person concerned as vendor (or as having an interest in the proceeds of sale) is the same as or connected with any person concerned as purchaser (or as having an interest in the purchase); and

(d) neither the vendors nor any other person having an interest in the proceeds of sale obtain in connection with the sale a right to acquire the property sold or any interest in or created out of it.

176(4) Subsection (2) above shall not apply unless the price obtained on the sale, with any adjustment needed to take account of any difference in circumstances at the date of the sale and at the date of the death, is less than the value which, apart from this section and apart from Chapter IV of this Part of this Act, would be the value of the property concerned determined as mentioned in subsection (1) above.

176(5) Where the property concerned consists of shares in or securities of a close company, subsection (2) above shall not apply if at any time between the death and the qualifying sale the value of the shares or securities is reduced by more than 5 per cent as a result of an alteration in the company's share or loan capital or in any rights attaching to shares in or securities of the company; and for the purposes of this subsection–

"alteration" includes extinguishment, and

"close company" has the same meaning as in Part IV of this Act.

Cross references – S. 105(2A): circumstances in which shares of a company whose value is reduced under s. 176 fail to qualify as relevant business property under s. 105(1)(bb).
S. 122(2): circumstances in which shares of a company whose value is reduced under s. 176 fail to qualify for agricultural property relief.
S. 161: valuation of related property – general.

177 Scottish agricultural leases

177(1) Where any part of the value of a person's estate immediately before his death is attributable to the interest of a tenant in an unexpired portion of a lease for a fixed term of agricultural property in Scotland then, subject to subsection (3) below, there shall be left out of account in determining that value any value associated with any prospect of renewal of the lease by tacit relocation.

177(2) Where any part of the value of a person's estate immediately before his death is attributable to the interest of a tenant of agricultural property in Scotland, being an interest which is–

(a) held by virtue of tacit relocation, and

(b) acquired on the death by a new tenant,

then, subject to subsection (3) below, the value of the interest shall be left out of account in determining the value of that estate.

177(3) Subsections (1) and (2) above shall not apply unless the deceased had been tenant of the property in question continuously for a period of at least two years immediately preceding his death or had become tenant by succession.

177(4) The value to be left out of account by virtue of subsection (2) above shall not include the value of any rights to compensation in respect of tenant's improvements.

Chapter III – Sale of Shares etc. from Deceased's Estate

178 Preliminary

178(1) In this Chapter–

"the appropriate person", in relation to any qualifying investments comprised in a person's estate immediately before his death, means the person liable for capital transfer tax attributable to the value of those investments or, if there is more than one such person, and one of them is in fact paying the tax, that person;

"the loss on sale" means the amount determined in accordance with section 179(1) below;

"qualifying investments" means (subject to subsection (2) below) shares or securities which are quoted at the date of death in question, holdings in a unit trust which at that date is an authorised unit trust, shares in an open-ended investment company and shares in any common investment fund established under section 42 of the Administration of Justice Act 1982;

"relevant proportion", in relation to the investments to which a claim relates, or any of them, means the proportion by which the loss on sale is reduced under section 180 below;

"sale value", in relation to any qualifying investments, means their value for the purposes of section 179(1)(b) below;

"value on death", in relation to any qualifying investments, means their value for the purposes of section 179(1)(a) below.

178(2) Shares or securities which are comprised in a person's estate immediately before his death and in respect of which listing on a recognised stock exchange or dealing on the Unlisted Securities Market is suspended at that time shall be qualifying investments for the purposes of this Chapter if they are again so listed or dealt in when they are sold as mentioned in section 179(1) below or exchanged as mentioned in section 184 below.

178(3) Any reference in this Chapter to the **investments to which a claim relates** is a reference to all the qualifying investments which, on the making of the claim, are taken into account under section 179(1) below in determining the loss on sale.

IHT Statutes

178(4) For the purposes of this Chapter–

(a) the personal representatives of the deceased, and

(b) the trustees of a settlement,

shall each be treated as a single and continuing body of persons (distinct from the persons who may from time to time be the personal representatives or trustees).

178(5) In any case where, for the purposes of this Chapter, it is necessary to determine the price at which any investments were purchased or sold or the best consideration that could reasonably have been obtained on the sale of any investments, no account shall be taken of expenses (whether by way of commission, stamp duty or otherwise) which are incidental to the sale or purchase.

History – In s. 178(1), in the definition of "qualifying investments", immediately after the words "authorised unit trust", the words "(as defined in section 468 of the Taxes Act 1988)" were repealed by FA 2003, s. 216 and Sch. 43, Pt. 4(1), with effect in relation to transfers of value and other events occurring on or after 16 October 2002.

In s. 178(1), in the definition of "qualifying investments", the words ", shares in an open-ended investment company" inserted and the words "section 42 of the Administration of Justice Act 1982" substituted for the words "section 1 of the Administration of Justice Act 1965" by FA 2003, s. 186(4), with effect in relation to transfers of value or other events occurring on or after 16 October 2002.

In s. 178(1), in the definition of "qualifying investments", the words "are quoted…in question" substituted by FA 1987, s. 58 and Sch. 8, para. 13(1), with effect in relation to transfers of value made, and other events occurring, on or after 17 March 1987.

In s. 178(2), the word "listing" substituted for the previous word "quotation", and words "so listed or dealt in" substituted for the previous word "quoted", by FA 1996, s. 199 and Sch. 38, para. 4(1), with effect in relation to investments sold, or treated as sold, on or after 1 April 1996.

In s. 178(2), the words "or dealing on the Unlisted Securities Market" were inserted, and the words "on a recognised stock exchange" which occurred between "again quoted" and "when they are sold" were omitted, by FA 1987, s. 58 and Sch. 8, para. 13(2), with effect in relation to transfers of value made, and other events occurring, on or after 17 March 1987.

See ICTA 1988, Sch. 29, para. 32, for substitution of reference to that Act.

Cross references – FA 1986, s. 100(1)(b): any reference to capital transfer tax (except where it relates to a liability to tax arising before 25 July 1986) has effect as a reference to inheritance tax.

179 The relief

179(1) On a claim being made in that behalf by the appropriate person there shall be determined for the purposes of this Chapter the amount (if any) by which–

(a) the aggregate of the values which, apart from this Chapter, would be the values for the purposes of tax of all the qualifying investments comprised in a person's estate immediately before his death which are sold by the appropriate person within the period of twelve months immediately following the date of the death

exceeds

(b) the aggregate of the values of those investments at the time they were so sold, taking the value of any particular investments for this purpose as the price for which they were so sold or, if it is greater, the best consideration which could reasonably have been obtained for them at the time of the sale.

179(2) Subject to the following provisions of the Chapter, in determining the tax chargeable on the death in question, the value of the investments to which the claim relates shall be treated as reduced by an amount equal to the loss on sale.

179(2A) A claim under this Chapter must be made not more than 4 years after the end of the period mentioned in subsection (1)(a).

179(3) A claim made by the appropriate person under this Chapter shall specify the capacity in which he makes the claim, and the reference in subsection (1) above to **qualifying investments** which are sold by him is a reference to investments which, immediately before their sale, were held by him in the capacity in which he makes the claim.

History – S. 179(2A) inserted by FA 2009, s. 99 and Sch. 51, para. 9, with effect from 1 April 2011 (SI 2010/867, art. 2(2)).

180 Effect of purchases

180(1) If a claim is made under this Chapter and, at any time during the period beginning on the date of the death in question and ending two months after the date of the last sale made as mentioned in section 179(1)(a) above, the person making the claim purchases any qualifying investments in the same capacity as that in which he makes the claim, the loss on sale of the investments to which the claim relates shall be treated for the purposes of section 179(2) above as reduced by the proportion which the aggregate of the purchase prices of all the qualifying investments so purchased bears to the aggregate of the values referred to in section 179(1)(b) above (or, if the aggregate of those purchase prices equals or exceeds the aggregate of those values, the loss on sale shall be extinguished).

180(2) If a claim is made under this Chapter by any person in a capacity other than that of personal representative or trustee–

(a) subsection (1) above shall have effect in his case as if for the words "in the same capacity as that in which he makes the claim" there were substituted the words "otherwise than in the capacity of personal representative or trustee", and

(b) no account shall be taken under that subsection of any qualifying investments purchased by him unless they are of the same description as one of the qualifying investments to which the claim relates.

180(3) For the purposes of subsection (2) above, two investments, not being investments in an authorised unit trust or common investment fund, shall not be treated as of the same description if they are separately listed on a recognised stock exchange or separately dealt in on the Unlisted Securities Market, and an investment in one authorised unit trust or common investment fund shall not be treated as of the same description as an investment in another authorised unit trust or common investment fund.

History – In s. 180(3) the word "listed" substituted for the previous word "quoted" by FA 1996, s. 199 and Sch. 38, para. 3, with effect in relation to any time falling on or after 1 April 1996.

In s. 180(3), the words "or separately dealt in on the Unlisted Securities Market" were inserted by FA 1987, s. 58 and Sch. 8, para. 14, in relation to transfers of value made, and other events occurring, on or after 17 March 1987.

181 Capital receipts

181(1) For the purposes of section 179(1)(b) above, if–

(a) at any time after the death in question (whether during or after the period of twelve months immediately following the date of the death) the appropriate person receives any capital payment or payments which is or are attributable to any qualifying investments comprised in the deceased's estate immediately before his death, and

(b) those investments are sold by him within that period,

the price for which those investments were sold or, as the case may be, the best consideration referred to in section 179(1)(b) shall be taken to be increased by an amount equal to the capital payment or, as the case may be, the aggregate of the capital payments, referred to in paragraph (a) above.

181(2) If the appropriate person receives or becomes entitled to receive in respect of any qualifying investments a provisional allotment of shares in or debentures of a company and he disposes of his rights, the amount of the consideration for the disposal shall be treated for the purposes of this section as a capital payment attributable to those investments.

181(3) In this section **"capital payment"**, in relation to any investment, does not include the price paid on the sale of the investment but, subject to that, includes any money or money's worth which does not constitute income for the purposes of income tax.

182 Payment of calls

182 For the purposes of section 179(1)(a) above, if–

(a) at any time after the death in question (whether during or after the period of twelve months immediately following the date of the death) the appropriate person pays an amount in pursuance of a call in respect of any qualifying investments comprised in the deceased's estate immediately before his death, and

(b) those investments are sold by the appropriate person within that period,

the value on death of those investments shall be the aggregate of the amount so paid and their value as determined apart from this Chapter.

183 Changes in holdings

183(1) This section applies in any case where, within the period of twelve months immediately following the date of the death in question, there occurs in relation to any qualifying investments comprised in the deceased's estate immediately before his death (in this section referred to as **"the original holding"**) a transaction to which section 127 of the 1992 Act applies, that is to say–

(a) a reorganisation, within the meaning of section 126(1) of that Act; or

(b) the conversion of securities within the meaning of section 132 of that Act; or

(c) the issue by a company of shares or debentures in exchange for shares in or debentures of another company in such circumstances that section 135 of that Act applies; or

(d) the issue by a company of shares or debentures under such an arrangement as is referred to in section 136 of that Act;

or any transaction relating to a unit trust scheme which corresponds to any of the transactions referred to in paragraphs (a) to (d) above and to which section 127 of that Act applies by virtue of section 99 of that Act.

183(2) Where this section applies, the holding of investments which, as the result of the transaction, constitutes a new holding within the meaning of section 126(1) shall be treated for the purposes of this Chapter as being the same as the original holding; and references in the following provisions of this section to the new holding shall be construed accordingly.

183(3) If the appropriate person gives, or becomes liable to give, as part of or in connection with the transaction concerned, any consideration for the new holding or any part of it, then, for the purposes of subsection (5) below, the value on death of the new holding shall be treated as the aggregate of–

(a) the value on death of the original holding, and

(b) an amount equal to that consideration,

and in any other case the value on death of the new holding shall be taken to be the same as the value on death of the original holding.

183(4) For the purposes of subsection (3) above, there shall not be treated as consideration given for the new holding or any part of it–

(a) any surrender, cancellation or other alteration of any of the investments comprised in the original holding or of the rights attached thereto, or

(b) any consideration consisting of any application, in paying up the new holding or any part of it, of assets of the company concerned or of any dividend or other distribution declared out of those assets but not made.

183(5) If, within the period referred to in subsection (1) above, the appropriate person sells any investments comprised in the new holding, the value on death of those investments shall be determined by the formula–

$$\frac{Vs(H - S)}{(Vs + Vr)}$$

where–

Vs is the sale value of the investments,

Vr is the market value at the time of the sale of any investments remaining in the new holding after the sale,

H is the value on death of the new holding, and

S is the value on death of any investments which were originally comprised in the new holding but have been sold on a previous occasion or occasions.

183(6) For the purposes of subsection (5) above the **market value** of any investments at any time means the value which they would (apart from this Chapter) have for the purposes of this Act if they were comprised in the estate of a person who died at that time.

History – References to provisions of the "1992 Act" substituted by TCGA 1992, s. 290 and Sch. 10, para. 8(9).

Cross references – TCGA 1992, s. 126(1), 127, 132, 135, 136: equation of original and new holdings on a reorganisation, conversion of securities (excluding compensation for compulsory purchase: s. 134), exchange of securities and reconstruction involving the issue of securities.

Notes – In s. 183(2), reference to "section 126(1)" is a reference to that section of the 1992 Act.

184 Exchanges

184(1) If–

(a) within the period of twelve months immediately following the date of the death in question, the appropriate person exchanges (with or without any payment by way of equality of exchange) any qualifying investments comprised in the deceased's estate immediately before his death, and

(b) the market value of those investments is at the date of the exchange greater than their value on death,

then, regardless of the nature of the property taken in exchange, they shall be treated for the purposes of this Chapter as having been sold at the date of the exchange for a price equal to that market value.

184(2) This section shall not apply in any case where the exchange falls within section 183(1) above; and section 183(6) shall apply for the purposes of subsection (1) above as it applies for the purposes of section 183(5).

185 Acquisition of like investments

185(1) If, at any time within the period of twelve months immediately following the date of the death in *question, the appropriate person sells* any investments which form part of a holding of investments which are all of the same description and consist of–

(a) investments comprised in the deceased's estate immediately before his death, and

(b) investments acquired by the appropriate person, by purchase or otherwise, after the death but not in the circumstances in which section 183 above applies, the investments so sold shall be apportioned for the purposes of this Chapter between those falling within paragraph (a) and those falling within paragraph (b) above in the same proportion as, immediately before the sale, the investments comprised in the holding and falling within paragraph (a) above bore to the investments so comprised and falling within paragraph (b) above.

185(2) For the purposes of this section, if the appropriate person holds investments of any description in the capacity of personal representative or trustee, the investments shall not be treated as forming part of the same holding as investments which, though of the same description, are held by him otherwise than in that capacity.

185(3) Section 180(3) above shall have effect for the purposes of this section as it has effect for the purposes of section 180(2).

186 Value of part of a fund

186(1) In any case where–

(a) part only of a holding of qualifying investments is comprised in a person's estate, and

(b) investments included in that holding are sold by the appropriate person within the period of twelve months immediately following the date of the death,

this Chapter shall apply as if the entirety of the holding were comprised in the estate and, if a claim is made in respect of the investments referred to in paragraph (b) above, the taxable fraction of the value of the investments to which the claim relates, as determined under this Chapter, shall be the value of that part of those investments which is comprised in the estate.

186(2) In subsection (1) above, **"taxable fraction"** means the fraction of which the numerator is the value, as determined apart from this Chapter, of the part of the holding referred to in paragraph (a) of that subsection and the denominator is the value, as so determined, of the entirety of that holding.

186A Cancelled investments

186A(1) Where any qualifying investments comprised in a person's estate immediately before his death are–

(a) cancelled within the period of twelve months immediately following the date of the death without being replaced by other shares or securities, and

(b) held, immediately before cancellation, by the appropriate person,

they shall be treated for the purposes of this Chapter as having been sold by the appropriate person for a nominal consideration (one pound) immediately before cancellation.

186A(2) Where any qualifying investments are included in the calculation under section 179(1) above by virtue of this section, paragraph (b) of that subsection shall have effect, so far as relating to those investments, with the omission of the words from "or" to the end.

History – S. 186A inserted by FA 1993, s. 198(1), in relation to deaths occurring on or after 16 March 1992.

186B Suspended investments

186B(1) This section applies to any qualifying investments comprised in a person's estate immediately before his death in respect of which listing on a recognised stock exchange or dealing on the Unlisted Securities Market is suspended at the end of the period of twelve months immediately following the date of the death (**"the relevant period"**).

186B(2) Where–

(a) any qualifying investments to which this section applies are, at the end of the relevant period, held by the appropriate person, and

(b) the value on death of those investments exceeds their value at the end of that period,

they shall be treated for the purposes of this Chapter as having been sold by the appropriate person immediately before the end of that period for a price equal to their value at that time.

186B(3) Where any qualifying investments are included in the calculation under section 179(1) above by virtue of this section, paragraph (b) of that subsection shall have effect, so far as relating to those investments, with the omission of the words from "or" to the end.

History – In s. 186B(1), the word "listing" substituted for the previous word "quotation", by FA 1996, s. 199 and Sch. 38, para. 4(2), with effect in relation to investments sold, or treated as sold, on or after 1 April 1996.
S. 186B inserted by FA 1993, s. 198(1), in relation to deaths occurring on or after 16 March 1992.

187 Attribution of values to specific investments

187(1) This section shall have effect in determining the value for the purposes of this Act (and, accordingly, the market value for the purposes of capital gains tax under section 274 of the 1992 Act) of any investment (in this section referred to as a **"specific investment"**) which is included among the investments to which a claim relates.

187(2) Subject to the following provisions of this section, the value of a specific investment shall be its sale value.

187(3) Subject to the following provisions of this section, in a case where the calculation of the loss on sale of the investments to which a claim relates is affected by section 180 above–

(a) if the value on death of a specific investment exceeds its sale price, the value of that investment shall be the aggregate of its sale value and an amount equal to the relevant proportion of the difference between its sale price and its value on death; and

(b) if the sale price of a specific investment exceeds its value on death, the value of the investment shall be its sale value less an amount equal to the relevant proportion of the difference between its value on death and its sale price.

187(4) For the purposes of subsections (2) and (3) above, the sale value of a specific investment in respect of which an amount has been paid in pursuance of a call, as mentioned in section 182 above, shall be reduced by the amount so paid in respect of that investment.

187(5) In a case where, by virtue of subsection (3) of section 183 above, the value on death of the new holding, within the meaning of that section, includes an amount equal to the consideration referred to in that subsection, the sale value of any specific investment comprised in the new holding shall be reduced, for the purposes of subsections (2) and (3) above, by an amount which bears to that consideration the like proportion as the value on death of the specific investment sold bears to the value on death of the whole of the new holding.

187(6) In subsection (3) above **"sale price"**, in relation to a specific investment, means the price for which the investment was sold by the appropriate person or, if it is greater, the best consideration which could reasonably have been obtained for the specific investment at the time of the sale; and section 181 above shall apply for the purposes of this subsection as it applies for the purposes of section 179(1)(b).

History – Reference to the "1992 Act" substituted by TCGA 1992, s. 290 and Sch. 10, para. 8(10).

Cross references – TCGA 1992, s. 274: value determined for inheritance tax taken to be the market value at the date of death for capital gains tax.

188 Limitation of loss on sale

188 In any case where, apart from this section, the loss on sale of any investments–

(a) in respect of which an amount has been paid in pursuance of a call as mentioned in section 182 above, or

(b) which are sold as mentioned in section 183(5) above,

would exceed their value as determined apart from this Chapter, their sale value shall be treated for the purposes of sections 179(2) and 187 above as being of such an amount that the loss on sale would be equal to their value as so determined.

189 Date of sale or purchase

189(1) Subject to subsection (2) below, for the purposes of this Chapter where any investments are sold or purchased by the appropriate person the date on which they are sold or purchased shall be taken to be the date on which he entered into a contract to sell or purchase them.

189(2) If the sale or purchase of any investments by the appropriate person results from the exercise (whether by him or by any other person) of an option, then, for the purposes of this Chapter, the date on which the investments are sold or purchased shall be taken to be the date on which the option was granted.

Chapter IV – Sale of Land from Deceased's Estate

190 Preliminary

190(1) In this Chapter–

"the appropriate person", in relation to any interest in land comprised in a person's estate immediately before his death, means the person liable for capital transfer tax attributable to the value of that interest or, if there is more than one such person and one of them is in fact paying *the tax, that person;*

"interest in land" does not include any estate, interest or right by way of mortgage or other security;

"sale price", in relation to any interest in land, means the price for which it is sold or, if greater, the best consideration that could reasonably have been obtained for it at the time of the sale;

"sale value", in relation to any interest in land, means its sale price as increased or reduced under the following provisions of this Chapter;

"value on death", in relation to any interest in land comprised in a person's estate immediately before his death, means the value which, apart from this Chapter, (and apart from section 176 above) would be its value as part of that estate for the purposes of this Act.

190(2) Any reference in this Chapter to the **interests to which a claim relates** is a reference to the interests to which section 191(1) below applies by virtue of the claim.

190(3) For the purposes of this Chapter–

(a) the personal representatives of the deceased, and

(b) the trustees of a settlement,

shall each be treated as a single and continuing body of persons (distinct from the persons who may from time to time be the personal representatives or trustees).

190(4) In any case where, for the purposes of this Chapter, it is necessary to determine the price at which any interest was purchased or sold or the best consideration that could reasonably have been obtained on the sale of any interest, no account shall be taken of expenses (whether by way of commission, stamp duty or stamp duty land tax or otherwise) which are incidental to the sale or purchase.

History – In s. 190(4), the words "or stamp duty land tax" inserted after the words "stamp duty" by FA 2003, s. 123 and Sch. 18, para. 2 with effect from 10 July 2003 (date of Royal Assent to FA 2003) for transactions which are within the charge to stamp duty land tax from 1 December 2003 (the appointed day by virtue of SI 2003/2899 (C. 106)).

Cross references – FA 2004, Sch. 15, para. 1: charge to income tax on benefits received by former owner of property, application of term "interest in land" (in s. 190(1)).
S. 176: sales of related property etc.

Notes – FA 1986, s. 100(1)(b): any reference to capital transfer tax (except where it relates to a liability to tax arising before 25 July 1986) has effect as a reference to inheritance tax.

191 The relief

191(1) Where–

(a) an interest in land is comprised in a person's estate immediately before his death and is sold by the appropriate person within the period of three years immediately following the date of the death, and

(b) the appropriate person makes a claim under this Chapter stating the capacity in which he makes it,

the value for the purposes of this Act of that interest and of any other interest in land comprised in that estate and sold within that period by the person making the claim acting in the same capacity shall, subject to the following provisions of this Chapter, be its sale value.

191(1A) A claim under this Chapter must be made not more than 4 years after the end of the period mentioned in subsection (1)(a).

191(2) Subsection (1) above shall not apply to an interest if its sale value would differ from its value on death by less than the lower of–

(a) £1,000, and

(b) 5 per cent of its value on death.

191(3) Subsection (1) above shall not apply to an interest if its sale is–

(a) a sale by a personal representative or trustee to–

(i) a person who, at any time between the death and the sale, has been beneficially entitled to, or to an interest in possession in, property comprising the interest sold, or

(ii) the spouse or civil partner or a child or remoter descendant of a person within sub-paragraph (i) above, or

(iii) trustees of a settlement under which a person within sub-paragraph (i) or (ii) above has an interest in possession in property comprising the interest sold; or

(b) a sale in connection with which the vendor or any person within sub-paragraph (i), (ii) or (iii) of paragraph (a) above obtains a right to acquire the interest sold or any other interest in the same land;

and for the purposes of this subsection a person shall be treated as having in the property comprised in an unadministered estate (within the meaning of section 91(2) above) the same interest as he would have if the administration of the estate had been completed.

History – S. 191(1A) inserted by FA 2009, s. 99 and Sch. 51, para. 10, with effect from 1 April 2011 (SI 2010/867, art. 2(2)).
In s. 191(3)(a)(ii) the words "or civil partner" inserted by SI 2005/3229, reg. 35, with effect from 5 December 2005.

Other material – Law Society's Gazette, 12 January 1994: circumstances in which CTO will process a claim for loss on sale relief and make provisional repayment of inheritance tax before expiry of four months from date of last sale.

192 Effect of purchases

192(1) This section applies where a claim is made under this Chapter and, at any time during the period beginning on the date of the death and ending four months after the last of the sales referred to in section 191(1) above, the person making the claim purchases any interests in land in the same capacity as that in which he makes the claim.

192(2) If the aggregate of the purchase prices of all the interests purchased as mentioned in subsection (1) above equals or exceeds the aggregate of the sale prices (as adjusted under sections 193 to 195 below) of all the interests to which the claim relates, this Chapter shall not apply in relation to the claim; but otherwise subsection (3) below shall have effect, and in that subsection **"the appropriate fraction"** means the fraction of which–

(a) the numerator is the aggregate of the said purchase prices, and

(b) the denominator is the aggregate of the said sale prices.

192(3) Subject to subsection (4) below, where this subsection has effect an addition shall be made to the sale price of every interest to which the claim relates; and the amount of the addition shall be equal to the appropriate fraction of the difference between the value on death of the interest and its sale price (as adjusted under sections 193 to 196 below).

192(4) Where the value on death of an interest is less than its sale price (as adjusted under sections 193 to 196 below) subsection (3) above shall apply as if it provided for a reduction instead of an increase in the sale price.

193 Changes between death and sale

193(1) Where the conditions mentioned in subsection (2) below are not satisfied in relation to any interest to which the claim relates then, subject to subsections (3) and (4) below, an addition shall be made to the sale price of the interest; and the amount of the addition shall be equal to the difference between–

(a) the value on death of the interest, and

(b) what that value would have been if the circumstances prevailing at the date of the sale and by reason of which the conditions are not satisfied had prevailed immediately before the death.

193(2) The conditions referred to in subsection (1) above are–

(a) that the interest was the same in all respects and with the same incidents at the date of the death and at the date of the sale; and

(b) that the land in which the interest subsists was in the same state and with the same incidents at the date of the death and at the date of the sale.

193(3) If after the date of the death but before the date of the sale compensation becomes payable under any enactment to the appropriate person or any other person liable for tax attributable to the value of the interest–

(a) because of the imposition of a restriction on the use or development of the land in which the interest subsists, or

(b) because the value of the interest is reduced for any other reason,

the imposition of the restriction or the other cause of the reduction in value shall be ignored for the purposes of subsections (1) and (2) above, but there shall be added to the sale price of the interest an amount equal to the amount of compensation.

193(4) Where the value on death of an interest is less than it would have been as mentioned in subsection (1) above, that subsection shall apply as if, instead of providing for an addition to be made to the sale price, it provided for that price to be reduced to what it would have been if the change in circumstances by reason of which the conditions mentioned in subsection (2) above are not satisfied had not occurred.

194 Leases

194(1) Where the claim relates to an interest which is the interest of a lessee under a lease the duration of which at the date of the death does not exceed fifty years, an addition shall be made to the sale price of the interest; and the amount of the addition shall be equal to the appropriate fraction of the value on death of the interest.

194(2) In subsection (1) above, **"the appropriate fraction"** means the fraction–

$$\frac{P(1) - P(2)}{P(1)}$$

where–

P(1) is the percentage that would be derived from the Table in paragraph 1 of Schedule 8 to the 1992 Act for the duration of the lease at the date of the death, and

P(2) is the percentage that would be so derived for the duration of the lease at the date of the sale.

History – Reference to the "1992 Act" substituted by TCGA 1992, s. 290 and Sch. 10, para. 8(11).

Cross references – TCGA 1992, Sch. 8, para. 1(6): Table for calculating the curved line write-off of expenditure on leases.

195 Valuation by reference to other interests

195 If in determining the value on death of any interest to which the claim relates, any other interests, whether in the same or other land, were taken into account, an addition shall be made to the sale price of the interest; and the amount of the addition shall be equal to the difference between the value on death of the interest and the value which would have been the value on death if no other interests had been taken into account.

196 Sales to beneficiaries etc. and exchanges

196(1) This section applies where a person who makes a claim under this Chapter, acting in the same capacity as that in which he makes the claim–

(a) sells an interest to which section 191(1) would apply but for section 191(3), or

(b) within the period of three years immediately following the date of the death exchanges (with or without any payment by way of equality of exchange) any interest in land which was comprised in the deceased's estate immediately before his death,

and the sale price of the interest, or in the case of an exchange its market value at the date of the exchange, exceeds its value on death.

196(2) Where this section applies, an addition shall be made to the sale price of any interest to which the claim relates; and the amount of the addition–

(a) if the claim relates to one interest only, shall be equal to the excess referred to in subsection (1) above, and

(b) if the claim relates to more than one interest, shall be equal to the appropriate fraction of that excess.

196(3) In subsection (2) above **"the appropriate fraction"** in relation to any interest to which the claim relates is the fraction of which–

(a) the numerator is the difference between the value on death of that interest and its sale price (as adjusted under sections 193 to 195 above) and

(b) the denominator is the aggregate of that difference and the corresponding differences for all the other interests to which the claim relates;

and the aggregate referred to in paragraph (b) above shall be calculated without regard to which is the greater, in the case of any particular interest, of its value on death and its sale price.

197 Compulsory acquisition more than three years after death

197(1) If after the end of the period of three years immediately following the date of the death an interest in land is acquired from the appropriate person in pursuance of a notice to treat served before the death or within that period by an authority possessing powers of compulsory acquisition, this Chapter shall apply in relation to the interest as it applies in relation to interests sold within that period.

197(2) Subsection (1) above shall not have effect in relation to an interest if its sale value would exceed its value on death.

197(3) In determining the period referred to in section 192(1) above, no account shall be taken of the sale of an interest in relation to which subsection (1) above has effect; and if the claim relates only to such interests, section 192 shall not apply in relation to the claim.

197A Sales in fourth year after death

197A(1) Where an interest in land–

(a) is comprised in a person's estate immediately before his death, and

(b) is sold by the appropriate person in the fourth year immediately following the date of the death, otherwise than in circumstances in which section 197(1) above has effect,

the interest shall be treated, for the purposes of section 191(1) above, as having been sold within the period of three years immediately following the date of the death.

197A(2) Subsection (1) above shall not have effect in relation to an interest if its sale value would exceed its value on death.

197A(3) In determining the period referred to in section 192(1) above, no account shall be taken of the sale of an interest in relation to which subsection (1) above has effect; and if the claim relates only to such interests, section 192 shall not apply in relation to the claim.

197A(4) In applying section 196(1) above, no account shall be taken, for the purposes of paragraph (a) of that subsection, of an interest in relation to which subsection (1) above has effect.

History – S. 197A inserted by FA 1993, s. 199(1) in relation to deaths occurring on or after 16 March 1990.

198 Date of sale or purchase

198(1) Subject to the following subsections, the date on which an interest in land is sold or purchased by the appropriate person shall for the purposes of this Chapter be taken to be the date on which he enters into a contract to sell or purchase it.

198(2) If the sale or purchase of any interest by the appropriate person results from the exercise (whether by him or by any other person) of an option granted not more than six months earlier, the date on which the interest is sold or purchased shall be taken to be the date on which the option was granted.

198(3) If an interest is acquired from the appropriate person in pursuance of a notice to treat served by an authority possessing powers of compulsory acquisition, the date on which the interest is sold shall, subject to subsection (4) below, be taken to be the date on which compensation for the acquisition is agreed or otherwise determined (variations on appeal being disregarded for this purpose) or, if earlier, the date when the authority enter on the land in pursuance of their powers.

198(4) If an interest in land is acquired from the appropriate person–

(a) in England, Scotland or Wales by virtue of a general vesting declaration within the meaning of the Compulsory Purchase (Vesting Declarations) Act 1981 or, in Scotland, Schedule 24 to the Town and Country Planning (Scotland) Act 1972, or

(b) in Northern Ireland, by way of a vesting order,

the date on which it is sold by the appropriate person shall be taken to be the last day of the period specified in the declaration or, in Northern Ireland, the date on which the vesting order becomes operative.

PART VII – LIABILITY

GENERAL RULES

199 Dispositions by transferor

199(1) The persons liable for the tax on the value transferred by a chargeable transfer made by a disposition (including any omission treated as a disposition under section 3(3) above) of the transferor are–

(a) the transferor;

(b) any person the value of whose estate is increased by the transfer;

(c) so far as the tax is attributable to the value of any property, any person in whom the property is vested (whether beneficially or otherwise) at any time after the transfer, or who at any such time is beneficially entitled to an interest in possession in the property;

(d) where by the chargeable transfer any property becomes comprised in a settlement, any person for whose benefit any of the property or income from it is applied.

199(2) Subsection (1)(a) above shall apply in relation to–

(a) the tax on the value transferred by a potentially exempt transfer; and

(b) so much of the tax on the value transferred by any other chargeable transfer made within seven years of the transferor's death as exceeds what it would have been had the transferor died more than seven years after the transfer,

with the substitution for the reference to the transferor of a reference to his personal representatives.

199(3) A purchaser of property, and a person deriving title from or under such a purchaser, shall not by virtue of subsection (1)(c) above be liable for tax attributable to the value of the property unless the property is subject to an Inland Revenue charge.

199(4) For the purposes of this section–

(a) any person who takes possession of or intermeddles with, or otherwise acts in relation to, property so as to become liable as executor or trustee (or, in Scotland, any person who intromits with property or has become liable as a vitious intromitter), and

(b) any person to whom the management of property is entrusted on behalf of a person not of full legal capacity, shall be treated as a person in whom the property is vested.

199(5) References in this section to any **property** include references to any property directly or indirectly representing it.

History – S. 199(2) substituted by FA 1986, s. 101 and Sch. 19, para. 26, with respect to transfers of value made, and other events occurring, on or after 18 March 1986.

Cross references – S. 3(3): omission to exercise a right.
S. 216(1)(b): duty of person liable under s. 199(1)(b) to deliver account.
FA 1986, Sch. 19, para. 40(1): transitional – transfer of value occurring before, and death or other event occurring after, 18 March 1986.

Statements of practice – SP 1/82: income tax position where trustees pay tax on assets put into settlement.

Other material – Law Society's Gazette, 7 March 1990: extent of indemnity offered by Solicitors' Indemnity Fund Ltd where solicitor incurs civil liability in course of his private practice by reason of s. 199(2) (but see below).
Law Society's Gazette, 13 March 1991: circumstances in which Capital Taxes Office will not pursue a personal representative for IHT when a chargeable lifetime transfer comes to light after a certificate of discharge obtained and the estate distributed.

200 Transfer on death

200(1) The persons liable for the tax on the value transferred by a chargeable transfer made (under section 4 above) on the death of any person are–

(a) so far as the tax is attributable to the value of property which either–
  (i) was not immediately before the death comprised in a settlement, or
  (ii) was so comprised and consists of land in the United Kingdom which devolves upon or vests in the deceased's personal representatives,

the deceased's personal representatives;

(b) so far as the tax is attributable to the value of property which, immediately before the death, was comprised in a settlement, the trustees of the settlement;

(c) so far as the tax is attributable to the value of any property, any person in whom the property is vested (whether beneficially or otherwise) at any time after the death, or who at any such time is beneficially entitled to an interest in possession in the property;

(d) so far as the tax is attributable to the value of any property which, immediately before the death, was comprised in a settlement, any person for whose benefit any of the property or income from it is applied after the death.

200(1A) [Omitted by FA 2011, s. 65 and Sch. 16, para. 52(b).]

200(2) A purchaser of property, and a person deriving title from or under such a purchaser, shall not by virtue of subsection (1)(c) above be liable for tax attributable to the value of the property unless the property is subject to an Inland Revenue charge.

200(3) For the purposes of subsection (1) above a person entitled to part only of the income of any property shall, notwithstanding anything in section 50 above, be deemed to be entitled to an interest in the whole of the property.

200(4) Subsections (4) and (5) of section 199 above shall have effect for the purposes of this section as they have effect for the purposes of that section.

History – In s. 200(1), the words "(subject to subsection (1A) below)", which appeared after the words "on the death of any person are", omitted by FA 2011, s. 65 and Sch. 16, para. 52(a), with effect in relation to deaths occurring on or after 6 April 2011.
In s. 200(1) the words "(subject to subsection (1A) below)" inserted by FA 2006, s. 160 and Sch. 22, para. 5(2), with effect from 6 April 2006.
S. 200(1A) omitted by FA 2011, s. 65 and Sch. 16, para. 52(b), with effect in relation to deaths occurring on or after 6 April 2011.
Former s. 200(1A) inserted by FA 2006, s. 160 and Sch. 22, para. 5(3), with effect from 6 April 2006.

Cross references – S. 4: charge to tax for transfers on death.
S. 50: interest in part of income from property generally taken as indication of proportionate share in property.
S. 216(1)(bc): duty of person liable under s. 200(1)(c) to deliver account.

Extra-statutory concessions – F6: if executors cannot transfer to this country sufficient of the deceased's foreign assets for the payment of the IHT attributable to them, due to foreign government restrictions, they may defer payment. If the executors succeed in bringing to this country less than the amount of the tax, the balance is waived.

201 Settled property

201(1) The persons liable for the tax on the value transferred by a chargeable transfer made under Part III of this Act are–

(a) the trustees of the settlement;

(b) any person entitled (whether beneficially or not) to an interest in possession in the settled property;

(c) any person for whose benefit any of the settled property or income from it is applied at or after the time of the transfer;

(d) where the transfer is made during the life of the settlor and the trustees are not for the time being resident in the United Kingdom, the settlor.

201(2) Where the chargeable transfer is made within seven years of the transferor's death but is not a potentially exempt transfer, subsection (1)(d) above shall not apply in relation to so much of the tax as exceeds what it would have been had the transferor died more than seven years after the transfer.

201(3) Subsection (1)(d) above shall not apply in relation to a settlement made before 11th December 1974 if the trustees were resident in the United Kingdom when the settlement was made, but have not been resident there at any time during the period between 10th December 1974 and the time of the transfer.

201(3A) Subsection (1)(d) above shall not apply in relation to the tax chargeable on the value transferred by a potentially exempt transfer which proves to be a chargeable transfer in a case where the settlement was made before 17th March 1987 if the trustees were resident in the United Kingdom when the settlement was made, but have not been resident there at any time between 16th March 1987 and the death of the transferor.

201(4) Where more than one person is a settlor in relation to a settlement and the circumstances so require, subsection (1)(d) above shall have effect in relation to it as if the settled property were comprised in separate settlements.

201(4A) Where–

(a) a charge to tax arises under or by virtue of section 74A, or

(b) in a case where paragraphs (a) to (d) of section 74A are satisfied, a charge to tax arises under section 64 or 65 in respect of the relevant settled property (within the meaning of section 74A),

subsection (1) of this section has effect as if the persons listed in that subsection included the individual mentioned in section 74A(1)(b)(i).

201(5) For the purposes of this section trustees of a settlement shall be regarded as not resident in the United Kingdom unless the general administration of the settlement is ordinarily carried on in the United Kingdom and the trustees or a majority of them (and, where there is more than one class of trustees, a majority of each class) are for the time being resident in the United Kingdom.

201(6) References in this section to any property include references to any property directly or indirectly representing it.

History – In s. 201(2), the words "but … transfer" inserted by F(No. 2)A 1987, s. 96 and Sch. 7, para. 3(2), (3), with respect to transfers of value made, and other events occurring, on or after 17 March 1987.

In s. 201(2), the words "seven years" were substituted by FA 1986, s. 101 and Sch. 19, para. 27, with respect to transfers of value made, and other events occurring, on or after 18 March 1986.

S. 201(3A) inserted by F(No. 2)A 1987, s. 96 and Sch. 7, para. 3(2), (3), with respect to transfers of value made, and other events occurring, on or after 17 March 1987.

S. 201(4A) inserted by FA 2012, s. 210(4), with effect in relation to arrangements entered into on or after 20 June 2012.

Cross references – S. 216(1)(bd): duty of person liable under s. 201(1)(b)–(d) to deliver account.

FA 1986, Sch. 19, para. 40(1): transitional – transfer of value occurring before, and death or other event occurring after, 18 March 1986.

Statements of practice – SP 1/82: income tax position where trustees pay tax on assets put into settlement.

Other material – HMRC Brief 18/11: HMRC view on IHT position in relation to Employee Benefit Trusts: identity of settlor for the purposes of s. 201.

202 Close companies

202(1) The persons liable for tax chargeable by virtue of section 94(1) or section 99(2) above are–

(a) the company making the transfer of value concerned, and

(b) so far as the tax remains unpaid after it ought to have been paid, the persons to whom any amounts have been apportioned under section 94 above and any individual (whether such a person or not) the value of whose estate is increased by the company's transfer.

202(2) A person to whom not more than 5 per cent of the value transferred by the company's transfer is apportioned shall not as such be liable for any of the tax; and each of the other persons to whom any part of that value has been apportioned shall be so liable only for such part of the tax as corresponds to that part of that value.

202(3) A person the value of whose estate is increased by the company's transfer shall not as such be liable for a greater amount than the amount of the increase.

202(4) No person other than those liable under this section shall be liable for any tax chargeable by virtue of section 94(1) or section 99(2) above.

Cross references – S. 94(1), 99(2): transfers of value by close company apportioned to participators.

203 Liability of *spouse or civil partner*

History – In the heading to s. 203 the words "or civil partner" inserted by SI 2005/3229, reg. 36(b), with effect from 5 December 2005.

203(1) Where–

(a) a transferor is liable for any tax on the value transferred by a chargeable transfer, and

(b) by another transfer of value made by him on or after 27th March 1974 (**"the spouse or civil partner transfer"**) any property became the property of a person (**"the transferee"**) who at the time of both transfers was his spouse or civil partner,

the transferee is liable for so much of the tax as does not exceed the market value of the property at the time of the spouse or civil partner transfer or, in a case where subsection (2) below applies, the lower market value mentioned in paragraph (c) of that subsection.

203(2) This subsection applies where–

(a) the chargeable transfer is made after the spouse or civil partner transfer; and

(b) the property (**"the transferred property"**) which became the property of the transferee either remains the transferee's property at the date of the chargeable transfer or has before that date been sold by the transferee by a qualifying sale; and

(c) the market value of the transferred property on the relevant date (that is to say, the date of the chargeable transfer or, as the case may be, of the qualifying sale) is lower than its market value at the time of the spouse or civil partner transfer; and

(d) the transferred property is not tangible movable property.

203(3) In this section **"qualifying sale"** has the same meaning as in section 131 above; and, subject to subsection (4) below, sections 133 to 140 above shall have effect for the purposes of this section as they have effect for the purposes of section 131.

203(4) In their application by virtue of subsection (3) above, sections 133 to 140 above shall have effect as if–

(a) references to the chargeable transfer were references to the spouse transfer,

(b) references to the transferee's spouse or civil partner were omitted, and

(c) references to section 131 above were references to this section.

History – In s. 203(1), (2) and (4) the words "or civil partner" inserted by SI 2005/3229, reg. 36(a), with effect from 5 December 2005.

Cross references – S. 133–140: adjustments of market value in respect of chargeable transfer involving capital receipts on shares, calls, reorganisation of share capital, close company transactions, interests in land, leases etc.
S. 162(3): treatment of tax liabilities in determining value of an estate.

204 Limitation of liability

204(1) A person shall not be liable under section 200(1)(a) above for any tax as a personal representative of a deceased person, except to the extent of the following assets, namely–

(a) so far as the tax is attributable to the value of any property other than such as is mentioned in paragraph (b) below, the assets (other than property so mentioned) which he has received as personal representative or might have so received but for his own neglect or default; and

(b) so far as the tax is attributable to property which, immediately before the death, was comprised in a settlement and consists of land in the United Kingdom, so much of that property as is at any time available in his hands for the payment of the tax, or might have been so available but for his own neglect or default.

204(2) A person shall not be liable for tax as trustee in relation to any property, except to the extent of–

(a) so much of the property as he has actually received or disposed of or as he has become liable to account for to the persons beneficially entitled thereto, and

(b) so much of any other property as is for the time being available in his hands as trustee for the payment of the tax or might have been so available but for his own neglect or default.

204(3) A person not liable as mentioned in subsection (1) or (2) above but liable for tax as a person in whom property is vested or liable for tax as a person entitled to a beneficial interest in possession in any property shall not be liable for the tax except to the extent of that property.

204(4) [Repealed by FA 1986, s. 101 and Sch. 19, para. 28(1) and s. 114 and Sch. 23, Pt. X.]

204(5) A person liable for tax as a person for whose benefit any settled property, or income from any settled property, is applied, shall not be liable for the tax except to the extent of the amount of the property or income (reduced in the case of income by the amount of any income tax borne by him in respect of it, and in the case of other property in respect of which he has borne income tax by virtue of Chapter 2 of Part 13 of the Income Tax Act 2007 by the amount of that tax).

204(6) Where a person is liable for any tax–

(a) under section 199 above otherwise than as transferor or personal representative of the transferor, or

(b) under section 201 above otherwise than as trustee of the settlement,

he shall be liable only if the tax remains unpaid after it ought to have been paid and, in a case where any part of the value transferred is attributable to the tax on it, shall be liable to no greater extent than he would have been had the value transferred been reduced by the tax remaining unpaid.

204(7) Where the tax exceeds what it would have been had the transferor died more than seven years after the transfer, subsection (6) above shall not apply in relation to the excess.

204(8) A person liable by virtue of section 199(2) above for any tax as personal representative of the transferor shall be liable only to the extent that either–

(a) in consequence of subsections (2), (3) and (5) above, no person falling within paragraphs (b) to (d) of section 199(1) above is liable for the tax, or

(b) the tax remains unpaid twelve months after the end of the month in which the death of the transferor occurs,

and, subject to that, shall be liable only to the extent of the assets mentioned in subsection (1) above.

204(9) Where by virtue of subsection (3) of section 102 of the Finance Act 1986 the estate of a deceased person is treated as including property which would not apart from that subsection form part of his estate, a person shall be liable under section 200(1)(a) above as personal representative for tax attributable to the value of that property only if the tax remains unpaid twelve months after the end of the month in which the death occurs and subject to that, only to the extent of the assets mentioned in subsection (1) above.

History – S. 204(4) repealed by FA 1986, s. 101 and Sch. 19, para. 28(1) and s. 114 and Sch. 23, Pt. X with effect with respect to transfers of value made, and other events occurring, on or after 18 March 1986.
In s. 204(5), reference to ICTA 1988 substituted by Sch. 29, para. 32 of that Act.
In s. 204(5) the words "Chapter 2 of Part 13 of the Income Tax Act 2007" substituted for the words "section 739 or 740 of the Taxes Act 1988" by ITA 2007, s. 1027 and Sch. 1, para. 270, with effect from 6 April 2007.
In s. 204(6), the words "or personal representative of the transferor" in para. (a) were inserted by FA 1986, s. 101 and Sch. 19, para. 28(2), with respect to transfers of value made, and other events occurring, on or after 18 March 1986.
s. 204(7)–(9) substituted by FA 1986, s. 101 and Sch. 19, para. 28(3), with respect to transfers of value made, and other events occurring, on or after 18 March 1986.

Cross references – FA 1986, s. 102: gifts with reservation.
FA 1986, Sch. 19, para. 40(1): transitional – transfer of value occurring before, and death or other event occurring after, 18 March 1986.
ICTA 1988, s. 739, 740: transfer of assets abroad by UK residents – anti-avoidance.

205 More than one person liable

205 Except as otherwise provided, where under this Act two or more persons are liable for the same tax, each of them shall be liable for the whole of it.

SPECIAL CASES

206 Gifts to political parties

206 [Repealed by FA 1988, s. 148 and Sch. 14, Pt. X, in relation to transfers of value made on or after 15 March 1988.]

207 Conditional exemption, etc.

207(1) Where tax is chargeable under section 32 above on the occurrence of an event which is a chargeable event with respect to any property by virtue of subsection (2) or subsection (3)(a) of that section, the person liable for the tax is the person who, if the property were sold–

(a) in a case within subsection (2) of that section, at the time the tax becomes chargeable, and

(b) in a case within subsection (3)(a), immediately after the death,

would be entitled to receive (whether for his benefit or not) the proceeds of sale or any income arising from them.

207(2) Where tax is chargeable under section 32 above on the occurrence of an event which is a chargeable event with respect to any property by virtue of subsection (3)(b) of that section, the person liable for the tax is the person by whom or for whose benefit the property is disposed of.

207(2A) Where tax is chargeable under section 32A above on the occurrence of an event which is a chargeable event with respect to any property by virtue of subsection (3) or subsection (4)(a) of that section, the person liable for the tax is the person who, if the property were sold–

(a) in a case within subsection (3) of that section, at the time the tax becomes chargeable, and

(b) in a case within subsection (4)(a), immediately after the death,

would be entitled to receive (whether for his benefit or not) the proceeds of sale or any income arising from them.

207(2B) Where tax is chargeable under section 32A above on the occurrence of an event which is a chargeable event with respect to any property by virtue of subsection (4)(b) of that section, the person liable for the tax is the person by whom or for whose benefit the property is disposed of.

207(3) The persons liable for tax charged under section 79(3A) above are–

(a) the trustees of the settlement concerned, and

(b) any person for whose benefit any of the property or income from it is applied at or after the time of the event occasioning the charge.

207(4) The person liable for tax chargeable under paragraph 1(1) or 3(1) of Schedule 5 to this Act is the person who, if the property were sold at the time the tax becomes chargeable, would be entitled to receive (whether for his benefit or not) the proceeds of sale or any income arising from them.

207(5) The person liable for tax chargeable under paragraph 1(2) or 3(2) of Schedule 5 to this Act is the person by whom or for whose benefit the property is disposed of.

History – S. 207(2A) and (2B) inserted by FA 1985, Sch. 26, para. 10, in relation to events on or after 19 March 1985.
In s. 207(3), the words "section 79(3A)" substituted for the words "section 79(3)" by F(No. 2)A 2015, s. 12(8)(a), with effect in relation to occasions on which tax would (ignoring the effect of the amendments) fall to be charged under IHTA 1984, s. 64 on or after 18 November 2015 (Royal Assent).

Cross references – S. 32, 32A: following conditionally exempt transfer of property, charge on certain events in relation to that property or associated property.
S. 79(3): deferral of ten-yearly charge until chargeable event.
Sch. 5, para. 1, 3: certain events by reference to conditional exemption for deaths before 7 April 1976.

208 Woodlands

208 The person liable for tax chargeable under section 126 above in relation to a disposal is the person who is entitled to the proceeds of sale or would be so entitled if the disposal were a sale.

Cross references – S. 126: special charge on disposal of certain trees or underwood.

209 Succession in Scotland

209(1) A person shall not be liable under section 200(1)(a) above for tax attributable to the value of any heritable property in Scotland which is vested in him as executor in the circumstances and for the purposes mentioned in subsection (1) or (2) of section 18 of the Succession (Scotland) Act 1964.

209(2) The persons liable for tax chargeable under section 147(4) above are the person who claims legitim or rights under section 131 of the Civil Partnership Act 2004 and any person mentioned in section 200(1)(c) above.

209(3) Section 200(1)(a) shall not apply in relation to tax chargeable under section 147(4) above, but section 204(1) shall apply in relation to the person who claims legitim or rights under section 131 of the Civil Partnership Act 2004 as it applies in relation to the personal representatives of a deceased person.

History – In s. 209(2) and (3) the words "or rights under section 131 of the Civil Partnership Act 2004" inserted by SI 2005/3229, reg. 37, with effect from 5 December 2005.

Cross references – S. 147(4): tax charge on the amount claimed on the basis that the legitim fund had been paid out in full.
Civil Partnership Act 2004, s. 131: reproduced in the annotations to IHTA 1984, s. 147.

210 Pension rights, etc.

210(1) Where any tax chargeable on a transfer of value is attributable to the value of an interest satisfying the conditions of paragraphs (a) and (b) of section 151(2) above, the persons liable for the tax shall not include the trustees of the scheme or fund concerned but shall, if the transfer is made on the death of the person entitled to the interest, include his personal representatives.

210(2) [Omitted by FA 2011, s. 65 and Sch. 16, para. 53.]

210(3) [Omitted by FA 2011, s. 65 and Sch. 16, para. 53.]

History – Existing text renumbered as s. 210(1) and former s. 210(2) inserted by FA 2006, s. 160 and Sch. 22, para. 6, with effect from 6 April 2006.
S. 210(2) and (3) omitted by FA 2011, s. 65 and Sch. 16, para. 53, with effect in relation to deaths occurring on or after 6 April 2011.
Former s. 210(3) inserted by FA 2008, s. 91 and Sch. 28, para. 11, with effect in relation to deaths occurring on or after 6 April 2008.

Cross references – S. 151(2)(a) and (b): pension as annuity.

BURDEN OF TAX, ETC.

211 Burden of tax on death

211(1) Where personal representatives are liable for tax on the value transferred by the chargeable transfer made on death, the tax shall be treated as part of the general testamentary and administration expenses of the estate, but only so far as it is attributable to the value of property in the United Kingdom which–

(a) vests in the deceased's personal representatives, and

(b) was not immediately before the death comprised in a settlement.

211(2) Subsection (1) above shall have effect subject to any contrary intention shown by the deceased in his will.

211(3) Where any amount of tax paid by personal representatives on the value transferred by a chargeable transfer made on death does not fall to be borne as part of the general testamentary and administration expenses of the estate, that amount shall, where occasion requires, be repaid to them by the person in whom the property to the value of which the tax is attributable is vested.

211(4) References in this section to **tax** include references to interest on tax.

212 Powers to raise tax

212(1) Where a person is liable, otherwise than as transferor, and otherwise than under section 203 above, for tax attributable to the value of any property he shall, for the purpose of paying the tax or raising the amount of it when paid, have power, whether or not the property is vested in him, to raise the amount of the tax by sale or mortgage of, or a terminable charge on, that property or any part of it.

212(2) A person having a limited interest in any property who pays the tax attributable to the value of that property shall be entitled to the like charge as if the tax so attributable had been raised by means of a mortgage to him.

212(3) Any money held on the trusts of a settlement may be expended in paying the tax attributable to the value of any property comprised in the settlement and held on the same trusts.

212(4) References in this section to **tax** include references to interest on tax and to costs properly incurred in respect of tax.

213 Refund by instalments

213 Where a person has paid to the Board any tax which is or might at his option have been payable by instalments and he is entitled to recover the whole or part of it from another person, that other person shall, unless otherwise agreed between them, be entitled to refund the tax or that part by the same instalments (with the same interest thereon) as those by which it might have been paid to the Board.

214 Certificates of tax paid

214(1) On an application being made in such form as the Board may prescribe by a person who has paid or borne the tax attributable to the value of any property, being tax for which he is not ultimately liable, the Board shall grant a certificate specifying the tax paid and the debts and incumbrances allowed in valuing the property.

214(2) Except to the extent of any repayment which may be or become due from the Board, a certificate under subsection (1) above shall be conclusive as between any person by whom the tax specified in the certificate falls to be borne and the person seeking to recover the tax from him; and any repayment of the tax falling to be made by the Board shall be duly made if made to the person producing the certificate.

214(3) References in this section to **tax** include references to interest on tax.

PART VIII – ADMINISTRATION AND COLLECTION

MANAGEMENT

215 General

215 The tax shall be under the care and management of the Board.

ACCOUNTS AND INFORMATION

216 Delivery of accounts

216(1) Except as otherwise provided by this section or by regulations under section 256 below, the personal representatives of a deceased person and every person who–

(a) is liable as transferor for tax on the value transferred by a chargeable transfer, or would be so liable if tax were chargeable on that value, or

(b) is liable as trustee of a settlement for tax on the value transferred by a transfer of value, or would be so liable if tax were chargeable on that value, or

(bb) is liable under section 199(1)(b) above for tax on the value transferred by a potentially exempt transfer which proves to be a chargeable transfer, or would be so liable if tax were chargeable on that value, or

(bc) is liable under section 200(1)(c) above for tax on the value transferred by a chargeable transfer made on death, so far as the tax is attributable to the value of property which, apart from section 102(3) of the Finance Act 1986, would not form part of the deceased's estate, or would be so liable if tax were chargeable on the value transferred on the death, or

(bca) [omitted by FA 2011, s. 65 and Sch. 16, para. 54(2),]

(bd) is liable under section 201(1)(b), (c) or (d) above for tax on the value transferred by a potentially exempt transfer which is made under section 52 above and which proves to be a chargeable transfer, or would be so liable if tax were chargeable on that value, or

(c) is liable as trustee of a settlement for tax on an occasion on which tax is chargeable under Chapter III of Part III of this Act (apart from section 79), or would be so liable if tax were chargeable on the occasion,

shall deliver to the Board an account specifying to the best of his knowledge and belief all appropriate property and the value of that property.

216(2) Where in the case of the estate of a deceased person no grant of representation or confirmation has been obtained in the United Kingdom before the expiration of the period of twelve months from the end of the month in which the death occurred–

(a) every person in whom any of the property forming part of the estate vests (whether beneficially or otherwise) on or at any time after the deceased's death or who at any such time is beneficially entitled to an interest in possession in any such property, and

(b) where any of the property is at any such time comprised in a settlement and there is no person beneficially entitled to an interest in possession in that property, every person for whose benefit any of that property (or income from it) is applied at any such time,

shall deliver to the Board an account specifying to the best of his knowledge and belief the appropriate property vested in him, in which he has an interest or which (or income from which) is applicable for his benefit and the value of that property.

216(3) Subject to subsections (3A) and (3B) below, where an account is to be delivered by personal representatives (but not where it is to be delivered by a person who is an executor of the deceased only in respect of settled land in England and Wales), the appropriate property is–

(a) all property which formed part of the deceased's estate immediately before his death, other than property which would not, apart from section 102(3) of the Finance Act 1986, form part of his estate; and

(b) all property to which was attributable the value transferred by any chargeable transfers made by the deceased within seven years of his death.

216(3A) If the personal representatives, after making the fullest enquiries that are reasonably practicable in the circumstances, are unable to ascertain the exact value of any particular property, their account shall in the first instance be sufficient as regards that property if it contains–

(a) a statement to that effect;

(b) a provisional estimate of the value of the property; and

(c) an undertaking to deliver a further account of it as soon as its value is ascertained.

216(3B) The Board may from time to time give such general or special directions as they think fit for restricting the property to be specified in pursuance of subsection (3) above by any class of personal representatives.

216(4) Where subsection (3) above does not apply the appropriate property is any property to the value of which the tax is or would be attributable.

216(5) Except in the case of an account to be delivered by personal representatives, a person shall not be required to deliver an account under this section with respect to any property if a full and proper account of the property, specifying its value, has already been delivered to the Board by some other person who–

(a) is or would be liable for the tax attributable to the value of the property, and

(b) is not or would not be liable with him jointly as trustee;

and a person within subsection (2) above shall not be required to deliver an account under that subsection if he or another person within that subsection has satisfied the Board that an account will in due course be delivered by the personal representatives.

216(6) An account under the preceding provisions of this section shall be delivered–

(a) in the case of an account to be delivered by personal representatives, before the expiration of the period of twelve months from the end of the month in which the death occurs, or, if it expires later, the period of three months beginning with the date on which the personal representatives first act as such;

(aa) in the case of an account to be delivered by a person within subsection (1)(bb) or (bd) above, before the expiration of the period of twelve months from the end of the month in which the death of the transferor occurs;

(ab) in the case of an account to be delivered by a person within subsection (1)(bc) above, before the expiration of the period of twelve months from the end of the month in which the death occurs;

(ac) [omitted by FA 2011, s. 65 and Sch. 16, para. 54(5),]

(ad) in the case of an account to be delivered by a person within subsection (1)(c) above, before the expiration of the period of six months from the end of the month in which the occasion concerned occurs;

(b) in the case of an account to be delivered by a person within subsection (2) above, before the expiration of the period of three months from the time when he first has reason to believe that he is required to deliver an account under that subsection;

(c) in the case of an account to be delivered by any other person, before the expiration of the period of twelve months from the end of the month in which the transfer is made or, if it expires later, the period of three months beginning with the date on which he first becomes liable for tax.

216(7) A person liable for tax under section 32, 32A, 79 or 126 above or under Schedule 5 to this Act shall deliver an account under this section before the expiration of the period of six months from the end of the month in which the event by reason of which the tax is chargeable occurs.

History – S. 216(1)(bca) omitted by FA 2011, s. 65 and Sch. 16, para. 54(2), with effect in relation to deaths occurring on or after 6 April 2011.
In former s. 216(1)(bca) the words "or (3)" inserted by FA 2008, s. 91 and Sch. 28, para. 12(2), with effect in relation to deaths occurring on or after 6 April 2008.
Former s. 216(1)(bca) inserted by FA 2006, s. 160 and Sch. 22, para. 7(2), with effect from 6 April 2006.
S. 216(1)(bb) and (bc) were inserted by FA 1986, s. 101 and Sch. 19, para. 29(1), with respect to transfers of value made, and other events occurring, on or after 18 March 1986.
S. 216(1)(bd), was inserted by F(No. 2)A 1987, s. 96 and Sch. 7, para. 4(2), with respect to transfers of value made, and other events occurring, on or after 17 March 1987.
In s. 216(3)(a), the words "(or would do apart from section 151A(3)(b) or 151C(3)(b) above)", which appeared after the words "immediately before his death", omitted by FA 2011, s. 65 and Sch. 16, para. 54(3), with effect in relation to deaths occurring on or after 6 April 2011.
In s. 216(3)(a) the words "(or would do apart from section 151A(3)(b) or 151C(3)(b) above)" inserted by FA 2006, s. 160 and Sch. 22, para. 7(3), with effect from 6 April 2006.
S. 216(3), (3A), (3B) substituted for s. 216(3) by FA 1999, s. 105, with effect in relation to deaths occurring on or after 9 March 1999.
In former s. 216(3)(aa), the words "other than property … of his estate" were inserted by FA 1986, s. 101 and Sch. 19, para. 29(2), with respect to transfers of value made, and other events occurring, on or after 18 March 1986.
In s. 216(4), the words "(or would be apart from section 151A(3)(b), 151C(3)(b) or 151B(4) above)", which appeared after the word "attributable", omitted by FA 2011, s. 65 and Sch. 16, para. 54(4), with effect in relation to deaths occurring on or after 6 April 2011.
In s. 216(4) the former words "(or would be apart from section 151A(3)(b), 151C(3)(b) or 151B(4) above)" inserted by FA 2006, s. 160 and Sch. 22, para. 7(4), with effect from 6 April 2006.
S. 216(6)(ac) omitted by FA 2011, s. 65 and Sch. 16, para. 54(5), with effect in relation to deaths occurring on or after 6 April 2011.
In former s. 216(6)(ac) the words "otherwise than by reason of a liability to tax under section 210(3)" inserted by FA 2008, s. 91 and Sch. 28, para. 12(3), with effect in relation to deaths occurring on or after 6 April 2008.
In former s. 216(6)(ac) the words ", the scheme administrator becomes aware of the death" and "(depending on which occasions the charge)" inserted by FA 2007, s. 69 and Sch. 19, para. 24, with effect in relation to deaths, cases where scheme administrators become aware of deaths and cessations of dependency occurring on or after 6 April 2007.
Former s. 216(6)(ac) inserted by FA 2006, s. 160 and Sch. 22, para. 7(5), with effect from6 April 2006.
S. 216(6)(ad) inserted by FA 2014, s. 117 and Sch. 25, para. 5(1), with effect in relation to chargeable transfers made on or after 6 April 2014.
In s. 216(6), the words "or (bd)" were inserted into para. (aa) by F(No. 2)A 1987, s. 96 and Sch. 7, para. 4(3) with respect to transfers of value made, and other events occurring, on or after 17 March 1987; and para. (aa) and (ab) were inserted by FA 1986, s. 101 and Sch. 19, para. 29(3), with respect to transfers of value made, and other events occurring, on or after 18 March 1986.
In s. 216(7), "or 126" substituted for ", 126 or 151D" by FA 2011, s. 65 and Sch. 16, para. 54(6), with effect in relation to deaths occurring on or after 6 April 2011.
In s. 216(7) the words ", 126 or 151D" substituted for the words "or 126" by FA 2008, s. 91 and Sch. 28, para. 12(4), with effect in relation to deaths occurring on or after 6 April 2008.
In s. 216(7), the reference to s. 32A was inserted by FA 1985, s. 94(1) and Sch. 26, para. 11, in relation to events on or after 19 March 1985.

Cross references – S. 245: failure to deliver accounts.
S. 32, 32A: following conditionally exempt transfer of property, charge where certain events in respect of property or associated property.
S. 52: charge on termination of interest in possession.
S. 79: deferral of ten-yearly charge until subsequent chargeable event.
S. 126: special charge on disposal of certain trees and underwood.
S. 199(1)(b), 200(1)(c): liability of person the value of whose estate is increased by a transfer; and of any person in whom property is vested following a death etc.
S. 201(1)(b), (c) and (d): in respect of settled property, liability of persons other than the trustees.
S. 264: transfers reported late.
Sch. 5: charge where certain events in relation to conditionally exempt transfer for death before 7 April 1976.
FA 1986, s. 102: gifts with reservation.
FA 1986, Sch. 19, para. 40(1): transitional – transfer of value occurring before, and death or other event occurring after, 18 March 1986.
FA 2009, Sch. 55: penalty for failure to make returns etc.
FA 2009, Sch. 56: penalty for failure to make payments on time.
FA 2014, s. 202(5)(a): an account delivered under s. 216 or s. 217 (including an account delivered in accordance with regulations under s. 256) is treated as a return for the purposes of FA 2014, Pt. 4 (follower notices and accelerated payments)
SI 2002/1731, reg. 3: accounts not required.
SI 2002/1732, reg. 4: accounts not required.
SI 2002/1733, reg. 4: accounts not required.

217 Defective accounts

217 If a person who has delivered an account under section 216 above discovers at any time that the account is defective in a material respect by reason of anything contained in or omitted from it he shall, within six months of that time, deliver to the Board a further account containing such information as may be necessary to remedy the defect.

Cross references – S. 245: failure to deliver accounts.
FA 2009, Sch. 55: penalty for failure to make returns etc.
FA 2014, s. 202(5)(a): an account delivered under s. 216 or s. 217 (including an account delivered in accordance with regulations under s. 256) is treated as a return for the purposes of FA 2014, Pt. 4 (follower notices and accelerated payments)

218 Non-resident trustees

218(1) Where any person, in the course of a trade or profession carried on by him, other than the profession of a barrister, has been concerned with the making of a settlement and knows or has reason to believe–

(a) that the settlor was domiciled in the United Kingdom, and

(b) that the trustees of the settlement are not or will not be resident in the United Kingdom,

he shall, within three months of the making of the settlement, make a return to the Board stating the names and addresses of the settlor and of the trustees of the settlement.

218(2) A person shall not be required to make a return under this section in relation to–

(a) any settlement made by will, or

(b) any other settlement, if such a return in relation to that settlement has already been made by another person or if an account has been delivered in relation to it under section 216 above.

218(3) For the purposes of this section trustees of a settlement shall be regarded as not resident in the United Kingdom unless the general administration of the settlement is ordinarily carried on in the United Kingdom and the trustees or a majority of them (and, where there is more than one class of trustees, a majority of each class) are for the time being resident in the United Kingdom.

218A Instruments varying dispositions taking effect on death

218A(1) Where–

(a) an instrument is made varying any of the dispositions of the property comprised in the estate of a deceased person immediately before his death,

(b) the instrument contains a statement under subsection (2) of section 142 above, and

(c) the variation results in additional tax being payable,

the relevant persons (within the meaning of that subsection) shall, within six months after the day on which the instrument is made, deliver a copy of it to the Board and notify them of the amount of the additional tax.

218A(2) To the extent that any of the relevant persons comply with the requirements of this section, the others are discharged from the duty to comply with them.

History – S. 218A inserted by FA 2002, s. 120(2) which applies in relation to instruments made on or after 1 August 2002.
Cross references – S. 245A: failure to provide information, etc.

219 Power to require information

219 [Omitted by SI 2009/3054, art. 3 and Schedule, para. 2(2).]

History – S. 219 omitted by SI 2009/3054, art. 3 and Schedule, para. 2(2), with effect from 1 April 2010.

219A Power to call for documents etc.

219A [Omitted by SI 2009/3054, art. 3 and Schedule, para. 2(2).]

History – S. 219A omitted by SI 2009/3054, art. 3 and Schedule, para. 2(2), with effect from 1 April 2010.

219B Appeal against requirement to produce documents etc.

219B [Omitted by SI 2009/3054, art. 3 and Schedule, para. 2(2).]

History – S. 219B omitted by SI 2009/3054, art. 3 and Schedule, para. 2(2), with effect from 1 April 2010, except in relation to a notice given under s. 219 or 219A before 1 April 2010, in which case s. 219B continues to have effect (SI 2009/3054, art. 4). Former s. 219B read as follows:

"219B Appeal against requirement to produce documents etc.

219B(1) An appeal may be brought against any requirement imposed by a notice under section 219A(1) above to produce any document or to furnish any accounts or particulars.

IHT Statutes

219B(2) Subject to the following provisions of this section, the provisions of this Act relating to appeals shall have effect in relation to an appeal under this section as they have effect in relation to an appeal against a determination specified in a notice under section 221 below.

219B(3) An appeal under this section must be brought within the period of thirty days beginning with the date on which the notice under section 219A(1) above is given.

219B(4) On an appeal under this section the tribunal may–

(a) if it appears that the production of the document or the furnishing of the accounts or particulars was reasonably required by the officer of the Board for any of the purposes mentioned in section 219A(2) above, confirm the notice under section 219A(1) above so far as relating to the requirement; or

(b) if it does not so appear, set aside that notice so far as so relating.

219B(5) Where, on an appeal under this section, the tribunal confirms the notice under section 219A(1) above so far as relating to any requirement, the notice shall have effect in relation to that requirement as if it had specified thirty days beginning with the determination of the appeal.

219B(6) Neither the person required to produce documents or furnish accounts or particulars nor the officer of the Board shall be entitled to appeal under sections 11 or 13 of the TCEA 2007 against the determination of an appeal under this section.

History – In s. 219B(4) the word "tribunal" substituted for the words "Special Commissioners" and in para. (a) and (b) the words "to them" omitted by SI 2009/56, art. 3 and Sch. 1, para. 113(2), with effect from 1 April 2009, subject to transitional and saving provisions in SI 2009/56, Sch. 3.
In s. 219B(5) the words "tribunal confirms" substituted for the words "Special Commissioners confirm" by SI 2009/56, art. 3 and Sch. 1, para. 113(3), with effect from 1 April 2009, subject to transitional and saving provisions in SI 2009/56, Sch. 3.
In s. 219B(6) the words "under sections 11 or 13 of the TCEA 2007" substituted for the words "under section 225 below" by SI 2009/56, art. 3 and Sch. 1, para. 113(4), with effect from 1 April 2009, subject to transitional and saving provisions in SI 2009/56, Sch. 3.
S. 219B inserted by FA 1999, s. 106, with effect from 27 July 1999."

220 Inspection of property

220 [Omitted by SI 2009/3054, art. 3 and Schedule, para. 2(3).]

History – S. 220 omitted by SI 2009/3054, art. 3 and Schedule, para. 2(3), with effect from 1 April 2010.

220A Exchange of information with other countries

220A [Repealed by FA 2006, s. 178 and Sch. 26, Pt. 8(2).]

History – S. 220A repealed by FA 2006, s. 178 and Sch. 26, Pt. 8(2), with effect from 19 July 2006 (Royal Assent).

DETERMINATIONS, REVIEWS AND APPEALS

History – In the above heading the word ", REVIEWS" inserted by SI 2009/56, art. 3 and Sch. 1, para. 114, with effect from 1 April 2009, subject to transitional and saving provisions in SI 2009/56, Sch. 3.

221 Notices of determination

221(1) Where it appears to the Board that a transfer of value has been made or where a claim under this Act is made to the Board in connection with a transfer of value, the Board may give notice in writing to any person who appears to the Board to be the transferor or the claimant or to be liable for any of the tax chargeable on the value transferred, stating that they have determined the matters specified in the notice.

221(2) The matters that may be specified in a notice under this section in relation to any transfer of value are all or any of the following–

(a) the date of the transfer;

(b) the value transferred and the value of any property to which the value transferred is wholly or partly attributable;

(c) the transferor;

(d) the tax chargeable (if any) and the persons who are liable for the whole or part of it;

(e) the amount of any payment made in excess of the tax for which a person is liable and the date from which and the rate at which tax or any repayment of tax overpaid carries interest; and

(f) any other matter that appears to the Board to be relevant for the purposes of this Act.

221(3) A determination for the purposes of a notice under this section of any fact relating to a transfer of value–

(a) shall, if that fact has been stated in an account or return under this Part of this Act and the Board are satisfied that the account or return is correct, be made by the Board in accordance with that account or return, but

(b) may, in any other case, be made by the Board to the best of their judgment.

221(4) A notice under this section shall state the time within which and the manner in which an appeal against any determination in it may be made.

221(5) Subject to any variation by agreement in writing or on appeal, a determination in a notice under this section shall be conclusive for the purposes of this Act against the person on whom the notice is served; and if the notice is served on the transferor and specifies a determination of the value transferred by the transfer of value or previous transfers of value, the determination, so far as relevant to the tax chargeable in respect of later transfers of value (whether or not made by the transferor) shall be conclusive also against any other person, subject however to any adjustment under section 240 or 241 below.

221(6) References in this section to **transfers of value** or to the values transferred by them shall be construed as including references to–

(a) chargeable events by reference to which tax is chargeable under section 32 or 32A of this Act,

(b) occasions on which tax is chargeable under Chapter III of Part III of this Act,

(c) disposals on which tax is chargeable under section 126 of this Act,

or to the amounts on which tax is then chargeable.

History – In s. 221(6)(a), the words "or 32A" were inserted by FA 1985, Sch. 26, para. 5, in relation to events on or after 19 March 1985.

Cross references – S. 32, 32A: following conditionally exempt transfer of property, charge where certain events occur in respect of property or associated property.
S. 126: charge on disposal of trees or underwood.

222 Appeals against determinations

222(1) A person on whom a notice under section 221 above has been served may, within thirty days of the service, appeal against any determination specified in it by notice in writing given to the Board and specifying the grounds of appeal.

222(2) Sections 223D, 223G and 223H provide for notification of the appeal to the tribunal.

222(3) Where–

(a) it is so agreed between the appellant and the Board, or

(b) the High Court, on an application made by the appellant, is satisfied that the matters to be decided on the appeal are likely to be substantially confined to questions of law and gives leave for that purpose,

the appeal may be notified to the High Court.

222(4) An appeal on any question as to the value of land in the United Kingdom may be notified to the appropriate [tribunal].

222(4ZA) The appeal may be notified under subsection (3) or (4) only if it could be notified to the tribunal under section 223D, 223G or 223H.

222(4A) If and so far as the question in dispute on any appeal under this section which has been notified to the tribunal or the High Court is a question as to the value of land in the United Kingdom, the question shall be determined on a reference to the appropriate [tribunal].

222(4B) In this section **"the appropriate tribunal"** means–

(a) where the land is in England or Wales, the Upper Tribunal;

(b) where the land is in Scotland, the Lands Tribunal for Scotland;

(c) where the land is in Northern Ireland, the Lands Tribunal for Northern Ireland.

222(5) In the application of this section to Scotland, for references to the High Court there shall be substituted references to the Court of Session.

History – S. 222(2) substituted by SI 2009/56, art. 3 and Sch. 1, para. 115(2), with effect from 1 April 2009, subject to transitional and saving provisions in SI 2009/56, Sch. 3. Former s. 222(2) read as follows:

"222(2) Subject to the following provisions of this section the appeal shall be to the Special Commissioners."

In s. 222(3) the word "notified" inserted by SI 2009/56, art. 3 and Sch. 1, para. 115(3), with effect from 1 April 2009, subject to transitional and saving provisions in SI 2009/56, Sch. 3.

In s. 222(4) the words "Land Tribunal" omitted by SI 2009/1307, art. 5(1) and (2) and Sch. 1, para. 167(a), with effect from 1 June 2009 (subject to transitional and savings provisions at SI 2009/1307, Sch. 5). Note the sentence as amended did not make sense so in the text Croner-i has replaced the omitted words with "[tribunal]".

In s. 222(4) the word "notified" and the word "Lands" inserted by SI 2009/56, art. 3 and Sch. 1, para. 115(4), with effect from 1 April 2009, subject to transitional and saving provisions in SI 2009/56, Sch. 3.

S. 222(4ZA) inserted by SI 2009/56, art. 3 and Sch. 1, para. 115(5), with effect from 1 April 2009, subject to transitional and saving provisions in SI 2009/56, Sch. 3.

In s. 222(4A) the words "Land Tribunal" omitted by SI 2009/1307, art. 5(1) and (2) and Sch. 1, para. 167(b), with effect from 1 June 2009 (subject to transitional and savings provisions at SI 2009/1307, Sch. 5). Note the sentence as amended did not make sense so in the text Croner-i has replaced the omitted words with "[tribunal]".

S. 222(4A) substituted by SI 2009/56, art. 3 and Sch. 1, para. 115(6), with effect from 1 April 2009, subject to transitional and saving provisions in SI 2009/56, Sch. 3. Former s. 222(4A) read as follows:

"222(4A) If and so far as the question in dispute on any appeal under this section to the Special Commissioners or the High Court is a question as to the value of land in the United Kingdom, the question shall be determined on a reference to the appropriate tribunal."

In s. 222(4B), the words "appropriate tribunal" substituted for the words "appropriate Lands tribunal" and the words "Upper Tribunal" substituted for the words "Lands Tribunal" by SI 2009/1307, art. 5(1) and (2) and Sch. 1, para. 167(c), with effect from 1 June 2009 (subject to transitional and savings provisions at SI 2009/1307, Sch. 5).

In s. 222(4B) the word "Lands" inserted by SI 2009/56, art. 3 and Sch. 1, para. 115(7), with effect from 1 April 2009, subject to transitional and saving provisions in SI 2009/56, Sch. 3.

S. 222(4)–(4B) substituted for the former s. 222(4) by FA 1993, s. 200(1) in relation to appeals made on or after 27 July 1993 or made but not begun to be heard before that day.

Cross references – FA 2014, s. 203(f): an appeal under s. 222 is treated as a tax appeal for the purposes of FA 2014, Pt. 4 (follower notices and accelerated payments).
SI 1994/1811, reg. 23: reference of a question in an appeal which is required to be determined under s. 222(4A) to the appropriate tribunal; determination of remaining questions in appeal without awaiting determination of question referred to other tribunal.
SI 1994/1811, reg. 24(4): penalties under reg. 24 for failure to comply with special commissioners' direction etc. in proceedings relating to an appeal under s. 222 treated for all purposes as if it were tax determined by the Board and due and payable.

223 Late notice of appeal

223(1) This section applies in a case where–

(a) notice of appeal may be given to HMRC under section 222, but

(b) no notice is given before the relevant time limit.

223(2) Notice may be given after the relevant time limit if–

(a) HMRC agree, or

(b) where HMRC do not agree, the tribunal gives permission.

223(3) If the following conditions are met, HMRC shall agree to notice being given after the relevant time limit.

223(4) Condition A is that the appellant has made a request in writing to HMRC to agree to the notice being given.

223(5) Condition B is that HMRC are satisfied that there was reasonable excuse for not giving the notice before the relevant time limit.

223(6) Condition C is that HMRC are satisfied that request under subsection (4) was made without unreasonable delay after the reasonable excuse ceased.

223(7) If a request of the kind referred to in subsection (4) is made, HMRC must notify the appellant whether or not HMRC agree to the appellant giving notice of appeal after the relevant time limit.

223(8) In this section **"relevant time limit"**, in relation to notice of appeal, means the time before which the notice is to be given (but for this section).

History – S. 223 substituted and s. 223A–223I inserted by SI 2009/56, art. 3 and Sch. 1, para. 116, with effect from 1 April 2009, subject to transitional and saving provisions in SI 2009/56, Sch. 3. Former s. 223 read as follows:

"223 Appeals out of time

223 An appeal under section 222 above may be brought out of time with the consent of the Board or the Special Commissioners; and the Board–

(a) shall give that consent if satisfied, on an application for the purpose, that there was a reasonable excuse for not bringing the appeal within the time limited and that the application was made thereafter without unreasonable delay, and

(b) shall, if not so satisfied, refer the application for determination by the Special Commissioners."

223A Appeal: HMRC review or determination by tribunal

223A(1) This section applies if notice of appeal has been given to HMRC.

223A(2) In such a case–

(a) the appellant may notify HMRC that the appellant requires HMRC to review the matter in question (see section 223B),

(b) HMRC may notify the appellant of an offer to review the matter in question (see section 223C), or

(c) the appellant may notify the appeal to the tribunal (see section 223D).

223A(3) See sections 223G and 223H for provision about notifying appeals to the tribunal after a review has been required by the appellant or offered by HMRC.

History – S. 223A inserted by SI 2009/56, art. 3 and Sch. 1, para. 117, with effect from 1 April 2009, subject to transitional and saving provisions in SI 2009/56, Sch. 3.

223B Appellant requires review by HMRC

223B(1) Subsections (2) and (3) apply if the appellant notifies HMRC that the appellant requires HMRC to review the matter in question.

223B(2) HMRC must, within the relevant period, notify the appellant of HMRC's view of the matter in question.

223B(3) HMRC must review the matter in question in accordance with section 223E.

223B(4) The appellant may not notify HMRC that the appellant requires HMRC to review the matter in question and HMRC shall not be required to conduct a review if–

(a) the appellant has already given a notification under this section in relation to the matter in question,

(b) HMRC have given a notification under section 223C in relation to the matter in question, or

(c) the appellant has notified the appeal to the court under section 222(3), the appropriate Lands tribunal under section 222(4), or the tribunal under section 223D.

223B(5) *In this section* ***"relevant period"*** means–

(a) the period of 30 days beginning with the day on which HMRC receive the notification from the appellant, or

(b) such longer period as is reasonable.

History – S. 223B inserted by SI 2009/56, art. 3 and Sch. 1, para. 117, with effect from 1 April 2009, subject to transitional and saving provisions in SI 2009/56, Sch. 3.

223C HMRC offer review

223C(1) Subsections (2) to (6) apply if HMRC notify the appellant of an offer to review the matter in question.

223C(2) When HMRC notify the appellant of the offer, HMRC must also notify the appellant of HMRC's view of the matter in question.

223C(3) If, within the acceptance period, the appellant notifies HMRC of acceptance of the offer, HMRC must review the matter in question in accordance with section 223E.

223C(4) If the appellant does not give HMRC such a notification within the acceptance period, HMRC's view of the matter in question shall be conclusive for the purposes of this Act.

223C(5) The same consequences shall follow for all purposes as would have followed if, on the date that HMRC gave notice of their view, the tribunal had determined the appeal in accordance with its terms.

223C(6) Subsection (4) does not apply to the matter in question if, or to the extent that, the appellant notifies the appeal to the tribunal under section 223H.

223C(7) HMRC may not notify the appellant of an offer to review the matter in question (and, accordingly, HMRC shall not be required to conduct a review) if–

(a) HMRC have already given a notification under this section in relation to the matter in question,

(b) the appellant has given a notification under section 223B in relation to the matter in question, or

(c) the appellant has notified the appeal to the court under section 222(3), the appropriate Lands tribunal under section 222(4) or the tribunal under section 223D.

223C(8) In this section **"acceptance period"** means the period of 30 days beginning with the date of the document by which HMRC notify the appellant of the offer to review the matter in question.

History – S. 223C inserted by SI 2009/56, art. 3 and Sch. 1, para. 117, with effect from 1 April 2009, subject to transitional and saving provisions in SI 2009/56, Sch. 3.

223D Notifying appeal to the tribunal

223D(1) This section applies if notice of appeal has been given to HMRC.

223D(2) The appellant may notify the appeal to the tribunal.

223D(3) If the appellant notifies the appeal to the tribunal, the tribunal is to decide the matter in question.

223D(4) Subsections (2) and (3) do not apply in a case where–

(a) HMRC have given a notification of their view of the matter in question under section 223B, or

(b) HMRC have given a notification under section 223C in relation to the matter in question.

223D(5) In a case falling within subsection (4)(a) or (b), the appellant may notify the appeal to the tribunal, but only if permitted to do so by section 223G or 223H.

History – S. 223D inserted by SI 2009/56, art. 3 and Sch. 1, para. 117, with effect from 1 April 2009, subject to transitional and saving provisions in SI 2009/56, Sch. 3.

223E Nature of review etc

223E(1) This section applies if HMRC are required by section 223B or 223C to review the matter in question.

223E(2) The nature and extent of the review are to be such as appear appropriate to HMRC in the circumstances.

223E(3) For the purpose of subsection (2), HMRC must, in particular, have regard to steps taken before the beginning of the review–

(a) by HMRC in deciding the matter in question, and

(b) by any person in seeking to resolve disagreement about the matter in question.

223E(4) The review must take account of any representations made by the appellant at a stage which gives HMRC a reasonable opportunity to consider them.

223E(5) The review may conclude that HMRC's view of the matter in question is to be–

(a) upheld,

(b) varied, or

(c) cancelled.

223E(6) HMRC must notify the appellant of the conclusions of the review and their reasoning within–

(a) the period of 45 days beginning with the relevant day, or

(b) such other period as may be agreed.

223E(7) In subsection (6) **"relevant day"** means–

(a) in a case where the appellant required the review, the day when HMRC notified the appellant of HMRC's view of the matter in question,

(b) in a case where HMRC offered the review, the day when HMRC received notification of the appellant's acceptance of the offer.

223E(8) Where HMRC are required to undertake a review but do not give notice of the conclusions within the time period specified in subsection (6), the review is to be treated as having concluded that HMRC's view of the matter in question (see sections 223B(2) and 223C(2)) is upheld.

223E(9) If subsection (8) applies, HMRC must notify the appellant of the conclusion which the review is treated as having reached.

History – S. 223E inserted by SI 2009/56, art. 3 and Sch. 1, para. 117, with effect from 1 April 2009, subject to transitional and saving provisions in SI 2009/56, Sch. 3.

223F Effect of conclusions of review

223F(1) This section applies if HMRC give notice of the conclusions of a review (see section 223E(6) and (9)).

223F(2) The conclusions of the review shall be conclusive for the purposes of this Act.

223F(3) Subsections (2) and (3) do not apply to the matter in question if, or to the extent that, the appellant notifies the appeal to the tribunal under section 223G.

History – S. 223F inserted by SI 2009/56, art. 3 and Sch. 1, para. 117, with effect from 1 April 2009, subject to transitional and saving provisions in SI 2009/56, Sch. 3.

223G Notifying appeal to tribunal after review concluded

223G(1) This section applies if–

(a) HMRC have given notice of the conclusions of a review in accordance with section 223E, or

(b) the period specified in section 223E(6) has ended and HMRC have not given notice of the conclusions of the review.

223G(2) The appellant may notify the appeal to the tribunal within the post-review period.

223G(3) If the post-review period has ended, the appellant may notify the appeal to the tribunal only if the tribunal gives permission.

223G(4) If the appellant notifies the appeal to the tribunal, the tribunal is to determine the matter in question.

223G(5) The appellant may not notify the appeal to the tribunal under this section if the appeal has been notified to the court under section 222(3) or the appropriate Lands tribunal under section 222(4).

223G(6) In this section **"post-review period"** means–

(a) in a case falling within subsection (1)(a), the period of 30 days beginning with the date of the document in which HMRC give notice of the conclusions of the review in accordance with section 223E(6), or

(b) in a case falling within subsection (1)(b), the period that–

(i) begins with the day following the last day of the period specified in section 223E(6), and

(ii) ends 30 days after the date of the document in which HMRC give notice of the conclusion of the review in accordance with section 223E(9).

History – S. 223G inserted by SI 2009/56, art. 3 and Sch. 1, para. 117, with effect from 1 April 2009, subject to transitional and saving provisions in SI 2009/56, Sch. 3.

223H Notifying appeal to tribunal after review offered but not accepted

223H(1) This section applies if–

(a) HMRC have offered to review the matter in question (see section 223C), and

(b) the appellant has not accepted the offer.

223H(2) The appellant may notify the appeal to the tribunal within the acceptance period.

223H(3) But if the acceptance period has ended, the appellant may notify the appeal to the tribunal only if the tribunal gives permission.

223H(4) *If the appellant notifies* the appeal to the tribunal, the tribunal is to determine the matter in question.

223H(5) The appellant may not notify the appeal to the tribunal under this section if the appeal has been notified to the court under section 222(3) or the appropriate Lands tribunal under section 222(4).

223H(6) In this section **"acceptance period"** has the same meaning as in section 223C.

History – S. 223H inserted by SI 2009/56, art. 3 and Sch. 1, para. 117, with effect from 1 April 2009, subject to transitional and saving provisions in SI 2009/56, Sch. 3.

223I Interpretation of sections 223A to 223I

223I(1) In sections 223A to 223H–

(a) **"matter in question"** means the matter to which an appeal relates;

(b) a reference to a notification is a reference to a notification in writing.

223I(2) In sections 223A to 223H, a reference to the appellant includes a person acting on behalf of the appellant except in relation to–

(a) notification of HMRC's view under section 223B(2);

(b) notification by HMRC of an offer of review (and of their view of the matter) under section 223C;

(c) notification of the conclusions of a review under section 223E(6); and

(d) notification of the conclusions of a review under section 223E(9).

223I(3) But if a notification falling within any of the paragraphs of subsection (2) is given to the appellant, a copy of the notification may also be given to a person acting on behalf of the appellant.

History – S. 223I inserted by SI 2009/56, art. 3 and Sch. 1, para. 117, with effect from 1 April 2009, subject to transitional and saving provisions in SI 2009/56, Sch. 3.

224 Determination of appeal by tribunal

224 If an appeal is notified to the tribunal, the tribunal must confirm the determination appealed against (or that determination as varied on a review under section 223E) unless the tribunal is satisfied that it ought to be varied (or further varied) or quashed.

History – S. 224 substituted by SI 2009/56, art. 3 and Sch. 1, para. 118, with effect from 1 April 2009, subject to transitional and saving provisions in SI 2009/56, Sch. 3. Former s. 224 read as follows:

"224 Procedure before Special Commissioners

224(1)–(3) [Omitted by SI 1994/1813, Sch. 1, para. 20, Sch. 2, Pt. I.]

224(4) On an appeal before the Special Commissioners, the Special Commissioners may allow the appellant to put forward any ground of appeal not specified in the notice of appeal and may take it into consideration if satisfied that the omission was not wilful or unreasonable.

224(5) The Special Commissioners shall on an appeal to them confirm the determination appealed against unless they are satisfied that the determination ought to be varied or quashed.

History – S. 224(1)–(3) omitted by SI 1994/1813, reg. 2(1) and Sch. 1, para. 20, Sch. 2, Pt. I, with effect from 1 September 1994."

225 Appeals from Special Commissioners

225 [Omitted by SI 2009/56, art. 3 and Sch. 1, para. 119.]

History – S. 225 omitted by SI 2009/56, art. 3 and Sch. 1, para. 119, with effect from 1 April 2009, subject to transitional and saving provisions in SI 2009/56, Sch. 3. Former s. 225 read as follows:

"225 Appeals from Special Commissioners

225(1) Any party to an appeal, if dissatisfied in point of law with the determination of that appeal by the Special Commissioners, may appeal against that determination to the High Court.

225(2) The High Court shall hear and determine any question of law arising on an appeal under subsection (1) above and may reverse, affirm or vary the determination appealed against, or remit the matter to the Special Commissioners with the court's opinion on it, or make such other order in relation to the matter as the court thinks fit.

225(3) This section shall have effect–

(a) in its application to Scotland, with the substitution of references to the Court of Session for references to the High Court; and

(b) in its application to Northern Ireland, with the substitution of references to the Court of Appeal in Northern Ireland for references to the High Court.

History – S. 225 substituted by SI 1994/1813, reg. 2(1) and Sch. 1, para. 21, with effect from 1 September 1994."

225A Extension of regulation-making powers

225A [Omitted by SI 2009/56, art. 3 and Sch. 1, para. 119.]

History – S. 225A omitted by SI 2009/56, art. 3 and Sch. 1, para. 119, with effect from 1 April 2009, subject to transitional and saving provisions in SI 2009/56, Sch. 3. Former s. 225A read as follows:

"225A Extension of regulation-making powers

225A(1) Section 46A of the Taxes Management Act 1970 (regulations about jurisdiction of General and Special Commissioners) shall apply in relation to appeals or other proceedings under this Part of this Act as it applies in relation to appeals or other proceedings under the Taxes Acts, but with the omission from subsection (1) of–

(a) paragraphs (a) and (b), and

(b) the words "General Commissioners or" in paragraph (c).

225A(2) Sections 56B, 56C and 56D of the Taxes Management Act 1970 (regulations about practice and procedure of General and Special Commissioners) shall apply in relation to appeals or other proceedings under this Part of this Act as they apply in relation to appeals or other proceedings under the Taxes Acts.

225A(3) In this section, **"the Taxes Acts"** has the meaning given in section 118(1) of the Taxes Management Act 1970.

History – S. 225A inserted by F(No. 2)A 1992, s. 76 and Sch. 16, para. 8."

PAYMENT

226 Payment: general rules

226(1) Except as otherwise provided by the following provisions of this Part of this Act, the tax on the value transferred by a chargeable transfer shall be due six months after the end of the month in which the chargeable transfer is made or, in the case of a transfer made after 5th April and before 1st October in any year otherwise than on death, at the end of April in the next year.

226(2) Personal representatives shall, on delivery of their account, pay all the tax for which they are liable and may, on delivery of that account, also pay any part of the tax chargeable on the death for which they are not liable, if the persons liable for it request them to make the payment.

226(3) So much of the tax chargeable on the value transferred by a chargeable transfer made within seven years of the death of the transferor as–

(a) exceeds what it would have been had the transferor died more than seven years after the transfer,

(b) [repealed by FA 1988, s. 148 and Sch. 14, Pt. X]

shall be due six months after the end of the month in which the death occurs.

226(3A) Without prejudice to subsection (3) above, the tax chargeable on the value transferred by a potentially exempt transfer which proves to be a chargeable transfer shall be due six months after the end of the month in which the transferor's death occurs.

226(3B) So much (if any) of the tax chargeable on the value transferred by a chargeable transfer made under Chapter III of Part III of this Act within the period of seven years ending with the settlor's death as exceeds what it would have been had the settlor died more than seven years after the date of the transfer shall be due six months after the end of the month in which the death occurs.

226(3C) Tax chargeable under Chapter 3 of Part 3 of this Act on the value transferred by a chargeable transfer, other than any for which the due date is given by subsection (3B) above, is due six months after the end of the month in which the chargeable transfer is made.

226(4) Tax chargeable under section 32, 32A, 79 or 126 above or under Schedule 5 to this Act shall be due six months after the end of the month in which the event by reason of which it is chargeable occurs.

226(5) The Board may in the first instance, and without prejudice to the recovery of the remainder of the tax, accept or demand payment of an amount by reference to the value stated in an account delivered to the Board under section 216 or 217 above.

226(6) Nothing in this section shall be taken to authorise the recovery from, or require the payment by, any person of tax in excess of his liability as limited by section 204 above.

History – In s. 226(3), certain words and para. (b) repealed by FA 1988, s. 148 and Sch. 14, Pt. X, in relation to transfers of value made on or after 15 March 1988.

In s. 226(3), words "seven years" in both places substituted by FA 1986, s. 101 and Sch. 19, para. 30(1), with respect to transfers of value made, and other events occurring, on or after 18 March 1986.

S. 226(3A), (3B) inserted by FA 1986, s. 101 and Sch. 19, para. 30(2), with respect to transfers of value made, and other events occurring, on or after 18 March 1986.

S. 226(3C) inserted by FA 2014, s. 117 and Sch. 25, para. 5(2), with effect in relation to chargeable transfers made on or after 6 April 2014.

In s. 226(4), "or 126" substituted for ", 126, 151B or 151D" by FA 2011, s. 65 and Sch. 16, para. 55(a), with effect in relation to deaths occurring on or after 6 April 2011.

In s. 226(4), the words ", or under section 151A above by virtue of subsection (6) of that section,", which appeared after the words "or under Schedule 5 to this Act", omitted by FA 2011, s. 65 and Sch. 16, para. 55(b), with effect in relation to deaths occurring on or after 6 April 2011.

In s. 226(4) the words ", 151B or 151D" substituted for the words "or 151B" by FA 2008, s. 91 and Sch. 28, para. 13, with effect in relation to deaths occurring on or after 6 April 2008.

In s. 226(4) the words ", or under section 151A above by virtue of subsection (6) of that section," inserted by FA 2007, s. 69 and Sch. 19, para. 25, with effect in relation to deaths, cases where scheme administrators become aware of deaths and cessations of dependency occurring on or after 6 April 2007.

In s. 226(4) the words ", 126 or 151B" substituted for the words "or 126" by FA 2006, s. 160 and Sch. 22, para. 8, with effect from 6 April 2006.

In s. 226(4), reference to s. 32A inserted by FA 1985, s. 94(1) and Sch. 26, para. 11, in relation to events on or after 19 March 1985.

Cross references – S. 32, 32A: following conditionally exempt transfer of property, charge where certain events occur in respect of property or associated property.

S. 79: conditionally exempt transfer of property held on discretionary trust – conditions for exemption from ten-year charge.

S. 126: charge on disposal of trees or underwood.

Sch. 5: conditional exemption – deaths before 7 April 1976.

FA 1986, Sch. 19, para. 40(1): transitional – transfer of value occurring before, and death or other event occurring after, 18 March 1986.

FA 2009, Sch. 56: penalty for failure to make payments on time.

Extra-statutory concessions – F6: if executors cannot transfer to this country sufficient of the deceased's foreign assets for the payment of the IHT attributable to them, due to foreign government restrictions, they may defer payment. If the executors succeed in bringing to this country less than the amount of the tax, the balance is waived.

227 Payment by instalments – land, shares and businesses

227(1) Where any of the tax payable on the value transferred by a chargeable transfer is attributable to the value of qualifying property and–

(a) the transfer is made on death, or

(b) the tax so attributable is borne by the person benefiting from the transfer, or

(c) the transfer is made under Part III of this Act and the property concerned continues to be comprised in the settlement,

the tax so attributable may, if the person paying it by notice in writing to the Board so elects, be paid by ten equal yearly instalments.

227(1A) Subsection (1) above does not apply to–

(a) tax payable on the value transferred by a potentially exempt transfer which proves to be a chargeable transfer, or

(b) additional tax becoming payable on the value transferred by any chargeable transfer by reason of the transferor's death within seven years of the transfer,

except to the extent that the tax is attributable to the value of property which satisfies one of the conditions specified in subsection (1C) below and, in the case of property consisting of unquoted shares or unquoted securities, the further condition specified in section 228(3A) below.

227(1AA) In subsection (1A) above **"unquoted"**, in relation to any shares or securities, means not listed on a recognised stock exchange.

227(1B) In this section **"the transferee"** means the person whose property the qualifying property became on the transfer or, where on the transfer the qualifying property became comprised in a settlement in which no qualifying interest in possession (within the meaning of Chapter III of Part III of this Act) subsists, the trustees of the settlement.

227(1C) The conditions referred to in subsection (1A) above are–

(a) that the property was owned by the transferee throughout the period beginning with the date of the chargeable transfer and ending with the death of the transferor (or, if earlier, the death of the transferee), or

(b) that for the purposes of determining the tax, or additional tax, due by reason of the death of the transferor, the value of the property is reduced in accordance with the provisions of Chapter I or Chapter II of Part V of this Act by virtue of section 113B or section 124B above.

227(2) In this section **"qualifying property"** means–

(a) land of any description, wherever situated;

(b) shares or securities to which section 228 below applies;

(c) a business or an interest in a business.

227(3) The first of the instalments referred to in subsection (1) above shall be payable–

(a) if the chargeable transfer was made on death, six months after the end of the month in which the death occurred, and

(b) in any other case, at the time when the tax would be due if it were not payable by instalments;

and interest under section 233 below on the unpaid portion of the tax shall be added to each instalment and paid accordingly, except as otherwise provided in section 234 below.

227(4) Notwithstanding the making of an election under this section, the tax for the time being unpaid, with interest to the time of payment, may be paid at any time; and if at any time (whether before or after the date when the first instalment is payable) the whole or any part of the property concerned is sold, the tax unpaid (or, in the case of a sale of part, the proportionate part of that tax) shall become payable forthwith (or, if the sale precedes the date when the first instalment is payable, on that date) together with any interest accrued under section 233 below.

227(5) References in subsection (4) above to the sale of property shall have effect–

(a) in a case within subsection (1)(b) above other than a case within subsection (1A) above where the transferee dies before the transferor, as if they included references to any chargeable transfer in which the value transferred is wholly or partly attributable to the value of the property, other than a transfer made on death, and

(b) in a case within subsection (1)(c) above, as references to the property ceasing to be comprised in the settlement.

227(6) For the purposes of subsection (4) above–

(a) the sale of an interest or part of an interest in a business shall be treated as a sale of part of the business, and

(b) the payment, under a partnership agreement or otherwise, of a sum in satisfaction of the whole or part of an interest in a business otherwise than on a sale shall be treated as a sale of the interest or part at the time of payment.

227(7) For the purposes of this section–

(a) the value of a business or of an interest in a business shall be taken to be its net value;

(b) the net value of a business is the value of the assets used in the business (including goodwill) reduced by the aggregate amount of any liabilities incurred for the purposes of the business;

(c) in ascertaining the net value of an interest in a business, no regard shall be had to assets or liabilities other than those by reference to which the net value of the business would have fallen to be ascertained if the tax had been attributable to the entire business; and

(d) **"business"** includes a business carried on in the exercise of a profession or vocation, but does not include a business carried on otherwise than for gain.

History – S. 227(1A) substituted by FA 1987, s. 58 and Sch. 8, para. 15(1), in relation to transfers of value made, and other events occurring, on or after 17 March 1987.
Former s. 227(1A) inserted by FA 1986, s. 101 and Sch. 19, para. 31(1), with respect to transfers of value made, and other events occurring, on or after 18 March 1986.
In s. 227(1AA), the word "listed" substituted for the previous word "quoted" by FA 1996, s. 199 and Sch. 38, para. 5, with effect in relation to transfers of value on or after 1 April 1996 and, for the purposes of any charge to tax by reason of an event occurring on or after 1 April 1996, in relation to transfers of value before that date.
S. 227(1AA) inserted by F(No. 2)A 1992, s. 73 and Sch. 14, para. 5, in relation to transfers of value made, and other events occurring, on or after 10 March 1992, but subject to the transitional provisions in F(No. 2)A 1992, Sch. 14, para. 9.
In s. 227(1B), the words "this section" were substituted by FA 1987, s. 58 and Sch. 8, para. 15(2), in relation to transfers of value made, and other events occurring, on or after 17 March 1987.
S. 227 (1B) inserted by FA 1986, s. 101 and Sch. 19, para. 31(1), with respect to transfers of value made, and other events occurring, on or after 18 March 1986.
S. 227(1C) inserted by FA 1987, s. 58 and Sch. 8, para. 15(3), in relation to transfers of value made, and other events occurring, on or after 17 March 1987.
In s. 227(5)(a), the words "other than a case … the transferor" were inserted by FA 1986, s. 101 and Sch. 19, para. 31(2), with respect to transfers of value made, and other events occurring, on or after 18 March 1986.

Cross references – S. 113B: transfer of business property within seven years of death – replacement property.
S. 124B: transfer of agricultural property within seven years of death – replacement property.
FA 1986, Sch. 19, para. 40(1): transitional – transfer of value occurring before, and death or other event occurring after, 18 March 1986.
FA 2009, Sch. 53, para. 7: late payment interest start dates.
FA 2009, Sch. 56: penalty for failure to make payments on time.

228 Shares, etc. within section 227

228(1) This section applies–

(a) to shares or securities of a company which immediately before the chargeable transfer gave control of the company–

  (i) in the case of a transfer on death, to the deceased,

  (ii) in the case of a transfer under Chapter III of Part III of this Act, to the trustees, and

  (iii) in any other case, to the transferor;

(b) to shares or securities of a company which do not fall under paragraph (a) above and are unquoted, if the chargeable transfer is made on death and the condition stated in subsection (2) below is satisfied;

(c) to shares or securities of a company which do not fall under paragraph (a) above and are unquoted, if the Board are satisfied that the tax attributable to their value cannot be paid in one sum without undue hardship (assuming, in the case of a chargeable transfer made otherwise than on death, that the shares or securities would be retained by the persons liable to pay the tax);

(d) to shares of a company which do not fall under paragraph (a) above and are unquoted, if the conditions stated in subsection (3) below are satisfied.

228(2) The condition mentioned in subsection (1)(b) above is that not less than 20 per cent of so much of the tax chargeable on the value transferred as is tax for which the person paying the tax attributable as mentioned in section 227(1) above is liable (in the same capacity) consists of tax attributable to the value of the shares or securities or such other tax (if any) as may by virtue of section 227 be paid by instalments.

228(3) The conditions mentioned in subsection (1)(d) above are that so much of the value transferred (calculated, if the transfer is not made on death, as if no tax were chargeable on it) as is attributable to the shares exceeds £20,000, and that either–

(a) the nominal value of the shares is not less than 10 per cent of the nominal value of all the shares of the company at the time of the transfer, or

(b) the shares are ordinary shares and their nominal value is not less than 10 per cent of the nominal value of all ordinary shares of the company at that time.

228(3A) The further condition referred to in section 227(1A) above is that the shares or securities remained unquoted throughout the period beginning with the date of the chargeable transfer and ending with the death of the transferor (or, if earlier, the death of the transferee).

228(4) In this section **"ordinary shares"** means shares which carry either–

(a) a right to dividends not restricted to dividends at a fixed rate, or

(b) a right to conversion into shares carrying such a right as is mentioned in paragraph (a) above.

228(5) In this section **"unquoted"**, in relation to any shares or securities, means not listed on a recognised stock exchange.

History – In s. 228(1), the words "which do not fall under paragraph (a) above and are unquoted" in each place were substituted by FA 1987, Sch. 8, para. 16(1), with effect in relation to transfers of value made, and other events occurring, on or after 17 March 1987. S. 228(3A) was inserted by FA 1987, Sch. 8, para. 16(2), with effect in relation to transfers of value made, and other events occurring, on or after 17 March 1987.
In s. 228(5) the word "listed" substituted for the previous word "quoted" by FA 1996, s. 199 and Sch. 38, para. 5, with effect in relation to transfers of value on or after 1 April 1996 and, for the purposes of any charge to tax by reason of an event occurring on or after 1 April 1996, in relation to transfers of value before that date.
S. 228(5) inserted by F(No. 2)A 1992, s. 73 and Sch. 14, para. 6, in relation to transfers of value made, and other events occurring, on and after 10 March 1992, but subject to the transitional provisions in F(No. 2)A 1992, Sch. 14, para. 9.

Other material – Taxline, 1991/13 (not reproduced): Capital Taxes Office confirmation that where a settlor creates a number of different discretionary settlements on the same day, the transfer into each settlement has to be considered separately for the purpose of the tests in s. 228(3); also, clarification of position where property leaves a discretionary settlement and is appointed in favour of several beneficiaries.

229 Payment by instalments – woodlands

229 Tax chargeable on such a chargeable transfer as is mentioned in section 129 above may, if the person paying the tax by notice in writing to the Board so elects, be paid by ten equal yearly instalments, of which the first shall be payable six months after the end of the month in which the transfer is made.

Cross references – S. 129: credit for tax charged under s. 126.
FA 2009, Sch. 53, para. 7: late payment interest start dates.
FA 2009, Sch. 56: penalty for failure to make payments on time.

Notes – S. 126: charge on disposal of trees or underwood.

230 Acceptance of property in satisfaction of tax

230(1) The Board may, if they think fit and the Secretary of State agrees, on the application of any person liable to pay tax or interest payable under section 233 below, accept in satisfaction of the whole or any part of it any property to which this section applies.

230(2) This section applies to any such land as may be agreed upon between the Board and the person liable to pay tax.

230(3) This section also applies to any objects which are or have been kept in any building–

(a) if the Board have determined to accept or have accepted that building in satisfaction or part satisfaction of tax or of estate duty, or

(b) if the building or any interest in it belongs to Her Majesty in right of the Crown or of the Duchy of Lancaster, or belongs to the Duchy of Cornwall or belongs to a Government department or is held for the purposes of a Government department, or

(c) if the building is one of which the Secretary of State is guardian under the Ancient Monuments and Archaeological Areas Act 1979 or of which the Department of the Environment for Northern Ireland is guardian under the Historic Monuments and Archaeological Objects (Northern Ireland) Order 1995, or

(d) if the building belongs to any body within Schedule 3 to this Act,

in any case where it appears to the Secretary of State desirable for the objects to remain associated with the building.

230(4) This section also applies to–

(a) any picture, print, book, manuscript, work of art, scientific object or other thing which the Secretary of State is satisfied is pre-eminent for its national, scientific, historic or artistic interest, and

(b) any collection or group of pictures, prints, books, manuscripts, works of art, scientific objects or other things if the Secretary of State is satisfied that the collection or group, taken as a whole, is pre-eminent for its national, scientific, historic or artistic interest.

230(5) In this section–

"national interest" includes interest within any part of the United Kingdom;

and in determining under subsection (4) above whether an object or collection or group of objects is pre-eminent, regard shall be had to any significant association of the object, collection or group with a particular place.

230(6) The functions of the Ministers under this section in relation to the acceptance, in satisfaction of tax, of property in which there is a Scottish interest may be exercised separately.

230(7) For the purposes of subsection (6) a Scottish interest in the property exists–

(a) where the property is located in Scotland; or

(b) the person liable to pay the tax has expressed a wish or imposed a condition on his offer of the property in satisfaction of tax that it be displayed in Scotland or disposed of or transferred to a body or institution in Scotland.

History – References to the Secretary of State substituted and definition of "the ministers" in s. 230(5) repealed by SI 1992/1311. Reference to the Historic Monuments and Archaeological Objects (Northern Ireland) Order 1995 substituted by SI 1995/1625 (NI 9).
S. 230(6) inserted by SI 1999/1756, art. 2, Schedule, para. 8, with effect from immediately before 1 July 1999 (by virtue of SI 1999/1756, art. 1(1) and SI 1998/3178, art. 3).
S. 230(7) inserted by SI 1999/1756, art. 2, Schedule, para. 8, with effect from immediately before 1 July 1999 (by virtue of SI 1999/1756, art. 1(1) and SI 1998/3178, art. 3).

Cross references – S. 26A: a PET proving to be chargeable is nevertheless exempt if designated under s. 31(1) and (inter alia) disposed of in pursuance of s. 230.
S. 32A: associated properties for conditional exemption purposes.
Sch. 3: eligible bodies – gifts for national purposes etc.
TCGA 1992, s. 258(2)(b): capital gains tax treatment of property disposed of to the Board under s. 230.
FA 1998, s. 145(2)(a): information about property accepted on or after 1 April 1998 in satisfaction of tax to be contained in accounts required to be rendered to Comptroller and Auditor General under Exchequer and Audit Departments Act 1866, s. 10.
SI 2005/1103: allows Secretary of State to authorise another person/that person's employees to exercise their functions under s. 230.
FA 2009, Sch. 53, para. 14: late payment interest start dates.

Statements of practice – SP 6/87: taxpayer may choose between "offer date" or "acceptance date" basis of valuation – see also s. 233(1A) (waiver of interest charges).

Other material – IR 67 (not reproduced): National Heritage booklet "Capital Taxation and the National Heritage". See particularly para. 11.12: guidelines for expert advisers on what would satisfy the "pre-eminent" test in s. 230:
(i) does the object have an especially close association with our history and national life?
(ii) is the object of especial artistic or art-historical interest?
(iii) is the object of especial importance for the study of some particular form of art, learning or history?
(iv) does the object have an especially close association with a particular historic setting?

Notes – National Heritage Act 1980, s. 9: disposal of property accepted by commissioners in lieu of tax.

231 Powers to transfer property in satisfaction of tax

231(1) Where a person has power to sell any property in order to raise money for the payment of tax, he may agree with the Board for the property to be accepted in satisfaction of that tax in pursuance of section 230 above; and, except as regards the nature of the consideration and its receipt and application, any such agreement shall be subject to the same provisions and shall be treated for all purposes as a sale made in the exercise of the said power, and any conveyance or transfer made or purporting to be made to give effect to such an agreement shall have effect accordingly.

231(2) The references in subsection (1) above to **tax** include references to interest payable under section 233 below.

231(3) This section shall not affect paragraph 1(4) or 3(4) of Schedule 5 to this Act.

Cross references – Sch. 5, para. 1(4), 3(4): acceptance of object under s. 230 is not a disposal.

232 Administration actions

232 Where proceedings are pending in any court for the administration of any property to the value of which any tax charged on the value transferred by a chargeable transfer is attributable, the court shall provide, out of any such property in the possession or control of the court, for the payment of any of the tax so attributable, or interest on it, which remains unpaid.

INTEREST

233 Interest on unpaid tax

233(1) If–

(a) an amount of tax charged on the value transferred by a chargeable transfer not within paragraph (aa) below and made after 5th April and before 1st October in any year and otherwise than on death remains unpaid after the end of the period ending with April in the next year, or

(aa) an amount of tax charged under Chapter 3 of Part 3 of this Act on the value transferred by a chargeable transfer remains unpaid after the end of the period of six months beginning with the end of the month in which the chargeable transfer was made, or

(b) an amount of tax charged on the value transferred by a chargeable transfer not within paragraph (a) or (aa) above remains unpaid after the end of the period of six months beginning with the end of the month in which the chargeable transfer was made, or

(c) an amount of tax chargeable under section 32, 32A, 79(3A) or 126 above or under Schedule 5 to this Act, remains unpaid after the end of the period of six months beginning with the end of the month in which the event occasioning the charge occurs, then, subject to subsection (1A) below, it shall carry interest from the end of that period at the rate applicable under section 178 of the Finance Act 1989.

233(1A) If, under section 230 above, the Board agree to accept property in satisfaction of any tax on terms that the value to be attributed to the property for the purposes of that acceptance is determined as at a date earlier than that on which the property is actually accepted, the terms may provide that the amount of tax which is satisfied by the acceptance of the property shall not carry interest under this section from that date.

233(2) [Repealed by FA 1989, s. 187 and Sch. 17, Pt. X.]

233(3) Interest payable under this section shall not be allowed as a deduction in computing any income, profits or losses for any tax purposes.

233(4) [Repealed by FA 1989, s. 187 and Sch. 17, Pt. X.]

History – In s. 233(1)(c), the words "79(3A)" substituted for the words "79(3)" by F(No. 2)A 2015, s. 12(8)(b), with effect in relation to occasions on which tax would (ignoring the effect of the amendments) fall to be charged under IHTA 1984, s. 64 on or after 18 November 2015 (Royal Assent).
In s. 233(1)(a), the words "not within paragraph (aa) below and" inserted by FA 2014, s. 117 and Sch. 25, para. 5(3)(a), with effect in relation to chargeable transfers made on or after 6 April 2014.
S. 233(1)(aa) inserted by FA 2014, s. 117 and Sch. 25, para. 5(3)(b), with effect in relation to chargeable transfers made on or after 6 April 2014.
In s. 233(1)(b), the words "a chargeable transfer not within paragraph (a) or (aa) above" substituted for the words "any other chargeable transfer" by FA 2014, s. 117 and Sch. 25, para. 5(3)(c), with effect in relation to chargeable transfers made on or after 6 April 2014.
In s. 233(1)(c), "or 126" substituted for ", 126, 151B or 151D" by FA 2011, s. 65 and Sch. 16, para. 56(a), with effect in relation to deaths occurring on or after 6 April 2011.
In s. 233(1)(c), the words ", or under section 151A above by virtue of subsection (6) of that section", which appeared after the words "or under Schedule 5 to this Act", omitted by FA 2011, s. 65 and Sch. 16, para. 56(b), with effect in relation to deaths occurring on or after 6 April 2011.
In s. 233(1)(c) the words ", 151B or 151D" substituted for the words "or 151B" by FA 2008, s. 91 and Sch. 28, para. 14, with effect in relation to deaths occurring on or after 6 April 2008.
In s. 233(1)(c) the words ", or under section 151A above by virtue of subsection (6) of that section," inserted by FA 2007, s. 69 and Sch. 19, para. 26, with effect in relation to deaths, cases where scheme administrators become aware of deaths and cessations of dependency occurring on or after 6 April 2007.
In s. 233(1)(c) the words ", 126 or 151B" substituted for the words "or 126" by FA 2006, s. 160 and Sch. 22, para. 9, with effect from 6 April 2006.
In s. 233(1)(c), the reference to s. 32A inserted by FA 1985, s. 94(1) and Sch. 26, para. 11, in relation to events on or after 19 March 1985.
In s. 233(1) the words "rate applicable under … Finance Act 1989" substituted, by FA 1989, s. 179(1)(d), 187 and Sch. 17, Pt. X, for periods beginning on or after 18 August 1989 by virtue of SI 1989/1298 (C. 44).
In s. 233(1), the words "then, subject to subsection (1A) below" inserted by FA 1987, s. 60(1), (2), effective where the acceptance referred to in s. 230 occurs on or after 17 March 1987.
S. 233(1A) inserted by FA 1987, s. 60(1), (2), effective where the acceptance referred toin s. 230 occurs on or after 17 March 1987.
S. 233(2) repealed by FA 1989, s. 187 and Sch. 17, Pt. X, for periods beginning on or after 18 August 1989 by virtue of SI 1989/1298 (C. 44).
Former s. 233(2)(a), (b) substituted by FA 1986, s. 101 and Sch. 19, para. 32, with respect to transfers of value made, and other events occurring, on or after 18 March 1986.
S. 233(4) repealed by FA 1989, s. 187 and Sch. 17, Pt. X, for periods beginning on or after 18 August 1989 by virtue of SI 1989/1298 (C. 44).

Cross references – S. 32, s. 32A: following conditionally exempt transfer of property, charge where certain events occur in respect of property or associated property.
S. 79(3): deferral of ten-yearly charge until subsequent chargeable event.
S. 126: special charge on disposal of certain trees and underwood.
Sch. 5: charge where certain events in relation to conditionally exempt transfer for death before 7 April 1976.
FA 1986, Sch. 19, para. 40(1): transitional – transfer of value occurring before, and death or other event occurring after, 18 March 1986.
FA 1989, s. 178: Treasury powers to set interest rates.

Statements of practice – SP 6/87: valuation as at date of offer – waiver of interest charges under s. 233(1A).

234 Interest on instalments

234(1) Where tax payable on the value transferred by a chargeable transfer–

(a) is payable by instalments under section 227 above and is attributable to the value of any shares, securities, business or interest in a business, or to value treated as reduced under Chapter II of Part V of this Act, or

(b) is payable by instalments under section 229 above,

it shall, for the purposes of any interest to be added to each instalment, be treated as carrying interest from the date at which the instalment is payable.

234(2) Subsection (1) above shall not apply to tax attributable to the value of shares or securities of a company falling within paragraph (a) of subsection (3) below (not being tax attributable to value treated as reduced under Chapter II of Part V of this Act) unless it also falls within paragraph (b) or (c) of that subsection.

234(3) The companies referred to in subsection (2) above are–

(a) any company whose business consists wholly or mainly of one or more of the following, that is to say, dealing in securities, stocks or shares, land or buildings, or making or holding investments;

(b) any company whose business consists wholly or mainly in being a holding company (as defined in section 1159 of and Schedule 6 to the Companies Act 2006) of one or more companies not falling within paragraph (a) above;

(c) any company–

(i) whose business is wholly that of a market maker or is that of a discount house and (in either case) is carried on in the United Kingdom, or

(ii) which is of a description set out in regulations under section 107(5) of the Finance Act 1986.

234(4) In this section **"market maker"** means a person who–

(a) holds himself out at all normal times in compliance with the rules of The Stock Exchange as willing to buy and sell securities, stocks or shares at a price specified by him, and

(b) is recognised as doing so by the Council of The Stock Exchange.

History – In s. 234(3)(b), the words "1159 of and Schedule 6 to" substituted for the words "736 of", and "2006" substituted for "1985", by SI 2009/1890, art. 4(1)(f), with effect from 1 October 2009.
In s. 234(3)(b), the words "as defined in section 736 of" were substituted by Companies Act 1989, s. 144(4) and Sch. 18, para. 30(1), (4), with effect from 1 November 1990. The reference to the Companies Act 1985 was substituted by Companies Consolidation (Consequential Provisions) Act 1985.
S. 234(3)(c) substituted by SI 2012/2903, reg. 5, with effect from 31 December 2012.
S. 234(3)(c) substituted by FA 1986, s. 107(1), (2), in relation to transfers of value made, and other events occurring, on or after 27 October 1986 (the day of The Stock Exchange reforms).
S. 234(4) inserted, by FA 1986, s. 107(1), (2), in relation to transfers of value made, and other events occurring, on or after 27 October 1986 (the day of The Stock Exchange reforms).

Cross references – FA 1986, s. 107(4) (as amended by SI 2001/3629, art. 11 which came into force on 1 December 2001), (5): power of Board to make regulations regarding interpretation, and amending s. 234 in certain respects.
SI 1992/3181: applicable from 23 March 1992, reference to "The Stock Exchange" in s. 234(4) reads as a reference to either of The Stock Exchange and LIFFE (Administration and Management).
SI 2012/2903, reg. 7: description of a company for the purposes of s. 234(3)(c)(ii).

235 Interest on overpaid tax

235(1) Any repayment of an amount paid in excess of a liability for tax or for interest on tax shall carry interest from the date on which the payment was made until the order for repayment is issued at the rate applicable under section 178 of the Finance Act 1989.

235(2) Interest paid under this section shall not constitute income for any tax purposes.

History – In s. 235(1) the words "the rate applicable under section 178 of the Finance Act 1989" substituted for the words "the same rate as that at which the tax, if outstanding, would have carried interest" by FA 2009, s. 105(4)(b), with effect from 21 July (Royal Assent).
In s. 235(1), the words "until the order for repayment is issued" were inserted by FA 1989, s. 180(4), with retrospective effect.

236 Special cases

236(1) Section 233 above shall apply in relation to–

(a) the amount by which tax chargeable on the value transferred by a chargeable transfer made within seven years of the transferor's death exceeds what it would have been had the transferor died more than seven years after the transfer,

(b) [Repealed by FA 1988, s. 148 and Sch. 14, Pt. X.]

as if the chargeable transfer had been made on the death of the transferor.

236(1A) Section 233 above shall apply in relation to the amount (if any) by which–

(a) the tax chargeable on the value transferred by a chargeable transfer made under Chapter III of Part III of this Act within the period of seven years ending with the settlor's death,

exceeds

(b) what that tax would have been had the settlor died more than seven years after the date of the transfer,

as if the chargeable transfer had been made on the death of the settlor.

236(2) Tax overpaid or underpaid in consequence of–

(a) section 146(1) above, or section 19(1) of the Inheritance (Provision for Family and Dependants) Act 1975, or

(b) the corresponding provision of the Inheritance (Provision for Family and Dependants) (Northern Ireland) Order 1979,

shall not carry interest for any period before the order there mentioned is made.

236(3) Tax repayable on a claim under section 146(2) or 150 above shall carry interest (which shall not constitute income for any tax purposes) at the rate applicable under section 178 of the Finance Act 1989 from the date on which the claim is made.

236(4) Tax repayable under section 147(2) above shall carry interest (which shall not constitute income for any tax purposes) at the rate applicable under section 178 of the Finance Act 1989 from the date on which the tax was paid; and tax charged by virtue of section 147(4) above shall carry interest at that rate from the end of the period mentioned in section 233(1)(b) above.

History – In s. 236(1)(a), the words "seven years" in each place substituted by FA 1986, Sch. 19, para. 33(1), (2), with respect to transfers of value made, and other events occurring, on or after 18 March 1986.
S. 236(1)(b) repealed by FA 1988, s. 148 and Sch. 14, Pt. X, with effect in relation to transfers of value made on or after 15 March 1988.
S. 236(1A) inserted, by FA 1986, Sch. 19, para. 33(1), (2), with respect to transfers of value made, and other events occurring, on or after 18 March 1986.
In s. 236(3), the reference to s. 149 between "146(2)" and "or 150" was removed by FA 1986, s. 101 and Sch. 19, para. 33(3), with effect where the donee's transfer was made on or after 18 March 1986.
The words "rate applicable under … Finance Act 1989" in s. 236(3), (4), and "from the end … section 233(1)(b) above" in s. 236(4), substituted by FA 1989, s. 179(1)(e) and s. 179(3) respectively, for periods beginning on or after 18 August 1989 by virtue of SI 1989/1298 (C. 44).

Cross references – S. 146(1), (2): claims under the Inheritance (Provision for Family and Dependants) Act 1975.
S. 147(2), (4): legitim claims in Scotland.
S. 150: repayments in relation to voidable transfers.
FA 1986, Sch. 19, para. 40(1): transitional – transfer of value occurring before, and death or other event occurring after, 18 March 1986.
FA 1989, s. 178: Treasury powers to set interest rates.

Notes – Inheritance (Provision for Family and Dependants) Act 1975, s. 19(1): court order under the Act deemed to have effect from the deceased's death.

INLAND REVENUE CHARGE FOR UNPAID TAX

237 Imposition of charge

237(1) Except as otherwise provided, where any tax charged on the value transferred by a chargeable transfer, or any interest on it, is for the time being unpaid a charge for the amount unpaid (to be known as an Inland Revenue charge) is by virtue of this section imposed in favour of the Board on–

(a) any property to the value of which the value transferred is wholly or partly attributable, and

(b) where the chargeable transfer is made by the making of a settlement or is made under Part III of this Act, any property comprised in the settlement.

237(2) References in subsection (1) above to any property include references to any property directly or indirectly representing it.

237(2A) Where tax is charged by virtue of Schedule A1 on the value transferred by a chargeable transfer, the reference in subsection (1)(a) to property to the value of which the value transferred is wholly or partly attributable includes the UK residential property interest (within the meaning of that Schedule) to which the charge to tax relates.

237(3) Where the chargeable transfer is made on death, personal or movable property situated in the United Kingdom which was beneficially owned by the deceased immediately before his death and vests in his personal representatives is not subject to the Inland Revenue charge; and for this purpose "personal property" does not include leaseholds and the question whether any property was beneficially owned by the deceased shall be determined without regard to section 49(1) above.

237(3A) In the case of a potentially exempt transfer which proves to be a chargeable transfer–

(a) property concerned, or an interest in property concerned, which has been disposed of to a purchaser before the transferor's death is not subject to the Inland Revenue charge, but

(b) property concerned which has been otherwise disposed of before the death and property which at the death represents any property or interest falling within paragraph (a) above shall be subject to the charge;

and in this subsection **"property concerned"** means property to the value of which the value transferred by the transfer is wholly or partly attributable.

237(3B) Subsection (3C) below applies to any tax charged–

(a) under section 32, 32A or 79(3A) above in respect of any property,

(b) under paragraph 8 of Schedule 4 to this Act in respect of any property, or

(c) under paragraph 1 or 3 of Schedule 5 to this Act with respect to any object or property.

237(3C) Where any tax to which this subsection applies, or any interest on it, is for the time being unpaid, a charge for the amount unpaid is also by virtue of this section imposed in favour of the Board–

(a) except where the event giving rise to the charge was a disposal to a purchaser of the property or object in question, on that property or object; and

(b) in the excepted case, on any property for the time being representing that property or object.

237(4) No heritable property situated in Scotland is subject to the Inland Revenue charge, but where such property is disposed of any other property for the time being representing it is subject to the charge to which the first-mentioned property would have been subject but for this subsection.

237(5) The Inland Revenue charge imposed on any property shall take effect subject to any incumbrance on it which is allowable as a deduction in valuing that property for the purposes of the tax.

237(6) Except as provided by section 238 below, a disposition of property subject to an Inland Revenue charge shall take effect subject to that charge.

History – S. 237(2A) inserted by F(No. 2)A 2017, s. 33 and Sch. 10, para. 7, with effect in relation to times after 5 April 2017 subject to Sch. 10, para. 9 and 10.

In s. 237(3), words "does not include" substituted for the word "includes" by FA 1999, s. 107, with effect in relation to deaths on or after 9 March 1999.

In s. 237(3), former words "and undivided shares in land held on trust for sale, whether statutory or not," which followed "leaseholds", repealed by Trusts of Land and Appointment of Trustees Act 1996, Sch. 4, with effect from 1 January 1997 by virtue of SI 1996/2974.

S. 237(3A) inserted by FA 1986, s. 101 and Sch. 19, para. 34, with respect to transfers of value made, and other events occurring, on or after 18 March 1986.

In s. 237(3B)(a), the words "or 79(3A)" substituted for the words "or 79(3)" by F(No. 2)A 2015, s. 12(8)(c), with effect in relation to occasions on which tax would (ignoring the effect of the amendments) fall to be charged under IHTA 1984, s. 64 on or after 18 November 2015 (Royal Assent).

S. 237(3B) and (3C) inserted by FA 1999, s. 107, with effect in relation to tax charged on or after 9 March 1999.

Cross references – FA 1986, Sch. 19, para. 40(1): transitional – transfer of value occurring before, and death or other event occurring after, 18 March 1986.

Land Registration Act 2002, s. 31 (not reproduced): the effect of a disposition of a registered estate or charge on a charge under s. 237 is determined, not in accordance with s. 28 to 30 of that Act, but in accordance with IHTA 1984, s. 237(6) and 238 (under which a purchaser in good faith for money or money's worth takes free from the charge in the absence of registration).

238 Effect of purchases

238(1) Where property subject to an Inland Revenue charge, or an interest in such property, is disposed of to a purchaser, then if at the time of the disposition–

(a) in the case of land in England and Wales, the charge was not registered as a land charge or, in the case of registered land, was not protected by notice on the register, or

(b) in the case of land in Northern Ireland the title to which is registered under the Land Registration Act (Northern Ireland) 1970, the charge was not entered as a burden on the appropriate register maintained under that Act or was not protected by a caution or inhibition under that Act or, in the case of other land in Northern Ireland, the purchaser had no notice of the facts giving rise to the charge, or

(c) in the case of personal property situated in the United Kingdom other than such property as is mentioned in paragraph (a) or (b) above, and of any property situated outside the United Kingdom, the purchaser had no notice of the facts giving rise to the charge, or

(d) in the case of any property, a certificate of discharge had been given by the Board under section 239 below and the purchaser had no notice of any fact invalidating the certificate,

the property or interest shall then cease to be subject to the charge but the property for the time being representing it shall be subject to it.

238(2) Where property subject to an Inland Revenue charge, or an interest in such property, is disposed of to a purchaser in circumstances where it does not then cease to be subject to the charge, it shall cease to be subject to it at the end of the period of six years beginning with the later of–

(a) the date on which the tax became due, and

(b) the date on which a full and proper account of the property was first delivered to the Board in connection with the chargeable transfer concerned.

238(3) In this section **"the time of the disposition"** means–

(a) in relation to registered land–

(i) if the disposition is required to be completed by registration, the time of registration, and

(ii) otherwise, the time of completion,

(b) in relation to other property, the time of completion.

History – S. 238(3)(a) substituted by Land Registration Act 2002, Sch. 11, para. 17, with effect from 13 October 2003 by virtue of SI 2003/1725, art. 2(1).

Cross references – Land Registration Act 2002, s. 31 (not reproduced): the effect of a disposition of a registered estate or charge on a charge under s. 237 is determined, not in accordance with s. 28 to 30 of that Act, but in accordance with IHTA 1984, s. 237(6) and 238 (under which a purchaser in good faith for money or money's worth takes free from the charge in the absence of registration).

CERTIFICATES OF DISCHARGE

239 Certificates of discharge

239(1) Where application is made to the Board by a person liable for any tax on the value transferred by a chargeable transfer which is attributable to the value of property specified in the application, the Board, on being satisfied that the tax so attributable has been or will be paid, may give a certificate to that effect, and shall do so if the chargeable transfer is one made on death or the transferor has died.

239(2) Where tax is or may be chargeable on the value transferred by a transfer of value and–

(a) application is made to the Board after the expiration of two years from the transfer (or, if the Board think fit to entertain the application, at an earlier time) by a person who is or might be liable for the whole or part of the tax, and

(b) the applicant delivers to the Board, if the transfer is one made on death, a full statement to the best of his knowledge and belief of all property included in the estate of the deceased immediately before his death and, in any other case, a full and proper account under this Part of this Act,

the Board may, as the case requires, determine the amount of the tax or determine that no tax is chargeable; and subject to the payment of any tax so determined to be chargeable the Board may give a certificate of their determination, and shall do so if the transfer of value is one made on death or the transferor has died.

239(2A) An application under subsection (1) or (2) above with respect to tax which is or may become chargeable on the value transferred by a potentially exempt transfer may not be made before the expiration of two years from the death of the transferor (except where the Board think fit to entertain the application at an earlier time after the death).

239(3) Subject to subsection (4) below,–

(a) a certificate under subsection (1) above shall discharge the property shown in it from the Inland Revenue charge on its acquisition by a purchaser, and

(b) a certificate under subsection (2) above shall discharge all persons from any further claim for the tax on the value transferred by the chargeable transfer concerned and extinguish any Inland Revenue charge for that tax.

239(4) A certificate under this section shall not discharge any person from tax in case of fraud or failure to disclose material facts and shall not affect any further tax–

(a) that may afterwards be shown to be payable by virtue of section 93, 142, 143, 144 or 145 above,

(aa) that may afterwards be shown to be payable by reason of too great an increase having been made under section 8A(3) above, or

(b) that may be payable if any further property is afterwards shown to have been included in the estate of a deceased person immediately before his death;

but in so far as the certificate shows any tax to be attributable to the value of any property it shall remain valid in favour of a purchaser of that property without notice of any fact invalidating the certificate.

239(5) References in this section to a **transfer of value**, or to the **value transferred by a transfer of value**, shall be construed as including references to an occasion on which tax is chargeable under Chapter III of Part III of this Act (apart from section 79) or to the amount on which tax is then chargeable.

History – S. 239(2A) inserted by FA 1986, s. 101 and Sch. 19, para. 35, with respect to transfers of value made, and other events occurring, on or after 18 March 1986.
S. 239(4)(aa) inserted by FA 2008, s. 10 and Sch. 4, para. 5, with effect from 9 October 2007.

Cross references – Pt. III, Ch. III: charge on settlements without an interest in possession, subject to exemption from ten-yearly charge in certain cases (s. 79).
S. 93: disclaimers.
S. 142: alteration of dispositions taking effect on death.
S. 143: compliance with testator's request.
S. 144: distribution etc. from property settled by will.
S. 145: redemption of surviving spouse's life interest.
S. 147(9): legitim claims in Scotland.
FA 1986, Sch. 19, para. 40(1): transitional – transfer of value occurring before, and death or other event occurring after, 18 March 1986.

ADJUSTMENTS

240 Underpayments

240(1) Where too little tax has been paid in respect of a chargeable transfer the tax underpaid shall be payable with interest under section 233 above, whether or not the amount that has been paid was that stated as payable in a notice under section 221 above; but subject to section 239 above and to the following provisions of this section.

240(2) Where tax attributable to the value of any property is paid in accordance with an account duly delivered to the Board under this Part of this Act and the payment is made and accepted in full satisfaction of the tax so attributable, no proceedings shall be brought for the recovery of any additional tax so attributable after the end of the period of 4 years beginning with the later of–

(a) the date on which the payment (or in the case of tax paid by instalments the last payment) was made and accepted, and

(b) the date on which the tax or the last instalment became due;

and at the end of that period any liability for the additional tax and any Inland Revenue charge for that tax shall be extinguished.

240(3) Subsection (2) has effect subject to subsections (4) to (5A).

240(4) Proceedings in a case involving a loss of tax brought about carelessly by a person liable for the tax (or a person acting on behalf of such a person) may be brought at any time not more than 6 years after the later of the dates in subsection (2)(a) and (b).

240(5) Proceedings in a case involving a loss of tax brought about deliberately by a person liable for the tax (or a person acting on behalf of such a person) may be brought at any time not more than 20 years after the later of the dates in subsection (2)(a) and (b).

240(5A) Proceedings in a case involving a loss of tax attributable to arrangements which were expected to give rise to a tax advantage in respect of which a person liable for the tax was under an obligation to make a report under section 253 of the Finance Act 2014 (duty to notify Commissioners of promoter reference number) but failed to do so, may be brought at any time not more than 20 years after the later of the dates in subsection (2)(a) and (b).

240(6) Subsection (7) applies to any case not falling within subsection (2) where too little tax has been paid in respect of a chargeable transfer, provided that the case does not involve a loss of tax brought about deliberately by a person liable for the tax (or a person acting on behalf of such a person).

240(7) Where this subsection applies–

(a) no proceedings are to be brought for the recovery of the tax after the end of the period of 20 years beginning with the date on which the chargeable transfer was made, and

(b) at the end of that period any liability for the tax and any Inland Revenue charge for that tax is extinguished.

240(8) In relation to cases of tax chargeable under Chapter 3 of Part 3 of this Act (apart from section 79), the references in subsections (4) to (6) to a person liable for the tax are to be treated as including references to a person who is the settlor in relation to the settlement.

History – In s. 240(2), the words "4 years" substituted for the words "six years" by FA 2009, s. 99 and Sch. 51, para. 11(2), with effect from 1 April 2011 (SI 2010/867, art. 2(2)), subject to transitional provisions in SI 2010/867, reg. 6.
In s. 240(3), "to (5A)" substituted for "and (5)" by FA 2014, s. 277(3)(a), with effect from 17 July 2014.
In s. 240(5), the words "the dates in subsection (2)(a) and (b)" substituted for the words "those dates" by FA 2014, s. 277(3)(b), with effect from 17 July 2014.
S. 240(5A) inserted by FA 2014, s. 277(3)(c), with effect from 17 July 2014.
In s. 240(8), "to (6)" substituted for ", (5) and (6)" by FA 2014, s. 277(3)(d), with effect from 17 July 2014.
S. 240(3)–(8) substituted for former s. 240(3) by FA 2009, s. 99 and Sch. 51, para. 11(3), with effect from 1 April 2011 (SI 2010/867, art. 2(2)), subject to transitional provisions in SI 2010/867, reg. 6.

Cross references – Pt. III, Ch. III: charge on settlements without interest in possession, subject to exemption from ten-yearly charge in certain cases (s. 79).
S. 147(9): legitim claims in Scotland.

240A Underpayments: supplementary

240A(1) This section applies for the purposes of section 240.

240A(2) A loss of tax is brought about carelessly by a person if the person fails to take reasonable care to avoid bringing about that loss.

240A(3) Where–

(a) information is provided to Her Majesty's Revenue and Customs,

(b) the person who provided the information, or the person on whose behalf the information was provided, discovers some time later that the information was inaccurate, and

(c) that person fails to take reasonable steps to inform Her Majesty's Revenue and Customs,

any loss of tax brought about by the inaccuracy is to be treated as having been brought about carelessly by that person.

240A(4) References to a loss of tax brought about deliberately by a person include a loss of tax brought about as a result of a deliberate inaccuracy in a document given to Her Majesty's Revenue and Customs by or on behalf of that person.

History – S. 240A inserted by FA 2009, s. 99 and Sch. 51, para. 12, with effect from 1 April 2011 (SI 2010/867, art. 2(2)).

241 Overpayments

241(1) If it is proved to the satisfaction of the Board that too much tax has been paid on the value transferred by a chargeable transfer or on so much of that value as is attributable to any property, the Board shall repay the excess unless the claim for repayment was made more than 4 years after the date on which *the payment or last payment* of the tax was made.

241(2) References in this section to tax include references to interest on tax.

History – In s. 241(1), the words "4 years" substituted for the words "six years" by FA 2009, s. 99 and Sch. 51, para. 13, with effect from 1 April 2011 (SI 2010/867, art. 2(2)).

Cross references – S. 147(8): Scotland – repayment due to estate on renunciation of claim to legitim may be made without limit of time. FA 2016, s. 94(6): where a repayment of inheritance tax or interest on inheritance tax arises as a result of the insertion of IHTA 1984, s. 12A, s. 241(1) applies as if the last date for making a claim for repayment of the amount were 5 April 2020 if that is later than what would otherwise be the last date for that purpose.

Statements of practice – SP 6/95: assessments that lead to repayments of sums overpaid are not initiated automatically unless the amount repayable is more than £25.

RECOVERY OF TAX

242 Recovery of tax

242(1) The Board shall not take any legal proceedings for the recovery of any amount of tax or of interest on tax which is due from any person unless the amount has been agreed in writing between that person and the Board or has been determined and specified in a notice under section 221 above.

242(2) Where an amount has been so determined and specified but an appeal to which this subsection applies is pending against the determination the Board shall not take any legal proceedings to recover the amount determined except such part of it as may be agreed in writing or determined and specified in a further notice under section 221 above to be a part not in dispute.

242(3) Subsection (2) above applies to any appeal under section 222 above but not to any further appeal; and section 222 above shall have effect, in relation to a determination made in pursuance of subsection (2) above, as if subsections (4) to (4B) of that section were omitted.

242(4) Where a person has been given an accelerated payment notice under Chapter 3 of Part 4 of the Finance Act 2014 and that notice has not been withdrawn, nothing in this section prevents legal proceedings being taken for the recovery of (as the case may be)–

(a) the understated tax to which the payment specified in the notice under section 220(2)(b) of that Act relates, or

(b) the disputed tax specified in the notice under section 221(2)(b) of that Act.

History – In s. 242(3) the words "subsections (4) to (4B)" substituted by FA 1993, s. 200(2), in relation to appeals made on or after 27 July 1993 or made but not begun to be heard before that date.
S. 242(4) inserted by FA 2014, s. 224(2), with effect from 17 July 2014.

243 Scotland: recovery of tax in sheriff court

243 In Scotland, tax and interest on tax may, without prejudice to any other remedy, and if the amount of the tax and interest does not exceed the sum for the time being specified in section 35(1)(a) of the Sheriff Courts (Scotland) Act 1971, be sued for and recovered in the sheriff court.

244 Right to address court

244 An officer of the Board who is authorised by the Board to do so may address the court in any proceedings in a sheriff court for the recovery of tax or interest on tax.

History – In s. 244, the words "county court or" which preceded "sheriff court" omitted by FA 2008, s. 137(4), with effect from 21 July 2008 (subject to FA 2008, s. 137(2)).

PENALTIES

245 Failure to deliver accounts

245(1) This section applies where a person ("the taxpayer") fails to deliver an account under section 216 or 217 above.

245(2) The taxpayer shall be liable–

(a) to a penalty of £100; and

(b) to a further penalty not exceeding £60 for every day after the day on which the failure has been declared by a court or the tribunal and before the day on which the account is delivered.

245(3) If–

(a) proceedings in which the failure could be declared are not commenced before the end of the relevant period, and

(b) the taxpayer has not delivered the account by the end of that period,

he shall be liable to a further penalty of £100.

245(4) In subsection (3) above **"the relevant period"** means the period of six months beginning immediately after the end of the period given by section 216(6) or (7) or section 217 above (whichever is applicable).

245(4A) Without prejudice to any penalties under subsections (2) and (3) above, if–

(a) the failure by the taxpayer to deliver the account continues after the anniversary of the end of the period given by section 216(6) or (7) (whichever is applicable), and

(b) there would have been a liability to tax shown in the account,

the taxpayer shall be liable to a penalty of an amount not exceeding £3,000.

245(5) If the taxpayer proves that his liability to tax does not exceed a particular amount, the penalty under subsection (2)(a) above, together with any penalty under subsection (3) above, shall not exceed that amount.

245(6) A person shall not be liable to a penalty under subsection (2)(b) above if he delivers the account required by section 216 or 217 before proceedings in which the failure could be declared are commenced.

245(7) A person who has a reasonable excuse for failing to deliver an account shall not be liable by reason of that failure to a penalty under this section, unless he fails to deliver the account without unreasonable delay after the excuse has ceased.

History – In s. 245(2)(b) the word "tribunal" substituted for the words "Special Commissioners" by SI 2009/56, art. 3 and Sch. 1, para. 120, with effect from 1 April 2009, subject to transitional and saving provisions in SI 2009/56, Sch. 3.

In s. 245(2)(a), the word "of" substituted for the former words "not exceeding" by FA 2004, s. 295(2)(a), with effect in relation to a failure by any person to deliver an account under s. 216 or s. 217 where the period under s. 216(6) or (7) or s. 217, within which the person is required to deliver the account, expires on or after 23 January 2005 (i.e. after six months from 22 July 2004, as per FA 2004, s. 295(5)).

In s. 245(3), the word "of" substituted for the former words "not exceeding" by FA 2004, s. 295(2)(a), with effect in relation to a failure by any person to deliver an account under s. 216 or s. 217 where the period under s. 216(6) or (7) or s. 217, within which the person is required to deliver the account, expires on or after 23 January 2005 (i.e. after six months from 22 July 2004, as per FA 2004, s. 295(5)).

S. 245(4A) inserted by FA 2004, s. 295(2)(b) with effect:

(a) in relation to a failure by any person to deliver an account under s. 216 where the period under s. 216(6) or s. 216(7) within which the person is required to deliver the account expires after 22 July 2004; and

(b) in relation to such a failure to deliver such an account where that period expires on or before 22 July 2004, as if, in s. 245(4A), for the words "anniversary of the end of the period given by section 216(6) or (7) (whichever is applicable)" there were substituted "end of the period of twelve months beginning with the day on which the Finance Act 2004 is passed" (Finance Act 2004 passed on 22 July 2004) (FA 2004, s. 295(6)).

S. 245 substituted by FA 1999, s. 108, with effect in relation to any failure by a person to comply with obligations under IHTA 1984, s. 216–219 that expire on or after 27 July 1999.

Former s. 245(1)(d) omitted by SI 1994/1813, reg. 2(1) and Sch. 1, para. 20, Sch. 2, Pt. I, with effect from 1 September 1994.

245A Failure to provide information etc.

245A(1) A person who fails to make a return under section 218 above shall be liable–

(a) to a penalty not exceeding £300; and

(b) to a further penalty not exceeding £60 for every day after the day on which the failure has been declared by a court or the tribunal and before the day on which the return is made.

245A(1A) A person who fails to comply with the requirements of section 218A above shall be liable–

(a) to a penalty not exceeding £100; and

(b) to a further penalty not exceeding £60 for every day after the day on which the failure has been declared by a court or the tribunal and before the day on which the requirements are complied with.

245A(1B) Without prejudice to any penalties under subsection (1A) above, if a person continues to fail to comply with the requirements of section 218A after the anniversary of the end of the period of six months referred to in section 218A(1), he shall be liable to a penalty of an amount not exceeding £3,000.

245A(2) [Omitted by SI 2009/3054, art. 3 and Schedule, para. 2(4)(a).]

245A(3) [Omitted by SI 2009/3054, art. 3 and Schedule, para. 2(4)(a).]

245A(4) A person shall not be liable to a penalty under subsection (1)(b) or (1A)(b) above if–

(a) he makes the return required by section 218 above,

(aa) he complies with the requirements of section 218A above,

(b) [omitted by SI 2009/3054, art. 3 and Schedule, para. 2(4)(b)(i) and (ii)),]

(c) [omitted by SI 2009/3054, art. 3 and Schedule, para. 2(4)(b)(i) and (ii)),]

before proceedings in which the failure could be declared are commenced.

245A(5) A person who has a reasonable excuse for failing to make a return or to comply with the requirements of section 218A shall not be liable by reason of that failure to a penalty under this section, unless he fails to make the return or to comply with those requirements without unreasonable delay after the excuse has ceased.

***History** – S. 245A(1A) inserted by FA 2002, s. 120(3) which applies in relation to instruments made on or after 1 August 2002.*

S. 245A(1B) inserted by FA 2004, s. 295(3)(a) with effect from:

(a) in relation to a failure to comply with the requirements of s. 218A where the period of six months referred to in s. 218A(1) of that section expires after 22 July 2004; and

(b) where that period expires on or before 22 July 2004, as if, in s. 245A(1B) for the words "anniversary of the end of the period of six months referred to in s. 218A(1)" read, end of the period of twelve months beginning with 22 July 2004 (FA 2004, s. 295(7)).

S. 245A(2) omitted by SI 2009/3054, art. 3 and Schedule, para. 2(4)(a), with effect from 1 April 2010, except in relation to a notice given under s. 219 or 219A before 1 April 2010, in which case s. 245A(2) continues to have effect (SI 2009/3054, art. 4). Former s. 245A(2) read as follows:

"245A(2) A person who fails to comply with a notice under section 219 above shall be liable–

(a) to a penalty not exceeding £300; and

(b) to a further penalty not exceeding £60 for every day after the day on which the failure has been declared by a court or the tribunal and before the day on which the notice is complied with."

S. 245A(3) omitted by SI 2009/3054, art. 3 and Schedule, para. 2(4)(a), with effect from 1 April 2010, except in relation to a notice given under s. 219 or 219A before 1 April 2010, in which case s. 245A(3) continues to have effect (SI 2009/3054, art. 4). Former s. 245A(3) read as follows:

"245A(3) A person who fails to comply with a notice under section 219A(1) or (4) above shall be liable–

(a) to a penalty not exceeding £50; and

(b) to a further penalty not exceeding £30 for every day after the day on which the failure has been declared by a court or the tribunal and before the day on which the notice is complied with."

In s. 245A(4), "or (1A)(b)" substituted for ", (1A)(b), (2)(b) or (3)(b)" by SI 2009/3054, art. 3 and Schedule, para. 2(4)(b)(i), with effect from 1 April 2010, except in relation to a notice given under s. 219 or 219A before 1 April 2010 (SI 2009/3054, art. 4).

S. 245A(4)(b) and (c) omitted (and the word "or" inserted at the end of s. 245A(4)(a)) by SI 2009/3054, art. 3 and Schedule, para. 2(4)(b)(ii) and (iii), with effect from 1 April 2010, except in relation to a notice given under s. 219 or 219A before 1 April 2010 (SI 2009/3054, art. 4). Former s. 245A(4)(b) and (c) read as follows:

"(b) he complies with the notice under section 219 above, or

(c) he complies with the notice under section 219A(1) or (4) above,"

In s. 245A(4), reference to subsection (1A)(b) was inserted by FA 2002, s. 120(3) which applies in relation to instruments made on or after 1 August 2002.

S. 245A(4)(aa) inserted by FA 2002, s. 120(3) which applies in relation to instruments made on or after 1 August 2002.

In s. 245A(5), the words "or to comply with the requirements of section 218A" substituted for the words ", to comply with the requirements of section 218A or to comply with a notice" by SI 2009/3054, art. 3 and Schedule, para. 2(4)(c)(i), with effect from 1 April 2010, except in relation to a notice given under s. 219 or 219A before 1 April 2010 (SI 2009/3054, art. 4).

In s. 245A(5), the words "or to comply with those requirements" substituted for the words ", to comply with the requirements of section 218A or to comply with the notice" by SI 2009/3054, art. 3 and Schedule, para. 2(4)(c)(ii), with effect from 1 April 2010, except in relation to a notice given under s. 219 or 219A before 1 April 2010 (SI 2009/3054, art. 4).

In s. 245A(5), the words "to comply with the requirements of s. 218A" inserted (twice) by FA 2004, s. 295(3)(b) with effect where the period of six months referred to in s. 218A(1) expires after 22 July 2004 (FA 2004, s. 295(8)).

In s. 245A the word "tribunal" substituted for the words "Special Commissioners" four times by SI 2009/56, art. 3 and Sch. 1, para. 121, with effect from 1 April 2009, subject to transitional and saving provisions in SI 2009/56, Sch. 3.

S. 245A inserted by FA 1999, s. 108, with effect in relation to any failure by a person to comply with obligations under IHTA 1984, s. 216–219 that expire on or after 27 July 1999.

246 Failure to appear before Special Commissioners, etc.

246 [Omitted by SI 1994/1813, reg. 2(1) and Sch. 1, para. 20, Sch. 2, Pt. I.]

History – S. 246 omitted by SI 1994/1813, reg. 2(1) and Sch. 1, para. 20, Sch. 2, Pt. I, with effect from 1 September 1994.

247 Provision of incorrect information

247(1) [Omitted by FA 2008, s. 122 and Sch. 40, para. 21(c)(i).]

247(2) [Omitted by FA 2008, s. 122 and Sch. 40, para. 21(c)(i).]

247(3) Any person not liable for tax on the value transferred by a chargeable transfer who fraudulently or negligently furnishes or produces to the Board any incorrect information or document in connection with the transfer shall be liable to a penalty not exceeding £3,000.

247(4) [Omitted by FA 2012, s. 223 and Sch. 38, para. 52.]

History – S. 247(1) omitted by FA 2008, s. 122 and Sch. 40, para. 21(c)(i), with effect from 1 April 2009 (SI 2009/571, art. 2 but subject to transitional provisions at SI 2009/571, art. 6 and 7). Former s. 247(1) read as follows:

"247(1) If any person liable for any tax on the value transferred by a chargeable transfer fraudulently or negligently delivers, furnishes or produces to the Board any incorrect account, information or document, he shall be liable to a penalty not exceeding the difference mentioned in subsection (2) below."

In former s. 247(1), the words "to a penalty not exceeding the difference mentioned in subsection (2) below" substituted for the former wording ", in the case of fraud, to a penalty not exceeding the aggregate of £3,000 and the difference mentioned in subsection (2) below and, in the case of negligence, to a penalty not exceeding the aggregate of £1,500 and that difference." by FA 2004, s. 295(4)(a), with effect in relation to incorrect accounts, information or documents delivered, furnished etc. after 22 July 2004 (FA 2004, s. 295(9)).

In. former s. 247(1), "£3,000 and the difference" substituted for "£50 and twice the difference" by FA 1999, s. 108, with effect in relation to incorrect accounts, information or documents delivered, furnished or produced on or after 27 July 1999.

S. 247(2) omitted by FA 2008, s. 122 and Sch. 40, para. 21(c)(i), with effect from 1 April 2009 (SI 2009/571, art. 2 but subject to transitional provisions at SI 2009/571, art. 6 and 7). Former s. 247(2) read as follows:

"247(2) The difference referred to in subsection (1) above is the amount by which the tax for which that person is liable, or for which any other person is liable by virtue of the operation of section 8A above, exceeds what would be the amount of that tax if the facts were as shown in the account, information or document."

In former s. 247(2), the words ", or for which any other person is liable by virtue of the operation of section 8A above," inserted by FA 2008, s. 10 and Sch. 4, para. 6, with effect from 21 July 2008.

In s. 247(3), the words "to a penalty not exceeding £3,000" substituted for the former wording ", in the case of fraud, to a penalty not exceeding £3,000 and, in the case of negligence, to a penalty not exceeding £1,500." by FA 2004, s. 295(4)(b) with effect in relation to incorrect accounts, information or documents delivered, furnished etc. after 22 July 2004 (FA 2004, s. 295(9)).

In s. 247(3), the figures of £3,000 and £1,500 substituted for £500 and £250 respectively, by FA 1999, s. 108, with effect in relation to incorrect accounts, information or documents delivered, furnished or produced on or after 27 July 1999.

S. 247(4) omitted by FA 2012, s. 223 and Sch. 38. para. 52, with effect from 1 April 2013 (SI 2013/279, art. 2). Former s. 247(4) read as follows:

"247(4) Any person who assists in or induces the delivery, furnishing or production in pursuance of this Part of this Act of any account, information or document which he knows to be incorrect shall be liable to a penalty not exceeding £3,000.".

In s. 247(4), the figure of £3,000 substituted for £500, by FA 1999, s. 108, with effect in relation to incorrect accounts, information or documents delivered, furnished or produced on or after 27 July 1999.

Cross references – FA 2004, s. 313(4)(c): no penalty under s. 247 for a failure to include the reference number of a notifiable tax avoidance scheme in any return; duty of parties to notifiable arrangements to notify Board of number, etc.

248 Failure to remedy errors

248(1) If after any information or document has been furnished or produced by any person without fraud or negligence it comes to his notice that it was incorrect in any material respect it shall be treated for the purposes of section 247 above as having been negligently furnished or produced unless the error is remedied without unreasonable delay.

248(2) If after any account, information or document has been delivered, furnished or produced by any person in pursuance of this Part of this Act it comes to the notice of any other person that it contains an error whereby tax for which that other person is liable has been or might be underpaid, that other person shall inform the Board of the error; and if he fails to do so without unreasonable delay he shall be liable to the penalty to which he would be liable if the account, information or document had been delivered, furnished or produced by him and the case were one of negligence.

History – In s. 248(1), the words "account," and "delivered," (twice) omitted by FA 2008, s. 122 and Sch. 40, para. 21(c)(ii), with effect from 1 April 2009 (SI 2009/571, art. 2 but subject to transitional provisions at SI 2009/571, art. 6 and 7).
In s. 248(2), the words "under section 247 above" omitted by FA 2008, s. 122 and Sch. 40, para. 21(c)(ii), with effect from 1 April 2009 (SI 2009/571, art. 2 but subject to transitional provisions at SI 2009/571, art. 6 and 7).

249 Recovery of penalties

249(1) All proceedings for the recovery of penalties under this Part of this Act shall be commenced by the Board or, in Scotland, by the Board or the Advocate General for Scotland.

249(2) Any such proceedings may be commenced either before the First-tier Tribunal or in the High Court or the Court of Session and shall, if brought in the High Court, be deemed to be civil proceedings by the Crown within the meaning of Part II of the Crown Proceedings Act 1947 or, as the case may be, that Part as for the time being in force in Northern Ireland.

249(3) Where any proceedings are brought before the First-tier Tribunal, in addition to any right of appeal on a point of law under section 11(2) of the TCEA 2007, the person liable to the penalty may appeal to the Upper Tribunal against the amount of a penalty which has been determined under this Part, but not against any decision which falls under section 11(5)(d) and (e) of the TCEA 2007 and was made in connection with the determination of the amount of the penalty.

249(3A) Section 11(3) and (4) of the TCEA 2007 applies to the right of appeal under subsection (3) as it applies to the right of appeal under section 11(2) of the TCEA 2007.

249(3B) On an appeal under this section the Upper Tribunal has the same powers as are conferred on the First-tier Tribunal by virtue of this section.

249(4) The person liable to the penalty shall be a party to the proceedings.

249(5) References in this section to the Court of Session are references to that Court as the Court of Exchequer in Scotland.

History – In s. 249(1) the words "Advocate General for Scotland" substituted for the words "Lord Advocate" by SI 1999/679, art. 2, Schedule, with effect from 20 May 1999.
In s. 249(2) the word "First-tier Tribunal" substituted for the words "Special Commissioners" by SI 2009/56, art. 3 and Sch. 1, para. 122(2), with effect from 1 April 2009, subject to transitional and saving provisions in SI 2009/56, Sch. 3.
S. 249(3)–(3B) substituted for former s. 249(3) by SI 2009/56, art. 3 and Sch. 1, para. 122(3), with effect from 1 April 2009, subject to transitional and saving provisions in SI 2009/56, Sch. 3. Former s. 249(3) read as follows:
"**249(3)** Where any such proceedings are brought before the Special Commissioners, an appeal shall lie from their decision to the High Court or, as the case may be, the Court of Session–
(a) by either party, on a question of law, and
(b) by the defendant (or, in Scotland, defender) against the amount of any penalty awarded;
and on an appeal under paragraph (b) above the Court may either confirm the decision or reduce or increase the sum awarded."
S. 249(4) substituted by SI 2009/56, art. 3 and Sch. 1, para. 122(3), with effect from 1 April 2009, subject to transitional and saving provisions in SI 2009/56, Sch. 3. Former s. 249(4) read as follows:
"**249(4)** Proceedings under this section before the Special Commissioners shall be by way of information writing made to them, and upon summons issued by them to the defendant (or defender) to appear before them at a time and place stated in the summons, and they shall hear and determine each case in a summary way."
Cross references – SI 1994/1811, reg. 3(1): procedure for listing and notice of hearing before special commissioners does not apply to proceedings under s. 249.

250 Time limit for recovery

250(1) No proceedings for the recovery of a penalty under this Part of this Act shall be brought after the end of the period of three years beginning with the date on which the amount of the tax properly payable in respect of the chargeable transfer concerned was notified by the Board to the person or one of the persons liable for the tax or any part of it.

250(2) [Omitted by FA 2008, s. 122 and Sch. 40, para. 21(c)(iii).]

History – *S. 250(2) omitted by FA 2008, s. 122 and Sch. 40, para. 21(c)(iii), with effect from 1 April 2009 (SI 2009/571, art. 2 but subject to transitional provisions at SI 2009/571, art. 6 and 7). Former s. 250(2) read as follows:*
"**250(2)** Where the person who has incurred any such penalty has died, any proceedings for the recovery of the penalty which have been or could have been commenced against him may be continued or commenced against his personal representatives, and any penalty awarded in proceedings so continued or commenced shall be a debt due from and payable out of his estate."

251 Appeals against summary determination of penalties

251 [Omitted by SI 2009/56, art. 3 and Sch. 1, para. 123.]

History – S. 251 omitted by SI 2009/56, art. 3 and Sch. 1, para. 123, with effect from 1 April 2009, subject to transitional and saving provisions in SI 2009/56, Sch. 3. Former s. 251 read as follows:

"251 Appeals against summary determination of penalties

251(1) An appeal shall lie to the High Court or the Court of Session against the summary determination by the Special Commissioners of a penalty under regulation 24 of the Special Commissioners (Jurisdiction and Procedure) Regulations 1994 in proceedings relating to inheritance tax.

251(2) On such an appeal the Court may either confirm or reverse the determination of the Special Commissioners or reduce or increase the sum determined.

History – S. 251 substituted by SI 1994/1813, reg. 2(1) and Sch. 1, para. 22, with effect from 1 September 1994."

252 Effect of award by tribunal

252 Any penalty awarded by the tribunal shall be recoverable by the Board as a debt due to the Crown.

History – In the heading to s. 252 the word "tribunal" substituted for the words "Special Commissioners" by SI 2009/56, art. 3 and Sch. 1, para. 124(2), with effect from 1 April 2009, subject to transitional and saving provisions in SI 2009/56, Sch. 3.
In s. 252 the word "tribunal" substituted for the words "Special Commissioners" by SI 2009/56, art. 3 and Sch. 1, para. 124(3), with effect from 1 April 2009, subject to transitional and saving provisions in SI 2009/56, Sch. 3.

253 Mitigation of penalties

253 The Board may in their discretion mitigate any penalty, or stay or compound any proceedings for recovery of any penalty, and may also, after judgment, further mitigate or entirely remit the penalty.

MISCELLANEOUS

254 Evidence

254(1) For the purposes of the preceding provisions of this Part of this Act, a notice under section 221 above specifying any determination which can no longer be varied or quashed on appeal shall be sufficient evidence of the matters determined.

254(2) [Omitted by FA 2008, s. 138 and Sch. 44, para. 3.]

History – S. 254(2) omitted by FA 2008, s. 138 and Sch. 44, para. 3, with effect from 21 July 2008.

255 Determination of questions on previous view of law

255 Where any payment has been made and accepted in satisfaction of any liability for tax and on a view of the law then generally received or adopted in practice, any question whether too little or too much has been paid or what was the right amount of tax payable shall be determined on the same view, notwithstanding that it appears from a subsequent legal decision or otherwise that the view was or may have been wrong.

256 Regulations about accounts, etc.

256(1) The Board may make regulations–

(a) dispensing with the delivery of accounts under section 216 above in such cases as may be specified in or determined under the regulations;

(aa) requiring persons who by virtue of regulations under paragraph (a) above are not required to deliver accounts under section 216 above to produce to the Board, in such manner as may be specified in or determined under the regulations, such information or documents as may be so specified or determined.

(b) discharging, subject to such restrictions as may be so specified or determined, property from an Inland Revenue charge and persons from further claims for tax in cases other than those mentioned in section 239 above;

(c) [ceases to have effect by virtue of FA 2004, s. 293(2)(d); and repealed by FA 2004, s. 326 and Sch. 42, Pt. 4(1);]

(d) modifying section 264(8) below in cases where the delivery of an account has been dispensed with under the regulations.

256(1A) Regulations under subsection (1)(aa) may in particular–

(a) provide that information or documents must be produced to the Board by producing it or them to–
   (i) a probate registry in England and Wales;
   (ii) the sheriff in Scotland;
   (iii) the Probate and Matrimonial Office in Northern Ireland;

IHT Statutes

(b) provide that information or documents produced as specified in paragraph (a) is or are to be treated for any or all purposes of this Act as produced to the Board;

(c) provide for the further transmission to the Board of information or documents produced as specified in paragraph (a).

256(2) [Ceases to have effect by virtue of FA 2004, s. 293(4); and repealed by FA 2004, s. 326 and Sch. 42, Pt. 4(1).]

256(3) Regulations under this section may contain such supplementary or incidental provisions as the Board think fit and may make different provision for different cases.

256(3A) Regulations under this section may only be made–

(a) in relation to England and Wales, after consulting the Lord Chancellor;

(b) in relation to Scotland, after consulting the Scottish Ministers;

(c) in relation to Northern Ireland, after consulting the Lord Chief Justice of Northern Ireland.

256(3B) The Lord Chief Justice of Northern Ireland may nominate any of the following to exercise his functions under subsection (3A)–

(a) the holder of one of the offices listed in Schedule 1 to the Justice (Northern Ireland) Act 2002;

(b) a Lord Justice of Appeal (as defined in section 88 of that Act).

256(4) The power to make regulations under this section shall be exercisable by statutory instrument, which shall be subject to annulment in pursuance of a resolution of the House of Commons.

History – In s. 256(1)(a), the words "determined under" inserted by FA 2004, s. 293(2)(a) with effect from 22 July 2004.
S. 256(1)(aa) inserted by FA 2004, s. 293(2)(b) with effect from 22 July 2004.
In s. 256(1)(b), the words "or determined" inserted by FA 2004, s. 293(2)(c) with effect from 22 July 2004.
S. 256(1)(c) ceased to have effect by virtue of FA 2004, s. 293(2)(d); and was repealed by FA 2004, s. 326 and Sch. 42, Pt. 4(1); with effect from 22 July 2004.
S. 256(1A) inserted by FA 2004, s. 293(3) with effect from 22 July 2004.
S. 256(2) ceased to have effect by virtue of FA 2004, s. 293(4); and was repealed by FA 2004, s. 326 and Sch. 42, Pt. 4(1); with effect from 22 July 2004.
In s. 256(3) the words "and may make different provision for different cases" inserted by FA 2004, s. 293(5) with effect from 22 July 2004.
S. 256(3A) and (3B) substituted for former (3A) by Constitutional Reform Act 2005, s. 15 and Sch. 4, para. 176, with effect from 3 April 2006 (by virtue of SI 2006/1014, art. 2(a), Sch. 1, para. 10 and 11).
Former s. 256(3A) inserted by FA 2004, s. 293(6) with effect from 22 July 2004.

Cross references – S. 239: certificates of discharge.
S. 264: transfers reported late.
Supreme Court Act 1981, s. 109(3): disapplication of s. 109(1) where delivery of accounts dispensed with by regulations made under s. 256(1).
FA 2014, s. 195(5): an account delivered under s. 216 or 217 (including an account delivered in accordance with regulations under s. 256), or information or a document provided in accordance with regulations under s. 256, is treated as a return for the purposes of FA 2014, Pt. 4 (follower notices and accelerated payments)

Statutory instruments – SI 2008/605: made under s. 256(1)(a).
SI 2008/606: made under s. 256(1)(a).
SI 2006/2141: made under s. 256(1), (1A) and (3).
SI 2004/2543: made under s. 256(1).
SI 2002/1731: made under s. 256(1)(a).
SI 2002/1732: made under s. 256(1)(a).
SI 2002/1733: made under s. 256(1)(a).

257 Form etc. of accounts

257(1) All accounts and other documents required for the purposes of this Act shall be in such form and shall contain such particulars as may be prescribed by the Board.

257(2) All accounts to be delivered to the Board under this Act shall be supported by such books, papers and other documents, and verified (whether on oath or otherwise) in such manner, as the Board may require.

257(3) For the purposes of this Act, an account delivered to a probate registry pursuant to arrangements made between the President of the Family Division and the Board or delivered to the Probate and Matrimonial Office in Northern Ireland pursuant to arrangements made between the Lord Chief Justice of Northern Ireland and the Board shall be treated as an account delivered to the Board.

257(4) The Lord Chief Justice of Northern Ireland may nominate any of the following to exercise his functions under subsection (3)–

(a) the holder of one of the offices listed in Schedule 1 to the Justice (Northern Ireland) Act 2002;

(b) a Lord Justice of Appeal (as defined in section 88 of that Act).

History – In s. 257(3) the words "Lord Chief Justice of Northern Ireland" substituted for the words "Lord Chancellor" by Constitutional Reform Act 2005, s. 15 and Sch. 4, para. 177(2), with effect from 3 April 2006 (by virtue of SI 2006/1014, art. 2(a) and Sch. 1, para. 10 and 11).
S. 257(4) inserted by Constitutional Reform Act 2005, s. 15 and Sch. 4, para. 177(3), with effect from 3 April 2006 (by virtue of SI 2006/1014, art. 2(a) and Sch. 1, para. 10 and 11).

Statements of practice – SP 2/93: HMRC's approach towards acceptance of facsimiles of inheritance tax accounts and forms as substitutes for officially produced documents.

Other material – Law Society's Gazette, 3 March 1993 (p. 32): guidance notes on Capital Taxes Office policy in relation to substitute accounts and forms.

258 Service of documents

258 A notice or other document which is to be served on a person under this Act may be delivered to him or left at his usual or last known place of residence or served by post, addressed to him at his usual or last known place of residence or his place of business or employment.

259 Inspection of records

259 Section 16 of the Stamp Act 1891, section 56 of the Finance Act 1946 and section 27 of the Finance (No. 2) Act (Northern Ireland) 1946 (inspection of public records and records of unit trusts) shall apply in relation to capital transfer tax as they apply in relation to stamp duties.

Cross references – FA 1986, s. 100(1)(b): any reference to capital transfer tax (except where it relates to a liability to tax arising before 25 July 1986) has effect as a reference to inheritance tax.

260 Inland Revenue Regulation Act 1890

260 Sections 21, 22 and 35 of the Inland Revenue Regulation Act 1890 (proceedings for fines, etc.) shall not apply in relation to capital transfer tax.

Cross references – FA 1986, s. 100(1)(b): any reference to capital transfer tax (except where it relates to a liability to tax arising before 25 July 1986) has effect as a reference to inheritance tax.

261 Scotland: inventories

261 In the application of this Part of this Act to Scotland, references to an account required to be delivered to the Board by the personal representatives of a deceased person, however expressed, shall be construed as references to such an inventory or additional inventory as is mentioned in section 38 of the Probate and Legacy Duties Act 1808 which has been duly exhibited as required by that section.

PART IX – MISCELLANEOUS AND SUPPLEMENTARY

MISCELLANEOUS

262 Tax chargeable in certain cases of future payments, etc.

262(1) Where a disposition made for a consideration in money or money's worth is a transfer of value and any payments made or assets transferred by the transferor in pursuance of the disposition are made or transferred more than one year after the disposition is made, tax (if any) shall be charged as if–

(a) any payment made or asset transferred in pursuance of the disposition were made or transferred in pursuance of a separate disposition made, without consideration, at the time the payment is made or the asset is transferred, and

(b) the amount of the payment made or the value of the asset transferred in pursuance of each of those separate dispositions were the chargeable portion of the payment or asset.

262(2) For the purposes of this section the **chargeable portion of any payment** made or any asset transferred at any time shall be such portion of its value at that time as is found by applying to it the fraction of which–

(a) the numerator is the value actually transferred by the disposition first mentioned in subsection (1) above (calculated as if no tax were payable on it), and

(b) the denominator is the value, at the time of that disposition, of the aggregate of the payments made or to be made and assets transferred or to be transferred by the transferor in pursuance of it.

Cross references – S. 175: computation of liability to make future payments etc. in determining value of a person's estate on death.

263 Annuity purchased in conjunction with life policy

263(1) Where–

(a) a policy of life insurance is issued in respect of an insurance made after 26th March 1974 or is after that date varied or substituted for an earlier policy, and

(b) at the time the insurance is made or at any earlier or later date an annuity on the life of the insured is purchased, and

(c) the benefit of the policy is vested in a person other than the person who purchased the annuity,

IHT Statutes

then, unless it is shown that the purchase of the annuity and the making of the insurance (or, as the case may be, the substitution or variation) were not associated operations, the person who purchased the annuity shall be treated as having made a transfer of value by a disposition made at the time the benefit of the policy became so vested (to the exclusion of any transfer of value which, apart from this section, he might have made as a result of the vesting, or of the purchase and the vesting being associated operations).

263(2) The value transferred by that transfer of value shall be equal to whichever of the following is less, namely,–

(a) the aggregate of–

(i) the value of the consideration given for the annuity, and

(ii) any premium paid or other consideration given under the policy on or before the transfer; and

(b) the value of the greatest benefit capable of being conferred at any time by the policy, calculated as if that time were the date of the transfer.

263(3) The preceding provisions of this section shall apply, with the necessary modifications, where a contract for an annuity payable on a person's death is after 26th March 1974 made or varied or substituted for or replaced by such a contract or a policy of life insurance as they apply where a policy of life insurance is issued, varied or substituted as mentioned in subsection (1) above.

Statements of practice – E4: policies and annuities not regarded as affected by the associated operations rule if policy was issued on full medical evidence of the assured's health, and would have been issued on the same terms if annuity had not been bought.

264 Transfers reported late

264(1) This section has effect where a person has made a transfer of value (**"the earlier transfer"**) which–

(a) is not notified to the Board in an account under section 216 above or by information furnished under section 219 above before the expiration of the period specified in section 216 for the delivery of accounts, and

(b) is not discovered until after payment has been accepted by the Board in full satisfaction of the tax on the value transferred by another transfer of value (**"the later transfer"**) made by him on or after the day on which he made the earlier transfer.

264(2) Where the earlier transfer is made in the period of ten years ending with the date of the later transfer there shall be charged on the value transferred by the earlier transfer, in addition to any tax chargeable on it apart from this section, an amount of tax equal to the difference, if any, between–

(a) the tax which, having regard to the earlier transfer, was properly chargeable on the value transferred by the later transfer, and

(b) the payment accepted by the Board in full satisfaction of the tax chargeable on that value;

and any such difference shall not be chargeable on the value transferred by the later transfer.

264(3) Where in the period mentioned in subsection (2) above there have been two or more earlier transfers the reference in paragraph (a) of that subsection to the earlier transfer shall be construed as a reference to both or all of those transfers, but the amount of tax chargeable under that subsection in respect of each of them shall, subject to subsection (4) below, be reduced in the proportion which the value transferred by it bears to the aggregate of the values transferred by it and the other or others.

264(4) Where the earlier transfers mentioned in subsection (3) above include a settled transfer, that is to say, a transfer in the case of which an amount in full satisfaction of the tax chargeable in respect of it under subsection (2) above has been paid to and accepted by the Board before the discovery of one or more of the other earlier transfers,–

(a) no further tax shall be chargeable under subsection (2) above in respect of the settled transfer in consequence of regard being had under paragraph (a) of that subsection to the subsequently discovered transfer or transfers;

(b) the amount so paid and accepted shall reduce the amount chargeable under subsection (2) above in respect of the subsequently discovered transfer or transfers; and

(c) if there are two or more subsequently discovered transfers, the value transferred by the settled transfer shall be disregarded in calculating under subsection (3) above the reduction in the amount of tax chargeable in respect of each of them.

264(5) Where the later transfer referred to in subsection (2) above is itself an earlier transfer in relation to another later transfer the references in paragraphs (a) and (b) of that subsection to tax chargeable on the value transferred by it are references to tax so chargeable apart from this section.

264(6) Subsection (2) above shall not increase the amount in respect of which interest is payable under section 233 above in relation to the earlier transfer in respect of any period falling before the expiration of six months from the date on which it was discovered.

264(7) Where, apart from this subsection, the earlier transfer would be wholly or partly exempt by reason of some or all of the value transferred by it falling within a limit applicable to an exemption, then, if tax has been accepted as mentioned in subsection (1)(b) above on the basis that the later transfer is partly exempt by reason of part of the value thereby transferred falling within that limit–

(a) tax shall not be chargeable on that part of the value transferred by the later transfer, but

(b) a corresponding part of the value transferred by the earlier transfer shall be treated as falling outside that limit.

264(8) Subsection (1)(b) above shall apply to a transfer in respect of which no tax is chargeable because the rate of tax applicable under section 7 above is nil as if payment had been accepted when the transfer was notified in an account under section 216 above, and subsection (2)(b) above shall apply in relation to any such transfer as if the amount of the payment were nil.

264(9) For the purposes of this section **a transfer is discovered**–

(a) if it is notified under the provisions mentioned in subsection (1)(a) above after the expiration of the period there mentioned, on the date on which it is so notified;

(b) in any other case, on the date on which the Board give notice of a determination in respect of the transfer under section 221 above.

Cross references – S. 216: delivery of accounts.
S. 219: information powers of Board.
S. 233: interest on unpaid tax.
S. 256(1)(d): power of Board to modify s. 264(8) in certain cases where delivery of an account has been dispensed with by regulations under s. 256(1).
SI 2002/1731, reg. 7: transfers reported late.
SI 2002/1732, reg. 8: transfers reported late.
SI 2002/1733, reg. 8: transfers reported late.

265 Chargeable transfers affecting more than one property

265 Where the value transferred by a chargeable transfer is determined by reference to the values of more than one property the tax chargeable on the value transferred shall be attributed to the respective values in the proportions which they bear to their aggregate, but subject to section 54B(3) above and to any provision reducing the amount of tax attributable to the value of any particular property.

History – In s. 265, the words "section 54B(3) above and to" inserted by F(No. 2)A 1987, s. 96 and Sch. 7, para. 5, with respect to transfers of value made, and other events occurring, on or after 17 March 1987.

Cross references – S. 54B(3): attribution of tax where settled property affected by potentially exempt transfer.

266 More than one chargeable transfer on one day

266(1) Where the value transferred by more than one chargeable transfer made by the same person on the same day depends on the order in which the transfers are made, they shall be treated as made in the order which results in the lowest value chargeable.

266(2) Subject to subsection (1) above, the rate at which the tax is charged on the values transferred by two or more chargeable transfers made by the same person on the same day shall be the effective rate at which tax would have been charged if those transfers had been a single chargeable transfer of the same total value.

266(3) The chargeable transfers referred to in subsections (1) and (2) above do not include a transfer made on the death of the transferor.

266(4) Chargeable transfers under Chapter III of Part III of this Act shall if they relate to the same settlement be treated for the purposes of subsections (1) and (2) above as made by the same person.

Cross references – Pt. III, Ch. III: charge on settlements without interest in possession.

267 Persons treated as domiciled in United Kingdom

267(1) A person not domiciled in the United Kingdom at any time (in this section referred to as **"the relevant time"**) shall be treated for the purposes of this Act as domiciled in the United Kingdom (and not elsewhere) at the relevant time if–

(a) he was domiciled in the United Kingdom within the three years immediately preceding the relevant time,

(aa) he is a formerly domiciled resident for the tax year in which the relevant time falls ("the relevant tax year"), or

(b) he was resident in the United Kingdom–

  (i) for at least fifteen of the twenty tax years immediately preceding the relevant tax year, and

  (ii) for at least one of the four tax years ending with the relevant tax year.

IHT Statutes

267(2) Subsection (1) above shall not apply for the purposes of section 6(2) or (3) or 48(4) above and shall not affect the interpretation of any such provision as is mentioned in section 158(6) above.

267(3) [Omitted by F(No. 2)A 2017, s. 30(2).]

267(4) For the purposes of this section the question whether a person was resident in the United Kingdom for any tax year shall be determined as for the purposes of income tax.

267(5) In determining for the purposes of this section whether a person is, or at any time was, domiciled in the United Kingdom, sections 267ZA and 267ZB are to be ignored.

History – S. 267(1)(aa) inserted (and the word "or" preceding it omitted) and s. 267(1)(b) substituted by F(No. 2)A 2017, s. 30(1), with effect in relation to times after 5 April 2017 subject to s. 30(10)–(17). Former s. 267(1)(b) read as follows:

"(b) he was resident in the United Kingdom in not less than seventeen of the twenty years of assessment ending with the year of assessment in which the relevant time falls."

S. 267(3) omitted by F(No. 2)A 2017, s. 30(2), with effect in relation to times after 5 April 2017 subject to s. 30(10)–(17). Former s. 267(3) read as follows:

"**267(3)** Paragraph (a) of subsection (1) above shall not apply in relation to a person who (apart from this section) has not been domiciled in the United Kingdom at any time since 9th December 1974, and paragraph (b) of that subsection shall not apply in relation to a person who has not been resident there at any time since that date; and that subsection shall be disregarded–

(a) in determining whether settled property which became comprised in the settlement on or before that date is excluded property,

(b) in determining the settlor's domicile for the purposes of section 65(8) above in relation to settled property which became comprised in the settlement on or before that date, and

(c) in determining for the purpose of section 65(8) above whether the condition in section 82(3) above is satisfied in relation to such settled property."

In s. 267(4) the words "for any tax year" substituted for the words "in any year of assessment" by F(No. 2)A 2017, s. 30(13), with effect in relation to times after 5 April 2017 subject to s. 30(10)–(17).

S. 267(4) partially repealed by FA 1993, s. 208(3), 213 and Sch. 23, Pt. V in relation to 1993–94 and subsequent years of assessment by omitting words which appeared after "tax".

S. 267(5) inserted by FA 2013, s. 177(2), with effect from 17 July 2013 (Royal Assent).

Cross references – S. 6(2), (3), 48(4), 65(8), 82(3): exclusion for certain securities etc. by reference to domicile.

S. 158(6): double tax conventions referable to estate duty.

FA 1996, s. 200(1): in determining for the purpose of s. 267(1)(a) where a person was domiciled at any time on or after 6 April 1993 there shall be disregarded any relevant action (see FA 1996, s. 200(2)) taken by that person in connection with electoral rights.

SI 2002/1733, reg. 3(3)(b): non-domicile.

Statements of practice – E9: for purposes of s. 267(3), property becomes comprised in a settlement when introduced by the settlor.

267ZA Election to be treated as domiciled in United Kingdom

267ZA(1) A person may, if condition A or B is met, elect to be treated for the purposes of this Act as domiciled in the United Kingdom (and not elsewhere).

267ZA(2) A person's personal representatives may, if condition B is met, elect for the person to be treated for the purposes of this Act as domiciled in the United Kingdom (and not elsewhere).

267ZA(3) Condition A is that, at any time on or after 6 April 2013 and during the period of 7 years ending with the date on which the election is made, the person had a spouse or civil partner who was domiciled in the United Kingdom.

267ZA(4) Condition B is that a person ("the deceased") dies and, at any time on or after 6 April 2013 and within the period of 7 years ending with the date of death, the deceased was–

(a) domiciled in the United Kingdom, and

(b) the spouse or civil partner of the person who would, by virtue of the election, be treated as domiciled in the United Kingdom.

267ZA(5) An election under this section does not affect a person's domicile for the purposes of section 6(2) or (3) or 48(4).

267ZA(6) An election under this section is to be ignored–

(a) in interpreting any such provision as is mentioned in section 158(6), and

(b) in determining the effect of any qualifying double taxation relief arrangements in relation to a transfer of value by the person making the election.

267ZA(7) For the purposes of subsection (6)(b) a qualifying double taxation relief arrangement is an arrangement which is specified in an Order in Council made under section 158 before the coming into force of this section (other than by way of amendment by an Order made on or after the coming into force of this section).

267ZA(8) In determining for the purposes of this section whether a person making an election under this section is or was domiciled in the United Kingdom, section 267 is to be ignored.

History – S. 267ZA inserted by FA 2013, s. 177(3), with effect from 17 July 2013 (Royal Assent).

267ZB Section 267ZA: further provision about election

267ZB(1) For the purposes of this section–

(a) references to a lifetime election are to an election made by virtue of section 267ZA(3), and

(b) references to a death election are to an election made by virtue of section 267ZA(4).

267ZB(2) A lifetime or death election is to be made by notice in writing to HMRC.

267ZB(3) A lifetime or death election is treated as having taken effect on a date specified, in accordance with subsection (4), in the notice.

267ZB(4) The date specified in a notice under subsection (3) must–

(a) be 6 April 2013 or a later date,

(b) be within the period of 7 years ending with–

(i) in the case of a lifetime election, the date on which the election is made, or

(ii) in the case of a death election, the date of the deceased's death, and

(c) meet the condition in subsection (5).

267ZB(5) The condition in this subsection is met by a date if, on the date–

(a) in the case of a lifetime election–

(i) the person making the election was married to, or in a civil partnership with, the spouse or civil partner, and

(ii) the spouse or civil partner was domiciled in the United Kingdom, or

(b) in the case of a death election–

(i) the person who is, by virtue of the election, to be treated as domiciled in the United Kingdom was married to, or in a civil partnership with, the deceased, and

(ii) the deceased was domiciled in the United Kingdom.

267ZB(6) A death election may only be made within 2 years of the death of the deceased or such longer period as an officer of Revenue and Customs may in the particular case allow.

267ZB(7) Subsection (8) applies if–

(a) a lifetime or death election is made,

(b) a disposition is made, or another event occurs, during the period beginning with the time when the election is treated by virtue of subsection (3) as having taken effect and ending at the time when the election is made, and

(c) the effect of the election being treated as having taken effect at that time is that the disposition or event gives rise to a transfer of value.

267ZB(8) This Act applies with the following modifications in relation to the transfer of value–

(a) subsections (1) and (6)(c) of section 216 have effect as if the period specified in subsection (6)(c) of that section were the period of 12 months from the end of the month in which the election is made, and

(b) sections 226 and 233 have effect as if the transfer were made at the time when the election is made.

267ZB(9) A lifetime or death election cannot be revoked.

267ZB(10) If a person who made an election under section 267ZA(1) is not resident in the United Kingdom for the purposes of income tax for a period of four successive tax years beginning at any time after the election is made, the election ceases to have effect at the end of that period.

History – S. 267ZB inserted by FA 2013, s. 177(3), with effect from 17 July 2013 (Royal Assent).

267A Limited liability partnerships

267A For the purposes of this Act and any other enactments relating to inheritance tax–

(a) property to which a limited liability partnership is entitled, or which it occupies or uses, shall be treated as property to which its members are entitled, or which they occupy or use, as partners,

(b) any business carried on by a limited liability partnership shall be treated as carried on in partnership by its members,

(c) incorporation, change in membership or dissolution of a limited liability partnership shall be treated as formation, alteration or dissolution of a partnership, and

(d) any transfer of value made by or to a limited liability partnership shall be treated as made by or to its members in partnership (and not by or to the limited liability partnership as such).

History – S. 267A inserted with effect from 6 April 2001, by Limited Liability Partnership Act 2000, s. 11, by virtue of SI 2000/3316 (C. 108).

INTERPRETATION

268 Associated operations

268(1) In this Act **"associated operations"** means, subject to subsection (2) below, any two or more operations of any kind, being–

IHT Statutes

(a) operations which affect the same property, or one of which affects some property and the other or others of which affect property which represents, whether directly or indirectly, that property, or income arising from that property, or any property representing accumulations of any such income, or

(b) any two operations of which one is effected with reference to the other, or with a view to enabling the other to be effected or facilitating its being effected, and any further operation having a like relation to any of those two, and so on,

whether those operations are effected by the same person or different persons, and whether or not they are simultaneous; and **"operation"** includes an omission.

268(2) The granting of a lease for full consideration in money or money's worth shall not be taken to be associated with any operation effected more than three years after the grant, and no operation effected on or after 27th March 1974 shall be taken to be associated with an operation effected before that date.

268(3) Where a transfer of value is made by associated operations carried out at different times it shall be treated as made at the time of the last of them; but where any one or more of the earlier operations also constitute a transfer of value made by the same transferor, the value transferred by the earlier operations shall be treated as reducing the value transferred by all the operations taken together, except to the extent that the transfer constituted by the earlier operations but not that made by all the operations taken together is exempt under section 18 above.

Cross references – FA 2004, Sch. 15, para. 11(7): charge to income tax on benefits received by former owner of property; excluded liability possible in some situations involving associated operations, with effect for 2005–06 onwards.
S. 18: transfers between spouses.

Hansard – HC Debates, vol. 888, col. 56, 10 March 1975: limited use of associated operations rule where one spouse makes gifts out of money received from the other.

Other material – Law Society's Gazette, 1 March 1978, (p. 214), Inland Revenue letter: applications of associated operations rule to schemes designed to maximise annual exemption.

269 Control of company

269(1) For the purposes of this Act a person has control of a company at any time if he then has the control of powers of voting on all questions affecting the company as a whole which if exercised would yield a majority of the votes capable of being exercised on them.

269(2) For the purposes of this Act shares or securities shall be deemed to give a person control of a company if, together with any shares or securities which are related property within the meaning of section 161 above, they would be sufficient to give him control of the company (as defined in subsection (1) above).

269(3) Where shares or securities are comprised in a settlement, any powers of voting which they give to the trustees of the settlement shall for the purposes of subsection (1) above be deemed to be given to the person beneficially entitled in possession to the shares or securities (except in a case where no individual is so entitled).

269(4) Where a company has shares or securities of any class giving powers of voting limited to either or both of–

(a) the question of winding up the company, and

(b) any question primarily affecting shares or securities of that class,

the reference in subsection (1) above to all questions affecting the company as a whole shall have effect as a reference to all such questions except any in relation to which those powers are capable of being exercised.

270 Connected persons

270 For the purposes of this Act any question whether a person is connected with another shall be determined as, for the purposes of the 1992 Act, it falls to be determined under section 286 of that Act, but as if in that section **"relative"** included uncle, aunt, nephew and niece and **"settlement"**, **"settlor"** and **"trustee"** had the same meanings as in this Act.

History – References to the "1992 Act" substituted by TCGA 1992, s. 290 and Sch. 10, para. 8(12).

Cross references – TCGA 1992, s. 286: individuals are connected by blood relationship with them or their spouse or a spousal bond to such a related person and there are special rules for trust and corporate relationships.

271 Property of corporations sole

271 *References in this Act* (except section 59) to property to which a person is **beneficially entitled** do not include references to property to which a person is entitled as a corporation sole.

Cross references – S. 59: qualifying interest in possession.

271A Qualifying non-UK pension scheme

271A(1) For the purposes of this Act **"qualifying non-UK pension scheme"** means a pension scheme (other than a registered pension scheme) which–

(a) is established in a country or territory outside the United Kingdom, and

(b) satisfies any requirements prescribed for the purposes of this section by regulations made by the Commissioners for Her Majesty's Revenue and Customs.

271A(2) **"Pension scheme"** has the same meaning as in Part 4 of the Finance Act 2004 (see section 150 of that Act).

271A(3) Regulations under this section may include provision having effect in relation to times before the regulations are made if it does not increase any person's liability to tax.

271A(4) The power to make regulations under this section is exercisable by statutory instrument, which is subject to annulment in pursuance of a resolution of the House of Commons.

History – S. 271A inserted by FA 2008, s. 92 and Sch. 29, para. 18(6), with effect from 6 April 2006.

Statutory instruments – SI 2010/51: made under s. 271A.

272 General interpretation

272 In this Act, except where the context otherwise requires,–

"amount" includes value;

"authorised unit trust" means a scheme which is a unit trust scheme for the purposes of the Income Tax Acts (see section 1007 of the Income Tax Act 2007) and in the case of which an order under section 243 of the Financial Services and Markets Act 2000 is in force;

"barrister" includes a member of the Faculty of Advocates;

"the Board" means the Commissioners of Inland Revenue;

"conditionally exempt transfer" shall be construed in accordance with section 30(2) above;

"disabled person's interest" has the meaning given by section 89B above;

"disposition" includes a disposition effected by associated operations;

"estate" shall be construed in accordance with sections 5, 55 and 151(4) above;

"estate duty" includes estate duty under the law of Northern Ireland;

"excluded property" shall be construed in accordance with section 6 and 48 above and Schedule A1;

"foreign-owned", in relation to property at any time, means property–

(a) in the case of which the person beneficially entitled to it is at that time domiciled outside the United Kingdom, or

(b) if the property is comprised in a settlement, in the case of which the settlor–

(i) is not a formerly domiciled resident for the tax year in which that time falls, and

(ii) was domiciled outside the United Kingdom when the property became comprised in the settlement;

"formerly domiciled resident", in relation to a tax year, means a person–

(a) who was born in the United Kingdom,

(b) whose domicile of origin was in the United Kingdom,

(c) who was resident in the United Kingdom for that tax year, and

(d) who was resident in the United Kingdom for at least one of the two tax years immediately preceding that tax year;

"Government department" includes a Northern Ireland department;

"heritable security" means any security capable of being constituted over any interest in land by disposition or assignation of that interest in security of any debt and of being recorded in the General Register of Sasines;

"HMRC" means Her Majesty's Revenue and Customs;

"immediate post-death interest" means an immediate post-death interest for the purposes of Chapter 2 of Part 3 (see section 49A above);

"incumbrance" includes any heritable security, or other debt or payment secured upon heritage;

"Inland Revenue charge" means a charge imposed by virtue of section 237 above;

"land" does not include any estate, interest or right by way of mortgage or other security;

"local authority" has the meaning given by section 1130 of the Corporation Tax Act 2010;

"member", in relation to a registered pension scheme, has the same meaning as in Part 4 of the Finance Act 2004 (see section 151 of that Act);

"mortgage" includes a heritable security and a security constituted over any interest in movable property;

"nil-rate band maximum" has the meaning given by section 8A(7);

"open-ended investment company" means an open-ended investment company within the meaning given by section 236 of the Financial Services and Markets Act 2000 which is incorporated in the United Kingdom;

"personal representatives" includes any person by whom or on whose behalf application for a grant of administration or for the resealing of a grant made outside the United Kingdom is made, and any such person as mentioned in section 199(4)(a) above;

"property" includes rights and interests of any description but does not include a settlement power;

"public display" means display to which the public are admitted, on payment or not, but does not include display with a view to sale;

"purchaser" means a purchaser in good faith for consideration in money or money's worth other than a nominal consideration and includes a lessee, mortgagee or other person who for such consideration acquires an interest in the property in question;

"quoted", in relation to any shares or securities, means listed on a recognised stock exchange or dealt in on the Unlisted Securities Market and **"unquoted"**, in relation to any shares or securities, means neither so listed nor so dealt in.

"registered pension scheme" has the same meaning as in Part 4 of the Finance Act 2004;

"reversionary interest" has the meaning given by section 47 above;

"section 615(3) scheme" means a superannuation fund to which section 615(3) of the Taxes Act applies;

"settlement" and **"settled property"** shall be construed in accordance with section 43 above;

"settlement power" has the meaning given by section 47A above;

"settlor" shall be construed in accordance with section 44 above;

"step-child", in relation to a civil partner, shall be construed in accordance with section 246 of the Civil Partnership Act 2004;

"tax" means capital transfer tax;

"the Taxes Act 1970" means the Income and Corporation Taxes Act 1970;

"the Taxes Act 1988" means the Income and Corporation Taxes Act 1988;

"the TCEA 2007" means the Tribunals, Courts and Enforcement Act 2007;

"transitional serial interest" means an immediate post-death interest for the purposes of Chapter 2 of Part 3 (see section 49A above);

"the tribunal" means the First-tier Tribunal or, where determined by or under Tribunal Procedure Rules, the Upper Tribunal,

"trustee" shall be construed in accordance with section 45 above; and

"the 1992 Act" means the Taxation of Chargeable Gains Act 1992.

History – In the definition of "authorised unit trust" the words "the Income Tax Acts (see section 1007 of the Income Tax Act 2007)" substituted for the words "section 469 of the Taxes Act 1988 (see subsection (7) of that section)" by ITA 2007, s. 1027 and Sch. 1, para. 271, with effect from 6 April 2007.

Definition of "authorised unit trust" inserted by FA 2003, s. 186(6), with effect in relation to transfers of value or other events occurring on or after 16 October 2002.

In s. 272, the definitions of "charity" and "charitable" omitted by FA 2010, s. 30 and Sch. 6, para. 10, with effect in relation to a transfer of value (as defined at IHTA 1984, s. 3) made on or after 1 April 2012 (SI 2012/736, art. 5).

Definition of "disabled person's interest" inserted by FA 2006, s. 156 and Sch. 20, para. 28, with effect from 22 March 2006.

In the definition of "excluded property" the words "and Schedule A1" inserted by F(No. 2)A 2017, s. 33 and Sch. 10, para. 8, with effect in relation to times after 5 April 2017 subject to Sch. 10, para. 9 and 10.

Definition of "foreign-owned" substituted by F(No. 2)A 2017, s. 30(8)(a), with effect in relation to times after 5 April 2017 subject to s. 30(10)–(17). Former definition read as follows:

> "**"foreign-owned"**, in relation to property, means property in the case of which the person beneficially entitled to it is domiciled outside the United Kingdom or, if the property is comprised in a settlement, in the case of which the settlor was domiciled outside the United Kingdom when the property became comprised in the settlement;"

Former definition of "foreign-owned" inserted by SI 2009/730, art. 13(4), with effect in relation to deaths and ten-year anniversaries occurring on or after 6 April 2009.

Definition of "formerly domiciled resident" inserted by F(No. 2)A 2017, s. 30(8)(b), with effect in relation to times after 5 April 2017 *subject to s. 30(10)–(17).*

Definition of "HMRC" inserted by SI 2009/56, art. 3 and Sch. 1, para. 125(3), with effect from 1 April 2009, subject to transitional and saving provisions in SI 2009/56, Sch. 3.

Definition of "immediate post-death interest" inserted by FA 2006, s. 156 and Sch. 20, para. 28, with effect from 22 March 2006.

In the definition of "local authority", the words "section 1130 of the Corporation Tax Act 2010" substituted for the words "section 842A of the Taxes Act 1988" by SI 2013/463, art. 2(1), with effect from 1 April 2013.

In the definition of "local authority", reference to "842A" substituted by FA 1990, s. 127 and Sch. 18, para. 4, with deemed effect from 1 April 1990.
Definition of "member" inserted by FA 2006, s. 160 and Sch. 22, para. 10(2), with effect from 6 April 2006.
Definition of "nil-rate band maximum" inserted by FA 2008, s. 10 and Sch. 4, para. 7, with effect from 9 October 2007.
Definition of "open-ended investent company" inserted by FA 2003, s. 186(7), with effect in relation to transfers of value or other events occurring on or after 16 October 2002.
In the definition of "property" the words "but does not include a settlement power" inserted by FA 2002, s. 119(4). The amendment made by FA 2002, s. 119(4)(b) has effect in relation to transfers of value on or after 17 April 2002. This amendment is deemed always to have effect (subject to and in accordance with the other provisions of the IHTA 1984) for the purpose of determining the value, immediately before his or her death, of the estate of any person who died before 17 April 2002, for the purposes of the transfer of value which that person is treated by section 4(1) of that Act as having made immediately before his or her death.
Definition of "public display" inserted by SI 2009/730, art. 13(4), with effect in relation to deaths and ten-year anniversaries occurring on or after 6 April 2009.
Definition of "quoted" inserted by FA 1987, Sch. 8, para. 17, in relation to transfers of value made, and other events occurring, on or after 17 March 1987. The references in that definition to "listed" were substituted for the previous word "quoted" by FA 1996, s. 199 and Sch. 38, para. 2, with effect in relation to transfers of value on or after 1April 1996 and, for the purposes of any charge to tax by reason of an event occurring on or after 1 April 1996, in relation to transfers of value before that date.
Definition of "registered pension scheme" inserted by FA 2004, s. 203(6), with effect from 6 April 2006 (FA 2004, s. 284(1)).
Definition of "scheme administrator" omitted by FA 2011, s. 65 and Sch. 16, para. 57, with effect in relation to deaths occurring on or after 6 April 2011.
Former definition of "scheme administrator" inserted by FA 2006, s. 160 and Sch. 22, para. 10(3), with effect from 6 April 2006.
Definition of "section 615(3) scheme" inserted by FA 2004, s. 203(6), with effect from 6 April 2006 (FA 2004, s. 284(1)).
Definition of "settlement power" inserted by FA 2002, s. 119(4)(a). The amendment made by FA 2002, s. 119(4) has effect in relation to transfers of value on or after 17 April 2002. This amendment is deemed always to have effect (subject to and in accordance with the other provisions of IHTA 1984) for the purpose of determining the value, immediately before his or her death, of the estate of any person who died before 17 April 2002, for the purposes of the transfer of value which that person is treated by section 4(1) of that Act as having made immediately before his or her death.
Definition of "Special Commissioners" omitted by SI 2009/56, art. 3 and Sch. 1, para. 125(2), with effect from 1 April 2009, subject to transitional and saving provisions in SI 2009/56, Sch. 3. Former definition read as follows:

""**Special Commissioners**" has the same meaning as in the Taxes Management Act 1970;"

Definition of "step-child" inserted by SI 2005/3229, reg. 38, with effect from 5 December 2005 (see Note below).
Definition of "transitional serial interest" inserted by FA 2006, s. 156 and Sch. 20, para. 28, with effect from 22 March 2006.
Definition of "the TCEA 2007" inserted by SI 2009/56, art. 3 and Sch. 1, para. 125(3), with effect from 1 April 2009, subject to transitional and saving provisions in SI 2009/56, Sch. 3.
Definition of "the tribunal" inserted by SI 2009/56, art. 3 and Sch. 1, para. 125(3), with effect from 1 April 2009, subject to transitional and saving provisions in SI 2009/56, Sch. 3.
Definition of "the 1992 Act" inserted by TCGA 1992, s. 290 and Sch. 10, para. 8(13).
See ICTA 1988, Sch. 29, para. 32 for substitution of reference to that Act in the definition of "local authority", and of the definitions of "the Taxes Act 1970" and "the Taxes Act 1988".

Cross references – FA 1986, s. 100(1)(b): any reference to capital transfer tax (except where it relates to a liability to tax arising before 25 July 1986) has effect as a reference to inheritance tax.

Notes – For the purposes of the definition of "step-child", s. 246 of the Civil Partnership Act 2004 reads as follows:

"**246 Interpretation of statutory references to stepchildren etc.**

246(1) In any provision to which this section applies, references to a stepchild or step-parent of a person (here, "A"), and cognate expressions, are to be read as follows–

A's stepchild includes a person who is the child of A's civil partner (but is not A's child);
A's step-parent includes a person who is the civil partner of A's parent (but is not A's parent);
A's stepdaughter includes a person who is the daughter of A's civil partner (but is not A's daughter);
A's stepson includes a person who is the son of A's civil partner (but is not A's son);
A's stepfather includes a person who is the civil partner of A's father (but is not A's parent);
A's stepmother includes a person who is the civil partner of A's mother (but is not A's parent);
A's stepbrother includes a person who is the son of the civil partner of A's parent (but is not the son of either of A's parents);
A's stepsister includes a person who is the daughter of the civil partner of A's parent (but is not the daughter of either of A's parents).

246(2) For the purposes of any provision to which this section applies–

"brother-in-law" includes civil partner's brother,
"daughter-in-law" includes daughter's civil partner,
"father-in-law" includes civil partner's father,
"mother-in-law" includes civil partner's mother,
"parent-in-law" includes civil partner's parent,
"sister-in-law" includes civil partner's sister, and
"son-in-law" includes son's civil partner."

SUPPLEMENTARY

273 Transition from estate duty

273 Schedule 6 to this Act shall have effect.

274 Commencement

274(1) This Act shall come into force on 1st January 1985 but shall not apply to transfers of value made before that date or to other events before that date on which capital transfer tax is chargeable or would be chargeable but for an exemption, exception or relief.

274(2) Subsection (1) above shall have effect subject to section 275 below, to Schedule 7 to this Act and to any other provision to the contrary.

Cross references – FA 1986, s. 100(1)(b): any reference to capital transfer tax (except where it relates to a liability to tax arising before 25 July 1986) has effect as a reference to inheritance tax.

275 Continuity and construction of references to old and new law

275(1) The continuity of the operation of the law relating to capital transfer tax shall not be affected by the substitution of this Act for the repealed enactments.

275(2) Any reference, whether express or implied, in any enactment, instrument or document (including this Act and any enactment amended by Schedule 8 to this Act) to, or to things done or falling to be done under or for the purposes of, any provision of this Act shall, if and so far as the nature of the reference permits, be construed as including, in relation to the times, circumstances or purposes in relation to which the corresponding provision in the repealed enactments has or had effect, a reference to, or as the case may be, to things done or falling to be done under or for the purposes of, that corresponding provision.

275(3) Any reference, whether express or implied, in any enactment, instrument or document (including the repealed enactments and enactments, instruments and documents passed or made after the passing of this Act) to, or to things done or falling to be done under or for the purposes of, any of the repealed enactments shall, if and so far as the nature of the reference permits, be construed as including, in relation to the times, circumstances or purposes in relation to which the corresponding provision of this Act has effect, a reference to, or as the case may be, to things done or falling to be done under or for the purposes of, that corresponding provision.

275(4) Subsection (2) above shall have effect without prejudice to section 17(2) of the Interpretation Act 1978.

275(5) In this section **"the repealed enactments"** means the enactments repealed by this Act.

Cross references – FA 1986, s. 100(1)(b): any reference to capital transfer tax (except where it relates to a liability to tax arising before 25 July 1986) has effect as a reference to inheritance tax.

Notes – Interpretation Act 1978, s. 17(2):

"**17(2)** Where an Act repeals and re-enacts, with or without modification, a previous enactment then, unless the contrary intention appears–

(a) any reference in any other enactment to the enactment so repealed shall be construed as a reference to the provision re-enacted;

(b) in so far as any subordinate legislation made or other thing done under the enactment so repealed, or having effect as if so made or done, could have been made or done under the provision re-enacted, it shall have effect as if made or done under that provision."

278 Short title

278 This Act may be cited as the Inheritance Tax Act 1984.

History – Words "Inheritance Tax Act 1984" substituted by FA 1986, s. 100(1)(a).

Cross references – FA 1986, s. 100(1)(b): any reference to capital transfer tax (except where it relates to a liability to tax arising before 25 July 1986) has effect as a reference to inheritance tax.

SCHEDULES

SCHEDULE A1 – NON-EXCLUDED OVERSEAS PROPERTY

History – Sch. A1 inserted by F(No. 2)A 2017, s. 33 and Sch. 10, para. 1, with effect in relation to times after 5 April 2017 subject to Sch. 10, para. 9 and 10.

Part 1 – Overseas Property with Value Attributable to UK Residential Property

INTRODUCTORY

1 Property is not excluded property by virtue of section 6(1) or 48(3)(a) if and to the extent that paragraph 2 or 3 applies to it.

CLOSE COMPANY AND PARTNERSHIP INTERESTS

2(1) This paragraph applies to an interest in a close company or in a partnership, if and to the extent that the interest meets the condition in sub-paragraph (2).

2(2) The condition is that the value of the interest is–

(a) directly attributable to a UK residential property interest, or

(b) attributable to a UK residential property interest by virtue only of one or more of the following–

(i) an interest in a close company;

(ii) an interest in a partnership;

(iii) property to which paragraph 3 (loans) applies.

2(3) For the purposes of sub-paragraphs (1) and (2) disregard–

(a) an interest in a close company, if the value of the interest is less than 5% of the total value of all the interests in the close company;

(b) an interest in a partnership, if the value of the interest is less than 5% of the total value of all the interests in the partnership.

2(4) In determining under sub-paragraph (3) whether to disregard a person's interest in a close company or partnership, treat the value of the person's interest as increased by the value of any connected person's interest in the close company or partnership.

2(5) In determining whether or to what extent the value of an interest in a close company or in a partnership is attributable to a UK residential property interest for the purposes of sub-paragraph (1), liabilities of a close company or partnership are to be attributed rateably to all of its property, whether or not they would otherwise be attributed to any particular property.

LOANS

3 This paragraph applies to–

(a) the rights of a creditor in respect of a loan which is a relevant loan (see paragraph 4), and

(b) money or money's worth held or otherwise made available as security, collateral or guarantee for a loan which is a relevant loan, to the extent that it does not exceed the value of the relevant loan.

4(1) For the purposes of this Schedule a loan is a relevant loan if and to the extent that money or money's worth made available under the loan is used to finance, directly or indirectly–

(a) the acquisition by an individual, a partnership or the trustees of a settlement of–

(i) a UK residential property interest, or

(ii) property to which paragraph 2 to any extent applies, or

(b) the acquisition by an individual, a partnership or the trustees of a settlement of an interest in a close company or a partnership ("the intermediary") and the acquisition by the intermediary of property within paragraph (a)(i) or (ii).

4(2) In this paragraph references to money or money's worth made available under a loan or sale proceeds being used **"indirectly"** to finance the acquisition of something include the money or money's worth or sale proceeds being used to finance–

(a) the acquisition of any property the proceeds of sale of which are used directly or indirectly to finance the acquisition of that thing, or

(b) the making, or repayment, of a loan to finance the acquisition of that thing.

4(3) In this paragraph references to the acquisition of a UK residential property interest by an individual, a partnership, the trustees of a settlement or a close company include the maintenance, or an enhancement, of the value of a UK residential property interest which is (as the case may be) the property of the individual, property comprised in the settlement or property of the partnership or close company.

4(4) Where the UK residential property interest by virtue of which a loan is a relevant loan is disposed of, the loan ceases to be a relevant loan.

4(5) Where a proportion of the UK residential property interest by virtue of which a loan is a relevant loan is disposed of, the loan ceases to be a relevant loan by the same proportion.

4(6) In this Schedule, references to a loan include an acknowledgment of debt by a person or any other arrangement under which a debt arises; and in such a case references to money or money's worth made available under the loan are to the amount of the debt.

Part 2 – Supplementary

DISPOSALS AND REPAYMENTS

5(1) This paragraph applies to–

(a) property which constitutes consideration in money or money's worth for the disposal of property to which paragraph 2 or paragraph 3(a) applies;

(b) any money or money's worth paid in respect of a creditor's rights falling within paragraph 3(a);

(c) any property directly or indirectly representing property within paragraph (a) or (b).

5(2) If and to the extent that this paragraph applies to any property–

(a) for the two-year period it is not excluded property by virtue of section 6(1), (1A) or (2) or 48(3)(a), (3A) or (4), and

(b) if it is held in a qualifying foreign currency account within the meaning of section 157 (non-residents' bank accounts), that section does not apply to it for the two-year period.

5(3) The two-year period is the period of two years beginning with the date of–

(a) the disposal referred to in sub-paragraph (1)(a), or

(b) the payment referred to in sub-paragraph (1)(b).

5(4) The value of any property within sub-paragraph (1)(c) is to be treated as not exceeding the relevant amount.

5(5) The relevant amount is–

(a) where the property within sub-paragraph (1)(c) directly or indirectly represents property within sub-paragraph (1)(a) ("the consideration"), the value of the consideration at the time of the disposal referred to in that sub-paragraph, and

(b) where the property within sub-paragraph (1)(c) directly or indirectly represents property within sub-paragraph (1)(b), the amount of the money or money's worth paid as mentioned in that sub-paragraph.

TAX AVOIDANCE ARRANGEMENTS

6(1) In determining whether or to what extent property situated outside the United Kingdom is excluded property, no regard is to be had to any arrangements the purpose or one of the main purposes of which is to secure a tax advantage by avoiding or minimising the effect of paragraph 1 or 5.

6(2) In this paragraph–

"tax advantage" has the meaning given in section 208 of the Finance Act 2013;

"arrangements" includes any scheme, transaction or series of transactions, agreement or understanding (whether or not legally enforceable and whenever entered into) and any associated operations.

DOUBLE TAXATION RELIEF ARRANGEMENTS

7(1) Nothing in any double taxation relief arrangements made with the government of a territory outside the United Kingdom is to be read as preventing a person from being liable for any amount of inheritance tax by virtue of paragraph 1 or 5 in relation to any chargeable transfer if under the law of that territory–

(a) no tax of a character similar to inheritance tax is charged on that chargeable transfer, or

(b) a tax of a character similar to inheritance tax is charged in relation to that chargeable transfer at an effective rate of 0% (otherwise than by virtue of a relief or exemption).

7(2) In this paragraph–

"double taxation relief arrangements" means arrangements having effect under section 158(1);

"effective rate" means the rate found by expressing the tax chargeable as a percentage of the amount by reference to which it is charged.

Part 3 – Interpretation

UK RESIDENTIAL PROPERTY INTEREST

8(1) In this Schedule **"UK residential property interest"** means an interest in UK land–

(a) where the land consists of a dwelling,

(b) where and to the extent that the land includes a dwelling, or

(c) where the interest subsists under a contract for an off-plan purchase.

8(2) For the purposes of sub-paragraph (1)(b), the extent to which land includes a dwelling is to be determined on a just and reasonable basis.

8(3) In this paragraph–

"interest in UK land" has the meaning given by paragraph 2 of Schedule B1 to the 1992 Act (and the power in sub-paragraph (5) of that paragraph applies for the purposes of this Schedule);

"the land", in relation to an interest in UK land which is an interest subsisting for the benefit of land, is a reference to the land for the benefit of which the interest subsists;

"dwelling" has the meaning given by paragraph 4 of Schedule B1 to the 1992 Act (and the power in paragraph 5 of that Schedule applies for the purposes of this Schedule);

"contract for an off-plan purchase" has the meaning given by paragraph 1(6) of Schedule B1 to the 1992 Act.

CLOSE COMPANIES

9(1) In this Schedule–

"close company" means a company within the meaning of the Corporation Tax Acts which is (or would be if resident in the United Kingdom) a close company for the purposes of those Acts;

references to an interest in a close company are to the rights and interests that a participator in a close company has in that company.

9(2) In this paragraph–

"participator", in relation to a close company, means any person who is (or would be if the company were resident in the United Kingdom) a participator in relation to that company within the meaning given by section 454 of the Corporation Tax Act 2010;

references to rights and interests in a close company include references to rights and interests in the assets of the company available for distribution among the participators in the event of a winding-up or in any other circumstances.

PARTNERSHIPS

10 In this Schedule **"partnership"** means–

(a) a partnership within the Partnership Act 1890,

(b) a limited partnership registered under the Limited Partnerships Act 1907,

(c) a limited liability partnership formed under the Limited Liability Partnerships Act 2000 or the Limited Liability Partnerships Act (Northern Ireland) 2002, or

(d) a firm or entity of a similar character to either of those mentioned in paragraph (a) or (b) formed under the law of a country or territory outside the United Kingdom.

SCHEDULE 1 – TABLE OF RATES OF TAX

Section 7

TABLE OF RATES OF TAX

Portion of value		*Rate of tax*
Lower limit (£)	Upper limit (£)	Per cent.
0	325,000	Nil
325,000	–	40

History – Table for 2009–10 in relation to chargeable transfers made on or after 6 April 2009 substituted by FA 2006, s. 155(1) and extended in relation to chargeable transfers made on or after 6 April 2010 by FA 2010, s. 8(1).
Previously substituted by FA 2006, s. 155(1) in relation to chargeable transfers made on or after 6 April 2008. Previously substituted by FA 2005, s. 81 in relation to chargeable transfers made on or after 6 April 2007. Previously substituted by FA 2005, s. 98(1) in relation to chargeable transfers made on or after 6 April 2006. Previously substituted by FA 2005, s. 98(1) in relation to chargeable transfers made on or after 6 April 2005. Previously substituted by SI 2004/771 in relation to chargeable transfers made on or after 6 April 2004. Previously substituted by SI 2003/841 with effect for any chargeable transfer made on or after 6 April 2003. Previously substituted by FA 2002, s. 118(1) and by SI 2002/701, with effect for any chargeable transfer made on or after 6 April 2002. Previously substituted by SI 2001/639, with effect for any chargeable transfer made on or after 6 April 2001, by SI 2000/803, with effect for any chargeable transfer made on or after 6 April 2000, by SI 1999/596, with effect for any chargeable transfer made on or after 6 April 1999, by SI 1998/756, with effect for any chargeable transfer made on or after 6 April 1998 and by FA 1997, s. 93, with effect for any chargeable transfer made on or after 6 April 1997 (s. 8 disapplied as respects the difference in the retail prices index between September 1995 and September 1996).

Cross references – S. 8: indexation of rate and bands on or after 6 April in each year (disapplication of s. 8(1) for chargeable transfers made in the year 1997–98, by virtue of FA 1997, s. 93.
FA 1986, Sch. 19, para. 40(1): transitional – transfer of value occurring before, and death or other event occurring after, 18 March 1986.

SCHEDULE 1A – GIFTS TO CHARITIES ETC: TAX CHARGED AT LOWER RATE

APPLICATION OF THIS SCHEDULE

1(1) This Schedule applies if–

(a) a chargeable transfer is made (under section 4) on the death of a person ("D"), and

(b) all or part of the value transferred by the chargeable transfer is chargeable to tax at a rate other than nil per cent.

1(2) The part of the value transferred that is chargeable to tax at a rate other than nil per cent is referred to in this Schedule as "TP".

THE RELIEF

2(1) If the charitable giving condition is met–

(a) the tax charged on the part of TP that qualifies for the lower rate of tax is to be charged at the lower rate of tax, and

(b) the tax charged on any remaining part of TP is to be charged at the rate at which it would (but for this Schedule) have been charged on the whole of TP in accordance with section 7.

2(2) For the purposes of this paragraph, the charitable giving condition is met if, for one or more components of the estate (taking each component separately), the donated amount is at least 10% of the baseline amount.

2(3) Paragraph 3 defines the components of the estate.

2(4) Paragraphs 4 and 5 explain how to calculate the donated amount and the baseline amount for each component.

2(5) The part of TP that **"qualifies for the lower rate of tax"** is the part attributable to all the property in each of the components for which the donated amount is at least 10% of the baseline amount.

2(6) The lower rate of tax is 36%.

THE COMPONENTS OF THE ESTATE

3(1) For the purposes of paragraph 2, the components of the estate are–

(a) the survivorship component,

(b) the settled property component, and

(c) the general component.

3(2) The survivorship component is made up of all the property comprised in the estate that, immediately before D's death, was joint (or common) property liable to pass on D's death–

(a) by survivorship (in England and Wales or Northern Ireland),

(b) under a special destination (in Scotland), or

(c) by or under anything corresponding to survivorship or a special destination under the law of a country or territory outside the United Kingdom.

3(3) The settled property component is made up of all the settled property comprised in the estate in which there subsisted, immediately before D's death, an interest in possession to which D was beneficially entitled immediately before death.

3(4) The general component is made up of all the property comprised in the estate other than–

(a) property in the survivorship component,

(b) property in the settled property component, and

(c) property that forms part of the estate by virtue of section 102(3) of the Finance Act 1986 (gifts with reservation).

THE DONATED AMOUNT

4 The donated amount, for a component of the estate, is so much of the value transferred by the relevant transfer as (in total) is attributable to property that–

(a) forms part of that component, and

(b) is property in relation to which section 23(1) applies.

THE BASELINE AMOUNT

5 The baseline amount, for a component of the estate, is the amount calculated in accordance with the following steps–

Step 1

Determine the part of the value transferred by the chargeable transfer that is attributable to property in that component.

Step 2

Deduct from the amount determined under Step 1 the appropriate proportion of the available nil-rate band.

"The appropriate proportion" is a proportion equal to the proportion that the amount determined under Step 1 bears to the value transferred by the chargeable transfer as a whole.

"The available nil-rate band" is the amount (if any) by which–

(a) the nil-rate band maximum (increased, where applicable, in accordance with section 8A), exceeds

(b) the sum of the values transferred by previous chargeable transfers made by D in the period of 7 years ending with the date of the relevant transfer.

Step 3

Add to the amount determined under Step 2 an amount equal to so much of the value transferred by the relevant transfer as (in total) is attributable to property that–

(a) forms part of that component, and

(b) is property in relation to which section 23(1) applies.

The result is the baseline amount for that component.

RULES FOR DETERMINING WHETHER CHARITABLE GIVING CONDITION IS MET

6(1) For the purpose of calculating the donated amount and the baseline amount, any amount to be arrived at in accordance with section 38(3) or (5) is to be arrived at assuming the rate of tax is the lower rate of tax (see paragraph 2(6)).

6(2) For the purpose of calculating the donated amount, section 39A does not apply to a specific gift of property in relation to which section 23(1) applies (but that section does apply to such a gift for the purpose of calculating the baseline amount).

6(3) Subject to sub-paragraphs (1) and (2), the provisions of this Act apply for the purpose of calculating the donated amount and the baseline amount as for the purpose of calculating the tax to be charged on the value transferred by the chargeable transfer.

ELECTION TO MERGE PARTS OF THE ESTATE

7(1) An election may be made under this paragraph if, for a component of the estate, the donated amount is at least 10% of the baseline amount.

7(2) That component is referred to as **"the qualifying component"**.

7(3) The effect of the election is that the qualifying component and one or more eligible parts of the estate (as specified in the election) are to be treated for the purposes of this Schedule as if they were a single component.

7(4) Accordingly, if the donated amount for that deemed single component is at least 10% of the baseline amount for it, the property in that component is to be included in the part of TP that qualifies for the lower rate of tax.

7(5) In relation to the qualifying component–

(a) each one of the other two components of the estate is an **"eligible part"** of the estate, and

(b) all the property that forms part of the estate by virtue of section 102(3) of the Finance Act 1986 (gifts with reservation) is also an **"eligible part"** of the estate.

7(6) The election must be made by all those who are appropriate persons with respect to the qualifying component and each of the eligible parts to be treated as a single component.

7(7) **"Appropriate persons"** means–

(a) with respect to the survivorship component, all those to whom the property in that component passes on D's death (or, if they have subsequently died, their personal representatives),

(b) with respect to the settled property component, the trustees of all the settled property in that component,

(c) with respect to the general component, all the personal representatives of D or, if there are none, all those who are liable for the tax attributable to the property in that component, and

(d) with respect to property within paragraph (b) of sub-paragraph (5), all those in whom the property within that paragraph is vested when the election is to be made.

OPTING OUT

8(1) If an election is made under this paragraph in relation to a component of the estate, this Schedule is to apply as if the donated amount for that component were less than 10% of the baseline amount for it (whether or not it actually is).

8(2) The election must be made by all those who are appropriate persons (as defined in paragraph 7(7)) with respect to the component.

ELECTIONS: PROCEDURE

9(1) An election under this Schedule must be made by notice in writing to HMRC within two years after D's death.

9(2) An election under this Schedule may be withdrawn by notice in writing to HMRC given–

(a) by all those who would be entitled to make such an election, and

(b) no later than the end of the period of two years and one month after D's death.

9(3) An officer of Revenue and Customs may agree in a particular case to extend the time limit in sub-paragraph (1) or (2)(b) by such period as the officer may allow.

GENERAL INTERPRETATION

10 In this Schedule, in relation to D–

"the chargeable transfer" means the chargeable transfer mentioned in paragraph 1(1);

"the estate" means D's estate immediately before death;

"the relevant transfer" means the transfer of value that D is treated (under section 4) as having made immediately before death.

History – Sch. 1A inserted by FA 2012, s. 209 and Sch. 33, para. 1, with effect in cases where D's death occurs on or after 6 April 2012.

SCHEDULE 2 – PROVISIONS APPLYING ON REDUCTION OF TAX

Section 9

Cross references – FA 1986, Sch. 19, para. 40(1): transitional – transfer of value occurring before, and death or other event occurring after, 18 March 1986.

INTERPRETATION

1 In this Schedule–

(a) references to a reduction are to a reduction of tax by the substitution of a new Table in Schedule 1 to this Act, and

(b) references to something happening before or after a reduction are to its happening before or, as the case may be, on or after the date on which the Table giving effect to the reduction comes into force.

History – The words "a new Table" in para. 1(a), and "the Table" and "comes" in para. 1(b), were substituted by FA 1986, s. 101 and Sch. 19, para. 37(1), (2), with respect to transfers of value made, and other events occurring, on or after 18 March 1986.

DEATH WITHIN SEVEN YEARS OF POTENTIALLY EXEMPT TRANSFER

1A Where a person who has made a potentially exempt transfer before a reduction dies after that reduction (or after that and one or more subsequent reductions) and within the period of seven years beginning with the date of the transfer, tax shall be chargeable by reason of the transfer proving to be a chargeable transfer only if, and to the extent that, it would have been so chargeable if the Table in Schedule 1 as substituted by that reduction (or by the most recent of those reductions) had applied to that transfer.

History – Para. 1A inserted by FA 1986, s. 101 and Sch. 19, para. 37(3), with respect to transfers of value made, and other events occurring, on or after 18 March 1986.

DEATH WITHIN SEVEN YEARS OF CHARGEABLE TRANSFER

2 Where a person who has made a chargeable transfer (other than a potentially exempt transfer) before a reduction dies after that reduction (or after that and one or more subsequent reductions) and within seven years of the transfer, additional tax shall be chargeable by reason of his death only if, and to the extent that, it would have been so chargeable if the Table in Schedule 1 as substituted by that reduction (or by the most recent of those reductions) had applied to that transfer.

History – In para. 2 the words "seven years" and "the Table" were substituted, the words "(other than a potentially exempt transfer)" were inserted, and words which preceded "the tables" were repealed, by FA 1986, s. 101 and Sch. 19, para. 37(1), (4), with respect to transfers of value made, and other events occurring, on or after 18 March 1986.

Cross references – FA 1986, Sch. 19, para. 44: modifications of para. 2 in relation to a death on or after 18 March 1986 in a case where *the chargeable transfer* was made before that date.

SETTLEMENT WITHOUT INTEREST IN POSSESSION

3 Where tax is chargeable under section 65 of this Act on any occasion after a reduction and the rate at which it is charged is determined under section 69 by reference to the rate that was (or would have been) charged under section 64 on an occasion before that reduction (or before that and one or more other reductions), the rate charged on the later occasion shall be determined as if the Table in Schedule 1 as substituted by that reduction (or by the most recent of those reductions) had been in force on the earlier occasion.

History – In para. 3, the words "The Table" were substituted, and the words "the second of" before the former words "the Tables" were omitted, by FA 1986, s. 101 and Sch. 19, para. 37(1), (5), with respect to transfers of value made, and other events occurring, on or after 18 March 1986.

Cross references – S. 64: ten-year anniversary charge on discretionary trusts.
S. 65: charges on discretionary trusts other than on ten-year anniversaries.
S. 69: rate of tax on charges on discretionary trusts between ten-year anniversaries.
FA 1986, Sch. 19, para. 43(3): transitional provisions where rate of tax on an occasion on or after 18 March 1986 falls to be determined with reference to a ten-year anniversary falling before that date – modifications of para. 3.

DISPOSAL OF TREES ETC. FOLLOWING EXEMPTION ON DEATH

4 Where the value of any trees or underwood has been left out of account under Chapter III of Part V of this Act in determining the value transferred by the chargeable transfer made on a death before a reduction and tax is chargeable under section 126 on a disposal of the trees or underwood after that reduction (or after that and one or more subsequent reductions) the rate or rates mentioned in section 128 shall be determined as if the Table in Schedule 1 as substituted by that reduction (or by the most recent of those reductions) had applied to that transfer.

History – In para. 4 the words "the Table" were substituted, and words before the former words "the Tables" were omitted, by FA 1986, s. 101 and Sch. 19, para. 37(1), (6), with respect to transfers of value made, and other events occurring, on or after 18 March 1986.

Cross references – S. 128: rate of charge on disposal of trees or underwood.
FA 1986, Sch. 19, para. 45: modifications of para. 4 in relation to a disposal of trees or underwood on or after 18 March 1986 where the death occurred before that date.

CONDITIONALLY EXEMPT TRANSFERS

5 Where tax is chargeable under section 32 or 32A of this Act by reason of a chargeable event occurring after a reduction and the rate or rates at which it is charged fall to be determined under the provisions of section 33(1)(b)(ii) by reference to a death which occurred before that reduction (or before that and one or more other reductions) those provisions shall apply as if the Table in Schedule 1 as substituted by that reduction (or by the most recent of those reductions) had been in force at the time of the death.

History – In para. 5, the words "or 32A" inserted by FA 1985, Sch. 26, para. 5 in relation to events occurring after 18 March 1985.
In para. 5 the words "The Table" were substituted by FA 1986, s. 101 and Sch. 19, para. 37(1), with respect to transfers of value made, and other events occurring, on or after 18 March 1986.

Cross references – S. 33(1)(b)(ii): rate of charge where tax is payable on first occurrence of a chargeable event in respect of property previously the subject of a conditionally exempt transfer.

MAINTENANCE FUNDS FOR HISTORIC BUILDINGS

6 Where tax is chargeable under paragraph 8 of Schedule 4 to this Act on any occasion after a reduction and the rate at which it is charged falls to be determined under paragraph 14 of that Schedule by reference to a death which occurred before that reduction (or before that and one or more other reductions) paragraph 14 shall apply as if the Table in Schedule 1 as substituted by that reduction (or by the most recent of those reductions) had been in force at the time of the death.

History – In para. 6 the words "the Table" were substituted by FA 1986, s. 101 and Sch. 19, para. 37(1), with respect to transfers of value made, and other events occurring, on or after 18 March 1986.

Cross references – Sch. 4, para. 14: rate of tax where property previously comprised in a maintenance fund.

RELEVANT DEPENDANT WITH PENSION FUND INHERITED FROM MEMBER OVER 75

6A [Omitted by FA 2007, s. 69 and Sch. 19, para. 27; and repealed by FA 2007, s. 114 and Sch. 27, Pt. 3(1).]

History – Para. 6A omitted and repealed by FA 2007, s. 69 and Sch. 19, para. 27, and FA 2007, s. 114 and Sch. 27, Pt. 3(1) with effect in relation to deaths, cases where scheme administrators become aware of deaths and cessations of dependency occurring on or after 6 April 2007. Para. 6A read as follows:
"**6A** Where tax is chargeable under section 151B of this Act on an occasion after a reduction and the rate or rates at which it is charged fall to be determined by reference to the death of a person which occurred before that reduction (or before that and one or more other reductions) that section applies as if the Table in Schedule 1 as substituted by that reduction (or by the most recent of those reductions) had been in force at the time of that person's death.".

7 [Repealed by FA 1986, s. 114 and Sch. 23, Pt. X, where the donee's transfer was made on or after 18 March 1986.]

SCHEDULE 3 – GIFTS FOR NATIONAL PURPOSES, ETC.

Sections 25, 32, 230 etc.

Cross references – FA 2016, s. 96(1)–(3): transfer of Sch. 3 approval function to the Treasury, with effect in relation to approvals given on or after 15 September 2016.

The National Gallery.

The British Museum.

The National Museums of Scotland.

The National Museum of Wales.

The Ulster Museum.

Any other similar national institution which exists wholly or mainly for the purpose of preserving for the public benefit a collection of scientific, historic or artistic interest and which is approved for the purposes of this Schedule by the Treasury.

Any museum or art gallery in the United Kingdom which exists wholly or mainly for that purpose and is or has been maintained by a local authority or university in the United Kingdom.

Any library the main function of which is to serve the needs of teaching and research at a university in the United Kingdom.

The Historic Buildings and Monuments Commission for England.

The National Trust for Places of Historic Interest or Natural Beauty.

The National Trust for Scotland for Places of Historic Interest or Natural Beauty.

The National Art Collections Fund.

The Trustees of the National Heritage Memorial Fund.

The National Endowment for Science, Technology and the Arts.

The Friends of the National Libraries.

The Historic Churches Preservation Trust.

Commission for Rural Communities.

Natural England.

Scottish Natural Heritage.

Countryside Council for Wales.

Any local authority.

Any Government department (including the National Debt Commissioners).

Any university or university college in the United Kingdom.

A health service body, within the meaning of section 986 of the Corporation Tax Act 2010.

History – The entry for "The National Museums of Scotland" substituted by National Heritage (Scotland) Act 1985, Sch. 2, para. 4, with effect from 1 October 1985 (SI 1985/851).

In the entry beginning "Any museum", the words "or has been" inserted by FA 2016, s. 96(4), with effect from 15 September 2016 (Royal Assent).

Reference to the National Endowment for Science, Technology and the Arts inserted by National Lottery Act 1998, s. 24(3), with effect from 2 July 1998.

The entry for "Commission for Rural Communities" inserted by the Natural Environment and Rural Communities Act 2006, s. 105(1) and Sch. 11, Pt. 1, para. 105, with effect from 1 October 2006 (SI 2006/2541, reg. 2).

The entry for "Natural England" inserted by the Natural Environment and Rural Communities Act 2006, s. 105(1) and Sch. 11, Pt. 1, para. 105, with effect from 2 May 2006, by virtue of SI 2006/1176, art. 4.

The entry for "Scottish Natural Heritage" substituted by Natural Heritage (Scotland) Act 1991, s. 4(10) and Sch. 2, para. 9, with effect from 1 April 1992 (SI 1991/2633).

The words "English Nature" revoked inserted by the Natural Environment and Rural Communities Act 2006, s. 105(1) and Sch. 11, Pt. 1, para. 105, with effect from 2 May 2006, for the purposes of the words "Natural England", by virtue of SI 2006/1176, art. 4 and for the purposes of the words "Commission for Rural Communities", with effect from 1 October 2006 (SI 2006/2541, reg. 2).

The words "English Nature" substituted for "Nature Conservancy Council for England" by Countryside and Rights of Way Act 2000, Sch. 8, para. 1, with effect from 31 January 2001.

Nature Conservancy Council for England, Nature Conservancy Council for Scotland, and Countryside Council for Wales, substituted by Environmental Protection Act 1990, s. 128(5) and Sch. 6, para. 25, with effect from 1 April 1991 (SI 1991/685).

In the entry for "health service body", the words "section 986 of the Corporation Tax Act 2010" substituted for the words "section 519A of the Income and Corporation Taxes Act 1988" by CTA 2010, s. 1177 and Sch. 1, para. 192, with effect for corporation tax purposes for accounting periods ending on or after 1 April 2010, and for income tax and capital gains tax purposes for the tax year 2010–11 and subsequent tax years.

The entry for "health service body" added by National Health Service and Community Care Act 1990, s. 61(5), with effect from 17 September 1990 (SI 1990/1329, art. 2(5)).

Cross references – S. 76: exemption for property which ceases to be relevant property within Pt. III, Ch. III on becoming the property of a body within Sch. 3.

FA 1985, s. 95(1): Treasury functions under Pt. II transferred to the Commissioners of Inland Revenue ("the Board") from 25 July 1985.

TCGA 1992, s. 258(2)(a): capital gains tax treatment of property disposed of to a body mentioned in Sch. 3.

SI 2013/489 (not reproduced): for the purposes of the Tax Acts the Natural Resources Body for Wales and the Countryside Council for Wales are to be treated as the same person.

SCHEDULE 4 – MAINTENANCE FUNDS FOR HISTORIC BUILDINGS, ETC.

Sections 27, 58, 77 etc.

Cross references – FA 1985, s. 95(1): Treasury functions under Pt. II transferred to the Commissioners of Inland Revenue ("the Board") from 25 July 1985.

Part I – Treasury Directions

GIVING OF DIRECTIONS

1(1) If the conditions mentioned in paragraph 2(1) below are fulfilled in respect of settled property, the Treasury shall, on a claim made for the purpose, give a direction under this paragraph in respect of the property.

1(2) The Treasury may give a direction under this paragraph in respect of property proposed to be comprised in a settlement or to be held on particular trusts in any case where, if the property were already so comprised or held, they would be obliged to give the direction.

1(3) Property comprised in a settlement by virtue of a transfer of value made before the coming into force of section 94 of the Finance Act 1982 and exempt under section 84 of the Finance Act 1976 shall be treated as property in respect of which a direction has been given under this paragraph.

CONDITIONS

2(1) The conditions referred to in paragraph 1 above are–

(a) that the Treasury are satisfied–

(i) that the trusts on which the property is held comply with the requirements mentioned in paragraph 3 below, and

(ii) that the property is of a character and amount appropriate for the purposes of those trusts; and

(b) that the trustees–

(i) are approved by the Treasury,

(ii) include a trust corporation, a solicitor, an accountant or a member of such other professional body as the Treasury may allow in the case of the property concerned, and

(iii) are, at the time the direction is given, resident in the United Kingdom.

2(2) For the purposes of this paragraph trustees shall be regarded as **"resident in the United Kingdom"** if–

(a) the general administration of the trusts is ordinarily carried on in the United Kingdom, and

(b) the trustees or a majority of them (and, where there is more than one class of trustees, a majority of each class) are resident in the United Kingdom;

and where a trustee is a trust corporation, the question whether the trustee is resident in the United Kingdom shall, for the purposes of paragraph (b) above, be determined as for the purposes of corporation tax.

2(3) In this paragraph–

"accountant" means a member of an incorporated society of accountants;

"trust corporation" means a person that is a trust corporation for the purposes of the Law of Property Act 1925 or for the purposes of Article 9 of the Administration of Estates (Northern Ireland) Order 1979.

3(1) The requirements referred to in paragraph 2(1)(a)(i) above are (subject to paragraph 4 below)–

(a) that none of the property held on the trusts can at any time in the period of six years beginning with the date on which it became so held be applied otherwise than–

(i) for the maintenance, repair or preservation of, or making provision for public access to, property which is for the time being qualifying property, for the maintenance, repair or preservation of property held on the trusts or for such improvement of property so held as is reasonable having regard to the purposes of the trusts, or for defraying the expenses of the trustees in relation to the property so held;

(ii) as respects income not so applied and not accumulated, for the benefit of a body within Schedule 3 to this Act or of a qualifying charity; and

IHT Statutes

(b) that none of the property can, on ceasing to be held on the trusts at any time in that period or, if the settlor dies in that period, at any time before his death, devolve otherwise than on any such body or charity; and

(c) that income arising from property held on the trusts cannot at any time after the end of that period be applied except as mentioned in paragraph (a)(i) or (ii) above.

3(2) Property is **"qualifying property"** for the purposes of sub-paragraph (1) above if–

(a) it has been designated under section 34(1) of the Finance Act 1975 or section 77(1)(b), (c), (d) or (e) of the Finance Act 1976 or section 31(1)(b), (c), (d) or (e) of this Act; and

(b) the requisite undertaking has been given with respect to it under section 34 of the Finance Act 1975 or under section 76, 78(5)(b) or 82(3) of the Finance Act 1976 or under section 30, 32(5)(b), 32A(6), (8)(b) or (9)(b) or 79(3) of this Act or paragraph 5 of Schedule 5 to this Act; and

(c) tax has not (since the last occasion on which such an undertaking was given) become chargeable with respect to it under the said section 34 or under section 78 or 82(3) of the Finance Act 1976 or under section 32, 32A or 79(3A) of this Act or paragraph 3 of Schedule 5 to this Act.

3(3) If it appears to the Treasury that provision is, or is to be, made by a settlement for the maintenance, repair or preservation of any such property as is mentioned in subsection (1)(b), (c), (d), or (e) of section 31 of this Act they may, on a claim made for the purpose–

(a) designate that property under this sub-paragraph, and

(b) accept with respect to it an undertaking such as is described in subsection (4), or (as the case may be) undertakings such as are described in subsections (4) and (4A), of that section;

and, if they do so, sub-paragraph (2) above shall have effect as if the designation were under that section and the undertaking or undertakings under section 30 of this Act and as if the reference to tax becoming chargeable were a reference to the occurrence of an event on which tax would become chargeable under section 32 or 32A of this Act if there had been a conditionally exempt transfer of the property when the claim was made and the undertaking or undertakings had been given under section 30.

3(3A) Section 35A of this Act shall apply in relation to an undertaking given under sub-paragraph (3) above as it applies in relation to an undertaking given under section 30 of this Act.

3(4) A charity is a **"qualifying charity"** for the purposes of sub-paragraph (1) above if it exists wholly or mainly for maintaining, repairing or preserving for the public benefit buildings of historic or architectural interest, land of scenic, historic or scientific interest or objects of national, scientific, historic or artistic interest; and in this sub-paragraph **"national interest"** includes interest within any part of the United Kingdom.

3(5) Designations, undertakings and acceptances made under section 84(6) of the Finance Act 1976 or section 94(3) of the Finance Act 1982 shall be treated as made under sub-paragraph (3) above.

3(5A) In the case of property which, if a direction is given under paragraph 1 above, will be property to which paragraph 15A below applies, sub-paragraph (1)(b) above shall have effect as if for the reference to the settlor there weresubstituted a reference to either the settlor or the person referred to in paragraph 15A(2).

History – References to s. 32A were added to para. 3(2), (3), and in para. 3(3) the words ", or (as the … 4A)", and "or undertakings" in both places, were inserted, by FA 1985, s. 94(1) and Sch. 26, para. 12, in relation to events on or after 19 March 1985.

In para. 3(2)(c), the words "or 79(3A)" substituted for the words "or 79(3)" by F(No. 2)A 2015, s. 12(8)(d), with effect in relation to occasions on which tax would (ignoring the effect of the amendments) fall to be charged under IHTA 1984, s. 64 on or after 18 November 2015 (Royal Assent).

Para. 3(3A) inserted by FA 1998, s. 142 and Sch. 25, para. 8(3), with effect in relation to undertakings given on or after 31 July 1998.

Para. 3(5A) was inserted by FA 1987, s. 59 and Sch. 9, para. 2, in relation to directions given on or after 17 March 1987.

Cross references – FA 2004, Sch. 15, para. 11(10): charge to income tax on benefits received by former owner of property, conditions for exemption from the charge, effective from 2005–06 onwards.

S. 31(4G): potentially exempt transfer proving chargeable: undertaking in force at transferor's death.

FA 1998, Sch. 25, para. 10: variation of undertakings given under para. 3(3) with respect to any property before 31 July 1998.

4(1) Paragraphs (a) and (b) of paragraph 3(1) above do not apply to property which–

(a) was previously comprised in another settlement, and

(b) ceased to be comprised in that settlement and became comprised in the current settlement in circumstances such that by virtue of paragraph 9(1) below there was no charge (or, but for paragraph 9(4), there would have been no charge) to tax in respect of it;

and in relation to any such property paragraph 3(1)(c) above shall apply with the omission of the words "at any time after the end of that period".

4(2) *Sub-paragraph (1) above shall* not have effect if the time when the property comprised in the previous settlement devolved otherwise than on any such body or charity as is mentioned in paragraph 3(1)(a) above fell before the expiration of the period of six years there mentioned; but in such a case paragraph 3(1) above shall apply to the current settlement as if for the references to that period of six years there were substituted references to the period beginning with the date on which the property became comprised in the current settlement and ending six years after the date on which it became held on the relevant trusts of the previous settlement (or, where this sub-paragraph has already had effect in relation to the property, the date on which it became held on the relevant trusts of the first settlement in the series).

WITHDRAWAL

5 If in the Treasury's opinion the facts concerning any property or its administration cease to warrant the continuance of the effect of a direction given under paragraph 1 above in respect of the property, they may at any time by notice in writing to the trustees withdraw the direction on such grounds, and from such date, as may be specified in the notice; and the direction shall cease to have effect accordingly.

INFORMATION

6 Where a direction under paragraph 1 above has effect in respect of property, the trustees shall from time to time furnish the Treasury with such accounts and other information relating to the property as the Treasury may reasonably require.

ENFORCEMENT OF TRUSTS

7 Where a direction under paragraph 1 above has effect in respect of property, the trusts on which the property is held shall be enforceable at the suit of the Treasury and the Treasury shall, as respects the appointment, removal and retirement of trustees, have the rights and powers of a beneficiary.

Part II – Property Leaving Maintenance Funds

CHARGE TO TAX

8(1) This paragraph applies to settled property which is held on trusts which comply with the requirements mentioned in paragraph 3(1) above, and in respect of which a direction given under paragraph 1 above has effect.

8(2) Subject to paragraphs 9 and 10 below, there shall be a charge to tax under this paragraph–

(a) where settled property ceases to be property to which this paragraph applies, otherwise than by virtue of an application of the kind mentioned in paragraph 3(1)(a)(i) or (ii) above or by devolving on any such body or charity as is mentioned in paragraph 3(1)(a)(ii);

(b) in a case in which paragraph (a) above does not apply, where the trustees make a disposition (otherwise than by such an application) as a result of which the value of settled property to which this paragraph applies is less than it would be but for the disposition.

8(3) Subsections (4), (5) and (10) of section 70 of this Act shall apply for the purposes of this paragraph as they apply for the purposes of that section (with the substitution of a reference to sub-paragraph (2)(b) above for the reference in section 70(4) to section 70(2)(b)).

8(4) The rate at which tax is charged under this paragraph shall be determined in accordance with paragraphs 11 to 15 below.

8(5) The devolution of property on a body or charity shall not be free from charge by virtue of sub-paragraph (2)(a) above if, at or before the time of devolution, an interest under the settlement in which the property was comprised immediately before the devolution is or has been acquired for a consideration in money or money's worth by that or another such body or charity; but for the purposes of this sub-paragraph any acquisition from another such body or charity shall be disregarded.

8(6) For the purposes of sub-paragraph (5) above a body or charity shall be treated as acquiring an interest for a consideration in money or money's worth if it becomes entitled to the interest as a result of transactions which include a disposition for such consideration (whether to that body or charity or to another person) of that interest or of other property.

Cross references – S. 70(4), (5), (10): conditions in respect of charge to tax on property leaving temporary charitable trusts.
FA 1986, Sch. 19, para. 42: transitional rules where rate of tax on chargeable occasion under para. 8 falls to be determined by reference to a death which occurred before 18 March 1986.

EXCEPTIONS FROM CHARGE

9(1) Tax shall not be charged under paragraph 8 above in respect of property which, within the permitted period after the occasion on which tax would be chargeable under that paragraph, becomes comprised in another settlement as a result of a transfer of value which is exempt under section 27 of this Act.

9(2) In sub-paragraph (1) above **"the permitted period"** means the period of thirty days except in a case where the occasion referred to is the death of the settlor, and in such a case means the period of two years.

9(3) Sub-paragraph (1) above shall not apply to any property if the person who makes the transfer of value has acquired it for a consideration in money or money's worth; and for the purposes of this sub-paragraph a person shall be treated as acquiring any property for such consideration if he becomes entitled to it as a result of transactions which include a disposition for such consideration (whether to him or another) of that or other property.

9(4) If the amount on which tax would be charged apart from sub-paragraph (1) above in respect of any property exceeds the value of the property immediately after it becomes comprised in the other settlement (less the amount of any consideration for its transfer received by the person who makes the transfer of value), that sub-paragraph shall not apply but the amount on which tax is charged shall be equal to the excess.

9(5) The reference in sub-paragraph (4) above to the amount on which tax would be charged is a reference to the amount on which it would be charged apart from–

(a) section 70(5)(b) of this Act (as applied by paragraph 8(3) above), and

(b) Chapters I and II of Part V of this Act;

and the reference in that sub-paragraph to the amount on which tax is charged is a reference to the amount on which it would be charged apart from section 70(5)(b) and those Chapters.

Cross references – TCGA 1992, s. 260: capital gains tax consequences where para. 9 applies.

10(1) Tax shall not be charged under paragraph 8 above in respect of property which ceases to be property to which that paragraph applies on becoming–

(a) property to which the settlor or his spouse or civil partner is beneficially entitled, or

(b) property to which the settlor's widow or widower or surviving civil partner is beneficially entitled if the settlor has died in the two years preceding the time when it becomes such property.

10(2) If the amount on which tax would be charged apart from sub-paragraph (1) above in respect of any property exceeds the value of the property immediately after it becomes property of a description specified in paragraph (a) or (b) of that sub-paragraph (less the amount of any consideration for its transfer received by the trustees), that sub-paragraph shall not apply but the amount on which tax is charged shall be equal to the excess.

10(3) The reference in sub-paragraph (2) above to the **amount on which tax would be charged** is a reference to the amount on which it would be charged apart from–

(a) section 70(5)(b) of this Act (as applied by paragraph 8(3) above), and

(b) Chapters I and II of Part V of this Act;

and the reference in sub-paragraph (2) above to the **amount on which tax is charged** is a reference to the amount on which it would be charged apart from section 70(5)(b) and those Chapters.

10(4) Sub-paragraph (1) above shall not apply in relation to any property if, at or before the time when it becomes property of a description specified in paragraph (a) or (b) of that sub-paragraph, an interest under the settlement in which the property was comprised immediately before it ceased to be property to which paragraph 8 above applies is or has been acquired for a consideration in money or money's worth by the person who becomes beneficially entitled.

10(5) For the purposes of sub-paragraph (4) above a person shall be treated as **acquiring an interest for a consideration** in money or money's worth if he becomes entitled to the interest as a result of transactions which include a disposition for such consideration (whether to him or to another person) of that interest or of other property.

10(6) Sub-paragraph (1) above shall not apply in respect of property if it was relevant property before it became (or last became) property to which paragraph 8 above applies and, by virtue of paragraph 16(1) or 17(1) below, tax was not chargeable (or, but for paragraph 16(2) or 17(4), would not have been chargeable) under section 65 of this Act in respect of its ceasing to be relevant property before becoming (or last becoming) property to which paragraph 8 above applies.

10(7) Sub-paragraph (1) above shall not apply in respect of property if–

(a) before it last become property to which paragraph 8 above applies it was comprised in another settlement in which it was property to which that paragraph applies, and

(b) it ceased to be comprised in the other settlement and last became property to which that paragraph applies in circumstances such that by virtue of paragraph 9(1) above there was no charge (or, but for paragraph 9(4), *there would have been no* charge) to tax in respect of it.

10(8) *Sub-paragraph* (1) above shall not apply unless the person who becomes beneficially entitled to the property is domiciled in the United Kingdom at the time when he becomes so entitled.

History – In para. 10(1) the words "or civil partner" and "or surviving civil partner" inserted by SI 2005/3229, reg. 39(2), with effect from 5 December 2005.

RATES OF CHARGE

11(1) This paragraph applies where tax is chargeable under paragraph 8 above and–

(a) the property in respect of which the tax is chargeable was relevant property before it became (or last became) property to which that paragraph applies, and

(b) by virtue of paragraph 16(1) or 17(1) below tax was not chargeable (or, but for paragraph 16(2) or 17(4), would not have been chargeable) under section 65 of this Act in respect of its ceasing to be relevant property on or before becoming (or last becoming) property to which paragraph 8 above applies.

11(2) Where this paragraph applies, the rate at which the tax is charged shall be the aggregate of the following percentages–

(a) 0.25 per cent for each of the first forty complete successive quarters in the relevant period,

(b) 0.20 per cent for each of the next forty,

(c) 0.15 per cent for each of the next forty,

(d) 0.10 per cent for each of the next forty, and

(e) 0.05 per cent for each of the next forty.

11(3) In sub-paragraph (2) above **"the relevant period"** means the period beginning with the latest of–

(a) the date of the last ten-year anniversary of the settlement in which the property was comprised before it ceased (or last ceased) to be relevant property,

(b) the day on which the property became (or last became) relevant property before it ceased (or last ceased) to be such property, and

(c) 13th March 1975,

and ending with the day before the event giving rise to the charge.

11(4) Where the property in respect of which the tax is chargeable has at any time ceased to be and again become property to which paragraph 8 above applies in circumstances such that by virtue of paragraph 9(1) above there was no charge to tax in respect of it (or, but for paragraph 9(4), there would have been no charge), it shall for the purposes of this paragraph be treated as having been property to which paragraph 8 above applies throughout the period mentioned in paragraph 9(1).

12(1) This paragraph applies where tax is chargeable under paragraph 8 above and paragraph 11 above does not apply.

12(2) Where this paragraph applies, the rate at which the tax is charged shall be the higher of–

(a) the first rate (as determined in accordance with paragraph 13 below), and

(b) the second rate (as determined in accordance with paragraph 14 below).

13(1) The first rate is the aggregate of the following percentages–

(a) 0.25 per cent for each of the first forty complete successive quarters in the relevant period,

(b) 0.20 per cent for each of the next forty,

(c) 0.15 per cent for each of the next forty,

(d) 0.10 per cent for each of the next forty, and

(e) 0.05 per cent for each of the next forty.

13(2) In sub-paragraph (1) above **"the relevant period"** means the period beginning with the day on which the property in respect of which the tax is chargeable became (or first became) property to which paragraph 8 above applies, and ending with the day before the event giving rise to the charge.

13(3) For the purposes of sub-paragraph (2) above, any occasion on which property became property to which paragraph 8 above applies, and which occurred before an occasion of charge to tax under that paragraph in respect of the property, shall be disregarded.

13(4) The reference in sub-paragraph (3) above to an occasion of charge to tax under paragraph 8 does not include a reference to–

(a) the occasion by reference to which the rate is being determined in accordance with this Schedule, or

(b) an occasion which would not be an occasion of charge but for paragraph 9(4) above.

14(1) If the settlor is alive, the second rate is the effective rate at which tax would be charged, on the amount on which it is chargeable, in accordance with the appropriate provision of section 7 of this Act if the amount were the value transferred by a chargeable transfer made by him on the occasion on which the tax becomes chargeable.

14(1A) The rate or rates of tax determined under sub-paragraph (1) above in respect of any occasion shall not be affected by the death of the settlor after that occasion.

IHT Statutes

14(2) If the settlor is dead, the second rate is (subject to sub-paragraph (3) below) the effective rate at which tax would have been charged, on the amount on which it is chargeable, in accordance with the appropriate provision of section 7 of this Act if the amount had been added to the value transferred on his death and had formed the highest part of it.

14(2A) In determining for the purposes of sub-paragraph (2) the effective rate or rates at which tax would have been charged on the amount in accordance with section 7(1), the effect of Schedule 1A (if it would have applied) is to be disregarded.

14(3) If the settlor died before 13th March 1975, the second rate is the effective rate at which tax would have been charged, on the amount on which it is chargeable (**"the chargeable amount"**), in accordance with the appropriate provision of section 7 of this Act if the settlor had died when the event occasioning the charge under paragraph 8 above occurred, the value transferred on his death had been equal to the amount on which estate duty was chargeable when he in fact died, and the chargeable amount had been added to that value and had formed the highest part of it.

14(4) Where, in the case of a settlement (**"the current settlement"**), tax is chargeable under paragraph 8 above in respect of property which–

(a) was previously comprised in another settlement, and

(b) ceased to be comprised in that settlement and became comprised in the current settlement in circumstances such that by virtue of paragraph 9(1) above there was no charge (or, but for paragraph 9(4), there would have been no charge) to tax in respect of it,

then, subject to sub-paragraph (5) below, references in sub-paragraphs (1) to (3) above to the settlor shall be construed as references to the person who was the settlor in relation to the settlement mentioned in paragraph (a) above (or, if the Board so determine, the person who was the settlor in relation to the current settlement).

14(5) Where, in the case of a settlement (**"the current settlement"**), tax is chargeable under paragraph 8 above in respect of property which–

(a) was previously comprised at different times in other settlements (**"the previous settlements"**), and

(b) ceased to be comprised in each of them, and became comprised in another of them or in the current settlement, in circumstances such that by virtue of paragraph 9(1) above there was no charge (or, but for paragraph 9(4), there would have been no charge) to tax in respect of it,

references in sub-paragraphs (1) to (3) above to the settlor shall be construed as references to the person who was the settlor in relation to the previous settlement in which the property was first comprised (or, if the Board so determine, any person selected by them who was the settlor in relation to any of the other previous settlements or the current settlement).

14(6) Sub-paragraph (7) below shall apply if–

(a) in the period of seven years preceding a charge under paragraph 8 above (the **"current charge"**), there has been another charge under that paragraph where tax was charged at the second rate, and

(b) the person who is the settlor for the purposes of the current charge is the settlor for the purposes of the other charge (whether or not the settlements are the same and, if the settlor is dead, whether or not he has died since the other charge);

and in sub-paragraph (7) below the other charge is referred to as the **"previous charge"**.

14(7) Where this sub-paragraph applies, the amount on which tax was charged on the previous charge (or, if there have been more than one, the aggregate of the amounts on which tax was charged on each)–

(a) shall, for the purposes of calculating the rate of the current charge under sub-paragraph (1) above, be taken to be the value transferred by a chargeable transfer made by the settlor immediately before the occasion of the current charge, and

(b) shall, for the purposes of calculating the rate of the current charge under sub-paragraph (2) or (3) above, be taken to increase the value there mentioned by an amount equal to that amount (or aggregate).

14(8) References in sub-paragraphs (1) to (3) above to the **effective rate** are to the rate found by expressing the tax chargeable as a percentage of the amount on which it is charged.

14(9) For the purposes of sub-paragraph (1) above the appropriate provision of section 7 of this Act is subsection (2), and for the purposes of sub-paragraphs (2) and (3) above it is (if the settlement was made on death) subsection (1) and (if not) subsection (2).

History – In para. 14(1), the words "in accordance with the appropriate provision of section 7 of this Act" were inserted by FA 1986, *s. 101 and Sch. 19, para. 38(1)*.

Para. 14(1A) was inserted by FA 1986, s. 101 and Sch. 19, para. 38(2).

In para. 14(2), the words "in accordance with the appropriate provision of section 7 of this Act" were inserted by FA 1986, s. 101 and Sch. 19, para. 38(1).

Para. 14(2A) inserted by FA 2012, s. 209 and Sch. 33, para. 8, with effect in cases where D's death occurs on or after 6 April 2012.

In para. 14(3), the words "in accordance with the appropriate provision of section 7 of this Act" were inserted by FA 1986, s. 101 and Sch. 19, para. 38(1).

In para. 14(6), the words "seven years" were substituted by FA 1986, s. 101 and Sch. 19, para. 38(3).
Para. 14(9) was substituted by FA 1986, s. 101 and Sch. 19, para. 38(4).
The above amendments have effect with respect to transfers of value made, and other events occurring on or after 18 March 1986.
Cross references – S. 7: rates of tax.
Sch. 2, para. 6: rate determined under para. 14 where there has been a reduction in the rate charged under Sch. 1 between the death of the settlor and the chargeable event.
FA 1986, Sch. 19, para. 40(1): transitional – transfer of value occurring before, and death or other event occurring after, 18 March 1986.

15 Where property is, by virtue of paragraph 1(3) above, treated as property in respect of which a direction has been given under paragraph 1, it shall for the purposes of paragraphs 11 to 14 above be treated as having become property to which paragraph 8 above applies when the transfer of value mentioned in paragraph 1(3) was made.

MAINTENANCE FUND FOLLOWING INTEREST IN POSSESSION

15A(1) In relation to settled property to which this paragraph applies, the provisions of this Part of this Schedule shall have effect with the modifications set out in the following sub-paragraphs.

15A(2) This paragraph applies to property which became property to which paragraph 8 above applies on the occasion of a transfer of value which was made by a person beneficially entitled to an interest in possession in the property, and which (so far as the value transferred by it was attributable to the property)–

(a) was an exempt transfer by virtue of the combined effect of either–

(i) sections 27 and 57(5) of this Act, or

(ii) sections 27 and 57A of this Act, and

(b) would but for those sections have been a chargeable transfer;

and in the following sub-paragraphs **"the person entitled to the interest in possession"** means the person above referred to.

15A(3) Paragraph 9(2) shall have effect as if for the reference to the settlor there were substituted a reference to either the settlor or the person entitled to the interest in possession.

15A(4) Paragraph 10 shall not apply if the person entitled to the interest in possession had died at or before the time when the property became property to which paragraph 8 above applies; and in any other case shall have effect with the substitution in sub-paragraph (1) of the following words for the words from "on becoming" onwards–

"(a) on becoming property to which the person entitled to the interest in possession is beneficially entitled, or

(b) on becoming–

(i) property to which that person's spouse or civil partner is beneficially entitled, or

(ii) property to which that person's widow or widower or surviving civil partner is beneficially entitled if that person has died in the two years preceding the time when it becomes such property;

but paragraph (b) above applies only where the spouse or civil partner, or widow or widower or surviving civil partner, would have become beneficially entitled to the property on the termination of the interest in possession had the property not then become property to which paragraph 8 above applies."

15A(5) Paragraph 11 shall not apply.

15A(6) Sub-paragraphs (1) to (3) of paragraph 14 shall have effect as if for the references to the settlor there were substituted references to the person entitled to the interest in possession.

15A(7) Sub-paragraph (4) of paragraph 14 shall have effect with the insertion after paragraph (b) of the words "and

(c) was, in relation to either of those settlements, property to which paragraph 15A below applied,",

and with the substitution for the words from "settlor shall" onwards of the words "person entitled to the interest in possession shall, if the Board so determine, be construed as references to the person who was the settlor *in relation to the current* settlement."

15A(8) Sub-paragraph (5) of paragraph 14 shall have effect with the insertion after paragraph (b) of the words "and

(c) was, in relation to any of those settlements, property to which paragraph 15A below applied,",

and with the substitution for the words from "settlor shall" onwards of the words "person entitled to the interest in possession shall, if the Board so determine, be construed as references to any person selected by them who was the settlor in relation to any of the previous settlements or the current settlement."

15A(9) Except in a case where the Board have made a determination under sub-paragraph (4) or (5) of paragraph 14, sub-paragraphs (6) and (7) of that paragraph shall have effect as if for the references to the settlor there were substituted references to the person entitled to the interest in possession.

15A(10) Sub-paragraph (9) of paragraph 14 shall have effect with the substitution for the words "(if the settlement was made on death)" of the words "(if the person entitled to the interest in possession had died at or before the time when the property became property to which paragraph 8 above applies)".

History – In para. 15A(4), in the words substituted in para. 10(1), the words "or civil partner" and "or surviving civil partner" inserted and the words "spouse or civil partner, or widow or widower or surviving civil partner," substituted for the words "spouse, widow or widower" by SI 2005/3229, reg. 39(3), with effect from 5 December 2005.
Para. 15A inserted by FA 1987, s. 59 and Sch. 9, para. 3, effective where the occasion of the charge or potential charge to tax under Sch. 4, para. 8 falls on or after 17 March 1987.

Part III – Property Becoming Comprised in Maintenance Funds

16(1) Tax shall not be charged under section 65 of this Act in respect of property which ceases to be relevant property on becoming property in respect of which a direction under paragraph 1 above then has effect.

16(2) If the amount on which tax would be charged apart from sub-paragraph (1) above in respect of any property exceeds the value of the property immediately after it becomes property in respect of which the direction has effect (less the amount of any consideration for its transfer received by the trustees of the settlement in which it was comprised immediately before it ceased to be relevant property), that sub-paragraph shall not apply but the amount on which tax is charged shall be equal to the excess.

16(3) Sub-paragraph (1) above shall not apply in relation to any property if, at or before the time when it becomes property in respect of which the direction has effect, an interest under the settlement in which it was comprised immediately before it ceased to be relevant property is or has been acquired for a consideration in money or money's worth by the trustees of the settlement in which it becomes comprised on ceasing to be relevant property.

16(4) For the purposes of sub-paragraph (3) above trustees shall be treated as acquiring an interest for a consideration in money or money's worth if they become entitled to the interest as a result of transactions which include a disposition for such consideration (whether to them or to another person) of that interest or of other property.

Cross references – S. 65: charge on discretionary trusts between ten-year anniversaries.
S. 144: distributions etc. from property settled by will.
TCGA 1992, s. 260: capital gains tax consequences where para. 16 applies.

17(1) Tax shall not be charged under section 65 of this Act in respect of property which ceases to be relevant property if within the permitted period an individual makes a transfer of value–

(a) which is exempt under section 27 of this Act, and

(b) the value transferred by which is attributable to that property.

17(2) In sub-paragraph (1) above **"the permitted period"** means the period of thirty days beginning with the day on which the property ceases to be relevant property except in a case where it does so on the death of any person, and in such a case means the period of two years beginning with that day.

17(3) Sub-paragraph (1) above shall not apply if the individual has acquired the property concerned for a consideration in money or money's worth; and for the purposes of this sub-paragraph an individual shall be treated as acquiring any property for such consideration if he becomes entitled to it as a result of transactions which include a disposition for such consideration (whether to him or another) of that or other property.

17(4) If the amount on which tax would be charged apart from sub-paragraph (1) above in respect of any property exceeds the value of the property immediately after the transfer there referred to (less the amount of any consideration for its transfer received by the individual), that sub-paragraph shall not apply but the amount on which tax is charged shall be equal to the excess.

Cross references – S. 65: charge on discretionary trusts between ten-year anniversaries.
TCGA 1992, s. 260: capital gains tax consequences where para. 17 applies.

18 In paragraphs 16(2) and 17(4) above the references to the amount on which tax would be charged are references to the amount on which it would be charged apart from–

(a) paragraph (b) of section 65(2) of this Act, and

(b) Chapters I and II of Part V of this Act;

and the references to the amount on which tax is charged are references to the amount on which it would be charged apart from that paragraph and those Chapters.

SCHEDULE 5 – CONDITIONAL EXEMPTION: DEATHS BEFORE 7TH APRIL 1976

Section 35

Cross references – S. 79: exemption from ten-yearly charge on settlements without an interest in possession.
S. 216(7): time within which a person liable under Sch. 5 must deliver an account.
S. 226(4): due date for payment of tax as a chargeable event under Sch. 5.
S. 233(1)(c): interest on unpaid tax chargeable under Sch. 5.
FA 1985, s. 95(1): Treasury functions under Sch. 5 transferred to the Commissioners of Inland Revenue ("the Board") from 25 July 1985.
FA 2012, Sch. 14, para. 33: amount of tax chargeable under Sch. 5 if a person makes a qualifying gift.

CHARGE ON FAILURE OF CONDITION OF EXEMPTION – OBJECTS

1(1) Where, under section 31 of the Finance Act 1975, the value of an object has been left out of account and the Treasury are satisfied that at any time the undertaking given under that section or under paragraph 5 below with respect to the object has not been observed in a material respect, tax shall be chargeable with respect to the object in accordance with paragraph 2 below.

1(2) Where, under section 31 of the Finance Act 1975, the value of any object has been left out of account and–

(a) sub-paragraph (1) above does not apply, but

(b) the object is disposed of, whether on sale or otherwise,

then, subject to the following provisions of this paragraph, tax shall be chargeable with respect to the object in accordance with paragraph 2 below; but where the value of an object has been so left out of account on the death of more than one person, the tax chargeable under this sub-paragraph shall be chargeable only by reference to the last death.

1(3) Tax shall not be chargeable by virtue of sub-paragraph (2) above with respect to an object–

(a) on its being sold by private treaty to a body mentioned in Schedule 3 to this Act or on its being disposed of to such a body otherwise than by sale, or

(b) if it is disposed of otherwise than by sale and the undertaking previously given with respect to it is replaced by a further undertaking under paragraph 5 below.

1(4) For the purposes of sub-paragraph (2) above, the acceptance of an object under section 230 of this Act shall not be treated as a disposal of the object.

Cross references – S. 207(4), (5): liability for tax charged under para. 1(1), (2).
S. 231: power to transfer property in satisfaction of tax does not affect para. 1(4).

2(1) The following provisions of this paragraph shall have effect where, under section 31 of the Finance Act 1975, the value of any object has been left out of account in determining the value transferred by the transfer of value made on the death of any person (in this paragraph referred to as the value transferred on death) and tax becomes chargeable with respect to the object under paragraph 1 above by reason of the disposal of the object or the non-observance of an undertaking (in this paragraph referred to as a chargeable event).

2(2) The tax chargeable under paragraph 1 above with respect to an object shall be so much of the tax that would have been chargeable on the value transferred on death as would have been attributable to the value of the object if–

(a) section 31 of the Finance Act 1975 had not applied to the object, and

(b) the value of the object at the time of the death had been equal to its value at the time of the chargeable event and, if the chargeable event was a disposal on sale complying with paragraph 6 below, that value had been equal to the proceeds of sale.

2(3) Where–

(a) under section 31 of the Finance Act 1975 the value of two or more objects has been left out of account in determining the value transferred on death, and

(b) those objects formed a set at the time of the death, and

(c) tax becomes chargeable under paragraph 1 above with respect to two or more of the objects by reason of chargeable events occurring at different times,

the preceding provisions of this paragraph shall apply as if both or all the chargeable events had occurred at the time of the earlier or earliest one, and the tax chargeable with respect to the objects shall be adjusted accordingly on the occurrence of each of the subsequent chargeable events.

2(4) Sub-paragraph (3) above shall not apply with respect to two or more chargeable events which are disposals to different persons who are neither acting in concert nor connected with each other.

CHARGE ON FAILURE OF CONDITION OF EXEMPTION – BUILDINGS ETC.

3(1) Where, under subsection (2) of section 34 of the Finance Act 1975, the value of any property has been left out of account and the Treasury are satisfied that at any time the undertaking given under that subsection or under paragraph 5 below in respect of that property has not been observed in a material respect, then, subject to sub-paragraph (3) below, tax shall be chargeable in accordance with paragraph 4 below with respect to the property and any property associated with it.

3(2) Where, under section 34(2) of the Finance Act 1975, the value of any property has been left out of account in determining the value transferred on the death of any person and–

(a) sub-paragraph (1) above does not apply, but

(b) the property is disposed of, whether on sale or otherwise,

then, subject to sub-paragraphs (3) and (4) below, tax shall be chargeable in accordance with paragraph 4 below with respect to the property and any property associated with it; but where the value of the property has been left out of account on the death of more than one person, the tax chargeable under this sub-paragraph shall be chargeable only by reference to the last death.

3(3) The Treasury may direct that the tax chargeable under this paragraph on a failure to observe an undertaking with respect to any property or on the disposal of any property shall be chargeable with respect only to that property, if it appears to them that the entity consisting of the building, land and objects concerned has not been materially affected.

3(4) Tax shall not be chargeable under sub-paragraph (2) above with respect to any property–

(a) on its being sold by private treaty to a body mentioned in Schedule 3 to this Act or on its being disposed of to such a body otherwise than by sale, or

(b) if it is disposed of otherwise than by sale and the undertaking previously given with respect to it is replaced by a further undertaking under paragraph 5 below;

and for the purposes of sub-paragraph (2) above the acceptance of any property under section 230 of this Act shall not be treated as a disposal of the property.

3(5) For the purposes of this paragraph, two or more properties are **associated** with each other if one of them is a building falling within subsection (1)(b) of section 34 of the Finance Act 1975 and the other or others such land or objects as, in relation to that building, fall within subsection (1)(c) or (d) of that section.

Cross references – S. 207(4), (5): liability for tax charged under para. 3(1), (2).
S. 231: power to transfer property in satisfaction of tax does not affect para. 3(4).

4 The tax chargeable under paragraph 3 above with respect to any property shall be so much of the tax that would have been chargeable on the value transferred on the death as would have been attributable to the value of the property if–

(a) section 34 of the Finance Act 1975 had not applied to the property; and

(b) the value of the property at the time of the death had been equal to its value at the time the tax becomes chargeable and, if it becomes chargeable on a sale complying with paragraph 6 below, that value had been equal to the proceeds of sale.

FURTHER UNDERTAKING ON DISPOSAL

5(1) The further undertaking referred to in paragraph 1 above is the requisite undertaking described in section 31(2) of this Act given with respect to the object in question by such person as the Board think appropriate in the circumstances of the case.

5(2) Subsection (3) of section 31 of this Act shall apply in relation to documents which are designated as objects to which section 31 of the Finance Act 1975 applies as that subsection applies in relation to documents designated under section 31(1)(a) of this Act.

5(3) The further undertaking referred to in paragraph 3 above is–

(a) the requisite undertaking described in subsection (4) of section 31 of this Act given with respect to the property in question by such person as the Board think appropriate in the circumstances of the case, or

(b) (where applicable) the requisite undertakings described in subsections (4) and (4A) of that section given with respect to the property in question by such person or persons as the Board think appropriate in the circumstances of the case.

History – Para. 5 substituted by FA 1998, s. 142 and Sch. 25, para. 7(8), with effect in relation to the giving of any undertaking on or after *31 July 1998*.

Cross references – S. 35A: variation of undertakings given under para. 5 on or after 31 July 1998.
FA 1998, Sch. 25, para. 10: variation of undertakings given under para. 5 before 31 July 1998.

REQUIREMENTS OF SALE

6 A sale complies with this paragraph if–

(a) it was not intended to confer any gratuitous benefit on any person, and

(b) it was either a transaction at arm's length between persons not connected with each other or a transaction such as might be expected to be made at arm's length between persons not connected with each other.

SCHEDULE 5A – QUALIFYING PAYMENTS: VICTIMS OF PERSECUTION DURING SECOND WORLD WAR ERA

Section 153ZA

History – Sch. 5A inserted by FA 2016, s. 95(2), with effect in relation to deaths occurring on or after 1 January 2015.

Part 1 – Compensation Payments

1 A payment of a fixed amount from the German foundation known as **"Remembrance, Responsibility and Future"** (*Stiftung EVZ*) in respect of a person who was a slave or forced labourer.

2 A payment of a fixed amount in accordance with the arrangements made under the Swiss Bank Settlement (Holocaust Victim Assets Litigation) in respect of the slave or forced labourers qualifying for compensation under the Remembrance, Responsibility and Future scheme.

3 A payment of a fixed amount from the Hardship Fund established by the Government of the Federal Republic of Germany.

4 A payment of a fixed amount from the National Fund of the Republic of Austria for Victims of National-Socialism under the terms of the scheme as at June 1995.

5 A payment of a fixed amount in respect of a slave or forced labourer from the Austrian Reconciliation Fund.

6 A payment of a fixed amount by the Swiss Refugee Programme in accordance with the arrangements made under the Swiss Bank Settlement (Holocaust Victim Assets Litigation) in respect of refugees.

7 A payment of a fixed amount under the foundation established in the Netherlands and known as the Dutch Maror Fund (*Stichting Maror-Gelden Overheid*).

8 A one-off payment of a fixed amount from the scheme established by the Government of the French Republic and known as the French Orphan Scheme.

9 A payment of a fixed amount from the Child Survivor Fund established by the Government of the Federal Republic of Germany.

Part 2 – Ex-gratia Payments

10 A payment of a fixed amount made from the scheme established by the United Kingdom Government and known as the Far Eastern Prisoners of War Ex Gratia Scheme.

SCHEDULE 6 – TRANSITION FROM ESTATE DUTY

Section 273

GENERAL

1 References in any enactment, in any instrument made under any enactment, or in any document (whether executed before or after the passing of this Act) to **estate duty** or to **death duties** shall have effect, as far as may be, as if they included references to capital transfer tax chargeable under section 4 of this Act (or under section 22 of the Finance Act 1975).

Cross references – S. 79: exemption from ten-yearly charge on settlements without an interest in possession.

Notes – FA 1986, s. 100(1)(b): any reference to capital transfer tax (except where it relates to a liability to tax arising before 25 July 1986) has effect as a reference to inheritance tax.

SURVIVING SPOUSE OR FORMER SPOUSE

2 In determining for the purposes of this Act the value of the estate, immediately before his death, of a person whose spouse (or former spouse) died before 13th November 1974, there shall be left out

IHT Statutes

of account the value of any property which, if estate duty were chargeable on the later death, would be excluded from the charge by section 5(2) of the Finance Act 1894 (relief on death of surviving spouse); and tax shall not be chargeable under section 52 of this Act on the coming to an end of an interest in possession in settled property if –

(a) the spouse (or former spouse) of the person beneficially entitled to the interest died before 13th November 1974, and

(b) the value of the property in which the interest subsists would by virtue of the preceding provisions of this paragraph have been left out of account in determining the value of the survivor's estate had he died immediately before the interest came to an end.

Cross references – S. 52: charge on termination of interest in possession.

Other material – The Law Society/Inland Revenue meeting notes, 7 February 1978 (not reproduced): exemption lost where protective trusts and the life interest is forfeited.

Notes – FA 1894, s. 5(2) read as follows:

"**5(2)** If Estate duty has already been paid in respect of any settled property since the date of the settlement, the Estate duty shall not, nor shall any of the duties mentioned in the fifth paragraph of the First Schedule to this Act, be payable in respect thereof, until the death of a person who was at the time of his death or had been at any time during the continuance of the settlement competent to dispose of such property and who if on his death subsequent limitations under the settlement take effect in respect of such property was sui juris at the time of his death or had been sui juris at any time while so competent to dispose of the property."

The duties mentioned in Sch. 1, para. 5 were legacy duty and succession duty. That provision was repealed by FA 1949.

SALES AND MORTGAGES OF REVERSIONARY INTERESTS

3(1) Where a reversionary interest in settled property was before 27th March 1974 sold or mortgaged for full consideration in money or money's worth, no greater amount of tax shall be payable by the purchaser or mortgagee when the interest falls into possession than the amounts of estate duty that would have been payable by him if none of the provisions of the Finance Act 1975 or this Act had been passed; and any tax which, by virtue of this paragraph, is not payable by the mortgagee but which is payable by the mortgagor shall rank as a charge subsequent to that of the mortgagee.

3(2) Where the interest referred to in sub-paragraph (1) above was sold or mortgaged to a close company in relation to which the person entitled to the interest was a participator, sub-paragraph (1) above shall apply only to the extent that other persons had rights and interests in the company; and this sub-paragraph shall be construed as if contained in Part IV of this Act.

OBJECTS OF NATIONAL ETC. INTEREST LEFT OUT OF ACCOUNT ON DEATH

4(1) In its application to a sale which does not comply with paragraph 6 of Schedule 5 to this Act, subsection (2) of section 40 of the Finance Act 1930 shall have effect as if the reference to the proceeds of sale were a reference to the value of the objects on that date.

4(2) Where there has been a death in relation to which the value of any property has been left out of account under section 40 of the Finance Act 1930 and, before any estate duty has become chargeable under the provisions of that section or of section 48 of the Finance Act 1950, there is a conditionally exempt transfer of that property, then, on the occurrence of a chargeable event in respect of that property–

(a) tax shall be chargeable under section 32 or 32A of this Act (as the case may be), or

(b) estate duty shall be chargeable under those provisions,

as the Board may elect,

and in this sub-paragraph **"conditionally exempt transfer"** includes a conditionally exempt occasion within the meaning of section 78(2) of this Act.

4(3) In sections 33(7) and (8) and 79(1) of this Act, references to a conditionally exempt transfer of any property include references to a death in relation to which the value of any property has been left out of account under section 40 of the Finance Act 1930 and, in relation to such property, references to a chargeable event or to the tax chargeable in accordance with section 33 of this Act by reference to a chargeable event include references to an event on the occurrence of which estate duty becomes chargeable under section 40 of the Finance Act 1930 or section 48 of the Finance Act 1950 or to the estate duty so chargeable.

4(4) In determining for the purposes of section 40(2) or (2A) of the Finance Act 1930 what is the last death on which the objects passed, there shall be disregarded any death after 6th April 1976.

4(5) In the application of this paragraph to Northern Ireland for references to section 40 of the Finance Act 1930 and section 48 of the Finance Act 1950 there shall be substituted references to section 2 of *the Finance Act* (Northern Ireland) 1931 and Article 6 of the Finance (Northern Ireland) Order 1972 respectively.

History – Para. 4(2)(a) and (b) (and the words "as the Board may elect," following (b)) substituted for (a) and (b) by FA 2016, s. 97(7)(a), with effect in relation to a chargeable event where the conditionally exempt transfer referred to in IHTA 1984, s. 35(2) or Sch. 6, para. 4(2) occurred after 16 March 2016. Former para. 4(2)(a) and (b) read as follows:

"(a) if there has been no conditionally exempt transfer of the property on death, either–
(i) tax shall be chargeable under section 32 or 32A of this Act (as the case may be), or
(ii) estate duty shall be chargeable under those provisions,
as the Board may elect, and
(b) if there has been such a conditionally exempt transfer, there shall be a charge under section 32 or 32A of this Act (as the case may be) and not under those provisions;"
Former para. 4(2)(a) and (b) substituted by FA 1985, s. 94(1) and Sch. 26, para. 13, in relation to events on or after 19 March 1985.
In para. 4(3), the words "and (8)" were inserted by FA 1986, s. 101 and Sch. 19, para. 39, in respect of transfers of value made, and other events occurring, on or after 18 March 1986.
In para. 4(4), the words "or (2A)" inserted by FA 2016, s. 97(7)(b), with effect in relation to a chargeable event where the conditionally exempt transfer referred to in IHTA 1984, s. 35(2) or Sch. 6, para. 4(2) occurred after 16 March 2016.

Cross references – S. 32: tax charge on first occurrence of chargeable event in respect of property previously subject to conditionally exempt transfer.
S. 32A: associated properties in respect of conditional exemption.
FA 1986, Sch. 19, para. 40(1): transitional – transfer of value occurring before, and death or other event occurring after, 18 March 1986.

Notes – FA 1894, s. 15(2): power of Treasury to remit estate duty on objects of national, scientific or historic interest, to be given or bequeathed for national purposes etc.
FA 1930, s. 40 (exemption from death duties of objects of national, scientific, historic or artistic interest) formerly read as follows:
"**40(1)** Where there pass on the death of a person dying after the commencement of this Act any objects to which this section applies, the value of those objects shall not be taken into account for the purpose of estimating the principal value of the estate passing on the death or the rate at which estate duty is chargeable thereon, and those objects shall, while enjoyed in kind, be exempt from death duties.
40(2) In the event of the sale of any objects to which this section applies, death duties shall, subject as hereinafter provided, become chargeable on the proceeds of sale in respect of the last death on which the objects passed and, as respects estate duty, at the rate appropriate to the principal value of the estate passing on that death upon which estate duty is leviable, and with which the objects would have been aggregated if they had not been objects to which this section applies, and the person by whom or for whose benefit the objects were sold shall be accountable for the duties and shall deliver an account for the purposes thereof within one month after the sale:
Provided that death duties shall not become chargeable as aforesaid if the sale is to the National Gallery, British Museum, or any other similar national institution, any university, county council or municipal corporation in Great Britain, or the National Art Collections Fund.
40(3) The objects to which this section applies are such pictures, prints, books, manuscripts, works of art, scientific collections or other things not yielding income as on a claim being made to the Treasury under this section appear to them to be of national, scientific, historic or artistic interest.
40(4) Nothing in this section shall affect the power of the Treasury under subsection (2) of section fifteen of the principal Act to remit death duties chargeable in respect of any objects to which that section applies."
FA 1950, s. 48 (objects of national, scientific, historic or artistic interest) formerly read as follows:
"**48(1)** Subject to the next following subsection, section 40 of the Finance Act, 1930 (which exempts from estate duty objects of national, scientific, historic or artistic interest), shall apply to objects which pass on a death occurring after the date of the passing of this Act only if an undertaking is given, by such person as the Treasury think appropriate in the circumstances of the case, that, until the objects again pass on a death or are sold,–
(a) the objects will be kept permanently in the United Kingdom, and will not leave it temporarily except for a purpose and a period approved by the Treasury; and
(b) reasonable steps will be taken for the preservation of the objects; and
(c) reasonable facilities for examining the objects for the purpose of seeing the steps taken for their preservation, or for purposes of research, will be allowed to any person authorised by the Treasury so to examine them.
48(2) If on a claim for exemption under the said section forty it is made to appear to the Treasury that any documents for which the exemption is claimed contain information which for personal or other reasons ought to be treated as confidential, the Treasury may exclude those documents either altogether or to such extent as they think fit from any undertaking under the foregoing subsection so far as the undertaking relates to the examination of the documents for purposes of research.
48(3) Where any objects are exempted from estate duty in pursuance of an undertaking under subsection (1) of this section, and the Treasury are satisfied that at any time during the period for which the undertaking was given it had not been observed in a material respect, then estate duty shall become chargeable, on the value at that time of those objects, in respect of the death on which the exemption was given and at the rate appropriate to the principal value of the estate passing on that death upon which estate duty is leviable, and with which the objects would have been aggregated if: they had not been objects to which the said section forty applies; and any person who, if the objects were sold when the duty becomes chargeable, would be entitled to receive (whether for his own benefit or not) the proceeds of sale or any income arising therefrom shall be accountable for the duty.
48(4) Where any objects are sold after becoming chargeable with estate duty under this section in respect of any death, the proceeds of sale shall not be chargeable with estate duty in respect of the same death under subsection (2) of the said section forty."

SCHEDULE 7 – COMMENCEMENT: SUPPLEMENTARY RULES

Section 274

1 In this Schedule **"the repealed enactments"** means the enactments repealed by this Act.

2 Sections 126 to 130 of this Act shall have effect (to the exclusion of the corresponding repealed enactments) in relation to any disposal after the end of 1984, whether the death in respect of which relief was given occurred before or after that time.

3 Where section 146 of this Act has effect in relation to a death after the end of 1984, it shall also have effect (to the exclusion of section 122 of the Finance Act 1976) in relation to any chargeable transfer of the kind referred to in section 146(2), whether made before or after that time.

4 Section 147 of this Act, so far as it relates to charges to tax in respect of claims to legitim made in the circumstances described in subsection (4) of that section, shall have effect (to the exclusion of the corresponding repealed enactments) in relation to claims made after the end of 1984, whether the testator died before or after that time.

5 Sections 148 and 149 of this Act shall have effect (to the exclusion of the corresponding repealed enactments) in any case where the donee's transfer is made after the end of 1984, whether the donor's transfer was made before or after that time.

6 Section 150 of this Act shall have effect (to the exclusion of section 88 of the Finance Act 1976) in relation to any claim made after the end of 1984.

7 Section 203 of this Act shall have effect (to the exclusion of the corresponding repealed enactments) in relation to any chargeable transfer made after the end of 1984 (whether the spouse transfer concerned was made before or after that time).

8 Section 218 of this Act, and section 245 so far as it relates to section 218, shall have effect in relation to settlements made after the end of 1984 to the exclusion of the corresponding repealed enactments, and those enactments shall continue to have effect in relation to settlements made before that time.

9 Section 219 of this Act, and section 245 so far as it relates to section 219, shall come into force on 1st January 1985 for all purposes to the exclusion of the corresponding repealed enactments, except that those enactments shall continue to have effect in relation to notices given before that time.

10 Section 220 of this Act shall come into force on 1st January 1985 for all purposes to the exclusion of the corresponding repealed enactments, except that those enactments shall continue to have effect in relation to authorisations given before that time.

11 Any order made under section 233 of this Act shall have effect in relation to interest chargeable (under the repealed enactments) in respect of chargeable transfers and other events before the end of 1984 as it has effect in relation to interest chargeable (under this Act) in respect of transfers and other events after that time.

12 Where payments are made or assets transferred after the end of 1984 in the circumstances described in section 262 of this Act, that section shall have effect (to the exclusion of the corresponding repealed enactments) whether the disposition first mentioned in that section was made before or after that time.

13 Section 264 of this Act shall have effect (to the exclusion of section 114 of the Finance Act 1976) in any case where the later transfer is made after the end of 1984, whether the earlier transfer was made before or after that date.

14 This Act shall not have effect in a case which would otherwise fall within paragraph 2(3) of Schedule 5 if the first chargeable event occurred before the end of 1984.

FINANCE ACT 1985

(1985 Chapter 54)

[*25th July 1985*]

ARRANGEMENT OF SECTIONS

PART V – MISCELLANEOUS AND SUPPLEMENTARY

SCHEDULES

PART V – MISCELLANEOUS AND SUPPLEMENTARY

94 Capital transfer tax: conditional exemption

94(1) Schedule 26 to this Act (which contains amendments about conditional exemption) shall have effect.

94(2) Those amendments have effect in relation to events on or after 19th March 1985.

Notes – FA 1986, s. 100(1)(b): any reference to capital transfer tax (except where it relates to a liability to tax arising before 25 July 1986) has effect as a reference to inheritance tax.

95 The national heritage: transfer of Treasury functions to Board

95(1) The functions of the Treasury under–

(a) Part II, and section 76 of, and Schedules 3 to 5 to, the Capital Transfer Tax Act 1984 (exempt transfers);

(b) [repealed by TCGA 1992, s. 290(3) and Sch. 12;]

(c) the enactments re-enacted by those provisions;

and the corresponding functions of the Treasury under any earlier enactments relating to capital transfer tax or estate duty, are hereby transferred to the Commissioners of Inland Revenue (**"the Board"**).

95(2) This section shall not affect the validity of anything done by or in relation to the Treasury before the passing of this Act; and anything which at that date is in the process of being done by or in relation to the Treasury may, if it relates to functions transferred by this section to the Board, be continued by or in relation to the Board.

95(3) Any authorisation, designation, direction, approval, determination, or other thing given, made or done by the Treasury in connection with functions transferred by this section shall have effect as if given, made or done by the Board in so far as that is required for continuing its effect after the passing of this Act.

95(4) Any enactment passed or instrument or other document made before the coming into operation of this section shall have effect, so far as may be necessary, for the purpose or in consequence of the transfer of functions effected by this section as if any reference to the Treasury were or included a reference to the Board.

History – S. 95(1)(b) repealed by TCGA 1992, s. 290(3) and Sch. 12.

Cross references – TCGA 1992, s. 258: exemption for gains accruing on disposal of works of art.

Hansard – Standing Committee B, 13 June 1985, col. 568 (not reproduced): statement by the Chief Secretary to the Treasury that transfer was not intended to result in any change in approach.

Notes – FA 1986, s. 100(1)(b): any reference to capital transfer tax (except where it relates to a liability to tax arising before 25 July 1986) has effect as a reference to inheritance tax. See also FA 1986, s. 100(1)(a) for citation of the Capital Transfer Tax Act 1984 as the Inheritance Tax Act 1984.

SCHEDULE 26 – CAPITAL TRANSFER TAX: CONDITIONAL EXEMPTION

Section 94

[Amendments to IHTA 1984, s. 30–35, 78, 79, 207, 216, 221, 226, 233 and Sch. 6, para. 4; insertion of IHTA 1984, s. 32A.]

Notes – FA 1986, s. 100(1)(b): any reference to capital transfer tax (except where it relates to a liability to tax arising before 25 July 1986) has effect as a reference to inheritance tax.

BANKRUPTCY (SCOTLAND) ACT 1985

(1985 Chapter 66)

[*30th October 1985*]

ARRANGEMENT OF SECTIONS

SAFEGUARDING OF INTERESTS OF CREDITORS OF INSOLVENT PERSONS

34 Gratuitous alienations

34(1) Where this subsection applies, an alienation by a debtor shall be challengeable by–

(a) any creditor who is a creditor by virtue of a debt incurred on or before the date of sequestration, or before the granting of the trust deed or the debtor's death, as the case may be; or

(b) the permanent trustee, the trustee acting under the trust deed or the judicial factor, as the case may be.

34(2) Subsection (1) above applies where–

(a) by the alienation, whether before or after the coming into force of this section, any of the debtor's property has been transferred or any claim or right of the debtor has been discharged or renounced; and

(b) any of the following has occurred–

(i) his estate has been sequestrated (other than, in the case of a natural person, after his death); or

(ii) he has granted a trust deed which has become a protected trust deed; or

(iii) he has died and within 12 months after his death, his estate has been sequestrated; or

(iv) he has died and within the said 12 months, a judicial factor has been appointed under section 11A of the Judicial Fators (Scotland) Act 1889 to administer his estate and the estate was absolutely insolvent at the date of death; and

(c) the alienation took place on a relevant day.

34(3) For the purposes of paragraph (c) of subsection (2) above, the day on which an alienation took place shall be the day on which the alienation became completely effectual; and in that paragraph "relevant day" means, if the alienation has the effect of favouring–

(a) a person who is an associate of the debtor, a day not earlier than 5 years before the date of sequestration, the granting of the trust deed or the debtor's death, as the case may be; or

(b) any other person, a day not earlier than 2 years before the said date.

34(4) On a challenge being brought under subsection (1) above, the court shall grant decree of reduction or for such restoration of property to the debtor's estate or other redress as may be appropriate, but the court shall not grant such a decree if the person seeking to uphold the alienation establishes–

(a) that immediately, or at any other time, after the alienation the debtor's assets were greater than his liabilities; or

(b) that the alienation was made for adequate consideration; or

(c) *that the alienation*–

(i) was a birthday, Christmas or other conventional gift; or

(ii) was a gift made, for a charitable purpose, to a person who is not an associate of the debtor, which having regard to all the circumstances, it was reasonable for the debtor to make:

Provided that this subsection shall be without prejudice to any right or interest acquired in good faith and for value from or through the transferee in the alienation.

34(5) In subsection (4) above, **"charitable purpose"** means any charitable, benevolent or philanthropic purpose whether or not it is charitable within the meaning of any rule of law.

34(6) For the purposes of the foregoing provisions of this section, an alienation in implementation of a prior obligation shall be deemed to be one for which there was no consideration or no adequate consideration to the extent that the prior obligation was undertaken for no consideration or no adequate consideration.

34(7) This section is without prejudice to the operation of section 2 of the Married Women's Policies of Assurance (Scotland) Act 1880 (policy of assurance may be effected in trust for spouse, future spouse and children) including the operation of that section as applied by section 132 of the Civil Partnership Act 2004.

34(8) A permanent trustee, the trustee acting under a protected trust deed and a judicial factor appointed under section 11A of the Judicial Factors (Scotland) Act 1889 shall have the same right as a creditor has under any rule of law to challenge an alienation of a debtor made for no consideration or for no adequate consideration.

34(9) The permanent trustee shall insert in the sederunt book a copy of any decree under this section affecting the sequestrated estate.

History – In s. 34(7), the words "including the operation of that section as applied by section 132 of the Civil Partnership Act 2004" inserted by CPA 2004, s. 261(2) and Sch. 28, para. 35, with effect from 5 December 2005 (SSI 2005/604, art. 2(a)).

DISTRIBUTION OF DEBTOR'S ESTATE

51 Order of priority in distribution

51(1) The funds of the debtor's estate shall be distributed by the trustee to meet the following debts in the order in which they are mentioned–

(a) the outlays and remuneration of the interim trustee in the administration of the debtor's estate;

(b) the outlays and remuneration of the trustee in the administration of the debtor's estate;

(c) where the debtor is a deceased debtor, deathbed and funeral expenses reasonably incurred and expenses reasonably incurred in administering the deceased's estate;

(d) the expenses reasonably incurred by a creditor who is a petitioner, or concurs in a debtor application, for sequestration;

(e) ordinary preferred debts (excluding any interest which has accrued thereon to the date of sequestration);

(ea) secondary preferred debts (excluding any interest which has accrued thereon to the date of sequestration);

(f) ordinary debts, that is to say a debt which is neither a secured debt nor a debt mentioned in any other paragraph of this subsection;

(g) interest at the rate specified in subsection (7) below on–

(i) the ordinary preferred debts;

(ia) the secondary preferred debts;

(ii) the ordinary debts,

between the date of sequestration and the date of payment of the debt;

(h) any postponed debt.

51(2) In this Act—

(a) **"preferred debt"** means a debt listed in Part I of Schedule 3 to this Act,

(b) **"ordinary preferred debt"** means a debt within any of paragraphs 4 to 6B of Part I of Schedule 3 to this Act,

(c) **"secondary preferred debt"** means a debt within paragraph 6C or 6D of Part 1 of Schedule 3 to this Act, and

Part II of that Schedule shall have effect for the interpretation of Part I.

51(3) In this Act **"postponed debt"** means–

(a) a loan made to the debtor, in consideration of a share of the profits in his business, which is postponed under section 3 of the Partnership Act 1890 to the claims of other creditors;

(b) a loan made to the debtor by the debtor's spouse or civil partner;

(c) a creditor's right to anything vesting in the trustee by virtue of a successful challenge under section 34 of this Act or to the proceeds of sale of such a thing.

51(4) Any debt falling within any of paragraphs (c) to (h) of subsection (1) above shall have the same priority as any other debt falling within the same paragraph and, where the funds of the estate are inadequate to enable the debts mentioned in the paragraph to be paid in full, they shall abate in equal proportions.

51(5) Any surplus remaining, after all the debts mentioned in this section have been paid in full, shall be made over to the debtor or to his successors or assignees; and in this subsection **"surplus"** includes any kind of estate but does not include any unclaimed dividend.

51(5A) Subsection (5) above is subject to Article 35 of the EC Regulation (surplus in secondary proceedings to be transferred to main proceedings).

51(6) Nothing in this section shall affect–

(a) the right of a secured creditor which is preferable to the rights of the trustee; or

(b) any preference of the holder of a lien over a title deed or other document which has been delivered to the trustee in accordance with a requirement under section 38(4) of this Act.

51(7) The rate of interest referred to in paragraph (g) of subsection (1) above shall be whichever is the greater of–

(a) the prescribed rate at the date of sequestration; and

(b) the rate applicable to that debt apart from the sequestration.

History – In s. 51(1)(d), the words "a debtor application" substituted for the words "the petition" by Bankruptcy and Diligence etc. (Scotland) Act 2007, s. 36 and Sch. 1, para. 43, with effect from 1 April 2008 (SI 2008/115, art. 3).
S. 51(1)(e) and (ea) substituted for (e) by SI 2014/3486, art. 28(2)(a), with effect from 1 January 2015, subject to the transitional provision in SI 2014/3486, art. 3 (amendments have no effect in relation to any insolvency proceedings commenced before that date).
In s. 51(1)(g)(i), the word "ordinary" inserted by SI 2014/3486, art. 28(2)(a), with effect from 1 January 2015, subject to the transitional provision in SI 2014/3486, art. 3 (amendments have no effect in relation to any insolvency proceedings commenced before that date).
S. 51(1)(g)(ia) inserted by SI 2014/3486, art. 28(2)(a), with effect from 1 January 2015, subject to the transitional provision in SI 2014/3486, art. 3 (amendments have no effect in relation to any insolvency proceedings commenced before that date).
S. 51(2) substituted by SI 2014/3486, art. 28(2)(b), with effect from 1 January 2015, subject to the transitional provision in SI 2014/3486, art. 3 (amendments have no effect in relation to any insolvency proceedings commenced before that date).
In s. 51(3)(b) words "or civil partner" inserted at end by Civil Partnership Act 2004, Sch. 28, para. 39, with effect from 5 December 2005 (by virtue of Scottish SI 2005/604, art. 2(c)).
S. 51(5A) inserted by SI 2003/2109, reg. 14, with effect from 8 September 2003.
In s. 51 the word "permanent" which appeared before the word "trustee" in five places, omitted by the Bankruptcy and Diligence etc. (Scotland) Act 2007, s. 226(2) and Sch. 6, Pt. 1, with effect from 1 April 2008 (SSI 2008/115, art. 3 and Sch. 2, para. 8) subject to transitional provisions and savings at SSI 2008/115, art. 4–7, 10 and 15.

Notes – The commencement date for s. 51 is 29 December 1986 (s. 78(2), SI 1986/1913).

MISCELLANEOUS AND SUPPLEMENTARY

78 Short title, commencement and extent

78(1) This Act may be cited as the Bankruptcy (Scotland) Act 1985.

78(2) This Act, except this section, shall come into force on such day as the Secretary of State may by order made by statutory instrument appoint; and different days may be so appointed for different purposes and for different provisions.

78(3)–(4) [Transitional and saving provisions.]

78(5) This Act, except the provisions mentioned in subsection (6) below, extends to Scotland only.

78(6) [Not reproduced.]

Notes – The commencement date for s. 78 is 30 October 1985 (s. 78(2)).

SCHEDULE 3 – PREFERRED DEBTS

Section 51

Part I – List of Preferred Debts

DEBTS TO INLAND REVENUE

1 [Sch. 3, para. 1 repealed by the Enterprise Act 2002, s. 251(2)(a), s. 278(2), and Sch. 26.]

History – Sch. 3, para. 1 repealed by the Enterprise Act 2002, s. 251(2)(a), s. 278(2), and Sch. 26, with effect from 15 September 2003, by virtue of SI 2003/2093, art. 2 and Sch. 1. Art. 4 contains transitional provisions.
Previously, in Sch. 3, para. 1 the words "PAYE regulations" substituted for "section 203 of the Income and Corporation Taxes Act 1988 (pay as you earn)" by ITEPA 2003, s. 722 and Sch. 6, para. 153, with effect for income tax purposes, for the tax year 2003–2004 and *subsequent* tax years, and for corporation tax purposes, for accounting periods ending after 5 April 2003.
References to ICTA 1988 substituted by ICTA 1988, s. 844 and Sch. 29, para. 32.

Transitional – Enterprise Act 2002 (Commencement No. 4 and Transitional Provisions and Savings) Order 2003, SI 2003/2093, art. 4, contains transitional provisions so that the former rules remain in effect where insolvency arrangements are in place prior to 15 September 2003.

Notes – The commencement date for Sch. 3 is 29 December 1986 (s. 78(2), SI 1986/1913).

FINANCE ACT 1986

(1986 Chapter 41)

[25th July 1986]

ARRANGEMENT OF SECTIONS

PART V – INHERITANCE TAX

100 Capital transfer tax to be known as inheritance tax

100(1) On and after the passing of this Act, the tax charged under the Capital Transfer Tax Act 1984 (in this Part of this Act referred to as **"the 1984 Act"**) shall be known as inheritance tax and, accordingly, on and after that passing,–

(a) the 1984 Act may be cited as the Inheritance Tax Act 1984; and

(b) subject to subsection (2) below, any reference to capital transfer tax in the 1984 Act, in any other enactment passed before or in the same Session as this Act or in any document executed, made, served or issued on or before the passing of this Act or at any time thereafter shall have effect as a reference to inheritance tax.

100(2) Subsection (1)(b) above does not apply where the reference to capital transfer tax relates to a liability to tax arising before the passing of this Act.

100(3) In the following provisions of this Part of this Act, any reference to **"tax"** except where it is a reference to a named tax is a reference to inheritance tax and, in so far as it occurs in a provision which relates to a time before the passing of this Act, includes a reference to capital transfer tax.

101 Lifetime transfers potentially exempt etc.

101(1) The 1984 Act shall have effect subject to the amendments in Part I of Schedule 19 to this Act, being amendments–

(a) removing liability for tax on certain transfers of value where the transfer occurs at least seven years before the transferor's death;

(b) providing for one Table of rates of tax;

(c) abolishing exemptions for mutual transfers;

(d) making provision with respect to the amounts of tax to be charged on transfers occurring before the death of the transferor;

IHT Statutes

(e) making provision with respect to the application of relief under Chapter I (business property) and Chapter II (agricultural property) of Part V of the 1984 Act to such transfers; and

(f) reducing the period during which the values transferred by chargeable transfers are aggregated from ten years to seven;

and amendments making provisions consequential on or incidental to the matters referred to above and to sections 102 and 103 below.

101(2) [Repealed by FA 1989, s. 187 and Sch. 17, Pt. VII.]

101(3) Part I of Schedule 19 to this Act has effect, subject to Part II of that Schedule, with respect to transfers of value made, and other events occurring, on or after 18th March 1986.

101(4) The transitional provisions in Part II of Schedule 19 to this Act shall have effect.

History – The repeal of s. 101(2) by FA 1989, s. 187 and Sch. 17, Pt. VII is consequential on the repeal, in relation to disposals on or after 14 March 1989, of FA 1980, s. 79, which s. 101(2) amended.

102 Gifts with reservation

102(1) Subject to subsections (5) and (6) below, this section applies where, on or after 18th March 1986, an individual disposes of any property by way of gift and either–

(a) possession and enjoyment of the property is not bona fide assumed by the donee at or before the beginning of the relevant period; or

(b) at any time in the relevant period the property is not enjoyed to the entire exclusion, or virtually to the entire exclusion, of the donor and of any benefit to him by contract or otherwise;

and in this section **"the relevant period"** means a period ending on the date of the donor's death and beginning seven years before that date or, if it is later, on the date of the gift.

102(2) If and so long as–

(a) possession and enjoyment of any property is not bona fide assumed as mentioned in subsection (1)(a) above, or

(b) any property is not enjoyed as mentioned in subsection (1)(b) above,

the property is referred to (in relation to the gift and the donor) as **"property subject to a reservation"**.

102(3) If, immediately before the death of the donor, there is any property which, in relation to him, is property subject to a reservation then, to the extent that the property would not, apart from this section, form part of the donor's estate immediately before his death, that property shall be treated for the purposes of the 1984 Act as property to which he was beneficially entitled immediately before his death.

102(4) If, at a time before the end of the relevant period, any property ceases to be property subject to a reservation, the donor shall be treated for the purposes of the 1984 Act as having at that time made a disposition of the property by a disposition which is a potentially exempt transfer.

102(5) This section does not apply if or, as the case may be, to the extent that the disposal of property by way of gift is an exempt transfer by virtue of any of the following provisions of Part II of the 1984 Act,–

(a) section 18 (transfers between spouses or civil partners), except as provided by subsections (5A) and (5B) below;

(b) section 20 (small gifts);

(c) section 22 (gifts in consideration of marriage or civil partnership);

(d) section 23 (gifts to charities);

(e) section 24 (gifts to political parties);

(ee) section 24A (gifts to housing associations);

(f) section 25 (gifts for national purposes, etc.);

(g) [repealed by FA 1998, s. 165 and Sch. 27, Pt. IV]

(h) section 27 (maintenance funds for historic buildings);

(i) section 28 (employee trusts); and

(j) section 28A (employee-ownership trusts).

102(5A) Subsection (5)(a) above does not prevent this section from applying if or, as the case may be, to the extent that–

(a) the property becomes settled property by virtue of the gift,

(b) by reason of the donor's spouse or civil partner ("the relevant beneficiary") becoming beneficially entitled to an interest in possession in the settled property, the disposal is or, as the case may be, is to any extent an exempt transfer by virtue of section 18 of the 1984 Act in consequence of the operation of section 49 of that Act (treatment of interests in possession),

(c) at some time after the disposal, but before the death of the donor, the relevant beneficiary's interest in possession comes to an end, and

(d) on the occasion on which that interest comes to an end, the relevant beneficiary does not become beneficially entitled to the settled property or to another interest in possession in the settled property.

102(5B) If or, as the case may be, to the extent that this section applies by virtue of subsection (5A) above, it has effect as if the disposal by way of gift had been made immediately after the relevant beneficiary's interest in possession came to an end.

102(5C) For the purposes of subsections (5A) and (5B) above—

(a) section 51(1)(b) of the 1984 Act (disposal of interest in possession treated as coming to end of interest) applies as it applies for the purposes of Chapter 2 of Part 3 of that Act; and

(b) references to any property or to an interest in any property include references to part of any property or interest.".

102(6) This section does not apply if the disposal of property by way of gift is made under the terms of a policy issued in respect of an insurance made before 18th March 1986 unless the policy is varied on or after the date so as to increase the benefits secured or to extend the term of the insurance; and, for this purpose, any change in the terms of the policy which is made in pursuance of an option or other power conferred by the policy shall be deemed to be a variation of the policy.

102(7) If a policy issued as mentioned in subsection (6) above confers an option or other power under which benefits and premiums may be increased to take account of increases in the retail prices index (as defined in section 8(3) of the 1984 Act) or any similar index specified in the policy, then, to the extent that the right to exercise that option or power would have been lost if it had not been exercised on or before 1st August 1986, the exercise of that option or power before that date shall be disregarded for the purposes of subsection (6) above.

102(8) Schedule 20 to this Act has effect for supplementing this section.

History – In s. 102(5) the words "or civil partners" and "or civil partnership" inserted by SI 2005/3229, reg. 44(2), with effect from 5 December 2005.

In s. 102(5)(a), the words ", except as provided by subsections (5A) and (5B) below" inserted by FA 2003, s. 185(2), with effect in relation to disposals made on or after 20 June 2003.

S. 102(5)(ee) inserted by FA 1989, s. 171(5), with respect to transfers of value made after 13 March 1989.

S. 102(5)(g) repealed by FA 1998, s. 165 and Sch. 27, Pt. IV, with effect in relation to any transfer of value made on or after 17 March 1988.

S. 102(5)(j) inserted (and the "; and" after s. 102(5)(i) inserted, and the "and" after s. 102(5)(h) omitted) by FA 2014, s. 290 and Sch. 37, para. 17(1), with effect in relation to disposals made on or after 6 April 2014.

In s. 102(5A) the words "or civil partner" inserted by SI 2005/3229, reg. 44(3), with effect from 5 December 2005.

S. 102(5A)–(5C) inserted by FA 2003, s. 185(3), with effect in relation to disposals made on or after 20 June 2003.

Cross references – FA 2004, Sch. 15, para. 11: exemptions from charge to income tax on benefits received by former owner of property where any of para. (d) to (i) of s. 102(5) applies.

IHTA 1984, s. 142(5): property subject to a reservation is not included in a person's estate for the purposes of varying or disclaiming dispositions within two years of death.

IHTA 1984, s. 204(9): limitation of liability of personal representatives for tax attributable to property subject to a reservation.

IHTA 1984, s. 216(1)(bc) and (3): delivery of accounts in respect of property which apart from s. 102(3) would not form part of the deceased's estate.

SI 1987/1130, reg. 5: relief from double charges on release of reservation, or where property subject to a reservation is deemed to be part of deceased's estate on death.

SI 2002/1733, reg. 3(4)(c)(i): Inheritance Tax (Delivery of Accounts) (Excepted Estates) Regulations 2002: excepted estates and specified transfers.

Statements of practice – SP 5/92: right under TCGA 1992, Sch. 5, para. 6 (settlor's right of recovery of tax from trustee in certain cases) is not regarded as a reservation of benefit.

HMRC interpretations – IR Int. 1001: Revenue views on:

- interpretation of "virtually to the entire exclusion";
- exclusion from GWR provisions where donor pays full consideration for any use of the property; and
- position of annual exemption under IHTA 1984, s. 19 where reservation of benefit ceases.

Hansard – Official Report Standing Committee G, 10 June 1986, col. 419–420 (not reproduced): statement by Treasury Minister of State that s. 102(5)(a) included as it makes no sense to tax a gift with reservation to spouse when a gift of the whole would be exempt.

Official Report Standing Committee G, 10 June 1986, col. 425 (not reproduced): Statement by the Treasury Minister of State that gift with reservation rules will not be applied to an unconditional gift of an undivided share in land merely because property is occupied by all the joint owners or tenants in common, including the donor.

Other material – Law Society's *Gazette*, 1 June 1988: Revenue letter on aspects of GWR provisions in response to Law Society's reform memorandum.

Law Society's *Gazette*, 7 March 1990: extent of indemnity offered by Solicitors' Indemnity Fund Ltd where a solicitor incurs civil liability by reason of s. 102(3) in course of his private practice.

102ZA Gifts with reservation: termination of interests in possession

102ZA(1) Subsection (2) below applies where–

(a) an individual is beneficially entitled to an interest in possession in settled property,

(b) either–

(i) the individual became beneficially entitled to the interest in possession before 22nd March 2006, or

(ii) the individual became beneficially entitled to the interest in possession on or after 22nd March 2006 and the interest is an immediate post-death interest, a disabled person's interest or a transitional serial interest or falls within section 5(1B) of the 1984 Act, and

(c) the interest in possession comes to an end during the individual's life.

102ZA(2) For the purposes of–

(a) section 102 above, and

(b) Schedule 20 to this Act,

the individual shall be taken (if, or so far as, he would not otherwise be) to dispose, on the coming to an end of the interest in possession, of the no-longer-possessed property by way of gift.

102ZA(3) In subsection (2) above **"the no-longer-possessed property"** means the property in which the interest in possession subsisted immediately before it came to an end, other than any of it to which the individual becomes absolutely and beneficially entitled in possession on the coming to an end of the interest in possession.

History – In s. 102ZA(1)(b)(ii) the words "or falls within section 5(1B) of the 1984 Act" inserted by FA 2010, s. 53(8), with effect in relation to an interest in possession to which a person is beneficially entitled if the person becomes beneficially entitled to it on or after 9 December 2009.

S. 102ZA inserted by FA 2006, s.156 and Sch. 20, para. 33(2), with effect from 22 March 2006, but only as respects cases where an interest in possession comes to an end on or after that day.

102A Gifts with reservation: interest in land

102A(1) This section applies where an individual disposes of an interest in land by way of gift on or after 9th March 1999.

102A(2) At any time in the relevant period when the donor or his spouse or civil partner enjoys a significant right or interest, or is party to a significant arrangement, in relation to the land–

(a) the interest disposed of is referred to (in relation to the gift and the donor) as property subject to a reservation; and

(b) section 102(3) and (4) above shall apply.

102A(3) Subject to subsections (4) and (5) below, a right, interest or arrangement in relation to land is significant for the purposes of subsection (2) above if (and only if) it entitles or enables the donor to occupy all or part of the land, or to enjoy some right in relation to all or part of the land, otherwise than for full consideration in money or money's worth.

102A(4) A right, interest or arrangement is not significant for the purposes of subsection (2) above if–

(a) it does not and cannot prevent the enjoyment of the land to the entire exclusion, or virtually to the entire exclusion, of the donor; or

(b) it does not entitle or enable the donor to occupy all or part of the land immediately after the disposal, but would do so were it not for the interest disposed of.

102A(5) A right or interest is not significant for the purposes of subsection (2) above if it was granted or acquired before the period of seven years ending with the date of the gift.

102A(6) Where an individual disposes of more than one interest in land by way of gift, whether or not at the same time or to the same donee, this section shall apply separately in relation to each interest.

History – In s. 102A(2) the words "or civil partner" inserted by SI 2005/3229, reg. 45, with effect from 5 December 2005.

S. 102A inserted by FA 1999, s. 104, with effect in relation to gifts of interests in land made by an individual on or after 9 March 1999.

Cross references – SI 2002/1733, reg. 3(4)(c)(i): Inheritance Tax (Delivery of Accounts) (Excepted Estates) Regulations 2002: excepted estates and specified transfers.

102B Gifts with reservation: share of interest in land

102B(1) This section applies where an individual disposes, by way of gift on or after 9th March 1999, of an undivided share of an interest in land.

102B(2) At any time in the relevant period, except when subsection (3) or (4) below applies–

(a) the share disposed of is referred to (in relation to the gift and the donor) as property subject to a reservation; and

(b) section 102(3) and (4) above shall apply.

102B(3) This subsection applies when the donor–

(a) does not occupy the land; or

(b) occupies the land to the exclusion of the donee for full consideration in money or money's worth.

102B(4) This subsection applies when–

(a) the donor and the donee occupy the land; and

(b) the donor does not receive any benefit, other than a negligible one, which is provided by or at the expense of the donee for some reason connected with the gift.

History – S. 102B inserted by FA 1999, s. 104, with effect in relation to gifts of an undivided share of an interest in land made by an individual on or after 9 March 1999.

Cross references – FA 2004, Sch. 15, para. 11: exemptions from charge to income tax for benefits received by former owner of property where s. 102B(4) applies.

Hansard – Official Report Standing Committee B, 15 June 1999, col. 552–556: assurance by Paymaster General that what was said by the Treasury Minister in 1986 about undivided shares (see note to s. 102) still held good following enactment of s. 102B.

102C Sections 102A and 102B: supplemental

102C(1) In sections 102A and 102B above "the relevant period" has the same meaning as in section 102 above.

102C(2) An interest or share disposed of is not property subject to a reservation under section 102A(2) or 102B(2) above if or, as the case may be, to the extent that the disposal is an exempt transfer by virtue of any of the provisions listed in section 102(5) above.

102C(3) In applying sections 102A and 102B above no account shall be taken of–

(a) occupation of land by a donor, or

(b) an arrangement which enables land to be occupied by a donor,

in circumstances where the occupation, or occupation pursuant to the arrangement, would be disregarded in accordance with paragraph 6(1)(b) of Schedule 20 to this Act.

102C(4) The provisions of Schedule 20 to this Act, apart from paragraph 6, shall have effect for the purposes of sections 102A and 102B above as they have effect for the purposes of section 102 above; and any question which falls to be answered under section 102A or 102B above in relation to an interest in land shall be determined by reference to the interest which is at that time treated as property comprised in the gift.

102C(5) Where property other than an interest in land is treated by virtue of paragraph 2 of that Schedule as property comprised in a gift, the provisions of section 102 above shall apply to determine whether or not that property is property subject to a reservation.

102C(6) Sections 102 and 102A above shall not apply to a case to which section 102B above applies.

102C(7) Section 102A above shall not apply to a case to which section 102 above applies.

History – S. 102C inserted by FA 1999, s. 104, with effect in relation to gifts of interests in land made on or after 9 March 1999.

Cross references – FA 2004, Sch. 15, para. 11: exemptions from charge to income tax for benefits received by former owner of property where s. 102C(3) and FA 1986, Sch. 20, para. 6 apply.

103 Treatment of certain debts and incumbrances

103(1) Subject to subsection (2) below, if, in determining the value of a person's estate immediately before his death, account would be taken, apart from this subsection, of a liability consisting of a debt incurred by him or an incumbrance created by a disposition made by him, that liability shall be subject to abatement to an extent proportionate to the value of any of the consideration given for the debt or incumbrance which consisted of–

(a) property derived from the deceased; or

(b) consideration (not being property derived from the deceased) given by any person who was at any time entitled to, or amongst whose resources there was at any time included, any property derived from the deceased.

103(2) If, in a case where the whole or a part of the consideration given for a debt or incumbrance consisted of such consideration as is mentioned in subsection (1)(b) above, it is shown that the value of the consideration given, or of that part thereof, as the case may be, exceeded that which could have been rendered available by application of all the property derived from the deceased, other than such (if any) of that property–

(a) as is included in the consideration given, or

(b) as to which it is shown that the disposition of which it, or the property which it represented, was the subject matter was not made with reference to, or with a view to enabling or facilitating, the giving of the consideration or the recoupment in any manner of the cost thereof,

no abatement shall be made under subsection (1) above in respect of the excess.

103(3) In subsections (1) and (2) above **"property derived from the deceased"** means, subject to subsection (4) below, any property which was the subject matter of a disposition made by the deceased, either by himself alone or in concert or by arrangement with any other person or which represented any of the subject matter of such a disposition, whether directly or indirectly, and whether by virtue of one or more intermediate dispositions.

103(4) If the disposition first-mentioned in subsection (3) above was not a transfer of value and it is shown that the disposition was not part of associated operations which included–

(a) a disposition by the deceased, either alone or in concert or by arrangement with any other person, otherwise than for full consideration in money or money's worth paid to the deceased for his own use or benefit; or

(b) a disposition by any other person operating to reduce the value of the property of the deceased,

that first-mentioned disposition shall be left out of account for the purposes of subsections (1) to (3) above.

103(5) If, before a person's death but on or after 18th March 1986, money or money's worth is paid or applied by him–

(a) in or towards the satisfaction or discharge or a debt or incumbrance in the case of which subsection (1) above would have effect on his death if the debt or incumbrance had not been satisfied or discharged, or

(b) in reduction of a debt or incumbrance in the case of which that subsection has effect on his death,

the 1984 Act shall have effect as if, at the time of the payment or application, the person concerned had made a transfer of value equal to the money or money's worth and that transfer were a potentially exempt transfer.

103(6) Any reference in this section to a **"debt incurred"** is a reference to a debt incurred on or after 18th March 1986 and any reference to an **"incumbrance created by a disposition"** is a reference to an incumbrance created by a disposition made on or after that date; and in this section **"subject matter"** includes, in relation to any disposition, any annual or periodical payment made or payable under or by virtue of the disposition.

103(7) In determining the value of a person's estate immediately before his death, no account shall be taken (by virtue of section 5 of the 1984 Act) of any liability arising under or in connection with a policy of life insurance issued in respect of an insurance made on or after 1st July 1986 unless the whole of the sums assured under that policy form part of that person's estate immediately before his death.

Cross references – IHTA 1984, s. 5: a person's estate is the aggregate of all the property to which he is beneficially entitled.
IHTA 1984, s. 38(6): any liability of the transferor abated under s. 103 to be treated as a specific gift for the purposes of s. 38 (attribution of value to specific gifts).
SI 1987/1130, reg. 6: relief from double charges (liabilities subject to abatement and death).

104 Regulations for avoiding double charges etc.

104(1) For the purposes of the 1984 Act the Board may by regulations make such provision as is mentioned in subsection (2) below with respect to transfers of value made, and other events occurring, on or after 18th March 1986 where–

(a) a potentially exempt transfer proves to be a chargeable transfer and, immediately before the death of the transferor, his estate includes property acquired by him from the transferee otherwise than for full consideration in money or money's worth;

(b) an individual disposes of property by a transfer of value which is or proves to be a chargeable transfer and the circumstances are such that subsection (3) or subsection (4) of section 102 above applies to the property as being or having been property subject to a reservation;

(c) in determining the value of a person's estate immediately before his death, a liability of his to any person is abated as mentioned in section 103 above and, before his death, the deceased made a transfer of value by virtue of which the estate of that other person was increased or by virtue of which property becomes comprised in a settlement of which that other person is a trustee; or

(d) the circumstances are such as may be specified in the regulations for the purposes of this subsection, being circumstances appearing to the Board to be similar to those referred to in paragraphs (a) to (c) above.

104(2) The provision which may be made by regulations under this section is provision for either or both of the following,–

(a) treating the value transferred by a transfer of value as reduced by reference to the value transferred by another transfer of value; and

(b) treating the whole or any part of the tax paid or payable on the value transferred by a transfer of value as a credit against the tax payable on the value transferred by another transfer of value.

104(3) The power to make regulations under this section shall be exercisable by statutory instrument subject to annulment *in pursuance of a resolution* of the Commons House of Parliament.

Statutory instruments – SI 2005/3441 made under s. 104.
SI 1987/1130 made under s. 104(3).

105 Application of business and agricultural relief where transfer partly exempt

105 [Inserts IHTA 1984, s. 39A.]

106 Changes in financial institutions: business property

106(1) [Substitutes IHTA 1984, s. 105(4)(a).]

106(2) [Inserts IHTA 1984, s. 105(7).]

106(3) Subsections (1) and (2) above apply in relation to transfers of value made, and other events occurring, on or after the day of The Stock Exchange reforms.

106(4) The Board may by regulations provide that section 105(7) of the 1984 Act (as inserted by subsection (2) above) shall have effect–

(a) as if the reference to The Stock Exchange in paragraph (a) were to any recognised investment exchange (within the meaning given by section 285(1)(a) of the Financial Services and Markets Act 2001) or to any of those exchanges specified in the regulations, and

(b) as if the reference to the Council of The Stock Exchange in paragraph (b) were to the investment exchange concerned.

106(5) The Board may by regulations amend section 105 of the 1984 Act so as to secure that section 105(3) does not apply to any property if the business concerned is of such a description as is set out in the regulations; and the regulations may include such incidental and consequential provisions as the Board think fit.

106(6) Regulations under subsection (4) or (5) above shall apply in relation to transfers of value made, and other events occurring, on or after such day, after the day of The Stock Exchange reforms, as is specified in the regulations.

106(7) The power to make regulations under subsection (4) or (5) above shall be exercisable by statutory instrument subject to annulment in pursuance of a resolution of the Commons House of Parliament.

106(8) In this section **"the day of The Stock Exchange reforms"** means the day on which the rule of The Stock Exchange that prohibits a person from carrying on business as both a broker and a jobber is abolished.

History – In FA 1986, s. 106(4)(a) the words "of the Financial Services Act 1986" were substituted by the words "given by section 285(1)(a) of the Financial Services and Markets Act 2000", by virtue of SI 2001/3629, article 11 which came into force on 1 December 2001.

Statutory instruments – SI 2012/2903: Inheritance Tax (Market Makers And Discount Houses) Regulations 2012, partly made under s. 106(5).
SI 1992/3181 made under s. 106(4), (6), (8).

Notes – The day of The Stock Exchange reforms was 27 October 1986.
Section 285(1) of the Financial Services and Markets Act 2000 provides that:
"285(1) In this Act–

(a) **"recognised investment exchange"** means an investment exchange in relation to which a recognition order is in force; and

(b) **"recognised clearing house"** means a clearing house in relation to which a recognition order is in force."

107 Changes in financial institutions: interest

107(1) [Substitutes IHTA 1984, s. 234(3)(c).]

107(2) [Inserts IHTA 1984, s. 234(4).]

107(3) Subsections (1) and (2) above apply in relation to chargeable transfers made, and other events occurring, on or after the day of The Stock Exchange reforms.

107(4) The Board may by regulations provide that section 234(4) of the 1984 Act (as inserted by subsection (2) above) shall have effect–

(a) as if the reference to The Stock Exchange in paragraph (a) were to any recognised investment exchange (within the meaning given by section 285(1)(a) of the Financial Services and Markets Act 2000) or to any of those exchanges specified in the regulations, and

(b) as if the reference to the Council of The Stock Exchange in paragraph (b) were to the investment exchange concerned.

107(5) The Board may by regulations amend section 234 of the 1984 Act so as to secure that companies of a description set out in the regulations fall within section 234(3)(c); and the regulations may include such incidental and consequential provisions as the Board think fit.

107(6) Regulations under subsection (4) or (5) above shall apply in relation to chargeable transfers made, and other events occurring, on or after such day, after the day of The Stock Exchange reforms, as is specified in the regulations.

107(7) The power to make regulations under subsection (4) or (5) above shall be exercisable by statutory instrument subject to annulment in pursuance of a resolution of the Commons House of Parliament.

107(8) In this section **"the day of The Stock Exchange reforms"** has the same meaning as in section 106 above.

Prospective amendments – In s. 107(4), the words "paragraph 7(8) of Schedule 53 to the Finance Act 2009 (late payment interest: inheritance tax payable by instalments)" substituted for the words "section 234(4) of the 1984 Act (as inserted by subsection (2) above)" by F(No. 2)A 2015, s. 15(1)(a), with effect from a day to be appointed.
In s. 107(5), the words "set out one or more descriptions of company for the purposes of paragraph 7(7) of Schedule 53 to the Finance Act 2009" substituted for the words "amend section 234 of the 1984 Act so as to secure that companies of a description set out in the regulations fall within section 234(3)(c)" by F(No. 2)A 2015, s. 15(1)(b), with effect from a day to be appointed.

History – In FA 1986, s. 107(4)(a), the words "of the Financial Services Act 1986" were substituted by the words "given by section 235(1)(a) of the Financial Services and Markets Act 2000", by virtue of SI 2001/3629, article 11 which came into force on 1 December 2001.

Statutory instruments – SI 2012/2903: Inheritance Tax (Market Makers And Discount Houses) Regulations 2012, partly made under s. 107(5).
SI 1992/3181 made under s. 107(4), (6), (8).

Notes – The day of the Stock Exchange reforms was 27 October 1986.
Section 285(1) of the Financial Services and Markets Act 2000 provides that:
"**285(1)** In this Act–
(a) **"recognised investment exchange"** means an investment exchange in relation to which a recognition order is in force; and
(a) **"recognised clearing house"** means a clearing house in relation to which a recognition order is in force."

PART VII – MISCELLANEOUS AND SUPPLEMENTARY

114 Short title, interpretation, construction and repeals

114(1) This Act may be cited as the Finance Act 1986.

114(2) [Not relevant to inheritance tax.]

114(3) [Not relevant to inheritance tax.]

114(4) [Not relevant to inheritance tax.]

114(5) Part V of this Act, other than section 100, shall be construed as one with the Capital Transfer Tax Act 1984.

114(6) The enactments and Orders specified in Schedule 23 to this Act are hereby repealed to the extent specified in the third column of that Schedule, but subject to any provision at the end of any Part of that Schedule.

SCHEDULE 19 – INHERITANCE TAX

Section 101

Part I – Amendments of 1984 Act

1 [Inserts s. 3A.]

2 [Amends s. 7.]

3 [Amends s. 8; para. 3(2) repealed by FA 1988, s. 137 and Sch. 14, Pt. X.]

4 [Amends s. 9.]

5 [Inserts s. 19(3A).]

6 [Inserts s. 26A.]

7 [Inserts s. 30(3A)–(3C).]

8 [Inserts s. 31(1A), (4G).]

9 [Amends s. 32(1).]

10 [Amends s. 32A(2).]

11 [Amends s. 33.]

12 [Amends s. 35(3).]

13 [Amends s. 38(6).]

14 [Amends s. 49(3); repealed by F(No. 2)A 1987, s. 104 and Sch. 9, Pt. III.]

15 [Amends s. 55(2); repealed by F(No. 2)A 1987, s. 104 and Sch. 9, Pt. III.]

16 [Amends s. 66.]

17 [Amends s. 67.]

18 [Amends s. 68.]

19 [Amends s. 78.]

20 [Inserts s. 98(3).]

21 [Inserts s. 113A, 113B.]

22 [Inserts s. 124A, 124B.]
23 [Amends s. 131.]
24 [Amends s. 142(5).]
25 [Repeals s. 148, 149.]
26 [Substitutes s. 199(2).]
27 [Amends s. 201(2).]
28 [Amends s. 204.]
29 [Amends s. 216.]
30 [Amends s. 226.]
31 [Inserts s. 277(1A), (1B).]
32 [Amends s. 233.]
33 [Amends s. 236.]
34 [Inserts s. 237(3A).]
35 [Inserts s. 239(2A).]
36 [Substitutes Sch. 1.]
37 [Amends Sch. 2.]
38 [Amends Sch. 4, para. 14.]
39 [Amends Sch. 6, para. 4(3).]

Part II – Transitional Provisions

40(1) Notwithstanding that Part I of this Schedule has effect with respect to events occurring on or after 18th March 1986, where a death or other event occurs on or after that date, nothing in that Part shall affect the tax chargeable on a transfer of value occurring before that date.

40(2) Sub-paragraph (1) above does not authorise the making of a claim under section 149 of the 1984 Act where the donee's transfer, as defined in section 148 of that Act, occurs on or after 18th March 1986.

41 Where tax is chargeable under section 32 or section 32A of the 1984 Act by reason of a chargeable event occurring on or after 18th March 1986 and the rate or rates at which it is charged fall to be determined under the provisions of sections 33(1)(b)(ii) of the 1984 Act by reference to a death which occurred before that date, those provisions shall apply (subject to paragraph 5 of Schedule 2 to that Act) as if the amendments of section 7 of, and Schedule 1 to, that Act contained in Part I of this Schedule had been in force at the time of the death.

42 Where tax is chargeable under paragraph 8 of Schedule 4 to the 1984 Act on any occasion on or after 18th March 1986 and the rate at which it is charged falls to be determined under paragraph 14 of that Schedule by reference to a death which occurred before that date, that paragraph shall apply (subject to paragraph 6 of Schedule 2 to the 1984 Act) as if the amendments of section 7 of, and Schedule 1 to, the 1984 Act contained in Part I of this Schedule had been in force at the time of the death.

43(1) This paragraph applies if, in the case of a settlement,–

(a) tax is charged under section 65 of the 1984 Act on an occasion falling on or after 18th March 1986; and

(b) the rate at which tax is so charged falls to be determined under section 69 of that Act (rate between ten-year anniversaries) by reference to the rate (in this paragraph referred to as **"the last ten-year rate"**) at which tax was last charged under section 64 of that Act (or would have been charged apart from section 66(2) thereof); and

(c) the most recent ten-year anniversary fell before 18th March 1986.

43(2) For the purpose of determining the rate of which tax is charged on the occasion referred to in sub-paragraph (1)(a) above, it shall be assumed that the last ten-year rate was what that rate would have been if, immediately before the ten-year anniversary referred to in sub-paragraph (1)(c) above, the amendments of sections 66 and 67 of the 1984 Act contained in Part I of this Schedule had been in force.

43(3) Where this paragraph applies, paragraph 3 of Schedule 2 to the 1984 Act shall have effect as if–

(a) references to a reduction included references to a reduction by the substitution of a new Table in Schedule 1 to the 1984 Act; and

(b) in relation to a reduction resulting from the substitution of such a new Table, the reference to the second of the Tables in Schedule 1 to the 1984 Act were a reference to a Table in which the rates of tax were one-half of those specified in the new Table.

43(4) In this paragraph **"ten-year anniversary"** has the same meaning as in Chapter III of Part III of the 1984 Act.

44 In relation to a death on or after 18th March 1986, paragraph 2 of Schedule 2 to the 1984 Act (provisions applying on reduction of tax) shall have effect, in a case where the chargeable transfer in question was made before 18th March 1986, as if–

(a) references to a reduction included references to a reduction by the substitution of a new Table in Schedule 1 to the 1984 Act; and

(b) the Table in Schedule 1 to the Act was the first Table in that Schedule.

45 In relation to a disposal of trees or underwood on or after 18th March 1986, paragraph 4 of Schedule 2 to the 1984 Act shall have effect, in a case where the death in question occurred before 18th March 1986, as mentioned in paragraphs (a) and (b) of paragraph 44 above.

46 Notwithstanding anything in section 3A of the 1984 Act, a transfer of value which is made on or after 1st July 1986 and which, by virtue of subsection (4) of section 49 of the Finance Act 1975 (transitional provision relating to estate duty deferment in respect of timber etc.), brings to an end the period during which estate duty is payable on the net moneys received from the sale of timber etc. is not a potentially exempt transfer to the extent that the value transferred is attributable to the land concerned.

History – In para. 46, the words "to the extent that the value transferred is attributable to the land concerned" inserted by SI 2017/495, art. 2, with effect in relation to transfers of value made on or after 6 April 2017.

Cross references – IHTA 1984, s. 3A: potentially exempt transfers.

Extra-statutory concessions – F15: potential exemption denied only to that part of value transferred which is attributable to woodlands which are the subject of the deferred charge (enacted by SI 2017/495, art. 2).

SCHEDULE 20 – GIFTS WITH RESERVATION

Section 102

INTERPRETATION AND APPLICATION

1 In this Schedule–

"the material date", in relation to any property means, in the case of property falling within subsection (3) of the principal section, the date of the donor's death and, in the case of property falling within subsection (4) of that section, the date on which the property ceases to be property subject to a reservation;

"the principal section" means section 102 of this Act; and

"property subject to a reservation" has the same meaning as in the principal section.

1(2) Any reference in this Schedule to a **"disposal by way of gift"** is a reference to such a disposal which is made on or after 18th March 1986.

1(3) This Schedule has effect for the purposes of the principal section and the 1984 Act.

SUBSTITUTIONS AND ACCRETIONS

2(1) Where there is a disposal by way of gift and, at any time before the material date, the donee ceases to have the possession and enjoyment of any of the property comprised in the gift, then on and after that time the principal section and the following provisions of this Schedule shall apply as if the property, if any, received by the donee in substitution for that property had been comprised in the gift instead of that property (but in addition to any other property comprised in the gift).

2(2) This paragraph does not apply if the property disposed of by the gift–

(a) becomes settled property by virtue of the gift; or

(b) is a sum of money in sterling or any other currency.

2(3) In sub-paragraph (1) above the reference to property received by the donee in substitution for property comprised in the gift includes in particular–

(a) in relation to property sold, exchanged or otherwise disposed of by the donee, any benefit received by him by way of consideration for the sale, exchange or other disposition; and

(b) in relation to a debt or security, any benefit received by the donee in or towards the satisfaction or redemption thereof; and

(c) in relation to any right to acquire property, any property acquired in pursuance of that right.

2(4) Where, at a time before the material date, the donee makes a gift of property comprised in the gift to him, or otherwise voluntarily divests himself of any such property otherwise than for a consideration in money or money's worth not less than the value of the property at that time, then, unless he does so in favour of the donor, he shall be treated for the purposes of the principal section and sub-paragraph (1) above as continuing to have the possession and enjoyment of that property.

2(5) For the purposes of sub-paragraph (4) above–

(a) a disposition made by the donee by agreement shall not be deemed to be made voluntarily if it is made to any authority who, when the agreement is made, is authorised by, or is or can be authorised under, any enactment to acquire the property compulsorily; and

(b) a donee shall be treated as divesting himself, voluntarily and without consideration, of any interest in property which merges or is extinguished in another interest held or acquired by him in the same property.

2(6) Where any shares in or debentures of a body corporate are comprised in a gift and the donee is, as the holder of those shares or debentures, issued with shares in or debentures of the same or any other body corporate, or granted any right to acquire any such shares or debentures, then, unless the issue or grant is made by way of exchange for the first-mentioned shares or debentures so issued, or the right granted, shall be treated for the purposes of the principal section and this Schedule as having been comprised in the gift in addition to any other property so comprised.

2(7) In sub-paragraph (6) above the reference to an issue being made or right being granted to the donee as the holder of shares or debentures shall be taken to include any case in which an issue or grant is made to him as having been the holder of those shares or debentures, or is made to him in pursuance of an offer or invitation made to him as being or having been the holder of those shares or debentures, or of an offer or invitation in connection with which any preference is given to him as being or having been the holder thereof.

Cross references – FA 2004, Sch. 15, para. 11: exemptions from charge to income tax for benefits received by former owner of property (in determining whether any property falls within FA 2004, Sch. 15, para. (5), para. 2(2)(b) is to be disregarded).

3(1) Where either sub-paragraph (3)(c) or sub-paragraph (6) of paragraph 2 above applies to determine, for the purposes of the principal section, the property comprised in a gift made by a donor–

(a) the value of any consideration in money or money's worth given by the donee for the acquisition in pursuance of the right referred to in the said sub-paragraph (3)(c) or for the issue or grant referred to in the said sub-paragraph (6), as the case may be, shall be allowed as a deduction in valuing the property comprised in a gift at any time after the consideration is given, but

(b) if any part (not being a sum of money) of that consideration consists of property comprised in the same or another gift from the donor and treated for the purposes of the 1984 Act as forming part of the donor's estate immediately before his death or as being attributable to the value transferred by a potentially exempt transfer made by him, no deduction shall be made in respect of it under this sub-paragraph.

3(2) For the purposes of sub-paragraph (1) above, there shall be left out of account so much (if any) of the consideration for any shares in or debentures of a body corporate, or for the grant of any right to be issued with any such shares or debentures, as consists in the capitalisation of reserves of that body corporate, or in the retention by that body corporate, by way of set-off or otherwise, of any property distributable by it, or is otherwise provided directly or indirectly out of the assets or at the expense of that or any associated body corporate.

3(3) For the purposes of sub-paragraph (2) above, two bodies corporate shall be deemed to be **"associated"** if one has control of the other or if another person has control of both.

DONEE PREDECEASING THE MATERIAL DATE

4 Where there is a disposal by way of gift and the donee dies before the date which is the material date in relation to any property comprised in the gift, paragraphs 2 and 3 above shall apply as if–

(a) he had not died and the acts of his personal representatives were his acts; and

(b) property taken by any person under his testamentary dispositions or his intestacy (or partial intestacy) were taken under a gift made by him at the time of his death.

TERMINATION OF INTERESTS IN POSSESSION

4A(1) This paragraph applies where–

(a) under section 102ZA of this Act, an individual ("D") is taken to dispose of property by way of gift, and

(b) the property continues to be settled property immediately after the disposal.

4A(2) Paragraphs 2 to 4 above shall not apply but, subject to the following provisions of this paragraph, the principal section and the following provisions of this Schedule shall apply as if the property comprised in the gift consisted of the property comprised in the settlement on the material date, except in so far as that property neither is, nor represents, nor is derived from, property originally comprised in the gift.

4A(3) Any property which–

(a) on the material date is comprised in the settlement, and

(b) is derived, directly or indirectly, from a loan made by D to the trustees of the settlement,

shall be treated for the purposes of sub-paragraph (2) above as derived from property originally comprised in the gift.

4A(4) If the settlement comes to an end at some time before the material date as respects all or any of the property which, if D had died immediately before that time, would be treated as comprised in the gift,–

(a) the property in question, other than property to which D then becomes absolutely and beneficially entitled in possession, and

(b) any consideration (not consisting of rights under the settlement) given by D for any of the property to which D so becomes entitled,

shall be treated as comprised in the gift (in addition to any other property so comprised).

4A(5) Where, under any trust or power relating to settled property, income arising from that property after the material date is accumulated, the accumulations shall not be treated for the purposes of sub-paragraph (2) above as derived from that property.

History – Para. 4A inserted by FA 2006, s. 156 and Sch. 20, para. 33(3), with effect from 22 March 2006, but only as respects cases where an interest in possession comes to an end on or after that day.

SETTLED GIFTS

5(1) Where there is a disposal by way of gift and the property comprised in the gift becomes settled property by virtue of the gift, paragraphs 2 to 4 above shall not apply but, subject to the following provisions of this paragraph, the principal section and the following provisions of this Schedule shall apply as if the property comprised in the gift consisted of the property comprised in the settlement on the material date, except in so far as that property neither is, nor represents, nor is derived from, property originally comprised in the gift.

5(2) If the settlement comes to an end at some time before the material date as respects all or any of the property which, if the donor has died immediately before that time would be treated as comprised in the gift,–

(a) the property in question, other than property to which the donor then becomes absolutely and beneficially entitled in possession, and

(b) any consideration (not consisting of rights under the settlement) given by the donor for any of the property to which he so becomes entitled,

shall be treated as comprised in the gift (in addition to any other property so comprised).

5(3) Where property comprised in a gift does not become settled property by virtue of the gift, but is before the material date settled by the donee, sub-paragraphs (1) and (2) above shall apply in relation to property comprised in the settlement as if the settlement had been made by the gift; and for this purpose property which becomes settled property under any testamentary disposition of the donee or on his intestacy (or partial intestacy) shall be treated as settled by him.

5(4) Where property comprised in a gift becomes settled property either by virtue of the gift or as mentioned in sub-paragraph (3) above, any property which–

(a) on the material date is comprised in the settlement, and

(b) is derived, directly or indirectly, from a loan made by the donor to the trustees of the settlement,

shall be treated for the purposes of sub-paragraph (1) above as **"derived from property"** originally comprised in the gift.

5(5) Where, under any trust or power relating to settled property, income arising from that property after the material date is accumulated, the accumulations shall not be treated for the purposes of sub-paragraph (1) above as derived from that property.

EXCLUSION OF BENEFIT

6(1) In determining whether any property which is disposed of by way of gift is enjoyed to the entire exclusion, or virtually to the entire exclusion, of the donor and of any benefit to him by contract or otherwise–

(a) in the case of property which is an interest in land or a chattel, retention or assumption by the donor of actual occupation of the land or actual enjoyment of an incorporeal right over the land, or actual possession of the chattel shall be disregarded if it is for full consideration in money or money's worth;

(b) in the case of property which is an interest in land, any occupation by the donor of the whole or any part of the land shall be disregarded if–

(i) it results from a change in the circumstances of the donor since the time of the gift, being a change which was unforseen at that time and was not brought about by a donor to receive the benefit of this provision; and

(ii) it occurs at a time when the donor has become unable to maintain himself through old age, infirmity or otherwise; and

(iii) it represents a reasonable provision by the donee for the care and maintenance of the donor; and

(iv) the donee is a relative of the donor or his spouse or civil partner;

(c) a benefit which the donor obtained by virtue of any associated operations (as defined in section 268 of the 1984 Act) of which the disposal by way of gift is one shall be treated as a benefit to him by contract or otherwise.

6(2) Any question whether any property comprised in a gift was at any time enjoyed to the entire exclusion, or virtually to the entire exclusion of the donor and of any benefit to him shall (so far as that question depends upon the identity of the property) be determined by reference to the property which is at that time treated as property comprised in the gift.

6(3) In the application of this paragraph to Scotland, references to a chattel shall be construed as references to a corporeal moveable.

History – In para. 6(1)(b)(iv) the words "or civil partner" inserted by SI 2005/3229, reg. 46, with effect from 5 December 2005.

Cross references – FA 2004, Sch. 15, para. 11: exemptions from charge to income tax for benefits received by former owner of property where para. 6 and FA 1986, s. 102C(3) apply.

7(1) Where arrangements are entered into under which–

(a) there is a disposal by way of gift which consists of or includes, or is made in connection with, a policy of insurance on the life of the donor or his spouse or civil partner or on their joint lives, and

(b) the benefits which will or may accrue to the donee as a result of the gift vary by reference to benefits accruing to the donor or his spouse or civil partner (or both of them) under that policy or under another policy (whether issued before, at the same time as or after that referred to in paragraph (a) above),

the property comprised in the gift shall be treated for the purposes of the principal section as not enjoyed to the entire exclusion, or virtually to the entire exclusion, of the donor.

7(2) In sub-paragraph (1) above–

(a) the reference in paragraph (a) to a policy on the joint lives of the donor and his spouse or civil partner includes a reference to a policy on their joint lives and on the life of the survivor; and

(b) the reference in paragraph (b) to benefits accruing to the donor or his spouse or civil partner (or both of them) includes a reference to benefits which accrue by virtue of the exercise of rights conferred on either or both of them.

History – In para. 7(1) and (2) the words "or civil partner" inserted by SI 2005/3229, reg. 46, with effect from 5 December 2005.

AGRICULTURAL PROPERTY AND BUSINESS PROPERTY

8(1) This paragraph applies where there is a disposal by way of gift of property which, in relation to the donor, is at that time–

(a) relevant business property within the meaning of Chapter I of Part V of the 1984 Act, or

(b) agricultural property, within the meaning of Chapter II of that Part, to which section 116 of that Act applies, or

(c) shares or securities to which section 122(1) of that Act applies (agricultural property of companies),

and that property is property subject to a reservation.

8(1A) Where this paragraph applies–

(a) any question whether, on the material transfer of value, any shares or securities fall within paragraph (b), (bb) or (cc) of section 105(1) of the 1984 Act (certain shares or securities qualifying for relief) shall be determined, subject to the following provisions of this paragraph, as if the shares or securities were owned by the donor and had been owned by him since the disposal by way of gift; and

(b) subject to paragraph (a) above, any question whether, on the material transfer of value, relief is available by virtue of Chapter I or Chapter II of Part V of the 1984 Act and, if relief is available by virtue of Chapter II, what is the appropriate percentage for that relief, shall be determined, subject to the following provisions of this paragraph, as if, so far as it is attributable to the property comprised in the gift, that transfer were a transfer of value by the donee.

8(2) For the purpose only of determining whether, on the transfer of value which, by virtue of sub-paragraph (1A)(b) above, the donee is assumed to make, the requirement of section 106 or, as the case may be, section 117 of the 1984 Act (minimum period of ownership or occupation) is fulfilled,–

(a) ownership by the donor prior to the disposal by way of gift shall be treated as ownership by the donee; and

(b) occupation by the donor prior to the disposal and any occupation by him after that disposal shall be treated as occupation by the donee.

8(3) Where the property disposed of by the gift consists of shares or securities falling within paragraph (c) of sub-paragraph (1) above, relief shall not be available by virtue of Chapter II of Part V of the 1984 Act on the material transfer of value unless–

(a) section 116 of the 1984 Act applied in relation to the value transferred by the disposal, and

(b) throughout the period beginning with the disposal and ending on the material date, the shares or securities are owned by the donee,

and for the purpose only of determining whether, on the transfer of value which, by virtue of sub-paragraph (1A)(b) above, the donee is assumed to make, the requirements of subsection (1) of section 123 of the 1984 Act are fulfilled, it shall be assumed that the requirement in paragraph (b) of that subsection (as to the ownership of the shares or securities) is fulfilled.

8(4) In this paragraph, **"the material transfer of value"** means, as the case may require,–

(a) the transfer of value under section 4 of the 1984 Act on the death of the donor; or

(b) the transfer of value under subsection (4) of the principal section on the property concerned ceasing to be subject to a reservation.

8(5) If the donee dies before the material transfer of value, then, as respects any time after his death, any reference in the preceding provisions of this paragraph to the donee shall be construed as a reference to his personal representatives or, as the case may require, the person (if any) by whom the property, shares or securities concerned were taken under a testamentary disposition made by the donee or under his intestacy (or partial intestacy).

History – In para. 8(1), words "This paragraph applies where" substituted and words following "subject to a reservation" omitted, by FA 1987, s. 58 and Sch. 8, para. 18(2), with effect in relation to transfers of value made, and other events occurring, on or after 17 March 1987.

In para. 8(1A)(a), words "within paragraph (b) … relief)" substituted by F(No. 2)A 1992, s. 73 and Sch. 14, para. 7, in relation to transfers of value made, and other events occurring, on and after 10 March 1992, but subject to the transitional provisions in Sch. 14, para. 9.

Para. 8(1A) inserted by FA 1987, s. 58 and Sch. 8, para. 18(3), with effect in relation to transfers of value made, and other events occurring, on or after 17 March 1987.

In para. 8(2), words "sub-paragraph (1A)(b)" substituted by FA 1987, s. 58 and Sch. 8, para. 18(4), with effect in relation to transfers of value made, and other events occurring, on or after 17 March 1987.

In para. 8(3), words "relief shall not … material transfer of value", and "by virtue of sub-paragraph (1A)(b) above", substituted by FA 1987, s. 58 and Sch. 8, para. 18(5), with effect in relation to transfers of value made, and other events occurring, on or after 17 March 1987.

FINANCE ACT 1987

(1987 Chapter 16)

[*15th May 1987*]

ARRANGEMENT OF SECTIONS

PART IV – INHERITANCE TAX

58 Securities, other business property and agricultural property

58(1) The 1984 Act and Schedule 20 to the Finance Act 1986 (gifts with reservation) shall have effect subject to the amendments in Schedule 8 to this Act, being amendments–

(a) making provision with respect to the treatment for the purposes of the 1984 Act of shares and securities dealt in on the Unlisted Securities Market;

(b) making other amendments of Chapter I of Part V of the 1984 Act (business property);

(c) making provision with respect to the application to certain transfers of relief under that Chapter and under Chapter II of that Part (agricultural property); and

(d) making provision with respect to the payment of tax by instalments.

58(2) Subject to subsection (3) below, Schedule 8 to this Act shall have effect in relation to transfers of value made, and other events occurring, on or after 17th March 1987.

58(3) The amendments of the 1984 Act made by Schedule 8 to this Act shall be disregarded in determining under section 113A(3) or section 113B(3) of the 1984 Act whether any property acquired by the transferee before 17th March 1987 would be relevant business property in relation to an notional transfer of value made on or after that date.

59 Maintenance funds for historic buildings etc.

59 Schedule 9 to this Act shall have effect.

60 Acceptance in lieu: waiver of interest

60 [Amends IHTA 1984, s. 233.]

PART VI – MISCELLANEOUS AND SUPPLEMENTARY

70 Arrangements specified in Orders in Council relating to double taxation relief etc.

70(1) [Not relevant to inheritance tax.]

70(2) [Repealed by FA 2006, s. 178 and Sch. 26, Pt. 8(2), with effect from 19 July 2006 (Royal Assent). Previously inserted 1984 Act, s. 158(1A).]

72 Short title, interpretation, construction and repeals

72(1) This Act may be cited as the Finance Act 1987.

72(2)–(4) [Not relevant to inheritance tax.]

72(5) In Part IV of this Act **"the 1984 Act"** means the Inheritance Tax Act 1984.

SCHEDULES

SCHEDULE 8 – SECURITIES, OTHER BUSINESS PROPERTY AND AGRICULTURAL PROPERTY

Section 58

1 [Amends IHTA 1984, s. 10(2).]

2 [Amends IHTA 1984, s. 98(1).]

3 [Amends IHTA 1984, s. 100(1)(c).]

4 [Amends IHTA 1984, s. 104(1)(a).]

5 [Amends IHTA 1984, s. 105; repealed by FA 1996, s. 205 and Sch. 41, Pt. VI.]

6 [Amends IHTA 1984, s. 107(4); repealed by FA 1996, s. 205 and Sch. 41, Pt. VI.]

7 [Inserts IHTA 1984, s. 109A; repealed by FA 1996, s. 205 and Sch. 41, Pt. VI.]

8 [Amends IHTA 1984, s. 113A(3); inserts s. 113A(3A).]

9 [Amends IHTA 1984, s. 124A(6).]

10 [Amends IHTA 1984, s. 136(1)(b).]

11 [Amends IHTA 1984, s. 140(2)(b).]

12 [Amends IHTA 1984, s. 168(1); repeals s. 168(2).]

13 [Amends IHTA 1984, s. 178(1), (2).]

14 [Amends IHTA 1984, s. 180(3).]

15 [Substitutes IHTA 1984, s. 227(1A); amends s. 227(1B); inserts s. 227(1C).]

16 [Amends IHTA 1984, s. 228(1); inserts s. 228(3A).]

17 [Amends IHTA 1984, s. 272.]

18 [Amends FA 1986, Sch. 20, para. 8.]

SCHEDULE 9 – MAINTENANCE FUNDS FOR HISTORIC BUILDINGS ETC.

Section 59

1 [Inserts IHTA 1984, s. 57A.]

2 [Inserts IHTA 1984, Sch. 4, para. 5A.]

3 [Inserts IHTA 1984, Sch. 4, para. 15A.]

4–6 [Effective dates for para. 1–3 respectively.]

FINANCE (NO. 2) ACT 1987

(1987 Chapter 51)

[23rd July 1987]

ARRANGEMENT OF SECTIONS

PART II – INHERITANCE TAX ETC.

SCHEDULES

PART II – INHERITANCE TAX ETC.

96 Interests in possession

96(1) With respect to transfers of value made, and other events occurring, on or after 17th March 1987, the Inheritance Tax Act 1984 shall be amended in accordance with this section.

96(2) [Amends IHTA 1984, s. 3A(2), (6). Para. (c) omitted by FA 2010, s. 53(9).]

96(3) [Inserts IHTA 1984, s. 3A(7).]

96(4) [Repeals IHTA 1984, s. 49(3).]

96(5) [Amends IHTA 1984, s. 55(2).]

96(6) Schedule 7 to this Act shall have effect for the purpose of making further amendments of the Inheritance Tax Act 1984 relating to interests in possession in settled property.

History – S. 96(2)(c) omitted by FA 2010, s. 53(9), with effect in relation to an interest in possession to which a person is beneficially entitled if the person becomes beneficially entitled to it on or after 9 December 2009.

97 Acceptance in lieu: capital transfer tax and estate duty

97(1) If, under paragraph 17 of Schedule 4 to the Finance Act 1975, the Commissioners of Inland Revenue agree to accept property in satisfaction of an amount of capital transfer tax on terms that the value to be attributed to the property for the purposes of that acceptance is determined as at a date earlier than that on which the property is actually accepted, the terms may provide that the amount of capital transfer tax which is satisfied by the acceptance of that property shall not carry interest under paragraph 19 of that Schedule from that date.

97(2) If, under any of the enactments set out in paragraphs (a) to (c) of subsection (3) of section 8 of the National Heritage Act 1980, the Commissioners of Inland Revenue agree to accept property in satisfaction of an amount of estate duty on terms that the value to be attributed to the property for the purposes of that acceptance is determined as at a date earlier than that on which the property is actually accepted, the terms may provide that the amount of estate duty which is satisfied by the acceptance of that property shall not carry interest under section 18 of the Finance Act 1896 from that date.

97(3) Subsections (1) and (2) above apply in any case where the acceptance of the property in question occurs on or after 17th March 1987 and paragraph 19 of Schedule 4 to the Finance Act 1975 or, as the case may be, section 18 of the Finance Act 1896 shall have effect subject to any such terms as are referred to in subsection (1) or subsection (2) above.

97(4) In this section **"estate duty"** and **"property"** have the meaning assigned by section 272 of the Inheritance Tax Act 1984.

98 Personal pension schemes

98 [S. 98 repealed by FA 2004, s. 326 and Sch. 42, Pt. 3.]

History – S. 98 repealed by FA 2004, s. 326 and Sch. 42, Pt. 3, with effect from 6 April 2006, subject to the transitional provisions at FA 2004, Sch. 36.

IHT Statutes

SCHEDULE 7 – INHERITANCE TAX: INTERESTS IN POSSESSION

Section 96

1 [Inserts IHTA 1984, s. 54A, 54B.]

2 [Amends IHTA 1984, s. 56(5).]

3 [Amends IHTA 1984, s. 201(2); inserts s. 201(3A).]

4 [Amends IHTA 1984, s. 216(1), (6)(aa).]

5 [Amends IHTA 1984, s. 265.]

FINANCE ACT 1989

(1989 Chapter 26)

[*27th July 1989*]

ARRANGEMENT OF SECTIONS

PART III – MISCELLANEOUS AND GENERAL

PART III – MISCELLANEOUS AND GENERAL

INHERITANCE TAX

171 Gifts to housing associations

171(1) [Inserts IHTA 1984, s. 24A.]

171(2) [Amends IHTA 1984, s. 23(5).]

171(3) [Amends IHTA 1984, s. 29(5).]

171(4) [Amends IHTA 1984, s. 161(2)(b)(ii).]

171(5) [Inserts IHTA 1984, s. 102(5)(ee).]

171(6) This section shall apply to transfers of value made on or after 14th March 1989.

172 Abatement of exemption where claim settled out of beneficiary's own resources

172(1) [Inserts IHTA 1984, s. 29A.]

172(2) This section shall have effect in relation to deaths occurring on or after the day on which this Act is passed.

INTEREST ETC.

178 Setting of rates of interest

178(1) The rate of interest applicable for the purposes of an enactment to which this section applies shall be the rate which for the purposes of that enactment is provided for by regulations made by the Treasury under this section.

178(2) This section applies to–

(aa) [not relevant to inheritance tax,]

(a) section 8(9) of the Finance Act 1894,

(b) section 18 of the Finance Act 1896,

(c) section 61(5) of the Finance (1909–10) Act 1910,

(d) section 17(3) of the Law of Property Act 1925,

(e) [not relevant to inheritance tax,]

(f) [not relevant to inheritance tax,]

(g) [not relevant to inheritance tax,]

(ga) [not relevant to inheritance tax,]

(gg) [not relevant to inheritance tax,]

(gh) [not relevant to inheritance tax,]

(h) [not relevant to inheritance tax,]

(i) [not relevant to inheritance tax,]
(j) [not relevant to inheritance tax,]
(k) sections 233, 235(1) and 236(3) and (4) of the Inheritance Tax Act 1984,
(l) [not relevant to inheritance tax,]
(m) [not relevant to inheritance tax,]
(n) [repealed by FA 1995, s. 153 and Sch. 29, Pt. XII,]
(o) [not relevant to inheritance tax,]
(p) [not relevant to inheritance tax,]
(q) [not relevant to inheritance tax,]
(r) [not relevant to inheritance tax,]
(s) [not relevant to inheritance tax,]
(t) [not relevant to inheritance tax.]
(u) paragraph 11 of Schedule 35 to the Finance Act 2014.
(v) [not relevant to inheritance tax.]

178(3) Regulations under this section may–

(a) make different provision for different enactments or for different purposes of the same enactment,
(b) either themselves specify a rate of interest for the purposes of an enactment or make provision for any such rate to be determined by reference to such rate or the average of such rates as may be referred to in the regulations,
(c) provide for rates to be reduced below, or increased above, what they otherwise would be by specified amounts or by reference to specified formulae,
(d) provide for rates arrived at by reference to averages to be rounded up or down,
(e) provide for circumstances in which alteration of a rate of interest is or is not to take place, and
(f) provide that alterations of rates are to have effect for periods beginning on or after a day determined in accordance with the regulations in relation to interest running from before that day as well as from or from after that day.

178(4) The power to make regulations under this section shall be exercisable by statutory instrument which shall be subject to annulment in pursuance of a resolution of the House of Commons.

178(5) [Omitted by FA 2009, s. 105(6)(a).]

178(6) [Not relevant to inheritance tax.]

178(7) Subsection (1) shall have effect for periods beginning on or after such day as the Treasury may by order made by statutory instrument appoint and shall have effect in relation to interest running from before that day as well as from or from after that day; and different days may be appointed for different enactments.

History – In s. 178(2)(k), the words ", 235(1)" inserted by FA 2009, s. 105(5)(b), with effect from 21 July 2009.
S. 178(2)(u) inserted by FA 2014, s. 274 and Sch. 35, para. 11(2), with effect from 17 July 2014.
S. 178(2)(v) inserted by FA 2015, s. 115(4) with effect in relation to accounting periods beginning on or after 1 April 2015 (subject to the provisions of FA 2015, s. 116(2)–(5)).
S. 178(5) omitted by FA 2009, s. 105(6)(a), with effect from 21 July 2009.

Notes – This version of s. 178 contains only material relevant to inheritance tax. A complete version of s. 178 is included in the Income Tax, Corporation Tax and Capital Gains Tax section (Vol. 1A).

GENERAL

188 Short title

188 This Act may be cited as the Finance Act 1989.

FINANCE ACT 1990

(1990 Chapter 29)

[*26th July 1990*]

ARRANGEMENT OF SECTIONS

PART IV – MISCELLANEOUS AND GENERAL

MISCELLANEOUS

PART IV – MISCELLANEOUS AND GENERAL

MISCELLANEOUS

124 Inheritance tax: restriction on power to require information

124 [Omitted by SI 2009/3054, art. 3 and Schedule, para. 16(a).]

History – S. 124 omitted by SI 2009/3054, art. 3 and Schedule, para. 16(a), with effect from 1 April 2010.

125 Information for tax authorities in other member States

125(1), (2) [Not relevant to inheritance tax.]

125(3) [Repealed by SI 2009/2035, art. 2 and Sch., para. 26.]

125(4) [Repealed by SI 2009/2035, art. 2 and Sch., para. 26.]

125(5) [Repealed by FA 2003, s. 216 and Sch. 43, Pt. 5(1).]

125(6) [Repealed by SI 2009/2035, art. 2 and Sch., para. 26.]

History – S. 125(3) omitted by SI 2009/2035, art. 2 and Sch, para. 26, with effect from 13 August 2009.
In former s. 125(3), the words "the Directive of the Council of the European Communities dated 19 December 1977 No. 77/799/EEC (the "1977 Directive")" substituted for the words "the Directive mentioned in subsection (1) above" by FA 2008, s. 113 and Sch. 36, para. 83(b), with effect from 1 April 2009 (SI 2009/404, art. 2, subject to savings at SI 2009/404, art. 3).
S. 125(4) omitted by SI 2009/2035, art. 2 and Sch, para. 26, with effect from 13 August 2009.
In former s. 125(4), the words "which is covered by the provisions for the exchange of information under the 1977 Directive" substituted for the words "such as is mentioned in subsection (1) above" by FA 2008, s. 113 and Sch. 36, para. 83(c), with effect from 1 April 2009 (SI 2009/404, art. 2, subject to savings at SI 2009/404, art. 3).
S. 125(5) repealed by FA 2003, s. 216 and Sch. 43, Pt. 5(1), with effect from 10 July 2003 (Royal Assent).
S. 125(6) omitted by SI 2009/2035, art. 2 and Sch, para. 26, with effect from 13 August 2009.
In former s. 125(6), the words "Subsections (1) and (2) above shall apply with respect to notices given on or after the day on which this Act is passed," omitted by FA 2008, s. 113 and Sch. 36, para. 83(d), with effect from 1 April 2009 (SI 2009/404, art. 2, subject to savings at SI 2009/404, art. 3).
In s. 125(6) the words " and subsection (5) above shall come into force on that day" repealed by FA 2003, s. 216 and Sch. 43, Pt. 5(1), with effect from 10 July 2003 (Royal Assent).

Cross references – FA 2000, s. 147(2).

European material – The directive mentioned in s. 125(1) is the Directive of the Council of the European Communities, dated 19 December 1977, 77/799 (OJ 1977/L336, p. 15).

126 Pools payments for football ground improvements

126 [Repealed by FA 2012, s. 227 and Sch. 39, para. 19(1).]

History – S. 126 repealed by FA 2012, s. 227 and Sch. 39, para. 19(1), with effect for inheritance tax purposes from 6 April 2013 (and in relation to payments whenever made).

133 Short title

133 This Act may be cited as the Finance Act 1990.

FINANCE ACT 1991

(1991 Chapter 31)

[*25th July 1991*]

PART V – MISCELLANEOUS AND GENERAL

MISCELLANEOUS

121 Pools payments to support games etc.

121 [Repealed by FA 2012, s. 227 and Sch. 39. para. 20(1).]

History – S. 121 repealed by FA 2012, s. 227 and Sch. 39. para. 20(1), with effect from 6 April 2013 (and in relation to payments whenever made).

FINANCE (NO. 2) ACT 1992

(1992 Chapter 48)

[16th July 1992]

ARRANGEMENT OF SECTIONS

PART III – MISCELLANEOUS AND GENERAL

PART III – MISCELLANEOUS AND GENERAL

INHERITANCE TAX

72 Increase of rate bands

72(1) [Spent, substituted new Table in IHTA 1984, Sch. 1.]

72(2) Subsection (1) above shall apply to any chargeable transfer made on or after 10th March 1992, and section 8(1) of the Inheritance Tax Act 1984 (indexation of rate bands) shall not apply to chargeable transfers made in the year beginning 6th April 1992.

Cross references – FA 1994, s. 246: no indexation of rate bands for the year beginning 6 April 1994.

73 Business and agricultural property relief

73 Schedule 14 to this Act (which makes provision in relation to relief in respect of business property and agricultural property) shall have effect.

76 Miscellaneous

76 [Omitted by SI 2009/56, art. 3 and Sch. 1, para. 186.]

History – S. 76 and the cross-heading which preceded it omitted by SI 2009/56, art. 3 and Sch. 1, para. 186, with effect from 1 April 2009, subject to transitional and saving provisions in SI 2009/56, Sch. 3. Former s. 76 and the heading read as follows:

"GENERAL AND SPECIAL COMMISSIONERS

76 Miscellaneous

76 Schedule 16 to this Act (which makes provision in relation to the remuneration, jurisdiction, practice and procedure of the General and Special Commissioners etc.) shall have effect."

GENERAL

83 Short title

83 This Act may be cited as the Finance (No. 2) Act 1992.

SCHEDULE 14 – INHERITANCE TAX

Section 73

BUSINESS PROPERTY

1 [Amends IHTA 1984, s. 104(1)(a), (1)(b).]

2(1) [Amends provisions as below.]

2(2) [Amends IHTA 1984, s. 105(1)(b).]

IHT Statutes

2(3) [Inserts IHTA 1984, s. 105(1)(cc).]

2(4) [Inserts IHTA 1984, s. 105(12A).]

2(3) [Amends IHTA 1984, s. 105(2).]

3 [Inserts IHTA 1984, s. 113A(3B).]

AGRICULTURAL PROPERTY

4 [Amends IHTA 1984, s. 116(2), (4).]

PAYMENT BY INSTALMENTS

5 [Inserts IHTA 1984, s. 227(1AA).]

6 [Inserts IHTA 1984, s. 228(5).]

GIFTS WITH RESERVATION

7 [Amends FA 1986, Sch. 20, para. 8(1A)(a).]

COMMENCEMENT

8 Subject to paragraph 9 below, the amendments made by this Schedule shall have effect in relation to transfers of value made, and other events occurring, on or after 10th March 1992.

9(1) This paragraph applies where by reason of a death occurring on or after 10th March 1992–

(a) a potentially exempt transfer made before that date proves to be a chargeable transfer, or

(b) additional tax falls to be calculated in respect of a chargeable transfer (other than a potentially exempt transfer) made before that date and within seven years of the death.

9(2) Subject to sub-paragraph (3) below, for the purposes of sections 113A and 113B of the Inheritance Tax Act 1984, it shall be assumed–

(a) that the amendments made by this Schedule came into effect at the time the transfer was made, and

(b) (in a case within sub-paragraph (1)(b) above) that so much of the value transferred as would have been reduced in accordance with Chapter I of Part V of that Act as amended by this Schedule was so reduced.

9(3) Where, disregarding the amendments made by this Schedule, any shares or securities transferred fell within section 105(1)(b) of that Act in relation to the transfer, those amendments shall be disregarded in determining whether section 113A(3A) applies to the shares or securities.

9(4) This paragraph shall be construed as if it were contained in Chapter I of Part V of that Act.

SCHEDULE 16 – GENERAL AND SPECIAL COMMISSIONERS

Section 76

[Omitted by SI 2009/56, art. 3 and Sch. 1, para. 186.]

History – Sch. 16 omitted by SI 2009/56, art. 3 and Sch. 1, para. 186, with effect from 1 April 2009, subject to transitional and saving provisions in SI 2009/56, Sch. 3. Former Sch. 16, para. 8 inserted IHTA 1984, s. 225A.

FINANCE ACT 1993

(1993 Chapter 34)

[27th July 1993]

ARRANGEMENT OF SECTIONS

PART IV – INHERITANCE TAX

196 Rate bands: no indexation in 1993

196 The Table substituted by section 72(1) of the Finance (No. 2) Act 1992 shall apply to chargeable transfers made in the year beginning 6th April 1993, and accordingly section 8(1) of the Inheritance Tax Act 1984 (indexation of rate bands) shall not apply to such transfers.

Cross references – IHTA 1984, s. 8(1): indexation of rate bands.

197 Rate bands: indexation for 1994 onwards

197(1) [Amends IHTA 1984, s. 8(1), (3) and (4).]

197(2) This section shall apply in relation to chargeable transfers made on or after 6th April 1994.

198 Fall in value relief: qualifying investments

198(1) [Inserts IHTA 1984, s. 186A and 186B.]

198(2) This section shall have effect in relation to deaths occurring on or after 16th March 1992.

199 Fall in value relief: interests in land

199(1) [Inserts IHTA 1984, s. 197A.]

199(2) This section shall have effect in relation to deaths occurring on or after 16th March 1990.

200 Appeals: questions as to value of land

200(1) [Substitutes IHTA 1984, s. 222(4), (4A) and (4B).]

200(2) [Amends IHTA 1984, s. 242(3).]

200(3) This section shall apply in relation to any appeal which–

(a) is made on or after the day on which this Act is passed, or

(b) is made, but has not begun to be heard, before that day.

PART VI – MISCELLANEOUS AND GENERAL

MISCELLANEOUS

208 Residence: available accommodation

208(1), (2) [Not relevant to inheritance tax.]

208(3) [Amends IHTA 1984, s. 267(4).]

208(4) [Not relevant to inheritance tax.]

208(5) Subsection (3) above shall have effect where the year of assessment concerned is 1993–94 or a subsequent year of assessment.

Notes – S. 208(1) inserts ICTA 1988, s. 336(3) (question of individual's residence to be determined without regard to availability of living accommodation in the UK for his use).

GENERAL

213 Repeals

213 The enactments specified in Schedule 23 to this Act (which include provisions which are already spent) are hereby repealed to the extent specified in the third column of that Schedule, but subject to any provision of that Schedule.

214 Short title

214 This Act may be cited as the Finance Act 1993.

FINANCE ACT 1994

(1994 Chapter 9)

[*3rd May 1994*]

ARRANGEMENT OF SECTIONS

PART VII – INHERITANCE TAX

PART VII – INHERITANCE TAX

246 Rate bands: no indexation in 1994

246 The Table substituted by section 72(1) of the Finance (No. 2) Act 1992 shall apply to chargeable transfers made in the year beginning 6th April 1994, and accordingly section 8(1) of the Inheritance Tax Act 1984 (indexation of rate bands) shall not apply to such transfers.

247 Business and agricultural relief

247(1) [Amends IHTA 1984, s. 113B(2)(a), (5)(b), (8).]

247(2) [Amends IHTA 1984, s. 124B(2)(a), (5)(b), (8).]

247(3) This section applies in relation to transfers of value made, and other events occurring, on or after 30th November 1993.

248 Corporate Lloyd's underwriters

248(1) No property forming part of a premiums trust fund or ancillary trust fund of a corporate member shall be relevant property for the purposes of Chapter III of Part III of the Inheritance Tax Act 1984 (settlements without interests in possession).

248(2) In this section **"ancillary trust fund"**, **"corporate member"** and **"premiums trust fund"** have the same meanings as in Chapter V of Part IV of this Act (Lloyd's underwriters: corporations etc.).

FINANCE ACT 1995

(1995 Chapter 4)

[*1st May 1995*]

ARRANGEMENT OF SECTIONS

PART VI – MISCELLANEOUS AND GENERAL

MISCELLANEOUS

PART VI – MISCELLANEOUS AND GENERAL

MISCELLANEOUS

154 Short rotation coppice

Notes – ITTOIA 2005, Sch. 1 amends s. 154 leaving it ineffective for income tax purposes, for 2005–06 onward. The omitted income tax material is principally rewritten at ITTOIA 2005, s. 876.

154(1) [Not relevant to inheritance tax.]

154(1A) [Not relevant to inheritance tax.]

154(2) For the purposes of the Inheritance Tax Act 1984 the cultivation of short rotation coppice shall be regarded as agriculture; and accordingly for those purposes–

(a) land on which short rotation coppice is cultivated shall be regarded as agricultural land, and

(b) buildings used in connection with the cultivation of short rotation coppice shall be regarded as farm buildings.

154(3) In subsections (1) and (2) **"short rotation coppice"** means a perennial crop of tree species planted at high density, the stems of which are harvested above ground level at intervals of less than ten years.

154(4) [Not relevant to inheritance tax.]

154(5) Subsection (2) and subsection (3) so far as relating to subsection (2) shall have effect in relation to transfers of value or other events occurring on or after 6th April 1995.

Other material – Taxline 2005/6 (not reproduced): land cultivated for the growing of energy crops is also brought within the definition of agricultural land attracting APR for the purposes of IHT 1984.

155 Inheritance tax: agricultural property

155(1) [Amends IHTA 1984, s. 116.]

155(2) [Inserts IHTA 1984, s. 116(2A); repealed by FA 1996, s. 205 and Sch. 41, Pt. VI.]

155(3) Subsections (1) and (2) above shall apply in relation to transfers of value made, and other events occurring, on or after 1st September 1995.

FINANCE ACT 1996

(1996 Chapter 8)

[*29th April 1996*]

ARRANGEMENT OF SECTIONS

PART V – INHERITANCE TAX

PART VII – MISCELLANEOUS AND SUPPLEMENTAL

MISCELLANEOUS: DIRECT TAXATION

MISCELLANEOUS: OTHER MATTERS

SCHEDULES

PART V – INHERITANCE TAX

183 Rate bands

183(1) [Spent: substituted table in IHTA 1984, Sch. 1.]

183(2) [Spent: disapplied indexation for 1996–97.]

184 Business property relief

184(1) The Inheritance Tax Act 1984 shall be amended as follows.

184(2) In section 105(1) (relevant business property for the purposes of business property relief)–

(a) [amends s. 105(1)(b);]

(b) [substitutes s. 105(1)(bb); and]

(c) [omits s. 105(c).]

184(3) [Amends IHTA 1984, s. 107(4).]

184(4) [Amends IHTA 1984, s. 113A(3A)(b).]

184(5) [Inserts IHTA 1984, s. 113A(7A).]

184(6) This section–

(a) so far is it inserts a new subsection (7A) in section 113A, has effect in relation to any transfer of value on or after 28th November 1995; and

(b) so far as it makes any other provision, has effect–

(i) in relation to any transfer of value on or after 6th April 1996, and

(ii) for the purposes of any charge to tax by reason of an event occurring on or after 6th April 1996, in relation to transfers of value before that date.

185 Agricultural property relief

185(1) Chapter II of Part V of the Inheritance Tax Act 1984 (agricultural property) shall be amended as follows.

185(2) [Inserts IHTA 1984, s. 116(5A)–(5E).]

185(3) In consequence of subsection (2) above, subsection (2A) of that section (which made, in relation to Scotland, provision which is superseded by the subsection (5A) inserted by subsection (2) above) shall cease to have effect.

185(4) [Inserts IHTA 1984, s. 124A(7A).]

185(5) Subsection (2) above–

(a) so far as relating to subsections (5A) to (5C) of section 116 of the Inheritance Tax Act 1984, has effect in any case where the death of the tenant or, as the case may be, the sole surviving tenant, occurs on or after 1st September 1995; and

(b) so far as relating to subsections (5D) and (5E) of that section, has effect in any case where the death of the transferor occurs on or after 1st September 1995.

185(6) Subsection (3) above has effect in any case where the death of the tenant or, as the case may be, the sole surviving tenant, occurs on or after 1st September 1995.

185(7) Subsection (4) above has effect in relation to any transfer of value on or after 28th November 1995.

PART VII – MISCELLANEOUS AND SUPPLEMENTAL

MISCELLANEOUS: DIRECT TAXATION

198 Banks

198 Schedule 37 to this Act (which re-defines "bank" for certain purposes, and makes related amendments) shall have effect.

199 Quotation or listing of securities

199 Schedule 38 to this Act (which contains amendments of enactments referring to the quotation or listing of securities) shall have effect.

200 Domicile for tax purposes of overseas electors

200(1) In determining–

(a) for the purposes of inheritance tax, income tax or capital gains tax where a person is domiciled at any time on or after 6th April 1996, or

(b) for the purposes of section 267(1)(a) of the Inheritance Tax Act 1984 (deemed UK domicile for three years after ceasing to be so domiciled) where a person was domiciled at any time on or after 6th April 1993,

there shall be disregarded any relevant action taken by that person (whether before, on or after that date) in connection with electoral rights.

200(2) Relevant action is taken by a person in connection with electoral rights where–

(a) he does anything with a view to, or in connection with, being registered as an overseas elector; or

(b) when registered as an overseas elector, he votes in any election at which he is entitled to vote by virtue of being so registered.

200(3) For the purposes of this section, a person is registered as an overseas elector if he is–

(a) registered in any register of parliamentary electors in pursuance of such a declaration as is mentioned in section 1(1)(a) of the Representation of the People Act 1985 (extension of parliamentary franchise to certain non-resident British citizens); or

(b) registered under section 3 of that Act of 1985 (certain non-resident peers entitled to vote at European Parliamentary elections).

200(4) Nothing in subsection (1) above prevents regard being had, in determining the domicile of a person at any time, to any relevant action taken by him in connection with electoral rights if–

(a) his domicile at that time falls to be determined for the purpose of ascertaining his or any other person's liability to any of the taxes mentioned in subsection (1)(a) above; and

(b) the person whose liability is being ascertained wishes regard to be had to that action;

and a person's domicile determined in accordance with any such wishes shall be taken to have been so determined for the purpose only of ascertaining the liability in question.

History – In s. *200(3)(a) the words "of parliamentary electors in pursuance of such a declaration as is mentioned in section 1(1)(a)" substituted* for the words "mentioned in section 12(10) of the Representation of the People Act 1993 (right to be registered of persons entitled to vote at parliamentary elections) on account of any entitlement to vote conferred on him by section 1" by the Representation of the People Act 2000, s. 15 and Sch. 6, para. 19 with effect from 16 February 2001.

MISCELLANEOUS: OTHER MATTERS

202 Gilt stripping

202(1)–(4) [Not relevant to inheritance tax.]

202(5) The Treasury may by regulations make provision for securing that enactments and subordinate legislation which–

(a) apply in relation to government securities or to any description of such securities, or

(b) for any other purpose refer (in whatever terms) to such securities or to any description of them,

have effect with such modifications as the Treasury may think appropriate in consequence of the making of any provision or arrangements for, or in connection with, the issue or transfer of strips of government securities or the consolidation of such strips into other securities.

202(6) Regulations under subsection (5) above may–

(a) impose a charge to income tax, corporation tax, capital gains tax, inheritance tax, stamp duty or stamp duty reserve tax;

(b) include provision applying generally to, or to any description of, enactments or subordinate legislation;

(c) make different provision for different cases; and

(d) contain such incidental, supplemental, consequential and transitional provision as the Treasury think appropriate.

202(7) The power to make regulations under subsection (5) above shall be exercisable by statutory instrument subject to annulment in pursuance of a resolution of the House of Commons.

202(8), (9) [Not relevant to inheritance tax.]

202(10) In this section–

"government securities" means any securities included in Part I of Schedule 11 to the Finance Act 1942;

"modifications" includes amendments, additions and omissions; and

"subordinate legislation" has the same meaning as in the Interpretation Act 1978;

and expressions used in this section and in section 47 of the Finance Act 1942 have the same meanings in this section as in that section.

SCHEDULES

SCHEDULE 37 – BANKS

Part III – Other amendments

AMENDMENTS OF THE INHERITANCE TAX ACT 1984

12(1) [Amends IHTA 1984, s. 157(5).]

12(2) [Inserts IHTA 1984, s. 157(6).]

12(3) This paragraph applies in relation to deaths occurring on or after the day on which this Act is passed.

Notes – FA 1996 was passed on 29 April 1996.

SCHEDULE 38 – QUOTATION OR LISTING OF SECURITIES

THE INHERITANCE TAX ACT 1984

2(1) [Amends IHTA 1984, s. 105(1ZA), 113A(3B) and s. 272.]

2(2) This paragraph has effect–

(a) in relation to transfers of value on or after 1st April 1996; and

(b) for the purposes of any charge to tax by reason of an event occurring on or after 1st April 1996, in relation to transfers of value before that date.

3(1) [Amends IHTA 1984, s. 180(3).]

3(2) This paragraph has effect in relation to any time falling on or after 1st April 1996.

4(1) [Amends IHTA 1984, s. 178(2).]

4(2) [Amends IHTA 1984, s. 186B(1)).]

4(3) This paragraph has effect in relation to investments sold, or treated as sold, on or after 1st April 1996.

5(1) [Amends IHTA 1984, s. 227(1AA) and 228(5).]

5(2) This paragraph has effect–

(a) in relation to transfers of value on or after 1st April 1996; and

(b) for the purposes of any charge to tax by reason of an event occurring on or after 1st April 1996, in relation to transfers of value before that date.

FINANCE ACT 1997

(1997 Chapter 16)

[*19th March 1997*]

ARRANGEMENT OF SECTIONS

PART VI – INHERITANCE TAX

PART VIII – MISCELLANEOUS AND SUPPLEMENTAL

SUPPLEMENTAL

PART VI – INHERITANCE TAX

93 Rate bands

93(1)–(2) [Spent: substituted Table in IHTA 1984, Sch. 1 for 1997–98 and disapplied s. 8.]

94 Agricultural property relief

94 [Inserts IHTA 1984, s. 124C.]

PART VIII – MISCELLANEOUS AND SUPPLEMENTAL

SUPPLEMENTAL

114 Short title

114 This Act may be cited as the Finance Act 1997.

FINANCE ACT 1998

(1998 Chapter 36)

[*31st July 1998*]

ARRANGEMENT OF SECTIONS

PART IV – INHERITANCE TAX ETC.

PART VI – MISCELLANEOUS AND SUPPLEMENTAL

GOVERNMENT BORROWING

SCHEDULES

PART IV – INHERITANCE TAX ETC.

142 Property of historic interest etc.

142 Schedule 25 to this Act (which makes provision about the designation of property of historic interest, etc. and about undertakings in relation to such property) shall have effect.

143 Removal of exemption for gifts for public benefit

143(1) [Repeals IHTA 1984, s. 26 with respect to any transfer of value made on or after 17th March 1998.]

143(2) Accordingly, in that Act, in relation to any transfer of value made on or after 17th March 1998–

(a) [amends IHTA 1984, s. 23(5), 29A(6);]

(b) [amends IHTA 1984, s. 29(5).]

143(3) [Amends IHTA 1984, s. 56(4), (7).]

143(4) [Amends IHTA 1984, s. 76.]

143(5) Subsection (4) above has effect in relation to property which ceases to be relevant property, or to be property to which any of sections 70 to 74 of the Inheritance Tax Act 1984 or paragraph 8 of Schedule 4 to that Act applies, on or after 17th March 1998.

143(6) [Amends IHTA 1984, s. 161(2).]

143(7) [Amends TCGA 1992, s. 258(2).]

144 Maintenance funds for historic buildings, etc.

144(1) [Amends IHTA 1984, s. 27(1); inserts s. 27(1A).]

144(2) This section has effect in relation to transfers of value made on or after 17th March 1998.

145 Accounting for property accepted in satisfaction of tax

145 [Omitted by CRCA 2005, Sch. 4, para. 67 and repealed by CRCA 2005, s. 52 and Sch. 5.]

History – S. 145 omitted by CRCA 2005, Sch. 4, para. 67 and repealed by CRCA 2005, s. 52 and Sch. 5, with effect from 18 April 2005 (by virtue of SI 2005/1126, reg. 2(2)).

PART VI – MISCELLANEOUS AND SUPPLEMENTAL

GOVERNMENT BORROWING

161 Non-FOTRA securities

161(1) Subject to the following provisions of this section, any gilt-edged security issued before 6th April 1998 without FOTRA conditions shall be treated in relation to times on or after that date as if–

(a) it were a security issued with the post-1996 Act conditions; and

(b) those conditions had been authorised in relation to the issue of that security by virtue of section 22 of the Finance (No. 2) Act 1931.

161(2) Where a gilt-edged security falls to be treated as mentioned in subsection (1) above that treatment shall have effect–

(a) for the purposes of sections 711 to 728 of the Taxes Act 1988 (accrued income scheme), in relation only to amounts which a person is treated under those sections as receiving on or after 6th April 1998;

(b) for the other purposes of the Tax Acts, in relation only to payments of interest falling due on or after that date; and

(c) for the purposes of the Inheritance Tax Act 1984, in relation only to a determination of whether property is excluded property at a time falling on or after that date.

161(3) No charge to tax shall be treated as arising under section 65 of the Inheritance Tax Act 1984 (property becoming excluded property) by reason only of the coming into force of this section.

161(4) In this section **"FOTRA conditions"** means any such conditions about exemption from taxation as are authorised in relation to the issue of a gilt-edged security by virtue of section 22 of the Finance (No. 2) Act 1931.

161(5) In this section **"the post-1996 Act conditions"** means the FOTRA conditions with which 7.25% Treasury Stock 2007 was first issued by virtue of section 22 of the Finance (No. 2) Act 1931.

161(6) In this section **"gilt-edged securities"** means any securities which are gilt-edged securities for the purposes of the Taxation of Chargeable Gains Act 1992.

161(7) This section does not apply to any 31/2% War Loan 1952 Or After which was issued with a condition authorised by virtue of section 47 of the Finance (No. 2) Act 1915.

SCHEDULES

SCHEDULE 25 – PROPERTY OF HISTORIC INTEREST ETC.

MEANING OF "THE 1984 ACT"

1 In this Schedule **"the 1984 Act"** means the Inheritance Tax Act 1984.

CLAIMS FOR DESIGNATION

2(1) [Inserts IHTA 1984, section 30(3BA).]

2(2) This paragraph has effect in relation to any transfer of value or death on or after 17th March 1998.

3(1) [Inserts IHTA 1984, s. 78(1A).]

3(2) This paragraph has effect in relation to transfers of property made, and other events occurring, on or after 17th March 1998.

PROPERTY CAPABLE OF DESIGNATION

4(1) [Substitutes IHTA 1984, s. 31(1)(a).]

4(2) [Substitutes IHTA 1984, s. 31(2), (3).]

4(3) [Substitutes IHTA 1984, s. 31(5).]

4(4) This paragraph has effect in relation to the making of any designation on a claim made on or after the day on which this Act is passed.

ACCESS TO DESIGNATED PROPERTY

5(1) [Inserts IHTA 1984, s. 31(4FA).]

5(2) This paragraph has effect in relation to the giving of any undertaking on or after the day on which this Act is passed.

PUBLICATION OF INFORMATION ABOUT DESIGNATED PROPERTY

6(1) [Inserts IHTA 1984, s. 31(4FB).]

6(2) This paragraph has effect in relation to the giving of any undertaking on or after the day on which this Act is passed.

UNDERTAKINGS ON DEATH, DISPOSAL OF PROPERTY, ETC.

7(1) [Amends IHTA 1984, s. 32(2).]

7(2) [Substitutes IHTA 1984, s. 32(5)(b).]

7(3) [Inserts IHTA 1984, s. 32(5AA).]

7(4) [Substitutes IHTA 1984, s. 32A(6).]

7(5) [Substitutes IHTA 1984, s. 32A(8)(b).]

7(6) [Inserts IHTA 1984, s. 32A(8A).]

7(7) [Substitutes IHTA 1984, s. 32A(9).]

7(8) [Substitutes IHTA 1984, Sch. 5, para. 5.]

7(9) This paragraph has effect in relation to the giving of any undertaking on or after the day on which this Act is passed.

VARIATION OF UNDERTAKINGS

8(1) [Inserts IHTA 1984, s. 35A.]

8(2) [Inserts IHTA 1984, s. 79A(8)(b).]

8(3) [Inserts IHTA 1984, Sch. 4, para. 3(3A).]

8(4) Subject to paragraph 10 below, this paragraph has effect in relation to undertakings given on or after the day on which this Act is passed.

9(1) [Inserts TCGA 1992, s. 258(8A).]

9(2) Subject to paragraph 10 below, this paragraph has effect in relation to undertakings given on or after the day on which this Act is passed.

10(1) Section 35A of the 1984 Act applies in relation to a relevant undertaking given with respect to any property before the day on which this Act is passed except in a case where there has been a chargeable event with respect to that property at any time after the giving of the undertaking but before that day.

10(2) In its application to such a relevant undertaking, section 35A of the 1984 Act applies with the modifications set out in sub-paragraphs (3) and (4) below.

10(3) [Substitutes IHTA 1984, s. 35A(2)(a).]

10(4) [Inserts IHTA 1984, s. 35A(5), (6).]

10(5) In this paragraph **"relevant undertaking"** means any of the following–

(a) an undertaking given under section 30, 32, 32A, 78 or 79 of the 1984 Act;

(b) an undertaking given under paragraph 3(3) of Schedule 4 to the 1984 Act or paragraph 5(2) of Schedule 5 to that Act;

(c) an undertaking given under section 76, 78, 81 or 82 of the Finance Act 1976;

(d) an undertaking given under section 34(2) of the Finance Act 1975;

(e) an undertaking given under section 258 of the Taxation of Chargeable Gains Act 1992.

10(6) In this paragraph **"chargeable event"**, in relation to any property means–

(a) an event which under section 32 or 32A of the 1984 Act is a chargeable event with respect to that property; or

(b) an event which under *either of those sections* would be such an event if (where it is not the case) the undertaking in question had been given under section 30 of that Act.

FINANCE ACT 1999

(1999 Chapter 16)

[*27th July 1999*]

ARRANGEMENT OF SECTIONS

PART V – INHERITANCE TAX

PART VIII – GENERAL ADMINISTRATION OF TAX

PART V – INHERITANCE TAX

104 Gifts

104 [Inserts FA 1986, s. 102A, s. 102B, s. 102C.]

105 Delivery of accounts

105(1) [Substitutes IHTA 1984, s. 216(3); inserts IHTA 1984, s. 216(3A), (3B).]

105(2) This section has effect in relation to deaths occurring on or after 9th March 1999.

106 Power to call for documents etc.

106 [Omitted by SI 2009/3054, art. 3 and Schedule, para. 16(b).]

History – S. 106 omitted by SI 2009/3054, art. 3 and Schedule, para. 16(b), with effect from 1 April 2010.

107 Inland revenue charge

107(1) [Amends IHTA 1984, s. 237(3).]

107(2) [Inserts IHTA 1984, s. 237(3B), (3C).]

107(3) Subsection (1) above has effect in relation to deaths occurring on or after 9th March 1999; and subsection (2) above has effect in relation to tax charged on or after that day.

108 Penalties

108(1) [Substitutes IHTA 1984, s. 245. Inserts IHTA 1984, s. 245A.]

108(2) [Amends IHTA 1984, s. 247(3), (4).]

108(3) Subsection (1) above does not have effect in relation to a failure by any person–

(a) to deliver an account under section 216 or 217 of the Inheritance Tax Act 1984,

(b) to make a return under section 218 of that Act, or

(c) to comply with a notice under section 219 of that Act,

where the period within which the person is required to perform the obligation in question expires before the day on which this Act is passed.

108(4) Subsection (2) above has effect in relation to incorrect accounts, information or documents delivered, furnished or produced on or after the day on which this Act is passed.

History – S. 108(2)(a) omitted by FA 2008, s. 122 and Sch. 40, para. 21(g), with effect from 1 April 2009 (SI 2009/571).

PART VIII – GENERAL ADMINISTRATION OF TAX

132 Power to provide for use of electronic communications

132(1) Regulations may be made, in accordance with this section, for facilitating the use of electronic communications for–

(a) the delivery of information the delivery of which is authorised or required by or under any legislation relating to a taxation matter;

(b) the making of payments under any such legislation.

IHT Statutes

132(2) The power to make regulations under this section is conferred–

(a) on the Commissioners of Inland Revenue in relation to matters which are under their care and management; and

(b) on the Commissioners of Customs and Excise in relation to matters which are under their care and management.

132(3) For the purposes of this section provision for facilitating the use of electronic communications includes any of the following–

(a) provision authorising persons to use electronic communications for the delivery of information to tax authorities, or for the making of payments to tax authorities;

(b) provision requiring electronic communications to be used for the making to tax authorities of payments due from persons using such communications for the delivery of information to those authorities;

(c) provision authorising tax authorities to use electronic communications for the delivery of information to other persons or for the making of any payments;

(d) provision as to the electronic form to be taken by any information that is delivered to any tax authorities using electronic communications;

(e) provision requiring persons to prepare and keep records of information delivered to tax authorities by means of electronic communications, and of payments made to any such authorities by any such means;

(f) provision for the production of the contents of records kept in accordance with any regulations under this section;

(g) provision imposing conditions that must be complied with in connection with any use of electronic communications for the delivery of information or the making of any payment;

(h) provision, in relation to cases where use is made of electronic communications, for treating information as not having been delivered, or a payment as not having been made, unless conditions imposed by any such regulations are satisfied;

(i) provision, in relation to such cases, for determining the time when information is delivered or a payment is made;

(j) provision, in relation to such cases, for determining the person by whom information is to be taken to have been delivered or by whom a payment is to be taken to have been made;

(k) provision, in relation to cases where information is delivered by means of electronic communications, for authenticating whatever is delivered.

132(4) The power to make provision under this section for facilitating the use of electronic communications shall also include power to make such provision as the persons exercising the power think fit (including provision for the application of conclusive or other presumptions) as to the manner of proving for any purpose–

(a) whether any use of electronic communications is to be taken as having resulted in the delivery of information or the making of a payment;

(b) the time of delivery of any information for the delivery of which electronic communications have been used;

(c) the time of the making of any payment for the making of which electronic communications have been used;

(d) the person by whom information delivered by means of electronic communications was delivered;

(e) the contents of anything so delivered;

(f) the contents of any records;

(g) any other matter for which provision may be made by regulations under this section.

132(5) Regulations under this section may–

(a) allow any authorisation or requirement for which such regulations may provide to be given or imposed by means of a specific or general direction given by the Commissioners of Inland Revenue or the Commissioners of Customs and Excise;

(b) provide that the conditions of any such authorisation or requirement are to be taken to be satisfied only where such tax authorities as may be determined under the regulations are satisfied as to specified matters;

(c) allow a person to refuse to accept delivery of information in an electronic form or by means of electronic communications except in such circumstances as may be specified in or determined under the regulations;

(d) allow or require use to be made of intermediaries in connection with–

(i) the delivery of information, or the making of payments, by means of electronic communications; or

(ii) the authentication or security of anything transmitted by any such means.

132(6) Power to make provision by regulations under this section shall include power–

(a) to provide for a contravention of, or any failure to comply with, a specified provision of any such regulations to attract a penalty of a specified amount not exceeding £1,000;

(b) to provide that specified enactments relating to penalties imposed for the purposes of any taxation matter (including enactments relating to assessments, review and appeal) are to apply, with or without modifications, in relation to penalties under such regulations;

(c) to make different provision for different cases;

(d) to make such incidental, supplemental, consequential and transitional provision in connection with any provision contained in any such regulations as the persons exercising the power think fit.

132(7) The power to make regulations under this section shall be exercisable by statutory instrument subject to annulment in pursuance of a resolution of the House of Commons.

132(8) References in this section to the delivery of information include references to any of the following (however referred to)–

(a) the production or furnishing to a person of any information, account, record or document;

(b) the giving, making, issue or surrender to, or service on, any person of any notice, notification, statement, declaration, certificate or direction;

(c) the imposition on any person of any requirement or the issue to any person of any request;

(d) the making of any return, claim, election or application;

(e) the amendment or withdrawal of anything mentioned in paragraphs (a) to (d) above.

132(9) References in this section to a taxation matter are references to any of the matters which are under the care and management of the Commissioners of Inland Revenue or of the Commissioners of Customs and Excise.

132(10) In this section–

"electronic communications" includes any communications by means of an electronic communications service;

"legislation" means any enactment, Community legislation or subordinate legislation;

"payment" includes a repayment;

"records" includes records in electronic form;

"subordinate legislation" has the same meaning as in the Interpretation Act 1978;

"tax authorities" means–

(a) the Commissioners of Inland Revenue or the Commissioners of Customs and Excise,

(b) any officer of either body of Commissioners; or

(c) any other person who for the purposes of electronic communications is acting under the authority of either body of Commissioners.

History – In s. 132(10), in the definition of "electronic communications", the words "an electronic communications service" substituted for the words "a telecommunication system (within the meaning of the Telecommunications Act 1984)" by the Communications Act 2003, s. 406(1) and Sch. 17, para. 156, with effect for the purpose only of enabling the networks and services functions and the spectrum functions to be carried out by the Director General of Telecommunications and the Secretary of State respectively, during the transitional period (as provided for by the Communications Act 2003, s. 408(6)) from 25 July 2003–29 December 2003 (by virtue of SI 2003/1900, art. 2(1), 3(1), Sch. 1 and the Communications Act 2003, s. 406(6), 408, Sch. 18, para. 2); and with effect for the purpose of conferring the networks and services functions and the spectrum functions on OFCOM from 29 December 2003 (by virtue of SI 2003/3142, art. 3(2)).

Cross references – FA 2000, Sch. 38, para. 1: power to make regulations for providing incentives to use electronic communications.

Statutory instruments – SI 2015/1378.

FINANCE ACT 2000

(2000 Chapter 17) [*28th July 2000*]

ARRANGEMENT OF SECTIONS

PART V – OTHER TAXES

INHERITANCE TAX

PART VI – MISCELLANEOUS AND SUPPLEMENTARY PROVISIONS

INFORMATION POWERS

SCHEDULES

PART V – OTHER TAXES

INHERITANCE TAX

138 Treatment of employee share ownership trusts

138(1) The Inheritance Tax Act 1984 is amended as follows.

138(2) [Inserts IHTA 1984, s. 13(4)(c).]

138(3) [Amends IHTA 1984, s. 72(2) and inserts IHTA 1984, s. 72(4A).]

138(4) [Inserts IHTA 1984, s. 86(3)(c).]

PART VI – MISCELLANEOUS AND SUPPLEMENTARY PROVISIONS

INFORMATION POWERS

147 International exchange of information: inheritance tax

147 [Repealed by FA 2006, s. 178 and Sch. 26, Pt. 8(2).]

History – S. 147 repealed by FA 2006, s. 178 and Sch. 26, Pt. 8(2) with effect from 25 July 2006 (Royal Assent).

SCHEDULES

SCHEDULE 29 – CHARGEABLE GAINS: NON-RESIDENT COMPANIES AND GROUPS ETC.

Section 101

Part II – Minor and Consequential Amendments

SECTION 97 OF THE INHERITANCE TAX ACT 1984

14 The *main amendments* have effect for the purposes of section 97 of the Inheritance Tax Act 1984 (transfer of asset within a group of companies) in relation to disposals on or after 1st April 2000.

FINANCE ACT 2001

(2001 Chapter 9)

[*11th May 2001*]

PART 4 – OTHER TAXES

INHERITANCE TAX

106 Transfers within group etc.

106(1) Section 97 of the Inheritance Tax Act 1984 (c. 51) (transfers within group etc.) is amended as follows.

106(2) [Substitutes IHTA 1984, s. 97(1)(a) and inserts IHTA 1984, s. 97(1)(aa).]

106(3) The amendment made by this section has effect, and shall be taken always to have had effect, in relation to disposals made, or transfers deemed to have been made, on or after 1st April 2000.

FINANCE ACT 2002

(2002 Chapter 23)

[*24th July 2002*]

ARRANGEMENT OF SECTIONS

PART 3 – INCOME TAX, CORPORATION TAX AND CAPITAL GAINS TAX

CHARGEABLE GAINS

42 Reallocation within group of gain or loss accruing under section 179

42(1)–(2) [Not relevant to inheritance tax.]

42(3) [Inserts IHTA 1984, s. 97(1)(a)(iii) and amends s. 97(1)(aa).]

42(4) [Not relevant to inheritance tax.]

PART 5 – OTHER TAXES

INHERITANCE TAX

118 IHT: rate bands

118(1) [Spent – substituted new Table in IHTA 1984, Sch. 1.]

118(2) Subsection (1) shall apply to any chargeable transfer made on or after 6th April 2002; and section 8(1) of that Act (indexation of rate bands) shall not have effect as respects any difference between the retail prices index for the month of September 2000 and that for the month of September 2001.

119 IHT: powers over, or exercisable in relation to, settled property or a settlement

119(1) The Inheritance Tax Act 1984 is amended in accordance with the following provisions of this section.

119(2) [Inserts IHTA 1984, s. 47A.]

119(3) [Inserts IHTA 1984, s. 55A.]

119(4) [Amends IHTA 1984, s. 272.]

119(5) In consequence of the amendments made by this section, the title of Chapter 2 of Part 3 of the Inheritance Tax Act 1984 (c. 51) becomes "Interests in possession, reversionary interests and settlement powers".

119(6) The amendments made by this section have effect in relation to transfers of value on or after 17th April 2002.

119(7) The amendments made by subsections (2) and (4) shall also be deemed always to have had effect (subject to and in accordance with the other provisions of the Inheritance Tax Act 1984) for the purpose of determining the value, immediately before his death, of the estate of any person who died before 17th April 2002, for the purposes of the transfer of value which that person is treated by section 4(1) of that Act as having made immediately before his death.

120 IHT: variation of dispositions taking effect on death

120(1) [Substitutes IHTA 1984, s. 142(2) and (2A).]

120(2) [Inserts IHTA 1984, s. 218A.]

120(3) [Inserts IHTA 1984, s. 245A(1A), amends s. 245A(4) and inserts s. 245A(4)(aa).]

120(4) This section applies in relation to instruments made on or after 1st August 2002.

FINANCE ACT 2003

(2003 Chapter 14)

[*10th July 2003*]

ARRANGEMENT OF SECTIONS

PART 8 – OTHER TAXES

INHERITANCE TAX

PART 9 – MISCELLANEOUS AND SUPPLEMENTARY PROVISIONS

INTERNATIONAL MATTERS

SUPPLEMENTARY

PART 8 – OTHER TAXES

INHERITANCE TAX

185 Inheritance tax: Gifts with reservation

185(1) Section 102 of the Finance Act 1986 (c. 41) (gifts with reservation) is amended as follows.

185(2) [Amends FA 1986, s. 102(5)(a).]

185(3) [Inserts FA 1986, s. 102(5A)–(5C).]

185(4) The amendments made by this section have effect in relation to disposals made on or after 20th June 2003.

186 Authorised unit trusts, OEICs and common investment funds

186(1) The Inheritance Tax Act 1984 (c. 51) is amended as follows.

186(2) [Inserts IHTA 1984, s. 6(1A).]

186(3) [Inserts IHTA 1984, s. 48(3A).]

186(4) [Amends IHTA 1984, s. 178(1).]

186(5) Section 272 (general interpretation) is amended as follows.

186(6) [Amends IHTA 1984, s. 272.]

186(7) [Amends IHTA 1984, s. 272.]

186(8) This section has effect in relation to transfers of value or other events occurring on or after 16th October 2002.

PART 9 – MISCELLANEOUS AND SUPPLEMENTARY PROVISIONS

INTERNATIONAL MATTERS

197 Exchange of information between tax authorities of member States

197 [Repealed by *SI 2012/3062*, reg. 7 and Sch. 1.]

History – S. 197 repealed by SI 2012/3062, reg. 7 and Sch. 1, with effect from 1 January 2013.

198 Arrangements for mutual exchange of tax information

198 [Repealed by FA 2006, s. 178 and Sch. 26, Pt. 8(2).]

History – S. 198 repealed by FA 2006, s. 178 and Sch. 26, Pt. 8(2), with effect from 19 July 2006.

SUPPLEMENTARY

215 Interpretation

215 In this Act **"the Taxes Act 1988"** means the Income and Corporation Taxes Act 1988 (c. 1).

217 Short title

217 This Act may be cited as the Finance Act 2003.

FINANCE ACT 2004

(2004 Chapter 12)

[*22nd July 2004*]

ARRANGEMENT OF SECTIONS

PART 4 – PENSION SCHEMES ETC

CHAPTER 4 – REGISTERED PENSION SCHEMES: TAX RELIEFS AND EXEMPTIONS

INHERITANCE TAX EXEMPTIONS

PART 6 – OTHER TAXES

INHERITANCE TAX

PART 7 – DISCLOSURE OF TAX AVOIDANCE SCHEMES

SCHEDULES
36. PENSION SCHEMES ETC: TRANSITIONAL PROVISIONS AND SAVINGS
Part 4 – Other Provisions

PART 4 – PENSION SCHEMES ETC

Chapter 4 – Registered Pension Schemes: Tax Reliefs and Exemptions

INHERITANCE TAX EXEMPTIONS

203 Inheritance tax exemptions

203(1) The Inheritance Tax Act 1984 (c. 51) is amended as follows.
203(2) [Amends IHTA 1984, s. 12(2) and omits IHTA 1984, s. 12(3) and (4).]
203(3) [Substitutes IHTA 1984, s. 58(1)(d).]
203(4) [Omits IHTA 1984, s. 151(1) and (1A) and amends IHTA 1984, s. 151(2), (4) and (5).]
203(5) [Amends IHTA 1984, s. 152.]
203(6) [Amends IHTA 1984, s. 272.]

PART 6 – OTHER TAXES

INHERITANCE TAX

293 Delivery of accounts etc

293(1) Section 256 of the Inheritance Tax Act 1984 (c. 51) (regulations about information to be furnished to the Board) is amended as follows.
293(2) [Amends IHTA 1984, s. 256(1).]
293(3) [Inserts IHTA 1984, s. 256(1A).]
293(4) [Amends IHTA 1984, s. 256(2).]
293(5) [Amends IHTA 1984, s. 256(3).]
293(6) [Inserts IHTA 1984, s. 256(3A).]

294 Grant of probate

294(1) In section 109 of the Supreme Court Act 1981 (c. 54) (refusal of grant of probate where inheritance tax unpaid)–
(a) [substitutes SCA 1981, s. 109(1);]
(b) [amends SCA 1981, s. 109(2);]
(c) [inserts SCA 1981, s. 109(2A);]
(d) [omits SCA 1981, s. 109(3).]
294(2) [Amends PLDA 1808, s. 42.]
294(3) In Article 20 of the Administration of Estates (Northern Ireland) Order 1979 (S.I.1979/1575 (N.I.14)) (inheritance tax accounts)–
(a) for paragraph (1) substitute–
"(1) The High Court shall not make any grant, or reseal any grant made outside the United Kingdom, except–
(a) on the production of information or documents under regulations under section 256(1)(aa) of the Inheritance Tax Act 1984 (excepted estates); or
(b) on the production of an account prepared in pursuance of that Act showing by means of such receipt or certification as may be prescribed by the Commissioners of Inland Revenue either–
(i) that the inheritance tax payable on the delivery of the account has been paid; or
(ii) that no such tax is so payable.";
(b) in paragraph (2) of that Article, for "this Article" substitute "paragraph (1)(b)".

IHT Statutes

294(4) Subsection (1) shall come into force on such day as the Treasury may after consulting the Lord Chancellor by order made by statutory instrument appoint.

294(5) Subsection (2) shall come into force on such day as the Treasury may after consulting the Scottish Ministers by order made by statutory instrument appoint.

294(6) Subsection (3) shall come into force on such day as the Treasury may after consulting the Lord Chancellor by order made by statutory instrument appoint.

Notes – The day appointed for the purposes of s. 294(1), (2) and (3) is 1 November 2004 (SI 2004/2571, reg. 2).

295 Amendments to penalty regime

295(1) The Inheritance Tax Act 1984 is amended as specified in subsections (2) to (4).

295(2) In section 245 (failure to deliver accounts)–

(a) [amends IHTA 1984, s. 245(2)(a) and (3);]

(b) [inserts IHTA 1984, s. 245(4A).]

295(3) In section 245A (failure to provide information etc)–

(a) [inserts IHTA 1984, s. 245A(1B);]

(b) [amends IHTA 1984, s. 245A(5).]

295(4) [Partially omitted by FA 2008, s. 122 and Sch. 40, para. 21(1). Amends IHTA 1984, s. 247.]

295(5) Subsection (2)(a) above has effect in relation to a failure by any person to deliver an account under section 216 or 217 of the Inheritance Tax Act 1984 (c. 51) where the period under section 216(6) or (7) or 217 of that Act (whichever is applicable) within which the person is required to deliver the account expires after six months from the day on which this Act is passed.

295(6) Subsection (2)(b) above has effect–

(a) in relation to a failure by any person to deliver an account under section 216 of the Inheritance Tax Act 1984 where the period under section 216(6) or (7) of that Act (whichever is applicable) within which the person is required to deliver the account expires after the day on which this Act is passed; and

(b) in relation to such a failure to deliver such an account where that period expires on or before the day on which this Act is passed, as if, in the subsection (4A) inserted in section 245 of that Act by subsection (2)(b) above, for the words "anniversary of the end of the period given by section 216(6) or (7) (whichever is applicable)" there were substituted "end of the period of twelve months beginning with the day on which the Finance Act 2004 is passed".

295(7) Subsection (3)(a) above has effect–

(a) in relation to a failure to comply with the requirements of section 218A of the Inheritance Tax Act 1984 (c. 51) where the period of six months referred to in subsection (1) of that section expires after the day on which this Act is passed; and

(b) in relation to such a failure to comply with those requirements where that period expires on or before the day on which this Act is passed, as if, in the subsection (1B) inserted in section 245A of that Act by subsection (3)(a) above, for the words "anniversary of the end of the period of six months referred to in section 218A(1)" there were substituted "end of the period of twelve months beginning with the day on which the Finance Act 2004 is passed".

295(8) Subsection (3)(b) above has effect in relation to a failure to comply with the requirements of section 218A of the Inheritance Tax Act 1984 (c. 51) where the period of six months referred to in subsection (1) of that section expires after the day on which this Act is passed.

295(9) Subsection (4) above has effect in relation to incorrect accounts, information or documents delivered, furnished or produced after the day on which this Act is passed.

History – S. 295(4)(a) omitted by FA 2008, s. 122 and Sch. 40, para. 21(1), with effect on 1 April 2009 (SI 2009/571, art. 2, but subject to transitional provisions at SI 2009/571, art. 6 and 7).

PART 7 – DISCLOSURE OF TAX AVOIDANCE SCHEMES

Cross references – SI 2004/1863: prescribed descriptions of arrangements, where the main benefit which might be expected to arise is the obtaining of a tax advantage, resulting in the promoter's duty to notify HMRC.

SI 2004/1864: details of the information that must be provided to HMRC – entered into force on 1 August 2004, but which generally do not impose a requirement to provide information relating to proposals or arrangements where the "relevant date" (see s. 308(2)) is before 22 July 2004).

SI 2004/1865: circumstances in which a person is not to be regarded as a promoter in relation to tax avoidance schemes for the purposes of s. 307.

SI 2007/785: provisions corresponding to Pt. 7, other than s. 314.

SI 2011/170: prescribed descriptions of inheritance tax arrangements for the purposes of Pt. 7.

306 Meaning of "notifiable arrangements" and "notifiable proposal"

306(1) In this Part **"notifiable arrangements"** means any arrangements which–

(a) fall within any description prescribed by the Treasury by regulations,

(b) enable, or might be expected to enable, any person to obtain an advantage in relation to any tax that is so prescribed in relation to arrangements of that description, and

(c) are such that the main benefit, or one of the main benefits, that might be expected to arise from the arrangements is the obtaining of that advantage.

306(2) In this Part **"notifiable proposal"** means a proposal for arrangements which, if entered into, would be notifiable arrangements (whether the proposal relates to a particular person or to any person who may seek to take advantage of it).

Statutory instruments – SI 2004/1863: made under s. 306(1)(a) and (b).
SI 2006/1543: made under s. 306(1)(a) and (b).
SI 2011/170: made under s. 306(1)(a) and (b).
Other material – M04/2006: HMRC guidance on the disclosure of tax avoidance schemes.

306A Doubt as to notifiability

306A(1) HMRC may apply to the tribunal for an order that–

(a) a proposal is to be treated as notifiable, or

(b) arrangements are to be treated as notifiable.

306A(2) An application must specify–

(a) the proposal or arrangements in respect of which the order is sought, and

(b) the promoter.

306A(3) On an application the tribunal may make the order only if satisfied that HMRC–

(a) have taken all reasonable steps to establish whether the proposal or arrangements are notifiable, and

(b) have reasonable grounds for suspecting that the proposal or arrangements may be notifiable.

306A(4) Reasonable steps under subsection (3)(a) may (but need not) include taking action under section 313A or 313B.

306A(5) Grounds for suspicion under subsection (3)(b) may include–

(a) the fact that the relevant arrangements fall within a description prescribed under section 306(1)(a);

(b) an attempt by the promoter to avoid or delay providing information or documents about the proposal or arrangements under or by virtue of section 313A or 313B;

(c) the promoter's failure to comply with a requirement under or by virtue of section 313A or 313B in relation to another proposal or other arrangements.

306A(6) Where an order is made under this section in respect of a proposal or arrangements, the prescribed period for the purposes of section 308(1) or (3) in so far as it applies by virtue of the order–

(a) shall begin after a date prescribed for the purpose, and

(b) may be of a different length than the prescribed period for the purpose of other applications of section 308(1) or (3).

306A(7) An order under this section in relation to a proposal or arrangements is without prejudice to the possible application of section 308, other than by virtue of this section, to the proposal or arrangements.

History – In s. 306A(1) and (3), "tribunal" substituted for "Special Commissioners" by SI 2009/56, art. 3(1) and Sch. 1, para. 429, operative from 1 April 2009, subject to transitional and saving provisions in SI 2009/56, Sch. 3.
S. 306A inserted by FA 2007, s. 108(2) with effect from 19 July 2007.

Cross references – SI 2009/275, art. 3(i): any decision under s. 306A is an excluded decision for the purposes of TCEA 2007, s. 11(1) and 13(1).
SI 2007/3104: where a penalty is imposed under TMA 1970, s. 98C(1) following an order under FA 2004, s. 306A, or s. 314A the amount specified in s. 98C(1)(b) is increased to £5,000.
Other material – M04/2006: HMRC guidance on the disclosure of tax avoidance schemes.

307 Meaning of "promoter"

307(1) For the purposes of this Part a person is a promoter–

(a) in relation to a notifiable proposal, if, in the course of a relevant business, the person ("P")–

 (i) is to any extent responsible for the design of the proposed arrangements,

 (ii) makes a firm approach to another person ("C") in relation to the notifiable proposal with a view to P making the notifiable proposal available for implementation by C or any other person, or

 (iii) makes the notifiable proposal available for implementation by other persons, and

IHT Statutes

(b) in relation to notifiable arrangements, if he is by virtue of paragraph (a)(ii) or (iii) a promoter in relation to a notifiable proposal which is implemented by those arrangements or if, in the course of a relevant business, he is to any extent responsible for–

(i) the design of the arrangements, or

(ii) the organisation or management of the arrangements.

307(1A) For the purposes of this Part a person is an introducer in relation to a notifiable proposal if the person makes a marketing contact with another person in relation to the notifiable proposal.

307(2) In this section **"relevant business"** means any trade, profession or business which–

(a) involves the provision to other persons of services relating to taxation, or

(b) is carried on by a bank, as defined by section 1120 of the Corporation Tax Act 2010, or by a securities house, as defined by section 1009(3) of that Act.

307(3) For the purposes of this section anything done by a company is to be taken to be done in the course of a relevant business if it is done for the purposes of a relevant business falling within subsection (2)(b) carried on by another company which is a member of the same group.

307(4) Section 170 of the Taxation of Chargeable Gains Act 1992 has effect for determining for the purposes of subsection (3) whether two companies are members of the same group, but as if in that section–

(a) for each of the references to a 75 per cent subsidiary there were substituted a reference to a 51 per cent subsidiary, and

(b) subsection (3)(b) and subsections (6) to (8) were omitted.

307(4A) For the purposes of this Part a person makes a firm approach to another person in relation to a notifiable proposal if the person makes a marketing contact with the other person in relation to the notifiable proposal at a time when the proposed arrangements have been substantially designed.

307(4B) For the purposes of this Part a person makes a marketing contact with another person in relation to a notifiable proposal if–

(a) the person communicates information about the notifiable proposal to the other person,

(b) the communication is made with a view to that other person, or any other person, entering into transactions forming part of the proposed arrangements, and

(c) the information communicated includes an explanation of the advantage in relation to any tax that might be expected to be obtained from the proposed arrangements.

307(4C) For the purposes of subsection (4A) proposed arrangements have been substantially designed at any time if by that time the nature of the transactions to form part of them has been sufficiently developed for it to be reasonable to believe that a person who wished to obtain the advantage mentioned in subsection (4B)(c) might enter into–

(a) transactions of the nature developed, or

(b) transactions not substantially different from transactions of that nature.

307(5) A person is not to be treated as a promoter or introducer for the purposes of this Part by reason of anything done in prescribed circumstances.

307(6) In the application of this Part to a proposal or arrangements which are not notifiable, a reference to a promoter or introducer is a reference to a person who would be a promoter or introducer under subsections (1) to (5) if the proposal or arrangements were notifiable.

History – In s. 307(1)(a), the words from "business, the person ("P")–" to "makes" (in s. 307(1)(a)(iii)) substituted for the former words by FA 2010, s. 56 and Sch. 17, para. 2(2), with effect from 1 January 2011 (2010/3019).
In s. 307(1)(b), "or (iii)" inserted after "(a)(ii)" by FA 2010, s. 56 and Sch. 17, para. 2(3), with effect from 1 January 2011 (2010/3019).
S. 307(1A) inserted by FA 2010, s. 56 and Sch. 17, para. 2(4), with effect from 1 January 2011 (2010/3019).
In s. 307(2)(b), the words "section 1120 of the Corporation Tax Act 2010" substituted for the words "section 840A of the Taxes Act 1988", and the words "section 1009(3)" substituted for the words "section 209A(4)", by CTA 2010, s. 1177 and Sch. 1, para. 429, with effect for corporation tax purposes for accounting periods ending on or after 1 April 2010, and for income tax and capital gains tax purposes for the tax year 2010–11 and subsequent tax years.
S. 307(4A) inserted by FA 2010, s. 56 and Sch. 17, para. 2(5), with effect from 1 January 2011 (SI 2010/3019).
S. 307(4B) inserted by FA 2010, s. 56 and Sch. 17, para. 2(5), with effect from 1 January 2011 (SI 2010/3019).
S. 307(4C) inserted by FA 2010, s. 56 and Sch. 17, para. 2(5), with effect from 1 January 2011 (SI 2010/3019).
In s. 307(5), the words "or introducer" inserted after "promoter" by FA 2010, s. 56 and Sch. 17, para. 2(6), with effect from 1 January 2011 (SI 2010/3019).
In s. 307(6), the words "or introducer" inserted after "promoter" in both places by FA 2010, s. 56 and Sch. 17, para. 2(7), with effect from 1 January 2011 (SI 2010/3019).
S. 307(6) inserted by FA 2007, s. 108(3) with effect from 19 July 2007.

***Cross references** – SI 2004/1865.*

Statutory instruments – SI 2004/1865: made under s. 307(5).

Other material – M04/2006: HMRC guidance on the disclosure of tax avoidance schemes.

308 Duties of promoter

308(1) A person who is a promoter in relation to a notifiable proposal must, within the prescribed period after the relevant date, provide the Board with prescribed information relating to the notifiable proposal.

308(2) In subsection (1) **"the relevant date"** means the earliest of the following–

(za) the date on which the promoter first makes a firm approach to another person in relation to a notifiable proposal,

(a) the date on which the promoter makes the notifiable proposal available for implementation by any other person, or

(b) the date on which the promoter first becomes aware of any transaction forming part of notifiable arrangements implementing the notifiable proposal.

308(3) A person who is a promoter in relation to notifiable arrangements must, within the prescribed period after the date on which he first becomes aware of any transaction forming part of the notifiable arrangements, provide the Board with prescribed information relating to those arrangements, unless those arrangements implement a proposal in respect of which notice has been given under subsection (1).

308(4) Subsection (4A) applies where a person complies with subsection (1) in relation to a notifiable proposal for arrangements and another person is–

(a) also a promoter in relation to the notifiable proposal or is a promoter in relation to a notifiable proposal for arrangements which are substantially the same as the proposed arrangements (whether they relate to the same or different parties), or

(b) a promoter in relation to notifiable arrangements implementing the notifiable proposal or notifiable arrangements which are substantially the same as notifiable arrangements implementing the notifiable proposal (whether they relate to the same or different parties).

308(4A) Any duty of the other person under subsection (1) or (3) in relation to the notifiable proposal or notifiable arrangements is discharged if–

(a) the person who complied with subsection (1) has notified the identity and address of the other person to HMRC or the other person holds the reference number allocated to the proposed notifiable arrangements under section 311, and

(b) the other person holds the information provided to HMRC in compliance with subsection (1).

308(4B) Subsection (4C) applies where a person complies with subsection (3) in relation to notifiable arrangements and another person is–

(a) a promoter in relation to a notifiable proposal for arrangements which are substantially the same as the notifiable arrangements (whether they relate to the same or different parties), or

(b) also a promoter in relation to the notifiable arrangements or notifiable arrangements which are substantially the same (whether they relate to the same or different parties).

308(4C) Any duty of the other person under subsection (1) or (3) in relation to the notifiable proposal or notifiable arrangements is discharged if–

(a) the person who complied with subsection (3) has notified the identity and address of the other person to HMRC or the other person holds the reference number allocated to the notifiable arrangements under section 311, and

(b) the other person holds the information provided to HMRC in compliance with subsection (3).

308(5) Where a person is a promoter in relation to two or more notifiable proposals or sets of notifiable arrangements which are substantially the same (whether they relate to the same parties or different parties), he need not provide information under subsection (1) or (3) if he has already provided information under either of those subsections in relation to any of the other proposals or arrangements.

308(6) [Not relevant to inheritance tax.]

History – In s. 308(1), the words "A person who is a promoter in relation to a notifiable proposal" substituted for the words "The promoter", and the word "the" substituted for the word "any" (before "notifiable"), by FA 2008, s. 116 and Sch. 38, para. 2, with effect from 1 November 2008, for purposes other than stamp duty land tax (by virtue of SI 2008/1935).

In s. 308(2), the word "earliest" substituted for the word "earlier" by FA 2010, s. 56 and Sch. 17, para. 3(2), with effect from 1 January 2011 (SI 2010/3019).

S. 308(2)(za) inserted by FA 2010, s. 56 and Sch. 17, para. 3(3), with effect from 1 January 2011 (SI 2010/3019).

In s. 308(2)(a), the word "the" substituted for the word "a" (before "notifiable"), by FA 2008, s. 116 and Sch. 38, para. 3, with effect from 1 November 2008, for purposes other than stamp duty land tax (by virtue of SI 2008/1935).

In s. 308(3), the words "A person who is a promoter in relation to notifiable arrangements" substituted for the words "The promoter", and the words "the notifiable" substituted for the words "any notifiable", by FA 2008, s. 116 and Sch. 38, para. 4, with effect from 1 November 2008, for purposes other than stamp duty land tax (by virtue of SI 2008/1935).

S. 308(4), (4A), (4B) and (4C) substituted for former s. 308(4) by FA 2008, s. 116 and Sch. 38, para. 5, with effect from 1 November 2008, for purposes other than stamp duty land tax (by virtue of SI 2008/1935).

Cross references – SI 2004/1864.
SI 2004/1865.

Statutory instruments – SI 2004/1864: made under s. 308(1) and (3).

SI 2011/171: made partly under s. 308(1) and (3).
Other material – M04/2006: HMRC guidance on the disclosure of tax avoidance schemes.

308A Supplemental information

308A(1) This section applies where–

(a) a promoter (P) has provided information in purported compliance with section 308(1) or (3), but

(b) HMRC believe that P has not provided all the prescribed information.

308A(2) HMRC may apply to the tribunal for an order requiring P to provide specified information about, or documents relating to, the notifiable proposal or arrangements.

308A(3) The tribunal may make an order under subsection (2) in respect of information or documents only if satisfied that HMRC have reasonable grounds for suspecting that the information or documents–

(a) form part of the prescribed information, or

(b) will support or explain the prescribed information.

308A(4) A requirement by virtue of subsection (2) shall be treated as part of P's duty under section 308(1) or (3).

308A(5) In so far as P's duty under section 308(1) or (3) arises out of a requirement by virtue of subsection (2) above, the prescribed period shall begin after a date prescribed for the purpose.

308A(6) In so far as P's duty under section 308(1) or (3) arises out of a requirement by virtue of subsection (2) above, the prescribed period–

(a) may be of a different length than the prescribed period for the purpose of other applications of section 308(1) or (3), and

(b) may be extended by HMRC by direction.

History – In s. 308A(2) and (3), "tribunal" substituted for "Special Commissioners" by SI 2009/56, art. 3(1) and Sch. 1, para. 430, operative from 1 April 2009, subject to transitional and saving provisions in SI 2009/56, Sch. 3.
S. 308A inserted by FA 2007, s. 108(4) with effect from 19 July 2007.

Cross references – SI 2009/275, art. 3(i): any decision under s. 308A is an excluded decision for the purposes of TCEA 2007, s. 11(1) and 13(1).

Other material – M04/2006: HMRC guidance on the disclosure of tax avoidance schemes.

309 Duty of person dealing with promoter outside United Kingdom

309(1) Any person ("the client") who enters into any transaction forming part of any notifiable arrangements in relation to which–

(a) a promoter is resident outside the United Kingdom, and

(b) no promoter is resident in the United Kingdom,

must, within the prescribed period after doing so, provide the Board with prescribed information relating to the notifiable arrangements.

309(2) Compliance with section 308(1) by any promoter in relation to the notifiable arrangements discharges the duty of the client under subsection (1).

Cross references – SI 2004/1864.

Statutory instruments – SI 2004/1864 made under 309(1).
SI 2011/171: made partly under s. 309(1).

Other material – M04/2006: HMRC guidance on the disclosure of tax avoidance schemes.

310 Duty of parties to notifiable arrangements not involving promoter

310 Any person who enters into any transaction forming part of notifiable arrangements as respects which neither he nor any other person in the United Kingdom is liable to comply with section 308 (duties of promoter) or section 309 (duty of person dealing with promoter outside the United Kingdom) must at the prescribed time provide the Board with prescribed information relating to the notifiable arrangements.

Cross references – SI 2004/1864.

Statutory instruments – SI 2004/1864 made under s. 310.
SI 2011/171: made partly under s. 310.

Other material – M04/2006: HMRC guidance on the disclosure of tax avoidance schemes.

310A Duty to provide further information requested by HMRC

310A(1) This section applies where–

(a) a person has provided the prescribed information about notifiable proposals or arrangements in compliance with section 308, 309 or 310, or

(b) a person has provided information in purported compliance with section 309 or 310 but HMRC believe that the person has not provided all the prescribed information.

310A(2) HMRC may require the person to provide–

(a) further specified information about the notifiable proposals or arrangements (in addition to the prescribed information under section 308, 309 or 310);

(b) documents relating to the notifiable proposals or arrangements.

310A(3) Where HMRC impose a requirement on a person under this section, the person must comply with the requirement within–

(a) the period of 10 working days beginning with the day on which HMRC imposed the requirement, or

(b) such longer period as HMRC may direct.

Commencement Date – Under FA 2014, s. 284(11), s. 310A applies to a person who provides the prescribed information about notifiable proposals or arrangements in compliance or purported compliance with section 308, 309 or 310 on or after 17 July 2014.

History – S. 310A inserted by FA 2014, s. 284(2), with effect from 17 July 2014.

310B Failure to provide information under section 310A: application to the Tribunal

310B(1) This section applies where HMRC–

(a) have required a person to provide information or documents under section 310A, but

(b) believe that the person has failed to provide the information or documents required.

310B(2) HMRC may apply to the tribunal for an order requiring the person to provide the information or documents required.

310B(3) The tribunal may make an order under subsection (2) only if satisfied that HMRC have reasonable grounds for suspecting that the information or documents will assist HMRC in considering the notifiable proposals or arrangements.

310B(4) Where the tribunal makes an order under subsection (2), the person must comply with it within–

(a) the period of 10 working days beginning with the day on which the tribunal made the order, or

(b) such longer period as HMRC may direct.

History – S. 310B inserted by FA 2014, s. 284(2), with effect from 17 July 2014.

310C Duty of promoters to provide updated information

310C(1) This section applies where–

(a) information has been provided under section 308 about any notifiable arrangements, or proposed notifiable arrangements, to which a reference number is allocated under section 311, and

(b) after the provision of the information, there is a change in relation to the arrangements of a kind mentioned in subsection (2).

310C(2) The changes referred to in subsection (1)(b) are–

(a) a change in the name by which the notifiable arrangements, or proposed notifiable arrangements, are known;

(b) a change in the name or address of any person who is a promoter in relation to the notifiable arrangements or, in the case of proposed notifiable arrangements, the notifiable proposal.

310C(3) A person who is a promoter in relation to the notifiable arrangements or, in the case of proposed notifiable arrangements, the notifiable proposal must inform HMRC of the change mentioned in subsection (1)(b) within 30 days after it is made.

310C(4) Subsections (5) and (6) apply for the purposes of subsection (3) where there is more than one person who is a promoter in relation to the notifiable arrangements or proposal.

310C(5) If the change in question is a change in the name or address of a person who is a promoter in relation to the notifiable arrangements or proposal, it is the duty of that person to comply with subsection (3).

310C(6) If a person provides information in compliance with subsection (3), the duty imposed by that subsection on any other person, so far as relating to the provision of that information, is discharged.

History – S. 310C inserted by FA 2015, s. 117 and Sch. 17, para. 1, with effect from 26 March 2015 subject to the transitional provisions at Sch. 17, para. 19.

311 Arrangements to be given reference number

311(1) Where a person complies or purports to comply with section 308(1) or (3), 309(1) or 310 in relation to any notifiable proposal or notifiable arrangements, the Board–

(a) may within 90 days allocate a reference number to the notifiable arrangements or, in the case of a notifiable proposal, to the proposed notifiable arrangements, and

(b) if it does so, must notify that number to the person and (where the person is one who has complied or purported to comply with section 308(1) or (3)) to any other person–

(i) who is a promoter in relation to the notifiable proposal (or arrangements implementing the notifiable proposal) or the notifiable arrangements (or proposal implemented by the notifiable arrangements), and

(ii) whose identity and address has been notified to HMRC by the person.

311(2) The allocation of a reference number to any notifiable arrangements (or proposed notifiable arrangements) is not to be regarded as constituting any indication by the Board that the arrangements could as a matter of law result in the obtaining by any person of a tax advantage.

311(3) In this Part **"reference number"**, in relation to any notifiable arrangements, means the reference number allocated under this section.

History – In s. 311(1), the words "or purports to comply" inserted by FA 2008, s. 116 and Sch. 38, para. 3(a), with effect from 1 November 2008, for purposes other than stamp duty land tax (by virtue of SI 2008/1935).

In s. 311(1), the words "may within 30 days", which followed "the Board", omitted by FA 2008, s. 116 and Sch. 38, para. 3(b), with effect from 1 November 2008, for purposes other than stamp duty land tax (by virtue of SI 2008/1935).

In s. 311(1)(a) the words "90 days" substituted for the words "30 days" by FA 2015, s. 117 and Sch. 17, para. 4, with effect from 26 March 2015.

In s. 311(1)(a), the words "may within 30 days" inserted by FA 2008, s. 116 and Sch. 38, para. 3(c), with effect from 1 November 2008, for purposes other than stamp duty land tax (by virtue of SI 2008/1935).

In s. 311(1) the words from "must notify that number to the person" to the end of sub-para. (ii) substituted for the words "notify the person of that number" by FA 2008, s. 116 and Sch. 38, para. 3(d), with effect from 1 November 2008, for purposes other than stamp duty land tax (by virtue of SI 2008/1935).

Cross references – SI 2004/1864.

Other material – M04/2006: HMRC guidance on the disclosure of tax avoidance schemes.

312 Duty of promoter to notify client of number

312(1) This section applies where a person who is a promoter in relation to notifiable arrangements is providing (or has provided) services to any person ("the client") in connection with the notifiable arrangements.

312(2) The promoter must, within 30 days after the relevant date, provide the client with prescribed information relating to any reference number (or, if more than one, any one reference number) that has been notified to the promoter (whether by HMRC or any other person) in relation to–

(a) the notifiable arrangements, or

(b) any arrangements substantially the same as the notifiable arrangements (whether involving the same or different parties).

312(3) In subsection (2) **"the relevant date"** means the later of–

(a) the date on which the promoter becomes aware of any transaction which forms part of the notifiable arrangements, and

(b) the date on which the reference number is notified to the promoter.

312(4) But where the conditions in subsection (5) are met the duty imposed on the promoter under subsection (2) to provide the client with information in relation to notifiable arrangements is discharged.

312(5) Those conditions are–

(a) that the promoter is also a promoter in relation to a notifiable proposal and provides services to the client in connection with them both,

(b) the notifiable proposal and the notifiable arrangements are substantially the same, and

(c) the promoter has provided to the client, in a form and manner specified by HMRC, prescribed information relating to the reference number that has been notified to the promoter in relation to the proposed notifiable arrangements.

312(6) HMRC may give notice that, in relation to notifiable arrangements specified in the notice, promoters are not under the duty under subsection (2) after the date specified in the notice.

History – S. 312 (together with s. 312A) substituted for former s. 312 by FA 2008, s. 116 and Sch. 38, para. 4, with effect from 1 November 2008, for purposes other than stamp duty land tax (by virtue of SI 2008/1935).

Cross references – SI 2004/1864: prescribed information under s. 312.

Statutory instruments – SI 2004/1864: made under s. 312.

Other material – M04/2006: HMRC guidance on the disclosure of tax avoidance schemes.

312A Duty of client to notify parties of number

312A(1) This section applies where a person (a "client") to whom a person who is a promoter in relation to notifiable arrangements or a notifiable proposal is providing (or has provided) services in connection with the notifiable *arrangements or notifiable* proposal receives prescribed information relating to the *reference number* allocated to the notifiable arrangements or proposed notifiable arrangements.

312A(2) The client must, within the prescribed period, provide prescribed information relating to the reference number to any other person–

313ZB(2) HMRC may by written notice require the promoter to provide prescribed information in relation to any person other than the client who the promoter might reasonably be expected to know is or is likely to be a party to the arrangements.

313ZB(3) The promoter must comply with a requirement under or by virtue of subsection (2) within–

(a) the prescribed period, or

(b) such longer period as HMRC may direct.

History – S. 313ZB inserted by FA 2013, s. 223(3), with effect from 17 July 2013 (Royal Assent).

313ZC Duty of employer to notify HMRC of details of employees etc

313ZC(1) This section applies if conditions A, B and C are met.

313ZC(2) Condition A is that a person who is a promoter in relation to notifiable arrangements or a notifiable proposal is providing (or has provided) services in connection with the notifiable arrangements or notifiable proposal to a person ("the client").

313ZC(3) Condition B is that the client receives information under section 312(2) or as mentioned in section 312(5).

313ZC(4) Condition C is that the client is an employer in circumstances where, as a result of the notifiable arrangement or proposed notifiable arrangement–

(a) one or more of the client's employees receive, or might reasonably be expected to receive, in relation to their employment, an advantage in relation to any relevant tax, or

(b) the client receives or might reasonably be expected to receive such an advantage in relation to the employment of one or more of the client's employees.

313ZC(5) Where an employee is within subsection (4)(a), or is an employee mentioned in subsection (4)(b), the client must provide HMRC with prescribed information relating to the employee at the prescribed time or times.

313ZC(6) The client need not comply with subsection (5) in relation to any notifiable arrangements at any time after HMRC have given notice under section 312(6) or 313(5) in relation to the notifiable arrangements.

313ZC(7) The duty under subsection (5) does not apply in prescribed circumstances.

313ZC(8) Section 312A(3) applies for the purposes of this section as it applies for the purposes of that section.

History – S. 313ZC inserted by FA 2015, s. 117 and Sch. 17, para. 9, with effect from 26 March 2015.

313A Pre-disclosure enquiry

313A(1) Where HMRC suspect that a person (P) is the promoter or introducer of a proposal, or the promoter of arrangements, which may be notifiable, they may by written notice require P to state–

(a) whether in P's opinion the proposal or arrangements are notifiable by P, and

(b) if not, the reasons for P's opinion.

313A(2) A notice must specify the proposal or arrangements to which it relates.

313A(3) For the purpose of subsection (1)(b)–

(a) it is not sufficient to refer to the fact that a lawyer or other professional has given an opinion,

(b) the reasons must show, by reference to this Part and regulations under it, why P thinks the proposal or arrangements are not notifiable by P, and

(c) in particular, if P asserts that the arrangements do not fall within any description prescribed under section 306(1)(a), the reasons must provide sufficient information to enable HMRC to confirm the assertion.

313A(4) P must comply with a requirement under or by virtue of subsection (1) within–

(a) the prescribed period, or

(b) such longer period as HMRC may direct.

History – In s. 313A(1), the words "or introducer of a proposal, or the promoter of arrangements," substituted for the words "of a proposal or arrangements" by FA 2010, s. 56 and Sch. 17, para. 4, with effect from 1 January 2011 (SI 2010/3019).
S. 313A inserted by FA 2007, s. 108(5) with effect from 19 July 2007.

Other material – M04/2006: HMRC guidance on the disclosure of tax avoidance schemes.

313B Reasons for non-disclosure: supporting information

313B(1) Where HMRC receive from a person (P) a statement of reasons why a proposal or arrangements are not notifiable by P, HMRC may apply to the tribunal for an order requiring P to provide specified information or documents in support of the reasons.

313B(2) P must comply with a requirement under or by virtue of subsection (1) within–

(a) the prescribed period, or

(b) such longer period as HMRC may direct.

313B(3) The power under subsection (1)–

(a) may be exercised more than once, and

(b) applies whether or not the statement of reasons was received under section 313A(1)(b).

History – In s. 313B(1), "tribunal" substituted for "Special Commissioners" by SI 2009/56, art. 3(1) and Sch. 1, para. 431, operative from 1 April 2009, subject to transitional and saving provisions in SI 2009/56, Sch. 3.
S. 313B inserted by FA 2007, s. 108(5) with effect from 19 July 2007.

Other material – M04/2006: HMRC guidance on the disclosure of tax avoidance schemes.

313C Provision of information to HMRC by introducers

History – The heading for former wording "Information provided to introducers" by FA 2015, s. 117 and Sch. 17, para. 12(4), with effect from 26 March 2015.

313C(1) This section applies where HMRC suspect–

(a) that a person ("P") is an introducer in relation to a proposal, and

(b) that the proposal may be notifiable.

313C(1A) HMRC may by written notice require P to provide HMRC with one or both of the following–

(a) prescribed information in relation to each person who has provided P with any information relating to the proposal;

(b) prescribed information in relation to each person with whom P has made a marketing contact in relation to the proposal.

313C(2) A notice must specify the proposal to which it relates.

313C(3) P must comply with a requirement under subsection (1A) within–

(a) the prescribed period, or

(b) such longer period as HMRC may direct.

History – S. 313C(1) and (1A) substituted for former s. 313C(1) by FA 2015, s. 117 and Sch. 17, para. 12(2), with effect from 26 March 2015.
In s. 313C(3) the words "subsection (1A)" substituted for the words "or by virtue of subsection (1)" by FA 2015, s. 117 and Sch. 17, para. 12(3), with effect from 26 March 2015.
S. 313C inserted by FA 2010, s. 56 and Sch. 17, para. 9, with effect from 1 January 2011 (SI 2010/3019).

314 Legal professional privilege

314(1) Nothing in this Part requires any person to disclose to the Board any privileged information.

314(2) In this Part **"privileged information"** means information with respect to which a claim to legal professional privilege, or, in Scotland, to confidentiality of communications, could be maintained in legal proceedings.

Cross references – SI 2004/1865, reg. 6: persons not to be treated as promoters if information to be provided is subject wholly or partly subject to legal professional privilege.

Other material – M04/2006: HMRC guidance on the disclosure of tax avoidance schemes.

314A Order to disclose

314A(1) HMRC may apply to the tribunal for an order that–

(a) a proposal is notifiable, or

(b) arrangements are notifiable.

314A(2) An application must specify–

(a) the proposal or arrangements in respect of which the order is sought, and

(b) the promoter.

314A(3) On an application the tribunal may make the order only if satisfied that section 306(1)(a) to (c) applies to the relevant arrangements.

History – In s. 314A(1) and (3), "tribunal" substituted for "Special Commissioners" by SI 2009/56, art. 3(1) and Sch. 1, para. 432, operative from 1 April 2009, subject to transitional and saving provisions in SI 2009/56, Sch. 3.
S. 314A inserted by FA 2007, s. 108(6) with effect from 19 July 2007.

Cross references – SI 2009/275, art. 3(i): any decision under s. 314A is an excluded decision for the purposes of TCEA 2007, s. 11(1) and 13(1).
SI 2007/3104: where a penalty is imposed under TMA 1970, s. 98C(1) following an order under FA 2004, s. 306A, or s. 314A the amount specified in s. 98C(1)(b) is increased to £5,000.

Other material – M04/2006: HMRC guidance on the disclosure of tax avoidance schemes.

315 Penalties

315(1) [Inserts TMA 1970, s. 98C.]

315(2) [Amends TMA 1970, s. 100(2).]

315(3) [Inserts TMA 1970, s. 100C(1A).]

316 Information to be provided in form and manner specified by HMRC

316(1) HMRC may specify the form and manner in which information required to be provided by any of the information provisions must be provided if the provision is to be complied with.

316(2) The **"information provisions"** are sections 308(1) and (3), 309(1), 310, 310A, 310C, 312(2), 312A(2) and (2A), 313(1) and (3), 313ZA(3) and 313ZC(5).

History – In s. 316(2) the words ", 313ZA(3) and 313ZC(5)" substituted for the words "and 313ZA(3)" by FA 2015, s. 117 and Sch. 17, para. 10, with effect from 26 March 2015.
In s. 316(2) the words "and (2A)" inserted by FA 2015, s. 117 and Sch. 17, para. 7, with effect from 26 March 2015.
In s. 316(2) the words "310C," inserted by FA 2015, s. 117 and Sch. 17, para. 2, with effect from 26 March 2015.
In s. 316(2), "310A," inserted by FA 2014, s. 284(3) with effect from 17 July 2014.
In s. 316, the words ", 313(1) and (3) and 313ZA(3)" substituted for the words "and 313(1) and (3)" by FA 2010, s. 56 and Sch. 17, para. 7, with effect from 1 January 2011 (SI 2010/3019).
S. 316 substituted by FA 2008, s. 116 and Sch. 38, para. 6, with effect from 1 November 2008, for purposes other than stamp duty land tax (by virtue of SI 2008/1935).

Other material – M04/2006: HMRC guidance on the disclosure of tax avoidance schemes.

316A Duty to provide additional information

316A(1) This section applies where a person is required to provide information under section 312(2) or 312A(2) or (2A).

316A(2) HMRC may specify additional information which must be provided by that person to the recipients under section 312(2) or 312A(2) or (2A) at the same time as the information referred to in subsection (1).

316A(3) HMRC may specify the form and manner in which the additional information is to be provided.

316A(4) For the purposes of this section **"additional information"** means information supplied by HMRC which relates to notifiable proposals or notifiable arrangements in general.

History – S. 316A inserted by FA 2015, s. 117 and Sch. 17, para. 14, with effect from 26 March 2015.

316B Confidentiality

316B No duty of confidentiality or other restriction on disclosure (however imposed) prevents the voluntary disclosure by any person to HMRC of information or documents which the person has reasonable grounds for suspecting will assist HMRC in determining whether there has been a breach of any requirement imposed by or under this Part.

History – S. 316B inserted by FA 2015, s. 117 and Sch. 17, para. 16, with effect from 26 March 2015.

316C Publication by HMRC

316C(1) HMRC may publish information about–

(a) any notifiable arrangements, or proposed notifiable arrangements, to which a reference number is allocated under section 311;

(b) any person who is a promoter in relation to the notifiable arrangements or, in the case of proposed notifiable arrangements, the notifiable proposal.

316C(2) The information that may be published is (subject to subsection (4))–

(a) any information relating to arrangements within subsection (1)(a), or a person within subsection (1)(b), that is prescribed information for the purposes of section 308, 309 or 310;

(b) any ruling of a court or tribunal relating to any such arrangements or person (in that person's capacity as a promoter in relation to a notifiable proposal or arrangements);

(c) the number of persons in any period who enter into transactions forming part of notifiable arrangements within subsection (1)(a);

(d) whether arrangements within subsection (1)(a) are APN relevant (see subsection (7));

(e) any other information that HMRC considers it appropriate to publish for the purpose of identifying arrangements within subsection (1)(a) or a person within subsection (1)(b).

316C(3) The information may be published in any manner that HMRC considers appropriate.

316C(4) No information may be published under this section that identifies a person who enters into a transaction forming part of notifiable arrangements within subsection (1)(a).

316C(5) But where a person who is a promoter within subsection (1)(b) is also a person mentioned in subsection (4), nothing in subsection (4) is to be taken as preventing the publication under this section of information so far as relating to the person's activities as a promoter.

316C(6) Before publishing any information under this section that identifies a person as a promoter within subsection (1)(b), HMRC must–

IHT Statutes

(a) inform the person that they are considering doing so, and

(b) give the person reasonable opportunity to make representations about whether it should be published.

316C(7) Arrangements are **"APN relevant"** for the purposes of subsection (2)(d) if HMRC has indicated in a publication that it may exercise (or has exercised) its power under section 219 of the Finance Act 2014 (accelerated payment notices) by virtue of the arrangements being DOTAS arrangements within the meaning of that section.

History – S. 316C inserted by FA 2015, s. 117 and Sch. 17, para. 17, with effect from 26 March 2015 subject to the transitional provisions at Sch. 17, para. 21.

316D Section 316C: subsequent judicial rulings

316D(1) This section applies if–

(a) information about notifiable arrangements, or proposed notifiable arrangements, is published under section 316C,

(b) at any time after the information is published, a ruling of a court or tribunal is made in relation to tax arrangements, and

(c) HMRC is of the opinion that the ruling is relevant to the arrangements mentioned in paragraph (a).

316D(2) A ruling is **"relevant"** to the arrangements if–

(a) the principles laid down, or reasoning given, in the ruling would, if applied to the arrangements, allow the purported advantage arising from the arrangements in relation to tax, and

(b) the ruling is final.

316D(3) HMRC must publish information about the ruling.

316D(4) The information must be published in the same manner as HMRC published the information mentioned in subsection (1)(a) (and may also be published in any other manner that HMRC considers appropriate).

316D(5) A ruling is **"final"** if it is–

(a) a ruling of the Supreme Court, or

(b) a ruling of any other court or tribunal in circumstances where–

  (i) no appeal may be made against the ruling,

  (ii) if an appeal may be made against the ruling with permission, the time limit for applications has expired and either no application has been made or permission has been refused,

  (iii) if such permission to appeal against the ruling has been granted or is not required, no appeal has been made within the time limit for appeals, or

  (iv) if an appeal was made, it was abandoned or otherwise disposed of before it was determined by the court or tribunal to which it was addressed.

316D(6) Where a ruling is final by virtue of sub-paragraph (ii), (iii) or (iv) of subsection (5)(b), the ruling is to be treated as made at the time when the sub-paragraph in question is first satisfied.

316D(7) In this section **"tax arrangements"** means arrangements in respect of which it would be reasonable to conclude (having regard to all the circumstances) that the obtaining of an advantage in relation to tax was the main purpose, or one of the main purposes.

History – S. 316D inserted by FA 2015, s. 117 and Sch. 17, para. 17, with effect from 26 March 2015.

317 Regulations under Part 7

317(1) Any power of the Treasury or the Board to make regulations under this Part is exercisable by statutory instrument.

317(2) Regulations made by the Treasury or the Board under this Part may make different provision for different cases and may contain transitional provisions and savings.

317(3) A statutory instrument containing regulations made by the Treasury or the Board under any provision of this Part is subject to annulment in pursuance of a resolution of the House of Commons.

History – In s. 317(2), the words "make different provision for different cases and may" inserted by FA 2010, s. 56 and Sch. 17, para. 8, with effect from 1 January 2011 (SI 2010/3019).

Statutory instruments – SI 2004/1864: made under s. 317(2).

Other material – M04/2006: HMRC guidance on the disclosure of tax avoidance schemes.

317A Special Commissioners: procedure

317A [Omitted by SI 2009/56, art. 3(1) and Sch. 1, para. 433.]

History – S. 317A omitted by SI 2009/56, art. 3(1) and Sch. 1, para. 433, operative from 1 April 2009, subject to transitional and saving provisions in SI 2009/56, Sch. 3. Former s. 317A read as follows:

"317A Special Commissioners: procedure

317A Sections 56B to 56D of the Taxes Management Act 1970 (procedure) shall apply (with any necessary modifications) to applications under this Part as to appeals.".

Former s. 317A inserted by FA 2007, s. 108(7) with effect from 19 July 2007.

Other material – M04/2006: HMRC guidance on the disclosure of tax avoidance schemes.

318 Interpretation of Part 7

318(1) In this Part–

"advantage", in relation to any tax, means–

(a) relief or increased relief from, or repayment or increased repayment of, that tax, or the avoidance or reduction of a charge to that tax or an assessment to that tax or the avoidance of a possible assessment to that tax,

(b) the deferral of any payment of tax or the advancement of any repayment of tax, or

(c) the avoidance of any obligation to deduct or account for any tax;

"arrangements" includes any scheme, transaction or series of transactions;

"company" has the meaning given by section 1121 of the Corporation Tax Act 2010;

"corporation tax" includes any amount which, by virtue of any of the provisions mentioned in paragraph 1 of Schedule 18 to the Finance Act 1998 (c. 36) (company tax returns, assessments and related matters) is assessable and chargeable as if it were corporation tax;

"HMRC" means the Commissioners for Her Majesty's Revenue and Customs;

"introducer", in relation to a notifiable proposal, has the meaning given by section 307;

"make a firm approach" has the meaning given by section 307(4A);

"make a marketing contact" has the meaning given by section 307(4B);

"notifiable arrangements" has the meaning given by section 306(1);

"notifiable proposal" has the meaning given by section 306(2);

"prescribed", except in section 306, means prescribed by regulations made by the Board;

"promoter", in relation to notifiable arrangements or a notifiable proposal, has the meaning given by section 307;

"reference number", in relation to notifiable arrangements, has the meaning given by section 311(3);

"tax" means–

(a) income tax,

(b) capital gains tax,

(c) corporation tax,

(d) petroleum revenue tax,

(da) apprenticeship levy,

(e) inheritance tax,

(f) stamp duty land tax, or

(g) stamp duty reserve tax.

"trade" includes every venture in the nature of trade.

"tribunal" means the First-tier tribunal, or where determined by or under Tribunal Procedure Rules, the Upper Tribunal.

"working day" means a day which is not a Saturday or a Sunday, Christmas Day, Good Friday or a bank holiday under the Banking and Financial Dealings Act 1971 in any part of the United Kingdom.

318(2) [Omitted by TIOPA 2010, s. 374 and Sch. 8, para. 302(3) and repealed by TIOPA 2010, s. 378 and Sch. 10, Pt. 13.]

History – In s. 318(1), the definition of "working day" inserted by FA 2014, s. 284(4), with effect from 17 July 2014.

In s. 318(1), the definition of "company" inserted by TIOPA 2010, s. 374 and Sch. 8, para. 302(2)(a), with effect for corporation tax purposes for accounting periods ending on or after 1 April 2010, for income tax and capital gains tax purposes for the tax year 2010–11 and subsequent tax years, and for petroleum revenue tax purposes for chargeable periods beginning on or after 1 July 2010.

In s. 318(1), definitions of "introducer", "make a firm approach" and "make a marketing contact" inserted by FA 2010, s. 56 and Sch. 17, para. 5, with effect from 1 January 2011 (SI 2010/3019).

In s. 318(1), in the definition of "tax", para. (da) inserted by FA 2016, s. 104(1), with effect from 15 September 2016 (Royal Assent).

In s. 318(1), the definition of "trade" inserted by TIOPA 2010, s. 374 and Sch. 8, para. 302(2)(b), with effect for corporation tax purposes for accounting periods ending on or after 1 April 2010, for income tax and capital gains tax purposes for the tax year 2010–11 and subsequent tax years, and for petroleum revenue tax purposes for chargeable periods beginning on or after 1 July 2010.

In s. 318(1), the definition of "the Special Commissioners" omitted by SI 2009/56, art. 3(1) and Sch. 1, para. 434(2), operative from 1 April 2009, subject to transitional and saving provisions in SI 2009/56, Sch. 3.

In s. 318(1), the definition of "tribunal" inserted by SI 2009/56, art. 3(1) and Sch. 1, para. 434(3), operative from 1 April 2009, subject to transitional and saving provisions in SI 2009/56, Sch. 3.
In s. 318(1), the definitions of "HMRC" and "the Special Commissioners" inserted by FA 2007, s. 108(8) with effect from 19 July 2007.
S. 318(2) omitted by TIOPA 2010, s. 374 and Sch. 8, para. 302(3) and repealed by TIOPA 2010, s. 378 and Sch. 10, Pt. 13, with effect for corporation tax purposes for accounting periods ending on or after 1 April 2010, for income tax and capital gains tax purposes for the tax year 2010–11 and subsequent tax years, and for petroleum revenue tax purposes for chargeable periods beginning on or after 1 July 2010.

Statutory instruments – SI 2004/1864: made under s. 318(1).
SI 2004/1865: made under s. 318(1).
SI 2011/171: made partly under s. 318(1).

Other material – M04/2006: HMRC guidance on the disclosure of tax avoidance schemes.

Notes – S. 318(2) not rewritten, as its effect is preserved in the amendments made in s. 318(1) by TIOPA 2010, Sch. 8, para. 302.

319 Part 7: commencement and savings

319(1) The following provisions of this Part come into force on the passing of this Act–

sections 306 to 315, so far as is necessary for enabling the making of any regulations for which they provide, and

sections 317 and 318 and this section.

319(2) Except as provided by subsection (1), the provisions of this Part come into force on 1st August 2004.

319(3) Section 308 does not apply to a promoter in the case of–

(a) any notifiable proposal as respects which the relevant date, as defined by subsection (2) of that section, fell before 18th March 2004,

(b) any notifiable arrangements which implement such a proposal, or

(c) any notifiable arrangements which include any transaction entered into before 18th March 2004.

319(4) Sections 309 and 310 do not apply in relation to notifiable arrangements which include any transaction entered into before 23rd April 2004.

319(5) Section 313 does not apply in relation to any notifiable arrangements in respect of which, by virtue of subsection (3) or (4), none of the duties imposed by sections 308 to 310 arises.

Other material – M04/2006: HMRC guidance on the disclosure of tax avoidance schemes.

SCHEDULES

SCHEDULE 36 – PENSION SCHEMES ETC: TRANSITIONAL PROVISIONS AND SAVINGS

Section 283

Part 4 – Other Provisions

INHERITANCE TAX

56(1) This paragraph applies in relation to a fund or scheme–

(a) which is not a registered pension scheme, a qualifying non-UK pension scheme or a superannuation fund to which section 615(3) of ICTA applies, but

(b) to which section 151 of the Inheritance Tax Act 1984 (c. 51) (treatment of pension rights) applied immediately before 6th April 2006.

56(2) If no contributions are made under the fund or scheme on or after that date–

(a) section 151 of the Inheritance Tax Act 1984 continues to apply to the fund or scheme on and after that date for all purposes of that Act, and

(b) property which is part of or held for the purposes of the fund or scheme does not constitute relevant property for the purposes of Chapter 3 of Part 3 of that Act (settlements without interest in possession).

56(3) In any other case, paragraphs 57 and 58 apply to the fund or scheme on and after that date.

56(4) In this paragraph **"qualifying non-UK pension scheme"** has the same meaning as in the Inheritance Tax Act 1984 (see section 271A of that Act).

History – In para. 56(1)(a) the words ", a qualifying non-UK pension scheme" inserted by FA 2008, s. 92 and Sch. 29, para. 18(7)(a), with effect from 6 April 2006.
Para. 56(4) inserted by FA 2008, s. 92 and Sch. 29, para. 18(7)(b), with effect from 6 April 2006.

57(1) The proportion of the assets of the fund or scheme which at any time is the protected proportion of those assets does not at that time constitute relevant property for the purposes of Chapter 3 of Part 3 of the Inheritance Tax Act 1984 (settlements without interest in possession).

57(2) **"The protected proportion"** of the assets of the fund or scheme at a time is–

$$\frac{ACV}{V} \times 100$$

where–

V is the market value of the assets of the fund or scheme at that time, and

ACV is the adjusted commencement value, that is an amount equal to the market value of the assets of the fund or scheme on 5th April 2006, but subject to the adjustments provided by sub-paragraph (3).

57(3) The adjustments are–

(a) an increase by the percentage by which the retail prices index for the month of September immediately preceding the time in question is greater than that for April 2006, and

(b) a reduction by the amount of any relevant payments made under the fund or scheme on or after 6th April 2006 and before that time.

57(4) **"Relevant payments"** are payments other than–

(a) payments of costs or expenses, or

(b) payments which are (or will be) income of any person for any of the purposes of income tax.

58(1) Section 151 of the Inheritance Tax Act 1984 (c. 51) (treatment of pension rights) continues to apply to so much of the assets of the fund or scheme at any time as does not exceed the amount that is the protected amount at that time.

58(2) But sub-paragraph (1) does not affect the operation of subsection (1)(d) of section 58 of that Act (because paragraph 57 makes provision about the extent to which the assets of the fund or scheme constitute relevant property within the meaning given by that section).

58(3) If inheritance tax has not previously been chargeable (otherwise than only because of this paragraph) by reference to the value of the assets of the fund or scheme on or after 6th April 2006, the protected amount is an amount equal to the amount of the market value of the assets of the fund or scheme on 5th April 2006, but subject to the adjustments provided by sub-paragraph (4).

58(4) The adjustments are–

(a) an increase by the percentage by which the retail prices index for the month of September immediately preceding the time in question is greater than that for April 2006, and

(b) a reduction by the amount of any relevant payments made under the fund or scheme on or after 6th April 2006 and before that time.

58(5) If inheritance tax would (apart from this paragraph) have previously been chargeable by reference to the value of the assets of the fund or scheme on one or more occasions on or after 6th April 2006, the protected amount is what it was immediately before the occasion, or (where there has been more than one) the last occasion, on which inheritance tax would have been so chargeable ("the relevant tax occasion"), but–

(a) reduced by the value of the property on which inheritance tax would have been chargeable on the relevant tax occasion, and

(b) subject to the adjustments provided by sub-paragraph (6).

58(6) The adjustments are –

(a) an increase by the percentage by which the retail prices index for the month of September immediately preceding the time in question is greater than that for the month in which the relevant tax occasion fell, and

(b) a reduction by the amount of any payments made under the fund or scheme since the relevant tax occasion.

58(7) **"Relevant payments"** are payments other than–

(a) payments of costs or expenses, or

(b) payments which are (or will be) income of any person for any of the purposes of income tax.

INCOME TAX (TRADING AND OTHER INCOME) ACT 2005

(2005 Chapter 5)

[*24th March 2005*]

SCHEDULES

SCHEDULE 1 – CONSEQUENTIAL AMENDMENTS

INHERITANCE TAX ACT 1984 (c. 51)

393 The Inheritance Tax Act 1984 is amended as follows.

394 [Amends IHTA 1984, s. 6(3)(e).]

395 [Amends IHTA 1984, s. 21(3).]

396 [Amends IHTA 1984, s. 174(1).]

FINANCE ACT 2005

(2005 Chapter 7) [*7th April 2005*]

ARRANGEMENT OF SECTIONS

PART 4 – OTHER TAXES

INHERITANCE TAX

98 Rates and rate bands for the next three years

98(1) For the Table in Schedule 1 to IHTA 1984 (rates and rate bands), as it has effect from time to time, there shall be successively substituted–

(a) [substituted 2005–06 table at IHTA 1984, Sch. 1,]

(b) [substitutes 2006–07 table at IHTA 1984, Sch. 1,]

(c) the 2007–08 Table, which shall apply to any chargeable transfer made on or after 6th April 2007.

98(2) Subsection (1)(c) is without prejudice to the application of section 8 of IHTA 1984 (indexation) by virtue of the difference between the retail prices index for the month of September in 2006 or any later year and that for the month of September in the following year.

98(3) [2005–06 table substituted at IHTA 1984, Sch. 1.]

98(4) [2006–07 table substituted at IHTA 1984, Sch. 1.]

98(5) [2007–08 table substituted at IHTA 1984, Sch. 1.]

98(6) Section 8(1) of IHTA 1984 (indexation of rate bands) shall not have effect as respects any difference between the retail prices index–

(a) for the month of September 2003 and that for the month of September 2004,

(b) for the month of September 2004 and that for the month of September 2005, or

(c) for the month of September 2005 and that for the month of September 2006.

PART 7 – SUPPLEMENTARY PROVISIONS

104 Repeals

104(1) The enactments mentioned in Schedule 11 (which include provisions that are spent or of no practical utility) are repealed to the extent specified.

104(2) The repeals specified in that Schedule have effect subject to the commencement provisions and savings contained or referred to in the notes set out in that Schedule.

105 Interpretation

105 In this Act–

"ALDA 1979" means the Alcoholic Liquor Duties Act 1979 (c. 4);

"CAA 2001" means the Capital Allowances Act 2001 (c. 2);

"CTA 2009" means the Corporation Tax Act 2009;

"FA", followed by a year, means the Finance Act of that year;

"F(No. 2)A", followed by a year, means the Finance (No.2) Act of that year;

IHT Statutes

"HODA 1979" means the Hydrocarbon Oil Duties Act 1979 (c. 5);

"ICTA" means the Income and Corporation Taxes Act 1988 (c. 1);

"IHTA 1984" means the Inheritance Tax Act 1984 (c. 51);

"ITEPA 2003" means the Income Tax (Earnings and Pensions) Act 2003 (c. 1);

"ITTOIA 2005" means the Income Tax (Trading and Other Income) Act 2005 (c. 5);

"TCGA 1992" means the Taxation of Chargeable Gains Act 1992 (c. 12);

"TMA 1970" means the Taxes Management Act 1970 (c. 9);

"VERA 1994" means the Vehicle Excise and Registration Act 1994 (c. 22).

History – In s. 105, the definition of "CTA 2009" inserted by CTA 2009, s. 1322 and Sch. 1, para. 663, with effect for corporation tax purposes for accounting periods ending on or after 1 April 2009, and for income tax and capital gains tax purposes for the tax year 2009–10 and subsequent tax years.

106 Short title

106 This Act may be cited as the Finance Act 2005.

COMMISSIONERS FOR REVENUE AND CUSTOMS ACT 2005

(2005 Chapter 11)

[*7th April 2005*]

Only those parts of CRCA 2005 which directly affect material in this division are reproduced here. The full text of CRCA 2005 is reproduced in the Income, Corporation and Capital Gains Taxes division (Vol. 1B).

SCHEDULES

SCHEDULE 4 – CONSEQUENTIAL AMENDMENTS ETC.

FINANCE ACT 1998 (C. 36)

67 [Ceases FA 1998, s. 145 to have effect.]

FINANCE ACT 2006

(2006 Chapter 25)

[*19th July 2006*]

ARRANGEMENT OF SECTIONS

PART 6 – INHERITANCE TAX

FUTURE RATES AND BANDS

155 Rates and rate bands for 2008–09 and 2009–10

155(1) For the Table in Schedule 1 to IHTA 1984 (rates and rate bands), as it has effect in relation to chargeable transfers made on or after 6th April 2008, there shall be successively substituted–

(a) the 2008–09 Table, which shall apply to any chargeable transfer made on or after 6th April 2008 (but before 6th April 2009), and

(b) the 2009–10 Table, which shall apply to any chargeable transfer made on or after 6th April 2009.

155(2) Subsection (1)(b) is without prejudice to the application of section 8 of IHTA 1984 (indexation) by virtue of the difference between the retail prices index for the month of September in 2008 or any later year and that for the month of September in the following year.

155(3) [2008–09 table substituted at IHTA 1984, Sch. 1.]

155(4) [2009–10 table substituted at IHTA 1984, Sch. 1.]

155(5) Section 8(1) of IHTA 1984 (indexation of rate bands) shall not have effect as respects any difference between the retail prices index–

(a) for the month of September 2006 and that for the month of September 2007, or

(b) for the month of September 2007 and that for the month of September 2008.

TRUSTS

156 Rules for trusts etc

156(1) Schedule 20 contains–

(a) amendments of provisions of IHTA 1984 relating to settled property,

(b) amendments of provisions relating to property that, for purposes of that Act, is property subject to a reservation, and

(c) related amendments of provisions relating to chargeable gains.

156(2) Those amendments have effect as mentioned in that Schedule.

157 Purchase of interests in foreign trusts

157(1) Section 48 of IHTA 1984 (settled property: excluded property) is amended as follows.

157(2) [Amends IHTA 1984, s. 48(3).]

157(3) [Amends IHTA 1984, s. 48(3A).]

157(4) [Inserts IHTA 1984, s. 48(3B) and (3C).]

157(5) If, in consequence of the amendments made by this section, an amount of inheritance tax would (but for this subsection) fall due before the day on which this Act is passed, that amount is to be treated instead as falling due at the end of the period of 14 days beginning with that day.

157(6) This section is deemed to have come into force on 5th December 2005.

PART 7 – PENSIONS

160 Inheritance tax

160(1) Schedule 22 (provisions about inheritance tax in relation to registered pension schemes) has effect.

160(2) This section and that Schedule are deemed to have come into force on 6th April 2006.

PART 10 – SUPPLEMENTARY PROVISIONS

178 Repeals

178(1) The enactments mentioned in Schedule 26 (which include provisions that are spent or of no practical utility) are repealed to the extent specified.

178(2) The repeals specified in that Schedule have effect subject to the commencement provisions and savings contained or referred to in the notes set out in that Schedule.

179 Interpretation

179 In this Act–

"ALDA 1979" means the Alcoholic Liquor Duties Act 1979 (c. 4);

"CAA 2001" means the Capital Allowances Act 2001 (c. 2);

"CTA 2009" means the Corporation Tax Act 2009;

"FA", followed by a year, means the Finance Act of that year;

"F(No.2)A", followed by a year, means the Finance (No.2) Act of that year;

"HODA 1979" means the Hydrocarbon Oil Duties Act 1979 (c. 5);

"ICTA" means the Income and Corporation Taxes Act 1988 (c. 1);

"IHTA 1984" means the Inheritance Tax Act 1984 (c. 51);

"ITEPA 2003" means the Income Tax (Earnings and Pensions) Act 2003 (c. 1);

"ITTOIA 2005" means the Income Tax (Trading and Other Income) Act 2005 (c. 5);

"OTA 1975" means the Oil Taxation Act 1975 (c. 22);

"TCGA 1992" means the Taxation of Chargeable Gains Act 1992 (c. 12);

"TMA 1970" means the Taxes Management Act 1970 (c. 9);

"VATA 1994" means the Value Added Tax Act 1994 (c. 23);

"VERA 1994" means the Vehicle Excise and Registration Act 1994 (c. 22).

History – In s. 179, the definition of "CTA 2009" inserted by CTA 2009, s. 1322 and Sch. 1, para. 692, with effect for corporation tax purposes for accounting periods ending on or after 1 April 2009, and for income tax and capital gains tax purposes for the tax year 2009–10 and subsequent tax years.

180 Short title

180 This Act may be cited as the Finance Act 2006.

SCHEDULES

SCHEDULE 20 – INHERITANCE TAX: RULES FOR TRUSTS ETC

Section 156

Other material – Misc. 119: STEP/CIOT correspondence with HMRC re Sch. 20.

Part 1 – "Trusts for Bereaved Minors", "Age 18-to-25 Trusts" and "Accumulation and Maintenance" Trusts

TRUSTS FOR BEREAVED MINORS AND AGE 18-TO-25 TRUSTS

1(1) [Inserts IHTA 1984, s. 71A–71H.]

1(2) Sub-paragraph (1) shall be deemed to have come into force on 22nd March 2006.

SECTION 71 OF IHTA 1984 NOT TO APPLY TO PROPERTY SETTLED ON OR AFTER 22ND MARCH 2006

2(1) Section 71 of IHTA 1984 (accumulation and maintenance trusts) is amended as follows.

2(2) [Amends IHTA 1984, s. 71(1).]

2(3) [Inserts IHTA 1984, s. 71(1A) and (1B).]

2(4) Where a chargeable transfer to which section 54A of IHTA 1984 applies was made before 22nd March 2006, that section has effect in relation to that transfer as if references in that section to section 71 of IHTA 1984 were to section 71 of IHTA 1984 without the amendments made by sub-paragraphs (2) and (3).

2(5) There is no charge to tax under section 71 of IHTA 1984 in a case where settled property ceases, by the operation of the subsection (1B) inserted into that section by this paragraph, to be property to which that section applies.

2(6) Sub-paragraphs (1) to (5) shall be deemed to have come into force on 22nd March 2006.

SECTION 71 OF IHTA 1984 TO CEASE TO APPLY TO CERTAIN SETTLED PROPERTY FROM 6TH APRIL 2008

3(1) In section 71(1)(a) of IHTA 1984 (section applies to settled property only if one or more persons will become beneficially entitled on or before reaching a specified age not exceeding 25)–

(a) for "twenty-five" substitute "eighteen", and

(b) omit "or to an interest in possession in it".

3(2) Sub-paragraph (1) comes into force on 6th April 2008 but only for the purpose of determining whether, at a time on or after that day, section 71 of IHTA 1984 applies to settled property.

3(3) There is no charge to tax under section 71 of IHTA 1984 in a case where–

(a) settled property ceases, on the coming into force of sub-paragraph (1), to be property to which that section applies, but

(b) that section would immediately after the coming into force of sub-paragraph (1) apply to the settled property but for the amendments made by sub-paragraph (1).

Part 2 – Interests in Possession: When Settled Property is Part of Beneficiary's Estate

AGGREGATION WITH PERSON'S ESTATE OF PROPERTY IN WHICH INTEREST IN POSSESSION SUBSISTS

4(1) *[Inserts* IHTA 1984, s. 49(1A) and (1B).]

4(2) Sub-paragraph (1) shall be deemed to have come into force on 22nd March 2006.

"IMMEDIATE POST-DEATH INTERESTS" AND "TRANSITIONAL SERIAL INTERESTS"

5(1) [Inserts IHTA 1984, s. 49A–49E .]

5(2) Sub-paragraph (1) shall be deemed to have come into force on 22nd March 2006.

DISABLED PERSONS' TRUSTS: MEANING OF "DISABLED PERSON'S INTEREST" AND "DISABLED PERSON"

6(1) [Inserts IHTA 1984, s. 89A and 89B.]

6(2) [Inserts IHTA 1984,s. 89(5) and (6).]

6(3) Sub-paragraph (1) shall be deemed to have come into force on 22nd March 2006.

6(4) Sub-paragraph (2) shall be deemed to have come into force on 22nd March 2006, but only in respect of property transferred into settlement on or after that day.

Part 3 – Related Amendments in IHTA 1984

COMMENCEMENT

7 The following paragraphs of this Part of this Schedule shall be deemed to have come into force on 22nd March 2006.

DEEMED DISPOSITION WHERE OMISSION TO EXERCISE A RIGHT INCREASES VALUE OF ANOTHER PERSON'S ESTATE OR OF SETTLED PROPERTY NOT AGGREGATED WITH A PERSON'S ESTATE

8 [Amends IHTA 1984, s. 3(3).]

POTENTIALLY EXEMPT TRANSFERS: PROVISION IN CONSEQUENCE OF SECTION 71 OF IHTA 1984 NOT APPLYING TO PROPERTY SETTLED ON OR AFTER 22ND MARCH 2006

9(1) Section 3A of IHTA 1984 (potentially exempt transfers) is amended as follows.

9(2) [Amends IHTA 1984, s. 3A(1)(a).]

9(3) [Inserts IHTA 1984, s. 3A(1A) and (1B).]

9(4) [Amends IHTA 1984, s. 3A(2).]

9(5) [Inserts IHTA 1984, s. 3A(3A) and (3B).]

9(6) [Amends IHTA 1984, s. 3A(7).]

PERSON'S "ESTATE" NOT TO INCLUDE CERTAIN INTERESTS IN POSSESSION

10(1) Section 5 of IHTA 1984 (meaning of "estate") is amended as follows.

10(2) [Amends IHTA 1984, s. 5(1).]

10(3) [Inserts IHTA 1984, s. 5(1A).]

LIFE ASSURANCE POLICIES ENTERED INTO BEFORE 22ND MARCH 2006

11(1) [Inserts IHTA 1984, s. 46A and 46B.]

11(2) Sub-paragraph (1) shall be deemed to have come into force on 22nd March 2006.

TAX WHERE INTEREST IN POSSESSION ENDS, OR IS TREATED AS ENDING, DURING BENEFICIARY'S LIFE

12 [Inserts IHTA 1984, s. 51(1A).]

13 [Inserts IHTA 1984, s. 52(2A) and (3A).]

14 [Inserts IHTA 1984, s. 53(1A) and (2A).]

NON-AGGREGATION WITH DECEASED PERSON'S ESTATE OF PROPERTY IN WHICH HE HAD INTEREST IN POSSESSION IF PROPERTY REVERTS TO SETTLOR OR PASSES TO SETTLOR'S SPOUSE OR CIVIL PARTNER ETC

15 [Inserts IHTA 1984, s. 54(2A) and (2B) and amends s. 54(3).]

RATE OF TAX ON ENDING OF INTEREST IN POSSESSION IN PROPERTY SETTLED DURING SETTLOR'S LIFE

16(1) Section 54A of IHTA 1984 (special rate of charge on coming to end of interest in possession in settled property affected by potentially exempt transfer) is amended as follows.

16(2) [Inserts IHTA 1984, s. 54A(1A).]

16(3) [Amends IHTA 1984, s. 54A(2).]

16(4) Where a chargeable transfer to which section 54A of IHTA 1984 applies was made before 22nd March 2006, that section has effect in relation to that transfer without the amendments made by sub-paragraph (3).

PROPERTY ENTERING MAINTENANCE FUND AFTER DEATH OF PERSON ENTITLED TO INTEREST IN POSSESSION

17 [Inserts IHTA 1984, s. 57A(1A).]

"RELEVANT PROPERTY" NOT TO INCLUDE PROPERTY HELD ON TRUST FOR A BEREAVED CHILD

18 [Amends IHTA 1984, s. 58(1)(b).]

"RELEVANT PROPERTY" TO INCLUDE PROPERTY HELD ON EMPLOYEE TRUSTS OR NEWSPAPER TRUSTS IF CERTAIN INTERESTS IN POSSESSION SUBSIST IN THE PROPERTY

19(1) Section 58 of IHTA 1984 (meaning of "relevant property" in Chapter 3 of Part 3) is amended as follows.

19(2) [Amends IHTA 1984, s. 58(1)(b).]

19(3) [Inserts IHTA 1984, s. 58(1A)–(1C).]

CERTAIN INTERESTS IN POSSESSION TO WHICH A PERSON BECOMES ENTITLED ON OR AFTER 22ND MARCH 2006 NOT TO BE "QUALIFYING INTERESTS IN POSSESSION" FOR PURPOSES OF CHAPTER 3 OF PART 3 OF IHTA 1984

20(1) Section 59 of IHTA 1984 (settlements without interests in possession: meaning of "qualifying interest in possession") is amended as follows.

20(2) [Substitutes IHTA 1984, s. 59(1).]

20(3) [Inserts IHTA 1984, s. 59(2)(c).]

20(4) Where a chargeable transfer to which section 54A of IHTA 1984 applies was made before 22nd March 2006, that section has effect in relation to that transfer as if in that section "qualifying interest in possession" has the meaning it would have apart from sub-paragraphs (1) to (3).

20(5) [Amends the heading toIHTA 1984, Pt. 3, Ch. 3.]

NEW MEANING OF "QUALIFYING INTEREST IN POSSESSION" NOT TO APPLY IN SECTION 72 OF IHTA 1984

21(1) Section 72 of IHTA 1984 (property leaving employee trusts and newspaper trusts) is amended as follows.

21(2) [Amends IHTA 1984, s. 72(1).]

21(3) [Inserts IHTA 1984, s. 72(1A) and (1B).]

NO CHARGE UNDER SECTIONS 71B, 71E ETC WHERE PROPERTY HELD ON TRUSTS FOR BEREAVED CHILD BECOMES HELD ON TRUSTS FOR CHARITABLE PURPOSES ETC

22 [Amends IHTA 1984, s. 76(1).]

NO POSTPONEMENT OF COMMENCEMENT DATE OF SETTLEMENT WHERE PROPERTY SETTLED ON OR AFTER 22ND MARCH 2006 UNLESS SETTLOR, OR SPOUSE OR CIVIL PARTNER, HAS IMMEDIATE POST-DEATH INTEREST

23 [Inserts IHTA 1984, s. 80(4).]

PROTECTIVE TRUSTS

24 [Inserts IHTA 1984, s. 88(3)–(6).]

ALTERATIONS OF CAPITAL ETC OF CLOSE COMPANY WHERE PARTICIPATOR HOLDS SHARES ETC IN COMPANY AS TRUSTEE OF SETTLED PROPERTY IN WHICH AN INTEREST IN POSSESSION SUBSISTS

25 [Inserts IHTA 1984, s. 100(1A).]

CLOSE COMPANY'S INTEREST IN POSSESSION TREATED AS INTEREST OF ITS PARTICIPATORS

26 [Inserts IHTA 1984, s. 101(1A)–(1C).]

DISTRIBUTIONS WITHIN TWO YEARS OF PERSON'S DEATH OUT OF PROPERTY SETTLED BY HIS WILL

27(1) Section 144 of IHTA 1984 (distribution etc from property settled by will) is amended as follows.

27(2) [Amends IHTA 1984, s. 144(1).]

27(3) [Inserts IHTA 1984, s. 144(1A).]

27(4) [Amends IHTA 1984, s. 144(2).]

27(5) [Inserts IHTA 1984, s. 144(3)–(6).]

INTERPRETATION OF IHTA 1984

28 [Amends IHTA 1984, s. 272.]

Part 5 – Property Subject to a Reservation

33(1) FA 1986 is amended as follows.

33(2) [Inserts FA 1986, s. 102ZA.]

33(3) [Inserts FA 1986, Sch. 20, para. 4A.]

33(4) Sub-paragraphs (1) to (3) shall be deemed to have come into force on 22nd March 2006, but only as respects cases where an interest in possession comes to an end on or after that day.

Part 6 – Conditional Exemption: Relief from Charges

34(1) Section 79 of IHTA 1984 (subsection (3) of which provides for charges to tax where, in the case of settled property designated under section 31 on a claim under section 79, an event occurs that would be chargeable under section 32 or 32A if the claim had been under section 30) is amended as follows.

34(2) *[Inserts IHTA 1984, s. 79(5A).]*

34(3) [Substitutes IHTA 1984, s. 79(7)–(7C).]

34(4) [Inserts IHTA 1984, s. 79(9A) and (9B).]

SCHEDULE 22 – PENSION SCHEMES: INHERITANCE TAX

Section 161

INTRODUCTORY

1 IHTA 1984 is amended as follows.

DISPOSITIONS

2 [Inserts IHTA 1984, s. 12(2A)–(2G).]

SECURED PENSION FUNDS

3 [Omitted by FA 2011, s. 65 and Sch. 16, para. 84(b)(i).]

History – Para. 3 omitted by FA 2011, s. 65 and Sch. 16, para. 84(b)(i), with effect in relation to deaths occurring on or after 6 April 2011.

4 [Omitted by FA 2011, s. 65 and Sch. 16, para. 84(b)(i).]

History – Para. 4 omitted by FA 2011, s. 65 and Sch. 16, para. 84(b)(i), with effect in relation to deaths occurring on or after 6 April 2011.

LIABILITY

5 [Omitted by FA 2011, s. 65 and Sch. 16, para. 84(b)(i).]

History – Para. 5 omitted by FA 2011, s. 65 and Sch. 16, para. 84(b)(i), with effect in relation to deaths occurring on or after 6 April 2011.

6 [Omitted by FA 2011, s. 65 and Sch. 16, para. 84(b)(i).]

History – Para. 6 omitted by FA 2011, s. 65 and Sch. 16, para. 84(b)(i), with effect in relation to deaths occurring on or after 6 April 2011.

DELIVERY OF ACCOUNTS

7 [Omitted by FA 2011, s. 65 and Sch. 16, para. 84(b)(i).]

History – Para. 7 omitted by FA 2011, s. 65 and Sch. 16, para. 84(b)(i), with effect in relation to deaths occurring on or after 6 April 2011.

PAYMENT

8 [Omitted by FA 2011, s. 65 and Sch. 16, para. 84(b)(i).]

History – Para. 8 omitted by FA 2011, s. 65 and Sch. 16, para. 84(b)(i), with effect in relation to deaths occurring on or after 6 April 2011.

INTEREST

9 [Omitted by FA 2011, s. 65 and Sch. 16, para. 84(b)(i).]

History – Para. 9 omitted by FA 2011, s. 65 and Sch. 16, para. 84(b)(i), with effect in relation to deaths occurring on or after 6 April 2011.

INTERPRETATION

10(1) Section 272 (general interpretation) is amended as follows.

10(2) [Amends IHTA 1984, s. 272.]

10(3) [Omitted by FA 2011, s. 65 and Sch. 16, para. 84(b)(i).]

History – Para. 10(3) omitted by FA 2011, s. 65 and Sch. 16, para. 84(b)(i), with effect in relation to deaths occurring on or after 6 April 2011.

RATES OF TAX

11 [Inserts IHTA 1984, Sch. 2, para. 6A.]

TRANSITIONAL

12 [Omitted by FA 2011, s. 65 and Sch. 16, para. 84(b)(i).]

History – Para. 12 omitted by FA 2011, s. 65 and Sch. 16, para. 84(b)(i), with effect in relation to dispositions made (or treated as made) on or after 6 April 2011.

INCOME TAX ACT 2007

(2007 Chapter 3)

[*20th March 2007*]

ARRANGEMENT OF SECTIONS

PART 17 – DEFINITIONS FOR PURPOSES OF ACT AND FINAL PROVISIONS

FINAL PROVISIONS

SCHEDULES

PART 17 – DEFINITIONS FOR PURPOSES OF ACT AND FINAL PROVISIONS

FINAL PROVISIONS

1027 Minor and consequential amendments

1027 Schedule 1 (minor and consequential amendments) has effect.

Origin – S. 1027: Drafting.

1033 Extent

1033(1) This Act extends to England and Wales, Scotland and Northern Ireland (but see subsection (2)).

1033(2) An amendment, repeal or revocation contained in Schedule 1 or 3 has the same extent as the provision amended, repealed or revoked.

Origin – S. 1033: Drafting.

1034 Commencement

1034(1) This Act comes into force on 6 April 2007 and has effect–

(a) for income tax purposes, for the tax year 2007–08 and subsequent tax years, and

(b) for corporation tax purposes, for accounting periods ending after 5 April 2007.

1034(2) Subsection (1) is subject to subsections (3) and (4).

1034(3) The following–

(a) Part 5 (enterprise investment scheme),

(b) Part 3 of Schedule 1 (consequential amendment associated with Part 5), and

(c) Part 2 of Schedule 3 (repeals so associated),

do not have effect in relation to shares issued before 6 April 2007.

This is subject to Schedule 2 (transitional provisions and savings).

1034(4) Subsection (1) does not apply to the following provisions of this Act (which therefore come into force on the day on which this Act is passed)–

(a) in Part 15, section 852, and

(b) in this Part, sections 1017, 1018, 1028, 1029, 1030(2) to (4) and 1033, this section and section 1035.

Origin – S. 1034: Drafting.

1035 Short title

1035 This Act may be cited as the Income Tax Act 2007.

Origin – S. 1035: Drafting.

SCHEDULES

SCHEDULE 1 – MINOR AND CONSEQUENTIAL AMENDMENTS

Section 1027

Part 2 – Other enactments

INHERITANCE TAX ACT 1984 (C. 51)

268 The Inheritance Tax Act 1984 is amended as follows.

269 In section 157(6) (non-residents' bank accounts) for "section 840A of the Taxes Act 1988" substitute "section 991 of the Income Tax Act 2007".

270 In section 204(5) (limitation of liability) for "section 739 or 740 of the Taxes Act 1988" substitute "Chapter 2 of Part 13 of the Income Tax Act 2007".

271 In section 272 (general interpretation) in the definition of "authorised unit trust" for the words from "section 469" to "section)" substitute "the Income Tax Acts (see section 1007 of the Income Tax Act 2007)".

FINANCE ACT 2007

(2007 Chapter 11)

[*19th July 2007*]

ARRANGEMENT OF SECTIONS

PART 1 – CHARGES, RATES, THRESHOLDS ETC

INHERITANCE TAX

4 Rates and rate bands for 2010–11

4 [Omitted by FA 2010, s. 8(2)(b).]

History – S. 4 omitted (before coming into effect) by FA 2010, s. 8(2)(b), with effect for chargeable transfers made on or after 6 April 2010.

PART 4 – PENSIONS

69 Alternatively secured pensions etc

69 Schedule 19 contains provisions about alternatively secured pensions and transfer lump sum death benefit etc.

70 Miscellaneous

70 Schedule 20 contains miscellaneous provisions about registered pension schemes and employer-financed retirement benefits schemes.

PART 6 – INVESTIGATION, ADMINISTRATION ETC

OTHER ADMINISTRATION

97 Penalties for errors

97(1) Schedule 24 contains provisions imposing penalties on taxpayers who–

(a) make errors in certain documents sent to HMRC, or

(b) unreasonably fail to report errors in assessments by HMRC.

97(2) That Schedule comes into force in accordance with provision made by the Treasury by order.

97(3) An order–

(a) may commence a provision generally or only for specified purposes,

(b) may make different provision for different purposes, and

(c) may include incidental, consequential or transitional provision.

97(4) The power to make an order is exercisable by statutory instrument.

PART 8 – FINAL PROVISIONS

115 Short title

115 This Act may be cited as the Finance Act 2007.

SCHEDULES

SCHEDULE 19 – ALTERNATIVELY SECURED PENSIONS AND TRANSFER LUMP SUM DEATH BENEFITS

Section 69

INHERITANCE TAX

19 IHTA 1984 is amended as follows.

20(1) Section 151A (person dying with alternatively secured pension fund) is amended as follows.

20(2) [Substitutes IHTA 1984, s. 151A(2).]

20(3) [Amends IHTA 1984, s. 151A(3)(a).]

20(4) [Inserts IHTA 1984, s. 151A(4A)–(4C).]

20(5) [Amends IHTA 1984, s. 151A(5).]

20(6) [Inserts IHTA 1984, s. 151A(6) and (7).]

21(1) Section 151B (relevant dependant with pension fund inherited from member over 75) is amended as follows.

21(2) [Amends IHTA 1984, s. 151B(1)(b).]

21(3) [Omits IHTA 1984, s. 151B(5).]

22 [Inserts IHTA 1984, s. 151BA.]

23(1) Section 151C (dependant dying with other pension fund) is amended as follows.

23(2) [Substitutes IHTA 1984, s. 151C(2).]

23(3) [Amends IHTA 1984, s. 151C(3)(a).]

23(4) [Inserts IHTA 1984, s. 151C(3A)–(3D).]

23(5) [Amends IHTA 1984, s. 151C(4).]

24 [Amends IHTA 1984, s. 216(6)(ac).]

25 [Amends IHTA 1984, s. 226(4).]

26 [Amends IHTA 1984, s. 233(1)(c).]

27 [Omits IHTA 1984, Sch. 2, para. 6A.]

COMMENCEMENT

29(8) The amendments made by paragraphs 19 to 27 have effect in relation to deaths, cases where scheme administrators become aware of deaths and cessations of dependency occurring on or after 6th April 2007.

SCHEDULE 20 – PENSION SCHEMES ETC: MISCELLANEOUS

Section 70

INHERITANCE TAX: LUMP SUM DEATH BENEFITS

20 [Inserts IHTA 1984, s. 58(2A).]

COMMENCEMENT

24(9) The amendment made by paragraph 20 has effect in relation to lump sum death benefits paid on or after 6th April 2006.

SCHEDULE 24 – PENALTIES FOR ERRORS

Section 97

Commencement Date – Sch. 24 has effect as follows by virtue of SI 2008/568, art. 2:

- 1 April 2008 in relation to relevant documents relating to tax periods commencing on or after that date;
- 1 April 2008 in relation to assessments falling within paragraph 2 for tax periods commencing on or after that date;
- 1 April 2009 in relation to documents relating to all other claims for repayments of relevant tax made on or after 1 April 2009 which are not related to a tax period; and
- in any other case, 1 April 2009 in relation to documents given where a person's liability to pay relevant tax arises on or after that date.

However, no person will be liable to a penalty under Sch. 24 in respect of any tax period for which a return is required to be made before 1 April 2009.

Cross references – FA 2009, s. 94: Publishing details of deliberate tax defaulters.

Other material – HMRC Brief 14/11: Penalty for failure to disclose offshore income or gains.

Notes – This is an edited version of Sch. 24, containing only the provisions relevant to inheritance tax.

Part 1 – Liability for Penalty

ERROR IN TAXPAYER'S DOCUMENT

1(1) A penalty is payable by a person (P) where–

(a) P gives HMRC a document of a kind listed in the Table below, and

(b) Conditions 1 and 2 are satisfied.

1(2) Condition 1 is that the document contains an inaccuracy which amounts to, or leads to–

(a) an understatement of a liability to tax,

(b) a false or inflated statement of a loss, or

(c) a false or inflated claim to repayment of tax.

1(3) Condition 2 is that the inaccuracy was careless (within the meaning of paragraph 3) or deliberate on P's part.

1(4) Where a document contains more than one inaccuracy, a penalty is payable for each inaccuracy.

Tax	Document
Inheritance tax	Account under section 216 or 217 of IHTA 1984.
Inheritance tax	Information or document under regulations under section 256 of IHTA 1984.
Inheritance tax	Statement or declaration in connection with a deduction, exemption or relief.
Any of the taxes mentioned above	Any document which is likely to be relied upon by HMRC to determine, without further inquiry, a question about– (a) P's liability to tax, (b) payments by P by way of or in connection with tax, (c) any other payment by P (including penalties), or (d) repayments, or any other kind of payment or credit, to P.

IHT Statutes

1(5) [Not relevant to inheritance tax.]

Commencement Date – See headnote to Sch. 24.

History – In para. 1(2)(a) the word "a" substituted for the word "P's" and in para. (b) the words "by P" omitted by FA 2008, s. 122 and Sch. 40, para. 2(2), with effect from 1 April 2009 (SI 2009/571, art. 2).
In para. 1(3), the words "careless (within the meaning of paragraph 3) or deliberate on P's part" substituted for the words "careless or deliberate (within the meaning of paragraph 3)" by FA 2008, s. 122 and Sch. 40, para. 2(3), with effect from 1 April 2009 (SI 2009/571, art. 2).
In para. 1(4), in the Table, the entries for inheritance tax inserted by FA 2008, s. 122 and Sch. 40, para. 2(4), with effect from 1 April 2009 (SI 2009/571, art. 2) but subject to the provisions of SI 2009/571, art. 3–5. (Note that the Table as reproduced here shows only those entries relevant to inheritance tax. The Table as it relates to other taxes is reproduced in the version of para. 1 for those other taxes in the relevant division of this publication).
In para. 1(4), in the Table, in the last entry the words "Any of the taxes mentioned above" in column 1 substituted for the words "Income tax, capital gains tax, corporation tax or VAT" by FA 2008, s. 122 and Sch. 40, para. 2(6), with effect from 1 April 2009 (SI 2009/571, art. 2) but subject to the provisions of SI 2009/571, art. 3–5.
Para. 1(5) inserted by FA 2008, s. 122 and Sch. 40, para. 2(7), with effect from 1 April 2009 (SI 2009/571, art. 2).

Cross references – FA 2009, s. 94(2)(a): Publishing details of deliberate tax defaulters.

ERROR IN TAXPAYER'S DOCUMENT ATTRIBUTABLE TO ANOTHER PERSON

1A(1) A penalty is payable by a person (T) where–

(a) another person (P) gives HMRC a document of a kind listed in the Table in paragraph 1,

(b) the document contains a relevant inaccuracy, and

(c) the inaccuracy was attributable to T deliberately supplying false information to P (whether directly or indirectly), or to T deliberately withholding information from P, with the intention of the document containing the inaccuracy.

1A(2) A **"relevant inaccuracy"** is an inaccuracy which amounts to, or leads to–

(a) an understatement of a liability to tax,

(b) a false or inflated statement of a loss, or

(c) a false or inflated claim to repayment of tax.

1A(3) A penalty is payable under this paragraph in respect of an inaccuracy whether or not P is liable to a penalty under paragraph 1 in respect of the same inaccuracy.

History – Para. 1A inserted by FA 2008, s. 122 and Sch. 40, para. 3, with effect from 1 April 2009 (SI 2009/571, art. 2).

Cross references – FA 2009, s. 94(2)(b): Publishing details of deliberate tax defaulters.

UNDER-ASSESSMENT BY HMRC

2(1) A penalty is payable by a person (P) where–

(a) an assessment issued to P by HMRC understates P's liability to a relevant tax, and

(b) P has failed to take reasonable steps to notify HMRC, within the period of 30 days beginning with the date of the assessment, that it is an under-assessment.

2(2) In deciding what steps (if any) were reasonable HMRC must consider–

(a) whether P knew, or should have known, about the under-assessment, and

(b) what steps would have been reasonable to take to notify HMRC.

2(3) In sub-paragraph (1) **"relevant tax"** means any tax mentioned in the Table in paragraph 1.

2(4) In this paragraph (and in Part 2 of this Schedule so far as relating to this paragraph)–

(a) **"assessment"** includes determination, and

(b) accordingly, references to an under-assessment include an under-determination.

Commencement Date – See headnote to Sch. 24.

History – In para. 2(1)(a) the words "a relevant tax" substituted for the word "tax" by FA 2008, s. 122 and Sch. 40, para. 4(2), with effect from 1 April 2009 (SI 2009/571, art. 2).
Para. 2(3) substituted by FA 2008, s. 122 and Sch. 40, para. 4(3), with effect from 1 April 2009 (SI 2009/571, art. 2).
Para. 2(4) inserted by FA 2009. s. 109 and Sch. 57, para. 2, with effect from 21 July 2009.

DEGREES OF CULPABILITY

3(1) For the purposes of a penalty under paragraph 1, inaccuracy in a document given by P to HMRC is–

(a) "careless" if the inaccuracy is due to failure by P to take reasonable care,

(b) "deliberate but not concealed" if the inaccuracy is deliberate on P's part but P does not make arrangements to conceal it, and

(c) "deliberate and concealed" if the inaccuracy is deliberate on P's part and P makes arrangements to conceal it (for example, by submitting false evidence in support of an inaccurate figure).

3(2) An inaccuracy in a document given by P to HMRC, which was neither careless nor deliberate on P's part when the document was given, is to be treated as careless if P–

(a) discovered the inaccuracy at some later time, and

(b) did not take reasonable steps to inform HMRC.

3(3) Paragraph 47 of Schedule 19 to FA 2016 (special measures for persistently unco-operative large businesses) provides for certain inaccuracies to be treated, for the purposes of this Schedule, as being due to a failure by P to take reasonable care.

Commencement Date – See headnote to Sch. 24.

History – In para. 3(1) the words "For the purposes of a penalty under paragraph 1, inaccuracy in" substituted for the words "Inaccuracy in" and the words "on P's part" inserted twice by FA 2008, s. 122 and Sch. 40, para. 5(2), with effect from 1 April 2009 (SI 2009/571, art. 2).

In para. 3(2) the words "on P's part" inserted by FA 2008, s. 122 and Sch. 40, para. 5(3), with effect from 1 April 2009 (SI 2009/571, art. 2).

Para. 3(3) inserted by FA 2016, s. 161 and Sch. 19, para. 48, with effect, so far as relating to the publication of a tax strategy for a financial year of a relevant body or other entity, for financial years beginning on or after 15 September 2016.

ERRORS RELATED TO AVOIDANCE ARRANGEMENTS

3A(1) This paragraph applies where a document of a kind listed in the Table in paragraph 1 is given to HMRC by a person ("P") and the document contains an inaccuracy which–

(a) falls within paragraph 1(2), and

(b) arises because the document is submitted on the basis that particular avoidance arrangements (within the meaning of paragraph 3B) had an effect which in fact they did not have.

3A(2) It is to be presumed that the inaccuracy was careless, within the meaning of paragraph 3, unless–

(a) the inaccuracy was deliberate on P's part, or

(b) P satisfies HMRC or (on an appeal notified to the tribunal) the tribunal that P took reasonable care to avoid inaccuracy.

3A(3) In considering whether P took reasonable care to avoid inaccuracy, HMRC and (on an appeal notified to the tribunal) the tribunal must take no account of any evidence of any reliance by P on advice where the advice is disqualified.

3A(4) Advice is **"disqualified"** if any of the following applies–

(a) the advice was given to P by an interested person;

(b) the advice was given to P as a result of arrangements made between an interested person and the person who gave the advice;

(c) the person who gave the advice did not have appropriate expertise for giving the advice;

(d) the advice took no account of P's individual circumstances;

(e) the advice was addressed to, or given to, a person other than P;

but this is subject to sub-paragraphs (5) and (7).

3A(5) Where (but for this sub-paragraph) advice would be disqualified under any of paragraphs (a) to (c) of sub-paragraph (4), the advice is not disqualified under that paragraph if at the relevant time P–

(a) has taken reasonable steps to find out whether the advice falls within that paragraph, and

(b) reasonably believes that it does not.

3A(6) In sub-paragraph (4) **"an interested person"** means–

(a) a person, other than P, who participated in the avoidance arrangements or any transaction forming part of them, or

(b) a person who for any consideration (whether or not in money) facilitated P's entering into the avoidance arrangements.

3A(7) Where (but for this sub-paragraph) advice would be disqualified under paragraph (a) of sub-paragraph (4) because it was given by a person within sub-paragraph (6)(b), the advice is not disqualified under that paragraph if–

(a) the person giving the advice had appropriate expertise for giving it,

(b) the advice took account of P's individual circumstances, and

(c) at the time when the question whether the advice is disqualified arises–

(i) Condition E in paragraph 3B(5) is met in relation to the avoidance arrangements, but

(ii) none of Conditions A to D in paragraph 3B(5) is or has at any time been met in relation to them.

3A(8) If the document mentioned in sub-paragraph (1) is given to HMRC by P as a personal representative of a deceased person ("D")–

(a) sub-paragraph (4) is to be read as if–

(i) the references in paragraphs (a) and (b) to P were to P or D;

(ii) the reference in paragraph (d) to P were to D, and

(iii) the reference in paragraph (e) to a person other than P were to a person who is neither P nor D,

(b) sub-paragraph (6) is to be read as if–

(i) the reference in paragraph (a) to P were a reference to the person to whom the advice was given, and

(ii) the reference in paragraph (b) to P were to D (or, where P also participated in the avoidance arrangements, P or D), and

(c) sub-paragraph (7) is to be read as if the reference in paragraph (b) to P were to D.

3A(9) In this paragraph–

"arrangements" includes any agreement, understanding, scheme, transaction or series of transactions (whether or not legally enforceable);

"the relevant time" means the time when the document mentioned in sub-paragraph (1) is given to HMRC;

"the tribunal" has the same meaning as in paragraph 17 (see paragraph 17(5A)).

History – Para. 3A inserted by F(No. 2)A 2017, s. 64(2), with effect in relation to any document of a kind listed in the Table at para. 1 which is given to HMRC on or after 16 November 2017 (Royal Assent) and relates to a tax period that begins on or after 6 April 2017 and ends on or after 16 November 2017 (Royal Assent).

3B(1) In paragraph 3A **"avoidance arrangements"** means, subject to sub-paragraph (3), arrangements which fall within sub-paragraph (2).

3B(2) Arrangements fall within this sub-paragraph if, having regard to all the circumstances, it would be reasonable to conclude that the obtaining of a tax advantage was the main purpose, or one of the main purposes, of the arrangements.

3B(3) Arrangements are not avoidance arrangements for the purposes of paragraph 3A if (although they fall within sub-paragraph (2))–

(a) they are arrangements which accord with established practice, and

(b) HMRC had, at the time the arrangements were entered into, indicated its acceptance of that practice.

3B(4) If, at any time, any of Conditions A to E is met in relation to particular arrangements–

(a) for the purposes of this Schedule the arrangements are to be taken to fall within (and always to have fallen within) sub-paragraph (2), and

(b) in relation to the arrangements, sub-paragraph (3) (and the reference to it in sub-paragraph (1)) are to be treated as omitted.

This does not prevent arrangements from falling within sub-paragraph (2) other than by reason of one or more of Conditions A to E being met.

3B(5) Conditions A to E are as follows–

(a) Condition A is that the arrangements are DOTAS arrangements within the meaning given by section 219(5) and (6) of FA 2014;

(b) Condition B is that the arrangements are disclosable VAT arrangements or disclosable indirect tax arrangements for the purposes of Schedule 18 to FA 2016 (see paragraphs 8A to 9A of that Schedule);

(c) Condition C is that both of the following apply–

(i) P has been given a notice under a provision mentioned in sub-paragraph (6) stating that a tax advantage arising from the arrangements is to be counteracted, and

(ii) that tax advantage has been counteracted under section 209 of FA 2013;

(d) Condition D is that a follower notice under section 204 of FA 2014 has been given to P by reference to the arrangements (and not withdrawn) and–

(i) the necessary corrective action for the purposes of section 208 of FA 2014 has been taken in respect of the denied advantage, or

(ii) the denied advantage has been counteracted otherwise than as mentioned in sub-paragraph (i);

(e) Condition E is that a tax advantage asserted by reference to the arrangements has been counteracted (by an assessment, an amendment of a return or claim, or otherwise) on the basis that an avoidance-related rule applies in relation to P's affairs.

3B(6) The provisions referred to in sub-paragraph (5)(c)(i) are–

(a) paragraph 12 of Schedule 43 to FA 2013 (general anti-abuse rule: notice of final decision);

(b) paragraph 8 or 9 of Schedule 43A to that Act (pooled or bound arrangements: notice of final decision);

(c) paragraph 8 of Schedule 43B to that Act (generic referrals: notice of final decision).

3B(7) In sub-paragraph (5)(d) the reference to giving a follower notice to P includes giving a partnership follower notice in respect of a partnership return in relation to which P is a relevant partner; and for the purposes of this sub-paragraph–

(a) **"relevant partner"** has the meaning given by paragraph 2(5) of Schedule 31 to FA 2014;

(b) a partnership follower notice is given "in respect of" the partnership return mentioned in paragraph 2(2)(a) or (b) of that Schedule.

3B(8) For the purposes of sub-paragraph (5)(d) it does not matter whether the denied advantage has been dealt with–

(a) wholly as mentioned in one or other of sub-paragraphs (i) and (ii) of sub-paragraph (5)(d), or

(b) partly as mentioned in one of those sub-paragraphs and partly as mentioned in the other;

and **"the denied advantage"** has the same meaning as in Chapter 2 of Part 4 of FA 2014 (see section 208(3) of and paragraph 4(3) of Schedule 31 to that Act).

3B(9) For the purposes of sub-paragraph (5)(e) a tax advantage has been **"asserted by reference to"** the arrangements if a return, claim or appeal has been made by P on the basis that the tax advantage results from the arrangements.

3B(10) In this paragraph–

"arrangements" has the same meaning as in paragraph 3A;

"avoidance-related rule" has the same meaning as in Part 4 of Schedule 18 to FA 2016 (see paragraph 25 of that Schedule);

a **"tax advantage"** includes–

(a) relief or increased relief from tax,

(b) repayment or increased repayment of tax,

(c) avoidance or reduction of a charge to tax or an assessment to tax,

(d) avoidance of a possible assessment to tax,

(e) deferral of a payment of tax or advancement of a repayment of tax,

(f) avoidance of an obligation to deduct or account for tax, and

(g) in relation to VAT, anything which is a tax advantage for the purposes of Schedule 18 to FA 2016 under paragraph 5 of that Schedule.

History – Para. 3B inserted by F(No. 2)A 2017, s. 64(2), with effect in relation to any document of a kind listed in the Table at para. 1 which is given to HMRC on or after 16 November 2017 (Royal Assent) and relates to a tax period that begins on or after 6 April 2017 and ends on or after 16 November 2017 (Royal Assent).

Part 2 – Amount of Penalty

STANDARD AMOUNT

4(1) This paragraph sets out the penalty payable under paragraph 1.

4(2) If the inaccuracy is in category 1, the penalty is–

(a) for careless action, 30% of the potential lost revenue,

(b) for deliberate but not concealed action, 70% of the potential lost revenue, and

(c) for deliberate and concealed action, 100% of the potential lost revenue.

4(3) If the inaccuracy is in category 2, the penalty is–

(a) for careless action, 45% of the potential lost revenue,

(b) for deliberate but not concealed action, 105% of the potential lost revenue, and

(c) for deliberate and concealed action, 150% of the potential lost revenue.

4(4) If the inaccuracy is in category 3, the penalty is–

(a) for careless action, 60% of the potential lost revenue,

(b) for deliberate but not concealed action, 140% of the potential lost revenue, and

(c) for deliberate and concealed action, 200% of the potential lost revenue.

4(5) Paragraph 4A explains the 3 categories of inaccuracy.

Commencement Date – See headnote to Sch. 24 for commencement date of former para. 4.

Prospective amendments – Para. 4(1A) inserted by FA 2015, s. 120 and Sch. 20, para. 2(2), with effect from a day to be appointed under FA 2015, s. 120(2).

In para. 4(2)(a) "37.5%" substituted for "30%", in para. 4(2)(b) "87.5%" substituted for "70%" and in para. 4(2)(c) "125%" substituted for "100%" by FA 2015, s. 120 and Sch. 20, para. 2(3), with effect from a day to be appointed under FA 2015, s. 120(2).
In para. 4(2)(a) "4" substituted for "3" by FA 2015, s. 120 and Sch. 20, para. 2(4), with effect from a day to be appointed under FA 2015, s. 120(2).

History – Para. 4, 4A, 4B, 4C and 4D substituted for former para. 4 by FA 2010, s. 35 and Sch. 10, para 2, with effect from 6 April 2011, but the substitution does not have effect in relation to documents given to HMRC and assessments issued by HMRC in relation to a tax period (as defined in para. 28(g)) commencing on or before 5 April 2011 (SI 2011/975). Former para. 4 read as follows:
"**4(1)** The penalty payable under paragraph 1 is–
(a) for careless action, 30% of the potential lost revenue,
(b) for deliberate but not concealed action, 70% of the potential lost revenue, and
(c) for deliberate and concealed action, 100% of the potential lost revenue.
4(1A) The penalty payable under paragraph 1A is 100% of the potential lost revenue.
4(2) The penalty payable under paragraph 2 is 30% of the potential lost revenue.
4(3) Paragraphs 5 to 8 define "potential lost revenue".".
Former para. 4(1A) inserted by FA 2008, s. 122 and Sch. 40, para. 6, with effect from 1 April 2009 (SI 2009/571, art. 2).

4A(1) An inaccuracy is in category 1 if–
(a) it involves a domestic matter, or
(b) it involves an offshore matter and–
  (i) the territory in question is a category 1 territory, or
  (ii) the tax at stake is a tax other than income tax or capital gains tax.

4A(2) An inaccuracy is in category 2 if–
(a) it involves an offshore matter or an offshore transfer,
(b) the territory in question is a category 2 territory, and
(c) the tax at stake is income tax, capital gains tax or inheritance tax.

4A(3) An inaccuracy is in category 3 if–
(a) it involves an offshore matter or an offshore transfer,
(b) the territory in question is a category 3 territory, and
(c) the tax at stake is income tax, capital gains tax or inheritance tax.

4A(4) An inaccuracy **"involves an offshore matter"** if it results in a potential loss of revenue that is charged on or by reference to–
(a) income arising from a source in a territory outside the UK,
(b) assets situated or held in a territory outside the UK,
(c) activities carried on wholly or mainly in a territory outside the UK, or
(d) anything having effect as if it were income, assets or activities of a kind described above.

4A(4A) Where the tax at stake is inheritance tax, assets are treated for the purposes of sub-paragraph (4) as situated or held in a territory outside the UK if they are so situated or held immediately after the transfer of value by reason of which inheritance tax becomes chargeable.

4A(4B) An inaccuracy **"involves an offshore transfer"** if–
(a) it does not involve an offshore matter,
(b) it is deliberate (whether or not concealed) and results in a potential loss of revenue,
(c) the tax at stake is income tax, capital gains tax or inheritance tax, and
(d) the applicable condition in paragraph 4AA is satisfied.

4A(5) An inaccuracy **"involves a domestic matter"** if it results in a potential loss of revenue and does not involve either an offshore matter or an offshore transfer.

4A(6) If a single inaccuracy is in more than one category (each referred to as a "relevant category")–
(a) it is to be treated for the purposes of this Schedule as if it were separate inaccuracies, one in each relevant category according to the matters or transfers that it involves, and
(b) the potential lost revenue is to be calculated separately in respect of each separate inaccuracy.

4A(7) **"Category 1 territory"**, **"category 2 territory"** and **"category 3 territory"** are defined in paragraph 21A.

4A(8) **"Assets"** has the meaning given in section 21(1) of TCGA 1992, but also includes sterling.

Prospective amendments – Para. 4A(1A) and (1) substituted for para. 4A(1) by FA 2015, s. 120 and Sch. 20, para. 3(2), with effect from a day to be appointed under FA 2015, s. 120(2).
In para. 4A(7) the words "Category 0 territory", "category 1" substituted for the words "Category 1" by FA 2015, s. 120 and Sch. 20, para. 3(8), with effect from a day to be appointed under FA 2015, s. 120(2).

History – *In para.* 4A(2)(a) the words "or an offshore transfer" inserted and in para. 4A(2)(c) the words ", capital gains tax or inheritance tax" substituted for the words "or capital gains tax" by FA 2015, s. 120 and Sch. 20, para. 3(3), with effect in relation to documents given to HMRC relating to a transfer of value made on or after 6 April 2016 for the purposes of inheritance tax (SI 2016/456, art. 3).
In para. 4A(3)(a) the words "or an offshore transfer" inserted and in para. 4A(3)(b) the words ", capital gains tax or inheritance tax" substituted for the words "or capital gains tax" by FA 2015, s. 120 and Sch. 20, para. 3(4), with effect in relation to documents given to HMRC relating to a transfer of value made on or after 6 April 2016 for the purposes of inheritance tax (SI 2016/456, art. 3).

Para. 4A(4A) and (4B) inserted by FA 2015, s. 120 and Sch. 20, para. 3(5), with effect in relation to documents given to HMRC relating to a transfer of value made on or after 6 April 2016 for the purposes of inheritance tax (SI 2016/456, art. 3).
In para. 4A(5) the words "and does not involve either an offshore matter or an offshore transfer" substituted for the words "that is charged on or by reference to anything not mentioned in sub-paragraph (4)(a) to (d)" by FA 2015, s. 120 and Sch. 20, para. 3(6), with effect in relation to documents given to HMRC relating to a transfer of value made on or after 6 April 2016 for the purposes of inheritance tax (SI 2016/456, art. 3).
In para. 4A(6)(a) the words "or transfers" inserted by FA 2015, s. 120 and Sch. 20, para. 3(7), with effect in relation to documents given to HMRC relating to a transfer of value made on or after 6 April 2016 for the purposes of inheritance tax (SI 2016/456, art. 3).
Para. 4, 4A, 4B, 4C and 4D substituted for former para. 4 by FA 2010, s. 35 and Sch. 10, para 2, with effect from 6 April 2011, but the substitution does not have effect in relation to documents given to HMRC and assessments issued by HMRC in relation to a tax period (as defined in para. 28(g)) commencing on or before 5 April 2011 (SI 2011/975).

4AA(1) This paragraph makes provision in relation to offshore transfers.

4AA(2) Where the tax at stake is income tax, the applicable condition is satisfied if the income on or by reference to which the tax is charged, or any part of the income–

(a) is received in a territory outside the UK, or

(b) is transferred before the filing date to a territory outside the UK.

4AA(3) Where the tax at stake is capital gains tax, the applicable condition is satisfied if the proceeds of the disposal on or by reference to which the tax is charged, or any part of the proceeds–

(a) are received in a territory outside the UK, or

(b) are transferred before the filing date to a territory outside the UK.

4AA(4) Where the tax at stake is inheritance tax, the applicable condition is satisfied if–

(a) the disposition that gives rise to the transfer of value by reason of which the tax becomes chargeable involves a transfer of assets, and

(b) after that disposition but before the filing date the assets, or any part of the assets, are transferred to a territory outside the UK.

4AA(5) In the case of a transfer falling within sub-paragraph (2)(b), (3)(b) or (4)(b), references to the income, proceeds or assets transferred are to be read as including references to any assets derived from or representing the income, proceeds or assets.

4AA(6) In relation to an offshore transfer, the territory in question for the purposes of paragraph 4A is the highest category of territory by virtue of which the inaccuracy involves an offshore transfer.

4AA(7) **"Filing date"** means the date when the document containing the inaccuracy is given to HMRC.

4AA(8) **"Assets"** has the same meaning as in paragraph 4A.

History – Para. 4AA inserted by FA 2015, s. 120 and Sch. 20, para. 4, with effect from in relation to documents given to HMRC relating to a transfer of value made on or after 6 April 2016 for the purposes of inheritance tax (SI 2016/456, art. 3).

4B The penalty payable under paragraph 1A is 100% of the potential lost revenue.

History – Para. 4, 4A, 4B, 4C and 4D substituted for former para. 4 by FA 2010, s. 35 and Sch. 10, para 2, with effect from 6 April 2011, but the substitution does not have effect in relation to documents given to HMRC and assessments issued by HMRC in relation to a tax period (as defined in para. 28(g)) commencing on or before 5 April 2011 (SI 2011/975).

4C The penalty payable under paragraph 2 is 30% of the potential lost revenue.

History – Para. 4, 4A, 4B, 4C and 4D substituted for former para. 4 by FA 2010, s. 35 and Sch. 10, para 2, with effect from 6 April 2011, but the substitution does not have effect in relation to documents given to HMRC and assessments issued by HMRC in relation to a tax period (as defined in para. 28(g)) commencing on or before 5 April 2011 (SI 2011/975).

4D Paragraphs 5 to 8 define **"potential lost revenue"**.

History – Para. 4, 4A, 4B, 4C and 4D substituted for former para. 4 by FA 2010, s. 35 and Sch. 10, para 2, with effect from 6 April 2011, but the substitution does not have effect in relation to documents given to HMRC and assessments issued by HMRC in relation to a tax period (as defined in para. 28(g)) commencing on or before 5 April 2011 (SI 2011/975).

POTENTIAL LOST REVENUE: NORMAL RULE

5 [Not relevant to inheritance tax.]

POTENTIAL LOST REVENUE: MULTIPLE ERRORS

6(1) Where P is liable to a penalty under paragraph 1 in respect of more than one inaccuracy, and the calculation of potential lost revenue under paragraph 5 in respect of each inaccuracy depends on the order in which they are corrected–

(a) careless inaccuracies shall be taken to be corrected before deliberate inaccuracies, and

(b) deliberate but not concealed inaccuracies shall be taken to be corrected before deliberate and concealed inaccuracies.

6(2) In calculating potential lost revenue where P is liable to a penalty under paragraph 1 in respect of one or more understatements in one or more documents relating to a tax period, account shall be taken of any overstatement in any document given by P which relates to the same tax period.

6(3) In sub-paragraph (2)–

(a) **"understatement"** means an inaccuracy that satisfies Condition 1 of paragraph 1, and

(b) **"overstatement"** means an inaccuracy that does not satisfy that condition.

6(4) For the purposes of sub-paragraph (2) overstatements shall be set against understatements in the following order–

(a) understatements in respect of which P is not liable to a penalty,

(b) careless understatements,

(c) deliberate but not concealed understatements, and

(d) deliberate and concealed understatements.

6(5) In calculating for the purposes of a penalty under paragraph 1 potential lost revenue in respect of a document given by or on behalf of P no account shall be taken of the fact that a potential loss of revenue from P is or may be balanced by a potential over-payment by another person (except to the extent that an enactment requires or permits a person's tax liability to be adjusted by reference to P's).

Commencement Date – See headnote to Sch. 24.

History – In para. 6(1) the words "under paragraph 1" inserted by FA 2008, s. 122 and Sch. 40, para. 8(2), with effect from 1 April 2009 (SI 2009/571, art. 2).

In para. 6(2) the words "under paragraph 1" inserted by FA 2008, s. 122 and Sch. 40, para. 8(2), with effect from 1 April 2009 (SI 2009/571, art. 2).

In para. 6(5) the words "for the purposes of a penalty under paragraph 1" inserted by FA 2008, s. 122 and Sch. 40, para. 8(3), with effect from 1 April 2009 (SI 2009/571, art. 2).

POTENTIAL LOST REVENUE: LOSSES

7(1) Where an inaccuracy has the result that a loss is wrongly recorded for purposes of direct tax and the loss has been wholly used to reduce the amount due or payable in respect of tax, the potential lost revenue is calculated in accordance with paragraph 5.

7(2) Where an inaccuracy has the result that a loss is wrongly recorded for purposes of direct tax and the loss has not been wholly used to reduce the amount due or payable in respect of tax, the potential lost revenue is–

(a) the potential lost revenue calculated in accordance with paragraph 5 in respect of any part of the loss that has been used to reduce the amount due or payable in respect of tax, plus

(b) 10% of any part that has not.

7(3) Sub-paragraphs (1) and (2) apply both–

(a) to a case where no loss would have been recorded but for the inaccuracy, and

(b) to a case where a loss of a different amount would have been recorded (but in that case sub-paragraphs (1) and (2) apply only to the difference between the amount recorded and the true amount).

7(4) Where an inaccuracy has the effect of creating or increasing an aggregate loss recorded for a group of companies–

(a) the potential lost revenue shall be calculated in accordance with this paragraph, and

(b) in applying paragraph 5 in accordance with sub-paragraphs (1) and (2) above, group relief may be taken into account (despite paragraph 5(4)(a)).

7(5) The potential lost revenue in respect of a loss is nil where, because of the nature of the loss or P's circumstances, there is no reasonable prospect of the loss being used to support a claim to reduce a tax liability (of any person).

Commencement Date – See headnote to Sch. 24.

POTENTIAL LOST REVENUE: DELAYED TAX

8(1) Where an inaccuracy resulted in an amount of tax being declared later than it should have been ("the delayed tax"), the potential lost revenue is–

(a) 5% of the delayed tax for each year of the delay, or

(b) a percentage of the delayed tax, for each separate period of delay of less than a year, equating to 5% per year.

8(2) *This paragraph* does not apply to a case to which paragraph 7 applies.

Commencement Date – See headnote to Sch. 24.

Other material – HMRC Brief 15/11: change in HMRC's view of the operation of the delayed tax provisions for inaccuracy penalties.

REDUCTIONS FOR DISCLOSURE

9(A1) Paragraph 10 provides for reductions in penalties–

(a) under paragraph 1 where a person discloses an inaccuracy that involves a domestic matter,

(b) under paragraph 1A where a person discloses a supply of false information or withholding of information, and

(c) under paragraph 2 where a person discloses a failure to disclose an under-assessment.

9(A2) Paragraph 10A provides for reductions in penalties under paragraph 1 where a person discloses an inaccuracy that involves an offshore matter or an offshore transfer.

9(A3) Sub-paragraph (1) applies where a person discloses–

(a) an inaccuracy that involves a domestic matter,

(b) a careless inaccuracy that involves an offshore matter,

(c) a supply of false information or withholding of information, or

(d) a failure to disclose an under-assessment.

9(1) A person discloses the matter by–

(a) telling HMRC about it,

(b) giving HMRC reasonable help in quantifying the inaccuracy, the inaccuracy attributable to the supply of false information or withholding of information, or the under-assessment, and

(c) allowing HMRC access to records for the purpose of ensuring that the inaccuracy, the inaccuracy attributable to the supply of false information or withholding of information, or the under-assessment is fully corrected.

9(1A) Sub-paragraph (1B) applies where a person discloses–

(a) a deliberate inaccuracy (whether concealed or not) that involves an offshore matter, or

(b) an inaccuracy that involves an offshore transfer.

9(1B) A person discloses the inaccuracy by–

(a) telling HMRC about it,

(b) giving HMRC reasonable help in quantifying the inaccuracy,

(c) allowing HMRC access to records for the purpose of ensuring that the inaccuracy is fully corrected, and

(d) providing HMRC with additional information.

9(1C) The Treasury must make regulations setting out what is meant by **"additional information"** for the purposes of sub-paragraph (1B)(d).

9(1D) Regulations under sub-paragraph (1C) are to be made by statutory instrument.

9(1E) An instrument containing regulations under sub-paragraph (1C) is subject to annulment in pursuance of a resolution of the House of Commons.

9(2) Disclosure–

(a) is "unprompted" if made at a time when the person making it has no reason to believe that HMRC have discovered or are about to discover the inaccuracy, the supply of false information or withholding of information, or the under assessment, and

(b) otherwise, is "prompted".

9(3) In relation to disclosure **"quality"** includes timing, nature and extent.

9(4) Paragraph 4A(4) to (5) applies to determine whether an inaccuracy involves an offshore matter, an offshore transfer or a domestic matter for the purposes of this paragraph.

Commencement Date – See headnote to Sch. 24.

History – Para. 9(A1) to (A3) substituted for (A1) by FA 2016, s. 163(1) and Sch. 21, para. 2(2), with effect for inheritance tax purposes in relation to transfers of value made on or after 1 April 2017 (SI 2017/259, reg. 2(a)). Former para. 9(A1) read as follows:

"**9(A1)** Paragraph 10 provides for reductions in penalties under paragraphs 1, 1A and 2 where a person discloses an inaccuracy, *a supply of false information or withholding of information*, or a failure to disclose an under-assessment.".

Para. 9(A1) inserted by FA 2008, s. 122 and Sch. 40, para. 9(2), with effect from 1 April 2009 (SI 2009/571, art. 2).

In para. 9(1), the words "the matter" substituted for the words "an inaccuracy, a supply of false information or withholding of information, or a failure to disclose an under-assessment" by FA 2016, s. 163(1) and Sch. 21, para. 2(3), with effect for inheritance tax purposes in relation to transfers of value made on or after 1 April 2017 (SI 2017/259, reg. 2(a)).

In para. 9(1)(b), the words "supply of false information" substituted for "supply or false information" by FA 2009, s. 109 and Sch. 57, para. 4, with effect from 21 July 2009.

In para. 9(1)(c), the words "supply of false information" substituted for "supply or false information" by FA 2009, s. 109 and Sch. 57, para. 4, with effect from 21 July 2009.

In para. 9(1) the words ", a supply of false information or withholding of information," inserted and in para. (b) and (c) the words ", the inaccuracy attributable to the supply or false information or withholding of information, or the" substituted for the word "or" by FA 2008, s. 122 and Sch. 40, para. 9(3), with effect from 1 April 2009 (SI 2009/571, art. 2).

Para. 9(1A) to (1E) inserted by FA 2016, s. 163(1) and Sch. 21, para. 2(4), with effect from 8 March 2017 for the purpose of making the regulations and for inheritance tax purposes in relation to transfers of value made on or after 1 April 2017 (SI 2017/259, reg. 2(a)).

In para. 9(2)(a) the words ", the supply of false information or withholding of information, or the under assessment" substituted for the word "or under-assessment" by FA 2008, s. 122 and Sch. 40, para. 9(3), with effect from 1 April 2009 (SI 2009/571, art. 2).
Para. 9(4) inserted by FA 2016, s. 163(1) and Sch. 21, para. 2(5), with effect for inheritance tax purposes in relation to transfers of value made on or after 1 April 2017 (SI 2017/259, reg. 2(a)).
Statutory instruments – SI 2017/345: partly made under para. 9(1C).

10(1) If a person who would otherwise be liable to a penalty of a percentage shown in column 1 of the Table (a "standard percentage") has made a disclosure, HMRC must reduce the standard percentage to one that reflects the quality of the disclosure.

10(2) But the standard percentage may not be reduced to a percentage that is below the minimum shown for it–

(a) in the case of a prompted disclosure, in column 2 of the Table, and

(b) in the case of an unprompted disclosure, in column 3 of the Table.

Standard %	*Minimum % for prompted disclosure*	*Minimum % for unprompted disclosure*
30%	15%	0%
70%	35%	20%
100%	50%	30%

Commencement Date – See headnote to Sch. 24 for commencement of former para. 10.
Prospective amendments – Table in para. 10(2) amended by FA 2015, s. 120 and Sch. 20, para. 5, with effect from a day to be appointed under FA 2015, s. 120(2).
History – Table in para. 10(2) substituted by FA 2016, s. 163(1) and Sch. 21, para. 3, with effect for inheritance tax purposes in relation to transfers of value made on or after 1 April 2017 (SI 2017/259, reg. 2(a)). Former table read as follows:

"Standard %	*Minimum % for prompted disclosure*	*Minimum % for unprompted disclosure*
30%	15%	0%
45%	22.5%	0%
60%	30%	0%
70%	35%	20%
105%	52.5%	30%
140%	70%	40%
100%	50%	30%
150%	75%	45%
200%	100%	60%".

Para. 10 substituted by FA 2010, s. 35 and Sch. 10, para. 3, with effect from 6 April 2011, but the substitution does not have effect in relation to documents given to HMRC and assessments issued by HMRC in relation to a tax period (as defined in para. 28(g)) commencing on or before 5 April 2011 (SI 2011/975). Former para. 10 read as follows:
"10(1) Where a person who would otherwise be liable to a 30% penalty has made an unprompted disclosure, HMRC shall reduce the 30% to a percentage (which may be 0%) which reflects the quality of the disclosure.
10(2) Where a person who would otherwise be liable to a 30% penalty has made a prompted disclosure, HMRC shall reduce the 30% to a percentage, not below 15%, which reflects the quality of the disclosure.
10(3) Where a person who would otherwise be liable to a 70% penalty has made an unprompted disclosure, HMRC shall reduce the 70% to a percentage, not below 20%, which reflects the quality of the disclosure.
10(4) Where a person who would otherwise be liable to a 70% penalty has made a prompted disclosure, HMRC shall reduce the 70% to a percentage, not below 35%, which reflects the quality of the disclosure.
10(5) Where a person who would otherwise be liable to a 100% penalty has made an unprompted disclosure, HMRC shall reduce the 100% to a percentage, not below 30%, which reflects the quality of the disclosure.
10(6) Where a person who would otherwise be liable to a 100% penalty has made a prompted disclosure, HMRC shall reduce the 100% to a percentage, not below 50%, which reflects the quality of the disclosure.".
Cross references – FA 2009, s. 94(10)(a): no information may be published if the amount of the penalty is reduced to the full extent permitted.

10A(1) If a person who would otherwise be liable to a penalty of a percentage shown in column 1 of the Table (a "standard percentage") has made a disclosure, HMRC must reduce the standard percentage to one that reflects the quality of the disclosure.

10A(2) But the standard percentage may not be reduced to a percentage that is below the minimum shown for it–

(a) in the case of a prompted disclosure, in column 2 of the Table, and

(b) in the case of an unprompted disclosure, in column 3 of the Table.

Standard %	*Minimum % for prompted disclosure*	*Minimum % for unprompted* disclosure
30%	15%	0%
37.5%	18.75%	0%
45%	22.5%	0%

Standard %	*Minimum % for prompted disclosure*	*Minimum % for unprompted disclosure*
60%	30%	0%
70%	45%	30%
87.5%	53.75%	35%
100%	60%	40%
105%	62.5%	40%
125%	72.5%	50%
140%	80%	50%
150%	85%	55%
200%	110%	70%

History – Para. 10A inserted by FA 2016, s. 163(1) and Sch. 21, para. 4, with effect for inheritance tax purposes in relation to transfers of value made on or after 1 April 2017 (SI 2017/259, reg. 2(a)).

SPECIAL REDUCTION

11(1) If they think it right because of special circumstances, HMRC may reduce a penalty under paragraph 1, 1A or 2.

11(2) In sub-paragraph (1) **"special circumstances"** does not include–

(a) ability to pay, or

(b) the fact that a potential loss of revenue from one taxpayer is balanced by a potential over-payment by another.

11(3) In sub-paragraph (1) the reference to reducing a penalty includes a reference to–

(a) staying a penalty, and

(b) agreeing a compromise in relation to proceedings for a penalty.

Commencement Date – See headnote to Sch. 24.

History – In para. 11(1) ", (1A)" inserted by FA 2008, s. 122 and Sch. 40, para. 10, with effect from 1 April 2009 (SI 2009/571, art. 2).

INTERACTION WITH OTHER PENALTIES AND LATE PAYMENT SURCHARGES

History – In above heading the words "AND LATE PAYMENT SURCHARGES" inserted by FA 2008, s. 122 and Sch. 40, para. 11(4), with effect from 1 April 2009 (SI 2009/571, art. 2).

12(1) The final entry in the Table in paragraph 1 excludes a document in respect of which a penalty is payable under section 98 of TMA 1970 (special returns).

12(2) The amount of a penalty for which P is liable under paragraph 1 or 2 in respect of a document relating to a tax period shall be reduced by the amount of any other penalty incurred by P, or any surcharge for late payment of tax imposed on P, if the amount of the penalty or surcharge is determined by reference to the same tax liability.

12(2A) In sub-paragraph (2) **"any other penalty"** does not include a penalty under Part 4 of FA 2014 (penalty where corrective action not taken after follower notice etc) or Schedule 22 to FA 2016 (asset-based penalty).

12(3) In the application of section 97A of TMA 1970 (multiple penalties) no account shall be taken of a penalty under paragraph 1 or 2.

12(4) Where penalties are imposed under paragraphs 1 and 1A in respect of the same inaccuracy, the aggregate of the amounts of the penalties must not exceed the relevant percentage of the potential lost revenue.

12(5) The relevant percentage is–

(a) *if the penalty imposed* under paragraph 1 is for an inaccuracy in category 1, 100%,

(b) if the penalty imposed under paragraph 1 is for an inaccuracy in category 2, 150%, and

(c) if the penalty imposed under paragraph 1 is for an inaccuracy in category 3, 200%.

Commencement Date – See headnote to Sch. 24.

Prospective amendments – Para. 12(5)(za) inserted and in para. 12(5)(a) "125%" substituted for "100%" amended by FA 2015, s. 120 and Sch. 20, para. 6, with effect from a day to be appointed under FA 2015, s. 120(2).

History – In para. 12(2) the words "incurred by P, or any surcharge for late payment of tax imposed on P, if the amount of the penalty or surcharge is determined by reference to the same tax liability." substituted for the words "which P has incurred and the amount of which is determined by reference to P's tax liability for that period." by FA 2008, s. 122 and Sch. 40, para. 11(2), with effect from 1 April 2009 (SI 2009/571, art. 2).

In para. 12(2A), the words "or Schedule 22 to FA 2016 (asset-based penalty)" inserted by FA 2016, s. 165(1) and Sch. 22, para. 20(3), with effect for inheritance tax purposes, in relation to transfers of value made on or after 1 April 2017 (SI 2017/277, reg. 2).
Para. 12(2A) inserted by FA 2014, s. 233 and Sch. 33, para. 3, with effect from 17 July 2014.
Para. 12(4) and (5) substituted for former para. 12(4) by FA 2010, s. 35 and Sch. 10, para. 4, with effect from 6 April 2011, but the substitution does not have effect in relation to documents given to HMRC and assessments issued by HMRC in relation to a tax period (as defined in para. 28(g)) commencing on or before 5 April 2011 (SI 2011/975). Former para. 12(4) read as follows:
"**12(4)** Where penalties are imposed under paragraphs 1 and 1A in respect of the same inaccuracy, the aggregate of the amounts of the penalties must not exceed 100% of the potential lost revenue.".
Former para. 12(4) inserted by FA 2008, s. 122 and Sch. 40, para. 11(2), with effect from 1 April 2009 (SI 2009/571, art. 2).

Part 3 – Procedure

ASSESSMENT

13(1) Where a person becomes liable for a penalty under paragraph 1, 1A or 2 HMRC shall–

(a) assess the penalty,

(b) notify the person, and

(c) state in the notice a tax period in respect of which the penalty is assessed (subject to sub-paragraph (1ZB)).

13(1ZA)–(1ZD) [Not relevant to inheritance tax.]

13(1A) A penalty under paragraph 1, 1A or 2 must be paid before the end of the period of 30 days beginning with the day on which notification of the penalty is issued.

13(2) An assessment–

(a) shall be treated for procedural purposes in the same way as an assessment to tax (except in respect of a matter expressly provided for by this Act),

(b) may be enforced as if it were an assessment to tax, and

(c) may be combined with an assessment to tax.

13(3) An assessment of a penalty under paragraph 1 or 1A must be made before the end of the period of 12 months beginning with–

(a) the end of the appeal period for the decision correcting the inaccuracy, or

(b) if there is no assessment to the tax concerned within paragraph (a), the date on which the inaccuracy is corrected.

13(4) An assessment of a penalty under paragraph 2 must be made before the end of the period of 12 months beginning with–

(a) the end of the appeal period for the assessment of tax which corrected the understatement, or

(b) if there is no assessment within paragraph (a), the date on which the understatement is corrected.

13(5) For the purpose of sub-paragraphs (3) and (4) a reference to an appeal period is a reference to the period during which–

(a) an appeal could be brought, or

(b) an appeal that has been brought has not been determined or withdrawn.

13(6) Subject to sub-paragraphs (3) and (4), a supplementary assessment may be made in respect of a penalty if an earlier assessment operated by reference to an underestimate of potential lost revenue.

13(7) In this Part of this Schedule references to an assessment to tax, in relation to inheritance tax and stamp duty reserve tax, are to a determination.

Commencement Date – See headnote to Sch. 24.

History – In para. 13(1) the words "Where a person" substituted for the words "Where P", ", (1A)" inserted and the words "notify the person" substituted for the words "notify P" by FA 2008, s. 122 and Sch. 40, para. 12(2), with effect from 1 April 2009 (SI 2009/571, art. 2).
In para. 13(1)(c), the words "(subject to sub-paragraph (1ZB))" inserted by FA 2013, s. 230 and Sch. 50, para. 1(2), with effect in relation to any assessment of a penalty under Sch. 24 made on or after 17 July 2013 (Royal Assent).
Para. 13(1ZA)–(1ZD) inserted by FA 2013, s. 230 and Sch. 50, para. 1(3), with effect in relation to any assessment of a penalty under Sch. 24 made on or after 17 July 2013 (Royal Assent).
Para. 13(1A) inserted by FA 2008, s. 122 and Sch. 40, para. 12(3), with effect from 1 April 2009 (SI 2009/571, art. 2).
In para. 13(3) "or (1A)" inserted, the words "before the end of the" substituted for the words "within the" and the words "to the tax concerned" inserted by FA 2008, s. 122 and Sch. 40, para. 12(4), with effect from 1 April 2009 (SI 2009/571, art. 2).
In para. 13(4) the words from "before the end" to the end substituted for the words "within the period of 12 months beginning with the end of the appeal period for the assessment of tax which corrected the understatement." by FA 2008, s. 122 and Sch. 40, para. 12(5), with effect from 1 April 2009 (SI 2009/571, art. 2).
Para. 13(7) inserted by FA 2009, s. 109 and Sch. 57, para. 5, with effect from 21 July 2009.

SUSPENSION

14(1) HMRC may suspend all or part of a penalty for a careless inaccuracy under paragraph 1 by notice in writing to P.

14(2) A notice must specify–

(a) what part of the penalty is to be suspended,

(b) a period of suspension not exceeding two years, and

(c) conditions of suspension to be complied with by P.

14(3) HMRC may suspend all or part of a penalty only if compliance with a condition of suspension would help P to avoid becoming liable to further penalties under paragraph 1 for careless inaccuracy.

14(4) A condition of suspension may specify–

(a) action to be taken, and

(b) a period within which it must be taken.

14(5) On the expiry of the period of suspension–

(a) if P satisfies HMRC that the conditions of suspension have been complied with, the suspended penalty or part is cancelled, and

(b) otherwise, the suspended penalty or part becomes payable.

14(6) If, during the period of suspension of all or part of a penalty under paragraph 1, P becomes liable for another penalty under that paragraph, the suspended penalty or part becomes payable.

Commencement Date – See headnote to Sch. 24.

APPEAL

15(1) A person may appeal against a decision of HMRC that a penalty is payable by the person.

15(2) A person may appeal against a decision of HMRC as to the amount of a penalty payable by the person.

15(3) A person may appeal against a decision of HMRC not to suspend a penalty payable by the person.

15(4) A person may appeal against a decision of HMRC setting conditions of suspension of a penalty payable by the person.

Commencement Date – See headnote to Sch. 24.

History – In para. 15 the words "A person may" substituted for the words "P may" (four times) and the words "by the person" substituted for the words "by P" (four times) by FA 2008, s. 122 and Sch. 40, para. 13, with effect from 1 April 2009 (SI 2009/571, art. 2).

16(1) An appeal under this Part of this Schedule shall be treated in the same way as an appeal against an assessment to the tax concerned (including by the application of any provision about bringing the appeal by notice to HMRC, about HMRC review of the decision or about determination of the appeal by the First-tier Tribunal or Upper Tribunal).

16(2) Sub-paragraph (1) does not apply–

(a) so as to require P to pay a penalty before an appeal against the assessment of the penalty is determined, or

(b) in respect of any other matter expressly provided for by this Act.

Commencement Date – See headnote to Sch. 24.

History – Para. 16(2) substituted by FA 2009, s. 109 and Sch. 57, para. 6, with effect from 21 July 2009.

Para. 16 substituted by SI 2009/56, art. 3(1) and Sch. 1, para. 466, operative from 1 April 2009, subject to transitional and saving provisions in SI 2009/56, Sch. 3.

Para. 16 also substituted by FA 2008, s. 122 and Sch. 40, para. 14, with effect from 1 April 2009 (SI 2009/571, art. 2). The version of para. 16 inserted by FA 2008 reads as follows:

"**16(1)** An appeal is to be brought to the First-tier tribunal.

16(2) An appeal shall be treated for procedural purposes in the same way as an appeal against an assessment to the tax concerned (except in respect of a matter expressly provided for by this Act)."

Before these substitutions para. 16 read as follows:

"**16** An appeal may be brought to–

(a) the General Commissioners, in so far as the penalty relates to direct tax, or

(b) a VAT and duties tribunal, in so far as the penalty relates to VAT.".

17(1) On an appeal under paragraph 15(1) the tribunal may affirm or cancel HMRC's decision.

17(2) On an appeal under paragraph 15(2) the tribunal may–

(a) affirm HMRC's decision, or

(b) substitute for HMRC's decision another decision that HMRC had power to make.

17(3) If the tribunal substitutes its decision for HMRC's, the appellate tribunal may rely on paragraph 11–

(a) to the same extent as HMRC (which may mean applying the same percentage reduction as HMRC to a different starting point), or

(b) to a different extent, but only if the appellate tribunal thinks that HMRC's decision in respect of the application of paragraph 11 was flawed.

17(4) On an appeal under paragraph 15(3)–

(a) the tribunal may order HMRC to suspend the penalty only if it thinks that HMRC's decision not to suspend was flawed, and

(b) if the tribunal orders HMRC to suspend the penalty–

(i) P may appeal against a provision of the notice of suspension, and

(ii) the tribunal may order HMRC to amend the notice.

17(5) On an appeal under paragraph 15(4) the tribunal–

(a) may affirm the conditions of suspension, or

(b) may vary the conditions of suspension, but only if the tribunal thinks that HMRC's decision in respect of the conditions was flawed.

17(5A) In this paragraph **"tribunal"** means the First-tier Tribunal or Upper Tribunal (as appropriate by virtue of paragraph 16(1)).

17(6) In sub-paragraphs (3)(b), (4)(a) and (5)(b) **"flawed"** means flawed when considered in the light of the principles applicable in proceedings for judicial review.

17(7) Paragraph 14 (see in particular paragraph 14(3)) is subject to the possibility of an order under this paragraph.

Commencement Date – See headnote to Sch. 24.

History – In para. 17(1), (2) and (3), the word "appellate", which appeared before the word "tribunal", omitted by SI 2009/56, art. 3(1) and Sch. 1, para. 467(2), operative from 1 April 2009, subject to transitional and saving provisions in SI 2009/56, Sch. 3.
In para. 17(4)(a) and (b), the word "appellate", which appeared before the word "tribunal", omitted by SI 2009/56, art. 3(1) and Sch. 1, para. 467(3)(a) and (b)(i), operative from 1 April 2009, subject to transitional and saving provisions in SI 2009/56, Sch. 3.
In para. 17(4)(b)(i), the words "to the appellate tribunal", which appeared after the word "appeal", omitted by SI 2009/56, art. 3(1) and Sch. 1, para. 467(3)(b)(ii), operative from 1 April 2009, subject to transitional and saving provisions in SI 2009/56, Sch. 3.
In para. 17(4)(b)(ii), the word "appellate", which appeared before the word "tribunal", omitted by SI 2009/56, art. 3(1) and Sch. 1, para. 467(3)(b)(iii), operative from 1 April 2009, subject to transitional and saving provisions in SI 2009/56, Sch. 3.
In para. 17(5), the word "appellate", which appeared before the word "tribunal" in each place, omitted by SI 2009/56, art. 3(1) and Sch. 1, para. 467(4), operative from 1 April 2009, subject to transitional and saving provisions in SI 2009/56, Sch. 3.
Para. 17(5A) inserted by SI 2009/56, art. 3(1) and Sch. 1, para. 467(5), operative from 1 April 2009, subject to transitional and saving provisions in SI 2009/56, Sch. 3.

Part 4 – Miscellaneous

AGENCY

18(1) P is liable under paragraph 1(1)(a) where a document which contains a careless inaccuracy (within the meaning of paragraph 3) is given to HMRC on P's behalf.

18(2) In paragraph 2(1)(b) and (2)(a) a reference to P includes a reference to a person who acts on P's behalf in relation to tax.

18(3) Despite sub-paragraphs (1) and (2), P is not liable to a penalty under paragraph 1 or 2 in respect of anything done or omitted by P's agent where P satisfies HMRC that P took reasonable care to avoid inaccuracy (in relation to paragraph 1) or unreasonable failure (in relation to paragraph 2).

18(4) In paragraph 3(1)(a) (whether in its application to a document given by P or, by virtue of sub-paragraph (1) above, in its application to a document given on P's behalf) a reference to P includes a reference to a person who acts on P's behalf in relation to tax.

18(5) In paragraph 3(2) a reference to P includes a reference to a person who acts on P's behalf in relation to tax.

18(6) Paragraph 3A applies where a document is given to HMRC on behalf of P as it applies where a document is given to HMRC by P (and in paragraph 3B(9) the reference to P includes a person acting on behalf of P).

Commencement Date – See headnote to Sch. 24.

History – In para. 18(3) the words "under paragraph 1 or 2" inserted by FA 2008, s. 122 and Sch. 40, para. 15, with effect from 1 April 2009 (SI 2009/571, art. 2).
Para. 18(6) inserted by F(No. 2)A 2017, s. 64(3), with effect in relation to any document of a kind listed in the Table at para. 1 which is given to HMRC on or after 16 November 2017 (Royal Assent) and relates to a tax period that begins on or after 6 April 2017 and ends on or after 16 November 2017 (Royal Assent).

COMPANIES: OFFICERS' LIABILITY

19(1) Where a penalty under paragraph 1 is payable by a company for a deliberate inaccuracy which was attributable to an officer of the company, the officer is liable to pay such portion of the penalty (which may be 100%) as HMRC may specify by written notice to the officer.

(a) the officer as well as the company shall be liable to pay the penalty, and

(b) HMRC may pursue the officer for such portion of the penalty (which may be 100%) as they may specify by written notice to the officer.

19(2) Sub-paragraph (1) does not allow HMRC to recover more than 100% of a penalty.

19(3) In the application of sub-paragraph (1) to a body corporate other than a limited liability partnership **"officer"** means–

(a) a director (including a shadow director within the meaning of section 251 of the Companies Act 2006 (c. 46)),

(aa) a manager, and

(b) a secretary.

19(3A) In the application of sub-paragraph (1) to a limited liability partnership **"officer"** means a member.

19(4) In the application of sub-paragraph (1) in any other case **"officer"** means–

(a) a director,

(b) a manager,

(c) a secretary, and

(d) any other person managing or purporting to manage any of the company's affairs.

19(5) Where HMRC have specified a portion of a penalty in a notice given to an officer under sub-paragraph (1)–

(a) paragraph 11 applies to the specified portion as to a penalty,

(b) the officer must pay the specified portion before the end of the period of 30 days beginning with the day on which the notice is given,

(c) paragraph 13(2), (3) and (5) apply as if the notice were an assessment of a penalty,

(d) a further notice may be given in respect of a portion of any additional amount assessed in a supplementary assessment in respect of the penalty under paragraph 13(6),

(e) paragraphs 15(1) and (2), 16 and 17(1) to (3) and (6) apply as if HMRC had decided that a penalty of the amount of the specified portion is payable by the officer, and

(f) paragraph 21 applies as if the officer were liable to a penalty.

19(6) In this paragraph **"company"** means any body corporate or unincorporated association, but does not include a partnership, a local authority or a local authority association.

Commencement Date – See headnote to Sch. 24.

History – In para. 19(1) the words "of the company, the officer is liable to pay such portion of the penalty (which may be 100%) as HMRC" substituted for the following words by FA 2008, s. 122 and Sch. 40, para. 16(2), with effect from 1 April 2009 (SI 2009/571, art. 2).

In para. 19(3), the words "other than a limited liability partnership" inserted by FA 2009, s. 109 and Sch. 57, para. 7(2)(a), with effect from 21 July 2009.

In para. 19(3)(a), the word "or" at the end omitted by FA 2009, s. 109 and Sch. 57, para. 7(2)(b), with effect from 21 July 2009.

Para. 19(3)(aa) inserted by FA 2009, s. 109 and Sch. 57, para. 7(2)(c), with effect from 21 July 2009.

Para. 19(3A) inserted by FA 2009, s. 109 and Sch. 57, para. 7(3), with effect from 21 July 2009.

Para. 19(6) inserted by FA 2009, s. 109 and Sch. 57, para. 7(4), with effect from 21 July 2009.

Para. 19(5) substituted by FA 2008, s. 122 and Sch. 40, para. 16(3), with effect from 1 April 2009 (SI 2009/571, art. 2).

PARTNERSHIPS

20(1) This paragraph applies where P is liable to a penalty under paragraph 1 for an inaccuracy in or in connection with a partnership return.

20(2) Where the inaccuracy affects the amount of tax due or payable by a partner of P, the partner is also liable to a penalty ("a partner's penalty").

20(3) Paragraphs 4 to 13 and 19 shall apply in relation to a partner's penalty (for which purpose a reference to P shall be taken as a reference to the partner).

20(4) Potential lost revenue shall be calculated separately for the purpose of P's penalty and any partner's penalty, by reference to the proportions of any tax liability that would be borne by each partner.

20(5) Paragraph 14 shall apply jointly to P's penalty and any partner's penalties.

20(6) P may bring an appeal under paragraph 15 in respect of a partner's penalty (in addition to any appeal that P may bring in connection with the penalty for which P is liable).

Commencement Date – See headnote to Sch. 24.

DOUBLE JEOPARDY

21 A person is not liable to a penalty under paragraph 1, 1A or 2 in respect of an inaccuracy or failure in respect of which the person has been convicted of an offence.

Commencement Date – See headnote to Sch. 24.

History – In para. 21 the words "A person is" substituted for the words "P is", ", 1A" inserted and the words "the person has" substituted for the words "P has" by FA 2008, s. 122 and Sch. 40, para. 17, with effect from 1 April 2009 (SI 2009/571, art. 2).

21ZA(1) A person is not liable to a penalty under paragraph 1 in respect of an inaccuracy if–

(a) the inaccuracy involves a claim by the person to exercise or rely on a VAT right (in relation to a supply) that has been denied or refused by HMRC as mentioned in subsection (4) of section 69C of VATA 1994, and

(b) the person has been assessed to a penalty under that section (and the assessment has not been successfully appealed against or withdrawn).

21ZA(2) In sub-paragraph (1)(a) **"VAT right"** has the same meaning as in section 69C of VATA 1994.

History – Para. 21ZA inserted by F(No. 2)A 2017, s. 68(6), with effect from 16 November 2017 (Royal Assent).

Part 5 – General

CLASSIFICATION OF TERRITORIES

21A(1) A category 1 territory is a territory designated as a category 1 territory by order made by the Treasury.

21A(2) A category 2 territory is a territory that is neither–

(a) a category 1 territory, nor

(b) a category 3 territory.

21A(3) A category 3 territory is a territory designated as a category 3 territory by order made by the Treasury.

21A(4) In considering how to classify a territory for the purposes of this paragraph, the Treasury must have regard to–

(a) the existence of any arrangements between the UK and that territory for the exchange of information for tax enforcement purposes,

(b) the quality of any such arrangements (in particular, whether they provide for information to be exchanged automatically or on request),

(c) the benefit that the UK would be likely to obtain from receiving information from that territory, were such arrangements to exist with it,

(d) the existence of any other arrangements between the UK and that territory for co-operation in the area of taxation, and

(e) the quality of any such other arrangements (in particular, the extent to which the co-operation provided for in them assists or is likely to assist in the protection of revenue raised from taxation in the UK).

21A(5) An order under this paragraph is to be made by statutory instrument.

21A(6) Subject to sub-paragraph (7), an instrument containing an order under this paragraph is subject to annulment in pursuance of a resolution of the House of Commons.

21A(7) If the order is–

(a) the first order to be made under sub-paragraph (1), or

(b) the first order to be made under sub-paragraph (3),

it may not be made unless a draft of the instrument containing it has been laid before, and approved by a resolution of, the House of Commons.

21A(8) An order under this paragraph does not apply to inaccuracies in a document given to HMRC (or, in a case within paragraph 3(2), inaccuracies discovered by P) before the date on which the order comes into force.

Prospective amendments – Para. 21A(A1) inserted by FA 2015, s. 120 and Sch. 20, para. 7(2), with effect from a day to be appointed under FA 2015, s. 120(2).

Para. 21A(2) substituted by FA 2015, s. 120 and Sch. 20, para. 7(3), with effect from a day to be appointed under FA 2015, s. 120(2).
Para. 21A(7) substituted by FA 2015, s. 120 and Sch. 20, para. 7(4), with effect from a day to be appointed under FA 2015, s. 120(2).

History – In para. 21A(4)(b), the word "and" at the end omitted by FA 2012, s. 219(a), with effect from 17 July 2012.

Para. 21A(4)(d) inserted by FA 2012, s. 219(b), with effect from 17 July 2012.

Para. 21A(4)(e) inserted by FA 2012, s. 219(b), with effect from 17 July 2012.

Para. 21A and the heading before it inserted by FA 2010, s. 35 and Sch. 10, para. 5, with effect from 6 April 2011, but the insertion does not have effect in relation to documents given to HMRC and assessments issued by HMRC in relation to a tax period (as defined in para. 28(g)) commencing on or before 5 April 2011 (SI 2011/975).

Statutory instruments – SI 2011/976: made under para. 21A(1)–(4).
Notes – The comma at the end of para. 21A(4)(c) substituted for full point by Croner-i editors as this was apparently omitted in error by FA 2012, s. 219(b).

LOCATION OF ASSETS ETC

21B(1) The Treasury may by regulations make provision for determining for the purposes of paragraph 4A where–

(a) a source of income is located,

(b) an asset is situated or held, or

(c) activities are wholly or mainly carried on.

21B(1A) The Treasury may by regulations make provision for determining for the purposes of paragraph 4AA where–

(a) income is received or transferred,

(b) the proceeds of a disposal are received or transferred, or

(c) assets are transferred.

21B(2) Different provision may be made for different cases and for income tax, capital gains tax and inheritance tax.

21B(3) Regulations under this paragraph are to be made by statutory instrument.

21B(4) An instrument containing regulations under this paragraph is subject to annulment in pursuance of a resolution of the House of Commons.

History – Para. 21B(1A) inserted by FA 2015, s. 120 and Sch. 20, para. 8(2), with effect in relation to documents given to HMRC relating to a transfer of value made on or after 6 April 2016 for the purposes of inheritance tax (SI 2016/456, art. 3).
In para. 21B(2) the words ", capital gains tax and inheritance tax" substituted for the words "and capital gains tax" by FA 2015, s. 120 and Sch. 20, para. 8(3), with effect in relation to documents given to HMRC relating to a transfer of value made on or after 6 April 2016 for the purposes of inheritance tax (SI 2016/456, art. 3).
Para. 21B and the heading before it inserted by FA 2010, s. 35 and Sch. 10, para. 5, with effect from 6 April 2011, but the insertion does not have effect in relation to documents given to HMRC and assessments issued by HMRC in relation to a tax period (as defined in para. 28(g)) commencing on or before 5 April 2011 (SI 2011/975).

TREATMENT OF CERTAIN PAYMENTS ON ACCOUNT OF TAX

21C In paragraphs 1(2) and 5 references to "tax" are to be interpreted as if amounts payable under section 59AA(2) of TMA 1970 (non-resident CGT disposals: payments on account of capital gains tax) were tax.

Prospective amendments – In para. 21C, the words "and amounts payable on account of apprenticeship levy" inserted (after the words "capital gains tax)") by FA 2016, s. 113(4), with effect in accordance with regulations made under FA 2016, s. 113(16).

History – Para. 21C inserted by FA 2015, s. 37 and Sch. 7, para. 56(3), with effect in relation to disposals made on or after 6 April 2015.

INTERPRETATION

22 Paragraphs 23 to 27 apply for the construction of this Schedule.

Commencement Date – See headnote to Sch. 24.

History – In para. 22 "27" substituted for "26" by FA 2008, s. 122 and Sch. 40, para. 18, with effect from 1 April 2009 (SI 2009/571, art. 2).

23 **HMRC** means Her Majesty's Revenue and Customs.

Commencement Date – See headnote to Sch. 24.

23A **"Tax"**, without more, includes duty.

History – Para. 23A inserted by FA 2008, s. 122 and Sch. 40, para. 19, with effect from 1 April 2009 (SI 2009/571, art. 2).

23B **"UK"** means the United Kingdom, including the territorial sea of the United Kingdom.

History – Para. 23B inserted by FA 2010, s. 35 and Sch. 10, para. 6, with effect from 6 April 2011, but the insertion does not have effect in relation to documents given to HMRC and assessments issued by HMRC in relation to a tax period (as defined in para. 28(g)) commencing on or before 5 April 2011 (SI 2011/975).

24–27 [Not relevant to inheritance tax.]

28 In this Schedule–

(a) [not relevant to inheritance tax.]

(b) [not relevant to inheritance tax.]

(c) [not relevant to inheritance tax.]

(d) [not relevant to inheritance tax.]

(da) [omitted by FA 2009, s. 109 and Sch. 57, para. 8,]

(e) [not relevant to inheritance tax.]

(f) a reference to repayment of tax includes a reference to allowing a credit against tax or to a payment of a corporation tax credit,

(fa) [not relevant to inheritance tax.]

(g) **"tax period"** means a tax year, accounting period or other period in respect of which tax is charged,

(h) a reference to giving a document to HMRC includes a reference to communicating information to HMRC in any form and by any method (whether by post, fax, email, telephone or otherwise),

(i) a reference to giving a document to HMRC includes a reference to making a statement or declaration in a document,

(j) a reference to making a return or doing anything in relation to a return includes a reference to amending a return or doing anything in relation to an amended return, and

(k) a reference to action includes a reference to omission.

Commencement Date – See headnote to Sch. 24.

History – Para. 28(da) omitted by FA 2009, s. 109 and Sch. 57, para. 8, with effect from 21 July 2009.

FINANCE ACT 2008

(2008 Chapter 9)

[*21st July 2008*]

ARRANGEMENT OF SECTIONS

PART 1 – CHARGES, RATES, ALLOWANCES, RELIEFS ETC

INHERITANCE TAX

10 Transfer of unused nil-rate band etc

10 Schedule 4 contains provisions about the transfer of unused nil-rate band between spouses and civil partners for the purposes of the charge to inheritance tax etc.

PART 4 – PENSIONS

91 Inheritance etc of tax-relieved pension savings

91 Schedule 28 contains provision about the inheritance etc of tax-relieved pension savings.

92 Pension schemes: further provision

92 Schedule 29 contains further provision about pension schemes.

PART 7 – ADMINISTRATION

Chapter 1 – Information etc

NEW INFORMATION ETC POWERS

113 Information and inspection powers

113(1) Schedule 36 contains provision about the powers of officers of Revenue and Customs to obtain information and to inspect businesses.

113(2) That Schedule comes into force on such day as the Treasury may by order made by statutory instrument appoint.

113(3) An order under subsection (2) may contain transitional provision and savings.

Chapter 3 – Penalties

122 Penalties for errors

122(1) Schedule 40 contains provisions amending Schedule 24 to FA 2007 (penalties for errors in returns etc).

122(2) That Schedule comes into force on such day as the Treasury may by order appoint.

122(3) An order under subsection (2)–

(a) may commence a provision generally or only for specified purposes, and

(b) may appoint different days for different provisions or for different purposes.

122(4) The Treasury may by order make any incidental, supplemental, consequential, transitional, transitory or saving provision which may appear appropriate in consequence of, or otherwise in connection with, Schedule 24 to FA 2007 or Schedule 40.

122(5) An order under subsection (4) may include provision amending, repealing or revoking any provision of any Act or subordinate legislation whenever passed or made (including this Act and any Act amended by it).

122(6) An order under subsection (4) may make different provision for different purposes.

122(7) The power to make an order under this section is exercisable by statutory instrument.

122(8) A statutory instrument containing an order under subsection (4) which includes provision amending or repealing any provision of an Act is subject to annulment in pursuance of a resolution of the House of Commons.

Chapter 5 – Payment and Enforcement

OTHER MEASURES

137 County court proceedings

137(1) [Not relevant to inheritance tax.]

137(2) [Not relevant to inheritance tax.]

137(3) [Not relevant to inheritance tax.]

137(4) [Amends IHTA 1984, s. 244.]

137(5) [Not relevant to inheritance tax.]

137(6) [Not relevant to inheritance tax.]

137(7) Nothing in subsections (2) to (6) affects proceedings commenced or brought in the name of a collector or authorised officer before this Act is passed.

138 Certificates of debt

138(1) [Not relevant to inheritance tax.]

138(2) Schedule 44 contains provisions consequential on this section.

PART 8 – MISCELLANEOUS

INHERITANCE TAX

140 Charge on termination of interest in possession where new interest acquired

140(1) [Substitutes IHTA 1984, s. 53(2A).]

140(2) The amendment made by subsection (1) is treated as having come into force on 22 March 2006 (so that paragraph 14(3) of Schedule 20 to FA 2006 is treated as never having had effect).

141 Interest in possession settlements: extension of transitional period

141(1) In Chapter 2 of Part 3 of IHTA 1984 (interests in possession etc)–

(a) [amends IHTA 1984, s. 49C;]

(b) [amends IHTA 1984, s. 49D;]

(c) [amends IHTA 1984, s. 49E.]

141(2) The amendments made by subsection (1) are treated as having come into force on 6 April 2008.

IHT Statutes

PART 9 – FINAL PROVISIONS

165 Interpretation

165(1) In this Act–

"ALDA 1979" means the Alcoholic Liquor Duties Act 1979 (c. 4),

"BGDA 1981" means the Betting and Gaming Duties Act 1981 (c. 63),

"CAA 2001" means the Capital Allowances Act 2001 (c. 2),

"CEMA 1979" means the Customs and Excise Management Act 1979 (c. 2),

"CRCA 2005" means the Commissioners for Revenue and Customs Act 2005 (c. 11),

"CTA 2009" means the Corporation Tax Act 2009,

"CTA 2010" means the Corporation Tax Act 2010,

"CTTA 1984" means the Capital Transfer Tax Act 1984 (c. 51),

"HODA 1979" means the Hydrocarbon Oil Duties Act 1979 (c. 5),

"ICTA" means the Income and Corporation Taxes Act 1988 (c. 1),

"IHTA 1984" means the Inheritance Tax Act 1984 (c. 51),

"ITA 2007" means the Income Tax Act 2007 (c. 3),

"ITEPA 2003" means the Income Tax (Earnings and Pensions) Act 2003 (c. 1),

"ITTOIA 2005" means the Income Tax (Trading and Other Income) Act 2005 (c. 5),

"OTA 1975" means the Oil Taxation Act 1975 (c. 22),

"TCGA 1992" means the Taxation of Chargeable Gains Act 1992 (c. 12),

"TMA 1970" means the Taxes Management Act 1970 (c. 9),

"TPDA 1979" means the Tobacco Products Duty Act 1979 (c. 7),

"VATA 1994" means the Value Added Tax Act 1994 (c. 23), and

"VERA 1994" means the Vehicle Excise and Registration Act 1994 (c. 22).

165(2) In this Act–

"FA", followed by a year, means the Finance Act of that year, and

"F(No. 2)A", followed by a year, means the Finance (No. 2) Act of that year.

History – In s. 165(1), the definition of "CTA 2010" inserted by CTA 2010, s. 1177 and Sch. 1, para. 579, with effect for corporation tax purposes for accounting periods ending on or after 1 April 2010, and for income tax and capital gains tax purposes for the tax year 2010–11 and subsequent tax years.

In s. 165(1), the definition of "CTA 2009" inserted by CTA 2009, s. 1322 and Sch. 1, para. 733, with effect for corporation tax purposes for accounting periods ending on or after 1 April 2009, and for income tax and capital gains tax purposes for the tax year 2009–10 and subsequent tax years.

166 Short title

166 This Act may be cited as the Finance Act 2008.

SCHEDULES

SCHEDULE 4 – INHERITANCE TAX: TRANSFER OF NIL-RATE BAND ETC

Section 10

AMENDMENTS OF IHTA 1984

1 IHTA 1984 is amended as follows.

2 [Inserts IHTA 1984, s. 8A–8C.]

3 [Inserts IHTA 1984, s. 147(10).]

4 [Omitted by FA 2011, s. 65 and Sch. 16, para. 84(d)(i).]

History – Para. 4 omitted by FA 2011, s. 65 and Sch. 16, para. 84(d)(i), with effect in relation to deaths occurring on or after 6 April 2011.

5 [Inserts IHTA 1984, s. 239(4)(aa).]

6 [Amends IHTA 1984, s. 247(2).]

7 [Amends IHTA 1984, s. 272.]

COMMENCEMENT

9(1) The amendments made by paragraphs 2, 3 and 4(4) have effect in relation to cases where the survivor's death occurs on or after 9 October 2007.

9(2) [Omitted by FA 2011, s. 65 and Sch. 16, para. 84(d)(i).]

9(3) The amendments made by paragraphs 5 and 7 are to be treated as having come into force on 9 October 2007.

9(4) The amendment made by paragraph 8 has effect in relation to any ascertainment of value made on or after 6 April 2008.

History – Para. 9(2) omitted by FA 2011, s. 65 and Sch. 16, para. 84(d)(i), with effect in relation to deaths occurring on or after 6 April 2011.

MODIFICATIONS FOR CASES WHERE DECEASED PERSON DIED BEFORE 25 JULY 1986

10(1) Section 8A of IHTA 1984 (as inserted by paragraph 2) have effect in relation to cases where the deceased person died before 25 July 1986 (and the survivor dies on or after 9 October 2007) subject as follows.

10(2) Where the deceased person died on or after 1 January 1985–

(a) the references in subsection (2) to a chargeable transfer made under section 4 of IHTA 1984 is to a chargeable transfer made under section 4 of CTTA 1984, and

(b) the reference in subsection (4) to the nil-rate band maximum is to the amount shown in the second column of the first row, and the first column of the second row, of the First Table in Schedule 1 to that Act.

10(3) Where the deceased person died on or after 13 March 1975 and before 1 January 1985–

(a) the references in subsection (2) to a chargeable transfer made under section 4 of IHTA 1984 is to a chargeable transfer made under section 22 of FA 1975, and

(b) the reference in subsection (4) to the nil-rate band maximum is to the amount shown in the second column of the first row, and in the first column of the second row, of the First Table in section 37 of that Act.

10(4) Where the deceased person died on or after 16 April 1969 and before 13 March 1975, section 8A applies as if–

(a) M were the amount specified in paragraph (a) in Part 1 of Schedule 17 to FA 1969 at the time of the deceased person's death,

(b) VT were the aggregate principal value of all property comprised in the estate of the deceased person for the purposes of estate duty, and

(c) the reference in subsection (4) to the nil-rate band maximum were to the amount mentioned in paragraph (a).

10(5) Where the deceased person died before 16 April 1969, section 8A applies as if–

(a) M were the amount specified as the higher figure in the first line, and the lower figure in the second line, in the first column of the scale in section 17 of FA 1894 at the time of the deceased person's death,

(b) VT were the principal value of the estate of the deceased person for the purposes of estate duty, and

(c) the reference in subsection (4) to the nil-rate band maximum were to the figure mentioned in paragraph (a).

11(1) Section 8C of IHTA 1984 (as inserted by paragraph 2) has effect in relation to cases where the deceased person died before 25 July 1986 but on or after 13 March 1975 (and the survivor dies on or after 9 October 2007) subject as follows.

11(2) Where the deceased person died on or after 1 January 1985–

(a) the reference in subsection (1) to sections 32, 32A and 126 of IHTA 1984 includes sections 32, 32A and 126 of CTTA 1984,

(b) the reference in that subsection to section 4 of IHTA 1984 is to section 4 of CTTA 1984,

(c) the reference in subsection (2) to the nil-rate band maximum includes the amount shown in the second column of the first row, and the first column of the second row, of the First Table in Schedule 1 to that Act,

(d) the first reference in subsection (5) to the nil-rate band maximum is to that amount, and

(e) the reference in subsection (5) to Schedule 2 to IHTA 1984 includes Schedule 2 to CTTA 1984.

11(3) Where the deceased person died on or after 7 April 1976 and before 1 January 1985–

(a) the reference in subsection (1) to sections 32, 32A and 126 of IHTA 1984 includes sections 32, 32A and 126 of CTTA 1984, section 78 of FA 1976 and paragraph 2 of Schedule 9 to FA 1975,

(b) the reference in that subsection to section 4 of IHTA is to section 22 of FA 1975,

(c) the reference in subsection (2) to the nil-rate band maximum includes the amount shown in the second column of the first row, and the first column of the second row, of the First Table in Schedule 1 to CTTA 1984 and the amount shown in the second column of the first row, and in the first column of the second row, of the First Table in section 37 of FA 1975,

(d) the first reference in subsection (5) to the nil-rate band maximum is to that amount, and

(e) the reference in subsection (5) to Schedule 2 to IHTA 1984 includes Schedule 2 to CTTA 1984, Schedule 15 to FA 1980 and section 62 of FA 1978;

but, if the event occasioning the charge occurred before 27 October 1977, the reference in subsection (4) to the personal nil-rate band maximum is to the amount shown in the second column of the first row, and in the first column of the second row, of the First Table in section 37 of FA 1975 at the time of the deceased person's death.

11(4) Where the deceased person died on or after 13 March 1975 and before 7 April 1976–

(a) the reference in subsection (1) to sections 32, 32A and 126 of IHTA 1984 includes paragraph 1 of Schedule 5 to that Act, section 126 of CTTA 1984 and paragraph 2 of Schedule 9 to FA 1975,

(b) the reference in that subsection to section 4 of IHTA is to section 22 of FA 1975,

(c) the reference in subsection (2) to the nil-rate band maximum includes the amount shown in the second column of the first row, and the first column of the second row, of the First Table in Schedule 1 to CTTA 1984 and the amount shown in the second column of the first row, and in the first column of the second row, of the First Table in section 37 of FA 1975, and

(d) the reference in subsection (4) to the personal nil-rate band maximum is to the amount shown in the second column of the first row, and in the first column of the second row, of the First Table in section 37 of FA 1975 at the time of the deceased person's death.

SCHEDULE 28 – INHERITANCE OF TAX-RELIEVED PENSION SAVINGS

Section 91

AMENDMENTS OF IHTA 1984

6 [Omitted by FA 2011, s. 65 and Sch. 16, para. 84(d)(ii).]

History – Para. 6 omitted by FA 2011, s. 65 and Sch. 16, para. 84(d)(ii), with effect in relation to deaths occurring on or after 6 April 2011.

7 [Omitted by FA 2011, s. 65 and Sch. 16, para. 84(d)(ii).]

History – Para. 7 omitted by FA 2011, s. 65 and Sch. 16, para. 84(d)(ii), with effect in relation to deaths occurring on or after 6 April 2011.

8 [Omitted by FA 2011, s. 65 and Sch. 16, para. 84(d)(ii).]

History – Para. 8 omitted by FA 2011, s. 65 and Sch. 16, para. 84(d)(ii), with effect in relation to deaths occurring on or after 6 April 2011.

9 [Omitted by FA 2011, s. 65 and Sch. 16, para. 84(d)(ii).]

History – Para. 9 omitted by FA 2011, s. 65 and Sch. 16, para. 84(d)(ii), with effect in relation to deaths occurring on or after 6 April 2011.

10 [Omitted by FA 2011, s. 65 and Sch. 16, para. 84(d)(ii).]

History – Para. 10 omitted by FA 2011, s. 65 and Sch. 16, para. 84(d)(ii), with effect in relation to deaths occurring on or after 6 April 2011.

11 [Omitted by FA 2011, s. 65 and Sch. 16, para. 84(d)(ii).]

History – Para. 11 omitted by FA 2011, s. 65 and Sch. 16, para. 84(d)(ii), with effect in relation to deaths occurring on or after 6 April 2011.

12 [Omitted by FA 2011, s. 65 and Sch. 16, para. 84(d)(ii).]

History – Para. 12 omitted by FA 2011, s. 65 and Sch. 16, para. 84(d)(ii), with effect in relation to deaths occurring on or after 6 April 2011.

13 [Omitted by FA 2011, s. 65 and Sch. 16, para. 84(d)(ii).]

History – Para. 13 omitted by FA 2011, s. 65 and Sch. 16, para. 84(d)(ii), with effect in relation to deaths occurring on or after 6 April 2011.

14 [Omitted by FA 2011, s. 65 and Sch. 16, para. 84(d)(ii).]

History – Para. 14 omitted by FA 2011, s. 65 and Sch. 16, para. 84(d)(ii), with effect in relation to deaths occurring on or after 6 April 2011.

COMMENCEMENT

15(1) The amendments made by paragraph 2 have effect in relation to assignments or agreements to assign made on or after 10 October 2007.

15(2) The amendments made by paragraph 3 have effect in relation to surrenders and agreements to surrender made on or after that date.

15(3) The amendments made by paragraphs 4, 7(2), 8, 10 and 11 to 14 have effect in relation to deaths occurring on or after 6 April 2008.

SCHEDULE 29 – FURTHER PROVISION ABOUT PENSION SCHEMES

Section 92

INHERITANCE TAX TREATMENT OF NON-UK PENSION SCHEMES

18(1) IHTA 1984 is amended as follows.

18(2) [Amends IHTA 1984, s. 12(2).]

18(3) [Amends IHTA 1984, s. 58(12).]

18(4) [Amends IHTA 1984, s. 151(2), (4) and (5).]
18(5) [Amends IHTA 1984, s. 152.]
18(6) [Inserts IHTA 1984, s. 271A.]
18(7) [Amends FA 2004, Sch. 36, para. 56(1)(a); inserts para. 56(4).]
18(8) The amendments made by this paragraph are treated as having come into force on 6 April 2006.

SCHEDULE 36 – INFORMATION AND INSPECTION POWERS

Section 113

Commencement Date – Sch. 36 came into effect for the purpose of inheritance tax by virtue of FA 2009, s. 96(1), with effect from 1 April 2010 (SI 2009/3054).

Notes – Amendments made to Sch. 38 which took effect before 1 April 2010 are reflected in the text of the Schedule reproduced here, but history annotations for those amendments are not included here as they are not relevant for inheritance tax purposes.

Part 1 – Powers to Obtain Information and Documents

POWER TO OBTAIN INFORMATION AND DOCUMENTS FROM TAXPAYER

1(1) An officer of Revenue and Customs may by notice in writing require a person ("the taxpayer")–
(a) to provide information, or
(b) to produce a document,
if the information or document is reasonably required by the officer for the purpose of checking the taxpayer's tax position.

1(2) In this Schedule, **"taxpayer notice"** means a notice under this paragraph.

POWER TO OBTAIN INFORMATION AND DOCUMENTS FROM THIRD PARTY

2(1) An officer of Revenue and Customs may by notice in writing require a person–
(a) to provide information, or
(b) to produce a document,
if the information or document is reasonably required by the officer for the purpose of checking the tax position of another person whose identity is known to the officer ("the taxpayer").

2(2) A third party notice must name the taxpayer to whom it relates, unless the tribunal has approved the giving of the notice and disapplied this requirement under paragraph 3.

2(3) In this Schedule, **"third party notice"** means a notice under this paragraph.

APPROVAL ETC OF TAXPAYER NOTICES AND THIRD PARTY NOTICES

3(1) An officer of Revenue and Customs may not give a third party notice without–
(a) the agreement of the taxpayer, or
(b) the approval of the tribunal.

3(2) An officer of Revenue and Customs may ask for the approval of the tribunal to the giving of any taxpayer notice or third party notice (and for the effect of obtaining such approval see paragraphs 29, 30 and 53 (appeals against notices and offence)).

3(2A) An application for approval under this paragraph may be made without notice (except as required under sub-paragraph (3)).

3(3) The tribunal may not approve the giving of a taxpayer notice or third party notice unless–
(a) an application for approval is made by, or with the agreement of, an authorised officer of Revenue and Customs,
(b) the tribunal is satisfied that, in the circumstances, the officer giving the notice is justified in doing so,
(c) the person to whom the notice is to be addressed has been told that the information or documents referred to in the notice are required and given a reasonable opportunity to make representations to an officer of Revenue and Customs,
(d) the tribunal has been given a summary of any representations made by that person, and
(e) in the case of a third party notice, the taxpayer has been given a summary of the reasons why an officer of Revenue and Customs requires the information and documents.

3(4) Paragraphs (c) to (e) of sub-paragraph (3) do not apply to the extent that the tribunal is satisfied that taking the action specified in those paragraphs might prejudice the assessment or collection of tax.

3(5) Where the tribunal approves the giving of a third party notice under this paragraph, it may also disapply the requirement to name the taxpayer in the notice if it is satisfied that the officer has reasonable grounds for believing that naming the taxpayer might seriously prejudice the assessment or collection of tax.

COPYING THIRD PARTY NOTICE TO TAXPAYER

4(1) An officer of Revenue and Customs who gives a third party notice must give a copy of the notice to the taxpayer to whom it relates, unless the tribunal has disapplied this requirement.

4(2) The tribunal may not disapply that requirement unless–

(a) an application for approval is made by, or with the agreement of, an authorised officer of Revenue and Customs, and

(b) the tribunal is satisfied that the officer has reasonable grounds for believing that giving a copy of the notice to the taxpayer might prejudice the assessment or collection of tax.

POWER TO OBTAIN INFORMATION AND DOCUMENTS ABOUT PERSONS WHOSE IDENTITY IS NOT KNOWN

5(1) An authorised officer of Revenue and Customs may by notice in writing require a person–

(a) to provide information, or

(b) to produce a document,

if the condition in sub-paragraph (2) is met.

5(2) That condition is that the information or document is reasonably required by the officer for the purpose of checking the tax position of–

(a) a person whose identity is not known to the officer, or

(b) a class of persons whose individual identities are not known to the officer.

5(3) An officer of Revenue and Customs may not give a notice under this paragraph without the approval of the tribunal.

5(3A) An application for approval under this paragraph may be made without notice.

5(4) The tribunal may not approve the giving of a notice under this paragraph unless it is satisfied that–

(a) the notice would meet the condition in sub-paragraph (2),

(b) there are reasonable grounds for believing that the person or any of the class of persons to whom the notice relates may have failed or may fail to comply with any provision of the law (including the law of a territory outside the United Kingdom) relating to tax,

(c) any such failure is likely to have led or to lead to serious prejudice to the assessment or collection of tax, and

(d) the information or document to which the notice relates is not readily available from another source.

5(5) [Omitted by FA 2011, s. 86 and Sch. 24, para. 2(4).]

History – In para. 5(2), "UK" omitted by FA 2011, s. 86 and Sch. 24, para. 2(2), with effect from 1 April 2012 in relation to tax regardless of when the tax became due (whether before, on or after that date).

In para. 5(4)(b), the words "the law (including the law of a territory outside the United Kingdom) relating to tax," substituted for the words "the Taxes Acts, or any other enactment relating to UK tax," by FA 2011, s. 86 and Sch. 24, para. 2(3)(a), with effect from 1 April 2012 in relation to tax regardless of when the tax became due (whether before, on or after that date).

In para. 5(4)(c), "UK" omitted by FA 2011, s. 86 and Sch. 24, para. 2(3)(b), with effect from 1 April 2012 in relation to tax regardless of when the tax became due (whether before, on or after that date).

Para. 5(5) omitted by FA 2011, s. 86 and Sch. 24, para. 2(4), with effect from 1 April 2012 in relation to tax regardless of when the tax became due (whether before, on or after that date).

POWER TO OBTAIN INFORMATION ABOUT PERSONS WHOSE IDENTITY CAN BE ASCERTAINED

5A(1) An authorised officer of Revenue and Customs may by notice in writing require a person to provide relevant information about another person ("the taxpayer") if conditions A to D are met.

5A(2) Condition A is that the information is reasonably required by the officer for the purpose of checking the tax position of the taxpayer.

5A(3) Condition B is that–

(a) the taxpayer's identity is not known to the officer, but

(b) the officer holds information from which the taxpayer's identity can be ascertained.

5A(4) Condition C is that the officer has reason to believe that–

(a) the person will be able to ascertain the taxpayer's identity from the information held by the officer, and

(b) the person obtained relevant information about the taxpayer in the course of carrying on a business.

5A(5) Condition D is that the taxpayer's identity cannot readily be ascertained by other means from the information held by the officer.

5A(6) **"Relevant information"** means all or any of the following–

(a) name,

(b) last known address, and

(c) date of birth (in the case of an individual).

5A(7) This paragraph applies for the purpose of checking the tax position of a class of persons as for the purpose of checking the tax position of a single person (and references to "the taxpayer" are to be read accordingly).

History – Para. 5A inserted by FA 2012, s. 224(2), with effect from 17 July 2012, subject to the transitional provisions in FA 2012, s. 224(7).

NOTICES

6(1) In this Schedule, **"information notice"** means a notice under paragraph 1, 2, 5 or 5A.

6(2) An information notice may specify or describe the information or documents to be provided or produced.

6(3) If an information notice is given with the approval of the tribunal, it must state that it is given with that approval.

6(4) A decision of the tribunal under paragraph 3, 4 or 5 is final (despite the provisions of sections 11 and 13 of the Tribunals, Courts and Enforcement Act 2007).

History – In para. 6(1), the words ", 5 or 5A" substituted for "or 5" by FA 2012, s. 222(3), with effect from 17 July 2012, subject to the transitional provisions in FA 2012, s. 222(7).

COMPLYING WITH NOTICES

7(1) Where a person is required by an information notice to provide information or produce a document, the person must do so–

(a) within such period, and

(b) at such time, by such means and in such form (if any),

as is reasonably specified or described in the notice.

7(2) Where an information notice requires a person to produce a document, it must be produced for inspection–

(a) at a place agreed to by that person and an officer of Revenue and Customs, or

(b) at such place as an officer of Revenue and Customs may reasonably specify.

7(3) An officer of Revenue and Customs must not specify a place that is used solely as a dwelling.

7(4) The production of a document in compliance with an information notice is not to be regarded as breaking any lien claimed on the document.

PRODUCING COPIES OF DOCUMENTS

8(1) Where an information notice requires a person to produce a document, the person may comply with the notice by producing a copy of the document, subject to any conditions or exceptions set out in regulations made by the Commissioners.

8(2) Sub-paragraph (1) does not apply where–

(a) the notice requires the person to produce the original document, or

(b) an officer of Revenue and Customs subsequently makes a request in writing to the person for the original document.

8(3) Where an officer of Revenue and Customs requests a document under sub-paragraph (2)(b), the person to whom the request is made must produce the document–

(a) within such period, and

(b) at such time and by such means (if any),

as is reasonably requested by the officer.

RESTRICTIONS AND SPECIAL CASES

9 This Part of this Schedule has effect subject to Parts 4 and 6 of this Schedule.

Part 2 – Powers to Inspect Premises and Other Property

History – In the heading to Part 2, the words "Premises and Other Property" substituted for the words "Businesses etc" by SI 2009/3054, art. 3 and Schedule, para. 15, with effect from 1 April 2010.

POWER TO INSPECT BUSINESS PREMISES ETC

10(1) An officer of Revenue and Customs may enter a person's business premises and inspect–

(a) the premises,

(b) business assets that are on the premises, and

(c) business documents that are on the premises,

if the inspection is reasonably required for the purpose of checking that person's tax position.

10(2) The powers under this paragraph do not include power to enter or inspect any part of the premises that is used solely as a dwelling.

10(3) In this Schedule–

"business assets" means assets that an officer of Revenue and Customs has reason to believe are owned, leased or used in connection with the carrying on of a business by any person (but see sub-paragraph (4)),

"business documents" means documents (or copies of documents)–

(a) that relate to the carrying on of a business by any person, and

(b) that form part of any person's statutory records, and

"business premises", in relation to a person, means premises (or any part of premises) that an officer of Revenue and Customs has reason to believe are (or is) used in connection with the carrying on of a business by or on behalf of the person.

10(4) For the purposes of this Schedule, **"business assets"** does not include documents, other than–

(a) documents that are trading stock for the purposes of Chapter 11A of Part 2 of ITTOIA 2005 (see section 172A of that Act), and

(b) documents that are plant for the purposes of Part 2 of CAA 2001.

Prospective amendments – Para. 10(5) inserted by FA 2017, s. 56 and Sch. 11, para. 1(2), with effect from a day to be appointed under FA 2017, s. 61(1). Para. 10(5) to read as follows:

"**10(5)** In sub-paragraph (1), the reference to a person's tax position does not include a reference to a person's position as regards soft drinks industry levy."

POWER TO INSPECT BUSINESS PREMISES ETC OF INVOLVED THIRD PARTIES

10A(1) An officer of Revenue and Customs may enter business premises of an involved third party (see paragraph 61A) and inspect–

(a) the premises,

(b) business assets that are on the premises, and

(c) relevant documents that are on the premises,

if the inspection is reasonably required by the officer for the purpose of checking the position of any person or class of persons as regards a relevant tax.

10A(2) The powers under this paragraph may be exercised whether or not the identity of that person is, or the individual identities of those persons are, known to the officer.

10A(3) The powers under this paragraph do not include power to enter or inspect any part of the premises that is used solely as a dwelling.

10A(4) In relation to an involved third party, **"relevant documents"** and **"relevant tax"** are defined in paragraph 61A.

History – Para. 10A inserted by FA 2009, s. 96 and Sch. 48, para. 3, with effect from 1 April 2010, by virtue of SI 2009/3054.

POWER TO INSPECT PREMISES USED IN CONNECTION WITH TAXABLE SUPPLIES ETC

11(1) This paragraph applies where an officer of Revenue and Customs has reason to believe that–

(a) premises are used in connection with the supply of goods under taxable supplies and goods to be so supplied or documents relating to such goods are on those premises,

(b) premises are used in connection with the acquisition of goods from other member States under taxable acquisitions and goods to be so acquired or documents relating to such goods are on those premises, or

(c) premises are used as or in connection with a fiscal warehouse.

11(2) An officer of Revenue and Customs may enter the premises and inspect–

(a) the premises,

(b) any goods that are on the premises, and

(c) any documents on the premises that appear to the officer to relate to the supply of goods under taxable supplies, the acquisition of goods from other member States under taxable acquisitions or fiscal warehousing.

11(3) The powers under this paragraph do not include power to enter or inspect any part of the premises that is used solely as a dwelling.

11(4) Terms used both in this paragraph and in VATA 1994 have the same meaning here as they have in that Act.

CARRYING OUT INSPECTIONS UNDER PARAGRAPH 10, 10A OR 11

History – In the heading to para. 12, the words "under paragraph 10, 10A or 11" inserted by FA 2009, s. 96 and Sch. 48, para. 4(3), with effect from 1 April 2010, by virtue of SI 2009/3054.

12(1) An inspection under paragraph 10, 10A or 11 may be carried out only–

(a) at a time agreed to by the occupier of the premises, or

(b) if sub-paragraph (2) is satisfied, at any reasonable time.

12(2) This sub-paragraph is satisfied if–

(a) the occupier of the premises has been given at least 7 days' notice of the time of the inspection (whether in writing or otherwise), or

(b) the inspection is carried out by, or with the agreement of, an authorised officer of Revenue and Customs.

12(3) An officer of Revenue and Customs seeking to carry out an inspection under sub-paragraph (2)(b) must provide a notice in writing as follows–

(a) if the occupier of the premises is present at the time the inspection is to begin, the notice must be provided to the occupier,

(b) if the occupier of the premises is not present but a person who appears to the officer to be in charge of the premises is present, the notice must be provided to that person, and

(c) in any other case, the notice must be left in a prominent place on the premises.

12(4) The notice referred to in sub-paragraph (3) must state the possible consequences of obstructing the officer in the exercise of the power.

12(5) If a notice referred to in sub-paragraph (3) is given in respect of an inspection approved by the tribunal (see paragraph 13), it must state that the inspection has been so approved.

History – In para. 12(1), the words "paragraph 10, 10A or 11" substituted for the words "this Part of this Schedule" by FA 2009, s. 96 and Sch. 48, para. 4(2) with effect from 1 April 2010, by virtue of SI 2009/3054.

POWERS TO INSPECT PROPERTY FOR VALUATION ETC

12A(1) An officer of Revenue and Customs may enter and inspect premises for the purpose of valuing the premises if the valuation is reasonably required for the purpose of checking any person's position as regards income tax or corporation tax.

12A(2) An officer of Revenue and Customs may enter premises and inspect–

(a) the premises, and

(b) any other property on the premises,

for the purpose of valuing, measuring or determining the character of the premises or property.

12A(3) Sub-paragraph (2) only applies if the valuation, measurement or determination is reasonably required for the purpose of checking any person's position as regards–

(a) capital gains tax,

(b) corporation tax in respect of chargeable gains,

(c) inheritance tax,

(d) stamp duty land tax,

(e) stamp duty reserve tax, or

(f) annual tax on enveloped dwellings.

12A(4) A person who the officer considers is needed to assist with the valuation, measurement or determination may enter and inspect the premises or property with the officer.

History – Para. 12A(3)(f) (and the ", or" before it) inserted (and the "or" after (d) omitted) by FA 2013, s. 164 and Sch. 34, para. 2, with effect from 17 July 2013 (Royal Assent).
Para. 12A inserted by FA 2009, s. 96 and Sch. 48, para. 5, with effect from 1 April 2010, by virtue of SI 2009/3054.

CARRYING OUT INSPECTIONS UNDER PARAGRAPH 12A

12B(1) An inspection under paragraph 12A may be carried out only if condition A or B is satisfied.

12B(2) Condition A is that–

(a) the inspection is carried out at a time agreed to by a relevant person, and

(b) the relevant person has been given notice in writing of the agreed time of the inspection.

12B(3) **"Relevant person"** means–

(a) the occupier of the premises, or

(b) if the occupier cannot be identified or the premises are vacant, a person who controls the premises.

12B(4) Condition B is that–

(a) the inspection has been approved by the tribunal, and

(b) any relevant person specified by the tribunal has been given at least 7 days' notice in writing of the time of the inspection.

12B(5) A notice under sub-paragraph (4)(b) must state the possible consequences of obstructing the officer in the exercise of the power.

12B(6) If a notice is given under this paragraph in respect of an inspection approved by the tribunal (see paragraph 13), it must state that the inspection has been so approved.

12B(7) An officer of Revenue and Customs seeking to carry out an inspection under paragraph 12A must produce evidence of authority to carry out the inspection if asked to do so by–

(a) the occupier of the premises, or

(b) any other person who appears to the officer to be in charge of the premises or property.

History – Para. 12B inserted by FA 2009, s. 96 and Sch. 48, para. 5, with effect from 1 April 2010, by virtue of SI 2009/3054.

APPROVAL OF TRIBUNAL

13(1) An officer of Revenue and Customs may ask the tribunal to approve an inspection under this Part of this Schedule (and for the effect of obtaining such approval see paragraph 39 (penalties)).

13(1A) An application for approval under this paragraph may be made without notice (except as required under sub-paragraph (2A)).

13(2) The tribunal may not approve an inspection under paragraph 10, 10A or 11unless–

(a) an application for approval is made by, or with the agreement of, an authorised officer of Revenue and Customs, and

(b) the tribunal is satisfied that, in the circumstances, the inspection is justified.

13(2A) The tribunal may not approve an inspection under paragraph 12A unless–

(a) an application for approval is made by, or with the agreement of, an authorised officer of Revenue and Customs,

(b) the person whose tax position is the subject of the proposed inspection has been given a reasonable opportunity to make representations to the officer of Revenue and Customs about that inspection,

(c) the occupier of the premises has been given a reasonable opportunity to make such representations,

(d) the tribunal has been given a summary of any representations made, and

(e) the tribunal is satisfied that, in the circumstances, the inspection is justified.

13(2B) Paragraph (c) of sub-paragraph (2A) does not apply if the tribunal is satisfied that the occupier of the premises cannot be identified.

13(3) A decision of the tribunal under this paragraph is final (despite the provisions of sections 11 and 13 of the Tribunals, Courts and Enforcement Act 2007).

History – In para. 13(1), the words "(and for the effect of obtaining such approval see paragraph 39 (penalties))" inserted by FA 2009, s. 96 and Sch. 48, para. 6(2), with effect from 1 April 2010, by virtue of SI 2009/3054.
In para. 13(1), the word "tribunal" substituted for the words "First-tier Tribunal" and in para. 13(2)(b), the word "tribunal" substituted for the word "Tribunal" by SI 2009/56, art. 3(1) and Sch. 1, para. 471(5)(b) and (c), operative from 1 April 2009, subject to transitional and saving provisions in SI 2009/56, Sch. 3.
In para. 13(1A), the words "(except as required under sub-paragraph (2A))" inserted by FA 2009, s. 96 and Sch. 48, para. 6(3), with effect from 1 April 2010, by virtue of SI 2009/3054.
Para. 13(1A) inserted by FA 2009, s. 95 and Sch. 47, para. 8(2), with effect from 21 July 2009 (subject to FA 2009, s. 95(2)–(5)).

In para. 13(2), the words "under paragraph 10, 10A or 11" inserted by FA 2009, s. 96 and Sch. 48, para. 6(4), with effect from 1 April 2010, by virtue of SI 2009/3054.
Para. 13(2A) and (2B) inserted by FA 2009, s. 96 and Sch. 48, para. 6(5), with effect from 1 April 2010, by virtue of SI 2009/3054.
Para. 13(3) inserted by FA 2009, s. 95 and Sch. 47, para. 8(3), with effect from 21 July 2009 (subject to FA 2009, s. 95(2)–(5)).

RESTRICTIONS AND SPECIAL CASES

14 This Part of this Schedule has effect subject to Parts 4 and 6 of this Schedule.

Part 3 – Further Powers

POWER TO COPY DOCUMENTS

15 Where a document (or a copy of a document) is produced to, or inspected by, an officer of Revenue and Customs, such an officer may take copies of, or make extracts from, the document.

POWER TO REMOVE DOCUMENTS

16(1) Where a document is produced to, or inspected by, an officer of Revenue and Customs, such an officer may–

(a) remove the document at a reasonable time, and

(b) retain it for a reasonable period,

if it appears to the officer to be necessary to do so.

16(2) Where a document is removed in accordance with sub-paragraph (1), the person who produced the document may request–

(a) a receipt for the document, and

(b) if the document is reasonably required for any purpose, a copy of the document,

and an officer of Revenue and Customs must comply with such a request without charge.

16(3) The removal of a document under this paragraph is not to be regarded as breaking any lien claimed on the document.

16(4) Where a document removed under this paragraph is lost or damaged, the Commissioners are liable to compensate the owner of the document for any expenses reasonably incurred in replacing or repairing the document.

16(5) In this paragraph, references to a document include a copy of a document.

POWER TO MARK ASSETS AND TO RECORD INFORMATION

17 The powers under Part 2 of this Schedule include–

(a) power to mark business assets, and anything containing business assets, for the purpose of indicating that they have been inspected, and

(b) power to obtain and record information (whether electronically or otherwise) relating to the premises, property, goods, assets and documents that have been inspected.

History – In para. 17(b), the words "property, goods," inserted by FA 2009, s. 96 and Sch. 48, para. 7 with effect from 1 April 2010, by virtue of SI 2009/3054.

Part 4 – Restrictions on Powers

DOCUMENTS NOT IN PERSON'S POSSESSION OR POWER

18 An information notice only requires a person to produce a document if it is in the person's possession or power.

TYPES OF INFORMATION

19(1) An information notice does not require a person to provide or produce–

(a) information that relates to the conduct of a pending appeal relating to tax or any part of a document containing such information,

(aa) information that relates to the conduct of a pending appeal under the Savings (Government Contributions) Act 2017 or any part of a document containing such information, or

(b) journalistic material (as defined in section 13 of the Police and Criminal Evidence Act 1984 (c. 60)) or information contained in such material.

19(2) An information notice does not require a person to provide or produce personal records (as defined in section 12 of the Police and Criminal Evidence Act 1984) or information contained in such records, subject to sub-paragraph (3).

19(3) An information notice may require a person–

(a) to produce documents, or copies of documents, that are personal records, omitting any information whose inclusion (whether alone or with other information) makes the original documents personal records ("personal information"), and

(b) to provide any information contained in such records that is not personal information.

Prospective amendments – Para. 19(4) and (5) inserted by Investigatory Powers Act 2016, s. 12(1) and Sch. 2, para. 10, with effect from such day as the Secretary of State may by regulations appoint. Para. 19(4) and (5) to read:

"**19(4)** An information notice does not require a telecommunications operator or postal operator to provide or produce communications data.

19(5) In sub-paragraph (4) **"communications data"**, **"postal operator"** and **"telecommunications operator"** have the same meanings as in the Investigatory Powers Act 2016 (see sections 261 and 262 of that Act)."

History – Para. 19(1)(aa) inserted by SGCA 2017, s. 3(1), with effect from 17 January 2017.

OLD DOCUMENTS

20 An information notice may not require a person to produce a document if the whole of the document originates more than 6 years before the date of the notice, unless the notice is given by, or with the agreement of, an authorised officer.

TAXPAYER NOTICES FOLLOWING TAX RETURN

History – In the heading to para. 21, the words "following tax return" inserted by FA 2009, s. 96 and Sch. 48, para. 8(3), with effect from 1 April 2010, by virtue of SI 2009/3054.

21(1) Where a person has made a tax return in respect of a chargeable period under section 8, 8A or 12AA of TMA 1970 (returns for purpose of income tax and capital gains tax), a taxpayer notice may not be given for the purpose of checking that person's income tax position or capital gains tax position in relation to the chargeable period.

21(2) Where a person has made a tax return in respect of a chargeable period under paragraph 3 of Schedule 18 to FA 1998 (company tax returns), a taxpayer notice may not be given for the purpose of checking that person's corporation tax position in relation to the chargeable period

21(3) Sub-paragraphs (1) and (2) do not apply where, or to the extent that, any of conditions A to D is met.

21(4) Condition A is that a notice of enquiry has been given in respect of–

(a) the return, or

(b) a claim or election (or an amendment of a claim or election) made by the person in relation to the chargeable period in respect of the tax (or one of the taxes) to which the return relates ("relevant tax"),

and the enquiry has not been completed so far as relating to the matters to which the taxpayer notice relates.

21(5) In sub-paragraph (4), **"notice of enquiry"** means a notice under–

(a) section 9A or 12AC of, or paragraph 5 of Schedule 1A to, TMA 1970, or

(b) paragraph 24 of Schedule 18 to FA 1998.

21(6) Condition B is that, as regards the person, an officer of Revenue and Customs has reason to suspect that–

(a) an amount that ought to have been assessed to relevant tax for the chargeable period may not have been assessed,

(b) an assessment to relevant tax for the chargeable period may be or have become insufficient, or

(c) relief from relevant tax given for the chargeable period may be or have become excessive.

21(7) Condition C is that the notice is given for the purpose of obtaining any information or document that is also required for the purpose of checking the person's position as regards any tax other than income tax, capital gains tax or corporation tax.

21(8) Condition D is that the notice is given for the purpose of obtaining any information or document that is required (or also required) for the purpose of checking the person's position as regards any deductions or repayments of tax or withholding of income referred to in paragraph 64(2) or (2A) (PAYE etc).

21(9) In this paragraph, references to the person who made the return are only to that person in the capacity in which the return was made.

Prospective amendments – In para. 21(1) the words ", or regulations under paragraph 10 of Schedule A1 to," inserted after the words "12AA of" by F(No. 2)A 2017, s. 61 and Sch. 14, para. 38(2), with effect from a day to be appointed under F(No. 2)A 2017, s. 61(6).
History – In para. 21(4) the words "so far as relating to the matters to which the taxpayer notice relates" inserted by F(No. 2)A 2017, s. 63 and Sch. 15, para. 36, with effect in relation to an enquiry under TMA 1970, s. 9A, 12ZM or 12AC or FA 1998, Sch. 18 where the notice of enquiry is given on or after 16 November 2017 (Royal Assent) or the enquiry is in progress immediately before that day. In para. 21(7), the words "position as regards any tax other than income tax, capital gains tax or corporation tax" substituted for the words "VAT position" by FA 2009, s. 96 and Sch. 48, para. 8(2), with effect from 1 April 2010, by virtue of SI 2009/3054.

TAXPAYER NOTICES FOLLOWING NRCGT RETURN

21ZA [Not relevant to inheritance tax.]

TAXPAYER NOTICES FOLLOWING LAND TRANSACTION RETURN

21A(1) Where a person has delivered a land transaction return under section 76 of FA 2003 (returns for purposes of stamp duty land tax) in respect of a transaction, a taxpayer notice may not be given for the purpose of checking that person's stamp duty land tax position in relation to that transaction.

21A(2) Sub-paragraph (1) does not apply where, or to the extent that, any of conditions A to C is met.

21A(3) Condition A is that a notice of enquiry has been given in respect of–

(a) the return, or

(b) a claim (or an amendment of a claim) made by the person in connection with the transaction,

and the enquiry has not been completed.

21A(4) In sub-paragraph (3) **"notice of enquiry"** means a notice under paragraph 12 of Schedule 10, or paragraph 7 of Schedule 11A, to FA 2003.

21A(5) Condition B is that, as regards the person, an officer of Revenue and Customs has reason to suspect that–

(a) an amount that ought to have been assessed to stamp duty land tax in respect of the transaction may not have been assessed,

(b) an assessment to stamp duty land tax in respect of the transaction may be or have become insufficient, or

(c) relief from stamp duty land tax in respect of the transaction may be or have become excessive.

21A(6) Condition C is that the notice is given for the purpose of obtaining any information or document that is also required for the purpose of checking that person's position as regards a tax other than stamp duty land tax.

History – Para. 21A inserted by FA 2009, s. 96 and Sch. 48, para. 9, with effect from 1 April 2010, by virtue of SI 2009/3054.

ANNUAL TAX ON ENVELOPED DWELLINGS: TAXPAYER NOTICES FOLLOWING RETURN

21B(1) Where a person has delivered, for a chargeable period with respect to a single-dwelling interest–

(a) an annual tax on enveloped dwellings return, or

(b) a return of the adjusted chargeable amount,

a taxpayer notice may not be given for the purpose of checking the person's annual tax on enveloped dwellings position as regards the matters dealt with in that return.

21B(2) Sub-paragraph (1) does not apply where, or to the extent that, any of conditions A to C is met.

21B(3) Condition A is that notice of enquiry has been given in respect of–

(a) the return, or

(b) a claim (or an amendment of a claim) made by the person in relation to the chargeable period,

and the enquiry has not been completed.

21B(4) In sub-paragraph (3) **"notice of enquiry"** means a notice under paragraph 8 of Schedule 33 to FA 2013 or paragraph 7 of Schedule 11A to FA 2003 (as applied by paragraphs 28(2) and 31(3) of Schedule 33 to FA 2013).

21B(5) Condition B is that, as regards the person, an officer of Revenue and Customs has reason to suspect that–

(a) an amount that ought to have been assessed to annual tax on enveloped dwellings for the chargeable period may not have been assessed,

(b) an assessment to annual tax on enveloped dwellings for the chargeable period may be or have become insufficient, or

(c) relief from annual tax on enveloped dwellings for the chargeable period may be or have become excessive.

21B(6) Condition C is that the notice is given for the purpose of obtaining any information or document that is also required for the purpose of checking that person's position as regards a tax other than annual tax on enveloped dwellings.

21B(7) In this Schedule references to a **"single-dwelling interest"** are to be read in accordance with section 108 of FA 2013.

History – Para. 21B inserted by FA 2013, s. 164 and Sch. 34, para. 3, with effect from 17 July 2013 (Royal Assent).

DECEASED PERSONS

22 An information notice given for the purpose of checking the tax position of a person who has died may not be given more than 4 years after the person's death.

PRIVILEGED COMMUNICATIONS BETWEEN PROFESSIONAL LEGAL ADVISERS AND CLIENTS

23(1) An information notice does not require a person–

(a) to provide privileged information, or

(b) to produce any part of a document that is privileged.

23(2) For the purpose of this Schedule, information or a document is privileged if it is information or a document in respect of which a claim to legal professional privilege or, (in Scotland) to confidentiality of communications as between client and professional legal adviser, could be maintained in legal proceedings.

23(3) The Commissioners may by regulations make provision for the resolution by the tribunal of disputes as to whether any information or document is privileged.

23(4) The regulations may, in particular, make provision as to–

(a) the custody of a document while its status is being decided,

(b) [omitted by SI 2009/56, art. 3(1) and Sch. 1, para. 471(6)(b).]

Cross references – SI 2009/1916: resolution of disputes as to privileged communications.

Statutory instruments – SI 2009/1916: made under para. 23(3) and (4).

AUDITORS

24(1) An information notice does not require a person who has been appointed as an auditor for the purpose of an enactment–

(a) to provide information held in connection with the performance of the person's functions under that enactment, or

(b) to produce documents which are that person's property and which were created by that person or on that person's behalf for or in connection with the performance of those functions.

24(2) Sub-paragraph (1) has effect subject to paragraph 26.

TAX ADVISERS

25(1) An information notice does not require a tax adviser–

(a) to provide information about relevant communications, or

(b) to produce documents which are the tax adviser's property and consist of relevant communications.

25(2) Sub-paragraph (1) has effect subject to paragraph 26.

25(3) In this paragraph–

"relevant communications" means communications between the tax adviser and–

(a) a person in relation to whose tax affairs he has been appointed, or

(b) any other tax adviser of such a person,

the purpose of which is the giving or obtaining of advice about any of those tax affairs, and

"tax adviser" means a person appointed to give advice about the tax affairs of another person (whether appointed directly by that person or by another tax adviser of that person).

AUDITORS AND TAX ADVISERS: SUPPLEMENTARY

26(1) Paragraphs 24(1) and 25(1) do not have effect in relation to–

(a) information explaining any information or document which the person to whom the notice is given has, as tax accountant, assisted any client in preparing for, or delivering to, HMRC, or

(b) a document which contains such information.

26(2) In the case of a notice given under paragraph 5, paragraphs 24(1) and 25(1) do not have effect in relation to–

(a) any information giving the identity or address of a person to whom the notice relates or of a person who has acted on behalf of such a person, or

(b) a document which contains such information.

26(3) Paragraphs 24(1) and 25(1) are not disapplied by sub-paragraph (1) or (2) if the information in question has already been provided, or a document containing the information in question has already been produced, to an officer of Revenue and Customs.

27(1) This paragraph applies where paragraph 24(1) or 25(1) is disapplied in relation to a document by paragraph 26(1) or (2).

27(2) An information notice that requires the document to be produced has effect as if it required any part or parts of the document containing the information mentioned in paragraph 26(1) or (2) to be produced.

CORRESPONDING RESTRICTIONS ON INSPECTION OF DOCUMENTS

History – In the heading before para. 28, the word "business" (which appeared before the word "documents") omitted by FA 2009, s. 96 and Sch. 48, para. 10, with effect from 1 April 2010, by virtue of SI 2009/3054.

28 An officer of Revenue and Customs may not inspect a document under Part 2 of this Schedule if or to the extent that, by virtue of this Part of this Schedule, an information notice given at the time of the inspection to the occupier of the premises could not require the occupier to produce the document.

History – In para. 28, the word "business" (which appeared before the word "document") omitted by FA 2009, s. 96 and Sch. 48, para. 10, with effect from 1 April 2010, by virtue of SI 2009/3054.

Part 5 – Appeals Against Information Notices

RIGHT TO APPEAL AGAINST TAXPAYER NOTICE

29(1) Where a taxpayer is given a taxpayer notice, the taxpayer may appeal against the notice or any requirement in the notice.

29(2) Sub-paragraph (1) does not apply to a requirement in a taxpayer notice to provide any information, or produce any document, that forms part of the taxpayer's statutory records.

29(3) Sub-paragraph (1) does not apply if the tribunal approved the giving of the notice in accordance with paragraph 3.

RIGHT TO APPEAL AGAINST THIRD PARTY NOTICE

30(1) Where a person is given a third party notice, the person may appeal against the notice or any requirement in the notice on the ground that it would be unduly onerous to comply with the notice or requirement.

30(2) Sub-paragraph (1) does not apply to a requirement in a third party notice to provide any information, or produce any document, that forms part of the taxpayer's statutory records.

30(3) Sub-paragraph (1) does not apply if the tribunal approved the giving of the notice in accordance with paragraph 3.

RIGHT TO APPEAL AGAINST NOTICE GIVEN UNDER PARAGRAPH 5 OR 5A

31 Where a person is given a notice under paragraph 5 or 5A, the person may appeal against the notice or any requirement in the notice on the ground that it would be unduly onerous to comply with the notice or requirement.

History – In para. 31, in the heading, the words "or 5A" inserted by FA 2012, s. 222(5), with effect from 17 July 2012, subject to the transitional provisions in FA 2012, s. 222(7).
In para. 31, the words "or 5A" inserted by FA 2012, s. 222(4), with effect from 17 July 2012, subject to the transitional provisions in FA 2012, s. 222(7).

PROCEDURE

32(1) Notice of an appeal under this Part of this Schedule must be given–

(a) in writing,

(b) before the end of the period of 30 days beginning with the date on which the information notice is given, and

(c) to the officer of Revenue and Customs by whom the information notice was given.

IHT Statutes

32(2) Notice of an appeal under this Part of this Schedule must state the grounds of appeal.

32(3) On an appeal that is notified to the tribunal, the tribunal may–

(a) confirm the information notice or a requirement in the information notice,

(b) vary the information notice or such a requirement, or

(c) set aside the information notice or such a requirement.

32(4) Where the tribunal confirms or varies the information notice or a requirement, the person to whom the information notice was given must comply with the notice or requirement–

(a) within such period as is specified by the tribunal, or

(b) if the tribunal does not specify a period, within such period as is reasonably specified in writing by an officer of Revenue and Customs following the tribunal's decision.

32(5) Notwithstanding the provisions of sections 11 and 13 of the Tribunals, Courts and Enforcement Act 2007 a decision of the tribunal on an appeal under this Part of this Schedule is final.

32(6) Subject to this paragraph, the provisions of Part 5 of TMA 1970 relating to appeals have effect in relation to appeals under this Part of this Schedule as they have effect in relation to an appeal against an assessment to income tax.

SPECIAL CASES

33 This Part of this Schedule has effect subject to Part 6 of this Schedule.

Part 6 – Special Cases

SUPPLY OF GOODS OR SERVICES ETC

34(1) This paragraph applies to a taxpayer notice or third party notice that refers only to information or documents that form part of any person's statutory records and relate to–

(a) the supply of goods or services,

(b) the acquisition of goods from another member State, or

(c) the importation of goods from a place outside the member States in the course of carrying on a business.

34(2) Paragraph 3(1) (requirement for consent to, or approval of, third party notice) does not apply to such a notice.

34(3) Where a person is given such a notice, the person may not appeal against the notice or any requirement in the notice.

34(4) Sections 5, 11 and 15 of, and Schedule 4 to, VATA 1994, and any orders made under those provisions, apply for the purposes of this paragraph as if it were part of that Act.

INVOLVED THIRD PARTIES

34A [Omitted by FA 2011, s. 86 and Sch. 23, para. 62(2).]

History – Para. 34A omitted by FA 2011, s. 86 and Sch. 23, para. 62(2), with effect from 1 April 2012, subject to transitional provisions in FA 2011, Sch. 23, para. 65. Former para. 34A read as follows:

"**34A(1)** This paragraph applies to a third party notice or a notice under paragraph 5 if–

(a) it is given to an involved third party (see paragraph 61A),

(b) it is given for the purpose of checking the position of a person, or a class of persons, as regards the relevant tax, and

(c) it refers only to relevant information or relevant documents.

34A(2) In relation to such a third party notice–

(a) paragraph 3(1) (approval etc of third party notices) does not apply,

(b) paragraph 4(1) (copying third party notices to taxpayer) does not apply, and

(c) paragraph 30(1) (appeal) has effect as if it permitted an appeal on any grounds.

34A(3) In relation to such a notice under paragraph 5–

(a) sub-paragraphs (3) and (4) of that paragraph (approval of tribunal) have effect as if they permitted, but did not require, an authorised officer of Revenue and Customs to obtain the approval of the tribunal, and

(b) paragraph 31 (appeal) has effect as if it permitted an appeal on any grounds.

34A(4) The involved third party may not appeal against a requirement in the notice to provide any information, or produce any document, that forms part of the involved third party's statutory records.

34A(5) In relation to an involved third party, **"relevant documents"**, **"relevant information"** and **"relevant tax"** are defined in paragraph 61A.".

REGISTERED PENSION SCHEMES ETC

34B(1) This paragraph applies to a third party notice or a notice under paragraph 5 if it refers only to information or documents that relate to any pensions matter.

34B(2) **"Pensions matter"** means any matter relating to–

(a) a registered pension scheme,

(b) an annuity purchased with sums or assets held for the purposes of a registered pension scheme or a pre-2006 pension scheme, or

(c) an employer-financed retirement benefits scheme.

34B(3) In relation to such a third party notice–

(a) paragraph 3(1) (approval etc of third party notices) does not apply,

(b) paragraph 4(1) (copying third party notices to taxpayer) does not apply, and

(c) paragraph 30(1) (appeal) has effect as if it permitted an appeal on any grounds.

34B(4) In relation to such a notice under paragraph 5–

(a) sub-paragraphs (3) and (4) of that paragraph (approval of tribunal) have effect as if they permitted, but did not require, an authorised officer of Revenue and Customs to obtain the approval of the tribunal, and

(b) paragraph 31 (appeal) has effect as if it permitted an appeal on any grounds.

34B(5) A person may not appeal against a requirement in the notice to provide any information, or produce any document, that forms part of any person's statutory records.

34B(6) Where the notice relates to a matter within sub-paragraph (2)(a) or (b), the officer of Revenue and Customs who gives the notice must give a copy of the notice to the scheme administrator in relation to the pension scheme.

34B(7) Where the notice relates to a matter within sub-paragraph (2)(c), the officer of Revenue and Customs who gives the notice must give a copy of the notice to the responsible person in relation to the employer-financed retirement benefits scheme.

34B(8) Sub-paragraphs (6) and (7) do not apply if the notice is given to a person who, in relation to the scheme or annuity to which the notice relates, is a prescribed description of person.

History – Para. 34B inserted by FA 2009, s. 96 and Sch. 48, para. 11, with effect from 1 April 2010, by virtue of SI 2009/3054.

REGISTERED PENSION SCHEMES ETC: INTERPRETATION

34C In paragraph 34B–

"employer-financed retirement benefits scheme" has the same meaning as in Chapter 2 of Part 6 of ITEPA 2003 (see sections 393A and 393B of that Act);

"pension scheme" has the same meaning as in Part 4 of FA 2004;

"pre-2006 pension scheme" means a scheme that, at or in respect of any time before 6 April 2006, was–

(a) a retirement benefits scheme approved for the purposes of Chapter 1 of Part 14 of ICTA,

(b) a former approved superannuation fund (as defined in paragraph 1(3) of Schedule 36 to FA 2004),

(c) a relevant statutory scheme (as defined in section 611A of ICTA) or a pension scheme treated as if it were such a scheme, or

(d) a personal pension scheme approved under Chapter 4 of Part 14 of ICTA;

"prescribed" means prescribed by regulations made by the Commissioners;

"registered pension scheme" means a pension scheme that is or has been a registered pension scheme within the meaning of Part 4 of FA 2004 or in relation to which an application for registration under that Part of that Act has been made;

"responsible person", in relation to an employer-financed retirement benefits scheme, has the same meaning as in Chapter 2 of Part 6 of ITEPA 2003 (see section 399A of that Act);

"scheme administrator", in relation to a pension scheme, has the same meaning as in Part 4 of FA 2004 (see section 270 of that Act).

History – Para. 34C inserted by FA 2009, s. 96 and Sch. 48, para. 11, with effect from 1 April 2010, by virtue of SI 2009/3054.

GROUPS OF UNDERTAKINGS

35(1) This paragraph applies where an undertaking is a parent undertaking in relation to another undertaking (a subsidiary undertaking).

35(2) Where a third party notice is given to any person for the purpose of checking the tax position of the parent undertaking and any of its subsidiary undertakings–

(a) paragraph 2(2) only requires the notice to state this and name the parent undertaking, and

(b) the references in paragraph 3(5) to naming the taxpayer are to making that statement and naming the parent undertaking.

35(3) In relation to such a notice–

(a) in paragraphs 3 and 4 (approval etc of notices and copying third party notices to taxpayer), the references to the taxpayer have effect as if they were references to the parent undertaking, but

(b) in paragraph 30(2) (no appeal in relation to taxpayer's statutory records), the reference to the taxpayer has effect as if it were a reference to the parent undertaking and each of its subsidiary undertakings.

35(4) Where a third party notice is given to the parent undertaking for the purpose of checking the tax position of more than one subsidiary undertaking–

(a) paragraph 2(2) only requires the notice to state this, and

(b) the references in paragraph 3(5) to naming the taxpayer are to making that statement.

35(4A) In relation to such a notice–

(a) in paragraph 3 (approval etc of notices), sub-paragraphs (1) and (3)(e) do not apply,

(b) paragraph 4(1) (copying third party notices to taxpayer) does not apply,

(c) paragraphs 21 and 21A (restrictions on giving taxpayer notice where taxpayer has made return) apply as if the notice was a taxpayer notice or taxpayer notices given to each subsidiary undertaking (or, if the notice names the subsidiary undertakings to which it relates, to each of those undertakings),

(d) paragraph 30(1) (appeal) has effect as if it permitted an appeal on any grounds, and

(e) in paragraph 30(2) (no appeal in relation to taxpayer's statutory records), the reference to the taxpayer has effect as if it were a reference to the parent undertaking or any of its subsidiary undertakings.

35(5) Where a notice is given under paragraph 5 to the parent undertaking for the purpose of checking the tax position of one or more subsidiary undertakings whose identities are not known to the officer giving the notice–

(a) sub-paragraphs (3) and (4) of that paragraph (approval of tribunal) have effect as if they permitted, but did not require, the officer to obtain the approval of the tribunal, and

(b) paragraph 31 (appeal) has effect as if it permitted an appeal on any grounds, but the parent undertaking may not appeal against a requirement in the notice to produce any document that forms part of the statutory records of the parent undertaking or any of its subsidiary undertakings.

35(6) [Omitted by FA 2009, s. 95 and Sch. 47, para. 10(5).]

35(7) In this paragraph, **"parent undertaking"**, **"subsidiary undertaking"** and **"undertaking"** have the same meaning as in the Companies Acts (see sections 1161 and 1162 of, and Schedule 7 to, the Companies Act 2006 (c. 46)).

History – In para. 35(4A)(c), the words "paragraphs 21 and 21A" substituted for the words "paragraph 21" and the word "apply" substituted for the word "applies" by FA 2009, s. 96 and Sch. 48, para. 12, with effect from 1 April 2010, by virtue of SI 2009/3054. Para. 35(6) omitted by FA 2009, s. 95 and Sch. 47, para. 10(5), with effect from 21 July 2009.

CHANGE OF OWNERSHIP OF COMPANIES

36 [Not relevant to inheritance tax.]

PARTNERSHIPS

37(1) This paragraph applies where a business is carried on by two or more persons in partnership.

37(2) Where, in respect of a chargeable period, any of the partners has–

(a) made a tax return under section 12AA of TMA 1970 (partnership returns), or

(b) made a claim or election in accordance with section 42(6)(b) of TMA 1970 (partnership claims and elections),

paragraph 21 (restrictions where taxpayer has made tax return) has effect as if that return, claim or election had been made by each of the partners.

37(2A) Where, in respect of a transaction entered into as purchaser by or on behalf of the members of the partnership, any of the partners has–

(a) delivered a land transaction return under Part 4 of FA 2003 (stamp duty land tax), or

(b) made a claim under that Part of that Act,

paragraph 21A (restrictions where taxpayer has delivered land transaction return) has effect as if that return had been delivered, or that claim had been made, by each of the partners.

37(2B) Where, in respect of a single-dwelling interest (see paragraph 21B(7)) to which one or more companies are or were entitled as members of a partnership, any member of the partnership has–

(a) delivered an annual tax on enveloped dwellings return or a return of the adjusted chargeable amount under Part 3 of FA 2013, or

(b) made a claim under that Part of that Act,

paragraph 21B (restrictions where taxpayer has delivered return) has effect as if that return had been delivered, or that claim had been made, by each member of the partnership.

37(3) Where a third party notice is given for the purpose of checking the tax position of more than one of the partners (in their capacity as such)–

(a) paragraph 2(2) only requires the notice to state this and give a name in which the partnership is registered for any purpose, and

(b) the references in paragraph 3(5) to naming the taxpayer are to making that statement and naming the partnership.

37(4) In relation to such a notice given to a person other than one of the partners–

(a) in paragraphs 3 and 4 (approval etc of notices and copying third party notices to taxpayer), the references to the taxpayer have effect as if they were references to at least one of the partners, and

(b) in paragraph 30(2) (no appeal in relation to taxpayer's statutory records), the reference to the taxpayer has effect as if it were a reference to any of the partners in the partnership.

37(5) In relation to a third party notice given to one of the partners for the purpose of checking the tax position of one or more of the other partners (in their capacity as such)–

(a) in paragraph 3 (approval etc of notices), sub-paragraphs (1) and (3)(e) do not apply,

(b) paragraph 4(1) (copying third party notices to taxpayer) does not apply,

(c) paragraph 30(1) (appeal) has effect as if it permitted an appeal on any grounds, and

(d) in paragraph 30(2) (no appeal in relation to taxpayer's statutory records), the reference to the taxpayer has effect as if it were a reference to any of the partners in the partnership.

37(6) Where a notice is given under paragraph 5 to one of the partners for the purpose of checking the tax position of one or more of the other partners whose identities are not known to the officer giving the notice–

(a) sub-paragraphs (3) and (4) of that paragraph (approval of tribunal) have effect as if they permitted, but did not require, the officer to obtain the approval of the tribunal, and

(b) paragraph 31 (appeal) has effect as if it permitted an appeal on any grounds, but the partner to whom the notice is given may not appeal against a requirement in the notice to produce any document that forms part of that partner's statutory records.

37(7) [Omitted by FA 2009, s. 95 and Sch. 47, para. 11(7).]

Prospective amendments – In para. 37(2)(a) the words ", or regulations under paragraph 10 of Schedule A1 to," inserted after the words "section 12AA of" by F(No. 2)A 2017, s. 61 and Sch. 14, para. 38(3), with effect from a day to be appointed under F(No. 2)A 2017, s. 61(6).

History – Para. 37(2A) inserted by FA 2009, s. 96 and Sch. 48, para. 13, with effect from 1 April 2010, by virtue of SI 2009/3054. Para. 37(2B) inserted by FA 2013, s. 164 and Sch. 34, para. 4, with effect from 17 July 2013 (Royal Assent).

INFORMATION IN CONNECTION WITH HERD BASIS ELECTION

37A(1) This paragraph applies to a taxpayer notice given to a person carrying on a trade in relation to which a herd basis election is made if the notice refers only to information or documents that relate to–

(a) the animals kept for the purposes of the trade, or

(b) the products of those animals.

37A(2) Paragraph 21 (restrictions on giving taxpayer notice where taxpayer has made tax return) does not apply in relation to the notice.

37A(3) **"Herd basis election"** means an election under Chapter 8 of Part 2 of ITTOIA 2005 or Chapter 8 of Part 3 of CTA 2009.

INFORMATION FROM PERSONS LIABLE TO COUNTERACTION OF TAX ADVANTAGE

37B(1) This paragraph applies to a taxpayer notice given to a person if–

(a) it appears to an officer of Revenue and Customs that a counteraction provision may apply to the person by reason of one or more transactions, and

(b) the notice refers only to information or documents relating to the transaction (or, if there are two or more transactions, any of them).

37B(2) Paragraph 21 (restrictions on giving taxpayer notice where taxpayer has made tax return) does not apply in relation to the notice.

37B(3) "Counteraction provision" means–

(a) [omitted by CTA 2010, s. 1177 and Sch. 1, para. 582(3)(a) and repealed by CTA 2010, s. 1181 and Sch. 3, Pt. 1,]

(b) section 684 of ITA 2007 (person liable to counteraction of income tax advantage) or

(c) section 733 of CTA 2010 (company liable to counteraction of corporation tax advantage).

History – Para. 37B(3)(a) omitted by CTA 2010, s. 1177 and Sch. 1, para. 582(3)(a) and repealed by CTA 2010, s. 1181 and Sch. 3, Pt. 1, with effect for corporation tax purposes for accounting periods ending on or after 1 April 2010, and for income tax and capital gains tax purposes for the tax year 2010–11 and subsequent tax years.

Para. 37B(3)(c) (and the "or" at the end of para. 37B(3)(b)) inserted by CTA 2010, s. 1177 and Sch. 1, para. 582(3)(b), with effect for corporation tax purposes for accounting periods ending on or after 1 April 2010, and for income tax and capital gains tax purposes for the tax year 2010–11 and subsequent tax years.

APPLICATION TO THE CROWN

38 This Schedule (other than Part 8) applies to the Crown, but not to Her Majesty in Her private capacity (within the meaning of the Crown Proceedings Act 1947 (c. 44)).

Part 7 – Penalties

PENALTIES FOR FAILURE TO COMPLY OR OBSTRUCTION

39(1) This paragraph applies to a person who–

(a) fails to comply with an information notice, or

(b) deliberately obstructs an officer of Revenue and Customs in the course of an inspection under Part 2 of this Schedule that has been approved by the tribunal.

39(2) The person is liable to a penalty of £300.

39(3) The reference in this paragraph to a person who fails to comply with an information notice includes a person who conceals, destroys or otherwise disposes of, or arranges for the concealment, destruction or disposal of, a document in breach of paragraph 42 or 43.

DAILY DEFAULT PENALTIES FOR FAILURE TO COMPLY OR OBSTRUCTION

40(1) This paragraph applies if the failure or obstruction mentioned in paragraph 39(1) continues after the date on which a penalty is imposed under that paragraph in respect of the failure or obstruction.

40(2) The person is liable to a further penalty or penalties not exceeding £60 for each subsequent day on which the failure or obstruction continues.

PENALTIES FOR INACCURATE INFORMATION AND DOCUMENTS

40A(1) This paragraph applies if–

(a) in complying with an information notice, a person provides inaccurate information or produces a document that contains an inaccuracy, and

(b) condition A, B or C is met.

40A(2) Condition A is that the inaccuracy is careless or deliberate.

40A(3) An inaccuracy is careless if it is due to a failure by the person to take reasonable care.

40A(3A) Condition B is that the person knows of the inaccuracy at the time the information is provided or the document produced but does not inform HMRC at that time.

40A(4) Condition C is that the person–

(a) discovers the inaccuracy some time later, and

(b) fails to take reasonable steps to inform HMRC.

40A(5) The person is liable to a penalty not exceeding £3,000.

40A(6) Where the information or document contains more than one inaccuracy, a penalty is payable for each inaccuracy.

History – In para. 40A(1)(b), "A, B or C" substituted for "A or B" by FA 2011, s. 86 and Sch. 24, para. 3(2), with effect in relation to any inaccuracy in information provided, or in documents produced, on or after 1 April 2012.

Para. 40A(3A) inserted by FA 2011, s. 86 and Sch. 24, para. 3(3), with effect in relation to any inaccuracy in information provided, or in documents produced, on or after 1 April 2012.

In para. 40A(4), "C" substituted for "B" by FA 2011, s. 86 and Sch. 24, para. 3(4), with effect in relation to any inaccuracy in information provided, or in documents produced, on or after 1 April 2012.

POWER TO CHANGE AMOUNT OF PENALTIES

41(1) If it appears to the Treasury that there has been a change in the value of money since the last relevant date, they may by regulations substitute for the sums for the time being specified in paragraphs 39(2), 40(2) and 40A(5) such other sums as appear to them to be justified by the change.

41(2) In sub-paragraph (1), in relation to a specified sum, **"relevant date"** means–

(a) the date on which this Act is passed, and

(b) each date on which the power conferred by that sub-paragraph has been exercised in relation to that sum.

41(3) Regulations under this paragraph do not apply to–

(a) any failure or obstruction which began before the date on which they come into force, or

(b) an inaccuracy in any information or document provided to HMRC before that date.

CONCEALING, DESTROYING ETC DOCUMENTS FOLLOWING INFORMATION NOTICE

42(1) A person must not conceal, destroy or otherwise dispose of, or arrange for the concealment, destruction or disposal of, a document that is the subject of an information notice addressed to the person (subject to sub-paragraphs (2) and (3)).

42(2) Sub-paragraph (1) does not apply if the person acts after the document has been produced to an officer of Revenue and Customs in accordance with the information notice, unless an officer of Revenue and Customs has notified the person in writing that the document must continue to be available for inspection (and has not withdrawn the notification).

42(3) Sub-paragraph (1) does not apply, in a case to which paragraph 8(1) applies, if the person acts after the expiry of the period of 6 months beginning with the day on which a copy of the document was produced in accordance with that paragraph unless, before the expiry of that period, an officer of Revenue and Customs made a request for the original document under paragraph 8(2)(b).

CONCEALING, DESTROYING ETC DOCUMENTS FOLLOWING INFORMAL NOTIFICATION

43(1) A person must not conceal, destroy or otherwise dispose of, or arrange for the concealment, destruction or disposal of, a document if an officer of Revenue and Customs has informed the person that the document is, or is likely, to be the subject of an information notice addressed to that person (subject to sub-paragraph (2)).

43(2) Sub-paragraph (1) does not apply if the person acts after–

(a) at least 6 months has expired since the person was, or was last, so informed, or

(b) an information notice has been given to the person requiring the document to be produced.

FAILURE TO COMPLY WITH TIME LIMIT

44 A failure by a person to do anything required to be done within a limited period of time does not give rise to liability to a penalty under paragraph 39 or 40 if the person did it within such further time, if any, as an officer of Revenue and Customs may have allowed.

REASONABLE EXCUSE

45(1) Liability to a penalty under paragraph 39 or 40 does not arise if the person satisfies HMRC or (on an appeal notified to the tribunal) the tribunal that there is a reasonable excuse for the failure or the obstruction of an officer of Revenue and Customs.

45(2) For the purposes of this paragraph–

(a) an insufficiency of funds is not a reasonable excuse unless attributable to events outside the person's control,

(b) where the person relies on any other person to do anything, that is not a reasonable excuse unless the first person took reasonable care to avoid the failure or obstruction, and

(c) where the person had a reasonable excuse for the failure or obstruction but the excuse has ceased, the person is to be treated as having continued to have the excuse if the failure is remedied, or the obstruction stops, without unreasonable delay after the excuse ceased.

ASSESSMENT OF PENALTY

46(1) Where a person becomes liable for a penalty under paragraph 39, 40 or 40A, –

(a) HMRC may assess the penalty, and

(b) if they do so, they must notify the person.

46(2) An assessment of a penalty under paragraph 39 or 40 must be made within the period of 12 months beginning with the date on which the person became liable to the penalty, subject to sub-paragraph (3).

46(3) In a case involving an information notice against which a person may appeal, an assessment of a penalty under paragraph 39 or 40 must be made within the period of 12 months beginning with the latest of the following–

(a) the date on which the person became liable to the penalty,

(b) the end of the period in which notice of an appeal against the information notice could have been given, and

(c) if notice of such an appeal is given, the date on which the appeal is determined or withdrawn.

46(4) An assessment of a penalty under paragraph 40A must be made–

(a) within the period of 12 months beginning with the date on which the inaccuracy first came to the attention of an officer of Revenue and Customs, and

(b) within the period of 6 years beginning with the date on which the person became liable to the penalty.

RIGHT TO APPEAL AGAINST PENALTY

47 A person may appeal against any of the following decisions of an officer of Revenue and Customs–

(a) a decision that a penalty is payable by that person under paragraph 39, 40 or 40A, or

(b) a decision as to the amount of such a penalty.

PROCEDURE ON APPEAL AGAINST PENALTY

48(1) Notice of an appeal under paragraph 47 must be given–

(a) in writing,

(b) before the end of the period of 30 days beginning with the date on which the notification under paragraph 46 was issued, and

(c) to HMRC.

48(2) Notice of an appeal under paragraph 47 must state the grounds of appeal.

48(3) On an appeal under paragraph 47(a), that is notified to the tribunal, the tribunal may confirm or cancel the decision.

48(4) On an appeal under paragraph 47(b), the First-tier Tribunal may–

(a) confirm the decision, or

(b) substitute for the decision another decision that the officer of Revenue and Customs had power to make.

48(5) Subject to this paragraph and paragraph 49, the provisions of Part 5 of TMA 1970 relating to appeals have effect in relation to appeals under this Part of this Schedule as they have effect in relation to an appeal against an assessment to income tax.

ENFORCEMENT OF PENALTY

49(1) A penalty under paragraph 39, 40 or 40A must be paid–

(a) before the end of the period of 30 days beginning with the date on which the notification under paragraph 46 was issued, or

(b) if a notice of an appeal against the penalty is given, before the end of the period of 30 days beginning with the date on which the appeal is determined or withdrawn.

49(2) A penalty under paragraph 39, 40 or 40A may be enforced as if it were income tax charged in an assessment and due and payable.

INCREASED DAILY DEFAULT PENALTY

49A(1) This paragraph applies if–

(a) a penalty under paragraph 40 is assessed under paragraph 46 in respect of a person's failure to comply with a notice under paragraph 5,

(b) the failure continues for more than 30 days beginning with the date on which notification of that assessment was issued, and

(c) the person has been told that an application may be made under this paragraph for an increased daily penalty to be imposed.

49A(2) If this paragraph applies, an officer of Revenue and Customs may make an application to the tribunal for an increased daily penalty to be imposed on the person.

49A(3) If the tribunal decides that an increased daily penalty should be imposed, then for each applicable day (see paragraph 49B) on which the failure continues–

(a) the person is not liable to a penalty under paragraph 40 in respect of the failure, and

(b) the person is liable instead to a penalty under this paragraph of an amount determined by the tribunal.

49A(4) The tribunal may not determine an amount exceeding £1,000 for each applicable day.

49A(5) But subject to that, in determining the amount the tribunal must have regard to–

(a) the likely cost to the person of complying with the notice,

(b) any benefits to the person of not complying with it, and

(c) any benefits to anyone else resulting from the person's non-compliance.

49A(6) Paragraph 41 applies in relation to the sum specified in sub-paragraph (4) as it applies in relation to the sums mentioned in paragraph 41(1).

History – Para. 49A and the heading before it inserted by FA 2011, s. 86 and Sch. 24, para. 4(1), with effect in relation to failures to comply with a notice under para. 5 that begin on or after 1 April 2012.

49B(1) If a person becomes liable to a penalty under paragraph 49A, HMRC must notify the person.

49B(2) The notification must specify the day from which the increased penalty is to apply.

49B(3) That day and any subsequent day is an **"applicable day"** for the purposes of paragraph 49A(3).

History – Inserted by FA 2011, s. 86 and Sch. 24, para. 4(1), with effect in relation to failures to comply with a notice under para. 5 that begin on or after 1 April 2012.

49C(1) A penalty under paragraph 49A must be paid before the end of the period of 30 days beginning with the date on which the notification under paragraph 49B is issued.

49C(2) A penalty under paragraph 49A may be enforced as if it were income tax charged in an assessment and due and payable.

History – Para. 49C inserted by FA 2011, s. 86 and Sch. 24, para. 4(1), with effect in relation to failures to comply with a notice under para. 5 that begin on or after 1 April 2012.

TAX-RELATED PENALTY

50(1) This paragraph applies where–

(a) a person becomes liable to a penalty under paragraph 39,

(b) the failure or obstruction continues after a penalty is imposed under that paragraph,

(c) an officer of Revenue and Customs has reason to believe that, as a result of the failure or obstruction, the amount of tax that the person has paid, or is likely to pay, is significantly less than it would otherwise have been,

(d) before the end of the period of 12 months beginning with the relevant date, an officer of Revenue and Customs makes an application to the Upper Tribunal for an additional penalty to be imposed on the person, and

(e) the Upper Tribunal decides that it is appropriate for an additional penalty to be imposed.

50(2) The person is liable to a penalty of an amount decided by the Upper Tribunal.

50(3) In deciding the amount of the penalty, the Upper Tribunal must have regard to the amount of tax which has not been, or is not likely to be, paid by the person.

50(4) Where a person becomes liable to a penalty under this paragraph, HMRC must notify the person.

50(5) Any penalty under this paragraph is in addition to the penalty or penalties under paragraph 39 or 40.

50(6) In the application of the following provisions, no account shall be taken of a penalty under this paragraph–

(a) section 97A of TMA 1970 (multiple penalties),

(b) paragraph 12(2) of Schedule 24 to FA 2007 (interaction with other penalties), and

(c) paragraph 15(1) of Schedule 41 (interaction with other penalties).

50(7) In sub-paragraph (1)(d) **"the relevant date"** means–

(a) in a case involving an information notice against which a person may appeal, the latest of–

(i) the date on which the person became liable to the penalty under paragraph 39,

(ii) the end of the period in which notice of an appeal against the information notice could have been given, and

(iii) if notice of such an appeal is given, the date on which the appeal is determined or withdrawn, and

(b) in any other case, the date on which the person became liable to the penalty under paragraph 39.

History – In para. 50(1)(d), the words "(within the meaning of paragraph 46)", which appeared after the words "relevant date", omitted by FA 2011, s. 86 and Sch. 24, para. 5(2), with effect where a person becomes liable to a penalty under para. 39 on or after 19 July 2011.

Para. 50(7) inserted by FA 2011, s. 86 and Sch. 24, para. 5(3), with effect where a person becomes liable to a penalty under para. 39 on or after 19 July 2011.

ENFORCEMENT OF TAX-RELATED PENALTY

51(1) A penalty under paragraph 50 must be paid before the end of the period of 30 days beginning with the date on which the notification of the penalty is issued.

51(2) A penalty under paragraph 50 may be enforced as if it were income tax charged in an assessment and due and payable.

DOUBLE JEOPARDY

52 A person is not liable to a penalty under this Schedule in respect of anything in respect of which the person has been convicted of an offence.

Part 8 – Offence

CONCEALING ETC DOCUMENTS FOLLOWING INFORMATION NOTICE

53(1) A person is guilty of an offence (subject to sub-paragraphs (2) and (3)) if–

(a) the person is required to produce a document by an information notice,

(b) the tribunal approved the giving of the notice in accordance with paragraph 3 or 5, and

(c) the person conceals, destroys or otherwise disposes of, or arranges for the concealment, destruction or disposal of, that document.

53(2) Sub-paragraph (1) does not apply if the person acts after the document has been produced to an officer of Revenue and Customs in accordance with the information notice, unless an officer of Revenue and Customs has notified the person in writing that the document must continue to be available for inspection (and has not withdrawn the notification).

53(3) Sub-paragraph (1) does not apply, in a case to which paragraph 8(1) applies, if the person acts after the expiry of the period of 6 months beginning with the day on which a copy of the document was so produced unless, before the expiry of that period, an officer of Revenue and Customs made a request for the original document under paragraph 8(2)(b).

CONCEALING ETC DOCUMENTS FOLLOWING INFORMAL NOTIFICATION

54(1) A person is also guilty of an offence (subject to sub-paragraph (2)) if the person conceals, destroys or otherwise disposes of, or arranges for the concealment, destruction or disposal of a document after the person has been informed by an officer of Revenue and Customs in writing that–

(a) the document is, or is likely, to be the subject of an information notice addressed to that person, and

(b) an officer of Revenue and Customs intends to seek the approval of the tribunal to the giving of the notice under paragraph 3 or 5 in respect of the document.

54(2) A person is not guilty of an offence under this paragraph if the person acts after–

(a) at least 6 months has expired since the person was, or was last, so informed, or

(b) an information notice has been given to the person requiring the document to be produced.

FINE OR IMPRISONMENT

55 A person who is guilty of an offence under this Part of this Schedule is liable–

(a) on summary conviction, to a fine not exceeding the statutory maximum, and

(b) on conviction on indictment, to imprisonment for a term not exceeding 2 years or to a fine, or both.

Part 9 – Miscellaneous Provisions and Interpretation

APPLICATION OF PROVISIONS OF TMA 1970

56 Subject to the provisions of this Schedule, the following provisions of TMA 1970 apply for the purposes of this Schedule as they apply for the purposes of the Taxes Acts–

(a) section 108 (responsibility of company officers),

(b) section 114 (want of form), and

(c) section 115 (delivery and service of documents).

REGULATIONS UNDER THIS SCHEDULE

57(1) Regulations made by the Commissioners or the Treasury under this Schedule are to be made by statutory instrument.

57(2) A statutory instrument containing regulations under this Schedule is subject to annulment in pursuance of a resolution of the House of Commons.

GENERAL INTERPRETATION

58 In this Schedule–

"checking" includes carrying out an investigation or enquiry of any kind,

"the Commissioners" means the Commissioners for Her Majesty's Revenue and Customs,

"document" includes a part of a document (except where the context otherwise requires),

"enactment" includes subordinate legislation (within the meaning of the Interpretation Act 1978 (c. 30)),

"HMRC" means Her Majesty's Revenue and Customs,

"premises" includes–

(a) any building or structure,

(b) any land, and

(c) any means of transport,

"the Taxes Acts" means–

(a) TMA 1970,

(b) the Tax Acts, and

(c) TCGA 1992 and all other enactments relating to capital gains tax

"taxpayer", in relation to a taxpayer notice or a third party notice, has the meaning given in paragraph 1(1) or 2(1) (as appropriate), and

"tribunal" means the First-tier Tribunal or, where determined by or under Tribunal Procedure Rules, the Upper Tribunal.

AUTHORISED OFFICER OF REVENUE AND CUSTOMS

59 A reference in a provision of this Schedule to an authorised officer of Revenue and Customs is a reference to an officer of Revenue and Customs who is, or is a member of a class of officers who are, authorised by the Commissioners for the purpose of that provision.

BUSINESS

60(1) In this Schedule (subject to regulations under this paragraph), references to carrying on a business include–

(a) the letting of property,

(b) the activities of a charity, and

(c) the activities of a government department, a local authority, a local authority association and any other public authority.

60(2) In sub-paragraph (1)–

"local authority" has the meaning given in section 999 of ITA 2007, and

"local authority association" has the meaning given in section 1000 of that Act.

60(3) The Commissioners may by regulations provide that for the purposes of this Schedule–

(a) the carrying on of an activity specified in the regulations, or

(b) the carrying on of such an activity (or any activity) by a person specified in the regulations,

is or is not to be treated as the carrying on of a business.

History – In para. 60(2), the definition of "charity" omitted by FA 2010, s. 30 and Sch. 6, para. 24, with effect from 1 April 2012 (SI 2012/736, art. 19).

CHARGEABLE PERIOD

61 In this Schedule, **"chargeable period"** means–

(a) in relation to income tax or capital gains tax, a tax year, and

(b) in relation to corporation tax, an accounting period.

INVOLVED THIRD PARTIES

61A(1) In this Schedule, **"involved third party"** means a person described in the first column of the Table below.

61A(2) In this Schedule, in relation to an involved third party, **"relevant information"**, **"relevant document"** and **"relevant tax"** have the meaning given in the corresponding entries in that Table.

	Involved third party	*Relevant documents*	*Relevant tax*
1.	A body approved by an officer of Revenue and Customs for the purpose of paying donations within the meaning of Part 12 of ITEPA 2003 (donations to charity: payroll giving) (see section 714 of that Act)	Documents relating to the donations	Income tax
2.	A plan manager (see section 696 of ITTOIA 2005 (managers of individual investment plans))	Documents relating to the plan, including investments which are or have been held under the plan	Income tax
3.	An account provider in relation to a child trust fund (as defined in section 3 of the Child Trust Funds Act 2004)	Documents relating to the fund, including investments which are or have been held under the fund	Income tax
4.	A person who is or has been registered as a managing agent at Lloyd's in relation to a syndicate of underwriting members of Lloyd's	Documents relating to, and to the activities of, the syndicate	Income tax Capital gains tax Corporation tax
5.	A person involved (in any capacity) in an insurance business (as defined for the purposes of Part 3 of FA 1994)	Documents relating to contracts of insurance entered into in the course of the business	Insurance premium tax
6.	A person who makes arrangements for persons to enter into contracts of insurance	Documents relating to the contracts	Insurance premium tax
7.	A person who– (a) is concerned in a business that is not an insurance business (as defined for the purposes of Part 3 of FA 1994), and (b) has been involved in the entry into a contract of insurance providing cover for any matter associated with that business	Documents relating to the contracts	Insurance premium tax

	Involved third party	*Relevant documents*	*Relevant tax*
8.	A person who, in relation to a charge to stamp duty reserve tax on an agreement, transfer, issue, appropriation or surrender, is an accountable person (as defined in regulation 2 of the Stamp Duty Reserve Tax Regulations S.I. 1986/1711 (as amended from time to time))	Documents relating to the agreement, transfer, issue, appropriation or surrender	Stamp duty reserve tax
9.	A responsible person in relation to an oil field (as defined for the purposes of Part 1 of OTA 1975)	Documents relating to the oil field	Petroleum revenue tax
10.	A person involved (in any capacity) in subjecting aggregate to exploitation in the United Kingdom (as defined for the purposes of Part 2 of FA 2001) or in connected activities	Documents relating to matters in which the person is or has been involved	Aggregates levy
11.	A person involved (in any capacity) in making or receiving supplies of taxable commodities (as defined for the purposes of Schedule 6 to FA 2000) or in connected activities	Documents relating to matters in which the person is or has been involved	Climate change levy
12.	A person involved (in any capacity) with any landfill disposal (as defined for the purposes of Part 3 of FA 1996)	Documents relating to the disposal	Landfill tax.

History – In para. 61A(2), the words "“relevant information”," omitted by FA 2011, s. 86 and Sch. 23, para. 62(3)(a), with effect from 1 April 2012, subject to transitional provisions in FA 2011, Sch. 23, para. 65.
In para. 61A(2), in each entry in the second column of the Table, the word “Documents” substituted for the words “Information and documents” by FA 2011, s. 86 and Sch. 23, para. 62(3)(b), with effect from 1 April 2012, subject to transitional provisions in FA 2011, Sch. 23, para. 65.
In para. 61A(2), in the heading to the second column of the Table, the words “information and relevant” omitted by FA 2011, s. 86 and Sch. 23, para. 62(3)(c), with effect from 1 April 2012, subject to transitional provisions in FA 2011, Sch. 23, para. 65.
In para. 61A(2), in the first column of item 11 of the Table, the words “supplies of” inserted by FA 2011, s. 86 and Sch. 24, para. 6, with effect from 19 July 2011.
Para. 61A inserted by FA 2009, s. 96 and Sch. 48, para. 14 with effect from 1 April 2010, by virtue of SI 2009/3054.

STATUTORY RECORDS

62(1) For the purposes of this Schedule, information or a document forms part of a person’s statutory records if it is information or a document which the person is required to keep and preserve under or by virtue of–

(a) the Taxes Acts, or

(b) any other enactment relating to a tax,

subject to the following provisions of this paragraph.

62(2) To the extent that any information or document that is required to be kept and preserved under or by virtue of the Taxes Acts–

(a) does not relate to the carrying on of a business, and

(b) is not also required to be kept or preserved under or by virtue of any other enactment relating to a tax,

it only forms part of a person’s statutory records to the extent that the chargeable period or periods to which it relates has or have ended.

62(3) Information and documents cease to form part of a person’s statutory records when the period for which they are required to be preserved by the enactments mentioned in sub-paragraph (1) has expired.

History – Para. 62(1)(b) substituted by FA 2009, s. 96 and Sch. 48, para. 15(2) with effect from 1 April 2010, by virtue of SI 2009/3054.
In para. 62(2)(b), the words “any other enactment relating to a tax” substituted for the words “VATA 1994 or any other enactment relating to value added tax” by FA 2009, s. 96 and Sch. 48, para. 15(3), with effect from 1 April 2010, by virtue of SI 2009/3054.

TAX

63(1) In this Schedule, except where the context otherwise requires, **"tax"** means all or any of the following–

(a) income tax,

(b) capital gains tax,

(c) corporation tax,

(ca) diverted profits tax,

(cb) apprenticeship levy,

(d) VAT,

(e) insurance premium tax,

(f) inheritance tax,

(g) stamp duty land tax,

(h) stamp duty reserve tax,

(ha) annual tax on enveloped dwellings,

(i) petroleum revenue tax,

(j) aggregates levy,

(k) climate change levy,

(l) landfill tax, and

(m) relevant foreign tax,

and references to **"a tax"** are to be interpreted accordingly.

63(2) In this Schedule, **"corporation tax"** includes any amount assessable or chargeable as if it were corporation tax.

63(3) In this Schedule, **"VAT"** means–

(a) value added tax charged in accordance with VATA 1994,

(b) value added tax charged in accordance with the law of another member State, and

(c) amounts listed in sub-paragraph (3A).

63(3A) Those amounts are–

(a) any amount that is recoverable under paragraph 5(2) of Schedule 11 to VATA 1994 (amounts shown on invoices as VAT), and

(b) any amount that is treated as VAT by virtue of regulations under section 54 of VATA 1994 (farmers etc).

63(4) In this Schedule, **"relevant foreign tax"** means–

(a) a tax of a member State, other than the United Kingdom, which is covered by the provisions for the exchange of information under Council Directive 2011/16/EU of 15 February 2011 on administrative cooperation in the field of taxation (as amended from time to time), and

(b) any tax or duty which is imposed under the law of a territory in relation to which arrangements having effect by virtue of section 173 of FA 2006 (international tax enforcement arrangements) have been made and which is covered by the arrangements.

Prospective amendments – Para. 63(1)(ia) inserted by FA 2017, s. 56 and Sch. 11, para. 1(3), with effect from a day to be appointed under FA 2017, s. 61(1). Para. 63(1)(ia) to read as follows:

"(ia) soft drinks industry levy,"

History – Para. 63(1)(ca) inserted by FA 2015, s. 105(2), with effect in relation to accounting periods beginning on or after 1 April 2015 (subject to the provisions of FA 2015, s. 116(2)–(5)).

Para. 63(1)(cb) inserted by FA 2016, s. 112, with effect from 15 September 2016 (Royal Assent).

Para. 63(1)(e)–(m) substituted for former s. 63(1)(e) (and the "and" before it) by FA 2009, s. 96(1), with effect from 1 April 2010, by virtue of SI 2009/3054. The wording of former s. 63(1)(e) was "relevant foreign tax".

Para. 63(1)(ha) inserted by FA 2013, s. 164 and Sch. 34, para. 5, with effect from 17 July 2013 (Royal Assent).

In para. 63(4), the words "Council Directive 2011/16/EU of 15 February 2011 on administrative cooperation in the field of taxation" substituted for the words "the Directive of the Council of the European Communities dated 19 December 1977 No. 77/799/EEC" by SI 2012/3062, reg. 6(1), with effect from 1 January 2013.

TAX POSITION

64(1) In this Schedule, except as otherwise provided, **"tax position"**, in relation to a person, means the person's position as regards any tax, including the person's position as regards–

(a) past, present and future liability to pay any tax,

(b) penalties and other amounts that have been paid, or are or may be payable, by or to the person in connection with any tax, and

(c) claims, elections, applications and notices that have been or may be made or given in connection with the person's liability to pay any tax,

and references to a person's position as regards a particular tax (however expressed) are to be interpreted accordingly.

64(2) References in this Schedule to a person's tax position include, where appropriate, a reference to the person's position as regards any deductions or repayments of tax, or of sums representing tax, that the person is required to make–

(a) under PAYE regulations,

(b) under Chapter 3 of Part 3 of FA 2004 or regulations made under that Chapter (construction industry scheme), or

(c) by or under any other provision of the Taxes Acts.

64(2A) References in this Schedule to a person's tax position also include, where appropriate, a reference to the person's position as regards the withholding by the person of another person's PAYE income (as defined in section 683 of ITEPA 2003).

64(3) References in this Schedule to the tax position of a person include the tax position of–

(a) a company that has ceased to exist, and

(b) an individual who has died.

64(4) References in this Schedule to a person's tax position are to the person's tax position at any time or in relation to any period, unless otherwise stated.

Part 10 – Consequential Provisions

TMA 1970

65 TMA 1970 is amended as follows.

66 [Omits TMA 1970, s. 19A.]

67 [Omits TMA 1970, s. 20.]

68(1) Section 20B (restrictions on powers to call for documents under ss20 and 20A) is amended as follows.

68(2) [Amends heading to TMA 1970, s. 20B.]

68(3) [Amends TMA 1970, s. 20B(1).]

68(4) [Omits TMA 1970, s. 20B(1A), (1B).]

68(5) [Amends TMA 1970, s. 20B(2).]

68(6) [Amends TMA 1970, s. 20B(3).]

68(7) [Omits TMA 1970, s. 20B(4).]

68(8) [Omits TMA 1970, s. 20B(5), (6), (7).]

68(9) [Amends TMA 1970, s. 20B(8).]

68(10) [Omits TMA 1970, s. 20B(9)–(14).]

69(1) Section 20BB (falsification etc. of documents) is amended as follows.

69(2) [Amends TMA 1970, s. 20BB(1)(a).]

69(3) [Amends TMA 1970, s. 20BB(2)(b).]

70(1) Section 20D (interpretation) is amended as follows.

70(2) [Amends TMA 1970, s. 20D(2).]

70(3) [Omits TMA 1970, s. 20D(3).]

71 [Amends TMA 1970, s. 29(6)(c).]

72 [Omits TMA 1970, s. 97AA.]

73 [Amends TMA 1970, s. 98.]

74 [Omitted by FA 2009, s. 109 and Sch. 57, para. 14(a).]

75(1) Section 107A (relevant trustees) is amended as follows.

75(2) [Amends TMA 1970, s. 107A(2)(a).]

75(3) [Omits TMA 1970, s. 107A(3)(a).]

76 [Amends TMA 1970, s. 118.]

77 [Amends TMA 1970, Sch. 1A, para. 6, 6A.]

NATIONAL SAVINGS BANK ACT 1971 (C. 29)

78 [Amends National Savings Bank Act 1971, s. 12(3).]

ICTA

79 ICTA is amended as follows.

80 [Repealed by CTA 2010, s. 1181 and Sch. 3, Pt. 1.]

History – Para. 80 repealed by CTA 2010, s. 1181 and Sch. 3, Pt. 1, with effect for corporation tax purposes for accounting periods ending on or after 1 April 2010, and for income tax and capital gains tax purposes for the tax year 2010–11 and subsequent tax years.

81 [Omits ICTA 1988, s. 767C.]

82 [Repealed by CTA 2010, s. 1181 and Sch. 3, Pt. 1.]

History – Para. 82 repealed by CTA 2010, s. 1181 and Sch. 3, Pt. 1, with effect for corporation tax purposes for accounting periods ending on or after 1 April 2010, and for income tax and capital gains tax purposes for the tax year 2010–11 and subsequent tax years.

FA 1990

83 [Amends FA 1990, s. 125(1), (2), (3), (4), (6); partially omitted by SI 2009/2035, art. 2 and Sch., para. 60(p).]

SOCIAL SECURITY ADMINISTRATION ACT 1992 (C. 5)

84 [Amends SSAA 1992, s. 110ZA.]

SOCIAL SECURITY ADMINISTRATION (NORTHERN IRELAND) ACT 1992 (C. 8)

85 [Amends Social Security (Northern Ireland) Act 1992, s. 104ZA.]

F(NO. 2)A 1992

86 [Omits F(No. 2)A 1992, s. 28(1)–(3).]

VATA 1994

87 [Amends VATA 1994, Sch. 11, para. 7, 10.]

FA 1998

88 [Omits FA 1998, Sch. 18, para. 27, 28, 29.]

FA 1999

89 [Omits FA 1990, s. 13(5)(c).]

TAX CREDITS ACT 2002 (C. 21)

90 [Omits TCA 2002, s. 25(3), (4).]

FA 2006

91 [Omits FA 2006, s. 174.]

OTHER REPEALS

92 In consequence of the preceding provisions of this Part of this Schedule, omit the following–

(a) [omits FA 1988, s. 126;]

(b) [omits FA 1989, s. 142(2), (3), (4), (6)(a), (7), (8), (9) and 144(3), (5), (7);]

(c) [omits FA 1994, s. 187, 255, Sch. 19, para. 29;]

(d) [omits Civil Evidence Act 1995, Sch. 1, para. 6;]

(e) [omits FA 1996, Sch. 3, para. 17, Sch. 19, para. 3 and Sch. 22, para. 2;]

(f) [omits FA 1998, s. 115, Sch. 19, para. 36, 42(6), (7);]

(g) [omits FA 1999, s. 15(3);]

(h) [omits FA 2001, Sch. 29, para. 21, 38(4);]

(i) [omits FA 2006, s. 20;]

(j) [omits ITA 2007, Sch. 1, para. 350.]

SCHEDULE 38 – DISCLOSURE OF TAX AVOIDANCE SCHEMES

Section 116

Commencement Date – The day appointed for the amendments made by Sch. 38 is 1 November 2008, for purposes other than stamp duty land tax (SI 2008/1935).

AMENDMENTS OF PART 7 OF FA 2004

1 Part 7 of FA 2004 (disclosure of tax avoidance schemes) is amended as follows.

Commencement Date – See headnote to Sch. 38.

2(1) Section 308 (duties of promoter) is amended as follows.

2(2) [Amends FA 2004, s. 308(1).]

2(3) [Amends FA 1998, s. 308(2)(a).]

2(4) [Amends FA 1998, s. 308(3).]

2(5) [Substitutes FA 1998, s. 308(4), (4A), (4B), (4C).]

Commencement Date – See headnote to Sch. 38.

3 [Amends FA 2004, s. 311(1).]

Commencement Date – See headnote to Sch. 38.

4 [Substitutes FA 2004, s. 312, 312A.]

Commencement Date – See headnote to Sch. 38.

5(1) Section 313 (duty of parties to notifiable arrangements to notify HMRC of number etc) is amended as follows.

5(2) [Amends FA 2004, s. 313(1)(a).]

5(3) [Amends FA 2004, s. 313(3).]

5(4) [Inserts FA 2004, s. 313(5).]

Commencement Date – See headnote to Sch. 38.

6 [Substitutes FA 2004, s. 316.]

Commencement Date – See headnote to Sch. 38.

AMENDMENTS OF TMA 1970

7(1) Section 98C of TMA 1970 (penalties for failure to comply with duties under Part 7 of FA 2004) is amended as follows.

7(2) [Amends TMA 1970, s. 98C(2).]

7(3) [Amends FA 1998, s. 98C(3).]

7(4) [Amends TMA 1970, s. 98C(4).]

Commencement Date – See headnote to Sch. 38.

SCHEDULE 40 – PENALTIES: AMENDMENTS OF SCHEDULE 24 TO FA 2007

Section 122

Commencement Date – Sch. 40 came into effect on 1 April 2009 (SI 2009/571, art. 2–5 subject to transitional rules at SI 2009/571, art. 6 and 7).

1 Schedule 24 to FA 2007 (penalties for errors) is amended as follows.

2(1) Paragraph 1 (error in taxpayer's document) is amended as follows.

2(2) [Amends FA 2007, Sch. 24, para. 1(2).]

2(3) [Amends FA 2007, Sch. 24, para. 1(3).]

2(4) [Amends FA 2007, Sch. 24, para. 1, Table.]

2(5) [Amends FA 2007, Sch. 24, para. 1, Table.]

2(6) [Amends FA 2007, Sch. 24, para. 1, Table.]

2(7) [Inserts FA 2007, Sch. 24, para. 1(5).]

3 [Inserts FA 2007, Sch. 24, para. 1A.]

4(1) Paragraph 2 (under-assessment by HMRC) is amended as follows.

4(2) [Amends FA 2007, Sch. 24, para. 2(1).]

4(3) [Substitutes FA 2007, Sch. 24, para. 1(3).]

5(1) Paragraph 3 (degrees of culpability) is amended as follows.

5(2) [Amends FA 2007, Sch. 24, para. 3(1).]

5(3) [Amends FA 2007, Sch. 24, para. 3(2).]

6 [Inserts FA 2007, Sch. 24, para. 4(1A).]

7 [Amends FA 2007, Sch. 24, para. 5(1).]

8(1) Paragraph 6 (potential lost revenue: multiple errors) is amended as follows.

8(2) [Amends FA 2007, Sch. 24, para. 6(1), (2).]

8(3) [Amends FA 2007, Sch. 24, para. 6(5).]

9(1) Paragraph 9 (reductions for disclosure) is amended as follows.

9(2) [Inserts FA 2007, Sch. 24, para. 9(A1).]

9(3) [Amends FA 2007, Sch. 24, para. 9(1).]

9(4) [Amends FA 2007, Sch. 24, para. 9(2)(a).]

10 [Amends FA 2007, Sch. 24, para. 11(1).]

11(1) Paragraph 12 (interaction with other penalties) is amended as follows.

11(2) [Amends FA 2007, Sch. 24, para. 12(2).]

11(3) [Inserts FA 2007, Sch. 24, para. 12(4).]

11(4) [Amends heading before FA 2007, Sch. 24, para. 12.]

12(1) Paragraph 13 (assessment) is amended as follows.

12(2) [Amends FA 2007, Sch. 24, para. 13(1).]

12(3) [Inserts FA 2007, Sch. 24, para. 13(1A).]

12(4) [Amends FA 2007, Sch. 24, para. 13(3).]

12(5) [Amends FA 2007, Sch. 24, para. 13(4).]

13 [Amends FA 2007, Sch. 24, para. 15.]

14 [Omitted by SI 2009/56, art. 3(1) and Sch. 1, para. 472.]

History – Para. 14 omitted by SI 2009/56, art. 3(1) and Sch. 1, para. 472, operative from 1 April 2009, subject to transitional and saving provisions in SI 2009/56, Sch. 3. Former para. 14 read as follows:

"**14** For paragraph 16 substitute–

"**16(1)** An appeal is to be brought to the First-tier tribunal.

16(2) An appeal shall be treated for procedural purposes in the same way as an appeal against an assessment to the tax concerned (except in respect of a matter expressly provided for by this Act).""."

15 [Amends FA 2007, Sch. 24, para. 18(3).]

16(1) Paragraph 19 (companies: officers' liability) is amended as follows.

16(2) [Amends FA 2007, Sch. 24, para. 19(1).]

16(3) [Substitutes FA 2007, Sch. 24, para. 19(5).]

17 [Amends FA 2007, Sch. 24, para. 21.]

18 [Amends FA 2007, Sch. 24, para. 22.]

19 [Inserts FA 2007, Sch. 24, para. 23.]

20(1) Paragraph 28 (interpretation) is amended as follows.

20(2) [Amends FA 2007, Sch. 24, para. 28(c).]

20(3) [Omitted by FA 2009, s. 109 and Sch. 57, para. 14(b).]

20(4) [Amends FA 2007, Sch. 24, para. 28(f).]

20(5) [Inserts FA 2007, Sch. 24, para. 28(fa).]

History – Para. 20(3) omitted by FA 2009, s. 109 and Sch. 57, para. 14(b), with effect from 21 July 2009.

21 In consequence of this Schedule the following provisions are omitted–

(a) [not relevant to inheritance tax;]

(b) [not relevant to inheritance tax;]

(c) [omits IHTA 1984, s. 247(1) and (2), 250(2); amends IHTA 1984, s. 248(1) and (2);]

(d) [not relevant to inheritance tax;]

(e) [not relevant to inheritance tax;]

(f) [not relevant to inheritance tax;]

(g) [omits FA 1999, s. 108(2)(a);]

(h) [not relevant to inheritance tax;]

(i) [not relevant to inheritance tax;]

(j) [not relevant to inheritance tax;]

(k) [not relevant to inheritance tax;]

(l) [omits FA 2004, s. 295(4)(a).]

SCHEDULE 44 – CERTIFICATES OF DEBT: CONSEQUENTIAL PROVISION

Section 138

IHTA 1984

3 [Amends IHTA 1984, s. 254(3).]

FINANCE ACT 2009

(2009 Chapter 10)

[*21st July 2009*]

ARRANGEMENT OF SECTIONS

PART 7 – ADMINISTRATION

PART 7 – ADMINISTRATION

STANDARDS AND VALUES

94 Publishing details of deliberate tax defaulters

94(1) *The Commissioners may publish* information about any person if–

(a) in consequence of an investigation conducted by the Commissioners, one or more relevant tax penalties is found to have been incurred by the person, and

(b) the potential lost revenue in relation to the penalty (or the aggregate of the potential lost revenue in relation to each of the penalties) exceeds £25,000.

94(2) A **"relevant tax penalty"** is–

(a) a penalty under paragraph 1 of Schedule 24 to FA 2007 (inaccuracy in taxpayer's document) in respect of a deliberate inaccuracy on the part of the person,

(b) a penalty under paragraph 1A of that Schedule (inaccuracy in taxpayer's document attributable to deliberate supply of false information or deliberate withholding of information by person),

(c) a penalty under paragraph 1 of Schedule 41 to FA 2008 (failure to notify) in respect of a deliberate failure on the part of the person, or

(d) a penalty under paragraph 2 (unauthorised VAT invoice), 3 (putting product to use attracting higher duty etc) or 4 (handling goods subject to unpaid excise duty) of that Schedule in respect of deliberate action by the person.

94(3) **"Potential lost revenue"**, in relation to a penalty, has the meaning given by–

(a) paragraphs 5 to 8 of Schedule 24 to FA 2007, or

(b) paragraphs 7 to 11 of Schedule 41 to FA 2008,

in relation to the inaccuracy, failure or action to which the penalty relates.

94(4) The information that may be published is–

(a) the person's name (including any trading name, previous name or pseudonym),

(b) the person's address (or registered office),

(c) the nature of any business carried on by the person,

(d) the amount of the penalty or penalties and the potential lost revenue in relation to the penalty (or the aggregate of the potential lost revenue in relation to each of the penalties),

(e) the periods or times to which the inaccuracy, failure or action giving rise to the penalty (or any of the penalties) relates, and

(f) any such other information as the Commissioners consider it appropriate to publish in order to make clear the person's identity.

94(4A) Subsection (4B) applies where a person who is a body corporate or a partnership has incurred–

(a) a penalty under paragraph 1 of Schedule 24 to FA 2007 in respect of a deliberate inaccuracy which involves an offshore matter or an offshore transfer (within the meaning of paragraph 4A of that Schedule), or

(b) a penalty under paragraph 1 of Schedule 41 to FA 2008 in respect of a deliberate failure which involves an offshore matter or an offshore transfer (within the meaning of paragraph 6A of that Schedule).

94(4B) The Commissioners may publish the information mentioned in subsection (4) in respect of any individual who–

(a) controls the body corporate or the partnership (within the meaning of section 1124 of CTA 2010), and

(b) has obtained a tax advantage as a result of the inaccuracy or failure.

94(4C) Subsection (4D) applies where one or more trustees of a settlement have incurred–

(a) a penalty under paragraph 1 of Schedule 24 to FA 2007 in respect of a deliberate inaccuracy which involves an offshore matter or an offshore transfer (within the meaning of paragraph 4A of that Schedule), or

(b) a penalty under paragraph 1 of Schedule 41 to FA 2008 in respect of a deliberate failure which involves an offshore matter or an offshore transfer (within the meaning of paragraph 6A of that Schedule).

94(4D) The Commissioners may publish the information mentioned in subsection (4) in respect of any trustee who is an individual and who has obtained a tax advantage as a result of the inaccuracy or failure.

94(5) The information may be published in any manner that the Commissioners consider appropriate.

94(6) Before publishing any information about a person under subsection (1), the Commissioners–

(a) must inform the person that they are considering doing so, and

(b) afford the person reasonable opportunity to make representations about whether it should be published.

94(6A) Before publishing any information about an individual under subsection (4B) or (4D), the Commissioners–

(a) must inform the individual that they are considering doing so, and

(b) afford the individual reasonable opportunity to make representations about whether it should be published.

94(7) No information may be published before the day when the penalty becomes final (or the latest day when any of the penalties becomes final).

94(8) No information may be published for the first time after the end of the period of one year beginning with that day (or that latest day).

94(9) No information may be published (or continue to be published) after the end of the period of one year beginning with the day on which it is first published.

94(10) No information may be published if the amount of the penalty is reduced under–

(a) paragraph 10 of Schedule 24 to FA 2007,

(aa) paragraph 10A of that Schedule to the full extent permitted following an unprompted disclosure,

(b) paragraph 13 of Schedule 41 to FA 2008, or

(c) paragraph 13A of that Schedule to the full extent permitted following an unprompted disclosure.

(reductions for disclosure) to the full extent permitted.

94(11) For the purposes of this section, a penalty becomes final–

(a) if it has been assessed, when the time for any appeal or further appeal relating to it expires or, if later, any appeal or final appeal relating to it is finally determined, or

(b) if a contract is made between the Commissioners and the person under which the Commissioners undertake not to assess the penalty or (if it has been assessed) not to take proceedings to recover it, at the time when the contract is made.

94(12) The Treasury may by order vary the amount for the time being specified in subsection (1).

94(13) This section comes into force on a day appointed by order made by the Treasury.

94(14) Orders under this section are to be made by statutory instrument.

94(15) A statutory instrument containing an order under subsection (12) is subject to annulment in pursuance of a resolution of the House of Commons.

94(16) In this section–

"the Commissioners" means the Commissioners for Her Majesty's Revenue and Customs;

"tax advantage" has the meaning given by section 208 of FA 2013.

History – S. 94(4A)–(4D) inserted by FA 2016, s. 164(2), with effect from 1 April 2017 (SI 2017/261, reg. 2).
In s. 94(6), the words "about a person under subsection (1)," inserted by FA 2016, s. 164(3), with effect from 1 April 2017 (SI 2017/261, reg. 2).
S. 94(6A) inserted by FA 2016, s. 164(4), with effect from 1 April 2017 (SI 2017/261, reg. 2).
S. 94(10)(aa) inserted (and the "or" after (a) omitted) by FA 2016, s. 164(5)(a), with effect from 1 April 2017 (SI 2017/261, reg. 2).
S. 94(10)(c) (and the ", or" before it) inserted by FA 2016, s. 164(5)(b), with effect from 1 April 2017 (SI 2017/261, reg. 2).
S. 94(16) substituted by FA 2016, s. 164(6), with effect from 1 April 2017 (SI 2017/261, reg. 2). Former s. 94(16) read as follows:
"**94(16)** In this section **"the Commissioners"** means the Commissioners for Her Majesty's Revenue and Customs.".

INFORMATION ETC

96 Extension of information and inspection powers to further taxes

96(1) [Amends FA 2008, Sch. 36, para. 63(1).]

96(2) Schedule 48 contains further amendments of that Schedule.

96(3) The amendments made by this section and Schedule 48 come into force on such day as the Treasury may by order appoint.

96(4) An order under subsection (3) may–

(a) appoint different days for different purposes, and

(b) contain transitional provision and savings.

96(5) The Treasury may by order make any incidental, supplemental, consequential, transitional or transitory provision or saving which appears appropriate in consequence of, or otherwise in connection with, this section and Schedule 48.

96(6) An order under subsection (5) may–

(a) make different provision for different purposes, and

(b) make provision amending, repealing or revoking an enactment or instrument (whenever passed or made).

96(7) An order under this section is to be made by statutory instrument.

96(8) A statutory instrument containing an order under subsection (5) is subject to annulment in pursuance of a resolution of the House of Commons.

Commencement Date – SI 2009/3054 sets 1 April 2010 as the appointed day for the amendments made by s. 96 and Sch. 48 and contains savings provisions.

Statutory instruments – SI 2009/3054: made under s. 96(3)–(6).

ASSESSMENTS, CLAIMS ETC

99 Time limits for assessments, claims etc

99(1) Schedule 51 contains provision about time limits for assessments, claims etc.

99(2) The amendments made by that Schedule come into force on such day as the Treasury may by order made by statutory instrument appoint.

99(3) An order under subsection (2)–

(a) may make different provision for different purposes, and

(b) may include transitional provision and savings.

Statutory instruments – SI 2010/867: made under s. 99(2) and (3).

INTEREST

101 Late payment interest on sums due to HMRC

101(1) This section applies to any amount that is payable by a person to HMRC under or by virtue of an enactment.

101(2) But this section does not apply to–

(a) [not relevant to inheritance tax,]

(b) [not relevant to inheritance tax,]

(c) an amount of any description specified in an order made by the Treasury.

101(3) An amount to which this section applies carries interest at the late payment interest rate from the late payment interest start date until the date of payment.

101(4) The late payment interest start date in respect of any amount is the date on which that amount becomes due and payable.

101(5) In Schedule 53–

(a) Part 1 makes special provision as to the amount on which late payment interest is calculated,

(b) Part 2 makes special provision as to the late payment interest start date,

(c) Part 3 makes special provision as to the date to which late payment interest runs, and

(d) Part 4 makes provision about the effect that the giving of a relief has on late payment interest.

101(6) Subsection (3) applies even if the late payment interest start date is a non-business day within the meaning of section 92 of the Bills of Exchange Act 1882.

101(7) Late payment interest is to be paid without any deduction of income tax.

101(8) Late payment interest is not payable on late payment interest.

101(9) For the purposes of this section any reference to the payment of an amount to HMRC includes a reference to its being set off against an amount payable by HMRC (and, accordingly, the reference to the date on which an amount is paid includes a reference to the date from which the set-off takes effect).

Commencement Date – The day appointed as the day on which s. 101 comes into force for the purposes of penalties assessed under FA 2012, Sch. 38, Pt. 3–5 (tax agents dishonest conduct) is 1 April 2013 (SI 2013/280).

Cross references – SI 2010/1878, art. 3: interest charged under s. 101 on an amount enforceable as if it were bank payroll tax may be enforced as if it were an amount of bank payroll tax.
SI 2010/1879, reg. 3: sets late payment interest rate for the purposes of s. 101.

102 Repayment interest on sums to be paid by HMRC

102(1) This section applies to–

(a) any amount that is payable by HMRC to any person under or by virtue of an enactment, and

(b) a relevant amount paid by a person to HMRC that is repaid by HMRC to that person or to another person.

102(2) But this section does not apply to–

(a) [not relevant to inheritance tax,]

(b) [not relevant to inheritance tax,]

(c) an amount of any description specified in an order made by the Treasury.

102(3) An amount to which this section applies carries interest at the repayment interest rate from the repayment interest start date until the date on which the payment or repayment is made.

102(4) In Schedule 54–

(a) Parts 1 and 2 define the repayment interest start date, and

(b) Part 3 makes supplementary provision.

IHT Statutes

102(5) Subsection (3) applies even if the repayment interest start date is a non-business day within the meaning of section 92 of the Bills of Exchange Act 1882.

102(6) Repayment interest is not payable on an amount payable in consequence of an order or judgment of a court having power to allow interest on the amount.

102(7) Repayment interest is not payable on repayment interest.

102(8) For the purposes of this section–

(a) **"relevant amount"** means any sum that was paid in connection with any liability (including any purported or anticipated liability) to make a payment to HMRC under or by virtue of an enactment, and

(b) any reference to the payment or repayment of an amount by HMRC includes a reference to its being set off against an amount owed to HMRC (and, accordingly, the reference to the date on which an amount is paid or repaid by HMRC includes a reference to the date from which the set-off takes effect).

Cross references – SI 2010/1879, reg. 4: sets repayment interest rate for the purposes of s. 102.

103 Rates of interest

103(1) The late payment interest rate is the rate provided for in regulations made by the Treasury under this subsection.

103(2) The repayment interest rate is the rate provided for in regulations made by the Treasury under this subsection.

103(3) Regulations under subsection (1) or (2)–

(a) may make different provision for different purposes,

(b) may either themselves specify a rate of interest or make provision for such a rate to be determined (and to change from time to time) by reference to such rate, or the average of such rates, as may be referred to in the regulations,

(c) may provide for rates to be reduced below, or increased above, what they otherwise would be by specified amounts or by reference to specified formulae,

(d) may provide for rates arrived at by reference to averages to be rounded up or down,

(e) may provide for circumstances in which alteration of a rate of interest is or is not to be take place, and

(f) may provide that alterations of rates are to have effect for periods beginning on or after a day determined in accordance with the regulations in relation to interest running from before that day as well as from or from after that day.

Commencement Date – S. 103 came into force generally on 6 October 2011 (SI 2011/2401).

Cross references – F(No. 2)A 2015, s. 52(3), (4), (5): application of late payment interest rate provided for in regulations made under s. 103(1) (in substitution for the rate specified in section 17(1) of the Judgments Act 1838 and any other rate specified in an order under section 74 of the County Courts Act 1984) in relation to tax-related judgment debts payable to the Commissioners.

Statutory instruments – SI 2011/2446: made under s. 103.

103A Further provision as to late payment interest and repayment interest

103A [Not relevant to inheritance tax.]

104 Supplementary

104(1) In sections 101 to 103–

"HMRC" means Her Majesty's Revenue and Customs;

"late payment interest" means interest payable under section 101;

"repayment interest" means interest payable under section 102;

"revenue" has the meaning given in section 5(4) of CRCA 2005.

104(2) A reference to the date on which an amount becomes due and payable is a reference to the date (however described) on or before which the amount must be paid.

104(3) Sections 101 to 103 come into force on such day as the Treasury may by order appoint.

104(4) An order under subsection (3)–

(a) may commence a provision generally or only for specified purposes, and

(b) may appoint different days for different provisions or for different purposes.

104(5) The Treasury may by order make any incidental, supplemental, consequential, transitional, transitory or saving provision which may appear appropriate in consequence of, or otherwise in connection with, those sections.

104(6) An order under subsection (5) may include provision amending, repealing or revoking any provision of any Act or subordinate legislation whenever passed or made (including this Act and any Act amended by it).

104(7) An order under subsection (5) may make different provision for different purposes.

104(8) The following are to be made by statutory instrument–

(a) orders under section 101(2) or 102(2),

(b) regulations under section 103(1) or (2), and

(c) orders under subsection (3) or (5).

104(9) A statutory instrument containing–

(a) an order under section 101(2) or 102(2),

(b) regulations under section 103(1) or (2),

(c) an order under subsection (5) which includes provision amending or repealing any provision of an Act,

is subject to annulment in pursuance of a resolution of the House of Commons.

Prospective amendments – In s. 104(1), "103A (and Schedules 53 to 54A)" substituted for "103" by F(No. 3)A 2010, s. 25 and Sch. 9, para. 5, with effect from a day to be appointed by Treasury order.

Statutory instruments – SI 2010/1878: made under s. 104(3)–(5).
SI 2011/2401 (not reproduced): made partly under s. 104(3)–(5).

INTEREST

105 Miscellaneous amendments

105(1) [Not relevant to inheritance tax.]

105(2) [Not relevant to inheritance tax.]

105(3) [Not relevant to inheritance tax.]

105(4) [Amends IHTA 1984, s. 235(1).]

105(5) [Not relevant to inheritance tax.]

105(6) [Omits FA 1989, s. 178(5).]

PENALTIES

106 Penalties for failure to make returns etc

106(1) Schedule 55 contains provision for imposing penalties on persons in respect of failures to make returns and other documents relating to liabilities for tax.

106(2) That Schedule comes into force on such day as the Treasury may by order appoint.

106(3) An order under subsection (2)–

(a) may commence a provision generally or only for specified purposes, and

(b) may appoint different days for different provisions or for different purposes.

106(4) The Treasury may by order make any incidental, supplemental, consequential, transitional, transitory or saving provision which may appear appropriate in consequence of, or otherwise in connection with, Schedule 55.

106(5) An order under subsection (4) may include provision amending, repealing or revoking any provision of any Act or subordinate legislation whenever passed or made (including this Act and any Act amended by it).

106(6) An order under subsection (4) may make different provision for different purposes.

106(7) An order under this section is to be made by statutory instrument.

106(8) A statutory instrument containing an order under subsection (4) which includes provision amending or repealing any provision of an Act is subject to annulment in pursuance of a resolution of the House of Commons.

107 Penalties for failure to pay tax

107(1) Schedule 56 contains provision for imposing penalties on persons in respect of failures to comply with obligations to pay tax.

107(2) That Schedule comes into force on such day as the Treasury may by order appoint.

107(3) An order under subsection (2)–

(a) may commence a provision generally or only for specified purposes, and

(b) may appoint different days for different provisions or for different purposes.

107(4) The Treasury may by order make any incidental, supplemental, consequential, transitional, transitory or saving provision which may appear appropriate in consequence of, or otherwise in connection with, Schedule 56.

107(5) An order under subsection (4) may include provision amending, repealing or revoking any provision of any Act or subordinate legislation whenever passed or made (including this Act and any Act amended by it).

107(6) An order under subsection (4) may make different provision for different purposes.

107(7) An order under this section is to be made by statutory instrument.

107(8) A statutory instrument containing an order under subsection (4) which includes provision amending or repealing any provision of an Act is subject to annulment in pursuance of a resolution of the House of Commons.

PART 8 – MISCELLANEOUS

OTHER MATTERS

122 Inheritance tax: agricultural property and woodlands relief for EEA land

122(1) Part 5 of IHTA 1984 (miscellaneous reliefs) is amended as follows.

122(2) [Amends IHTA 1984, s. 115(3).]

122(3) [Substitutes IHTA 1984, s. 115(5).]

122(4) [Inserts IHTA 1984, s. 116(8).]

122(5) [Amends IHTA 1984, s. 125(1)(a).]

122(6) [Inserts IHTA 1984, s. 125(1A).]

122(7) The amendments made by this section have effect in relation to transfers of value where the tax payable but for this section (or, in the case of tax payable by instalments, the last instalment of that tax)–

(a) would have been due on or after 22 April 2009, or

(b) was paid or due on or after 23 April 2003.

122(8) Where tax falling within subsection (7) has been paid, Her Majesty's Revenue and Customs must repay the tax (together with interest under section 235(1) of IHTA 1984) if, but only if, a claim for repayment is made on or before–

(a) the date determined under section 241(1) of that Act as the last date on which the claim may be made, or

(b) 21 April 2010,

whichever is later.

122(9) Where, by virtue of the amendments made by subsections (5) and (6), an election is made under section 125 of IHTA 1984, that election must be made on or before–

(a) the date determined under section 125(3) as the last date on which the election may be made, or

(b) 21 April 2010,

whichever is later.

SCHEDULES

SCHEDULE 48 – EXTENSION OF INFORMATION AND INSPECTION POWERS

Section 96

Commencement Date – SI 2009/3054 sets 1 April 2010 as the appointed day for the amendments made by s. 96 and Sch. 48 and contains savings provisions.

[Amends FA 2008, Sch. 36 which is reproduced in full in the Income Tax, Corporation Tax and Capital Gains Tax section (Vol. 1C in print).]

SCHEDULE 51 – TIME LIMITS FOR ASSESSMENTS, CLAIMS ETC

Section 99

Commencement Date – SI 2010/867: amendments made by Sch. 51, para. 5–13 come into force on 1 April 2011, subject to transitional provision in SI 2010/867, art. 6.

INHERITANCE TAX

5 IHTA 1984 is amended as follows.

6 [Inserts IHTA 1984, s. 131(2ZA).]

7 [Amends IHTA 1984, s. 146(2)(a).]

8 [Inserts IHTA 1984, s. 150(3).]

9 [Inserts IHTA 1984, s. 179(2A).]

10 [Inserts IHTA 1984, s. 191(1A).]

11(1) Section 240 (underpayments) is amended as follows.

11(2) [Amends IHTA 1984, s. 240(2).]

11(3) [Substitutes IHTA 1984, s. 240(3)–(8).]

12 [Inserts IHTA 1984, s. 240A.]

13 [Amends IHTA 1984, s. 241.]

SCHEDULE 53 – LATE PAYMENT INTEREST

Section 101

Commencement Date – The day appointed as the day on which s. 101 and Sch. 53 comes into force for the purposes of penalties assessed under FA 2012, Sch. 38, Pt. 3–5 (tax agents dishonest conduct) is 1 April 2013 (SI 2013/280).

Notes – This is an edited version of Sch. 53, containing only those provisions that are relevant to inheritance tax.

Part 2 – Special Provision: Late Payment Interest Start Date

INHERITANCE TAX PAYABLE BY INSTALMENTS

7(1) The late payment interest start date for each instalment of an amount to which this paragraph applies is the date on which that instalment is to be paid.

7(2) This paragraph applies to any amount of inheritance tax which is payable by instalments under section 229 of IHTA 1984.

7(3) This paragraph also applies to any amount of inheritance tax which is payable by instalments under section 227 of IHTA 1984 if the value on which the amount is payable is attributable to–

(a) the value of qualifying property within subsection (2)(b) or (c) of that section (shares or securities, or business or interest in a business), or

(b) value treated as reduced under Chapter 2 of Part 5 of that Act.

7(4) But this paragraph does not apply to an amount by virtue of sub-paragraph (3)(a) if the qualifying property is shares or securities of a company which–

(a) falls within sub-paragraph (5), but

(b) does not fall within sub-paragraph (6) or (7).

7(5) A company falls within this sub-paragraph if its business consists wholly or mainly of one or more of the following–

(a) dealing in securities, stocks or shares, land or buildings, or

(b) making or holding investments.

7(6) A company falls within this sub-paragraph if its business consists wholly or mainly in being a holding company (as defined in section 1159 of the Companies Act 2006) of one or more companies not falling within sub-paragraph (5).

7(7) A company falls within this sub-paragraph if its business is carried on in the United Kingdom and is–

(a) wholly that of a market maker, or

(b) that of a discount house.

7(8) A company is a market maker if–

(a) it holds itself out at all normal times in compliance with the rules of The Stock Exchange as willing to buy and sell securities, stocks or shares at a price specified by it, and

(b) it is recognised as doing so by the Council of The Stock Exchange.

Prospective amendments – Para. 7(7) substituted by F(No. 2)A 2015, s. 15(2)(a), with effect from a day to be appointed.

CERTAIN OTHER AMOUNTS OF INHERITANCE TAX

8 An amount of inheritance tax which is underpaid in consequence of any of the following provisions–

(a) section 146(1) of IHTA 1984,

(b) section 19 of the Inheritance (Provision for Family and Dependants) Act 1975, or

(c) Article 21 of the Inheritance (Provision for Family and Dependants) (Northern Ireland) Order 1979,

does not carry late payment interest before the order mentioned in that provision is made.

9 In the case of an amount which is payable under section 147(4) of IHTA 1984, the late payment interest start date is the day after the end of the period of 6 months beginning with the date of the testator's death.

Prospective amendments – In para. 9, the words "end of the month in which the testator died" substituted for the words "date of the testator's death" by F(No. 2)A 2015, s. 15(2)(b), with effect from a day to be appointed.

DEATH OF TAXPAYER

12(1) This paragraph applies if–

(a) a person chargeable to an amount of revenue dies before the amount becomes due and payable, and

(b) the executor or administrator is unable to pay the amount before obtaining probate or letters of administration or (in Scotland) the executor is unable to pay the amount before obtaining confirmation.

12(2) The late payment interest start date in respect of that amount is the later of the following–

(a) the date which would be the late payment interest start date apart from this paragraph, and

(b) the day after the end of the period of 30 days beginning with the grant of probate or letters of administration or (in Scotland) the grant of confirmation.

Part 3 – Special Provision: Date to Which Late Payment Interest Runs

PROPERTY ACCEPTED IN LIEU OF INHERITANCE TAX

14 If, in the case of any amount of inheritance tax–

(a) HMRC agree under section 230 of IHTA 1984 to accept property in satisfaction of the amount, and

(b) under terms of that acceptance the value to be attributed to the property for the purposes of the acceptance is determined as at a date earlier than that on which the property is actually accepted,

the terms may provide that the amount of tax which is satisfied by the acceptance of the property does not carry late payment interest after that date.

SCHEDULE 54 – REPAYMENT INTEREST

Section 102

Notes – This is an edited version of Sch. 54, containing only the provisions relevant to inheritance tax.

Part 1 – Repayment Interest Start Date: General Rule

INTRODUCTORY

1(1) This Part sets out the general rule for determining the repayment interest start date.

1(2) The general rule is subject to the special provision made by Part 2.

REPAYMENT OF AMOUNTS PAID TO HMRC

2 In the case of an amount which has been paid to HMRC, the repayment interest start date is the later of date A and (where applicable) date B.

3 Date A is the date on which the amount was paid to HMRC.

4 Date B is, in the case of an amount which–

(a) has been paid in connection with a liability to make a payment to HMRC, and

(b) is to be repaid by them,

the date on which the payment became due and payable to HMRC.

PAYMENT OF AMOUNTS ON RETURN OR CLAIM

5(1) In the case of an amount which–

(a) has not been paid to HMRC, and

(b) is payable by virtue of a return having been filed or a claim having been made,

the repayment interest start date is the later of the dates mentioned in sub-paragraph (2).

5(2) The dates are–

(a) the date (if any) on which the return was required to be filed or the claim was required to be made, and

(b) the date on which the return was in fact filed or the claim was in fact made.

Part 2 – Special Provision as to Repayment Interest Start Date

CERTAIN AMOUNTS OF INHERITANCE TAX

10 An amount of inheritance tax which is overpaid in consequence of any of the following provisions–

(a) section 146(1) of IHTA 1984,

(b) section 19 of the Inheritance (Provision for Family and Dependants) Act 1975, or

(c) Article 21 of the Inheritance (Provision for Family and Dependants) (Northern Ireland) Order 1979,

does not carry repayment interest before the order mentioned in that provision is made.

11 In the case of an amount which is repayable on a claim under section 146(2) or 150 of IHTA 1984, the repayment interest start date is the date on which the claim is made.

12 In the case of an amount which is repayable under section 147(2) of IHTA 1984, the repayment interest start date is the date on which the tax was paid.

SCHEDULE 55 – PENALTY FOR FAILURE TO MAKE RETURNS ETC

Section 106

Other material – HMRC Brief 14/11: Penalty for failure to disclose offshore income or gains.

Notes – This is an edited version of Sch. 55, containing only the provisions relevant to inheritance tax.

PENALTY FOR FAILURE TO MAKE RETURNS ETC

1(1) A penalty is payable by a person ("P") where P fails to make or deliver a return, or to deliver any other document, specified in the Table below on or before the filing date.

1(2) Paragraphs 2 to 13 set out–

(a) the circumstances in which a penalty is payable, and

(b) subject to paragraphs 14 to 17, the amount of the penalty.

1(3) If P's failure falls within more than one paragraph of this Schedule, P is liable to a penalty under each of those paragraphs (but this is subject to paragraph 17(3)).

1(4) *In this Schedule*–

"filing date", in relation to a return or other document, means the date by which it is required to be made or delivered to HMRC;

"penalty date", in relation to a return or other document falling within any of items 1 to 3 and 5 to 13 in the Table, means the date on which a penalty is first payable for failing to make or deliver it (that is to say, the day after the filing date).

1(4A) [Not relevant to inheritance tax.]

1(5) In the provisions of this Schedule which follow the Table–

(a) any reference to a return includes a reference to any other document specified in the Table, and

(b) any reference to making a return includes a reference to delivering a return or to delivering any such document.

	Tax to which return etc relates	*Return or other document*
8	Inheritance tax	Account under section 216 or 217 of IHTA 1984

Prospective amendments – In para. 1(2), "13J" substituted for "13" by F(No. 3)A 2010, s. 26 and Sch. 10, para. 2(2), with effect from a day to be appointed by Treasury order.
In para. 1(4), in the definition of "penalty date", "13A" substituted for "13" by FA 2017, s. 56 and Sch. 11, para. 4(2), with effect from a day to be appointed under FA 2017, s. 61(1).
In para. 1(4), in the definition of "filing date", the words "(or, in the case of a return mentioned in item 7AA or 7AB of the Table, to the tax authorities to whom the return is required to be delivered)" inserted (at the end) by F(No. 3)A 2010, s. 26 and Sch. 10, para. 2(2A) (as inserted by FA 2014, s. 103 and Sch. 22, para. 2(a)), with effect from a date to be appointed under F(No. 3)A 2010, s. 26(2).
History – In para. 1(4), in the definition of "penalty date", the words "falling within any of items 1 to 3 and 5 to 13 in the Table" inserted by FA 2013, s. 230 and Sch. 50, para. 3(a), with effect for the tax year 2014–15 and subsequent tax years in relation to failures to make returns with a filing date (as defined in para. 1(4)) on or after 6 April 2014.
Para. 1(4A) inserted by FA 2013, s. 230 and Sch. 50, para. 3, with effect for the tax year 2014–15 and subsequent tax years in relation to failures to make returns with a filing date (as defined in para. 1(4)) on or after 6 April 2014.

AMOUNT OF PENALTY: OCCASIONAL RETURNS AND ANNUAL RETURNS

2 Paragraphs 3 to 6 apply in the case of a return falling within any of items 1 to 3, 5 and 7 to 13 in the Table.

Prospective amendments – Para. 2 and the heading before it substituted by F(No. 3)A 2010, s. 26 and Sch. 10, para. 3, with effect from a day to be appointed by Treasury order. The substituted text reads as follows:

"AMOUNT OF PENALTY: OCCASIONAL RETURNS AND RETURNS FOR PERIODS OF 6 MONTHS OR MORE

2(1) Paragraphs 3 to 6 apply in the case of–
(a) a return falling within any of items 1 to 5, 7 and 8 to 13 in the Table,
(b) [not relevant to inheritance tax,]
(c) [not relevant to inheritance tax.]
2(2) [Not relevant to inheritance tax.]".

History – In para. 2, the words "1 to 3, 5" substituted for the words "1 to 5" by FA 2013, s. 230 and Sch. 50, para. 5, with effect for the tax year 2014–15 and subsequent tax years in relation to failures to make returns with a filing date (as defined in para. 1(4)) on or after 6 April 2014.

3 P is liable to a penalty under this paragraph of £100.

4(1) P is liable to a penalty under this paragraph if (and only if)–
(a) P's failure continues after the end of the period of 3 months beginning with the penalty date,
(b) HMRC decide that such a penalty should be payable, and
(c) HMRC give notice to P specifying the date from which the penalty is payable.

4(2) The penalty under this paragraph is £10 for each day that the failure continues during the period of 90 days beginning with the date specified in the notice given under sub-paragraph (1)(c).

4(3) The date specified in the notice under sub-paragraph (1)(c)–
(a) may be earlier than the date on which the notice is given, but
(b) may not be earlier than the end of the period mentioned in sub-paragraph (1)(a).

5(1) P is liable to a penalty under this paragraph if (and only if) P's failure continues after the end of the period of 6 months beginning with the penalty date.

5(2) The penalty under this paragraph is the greater of–
(a) 5% of any liability to tax which would have been shown in the return in question, and
(b) £300.

6(1) P is liable to a penalty under this paragraph if (and only if) P's failure continues after the end of the period of 12 months beginning with the penalty date.

6(2) Where, by failing to make the return, P withholds information which would enable or assist HMRC to assess P's liability to tax, the penalty under this paragraph is determined in accordance with sub-paragraphs (3) and (4).

6(3) If the withholding of the information is deliberate and concealed, the penalty is the greater of–
(a) 100% of any liability to tax which would have been shown in the return in question, and
(b) £300.

6(4) If the withholding of the information is deliberate but not concealed, the penalty is the greater of–
(a) 70% of any liability to tax which would have been shown in the return in question, and
(b) £300.

6(5) In any other case, the penalty under this paragraph is the greater of–
(a) 5% of any liability to tax which would have been shown in the return in question, and

(b) £300.

Prospective amendments – In para. 6(2), after "P" in the first place it occurs, the word "deliberately" inserted by F(No. 3)A 2010, s. 26 and Sch. 10, para. 4(2), with effect from a day to be appointed by Treasury order.
In para. 6(3)(a), the words "the relevant percentage" substituted for "100%" by FA 2010, s. 35 and Sch. 10, para. 11(2), with effect from a date to be appointed.
Para. 6(3A)(za) inserted and in para. 6(3A)(a) "125%" substituted for "100%" by FA 2015, s. 120 and Sch. 20, para. 15(2), with effect from a day to be appointed under FA 2015, s. 120(2).
Para. 6(3A) inserted by FA 2010, s. 35 and Sch. 10, para. 11(3), with effect from a date to be appointed. Para. 6(3A) reads:
"6(3A) For the purposes of sub-paragraph (3)(a), the relevant percentage is–
(a) for the withholding of category 1 information, 100%,
(b) for the withholding of category 2 information, 150%, and
(c) for the withholding of category 3 information, 200%."
In para. 6(4)(a), the words "the relevant percentage" substituted for "70%" by FA 2010, s. 35 and Sch. 10, para. 11(4), with effect from a date to be appointed.
Para. 6(4A)(za) inserted and in para. 6(4A)(a) "87.5%" substituted for "70%" by FA 2015, s. 120 and Sch. 20, para. 15(3), with effect from a day to be appointed under FA 2015, s. 120(2).
Para. 6(4A) inserted by FA 2010, s. 35 and Sch. 10, para. 11(5), with effect from a date to be appointed. Para. 6(4A) reads:
"6(4A) For the purposes of sub-paragraph (4)(a), the **relevant percentage** is–
(a) for the withholding of category 1 information, 70%,
(b) for the withholding of category 2 information, 105%, and
(c) for the withholding of category 3 information, 140%."
In para. 6(5), the words "any case not falling within sub-paragraph (2)" substituted for the words "any other case" by F(No. 3)A 2010, s. 26 and Sch. 10, para. 4(3), with effect from a day to be appointed by Treasury order.
In para. 6(6) "4" substituted for "3" by FA 2015, s. 120 and Sch. 20, para. 15(4), with effect from a day to be appointed under FA 2015, s. 120(2).
Para. 6(6) inserted by FA 2010, s. 35 and Sch. 10, para. 11(6), with effect from a date to be appointed. Para. 6(6) reads:
"6(6) Paragraph 6A explains the 3 categories of information."

Notes – The amendments by FA 2010, Sch. 10, para. 10 to 14 were brought into effect from 6 April 2011 but only in relation to items 1, 2 or 3 in the Table in para. 1 (which relate to income tax, capital gains tax and corporation tax) (SI 2011/975).
The amendments by F(No. 3)A 2010, s. 27 and Sch. 10, para. 4, were brought into effect from 6 April 2011 in relation to items 1, 2 or 3 in the Table in para. 1 (which relate to income tax, capital gains tax and corporation tax) and from 1 April 2011 in relation to a return under FA 2004, s. 254 (pension schemes; accounting for tax) (SI 2011/703).

6A [Para. 6A prospectively inserted by FA 2010, s. 35 and Sch. 10, para. 12.]

Prospective amendments – Para. 6A inserted by FA 2010, s. 35 and Sch. 10, para. 12, with effect from a date to be appointed. Para. 6A (as amended by FA 2015, s. 120 and Sch. 20, para. 16(3)–(9) (see history notes below)) reads:
"6A(1) Information is **category 1** information if–
(a) it involves a domestic matter, or
(b) it involves an offshore matter and–
(i) the territory in question is a category 1 territory, or
(ii) it is information which would enable or assist HMRC to assess P's liability to a tax other than income tax or capital gains tax.
6A(2) Information is **category 2** information if–
(a) it involves an offshore matter or an offshore transfer,
(b) the territory in question is a category 2 territory, and
(c) it is information which would enable or assist HMRC to assess P's liability to income tax, capital gains tax or inheritance tax.
6A(3) Information is **category 3** information if–
(a) it involves an offshore matter or an offshore transfer,
(b) the territory in question is a category 3 territory, and
(c) it is information which would enable or assist HMRC to assess P's liability to income tax, capital gains tax or inheritance tax.
6A(4) Information **"involves an offshore matter"** if the liability to tax which would have been shown in the return includes a liability to tax charged on or by reference to–
(a) income arising from a source in a territory outside the UK,
(b) assets situated or held in a territory outside the UK,
(c) activities carried on wholly or mainly in a territory outside the UK, or
(d) anything having effect as if it were income, assets or activities of a kind described above.
6A(4A) If the liability to tax which would have been shown in the return is a liability to inheritance tax, assets are treated for the purposes of sub-paragraph (4) as situated or held in a territory outside the UK if they are so situated or held immediately after the transfer of value by reason of which inheritance tax becomes chargeable.
6A(4B) Information **"involves an offshore transfer"** if–
(a) it does not involve an offshore matter,
(b) it is information which would enable or assist HMRC to assess P's liability to income tax, capital gains tax or inheritance tax,
(c) by failing to make the return, P deliberately withholds the information (whether or not the withholding of the information is also concealed), and
(d) the applicable condition in paragraph 6AA is satisfied.
6A(5) Information **"involves a domestic matter"** if it does not involve an offshore matter or an offshore transfer.
6A(6) If the information which P withholds falls into more than one category–
(a) P's failure to make the return is to be treated for the purposes of this Schedule as if it were separate failures, one for each category of information according to the matters or transfers which the information involves, and
(b) for each separate failure, the liability to tax which would have been shown in the return in question is taken to be such share of the liability to tax which would have been shown in the return mentioned in paragraph (a) as is just and reasonable.
6A(7) For the purposes of this Schedule–
(a) paragraph 21A of Schedule 24 to FA 2007 (classification of territories) has effect, but
(b) an order under that paragraph does not apply to a failure if the filing date is before the date on which the order comes into force.
6A(8) [Omitted by FA 2015, s. 120 and Sch. 20, para. 16(8).]
6A(9) In this paragraph and paragraph 6AA–
"assets" has the meaning given in section 21(1) of TCGA 1992, but also includes sterling;
"UK" means the United Kingdom, including the territorial sea of the United Kingdom."
Para. 6A(A1) and (1) substituted for para. 6A(1) by FA 2015, s. 120 and Sch. 20, para. 16(2), with effect from a day to be appointed under FA 2015, s. 120(2).

History – In para. 6A(2)(a) the words "or an offshore transfer" inserted and in para. 6A(2)(c) the words ", capital gains tax or inheritance tax" substituted for the words "or capital gains tax" by FA 2015, s. 120 and Sch. 20, para. 16(3), with effect from 6 April 2016 (and the

IHT Statutes

amendments have effect in relation to a return or other document which: is required to be made or delivered to HMRC in relation to a tax year commencing on or after 6 April 2016; and falls within item 1, 2 or 3 of the Table in para. 1(5)) (SI 2016/456, art. 5).
In para. 6A(3)(a) the words "or an offshore transfer" inserted and in para. 6A(3)(c) the words ", capital gains tax or inheritance tax" substituted for the words "or capital gains tax" by FA 2015, s. 120 and Sch. 20, para. 16(4), with effect from 6 April 2016 (and the amendments have effect in relation to a return or other document which: is required to be made or delivered to HMRC in relation to a tax year commencing on or after 6 April 2016; and falls within item 1, 2 or 3 of the Table in para. 1(5)) (SI 2016/456, art. 5).
Para. 6A(4A) and (4B) inserted by FA 2015, s. 120 and Sch. 20, para. 16(5), with effect from 6 April 2016 (and the amendments have effect in relation to a return or other document which: is required to be made or delivered to HMRC in relation to a tax year commencing on or after 6 April 2016; and falls within item 1, 2 or 3 of the Table in para. 1(5)) (SI 2016/456, art. 5).
In para. 6A(5) the words "it does not involve an offshore matter or an offshore transfer" substituted for the words "the liability to tax which would have been shown in the return includes a liability to tax charged on or by reference to anything not mentioned in sub-paragraph (4)(a) to (d)" by FA 2015, s. 120 and Sch. 20, para. 16(6), with effect from 6 April 2016 (and the amendments have effect in relation to a return or other document which: is required to be made or delivered to HMRC in relation to a tax year commencing on or after 6 April 2016; and falls within item 1, 2 or 3 of the Table in para. 1(5)) (SI 2016/456, art. 5).
In para. 6A(6)(a) the words "or transfers" inserted by FA 2015, s. 120 and Sch. 20, para. 16(7), with effect from 6 April 2016 (and the amendments have effect in relation to a return or other document which: is required to be made or delivered to HMRC in relation to a tax year commencing on or after 6 April 2016; and falls within item 1, 2 or 3 of the Table in para. 1(5)) (SI 2016/456, art. 5).
Para. 6A(8) omitted by FA 2015, s. 120 and Sch. 20, para. 16(8), with effect from 6 April 2016 (and the amendments have effect in relation to a return or other document which: is required to be made or delivered to HMRC in relation to a tax year commencing on or after 6 April 2016; and falls within item 1, 2 or 3 of the Table in para. 1(5)) (SI 2016/456, art. 5).
In para. 6A(9) the words "and paragraph 6AA" insertedby FA 2015, s. 120 and Sch. 20, para. 16(9), with effect from 6 April 2016 (and the amendments have effect in relation to a return or other document which: is required to be made or delivered to HMRC in relation to a tax year commencing on or after 6 April 2016; and falls within item 1, 2 or 3 of the Table in para. 1(5)) (SI 2016/456, art. 5).

Notes – The amendments by FA 2010, Sch. 10, para. 10 to 14 were brought into effect from 6 April 2011 but only in relation to items 1, 2 or 3 in the Table in para. 1 (which relate to income tax, capital gains tax and corporation tax) (SI 2011/975).
The amendments by FA 2015, Sch. 20, para. 16(3)–(9) were brought into effect from 6 April 2016 in relation to a return or other document which is required to be made or delivered to HMRC in relation to a tax year commencing on or after 6 April 2016; and falls within item 1, 2 or 3 of the Table in para. 1(5) (SI 2016/456, art. 5).

6AA(1) This paragraph makes provision in relation to offshore transfers.

6AA(2) Where the liability to tax which would have been shown in the return is a liability to income tax, the applicable condition is satisfied if the income on or by reference to which the tax is charged, or any part of the income–

(a) is received in a territory outside the UK, or

(b) is transferred before the relevant date to a territory outside the UK.

6AA(3) Where the liability to tax which would have been shown in the return is a liability to capital gains tax, the applicable condition is satisfied if the proceeds of the disposal on or by reference to which the tax is charged, or any part of the proceeds–

(a) are received in a territory outside the UK, or

(b) are transferred before the relevant date to a territory outside the UK.

6AA(4) Where the liability to tax which would have been shown in the return is a liability to inheritance tax, the applicable condition is satisfied if–

(a) the disposition that gives rise to the transfer of value by reason of which the tax becomes chargeable involves a transfer of assets, and

(b) after that disposition but before the relevant date the assets, or any part of the assets, are transferred to a territory outside the UK.

6AA(5) In the case of a transfer falling within sub-paragraph (2)(b), (3)(b) or (4)(b), references to the income, proceeds or assets transferred are to be read as including references to any assets derived from or representing the income, proceeds or assets.

6AA(6) In relation to an offshore transfer, the territory in question for the purposes of paragraph 6A is the highest category of territory by virtue of which the information involves an offshore transfer.

6AA(7) **"Relevant date"** means the date on which P becomes liable to a penalty under paragraph 6.

History – Para. 6AA inserted by FA 2015, s. 120 and Sch. 20, para. 17, with effect from 6 April 2016 (in relation to a return or other document which: is required to be made or delivered to HMRC in relation to a tax year commencing on or after 6 April 2016; and falls within item 1, 2 or 3 of the Table in para. 1(5)) (SI 2016/456, art. 5).

6AB Regulations under paragraph 21B of Schedule 24 to FA 2007 (location of assets etc) apply for the purposes of paragraphs 6A and 6AA of this Schedule as they apply for the purposes of paragraphs 4A and 4AA of that Schedule.

History – Para. 6AB inserted by FA 2015, s. 120 and Sch. 20, para. 17, with effect from 6 April 2016 (in relation to a return or other document which: is required to be made or delivered to HMRC in relation to a tax year commencing on or after 6 April 2016; and falls within item 1, 2 or 3 of the Table in para. 1(5)) (SI 2016/456, art. 5).

AMOUNT OF PENALTY: REAL TIME INFORMATION FOR PAYE AND APPRENTICESHIP LEVY

History – In heading before para. 6B, the words "and apprenticeship levy" inserted by FA 2016, s. 113(8), with effect from 15 September 2016 (Royal Assent).

6B–6D [Not relevant to inheritance tax.]

AMOUNT OF PENALTY: CIS RETURNS

7–13 [Not relevant to inheritance tax.]

AMOUNT OF PENALTY: RETURNS FOR PERIODS OF BETWEEN 2 AND 6 MONTHS

13A–13E [Not relevant to inheritance tax.]

AMOUNT OF PENALTY: RETURNS FOR PERIODS OF 2 MONTHS OR LESS

13F–13J [Not relevant to inheritance tax.]

REDUCTIONS FOR DISCLOSURE

14(A1) In this paragraph, **"relevant information"** means information which has been withheld by a failure to make a return.

14(1) Paragraph 15 provides for reductions in the penalty under paragraph 6(3) or (4) where P discloses relevant information that involves a domestic matter or 11(3) or (4) where P discloses relevant information.

14(1A) Paragraph 15A provides for reductions in the penalty under paragraph 6(3) or (4) where P discloses relevant information that involves an offshore matter or an offshore transfer.

14(1B) Sub-paragraph (2) applies where–

(a) P is liable to a penalty under paragraph 6(3) or (4) and P discloses relevant information that involves a domestic matter, or

(b) P is liable to a penalty under any of the other provisions mentioned in sub-paragraph (1) and P discloses relevant information.

14(2) P discloses relevant information by–

(a) telling HMRC about it,

(b) giving HMRC reasonable help in quantifying any tax unpaid by reason of its having been withheld, and

(c) allowing HMRC access to records for the purpose of checking how much tax is so unpaid.

14(2A) Sub-paragraph (2B) applies where P is liable to a penalty under paragraph 6(3) or (4) and P discloses relevant information that involves an offshore matter or an offshore transfer.

14(2B) P discloses relevant information by–

(a) telling HMRC about it,

(b) giving HMRC reasonable help in quantifying any tax unpaid by reason of its having been withheld,

(c) allowing HMRC access to records for the purpose of checking how much tax is so unpaid, and

(d) providing HMRC with additional information.

14(2C) The Treasury must make regulations setting out what is meant by **"additional information"** for the purposes of sub-paragraph (2B)(d).

14(2D) Regulations under sub-paragraph (2C) are to be made by statutory instrument.

14(2E) An instrument containing regulations under sub-paragraph (2C) is subject to annulment in pursuance of a resolution of the House of Commons.

14(3) Disclosure of relevant information–

(a) is "unprompted" if made at a time when P has no reason to believe that HMRC have discovered or are about to discover the relevant information, and

(b) otherwise, is "prompted".

14(4) In relation to disclosure **"quality"** includes timing, nature and extent.

14(5) Paragraph 6A(4) to (5) applies to determine whether relevant information involves an offshore matter, an offshore transfer or a domestic matter for the purposes of this paragraph.

Prospective amendments – In para. 14(1), ", 11(3) or (4), 13E(3) or (4) or 13J(3) or (4)" substituted for "or 11(3) or (4)" by F(No. 3)A 2010, s. 26 and Sch. 10, para. 8, with effect from a day to be appointed by Treasury Order.

History – Para. 14(A1) inserted by FA 2016, s. 163(1) and Sch. 21, para. 10(2), with effect for inheritance tax purposes in relation to transfers of value made on or after 1 April 2017 (SI 2017/259, reg. 2(a)).

In para. 14(1), the words "where P discloses relevant information that involves a domestic matter" inserted and the words "relevant information" substituted for the words "information which has been withheld by a failure to make a return ("relevant information")" by FA 2016, s. 163(1) and Sch. 21, para. 10(3), with effect for inheritance tax purposes in relation to in relation to transfers of value made on or after 1 April 2017 (SI 2017/259, reg. 2(a)).

Para. 14(1A) and (1B) inserted by FA 2016, s. 163(1) and Sch. 21, para. 10(4), with effect in relation to transfers of value made on or after 1 April 2017 (SI 2017/259, reg. 2(a)).

Para. 14(2A)–(2E) inserted by FA 2016, s. 163(1) and Sch. 21, para. 10(5), with effect from 8 March 2017 for the purpose of making the regulations and for inheritance tax purposes in relation to transfers of value made on or after 1 April 2017 (SI 2017/259, reg. 2 and 3).

Para. 14(5) inserted by FA 2016, s. 163(1) and Sch. 21, para. 10(6), with effect for inheritance tax purposes in relation to transfers of value made on or after 1 April 2017 (SI 2017/259, reg. 2(a)).

Statutory instruments – SI 2017/345: partly made under para. 14(2C).

15(1) Where a person who would otherwise be liable to a 100% penalty has made an unprompted disclosure, HMRC must reduce the 100% to a percentage, not below 30%, which reflects the quality of the disclosure.

15(2) Where a person who would otherwise be liable to a 100% penalty has made a prompted disclosure, HMRC must reduce the 100% to a percentage, not below 50%, which reflects the quality of the disclosure.

15(3) Where a person who would otherwise be liable to a 70% penalty has made an unprompted disclosure, HMRC must reduce the 70% to a percentage, not below 20%, which reflects the quality of the disclosure.

15(4) Where a person who would otherwise be liable to a 70% penalty has made a prompted disclosure, HMRC must reduce the 70% to a percentage, not below 35%, which reflects the quality of the disclosure.

15(5) But HMRC must not under this paragraph–

(a) reduce a penalty under paragraph 6(3) or (4) below £300, or

(b) reduce a penalty under paragraph 11(3) or (4) below the amount set by paragraph 11(3)(b) or (4)(b) (as the case may be).

Prospective amendments – Para. 15(1) substituted by FA 2010, s. 35 and Sch. 10, para. 13(2), with effect from a date to be appointed. Para. 15(1) reads:

"15(1) If a person who would otherwise be liable to a penalty of a percentage shown in column 1 of the Table (a "standard percentage") has made a disclosure, HMRC must reduce the standard percentage to one that reflects the quality of the disclosure."

The Table in para. 15(2) amended by FA 2015, s. 120 and Sch. 20, para. 18, with effect from a day to be appointed under FA 2015, s. 120(2).

Para. 15(2) substituted by FA 2010, s. 35 and Sch. 10, para. 13(2), with effect from a date to be appointed. Para. 15(2) (as amended by by FA 2016, s. 163(1) and Sch. 21, para. 11 (see history notes below)) reads:

"15(2) But the standard percentage may not be reduced to a percentage that is below the minimum shown for it–

(a) in the case of a prompted disclosure, in column 2 of the Table, and

(b) in the case of an unprompted disclosure, in column 3 of the Table.

Standard %	*Minimum % for prompted disclosure*	*Minimum % for unprompted disclosure*
70%	35%	20%
100%	50%	30%"

Para. 15(3) omitted by FA 2010, s. 35 and Sch. 10, para. 13(3), with effect from a date to be appointed.

Para. 15(4) omitted by FA 2010, s. 35 and Sch. 10, para. 13(3), with effect from a date to be appointed.

In para. 15(5), the words "sub-paragraph (3) or (4) of any of paragraphs 11, 13E and 13J" substituted for the words "paragraph 11(3) or (4)" by F(No. 3)A 2010, s. 26 and Sch. 10, para. 9(a), with effect from a day to be appointed by Treasury order.

In para. 15(5), the words "paragraph (b) of that sub-paragraph" substituted for the words "paragraph 11(3)(b) or (4)(b) (as the case may be)" by F(No. 3)A 2010, s. 26 and Sch. 10, para. 9(b), with effect from a day to be appointed by Treasury order.

History – The Table in para. 15(2) substituted by FA 2016, s. 163(1) and Sch. 21, para. 11, with effect with effect from 1 April 2017 for all purposes and has effect for inheritance tax purposes in relation to transfers of value on or after that date and for income tax and capital gains tax in relation to any tax year commencing on or after 6 April 2016 (SI 2017/259, reg. 2).

Notes – The amendments by FA 2010, Sch. 10, para. 10 to 14 were brought into effect from 6 April 2011 but only in relation to items 1, 2 or 3 in the Table in para. 1 (which relate to income tax, capital gains tax and corporation tax) (SI 2011/975).

15A(1) If a person who would otherwise be liable to a penalty of a percentage shown in column 1 of the Table (a "standard percentage") has made a disclosure, HMRC must reduce the standard percentage to one that reflects the quality of the disclosure.

15A(2) But the standard percentage may not be reduced to a percentage that is below the minimum shown for it–

(a) in the case of a prompted disclosure, in column 2 of the Table, and

(b) in the case of an unprompted disclosure, in column 3 of the Table.

Standard %	*Minimum % for prompted disclosure*	*Minimum % for unprompted disclosure*
70%	45%	30%
87.5%	53.75%	35%
100%	60%	40%
105%	62.5%	40%
125%	72.5%	50%
140%	80%	50%
150%	85%	55%
200%	110%	70%

15A(3) But HMRC must not under this paragraph reduce a penalty below £300.

History – Para. 15A inserted by FA 2016, s. 163(1) and Sch. 21, para. 12, with effect for inheritance tax purposes in relation to transfers of value made on or after 1 April 2017 (SI 2017/259, reg. 2).

SPECIAL REDUCTION

16(1) If HMRC think it right because of special circumstances, they may reduce a penalty under any paragraph of this Schedule.

16(2) In sub-paragraph (1) **"special circumstances"** does not include–

(a) ability to pay, or

(b) the fact that a potential loss of revenue from one taxpayer is balanced by a potential over-payment by another.

16(3) In sub-paragraph (1) the reference to reducing a penalty includes a reference to–

(a) staying a penalty, and

(b) agreeing a compromise in relation to proceedings for a penalty.

INTERACTION WITH OTHER PENALTIES AND LATE PAYMENT SURCHARGES

17(1) Where P is liable for a penalty under any paragraph of this Schedule which is determined by reference to a liability to tax, the amount of that penalty is to be reduced by the amount of any other penalty incurred by P, if the amount of the penalty is determined by reference to the same liability to tax.

17(2) In sub-paragraph (1) the reference to **"any other penalty"** does not include–

(a) a penalty under any other paragraph of this Schedule, or

(b) a penalty under Schedule 56 (penalty for late payment of tax), or

(c) a penalty under Part 4 of FA 2014 (penalty where corrective action not taken after follower notice etc), or

(d) a penalty under Schedule 22 to FA 2016 (asset-based penalty).

17(3) Where P is liable for a penalty under more than one paragraph of this Schedule which is determined by reference to a liability to tax, the aggregate of the amounts of those penalties must not exceed 100% of the liability to tax.

Prospective amendments – In para. 17(3), the words "the relevant percentage" substituted for "100%" by FA 2010, s. 35 and Sch. 10, para. 14(a), with effect from a day to be appointed.

Para. 17(4)(ba) (and the word "and" immediately after it) inserted and the words "and" at the end of para. (b) omitted by FA 2015, s. 120 and Sch. 20, para. 19, with effect from a day to be appointed under FA 2015, s. 120(2).

Para. 17(4) inserted by FA 2010, s. 35 and Sch. 10, para. 14(b), with effect from a day to be appointed. Para. 17(4) reads:

"17(4) The **relevant percentage** is–

(a) if one of the penalties is a penalty under paragraph 6(3) or (4) and the information withheld is category 3 information, 200%,

(b) if one of the penalties is a penalty under paragraph 6(3) or (4) and the information withheld is category 2 information, 150%, and

(c) in all other cases, 100%."

History – Para. 17(2)(c) (and the ", or" before it) inserted by FA 2014, s. 233 and Sch. 33, para. 5, with effect from 17 July 2014. Para. 17(2)(d) (and the ", or" before it) inserted by FA 2016, s. 165(1) and Sch. 22, para. 20(5), with effect for inheritance tax purposes, in relation to transfers of value made on or after 1 April 2017 (SI 2017/277, reg. 2).

Notes – The amendments by FA 2010, Sch. 10, para. 10–14 were brought into effect from 6 April 2011 but only in relation to items 1, 2 or 3 in the Table in para. 1 (which relate to income tax, capital gains tax and corporation tax) (SI 2011/975).

CANCELLATION OF PENALTY

17A [Not relevant to inheritance tax.]

17B [Not relevant to inheritance tax.]

ASSESSMENT

18(1) Where P is liable for a penalty under any paragraph of this Schedule HMRC must–

(a) assess the penalty,

(b) notify P, and

(c) state in the notice the period in respect of which the penalty is assessed.

18(2) A penalty under any paragraph of this Schedule must be paid before the end of the period of 30 days beginning with the day on which notification of the penalty is issued.

18(3) An assessment of a penalty under any paragraph of this Schedule–

(a) is to be treated for procedural purposes in the same way as an assessment to tax (except in respect of a matter expressly provided for by this Schedule),

(b) may be enforced as if it were an assessment to tax, and

(c) may be combined with an assessment to tax.

18(4) A supplementary assessment may be made in respect of a penalty if an earlier assessment operated by reference to an underestimate of the liability to tax which would have been shown in a return.

18(5) Sub-paragraph (6) applies if–

(a) an assessment in respect of a penalty is based on a liability to tax that would have been shown in a return, and

(b) that liability is found by HMRC to be excessive.

18(6) HMRC may by notice to P amend the assessment so that it is based upon the correct amount.

18(7) An amendment under sub-paragraph (6)–

(a) does not affect when the penalty must be paid;

(b) may be made after the last day on which the assessment in question could have been made under paragraph 19.

History – Para. 18(5), (6) and (7) substituted for para. 18(5) by FA 2013, s. 230 and Sch. 50, para. 7, with effect for the tax year 2014–15 and subsequent tax years in relation to failures to make returns with a filing date (as defined in para. 1(4)) on or after 6 April 2014.

Notes – Para. 18(5) was inserted by F(No. 3)A 2010, s. 27 and Sch. 10, para. 10, which was brought into effect from 6 April 2011 in relation to items 1, 2 or 3 in the Table in para. 1 (which relate to income tax, capital gains tax and corporation tax) and from 1 April 2011 in relation to a return under FA 2004, s. 254 (pension schemes; accounting for tax) (SI 2011/703), and from 6 October 2011 in relation to item 6 (CIS returns) (SI 2011/2391) but remained prospective for other purposes. As a consequence of the substitution of para. 18(5)–(7) by FA 2013, s. 230 and Sch. 50, para. 7 (see history note above) (which applies for all purposes), F(No. 3)A 2010, Sch. 10, para. 10 was repealed by FA 2013, s. 230 and Sch. 50, para. 15, with effect for the tax year 2014–15 and subsequent tax years in relation to failures to make returns with a filing date (as defined in para. 1(4)) on or after 6 April 2014.

19(1) An assessment of a penalty under any paragraph of this Schedule in respect of any amount must be made on or before the later of date A and (where it applies) date B.

19(2) Date A is–

(a) [not relevant to inheritance tax,]

(b) [not relevant to inheritance tax,]

(c) in any other case, the last day of the period of 2 years beginning with the filing date.

19(3) Date B is the last day of the period of 12 months beginning with–

(a) the end of the appeal period for the assessment of the liability to tax which would have been shown in the return or returns (as the case may be in relation to penalties under section 6C or 6D), or

(b) if there is no such assessment, the date on which that liability is ascertained or it is ascertained that the liability is nil.

19(4) In sub-paragraph (3)(a) **"appeal period"** means the period during which–

(a) an appeal could be brought, or

(b) an appeal that has been brought has not been determined or withdrawn.

19(5) Sub-paragraph (1) does not apply to a re-assessment under paragraph 24(2)(b).

History – In para. 19(2), the words " – (a) in the case of an assessment of a penalty under paragraph 6C, the last day of the period of 2 years beginning with the end of the tax month in respect of which the penalty is payable, (b) in the case of an assessment of a penalty under paragraph 6D, the last day of the period of 2 years beginning with the filing date for the relevant extended failure (as defined in paragraph 6D(10)), and (c) in any other case," inserted by FA 2013, s. 230 and Sch. 50, para. 8(2), with effect for the tax year 2014–15 and subsequent tax years in relation to failures to make returns with a filing date (as defined in para. 1(4)) on or after 6 April 2014.
In para. 19(3)(a), the words "or returns (as the case may be in relation to penalties under section 6C or 6D)" inserted by FA 2013, s. 230 and Sch. 50, para. 8(3), with effect for the tax year 2014–15 and subsequent tax years in relation to failures to make returns with a filing date (as defined in para. 1(4)) on or after 6 April 2014.

APPEAL

20(1) P may appeal against a decision of HMRC that a penalty is payable by P.

20(2) P may appeal against a decision of HMRC as to the amount of a penalty payable by P.

21(1) An appeal under paragraph 20 is to be treated in the same way as an appeal against an assessment to the tax concerned (including by the application of any provision about bringing the appeal by notice to HMRC, about HMRC review of the decision or about determination of the appeal by the First-tier Tribunal or Upper Tribunal).

21(2) Sub-paragraph (1) does not apply–

(a) so as to require P to pay a penalty before an appeal against the assessment of the penalty is determined, or

(b) in respect of any other matter expressly provided for by this Act.

22(1) On an appeal under paragraph 20(1) that is notified to the tribunal, the tribunal may affirm or cancel HMRC's decision.

22(2) On an appeal under paragraph 20(2) that is notified to the tribunal, the tribunal may–

(a) affirm HMRC's decision, or

(b) substitute for HMRC's decision another decision that HMRC had power to make.

22(3) If the tribunal substitutes its decision for HMRC's, the tribunal may rely on paragraph 16–

(a) to the same extent as HMRC (which may mean applying the same percentage reduction as HMRC to a different starting point), or

(b) to a different extent, but only if the tribunal thinks that HMRC's decision in respect of the application of paragraph 16 was flawed.

22(4) In sub-paragraph (3)(b) **"flawed"** means flawed when considered in the light of the principles applicable in proceedings for judicial review.

22(5) In this paragraph **"tribunal"** means the First-tier Tribunal or Upper Tribunal (as appropriate by virtue of paragraph 21(1)).

REASONABLE EXCUSE

23(1) Liability to a penalty under any paragraph of this Schedule does not arise in relation to a failure to make a return if P satisfies HMRC or (on appeal) the First-tier Tribunal or Upper Tribunal that there is a reasonable excuse for the failure.

23(2) For the purposes of sub-paragraph (1)–

(a) an insufficiency of funds is not a reasonable excuse, unless attributable to events outside P's control,

(b) where P relies on any other person to do anything, that is not a reasonable excuse unless P took reasonable care to avoid the failure, and

(c) where P had a reasonable excuse for the failure but the excuse has ceased, P is to be treated as having continued to have the excuse if the failure is remedied without unreasonable delay after the excuse ceased.

Prospective amendments – Para. 23(1) substituted by F(No. 3)A 2010, s. 26 and Sch. 10, para. 11, with effect from a day to be appointed by Treasury Order. The substituted para. 23(1) to read as follows:

"**23(1)** If P satisfies HMRC or (on appeal) the First-tier Tribunal or Upper Tribunal that there is a reasonable excuse for a failure to make a return–

(a) liability to a penalty under any paragraph of this Schedule does not arise in relation to that failure, and

(b) [not relevant to inheritance tax.]"

DETERMINATION OF PENALTY GEARED TO TAX LIABILITY WHERE NO RETURN MADE

24(1) References to a liability to tax which would have been shown in a return are references to the amount which, if a complete and accurate return had been delivered on the filing date, would have been shown to be due or payable by the taxpayer in respect of the tax concerned for the period to which the return relates.

24(2) In the case of a penalty which is assessed at a time before P makes the return to which the penalty relates–

(a) HMRC is to determine the amount mentioned in sub-paragraph (1) to the best of HMRC's information and belief, and

(b) if P subsequently makes a return, the penalty must be re-assessed by reference to the amount of tax shown to be due and payable in that return (but subject to any amendments or corrections to the return).

24(3) In calculating a liability to tax which would have been shown in a return, no account is to be taken of any relief under section 458 of CTA 2010 (relief in respect of repayment etc of loan) which is deferred under subsection (5) of that section.

History – In para. 24(3), the words "section 458 of CTA 2010" substituted for the words "subsection (4) of section 419 of ICTA" and the words "subsection (5)" substituted for the words "subsection (4A)" by CTA 2010, s. 1177 and Sch. 1, para. 723, with effect for corporation tax purposes for accounting periods ending on or after 1 April 2010, and for income tax and capital gains tax purposes for the tax year 2010–11 and subsequent tax years.

PARTNERSHIPS

25 *[Not relevant to inheritance tax.]*

DOUBLE JEOPARDY

26 P is not liable to a penalty under any paragraph of this Schedule in respect of a failure or action in respect of which P has been convicted of an offence.

INTERPRETATION

27(1) This paragraph applies for the construction of this Schedule.

27(2) The withholding of information by P is–

(a) **"deliberate and concealed"** if P deliberately withholds the information and makes arrangements to conceal the fact that the information has been withheld, and

(b) **"deliberate but not concealed"** if P deliberately withholds the information but does not make arrangements to conceal the fact that the information has been withheld.

27(2A) **"The Commissioners"** means the Commissioners for Her Majesty's Revenue and Customs.

27(3) **"HMRC"** means Her Majesty's Revenue and Customs.

27(3A) **"Tax month"** means the period beginning with the 6th day of a month and ending with the 5th day of the following month.

27(4) References to a liability to tax, in relation to a return falling within item 6 in the Table (construction industry scheme), are to a liability to make payments in accordance with Chapter 3 of Part 3 of FA 2004.

27(5) References to an assessment to tax, in relation to inheritance tax and stamp duty reserve tax, are to a determination.

History – Para. 27(2A) inserted by FA 2013, s. 230 and Sch. 50, para. 9(2), with effect for the tax year 2014–15 and subsequent tax years in relation to failures to make returns with a filing date (FA 2009, Sch. 55, para. 1(4)) on or after 6 April 2014.
Para. 27(3A) inserted by FA 2013, s. 230 and Sch. 50, para. 9(3), with effect for the tax year 2014–15 and subsequent tax years in relation to failures to make returns with a filing date (FA 2009, Sch. 55, para. 1(4)) on or after 6 April 2014.

Notes – This is an edited version of Sch. 55, containing only the provisions relevant to inheritance tax.

SCHEDULE 56 – PENALTY FOR FAILURE TO MAKE PAYMENTS ON TIME

Section 107

Notes – This is an edited version of Sch. 56, containing only the provisions relevant to inheritance tax.

PENALTY FOR FAILURE TO PAY TAX

1(1) A penalty is payable by a person ("P") where P fails to pay an amount of tax specified in column 3 of the Table below on or before the date specified in column 4.

1(2) Paragraphs 3 to 8 set out–

(a) the circumstances in which a penalty is payable, and

(b) subject to paragraph 9, the amount of the penalty.

1(3) If P's failure falls within more than one provision of this Schedule, P is liable to a penalty under each of those provisions.

1(4) In the following provisions of this Schedule, the **"penalty date"**, in relation to an amount of tax, means the day after the date specified in or for the purposes of column 4 of the Table in relation to that amount.

1(5) [Not relevant to inheritance tax.]

	Tax to which payment relates	*Amount of tax payable*	*Date after which penalty is incurred*
		PRINCIPAL AMOUNTS	
7	Inheritance tax	Amount payable under section 226 of IHTA 1984 (except an amount falling within item 14 or 21)	The filing date (determined under section 216 of IHTA 1984) for the account in respect of the liability for that amount
8	Inheritance tax	Amount payable under section 227 or 229 of IHTA 1984 (except an amount falling within item 14 or 21)	For the first instalment, the filing date (determined under section 216 of IHTA 1984) for the account in respect of the liability for that amount For any later instalment, the date falling 30 days after the date determined under section 227 or 229 of IHTA 1984 as the date by which the instalment must be paid
		AMOUNTS PAYABLE IN DEFAULT OF A RETURN BEING MADE	
14	*Inheritance tax*	Amount shown in a determination made by HMRC in the circumstances set out in paragraph 2	The filing date (determined under section 216 of IHTA 1984) for the account in respect of the liability for that amount

Tax to which payment relates		Amount of tax payable	Date after which penalty is incurred
	AMOUNTS SHOWN TO BE DUE IN OTHER ASSESSMENTS, DETERMINATIONS, ETC		
21	Inheritance tax	Amount shown in–	The later of–
		(a) an amendment or correction of a return showing an amount falling within item 7 or 8, or	(a) the filing date (determined under section 216 of IHTA 1984) for the account in respect of the liability for that amount, and
		(b) a determination made by HMRC in circumstances other than those set out in paragraph 2	(b) the date falling 30 days after the date on which the amendment, correction, assessment or determination is made

Prospective amendments – In para. 1(2), "8J" substituted for "8" by F(No. 3)A 2010, s. 27 and Sch. 11, para. 2(2), with effect from a day to be appointed by Treasury order.

History – In para. 1(4), the words "the day after the date specified in or for the purposes of column 4 of the Table in relation to that amount." substituted for the words "the date on which a penalty is first payable for failing to pay the amount (that is to say, the day after the date specified in or for the purposes of column 4 of the Table)." by FA 2013, s. 230 and Sch. 50, para. 11, with effect for defaults made in relation to the tax year 2014–15 and subsequent tax years (see FA 2009, Sch. 56, para. 6(2) as to when a default is made in relation to a tax year).

Para. 1(5) inserted by F(No. 3)A 2010, s. 27 and Sch. 11, para. 2(3), with effect from 25 January 2011 (SI 2011/132, art. 2(a)).

ASSESSMENTS AND DETERMINATIONS IN DEFAULT OF RETURN

2 The circumstances referred to in items 14, 17, 21 and 24 are where–

(a) P or another person is required to make or deliver a return falling within any item in the Table in Schedule 55,

(b) that person fails to make or deliver the return on or before the date by which it is required to be made or delivered, and

(c) if the return had been made or delivered as required, the return would have shown that an amount falling within any of items 1 to 10 was due and payable.

Prospective amendments – In para. 2(c), "11M" substituted for "10" by F(No. 3)A 2010, s. 27 and Sch. 11, para. 3, with effect from a day to be appointed by Treasury order.

DIFFERENT PENALTY DATE FOR CERTAIN PAYE PAYMENTS

2A [Not relevant to inheritance tax.]

AMOUNT OF PENALTY: OCCASIONAL AMOUNTS AND AMOUNTS IN RESPECT OF PERIODS OF 6 MONTHS OR MORE

3(1) This paragraph applies in the case of–

(a) a payment of tax falling within any of items 1, 3 and 7 to 24 in the Table,

(aa) [not relevant to inheritance tax,]

(b) [not relevant to inheritance tax,]

(c) [not relevant to inheritance tax,]

(ca) [not relevant to inheritance tax,]

3(2) P is liable to a penalty of 5% of the unpaid tax.

3(3) If any amount of the tax is unpaid after the end of the period of 5 months beginning with the penalty date, P is liable to a penalty of 5% of that amount.

3(4) If any amount of the tax is unpaid after the end of the period of 11 months beginning with the penalty date, P is liable to a penalty of 5% of that amount.

Prospective amendments – In para. 3(1)(a), "1A," inserted (after the words "items 1,") by FA 2016, s. 167(1) and Sch. 23, para. 9(3), with effect from a day to be appointed under FA 2016, s. 167(3).

In para. 3(1)(a), "items 1, 3, 6B, 7 to 11 and 12 to 24" substituted for "items 1, 3 and 7 to 24" by F(No. 3)A 2010, s. 27 and Sch. 11, para. 5(3), with effect from a day to be appointed by Treasury order.

Para. 3(1)(d) inserted by F(No. 3)A 2010, s. 27 and Sch. 11, para. 5(5), with effect from a day to be appointed by Treasury order. Para. 3(1)(d) is not relevant to inheritance tax.

Para. 3(1A) inserted by F(No. 3)A 2010, s. 27 and Sch. 11, para. 5(6), with effect from a day to be appointed by Treasury order. Para. 3(1A) relates to VAT and will not be reproduced here.

History – Para. 3(1)(aa) inserted by FA 2015, s. 104(3), with effect in relation to accounting periods beginning on or after 1 April 2015 (subject to FA 2015, s. 116(2)–(5)).

Para. 3(1)(ca) inserted by FA 2016, s. 113(11)(b), with effect from 15 September 2016 (Royal Assent).

4 [Not relevant to inheritance tax.]

AMOUNT OF PENALTY: PAYE AND CIS AMOUNTS ETC.

History – In the heading before para. 5, the word "etc." inserted by FA 2016, s. 113(15), with effect from 15 September 2016 (Royal Assent).

5–8 [Not relevant to inheritance tax.]

AMOUNT OF PENALTY: AMOUNTS IN RESPECT OF PERIODS OF BETWEEN 2 AND 6 MONTHS

8A–8J [Not relevant to inheritance tax.]

CALCULATION OF UNPAID VAT: TREATMENT OF PAYMENTS ON ACCOUNT

8K [Prospectively inserted (see note below).]

Prospective amendments – Para. 8K inserted by F(No. 3)A 2010, s. 27 and Sch. 11, para. 8, with effect from a day to be appointed. Para. 8K relates to VAT and will not be reproduced here.

SPECIAL REDUCTION

9(1) If HMRC think it right because of special circumstances, they may reduce a penalty under any paragraph of this Schedule.

9(2) In sub-paragraph (1) **"special circumstances"** does not include–

(a) ability to pay, or

(b) the fact that a potential loss of revenue from one taxpayer is balanced by a potential over-payment by another.

9(3) In sub-paragraph (1) the reference to reducing a penalty includes a reference to–

(a) staying a penalty, and

(b) agreeing a compromise in relation to proceedings for a penalty.

INTERACTION WITH OTHER PENALTIES AND LATE PAYMENT SURCHARGES

9A In the application of the following provisions, no account shall be taken of a penalty under this Schedule–

(a) [not relevant to inheritance tax,]

(b) paragraph 12(2) of Schedule 24 to FA 2007 (interaction with other penalties), and

(c) paragraph 15(1) of Schedule 41 to FA 2008 (interaction with other penalties).

History – Para. 9A inserted by FA 2013, s. 230 and Sch. 50, para. 13, with effect for defaults made in relation to the tax year 2014–15 and subsequent tax years (see FA 2009, Sch. 56, para. 6(2) as to when a default is made in relation to a tax year).

SUSPENSION OF PENALTY DURING CURRENCY OF AGREEMENT FOR DEFERRED PAYMENT

10(1) This paragraph applies if–

(a) P fails to pay an amount of tax when it becomes due and payable,

(b) P makes a request to HMRC that payment of the amount of tax be deferred, and

(c) HMRC agrees that payment of that amount may be deferred for a period ("the deferral period").

10(2) If P would (apart from this sub-paragraph) become liable, between the date on which P makes the request and the end of the deferral period, to a penalty under any paragraph of this Schedule for failing to pay that amount, P is not liable to that penalty.

10(3) But if–

(a) P breaks the agreement (see sub-paragraph (4)), and

(b) HMRC serves on P a notice specifying any penalty to which P would become liable apart from sub-paragraph (2),

P becomes liable, at the date of the notice, to that penalty.

10(4) P breaks an agreement if–

(a) P fails to pay the amount of tax in question when the deferral period ends, or

(b) the deferral is subject to P complying with a condition (including a condition that part of the amount be paid during the deferral period) and P fails to comply with it.

10(5) If the agreement mentioned in sub-paragraph (1)(c) is varied at any time by a further agreement between P and HMRC this paragraph applies from that time to the agreement as varied.

ASSESSMENT

11(1) Where P is liable for a penalty under any paragraph of this Schedule HMRC must–

(a) assess the penalty,

(b) notify P, and

(c) state in the notice the period in respect of which the penalty is assessed.

11(2) A penalty under any paragraph of this Schedule must be paid before the end of the period of 30 days beginning with the day on which notice of the assessment of the penalty is issued.

11(3) An assessment of a penalty under any paragraph of this Schedule–

(a) is to be treated for procedural purposes in the same way as an assessment to tax (except in respect of a matter expressly provided for by this Schedule),

(b) may be enforced as if it were an assessment to tax, and

(c) may be combined with an assessment to tax.

11(4) A supplementary assessment may be made in respect of a penalty if an earlier assessment operated by reference to an underestimate of an amount of unpaid tax.

11(5) [Omitted by FA 2013, s. 230 and Sch. 50, para. 14(3).]

Prospective amendments – In para. 11(4), the words "tax which was due or payable" substituted for the words "unpaid tax" by F(No. 3)A 2010, s. 27 and Sch. 11, para. 9(2), with effect from a day to be appointed by Treasury order.
Para. 11(4A) inserted by F(No. 3)A 2010, s. 27 and Sch. 11, para. 9(3), with effect from a day to be appointed by Treasury order.
Para. 11(4A), as amended by FA 2013, s. 230 and Sch. 50, para. 14(2), to read as follows:

"**11(4A)** If an assessment in respect of a penalty is based on an amount of tax due or payable that is found by HMRC to be excessive, HMRC may by notice to P amend the assessment so that it is based upon the correct amount.

11(4B) An amendment made under sub-paragraph (4A)–

(a) does not affect when the penalty must be paid;

(b) may be made after the last day on which the assessment in question could have been made under paragraph 12.".

History – Para. 11(4A) and (4B) substituted for para. 11(4A) by FA 2013, s. 230 and Sch. 50, para. 14(2) with effect for defaults made in relation to the tax year 2014–15 and subsequent tax years (see FA 2009, Sch. 56, para. 6(2) as to when a default is made in relation to a tax year).
Para. 11(5) omitted by FA 2013, s. 230 and Sch. 50, para. 14(3), with effect for defaults made in relation to the tax year 2014–15 and subsequent tax years (see FA 2009, Sch. 56, para. 6(2) as to when a default is made in relation to a tax year).

Notes – The amendments made by F(No. 3)A 2010, s. 27 and Sch. 11, para. 9(2) and (3), were brought into effect from 6 April 2011 for the purposes of items 1, 12, 18 or 19 of the Table in para. 1 (income tax self assessment) (and insofar as the tax falls within item 1 of that Table, item 17, 23 or 24 of that Table) (SI 2011/703, art. 3).

12(1) An assessment of a penalty under any paragraph of this Schedule in respect of any amount must be made on or before the later of date A and (where it applies) date B.

12(2) Date A is the last day of the period of 2 years beginning with the date specified in or for the purposes of column 4 of the Table (that is to say, the last date on which payment may be made without incurring a penalty).

12(3) Date B is the last day of the period of 12 months beginning with–

(a) the end of the appeal period for the assessment of the amount of tax in respect of which the penalty is assessed, or

(b) if there is no such assessment, the date on which that amount of tax is ascertained.

12(4) In sub-paragraph (3)(a) **"appeal period"** means the period during which–

(a) an appeal could be brought, or

(b) an appeal that has been brought has not been determined or withdrawn.

APPEAL

13(1) P may appeal against a decision of HMRC that a penalty is payable by P.

13(2) P may appeal against a decision of HMRC as to the amount of a penalty payable by P.

14(1) An appeal under paragraph 13 is to be treated in the same way as an appeal against an assessment to the tax concerned (including by the application of any provision about bringing the appeal by notice to HMRC, about HMRC review of the decision or about determination of the appeal by the First-tier Tribunal or Upper Tribunal).

14(2) Sub-paragraph (1) does not apply–

(a) so as to require P to pay a penalty before an appeal against the assessment of the penalty is determined, or

(b) in respect of any other matter expressly provided for by this Act.

15(1) On an appeal under paragraph 13(1) that is notified to the tribunal, the tribunal may affirm or cancel HMRC's decision.

15(2) On an appeal under paragraph 13(2) that is notified to the tribunal, the tribunal may–

(a) affirm HMRC's decision, or

(b) substitute for HMRC's decision another decision that HMRC had power to make.

15(3) If the tribunal substitutes its decision for HMRC's, the tribunal may rely on paragraph 9–

(a) to the same extent as HMRC (which may mean applying the same percentage reduction as HMRC to a different starting point), or

(b) to a different extent, but only if the tribunal thinks that HMRC's decision in respect of the application of paragraph 9 was flawed.

15(4) In sub-paragraph (3)(b) **"flawed"** means flawed when considered in the light of the principles applicable in proceedings for judicial review.

15(5) In this paragraph **"tribunal"** means the First-tier Tribunal or Upper Tribunal (as appropriate by virtue of paragraph 14(1)).

REASONABLE EXCUSE

16(1) Liability to a penalty under any paragraph of this Schedule does not arise in relation to a failure to make a payment if P satisfies HMRC or (on appeal) the First-tier Tribunal or Upper Tribunal that there is a reasonable excuse for the failure.

16(2) For the purposes of sub-paragraph (1)–

(a) an insufficiency of funds is not a reasonable excuse unless attributable to events outside P's control,

(b) where P relies on any other person to do anything, that is not a reasonable excuse unless P took reasonable care to avoid the failure, and

(c) where P had a reasonable excuse for the failure but the excuse has ceased, P is to be treated as having continued to have the excuse if the failure is remedied without unreasonable delay after the excuse ceased.

Prospective amendments – Para. 16(1) substituted by F(No. 3)A 2010, s. 27 and Sch. 11, para. 10, with effect from a day to be appointed by Treasury order. The substituted para. 16(1) to read as follows:

"**16(1)** If P satisfies HMRC or (on appeal) the First-tier Tribunal or Upper Tribunal that there is a reasonable excuse for a failure to make a payment–

(a) liability to a penalty under any paragraph of this Schedule does not arise in relation to that failure, and

(b) the failure does not count as a default for the purposes of paragraphs 6, 8B, 8C, 8G and 8H.".

Notes – The substitution of para. 16(1) made by F(No. 3)A 2010, s. 27 and Sch. 11, para. 10 was brought into effect from 25 January 2011 for the purposes of item 2 (PAYE regulations), item 3 (returns under FA 2004, s. 254(1)) and item 4 (FA 2004, s. 62) of the Table in para. 1 and items 17, 23 and 24 but only insofar as the tax falls within any of items 2, 3 or 4 (SI 2011/132, art. 3).

DOUBLE JEOPARDY

17 P is not liable to a penalty under any paragraph of this Schedule in respect of a failure or action in respect of which P has been convicted of an offence.

INTERPRETATION

18(1) This paragraph applies for the construction of this Schedule.

18(2) **"HMRC"** means Her Majesty's Revenue and Customs.

18(3) [Not relevant to inheritance tax.]

18(4) [Not relevant to inheritance tax.]

18(5) References to an assessment to tax, in relation to inheritance tax and stamp duty reserve tax, are to a determination.

PERPETUITIES AND ACCUMULATIONS ACT 2009

(2009 Chapter 18)

[*12th November 2009*]

ARRANGEMENT OF SECTIONS

APPLICATION OF RULE AGAINST PERPETUITIES

1 Application of the rule

1(1) The rule against perpetuities applies (and applies only) as provided by this section.

1(2) If an instrument limits property in trust so as to create successive estates or interests the rule applies to each of the estates or interests.

IHT Statutes

1(3) If an instrument limits property in trust so as to create an estate or interest which is subject to a condition precedent and which is not one of successive estates or interests, the rule applies to the estate or interest.

1(4) If an instrument limits property in trust so as to create an estate or interest subject to a condition subsequent the rule applies to–

(a) any right of re-entry exercisable if the condition is broken, or

(b) any equivalent right exercisable in the case of property other than land if the condition is broken.

1(5) If an instrument which is a will limits personal property so as to create successive interests under the doctrine of executory bequests, the rule applies to each of the interests.

1(6) If an instrument creates a power of appointment the rule applies to the power.

1(7) For the purposes of subsection (2) an estate or interest includes an estate or interest–

(a) which arises under a right of reverter on the determination of a determinable fee simple, or

(b) which arises under a resulting trust on the determination of a determinable interest.

1(8) This section has effect subject to the exceptions made by section 2 and to any exceptions made under section 3.

1(9) In section 4(3) of the Law of Property Act 1925 (c. 20) (rights of entry affecting a legal estate) omit the words from "but" to the end.

Commencement Date – S. 1 came into force on 6 April 2010 (SI 2010/37, art. 2).

2 Exceptions to rule's application

2(1) This section contains exceptions to the application of the rule against perpetuities.

2(2) The rule does not apply to an estate or interest created so as to vest in a charity on the occurrence of an event if immediately before the occurrence an estate or interest in the property concerned is vested in another charity.

2(3) The rule does not apply to a right exercisable by a charity on the occurrence of an event if immediately before the occurrence an estate or interest in the property concerned is vested in another charity.

2(4) The rule does not apply to an interest or right arising under a relevant pension scheme.

2(5) The exception in subsection (4) does not apply if the interest or right arises under–

(a) an instrument nominating benefits under the scheme, or

(b) an instrument made in the exercise of a power of advancement arising under the scheme.

Commencement Date – S. 2 came into force on 6 April 2010 (SI 2010/37, art. 2).

3 Power to specify exceptions

3(1) The Lord Chancellor may by order provide that the rule against perpetuities is not to apply–

(a) in cases of a specified description, or

(b) if specified conditions are fulfilled.

3(2) Different descriptions and conditions may be specified for different purposes.

3(3) Any order under this section may include such supplementary, incidental, consequential or transitional provisions as appear to the Lord Chancellor to be necessary or expedient.

3(4) In this section **"specified"** means specified in the order.

3(5) The power to make an order under this section is exercisable by statutory instrument.

3(6) A statutory instrument containing an order under this section may not be made unless a draft of the instrument has been laid before and approved by a resolution of each House of Parliament.

Commencement Date – S. 3 came into force on 6 April 2010 (SI 2010/37, art. 2).

4 Abolition of existing exceptions

4(1) These provisions cease to have effect–

(a) section 121(6) of the Law of Property Act 1925 (c. 20) (rule against perpetuities not to apply to certain powers and remedies);

(b) section 162 of that Act (declaration that rule does not apply in certain cases);

(c) section 163 of the Pension Schemes Act 1993 (c. 48) (rule not to apply to trusts and dispositions concerning certain pension schemes).

Commencement Date – S. 4 came into force on 6 April 2010 (SI 2010/37, art. 2).

PERPETUITY PERIOD

5 Perpetuity period

5(1) The perpetuity period is 125 years (and no other period).

5(2) Subsection (1) applies whether or not the instrument referred to in section 1(2) to (6) specifies a perpetuity period; and a specification of a perpetuity period in that instrument is ineffective.

Commencement Date – S. 5 came into force on 6 April 2010 (SI 2010/37, art. 2).

PERPETUITIES: MISCELLANEOUS

6 Start of perpetuity period

6(1) The perpetuity period starts when the instrument referred to in section 1(2) to (6) takes effect; but this is subject to subsections (2) and (3).

6(2) If section 1(2), (3) or (4) applies and the instrument is made in the exercise of a special power of appointment the perpetuity period starts when the instrument creating the power takes effect; but this is subject to subsection (3).

6(3) If section 1(2), (3) or (4) applies and–

(a) the instrument nominates benefits under a relevant pension scheme, or

(b) the instrument is made in the exercise of a power of advancement arising under a relevant pension scheme,

the perpetuity period starts when the member concerned became a member of the scheme.

6(4) The member concerned is the member in respect of whose interest in the scheme the instrument is made.

Commencement Date – S. 6 came into force on 6 April 2010 (SI 2010/37, art. 2).

7 Wait and see rule

7(1) Subsection (2) applies if (apart from this section and section 8) an estate or interest would be void on the ground that it might not become vested until too remote a time.

7(2) In such a case–

(a) until such time (if any) as it becomes established that the vesting must occur (if at all) after the end of the perpetuity period the estate or interest must be treated as if it were not subject to the rule against perpetuities, and

(b) if it becomes so established, that does not affect the validity of anything previously done (whether by way of advancement, application of intermediate income or otherwise) in relation to the estate or interest.

7(3) Subsection (4) applies if (apart from this section) any of the following would be void on the ground that it might be exercised at too remote a time–

(a) a right of re-entry exercisable if a condition subsequent is broken;

(b) an equivalent right exercisable in the case of property other than land if a condition subsequent is broken;

(c) a special power of appointment.

7(4) In such a case–

(a) the right or power must be treated as regards any exercise of it within the perpetuity period as if it were not subject to the rule against perpetuities, and

(b) the right or power must be treated as void for remoteness only if and so far as it is not fully exercised within the perpetuity period.

7(5) Subsection (6) applies if (apart from this section) a general power of appointment would be void on the ground that it might not become exercisable until too remote a time.

7(6) Until such time (if any) as it becomes established that the power will not be exercisable within the perpetuity period, it must be treated as if it were not subject to the rule against perpetuities.

Commencement Date – S. 7 came into force on 6 April 2010 (SI 2010/37, art. 2).

8 Exclusion of class members to avoid remoteness

8(1) This section applies if–

(a) it is apparent at the time an instrument takes effect or becomes apparent at a later time that (apart from this section) the inclusion of certain persons as members of a class would cause an estate or interest to be treated as void for remoteness, and

(b) those persons are potential members of the class or unborn persons who at birth would become members or potential members of the class.

8(2) From the time it is or becomes so apparent those persons must be treated for all the purposes of the instrument as excluded from the class unless their exclusion would exhaust the class.

8(3) If this section applies in relation to an estate or interest to which section 7 applies, this section does not affect the validity of anything previously done (whether by way of advancement, application of intermediate income or otherwise) in relation to the estate or interest.

8(4) For the purposes of this section–

(a) a person is a member of a class if in that person's case all the conditions identifying a member of the class are satisfied, and

(b) a person is a potential member of a class if in that person's case some only of those conditions are satisfied but there is a possibility that the remainder will in time be satisfied.

Commencement Date – S. 8 came into force on 6 April 2010 (SI 2010/37, art. 2).

9 Saving and acceleration of expectant interests

9(1) An estate or interest is not void for remoteness by reason only that it is ulterior to and dependent on an estate or interest which is so void.

9(2) The vesting of an estate or interest is not prevented from being accelerated on the failure of a prior estate or interest by reason only that the failure arises because of remoteness.

Commencement Date – S. 9 came into force on 6 April 2010 (SI 2010/37, art. 2).

10 Determinable interests becoming absolute

10(1) If an estate arising under a right of reverter on the determination of a determinable fee simple is void for remoteness the determinable fee simple becomes absolute.

10(2) If an interest arising under a resulting trust on the determination of a determinable interest is void for remoteness the determinable interest becomes absolute.

Commencement Date – S. 10 came into force on 6 April 2010 (SI 2010/37, art. 2).

11 Powers of appointment

11(1) Subsection (2) applies to a power of appointment exercisable otherwise than by will (whether or not it is also exercisable by will).

11(2) For the purposes of the rule against perpetuities the power is a special power unless–

(a) the instrument creating it expresses it to be exercisable by one person only, and

(b) at all times during its currency when that person is of full age and capacity it could be exercised by that person so as immediately to transfer to that person the whole of the interest governed by the power without the consent of any other person or compliance with any other condition (ignoring a formal condition relating only to the mode of exercise of the power).

11(3) Subsection (4) applies to a power of appointment exercisable by will (whether or not it is also exercisable otherwise than by will).

11(4) For the purposes of the rule against perpetuities the power is a special power unless–

(a) the instrument creating it expresses it to be exercisable by one person only, and

(b) that person could exercise it so as to transfer to that person's personal representatives the whole of the estate or interest to which it relates.

11(5) Subsection (6) applies to a power of appointment exercisable by will or otherwise.

11(6) If for the purposes of the rule against perpetuities the power would be a special power under one but not both of subsections (2) and (4), for the purposes of the rule it is a special power.

Commencement Date – S. 11 came into force on 6 April 2010 (SI 2010/37, art. 2).

12 Pre-commencement instruments: period difficult to ascertain

12(1) If–

(a) an instrument specifies for the purposes of property limited in trust a perpetuity period by reference to the lives of persons in being when the instrument takes effect,

(b) the trustees believe that it is difficult or not reasonably practicable for them to ascertain whether the lives have ended and therefore whether the perpetuity period has ended, and

(c) they execute a deed stating that they so believe and that subsection (2) is to apply to the instrument,

that subsection applies to the instrument.

12(2) If this subsection applies to an instrument–

(a) the instrument has effect as if it specified a perpetuity period of 100 years (and no other period);

(b) the rule against perpetuities has effect as if the only perpetuity period applicable to the instrument were 100 years;

(c) sections 6 to 11 of this Act are to be treated as if they applied (and always applied) in relation to the instrument;

(d) sections 1 to 12 of the Perpetuities and Accumulations Act 1964 (c. 55) are to be treated as if they did not apply (and never applied) in relation to the instrument.

12(3) A deed executed under this section cannot be revoked.

Commencement Date – S. 12 came into force on 6 April 2010 (SI 2010/37, art. 2).

ACCUMULATIONS

13 Abolition of restrictions

13 These provisions cease to have effect–

(a) sections 164 to 166 of the Law of Property Act 1925 (c. 20) (which impose restrictions on accumulating income, subject to qualifications);

(b) section 13 of the Perpetuities and Accumulations Act 1964 (which amends section 164 of the 1925 Act).

Commencement Date – S. 13 came into force on 6 April 2010 (SI 2010/37, art. 2).

14 Restriction on accumulation for charitable trusts

14(1) This section applies to an instrument to the extent that it provides for property to be held on trust for charitable purposes.

14(2) But it does not apply where the provision is made by a court or the Charity Commission for England and Wales.

14(3) If the instrument imposes or confers on the trustees a duty or power to accumulate income, and apart from this section the duty or power would last beyond the end of the statutory period, it ceases to have effect at the end of that period unless subsection (5) applies.

14(4) The statutory period is a period of 21 years starting with the first day when the income must or may be accumulated (as the case may be).

14(5) This subsection applies if the instrument provides for the duty or power to cease to have effect–

(a) on the death of the settlor, or

(b) on the death of one of the settlors, determined by name or by the order of their deaths.

14(6) If a duty or power ceases to have effect under this section the income to which the duty or power would have applied apart from this section must–

(a) go to the person who would have been entitled to it if there had been no duty or power to accumulate, or

(b) be applied for the purposes for which it would have had to be applied if there had been no such duty or power.

14(7) This section applies whether or not the duty or power to accumulate extends to income produced by the investment of income previously accumulated.

Commencement Date – S. 14 came into force on 6 April 2010 (SI 2010/37, art. 2).

APPLICATION OF STATUTORY PROVISIONS

15 Application of this Act

15(1) Sections 1, 2, 4 to 11, 13 and 14 apply in relation to an instrument taking effect on or after the commencement day, except that–

(a) those sections do not apply in relation to a will executed before that day, and

(b) those sections apply in relation to an instrument made in the exercise of a special power of appointment only if the instrument creating the power takes effect on or after that day.

15(2) Section 12 applies (except as provided by subsection (3)) in relation to–

(a) a will executed before the commencement day (whether or not it takes effect before that day);

(b) an instrument, other than a will, taking effect before that day.

15(3) Section 12 does not apply if–

(a) the terms of the trust were exhausted before the commencement day, or

(b) before that day the property became held on trust for charitable purposes by way of a final disposition of the property.

15(4) The commencement day is the day appointed under section 22(2).

Commencement Date – S. 15 came into force on 6 April 2010 (SI 2010/37, art. 2).

16 Limitation of 1964 Act to existing instruments

16 In section 15 of the Perpetuities and Accumulations Act 1964 (c. 55) the following subsections are inserted after subsection (5) (which makes provision as to the instruments to which the Act applies)–

> "**15(5A)** The foregoing sections of this Act shall not apply in relation to an instrument taking effect on or after the day appointed under section 22(2) of the Perpetuities and Accumulations Act 2009 (commencement), but this shall not prevent those sections applying in relation to an instrument so taking effect if–
>
> (a) it is a will executed before that day, or
>
> (b) it is an instrument made in the exercise of a special power of appointment, and the instrument creating the power took effect before that day.
>
> **15(5B)** Subsection (5A) above shall not affect the operation of sections 4(6) and 11(2) above."

Commencement Date – S. 16 came into force on 6 April 2010 (SI 2010/37, art. 2).

GENERAL

17 The Crown

17(1) This Act does not extend the application of the rule against perpetuities in relation to the Crown.

17(2) Subject to that, this Act binds the Crown.

Commencement Date – S. 17 came into force on 6 April 2010 (SI 2010/37, art. 2).

18 Rule as to duration not affected

18 This Act does not affect the rule of law which limits the duration of noncharitable purpose trusts.

Commencement Date – S. 18 came into force on 6 April 2010 (SI 2010/37, art. 2).

19 Provision made otherwise than by instrument

19 If provision is made in relation to property otherwise than by an instrument, this Act applies as if the provision were contained in an instrument taking effect on the making of the provision.

Commencement Date – S. 19 came into force on 6 April 2010 (SI 2010/37, art. 2).

20 Interpretation

20(1) For the purposes of this Act this section contains provisions relating to the interpretation of these expressions–

(a) power of appointment, general power of appointment and special power of appointment;

(b) relevant pension scheme;

(c) taking effect (in relation to a will);

(d) will.

20(2) A power of appointment includes–

(a) a discretionary power to create a beneficial interest in property without the provision of valuable consideration;

(b) a discretionary power to transfer a beneficial interest in property without the provision of valuable consideration.

20(3) Section 11 applies to interpret references to a general or special power of appointment.

20(4) Each of these is a relevant pension scheme–

(a) an occupational pension scheme;

(b) a personal pension scheme;

(c) a public service pension scheme.

20(5) The expressions in subsection (4)(a) to (c) have the meanings given by sections 1 and 181(1) of the Pension Schemes Act 1993 (c. 48).

20(6) An instrument which is a will takes effect at the testator's death.

20(7) A reference to a will includes a reference to a codicil.
Commencement Date – S. 20 came into force on 6 April 2010 (SI 2010/37, art. 2).

21 Repeals

21 The enactments mentioned in the Schedule are repealed to the extent specified, but subject to the provision at the end of the Schedule.
Commencement Date – S. 21 came into force on 6 April 2010 (SI 2010/37, art. 2).

22 Commencement

22(1) This section and sections 23 and 24 come into force on the day on which this Act is passed.

22(2) The other provisions of this Act come into force on such day as the Lord Chancellor may appoint by order made by statutory instrument.

23 Extent

23 This Act extends to England and Wales only.

24 Short title

24 This Act may be cited as the Perpetuities and Accumulations Act 2009.

SCHEDULES

SCHEDULE

Commencement Date – Schedule came into force on 6 April 2010 (SI 2010/37, art. 2).

REPEALS

Short title and chapter	*Extent of repeal*
Law of Property Act 1925 (c. 20)	In section 4(3), the words from "but" to the end.
	Section 121(6).
	Section 162.
	Sections 164 to 166.
Perpetuities and Accumulations Act 1964 (c. 55)	Section 13.
Pension Schemes Act 1993 (c. 48)	Section 163.

FINANCE ACT 2010

(2010 Chapter 13)

[*8th April 2010*]

ARRANGEMENT OF SECTIONS

PART 1 – CHARGES, RATES ETC

INHERITANCE TAX

8 Rate bands

8(1) The Table substituted in Schedule 1 to IHTA 1984 by section 155(1)(b) and (4) of FA 2006 (which provides for a rate of nil per cent on such portion of the value concerned as does not exceed £325,000 and a rate of 40 per cent on such portion as exceeds that amount) has effect in relation to chargeable transfers made on or after 6 April 2010.

8(2) Accordingly, omit–

(a) [*omits Table substituted* in IHTA 1984, Sch. 1 by FA 2007, s. 4;]

(b) [omits FA 2007, s. 4.]

8(3) Section 8 of IHTA 1984 (indexation) does not have effect by virtue of any difference between the retail prices index for the month of September in 2010, 2011, 2012 or 2013 and the previous September.

PART 2 – ANTI-AVOIDANCE AND REVENUE PROTECTION

CHARITIES ETC

30 Charities and community amateur sports clubs: definitions

30 Schedule 6 contains provision about the meaning of **"charity"** (and related expressions) and **"community amateur sports club"**.

OTHER INTERNATIONAL MATTERS

35 Penalties: offshore income etc

35(1) Schedule 10 contains provision about penalties in respect of offshore income etc.

35(2) Schedule 10 comes into force on such day as the Treasury may by order appoint.

35(3) An order under subsection (2)–

(a) may make different provision for different purposes, and

(b) may include transitional provisions and savings.

35(4) The Treasury may by order make any incidental, supplemental, consequential, transitional or transitory provision or saving that appears appropriate in consequence of, or otherwise in connection with, Schedule 10.

35(5) An order under subsection (4) may–

(a) make different provision for different purposes, and

(b) make provision amending, repealing or revoking an enactment or instrument (whenever passed or made).

35(6) An order under this section is to be made by statutory instrument.

35(7) A statutory instrument containing an order under subsection (4) is subject to annulment in pursuance of a resolution of the House of Commons.

Statutory instruments – SI 2011/975 (not reproduced): made under s. 35(2) and (3).

INHERITANCE TAX

52 Reversionary interests of purchaser or settlor etc in relevant property

52(1) [Inserts IHTA 1984, s. 81A.]

52(2) The amendment made by subsection (1) has effect in relation to reversionary interests to which a relevant reversioner becomes beneficially entitled on or after 9 December 2009.

53 Interests in possession

53(1) IHTA 1984 is amended as follows.

53(2) In section 3A (potentially exempt transfers)–

(a) [amends IHTA 1984, s. 3A(6),]

(b) [inserts IHTA 1984, s. 3A(6A).]

53(3) In section 5 (meaning of estate)–

(a) [amends IHTA 1984, s. 5(1)(a)(ii),]

(b) [inserts IHTA 1984, s. 5(1B).]

53(4)

(a) [amends IHTA 1984, s. 49(1A),]

(b) [amends IHTA 1984, s. 51(1A),]

(c) [amends IHTA 1984, s. 52(2A) and (3A).]

53(5) [Amends IHTA 1984, s. 57A(1A).]

53(6) [Amends IHTA 1984, s. 100(1A).]

53(7) [Amends IHTA 1984, s. 101(1A).]

53(8) [Amends FA 1986, s. 102ZA(1)(b)(ii).]

53(9) [Amends F(No. 2)A 1987, s. 96(2)(c).]

IHT Statutes

53(10) The amendments made by this section have effect in relation to an interest in possession to which a person is beneficially entitled if the person becomes beneficially entitled to it on or after 9 December 2009.

ADMINISTRATION

56 Disclosure of tax avoidance schemes

56 Schedule 17 contains amendments of the provisions relating to the disclosure of tax avoidance schemes.

PART 3 – OTHER PROVISIONS

MISCELLANEOUS

64 FSCS intervention in relation to insurance contracts

64(1) The Treasury may by regulations make provision for and in connection with the application of the relevant taxes in relation to circumstances in which there is relevant intervention under the FSCS.

64(2) **"Relevant intervention"** means–

(a) anything done under, or while seeking to make, arrangements for securing continuity of insurance in connection with protected contracts of insurance,

(b) anything done as part of measures for safeguarding policyholders in connection with protected contracts of insurance, or

(c) the payment of compensation in connection with protected contracts of insurance.

64(3) In this section–

"the FSCS" means the Financial Services Compensation Scheme (established under Part 15 of FISMA 2000);

"protected contracts of insurance" has the same meaning as in the Handbook made by the Financial Services Authority under that Act as it has effect from time to time.

64(4) The provision that may be made by regulations under this section includes provision imposing any of the relevant taxes (as well as provisions for exemptions or reliefs).

64(5) The relevant taxes are–

(a) income tax,

(b) capital gains tax,

(c) corporation tax,

(d) inheritance tax,

(e) stamp duty land tax,

(f) stamp duty,

(g) stamp duty reserve tax, and

(h) insurance premium tax.

64(6) Regulations under this section may include provision having effect in relation to any time before they are made if the provision does not increase any person's liability to tax.

64(7) The provision made by regulations under this section may be framed as provision modifying, or applying with appropriate modifications, provisions having effect in relation to protected contracts of insurance.

64(8) Regulations under this section may, in particular–

(a) amend, repeal or revoke or otherwise modify any enactment or instrument (whenever passed or made),

(b) make different provision for different cases or otherwise for different purposes, and

(c) make incidental, consequential, supplementary or transitional provision.

64(9) Regulations under this section are to be made by statutory instrument.

64(10) A statutory instrument containing regulations under this section is subject to annulment in *pursuance of a resolution of the House of Commons.*

FINAL PROVISIONS

69 Interpretation

69(1) In this Act–

"ALDA 1979" means the Alcoholic Liquor Duties Act 1979;

"BGDA 1981" means the Betting and Gaming Duties Act 1981;

"CAA 2001" means the Capital Allowances Act 2001;

"CTA 2009" means the Corporation Tax Act 2009;

"CTA 2010" means the Corporation Tax Act 2010;

"FISMA 2000" means the Financial Services and Markets Act 2000;

"HODA 1979" means the Hydrocarbon Oil Duties Act 1979;

"ICTA" means the Income and Corporation Taxes Act 1988;

"IHTA 1984" means the Inheritance Tax Act 1984;

"ITA 2007" means the Income Tax Act 2007;

"ITEPA 2003" means the Income Tax (Earnings and Pensions) Act 2003;

"ITTOIA 2005" means the Income Tax (Trading and Other Income) Act 2005;

"TCGA 1992" means the Taxation of Chargeable Gains Act 1992;

"TIOPA 2010" means the Taxation (International and Other Provisions) Act 2010;

"TMA 1970" means the Taxes Management Act 1970;

"TPDA 1979" means the Tobacco Products Duty Act 1979;

"VATA 1994" means the Value Added Tax Act 1994;

"VERA 1994" means the Vehicle Excise and Registration Act 1994.

69(2) In this Act–

"FA", followed by a year, means the Finance Act of that year;

"F(No. 2)A", followed by a year, means the Finance (No. 2) Act of that year.

70 Short title

70 This Act may be cited as the Finance Act 2010.

SCHEDULES

SCHEDULE 6 – CHARITIES AND COMMUNITY AMATEUR SPORTS CLUBS: DEFINITIONS

Section 30

Part 1 – Definition of "Charity", "Charitable Company" and "Charitable Trust"

DEFINITION OF "CHARITY" ETC

1(1) For the purposes of the enactments to which this Part applies **"charity"** means a body of persons or trust that–

(a) is established for charitable purposes only,

(b) meets the jurisdiction condition (see paragraph 2),

(c) meets the registration condition (see paragraph 3), and

(d) meets the management condition (see paragraph 4).

1(2) For the purposes of the enactments to which this Part applies–

"charitable company" means a charity that is a body of persons;

"charitable trust" means a charity that is a trust.

1(3) Sub-paragraphs (1) and (2) are subject to any express provision to the contrary.

1(4) For the meaning of **"charitable purpose"**, see section 2 of the Charities Act 2011 (which–

(a) applies regardless of where the body of persons or trust in question is established, and

(b) for this purpose forms part of the law of each part of the United Kingdom (see sections 7 and 8 of that Act)).

History – In para. 1(4), the words "see section 2 of the Charities Act 2011" substituted for the words "see section 2 of the Charities Act 2006" by Charities Act 2011, s. 354 and Sch. 7, para. 143(2)(a), with effect from the end of the period of 3 months beginning with 14 December 2011.

In para. 1(4)(b), the words "(see sections 7 and 8 of that Act)" substituted for the words "(see section 80(3) to (6) of that Act)" by Charities Act 2011, s. 354 and Sch. 7, para. 143(2)(b), with effect from the end of the period of 3 months beginning with 14 December 2011.

JURISDICTION CONDITION

2(1) A body of persons or trust meets the jurisdiction condition if it falls to be subject to the control of–

(a) a relevant UK court in the exercise of its jurisdiction with respect to charities, or

(b) any other court in the exercise of a corresponding jurisdiction under the law of a relevant territory.

2(2) In sub-paragraph (1)(a) **"a relevant UK court"** means–

(a) the High Court,

(b) the Court of Session, or

(c) the High Court in Northern Ireland.

2(3) In sub-paragraph (1)(b) **"a relevant territory"** means–

(a) a member State other than the United Kingdom, or

(b) a territory specified in regulations made by the Commissioners for Her Majesty's Revenue and Customs.

2(4) Regulations under this paragraph are to be made by statutory instrument.

2(5) A statutory instrument containing regulations under this paragraph is subject to annulment in pursuance of a resolution of the House of Commons.

Statutory instruments – SI 2010/1904: made under para. 2.

REGISTRATION CONDITION

3(1) A body of persons or trust meets the registration condition if–

(a) in the case of a body of persons or trust that is a charity within the meaning of section 10 of the Charities Act 2011, condition A is met, and

(b) in the case of any other body of persons or trust, condition B is met.

3(2) Condition A is that the body of persons or trust has complied with any requirement to be registered in the register of charities kept under section 29 of the Charities Act 2011.

3(3) Condition B is that the body of persons or trust has complied with any requirement under the law of a territory outside England and Wales to be registered in a register corresponding to that mentioned in sub-paragraph (2).

History – In para. 3(1)(a), the words "within the meaning of section 10 of the Charities Act 2011" substituted for the words "within the meaning of the Charities Act 1993" by Charities Act 2011, s. 354 and Sch. 7, para. 143(3), with effect from the end of the period of 3 months beginning with 14 December 2011.

In para. 3(2), the words "section 29 of the Charities Act 2011" substituted for the words "section 3 of the Charities Act 1993" by Charities Act 2011, s. 354 and Sch. 7, para. 143(4), with effect from the end of the period of 3 months beginning with 14 December 2011.

MANAGEMENT CONDITION

4(1) A body of persons or trust meets the management condition if its managers are fit and proper persons to be managers of the body or trust.

4(2) In this paragraph **"managers"**, in relation to a body of persons or trust, means the persons having the general control and management of the administration of the body or trust.

PERIODS OVER WHICH MANAGEMENT CONDITION TREATED AS MET

5(1) This paragraph applies in relation to any period throughout which the management condition is not met.

5(2) The management condition is treated as met throughout the period if the Commissioners for Her Majesty's Revenue and Customs consider that–

(a) the failure to meet the management condition has not prejudiced the charitable purposes of the body or trust, or

(b) it is just and reasonable in all the circumstances for the condition to be treated as met throughout the period.

PUBLICATION OF NAMES AND ADDRESSES OF BODIES OR TRUSTS REGARDED BY HMRC AS CHARITIES

6 Her Majesty's Revenue and Customs may publish the name and address of any body of persons or trust that appears to them to meet, or at any time to have met, the definition of a charity in paragraph 1.

ENACTMENTS TO WHICH THIS PART APPLIES

7 The enactments to which this Part applies are the enactments relating to–

(a) income tax

(b) capital gains tax,

(c) corporation tax,

(d) value added tax,

(e) inheritance tax,

(f) stamp duty,

(g) stamp duty land tax,

(h) stamp duty reserve tax.

(i) annual tax on enveloped dwellings, and

(j) diverted profits tax.

History – Para. 7(i) (and the word ", and" before it) inserted (and the word "and" formerly at end of para. 7(g) omitted) by FA 2013, s. 168 and Sch. 35, para. 3, with effect from 17 July 2013 (Royal Assent).
Para. 7(j) (and the word ", and" before it) inserted (and the word "and" formerly at end of para. 7(h) omitted) by FA 2015, s. 115(2), with effect in relation to accounting periods beginning on or after 1 April 2015 (subject to provisions of FA 2015, s. 116(2)–(5)).

Part 2 – Repeals of Superseded Definitions and Other Consequential Amendments

Notes – Only paragraphs relating to inheritance tax reproduced here.

IHTA 1984

10 [Amends IHTA 1984, s. 272.]

FA 2008

24 [Amends FA 2008, Sch. 36, para. 60(2).]

POWER TO MAKE FURTHER CONSEQUENTIAL PROVISION

29(1) The Commissioners for Her Majesty's Revenue and Customs may by order make such further consequential, incidental, supplemental, transitional or transitory provision or saving as appears appropriate in consequence of, or otherwise in connection with, Part 1.

29(2) An order under this paragraph may–

(a) make different provision for different purposes, and

(b) make provision repealing, revoking or otherwise amending any enactment or instrument (whenever passed or made).

29(3) An order under this paragraph is to be made by statutory instrument.

29(4) A statutory instrument containing an order under this paragraph is subject to annulment in pursuance of an order of the House of Commons.

Part 4 – Commencement

COMMENCEMENT OF PART 1

33(1) Part 1 is treated as having come into force on 6 April 2010.

33(2) But the definitions of **"charity"**, **"charitable company"** and **"charitable trust"** in that Part do not apply for the purposes of an enactment in relation to which, on that date, another definition applies until such time as that other definition ceases to have effect on the coming into force of provision made by or under Part 2.

33(3) For provision about the coming into force of provision made by that Part, see paragraph 34.

COMMENCEMENT OF PART 2

34(1) The repeal of the definition of **"charity"** in section 989 of ITA 2007 made by paragraph 23(6) above has effect–

(a) so far as it applies for the purposes of Chapter 2 of Part 8 of that Act (gift aid), in relation to gifts made on or after 6 April 2010, and

(b) so far as it applies for other purposes, in accordance with such provision as the Treasury may make by order.

34(2) The other amendments made by Part 2 come into force in accordance with such provision as the Treasury may make by order.

34(3) An order under this paragraph may–

(a) make different provision for different purposes, and

(b) include transitional provision and savings.

34(4) An order under this paragraph is to be made by statutory instrument.

Statutory instruments – SI 2012/736 (not reproduced): made under para. 34(1)(b), (2) and (3).

SCHEDULE 10 – PENALTIES: OFFSHORE INCOME ETC

Section 35

Other material – HMRC Brief 14/11: Penalty for failure to disclose offshore income or gains.

SCHEDULE 24 TO FA 2007

1 Schedule 24 to FA 2007 (penalties for errors) is amended as follows.

2 [Substitutes FA 2007, Sch. 24, para. 4, 4A, 4B, 4C, 4D.]

3 [Substitutes FA 2007, Sch. 24, para. 10.]

4 [Substitutes FA 2007, Sch. 24, para. 12(4), (5).]

5 [Inserts FA 2007, Sch. 24, para. 21A, 21B.]

6 [Inserts FA 2007, Sch. 24, para. 23B.]

SCHEDULE 55 TO FA 2009

10 Schedule 55 to FA 2009 (penalties for failure to make returns etc) is amended as follows.

14 In paragraph 17 (interaction with other penalties)–

(a) in sub-paragraph (3), for "100%" substitute "the relevant percentage", and

(b) after that sub-paragraph insert–

"**17(4)** The relevant percentage is–

(a) if one of the penalties is a penalty under paragraph 6(3) or (4) and the information withheld is category 3 information, 200%,

(b) if one of the penalties is a penalty under paragraph 6(3) or (4) and the information withheld is category 2 information, 150%, and

(c) in all other cases, 100%."

SCHEDULE 17 – DISCLOSURE OF TAX AVOIDANCE SCHEMES

Section 56

INTRODUCTION

1 Part 7 of FA 2004 (disclosure of tax avoidance schemes) is amended as follows.

INITIAL MARKETING

2(1) Section 307 (meaning of **"promoter"**) is amended as follows.

2(2) [Amends FA 2004, s. 307(1)(a).]

2(3) [Amends FA 2004, s. 307(1)(b).]

2(4) [Inserts FA 2004, s. 307(1A).]

2(5) [Inserts FA 2004, s. 307(4A), (4B) and (4C).]

2(6) [Amends FA 2004, s. 307(5).]

2(7) [Amends FA 2004, s. 307(6).]

3(1) Section 308(2) (duties of promoter) is amended as follows.

3(2) [Amends FA 2004, s. 308(2).]

3(3) [Inserts FA 2004, s. 308(2)(za).]

4 [Amends FA 2004, s. 313A(1).]

5 [Amends FA 2004, s. 318(1).]

PROMOTERS TO PROVIDE CLIENT LISTS

6 [Inserts FA 2004, s. 313ZA.]

7 [Amends FA 2004, s. 316.]

8 [Amends FA 2004, s. 317(2).]

INFORMATION PROVIDED TO INTRODUCERS

9 [Inserts FA 2004, s. 313C.]

PENALTIES

10(1) Section 98C of TMA 1970 (penalties for failures to comply with duties relating to disclosure of tax avoidance schemes) is amended as follows.

10(2) [Amends TMA 1970, s. 98C(1)(a).]

10(3) In subsection (2)–

(a) [amends TMA 1970, s. 98C(2)(da),]

(b) [inserts TMA 1970, s. 98C(2)(db),]

(c) [inserts TMA 1970, s. 98C(2)(f).]

10(4) [Inserts TMA 1970, s. 98C(2ZA), (2ZB), (2ZC), (2ZD) and (2ZE).]

10(5) [Amends TMA 1970, s. 98C(2A).]

10(6) [Amends TMA 1970, s. 98C(2B).]

10(7) [Amends TMA 1970, s. 98C(2C)(b).]

10(8) [Amends TMA 1970, s. 98C(2D).]

10(9) [Amends TMA 1970, s. 98C(2E).]

10(10) In subsection (2F)–

(a) [amends TMA 1970, s. 98C(2C),]

(b) [amends TMA 1970, s. 98C(2C)(c).]

COMMENCEMENT

11(1) The amendments made by this Schedule come into force on such day as the Treasury may by order made by statutory instrument appoint.

11(2) An order may appoint different days for different provisions or for different purposes.

Statutory instruments – SI 2010/3019 (not reproduced): appoints 1 January 2011 as the commencement day for the amendments made by Sch. 17.

IHT Statutes

FINANCE (NO. 3) ACT 2010

(2010 Chapter 33) [*16th December 2010*]

ARRANGEMENT OF SECTIONS

PART 3 – ADMINISTRATION

PART 4 – MISCELLANEOUS PROVISIONS

PART 5 – FINAL PROVISIONS

SCHEDULES

PART 3 – ADMINISTRATION

25 Interest: corporation tax and petroleum revenue tax

25(1) Schedule 9 contains amendments of FA 2009 relating to late payment interest and repayment interest on amounts of corporation tax and petroleum revenue tax.

25(2) That Schedule comes into force on such day as the Treasury may by order appoint.

25(3) An order under subsection (2)–

(a) may commence a provision generally or only for specified purposes, and

(b) may appoint different days for different provisions or for different purposes.

25(4) The Treasury may by order make any incidental, supplemental, consequential, transitional, transitory or saving provision which appears appropriate in consequence of, or otherwise in connection with, that Schedule.

25(5) An order under subsection (4) may–

(a) make different provision for different purposes, and

(b) make provision amending, repealing or revoking any Act or subordinate legislation whenever passed or made (including this Act and any Act amended by it).

25(6) An order under this section is to be made by statutory instrument.

25(7) A statutory instrument containing an order under subsection (4) which includes provision amending or repealing any provision of an Act is subject to annulment in pursuance of a resolution of the House of Commons.

26 Penalties for failure to make returns etc

26(1) Schedule 10 contains provision amending Schedule 55 to FA 2009 (penalties in respect of failures to make returns and other documents relating to liabilities for tax).

26(2) Schedule 10 comes into force on such day as the Treasury may by order appoint.

26(3) An order under subsection (2)–

(a) may commence a provision generally or only for specified purposes, and

(b) may appoint different days for different provisions or for different purposes.

26(4) The Treasury may by order make any incidental, supplemental, consequential, transitional, transitory or saving provision which appears appropriate in consequence of, or otherwise in connection with, that Schedule.

26(5) An order under subsection (4) may–

(a) make different provision for different purposes, and

(b) make provision amending, repealing or revoking any Act or subordinate legislation whenever passed or made (including this Act and any Act amended by it).

26(6) An order under this section is to be made by statutory instrument.

26(7) A statutory instrument containing an order under subsection (4) which includes provision amending or repealing any provision of an Act is subject to annulment in pursuance of a resolution of the House of Commons.

27 Penalties for failure to pay tax

27(1) Schedule 11 contains provision amending Schedule 56 to FA 2009 (penalties in respect of failures to comply with obligations to pay tax).

27(2) Schedule 11 comes into force on such day as the Treasury may by order appoint.

27(3) An order under subsection (2)–

(a) may commence a provision generally or only for specified purposes, and

(b) may appoint different days for different provisions or for different purposes.

27(4) The Treasury may by order make any incidental, supplemental, consequential, transitional, transitory or saving provision which appears appropriate in consequence of, or otherwise in connection with, that Schedule.

27(5) An order under subsection (4) may–

(a) make different provision for different purposes, and

(b) make provision amending, repealing or revoking any Act or subordinate legislation whenever passed or made (including this Act and any Act amended by it).

27(6) An order under this section is to be made by statutory instrument.

27(7) A statutory instrument containing an order under subsection (4) which includes provision amending or repealing any provision of an Act is subject to annulment in pursuance of a resolution of the House of Commons.

PART 4 – MISCELLANEOUS PROVISIONS

31 Asbestos compensation settlements

Schedule 14 contains provision about the taxation of settlements the purpose of which is to make compensation payments to or in respect of individuals affected by an asbestos-related condition.

PART 5 – FINAL PROVISIONS

32 Interpretation

32(1) In this Act–

"BGDA 1981" means the Betting and Gaming Duties Act 1981;

"CAA 2001" means the Capital Allowances Act 2001;

"CTA 2009" means the Corporation Tax Act 2009;

"CTA 2010" means the Corporation Tax Act 2010;

"HODA 1979" means the Hydrocarbon Oil Duties Act 1979;

"ICTA" means the Income and Corporation Taxes Act 1988;

"IHTA 1984" means the Inheritance Tax Act 1984;

"ITA 2007" means the Income Tax Act 2007;

"ITEPA 2003" means the Income Tax (Earnings and Pensions) Act 2003;

"ITTOIA 2005" means the Income Tax (Trading and Other Income) Act 2005;

"OTA 1975" means the Oil Taxation Act 1975;

"TCGA 1992" means the Taxation of Chargeable Gains Act 1992;

"**TIOPA 2010**" means the Taxation (International and Other Provisions) Act 2010;

"**TMA 1970**" means the Taxes Management Act 1970;

"**TPDA 1979**" means the Tobacco Products Duty Act 1979;

"**VATA 1994**" means the Value Added Tax Act 1994;

"**VERA 1994**" means the Vehicle Excise and Registration Act 1994.

32(2) In this Act–

"**FA**", followed by a year, means the Finance Act of that year;

"**F(No. 2)A**", followed by a year, means the Finance (No. 2) Act of that year.

33 Short title

This Act may be cited as the Finance (No. 3) Act 2010.

SCHEDULES

SCHEDULE 9 – INTEREST

Section 25

Part 1 – Corporation Tax

AMENDMENTS OF SECTIONS 101 TO 104

1 FA 2009 is amended as follows.

2 In section 101 (late payment interest on sums due to HMRC), omit subsection (2)(a).

3(1) Section 102 (repayment interest on sums to be paid by HMRC) is amended as follows.

3(2) Omit subsection (2)(a).

3(3) [Not relevant to inheritance tax.]

Part 2 – Petroleum Revenue Tax

13 FA 2009 is amended as follows.

14 In section 101 (late payment interest on sums due to HMRC), omit subsection (2)(b).

15 In section 102 (repayment interest on sums to be paid by HMRC), omit subsection (2)(b).

SCHEDULE 10 – PENALTY FOR FAILURE TO MAKE RETURNS ETC

Section 26

1 Schedule 55 to FA 2009 (penalty for failure to make returns etc) is amended as follows.

2(1) Paragraph 1 (penalty for failure) is amended as follows.

2(2) In sub-paragraph (2), for "13" substitute "13J".

2(3) The Table is amended as follows.

2(4) [Not relevant to inheritance tax.]

2(5) [Not relevant to inheritance tax.]

3 For paragraph 2 (amount of penalty for occasional or annual returns) and the italic heading preceding it substitute–

"AMOUNT OF PENALTY: OCCASIONAL RETURNS AND RETURNS FOR PERIODS OF 6 MONTHS OR MORE

2(1) Paragraphs 3 to 6 apply in the case of–

(a) a return falling within any of items 1 to 5, 7 and 8 to 13 in the Table,

(b) a return falling within any of items 7A, 7B and 14 to 28 which relates to a period of 6 months or more, and

(c) a return falling within item 7A which relates to a transitional period for the purposes of the annual accounting scheme.

2(2) In sub-paragraph (1)(c), a transitional period for the purposes of the annual accounting scheme is a prescribed accounting period (within the meaning of section 25(1) of VATA 1994) which–

(a) ends on the day immediately preceding the date indicated by the Commissioners for Her Majesty's Revenue and Customs in a notification of authorisation under regulation 50 of the Value Added Tax Regulations 1995 (S.I. 1995/2518) (admission to annual accounting scheme), or

(b) begins on the day immediately following the end of the last period of 12 months for which such an authorisation has effect."

4(1) Paragraph 6 (amount of penalty for occasional returns and annual returns) is amended as follows.

4(2) In sub-paragraph (2), after "P" in the first place it occurs insert "deliberately".

4(3) In sub-paragraph (5), for "any other case" substitute "any case not falling within sub-paragraph (2)".

8 In paragraph 14(1) (reductions for disclosure), for "or 11(3) or (4)" substitute ", 11(3) or (4), 13E(3) or (4) or 13J(3) or (4)".

9 In paragraph 15(5) (reductions for disclosure not below certain amounts)–

(a) for "paragraph 11(3) or (4)" substitute "sub-paragraph (3) or (4) of any of paragraphs 11, 13E and 13J", and

(b) for "paragraph 11(3)(b) or (4)(b) (as the case may be)" substitute "paragraph (b) of that sub-paragraph".

10 [Repealed by FA 2013, s. 230 and Sch. 50, para. 15.]

History – Para. 10 repealed by FA 2013, s. 230 and Sch. 50, para. 15, with effect for the tax year 2014–15 and subsequent tax years in relation to failures to make returns with a filing date (as defined in FA 2009, Sch. 55, para. 1(4)) on or after 6 April 2014. Former para. 10 inserted FA 2009, Sch. 55, para. 18(5).

11 For paragraph 23(1) (no liability where there is reasonable excuse for failure) substitute–

"**23(1)** If P satisfies HMRC or (on appeal) the First-tier Tribunal or Upper Tribunal that there is a reasonable excuse for a failure to make a return–

(a) liability to a penalty under any paragraph of this Schedule does not arise in relation to that failure, and

(b) the failure does not count for the purposes of paragraphs 13B(2), 13C, 13G(2) and 13H."

SCHEDULE 11 – PENALTY FOR FAILURE TO MAKE PAYMENTS ON TIME

Section 27

1 Schedule 56 to FA 2009 (penalty for failure to make payments on time) is amended as follows.

2(1) Paragraph 1 (penalty for failure) is amended as follows.

2(2) In sub-paragraph (2), for "8" substitute "8J".

2(3)–(14) [Not relevant to inheritance tax.]

3 In paragraph 2 (assessments and determinations in default of return), in paragraph (c), for "10" substitute "11M".

5(1) Paragraph 3 (amount of penalty for occasional amounts and amounts due for periods of 6 months or more) is amended as follows.

5(2) Sub-paragraph (1) is amended as follows.

5(3) In paragraph (a), for "items 1, 3 and 7 to 24" substitute "items 1, 3, 6B, 7 to 11 and 12 to 24".

5(4)–(6) [Not relevant to inheritance tax.]

9(1) Paragraph 11 (assessment) is amended as follows.

9(2) In sub-paragraph (4), for "unpaid tax" substitute "tax which was due or payable".

9(3) After sub-paragraph (4) insert–

"**11(4A)** A replacement assessment may be made in respect of a penalty if an earlier assessment operated by reference to an overestimate of an amount of tax which was due or payable."

10 For paragraph 16(1) (no liability where there is reasonable excuse for failure) substitute–

"**16(1)** If P satisfies HMRC or (on appeal) the First-tier Tribunal or Upper Tribunal that there is a reasonable excuse for a failure to make a payment–

(a) liability to a penalty under any paragraph of this Schedule does not arise in relation to that failure, and

(b) the failure does not count as a default for the purposes of paragraphs 6, 8B, 8C, 8G and 8H."

SCHEDULE 14 – ASBESTOS COMPENSATION SETTLEMENTS

Section 31

INHERITANCE TAX

1(1) Section 58 of IHTA 1984 (relevant property) is amended as follows.

1(2) [Amends IHTA 1984, s. 58(1).]

1(3) [Inserts IHTA 1984, s. 58(4) and (5).]

1(4) The amendments made by this paragraph are treated as having come into force on 6 April 2006.

FINANCE ACT 2011

(2011 Chapter 11)

[19th July 2011]

ARRANGEMENT OF SECTIONS

PART 2 – INCOME TAX, CORPORATION TAX AND CAPITAL GAINS TAX

CHARGEABLE GAINS

PART 4 – PENSIONS

PART 7 – ADMINISTRATION ETC

PART 9 – FINAL PROVISIONS

SCHEDULES

PART 2 – INCOME TAX, CORPORATION TAX AND CAPITAL GAINS TAX

CHARGEABLE GAINS

45 Company ceasing to be member of a group

45 Schedule 10 contains provision about the consequences, for the purposes of corporation tax on chargeable gains, of a company ceasing to be a member of a group.

PART 4 – PENSIONS

65 Benefits under pension schemes

65 Schedule 16 contains provision about the benefits available under pension schemes and related matters.

IHT Statutes

70 Power to make further provision about section 67 pension scheme

70(1) The Treasury may by regulations make provision for and in connection with–

(a) the application of the relevant taxes in relation to a pension scheme established under section 67 of the Pensions Act 2008, and

(b) the application of the relevant taxes in relation to any person in connection with such a pension scheme.

70(2) The provision that may be made by regulations under this section includes provision imposing any of the relevant taxes (as well as provisions for exemptions or reliefs).

70(3) The relevant taxes are–

(a) [not relevant to inheritance tax,]

(b) [not relevant to inheritance tax,]

(c) [not relevant to inheritance tax,]

(d) inheritance tax.

70(4) Regulations under this section may include provision having effect in relation to any time before they are made if the provision does not increase any person's liability to tax.

70(5) Regulations under this section may include–

(a) provision amending any enactment or instrument, and

(b) consequential, supplementary and transitional provision.

70(6) Regulations under this section are to be made by statutory instrument.

70(7) A statutory instrument containing regulations under this section is subject to annulment in pursuance of a resolution of the House of Commons.

71 Tax provision consequential on Part 1 of Pensions Act 2008 etc

71(1) The Treasury may by regulations make provision in relation to any of the relevant taxes in consequence of Part 1 of the Pensions Act 2008 or Part 1 of the Pensions (No. 2) Act (Northern Ireland) 2008.

71(2) The provision that may be made by regulations under this section includes provision imposing any of the relevant taxes (as well as provisions for exemptions or reliefs).

71(3) The relevant taxes are–

(a) [not relevant to inheritance tax,]

(b) [not relevant to inheritance tax,]

(c) [not relevant to inheritance tax,]

(d) inheritance tax,

(e) [not relevant to inheritance tax,]

(f) [not relevant to inheritance tax,]

(g) [not relevant to inheritance tax,]

(h) [not relevant to inheritance tax.]

71(4) Regulations under this section may include provision having effect in relation to any time before they are made if the provision does not increase any person's liability to tax.

71(5) Regulations under this section may make different provision for different cases.

71(6) Regulations under this section may include–

(a) provision amending any enactment or instrument, and

(b) consequential, supplementary and transitional provision.

71(7) Regulations under this section are to be made by statutory instrument.

71(8) A statutory instrument containing regulations under this section is subject to annulment in pursuance of a resolution of the House of Commons.

PART 7 – ADMINISTRATION ETC

86 *Data-gathering powers*

86(1) Schedule 23 contains provision for officers of Revenue and Customs to obtain data from data-holders.

86(2) Schedule 24 contains amendments of Schedule 36 to FA 2008 (information and inspection powers).

PART 9 – FINAL PROVISIONS

92 Interpretation

92(1) In this Act–

"ALDA 1979" means the Alcoholic Liquor Duties Act 1979,

"BGDA 1981" means the Betting and Gaming Duties Act 1981,

"CAA 2001" means the Capital Allowances Act 2001,

"CRCA 2005" means the Commissioners for Revenue and Customs Act 2005,

"CTA 2009" means the Corporation Tax Act 2009,

"CTA 2010" means the Corporation Tax Act 2010,

"FISMA 2000" means the Financial Services and Markets Act 2000,

"HODA 1979" means the Hydrocarbon Oil Duties Act 1979,

"ICTA" means the Income and Corporation Taxes Act 1988,

"IHTA 1984" means the Inheritance Tax Act 1984,

"ITA 2007" means the Income Tax Act 2007,

"ITEPA 2003" means the Income Tax (Earnings and Pensions) Act 2003,

"ITTOIA 2005" means the Income Tax (Trading and Other Income) Act 2005,

"OTA 1975" means the Oil Taxation Act 1975,

"PRTA 1980" means the Petroleum Revenue Tax Act 1980,

"TCGA 1992" means the Taxation of Chargeable Gains Act 1992,

"TIOPA 2010" means the Taxation (International and Other Provisions) Act 2010,

"TMA 1970" means the Taxes Management Act 1970,

"TPDA 1979" means the Tobacco Products Duty Act 1979,

"VATA 1994" means the Value Added Tax Act 1994, and

"VERA 1994" means the Vehicle Excise and Registration Act 1994.

92(2) In this Act–

"FA", followed by a year, means the Finance Act of that year;

"F(No. 2)A", followed by a year, means the Finance (No. 2) Act of that year.

93 Short title

93 This Act may be cited as the Finance Act 2011.

SCHEDULES

SCHEDULE 10 – COMPANY CEASING TO BE MEMBER OF GROUP

Section 45

CONSEQUENTIAL REPEALS

8 In consequence of the repeals made by paragraph 5, the following are also repealed–

(a) [repeals IHTA 1984, section 97(1)(a)(iii),]

(b) [not relevant to inheritance tax,]

(c) *[not relevant to inheritance tax,]*

(d) [not relevant to inheritance tax.]

COMMENCEMENT

9(1) The amendments made by paragraphs 1 to 5 and 8 have effect in relation to any disposal of an asset by one company ("company B") to another company ("company A") made at a time when company B is a member of a group, if–

(a) company A ceases to be a member of the group on or after the passing of this Act, or

(b) where company A ceased to be such a member before the passing of this Act in circumstances where section 179(6) to (8) of TCGA 1992 applied, company A ceases to satisfy the conditions in section 179(7) of that Act on or after the passing of this Act.

9(2) [Not relevant to inheritance tax.]

9(3) [Not relevant to inheritance tax.]

9(4) But where an early commencement election is made in relation to a group–

(a) sub-paragraphs (1) and (3) apply in relation to that group as if the references in those sub-paragraphs to the passing of this Act were references to 1 April 2011, and

(b) sub-paragraph (2) applies in relation to any disposal of shares by a member of that group as if the reference in that sub-paragraph to the passing of this Act were a reference to 1 April 2011.

9(5) An early commencement election in relation to a group means an election made for the purposes of this paragraph by the principal company of the group.

9(6) If a company ceases to be a member of a group in the period which begins with 1 April 2011 and ends with the passing of this Act, an early commencement election may be made or revoked in relation to the group only with the consent of that company contained in a notice which accompanies the election or revocation.

9(7) Where an early commencement election is revoked, the election is treated as never having had effect.

9(8) An early commencement election may not be made or revoked after 31 March 2012 (and paragraph 3(1)(b) of Schedule 1A to the Management Act (amendment of elections etc) does not apply in relation to an early commencement election).

SCHEDULE 16 – BENEFITS UNDER PENSION SCHEMES

Section 65

Part 1 – Changes to Benefits Available Under Pension Schemes Etc

REMOVAL OF CERTAIN CHARGES TO INHERITANCE TAX IN RESPECT OF PENSION SCHEMES

46 IHTA 1984 is amended as follows.

47(1) Section 12 (dispositions allowable for income tax or conferring benefits under pension scheme) is amended as follows.

47(2) [Inserts IHTA 1984, s. 12(2ZA).]

47(3) [Omits IHTA 1984, s. 12(2A)–(2E).]

48 Omit the following provisions–

(a) [omits IHTA 1984, s. 151A;]

(b) [omits IHTA 1984, s. 151B;]

(c) [omits IHTA 1984, s. 151BA;]

(d) [omits IHTA 1984, s. 151C;]

(e) [omits IHTA 1984, s. 151D;]

(f) [omits IHTA 1984, s. 151E.]

Part 2 – Consequential Amendments

INHERITANCE TAX ACT 1984

49 IHTA 1984 is amended as follows.

50(1) Section 12 (dispositions allowable for income tax or conferring benefits under pension scheme) is amended as follows.

50(2) [Omits IHTA 1984, s. 12(2F)(b).]

50(3) *[Amends IHTA 1984, s. 12(2G).]*

51 [Amends IHTA 1984, s. 151(2).]

52 In section 200 (transfer on death)–

(a) [amends IHTA 1984, s. 200(1);]

(b) [omits IHTA 1984, s. 200(1A).]

53 [Omits IHTA 1984, s. 210(2) and (3).]

54(1) Section 216 (delivery of accounts) is amended as follows.

54(2) [Omits IHTA 1984, s. 216(1)(bca).]

54(3) [Amends IHTA 1984, s. 216(3)(a).]

54(4) [Amends IHTA 1984, s. 216(4).]

54(5) [Omits IHTA 1984, s. 216(6)(ac).]

54(6) [Amends IHTA 1984, s. 216(7).]

55 [Amends IHTA 1984, s. 226(4).]

56 [Amends IHTA 1984, s. 233(1)(c).]

57 [Amends IHTA 1984, s. 272.]

CONSEQUENTIAL REPEALS

84 In consequence of the amendments made by this Schedule, omit the following provisions–

(a) [not relevant to inheritance tax,]

(b) in FA 2006–

(i) [omits FA 2006, Sch. 22, para. 3–9, 10(3) and 12,]

(ii) [not relevant to inheritance tax,]

(c) [not relevant to inheritance tax,]

(d) in FA 2008–

(i) [omits FA 2008, Sch. 4, para. 4 and 9(2),]

(ii) [omits FA 2008, Sch. 28, para. 6–14,]

(iii) [omits FA 2008, Sch. 29, para. 16.]

(e) [not relevant to inheritance tax.]

Part 3 – Commencement and Transitional Provision

INHERITANCE TAX

105 The amendments made by paragraphs 47 and 50 have effect in relation to dispositions made (or treated as made) on or after 6 April 2011.

106 The amendments made by paragraphs 48 and 51 to 57 have effect in relation to deaths occurring on or after 6 April 2011.

CONSEQUENTIAL REPEALS

107 Any repeal in paragraph 84 has effect to the same extent as the provision of this Schedule to which the repeal relates.

SCHEDULE 23 – DATA-GATHERING POWERS

Section 86(1)

Part 1 – Power to Obtain Data

POWER TO GIVE NOTICE

1(1) An officer of Revenue and Customs may by notice in writing require a relevant data-holder to provide relevant data.

1(2) Part 2 of this Schedule sets out who is a relevant data-holder.

1(3) In relation to a relevant data-holder, **"relevant data"** means data of a kind specified for that type of data-holder in regulations made by the Treasury.

1(4) The data that a relevant data-holder may be required to provide–

(a) may be general data or data relating to particular persons or matters, and

(b) may include personal data (such as names and addresses of individuals).

1(5) A notice under this paragraph is referred to as a data-holder notice.

PURPOSE OF POWER

2(1) The power in paragraph 1(1) is exercisable to assist with the efficient and effective discharge of HMRC's tax functions–

(a) whether a particular function or more generally, and

(b) whether involving a particular taxpayer or taxpayers generally.

2(2) It is additional to and is not limited by other powers that HMRC may have to obtain data (for example, in Schedule 36 to FA 2008).

2(3) But it may not be used (in place of the power in paragraph 1 of that Schedule) to obtain data required for the purpose of checking the relevant data-holder's own tax position.

2(4) Sub-paragraph (3) does not prevent use of the power in paragraph 1(1) of this Schedule to obtain data about a matter mentioned in paragraph 14(3)(a) (beneficial ownership of certain payments etc).

2(5) Nothing in this paragraph limits the use that may be made of data that have been obtained under this Schedule (see section 17(1) of CRCA 2005).

SPECIFYING RELEVANT DATA

3(1) A data-holder notice must specify the relevant data to be provided.

3(2) Relevant data may not be specified in a data-holder notice unless an officer of Revenue and Customs has reason to believe that the data could have a bearing on chargeable or other periods ending on or after the applicable day.

3(3) The applicable day is the first day of the period of 4 years ending with the day on which the notice is given.

COMPLIANCE

4(1) Relevant data specified in a data-holder notice must be provided by such means and in such form as is reasonably specified in the notice.

4(2) If the notice specifies that the data are to be provided by sending them somewhere, the data must be sent to such address and within such period as is reasonably specified in the notice.

4(3) If the notice specifies that the data are to be provided by making documents available for inspection somewhere, the documents must be made available for inspection at such place and time as is–

(a) reasonably specified in the notice, or

(b) agreed between an officer of Revenue and Customs and the data-holder.

4(4) A place used solely as a dwelling may not be specified under sub-paragraph (3)(a).

4(5) A data-holder notice requiring the provision of specified documents requires the documents to be provided only if they are in the data-holder's possession or power.

4(6) A power in this paragraph to specify something in a notice includes power to specify it in a document referred to in the notice.

APPROVAL BY TRIBUNAL

5(1) An officer of Revenue and Customs may ask for the approval of the tribunal before giving a data-holder notice.

5(2) This does not require an officer to do so (but see paragraph 28(3) for the effect of obtaining approval).

5(3) An application for approval under this paragraph may be made without notice (except as required under sub-paragraph (4)).

5(4) The tribunal may not approve the giving of a data-holder notice unless–

(a) the application for approval is made by, or with the agreement of, an authorised officer,

(b) the tribunal is satisfied that, in the circumstances, the officer giving the notice is justified in doing so,

(c) the data-holder has been told that the data are to be required and given a reasonable opportunity to make representations to an officer of Revenue and Customs, and

(d) the tribunal has been given a summary of any representations made by the data-holder.

5(5) Paragraphs (c) and (d) of sub-paragraph (4) do not apply to the extent that the tribunal is satisfied that taking the action specified in those paragraphs might prejudice any purpose for which the data are required.

5(6) A decision by the tribunal under this paragraph is final (despite the provisions of sections 11 and 13 of the Tribunals, Courts and Enforcement Act 2007).

5(7) **"Authorised officer"** means an officer of Revenue and Customs who is, or is a member of a class of officers who are, authorised by the Commissioners for the purposes of this paragraph.

POWER TO COPY DOCUMENTS

6 An officer of Revenue and Customs may take copies of or make extracts from any document provided pursuant to a data-holder notice.

POWER TO RETAIN DOCUMENTS

7(1) If an officer of Revenue and Customs thinks it reasonable to do so, HMRC may retain documents provided pursuant to a data-holder notice for a reasonable period.

7(2) While a document is being retained, the data-holder may, if the document is reasonably required for any purpose, request a copy of it.

7(3) The retention of a document under this paragraph is not to be regarded as breaking any lien claimed on the document.

7(4) If a document retained under this paragraph is lost or damaged, the Commissioners are liable to compensate the owner of the document for any expenses reasonably incurred in replacing or repairing the document.

Part 2 – Relevant Data-Holders

INTRODUCTION

8(1) This Part of this Schedule sets out who is a relevant data-holder for the purposes of this Schedule.

8(2) Descriptions of the various types of data-holder are to be read as including anyone who was previously of such a description.

INCOME, ASSETS ETC BELONGING TO OTHERS

13 A person who (in whatever capacity) is in receipt of money or value of or belonging to another is a relevant data-holder.

Cross references – SI 2012/847, reg. 11: relevant data.

MERCHANT ACQUIRERS ETC

13A(1) A person who has a contractual obligation to make payments to retailers in settlement of payment card transactions is a relevant data-holder.

13A(2) In this paragraph–

"payment card" includes a credit card, a charge card and a debit card;

"payment card transaction" means any transaction in which a payment card is accepted as payment;

"retailer" means a person who accepts a payment card as payment for any transaction.

13A(3) In this paragraph any reference to a payment card being accepted as payment includes a reference to any account number or other indicators associated with a payment card being accepted as payment.

History – Para. 13A inserted by FA 2013, s. 228(1), with effect in relation to relevant data with a bearing on any period (whether before, on or after 17 July 2013 (Royal Assent)).

PROVIDERS OF ELECTRONIC STORED-VALUE PAYMENT SERVICES

13B(1) A person who provides electronic stored-value payment services is a relevant data-holder.

13B(2) In this paragraph **"electronic stored-value payment services"** means services by means of which monetary value is stored electronically for the purpose of payments being made in respect of transactions to which the provider of those services is not a party.

History – Para. 13B (and the heading before it) inserted by FA 2016, s. 176(1), with effect in relation to relevant data with a bearing on any period (whether before, on or after 15 September 2016).

BUSINESS INTERMEDIARIES

13C(1) A person who–

(a) provides services to enable or facilitate transactions between suppliers and their customers or clients (other than services provided solely to enable payments to be made), and

(b) receives information about such transactions in the course of doing so,

is a relevant data-holder.

13C(2) In this paragraph **"suppliers"** means persons supplying goods or services in the course of business.

13C(3) For the purposes of this paragraph, information about transactions includes information that is capable of indicating the likely quantity or value of transactions.

History – Para. 13C (and the heading before it) inserted by FA 2016, s. 176(1), with effect in relation to relevant data with a bearing on any period (whether before, on or after 15 September 2016).

MONEY SERVICE BUSINESSES

13D(1) A person is a relevant data-holder if the person–

(a) carries on any of the activities in sub-paragraph (2) by way of business,

(b) is a relevant person within the meaning of regulation 8(1) of the Money Laundering, Terrorist Financing and Transfer of Funds (Information on the Payer) Regulations 2017 (S.I. 2017/692), and

(c) is not an excluded credit institution.

13D(2) The activities referred to in sub-paragraph (1)(a) are–

(a) operating a currency exchange office;

(b) transmitting money (or any representation of monetary value) by any means;

(c) cashing cheques which are made payable to customers.

13D(3) An excluded credit institution is a credit institution which has permission to carry on the regulated activity of accepting deposits–

(a) under Part 4A of the Financial Services and Markets Act 2000 (permission to carry on regulated activities), or

(b) resulting from Part 2 of Schedule 3 to that Act (exercise of passport rights by EEA firms).

13D(4) Sub-paragraph (3) is to be read with section 22 of and Schedule 2 to the Financial Services and Markets Act 2000, and any order under that section (classes of regulated activities).

13D(5) In this paragraph **"credit institution"** has the meaning given by Article 4.1(1) of Regulation (EU) No 575/2013 of the European Parliament and of the Council of 26 June 2013 on prudential requirements for credit institutions and investment firms.

History – Para. 13D inserted by F(No. 2)A 2017, s. 69(1), with effect in relation to relevant data with a bearing on any period (whether before, on or after 16 November 2017 (Royal Assent)).

SETTLEMENTS

26(1) Each of the following is a relevant data-holder–

(a) a person who makes a settlement,

(b) the trustees of a settlement,

(c) a beneficiary under a settlement, and

(d) any other person to whom income is payable under a settlement.

26(2) Section 620 of ITTOIA 2005 (meaning of "settlement" etc) applies for the purposes of this paragraph.

Cross references – SI 2012/847, reg. 24: relevant data.

Part 3 – Appeals Against Data-Holder Notices

RIGHT OF APPEAL

28(1) The data-holder may appeal against a data-holder notice, or any requirement in such a notice, on any of the following grounds–

(a) it is unduly onerous to comply with the notice or requirement,

(b) the data-holder is not a relevant data-holder, or

(c) data specified in the notice are not relevant data.

28(2) Sub-paragraph (1)(a) does not apply to a requirement to provide data that form part of the data-holder's statutory records.

28(3) Sub-paragraph (1) does not apply if the tribunal approved the giving of the notice in accordance with paragraph 5.

PROCEDURE FOR APPEAL

29(1) Notice of an appeal under paragraph 28 must be given–

(a) in writing,

(b) before the end of the period of 30 days beginning with the date on which the data-holder notice was given, and

(c) to the officer of Revenue and Customs by whom the data-holder notice was given.

29(2) It must state the grounds of appeal.

29(3) On an appeal that is notified to the tribunal, the tribunal may confirm, vary or set aside the data-holder notice or a requirement in it.

29(4) If the tribunal confirms or varies the notice or a requirement in it, the data-holder must comply with the notice or requirement–

(a) within such period as is specified by the tribunal, or

(b) if the tribunal does not specify a period, within such period as is reasonably specified in writing by an officer of Revenue and Customs following the tribunal's decision.

29(5) A decision by the tribunal under this Part is final (despite the provisions of sections 11 and 13 of the Tribunals, Courts and Enforcement Act 2007).

29(6) Subject to this paragraph, the provisions of Part 5 of TMA 1970 relating to appeals have effect in relation to appeals under paragraph 28 as they have effect in relation to an appeal against an assessment to income tax.

Part 4 – Penalties

PENALTIES FOR FAILURE TO COMPLY

30(1) If the data-holder fails to comply with a data-holder notice, the data-holder is liable to a penalty of £300.

30(2) A reference in this Schedule to failing to comply with a data-holder notice includes–

(a) concealing, destroying or otherwise disposing of a material document, or

(b) arranging for any such concealment, destruction or disposal.

30(3) A document is a material document if, at the time when the data-holder acts–

(a) the data-holder has received a data-holder notice requiring the data-holder to provide the document or data contained in the document, or

(b) the data-holder has not received such a notice but has been informed by an officer of Revenue and Customs that the data-holder will do so or is likely to do so.

30(4) A document is not a material document by virtue of sub-paragraph (3)(a) if the data-holder notice has already been complied with, unless–

(a) the data-holder has been notified in writing by an officer of Revenue and Customs that the data-holder must continue to preserve the document, and

(b) the notification has not been withdrawn.

30(5) A document is not a material document by virtue of sub-paragraph (3)(b) if more than 6 months have elapsed since the data-holder was (or was last) informed.

DAILY DEFAULT PENALTIES FOR FAILURE TO COMPLY

31 If–

(a) a penalty under paragraph 30 is assessed, and

(b) the failure in question continues after the data-holder has been notified of the assessment,

the data-holder is liable to a further penalty, for each subsequent day on which the failure continues, of an amount not exceeding £60 for each such day.

PENALTIES FOR INACCURATE INFORMATION OR DOCUMENTS

32(1) This paragraph applies if–

(a) in complying with a data-holder notice, the data-holder provides inaccurate data, and

(b) condition A, B or C is met.

32(2) Condition A is that the inaccuracy is–

(a) due to a failure by the data-holder to take reasonable care, or

(b) deliberate on the data-holder's part.

32(3) Condition B is that the data-holder knows of the inaccuracy at the time the data are provided but does not inform HMRC at that time.

32(4) Condition C is that the data-holder–

(a) discovers the inaccuracy some time later, and

(b) fails to take reasonable steps to inform HMRC.

32(5) If this paragraph applies, the data-holder is liable to a penalty not exceeding £3,000.

FAILURE TO COMPLY WITH TIME LIMIT

33 A failure to do anything required to be done within a limited period of time does not give rise to liability under paragraph 30 or 31 if the thing was done within such further time (if any) as an officer of Revenue and Customs may have allowed.

REASONABLE EXCUSE

34(1) Liability to a penalty under paragraph 30 or 31 does not arise if the data-holder satisfies HMRC or (on an appeal notified to the tribunal) the tribunal that there is a reasonable excuse for the failure.

34(2) For the purposes of this paragraph–

(a) an insufficiency of funds is not a reasonable excuse unless attributable to events outside the data-holder's control,

(b) if the data-holder relies on another person to do anything, that is not a reasonable excuse unless the data-holder took reasonable care to avoid the failure,

(c) if the data-holder had a reasonable excuse for the failure but the excuse has ceased, the data-holder is to be treated as having continued to have the excuse if the failure is remedied without unreasonable delay after the excuse ceased.

ASSESSMENT OF PENALTIES

35(1) If the data-holder becomes liable to a penalty under paragraph 30, 31 or 32, HMRC may assess the penalty.

35(2) If they do so, they must notify the data-holder.

35(3) An assessment of a penalty under paragraph 30 or 31 must be made within the period of 12 months beginning with the latest of the following–

(a) the date on which the data-holder became liable to the penalty,

(b) the end of the period in which notice of an appeal against the data-holder notice (or a requirement in it) could have been given, and

(c) if notice of such an appeal is given, the date on which the appeal is determined or withdrawn.

35(4) An assessment of a penalty under paragraph 32 must be made–

(a) within the period of 12 months beginning with the date on which the inaccuracy first came to the attention of an officer of Revenue and Customs, and

(b) within the period of 6 years beginning with the date on which the data-holder became liable to the penalty.

RIGHT TO APPEAL AGAINST PENALTY

36(1) The data-holder may appeal against a decision by an officer of Revenue and Customs–

(a) that a penalty is payable under paragraph 30, 31 or 32, or

(b) as to the amount of such a penalty.

36(2) But sub-paragraph (1)(b) does not give a right of appeal against the amount of an increased daily penalty payable by virtue of paragraph 38.

History – Para. 36(1) created from existing text by FA 2016, s. 177(5), with effect from 15 September 2016 (Royal Assent). Para. 36(2) inserted by FA 2016, s. 177(5), with effect from 15 September 2016 (Royal Assent).

PROCEDURE ON APPEAL AGAINST PENALTY

37(1) Notice of an appeal under paragraph 36 must be given–

(a) in writing,

(b) before the end of the period of 30 days beginning with the date on which notification under paragraph 35 was given, and

(c) to HMRC.

37(2) It must state the grounds of appeal.

37(3) On an appeal under paragraph 36(a) that is notified to the tribunal, the tribunal may confirm or cancel the decision.

37(4) On an appeal under paragraph 36(b) that is notified to the tribunal, the tribunal may–

(a) confirm the decision, or

(b) substitute for the decision another decision that the officer of Revenue and Customs had power to make.

37(5) Subject to this paragraph and paragraph 40, the provisions of Part 5 of TMA 1970 relating to appeals have effect in relation to appeals under paragraph 36 as they have effect in relation to an appeal against an assessment to income tax.

INCREASED DAILY DEFAULT PENALTY

38(1) This paragraph applies if–

(a) a penalty under paragraph 31 is assessed under paragraph 35,

(b) the failure in respect of which that assessment is made continues for more than 30 days beginning with the date on which notification of that assessment is given, and

(c) the data-holder has been told that an application may be made under this paragraph for an increased daily penalty to be assessable.

38(2) If this paragraph applies, an officer of Revenue and Customs may make an application to the tribunal for an increased daily penalty to be assessable on the data-holder.

38(3) If the tribunal decides that an increased daily penalty should be assessable–

(a) the tribunal must determine the day from which the increased daily penalty is to apply and the maximum amount of that penalty ("the new maximum amount");

(b) from that day, paragraph 31 has effect in the data-holder's case as if "the new maximum amount" were substituted for "£60".

38(4) The new maximum amount may not be more than £1,000.

38(5) But subject to that, in determining the new maximum amount the tribunal must have regard to–

(a) the likely cost to the data-holder of complying with the data-holder notice,

(b) any benefits to the data-holder of not complying with it, and

(c) any benefits to anyone else resulting from the data-holder's non-compliance.

History – In para. 38(1)(c) and (2), the word "assessable" substituted for the word "imposed" by FA 2016, s. 177(2)(a), with effect from 15 September 2016 (Royal Assent).

Para. 38(3) and (4) substituted by FA 2016, s. 177(2)(b), with effect from 15 September 2016 (Royal Assent). Former para. 38(3) and (4) read as follows:

"**38(3)** If the tribunal decides that an increased daily penalty should be imposed, then for each applicable day (see paragraph 39) on which the failure continues–

(a) the data-holder is not liable to a penalty under paragraph 31 in respect of the failure, and

(b) the data-holder is liable instead to a penalty under this paragraph of an amount determined by the tribunal.

38(4) The tribunal may not determine an amount exceeding £1,000 for each applicable day.".

In para. 38(5), the words "the new maximum amount" substituted for the words "the amount" by FA 2016, s. 177(2)(c), with effect from 15 September 2016 (Royal Assent).

39(1) If the tribunal makes a determination under paragraph 38, HMRC must notify the data-holder.

39(2) The notification must specify [the] new maximum amount and the day from which it applies.

39(3) [Omitted by FA 2016, s. 177(3)(c).]

History – In para. 39(1), the words "the tribunal makes a determination" substituted for the words "a data-holder becomes liable to a penalty" by FA 2016, s. 177(3)(a), with effect from 15 September 2016 (Royal Assent).

In para. 39(2), the words "[the] new maximum amount and the day from which it applies" (the word in square brackets added by Croner-i) substituted for the words "the day from which the increased penalty is to apply" by FA 2016, s. 177(3)(b), with effect from 15 September 2016 (Royal Assent).

Para. 39(3) omitted by FA 2016, s. 177(3)(c), with effect from 15 September 2016 (Royal Assent). Former para. 39(3) read as follows: "**39(3)** That day and any subsequent day is an **"applicable day"** for the purposes of paragraph 38(3).".

ENFORCEMENT OF PENALTIES

40(1) A penalty under this Schedule must be paid before the end of the period of 30 days beginning with the date mentioned in sub-paragraph (2).

40(2) That date is–

(a) the date on which notification under paragraph 35 is given in respect of the penalty, or

(b) if (in the case of a penalty under paragraph 30, 31 or 32) a notice of appeal under paragraph 36 is given, the date on which the appeal is finally determined or withdrawn.

40(3) A penalty under this Schedule may be enforced as if it were income tax charged in an assessment and due and payable.

History – In para. 40(2)(a), the words "or 39" (which appeared after the words "paragraph 35") omitted by FA 2016, s. 177(4), with effect from 15 September 2016 (Royal Assent).

POWER TO CHANGE AMOUNT OF PENALTIES

41(1) If it appears to the Treasury that there has been a change in the value of money since the last relevant date, they may by regulations substitute for the sums for the time being specified in paragraphs 30(1), 31, 32(5) and 38(4) such other sums as appear to them to be justified by the change.

41(2) **"Relevant date"**, in relation to a specified sum, means–

(a) the day on which this Act is passed, and

(b) each date on which the power conferred by sub-paragraph (1) has been exercised in relation to that sum.

41(3) Regulations under this paragraph do not apply to–

(a) a failure which began before the date on which they come into force, or

(b) an inaccuracy in any data or document provided to HMRC before that date.

DOUBLE JEOPARDY

42 The data-holder is not liable to a penalty under this Schedule in respect of anything in respect of which the data-holder has been convicted of an offence.

Part 5 – Miscellaneous Provision and Interpretation

APPLICATION OF PROVISIONS OF TMA 1970

43 Subject to the provisions of this Schedule, the following provisions of TMA 1970 apply for the purposes of this Schedule as they apply for the purposes of the Taxes Acts–

(a) section 108 (responsibility of company officers),

(b) section 114 (want of form), and

(c) section 115 (delivery and service of documents).

REGULATIONS

44(1) Regulations under this Schedule are to be made by statutory instrument.

44(2) The first regulations to be made under paragraph 1(3) may not be made unless the instrument containing them has been laid in draft before, and approved by a resolution of, the House of Commons.

44(3) Subject to sub-paragraph (2), a statutory instrument containing regulations under this Schedule is subject to annulment in pursuance of a resolution of the House of Commons.

Statutory instruments – SI 2012/847: made under para. 44(2).

TAX

45(1) In this Schedule **"tax"** means any or all of the following–

(a)–(e) [not relevant to inheritance tax,]

(f) inheritance tax,

(g)–(l) [not relevant to inheritance tax,]

(m) relevant foreign tax.

45(2) [Not relevant to inheritance tax.]

45(3) [Not relevant to inheritance tax.]

45(4) **"Relevant foreign tax"** means–

(a) a tax of a member State, other than the United Kingdom, which is covered by the provisions for the exchange of information under the Council Directive 2011/16/EU of 15 February 2011 on administrative cooperation in the field of taxation (as amended from time to time), and

(b) any tax or duty which is imposed under the law of a territory in relation to which arrangements having effect by virtue of section 173 of FA 2006 (international tax enforcement arrangements) have been made and which is covered by the arrangements.

History – Para. 45(1)(ca) inserted by FA 2015, s. 105(1), with effect in relation to accounting periods beginning on or after 1 April 2015 (subject to the provisions of FA 2015, s. 116(2)–(5)).
In para. 45(4), the words "Council Directive 2011/16/EU of 15 February 2011 on administrative cooperation in the field of taxation" substituted for the words "Directive of the Council of the European Communities No 77/799/EEC" by SI 2012/3062, reg. 6(2), with effect from 1 January 2013.

STATUTORY RECORDS

46(1) For the purposes of this Schedule data form part of a data-holder's statutory records if they are data that the data-holder is required to keep and preserve under or by virtue of any enactment relating to tax.

46(2) Data cease to form part of a data-holder's statutory records when the period for which the data are required to be preserved under or by virtue of that enactment has expired.

GENERAL INTERPRETATION

47 In this Schedule–

"address" includes an electronic address;

"body of persons" has the same meaning as in TMA 1970;

"chargeable period" means a tax year, accounting period or other period for which a tax is charged;

"charity" has the meaning given by paragraph 1(1) of Schedule 6 to FA 2010;

"the Commissioners" means the Commissioners for Her Majesty's Revenue and Customs;

"company" has the meaning given by section 288(1) of TCGA 1992;

"data" includes information held in any form;

"the data-holder", in relation to a data-holder notice, means the person to whom the notice is addressed;

"data-holder notice" is defined in paragraph 1;

"dividend" includes any kind of distribution;

"document" includes a copy of a document (see also section 114 of FA 2008);

"employment", **"employee"** and **"employer"** have the same meaning as in Parts 2 to 7 of ITEPA 2003 (see, in particular, sections 4 and 5 of that Act);

"HMRC" means Her Majesty's Revenue and Customs;

"local authority" has the meaning given in section 999 of ITA 2007;

"provide" includes make available for inspection;

"specify" includes describe;

"securities" includes–

(a) shares and stock,

(b) debentures, including debenture stock, loan stock, bonds, certificates of deposit and other instruments creating or acknowledging indebtedness, and

(c) warrants or other instruments entitling the holder to subscribe for or otherwise acquire anything within paragraph (a) or (b),

issued by or on behalf of a person resident in, or a government or public or local authority of, any country (including a country outside the United Kingdom);

"shares" is to be construed in accordance with sections 99 of TCGA 1992;

"tax functions" means functions relating to tax;

"the tribunal" means the First-tier Tribunal or, where determined by or under the Tribunal Procedure Rules, the Upper Tribunal.

History – In para. 47, in definition of "shares", the words "section 99" substituted for the words "sections 99 and 103A" by SI 2017/1204, reg. 15, with effect from 1 January 2018.

48 A reference in this Schedule to providing data includes–

(a) preparing and delivering a return, statement or declaration, and

(b) providing documents.

49(1) A reference in this Schedule to the carrying on of a business also includes–

(a) the letting of property,

(b) the activities of a charity, and

(c) the activities of a government department, a local authority, a local authority association or any other public authority.

49(2) **"Local authority association"** has the meaning given in section 1000 of ITA 2007.

CROWN APPLICATION

50 This Schedule applies to the Crown but not to Her Majesty in Her private capacity (within the meaning of the Crown Proceedings Act 1947).

Part 6 – Consequential Provisions

FA 2008

60 FA 2008 is amended as follows.

61 [Not relevant to inheritance tax.]

62(1) Schedule 36 (information and inspection powers) is amended as follows.

62(2) [Omits FA 2008, Sch. 36, para. 34A.]

62(3) [Amends FA 2008, Sch. 36, para. 61A.]

Part 7 – Application of this Schedule

65(1) This Schedule–

(a) comes into force on 1 April 2012, and

(b) applies from then on to relevant data with a bearing on any period (whether before, on or after that date), subject to paragraph 3(2).

65(2) The provisions repealed or otherwise amended by Part 6 of this Schedule continue to have effect in relation to notices given, or requests made, pursuant to any of the repealed provisions before 1 April 2012 as if the repeals and other amendments had not been made.

SCHEDULE 24 – AMENDMENTS OF SCHEDULE 36 FA 2008

Section 86(2)

1 Schedule 36 to FA 2008 (information and inspection powers) is amended as follows.

2(1) Paragraph 5 (power to obtain information and documents about persons whose identity is not known) is amended as follows.

2(2) [Amends FA 2008, Sch. 36, para. 5(2).]

2(3) [Amends FA 2008, Sch. 36, para. 5(4).]

2(4) [Omits FA 2008, Sch. 36, para. 5(5).]

2(5) The amendments made by this paragraph–

(a) come into force on 1 April 2012, and

(b) apply from then on in relation to tax regardless of when the tax became due (whether before, on or after that date).

3(1) Paragraph 40A (penalties for inaccurate information and documents) is amended as follows.

3(2) [Amends FA 2008, Sch. 36, para. 40A(1)(b).]

3(3) [Inserts FA 2008, Sch. 36, para. 40A(3A).]

3(4) [Amends FA 2008, Sch. 36, para. 40A(4).]

3(5) The amendments made by this paragraph have effect in relation to any inaccuracy in information provided, or in documents produced, on or after 1 April 2012.

4(1) [Inserts FA 2008, Sch. 36, para. 49A–49C.]

4(2) The amendment made by this paragraph has effect in relation to failures to comply with a notice under paragraph 5 that begin on or after 1 April 2012.

5(1) Paragraph 50 (tax-related penalty) is amended as follows.

5(2) [Amends FA 2008, Sch. 36, para. 50(1)(d).]

5(3) [Inserts FA 2008, Sch. 36, para. 50(7).]

5(4) The amendments made by this paragraph have effect where a person becomes liable to a penalty under paragraph 39 of Schedule 36 to FA 2008 on or after the day on which this Act is passed.

6 [Amends FA 2008, Sch. 36, para. 61A.]

FINANCE ACT 2012

(2012 Chapter 14)

[*17th July 2012*]

ARRANGEMENT OF SECTIONS

PART 1 – INCOME TAX, CORPORATION TAX AND CAPITAL GAINS TAX

Chapter 5 – Miscellaneous

CHARITABLE GIVING ETC

49 Gifts to the nation

49 Schedule 14 contains provision for a person's tax liability to be reduced in return for giving pre-eminent property to the nation.

PART 2 – INSURANCE COMPANIES CARRYING ON LONG-TERM BUSINESS

Chapter 12 – Supplementary

MINOR AND CONSEQUENTIAL AMENDMENTS AND TRANSITIONAL PROVISION

146 Minor and consequential amendments

146 Schedule 16 contains minor and consequential amendments.

147 Transitional provision

147 Schedule 17 contains transitional provision in connection with the coming into force of this Part.

COMMENCEMENT ETC

148 Commencement

148(1) The provisions of this Part (other than section 149) have effect in relation to accounting periods of companies beginning on or after 1 January 2013.

148(2) Subsection (1) is subject to the operation of any provision of Schedule 17 in relation to times before that date.

149 Accounting periods straddling 1 January 2013

149(1) If, apart from this section, an insurance company would have had an accounting period beginning before 1 January 2013 and ending on or after that date, the accounting period of the company is to end instead on 31 December 2012.

149(2) Accordingly, the rules in section 10 of CTA 2009 (end of accounting period) are subject to this section.

PART 8 – OTHER TAXES

INHERITANCE TAX

208 Indexation of rate bands

208(1) Section 8 of IHTA 1984 (indexation of rate bands) is amended as follows.

208(2) [Amends IHTA 1984, s. 8(1).]

208(3) [Amends IHTA 1984, s. 8(2).]

208(4) [Substitutes IHTA 1984, s. 8(3).]

208(5) The amendments made by this section have effect for the purposes of chargeable transfers made on or after 6 April 2015.

209 Gifts to charities etc

209 Schedule 33 contains provision for a lower rate of inheritance tax to be charged on transfers made on death that include sufficient gifts to charities or registered clubs.

210 Settled excluded property: effect of certain arrangements

210(1) IHTA 1984 is amended as follows.

210(2) In section 48 (settled property: excluded property)–

(a) [inserts IHTA 1984, s. 48(1)(d),]

(b) [amends IHTA 1984, s. 48(3),]

(c) [inserts IHTA 1984, s. 48(3D).]

210(3) [Inserts IHTA 1984, s. 74A, 74B and 74C.]

210(4) [Inserts IHTA 1984, s. 201(4A).]

210(5) The amendments made by this section are treated as having come into force on 20 June 2012 and have effect in relation to arrangements entered into on or after that day.

PART 9 – MISCELLANEOUS MATTERS

INTERNATIONAL MATTERS

218 Agreement between UK and Switzerland

218(1) Schedule 36 contains provision giving effect to–

(a) an agreement signed on 6 October 2011 between the United Kingdom and the Swiss Confederation on co-operation in the area of taxation, as amended by a protocol signed by them on 20 March 2012 and by a mutual agreement signed by them on 18 April 2012 implementing article XVIII of that protocol, and

(b) the joint declaration (concerning a tax finality payment) forming an integral part of that protocol.

218(2) Schedule 36 comes into force on the day on which the agreement of 6 October 2011 enters into force.

218(3) In section 23 of the Constitutional Reform and Governance Act 2010, after subsection (2A) insert–

"**23(2B)** Section 20 does not apply to any treaty referred to in section 218(1) of the Finance Act 2012."

219 Penalties: offshore income etc

219 [Inserts FA 2007, Sch. 24, para. 21A(4)(d) and (e).]

220 International military headquarters, EU forces, etc

220 Schedule 37 contains provision about the tax treatment of international military headquarters, EU forces, etc.

ADMINISTRATION

223 Tax agents: dishonest conduct

223(1) Schedule 38 contains provision about tax agents who engage in dishonest conduct.

223(2) That Schedule comes into force on such day as the Treasury may by order appoint.

223(3) An order under subsection (2)–

(a) may make different provision for different purposes, and

(b) may include transitional provision and savings.

223(4) The Treasury may by order make any incidental, supplemental, consequential, transitional or saving provision in consequence of Schedule 38.

223(5) An order under subsection (4) may–

(a) make different provision for different purposes, and

(b) make provision amending, repealing or revoking any provision made by or under an Act (whenever passed or made).

223(6) An order under this section is to be made by statutory instrument.

223(7) A statutory instrument containing an order under subsection (4) is subject to annulment in pursuance of a resolution of the House of Commons.

Commencement Date – The day appointed as the day on which Sch. 38 comes into force is 1 April 2013 (SI 2013/279, made under s. 223(2) and (3)).

224 Information powers

224(1) Schedule 36 to FA 2008 (information and inspection powers) is amended as follows.

224(2) [Inserts FA 2008, Sch. 36, para. 5A.]

224(3) [Amends FA 2008, Sch. 36, para. 6(1).]

224(4) [Amends FA 2008, Sch. 36, para. 31.]

224(5) [Amends heading to FA 2008, Sch. 36, para. 31.]

224(6) [Amends TMA 1970, s. 18D(1).]

224(7) The amendments made by subsections (1) to (5) apply for the purpose of checking the tax position of a taxpayer as regards periods or tax liabilities whenever arising (whether before, on or after the day on which this Act is passed).

224(8) The amendment made by subsection (6) is treated as having come into force on 1 April 2012.

MISCELLANEOUS RELIEFS ETC

227 Repeals of miscellaneous reliefs etc

227 Schedule 39 contains repeals of miscellaneous reliefs etc.

PART 10 – FINAL PROVISIONS

228 Interpretation

228(1) In this Act–

"ALDA 1979" means the Alcoholic Liquor Duties Act 1979,

"BGDA 1981" means the Betting and Gaming Duties Act 1981,

"CAA 2001" means the Capital Allowances Act 2001,

"CEMA 1979" means the Customs and Excise Management Act 1979,

"CRCA 2005" means the Commissioners for Revenue and Customs Act 2005,

"CTA 2009" means the Corporation Tax Act 2009,

"CTA 2010" means the Corporation Tax Act 2010,

"F(No. 3)A 2010" means the Finance (No. 3) Act 2010,

"HODA 1979" means the Hydrocarbon Oil Duties Act 1979,

"ICTA" means the Income and Corporation Taxes Act 1988,

"IHTA 1984" means the Inheritance Tax Act 1984,

"ITA 2007" means the Income Tax Act 2007,

"ITEPA 2003" means the Income Tax (Earnings and Pensions) Act 2003,

"ITTOIA 2005" means the Income Tax (Trading and Other Income) Act 2005,

"OTA 1975" means the Oil Taxation Act 1975,

"PRTA 1980" means the Petroleum Revenue Tax Act 1980,

"TCGA 1992" means the Taxation of Chargeable Gains Act 1992,

"TIOPA 2010" means the Taxation (International and Other Provisions) Act 2010,

"TMA 1970" means the Taxes Management Act 1970,

"TPDA 1979" means the Tobacco Products Duty Act 1979,

"VATA 1994" means the Value Added Tax Act 1994, and

"VERA 1994" means the Vehicle Excise and Registration Act 1994.

228(2) In this Act–

"FA", followed by a year, means the Finance Act of that year;

"F(No. 2)A", followed by a year, means the Finance (No. 2) Act of that year.

229 Short title

229 This Act may be cited as the Finance Act 2012.

SCHEDULES

SCHEDULE 14 – GIFTS TO THE NATION

Section 49

Part 5 – Related Changes

IHTA 1984

26 IHTA 1984 is amended as follows.

27 [Inserts IHTA 1984, s. 25(3).]

28 [Amends IHTA 1984, s. 26A(b).]

29(1) Section 32 (conditionally exempt transfers: chargeable events) is amended as follows.

29(2) [Amends IHTA 1984, s. 32(3).]

29(3) [Inserts IHTA 1984, s. 32(4A).]

30(1) Section 32A (associated properties) is amended as follows.

30(2) [Inserts IHTA 1984, s. 32A(5A).]

30(3) [Amends IHTA 1984, s. 32A(7).]

31 [Amends IHTA 1984, s. 33(6).]

32 [Amends IHTA 1984, s. 34(4).]

ESTATE DUTY ETC

32A(1) This paragraph applies where a person ("the donor") makes a qualifying gift of an object in circumstances where, had the donor instead sold the object to an individual at market value, a charge to estate duty would have arisen under section 40 of FA 1930 on the proceeds of sale.

32A(2) At the time when the gift is made, estate duty becomes chargeable under that section as if the gift were such a sale (subject to any limitation imposed by paragraph 33(2)).

32A(3) In the application of this paragraph to Northern Ireland, the references to section 40 of FA 1930 are to be read as references to section 2 of the Finance Act (Northern Ireland) 1931.

History – Para. 32A inserted by FA 2014, s. 118(1), with effect from 17 July 2014, subject to the restriction in FA 2014, s. 118(2) and (3) for gifts made before 17 July 2014.

33(1) This paragraph applies if a person makes a qualifying gift and as a result–

(a) estate duty becomes chargeable under section 40 of FA 1930 (exemption from death duties of objects of national etc interest), or

(b) tax becomes chargeable under Schedule 5 to IHTA 1984 (conditional exemption: deaths before 7 April 1976).

33(2) Despite any other enactment, the amount of duty or tax that becomes so chargeable as a result of the gift is to be limited to the amount (if any) by which A exceeds B.

33(3) For these purposes–

"A" is the amount of duty or tax that becomes so chargeable as a result of the gift (absent this paragraph), and

"B" is what that amount would be if the effective rate at which the duty or tax is charged were the highest rate specified in column 3 of the Table in Schedule 1 to IHTA 1984.

33(4) References in this paragraph to the amount of duty or tax that becomes so chargeable are to the amount before applying any credit allowable against it under section 33(7) of IHTA 1984.

33(5) Nothing in this paragraph entitles a person to any repayment of inheritance tax if the amount of any such credit exceeds the amount (if any) chargeable in accordance with sub-paragraph (2).

33(6) In the application of this paragraph to Northern Ireland, for the reference to section 40 of FA 1930 substitute a reference to section 2 of the Finance Act (Northern Ireland) 1931.

Part 6 – Commencement

36(1) Parts 2 and 3 of this Schedule have effect in relation to liabilities for tax years and accounting periods beginning on or after such day as the Treasury may by order appoint.

36(2) The power of the Treasury under sub-paragraph (1) includes power to appoint a day that is earlier than the day on which the order is made, but no earlier than 1 April 2012.

36(3) An order under this paragraph is to be made by statutory instrument.

SCHEDULE 16 – PART 2: MINOR AND CONSEQUENTIAL AMENDMENTS

Section 146

Part 3 – Amendments of Other Acts

INHERITANCE TAX ACT 1984

68 IHTA 1984 is amended as follows.

69 [Amends IHTA 1984, s. 59(3)(b).]

SCHEDULE 17 – PART 2: TRANSITIONAL PROVISION

Section 147

Part 3 – Supplementary

GENERAL TRANSITIONAL PROVISION IN RELATION TO PROVISIONS RE-ENACTED IN PART 2 OF THIS ACT

36(1) This paragraph applies where any provision of this Part of this Act re-enacts (with or without modification) an enactment repealed by this Part of this Act.

36(2) The repeal and re-enactment does not affect the continuity of the law.

36(3) Any subordinate legislation or other thing which–

(a) has been made or done, or has effect as if made or done, under or for the purposes of the repealed provision, and

(b) is in force or effective in relation to accounting periods of insurance companies ending on 31 December 2012,

has effect in relation to subsequent accounting periods of insurance companies as if made or done under or for the purposes of the corresponding provision of this Part of this Act.

36(4) Any reference (express or implied) in any enactment, instrument or document to a provision of this Part of this Act is to be read as including, in relation to times, circumstances or purposes in relation to which the corresponding repealed provision had effect, a reference to that corresponding provision. This sub-paragraph applies only so far as the context permits.

36(5) Any reference (express or implied) in any enactment, instrument or document to a repealed provision is to be read, in relation to times, circumstances or purposes in relation to which the corresponding provision of this Part of this Act has effect, as a reference or (as the context may require) as including a reference to that corresponding provision.
This sub-paragraph applies only so far as the context permits.

36(6) This paragraph is subject to any specific transitional, transitory or saving provision made by or under this Schedule.

36(7) The generality of this paragraph is not to be affected by specific transitional, transitory or saving provision made by or under this Schedule.

36(8) This paragraph has effect instead of section 17(2) of the Interpretation Act 1978.

POWER TO MAKE SUPPLEMENTARY TRANSITIONAL PROVISION ETC

37(1) The Treasury may by regulations make further transitional, transitory or saving provision in connection with the coming into force of any of the provisions of this Part of this Act.

37(2) The provision that may be made by the regulations includes provision (whether by way of textual amendment or otherwise) altering or supplementing the effect of any provision made by or under this Schedule.

37(3) The regulations may be made so as to have effect in relation to any period beginning before but ending on or after the day on which the regulations are made (as well as in relation to periods no part of which falls before that day).

38 Any regulations made by the Treasury under any provision of this Schedule may–

(a) make different provision for different cases or circumstances, and

(b) contain incidental, supplementary, consequential, transitional, transitory or saving provision.

INTERPRETATION

39 The following expressions have the same meaning in this Schedule as they have in Chapter 1 of Part 12 of ICTA–

"brought into account" (except in paragraph 24),
"gross roll-up business",
"the I minus E basis",
"the life assurance trade profits provisions",
"non-profit fund",
"period of account",
"periodical return", and
"PHI business".

SCHEDULE 33 – INHERITANCE TAX: GIFTS TO CHARITIES ETC

Section 209

REDUCED RATE OF INHERITANCE TAX

1 [Inserts IHTA 1984, Sch. 1A.]

CONSEQUENTIAL AMENDMENTS

2 IHTA 1984 is amended as follows in consequence of paragraph 1.

3 [Amends IHTA 1984, s. 7(1).]

4 [Inserts IHTA 1984, s. 33(2ZA).]

5 [Amends IHTA 1984, s. 78(3).]

6 In section 128 (rate of charge: woodlands)–

(a) [amends IHTA 1984, s. 128,]

(b) [inserts IHTA 1984, s. 128(2).]

7 [Inserts IHTA 1984, s. 141A.]

8 [Inserts IHTA 1984, Sch. 4, para. 14(2A).]

INSTRUMENTS OF VARIATION TO BE NOTIFIED TO CHARITIES ETC

9 [Inserts IHTA 1984, s. 142(3A).]

COMMENCEMENT

10(1) The Schedule inserted by paragraph 1 has effect in cases where D's death occurs on or after 6 April 2012 (and the amendments made by paragraphs 3 to 8 are to be read accordingly).

10(2) The amendment made by paragraph 9 has effect in cases where the person's death occurs on or after 6 April 2012.

SCHEDULE 36 – AGREEMENT BETWEEN UK AND SWITZERLAND

Section 218

Part 1 – Introduction

THE AGREEMENT AND THE JOINT DECLARATION

1 In this Schedule–

(a) **"the Agreement"** means the agreement signed on 6 October 2011 between the United Kingdom and the Swiss Confederation on cooperation in the area of taxation, as amended by a protocol signed by them on 20 March 2012 and by a mutual agreement signed by them on 18 April 2012 implementing article XVIII of that protocol,

(b) **"the Joint Declaration"** means the joint declaration (concerning a tax finality payment) forming an integral part of that protocol,

(c) **"the start date"** is the date on which the Agreement enters into force in accordance with its terms (see Article 44), and

(d) references to a numbered Article are to the Article of that number in the Agreement.

Part 2 – The Past

TAXES AFFECTED

2(1) The taxes affected by this Part are–

(a) income tax,

(b) capital gains tax,

(c) inheritance tax, and

(d) VAT.

2(2) Accordingly, this Part affects–

(a) amounts of income on which income tax is charged,

(b) *chargeable gains,*

(c) the value of property forming part of the value transferred by a chargeable transfer, and

(d) the value of supplies on which VAT is charged.

2(3) An amount falling within one (or more) of those descriptions is referred to as a **"taxable amount"** and, in relation to such an amount, **"tax"** means whichever of the taxes mentioned in sub-paragraph (1) is (or are) charged on it.

APPLICATION OF THIS PART

3(1) This Part applies if–

(a) a one-off payment is levied in accordance with Part 2 of the Agreement,

(b) a certificate is issued under Article 9(4) to a person ("P") in respect of that payment, and

(c) the certificate is approved by P or considered approved by virtue of that Article.

3(2) The certificate is referred to in this Part as **"the Part 2 certificate"**.

QUALIFYING AMOUNTS

4(1) The Part 2 certificate applies to taxable amounts in respect of which the conditions in sub-paragraph (2) are met.

4(2) The conditions are–

(a) P is liable to tax on the amount,

(b) the amount is untaxed,

(c) the taxable event took place before the start date, and

(d) the necessary link with the certificate can be demonstrated.

4(3) The necessary link is–

(a) in a case falling within Article 9(3) (non-UK domiciled individuals opting for self-assessment method), that the amount is included in the omitted taxable base by reference to which the one-off payment was calculated, and

(b) in any other case, that the amount forms part of or is represented by the assets comprised in the relevant capital by reference to which the one-off payment was calculated (referred to in the Agreement as C_r).

4(4) For the purposes of sub-paragraph (3)(b), amounts are assumed to be attributed to assets in the way that produces the most beneficial outcome for P.

4(5) Paragraph 11 makes further provision about the interpretation of sub-paragraph (2).

4(6) Amounts to which the Part 2 certificate applies in accordance with this paragraph are referred to in this Part as **"qualifying amounts"**.

ELIGIBILITY FOR CLEARANCE

5(1) The effect of the Part 2 certificate depends on whether P is eligible for clearance.

5(2) P is **"eligible for clearance"** if–

(a) none of the circumstances listed in Article 9(13)(a) to (e) apply (tax investigations etc), and

(b) Article 12(1) does not apply (wrongful behaviour in relation to non-UK domiciled status).

5(3) Otherwise, P is **"not eligible for clearance"**.

EFFECT IF P ELIGIBLE FOR CLEARANCE

6(1) This paragraph sets out the effect of the Part 2 certificate if P is eligible for clearance.

6(2) P ceases to be liable to tax on qualifying amounts.

6(3) Sub-paragraph (2) does not apply to a qualifying amount if–

(a) the amount was held in the United Kingdom,

(b) at some point during the period beginning with 6 October 2011 and ending immediately before the start date, it ceased to be held in the United Kingdom, and

(c) after that point (but before the start date) it began to be held in Switzerland.

6(4) Instead, such part of the one-off payment as is attributable (on a just and reasonable basis) to the qualifying amount is to be treated as if it were a credit allowable against the tax due from P taking account of that amount.

6(5) The meaning of tax due **"taking account of"** an amount is explained in Part 5 of this Schedule.

6(6) The form in which a qualifying amount was held in the United Kingdom is irrelevant (so references *in sub-paragraph (3) to the amount* include an asset representing the amount).

6(7) The total qualifying amounts to which sub-paragraphs (2) and (4) can apply as a result of the Part 2 certificate is limited to X.

6(8) If the total exceeds X, the particular qualifying amounts to which those sub-paragraphs apply are assumed to be those that would produce the most beneficial outcome for P.

6(9) X is–

(a) in a case falling within Article 9(3), the value of the omitted taxable base by reference to which the one-off payment was calculated, and

(b) in any other case, the value shown in the Part 2 certificate as the value of the relevant capital (C_r).

CEASING TO BE LIABLE TO TAX

7(1) The result of **"ceasing to be liable"** to tax on a qualifying amount depends on the tax (or taxes) in respect of which the amount is untaxed.

7(2) For income tax or capital gains tax, the result is that the amount is no longer liable to be brought into account in assessing the income tax or capital gains tax due from P for the tax year in which the amount would otherwise be liable to be brought into account.

7(3) For inheritance tax, the result is that any inheritance tax due from P in respect of the chargeable transfer and attributable to the property whose value is included in the amount is no longer due from P.

7(4) For VAT, the result is that P is no longer required to account for output tax on the amount in determining the VAT payable by P for the prescribed accounting period in which P would otherwise be required to account for output tax on the amount.

7(5) But–

(a) ceasing to be liable to tax on a qualifying amount does not affect P's liability to tax on any other amount, and

(b) P's liability to tax on any other amount remains what it would have been, had the qualifying amount been brought into account in calculating that liability.

7(6) Accordingly, if the qualifying amount were ever to be brought into account and it were found that the tax assessed on any other amount should have been higher as a result, P would remain liable for the extra tax due on that other amount and for any associated ancillary charge.

7(7) For the purposes of sub-paragraphs (5) and (6), the qualifying amount is assumed to form the top slice of the total sum on which P is liable to tax.

EFFECT IF P NOT ELIGIBLE FOR CLEARANCE

8(1) This paragraph sets out the effect of the Part 2 certificate if P is not eligible for clearance.

8(2) The one-off payment is to be treated as if it were a credit allowable against the tax due from P taking account of qualifying amounts.

8(3) The one-off payment is to be applied for the purposes of sub-paragraph (2)–

(a) in the order specified in sub-paragraph (4), and

(b) subject to that, in the way that produces the most beneficial outcome for P.

8(4) The order is–

(a) first, for VAT,

(b) then, for income tax,

(c) then, for capital gains tax, and

(d) finally, for inheritance tax.

INTEREST, PENALTIES ETC

9(1) Where, by virtue of this Part, P ceases to be liable to tax on a qualifying amount, P also ceases to be liable to any ancillary charge directly connected with that amount.

9(2) Where, by virtue of this Part, all or part of a one-off payment is treated as if it were a credit allowable against the tax due from P taking account of a qualifying amount, the credit may also be used to offset any ancillary charge directly connected with that amount.

9(3) Sub-paragraph (4) applies in the case of a qualifying amount that is part only of–

(a) an amount of income on which income tax is charged,

(b) a chargeable gain,

(c) the value of property forming part of the value transferred by a chargeable transfer, or

(d) the value of a supply on which VAT is charged.

9(4) The amount of any ancillary charge directly connected with that qualifying amount is determined by apportioning the ancillary charge directly connected with the income, gain or value on a just and reasonable basis.

REPAYMENTS

10 Nothing in this Part entitles any person to a repayment or refund of tax, save for any repayment or refund to which P may be entitled by virtue of paragraph 6(4) or 8(2) if the credit allowable under that paragraph exceeds the total amount of tax against which the credit is allowable.

PARAGRAPH 4: SUPPLEMENTARY PROVISION

11(1) This paragraph explains how paragraph 4(2) is to be read for each description of taxable amount.

11(2) For income and chargeable gains–

(a) the reference to P being **"liable to tax"** includes a case where P would be so liable if the income or gain were to be remitted to the United Kingdom,

(b) **"the taxable event"** takes place when the income arises or the gain accrues (whether or not, in a remittance basis case, it is remitted to the United Kingdom), and

(c) the income or gain is **"untaxed"** if it has not been brought into account in an assessment to income tax or, as the case may be, capital gains tax for the tax year in which it is required to be brought into account.

11(3) For the value of property forming part of the value transferred by a chargeable transfer–

(a) **"the taxable event"** takes place when the chargeable transfer is made (or, in the case of a potentially exempt transfer, when death occurs), and

(b) the value of the property is **"untaxed"** if it has not been brought into account in determining the value transferred by the chargeable transfer.

11(4) For the value of supplies on which VAT is charged–

(a) **"the taxable event"** takes place when P makes the supply, and

(b) the value of the supply is **"untaxed"** if output tax on the supply has not been accounted for in determining the VAT payable by P for the prescribed accounting period in which P is required to account for output tax on the supply.

11(5) Paragraph 4(2)(a) is not satisfied in a case where P is liable to tax only because the liability has been transferred to P as a result of action taken by HMRC (for example, as a result of a notice given under section 77A of VATA 1994 or a direction given under regulation 81 of the Income Tax (PAYE) Regulations 2003 (S.I. 2003/2682)).

REFUND OF ONE-OFF PAYMENT

12 If a one-off payment is refunded by HMRC in accordance with Article 15(3), this Part ceases to apply with respect to that payment.

Part 4 – The Future: Inheritance Tax

TAXES AFFECTED

20 This Part affects inheritance tax.

APPLICATION OF THIS PART

21(1) This Part applies if–

(a) an amount is withheld under Article 32(2) in respect of relevant assets of a deceased person ("P"), and

(b) a certificate is issued under Article 32(6) in respect of the withholding of that amount.

21(2) The certificate is referred to in this Part as **"the Article 32 certificate"**.

21(3) The relevant assets in relation to which the Article 32 certificate is issued are referred to as **"the cleared assets"**.

21(4) Any reference in this Part to **"the chargeable transfer"** is to the transfer made (under section 4 of IHTA 1984) on P's death.

EFFECT OF ARTICLE 32 CERTIFICATE

22(1) The cleared assets are to be treated as if they were excluded property in determining the value of P's estate immediately before P's death.

22(2) As a result, any ancillary charge directly connected with those assets is also extinguished.

22(3) But–

(a) treating the cleared assets as if they were excluded property does not affect any liability to inheritance tax on the rest of P's estate, and

(b) that liability remains what it would have been, had the cleared assets not been treated as excluded property.

22(4) Accordingly, if the cleared assets were ever to be included in an account or further account under section 216 or 217 of IHTA 1984 in respect of the chargeable transfer and it were found that the inheritance tax charged on the value of the property in P's estate other than the cleared assets should have been higher, the extra tax charged on the value of that other property remains due, together with any associated ancillary charge.

22(5) For the purposes of sub-paragraphs (3) and (4), the value of the cleared assets is assumed to form the highest part of the value transferred by the chargeable transfer.

ELECTION IN RESPECT OF ARTICLE 32 CERTIFICATES

23(1) This paragraph applies if the cleared assets for each of the Article 32 certificates issued in respect of P's death are included in full in an account or further account delivered in respect of P's death under section 216 or 217 of IHTA 1984 within the time permitted for delivering such an account or further account.

23(2) The person who delivers the account or further account may elect to disapply paragraph 22.

23(3) An election under this paragraph must be made in writing at the same time as the account or further account in which all the cleared assets are included, and signed by each person delivering the account or further account.

23(4) An election may only be made under this paragraph if it is accompanied by each of the Article 32 certificates.

23(5) If an election is made under this paragraph–

(a) paragraph 22 does not apply to the cleared assets for any of the Article 32 certificates issued in respect of P's death, and

(b) the amounts withheld under Article 32(2) are instead to be treated as if they were credits allowable against the inheritance tax due on the value transferred by the chargeable transfer (calculated with the value of all those cleared assets brought into account).

REPAYMENTS

24 Nothing in this Part entitles any person to a repayment or refund of tax, save for any repayment to which a person may be entitled as a result of paragraph 23 if the credit allowable under that paragraph exceeds the inheritance tax due from the person on the value transferred by the chargeable transfer.

Part 5 – General Provisions

INFORMATION EXCHANGE

25 No obligation of secrecy (whether imposed by statute or otherwise) prevents HMRC from disclosing information pursuant to a request made by virtue of Article 36 (reciprocity measures of the United Kingdom).

AMOUNTS RECOVERABLE AS IF THEY WERE VAT

26(1) Part 2 of this Schedule applies to amounts otherwise recoverable under paragraph 5(3) of Schedule 11 to VATA 1994 as a debt due to the Crown (amounts shown on invoices as VAT etc) in the same way as it applies to VAT.

26(2) But in the application of Part 2 to such amounts–

(a) a reference to the value of a supply on which VAT is charged is a reference to the value of the supply shown in the invoice mentioned in paragraph 5(2) of that Schedule,

(b) **"the taxable event"** takes place when the invoice is issued,

(c) the value of the supply shown in the invoice is **"untaxed"** if the amount otherwise recoverable under paragraph 5(3) of that Schedule has not been recovered, and

(d) **"ceasing to be liable"** to tax on the value of that supply means that the amount otherwise recoverable is no longer recoverable.

TRANSFERS TO HMRC UNDER AGREEMENT

26A(1) Income or chargeable gains of a person are to be treated as not remitted to the United Kingdom if conditions A to D are met.

26A(2) Condition A is that (but for sub-paragraph (1)) the income or gains would be regarded as remitted to the United Kingdom by virtue of the bringing of money to the United Kingdom.

26A(3) Condition B is that the money is brought to the United Kingdom pursuant to a transfer made to HMRC in accordance with the Agreement.

26A(4) Condition C (which applies only if the money brought to the United Kingdom is a sum levied under Article 19(2)(b)) is that the sum was levied within the period of 45 days beginning with the day on which the amount derived from the income or gain in question was remitted as mentioned in Article 19(2)(b).

26A(5) Condition D is that the transfer is made in relation to a tax year in which section 809B, 809D or 809E of ITA 2007 (application of remittance basis) applies to the person.

26A(6) Sub-paragraph (1) does not apply in relation to money brought to the United Kingdom if or to the extent that–

(a) paragraph 18(2), or section 138(4)(a) or 140(5)(a) of TIOPA 2010, is applied in relation to it (set-off against other tax liabilities), or

(b) it is repaid or refunded by HMRC.

History – Para. 26A inserted by FA 2013, s. 221(1), with effect from 1 January 2013.

26B(1) This paragraph applies if–

(a) but for paragraph 26A(1), income or chargeable gains would have been regarded as remitted to the United Kingdom by virtue of the bringing of money to the United Kingdom, and

(b) section 809Q of ITA 2007 (transfers from mixed funds) would have applied in determining the amount that would have been so remitted.

26B(2) The bringing of the money to the United Kingdom counts as an offshore transfer for the purposes of section 809R(4) of ITA 2007 (composition of mixed fund).

History – Para. 26B inserted by FA 2013, s. 221(1), with effect from 1 January 2013.

GENERAL INTERPRETATION

27(1) In this Schedule–

"ancillary charge" means any interest, penalty, surcharge or other ancillary charge;

"assessment", in relation to a tax, includes a determination and also includes an amended assessment or determination (and "assess" is to be read accordingly);

"chargeable gain" means a gain that is a chargeable gain for the purposes of TCGA 1992;

"chargeable transfer" has the meaning given in section 2 of IHTA 1984;

"EUSA" means the agreement dated 26 October 2004 between the European Community and the Swiss Confederation providing for measures equivalent to those laid down in Council Directive 2003/ 48/EC on taxation on savings income in the form of interest payments;

"HMRC" means Her Majesty's Revenue and Customs;

"qualifying amount" is defined in paragraph 4;

"remitted to the United Kingdom" means remitted to the United Kingdom within the meaning of Chapter A1 of Part 14 of ITA 2007;

"the value transferred", in relation to a chargeable transfer, has the meaning given in section 3 of IHTA 1984;

"taxable amount" is defined in paragraph 2;

"VAT" means value added tax charged in accordance with VATA 1994.

27(2) An expression used in relation to a tax has the same meaning as in enactments relating to that tax.

27(3) A reference to a person being **"liable"** includes being liable jointly with others.

27(4) A reference to the most beneficial outcome for P is a reference to the most beneficial outcome for P with respect to P's liability to tax.

27(5) *A reference to the tax due* **"taking account of"** a qualifying amount is–

(a) if the amount is an amount of income or a chargeable gain, a reference to the income tax or capital gains tax due for the tax year in which the amount is required to be brought into account (calculated with that amount brought into account),

(b) if the amount is the value of property forming part of the value transferred by a chargeable transfer, a reference to the inheritance tax due on the value transferred by the chargeable transfer (calculated with that amount brought into account),

(c) if the amount is the value of a supply on which VAT is charged, a reference to the VAT payable for the prescribed accounting period in which output tax on the supply is required to be brought into account (calculated with that output tax brought into account), and

(d) if the amount is the value of a supply to which Part 2 applies by virtue of paragraph 26, a reference to the amount otherwise recoverable under paragraph 5(3) of Schedule 11 to VATA 1994 in respect of that supply.

SCHEDULE 37 – INTERNATIONAL MILITARY HEADQUARTERS, EU FORCES, ETC

Section 220

IHTA 1984

2 [Amends IHTA 1984, s. 6(4).]

3(1) Section 155 of that Act (visiting forces and allied headquarters: residence, etc) is amended as follows.

3(2) [Amends IHTA 1984, s. 155(4).]

3(3) [Inserts IHTA 1984, s. 155(5A) and (5B).]

3(4) [Amends IHTA 1984, s. 155(6).]

SCHEDULE 38 – TAX AGENTS: DISHONEST CONDUCT

Section 223

Commencement Date – The day appointed as the day on which Sch. 38 comes into force is 1 April 2013 (SI 2013/279).
Other material – HMRC Factsheet TA/FS1: Tax agents: dishonest conduct.

Part 1 – Introduction

OVERVIEW

1 This Schedule is arranged as follows–

(a) this Part explains who is a tax agent and what it means to engage in dishonest conduct,

(b) Part 2 sets out the process for establishing whether someone is engaging in or has engaged in dishonest conduct,

(c) Part 3 confers power on HMRC to obtain relevant documents,

(d) Part 4 sets out sanctions for engaging in dishonest conduct,

(e) Part 5 provides for assessment of and appeals against penalties, and

(f) Parts 6 and 7 contain miscellaneous provisions and consequential amendments.

TAX AGENT

2(1) A **"tax agent"** is an individual who, in the course of business, assists other persons ("clients") with their tax affairs.

2(2) Individuals can be tax agents even if they (or the organisations for which they work) are appointed–

(a) indirectly, or

(b) at the request of someone other than the client.

2(3) Assistance with a client's tax affairs includes–

(a) advising a client in relation to tax, and

(b) acting or purporting to act as agent on behalf of a client in relation to tax.

2(4) Assistance with a client's tax affairs also includes assistance with any document that is likely to be relied on by HMRC to determine a client's tax position.

2(5) Assistance given for non-tax purposes counts as assistance with a client's tax affairs if it is given in the knowledge that it will be, or is likely to be, used by a client in connection with the client's tax affairs.

DISHONEST CONDUCT

3(1) An individual **"engages in dishonest conduct"** if, in the course of acting as a tax agent, the individual does something dishonest with a view to bringing about a loss of tax revenue.

3(2) It does not matter whether a loss is actually brought about.

3(3) Nor does it matter whether the individual is acting on the instruction of clients.

3(4) A loss of tax revenue would be brought about for these purposes if clients were to–

(a) account for less tax than they are required to account for by law,

(b) obtain more tax relief than they are entitled to obtain by law,

(c) account for tax later than they are required to account for it by law, or

(d) obtain tax relief earlier than they are entitled to obtain it by law.

3(5) **"Tax"** is defined in Part 6 of this Schedule.

3(6) **"Tax relief"** includes–

(a) any exemption from or deduction or credit against or in respect of tax, and

(b) any repayment of tax.

3(7) A reference in this paragraph to doing something dishonest includes–

(a) dishonestly omitting to do something, and

(b) advising or assisting a client to do something that the individual knows to be dishonest.

Part 2 – Establishing Dishonest Conduct

CONDUCT NOTICE

4(1) This paragraph applies if HMRC determine that an individual is engaging in or has engaged in dishonest conduct.

4(2) An authorised officer (or an officer of Revenue and Customs with the approval of an authorised officer) may notify the individual of that determination.

4(3) The notice must state the grounds on which the determination was made.

4(4) For the effect of notifying the individual, see paragraphs 7(2) and 29(2).

4(5) A notice under this paragraph is referred to as a **"conduct notice"**.

4(6) In relation to a conduct notice, a reference to **"the determination"** is to the determination forming the subject of the notice.

APPEAL AGAINST DETERMINATION

5(1) An individual to whom a conduct notice is given may appeal against the determination.

5(2) Notice of appeal must be given–

(a) in writing to the officer who gave the conduct notice, and

(b) within the period of 30 days beginning with the day on which the conduct notice was given.

5(3) It must state the grounds of appeal.

5(4) On an appeal that is notified to the tribunal, the tribunal may confirm or set aside the determination.

5(5) Subject to this paragraph, the provisions of Part 5 of TMA 1970 relating to appeals have effect in relation to an appeal under this paragraph as they have effect in relation to an appeal against an assessment to income tax.

5(6) Setting aside a determination does not prevent a further conduct notice being given in respect of the same conduct if further evidence emerges.

OFFENCE OF CONCEALMENT ETC IN CONNECTION WITH CONDUCT NOTICE

6(1) A person ("P") commits an offence if, after a relevant event has occurred, P–

(a) conceals, destroys or otherwise disposes of a material document, or

(b) arranges for the concealment, destruction or disposal of a material document.

6(2) A **"relevant event"** occurs if–

(a) a conduct notice is given to an individual, or

(b) an individual is informed by an officer of Revenue and Customs that a conduct notice will be or is likely to be given to the individual.

6(3) A **"material document"** is any document that could be sought under paragraph 8 as a result of the giving of the conduct notice.

6(4) If P acts after the event described in sub-paragraph (2)(a), no offence is committed if P acts–

(a) after the determination has been set aside,

(b) more than 4 years after the conduct notice was given, or

(c) without knowledge of that event.

6(5) If P acts before that event but after the event described in sub-paragraph (2)(b), no offence is committed if P acts–

(a) more than 2 years after the individual was, or was last, so informed, or

(b) without knowledge of the event described in sub-paragraph (2)(b).

6(6) P acts without knowledge of an event if P–

(a) is not the individual with respect to whom the event has occurred, and

(b) does not know, and could not reasonably be expected to know, that the event has occurred.

6(7) A person guilty of an offence under this paragraph is liable–

(a) on summary conviction, to a fine not exceeding the statutory maximum, and

(b) on conviction on indictment, to imprisonment for a term not exceeding 2 years or to a fine, or both.

Part 3 – Power to Obtain Tax Agent's Files etc

CIRCUMSTANCES IN WHICH POWER IS EXERCISABLE

7(1) The power in paragraph 8 is exercisable only in case A or case B and only with the approval of the tribunal.

7(2) Case A is where a conduct notice has been given to an individual and either–

(a) the time allowed for giving notice of appeal against the determination has expired without any such notice being given, or

(b) notice of appeal against the determination was given within that time, but the appeal has been withdrawn or the determination confirmed.

7(3) Case B is where–

(a) an individual has been convicted of an offence relating to tax that involves fraud or dishonesty,

(b) the offence was committed after the individual became a tax agent (whether or not the individual was still a tax agent when it was committed and regardless of the capacity in which it was committed),

(c) either–

(i) the time allowed for appealing against the conviction has expired without any such appeal being brought, or

(ii) an appeal against the conviction was brought within that time, but the appeal has been withdrawn or the conviction upheld, and

(d) no more than 12 months have elapsed since the date on which paragraph (c) was satisfied.

7(4) For the purposes of this paragraph, a determination or conviction that is appealed is not considered to have been confirmed or upheld until–

(a) the time allowed for bringing any further appeal has expired, or

(b) if a further appeal is brought within that time, that further appeal has been withdrawn or determined.

7(5) In this Schedule, a reference to **"the tax agent"** is–

(a) in a case falling within case A, a reference to the individual mentioned in sub-paragraph (2), and

(b) in a case falling within case B, a reference to the individual mentioned in sub-paragraph (3).

7(6) It does not matter whether the individual is still a tax agent when the power in paragraph 8 is to be exercised.

FILE ACCESS NOTICE

8(1) Subject to paragraph 7, an officer of Revenue and Customs may by notice in writing require any person mentioned in sub-paragraph (2) to provide relevant documents.

8(2) The persons are–

(a) the tax agent, and

(b) any other person the officer believes may hold relevant documents.

8(3) **"Relevant documents"** is defined in paragraph 9.

8(4) A notice under this paragraph is referred to as a **"file access notice"**.

8(5) The person to whom a file access notice is given is referred to as **"the document-holder"**.

RELEVANT DOCUMENTS

9(1) **"Relevant documents"** means the tax agent's working papers (whenever acting as a tax agent) and any other documents received, created, prepared or used by the tax agent for the purposes of or in the course of assisting clients with their tax affairs.

9(2) It does not matter who owns the papers or other documents.

9(3) The reference in sub-paragraph (1) to clients–

(a) includes former clients, and

(b) is not limited to the clients with respect to whom the tax agent is engaging in or has engaged in dishonest conduct.

CONTENT OF NOTICE

10(1) A file access notice may require the provision of–

(a) particular relevant documents specified in the notice, or

(b) all relevant documents in the document-holder's possession or power.

10(2) A file access notice does not need to identify the clients of the tax agent.

10(3) A file access notice addressed to anyone other than the tax agent must name the tax agent.

COMPLIANCE

11 A file access notice may require documents to be provided–

(a) within such period,

(b) by such means and in such form, and

(c) to such person and at such place,

as is reasonably specified in the notice or in a document referred to in the notice.

12 Unless otherwise specified in the notice, a file access notice may be complied with by providing copies of the relevant documents.

APPROVAL BY TRIBUNAL

13(1) The tribunal may not approve the giving of a file access notice unless–

(a) the application for approval is made by or with the agreement of an authorised officer,

(b) the tribunal is satisfied that the case falls within case A or case B (see paragraph 7),

(c) the tribunal is satisfied that, in the circumstances, the officer giving the notice is justified in doing so,

(d) the document-holder and (where different) the tax agent have been told that relevant documents are to be required and given a reasonable opportunity to make representations to an officer of Revenue and Customs, and

(e) the tribunal has been given a summary of any representations so made.

13(2) Nothing in sub-paragraph (1) requires the tribunal to determine whether an individual is engaging in or has engaged in dishonest conduct.

13(3) A decision by the tribunal under this paragraph is final (despite the provisions of sections 11 and 13 of the Tribunals, Courts and Enforcement Act 2007).

DOCUMENTS NOT IN PERSON'S POSSESSION OR POWER

14 A file access notice only requires the document-holder to provide a document if it is in the document-holder's possession or power.

TYPES OF INFORMATION

15(1) A file access notice does not require the document-holder to provide–

(a) parts of a document that contain information relating to the conduct of a pending appeal relating to tax, or

(b) journalistic material (as defined in section 13 of the Police and Criminal Evidence Act 1984).

15(2) A file access notice does not require the document-holder to provide personal records (as defined in section 12 of the Police and Criminal Evidence Act 1984).

15(3) But a file access notice may require the document-holder to provide documents that are personal records, omitting any information whose inclusion (whether alone or with other information) makes the original documents personal records.

OLD DOCUMENTS

16(1) A file access notice does not require the document-holder to provide a relevant document if–

(a) the whole of the document originated before the back-stop day, and

(b) no part of it has a bearing on tax periods ending on or after that day.

16(2) **"The back-stop day"** is the first day of the period of 20 years ending with the day on which the file access notice is given.

PRIVILEGED COMMUNICATIONS BETWEEN PROFESSIONAL LEGAL ADVISERS AND CLIENTS

17(1) A file access notice does not require the document-holder to provide any part of a document that is privileged.

17(2) For the purposes of this paragraph a document is privileged if it is a document in respect of which a claim to legal professional privilege, or (in Scotland) to confidentiality of communications between client and professional legal adviser, could be maintained in legal proceedings.

17(3) Regulations under paragraph 23 of Schedule 36 to FA 2008 (information powers: privileged communications) apply (with any necessary modifications) to disputes under this paragraph as to whether a document is privileged.

POWER TO COPY DOCUMENTS

18 If a document is provided pursuant to a file access notice, an officer of Revenue and Customs may take copies of or make extracts from the document.

POWER TO RETAIN DOCUMENTS

19(1) If a document is provided pursuant to a file access notice, HMRC may retain the document for a reasonable period if an officer of Revenue and Customs thinks it necessary to do so.

19(2) While a document is retained–

(a) the document-holder may, if the document is reasonably required for any purpose, request a copy of it, and

(b) an officer of Revenue and Customs must comply with such a request without charge.

19(3) The retention of a document under this paragraph is not to be regarded as breaking any lien claimed on the document.

19(4) If a document retained under this paragraph is lost or damaged, the Commissioners are liable to compensate the owner of the document for any expenses reasonably incurred in replacing or repairing the document.

APPEAL AGAINST FILE ACCESS NOTICE

20(1) If the document-holder is a person other than the tax agent, the document-holder may appeal against the file access notice, or any requirement in it, on the ground that it would be unduly onerous to comply with the notice or requirement.

20(2) Notice of appeal must be given–

(a) in writing to the officer by whom the file access notice was given, and

(b) within the period of 30 days beginning with the day on which the file access notice was given.

20(3) It must state the grounds of appeal.

20(4) On an appeal that is notified to the tribunal, the tribunal may confirm, vary or set aside the file access notice or a requirement in it.

20(5) If the tribunal confirms or varies the notice or a requirement in it, the document-holder must comply with the notice or requirement–

(a) within such period as is specified by the tribunal, or

(b) if the tribunal does not specify a period, within such period as is reasonably specified in writing by an officer of Revenue and Customs following the tribunal's decision.

20(6) A decision by the tribunal under this paragraph is final (despite the provisions of sections 11 and 13 of the Tribunals, Courts and Enforcement Act 2007).

20(7) Subject to this paragraph, the provisions of Part 5 of TMA 1970 relating to appeals have effect in relation to an appeal under this paragraph as they have effect in relation to an appeal against an assessment to income tax.

OFFENCE OF CONCEALMENT ETC IN CONNECTION WITH FILE ACCESS NOTICE

21(1) A person ("P") commits an offence if P–

(a) conceals, destroys or otherwise disposes of a required document, or

(b) arranges for the concealment, destruction or disposal of a required document.

21(2) A **"required document"** is a document within sub-paragraph (3) or sub-paragraph (4).

21(3) A document is within this sub-paragraph if at the time when P acts–

(a) P is required to provide the document by a file access notice, and

(b) either–

  (i) the notice has not been complied with, or

  (ii) it has been complied with, but P has been notified in writing by an officer of Revenue and Customs that P must continue to preserve the document (and the notification has not been withdrawn).

21(4) A document is within this sub-paragraph if at the time when P acts–

(a) P is not required to provide the document by a file access notice,

(b) P has been informed by an officer of Revenue and Customs that P will be or is likely to be so required, and

(c) no more than 6 months have elapsed since P was, or was last, so informed.

21(5) A person guilty of an offence under this paragraph is liable–

(a) on summary conviction, to a fine not exceeding the statutory maximum, and

(b) on conviction on indictment, to imprisonment for a term not exceeding 2 years or to a fine, or both.

PENALTY FOR FAILURE TO COMPLY

22(1) A person who fails to comply with a file access notice is liable to a penalty of £300.

22(2) Failing to comply with a file access notice also includes–

(a) concealing, destroying or otherwise disposing of a required document, or

(b) arranging for any such concealment, destruction or disposal.

22(3) **"Required document"** has the same meaning as in paragraph 21.

DAILY PENALTY FOR FAILURE TO COMPLY

23 If the failure continues after notification of a penalty under paragraph 22 has been issued, the person is liable to a further penalty, for each subsequent day on which the failure continues, of an amount not exceeding £60 for each such day.

FAILURE TO COMPLY WITH TIME LIMIT

24 A failure to do anything required to be done within a limited period of time does not give rise to liability to a penalty under paragraph 22 or 23 if the thing was done within such further time (if any) as an officer of Revenue and Customs may have allowed.

REASONABLE EXCUSE

25(1) Liability to a penalty under paragraph 22 or 23 does not arise if the person satisfies HMRC or (on an appeal notified to the tribunal) the tribunal that there is a reasonable excuse for the failure.

25(2) For the purposes of this paragraph–

(a) an insufficiency of funds is not a reasonable excuse unless attributable to events outside the person's control,

(b) if the person relies on another person to do anything, that is not a reasonable excuse unless the first person took reasonable care to avoid the failure,

(c) if the person had a reasonable excuse for the failure but the excuse has ceased, the person is to be treated as having continued to have the excuse if the failure is remedied without unreasonable delay after the excuse ceased.

Part 4 – Sanctions for Dishonest Conduct

PENALTY FOR DISHONEST CONDUCT

26(1) An individual who engages in dishonest conduct is liable to a penalty.

26(2) Subject to paragraph 27, the penalty to which the individual is liable is to be–

(a) no less than £5,000, and

(b) no more than £50,000.

26(3) In assessing the amount of the penalty, regard must be had to–

(a) whether the individual disclosed the dishonest conduct,

(b) whether that disclosure was prompted or unprompted,

(c) the quality of that disclosure, and

(d) the quality of the individual's compliance with any file access notice in connection with the dishonest conduct.

26(4) An individual **"discloses"** dishonest conduct by–

(a) telling HMRC about it,

(b) giving HMRC reasonable help in identifying the client or clients concerned and in quantifying the loss of tax revenue (if any) brought about by it, and

(c) allowing HMRC access to records for the purpose of ensuring that any such loss is recovered or otherwise properly accounted for.

26(5) A disclosure is **"unprompted"** if it is made at a time when the individual has no reason to believe that HMRC have discovered or are about to discover the dishonest conduct.

26(6) Otherwise, a disclosure is **"prompted"**.

26(7) In relation to disclosure or compliance, **"quality"** includes timing, nature and extent.

SPECIAL REDUCTION

27(1) This paragraph applies if HMRC propose to assess an individual to a penalty under paragraph 26 of £5,000.

27(2) If they think it right because of special circumstances, HMRC may take one or more of the following steps–

(a) reduce the penalty to an amount below £5,000 (which may be nil),

(b) stay the penalty, or

(c) agree a compromise in relation to proceedings for the penalty.

27(3) **"Special circumstances"** does not include–

(a) ability to pay, or

(b) the fact that a loss of tax revenue from a client is balanced by an overpayment by another person (whether or not a client).

POWER TO PUBLISH DETAILS

28(1) The Commissioners may publish information about an individual if the individual incurs a penalty under paragraph 26.

28(2) The information that may be published is–

(a) the individual's name (including any trading name, previous name or pseudonym),

(b) the individual's address,

(c) the nature of any business carried on by the individual,

(d) the amount of the penalty,

(e) the periods or times to which the dishonest conduct relates,

(f) any other information the Commissioners consider it appropriate to publish in order to make clear the individual's identity, and

(g) the link (if there is one) between the dishonest conduct and any inaccuracy, failure or action as a result of which information is published under section 94 of FA 2009 (which relates to deliberate tax defaulters).

28(3) No information may be published under this paragraph if the penalty incurred by the individual is £5,000 or less.

28(4) Subsections (5) to (9) and (11) of section 94 of FA 2009 apply to publishing information about an individual under this paragraph as they apply to publishing information about a person under that section.

28(5) If, in acting as a tax agent, the individual works or worked for an organisation, sub-paragraph (2)(f) includes power to publish such information about that organisation as the Commissioners consider appropriate in order to make clear the individual's identity.

28(6) Before publishing information about the organisation, the Commissioners must–

(a) inform the organisation that they are considering doing so, and

(b) afford the organisation reasonable opportunity to make representations about whether it should be published.

Part 5 – Penalties: Assessment etc

ASSESSMENT OF PENALTIES

29(1) If a person becomes liable to a penalty under Part 3 or 4 of this Schedule, HMRC may assess the penalty.

29(2) But, in the case of a penalty under Part 4, they may only do so if a conduct notice has been given to the person and either–

(a) the time allowed for giving notice of appeal against the determination has expired without notice of appeal being given, or

(b) notice of appeal against the determination was given within the time allowed, but the appeal has been withdrawn or the determination confirmed.

29(3) Paragraph 7(4) applies for the purposes of sub-paragraph (2)(b).

29(4) If HMRC assess a penalty, they must notify the person.

30(1) HMRC may not assess a penalty under this Schedule after the applicable deadline.

30(2) For a penalty under Part 3, the applicable deadline is the end of the period of 12 months beginning with the day on which the person became liable to the penalty.

30(3) For a penalty under Part 4, the applicable deadline is the end of the period of 12 months beginning with the later of–

(a) the first day on which HMRC may assess the penalty (see paragraph 29(2)), and

(b) day X.

30(4) If a loss of tax revenue is brought about by the dishonest conduct, day X is–

(a) the day immediately following the end of the appeal period for the assessment or determination of the tax revenue lost (or, if more than one client is involved, the end of the last such period), or

(b) if there is no such assessment or determination, the day on which the amount of tax revenue lost is ascertained.

30(5) Otherwise, day X is the day on which HMRC ascertain that no loss of tax revenue has been brought about by the dishonest conduct.

30(6) In sub-paragraph (4), **"appeal period"** means the period during which–

(a) an appeal could be brought, or

(b) an appeal that has been brought has not been withdrawn or determined.

APPEAL AGAINST PENALTY

31(1) A person may appeal against a decision of HMRC–

(a) that a penalty is payable under Part 3 of this Schedule, or

(b) as to the amount of a penalty payable under Part 3 or 4 of this Schedule.

31(2) Notice of appeal must be given–

(a) in writing to HMRC, and

(b) before the end of the period of 30 days beginning with the day on which notification of the penalty was issued.

31(3) It must state the grounds of appeal.

31(4) On an appeal under sub-paragraph (1)(a) that is notified to the tribunal, the tribunal may confirm or cancel the decision.

31(5) On an appeal under sub-paragraph (1)(b) that is notified to the tribunal, the tribunal may–

(a) confirm the decision, or

(b) substitute for the decision another decision that HMRC had power to make.

31(6) If, in the case of an appeal against a penalty under Part 4, the tribunal substitutes its decision for HMRC's, the tribunal may rely on paragraph 27 (special reduction)–

(a) to the same extent as HMRC (which may mean applying the same reduction as HMRC to a different starting point), or

(b) to a different extent, but only if the tribunal thinks that HMRC's decision in respect of the application of that paragraph was flawed (when considered in the light of the principles applicable in proceedings for judicial review).

31(7) Subject to this paragraph and paragraph 32, the provisions of Part 5 of TMA 1970 relating to appeals have effect in relation to an appeal under this paragraph as they have effect in relation to an appeal against an assessment to income tax.

ENFORCEMENT OF PENALTY

32(1) A penalty under this Schedule must be paid–

(a) before the end of the period of 30 days beginning with the day on which notification of the penalty was issued, or

(b) if a notice of appeal under paragraph 31 is given, before the end of the period of 30 days beginning with the day on which the appeal is withdrawn or determined.

32(2) A penalty under this Schedule may be enforced as if it were income tax charged in an assessment and due and payable.

DOUBLE JEOPARDY

33 A person is not liable to a penalty under this Schedule in respect of anything in respect of which the person has been convicted of an offence.

34(1) A person is not liable to a penalty under this Schedule in respect of anything in respect of which the person is personally liable to a penalty under–

(a) Schedule 24 to FA 2007 (penalties for errors),

(b) Schedule 41 to FA 2008 (penalties for failure to notify etc), or

(c) Schedule 55 to FA 2009 (penalties for failure to make a return etc).

34(2) Sub-paragraph (1) applies where, for example, the person is personally liable by virtue of section 48(3) of VATA 1994 (VAT representatives).

POWER TO CHANGE AMOUNT OF PENALTIES

35(1) If it appears to the Treasury that there has been a change in the value of money since the last relevant day, they may by regulations substitute for the sums for the time being specified in paragraphs 22(1), 23, 26(2), 27(1) and (2)(a) and 28(3) such other sums as appear to them to be justified by the change.

35(2) **"Relevant day"**, in relation to a specified sum, means–

(a) the day on which this Act is passed, and

(b) each day on which the power conferred by sub-paragraph (1) has been exercised in relation to that sum.

35(3) Regulations under this paragraph do not apply to a failure or conduct that began before the day on which they come into force.

35(4) The power to make regulations under this paragraph is exercisable by statutory instrument.

35(5) A statutory instrument containing regulations under this paragraph is subject to annulment in pursuance of a resolution of the House of Commons.

Part 6 – Miscellaneous Provision and Interpretation

APPLICATION OF PROVISIONS OF TMA 1970

36 Subject to the provisions of this Schedule, the following provisions of TMA 1970 apply for the purposes of this Schedule as they apply for the purposes of the Taxes Acts–

(a) section 108 (responsibility of company officers),

(b) section 114 (want of form), and

(c) section 115 (delivery and service of documents).

TAX

37(1) **"Tax"** means–

(a) income tax,

(b) capital gains tax,

(c) corporation tax,

(d) construction industry deductions,

(e) VAT,

(f) insurance premium tax,

(g) inheritance tax,

(h) stamp duty land tax,

(i) stamp duty reserve tax,

(j) petroleum revenue tax,

(k) aggregates levy,

(l) climate change levy,

(la) apprenticeship levy,

(m) landfill tax, and

(n) any duty of excise other than vehicle excise duty.

37(2) **"Construction industry deductions"** means construction industry deductions under Chapter 3 of Part 3 of FA 2004.

37(3) **"Corporation tax"** includes an amount assessable or chargeable as if it were corporation tax.

37(4) **"VAT"** means–

(a) value added tax charged in accordance with VATA 1994,

(b) amounts recoverable under paragraph 5(2) of Schedule 11 to that Act (amounts shown on invoices as VAT), and

(c) amounts treated as VAT by virtue of regulations under section 54 of that Act (farmers etc).

History – S. 37(1)(la) inserted by FA 2016, s. 115, with effect from 15 September 2016 (Royal Assent).

GENERAL INTERPRETATION

38 In this Schedule–

"appointed" includes engaged;

"client" (except in paragraph 17)–

(a) has the meaning given in paragraph 2(1), and

(b) in relation to a particular tax agent, means a client of that tax agent;

"the Commissioners" means the Commissioners for Her Majesty's Revenue and Customs;

"conduct notice" has the meaning given in paragraph 4;

"the document-holder" has the meaning given in paragraph 8;

"document" includes a copy of a document (see also section 114 of FA 2008);

"file access notice" has the meaning given in paragraph 8;

"HMRC" means Her Majesty's Revenue and Customs;

"organisation" includes any person or firm carrying on a business;

"specify" includes describe;

"tax period" means a tax year, accounting period or other period in respect of which tax is charged;

"the tribunal" means the First-tier Tribunal or, where determined by or under the Tribunal Procedure Rules, the Upper Tribunal.

39(1) A reference in this Schedule to clients of a tax agent (or to a tax agent's clients) is a reference to the persons whom the agent assists with their tax affairs.

39(2) Sub-paragraph (1) applies even if–

(a) the agent works for an organisation, and

(b) it is the organisation that is appointed to give the assistance.

40 A loss of tax revenue is taken for the purposes of this Schedule to be (or to be capable of being) brought about by dishonest conduct despite the fact that the loss can be recovered or properly accounted for (following discovery of the conduct or otherwise).

41 A reference in this Schedule to working for an organisation includes being a partner or member of an organisation.

42 A reference in a provision of this Schedule to an authorised officer is to an officer of Revenue and Customs who is, or is a member of a class of officers who are, authorised by the Commissioners for the purposes of that provision.

RELATIONSHIP WITH OTHER ENACTMENTS

43 Nothing in this Schedule limits–

(a) any liability a person may have under any other enactment in respect of conduct in respect of which a person is liable to a penalty under this Schedule, or

(b) any power a person may have under any other enactment to obtain relevant documents.

Part 7 – Consequential Provisions

IHTA 1984

52 [Omits IHTA 1984, s. 247(4).]

SCHEDULE 39 – REPEAL OF MISCELLANEOUS RELIEFS ETC

Section 227

Part 3 – Payments Relating to Reductions in Pool Betting Duty

19(1) [Repeals FA 1990, s. 126.]

19(2) Accordingly, the following are also repealed–

(a) [not relevant to inheritance tax,]

(b) [not relevant to inheritance tax,]

19(3) The repeals made by this paragraph–

(a) *for corporation tax purposes*, have effect in relation to payments made on or after 1 April 2013,

(b) for income tax purposes, have effect in relation to payments made on or after 6 April 2013, and

(c) for inheritance tax purposes, come into force on 6 April 2013 (and have effect in relation to payments whenever made).

20(1) [Repeals FA 1991, s. 121.]

20(2) The repeal made by this paragraph comes into force on 6 April 2013 (and has effect in relation to payments whenever made).

21 [Not relevant to inheritance tax.]

22 [Not relevant to inheritance tax.]

FINANCE ACT 2013

(2013 Chapter 29)

[*17th July 2013*]

ARRANGEMENT OF SECTIONS

PART 2 – OIL

DECOMMISSIONING SECURITY SETTLEMENTS

PART 3 – ANNUAL TAX ON ENVELOPED DWELLINGS

ADMINISTRATION AND PAYMENT OF TAX

PART 4 – EXCISE DUTIES AND OTHER TAXES

INHERITANCE TAX

PART 5 – GENERAL ANTI-ABUSE RULE

PART 6 – OTHER PROVISIONS

TRUSTS

RESIDENCE

INTERNATIONAL MATTERS

DISCLOSURE

PART 2 – OIL

DECOMMISSIONING SECURITY SETTLEMENTS

86 Removal of IHT charges in respect of decommissioning security settlements

86(1) In Chapter 3 of Part 3 of IHTA 1984 (settled property: settlements without interests in possession etc), section 58 (relevant property) is amended as follows.

86(2) [Inserts IHTA 1984, s. 58(1)(eb).]

86(3) [Inserts IHTA 1984, s. 58(6) and (7).]

86(4) This section is treated as having come into force on 20 March 1993.

86(5) For the purposes of section 58 of IHTA 1984–

(a) any reference in that section to Part 4 of the Petroleum Act 1998 has effect, in relation to any period before the coming into force of that Part, as a reference to Part 1 of the Petroleum Act 1987, and

(b) section 38A of the Petroleum Act 1998 is to be treated as having come into force at the same time as this section.

86(6) There is to be no charge to tax under section 65 of IHTA 1984 if the only reason for such a charge would be that property ceases to be relevant property by virtue of the coming into force of this section.

PART 3 – ANNUAL TAX ON ENVELOPED DWELLINGS

ADMINISTRATION AND PAYMENT OF TAX

164 Information and enforcement

164 In Schedule 34–

(a) Part 1 contains provision about information and inspection powers, and

(b) [not relevant to inheritance tax.]

IHT Statutes

PART 4 – EXCISE DUTIES AND OTHER TAXES

INHERITANCE TAX

175 Open-ended investment companies and authorised unit trusts

175(1) [Inserts IHTA 1984, s. 65(7A).]

175(2) The amendment made by this section is treated as having come into force on 16 October 2002.

176 Treatment of liabilities for inheritance tax purposes

176 Schedule 36 makes provision in relation to the treatment of liabilities for the purposes of inheritance tax.

177 Election to be treated as domiciled in United Kingdom

177(1) IHTA 1984 is amended as follows.

177(2) [Inserts IHTA 1984, s. 267(5).]

177(3) [Inserts IHTA 1984, s. 267ZA and 267ZB.]

178 Transfer to spouse or civil partner not domiciled in United Kingdom

178(1) Section 18 of IHTA 1984 (transfers between spouses or civil partners) is amended as follows.

178(2) [Amends IHTA 1984, s. 18(2).]

178(3) [Inserts IHTA 1984, s. 18(2A).]

178(4) The amendments made by this section have effect in relation to transfers of value made on or after 6 April 2013.

PART 5 – GENERAL ANTI-ABUSE RULE

Other material – Misc. 02/2015: HMRC general anti-abuse rule (GAAR) guidance.

206 General anti-abuse rule

206(1) This Part has effect for the purpose of counteracting tax advantages arising from tax arrangements that are abusive.

206(2) The rules of this Part are collectively to be known as "the general anti-abuse rule".

206(3) The general anti-abuse rule applies to the following taxes–

(a) income tax,

(b) corporation tax, including any amount chargeable as if it were corporation tax or treated as if it were corporation tax,

(c) capital gains tax,

(d) petroleum revenue tax,

(da) diverted profits tax,

(db) apprenticeship levy,

(e) inheritance tax,

(f) stamp duty land tax, and

(g) annual tax on enveloped dwellings.

History – S. 206(3)(da) inserted by FA 2015, s. 115(1), with effect in relation to accounting periods beginning on or after 1 April 2015 (subject to provisions of FA 2015, s. 116(2)–(5)).
S. 206(3)(db) inserted by FA 2016, s. 104(2), with effect from 15 September 2016 (Royal Assent).

207 Meaning of "tax arrangements" and "abusive"

207(1) Arrangements are **"tax arrangements"** if, having regard to all the circumstances, it would be reasonable to conclude that the obtaining of a tax advantage was the main purpose, or one of the main purposes, of the arrangements.

207(2) Tax arrangements are **"abusive"** if they are arrangements the entering into or carrying out of which cannot reasonably be regarded as a reasonable course of action in relation to the relevant tax provisions, having regard to all the circumstances including–

(a) whether the substantive results of the arrangements are consistent with any principles on which those provisions are based (whether express or implied) and the policy objectives of those provisions,

(b) whether the means of achieving those results involves one or more contrived or abnormal steps, and

(c) whether the arrangements are intended to exploit any shortcomings in those provisions.

207(3) Where the tax arrangements form part of any other arrangements regard must also be had to those other arrangements.

207(4) Each of the following is an example of something which might indicate that tax arrangements are abusive–

(a) the arrangements result in an amount of income, profits or gains for tax purposes that is significantly less than the amount for economic purposes,

(b) the arrangements result in deductions or losses of an amount for tax purposes that is significantly greater than the amount for economic purposes, and

(c) the arrangements result in a claim for the repayment or crediting of tax (including foreign tax) that has not been, and is unlikely to be, paid,

but in each case only if it is reasonable to assume that such a result was not the anticipated result when the relevant tax provisions were enacted.

207(5) The fact that tax arrangements accord with established practice, and HMRC had, at the time the arrangements were entered into, indicated its acceptance of that practice, is an example of something which might indicate that the arrangements are not abusive.

207(6) The examples given in subsections (4) and (5) are not exhaustive.

208 Meaning of "tax advantage"

208 A **"tax advantage"** includes–

(a) relief or increased relief from tax,

(b) repayment or increased repayment of tax,

(c) avoidance or reduction of a charge to tax or an assessment to tax,

(d) avoidance of a possible assessment to tax,

(e) deferral of a payment of tax or advancement of a repayment of tax, and

(f) avoidance of an obligation to deduct or account for tax.

209 Counteracting the tax advantages

209(1) If there are tax arrangements that are abusive, the tax advantages that would (ignoring this Part) arise from the arrangements are to be counteracted by the making of adjustments.

209(2) The adjustments required to be made to counteract the tax advantages are such as are just and reasonable.

209(3) The adjustments may be made in respect of the tax in question or any other tax to which the general anti-abuse rule applies.

209(4) The adjustments that may be made include those that impose or increase a liability to tax in any case where (ignoring this Part) there would be no liability or a smaller liability, and tax is to be charged in accordance with any such adjustment.

209(5) Any adjustments required to be made under this section (whether by an officer of Revenue and Customs or the person to whom the tax advantage would arise) may be made by way of an assessment, the modification of an assessment, amendment or disallowance of a claim, or otherwise.

209(6) But–

(a) no steps may be taken by an officer of Revenue and Customs by virtue of this section unless the procedural requirements of Schedule 43, 43A or 43B have been complied with, and

(b) the power to make adjustments by virtue of this section is subject to any time limit imposed by or under any enactment other than this Part.

209(7) Any adjustments made under this section have effect for all purposes.

209(8) Where a matter is referred to the GAAR Advisory Panel under paragraph 5 or 6 of Schedule 43, the taxpayer (as defined in paragraph 3 of that Schedule) must not make any GAAR-related adjustments in relation to the taxpayer's tax affairs in the period (the "closed period") which–

(a) begins with the 31st day after the end of the 45 day period mentioned in paragraph 4(1) of that Schedule, and

(b) ends immediately before the day on which the taxpayer is given the notice under paragraph 12 of Schedule 43 (notice of final decision after considering opinion of GAAR Advisory Panel).

209(9) Where a person has been given a pooling notice or a notice of binding under Schedule 43A in relation to any tax arrangements, the person must not make any GAAR-related adjustments in the period ("the closed period") that–

IHT Statutes

(a) begins with the 31st day after that on which that notice is given, and

(b) ends–

(i) in the case of a pooling notice, immediately before the day on which the person is given a notice under paragraph 8(2) or 9(2) of Schedule 43A, or a notice under paragraph 8(2) of Schedule 43B, in relation to the tax arrangements (notice of final decision after considering opinion of GAAR Advisory Panel), or

(ii) in the case of a notice of binding, with the 30th day after the day on which the notice is given.

209(10) In this section **"GAAR-related adjustments"** means–

(a) for the purposes of subsection (8), adjustments which give effect (wholly or in part) to the proposed counteraction set out in the notice under paragraph 3 of Schedule 43;

(b) for the purposes of subsection (9), adjustments which give effect (wholly or partly) to the proposed counteraction set out in the notice of pooling or binding (as the case may be).

History – In s. 209(6)(a), the words", 43A or 43B" inserted by FA 2016, s. 157(4), with effect in relation to tax arrangements (within the meaning of FA 2013, Pt. 5) entered into at any time (whether before or on or after 15 September 2016).
S. 209(8)–(10) inserted by FA 2016, s. 158(4), with effect in relation to tax arrangements (within the meaning of FA 2013, Pt. 5) entered into on or after 15 September 2016.

209A Effect of adjustments specified in a provisional counteraction notice

209A(1) Adjustments made by an officer of Revenue and Customs which–

(a) are specified in a provisional counteraction notice given to a person by the officer (and have not been cancelled: see sections 209B to 209E),

(b) are made in respect of a tax advantage that would (ignoring this Part) arise from tax arrangements that are abusive, and

(c) but for section 209(6)(a), would have effected a valid counteraction of that tax advantage under section 209,

are treated for all purposes as effecting a valid counteraction of the tax advantage under that section.

209A(2) A **"provisional counteraction notice"** is a notice which–

(a) specifies adjustments (the "notified adjustments") which the officer reasonably believes may be required under section 209(1) to counteract a tax advantage that would (ignoring this Part) arise to the person from tax arrangements;

(b) specifies the arrangements and the tax advantage concerned, and

(c) notifies the person of the person's rights of appeal with respect to the notified adjustments (when made) and contains a statement that if an appeal is made against the making of the adjustments–

(i) no steps may be taken in relation to the appeal unless and until the person is given a notice referred to in section 209F(2), and

(ii) the notified adjustments will be cancelled if HMRC fails to take at least one of the actions mentioned in section 209B(4) within the period specified in section 209B(2).

209A(3) It does not matter whether the notice is given before or at the same time as the making of the adjustments.

209A(4) In this section **"adjustments"** includes adjustments made in any way permitted by section 209(5).

History – S. 209A inserted by FA 2016, s. 156(1), with effect in relation to tax arrangements (within the meaning of FA 2013, Pt. 5) entered into at any time (whether before or on or after 15 September 2016).

209B Notified adjustments: 12 month period for taking action if appeal made

209B(1) This section applies where a person (the "taxpayer") to whom a provisional counteraction notice has been given appeals against the making of the notified adjustments.

209B(2) The notified adjustments are to be treated as cancelled with effect from the end of the period of 12 months beginning with the day on which the provisional counteraction notice is given unless an action mentioned in subsection (4) is taken before that time.

209B(3) For the purposes of subsection (2) it does not matter whether the action mentioned in subsection (4)(c), (d) or (e) is taken before or after the provisional counteraction notice is given (but if that action is taken before the provisional counteraction notice is given subsection (5) does not have effect).

209B(4) *The actions are–*

(a) an officer of Revenue and Customs notifying the taxpayer that the notified adjustments are cancelled;

(b) an officer of Revenue and Customs giving the taxpayer written notice of the withdrawal of the provisional counteraction notice (without cancelling the notified adjustments);

(c) a designated HMRC officer giving the taxpayer a notice under paragraph 3 of Schedule 43 which–
 (i) specifies the arrangements and the tax advantage which are specified in the provisional counteraction notice, and
 (ii) specifies the notified adjustments (or lesser adjustments) as the counteraction that the officer considers ought to be taken (see paragraph 3(2)(c) of that Schedule);
(d) a designated HMRC officer giving the taxpayer a notice of binding under paragraph 1 of Schedule 43A which–
 (i) specifies the arrangements and the tax advantage which are specified in the provisional counteraction notice, and
 (ii) specifies the notified adjustments (or lesser adjustments) as the counteraction that the officer considers ought to be taken (see paragraph 1(4)(c) of that Schedule);
(e) a designated HMRC officer giving the taxpayer a notice under paragraph 1(2) of Schedule 43B which–
 (i) specifies the arrangements and the tax advantage which are specified in the provisional counteraction notice, and
 (ii) specifies the notified adjustments (or lesser adjustments) as the counteraction that the officer considers ought to be taken.

209B(5) In a case within subsection (4)(c), (d) or (e), if–
(a) the notice under paragraph 3 of Schedule 43, or
(b) the pooling notice or notice of binding, or
(c) the notice under paragraph 1(2) of Schedule 43B,
(as the case may be) specifies lesser adjustments the officer must modify the notified adjustments accordingly.

209B(6) The officer may not take the action in subsection (4)(b) unless the officer was authorised to make the notified adjustments otherwise than under this Part.

209B(7) In this section **"lesser adjustments"** means adjustments which assume a smaller tax advantage than was assumed in the provisional counteraction notice.

History – S. 209B inserted by FA 2016, s. 156(1), with effect in relation to tax arrangements (within the meaning of FA 2013, Pt. 5) entered into at any time (whether before or on or after 15 September 2016).

209C Notified adjustments: case within section 209B(4)(c)

209C(1) This section applies if the action in section 209B(4)(c) (notice to taxpayer of proposed counteraction of tax advantage) is taken.

209C(2) If the matter is not referred to the GAAR Advisory Panel, the notified adjustments are to be treated as cancelled with effect from the date of the designated HMRC officer's decision under paragraph 6(2) of Schedule 43 unless the notice under paragraph 6(3) of Schedule 43 states that the adjustments are not to be treated as cancelled under this section.

209C(3) A notice under paragraph 6(3) of Schedule 43 may not contain the statement referred to in subsection (2) unless HMRC would have been authorised to make the adjustments if the general anti-abuse rule did not have effect.

209C(4) If the taxpayer is given a notice under paragraph 12 of Schedule 43 which states that the specified tax advantage is not to be counteracted under the general anti-abuse rule, the notified adjustments are to be treated as cancelled unless that notice states that those adjustments are not to be treated as cancelled under this section.

209C(5) A notice under paragraph 12 of Schedule 43 may not contain the statement referred to in subsection (4) unless HMRC would have been authorised to make the adjustments if the general anti-abuse rule did not have effect.

209C(6) If the taxpayer is given a notice under paragraph 12 of Schedule 43 stating that the specified tax advantage is to be counteracted–
(a) the notified adjustments are confirmed only so far as they are specified in that notice as adjustments required to give effect to the counteraction, and
(b) so far as they are not confirmed, the notified adjustments are to be treated as cancelled.

History – S. 209C inserted by FA 2016, s. 156(1), with effect in relation to tax arrangements (within the meaning of FA 2013, Pt. 5) entered into at any time (whether before or on or after 15 September 2016).

209D Notified adjustments: case within section 209B(4)(d)

209D(1) This section applies if the action in section 209B(4)(d) (notice of binding) is taken.

209D(2) If the taxpayer is given a notice under paragraph 8(2) or 9(2) of Schedule 43A which states that the specified tax advantage is not to be counteracted under the general anti-abuse rule, the notified adjustments are to be treated as cancelled, unless that notice states that those adjustments are not to be treated as cancelled under this section.

209D(3) A notice under paragraph 8(2) or 9(2) of Schedule 43A may not contain the statement referred to in subsection (2) unless HMRC would have been authorised to make the adjustments if the general anti-abuse rule did not have effect.

209D(4) If the taxpayer is given a notice under paragraph 8(2) or 9(2) of Schedule 43A stating that the specified tax advantage is to be counteracted–

(a) the notified adjustments are confirmed only so far as they are specified in that notice as adjustments required to give effect to the counteraction, and

(b) so far as they are not confirmed, the notified adjustments are to be treated as cancelled.

History – S. 209D inserted by FA 2016, s. 156(1), with effect in relation to tax arrangements (within the meaning of FA 2013, Pt. 5) entered into at any time (whether before or on or after 15 September 2016).

209E Notified adjustments: case within section 209B(4)(e)

209E(1) This section applies if the action in section 209B(4)(e) (notice of proposal to make generic referral) is taken.

209E(2) If the notice under paragraph 1(2) of Schedule 43B is withdrawn, the notified adjustments are to be treated as cancelled unless the notice of withdrawal states that the adjustments are not to be treated as cancelled under this section.

209E(3) The notice of withdrawal may not contain the statement referred to in subsection (2) unless HMRC was authorised to make the notified adjustments otherwise than under this Part.

209E(4) If the taxpayer is given a notice under paragraph 8(2) of Schedule 43B, which states that the specified tax advantage is not to be counteracted under the general anti-abuse rule, the notified adjustments are to be treated as cancelled, unless that notice states that those adjustments are not to be treated as cancelled under this section.

209E(5) A notice under paragraph 8(2) of Schedule 43B may not contain the statement referred to in subsection (4) unless HMRC was authorised to make the adjustments otherwise than under this Part.

209E(6) If the taxpayer is given a notice under paragraph 8(2) of Schedule 43B stating that the specified tax advantage is to be counteracted–

(a) the notified adjustments are confirmed only so far as they are specified in that notice as adjustments required to give effect to the counteraction, and

(b) so far as they are not confirmed, the notified adjustments are to be treated as cancelled.

History – S. 209E inserted by FA 2016, s. 156(1), with effect in relation to tax arrangements (within the meaning of FA 2013, Pt. 5) entered into at any time (whether before or on or after 15 September 2016).

209F Appeals against provisional counteractions: further provision

209F(1) Subsections (2) to (5) have effect in relation to an appeal by a person ("the taxpayer") against the making of adjustments which are specified in a provisional counteraction notice.

209F(2) No steps after the initial notice of appeal are to be taken in relation to the appeal unless and until the taxpayer is given–

(a) a notice under section 209B(4)(b),

(b) a notice under paragraph 6(3) of Schedule 43 (notice of decision not to refer matter to GAAR advisory panel) containing the statement described in section 209C(2) (statement that adjustments are not to be treated as cancelled),

(c) a notice under paragraph 12 of Schedule 43, or

(d) a notice under paragraph 8(2) or 9(2) of Schedule 43A,

(e) a notice under paragraph 8 of Schedule 43B,

in respect of the tax arrangements concerned.

209F(3) The taxpayer has until the end of the period mentioned in subsection (4) to comply with any requirement to specify the grounds of appeal.

209F(4) The period mentioned in subsection (3) is the 30 days beginning with the day on which the taxpayer receives the notice mentioned in subsection (2).

209F(5) In subsection (2) the reference to **"steps"** does not include the withdrawal of the appeal.

History – S. 209F inserted by FA 2016, s. 156(1), with effect in relation to tax arrangements (within the meaning of FA 2013, Pt. 5) entered into at any time (whether before or on or after 15 September 2016).

210 Consequential relieving adjustments

210(1) This section applies where–

(a) the counteraction of a tax advantage under section 209 is final, and

(b) if the case is not one in which notice of the counteraction was given under paragraph 12 of Schedule 43, paragraph 8 or 9 of Schedule 43A or paragraph 8 of Schedule 43B, HMRC have been notified of the counteraction by the taxpayer.

210(2) A person has 12 months, beginning with the day on which the counteraction becomes final, to make a claim for one or more consequential adjustments to be made in respect of any tax to which the general anti-abuse rule applies.

210(3) On a claim under this section, an officer of Revenue and Customs must make such of the consequential adjustments claimed (if any) as are just and reasonable.

210(4) Consequential adjustments–

(a) may be made in respect of any period, and

(b) may affect any person (whether or not a party to the tax arrangements).

210(5) But nothing in this section requires or permits an officer to make a consequential adjustment the effect of which is to increase a person's liability to any tax.

210(6) For the purposes of this section–

(a) if the claim relates to income tax or capital gains tax, Schedule 1A to TMA 1970 applies to it;

(b) if the claim relates to corporation tax, Schedule 1A to TMA 1970 (and not Schedule 18 to FA 1998) applies to it;

(c) if the claim relates to petroleum revenue tax, Schedule 1A to TMA 1970 applies to it, but as if the reference in paragraph 2A(4) of that Schedule to a year of assessment included a reference to a chargeable period within the meaning of OTA 1975 (see section 1(3) and (4) of that Act);

(d) if the claim relates to inheritance tax it must be made in writing to HMRC and section 221 of IHTA 1984 applies as if the claim were a claim under that Act;

(e) if the claim relates to stamp duty land tax or annual tax on enveloped dwellings, Schedule 11A to FA 2003 applies to it as if it were a claim to which paragraph 1 of that Schedule applies.

210(7) Where an officer of Revenue and Customs makes a consequential adjustment under this section, the officer must give the person who made the claim written notice describing the adjustment which has been made.

210(8) For the purposes of this section the counteraction of a tax advantage is final when the adjustments made to effect the counteraction, and any amounts arising as a result of those adjustments, can no longer be varied, on appeal or otherwise.

210(9) Any adjustments required to be made under this section may be made–

(a) by way of an assessment, the modification of an assessment, the amendment of a claim, or otherwise, and

(b) despite any time limit imposed by or under any enactment other than this Part.

210(10) In this section **"the taxpayer"**, in relation to a counteraction of a tax advantage under section 209, means the person to whom the tax advantage would have arisen.

History – In s. 210(1)(b), the words "paragraph 8 or 9 of Schedule 43A or paragraph 8 of Schedule 43B," inserted by FA 2016, s. 157(5), with effect in relation to tax arrangements (within the meaning of FA 2013, Pt. 5) entered into at any time (whether before or on or after 15 September 2016).

211 Proceedings before a court or tribunal

211(1) In proceedings before a court or tribunal in connection with the general anti-abuse rule, HMRC must show–

(a) that there are tax arrangements that are abusive, and

(b) that the adjustments made to counteract the tax advantages arising from the arrangements are just and reasonable.

211(2) In determining any issue in connection with the general anti-abuse rule, a court or tribunal must take into account–

(a) HMRC's guidance about the general anti-abuse rule that was approved by the GAAR Advisory Panel at the time the tax arrangements were entered into, and

(b) any opinion of the GAAR Advisory Panel given–

(i) under paragraph 11 of Schedule 43 about the arrangements or any tax arrangements which are, as a result of a notice under paragraph 1 or 2 of Schedule 43A, the referred or (as the case may be) counteracted arrangements in relation to the arrangements, or

(ii) under paragraph 6 of Schedule 43B in respect of a generic referral of the arrangements.

211(3) In determining any issue in connection with the general anti-abuse rule, a court or tribunal may take into account–

(a) guidance, statements or other material (whether of HMRC, a Minister of the Crown or anyone else) that was in the public domain at the time the arrangements were entered into, and

(b) evidence of established practice at that time.

History – S. 211(2)(b)(i) and (ii) and the words "Panel given–" before them substituted for the words "Panel about the arrangements (see paragraph 11 of Schedule 43)." by FA 2016, s. 157(6), with effect in relation to tax arrangements (within the meaning of FA 2013, Pt. 5) entered into at any time (whether before or on or after 15 September 2016).

212 Relationship between the GAAR and priority rules

212(1) Any priority rule has effect subject to the general anti-abuse rule (despite the terms of the priority rule).

212(2) A **"priority rule"** means a rule (however expressed) to the effect that particular provisions have effect to the exclusion of, or otherwise in priority to, anything else.

212(3) Examples of priority rules are–

(a) the rule in section 464, 699 or 906 of CTA 2009 (priority of loan relationships rules, derivative contracts rules and intangible fixed assets rules for corporation tax purposes), and

(b) the rule in section 6(1) of TIOPA 2010 (effect to be given to double taxation arrangements despite anything in any enactment).

212A Penalty

212A(1) A person (P) is liable to pay a penalty if–

(a) (P) has been given a notice under

(i) paragraph 12 of Schedule 43,

(ii) paragraph 8 or 9 of Schedule 43A, or

(iii) paragraph 8 of Schedule 43B,

stating that a tax advantage arising from particular tax arrangements is to be counteracted,

(b) a tax document has been given to HMRC on the basis that the tax advantage arises to P from those arrangements,

(c) that document was given to HMRC–

(i) by P, or

(ii) by another person in circumstances where P knew, or ought to have known, that the other person gave the document on the basis mentioned in paragraph (c), and

(d) the tax advantage has been counteracted by the making of adjustments under section 209.

212A(2) The penalty is 60% of the value of the counteracted advantage.

212A(3) Schedule 43C–

(a) gives the meaning of **"the value of the counteracted advantage"**, and

(b) makes other provision in relation to penalties under this section.

212A(4) In this section **"tax document"** means any return, claim or other document submitted in compliance (or purported compliance) with any provision of, or made under, an Act.

212A(5) In this section the reference to giving a tax document to HMRC is to be interpreted in accordance with paragraph 11(g) and (h) of Schedule 43C.

History – S. 212A inserted by FA 2016, s. 158(2), with effect in relation to tax arrangements (within the meaning of FA 2013, Pt. 5) entered into on or after 15 September 2016.

214 Interpretation of Part 5

214(1) In this Part–

"abusive", in relation to tax arrangements, has the meaning given by section 207(2) to (6);

"arrangements" includes any agreement, understanding, scheme, transaction or series of transactions (whether or not legally enforceable);

"the Commissioners" means the Commissioners for Her Majesty's Revenue and Customs;

"designated HMRC officer" has the meaning given by paragraph 2 of Schedule 43;
"the GAAR Advisory Panel" has the meaning given by paragraph 1 of Schedule 43;
"the general anti-abuse rule" has the meaning given by section 206;
"HMRC" means Her Majesty's Revenue and Customs;
"notice of binding" has the meaning given by paragraph 2(2) of Schedule 43A;
"notified adjustments", in relation to a provisional counteraction notice, has the meaning given by section 209A(2);
"pooling notice" has the meaning given by paragraph 1(4) of Schedule 43A;
"provisional counteraction notice" has the meaning given by section 209A(2);
"tax advantage" has the meaning given by section 208;
"tax appeal" has the meaning given by paragraph 1A of Schedule 43;
"tax arrangements" has the meaning given by section 207(1).
"tax enquiry" has the meaning given by section 202(2) of FA 2014.

214(2) In this Part references to any **"opinion of the GAAR Advisory Panel"** about any tax arrangements are to be interpreted in accordance with paragraph 11(5) of Schedule 43.

214(3) In this Part references to tax arrangements which are **"equivalent"** to one another are to be interpreted in accordance with paragraph 11 of Schedule 43A.

History – In s. 214(1), definitions of "notified adjustments" and "provisional counteraction notice" inserted by FA 2016, s. 156(2), with effect in relation to tax arrangements (within the meaning of FA 2013, Pt. 5) entered into at any time (whether before or on or after 15 September 2016).
In s. 214(1), definitions of "designated HMRC officer", "notice of binding", "pooling notice", "tax appeal" and "tax enquiry" inserted by FA 2016, s. 157(9), with effect in relation to tax arrangements (within the meaning of FA 2013, Pt. 5) entered into at any time (whether before or on or after 15 September 2016).
S. 214(1) created from existing text by FA 2016, s. 157(8), with effect in relation to tax arrangements (within the meaning of FA 2013, Pt. 5) entered into at any time (whether before or on or after 15 September 2016).
S. 214(2) and (3) inserted by FA 2016, s. 157(10), with effect in relation to tax arrangements (within the meaning of FA 2013, Pt. 5) entered into at any time (whether before or on or after 15 September 2016).

215 Commencement and transitional provision

215(1) The general anti-abuse rule has effect in relation to any tax arrangements entered into on or after the day on which this Act is passed.

215(2) Where the tax arrangements form part of any other arrangements entered into before that day those other arrangements are to be ignored for the purposes of section 207(3), subject to subsection (3).

215(3) Account is to be taken of those other arrangements for the purposes of section 207(3) if, as a result, the tax arrangements would not be abusive.

PART 6 – OTHER PROVISIONS

TRUSTS

216 Trusts with vulnerable beneficiary

216 Schedule 44 contains provision about trusts which have a vulnerable beneficiary.

RESIDENCE

218 Statutory residence test

218(1) Schedule 45 contains–

(a) provision for determining whether individuals are resident in the United Kingdom for the purposes of income tax, capital gains tax and (where relevant) inheritance tax and corporation tax,

(b) *provision about split years, and*

(c) provision about periods when individuals are temporarily non-resident.

218(2) The Treasury may by order make any incidental, supplemental, consequential, transitional or saving provision in consequence of Schedule 45.

218(3) An order under subsection (2) may–

(a) make different provision for different purposes, and

(b) make provision amending, repealing or revoking any provision made by or under an Act (whenever passed or made).

218(4) An order under subsection (2) is to be made by statutory instrument.

218(5) A statutory instrument containing an order under subsection (2) is subject to annulment in pursuance of a resolution of the House of Commons.

219 Ordinary residence

219(1) Schedule 46 contains provision removing or replacing rules relating to ordinary residence.

219(2) The Treasury may by order make further provision removing or replacing rules relating to ordinary residence with respect to–

(a) [not relevant to inheritance tax,]

(b) [not relevant to inheritance tax,]

(c) (so far as the ordinary residence status of individuals is relevant to them) inheritance tax and corporation tax.

219(3) An order under subsection (2) may take effect from the start of the tax year in which the order is made.

219(4) The Treasury may by order make any incidental, supplemental, consequential, transitional or saving provision in consequence of Schedule 46 or in consequence of any further provision made under subsection (2).

219(5) An order under this section may–

(a) make different provision for different purposes, and

(b) make provision amending, repealing or revoking any provision made by or under an Act (whenever passed or made).

219(6) An order under this section is to be made by statutory instrument.

219(7) A statutory instrument containing an order under subsection (2) (whether alone or with other provisions) may not be made unless a draft of the instrument has been laid before, and approved by a resolution of, the House of Commons.

219(8) Subject to subsection (7), a statutory instrument containing an order under this section is subject to annulment in pursuance of a resolution of the House of Commons.

INTERNATIONAL MATTERS

221 Agreement between UK and Switzerland

221(1) [Inserts FA 2012, Sch. 36, para. 26A and 26B.]

221(2) The amendment made by this section is to be treated as having come into force on 1 January 2013.

DISCLOSURE

223 Disclosure of tax avoidance schemes

223(1) Part 7 of FA 2004 (disclosure of tax avoidance schemes) is amended in accordance with subsections (2) and (3).

223(2) [Inserts FA 2004, s. 312B.]

223(3) [Inserts FA 2004, s. 313ZB.]

223(4) [not relevant to inheritance tax.]

POWERS

228 Data-gathering from merchant acquirers etc

228(1) [Inserts FA 2011, Sch. 23, para. 13A.]

228(2) This section applies in relation to relevant data with a bearing on any period (whether before, on or after the day on which this Act is passed).

PAYMENT

230 Penalties: late filing, late payment and errors

230 Schedule 50 contains provision for, and in connection with, penalties for late filing, late payment and errors.

PART 7 – FINAL PROVISIONS

235 Interpretation

235(1) In this Act–

"ALDA 1979" means the Alcoholic Liquor Duties Act 1979,

"BGDA 1981" means the Betting and Gaming Duties Act 1981,

"CAA 2001" means the Capital Allowances Act 2001,

"CEMA 1979" means the Customs and Excise Management Act 1979,

"CRCA 2005" means the Commissioners for Revenue and Customs Act 2005,

"CTA 2009" means the Corporation Tax Act 2009,

"CTA 2010" means the Corporation Tax Act 2010,

"F(No. 3)A 2010" means the Finance (No. 3) Act 2010,

"HODA 1979" means the Hydrocarbon Oil Duties Act 1979,

"ICTA" means the Income and Corporation Taxes Act 1988,

"IHTA 1984" means the Inheritance Tax Act 1984,

"ITA 2007" means the Income Tax Act 2007,

"ITEPA 2003" means the Income Tax (Earnings and Pensions) Act 2003,

"ITTOIA 2005" means the Income Tax (Trading and Other Income) Act 2005,

"OTA 1975" means the Oil Taxation Act 1975,

"TCGA 1992" means the Taxation of Chargeable Gains Act 1992,

"TIOPA 2010" means the Taxation (International and Other Provisions) Act 2010,

"TMA 1970" means the Taxes Management Act 1970,

"TPDA 1979" means the Tobacco Products Duty Act 1979,

"VATA 1994" means the Value Added Tax Act 1994, and

"VERA 1994" means the Vehicle Excise and Registration Act 1994.

235(2) In this Act–

"FA", followed by a year, means the Finance Act of that year;

"F(No. 2)A", followed by a year, means the Finance (No. 2) Act of that year.

236 Short title

236 This Act may be cited as the Finance Act 2013.

SCHEDULES

SCHEDULE 34 – ANNUAL TAX ON ENVELOPED DWELLINGS: INFORMATION AND ENFORCEMENT

Section 164

Part 1 – Information and Inspection Powers

1 Schedule 36 to FA 2008 (information and inspection powers) is amended as follows.

2 [Inserts FA 2008, Sch. 36, para. 12A(3)(f).]

3 [Inserts FA 2008, Sch. 36, para. 21B.]

4 [Inserts FA 2008, Sch. 36, para. 37(2B).]

5 [Inserts FA 2008, Sch. 36, para. 63(1)(ha).]

SCHEDULE 36 – TREATMENT OF LIABILITIES FOR INHERITANCE TAX PURPOSES

Section 176

IHTA 1984

1 IHTA 1984 is amended as follows.

2(1) Section 162 (liabilities) is amended as follows.

2(2) [Amends IHTA 1984, s. 162(4).]

2(3) [Amends IHTA 1984, s. 162(5).]

3 [Inserts IHTA 1984, s. 162A–162C.]

4 [Inserts IHTA 1984, s. 175A.]

COMMENCEMENT

5(1) Subject to sub-paragraph (2), the amendments made by this Schedule have effect in relation to transfers of value made, or treated as made, on or after the day on which this Act is passed.

5(2) Section 162B of IHTA 1984 (inserted by paragraph 3) only has effect in relation to liabilities incurred on or after 6 April 2013.

5(3) For the purposes of sub-paragraph (2), where a liability is incurred under an agreement–

(a) if the agreement was varied so that the liability could be incurred under it, the liability is to be treated as having been incurred on the date of the variation, and

(b) in any other case, the liability is to be treated as having been incurred on the date the agreement was made.

SCHEDULE 43 – GENERAL ANTI-ABUSE RULE: PROCEDURAL REQUIREMENTS

Section 209

Other material – HMRC guidance: the general anti-abuse rule.

THE GAAR ADVISORY PANEL

1(1) In this Part **"the GAAR Advisory Panel"** means the panel of persons established by the Commissioners for the purposes of the general anti-abuse rule.

1(2) In this Schedule **"the Chair"** means any member of the GAAR Advisory Panel appointed by the Commissioners to chair it.

MEANING OF "TAX APPEAL"

1A In this Part **"tax appeal"** means–

(a) an appeal under section 31 of TMA 1970 (income tax: appeals against amendments of self-assessment, amendments made by closure notices under section 28A or 28B of that Act, etc), including an appeal under that section by virtue of regulations under Part 11 of ITEPA 2003 (PAYE),

(b) an appeal under paragraph 9 of Schedule 1A to TMA 1970 (income tax: appeals against amendments made by closure notices under paragraph 7(2) of that Schedule, etc),

(c) an appeal under section 705 of ITA 2007 (income tax: appeals against counteraction notices),

(d) an appeal under paragraph 34(3) or 48 of Schedule 18 to FA 1998 (corporation tax: appeals against amendment of a company's return made by closure notice, assessments other than self-assessments, etc),

(e) an appeal under section 750 of CTA 2010 (corporation tax: appeals against counteraction notices),

(f) an appeal under section 222 of IHTA 1984 (appeals against HMRC determinations) other than an appeal made by a person against a determination in respect of a transfer of value at a time when a tax enquiry is in progress in respect of a return made by that person in respect of that transfer,

(g) an appeal under paragraph 35 of Schedule 10 to FA 2003 (stamp duty land tax: appeals against amendment of self-assessment, discovery assessments, etc),

(h) an appeal under paragraph 35 of Schedule 33 to FA 2013 (annual tax on enveloped dwellings: appeals against amendment of self-assessment, discovery assessments, etc),
(i) an appeal under paragraph 14 of Schedule 2 to the Oil Taxation Act 1975 (petroleum revenue tax: appeal against assessment, determination etc),
(j) an appeal under section 102 of FA 2015 (diverted profits tax: appeal against charging notice etc),
(k) an appeal under section 114 of FA 2016 (apprenticeship levy: appeal against an assessment), or
(l) an appeal against any determination of–
(i) an appeal within paragraphs (a) to (k), or
(ii) an appeal within this paragraph.

History – Para. 1A (and the heading before it) inserted by FA 2016, s. 158(6), with effect in relation to tax arrangements (within the meaning of FA 2013, Pt. 5) entered into on or after 15 September 2016.

MEANING OF "DESIGNATED HMRC OFFICER"

2 In this Schedule a **"designated HMRC officer"** means an officer of Revenue and Customs who has been designated by the Commissioners for the purposes of the general anti-abuse rule.

NOTICE TO TAXPAYER OF PROPOSED COUNTERACTION OF TAX ADVANTAGE

3(1) If a designated HMRC officer considers–
(a) that a tax advantage has arisen to a person ("the taxpayer") from tax arrangements that are abusive, and
(b) that the advantage ought to be counteracted under section 209,
the officer must give the taxpayer a written notice to that effect.

3(2) The notice must–
(a) specify the arrangements and the tax advantage,
(b) explain why the officer considers that a tax advantage has arisen to the taxpayer from tax arrangements that are abusive,
(c) set out the counteraction that the officer considers ought to be taken,
(d) inform the taxpayer of the period under paragraph 4 for making representations, and
(e) explain the effect of–
(i) paragraphs 5 and 6, and
(ii) sections 209(8) and (9) and 212A.

3(3) The notice may set out steps that the taxpayer may take to avoid the proposed counteraction.

History – Para. 3(2)(e)(i) and (ii) and the word "of–" before them substituted for the words "of paragraphs 5 and 6" by FA 2016, s. 158(7), with effect in relation to tax arrangements (within the meaning of FA 2013, Pt. 5) entered into on or after 15 September 2016.

4(1) If a notice is given to the taxpayer under paragraph 3, the taxpayer has 45 days beginning with the day on which the notice is given to send written representations in response to the notice to the designated HMRC officer.

4(2) The designated officer may, on a written request made by the taxpayer, extend the period during which representations may be made.

CORRECTIVE ACTION BY TAXPAYER

4A(1) If the taxpayer takes the relevant corrective action before the beginning of the closed period mentioned in section 209(8), the matter is not to be referred to the GAAR Advisory Panel.

4A(2) For the purposes of this Schedule the "relevant corrective action" is taken if (and only if) the taxpayer takes the steps set out in sub-paragraphs (3) and (4).

4A(3) The first step is that–
(a) the taxpayer amends a return or claim to counteract the tax advantage specified in the notice under paragraph 3, or
(b) if the taxpayer has made a tax appeal (by notifying HMRC or otherwise) on the basis that the tax advantage specified in the notice under paragraph 3 arises from the tax arrangements specified in that notice, the taxpayer takes all necessary action to enter into an agreement with HMRC (in writing) for the purpose of relinquishing that advantage.

4A(4) The second step is that the taxpayer notifies HMRC–

(a) that the taxpayer has taken the first step, and

(b) of any additional amount which has or will become due and payable in respect of tax by reason of the first step being taken.

4A(5) Where the taxpayer takes the first step described in sub-paragraph (3)(b), HMRC may proceed as if the taxpayer had not taken the relevant corrective action if the taxpayer fails to enter into the written agreement.

4A(6) In determining the additional amount which has or will become due and payable in respect of tax for the purposes of sub-paragraph (4)(b), it is to be assumed that, where P takes the necessary action as mentioned in sub-paragraph (3)(b), the agreement is then entered into.

4A(7) No enactment limiting the time during which amendments may be made to returns or claims operates to prevent P taking the first step mentioned in sub-paragraph (3)(a) before the tax enquiry is closed (whether or not before the specified time).

4A(8) No appeal may be brought, by virtue of a provision mentioned in sub-paragraph (9), against an amendment made by a closure notice in respect of a tax enquiry to the extent that the amendment takes into account an amendment made by the taxpayer to a return or claim in taking the first step mentioned in sub-paragraph (3)(a).

4A(9) The provisions are–

(a) section 31(1)(b) or (c) of TMA 1970,

(b) paragraph 9 of Schedule 1A to TMA 1970,

(c) paragraph 34(3) of Schedule 18 to FA 1998,

(d) paragraph 35(1)(b) of Schedule 10 to FA 2003, and

(e) paragraph 35(1)(b) of Schedule 33 to FA 2013.

History – Para. 4A (and the heading before it) inserted by FA 2016, s. 158(8), with effect in relation to tax arrangements (within the meaning of FA 2013, Pt. 5) entered into on or after 15 September 2016.

REFERRAL TO GAAR ADVISORY PANEL

4B Paragraphs 5 and 6 apply if the taxpayer does not take the relevant corrective action (see paragraph 4A) by the beginning of the closed period mentioned in section 209(8).

History – Para. 4B inserted by FA 2016, s. 158(9), with effect in relation to tax arrangements (within the meaning of FA 2013, Pt. 5) entered into on or after 15 September 2016.

5 If no representations are made in accordance with paragraph 4, a designated HMRC officer must refer the matter to the GAAR Advisory Panel.

6(1) If representations are made in accordance with paragraph 4, a designated HMRC officer must consider them.

6(2) If, after considering them, the designated HMRC officer considers that the tax advantage ought to be counteracted under section 209, the officer must refer the matter to the GAAR Advisory Panel.

6(3) The officer must, as soon as reasonably practicable after deciding whether or not the matter is to be referred to the GAAR Advisory Panel, give the taxpayer written notice of the decision.

History – Para. 6(3) inserted by FA 2016, s. 157(11), with effect in relation to tax arrangements (within the meaning of FA 2013, Pt. 5) entered into at any time (whether before or on or after 15 September 2016).

7 If the matter is referred to the GAAR Advisory Panel, the designated HMRC officer must at the same time provide it with–

(a) a copy of the notice given to the taxpayer under paragraph 3,

(b) a copy of any representations made in accordance with paragraph 4 and any comments that the officer has on those representations, and

(c) a copy of the notice given to the taxpayer under paragraph 8.

8 If the matter is referred to the GAAR Advisory Panel, the designated HMRC officer must at the same time give the taxpayer a notice which–

(a) specifies that the matter is being referred,

(b) is accompanied by a copy of any comments provided to the GAAR Advisory Panel under paragraph 7(b), and

(c) informs the taxpayer of the period under paragraph 9 for making representations, and of the requirement under that paragraph to send any representations to the officer.

9(1) The taxpayer has 21 days beginning with the day on which a notice is given under paragraph 8 to send the GAAR Advisory Panel written representations about–

(a) the notice given to the taxpayer under paragraph 3, or

(b) any comments provided under paragraph 7(b).

9(2) The GAAR Advisory Panel may, on a written request made by the taxpayer, extend the period during which representations may be made.

9(3) The taxpayer must send a copy of any representations to the designated HMRC officer at the same time as the representations are sent to the GAAR Advisory Panel.

9(4) If no representations were made in accordance with paragraph 4, the designated HMRC officer–

(a) may provide the GAAR Advisory Panel with comments on any representations made under this paragraph, and

(b) if comments are provided, must at the same time send a copy of them to the taxpayer.

DECISION OF GAAR ADVISORY PANEL AND OPINION NOTICES

10(1) If the matter is referred to the GAAR Advisory Panel, the Chair must arrange for a sub-panel consisting of 3 members of the GAAR Advisory Panel (one of whom may be the Chair) to consider it.

10(2) The sub-panel may invite the taxpayer or the designated HMRC officer (or both) to supply the sub-panel with further information within a period specified in the invitation.

10(3) Invitations must explain the effect of sub-paragraph (4) or (5) (as appropriate).

10(4) If the taxpayer supplies information to the sub-panel under this paragraph, the taxpayer must at the same time send a copy of the information to the designated HMRC officer.

10(5) If the designated HMRC officer supplies information to the sub-panel under this paragraph, the officer must at the same time send a copy of the information to the taxpayer.

11(1) Where the matter is referred to the GAAR Advisory Panel, the sub-panel must produce–

(a) one opinion notice stating the joint opinion of all the members of the sub-panel, or

(b) two or three opinion notices which taken together state the opinions of all the members.

11(2) The sub-panel must give a copy of the opinion notice or notices to–

(a) the designated HMRC officer, and

(b) the taxpayer.

11(3) An opinion notice is a notice which states that in the opinion of the members of the sub-panel, or one or more of those members–

(a) the entering into and carrying out of the tax arrangements is a reasonable course of action in relation to the relevant tax provisions–

  (i) having regard to all the circumstances (including the matters mentioned in subsections (2)(a) to (c) and (3) of section 207), and

  (ii) taking account of subsections (4) to (6) of that section, or

(b) the entering into or carrying out of the tax arrangements is not a reasonable course of action in relation to the relevant tax provisions having regard to those circumstances and taking account of those subsections, or

(c) it is not possible, on the information available, to reach a view on that matter,

and the reasons for that opinion.

11(4) For the purposes of the giving of an opinion under this paragraph, the arrangements are to be assumed to be tax arrangements.

11(5) In this Part, a reference to any opinion of the GAAR Advisory Panel about any tax arrangements is a reference to the contents of any opinion notice about the arrangements.

NOTICE OF FINAL DECISION AFTER CONSIDERING OPINION OF GAAR ADVISORY PANEL

12(1) A designated HMRC officer who has received a notice or notices under paragraph 11 must, having considered any opinion of the GAAR Advisory Panel about the tax arrangements, give the taxpayer a written notice setting out whether the tax advantage arising from the arrangements is to be counteracted under the general anti-abuse rule.

12(2) If the notice states that a tax advantage is to be counteracted, it must also set out–

(a) the adjustments required to give effect to the counteraction, and

(b) if relevant, any steps that the taxpayer is required to take to give effect to it.

IHT Statutes

NOTICES MAY BE GIVEN ON ASSUMPTION THAT TAX ADVANTAGE DOES ARISE

13(1) A designated HMRC officer may give a notice, or do anything else, under this Schedule where the officer considers that a tax advantage might have arisen to the taxpayer.

13(2) Accordingly, any notice given by a designated HMRC officer under this Schedule may be expressed to be given on the assumption that the tax advantage does arise (without agreeing that it does).

SCHEDULE 43A – PROCEDURAL REQUIREMENTS: POOLING NOTICES AND NOTICES OF BINDING

History – Sch. 43A inserted by FA 2016, s. 157(2), with effect in relation to tax arrangements (within the meaning of FA 2013, Pt. 5) entered into at any time (whether before or on or after 15 September 2016).

POOLING NOTICES

1(1) This paragraph applies where a person has been given a notice under paragraph 3 of Schedule 43 in relation to any tax arrangements (the "lead arrangements") and the condition in sub-paragraph (2) is met.

1(2) The condition is that the period of 45 days mentioned in paragraph 4(1) of Schedule 43 has expired but no notice under paragraph 12 of Schedule 43 or paragraph 8 of Schedule 43B has yet been given in respect of the matter.

1(3) If a designated HMRC officer considers–

(a) that a tax advantage has arisen to a person ("R") from tax arrangements (other than the lead arrangements) that are abusive,

(b) that those tax arrangements ("R's arrangements") are equivalent to the lead arrangements, and

(c) that the advantage ought to be counteracted under section 209,

the officer may give R a notice (a "pooling notice") to that effect.

1(3A) For the purposes of this Schedule and Schedule 43B, all the tax arrangements in relation to which pooling notices have been served in respect of the same lead arrangements are to be regarded as being in a "pool" together.

1(4) [Omitted by SI 2017/1090, reg. 3(4).]

1(5) [Omitted by SI 2017/1090, reg. 3(4).]

1(6) The officer may not give R a pooling notice if R has been given in respect of R's arrangements a notice under paragraph 3 of Schedule 43.

History – In para. 1(3)(a), the word "a" substituted for the word "another" and the words "(other than the lead arrangements)" inserted by SI 2017/1090, reg. 3(2)(a), with effect from 5 December 2017.
In para. 1, the words "to that effect" substituted for the words "which places R's arrangements in a pool with the lead arrangements." by SI 2017/1090, reg. 3(2)(b), with effect from 5 December 2017.
Para. 1(3A) inserted by SI 2017/1090, reg. 3(3), with effect from 5 December 2017.
Para. 1(4) and (5) omitted by SI 2017/1090, reg. 3(4), with effect from 5 December 2017.

NOTICE OF PROPOSAL TO BIND ARRANGEMENTS TO COUNTERACTED ARRANGEMENTS

2(1) This paragraph applies where a counteraction notice has been given to a person in relation to any tax arrangements (the "counteracted arrangements").

2(2) If a designated HMRC officer considers–

(a) that a tax advantage has arisen to a person ("R") from tax arrangements (other than the counteracted arrangements) that are abusive,

(b) that those tax arrangements ("R's arrangements") are equivalent to the counteracted arrangements, and

(c) that the advantage ought to be counteracted under section 209,

the officer may give R a notice (a "notice of binding") in relation to R's arrangements.

2(3) The officer may not give R a notice of binding if R has been given in respect of R's arrangements a notice under–

(a) paragraph 1, or

(b) paragraph 3 of Schedule 43.

2(4) In this paragraph **"counteraction notice"** means a notice such as is mentioned in sub-paragraph (2) of paragraph 12 of Schedule 43 or sub-paragraph (3) of paragraph 8 of Schedule 43B (notice of final decision to counteract).

History – In para. 2(1), the words "which are in a pool created under paragraph 1" (which appeared after the words "(the "counteracted arrangements")") omitted by SI 2017/1090, reg. 4(2), with effect from 5 December 2017.
In para. 2(2)(a), the word "a" substituted for the word "another" and the words "(other than the counteracted arrangements)" inserted by SI 2017/1090, reg. 4(3), with effect from 5 December 2017.

3(1) The decision of a designated HMRC officer whether or not to give R a pooling notice or notice of binding must be taken, and any notice must be given, as soon as is reasonably practicable after the officer becomes aware of the relevant facts.

3(2) A pooling notice or notice of binding must–

(a) specify the tax arrangements in relation to which the notice is given and the tax advantage,

(b) explain why the officer considers R's arrangements to be equivalent to the lead arrangements or the counteracted arrangements (as the case may be),

(c) explain why the officer considers that a tax advantage has arisen to R from tax arrangements that are abusive,

(d) set out the counteraction that the officer considers ought to be taken, and

(e) explain the effect of–

(i) paragraphs 4 to 10,

(ii) subsection (9) of section 209, and

(iii) section 212A.

3(3) A pooling notice or notice of binding may set out steps that R may (subject to subsection (9) of section 209) take to avoid the proposed counteraction.

History – In para. 3(1), the words "of a designated HMRC officer" inserted and the words "the officer" substituted for the word "HMRC" by SI 2017/1090, reg. 5, with effect from 5 December 2017.

CORRECTIVE ACTION BY A NOTIFIED TAXPAYER

4(1) If a person to whom a pooling notice or notice of binding has been given takes the relevant corrective action in relation to the tax arrangements and tax advantage specified in the notice before the beginning of the closed period mentioned in section 209(9), the person is to be treated for the purposes of paragraphs 6 to 8 and 9 and Schedule 43B (generic referral of tax arrangements) as not having been given the notice in question (and accordingly the tax arrangements in question are no longer in the pool).

4(2) For the purposes of this Schedule the **"relevant corrective action"** is taken if (and only if) the person takes the steps set out in sub-paragraphs (3) and (4).

4(3) The first step is that–

(a) the person amends a return or claim to counteract the tax advantage specified in the pooling notice or notice of binding, or

(b) P takes all necessary action to enter into an agreement with HMRC (in writing) for the purpose of relinquishing that advantage.

4(4) The second step is that the person notifies HMRC–

(a) that the first step has been taken, and

(b) of any additional amount which has or will become due and payable in respect of tax by reason of the first step being taken.

4(5) Where a person takes the first step described in sub-paragraph (3)(b), HMRC may proceed as if the person had not taken the relevant corrective action if the person fails to enter into the written agreement.

4(6) In determining the additional amount which has or will become due and payable in respect of tax for the purposes of sub-paragraph (4)(b), it is to be assumed that, where P takes the necessary action as mentioned in sub-paragraph (3)(b), the agreement is then entered into.

4(7) No enactment limiting the time during which amendments may be made to returns or claims operates to prevent P taking the first step mentioned in sub-paragraph (3)(a) before the tax enquiry is closed.

4(8) No appeal may be brought, by virtue of a provision mentioned in sub-paragraph (9), against an amendment made by a closure notice in respect of a tax enquiry to the extent that the amendment takes into account an amendment made by the taxpayer to a return or claim in taking the first step mentioned in sub-paragraph (3)(a).

4(9) The provisions are–

(a) paragraph 35(1)(b) of Schedule 33,

(b) section 31(1)(b) or (c) of TMA 1970,

(c) paragraph 9 of Schedule 1A to TMA 1970,

(d) paragraph 34(3) of Schedule 18 to FA 1998, and

(e) paragraph 35(1)(b) of Schedule 10 to FA 2003.

History – In para. 4(1), the words "6 to" inserted by SI 2017/1090, reg. 6(2), with effect from 5 December 2017.

In para. 4(3)(b), the words "if the person has made a tax appeal (by notifying HMRC or otherwise) on the basis that the tax advantage specified in the pooling notice or notice of binding arises from the tax arrangements specified in that notice," (which appeared before the words "P takes all") omitted by SI 2017/1090, reg. 6(3), with effect from 5 December 2017.

CORRECTIVE ACTION BY LEAD TAXPAYER

5 [Omitted by SI 2017/1090, reg. 7.]

History – Para. 5 omitted by SI 2017/1090, reg. 7, with effect from 5 December 2017. Former para. 5 read as follows:

"5 If the person mentioned in paragraph 1(1) takes the relevant corrective action (as defined in paragraph 4A of Schedule 43) before the end of the period of 75 days beginning with the day on which the notice mentioned in paragraph 1(1) was given to that person, the lead arrangements are treated as ceasing to be in the pool.".

OPINION NOTICES AND RIGHT TO MAKE REPRESENTATIONS

6(1) Sub-paragraph (2) applies where–

(a) a pooling notice is given to a person in relation to any tax arrangements, and

(b) an opinion notice (or opinion notices) under paragraph 11(2) of Schedule 43 aboutanother set of tax arrangements in the pool or the lead arrangements ("the referred arrangements") is subsequently given to a designated HMRC officer.

6(2) The officer must give the person a pooled arrangements opinion notice.

6(3) No more than one pooled arrangements opinion notice may be given to a person in respect of the same tax arrangements.

6(4) Where a designated HMRC officer gives a person a notice of binding, the officer must, at the same time, give the person a bound arrangements opinion notice.

History – In para. 6(1)(b), the words "or the lead arrangements" inserted by SI 2017/1090, reg. 8, with effect from 5 December 2017.

7(1) In relation to a person who is, or has been, given a pooling notice, **"pooled arrangements opinion notice"** means a written notice which–

(a) sets out a report prepared by HMRC of any opinion of the GAAR Advisory Panel about the referred arrangements,

(b) explains the person's right to make representations falling within sub-paragraph (3), and

(c) sets out the period in which those representations may be made.

7(2) In relation to a person who is given a notice of binding **"bound arrangements opinion notice"** means a written notice which–

(a) sets out a report prepared by HMRC of any opinion of the GAAR Advisory Panel about the counteracted arrangements (see paragraph 2(1)),

(b) explains the person's right to make representations falling within sub-paragraph (3), and

(c) sets out the period in which those representations may be made.

7(3) A person who is given a pooled arrangements opinion notice or a bound arrangements opinion notice has 30 days beginning with the day on which the notice is given to make representations in any of the following categories–

(a) representations that no tax advantage has arisen to the person from the arrangements to which the notice relates;

(b) representations as to why the arrangements to which the notice relates are or may be materially different from–

 (i) the referred arrangements (in the case of a pooled arrangements opinion notice), or

 (ii) the counteracted arrangements (in the case of a bound arrangements opinion notice).

7(4) In sub-paragraph (3)(b) references to **"arrangements"** include any circumstances which would be relevant in accordance with section 207 to a determination of whether the tax arrangements in question are abusive.

NOTICE OF FINAL DECISION

8(1) This paragraph applies where–

(a) further to a pooling notice given under paragraph 1(3), a set of tax arrangements is in a pool relating to any lead arrangements, and

(b) a designated HMRC officer has given a notice under paragraph 12 of Schedule 43 in relation to any other arrangements in the pool or the lead arrangements (the "referred arrangements").

8(2) The officer must, having considered any opinion of the GAAR Advisory Panel about the referred arrangements and any representations made under paragraph 7(3) in relation to the arrangements mentioned in sub-paragraph (1)(a), give the person a written notice setting out whether the tax advantage arising from those arrangements is to be counteracted under the general anti-abuse rule.

History – Para. 8(1)(a) substituted by SI 2017/1090, reg. 9(a), with effect from 5 December 2017.
In para. 8(1)(b), the words "or the lead arrangements " inserted by SI 2017/1090, reg. 9(b), with effect from 5 December 2017.

9(1) This paragraph applies where–

(a) a person has been given a notice of binding under paragraph 2, and

(b) the period of 30 days for making representations under paragraph 7(3) has expired.

9(2) A designated HMRC officer must, having considered any opinion of the GAAR Advisory Panel about the counteracted arrangements and any representations made under paragraph 7(3) in relation to the arrangements specified in the notice of binding, give the person a written notice setting out whether the tax advantage arising from the arrangements specified in the notice of binding is to be counteracted under the general anti-abuse rule.

10 If a notice under paragraph 8(2) or 9(2) states that a tax advantage is to be counteracted, it must also set out–

(a) the adjustments required to give effect to the counteraction, and

(b) if relevant, any steps the person concerned is required to take to give effect to it.

"EQUIVALENT ARRANGEMENTS"

11(1) For the purposes of paragraph 1, tax arrangements are **"equivalent"** to one another if they are substantially the same as one another having regard to–

(a) their substantive results,

(b) the means of achieving those results, and

(c) the characteristics on the basis of which it could reasonably be argued, in each case, that the arrangements are abusive tax arrangements under which a tax advantage has arisen to a person.

NOTICES MAY BE GIVEN ON ASSUMPTION THAT TAX ADVANTAGE DOES ARISE

12(1) A designated HMRC officer may give a notice, or do anything else, under this Schedule where the officer considers that a tax advantage might have arisen to the person concerned.

12(2) Accordingly, any notice given by a designated HMRC officer under this Schedule may be expressed to be given on the assumption that a tax advantage does arise (without conceding that it does).

HMRC OFFICERS

12A Anything that may or must be done by a given designated HMRC officer under this Schedule may be done instead by any other designated HMRC officer.

History – Para. 12A inserted by SI 2017/1090, reg. 10, with effect from 5 December 2017.

POWER TO AMEND

13(1) The Treasury may by regulations amend this Schedule (apart from this paragraph).

13(2) *Regulations under sub-paragraph (1) may include–*

(a) any amendment of this Part that is appropriate in consequence of an amendment by virtue of sub-paragraph (1);

(b) transitional provision.

13(3) Regulations under sub-paragraph (1) are to be made by statutory instrument.

13(4) A statutory instrument containing regulations under sub-paragraph (1) is subject to annulment in pursuance of a resolution of the House of Commons.

SCHEDULE 43B – PROCEDURAL REQUIREMENTS: GENERIC REFERRAL OF TAX ARRANGEMENTS

History – Sch. 43B inserted by FA 2016, s. 157(3), with effect in relation to tax arrangements (within the meaning of FA 2013, Pt. 5) entered into at any time (whether before or on or after 15 September 2016).

NOTICE OF PROPOSAL TO MAKE GENERIC REFERRAL OF TAX ARRANGEMENTS

1(1) Sub-paragraph (2) applies if–

(a) further to pooling notices given under paragraph 1(3) of Schedule 43A, two or more sets of tax arrangements are in a pool relating to any lead arrangements,

(b) the person to whom the notice mentioned in paragraph 1(1) of Schedule 43A was given takes the relevant corrective action (as defined in paragraph 4A of Schedule 43) before–

(i) the end of the period of 75 days beginning with the day on which that notice was given, or

(ii) such later time as that person and HMRC may agree, and

(c) no referral under paragraph 5 or 6 of Schedule 43 has been made in respect of any arrangements in the pool.

1(2) A designated HMRC officer may determine that, in respect of each of the tax arrangements that are in the pool, there is to be given (to the person to whom the pooling notice in question was given) a written notice of a proposal to make a generic referral to the GAAR Advisory Panel in respect of the arrangements in the pool.

1(3) Only one determination under sub-paragraph (2) may be made in relation to any one pool.

1(4) The persons to whom those notices are given are **"the notified taxpayers"**.

1(5) A notice given to a person ("T") under sub-paragraph (2) must–

(a) specify the arrangements (the "specified arrangements") and the tax advantage (the "specified advantage") to which the notice relates,

(b) inform T of the period under paragraph 2 for making a proposal.

History – Para. 1(1)(a) and (b) substituted by SI 2017/1090, reg. 12(2), with effect from 5 December 2017.

2(1) T has 30 days beginning with the day on which the notice under paragraph 1 is given to propose to HMRC that it–

(a) should give T a notice under paragraph 3 of Schedule 43 in respect of the arrangements to which the notice under paragraph 1 relates, and

(b) should not proceed with the proposal to make a generic referral to the GAAR Advisory Panel in respect of those arrangements.

2(2) If a proposal is made in accordance with sub-paragraph (1) a designated HMRC officer must consider it.

GENERIC REFERRAL

3(1) This paragraph applies where a designated HMRC officer has given notices to the notified taxpayers in accordance with paragraph 1(2).

3(2) If none of the notified taxpayers has made a proposal under paragraph 2 by the end of the 30 day period mentioned in that paragraph, the officer must make a referral to the GAAR Advisory Panel in respect of the notified taxpayers and the arrangements which are specified arrangements in relation to them.

3(3) If at least one of the notified taxpayers makes a proposal in accordance with paragraph 2, the designated HMRC officer must, after the end of that 30 day period, decide whether to–

(a) give a notice under paragraph 3 of Schedule 43 in respect of one set of tax arrangements in the relevant pool in relation to which such a proposal has been made, or

(b) make a referral to the GAAR Advisory Panel in respect of the tax arrangements in the relevant pool.

3(3A) If under sub-paragraph (3)(a) a notice is given under paragraph 3 of Schedule 43 in respect of one set of tax arrangements but (by virtue of paragraph 4A of that Schedule) the matter is not referred to the GAAR Advisory Panel, a designated officer must make a referral to the GAAR Advisory Panel in respect of the notified taxpayers and the arrangements which are specified arrangements in relation to them.

3(4) A referral under this paragraph is a **"generic referral"**.

History – In para. 3(3)(a), the words " in relation to which such a proposal has been made" inserted by SI 2017/1090, reg. 13(2), with effect from 5 December 2017.
Para. 3(3A) inserted by SI 2017/1090, reg. 13(3), with effect from 5 December 2017.

4(1) If a generic referral is made to the GAAR Advisory Panel, the designated HMRC officer must at the same time provide it with–

(a) a general statement of the material characteristics of the specified arrangements, and

(b) a declaration that–

(i) the statement under paragraph (a) is applicable to all the specified arrangements, and

(ii) as far as HMRC is aware, nothing which is material to the GAAR Advisory Panel's consideration of the matter has been omitted.

4(2) The general statement under sub-paragraph (1)(a) must–

(a) contain a factual description of the tax arrangements;

(b) set out HMRC's view as to whether the tax arrangements accord with established practice (when the arrangements were entered into);

(c) explain why it is the designated HMRC officer's view that a tax advantage of the nature described in the statement and arising from tax arrangements having the characteristics described in the statement would be a tax advantage arising from arrangements that are abusive;

(d) set out any matters the designated officer is aware of which may suggest that any view of HMRC or the designated HMRC officer expressed in the general statement is not correct;

(e) set out any other matters which the designated officer considers are required for the purposes of the exercise of the GAAR Advisory Panel's functions under paragraph 6.

5 If a generic referral is made the designated HMRC officer must at the same time give each of the notified taxpayers a notice which–

(a) specifies that a generic referral is being made, and

(b) is accompanied by a copy of the statement given to the GAAR Advisory Panel in accordance with paragraph 4(1)(a).

DECISION OF GAAR ADVISORY PANEL AND OPINION NOTICES

6(1) If a generic referral is made to the GAAR Advisory Panel under paragraph 3, the Chair must arrange for a sub-panel consisting of 3 members of the GAAR Advisory Panel (one of whom may be the Chair) to consider it.

6(2) The sub-panel must produce–

(a) one opinion notice stating the joint opinion of all the members of the sub-panel, or

(b) two or three opinion notices which taken together state the opinions of all the members.

6(3) The sub-panel must give a copy of the opinion notice or notices to the designated HMRC officer.

6(4) An opinion notice is a notice which states that in the opinion of the members of the sub-panel, or one or more of those members–

(a) the entering into and carrying out of tax arrangements such as are described in the general statement under paragraph 4(1)(a) is a reasonable course of action in relation to the relevant tax provisions,

(b) the entering into or carrying out of such tax arrangements is not a reasonable course of action in relation to the relevant tax provisions, or

(c) it is not possible, on the information available, to reach a view on that matter,

and the reasons for that opinion.

6(5) In forming their opinions for the purposes of sub-paragraph (4) members of the sub-panel must–

(a) have regard to all the matters set out in the statement under paragraph 4(1)(a),

(b) assume (unless the contrary is stated in the statement under paragraph 4(1)(a)) that the tax arrangements do not form part of any other arrangements,

(c) have regard to the matters mentioned in paragraphs (a) to (c) of section 207(2), and

(d) take account of subsections (4) to (6) of section 207.

6(6) For the purposes of the giving of an opinion under this paragraph, the arrangements are to be assumed to be tax arrangements.

6(7) In this Part, a reference to any opinion of the GAAR Advisory Panel in respect of a generic referral of any tax arrangements is a reference to the contents of any opinion notice given in relation to a generic referral in respect of the arrangements.

NOTICE OF RIGHT TO MAKE REPRESENTATIONS

7(1) Where a designated HMRC officer is given an opinion notice (or opinion notices) under paragraph 6, the officer must give each of the notified taxpayers a copy of the opinion notice (or notices) and a written notice which–

(a) explains the notified taxpayer's right to make representations falling within sub-paragraph (2), and

(b) sets out the period in which those representations may be made.

7(2) A notified taxpayer ("T") who is given a notice under sub-paragraph (1) has 30 days beginning with the day on which the notice is given to make representations in any of the following categories–

(a) representations that no tax advantage has arisen from the specified arrangements;

(b) representations that T has already been given a notice under paragraph 6 of Schedule 43A in relation to the specified arrangements;

(c) representations that any matter set out in the statement under paragraph 4(1)(a) is materially inaccurate as regards the specified arrangements (having regard to all circumstances which would be relevant in accordance with section 207 to a determination of whether the tax arrangements in question are abusive).

NOTICE OF FINAL DECISION AFTER CONSIDERING OPINION OF GAAR ADVISORY PANEL

8(1) A designated HMRC officer who has received a notice or notices under paragraph 6(3) in respect of a generic referral must consider the case of each notified taxpayer in accordance with sub-paragraph (2).

8(2) The officer must, having considered–

(a) any opinion of the GAAR Advisory Panel about the matters referred to it, and

(b) any representations made by the notified taxpayer under paragraph 7,

give to the notified taxpayer a written notice setting out whether the specified advantage is to be counteracted under the general anti-abuse rule.

8(3) If the notice states that a tax advantage is to be counteracted, it must also set out–

(a) the adjustments required to give effect to the counteraction, and

(b) if relevant, any steps that the taxpayer is required to take to give effect to it.

NOTICES MAY BE GIVEN ON ASSUMPTION THAT TAX ADVANTAGE DOES ARISE

9(1) A designated HMRC officer may give a notice, or do anything else, under this Schedule where the officer considers that a tax advantage might have arisen to the person concerned.

9(2) Accordingly, any notice given by a designated HMRC officer under this Schedule may be expressed to be given on the assumption that a tax advantage does arise (without conceding that it does).

HMRC OFFICERS

9A Anything that may or must be done by a given designated HMRC officer under this Schedule may be done instead by any other designated HMRC officer.

History – Para. 9A inserted by SI 2017/1090, reg. 14, with effect from 5 December 2017.

POWER TO AMEND

10(1) The Treasury may by regulations amend this Schedule (apart from this paragraph).

10(2) Regulations under sub-paragraph (1) may include–

(a) any amendment of this Part that is appropriate in consequence of an amendment by virtue of sub-paragraph (1);

(b) transitional provision.

10(3) Regulations under sub-paragraph (1) are to be made by statutory instrument.

10(4) A statutory instrument containing regulations under sub-paragraph (1) is subject to annulment in pursuance of a resolution of the House of Commons.

SCHEDULE 43C – PENALTY UNDER SECTION 212A: SUPPLEMENTARY PROVISION

History – Sch. 43C inserted by FA 2016, s. 158(3), with effect in relation to tax arrangements (within the meaning of FA 2013, Pt. 5) entered into on or after 15 September 2016.

VALUE OF THE COUNTERACTED ADVANTAGE: INTRODUCTION

1 Paragraphs 2 to 4 set out how to calculate the **"value of the counteracted advantage"** for the purposes of section 212A.

VALUE OF THE COUNTERACTED ADVANTAGE: BASIC RULE

2(1) The **"value of the counteracted advantage"** is the additional amount due or payable in respect of tax as a result of the counteraction mentioned in section 212A(1)(c).

2(2) The reference in sub-paragraph (1) to the additional amount due and payable includes a reference to–

(a) an amount payable to HMRC having erroneously been paid by way of repayment of tax, and

(b) an amount which would be repayable by HMRC if the counteraction were not made.

2(3) The following are ignored in calculating the value of the counteracted advantage–

(a) group relief, and

(b) any relief under section 458 of CTA 2010 (relief in respect of repayment etc of loan) which is deferred under subsection (5) of that section.

2(4) For the purposes of this paragraph consequential adjustments under section 210 are regarded as part of the counteraction in question.

2(5) If the counteraction affects the person's liability to two or more taxes, the taxes concerned are to be considered together for the purpose of determining the value of the counteracted advantage.

2(6) This paragraph is subject to paragraphs 3 and 4.

VALUE OF COUNTERACTED ADVANTAGE: LOSSES

3(1) To the extent that the tax advantage mentioned in section 212A(1)(b) ("the tax advantage") resulted in the wrong recording of a loss for the purposes of direct tax and the loss has been wholly used to reduce the amount due or payable in respect of tax, the value of the counteracted advantage is determined in accordance with paragraph 2.

3(2) To the extent that the tax advantage resulted in the wrong recording of a loss for purposes of direct tax and the loss has not been wholly used to reduce the amount due or payable in respect of tax, the value of the counteracted advantage is–

(a) the value under paragraph 2 of so much of the tax advantage as results (or would in the absence of the counteraction result) from the part (if any) of the loss which was used to reduce the amount due or payable in respect of tax, plus

(b) 10% of the part of the loss not so used.

3(3) Sub-paragraphs (1) and (2) apply both–

(a) to a case where no loss would have been recorded but for the tax advantage, and

(b) to a case where a loss of a different amount would have been recorded (but in that case sub-paragraphs (1) and (2) apply only to the difference between the amount recorded and the true amount).

3(4) To the extent that the tax advantage creates or increases (or would in the absence of the counteraction create or increase) an aggregate loss recorded for a group of companies–

(a) the value of the counteracted advantage is calculated in accordance with this paragraph, and

(b) in applying paragraph 2 in accordance with sub-paragraphs (1) and (2), group relief may be taken into account (despite paragraph 2(3)).

3(5) To the extent that the tax advantage results (or would in the absence of the counteraction result) in a loss, the value of it is nil where, because of the nature of the loss or the person's circumstances, there was no reasonable prospect of the loss being used to support a claim to reduce a tax liability (of any person).

VALUE OF COUNTERACTED ADVANTAGE: DEFERRED TAX

4(1) To the extent that the tax advantage mentioned in section 212A is a deferral of tax, the value of the counteracted advantage is–

(a) 25% of the amount of the deferred tax for each year of the deferral, or
(b) a percentage of the amount of the deferred tax, for each separate period of deferral of less than a year, equating to 25% per year,

or, if less, 100% of the amount of the deferred tax.

4(2) This paragraph does not apply to a case to the extent that paragraph 3 applies.

ASSESSMENT OF PENALTY

5(1) Where a person is liable for a penalty under section 212A, HMRC must assess the penalty.

5(2) Where HMRC assess the penalty, HMRC must–
(a) notify the person who is liable for the penalty, and
(b) state in the notice a tax period in respect of which the penalty is assessed.

5(3) A penalty under this paragraph must be paid before the end of the period of 30 days beginning with the day on which notification of the penalty is issued.

5(4) An assessment–
(a) is to be treated for procedural purposes as if it were an assessment to tax,
(b) may be enforced as if it were an assessment to tax, and
(c) may be combined with an assessment to tax.

5(5) An assessment of a penalty under this paragraph must be made before the end of the period of 12 months beginning with–
(a) the end of the appeal period for the assessment which gave effect to the counteraction mentioned in section 212A(1)(b), or
(b) if there is no assessment within paragraph (a), the date (or the latest of the dates) on which that counteraction becomes final.

5(6) The reference in sub-paragraph (5)(b) to the counteraction becoming final is to be interpreted in accordance with section 210(8).

ALTERATION OF ASSESSMENT OF PENALTY

6(1) After notification of an assessment has been given to a person under paragraph 5(2), the assessment may not be altered except in accordance with this paragraph or paragraph 7, or on appeal.

6(2) A supplementary assessment may be made in respect of a penalty if an earlier assessment operated by reference to an underestimate of the value of the counteracted advantage.

6(3) An assessment may be revised as necessary if it operated by reference to an overestimate of the value of the counteracted advantage.

REVISION OF ASSESSMENT FOLLOWING CONSEQUENTIAL RELIEVING ADJUSTMENT

7(1) Sub-paragraph (2) applies where a person–
(a) is notified under section 210(7) of a consequential adjustment relating to a counteraction under section 209, and
(b) an assessment to a penalty in respect of that counteraction of which the person has been notified under paragraph 5(2) does not take account of that consequential adjustment.

7(2) HMRC must make any alterations of the assessment that appear to HMRC to be just and reasonable in connection with the consequential amendment.

7(3) Alterations under this paragraph may be made despite any time limit imposed by or under an enactment.

AGGREGATE PENALTIES

8(1) Sub-paragraph (3) applies where–
(a) two or more penalties are incurred by the same person and fall to be determined by reference to an amount of tax to which that person is chargeable,
(b) one of those penalties is incurred under section 212A, and
(c) one or more of the other penalties are incurred under a relevant penalty provision.

8(2) But sub-paragraph (3) does not apply if section 212(2) of FA 2014 (follower notices: aggregate penalties) applies in relation to the amount of tax in question.

8(3) The aggregate of the amounts of the penalties mentioned in subsection (1)(b) and (c), so far as determined by reference to that amount of tax, must not exceed–

(a) the relevant percentage of that amount, or

(b) in a case where at least one of the penalties is under paragraph 5(2)(b) of, or sub-paragraph (3)(b), (4)(b) or (5)(b) of paragraph 6 of, Schedule 55 to FA 2009, £300 (if greater).

8(4) In the application of section 97A of TMA 1970 (multiple penalties) no account shall be taken of a penalty under section 212A.

8(5) **"Relevant penalty provision"** means–

(a) Schedule 24 to FA 2007 (penalties for errors),

(b) Schedule 41 to FA 2008 (penalties: failure to notify etc),

(c) Schedule 55 to FA 2009 (penalties for failure to make returns etc), or

(d) Part 5 of Schedule 18 to FA 2016 (penalty under serial tax avoidance regime).

8(6) **"The relevant percentage"** means–

(a) 200% in a case where at least one of the penalties is determined by reference to the percentage in–

  (i) paragraph 4(4)(c) of Schedule 24 to FA 2007,

  (ii) paragraph 6(4)(a) of Schedule 41 to FA 2008, or

  (iii) paragraph 6(3A)(c) of Schedule 55 to FA 2009,

(b) 150% in a case where paragraph (a) does not apply and at least one of the penalties is determined by reference to the percentage in–

  (i) paragraph 4(3)(c) of Schedule 24 to FA 2007,

  (ii) paragraph 6(3)(a) of Schedule 41 to FA 2008, or

  (iii) paragraph 6(3A)(b) of Schedule 55 to FA 2009,

(c) 140% in a case where neither paragraph (a) nor paragraph (b) applies and at least one of the penalties is determined by reference to the percentage in–

  (i) paragraph 4(4)(b) of Schedule 24 to FA 2007,

  (ii) paragraph 6(4)(b) of Schedule 41 to FA 2008, or

  (iii) paragraph 6(4A)(c) of Schedule 55 to FA 2009,

(d) 105% in a case where at none of paragraphs (a), (b) and (c) applies and at least one of the penalties is determined by reference to the percentage in–

  (i) paragraph 4(3)(b) of Schedule 24 to FA 2007,

  (ii) paragraph 6(3)(b) of Schedule 41 to FA 2008, or

  (iii) paragraph 6(4A)(b) of Schedule 55 to FA 2009, and

(e) in any other case, 100%.

Prospective amendments – Para. 8(6)(ba) inserted by FA 2015, s. 120 and Sch. 20, para. 20(2), with effect from a day to be appointed under s. 120(2).

In para. 8(6)(c), the words "none of paragraphs (a) to (ba) applies" substituted for the words "neither paragraph (a) nor paragraph (b) applies" by FA 2015, s. 120 and Sch. 20, para. 20(3), with effect from a day to be appointed under s. 120(2).

In para. 8(6)(d), the words "none of paragraphs (a) to (c) applies" substituted for the words "none of paragraphs (a), (b) and (c) applies" by FA 2015, s. 120 and Sch. 20, para. 20(4), with effect from a day to be appointed under s. 120(2).

APPEAL AGAINST PENALTY

9(1) A person may appeal against–

(a) the imposition of a penalty under section 212A, or

(b) the amount assessed under paragraph 5.

9(2) An appeal under sub-paragraph (1)(a) may only be made on the grounds that the arrangements were not abusive or there was no tax advantage to be counteracted.

9(3) An appeal under sub-paragraph (1)(b) may only be made on the grounds that the assessment was based on an overestimate of the value of the counteracted advantage (whether because the estimate was made by reference to adjustments which were not just and reasonable or for any other reason).

9(4) An appeal under this paragraph must be made within the period of 30 days beginning with the day on which notification of the penalty is given under paragraph 5(2).

9(5) An appeal under this paragraph is to be treated in the same way as an appeal against an assessment to the tax concerned (including by the application of any provision about bringing the appeal by notice to HMRC, about HMRC's review of the decision or about determination of the appeal by the First-tier Tribunal or Upper Tribunal).

9(6) Sub-paragraph (5) does not apply–

(a) so as to require a person to pay a penalty before an appeal against the assessment of the penalty is determined, or

(b) in respect of any other matter expressly provided for by this Part.

9(7) On an appeal against the penalty the tribunal may affirm or cancel HMRC's decision.

9(8) On an appeal against the amount of the penalty the tribunal may–

(a) affirm HMRC's decision, or

(b) substitute for HMRC's decision another decision that HMRC has power to make.

9(9) In this paragraph **"tribunal"** means the First-tier Tribunal or Upper Tribunal (as appropriate by virtue of sub-paragraph (5)).

MITIGATION OF PENALTIES

10(1) The Commissioners may in their discretion mitigate a penalty under section 212A, or stay or compound any proceedings for such a penalty.

10(2) They may also, after judgment, further mitigate or entirely remit the penalty.

INTERPRETATION

11 In this Schedule–

(a) a reference to an **"assessment"** to tax is to be interpreted, in relation to inheritance tax, as a reference to a determination;

(b) **"direct tax"** means–

- (i) income tax,
- (ii) capital gains tax,
- (iii) corporation tax (including any amount chargeable as if it were corporation tax or treated as corporation tax), and
- (iv) petroleum revenue tax;
- (v) diverted profits tax;

(c) a reference to a loss includes a reference to a charge, expense, deficit and any other amount which may be available for, or relied on to claim, a deduction or relief;

(d) a reference to a repayment of tax includes a reference to allowing a credit against tax or to a payment of a corporation tax credit;

(e) **"corporation tax credit"** means–

- (i) an R&D tax credit under Chapter 2 or 7 of Part 13 of CTA 2009,
- (ii) an R&D expenditure credit under Chapter 6A of Part 3 of CTA 2009,
- (iii) a land remediation tax credit or life assurance company tax credit under Chapter 3 or 4 respectively of Part 14 of CTA 2009,
- (iv) a film tax credit under Chapter 3 of Part 15 of CTA 2009,
- (v) a television tax credit under Chapter 3 of Part 15A of CTA 2009,
- (vi) a video game tax credit under Chapter 3 of Part 15B of CTA 2009,
- (vii) a theatre tax credit under section 1217K of CTA 2009,
- (viii) an orchestra tax credit under Chapter 3 of Part 15D of CTA 2009, or
- (ix) a first-year tax credit under Schedule A1 to CAA 2001;

(f) **"tax period"** means a tax year, accounting period or other period in respect of which tax is charged;

(g) a reference to giving a document to HMRC includes a reference to communicating information to HMRC in any form and by any method (whether by post, fax, email, telephone or otherwise),

(h) a reference to giving a document to HMRC includes a reference to making a statement or declaration in a document.

SCHEDULE 44 – TRUSTS WITH VULNERABLE BENEFICIARY

Section 216

INHERITANCE TAX ACT 1984

1 IHTA 1984 is amended as follows.

2(1) Section 71A (trusts for bereaved minors) is amended as follows.

2(2) [Substitutes IHTA 1984, s. 71A(3)(c)(ii).]

2(3) [Inserts IHTA 1984, s. 71A(4)(za).]

2(4) [Inserts IHTA 1984, s. 71A(4A)–(4E).]

3(1) Section 71B (charge to tax on property to which section 71A applies) is amended as follows.

3(2) [Amends IHTA 1984, s. 71B(1).]

3(3) [Inserts IHTA 1984, s. 71B(2A) and (2B).]

4(1) Section 71D (age 18-to-25 trusts) is amended as follows.

4(2) [Substitutes IHTA 1984, s. 71D(6)(c)(ii).]

4(3) [Inserts IHTA 1984, s. 71D(6A).]

4(4) [Inserts IHTA 1984, s. 71D(7)(za).]

4(5) [Inserts IHTA 1984, s. 71D(7A)–(7E).]

5(1) Section 71E (charge to tax on property to which section 71D applies) is amended as follows.

5(2) [Amends IHTA 1984, s. 71E(1).]

5(3) [Inserts IHTA 1984, s. 71E(4A).]

6(1) Section 89 (trusts for disabled persons) is amended as follows.

6(2) [Substitutes IHTA 1984, s. 89(1)(b).]

6(3) [Substitutes IHTA 1984, s. 89(3) and inserts (3A)–(3E).]

6(4) [Amends IHTA 1984, s. 89(4).]

6(5) [Substitutes IHTA 1984, s. 89(4A).]

7(1) Section 89A (self-settlement by person with condition expected to lead to disability) is amended as follows.

7(2) [Amends IHTA 1984, s. 89A(1)(b).]

7(3) [Amends IHTA 1984, s. 89A(2).]

7(4) [Substitutes IHTA 1984, s. 89A(5) and (6).]

7(5) [Inserts IHTA 1984, s. 89A(6A)–(6F).]

7(6) [Substitutes IHTA 1984, s. 89A(8).]

7(7) [Amends heading to IHTA 1984, s. 89A.]

8(1) Section 89B (meaning of "disabled person's interest") is amended as follows.

8(2) [Substitutes IHTA 1984, s. 89B(2).]

8(3) [Inserts IHTA 1984, s. 89B(2A).]

9(1) The amendments made by paragraphs 2 to 8 have effect in relation to property transferred into settlement on or after 8 April 2013.

9(2) Nothing in paragraphs 6 to 8 is to be read as preventing property transferred into a relevant settlement on or after 8 April 2013 from being property to which section 89 or 89A of IHTA 1984 applies.

10(1) [Amends IHTA 1984, s. 89B(1)(c).]

10(2) *[Inserts IHTA 1984, s. 89C.]*

10(3) The amendments made by this paragraph have effect in relation to property transferred into settlement on or after the day on which this Act is passed.

10(4) Nothing in this paragraph is to be read as preventing property transferred into a settlement to which sub-paragraph (5) applies from being settled property for the purposes of section 89B(1)(c) or (d) of IHTA 1984.

10(5) This sub-paragraph applies to a settlement–

(a) created before the day on which this Act is passed the trusts of which have not been altered on or after that day, or

(b) arising on or after the day on which this Act is passed under the will of a testator, if–

  (i) the will was executed before the day on which this Act is passed and its provisions, so far as relating to the settlement, have not been altered on or after that day, or

  (ii) the will was executed or confirmed on or after the day on which this Act is passed and its provisions, so far as relating to the settlement, are in the same terms as those contained in a will executed by the same testator before that day.

INTERPRETATION: RELEVANT SETTLEMENT

20(1) In this Schedule, **"relevant settlement"** means–

(a) a settlement created before 8 April 2013 the trusts of which have not been altered on or after that date, or

(b) a settlement arising on or after 8 April 2013 under the will of a testator, if–

  (i) the will was executed before 8 April 2013 and its provisions, so far as relating to the settlement, have not been altered on or after that date, or

  (ii) the will was executed or confirmed on or after 8 April 2013 and its provisions, so far as relating to the settlement, are in the same terms as those contained in a will executed by the same testator before that date.

20(2) In this Schedule a reference to a will includes a reference to a codicil.

SCHEDULE 45 – STATUTORY RESIDENCE TEST

Section 218

Part 1 – The Rules

INTRODUCTION

1(1) This Part of this Schedule sets out the rules for determining for the purposes of relevant tax whether individuals are resident or not resident in the UK.

1(2) The rules are referred to collectively as **"the statutory residence test"**.

1(2) The rules do not apply in determining for the purposes of relevant tax whether individuals are resident or not resident in England, Wales, Scotland or Northern Ireland specifically (rather than in the UK as a whole).

1(4) **"Relevant tax"** means–

(a) [not relevant to inheritance tax]

(b) [not relevant to inheritance tax]

(c) (so far as the residence status of individuals is relevant to them) inheritance tax and corporation tax.

1(5) Key concepts used in the rules are defined in Part 2 of this Schedule.

INTERPRETATION OF ENACTMENTS

2(1) In enactments relating to relevant tax, a reference to being resident (or not resident) in the UK is, in the case of individuals, a reference to being resident (or not resident) in the UK in accordance with the statutory residence test.

2(2) Sub-paragraph (1) applies even if the reference relates to the tax liability of an actual or deemed person that is not an individual (for example, where the liability of another person depends on the residence status of an individual).

2(3) An individual who, in accordance with the statutory residence test, is resident (or not resident) in the UK "for" a tax year is taken for the purposes of any enactment relating to relevant tax to be resident (or not resident) there at all times in that tax year.

2(4) But see Part 3 of this Schedule (split year treatment) for cases where the effect of sub-paragraph (3) is relaxed in certain circumstances.

2(5) This Schedule has effect subject to any express provision to the contrary in (or falling to be recognised and acknowledged in law by virtue of) any enactment.

THE BASIC RULE

3 An individual ("P") is resident in the UK for a tax year ("year X") if–
(a) the automatic residence test is met for that year, or
(b) the sufficient ties test is met for that year.

4 If neither of those tests is met for that year, P is not resident in the UK for that year.

THE AUTOMATIC RESIDENCE TEST

5 The automatic residence test is met for year X if P meets–
(a) at least one of the automatic UK tests, and
(b) none of the automatic overseas tests.

THE AUTOMATIC UK TESTS

6 There are 4 automatic UK tests.

7 The first automatic UK test is that P spends at least 183 days in the UK in year X.

8(1) The second automatic UK test is that–
(a) P has a home in the UK during all or part of year X,
(b) that home is one where P spends a sufficient amount of time in year X, and
(c) there is at least one period of 91 (consecutive) days in respect of which the following conditions are met–
  (i) the 91-day period in question occurs while P has that home,
  (ii) at least 30 days of that 91-day period fall within year X, and
  (iii) throughout that 91-day period, condition A or condition B is met or a combination of those conditions is met.

8(2) Condition A is that P has no home overseas.

8(3) Condition B is that–
(a) P has one or more homes overseas, but
(b) each of those homes is a home where P spends no more than a permitted amount of time in year X.

8(4) In relation to a home of P's in the UK, P "spends a sufficient amount of time" there in year X if there are at least 30 days in year X when P is present there on that day for at least some of the time (no matter how short a time).

8(5) In relation to a home of P's overseas, P "spends no more than a permitted amount of time" there in year X if there are fewer than 30 days in year X when P is present there on that day for at least some of the time (no matter how short a time).

8(6) In sub-paragraphs (4) and (5)–
(a) a reference to 30 days is to 30 days in aggregate, whether the days are consecutive or intermittent, and
(b) a reference to P being present at the home is to P being present there at a time when it is a home of P's (so presence there on any other occasion, for example to look round the property with a view to buying it, is to be disregarded).

8(7) Sub-paragraph (1)(c) is satisfied so long as there is a period of 91 days in respect of which the conditions described there are met, even if those conditions are in fact met for longer than that.

8(8) If P has more than one home in the UK–
(a) each of those homes must be looked at separately to see if the second automatic UK test is met, and
(b) the second automatic UK test is then met so long as it is met in relation to at least one of those homes.

9(1) The third automatic UK test is that–
(a) P works sufficient hours in the UK, as assessed over a period of 365 days,
(b) during that period, there are no significant breaks from UK work,
(c) all or part of that period falls within year X,
(d) more than 75% of the total number of days in the 365-day period on which P does more than 3 hours' work are days on which P does more than 3 hours' work in the UK, and

IHT Statutes

(e) at least one day which falls in both that period and year X is a day on which P does more than 3 hours' work in the UK.

9(2) Take the following steps to work out, for any given period of 365 days, whether P works "sufficient hours in the UK" as assessed over that period–

Step 1

Identify any days in the period on which P does more than 3 hours' work overseas, including ones on which P also does work in the UK on the same day.

The days so identified are referred to as "disregarded days".

Step 2

Add up (for all employments held and trades carried on by P) the total number of hours that P works in the UK during the period, but ignoring any hours that P works in the UK on disregarded days.

The result is referred to as P's "net UK hours".

Step 3

Subtract from 365–

(a) the total number of disregarded days, and

(b) any days that are allowed to be subtracted, in accordance with the rules in paragraph 28 of this Schedule, to take account of periods of leave and gaps between employments.

The result is referred to as the "reference period".

Step 4

Divide the reference period by 7. If the answer is more than 1 and is not a whole number, round down to the nearest whole number. If the answer is less than 1, round up to 1.

Step 5

Divide P's net UK hours by the number resulting from step 4.

If the answer is 35 or more, P is considered to work "sufficient hours in the UK" as assessed over the 365-day period in question.

9(3) This paragraph does not apply to P if–

(a) P has a relevant job on board a vehicle, aircraft or ship at any time in year X, and

(b) at least 6 of the trips that P makes in year X as part of that job are cross-border trips that either begin in the UK, end in the UK or begin and end in the UK.

10(1) The fourth automatic UK test is that–

(a) P dies in year X,

(b) for each of the previous 3 tax years, P was resident in the UK by virtue of meeting the automatic residence test,

(c) even assuming P were not resident in the UK for year X, the tax year preceding year X would not be a split year as respects P (see Part 3 of this Schedule),

(d) when P died, either–

  (i) P's home was in the UK, or

  (ii) P had more than one home and at least one of them was in the UK, and

(e) if P had a home overseas during all or part of year X, P did not spend a sufficient amount of time there in year X.

10(2) In relation to a home of P's overseas, P "spent a sufficient amount of time there" in year X if–

(a) there were at least 30 days in year X when P was present there on that day for at least some of the time (no matter how short a time), or

(b) P was present there for at least some of the time (no matter how short a time) on each day of year X up to and including the day on which P died.

10(3) In sub-paragraph (2)–

(a) the reference to 30 days is to 30 days in aggregate, whether the days were consecutive or intermittent, and

(b) the reference to P being present at the home is to P being present there at a time when it was a home of P's.

10(4) If P had more than one home overseas–

(a) each of those homes must be looked at separately to see if the requirement of sub-paragraph (1)(e) *is met, and*

(b) that requirement is then met so long as it is met in relation to each of them.

THE AUTOMATIC OVERSEAS TESTS

11 There are 5 automatic overseas tests.

12 The first automatic overseas test is that–

(a) P was resident in the UK for one or more of the 3 tax years preceding year X,

(b) the number of days in year X that P spends in the UK is less than 16, and

(c) P does not die in year X.

13 The second automatic overseas test is that–

(a) P was resident in the UK for none of the 3 tax years preceding year X, and

(b) the number of days that P spends in the UK in year X is less than 46.

14(1) The third automatic overseas test is that–

(a) P works sufficient hours overseas, as assessed over year X,

(b) during year X, there are no significant breaks from overseas work,

(c) the number of days in year X on which P does more than 3 hours' work in the UK is less than 31, and

(d) the number of days in year X falling within sub-paragraph (2) is less than 91.

14(2) A day falls within this sub-paragraph if–

(a) it is a day spent by P in the UK, but

(b) it is not a day that is treated under paragraph 23(4) as a day spent by P in the UK.

14(3) Take the following steps to work out whether P works "sufficient hours overseas" as assessed over year X–

Step 1

Identify any days in year X on which P does more than 3 hours' work in the UK, including ones on which P also does work overseas on the same day.

The days so identified are referred to as "disregarded days".

Step 2

Add up (for all employments held and trades carried on by P) the total number of hours that P works overseas in year X, but ignoring any hours that P works overseas on disregarded days. The result is referred to as P's "net overseas hours".

Step 3

Subtract from 365 (or 366 if year X includes 29 February)–

(a) the total number of disregarded days, and

(b) any days that are allowed to be subtracted, in accordance with the rules in paragraph 28 of this Schedule, to take account of periods of leave and gaps between employments.

The result is referred to as the "reference period".

Step 4

Divide the reference period by 7. If the answer is more than 1 and is not a whole number, round down to the nearest whole number. If the answer is less than 1, round up to 1.

Step 5

Divide P's net overseas hours by the number resulting from step 4.

If the answer is 35 or more, P is considered to work "sufficient hours overseas" as assessed over year X.

14(4) This paragraph does not apply to P if–

(a) P has a relevant job on board a vehicle, aircraft or ship at any time in year X, and

(b) at least 6 of the trips that P makes in year X as part of that job are cross-border trips that either begin in the UK, end in the UK or begin and end in the UK.

15(1) The fourth automatic overseas test is that–

(a) P dies in year X,

(b) P was resident in the UK for neither of the 2 tax years preceding year X or, alternatively, P's case falls within sub-paragraph (2), and

(c) the number of days that P spends in the UK in year X is less than 46.

15(2) P's case falls within this sub-paragraph if–

(a) P was not resident in the UK for the tax year preceding year X, and

(b) the tax year before that was a split year as respects P because the circumstances of the case fell within Case 1, Case 2 or Case 3 (see Part 3 of this Schedule).

16(1) The fifth automatic overseas test is that–

(a) P dies in year X,

(b) P was resident in the UK for neither of the 2 tax years preceding year X because P met the third automatic overseas test for each of those years or, alternatively, P's case falls within sub-paragraph (2), and

(c) P would meet the third automatic overseas test for year X if paragraph 14 were read with the relevant modifications.

16(2) P's case falls within this sub-paragraph if–

(a) P was not resident in the UK for the tax year preceding year X because P met the third automatic overseas test for that year, and

(b) the tax year before that was a split year as respects P because the circumstances of the case fell within Case 1 (see Part 3 of this Schedule).

16(3) The relevant modifications of paragraph 14 are–

(a) in sub-paragraph (1)(a) and (b) and sub-paragraph (3), for "year X" read "the period from the start of year X up to and including the day before the day of P's death", and

(b) in step 3 of sub-paragraph (3), for "365 (or 366 if year X includes 29 February)" read "the number of days in the period from the start of year X up to and including the day before the day of P's death".

THE SUFFICIENT TIES TEST

17(1) The sufficient ties test is met for year X if–

(a) P meets none of the automatic UK tests and none of the automatic overseas tests, but

(b) P has sufficient UK ties for that year.

17(2) **"UK ties"** is defined in Part 2 of this Schedule.

17(3) Whether P has "sufficient" UK ties for year X will depend on–

(a) whether P was resident in the UK for any of the previous 3 tax years, and

(b) the number of days that P spends in the UK in year X.

17(4) The Tables in paragraphs 18 and 19 show how many ties are sufficient in each case.

SUFFICIENT UK TIES

18 The Table below shows how many UK ties are sufficient in a case where P was resident in the UK for one or more of the 3 tax years preceding year X–

Days spent by P in the UK in year X	*Number of ties that are sufficient*
More than 15 but not more than 45	At least 4
More than 45 but not more than 90	At least 3
More than 90 but not more than 120	At least 2
More than 120	At least 1

19 The Table below shows how many UK ties are sufficient in a case where P was resident in the UK for none of the 3 tax years preceding year X–

Days spent by P in the UK in year X	*Number of ties that are sufficient*
More than 45 but not more than 90	All 4
More than 90 but not more than 120	At least 3
More than 120	At least 2

20(1) If P dies in year X, paragraph 18 has effect as if the words "More than 15 but" were omitted from the first column of the Table.

20(2) In addition to that modification, if the death occurs before 1 March in year X, paragraphs 18 and 19 have effect as if each number of days mentioned in the first column of the Table were reduced by the appropriate number.

20(3) The appropriate number is found by multiplying the number of days, in each case, by–

where "A" is the number of whole months in year X after the month in which P dies.

20(4) If, for any number of days, the appropriate number is not a whole number, the appropriate number is to be rounded up or down as follows–

(a) if the first figure after the decimal point is 5 or more, round the appropriate number up to the nearest whole number,

(b) otherwise, round it down to the nearest whole number.

Part 2 – Key Concepts

INTRODUCTION

21 This Part of this Schedule defines some key concepts for the purposes of this Schedule.

DAYS SPENT

22(1) If P is present in the UK at the end of a day, that day counts as a day spent by P in the UK.

22(2) But it does not do so in the following two cases.

22(3) The first case is where–

(a) P only arrives in the UK as a passenger on that day,

(b) P leaves the UK the next day, and

(c) between arrival and departure, P does not engage in activities that are to a substantial extent unrelated to P's passage through the UK.

22(4) The second case is where–

(a) P would not be present in the UK at the end of that day but for exceptional circumstances beyond P's control that prevent P from leaving the UK, and

(b) P intends to leave the UK as soon as those circumstances permit.

22(5) Examples of circumstances that may be "exceptional" are–

(a) national or local emergencies such as war, civil unrest or natural disasters, and

(b) a sudden or life-threatening illness or injury.

22(6) For a tax year–

(a) the maximum number of days to which sub-paragraph (2) may apply in reliance on sub-paragraph (4) is limited to 60, and

(b) accordingly, once the number of days within sub-paragraph (4) reaches 60 (counting forward from the start of the tax year), any subsequent days within that sub-paragraph, whether involving the same or different exceptional circumstances, will count as days spent by P in the UK.

23(1) If P is not present in the UK at the end of a day, that day does not count as a day spent by P in the UK.

23(2) This is subject to the deeming rule.

23(3) The deeming rule applies if–

(a) P has at least 3 UK ties for a tax year,

(b) the number of days in that tax year when P is present in the UK at some point in the day but not at the end of the day ("qualifying days") is more than 30, and

(c) P was resident in the UK for at least one of the 3 tax years preceding that tax year.

23(4) The deeming rule is that, once the number of qualifying days in the tax year reaches 30 (counting forward from the start of the tax year), each subsequent qualifying day in the tax year is to be treated as a day spent by P in the UK.

23(5) The deeming rule does not apply for the purposes of sub-paragraph (3)(a) (so, in deciding for those purposes whether P has a 90-day tie, qualifying days in excess of 30 are not to be treated as days spent by P in the UK).

DAYS SPENT "IN" A PERIOD

24 Any reference to a number of days spent in the UK "in" a given period is a reference to the total number of days spent there (in aggregate) in that period, whether continuously or intermittently.

HOME

25(1) A person's home could be a building or part of a building or, for example, a vehicle, vessel or structure of any kind.

25(2) Whether, for a given building, vehicle, vessel, structure or the like, there is a sufficient degree of permanence or stability about P's arrangements there for the place to count as P's home (or one of P's homes) will depend on all the circumstances of the case.

25(3) But somewhere that P uses periodically as nothing more than a holiday home or temporary retreat (or something similar) does not count as a home of P's.

25(4) A place may count as a home of P's whether or not P holds any estate or interest in it (and references to "having" a home are to be read accordingly).

25(5) Somewhere that was P's home does not continue to count as such merely because P continues to hold an estate or interest in it after P has moved out (for example, if P is in the process of selling it or has let or sub-let it, having set up home elsewhere).

WORK

26(1) P is considered to be "working" (or doing "work") at any time when P is doing something–

(a) in the performance of duties of an employment held by P, or

(b) in the course of a trade carried on by P (alone or in partnership).

26(2) In deciding whether something is being done in the performance of duties of an employment, regard must be had to whether, if value were received by P for doing the thing, it would fall within the definition of employment income in section 7 of ITEPA 2003.

26(3) In deciding whether something is being done in the course of a trade, regard must be had to whether, if expenses were incurred by P in doing the thing, the expenses could be deducted in calculating the profits of the trade for income tax purposes.

26(4) Time spent travelling counts as time spent working–

(a) if the cost of the journey could, if it were incurred by P, be deducted in calculating P's earnings from that employment under section 337, 338, 340 or 342 of ITEPA 2003 or, as the case may be, in calculating the profits of the trade under ITTOIA 2005, or

(b) to the extent that P does something else during the journey that would itself count as work in accordance with this paragraph.

26(5) Time spent undertaking training counts as time spent working if–

(a) in the case of an employment held by P, the training is provided or paid for by the employer and is undertaken to help P in performing duties of the employment, and

(b) in the case of a trade carried on by P, the cost of the training could be deducted in calculating the profits of the trade for income tax purposes.

26(6) Sub-paragraphs (4) and (5) have effect without prejudice to the generality of sub-paragraphs (2) and (3).

26(7) Assume for the purposes of sub-paragraphs (2) to (5) that P is someone who is chargeable to income tax under ITEPA 2003 or ITTOIA 2005.

26(8) A voluntary post for which P has no contract of service does not count as an employment for the purposes of this Schedule.

LOCATION OF WORK

27(1) Work is done where it is actually done, regardless of where the employment is held or the trade is carried on by P.

27(2) But work done by way of or in the course of travelling to or from the UK by air or sea or via a tunnel under the sea is assumed to be done overseas even during the part of the journey in or over the UK.

27(3) For these purposes, travelling to or from the UK is taken to–

(a) begin when P boards the aircraft, ship or train that is bound for a destination in the UK or (as the case may be) overseas, and

(b) *end when P disembarks* from that aircraft, ship or train.

27(4) This paragraph is subject to express provisions in this Schedule about the location of work done by people with relevant jobs on board vehicles, aircraft or ships.

RULES FOR CALCULATING THE REFERENCE PERIOD

28(1) This paragraph applies in calculating the "reference period" (which is a step taken in determining whether P works "sufficient hours in the UK" or "sufficient hours overseas" as assessed over a given period of days).

28(2) The number of days in the given period may be reduced to take account of–

(a) reasonable amounts of annual leave or parenting leave taken by P during the period (for all employments held and trades carried on by P during the period, whether in the UK or overseas),

(b) absences from work at times during the period when P is on sick leave and cannot reasonably be expected to work as a result of the illness or injury in question, and

(c) non-working days embedded within a block of leave for which a reduction is made under paragraph (a) or (b).

28(3) But no reduction may be made in respect of any day that is a "disregarded day" (see paragraphs 9(2) and 14(3) in Part 1 of this Schedule).

28(4) For any particular employment or trade, "reasonable" amounts of annual leave or parenting leave are to be assessed having regard to (among other things)–

(a) the nature of the work, and

(b) the country or countries where P is working.

28(5) Non-working days are "embedded within" a block of leave only if there are, as part of that block of leave–

(a) at least 3 consecutive days of leave taken before the non-working day or series of non-working days in question, and

(b) at least 3 consecutive days of leave taken after the non-working day or series of non-working days in question.

28(6) A "non-working day" is any day of the week, month or year on which P–

(a) is not normally expected to work (according to P's contract of employment or usual pattern of work), and

(b) does not in fact work.

28(7) In calculating the reductions to be made under sub-paragraph (2)–

(a) if it turns out, after applying sub-paragraph (3), that the reasonable amounts of annual leave or parenting leave or, as the case may be, the absences from work on sick leave do not add up (across the period) to a whole number of days, the number in that case is to be rounded down to the nearest whole number, but

(b) any such rounding is to be ignored for the purposes of sub-paragraph (2)(c).

28(8) If–

(a) P changes employment during the given period,

(b) there is a gap between the two employments, and

(c) P does not work at all at any time between the two employments,

the number of days in the given period may be reduced by the number of days in that gap.

28(9) But–

(a) if the gap lasts for more than 15 days, only 15 days may be subtracted, and

(b) if there is more than one change of employment during the period, the maximum number of days that may be subtracted under sub-paragraph (8) for all the gaps in total is 30.

SIGNIFICANT BREAKS FROM UK OR OVERSEAS WORK

29(1) There is a "significant break from UK work" if at least 31 days go by and not one of those days is–

(a) a day on which P does more than 3 hours' work in the UK, or

(b) a day on which P would have done more than 3 hours' work in the UK but for being on annual leave, sick leave or parenting leave.

29(2) There is a "significant break from overseas work" if at least 31 days go by and not one of those days is–

(a) a day on which P does more than 3 hours' work overseas, or

(b) a day on which P would have done more than 3 hours' work overseas but for being on annual leave, sick leave or parenting leave.

RELEVANT JOBS ON BOARD VEHICLES, AIRCRAFT OR SHIPS

30(1) P has a "relevant" job on board a vehicle, aircraft or ship if condition A and condition B are met.

30(2) Condition A is that P either–

(a) holds an employment, the duties of which consist of duties to be performed on board a vehicle, aircraft or ship while it is travelling, or

(b) carries on a trade, the activities of which consist of work to be done or services to be provided on board a vehicle, aircraft or ship while it is travelling.

30(3) Condition B is that substantially all of the trips made in performing those duties or carrying on those activities are ones that involve crossing an international boundary at sea, in the air or on land (referred to as "cross-border trips").

30(4) Sub-paragraph (2)(b) is not satisfied unless, in order to do the work or provide the services, P has to be present (in person) on board the vehicle, aircraft or ship while it is travelling.

30(5) Duties or activities of a purely incidental nature are to be ignored in deciding whether the duties of an employment or the activities of a trade consist of duties or activities of a kind described in sub-paragraph (2)(a) or (b).

UK TIES

31(1) What counts as a "UK tie" depends on whether P was resident in the UK for one or more of the 3 tax years preceding year X.

31(2) If P was resident in the UK for one or more of those 3 tax years, each of the following types of tie counts as a UK tie–

(a) a family tie,

(b) an accommodation tie,

(c) a work tie,

(d) a 90-day tie, and

(e) a country tie.

31(3) Otherwise, each of the following types of tie counts as a UK tie–

(a) a family tie,

(b) an accommodation tie,

(c) a work tie, and

(d) a 90-day tie.

31(4) In order to have the requisite number of UK ties for year X, each tie of P's must be of a different type.

FAMILY TIE

32(1) P has a family tie for year X if–

(a) in year X, a relevant relationship exists at any time between P and another person, and

(b) that other person is someone who is resident in the UK for year X.

32(2) A relevant relationship exists at any time between P and another person if at the time–

(a) P and the other person are husband and wife or civil partners and, in either case, are not separated,

(b) P and the other person are living together as husband and wife or, if they are of the same sex, as if they were civil partners, or

(c) the other person is a child of P's and is under the age of 18.

32(3) P does not have a family tie for year X by virtue of sub-paragraph (2)(c) if P sees the child in the UK on fewer than 61 days (in total) in–

(a) year X, or

(b) if the child turns 18 during year X, the part of year X before the day on which the child turns 18.

32(4) A day counts as a day on which P sees the child if P sees the child in person for all or part of the day.

32(5) **"Separated"** means separated–

(a) under an order of a court of competent jurisdiction,

(b) by deed of separation, or

(c) in circumstances where the separation is likely to be permanent.

33(1) This paragraph applies in deciding for the purposes (only) of paragraph 32(1)(b) whether a person with whom P has a relevant relationship (a "family member") is someone who is resident in the UK for year X.

33(2) A family tie based on the fact that a family member has, by the same token, a relevant relationship with P is to be disregarded in deciding whether that family member is someone who is resident in the UK for year X.

33(3) A family member falling within sub-paragraph (4) is to be treated as being not resident in the UK for year X if the number of days that he or she spends in the UK in the part of year X outside term-time is less than 21.

33(4) A family member falls within this sub-paragraph if he or she–

(a) is a child of P's who is under the age of 18,

(b) is in full-time education in the UK at any time in year X, and

(c) is resident in the UK for year X but would not be so resident if the time spent in full-time education in the UK in that year were disregarded.

33(5) In sub-paragraph (4)–

(a) references to full-time education in the UK are to full-time education at a university, college, school or other educational establishment in the UK, and

(b) the reference to the time spent in full-time education in the UK is to the time spent there during term-time.

33(6) For the purposes of this paragraph, half-term breaks and other breaks when teaching is not provided during a term are considered to form part of "term-time".

ACCOMMODATION TIE

34(1) P has an accommodation tie for year X if–

(a) P has a place to live in the UK,

(b) that place is available to P during year X for a continuous period of at least 91 days, and

(c) P spends at least one night at that place in that year.

34(2) If there is a gap of fewer than 16 days between periods in year X when a particular place is available to P, that place is to be treated as continuing to be available to P during the gap.

34(3) P is considered to have a "place to live" in the UK if–

(a) P's home or at least one of P's homes (if P has more than one) is in the UK, or

(b) P has a holiday home or temporary retreat (or something similar) in the UK, or

(c) accommodation is otherwise available to P where P can live when P is in the UK.

34(4) Accommodation may be "available" to P even if P holds no estate or interest in it and even if P has no legal right to occupy it.

34(5) If the accommodation is the home of a close relative of P's, sub-paragraph (1)(c) has effect as if for "at least one night" there were substituted "a total of at least 16 nights".

34(6) A **"close relative"** is–

(a) a parent or grandparent,

(b) a brother or sister,

(c) a child aged 18 or over, or

(d) a grandchild aged 18 or over,

in each case, including by half-blood or by marriage or civil partnership.

WORK TIE

35(1) P has a work tie for year X if P works in the UK for at least 40 days (whether continuously or intermittently) in year X.

35(2) For these purposes, P works in the UK for a day if P does more than 3 hours' work in the UK on that day.

36(1) This paragraph applies for the purposes of paragraph 35.

36(2) It applies in cases where P has a relevant job on board a vehicle, aircraft or ship.

36(3) When making a cross-border trip as part of that job–

(a) if the trip begins in the UK, P is assumed to do more than 3 hours' work in the UK on the day on which it begins,

(b) if the trip ends in the UK, P is assumed to do fewer than 3 hours' work in the UK on the day on which it ends.

36(4) Those assumptions apply regardless of how late in the day the trip begins or ends (even if it begins or ends just before midnight).

36(5) For the purposes of sub-paragraph (3)(a), it does not matter whether the trip ends on that same day.

36(6) A day that falls within both paragraph (a) and paragraph (b) of sub-paragraph (3) is to be treated as if it fell only within paragraph (a).

36(7) In the case of a cross-border trip to or from the UK that is undertaken in stages–

(a) the day on which the trip begins or, as the case may be, ends is the day on which the stage of the trip that involves crossing the UK border begins or ends, and

(b) accordingly, any day on which a stage is undertaken by P solely within the UK must (if it lasts for more than 3 hours) be counted separately as a day on which P does more than 3 hours' work in the UK.

90-DAY TIE

37 P has a 90-day tie for year X if P has spent more than 90 days in the UK in–

(a) the tax year preceding year X,

(b) the tax year preceding that tax year, or

(c) each of those tax years separately.

COUNTRY TIE

38(1) P has a country tie for year X if the country in which P meets the midnight test for the greatest number of days in year X is the UK.

38(2) If–

(a) P meets the midnight test for the same number of days in year X in two or more countries, and

(b) that number is the greatest number of days for which P meets the midnight test in any country in year X,

P has a country tie for year X if one of those countries is the UK.

38(3) P meets the "midnight test" in a country for a day if P is present in that country at the end of that day.

Part 5 – Miscellaneous

INTERPRETATION

145 In this Schedule–

"corporation tax" includes any amount assessable or chargeable as if it were corporation tax;

"country" includes a state or territory;

"cross-border trip" is defined in paragraph 30;

"double taxation arrangements" means arrangements that have effect under section 2(1) of TIOPA 2010;

"employment"–

(a) has the meaning given in section 4 of ITEPA 2003, and

(b) includes an office within the meaning of section 5(3) of that Act;

"enactment" means an enactment whenever passed (including this Act) and includes–

(a) an Act of the Scottish Parliament,

(b) a Measure or Act of the National Assembly for Wales,

(c) any Northern Ireland legislation as defined by section 24(5) of the Interpretation Act 1978, and

(d) any Orders in Council, orders, rules, regulations, schemes warrants, byelaws and other instruments made under an enactment (including anything mentioned in paragraphs (a) to (c) of this definition);

"home" is to be construed in accordance with paragraph 25;

"individual" means an individual acting in any capacity (including as trustee or personal representative);

"overseas" means anywhere outside the UK;

"parenting leave" means maternity leave, paternity leave, adoption leave or parental leave (whether statutory or otherwise);

"relevant job on board a vehicle, aircraft or ship" is defined in paragraph 30;

"ship" includes any kind of vessel (including a hovercraft);

"significant break from overseas work" is defined in paragraph 29;

"significant break from UK work" is defined in paragraph 29;

"split year", as respects an individual, means a tax year that is, as respects that individual, a split year within the meaning of Part 3 of this Schedule;

"trade" also includes–

(a) a profession or vocation,

(b) anything that is treated as a trade for income tax purposes, and

(c) the commercial occupation of woodlands (within the meaning of section 11(2) of ITTOIA 2005);

"work" is defined in paragraph 26;

"UK" means the United Kingdom, including the territorial sea of the United Kingdom;

"UK tie" is defined in paragraph 31;

"whole month" means the whole of January, the whole of February and so on, except that the period from the start of a tax year to the end of April is to count as a whole month.

146 In relation to an individual who carries on a trade–

(a) a reference in this Schedule to annual leave or parenting leave is to reasonable amounts of time off from work for the same purposes as the purposes for which annual leave or parenting leave is taken, and

(b) what are "reasonable amounts" is to be assessed having regard to the annual leave or parenting leave to which an employee might reasonably expect to be entitled if doing similar work.

147 A reference in this Schedule to a number of days being less than a specified number includes a case where the number of days is zero.

COMMENCEMENT

153(1) Parts 1 and 2 of this Schedule have effect for determining whether individuals are resident or not resident in the UK for the tax year 2013–14 or any subsequent tax year.

153(2) [Not relevant to inheritance tax.]

153(3) [Not relevant to inheritance tax.]

SCHEDULE 46 – ORDINARY RESIDENCE

Section 219

Part 4 – Other Amendments

F(No. 2)A 1931

114(1) [Amends F(No. 2)A 1931, s. 22(1)(a) and (b).]

114(2) Nothing in sub-paragraph (1) limits the power conferred by section 60(1) of FA 1940.

114(3) *Subject to sub-paragraph* (5), the amendment made by sub-paragraph (1) does not affect a pre-commencement security (nor the availability of the relevant exemption).

114(4) Sub-paragraph (5) applies to a person who becomes the beneficial owner of a pre-commencement security (or an interest in such a security) on or after 6 April 2013.

114(5) If obtaining the relevant exemption is conditional on being not ordinarily resident in the United Kingdom, any enactment conferring the exemption is to have effect (in relation to a person to whom this sub-paragraph applies) as if obtaining the exemption were conditional instead on being not resident in the United Kingdom.

114(5) In this paragraph–

"pre-commencement security" means a FOTRA security (as defined in section 713 of ITTOIA 2005) issued before the day on which this Act is passed;

"the relevant exemption", in relation to a pre-commencement security, means the exemption for which provision is made in the exemption condition (as defined in that section).

IHTA 1984

118(1) Section 157 of IHTA 1984 (non-residents' bank accounts) is amended as follows.

118(2) [Substitutes IHTA 1984, s. 157(2).]

118(3) [Amends IHTA 1984, s. 157(3).]

118(4) [Amends IHTA 1984, s. 157(4)(a) and (b).]

118(5) The amendments made by this paragraph do not apply if the person dies before 6 April 2013.

SCHEDULE 50 – PENALTIES: LATE FILING, LATE PAYMENT AND ERRORS

Section 230

AMENDMENTS TO SCHEDULE 24 TO FA 2007: PENALTIES FOR ERRORS

1(1) In Schedule 24 to FA 2007 (penalties for errors), paragraph 13 (procedure: assessment) is amended as follows.

1(2) [Amends FA 2007, Sch. 24, para. 13(1)(c).]

1(3) [Inserts FA 2007, Sch. 24, para. 13(1ZA)–(1ZD).]

AMENDMENTS TO SCHEDULE 55 TO FA 2009: PENALTY FOR FAILURE TO MAKE RETURNS

2 Schedule 55 (penalty for failure to make returns etc) to FA 2009 is amended in accordance with paragraphs 3 to 9.

3 In paragraph 1 (returns etc in respect of which penalties are to be paid under that Schedule)–

(a) [amends FA 2009, Sch. 55, para. 1;]

(b) [inserts FA 2009, Sch. 55, para. 1(4A).]

5 [Amends FA 2009, Sch. 55, para. 2.]

7 [Substitutes FA 2009, Sch. 55, para. 18(5)–(7).]

8(1) Paragraph 19 (assessment) is amended as follows.

8(2) [Amends FA 2009, Sch. 55, para. 19(2).]

8(3) [Amends FA 2009, Sch. 55, para. 19(3)(a).]

9(1) Paragraph 27 (interpretation) is amended as follows.

9(2) [Inserts FA 2009, Sch. 55, para. 27(2A).]

9(3) [Inserts FA 2009, Sch. 55, para. 27(3A).]

AMENDMENTS TO SCHEDULE 56 TO FA 2009: PENALTY FOR FAILURE TO MAKE PAYMENTS ON TIME

10 Schedule 56 (penalty for failure to make payments on time) to FA 2009 is amended in accordance with paragraphs 11 to 14.

11 [Amends FA 2009, Sch. 56, para. 1(4).]

13 [Inserts FA 2009, Sch. 56, para. 9A.]

14(1) Paragraph 11 (assessment of penalty) is amended as follows.

14(2) [Substitutes FA 2009, Sch. 56, para. 11(4A) and (4B).]

14(3) [Omits FA 2009, Sch. 56, para. 11(5).]

CONSEQUENTIAL AMENDMENT

15 [Repeals F(No. 3)A 2010, Sch. 10, para. 10.]

COMMENCEMENT

16(1) The amendments made by paragraph 1 have effect in relation to any assessment of a penalty under Schedule 24 to FA 2007 made on or after the day on which this Act is passed.

16(2) The amendments made by paragraphs 2 to 9 and 15 have effect for the tax year 2014–15 and subsequent tax years in relation to failures to make returns with a filing date (as defined in paragraph 1(4) of Schedule 55 to FA 2009) on or after 6 April 2014.

16(3) The amendments made by paragraphs 10 to 14 have effect for defaults made in relation to the tax year 2014–15 and subsequent tax years (see paragraph 6(2) of Sch. 56 to FA 2009 (as amended by paragraph 12(3) of this Schedule) as to when a default is made in relation to a tax year).

INHERITANCE AND TRUSTEES' POWERS ACT 2014

(2014 Chapter 16)

[14th May 2014]

ARRANGEMENT OF SECTIONS

1 Intestacy: surviving spouse or civil partner

1(1) Section 46 of the Administration of Estates Act 1925 (succession to real and personal estate on intestacy) is amended as follows.

1(2) [Substitutes Table in AEA 1925, s. 46(1)(i).]

1(3) [Substitutes AEA 1925, s. 46(1A).]

1(4) [Inserts AEA 1925, s. 46(5) to (9).]

11 Minor and consequential amendments

11 Schedule 4 makes minor and consequential amendments.

12 Short title, commencement, application and extent

12(1) This Act may be cited as the Inheritance and Trustees' Powers Act 2014.

12(2) This section comes into force on the day on which this Act is passed, but otherwise this Act comes into force on such day as the Lord Chancellor may by order made by statutory instrument appoint.

12(3) An order under subsection (2) may appoint different days for different purposes.

12(4) The provisions of this Act, except sections 4 and 8 to 10, apply only in relation to deaths occurring after the coming into force of the provision concerned.

12(5) Subject to subsection (6), this Act extends to England and Wales only.

12(6) The repeals made by paragraph 4 of Schedule 4 extend to the United Kingdom.

Commencement Date – IHTPA 2014, so far as not already in force, comes into force on 1 October 2014 (SI 2014/2039, art. 2).

SCHEDULES

SCHEDULE 4 – MINOR AND CONSEQUENTIAL AMENDMENTS

Section 11

ADMINISTRATION OF ESTATES ACT 1925

1(1) The Administration of Estates Act 1925 is amended as follows.

1(2) [Omits AEA 1925, s. 46(3).]

1(3) [Omits AEA 1925, s. 47A.]

1(4) [Not relevant to inheritance tax.]

1(5) [Not relevant to inheritance tax.]

INHERITANCE TAX ACT 1984

4 In the Inheritance Tax Act 1984–

(a) [omits IHTA 1984, s. 17(c);]

(b) [omits IHTA 1984, s. 145.]

FINANCE ACT 2014

(2014 Chapter 26)

[*17th July 2014*]

ARRANGEMENT OF SECTIONS

PART 2 – EXCISE DUTIES AND OTHER TAXES

PART 4 – FOLLOWER NOTICES AND ACCELERATED PAYMENTS

CHAPTER 1 – INTRODUCTION

CHAPTER 2 – FOLLOWER NOTICES

CHAPTER 3 – ACCELERATED PAYMENT

CHAPTER 4 – MISCELLANEOUS AND GENERAL PROVISION

PART 5 – PROMOTERS OF TAX AVOIDANCE SCHEMES

PART 2 – EXCISE DUTIES AND OTHER TAXES

INHERITANCE TAX

117 Inheritance tax

117 Schedule 25 contains provision about inheritance tax.

ESTATE DUTY

118 Gifts to the nation: estate duty

118(1) [Inserts FA 2012, Sch. 14, para. 32A.]

118(2) Subsection (3) applies where a person ("the donor") has, before the day on which this Act is passed, made a qualifying gift of an object in circumstances where, had the donor instead sold the object to an individual at market value, a charge to estate duty would have arisen under section 40 of FA 1930 on the proceeds of sale.

118(3) No liability to estate duty under section 40 of FA 1930 arises in respect of the object on or after the day on which this Act is passed.

118(4) In subsection (2) **"qualifying gift"** has the same meaning as in Schedule 14 to FA 2012.

118(5) In the application of subsections (2) and (3) to Northern Ireland, the references to section 40 of FA 1930 are to be read as references to section 2 of the Finance Act (Northern Ireland) 1931.

PART 4 – FOLLOWER NOTICES AND ACCELERATED PAYMENTS

Chapter 1 – Introduction

OVERVIEW

199 Overview of Part 4

199 In this Part–

(a) sections 200 to 203 set out the main defined terms used in the Part,

(b) Chapter 2 makes provision for follower notices and for penalties if account is not taken of judicial rulings which lay down principles or give reasoning relevant to tax cases,

(c) Chapter 3 makes–

(i) provision for accelerated payments to be made on account of tax,

(ii) provision restricting the circumstances in which payments of tax can be postponed pending an appeal,

(iii) provision to enable a court to prevent repayment of tax, for the purpose of protecting the public revenue, and

(iv) provision restricting the surrender of losses and other amounts for the purposes of group relief.

(d) Chapter 4–

(i) makes special provision about the application of this Part in relation to stamp duty land tax and annual tax for enveloped dwellings,

(ii) confers a power to extend the provisions of this Part to other taxes, and

(iii) makes amendments consequential on this Part.

History – S. 199(c)(iv) (and the ", and" preceding it) inserted and the word "and" at the end of s. 199(c)(ii) omitted by FA 2015, s. 118 and Sch. 18, para. 2, with effect from 26 March 2015.

MAIN DEFINITIONS

200 "Relevant tax"

200 In this Part, **"relevant tax"** means–

(a) income tax,

(b) capital gains tax,

(c) corporation tax, including any amount chargeable as if it were corporation tax or treated as if it were corporation tax,

(ca) apprenticeship levy,

(d) inheritance tax,

(e) stamp duty land tax, and

(f) annual tax on enveloped dwellings.

History – S. 200(ca) inserted by FA 2016, s. 104(4), with effect from 15 September 2016 (Royal Assent).

201 "Tax advantage" and "tax arrangements"

201(1) This section applies for the purposes of this Part.

201(2) **"Tax advantage"** includes–

(a) relief or increased relief from tax,

(b) repayment or increased repayment of tax,

(c) avoidance or reduction of a charge to tax or an assessment to tax,

(d) avoidance of a possible assessment to tax,

(e) deferral of a payment of tax or advancement of a repayment of tax, and

(f) avoidance of an obligation to deduct or account for tax.

201(3) Arrangements are **"tax arrangements"** if, having regard to all the circumstances, it would be reasonable to conclude that the obtaining of a tax advantage was the main purpose, or one of the main purposes, of the arrangements.

201(4) **"Arrangements"** includes any agreement, understanding, scheme, transaction or series of transactions (whether or not legally enforceable).

202 "Tax enquiry" and "return"

202(1) This section applies for the purposes of this Part.

202(2) [Not relevant to inheritance tax.]

202(3) [Not relevant to inheritance tax.]

202(4) [Not relevant to inheritance tax.]

202(5) In the case of inheritance tax, each of the following is to be treated as a return–

(a) an account delivered by a person under section 216 or 217 of IHTA 1984 (including an account delivered in accordance with regulations under section 256 of that Act);

(b) a statement or declaration which amends or is otherwise connected with such an account produced by the person who delivered the account;

(c) information or a document provided by a person in accordance with regulations under section 256 of that Act;

and such a return is to be treated as made by the person in question.

202(6) An enquiry is deemed to be in progress, in relation to a return to which subsection (5) applies, during the period which–

(a) begins with the time the account is delivered or (as the case may be) the statement, declaration, information or document is produced, and

(b) ends when the person is issued with a certificate of discharge under section 239 of that Act, or is discharged by virtue of section 256(1)(b) of that Act, in respect of the return (at which point the enquiry is to be treated as completed).

203 "Tax appeal"

203 In this Part **"tax appeal"** means–

(a) [not relevant to inheritance tax,]

(b) [not relevant to inheritance tax,]

(c) [not relevant to inheritance tax,]

(d) [not relevant to inheritance tax,]

(e) [not relevant to inheritance tax,]

(ea) [not relevant to inheritance tax,]

(f) an appeal under section 222 of IHTA 1984 (appeals against HMRC determinations) other than an appeal made by a person against a determination in respect of a transfer of value at a time when a tax enquiry is in progress in respect of a return made by that person in respect of that transfer,

(g) [not relevant to inheritance tax,]

(h) [not relevant to inheritance tax,]

(i) an appeal against any determination of–

(i) an appeal within paragraphs (a) to (h), or

(ii) an appeal within this paragraph.

History – S. 203(ea) inserted by FA 2016, s. 104(5), with effect from 15 September 2016.

Chapter 2 – Follower Notices

GIVING OF FOLLOWER NOTICES

204 Circumstances in which a follower notice may be given

204(1) HMRC may give a notice (a "follower notice") to a person ("P") if Conditions A to D are met.

204(2) Condition A is that–

(a) a tax enquiry is in progress into a return or claim made by P in relation to a relevant tax, or

(b) P has made a tax appeal (by notifying HMRC or otherwise) in relation to a relevant tax, but that appeal has not yet been–

(i) determined by the tribunal or court to which it is addressed, or

(ii) abandoned or otherwise disposed of.

204(3) Condition B is that the return or claim or, as the case may be, appeal is made on the basis that a particular tax advantage ("the asserted advantage") results from particular tax arrangements ("the chosen arrangements").

204(4) Condition C is that HMRC is of the opinion that there is a judicial ruling which is relevant to the chosen arrangements.

204(5) Condition D is that no previous follower notice has been given to the same person (and not withdrawn) by reference to the same tax advantage, tax arrangements, judicial ruling and tax period.

204(6) A follower notice may not be given after the end of the period of 12 months beginning with the later of–

(a) the day on which the judicial ruling mentioned in Condition C is made, and

(b) the day the return or claim to which subsection (2)(a) refers was received by HMRC or (as the case may be) the day the tax appeal to which subsection (2)(b) refers was made.

205 "Judicial ruling" and circumstances in which a ruling is "relevant"

205(1) This section applies for the purposes of this Chapter.

205(2) **"Judicial ruling"** means a ruling of a court or tribunal on one or more issues.

205(3) A judicial ruling is **"relevant"** to the chosen arrangements if–

(a) it relates to tax arrangements,

(b) the principles laid down, or reasoning given, in the ruling would, if applied to the chosen arrangements, deny the asserted advantage or a part of that advantage, and

(c) it is a final ruling.

205(4) A judicial ruling is a **"final ruling"** if it is–

(a) a ruling of the Supreme Court, or

(b) a ruling of any other court or tribunal in circumstances where–

(i) no appeal may be made against the ruling,

(ii) if an appeal may be made against the ruling with permission, the time limit for applications has expired and either no application has been made or permission has been refused,

(iii) if such permission to appeal against the ruling has been granted or is not required, no appeal has been made within the time limit for appeals, or

(iv) if an appeal was made, it was abandoned or otherwise disposed of before it was determined by the court or tribunal to which it was addressed.

205(5) Where a judicial ruling is final by virtue of sub-paragraph (ii), (iii) or (iv) of subsection (4)(b), the ruling is treated as made at the time when the sub-paragraph in question is first satisfied.

206 Content of a follower notice

206 A follower notice must–

(a) identify the judicial ruling in respect of which Condition C in section 204 is met,

(b) explain why HMRC considers that the ruling meets the requirements of section 205(3), and

(c) explain the effects of sections 207 to 210.

REPRESENTATIONS

207 Representations about a follower notice

207(1) Where a follower notice is given under section 204, P has 90 days beginning with the day that notice is given to send written representations to HMRC objecting to the notice on the grounds that–

(a) Condition A, B or D in section 204 was not met,

(b) the judicial ruling specified in the notice is not one which is relevant to the chosen arrangements, or

(c) the notice was not given within the period specified in subsection (6) of that section.

207(2) HMRC must consider any representations made in accordance with subsection (1).

207(3) Having considered the representations, HMRC must determine whether to–

(a) confirm the follower notice (with or without amendment), or

(b) withdraw the follower notice,

and notify P accordingly.

PENALTIES

208 Penalty if corrective action not taken in response to follower notice

208(1) This section applies where a follower notice is given to P (and not withdrawn).

208(2) P is liable to pay a penalty if the necessary corrective action is not taken in respect of the denied advantage (if any) before the specified time.

208(3) In this Chapter **"the denied advantage"** means so much of the asserted advantage (see section 204(3)) as is denied by the application of the principles laid down, or reasoning given, in the judicial ruling identified in the follower notice under section 206(a).

208(4) The necessary corrective action is taken in respect of the denied advantage if (and only if) P takes the steps set out in subsections (5) and (6).

208(5) The first step is that–

(a) in the case of a follower notice given by virtue of section 204(2)(a), P amends a return or claim to counteract the denied advantage;

(b) in the case of a follower notice given by virtue of section 204(2)(b), P takes all necessary action to enter into an agreement with HMRC (in writing) for the purpose of relinquishing the denied advantage.

208(6) The second step is that P notifies HMRC–

(a) that P has taken the first step, and

(b) of the denied advantage and (where different) the additional amount which has or will become due and payable in respect of tax by reason of the first step being taken.

208(7) In determining the additional amount which has or will become due and payable in respect of tax for the purposes of subsection (6)(b), it is to be assumed that, where P takes the necessary action as mentioned in subsection (5)(b), the agreement is then entered into.

208(8) In this Chapter–

"the specified time" means–

(a) if no representations objecting to the follower notice were made by P in accordance with subsection (1) of section 207, the end of the 90 day post-notice period;

(b) if such representations were made and the notice is confirmed under that section (with or without amendment), the later of–

(i) the end of the 90 day post-notice period, and

(ii) the end of the 30 day post-representations period;

"the 90 day post-notice period" means the period of 90 days beginning with the day on which the follower notice is given;

"the 30 day post-representations period" means the period of 30 days beginning with the day on which P is notified of HMRC's determination under section 207.

208(9) No enactment limiting the time during which amendments may be made to returns or claims operates to prevent P taking the first step mentioned in subsection (5)(a) before the tax enquiry is closed (whether or not before the specified time).

208(10) No appeal may be brought, by virtue of a provision mentioned in subsection (11), against an amendment made by a closure notice in respect of a tax enquiry to the extent that the amendment takes into account an amendment made by P to a return or claim in taking the first step mentioned in subsection (5)(a) (whether or not that amendment was made before the specified time).

208(11) The provisions are–

(a) section 31(1)(b) or (c) of TMA 1970,

(b) paragraph 9 of Schedule 1A to TMA 1970,

(c) paragraph 34(3) of Schedule 18 to FA 1998,

(d) paragraph 35(1)(b) of Schedule 10 to FA 2003, and

(e) paragraph 35(1)(b) of Schedule 33 to FA 2013.

209 Amount of a section 208 penalty

209(1) The penalty under section 208 is 50% of the value of the denied advantage.

209(2) Schedule 30 contains provision about how the denied advantage is valued for the purposes of calculating penalties under this section.

209(3) Where P before the specified time–

(a) amends a return or claim to counteract part of the denied advantage only, or

(b) takes all necessary action to enter into an agreement with HMRC (in writing) for the purposes of relinquishing part of the denied advantage only,

in subsections (1) and (2) the references to the denied advantage are to be read as references to the remainder of the denied advantage.

210 Reduction of a section 208 penalty for co-operation

210(1) Where–

(a) P is liable to pay a penalty under section 208 of the amount specified in section 209(1),

(b) the penalty has not yet been assessed, and

(c) P has co-operated with HMRC,

HMRC may reduce the amount of that penalty to reflect the quality of that co-operation.

210(2) In relation to co-operation, **"quality"** includes timing, nature and extent.

210(3) P has co-operated with HMRC only if P has done one or more of the following–

(a) provided reasonable assistance to HMRC in quantifying the tax advantage;

(b) counteracted the denied advantage;

(c) provided HMRC with information enabling corrective action to be taken by HMRC;

(d) provided HMRC with information enabling HMRC to enter an agreement with P for the purpose of counteracting the denied advantage;

(e) allowed HMRC to access tax records for the purpose of ensuring that the denied advantage is fully counteracted.

210(4) But nothing in this section permits HMRC to reduce a penalty to less than 10% of the value of the denied advantage.

211 Assessment of a section 208 penalty

211(1) Where a person is liable for a penalty under section 208, HMRC may assess the penalty.

211(2) Where HMRC assess the penalty, HMRC must–

(a) notify the person who is liable for the penalty, and

(b) state in the notice a tax period in respect of which the penalty is assessed.

211(3) A penalty under section 208 must be paid before the end of the period of 30 days beginning with the day on which the person is notified of the penalty under subsection (2).

211(4) An assessment–

(a) is to be treated for procedural purposes in the same way as an assessment to tax (except in respect of a matter expressly provided for by this Chapter),

(b) may be enforced as if it were an assessment to tax, and

(c) may be combined with an assessment to tax.

211(5) No penalty under section 208 may be notified under subsection (2) later than–

(a) in the case of a follower notice given by virtue of section 204(2)(a) (tax enquiry in progress), the end of the period of 90 days beginning with the day the tax enquiry is completed, and

(b) in the case of a follower notice given by virtue of section 204(2)(b) (tax appeal pending), the end of the period of 90 days beginning with the earliest of–

(i) the day on which P takes the necessary corrective action (within the meaning of section 208(4)),

(ii) the day on which a ruling is made on the tax appeal by P, or any further appeal in that case, which is a final ruling (see section 205(4)), and

(iii) the day on which that appeal, or any further appeal, is abandoned or otherwise disposed of before it is determined by the court or tribunal to which it is addressed.

211(6) In this section a reference to an assessment to tax, in relation to inheritance tax, is to a determination.

212 Aggregate penalties

212(1) Subsection (2) applies where–

(a) two or more penalties are incurred by the same person and fall to be determined by reference to an amount of tax to which that person is chargeable,

(b) one of those penalties is incurred under section 208, and

(c) one or more of the other penalties are incurred under a relevant penalty provision.

212(2) The aggregate of the amounts of the penalties mentioned in subsection (1)(b) and (c), so far as determined by reference to that amount of tax, must not exceed–

(a) the relevant percentage of that amount, or

(b) in a case where at least one of the penalties is under paragraph 5(2)(b) or 6(3)(b), (4)(b) or (5)(b) of Schedule 55 to FA 2009, £300 (if greater).

212(3) In the application of section 97A of TMA 1970 (multiple penalties), no account is to be taken of a penalty under section 208.

212(4) **"Relevant penalty provision"** means–

(a) Schedule 24 to FA 2007 (penalties for errors),

(b) Schedule 41 to FA 2008 (penalties: failure to notify etc),

(c) Schedule 55 to FA 2009 (penalties for failure to make returns etc),

(d) Part 5 of Schedule 18 to FA 2016 (serial tax avoidance), or

(e) section 212A of FA 2013 (general anti-abuse rule).

212(5) **"The relevant percentage"** means–

(a) 200% in a case where at least one of the penalties is determined by reference to the percentage in–

(i) paragraph 4(4)(c) of Schedule 24 to FA 2007,

(ii) paragraph 6(4)(a) of Schedule 41 to FA 2008, or

(iii) paragraph 6(3A)(c) of Schedule 55 to FA 2009,

(b) 150% in a case where paragraph (a) does not apply and at least one of the penalties is determined by reference to the percentage in–

(i) paragraph 4(3)(c) of Schedule 24 to FA 2007,

(ii) paragraph 6(3)(a) of Schedule 41 to FA 2008, or

(iii) paragraph 6(3A)(b) of Schedule 55 to FA 2009,

(c) 140% in a case where neither paragraph (a) nor paragraph (b) applies and at least one the penalties is determined by reference to the percentage in–

(i) paragraph 4(4)(b) of Schedule 24 to FA 2007,

(ii) paragraph 6(4)(b) of Schedule 41 to FA 2008,

(iii) paragraph 6(4A)(c) of Schedule 55 to FA 2009,

(d) 105% in a case where none of paragraphs (a), (b) and (c) applies and at least one of the penalties is determined by reference to the percentage in–

(i) paragraph 4(3)(b) of Schedule 24 to FA 2007,

(ii) paragraph 6(3)(b) of Schedule 41 to FA 2008,

(iii) paragraph 6(4A)(b) of Schedule 55 to FA 2009, and

(e) in any other case, 100%.

History – S. 212(4)(d) (and the ", or" before it) inserted (and the "or" after (b) omitted) by FA 2016, s. 159 and Sch. 18, para. 60, with effect in relation to relevant defeats incurred after 15 September 2016 (Royal Assent), subject to transitional provisions in Sch. 18, para. 64 and 65 (in relation to arrangements entered into before 15 September 2016 relevant defeats incurred before 6 April 2017 and certain relevant defeats incurred on or after 6 April 2017 are disregarded).

S. 212(4)(e) (and the ", or" before it) inserted (and the "or" after (c) omitted) by FA 2016, s. 158(11), with effect in relation to tax arrangements (within the meaning of FA 2013, Pt. 5) entered into on or after 15 September 2016.

213 Alteration of assessment of a section 208 penalty

213(1) After notification of an assessment has been given to a person under section 211(2), the assessment may not be altered except in accordance with this section or on appeal.

213(2) A supplementary assessment may be made in respect of a penalty if an earlier assessment operated by reference to an underestimate of the value of the denied advantage.

213(3) An assessment or supplementary assessment may be revised as necessary if it operated by reference to an overestimate of the denied advantage; and, where more than the resulting assessed penalty has already been paid by the person to HMRC, the excess must be repaid.

214 Appeal against a section 208 penalty

214(1) P *may appeal against* a *decision* of HMRC that a penalty is payable by P under section 208.

214(2) P may appeal against a decision of HMRC as to the amount of a penalty payable by P under section 208.

214(3) The grounds on which an appeal under subsection (1) may be made include in particular–

(a) that Condition A, B or D in section 204 was not met in relation to the follower notice,

(b) that the judicial ruling specified in the notice is not one which is relevant to the chosen arrangements,

(c) that the notice was not given within the period specified in subsection (6) of that section, or

(d) that it was reasonable in all the circumstances for P not to have taken the necessary corrective action (see section 208(4)) in respect of the denied advantage.

214(4) An appeal under this section must be made within the period of 30 days beginning with the day on which notification of the penalty is given under section 211.

214(5) An appeal under this section is to be treated in the same way as an appeal against an assessment to the tax concerned (including by the application of any provision about bringing the appeal by notice to HMRC, about HMRC's review of the decision or about determination of the appeal by the First-tier Tribunal or Upper Tribunal).

214(6) Subsection (5) does not apply–

(a) so as to require a person to pay a penalty before an appeal against the assessment of the penalty is determined, or

(b) in respect of any other matter expressly provided for by this Part.

214(7) In this section a reference to an assessment to tax, in relation to inheritance tax, is to a determination.

214(8) On an appeal under subsection (1), the tribunal may affirm or cancel HMRC's decision.

214(9) On an appeal under subsection (2), the tribunal may–

(a) affirm HMRC's decision, or

(b) substitute for HMRC's decision another decision that HMRC had power to make.

214(10) The cancellation under subsection (8) of HMRC's decision on the ground specified in subsection (3)(d) does not affect the validity of the follower notice, or of any accelerated payment notice or partner payment notice under Chapter 3 related to the follower notice.

214(11) In this section **"tribunal"** means the First-tier Tribunal or Upper Tribunal (as appropriate by virtue of subsection (5)).

PARTNERS AND PARTNERSHIPS

215 Follower notices: treatment of partners and partnerships

215 Schedule 31 makes provision about the application of this Chapter in relation to partners and partnerships.

APPEALS OUT OF TIME

216 Late appeal against final judicial ruling

216(1) This section applies where a final judicial ruling ("the original ruling") is the subject of an appeal by reason of a court or tribunal granting leave to appeal out of time.

216(2) If a follower notice has been given identifying the original ruling under section 206(a), the notice is suspended until such time as HMRC notify P that–

(a) the appeal has resulted in a judicial ruling which is a final ruling, or

(b) the appeal has been abandoned or otherwise disposed of (before it was determined).

216(3) Accordingly the period during which the notice is suspended does not count towards the periods mentioned in section 208(8).

216(4) When a follower notice is suspended under subsection (2), HMRC must notify P as soon as reasonably practicable.

216(5) If the new final ruling resulting from the appeal is not a judicial ruling which is relevant to the chosen arrangements (see section 205), the follower notice ceases to have effect at the end of the period of suspension.

216(6) In any other case, the follower notice continues to have effect after the end of the period of suspension and, in a case within subsection (2)(a), is treated as if it were in respect of the new final ruling resulting from the appeal.

216(7) The notice given under subsection (2) must–

(a) state whether subsection (5) or (6) applies, and

(b) where subsection (6) applies in a case within subsection (2)(a), make any amendments to the follower notice required to reflect the new final ruling.

216(8) No new follower notice may be given in respect of the original ruling unless the appeal has been abandoned or otherwise disposed of before it is determined by the court or tribunal to which it is addressed.

216(9) Nothing in this section prevents a follower notice being given in respect of a new final ruling resulting from the appeal.

216(10) Where the appeal is abandoned or otherwise disposed of before it is determined by the court or tribunal to which it is addressed, for the purposes of the original ruling the period beginning when leave to appeal out of time was granted, and ending when the appeal is disposed of, does not count towards the period of 12 months mentioned in section 204(6).

TRANSITIONAL PROVISION

217 Transitional provision

217(1) In the case of judicial rulings made before the day on which this Act is passed, this Chapter has effect as if for section 204(6) there were substituted–

"**204(6)** A follower notice may not be given after–

(a) the end of the period of 24 months beginning with the day on which this Act is passed, or

(b) the end of the period of 12 months beginning with the day the return or claim to which subsection (2)(a) refers was received by HMRC or (as the case may be) with the day the tax appeal to which subsection (2)(b) refers was made,

whichever is later."

217(2) Accordingly, the reference in section 216(10) to the period of 12 months includes a reference to the period of 24 months mentioned in the version of section 204(6) set out in subsection (1) above.

DEFINED TERMS

218 Defined terms used in Chapter 2

218 For the purposes of this Chapter–

"arrangements" has the meaning given by section 201(4);

"the asserted advantage" has the meaning given by section 204(3);

"the chosen arrangements" has the meaning given by section 204(3);

"the denied advantage" has the meaning given by section 208(3);

"follower notice" has the meaning given by section 204(1);

"HMRC" means Her Majesty's Revenue and Customs;

"judicial ruling", and **"relevant"** in relation to a judicial ruling and the chosen arrangements, have the meaning given by section 205;

"relevant tax" has the meaning given by section 200;

"the specified time" has the meaning given by section 208(8);

"tax advantage" has the meaning given by section 201(2);

"tax appeal" has the meaning given by section 203;

"tax arrangements" has the meaning given by section 201(3);

"tax enquiry" has the meaning given by section 202(2);

"tax period" means a tax year, accounting period or other period in respect of which tax is charged;

"P" has the meaning given by section 204(1);

"the 30 day post-representations period" has the meaning given by section 208(8);

"the 90 day post-notice period" has the meaning given by section 208(8).

Chapter 3 – Accelerated Payment

ACCELERATED PAYMENT NOTICES

219 Circumstances in which an accelerated payment notice may be given

219(1) HMRC may give a notice (an "accelerated payment notice") to a person ("P") if Conditions A to C are met.

219(2) Condition A is that–

(a) a tax enquiry is in progress into a return or claim made by P in relation to a relevant tax, or

(b) P has made a tax appeal (by notifying HMRC or otherwise) in relation to a relevant tax but that appeal has not yet been–
(i) determined by the tribunal or court to which it is addressed, or
(ii) abandoned or otherwise disposed of.

219(3) Condition B is that the return or claim or, as the case may be, appeal is made on the basis that a particular tax advantage ("the asserted advantage") results from particular arrangements ("the chosen arrangements").

219(4) Condition C is that one or more of the following requirements are met–

(a) HMRC has given (or, at the same time as giving the accelerated payment notice, gives) P a follower notice under Chapter 2–
(i) in relation to the same return or claim or, as the case may be, appeal, and
(ii) by reason of the same tax advantage and the chosen arrangements;

(b) the chosen arrangements are DOTAS arrangements;

(c) a GAAR counteraction notice has been given in relation to the asserted advantage or part of it and the chosen arrangements (or is so given at the same time as the accelerated payment notice) in a case where the stated opinion of at least two of the members of the sub-panel of the GAAR Advisory Panel which considered the matter under paragraph 10 of Schedule 43 to FA 2013 was as set out in paragraph 11(3)(b) of that Schedule (entering into tax arrangements not reasonable course of action etc);

(d) a notice has been given under paragraph 8(2) or 9(2) of Schedule 43A to FA 2013 (notice of final decision after considering Panel's opinion about referred or counteracted arrangements) in relation to the asserted advantage or part of it and the chosen arrangements (or is so given at the same time as the accelerated payment notice) in a case where the stated opinion of at least two of the members of the sub-panel of the GAAR Advisory Panel about the other arrangements (see subsection (8)) was as set out in paragraph 11(3)(b) of Schedule 43 to FA 2013;

(e) a notice under paragraph 8(2) of Schedule 43B to FA 2013 (GAAR: generic referral of tax arrangements) has been given in relation to the asserted advantage or part of it and the chosen arrangements (or is so given at the same time as the accelerated payment notice) in a case where the stated opinion of at least two of the members of the sub-panel of the GAAR Advisory Panel which considered the generic referral in respect of those arrangements under paragraph 6 of Schedule 43B to FA 2013 was as set out in paragraph 6(4)(b) of that Schedule.

219(5) **"DOTAS arrangements"** means–

(a) notifiable arrangements to which HMRC has allocated a reference number under section 311 of FA 2004,

(b) notifiable arrangements implementing a notifiable proposal where HMRC has allocated a reference number under that section to the proposed notifiable arrangements, or

(c) arrangements in respect of which the promoter must provide prescribed information under section 312(2) of that Act by reason of the arrangements being substantially the same as notifiable arrangements within paragraph (a) or (b).

219(6) But the notifiable arrangements within subsection (5) do not include arrangements in relation to which HMRC has given notice under section 312(6) of FA 2004 (notice that promoters not under duty imposed to notify client of reference number).

219(7) **"GAAR counteraction notice"** means a notice under paragraph 12 of Schedule 43 to FA 2013 (notice of final decision to counteract under the general anti-abuse rule).

219(8) In subsection (4)(d) **"other arrangements"** means–

(a) in relation to a notice under paragraph 8(2) of Schedule 43A to FA 2013, the referred arrangements (as defined in that paragraph);

(b) in relation to a notice under paragraph 9(2) of that Schedule, the counteracted arrangements (as defined in paragraph 2 of that Schedule).

History – S. 219(4)(d) and (e) inserted by FA 2016, s. 157(19), with effect in relation to tax arrangements (within the meaning of FA 2013, Pt. 5) entered into at any time (whether before or on or after 15 September 2016).
S. 219(8) inserted by FA 2016, s. 157(20), with effect in relation to tax arrangements (within the meaning of FA 2013, Pt. 5) entered into at any time (whether before or on or after 15 September 2016).

220 Content of notice given while a tax enquiry is in progress

220(1) This section applies where an accelerated payment notice is given by virtue of section 219(2)(a) (notice given while a tax enquiry is in progress).

220(2) The notice must–

(a) specify the paragraph or paragraphs of section 219(4) by virtue of which the notice is given,

(b) specify the payment (if any) required to be made under section 223 and the requirements of that section,

(c) explain the effect of sections 222 and 226, and of the amendments made by sections 224 and 225 (so far as relating to the relevant tax in relation to which the accelerated payment notice is given), and

(d) if the denied advantage consists of or includes an asserted surrenderable amount, specify that amount and any action which is required to be taken in respect of it under section 225A.

220(3) The payment required to be made under section 223 is an amount equal to the amount which a designated HMRC officer determines, to the best of that officer's information and belief, as the understated tax.

220(4) **"The understated tax"** means the additional amount that would be due and payable in respect of tax if–

(a) in the case of a notice given by virtue of section 219(4)(a) (cases where a follower notice is given)–

(i) it were assumed that the explanation given in the follower notice in question under section 206(b) is correct, and

(ii) the necessary corrective action were taken under section 208 in respect of what the designated HMRC officer determines, to the best of that officer's information and belief, as the denied advantage;

(b) in the case of a notice given by virtue of section 219(4)(b) (cases where the DOTAS requirements are met), such adjustments were made as are required to counteract what the designated HMRC officer determines, to the best of that officer's information and belief, as the denied advantage;

(c) in the case of a notice given by virtue of section 219(4)(c), (d) or (e) (cases involving counteraction under the general anti-abuse rule), such of the adjustments set out in the GAAR counteraction notice as have effect to counteract the denied advantage were made.

220(4A) **"Asserted surrenderable amount"** means so much of a surrenderable loss as a designated HMRC officer determines, to the best of that officer's information and belief, to be an amount–

(a) which would not be a surrenderable loss of P if the position were as stated in paragraphs (a), (b) or (c) of subsection (4), and

(b) which is not the subject of a claim by P for relief from corporation tax reflected in the understated tax amount (and hence in the payment required to be made under section 223).

220(4B) **"Surrenderable loss"** means a loss or other amount within section 99(1) of CTA 2010 (or part of such a loss or other amount).

220(5) **"The denied advantage"**–

(a) in the case of a notice given by virtue of section 219(4)(a), has the meaning given by section 208(3),

(b) in the case of a notice given by virtue of section 219(4)(b), means so much of the asserted advantage as is not a tax advantage which results from the chosen arrangements or otherwise, and

(c) in the case of a notice given by virtue of section 219(4)(c), (d) or (e), means so much of the asserted advantage as would be counteracted by making the adjustments set out in the GAAR counteraction notice.

220(6) If a notice is given by reason of two or all of the requirements in section 219(4) being met, any payment specified under subsection (2)(b) or amount specified under subsection (2)(d) is to be determined as if the notice were given by virtue of such one of them as is stated in the notice as being used for this purpose.

220(7) **"The GAAR counteraction notice"** means the notice under–

(a) paragraph 12 of Schedule 43 to FA 2013,

(b) paragraph 8 or 9 of Schedule 43A to that Act, or

(c) paragraph 8 of Schedule 43B to that Act,

as the case may be.

History – In s. 220(2)(b) the words "(if any)" inserted and s. 220(2)(d) (and the word ", and" preceding it) inserted and the word "and" at the end of s. 220(2)(b) omitted by FA 2015, s. 118 and Sch. 18, para. 3(2), with effect from 26 March 2015.

In s. 220(4)(c), the words ", (d) or (e)" inserted by FA 2016, s. 157(21)(a), with effect in relation to tax arrangements (within the meaning of FA 2013, Pt. 5) entered into at any time (whether before or on or after 15 September 2016).

S. 220(4A) and (4B) inserted by FA 2015, s. 118 and Sch. 18, para. 3(3), with effect from 26 March 2015.

In s. 220(5)(c), the words ", (d) or (e)" inserted by FA 2016, s. 157(21)(b), with effect in relation to tax arrangements (within the meaning of FA 2013, Pt. 5) entered into at any time (whether before or on or after 15 September 2016).

In s. 220(6) the words "any payment specified under subsection (2)(b) or amount specified under subsection (2)(d)" substituted for the words "the payment specified under subsection (2)(b)" by FA 2015, s. 118 and Sch. 18, para. 3(4), with effect from 26 March 2015.

S. 220(7)(a)–(c) and the word "under–" before them substituted for the words "under paragraph 12 of Schedule 43 to FA 2013 (notice of final decision to counteract under the general anti-abuse rule)." by FA 2016, s. 157(21)(c), with effect in relation to tax arrangements (within the meaning of FA 2013, Pt. 5) entered into at any time (whether before or on or after 15 September 2016).

221 Content of notice given pending an appeal

221(1) This section applies where an accelerated payment notice is given by virtue of section 219(2)(b) (notice given pending an appeal).

221(2) The notice must–

(a) specify the paragraph or paragraphs of section 219(4) by virtue of which the notice is given,

(b) specify the disputed tax (if any),

(c) explain the effect of section 222 and of the amendments made by sections 224 and 225 so far as relating to the relevant tax in relation to which the accelerated payment notice is given, and

(d) if the denied advantage consists of or includes an asserted surrenderable amount (within the meaning of section 220(4A)), specify that amount and any action which is required to be taken in respect of it under section 225A.

221(3) **"The disputed tax"** means so much of the amount of the charge to tax arising in consequence of–

(a) the amendment or assessment to tax appealed against, or

(b) where the appeal is against a conclusion stated by a closure notice, that conclusion,

as a designated HMRC officer determines, to the best of the officer's information and belief, as the amount required to ensure the counteraction of what that officer so determines as the denied advantage.

221(4) **"The denied advantage"** has the same meaning as in section 220(5).

221(5) If a notice is given by reason of two or all of the requirements in section 219(4) being met, the denied advantage is to be determined as if the notice were given by virtue of such one of them as is stated in the notice as being used for this purpose.

221(6) In this section a reference to an assessment to tax, in relation to inheritance tax, is to a determination.

History – In s. 221(2)(b) the words "(if any)" inserted and s. 221(2)(d) (and the word ", and" preceding it) inserted and the word "and" at the end of s. 221(2)(b) omitted by FA 2015, s. 118 and Sch. 18, para. 4(2), with effect from 26 March 2015.

222 Representations about a notice

222(1) This section applies where an accelerated payment notice has been given under section 219 (and not withdrawn).

222(2) P has 90 days beginning with the day that notice is given to send written representations to HMRC–

(a) objecting to the notice on the grounds that Condition A, B or C in section 219 was not met,

(b) objecting to the amount specified in the notice under section 220(2)(b) or section 221(2)(b), or

(c) objecting to the amount specified in the notice under section 220(2)(d) or section 221(2)(d).

222(3) HMRC must consider any representations made in accordance with subsection (2).

222(4) Having considered the representations, HMRC must–

(a) if representations were made under subsection (2)(a), determine whether–

(i) to confirm the accelerated payment notice (with or without amendment), or

(ii) to withdraw the accelerated payment notice,

(b) if representations were made under subsection (2)(b) (and the notice is not withdrawn under paragraph (a)), determine whether a different amount (or no amount) ought to have been specified under section 220(2)(b) or section 221(2)(b), and then–

(i) confirm the amount specified in the notice,

(ii) amend the notice to specify a different amount, or

(iii) remove from the notice the provision made under section 220(2)(b) or section 221(2)(b), and

(c) if representations were made under subsection (2)(c) (and the notice is not withdrawn under paragraph (a)), determine whether a different amount (or no amount) ought to have been specified under section 220(2)(d) or 221(2)(d), and then–

(i) confirm the amount specified in the notice,

(ii) amend the notice to specify a different amount, or

(iii) remove from the notice the provision made under section 220(2)(d) or section 221(2)(d),

and notify P accordingly.

History – S. 222(2)(c) (and the word ", or" preceding it) inserted and the word "or" at the end of s. 222(2)(a) omitted by FA 2015, s. 118 and Sch. 18, para. 5(2), with effect from 26 March 2015.

In s. 222(4)(b) the words "(or no amount)" inserted, the word "and" at the end of para. (4)(a) omitted, the word or at the end of para. (4)(b)(i) omitted and para. (4)(b)(iii) (and the word ", or" preceding it) and (4)(c) inserted by FA 2015, s. 118 and Sch. 18, para. 5(3), with effect from 26 March 2015.

FORMS OF ACCELERATED PAYMENT

223 Effect of notice given while tax enquiry is in progress: accelerated payment

History – In the heading to s. 223 the words ": accelerated payment" inserted by FA 2015, s. 118 and Sch. 18, para. 6(4), with effect from 26 March 2015.

223(1) This section applies where–

(a) an accelerated payment notice is given by virtue of section 219(2)(a) (notice given while a tax enquiry is in progress) (and not withdrawn), and

(b) an amount is stated in the notice in accordance with section 220(2)(b).

223(2) P must make a payment ("the accelerated payment") to HMRC of that amount.

223(3) The accelerated payment is to be treated as a payment on account of the understated tax (see section 220).

223(4) The accelerated payment must be made before the end of the payment period.

223(5) **"The payment period"** means–

(a) if P made no representations under section 222, the period of 90 days beginning with the day on which the accelerated payment notice is given, and

(b) if P made such representations, whichever of the following periods ends later–

(i) the 90 day period mentioned in paragraph (a);

(ii) the period of 30 days beginning with the day on which P is notified under section 222 of HMRC's determination.

223(6) But where the understated tax would be payable by instalments by virtue of an election made under section 227 of IHTA 1984, to the extent that the accelerated payment relates to tax payable by an instalment which falls to be paid at a time after the payment period, the accelerated payment must be made no later than that time.

223(7) If P pays any part of the understated tax before the accelerated payment in respect of it, the accelerated payment is treated to that extent as having been paid at the same time.

223(8) Any tax enactment which relates to the recovery of a relevant tax applies to an amount to be paid on account of the relevant tax under this section in the same manner as it applies to an amount of the relevant tax.

223(9) **"Tax enactment"** means provisions of or made under–

(a) [not relevant to inheritance tax,]

(b) [not relevant to inheritance tax,]

(c) IHTA 1984 or any other enactment relating to inheritance tax,

(d) [not relevant to inheritance tax,]

(e) [not relevant to inheritance tax.]

History – S. 223(1) substituted by FA 2015, s. 118 and Sch. 18, para. 6(2), with effect from 26 March 2015.
In s. 223(2) the words "that amount" substituted for the words "the amount specified in the notice in accordance with section 220(2)(b)" by FA 2015, s. 118 and Sch. 18, para. 6(3), with effect from 26 March 2015.

224 Restriction on powers to postpone tax payments pending initial appeal

224(1) [Not relevant to inheritance tax.]

224(2) [Inserts IHTA 1984, s. 242(4).]

224(3) [Not relevant to inheritance tax.]

224(4) [Not relevant to inheritance tax.]

224(5) [Not relevant to inheritance tax.]

224(6) [Not relevant to inheritance tax.]

PREVENTION OF SURRENDER OF LOSSES

225A Effect of notice: surrender of losses ineffective, etc

225A(1) This section applies where–

(a) an accelerated payment notice is given (and not withdrawn), and

(b) an amount is specified in the notice in accordance with section 220(2)(d) or 221(2)(d).

225A(2) P may not consent to any claim for group relief in respect of the amount so specified.

225A(3) Subject to subsection (2), paragraph 75 (other than sub-paragraphs (7) and (8)) of Schedule 18 to FA 1998 (reduction in amount available for surrender) has effect as if the amount so specified ceased to be an amount available for surrender at the time the notice was given to P.

225A(4) For the purposes of subsection (3), paragraph 75 of that Schedule has effect as if, in sub-paragraph (2) of that paragraph for "within 30 days" there were substituted "before the end of the payment period (within the meaning of section 223(5) of the Finance Act 2014)".

225A(5) The time limits otherwise applicable to amendment of a company tax return do not prevent an amendment being made in accordance with paragraph 75(6) of Schedule 18 to FA 1998 where, pursuant to subsection (3), a claimant company receives–

(a) notice of the withdrawal of consent under paragraph 75(3) of that Schedule, or

(b) a copy of a notice containing directions under paragraph 75(4) of that Schedule.

225A(6) Subsection (7) applies where–

(a) a company makes such an amendment to its company tax return at a time when an enquiry is in progress into the return, and

(b) paragraph 31(3) of that Schedule prevents the amendment from taking effect until the enquiry is completed.

225A(7) Section 219 (circumstances in which an accelerated payment notice may be given) has effect, in its application to that company in a case where section 219(2)(a) applies (tax enquiry in progress), as if–

(a) for the purposes of section 219(3), that amendment to the return had not been made,

(b) in section 219(4), after paragraph (c) there were inserted–

"(d) P has amended its company tax return, in accordance with paragraph 75(6) of Schedule 18 to FA 1998, in circumstances where pursuant to section 225A(3), P has received–

(i) notice of the withdrawal of consent under paragraph 75(3) of that Schedule, or

(ii) a copy of a notice containing directions under paragraph 75(4) of that Schedule,

but paragraph 31(3) of that Schedule prevents that amendment having effect.",

(c) in section 220(4), after paragraph (c) there were inserted–

"(d) in the case of a notice given by virtue of section 219(4)(d) (cases involving withdrawal of consent for losses claimed), it were assumed that P had never made the claim to group relief to which the amendment to its company tax return relates.", and

(d) in section 227(10), for "or (c)" there were substituted ", (c) or (d)".

225A(8) Subsections (2) and (3) are subject to–

(a) section 227(14) to (16) (provision about claims for group relief, and consents to claims, following amendment or withdrawal of an accelerated payment notice), and

(b) section 227A (provision about claims for group relief, and consents to claims, once tax position finally determined).

History – S. 225A inserted by FA 2015, s. 118 and Sch. 18, para. 7, with effect from 26 March 2015 subject to the transitional provisions at FA 2015, Sch. 18, para. 12(1).

PENALTIES

226 Penalty for failure to pay accelerated payment

226(1) This section applies where an accelerated payment notice is given by virtue of section 219(2)(a) (notice given while tax enquiry is in progress) (and not withdrawn).

226(2) If any amount of the accelerated payment is unpaid at the end of the payment period, P is liable to a penalty of 5% of that amount.

226(3) If any amount of the accelerated payment is unpaid after the end of the period of 5 months beginning with the penalty day, P is liable to a penalty of 5% of that amount.

226(4) If any amount of the accelerated payment is unpaid after the end of the period of 11 months beginning with the penalty day, P is liable to a penalty of 5% of that amount.

226(5) **"The penalty day"** means the day immediately following the end of the payment period.

226(6) Where section 223(6) (accelerated payment payable by instalments when it relates to inheritance tax payable by instalments) applies to require an amount of the accelerated payment to be paid before a later time than the end of the payment period, references in subsections (2) and (5) to the end of that period are to be read, in relation to that amount, as references to that later time.

226(7) Paragraphs 9 to 18 (other than paragraph 11(5)) of Schedule 56 to FA 2009 (provisions which apply to penalties for failures to make payments of tax on time) apply, with any necessary modifications, to a penalty under this section in relation to a failure by P to pay an amount of the accelerated payment as they apply to a penalty under that Schedule in relation to a failure by a person to pay an amount of tax.

WITHDRAWAL ETC OF ACCELERATED PAYMENT NOTICE

227 Withdrawal, modification or suspension of accelerated payment notice

227(1) In this section a **"Condition C requirement"** means one of the requirements set out in Condition C in section 219.

227(2) Where an accelerated payment notice has been given, HMRC may, at any time, by notice given to P–

(a) withdraw the notice,

(b) where the notice is given by virtue of more than one Condition C requirement being met, withdraw it to the extent it is given by virtue of one of those requirements (leaving the notice effective to the extent that it was also given by virtue of any other Condition C requirement and has not been withdrawn),

(c) reduce the amount specified in the accelerated payment notice under section 220(2)(b) or 221(2)(b), or

(d) reduce the amount specified in the accelerated payment notice under section 220(2)(d) or 221(2)(d).

227(3) Where–

(a) an accelerated payment notice is given by virtue of the Condition C requirement in section 219(4)(a), and

(b) the follower notice to which it relates is withdrawn,

HMRC must withdraw the accelerated payment notice to the extent it was given by virtue of that requirement.

227(4) Where–

(a) an accelerated payment notice is given by virtue of the Condition C requirement in section 219(4)(a), and

(b) the follower notice to which it relates is amended under section 216(7)(b) (cases where there is a new relevant final judicial ruling following a late appeal),

HMRC may by notice given to P make consequential amendments (whether under subsection (2)(c) or (d) or otherwise) to the accelerated payment notice.

227(5) Where–

(a) an accelerated payment notice is given by virtue of the Condition C requirement in section 219(4)(b), and

(b) HMRC give notice under section 312(6) of FA 2004 with the result that promoters are no longer under the duty in section 312(2) of that Act in relation to the chosen arrangements,

HMRC must withdraw the notice to the extent it was given by virtue of that requirement.

227(6) Subsection (7) applies where–

(a) an accelerated payment notice is withdrawn to the extent that it was given by virtue of a Condition C requirement,

(b) that requirement is the one stated in the notice for the purposes of section 220(6) or 221(5) (calculation of amount of the accelerated payment or of the denied advantage etc), and

(c) the notice remains effective to the extent that it was also given by virtue of any other Condition C requirement.

227(7) HMRC must, by notice given to P–

(a) modify the accelerated payment notice so as to state the remaining, or one of the remaining, Condition C requirements for the purposes of section 220(6) or 221(5),

(b) if the amount of the accelerated payment or (as the case may be) the amount of the disputed tax determined on the basis of the substituted Condition C requirement is less than the amount specified in the notice, amend that notice under subsection (2)(c) to substitute the lower amount, and

(c) if the amount of the asserted surrenderable amount is less than the amount specified in the notice, amend the notice under subsection (2)(d) to substitute the lower amount.

227(8) If a follower notice is suspended under section 216 (appeals against final rulings made out of time) for any period, an accelerated payment notice in respect of the follower notice is also suspended for that period.

227(9) Accordingly, the period during which the accelerated payment notice is suspended does not count towards the periods mentioned in the following provisions–

(a) section 223;

(b) section 55(8D) of TMA 1970;

(c) paragraph 39(11) of Schedule 10 to FA 2003;

(d) paragraph 48(8C) of Schedule 33 to FA 2013.

227(10) But the accelerated payment notice is not suspended under subsection (8) if it was also given by virtue of section 219(4)(b) or (c) and has not, to that extent, been withdrawn.

227(11) In a case within subsection (10), subsections (6) and (7) apply as they would apply were the notice withdrawn to the extent that it was given by virtue of section 219(4)(a), except that any change made to the notice under subsection (7) has effect during the period of suspension only.

227(12) Where an accelerated payment notice is withdrawn, it is to be treated as never having had effect (and any accelerated payment made in accordance with, or penalties paid by virtue of, the notice are to be repaid).

227(12A) Where, as a result of an accelerated payment notice specifying an amount under section 220(2)(d) or 221(2)(d), a notice of consent by P to a claim for group relief in respect of the amount specified (or part of it) became ineffective by virtue of section 225A(3), nothing in subsection (12) operates to revive that notice.

227(13) If, as a result of a modification made under subsection (2)(c), more than the resulting amount of the accelerated payment has already been paid by P, the excess must be repaid.

227(14) If the accelerated payment notice is amended under subsection (2)(d) or withdrawn–

(a) section 225A(2) and (3) (which prevents consent being given to group relief claims) cease to apply in relation to the released amount, and

(b) a claim for group relief may be made in respect of any part of the released amount within the period of 30 days after the day on which the notice is amended or withdrawn.

227(15) The time limits otherwise applicable to amendment of a company tax return do not apply to the extent that it makes a claim for group relief within the time allowed by subsection (14).

227(16) **"The released amount"** means–

(a) in a case where the accelerated payment notice is amended under subsection (2)(d), the amount represented by the reduction, and

(b) in a case where the accelerated payment notice is withdrawn, the amount specified under section 220(2)(d) or 221(2)(d).

History – S. 227(2)(d) (and the word ", or" preceding it) inserted and the word "or" at end para. (b) omitted by FA 2015, s. 118 and Sch. 18, para. 8(2), with effect from 26 March 2015.
In s. 227(4) the words "or (d)" inserted by FA 2015, s. 118 and Sch. 18, para. 8(3), with effect from 26 March 2015.
In s. 227(6) the word "etc" inserted by FA 2015, s. 118 and Sch. 18, para. 8(4), with effect from 26 March 2015.
S. 227(7)(c) (and the word ", and" preceding it) inserted and the word "and" at end para. (a) omitted by FA 2015, s. 118 and Sch. 18, para. 8(5), with effect from 26 March 2015.
S. 227(12A) inserted by FA 2015, s. 118 and Sch. 18, para. 8(6), with effect from 26 March 2015.
S. 227(14)–(16) inserted by FA 2015, s. 118 and Sch. 18, para. 8(7), with effect from 26 March 2015.

GROUP RELIEF CLAIMS AFTER ACCELERATED PAYMENT NOTICES

227A Group relief claims after accelerated payment notices

227A(1) This section applies where as a result of an accelerated payment notice given to P–

(a) P was prevented from consenting to a claim for group relief in respect of an amount under section 225A(2), or

(b) pursuant to section 225A(3), a consent given by P to a claim for group relief in respect of an amount was ineffective.

227A(2) If a final determination establishes that the amount P has available to surrender consists of or includes the amount referred to in subsection (1)(a) or (b) or a part of it ("the allowed amount")–

(a) section 225A(2) and (3) (which prevents consent being given to group relief claims) ceases to apply in relation to the allowed amount, and

(b) a claim for group relief in respect of any part of the allowed amount may be made within the period of 30 days after the relevant time.

227A(3) The time limits otherwise applicable to amendment of a company tax return do not apply to an amendment to the extent that it makes a claim for group relief in respect of any part of the allowed amount within the time limit allowed by subsection (2)(b).

227A(4) In this section–

"final determination" means–

(a) a conclusion stated in a closure notice under paragraph 34 of Schedule 18 to FA 1998 against which no appeal is made;

(b) the final determination of a tax appeal within paragraph (d) or (e) of section 203;

"relevant time" means–

(a) in a case within paragraph (a) above, the end of the period during which the appeal could have been made;

(b) in the case within paragraph (b) above, the end of the day on which the final determination occurs.

History – S. 227A inserted by FA 2015, s. 118 and Sch. 18, para. 9, with effect from 26 March 2015.

PARTNERS AND PARTNERSHIPS

228 Accelerated partner payments

228 Schedule 32 makes provision for accelerated partner payments and modifies this Chapter in relation to partnerships.

DEFINED TERMS

229 Defined terms used in Chapter 3

229 In this Chapter–

"the accelerated payment" has the meaning given by section 223(2);

"accelerated payment notice" has the meaning given by section 219(1);

"arrangements" has the meaning given by section 201(4);

"the asserted advantage" has the meaning given by section 219(3);

"the chosen arrangements" has the meaning given by section 219(3), except in Schedule 32 where it has the meaning given by paragraph 3(3) of that Schedule;

"the denied advantage" has the meaning given by section 220(5), except in paragraph 4 of Schedule 32 where it has the meaning given by paragraph 4(4) of that Schedule;

"designated HMRC officer" means an officer of Revenue and Customs who has been designated by the Commissioners for the purposes of this Part;

"follower notice" has the meaning given by section 204(1);

"HMRC" means Her Majesty's Revenue and Customs;

"P" has the meaning given by section 219(1);

"partner payment notice" has the meaning given by paragraph 3 of Schedule 32;

"relevant tax" has the meaning given by section 200;

"tax advantage" has the meaning given by section 201(2);

"tax appeal" has the meaning given by section 203;

"tax enquiry" has the meaning given by section 202(2).

Chapter 4 – Miscellaneous and General Provision

EXTENSION OF PART BY ORDER

232 Extension of this Part by order

232(1) The Treasury may by order amend section 200 (definition of "relevant tax") so as to extend this Part to any other tax.

232(2) An order under this section may include–

(a) provision in respect of that other tax corresponding to the provision made by sections 224 and 225,

(b) consequential and supplemental provision, and

(c) transitional and transitory provision and savings.

232(3) For the purposes of subsection (1) or (2) an order under this section may amend this Part (other than this section) or any other enactment whenever passed or made.

232(4) The power to make orders under this section is exercisable by statutory instrument.

232(5) An order under this section may only be made if a draft of the instrument containing the order has been laid before and approved by a resolution of the House of Commons.

232(6) In this section **"tax"** includes duty.

CONSEQUENTIAL AMENDMENTS

233 Consequential amendments

233 Schedule 33 contains consequential amendments.

PART 5 – PROMOTERS OF TAX AVOIDANCE SCHEMES

INTRODUCTION

234 Meaning of "relevant proposal" and "relevant arrangements"

234(1) **"Relevant proposal"** means a proposal for arrangements which (if entered into) would be relevant arrangements (whether the proposal relates to a particular person or to any person who may seek to take advantage of it).

234(2) Arrangements are **"relevant arrangements"** if–

(a) they enable, or might be expected to enable, any person to obtain a tax advantage, and

(b) the main benefit, or one of the main benefits, that might be expected to arise from the arrangements is the obtaining of that advantage.

234(3) **"Tax advantage"** includes–

(a) relief or increased relief from tax,

(b) repayment or increased repayment of tax,

(c) avoidance or reduction of a charge to tax or an assessment to tax,

(d) avoidance of a possible assessment to tax,

(e) deferral of a payment of tax or advancement of a repayment of tax, and

(f) avoidance of an obligation to deduct or account for tax.

234(4) **"Arrangements"** includes any agreement, scheme, arrangement or understanding of any kind, whether or not legally enforceable, involving a single transaction or two or more transactions.

235 Carrying on a business "as a promoter"

235(1) A person carrying on a business in the course of which the person is, or has been, a promoter in relation to a relevant proposal or relevant arrangements carries on that business "as a promoter".

235(2) A person is a **"promoter"** in relation to a relevant proposal if the person–

(a) is to any extent responsible for the design of the proposed arrangements,

(b) makes a firm approach to another person in relation to the relevant proposal with a view to making the proposal available for implementation by that person or any other person, or

(c) makes the relevant proposal available for implementation by other persons.

235(3) A person is a **"promoter"** in relation to relevant arrangements if the person–

(a) is by virtue of subsection (2)(b) or (c), a promoter in relation to a relevant proposal which is implemented by the arrangements, or

(b) is responsible to any extent for the design, organisation or management of the arrangements.

235(4) For the purposes of this Part a person makes a firm approach to another person in relation to a relevant proposal if–

(a) the person communicates information about the relevant proposal to the other person at a time when the proposed arrangements have been substantially designed,

(b) the communication is made with a view to that other person or any other person entering into transactions forming part of the proposed arrangements, and

(c) the information communicated includes an explanation of the tax advantage that might be expected to be obtained from the proposed arrangements.

235(5) For the purposes of subsection (4) proposed arrangements have been substantially designed at any time if by that time the nature of the transactions to form them (or part of them) has been sufficiently developed for it to be reasonable to believe that a person who wished to obtain the tax advantage mentioned in subsection (4)(c) might enter into–

(a) transactions of the nature developed, or

(b) transactions not substantially different from transactions of that nature.

235(6) A person is not a promoter in relation to a relevant proposal or relevant arrangements by reason of anything done in prescribed circumstances.

235(7) Regulations under subsection (6) may contain provision having retrospective effect.

Statutory instruments – SI 2015/130: partly made under s. 235(6) and (7).

236 Meaning of "intermediary"

236 For the purposes of this Part a person ("A") is an intermediary in relation to a relevant proposal if–

(a) A communicates information about the relevant proposal to another person in the course of a business,

(b) the communication is made with a view to that other person, or any other person, entering into transactions forming part of the proposed arrangements, and

(c) A is not a promoter in relation to the relevant proposal.

CONDUCT NOTICES

237 Duty to give conduct notice

237(1) Subsections (5) to (9) apply if an authorised officer becomes aware at any time that a person ("P") who is carrying on a business as a promoter–

(a) has, in the period of 3 years ending with that time, met one or more threshold conditions, and

(b) was carrying on a business as a promoter when P met that condition.

237(1A) Subsections (5) to (9) also apply if an authorised officer becomes aware at any time ("the relevant time") that–

(a) a person has, in the period of 3 years ending with the relevant time, met one or more threshold conditions,

(b) at the relevant time another person ("P") meets one or more of those conditions by virtue of Part 2 of Schedule 34 (meeting the threshold conditions: bodies corporate and partnerships), and

(c) P is, at the relevant time, carrying on a business as a promoter.

237(2) Part 1 of Schedule 34 sets out the threshold conditions and describes how they are met.

237(3) Part 2 of that Schedule contains provision about when a person is treated as meeting a threshold condition.

237(4) See also Schedule 36 (which contains provision about the meeting of threshold conditions and other conditions by partnerships).

237(5) The authorised officer must determine–

(a) *in a case within subsection* (1), whether or not P's meeting of the condition mentioned in subsection (1)(a) (or, if more than one condition is met, the meeting of all of those conditions, taken together) should be regarded as significant in view of the purposes of this Part, or

(b) in a case within subsection (1A), whether or not–
(i) the meeting of the condition by the person as mentioned in subsection (1A)(a) (or, if more than one condition is met, the meeting of all of those conditions, taken together), and
(ii) P's meeting of the condition (or conditions) as mentioned in subsection (1A)(b),
should be regarded as significant in view of those purposes.

237(6) Subsection (5) does not apply if a conduct notice or a monitoring notice already has effect in relation to P.

237(7) If the authorised officer determines under subsection (5)(a) that P's meeting of the condition or conditions in question should be regarded as significant, the officer must give P a conduct notice, unless subsection (8) applies.

237(7A) If the authorised officer determines under subsection (5)(b) that both–
(a) the meeting of the condition or conditions by the person as mentioned in subsection (1A)(a), and
(b) P's meeting of the condition or conditions as mentioned in subsection (1A)(b),
should be regarded as significant, the officer must give P a conduct notice, unless subsection (8) applies.

237(8) This subsection applies if the authorised officer determines that, having regard to the extent of the impact that P's activities as a promoter are likely to have on the collection of tax, it is inappropriate to give P a conduct notice.

237(9) The authorised officer must determine under subsection (5) that the meeting of the condition (or all the conditions) should be regarded as significant if the condition (or any of the conditions) is in any of the following paragraphs of Schedule 34–
(a) paragraph 2 (deliberate tax defaulters);
(b) paragraph 3 (breach of Banking Code of Practice);
(c) paragraph 4 (dishonest tax agents);
(d) paragraph 6 (persons charged with certain offences);
(e) paragraph 7 (opinion notice of GAAR Advisory Panel).

237(10) If, as a result of subsection (1A), subsections (5) to (9) apply to a person, this does not prevent the giving of a conduct notice to the person mentioned in subsection (1A)(a).

History – S. 237(1A) inserted by FA 2015, s. 119 and Sch. 19, para. 2(2), with effect for the purposes of determining whether a person meets a threshold condition in a period of three years ending on or after 26 March 2015 (Royal Assent).
In s. 237(3) the words "when a person is treated as meeting a threshold condition" substituted for the words "the meeting of threshold conditions by bodies corporate" by FA 2015, s. 119 and Sch. 19, para. 2(3), with effect for the purposes of determining whether a person meets a threshold condition in a period of three years ending on or after 26 March 2015 (Royal Assent).
S. 237(5) substituted by FA 2015, s. 119 and Sch. 19, para. 2(4), with effect for the purposes of determining whether a person meets a threshold condition in a period of three years ending on or after 26 March 2015 (Royal Assent). Former s. 237(5) read as follows:
"**237(5)** The authorised officer must determine whether or not P's meeting of the condition mentioned in subsection (1)(a) (or, as the case requires, P's meeting of all those conditions, taken together) should be regarded as significant in view of the purposes of this Part."
In s. 237(7) the words "subsection (5)(a)" substituted for the words "subsection (5)" by FA 2015, s. 119 and Sch. 19, para. 2(5), with effect for the purposes of determining whether a person meets a threshold condition in a period of three years ending on or after 26 March 2015 (Royal Assent).
S. 237(7A) inserted by FA 2015, s. 119 and Sch. 19, para. 2(6), with effect for the purposes of determining whether a person meets a threshold condition in a period of three years ending on or after 26 March 2015 (Royal Assent).
In s. 237(9) the words "mentioned in subsection (1)(a)" omitted by FA 2015, s. 119 and Sch. 19, para. 2(7), with effect for the purposes of determining whether a person meets a threshold condition in a period of three years ending on or after 26 March 2015 (Royal Assent).
S. 237(10) inserted by FA 2015, s. 119 and Sch. 19, para. 2(8), with effect for the purposes of determining whether a person meets a threshold condition in a period of three years ending on or after 26 March 2015 (Royal Assent).

237A Duty to give conduct notice: defeat of promoted arrangements

237A(1) If an authorised officer becomes aware at any time ("the relevant time") that a person ("P") who is carrying on a business as a promoter meets any of the conditions in subsections (11) to (13), the officer must determine whether or not P's meeting of that condition should be regarded as significant in view of the purposes of this Part.
But see also subsection (14).

237A(2) An authorised officer must make the determination set out in subsection (3) if the officer becomes aware at any time ("the section 237A(2) relevant time") that–
(a) a person meets a condition in subsection (11), (12) or (13), and
(b) at the section 237A(2) relevant time another person ("P"), who is carrying on a business as a promoter, meets that condition by virtue of Part 4 of Schedule 34A (meeting the section 237A conditions: bodies corporate and partnerships).

237A(3) The authorised officer must determine whether or not–
(a) the meeting of the condition by the person as mentioned in subsection (2)(a), and
(b) P's meeting of the condition as mentioned in subsection (2)(b),
should be regarded as significant in view of the purposes of this Part.

237A(4) Subsections (1) and (2) do not apply if a conduct notice or monitoring notice already has effect in relation to P.

237A(5) Subsection (1) does not apply if, at the relevant time, an authorised officer is under a duty to make a determination under section 237(5) in relation to P.

237A(6) Subsection (2) does not apply if, at the section 237A(2) relevant time, an authorised officer is under a duty to make a determination under section 237(5) in relation to P.

237A(7) But in a case where subsection (1) does not apply because of subsection (5), or subsection (2) does not apply because of subsection (6), subsection (5) of section 237 has effect as if–

(a) the references in paragraph (a) of that subsection to "subsection (1)", and "subsection (1)(a)" included subsection (1) of this section, and

(b) in paragraph (b) of that subsection the reference to "subsection (2)(a)" included a reference to subsection (2)(a) of this section and the reference to subsection (2)(b) included a reference to subsection (2)(b) of this section.

237A(8) If the authorised officer determines under subsection (1) that P's meeting of the condition in question should be regarded as significant, the officer must give P a conduct notice, unless subsection (10) applies.

237A(9) If the authorised officer determines under subsection (3) that–

(a) the meeting of the condition by the person as mentioned in subsection (2)(a), and

(b) P's meeting of the condition as mentioned in subsection (2)(b),

should be regarded as significant in view of the purposes of this Part, the officer must give P a conduct notice, unless subsection (10) applies.

237A(10) This subsection applies if the authorised officer determines that, having regard to the extent of the impact that P's activities as a promoter are likely to have on the collection of tax, it is inappropriate to give P a conduct notice.

237A(11) The condition in this subsection is that in the period of 3 years ending with the relevant time at least 3 relevant defeats have occurred in relation to P.

237A(12) The condition in this subsection is that at least two relevant defeats have occurred in relation to P at times when a single defeat notice under section 241A(2) or (6) had effect in relation to P.

237A(13) The condition in this subsection is that at least one relevant defeat has occurred in relation to P at a time when a double defeat notice under section 241A(3) had effect in relation to P.

237A(14) A determination that the condition in subsection (12) or (13) is met cannot be made unless–

(a) the defeat notice in question still has effect when the determination is made, or

(b) the determination is made on or before the 90th day after the day on which the defeat notice in question ceased to have effect.

237A(15) Schedule 34A sets out the circumstances in which a **"relevant defeat"** occurs in relation to a person and includes provision limiting what can amount to a further relevant defeat in relation to a person (see paragraph 6).

History – S. 237A inserted by FA 2016, s. 160(2), with effect from 15 September 2016 (Royal Assent).

Cross references – FA 2016, s. 160(20)–(25): defeats treated as not having occurred.

237B Duty to give further conduct notice where provisional notice not complied with

237B(1) An authorised officer must give a conduct notice to a person ("P") who is carrying on a business as a promoter if–

(a) a conduct notice given to P under section 237A(8)–

  (i) has ceased to have effect otherwise than as a result of section 237D(2) or 241(3) or (4), and

  (ii) was provisional immediately before it ceased to have effect,

(b) the officer determines that P had failed to comply with one or more conditions in the conduct notice,

(c) the conduct notice relied on a Case 3 relevant defeat,

(d) since the time when the conduct notice ceased to have effect, one or more relevant defeats falling within subsection (2) have occurred in relation to–

  (i) P, and

  (ii) any arrangements to which the Case 3 relevant defeat also relates, and

(e) had that relevant defeat or (as the case may be) those relevant defeats, occurred before the conduct notice ceased to have effect, an authorised officer would have been required to notify the person under section 237C(3) that the notice was no longer provisional.

237B(2) A relevant defeat falls within this subsection if it occurs by virtue of Case 1 or Case 2 in Schedule 34A.

237B(3) Subsection (1) does not apply if the authorised officer determines that, having regard to the extent of the impact that the person's activities as a promoter are likely to have on the collection of tax, it is inappropriate to give the person a conduct notice.

237B(4) Subsection (1) does not apply if a conduct notice or monitoring notice already has effect in relation to the person.

237B(5) For the purposes of this Part a conduct notice **"relies on a Case 3 relevant defeat"** if it could not have been given under the following condition.

The condition is that paragraph 9 of Schedule 34A had effect with the substitution of "100% of the tested arrangements" for "75% of the tested arrangements".

History – S. 237B inserted by FA 2016, s. 160(2), with effect from 15 September 2016 (Royal Assent).

237C When a conduct notice given under section 237A(8) is "provisional"

237C(1) This section applies to a conduct notice which–

(a) is given to a person under section 237A(8), and

(b) relies on a Case 3 relevant defeat.

237C(2) The notice is **"provisional"** at all times when it has effect, unless an authorised officer notifies the person that the notice is no longer provisional.

237C(3) An authorised officer must notify the person that the notice is no longer provisional if subsection (4) or (5) applies.

237C(4) This subsection applies if–

(a) the condition in subsection (5)(a) is not met, and

(b) a full relevant defeat occurs in relation to P.

237C(5) This subsection applies if–

(a) two, or all three, of the relevant defeats by reference to which the conduct notice is given would not have been relevant defeats if paragraph 9 of Schedule 34A had effect with the substitution of "100% of the tested arrangements" for "75% of the tested arrangements", and

(b) the same number of full relevant defeats occur in relation to P.

237C(6) A **"full relevant defeat"** occurs in relation to P if–

(a) a relevant defeat occurs in relation to P otherwise than by virtue of Case 3 in paragraph 9 of Schedule 34A, or

(b) circumstances arise which would be a relevant defeat in relation to P by virtue of paragraph 9 of Schedule 34A if that paragraph had effect with the substitution of "100% of the tested arrangements" for "75% of the tested arrangements".

237C(7) In determining under subsection (6) whether a full relevant defeat has occurred in relation to P, assume that in paragraph 6 of Schedule 34A (provision limiting what can amount to a further relevant defeat in relation to a person) the first reference to a **"relevant defeat"** does not include a relevant defeat by virtue of Case 3 in paragraph 9 of Schedule 34A.

History – S. 237C inserted by FA 2016, s. 160(2), with effect from 15 September 2016 (Royal Assent).

237D Judicial ruling upholding asserted tax advantage: effect on conduct notice which is provisional

237D(1) Subsection (2) applies if at any time–

(a) a conduct notice which relies on a Case 3 relevant defeat (see section 237B(5)) is provisional, and

(b) a court or tribunal upholds a corresponding tax advantage which has been asserted in connection with any of the related arrangements to which that relevant defeat relates (see paragraph 5(2) of Schedule 34A).

237D(2) The conduct notice ceases to have effect when that judicial ruling becomes final.

237D(3) An authorised officer must give the person to whom the conduct notice was given a written notice stating that the conduct notice has ceased to have effect.

237D(4) For the purposes of this section, a tax advantage is **"asserted"** in connection with any arrangements if a person makes a return, claim or election on the basis that the tax advantage arises from those arrangements.

In relation to the arrangements mentioned in paragraph (b) of subsection (1) **"corresponding tax advantage"** means a tax advantage corresponding to any tax advantage the counteraction of which contributed to the relevant defeat mentioned in that paragraph.

237D(5) For the purposes of this section a court or tribunal **"upholds"** a tax advantage if–

(a) the court or tribunal makes a ruling to the effect that no part of the tax advantage is to be counteracted, and

(b) that judicial ruling is final.

237D(6) For the purposes of this Part of this Act a judicial ruling is **"final"** if it is–

(a) a ruling of the Supreme Court, or

(b) a ruling of any other court or tribunal in circumstances where–

(i) no appeal may be made against the ruling,

(ii) if an appeal may be made against the ruling with permission, the time limit for applications has expired and either no application has been made or permission has been refused,

(iii) if such permission to appeal against the ruling has been granted or is not required, no appeal has been made within the time limit for appeals, or

(iv) if an appeal was made, it was abandoned or otherwise disposed of before it was determined by the court or tribunal to which it was addressed.

237D(7) In this section references to **"counteraction"** include anything referred to as a counteraction in any of Conditions A to F in paragraphs 11 to 16 of Schedule 34A.

History – S. 237D inserted by FA 2016, s. 160(2), with effect from 15 September 2016 (Royal Assent).

238 Contents of a conduct notice

238(1) A conduct notice is a notice requiring the person to whom it has been given ("the recipient") to comply with conditions specified in the notice.

238(2) Before deciding on the terms of a conduct notice, the authorised officer must give the person to whom the notice is to be given an opportunity to comment on the proposed terms of the notice.

238(3) A notice may include only conditions that it is reasonable to impose for any of the following purposes–

(a) to ensure that the recipient provides adequate information to its clients about relevant proposals, and relevant arrangements, in relation to which the recipient is a promoter;

(b) to ensure that the recipient provides adequate information about relevant proposals in relation to which it is a promoter to persons who are intermediaries in relation to those proposals;

(c) to ensure that the recipient does not fail to comply with any duty under a specified disclosure provision;

(d) to ensure that the recipient does not discourage others from complying with any obligation to disclose to HMRC information of a description specified in the notice;

(e) to ensure that the recipient does not enter into an agreement with another person ("C") which relates to a relevant proposal or relevant arrangements in relation to which the recipient is a promoter, on terms which–

(i) impose a contractual obligation on C which falls within paragraph 11(2) or (3) of Schedule 34 (contractual terms restricting disclosure), or

(ii) impose on C obligations within both paragraph 11(4) and (5) of that Schedule (contractual terms requiring contribution to fighting funds and restricting settlement of proceedings);

(f) to ensure that the recipient does not promote relevant proposals or relevant arrangements which rely on, or involve a proposal to rely on, one or more contrived or abnormal steps to produce a tax advantage;

(g) to ensure that the recipient does not fail to comply with any stop notice which has effect under paragraph 12 of Schedule 34.

238(4) References in subsection (3) to ensuring that adequate information is provided about proposals or arrangements include–

(a) ensuring the adequacy of the description of the arrangements or proposed arrangements;

(b) ensuring that the information includes an adequate assessment of the risk that the arrangements or proposed arrangements will fail;

(c) ensuring that the information does not falsely state, and is not likely to create a false impression, that HMRC have (formally or informally) considered, approved or expressed a particular opinion in relation to the proposal or arrangements.

238(5) In subsection (3)(c) **"specified disclosure provision"** means a disclosure provision that is specified in the notice; and for this purpose **"disclosure provision"** means any of the following–

(a) section 308 of FA 2004 (disclosure of tax avoidance schemes: duties of promoter);

(b) section 312 of FA 2004 (duty of promoter to notify client of number);

(c) sections 313ZA and 313ZB of FA 2004 (duties to provide details of clients and certain others);

(d) Part 1 of Schedule 36 to FA 2008 (duties to provide information and produce documents).

238(6) In subsection (4)(b) **"fail"**, in relation to arrangements or proposed arrangements, means not result in a tax advantage which the arrangements or (as the case may be) proposed arrangements might be expected to result in.

238(7) The Treasury may by regulations amend the definition of **"disclosure provision"** in subsection (5).

239 Section 238: supplementary

239(1) In section 238 the following expressions are to be interpreted as follows.

239(2) **"Adequate"** means adequate having regard to what it might be reasonable for a client or (as the case may be) an intermediary to expect; and **"adequacy"** is to be interpreted accordingly.

239(3) A person ("C") is a "client" of a promoter, if at any time when a conduct notice has effect, the promoter–

(a) makes a firm approach to C in relation to a relevant proposal with a view to the promoter making the proposal available for implementation by C or another person;

(b) makes a relevant proposal available for implementation by C;

(c) takes part in the organisation or management of relevant arrangements entered into by C.

239(4) The recipient of a conduct notice **"promotes"** a relevant proposal if it–

(a) takes part in designing the proposal,

(b) makes a firm approach to a person in relation to the proposal with a view to making the proposal available for implementation by that person or another person, or

(c) makes the proposal available for implementation by persons (other than the recipient).

239(5) The recipient of a conduct notice **"promotes"** relevant arrangements if it takes part in designing, organising or managing the arrangements.

240 Amendment or withdrawal of conduct notice

240(1) This section applies where a conduct notice has been given to a person.

240(2) An authorised officer may at any time amend the notice.

240(3) An authorised officer–

(a) may withdraw the notice if the officer thinks it is not necessary for it to continue to have effect, and

(b) in considering whether or not that is necessary must take into account the person's record of compliance, or failure to comply, with the conditions in the notice.

241 Duration of conduct notice

241(1) A conduct notice has effect from the date specified in it as its commencement date.

241(2) A conduct notice ceases to have effect–

(a) at the end of the period of two years beginning with its commencement date, or

(b) if an earlier date is specified in it as its termination date, at the end of that day.

241(3) A conduct notice ceases to have effect if withdrawn by an authorised officer under section 240.

241(4) A conduct notice ceases to have effect in relation to a person when a monitoring notice takes effect in relation to that person.

241(5) See also section 237D(2) (provisional conduct notice affected by judicial ruling).

History – S. 241(5) inserted by FA 2016, s. 160(6), with effect from 15 September 2016 (Royal Assent).

DEFEAT NOTICES

History – Heading inserted by FA 2016, s. 160(3), with effect from 15 September 2016 (Royal Assent).

241A Defeat notices

241A(1) This section applies in relation to a person ("P") only if P is carrying on a business as a promoter.

241A(2) An authorised officer, or an officer of Revenue and Customs with the approval of an authorised officer, may give P a notice if the officer concerned has become aware of one (and only one) relevant defeat which has occurred in relation to P in the period of 3 years ending with the day on which the notice is given.

241A(3) An authorised officer, or an officer of Revenue and Customs with the approval of an authorised officer, may give P a notice if the officer concerned has become aware of two (but not more than two) relevant defeats which have occurred in relation to P in the period of 3 years ending with the day on which the notice is given.

241A(4) A notice under this section must be given by the end of the 90 days beginning with the day on which the matters mentioned in subsection (2) or (as the case may be) (3) come to the attention of HMRC.

241A(5) Subsection (6) applies if–

(a) a single defeat notice which had been given to P (under subsection (2) or (6)) ceases to have effect as a result of section 241B(1), and

(b) in the period when the defeat notice had effect a relevant defeat ("the further relevant defeat") occurred in relation to P.

241A(6) An authorised officer or an officer of Revenue and Customs with the approval of an authorised officer may give P a notice in respect of the further relevant defeat (regardless of whether or not it occurred in the period of 3 years ending with the day on which the notice is given).

241A(7) In this Part–

(a) **"single defeat notice"** means a notice under subsection (2) or (6);

(b) **"double defeat notice"** means a notice under subsection (3);

(c) **"defeat notice"** means a single defeat notice or a double defeat notice.

241A(8) A defeat notice must–

(a) set out the dates on which the look-forward period for the notice begins and ends;

(b) in the case of a single defeat notice, explain the effect of section 237A(12);

(c) in the case of a double defeat notice, explain the effect of section 237A(13).

241A(9) HMRC may specify what further information must be included in a defeat notice.

241A(10) **"Look-forward period"**–

(a) in relation to a defeat notice under subsection (2) or (3), means the period of 5 years beginning with the day after the day on which the notice is given;

(b) in relation to a defeat notice under subsection (6), means the period beginning with the day after the day on which the notice is given and ending at the end of the period of 5 years beginning with the day on which the further relevant defeat mentioned in subsection (6) occurred in relation to P.

241A(11) A defeat notice has effect throughout its look-forward period unless it ceases to have effect earlier in accordance with section 241B(1) or (4).

History – S. 241A inserted by FA 2016, s. 160(3), with effect from 15 September 2016 (Royal Assent).

Cross references – FA 2016, s. 160(20)–(25): defeats treated as not having occurred.

241B Judicial ruling upholding asserted tax advantage: effect on defeat notice

241B(1) If the relevant defeat to which a single defeat notice relates is overturned (see subsection (5)), the notice has no further effect on and after the day on which it is overturned.

241B(2) Subsection (3) applies if one (and only one) of the relevant defeats in respect of which a double defeat notice was given is overturned.

241B(3) The notice is to be treated for the purposes of this Part (including this section) as if it had always been a single defeat notice given (in respect of the other of the two relevant defeats) on the date on which *the notice was in fact given.*

The look-forward period for the notice is accordingly unchanged.

241B(4) If both the relevant defeats to which a double defeat notice relates are overturned (on the same date), that notice has no further effect on and after that date.

241B(5) A relevant defeat specified in a defeat notice is **"overturned"** if–

(a) the notice could not have specified that relevant defeat if paragraph 9 of Schedule 34A had effect with the substitution of "100% of the tested arrangements" for "75% of the tested arrangements", and

(b) at a time when the notice has effect a court or tribunal upholds a corresponding tax advantage which has been asserted in connection with any of the related arrangements to which the relevant defeat relates (see paragraph 5(2) of Schedule 34A).

Accordingly the relevant defeat is overturned on the day on which the judicial ruling mentioned in paragraph (b) becomes final.

241B(6) If a defeat notice ceases to have effect as a result of subsection (1) or (4) an authorised officer, or an officer of Revenue and Customs with the approval of an authorised officer, must notify the person to whom the notice was given that it has ceased to have effect.

241B(7) If subsection (3) has effect in relation to a defeat notice, an authorised officer, or an officer of Revenue and Customs with the approval of an authorised officer, must notify the person of the effect of that subsection.

241B(8) For the purposes of this section, a tax advantage is **"asserted"** in connection with any arrangements if a person makes a return, claim or election on the basis that the tax advantage arises from those arrangements.

241B(9) In relation to the arrangements mentioned in paragraph (b) of subsection (5) **"corresponding tax advantage"** means a tax advantage corresponding to any tax advantage the counteraction of which contributed to the relevant defeat mentioned in that paragraph.

241B(10) For the purposes of this section a court or tribunal **"upholds"** a tax advantage if–

(a) the court or tribunal makes a ruling to the effect that no part of the tax advantage is to be counteracted, and

(b) that judicial ruling is final.

241B(11) In this section references to **"counteraction"** include anything referred to as a counteraction in any of Conditions A to F in paragraphs 11 to 16 of Schedule 34A.

History – S. 241B inserted by FA 2016, s. 160(3), with effect from 15 September 2016 (Royal Assent).

MONITORING NOTICES: PROCEDURE AND PUBLICATION

242 Monitoring notices: duty to apply to tribunal

242(1) If–

(a) a conduct notice has effect in relation to a person who is carrying on a business as a promoter, and

(b) an authorised officer determines that the person has failed to comply with one or more conditions in the notice,

the authorised officer must apply to the tribunal for approval to give the person a monitoring notice.

242(2) An application under subsection (1) must include a draft of the monitoring notice.

242(3) Subsection (1) does not apply if–

(a) the condition (or all the conditions) mentioned in subsection (1)(b) were imposed under subsection (3)(a), (b) or (c) of section 238, and

(b) the authorised officer considers that the failure to comply with the condition (or all the conditions, taken together) is such a minor matter that it should be disregarded for the purposes of this section.

242(4) Where an authorised officer makes an application to the tribunal under subsection (1), the officer must at the same time give notice to the person to whom the application relates.

242(5) The notice under subsection (4) must state which condition (or conditions) the authorised officer has determined under subsection (1)(b) that the person has failed to comply with and the reasons for that determination.

242(6) At a time when a notice given under section 237A is provisional, no determination is to be made under subsection (1) in respect of the notice.

242(7) If a promoter fails to comply with conditions in a conduct notice at a time when the conduct notice is provisional, nothing in subsection (6) prevents those failures from being taken into account under subsection (1) at any subsequent time when the conduct notice is not provisional.

History – S. 242(6) and (7) inserted by FA 2016, s. 160(4), with effect from 15 September 2016 (Royal Assent).

243 Monitoring notices: tribunal approval

243(1) On an application under section 242, the tribunal may approve the giving of a monitoring notice only if–

(a) the tribunal is satisfied that, in the circumstances, the authorised officer would be justified in giving the monitoring notice, and

(b) the person to whom the monitoring notice is to be given ("the affected person") has been given a reasonable opportunity to make representations to the tribunal.

243(2) The tribunal may amend the draft notice included with the application under section 242.

243(3) If the representations that the affected person makes to the tribunal include a statement that in the affected person's view it was not reasonable to include the condition mentioned in section 242(1)(b) in the conduct notice, the tribunal must refuse to approve the giving of the monitoring notice if it is satisfied that it was not reasonable to include that condition (but see subsection (4)).

243(4) If the representations made to the tribunal include the statement described in subsection (3) and the determination under section 242(1)(b) is a determination that there has been a failure to comply with more than one condition in the conduct notice–

(a) subsection (3) does not apply, but

(b) in deciding whether or not to approve the giving of the monitoring notice, the tribunal is to assume, in the case of any condition that the tribunal considers it was not reasonable to include in the conduct notice, that there has been no failure to comply with that condition.

244 Monitoring notices: content and issuing

244(1) Where the tribunal has approved the giving of a monitoring notice, the authorised officer must give the notice to the person to whom it relates.

244(2) A monitoring notice given under subsection (1) or paragraph 9 or 10 of Schedule 36 must–

(a) explain the effect of the monitoring notice and specify the date from which it takes effect;

(b) inform the recipient of the right to request the withdrawal of the monitoring notice under section 245.

244(3) In addition, a monitoring notice must–

(a) if given under subsection (1), state which condition (or conditions) it has been determined the person has failed to comply with and the reasons for that determination;

(b) if given under paragraph 9 or 10 of Schedule 36, state the date of the original monitoring notice and name the partnership to which that notice was given.

244(4) The date specified under subsection (2)(a) must not be earlier than the date on which the monitoring notice is given.

244(5) In this Part, a person in relation to whom a monitoring notice has effect is called a "monitored promoter".

245 Withdrawal of monitoring notice

245(1) A person in relation to whom a monitoring notice has effect may, at any time after the end of the period of 12 months beginning with the end of the appeal period, request that the notice should cease to have effect.

245(2) The **"appeal period"** means–

(a) the period during which an appeal could be brought against the approval by the tribunal of the giving of the monitoring notice, or

(b) where an appeal mentioned in paragraph (a) has been brought, the period during which that appeal has not been finally determined, withdrawn or otherwise disposed of.

245(3) A request under this section is to be made in writing to an authorised officer.

245(4) Where a request is made under this section, an authorised officer must within 30 days beginning with the day on which the request is received determine either–

(a) that the monitoring notice is to cease to have effect, or

(b) that the request is to be refused.

245(5) The matters to be taken into account by an authorised officer in making a determination under subsection (4) include–

(a) whether or not the person subject to the monitoring notice has, since the time when the notice took effect, engaged in behaviour of a sort that conditions included in a conduct notice in accordance with section 238(3) could be used to regulate;

(b) whether or not it appears likely that the person will in the future engage in such behaviour;

(c) the person's record of compliance, or failure to comply, with obligations imposed on it under this Part, since the time when the monitoring notice took effect.

245(6) An authorised officer–

(a) may withdraw a monitoring notice if the officer thinks it is not necessary for it to continue to have effect, and

(b) in considering whether or not that is necessary, the officer must take into account the matters in paragraphs (a) to (c) of subsection (5).

245(7) If the authorised officer makes a determination under subsection (4)(a), or decides to withdraw a monitoring notice under subsection (6), the officer must also determine that the person is, or is not, to be given a follow-on conduct notice.

245(8) **"Follow-on conduct notice"** means a conduct notice taking effect immediately after the monitoring notice ceases to have effect.

245(9) Where the monitoring notice mentioned in subsection (1) is a replacement monitoring notice–

(a) in subsection (1) the reference to the end of the appeal period is to be read as a reference to whichever is the later of the end of the appeal period for the original monitoring notice and the date the replacement monitoring notice takes effect, and

(b) in subsection (5)(a) and (c) the time referred to is to be read as the time when the original monitoring notice (see paragraph 11(2) of Schedule 36) took effect.

246 Notification of determination under section 245

246(1) Where an authorised officer makes a determination under section 245(4), that officer, or an officer of Revenue and Customs with that officer's approval, must notify the person who made the request of the determination.

246(2) If the determination is that the monitoring notice is to cease to have effect, the notice must–

(a) specify the date from which the monitoring notice is to cease to have effect, and

(b) inform the person of the determination made under section 245(7).

246(3) If the determination is that the request is to be refused, the notice must inform the person who made the request–

(a) of the reasons for the refusal, and

(b) of the right to appeal under section 247.

247 Appeal against refusal to withdraw monitoring notice

247(1) A person may appeal against a refusal by an authorised officer of a request that a monitoring notice should cease to have effect.

247(2) Notice of appeal must be given–

(a) in writing to the officer who gave the notice of the refusal under section 245, and

(b) within the period of 30 days beginning with the day on which notice of the refusal was given.

247(3) The notice of appeal must state the grounds of appeal.

247(4) On an appeal that is notified to the tribunal, the tribunal may–

(a) confirm the refusal, or

(b) direct that the monitoring notice is to cease to have effect.

247(5) Subject to this section, the provisions of Part 5 of TMA 1970 relating to appeals have effect in relation to an appeal under this section.

248 Publication by HMRC

248(1) An authorised officer may publish the fact that a person is a monitored promoter.

248(2) Publication under subsection (1) may also include the following information about the monitored promoter–

(a) its name;

(b) its business address or registered office;

(c) the nature of the business mentioned in section 242(1)(a);

(d) any other information that the authorised officer considers it appropriate to publish in order to make clear the monitored promoter's identity.

248(3) The reference in subsection (2)(a) to the monitored promoter's name includes any name under which it carries on a business as a promoter and any previous name or pseudonym.

248(4) Publication under subsection (1) may also include a statement of which of the conditions in a conduct notice it has been determined that the person (or, in the case of a replacement monitoring notice, the person to whom the original monitoring notice was given) has failed to comply with.

248(5) Publication may not take place before the end of the appeal period (or, in the case of a replacement monitoring notice, the appeal period for the original monitoring notice).

248(6) The **"appeal period"**, in relation to a monitoring notice, means–

(a) the period during which an appeal could be brought against the approval by the tribunal of the giving of the notice, or

(b) where an appeal mentioned in paragraph (a) has been brought, the period during which that appeal has not been finally determined, withdrawn or otherwise disposed of.

248(7) Publication under this section is to be in such manner as the authorised officer thinks fit; but see subsection (8).

248(8) If an authorised officer publishes the fact that a person is a monitored promoter and the monitoring notice is withdrawn, the officer must publish the fact of the withdrawal in the same way as the officer published the fact that the person was a monitored promoter.

249 Publication by monitored promoter

249(1) A person who is given a monitoring notice ("the monitored promoter") must give the persons mentioned in subsection (6) a notice stating–

(a) that it is a monitored promoter, and

(b) which of the conditions in a conduct notice it has been determined that it (or, if the monitoring notice is a replacement monitoring notice, the person to whom that notice was given) has failed to comply with.

249(2) If the monitoring notice is a replacement monitoring notice, the notice under subsection (1) must also identify the original monitoring notice.

249(3) If regulations made by the Commissioners so require, the monitored promoter must publish on the internet–

(a) the information mentioned in paragraph (a) and (b) of subsection (1), and

(b) its promoter reference number (see section 250).

249(4) Subsection (1) and any duty imposed under subsection (3) or (10) do not apply until the end of the period of 10 days beginning with the end of the appeal period (and also see subsection (9)).

249(5) The **"appeal period"** means–

(a) the period during which an appeal could be brought against the approval by the tribunal of the giving of the monitoring notice, or

(b) where an appeal mentioned in paragraph (a) has been brought, the period during which that appeal has not been finally determined, withdrawn or otherwise disposed of.

249(6) The notice under subsection (1) must be given–

(a) to any person who becomes a client of the monitored promoter while the monitoring notice has effect, and

(b) (except in a case where the monitoring notice is a replacement monitoring notice) any person who is a client of the monitored promoter at the time the monitoring notice takes effect.

249(7) A person ("C") is a client of a monitored promoter at the time a monitoring notice takes effect if during the period beginning with the date the conduct notice mentioned in subsection (1)(b) takes effect and ending with that time the promoter–

(a) made a firm approach to C in relation to a relevant proposal with a view to the promoter making the proposal available for implementation by C or another person;

(b) made a relevant proposal available for implementation by C;

(c) took part in the organisation or management of relevant arrangements entered into by C.

249(8) A person becomes a client of a monitored promoter if the promoter does any of the things mentioned in paragraph (a) to (c) of subsection (7) in relation to that person.

249(9) In the case of a person falling within subsection (6)(a), notice under subsection (1) may be given within the period of 10 days beginning with the day on which the person first became a client of the monitored promoter if that period would expire at a later date than the date on which notification would otherwise be required by virtue of subsection (4).

249(10) A monitored promoter must also include in any prescribed publication or prescribed correspondence–

(a) the information mentioned in paragraph (a) and (b) of subsection (1), and

(b) its promoter reference number (see section 250).

249(11) Notification under subsection (1), publication under subsection (3) or inclusion of the information required by subsection (10) is to be in such form and manner as is prescribed.

249(12) Where the monitoring notice mentioned in subsection (1) is a replacement monitoring notice, the reference in subsection (4) to the end of the appeal period is to be read as a reference to whichever is the later of the end of the appeal period for the original monitoring notice and the date the replacement monitoring notice takes effect.

Statutory instruments – SI 2015/549: partly made under s. 249(3), (10), and (11).

ALLOCATION AND DISTRIBUTION OF PROMOTER REFERENCE NUMBER

250 Allocation of promoter reference number

250(1) Where a monitoring notice is given to a person ("the monitored promoter") HMRC must as soon as practicable after the end of the appeal period–

(a) allocate the monitored promoter a reference number, and

(b) notify the relevant persons of that number.

250(2) **"Relevant persons"** means–

(a) the monitored promoter, and

(b) if the monitored promoter is resident outside the United Kingdom, any person who HMRC know is an intermediary in relation to a relevant proposal of the monitored promoter.

250(3) The **"appeal period"** means–

(a) the period during which an appeal could be brought against the approval by the tribunal of the giving of the monitoring notice, or

(b) where an appeal mentioned in paragraph (a) has been brought, the period during which that appeal has not been finally determined, withdrawn or otherwise disposed of.

250(4) The duty in subsection (1) does not apply if the monitoring notice is set aside following an appeal.

250(5) A number allocated to a person under this section is referred to in this Part as a "promoter reference number".

250(6) Where the monitoring notice mentioned in subsection (1) is a replacement monitoring notice–

(a) in subsection (1) the reference to the end of the appeal period is to be read as a reference to whichever is the later of the end of the appeal period for the original monitoring notice and the date the replacement monitoring notice takes effect, and

(b) in subsection (4) the reference to the monitoring notice is to be read as a reference to the original monitoring notice.

251 Duty of monitored promoter to notify clients and intermediaries of number

251(1) This section applies where a person who is a monitored promoter ("the monitored promoter") is notified under section 250 of a promoter reference number.

251(2) The monitored promoter must, within the relevant period, notify the promoter reference number to–

(a) any person who has become its client at any time in the period beginning with the day on which the monitoring notice in relation to the monitored promoter took effect and ending with the day on which the monitored promoter was notified of that number,

(b) any person who becomes its client after the end of the period mentioned in paragraph (a) but while the monitoring notice has effect,

(c) any person who the monitored promoter could reasonably be expected to know falls within subsection (4), and

(d) any person who the monitored promoter could reasonably be expected to know is a relevant intermediary in relation to a relevant proposal of the monitored promoter.

251(3) A person ("C") becomes a client of a monitored promoter if the promoter does any of the following in relation to C–

(a) makes a firm approach to C in relation to a relevant proposal with a view to the promoter making the proposal available for implementation by C or another person;

(b) makes a relevant proposal available for implementation by C;

(c) takes part in the organisation or management of relevant arrangements entered into by C.

251(4) A person falls within this subsection if during the period beginning with the date the conduct notice took effect and ending with the date on which the monitoring notice took effect the person has entered into transactions forming part of relevant arrangements and those arrangements–

(a) enable, or are likely to enable, the person to obtain a tax advantage during the time a monitoring notice has effect, and

(b) are either relevant arrangements in relation to which the monitored promoter is or was a promoter or implement a relevant proposal in relation to which the monitored promoter was a promoter.

251(5) A person is a relevant intermediary in relation to a relevant proposal of a monitored promoter if the person meets the conditions in section 236(a) to (c) (meaning of "intermediary") at any time while the monitoring notice in relation to the monitored promoter has effect.

251(6) The **"relevant period"** means–

(a) in the case of a person falling within subsection (2)(a), the period of 30 days beginning with the day of the notification mentioned in subsection (1),

(b) in the case of a person falling within subsection (2)(b), the period of 30 days beginning with the day on which the person first became a client in relation to the monitored promoter,

(c) in the case of a person falling within subsection (2)(c), the period of 30 days beginning with the later of the day of the notification mentioned in subsection (1) and the first day on which the monitored promoter could reasonably be expected to know that the person fell within subsection (4), and

(d) in the case of a person falling within subsection (2)(d), the period of 30 days beginning with the later of the day of the notification mentioned in subsection (1) and the first day on which the monitored promoter could reasonably be expected to know that the person was a relevant intermediary in relation to a relevant proposal of the monitored promoter.

251(7) In this section **"the conduct notice"** means the conduct notice that the monitored promoter failed to comply with which resulted in the monitoring notice being given to the monitored promoter.

251(8) Subsection (2)(c) is to be ignored in a case where the monitoring notice is a replacement monitoring notice.

252 Duty of those notified to notify others of promoter's number

252(1) In this section **"notified client"** means–

(a) a person who is notified of a promoter reference number under section 250 by reason of being a person falling within subsection (2)(b) of that section, and

(b) a person who is notified of a promoter reference number under section 251.

252(2) A notified client must, within 30 days of being notified as described in subsection (1), provide the promoter reference number to any other person who the notified client might reasonably be expected to know has become, or is likely to have become, a client in relation to the monitored promoter concerned at a time when the monitoring notice in relation to that monitored promoter had effect.

252(3) A person ("C") becomes a client of a monitored promoter if the promoter does any of the following in relation to C–

(a) makes a firm approach to C in relation to a relevant proposal with a view to the promoter making the proposal available for implementation by C or another person;

(b) makes a relevant proposal available for implementation by C;

(c) takes part in the organisation or management of relevant arrangements entered into by C.

252(4) Where the notified client is an intermediary in relation to a relevant proposal of the monitored promoter concerned, the notified client must also, within 30 days, provide the promoter reference number to–

(a) any person to whom the notified client has, since the monitoring notice in relation to the monitored promoter concerned took effect, communicated in the course of a business information about a relevant proposal of the monitored promoter, and

(b) any person who the notified client might reasonably be expected to know has, since that monitoring notice took effect, entered into, or is likely to enter into, transactions forming part of relevant arrangements in relation to which that monitored promoter is a promoter.

252(5) Subsection (2) or (4) does not impose a duty on a notified client to notify a person of a promoter reference number if the notified client reasonably believes that the person has already been notified of the promoter reference number (whether as a result of a duty under this section or as a result of any of the other provision of this Part).

253 Duty of persons to notify the Commissioners

253(1) If a person ("N") is notified of a promoter reference number under section 250, 251 or 252, N must report the number to the Commissioners if N expects to obtain a tax advantage from relevant arrangements in relation to which the monitored promoter to whom the reference number relates (whether that is N or another person) is the promoter.

253(2) A report under this section–

(a) must be made in (or, if prescribed circumstances exist, submitted with) each tax return made by N for a period that is or includes a period for which the arrangements enable N to obtain a tax advantage (whether in relation to the tax to which the return relates or another tax);

(b) if no tax return falls within paragraph (a), or in the case mentioned in subsection (3), must contain such information, and be made in such form and manner and within such time, as is prescribed.

253(3) The case is that the tax return in which the report would (apart from this subsection) have been made is not submitted–

(a) by the filing date, or

(b) if there is no filing date in relation to the tax return concerned, by such other time that the tax return is required to be submitted by or under any enactment.

253(4) Where N expects to obtain the tax advantage referred to in subsection (1) in respect of inheritance tax, stamp duty land tax, stamp duty reserve tax or petroleum revenue tax–

(a) subsection (2) does not apply in relation to that tax advantage, and

(b) a report under this section in respect of that tax must be in such form and manner and contain such information and be made within such time as is prescribed.

253(5) Where the relevant arrangements referred to in subsection (1) give rise to N making a claim under section 261B of TCGA 1992 (treating trade loss as CGT loss) or for loss relief under Part 4 of ITA 2007 and that claim is not contained in a tax return, a report under this section must also be made in that claim.

253(6) In this section **"tax return"** means any of the following–

(a) a return under section 8 of TMA 1970 (income tax and capital gains tax: personal return);

(b) a return under section 8A of TMA 1970 (income tax and capital gains tax: trustee's return);

(c) a return under section 12AA of TMA 1970 (income tax and corporation tax: partnership return);

(d) a company tax return under paragraph 3 of Schedule 18 to the FA 1998 (company tax return);

(da) a return under regulations made under section 105 of FA 2016 (apprenticeship levy);

(e) a return under section 159 or 160 of FA 2013 (returns and further returns for annual tax on enveloped dwellings).

Prospective amendments – In s. 253(6)(c) the words ", or regulations under paragraph 10 of Schedule A1 to," inserted after the words "section 12AA of" by F(No. 2)A 2017, s. 61 and Sch. 14, para. 44, with effect from a day to be appointed under F(No. 2)A 2017, s. 61(6).

History – S. 253(6)(da) inserted by FA 2016, s. 104(7), with effect from 15 September 2016 (Royal Assent).

Statutory instruments – SI 2015/549: partly made under s. 253(2) and (4).

OBTAINING INFORMATION AND DOCUMENTS

254 Meaning of "monitored proposal" and "monitored arrangements"

254(1) For the purposes of this Part a relevant proposal in relation to which a person ("P") is a promoter is a "monitored proposal" in relation to P if any of the following dates fell on or after the date on which a monitoring notice took effect–

(a) the date on which P first made a firm approach to another person in relation to the relevant proposal;

(b) the date on which P first made the relevant proposal available for implementation by any other person;

(c) the date on which P first became aware of any transaction forming part of the proposed arrangements being entered into by any person.

254(2) For the purposes of this Part relevant arrangements in relation to which a person ("P") is a promoter are "monitored arrangements" in relation to P if–

(a) P was by virtue of section 235(2)(b) or (c) a promoter in relation to a relevant proposal which was implemented by the arrangements and any of the following fell on or after the date on which the monitoring notice took effect–

IHT Statutes

(i) the date on which P first made a firm approach to another person in relation to the relevant proposal;

(ii) the date on which P first made the relevant proposal available for implementation by any other person;

(iii) the date on which P first became aware of any transaction forming part of the proposed arrangements being entered into by any person,

(b) the date on which P first took part in designing, organising or managing the arrangements fell on or after the date on which a monitoring notice took effect, or

(c) the arrangements enable, or are likely to enable, the person who has entered into transactions forming them to obtain the tax advantage by reason of which they are relevant arrangements, at any time on or after the date on which a monitoring notice took effect.

255 Power to obtain information and documents

255(1) An authorised officer, or an officer of Revenue and Customs with the approval of an authorised officer, may by notice in writing require any person ("P") to whom this section applies–

(a) to provide information, or

(b) to produce a document,

if the information or document is reasonably required by the officer for any of the purposes in subsection (3).

255(2) This section applies to–

(a) any person who is a monitored promoter, and

(b) any person who is a relevant intermediary in relation to a monitored proposal of a monitored promoter,

and in either case that monitored promoter is referred to below as "the relevant monitored promoter".

255(3) The purposes mentioned in subsection (1) are–

(a) considering the possible consequences of implementing a monitored proposal of the relevant monitored promoter for the tax position of persons implementing the proposal,

(b) checking the tax position of any person who the officer reasonably believes has implemented a monitored proposal of the relevant monitored promoter, or

(c) checking the tax position of any person who the officer reasonably believes has entered into transactions forming monitored arrangements of the relevant monitored promoter.

255(4) A person is a **"relevant intermediary"** in relation to a monitored proposal if the person meets the conditions in section 236(a) to (c) (meaning of "intermediary") in relation to the proposal at any time after the person has been notified of a promoter reference number of a person who is a promoter in relation to the proposal.

255(5) In this section **"checking"** includes carrying out an investigation or enquiry of any kind.

255(6) In this section **"tax position"**, in relation to a person, means the person's position as regards any tax, including the person's position as regards–

(a) past, present and future liability to pay any tax,

(b) penalties and other amounts that have been paid, or are or may be payable, by or to the person in connection with any tax,

(c) claims, elections, applications and notices that have been or may be made or given in connection with the person's liability to pay any tax,

(d) deductions or repayments of tax, or of sums representing tax, that the person is required to make–

(i) under PAYE regulations, or

(ii) by or under any other provision of the Taxes Acts, and

(e) the withholding by the person of another person's PAYE income (as defined in section 683 of ITEPA 2003).

255(7) In this section the reference to the tax position of a person–

(a) includes the tax position of a company that has ceased to exist and an individual who has died, and

(b) is to the person's tax position at any time or in relation to any period.

255(8) A *notice under subsection* (1) which is given for the purpose of checking the tax position of a person mentioned in subsection (3)(b) or (c) may not be given more than 4 years after the person's death.

255(9) A notice under subsection (1) may specify or describe the information or documents to be provided or produced.

255(10) Information or a document required as a result of a notice under subsection (1) must be provided or produced within–

(a) the period of 10 days beginning with the day on which the notice was given, or

(b) such longer period as the officer who gives the notice may direct.

256 Tribunal approval for certain uses of power under section 255

256(1) An officer of Revenue and Customs may not, without the approval of the tribunal, give a notice under section 255 requiring a person ("A") to provide information or produce a document which relates (in whole or in part) to a person who is neither A nor an undertaking in relation to which A is a parent undertaking.

256(2) An officer of Revenue and Customs may apply to the tribunal for the approval required by subsection (1); and an application for approval may be made without notice.

256(3) The tribunal may approve the giving of the notice only if–

(a) the application for approval is made by, or with the agreement of, an authorised officer,

(b) the tribunal is satisfied that, in the circumstances, the officer giving the notice is justified in doing so,

(c) the person to whom the notice is to be given has been informed that the information or documents referred to in the notice are required and given a reasonable opportunity to make representations to an officer of Revenue and Customs, and

(d) the tribunal has been given a summary of any representations made by that person.

256(4) Where a notice is given under section 255 with the approval of the tribunal, it must state that it is given with that approval.

256(5) Paragraphs (c) and (d) of subsection (3) do not apply to the extent that the tribunal is satisfied that taking the action specified in those paragraphs might prejudice the assessment or collection of tax.

256(6) In subsection (1) **"parent undertaking"** and **"undertaking"** have the same meaning as in the Companies Acts (see section 1161 and 1162 of, and Schedule 7 to, the Companies Act 2006).

256(7) A decision of the tribunal under this section is final (despite the provisions of sections 11 and 13 of the Tribunals, Courts and Enforcement Act 2007).

257 Ongoing duty to provide information following HMRC notice

257(1) An authorised officer, or an officer of Revenue and Customs with the approval of an authorised officer, may give a notice to a person ("P") in relation to whom a monitoring notice has effect.

257(2) A person to whom a notice is given under subsection (1) must provide prescribed information and produce prescribed documents relating to–

(a) all the monitored proposals and all the monitored arrangements in relation to which the person is a promoter at the time of the notice, and

(b) all the monitored proposals and all the monitored arrangements in relation to which the person becomes a promoter after that time.

257(3) The duty under subsection (2)(b) does not apply in relation to any proposals or arrangements in relation to which the person first becomes a promoter after the monitoring notice ceases to have effect.

257(4) A notice under subsection (1) must specify the time within which information must be provided or a document produced and different times may be specified for different cases.

Statutory instruments – SI 2015/549: partly made under s. 257(2).

258 Duty of person dealing with non-resident monitored promoter

258(1) This section applies where a monitored promoter who is resident outside the United Kingdom has failed to comply with a duty under section 255 or 257 to provide information about a monitored proposal or monitored arrangements.

258(2) An authorised officer, or an officer of Revenue and Customs with the approval of an authorised officer, may give a notice to a relevant person which–

(a) specifies or describes the information which the monitored promoter has failed to provide, and

(b) requires the person to provide the information.

258(3) A **"relevant person"** means–

(a) any person who is an intermediary in relation to the monitored proposal concerned, and

(b) any person ("A") to whom the monitored promoter has made a firm approach in relation to the monitored proposal concerned with a view to making the proposal available for implementation by a person other than A.

258(4) If an authorised officer is not aware of any person to whom a notice could be given under subsection (2) the authorised officer, or an officer of Revenue and Customs with the approval of the authorised officer, may give a notice to any person who has implemented the proposal which–

(a) specifies or describes the information which the monitored promoter has failed to provide, and

(b) requires the person to provide the information.

258(5) If the duty mentioned in subsection (1) relates to monitored arrangements an authorised officer, or an officer of Revenue and Customs with the approval of an authorised officer, may give a notice to any person who has entered into any transaction forming part of the monitored arrangements concerned which–

(a) specifies or describes the information which the monitored promoter has failed to provide, and

(b) requires the person to provide the information.

258(6) A notice under this section may be given only if the officer giving the notice reasonably believes that the person to whom the notice is given is able to provide the information requested.

258(7) Information required as a result of a notice under this section must be provided within–

(a) the period of 10 days beginning with the day on which the notice was given, or

(b) such longer period as the officer who gives the notice may direct.

259 Monitored promoters: duty to provide information about clients

259(1) An authorised officer, or an officer of Revenue and Customs with the approval of an authorised officer, may give notice to a person in relation to whom a monitoring notice has effect ("the monitored promoter").

259(2) A person to whom a notice is given under subsection (1) must, for each relevant period, give the officer who gave the notice the information set out in subsection (9) in respect of each person who was its client with reference to that relevant period (see subsections (5) to (8)).

259(3) Each of the following is a "relevant period"–

(a) the calendar quarter in which the notice under subsection (1) was given but not including any time before the monitoring notice takes effect,

(b) the period (if any) beginning with the date the monitoring notice takes effect and ending immediately before the beginning of the period described in paragraph (a), and

(c) each calendar quarter after the period described in paragraph (a) but not including any time after the monitoring notice ceases to have effect.

259(4) Information required as a result of a notice under subsection (1) must be given–

(a) within the period of 30 days beginning with the end of the relevant period concerned, or

(b) in the case of a relevant period within subsection (3)(b), within the period of 30 days beginning with the day on which the notice under subsection (1) was given if that period would expire at a later time than the period given by paragraph (a).

259(5) A person ("C") is a client of the monitored promoter with reference to a relevant period if–

(a) the promoter did any of the things mentioned in subsection (6) in relation to C at any time during that period, or

(b) the person falls within subsection (7).

259(6) Those things are that the monitored promoter–

(a) made a firm approach to C in relation to a relevant proposal with a view to the promoter making the proposal available for implementation by C or another person;

(b) made a relevant proposal available for implementation by C;

(c) took part in the organisation or management of relevant arrangements entered into by C.

259(7) A person falls within this subsection if the person has entered into transactions forming part of relevant arrangements and those arrangements–

(a) enable the person to obtain a tax advantage either in that relevant period or a later relevant period, and

(b) are either relevant arrangements in relation to which the monitored promoter is or was a promoter, or implement a relevant proposal in relation to which the monitored promoter was a promoter.

259(8) But a person is not a client of the monitored promoter with reference to a relevant period if–

(a) the person has previously been a client of the monitored promoter with reference to a different relevant period,

(b) the promoter complied with the duty in subsection (2) in respect of the person for that relevant period, and

(c) the information provided as a result of complying with that duty remains accurate.

259(9) The information mentioned in subsection (2) is–

(a) the person's name and address, and

(b) such other information about the person as may be prescribed.

259(10) Where the monitoring notice mentioned in subsection (1) is a replacement monitoring notice, subsection (5)(b) does not impose a duty on the monitored promoter concerned to provide information about a person who has entered into transactions forming part of relevant arrangements (as described in subsection (7)) if the monitored promoter reasonably believes that information about that person has, in relation to those arrangements, already been provided under the original monitoring notice.

Statutory instruments – SI 2015/549: partly made under s. 259(9).

260 Intermediaries: duty to provide information about clients

260(1) An authorised officer, or an officer of Revenue and Customs with the approval of an authorised officer, may give notice to a person ("the intermediary") who is an intermediary in relation to a relevant proposal which is a monitored proposal of a person in relation to whom a monitoring notice has effect ("the monitored promoter").

260(2) A person to whom a notice is given under subsection (1) must, for each relevant period, give the officer who gave the notice the information set out in subsection (7) in respect of each person who was its client with reference to that relevant period (see subsections (5) to (6)).

260(3) Each of the following is a "relevant period"–

(a) the calendar quarter in which the notice under subsection (1) was given but not including any time before the intermediary was first notified under section 250, 251 or 252 of the promoter reference number of the monitored promoter,

(b) the period (if any) beginning with the date of the notification under section 250, 251 or 252 and ending immediately before the beginning of the period described in paragraph (a), and

(c) each calendar quarter after the period described in paragraph (a) but not including any time after the monitoring notice mentioned in subsection (1) ceases to have effect.

260(4) Information required as a result of a notice under subsection (1) must be given–

(a) within the period of 30 days beginning with the end of the relevant period concerned, or

(b) in the case of a relevant period within subsection (3)(b), within the period of 30 days beginning with the day on which the notice under subsection (1) was given if that period would expire at a later time than the period given by paragraph (a).

260(5) A person ("C") is a client of the intermediary with reference to a relevant period if during that period–

(a) the intermediary communicated information to C about a monitored proposal in the course of a business, and

(b) the communication was made with a view to C, or any other person, entering into transactions forming part of the proposed arrangements.

260(6) But a person is not a client of the intermediary with reference to a relevant period if–

(a) the person has previously been a client of the intermediary with reference to a different relevant period,

(b) the intermediary complied with the duty in subsection (2) in respect of the person for that relevant period, and

(c) the information provided as a result of complying with that duty remains accurate.

260(7) The information mentioned in subsection (2) is–

(a) the person's name and address, and

(b) such other information about the person as may be prescribed.

Statutory instruments – SI 2015/549: partly made under s. 260(7).

IHT Statutes

261 Enquiry following provision of client information

261(1) This section applies where–

(a) a person ("the notifying person") has provided information under section 259 or 260 about a person who was a client of the notifying person with reference to a relevant period (within the meaning of the section concerned) in connection with a particular relevant proposal or particular relevant arrangements, and

(b) an authorised officer suspects that a person in respect of whom information has not been provided under section 259 or 260–

(i) has at any time been, or is likely to be, a party to transactions implementing the proposal, or

(ii) is a party to a transaction forming (in whole or in part) particular relevant arrangements.

261(2) The authorised officer may by notice in writing require the notifying person to provide prescribed information in relation to any person whom the notifying person might reasonably be expected to know–

(a) has been, or is likely to be, a party to transactions implementing the proposal, or

(b) is a party to a transaction forming (in whole or in part) the relevant arrangements.

261(3) But a notice under subsection (2) does not impose a requirement on the notifying person to provide information which the notifying person has already provided to an authorised officer under section 259 or 260.

261(4) The notifying person must comply with a requirement under subsection (2) within–

(a) 10 days of the notice, or

(b) such longer period as the authorised officer may direct.

Statutory instruments – SI 2015/549: partly made under s. 261(2).

262 Information required for monitoring compliance with conduct notice

262(1) This section applies where a conduct notice has effect in relation to a person.

262(2) An authorised officer, or an officer of Revenue and Customs with the approval of an authorised officer, may (as often as is necessary for the purpose mentioned below) by notice in writing require the person–

(a) to provide information, or

(b) to produce a document,

if the information or document is reasonably required for the purpose of monitoring whether and to what extent the person is complying with the conditions in the conduct notice.

263 Duty to notify HMRC of address

263 If, on the last day of a calendar quarter, a monitoring notice has effect in relation to a person ("the monitored promoter") the monitored promoter must within 30 days of the end of the calendar quarter inform an authorised officer of its current address.

264 Failure to provide information: application to tribunal

264(1) This section applies where–

(a) a person ("P") has provided information or produced a document in purported compliance with section 255, 257, 258, 259, 260, 261 or 262, but

(b) an authorised officer suspects that P has not provided all the information or produced all the documents required under the section concerned.

264(2) The authorised officer, or an officer of Revenue and Customs with the approval of the authorised officer, may apply to the tribunal for an order requiring P to–

(a) provide specified information about persons who are its clients for the purposes of the section to which the application relates,

(b) provide specified information, or information of a specified description, about a monitored proposal or monitored arrangements,

(c) produce specified documents relating to a monitored proposal or monitored arrangements.

264(3) The tribunal may make an order under subsection (2) in respect of information or documents only if satisfied that the officer has reasonable grounds for suspecting that the information or documents–

(a) are required under section 255, 257, 258, 259, 260, 261 or 262 (as the case may be), or

(b) will support or explain information required under the section concerned.

264(4) A requirement by virtue of an order under subsection (2) is to be treated as part of P's duty under section 255, 257, 258, 259, 260, 261 or 262 (as the case may be).

264(5) Information or a document required as a result of subsection (2) must be provided, or the document produced, within the period of 10 days beginning with the day on which the order under subsection (2) was made.

264(6) An authorised officer may, by direction, extend the 10 day period mentioned in subsection (5).

265 Duty to provide information to monitored promoter

265(1) This section applies where a person has been notified of a promoter reference number–

(a) under section 250 by reason of being a person falling within subsection (2)(b) of that section, or

(b) under section 251 or 252.

265(2) The person notified ("C") must within 10 days notify the person whose promoter reference number it is of–

(a) C's national insurance number (if C has one), and

(b) C's unique tax reference number (if C has one).

265(3) If C has neither a national insurance number nor a unique tax reference number, C must within 10 days inform the person whose promoter reference number it is of that fact.

265(4) A unique tax reference number is an identification number allocated to a person by HMRC.

265(5) Subsection (2) or (3) does not impose a duty on C to provide information which C has already provided to the person whose promoter reference number it is.

OBTAINING INFORMATION AND DOCUMENTS: APPEALS

266 Appeals against notices imposing information etc requirements

266(1) This section applies where a person is given a notice under section 255, 257, 258, 259, 260, 261 or 262.

266(2) The person to whom the notice is given may appeal against the notice or any requirement under the notice.

266(3) Subsection (2) does not apply–

(a) to a requirement to provide any information or produce any document that forms part of the person's statutory records, or

(b) if the tribunal has approved the giving of the notice under section 256.

266(4) For the purposes of this section, information or a document forms part of a person's statutory records if it is information or a document which the person is required to keep and preserve under or by virtue of–

(a) the Taxes Acts, or

(b) any other enactment relating to a tax.

266(5) Information and documents cease to form part of a person's statutory records when the period for which they are required to be preserved by the enactments mentioned in subsection (4) has expired.

266(6) Notice of appeal must be given–

(a) in writing to the officer who gave the notice, and

(b) within the period of 30 days beginning with the day on which the notice was given.

266(7) The notice of appeal must state the grounds of the appeal.

266(8) On an appeal that is notified to the tribunal, the tribunal may–

(a) confirm the notice or a requirement under the notice,

(b) vary the notice or such a requirement, or

(c) set aside the notice or such a requirement.

266(9) Where the tribunal confirms or varies the notice or a requirement, the person to whom the notice was given must comply with the notice or requirement–

(a) within such period as is specified by the tribunal, or

(b) if the tribunal does not specify a period, within such period as is reasonably specified in writing by an officer of Revenue and Customs following the tribunal's decision.

266(10) A decision of the tribunal on an appeal under this section is final (despite the provisions of sections 11 and 13 of the Tribunals, Courts and Enforcement Act 2007).

266(11) Subject to this section, the provisions of Part 5 of TMA 1970 relating to appeals have effect in relation to an appeal under this section.

OBTAINING INFORMATION AND DOCUMENTS: SUPPLEMENTARY

267 Form and manner of providing information

267(1) The Commissioners may specify the form and manner in which information required to be provided or documents required to be produced by sections 255 to 264 must be provided or produced if the provision is to be complied with.

267(2) The Commissioners may specify that a document must be produced for inspection–

(a) at a place agreed between the person and an officer of Revenue and Customs, or

(b) at such place (which must not be a place used solely as a dwelling) as an officer of Revenue and Customs may reasonably specify.

267(3) The production of a document in compliance with a notice under this Part is not to be regarded as breaking any lien claimed on the document.

268 Production of documents: compliance

268(1) Where the effect of a notice under section 255, 257 or 262 is to require a person to produce a document, the person may comply with the requirement by producing a copy of the document, subject to any conditions or exceptions that may be prescribed.

268(2) Subsection (1) does not apply where–

(a) the effect of the notice is to require the person to produce the original document, or

(b) an authorised officer, or an officer of Revenue and Customs with the approval of an authorised officer, subsequently makes a request in writing to the person for the original document.

268(3) Where an officer requests a document under subsection (2)(b), the person to whom the request is made must produce the document–

(a) within such period, and

(b) at such time and by such means,

as is reasonably requested by the officer.

Statutory instruments – SI 2015/549: partly made under s. 268(1).

269 Exception for certain documents or information

269(1) Nothing in this Part requires a person to provide or produce–

(a) information that relates to the conduct of a pending appeal relating to tax or any part of a document containing such information,

(b) journalistic material (as defined in section 13 of the Police and Criminal Evidence Act 1984) or information contained in such material, or

(c) personal records (as defined in section 12 of the Police and Criminal Evidence Act 1984) or information contained in such records (but see subsection (2)).

269(2) A notice under this Part may require a person–

(a) to produce documents, or copies of documents, that are personal records, omitting any information whose inclusion (whether alone or with other information) makes the original documents personal records ("personal information"), and

(b) to provide any information contained in such records that is not personal information.

270 Limitation on duty to produce documents

270 Nothing in this Part requires a person to produce a document–

(a) which is not in the possession or power of that person, or

(b) if the whole of the document originates more than 6 years before the requirement to produce it would, if it were not for this section, arise.

271 Legal professional privilege

271(1) Nothing in this Part requires any person to disclose to HMRC any privileged information.

271(2) **"Privileged information"** means information with respect to which a claim to legal professional privilege by the person who would (ignoring the effect of this section) be required to disclose it, could be maintained in legal proceedings.

271(3) In the case of legal proceedings in Scotland, the reference in subsection (2) to legal professional privilege is to be read as a reference to confidentiality of communications.

272 Tax advisers

272(1) This section applies where a notice is given under section 258(4) or (5) and the person to whom the notice is given is a tax adviser.

272(2) The notice does not require a tax adviser–

(a) to provide information about relevant communications, or

(b) to produce documents which are the tax adviser's property and consist of relevant communications.

272(3) Subsection (2) does not have effect in relation to–

(a) information explaining any information or document which the person to whom the notice is given has, as tax accountant, assisted any person in preparing for, or delivering to, HMRC, or

(b) a document which contains such information.

272(4) But subsection (2) is not disapplied by subsection (3) if the information in question has already been provided, or a document containing the information has already been produced, to an officer of Revenue and Customs.

272(5) In this section–

"relevant communications" means communications between the tax adviser and–

(a) a person in relation to whose tax affairs the tax adviser has been appointed, or

(b) any other tax adviser of such a person,

the purpose of which is the giving or obtaining of advice about any of those tax affairs, and

"tax adviser" means a person appointed to give advice about the tax affairs of another person (whether appointed directly by that person or by another tax adviser of that person).

273 Confidentiality

273(1) No duty of confidentiality or other restriction on disclosure (however imposed) prevents the voluntary disclosure by a relevant client or a relevant intermediary to HMRC of information or documents about–

(a) a monitored promoter, or

(b) relevant proposals or relevant arrangements in relation to which a monitored promoter is a promoter.

273(2) **"Relevant client"** means a person in relation to whom the monitored promoter mentioned in subsection (1)(a) or (b)–

(a) has made a firm approach in relation to a relevant proposal with a view to making the proposal available for implementation by that person or another person;

(b) has made a relevant proposal available for implementation by that person;

(c) took part in the organisation or management of relevant arrangements entered into by that person.

273(3) **"Relevant intermediary"** means a person who is an intermediary in relation to a relevant proposal in relation to which the monitored promoter mentioned in subsection (1)(a) or (b) is a promoter.

273(4) The relevant proposal or relevant arrangements mentioned in subsection (2) or (3) need not be the relevant proposals or relevant arrangements to which the disclosure relates.

PENALTIES

274 Penalties

274 Schedule 35 contains provision about penalties for failure to comply with provisions of this Part.

276 Limitation of defence of reasonable care

276 [Omitted by F(No. 2)A 2017, s. 64(4).]

History – Omitted by F(No. 2)A 2017, s. 64(4), with effect in relation to any document of a kind listed in the Table at FA 2007, Sch. 24, para. 1 which is given to HMRC on or after 16 November 2017 (Royal Assent) and relates to a tax period that begins on or after 6 April 2017 and ends on or after 16 November 2017 (Royal Assent). Former s. 276 read as follows:

"276 Limitation of defence of reasonable care

276(1) Subsection (2) applies where–

(a) a person gives HMRC a document of a kind listed in the Table in paragraph 1 of Schedule 24 to FA 2007 (penalties for providing inaccurate documents to HMRC), and

(b) the document contains an inaccuracy.

276(2) In determining whether or not the inaccuracy was careless for the purposes of paragraph 3(1)(a) of Schedule 24 to FA 2007, reliance by the person on legal advice relating to relevant arrangements in relation to which a monitored promoter is a promoter is to be disregarded if the advice was given or procured by a person who was a monitored promoter in relation to the arrangements."

277 Extended time limit for assessment

277(1) [Not relevant to inheritance tax.]

277(2) [Not relevant to inheritance tax.]

277(3) In section 240 of IHTA 1984 (underpayments)–

(a) [amends IHTA 1984, s. 240(3),]

(b) [amends IHTA 1984, s. 240(5),]

(c) [inserts IHTA 1984, s. 240(5A),]

(d) [amends IHTA 1984, s. 240(8).]

277(4) [Not relevant to inheritance tax.]

277(5) [Not relevant to inheritance tax.]

277(6) [Not relevant to inheritance tax.]

OFFENCES

278 Offence of concealing etc documents

278(1) A person is guilty of an offence if–

(a) the person is required to produce a document by a notice given under section 255,

(b) the tribunal approved the giving of the notice under section 256, and

(c) the person conceals, destroys or otherwise disposes of, or arranges for the concealment, destruction or disposal of, that document.

278(2) Subsection (1) does not apply if the person acts after the document has been produced to an officer of Revenue and Customs in accordance with section 255, unless the officer has notified the person in writing that the document must continue to be available for inspection (and has not withdrawn the notification).

278(3) Subsection (1) does not apply, in a case to which section 268(1) applies, if the person acts after the end of the expiry of 6 months beginning with the day on which a copy of the document was produced in accordance with that section unless, before the expiry of that period, an officer of Revenue and Customs makes a request for the original document under section 268(2)(b).

279 Offence of concealing etc documents following informal notification

279(1) A person is guilty of an offence if the person conceals, destroys or otherwise disposes of, or arranges for the concealment, destruction or disposal of, a document after an officer of Revenue and Customs has informed the person in writing that–

(a) the document is, or is likely, to be the subject of a notice under section 255, and

(b) the officer of Revenue and Customs intends to seek the approval of the tribunal to the giving of the notice.

279(2) A person is not guilty of an offence under this section if the person acts after–

(a) at least 6 months has expired since the person was, or was last, informed as described in subsection (1), or

(b) a notice has been given to the person under section 255, requiring the document to be produced.

280 Penalties for offences

280(1) A person who is guilty of an offence under section 278 or 279 is liable–

(a) on summary conviction, to–

(i) in England and Wales, a fine, or

(ii) in Scotland or Northern Ireland, a fine not exceeding the statutory maximum, or

(b) on conviction on indictment, to imprisonment for a term not exceeding 2 years or to a fine or both.

280(2) In relation to an offence committed before section 85(1) of the Legal Aid, Sentencing and Punishment of Offenders Act 2012 comes into force, subsection (1)(a)(i) has effect as if the reference to "a fine" were a reference to "a fine not exceeding the statutory maximum".

SUPPLEMENTAL

281 Partnerships

281 Schedule 36 contains provision about the application of this Part to partnerships.

281A VAT and other indirect taxes

History – In the heading to s. 281A the words "and other indirect taxes" inserted by F(No. 2)A 2017, s. 66 and Sch. 17, para. 53(2), with effect so far as necessary for enabling the making of regulations under that Schedule from 16 November 2017 (Royal Assent) and from 1 January 2018 for all other purposes.

281A [Not relevant to inheritance tax.]

History – S. 281A inserted by FA 2016, s. 160(7), with effect from 15 September 2016 (Royal Assent).

282 Regulations under this Part

282(1) Regulations under this Part are to be made by statutory instrument.

282(2) Apart from an instrument to which subsection (3) applies, a statutory instrument containing regulations made under this Part is subject to annulment in pursuance of a resolution of the House of Commons.

282(3) A statutory instrument containing (whether alone or with other provision) regulations made under–

(a) section 238(7),

(b) paragraph 14 of Schedule 34,

(ba) paragraph 31 of Schedule 34A,

(c) paragraph 5(1) of Schedule 35, or

(d) paragraph 21 of Schedule 36,

may not be made unless a draft of the instrument has been laid before and approved by a resolution of the House of Commons.

282(4) Regulations under this Part–

(a) may make different provision for different purposes;

(b) may include transitional provision and savings.

History – S. 282(3)(ba) inserted by FA 2016, s. 160(8), with effect from 15 September 2016 (Royal Assent).

Statutory instruments – SI 2015/549: partly made under s. 282(4).

283 Interpretation of this Part

283(1) In this Part–

"arrangements" has the meaning given by section 234(4);

"the Commissioners" means the Commissioners for Her Majesty's Revenue and Customs;

"calendar quarter" means a period of 3 months beginning with 1 January, 1 April, 1 July or 1 October;

"conduct notice" means a notice of the description in section 238 that is given under–

(a) section 237(7) or (7A),

(aa) section 237A(8),

(ab) section 237B(1),

(b) section 245(7), or

(c) paragraph 8(2) or (3) or 10(3)(a) or (4)(a) of Schedule 36;

"contract settlement" means an agreement in connection with a person's liability to make a payment to the Commissioners under or by virtue of an enactment;

"defeat", in relation to arrangements, has the meaning given by paragraph 10 of Schedule 34A;

"defeat notice" has the meaning given by section 241A(7);

"double defeat notice" has the meaning given by section 241A(7);

"final", in relation to a judicial ruling, is to be interpreted in accordance with section 237D(6);

"HMRC" means Her Majesty's Revenue and Customs;

"firm approach" has the meaning given by section 235(4);

"judicial ruling" means a ruling of a court or tribunal on one or more issues;

"look-forward period", in relation to a defeat notice, has the meaning given by section 241A(10);

"monitored promoter" has the meaning given by section 244(5);

"monitored proposal" and **"monitored arrangements"** have the meaning given by section 254;

"monitoring notice" means a notice given under section 244(1) or paragraph 9(2) or (3) or 10(3)(b) or (4)(b) of Schedule 36;

"the original monitoring notice" has the meaning given by paragraph 11(2) of Schedule 36;

"prescribed" means prescribed, or of a description prescribed, in regulations made by the Commissioners;

"promoter reference number" has the meaning given by section 250(5);

"provisional", in relation to a conduct notice given under section 237A(8), is to be interpreted in accordance with section 237C;

"related", in relation to arrangements, is to be interpreted in accordance with paragraph 2 of Schedule 34A;

"relevant arrangements" has the meaning given by section 234(2);

"relevant defeat", in relation to a person, is to be interpreted in accordance with Schedule 34A;

"relevant proposal" has the meaning given by section 234(1);

""relies on a Case 3 relevant defeat" is to be interpreted in accordance section 237B(5);"

"replacement conduct notice" has the meaning given by paragraph 11(1) of Schedule 36;

"replacement monitoring notice" has the meaning given by paragraph 11(1) of Schedule 36;

"single defeat notice" has the meaning given by section 241A(7).

"tax" (except in provisions to which section 281A applies) means–

(a) income tax,

(b) capital gains tax,

(c) corporation tax,

(d) petroleum revenue tax,

(da) apprenticeship levy,

(e) inheritance tax,

(f) stamp duty land tax,

(g) stamp duty reserve tax, or

(h) annual tax on enveloped dwellings;

"tax advantage" has the meaning given by section 234(3) (but see also section 281A);

"Taxes Acts" has the same meaning as in TMA 1970 (see section 118(1) of that Act);

"the tribunal" means the First-tier Tribunal or, where determined by or under Tribunal Procedure Rules, the Upper Tribunal.

283(2) A reference in a provision of this Part to an authorised officer is to an officer of Revenue and Customs who is, or is a member of a class of officers who are, authorised by the Commissioners for the purposes of that provision.

283(3) A reference in a provision of this Part to meeting a threshold condition is to meeting one of the conditions described in paragraphs 2 to 12 of Schedule 34.

History – In s. 283(1), in the definition of "conduct notice", para. (aa) and (ab) inserted by FA 2016, s. 160(9)(a), with effect from 15 September 2016 (Royal Assent).

In s. 283(1), in the definition of "conduct notice", the words "or (7A)" inserted by FA 2015, s. 119 and Sch. 19, para. 3, with effect for the purposes of determining whether a person meets a threshold condition in a period of three years ending on or after 26 March 2015 (Royal Assent).

In s. 283(1), definitions of "contract settlement", "defeat", "defeat notice", "double defeat notice", "final", "judicial ruling", "look-forward period", "provisional", "relevant defeat", "related", "relies on a Case 3 relevant defeat" and "single defeat notice" inserted by FA 2016, s. 160(9)(d), with effect from 15 September 2016 (Royal Assent).

In s. 283(1), in the definition of "tax", the words "(except in provisions to which section 281A applies)" inserted by FA 2016, s. 160(9)(b), with effect from 15 September 2016 (Royal Assent).

In s. 283(1), in the definition of "tax", para. (da) inserted by FA 2016, s. 104(8), with effect from 15 September 2016 (Royal Assent).

In s. 283(1), in the definition of "tax advantage", the words "(but see also section 281A)" inserted by FA 2016, s. 160(9)(c), with effect from 15 September 2016 (Royal Assent).

Statutory instruments – SI 2015/130: partly made under s. 283(1).

SI 2015/131: partly made under s. 283(1).

SI 2015/549: partly made under s. 283(1).

PART 6 – OTHER PROVISIONS

ANTI-AVOIDANCE

284 Disclosure of tax avoidance schemes: information powers

284(1) Part 7 of FA 2004 (disclosure of tax avoidance schemes) is amended as set out in subsections (2) to (4).

284(2) [Inserts FA 2004, s. 310A and 310B.]

284(3) [Amends FA 2004, s. 316(2).]

284(4) [Amends FA 2004, s. 318(1).]

284(5)–(10) [Not relevant to inheritance tax.]

284(11) Section 310A of FA 2004 applies to a person who provides the prescribed information about notifiable proposals or arrangements in compliance or purported compliance with section 308, 309 or 310 on or after the day on which this Act is passed.

EMPLOYEE-OWNERSHIP TRUSTS

290 Companies owned by employee-ownership trusts

290 Schedule 37 contains provision about tax reliefs in connection with companies owned by employee-ownership trusts.

PART 7 – FINAL PROVISIONS

301 Power to update indexes of defined terms

301(1) The Treasury may by order amend any index of defined expressions contained in an Act relating to taxation, so as to make amendments consequential on any enactment.

301(2) In this section–

"enactment" means any provision made by or under an Act (whether before or after the passing of this Act);

"index of defined expressions" means a provision contained in an Act relating to taxation which lists where expressions used in the Act, or in a particular part of the Act, are defined or otherwise explained.

301(3) The power to make an order under this section is exercisable by statutory instrument.

301(4) An order under this section is subject to annulment in pursuance of a resolution of the House of Commons.

302 Interpretation

302(1) In this Act–

"ALDA 1979" means the Alcoholic Liquor Duties Act 1979,

"BGDA 1981" means the Betting and Gaming Duties Act 1981,

"CAA 2001" means the Capital Allowances Act 2001,

"CEMA 1979" means the Customs and Excise Management Act 1979,

"CRCA 2005" means the Commissioners for Revenue and Customs Act 2005,

"CTA 2009" means the Corporation Tax Act 2009,

"CTA 2010" means the Corporation Tax Act 2010,

"F(No. 3)A 2010" means the Finance (No. 3) Act 2010,

"IHTA 1984" means the Inheritance Tax Act 1984,

"ITA 2007" means the Income Tax Act 2007,

"ITEPA 2003" means the Income Tax (Earnings and Pensions) Act 2003,

"ITTOIA 2005" means the Income Tax (Trading and Other Income) Act 2005,

"OTA 1975" means the Oil Taxation Act 1975,

"TCGA 1992" means the Taxation of Chargeable Gains Act 1992,

"TIOPA 2010" means the Taxation (International and Other Provisions) Act 2010,

"TMA 1970" means the Taxes Management Act 1970,

"TPDA 1979" means the Tobacco Products Duty Act 1979,

"VATA 1994" means the Value Added Tax Act 1994, and

"VERA 1994" means the Vehicle Excise and Registration Act 1994.

302(2) In this Act–

"FA", followed by a year, means the Finance Act of that year, and

"F(No. 2)A", followed by a year, means the Finance (No. 2) Act of that year.

303 Short title

303 This Act may be cited as the Finance Act 2014.

SCHEDULE 25 – INHERITANCE TAX

Section 117

INTRODUCTORY

1 IHTA 1984 is amended as follows.

RATE BANDS FOR TAX YEARS 2015–16, 2016–17 AND 2017–18

2 Section 8 (indexation) does not have effect by virtue of any difference between the consumer prices index for the month of September in 2014, 2015 or 2016 and the previous September.

TREATMENT OF CERTAIN LIABILITIES

3(1) [Inserts IHTA 1984, s. 162AA.]

3(2) Section 162C (sections 162A and 162B: supplementary provision) is amended as follows.

3(3) [Amends heading to IHTA 1984, s. 162C.]

3(4) [Amends IHTA 1984, s. 162C(1).]

3(5) [Inserts IHTA 1984, s. 162C(1A).]

3(6) [Amends IHTA 1984, s. 162C(2).]

3(7) In section 175A (discharge of liabilities after death), in subsection (7)–

(a) [inserts IHTA 1984, s. 175A(7)(aa),]

(b) [amends IHTA 1984, s. 175A(7)(b),]

(c) [amends IHTA 1984, s. 175A(7)(c).]

3(8) The amendments made by this paragraph have effect in relation to transfers of value made, or treated as made, on or after the day on which this Act is passed.

TEN-YEAR ANNIVERSARY CHARGE

4(1) [Inserts IHTA 1984, s. 64(1A)–(1C).]

4(2) [Inserts IHTA 1984, s. 66(2A).]

4(3) The amendments made by this paragraph have effect in relation to occasions on which tax falls to be charged under section 64 of IHTA 1984 on or after 6 April 2014.

DELIVERY OF ACCOUNT AND PAYMENT OF TAX

5(1) [Inserts IHTA 1984, s. 216(6)(ad).]

5(2) [Inserts IHTA 1984, s. 226(3C).]

5(3) In section 233 (interest on unpaid tax)–

(a) [amends IHTA 1984, s. 233(1)(a),]

(b) [inserts IHTA 1984, s. 233(1)(aa),]

(c) [amends IHTA 1984, s. 233(1)(b).]

5(4) The amendments made by this paragraph have effect in relation to chargeable transfers made on or after 6 April 2014.

SCHEDULE 30 – SECTION 208 PENALTY: VALUE OF THE DENIED ADVANTAGE

Section 209

INTRODUCTION

1 This Schedule applies for the purposes of calculating penalties under section 209.

VALUE OF DENIED ADVANTAGE: NORMAL RULE

2(1) The value of the denied advantage is the additional amount due or payable in respect of tax as a result of counteracting the denied advantage.

2(2) The reference in sub-paragraph (1) to the additional amount due or payable includes a reference to–

(a) an amount payable to HMRC having erroneously been paid by way of repayment of tax, and

(b) an amount which would be repayable by HMRC if the denied advantage were not counteracted.

2(3) The following are ignored in calculating the value of the denied advantage–

(a) group relief, and

(b) any relief under section 458 of CTA 2010 (relief in respect of repayment etc of loan) which is deferred under subsection (5) of that section.

2(4) This paragraph is subject to paragraphs 3 and 4.

VALUE OF DENIED ADVANTAGE: LOSSES

3(1) To the extent that the denied advantage has the result that a loss is wrongly recorded for purposes of direct tax and the loss has been wholly used to reduce the amount due or payable in respect of tax, the value of the denied advantage is determined in accordance with paragraph 2.

3(2) To the extent that the denied advantage has the result that a loss is wrongly recorded for purposes of direct tax and the loss has not been wholly used to reduce the amount due or payable in respect of tax, the value of the denied advantage is–

(a) the value under paragraph 2 of so much of the denied advantage as results from the part (if any) of the loss which is used to reduce the amount due or payable in respect of tax, plus

(b) 10% of the part of the loss not so used.

3(3) Sub-paragraphs (1) and (2) apply both–

(a) to a case where no loss would have been recorded but for the denied advantage, and

(b) to a case where a loss of a different amount would have been recorded (but in that case sub-paragraphs (1) and (2) apply only to the difference between the amount recorded and the true amount).

3(4) To the extent that a denied advantage creates or increases an aggregate loss recorded for a group of companies–

(a) the value of the denied advantage is calculated in accordance with this paragraph, and

(b) in applying paragraph 2 in accordance with sub-paragraphs (1) and (2), group relief may be taken into account (despite paragraph 2(3)).

3(5) To the extent that the denied advantage results in a loss, the value of it is nil where, because of the nature of the loss or P's circumstances, there is no reasonable prospect of the loss being used to support a claim to reduce a tax liability (of any person).

VALUE OF DENIED ADVANTAGE: DEFERRED TAX

4(1) To the extent that the denied advantage is a deferral of tax, the value of that advantage is–

(a) 25% of the amount of the deferred tax for each year of the deferral, or

(b) a percentage of the amount of the deferred tax, for each separate period of deferral of less than a year, equating to 25% per year,

or, if less, 100% of the amount of the deferred tax.

4(2) This paragraph does not apply to a case to the extent that paragraph 3 applies.

SCHEDULE 31 – FOLLOWER NOTICES AND PARTNERSHIPS

Section 215

INTRODUCTION

1 This Schedule makes special provision about the application of Chapter 2 to partners and partnerships.

INTERPRETATION

2(1) This paragraph applies for the purposes of this Schedule.

2(2) **"Partnership follower notice"** means a follower notice given by reason of–

(a) a tax enquiry being in progress into a partnership return, or

(b) an appeal having been made in relation to an amendment of a partnership return or against a conclusion stated by a closure notice in relation to a tax enquiry into a partnership return.

2(3) **"Partnership return"** means a return in pursuance of a notice under section 12AA(2) or (3) of TMA 1970.

2(4) **"The representative partner"**, in relation to a partnership return, means the person who was required by a notice served under or for the purposes of section 12AA(2) or (3) of TMA 1970 to deliver the return.

2(5) **"Relevant partner"**, in relation to a partnership return, means a person who was a partner in the partnership to which the return relates at any time during the period in respect of which the return was required.

2(6) References to a **"successor"**, in relation to the representative partner are to be construed in accordance with section 12AA(11) of TMA 1970.

Prospective amendments – Para. 2(3)(a) created form existing text, the words "(a "section 12AA partnership return"), or" inserted at the end of para. 2(3)(a) and para. 2(3)(b) inserted by F(No. 2)A 2017, s. 61 and Sch. 14, para. 45(2)(a), with effect from a day to be appointed under F(No. 2)A 2017, s. 61(6).

In para. 2(4) the words "section 12AA" inserted after the words "in relation to a" by F(No. 2)A 2017, s. 61 and Sch. 14, para. 45(2)(b), with effect from a day to be appointed under F(No. 2)A 2017, s. 61(6).

Para. 2(4A) inserted by F(No. 2)A 2017, s. 61 and Sch. 14, para. 45(2)(c), with effect from a day to be appointed under F(No. 2)A 2017, s. 61(6).

GIVING OF FOLLOWER NOTICES IN RELATION TO PARTNERSHIP RETURNS

3(1) If the representative partner in relation to a partnership return is no longer available, then, for the purposes of section 204 the return, or an appeal in respect of the return, is to be regarded as made by the person who is for the time being the successor of that partner (if that would not otherwise be the case).

3(2) Where, at any time after a partnership follower notice is given to P, P is no longer available, any reference in this Chapter (other than section 204 and this sub-paragraph) to P is to be read as a reference to the person who is, for the time being, the successor of the representative partner.

3(3) For the purposes of Condition B in section 204 a partnership return, or appeal in respect of a partnership return, is made on the basis that a particular tax advantage results from particular tax arrangements if–

(a) it is made on the basis that an increase or reduction in one or more of the amounts mentioned in section 12AB(1) of TMA 1970 (amounts in the partnership statement in a partnership return) results from those tax arrangements, and

(b) that increase or reduction results in that tax advantage for one or more of the relevant partners.

3(4) For the purposes of Condition D in section 204–

(a) a notice given to a person in the person's capacity as the representative partner of a partnership, or a successor of that partner, and a notice given to that person otherwise than in that capacity are not to be treated as given to the same person, and

(b) all notices given to the representative partner and successors of that partner, in that capacity, are to be treated as given to the same person.

3(5) In this paragraph references to a person being **"no longer available"** have the same meaning as in *section 12AA(11) of TMA 1970*.

Prospective amendments – In para. 3(1) the words "section 12AA" inserted after the words "in relation to a" by F(No. 2)A 2017, s. 61 and Sch. 14, para. 45(3)(a), with effect from a day to be appointed under F(No. 2)A 2017, s. 61(6).

Para. 3(1A) inserted by F(No. 2)A 2017, s. 61 and Sch. 14, para. 45(3(b), with effect from a day to be appointed under F(No. 2)A 2017, s. 61(6).

In para. 3(2) the words ", or the nominated partner (as the case may be)." inserted at the end by F(No. 2)A 2017, s. 61 and Sch. 14, para. 45(3)(c), with effect from a day to be appointed under F(No. 2)A 2017, s. 61(6).
In para. 3(4)(a) the words "or as the nominated partner of a partnership," inserted after the words "or a successor of that partner," and in para. 3(4)(b) the words "or to a nominated partner" inserted after the words "successors of that partner" by F(No. 2)A 2017, s. 61 and Sch. 14, para. 45(3)(d), with effect from a day to be appointed under F(No. 2)A 2017, s. 61(6).

PENALTY IF CORRECTIVE ACTION NOT TAKEN IN RESPONSE TO PARTNERSHIP FOLLOWER NOTICE

4(1) Section 208 applies, in relation to a partnership follower notice, in accordance with this paragraph.

4(2) Subsection (2) applies as if the reference to P were to each relevant partner.

4(3) References to the denied advantage are to be read as references to the increase or reduction in an amount in the partnership statement mentioned in paragraph 3(3) which is denied by the application of the principles laid down or the reasoning given in the judicial ruling identified in the partnership follower notice under section 206(a) or, if only part of any increase or reduction is so denied, that part.

4(4) In subsection (6)(b) the words from "and (where different)" to the end are to be ignored, and accordingly subsection (7) does not apply.

CALCULATION OF PENALTY ETC

5(1) This paragraph applies in relation to a partnership follower notice.

5(2) Section 209 applies subject to the following modifications–

(a) the total amount of the penalties under section 208(2) for which the relevant partners are liable is 20% of the value of the denied advantage,

(b) the amount of the penalty for which each relevant partner is liable is that partner's appropriate share of that total amount, and

(c) the value of the denied advantage for the purposes of calculating the total amount of the penalties is–

(i) in the case of a notice given under section 204(2)(a), the net amount of the amendments required to be made to the partnership return to counteract the denied advantage, and

(ii) in the case of a notice given under section 204(2)(b), the net amount of the amendments that have been made to the partnership return to counteract the denied advantage,

(and, accordingly, Schedule 30 does not apply).

5(3) For the purposes of sub-paragraph (2), a relevant partner's appropriate share is–

(a) the same share as the share in which any profits or loss for the period to which the return relates would be apportioned to that partner in accordance with the firm's profit-sharing arrangements, or

(b) if HMRC do not have sufficient information from P to establish that share, such share as is determined for the purposes of this paragraph by an officer of HMRC.

5(4) Where–

(a) the relevant partners are liable to pay a penalty under section 208(2) (as modified by this paragraph),

(b) the penalties have not yet been assessed, and

(c) P has co-operated with HMRC,

section 210(1) does not apply, but HMRC may reduce the total amount of the penalties determined in accordance with sub-paragraph (2)(a) to reflect the quality of that co-operation.
Section 210(2) and (3) apply for the purposes of this sub-paragraph.

5(5) Nothing in sub-paragraph (4) permits HMRC to reduce the total amount of the penalties to less than 4% of the value of the denied advantage (as determined in accordance with sub-paragraph (2)(c)).

5(6) For the purposes of section 212, a penalty imposed on a relevant partner by virtue of paragraph 4(2) is to be treated as if it were determined by reference to such additional amount of tax as is due and payable by the relevant partner as a result of the counteraction of the denied advantage.

5(7) The right of appeal under section 214 extends to–

(a) a decision that penalties are payable by the relevant partners by virtue of this paragraph, and

(b) a decision as to the total amount of those penalties payable by those partners,

but not to a decision as to the appropriate share of, or the amount of a penalty payable by, a relevant partner.

5(8) Section 214(3) applies to an appeal by virtue of sub-paragraph (7)(a) as it applies to an appeal under section 214(1).

5(9) Section 214(8) applies to an appeal by virtue of sub-paragraph (7)(a), and section 214(9) to an appeal by virtue of sub-paragraph (7)(b).

5(10) An appeal by virtue of sub-paragraph (7) may be brought only by the representative partner or, if that partner is no longer available, the person who is for the time being the successor of that partner.

5(11) The Treasury may by order made by statutory instrument vary the rates for the time being specified in sub-paragraphs (2)(a) and (5).

5(12) Any statutory instrument containing an order under sub-paragraph (10) is subject to annulment in pursuance of a resolution of the House of Commons.

Prospective amendments – Para. 5(10)(a) created form existing text, the words "(in relation to a section 12AA partnership return), or" inserted at the end of para. 5(10)(a) and para. 5(10)(b) inserted by F(No. 2)A 2017, s. 61 and Sch. 14, para. 45(4), with effect from a day to be appointed under F(No. 2)A 2017, s. 61(6).

SCHEDULE 32 – ACCELERATED PAYMENTS AND PARTNERSHIPS

Section 228

INTERPRETATION

1(1) This paragraph applies for the purposes of this Schedule.

1(2) **"Partnership return"** means a return in pursuance of a notice under section 12AA(2) or (3) of TMA 1970.

1(3) **"The representative partner"**, in relation to a partnership return, means the person who was required by a notice served under or for the purposes of section 12AA(2) or (3) of TMA 1970 to deliver the return.

1(4) **"Relevant partner"**, in relation to a partnership return, means a person who was a partner in the partnership to which the return relates at any time during the period in respect of which the return was required.

1(5) References to a **"successor"**, in relation to the representative partner, are to be construed in accordance with section 12AA(11) of TMA 1970.

Prospective amendments – Para. 1(2)(a) created form existing text, the words "(a "section 12AA partnership return"), or" inserted at the end of para. 1(2)(a) and para. 1(2)(b) inserted by F(No. 2)A 2017, s. 61 and Sch. 14, para. 46(2)(a), with effect from a day to be appointed under F(No. 2)A 2017, s. 61(6).

In para. 1(3) the words "section 12AA" inserted after the words "in relation to a" by F(No. 2)A 2017, s. 61 and Sch. 14, para. 46(2)(b), with effect from a day to be appointed under F(No. 2)A 2017, s. 61(6).

Para. 1(3A) inserted by F(No. 2)A 2017, s. 61 and Sch. 14, para. 46(2)(c), with effect from a day to be appointed under F(No. 2) A 2017, s. 61(6).

RESTRICTION ON CIRCUMSTANCES WHEN ACCELERATED PAYMENT NOTICES CAN BE GIVEN

2(1) This paragraph applies where–

(a) a tax enquiry is in progress in relation to a partnership return, or

(b) an appeal has been made in relation to an amendment of such a return or against a conclusion stated by a closure notice in relation to a tax enquiry into such a return.

2(2) No accelerated payment notice may be given to the representative partner of the partnership, or a successor of that partner, by reason of that enquiry or appeal.

2(3) But this Schedule makes provision for partner payment notices and accelerated partner payments in such cases.

Prospective amendments – In para. 2(2) the words "(in relation to a section 12AA partnership return), or to the nominated partner of the partnership (in relation to a Schedule A1 partnership return)" inserted after the words "a successor of that partner" by F(No. 2)A 2017, s. 61 and Sch. 14, para. 46(3), with effect from a day to be appointed under F(No. 2)A 2017, s. 61(6).

CIRCUMSTANCES IN WHICH PARTNER PAYMENT NOTICES MAY BE GIVEN

3(1) Where a partnership return has been made in respect of a partnership, HMRC may give a notice (a "partner payment notice") to each relevant partner of the partnership if Conditions A to C are met.

3(2) Condition A is that–

(a) a tax enquiry is in progress in relation to the partnership return, or

(b) an appeal has been made in relation to an amendment of the return or against a conclusion stated by a closure notice in relation to a tax enquiry into the return.

3(3) Condition B is that the return or, as the case may be, appeal is made on the basis that a particular tax advantage ("the asserted advantage") results from particular arrangements ("the chosen arrangements").

3(4) Paragraph 3(3) of Schedule 31 applies for the purposes of sub-paragraph (3) as it applies for the purposes of Condition B in section 204(3).

3(5) Condition C is that one or more of the following requirements are met–

(a) HMRC has given (or, at the same time as giving the partner payment notice, gives) the representative partner, or a successor of that partner, a follower notice under Chapter 2–

(i) in relation to the same return or, as the case may be, appeal, and

(ii) by reason of the same tax advantage and the chosen arrangements;

(b) the chosen arrangements are DOTAS arrangements (within the meaning of section 219(5) and (6));

(c) the relevant partner in question has been given a GAAR counteraction notice in respect of any tax advantage resulting from the asserted advantage or part of it and the chosen arrangements (or is given such a notice at the same time as the partner payment notice) in a case where the stated opinion of at least two of the members of the sub-panel of the GAAR Advisory Panel which considered the matter under paragraph 10 of Schedule 43 to FA 2013 was as set out in paragraph 11(3)(b) of that Schedule (entering into tax arrangements not reasonable course of action etc);

(d) the relevant partner in question has been given a notice under paragraph 8(2) or 9(2) of Schedule 43A to FA 2013 (notice of final decision after considering Panel's opinion about referred or counteracted arrangements) in respect of any tax advantage resulting from the asserted advantage or part of it and the chosen arrangements (or is given such a notice at the same time as the partner payment notice) in a case where the stated opinion of at least two of the members of the sub-panel of the GAAR Advisory Panel about the other arrangements (see sub-paragraph (7)) was as set out in paragraph 11(3)(b) of Schedule 43 to FA 2013;

(e) the relevant partner in question has been given a notice under paragraph 8(2) of Schedule 43B to FA 2013 (GAAR: generic referral of arrangements) in respect of any tax advantage resulting from the asserted advantage or part of it and the chosen arrangements (or is given such a notice at the same time as the partner payment notice) in a case where the stated opinion of at least two of the members of the sub-panel of the GAAR Advisory Panel which considered the generic referral in respect of those arrangements was as set out in paragraph 6(4)(b) of that Schedule.

3(6) **"GAAR counteraction notice"** has the meaning given by section 219(7).

3(7) **"Other arrangements"** means–

(a) in relation to a notice under paragraph 8(2) of Schedule 43A to FA 2013, the referred arrangements (as defined in that paragraph);

(b) in relation to a notice under paragraph 9(2) of that Schedule, the counteracted arrangements (as defined in paragraph 2 of that Schedule).

Prospective amendments – In para. 3(5)(a) the words "(in relation to a section 12AA partnership return), or the nominated partner (in relation to a Schedule A1 partnership return)" inserted after the words "or a successor of that partner" by F(No. 2)A 2017, s. 61 and Sch. 14, para. 46(4), with effect from a day to be appointed under F(No. 2)A 2017, s. 61(6).

History – Para. 3(5)(d) and (e) inserted by FA 2016, s. 157(27), with effect in relation to tax arrangements (within the meaning of FA 2013, Pt. 5) entered into at any time (whether before or on or after 15 September 2016).

Para. 3(7) inserted by FA 2016, s. 157(28), with effect in relation to tax arrangements (within the meaning of FA 2013, Pt. 5) entered into at any time (whether before or on or after 15 September 2016).

CONTENT OF PARTNER PAYMENT NOTICES

4(1) The partner payment notice given to a relevant partner must–

(a) specify the paragraph or paragraphs of paragraph 3(5) by virtue of which the notice is given,

(b) specify the payment (if any) required to be made under paragraph 6,

(c) explain the effect of paragraphs 5 and 6, and of the amendments made by sections 224 and 225 (so far as relating to the relevant tax in relation to which the partner payment notice is given), and

(d) if the denied advantage consists of or includes an asserted surrenderable amount, specify that amount and any action which is required to be taken in respect of it under paragraph 6A.

4(2) The payment required to be made under paragraph 6 is an amount equal to the amount which a designated HMRC officer determines, to the best of the officer's information and belief, as the understated partner tax.

4(3) **"The understated partner tax"** means the additional amount that would become due and payable by the relevant partner in respect of tax if–

(a) in the case of a notice given by virtue of paragraph 3(5)(a) (case where a partnership follower notice is given)–

(i) it were assumed that the explanation given in the follower notice in question under section 206(b) is correct, and

(ii) what the officer may determine to the best of the officer's information and belief as the denied advantage is counteracted to the extent that it is reflected in a return or claim of the relevant partner;

(b) in the case of a notice given by virtue of paragraph 3(5)(b) (cases where the DOTAS arrangements are met), such adjustments were made as are required to counteract so much of what the designated HMRC officer so determines as the denied advantage as is reflected in a return or claim of the relevant partner;

(c) in the case of a notice given by virtue of paragraph 3(5)(c) (cases involving counteraction under the general anti-abuse rule), such of the adjustments set out in the GAAR counteraction notice are made as have effect to counteract so much of the denied advantage as is reflected in a return or claim of the relevant partner.

4(4) "The denied advantage"–

(a) in the case of the notice given by virtue of paragraph 3(5)(a), has the meaning given by paragraph 4(3) of Schedule 31,

(b) in the case of a notice given by virtue of paragraph 3(5)(b), means so much of the asserted advantage as is not a tax advantage which results from the chosen arrangements or otherwise, and

(c) in the case of a notice given by virtue of paragraph 3(5)(c), means so much of the asserted advantage as would be counteracted by making the adjustments set out in the GAAR counteraction notice.

4(4A) "Asserted surrenderable amount" means so much of a surrenderable loss which the relevant partner asserts to have as a designated HMRC officer determines, to the best of that officer's information and belief, to be an amount–

(a) which would not be a surrenderable loss of that partner if the position were as stated in paragraphs (a), (b) or (c) of sub-paragraph (3), and

(b) which is not the subject of a claim by the relevant partner to relief from corporation tax which is reflected in the amount of the understated partner tax of that partner (and hence in the payment required to be made under paragraph 6).

4(4B) "Surrenderable loss" means a loss or other amount within section 99(1) of CTA 2010 (or part of such a loss or other amount).

4(5) If a notice is given by reason of two or all of the requirements of paragraph 3(5) being met, any payment specified under sub-paragraph (1)(b) or amount specified under sub-paragraph (1)(d) is to be determined as if the notice were given by virtue of such one of them as is stated in the notice as being used for this purpose.

History – In para. 4(1)(b) the words "(if any)" inserted by FA 2015, s. 118 and Sch. 18, para. 10(2), with effect from 26 March 2015. Para. 4(1)(d) (and the word ", and" preceding) inserted and the word "and" at the end of para. (b) omitted by FA 2015, s. 118 and Sch. 18, para. 10(2), with effect from 26 March 2015.
Para. 4(4A) and (4B) inserted by FA 2015, s. 118 and Sch. 18, para. 10(2), with effect from 26 March 2015.
In para. 4(5) the words "any payment specified under sub-paragraph (1)(b) or amount specified under sub-paragraph (1)(d)" substituted for the words "the payment specified under sub-paragraph (1)(b)" by FA 2015, s. 118 and Sch. 18, para. 10(2), with effect from 26 March 2015.

REPRESENTATIONS ABOUT A PARTNER PAYMENT NOTICE

5(1) This paragraph applies where a partner payment notice has been given to a relevant partner under paragraph 3 (and not withdrawn).

5(2) The relevant partner has 90 days beginning with the day that notice is given to send written representations to HMRC–

(a) objecting to the notice on the grounds that Condition A, B or C in that paragraph was not met,

(b) objecting to the amount specified in the notice under paragraph 4(1)(b), or

(c) objecting to the amount specified in the notice under paragraph 4(1)(d).

5(3) HMRC must consider any representations made in accordance with sub-paragraph (2).

5(4) Having considered the representations, HMRC must–

(a) if representations were made under sub-paragraph (2)(a), determine whether–

(i) to confirm the partner payment notice (with or without amendment), or

(ii) to withdraw the partner payment notice,

(b) if representations were made under sub-paragraph (2)(b) (and the notice is not withdrawn under paragraph (a)), determine whether a different amount (or no amount) ought to have been specified as the understated partner tax, and then–

(i) confirm the amount specified in the notice,

(ii) amend the notice to specify a different amount, or

(iii) remove from the notice the provision made under paragraph 4(1)(b), and

(c) if representations were made under sub-paragraph (2)(c) (and the notice is not withdrawn under paragraph (a)), determine whether a different amount (or no amount) ought to have been specified under paragraph 4(1)(d), and then–

(i) confirm the amount specified in the notice,

(ii) amend the notice to specify a different amount, or

(iii) remove from the notice the provision made under paragraph 4(1)(d),

5(4) and notify P accordingly.

History – Para. 5(2)(c) (and the word ", or" preceding) inserted and the word "or" at the end of para. (a) omitted by FA 2015, s. 118 and Sch. 18, para. 10(3), with effect from 26 March 2015.
In para. 5(4) the word "or" at the end of para. (a) omitted by FA 2015, s. 118 and Sch. 18, para. 10(3), with effect from 26 March 2015.
In para. 5(4)(b) the words "(or no amount)" inserted by FA 2015, s. 118 and Sch. 18, para. 10(3), with effect from 26 March 2015.
Para. 5(4)(b)(iii) (and the word ", or" preceding) inserted and the word "or" at the end of para. (b)(i) omitted and para. (4)(c) (and the word ", and" preceding it) inserted by FA 2015, s. 118 and Sch. 18, para. 10(3), with effect from 26 March 2015.

EFFECT OF PARTNER PAYMENT NOTICE

6(1) This paragraph applies where–

(a) a partner payment notice has been given to a relevant partner (and not withdrawn), and

(b) an amount is stated in the notice in accordance with paragraph 4(1)(b).

6(2) The relevant partner must make a payment ("the accelerated partner payment") to HMRC of that amount.

6(3) The accelerated partner payment is to be treated as a payment on account of the understated partner tax (see paragraph 4).

6(4) The accelerated partner payment must be made before the end of the payment period.

6(5) **"The payment period"** means–

(a) if the relevant partner made no representations under paragraph 5, the period of 90 days beginning with the day on which the partner payment notice is given;

(b) if the relevant partner made such representations, whichever of the following ends later–

(i) the 90 day period mentioned in paragraph (a);

(ii) the period of 30 days beginning with the day on which the relevant partner is notified under paragraph 5 of HMRC's determination.

6(6) If the relevant partner pays any part of the understated partner tax before the accelerated partner payment in respect of it, the accelerated partner payment is treated to that extent as having been paid at the same time.

6(7) Subsections (8) and (9) of section 223 apply in relation to a payment under this paragraph as they apply to a payment under that section.

History – Para. 6(1) substituted by FA 2015, s. 118 and Sch. 18, para. 10(4), with effect from 26 March 2015. Former para. 6(1) read as follows:
"6(1) This paragraph applies where a partner payment notice has been given to a relevant partner (and not withdrawn)."
In para. 6(2) the words "that amount" substituted for the words "the amount specified in the notice in accordance with paragraph 4(1)(b)" by FA 2015, s. 118 and Sch. 18, para. 10(4), with effect from 26 March 2015.

6A(1) This paragraph applies where–

(a) an accelerated payment notice is given (and not withdrawn), and

(b) an amount is specified in the notice in accordance with paragraph 4(1)(d).

6A(2) The relevant partner may not at any time when the notice has effect consent to any claim for group relief in respect of the amount so specified.

6A(3) Subject to sub-paragraph (2), paragraph 75 (other than sub-paragraphs (7) and (8)) of Schedule 18 to FA 1998 (reduction in amount available for surrender) has effect at any time when the notice has effect as if that specified amount ceased to be an amount available for surrender at the time the notice was given to the relevant partner.

6A(4) For the purposes of sub-paragraph (3), paragraph 75 of that Schedule has effect as if, in sub-paragraph (2) of that paragraph for "within 30 days" there were substituted "before the end of the payment period (within the meaning of paragraph 6(5) of Schedule 32 to the Finance Act 2014)".

6A(5) The time limits otherwise applicable to amendment of a company tax return do not prevent an amendment being made in accordance with paragraph 75(6) of Schedule 18 to FA 1998 where the relevant partner withdraws consent by virtue of sub-paragraph (3).

History – Para. 6A inserted by FA 2015, s. 118 and Sch. 18, para. 10(5), with effect from 26 March 2015 subject to the transitional provision at Sch. 18, para. 12(2).

PENALTY FOR FAILURE TO COMPLY WITH PARTNER PAYMENT NOTICE

7 Section 226 (penalty for failure to make accelerated payment on time) applies to accelerated partner payments as if–

(a) references in that section to the accelerated payment were to the accelerated partner payment,

(b) references to P were to the relevant partner, and

(c) **"the payment period"** had the meaning given by paragraph 6(5).

WITHDRAWAL, SUSPENSION OR MODIFICATION OF PARTNER PAYMENT NOTICES

8(1) Section 227 (withdrawal, modification or suspension of accelerated payment notice) applies in relation to a relevant partner, a partner payment notice, Condition C in paragraph 3 and an accelerated partner payment as it applies in relation to P, an accelerated payment notice, Condition C in section 219 and an accelerated payment.

8(2) Accordingly, for this purpose–

(za) section 227(2)(d), (12A) and (16) has effect as if the references to section 220(2)(d) or 221(2)(d) were to paragraph 4(1)(d) of this Schedule,

(a) section 227(6)(b) and (7)(a) has effect as if the references to section 220(6) were to paragraph 4(5) of this Schedule,

(b) the provisions listed in section 227(9) are to be read as including paragraph 6(5) of this Schedule, and

(c) section 227(12A) has effect as if the reference to section 225A(3) were to paragraph 6A(3) of this Schedule.

History – Para. 8(2)(za) inserted by FA 2015, s. 118 and Sch. 18, para. 10(6), with effect from 26 March 2015 subject to the transitional provision at Sch. 18, para. 12(2).

Para. 8(2)(c) (and the word "; and" preceding it) inserted and the word "and" after para. (a) omitted by FA 2015, s. 118 and Sch. 18, para. 10(6), with effect from 26 March 2015 subject to the transitional provision at Sch. 18, para. 12(2).

SCHEDULE 33 – PART 4: CONSEQUENTIAL AMENDMENTS

Section 233

TAXES MANAGEMENT ACT 1970

1 [Not relevant to inheritance tax.]

2 [Not relevant to inheritance tax.]

FINANCE ACT 2007

3 [Inserts FA 2007, Sch. 24, para. 12(2A).]

FINANCE ACT 2009

5 [Inserts FA 2009, Sch. 55, para. 17(2)(c).]

SCHEDULE 34 – PROMOTERS OF TAX AVOIDANCE SCHEMES: THRESHOLD CONDITIONS

Section 237

Part 1 – Meeting the Threshold Conditions: General

MEANING OF "THRESHOLD CONDITION"

1 Each of the conditions described in paragraphs 2 to 12 is a "threshold condition".

DELIBERATE TAX DEFAULTERS

2 A person meets this condition if the Commissioners publish information about the person in reliance on section 94 of FA 2009 (publishing details of deliberate tax defaulters).

BREACH OF THE BANKING CODE OF PRACTICE

3 A person meets this condition if the person is named in a report under section 285 as a result of the Commissioners determining that the person breached the Code of Practice on Taxation for Banks by reason of promoting arrangements which the person cannot have reasonably believed achieved a tax result which was intended by Parliament.

DISHONEST TAX AGENTS

4 A person meets this condition if the person is given a conduct notice under paragraph 4 of Schedule 38 to FA 2012 (tax agents: dishonest conduct) and either–

(a) the time period during which a notice of appeal may be given in relation to the notice has expired, or

(b) an appeal against the notice has been made and the tribunal has confirmed the determination referred to in sub-paragraph (1) of paragraph 4 of that Schedule.

NON-COMPLIANCE WITH PART 7 OF FA 2004

5(1) A person meets this condition if the person fails to comply with any of the following provisions of Part 7 of FA 2004 (disclosure of tax avoidance schemes)–

(a) section 308(1) and (3) (duty of promoter in relation to notifiable proposals and notifiable arrangements);

(b) section 309(1) (duty of person dealing with promoter outside the United Kingdom);

(c) section 310 (duty of parties to notifiable arrangements not involving promoter);

(d) section 313ZA (duty of promoter to provide details of clients).

5(2) For the purposes of sub-paragraph (1), a person ("P") fails to comply with a provision mentioned in that sub-paragraph if and only if any of conditions A to C are met.

5(3) Condition A is met if–

(a) the tribunal has determined that P has failed to comply with the provision concerned,

(b) the appeal period has ended, and

(c) the determination has not been overturned on appeal.

5(4) Condition B is met if–

(a) the tribunal has determined for the purposes of section 118(2) of TMA 1970 that P is to be deemed not to have failed to comply with the provision concerned as P had a reasonable excuse for not doing the thing required to be done,

(b) the appeal period has ended, and

(c) the determination has not been overturned on appeal.

5(5) Condition C is met if P has admitted in writing to HMRC that P has failed to comply with the provision concerned.

5(6) The **"appeal period"** means–

(a) the period during which an appeal could be brought against the determination of the tribunal, or

(b) where an appeal mentioned in paragraph (a) has been brought, the period during which that appeal has not been finally determined, withdrawn or otherwise disposed of.

History – Para. 5(2)–(6) substituted for former para. 5(2) by FA 2015, s. 119 and Sch. 19, para. 6, with effect for the purposes of determining whether a person meets a threshold condition in a period of three years ending on or after 26 March 2015 (Royal Assent). Former para. 5(2) read as follows:

"**5(2)** For the purposes of sub-paragraph (1), failure to comply includes cases (despite section 118(2) of TMA 1970) where a person had a reasonable excuse for not doing the thing required to be done."

CRIMINAL OFFENCES

6(1) A person meets this condition if the person is charged with a relevant offence.

6(2) The fact that a person has been charged with an offence is disregarded for the purposes of this paragraph if–

(a) the person has been acquitted of the offence, or

(b) the charge has been dismissed or the proceedings have been discontinued.

6(3) An acquittal is not taken into account for the purposes of sub-paragraph (2) if an appeal has been brought against the acquittal and has not yet been disposed of.

6(4) **"Relevant offence"** means any of the following–

(a) an offence at common law of cheating in relation to the public revenue;
(b) in Scotland, an offence at common law of–
  (i) fraud;
  (ii) uttering;
(c) an offence under section 17(1) of the Theft Act 1968 or section 17 of the Theft Act (Northern Ireland) 1969 (c. 16 (N.I.)) (false accounting);
(d) an offence under section 106A of TMA 1970 (fraudulent evasion of income tax);
(e) an offence under section 107 of TMA 1970 (false statements: Scotland);
(f) [Not relevant to inheritance tax.]
(g) [Not relevant to inheritance tax.]
(h) an offence under section 1 of the Fraud Act 2006 (fraud);
(i) an offence under any of the following provisions of CRCA 2005–
  (i) section 30 (impersonating a Commissioner or officer of Revenue and Customs);
  (ii) section 31 (obstruction of officer of Revenue and Customs etc);
  (iii) section 32 (assault of officer of Revenue and Customs);
(j) an offence under regulation 86(1) of the Money Laundering, Terrorist Financing and Transfer of Funds (Information on the Payer) Regulations 2017;
(k) an offence under section 49(1) of the Criminal Justice and Licensing (Scotland) Act 2010 (asp 13) (possession of articles for use in fraud).

History – In para. 6(4)(j), the words "regulation 86(1) of the Money Laundering, Terrorist Financing and Transfer of Funds (Information on the Payer) Regulations 2017" substituted for the words "regulation 45(1) of the Money Laundering Regulations 2007 (S.I. 2007/2157)" by SI 2017/692, Sch. 7, para. 10, with effect from 26 June 2017.

OPINION NOTICE OF GAAR ADVISORY PANEL

7 A person meets this condition if–
(a) arrangements in relation to which the person is a promoter–
  (i) have been referred to the GAAR Advisory Panel under Schedule 43 to FA 2013 (referrals of single schemes),
  (ii) are in a pool in respect of which a referral has been made to that Panel under Schedule 43B to that Act (generic referrals), or
  (iii) have been referred to that Panel under paragraph 26 of Schedule 16 to F(No. 2)A 2017 (referrals in relation to penalties for enablers of defeated tax avoidance),
(b) one or more opinion notices are given in respect of the referral under (as the case may be)–
  (i) paragraph 11(3)(b) of Schedule 43 to FA 2013,
  (ii) paragraph 6(4)(b) of Schedule 43B to that Act, or
  (iii) paragraph 34(3)(b) of Schedule 16 to F(No. 2)A 2017,

(opinion of sub-panel of GAAR Advisory Panel that arrangements are not reasonable), and
(c) the notice, or the notices taken together, either–
  (i) state the joint opinion of all the members of the sub-panel arranged under that Schedule, or
  (ii) state the opinion of two or more members of that sub-panel.

History – Para. 7(a)(i)–(iii) (and the "–" preceding them) substituted for the words "have been referred to the GAAR Advisory Panel under Schedule 43 to FA 2013, (referrals of single schemes) or are in a pool in respect of which a referral has been made to that Panel under Schedule 43B to that Act (generic referrals)," by F(No. 2)A 2017, s. 65 and Sch. 16, para. 61(a), with effect in relation to arrangements entered into on or after 16 November 2017 (Royal Assent).
In para. 7(a), the words "(referrals of single schemes) or are in a pool in respect of which a referral has been made to that Panel under Schedule 43B to that Act (generic referrals)," inserted by FA 2016, s. 157(29)(a), with effect in relation to tax arrangements (within the meaning of FA 2013, Pt. 5) entered into at any time (whether before or on or after 15 September 2016).
Para. 7(b)(i)–(iii) (and the "under (as the case may be)–" preceding them and the end words after them) substituted for the words "under paragraph 11(3)(b) or (as the case may be) 6(4)(b) of that Schedule (opinion of sub-panel of GAAR Advisory Panel that arrangements are not reasonable), and" by F(No. 2)A 2017, s. 65 and Sch. 16, para. 61(b), with effect in relation to arrangements entered into on or after 16 November 2017 (Royal Assent).
In para. 7(b), the words "in respect of the referral" substituted for the words "in relation to the arrangements" and the words "or (as the case may be) 6(4)(b)" inserted by FA 2016, s. 157(29)(b), with effect in relation to tax arrangements (within the meaning of FA 2013, Pt. 5) entered into at any time (whether before or on or after 15 September 2016).
In para. 7(c), the words "paragraph 10 of" (which appeared before the words "that Schedule") omitted by FA 2016, s. 157(29)(c), with *effect in relation to tax arrangements* (within the meaning of FA 2013, Pt. 5) entered into at any time (whether before or on or after 15 September 2016).

DISCIPLINARY ACTION AGAINST A MEMBER OF A TRADE OR PROFESSION

History – In the heading the words "AGAINST A MEMBER OF A TRADE OR PROFESSION" substituted for the words "BY A PROFESSIONAL BODY" by FA 2015, s. 119 and Sch. 19, para. 7(3), with effect for the purposes of determining whether a person meets a threshold condition in a period of three years ending on or after 26 March 2015 (Royal Assent).

8(1) A person who carries on a trade or profession that is regulated by a professional body meets this condition if all of the following conditions are met–

(a) the person is found guilty of misconduct of a prescribed kind,

(b) action of a prescribed kind is taken against the person in relation to that misconduct, and

(c) a penalty of a prescribed kind is imposed on the person as a result of that misconduct.

8(2) Misconduct may only be prescribed for the purposes of sub-paragraph (1)(a) if it is misconduct other than misconduct in matters (such as the payment of fees) that relate solely or mainly to the person's relationship with the professional body.

8(3) A **"professional body"** means–

(a) the Institute of Chartered Accountants in England and Wales;

(b) the Institute of Chartered Accountants of Scotland;

(c) the General Council of the Bar;

(d) the Faculty of Advocates;

(e) the General Council of the Bar of Northern Ireland;

(f) the Law Society;

(g) the Law Society of Scotland;

(h) the Law Society of Northern Ireland;

(i) the Association of Accounting Technicians;

(j) the Association of Chartered Certified Accountants;

(k) the Association of Taxation Technicians;

(l) any other prescribed body with functions relating to the regulation of a trade or profession.

History – Para. 8(1) substituted by FA 2015, s. 119 and Sch. 19, para. 7(2), with effect for the purposes of determining whether a person meets a threshold condition in a period of three years ending on or after 26 March 2015 (Royal Assent). Former para. 8(1) read as follows:

"8(1) A person meets this condition if a professional body–

(a) determines that the person is guilty of misconduct of a kind prescribed for the purposes of this paragraph, and

(b) takes in relation to that misconduct action of a kind so prescribed, and

(c) imposes on the person a penalty of a kind so prescribed."

In para. 8(3)(h) the word "of" substituted for the word "for" by FA 2015, s. 119 and Sch. 19, para. 7(2)4 with effect for the purposes of determining whether a person meets a threshold condition in a period of three years ending on or after 26 March 2015 (Royal Assent).

Statutory instruments – SI 2015/131: partly made under para. 8(1) and (3).

DISCIPLINARY ACTION BY A REGULATORY AUTHORITY

9(1) A person meets this condition if a regulatory authority imposes a relevant sanction on the person.

9(2) A **"relevant sanction"** is a sanction which is–

(a) imposed in relation to misconduct other than misconduct in matters (such as the payment of fees) that relate solely or mainly to the person's relationship with the regulatory authority, and

(b) prescribed.

9(3) The following are regulatory authorities for the purposes of this paragraph–

(a) the Financial Conduct Authority;

(b) the Financial Services Authority;

(c) any other authority that may be prescribed.

9(4) Only authorities that have functions relating to the regulation of financial institutions may be prescribed under sub-paragraph (3)(c).

Statutory instruments – SI 2015/131: partly made under para. 9(2).

EXERCISE OF INFORMATION POWERS

10(1) A person meets this condition if the person fails to comply with an information notice given under any of paragraphs 1, 2, 5 and 5A of Schedule 36 to FA 2008.

10(2) For the purposes of section 237, the failure to comply is taken to occur when the period within which the person is required to comply with the notice expires (without the person having complied with it).

RESTRICTIVE CONTRACTUAL TERMS

11(1) A person ("P") meets this condition if P enters into an agreement with another person ("C") which relates to a relevant proposal or relevant arrangements in relation to which P is a promoter, on terms which–

(a) impose a contractual obligation on C which falls within sub-paragraph (2) or (3), or

(b) impose on C both obligations within sub-paragraph (4) and obligations within sub-paragraph (5).

11(2) A contractual obligation falls within this sub-paragraph if it prevents or restricts the disclosure by C to HMRC of information relating to the proposals or arrangements, whether or not by referring to a wider class of persons.

11(3) A contractual obligation falls within this sub-paragraph if it requires C to impose on any tax adviser to whom C discloses information relating to the proposals or arrangements a contractual obligation which prevents or restricts the disclosure of that information to HMRC by the adviser.

11(4) A contractual obligation falls within this sub-paragraph if it requires C to–

(a) meet (in whole or in part) the costs of, or contribute to a fund to be used to meet the costs of, any proceedings relating to arrangements in relation to which P is a promoter (whether or not implemented by C), or

(b) take out an insurance policy which insures against the risk of having to meet the costs connected with proceedings relating to arrangements which C has implemented and in relation to which P is a promoter.

11(5) A contractual obligation falls within this paragraph if it requires C to obtain the consent of P before–

(a) entering into any agreement with HMRC regarding arrangements which C has implemented and in relation to which P is a promoter, or

(b) withdrawing or discontinuing any appeal against any decision regarding such arrangements.

11(6) In sub-paragraph (5)(b), the reference to withdrawing or discontinuing an appeal includes any action or inaction which results in an appeal being discontinued.

11(7) In this paragraph–

"proceedings" includes any sort of proceedings for resolving disputes (and not just proceedings in court), whether commenced or contemplated;

"tax adviser" means a person appointed to give advice about the tax affairs of another person (whether appointed directly by that person or by another tax adviser of that person).

CONTINUING TO PROMOTE CERTAIN ARRANGEMENTS

12(1) A person ("P") meets this condition if P has been given a stop notice and after the end of the notice period P–

(a) makes a firm approach to another person ("C") in relation to an affected proposal with a view to making the affected proposal available for implementation by C or another person, or

(b) makes an affected proposal available for implementation by other persons.

12(2) **"Affected proposal"** means a relevant proposal that is in substance the same as the relevant proposal specified in the stop notice in accordance with sub-paragraph (4)(c).

12(3) An authorised officer may give a person ("P") a notice (a "stop notice") if each of these conditions is met–

(a) a person has been given a follower notice under section 204 (circumstances in which a follower notice may be given) in relation to particular relevant arrangements;

(b) P is a promoter in relation to a relevant proposal that is implemented by those arrangements;

(c) 90 days have elapsed since the follower notice was given and–

(i) the follower notice has not been withdrawn, and

(ii) if representations objecting to the follower notice were made under section 207 (representations about a follower notice), HMRC have confirmed the follower notice.

12(4) A stop notice must–

(a) *specify the arrangements* which are the subject of the follower notice mentioned in sub-paragraph (3)(a),

(b) specify the judicial ruling identified in that follower notice,

(c) specify a relevant proposal in relation to which the condition in sub-paragraph (3)(b) is met, and

(d) explain the effect of the stop notice.

12(5) An authorised officer may determine that a stop notice given to a person is to cease to have effect.

12(6) If an authorised officer makes a determination under sub-paragraph (5) the officer must give the person written notice of the determination.

12(7) The notice must specify the date from which it takes effect, which may be earlier than the date on which the notice is given.

12(8) In this paragraph–

"the notice period" means the period of 30 days beginning with the day on which a stop notice is given;

"judicial ruling" means a ruling of a court or tribunal.

Part 2 – Meeting the Threshold Conditions: Bodies Corporate and Partnerships

History – In the heading the words "and Partnerships" inserted by FA 2015, s. 119 and Sch. 19, para. 4(2), with effect for the purposes of determining whether a person meets a threshold condition in a period of three years ending on or after 26 March 2015 (Royal Assent).

13 [Substituted by para. 13A–13D by FA 2015, s. 119 and Sch. 19, para. 4(3).]

History – Para. 13 substituted by former para 13A–13D by FA 2015, s. 119 and Sch. 19, para. 4(3), with effect for the purposes of determining whether a person meets a threshold condition in a period of three years ending on or after 26 March 2015 (Royal Assent). Former para. 13 read as follows:

"13(1) Sub-paragraph (2) applies where–

(a) a relevant threshold condition is met by a person ("P") at a time ("the earlier time") when P has control of a body corporate,

(b) a determination under section 237 is made at a later time in relation to the body corporate, and

(c) P has control of the body corporate at the time of the determination.

13(2) The body corporate is regarded as having met the threshold condition at the earlier time.

13(3) **"Relevant threshold condition"** means a threshold condition specified in any of the following paragraphs of Schedule 34–

(a) paragraph 2 (deliberate tax defaulters);

(b) paragraph 4 (dishonest tax agents);

(c) paragraph 6 (criminal offences);

(d) paragraph 7 (opinion notice of GAAR advisory panel);

(e) paragraph 8 (disciplinary action by professional body);

(f) paragraph 9 (disciplinary action by regulatory authority);

(g) paragraph 10 (failure to comply with information notice).

13(4) For the purposes of this paragraph a person ("P") has control of a body corporate ("B") if P has power to secure–

(a) by means of the holding of shares or the possession of voting power in relation to B or any other body corporate, or

(b) as a result of any powers conferred by the articles of association or other document regulating B or any other body corporate,

that the affairs of B are conducted in accordance with P's wishes."

INTERPRETATION

13A(1) This paragraph contains definitions for the purposes of this Part of this Schedule.

13A(2) Each of the following is a **"relevant body"**–

(a) a body corporate, and

(b) a partnership.

13A(3) **"Relevant time"** means the time referred to in section 237(1A) (duty to give conduct notice to person treated as meeting threshold condition).

13A(4) **"Relevant threshold condition"** means a threshold condition specified in any of the following paragraphs of this Schedule–

(a) paragraph 2 (deliberate tax defaulters);

(b) paragraph 4 (dishonest tax agents);

(c) paragraph 6 (criminal offences);

(d) paragraph 7 (opinion notice of GAAR advisory panel);

(e) paragraph 8 (disciplinary action against a member of a trade or profession);

(f) paragraph 9 (disciplinary action by regulatory authority);

(g) paragraph 10 (failure to comply with information notice).

13A(5) A person controls a body corporate if the person has power to secure that the affairs of the body corporate are conducted in accordance with the person's wishes–

(a) by means of the holding of shares or the possession of voting power in relation to the body corporate or any other relevant body,

(b) as a result of any powers conferred by the articles of association or other document regulating the body corporate or any other relevant body, or

(c) by means of controlling a partnership.

13A(6) Two or more persons together control a body corporate if together they have the power to secure that the affairs of the body corporate are conducted in accordance with their wishes in any way specified in sub-paragraph (5)(a) to (c).

13A(7) A person controls a partnership if the person is a member of the partnership and–

(a) has the right to a share of more than half the assets, or more than half the income, of the partnership, or

(b) directs, or is on a day-to-day level in control of, the management of the business of the partnership.

13A(8) Two or more persons together control a partnership if they are members of the partnership and together they–

(a) have the right to a share of more than half the assets, or of more than half the income, of the partnership, or

(b) direct, or are on a day-to-day level in control of, the management of the business of the partnership.

13A(9) Paragraph 19(2) to (5) of Schedule 36 (connected persons etc) applies to a person referred to in sub-paragraph (7) or (8) as if references to "P" were to that person.

13A(10) A person has significant influence over a body corporate or partnership if the person–

(a) does not control the body corporate or partnership, but

(b) is able to, or actually does, exercise significant influence over it (whether or not as the result of a legal entitlement).

13A(11) Two or more persons together have significant influence over a body corporate or partnership if together those persons–

(a) do not control the body corporate or partnership, but

(b) are able to, or actually do, exercise significant influence over it (whether or not as the result of a legal entitlement).

13A(12) References to a person being a promoter are to the person carrying on business as a promoter.

History – Para. 13A(6)–(12) substituted for para. 13A(6)–(8), by FA 2017, s. 24(1), with effect for the purposes of determining whether a person meets a threshold condition in a period of three years ending on or after 8 March 2017. Former para. 13A(6)–(8) read as follows:

"**13A(6)** A person controls a partnership if the person is a controlling member or the managing partner of the partnership.

13A(7) **"Controlling member"** has the same meaning as in Schedule 36 (partnerships).

13A(8) **"Managing partner"**, in relation to a partnership, means the member of the partnership who directs, or is on a day-to-day level in control of, the management of the business of the partnership.".

Para. 13A–13D substituted for former para 13 by FA 2015, s. 119 and Sch. 19, para. 4(3), with effect for the purposes of determining whether a person meets a threshold condition in a period of three years ending on or after 26 March 2015 (Royal Assent).

RELEVANT BODIES CONTROLLED ETC BY OTHER PERSONS TREATED AS MEETING A THRESHOLD CONDITION

13B(1) A relevant body is treated as meeting a threshold condition at the relevant time if any of Conditions A to C is met.

13B(2) Condition A is that–

(a) a person met the threshold condition at a time when the person was a promoter, and

(b) the person controls or has significant influence over the relevant body at the relevant time.

13B(3) Condition B is that–

(a) a person met the threshold condition at a time when the person controlled or had significant influence over the relevant body,

(b) the relevant body was a promoter at that time, and

(c) the person controls or has significant influence over the relevant body at the relevant time.

13B(4) Condition C is that–

(a) two or more persons together controlled or had significant influence over the relevant body at a time when one of those persons met the threshold condition,

(b) the relevant body was a promoter at that time, and

(c) those persons together control or have significant influence over the relevant body at the relevant time.

13B(5) Where the person referred to in sub-paragraph (2)(a) or (3)(a) or (4)(a) as meeting a threshold condition is an individual, sub-paragraph (1) only applies if the threshold condition is a relevant threshold condition.

13B(6) For the purposes of sub-paragraph (2) it does not matter whether the relevant body existed at the time referred to in sub-paragraph (2)(a).

History – Para. 13B substituted by FA 2017, s. 24(2), with effect for the purposes of determining whether a person meets a threshold condition in a period of three years ending on or after 8 March 2017. Former para. 13B read as follows:

"TREATING PERSONS UNDER ANOTHER'S CONTROL AS MEETING A THRESHOLD CONDITION

13B(1) A relevant body ("RB") is treated as meeting a threshold condition at the relevant time if–

(a) the threshold condition was met by a person ("C") at a time when–

(i) C was carrying on a business as a promoter, or

(ii) RB was carrying on a business as a promoter and C controlled RB, and

(b) RB is controlled by C at the relevant time.

13B(2) Where C is an individual sub-paragraph (1) applies only if the threshold condition mentioned in sub-paragraph (1)(a) is a relevant threshold condition.

13B(3) For the purposes of determining whether the requirements of sub-paragraph (1) are met by reason of meeting the requirement in sub-paragraph (1)(a)(i), it does not matter whether RB existed at the time when the threshold condition was met by C.".

Para. 13A and former para. 13B–13D substituted for former para. 13 by FA 2015, s. 119 and Sch. 19, para. 4(3), with effect for the purposes of determining whether a person meets a threshold condition in a period of three years ending on or after 26 March 2015 (Royal Assent).

PERSONS WHO CONTROL ETC A RELEVANT BODY TREATED AS MEETING A THRESHOLD CONDITION

13C(1) If at a time when a person controlled or had significant influence over a relevant body–

(a) the relevant body met a threshold condition, and

(b) the relevant body, or another relevant body which the person controlled or had significant influence over, was a promoter,

the person is treated as meeting the threshold condition at the relevant time.

13C(2) It does not matter whether any relevant body referred to sub-paragraph (1) exists at the relevant time.

History – Para. 13C substituted by FA 2017, s. 24(2), with effect for the purposes of determining whether a person meets a threshold condition in a period of three years ending on or after 8 March 2017. Former para. 13C read as follows:

"TREATING PERSONS IN CONTROL OF OTHERS AS MEETING A THRESHOLD CONDITION

13C(1) A person other than an individual is treated as meeting a threshold condition at the relevant time if–

(a) a relevant body ("A") met the threshold condition at a time when A was controlled by the person, and

(b) at the time mentioned in paragraph (a) A, or another relevant body ("B") which was also at that time controlled by the person, carried on a business as a promoter.

13C(2) For the purposes of determining whether the requirements of sub-paragraph (1) are met it does not matter whether A or B (or neither) exists at the relevant time.".

Para. 13A and former para. 13B–13D substituted for former para. 13 by FA 2015, s. 119 and Sch. 19, para. 4(3), with effect for the purposes of determining whether a person meets a threshold condition in a period of three years ending on or after 26 March 2015 (Royal Assent).

RELEVANT BODIES CONTROLLED ETC BY THE SAME PERSON TREATED AS MEETING A THRESHOLD CONDITION

13D(1) If–

(a) a person controlled or had significant influence over a relevant body at a time when it met a threshold condition, and

(b) at that time that body, or another relevant body which the person controlled or had significant influence over, was a promoter,

any relevant body which the person controls or has significant influence over at the relevant time is treated as meeting the threshold condition at the relevant time.

13D(2) If–

(a) two or more persons together controlled or had significant influence over a relevant body at a time when it met a threshold condition, and

(b) at that time that body, or another relevant body which those persons together controlled or had significant influence over, was a promoter,

any relevant body which those persons together control or have significant influence over at the relevant time is treated as meeting the threshold condition at the relevant time.

13D(3) It does not matter whether–

(a) a relevant body referred to in sub-paragraph (1)(a) or (b) or (2)(a) or (b) exists at the relevant time, or

(b) a relevant body existing at the relevant time existed at the time referred to in sub-paragraph (1)(a) or (2)(a).

History – Para. 13D substituted by FA 2017, s. 24(2), with effect for the purposes of determining whether a person meets a threshold condition in a period of three years ending on or after 8 March 2017. Former para. 13D read as follows:

"TREATING PERSONS CONTROLLED BY THE SAME PERSON AS MEETING A THRESHOLD CONDITION

13D(1) A relevant body ("RB") is treated as meeting a threshold condition at the relevant time if–

(a) RB or another relevant body met the threshold condition at a time ("time T") when it was controlled by a person ("C"),

(b) at time T, there was a relevant body controlled by C which carried on a business as a promoter, and

(c) RB is controlled by C at the relevant time.

13D(2) For the purposes of determining whether the requirements of sub-paragraph (1) are met it does not matter whether–
(a) RB existed at time T, or
(b) any relevant body (other than RB) by reason of which the requirements of sub-paragraph (1) are met exists at the relevant time.".
Para. 13A and former para. 13B–13D substituted for former para. 13 by FA 2015, s. 119 and Sch. 19, para. 4(3), with effect for the purposes of determining whether a person meets a threshold condition in a period of three years ending on or after 26 March 2015 (Royal Assent).

Part 3 – Power to Amend

14(1) The Treasury may by regulations amend this Schedule.

14(2) An amendment made by virtue of sub-paragraph (1) may, in particular–

(a) vary or remove any of the conditions set out in paragraphs 2 to 12;
(b) add new conditions.
(c) vary any of the circumstances described in paragraphs 13B to 13D in which a person is treated as meeting a threshold condition (including by amending paragraph 13A);
(d) add new circumstances in which a person will be so treated.

14(3) Regulations under sub-paragraph (1) may include any amendment of this Part of this Act that is appropriate in consequence of an amendment made by virtue of sub-paragraph (1).

History – Para. 14(2)(c) and (d) inserted by FA 2015, s. 119 and Sch. 19, para. 8 with effect from 26 March 2015 (Royal Assent).

SCHEDULE 34A – PROMOTERS OF TAX AVOIDANCE SCHEMES: DEFEATED ARRANGEMENTS

History – Sch. 34A inserted by FA 2016, s. 160(5), with effect from 15 September 2016 (Royal Assent).

Part 1 – Introduction

1 In this Schedule–

(a) Part 2 is about the meaning of **"relevant defeat"**;
(b) Part 3 contains provision about when a relevant defeat is treated as occurring in relation to a person;
(c) Part 4 contains provision about when a person is treated as meeting a condition in subsection (11), (12) or (13) of section 237A;
(d) Part 5 contains definitions and other supplementary provisions.

Part 2 – Meaning of "Relevant Defeat"

"RELATED" ARRANGEMENTS

2(1) For the purposes of this Part of this Act, separate arrangements which persons have entered into are **"related"** to one another if (and only if) they are substantially the same.

2(2) Sub-paragraphs (3) to (6) set out cases in which arrangements are to be treated as being **"substantially the same"** (if they would not otherwise be so treated under sub-paragraph (1)).

2(3) Arrangements to which the same reference number has been allocated under Part 7 of FA 2004 (disclosure of tax avoidance schemes) are treated as being substantially the same.
For this purpose arrangements in relation to which information relating to a reference number has been provided in compliance with section 312 of FA 2004 are treated as arrangements to which that reference number has been allocated under Part 7 of that Act.

2(4) Arrangements to which the same reference number has been allocated under paragraph 9 of Schedule 11A to VATA 1994 (disclosure of avoidance schemes) or paragraph 22 of Schedule 17 to F[(No. 2)]A 2017 (disclosure of avoidance schemes: VAT and other indirect taxes) are treated as being substantially the same.

2(5) Any two or more sets of arrangements which are the subject of follower notices given by reference to the same judicial ruling are treated as being substantially the same.

2(6) Where a notice of binding has been given in relation to any arrangements ("the bound arrangements") on the basis that they are, for the purposes of Schedule 43A to FA 2013, equivalent arrangements in relation to another set of arrangements (the "lead arrangements")–

(a) the bound arrangements and the lead arrangements are treated as being substantially the same, and
(b) the bound arrangements are treated as being substantially the same as any other arrangements which, as a result of this sub-paragraph, are treated as substantially the same as the lead arrangements.

History – In para. 2(4) the words "or paragraph 22 of Schedule 17 to FA 2017 (disclosure of avoidance schemes: VAT and other indirect taxes)" inserted by F(No. 2)A 2017, s. 66 and Sch. 17, para. 54(2), with effect so far as necessary for enabling the making of regulations under that Schedule from 16 November 2017 (Royal Assent) and from 1 January 2018 for all other purposes.

"PROMOTED ARRANGEMENTS"

3(1) For the purposes of this Schedule arrangements are **"promoted arrangements"** in relation to a person if–

(a) they are relevant arrangements or would be relevant arrangements under the condition stated in sub-paragraph (2), and

(b) the person is carrying on a business as a promoter and–

(i) the person is or has been a promoter in relation to the arrangements, or

(ii) that would be the case if the condition in sub-paragraph (2) were met.

3(2) That condition is that the definition of **"tax"** in section 283 includes, and has always included, value added tax.

RELEVANT DEFEAT OF SINGLE ARRANGEMENTS

4(1) A defeat of arrangements (entered into by any person) which are promoted arrangements in relation to a person ("the promoter") is a **"relevant defeat"** in relation to the promoter if the condition in sub-paragraph (2) is met.

4(2) The condition is that the arrangements are not related to any other arrangements which are promoted arrangements in relation to the promoter.

4(3) For the meaning of **"defeat"** see paragraphs 10 to 16.

RELEVANT DEFEAT OF RELATED ARRANGEMENTS

5(1) This paragraph applies if arrangements (entered into by any person) ("Set A")–

(a) are promoted arrangements in relation to a person ("P"), and

(b) are related to other arrangements which are promoted arrangements in relation to P.

5(2) If Case 1, 2 or 3 applies (see paragraphs 7 to 9) a relevant defeat occurs in relation to P and each of the related arrangements.

5(3) **"The related arrangements"** means Set A and the arrangements mentioned in sub-paragraph (1)(b).

LIMIT ON NUMBER OF SEPARATE RELEVANT DEFEATS IN RELATION TO THE SAME, OR RELATED, ARRANGEMENTS

6 In relation to a person, if there has been a relevant defeat of arrangements (whether under paragraph 4 or 5) there cannot be a further relevant defeat of–

(a) those particular arrangements, or

(b) arrangements which are related to those arrangements.

CASE 1: COUNTERACTION UPHELD BY JUDICIAL RULING

7(1) Case 1 applies if–

(a) any of Conditions A to E is met in relation to any of the related arrangements, and

(b) in the case of those arrangements the decision to make the relevant counteraction has been upheld by a judicial ruling (which is final).

7(2) In sub-paragraph (1) **"the relevant counteraction"** means the counteraction mentioned in paragraph 11(d), 12(1)(b), 13(1)(d), 14(1)(d) or 15(1)(d) (as the case requires).

CASE 2: JUDICIAL RULING THAT AVOIDANCE-RELATED RULE APPLIES

8 Case 2 applies if Condition F is met in relation to any of the related arrangements.

CASE 3: PROPORTION-BASED RELEVANT DEFEAT

9(1) Case 3 applies if–

(a) at least 75% of the tested arrangements have been defeated, and

(b) no final judicial ruling in relation to any of the related arrangements has upheld a corresponding tax advantage which has been asserted in connection with any of the related arrangements.

9(2) In this paragraph **"the tested arrangements"** means so many of the related arrangements (as defined in paragraph 5(3)) as meet the condition in sub-paragraph (3) or (4).

9(3) Particular arrangements meet this condition if a person has made a return, claim or election on the basis that a tax advantage results from those arrangements and–

(a) there has been an enquiry or investigation by HMRC into the return, claim or election, or

(b) HMRC assesses the person to tax on the basis that the tax advantage (or any part of it) does not arise, or

(c) a GAAR counteraction notice has been given in relation to the tax advantage or part of it and the arrangements.

9(4) Particular arrangements meet this condition if HMRC takes other action on the basis that a tax advantage which might be expected to arise from those arrangements, or is asserted in connection with them, does not arise.

9(5) For the purposes of this paragraph a tax advantage has been **"asserted"** in connection with particular arrangements if a person has made a return, claim or election on the basis that the tax advantage arises from those arrangements.

9(6) In sub-paragraph (1)(b) **"corresponding tax advantage"** means a tax advantage corresponding to any tax advantage the counteraction of which is taken into account by HMRC for the purposes of sub-paragraph (1)(a).

9(7) For the purposes of this paragraph a court or tribunal **"upholds"** a tax advantage if–

(a) the court or tribunal makes a ruling to the effect that no part of the tax advantage is to be counteracted, and

(b) that judicial ruling is final.

9(8) In this paragraph references to **"counteraction"** include anything referred to as a counteraction in any of Conditions A to F in paragraphs 11 to 16.

9(9) In this paragraph **"GAAR counteraction notice"** means–

(a) a notice such as is mentioned in sub-paragraph (2) of paragraph 12 of Schedule 43 to FA 2013 (notice of final decision to counteract),

(b) a notice under paragraph 8(2) or 9(2) of Schedule 43A to that Act (binding of arrangements to lead arrangements) stating that the tax advantage is to be counteracted under the general anti-abuse rule, or

(c) a notice under paragraph 8(2) of Schedule 43B to that Act (generic referrals) stating that the tax advantage is to be counteracted under the general anti-abuse rule.

"DEFEAT" OF ARRANGEMENTS

10 For the purposes of this Part of this Act a **"defeat"** of arrangements occurs if any of Conditions A to F (in paragraphs 11 to 16) is met in relation to the arrangements.

11 Condition A is that–

(a) a person has made a return, claim or election on the basis that a tax advantage arises from the arrangements,

(b) a notice given to the person under paragraph 12 of Schedule 43 to, paragraph 8(2) or 9(2) of Schedule 43A to or paragraph 8(2) of Schedule 43B to FA 2013 stated that the tax advantage was to be counteracted under the general anti-abuse rule,

(c) the tax advantage has been counteracted (in whole or in part) under the general anti-abuse rule, and

(d) the counteraction is final.

12(1) Condition B is that a follower notice has been given to a person by reference to the arrangements (and not withdrawn) and–

(a) the person has complied with subsection (2) of section 208 of FA 2014 by taking the action specified in subsections (4) to (6) of that section in respect of the denied tax advantage (or part of it), or

(b) the denied tax advantage has been counteracted (in whole or in part) otherwise than as mentioned in paragraph (a) and the counteraction is final.

12(2) In this paragraph **"the denied tax advantage"** is to be interpreted in accordance with section 208(3) *of FA 2014.*

12(3) In this Schedule **"follower notice"** means a follower notice under Chapter 2 of Part 4 of FA 2014.

13(1) Condition C is that–

(a) the arrangements are DOTAS arrangements,
(b) a person ("the taxpayer") has made a return, claim or election on the basis that a relevant tax advantage arises,
(c) the relevant tax advantage has been counteracted, and
(d) the counteraction is final.

13(2) For the purposes of sub-paragraph (1) **"relevant tax advantage"** means a tax advantage which the arrangements might be expected to enable the taxpayer to obtain.

13(3) For the purposes of this paragraph the relevant tax advantage is **"counteracted"** if adjustments are made in respect of the taxpayer's tax position on the basis that the whole or part of that tax advantage does not arise.

14(1) Condition D is that–
(a) the arrangements are disclosable VAT or other indirect tax arrangements to which a person is a party,
(b) the person has made a return or claim on the basis that a relevant tax advantage arises,
(c) the relevant tax advantage has been counteracted, and
(d) the counteraction is final.

14(2) For the purposes of sub-paragraph (1) **"relevant tax advantage"** means a tax advantage which the arrangements might be expected to enable the person to obtain.

14(3) For the purposes of this paragraph the relevant tax advantage is **"counteracted"** if adjustments are made in respect of the person's tax position on the basis that the whole or part of that tax advantage does not arise.

History – In para. 14(1)(a) the words "or other indirect tax" inserted by F(No. 2)A 2017, s. 66 and Sch. 17, para. 54(3)(a), with effect so far as necessary for enabling the making of regulations under that Schedule from 16 November 2017 (Royal Assent) and from 1 January 2018 for all other purposes.
In para. 14(1)(a)and (b) the word "taxable" (which appeared before the word "person") omitted by F(No. 2)A 2017, s. 66 and Sch. 17, para. 54(3)(b), with effect so far as necessary for enabling the making of regulations under that Schedule from 16 November 2017 (Royal Assent) and from 1 January 2018 for all other purposes.
In para. 14(2) the word "taxable" (which appeared before the word "person") omitted by F(No. 2)A 2017, s. 66 and Sch. 17, para. 54(3)(b), with effect so far as necessary for enabling the making of regulations under that Schedule from 16 November 2017 (Royal Assent) and from 1 January 2018 for all other purposes.
In para. 14(3) the word "taxable" (which appeared before the word "person") omitted by F(No. 2)A 2017, s. 66 and Sch. 17, para. 54(3)(b), with effect so far as necessary for enabling the making of regulations under that Schedule from 16 November 2017 (Royal Assent) and from 1 January 2018 for all other purposes.

15(1) Condition E is that the arrangements are disclosable VAT arrangements to which a taxable person ("T") is a party and–
(a) the arrangements relate to the position with respect to VAT of a person other than T ("S") who has made supplies of goods or services to T,
(b) the arrangements might be expected to enable T to obtain a tax advantage in connection with those supplies of goods or services,
(c) the arrangements have been counteracted, and
(d) the counteraction is final.

15(2) For the purposes of this paragraph the arrangements are **"counteracted"** if–
(a) HMRC assess S to tax or take any other action on a basis which prevents T from obtaining (or obtaining the whole of) the tax advantage in question, or
(b) adjustments are made on a basis such as is mentioned in paragraph (a).

16(1) Condition F is that–
(a) a person has made a return, claim or election on the basis that a relevant tax advantage arises,
(b) the tax advantage, or part of the tax advantage would not arise if a particular avoidance-related rule (see paragraph 25) applies in relation to the person's tax affairs,
(c) it is held in a judicial ruling that the relevant avoidance-related rule applies in relation to the person's tax affairs, and
(d) the judicial ruling is final.

16(2) For the purposes of sub-paragraph (1) **"relevant tax advantage"** means a tax advantage which the arrangements might be expected to enable the person to obtain.

Part 3 – Relevant Defeats: Associated Persons

ATTRIBUTION OF RELEVANT DEFEATS

17(1) Sub-paragraph (2) applies if–

(a) there is (or has been) a person ("Q"),

(b) arrangements ("the defeated arrangements") have been entered into,

(c) an event occurs such that either–

  (i) there is a relevant defeat in relation to Q and the defeated arrangements, or

  (ii) the condition in sub-paragraph (i) would be met if Q had not ceased to exist,

(d) at the time of that event a person ("P") is carrying on a business as a promoter (or is carrying on what would be such a business under the condition in paragraph 3(2)), and

(e) Condition 1 or 2 is met in relation to Q and P.

17(2) The event is treated for all purposes of this Part of this Act as a relevant defeat in relation to P and the defeated arrangements (whether or not it is also a relevant defeat in relation to Q, and regardless of whether or not P existed at any time when those arrangements were promoted arrangements in relation to Q).

17(3) Condition 1 is that–

(a) P is not an individual,

(b) at a time when the defeated arrangements were promoted arrangements in relation to Q–

  (i) P was a relevant body controlled by Q, or

  (ii) Q was a relevant body controlled by P, and

(c) at the time of the event mentioned in sub-paragraph (1)(c)–

  (i) Q is a relevant body controlled by P,

  (ii) P is a relevant body controlled by Q, or

  (iii) P and Q are relevant bodies controlled by a third person.

17(4) Condition 2 is that–

(a) P and Q are relevant bodies,

(b) at a time when the defeated arrangements were promoted arrangements in relation to Q, a third person ("C") controlled Q, and

(c) C controls P at the time of the event mentioned in sub-paragraph (1)(c).

17(5) For the purposes of sub-paragraphs (3)(b) and (4)(b), the question whether arrangements are promoted arrangements in relation to Q at any time is to be determined on the assumption that the reference to **"design"** in paragraph (b) of section 235(3) (definition of "promoter" in relation to relevant arrangements) is omitted.

DEEMED DEFEAT NOTICES

18(1) This paragraph applies if–

(a) an authorised officer becomes aware at any time ("the relevant time") that a relevant defeat has occurred in relation to a person ("P") who is carrying on a business as a promoter,

(b) there have occurred, more than 3 years before the relevant time–

  (i) one third party defeat, or

  (ii) two third party defeats, and

(c) conditions A1 and B1 (in a case within paragraph (b)(i)), or conditions A2 and B2 (in a case within paragraph (b)(ii)), are met.

18(2) Where this paragraph applies by virtue of sub-paragraph (1)(b)(i), this Part of this Act has effect as if an authorised officer had (with due authority), at the time of the time of the third party defeat, given P a single defeat notice under section 241A(2) in respect of it.

18(3) Where this paragraph applies by virtue of sub-paragraph (1)(b)(ii), this Part of this Act has effect as if an authorised officer had (with due authority), at the time of the second of the two third party defeats, given P a double defeat notice under section 241A(3) in respect of the two third party defeats.

18(4) Section 241A(8) has no effect in relation to a notice treated as given as mentioned in subsection (2) or (3).

18(5) Condition A1 is that–

(a) a conduct notice or a single or double defeat notice has been given to the other person (see sub-paragraph (9)) in respect of the third party defeat,

(b) at the time of the third party defeat an authorised officer would have had power by virtue of paragraph 17 to give P a defeat notice in respect of the third party defeat, had the officer been aware that it was a relevant defeat in relation to P, and

(c) so far as the authorised officer mentioned in sub-paragraph (1)(a) is aware, the conditions for giving P a defeat notice in respect of the third party defeat have never been met (ignoring this paragraph).

18(6) Condition A2 is that–

(a) a conduct notice or a single or double defeat notice has been given to the other person (see sub-paragraph (9)) in respect of each, or both, of the third party defeats,

(b) at the time of the second third party defeat an authorised officer would have had power by virtue of paragraph 17 to give P a double defeat notice in respect of the third party defeats, had the officer been aware that either of the third party defeats was a relevant defeat in relation to P, and

(c) so far as the authorised officer mentioned in sub-paragraph (1)(a) is aware, the conditions for giving P a defeat notice in respect of those third party defeats (or either of them) have never been met (ignoring this paragraph).

18(7) Condition B1 is that, had an authorised officer given P a defeat notice in respect of the third party defeat at the time of that relevant defeat, that defeat notice would still have effect at the relevant time (see sub-paragraph (1)).

18(8) Condition B2 is that, had an authorised officer given P a defeat notice in respect of the two third party defeats at the time of the second of those relevant defeats, that defeat notice would still have effect at the relevant time.

18(9) In this paragraph **"third party defeat"** means a relevant defeat which has occurred in relation to a person other than P.

MEANING OF "RELEVANT BODY" AND "CONTROL"

19(1) In this Part of this Schedule **"relevant body"** means–

(a) a body corporate, or

(b) a partnership.

19(2) For the purposes of this Part of this Schedule a person controls a body corporate if the person has power to secure that the affairs of the body corporate are conducted in accordance with the person's wishes–

(a) by means of the holding of shares or the possession of voting power in relation to the body corporate or any other relevant body,

(b) as a result of any powers conferred by the articles of association or other document regulating the body corporate or any other relevant body, or

(c) by means of controlling a partnership.

19(3) For the purposes of this Part of this Schedule a person controls a partnership if the person is a controlling member or the managing partner of the partnership.

19(4) In this paragraph **"controlling member"** has the same meaning as in Schedule 36 (partnerships).

19(5) In this section **"managing partner"**, in relation to a partnership, means the member of the partnership who directs, or is on a day-to-day level in control of, the management of the business of the partnership.

Part 4 – Meeting Section 237A Conditions: Bodies Corporate and Partnerships

RELEVANT BODIES CONTROLLED ETC BY OTHER PERSONS TREATED AS MEETING SECTION 237A CONDITION

20(1) A relevant body is treated as meeting a section 237A condition at the section 237A(2) relevant time if any of Conditions A to C is met.

20(2) Condition A is that–

(a) a person met the section 237A condition at a time when the person was a promoter, and

(b) the person controls or has significant influence over the relevant body at the section 237A(2) relevant time.

20(3) Condition B is that–

(a) a person met the section 237A condition at a time when the person controlled or had significant influence over the relevant body,

(b) the relevant body was a promoter at that time, and

(c) the person controls or has significant influence over the relevant body at the section 237A(2) relevant time.

20(4) Condition C is that–

(a) two or more persons together controlled or had significant influence over the relevant body at a time when one of those persons met the section 237A condition,

(b) the relevant body was a promoter at that time, and

(c) those persons together control or have significant influence over the relevant body at the section 237A(2) relevant time.

20(5) Sub-paragraph (1) does not apply where the person referred to in sub-paragraph (2)(a), (3)(a), or (4)(a) as meeting a section 237A condition is an individual.

20(6) For the purposes of sub-paragraph (2) it does not matter whether the relevant body existed at the time referred to in sub-paragraph (2)(a).

History – Para. 20 substituted by FA 2017, s. 24(3), with effect for the purposes of determining whether a person meets a FA 2014, s. 237A condition in a period of three years ending on or after 8 March 2017. Former para. 20 read as follows:

"TREATING PERSONS UNDER ANOTHER'S CONTROL AS MEETING SECTION 237A CONDITION

20(1) A relevant body ("RB") is treated as meeting a section 237A condition at the section 237A(2) relevant time if–

(a) that condition was met by a person ("C") at a time when–

(i) C was carrying on a business as a promoter, or

(ii) RB was carrying on a business as a promoter and C controlled RB, and

(b) RB is controlled by C at the section 237A(2) relevant time.

20(2) Sub-paragraph (1) does not apply if C is an individual.

20(3) For the purposes of determining whether the requirements of sub-paragraph (1) are met by reason of meeting the requirement in sub-paragraph (1)(a)(i), it does not matter whether RB existed at the time when C met the section 237A condition.".

PERSONS WHO CONTROL ETC A RELEVANT BODY TREATED AS MEETING A SECTION 237A CONDITION

21(1) If at a time when a person controlled or had significant influence over a relevant body–

(a) the relevant body met a section 237A condition, and

(b) the relevant body, or another relevant body which the person controlled or had significant influence over, was a promoter,

the person is treated as meeting the section 237A condition at the section 237A(2) relevant time.

21(2) It does not matter whether any relevant body referred to in sub-paragraph (1) exists at the section 237A(2) relevant time.

History – Para. 21 substituted by FA 2017, s. 24(3), with effect for the purposes of determining whether a person meets a FA 2014, s. 237A condition in a period of three years ending on or after 8 March 2017. Former para. 21 read as follows:

"TREATING PERSONS IN CONTROL OF OTHERS AS MEETING SECTION 237A CONDITION

21(1) A person other than an individual is treated as meeting a section 237A condition at the section 237A(2) relevant time if–

(a) a relevant body ("A") met the condition at a time when A was controlled by the person, and

(b) at the time mentioned in paragraph (a) A, or another relevant body ("B") which was also at that time controlled by the person, carried on a business as a promoter.

21(2) For the purposes of determining whether the requirements of sub-paragraph (1) are met it does not matter whether A or B (or neither) exists at the section 237A(2) relevant time.".

RELEVANT BODIES CONTROLLED ETC BY THE SAME PERSON TREATED AS MEETING A SECTION 237A CONDITION

22(1) If–

(a) a person controlled or had significant influence over a relevant body at a time when it met a section 237A condition, and

(b) at that time that body, or another relevant body which the person controlled or had significant influence over, was a promoter,

any relevant body which the person controls or has significant influence over at the section 237A(2) relevant time is treated as meeting the section 237A condition at the section 237A(2) relevant time.

22(2) *If–*

(a) two or more persons together controlled or had significant influence over a relevant body at a time when it met a section 237A condition, and

(b) at that time that body, or another relevant body which those persons together controlled or had significant influence over, was a promoter, any relevant body which those persons together control or have significant influence over at the section 237A(2) relevant time is treated as meeting the section 237A condition at the section 237A(2) relevant time.

22(3) It does not matter whether–

(a) a relevant body referred to in sub-paragraph (1)(a) or (b) or (2)(a) or (b) exists at the section 237A(2) relevant time, or

(b) a relevant body existing at the section 237A(2) relevant time existed at the time referred to in sub-paragraph (1)(a) or (2)(a).

History – Para. 22 substituted by FA 2017, s. 24(3), with effect for the purposes of determining whether a person meets a FA 2014, s. 237A condition in a period of three years ending on or after 8 March 2017. Former para. 22 read as follows:

"TREATING PERSONS CONTROLLED BY THE SAME PERSON AS MEETING SECTION 237A CONDITION

22(1) A relevant body ("RB") is treated as meeting a section 237A condition at the section 237A(2) relevant time if–

(a) another relevant body met that condition at a time ("time T") when it was controlled by a person ("C"),

(b) at time T, there was a relevant body controlled by C which carried on a business as a promoter, and

(c) RB is controlled by C at the section 237A(2) relevant time.

22(2) For the purposes of determining whether the requirements of sub-paragraph (1) are met it does not matter whether–

(a) RB existed at time T, or

(b) any relevant body (other than RB) by reason of which the requirements of sub-paragraph (1) are met exists at the section 237A(2) relevant time.".

INTERPRETATION

23(1) In this Part of this Schedule–

"control" and **"significant influence"** have the same meanings as in Part 4 of Schedule 34 (see paragraph 13A(5) to (11));

references to a person being a promoter are to the person carrying on business as a promoter;

"relevant body" has the same meaning as in Part 3 of this Schedule;

"section 237A(2) relevant time" means the time referred to in section 237A(2);

"section 237A condition" means any of the conditions in section 237A(11), (12) and (13).

23(2) For the purposes of paragraphs 20 to 22, the condition in section 237A(11) (occurrence of 3 relevant defeats in the 3 years ending with the relevant time) is taken to have been met by a person at any time if at least 3 relevant defeats have occurred in relation to the person in the period of 3 years ending with that time.

History – In para. 23(1), definition of "control" substituted by FA 2017, s. 24(4)(a), with effect for the purposes of determining whether a person meets a FA 2014, s. 237A condition in a period of three years ending on or after 8 March 2017.
In para. 23(2), the words "20 to 22" substituted for the words "20(1)(a), 21(1)(a) and 22(1)(a)" by FA 2017, s. 24(4)(b), with effect for the purposes of determining whether a person meets a FA 2014, s. 237A condition in a period of three years ending on or after 8 March 2017.

Part 5 – Supplementary

"ADJUSTMENTS"

24 In this Schedule **"adjustments"** means any adjustments, whether by way of an assessment, the modification of an assessment or return, the amendment or disallowance of a claim, the entering into of a contract settlement or otherwise (and references to **"making"** adjustments accordingly include securing that adjustments are made by entering into a contract settlement).

MEANING OF "AVOIDANCE-RELATED RULE"

25(1) In this Schedule **"avoidance-related rule"** means a rule in Category 1 or 2.

25(2) A rule is in Category 1 if–

(a) it refers (in whatever terms) to the purpose or main purpose or purposes of a transaction, arrangements or any other action or matter, and

(b) to whether or not the purpose in question is or involves the avoidance of tax or the obtaining of any advantage in relation to tax (however described).

25(3) A rule is also in Category 1 if it refers (in whatever terms) to–

(a) expectations as to what are, or may be, the expected benefits of a transaction, arrangements or any other action or matter, and

(b) whether or not the avoidance of tax or the obtaining of any advantage in relation to tax (however described) is such a benefit.

For the purposes of paragraph (b) it does not matter whether the reference is (for instance) to the **"sole or main benefit"** or **"one of the main benefits"** or any other reference to a benefit.

25(4) A rule falls within Category 2 if as a result of the rule a person may be treated differently for tax purposes depending on whether or not purposes referred to in the rule (for instance the purposes of an actual or contemplated action or enterprise) are (or are shown to be) commercial purposes.

25(5) For example, a rule in the following form would fall within Category 1 and within Category 2–

"Example rule

Section X does not apply to a company in respect of a transaction if the company shows that the transaction meets Condition A or B.

Condition A is that the transaction is effected–

(a) for genuine commercial reasons, or

(b) in the ordinary course of managing investments.

Condition B is that the avoidance of tax is not the main object or one of the main objects of the transaction."

"DOTAS ARRANGEMENTS"

26(1) For the purposes of this Schedule arrangements are **"DOTAS arrangements"** at any time if at that time a person–

(a) has provided, information in relation to the arrangements under section 308(3), 309 or 310 of FA 2004, or

(b) has failed to comply with any of those provisions in relation to the arrangements.

26(2) But for the purposes of this Schedule **"DOTAS arrangements"** does not include arrangements in respect of which HMRC has given notice under section 312(6) of FA 2004 (notice that promoters not under duty to notify client of reference number).

26(3) For the purposes of sub-paragraph (1) a person who would be required to provide information under subsection (3) of section 308 of FA 2004–

(a) but for the fact that the arrangements implement a proposal in respect of which notice has been given under subsection (1) of that section, or

(b) but for subsection (4A), (4C) or (5) of that section,

is treated as providing the information at the end of the period referred to in subsection (3) of that section.

DISCLOSABLE VAT OR OTHER INDIRECT TAX ARRANGEMENTS

26A(1) For the purposes of this Schedule arrangements are **"disclosable VAT or other indirect tax arrangements"** at any time if at that time–

(a) the arrangements are disclosable Schedule 11A arrangements, or

(b) sub-paragraph (2) applies.

26A(2) This sub-paragraph applies if a person–

(a) has provided information in relation to the arrangements under paragraph 12(1), 17(2) or 18(2) of Schedule 17 to F[(No. 2)]A 2017, or

(b) has failed to comply with any of those provisions in relation to the arrangements.

26A(3) But for the purposes of this Schedule arrangements in respect of which HMRC have given notice under paragraph 23(6) of that Schedule (notice that promoters not under duty to notify client of reference number) are not to be regarded as disclosable VAT or other indirect tax arrangements.

26A(4) For the purposes of sub-paragraph (2) a person who would be required to provide information under paragraph 12(1) of that Schedule–

(a) but for the fact that the arrangements implement a proposal in respect of which notice has been given under paragraph 11(1) of that Schedule, or

(b) but for paragraph 13, 14 or 15 of that Schedule,

is treated as providing the information at the end of the period referred to in paragraph 12(1).

History – Para. 26A inserted by F(No. 2)A 2017, s. 66 and Sch. 17, para. 54(4), with effect so far as necessary for enabling the making of regulations under that Schedule from 16 November 2017 (Royal Assent) and from 1 January 2018 for all other purposes.

"DISCLOSABLE SCHEDULE 11A VAT ARRANGEMENTS"

History – In the heading the words "Schedule 11A" inserted by F(No. 2)A 2017, s. 66 and Sch. 17, para. 54(5), with effect so far as necessary for enabling the making of regulations under that Schedule from 16 November 2017 (Royal Assent) and from 1 January 2018 for all other purposes.

27 For the purposes of paragraph 26A arrangements are **"disclosable Schedule 11A VAT arrangements"** at any time if at that time–

(a) a person has complied with paragraph 6 of Schedule 11A to VATA 1994 in relation to the arrangements (duty to notify Commissioners),

(b) a person under a duty to comply with that paragraph in relation to the arrangements has failed to do so, or

(c) a reference number has been allocated to the scheme under paragraph 9 of that Schedule (voluntary notification of avoidance scheme which is not a designated scheme).

History – In para. 27 the words "paragraph 26A" substituted for the words "this Schedule" and the words "Schedule 11A" inserted by F(No. 2)A 2017, s. 66 and Sch. 17, para. 54(6), with effect so far as necessary for enabling the making of regulations under that Schedule from 16 November 2017 (Royal Assent) and from 1 January 2018 for all other purposes.

PARAGRAPHS 26 TO 27: SUPPLEMENTARY

History – In the heading the words "to 27" substituted for the words "and 27" by F(No. 2)A 2017, s. 66 and Sch. 17, para. 54(7), with effect so far as necessary for enabling the making of regulations under that Schedule from 16 November 2017 (Royal Assent) and from 1 January 2018 for all other purposes.

28(1) A person **"fails to comply"** with any provision mentioned in paragraph 26(1)(a), 26A(2)(a) or 27(b) if and only if any of the conditions in sub-paragraphs (2) to (4) is met.

28(2) The condition in this sub-paragraph is that–

(a) the tribunal has determined that the person has failed to comply with the provision concerned,

(b) the appeal period has ended, and

(c) the determination has not been overturned on appeal.

28(3) The condition in this sub-paragraph is that–

(a) the tribunal has determined for the purposes of section 118(2) of TMA 1970 that the person is to be deemed not to have failed to comply with the provision concerned as the person had a reasonable excuse for not doing the thing required to be done,

(b) the appeal period has ended, and

(c) the determination has not been overturned on appeal.

28(4) The condition in this sub-paragraph is that the person admitted in writing to HMRC that the person has failed to comply with the provision concerned.

28(5) In this paragraph **"the appeal period"** means–

(a) the period during which an appeal could be brought against the determination of the tribunal, or

(b) where an appeal mentioned in paragraph (a) has been brought, the period during which that appeal has not been finally determined, withdrawn or otherwise disposed of.

History – In para. 28(1) the words ", 26A(2)(a)" (the comma assumed by Croner-i) inserted by F(No. 2)A 2017, s. 66 and Sch. 17, para. 54(8), with effect so far as necessary for enabling the making of regulations under that Schedule from 16 November 2017 (Royal Assent) and from 1 January 2018 for all other purposes.

"FINAL" COUNTERACTION

29 For the purposes of this Schedule the counteraction of a tax advantage or of arrangements is **"final"** when the assessment or adjustments made to effect the counteraction, and any amounts arising as a result of the assessment or adjustments, can no longer be varied, on appeal or otherwise.

INHERITANCE TAX, STAMP DUTY RESERVE TAX, VAT AND PETROLEUM REVENUE TAX

30(1) In this Schedule, in relation to inheritance tax, each of the following is treated as a return–

(a) an account delivered by a person under section 216 or 217 of IHTA 1984 (including an account delivered in accordance with regulations under section 256 of that Act);

(b) a statement or declaration which amends or is otherwise connected with such an account produced by the person who delivered the account;

(c) information or a document provided by a person in accordance with regulations under section 256 of that Act;

and such a return is treated as made by the person in question.

30(2) In this Schedule references to an assessment to tax, in relation to inheritance tax, stamp duty reserve tax and petroleum revenue tax, include a determination.

30(3) In this Schedule an expression used in relation to VAT has the same meaning as in VATA 1994.

POWER TO AMEND

31(1) The Treasury may by regulations amend this Schedule (apart from this paragraph).

31(2) An amendment by virtue of sub-paragraph (1) may, in particular, add, vary or remove conditions or categories (or otherwise vary the meaning of "avoidance-related rule").

31(3) Regulations under sub-paragraph (1) may include any amendment of this Part of this Act that is appropriate in consequence of an amendment made by virtue of sub-paragraph (1).

SCHEDULE 35 – PROMOTERS OF TAX AVOIDANCE SCHEMES: PENALTIES

Section 274

INTRODUCTION

1 In this Schedule a reference to an **"information duty"** is to a duty arising under any of the following provisions to provide information or produce a document–

(a) section 255 (duty to provide information or produce document);

(b) section 257 (ongoing duty to provide information);

(c) section 258 (duty of person dealing with non-resident promoter);

(d) section 259 (monitored promoter: duty to provide information about clients);

(e) section 260 (intermediaries: duty to provide information about clients);

(f) section 261 (duty to provide information about clients following enquiry);

(g) section 262 (information required for monitoring compliance with conduct notice);

(h) section 263 (information about monitored promoter's address).

PENALTIES FOR FAILURE TO COMPLY

2(1) A person who fails to comply with a duty imposed by or under this Part mentioned in column 1 of the Table is liable to a penalty not exceeding the amount shown in relation to that provision in column 2 of the Table.

Table

Column 1 *Provision*	*Column 2* *Maximum penalty (£)*
Section 249(1) (duty to notify clients of monitoring notice)	5,000
Section 249(3) (duty to publicise monitoring notice)	1,000,000
Section 249(10) (duty to include information on correspondence etc)	1,000,000
Section 251 (duty of promoter to notify clients and intermediaries of reference number)	5,000
Section 252 (duty of those notified to notify others of promoter's number)	5,000
Section 253 (duty to notify HMRC of reference number)	the relevant amount (see sub-paragraph (3))
Section 255 (duty to provide information or produce document)	1,000,000
Section 257 (ongoing duty to provide information or produce document)	1,000,000
Section 258 (duty of person dealing with non-resident promoter)	1,000,000
Section 259 (monitored promoter: duty to provide information about clients)	5,000
Section 260 (intermediaries: duty to provide information about clients)	5,000
Section 261 (duty to provide information about clients following an enquiry)	10,000
Section 262 (duty to provide information required to monitor compliance with conduct notice)	5,000
Section 263 (duty to provide information about address)	5,000
Section 265 (duty to provide information to promoter)	5,000

2(2) In relation to a failure to comply with section 249(1), 251, 252, 259 or 260 the maximum penalty specified in column 2 of the Table is a maximum penalty which may be imposed in respect of each person to whom the failure relates.

2(3) In relation to a failure to comply with section 253, the **"relevant amount"** is–

(a) £5,000, unless paragraph (b) or (c) applies;

(b) £7,500, where a person has previously failed to comply with section 253 on one (and only one) occasion during the period of 36 months ending with the date on which the current failure occurred;

(c) £10,000, where a person has previously failed to comply with section 253 on two or more occasions during the period mentioned in paragraph (b).

2(4) The amount of a penalty imposed under sub-paragraph (1) is to be arrived at after taking account of all relevant considerations, including the desirability of setting it at a level which appears appropriate for deterring the person, or other persons, from similar failures to comply on future occasions having regard (in particular)–

(a) in the case of a penalty imposed for a failure to comply with section 255 or 257, to the amount of fees received, or likely to have been received, by the person in connection with the monitored proposal, arrangements implementing the monitored proposal or monitored arrangements to which the information or document required as a result of section 255 or 257 relates;

(b) in the case of a penalty imposed in relation to a failure to comply with section 258(4) or (5), to the amount of any tax advantage gained, or sought to be gained, by the person in relation to the monitored arrangements or the arrangements implementing the monitored proposal.

DAILY DEFAULT PENALTIES FOR FAILURE TO COMPLY

3(1) If the failure to comply with an information duty continues after a penalty is imposed under paragraph 2(1), the person is liable to a further penalty or penalties not exceeding the relevant sum for each day on which the failure continues after the day on which the penalty under paragraph 2(1) was imposed.

3(2) In sub-paragraph (1) **"the relevant sum"** means–

(a) £10,000, in a case where the maximum penalty which could have been imposed for the failure was £1,000,000;

(b) £600, in cases not falling within paragraph (a).

PENALTIES FOR INACCURATE INFORMATION AND DOCUMENTS

4(1) If–

(a) in complying with an information duty, a person provides inaccurate information or produces a document that contains an inaccuracy, and

(b) condition A, B or C is met,

the person is liable to a penalty not exceeding the relevant sum.

4(2) Condition A is that the inaccuracy is careless or deliberate.

4(3) An inaccuracy is careless if it is due to a failure by the person to take reasonable care.

4(4) For the purpose of determining whether or not a person who is a monitored promoter took reasonable care, reliance on legal advice is to be disregarded if either–

(a) the advice was not based on a full and accurate description of the facts, or

(b) the conclusions in the advice that the person relied on were unreasonable.

4(5) For the purpose of determining whether or not a person who complies with a duty under section 258 took reasonable care, reliance on legal advice is to be disregarded if the advice was given or procured by the monitored promoter mentioned in subsection (1) of that section.

4(6) Condition B is that the person knows of the inaccuracy at the time the information is provided or the document produced but does not inform HMRC at that time.

4(7) Condition C is that the person–

(a) discovers the inaccuracy some time later, and

(b) fails to take reasonable steps to inform HMRC.

4(8) The **"relevant sum"** means–

(a) £1,000,000, where the information is provided or document produced in compliance with a duty under section 255, 257 or 258;

(b) £10,000, where the information is provided in compliance with a duty under section 261;

(c) £5,000, where the information is provided or document produced in compliance with a duty under section 259, 260, 262 or 263.

4(9) If the information or document contains more than one inaccuracy, one penalty is payable under this paragraph whatever the number of inaccuracies.

POWER TO CHANGE AMOUNT OF PENALTIES

5(1) If it appears to the Treasury that there has been a change in the value of money since the last relevant date, they may by regulations substitute for the sums for the time being specified in paragraph 2, 3 or 4 such other sums as appear to them to be justified by the change.

5(2) Regulations under sub-paragraph (1) may include any amendment of paragraph 10(b) that is appropriate in consequence of an amendment made by virtue of sub-paragraph (1).

5(3) The **"relevant date"**, in relation to a specified sum, means–

(a) the date on which this Act is passed, and

(b) each date on which the power conferred by sub-paragraph (1) has been exercised in relation to that sum.

CONCEALING, DESTROYING ETC DOCUMENTS FOLLOWING IMPOSITION OF A DUTY TO PROVIDE INFORMATION

6(1) A person must not conceal, destroy or otherwise dispose of, or arrange for the concealment, destruction or disposal of, a document which is subject to a duty under section 255, 257 or 262.

6(2) Sub-paragraph (1) does not apply if the person acts after the document has been produced to an officer of Revenue and Customs in accordance with the duty, unless the officer has notified the person in writing that the document must continue to be available for inspection (and has not withdrawn the notification).

6(3) Sub-paragraph (1) does not apply, in a case to which section 268(1) applies, if the person acts after the expiry of the period of 6 months beginning with the day on which a copy of the document was produced in accordance with that section unless, before the expiry of that period, an officer of Revenue and Customs makes a request for the original document under section 268(2)(b).

6(4) A person who conceals, destroys or otherwise disposes of, or arranges for the concealment, destruction or disposal of, a document in breach of sub-paragraph (1), is taken to have failed to comply with the duty to produce the document under the provision concerned (but see sub-paragraph (5)).

6(5) If a person conceals, destroys or otherwise disposes of, or arranges for the concealment, destruction or disposal of, a document which is subject to a duty under more than one of the provisions mentioned in sub-paragraph (1) then–

(a) in a case where a duty under section 255 applies, the person will be taken to have failed to comply only with that provision, or

(b) in a case where a duty under section 255 does not apply, the person will be taken to have failed to comply only with section 257.

CONCEALING, DESTROYING ETC DOCUMENTS FOLLOWING INFORMAL NOTIFICATION

7(1) A person must not conceal, destroy or otherwise dispose of, or arrange for the concealment, destruction or disposal of, a document if an officer of Revenue and Customs has informed the person in writing that the person is, or is likely, to be given a notice under 255, 257 or 262 the effect of which will, or is likely to, require the production of the document.

7(2) Sub-paragraph (1) does not apply if the person acts–

(a) at least 6 months after the person was, or was last, informed as described in sub-paragraph (1), or

(b) after the person becomes subject to a duty under 255, 257 or 262 which requires the document to be produced.

7(3) A person who conceals, destroys or otherwise disposes of, or arranges for the concealment, destruction or disposal of, a document in breach of sub-paragraph (1), is taken to have failed to comply with the duty to produce the document under the provision concerned (but see sub-paragraph (4)).

7(4) If a person conceals, destroys or otherwise disposes of, or arranges for the concealment, destruction or disposal of, a document which is subject to a duty under more than one of the provisions mentioned in sub-paragraph (1) then–

(a) in a case where a duty under section 255 applies, the person will be taken to have failed to comply only with that provision, or

(b) in a case where a duty under section 255 does not apply, the person will be taken to have failed to comply only with section 257.

FAILURE TO COMPLY WITH TIME LIMIT

8 A failure to do anything required to be done within a limited period of time does not give rise to liability to a penalty under this Schedule if the person did it within such further time, if any, as an officer of Revenue and Customs or the tribunal may have allowed.

REASONABLE EXCUSE

9(1) Liability to a penalty under this Schedule does not arise if there is a reasonable excuse for the failure.

9(2) For the purposes of this paragraph–

(a) an insufficiency of funds is not a reasonable excuse unless attributable to events outside the person's control,

(b) if the person relies on any other person to do anything, that is not a reasonable excuse unless the first person took reasonable care to avoid the failure,

(c) if the person had a reasonable excuse for the failure but the excuse has ceased, the person is to be treated as having continued to have the excuse if the failure is remedied without unreasonable delay after the excuse ceased,

(d) reliance on legal advice is to be taken automatically not to constitute a reasonable excuse where the person is a monitored promoter if either–

(i) the advice was not based on a full and accurate description of the facts, or

(ii) the conclusions in the advice that the person relied on were unreasonable, and

(e) reliance on legal advice is to be taken automatically not to constitute a reasonable excuse in the case of a penalty for failure to comply with section 258, if the advice was given or procured by the monitored promoter mentioned in subsection (1) of that section.

ASSESSMENT OF PENALTY AND APPEALS

10 Part 10 of TMA 1970 (penalties, etc) has effect as if–

(a) the reference in section 100(1) to the Taxes Acts were read as a reference to the Taxes Acts and this Schedule,

(b) in subsection (2) of section 100, there were inserted a reference to a penalty under this Schedule, other than a penalty under paragraph 3 of this Schedule in respect of which the relevant sum is £600.

INTEREST ON PENALTIES

11(1) A penalty under this Schedule is to carry interest at the rate applicable under section 178 of FA 1989 from the date it is determined until payment.

11(2) [Inserts FA 1989, s. 178(2)(u).]

DOUBLE JEOPARDY

12 A person is not liable to a penalty under this Schedule in respect of anything in respect of which the person has been convicted of an offence.

OVERLAPPING PENALTIES

13 A person is not liable to a penalty under–

(a) Schedule 24 to the FA 2007 (penalties for errors),

(b) Part 7 of FA 2004, or

(c) any other provision which is prescribed,

by reason of any failure to include in any return or account a reference number required by section 253.

SCHEDULE 36 – PROMOTERS OF TAX AVOIDANCE SCHEMES: PARTNERSHIPS

Section 281

Part 1 – Partnerships as Persons

"PERSON" INCLUDES A PARTNERSHIP

1(1) Persons carrying on a business in partnership–

(a) are regarded as a person for the purposes of this Part of this Act;

(b) are referred to in this Part as a **"partnership"**.

1(2) But in this Part of this Act **"partnership"** does not include a body of persons forming a legal person that is distinct from themselves (and paragraphs 2 to 21 may accordingly be disregarded in applying this Part of this Act to such a body of persons).

1(3) In the references in this Part to carrying on a business in partnership, **"partnership"** has the same meaning as in the Partnership Act 1890.

CONTINUITY OF PARTNERSHIPS

2 A partnership is regarded for the purposes of this Part of this Act as continuing to be the same partnership (and the same person) regardless of a change in membership, provided that a person who was a member before the change remains a member after the change.

MEETING OF CONDITIONS

3(1) Accordingly, for the purposes of this Part of this Act a partnership is taken–

(a) to have done any act that bound the members, and

(b) to have failed to comply with any obligation of the firm which the members failed to comply with;

but see sub-paragraph (3).

3(2) In sub-paragraph (1), **"the members"** means those who were the members of the partnership or (in the case of a limited partnership) the general partners of the partnership at the time when the act was done or the failure to comply occurred.

3(3) Where a member of a partnership ("M") has done, or failed to do, an act at any time ("the earlier time"), the partnership is not treated at any later time as having done, or failed to do, that act unless–

(a) M, or

(b) another person who was a member of the partnership at the earlier time,

is a member of the partnership at the later time.

3(4) In this paragraph **"firm"** has the same meaning as in the Partnership Act 1890.

THRESHOLD CONDITIONS: ACTIONS OF PARTNERS IN A PERSONAL CAPACITY

4 [Omitted by FA 2015, s. 119 and Sch. 19, para. 5(a).]

History – Para. 4 (and the heading before it) omitted by FA 2015, s. 119 and Sch. 19, para. 5(a), with effect for the purposes of determining whether a person meets a threshold condition in a period of three years ending on or after 26 March 2015 (Royal Assent). Former para. 4 read as follows:

"**4(1)** Sub-paragraph (2) applies where–

(a) a relevant threshold condition is met by a person ("P") at a time ("the earlier time") when P is a controlling member, or managing partner, of a partnership,

(b) a determination under section 237 is made at a later time in relation to the partnership, and

(c) P is a controlling member, or managing partner, of the partnership at the time of the determination.

4(2) The partnership is regarded as having met the threshold condition at the earlier time (regardless of whether or not the partnership was bound by the act or omission as a result of which P met the threshold condition).

4(3) **"Relevant threshold condition"** means a threshold condition specified in any of the following paragraphs of Schedule 34–

(a) paragraph 2 (deliberate tax defaulters);

(b) paragraph 4 (dishonest tax agents);

(c) paragraph 6 (criminal offences);

(d) paragraph 7 (opinion notice of GAAR advisory panel);

(e) paragraph 8 (disciplinary action by a professional body);

(f) paragraph 9 (disciplinary action by a regulatory authority);

(g) paragraph 10 (failure to comply with information notice)."

Part 2 – Conduct Notices and Monitoring Notices

DEFEAT NOTICES

4A A defeat notice that is given to a partnership must state that it is a partnership defeat notice.

History – Para. 4A (and the heading before it) inserted by FA 2016, s. 160(11), with effect from 15 September 2016 (Royal Assent).

CONDUCT NOTICES

5(1) A conduct notice that is given to a partnership must state that it is a partnership conduct notice.

5(2) In accordance with paragraphs 1 and 2, where the person to whom a conduct notice is given is a partnership, section 238 authorises the imposition of conditions relating to–

(a) the persons who are members of the partnership when the conduct notice is given, and

(b) any person who becomes a member of the partnership after the conduct notice is given.

MONITORING NOTICES

6 A monitoring notice that is given to a partnership must state that it is a partnership monitoring notice.

PERSON CONTINUING TO CARRY ON PARTNERSHIP BUSINESS AS A SOLE TRADER

7(1) This paragraph applies where–

(a) a person or persons have ceased to be members of a partnership,

(b) immediately before the cessation, a defeat notice, conduct notice or monitoring notice had effect in relation to the partnership, and

(c) immediately after the cessation, a person who was a member of the partnership immediately before the cessation is carrying on the business of the partnership, but not in partnership.

7(2) Where this paragraph applies, the defeat notice, conduct notice or monitoring notice continues (despite paragraphs 1 and 2) to have effect in relation to the person mentioned in sub-paragraph (1)(c) (but, in relation to times when the business is not being carried on in partnership, the notice is not regarded for the purposes of this Part of this Act as a notice that has been given to a partnership.)

History – In para. 7(1)(b), the words "defeat notice," inserted by FA 2016, s. 160(12), with effect from 15 September 2016 (Royal Assent).
In para. 7(2), the words "defeat notice," inserted by FA 2016, s. 160(13), with effect from 15 September 2016 (Royal Assent).

PERSONS LEAVING PARTNERSHIP: DEFEAT NOTICES

7A(1) Sub-paragraphs (2) and (3) apply where–

(a) a person ("P") who was a controlling member of a partnership at the time when a defeat notice ("the original notice") was given to the partnership has ceased to be a member of the partnership,

(b) the defeat notice had effect in relation to the partnership at the time of that cessation, and

(c) P is carrying on a business as a promoter.

7A(2) An authorised officer may give P a defeat notice.

7A(3) If P is carrying on a business as a promoter in partnership with one or more other persons and is a controlling member of that partnership ("the new partnership"), an authorised officer may give a defeat notice to the new partnership.

7A(4) A defeat notice given under sub-paragraph (3) ceases to have effect if P ceases to be a member of the new partnership.

7A(5) A notice under sub-paragraph (2) or (3) may not be given after the original notice has ceased to have effect.

7A(6) A defeat notice given under sub-paragraph (2) or (3) is given in respect of the relevant defeat or relevant defeats to which the original notice relates.

History – Para. 7A (and the heading before it) inserted by FA 2016, s. 160(14), with effect from 15 September 2016 (Royal Assent).

PERSONS LEAVING A PARTNERSHIP: CONDUCT NOTICES

8(1) Sub-paragraphs (2) and (3) apply where–

(a) a person ("P") who was a controlling member of a partnership at the time when a conduct notice ("the original notice") was given to the partnership has ceased to be a member of the partnership,

IHT Statutes

(b) the conduct notice had effect in relation to the partnership at the time of that cessation, and

(c) P is carrying on a business as a promoter.

8(2) An authorised officer may give P a conduct notice.

8(3) If P is carrying on a business as a promoter in partnership with one or more other persons and is a controlling member of that partnership ("the new partnership"), an authorised officer may give a conduct notice to the new partnership.

8(4) A conduct notice given under sub-paragraph (3) ceases to have effect if P ceases to be a member of the new partnership.

8(5) A notice under sub-paragraph (2) or (3) may not be given after the termination date of the original notice (under section 241(2)(a) or (b)).

PERSONS LEAVING A PARTNERSHIP: MONITORING NOTICES

9(1) Sub-paragraphs (2) and (3) apply where–

(a) a person ("P") who was a controlling member of a partnership at the time when a monitoring notice was given to the partnership has ceased to be a member of the partnership,

(b) the monitoring notice had effect in relation to the partnership at the time of that cessation, and

(c) P is carrying on a business as a promoter.

9(2) An authorised officer may give P a monitoring notice.

9(3) If P is carrying on a business as a promoter in partnership with one or more other persons, and is a controlling member of that partnership ("the new partnership"), an authorised officer may give a monitoring notice to the new partnership.

9(4) A monitoring notice given under sub-paragraph (3) ceases to have effect if P ceases to be a member of the new partnership.

DIVISION OF PARTNERSHIP BUSINESS

10(1) This paragraph applies if–

(a) a person ("a departing partner") who has been carrying on a business in partnership ceases to carry on the business in partnership,

(b) a defeat notice, conduct notice or monitoring notice had effect in relation to the partnership immediately before the departing partner ceased to carry on the business in partnership, and

(c) the departing partner is continuing to carry on part (but not the whole) of the business ("the transferred part").

10(2) The notice mentioned in sub-paragraph (1)(b) is referred to in this paragraph as "the original notice".

10(3) An authorised officer may give the departing partner–

(za) a defeat notice (if the original notice is a defeat notice);

(a) a conduct notice (if the original notice is a conduct notice);

(b) a monitoring notice (if the original notice is a monitoring notice).

10(4) If the departing partner is itself carrying on the transferred part of the business in partnership, the authorised officer may give that partnership ("the new partnership")–

(za) a defeat notice (if the original notice is a defeat notice);

(a) a conduct notice (if the original notice is a conduct notice);

(b) a monitoring notice (if the original notice is a monitoring notice).

10(5) A notice given under sub-paragraph (4) ceases to have effect if the departing partner ceases to be a member of the new partnership.

10(5A) A notice under sub-paragraph (3)(za) or (4)(za) may not be given after the end of the look-forward period of the original notice.

10(6) A notice under sub-paragraph (3)(a) or (4)(a) may not be given after the termination date of the original notice (under section 241(2)(a) or (b)).

10(7) It does not matter whether one, some or all of the persons who were carrying on the business in partnership are departing partners by virtue of sub-paragraph (1).

History – In para. 10(1)(b), the words ", defeat notice, conduct notice or" substituted for the words "conduct notice or a" by FA 2016, s. 160(15)(a), with effect from 15 September 2016 (Royal Assent).
Para. 10(3)(za) inserted by FA 2016, s. 160(15)(b), with effect from 15 September 2016 (Royal Assent).
Para. 10(4)(za) inserted by FA 2016, s. 160(15)(c), with effect from 15 September 2016 (Royal Assent).
Para. 10(5A) inserted by FA 2016, s. 160(15)(d), with effect from 15 September 2016 (Royal Assent).

NOTICES UNDER PARAGRAPHS 8 TO 10: GENERAL

11(1) In this Part of this Act–

"replacement conduct notice" means a notice under paragraph 8(2) or (3) or 10(3)(a) or (4)(a);

"replacement monitoring notice" means a notice given under paragraph 9(2) or (3) or 10(3)(b) or (4)(b).

11(2) In this Part of this Act, **"the original monitoring notice"** means–

(a) in relation to a replacement monitoring notice given under paragraph 9(2), the monitoring notice mentioned in paragraph 9(1), and

(b) in relation to a replacement monitoring notice given under paragraph 10(3)(b) or (4)(b), the monitoring notice mentioned in paragraph 10(2),

and that original monitoring notice is also the "original monitoring notice" in relation to any monitoring notice that (under paragraph 9(2) or (3) or 10(3)(b) or (4)(b)) replaces a replacement monitoring notice.

11A The look-forward period for a notice under paragraph 7A(2) or (3) or 10(3)(za) or (4)(za)–

(a) begins on the day after the day on which the notice is given, and

(b) continues to the end of the look-forward period for the original notice (as defined in paragraph 7A(1)(a) or 10(2), as the case may be).

History – Para. 11A inserted by FA 2016, s. 160(16), with effect from 15 September 2016 (Royal Assent).

12 A notice under paragraph 8(2) or (3) or 10(3)(a) or (4)(a)–

(a) has no effect after the termination date of the original notice;

(b) must state that that date is its termination date.

13 An authorised officer may not give a replacement conduct notice or replacement monitoring notice to a person if a conduct notice or monitoring notice previously given to the person still has effect in relation to the person.

PUBLICATION UNDER SECTION 248

14 Where the monitored promoter referred to in section 248(2) is a partnership, paragraphs (a), (b) and (d) of that subsection are to be read as referring to details of the partnership (for instance, the name under which the business of the partnership is carried on), not to details of particular partners.

Part 3 – Responsibility of Partners

RESPONSIBILITY OF PARTNERS

15(1) A notice given to a partnership under this Part of this Act has effect, at any time, in relation to the persons who are members of the partnership at that time ("the responsible partners").

15(2) Sub-paragraph (1) does not affect any liability of a person who has ceased to be a member of a partnership in respect of things that the responsible partners did or failed to do before that person ceased to be a member of the partnership.

15(3) Anything required to be done by the responsible partners under or by virtue of a provision of this Part of this Act is required to be done by all the responsible partners (but see paragraph 18).

15(4) In relation to any right (such as a right of appeal) conferred by this Part of this Act references to a person have the meaning that is appropriate in consequence of sub-paragraphs (1) to (3).

JOINT AND SEVERAL LIABILITY OF RESPONSIBLE PARTNERS

16(1) Where the responsible partners are liable to a penalty under this Part of this Act, or to interest on such a penalty, their liability is joint and several.

16(2) No amount may be recovered under sub-paragraph (1) from a person who did not become a responsible partner until after the relevant time.

16(3) **"The relevant time"** means–

(a) in relation to so much of the penalty as is payable in respect of any day, or to interest on so much of a penalty as is so payable, the beginning of that day;

(b) in relation to any other penalty, or interest on such a penalty, the time when the act or omission occurred that caused the penalty to become payable.

SERVICE OF NOTICES

17(1) Any notice given to a partnership by an officer of Revenue and Customs under this Part of this Act must be served either–

(a) on all the persons who are members of the partnership when the notice is given, or

(b) on a representative partner.

17(2) "Representative partner" means–

(a) a nominated partner, or

(b) if no partner has been nominated under paragraph 18(2), a partner designated by an authorised officer as a representative partner.

17(3) A designation under sub-paragraph (2), or the revocation of such a designation, has effect only when notice of the designation, or revocation, has been given to the partnership by an authorised officer.

NOMINATED PARTNERS

18(1) Anything required to be done by the responsible partners under this Part of this Act may instead be done by any nominated partner.

18(2) "Nominated partner" means a partner nominated by a majority of the partners to act as the representative of the partnership for the purposes of this Part of this Act.

18(3) A nomination under sub-paragraph (2), or the revocation of such a nomination, has effect only after notice of the nomination, or revocation, has been given to an authorised officer.

Part 4 – Interpretation

MEANING OF "CONTROLLING MEMBER"

19(1) For the purposes of this Schedule a person ("P") is a "controlling member" of a partnership at any time when the person has a right to a share of more than half the assets, or of more than half the income, of the partnership.

19(2) For that purpose there are to be attributed to P any interests or rights of–

(a) any individual who is connected with P (if P is an individual), and

(b) any body corporate that P controls.

19(3) An individual is "connected" with P if the individual is–

(a) P's spouse or civil partner;

(b) a relative of P;

(c) the spouse or civil partner of a relative of P;

(d) a relative of P's spouse or civil partner, or

(e) the spouse or civil partner of a relative of P's spouse or civil partner.

19(4) In sub-paragraph (3) **"relative"** means brother, sister, ancestor or lineal descendant.

19(5) P controls a body corporate ("B") if P has power to secure–

(a) by means of the holding of shares or the possession of voting power in relation to B or any other body corporate, or

(b) as a result of any powers conferred by the articles of association or other document regulating that or any other body corporate,

that the affairs of B are conducted in accordance with P's wishes.

MEANING OF "MANAGING PARTNER"

20 [Omitted by FA 2015, s. 119 and Sch. 19, para. 5(b).]

History – Para. 20 (and the heading before it) omitted by FA 2015, s. 119 and Sch. 19, para. 5(b), with effect for the purposes of determining whether a person meets a threshold condition in a period of three years ending on or after 26 March 2015 (Royal Assent). Former para. 20 read as follows:

"**20** In this Schedule **"managing partner"**, in relation to a partnership, means a member of the partnership who directs or is on a day-to-day level in control of, the management of the business of the partnership."

POWER TO AMEND DEFINITIONS

21(1) The Treasury may by regulations amend paragraph 19.

21(2) Regulations under sub-paragraph (1) may include any amendment of this Schedule that is necessary in consequence of any amendment made by virtue of sub-paragraph (1).

History – In para. 21 the words "or 20" omitted by FA 2015, s. 119 and Sch. 19, para. 5(c), with effect for the purposes of determining whether a person meets a threshold condition in a period of three years ending on or after 26 March 2015 (Royal Assent).

SCHEDULE 37 – COMPANIES OWNED BY EMPLOYEE-OWNERSHIP TRUSTS

Section 290

Part 3 – Inheritance Tax Relief

9 IHTA 1984 is amended as follows.

10(1) [Inserts IHTA 1984, s. 13A.]

10(2) The amendment made by this paragraph has effect in relation to dispositions of property made on or after 6 April 2014.

11(1) [Inserts IHTA 1984, s. 28A.]

11(2) The amendment made by this paragraph has effect in relation to transfers of value made on or after 6 April 2014.

12(1) [Amends IHTA 1984, s. 29A(6).]

12(2) The amendment made by this paragraph has effect in relation to transfers of value made on or after 6 April 2014.

13(1) Section 72 (property leaving employee trusts and newspaper trusts) is amended as follows.

13(2) [Amends IHTA 1984, s. 72(2).]

13(3) [Inserts IHTA 1984, s. 72(3A).]

13(4) The amendments made by this paragraph are treated as having come into force on 6 April 2014.

14(1) [Inserts IHTA 1984, s. 75A.]

14(2) The amendment made by this paragraph is treated as having come into force on 6 April 2014.

15(1) Section 86 (trusts for benefit of employees) is amended as follows.

15(2) [Inserts IHTA 1984, s. 86(3)(d).]

15(3) [Inserts IHTA 1984, s. 86(3A).]

15(4) The amendments made by this paragraph are treated as having come into force on 6 April 2014.

16(1) [Amends IHTA 1984, s. 144(1)(b).]

16(2) The amendment made by this section is treated as having come into force on 6 April 2014.

Part 4 – Miscellaneous Amendments

FINANCE ACT 1986

17(1) [Inserts FA 1986, s. 102(5)(j).]

17(2) The amendment made by this paragraph has effect in relation to disposals made on or after 6 April 2014.

FINANCE ACT 2015

(2015 Chapter 11)

[*26th March 2015*]

ARRANGEMENT OF SECTIONS

PART 2 – EXCISE DUTIES AND OTHER TAXES

INHERITANCE TAX

74 Inheritance tax: exemption for decorations and other awards

74(1) [Substitutes IHTA 1984, s. 6(1B) and inserts (1BA).]

74(2) The amendment made by subsection (1) has effect in relation to transfers of value made, or treated as made, on or after 3 December 2014.

75 Inheritance tax: exemption for emergency service personnel etc

75(1) IHTA 1984 is amended as follows.

75(2) [Inserts IHTA 1984, s. 153A.]

75(3) In section 154 (death on active service)–

(a) [amends IHTA 1984, s. 154(1),]

(b) [inserts IHTA 1984, s. 154(1A),]

(c) [amends IHTA 1984, s. 154(2)(b) and inserts (c),]

(d) [inserts IHTA 1984, s. 154(2A).]

75(4) [Inserts IHTA 1984, s. 155A.]

75(5) The amendments made by this section have effect in relation to deaths occurring on or after 19 March 2014.

PART 3 – DIVERTED PROFITS TAX

ADMINISTRATION OF TAX

105 Information and inspection powers etc

105(1) [Not relevant to inheritance tax.]

105(2) [Inserts FA 2008, Sch. 36, para. 63(1)(ca).]

FINAL PROVISIONS

115 Application of other enactments to diverted profits tax

115(1) [Inserts FA 2013, s. 206(3)(da).]

115(2) [Inserts FA 2010, Sch. 6, para. 7(i).]

115(3) [Not relevant to inheritance tax.]

115(4) [Not relevant to inheritance tax.]

115(5) [Not relevant to inheritance tax.]

116 Commencement and transitional provision

116(1) This Part has effect in relation to accounting periods beginning on or after 1 April 2015.

116(2) For the purposes of this Part, if an accounting period of a company begins before and ends on or after 1 April 2015 ("the straddling period")–

(a) so much of that accounting period as falls before 1 April 2015 and so much of it as falls on or after that date are treated as separate accounting periods, and

(b) where it is necessary to apportion amounts for the straddling period to the different parts of that period, that apportionment is to be made on a just and reasonable basis.

116(3) For the purposes of any accounting period which ends on or before 31 March 2016, section 92 has effect as if in subsection (2)(b) of that section the reference to 3 months were a reference to 6 months.

116(4) This Part does not apply in relation to any profits arising to a Lloyd's corporate member which are–

(a) mentioned in section 220(2) of FA 1994 (Lloyd's underwriters: accounting period in which certain profits or losses arise), and

(b) declared in the calendar year 2015 or a later calendar year,

to the extent that those profits are referable, on a just and reasonable basis, to times before 1 April 2015.

116(5) In subsection (4) **"Lloyd's corporate member"** means a body corporate which is a member of Lloyd's and is or has been an underwriting member.

PART 4 – OTHER PROVISIONS

ANTI-AVOIDANCE

117 Disclosure of tax avoidance schemes

117 Schedule 17 contains amendments relating to the disclosure of tax avoidance schemes.

118 Accelerated payments and group relief

118 Schedule 18 contains provision about the relationship between accelerated payments and group relief.

119 Promoters of tax avoidance schemes

119 Schedule 19 contains provision about promoters of tax avoidance schemes.

120 Penalties in connection with offshore matters and offshore transfers

120(1) Schedule 20 contains provisions amending–

(a) Schedule 24 to FA 2007 (penalties for errors),

(b) Schedule 41 to FA 2008 (penalties for failure to notify),

(c) Schedule 55 to FA 2009 (penalties for failure to make returns etc), and

(d) Schedule 43C to FA 2013 (as amended by FA 2016).

120(2) That Schedule comes into force on such day as the Treasury may by order appoint.

120(3) An order under subsection (2)–

(a) may commence a provision generally or only for specified purposes, and

(b) may appoint different days for different provisions or for different purposes.

120(4) The power to make an order under this section is exercisable by statutory instrument.

History – S. 120(1)(d) (and the ", and" before it) inserted (and the "and" after (b) omitted) by FA 2016, s. 158(13), with effect in relation to tax arrangements (within the meaning of FA 2013, Pt. 5) entered into on or after 15 September 2016 (Royal Assent).

121 Penalties in connection with offshore asset moves

121 Schedule 21 contains provision for imposing an additional penalty in cases where–

(a) a person is liable for a penalty for a failure to comply with an obligation or provide a document, or for providing an inaccurate document, relating to income tax, capital gains tax or inheritance tax, and

(b) there is a related transfer of, or change in the ownership arrangements for, an asset situated or held outside the United Kingdom.

PART 5 – FINAL PROVISIONS

126 Interpretation

126(1) In this Act–

"ALDA 1979" means the Alcoholic Liquor Duties Act 1979,

"CAA 2001" means the Capital Allowances Act 2001,

"CTA 2009" means the Corporation Tax Act 2009,

"CTA 2010" means the Corporation Tax Act 2010,

"IHTA 1984" means the Inheritance Tax Act 1984,

"ITA 2007" means the Income Tax Act 2007,

"ITEPA 2003" means the Income Tax (Earnings and Pensions) Act 2003,

"ITTOIA 2005" means the Income Tax (Trading and Other Income) Act 2005,

"OTA 1975" means the Oil Taxation Act 1975,

"TCGA 1992" means the Taxation of Chargeable Gains Act 1992,

"TIOPA 2010" means the Taxation (International and Other Provisions) Act 2010,

"TMA 1970" means the Taxes Management Act 1970,

"TPDA 1979" means the Tobacco Products Duty Act 1979,

"VATA 1994" means the Value Added Tax Act 1994, and

"VERA 1994" means the Vehicle Excise and Registration Act 1994.

126(2) In this Act **"FA"**, followed by a year, means the Finance Act of that year.

127 *Short title*

127 This Act may be cited as the Finance Act 2015.

SCHEDULES

SCHEDULE 7 – DISPOSALS OF UK RESIDENTIAL PROPERTY INTERESTS BY NON-RESIDENTS ETC

Section 37

Part 2 – Other Amendments

56(1) In FA 2007, Schedule 24 (penalties for errors) is amended as follows.

56(2) [Not relevant to inheritance tax.]

56(3) [Inserts FA 2007, Sch. 24, para. 21C.]

Part 3 – Commencement

60 The amendments made by this Schedule have effect in relation to disposals made on or after 6 April 2015.

SCHEDULE 17 – DISCLOSURE OF TAX AVOIDANCE SCHEMES

Section 117

REQUIREMENT TO UPDATE DOTAS INFORMATION

1 [Inserts FA 2004, s. 310C.]

2 [Amends FA 2004, s. 316(2).]

3 [Not relevant to inheritance tax.]

ARRANGEMENTS TO BE GIVEN REFERENCE NUMBER

4 [Amends FA 2004, s. 311(1)(a).]

NOTIFICATION OF EMPLOYEES

5(1) Section 312A of FA 2004 (duty of client to notify parties of number) is amended as follows.

5(2) [Inserts FA 2004, s. 312A(2A).]

5(3) [Substitutes FA 2004, s. 312A(3).]

5(4) [Amends FA 2004, s. 312A(4).]

5(5) [Amends FA 2004, s. 312A(5).]

6 [Inserts FA 2004, s. 313(6).]

7 [Amends FA 2004, s. 316(2).]

8 [Not relevant to inheritance tax.]

EMPLOYERS' DUTY OF DISCLOSURE

9 [Inserts FA 2004, s. 313ZC.]

10 [Amends FA 2004, s. 316(2).]

11 [Not relevant to inheritance tax.]

IDENTIFYING SCHEME USERS

12(1) Section 313C of FA 2004 (information provided to introducers) is amended as follows.

12(2) [Substitutes FA 2004, s. 313C(1) and inserts (1A).]

12(3) [Amends FA 2004, s. 313C(3).]

12(4) [Substitutes heading to FA 2004, s. 313C.]

13 [Not relevant to inheritance tax.]

ADDITIONAL INFORMATION

14 [Inserts FA 2004, s. 316A.]

15 [Not relevant to inheritance tax.]

PROTECTION OF PERSONS MAKING VOLUNTARY DISCLOSURES

16 [Inserts FA 2004, s. 316B.]

PUBLICATION OF DOTAS INFORMATION

17 [Inserts FA 2004, s. 316C and 316D.]

INCREASE IN PENALTIES FOR FAILURE TO COMPLY WITH SECTION 313 OF FA 2004

18 [Not relevant to inheritance tax.]

TRANSITIONAL PROVISIONS

19(1) Section 310C of FA 2004 applies in relation to notifiable arrangements, or proposed notifiable arrangements, only if a reference number under section 311 of that Act is allocated to the arrangements on or after the day on which this Act is passed.

19(2) But section 310C of FA 2004 does not apply in relation to notifiable arrangements, or proposed notifiable arrangements, where prescribed information relating to the arrangements was provided to HMRC before that day in compliance with section 308 of that Act.

20 Any notice given by HMRC under section 312A(4) of FA 2004 (notice that section 312A(2) duty does not apply) before the day on which this Act is passed is treated on and after that day as given also in relation to the duty under section 312A(2A) of that Act.

21(1) Section 316C of FA 2004 applies in relation to notifiable arrangements, or proposed notifiable arrangements, only if a reference number under section 311 of that Act is allocated to the arrangements on or after the day on which this Act is passed.

21(2) But section 316C of FA 2004 does not apply in relation to notifiable arrangements, or proposed notifiable arrangements, where prescribed information relating to the arrangements was provided to HMRC before that day in compliance with section 308, 309 or 310 of that Act.

21(3) Section 316C(2)(b) of FA 2004 applies in relation to a ruling of a court or tribunal only if the ruling is given on or after the day on which this Act is passed.

SCHEDULE 18 – ACCELERATED PAYMENTS: GROUP RELIEF

Section 118

AMENDMENTS OF PART 4 OF FA 2014

1 Part 4 of FA 2014 (accelerated payments etc) is amended as follows.

2 [Inserts FA 2014, s. 199(c)(iv).]

3(1) Section 220 (content of notice given while a tax enquiry is in progress) is amended as follows.

3(2) [Amends FA 2014, s. 220(2)(b) and inserts (d).]

3(3) [Inserts FA 2014, s. 220(4A).]

3(4) [Amends FA 2014, s. 220(6).]

4(1) Section 221 (content of notice given pending an appeal) is amended as follows.

4(2) [Amends FA 2014, s. 221(2)(b) and inserts (d).]

5(1) Section 222 (representations about a notice) is amended as follows.

5(2) [Inserts FA 2014, s. 222(2)(c).]

5(3) *[Amends FA 2014, s. 222(4).]*

6(1) Section 223 (effect of notice given while tax enquiry is in progress) is amended as follows.

6(2) [Substitutes FA 2014, s. 223(1).]

6(3) [Amends FA 2014, s. 223(2).]

6(4) [Amends heading to FA 2014, s. 223.]

7 [Inserts FA 2014, s. 225A.]

8(1) Section 227 (withdrawal, modification or suspension of accelerated payment notice) is amended as follows.

8(2) [Inserts FA 2014, s. 227(2)(d).]

8(3) [Amends FA 2014, s. 227(4).]

8(4) [Amends FA 2014, s. 227(6)(b).]

8(5) [Inserts FA 2014, s. 227(7)(c).]

8(6) [Inserts FA 2014, s. 227(12A).]

8(7) [Inserts FA 2014, s. 227(14)–(16).]

9 [Inserts FA 2014, s. 227A.]

10(1) Schedule 32 (accelerated payments and partnerships) is amended as follows.

10(2) In paragraph 4 (content of partner payment notice)–

(a) [amends FA 2014, Sch. 32, para. 4(1)(b),]

(b) [inserts FA 2014, Sch. 32, para. 4(1)(d),]

(c) [inserts FA 2014, Sch. 32, para. 4(4A) and (4B),]

(d) [amends FA 2014, Sch. 32, para. 4(5).]

10(3) In paragraph 5 (representations about a partner payment notice)–

(a) [inserts FA 2014, Sch. 32, para. 5(2)(c),]

(b) [amends FA 2014, Sch. 32, para. 5(4)(a),]

(c) [amends FA 2014, Sch. 32, para. 5(4)(b),]

(d) [inserts FA 2014, Sch. 32, para. 5(4)(b)(iii),]

(e) [inserts FA 2014, Sch. 32, para. 5(4)(c).]

10(4) In paragraph 6 (effect of partner payment notice)–

(a) [substitutes FA 2014, Sch. 32, para. 6(1),]

(b) [amends FA 2014, Sch. 32, para. 6(2).]

10(5) [Inserts FA 2014, Sch. 32, para. 6A.]

10(6) In paragraph 8 (withdrawal, suspension or modification of partner payment notices), in sub-paragraph (2)–

(a) [inserts FA 2014, Sch. 32, para. 8(2)(za),]

(b) [inserts FA 2014, Sch. 32, para. 8(2)(c).]

TRANSITIONAL PROVISION

12(1) Section 225A(3) of FA 2014 (effect of notices: surrender of losses ineffective) (inserted by paragraph 7 of this Schedule) has effect in relation to an amount specified in a notice in accordance with section 220(2)(d) or 221(2)(d) of that Act (inserted by paragraphs 3(2) and 4(2) of this Schedule) whether the consent to a claim for group relief was given, or the claim itself was made, before or on or after the day on which this Act is passed.

12(2) Paragraph 6A(3) of Schedule 32 to FA 2014 (partnerships: effect of notices: surrender of losses ineffective) (inserted by paragraph 10(5) of this Schedule) has effect in relation to an amount specified in a notice in accordance with paragraph 4(1)(d) of that Schedule (inserted by paragraph 10(2) of this Schedule) whether the consent to a claim for group relief was given, or the claim itself was made, before or on or after the day on which this Act is passed.

SCHEDULE 19 – PROMOTERS OF TAX AVOIDANCE SCHEMES

Section 119

1 Part 5 of FA 2014 (promoters of tax avoidance schemes) is amended as follows.

TREATING PERSONS AS MEETING A THRESHOLD CONDITION

2(1) Section 237 (duty to give conduct notice) is amended as follows.

2(2) [Inserts FA 2014, s. 237(1A).]

2(3) [Amends FA 2014, s. 237(3).]
2(4) [Substitutes FA 2014, s. 237(5).]
2(5) [Amends FA 2014, s. 237(7).]
2(6) [Inserts FA 2014, s. 237(7A).]
2(7) [Amends FA 2014, s. 237(9).]
2(8) [Inserts FA 2014, s. 237(10).]
3 [Amends FA 2014, s. 283.]
4(1) Part 2 of Schedule 34 (meeting the threshold conditions) is amended as follows.
4(2) [Amends heading to FA 2014, Sch. 34, Pt. 2.]
4(3) [Substitutes FA 2014, Sch. 34, para. 13A to 13D.]
5 In Schedule 36 (partnerships)–
(a) [Omits FA 2014, Sch. 36, para. 4.]
(b) [Omits FA 2014, Sch. 36, para. 20 (and the heading before it).]
(c) [Amends FA 2014, Sch. 36, para. 21.]

FAILURE TO COMPLY WITH PART 7 OF FA 2004

6 [Substitutes FA 2014, Sch. 34, para. 5(2)–(6).]

DISCIPLINARY ACTION IN RELATION TO PROFESSIONALS ETC

7(1) In Schedule 34 (threshold conditions), paragraph 8 (disciplinary action: professionals etc) is amended as follows.
7(2) [Substitutes FA 2014, Sch. 34, para. 8(1).]
7(3) [Amends heading to FA 2014, Sch. 34, para. 8.]
7(4) [Amends FA 2014, Sch. 34, para. 8(3).]

POWER TO AMEND SCHEDULE 34

8 [Inserts FA 2014, Sch. 34, para. 14(2)(c) and (d).]

COMMENCEMENT

9 The amendments made by paragraphs 2 to 7 have effect for the purposes of determining whether a person meets a threshold condition in a period of three years ending on or after the day on which this Act is passed.

SCHEDULE 20 – PENALTIES IN CONNECTION WITH OFFSHORE MATTERS AND OFFSHORE TRANSFERS

Section 120

Commencement Date – 1 April 2016 is the day appointed for the coming into force of Sch. 20, para. 3(3)–3(7), 4 and 8 and 6 April 2016 is the day appointed for the coming into force of Sch. 20, para. 16(3)–16(9) and 17 (SI 2016/456).

PENALTIES FOR ERRORS

1 Schedule 24 to FA 2007 is amended as follows.
2(1) Paragraph 4 (penalties payable under paragraph 1) is amended as follows.
2(2) After sub-paragraph (1) insert–

"**4(1A)** If the inaccuracy is in category 0, the penalty is–
(a) for careless action, 30% of the potential lost revenue,
(b) for deliberate but not concealed action, 70% of the potential lost revenue, and
(c) for deliberate and concealed action, 100% of the potential lost revenue."

2(3) *In sub-paragraph (2)–*
(a) in paragraph (a), for "30%" substitute "37.5%",
(b) in paragraph (b), for "70%" substitute "87.5%", and
(c) in paragraph (c), for "100%" substitute "125%".

2(4) In sub-paragraph (5), for "3" substitute "4".

3(1) Paragraph 4A (categorisation of inaccuracies) is amended as follows.

3(2) For sub-paragraph (1) substitute–

"**4A(A1)** An inaccuracy is in category 0 if–

(a) it involves a domestic matter,

(b) it involves an offshore matter or an offshore transfer, the territory in question is a category 0 territory and the tax at stake is income tax, capital gains tax or inheritance tax, or

(c) it involves an offshore matter and the tax at stake is a tax other than income tax, capital gains tax or inheritance tax.

4A(1) An inaccuracy is in category 1 if–

(a) it involves an offshore matter or an offshore transfer,

(b) the territory in question is a category 1 territory, and

(c) the tax at stake is income tax, capital gains tax or inheritance tax."

3(3) In sub-paragraph (2)–

(a) [amends FA 2007, Sch. 24, para. 4A(2)(a);]

(b) [amends FA 2007, Sch. 24, para. 4A(2)(c);]

3(4) In sub-paragraph (3)–

(a) [amends FA 2007, Sch. 24, para. 4A(3)(a);]

(b) [amends FA 2007, Sch. 24, para. 4A(3)(c);]

3(5) [Inserts FA 2007, Sch. 24, para. 4A(4A) and (4B).]

3(6) [Amends FA 2007, Sch. 24, para. 4A(5).]

3(7) [Amends FA 2007, Sch. 24, para. 4A(6)(a).]

3(8) In sub-paragraph (7), for "Category 1" substitute "Category 0 territory", "category 1".

Commencement Date – 1 April 2016 is the appointed day for the coming into force of para. 3(3)–3(7) (and the amendments have effect in relation to documents given to HMRC relating to: a transfer of value made on or after that date for the purposes of inheritance tax; and a tax year commencing on or after 6 April 2016 for the purposes of income tax and capital gains tax) (SI 2016/456, art. 3).

4 [Inserts FA 2007, Sch. 24, para. 4AA.]

Commencement Date – 1 April 2016 is the appointed day for the coming into force of para. 4 (and the amendments have effect in relation to documents given to HMRC relating to: a transfer of value made on or after that date for the purposes of inheritance tax; and a tax year commencing on or after 6 April 2016 for the purposes of income tax and capital gains tax) (SI 2016/456, art. 3).

5 In paragraph 10 (standard percentage reductions for disclosure), in the Table in sub-paragraph (2), at the appropriate places insert–

"37.5%	18.75%	0%",
"87.5%	43.75%	25%", and
"125%	62.5%	40%".

6 In paragraph 12(5) (interaction with other penalties and late payment surcharges: the relevant percentage)–

(a) before paragraph (a) insert–

"(za) if the penalty imposed under paragraph 1 is for an inaccuracy in category 0, 100%,", and

(b) in paragraph (a), for "100%" substitute "125%".

7(1) Paragraph 21A (classification of territories) is amended as follows.

7(2) Before sub-paragraph (1) insert–

"**21A(A1)** A category 0 territory is a territory designated as a category 0 territory by order made by the Treasury."

7(3) For sub-paragraph (2) substitute–

"**21A(2)** A category 2 territory is a territory that is not any of the following–

(a) a category 0 territory;

(b) a category 1 territory;

(c) a category 3 territory."

7(4) For sub-paragraph (7) substitute–

"**21A(7)** An instrument containing (whether alone or with other provisions) the first order to be made under sub-paragraph (A1) may not be made unless a draft of the instrument has been laid before, and approved by a resolution of, the House of Commons."

8(1) Paragraph 21B (location of assets etc) is amended as follows.

8(2) [Inserts FA 2007, Sch. 24, para. 21B(1A).]

8(3) [Amends FA 2007, Sch. 24, para. 21B(2).]

Commencement Date – 1 April 2016 is the appointed day for the coming into force of para. 8 (and the amendments have effect in relation to documents given to HMRC relating to: a transfer of value made on or after that date for the purposes of inheritance tax; and a tax year commencing on or after 6 April 2016 for the purposes of income tax and capital gains tax) (SI 2016/456, art. 3).

PENALTIES FOR FAILURE TO MAKE RETURNS ETC

14 Schedule 55 to FA 2009 is amended as follows.

15(1) Paragraph 6 (penalty for failure continuing 12 months after penalty date) is amended as follows.

15(2) In sub-paragraph (3A)–

(a) before paragraph (a) insert–

"(za) for the withholding of category 0 information, 100%,", and

(b) in paragraph (a), for "100%" substitute "125%".

15(3) In sub-paragraph (4A)–

(a) before paragraph (a) insert–

"(za) for the withholding of category 0 information, 70%,", and

(b) in paragraph (a), for "70%" substitute "87.5%".

15(4) In sub-paragraph (6), for "3" substitute "4".

16(1) Paragraph 6A (categorisation of information) is amended as follows.

16(2) For sub-paragraph (1) substitute–

"6A(A1) Information is category 0 information if–

(a) it involves a domestic matter,

(b) it involves an offshore matter or an offshore transfer, the territory in question is a category 0 territory and it is information which would enable or assist HMRC to assess P's liability to income tax, capital gains tax or inheritance tax, or

(c) it involves an offshore matter and it is information which would enable or assist HMRC to assess P's liability to a tax other than income tax, capital gains tax or inheritance tax.

6A(1) Information is category 1 information if–

(a) it involves an offshore matter or an offshore transfer,

(b) the territory in question is a category 1 territory, and

(c) it is information which would enable or assist HMRC to assess P's liability to income tax, capital gains tax or inheritance tax."

16(3) [Amends FA 2009, Sch. 55, para. 6A(2)(a) and (c).]

16(4) [Amends FA 2009, Sch. 55, para. 6A(3)(a) and (c).]

16(5) [Inserts FA 2009, Sch. 55, para. 6A(4A) and (4B).]

16(6) [Amends FA 2009, Sch. 55, para. 6A(5).]

16(7) [Amends FA 2009, Sch. 55, para. 6A(6)(a).]

16(8) [Omits FA 2009, Sch. 55, para. 6A(8).]

16(9) [Amends FA 2009, Sch. 55, para. 6A(9).]

Commencement Date – 6 April 2016 is the day appointed for the coming into force of para. 16(3)–(9) (and the amendments have effect in relation to a return or other document which: is required to be made or delivered to HMRC in relation to a tax year commencing on or after that date; and falls within item 1, 2 or 3 of the Table in Sch. 55, para. 1(5) (penalty for failure to make returns etc)) (SI 2016/456, art. 5).

17 [Inserts FA 2009, Sch. 55, para. 6AA and 6AB.]

Commencement Date – 6 April 2016 is the day appointed for the coming into force of para. 17 (and the amendments have effect in relation to a return or other document which: is required to be made or delivered to HMRC in relation to a tax year commencing on or after that date; and falls within item 1, 2 or 3 of the Table in Sch. 55, para. 1(5) (penalty for failure to make returns etc)) (SI 2016/456, art. 5).

18 In paragraph 15 (standard percentage reductions for disclosure), in the Table in sub-paragraph (2), at the appropriate places insert–

"87.5%	43.75%	25%", and
"125%	62.5%	40%".

19 In paragraph 17(4) (interaction with other penalties and late payment surcharges), omit the "and" at the end of paragraph (b) and after that paragraph insert–

"(ba) if one of the penalties is a penalty under paragraph 6(3) or (4) and the information withheld is category 1 information, 125%, and".

GENERAL ANTI-ABUSE RULE: AGGREGATE PENALTIES

20(1) In Schedule 43C to FA 2013 (general anti-abuse rule: supplementary provision about penalty), sub-paragraph (6) of paragraph 8 is amended as follows.

20(2) After paragraph (b) insert–

"(ba) 125% in a case where neither paragraph (a) nor paragraph (b) applies and at least one of the penalties is determined by reference to the percentage in–

(i) paragraph 4(2)(c) of Schedule 24 to FA 2007,

(ii) paragraph 6(2)(a) of Schedule 41 to FA 2008,

(iii) paragraph 6(3A)(a) of Schedule 55 to FA 2009,".

20(3) In sub-paragraph (c) for "neither paragraph (a) nor paragraph (b) applies" substitute "none of paragraphs (a) to (ba) applies".

20(4) In sub-paragraph (d) for "none of paragraphs (a), (b) and (c) applies" substitute "none of paragraphs (a) to (c) applies".

History – Para. 20 (and the heading before it) inserted by FA 2016, s. 158(14), with effect in relation to tax arrangements (within the meaning of FA 2013, Pt. 5) entered into on or after 15 September 2016.

SCHEDULE 21 – PENALTIES IN CONNECTION WITH OFFSHORE ASSET MOVES

Section 121

PENALTY LINKED TO OFFSHORE ASSET MOVES

1(1) A penalty is payable by a person ("P") where Conditions A, B and C are met.

1(2) Condition A is that–

(a) P is liable for a penalty specified in paragraph 2 ("the original penalty"), and

(b) the original penalty is for a deliberate failure (see paragraph 3).

1(3) Condition B is that there is a relevant offshore asset move (see paragraph 4) which occurs after the relevant time (see paragraph 5).

1(4) Condition C is that–

(a) the main purpose, or one of the main purposes, of the relevant offshore asset move is to prevent or delay the discovery by Her Majesty's Revenue and Customs ("HMRC") of a potential loss of revenue, and

(b) the original penalty relates to an inaccuracy or failure which relates to the same potential loss of revenue.

ORIGINAL PENALTIES TRIGGERING PENALTIES UNDER THIS SCHEDULE

2 The penalties referred to in paragraph 1(2) are–

(a) a penalty under paragraph 1 of Schedule 24 to FA 2007 (penalty for error in taxpayer's document) in relation to an inaccuracy in a document of a kind listed in the Table in paragraph 1 of that Schedule, where the tax at stake is income tax, capital gains tax or inheritance tax,

(b) [not relevant to inheritance tax;]

(c) a penalty under paragraph 6 of Schedule 55 to FA 2009 (penalty for failures to make return etc where failure continues after 12 months), where the tax at stake is income tax, capital gains tax or inheritance tax, and

(d) a penalty under paragraph 1 of Schedule 18 to F[(No. 2)]A 2017 (requirement to correct relevant offshore tax non-compliance).

History – Para. 2(d) and the word ", and" preceding it inserted (and the word "and" at the end of para. 2(b) omitted) by F(No. 2)A 2017, s. 67 and Sch. 18, para. 27(2), with effect from 16 November 2017 (Royal Assent).

"DELIBERATE FAILURE"

3 The original penalty is for a **"deliberate failure"** if–

(a) in the case of a penalty within paragraph 2(a), the inaccuracy to which it relates was deliberate on P's part (whether or not concealed);

(b) [not relevant to inheritance tax;]

(c) in the case of a penalty within paragraph 2(c), the withholding of the information, resulting from the failure to make the return, is deliberate (whether or not concealed).

(d) in the case of a penalty within paragraph 2(d), P was aware at any time during the RTC period that at the end of the 2016–17 tax year P had relevant offshore tax non-compliance to correct;

and terms used in paragraph (d) have the same meaning as in Schedule 18 to F[(No. 2)]A 2017.

History – Para. 3(d) and the end words following it inserted by F(No. 2)A 2017, s. 67 and Sch. 18, para. 27(3), with effect from 16 November 2017 (Royal Assent).

"RELEVANT OFFSHORE ASSET MOVE"

4(1) There is a **"relevant offshore asset move"** if, at a time when P is the beneficial owner of an asset ("the qualifying time")–

(a) the asset ceases to be situated or held in a specified territory and becomes situated or held in a non-specified territory,

(b) the person who holds the asset ceases to be resident in a specified territory and becomes resident in a non-specified territory, or

(c) there is a change in the arrangements for the ownership of the asset,

and P remains the beneficial owner of the asset, or any part of it, immediately after the qualifying time.

4(2) Whether a territory is a **"specified territory"** or **"non-specified territory"** is to be determined, for the purposes of sub-paragraph (1), as at the qualifying time.

4(3) Where–

(a) an asset of which P is the beneficial owner ("the original asset") is disposed of, and

(b) all or part of any proceeds from the sale of the asset are (directly or indirectly) reinvested in another asset of which P is also the beneficial owner ("the new asset"),

the original asset and the new asset are to be treated as the same asset for the purposes of determining whether there is a relevant offshore asset move.

4(4) **"Asset"** has the meaning given in section 21(1) of TCGA 1992, but also includes sterling.

4(5) **"Specified territory"** means a territory specified in regulations made by the Treasury by statutory instrument; and references to **"non-specified territory"** are to be construed accordingly.

4(6) Regulations under sub-paragraph (5) are subject to annulment in pursuance of a resolution of the House of Commons.

Statutory instruments – SI 2015/866: made under para. 4(5).

"RELEVANT TIME"

5(1) **"The relevant time"** has the meaning given by this paragraph.

5(2) Where the original penalty is under Schedule 24 to FA 2007, the relevant time is–

(a) if the tax at stake as a result of the inaccuracy is income tax or capital gains tax, the beginning of the tax year to which the document containing the inaccuracy relates, and

(b) if the tax at stake as a result of the inaccuracy is inheritance tax, the time when liability to the tax first arises.

5(3) [not relevant to inheritance tax;]

5(4) Where the original penalty is for a failure to make a return or deliver a document specified in the table in paragraph 1 of Schedule 55 to FA 2009, the relevant time is–

(a) if the tax at stake is income tax or capital gains tax, the beginning of the tax year to which the return or document relates, and

(b) if the tax at stake is inheritance tax, the time when liability to the tax first arises.

5(5) Where the original penalty is under paragraph 1 of Schedule 18 to F[(No. 2)]A 2017, the relevant time is the time when that Schedule comes into force.

History – Para. 5(5) inserted by F(No. 2)A 2017, s. 67 and Sch. 18, para. 27(4), with effect from 16 November 2017 (Royal Assent).

AMOUNT OF THE PENALTY

6(1) The penalty payable under paragraph 1(1) is 50% of the amount of the original penalty payable by P.

6(2) The penalty payable under paragraph 1(1) is not a penalty determined by reference to a liability to tax (despite the fact that the original penalty by reference to which it is calculated may be such a penalty).

ASSESSMENT

7(1) Where a person becomes liable for a penalty under paragraph 1(1), HMRC must–

(a) assess the penalty,

(b) notify the person, and

(c) state in the notice the tax period in respect of which the penalty is assessed.

7(2) A penalty under paragraph 1(1) must be paid before the end of the period of 30 days beginning with the day on which notification of the penalty is issued.

7(3) An assessment–

(a) is to be treated for procedural purposes in the same way as an assessment to tax (except in respect of a matter expressly provided for by this Schedule),

(b) may be enforced as if it were an assessment to tax, and

(c) may be combined with an assessment to tax.

7(4) An assessment of a penalty under paragraph 1(1) must be made within the same period as that allowed for the assessment of the original penalty.

7(5) If, after an assessment of a penalty is made under this paragraph, HMRC amends the assessment, or makes a supplementary assessment, in respect of the original penalty, it must also at the same time amend the assessment, or make a supplementary assessment, in respect of the penalty under paragraph 1(1) to ensure that it is based on the correct amount of the original penalty.

7(6) In this paragraph–

(a) a reference to an assessment to tax, in relation to inheritance tax, is to a determination, and

(b) **"tax period"** means a tax year, accounting period or other period in respect of which tax is charged.

APPEAL

8(1) A person may appeal against a decision of HMRC that a penalty is payable by the person.

8(2) An appeal under this paragraph is to be treated in the same way as an appeal against an assessment to, or determination of, the tax concerned (including by the application of any provision about bringing the appeal by notice to HMRC, about HMRC review of the decision or about determination of the appeal by the First-tier Tribunal or Upper Tribunal).

8(3) Sub-paragraph (2) does not apply in respect of a matter expressly provided for by this Schedule.

8(4) On an appeal under this paragraph, the tribunal may affirm or cancel HMRC's decision.

COMMENCEMENT AND TRANSITIONALS

9(1) This Schedule has effect in relation to relevant offshore asset moves occurring after the day on which this Act is passed.

9(2) For the purposes of this Schedule, it does not matter if liability for the original penalty first arose on or before that day, unless the case is one to which sub-paragraph (3) applies.

9(3) The original penalty is to be ignored if P's liability for it for arose before the day on which this Act is passed and before that day–

(a) if the original penalty was under Schedule 24 to FA 2007, any tax which was unpaid as a result of the inaccuracy has been assessed or determined;

(b) if the original penalty was under Schedule 41 to FA 2008 or Schedule 55 to FA 2009, the failure to which it related was remedied and any tax which was unpaid as a result of the failure has been assessed or determined.

FINANCE (NO. 2) ACT 2015

(2015 Chapter 33) [*18th November 2015*]

ARRANGEMENT OF SECTIONS

PART 2 – INHERITANCE TAX

RATE BANDS

9 Increased nil-rate band where home inherited by descendants

9(1) IHTA 1984 is amended as follows.

9(2) [Amends IHTA 1984, s. 7(1).]

9(3) [Amends IHTA 1984, s. 8A(2).]

9(4) [Inserts IHTA 1984, s. 8D–8M.]

10 Rate bands for tax years 2018–19, 2019–20 and 2020–21

10 Section 8 of IHTA 1984 (indexation) does not have effect by virtue of any difference between–

(a) the consumer prices index for the month of September in 2017, 2018 or 2019, and

(b) that index for the previous September.

SETTLEMENTS

11 Calculation of rate of inheritance tax on settled property

11 Schedule 1 contains provision about calculating the rate at which inheritance tax is charged under Chapter 3 of Part 3 of IHTA 1984.

12 Exemption from ten-yearly charge for heritage property

12(1) Section 79 of IHTA 1984 (exemption from ten-yearly charge) is amended as follows.

12(2) In subsection (3)–

(a) [amends IHTA 1984, s. 79(3),]

(b) [amends IHTA 1984, s. 79(3)(a),]

(c) [inserts IHTA 1984, s. 79(3)(aa),]

(d) [amends IHTA 1984, s. 79(3)(b),]

(e) [amends IHTA 1984, s. 79(3).]

12(3) [Inserts IHTA 1984, s. 79(3A).]

12(4) [Amends IHTA 1984, s. 79(4).]

12(5) [Amends IHTA 1984, s. 79(5), (5A), (6), (8)(a) and (9A)(a).]

12(6) [Amends IHTA 1984, s. 79(7A)(c).]

12(7) In subsection (8)–

(a) [amends IHTA 1984, s. 79(8)(a),]

(b) [amends IHTA 1984, s. 79(8)(c).]

12(8) Accordingly, in that Act–

(a) [amends IHTA 1984, s. 207(3),]

(b) [amends IHTA 1984, s. 233(1)(c),]

(c) [amends IHTA 1984, s. 237(3B)(a),]

(d) [amends IHTA 1984, Sch. 4, para. 3(2)(c).]

12(9) The amendments made by this section have effect in relation to occasions on which tax would (ignoring the effect of the amendments) fall to be charged under section 64 of IHTA 1984 on or after the day on which this Act is passed.

13 Settlements with initial interest in possession

13(1) [Amends IHTA 1984, s. 80.]

13(2) The amendments made by this section come into force on the day after the day on which this Act is passed subject to the saving provision in subsections (3) to (7).

13(3) Subsections (4) to (7) apply where–

(a) the occasion first referred to in subsection (1) of section 80 of IHTA 1984 occurred before 22 March 2006,

(b) on that occasion the settlor, or the settlor's spouse or civil partner, became beneficially entitled to an interest in possession in property which, as a result of that subsection, was treated as not becoming comprised in a settlement for the purposes of Chapter 3 of Part 3 of IHTA 1984 on that occasion, and

(c) at all times in the relevant period that property, or some particular part of it, has been property in which the settlor, or the settlor's spouse or civil partner, has been beneficially entitled to an interest in possession,

and in subsections (4) to (7) **"the protected property"** means that property or, as the case may be, that particular part of it.

13(4) The amendments made by subsection (1) do not have effect in relation to any particular part of the protected property for so long as the subsisting interest in possession continues to subsist in that part (but see subsections (5) and (6) for what happens afterwards).

13(5) As from immediately before the time when the subsisting interest in possession comes to an end so far as subsisting in any particular part of the protected property (whether or not it also comes to an end at the same time so far as subsisting in some or all of the rest of the protected property), section 80(1) of IHTA 1984 has effect in relation to that part as if the second appearance of "an interest in possession" were "a qualifying interest in possession".

13(6) If (ignoring this subsection), subsection (5) would have the consequence that a particular part of the protected property is treated as becoming comprised in a separate settlement at a time earlier than the time at which the subsisting interest in possession comes to an end so far as subsisting in that part, that part is to be treated as becoming comprised in a separate settlement at that later time.

13(7) In this section–

(a) **"the relevant period"** means the period beginning with the occasion first mentioned in section 80(1) of IHTA 1984 and ending with the day on which this Act is passed,

(b) **"qualifying interest in possession"** has the same meaning as in section 80(1) of IHTA 1984,

(c) **"subsisting interest in possession"**, in relation to a part of the protected property, means the interest in possession which subsisted in that part immediately before the end of the relevant period, and

(d) the reference in subsection (3)(c) to the spouse or civil partner of a settlor includes a reference to the widow or widower or surviving civil partner of the settlor.

14 Distributions etc from property settled by will

14(1) [Amends IHTA 1984, s. 144(1)(b).]

14(2) The amendment made by this section has effect in cases where the testator's death occurs on or after 10 December 2014.

INTEREST

15 Inheritance tax: interest

15(1) In section 107 of FA 1986 (changes in financial institutions: interest)–

(a) in subsection (4), for the words from "section 234(4)" to "above)" substitute "paragraph 7(8) of Schedule 53 to the Finance Act 2009 (late payment interest: inheritance tax payable by instalments)";

(b) in subsection (5), for the words from "amend" to "section 234(3)(c)" substitute "set out one or more descriptions of company for the purposes of paragraph 7(7) of Schedule 53 to the Finance Act 2009".

15(2) In Schedule 53 to FA 2009 (special provision: late payment interest start date)–

(a) in paragraph 7 (inheritance tax payable by instalments) for sub-paragraph (7) substitute–

"7(7) A company falls within this sub-paragraph if–

(a) its business is carried on in the United Kingdom and is–

(i) wholly that of a market maker, or

(ii) that of a discount house, or

(b) it is of a description set out in regulations under section 107(5) of FA 1986.";

(b) in paragraph 9 (certain other amounts of inheritance tax), for "date of the testator's death" substitute "end of the month in which the testator died".

15(3) The amendments made by this section come into force on such day or days as the Treasury may by regulations made by statutory instrument appoint.

15(4) Regulations under subsection (3) may–

(a) appoint different days for different purposes;

(b) make transitional or saving provision.

PART 6 – ADMINISTRATION AND ENFORCEMENT

51 Enforcement by deduction from accounts

51(1) Schedule 8 contains provision about the enforcement of debts owed to the Commissioners for Her Majesty's Revenue and Customs by making deductions from accounts held with deposit-takers.

51(2) The Treasury may, by regulations made by statutory instrument, make consequential, incidental or supplementary provision in connection with any provision made by that Schedule.

51(3) Regulations under subsection (2) may amend, repeal or revoke any enactment (whenever passed or made).

51(4) **"Enactment"** includes an enactment contained in subordinate legislation within the meaning of the Interpretation Act 1978.

51(5) A statutory instrument containing (whether alone or with other provision) provision amending or repealing an Act may not be made unless a draft of the instrument has been laid before and approved by a resolution of the House of Commons.

51(6) Any other statutory instrument containing regulations under subsection (2) is subject to annulment in pursuance of a resolution of the House of Commons.

52 Rate of interest applicable to judgment debts etc in taxation matters

52(1) This section applies if a sum payable to or by the Commissioners under a judgment or order given or made in any court proceedings relating to a taxation matter (a "tax-related judgment debt") carries interest as a result of a relevant enactment.

52(2) The **"relevant enactments"** are–

(a) section 17 of the Judgments Act 1838 (judgment debts to carry interest), and

(b) any order under section 74 of the County Courts Act 1984 (interest on judgment debts etc).

52(3) The relevant enactment is to have effect in relation to the tax-related judgment debt as if for the rate specified in section 17(1) of the Judgments Act 1838 and any other rate specified in an order under section 74 of the County Courts Act 1984 there were substituted–

(a) in the case of a sum payable to the Commissioners, the late payment interest rate provided for in regulations made by the Treasury under section 103(1) of FA 2009, and

(b) in the case of a sum payable by the Commissioners, the special repayment rate.

52(4) Subsection (3) does not affect any power of the court under the relevant enactment to prevent any sum from carrying interest or to provide for a rate of interest which is lower than (and incapable of exceeding) that for which the subsection provides.

52(5) If section 44A of the Administration of Justice Act 1970 (interest on judgment debts expressed otherwise than in sterling), or any corresponding provision made under section 74 of the County Courts Act 1984 in relation to the county court, applies to a tax-related judgment debt–

(a) subsection (3) does not apply, but

(b) the court may not specify in an order under section 44A of the Administration of Justice Act 1970, or under any provision corresponding to that section which has effect under section 74 of the County Courts Act 1984, an interest rate which exceeds (or is capable of exceeding)–

(i) in the case of a sum payable to the Commissioners, the rate mentioned in subsection (3)(a), or

(ii) in the case of a sum payable by the Commissioners, the special repayment rate.

52(6) The **"special repayment rate"** is the percentage per annum given by the formula–

$$BR + 2$$

where BR is the official Bank rate determined by the Bank of England Monetary Policy Committee at the operative meeting.

52(7) **"The operative meeting"**, in relation to the special repayment rate applicable in respect of any day, means the most recent meeting of the Bank of England Monetary Policy Committee apart from any meeting later than the 13th working day before that day.

52(8) The Treasury may by regulations made by statutory instrument–

(a) repeal subsections (6) and (7), and

(b) provide that the **"special repayment rate"** for the purposes of this section is the rate provided for in the regulations.

52(9) Regulations under subsection (8)–

(a) may make different provision for different purposes,

(b) may either themselves specify a rate of interest or make provision for such a rate to be determined (and to change from time to time) by reference to such rate, or the average of such rates, as may be referred to in the regulations,

(c) may provide for rates to be reduced below, or increased above, what they would otherwise be by specified amounts or by reference to specified formulae,

(d) may provide for rates arrived at by reference to averages to be rounded up or down,

(e) may provide for circumstances in which the alteration of a rate of interest is or is not to take place, and

(f) may provide that alterations of rates are to have effect for periods beginning on or after a day determined in accordance with the regulations ("the effective date") regardless of–

(i) the date of the judgment or order in question, and

(ii) whether interest begins to run on or after the effective date, or began to run before that date.

52(10) A statutory instrument containing regulations under subsection (8) is subject to annulment in pursuance of a resolution of the House of Commons.

52(11) To the extent that a tax-related judgment debt consists of an award of costs to or against the Commissioners, the reference in section 24(2) of the Crown Proceedings Act 1947 (which relates to interest on costs awarded to or against the Crown) to the rate at which interest is payable upon judgment debts due from or to the Crown is to be read as a reference to the rate at which interest is payable upon tax-related judgment debts.

52(12) This section has effect in relation to interest for periods beginning on or after 8 July 2015, regardless of–

(a) the date of the judgment or order in question, and

(b) whether interest begins to run on or after 8 July 2015, or began to run before that date.

52(13) Subsection (14) applies where, at any time during the period beginning with 8 July 2015 and ending immediately before the day on which this Act is passed ("the relevant period")–

(a) a payment is made in satisfaction of a tax-related judgment debt, and

(b) the payment includes interest under a relevant enactment in respect of any part of the relevant period.

52(14) The court by which the judgment or order in question was given or made must, on an application made to it under this subsection by the person who made the payment, order the repayment of the amount by which the interest paid under the relevant enactment in respect of days falling within the relevant period exceeds the interest payable under the relevant enactment in respect of those days in accordance with the provisions of this section.

52(15) In this section–

"the Commissioners" means the Commissioners for Her Majesty's Revenue and Customs;

"taxation matter" means anything the collection and management of which is the responsibility of the Commissioners (or was the responsibility of the Commissioners of Inland Revenue or Commissioners of Customs and Excise);

"working day" means any day other than a non-business day as defined in section 92 of the Bills of Exchange Act 1882.

52(16) This section extends to England and Wales only.

History – In s. 52(15), in the definition of "taxation matter", the words ", other than national insurance contributions," (which appeared after the words "means anything") omitted by FA 2016, s. 172(1), with effect (in England and Wales only) in relation to interest for periods beginning on or after 15 September 2016, regardless of— (a) the date of the judgment or order in question, and (b) whether interest begins to run on or after 15 September 2016, or began to run before that date

PART 7 – FINAL

53 Interpretation

53 In this Act–

"CAA 2001" means the Capital Allowances Act 2001,

"CTA 2009" means the Corporation Tax Act 2009,

"CTA 2010" means the Corporation Tax Act 2010,

"FA", followed by a year, means the Finance Act of that year,

"IHTA 1984" means the Inheritance Tax Act 1984,

"ITA 2007" means the Income Tax Act 2007,

"ITEPA 2003" means the Income Tax (Earnings and Pensions) Act 2003,

"ITTOIA 2005" means the Income Tax (Trading and Other Income) Act 2005,

"TCGA 1992" means the Taxation of Chargeable Gains Act 1992,

"TIOPA 2010" means the Taxation (International and Other Provisions) Act 2010,

"TMA 1970" means the Taxes Management Act 1970,

"VATA 1994" means the Value Added Tax Act 1994, and

"VERA 1994" means the Vehicle Excise and Registration Act 1994.

54 Short title

54 This Act may be cited as the Finance (No. 2) Act 2015.

SCHEDULES

SCHEDULE 1 – RATE OF TAX CHARGED UNDER CHAPTER 3 OF PART 3 IHTA 1984

Section 11

1 IHTA 1984 is amended as follows.

2 [Inserts IHTA 1984, s. 62A to 62C.]

3(1) Section 66 (rate of ten-yearly charge) is amended as follows.

3(2) In subsection (4)–

(a) [omits IHTA 1984, s. 66(4)(b),]

(b) [amends IHTA 1984, s. 66(4)(c),]

(c) [inserts IHTA 1984, s. 66(4)(d) and (e).]

3(3) [Amends IHTA 1984, s. 66(6)(a).]

4 In section 68 (rate before ten-year anniversary), in subsection (5)–

(a) [amends IHTA 1984, s. 68(5)(a) and (b),]

(b) [amends IHTA 1984, s. 68(5)(b),]

(c) [substitutes IHTA 1984, s. 68(5)(c) to (f).]

5(1) Section 69 (rate between ten-year anniversaries) is amended as follows.

5(2) [Amends IHTA 1984, s. 69(1).]

5(3) [Substitutes IHTA 1984, s. 69(2) and inserts (2A).]

5(4) [Amends IHTA 1984, s. 69(3).]

6 [Amends IHTA 1984, s. 71F(9)(b).]

7 The amendments made by this Schedule have effect in relation to occasions on which tax falls to be charged under Chapter 3 of Part 3 of IHTA 1984 on or after the day on which this Act is passed.

SCHEDULE 8 – ENFORCEMENT BY DEDUCTION FROM ACCOUNTS

Section 51

Part 1 – Scheme for Enforcement by Deduction from Accounts

INTRODUCTION

1 This Part of this Schedule contains provision about the collection of amounts due and payable to the Commissioners by the making of deductions from accounts held with deposit-takers.

"RELEVANT SUM"

2(1) In this Part of this Schedule **"relevant sum"**, in relation to a person, means a sum that is due and payable by the person to the Commissioners–

(a) under or by virtue of an enactment, or

(b) under a contract settlement,

and in relation to which Conditions A to C are met.

2(2) Condition A is that the sum is at least £1,000.

2(3) Condition B is that the sum is–

(a) an established debt (see sub-paragraph (5)),

(b) due under section 223 of, or paragraph 6 of Schedule 32 to, FA 2014 (accelerated payment notice or partner payment notice), or

(c) the disputed tax specified in a notice under section 221(2)(b) of FA 2014 (accelerated payment of tax: notice given pending appeal).

2(4) Condition C is that HMRC is satisfied that the person is aware that the sum is due and payable by the person to the Commissioners.

IHT Statutes

2(5) A sum that is due and payable to the Commissioners is an **"established debt"** if there is no possibility that the sum, or any part of it, will cease to be due and payable to the Commissioners on appeal.

2(6) For the purposes of sub-paragraph (5) it does not matter whether the reason that there is no such possibility is–

(a) that there is no right of appeal in relation to the sum,

(b) that a period for bringing an appeal has expired without an appeal having been brought, or

(c) that an appeal which was brought has been finally determined or withdrawn;

and any power to grant permission to appeal out of time is to be disregarded.

INFORMATION NOTICE

3(1) This paragraph applies if it appears to HMRC that–

(a) a person has failed to pay a relevant sum, and

(b) that person holds one or more accounts with a deposit-taker.

3(2) HMRC may give the deposit-taker a notice under this paragraph (an "information notice") requiring the deposit-taker to provide HMRC with–

(a) prescribed information about accounts held by the person with the deposit-taker,

(b) in relation to any joint account held by the person with the deposit-taker, prescribed information about the other holder or holders of the account, and

(c) any other prescribed information.

3(3) HMRC may exercise the power under sub-paragraph (2) only for the purposes of determining whether to give a hold notice to the deposit-taker in respect of the person concerned (see paragraph 4).

3(4) Where a deposit-taker is given an information notice, it must comply with the notice as soon as reasonably practicable and, in any event, within the period of 10 working days beginning with the day on which the notice is given to it.

3(5) An information notice must explain the effect of–

(a) sub-paragraph (4), and

(b) paragraph 14 (penalties).

Statutory instruments – SI 2015/1986: partly made under para. 3(2).

HOLD NOTICE

4(1) If it appears to HMRC that–

(a) a person ("P") has failed to pay a relevant sum, and

(b) P holds one or more accounts with a deposit-taker,

HMRC may give the deposit-taker a notice under this paragraph (a "hold notice").

4(2) The hold notice must–

(a) specify P's name and last known address,

(b) specify as the "specified amount" an amount that meets the conditions in sub-paragraph (4),

(c) specify as the "safeguarded amount" an amount that meets the requirements set out in sub-paragraphs (6) to (8),

(d) set out any rules which are to apply for the purposes of paragraph 7(5)(b) (priority of accounts subject to a hold notice),

(e) explain the effect of–

(i) paragraphs 6 to 13 (effect of hold notice, duty to notify account holders etc),

(ii) paragraph 14 (penalties), and

(iii) any regulations under paragraph 20(2)(c) or (d) (powers to restrict the accounts or amounts in relation to which a hold notice may have effect, in addition to the powers to make provision in the hold notice under sub-paragraph (3)(b) and (c)), and

(f) contain a statement about HMRC's compliance with paragraph 5 in relation to the notice.

For provision about the particular relevant sums to which a hold notice relates see paragraph 8(6)(a)(ii) and (7) (notice to be given by HMRC to P).

4(3) The hold notice may–

(a) specify any other information which HMRC considers might assist the deposit-taker in identifying accounts which P holds with it;

(b) specify an account, or description of account, which is to be treated for the purposes of the hold notice and this Part of this Schedule as not being an account held by P with the deposit-taker;

(c) require that an amount specified in the notice is to be treated for the purposes of the hold notice and this Part of this Schedule as if it were not an amount standing to the credit of a specified account held by P.

4(4) The amount specified as the specified amount in the hold notice ("the current hold notice") must not exceed so much of the notified sum (see paragraph 8(6) to (8)) as remains after deducting–

(a) the amount specified as the **"specified amount"** in any hold notice which relates to the same debts as the current hold notice (see sub-paragraph (5)) and is given to another deposit-taker on the same day as that notice, and

(b) the amount specified as the **"specified amount"** in any hold notice which relates to the same debts as the current hold notice and is given to a deposit-taker on an earlier day, (unless HMRC has received a notification under paragraph 8(4) in relation to that earlier hold notice).

4(5) For the purposes of this paragraph, any two hold notices given in respect of the same person **"relate to the same debts"** if at least one relevant sum specified in relation to one of those notices by virtue of paragraph 8(7)(a) is the same debt as a relevant sum so specified in relation to the other notice.

4(6) The amount specified in the hold notice as the safeguarded amount must be at least £5,000; but this is qualified by sub-paragraphs (7) and (8).

4(7) The safeguarded amount must be nil if–

(a) HMRC has previously given a deposit-taker a hold notice ("the earlier hold notice") relating to the same debts as the hold notice mentioned in sub-paragraph (2) ("the new hold notice"), and

(b) within the period of 30 days ending with the day on which the new hold notice is given to the deposit-taker, HMRC has received a notice under paragraph 8 which states that there is a held amount as a result of the earlier hold notice.

4(8) HMRC may (in a case not falling within sub-paragraph (7)) determine that an amount less than £5,000 (which may be nil) is to be the safeguarded amount if HMRC considers it appropriate to do so having regard to the value (or aggregate value) in sterling at the relevant time of any amounts which at that time stand to the credit of a qualifying non-sterling account or accounts.

4(9) In sub-paragraph (8) **"qualifying non-sterling account"** means an account which, but for paragraph 6(6)(b) (account not denominated in sterling), would be a relevant account in relation to the hold notice.

4(10) For the purposes of sub-paragraph (8), the value in sterling of any amount is to be determined in the prescribed manner; and regulations for the purposes of this sub-paragraph may specify circumstances in which the exchange rate is to be determined in accordance with a notice published by the Commissioners.

4(11) In sub-paragraph (8) **"the relevant time"** means the time when the Commissioners determine the amount to be specified as the **"safeguarded amount"** under sub-paragraph (2)(c).

4(12) HMRC must not on any one day give to a single deposit-taker more than one hold notice relating to the same debts.

PERSONS AT A PARTICULAR DISADVANTAGE IN DEALING WITH REVENUE AND CUSTOMS AFFAIRS

5(1) Before deciding whether or not to exercise the power under paragraph 3(2) or 4(1) in relation to a person, HMRC must consider whether or not, to the best of HMRC's knowledge, there are any matters as a result of which the person is, or may be, at a particular disadvantage in dealing with the person's Revenue and Customs affairs.

5(2) If HMRC determines that there are any such matters, HMRC must take those matters into account in deciding whether or not to exercise the power concerned in relation to the person.

5(3) The Commissioners must publish guidance as to the factors which are relevant to determining whether or not a person is at a particular disadvantage in dealing with the person's Revenue and Customs affairs for the purposes of this Schedule.

5(4) In this paragraph **"Revenue and Customs affairs"**, in relation to a person by whom a relevant sum is payable, means any affairs of the person which relate to the relevant sum.

EFFECT OF HOLD NOTICE

6(1) A deposit-taker to whom a hold notice is given under paragraph 4 must, for each relevant account (see sub-paragraph (6))–

(a) determine whether or not there is a held amount (greater than nil) in relation to that account, and

(b) if there is such a held amount in relation to that account, take the first or second type of action (see sub-paragraph (3)) in respect of that account.

See paragraph 7 for how to determine the held amount in relation to any relevant account.

6(2) The deposit-taker must comply with sub-paragraph (1) as soon as is reasonably practicable and, in any event, within the period of 5 working days beginning with the day on which the hold notice is given.

6(3) In relation to each affected account (see sub-paragraph (7))–

(a) the first type of action is to put in place such arrangements as are necessary to ensure that the deposit-taker does not do anything, or permit anything to be done, that would reduce the amount standing to the credit of that account below the held amount in relation to that account;

(b) the second type of action is to–

(i) transfer an amount equal to the held amount from the affected account into an account created by the deposit-taker for the sole purpose of containing that transferred amount (a "suspense account"), and

(ii) put in place such arrangements as are necessary to ensure that the deposit-taker does not do anything, or permit anything to be done, that would reduce the amount standing to the credit of that suspense account below the amount that is the held amount in relation to the affected account.

6(4) The deposit-taker must maintain any arrangements made under sub-paragraph (3) until the hold notice ceases to be in force.

6(5) A hold notice ceases to be in force when–

(a) the deposit-taker is given a notice cancelling it under paragraph 9 or 11 or the hold notice is cancelled under paragraph 12, or

(b) the deposit-taker is given a deduction notice in relation to the hold notice (see paragraph 13).

6(6) In this Part of this Schedule **"relevant account"**, in relation to a hold notice, means an account held with the deposit-taker by P, but not including–

(a) an account excluded under paragraph 4(3)(b) or by regulations under paragraph 20(2)(c),

(b) an account not denominated in sterling, or

(c) any suspense account.

6(7) For the purposes of this Part of this Schedule, a relevant account is an **"affected account"** if, as a result of the hold notice, an amount is the held amount in relation to that account (see paragraph 7(1) and (2)).

DETERMINATION OF HELD AMOUNTS

7(1) If there is only one relevant account (see paragraph 6(6)) in existence at the time the deposit-taker complies with paragraph 6(1), **"the held amount"** in relation to that account is–

(a) if the available amount in respect of the account (see sub-paragraph (3)) exceeds the safeguarded amount, so much of the amount of the excess as does not exceed the specified amount, and

(b) if the available amount does not exceed the safeguarded amount, nil.

For the meaning of **"the safeguarded amount"** and **"the specified amount"** see paragraph 23(1).

7(2) If there is more than one relevant account in existence at the time the deposit-taker complies with paragraph 6(1), "the held amount" in relation to each relevant account is determined as follows–

Step 1

Determine the available amount in respect of each relevant account.

Step 2

Determine the total of the available amounts in respect of all of the relevant accounts.

If that total does not exceed the safeguarded amount, the held amount in relation to each relevant account is nil (and no further steps are to be taken). In any other case, go to Step 3.

Step 3

Match the safeguarded amount against the available amounts in respect of the relevant accounts, taking those accounts in reverse priority order (see sub-paragraph (6)).

Step 4

Match the specified amount against what remains of the available amounts in respect of the relevant accounts by taking each relevant account in priority order (see sub-paragraph (5)) and matching the specified amount (or, as the case may be, what remains of the specified amount) against the available amount for each account until either–

(a) the specified amount has been fully matched, or

(b) what remains of the available amounts is exhausted.

Where this sub-paragraph applies, **"the held amount"**, in relation to a relevant account–

(i) is so much of the amount standing to the credit of the account as is matched against the specified amount under Step 4, and

(ii) accordingly, is nil if no amount standing to the credit of the account is so matched against the specified amount.

7(3) In this paragraph **"the available amount"** means–

(a) in the case of an account other than a joint account, the amount standing to the credit of that account at the time the deposit-taker complies with paragraph 6(1), or

(b) in the case of a joint account, the appropriate fraction of the amount standing to the credit of that account at that time;

so, if no amount stands to the credit of an account at that time, **"the available amount"** is nil.

7(4) In this paragraph **"the appropriate fraction"**, in relation to a joint account, means–

$$\frac{1}{N}$$

where N is the number of persons who together hold the joint account.

7(5) In this paragraph **"priority order"** means such order as the deposit-taker considers appropriate, but the deposit-taker must ensure–

(a) that accounts other than joint accounts always have a higher priority than joint accounts, and

(b) subject to paragraph (a), that any rule set out in the hold notice under paragraph 4(2)(d) is adhered to.

7(6) In this paragraph **"reverse priority order"** means the reverse of the order determined under sub-paragraph (5).

7(7) In this paragraph references to an amount standing to the credit of an account are to be read subject to any regulations under paragraph 20(2)(d).

DUTY TO NOTIFY HMRC AND ACCOUNT HOLDERS ETC

8(1) This paragraph applies where a deposit-taker receives a hold notice.

8(2) If the deposit-taker determines that there are one or more affected accounts (see paragraph 5(7)) as a result of the hold notice, the deposit-taker must give HMRC a notice which sets out–

(a) prescribed information about each of the affected accounts held by P,

(b) the amount of the held amount in relation to each such account,

(c) if any of the affected accounts is a joint account held by P and one or more other persons, prescribed information about the other person or persons, and

(d) any other prescribed information.

8(3) The notice under sub-paragraph (2) must be given within the period of 5 working days beginning with the day on which the deposit-taker complies with paragraph 6(1).

8(4) If the deposit-taker determines that there are no affected accounts as a result of the hold notice, it must give HMRC a notice which–

(a) states that this is the case, and

(b) sets out any other prescribed information.

8(5) The notice under sub-paragraph (4) must be given within the period of 5 working days beginning with the day on which the deposit-taker makes that determination.

8(6) If HMRC receives a notice under sub-paragraph (2) it must as soon as reasonably practicable–

(a) give P–

(i) a copy of the hold notice, and

(ii) a notice under sub-paragraph (7), and

(b) in relation to each affected account, give a notice to each person within sub-paragraph (9) explaining that a hold notice has been given in respect of the account, the effect of the hold notice so far as it relates to the account and the effect of paragraphs 10 to 12.

8(7) A notice under this sub-paragraph must comply with the following requirements–

(a) the notice must specify the particular relevant sums (see paragraph 2) to which the hold notice relates;

(b) the details given for that purpose must include a statement, to the best of HMRC's knowledge, of the amount of each of those sums (that is, the unpaid amount) at the date of the notice;

(c) the notice must state the total of the amounts stated under paragraph (b) (if more than one), and

IHT Statutes

(d) the notice must state that the notified sum for the purposes of the hold notice (see paragraph 4(4)) is equal to–

(i) the total amount specified under paragraph (c) or,

(ii) if paragraph (c) is not applicable, the amount specified under paragraph (b) as the amount of the relevant sum to which the hold notice relates.

8(8) In this Part of this Schedule **"the notified sum"**, in relation to a hold notice, means the amount identified as such (or that is to be identified as such) in the notice under sub-paragraph (7).

8(9) The persons mentioned in sub-paragraph (6)(b) are–

(a) in the case of a joint account, any holder of the account other than P, and

(b) any person (not falling within paragraph (a)) who is an interested third party in relation to the affected account,

in respect of whom prescribed information has been provided under sub-paragraph (2)(c) or sufficient information has otherwise been given in the notice under sub-paragraph (2) to enable HMRC to give a notice.

8(10) After the deposit-taker has complied with paragraph 6(1), the deposit-taker may, in relation to any affected account, give a notice to–

(a) P,

(b) if the account is a joint account, any other holder of the account, and

(c) any person (not falling within paragraph (b)) who is an interested third party in relation to the account,

which states that a hold notice has been received by the deposit-taker in respect of the account and the effect of that notice so far as it relates to that account.

8(11) In this Part of this Schedule **"interested third party"**, in relation to a relevant account, means a person other than P who has a beneficial interest in–

(a) an amount standing to the credit of the account, or

(b) an amount which has been transferred from that account to a suspense account.

8(12) But, in relation to a hold notice, an interest which comes into existence after any arrangements under paragraph 6(3) have been put into place is treated as not being a beneficial interest for the purposes of sub-paragraph (11).

Statutory instruments – SI 2015/1986: partly made under para. 8(2)(a), (2)(c), (2)(d) and 8(4)(b).

CANCELLATION OR VARIATION OF EFFECTS OF HOLD NOTICE

9(1) Where a hold notice has been given to a deposit-taker HMRC may, by a notice given to the deposit-taker (a "notice of cancellation or variation")–

(a) cancel the hold notice,

(b) cancel the effect of the hold notice in relation to one or more accounts, or

(c) cancel the effect of the hold notice in relation to any part of the held amount standing to the credit of a particular account or accounts.

In this sub-paragraph references to the effect of a hold notice are to its effect by virtue of paragraph 6(4).

9(2) Where HMRC gives a notice under sub-paragraph (1) it must give a copy of that notice to–

(a) P, and

(b) any other person who HMRC considers is affected by the giving of the notice of cancellation or variation and is–

(i) a person who holds a relevant account of which P is also a holder and in respect of whom prescribed information is provided under paragraph 8(2)(c), or

(ii) an interested third party in relation to a relevant account in respect of whom sufficient information has been given in the notice under paragraph 8(2) to enable HMRC to give a notice.

9(3) Where the deposit-taker is given a notice under sub-paragraph (1), it must as soon as reasonably practicable and, in any event, within the period of 5 working days beginning with the day the notice is given–

(a) if the notice is given under sub-paragraph (1)(a), cancel the arrangements made under paragraph 6(3) as a result of the notice, and

(b) if the notice is given under sub-paragraph (1)(b) or (c), make such adjustments to those arrangements as are necessary to give effect to the notice.

MAKING OBJECTIONS TO HOLD NOTICE

10(1) Where a hold notice is given to a deposit-taker, a person within sub-paragraph (2) may by a notice given to HMRC (a "notice of objection") object against the hold notice.

10(2) The persons who may object are–

(a) P,

(b) any interested third party in relation to an affected account, and

(c) any person (not falling within paragraph (a) or (b)) who is a holder of an affected account which is a joint account,

but only P may object on the ground in sub-paragraph (3)(a).

10(3) An objection may only be made on one or more of the following grounds–

(a) that the debts to which the hold notice relates (see paragraph 8(7)(a)) have been wholly or partly paid,

(b) that at the time when the hold notice was given, either there was no sum that was a relevant sum in relation to P or P did not hold any account with the deposit-taker,

(c) that the hold notice is causing or will cause exceptional hardship to the person making the objection or another person, or

(d) that there is an interested third party in relation to one or more of the affected accounts.

10(4) A notice of objection must state the grounds of the objection.

10(5) Objections under this paragraph may only be made within the period of 30 days beginning with–

(a) in the case of–

(i) P, or

(ii) a person within sub-paragraph (2)(b) or (c) who has not been given a notice under paragraph 8(6)(b),

the day on which a copy of the hold notice is given to P under paragraph 8(6)(a), and

(b) in the case of a person given a notice under paragraph 8(6)(b), the day on which that notice is given.

10(6) Sub-paragraph (5) does not apply if HMRC agree to the notice of objection being given after the end of the period mentioned in that sub-paragraph.

10(7) HMRC must agree to a notice of objection being given after the end of that period if the following conditions are met–

(a) the person seeking to make the objection has made a request in writing to HMRC to agree to the notice of objection being given;

(b) HMRC is satisfied that there was reasonable excuse for not giving the notice before the relevant time limit, and

(c) HMRC is satisfied that the person complied with paragraph (a) without unreasonable delay after the reasonable excuse ceased.

10(8) If a request of the kind referred to in sub-paragraph (7)(a) is made, HMRC must by a notice inform the person making the request whether or not HMRC agrees to the request.

10(9) Nothing in Part 5 of TMA 1970 (appeals and other proceedings) applies to an objection under this paragraph.

CONSIDERATION OF OBJECTIONS

11(1) HMRC must consider any objections made under paragraph 10 within 30 working days of being given the notice of objection.

11(2) Having considered the objections, HMRC must decide whether–

(a) to cancel the hold notice,

(b) *to cancel the effect of the hold notice in relation to the held amount, or any part of the held amount,* in respect of a particular account or accounts, or

(c) to dismiss the objection.

11(3) HMRC must give a notice stating its decision to–

(a) P,

(b) each person other than P who objected, and

(c) any other person who HMRC considers is affected by the decision and is–

IHT Statutes

(i) a person who holds a relevant account of which P is also a holder and in respect of whom prescribed information is provided under paragraph 8(2)(c), or

(ii) an interested third party in relation to a relevant account in respect of whom sufficient information has been given in the notice under paragraph 8(2) to enable HMRC to give a notice.

11(4) HMRC must, by a notice to the deposit-taker–

(a) if it makes a decision under sub-paragraph (2)(a), cancel the hold notice;

(b) if it makes a decision under sub-paragraph (2)(b), cancel the effect of the hold notice in relation to the accounts or amounts in question.

11(5) HMRC must give each person to whom HMRC is required to give a notice under sub-paragraph (3) a copy of any notice given to the deposit-taker under sub-paragraph (4).

11(6) Where the deposit-taker is given a notice under sub-paragraph (4), it must as soon as reasonably practicable and, in any event, within the period of 5 working days beginning with the day the notice is given–

(a) if the notice is given under sub-paragraph (4)(a), cancel the arrangements mentioned in paragraph 6(3), or

(b) if the notice is given under sub-paragraph (4)(b), make such adjustments to those arrangements as are necessary to give effect to the notice.

11(7) In this paragraph references to the effect of a hold notice are to its effect by virtue of paragraph 6(4).

APPEALS

12(1) Where HMRC makes a decision under paragraph (b) or (c) of paragraph 11(2), a person within sub-paragraph (2) may appeal against the hold notice.

12(2) The persons who may appeal are–

(a) P,

(b) any interested third party in relation to an affected account, and

(c) any person not falling within paragraph (a) or (b) who is a holder of an affected account which is a joint account.

12(3) An appeal may only be made on one or more of the grounds set out in paragraph 10(3) (and for this purpose the reference in paragraph 10(3)(c) to **"the objection"** is to be read as a reference to the appeal).

12(4) An appeal under sub-paragraph (1) must be made–

(a) in England and Wales, to the county court, and

(b) in Northern Ireland, to a county court.

12(5) An appeal under this paragraph may only be made within the period of 30 days beginning–

(a) in the case of a person given a notice of HMRC's decision under paragraph 11(3), with the day on which that notice is given to that person, and

(b) in the case of any person within sub-paragraph (2)(b) or (c) to whom such a notice has not been given, the day on which P is given such a notice.

12(6) A notice of appeal must state the grounds of appeal.

12(7) On an appeal under this paragraph, the court may–

(a) cancel the hold notice,

(b) cancel the effect of the hold notice in relation to the held amount, or any part of the held amount, in respect of a particular account or accounts, or

(c) dismiss the appeal.

12(8) Where the deposit-taker is served with an order made by the court under sub-paragraph (7)(a) or (b), the deposit-taker must as soon as reasonably practicable and, in any event, within the period of 5 working days beginning with the day the notice is given take such steps as are necessary to give effect to the order.

12(9) Where an appeal on the ground that the hold notice is causing or will cause the person making the appeal or another person exceptional hardship (or a further appeal following such an appeal) is pending, *the court to which the appeal* is made may, on an application made by the person who made the appeal–

(a) suspend the effect of the hold notice if adequate security is provided in respect of so much of the notified sum as remains unpaid,

(b) suspend the effect of the hold notice in relation to a particular account if adequate security is provided in respect of the held amount in relation to that account, or

(c) suspend the effect of the hold notice in relation to any part of the held amount standing to the credit of a particular account, if adequate security is provided in respect of that part.

12(10) In this paragraph references to the effect of a hold notice are to its effect by virtue of paragraph 6(4).

12(11) Nothing in Part 5 of TMA 1970 (appeals and other proceedings) applies to an appeal under this paragraph.

DEDUCTION NOTICE

13(1) If it appears to HMRC that a person in respect of whom a hold notice given to a deposit-taker is in force–

(a) has failed to pay a relevant sum, and

(b) holds an account (or more than one account) with the deposit-taker in respect of which there is a held amount in relation to that sum,

HMRC may give the deposit-taker a deduction notice in respect of that person.

13(2) A **"deduction notice"** is a notice which–

(a) specifies the name of the person concerned,

(b) specifies one or more affected accounts held by that person with the deposit-taker, and

(c) in relation to each such specified account requires the deposit-taker to deduct and pay a qualifying amount (see sub-paragraph (6)) to the Commissioners by a day specified in the notice.

13(3) Where a deduction notice specifies a particular affected account–

(a) the deduction required to be made in relation to that account by virtue of sub-paragraph (2)(c) must be made from the appropriate account, that is to say–

(i) if the deposit-taker has by virtue of the hold notice transferred an amount from the specified account into a suspense account, that suspense account, or

(ii) otherwise, the specified account, and

(b) the deposit-taker must not during the period in which the deduction notice is in force do anything, or permit anything to be done (except in accordance with paragraph (a)) that would reduce the amount standing to the credit of the appropriate account below the balance required for the purpose of making that deduction.

13(4) A deduction notice must explain the effect of sub-paragraph (3)(b) and paragraph 14 (penalties).

13(5) A deduction notice may not be given in respect of an account unless–

(a) the period for making an objection under paragraph 10 has expired and either no objections were made or any objection made has been decided or withdrawn, and

(b) if objections were made and decided, the period for appealing under paragraph 12 has expired and any appeal or further appeal has been finally determined.

13(6) In this paragraph **"qualifying amount"**, in relation to an affected account, means an amount not exceeding the held amount in relation to that account (as modified, where applicable, under paragraph 9(3)(b), 11(6)(b) or 12(7)(b)).

13(7) The total of the qualifying amounts specified in the deduction notice must not exceed the unpaid amount of the notified sum (see paragraph 8(8)).

13(8) HMRC must–

(a) give a copy of the deduction notice to the person in respect of whom it is given, and

(b) in the case of each account in respect of which the notice is given, give a notice to each person within sub-paragraph (9) explaining that a deduction notice has been given in respect of that account and the effect of the deduction notice so far as it relates to that account.

13(9) The persons mentioned in sub-paragraph (8)(b) are–

(a) if the account is a joint account, each person other than P who is a holder of the account, and

(b) any person (not falling within paragraph (a))–

(i) who is an interested third party in relation to the account whom HMRC knows will be affected by the deduction notice, and

(ii) about whom HMRC has sufficient information to enable it to give the notice under sub-paragraph (8)(b).

IHT Statutes

13(10) HMRC may, by a notice given to the deposit-taker, amend or cancel the deduction notice, and where it does so it must–

(a) give a copy of the notice under this sub-paragraph to the person in respect of whom the deduction notice was given, and

(b) in the case of each account affected by the amendment or cancellation, give a notice to each person within sub-paragraph (9) explaining the effect of the amendment or cancellation so far as it relates to that account.

13(11) The deduction notice–

(a) comes into force at the time it is given to the deposit-taker, and

(b) ceases to be in force at the time–

(i) the deposit-taker is given a notice cancelling it under sub-paragraph (10), or

(ii) the deposit-taker makes the final payment required by virtue of sub-paragraph (2)(c).

PENALTIES

14(1) This paragraph applies to a deposit-taker who–

(a) fails to comply with an information notice,

(b) fails to comply with a hold notice or a deduction notice,

(c) fails to comply with an obligation under paragraph 8(2) in accordance with paragraph 8(3) (obligation to notify HMRC of effects of hold notice),

(d) fails to comply with an obligation under paragraph 8(4) in accordance with paragraph 8(5) (obligation to notify HMRC if no affected accounts),

(e) fails to comply with an obligation under paragraph 9(3) (obligation to cancel or modify effects of hold notice),

(f) fails to comply with an obligation under paragraph 11(6) (obligation to cancel or adjust arrangements to give effect to HMRC's decision of objection), or

(g) following receipt of an information notice or hold notice in relation to an account or accounts held with the deposit-taker by a person ("the affected person"), makes a disclosure of information to the affected person or any other person in circumstances where that disclosure is likely to prejudice HMRC's ability to use the provisions of this Part of this Schedule to recover a relevant sum owed by the affected person.

14(2) In sub-paragraph (1)(g), the reference to a disclosure of information does not include the giving of a notice in accordance with paragraph 8(10) to the affected person in respect of a hold notice.

14(3) The deposit-taker is liable to a penalty of £300.

14(4) If a failure within sub-paragraph (1)(a) to (f) continues after the day on which notice is given under paragraph 15(1) of a penalty in respect of the failure, the deposit-taker is liable to a further penalty or penalties not exceeding £60 for each subsequent day on which the failure continues.

14(5) A failure by a deposit-taker to do anything required to be done within a limited period of time does not give rise to liability to a penalty under this paragraph if the deposit-taker did it within such further time, if any, as HMRC may have allowed.

14(6) Liability to a penalty under this paragraph does not arise if the person satisfies HMRC or (on an appeal notified to the tribunal) the tribunal that there is a reasonable excuse for the failure or (as the case may be) disclosure.

14(7) For the purposes of this paragraph–

(a) where the deposit-taker relies on any other person to do anything, that is not a reasonable excuse unless the deposit-taker took reasonable care to avoid the failure or disclosure, and

(b) where the deposit-taker had a reasonable excuse for the failure but the excuse has ceased, the deposit-taker is to be treated as having continued to have the excuse if the failure is remedied without unreasonable delay after the excuse ceased.

ASSESSMENT OF PENALTY

15(1) Where a deposit-taker becomes liable to a penalty under paragraph 14–

(a) HMRC must assess the penalty, and

(b) if HMRC does so, it must notify the deposit-taker in writing.

15(2) An assessment of a penalty by virtue of paragraph (a) of paragraph 14(1) must be made within the period of 12 months beginning with the day on which the deposit-taker becomes liable to the penalty.

15(3) An assessment of a penalty under any of paragraphs (b) to (g) of paragraph 14(1) must be made within the period of 12 months beginning with the latest of the following–

(a) the day on which the deposit-taker became liable to the penalty,

(b) the end of the period in which notice of an appeal in respect of the hold notice could have been given, and

(c) if notice of such an appeal is given, the day on which the appeal is finally determined or withdrawn.

APPEAL AGAINST PENALTY

16(1) A deposit-taker may appeal against–

(a) a decision that a penalty is payable by the deposit-taker under paragraph 14, or

(b) a decision as to the amount of such a penalty.

16(2) Notice of an appeal must be given to HMRC before the end of the period of 30 days beginning with the day on which the notification under paragraph 15 was given.

16(3) Notice of an appeal must state the grounds of appeal.

16(4) On an appeal under sub-paragraph (1)(a) that is notified to the tribunal (in accordance with Part 5 of TMA 1970: see below) the tribunal may confirm or cancel the decision.

16(5) On an appeal under sub-paragraph (1)(b) that is notified to the tribunal, the tribunal may–

(a) confirm the decision, or

(b) substitute for the decision another decision that HMRC had power to make.

16(6) Subject to this paragraph and paragraph 17, the provisions of Part 5 of TMA 1970 relating to appeals have effect in relation to appeals under this paragraph as they have effect in relation to an appeal against an assessment to income tax.

ENFORCEMENT OF PENALTY

17(1) A penalty under paragraph 14 must be paid–

(a) before the end of the period of 30 days beginning with the day on which the notification under paragraph 15 was given, or

(b) if notice of an appeal against the penalty is given, before the end of the period of 30 days beginning with the day on which the appeal is finally determined or withdrawn.

17(2) A penalty under paragraph 14 may be enforced as if it were income tax charged in an assessment and due and payable.

PROTECTION OF DEPOSIT-TAKERS ACTING IN GOOD FAITH

18 A deposit-taker is not liable for damages in respect of anything done in good faith for the purposes of complying with a hold notice or a deduction notice.

POWER TO MODIFY AMOUNTS AND TIME LIMITS

19(1) The Commissioners may by regulations amend any of the following provisions by substituting a different amount for the amount for the time being specified there–

(a) paragraph 2(2) (requirement that relevant sum is a minimum amount);

(b) paragraph 4(6) and (8) (threshold for safeguarded amount);

(c) paragraph 14(3) or (4) (level of penalties).

19(2) The Commissioners may by regulations amend any of the following provisions by substituting a different period for the period for the time being specified there–

(a) paragraph 3(4) (time limit for complying with information notices);

(b) paragraph 6(2) (time limit for complying with hold notices);

(c) paragraph 8(3) or (5) (time limit for notifying HMRC of effects of hold notice);

(d) paragraph 9(3) (cancellation etc of hold notice: time limit for cancelling or adjusting arrangements);

(e) paragraph 10(5) (time limit for making objections);

(f) paragraph 11(1) (time limit for consideration of objections);

(g) paragraph 11(6) (consideration of objections: time limit for cancelling or adjusting arrangements);

(h) paragraph 12(8) (appeals: time limit for compliance with court order).

IHT Statutes

POWER TO MAKE FURTHER PROVISION

20(1) The Commissioners may by regulations make provision supplementing this Part of this Schedule.

20(2) The regulations may, in particular, make provision–

(a) about the manner in which a notice or a copy of a notice is to be given under this Part of this Schedule, or the circumstances in which a notice or a copy of a notice is to be treated as given, for the purposes of this Part of this Schedule;

(b) specifying circumstances in which a notice under this Part of this Schedule may not be given;

(c) specifying descriptions of account in respect of which a hold notice or deduction notice has no effect;

(d) specifying circumstances in which amounts standing to the credit of an account are to be treated as not standing to the credit of the account for the purposes of a hold notice or deduction notice;

(e) about fees a deposit-taker may charge a person in respect of whom a notice is given under this Part of this Schedule towards administrative costs in complying with that notice;

(f) with respect to priority as between a notice under this Part of this Schedule and–

  (i) any other such notice, or

  (ii) any notice or order under any other enactment.

Statutory instruments – SI 2016/44: made under para. 20(2)(e).

REGULATIONS

21(1) Regulations under this Part of this Schedule may–

(a) make different provision for different purposes,

(b) include supplementary, incidental and consequential provision, or

(c) make transitional provision and savings.

21(2) Regulations under this Part of this Schedule are to be made by statutory instrument.

21(3) A statutory instrument containing only regulations within sub-paragraph (4) is subject to annulment in pursuance of a resolution of the House of Commons.

21(4) The regulations within this sub-paragraph are–

(a) regulations which prescribe information for the purposes of paragraph 3(2) or any provision of paragraph 8,

(b) regulations under paragraph 4(10),

(c) regulations under paragraph (a), (b), (c), (d), (g) or (h) of paragraph 19(2), or

(d) regulations under paragraph 20(2).

21(5) Any other statutory instrument containing regulations under this Part of this Schedule may not be made unless a draft of the instrument has been laid before, and approved by a resolution of, the House of Commons.

JOINT ACCOUNTS

22 In this Part of this Schedule a reference to an account held by a person includes a reference to a joint account held by that person and one or more other persons.

DEFINED TERMS

23(1) In this Part of this Schedule–

"affected account" has the meaning given by paragraph 6(7);

"the Commissioners" means the Commissioners for Her Majesty's Revenue and Customs;

"contract settlement" means an agreement made in connection with any person's liability to make a payment to the Commissioners under or by virtue of an enactment;

"deduction notice" has the meaning given by paragraph 13;

"deposit-taker" means a person who may lawfully accept deposits in the United Kingdom in the course of a business (see sub-paragraph (2));

"HMRC" means Her Majesty's Revenue and Customs;

"hold notice" has the meaning given by paragraph 4;

"information notice" has the meaning given by paragraph 3;

"interested third party", in relation to a relevant account, has the meaning given by paragraph 8(11);

"joint account", in relation to a person, means an account held by the person and one or more other persons;

"notice" means notice in writing;

"notified sum", in relation to a hold notice, has the meaning given by paragraph 8(8);

"prescribed" means prescribed by regulations made by the Commissioners;

"relevant account" (in relation to a hold notice) has the meaning given by paragraph 6(6);

"relevant sum", in relation to a person, has the meaning given by paragraph 2(1);

"the safeguarded amount" (in relation to a hold notice) means the amount specified as the safeguarded amount in the notice (see paragraph 4(2)(c));

"the specified amount" (in relation to a hold notice) means the amount specified as such in the notice (see paragraph 4(2)(b));

"suspense account" has the meaning given by paragraph 6(3)(b)(i);

"the tribunal" means the First-tier Tribunal;

"working day" means a day other than–

(a) Saturday or Sunday,

(b) Christmas Eve, Christmas Day or Good Friday, or

(c) a day which is a bank holiday under the Banking and Financial Dealings Act 1971 in England and Wales or Northern Ireland.

23(2) The definition of **"deposit-taker"** in sub-paragraph (1) is to be read with–

(a) section 22 of the Financial Services and Markets Act 2000 (regulated activities),

(b) any relevant order under that section, and

(c) Schedule 2 to that Act.

Statutory instruments – SI 2015/1986: partly made under para. 23(1).

EXTENT

24 This Part of this Schedule extends to England and Wales and Northern Ireland.

IHT Statutes

FINANCE ACT 2016

(2016 Chapter 24)

[*15th September 2016*]

ARRANGEMENT OF SECTIONS

PART 1 – INCOME TAX

PENSIONS

22 Pension flexibility

22 Schedule 5 makes amendments in connection with pension flexibility.

PART 5 – INHERITANCE TAX ETC

93 Inheritance tax: increased nil-rate band

93 Schedule 15 contains provision in connection with the increased nil-rate band provided for by section 8D of IHTA 1984 (extra nil-rate band on death if interest in home goes to descendants etc).

94 Inheritance tax: pension drawdown funds

94(1) IHTA 1984 is amended as follows.

94(2) [Amends heading before IHTA 1984, s. 10.]

94(3) [Amends IHTA 1984, s. 12(2G).]

94(4) [Inserts IHTA 1984, s. 12A.]

94(5) The amendment made by subsection (4)–

(a) so far as relating to a fund within the new section 12A(2)(a) or (c) (drawdown pension funds), or to a fund within the new section 12A(3) that corresponds to a fund within the new section 12A(2)(a) or (c)–

(i) has effect where the person who has the fund dies on or after 6 April 2011, and

(ii) is to be treated as having come into force on 6 April 2011, and

(b) so far as relating to a fund mentioned in the new section 12A(2)(b), (d), (e) or (f) (flexi-access drawdown funds), or to a fund within the new section 12A(3) that corresponds to a fund within the new section 12A(2)(b), (d), (e) or (f)–

(i) has effect where the person who has the fund dies on or after 6 April 2015, and

(ii) is to be treated as having come into force on 6 April 2015.

94(6) Where an amount paid by way of–

(a) inheritance tax, or

(b) interest on inheritance tax,

is repayable as a result of the amendment made by subsection (4), section 241(1) of IHTA 1984 applies as if the last date for making a claim for repayment of the amount were 5 April 2020 if that is later than what would otherwise be the last date for that purpose.

95 Inheritance tax: victims of persecution during Second World War era

95(1) [Inserts IHTA 1984, s. 153ZA.]

95(2) [Inserts IHTA 1984, Sch. 5A.]

95(3) The amendments made by this section have effect in relation to deaths occurring on or after 1 January 2015.

96 Inheritance tax: gifts for national purposes etc

96(1) The Schedule 3 IHTA approval function is transferred to the Treasury.

96(2) The **"Schedule 3 IHTA approval function"** is the function of approval conferred by Schedule 3 to IHTA 1984 in the entry beginning "Any other similar national institution" (and which was initially conferred on the Treasury but, along with other functions, transferred to the Commissioners of Inland Revenue under section 95 of FA 1985).

96(3) Subsection (1) does not affect any approval given under Schedule 3 to IHTA 1984 before this Act is passed.

96(4) In Schedule 3 to IHTA 1984 (gifts for national purposes, etc), in the entry beginning "Any museum", after "and is" insert "or has been".

97 Estate duty: objects of national, scientific, historic or artistic interest

97(1) Section 40 of FA 1930 and section 2 of the Finance Act (Northern Ireland) 1931 (exemption from death duties of objects of national etc interest), so far as continuing to have effect, have effect as if after subsection (2) there were inserted–

"**40(2A)** In the event of the loss of any objects to which this section applies, estate duty shall become chargeable on the value of those objects in respect of the last death on which the objects passed at the rate appropriate to the principal value of the estate passing on that death upon which estate duty is leviable, and with which the objects would have been aggregated if they had not been objects to which this section applies.

40(2B) Where subsection (2A) applies, any owner of the objects–

(a) shall be accountable for the estate duty, and

(b) shall deliver an account for the purposes thereof.

40(2C) The account under subsection (2B)(b) must be delivered within the period of one month beginning with–

(a) in the case of a loss occurring before the coming into force of subsection (2A)–

(i) the coming into force of subsection (2A), or

(ii) if later, the date when the owner became aware of the loss;

(b) in the case of a loss occurring after the coming into force of subsection (2A)–

(i) the date of the loss, or

(ii) if later, the date when the owner became aware of the loss.

This is subject to subsection (2E).

40(2D) Subsection (2E) applies if–

(a) no account has been delivered under subsection (2B),

(b) the Commissioners for Her Majesty's Revenue and Customs have by notice required an owner of the objects to confirm that the objects have not been lost,

(c) the owner has not so confirmed by the end of–

(i) the period of three months beginning with the day on which the notice was sent, or
(ii) such longer period as the Commissioners may allow, and

(d) the Commissioners are satisfied that the objects are lost.

40(2E) Where this subsection applies–

(a) the objects are to be treated as lost for the purposes of subsection (2A) on the day on which the Commissioners are satisfied as specified in subsection (2D)(d), and

(b) the account under subsection (2B)(b) must be delivered within the period of one month beginning with that date.

40(2F) The reference in subsection (2A) to the value of objects is to their value at the time they are lost (or treated as lost).

40(2G) Subsection (2A) does not apply in relation to a loss notified to the Commissioners before the coming into force of that subsection.

40(2H) In this section **"owner"**, in relation to any objects, means a person who, if the objects were sold, would be entitled to receive (whether for their own benefit or not) the proceeds of sale or any income arising therefrom.

40(2I) In this section references to the loss of objects include their theft or destruction; but do not include a loss which the Commissioners are satisfied was outside the owner's control."

97(2) Section 48 of FA 1950, so far as continuing to have effect, has effect as if–

(a) after subsection (3) there were inserted–

"**48(3A)** But where the value of any objects is chargeable with estate duty under subsection (2A) of the said section forty (loss of objects), no estate duty shall be chargeable under this section on that value.";

(b) after subsection (4) there were inserted–

"**48(5)** Where any objects are lost (within the meaning of the said section forty) after becoming chargeable with estate duty under this section in respect of any death, the value of those objects shall not be chargeable with estate duty under subsection (2A) of the said section forty."

97(3) Section 39 of FA 1969, so far as continuing to have effect, has effect as if–

(a) in subsection (1)–
(i) after "subsection (2)" there were inserted "or (2A)";
(ii) after "other disposal" there were inserted "or loss";

(b) in subsection (2), after "subsection (2)" there were inserted ", (2A)";

(c) in subsection (3)–
(i) after "subsection (2)" there were inserted ", (2A)";
(ii) for the words from "the amount" to the end there were substituted "the amount in respect of which estate duty is chargeable under the said subsection".

97(4) Section 6 of the Finance Act (Northern Ireland) 1969, so far as continuing to have effect as originally enacted, has effect as if–

(a) in subsection (1)–
(i) after "subsection (2)" there were inserted "or (2A)";
(ii) after "sale" there were inserted "or loss";

(b) in subsection (2)–
(i) for "sale" there were substituted "event";
(ii) after "subsection (2)" there were inserted "or (2A)";

(c) in subsection (3)–
(i) for "sale" there were substituted "event";
(ii) after "subsection (2)" there were inserted "or (2A)";
(iii) for "the amount of the proceeds of sale" there were substituted "the amount in respect of which estate duty is chargeable under the said subsection".

97(5) Section 6 of the Finance Act (Northern Ireland) 1969, so far as continuing to have effect as amended by Article 7 of the Finance (Northern Ireland) Order 1972 (S.I. 1972/1100 (N.I.11)) (deaths occurring after the making of that Order), has effect as if–

(a) in subsection (1)–
(i) after "subsection (2)" there were inserted "or (2A)";
(ii) after "sale" there were inserted "or loss";

(b) in subsection (2), after "subsection (2)" there were inserted "or (2A)";

(c) in subsection (3)–

(i) in the opening words, after "subsection (2)" there were inserted "or (2A)";

(ii) in paragraphs (a) and (b), after "otherwise than on sale" there were inserted "or at the time of the loss".

97(6) [Substitutes IHTA 1984, s. 35(2)(a) and (b).]

97(7) In Schedule 6 to IHTA 1984 (transition from estate duty), in paragraph 4 (objects of national etc interest left out of account on death)–

(a) [substitutes IHTA 1984, Sch. 6, para. 4(2)(a) and (b);]

(b) [amends IHTA 1984, Sch. 6, para. 4(4).]

97(8) Subsections (6) and (7) have effect in relation to a chargeable event where the conditionally exempt transfer referred to in section 35(2) of or paragraph 4(2) of Schedule 6 to IHTA 1984 occurred after 16 March 2016.

PART 6 – APPRENTICESHIP LEVY

ANTI-AVOIDANCE

104 Application of other regimes to apprenticeship levy

104(1) [Inserts FA 2004, s. 318(1)(da).]

104(2) [Inserts FA 2013, s. 206(3)(db).]

104(3) Part 4 of FA 2014 (follower notices and accelerated payments) is amended in accordance with subsections (4) and (5).

104(4) [Inserts FA 2014, s. 200(ca).]

104(5) [Inserts FA 2014, s. 203(ea).]

104(6) Part 5 of FA 2014 (promoters of tax avoidance schemes) is amended in accordance with subsections (7) and (8).

104(7) [Inserts FA 2014, s. 253(6)(da).]

104(8) [Inserts FA 2014, s. 283(1)(da).]

INFORMATION AND PENALTIES

112 Information and inspection powers

112 [Inserts FA 2008, Sch. 36, para. 63(1)(ca).]

113 Penalties

113(1) Schedule 24 to FA 2007 (penalties for errors) is amended in accordance with subsections (2) to (4).

113(2) [Not relevant to inheritance tax.]

113(3) [Not relevant to inheritance tax.]

113(4) [Amends FA 2007, Sch. 24, para. 21C.]

113(5) Schedule 55 to FA 2009 (penalty for failure to make returns etc) is amended in accordance with subsections (6) to (8).

113(6) [Not relevant to inheritance tax.]

113(7) [Not relevant to inheritance tax.]

113(8) [Not relevant to inheritance tax.]

113(9) Schedule 56 to FA 2009 (penalty for failure to make payments on time) is amended in accordance with subsections (10) to (15).

113(10) [Not relevant to inheritance tax.]

113(11) In paragraph 3(1)–

(a) in paragraph (b) after "within" insert "item 4A or";

(b) after paragraph (c) insert–

"(ca) an amount in respect of apprenticeship levy falling within item 4A which is payable by virtue of regulations under section 106 of FA 2016 (recovery from third parties)."

113(12)–(15) [Not relevant to inheritance tax.]

113(16) The amendments made by subsections (1) to (4) of this section come into force in accordance with provision made by the Treasury by regulations.

113(17) In subsections (2) and (4) of section 106 of FA 2009 (penalties for failure to make returns: commencement etc) references to Schedule 55 to that Act have effect as references to that Schedule as amended by subsections (5) to (8) of this section.

113(18) Schedule 56 to FA 2009, as amended by this section, is taken to come into force for the purposes of apprenticeship levy on the date on which this Act is passed.

Commencement Date – S. 113(1) to (4) comes into force on 6 April 2017 (SI 2017/355, reg. 2).

GENERAL

115 Tax agents: dishonest conduct

115 [Inserts FA 2012, Sch. 38, para. 37(1)(la).]

PART 10 – TAX AVOIDANCE AND EVASION

GENERAL ANTI-ABUSE RULE

156 General anti-abuse rule: provisional counteractions

156(1) [Inserts FA 2013, s. 209A to 209F.]

156(2) [Amends FA 2013, s. 214(1).]

156(3) The amendments made by this section have effect in relation to tax arrangements (within the meaning of Part 5 of FA 2013) entered into at any time (whether before or on or after the day on which this Act is passed).

157 General anti-abuse rule: binding of tax arrangements to lead arrangements

157(1) Part 5 of FA 2013 (general anti-abuse rule) is amended in accordance with subsections (2) to (11).

157(2) [Inserts FA 2013, Sch. 43A.]

157(3) [Inserts FA 2013, Sch. 43B.]

157(4) [Amends FA 2013, s. 209(6)(a).]

157(5) [Inserts FA 2013, s. 210(1)(b).]

157(6) [Substitutes FA 2013, s. 211(2)(b).]

157(7) Section 214 (interpretation of Part 5) is amended in accordance with subsections (8) to (10).

157(8) [Amends FA 2013, s. 214(1).]

157(9) [Amends FA 2013, s. 214(1).]

157(10) [Inserts FA 2013, s. 214(2) and (3).]

157(11) [Inserts FA 2013, Sch. 43, para. 6(3).]

157(12)–(17) [Not relevant to inheritance tax.]

157(18) Section 219 of FA 2014 (circumstances in which an accelerated payment notice may be given) is amended in accordance with subsections (19) and (20).

157(19) [Inserts FA 2014, s. 219(4)(d) and (e).]

157(20) [Inserts FA 2014, s. 219(8).]

157(21) In section 220 of FA 2014 (content of notice given while a tax enquiry is in progress)–

(a) [amends FA 2014, s. 220(4)(c);]

(b) [amends FA 2014, s. 220(5)(c);]

(c) [amends FA 2014, s. 220(7).]

157(22)–(25) [Not relevant to inheritance tax.]

157(26) In Schedule 32 to FA 2014 (accelerated payments and partnerships), paragraph 3 is amended in accordance with subsections (27) and (28).

157(27) [Inserts FA 2014, Sch. 32, para. 3(5)(d) and (e).]

157(28) [Inserts FA 2014, Sch. 32, para. 3(7).]

157(29) In Schedule 34 to FA 2014 (promoters of tax avoidance schemes: threshold conditions), in paragraph 7–

(a) [amends FA 2014, Sch. 34, para. 7(a);]

(b) [amends FA 2014, Sch. 34, para. 7(b);]

(c) [amends FA 2014, Sch. 34, para. 7(c).]

157(30) The amendments made by this section have effect in relation to tax arrangements (within the meaning of Part 5 of FA 2013) entered into at any time (whether before or on or after the day on which this Act is passed).

158 General anti-abuse rule: penalty

158(1) Part 5 of FA 2013 (general anti-abuse rule) is amended as follows.

158(2) [Inserts FA 2013, s. 212A.]

158(3) [Inserts FA 2013, Sch. 43C.]

158(4) [Inserts FA 2013, s. 209(8)–(10).]

158(5) Schedule 43 (general anti-abuse rule: procedural requirements) is amended in accordance with subsections (6) to (9).

158(6) [Inserts FA 2013, Sch. 43, para. 1A.]

158(7) [Amends FA 2013, Sch. 43, para. 3(2)(e).]

158(8) [Inserts FA 2013, Sch. 43, para. 4A.]

158(9) [Inserts FA 2013, Sch. 43, para. 4B.]

158(10) [Not relevant to inheritance tax.]

158(11) [Inserts FA 2014, s. 212(4)(e).]

158(12) FA 2015 is amended in accordance with subsections (13) and (14).

158(13) [Inserts FA 2015, s. 120(1)(d).]

158(14) [Inserts FA 2015, Sch. 20, para. 20.]

158(15) The amendments made by this section have effect in relation to tax arrangements (within the meaning of Part 5 of FA 2013) entered into on or after the day on which this Act is passed.

TACKLING FREQUENT AVOIDANCE

159 Serial tax avoidance

159 Schedule 18 contains provision about the issue of warning notices to, and further sanctions for, persons who incur a relevant defeat in relation to arrangements.

160 Promoters of tax avoidance schemes

160(1) Part 5 of FA 2014 (promoters of tax avoidance schemes) is amended as follows.

160(2) [Inserts FA 2014, s. 237A–237D.]

160(3) [Inserts FA 2014, s. 241A and 241B.]

160(4) [Inserts FA 2014, s. 242(6) and (7).]

160(5) [Inserts FA 2014, Sch. 34A.]

160(6) [Inserts FA 2014, s. 241(5).]

160(7) [Inserts FA 2014, s. 281A.]

160(8) [Inserts FA 2014, s. 282(3)(ba).]

160(9) [Amends FA 2014, s. 283(1).]

160(10) Schedule 36 (promoters of tax avoidance schemes: partnerships) is amended in accordance with subsections (11) to (16).

160(11) [Inserts FA 2014, Sch. 36, para. 4A.]

160(12) [Amends FA 2014, Sch. 36, para. 7(1)(b).]

160(13) [Amends FA 2014, Sch. 36, para. 7(2).]

160(14) *[Inserts FA 2014, Sch. 36, para. 7A.]*

160(15) In paragraph 10–

(a) [amends FA 2014, Sch. 36, para. 10(1)(b);]

(b) [inserts FA 2014, Sch. 36, para. 10(3)(za);]

(c) [inserts FA 2014, Sch. 36, para. 10(4)(za);]

(d) [inserts FA 2014, Sch. 36, para. 10(5A).]

160(16) [Inserts FA 2014, Sch. 36, para. 11A.]

160(17)–(19) [Not relevant to inheritance tax.]

160(20) For the purposes of sections 237A and 241A of FA 2014, a defeat (by virtue of any of Conditions A to F in Schedule 34A to that Act) of arrangements is treated as not having occurred if–

(a) there has been a final judicial ruling on or before the day on which this Act is passed as a result of which the counteraction referred to in paragraph 11(d), 12(1)(b), 13(1)(d), 14(1)(d) or 15(1)(d) (as the case may be) is final for the purposes of Schedule 34A of that Act, or

(b) (in the case of a defeat by virtue of Condition F in Schedule 34A) the judicial ruling mentioned in paragraph 16(1)(d) of that Schedule becomes final on or before the day on which this Act is passed.

160(21) Subsection (20) does not apply in relation to a person (who is carrying on a business as a promoter) if at any time after 17 July 2014 that person or an associated person takes action as a result of which the person taking the action–

(a) becomes a promoter in relation to the arrangements, or arrangements related to those arrangements, or

(b) would have become a promoter in relation to arrangements mentioned in paragraph (a) had the person not already been a promoter in relation to those arrangements.

160(22) For the purposes of sections 237A and 241A of FA 2014, a defeat of arrangements is treated as not having occurred if it would (ignoring this sub-paragraph) have occurred–

(a) on or before the first anniversary of the day on which this Act is passed, and

(b) by virtue of any of Conditions A to E in Schedule 34A to FA 2014, but otherwise than as a result of a final judicial ruling.

160(23) For the purposes of subsection (21) a person ("Q") is an "associated person" in relation to another person ("P") at any time when any of the following conditions is met–

(a) P is a relevant body which is controlled by Q;

(b) Q is a relevant body, P is not an individual and Q is controlled by P;

(c) P and Q are relevant bodies and a third person controls P and Q.

160(24) In subsection (23) "relevant body" and "control" are to be interpreted in accordance with paragraph 19 of Schedule 34A to FA 2014.

160(25) In subsections (20) to (22) expressions used in Part 5 of FA 2014 (as amended by this section) have the same meaning as in that Part.

161 Large businesses: tax strategies and sanctions for persistently unco-operative behaviour

161(1) Schedule 19 contains provisions relating to–

(a) the publication of tax strategies by bodies which are or are part of a large business,

(b) the imposition of sanctions for such bodies where there has been persistent unco-operative behaviour.

161(2) That Schedule, so far as relating to the publication of a tax strategy for a financial year of a relevant body or other entity, has effect only where the financial year begins on or after the day on which this Act is passed.

161(3) An officer of HMRC may not give a warning notice under Part 3 of that Schedule to a relevant body or other entity before the beginning of its first financial year beginning on or after the day on which this Act is passed.

161(4) In this section and Schedule 19 **"HMRC"** means Her Majesty's Revenue and Customs.

OFFSHORE ACTIVITIES

162 Penalties for enablers of offshore tax evasion or non-compliance

162(1) Schedule 20 makes provision for civil penalties for persons who enable offshore tax evasion by other persons.

162(2) Subsection (1) and that Schedule come into force on such day as the Treasury may appoint by regulations made by statutory instrument.

162(3) Regulations under this section may–

(a) commence a provision generally or only for specified purposes,

(b) appoint different days for different purposes, and

(c) make supplemental, incidental and transitional provision in connection with the coming into force of any provision of the Schedule.

Commencement Date – S. 162(1) and Sch. 20 come into force on 1 January 2017 (SI 2016/1249, reg. 2).

163 Penalties in connection with offshore matters and offshore transfers

163(1) Schedule 21 contains provisions amending–

(a) Schedule 24 to FA 2007 (penalties for errors in tax returns etc),

(b) Schedule 41 to FA 2008 (penalties for failure to notify etc), and

(c) Schedule 55 to FA 2009 (penalties for failure to make return etc).

163(2) That Schedule comes into force on such day as the Treasury may by regulations made by statutory instrument appoint.

163(3) Regulations under this section may–

(a) commence a provision generally or only for specified purposes,

(b) appoint different days for different provisions or for different purposes, and

(c) make supplemental, incidental and transitional provision.

164 Offshore tax errors etc: publishing details of deliberate tax defaulters

164(1) Section 94 of FA 2009 (publishing details of deliberate tax defaulters) is amended as follows.

164(2) [Inserts FA 2009, s. 94(4A)–(4D).]

164(3) [Amends FA 2009, s. 94(6).]

164(4) [Inserts FA 2009, s. 94(6A).]

164(5) [Inserts FA 2009, s. 94(10)(aa) and (c).]

164(6) [Substitutes FA 2009, s. 94(16).]

164(7) The amendments made by this section come into force on such day as the Treasury may by regulations made by statutory instrument appoint.

Commencement Date – 1 April 2017 is the appointed day for the coming into force of amendments made by s. 164 (SI 2017/261, reg. 2).

165 Asset-based penalties for offshore inaccuracies and failures

165(1) Schedule 22 contains provision imposing asset-based penalties on certain taxpayers who have been charged a penalty for deliberate offshore inaccuracies and failures.

165(2) That Schedule comes into force on such day as the Treasury may by regulations made by statutory instrument appoint.

165(3) Regulations under subsection (2) may–

(a) commence a provision generally or only for specified purposes,

(b) appoint different days for different provisions or for different purposes, and

(c) make supplemental, incidental and transitional provision.

PART 11 – ADMINISTRATION, ENFORCEMENT AND SUPPLEMENTARY POWERS

ASSESSMENT AND RETURNS

167 Simple assessments

167(1) Schedule 23 contains provisions about simple assessments by HMRC.

167(2) Paragraphs 1 to 8 of that Schedule have effect in relation to the 2016–17 tax year and subsequent years.

167(3) Paragraph 9 of that Schedule comes into force on such day as the Treasury may appoint by regulations made by statutory instrument.

167(4) Regulations under subsection (3) may–

(a) commence paragraph 9 generally or only for specified purposes, and

(b) appoint different days for different purposes.

JUDGMENT DEBTS

170 Rate of interest applicable to judgment debts etc: Scotland

170(1) This section applies if–

(a) a sum is payable to or by the Commissioners under a decree or extract issued in any court proceedings relating to a taxation matter (a "tax-related judgment debt"), and

(b) interest in relation to the tax-related judgment debt is included in or payable under the decree or extract.

170(2) In a case where the rate of interest in relation to the tax-related judgment debt is stated in the decree or extract, the rate stated in relation to that debt may not exceed (and may not be capable of exceeding)–

(a) in the case of a sum payable to the Commissioners, the late payment interest rate, and

(b) in the case of a sum payable by the Commissioners, the special repayment rate.

170(3) In a case where the rate of interest in relation to the tax-related judgment debt is not stated in the decree or extract but provided for by an enactment or rule of court (whenever passed or made), that enactment or rule is to have effect in relation to the debt as if for the rate for which it provides there were substituted–

(a) in the case of a sum payable to the Commissioners, the late payment interest rate, and

(b) in the case of a sum payable by the Commissioners, the special repayment rate.

170(4) This section has effect in relation to interest for periods beginning on or after the day on which this Act is passed, regardless of–

(a) the date of the decree or extract in question, and

(b) whether interest begins to run on or after the day on which this Act is passed, or began to run before that date.

170(5) In this section–

"the Commissioners" means the Commissioners for Her Majesty's Revenue and Customs;

"enactment" includes an Act of the Scottish Parliament or an instrument made under such an Act;

"late payment interest rate" means the rate provided for in regulations made by the Treasury under section 103(1) of FA 2009;

"special repayment rate" has the same meaning as in section 52 of F(No. 2)A 2015 (and subsections (7) to (10) of that section apply for the purposes of this section as they apply for the purposes of that section);

"taxation matter" means anything the collection and management of which is the responsibility of the Commissioners (or was the responsibility of the Commissioners of Inland Revenue or Commissioners of Customs and Excise);

"working day" means any day other than a non-business day as defined in section 92 of the Bills of Exchange Act 1882.

170(6) This section extends to Scotland only.

171 Rate of interest applicable to judgment debts etc: Northern Ireland

171(1) This section applies if a sum payable to or by the Commissioners under a judgment or order given or made in any court proceedings relating to a taxation matter (a "tax-related judgment debt") carries interest.

171(2) In a case where the rate of interest is specified in the judgment (in the case of the High Court) or directed by the judge (in the case of a county court), the rate specified or directed in relation to that debt may not exceed (and may not be capable of exceeding)–

(a) in the case of a sum payable to the Commissioners, the late payment interest rate, and

(b) in the case of a sum payable by the Commissioners, the special repayment rate.

171(3) In a case where the rate of interest in relation to the tax-related judgment debt is not specified in the judgment or directed by the judge but provided for by an enactment or rule of court (whenever passed or made), that enactment or rule is to have effect in relation to the debt as if for the rate for which it provides there were substituted–

(a) in the case of a sum payable to the Commissioners, the late payment interest rate, and

(b) in the case of a sum payable by the Commissioners, the special repayment rate.

171(4) This section has effect in relation to interest for periods beginning on or after the day on which this Act is passed, regardless of–

(a) the date of the judgment or order in question, and

(b) whether interest begins to run on or after the day on which this Act is passed, or began to run before that date.

171(5) In this section–

"the Commissioners" means the Commissioners for Her Majesty's Revenue and Customs;

"enactment" includes Northern Ireland legislation or an instrument made under such legislation;

"late payment interest rate" means the rate provided for in regulations made by the Treasury under section 103(1) of FA 2009;

"special repayment rate" has the same meaning as in section 52 of F(No. 2) A 2015 (and subsections (7) to (10) of that section apply for the purposes of this section as they apply for the purposes of that section);

"taxation matter" means anything the collection and management of which is the responsibility of the Commissioners (or was the responsibility of the Commissioners of Inland Revenue or Commissioners of Customs and Excise);

"working day" means any day other than a non-business day as defined in section 92 of the Bills of Exchange Act 1882.

171(6) This section extends to Northern Ireland only.

172 Rate of interest applicable to judgment debts etc: England and Wales

172(1) [Amends F(No. 2)A 2015, s. 52(15).]

172(2) This section has effect in relation to interest for periods beginning on or after the day on which this Act is passed, regardless of–

(a) the date of the judgment or order in question, and

(b) whether interest begins to run on or after the day on which this Act is passed, or began to run before that date.

172(3) This section extends to England and Wales only.

ENFORCEMENT POWERS

176 Data-gathering powers: providers of payment or intermediary services

176(1) [Inserts FA 2011, Sch. 23, para. 13B and 13C.]

176(2) This section applies in relation to relevant data with a bearing on any period (whether before, on or after the day on which this Act is passed).

177 Data-gathering powers: daily penalties for extended default

177(1) Part 4 of Schedule 23 to FA 2011 (data-gathering powers: penalties) is amended as follows.

177(2) In paragraph 38 (increased daily default penalty)–

(a) [amends FA 2011, Sch. 23, para. 38(1)(c) and (2);]

(b) [substitutes FA 2011, Sch. 23, para. 38(3) and (4);]

(c) [amends FA 2011, Sch. 23, para. 38(5).]

177(3) In paragraph 39–

(a) [amends FA 2011, Sch. 23, para. 39(1);]

(b) [amends FA 2011, Sch. 23, para. 39(2);]

(c) [omits FA 2011, Sch. 23, para. 39(3).]

177(4) [Amends FA 2011, Sch. 23, para. 40(2)(a).]

177(5) [Inserts FA 2011, Sch. 23, para. 36(2).]

PART 13 – FINAL

190 Interpretation

190 In this Act–

"ALDA 1979" means the Alcoholic Liquor Duties Act 1979;

"CAA 2001" means the Capital Allowances Act 2001;

"**CEMA 1979**" means the Customs and Excise Management Act 1979;
"**CTA 2009**" means the Corporation Tax Act 2009;
"**CTA 2010**" means the Corporation Tax Act 2010;
"**FA**", followed by a year, means the Finance Act of that year;
"**F(No. 2)A**", followed by a year means the Finance (No. 2) Act of that year;
"**F(No. 3)A**", followed by a year, means the Finance (No. 3) Act of that year;
"**HODA 1979**" means the Hydrocarbon Oil Duties Act 1979;
"**ICTA**" means the Income and Corporation Taxes Act 1988;
"**IHTA 1984**" means the Inheritance Tax Act 1984;
"**ITA 2007**" means the Income Tax Act 2007;
"**ITEPA 2003**" means the Income Tax (Earnings and Pensions) Act 2003;
"**ITTOIA 2005**" means the Income Tax (Trading and Other Income) Act 2005;
"**OTA 1975**" means the Oil Taxation Act 1975;
"**TCGA 1992**" means the Taxation of Chargeable Gains Act 1992;
"**TIOPA 2010**" means the Taxation (International and Other Provisions) Act 2010;
"**TMA 1970**" means the Taxes Management Act 1970;
"**TPDA 1979**" means the Tobacco Products Duty Act 1979;
"**VATA 1994**" means the Value Added Tax Act 1994;
"**VERA 1994**" means the Vehicle Excise and Registration Act 1994.

191 Short title

191 This Act may be cited as the Finance Act 2016.

SCHEDULES

SCHEDULE 5 – PENSION FLEXIBILITY

Section 22

INHERITANCE TAX AS RESPECTS CASH ALTERNATIVES TO ANNUITIES FOR DEPENDANTS ETC

11(1) [Amends IHTA 1984, s. 152.]

11(2) The amendment made by sub-paragraph (1)–

(a) is to be treated as having come into force on 6 April 2015, and

(b) has effect where the person on whose death an annuity is payable dies on or after that date.

SCHEDULE 15 – INHERITANCE TAX: INCREASED NIL-RATE BAND

Section 93

1 IHTA 1984 is amended as follows.

2(1) Section 8D (extra nil-rate band on death if interest in home goes to descendants etc) is amended as follows.

2(2) [Amends IHTA 1984, s. 8D(4).]

2(3) [Amends IHTA 1984, s. 8D(9).]

3(1) Section 8E (residence nil-rate amount: interest in home goes to descendants etc) is amended as follows.

3(2) [Amends IHTA 1984, s. 8E(6).]

3(3) [Amends IHTA 1984, s. 8E(7).]

3(4) [Amends IHTA 1984, s. 8E(8).]

4 [Amends IHTA 1984, s. 8F(4).]

5 [Inserts IHTA 1984, s. 8FA–8FE.]

6 [Amends IHTA 1984, s. 8G.]

7(1) Section 8H (meaning of "qualifying residential interest") is amended as follows.

7(2) [Amends heading to IHTA 1984, s. 8H.]

7(3) [Amends IHTA 1984, s. 8H(1).]

7(4) [Amends IHTA 1984, s. 8H(2).]

7(5) [Inserts IHTA 1984, s. 8H(4A)–(4G).]

8 [Inserts IHTA 1984, s. 8HA.]

9 [Amends IHTA 1984, s. 8J(1).]

10 [Amends IHTA 1984, s. 8K(1).]

11 In section 8L (claims for brought-forward allowance)–

(a) [amends heading to IHTA 1984, s. 8L,]

(b) [amends IHTA 1984, s. 8L(1).]

12(1) Section 8M (residence nil-rate amount: cases involving conditional exemption) is amended as follows.

12(2) [Substitutes IHTA 1984, s. 8M(1)–(2I).]

12(3) [Amends IHTA 1984, s. 8M(3).]

12(4) In subsection (3)–

(a) [amends IHTA 1984, s. 8M(3)(b),]

(b) [amends IHTA 1984, s. 8M(3)(b),]

(c) [amends IHTA 1984, s. 8M(3)(c),]

(d) [inserts IHTA 1984, s. 8M(3)(d).]

12(5) [Amends IHTA 1984, s. 8M(5).]

12(6) [Amends IHTA 1984, s. 8M(6).]

12(7) [Amends IHTA 1984, s. 8M(7).]

SCHEDULE 18 – SERIAL TAX AVOIDANCE

Section 159

Part 1 – Contents of Schedule

1 In this Schedule–

(a) Part 2 provides for HMRC to give warning notices to persons who incur relevant defeats and includes–

 (i) provision about the duration of warning periods under warning notices (see paragraph 3), and

 (ii) definitions of "relevant defeat" and other key terms;

(b) Part 3 contains provisions about persons to whom a warning notice has been given, and in particular–

 (i) imposes a duty to give information notices, and

 (ii) allows the Commissioners to publish information about such persons in certain cases involving repeated relevant defeats;

(c) Part 4 contains provision about the restriction of reliefs;

(d) Part 5 imposes liability to penalties on persons who incur relevant defeats in relation to arrangements used in warning periods;

(e) Part 6 contains provisions about corporate groups, associated persons and partnerships;

(f) Part 7 contains definitions and other supplementary provisions.

Part 2 – Entry into the Regime and Basic Concepts

DUTY TO GIVE WARNING NOTICE

2(1) This paragraph applies where a person incurs a relevant defeat in relation to any arrangements.

2(2) HMRC must give the person a written notice (a "warning notice").

2(3) The notice must be given within the period of 90 days beginning with the day on which the relevant defeat is incurred.

2(4) The notice must–

(a) set out when the warning period begins and ends (see paragraph 3),

(b) specify the relevant defeat to which the notice relates, and

(c) explain the effect of paragraphs 3 and 17 to 46.

2(5) A warning notice given by virtue of paragraph 49 must also explain the effect of paragraph 51 (information in certain cases involving partnerships).

2(6) In this Schedule **"arrangements"** includes any agreement, understanding, scheme, transaction or series of transactions (whether or not legally enforceable).

2(7) For the meaning of "relevant defeat" and provision about when a relevant defeat is incurred see paragraph 11.

WARNING PERIOD

3(1) If a person is given a warning notice with respect to a relevant defeat (and sub-paragraph (2) does not apply) the period of 5 years beginning with the day after the day on which the notice is given is a **"warning period"** in relation to that person.

3(2) If a person incurs a relevant defeat in relation to arrangements during a period which is a warning period in relation to that person, the warning period is extended to the end of the 5 years beginning with the day after the day on which the relevant defeat occurs.

3(3) In relation to a warning period which has been extended under this Schedule, references in this Schedule (including this paragraph) to the warning period are to be read as references to the warning period as extended.

MEANING OF "TAX"

4(1) In this Schedule **"tax"** includes any of the following taxes–

(a) income tax,

(b) corporation tax, including any amount chargeable as if it were corporation tax or treated as if it were corporation tax,

(c) capital gains tax,

(d) petroleum revenue tax,

(e) diverted profits tax,

(f) apprenticeship levy,

(g) inheritance tax,

(h) stamp duty land tax,

(i) annual tax on enveloped dwellings,

(j) VAT and other indirect taxes, and

(k) national insurance contributions.

4(2) [Not relevant to inheritance tax.]

History – Para. 4(1) created from existing text (with the insertion of the words "and other indirect taxes") by F(No. 2)A 2017, s. 66 and Sch. 17, para. 55(2) with effect so far as is necessary for enabling the making of regulations under that Schedule on 16 November 2017 (Royal Assent) and on 1 January 2018 for all other purposes.

Para. 4(2) inserted by F(No. 2)A 2017, s. 66 and Sch. 17, para. 55(2) with effect so far as is necessary for enabling the making of regulations under that Schedule on 16 November 2017 (Royal Assent) and on 1 January 2018 for all other purposes.

MEANING OF "TAX ADVANTAGE" IN RELATION TO VAT

5 [Not relevant to inheritance tax.]

MEANING OF "NON-DEDUCTIBLE TAX"

6 [Not relevant to inheritance tax.]

"TAX ADVANTAGE": OTHER TAXES

7 In relation to taxes other than VAT, **"tax advantage"** includes–

(a) relief or increased relief from tax,

(b) repayment or increased repayment of tax,

(c) receipt, or advancement of a receipt, of a tax credit,

(d) avoidance or reduction of a charge to tax, an assessment of tax or a liability to pay tax,

(e) avoidance of a possible assessment to tax or liability to pay tax,

(f) deferral of a payment of tax or advancement of a repayment of tax, and

(g) avoidance of an obligation to deduct or account for tax.

"DOTAS ARRANGEMENTS"

8(1) For the purposes of this Schedule arrangements are **"DOTAS arrangements"** at any time if they are notifiable arrangements at the time in question and a person–

(a) has provided information in relation to the arrangements under section 308(3), 309 or 310 of FA 2004, or

(b) has failed to comply with any of those provisions in relation to the arrangements.

8(2) But for the purposes of this Schedule **"DOTAS arrangements"** does not include arrangements in respect of which HMRC has given notice under section 312(6) of FA 2004 (notice that promoters not under duty to notify client of reference number).

8(3) For the purposes of sub-paragraph (1) a person who would be required to provide information under subsection (3) of section 308 of FA 2004–

(a) but for the fact that the arrangements implement a proposal in respect of which notice has been given under subsection (1) of that section, or

(b) but for subsection (4A), (4C) or (5) of that section,

is treated as providing the information at the end of the period referred to in subsection (3) of that section.

8(4) In this paragraph **"notifiable arrangements"** has the same meaning as in Part 7 of FA 2004.

"DISCLOSABLE SCHEDULE 11A VAT ARRANGEMENTS"

History – In the heading the words "SCHEDULE 11A" inserted by F(No. 2)A 2017, s. 66 and Sch. 17, para. 55(4) with effect so far as is necessary for enabling the making of regulations under that Schedule on 16 November 2017 (Royal Assent) and on 1 January 2018 for all other purposes.

8A [Not relevant to inheritance tax.]

History – Para. 8A inserted by F(No. 2)A 2017, s. 66 and Sch. 17, para. 55(3) with effect so far as is necessary for enabling the making of regulations under that Schedule on 16 November 2017 (Royal Assent) and on 1 January 2018 for all other purposes.

9 [Not relevant to inheritance tax.]

DISCLOSABLE INDIRECT TAX ARRANGEMENTS

9A [Not relevant to inheritance tax.]

History – Para. 9A inserted by F(No. 2)A 2017, s. 66 and Sch. 17, para. 55(6) with effect so far as is necessary for enabling the making of regulations under that Schedule on 16 November 2017 (Royal Assent) and on 1 January 2018 for all other purposes.

PARAGRAPHS 8 TO 9A: "FAILURE TO COMPLY"

History – In the heading the words "TO 9A" substituted for the words "AND 9" by F(No. 2)A 2017, s. 66 and Sch. 17, para. 55(7) with effect so far as is necessary for enabling the making of regulations under that Schedule on 16 November 2017 (Royal Assent) and on 1 January 2018 for all other purposes.

10(1) A person **"fails to comply"** with any provision mentioned in paragraph 8(1), 8A(2)(c), 9(a) or 9A(1)(c) if and only if any of the conditions in sub-paragraphs (2) to (4) is met.

10(2) The condition in this sub-paragraph is that–

(a) the tribunal has determined that the person has failed to comply with the provision concerned,

(b) the appeal period has ended, and

(c) the determination has not been overturned on appeal.

10(3) The condition in this sub-paragraph is that–

(a) the tribunal has determined for the purposes of section 118(2) of TMA 1970 that the person is to be deemed not to have failed to comply with the provision concerned as the person had a reasonable excuse for not doing the thing required to be done,

(b) the appeal period has ended, and

(c) the determination has not been overturned on appeal.

10(4) The condition in this sub-paragraph is that the person admitted in writing to HMRC that the person has failed to comply with the provision concerned.

10(5) In this paragraph **"the appeal period"** means–

(a) the period during which an appeal could be brought against the determination of the tribunal, or

(b) where an appeal mentioned in paragraph (a) has been brought, the period during which that appeal has not been finally determined, withdrawn or otherwise disposed of.

10(6) In this paragraph **"the tribunal"** means the First-tier tribunal or, where determined by or under Tribunal Procedure Rules, the Upper Tribunal.

History – In para. 10(1) the words ", 8A(2)(c), 9(a) or 9A(1)(c)" substituted for the words "or 9(a)" by F(No. 2)A 2017, s. 66 and Sch. 17, para. 55(8) with effect so far as is necessary for enabling the making of regulations under that Schedule on 16 November 2017 (Royal Assent) and on 1 January 2018 for all other purposes.

"RELEVANT DEFEAT"

11(1) A person ("P") incurs a **"relevant defeat"** in relation to arrangements if any of Conditions A to F is met in relation to P and the arrangements.

11(2) The relevant defeat is incurred when the condition in question is first met.

History – In para. 11(1) "F" substituted for "E" by F(No. 2)A 2017, s. 66 and Sch. 17, para. 55(9) with effect so far as is necessary for enabling the making of regulations under that Schedule on 16 November 2017 (Royal Assent) and on 1 January 2018 for all other purposes.

CONDITION A

12(1) Condition A is that–

(a) P has been given a notice under paragraph 12 of Schedule 43 to FA 2013 (general anti-abuse rule: notice of final decision), paragraph 8 or 9 of Schedule 43A to that Act (pooled arrangements: notice of final decision) or paragraph 8 of Schedule 43B to that Act (generic referrals: notice of final decision)stating that a tax advantage arising from the arrangements is to be counteracted,

(b) that tax advantage has been counteracted under section 209 of FA 2013, and

(c) the counteraction is final.

12(2) For the purposes of this paragraph the counteraction of a tax advantage is **"final"** when the adjustments made to effect the counteraction, and any amounts arising as a result of those adjustments, can no longer be varied, on appeal or otherwise.

CONDITION B

13(1) Condition B is that (in a case not falling within Condition A above) a follower notice has been given to P by reference to the arrangements (and not withdrawn) and–

(a) the necessary corrective action for the purposes of section 208 of FA 2014 has been taken in respect of the denied advantage, or

(b) the denied advantage has been counteracted otherwise than as mentioned in paragraph (a) and the counteraction of the denied advantage is final.

13(2) In sub-paragraph (1) the reference to giving a follower notice to P includes a reference to giving a partnership follower notice in respect of a partnership return in relation to which P is a relevant partner (as defined in paragraph 2(5) of Schedule 31 to FA 2014).

13(3) For the purposes of this paragraph it does not matter whether the denied advantage has been dealt with–

(a) wholly as mentioned in one or other of paragraphs (a) and (b) of sub-paragraph (1), or

(b) partly as mentioned in one and partly as mentioned in the other of those paragraphs.

13(4) In this paragraph **"the denied advantage"** has the same meaning as in Chapter 2 of Part 4 of FA 2014 (see section 208(3) of and paragraph 4(3) of Schedule 31 to that Act).

13(5) For the purposes of this paragraph the counteraction of a tax advantage is **"final"** when the adjustments made to effect the counteraction, and any amounts arising as a result of those adjustments, can no longer be varied, on appeal or otherwise.

13(6) In this Schedule **"follower notice"** means a follower notice under Chapter 2 of Part 4 of FA 2014.

13(7) For the purposes of this paragraph a partnership follower notice is given **"in respect of"** the partnership return mentioned in paragraph (a) or (b) of paragraph 2(2) of Schedule 31 to FA 2014.

CONDITION C

14(1) Condition C is that (in a case not falling within Condition A or B)–

(a) the arrangements are DOTAS arrangements,

(b) P has relied on the arrangements (see sub-paragraph (2))–

(c) the arrangements have been counteracted, and

(d) the counteraction is final.

14(2) For the purposes of sub-paragraph (1), P **"relies on the arrangements"** if–

(a) P makes a return, claim or election, or a partnership return is made, on the basis that a relevant tax advantage arises, or

(b) P fails to discharge a relevant obligation ("the disputed obligation") and there is reason to believe that P's failure to discharge that obligation is connected with the arrangements.

14(3) For the purposes of sub-paragraph (2) **"relevant tax advantage"** means a tax advantage which the arrangements might be expected to enable P to obtain.

14(4) For the purposes of sub-paragraph (2) an obligation is a **"relevant obligation"** if the arrangements might be expected to have the result that the obligation does not arise.

14(5) For the purposes of this paragraph the arrangements are **"counteracted"** if–

(a) adjustments, other than taxpayer emendations, are made in respect of P's tax position–

  (i) on the basis that the whole or part of the relevant tax advantage mentioned in sub-paragraph (2)(a) does not arise, or

  (ii) on the basis that the disputed obligation does (or did) arise, or

(b) an assessment to tax other than a self-assessment is made, or any other action is taken by HMRC, on the basis mentioned in paragraph (a)(i) or (ii) (otherwise than by way of an adjustment).

14(6) For the purposes of this paragraph a counteraction is **"final"** when the assessment, adjustments or action in question, and any amounts arising from the assessment, adjustments or action, can no longer be varied, on appeal or otherwise.

14(7) For the purposes of sub-paragraph (1) the time at which it falls to be determined whether or not the arrangements are DOTAS arrangements is when the counteraction becomes final.

14(8) The following are **"taxpayer emendations"** for the purposes of sub-paragraph (5)–

(a) an adjustment made by P at a time when P had no reason to believe that HMRC had begun or were about to begin enquiries into P's affairs relating to the tax in question;

(b) an adjustment (by way of an assessment or otherwise) made by HMRC with respect to P's tax position as a result of a disclosure made by P which meets the conditions in sub-paragraph (9).

For the purposes of paragraph (a) a payment in respect of a liability to pay national insurance contributions is not an adjustment unless it is a payment in full.

14(9) The conditions are that the disclosure–

(a) is a full and explicit disclosure of an inaccuracy in a return or other document or of a failure to comply with an obligation, and

(b) was made at a time when P had no reason to believe that HMRC were about to begin enquiries into P's affairs relating to the tax in question.

14(10) For the purposes of this paragraph a contract settlement which HMRC enters into with P is treated as an assessment to tax (other than a self-assessment); and in relation to contract settlements references in sub-paragraph (5) to the basis an which any assessment or adjustments are made, or any other action is taken, are to be read with any necessary modifications.

CONDITION D

15 [Not relevant to inheritance tax.]

CONDITION E

16 [Not relevant to inheritance tax.]

CONDITION F

16A [Not relevant to inheritance tax.]

History – Para. 16A inserted by F(No. 2)A 2017, s. 66 and Sch. 17, para. 55(10) with effect so far as is necessary for enabling the making of regulations under that Schedule on 16 November 2017 (Royal Assent) and on 1 January 2018 for all other purposes.

Part 3 – Annual Information Notices and Naming

ANNUAL INFORMATION NOTICES

17(1) A person ("P") who has been given a warning notice under this Schedule must give HMRC a written notice (an "information notice") in respect of each reporting period in the warning period (see sub-paragraph (11)).

17(2) An information notice must be given not later than the 30th day after the end of the reporting period to which it relates.

17(3) An information notice must state whether or not P–

(a) has in the reporting period delivered a return, or made a claim, election, declaration or application for approval, on the basis that a relevant tax advantage arises, or has since the end of the reporting period delivered on that basis a return which P was required to deliver before the end of that period,

(b) has in the reporting period failed to take action which P would be required to take under or by virtue of an enactment relating to tax but for particular disclosable arrangements to which P is a party,

(c) has in the reporting period become a party to arrangements which–

(i) relate to the position with respect to VAT of another person ("S") who has made supplies of goods or services to P, and

(ii) might be expected to enable P to obtain a relevant tax advantage ("the expected tax advantage") in connection with those supplies of goods or services,

(d) has failed to deliver a return which P was required to deliver by a date falling in the reporting period.

17(4) In this paragraph **"relevant tax advantage"** means a tax advantage which particular disclosable arrangements enable, or might be expected to enable, P to obtain.

17(5) If P has, in the reporting period concerned, made a return, claim, election, declaration or application for approval on the basis mentioned in sub-paragraph (3)(a) or failed to take action as mentioned in sub-paragraph (3)(b) the information notice must–

(a) explain (on the assumptions made by P in so acting or failing to act) how the disclosable arrangements enable P to obtain the tax advantage, or (as the case may be) have the result that P is not required to take the action in question, and

(b) state (on the same assumptions) the amount of the relevant tax advantage mentioned in sub-paragraph (3)(a) or (as the case may be) the amount of any tax advantage which arises in connection with the absence of a requirement to take the action mentioned in sub-paragraph (3)(b).

17(6) If P has, in the reporting period, become a party to arrangements such as are mentioned in sub-paragraph (3)(c), the information notice–

(a) must state whether or not it is P's view that the expected tax advantage arises to P, and

(b) if that is P's view, must explain how the arrangements enable P to obtain the tax advantage and state the amount of the tax advantage.

17(7) If the time by which P must deliver a return falls within a reporting period and P fails to deliver the return by that time, HMRC may require P to give HMRC a written notice (a "supplementary information notice") setting out any matters which P would have been required to set out in an information notice had P delivered the return in that reporting period.

17(8) A requirement under sub-paragraph (7) must be made by a written notice which states the period within which P must comply with the notice.

17(9) If P fails to comply with a requirement of (or imposed under) this paragraph HMRC may by written notice extend the warning period to the end of the period of 5 years beginning with–

(a) the day by which the information notice or supplementary information notice should have been given (see sub-paragraphs (2) and (8)) or, as the case requires,

(b) the day on which P gave the defective information notice or supplementary information notice to HMRC,

or, if earlier, the time when the warning period would have expired but for the extension.

17(10) HMRC may permit information notices given by members of the same group of companies (as defined in paragraph 46(9)) to be combined.

17(11) For the purposes of this paragraph–

(a) the first reporting period in any warning period begins with the first day of the warning period and ends with a day specified by HMRC ("the specified day"),

(b) the remainder of the warning period is divided into further reporting periods each of which begins immediately after the end of the preceding reporting period and is twelve months long or (if that would be shorter) ends at the end of the warning period.

17(12) In this paragraph **"disclosable arrangements"** means any of the following–

(a) DOTAS arrangements,

(b) disclosable VAT arrangements, and

(c) disclosable indirect tax arrangements.

History – In para. 17(3)(a) the words ", election, declaration or application for approval," (initial comma assumed by Croner-i) substituted for the words "or election," by F(No. 2)A 2017, s. 66 and Sch. 17, para. 55(11)(a) with effect so far as is necessary for enabling the making of regulations under that Schedule on 16 November 2017 (Royal Assent) and on 1 January 2018 for all other purposes.
In para. 17(3)(b) the words "disclosable" (initial comma assumed by Croner-i) substituted for the words "DOTAS arrangements or [disclosable] VAT" by F(No. 2)A 2017, s. 66 and Sch. 17, para. 55(11)(b) with effect so far as is necessary for enabling the making of regulations under that Schedule on 16 November 2017 (Royal Assent) and on 1 January 2018 for all other purposes.
In para. 17(4) the words "disclosable" (initial comma assumed by Croner-i) substituted for the words "DOTAS arrangements or [disclosable] VAT" by F(No. 2)A 2017, s. 66 and Sch. 17, para. 55(11)(b) with effect so far as is necessary for enabling the making of regulations under that Schedule on 16 November 2017 (Royal Assent) and on 1 January 2018 for all other purposes.
In para. 17(5)(a) the words "disclosable" (initial comma assumed by Croner-i) substituted for the words "DOTAS arrangements or [disclosable] VAT" by F(No. 2)A 2017, s. 66 and Sch. 17, para. 55(11)(b) with effect so far as is necessary for enabling the making of regulations under that Schedule on 16 November 2017 (Royal Assent) and on 1 January 2018 for all other purposes.
In para. 17(5) the words ", election, declaration or application for approval" (initial comma assumed by Croner-i) substituted for the words "or election" by F(No. 2)A 2017, s. 66 and Sch. 17, para. 55(11)(c) with effect so far as is necessary for enabling the making of regulations under that Schedule on 16 November 2017 (Royal Assent) and on 1 January 2018 for all other purposes.
Para. 17(12) inserted by F(No. 2)A 2017, s. 66 and Sch. 17, para. 55(11)(d) with effect so far as is necessary for enabling the making of regulations under that Schedule on 16 November 2017 (Royal Assent) and on 1 January 2018 for all other purposes.

NAMING

18(1) The Commissioners may publish information about a person if the person–

(a) incurs a relevant defeat in relation to arrangements which the person has used in a warning period, and

(b) has been given at least two warning notices in respect of other defeats of arrangements which were used in the same warning period.

18(2) Information published for the first time under sub-paragraph (1) must be published within the 12 months beginning with the day on which the most recent of the warning notices falling within that sub-paragraph has been given to the person.

18(3) No information may be published (or continue to be published) after the end of the period of 12 months beginning with the day on which it is first published.

18(4) The information that may be published is–

(a) the person's name (including any trading name, previous name or pseudonym),

(b) the person's address (or registered office),

(c) the nature of any business carried on by the person,

(d) information about the fiscal effect of the defeated arrangements (had they not been defeated), for instance information about total amounts of tax understated or total amounts by which claims, or statements of losses, have been adjusted,

(e) the amount of any penalty to which the person is liable under paragraph 30 in respect of the relevant defeat of any defeated arrangements,

(f) the periods in which or times when the defeated arrangements were used, and

(g) any other information the Commissioners may consider it appropriate to publish in order to make clear the person's identity.

18(5) If the person mentioned in sub-paragraph (1) is a member of a group of companies (as defined in paragraph 46(9)), the information which may be published also includes–

(a) any trading name of the group, and

(b) information about other members of the group of the kind described in sub-paragraph (4)(a), (b) or (c).

18(6) If the person mentioned in sub-paragraph (1) is a person carrying on a trade or business in partnership, the information which may be published also includes–

(a) any trading name of the partnership, and

(b) information about other members of the partnership of the kind described in sub-paragraph (4)(a) or (b).

18(7) The information may be published in any manner the Commissioners may consider appropriate.

18(8) Before publishing any information the Commissioners–

(a) must inform the person that they are considering doing so, and

(b) afford the person reasonable opportunity to make representations about whether or not it should be published.

18(9) Arrangements are **"defeated arrangements"** for the purposes of sub-paragraph (4) if the person used them in the warning period mentioned in sub-paragraph (1) and a warning notice specifying the defeat of those arrangements has been given to the person before the information is published.

18(10) If a person has been given a single warning notice in relation to two or more relevant defeats, the person is treated for the purposes of this paragraph as having been given a separate warning notice in relation to each of those relevant defeats.

18(11) Nothing in this paragraph prevents the power under sub-paragraph (1) from being exercised on a subsequent occasion in relation to arrangements used by the person in a different warning period.

Part 4 – Restriction of Reliefs

DUTY TO GIVE A RESTRICTION RELIEF NOTICE

19(1) HMRC must give a person a written notice (a "restriction of relief notice") if–

(a) the person incurs a relevant defeat in relation to arrangements which the person has used in a warning period,

(b) the person has been given at least two warning notices in respect of other relevant defeats of arrangements which were used in that same warning period, and

(c) the defeats mentioned in paragraphs (a) and (b) meet the conditions in sub-paragraph (2).

19(2) The conditions are–

(a) that each of the relevant defeats is by virtue of Condition A, B or C,

(b) that each of the relevant defeats relates to the misuse of a relief (see sub-paragraph (5)), and

(c) in the case of each of the relevant defeats, either–

(i) that the relevant counteraction (see sub-paragraph (7)) was made on the basis that a particular avoidance-related rule applies in relation to a person's affairs, or

(ii) that the misused relief is a loss relief.

19(3) In sub-paragraph (2)(c)–

(a) the **"misused relief"** means the relief mentioned in sub-paragraph (5), and

(b) **"loss relief"** means any relief under Part 4 of ITA 2007 or Part 4 or 5 of CTA 2010.

19(4) A restriction of relief notice must–

(a) explain the effect of paragraphs 20, 21 and 22, and

(b) set out when the restricted period is to begin and end.

19(5) For the purposes of this Part of this Schedule, a relevant defeat by virtue of Condition A, B or C **"relates to the misuse of a relief"** if–

(a) the tax advantage in question, or part of the tax advantage in question, is or results from (or would but for the counteraction be or result from) a relief or increased relief from tax, or

(b) it is reasonable to conclude that the making of a particular claim for relief, or the use of a particular relief, is a significant component of the arrangements in question.

19(6) In sub-paragraph (5) **"the tax advantage in question"** means–

(a) in relation to a defeat by virtue of Condition A, the tax advantage mentioned in paragraph 12(1)(a),

(b) in relation to a defeat by virtue of Condition B, the denied advantage (as defined in paragraph 13(4)), or

(c) in relation to a defeat by virtue of Condition C–

(i) the tax advantage mentioned in paragraph 14(2)(a), or, as the case requires,

(ii) the absence of the relevant obligation (as defined in paragraph 14(4)).

19(7) In this paragraph **"the relevant counteraction"**, in relation to a relevant defeat means–

(a) in the case of a defeat by virtue of Condition A, the counteraction referred to in paragraph 12(1)(c);

(b) in the case of a defeat by virtue of Condition B, the action referred to in paragraph 13(1);

(c) in the case of a defeat by virtue of Condition C, the counteraction referred to in paragraph 14(1)(d).

19(8) If a person has been given a single warning notice in relation to two or more relevant defeats, the person is treated for the purposes of this paragraph as having been given a separate warning notice in relation to each of those relevant defeats.

RESTRICTION OF RELIEF

20(1) Sub-paragraphs (2) to (15) have effect in relation to a person to whom a relief restriction notice has been given.

20(2) The person may not, in the restricted period, make any claim for relief.

20(3) Sub-paragraph (2) does not have effect in relation to–

(a) a claim for relief under Schedule 8 to FA 2003 (stamp duty land tax: charities relief);

(b) a claim for relief under Chapter 3 of Part 8 of ITA 2007 (gifts of shares, securities and real property to charities etc);

(c) a claim for relief under Part 10 of ITA 2007 (special rules about charitable trusts etc);

(d) a claim for relief under double taxation arrangements;

(e) an election under section 426 of ITA 2007 (gift aid: election to treat gift as made in previous year).

20(4) Claims under the following provisions in Part 4 of FA 2004 (registered pension schemes: tax reliefs etc) do not count as claims for relief for the purposes of this paragraph–

section 192(4) (increase of basic rate limit and higher rate limit);

section 193(4) (net pay arrangements: excess relief);

section 194(1) (relief on making of a claim).

20(5) The person may not, in the restricted period, surrender group relief under Part 5 of CTA 2010.

20(6) No deduction is to be made under section 83 of ITA 2007 (carry forward against subsequent trade profits) in calculating the person's net income for a relevant tax year.

20(7) No deduction is to be made under section 118 of ITA 2007 (carry-forward property loss relief) in calculating the person's net income for a relevant tax year.

20(8) The person is not entitled to relief under section 448 (annual payments: relief for individuals) or 449 (annual payments: relief for other persons) of ITA 2007 for any payment made in the restricted period.

20(9) No deduction of expenses referable to a relevant accounting period is to be made under section 1219(1) of CTA 2009 (expenses of management of a company's investment business).

20(10) No reduction is to be made under section 45(4) of CTA 2010 (carry-forward of trade loss relief) in calculating the profits for a relevant accounting period of a trade carried on by the person.

20(11) In calculating the total amount of chargeable gains accruing to a person in a relevant tax year (or part of a relevant tax year), no losses are to be deducted under subsections (2) to (2B) of section 2 of TCGA 1992 (persons and gains chargeable to capital gains tax, and allowable losses).

20(12) In calculating the total amount of ATED-related chargeable gains accruing to a person in a relevant tax year, no losses are to be deducted under subsection (3) of section 2B of TCGA 1992 (persons chargeable to capital gains tax on ATED-related gains).

20(13) In calculating the total amount of chargeable NRCGT gains accruing to a person in a relevant tax year on relevant high value disposals, no losses are to be deducted under subsection (2) of section 14D of TCGA 1992 (persons chargeable to capital gains tax on NRCGT gains).

20(14) If the person is a company, no deduction is to be made under section 62 of CTA 2010 (relief for losses made in UK property business) from the company's total profits of a relevant accounting period.

20(15) No deduction is to be made under regulation 18 of the Unauthorised Unit Trusts (Tax) Regulations 2013 (S.I. 2013/2819) (relief for deemed payments by trustees of an exempt unauthorised unit trust) in calculating the person's net income for a relevant tax year.

20(16) In this paragraph **"relevant tax year"** means any tax year the first day of which is in the restricted period.

20(17) In this paragraph **"relevant accounting period"** means an accounting period the first day of which is in the restricted period.

20(18) In this paragraph **"double taxation arrangements"** means arrangements which have effect under section 2(1) of TIOPA 2010 (double taxation relief by agreement with territories outside the UK).

THE RESTRICTED PERIOD

21(1) In paragraphs 19 and 20 (and this paragraph) **"the restricted period"** means the period of 3 years *beginning with the day on which the relief restriction notice is given.*

21(2) If during the restricted period (or the restricted period as extended under this sub-paragraph) the person to whom a relief restriction notice has been given incurs a further relevant defeat meeting the conditions in sub-paragraph (4), HMRC must give the person a written notice (a "restricted period extension notice").

21(3) A restricted period extension notice extends the restricted period to the end of the period of 3 years beginning with the day on which the further relevant defeat occurs.

21(4) The conditions mentioned in sub-paragraph (2) are that–

(a) the relevant defeat is incurred by virtue of Condition A, B or C in relation to arrangements which the person used in the warning period mentioned in paragraph 19(1)(a), and

(b) the warning notice given to the person in respect of the relevant defeat relates to the misuse of a relief.

21(5) If the person to whom a relief restriction notice has been given incurs a relevant defeat which meets the conditions in sub-paragraph (4) after the restricted period has expired but before the end of a concurrent warning period, HMRC must give the person a restriction of relief notice.

21(6) In sub-paragraph (5) **"concurrent warning period"** means a warning period which at some time ran concurrently with the restricted period.

REASONABLE EXCUSE

22(1) If a person who has incurred a relevant defeat satisfies HMRC or, on an appeal under paragraph 24, the First-tier Tribunal or Upper Tribunal that the person had a reasonable excuse for the matters to which that relevant defeat relates, then–

(a) for the purposes of paragraph 19(1)(a) and 21(2) and (5), the person is treated as not having incurred that relevant defeat, and

(b) for the purposes of paragraph 19(1)(b) and (c) any warning notice given to the person which relates to that relevant defeat is treated as not having been given to the person.

22(2) For the purposes of this paragraph, in the case of a person ("P")–

(a) an insufficiency of funds is not a reasonable excuse unless attributable to events outside P's control,

(b) where P relies on another person to do anything, that is not a reasonable excuse unless P took reasonable care to avoid the relevant failure, and

(c) where P had reasonable excuse for the relevant failure but the excuse had ceased, P is to be treated as having continued to have the excuse if the failure is remedied without unreasonable delay after the excuse ceased.

22(3) In determining for the purposes of this paragraph whether or not a person ("P") had a reasonable excuse for any action, failure or inaccuracy, reliance on advice is to be taken automatically not to constitute a reasonable excuse if the advice is addressed to, or was given to, a person other than P or takes no account of P's individual circumstances.

22(4) In this paragraph **"relevant failure"**, in relation to a relevant defeat, is to be interpreted in accordance with sub-paragraphs (2) to (7) of paragraph 43.

MITIGATION OF RESTRICTION OF RELIEF

23(1) The Commissioners may mitigate the effects of paragraph 20 in relation to a person ("P") so far as it appears to them that there are exceptional circumstances such that the operation of that paragraph would otherwise have an unduly serious impact with respect to the tax affairs of P or another person.

23(2) For the purposes of sub-paragraph (1) the Commissioners may modify the effects of paragraph 20 in any way they think appropriate, including by allowing P access to the whole or part of a relief to which P would otherwise not be entitled as a result of paragraph 20.

APPEAL

24(1) A person may appeal against–

(a) a relief restriction notice, or

(b) a restricted period extension notice.

24(2) An appeal under this paragraph must be made within the period of 30 days beginning with the day on which the notice is given.

24(3) An appeal under this paragraph is to be treated in the same way as an appeal against an assessment to income tax (including by the application of any provision about bringing the appeal by notice to HMRC, about HMRC's review of the decision or about determination of the appeal by the First-tier Tribunal or Upper Tribunal).

24(4) On an appeal the tribunal may–

(a) cancel HMRC's decision, or

(b) affirm that decision with or without any modifications in accordance with sub-paragraph (5).

24(5) On an appeal the tribunal may rely on paragraph 23 (mitigation of restriction of relief)–

(a) to the same extent as HMRC (which may mean applying the same mitigation as HMRC to a different starting point), or

(b) to a different extent, but only if the tribunal thinks that HMRC's decision in respect of the application of paragraph 23 was flawed.

24(6) In this paragraph **"tribunal"** means the First-tier Tribunal or Upper Tribunal (as appropriate by virtue of sub-paragraph (3)).

MEANING OF "AVOIDANCE-RELATED RULE"

25(1) In this Part of this Schedule **"avoidance-related rule"** means a rule in Category 1 or 2.

25(2) A rule is in Category 1 if it refers (in whatever terms)–

(a) to the purpose or main purpose or purposes of a transaction, arrangements or any other action or matter, and

(b) to whether or not the purpose in question is or involves the avoidance of tax or the obtaining of any advantage in relation to tax (however described).

25(3) A rule is also in Category 1 if it refers (in whatever terms) to–

(a) expectations as to what are, or may be, the expected benefits of a transaction, arrangements or any other action or matter, and

(b) whether or not the avoidance of tax or the obtaining of any advantage in relation to tax (however described) is such a benefit.

For the purposes of paragraph (b) it does not matter whether the reference is (for instance) to the "sole or main benefit" or "one of the main benefits" or any other reference to a benefit.

25(4) A rule falls within Category 2 if as a result of the rule a person may be treated differently for tax purposes depending on whether or not purposes referred to in the rule (for instance the purposes of an actual or contemplated action or enterprise) are (or are shown to be) commercial purposes.

25(5) For example, a rule in the following form would fall within Category 1 and within Category 2–

"Example rule

Section X does not apply to a company in respect of a transaction if the company shows that the transaction meets Condition A or B.

Condition A is that the transaction is effected–

(a) for genuine commercial reasons, or

(b) in the ordinary course of managing investments.

Condition B is that the avoidance of tax is not the main object or one of the main objects of the transaction."

MEANING OF "RELIEF"

26 The following are **"reliefs"** for the purposes of this Part of this Schedule–

(a) any relief from tax (however described) which must be claimed, or which is not available without making an election,

(b) relief under section 1219 of CTA 2009 (expenses of management of a company's investment business),

(c) any relief (not falling within paragraph (a)) under Part 4 of ITA 2007 (loss relief) or Part 4 or 5 of CTA 2010 (loss relief and group relief), and

(d) any relief (not falling within paragraph (a) or (b)) under a provision listed in section 24 of ITA 2007 (reliefs deductible at Step 2 of the calculation of income tax liability).

"CLAIM" FOR RELIEF

27 In this Part of this Schedule **"claim for relief"** includes any election or other similar action which is in substance a claim for relief.

VAT AND INDIRECT TAXES

History – In the heading the words "and indirect taxes" inserted by F(No. 2)A 2017, s. 66 and Sch. 17, para. 55(12) with effect so far as is necessary for enabling the making of regulations under that Schedule on 16 November 2017 (Royal Assent) and on 1 January 2018 for all other purposes.

28 In this Part of this Schedule **"tax"** does not include VAT or any other indirect tax.

History – In para. 28 the words "or any other indirect tax" inserted by F(No. 2)A 2017, s. 66 and Sch. 17, para. 55(13) with effect so far as is necessary for enabling the making of regulations under that Schedule on 16 November 2017 (Royal Assent) and on 1 January 2018 for all other purposes.

POWER TO AMEND

29(1) The Treasury may by regulations amend–

(a) amend paragraph 20;

(b) amend paragraph 26.

29(2) Regulations under sub-paragraph (1)(a) may, in particular, alter the application of paragraph 20 in relation to any relief, exclude any relief from its application or extend its application to further reliefs.

29(3) Regulations under sub-paragraph (1)(b) may amend the meaning of "relief" in any way (including by extending or limiting the meaning).

29(4) Regulations under this paragraph may–

(a) make supplementary, incidental and consequential provision;

(b) make transitional provision.

29(5) Regulations under this paragraph are to be made by statutory instrument.

29(6) A statutory instrument containing regulations under this Part may not be made unless a draft of the instrument has been laid before and approved by a resolution of the House of Commons.

Part 5 – Penalty

PENALTY

30(1) A person is liable to pay a penalty if the person incurs a relevant defeat in relation to any arrangements which the person has used in a warning period.

30(2) The penalty is 20% of the value of the counteracted advantage if neither sub-paragraph (3) nor sub-paragraph (4) applies.

30(3) The penalty is 40% of the value of the counteracted advantage if before the relevant defeat is incurred the person has been given, or become liable to be given, one (but not more than one) relevant prior warning notice.

30(4) The penalty is 60% of the value of the counteracted advantage if before the current defeat is incurred the person has been given, or become liable to be given, two or more relevant prior warning notices.

30(5) In this paragraph **"relevant prior warning notice"** means a warning notice in relation to the defeat of arrangements which the person has used in the warning period mentioned in sub-paragraph (1).

30(6) For the meaning of "the value of the counteracted advantage" see paragraphs 32 to 37.

SIMULTANEOUS DEFEATS ETC

31(1) If a person incurs simultaneously two or more relevant defeats in relation to different arrangements, sub-paragraphs (2) to (4) of paragraph 30 have effect as if the relevant defeat with the lowest value was incurred last, the relevant defeat with the next lowest value immediately before it, and so on.

31(2) For this purpose the **"value"** of a relevant defeat is taken to be equal to the value of the counteracted advantage.

31(3) If a person has been given a single warning notice in relation to two or more relevant defeats, the person is treated for the purposes of paragraph 30 as having been given a separate warning notice in relation to each of those relevant defeats.

VALUE OF THE COUNTERACTED ADVANTAGE: BASIC RULE FOR TAXES OTHER THAN VAT

32(1) In relation to a relevant defeat incurred by virtue of Condition A, B, C or F, the **"value of the counteracted advantage"** is–

(a) in the case of a relevant defeat incurred by virtue of Condition A, the additional amount due or payable in respect of tax as a result of the counteraction mentioned in paragraph 12(1)(c);

(b) in the case of a relevant defeat incurred by virtue of Condition B, the additional amount due or payable in respect of tax as a result of the action mentioned in paragraph 13(1);

(c) in the case of a relevant defeat incurred by virtue of Condition C, the additional amount due or payable in respect of tax as a result of the counteraction mentioned in paragraph 14(1)(d);

(d) in the case of a relevant defeat incurred by virtue of Condition F, the additional amount due or payable in respect of tax as a result of the counteraction mentioned in paragraph 16A(1)(d).

32(2) The reference in sub-paragraph (1) to the additional amount due and payable includes a reference to–

(a) an amount payable to HMRC having erroneously been paid by way of repayment of tax, and

(b) an amount which would be repayable by HMRC if the counteraction mentioned in paragraph (a), (c) or (d) of sub-paragraph (1) were not made or the action mentioned in paragraph (b) of that sub-paragraph were not taken (as the case may be).

32(3) The following are ignored in calculating the value of the counteracted advantage–

(a) group relief, and

(b) any relief under section 458 of CTA 2010 (relief in respect of repayment etc of loan) which is deferred under subsection (5) of that section.

32(4) This paragraph is subject to paragraphs 33 and 34.

History – In para. 32(1) the words ", C or F" (comma assumed by Croner-i) substituted for the words "or C" and para. 32(1)(d) inserted by F(No. 2)A 2017, s. 66 and Sch. 17, para. 55(14)(a) with effect so far as is necessary for enabling the making of regulations under that Schedule on 16 November 2017 (Royal Assent) and on 1 January 2018 for all other purposes.
In para. 32(2)(b) the words ", (c) or (d)" (comma assumed by Croner-i) substituted for the words "or (c)" and para. 32(1)(d) inserted by F(No. 2)A 2017, s. 66 and Sch. 17, para. 55(14)(b) with effect so far as is necessary for enabling the making of regulations under that Schedule on 16 November 2017 (Royal Assent) and on 1 January 2018 for all other purposes.

VALUE OF COUNTERACTED ADVANTAGE: LOSSES FOR PURPOSES OF DIRECT TAX

33(1) This paragraph has effect in relation to relevant defeats incurred by virtue of Condition A, B or C.

33(2) To the extent that the counteracted advantage (see paragraph 35) has the result that a loss is wrongly recorded for the purposes of direct tax and the loss has been wholly used to reduce the amount due or payable in respect of tax, the value of the counteracted advantage is determined in accordance with paragraph 32.

33(3) To the extent that the counteracted advantage has the result that a loss is wrongly recorded for purposes of direct tax and the loss has not been wholly used to reduce the amount due or payable in respect of tax, the value of the counteracted advantage is–

(a) the value under paragraph 32 of so much of the counteracted advantage as results from the part (if any) of the loss which is used to reduce the amount due or payable in respect of tax, plus

(b) 10% of the part of the loss not so used.

33(4) Sub-paragraphs (2) and (3) apply both–

(a) to a case where no loss would have been recorded but for the counteracted advantage, and

(b) to a case where a loss of a different amount would have been recorded (but in that case sub-paragraphs (2) and (3) apply only to the difference between the amount recorded and the true amount).

33(5) To the extent that a counteracted advantage creates or increases an aggregate loss recorded for a group of companies–

(a) the value of the counteracted advantage is calculated in accordance with this paragraph, and

(b) in applying paragraph 32 in accordance with sub-paragraphs (2) and (3), group relief may be taken into account (despite paragraph 32(3)).

33(6) To the extent that the counteracted advantage results in a loss, the value of it is nil where, because of the nature of the loss or the person's circumstances, there is no reasonable prospect of the loss being used to support a claim to reduce a tax liability (of any person).

VALUE OF COUNTERACTED ADVANTAGE: DEFERRED TAX

34(1) To the extent that the counteracted advantage (see paragraph 35) is a deferral of tax (other than VAT), the value of that advantage is–

(a) 25% of the amount of the deferred tax for each year of the deferral, or

(b) a percentage of the amount of the deferred tax, for each separate period of deferral of less than a year, equating to 25% per year,

or, if less, 100% of the amount of the deferred tax.

34(2) This paragraph does not apply to a case to the extent that paragraph 33 applies.

MEANING OF "THE COUNTERACTED ADVANTAGE" IN PARAGRAPHS 33 AND 34

35(1) In paragraphs 33 and 34 **"the counteracted advantage"** means–

(a) in relation to a relevant defeat incurred by virtue of Condition A, the tax advantage mentioned in paragraph 12(1)(b);

(b) in relation to a relevant defeat incurred by virtue of Condition B, the denied advantage in relation to which the action mentioned in paragraph 13(1) is taken;

(c) in relation to a relevant defeat incurred by virtue of Condition C, means any tax advantage in respect of which the counteraction mentioned in paragraph 14(1)(c) is made;

(d) in relation to a relevant defeat incurred by virtue of Condition F, means any tax advantage in respect of which the counteraction mentioned in paragraph 16A(1)(c) is made.

35(2) In sub-paragraph (1)(c) **"counteraction"** is to be interpreted in accordance with paragraph 14(5).

History – Para. 35(1)(d) inserted by F(No. 2)A 2017, s. 66 and Sch. 17, para. 55(15) with effect so far as is necessary for enabling the making of regulations under that Schedule on 16 November 2017 (Royal Assent) and on 1 January 2018 for all other purposes.

VALUE OF THE COUNTERACTED ADVANTAGE: CONDITIONS D AND E

36 [Not relevant to inheritance tax.]

VALUE OF COUNTERACTED ADVANTAGE: DELAYED VAT

37 [Not relevant to inheritance tax.]

ASSESSMENT OF PENALTY

38(1) Where a person is liable for a penalty under paragraph 30, HMRC must assess the penalty.

38(2) Where HMRC assess the penalty, HMRC must–

(a) notify the person who is liable for the penalty, and

(b) state in the notice a tax period in respect of which the penalty is assessed.

38(3) A penalty under this paragraph must be paid before the end of the period of 30 days beginning with the day on which the person is notified of the penalty under sub-paragraph (2).

38(4) An assessment–

(a) is to be treated for procedural purposes as if it were an assessment to tax,

(b) may be enforced as if it were an assessment to tax, and

(c) may be combined with an assessment to tax.

38(5) An assessment of a penalty under this paragraph must be made before the end of the period of 12 months beginning with the date of the defeat mentioned in paragraph 30(1).

ALTERATION OF ASSESSMENT OF PENALTY

39(1) After notification of an assessment has been given to a person under paragraph 38(2), the assessment may not be altered except in accordance with this paragraph or on appeal.

39(2) A supplementary assessment may be made in respect of a penalty if an earlier assessment operated by reference to an underestimate of the value of the counteracted advantage.

39(3) An assessment may be revised as necessary if operated by reference to an overestimate of the value of the counteracted advantage.

AGGREGATE PENALTIES

40(1) The amount of a penalty for which a person is liable under paragraph 30 is to be reduced by the amount of any other penalty incurred by the person, or any surcharge for late payment of tax imposed on the person, if the amount of the penalty or surcharge is determined by reference to the same tax liability.

40(2) In sub-paragraph (1) **"any other penalty"** does not include a penalty under section 212A of FA 2013 (GAAR penalty) or Part 4 of FA 2014 (penalty where corrective action not taken after follower notice etc).

40(3) In the application of section 97A of TMA 1970 (multiple penalties) no account shall be taken of a penalty under paragraph 30.

APPEAL AGAINST PENALTY

41(1) A person may appeal against a decision of HMRC that a penalty is payable under paragraph 30.

41(2) A person may appeal against a decision of HMRC as to the amount of a penalty payable by P under paragraph 30.

41(3) An appeal under this paragraph must be made within the period of 30 days beginning with the day on which notification of the penalty is given under paragraph 38.

41(4) An appeal under this paragraph is to be treated in the same way as an appeal against an assessment to the tax concerned (including by the application of any provision about bringing the appeal by notice to HMRC, about HMRC's review of the decision or about determination of the appeal by the First-tier Tribunal or Upper Tribunal).

41(5) Sub-paragraph (4) does not apply–

(a) so as to require a person to pay a penalty before an appeal against the assessment of the penalty is determined, or

(b) in respect of any other matter expressly provided for by this Part of this Schedule.

41(6) On an appeal under sub-paragraph (1) or (2) the tribunal may–

(a) affirm HMRC's decision, or

(b) substitute for HMRC's decision another decision that HMRC has power to make.

41(7) In this paragraph **"tribunal"** means the First-tier Tribunal or Upper Tribunal (as appropriate by virtue of sub-paragraph (4)).

PENALTIES: REASONABLE EXCUSE

42(1) A person is not liable to a penalty under paragraph 30 in respect of a relevant defeat if the person satisfies HMRC or (on appeal) the First-tier Tribunal or Upper Tribunal that the person had a reasonable excuse for the relevant failure to which that relevant defeat relates (see paragraph 43).

42(2) Sub-paragraph (3) applies if–

(a) a person has incurred a relevant defeat in respect of which the person is liable to a penalty under paragraph 30, and

(b) before incurring that defeat the person had been given, or become liable to be given, an excepted warning notice.

42(3) The person is treated for the purposes of sub-paragraphs (2) to (4) of paragraph 30 (rate of penalty) as not having been given, and not having become liable to be given, the excepted notice (so far as it relates to the relevant defeat in respect of which the person had a reasonable excuse).

42(4) A warning notice is **"excepted"** for the purposes of this paragraph if the person was not liable to a penalty in respect of the defeat specified in it because the person had a reasonable excuse for the relevant failure in question.

42(5) For the purposes of this paragraph, in the case of a person ("P")–

(a) an insufficiency of funds is not a reasonable excuse unless attributable to events outside P's control,

(b) where P relies on another person to do anything, that is not a reasonable excuse unless P took reasonable care to avoid the relevant failure, and

(c) where P had a reasonable excuse for the relevant failure but the excuse had ceased, P is to be treated as having continued to have the excuse if the failure is remedied without unreasonable delay after the excuse ceased.

42(6) In determining for the purposes of this paragraph whether or not a person ("P") had a reasonable excuse for any action, failure or inaccuracy, reliance on advice is to be taken automatically not to constitute a reasonable excuse if the advice is addressed to, or was given to, a person other than P or takes no account of P's individual circumstances.

PARAGRAPH 42: MEANING OF "THE RELEVANT FAILURE"

43(1) In paragraph 42 **"the relevant failure"**, in relation to a relevant defeat, is to be interpreted in accordance with sub-paragraphs (2) to (7).

43(2) In relation to a relevant defeat incurred by virtue of Condition A, **"the relevant failure"** means the failures or inaccuracies as a result of which the counteraction under section 209 of FA 2013 was necessary.

43(3) In relation to a relevant defeat incurred by virtue of Condition B, **"the relevant failure"** means the failures or inaccuracies in respect of which the action mentioned in paragraph 13(1) was taken.

43(4) In relation to a relevant defeat incurred by virtue of Condition C, **"the relevant failure"** means the failures of inaccuracies as a result of which the adjustments, assessments, or other action mentioned in paragraph 14(5) are required.

43(5) In relation to a relevant defeat incurred by virtue of Condition D, **"the relevant failure"** means the failures or inaccuracies as a result of which the adjustments, assessments or other action mentioned in paragraph 15(5) are required.

43(6) In relation to a relevant defeat incurred by virtue of Condition E, **"the relevant failure"** means P's actions (and failures to act), so far as they are connected with matters in respect of which the counteraction mentioned in paragraph 16(1) is required.

43(7) In sub-paragraph (6) **"counteraction"** is to be interpreted in accordance with paragraph 16(2).

43(8) In relation to a relevant defeat incurred by virtue of Condition F, **"the relevant failure"** means the failures or inaccuracies as a result of which the adjustments, assessments, or other actions mentioned in paragraph 16A(5) are required.

History – Para. 43(8) inserted by F(No. 2)A 2017, s. 66 and Sch. 17, para. 55(16) with effect so far as is necessary for enabling the making of regulations under that Schedule on 16 November 2017 (Royal Assent) and on 1 January 2018 for all other purposes.

MITIGATION OF PENALTIES

44(1) The Commissioners may in their discretion mitigate a penalty under paragraph 30, or stay or compound any proceedings for such a penalty.

44(2) They may also, after judgment, further mitigate or entirely remit the penalty.

Part 6 – Corporate Groups, Associated Persons and Partnerships

REPRESENTATIVE MEMBER OF A VAT GROUP

45 [Not relevant to inheritance tax.]

CORPORATE GROUPS

46(1) Sub-paragraphs (2) and (3) apply if HMRC has a duty under paragraph 2 to give a warning notice to a company ("C") which is a member of a group.

46(2) That duty has effect as a duty to give a warning notice to each current group member (see sub-paragraph (8)).

46(3) Any warning notice which has been given (or is treated as having been given) previously to any current group member is treated as having been given to each current group member (and any provision in this Schedule which refers to a **"warning period"** in relation to a person is to be interpreted accordingly). But see sub-paragraphs (4) and (5).

46(4) In relation to a company which incurs a relevant defeat, paragraph 19(1) (duty to give relief restriction notice) does not have effect unless the warning period mentioned in that sub-paragraph would be a warning period in relation to the company regardless of sub-paragraph (3).

46(5) A company which incurs a relevant defeat is not liable to pay a penalty under paragraph 30 unless the warning period mentioned in sub-paragraph (1) of that paragraph would be a warning period in relation to the company regardless of sub-paragraph (3).

46(6) HMRC may discharge any duty to give a warning notice to a current group member in accordance with sub-paragraph (2) by delivering the notice to C (and if it does so may combine one or more warning notices in a single notice).

46(7) If a company ceases to be a member of a group, and–

(a) immediately before it ceases to be a member of the group, a warning period has effect in relation to the company, but

(b) no warning period would have effect in relation to the company at that time but for sub-paragraph (2) or (3),

that warning period ceases to have effect in relation to the company when it ceases to be a member of that group.

46(8) In this paragraph **"current group member"** means a company which is a member of the group concerned at the time when the warning notice mentioned in sub-paragraph (1) is given.

IHT Statutes

46(9) For the purposes of this paragraph two companies are members of the same group of companies if–

(a) one is a 75% subsidiary of the other, or

(b) both are 75% subsidiaries of a third company.

46(10) In this paragraph **"75% subsidiary"** has the meaning given by section 1154 of CTA 2010.

46(11) In this paragraph **"company"** has the same meaning as in the Corporation Tax Acts (see section 1121 of CTA 2010).

ASSOCIATED PERSONS TREATED AS INCURRING RELEVANT DEFEATS

47(1) Sub-paragraph (2) applies if a person ("P") incurs a relevant defeat in relation to any arrangements (otherwise than by virtue of this paragraph).

47(2) Any person ("S") who is associated with P at the relevant time is also treated for the purposes of paragraphs 2 (duty to give warning notice) and 3(2) (warning period) as having incurred that relevant defeat in relation to those arrangements (but see sub-paragraph (3)).
For the meaning of "associated" see paragraph 48.

47(3) Sub-paragraph (2) does not apply if P and S are members of the same group of companies (as defined in paragraph 46(9)).

47(4) In relation to a warning notice given to S by virtue of sub-paragraph (2), paragraph 2(4)(c) (certain information to be included in warning notice) is to be read as referring only to paragraphs 3, 17 and 18.

47(5) A warning notice which is given to a person by virtue of sub-paragraph (2) is treated for the purposes of paragraphs 19(1) (duty to give relief restriction notice) and 30 (penalty) as not having been given to that person.

47(6) In sub-paragraph (2) **"the relevant time"** means the time when P is given a warning notice in respect of the relevant defeat.

MEANING OF "ASSOCIATED"

48(1) For the purposes of paragraph 47 two persons are associated with one another if–

(a) one of them is a body corporate which is controlled by the other, or

(b) they are bodies corporate under common control.

48(2) Two bodies corporate are under common control if both are controlled–

(a) by one person,

(b) by two or more, but fewer than six, individuals, or

(c) by any number of individuals carrying on business in partnership.

48(3) For the purposes of this section a body corporate ("H") is taken to control another body corporate ("B") if–

(a) H is empowered by statute to control B's activities, or

(b) H is B's holding company within the meaning of section 1159 of and Schedule 6 to the Companies Act 2006.

48(4) For the purposes of this section an individual or individuals are taken to control a body corporate ("B") if the individual or individuals, were they a body corporate, would be B's holding company within the meaning of those provisions.

PARTNERS TREATED AS INCURRING RELEVANT DEFEATS

49(1) Where paragraph 50 applies in relation to a partnership return, each relevant partner is treated for the purposes of this Part of this Act as having incurred the relevant defeat mentioned in paragraph 50(1)(b), (2) or (3)(b) (as the case may be).

49(2) In this paragraph **"relevant partner"** means any person who was a partner in the partnership at any time during the relevant reporting period (but see sub-paragraph (3)).

49(3) The **"relevant partners"** do not include–

(a) the person mentioned in sub-paragraph (1)(b), (2) or (3)(b) (as the case may be) of paragraph 50, or

(b) any other person who would, apart from this paragraph, incur a relevant defeat in connection with the subject matter of the partnership return mentioned in sub-paragraph (1).

49(4) In this paragraph the **"relevant reporting period"** means the period in respect of which the partnership return mentioned in sub-paragraph (1), (2) or (3) of paragraph 50 was required.

PARTNERSHIP RETURNS TO WHICH THIS PARAGRAPH APPLIES

50(1) This paragraph applies in relation to a partnership return if–

(a) that return has been made on the basis that a tax advantage arises to a partner from any arrangements, and

(b) that person has incurred, in relation to that tax advantage and those arrangements, a relevant defeat by virtue of Condition A (final counteraction of tax advantage under general anti-abuse rule).

50(2) Where a person has incurred a relevant defeat by virtue of sub-paragraph (2) of paragraph 13 (Condition B: case involving partnership follower notice) this paragraph applies in relation to the partnership return mentioned in that sub-paragraph.

50(3) This paragraph applies in relation to a partnership return if–

(a) that return has been made on the basis that a tax advantage arises to a partner from any arrangements, and

(b) that person has incurred, in relation to that tax advantage and those arrangements, a relevant defeat by virtue of Condition C (return, claim or election made in reliance on DOTAS arrangements).

50(4) The references in this paragraph to a relevant defeat do not include a relevant defeat incurred by virtue of paragraph 47(2).

PARTNERSHIPS: INFORMATION

51(1) If paragraph 50 applies in relation to a partnership return, the appropriate partner must give HMRC a written notice (a "partnership information notice") in respect of each sub-period in the information period.

51(2) The **"information period"** is the period of 5 years beginning with the day after the day of the relevant defeat mentioned in paragraph 50.

51(3) If, in the case of a partnership, a new information period (relating to another partnership return) begins during an existing information period, those periods are treated for the purposes of this paragraph as a single period (which includes all times that would otherwise fall within either period).

51(4) An information period under this paragraph ends if the partnership ceases.

51(5) A partnership information notice must be given not later than the 30th day after the end of the sub-period to which it relates.

51(6) A partnership information notice must state–

(a) whether or not any relevant partnership return which was, or was required to be, delivered in the sub-period has been made on the basis that a relevant tax advantage arises, and

(b) whether or not there has been a failure to deliver a relevant partnership return in the sub-period.

51(7) In this paragraph–

(a) **"relevant partnership return"** means a partnership return in respect of the partnership's trade, profession or business;

(b) **"relevant tax advantage"** means a tax advantage which particular DOTAS arrangements enable, or might be expected to enable, a person who is or has been a partner in the partnership to obtain.

51(8) If a partnership information notice states that a relevant partnership return has been made on the basis mentioned in sub-paragraph (6)(a) the notice must–

(a) explain (on the assumptions made for the purposes of the return) how the DOTAS arrangements enable the tax advantage concerned to be obtained, and

(b) describe any variation in the amounts required to be stated in the return under section 12AB(1) of TMA 1970 which results from those arrangements.

51(9) HMRC may require the appropriate partner to give HMRC a notice (a "supplementary information notice") setting out further information in relation to a partnership information notice.
In relation to a partnership information notice **"further information"** means information which would have been required to be set out in the notice by virtue of sub-paragraph (6)(a) or (8) had there not been a failure to deliver a relevant partnership return.

51(10) A requirement under sub-paragraph (9) must be made by a written notice and the notice must state the period within which the notice must be complied with.

51(11) If a person fails to comply with a requirement of (or imposed under) this paragraph, HMRC may by written notice extend the information period concerned to the end of the period of 5 years beginning with–

(a) the day by which the partnership information notice or supplementary information notice was required to be given to HMRC or, as the case requires,

(b) the day on which the person gave the defective notice to HMRC,

or, if earlier, the time when the information period would have expired but for the extension.

51(12) For the purposes of this paragraph–

(a) the first sub-period in an information period begins with the first day of the information period and ends with a day specified by HMRC,

(b) the remainder of the information period is divided into further sub-periods each of which begins immediately after the end of the preceding sub-period and is twelve months long or (if that would be shorter) ends at the end of the information period.

51(13) In this paragraph **"the appropriate partner"** means the partner in the partnership who is for the time being nominated by HMRC for the purposes of this paragraph.

Prospective amendments – In para. 51(8)(b) the words ", or under equivalent provision made by regulations under paragraph 10 of Schedule A1 to that Act," inserted after the words "TMA 1970" by F(No. 2)A 2017, s. 61 and Sch. 14, para. 48(2), with effect from a day to be appointed under F(No. 2)A 2017, s. 61(6).

PARTNERSHIPS: SPECIAL PROVISION ABOUT TAXPAYER EMENDATIONS

52(1) Sub-paragraph (2) applies if a partnership return is amended at any time under section 12ABA of TMA 1970 (amendment of partnership return by representative partner etc) on a basis that–

(a) results in an increase or decrease in, or

(b) otherwise affects the calculation of,

any amount stated under subsection (1)(b) of section 12AB of that Act (partnership statement) as a partner's share of any income, loss, consideration, tax or credit for any period.

52(2) For the purposes of paragraph 14 (Condition C: counteraction of DOTAS arrangements), the partner is treated as having at that time amended–

(a) the partner's return under section 8 or 8A of TMA 1970, or

(b) the partner's company tax return,

so as to give effect to the amendments of the partnership return.

52(3) Sub-paragraph (4) applies if a partnership return is amended at any time by HMRC as a result of a disclosure made by the representative partner or that person's successor on a basis that–

(a) results in an increase or decrease in, or

(b) otherwise affects the calculation of,

any amount stated under subsection (1)(b) of section 12AB (partnership statement) as the share of a particular partner (P) of any income, loss, consideration, tax or credit for any period.

52(4) If the conditions in sub-paragraph (5) are met, P is treated for the purposes of paragraph 14 as having at that time amended–

(a) P's return under section 8 or 8A of TMA 1970, or

(b) P's company tax return,

so as to give effect to the amendments of the partnership return.

52(5) The conditions are that the disclosure–

(a) is a full and explicit disclosure of an inaccuracy in the partnership return, and

(b) was made at a time when neither the person making the disclosure nor P had reason to believe that HMRC was about to begin enquiries into the partnership return.

Prospective amendments – In para. 52(1) the words "section 12AB(1)(b) of that Act or under equivalent provision made by regulations under paragraph 10 of Schedule A1 to that Act (partnership statement)" substituted for the words "subsection (1)(b) of section 12AB of that Act (partnership statement)" by F(No. 2)A 2017, s. 61 and Sch. 14, para. 48(3)(a), with effect from a day to be appointed under F(No. 2)A 2017, s. 61(6).

In para. 52(3)(a) the words "(in the case of a section 12AA partnership return) or the nominated partner (in the case of a Schedule A1 partnership return)" inserted after the words "that person's successor" and in the end words to para. 52(3) the words "section 12AB(1)(b) of TMA 1970 or under equivalent provision made by regulations under paragraph 10 of Schedule A1 to that Act (partnership statement)" substituted for the words "subsection (1)(b) of section 12AB of TMA 1970 (partnership statement)" by F(No. 2)A 2017, s. 61 and Sch. 14, para. 48(3)(b), with effect from a day to be appointed under F(No. 2)A 2017, s. 61(6).

SUPPLEMENTARY PROVISION RELATING TO PARTNERSHIPS

53(1) *In paragraphs 49 to 52 and this paragraph–*

"partnership" is to be interpreted in accordance with section 12AA of TMA 1970 (and includes a limited liability partnership);

"the representative partner", in relation to a partnership return, means the person who was required by a notice served under or for the purposes of section 12AA(2) or (3) of TMA 1970 to deliver the return;

"successor", in relation to a person who is the representative partner in the case of a partnership return, has the same meaning as in TMA 1970 (see section 118(1) of that Act).

53(2) For the purposes of this Part of this Act a partnership is treated as the same partnership notwithstanding a change in membership if any person who was a member before the change remains a member after the change.

Prospective amendments – In para. 53(1), in the definition of "the representative partner" the words "section 12AA" inserted after the words "in relation to a" by F(No. 2)A 2017, s. 61 and Sch. 14, para. 48(4)(a), with effect from a day to be appointed under F(No. 2)A 2017, s. 61(6).
In para. 53(1) the definition of "the nominated partner" inserted by F(No. 2)A 2017, s. 61 and Sch. 14, para. 48(4)(b), with effect from a day to be appointed under F(No. 2)A 2017, s. 61(6).

Part 7 – Supplemental

MEANING OF "ADJUSTMENTS"

54(1) In this Schedule **"adjustments"** means any adjustments, whether by way of an assessment, the modification of an assessment or return, amendment or disallowance of a claim, a payment, the entering into of a contract settlement, or otherwise (and references to "making" adjustments accordingly include securing that adjustments are made by entering into a contract settlement).

54(2) **"Adjustments"** also includes a payment in respect of a liability to pay national insurance contributions.

TIME OF "USE" OF DEFEATED ARRANGEMENTS

55(1) With reference to a particular relevant defeat incurred by a person in relation to arrangements, the person is treated as having "used" the arrangements on the dates set out in this paragraph.

55(2) If the person incurs the relevant defeat by virtue of Condition A, the person is treated as having **"used"** the arrangements on the following dates–

(a) the filing date of any return made by the person on the basis that the tax advantage mentioned in paragraph 12(1)(a) arises from the arrangements;

(b) the date on which the person makes any claim or election on that basis;

(c) the date of any relevant failure by the person to comply with an obligation.

55(3) For the purposes of sub-paragraph (2) a failure to comply with an obligation is a **"relevant failure"** if the whole or part of the tax advantage mentioned in paragraph 12(1)(b) arose as a result of, or in connection with, that failure.

55(4) If the person incurs the relevant defeat by virtue of Condition B, the person is treated as having **"used"** the arrangements on the following dates–

(a) the filing date of any return made by the person on the basis that the asserted advantage (see section 204(3) of FA 2014) results from the arrangements,

(b) the date on which any claim is made by the person on that basis,

(c) the date of any failure by the person to comply with a relevant obligation.

In this sub-paragraph **"relevant obligation"** means an obligation which would not have fallen on the person (or might have been expected not to do so), had the denied advantage arisen (see section 208(3) of FA 2014).

55(5) If the person incurs the relevant defeat by virtue of Condition C, the person is treated as having **"used"** the arrangements on the following dates–

(a) the filing date of any return made by the person on the basis mentioned in paragraph 14(2)(a);

(b) the date on which the person makes any claim or election on that basis;

(c) the date of any failure by the person to comply with a relevant obligation (as defined in paragraph 14(4)).

55(6) If the person incurs the relevant defeat by virtue of Condition D, the person is treated as having **"used"** the arrangements on the following dates–

(a) the filing date of any return made by the person on the basis mentioned in paragraph 15(2)(a);

(b) the date on which the person makes any claim on that basis;

(c) the date of any failure by the person to comply with a relevant obligation (as defined in paragraph 15(4)).

55(7) If the person incurs the relevant defeat by virtue of Condition E, the person is treated as having **"used"** the arrangements on the following dates–

(a) the filing date of any return made by S to which the counteraction mentioned in paragraph 16(1)(c) relates;

(b) the date on which S made any claim to which that counteraction relates;

(c) the date of any relevant failure by S to which that counteraction relates.

55(8) In sub-paragraph (7) **"relevant failure"** means a failure to comply with an obligation relating to VAT.

55(8A) If the person incurs the relevant defeat by virtue of Condition F, the person is treated as having **"used"** the arrangements on the following dates–

(a) the filing date of any return made by the person on the basis mentioned in paragraph 16A(2)(a);

(b) the date on which the person makes any claim, declaration or application for approval;

(c) the date of any failure by the person to comply with a relevant obligation (as defined in paragraph 16A(4)).

55(9) In this paragraph **"filing date"**, in relation to a return, means the earlier of–

(a) the day on which the return is delivered, or

(b) the last day of the period within which the return must be delivered.

55(10) References in this paragraph to the date on which a person fails to comply with an obligation are to the date on which the person is first in breach of the obligation.

History – Para. 55(8A) inserted by F(No. 2)A 2017, s. 66 and Sch. 17, para. 55(17) with effect so far as is necessary for enabling the making of regulations under that Schedule on 16 November 2017 (Royal Assent) and on 1 January 2018 for all other purposes.

INHERITANCE TAX

56(1) In the case of inheritance tax, each of the following is treated as a return for the purposes of this Schedule–

(a) an account delivered by a person under section 216 or 217 of IHTA 1984 (including an account delivered in accordance with regulations under section 256 of that Act);

(b) a statement or declaration which amends or is otherwise connected with such an account produced by the person who delivered the account;

(c) information or a document provided by a person in accordance with regulations under section 256 of that Act;

and such a return is treated as made by the person in question.

56(2) In this Schedule (except where the context requires otherwise) **"assessment"**, in relation to inheritance tax, includes a determination.

NATIONAL INSURANCE CONTRIBUTIONS

57 [Not relevant to inheritance tax.]

GENERAL INTERPRETATION

58(1) In this Schedule–

"arrangements" has the meaning given by paragraph 2(6);

"the Commissioners" means the Commissioners for Her Majesty's Revenue and Customs;

"contract settlement" means an agreement in connection with a person's liability to make a payment to the Commissioners under or by virtue of an enactment;

"disclosable indirect tax arrangements" is to be interpreted in accordance with paragraph 9A;

"disclosable Schedule 11A VAT arrangements" is to be interpreted in accordance with paragraph 9;

"disclosable VAT arrangements" is to be interpreted in accordance with paragraph 8A;

"DOTAS arrangements" is to be interpreted in accordance with paragraph 8 (and see also paragraph 57(2));

"follower notice" has the meaning given by paragraph 13(6);

"HMRC" means Her Majesty's Revenue and Customs;

"indirect tax" has the meaning given by paragraph 4(2);

"national insurance contributions" means contributions under Part 1 of the Social Security Contributions and Benefits Act 1992 or Part 1 of the Social Security Contributions and Benefits (Northern Ireland) Act 1992;

"net income" has the meaning given by section 23 of ITA 2007 (see Step 2 of that section);

"partnership follower notice" has the meaning given by paragraph 2(2) of Schedule 31 to FA 2014;

"partnership return" means a return under section 12AA of TMA 1970;

"relevant contributions" means the following contributions under Part 1 of the Social Security Contributions and Benefits Act 1992 or Part 1 of the Social Security Contributions and Benefits (Northern Ireland) Act 1992–

(a) Class 1 contributions;

(b) Class 1A contributions;

(c) Class 1B contributions;

(d) Class 2 contributions which must be paid but in relation to which section 11A of the Act in question (application of certain provisions of the Income Tax Acts in relation to Class 2 contributions under section 11(2) of that Act) does not apply;

"relevant defeat" is to be interpreted in accordance with paragraph 11;

"tax" has the meaning given by paragraph 4(1);

"tax advantage" has the meaning given by paragraph 7;

"warning notice" has the meaning given by paragraph 2.

58(2) In this Schedule an expression used in relation to VAT has the same meaning as in VATA 1994.

58(3) In this Schedule (except where the context requires otherwise) references, however expressed, to a person's affairs in relation to tax include the person's position as regards deductions or repayments of, or of sums representing, tax that the person is required to make by or under an enactment.

58(4) For the purposes of this Schedule a partnership return is regarded as made on the basis that a particular tax advantage arises to a person from particular arrangements if–

(a) it is made on the basis that an increase or reduction in one or more of the amounts mentioned in section 12AB(1) of TMA 1970 (amounts in the partnership statement in a partnership return) results from those arrangements, and

(b) that increase or reduction results in that tax advantage for the person.

Prospective amendments – In para. 58(1) the definition of "partnership return" substituted by F(No. 2)A 2017, s. 61 and Sch. 14, para. 48(5), with effect from a day to be appointed under F(No. 2)A 2017, s. 61(6).

History – In para. 58(1) the definition of "disclosable indirect tax arrangements" inserted by F(No. 2)A 2017, s. 66 and Sch. 17, para. 55(18)(a) with effect so far as is necessary for enabling the making of regulations under that Schedule on 16 November 2017 (Royal Assent) and on 1 January 2018 for all other purposes.

In para. 58(1) the definition of "disclosable Schedule 11A VAT arrangements" inserted by F(No. 2)A 2017, s. 66 and Sch. 17, para. 55(18)(a) with effect so far as is necessary for enabling the making of regulations under that Schedule on 16 November 2017 (Royal Assent) and on 1 January 2018 for all other purposes.

In para. 58(1) the definition of "indirect tax" inserted by F(No. 2)A 2017, s. 66 and Sch. 17, para. 55(18)(b) with effect so far as is necessary for enabling the making of regulations under that Schedule on 16 November 2017 (Royal Assent) and on 1 January 2018 for all other purposes.

In para. 58(1), in the definition of "disclosable VAT arrangements", "8A" substituted for "9" by F(No. 2)A 2017, s. 66 and Sch. 17, para. 55(18)(c) with effect so far as is necessary for enabling the making of regulations under that Schedule on 16 November 2017 (Royal Assent) and on 1 January 2018 for all other purposes.

In para. 58(1), in the definition of "tax", "4(1)" substituted for "4" by F(No. 2)A 2017, s. 66 and Sch. 17, para. 55(18)(d) with effect so far as is necessary for enabling the making of regulations under that Schedule on 16 November 2017 (Royal Assent) and on 1 January 2018 for all other purposes.

CONSEQUENTIAL AMENDMENTS

59 [Not relevant to inheritance tax.]

60 [Inserts FA 2014, s. 212(4)(d).]

61 [Not relevant to inheritance tax.]

62 [Not relevant to inheritance tax.]

COMMENCEMENT

63 Subject to paragraphs 64 and 65, paragraphs 1 to 62 of this Schedule have effect in relation to relevant defeats incurred after the day on which this Act is passed.

64(1) A relevant defeat is to be disregarded for the purposes of this Schedule if it is incurred before 6 April 2017 in relation to arrangements which the person has entered into before the day on which this Act is passed.

64(2) A relevant defeat incurred on or after 6 April 2017 is to be disregarded for the purposes of this Schedule if–

(a) the person entered into the arrangements concerned before the day on which this Act is passed, and

(b) before 6 April 2017–

(i) the person incurring the defeat fully discloses to HMRC the matters to which the relevant counteraction relates, or

(ii) that person gives HMRC notice of a firm intention to make a full disclosure of those matters and makes such a full disclosure within any time limit set by HMRC.

64(3) In sub-paragraph (2) **"the relevant counteraction"** means–

(a) in a case within Condition A, the counteraction mentioned in paragraph 12(1)(c);

(b) in a case within Condition B, the action mentioned in paragraph 13(1);

(c) in a case within Condition C, the counteraction mentioned in paragraph 14(1)(c);

(d) in a case within Condition D, the counteraction mentioned in paragraph 15(1)(d);

(e) in a case within Condition E, the counteraction mentioned in paragraph 16(1)(c).

64(4) In sub-paragraph (3)–

(a) in paragraph (c) **"counteraction"** is to be interpreted in accordance with paragraph 14(5);

(b) in paragraph (d) **"counteraction"** is to be interpreted in accordance with paragraph 15(5);

(c) in paragraph (e) **"counteraction"** is to be interpreted in accordance with paragraph 16(2).

64(5) See paragraph 11(2) for provision about when a relevant defeat is incurred.

65(1) A warning notice given to a person is to be disregarded for the purposes of–

(a) paragraph 18 (naming), and

(b) Part 4 of this Schedule (restriction of reliefs),

if the relevant defeat specified in the notice relates to arrangements which the person has entered into before the day on which this Act is passed.

65(2) Where a person has entered into any arrangements before the day on which this Act is passed–

(a) a relevant defeat incurred by a person in relation to the arrangements, and

(b) any warning notice specifying such a relevant defeat,

is to be disregarded for the purposes of paragraph 30 (penalty).

SCHEDULE 20 – PENALTIES FOR ENABLERS OF OFFSHORE TAX EVASION OR NON-COMPLIANCE

Section 162

Commencement Date – Sch. 20 comes into force on 1 January 2017 (SI 2016/1249, reg. 2).

Part 1 – Liability for Penalty

LIABILITY FOR PENALTY

1(1) A penalty is payable by a person (P) who has enabled another person (Q) to carry out offshore tax evasion or non-compliance, where conditions A and B are met.

1(2) For the purposes of this Schedule–

(a) Q carries out **"offshore tax evasion or non-compliance"** by–

(i) committing a relevant offence, or

(ii) engaging in conduct that makes Q liable (if the applicable conditions are met) to a relevant civil penalty,

where the tax at stake is income tax, capital gains tax or inheritance tax, and

(b) P "has enabled" Q to carry out offshore tax evasion or non-compliance if P has encouraged, assisted or otherwise facilitated conduct by Q that constitutes offshore tax evasion or non-compliance.

1(3) The relevant offences are–

(a) an offence of cheating the public revenue involving offshore activity, or

(b) an offence under section 106A of TMA 1970 (fraudulent evasion of income tax) involving offshore activity,

(c) an offence under section 106B, 106C or 106D of TMA 1970 (offences relating to certain failures to comply with section 7 or 8 by a taxpayer chargeable to income tax or capital gains tax on or by reference to offshore income, assets or liabilities).

1(4) The relevant civil penalties are–

(a) a penalty under paragraph 1 of Schedule 24 to FA 2007 (errors in taxpayer's document) involving an offshore matter or an offshore transfer (within the meaning of that Schedule),

(b) a penalty under paragraph 1 of Schedule 41 to FA 2008 (failure to notify etc) in relation to a failure to comply with section 7(1) of TMA 1970 involving offshore activity,

(c) a penalty under paragraph 6 of Schedule 55 to FA 2009 (failure to make return for 12 months) involving offshore activity,

(d) a penalty under paragraph 1 of Schedule 21 to FA 2015 (penalties in connection with relevant offshore asset moves).

1(5) Condition A is that P knew when P's actions were carried out that they enabled, or were likely to enable, Q to carry out offshore tax evasion or non-compliance.

1(6) Condition B is that–

(a) in the case of offshore tax evasion or non-compliance consisting of the commission of a relevant offence, Q has been convicted of the offence and the conviction is final, or

(b) in the case of offshore tax evasion or non-compliance consisting of conduct that makes Q liable to a relevant penalty–

(i) Q has been found to be liable to such a penalty, assessed and notified, and the penalty is final, or

(ii) a contract has been made between the Commissioners for Her Majesty's Revenue and Customs and Q under which the Commissioners undertake not to assess the penalty or (if it has been assessed) not to take proceedings to recover it.

1(7) For the purposes of sub-paragraph (6)(a)–

(a) **"convicted of the offence"** means convicted of the full offence (and not for example of an attempt), and

(b) a conviction becomes final when the time allowed for bringing an appeal against it expires or, if later, when any appeal against conviction has been determined.

1(8) For the purposes of sub-paragraph (6)(b)(i) a penalty becomes final when the time allowed for any appeal or further appeal relating to it expires or, if later, any appeal or final appeal relating to it is determined.

1(9) It is immaterial for the purposes of condition B that–

(a) any offence of which Q was convicted, or

(b) any penalty for which Q was found to be liable,

relates also to other tax evasion or non-compliance by Q.

1(10) In this Schedule **"other tax evasion or non-compliance by Q"** means conduct by Q that–

(a) constitutes an offence of cheating the public revenue or an offence of fraudulent evasion of tax, or

(b) makes Q liable to a penalty under any provision of the Taxes Acts,

but does not constitute offshore tax evasion or non-compliance.

1(11) Nothing in condition B affects the law of evidence as to the relevance if any of a conviction, assessment of a penalty or contract mentioned in sub-paragraph (6) for the purpose of proving that condition A is met in relation to P.

1(12) In this Schedule **"conduct"** includes a failure to act.

MEANING OF "INVOLVING OFFSHORE ACTIVITY" AND RELATED EXPRESSIONS

2(1) This paragraph has effect for the purposes of this Schedule.

2(2) Conduct involves offshore activity if it involves–

(a) an offshore matter,

(b) an offshore transfer, or

(c) a relevant offshore asset move.

2(3) Conduct involves an offshore matter if it results in a potential loss of revenue that is charged on or by reference to–

(a) income arising from a source in a territory outside the United Kingdom,

(b) assets situated or held in a territory outside the United Kingdom,

(c) activities carried on wholly or mainly in a territory outside the United Kingdom, or

(d) anything having effect as if it were income, assets or activities of the kind described above.

2(4) Where the tax at stake is inheritance tax, assets are treated for the purposes of sub-paragraph (3) as situated or held in a territory outside the United Kingdom if they are so held or situated immediately after the transfer of value by reason of which inheritance tax becomes chargeable.

2(5) Conduct involves an offshore transfer if–

(a) it does not involve an offshore matter,

(b) it is deliberate (whether or not concealed) and results in a potential loss of revenue,

(c) the condition set out in paragraph 4AA of Schedule 24 to FA 2007 is satisfied.

2(6) Conduct involves a relevant offshore asset move if at a time when Q is the beneficial owner of an asset ("the qualifying time")–

(a) the asset ceases to be situated or held in a specified territory and becomes situated or held in a non-specified territory,

(b) the person who holds the asset ceases to be resident in a specified territory and becomes resident in a non-specified territory, or

(c) there is a change in the arrangements for the ownership of the asset,

and Q remains the beneficial owner of the asset, or any part of it, immediately after the qualifying time.

2(7) Paragraphs 4(2) to (4) of Schedule 21 to FA 2015 apply for the purposes of sub-paragraph (6) above as they apply for purposes of paragraph 4 of that Schedule.

2(8) In sub-paragraph (6) above, **"specified territory"** has the same meaning as in paragraph 4(5) of Schedule 21 to FA 2015.

AMOUNT OF PENALTY

3(1) The penalty payable under paragraph 1 is (except in a case mentioned in sub-paragraph (2)) the higher of–

(a) 100% of the potential lost revenue, or

(b) £3,000.

3(2) In a case where P has enabled Q to engage in conduct which makes Q liable to a penalty under paragraph 1 of Schedule 21 to FA 2015, the penalty payable under paragraph 1 is the higher of–

(a) 50% of the potential lost revenue in respect of the original tax non-compliance, and

(b) £3,000.

3(3) In sub-paragraph (2)(a) **"the original tax non-compliance"** means the conduct that incurred the original penalty and **"the potential lost revenue"** (in respect of that non-compliance) is–

(a) the potential lost revenue under Schedule 24 to FA 2007,

(b) the potential lost revenue under Schedule 41 to FA 2008, or

(c) the liability to tax which would have been shown on the return (within the meaning of Schedule 55 to FA 2009),

according to whether the original penalty was incurred under paragraph 1 of Schedule 24, paragraph 1 of Schedule 41 or paragraph 6 of Schedule 55.

POTENTIAL LOST REVENUE: ENABLING Q TO COMMIT RELEVANT OFFENCE

4(1) The potential lost revenue in a case where P is liable to a penalty under paragraph 1 for enabling Q to commit a relevant offence is the same amount as the potential lost revenue applicable for the purposes of the corresponding relevant civil penalty (determined in accordance with the relevant sub-paragraph of paragraph 5).

4(2) Where Q's offending conduct is–

(a) an offence of cheating the public revenue involving offshore activity, or

(b) an offence under section 106A of TMA 1970 involving offshore activity,

the corresponding relevant civil penalty is the penalty which Q is liable for as a result of that offending conduct.

4(3) Where Q's offending conduct is an offence under section 106B, 106C or 106D of TMA 1970, the corresponding relevant civil penalty is–

(a) for an offence under section 106B of TMA 1970, a penalty under paragraph 1 of Schedule 41 to FA 2008,

(b) for an offence under section 106C of TMA 1970, a penalty under paragraph 6 of Schedule 55 to FA 2009, and

(c) for an offence under section 106D of TMA 1970, a penalty under paragraph 1 of Schedule 24 to FA 2007.

4(4) In determining any amount of potential lost revenue for the purposes of this paragraph, the fact Q has been prosecuted for the offending conduct is to be disregarded.

POTENTIAL LOST REVENUE: ENABLING Q TO ENGAGE IN CONDUCT INCURRING RELEVANT CIVIL PENALTY

5(1) The potential lost revenue in a case where P is liable to a penalty under paragraph 1 for enabling Q to engage in conduct that makes Q liable (if the applicable conditions are met) to a relevant civil penalty is to be determined as follows.

5(2) In the case of a penalty under paragraph 1 of Schedule 24 to FA 2007 involving an offshore matter or an offshore transfer, the potential lost revenue is the amount that under that Schedule is the potential lost revenue in respect of Q's conduct.

5(3) In the case of a penalty under paragraph 1 of Schedule 41 to FA 2008 in relation to a failure to comply with section 7(1) of TMA 1970 involving offshore activity, the potential lost revenue is the amount that under that Schedule is the potential lost revenue in respect of Q's conduct.

5(4) In the case of a penalty under paragraph 6 of Schedule 55 to FA 2009 involving offshore activity, the potential lost revenue is the liability to tax which would have been shown in the return in question (within the meaning of that Schedule).

TREATMENT OF POTENTIAL LOST REVENUE ATTRIBUTABLE TO BOTH OFFSHORE TAX EVASION OR NON-COMPLIANCE AND OTHER TAX EVASION OR NON-COMPLIANCE

6(1) This paragraph applies where any amount of potential lost revenue in a case falling within paragraph 4 or 5 is attributable not only to Q's offshore tax evasion or non-compliance but also to any other tax evasion or non-compliance by Q.

6(2) In that case the potential lost revenue in respect of Q's offshore tax evasion or non-compliance is to be taken for the purposes of assessing the penalty to which P is liable as being or (as the case may be) including such share as is just and reasonable of the amount mentioned in sub-paragraph (1).

REDUCTION OF PENALTY FOR DISCLOSURE ETC BY P

7(1) If P (who would otherwise be liable to a penalty under paragraph 1)–

(a) makes a disclosure to HMRC of–

  (i) a matter relating to an inaccuracy in a document, a supply of false information or a failure to disclose an under-assessment,

  (ii) P's enabling of actions by Q that constituted (or might constitute) a relevant offence or that made (or might make) Q liable to a relevant penalty, or

  (iii) any other matter HMRC regard as assisting them in relation to the assessment of P's liability to a penalty under paragraph 1, or

(b) assists HMRC in any investigation leading to Q being charged with a relevant offence or found liable to a relevant penalty,

HMRC must reduce the penalty to one that reflects the quality of the disclosure or assistance.

7(2) But the penalty may not be reduced–

(a) in the case of unprompted disclosure or assistance, below whichever is the higher of–

  (i) 10% of the potential lost revenue, or

  (ii) £1,000, or

(b) in the case of prompted disclosure or assistance, below whichever is the higher of–

  (i) 30% of the potential lost revenue, or

  (ii) £3,000.

8(1) This paragraph applies for the purposes of paragraph 7.

8(2) P discloses a matter by–

(a) telling HMRC about it,

(b) giving HMRC reasonable help in relation to the matter (for example by quantifying an inaccuracy in a document, an inaccuracy attributable to the supply of false information or withholding of information or an under-assessment), and

(c) allowing HMRC access to records for any reasonable purpose connected with resolving the matter (for example for the purpose of ensuring that an inaccuracy in a document, an inaccuracy attributable to the supply of false information or withholding of information or an under-assessment is fully corrected).

8(3) P assists HMRC in relation to an investigation leading to Q being charged with a relevant offence or found liable to a relevant penalty by–

(a) assisting or encouraging Q to disclose all relevant facts to HMRC,

(b) allowing HMRC access to records, or

(c) any other conduct which HMRC considers assisted them in investigating or assessing Q's liability to such a penalty.

8(4) Disclosure or assistance by P–

(a) is **"unprompted"** if made at a time when P has no reason to believe that HMRC have discovered or are about to discover Q's offshore tax evasion or non-compliance (including any inaccuracy in a document, supply of false information or withholding of information, or under-assessment), and

(b) otherwise is **"prompted"**.

8(5) In relation to disclosure or assistance, **"quality"** includes timing, nature and extent.

9(1) If they think it right because of special circumstances, HMRC may reduce a penalty under paragraph 1.

9(2) In sub-paragraph 1 **"special circumstances"** does not include–

(a) ability to pay, or

(b) the fact that a potential loss of revenue from one taxpayer is balanced by a potential overpayment by another.

9(3) In sub-paragraph (1) the reference to reducing a penalty includes a reference to–

(a) staying a penalty, or

(b) agreeing a compromise in relation to proceedings for a penalty.

PROCEDURE FOR ASSESSING PENALTY, ETC

10(1) Where a person is found liable for a penalty under paragraph 1 HMRC must–

(a) assess the penalty,

(b) notify the person, and

(c) state in the notice the period in respect of which the penalty is assessed.

10(2) A penalty must be paid before the end of the period of 30 days beginning with the day on which notification of the penalty is issued.

10(3) An assessment of a penalty–

(a) is to be treated for procedural purposes in the same way as an assessment to tax (except in respect of a matter expressly provided for by this Schedule), and

(b) may be enforced as if it were an assessment to tax.

10(4) A supplementary assessment may be made in respect of a penalty if an earlier assessment operated by reference to an underestimate of the liability to tax that would have been shown in a return.

10(5) Sub-paragraph (6) applies if–

(a) an assessment in respect of a penalty is based on a liability to tax that would have been shown on a return, and

(b) that liability is found by HMRC to have been excessive.

10(6) HMRC may amend the assessment so that it is based upon the correct amount.

10(7) But an amendment under sub-paragraph (6)–

(a) does not affect when the penalty must be paid, and

(b) may be made after the last day on which the assessment in question could have been made under paragraph 11.

11 An assessment of a person as liable to a penalty under paragraph 1 may not take place more than 2 years after the fulfilment of the conditions mentioned in paragraph 1(1) (in relation to that person) first came to the attention of an officer of Revenue and Customs.

APPEALS

12 A person may appeal against–

(a) a decision of HMRC that a penalty under paragraph 1 is payable by that person, or

(b) a decision of HMRC as to the amount of a penalty under paragraph 1 payable by the person.

13(1) An appeal under paragraph 12 is to be treated in the same way as an appeal against an assessment to the tax at stake (including by the application of any provision about bringing the appeal by notice to HMRC, about HMRC review of the decision or about determination of the appeal by the First-tier Tribunal or Upper Tribunal).

13(2) Sub-paragraph (1) does not apply–

(a) so as to require the person bringing the appeal to pay a penalty before an appeal against the assessment of the penalty is determined,

(b) in respect of any other matter expressly provided for by this Schedule.

14(1) On an appeal under paragraph 12(a) that is notified to the tribunal, the tribunal may affirm or cancel HMRC's decision.

14(2) On an appeal under paragraph 12(b) that is notified to the tribunal, the tribunal may–

(a) affirm HMRC's decision, or

(b) substitute for that decision another decision that HMRC had power to make.

14(3) If the tribunal substitutes its own decision for HMRC's, the tribunal may rely on paragraph 7 or 9 (or both)–

(a) to the same extent as HMRC (which may mean applying the same percentage reduction as HMRC to a different starting point),

(b) to a different extent, but only if the tribunal thinks that HMRC's decision in respect of the application of that paragraph was flawed.

14(4) In sub-paragraph (3)(b) **"flawed"** means flawed when considered in the light of the principles applicable in proceedings for judicial review.

14(5) In this paragraph **"tribunal"** means the First-tier Tribunal or Upper Tribunal (as appropriate by virtue of paragraph 13(1).

DOUBLE JEOPARDY

15 A person is not liable to a penalty under paragraph 1 in respect of conduct for which the person–

(a) has been convicted of an offence, or

(b) has been assessed to a penalty under any provision other than paragraph 1.

APPLICATION OF PROVISIONS OF TMA 1970

16 Subject to the provisions of this Part of this Schedule, the following provisions of TMA 1970 apply for the purposes of this Part of this Schedule as they apply for the purposes of the Taxes Acts–

(a) section 108 (responsibility of company officers),

(b) section 114 (want of form), and

(c) section 115 (delivery and service of documents).

History – In para. 16(c) "115" substituted for "114" by correction slip dated September 2017.

INTERPRETATION OF PART 1

17(1) This paragraph applies for the purposes of this Schedule.

17(2) References to an assessment to tax, in relation to inheritance tax, are to a determination.

Part 2 – Application of Schedule 36 to FA 2008: Information Powers

GENERAL APPLICATION OF INFORMATION AND INSPECTION POWERS TO SUSPECTED ENABLERS

18(1) Schedule 36 to FA 2008 (information and inspection powers) applies for the purpose of checking a relevant person's position as regards liability for a penalty under paragraph 1 as it applies for checking a person's tax position, subject to the modifications in paragraphs 19 to 21.

18(2) In this Part of this Schedule **"relevant person"** means a person an officer of Revenue and Customs has reason to suspect has or may have enabled offshore tax evasion or non-compliance by another person so as to be liable to a penalty under paragraph 1.

GENERAL MODIFICATIONS

19 In its application for the purpose mentioned in paragraph 18(1) Schedule 36 to FA 2008 has effect as if–

(a) any provisions which can have no application for that purpose, or are specifically excluded by paragraph 20, were omitted,

(b) references to **"the taxpayer"** were references to the relevant person whose position as regards liability for a penalty under paragraph 1 is to be checked, and references to **"a taxpayer"** were references to a relevant person,

(c) references to a person's **"tax position"** are to the relevant person's position as regards liability for a penalty under paragraph 1,

(d) references to prejudice to the assessment or collection of tax included a reference to prejudice to the investigation of the relevant person's position as regards liability for a penalty under paragraph 1,

(e) references to information relating to the conduct of a pending appeal relating to tax were references to information relating to the conduct of a pending appeal relating to an assessment of liability for a penalty under paragraph 1.

SPECIFIC MODIFICATIONS

20 The following provisions are excluded from the application of Schedule 36 to FA 2008 for the purpose mentioned in paragraph 18(1)–

(a) paragraph 24 (exception for auditors),

(b) paragraph 25 (exception for tax advisers),

(c) paragraphs 26 and 27 (provisions supplementary to paragraphs 24 and 25),

(d) paragraphs 50 and 51 (tax-related penalty).

21 In the application of Schedule 36 to FA 2008 for the purpose mentioned in paragraph 18(1), paragraph 10A (power to inspect business premises of involved third parties) has effect as if the reference in sub-paragraph (1) to the position of any person or class of persons as regards a relevant tax were a reference to the position of a relevant person as regards liability for a penalty under paragraph 1.

Part 3 – Publishing Details of Persons Found Liable to Penalties

NAMING ETC OF PERSONS ASSESSED TO PENALTY OR PENALTIES UNDER PARAGRAPH 1

22(1) The Commissioners for Her Majesty's Revenue and Customs ("the Commissioners") may publish information about a person if–

(a) in consequence of an investigation the person has been found to have incurred one or more penalties under paragraph 1 (and has been assessed or is the subject of a contract settlement), and

(b) the potential lost revenue in relation to the penalty (or the aggregate of the potential lost revenue in relation to each of the penalties) exceeds £25,000.

22(2) The Commissioners may also publish information about a person if the person has been found to have incurred 5 or more penalties under paragraph 1 in any 5 year period.

22(3) The information that may be published is–

(a) the person's name (including any trading name, previous name or pseudonym),

(b) the person's address (or registered office),

(c) the nature of any business carried on by the person,

(d) the amount of the penalty or penalties in question,

(e) the periods or times to which the actions giving rise to the penalty or penalties relate,

(f) any other information that the Commissioners consider it appropriate to publish in order to make clear the person's identity.

22(4) The information may be published in any manner that the Commissioners consider appropriate.

22(5) Before publishing any information the Commissioners must–

(a) inform the person that they are considering doing so, and
(b) afford the person the opportunity to make representations about whether it should be published.

22(6) No information may be published before the day on which the penalty becomes final or, where more than one penalty is involved, the latest day on which any of the penalties becomes final.

22(7) No information may be published for the first time after the end of the period of one year beginning with that day.

22(8) No information may be published if the amount of the penalty–
(a) is reduced under paragraph 7 to–
(i) 10% of the potential lost revenue (in a case of unprompted disclosure or assistance), or
(ii) 30% of potential lost revenue (in a case of prompted disclosure or assistance),
(b) would have been reduced to 10% or 30% of potential lost revenue but for the imposition of the minimum penalty,
(c) is reduced under paragraph 9 to nil or stayed.

22(9) For the purposes of this paragraph a penalty becomes final–
(a) if it has been assessed, when the time for any appeal or further appeal relating to it expires or, if later, any appeal or final appeal relating to it is finally determined, and
(b) if a contract settlement has been made, at the time when the contract is made.

22(10) In this paragraph **"contract settlement"**, in relation to a penalty, means a contract between the Commissioners and the person under which the Commissioners undertake not to assess the penalty or (if it has been assessed) not to take proceedings to recover it.

23(1) The Treasury may by regulations amend paragraph 22(1) to vary the amount for the time being specified in paragraph (b).

23(2) Regulations under this paragraph are to be made by statutory instrument.

23(3) A statutory instrument under this paragraph is subject to annulment in pursuance of a resolution of the House of Commons.

SCHEDULE 21 – PENALTIES RELATING TO OFFSHORE MATTERS AND OFFSHORE TRANSFERS

Section 163

Commencement Date – 1 April 2017 is the day appointed for the coming into force of amendments by Sch. 21 for all purposes except as noted below and the amendments have effect for inheritance tax purposes, in relation to transfers of value made on or after that day (SI 2017/259, reg. 2–3). Excepted commencement dates as follows:

- para. 2(4) comes into force on 8 March 2017 for the purpose of making the regulations required by FA 2007, Sch. 24, para. 9(1C) (penalties for errors);
- para. 10(5) comes into force on 8 March 2017 for the purpose of making the regulations required by FA 2009, Sch. 55, para. 14(2C) (penalty for failure to make returns etc).

AMENDMENTS TO SCHEDULE 24 TO THE FINANCE ACT 2007 (C. 11)

1 Schedule 24 to FA 2007 (penalties for errors) is amended as follows.

2(1) Paragraph 9 (reductions for disclosure) is amended as follows.

2(2) [Substitutes FA 2007, Sch. 24, para. 9(A1) to (A3).]

2(3) [Amends FA 2007, Sch. 24, para. 9(1).]

2(4) [Inserts FA 2007, Sch. 24, para. 9(1A) to (1E).]

2(5) [Inserts FA 2007, Sch. 24, para. 9(4).]

Commencement Date – Para. 2(4) comes into force on 8 March 2017 for the purpose of making the regulations required by FA 2007, Sch. 24, para. 9(1C) (penalties for errors) (SI 2017/259, reg. 3(a)).

3 [Substitutes Table in FA 2007, Sch. 24, para. 10(2).]

4 [Inserts FA 2007, Sch. 24, para. 10A.]

AMENDMENTS TO SCHEDULE 55 TO THE FINANCE ACT 2009 (C.10)

9 Schedule 55 to FA 2009 (penalty for failure to make returns etc) is amended as follows

10(1) Paragraph 14 (reductions for disclosure) is amended as follows.

10(2) [Inserts FA 2009, Sch. 55, para. 14(A1).]

10(3) [Amends FA 2009, Sch. 55, para. 14(1).]

10(4) [Inserts FA 2009, Sch. 55, para. 14(1A) and (1B).]

10(5) [Inserts FA 2009, Sch. 55, para. 14(2A) to (2E).]

10(6) [Inserts FA 2009, Sch. 55, para. 14(5).]

History – Para. 10(5) comes into force on 8 March 2017 for the purpose of making the regulations required by FA 2009, Sch. 55, para. 14(2C) (penalty for failure to make returns etc) (SI 2017/259, reg. 3(c)).

11 [Substitutes Table in FA 2009, Sch. 55, para. 15(2).]

12 [Inserts FA 2009, Sch. 55, para. 15A.]

SCHEDULE 22 – ASSET-BASED PENALTY FOR OFFSHORE INACCURACIES AND FAILURES

Section 165

Commencement Date – Sch. 22 comes into force on 1 April 2017 (except para. 8 which comes into force on 8 March 2017 for the purposes of making regulations) and has effect for inheritance tax purposes, in relation to transfers of value made on or after 1 April 2017 (SI 2017/277, reg. 2).

Part 1 – Liability for Penalty

CIRCUMSTANCES IN WHICH ASSET-BASED PENALTY IS PAYABLE

1(1) An asset-based penalty is payable by a person (P) where–

(a) one or more standard offshore tax penalties have been imposed on P in relation to a tax year (see paragraphs 2 and 3), and

(b) the potential lost revenue threshold is met in relation to that tax year (see paragraph 4).

1(2) But this is subject to paragraph 6 (restriction on imposition of multiple assetbased penalties in relation to the same asset).

MEANING OF STANDARD OFFSHORE TAX PENALTY

2(1) A standard offshore tax penalty is a penalty that falls within sub-paragraph (2), (3), (4) or (4A).

2(2) A penalty falls within this sub-paragraph if–

(a) it is imposed under paragraph 1 of Schedule 24 to FA 2007 (inaccuracy in taxpayer's document),

(b) the inaccuracy for which the penalty is imposed involves an offshore matter or an offshore transfer,

(c) it is imposed for deliberate action (whether concealed or not), and

(d) the tax at stake is (or includes) capital gains tax, inheritance tax or asset-based income tax.

2(3) A penalty falls within this sub-paragraph if–

(a) it is imposed under paragraph 1 of Schedule 41 to FA 2008 (penalty for failure to notify),

(b) the failure for which the penalty is imposed involves an offshore matter or an offshore transfer,

(c) it is imposed for a deliberate failure (whether concealed or not), and

(d) the tax at stake is (or includes) capital gains tax or asset-based income tax.

2(4) A penalty falls within this sub-paragraph if–

(a) it is imposed under paragraph 6 of Schedule 55 to FA 2009 (penalty for failure to make return more than 12 months after filing date),

(b) it is imposed for the withholding of information involving an offshore matter or an offshore transfer,

(c) it is imposed for a deliberate withholding of information (whether concealed or not), and

(d) the tax at stake is (or includes) capital gains tax, inheritance tax or asset-based income tax.

2(4A) A penalty falls within this paragraph if–

(a) it is imposed on a person under paragraph 1 of Schedule 18 to F[(No. 2)]A 2017 (requirement to correct relevant offshore tax non-compliance),

(b) the person was aware at any time during the RTC period that at the end of the 2016–17 tax year P had relevant offshore tax non-compliance to correct, and

(c) the tax at stake is (or includes) capital gains tax, inheritance tax or asset-based income tax.

2(5) In a case where the inaccuracy, failure or withholding of information for which a penalty is imposed involves both an offshore matter or an offshore transfer and a domestic matter, the standard offshore tax penalty is only that part of the penalty that involves the offshore matter or offshore transfer.

2(5A) Sub-paragraph (5) does not apply to a penalty imposed under paragraph 1 of Schedule 18 to F[(No. 2)]A 2017.

2(6) In a case where the tax at stake in relation to a penalty includes a tax other than capital gains tax, inheritance tax or asset-based income tax, the standard offshore tax penalty is only that part of the penalty which relates to capital gains tax, inheritance tax or asset-based income tax.

2(7) **"Asset-based income tax"** means income tax that is charged under any of the provisions mentioned in column 1 of the table in paragraph 13(2).

History – In para. 2(1) the words ", (4) or (4A)" (the comma assumed by Croner-i) substituted for the words "or (4)" by F(No. 2)A 2017, s. 67 and Sch. 18, para. 28(2)(a), with effect from 16 November 2017 (Royal Assent).
Para. 2(4A) inserted by F(No. 2)A 2017, s. 67 and Sch. 18, para. 28(2)(b), with effect from 16 November 2017 (Royal Assent).
Para. 2(5A) inserted by F(No. 2)A 2017, s. 67 and Sch. 18, para. 28(2)(b), with effect from 16 November 2017 (Royal Assent).

TAX YEAR TO WHICH STANDARD OFFSHORE TAX PENALTY RELATES

3(1) Where a standard offshore tax penalty is imposed under paragraph 1 of Schedule 24 to FA 2007, the tax year to which that penalty relates is–

(a) if the tax at stake as a result of the inaccuracy is income tax or capital gains tax, the tax year to which the document containing the inaccuracy relates;

(b) if the tax at stake as a result of the inaccuracy is inheritance tax, the year, beginning on 6 April and ending on the following 5 April, in which the liability to tax first arose.

3(2) Where a standard offshore tax penalty is imposed under paragraph 1 of Schedule 41 to FA 2008 for a failure to comply with an obligation specified in the table in that paragraph, the tax year to which that penalty relates is the tax year to which the obligation relates.

3(3) Where a standard offshore tax penalty is imposed under paragraph 6 of Schedule 55 to FA 2009 for a failure to make a return or deliver a document specified in the table of paragraph 1 of that Schedule, the tax year to which that penalty relates is–

(a) if the tax at stake is income tax or capital gains tax, the tax year to which the return or document relates;

(b) if the tax at stake is inheritance tax, the year, beginning on 6 April and ending on the following 5 April, in which the liability to tax first arose.

3(4) Where a standard offshore penalty is imposed under paragraph 1 of Schedule 18 to F[(No. 2)]A 2017, the tax year to which that penalty relates is–

(a) if the tax at stake in relation to the uncorrected relevant offshore tax non-compliance is income tax or capital gains tax, the tax year or years to which the failure or inaccuracy constituting the relevant offshore tax non-compliance in question relates;

(b) if the tax at stake in relation to the uncorrected relevant offshore tax non-compliance is inheritance tax, the year, beginning on 6 April and ending on the following 5 April, in which the liability to tax first arose.

3(5) In sub-paragraph (4) references to uncorrected relevant offshore tax non-compliance are to the relevant offshore tax non-compliance in respect of which the standard offshore penalty is imposed.

History – Para. 3(4) inserted by F(No. 2)A 2017, s. 67 and Sch. 18, para. 28(3), with effect from 16 November 2017 (Royal Assent).
Para. 3(5) inserted by F(No. 2)A 2017, s. 67 and Sch. 18, para. 28(3), with effect from 16 November 2017 (Royal Assent).

POTENTIAL LOST REVENUE THRESHOLD

4(1) The potential lost revenue threshold is reached where the offshore PLR in relation to a tax year exceeds £25,000.

4(2) The Treasury may by regulations change the figure for the time being specified in sub-paragraph (1).

4(3) Regulations under sub-paragraph (2) are to be made by statutory instrument.

4(4) A statutory instrument containing regulations under sub-paragraph (2) is subject to annulment in pursuance of a resolution of the House of Commons.

4(5) Regulations under sub-paragraph (2)–

(a) may make different provision for different purposes;

(b) may contain supplemental, incidental, consequential, transitional and transitory provision.

OFFSHORE PLR

5(1) The offshore PLR, in relation to a tax year, is the total of–

(a) the potential lost revenue (in the case of a standard offshore tax penalty imposed under Schedule 24 to FA 2007 or Schedule 41 to FA 2008 or Schedule 18 to F[(No. 2)]A 2017), and

(b) the liability to tax (in the case of a standard offshore tax penalty imposed under Schedule 55 to FA 2009), by reference to which all of the standard offshore tax penalties imposed on P in relation to the tax year are assessed.

5(2) Sub-paragraphs (3) to (5) apply where–

(a) a penalty is imposed on P under paragraph 1 of Schedule 24 to FA 2007, paragraph 1 of Schedule 41 to FA 2008 or paragraph 6 of Schedule 55 to FA 2009, and

(b) the potential lost revenue or liability to tax by reference to which the penalty is assessed relates to a standard offshore tax penalty and one or more other penalties.

In this paragraph, such a penalty is referred to as a **"combined penalty"**.

5(3) Only the potential lost revenue or liability to tax relating to the standard offshore tax penalty is to be taken into account in calculating the offshore PLR.

5(4) Where the calculation of the potential lost revenue or liability to tax by reference to which a combined penalty is assessed depends on the order in which income or gains are treated as having been taxed, for the purposes of calculating the offshore PLR–

(a) income and gains relating to domestic matters are to be taken to have been taxed before income and gains relating to offshore matters and offshore transfers;

(b) income and gains relating to taxes that are not capital gains tax, inheritance tax or asset-based income tax are to be taken to have been taxed before income and gains relating to capital gains tax, inheritance tax and asset-based income tax.

5(5) In a case where it cannot be determined–

(a) whether income or gains relate to an offshore matter or offshore transfer or to a domestic matter, or

(b) whether income or gains relate to capital gains tax, asset-based income tax or inheritance tax or not,

for the purposes of calculating the offshore PLR, the potential lost revenue or liability to tax relating to the standard offshore tax penalty is to be taken to be such share of the total potential lost revenue or liability to tax by reference to which the combined penalty was calculated as is just and reasonable.

5(6) Sub-paragraph (7) applies where–

(a) a standard offshore tax penalty or a combined penalty is imposed on P, and

(b) there are two or more taxes at stake, including capital gains tax and asset-based income tax.

5(7) Where the calculation of the potential lost revenue or liability to tax by reference to which the penalty is assessed depends on the order in which income or gains are treated as having been taxed, for the purposes of calculating the offshore PLR, income and gains relating to asset-based income tax are to be taken to have been taxed before income and gains relating to capital gains tax.

History – In para. 5(1)(a) the words "or Schedule 18 to FA 2017" inserted by F(No. 2)A 2017, s. 67 and Sch. 18, para. 28(4), with effect from 16 November 2017 (Royal Assent).

RESTRICTION ON IMPOSITION OF MULTIPLE ASSET-BASED PENALTIES IN RELATION TO THE SAME ASSET

6(1) Sub-paragraphs (2) and (3) apply where–

(a) a standard offshore tax penalty (other than one imposed under paragraph 1 of Schedule 18 to F[(No. 2)]A 2017) has been imposed on P, and

(b) the potential lost revenue threshold is met,

in relation to more than one tax year falling within the same investigation period.

6(2) Only one asset-based penalty is payable by P in the investigation period in relation to any given asset.

6(3) The asset-based penalty is to be charged by reference to the tax year in the investigation period with the highest offshore PLR.

6(4) An **"investigation period"** is–

(a) the period starting with the day on which this Schedule comes into force and ending with the last day of the last tax year before P was notified of an asset-based penalty in respect of an asset, and

(b) subsequent periods beginning with the day after the previous period ended and ending with the last day of the last tax year before P is notified of a subsequent asset-based penalty in respect of the asset,

and different investigation periods may apply in relation to different assets.

History – In para. 6(1)(a) the words "(other than one imposed under paragraph 1 of Schedule 18 to FA 2017)" inserted by F(No. 2)A 2017, s. 67 and Sch. 18, para. 28(5), with effect from 16 November 2017 (Royal Assent).

6A Where–

(a) a penalty has been imposed on a person under paragraph 1 of Schedule 18 to F[(No. 2)]A 2017, and

(b) the potential loss of revenue threshold has been met,

only one asset-based penalty is payable by the person in relation to any given asset.

History – Para. 6A inserted by F(No. 2)A 2017, s. 67 and Sch. 18, para. 28(6), with effect from 16 November 2017 (Royal Assent).

Part 2 – Amount of Penalty

STANDARD AMOUNT OF ASSET-BASED PENALTY

7(1) The standard amount of the asset-based penalty is the lower of–

(a) 10% of the value of the asset, and

(b) offshore PLR × 10.

7(2) See also–

(a) paragraphs 8 and 9, which provide for reductions in the standard amount, and

(b) Part 3, which makes provision about the identification and valuation of the asset.

REDUCTIONS FOR DISCLOSURE AND CO-OPERATION

8(1) HMRC must reduce the standard amount of the asset-based penalty where P does all of the following things–

(a) makes a disclosure of the inaccuracy or failure relating to the standard offshore tax penalty;

(b) provides HMRC with a reasonable valuation of the asset;

(c) provides HMRC with information or access to records that HMRC requires from P for the purposes of valuing the asset.

8(2) A reduction under sub-paragraph (1) must reflect the quality of the disclosure, valuation and information provided (and for these purposes **"quality"** includes timing, nature and extent).

8(3) The Treasury must make regulations setting out the maximum amount of the penalty reduction under sub-paragraph (1).

8(4) The maximum amount may differ according to whether the case involves only unprompted disclosures or involves prompted disclosures.

8(5) A case involves only unprompted disclosures where–

(a) in a case where the asset-based penalty relates to only one standard offshore tax penalty, that standard offshore tax penalty was reduced on the basis of an unprompted disclosure, or

(b) in a case where the asset-based penalty relates to more than one standard offshore tax penalty, all of those standard offshore tax penalties were reduced on the basis of unprompted disclosures.

8(6) A case involves prompted disclosures where any of the standard offshore tax penalties to which the asset-based penalty relates was reduced on the basis of a prompted disclosure.

8(7) Regulations under sub-paragraph (3) are to be made by statutory instrument.

8(8) A statutory instrument containing regulations under sub-paragraph (3) is subject to annulment in pursuance of a resolution of the House of Commons.

8(9) Regulations under sub-paragraph (3)–

(a) may make different provision for different purposes;

(b) may contain supplemental, incidental, consequential, transitional and transitory provision.

Commencement Date – Para. 8 comes into force on 8 March 2017 for the purpose of exercising any of the powers to make the regulations described in para. 8(3) (SI 2017/277, reg. 2(a)).

Cross references – SI 2017/334, reg. 2: maximum reduction of the asset-based penalty under para. 7.

Statutory instruments – SI 2017/334: made under para. 8(3) and (4).

SPECIAL REDUCTION

9(1) If HMRC think it right because of special circumstances, they may reduce the standard amount of the asset-based penalty.

9(2) In sub-paragraph (1) **"special circumstances"** does not include–

(a) ability to pay, or

(b) the fact that a potential loss of revenue from one taxpayer is balanced by a potential over-payment by another.

9(3) In sub-paragraph (1) the reference to reducing a penalty includes a reference to–

(a) staying a penalty, and

(b) agreeing a compromise in relation to proceedings for a penalty.

Part 3 – Identification and Valuation of Assets

INTRODUCTION

10(1) This Part makes provision about the identification and valuation of the asset for the purposes of calculating the amount of the asset-based penalty.

10(2) An asset-based penalty may relate to more than one asset.

10(3) The identification and valuation of the asset is to be determined–

(a) under paragraph 11 where the principal tax at stake is capital gains tax,

(b) under paragraph 12 where the principal tax at stake is inheritance tax, and

(c) under paragraph 13 where the principal tax at stake is asset-based income tax.

See also paragraph 14 (jointly held assets).

10(4) The principal tax at stake–

(a) in a case where the standard offshore tax penalty (or penalties) relates to only one type of tax, is the tax to which that standard offshore tax penalty (or penalties) relates;

(b) in a case where the standard offshore tax penalty (or penalties) relate to more than one type of tax, is the tax which gives rise to the highest offshore PLR value.

10(5) The offshore PLR value, in relation to a type of tax, is the potential lost revenue or liability to tax by reference to which the part of the penalty relating to that type of tax was assessed.

10(6) The rules in paragraph 5(2) to (7) apply for the purposes of calculating the offshore PLR value, in relation to a type of tax, as they apply for the purposes of calculating the offshore PLR.

CAPITAL GAINS TAX

11 [Not relevant to inheritance tax.]

INHERITANCE TAX

12(1) This paragraph applies where the principal tax at stake is inheritance tax.

12(2) The asset is the property the disposition of which gave rise to the transfer of value by reason of which the inheritance tax to which the standard offshore penalty relates became chargeable.

12(3) For the purposes of calculating the amount of the asset-based penalty, the value of the property is to be the value of the property used by HMRC in assessing the liability to inheritance tax.

12(4) Terms used in this paragraph have the same meaning as in IHTA 1984.

ASSET-BASED INCOME TAX

13 [Not relevant to inheritance tax.]

JOINTLY HELD ASSETS

14(1) This paragraph applies where an asset-based penalty is chargeable in relation to an asset that is jointly held by P and another person (A).

14(2) The value of the asset is to be taken to be the value of P's share of the asset.

14(3) In a case where P and A–

(a) are married to, or are civil partners of, each other, and

(b) live together,

the asset is to be taken to be jointly owned by P and A in equal shares, unless it appears to HMRC that this is not the case.

Part 4 – Procedure

ASSESSMENT

15(1) Where a person (P) becomes liable for an asset-based penalty under paragraph 1, HMRC must–

(a) assess the penalty,

(b) notify P, and

(c) state in the notice–

(i) the tax year to which the penalty relates, and

(ii) the investigation period within which that tax year falls (see paragraph 6).

15(2) A penalty under paragraph 1 must be paid before the end of the period of 30 days beginning with the day on which notification of the penalty is issued.

15(3) An assessment–

(a) is to be treated for procedural purposes in the same way as an assessment to tax (except in respect of a matter expressly provided for by this Schedule),

(b) may be enforced as if it were an assessment to tax, and

(c) may be combined with an assessment to tax.

15(4) An assessment of an asset-based penalty under paragraph 1 must be made within the period allowed for making an assessment of the standard offshore tax penalty to which the asset-based penalty relates (and where an asset-based penalty relates to more than one standard offshore tax penalty, the assessment must be made within the latest of those periods).

15(5) In this Part of this Schedule references to an assessment to tax, in relation to inheritance tax, are to a determination.

APPEAL

16(1) P may appeal against a decision of HMRC that a penalty is payable by P.

16(2) P may appeal against a decision of HMRC as to the amount of a penalty payable by P.

17(1) An appeal is to be treated in the same way as an appeal against an assessment to the tax concerned (including by the application of any provision about bringing the appeal by notice to HMRC, about HMRC review of the decision or about determination of the appeal by the First-tier Tribunal or the Upper Tribunal).

17(2) Sub-paragraph (1) does not apply–

(a) so as to require P to pay a penalty before an appeal against the assessment of the penalty is determined, or

(b) in respect of any other matter expressly provided for by this Schedule.

18(1) On an appeal under paragraph 16(1), the tribunal may affirm or cancel HMRC's decision.

18(2) On an appeal under paragraph 16(2), the tribunal may–

(a) affirm HMRC's decision, or

(b) substitute for HMRC's decision another decision that HMRC had power to make.

18(3) If the tribunal substitutes its decision for HMRC's, the tribunal may rely on paragraph 9–

(a) to the same extent as HMRC (which may mean applying the same percentage reduction as HMRC to a different starting point), or

(b) to a different extent, but only if the tribunal thinks that HMRC's decision in respect of the application of paragraph 9 was flawed.

18(4) In sub-paragraph (3), **"flawed"** means flawed when considered in the light of the principles applied in proceedings for judicial review.

18(5) In this paragraph **"tribunal"** means the First-tier Tribunal or the Upper Tribunal (as appropriate by virtue of paragraph 17(1)).

Part 5 – General

INTERPRETATION

19(1) In this Schedule–

"asset" has the same meaning as in TCGA 1992 (but also includes currency in sterling);

"asset-based income tax" has the meaning given in paragraph 2(7);

"HMRC" means Her Majesty's Revenue and Customs;

"investigation period" has the meaning given in paragraph 6(4);

"offshore PLR" has the meaning given in paragraph 5;

"standard amount of the asset-based penalty" has the meaning given in paragraph 7;

"standard offshore tax penalty" has the meaning given in paragraph 2.

19(2) Terms used in relation to a penalty imposed under Schedule 24 to FA 2007, Schedule 41 to FA 2008, Schedule 55 to FA 2009 or Part 1 of Schedule 18 to F[(No. 2)]A 2017 have the same meaning as in the Schedule under which the penalty was imposed.

19(3) References in this Schedule to capital gains tax do not include capital gains tax payable by companies in respect of chargeable gains accruing to them to the extent that those gains are NRCGT gains in respect of which the companies are chargeable to capital gains tax under section 14D or 188D of TCGA 1992 (see section 1(2A)(b) of that Act).

History – In para. 19(2) the words ", Schedule 55 to FA 2009 or Part 1 of Schedule 18 to FA 2017" (comma assumed by Croner-i) substituted for the words "or Schedule 55 to FA 2009" by F(No. 2)A 2017, s. 67 and Sch. 18, para. 28(8), with effect from 16 November 2017 (Royal Assent).

CONSEQUENTIAL AMENDMENTS ETC

20(1) [Not relevant to inheritance tax.]

20(2) [Not relevant to inheritance tax.]

20(3) [Amends FA 2007, Sch. 24, para. 12(2A).]

20(4) [Inserts FA 2009, Sch. 55, para. 17(2)(d).]

20(5) [Inserts FA 2009, Sch. 55, para. 17(2)(d).]

SCHEDULE 23 – SIMPLE ASSESSMENTS

Section 167

9(1) Schedule 56 to FA 2009 (penalty for failure to make payments on time) is amended as follows.

9(2) [Not relevant to inheritance tax.]

9(3) In paragraph 3(1)(a), after "items 1," insert "1A,".

FINANCE ACT 2017

(2017 Chapter 10)

[*27th April 2017*]

ARRANGEMENT OF SECTIONS

PART 1 – DIRECT AND INDIRECT TAXES

PART 3 – FINAL

SCHEDULES

PART 1 – DIRECT AND INDIRECT TAXES

AVOIDANCE

24 Promoters of tax avoidance schemes: threshold conditions etc

24(1) [Substitutes FA 2014, Sch. 34, para. 13A(6)–(12).]

24(2) [Substitutes FA 2014, Sch. 24, para. 13B–13D.]

24(3) [Substitutes FA 2014, Sch. 34A, para. 20–22.]

24(4) [Amends FA 2014, Sch. 34A, para. 23.]

24(5) The amendments made by subsections (1) and (2) have effect for the purposes of determining whether a person meets a threshold condition in a period of three years ending on or after 8 March 2017.

24(6) The amendments made by subsections (3) and (4) have effect for the purposes of determining whether a person meets a section 237A condition in a period of three years ending on or after 8 March 2017.

PART 3 – FINAL

62 Interpretation

62 In this Act the following abbreviations are references to the following Acts.

ALDA 1979	Alcoholic Liquor Duties Act 1979
CAA 2001	Capital Allowances Act 2001
CTA 2009	Corporation Tax Act 2009
CTA 2010	Corporation Tax Act 2010
FA, followed by a year	Finance Act of that year
ICTA	Income and Corporation Taxes Act 1988
IHTA 1984	Inheritance Tax Act 1984
ITA 2007	Income Tax Act 2007
ITEPA 2003	Income Tax (Earnings and Pensions) Act 2003
ITTOIA 2005	Income Tax (Trading and Other Income) Act 2005
TCGA 1992	Taxation of Chargeable Gains Act 1992
TMA 1970	Taxes Management Act 1970
TPDA 1979	Tobacco Products Duty Act 1979
VATA 1994	Value Added Tax Act 1994
VERA 1994	Vehicle Excise and Registration Act 1994

63 Short title

63 This Act may be cited as the Finance Act 2017.

SCHEDULES

SCHEDULE 11 – SOFT DRINKS INDUSTRY LEVY: SUPPLEMENTARY AMENDMENTS

Section 56

HMRC POWERS TO OBTAIN INFORMATION ETC.

1(1) Schedule 36 to FA 2008 (powers to obtain information etc.) is amended as follows.

1(2) In paragraph 10 (power to inspect business premises etc.), at the end insert–

"**10(5)** In sub-paragraph (1), the reference to a person's tax position does not include a reference to a person's position as regards soft drinks industry levy."

1(3) In paragraph 63(1) (meaning of "tax"), after paragraph (i) insert–

"(ia) soft drinks industry levy,".

PENALTIES: FAILURE TO COMPLY WITH REQUIREMENTS RELATING TO RETURNS

4(1) Schedule 55 to FA 2009 (penalty for failure to make returns etc) is amended in accordance with this paragraph.

4(2) In paragraph 1(4), in the definition of "penalty date", for "13" substitute "13A".

4(3) [Not relevant to inheritance tax.]

4(4) In subsections (2) and (4) of section 106 of FA 2009 (penalties for failure to make returns: commencement) references to Schedule 55 to that Act have effect as references to that Schedule as amended by this paragraph.

FINANCE (NO. 2) ACT 2017

(2017 Chapter 32)

[16th November 2017]

ARRANGEMENT OF SECTIONS

PART 1 – DIRECT TAXES

DOMICILE, OVERSEAS PROPERTY ETC

30 Deemed domicile: inheritance tax

30(1) [Amends IHTA 1984, s. 267(1).]

30(2) [Omits IHTA 1984, s. 267(3).]

30(3) [Amends IHTA 1984, s. 267(4).]

30(4) In section 48 of that Act (settlements: excluded property)–

(a) [amends IHTA 1984, s. 48(3);]

(b) [amends IHTA 1984, s. 48(3A);]

(c) [inserts IHTA 1984, s. 48(3E).]

30(5) [amends IHTA 1984, s. 64(1B).]

30(6) [Inserts IHTA 1984, s. 65(7B).]

30(7) In section 82 of that Act (excluded property)–

(a) [substitutes IHTA 1984, s. 82(1);]

(b) [amends IHTA 1984, s. 82(2);]

(c) [amends IHTA 1984, s. 82(3);]

(d) [inserts IHTA 1984, s. 82(4).]

30(8) [Amends IHTA 1984, s. 272.]

30(9) The amendments made by this section have effect in relation to times after 5 April 2017, subject to subsections (10) to (12).

30(10) The amendment to section 267(1) of IHTA 1984 made by subsection (1)(c) does not have effect in relation to a person if–

(a) the person is not resident in the United Kingdom for the relevant tax year, and

(b) there is no tax year beginning after 5 April 2017 and preceding the relevant tax year in which the person was resident in the United Kingdom.

In this subsection **"relevant tax year"** is to be construed in accordance with section 267(1) of IHTA 1984 as amended by subsection (1).

30(11) The amendment to section 267(1) of IHTA 1984 made by subsection (1)(c) also does not have effect in determining–

(a) whether settled property which became comprised in the settlement on or before that date is excluded property for the purposes of IHTA 1984;

(b) the settlor's domicile for the purposes of section 65(8) of that Act in relation to settled property which became comprised in the settlement on or before that date;

(c) whether, for the purpose of section 65(8) of that Act, the condition in section 82(3) of that Act is satisfied in relation to such settled property.

30(12) Despite subsection (2), section 267(1) of IHTA 1984, as originally enacted, shall continue to be disregarded in determining–

(a) whether settled property which became comprised in the settlement on or before 9 December 1974 is excluded property for the purposes of IHTA 1984;

(b) the settlor's domicile for the purposes of section 65(8) of that Act in relation to settled property which became comprised in the settlement on or before that date;

(c) whether, for the purpose of section 65(8) of that Act, the condition in section 82(3) of that Act is satisfied in relation to such settled property.

30(13) Subsections (14) and (15) apply if an amount of inheritance tax–

(a) would not be charged but for the amendments made by this section, or

(b) is, because of those amendments, greater than it would otherwise have been.

30(14) Section 233 of IHTA 1984 (interest on unpaid inheritance tax) applies in relation to the amount of inheritance tax as if the reference, in the closing words of subsection (1) of that section, to the end of the period mentioned in paragraph (a), (aa), (b) or (c) of that subsection were a reference to–

(a) the end of that period, or

(b) if later, the end of the month immediately following the month in which this Act is passed.

30(15) Subsection (1) of section 234 of IHTA 1984 (cases where inheritance tax payable by instalments carries interest only from instalment dates) applies in relation to the amount of inheritance tax as if the reference, in the closing words of that subsection, to the date at which an instalment is payable were a reference to–

(a) the date at which the instalment is payable, or

(b) if later, the end of the month immediately following the month in which this Act is passed.

30(16) Subsection (17) applies if–

(a) a person is liable as mentioned in section 216(1)(c) of IHTA 1984 (trustee liable on 10-year anniversary, and other trust cases) for an amount of inheritance tax charged on an occasion, and

(b) but for the amendments made by this section–

(i) no inheritance tax would be charged on that occasion, or

(ii) a lesser amount of inheritance tax would be charged on that occasion.

30(17) Section 216(6)(ad) of IHTA 1984 (delivery date for accounts required by section 216(1)(c)) applies in relation to the account to be delivered in connection with the occasion as if the reference to the expiration of the period of 6 months from the end of the month in which the occasion occurs were a reference to–

(a) the expiration of that period, or

(b) if later, the end of the month immediately following the month in which this Act is passed.

33 Inheritance tax on overseas property representing UK residential property

33 Schedule 10 makes provision about the extent to which overseas property is excluded property for the purposes of inheritance tax, in cases where the value of the overseas property is attributable to residential property in the United Kingdom.

PART 4 – ADMINISTRATION, AVOIDANCE AND ENFORCEMENT

REPORTING AND RECORD-KEEPING

61 Digital reporting and record-keeping for income tax etc: further amendments

61(1) Schedule 14 contains provision amending TMA 1970 and other Acts.

61(2) The Commissioners for Her Majesty's Revenue and Customs may by regulations amend or modify any provision of the Taxes Acts in consequence of the provision made by section 60 or Schedule 14.

61(3) Regulations under subsection (2) may make transitional, transitory or saving provision.

61(4) Regulations under subsection (2) must be made by statutory instrument.

61(5) A statutory instrument containing regulations under subsection (2) may not be made unless a draft of the instrument has been laid before, and approved by a resolution of, the House of Commons.

61(6) Subsections (1) to (5) and Schedule 14 come into force on such day as the Treasury may by regulations made by statutory instrument appoint.

61(7) Regulations under subsection (6) may appoint different days for different purposes.

ENQUIRIES

63 Partial closure notices

63 Schedule 15 makes provision for partial closure notices in respect of enquiries under sections 9A, 12ZM and 12AC of TMA 1970 and Schedule 18 to FA 1998.

AVOIDANCE ETC

64 Errors in taxpayers' documents

64(1) Schedule 24 to FA 2007 (penalties for errors) is amended as set out in subsections (2) and (3).

64(2) [Inserts FA 2007, Sch. 24, para. 3A and 3B.]

64(3) [Inserts FA 2007, Sch. 24, para. 18(6).]

64(4) [Omits FA 2014, s. 276.]

64(5) The amendments made by this section have effect in relation to any document of a kind listed in the Table in paragraph 1 of Schedule 24 to FA 2007 which–

(a) is given to HMRC on or after the day on which this Act is passed, and

(b) relates to a tax period that–

(i) begins on or after 6 April 2017, and

(ii) ends on or after the day on which this Act is passed.

64(6) In subsection (5) **"tax period"**, and the reference to giving a document to HMRC, have the same meaning as in Schedule 24 to FA 2007 (see paragraph 28 of that Schedule).

65 Penalties for enablers of defeated tax avoidance

65 Schedule 16 makes provision for penalties for persons who enable tax avoidance which is defeated.

66 Disclosure of tax avoidance schemes: VAT and other indirect taxes

66(1) Schedule 17 contains provision about the disclosure of tax avoidance schemes involving VAT or other indirect taxes.

66(2) In consequence of the provision made by Schedule 17, section 58A of, and Schedule 11A to, VATA 1994 (disclosure of VAT avoidance schemes) cease to have effect to require a person to disclose any scheme which–

(a) is first entered into by that person on or after 1 January 2018,

(b) constitutes notifiable arrangements under Schedule 17,

(c) implements proposals which are notifiable proposals under Schedule 17.

66(3) No scheme or proposed scheme may be notified to the Commissioners under paragraph 9 of Schedule 11A to VATA 1994 (voluntary notification of schemes) on or after 1 January 2018.

66(4) This section and Schedule 17 come into force–

(a) so far as is necessary for enabling the making of regulations under that Schedule, on the passing of this Act, and

(b) for all other purposes, on 1 January 2018.

67 Requirement to correct certain offshore tax non-compliance

67 Schedule 18 makes provision for and in connection with requiring persons to correct any offshore tax non-compliance subsisting on 6 April 2017.

68 Penalty for transactions connected with VAT fraud etc

68(6) [Inserts FA 2007, Sch. 24, para. 21ZA.]

INFORMATION

69 Data-gathering from money service businesses

69(1) [Inserts FA 2011, Sch. 23, para. 13D.]

69(2) This section applies in relation to relevant data with a bearing on any period (whether before, on or after the day on which this Act is passed).

PART 5 – FINAL

71 Interpretation

71 In this Act the following abbreviations are references to the following Acts.

CAA 2001	Capital Allowances Act 2001
CEMA 1979	Customs and Excise Management Act 1979
CTA 2009	Corporation Tax Act 2009
CTA 2010	Corporation Tax Act 2010
CT(NI)A 2015	Corporation Tax (Northern Ireland) Act 2015
FA, followed by a year	Finance Act of that year
F(No. 2)A, followed by a year	Finance (No. 2) Act of that year
F(No. 3)A, followed by a year	Finance (No. 3) Act of that year
ICTA	Income and Corporation Taxes Act 1988
IHTA 1984	Inheritance Tax Act 1984
ITA 2007	Income Tax Act 2007
ITEPA 2003	Income Tax (Earnings and Pensions) Act 2003
ITTOIA 2005	Income Tax (Trading and Other Income) Act 2005
OTA 1975	Oil Taxation Act 1975
TCGA 1992	Taxation of Chargeable Gains Act 1992
TIOPA 2010	Taxation (International and Other Provisions) Act 2010
TMA 1970	Taxes Management Act 1970
TPDA 1979	Tobacco Products Duty Act 1979
VATA 1994	Value Added Tax Act 1994

72 Short title

72 This Act may be cited as the Finance (No. 2) Act 2017.

SCHEDULES

SCHEDULE 10 – INHERITANCE TAX ON OVERSEAS PROPERTY REPRESENTING UK RESIDENTIAL PROPERTY

Section 33

NON-EXCLUDED OVERSEAS PROPERTY

1 [Inserts IHTA 1984, Sch. A1.]

CONSEQUENTIAL AND SUPPLEMENTARY AMENDMENTS

2 IHTA 1984 is amended as follows.

3 [Inserts IHTA 1984, s. 6(5).]

4 In section 48 (excluded property)–

(a) [amends IHTA 1984, s. 48(3) and (3A);]

(b) [amends IHTA 1984, s. 48(4).]

5 [Inserts IHTA 1984, s. 65(7C) and (7D).]

6 [Inserts IHTA 1984, s. 157(3A).]

7 [Inserts IHTA 1984, s. 237(2A).]

8 [Amends IHTA 1984, s. 272.]

COMMENCEMENT

9(1) The amendments made by this Schedule have effect in relation to times on or after 6 April 2017.

9(2) But for the purposes of paragraph 5(1) of Schedule A1 to IHTA 1984 as inserted by this Schedule–

(a) paragraph (a) of that paragraph does not apply in relation to a disposal of property occurring before 6 April 2017, and

(b) paragraph (b) of that paragraph does not apply in relation to a payment of money or money's worth occurring before 6 April 2017.

TRANSITIONAL PROVISION

10(1) Sub-paragraphs (2) and (3) apply if an amount of inheritance tax–

(a) would not be charged but for the amendments made by this Schedule, or

(b) is, because of those amendments, greater than it would otherwise have been.

10(2) Section 233 of IHTA 1984 (interest on unpaid inheritance tax) applies in relation to the amount of inheritance tax as if the reference, in the closing words of subsection (1) of that section, to the end of the period mentioned in paragraph (a), (aa), (b) or (c) of that subsection were a reference to–

(a) the end of that period, or

(b) if later, the end of the month immediately following the month in which this Act is passed.

10(3) Subsection (1) of section 234 of IHTA 1984 (cases where inheritance tax payable by instalments carries interest only from instalment dates) applies in relation to the amount of inheritance tax as if the reference, in the closing words of that subsection, to the date at which an instalment is payable were a reference to–

(a) the date at which the instalment is payable, or

(b) if later, the end of the month immediately following the month in which this Act is passed.

11(1) Sub-paragraph (2) applies if–

(a) a person is liable as mentioned in section 216(1)(c) of IHTA 1984 (trustee liable on 10-year anniversary, and other trust cases) for an amount of inheritance tax charged on an occasion, and

(b) but for the amendments made by this Schedule–

(i) no inheritance tax would be charged on that occasion, or

(ii) a lesser amount of inheritance tax would be charged on that occasion.

11(2) Section 216(6)(ad) of IHTA 1984 (delivery date for accounts required by section 216(1)(c)) applies in relation to the account to be delivered in connection with the occasion as if the reference to the expiration of the period of 6 months from the end of the month in which the occasion occurs were a reference to–

(a) the expiration of that period, or

(b) if later, the end of the month immediately following the month in which this Act is passed.

SCHEDULE 14 – DIGITAL REPORTING AND RECORD-KEEPING FOR INCOME TAX ETC: FURTHER AMENDMENTS

Section 61

Part 2 – Amendments of Other Acts

FA 2008

38(1) Schedule 36 to FA 2008 (information and inspection powers) is amended as follows.

38(2) In paragraph 21(1) (taxpayer notices) after "12AA of" insert ", or regulations under paragraph 10 of Schedule A1 to,".

38(3) In paragraph 37(2)(a) (partnerships) after "section 12AA of" insert ", or regulations under paragraph 10 of Schedule A1 to,".

FA 2014

43 FA 2014 is amended as follows.

44 In section 253(6)(c) (definition of "tax return") after "section 12AA of" insert ", or regulations under paragraph 10 of Schedule A1 to,".

45(1) Schedule 31 (follower notices and partnerships) is amended as follows.

45(2) In paragraph 2 (interpretation)–

(a) in sub-paragraph (3)–

(i) the words from "in pursuance" to the end become paragraph (a);

(ii) at the end of that paragraph insert "(a "section 12AA partnership return"), or";

(iii) after that paragraph insert–

"(b) required by regulations under paragraph 10 of Schedule A1 to TMA 1970 (a "Schedule A1 partnership return").";

(b) in sub-paragraph (4) after "in relation to a" insert "section 12AA";

(c) after sub-paragraph (4) insert–

"2(4A) **"The nominated partner"**, in relation to a Schedule A1 partnership return, has the meaning given by paragraph 5 of Schedule A1 to TMA 1970."

45(3) In paragraph 3 (giving of follower notices in relation to partnership returns)–

(a) in sub-paragraph (1), after "in relation to a" insert "section 12AA";

(b) after sub-paragraph (1) insert–

"3(1A) For the purposes of section 204 a Schedule A1 partnership return, or an appeal in respect of the return, is to be regarded as made by the person who is for the time being the nominated partner (if that would not otherwise be the case).";

(c) in sub-paragraph (2), at the end insert ", or the nominated partner (as the case may be).";

(d) in sub-paragraph (4)–

(i) in paragraph (a), after "or a successor of that partner," insert "or as the nominated partner of a partnership,";

(ii) in paragraph (b) after "successors of that partner" insert "or to a nominated partner".

45(4) In paragraph 5 (calculation of penalty etc) in sub-paragraph (10)–

(a) the words from "the representative partner" to the end become paragraph (a);

(b) at the end of that paragraph insert "(in relation to a section 12AA partnership return), or";

(c) after that paragraph insert–

"(b) the nominated partner (in relation to a Schedule A1 partnership return)."

46(1) Schedule 32 (accelerated payments and partnerships) is amended as follows.

46(2) In paragraph 1 (interpretation)–

(a) in sub-paragraph (2)–

(i) the words from "in pursuance" to the end become paragraph (a);

(ii) at the end of that paragraph insert "(a "section 12AA partnership return"), or";

(iii) after that paragraph insert–

"(b) required by regulations under paragraph 10 of Schedule A1 to TMA 1970 (a "Schedule A1 partnership return").";

(b) in sub-paragraph (3) after "in relation to a" insert "section 12AA";

(c) after sub-paragraph (3) insert–

"1(3A) **"The nominated partner"**, in relation to a Schedule A1 partnership return, has the meaning given by paragraph 5 of Schedule A1 to TMA 1970."

46(3) In paragraph 2(2) (restriction on circumstances when accelerated payment notices can be given) after "a successor of that partner" insert "(in relation to a section 12AA partnership return), or to the nominated partner of the partnership (in relation to a Schedule A1 partnership return)".

46(4) In paragraph 3(5)(a) (circumstances in which partner payment notices can be given) after "or a successor of that partner" insert "(in relation to a section 12AA partnership return), or the nominated partner (in relation to a Schedule A1 partnership return)".

FA 2016

47 FA 2016 is amended as follows.

48(1) Schedule 18 (serial tax avoidance) is amended as follows.

48(2) In paragraph 51(8)(b) (partnerships: information) after "TMA 1970" insert ", or under equivalent provision made by regulations under paragraph 10 of Schedule A1 to that Act,".

48(3) In paragraph 52 (partnerships: special provision about taxpayer emendations)–

IHT Statutes

(a) in sub-paragraph (1) for "subsection (1)(b) of section 12AB of that Act (partnership statement)" substitute "section 12AB(1)(b) of that Act or under equivalent provision made by regulations under paragraph 10 of Schedule A1 to that Act (partnership statement)";

(b) in sub-paragraph (3)–

(i) in the words before paragraph (a), after "that person's successor" insert "(in the case of a section 12AA partnership return) or the nominated partner (in the case of a Schedule A1 partnership return)";

(ii) for "subsection (1)(b) of section 12AB of TMA 1970 (partnership statement)" substitute "section 12AB(1)(b) of TMA 1970 or under equivalent provision made by regulations under paragraph 10 of Schedule A1 to that Act (partnership statement)".

48(4) In paragraph 53(1) (supplementary provision relating to partnerships)–

(a) in the definition of "the representative partner" after "in relation to a" insert "section 12AA";

(b) after the definition of "successor" insert–

""**the nominated partner**", in relation to a Schedule A1 partnership return, has the meaning given by paragraph 5 of Schedule A1 to TMA 1970."

48(5) In paragraph 58(1) (general interpretation), for the definition of "partnership return" substitute–

""**partnership return**" means a return–

(a) under section 12AA of TMA 1970 (a "section 12AA partnership return"), or

(b) required by regulations made under paragraph 10 of Schedule A1 to TMA 1970 (a "Schedule A1 partnership return");".

SCHEDULE 15 – PARTIAL CLOSURE NOTICES

Section 63

FA 2008

36 [Amends FA 2008, Sch. 36, para. 21(4) and 21ZA(3).]

COMMENCEMENT

44 The amendments made by this Schedule have effect in relation to an enquiry under section 9A, 12ZM or 12AC of TMA 1970 or Schedule 18 to FA 1998 where–

(a) notice of the enquiry is given on or after the day on which this Act is passed, or

(b) the enquiry is in progress immediately before that day.

SCHEDULE 16 – PENALTIES FOR ENABLERS OF DEFEATED TAX AVOIDANCE

Section 65

Part 1 – Liability to Penalty

1 Where–

(a) a person ("T") has entered into abusive tax arrangements, and

(b) T incurs a defeat in respect of the arrangements,

a penalty is payable by each person who enabled the arrangements.

2(1) Parts 2 to 4 of this Schedule define–

"**abusive tax arrangements**";

a "**defeat in respect of the arrangements**";

a "**person who enabled the arrangements**".

2(2) The other Parts of this Schedule make provision supplementing paragraph 1 as follows–

(a) *Part 5 makes provision* about the amount of a penalty;

(b) Parts 6 to 8 provide for the assessment of penalties, referrals to the GAAR Advisory Panel and appeals against assessments;

(c) Part 9 applies information and inspection powers, and makes provision about declarations relating to legally privileged communications;

(d) Part 10 confers power to publish details of persons who have incurred penalties;
(e) Parts 11 and 12 contain miscellaneous and general provisions.

Part 2 – "Abusive" and "Tax Arrangements": Meaning

3(1) Arrangements are **"tax arrangements"** for the purposes of this Schedule if, having regard to all the circumstances, it would be reasonable to conclude that the obtaining of a tax advantage was the main purpose, or one of the main purposes, of the arrangements.

3(2) Tax arrangements are **"abusive"** for the purposes of this Schedule if they are arrangements the entering into or carrying out of which cannot reasonably be regarded as a reasonable course of action in relation to the relevant tax provisions, having regard to all the circumstances.

3(3) The circumstances to which regard must be had under sub-paragraph (2) include–

(a) whether the substantive results, or the intended substantive results, of the arrangements are consistent with any principles on which the relevant tax provisions are based (whether express or implied) and the policy objectives of those provisions,
(b) whether the means of achieving those results involves one or more contrived or abnormal steps, and
(c) whether the arrangements are intended to exploit any shortcomings in those provisions.

3(4) Where the tax arrangements form part of any other arrangements regard must also be had to those other arrangements.

3(5) Each of the following is an example of something which might indicate that tax arrangements are abusive–

(a) the arrangements result in an amount of income, profits or gains for tax purposes that is significantly less than the amount for economic purposes;
(b) the arrangements result in deductions or losses of an amount for tax purposes that is significantly greater than the amount for economic purposes;
(c) the arrangements result in a claim for the repayment or crediting of tax (including foreign tax) that has not been, and is unlikely to be, paid;

but a result mentioned in paragraph (a), (b) or (c) is to be taken to be such an example only if it is reasonable to assume that such a result was not the anticipated result when the relevant tax provisions were enacted.

3(6) The fact that tax arrangements accord with established practice, and HMRC had, at the time the arrangements were entered into, indicated their acceptance of that practice, is an example of something which might indicate that the arrangements are not abusive.

3(7) The examples given in sub-paragraphs (5) and (6) are not exhaustive.

3(8) In sub-paragraph (5) the reference to income includes earnings, within the meaning of Part 1 of the Social Security Contributions and Benefits Act 1992 or Part 1 of the Social Security Contributions and Benefits (Northern Ireland) Act 1992.

Part 3 – "Defeat" in Respect of Abusive Tax Arrangements

"DEFEAT" IN RESPECT OF ABUSIVE TAX ARRANGEMENTS

4 T (within the meaning of paragraph 1) incurs a **"defeat"** in respect of abusive tax arrangements entered into by T ("the arrangements concerned") if–

(a) Condition A (in paragraph 5) is met, or
(b) Condition B (in paragraph 6) is met.

CONDITION A

5(1) Condition A is that–

(a) T, or a person on behalf of T, has given HMRC a document of a kind listed in the Table in paragraph 1 of Schedule 24 to FA 2007 (returns etc),
(b) the document was submitted on the basis that a tax advantage ("the relevant tax advantage") arose from the arrangements concerned,
(c) the relevant tax advantage has been counteracted, and
(d) the counteraction is final.

5(2) For the purposes of this paragraph the relevant tax advantage has been **"counteracted"** if adjustments have been made in respect of T's tax position on the basis that the whole or part of the relevant tax advantage does not arise.

5(3) For the purposes of this paragraph a counteraction is **"final"** when the adjustments in question, and any amounts arising from the adjustments, can no longer be varied, on appeal or otherwise.

5(4) In this paragraph **"adjustments"** means any adjustments, whether by way of an assessment, the modification of an assessment or return, the amendment or disallowance of a claim, a payment, the entering into of a contract settlement or otherwise.

Accordingly, references to "making" adjustments include securing that adjustments are made by entering into a contract settlement.

5(5) Any reference in this paragraph to giving HMRC a document includes–

(a) communicating information to HMRC in any form and by any method;

(b) making a statement or declaration in a document.

5(6) Any reference in this paragraph to a document of a kind listed in the Table in paragraph 1 of Schedule 24 to FA 2007 includes–

(a) a document amending a document of a kind so listed, and

(b) a document which–

(i) relates to national insurance contributions, and

(ii) is a document in relation to which that Schedule applies.

CONDITION B

6(1) Condition B is that (in a case not falling within Condition A)–

(a) HMRC have made an assessment in relation to tax,

(b) the assessment counteracts a tax advantage that it is reasonable to assume T expected to obtain from the arrangements concerned ("the expected tax advantage"), and

(c) the counteraction is final.

6(2) For the purposes of this paragraph an assessment **"counteracts"** the expected tax advantage if the assessment is on a basis which prevents T from obtaining (or obtaining the whole of) the expected tax advantage.

6(3) For the purposes of this paragraph a counteraction is **"final"**–

(a) when a relevant contract settlement is made, or

(b) if no contract settlement has been made, when the assessment in question and any amounts arising from the assessment can no longer be varied, on appeal or otherwise.

6(4) In sub-paragraph (3) a **"relevant contract settlement"** means a contract settlement on a basis which prevents T from obtaining (or obtaining the whole of) the expected tax advantage.

Part 4 – Persons Who "Enabled" the Arrangements

PERSONS WHO "ENABLED" THE ARRANGEMENTS

7(1) A person is a person who **"enabled"** the arrangements mentioned in paragraph 1 if that person is–

(a) a designer of the arrangements (see paragraph 8),

(b) a manager of the arrangements (see paragraph 9),

(c) a person who marketed the arrangements to T (see paragraph 10),

(d) an enabling participant in the arrangements (see paragraph 11), or

(e) a financial enabler in relation to the arrangements (see paragraph 12).

7(2) This paragraph is subject to paragraph 13 (excluded persons).

DESIGNERS OF ARRANGEMENTS

8(1) For the purposes of paragraph 7 a person is a **"designer"** of the arrangements if that person was, in *the course of a business carried* on by that person, to any extent responsible for the design of–

(a) the arrangements, or

(b) a proposal which was implemented by the arrangements;

but this is subject to sub-paragraph (2).

8(2) Where a person would (in the absence of this sub-paragraph) fall within sub-paragraph (1) because of having provided advice which was used in the design of the arrangements or of a proposal, that person does not because of that advice fall within that sub-paragraph unless–

(a) the advice is relevant advice, and

(b) the knowledge condition is met.

8(3) Advice is **"relevant advice"** if–

(a) the advice or any part of it suggests arrangements or an alteration of proposed arrangements, and

(b) it is reasonable to assume that the suggestion was made with a view to arrangements being designed in such a way that a tax advantage (or a greater tax advantage) might be expected to arise from them.

8(4) The knowledge condition is that, when the advice was provided, the person providing it knew or could reasonably be expected to know–

(a) that the advice would be used in the design of abusive tax arrangements or of a proposal for such arrangements, or

(b) that it was likely that the advice would be so used.

8(5) For the purposes of sub-paragraph (3), advice is not to be taken to "suggest" anything–

(a) which is put forward by the advice for consideration, but

(b) which the advice can reasonably be read as recommending against.

8(6) In sub-paragraph (3)–

(a) the reference in paragraph (a) to arrangements or an alteration of proposed arrangements includes a proposal for arrangements or an alteration of a proposal for arrangements, and

(b) the reference in paragraph (b) to arrangements includes arrangements proposed by a proposal.

8(7) For the purposes of this paragraph–

(a) references to advice include an opinion;

(b) advice is "used" in a design if the advice is taken account of in that design.

MANAGERS OF ARRANGEMENTS

9(1) For the purposes of paragraph 7 a person is a **"manager"** of the arrangements if that person–

(a) was, in the course of a business carried on by that person, to any extent responsible for the organisation or management of the arrangements, and

(b) when carrying out any functions in relation to the organisation or management of the arrangements, knew or could reasonably be expected to know that the arrangements involved were abusive tax arrangements.

9(2) Where–

(a) a person is, in the course of a business carried on by the person, to any extent responsible for facilitating T's withdrawal from the arrangements, and

(b) it is reasonable to assume that the obtaining of a tax advantage is not T's purpose (or one of T's purposes) in withdrawing from the arrangements,

that person is not because of anything done in the course of facilitating that withdrawal to be regarded as to any extent responsible for the organisation or management of the arrangements.

MARKETERS OF ARRANGEMENTS

10 For the purposes of paragraph 7 a person **"marketed"** the arrangements to T if, in the course of a business carried on by that person–

(a) that person made available for implementation by T a proposal which has since been implemented, *in relation to* T, *by the arrangements*, or

(b) that person–

(i) communicated information to T or another person about a proposal which has since been implemented, in relation to T, by the arrangements, and

(ii) did so with a view to T entering into the arrangements or transactions forming part of the arrangements.

ENABLING PARTICIPANTS

11 For the purposes of paragraph 7 a person is **"an enabling participant"** in the arrangements if–

(a) that person is a person (other than T) who enters into the arrangements or a transaction forming part of the arrangements,

(b) without that person's participation in the arrangements or transaction (or the participation of another person in the arrangements or transaction in the same capacity as that person), the arrangements could not be expected to result in a tax advantage for T, and

(c) when that person entered into the arrangements or transaction, that person knew or could reasonably be expected to know that what was being entered into was abusive tax arrangements or a transaction forming part of such arrangements.

FINANCIAL ENABLERS

12(1) For the purposes of paragraph 7 a person is a **"financial enabler"** in relation to the arrangements if–

(a) in the course of a business carried on by that person, that person provided a financial product (directly or indirectly) to a relevant party,

(b) it is reasonable to assume that the purpose (or a purpose) of the relevant party in obtaining the financial product was to participate in the arrangements, and

(c) when the financial product was provided, the person providing it knew or could reasonably be expected to know that the purpose (or a purpose) of obtaining it was to participate in abusive tax arrangements.

12(2) In this paragraph **"a relevant party"** means T or an enabling participant in the arrangements within the meaning given by paragraph 11.

12(3) Any reference in this paragraph to a person's providing a financial product to a relevant party includes (but is not limited to) the person's doing any of the following–

(a) providing a loan to a relevant party;

(b) issuing or transferring a share to a relevant party;

(c) entering into arrangements with a relevant party such that–

(i) the person becomes a party to a relevant contract within the meaning of section 577 of CTA 2009 (derivative contracts);

(ii) there is a repo in respect of securities within the meaning of section 263A(A1) of TCGA 1992;

(iii) the person or the relevant party has a creditor repo, creditor quasi-repo, debtor repo or debtor quasi-repo within the meaning of sections 543, 544, 548 and 549 of CTA 2009;

(d) entering into a stock lending arrangement, within the meaning of section 263B(1) of TCGA 1992, with a relevant party;

(e) entering into an alternative finance arrangement, within the meaning of Chapter 6 of Part 6 of CTA 2009 or Part 10A of ITA 2007, with a relevant party;

(f) entering into a contract with a relevant party which, whether alone or in combination with one or more other contracts–

(i) is in accordance with generally accepted accounting practice required to be treated as a loan, deposit or other financial asset or obligation, or

(ii) would be required to be so treated by the person if the person were a company to which the Companies Act 2006 applies;

and references to obtaining a financial product are to be read accordingly.

12(4) The Treasury may by regulations amend sub-paragraph (3).

EXCLUDED PERSONS

13(1) A person who–

(a) would (in the absence of this paragraph) be regarded for the purposes of this Schedule as having enabled particular arrangements mentioned in paragraph 1, but

(b) is a person within sub-paragraph (2),

is not to be regarded as having enabled those arrangements.

13(2) The persons within this sub-paragraph are–

(a) T;

(b) where T is a company, any company in the same group as T.

POWERS TO ADD CATEGORIES OF ENABLER AND TO PROVIDE EXCEPTIONS

14(1) The Treasury may by regulations add to the categories of persons who, in relation to arrangements mentioned in paragraph 1, are for the purposes of this Schedule persons who enabled the arrangements.

14(2) The Treasury may by regulations provide that a person who would otherwise be regarded for the purposes of this Schedule as having enabled arrangements is not to be so regarded where conditions prescribed by the regulations are met.

14(3) Regulations under this paragraph may–

(a) amend this Part of this Schedule;

(b) make supplementary, incidental, and consequential provision, including provision amending any other Part of this Schedule;

(c) make transitional provision.

Part 5 – Amount of Penalty

AMOUNT OF PENALTY

15(1) For each person who enabled the arrangements mentioned in paragraph 1, the penalty payable under paragraph 1 is the total amount or value of all the relevant consideration received or receivable by that person ("the person in question").

15(2) Particular consideration is **"relevant"** for the purposes of this paragraph if–

(a) it is consideration for anything done by the person in question which enabled the arrangements mentioned in paragraph 1, and

(b) it has not previously been taken into account in calculating the amount of a penalty payable under paragraph 1.

15(3) For the purposes of this paragraph a thing done by a person **"enabled"** the arrangements mentioned in paragraph 1 if, by doing that thing (alone or with anything else), the person fell within the definition in Part 4 of this Schedule of a person who enabled those arrangements.

16(1) This paragraph applies for the purposes of paragraph 15.

16(2) Where consideration for anything done by a person ("A") is, under any arrangements with A, paid or payable to a person other than A, it is to be taken to be received or receivable by A.

16(3) The **"consideration"** for anything done by a person does not include any amount charged by that person in respect of value added tax.

16(4) Consideration attributable to two or more transactions is to be apportioned on a just and reasonable basis.

16(5) Any consideration given for what is in substance one bargain is to be treated as attributable to all elements of the bargain, even though–

(a) separate consideration is, or purports to be, given for different elements of the bargain, or

(b) there are, or purport to be, separate transactions in respect of different elements of the bargain.

REDUCTION OF PENALTY WHERE OTHER PENALTIES INCURRED

17(1) The amount of a penalty for which a person is liable under paragraph 1 is to be reduced by the amount of any other penalty incurred by the person in respect of conduct for which the person is liable to the penalty under paragraph 1.

17(2) In this paragraph **"any other penalty"** means a penalty–

(a) which is a penalty under a provision other than paragraph 1, and

(b) which has been assessed.

MITIGATION OF PENALTY

18(1) HMRC may in their discretion reduce a penalty under paragraph 1.

18(2) In this paragraph the reference to reducing a penalty includes a reference to–

(a) entirely remitting the penalty, or

(b) staying, or agreeing a compromise in relation to, proceedings for the recovery of a penalty.

Part 6 – Assessment of Penalty

ASSESSMENT OF PENALTY

19(1) Where a person is liable for a penalty under paragraph 1 HMRC must–

(a) assess the penalty, and

(b) notify the person.

19(2) If–

(a) HMRC do not have all the information required to determine the amount or value of the relevant consideration within the meaning of paragraph 15, and

(b) HMRC have taken all reasonable steps to obtain that information,

HMRC may assess the penalty on the basis of a reasonable estimate by HMRC of that consideration.

19(3) This paragraph is subject to–

(a) paragraphs 21 and 22 (limits on when penalty may be assessed); and

(b) Part 7 of this Schedule (requirement for opinion of GAAR Advisory Panel before penalty may be assessed).

20(1) A penalty under paragraph 1 must be paid before the end of the period of 30 days beginning with the day on which notification of the penalty is issued.

20(2) An assessment of a penalty under paragraph 1–

(a) is to be treated for procedural purposes in the same way as an assessment to tax (except in respect of a matter expressly provided for by this Schedule), and

(b) may be enforced as if it were an assessment to tax.

SPECIAL PROVISION ABOUT ASSESSMENT FOR MULTI-USER SCHEMES

21(1) This paragraph applies where–

(a) a proposal for arrangements is implemented more than once, by a number of tax arrangements which are substantially the same as each other ("related arrangements"),

(b) paragraph 1 applies in relation to particular arrangements ("the arrangements concerned") which are one of the number of related arrangements implementing the proposal, and

(c) at the time when the person who entered into the arrangements concerned incurs a defeat in respect of them, the required percentage of relevant defeats has not been reached.

21(2) HMRC may not assess any penalty payable under paragraph 1 in respect of the arrangements concerned until the required percentage of relevant defeats is reached.

21(3) For the purposes of this paragraph the **"required percentage of relevant defeats"** is reached when HMRC reasonably believe that defeats have been incurred in the case of more than 50% of the related arrangements implementing the proposal.

21(4) Sub-paragraph (2) does not apply in relation to a penalty if the person liable to the penalty requests assessment of the penalty sooner than the time allowed by sub-paragraph (2).

TIME LIMIT FOR ASSESSMENT

22(1) An assessment of a person as liable to a penalty under paragraph 1 may not take place after the relevant time.

22(2) In this paragraph **"the relevant time"** means, subject to sub-paragraphs (3) to (6)–

(a) where a GAAR final decision notice within the meaning of paragraph 24(1) has been given in relation to the arrangements to which the penalty relates, the end of 12 months beginning with the date on which T incurs the defeat mentioned in paragraph 1;

(b) where a notice under paragraph 25 has been given to the person mentioned in sub-paragraph (1) above in respect of the arrangements to which the penalty relates, the end of 12 months beginning with the end of the time allowed for making representations in respect of that notice;

(c) where–

(i) a referral has been made under paragraph 26 in respect of the arrangements to which the penalty relates, and

(ii) paragraph (d) does not apply,

the end of 12 months beginning with the date on which the opinion of the GAAR Advisory Panel is given on the referral (within the meaning given by paragraph 34(6));

(d) where a notice under paragraph 35 has been given to the person mentioned in sub-paragraph (1) above in respect of the arrangements to which the penalty relates, the end of 12 months beginning with the end of the time allowed for making representations in respect of that notice.

22(3) Where–

(a) paragraph 21 prevented a penalty from being assessed before the required percentage of relevant defeats was reached, and

(b) the required percentage of relevant defeats (within the meaning of paragraph 21) has been reached,

the relevant time in relation to that penalty is whichever is the later of–

(i) the relevant time given by sub-paragraph (2), and

(ii) the end of 12 months beginning with the date on which that required percentage was reached.

22(4) Where under paragraph 21(4) a person requests assessment of a penalty, the relevant time in relation to that penalty is whichever is the later of–

(a) the relevant time given by sub-paragraph (2), and

(b) the end of 12 months beginning with the date on which the request is made,

and sub-paragraph (3) does not apply to the penalty even if the required percentage of relevant defeats is reached.

22(5) Sub-paragraph (6) applies where–

(a) at any time a declaration has been made under paragraph 44 for the purposes of any determination of whether a person is liable to a penalty under paragraph 1 in relation to particular arrangements ("the arrangements concerned"), and

(b) subsequently, facts that in the Commissioners' opinion are sufficient to indicate that the declaration contains a material inaccuracy have come to the Commissioners' knowledge.

22(6) The relevant time in respect of any penalty under paragraph 1 payable by that person in relation to the arrangements concerned is whichever is the later of–

(a) the relevant time given by the preceding provisions of this paragraph, and

(b) the end of 12 months beginning with the date on which such facts came to the Commissioners' knowledge.

Part 7 – GAAR Advisory Panel Opinion, and Representations

REQUIREMENT FOR OPINION OF GAAR ADVISORY PANEL

23(1) A penalty under paragraph 1 may not be assessed unless–

(a) the decision that it should be assessed is taken by a designated HMRC officer, and

(b) either the condition in sub-paragraph (2) or the condition in sub-paragraph (3) is met.

23(2) The condition in this sub-paragraph is that, when the assessment is made–

(a) a GAAR final decision notice has been given in relation to–

(i) the arrangements to which the penalty relates ("the relevant arrangements"), or

(ii) arrangements that are equivalent to the relevant arrangements,

(b) where a notice is required by paragraph 25 to be given to the person liable to the penalty, that notice has been given and the time allowed for making representations under that paragraph has expired, and

(c) a designated HMRC officer has, in deciding whether the penalty should be assessed, considered–

(i) the opinion of the GAAR Advisory Panel which was considered by HMRC in preparing that GAAR final decision notice, and

(ii) any representations made under paragraph 25.

23(3) The condition in this sub-paragraph is that, when the assessment is made–

(a) an opinion of the GAAR Advisory Panel which applies to the relevant arrangements has been given on a referral under paragraph 26,

(b) where a notice is required by paragraph 35 to be given to the person liable to the penalty, that notice has been given and the time allowed for making representations under that paragraph has expired, and

(c) a designated HMRC officer has, in deciding whether the penalty should be assessed, considered–

(i) that opinion of the GAAR Advisory Panel, and

(ii) any representations made under paragraph 35.

23(4) Where a notification of a penalty under paragraph 1 is given, the notification must be accompanied by a report prepared by HMRC of–

(a) if the condition in sub-paragraph (2) is met, the opinion of the GAAR Advisory Panel which was considered by HMRC in preparing the GAAR final decision notice;

(b) if the condition in sub-paragraph (3) is met, the opinion of the GAAR advisory panel mentioned in that sub-paragraph.

23(5) Paragraph 24 contains definitions of terms used in this paragraph.

24(1) In this Schedule a **"GAAR final decision notice"** means a notice under–

(a) paragraph 12 of Schedule 43 to FA 2013 (notice of final decision after considering opinion of GAAR Advisory Panel on referral under Schedule 43),

(b) paragraph 8 or 9 of Schedule 43A to FA 2013 (notice of final decision after considering opinion of GAAR Advisory Panel), or

(c) paragraph 8 of Schedule 43B to FA 2013 (notice of final decision after considering opinion of GAAR Advisory Panel on referral under Schedule 43B).

24(2) For the purposes of this Part of this Schedule, where the GAAR Advisory Panel gives an opinion on a referral under paragraph 26 the arrangements to which the opinion **"applies"** are–

(a) the arrangements in respect of which the referral was made (that is, "the arrangements in question" within the meaning given by paragraph 26(1)), and

(b) any arrangements that are equivalent to those arrangements.

24(3) For the purposes of this Part of this Schedule, arrangements are **"equivalent"** to one another if they are substantially the same as one another having regard to–

(a) their substantive results or intended substantive results,

(b) the means of achieving those results, and

(c) the characteristics on the basis of which it could reasonably be argued, in each case, that the arrangements are abusive tax arrangements.

NOTICE WHERE PANEL OPINION ALREADY OBTAINED IN RELATION TO EQUIVALENT ARRANGEMENTS

25(1) This paragraph applies where a designated HMRC officer is of the view that–

(a) a person is liable to a penalty under paragraph 1 in relation to particular arrangements ("the arrangements concerned"),

(b) no GAAR final decision notice has been given in relation to those arrangements, but those arrangements are equivalent to arrangements in relation to which a GAAR final decision notice has been given ("the GAAR decision arrangements"), and

(c) accordingly, the opinion of the GAAR Advisory Panel which was considered by HMRC in preparing that GAAR final decision notice is relevant to the arrangements concerned.

25(2) A designated HMRC officer must give the person mentioned in sub-paragraph (1) a notice in writing–

(a) explaining that the officer is of the view mentioned there,

(b) specifying the arrangements concerned,

(c) describing the material characteristics of the GAAR decision arrangements,

(d) setting out a report prepared by HMRC of the opinion of the GAAR Advisory Panel which was considered by HMRC in preparing the GAAR final decision notice, and

(e) explaining the effect of sub-paragraphs (3) and (4).

25(3) A person to whom a notice under this paragraph is given has 30 days, beginning with the day on which the notice is given, to send to the designated HMRC officer (in writing) any representations that that person wishes to make as to why the arrangements concerned are not equivalent to the GAAR decision arrangements.

25(4) A designated HMRC officer may, on a written request by that person, extend the period during which representations may be made by that person.

25(5) Paragraph 24 contains definitions of the following terms used in this paragraph–

"GAAR final decision notice";

"equivalent", in relation to arrangements.

REFERRAL TO GAAR ADVISORY PANEL

26(1) A designated HMRC officer may make a referral under this paragraph if–

(a) the officer considers that a person is liable to a penalty under paragraph 1 in relation to particular arrangements ("the arrangements in question"), and

(b) the requirements of paragraph 28 (procedure before making of referral) have been complied with.

26(2) But a referral may not be made under this paragraph if a GAAR final decision notice (within the meaning of paragraph 24(1)) has already been given in relation to–

(a) the arrangements in question, or

(b) arrangements that are equivalent to those arrangements.

26(3) A referral under this paragraph is a referral to the GAAR Advisory Panel of the question whether the entering into and carrying out of tax arrangements such as are described in the referral statement (see paragraph 27) is a reasonable course of action in relation to the relevant tax provisions.

27(1) In this Part of this Schedule **"the referral statement"**, in relation to a referral under paragraph 26, means a statement made by a designated HMRC officer which–

(a) accompanies the referral,

(b) is a general statement of the material characteristics of the arrangements in question (within the meaning given by paragraph 26(1)), and

(c) complies with sub-paragraph (2).

27(2) A statement under this paragraph must–

(a) contain a factual description of the arrangements in question,

(b) set out HMRC's view as to whether those arrangements accord with established practice (as it stood when those arrangements were entered into),

(c) explain why it is the designated HMRC officer's view that a tax advantage of the nature described in the statement and arising from tax arrangements having the characteristics described in the statement would be a tax advantage arising from arrangements that are abusive,

(d) set out any matters the designated HMRC officer is aware of which may suggest that any view of HMRC or the designated HMRC officer expressed in the statement is not correct, and

(e) set out any other matters which the designated HMRC officer considers are required for the purposes of the exercise of the GAAR Advisory Panel's functions under paragraphs 33 and 34.

NOTICE BEFORE DECISION WHETHER TO REFER

28(1) A referral must not be made under paragraph 26 unless–

(a) a designated HMRC officer has given each relevant person a notice under this paragraph,

(b) in the case of each relevant person, the time allowed for making representations has expired, and

(c) in deciding whether to make the referral, a designated HMRC officer has considered any representations made by a relevant person within the time allowed.

28(2) In this paragraph a **"relevant person"** means any person who at the time of the referral is considered by the officer making the referral to be liable to a penalty under paragraph 1 in relation to the arrangements in question (within the meaning given by paragraph 26(1)).

28(3) A notice under this paragraph is a notice in writing which–

(a) explains that the officer giving the notice considers that the person to whom the notice is given is liable to a penalty under paragraph 1 in relation to the arrangements in question (specifying those arrangements),

(b) explains why the officer considers those arrangements to be abusive tax arrangements,

(c) explains that HMRC are proposing to make a referral under paragraph 26 of the question whether the entering into and carrying out of tax arrangements that have the characteristics of the arrangements in question is a reasonable course of action in relation to the relevant tax provisions, and

(d) explains the effect of sub-paragraphs (4) and (5).

28(4) Each person to whom a notice under this paragraph is given has 45 days, beginning with the day on which the notice is given to that person, to send written representations to the designated HMRC officer in response to the notice.

28(5) A designated HMRC officer may, on a written request by a person to whom a notice is given, extend the period during which representations may be made by that person.

NOTICE OF DECISION WHETHER TO REFER

29 Where a designated HMRC officer decides whether to make a referral under paragraph 26, the officer must, as soon as reasonably practicable, give written notice of that decision to each person to whom notice under paragraph 28 was given.

INFORMATION TO ACCOMPANY REFERRAL

30 A referral under paragraph 26 must (as well as being accompanied by the referral statement under paragraph 27) be accompanied by–

(a) a declaration that, as far as HMRC are aware, nothing which is material to the GAAR Advisory Panel's consideration of the matter has been omitted from that statement,

(b) a copy of each notice given under paragraph 28 by HMRC in relation to the referral,

(c) a copy of any representations received under paragraph 28 and any comments that HMRC wish to make in respect of those representations, and

(d) a copy of each notice given under paragraph 31 by HMRC.

NOTICE ON MAKING OF REFERRAL

31(1) Where a referral is made under paragraph 26, a designated HMRC officer must at the same time give to each relevant person a notice in writing which–

(a) notifies the person of the referral,

(b) is accompanied by a copy of the referral statement,

(c) is accompanied by a copy of any comments provided to the GAAR Advisory Panel under paragraph 30(c) in respect of representations made by the person,

(d) notifies the person of the period under paragraph 32 for making representations, and

(e) notifies the person of the requirement under that paragraph to send any representations to the officer.

31(2) In this paragraph **"relevant person"** has the same meaning as in paragraph 28 (see sub-paragraph (2) of that paragraph).

RIGHT TO MAKE REPRESENTATIONS TO GAAR ADVISORY PANEL

32(1) A person who has received a notice under paragraph 31 has 21 days, beginning with the day on which that notice is given, to send to the GAAR Advisory Panel written representations about–

(a) the notice given to the person under paragraph 28, or

(b) any comments provided to the GAAR Advisory Panel under paragraph 30(c) in respect of representations made by the person.

32(2) The GAAR Advisory Panel may, on a written request made by the person, extend the period during which representations may be made.

32(3) If a person sends representations to the GAAR Advisory Panel under this paragraph, the person must at the same time send a copy of the representations to the designated HMRC officer.

32(4) If a person sends representations to the GAAR Advisory Panel under this paragraph and that person made no representations under paragraph 28, a designated HMRC officer–

(a) may provide the GAAR Advisory Panel with comments on that person's representations under this paragraph, and

(b) if such comments are provided, must at the same time send a copy of them to that person.

DECISION OF GAAR ADVISORY PANEL AND OPINION NOTICES

33(1) Where a referral is made to the GAAR Advisory Panel under paragraph 26, the Chair must arrange for a sub-panel consisting of 3 members of the GAAR Advisory Panel (one of whom may be the Chair) to consider it.

33(2) The sub-panel may invite–

(a) any person to whom notice under paragraph 28 was given, or

(b) the designated HMRC officer,

(or both) to supply the sub-panel with further information within a period specified in the invitation.

33(3) Invitations must explain the effect of sub-paragraph (4) or (5) (as appropriate).

33(4) If a person invited under sub-paragraph (2)(a) supplies information to the sub-panel under this paragraph, that person must at the same time send a copy of the information to the designated HMRC officer.

33(5) If a designated HMRC officer supplies information to the sub-panel under this paragraph, the officer must at the same time send a copy of the information to each person to whom notice under paragraph 28 was given.

34(1) The sub-panel must produce–

(a) one opinion notice stating the joint opinion of all the members of the sub-panel, or

(b) two or three opinion notices which taken together state the opinions of all the members.

34(2) The sub-panel must give a copy of the opinion notice or notices to the designated HMRC officer.

34(3) An opinion notice is a notice which states that in the opinion of the members of the sub-panel, or one or more of those members–

(a) the entering into and carrying out of tax arrangements such as are described in the referral statement is a reasonable course of action in relation to the relevant tax provisions,

(b) the entering into or carrying out of such tax arrangements is not a reasonable course of action in relation to the relevant tax provisions, or

(c) it is not possible, on the information available, to reach a view on that matter,

and the reasons for that opinion.

34(4) In forming their opinions for the purposes of sub-paragraph (3) members of the sub-panel must–

(a) have regard to all the matters set out in the referral statement,

(b) have regard to the matters mentioned in paragraphs (a) to (c) of paragraph 3(3) and paragraph 3(4), and

(c) take account of paragraph 3(5) to (7).

34(5) For the purposes of the giving of an opinion under this paragraph, the arrangements are to be assumed to be tax arrangements.

34(6) For the purposes of this Schedule–

(a) an opinion of the GAAR Advisory Panel is to be treated as having been given on a referral under paragraph 26 when an opinion notice (or notices) has been given under this paragraph in respect of the referral, and

(b) any requirement to consider the opinion of the GAAR Advisory Panel given on such a referral is a requirement to consider the contents of the opinion notice (or notices) given on the referral.

NOTICE BEFORE DECIDING THAT ARRANGEMENTS ARE ONES TO WHICH PANEL OPINION APPLIES

35(1) This paragraph applies where–

(a) an opinion of the GAAR Advisory Panel has been given on a referral under paragraph 26,

(b) a designated HMRC officer is of the view that a person is liable to a penalty under paragraph 1 in relation to particular arrangements ("the arrangements concerned") and that that opinion of the GAAR Advisory Panel applies to those arrangements, and

(c) that person is not a person to whom notice under paragraph 28 was given in connection with the referral.

35(2) A designated HMRC officer must give the person mentioned in sub-paragraph (1)(b) a notice in writing–

(a) explaining that the officer is of the view mentioned in that paragraph,

(b) specifying the arrangements concerned,

(c) setting out a report prepared by HMRC of the opinion mentioned in sub-paragraph (1)(a), and

(d) explaining the effect of sub-paragraphs (3) and (4).

35(3) A person to whom a notice under this paragraph is given has 30 days, beginning with the day on which the notice is given, to send the designated HMRC officer (in writing) any representations as to why the opinion does not apply to the arrangements concerned.

35(4) A designated HMRC officer may, on a written request by that person, extend the period during which representations may be made by that person.

35(5) Paragraph 24(2) defines the arrangements that an opinion given on a referral under paragraph 26 "applies to".

REQUIREMENT FOR COURT OR TRIBUNAL TO TAKE PANEL OPINION INTO ACCOUNT

36(1) In this paragraph **"enabler penalty proceedings"** means proceedings before a court or tribunal in connection with a penalty under paragraph 1.

36(2) In determining in enabler penalty proceedings any question whether tax arrangements to which the penalty relates were abusive, the court or tribunal–

(a) must take into account the relevant Panel opinion, and

(b) may also take into account any matter mentioned in sub-paragraph (4).

36(3) In sub-paragraph (2)(a) **"the relevant Panel opinion"** means the opinion of the GAAR Advisory Panel which under this Part of this Schedule was required to be considered by a designated HMRC officer in deciding whether the penalty should be assessed.

36(4) The matters mentioned in sub-paragraph (2)(b) are–

(a) guidance, statements or other material (whether of HMRC, a Minister of the Crown or anyone else) that was in the public domain at the time the arrangements were entered into, and

(b) evidence of established practice at that time.

Part 8 – Appeals

37 A person may appeal against–

(a) a decision of HMRC that a penalty under paragraph 1 is payable by that person, or

(b) a decision of HMRC as to the amount of a penalty under paragraph 1 payable by the person.

38(1) An appeal under paragraph 37 is to be treated in the same way as an appeal against an assessment to the tax to which the arrangements concerned relate (including by the application of any provision about bringing the appeal by notice to HMRC, about HMRC review of the decision or about determination of the appeal by the First-tier Tribunal or Upper Tribunal).

38(2) Sub-paragraph (1) does not apply–

(a) so as to require a person to pay a penalty under paragraph 1 before an appeal against the assessment of the penalty is determined;

(b) in respect of any other matter expressly provided for by this Schedule.

38(3) In this paragraph **"the arrangements concerned"** means the arrangements to which the penalty relates.

39(1) On an appeal under paragraph 37(a) that is notified to the tribunal, the tribunal may affirm or cancel HMRC's decision.

39(2) On an appeal under paragraph 37(b) that is notified to the tribunal, the tribunal may–

(a) affirm HMRC's decision, or

(b) substitute for that decision another decision that HMRC had power to make.

39(3) the tribunal substitutes its decision for HMRC's, the tribunal may rely on paragraph 18–

(a) to the same extent as HMRC (which may mean applying the same percentage reduction as HMRC to a different starting point), or

(b) to a different extent, but only if the tribunal thinks that HMRC's decision in respect of the application of paragraph 18 was flawed.

39(4) In sub-paragraph (3)(b) **"flawed"** means flawed when considered in the light of the principles applicable in proceedings for judicial review.

39(5) In this paragraph **"tribunal"** means the First-tier Tribunal or Upper Tribunal (as appropriate by virtue of paragraph 38(1)).

Part 9 – Information

INFORMATION AND INSPECTION POWERS: APPLICATION OF SCHEDULE 36 TO FA 2008

40(1) Schedule 36 to FA 2008 (information and inspection powers) applies for the purpose of checking a relevant person's position as regards liability for a penalty under paragraph 1 as it applies for checking a person's tax position, subject to the modifications in paragraphs 41 to 43.

40(2) In this paragraph and paragraphs 41 to 43–

"relevant person" means a person an officer of Revenue and Customs has reason to suspect is or may be liable to a penalty under paragraph 1;

"the Schedule" means Schedule 36 to FA 2008.

GENERAL MODIFICATIONS OF SCHEDULE 36 TO FA 2008 AS APPLIED

41 In its application for the purpose mentioned in paragraph 40(1) above, the Schedule has effect as if–

(a) any provisions which can have no application for that purpose were omitted,

(b) references to **"the taxpayer"** were references to the relevant person whose position as regards liability for a penalty under paragraph 1 is to be checked, and references to **"a taxpayer"** were references to a relevant person,

(c) references to a person's **"tax position"** were to the relevant person's position as regards liability for a penalty under paragraph 1,

(d) references to prejudice to the assessment or collection of tax included prejudice to the investigation of the relevant person's position as regards liability for a penalty under paragraph 1, and

(e) references to a pending appeal relating to tax were to a pending appeal relating to an assessment of liability for a penalty under paragraph 1.

SPECIFIC MODIFICATIONS OF SCHEDULE 36 TO FA 2008 AS APPLIED

42(1) The Schedule as it applies for the purpose mentioned in paragraph 40(1) above has effect with the modifications in sub-paragraphs (2) to (6).

42(2) Paragraph 10A (power to inspect business premises of involved third parties) has effect as if the reference in sub-paragraph (1) to the position of any person or class of persons as regards a relevant tax were to the position of a relevant person as regards liability for a penalty under paragraph 1.

42(3) Paragraph 47 (right to appeal against penalties under the Schedule) has effect as if after paragraph (b) (but not as part of that paragraph) there were inserted the words "but paragraph (b) does not give a right of appeal against the amount of an increased daily penalty payable by virtue of paragraph 49A."

42(4) Paragraph 49A (increased daily default penalty) has effect as if–

(a) in sub-paragraphs (1)(c) and (2) for "imposed" there were substituted "assessable";

(b) for sub-paragraphs (3) and (4) there were substituted–

> **"49A(3)** If the tribunal decides that an increased daily penalty should be assessable–
>
> (a) the tribunal must determine the day from which the increased daily penalty is to apply and the maximum amount of that penalty ("the new maximum amount");
>
> (b) from that day, paragraph 40 has effect in the person's case as if "the new maximum amount" were substituted for "£60".
>
> **49A(4)** The new maximum amount may not be more than £1,000.";

(c) in sub-paragraph (5) for "the amount" there were substituted "the new maximum amount".

42(5) Paragraph 49B (notification of increased daily default penalty) has effect as if–

(a) in sub-paragraph (1) for "a person becomes liable to a penalty" there were substituted "the tribunal makes a determination";

(b) in sub-paragraph (2) for "the day from which the increased penalty is to apply" there were substituted "the new maximum amount and the day from which it applies";

(c) sub-paragraph (3) were omitted.

42(6) Paragraph 49C is treated as omitted.

43 Paragraphs 50 and 51 are excluded from the application of the Schedule for the purpose mentioned in paragraph 40(1) above.

DECLARATIONS ABOUT CONTENTS OF LEGALLY PRIVILEGED COMMUNICATIONS

44(1) Subject to sub-paragraph (5), a declaration under this paragraph is to be treated by–

(a) HMRC, or

(b) in any proceedings before a court or tribunal in connection with a penalty under paragraph 1, the court or tribunal,

as conclusive evidence of the things stated in the declaration.

44(2) A declaration under this paragraph is a declaration which–

(a) is made by a relevant lawyer,

(b) relates to one or more communications falling within sub-paragraph (3), and

(c) meets such requirements as may be prescribed by regulations under sub-paragraph (4).

44(3) A communication falls within this sub-paragraph if–

(a) it was made by a relevant lawyer (whether or not the one making the declaration),

(b) it is legally privileged, and

(c) if it were not legally privileged, it would be relied on by a person for the purpose of establishing that that person is not liable to a penalty under paragraph 1 (whether or not that person is the person who made the communication or is making the declaration).

44(4) The Treasury may by regulations impose requirements as to the form and contents of declarations under this paragraph.

44(5) Sub-paragraph (1) does not apply where HMRC or (as the case may be) the court or tribunal is satisfied that the declaration contains information which is incorrect.

44(6) In this paragraph **"a relevant lawyer"** means a barrister, advocate, solicitor or other legal representative communications with whom may be the subject of a claim to legal professional privilege or, in Scotland, protected from disclosure in legal proceedings on the grounds of confidentiality of communication.

44(7) For the purpose of this paragraph, a communication is **"legally privileged"** if it is a communication in respect of which a claim to legal professional privilege, or (in Scotland) to confidentiality of communications as between client and professional legal adviser, could be maintained in legal proceedings.

Statutory instruments – SI 2017/1245: made under para. 44(4).

45(1) Where a person carelessly or deliberately gives any incorrect information in a declaration under paragraph 44, the person is liable to a penalty not exceeding £5,000.

45(2) For the purposes of this paragraph, incorrect information is carelessly given by a person if the information is incorrect because of a failure by the person to take reasonable care.

45(3) Paragraphs 19(1), 20, 22(1), 37, 38 and 39(1), (2) and (5) apply in relation to a penalty under this paragraph as they apply in relation to a penalty under paragraph 1, subject to the modifications in sub-paragraphs (4) and (5).

45(4) In its application to a penalty under this paragraph, paragraph 22(1) has effect as if for "the relevant time" there were substituted "the end of 12 months beginning with the date on which facts sufficient to indicate that the person is liable to the penalty came to the Commissioners' knowledge".

45(5) In its application to a penalty under this paragraph, paragraph 38(3) has effect as if the reference to the arrangements to which the penalty relates were to the arrangements to which the declaration under paragraph 44 relates.

45(6) In paragraph 44 any reference to a penalty under paragraph 1 includes a reference to a penalty under this paragraph.

Part 10 – Publishing Details of Persons Who Have Incurred Penalties

POWER TO PUBLISH DETAILS

46(1) The Commissioners may publish information about a person where–

(a) the person has incurred a penalty under paragraph 1,

(b) the penalty has become final, and

(c) either the condition in sub-paragraph (2) or the condition in sub-paragraph (3) is met.

46(2) The condition in this sub-paragraph is that, at the time when the penalty mentioned in sub-paragraph (1) becomes final, 50 or more other penalties which are reckonable penalties have been incurred by the person.

46(3) The condition in this sub-paragraph is that–

(a) the amount of the penalty mentioned in sub-paragraph (1), or

(b) the total amount of that penalty and any other penalties incurred by that person which are reckonable penalties,

is more than £25,000.

46(4) The information that may be published under this paragraph is–

(a) the person's name (including any trading name, previous name or pseudonym),

(b) the person's address (or registered office),

(c) the nature of any business carried on by the person,

(d) the total number of the penalties in question (that is, the penalty mentioned in sub-paragraph (1) and any penalties that are reckonable penalties in relation to that penalty),

(e) the total amount of the penalties in question, and

(f) any other information that the Commissioners consider it appropriate to publish in order to make clear the person's identity.

46(5) The information may be published in any way that the Commissioners consider appropriate.

46(6) For the purposes of this Part of this Schedule a penalty becomes **"final"**–

(a) if the penalty has been assessed and paragraph (b) does not apply, at the time when the period for any appeal or further appeal relating to the penalty expires or, if later, when any appeal or final appeal relating to it is finally determined;

(b) if a contract settlement has been made in relation to the penalty, at the time when the contract is made;

and **"contract settlement"** here means a contract between the Commissioners and the person under which the Commissioners undertake not to assess the penalty or (if it has been assessed) not to take proceedings to recover it.

46(7) **"Reckonable penalty"** has the meaning given by paragraph 47.

46(8) This paragraph is subject to paragraphs 48 to 50.

47(1) A penalty is a **"reckonable penalty"** for the purposes of paragraph 46 if–

(a) it is a penalty under paragraph 1 which becomes final at the same time as, or before, the penalty mentioned in paragraph 46(1),

(b) its entry date and the entry date of the penalty mentioned in paragraph 46(1) are not more than 12 months apart, and

(c) it is not a penalty which under paragraph 48(1) is to be disregarded.

47(2) For the purposes of this paragraph the **"entry date"** of a penalty under paragraph 1 is the date (or, if more than one, the latest date) on which the arrangements concerned or any agreement or transaction forming part of those arrangements was entered into by the taxpayer.

47(3) In sub-paragraph (2)–

"the arrangements concerned" means the arrangements to which the penalty relates, and

"the taxpayer" means the person whose defeat in respect of those arrangements resulted in the penalty being payable.

47(4) For the purposes of this paragraph, the entry date of a penalty is not more than 12 months apart from the entry date of another penalty if–

(a) the entry dates of those penalties are the same, or

(b) the period beginning with whichever of the entry dates is the earlier and ending with whichever of the entry dates is the later is 12 months or less.

RESTRICTIONS ON POWER

48(1) In determining at any time whether or what information may be published in relation to a person under paragraph 46, the following penalties incurred by the person are to be disregarded–

(a) a penalty which has been reduced to nil or stayed;

(b) a penalty by reference to which information has previously been published under paragraph 46;

(c) a penalty where–

(i) the arrangements to which the penalty relates ("the arrangements concerned") are related to other arrangements, and

(ii) the condition in sub-paragraph (3) is not met;

(d) a penalty that relates to arrangements which are related to arrangements that have already been dealt with (within the meaning given by sub-paragraph (4)).

48(2) For the purposes of sub-paragraph (1)(c) and (d) arrangements are **"related to"** each other if they–

(a) implement the same proposal for tax arrangements, and

(b) are substantially the same as each other.

48(3) The condition referred to in sub-paragraph (1)(c) is that HMRC reasonably believe that–

(a) defeats have been incurred in the case of all the arrangements that are related to the arrangements concerned ("the related arrangements"), and

(b) each penalty under paragraph 1 which relates to the arrangements concerned or to any of the related arrangements has become final.

48(4) For the purposes of sub-paragraph (1)(d) arrangements have **"already been dealt with"** if information about the person has already been published under paragraph 46 by reference to a penalty that relates to those arrangements.

49(1) Publication of information under paragraph 46 on the basis of a penalty or penalties incurred by a person may not take place after the relevant time.

49(2) In this paragraph **"the relevant time"** means the end of 12 months beginning with the date on which the penalty became final or, where more than one penalty is involved, the latest date on which any of them became final.

49(3) Sub-paragraph (1) is not to be taken to prevent the re-publishing, or continued publishing, after the relevant time of a set of information published under paragraph 46 before that time.

49(4) Information published under paragraph 46 may not be re-published, or continue to be published, after the end of 12 months beginning with the date on which it was first published.

49(5) Nothing in paragraph 48 applies in relation to determining whether to re-publish (or continue to publish) a set of information already published under paragraph 46.

50 Before publishing information under paragraph 46 the Commissioners must–

(a) inform the person that they are considering doing so, and

(b) afford the person the opportunity to make representations about whether it should be published.

POWER TO AMEND

51 The Treasury may by regulations amend this Part of this Schedule so as to alter any of the following–

(a) the figure for the time being specified in paragraph 46(2);

(b) the sum for the time being specified in paragraph 46(3);

(c) any period for the time being specified in paragraph 47(1)(b) or (4).

Part 11 – Miscellaneous

DOUBLE JEOPARDY

52 A person is not liable to a penalty under paragraph 1 in respect of conduct for which the person has been convicted of an offence.

APPLICATION OF PROVISIONS OF TMA 1970

53 Subject to the provisions of this Schedule, the following provisions of TMA 1970 apply for the purposes of this Schedule as they apply for the purposes of the Taxes Acts–

(a) section 108 (responsibility of company officers),

(b) section 114 (want of form), and

(c) section 115 (delivery and service of documents).

Part 12 – General

MEANING OF "TAX"

54(1) In this Schedule **"tax"** includes any of the following taxes–

(a) income tax,

(b) corporation tax, including any amount chargeable as if it were corporation tax or treated as if it were corporation tax,

(c) capital gains tax,

(d) petroleum revenue tax,

(e) diverted profits tax,

(f) apprenticeship levy,

(g) inheritance tax,
(h) stamp duty land tax, and
(i) annual tax on enveloped dwellings,
and also includes national insurance contributions.

54(2) The Treasury may by regulations amend sub-paragraph (1) so as to–
(a) add a tax to the list of taxes for the time being set out in that sub-paragraph;
(b) remove a tax for the time being set out in that sub-paragraph;
(c) remove the reference to national insurance contributions;
(d) substitute for that reference a reference to national insurance contributions of a particular class or classes;
(e) where provision has been made under paragraph (d)–
 (i) add a class or classes of national insurance contributions to those for the time being specified in that sub-paragraph;
 (ii) remove a class or classes of national insurance contributions for the time being so specified.

54(3) Regulations under this paragraph may–
(a) make supplementary, incidental, and consequential provision, including provision amending or repealing any provision of this Schedule;
(b) make transitional provision.

MEANING OF "TAX ADVANTAGE"

55 In this Schedule **"tax advantage"** includes–
(a) relief or increased relief from tax,
(b) repayment or increased repayment of tax,
(c) receipt, or advancement of a receipt, of a tax credit,
(d) avoidance or reduction of a charge to tax, an assessment of tax or a liability to pay tax,
(e) avoidance of a possible assessment to tax or liability to pay tax,
(f) deferral of a payment of tax or advancement of a repayment of tax, and
(g) avoidance of an obligation to deduct or account for tax.

OTHER DEFINITIONS

56(1) In this Schedule–

"abusive tax arrangements" has the meaning given by paragraph 3;

"arrangements" includes any agreement, understanding, scheme, transaction or series of transactions (whether or not legally enforceable);

"business" includes any trade or profession;

"the Commissioners" means the Commissioners for Her Majesty's Revenue and Customs;

"company" has the same meaning as in the Corporation Tax Acts (see section 1121 of CTA 2010);

"contract settlement" (except in paragraph 46(6)) means an agreement in connection with a person's liability to make a payment to the Commissioners under or by virtue of an enactment;

"a defeat", in relation to arrangements, is to be read in accordance with paragraph 4;

a **"designated HMRC officer"** means an officer of Revenue and Customs who has been designated by the Commissioners for the purposes of this Schedule;

"the GAAR Advisory Panel" has the meaning given by paragraph 1 of Schedule 43 to FA 2013;

"group" is to be read in accordance with sub-paragraph (2);

"HMRC" means Her Majesty's Revenue and Customs;

"national insurance contributions" means contributions under Part 1 of the Social Security Contributions and Benefits Act 1992 or Part 1 of the Social Security Contributions and Benefits (Northern Ireland) Act 1992;

a **"NICs decision"** means a decision under section 8 of the Social Security Contributions (Transfer of Functions, etc.) Act 1999 or Article 7 of the Social Security Contributions (Transfer of Functions, etc.) (Northern Ireland) Order 1999 (S.I. 1999/671) relating to a person's liability for relevant contributions;

"relevant contributions" means any of the following contributions under Part 1 of the Social Security Contributions and Benefits Act 1992 or Part 1 of the Social Security Contributions and Benefits (Northern Ireland) Act 1992–

(a) Class 1 contributions;

(b) Class 1A contributions;

(c) Class 1B contributions;

(d) Class 2 contributions which must be paid but in relation to which section 11A of the Act in question (application of certain provisions of the Income Tax Acts) does not apply;

"tax" is to be read in accordance with paragraph 54;

"tax advantage" is to be read in accordance with paragraph 55.

56(2) For the purposes of this Schedule two companies are members of the same group if–

(a) one is a 75% subsidiary of the other, or

(b) both are 75% subsidiaries of a third company;

and in this paragraph **"75% subsidiary"** has, subject to sub-paragraph (3), the meaning given by section 1154 of CTA 2010.

56(3) So far as relating to 75% subsidiaries, section 151(4) of CTA 2010 (requirements relating to beneficial ownership) applies for the purposes of this Schedule as it applies for the purposes of Part 5 of that Act.

56(4) In this Schedule references to an assessment to tax, however expressed–

(a) in relation to inheritance tax and petroleum revenue tax, include a determination;

(b) in relation to relevant contributions, include a NICs decision.

REGULATIONS

57(1) Any regulations under this Schedule must be made by statutory instrument.

57(2) A statutory instrument which contains (alone or with other provision) any regulations within sub-paragraph (3) may not be made unless a draft of the instrument has been laid before, and approved by a resolution of, the House of Commons.

57(3) Regulations within this sub-paragraph are–

(a) regulations under paragraph 12;

(b) regulations under paragraph 14(1);

(c) regulations under paragraph 14(2) which amend or repeal any provision of this Schedule;

(d) regulations under paragraph 51;

(e) regulations under paragraph 54.

57(4) A statutory instrument containing only–

(a) regulations under paragraph 14(2) which do not amend or repeal any provision of this Schedule, or

(b) regulations under paragraph 44,

is subject to annulment in pursuance of a resolution of the House of Commons.

CONSEQUENTIAL AMENDMENTS

61 In Schedule 34 to FA 2014 (promoters of tax avoidance schemes: threshold conditions), in paragraph 7–

(a) in paragraph (a), for the words after "promoter" substitute "–

(i) have been referred to the GAAR Advisory Panel under Schedule 43 to FA 2013 (referrals of single schemes),

(ii) are in a pool in respect of which a referral has been made to that Panel under Schedule 43B to that Act (generic referrals), or

(iii) have been referred to that Panel under paragraph 26 of Schedule 16 to F(No. 2)A 2017 (referrals in relation to penalties for enablers of defeated tax avoidance),";

(b) in paragraph (b), for the words after "referral" substitute"under (as the case may be)–

(i) paragraph 11(3)(b) of Schedule 43 to FA 2013,

(ii) paragraph 6(4)(b) of Schedule 43B to that Act, or

(iii) paragraph 34(3)(b) of Schedule 16 to F(No. 2)A 2017,

(opinion of sub-panel of GAAR Advisory Panel that arrangements are not reasonable), and".

COMMENCEMENT

62(1) Subject to sub-paragraphs (2) and (3), paragraphs 1 to 61 of this Schedule have effect in relation to arrangements entered into on or after the day on which this Act is passed.

62(2) In determining in relation to any particular arrangements whether a person is a person who enabled the arrangements, any action of the person carried out before the day on which this Act is passed is to be disregarded.

62(3) The amendments made by paragraph 61 do not apply in relation to a person who is a promoter in relation to arrangements if by virtue of sub-paragraph (2) above that person is not a person who enabled the arrangements.

SCHEDULE 17 – DISCLOSURE OF TAX AVOIDANCE SCHEMES: VAT AND OTHER INDIRECT TAXES

Section 66

Part 3 – Consequential Amendments

PROMOTERS OF TAX AVOIDANCE SCHEMES

52 Part 5 of FA 2014 (promoters of tax avoidance schemes) is amended as follows.

53 [Amends FA 2014, s. 281A.]

54(1) Schedule 34A (defeated arrangements) is amended as follows.

54(2) [Amends FA 2014, Sch. 34A, para. 2(4).]

54(3) [Amends FA 2014, Sch. 34A, para. 14.]

54(4) [Inserts FA 2014, Sch. 34A, para. 26A.]

54(5) [Amends heading before FA 2014, Sch. 34A, para. 27.]

54(6) [Amends FA 2014, Sch. 34A, para. 27.]

54(7) [Amends heading before FA 2014, Sch. 34A, para. 28.]

54(8) [Amends FA 2014, Sch. 34A, para. 28.]

SERIAL TAX AVOIDANCE

55(1) Schedule 18 to FA 2016 (serial tax avoidance) is amended as follows.

55(2) [Amends FA 2016, Sch. 18, para. 4.]

55(3) [Inserts FA 2016, Sch. 18, para. 8A.]

55(4) [Amends heading before FA 2016, Sch. 18, para. 9.]

55(5) [Amends FA 2016, Sch. 18, para. 9.]

55(6) [Inserts FA 2016, Sch. 18, para. 9A.]

55(7) [Amends heading before FA 2016, Sch. 18, para. 10.]

55(8) [Amends FA 2016, Sch. 18, para. 10(1).]

55(9) [Amends FA 2016, Sch. 18, para. 11(1).]

55(10) [Inserts FA 2016, Sch. 18, para. 16A.]

55(11) [Amends FA 2016, Sch. 18, para. 17.]

55(12) [Amends heading before FA 2016, Sch. 18, para. 28.]

55(13) [Amends FA 2016, Sch. 18, para. 28.]

55(14) [Amends FA 2016, Sch. 18, para. 32.]

55(15) [Inserts heading before FA 2016, Sch. 18, para. 35(1)(d).]

55(16) [Inserts FA 2016, Sch. 18, para. 43(8).]

55(17) [Inserts FA 2016, Sch. 18, para. 55(8A).]

55(18) [Amends FA 2016, Sch. 18, para. 58(1).]

Part 4 – Supplemental

REGULATIONS

56(1) Any power of the Treasury or the Commissioners to make regulations under this Schedule is exercisable by statutory instrument.

56(2) Regulations made under any such power may make different provision for different cases and may contain transitional provisions and savings.

56(3) A statutory instrument containing regulations made by the Treasury under paragraph 2(2) or 42(1) may not be made unless a draft of the instrument has been laid before and approved by a resolution of the House of Commons.

56(4) Any other statutory instrument containing regulations made under this Schedule, if made without a draft having been approved by a resolution of the House of Commons, is subject to annulment in pursuance of a resolution of the House of Commons.

INTERPRETATION

57 In this Schedule–

"arrangements" includes any scheme, transaction or series of transactions;

"the Commissioners" means the Commissioners for Her Majesty's Revenue and Customs;

"company" has the meaning given by section 1121 of the Corporation Tax Act 2010;

"HMRC" means Her Majesty's Revenue and Customs;

"indirect tax" has the meaning given by paragraph 2(1);

"introducer" is to be construed in accordance with paragraph 9;

"makes a firm approach" has the meaning given by paragraph 10(1);

"makes a marketing contact" has the meaning given by paragraph 10(2);

"marketing contact" has the meaning give by paragraph 10(2);

"notifiable arrangements" has the meaning given by paragraph 3(1);

"notifiable proposal" has the meaning given by paragraph 3(3);

"prescribed" (except in or in references to paragraph 3(1)(a)), means prescribed by regulations made by HMRC;

"promoter" is to be construed in accordance with paragraph 8;

"reference number", in relation to notifiable arrangements, has the meaning given by paragraph 22(4);

"TCEA 2007" means the Tribunals, Courts and Enforcement Act 2007;

"tax advantage" means a tax advantage within the meaning of–

(a) paragraph 6 (in relation to VAT), or

(b) paragraph 7 (in relation to indirect taxes other than VAT);

"trade" includes every venture in the nature of a trade;

"tribunal" means the First-tier tribunal, or where determined by or under Tribunal Procedure Rules, the Upper Tribunal;

"working day" means a day which is not a Saturday or a Sunday, Christmas Day, Good Friday or a bank holiday under the Banking and Financial Dealings Act 1971 in any part of the United Kingdom.

SCHEDULE 18 – REQUIREMENT TO CORRECT CERTAIN OFFSHORE TAX NON-COMPLIANCE

Section 67

Part 1 – Liability for Penalty for Failure to Correct

FAILURE TO CORRECT RELEVANT OFFSHORE TAX NON-COMPLIANCE

1 A penalty is payable by a person who–

(a) has any relevant offshore tax non-compliance to correct at the end of the tax year 2016–17, and

(b) fails to correct the relevant offshore tax non-compliance within the period beginning with 6 April 2017 and ending with 30 September 2018 (referred to in this Schedule as "the RTC period").

MAIN DEFINITIONS: GENERAL

2 Paragraphs 3 to 13 have effect for the purposes of this Schedule.

"RELEVANT OFFSHORE TAX NON-COMPLIANCE"

3(1) At the end of the 2016–17 tax year a person has **"relevant offshore tax non-compliance"** to correct if–

(a) Conditions A and B are satisfied in respect of any offshore tax non-compliance committed by that person on or before 5 April 2017 ("the original offshore tax non-compliance"), and

(b) Condition C will be satisfied on the relevant date (see paragraph 6).

3(2) Where the original offshore tax non-compliance committed by a person has been corrected in part by the end of the tax year 2016–17, the person's **"relevant offshore tax non-compliance"** is the uncorrected part of the original offshore tax non-compliance.

4 Condition A is that the original offshore tax non-compliance has not been fully corrected before the end of the tax year 2016–17 (see paragraph 13).

5 Condition B is that–

(a) the original offshore tax non-compliance involved a potential loss of revenue when it was committed, and

(b) if the original offshore tax non-compliance has been corrected in part by the end of the tax year 2016–17, the uncorrected part at that time involved a potential loss of revenue.

6(1) Condition C is that on the relevant date it is lawful, on the assumptions set out in sub-paragraph (2), for HMRC to assess the person concerned to any tax the liability to which would have been disclosed to or discovered by HMRC if on that date–

(a) where none of the original offshore tax non-compliance was corrected before the end of the 2016–17 tax year, HMRC were aware of the information missing as a result of the failure to correct that tax non-compliance, or

(b) where the original offshore tax non compliance was corrected in part before that time, HMRC were aware of the information missing as a result of the failure to correct the rest of that tax non-compliance.

6(2) The assumptions are–

(a) that paragraph 26 is to be disregarded, and

(b) where the tax at stake is inheritance tax, that the relevant offshore tax non-compliance is not corrected before the relevant date.

6(3) In this paragraph **"the relevant date"** is–

(a) where the tax at stake is income tax or capital gains tax, 6 April 2017, and

(b) where the tax at stake is inheritance tax, the day after the day on which this Act is passed.

"OFFSHORE TAX-NON COMPLIANCE" ETC

7(1) **"Offshore tax non-compliance"** means tax non-compliance which involves an offshore matter or an offshore transfer, whether or not it also involves an onshore matter.

7(2) Tax non-compliance **"involves an onshore matter"** if and to the extent that it does not involve an offshore matter or an offshore transfer.

7(3) For the meaning of **"involves an offshore matter or an offshore transfer"** (in relation to the different descriptions of tax non-compliance) see paragraphs 9 to 11.

"TAX NON-COMPLIANCE"

8(1) **"Tax non-compliance"** means any of the following–

(a) a failure to comply on or before the filing date with an obligation under section 7 of TMA 1970 to give notice of chargeability to income tax or capital gains tax,

(b) a failure to comply on or before the filing date with an obligation to deliver to HMRC a return or other document which is listed in sub-paragraph (3), or

(c) delivering to HMRC a return or other document which is listed in sub-paragraph (3) or (4) and contains an inaccuracy which amounts to, or leads to–

(i) an understatement of a liability to tax,

(ii) a false or inflated statement of a loss, or

(iii) a false or inflated claim to repayment of tax.

8(2) In sub-paragraph (1)–

(a) **"filing date"**, in relation to a notice of chargeability or a return or other document, means the date by which it is required to be given, made or delivered to HMRC,

(b) **"loss"** includes a charge, expense, deficit and any other amount which may be available for, or relied on to claim, a deduction or relief, and

(c) **"repayment of tax"** includes a reference to allowing a credit against tax.

8(3) The documents relevant for the purposes of both of paragraphs (b) and (c) of sub-paragraph (1) are (so far as they relate to the tax or taxes shown in the first column)–

Tax to which document relates	*Document*
Income tax or capital gains tax	Return, accounts, statement or document required under section 8(1) of TMA 1970 (personal return)
Income tax or capital gains tax	Return, accounts, statement or document required under section 8A(1) of TMA 1970 (trustee's return)
Income tax	Return, accounts, statement or document required under section 12AA(2) or (3) of TMA 1970 (partnership return)
Income tax	Return under section 254 of FA 2004 (pension schemes)
Income tax	Particulars or documents required under regulation 12 of the Retirement Benefits Schemes (Information Powers) Regulations 1995 (S.I. 1995/3101) (information relating to pension schemes)
Capital gains tax	NRCGT return under section 12ZB of TMA 1970
Inheritance tax	Account under section 216 or 217 of IHTA 1984.

8(4) The documents relevant for the purposes only of paragraph (c) of sub-paragraph (1) are (so far as they relate to the tax or taxes shown in the first column)–

Tax to which document relates	*Document*
Income tax or capital gains tax	Return, statement or declaration in connection with a claim for an allowance, deduction or relief
Income tax or capital gains tax	Accounts in connection with ascertaining liability to tax
Income tax or capital gains tax	Statement or declaration in connection with a partnership return
Income tax or capital gains tax	Accounts in connection with a partnership return
Inheritance tax	Information or document under regulations under section 256 of IHTA 1984
Inheritance tax	Statement or declaration in connection with a deduction, exemption or relief.
Income tax, capital gains tax or inheritance tax	Any other document given to HMRC by a person ("P") which is likely to be relied on by HMRC to determine, without further inquiry, a question about– (a) P's liability to tax; (b) payments by P by way of or in connection with tax; (c) any other payment by P (including penalties); (d) repayments, or any other kind of payment or credit, to P.

"INVOLVES AN OFFSHORE MATTER" AND "INVOLVES AN OFFSHORE TRANSFER"

9(1) This paragraph applies to any tax non-compliance consisting of a failure to comply with an obligation *under section* 7 *of TMA 1970 to notify* chargeability to income tax or capital gains tax.

9(2) The tax non-compliance **"involves an offshore matter"** if the potential loss of revenue is charged on or by reference to–

(a) income arising from a source in a territory outside the UK,

(b) assets situated or held in a territory outside the UK,

(c) activities carried on wholly or mainly in a territory outside the UK, or
(d) anything having effect as if it were income, assets or activities of a kind described above.

9(3) The tax non-compliance **"involves an offshore transfer"** if–
(a) it does not involve an offshore matter, and
(b) the applicable condition is satisfied (see sub-paragraphs (4) and (5)).

9(4) Where the tax at stake is income tax the applicable condition is satisfied if the income on or by reference to which tax is charged, or any part of the income–
(a) was received in a territory outside the UK, or
(b) was transferred on or before 5 April 2017 to a territory outside the UK.

9(5) Where the tax at stake is capital gains tax, the applicable condition is satisfied if the proceeds of the disposal on or by reference to which the tax is charged, or any part of the proceeds–
(a) were received in a territory outside the UK, or
(b) were transferred on or before 5 April 2017 to a territory outside the UK.

9(6) In the case of a transfer falling within sub-paragraph (4)(b) or (5)(b), references to the income or proceeds transferred are to be read as including references to any assets derived from or representing the income or proceeds.

9(7) In this paragraph and paragraphs 10 and 11 **"assets"** has the meaning given in section 21(1) of TCGA 1992, but also includes sterling.

10(1) This paragraph applies where–
(a) any tax non-compliance by a person consists of a failure to comply with an obligation to deliver a return or other document, and
(b) a complete and accurate return or other document would have included information that would have enabled or assisted HMRC to assess the person's liability to tax.

10(2) The tax non-compliance **"involves an offshore matter"** if the liability to tax that would have been shown in the return or other document is or includes a liability to tax charged on or by reference to–
(a) income arising from a source in a territory outside the UK,
(b) assets situated or held in a territory outside the UK,
(c) activities carried on wholly or mainly in a territory outside the UK, or
(d) anything having effect as if it were income, assets or activities of a kind described above.

10(3) Where the tax at stake is inheritance tax, assets are treated for the purposes of sub-paragraph (2) as situated or held in a territory outside the UK if they are so situated or held immediately after the transfer of value by reason of which inheritance tax becomes chargeable.

10(4) The tax non-compliance **"involves an offshore transfer"** if–
(a) it does not involve an offshore matter, and
(b) the applicable condition is satisfied in respect of the liability to tax that would have been shown by the return or other document (see sub-paragraphs (5) to (7)).

10(5) Where the tax at stake is income tax the applicable condition is satisfied if the income on or by reference to which tax is charged, or any part of the income–
(a) was received in a territory outside the UK, or
(b) was transferred on or before 5 April 2017 to a territory outside the UK.

10(6) Where the tax at stake is capital gains tax, the applicable condition is satisfied if the proceeds of the disposal on or by reference to which the tax is charged, or any part of the proceeds–
(a) was received in a territory outside the UK, or
(b) was transferred on or before 5 April 2017 to a territory outside the UK.

10(7) Where the liability to tax which would have been shown in the document is a liability to inheritance tax, the applicable condition is satisfied if–
(a) the disposition that gives rise to the transfer of value by reason of which the tax becomes chargeable involves a transfer of assets, and
(b) after that disposition but on or before 5 April 2017 the assets, or any part of the assets, are transferred to a territory outside the UK.

10(8) In the case of a transfer falling within sub-paragraph (5)(b), (6)(b) or (7)(b), references to the income or proceeds transferred are to be read as including references to any assets derived from or representing the income or proceeds.

11(1) This paragraph applies to any tax non-compliance by a person if–

(a) the tax non-compliance consists of delivering or giving HMRC a return or other document which contains an inaccuracy, and

(b) the inaccuracy relates to information that would have enabled or assisted HMRC to assess the person's liability to tax.

11(2) The tax non-compliance to which this paragraph applies **"involves an offshore matter"** if the information that should have been given in the tax document relates to–

(a) income arising from a source in a territory outside the UK,

(b) assets situated or held in a territory outside the UK,

(c) activities carried on wholly or mainly in a territory outside the UK, or

(d) anything having effect as if it were income, assets or activities of a kind described above.

11(3) Where the tax at stake is inheritance tax, assets are treated for the purposes of sub-paragraph (2) as situated or held in a territory outside the UK if they are so situated or held immediately after the transfer of value by reason of which inheritance tax becomes chargeable.

11(4) Tax non-compliance to which this paragraph applies **"involves an offshore transfer"** if–

(a) it does not involve an offshore matter, and

(b) the applicable condition is satisfied in respect of the liability to tax that would have been shown by the return or other document (see sub-paragraphs (5) to (7)).

11(5) Where the tax at stake is income tax the applicable condition is satisfied if the income on or by reference to which the tax is charged, or any part of the income–

(a) was received in a territory outside the UK, or

(b) was transferred on or before 5 April 2017 to a territory outside the UK.

11(6) Where the tax at stake is capital gains tax, the applicable condition is satisfied if–

(a) the information that should have been given in the tax document relates to the proceeds of the disposal on or by reference to which the tax is charged, and

(b) the proceeds, or any part of the proceeds–

  (i) were received in a territory outside the UK, or

  (ii) were transferred on or before 5 April 2017 to a territory outside the UK.

11(7) Where the tax at stake is inheritance tax, the applicable condition is satisfied if–

(a) the information that should have been given in the tax document relates to the disposition that gives rise to the transfer of value by reason of which the tax becomes payable relates to a transfer of assets, and

(b) after that disposition but on or before 5 April 2017 the assets or any part of the assets are transferred to a territory outside the UK.

11(8) In the case of a transfer falling within sub-paragraph (5)(b), (6)(b) or (7)(b), references to the income, proceeds or assets transferred are to be read as including references to any assets derived from or representing the income, proceeds or assets.

"TAX"

12(1) References to **"tax"** are (unless in the context the reference is more specific) to income tax, capital gains tax or inheritance tax.

12(2) References to **"capital gains tax"** do not include capital gains tax payable by companies in respect of chargeable gains accruing to them to the extent that those gains are NRCGT gains in respect of which the companies are chargeable to capital gains tax under section 14D or 188D of TCGA 1992 (see section 1(2A)(b) of that Act).

12(3) In sub-paragraph (2) **"company"** has the same meaning as in TCGA 1992.

CORRECTING OFFSHORE TAX NON-COMPLIANCE

13(1) This paragraph sets out how offshore tax non-compliance may be corrected.

13(2) References to the correction of offshore tax non-compliance of any description are to the taking of any action specified in this paragraph as a means of correcting offshore tax non-compliance of that description.

13(3) Offshore tax non-compliance consisting of a failure to notify chargeability may be corrected by–

(a) giving the requisite notice to HMRC (unless before doing so the person has received a notice requiring the person to make and deliver a tax return) and giving HMRC the relevant information by any means mentioned in paragraph (b),

(b) giving HMRC the relevant information–
(i) by making and delivering a tax return,
(ii) using the digital disclosure service or any other service provided by HMRC as a means of correcting tax non-compliance,
(iii) communicating it to an officer of Revenue and Customs in the course of an enquiry into the person's tax affairs, or
(iv) using a method agreed with an officer of Revenue and Customs.

13(4) In sub-paragraph (3) **"relevant information"** means information relating to offshore tax that–
(a) had the requisite notice been given in time and the person given a notice to make and deliver a tax return, would have been required to be included in the tax return, and
(b) would have enabled or assisted HMRC to calculate the offshore tax due.

13(5) Offshore tax non-compliance consisting of a failure to make or deliver a return or other document may be corrected by giving HMRC the relevant information by–
(a) making or delivering the requisite return or document,
(b) using the digital disclosure service or any other service provided by HMRC as a means of correcting tax non-compliance,
(c) communicating it to an officer of Revenue and Customs in the course of an enquiry into the person's tax affairs, or
(d) using a method agreed with an officer of Revenue and Customs.

13(6) In subsection (5) **"relevant information"** means information relating to offshore tax that–
(a) should have been included in the return or other document, and
(b) would have enabled or assisted HMRC to calculate the offshore tax due.

13(7) Offshore tax non-compliance consisting of making and delivering a return or other document containing an inaccuracy may be corrected by giving HMRC the relevant information by–
(a) in the case of an inaccurate tax document, amending the document or delivering a new document,
(b) using the digital disclosure service or any other service provided by HMRC as a means of correcting tax non-compliance,
(c) communicating it to an officer of Revenue and Customs in the course of an enquiry into the person's tax affairs, or
(d) using a method agreed with an officer of Revenue and Customs.

13(8) In sub-paragraph (7) **"relevant information"** means information relating to offshore tax that–
(a) should have been included in the return but was not (whether due to an omission or the giving of inaccurate information), and
(b) would have enabled or assisted HMRC to calculate the offshore tax due.

13(9) In this paragraph **"offshore tax"**, in relation to any offshore tax non-compliance, means tax corresponding to the offshore PLR in respect of the non-compliance.

Part 2 – Amount of Penalty

AMOUNT OF PENALTY

14(1) The penalty payable under paragraph 1 is 200% of the offshore PLR attributable to the uncorrected offshore tax non-compliance (subject to any reduction under a provision of this Part of this Schedule).

14(2) In this Part of this Schedule **"the uncorrected offshore tax non-compliance"** means–
(a) the relevant offshore tax non-compliance, in a case where none of it is corrected within the RTC period, or
(b) so much of the relevant offshore tax non-compliance as has not been corrected within the RTC period, in a case where part of it is corrected within that period.

OFFSHORE PLR

15(1) In this Schedule **"offshore PLR"**, in relation to any offshore tax non-compliance means the potential loss of revenue attributable to that non-compliance, to be determined as follows.

15(2) The potential lost revenue attributable to any offshore tax non-compliance is (subject to sub-paragraphs (5) and (6))–

(a) if the non-compliance is a failure to notify chargeability, the potential lost revenue under the applicable provisions of paragraph 7 of Schedule 41 to FA 2008 (or, where the original offshore tax non-compliance took place before 1 April 2010, the amount referred to in section 7(8) of TMA 1970),

(b) if the non-compliance is a failure to deliver a return or other document, the amount of the liability to tax under the applicable provisions of paragraph 24 of Schedule 55 to FA 2009 (or, where the original offshore tax non-compliance took place before 1 April 2011, the amount of liability to tax that would have been shown in the return as defined in section 93(9) of TMA 1970), and

(c) if the non-compliance is delivering a return or other document containing an inaccuracy, the potential lost revenue under the applicable provisions of paragraphs 5 to 8 of Schedule 24 to FA 2007 (or, where the original offshore tax non-compliance took place before 1 April 2008, the difference described in section 95(2) of TMA 1970).

15(3) In its application for the purposes of sub-paragraph (2)(c) above, paragraph 6 of Schedule 24 to FA 2007 has effect as if–

(a) for sub-paragraph (1) there were substituted–

"**6(1)** Where–

(a) P is liable to a penalty in respect of two or more inaccuracies (each being an inaccuracy in a return or other document listed in paragraph 8(3) or (4) of Schedule 18) to F(No. 2)A 2017) in relation to a tax year or, in the case of inheritance tax, a single transfer of value,

(b) in relation to any one (or more than one) of those inaccuracies, the delivery of the return or other document containing it constitutes offshore tax non-compliance, and

(c) the calculation of potential lost revenue attributable to each of those inaccuracies depends on the order in which they are corrected,

the potential lost revenue attributable to any offshore tax non-compliance constituted by any one of those inaccuracies is to be taken to be such amount as is just and reasonable.

6(1A) In sub-paragraph (1) **"offshore tax non-compliance"** has the same meaning as in Schedule 18 to F(No. 2)A 2017."; and

(b) in sub-paragraph (4), for paragraphs (b) to (d) there were substituted–

"(b) other understatements."

15(4) In sub-paragraphs (5) and (6) **"combined tax non-compliance"** is tax non-compliance that–

(a) involves an offshore matter or an offshore transfer, but

(b) also involves an onshore matter.

15(5) Any combined tax non-compliance is to be treated for the purposes of this Schedule as if it were two separate acts of tax non-compliance, namely–

(a) the combined tax non-compliance so far as it involves an offshore matter or an offshore transfer (which is then offshore tax non-compliance within the meaning of this Schedule), and

(b) the combined tax non-compliance so far as it involves an onshore matter.

15(6) The potential lost revenue attributable to the offshore tax non-compliance referred to in sub-paragraph (5)(a) is to be taken to be such share of the potential lost revenue attributable to the combined tax non-compliance as is just and reasonable.

REDUCTION OF PENALTY FOR DISCLOSURE ETC BY PERSON LIABLE TO PENALTY

16(1) This paragraph provides for a reduction in a penalty under paragraph 1 for any uncorrected relevant offshore tax non-compliance if the person ("P") who is liable to the penalty discloses any matter mentioned in sub-paragraph (2) that is relevant to the non-compliance or its correction or to the assessment or enforcement of the offshore tax attributable to it.

16(2) The matters are–

(a) chargeability to income tax or capital gains tax (where the tax non-compliance is a failure to notify chargeability),

(b) a missing tax return,

(c) an inaccuracy in a document,

(d) a supply of false information or a withholding of information, or

(e) a failure to disclose an under-assessment.

16(3) A person discloses a matter for the purposes of this paragraph only by–

(a) telling HMRC about it,

(b) giving HMRC reasonable help in relation to the matter (for example by quantifying an inaccuracy in a document),
(c) informing HMRC of any person who acted as an enabler of the relevant offshore tax non-compliance or the failure to correct it, and
(d) allowing HMRC access to records–
 (i) for any reasonable purpose connected with resolving the matter (for example for the purpose of ensuring that an inaccuracy in a document is fully corrected), and
 (ii) for the purpose of ensuring that HMRC can identify all persons who may have acted as an enabler of the relevant offshore tax non-compliance or the failure to correct it.

16(4) Where a person liable to a penalty under paragraph 1 discloses a matter HMRC must reduce the penalty to one that reflects the quality of the disclosure.

16(5) But the penalty may not be reduced below 100% of the offshore PLR.

16(6) In relation to disclosure or assistance, **"quality"** includes timing, nature and extent.

16(7) For the purposes of sub-paragraph (3) a person "acted as an enabler" of relevant offshore tax non-compliance by another if the person encouraged, assisted or otherwise facilitated the conduct by the other person that constituted the offshore tax non-compliance.

17(1) If they think it right because of special circumstances, HMRC may reduce a penalty under paragraph 1.

17(2) In sub-paragraph (1) **"special circumstances"** does not include–
(a) ability to pay, or
(b) the fact that a potential loss of revenue from one taxpayer is balanced by a potential overpayment by another.

17(3) In sub-paragraph (1) the reference to reducing a penalty includes a reference to–
(a) staying a penalty, or
(b) agreeing a compromise in relation to proceedings for a penalty.

PROCEDURE FOR ASSESSING PENALTY, ETC

18(1) Where a person is found liable for a penalty under paragraph 1 HMRC must–
(a) assess the penalty,
(b) notify the person, and
(c) state in the notice–
 (i) the uncorrected relevant offshore tax non-compliance to which the penalty relates, and
 (ii) the tax period to which that offshore tax non-compliance relates.

18(2) A penalty must be paid before the end of the period of 30 days beginning with the day on which notification of the penalty is issued.

18(3) An assessment of a penalty–
(a) is to be treated for procedural purposes in the same way as an assessment to tax (except in respect of a matter expressly provided for by this Schedule),
(b) may be enforced as if it were an assessment to tax, and
(c) may be combined with an assessment to tax.

18(4) A supplementary assessment may be made in respect of a penalty if an earlier assessment operated by reference to an underestimate of the liability to tax that would have been shown in a return.

18(5) Sub-paragraph (6) applies if–
(a) an assessment in respect of a penalty is based on a liability to offshore tax that would have been shown on a return, and
(b) that liability is found by HMRC to have been excessive.

18(6) HMRC may amend the assessment so that it is based upon the correct amount.

18(7) But an amendment under sub-paragraph (6)–
(a) does not affect when the penalty must be paid, and
(b) may be made after the last day on which the assessment in question could have been made under paragraph 19.

19(1) An assessment of a penalty under paragraph 1 in respect of uncorrected relevant offshore tax non-compliance must be made before the end of the relevant period for that non-compliance.

19(2) If the non-compliance consists of a failure to notify chargeability, the relevant period is the period of 12 months beginning with–

(a) the end of the appeal period for the assessment of tax unpaid by reason of the failure, or

(b) if there is no such assessment, the date on which the amount of tax unpaid by reason of the failure is ascertained.

19(3) If the non-compliance consists of a failure to submit a return or other document, the relevant period is the period of 12 months beginning with–

(a) the end of the appeal period for the assessment of the liability to tax which would have been shown in the return, or

(b) if there is no such assessment, the date on which that liability is ascertained.

19(4) If the non-compliance consists of making and delivering a tax document containing an inaccuracy, the relevant period is the period of 12 months beginning with–

(a) the end of the appeal period for the decision correcting the inaccuracy, or

(b) if there is no assessment to the tax concerned within paragraph (a), the date on which the inaccuracy is corrected.

19(5) In this paragraph references to the appeal period are to the period during which–

(a) an appeal could be brought, or

(b) an appeal that has been brought has not been finally determined or withdrawn.

APPEALS

20 A person may appeal against–

(a) a decision of HMRC that a penalty under paragraph 1 is payable by that person, or

(b) a decision of HMRC as to the amount of a penalty under paragraph 1 payable by the person.

21(1) An appeal under paragraph 20 is to be treated in the same way as an appeal against an assessment to the tax at stake (including by the application of any provision about bringing the appeal by notice to HMRC, about HMRC review of the decision or about determination of the appeal by the First-tier Tribunal or Upper Tribunal).

21(2) Sub-paragraph (1) does not apply–

(a) so as to require the person bringing the appeal to pay a penalty before an appeal against the assessment of the penalty is determined,

(b) in respect of any other matter expressly provided for by this Schedule.

22(1) On an appeal under paragraph 20(a) that is notified to the tribunal, the tribunal may affirm or cancel HMRC's decision.

22(2) On an appeal under paragraph 20(b) that is notified to the tribunal, the tribunal may–

(a) affirm HMRC's decision, or

(b) substitute for that decision another decision that HMRC had power to make.

22(3) If the tribunal substitutes its own decision for HMRC's, the tribunal may rely on paragraph 16 or 17 (or both)–

(a) to the same extent as HMRC (which may mean applying the same percentage reduction as HMRC to a different starting point),

(b) to a different extent, but only if the tribunal thinks that HMRC's decision in respect of the application of that paragraph was flawed.

22(4) In sub-paragraph (3)(b) **"flawed"** means flawed when considered in the light of the principles applicable in proceedings for judicial review.

22(5) In this paragraph **"tribunal"** means the First-tier Tribunal or Upper Tribunal (as appropriate by virtue of paragraph 21(1)).

REASONABLE EXCUSE

23(1) Liability to a penalty under paragraph 1 does not arise in relation to a particular failure to correct any relevant offshore tax non-compliance within the RTC period if the person concerned (P) satisfies HMRC or the relevant tribunal (as the case may be) that there is a reasonable excuse for the failure.

23(2) For this purpose–

(a) an insufficiency of funds is not a reasonable excuse, unless attributable to events outside P's control,

(b) where P relied on any other person to do anything, that cannot be a reasonable excuse unless P took reasonable care to avoid the failure,

(c) where P had a reasonable excuse but the excuse has ceased, P is to be treated as continuing to have the excuse if the failure is remedied without unreasonable delay after the excuse ceased, and

(d) reliance on advice is to be taken automatically not to be a reasonable excuse if it is disqualified under sub-paragraph (3).

23(3) Advice is disqualified (subject to sub-paragraph (4)) if–

(a) the advice was given to P by an interested person,

(b) the advice was given to P as a result of arrangements made between an interested person and the person who gave the advice,

(c) the person who gave the advice did not have appropriate expertise for giving the advice,

(d) the advice failed to take account of all P's individual circumstances (so far as relevant to the matters to which the advice relates), or

(e) the advice was addressed to, or was given to, a person other than P.

23(4) Where advice would otherwise be disqualified under any of paragraphs (a) to (d) of sub-paragraph (3) the advice is not disqualified if at the end of the RTC period P–

(a) has taken reasonable steps to find out whether or not the advice falls within that paragraph, and

(b) reasonably believes that it does not.

23(5) In sub-paragraph (3) **"an interested person"** means, in relation to any relevant offshore tax non-compliance–

(a) a person (other than P) who participated in relevant avoidance arrangements or any transaction forming part of them, or

(b) a person who for any consideration (whether or not in money) facilitated P's entering into relevant avoidance arrangements.

23(6) In this paragraph **"avoidance arrangements"** means arrangements as respects which, in all the circumstances, it would be reasonable to conclude that their main purpose, or one of their main purposes, is the obtaining of a tax advantage.

23(7) But arrangements are not avoidance arrangements for the purposes of this paragraph if (although they fall within sub-paragraph (6))–

(a) they are arrangements which accord with established practice, and

(b) HMRC had, at the time the arrangements were entered into, indicated its acceptance of that practice.

23(8) Where any relevant offshore tax non-compliance arose originally because information was submitted to HMRC on the basis that particular avoidance arrangements had an effect which they did not have, those avoidance arrangements are **"relevant avoidance arrangements"** in relation to that tax non-compliance.

23(9) In sub-paragraph (6)–

(a) **"arrangements"** includes any agreement, understanding, scheme, transaction or series of transactions (whether or not legally enforceable), and

(b) a **"tax advantage"** includes–

(i) relief or increased relief from tax,

(ii) repayment or increased repayment of tax,

(iii) avoidance or reduction of a charge to tax or an assessment to tax,

(iv) avoidance of a possible assessment to tax,

(v) deferral of a payment of tax or advancement of a repayment of tax.

DOUBLE JEOPARDY

24(1) Where by reason of any conduct a person–

(a) has been convicted of an offence, or

(b) is liable to a penalty otherwise than under paragraph 1 for which the person has been assessed (and the assessment has not been successfully appealed against or withdrawn),

that conduct does not give rise to liability to a penalty under paragraph 1.

24(2) In sub-paragraph (1) the reference to a penalty otherwise than under paragraph 1–

(a) includes a penalty under paragraph 6 of Schedule 55 to FA 2009, but does not include penalties under any other provision of that Schedule, and

(b) includes a penalty under subsection (5) of section 93 of TMA 1970 but, does not include penalties under any other provision of that section.

24(3) But the aggregate of–

(a) the amount of a penalty under paragraph 1, and

(b) the amount of a penalty under paragraph 5 of Schedule 55 which is determined by reference to a liability to tax,

must not exceed 200% of that liability to tax.

24(4) In sub-paragraph (1) **"conduct"** includes a failure to act.

APPLICATION OF PROVISIONS OF TMA 1970

25 Subject to the provisions of this Part of this Schedule, the following provisions of TMA 1970 apply for the purposes of this Part of this Schedule as they apply for the purposes of the Taxes Acts–

(a) section 108 (responsibility of company officers),

(b) section 114 (want of form), and

(c) section 115 (delivery and service of documents).

Part 3 – Further Provisions Relating to the Requirement to Correct

EXTENSION OF PERIOD FOR ASSESSMENT ETC OF OFFSHORE TAX

26(1) This paragraph applies where–

(a) at the end of the tax year 2016–17 a person has relevant offshore tax non-compliance to correct, and

(b) the last day on which it would (disregarding this paragraph) be lawful for HMRC to assess the person to any offshore tax falls within the period beginning with 6 April 2017 and ending with 4 April 2021.

26(2) The period in which it is lawful for HMRC to assess the person to the offshore tax is extended by virtue of this paragraph to end with 5 April 2021.

26(3) In this paragraph **"offshore tax"**, in relation to any relevant offshore tax non-compliance, means tax corresponding to the offshore PLR in respect of the non-compliance.

FURTHER PENALTY IN CONNECTION WITH OFFSHORE ASSET MOVES

27(1) Schedule 21 to FA 2015 (penalties in connection with offshore asset moves) is amended as follows.

27(2) [Inserts FA 2015, Sch. 21, para. 2(d).]

27(3) [Inserts FA 2015, Sch. 21, para. 3(d).]

27(4) [Inserts FA 2015, Sch. 21, para. 5(5).]

ASSET-BASED PENALTY IN ADDITION TO PENALTY UNDER PARAGRAPH 1

28(1) Schedule 22 to FA 2016 (asset-based penalty for offshore inaccuracies and failures) is amended as follows.

28(2) [Amends FA 2016, Sch. 22, para. 2.]

28(3) [Inserts FA 2016, Sch. 22, para. 3(4) and (5).]

28(4) [Amends FA 2016, Sch. 22, para. 5.]

28(5) [Amends FA 2016, Sch. 22, para. 6.]

28(6) [Inserts FA 2016, Sch. 22, para. 6A.]

28(7) [Inserts FA 2016, Sch. 22, para. 13(2A).]

28(8) [Amends FA 2016, Sch. 22, para. 19(2).]

PUBLISHING DETAILS OF PERSONS ASSESSED TO PENALTY OR PENALTIES UNDER PARAGRAPH 1

30(1) The Commissioners for Her Majesty's Revenue and Customs ("the Commissioners") may publish information about a person (P) if in consequence of an investigation they consider that sub-paragraph (2) or (3) applies in relation to P.

30(2) This sub-paragraph applies if–

(a) P has been found to have incurred one or more relevant penalties under paragraph 1 (and has been assessed or is the subject of a contract settlement), and

(b) the offshore potential lost revenue in relation to the penalty, or the aggregate of the offshore potential lost revenue in relation to each of the penalties, exceeds £25,000.

30(3) This sub-paragraph applies if P has been found to have incurred 5 or more relevant penalties under paragraph 1.

30(4) A penalty incurred by P under paragraph 1 is **"relevant"** if –

(a) P was aware at any time during the RTC period that at the end of the 2016–17 tax year the person had relevant offshore tax non-compliance to correct, and

(b) the penalty relates to the failure to correct that non-compliance.

30(5) The information that may be published is–

(a) P's name (including any trading name, previous name or pseudonym),

(b) P's address (or registered office),

(c) the nature of any business carried on by P,

(d) the amount of the penalty or penalties,

(e) the offshore potential lost revenue in relation to the penalty or the aggregate of the offshore potential lost revenue in relation to each of the penalties,

(f) the periods or times to which the uncorrected relevant offshore tax non-compliance relates,

(g) any other information that the Commissioners consider it appropriate to publish in order to make clear the person's identity.

30(6) In sub-paragraph (5)(f) the reference to the uncorrected relevant offshore tax non-compliance is to so much of P's relevant offshore tax non-compliance at the end of the 2016–17 tax year as P failed to correct within the RTC period.

30(7) The information may be published in any manner that the Commissioners consider appropriate.

30(8) Before publishing any information the Commissioners must–

(a) inform P that they are considering doing so, and

(b) afford P the opportunity to make representations about whether it should be published.

30(9) No information may be published before the day on which the penalty becomes final or, where more than one penalty is involved, the latest day on which any of the penalties becomes final.

30(10) No information may be published for the first time after the end of the period of one year beginning with that day.

30(11) No information may be published (or continue to be published) after the end of the period of one year beginning with the day on which it is first published.

30(12) No information may be published if the amount of the penalty–

(a) is reduced under paragraph 16 to the minimum permitted amount (being 100% of the offshore PLR), or

(b) is reduced under paragraph 17 to nil or stayed.

30(13) For the purposes of this paragraph a penalty becomes final–

(a) if it has been assessed, when the time for any appeal or further appeal relating to it expires or, if later, any appeal or final appeal relating to it is finally determined, and

(b) if a contract settlement has been made, at the time when the contract is made.

30(14) In this paragraph **"contract settlement"**, in relation to a penalty, means a contract between the Commissioners and the person under which the Commissioners undertake not to assess the penalty or (if it has been assessed) not to take proceedings to recover it.

31(1) The Treasury may by regulations amend paragraph 30(2) to vary the amount for the time being specified in paragraph (b).

31(2) Regulations under this paragraph are to be made by statutory instrument.

31(3) A statutory instrument under this paragraph is subject to annulment in pursuance of a resolution of the House of Commons.

Part 4 – Supplementary

INTERPRETATION: MINOR

32(1) In this Schedule (apart from the amendments made by Part 3)–

"HMRC" means Her Majesty's Revenue and Customs;

"tax period" means a tax year or other period in respect of which tax is charged (or in the case of inheritance tax, the year beginning with 6 April and ending on the following 5 April in which the liability to tax first arose);

"tax year", in relation to inheritance tax, means a period of 12 months beginning on 6 April and ending on the following 5 April;

"UK" means the United Kingdom, including its territorial sea.

32(2) A reference to making a return or doing anything in relation to a return includes a reference to amending a return or doing anything in relation to an amended return.

32(3) References to delivery (of a document) include giving, sending and any other similar expressions.

32(4) A reference to delivering a document to HMRC includes–

(a) a reference to communicating information to HMRC in any form and by any method (whether by post, fax, email, telephone or otherwise, and

(b) a reference to making a statement or declaration in a document.

32(5) References to an assessment to tax, in relation to inheritance tax, are to a determination.

32(6) An expression used in relation to income tax has the same meaning as in the Income Tax Acts.

32(7) An expression used in relation to capital gains tax has the same meaning as in the enactments relating to that tax.

32(8) An expression used in relation to inheritance tax has the same meaning as in IHTA 1984.

TERMS DEFINED OR EXPLAINED FOR PURPOSES OF MORE THAN ONE PARAGRAPH OF THIS SCHEDULE

Term	*Paragraph*
assets (in paragraphs 8 to 10)	paragraph 9(7)
capital gains tax	paragraph 12(2)
HMRC	paragraph 32(1)
involves an offshore matter (in relation to failure to notify chargeability)	paragraph 9(2)
involves an offshore matter (in relation to failure to deliver a return or other document)	paragraph 10(2) and (3)
involves an offshore matter (in relation to delivery of a return or other document containing an inaccuracy)	paragraph 11(2) and (3)
involves an offshore transfer (in relation to failure to notify chargeability)	paragraph 9(3) to (6)
involves an offshore transfer (in relation to failure to deliver a return or other document)	paragraph 10(4) to (8)
involves an offshore transfer (in relation to delivery of a return or other document containing an inaccuracy)	paragraph 11(4) to (8)
involves an onshore matter (in relation to any tax non-compliance)	paragraph 7(2)
offshore tax non-compliance	paragraph 7(1)
offshore PLR	paragraph 15(1)
potential lost revenue	paragraph 15(2)
RTC period	paragraph 1(b)

relevant offshore tax non-compliance	paragraph 3
tax non-compliance	paragraph 8(1)
tax period	paragraph 32(1)
tax year (in relation to inheritance tax)	paragraph 32(1)
tax	paragraph 12(1)
UK	paragraph 32(1)
uncorrected offshore tax non-compliance (in Part 2)	paragraph 14(2)

FINANCE ACT 2018

(2018 Chapter 3)

[*15th March 2018*]

ARRANGEMENT OF SECTIONS

PART 1 – DIRECT TAXES

DOUBLE TAXATION RELIEF

PART 3 – MISCELLANEOUS AND FINAL

FINAL

PART 1 – DIRECT TAXES

DOUBLE TAXATION RELIEF

32 Double taxation arrangements specified by Order in Council

32(1) [Not relevant to inheritance tax.]

32(2) [Not relevant to inheritance tax.]

32(3) In section 158 of IHTA 1984 (double taxation conventions), after subsection (1) insert–

"**158(1ZA)** For the purposes of this section, arrangements made with a view to affording relief from double taxation include any arrangements which modify the effect of arrangements so made.

158(1ZB) Arrangementsto which effect is given under this section may include provision conferring (with or without other functions) functions relating to the determination of matters arising under the arrangements on a public authority in the United Kingdom or in a territory outside the United Kingdom."

32(4) The amendments made by subsections (1) to (3) are to be regarded as always having had effect.

32(5) [Not relevant to inheritance tax.]

32(6) The provision made by section 158(1ZA) and (1ZB) of IHTA 1984 in relation to Orders under section 158 of that Act applies, and is to be regarded as always having applied, in relation to Orders in Council under any provision which that section replaces (directly or indirectly).

PART 3 – MISCELLANEOUS AND FINAL

FINAL

49 Interpretation

49 In this Act the following abbreviations are references to the followingActs.

CAA 2001	Capital Allowances Act 2001
CEMA 1979	Customs and Excise Management Act 1979
CTA 2009	Corporation Tax Act 2009
CTA 2010	Corporation Tax Act 2010
FA, followed by a year	Finance Act of that year
F(No. 2)A, followed by a year	Finance (No. 2) Act of that year
F(No. 3)A, followed by a year	Finance (No. 3) Act of that year
IHTA 1984	Inheritance Tax Act 1984
ITA 2007	Income Tax Act 2007
ITEPA 2003	Income Tax (Earnings and Pensions) Act 2003

ITTOIA 2005	Income Tax (Trading and Other Income) Act 2005
TCGA 1992	Taxation of Chargeable Gains Act 1992
TIOPA 2010	Taxation (International and Other Provisions) Act 2010
TMA 1970	Taxes Management Act 1970
TPDA 1979	Tobacco Products Duty Act 1979
VATA 1994	Value Added Tax Act 1994
VERA 1994	Vehicle Excise and Registration Act 1994

50 Short title

50 This Act may be cited as the Finance Act 2018.

INHERITANCE TAX STATUTORY INSTRUMENTS

Table of Contents

Those statutory instruments listed below which contain substantive provisions are reproduced in the following pages. Statutory instruments which do no more than amend other instruments are not reproduced; the amendments made by them have been consolidated in the relevant amended regulations. They are, however, listed below for convenience.

STATUTORY INSTRUMENTS **Page**

CHRONOLOGICAL LISTING

continued over

IHT Statutory Instruments

STATUTORY INSTRUMENTS | Page

continued over

continued over

STATUTORY INSTRUMENTS **Page**

ALPHABETICAL LISTING

continued over

STATUTORY INSTRUMENTS Page

continued over

INHERITANCE TAX (DOUBLE CHARGES RELIEF) REGULATIONS 1987

(SI 1987/1130)

Made on 30 June 1987 by the Commissioners of Inland Revenue, in exercise of the powers conferred on them by s. 104 of the Finance Act 1986.

CITATION AND COMMENCEMENT

1 These Regulations may be cited as the Inheritance Tax (Double Charges Relief) Regulations 1987 and shall come into force on 22nd July 1987.

INTERPRETATION

2 In these Regulations unless the context otherwise requires–

"PET" means potentially exempt transfer;

"property" includes part of any property;

"the 1984 Act" means the Inheritance Tax Act 1984;

"the 1986 Act" means Part V of the Finance Act 1986;

"section" means section of the 1984 Act.

INTRODUCTORY

3 These Regulations provide for the avoidance, to the extent specified, of double charges to tax arising with respect to specified transfers of value made, and other events occurring, on or after 18th March 1986.

DOUBLE CHARGES – POTENTIALLY EXEMPT TRANSFERS AND DEATH

4(1) This regulation applies in the circumstances to which paragraph (a) of section 104(1) of the 1986 Act refers where the conditions (**"specified conditions"**) of paragraph (2) are fulfilled.

4(2) The specified conditions to which paragraph (1) refers are–

(a) an individual (**"the deceased"**) makes a transfer of value to a person (**"the transferee"**) which is a PET,

(b) the transfer is made on or after 18th March 1986,

(c) the transfer proves to be a chargeable transfer, and

(d) the deceased immediately before his death was beneficially entitled to property to which paragraph (3) refers.

4(3) The property to which paragraph (2)(d) refers is property–

(a) which the deceased, after making the PET to which paragraph (2)(a) refers, acquired from the transferee otherwise than for full consideration in money or money's worth,

(b) which is property which was transferred to the transferee by the PET to which paragraph (2)(a) refers or which is property directly or indirectly representing that property, and

(c) which is property comprised in the estate of the deceased immediately before his death (within the meaning of section 5(1)), value attributable to which is transferred by a chargeable transfer (under section 4).

4(4) Where the specified conditions are fulfilled there shall be calculated, separately in accordance with sub-paragraphs (a) and (b), the total tax chargeable as a consequence of the death of the deceased–

(a) disregarding so much of the value transferred by the PET to which paragraph (2)(a) refers as is attributable to the property, value of which is transferred by the chargeable transfer to which paragraph (3)(c) refers, and

(b) disregarding so much of the value transferred by the chargeable transfer to which paragraph (3)(c) refers as is attributable to the property, value of which is transferred by the PET to which paragraph (2)(a) refers.

4(5)

(a) Whichever of the two amounts of tax calculated under paragraph (4)(a) or (b) is the lower amount shall be treated as reduced to nil but, subject to sub-paragraph (b), the higher amount shall be payable,

(b) where the amount calculated under paragraph (4)(a) is higher than the amount calculated under paragraph (4)(b)–

IHT Statutory Instruments

(i) so much of the tax chargeable on the value transferred by the chargeable transfer to which paragraph (2)(c) refers as is attributable to the amount of that value which falls to be disregarded by virtue of paragraph (ii) shall be treated as a nil amount, and

(ii) for all the purposes of the 1984 Act so much of the value transferred by the PET to which paragraph (2)(a) refers as is attributable to the property to which paragraph (3)(c) refers shall be disregarded.

4(6) Part I of the Schedule to these Regulations provides an example of the operation of this regulation.

DOUBLE CHARGES – GIFTS WITH RESERVATION AND DEATH

5(1) This regulation applies in the circumstances to which paragraph (b) of section 104(1) of the 1986 Act refers where the conditions (**"specified conditions"**) of paragraph (2) are fulfilled.

5(2) The specified conditions to which paragraph (1) refers are–

(a) an individual (**"the deceased"**) makes a transfer of value by way of gift of property,

(b) the transfer is made on or after 18th March 1986,

(c) the transfer is or proves to be a chargeable transfer,

(d) the deceased dies on or after 18th March 1986,

(e) the property in relation to the gift and the deceased is property subject to a reservation (within the meaning of section 102 of the 1986 Act),

(f)

(i) the property is by virtue of section 102(3) of the 1986 Act treated for the purposes of the 1984 Act as property to which the deceased was beneficially entitled immediately before his death, or,

(ii) the property ceases to be property subject to a reservation and is the subject of a PET by virtue of section 102(4) of the 1986 Act, and

(g)

(i) the property is comprised in the estate of the deceased immediately before his death (within the meaning of section 5(1)) and value attributable to it is transferred by a chargeable transfer (under section 4), or

(ii) the property is property transferred by the PET to which sub-paragraph (f)(ii) refers, value attributable to which is transferred by a chargeable transfer.

5(3) Where the specified conditions are fulfilled there shall be calculated, separately in accordance with sub-paragraphs (a) and (b), the total tax chargeable as a consequence of the death of the deceased–

(a) disregarding so much of the value transferred by the transfer of value to which paragraph (2)(a) refers as is attributable to property to which paragraph (2)(g) refers, and

(b) disregarding so much of the value of property to which paragraph (2)(g) refers as is attributable to property to which paragraph (2)(a) refers.

5(4) Where the amount calculated under paragraph (3)(a) is higher than the amount calculated under paragraph (3)(b)–

(a) only so much of that higher amount shall be payable as remains after deducting, as a credit, from the amount comprised in that higher amount which is attributable to the value of the property to which paragraph (2)(g) refers, a sum (not exceeding the amount so attributable) equal to so much of the tax paid–

(i) as became payable before the death of the deceased, and

(ii) as is attributable to the value disregarded under paragraph (3)(a), and

(b) so much of the value transferred by the transfer of value to which paragraph (2)(a) refers as is attributable to the property to which paragraph (2)(g) refers shall (except in relation to chargeable transfers which were chargeable to tax, when made by the deceased, for the purposes of an occasion which occurred before the death of the deceased on which tax was chargeable under section 64 or 65) be treated as reduced to a nil amount for all the purposes of the 1984 Act.

5(5) Where the amount calculated under paragraph (3)(a) is less than the amount calculated under paragraph (3)(b) the value of the property to which paragraph (2)(g) refers shall be reduced to nil for all the purposes of the 1984 Act.

5(6) For the purposes of the interpretation and application of this regulation section 102 of and Schedule 20 to the 1986 Act shall apply.

5(7) Part II of the Schedule to these Regulations provides examples of the operation of this regulation.

DOUBLE CHARGES – LIABILITIES SUBJECT TO ABATEMENT AND DEATH

6(1) This regulation applies in the circumstances to which paragraph (c) of section 104(1) of the 1986 Act refers where the conditions (**"specified conditions"**) of paragraph (2) are fulfilled.

6(2) The specified conditions to which paragraph (1) refers are–

(a) a transfer of value which is or proves to be a chargeable transfer (**"the transfer"**) is made on or after 18th March 1986 by an individual (**"the deceased"**) by virtue of which the estate of the transferee is increased or by virtue of which property becomes comprised in a settlement of which the transferee is a trustee, and

(b) at any time before his death the deceased incurs a liability to the transferee (**"the liability"**) which is a liability subject to abatement under the provisions of section 103 of the 1986 Act in determining the value transferred by a chargeable transfer (under section 4).

6(3) Where the specified conditions are fulfilled there shall be calculated, separately in accordance with sub-paragraphs (a) and (b), the total tax chargeable as a consequence of the death of the deceased–

(a) disregarding so much of the value transferred by the transfer–

(i) as is attributable to the property by reference to which the liability falls to be abated, and

(ii) as is equal to the amount of the abatement of the liability, and

(b) taking account both of the value transferred by the transfer and of the liability.

6(4)

(a) Whichever of the two amounts of tax calculated under paragraph (3)(a) or (b) is the lower amount shall be treated as reduced to nil but, subject to sub-paragraph (b), the higher amount shall be payable,

(b) where the amount calculated under paragraph (3)(a) is higher than the amount calculated under paragraph (3)(b)–

(i) only so much of that higher amount shall be payable as remains after deducting, as a credit, from that amount a sum equal to so much of the tax paid–

(a) as became payable before the death of the deceased, and

(b) as is attributable to the value disregarded under paragraph (3)(a), and

(c) as does not exceed the difference between the amount of tax calculated under paragraph (3)(a) and the amount of tax that would have fallen to be calculated under paragraph (3)(b) if the liability had been taken into account, and

(ii) so much of the value transferred by the transfer to which paragraph (2)(a) refers–

(a) as is attributable to property by reference to which the liability is abated, and

(b) as is equal to the amount of the abatement of the liability,

shall (except in relation to chargeable transfers which were chargeable to tax, when made by the deceased, for the purposes of an occasion which occurred before the death of the deceased on which tax was chargeable under section 64 or 65) be treated as reduced to a nil amount for all the purposes of the 1984 Act.

6(5) Where there is a number of transfers made by the deceased which are relevant to the liability to which paragraph (2)(b) applies the provisions of this regulation shall apply to those transfers taking them in reverse order of their making, that is to say, taking the latest first and the earliest last, but only to the extent that in aggregate the value of those transfers does not exceed the amount of the abatement to which paragraph (2)(b) refers.

6(6) Part III of the Schedule to these Regulations provides examples of the operation of this regulation.

DOUBLE CHARGES – CHARGEABLE TRANSFERS AND DEATH

7(1) This regulation applies in the circumstances specified (by this regulation) for the purposes of paragraph (d) of section 104(1) of the 1986 Act (being circumstances which appear to the Board to be similar to those referred to in paragraphs (a) to (c) of that subsection) where the conditions (**"specified conditions"**) of paragraph (2) are fulfilled.

7(2) The specified conditions to which paragraph (1) refers are–

(a) an individual (**"the deceased"**) makes a transfer of value to a person (**"the transferee"**) which is a chargeable transfer,

(b) the transfer is made on or after 18th March 1986,

(c) the deceased dies within 7 years after that chargeable transfer is made, and

(d) the deceased immediately before his death was beneficially entitled to property to which paragraph (3) refers.

IHT Statutory Instruments

7(3) The property to which paragraph (2)(d) refers is property–

(a) which the deceased, after making the chargeable transfer to which paragraph (2)(a) refers, acquired from the transferee otherwise than for full consideration in money or money's worth,

(b) which was transferred to the transferee by the chargeable transfer to which paragraph (2)(a) refers or which is property directly or indirectly representing that property, and

(c) which is property comprised in the estate of the deceased immediately before his death (within the meaning of section 5(1)), value attributable to which is transferred by a chargeable transfer (under section 4).

7(4) Where the specified conditions are fulfilled there shall be calculated, separately in accordance with sub-paragraphs (a) and (b), the total tax chargeable as a consequence of the death of the deceased–

(a) disregarding so much of the value transferred by the chargeable transfer to which paragraph (2)(a) refers as is attributable to the property, value of which is transferred by the chargeable transfer to which paragraph (3)(c) refers, and

(b) disregarding so much of the value transferred by the chargeable transfer to which paragraph (3)(c) refers as is attributable to the property, value of which is transferred by the chargeable transfer to which paragraph (2)(a) refers.

7(5)

(a) Whichever of the two amounts of tax calculated under paragraph (4)(a) or (b) is the lower amount shall be treated as reduced to nil but, subject to sub-paragraph (b), the higher amount shall be payable,

(b) where the amount calculated under paragraph (4)(a) is higher than the amount calculated under paragraph (4)(b)–

(i) only so much of that higher amount shall be payable as remains after deducting, as a credit, from the amount comprised in that higher amount which is attributable to the value of the property to which paragraph (2)(d) refers, a sum (not exceeding the amount so attributable) equal to so much of the tax paid–

(a) as became payable before the death of the deceased; and

(b) as is attributable to the value disregarded under paragraph (4)(a), and

(ii) so much of the value transferred by the chargeable transfer to which paragraph (2)(a) refers as is attributable to the property to which paragraph (3)(c) refers shall (except for the purposes of an occasion which occurred before the death of the deceased on which tax was chargeable under section 64 or 65) be treated as reduced to a nil amount for all the purposes of the 1984 Act.

7(6) Part IV of the Schedule to these Regulations provides an example of the operation of this regulation.

EQUAL CALCULATIONS OF TAX – SPECIAL RULE

8 Where the total tax chargeable as a consequence of death under the two separate calculations provided for by any of regulation 4(4), 5(3), 6(3) or 7(4) is equal in amount the first of those calculations shall be treated as producing a higher amount for the purposes of the regulation concerned.

SCHEDULE AND SAVING

9 The Schedule to these Regulations shall have effect only for providing examples of the operation of these Regulations and, in the event of any conflict between the Schedule and the Regulations, the Regulations shall prevail.

SCHEDULE

Regulation 9

INTRODUCTORY

1 This Schedule provides examples of the operation of the Regulations.

2 In this Schedule–

"cumulation" *means the inc*lusion of the total chargeable transfers made by the transferor in the 7 years preceding the current transfer;

"GWR" means gift with reservation;

"taper relief" means the reduction in tax provided under section 7(4) of the 1984 Act, inserted by paragraph 2(4) of Schedule 19 to the 1986 Act.

3 Except where otherwise stated, the examples assume that–

– tax rates and bands remain as at 18 March 1987;
– the transferor has made no other transfers than those shown in the examples;
– no exemptions (including annual exemption) or reliefs apply to the value transferred by the relevant transfer; and
– "grossing up" does not apply in determining any lifetime tax (the tax is not borne by the transferor).

PART I

Regulation 4: Example

Jul 1987	A makes PET of £100,000 to B	
Jul 1988	A makes gift into discretionary trust of £95,000	Tax paid £750
Jan 1989	A makes further gift into same trust of £45,000	Tax paid £6,750
Jan 1990	B dies and the 1987 PET returns to A	
Apr 1991	A dies. His death estate of £300,000 includes the 1987 PET returned to him in 1990, which is still worth £100,000	

First calculation under reg. 4(4)(a)

Charge the returned PET in A's death estate and ignore the PET made in 1987.

		Tax
Jul 1987	PET £100,000 ignored	NIL
Jul 1988	Gift £95,000	
	Tax £1,500 less £750 already paid	£750
Jan 1989	Gift £45,000 as top slice of £140,000	
	Tax £13,500 less £6,750 already paid	£6,750
Apr 1991	Death estate £300,000 as top slice of £440,000	£153,000*
	Total tax due as result of A's death	£160,500

* In first calculation the tax of £153,000 on death estate does not allow for any successive charges relief (under s. 141 IHTA 1984) that might be due in respect of "the returned PET" by reference to any tax charged on that "PET" in connection with B's death.

Second calculation under reg. 4(4)(b)

Charge the 1987 PET and ignore the value of the returned PET in A's death estate.

		Tax
Jul 1987	PET £100,000. Tax with taper relief	£2,400
Jul 1988	Gift £95,000 as top slice of £195,000	
	Tax £34,000 less £750 already paid	£33,250
Jan 1989	Gift £45,000 as top slice of £240,000	
	Tax £20,000 less £6,750 already paid	£13,250
Apr 1991	Death estate £200,000 as top slice of £440,000	£111,000
	Total tax due as result of A's death	£159,900

Result*

First calculation gives higher amount of tax. So PET reduced to nil and tax on other transfers is as in first calculation.

* If, after allowing any successive charges relief, the second calculation gives higher amount of tax, 1987 PET will be charged and tax on other transfers will be as in second calculation.

PART II

Regulation 5: Example 1

Jan 1988	A makes PET of £150,000 to B.	
Mar 1992	A makes gift of land worth £200,000 into a discretionary trust of which he is a potential beneficiary. The gift is a "GWR"	Tax paid £19,500
Feb 1995	A dies without having released his interest in the trust. His death estate valued at £400,000, includes the GWR land currently worth £300,000	

First calculation under reg. 5(3)(a)

Charge the GWR land in A's death estate and ignore the GWR.

		Tax
Jan 1988	PET (now exempt)	NIL
Mar 1992	GWR ignored	NIL
Feb 1995	Death estate £400,000	
	Tax £144,000 less £19,500 already paid on GWR*	£124,500
	Total tax due as result of A's death	£124,500

* Credit for the tax already paid cannot exceed the amount of the death tax attributable to the value of the GWR property. In this example the tax so attributable is £108,000 (ie 144,000/400,000 × 300,000). So credit is given for the full amount of £19,500.

Second calculation under reg. 5(3)(b)

Charge the GWR and ignore the GWR land in the death estate.

		Tax
Jan 1988	PET (now exempt)	NIL
March 1992	GWR £200,000	
	Tax £39,000 less £19,500 already paid	£19,500
Feb 1995	Death estate £100,000 (ignoring GWR property) as top slice of £300,000	£48,000
	Total tax due as result of A's death	£67,500

Result

First calculation yields higher amount of tax. So the value of the GWR transfer is reduced to nil and tax on death is charged as in first calculation with credit for the tax already paid.

PART II

Regulation 5: Example 2

Apr 1987	A makes gift into discretionary trust of £150,000	Tax paid £9,500
Jan 1988	A makes further gift into same trust of £50,000.	Tax paid £10,000
Mar 1993	A makes PET of shares valued at £150,000 to B	
Feb 1996	A dies. He had continued to enjoy the income of the shares he had given to B (the 1993 PET is a GWR). His death estate, valued at £300,000, includes those shares currently worth £200,000.	

[**Croner-i Note** – The government printer's edition of these regulations gives a figure for the April 1987 gift of £1,500,000. This would appear to be a typographical error as both calculations subsequently use the figure of £150,000 for the April 1987 gift.]

First calculation under reg. 5(3)(a)

Charge the GWR shares in the death estate and ignore the PET.

		Tax
Apr 1987	Gift £150,000. No adjustment to tax as gift made more than 7 years before death	NIL
Jan 1988	Gift £50,000. No adjustment to tax as gift made more than 7 years before death	NIL
Mar 1993	PET £150,000 now reduced to NIL	NIL
Feb 1996	Death estate including GWR shares £300,000. No previous cumulation	£87,000
	Total tax due as result of A's death	£87,000

Second calculation under reg. 5(3)(b)

Charge the PET and ignore the value of the GWR shares in the death estate.

		Tax
Apr 1987	Gift £150,000. No adjustment to tax as gift made more than 7 years before death	NIL
Jan 1988	Gift £50,000. No adjustment to tax as gift made more than 7 years before death	NIL
Mar 1993	GWR £150,000 as top slice of £350,000 (ie previous gifts totalling £200,000 + £150,000)	£75,000
Feb 1996	Death estate (excluding GWR shares) £100,000 as top slice of £250,000 (the 1987 and 1988 gifts drop out of cumulation)	£43,000
	Total tax due as result of A's death	£118,000

Result

Second calculation yields higher amount of tax. So tax is charged by reference to the PET and the value of the GWR shares in the death estate is reduced to NIL.

PART III

Regulation 6: Example 1

Nov 1987	X makes a PET of cash of £95,000 to Y
Dec 1987	Y makes a loan to X of £95,000
May 1988	X makes a gift into discretionary trust of £20,000
Apr 1993	X dies. His death estate is worth £182,000. A deduction of £95,000 is claimed for the loan from Y

First calculation under reg. 6(3)(a)

No charge on November 1987 gift, and no deduction against death estate.

		Tax
Nov 1987	PET ignored	NIL
May 1988	Gift £20,000	NIL
Apr 1993	Death estate £182,000 as top slice of £202,000	£39,800
	Total tax due as result of X's death	£39,800

IHT Statutory Instruments

Second calculation under reg. 6(3)(b)

Charge the November 1987 PET, and allow the deduction against the death estate.

		Tax
Nov 1987	PET £95,000. Tax with taper relief	£600
May 1988	Gift £20,000 as top slice of £115,000. Tax with taper relief	£3,600
Apr 1993	Death estate (£182,000 – loan of £95,000) £87,000 as top slice of £202,000	£32,300
	Total tax due as result of X's death	£36,500

Result

First calculation gives higher amount of tax. So debt is disallowed against death estate, but PET of £95,000 is not charged.

PART III

Regulation 6: Example 2

Aug 1988	P makes a PET of cash of £100,000 to Q	
Sept 1988	Q makes a loan to P of £100,000	
Oct 1989	P makes gift into discretionary trust of £98,000	Tax paid £1,200
Nov 1992	P dies. Death estate £110,000 less allowable liabilities of £80,000 (which do not include the debt of £100,000 owed to Q)	

First calculation under reg. 6(3)(a)

No charge on August 1988 PET, and no deduction against death estate for the £100,000 owed to Q.

		Tax
Aug 1988	PET ignored	NIL
Oct 1989	Gift £98,000	
	Tax (with taper relief) £1,920 less £1,200 already paid	£720
Nov 1992	Death estate £30,000 as top slice of £128,000	£9,000
	Total tax due as result of P's death	£9,720

Second calculation under reg. 6(3)(b)

Charge the August 1988 PET, and allow deduction against death estate for the £100,000 owed to Q.

		Tax
Aug 1988	PET £100,000. Tax with taper relief	£1,800
Oct 1989	Gift £98,000 as top slice of £198,000	
	Tax (with taper relief) £28,100 less £1,200 already paid	£26,960
Nov 1992	Death estate £30,000–£100,000 (owed to Q)	NIL
	Total tax due as result of P's death	£28,760

Result

Second calculation gives higher amount of tax. So the PET to Q is charged, and deduction is allowed against death estate for the debt of Q.

PART III

Regulation 6: Example 3

1 May 1987	A makes PET to B of £95,000	
1 Jan 1988	A makes PET to B of £40,000	
1 Jul 1988	A makes gift into discretionary trust of £100,000	Tax paid £1,500
1 Jan 1989	A makes PET to B of £30,000	
1 Jul 1989	B makes a loan to A of £100,000	
1 Dec 1990	A dies. Death estate £200,000, against which deduction is claimed for debt of £100,000 due to B	

First calculation under reg. 6(3)(a)

Disallow the debt and ignore corresponding amounts (£100,000) of PETs from A to B, starting with the latest PET.

		Tax
1 May 1987	PET now reduced to £65,000	NIL
1 Jan 1988	PET now reduced to NIL	NIL
1 Jul 1988	Gift into trust £100,000 as top slice of £165,000	
	Tax £25,000 less £1,500 already paid	£23,500
1 Jan 1989	PET now reduced to NIL	NIL
1 Dec 1990	Death estate £200,000 as top slice of £365,000	£98,000
	Total tax due as result of A's death	£121,500

Second calculation under reg. 6(3)(b)

Allow the debt and charge PETs to B in full.

		Tax
1 May 1987	PET £95,000. Tax with taper relief	£1,200
1 Jan 1988	PET £40,000 as top slice of £135,000	£12,000
1 Jul 1988	Gift into trust £100,000 as top slice of £235,000	
	Tax £41,000 less £1,500 already paid	£39,500
1 Jan 1989	PET £30,000 as top slice of £265,000	£15,000
1 Dec 1990	Death estate £100,000 as top slice of £365,000	£53,500
	Total tax due as result of A's death	£121,200

Result

First calculation yields higher amount of tax. So the debt is disallowed and corresponding amounts of PETs to B are ignored in determining the tax due as a result of the death.

PART III

Regulation 6: Example 4

1 Apr 1987	A makes gift into discretionary trust of £100,000	Tax paid £1,500
1 Jan 1990	A makes PET to B of £60,000	
1 Jan 1991	A makes further gift into same trust of £50,000	Tax paid £8,000
1 Jan 1992	Same trust makes a loan to A of £120,000	
1 Jun 1994	A dies. Death estate is £220,000, against which deduction is claimed for debt of £120,000 due to the trust	

First calculation under reg. 6(3)(a)

Disallow the debt and ignore corresponding amounts (£120,000) of gifts from A to trust, starting with the latest gift.

		Tax
1 Apr 1987	Gift now reduced to £30,000. No adjustment to tax already paid as gift made more than 7 years before death	NIL
1 Jan 1990	PET £60,000 as top slice of £90,000	NIL
1 Jan 1991	Gift now reduced to NIL. No adjustment to tax already paid	NIL
1 Jun 1994	Death estate £220,000 as top slice of £280,000 (the 1987 gift at £30,000 drops out of cumulation)	£77,000
		£77,000
	Less credit for tax already paid £1,500 + £8,000	£9,500
	Total tax due as result of A's death	£67,500

Second calculation under reg. 6(3)(b)

Allow the debt and no adjustment to gifts into the trust.

		Tax
1 Apr 1987	Gift £100,000. No adjustment to tax already paid as gift made more than 7 years before death	NIL
1 Jan 1990	PET £60,000 as top slice of £160,000. Tax with taper relief	£12,000
1 Jan 1991	Gift £50,000 as top slice of £210,000	
	Tax (with taper relief) £16,000 less £8,000 already paid	£8,000
1 Jun 1994	Death estate £100,000 as top slice of £210,000. (The 1987 gift drops out of cumulation. No credit for tax paid on that gift.)	£37,000
	Total tax due as result of A's death	£57,000

Result

First calculation yields higher amount tax. So the debt is disallowed and corresponding amounts of gifts into trust are ignored in determining the tax due as a result of the death.

PART IV

Regulation 7: Example

May 1986	S transfers into discretionary trust property worth £150,000. Immediate charge at the rates then in force	Tax paid £13,750
Oct 1986	S gives T a life interest in shares worth £85,000. Immediate charge at the rates then in force	Tax paid £19,500
Jan 1991	S makes a PET to R of £20,000	
Dec 1992	T dies, and the settled shares return to S who is the settlor and therefore no tax charge on the shares on T's death.	
Aug 1993	S dies. His death estate includes the shares returned from T which are currently worth £75,000, and other assets worth £144,000	

First calculation under reg. 7(4)(a)

Charge the returned shares in the death estate and ignore the October 1986 gift. Tax rates and bands are those in force at the date of S's death.

		Tax
May 1986	Gift into trust made more than 7 years before death. So no adjustment to tax already paid but the gift cumulates in calculating tax on other gifts	NIL
Oct 1986	Gift ignored and no adjustment to tax already paid	NIL
Jan 1991	PET of £20,000 as top slice of (£150,000 + £20,000) £170,000	£8,000
Nov 1993	Death estate £219,000 as top slice of £239,000	
	Tax £56,500 less £19,350 (part of tax already paid)*	£37,150
	Total tax due as result of S's death	£45,150

* £19,350 represents the amount of the death tax attributable to the value of the returned shares, and is lower than the amount of the lifetime tax charged on those shares. So credit against the death charge for the tax already paid is restricted to the lower amount.

[**Croner-i Note** – The figure of £37,150 representing tax on the value of S's estate at his death in November 1993 is only correct if tax due is £56,500 (less £19,350), and not £56,000 as set out in the government printer's edition of these regulations.]

Second calculation under reg. 7(4)(b)

Charge the October 1986 gift and ignore the returned shares in the death estate. Tax rates and bands are those in force at the date of S's death.

		Tax
May 1986	Gift into trust made more than 7 years before death. So no adjustment to tax already paid but the gift is taken into account in calculating the tax on the other gifts	NIL
Oct 1986	Gift of £85,000 as top slice of £235,000	
	Tax (with taper relief) £7,100 less £19,500 already paid	NIL*
Jan 1991	PET of £20,000 as top slice of £255,000	£10,000
Aug 1993	Death estate (excluding the returned shares) £144,000 as top slice of £249,000 (£85,000 + £20,000 + £144,000)	£57,000
	Total tax due as result of S's death	£67,000

* Credit for the tax already paid restricted to the (lower) amount of tax payable as result of the death. No repayment of the excess.

Result

Second calculation gives higher amount of tax. So tax is charged as in second calculation by excluding shares from the death estate.

TAXES (INTEREST RATE) REGULATIONS 1989

(SI 1989/1297, as amended by SI 1991/889, SI 1993/2212, SI 1994/1307, SI 1994/1567, SI 1996/2644, SI 1996/3187, SI 1997/1681, SI 1997/2707, SI 1998/310, SI 1998/3176, SI 1999/1928, SI 1999/2538, SI 1999/2637, SI 2000/893, SI 2001/204, SI 2001/254, SI 2005/2462, SI 2007/684, SI 2008/778, SI 2008/3234, SI 2009/199 and SI 2009/2032)

Made on 27 July 1989 by the Treasury, in exercise of the powers conferred on them by s. 178 of the Finance Act 1989.

CITATION AND COMMENCEMENT

1 These Regulations may be cited as the Taxes (Interest Rate) Regulations 1989 and shall come into force on 18th August 1989.

INTERPRETATION

2(1) In these Regulations unless the context otherwise requires–

"the 1998 Regulations" means the Corporation Tax (Instalment Payments) Regulations 1998;

"established rate" means–

(a) on the coming into force of these Regulations, 14 per cent per annum; and

(b) in relation to any date after the first reference date after the coming into force of these Regulations, the reference rate found on the immediately preceding reference date;

"operative date" means–

(a) the twelfth working day after the reference date, or

(b) where regulation 3ZA or 3BA applies–

(i) where the reference date is the first Tuesday, the day which is the Monday next following the first Tuesday, or

(ii) where the reference date is the second Tuesday, the day which is the Monday next following the second Tuesday;

"reference date" means–

(a) the working day following the day on which the most recent meeting of the Monetary Policy Committee of the Bank of England took place, or

(b) where regulation 3ZA or 3BA applies–

(i) the day which is the Tuesday next following the day on which that meeting took place ("the first Tuesday"), and

(ii) the day which is the Tuesday ("the second Tuesday") occurring two weeks after the first Tuesday;

"section 178" means section 178 of the Finance Act 1989;

"working day" means any day other than a non-business day within the meaning of section 92 of the Bills of Exchange Act 1882.

2(2) In these Regulations the reference rate found on a reference date is the official bank rate determined by the most recent meeting of the Monetary Policy Committee of the Bank of England.

History – In reg. 2(1), in para. (a) of the definition of "operative date", the word "twelfth" substituted for the word "eleventh" by SI 2009/2032, reg. 3(2)(a), with effect from 12 August 2009.
In reg. 2(1), the definition of "operative date" substituted by SI 2008/3234, reg. 2(2)(a), with effect from 7 January 2009.
In reg. 2(1), in para. (a) of the definition of "reference date", the word "second" (which appeared before the word "working") omitted by SI 2009/2032, reg. 3(2)(b), with effect from 12 August 2009.
In reg. 2(1), the definition of "reference date" substituted by SI 2008/3234, reg. 2(2)(b), with effect from 7 January 2009.
In reg. 2(1), definition of "the 1998 Regulations" inserted, words from "or, where regulation 3ZA" to the end added to each of the definitions of "operative date" and "reference date" by SI 1998/3176, reg. 3, and in reg. 2(2), para. (i), (ii) and (iii) substituted for former wording by SI 1998/3176, reg. 4, operative from 7 January 1999.
Reg. 2(2) substituted by SI 2009/2032, reg. 3(3), with effect from 12 August 2009.

APPLICABLE RATE OF INTEREST EQUAL TO ZERO

2A [Omitted by SI 2009/2032, reg. 4.]

History – Reg. 2A omitted by SI 2009/2032, reg. 4, with effect from 12 August 2009.

APPLICABLE RATE OF INTEREST ON UNPAID TAX, TAX REPAID AND REPAYMENT SUPPLEMENT

3–3BB [Not relevant to inheritance tax.]

APPLICABLE RATE OF INTEREST ON UNPAID INHERITANCE TAX, CAPITAL TRANSFER TAX AND ESTATE DUTY

4(1) For the purposes of–

(a) section 8(9) of the Finance Act 1894,

(b) section 18 of the Finance Act 1896,

(c) section 61(5) of the Finance Act (1909–10) Act 1910,

(d) section 17(3) of the Law of Property Act 1925,

(e) section 73(6) of the Land Registration Act 1925; and

(f) sections 233 of the Inheritance Tax Act 1984,

(g) section 236(4) of the Inheritance Tax Act 1984 so far as it relates to tax charged by virtue of section 147(4) of that Act.

the rate applicable under section 178 shall, subject to paragraph (2), be 11 per cent per annum.

4(2) Where, on a reference date after the coming into force of these Regulations, the reference rate found on that date differs from the established rate, the rate applicable under section 178 for the purposes of the enactments referred to in paragraph (1) shall, on and after the next operative date, be the percentage per annum found by applying the formula specified in paragraph (3).

4(3) The formula specified in this paragraph is–

$$RR + 2.5,$$

where RR is the reference rate referred to in paragraph (2).

History – In reg. 4(1) the words "[and] 236(3) and (4)" (the "and" in square brackets not actually specified in the amending provision) omitted and sub-para. (g) inserted by SI 2009/2032, reg. 12(2), with effect from 12 August 2009.
In reg. 4(2) the words "and, if the result is not a whole number, rounding the result down to the nearest such number" omitted by SI 2009/2032, reg. 12(3), with effect from 12 August 2009.
Reg. 4(3) substituted by SI 2009/2032, reg. 12(4), with effect from 12 August 2009.

APPLICABLE RATE ON REPAYMENTS OF INHERITANCE TAX, CAPITAL TRANSFER TAX AND ESTATE DUTY

4A(1) For the purposes of–

(a) section 48(1) of the Finance Act 1975,

(b) sections 235(1) of the Inheritance Tax Act 1984,

(c) section 236(3) of the Inheritance Tax Act, and

(d) section 236(4) of the Inheritance Tax Act so far as it relates to tax repayable under section 147(2) of that Act,

the rate applicable under section 178 shall, subject to paragraph (3), be the percentage per annum found by applying the formula specified in paragraph (2), but if the result is not a whole number the result shall be rounded down to the nearest such number.

4A(2) The formula specified for the purposes of paragraph (1) is–

$$\frac{(RR + 2) \times 80}{100} - 1,$$

where RR is the official bank rate determined at the meeting of the Monetary Policy Committee of the Bank of England which immediately preceded the coming into force of these Regulations.

4A(3) Where on a reference date after the coming into force of these Regulations, the reference rate found on that date differs from the established rate, the rate applicable under section 178 for the purposes of the enactments referred to in paragraph (1) shall, on and after the next operative date, be the higher of–

(a) 0.5% per annum, and

(b) the percentage per annum found by applying the formula specified in paragraph (4).

4A(4) The formula specified in this paragraph is–

$$RR - 1,$$

where RR is the reference rate referred to in paragraph (3).

History – Reg. 4A inserted by SI 2009/2032, reg. 13, with effect from 12 August 2009.

APPLICABLE RATE OF OFFICIAL RATE OF INTEREST

5 [Not relevant to inheritance tax.]

EFFECT OF CHANGE IN APPLICABLE RATE

6 Where the rate applicable under section 178 for the purpose of any of the enactments referred to in these Regulations changes on an operative date by virtue of these Regulations, that change shall have effect for periods beginning on or after the operative date in relation to interest running from before that date as well as from or from after that date.

History – In reg. 6 the words "these Regulations" substituted for the words "regulation 3(1) or 4(1)" by SI 2009/2032, reg. 14, with effect from 12 August 2009.
In reg. 6, reference to reg. 5(1) omitted by SI 1991/889, reg. 4, operative from 6 April 1991.

INHERITANCE TAX (MARKET MAKERS) REGULATIONS 1992

(SI 1992/3181 as amended by SI 2001/3629)

Made on 11 December 1992 by the Commissioners of Inland Revenue, in exercise of the powers conferred on them by s. 106(4), (6) and (8) and s. 107(4), (6) and (8) of the Finance Act 1986.

CITATION AND COMMENCEMENT

1 These Regulations may be cited as the Inheritance Tax (Market Makers) Regulations 1992 and shall come into force on 6th January 1993.

INTERPRETATION

2 In these Regulations **"subsection (7)"** and **"subsection (4)"** mean subsection (7) of section 105 and subsection (4) of section 234 respectively of the Inheritance Tax Act 1984.

APPLICATION OF REGULATIONS

3 The day specified for the application of these Regulations in accordance with sections 106(6) and 107(6) of the Finance Act 1986 is 23rd March 1992.

MODIFICATIONS OF SUBSECTION (7) AND SUBSECTION (4)

4 Subsection (7) and subsection (4) shall have effect as if–

(a) the reference to The Stock Exchange in paragraph (a) of each of those subsections were a reference to either of The Stock Exchange and LIFFE (Administration and Management) (both being recognised investment exchanges within the meaning given by section 285(1)(a) of the Financial Services and Markets Act 2000, and

(b) the reference to the Council of The Stock Exchange in paragraph (b) of each of those subsections were a reference to the investment exchange concerned.

History – In reg. 4(a) the words "given by section 285(1)(a) of the Financial Services and Markets Act 2000" substituted for "of the Financial Services Act 1986" by SI 2001/3629, reg. 135 which came into force on 1 December 2001.

Cross references – IHTA 1984, s. 105(7): "market maker" for the purposes of relevant business property.
IHTA 1984, s. 234(4): "market maker" for the purposes of interest on instalment payments.

INHERITANCE TAX (SETTLED PROPERTY INCOME YIELD) ORDER 2000

(SI 2000/174)

The Treasury in exercise of the powers conferred on them by s. 50(3) of the Inheritance Tax Act 1984 hereby make the following Order:

1(1) This Order may be cited as the Inheritance Tax (Settled Property Income Yield) Order 2000 and shall come into force on 18th February 2000.

1(2) This Order shall have effect in relation to transfers of value made on or after 18th February 2000.

2 In this Order references to "indices" are to the indices which are published in the Financial Times and produced in conjunction with the Institute of Actuaries and the Faculty of Actuaries.

3 The rate prescribed as the higher rate for the purposes of section 50 of the Inheritance Tax Act 1984 is the rate that is equal to the rate of the Irredeemables' yield shown in the indices which are known as the "FTSE Actuaries Government Securities UK Indices" and which are produced either–

(a) for the date on which the value in question is to be determined, or, if those indices are not produced for that date,

(b) for the latest date preceding that date for which those indices are produced.

4 The rate prescribed as the lower rate for the purposes of section 50 of the Inheritance Tax Act 1984 is the rate that is equal to the rate of the All-Share actual dividend yield shown in the indices which are known as the "FTSE Actuaries Share Indices" and which are produced either–

(a) for the date on which the value in question is to be determined, or, if those indices are not produced for that date,

(b) for the latest date preceding that date for which those indices are produced.

INHERITANCE TAX (DELIVERY OF ACCOUNTS) (EXCEPTED ESTATES) REGULATIONS 2004

(SI 2004/2543, as amended by SI 2005/3230, SI 2006/2141, SI 2011/214, SI 2011/2226 and SI 2014/488)

Made on 27 September 2004, after consultation with the Lord Chancellor and the Scottish Ministers, by the Commissioners of Inland Revenue, in exercise of the powers conferred on them by s. 256(1) of the Inheritance Tax Act 1984. Operative from 1 November 2004.

CITATION, COMMENCEMENT AND EFFECT

1 These Regulations may be cited as the Inheritance Tax (Delivery of Accounts) (Excepted Estates) Regulations 2004, shall come into force on 1st November 2004 and shall have effect in relation to deaths occurring on or after 6th April 2004.

INTERPRETATION

2 In these Regulations–

"the Board" means the Commissioners for Her Majesty's Revenue and Customs;

"the 1984 Act" means the Inheritance Tax Act 1984;

"an excepted estate" has the meaning given in regulation 4;

"IHT threshold" has the meaning given in regulation 5A;

"the prescribed period" in relation to any person is the period beginning with that person's death and ending–

(a) in England, Wales and Northern Ireland, 35 days after the making of the first grant of representation in respect of that person (not being a grant limited in duration, in respect of property or to any special purpose); or

(b) in Scotland, 60 days after the date on which confirmation to that person's estate was first issued;

"section 131 rights" means the rights of issue under section 131(2) of the Civil Partnership Act 2004;

"spouse, civil partner and charity transfer" has the meaning given in regulation 5;

"value" means value for the purpose of tax.

History – In reg. 2 in the definition of "Board" the words "Commissioners for Her Majesty's Revenue and Customs" substituted for the words "Commissioners of Inland Revenue" by SI 2006/2141, reg. 3 with effect from 1 September 2006 in relation to deaths occurring on or after that date.

In reg. 2, the definition of "IHT threshold" substituted by SI 2011/214, reg. 2, with effect from 1 March 2011 in relation to deaths occurring on or after 6 April 2010. The former definition read:

"**"IHT threshold"** means the lower limit shown in the Table in Schedule 1 of the 1984 Act applicable to–

(a) chargeable transfers made in the year before that in which a person's death occurred if–

(i) that person died on or after 6th April and before 6th August, and

(ii) an application for a grant of representation or, in Scotland, an application for confirmation, is made before 6th August in that year; or

(b) chargeable transfers made in the year in which a person's death occurred in any other case,

and for this purpose "year" means a period of twelve months ending with 5th April;".

In reg. 2, the definition of "section 131 rights" inserted by SI 2005/3230, reg. 15(2)(b), with effect from 5 December 2005.

In reg. 2 in the definition of "spouse and charity transfer" the words ", civil partner" inserted by SI 2005/3230, reg. 15(2)(a), with effect from 5 December 2005.

ACCOUNTS

3(1) No person is required to deliver an account under section 216 of the 1984 Act of the property comprised in an excepted estate.

3(2) If in reliance on these Regulations a person has not delivered an account paragraphs (3) and (4) apply.

3(3) If it is discovered at any time that the estate is not an excepted estate, the delivery to the Board within six months of that time of an account of the property comprised in that estate shall satisfy any requirement to deliver an account.

3(4) If the estate is no longer an excepted estate following an alteration of the dispositions taking effect on death within section 142 of the 1984 Act, the delivery to the Board within six months of the date of the instrument of variation of an account of the property comprised in that estate shall satisfy any requirement to deliver an account.

EXCEPTED ESTATES

4(1) An excepted estate means the estate of a person immediately before his death in the circumstances prescribed by paragraphs (2), (3) or (5).

4(2) The circumstances prescribed by this paragraph are that–

(a) the person died on or after 6th April 2004, domiciled in the United Kingdom;

(b) the value of that person's estate is attributable wholly to property passing–

(i) under his will or intestacy,

(ii) under a nomination of an asset taking effect on death,

(iii) under a single settlement in which he was entitled to an interest in possession in settled property, or

(iv) by survivorship in a beneficial joint tenancy or, in Scotland, by survivorship in a special destination;

(c) of that property–

(i) not more than £150,000 represented value attributable to property which, immediately before that person's death, was settled property; and

(ii) not more than £100,000 represented value attributable to property which, immediately before that person's death, was situated outside the United Kingdom;

(ca) that person was not a person by reason of whose death one of the alternatively secured pension fund provisions applies;

(d) subject to paragraph (7A), that person died without having made any chargeable transfers during the period of seven years ending with his death other than specified transfers where, subject to paragraph (7), the aggregate value transferred did not exceed £150,000; and

(e) the aggregate of–

(i) the gross value of that person's estate,

(ii) subject to paragraph (7), the value transferred by any specified transfers made by that person, and

(iii) the value transferred by any specified exempt transfers made by that person,

did not exceed the IHT threshold.

4(3) The circumstances prescribed by this paragraph are that–

(a) the person died on or after 6th April 2004, domiciled in the United Kingdom;

(b) the value of that person's estate is attributable wholly to property passing–

(i) under his will or intestacy,

(ii) under a nomination of an asset taking effect on death,

(iii) under a single settlement in which he was entitled to an interest in possession in settled property, or

(iv) by survivorship in a beneficial joint tenancy or, in Scotland, by survivorship in a special destination;

(c) of that property–

(i) subject to paragraph (8), not more than £150,000 represented value attributable to property which, immediately before that person's death, was settled property; and

(ii) not more than £100,000 represented value attributable to property which, immediately before that person's death, was situated outside the United Kingdom;

(ca) that person was not a person by reason of whose death one of the alternatively secured pension fund provisions applies;

(d) subject to paragraph (7A), that person died without having made any chargeable transfers during the period of seven years ending with his death other than specified transfers where, subject to paragraph (7), the aggregate value transferred did not exceed £150,000;

(e) the aggregate of–

(i) the gross value of that person's estate,

(ii) subject to paragraph (7), the value transferred by any specified transfers made by that person, and

(iii) the value transferred by any specified exempt transfers made by that person,

did not exceed £1,000,000;

(ea) the total value transferred on that person's death by a spouse, civil partner or charity transfer is greater than nil; and

(f) the aggregate of–

$$A - (B + C)$$

does not exceed the IHT threshold, where–

A is the aggregate of the values in sub-paragraph (e),

B, subject to paragraph (4), is the total value transferred on that person's death by a spouse, civil partner or charity transfer, and

C, subject to paragraph (7B), is the total liabilities of the estate.

4(4) In Scotland, if legitim or section 131 rights could be claimed which would reduce the value of the spouse, civil partner or charity transfer, the value of B is reduced–

(a) to take account of any legitim or section 131 rights claimed, and

(b) on the basis that any part of the remaining legitim fund, which has been neither claimed nor renounced at the time of the application for confirmation, will be claimed in full, and

(c) on the basis that all section 131 rights, which have been neither claimed nor renounced at the time of the application for confirmation, will be claimed in full.

4(5) The circumstances prescribed by this paragraph are that–

(a) the person died on or after 6th April 2004;

(b) that person was never domiciled in the United Kingdom or treated as domiciled in the United Kingdom by section 267 of the 1984 Act;

(ba) that person was not a person by reason of whose death one of the alternatively secured pension fund provisions applies; and

(c) the value of that person's estate situated in the United Kingdom is wholly attributable to cash or quoted shares or securities passing under his will or intestacy or by survivorship in a beneficial joint tenancy or, in Scotland, by survivorship in a special destination, the gross value of which does not exceed £150,000.

4(6) For the purposes of paragraphs (2) and (3)–

"specified transfers" means, subject to paragraph (7A), chargeable transfers made by a person during the period of seven years ending with that person's death where the value transferred is attributable to–

(a) cash;

(b) personal chattels or corporeal moveable property;

(c) quoted shares or securities; or

(d) an interest in or over land, save to the extent that sections 102 and 102A(2) of the Finance Act 1986 apply to that transfer or the land became settled property on that transfer;

"specified exempt transfers" means transfers of value made by a person during the period of seven years ending with that person's death which are exempt transfers only by reason of–

(a) section 18 (transfers between spouses or civil partners),

(b) section 23 (gifts to charities),

(c) section 24 (gifts to political parties),

(d) section 24A (gifts to housing associations),

(e) section 27 (maintenance funds for historic buildings, etc), or

(f) section 28 (employee trusts)

of the 1984 Act.

4(7) For the purpose of paragraphs (2)(d) and (e) and (3)(d) and (e), sections 104 (business property relief) and 116 (agricultural property relief) of the 1984 Act shall not apply in determining the value transferred by a chargeable transfer.

4(7A) For the purpose of paragraphs (2)(d) and (e), (3)(d) and (e) and (6) any transfers of value made by that person in any period from 6th April in any year until and including the following 5th April which–

(i) are exempt transfers by virtue of section 21 (normal expenditure out of income) of the 1984 Act,

(ii) are made less than seven years prior to the death of that person, and

(iii) are in total more than £3,000,

shall be treated as chargeable transfers.

4(7B) For the purpose of paragraph (3)(f) **"the total liabilities of the estate"** do not include liabilities of the estate to the extent that they–

(a) are not discharged as mentioned in section 175A(1)(a) of the 1984 Act (discharge of liabilities after death);

(b) are prevented from being taken into account as mentioned in section 175A(1)(b) of the 1984 Act (discharge of liabilities after death); or

(c) are attributable as mentioned in section 162A(1)(a) or (b), or section 162A(5), of the 1984 Act (liabilities attributable to financing excluded property).

4(8) Paragraph (3)(c)(i) does not apply to property which immediately before the person's death was settled property, to the extent that the property is transferred on that person's death by a spouse, civil partner or charity transfer.

4(9) In this regulation **"the alternatively secured pension fund provisions"** means the following sections of the 1984 Act–

(a) section 151A (person dying with alternatively secured pension fund);

(b) section 151B (relevant dependant with pension fund inherited from member over 75); and

(c) section 151C (dependant dying with other pension fund).

4(10) Paragraphs (2)(ca), (3)(ca) and (5)(ba)(a) shall not have effect in relation to deaths occurring on or after 6th April 2011.

History – In reg. 4(1) reference to para. "(5)" substituted for reference to para. "(4)" by SI 2006/2141, reg. 4(2) with effect from 1 September 2006 in relation to deaths occurring on or after that date.
In reg. 4(2)(c)(i) "£150,000" substituted for "£100,000" by SI 2006/2141, reg. 4(3)(a) with effect from 1 September 2006 in relation to deaths occurring on or after that date.
In reg. 4(2)(c)(ii) "£100,000" substituted for "£75,000" by SI 2006/2141, reg. 4(3)(b) with effect from 1 September 2006 in relation to deaths occurring on or after that date.
Reg. 4(2)(ca) inserted by SI 2006/2141, reg. 4(3)(c) with effect from 1 September 2006 in relation to deaths occurring on or after that date.
In reg. 4(2)(d) "£150,000" substituted for "£100,000" by SI 2006/2141, reg. 4(3)(d) with effect from 1 September 2006 in relation to deaths occurring on or after that date.
In reg. 4(3)(c)(i) "£150,000" substituted for "£100,000" by SI 2006/2141, reg. 4(3)(a) with effect from 1 September 2006 in relation to deaths occurring on or after that date.
In reg. 4(3)(c)(ii) "£100,000" substituted for "£75,000" by SI 2006/2141, reg. 4(3)(b) with effect from 1 September 2006 in relation to deaths occurring on or after that date.
Reg. 4(3)(ca) inserted by SI 2006/2141, reg. 4(3)(c) with effect from 1 September 2006 in relation to deaths occurring on or after that date.
In reg. 4(2)(d) the words "subject to paragraph (7A)," inserted by SI 2011/214, reg. 3(2), with effect from 1 March 2011 in relation to deaths occurring on or after that date.
In reg. 4(3)(d) the words "subject to paragraph (7A)," inserted by SI 2011/214, reg. 3(3)(a), with effect from 1 March 2011 in relation to deaths occurring on or after that date.
In reg. 4(3)(d) "£150,000" substituted for "£100,000" by SI 2006/2141, reg. 4(3)(d) with effect from 1 September 2006 in relation to deaths occurring on or after that date.
Reg. 4(3)(ea) inserted, and the "and" at the end of reg. 4(3)(e) omitted, by SI 2011/214, reg. 3(3)(c) and (b), with effect from 1 March 2011 in relation to deaths occurring on or after that date.
In reg. 4(3)(f), the words ", subject to paragraph (7B)," inserted by SI 2014/488, reg. 2(2), with effect from 1 April 2014.
In reg. 4(3)(f) in the definition of "B" the words ", civil partner" inserted by SI 2005/3230, reg. 15(3)(a), with effect from 5 December 2005.
Reg. 4(4) substituted by SI 2005/3230, reg. 15(3)(b), with effect from 5 December 2005.
In reg. 4(5), subpara. (b) and (ba) substituted for subpara. (b) by SI 2006/2141, reg. 4(4) with effect from 1 September 2006 in relation to deaths occurring on or after that date.
In reg. 4(5)(c) "£150,000" substituted for "£100,000" by SI 2006/2141,reg. 4(4)(b) with effect from 1 September 2006 in relation to deaths occurring on or after that date.
In reg. 4(6) the words ", subject to paragraph (7A)," inserted by SI 2011/214, reg. 3(4), with effect from 1 March 2011 in relation to deaths occurring on or after that date.
In reg. 4(6), in subpara. (a) of the definition of "specified exempt transfers" the words "or civil partners" inserted by SI 2005/3230, reg. 15(3)(c), with effect from 5 December 2005.
Reg. 4(7A) inserted by SI 2011/214, reg. 3(5), with effect from 1 March 2011 in relation to deaths occurring on or after that date.
Reg. 4(7B) inserted by SI 2014/488, reg. 2(3), with effect from 1 April 2014.
In reg. 4(8) the words ", civil partner" inserted by SI 2005/3230, reg. 15(3)(d), with effect from 5 December 2005.
Reg. 4(9) inserted by SI 2006/2141, reg. 4(5) with effect from 1 September 2006 in relation to deaths occurring on or after that date.
Reg. 4(10) inserted by SI 2011/2226, reg. 2, with effect from 1 October 2011.

SPOUSE, CIVIL PARTNER AND CHARITY TRANSFERS

History – In the heading to reg. 5 the words ", civil partner" inserted by SI 2005/3230, reg. 15(4)(c), with effect from 5 December 2005.

5(1) For the purposes of these Regulations, a spouse, civil partner or charity transfer means any disposition (whether effected by will, under the law relating to intestacy or otherwise) of property comprised in a person's estate–

(a) *subject to paragraph (2), to the person's spouse or civil partner within section 18(1) of the 1984 Act;* and

(b) subject to paragraph (3), to a charity within section 23(1) of the 1984 Act or for national purposes within section 25(1) of the 1984 Act.

5(2) A transfer is not a spouse or civil partner transfer within paragraph (1)(a) if either spouse or civil partner was not domiciled in the United Kingdom at any time prior to the transfer.

5(3) A transfer is not a charity transfer within paragraph (1)(b) if the property becomes comprised in a settlement as a result of the disposition.

History – In reg. 5(1) the words ", civil partner" and in para. (a) the words "or civil partner" inserted by SI 2005/3230, reg. 15(4)(a), with effect from 5 December 2005.

In reg. 5(2) the words "or civil partner" inserted twice by SI 2005/3230, reg. 15(4)(b), with effect from 5 December 2005.

IHT THRESHOLD

5A(1) Subject to paragraph (2), for the purposes of these Regulations **"IHT threshold"** means the amount shown in the second column in the first row of the Table in Schedule 1 to the 1984 Act (upper limit of portion of value charged at rate of nil per cent) and in the first column in the second row of that Table (lower limit of portion charged at next rate) applicable to–

(a) chargeable transfers made in the year before that in which a person's death occurred if–

(i) that person died on or after 6th April and before 6th August, and

(ii) an application for a grant of representation or, in Scotland, an application for confirmation, is made before 6th August in that year; or

(b) chargeable transfers made in the year in which a person's death occurred in any other case,

and for this purpose **"year"** means a period of twelve months ending with 5th April.

5A(2) Where the criteria specified in paragraphs (3) and (4) are met **"IHT threshold"** means the IHT threshold as defined in paragraph (1) as increased by 100 per cent.

5A(3) The criteria specified in this paragraph are as follows–

(a) immediately before the death of a person (referred to for the purposes of this paragraph and paragraphs (4), (5) and (6), as a **"first deceased person"**) that first deceased person was the spouse or civil partner of the person specified in regulation 4(2) or (3) (referred to for the purposes of this paragraph as "the survivor");

(b) the survivor survived the first deceased person;

(c) either–

(i) in a case where the first deceased person was the spouse of the survivor, the first deceased person died on or after 13th November 1974, or

(ii) in a case where the first deceased person was the civil partner of the survivor, the first deceased person died on or after 5th December 2005; and

(d) a claim is made pursuant to section 8A of the 1984 Act–

(i) by virtue of which the nil-rate band maximum at the time of the survivor's death is treated, for the purpose of the charge to tax on the death of the survivor, as increased by 100 per cent, and

(ii) which is made in respect of not more than one first deceased person.

5A(4) The criteria specified in this paragraph are as follows–

(a) the first deceased person died domiciled in the United Kingdom;

(b) the value of the first deceased person's estate is attributable wholly to property passing–

(i) under the first deceased person's will or intestacy, or

(ii) by survivorship in a beneficial joint tenancy or, in Scotland, by survivorship in a special destination;

(c) of that property, not more than £100,000 represented value attributable to property which immediately before the first deceased person's death was situated outside the United Kingdom;

(d) the first deceased person was not a person by reason of whose death one of the alternatively secured pension fund provisions applies;

(e) the first deceased person died without having made any chargeable transfers during the period of seven years ending with the first deceased person's death; and

(f) the value transferred by any chargeable transfer made on the death of the first deceased person was not reduced by virtue of section 104 (business property relief) or section 116 (agricultural property relief) of the 1984 Act.

5A(5) For the purpose of paragraph 4(e), sections 104 (business property relief) and 116 (agricultural property relief) of the 1984 Act shall not apply in determining whether the first deceased person has made a chargeable transfer.

5A(6) Subject to paragraph (8)(a), for the purpose of paragraph (4)(e) any transfers of value made by the first deceased person in any period from 6th April in any year until and including the following 5th April which–

(i) are exempt transfers by virtue of section 21 (normal expenditure out of income) of the 1984 Act,

(ii) are made less than seven years prior to the death of that person, and

(iii) are in total more than £3,000,

shall be treated as chargeable transfers.

5A(7) In this regulation **"the alternatively secured pension fund provisions"** means the following sections of the 1984 Act–

(a) section 151A (person dying with alternatively secured pension fund);

(b) section 151B (relevant dependant with pension fund inherited from member over 75); and

(c) section 151C (dependant dying with other pension fund).

5A(8) In this regulation–

(a) paragraph (6) shall have effect in relation to deaths occurring on or after 1st March 2011; and

(b) paragraph (7) shall have effect in relation to deaths occurring on or after 6th April 2010.

History – In reg. 5A(6), "(8)(a)" substituted for "(7)" by SI 2011/2226, reg. 3(1), with effect from 1 October 2011.
Reg. 5A(7) and (8) substituted for former reg. 5A(7) by SI 2011/2226, reg. 3(2), with effect from 1 October 2011. Former reg. 5A(7) read as follows:
Reg. 5A and the heading before it inserted by SI 2011/214, reg. 4, with effect from 1 March 2011 in relation to deaths occurring on or after 6 April 2010.

PRODUCTION OF INFORMATION

6(1) Subject to paragraphs (3) and (4), a person who by virtue of these Regulations is not required to deliver to the Board an account under section 216 of the 1984 Act of the property comprised in an excepted estate, must produce the information specified in paragraph (2) and, where the criteria specified in regulation 5A(3) and (4) are met, paragraph (2A), to the Board in such form as the Board may prescribe.

6(2) The information specified for the purpose of paragraph (1) is–

(a) the following details in relation to the deceased–

(i) full name;

(ii) date of death;

(iii) marital or civil partnership status;

(iv) occupation;

(v) any surviving spouse or civil partner, parent, brother or sister;

(vi) the number of surviving children, step-children, adopted children or grandchildren;

(vii) national insurance number, tax district and tax reference;

(viii) if the deceased was not domiciled in the United Kingdom at his date of death, his domicile and address;

(b) details of all property to which the deceased was beneficially entitled and the value of that property;

(c) details of any specified transfers, specified exempt transfers and the value of those transfers;

(d) the liabilities of the estate; and

(e) any spouse, civil partner or charity transfers and the value of those transfers.

6(2A) The information specified for the purpose of paragraph (1) is–

(a) the full name of the first deceased person,

(b) the last known address of the first deceased person,

(c) the date of death of the first deceased person,

(d) the date and place of the marriage or civil partnership (as the case may be) between the first deceased person and the survivor, and

(e) either–

(i) a statement specifying whether a grant of probate, grant of letters of administration or grant of confirmation was issued in relation to the estate of the first deceased person and the date and place of issue of such grant, or

(ii) a statement specifying that no grant of probate, grant of letters of administration or grant of confirmation was issued in relation to the estate of the first deceased person.

6(2B) In paragraph (2A) **"first deceased person"** and **"survivor"** shall have the meaning given to them in regulation 5A(3)(a).

6(3) Paragraph (1) does not apply to the extent that the information specified in paragraph (2) and, where applicable, paragraph (2A) has been produced in an account under section 216 of the 1984 Act of the property comprised in the excepted estate that has been delivered to the Board.

6(4) Paragraph (2)(a)(v) and (vi) shall not have effect in relation to information produced to the Board pursuant to paragraph (1) of this regulation on or after 1st March 2011.

History – In reg. 6(1), the words "paragraphs (3) and (4)" substituted for the words "paragraph (3)" by SI 2011/2226, reg. 4(2), with effect from 1 October 2011.
Reg. 6(1) substituted by SI 2011/214, reg. 5(2), with effect from 1 March 2011 in relation to deaths occurring on or after 6 April 2010. Former reg. 6(1) read as follows:
"**6(1)** Subject to paragraph (3), a person who by virtue of these Regulations is not required to deliver to the Board an account under section 216 of the 1984 Act of the property comprised in an excepted estate, must produce the information specified in paragraph (2) to the Board in such form as the Board may prescribe.".
In reg. 6(2)(a)(iii) the words "or civil partnership" and in reg. 6(2)(a)(v) the words "or civil partner" inserted by SI 2005/3230, reg. 15(5)(a), with effect from 5 December 2005.
In reg. 6(2)(e) the words ", civil partner" inserted by SI 2005/3230, reg. 15(5)(b), with effect from 5 December 2005.
Reg. 6(2A) inserted by SI 2011/214, reg. 5(3), with effect from 1 March 2011 in relation to deaths occurring on or after 6 April 2010.
Reg. 6(2B) inserted by SI 2011/214, reg. 5(3), with effect from 1 March 2011 in relation to deaths occurring on or after 6 April 2010.
In reg. 6(3) the words "to the extent that the information" substituted for the words "if the information" by SI 2011/214, reg. 5(4)(a), with effect from 1 March 2011 in relation to deaths occurring on or after 6 April 2010.
In reg. 6(3) the words "and, where applicable, paragraph (2A)" inserted by SI 2011/214, reg. 5(4)(b), with effect from 1 March 2011 in relation to deaths occurring on or after 6 April 2010.
Reg. 6(4) inserted by SI 2011/2226, reg. 4(3), with effect from 1 October 2011.

Cross references – Civil Partnership Act 2004, s. 246 (not reproduced): reference to an individual's step-children in reg. 6(2)(a) to include references to children of that individual's civil partner; in force from 5 December 2005 (by virtue of SI 2005/3137, art. 3).

7(1) The information specified in regulation 6(2) and (2A) must be produced to the Board by producing it to–

(a) a probate registry in England and Wales;

(b) the sheriff in Scotland;

(c) the Probate and Matrimonial Office in Northern Ireland.

7(2) Information produced in accordance with paragraph (1) is to be treated for all purposes of the 1984 Act as produced to the Board.

7(3) The person or body specified in paragraph (1) must transmit the information produced to them to the Board within one week of the issue of the grant of probate or confirmation.

History – In reg. 7(1) "and (2A)" inserted by SI 2011/214, reg. 6, with effect from 1 March 2011 in relation to deaths occurring on or after 6 April 2010.

DISCHARGE OF PERSONS AND PROPERTY FROM TAX

8(1) Subject to paragraph (2) and regulation 9, if the information specified in regulation 6 has been produced in accordance with these Regulations, all persons shall on the expiration of the prescribed period be discharged from any claim for tax on the value transferred by the chargeable transfer made on the deceased's death and attributable to the value of the property comprised in an excepted estate and any Inland Revenue charge for that tax shall then be extinguished.

8(2) Paragraph (1) shall not apply if within the prescribed period the Board issue a notice to–

(a) the person or persons who would apart from these Regulations be required to deliver an account under section 216 of the 1984 Act, or

(b) the solicitor or agent of that person or those persons who produced the specified information pursuant to regulation 6,

requiring additional information or documents to be produced in relation to the specified information produced pursuant to regulation 6.

9 Regulation 8 shall not discharge any person from tax in the case of fraud or failure to disclose material facts and shall not affect any tax that may be payable if further property is later shown to form part of the estate and, in consequence of that property, the estate is not an excepted estate.

History – In reg. 9 reference to reg. "8" substituted for reference to reg. "9" by SI 2006/2141, reg. 5 with effect from 1 September 2006 in relation to deaths occurring on or after that date.

TRANSFERS REPORTED LATE

10 An account of an excepted estate shall, for the purposes of section 264(8) of the 1984 Act (delivery of account to be treated as payment where tax rate nil), be treated as having been delivered on the last day of the prescribed period in relation to that person.

REVOCATION

11 The Inheritance Tax (Delivery of Accounts) (Excepted Estates) Regulations 2002 and the Inheritance Tax (Delivery of Accounts) (Excepted Estates) (Amendment) Regulations 2003(b) are revoked in relation to deaths occurring on or after 6th April 2004.

CONTRACTING OUT (FUNCTIONS IN RELATION TO CULTURAL OBJECTS) ORDER 2005

(SI 2005/1103)

Made on 24 March 2005 by the Secretary of State, in exercise of the powers conferred upon her by s. 69 of [the Deregulation and Contracting Out Act 1994]. Operative from 25 March 2005.

CITATION AND COMMENCEMENT

1 This Order may be cited as the Contracting Out (Functions in Relation to Cultural Objects) Order 2005 and shall come into force on the day after the day on which it is made.

2 In this Order–

"the functions" means the functions now vested in the Secretary of State under the following provisions–

(a) section 230 of the Inheritance Tax Act 1984;

(b) [not relevant to inheritance tax;]

(c) [not relevant to inheritance tax.]

CONTRACTING OUT OF FUNCTIONS

3 Subject to article 4 of this Order, the functions, or any of them, may be exercised by, or by employees of, such person (if any) as may be authorised in that behalf by the Secretary of State–

(a) either wholly or to such extent as may be specified in the authorisation;

(b) either generally or in such cases or areas as may be so specified; and

(c) either unconditionally or subject to the fulfilment of such conditions as may be so specified.

SUPPLEMENTARY

4 Where any person has been authorised to exercise any functions of the Secretary of State in relation to the Export of Objects of Cultural Interest (Control) Order 2003, the provisions of article 8 of that Order shall apply to information held by that person, or by any employee of that person, as they apply to information held by the Secretary of State.

INHERITANCE TAX (DOUBLE CHARGES RELIEF) REGULATIONS 2005

(SI 2005/3441)

Made on 14 December 2005 by the Commissioners for Her Majesty's Revenue and Customs, in exercise of the powers conferred by s. 104 of the Finance Act 1986. Operative from 4 January 2006.

CITATION, COMMENCEMENT AND INTERPRETATION

1(1) These Regulations may be cited as the Inheritance Tax (Double Charges Relief) Regulations 2005, and shall come into force on 4th January 2006.

1(2) In these Regulations–

"the Commissioners" means the Commissioners for Her Majesty's Revenue and Customs;

"the debt" means the debt mentioned in regulation 3(2);

"the relevant property" has the meaning given in regulation 3(6).

GENERAL

2(1) These Regulations apply in the circumstances specified in regulation 3.

2(2) They apply for the purposes of paragraph (d) of section 104(1) of the Finance Act 1986 (which refers to circumstances appearing to the Commissioners to be circumstances similar to those referred to in paragraphs (a) to (c) of that provision).

2(3) To the extent specified in regulation 4, these Regulations apply for the avoidance of double charges to tax.

CIRCUMSTANCES IN WHICH THESE REGULATIONS APPLY

3(1) These Regulations apply where conditions A to D are met.

3(2) Condition A is that an individual ("the deceased") enters into arrangements ("the arrangements") under which–

(a) the disposal condition or the contribution condition is met as respects the relevant property, and

(b) the deceased makes a transfer of value as a result of which a third party becomes entitled to the benefit of a debt ("the debt") owed to the deceased.

3(3) Condition B is that, before the deceased's death, any outstanding part of the debt is wholly written off, waived or released, and the write-off, waiver or release is made otherwise than for full consideration in money or money's worth.

3(4) Condition C is that the deceased dies on or after 6th April 2005.

3(5) Condition D is that–

(a) on the deceased's death, the transfer of value treated as made immediately before the deceased's death included the relevant property (or any property then representing the relevant property), and

(b) as a result of the deceased's death, the transfer of value referred to in paragraph (2)(b) has become a chargeable transfer.

3(6) In these Regulations **"the relevant property"** means property which, immediately after the carrying out of the arrangements, falls within the definition of "the relevant property" given in paragraph 11(9) of Schedule 15 to the Finance Act 2004.

3(7) In paragraph (2)(a) "the disposal condition" and "the contribution condition" are to be construed in accordance with Schedule 15 to the Finance Act 2004.

AVOIDANCE OF DOUBLE CHARGE: AMOUNTS TO BE CALCULATED

4(1) Where these Regulations apply, amounts A and B must be calculated separately.

4(2) Amount A is the total tax chargeable as a consequence of the death of the deceased, but disregarding the value transferred represented by the relevant property (or by any property which, at the time of the death, represents the relevant property).

4(3) Amount B is the total tax chargeable as a consequence of the death of the deceased, but disregarding the value transferred by the transfer of value specified in regulation 3(2)(b).

4(4) The total tax chargeable is reduced to amount A or to amount B (whichever is the greater).

INHERITANCE TAX (DELIVERY OF ACCOUNTS) (EXCEPTED TRANSFERS AND EXCEPTED TERMINATIONS) REGULATIONS 2008

(SI 2008/605)

Made on 6 March 2008 by the Commissioners for Her Majesty's Revenue and Customs in exercise of the powers conferred by s. 256(1)(a) of the Inheritance Tax Act 1984, after consultation with the Lord Chancellor, the Scottish Ministers and the Lord Chief Justice of Northern Ireland in accordance with s. 256(3A). Operative from 6 April 2008.

CITATION, COMMENCEMENT AND EFFECT

1 These Regulations may be cited as the Inheritance Tax (Delivery of Accounts) (Excepted Transfers and Excepted Terminations) Regulations 2008 and shall come into force on 6th April 2008.

INTERPRETATION

2(1) In these Regulations–

"the Commissioners" means the Commissioners for Her Majesty's Revenue and Customs;

"the 1984 Act" means the Inheritance Tax Act 1984;

"the IHT threshold" means the lower limit shown in the Table in Schedule 1 to the 1984 Act applicable in the year in which the chargeable transfer is made by the transferor;

"the net IHT threshold" means the IHT threshold less the aggregate of the values transferred by all previous chargeable transfers made by the transferor during the seven years preceding the chargeable transfer;

"a specified trust" means one of the following–

(a) a trust of settled property where a person became beneficially entitled to an interest in possession before 22nd March 2006;

(b) a trust for a bereaved minor within section 71A;

(c) a trust in which there is an immediate post-death interest within section 49A;

(d) a trust for a disabled person within section 89, a self-settlement within section 89A or a disabled person's interest within section 89B;

(e) a trust in which there is a transitional serial interest within sections 49B to 49E;

"value" means value for the purpose of tax.

2(2) In these Regulations, a reference to a section is a reference to the section of the 1984 Act bearing that number.

ACCOUNTS

3(1) Save as provided in paragraph (2), no person is required under section 216 to deliver an account of an excepted transfer or an excepted termination unless the Commissioners so require by notice in writing issued to that person.

3(2) Paragraph (1) does not apply to–

(a) The duty on trustees to deliver an account under section 216(1)(b) where the transferor dies within seven years of the chargeable transfer;

(b) The duty on trustees and persons to deliver an account under section 216(1)(bb) and (bd).

3(3) If any person who has not delivered an account in reliance on paragraph (1) discovers at any time that the transfer is not an excepted transfer, or that the termination is not an excepted termination, the delivery to the Commissioners within six months of that time of an account of that transfer or termination shall satisfy any requirement to deliver an account imposed on that person.

EXCEPTED TRANSFERS

4(1) For the purposes of regulation 3 an excepted transfer means a chargeable transfer made on or after 6th April 2007 which is a disposition made by an individual in the circumstances in paragraph (2) or (3), but not any other transaction that is treated as a disposition for the purposes of inheritance tax.

4(2) The circumstances are that–

(a) the value transferred by the chargeable transfer is attributable to either–

(i) cash; or

(ii) quoted shares or securities; and

(b) the value transferred by the chargeable transfer, together with the values transferred by any previous chargeable transfers made by the transferor during the seven years preceding the transfer does not exceed the IHT threshold.

4(3) The circumstances are that–

(a) the value transferred by the chargeable transfer, together with the values transferred by any previous chargeable transfers made by the transferor during the seven years preceding the transfer does not exceed 80% of the IHT threshold, and

(b) the value transferred by the transfer of value giving rise to the chargeable transfer does not exceed the net IHT threshold.

4(4) For the purpose of paragraph (3)(b), sections 104 (business property relief) and 116 (agricultural property relief) shall not apply in determining the value transferred by the chargeable transfer.

EXCEPTED TERMINATIONS

5(1) An excepted termination is the termination of an interest in possession in the settled property of a specified trust in any of the following circumstances.

5(2) The circumstances are that–

(a) the transferor has, in connection with the termination, given to the trustees of the settlement a notice under section 57(3) informing them of the availability of the exemption; and

(b) the value transferred in consequence of the termination does not exceed the amount of the exemption specified in the notice.

5(3) The circumstances are that–

(a) the value of the property in which the interest subsisted is attributable to either–

(i) cash; or

(ii) quoted shares or securities; and

(b) the value transferred in consequence of the termination, together with the values transferred by any previous chargeable transfers made by the transferor during the seven years preceding the transfer does not exceed the IHT threshold.

5(4) The circumstances are that–

(a) the value transferred in consequence of the termination, together with the values transferred by any previous chargeable transfers made by the transferor during the seven years preceding the termination does not exceed 80% of the IHT threshold; and

(b) the value transferred in consequence of the termination does not exceed the net IHT threshold.

5(5) For the purpose of paragraph (4)(b), sections 104 (business property relief) and 116 (agricultural property relief) shall not apply in determining the value transferred in consequence of the termination.

DISCHARGE OF TRUSTEES FROM TAX

6(1) This regulation applies to an excepted termination within regulation 5(2).

6(2) The trustees of the settlement shall, at the expiration of the period of six months beginning with the date of the excepted termination, be discharged from any claim for tax attributable to the value of the property in which the interest subsisted unless, within that period, the Commissioners issue a notice requiring an account of that property.

6(3) This regulation is subject to regulation 7.

7 Regulation 6 does not–

(a) discharge any person from tax in the case of fraud or failure to disclose material facts; or

(b) affect the liability to tax of any person other than the trustees of the settlement, or tax on any property other than that in which the interest subsisted.

TRANSFERS REPORTED LATE

8 Where no account of an excepted transfer is required by the Commissioners, an account of that transfer shall, for the purposes of section 264(8) (delivery of account to be treated as payment where tax rate nil), be treated as having been delivered twelve months after the end of the month in which that transfer is made.

REVOCATION

9 The Inheritance Tax (Delivery of Accounts) (Excepted Transfers and Terminations) Regulations 2002 are revoked in relation to any excepted transfer or excepted termination made on or after 6th April 2007.

INHERITANCE TAX (DELIVERY OF ACCOUNTS) (EXCEPTED SETTLEMENTS) REGULATIONS 2008

(SI 2008/606)

Made on 6 March 2008 by the Commissioners for Her Majesty's Revenue and Customs in exercise of the powers conferred by s. 256(1)(a) of the Inheritance Tax Act 1984, after consultation with the Lord Chancellor, the Scottish Ministers and the Lord Chief Justice of Northern Ireland in accordance with s. 256(3A). Operative from 6 April 2008.

CITATION, COMMENCEMENT AND EFFECT

1 These Regulations may be cited as the Inheritance Tax (Delivery of Accounts) (Excepted Settlements) Regulations 2008, shall come into force on 6th April 2008 and shall have effect in relation to chargeable events occurring on or after 6th April 2007.

INTERPRETATION

2(1) In these Regulations–

"the 1984 Act" means the Inheritance Tax Act 1984;

"the Commissioners" means the Commissioners for Her Majesty's Revenue and Customs;

"a chargeable event" means an occasion on which tax is chargeable under section 64 (charge at ten-year anniversary), section 65 (charge at other times) or section 71E (charge to tax on property to which section 71D applies);

"an excepted settlement" has the meaning given in regulation 4;

"the IHT threshold" means the lower limit shown in the Table in Schedule 1 to the 1984 Act applicable on the occasion of the chargeable event;

"qualifying interest in possession" has the meaning given in section 59;

"related settlement" has the meaning given in section 62;

"settlement" has the meaning given in section 43;

"settlor" has the meaning given in section 44;

"trustee" has the meaning given in section 45;

"value" means value for the purposes of tax.

2(2) In these Regulations, a reference to a section is a reference to the section of the 1984 Act bearing that number.

ACCOUNTS

3(1) No person is required to deliver an account under section 216 of the property comprised in an excepted settlement unless the Commissioners so require by notice in writing addressed to that person.

3(2) If in reliance on these Regulations a person has not delivered an account and it is discovered at any time that the settlement is not an excepted settlement, the delivery to the Commissioners within six months of that time of an account of the property comprised in that settlement shall satisfy any requirement to deliver an account imposed on that person.

EXCEPTED SETTLEMENT

4(1) An excepted settlement means a settlement in which no qualifying interest in possession subsists on an occasion of a chargeable event on or after 6th April 2007 in the circumstances in paragraph (2) or (3).

4(2) The circumstances are that–

(a) throughout the existence of the settlement, cash is the only property comprised in the settlement;

(b) after making the settlement, the settlor provided no further property which became comprised in the settlement;

(c) the trustees of the settlement are resident in the United Kingdom throughout the existence of the settlement;

(d) the gross value of the settled property throughout the existence of the settlement does not exceed £1,000; and

(e) there are no related settlements.

4(3) The circumstances are that–

(a) the settlor is domiciled in the United Kingdom at the time the settlement was made and throughout the existence of the settlement until either the chargeable event or the death of the settlor, whichever is earlier;

(b) the trustees of the settlement are resident in the United Kingdom throughout the existence of the settlement;

(c) there are no related settlements; and

(d) the relevant condition contained in paragraph (4), (6), (7) or (8) is met.

4(4) On the occasion of a chargeable event under section 64, the condition is that the value transferred by a chargeable transfer of the description specified in section 66(3) does not exceed 80% of the IHT threshold.

4(5) Where, in reliance on these Regulations, no person was required to deliver an account under section 216 of the property comprised in the settlement on an occasion of a chargeable event under section 65 in respect of the settlement in the ten years before the chargeable event in paragraph (4), the amounts on which any charges to tax were imposed under section 65 shall, for the purpose of determining the value transferred by a chargeable transfer of the description specified in section 66(3), be without deduction for liabilities or reliefs contained in the 1984 Act.

4(6) On the occasion of a chargeable event under section 65 preceding the first ten-year anniversary after the settlement's commencement, the condition is that the value transferred by a chargeable transfer of the description specified in section 68(4) does not exceed 80% of the IHT threshold.

4(7) On the occasion of a chargeable event under section 65 following one or more ten-year anniversaries after the settlement's commencement, the condition is that the value transferred by a chargeable transfer of the description specified in section 66(3), taking into account section 69, does not exceed 80% of the IHT threshold.

4(8) On the occasion of a chargeable event under section 71E by reason of the happening of an event within section 71F(2), the condition is that the value transferred by a chargeable transfer of the description specified in section 71F(8) does not exceed 80% of the IHT threshold.

4(9) For the purposes of this regulation–

(a) trustees of a settlement shall be regarded as resident in the United Kingdom if the general administration of the settlement is ordinarily carried on in the United Kingdom and the trustees or a majority of them (and, where there is more than one class of trustees, a majority of each class) are for the time being resident in the United Kingdom; and

(b) in determining value for the purposes of paragraph (4), (6), (7) or (8) disregard any liabilities or reliefs contained in the 1984 Act.

Other material – HMRC Brief 22/13: discounted gift schemes: ten year anniversary values for inheritance tax and updated guidance on the calculation of transfer values when discounted gift schemes are effected.

DISCHARGE OF TRUSTEES AND PROPERTY FROM TAX

5(1) Paragraph (2) shall apply to an excepted settlement within regulation 4(2).

5(2) The trustees of the settlement shall, on the expiration of the period of six months beginning with the date of the chargeable event, be discharged from any claim for tax on the occasion of the chargeable event and attributable to the value of the property comprised in the excepted settlement and any Inland Revenue charge for that tax shall then be extinguished unless, within that period, the Commissioners issue a notice requiring an account of that property.

5(3) This regulation is subject to regulation 6.

6 Regulation 5 does not–

(a) discharge any person from tax in the case of fraud or failure to disclose material facts; or

(b) affect the liability to tax of any persons other than the trustees of the settlement, or any tax that may be payable if the settlement is not an excepted settlement.

TRANSFERS REPORTED LATE

7 Where no account of an excepted settlement is required by the Commissioners, an account of that settlement shall, for the purposes of section 264(8) (delivery of account to be treated as payment where tax rate nil), be treated as having been delivered twelve months after the end of the month in which the chargeable event occurred.

REVOCATION

8 The Inheritance Tax (Delivery of Accounts) (Excepted Settlements) Regulations 2002 are revoked in relation to an occasion of a chargeable event on or after 6th April 2007.

TRANSFER OF TRIBUNAL FUNCTIONS AND REVENUE AND CUSTOMS APPEALS ORDER 2009

(SI 2009/56, as amended by SI 2009/777)

Made on 18 January 2009 by the Lord Chancellor and the Treasury in exercise of the powers conferred by s. 30(1) and (4), 31(1), (2) and (9) and 38 of, and para. 30 of Sch. 5 to, the Tribunals, Courts and Enforcement Act 2007 and s. 124(1)–(7) of the Finance Act 2008. Operative from 1 April 2009.

CITATION AND COMMENCEMENT

1(1) This Order may be cited as the Transfer of Tribunal Functions and Revenue and Customs Appeals Order 2009.

1(2) This Order comes into force on 1st April 2009.

THE EXISTING TRIBUNALS

2 In this Order **"existing tribunals"** means–

(a) the Commissioners for the general purposes of the income tax established under section 2 of the Taxes Management Act 1970;

(b) the Commissioners for the special purposes of the Income Tax Acts established under section 4 of the Taxes Management Act 1970;

(c) [not relevant to inheritance tax;]

(d) [not relevant to inheritance tax;]

(e) [not relevant to inheritance tax.]

TRANSFER OF FUNCTIONS, CONSEQUENTIAL AND OTHER AMENDMENTS

3(1) Schedule 1 contains amendments to primary legislation which–

(a) transfer functions of existing tribunals, and

(b) make consequential and other provision (including provision about reviews of decisions by Her Majesty's Revenue and Customs).

3(2) Schedule 2 contains amendments to secondary legislation which–

(a) transfer functions of existing tribunals, and

(b) make consequential and other provision (including provision about reviews of decisions by Her Majesty's Revenue and Customs).

ABOLITION OF EXISTING TRIBUNALS

4 The existing tribunals (apart from the Commissioners for the general purposes of the income tax) are abolished.

TRANSFER OF MEMBERS OF EXISTING TRIBUNALS

5 A person who, immediately before this Order comes into force, holds an office listed in column 1 of any of the following tables is to hold the office or offices listed in the corresponding entry in column 2 of that table–

THE SPECIAL COMMISSIONERS

1. Office held	2. Office or offices to be held
Commissioner for the special purposes of the Income Tax Acts appointed under section 4 of the Taxes Management Act 1970	Transferred-in judge of the Upper Tribunal
Deputy Commissioner for the special purposes of the Income Tax Acts appointed under section 4A of the Taxes Management Act 1970	Transferred-in judge of the First-tier Tribunal and deputy judge of the Upper Tribunal

TRANSITIONALS AND SAVINGS

6 Schedule 3 contains–

(a) transitional provision, and

(b) saving provision.

SCHEDULES

SCHEDULE 1 – CONSEQUENTIAL AMENDMENTS AND SUPPLEMENTAL PROVISIONS – PRIMARY LEGISLATION

Article 3

INHERITANCE TAX ACT 1984

108 The Inheritance Tax Act 1984 is amended as follows.

109 [Amends IHTA 1984, s. 35A.]

110 [Amends IHTA 1984, s. 54A(3).]

111 [Amends IHTA 1984, s. 79A.]

112 [Amends IHTA 1984, s. 219(1A).]

113 [Amends IHTA 1984, s. 219B.]

114 [Amends the heading before IHTA 1984, s. 221.]

115 [Amends IHTA 1984, s. 222.]

116 [Substitutes IHTA 1984, s. 223.]

117 [Inserts IHTA 1984, s. 223A–223I.]

118 [Substitutes IHTA 1984, s. 224.]

119 [Omits IHTA 1984, s. 225 and 225A.]

120 [Amends IHTA 1984, s. 245(2)(b).]

121 [Amends IHTA 1984, s. 245A.]

122 [Amends IHTA 1984, s. 249.]

123 [Omits IHTA 1984, s. 251.]

124 [Amends IHTA 1984, s. 252.]

125 [Amends IHTA 1984, s. 272.]

SCHEDULE 2 – CONSEQUENTIAL AMENDMENTS AND SUPPLEMENTAL PROVISIONS – SECONDARY LEGISLATION

Article 3

REVOCATIONS

187 The following instruments are revoked–

(a)–(d) [Not relevant to inheritance tax.]

(e) The Special Commissioners (Jurisdiction and Procedure) Regulations 1994.

(f) The General Commissioners (Jurisdiction and Procedure) Regulations 1994.

(h) The Retirement Age of General Commissioners Order 1995.

(i) The Special Commissioners (Jurisdiction and Procedure) (Amendment) Regulations 1999.

(j) The General Commissioners (Jurisdiction and Procedure) (Amendment) Regulations 1999.

(k) The Special Commissioners (Amendment of the Taxes Management Act 1970) Regulations 1999.

(l) The Special Commissioners (Jurisdiction and Procedure) (Amendment) Regulations 2000.

(o) The Referrals to the Special Commissioners Regulations 2001.

(p) The General Commissioners and Special Commissioners (Jurisdiction and Procedure) (Amendment) Regulations 2002.

(q) The Special Commissioners (Jurisdiction and Procedure) (Amendment) Regulations 2003.

(s) The General Commissioners (Jurisdiction and Procedure) (Amendment) Regulations 2005.

(t) The Special Commissioners (Jurisdiction and Procedure) (Amendment) Regulations 2005.

(v) The General Commissioners and Special Commissioners (Jurisdiction and Procedure) (Amendment) Regulations 2007.

SCHEDULE 3 – TRANSITIONAL AND SAVING PROVISIONS

Article 6

GENERAL

1(1) In this Schedule–

"commencement date" means the date on which this Order comes into force;

"enactment" includes subordinate legislation (within the meaning of the Interpretation Act 1978);

"HMRC" means Her Majesty's Revenue and Customs;

"tribunal" means the First-tier Tribunal or, where determined by or under Tribunal Procedure Rules, the Upper Tribunal.

1(2) For the purposes of this Schedule there are "current proceedings" if, before the commencement date–

(a) any party has served notice on an existing tribunal for the purpose of beginning proceedings before the existing tribunal, and

(b) the existing tribunal has not concluded proceedings arising by virtue of that notice.

FORMER VAT AND DUTIES TRIBUNALS MATTERS (EXCEPT VAT)

2(1) This paragraph applies in relation to the following decisions–

(a) any relevant decision which HMRC notify before the commencement date, unless–

(i) the period to require a review of the decision has expired before that date, or

(ii) a review of the decision has been required before that date;

(b) any relevant review decision which HMRC notify before the commencement date unless–

(i) the period to serve notice of appeal against the decision on an existing tribunal has expired before that date, or

(ii) notice of appeal against the decision has been served on an existing tribunal before that date.

2(2) On and after the commencement date, the following enactments continue to apply (subject to sub-paragraphs (3) and (4)) as they applied immediately before that date–

(a) the review and appeal provisions,

(b) rule 4(2) of the Value Added Tax Tribunals Rules 1986, and

(c) any other enactments that apply in relation to relevant decisions or relevant review decisions.

2(3) Those enactments apply subject to Tribunal Procedure Rules.

2(4) Any reference to an existing tribunal is to be substituted with a reference to the tribunal.

2(5) Any time period which has started to run before the commencement date and has not expired will continue to apply.

2(6) In this paragraph–

"relevant decision" means a decision to which a review and appeal provision applies (apart from a relevant review decision);

"relevant review decision" means a decision–

(a) that is made on a review of a relevant decision, and

(b) to which a review and appeal provision applies,

and includes a relevant decision that is treated as having been confirmed under a review and appeal provision.

"review and appeal provisions" means–

(a) sections 14 to 16 of the Finance Act 1994,

(b) sections 59 and 60 of the Finance Act 1994,

(c) sections 54 to 56 of the Finance Act 1996,

(d) paragraphs 121 to 123 of Schedule 6 to the Finance Act 2000,

(e) sections 40 to 42 of the Finance Act 2001,

(f) sections 33 to 37 of the Finance Act 2003,

(g) regulations 9 to 13 of the Export (Penalty) Regulations 2003,

(h) regulations 4 to 7 of the Control of Cash (Penalties) Regulations 2007,

(i) regulations 43 and 44 of the Money Laundering Regulations 2007, and
(j) regulations 12 and 13 of the Transfer of Funds (Information on the Payer) Regulations 2007.

3(1) This paragraph applies in relation to a relevant decision if, before the commencement date–
(a) HMRC have notified the relevant decision, and
(b) a review of the decision has begun under a review and appeal provision (whether or not a relevant review decision has been notified).

3(2) On and after the commencement date the following enactments continue to apply (subject to sub-paragraphs (3) and (4)), as they applied immediately before that date–
(a) the review and appeal provisions,
(b) rule 4(2) of the VAT Tribunals Rules 1986, and
(c) any other enactments that apply in relation to relevant decisions or relevant review decisions.

3(3) Those enactments apply subject to Tribunal Procedure Rules.

3(4) Any reference to an existing tribunal is to be substituted with a reference to the tribunal.

3(5) Any time period which has started to run before the commencement date and has not expired will continue to apply.

3(6) On and after the commencement date, no notification offering or requiring a review may be given under any review and appeal provision or any other enactments that are applicable to the decision as they apply after that date.

3(7) In this paragraph **"review and appeal provision"**, **"relevant decision"** and **"relevant review decision"** have the same meaning as in paragraph 2.

FORMER VAT AND DUTIES TRIBUNALS MATTERS: VAT

4(1) This paragraph applies if, before the commencement date–
(a) HMRC have notified a decision relating to a matter to which section 83 of the Value Added Tax Act 1994 applies, and
(b) no party has served notice on a VAT and duties tribunal for the purpose of beginning proceedings before such a tribunal in relation to that decision.

4(2) On and after the commencement date, the following enactments continue to apply (subject to sub-paragraphs (3) and (4)) as they applied immediately before that date–
(a) the Value Added Tax Act 1994,
(b) rule 4(2) of the VAT Tribunals Rules 1986, and
(c) any other enactments that are applicable to the decision.

4(3) Those enactments apply subject to Tribunal Procedure Rules.

4(4) Any reference to an existing tribunal is to be substituted with a reference to the tribunal.

4(5) Any time period which has started to run before the commencement date and has not expired will continue to apply.

MATTERS FORMERLY HEARD BY EXISTING TRIBUNALS (EXCEPT VAT AND DUTIES TRIBUNALS)

5(1) This paragraph applies if, before the commencement date–
(a) a notice of appeal has been given to HMRC; but
(b) no party has served notice on an existing tribunal for the purpose of beginning proceedings before the existing tribunal in relation to that appeal.

5(2) Where the date on which a review is required or offered falls on or before 31 March 2010, the period for HMRC to give notice of their conclusions for the purposes of the relevant provision is to be 90 days (but without prejudice to any power to agree to a different period).

5(3) In this paragraph–

"review" means a review under–

(a) section 49B or 49C of the Taxes Management Act 1970, or
(b) any other enactment which, as amended by this Order, contains provisions corresponding to section 49B or 49C for review to be required or offered;

"relevant provision" means–

(a) in the case of a review under section 49B or 49C of the Taxes Management Act 1970, section 49E(6) of that Act, or

(b) in the case of a review under any other enactment amended by this Order, the provision that corresponds to section 49E(6) of the Taxes Management Act 1970 in relation to that review.

CURRENT PROCEEDINGS

6 Any current proceedings are to continue on and after the commencement date as proceedings before the tribunal.

7(1) This paragraph applies to current proceedings that are continued before the tribunal by virtue of paragraph 6.

7(2) Where a hearing before an existing tribunal (except for the Commissioners for the general purposes of the income tax) began before the commencement date but was not completed by that date, the tribunal must be comprised for the continuation of that hearing of the person or persons who began it.

7(3) The tribunal may give any direction to ensure that proceedings are dealt with fairly and justly and, in particular, may–

(a) apply any provision in procedural rules which applied to the proceedings before the commencement date; or

(b) disapply any provision of Tribunal Procedure Rules.

7(4) In sub-paragraph (3) **"procedural rules"** means any provision (whether called rules or not) regulating practice or procedure before an existing tribunal.

7(5) Any direction or order made or given in proceedings which is in force immediately before the commencement date remains in force on and after that date as if it were a direction or order of the tribunal relating to proceedings before that tribunal.

7(6) A time period which has started to run before the commencement date and which has not expired will continue to apply.

7(7) An order for costs may only be made if, and to the extent that, an order could have been made before the commencement date (on the assumption, in the case of costs actually incurred after that date, that they had been incurred before that date).

CASES TO BE REMITTED BY COURTS

8 Any case to be remitted by a court on or after the commencement date in relation to an existing tribunal shall be remitted to the tribunal.

DECISIONS OF VAT AND DUTIES TRIBUNALS AND COURTS: INTEREST AND PAYMENT

9(1) This paragraph applies in relation to any decision of a VAT and duties tribunal made before the commencement date.

9(2) On and after that date, the following provisions continue to apply as they applied immediately before that date–

(a) section 84(8) of the Value Added Tax Act 1994 (VAT),

(b) section 60(6) to (8) of the Finance Act 1994 (insurance premium tax),

(c) paragraphs 8 and 10 of Schedule 6 to the Finance Act 1994 (air passenger duty),

(d) section 56(3) to (5) of the Finance Act 1996 (landfill tax),

(e) paragraph 123(4) to (6) of Schedule 6 to the Finance Act 2000 (climate change levy),

(f) section 42(4) to (6) of the Finance Act 2001 (aggregates levy),

(g) paragraph 14(4) of Schedule 3 to the Finance Act 2001 (excise and customs).

10(1) This paragraph applies if an appeal from a decision of a VAT and duties tribunal, or from a court, is made before the commencement date.

10(2) Section 85B of the Value Added Tax Act 1994 does not apply in relation to that decision.

DECISIONS OF EXISTING TRIBUNALS: RIGHTS OF APPEAL, REVIEWS AND IRREGULARITIES

11(1) This paragraph applies to a decision of an existing tribunal if, immediately before the commencement date–

(a) an appeal lies to a court from that decision,

(b) an application may be or has been made to an existing tribunal seeking a review of that decision, or

(c) the existing tribunal wishes to correct an irregularity.

11(2) Except as provided for in sub-paragraph (3), on and after the commencement date such rights of appeal shall lie from the decision as would lie from a decision of the First-tier Tribunal made on or after that date.

11(3) Subject to the modifications specified in sub-paragraphs (4) and (5) the following enactments continue to apply for the purposes of a case to be stated, a review, or for correcting an irregularity in respect of any decision of the Commissioners for the general purposes of the income tax made before the commencement date, as if the amendments in this Order had not been made–

(a) sections 56 and 58 of the Taxes Management Act 1970,

(b) regulations 17 and 20 to 24 of the General Commissioners (Jurisdiction and Procedure) Regulations 1994, and

(c) the General Commissioners of Income Tax (Costs) Regulations 2001.

11(4) Section 56(6) of the Taxes Management Act 1970 is modified so that for "the Commissioners" there is substituted "the tribunal".

11(5) Section 58 of the Taxes Management Act 1970 is modified as follows–

(a) omit subsection (2B); and

(b) in subsection (2C) omit "or on an appeal under section 56A of this Act".

11(6) In article 4 of the Tribunals, Courts and Enforcement Act 2007 (Commencement No. 6 and Transitional Provisions) Order 2008–

(a) for "section 56 of the 1970 Act (statement of case for opinion of the High Court)" substitute "sections 56(3) and (11) and 58 of the 1970 Act (statement of case for opinion of the High Court) and regulations 17 and 20 to 24 of the General Commissioners (Jurisdiction and Procedure) Regulations 1994 (review of tribunal's final determination, stated case procedures and correction of irregularities)"; and

(b) after "commenced" insert ", and the amendments to the 1970 Act and the revocation of the General Commissioners (Jurisdiction and Procedure) Regulations 1994, the General Commissioners (Jurisdiction and Procedure) (Amendment) Regulations 1999, the General Commissioners (Jurisdiction and Procedure) (Amendment) Regulations 2005 and the General Commissioners and Special Commissioners (Jurisdiction and Procedure) (Amendment) Regulations 2007 (as they relate to the General Commissioners) in the Transfer of Tribunal Functions and Revenue and Customs Appeals Order 2009 had not been made".

EXISTING TRIBUNALS – STAFF

12 Staff appointed to the existing tribunals (except to the Commissioners for the general purposes of the income tax) before the commencement date are, on and after that date, to be treated, for the purpose of any enactment, as if they had been appointed by the Lord Chancellor under section 40(1) of the Tribunals, Courts and Enforcement Act 2007 (tribunal staff and services).

TRANSITIONAL: GENERAL

13(1) In so far as appropriate in consequence of this Order, a reference in an enactment, instrument or other document to an existing tribunal, or a member or official of an existing tribunal (however expressed) is to be taken to be a reference to the tribunal.

13(2) Sub-paragraph (1) does not apply to any reference that is amended by Schedule 1 or 2.

FAMILY PROVISION (INTESTATE SUCCESSION) ORDER 2009

(SI 2009/135)

Made on 28 January 2009 by the Lord Chancellor in exercise of the powers conferred by s. 1(1)(a) and (b) of the Family Provision Act 1966. Operative from 1 February 2009.

CITATION AND COMMENCEMENT

1 This Order may be cited as the Family Provision (Intestate Succession) Order 2009 and shall come into force on 1st February 2009.

STATUTORY LEGACY

2 In the case of a person dying after this Order comes into force, section 46(1) of the Administration of Estates Act 1925(b) shall apply as if the net sums charged by paragraph (i) on the residuary estate were–

(a) under paragraph (2) of the Table, the sum of £250,000; and

(b) under paragraph (3) of the Table, the sum of £450,000.

INHERITANCE TAX (QUALIFYING NON-UK PENSION SCHEMES) REGULATIONS 2010

(SI 2010/51)

Made on 12 January 2010 by the Commissioners for Her Majesty's Revenue and Customs in exercise of the powers conferred by s. 271A of the Inheritance Tax Act 1984. Operative from 15 February 2010.

CITATION, COMMENCEMENT AND EFFECT

1(1) These Regulations may be cited as the Inheritance Tax (Qualifying Non-UK Pension Schemes) Regulations 2010 and shall come into force on 15th February 2010.

1(2) These Regulations shall have effect from 6th April 2006.

INTERPRETATION

2 In these Regulations–

"pension rule 1" means pension rule 1 in section 165 of the Finance Act 2004;

"relevant scheme funds" means any sums and assets held under a pension scheme–

(a) to which these Regulations apply, and

(b) which would be subject to inheritance tax if the scheme did not meet the requirements for a qualifying non-UK pension scheme.

SCOPE OF THESE REGULATIONS

3 These Regulations apply to pension schemes which are established in a country or territory outside the United Kingdom.

REQUIREMENTS FOR QUALIFYING NON-UK PENSION SCHEMES

4(1) For the purposes of section 271A of the Inheritance Tax Act 1984 (qualifying non-UK pension scheme) a pension scheme must–

(a) be recognised for tax purposes under the tax legislation of the country or territory in which it is established (see regulation 5) and satisfy regulation 6; or

(b) be established by an international organisation for the purpose of providing benefits for, or in respect of, past service as an employee of the organisation and satisfy regulation 7.

4(2) In this regulation **"international organisation"** means an organisation to which section 1 of the International Organisations Act 1968 applies by virtue of an Order in Council under subsection (1) of that section.

RECOGNITION FOR TAX PURPOSES

5(1) A scheme is recognised for tax purposes under the tax legislation of a country or territory in which it is established if it meets both Primary Condition 1 and Primary Condition 2 and either Condition A or Condition B.

Primary Condition 1

The scheme is open to persons resident in the country or territory in which it is established.

Primary Condition 2

The scheme is established in a country or territory where there is a system of taxation of personal income under which tax relief is available in respect of pensions and–

(a) tax relief is not available to the member on contributions made to the scheme by the member or, if the member is an employee, by their employer, in respect of earnings to which benefits under the scheme relate;

(b) the scheme is liable to taxation on its income and gains and is of a kind specified in the Schedule to these Regulations; or

(c) all or most of the benefits paid by the scheme to members who are not in serious ill-health are subject to taxation.

For the purposes of this condition **"tax relief"** includes the grant of an exemption from tax.

Condition A

5(2) The scheme is approved or recognised by, or registered with, the relevant tax authorities as a pension scheme in the country or territory in which it is established.

IHT Statutory Instruments

Condition B

5(3) If no system applies for the approval or recognition by, or registration with, relevant tax authorities of pension schemes in the country or territory in which it is established–

(a) the scheme must be resident there;

(b) the scheme rules must provide that at least 70% of a member's relevant scheme funds will be designated by the scheme manager for the purpose of providing the member with an income for life, or, in the case of a member who has died, so provided immediately before the member's death; and

(c) the pension benefits payable to the member under the scheme (and any lump sum associated with those benefits) must be payable no earlier than they would be if pension rule 1 applied.

REQUIREMENTS FOR SCHEMES RECOGNISED FOR TAX PURPOSES

6(1) This regulation is satisfied if paragraph (2), (3) or (4) applies.

6(2) This paragraph applies if the scheme is an occupational pension scheme and there is a body in the country or territory in which it is established–

(a) which regulates occupational pension schemes; and

(b) which regulates the scheme in question.

6(3) This paragraph applies if the scheme is not an occupational scheme and there is a body in the country or territory in which it is established–

(a) which regulates pension schemes other than occupational pension schemes; and

(b) which regulates the scheme in question.

6(4) This paragraph applies if neither paragraph (2) nor (3) applies by reason only that no such regulatory body exists in the country or territory and–

(a) the scheme is established in another member State, Norway, Iceland or Liechtenstein; or

(b) the scheme is one where–

(i) the scheme rules provide that at least 70% of a member's relevant scheme funds will be designated by the scheme manager for the purpose of providing the member with an income for life, or, in the case of a member who has died, so provided immediately before the member's death, and

(ii) the pension benefits payable to the member under the scheme (and any lump sum associated with those benefits) are payable no earlier than they would be if pension rule 1 applied.

6(5) In this regulation **"occupational pension scheme"** has the meaning given by section 150(5) of the Finance Act 2004.

REQUIREMENTS FOR SCHEMES ESTABLISHED BY INTERNATIONAL ORGANISATIONS

7 This regulation is satisfied if–

(a) the scheme rules provide that at least 70% of a member's relevant scheme funds will be designated by the scheme manager for the purpose of providing the member with an income for life, or, in the case of a member who has died, so provided immediately before the member's death, and

(b) the pension benefits payable to the member under the scheme (and any lump sum associated with those benefits) are payable no earlier than they would be if pension rule 1 applied.

SCHEDULE – SPECIFIED SCHEMES

Regulation 5

A complying superannuation plan as defined in section 995-1 (definitions) of the Income Tax Assessment Act 1997 of Australia (as amended by the Tax Law Amendment (Simplified Superannuation) Act 2007 of Australia).

FINANCE ACT 2009, SCHEDULE 51 (TIME LIMITS FOR ASSESSMENTS, CLAIMS, ETC.) (APPOINTED DAYS AND TRANSITIONAL PROVISIONS) ORDER 2010

(SI 2010/867)

Made on 18 March 2010 by the Treasury in exercise of the powers conferred by s. 99(2) and (3) of the Finance Act 2009.

PART 1 – APPOINTED DAYS AND PRELIMINARY PROVISIONS

CITATION AND INTERPRETATION

1(1) This Order may be cited as the Finance Act 2009, Schedule 51 (Time Limits for Assessments, Claims, etc.) (Appointed Days and Transitional Provisions) Order 2010.

1(2) In this Order a reference to a paragraph (without more) is a reference to that paragraph of Schedule 51 to the Finance Act 2009.

1(3) [Not relevant to inheritance tax.]

APPOINTED DAYS

2(1) [Not relevant to inheritance tax.]

2(2) The day appointed as the day on which the amendments made by paragraphs 5 to 26 (inheritance tax, stamp duty land tax and petroleum revenue tax) come into force is 1st April 2011.

PART 2 – TRANSITIONAL PROVISION

INHERITANCE TAX: UNDERPAYMENTS

6 In a case under section 240(2) IHTA 1984, where–

(a) the chargeable transfer took place on or before 31st March 2011, and

(b) a loss of tax was brought about deliberately by any person (or a person acting on behalf of such a person),

the period within which proceedings may be brought is the period of 6 years beginning when the deliberate conduct comes to the knowledge of Her Majesty's Revenue and Customs or the period of 20 years provided in section 240(5) IHTA 1984, whichever ends soonest.

FINANCE ACT 2009, SECTIONS 101 TO 103 (APPOINTED DAY AND SUPPLEMENTAL PROVISION) ORDER 2010

(SI 2010/1878)

Made on 21 July 2010 by the Treasury in exercise of the powers conferred by s. 104(3) to (5) of the Finance Act 2009.

CITATION

1 This Order may be cited as the Finance Act 2009, Sections 101 to 103 (Appointed Day and Supplemental Provision) Order 2010.

APPOINTED DAY

2 The day appointed as the day on which sections 101 to 103 of the Finance Act 2009 come into force for the purposes of bank payroll tax (including any penalties assessed in relation to that tax) is 31st August 2010.

SUPPLEMENTAL PROVISION

3 Interest charged under section 101 of the Finance Act 2009 (late payment interest on sums due to HMRC) on an amount enforceable as if it were bank payroll tax may be enforced as if it were an amount of bank payroll tax.

TAXES (DEFINITION OF CHARITY) (RELEVANT TERRITORIES) REGULATIONS 2010

(SI 2010/1904 as amended by SI 2014/1807)

Made on 23 July 2010 by the Commissioners for Her Majesty's Revenue and Customs in exercise of the powers conferred by para. 2 of Sch. 6 to the Finance Act 2010. Operative from 20 August 2010.

1 These Regulations may be cited as the Taxes (Definition of Charity) (Relevant Territories) Regulations 2010 and come into force on 20th August 2010.

2 The territories specified in the Schedule to these Regulations are relevant territories for the purposes of the meaning of a relevant territory in paragraph 2(3) of Schedule 6 to the Finance Act 2010 (the jurisdiction condition of the definition of "charity" in paragraph 1 of Schedule 6 to the Finance Act 2010).

SCHEDULE

Regulation 2

The Republic of Iceland

The Principality of Liechtenstein

The Kingdom of Norway

History – The words "The Principality of Liechtenstein" inserted by SI 2014/1807, reg. 2, with effect from 31 July 2014.

INHERITANCE TAX AVOIDANCE SCHEMES (PRESCRIBED DESCRIPTIONS OF ARRANGEMENTS) REGULATIONS 2011

(SI 2011/170 revoked by SI 2017/1172)

Made on 1 February 2011 by the Treasury in accordance with the powers conferred by s. 306(1)(a) and (b) of the Finance Act 2004. Operative from 6 April 2011.

History – SI 2011/170 revoked by SI 2017/1172, reg. 6(1), with effect from 1 April 2018. Former SI 2011/170 read as follows:

"CITATION AND COMMENCEMENT

1 These Regulations may be cited as the Inheritance Tax Avoidance Schemes (Prescribed Descriptions of Arrangements) Regulations 2011 and come into force on 6th April 2011.

PRESCRIBED DESCRIPTION OF ARRANGEMENTS IN RELATION TO INHERITANCE TAX

2(1) For the purposes of Part 7 of the Finance Act 2004 (disclosure of tax avoidance schemes) the arrangements specified in paragraph (2) are prescribed in relation to inheritance tax.

2(2) Arrangements are prescribed if–

(a) as a result of any element of the arrangements property becomes relevant property; and

(b) a main benefit of the arrangements is that an advantage is obtained in relation to a relevant property entry charge.

2(3) In this regulation–

"property" shall be construed in accordance with section 272 of the Inheritance Tax Act 1984;

"relevant property" has the meaning given by section 58(1) of the Inheritance Tax Act 1984;

"relevant property entry charge" means the charge to inheritance tax which arises on a transfer of value made by an individual during that individual's life as a result of which property becomes relevant property;

"transfer of value" has the meaning given by section 3(1) of the Inheritance Tax Act 1984.

3 Arrangements are excepted from disclosure under these Regulations if they are of the same, or substantially the same, description as arrangements–

(a) which were first made available for implementation before 6th April 2011; or

(b) in relation to which the date of any transaction forming part of the arrangements falls before 6th April 2011; or

(c) in relation to which a promoter first made a firm approach to another person before 6th April 2011."

TAXATION OF EQUITABLE LIFE (PAYMENTS) ORDER 2011

(SI 2011/1502)

Made on 15 June 2011 by the Treasury in exercise of the powers conferred by s. 1(3) and (4) of the Equitable Life (Payments) Act 2010. Operative from 16 June 2011.

Notes – This is an edited version of SI 2011/1502, containing only provisions relevant to inheritance tax.

CITATION, COMMENCEMENT, EFFECT AND INTERPRETATION

1(1) This Order may be cited as the Taxation of Equitable Life (Payments) Order 2011 and shall come into force on the day after the day on which it is made.

1(2) This Order has effect in relation to authorised payments made after the day on which this Order is made.

1(3) In this Order **"authorised payment"** means a payment to which section 1 of the Equitable Life (Payments) Act 2010 applies.

INHERITANCE TAX

5(1) For the purposes of the Inheritance Tax Act 1984–

(a) in determining the value of a person's estate immediately before that person's death, no account shall be taken of any value attributable to a right to, or interest in, an authorised payment made after that person's death; and

(b) in determining the value of relevant property immediately before a ten-year anniversary for the purposes of the charge under section 64 of the Inheritance Tax Act 1984, no account shall be taken of any value attributable to a right to, or interest in, an authorised payment made on or after that ten-year anniversary.

5(2) In this article–

"estate" has the meaning given by section 272 of the Inheritance Tax Act 1984;

"relevant property" has the meaning given by section 58 of that Act; and

"ten-year anniversary" has the meaning given by section 61 of that Act.

TAXES AND DUTIES, ETC (INTEREST RATE) REGULATIONS 2011

(SI 2011/2446)

Made on 10 October 2011 by the Treasury in exercise of the powers conferred by s. 103 of the Finance Act 2009. Operative from 31 October 2011.

CITATION AND COMMENCEMENT

1 These Regulations may be cited as the Taxes and Duties, etc (Interest Rate) Regulations 2011 and come into force on 31st October 2011.

INTERPRETATION

2 In these Regulations–

"Bank of England" rate means the official bank rate as announced at the relevant meeting;

"operative date" means the 13th working day following the relevant meeting;

"relevant meeting" means the most recent meeting of the Bank of England Monetary Policy Committee;

"working day" means any day other than a non-business day within the meaning of section 92 of the Bills of Exchange Act 1882.

LATE PAYMENT INTEREST RATE

3(1) Except where regulation 5 applies, the late payment interest rate for the purposes of section 101 of the Finance Act 2009 (late payment interest on sums due to HMRC), is the percentage per annum found by applying the following formula–

Bank of England rate + 2.5.

3(2) The interest rate found under paragraph (1) applies on and after the operative date.

REPAYMENT INTEREST RATE

4(1) Except where regulation 5 applies, the repayment interest rate for the purposes of section 102 of the Finance Act 2009 (repayment interest on sums to be paid by HMRC), is the higher of–

(a) 0.5% per annum; and

(b) the percentage per annum found by applying the following formula–

Bank of England rate – 1.

4(2) The interest rate found under paragraph (1) applies on and after the operative date.

INITIAL RATES OF INTEREST

5(1) This regulation applies immediately on the coming into force of these Regulations until the first operative date after the coming into force of these Regulations.

5(2) The late payment interest rate and repayment interest rate shall be the respective percentages per annum found by applying regulation 3(1) and regulation 4(1) as if the references in those regulations to the Bank of England rate were references to the official bank rate announced at the meeting of the Bank of England Monetary Policy Committee on, or most recently before, the 13th working day before the coming into force of these Regulations.

EFFECT OF CHANGE IN RATES OF INTEREST

6 Where the late payment interest rate or repayment interest rate changes in accordance with these Regulations with effect from an operative date, the change has effect in respect of interest running from before that date as well as interest running from or after that date.

EARLIER INSTRUMENT REVOKED

7 The Taxes and Duties (Interest Rate) Regulations 2010 are revoked.

DATA-GATHERING POWERS (RELEVANT DATA) REGULATIONS 2012

(SI 2012/847, as amended by SI 2016/979 and SI 2017/1175)

Made on 14 March 2012 by the Treasury, in exercise of the power conferred by para. 1(3) of Sch. 23 to the Finance Act 2011. Operative from 1 April 2012.

CITATION, COMMENCEMENT AND INTERPRETATION

1 These Regulations may be cited as the Data-gathering Powers (Relevant Data) Regulations 2012 and come into force on 1st April 2012.

2 In these Regulations–

"company registration number" has the same meaning as "registered number" in section 1066 of the Companies Act 2006;

"identifying information" means information which identifies a person or an account and includes–

(a) any unique or generic identifier or reference number allocated by, or used by, the data-holder for the purposes of identifying a person or account, or classifying the trade of a person or account;

(b) name, address (including email, website, and any other electronic address), and telephone number associated with a person or account;

(c) company registration number or national insurance number, unique taxpayer reference, VAT number, any other unique government-issued identifier associated with a person or account;

(d) in relation to a person, whether that person is an individual, partnership, limited company, or has any other legal status;

"Schedule 23" means Schedule 23 to the Finance Act 2011;

"VAT number" has the same meaning as "registration number" in paragraph (1) of regulation 2 of the Value Added Tax Regulations 1995.

History – Reg. 2 substituted by SI 2016/979, reg. 3, with effect from 1 November 2016. Former reg. 2 read as follows:
"**2** In these Regulations **"Schedule 23"** means Schedule 23 to the Finance Act 2011.".

INCOME, ASSETS ETC BELONGING TO OTHERS

11 The relevant data for a data-holder of the type described in paragraph 13 of Schedule 23 are–

(a) information relating to the money or value received; and

(b) the name and address of the beneficial owner of the money or value.

MONEY SERVICE BUSINESSES

11D(1) he relevant data for a data-holder of the type described in paragraph 13D of Schedule 23 are–

(a) records required to be kept by the data-holder under regulation 40 of the Money Laundering, Terrorist Financing and Transfer of Funds (Information on the Payer) Regulations 2017;

(b) the quantity and value of transactions carried out by the data-holder for a customer during any period;

(c) identifying information relating to a customer; and

(d) where, in a transaction carried out by the data-holder for a customer, there is a beneficial owner who is not the customer, identifying information relating to the beneficial owner.

11D(2) In this regulation **"beneficial owner"** has the meaning given by regulations 5 and 6 of the Money Laundering, Terrorist Financing and Transfer of Funds (Information on the Payer) Regulations 2017.

History – Reg. 11D inserted by SI 2017/1175, reg. 3, with effect from 21 December 2017.

SETTLEMENTS

24 The relevant data for a data-holder of the type described in paragraph 26 of Schedule 23 are information and documents relating to the settlement in question and to income or gains arising to the settlement.

TAX AVOIDANCE SCHEMES (INFORMATION) REGULATIONS 2012

(SI 2012/1836, as amended by SI 2013/2592, SI 2015/948 and SI 2017/1171)

Made on 12 July 2012 by the Commissioners for Her Majesty's Revenue and Customs, in exercise of the powers conferred by s. 98C(2A), (2B) and (2C)(b) of the Taxes Management Act 1970, s. 132 of the Finance Act 1999, s. 135 of the Finance Act 2002 and s. 306A(6), 307(5), 308(1) and (3), 308A(5) and (6)(a), 309(1), 310, 312(2) and (5), 312A(2) and (5), 313(1) and (3), 313ZA(3) and (4), 313A(4)(a), 313B(2)(a), 313C(1) and (3)(a), 317(2) and 318(1) of the Finance Act 2004. Operative from 1 September 2012.

CITATION AND COMMENCEMENT

1 These Regulations may be cited as the Tax Avoidance Schemes (Information) Regulations 2012 and shall come into force on 1st September 2012.

INTERPRETATION

2(1) In these Regulations a reference to a numbered section (without more) is a reference to the section of the Finance Act 2004 which is so numbered.

2(2) In these Regulations–

"employment" has the same meaning as it has for the purposes of the employment income Parts of the Income Tax (Earnings and Pensions) Act 2003 (see section 4 of that Act) and includes offices to which the provisions of those Parts that are expressed to apply to employments apply equally (see section 5 of that Act); and **"employee"** and **"employer"** have corresponding meanings;

"the filing date" is–

(a) whichever date in regulation 12(4)(a) to (c) applies to the relevant return or in the case of inheritance tax the last day of the period mentioned in regulation 9(5)(b); or

(b) in the case of regulation 10(7) the date by which the relevant return is required to be delivered;

"the prescribed taxes" means the apprenticeship levy, capital gains tax, corporation tax, income tax, inheritance tax, stamp duty land tax and annual tax on enveloped dwellings.

2(3) In reckoning any period under regulation 5 (apart from paragraph (8)), or regulations 8A, 13A,14, 15 and 16, any day which is a non-business day within the meaning of section 92 of the Bills of Exchange Act 1882 (computation of time) shall be disregarded.

2(4) In regulations 10(2) and (3), 11(4) and 12(2) expressions which are used in Part 4 of the Finance Act 2003 have the same meaning as in that Part.

History – In reg. 2(2), in definition of "the prescribed taxes", the words "the apprenticeship levy," inserted by SI 2017/1171, reg. 6, with effect from 21 December 2017, but the amendment does not have effect for the purposes of: FA 2004, s. 308(1), if the relevant date falls before 21 December 2017; or FA 2004, s. 308(3), if the date on which the promoter first becomes aware of any transaction forming part of notifiable arrangements falls before 21 December 2017; or FA 2004, s. 309(1) and 310, if the date on which any transaction forming part of notifiable arrangements is entered into falls before 21 December 2017.

In reg. 2(2), definition of "the prescribed taxes" substituted by SI 2013/2592, reg. 4, with effect from 4 November 2013.

In reg. 2(3), the words "8A, 13A," inserted by SI 2013/2592, reg. 15, with effect from 4 November 2013.

REVOCATIONS

3(1) The Regulations described in the Schedule to these Regulations are revoked.

3(2) Anything begun under or for the purpose of any Regulations revoked by these Regulations shall be continued under or, as the case may be, for the purpose of the corresponding provision of these Regulations.

3(3) Where any document refers to a provision of a regulation revoked by these Regulations, such reference shall, unless the context otherwise requires, be construed as a reference to the corresponding provision of these Regulations.

History – In reg. 3(2), "continued" substituted for "construed" by correction slip dated 31 January 2013.

PRESCRIBED INFORMATION IN RESPECT OF NOTIFIABLE PROPOSALS AND ARRANGEMENTS

4(1) The information which must be provided to HMRC by a promoter under section 308(1) or (3) (duties of promoter) in respect of a notifiable proposal or notifiable arrangements is sufficient information as might reasonably be expected to enable an officer of HMRC to comprehend the manner in which the proposal or arrangements are intended to operate, including–

(a) the promoter's name and address;

(b) details of the provision of the Arrangements Regulations, the ATED Arrangements Regulations, the IHT Arrangements Regulations or the SDLT Arrangements Regulations by virtue of which the arrangements or the proposed arrangements are notifiable;

(c) a summary of the arrangements or proposed arrangements and the name (if any) by which they are known;

(d) information explaining each element of the arrangements or proposed arrangements (including the way in which they are structured) from which the tax advantage expected to be obtained under those arrangements arises; and

(e) the statutory provisions, relating to any of the prescribed taxes, on which that tax advantage is based.

4(2) The information which must be provided to HMRC by a client under section 309 (duty of person dealing with promoter outside the United Kingdom) in respect of notifiable arrangements is sufficient information as might reasonably be expected to enable an officer of HMRC to comprehend the manner in which the arrangements are intended to operate, including–

(a) the client's name and address;

(b) the name and address of the promoter;

(c) details of the provision of the Arrangements Regulations, the ATED Arrangements Regulations, the IHT Arrangements Regulations or the SDLT Arrangements Regulations by virtue of which the arrangements are notifiable;

(d) a summary of the arrangements, and the name (if any) by which they are known;

(e) information explaining each element of the arrangements (including the way in which they are structured) from which the tax advantage expected to be obtained under the arrangements arises; and

(f) the statutory provisions, relating to any of the prescribed taxes, on which that tax advantage is based.

4(3) The information which must be provided to HMRC by a person obliged to do so by section 310 (duty of parties to notifiable arrangements not involving promoter) is sufficient information as might reasonably be expected to enable an officer of HMRC to comprehend the manner in which the arrangements of which that transaction forms part are intended to operate, including–

(a) the name and address of the person entering into the transaction;

(b) details of the provision of the Arrangements Regulations, the ATED Arrangements Regulations, the IHT Arrangements Regulations or the SDLT Arrangements Regulations by virtue of which the arrangements are notifiable;

(c) a summary of the arrangements and the name (if any) by which they are known;

(d) information explaining each element of the arrangements (including the way in which they are structured) from which the tax advantage expected to be obtained under the arrangements arises; and

(e) the statutory provisions, relating to any of the prescribed taxes, on which that tax advantage is based.

4(4) If, but for this paragraph–

(a) a person would be obliged to provide information in relation to two or more notifiable arrangements,

(b) those arrangements are substantially the same (whether they relate to the same parties or different parties), and

(c) the person has already provided information under paragraph (2) or (3) in relation to any of the other arrangements,

the person need not provide further information under paragraph (2) or (3).

4(5) In this regulation–

"the Arrangements Regulations" means the Tax Avoidance Schemes (Prescribed Descriptions of Arrangements) Regulations 2006;

"the ATED Arrangements Regulations" means the Annual Tax on Enveloped Dwellings Avoidance Schemes (Prescribed Descriptions of Arrangements) Regulations 2013;

"the IHT Arrangements Regulations" means the Inheritance Tax Avoidance Schemes (Prescribed Descriptions of Arrangements) Regulations 2017;

"the SDLT Arrangements Regulations" means the Stamp Duty Land Tax Avoidance Schemes (Prescribed Descriptions of Arrangements) Regulations 2005.

History – In reg. 4(1)(b), the words "the ATED Arrangements Regulations," inserted by SI 2013/2592, reg. 5, with effect from 4 November 2013.

In reg. 4(2)(c), the words "the ATED Arrangements Regulations," inserted by SI 2013/2592, reg. 6, with effect from 4 November 2013.

In reg. 4(3)(b), the words "the ATED Arrangements Regulations," inserted by SI 2013/2592, reg. 7, with effect from 4 November 2013.

In reg. 4(5) in the definition of "the IHT Arrangements Regulation", the word "2017" substituted for the word "2011" by SI 2017/1172, reg. 6(2), with effect from 1 April 2018.

In reg. 4(5), definition of "the ATED Arrangements Regulations" inserted by SI 2013/2592, reg. 8, with effect from 4 November 2013.

TIME FOR PROVIDING INFORMATION UNDER SECTION 308, 308A, 309 OR 310

5(1) The period or time (as the case may be) within which–

(a) the prescribed information under section 308, 309 or 310, and

(b) the information or documents which will support or explain the prescribed information under section 308A (supplemental information),

must be provided to HMRC is found in accordance with the following paragraphs of this regulation.

5(2) Where a proposal or arrangements (not being otherwise notifiable) is or are treated as notifiable by virtue of an order under section 306A(1) (doubt as to notifiability) the prescribed period is the period of 10 days beginning on the day after that on which the order is made.

5(3) In the case of a requirement to provide specified information about, or documents relating to, the notifiable proposal or arrangements which arises by virtue of an order under section 308A(2), the prescribed period is the period of 10 days beginning on the day after that on which the order is made.

5(4) In any other case of a notification under section 308(1), the prescribed period is the period of 5 days beginning on the day after the relevant date.

5(5) In any other case of a notification under section 308(3), the prescribed period is the period of 5 days beginning on the day after that on which the promoter first becomes aware of any transaction forming part of arrangements to which that subsection applies.

5(6) In the case of a notification under section 309(1), the prescribed period is the period of 5 days beginning on the day after that on which the client enters into the first transaction forming part of notifiable arrangements to which that subsection applies.

5(7) In the case of a notification under section 310 which arises by virtue of the application of regulation 6 of the Tax Avoidance Schemes (Promoters and Prescribed Circumstances) Regulations 2004 (persons not to be treated as promoters: legal professional privilege), the prescribed time is any time during the period of 5 days beginning on the day after that on which the person enters into the first transaction forming part of the notifiable arrangements.

5(8) In any other case of a notification under section 310 the prescribed time is any time during the period of 30 days beginning on the day after that on which the person enters into the first transaction forming part of the notifiable arrangements.

PRESCRIBED INFORMATION UNDER SECTIONS 312 AND 312A

6 For the purposes of sections 312(2) and (5) (duty of promoter to notify client of number) and 312A(2) and (2A) (duty of client to provide information to parties) the prescribed information is–

(a) the name and address of the promoter;

(b) the name, or a brief description of the notifiable arrangements or proposal;

(c) the reference number (or if more than one, any one reference number) allocated by HMRC under section 311 (arrangements to be given reference number) to the notifiable arrangements or proposed notifiable arrangements;

(d) the date that the reference number was–

(i) sent by the promoter to the client; or (as the case may be)

(ii) sent to any other person by the client under section 312A(2) or (2A).

History – In reg. 6, the words "and (2A) (duty of client to provide information to parties)" substituted for the words "(duty of client to notify parties of number)" by SI 2015/948, reg. 3(2), with effect from 16 April 2015.
In reg. 6(d)(ii), the words "or (2A)" inserted by SI 2015/948, reg. 3(3), with effect from 16 April 2015.

TIME FOR PROVIDING INFORMATION UNDER SECTION 312A

7 In the case of a notification under section 312A(2) or (2A) the prescribed period is the period of 30 days beginning on–

(a) the day on which the client first becomes aware of any transaction forming part of notifiable arrangements or proposed notifiable arrangements; or, if later,

(b) the day on which the prescribed information is notified to the client by the promoter under section 312.

History – In reg. 7, the words "or (2A)" inserted by SI 2015/948, reg. 4, with effect from 16 April 2015.

EXEMPTION FROM DUTY UNDER SECTION 312A

8 [Omitted by SI 2015/948, reg. 5.]

History – Reg. 8 omitted by SI 2015/948, reg. 5, with effect from 16 April 2015.
"**8** The duty of a client to notify other persons under section 312A(2) does not apply to an employer of an employee where the employee by reason of employment receives or expects to receive a tax advantage in respect of income tax or capital gains tax as a result of notifiable arrangements or proposed notifiable arrangements.".

PRESCRIBED INFORMATION UNDER SECTION 312B: INFORMATION AND TIMING

8A(1) For the purposes of section 312B (duty of client to provide information to promoter)–

(a) the prescribed period is 10 days from the later of the date that the client receives the reference number allocated by HMRC under section 311 to the notifiable arrangements, and the date the client first enters into a transaction which forms part of the notifiable arrangements; and

(b) the prescribed information is–

(i) any identification number allocated to the client by HMRC ("unique taxpayer number") and the client's national insurance number; or

(ii) confirmation that the client does not have a unique taxpayer number or a national insurance number or has neither number.

History – Reg. 8A inserted by SI 2013/2592, reg. 16, with effect from 4 November 2013.

EXEMPTION FROM DUTY UNDER SECTION 313

8B Where an employee receives prescribed information from an employer under section 312A(2) or (2A) in circumstances where the employer has a duty to notify HMRC under section 313ZC in respect of that employee, then no duty arises under section 313(1) in respect of that employee.

History – Reg. 8B inserted by SI 2015/948, reg. 6, with effect from 16 April 2015.

PRESCRIBED CASES UNDER SECTION 313(3)(A)

9(1) The prescribed cases for the purposes of section 313(3)(a) (cases in which the information is to be included in returns) are as follows.

9(2) Subject to regulation 10(7) and (8), in the case of a person who–

(a) expects an advantage to arise in respect of that person's liability to pay, entitlement to a repayment of, or to a deferment of the liability to pay, income tax or capital gains tax as a result of notifiable arrangements; and

(b) is required to make a return to HMRC by a notice under section 8 or 8A of the Taxes Management Act 1970 (income tax and capital gains tax: personal return and trustee's return), in respect of income tax or capital gains tax,

the prescribed information shall be included in the return (under the section which applies) which relates to the year of assessment in which the person first enters into a transaction forming part of the notifiable arrangements and in the return for each subsequent year of assessment until the advantage ceases to apply to that person.

9(3) Subject to regulation 10(7) and (8) in the case of a company which–

(a) expects a tax advantage to arise in respect of its liability to pay, entitlement to a repayment of, or to a deferment of its liability to pay, corporation tax as a result of notifiable arrangements; and

(b) is required to make a return to HMRC by a notice under paragraph 3 of Schedule 18 to the Finance Act 1998 (company tax return), in respect of corporation tax,

the prescribed information shall be included in the return under that paragraph covering the period in which the company first enters into a transaction forming part of the notifiable arrangements and in the return covering each subsequent period until the tax advantage ceases to apply to the company.

9(4) Subject to regulation 10(7) and (8) in the case of a partnership–

(a) which expects an advantage to arise in respect of a partner's liability to pay, entitlement to a repayment of, or to a deferment of the liability to pay income tax, capital gains tax or corporation tax in respect of partnership profits or gains as a result of notifiable arrangements; and

(b) in respect of which a return is required to be made to HMRC by virtue of a notice under section 12AA of the Taxes Management Act 1970(c) (partnership return) in respect of income tax, capital gains tax or corporation tax,

in addition to any duty under paragraph (2) or (3) the prescribed information shall be included in the return under that section covering the period in which the partnership first enters into a transaction forming part of the notifiable arrangements and in the returns covering each subsequent period until the tax advantage ceases to apply to the partner in question.

9(5) Subject to regulation 10(7) and (8) in the case of a person who–

(a) expects an advantage to arise in respect of that person's liability to pay, entitlement to a repayment of, or to a deferment of the liability to pay inheritance tax as a result of notifiable arrangements; and

(b) is required to make a return to HMRC under section 216 of the Inheritance Tax Act 1984 (accounts and information) in respect of a transaction forming part of the notifiable arrangements within a period of 12 months from the end of the month in which the first transaction forming part of the arrangements is entered into,

the prescribed information shall be included in the return under that section.

9(6) Subject to regulation 10(7) and (8) in the case of a person who–

(a) expects an advantage to arise in respect of that person's liability to pay, entitlement to a repayment of, or deferment of the liability to pay, annual tax on enveloped dwellings as a result of notifiable arrangements; and

(b) is required to make a return to HMRC under section 159 of the Finance Act 2013 in respect of annual tax on enveloped dwellings;

the prescribed information shall be included in the return under that section.

History – In reg. 9(2), (3) and (4), "10(7)" substituted for "10(4), (7)" by SI 2015/948, reg. 7, with effect from 16 April 2015. Reg. 9(6) inserted by SI 2013/2592, reg. 9, with effect from 4 November 2013.

PRESCRIBED CASES UNDER SECTION 313(3)(B)

10(1) The prescribed cases for the purposes of section 313(3)(b) (cases in which the information is to be provided separately) are as follows.

10(2) In a case where a purchaser expects an advantage to arise in respect of that person's liability to pay, entitlement to a repayment of, or to a deferment of the liability to pay stamp duty land tax as a result of notifiable arrangements the prescribed information shall be provided separately to HMRC in such form and manner as they may specify.

10(3) If paragraph (2) applies in relation to a land transaction entered into as purchaser by or on behalf of a partnership notification of the prescribed information by or in relation to the responsible partners may instead be done by or in relation to a representative partner or partners.

10(4) [Omitted by SI 2015/948, reg. 8.]

10(5) In the case of a person who would be obliged to comply with a duty under regulation 9(2) to (4), but is not required, in respect of a year of assessment, accounting period or tax year–

(a) in the case of notifiable arrangements to which regulation 9(2) applies, to make a return under either of the provisions referred to in regulation 9(2)(b);

(b) in the case of notifiable arrangements to which regulation 9(3) applies, to make a return under the provision referred to in regulation 9(3)(b); or

(c) in the case of notifiable arrangements to which regulation 9(4) applies, to make a return under the provision referred to in regulation 9(4)(b);

the prescribed information shall be provided separately to HMRC in such form and manner as they may specify.

10(6) In the case of a person who–

(a) expects an advantage to arise in respect of that person's liability to pay, entitlement to a repayment of, or to a deferment of the liability to pay inheritance tax as a result of notifiable arrangements; and

(b) is not required to make a return to HMRC under section 216 of the Inheritance Tax Act 1984 in respect of a transaction forming part of the notifiable arrangements within a period of 12 months from the end of the month in which the first transaction forming part of the arrangements is entered into,

the prescribed information shall be provided separately to HMRC in such form and manner as they may specify.

10(6A) In the case of a person who–

(a) expects an advantage to arise in respect of that person's liability to pay, entitlement to a repayment of, or deferment of the liability to pay, annual tax on enveloped dwellings as a result of notifiable arrangements; and

(b) is not required to make a return to HMRC under section 159 of the Finance Act 2013 in respect of a transaction forming part of the notifiable arrangements within a period of 30 days beginning with the later of–

(i) the effective date of the first transaction which forms part of the arrangements; or

(ii) the date of the receipt of the reference number allocated under the provisions of section 311;

the prescribed information shall be provided separately to HMRC.

10(6B) In the case of a person who expects an advantage to arise in respect of that person's liability to pay, entitlement to a repayment of, or deferment of the liability to pay, the apprenticeship levy as a result of notifiable arrangements, the prescribed information shall be provided separately to HMRC in such form and manner as they may specify.

10(7) In a case of a person who would, but for this paragraph, be obliged to comply with a duty under regulation 9 and–

(a) the relevant return is not delivered by the filing date; or

(b) the relevant return is delivered by the filing date but does not include the prescribed information;

the prescribed information shall be provided separately to HMRC in such form and manner as they may specify.

10(8) In a case where–

(a) a person is required to provide information relating to more than one reference number;

(b) the information is included in a return under regulation 9; and

(c) the number of reference numbers in relation to which information is required exceeds the number of spaces allocated to the information on the return form;

the information relating to so many of the reference numbers as exceeds the number of allocated spaces shall be provided separately to HMRC in such form and manner as they may specify.

10(9) In addition to the duty under any other paragraph above, or regulation 9, in a case where the arrangements give rise to a claim submitted separately from the return under–

(a) section 261B of the Taxation of Chargeable Gains Act 1992 (treating trade loss etc as CGT loss); or

(b) Part 4 of the Income Tax Act 2007 (loss relief);

the prescribed information shall be provided separately to HMRC in such form and manner as they may specify.

History – Reg. 10(4) omitted by SI 2015/948, reg. 8, with effect from 16 April 2015. Former reg. 10(4) read as follows:

"**10(4)** In the case of a person who is the employer of an employee, by reason of whose employment a tax advantage is expected to arise to any person in respect of income tax, corporation tax or capital gains tax as a result of notifiable arrangements, the prescribed information shall be provided separately to HMRC in such form and manner as they may specify.".

Reg. 10(6A) inserted by SI 2013/2592, reg. 10, with effect from 4 November 2013.

Reg. 10(6B) inserted by SI 2017/1171, reg. 7, with effect from 21 December 2017, but the amendment does not have effect for the purposes of: FA 2004, s. 308(1), if the relevant date falls before 21 December 2017; or FA 2004, s. 308(3), if the date on which the promoter first becomes aware of any transaction forming part of notifiable arrangements falls before 21 December 2017; or FA 2004, s. 309(1) and 310, if the date on which any transaction forming part of notifiable arrangements is entered into falls before 21 December 2017.

PRESCRIBED INFORMATION UNDER SECTION 313(1)

11(1) For the purposes of section 313(1) (duty of parties to notifiable arrangements to notify Board of number, etc) the prescribed information is that specified in whichever of paragraph (2), (3) or (4) is applicable.

11(2) In cases prescribed in regulation 9 the prescribed information is–

(a) the reference number (or if more than one, any one reference number) allocated by HMRC under section 311 to the notifiable arrangements or proposed notifiable arrangements; and

(b) the year of assessment, tax year or accounting period (as the case may be) in which, or the date on which, the person providing the information expects a tax advantage to be obtained.

11(3) In the cases prescribed in regulation 10 (apart from paragraph (2) and any case relating to annual tax on enveloped dwellings) the prescribed information is–

(a) the name and address of the person providing it;

(b) any National Insurance number, tax reference number, PAYE reference number or other personal identifier allocated by HMRC to the person to whom the information relates;

(c) the reference number (or if more than one, any one reference number) allocated by HMRC under section 311 to the notifiable arrangements or proposed notifiable arrangements;

(d) the year of assessment, tax year or accounting period (as the case may be) in which, or the date on which, the person providing the information or expects to obtain a tax advantage by virtue of the notifiable arrangements;

(e) the name of the person providing the declaration as to the accuracy and completeness of the notification; and

(f) the capacity in which the person mentioned in sub-paragraph (e) is acting.

11(4) In the case prescribed at regulation 10(2) the prescribed information is–

(a) the name and address of the purchaser;

(b) the reference number (or if more than one, any one reference number) allocated by HMRC under section 311 to the notifiable arrangements or proposed notifiable arrangements;

(c) the address of the property forming the subject of the arrangements ("the property");

(d) the title number of the property (if any is allocated);

IHT Statutory Instruments

(e) the unique transaction reference number (if a land transaction return has been submitted to HMRC at the time the prescribed information is provided);

(f) the market value of the property, taking into account all chargeable interests in the property held by the same person or connected persons;

(g) the effective date of the first land transaction which forms part of the arrangements;

(h) the name of the person providing the declaration as to the accuracy and completeness of the notification; and

(i) the capacity in which that person is acting.

11(5) In the cases prescribed in regulation 10(6A), (7) and (8), where they relate to annual tax on enveloped dwellings, the prescribed information is–

(a) the name and address of the person providing the information;

(b) any tax reference number or other personal identifier allocated by HMRC or a foreign tax authority to the person to whom the information relates;

(c) where a foreign tax authority has allocated a personal identifier, the name of the country on behalf of which that foreign tax authority acts;

(d) the reference number (or if more than one, any one reference number) allocated by HMRC under section 311 to the notifiable arrangements or proposed notifiable arrangements;

(e) the address of the property forming the subject of the arrangements ("the property");

(f) the title number of the property (if any is allocated);

(g) the first chargeable period (within the meaning of section 94(8) of the Finance Act 2013) in which the person providing the information expects to obtain a tax advantage by virtue of the notifable arrangements;

(h) the name of the person providing the declaration as to the accuracy and completeness of the notification, where different from information provided under sub-paragraph (a); and

(i) the capacity in which the person mentioned in sub-paragraph (h) is acting.

History – In reg. 11(3), the words "and any case relating to annual tax on enveloped dwellings" inserted by SI 2013/2592, reg. 11, with effect from 4 November 2013.

In reg. 11(3)(d), the words "or, in the case of regulation 10(4), an employee of that person," (which appeared after the words "information or") omitted by SI 2015/948, reg. 9, with effect from 16 April 2015.

Reg. 11(5) inserted by SI 2013/2592, reg. 12, with effect from 4 November 2013.

TIME FOR PROVIDING INFORMATION UNDER SECTION 313(3)(B)

12(1) The prescribed times for providing information in the cases prescribed in regulation 10 are as follows.

12(2) In the case of regulation 10(2) any time during the period of 30 days beginning with the later of–

(a) the effective date of the first land transaction which forms part of the arrangements; or

(b) the date of the receipt of the reference number allocated under the provisions of section 311.

12(3) [Omitted by SI 2015/948, reg. 10.]

12(4) In the case of regulation 10(5)–

(a) for regulation 10(5)(a), any time during the period ending on 31st January next following the end of the year of assessment in question;

(b) for regulation 10(5)(b), any time during the period ending on the date defined as the filing date for the purposes of paragraph 14 of Schedule 18 to the Finance Act 1998 in respect of the period of account in question;

(c) for regulation 10(5)(c), any time during the period ending on the earliest date by which the person in question could be required to file a return under section 12AA of the Taxes Management Act 1970, determined in accordance with whichever of subsections (4) and (5) of that section is applicable.

12(5) In the case of regulation 10(6) any time during the period of 12 months from the end of the month in which the first transaction forming part of the arrangements is entered into.

12(5A) In the cases of regulation 10(6A), (7) and (8), where it relates to annual tax on enveloped dwellings, any time during the period of 30 days beginning with the later of–

(a) the effective date of the first transaction which forms part of the arrangements; or

(b) the date of the receipt of the reference number allocated under the provisions of section 311.

12(5B) In the case of regulation 10(6B) 14 days after the end of the final tax period in respect of the tax year in which any person first enters into a transaction forming part of the notifiable arrangements and on the same date in each subsequent year until an advantage ceases to apply to any person.

12(5C) In paragraph (5B) **"tax period"** has the meaning given in regulation 2(1) (interpretation) of the Income Tax (Pay As You Earn) Regulations 2003.

12(6) In the case of regulation 10(7) and (8), except where they relate to annual tax on enveloped dwellings, any time during the period ending on the filing date for the relevant return.

12(7) In the case of regulation 10(9) the time that the claim is made.

History – Reg. 12(3) omitted by SI 2015/948, reg. 10, with effect from 16 April 2015. Former reg. 12(3) read as follows:

"**12(3)** In the case of regulation 10(4) whichever of (a) or (b) below applies in respect of the tax year in which the employer first enters into a transaction forming part of the notifiable arrangements and whichever applies in respect of each subsequent year until an advantage ceases to apply to any person–

(a) for a non-Real Time Information employer, any time during the period ending on the date on which the return under regulation 73 of the Income Tax (Pay As You Earn) Regulations 2003 (annual return of relevant payments liable to deduction of tax (Forms P35 and P14)) is or would be due; or

(b) for a Real Time Information employer, 14 days after the end of the final tax period of the tax year.

In this paragraph, **"non-Real Time Information employer"** and **"Real Time Information employer"** have the meanings given in regulation 2(1) (interpretation) of the Income Tax (Pay As You Earn) Regulations 2003.".

Reg. 12(5A) inserted by SI 2013/2592, reg. 13, with effect from 4 November 2013.

Reg. 12(5B) inserted by SI 2017/1171, reg. 8, with effect from 21 December 2017, but the amendment does not have effect for the purposes of: FA 2004, s. 308(1), if the relevant date falls before 21 December 2017; or FA 2004, s. 308(3), if the date on which the promoter first becomes aware of any transaction forming part of notifiable arrangements falls before 21 December 2017; or FA 2004, s. 309(1) and 310, if the date on which any transaction forming part of notifiable arrangements is entered into falls before 21 December 2017.

Reg. 12(5C) inserted by SI 2017/1171, reg. 8, with effect from 21 December 2017, but the amendment does not have effect for the purposes of: FA 2004, s. 308(1), if the relevant date falls before 21 December 2017; or FA 2004, s. 308(3), if the date on which the promoter first becomes aware of any transaction forming part of notifiable arrangements falls before 21 December 2017; or FA 2004, s. 309(1) and 310, if the date on which any transaction forming part of notifiable arrangements is entered into falls before 21 December 2017.

In reg. 12(6), the words ", except where they relate to annual tax on enveloped dwellings," inserted by SI 2013/2592, reg. 14, with effect from 4 November 2013.

PRESCRIBED INFORMATION UNDER SECTION 313ZA: INFORMATION AND TIMING

13(1) For the purposes of section 313ZA(3) (duty of promoter to provide client lists)–

(a) the prescribed period is–

(i) 30 days; or

(ii) where the circumstances in sub-paragraph (d)(iii) apply, 60 days in respect of the information prescribed under sub-paragraph (b)(iii) only.

(b) the prescribed information is–

(i) any reference number allocated by HMRC under section 311 to the arrangements (or to a proposal for them) to which the information provided relates;

(ii) the name and address of each client in relation to whom the relevant date (within the meaning of section 312(3)) occurs in the relevant period in relation to which the information is being provided;

(iii) any identification number allocated by HMRC ("unique taxpayer number") and national insurance number for each client in relation to whom the relevant date (within the meaning of section 312(3)) occurs in the relevant period in relation to which the information is being provided;

(iv) the promoter's name and address; and

(v) the end date of the relevant period in relation to which the information is being provided.

(c) in sub-paragraph (b)(ii) the address of the client is the address to which the promoter has sent or would have sent the prescribed information under section 312.

(d) at the end of the prescribed period under sub-paragraph (a)(i), where the promoter is unable to provide any unique taxpayer number or national insurance number, the prescribed information under sub-paragraph (b) must include confirmation that one of the following applies–

(i) the client has complied with section 312B and does not have a unique taxpayer number or national insurance number or has neither number;

(ii) the client has not complied with section 312B;

(iii) on the sixteenth day after the end of the relevant period, the prescribed period under regulation 8A(1)(a) had not yet expired;

(e) at the end of the prescribed period under sub-paragraph (a)(ii), where the promoter is unable to provide any unique taxpayer number or national insurance number, the prescribed information under sub-paragraph (b) must include confirmation that either sub-paragraph (d)(i) or sub-paragraph (d)(ii) applies.

13(2) For the purposes of section 313ZA(4) the relevant period is each calendar quarter.

History – Reg. 13(1)(a) substituted by SI 2013/2592, reg. 17, with effect from 4 November 2013.
Reg. 13(1)(b)(iii)–(v) substituted for (iii) and (iv) by SI 2013/2592, reg. 18, with effect from 4 November 2013.
Reg. 13(1)(d) and (e) inserted by SI 2013/2592, reg. 19, with effect from 4 November 2013.

PRESCRIBED INFORMATION UNDER SECTION 313ZB: INFORMATION AND TIMING

13A(1) For the purposes of section 313ZB (further information from promoters)–

(a) the prescribed period is 10 days from the date that the promoter receives the written notice under section 313ZB; and

(b) the prescribed information is–

(i) the name and address of any person described in section 313ZB(2) (but only those who will, or are likely to, either sell the arrangements to another person, or achieve a tax advantage by implementing the arrangements);

(ii) any identification number allocated by HMRC to any person mentioned at sub-paragraph (b)(i); and

(iii) sufficient information as might reasonably be expected to enable an officer of HMRC to comprehend the manner in which any person mentioned at subparagraph (b)(i) is involved in the arrangements.

13A(2) Paragraph (1)(b) only extends to information held by the promoter at the time of receipt of a written notice under section 313ZB(2).

History – Reg. 13A inserted by SI 2013/2592, reg. 20, with effect from 4 November 2013.

PRESCRIBED INFORMATION UNDER SECTION 313ZC: INFORMATION AND TIMING

13B(1) For the purposes of section 313ZC (duty of employer to notify HMRC of details of employees etc) the prescribed time for providing prescribed information is 14 days after the end of the final tax period in respect of the tax year in which any person first enters into a transaction forming part of the notifiable arrangements and on the same date in each subsequent year until an advantage ceases to apply to the employee and the employer.

In this paragraph, **"tax period"** has the meaning given in regulation 2(1) (interpretation) of the Income Tax (Pay As You Earn) Regulations 2003.

13B(2) For the purposes of section 313ZC the prescribed information is–

(a) the name, address and reference number of the employer;

(b) the name and any National Insurance Number of the employee;

(c) the reference number (or, if more than one, any one reference number) allocated by HMRC under section 311 (arrangements to be given reference number) to the notifiable arrangements or proposed notifiable arrangements;

(d) where the employee obtains or might reasonably be expected to obtain a tax advantage by virtue of the notifiable arrangements, the tax year in which the employee obtains or expects to obtain the tax advantage;

(e) where a tax advantage is obtained or might reasonably be expected to be obtained only by a person other than the employee by virtue of the notifiable arrangements, confirmation that the employee's tax advantage is expected to be nil; and

(f) the name and address of the promoter, and any name given to the notifiable arrangement when it was notified.

History – Reg. 13B inserted by SI 2015/948, reg. 11, with effect from 16 April 2015.

TIME FOR PROVIDING INFORMATION UNDER SECTION 313A AND 313B

14(1) In the case of a requirement under or by virtue of section 313A(1) (pre-disclosure enquiry), the prescribed period is the period of 10 days beginning on the day after that on which the notice is issued.

14(2) In the case of a requirement under or by virtue of section 313B(1) (reasons for nondisclosure: supporting information), the prescribed period is the period of 14 days beginning on the day after that on which the order is made.

PRESCRIBED INFORMATION UNDER SECTION 313C: INFORMATION AND TIMING

15(1) For the purposes of section 313C(1) (information provided to introducers) the prescribed information is–

(a) P's name and address;

(b) the name and address of each person who has provided P with any information relating to the proposal, and

(c) the name and address of each person with whom P has made a marketing contact.

15(2) For the purposes of section 313C(3)(a) the prescribed period is 10 days.

History – Reg. 15(1)(c) (and the ", and" before it) inserted (and the "and" after (a) omitted) by SI 2015/948, reg. 12(1), with effect from 16 April 2015.

HIGHER RATE OF PENALTY FOLLOWING A FAILURE TO COMPLY WITH AN ORDER UNDER SECTION 306A OR 314A

16(1) For the purposes of section 98C(2A) of the Taxes Management Act 1970 (higher rate of penalty after the making of an order under section 306A) the prescribed period is the period of 10 days beginning on the date on which the order is made.

16(2) For the purposes of section 98C(2B) of the Taxes Management Act 1970 (higher rate of penalty after the making of an order under section 314A) the prescribed period is the period of 10 days beginning on the date on which the order is made.

ELECTRONIC DELIVERY OF INFORMATION

17(1) Information required to be delivered to HMRC or to any other person by virtue of these Regulations may be delivered in such form and by such means of electronic communications as are for the time being authorised for that purpose.

17(2) The use of a particular means of electronic communications is authorised for the purposes of paragraph (1) only if–

(a) it is authorised by directions given by HMRC under section 132(5) of the Finance Act 1999 (voluntary filing by electronic means of returns and other documents); and

(b) the user complies with any conditions imposed by HMRC under that section.

17(3) Nothing in this regulation prevents the delivery of information by electronic communications if the information is contained in a return which is–

(a) authorised to be delivered electronically by virtue of regulations under section 132 of the Finance Act 1999; or

(b) required to be so delivered by virtue of regulations under section 135 of the Finance Act 2002 (mandatory e-filing).

AMENDMENT OF THE TAX AVOIDANCE SCHEMES (PROMOTERS AND PRESCRIBED CIRCUMSTANCES) REGULATIONS 2004

18 [Amends SI 2004/1865, reg. 6.]

SCHEDULE – REVOCATIONS

Regulation 3

[Revokes SI 2004/1864.]

INHERITANCE TAX (MARKET MAKERS AND DISCOUNT HOUSES) REGULATIONS 2012

(SI 2012/2903)

Made on 19 November 2012 by the Commissioners for Her Majesty's Revenue and Customs, in exercise of the powers conferred by s. 724(1)(c) of the Income Tax (Trading and Other Income) Act 2005. Operative from 21 December 2012.

CITATION AND COMMENCEMENT

1 These Regulations may be cited as the Inheritance Tax (Market Makers and Discount Houses) Regulations 2012 and come into force on 31st December 2012.

APPLICATION OF THESE REGULATIONS

2 The day specified for the purposes of sections 106(6) and 107(6) of the Finance Act 1986 for the application of these Regulations is 31st December 2012.

AMENDMENT OF THE INHERITANCE TAX ACT 1984

3 The Inheritance Tax Act 1984 is amended as follows.

4 [Inserts IHTA 1984, s. 105(4A).]

5 [Substitutes IHTA 1984, s. 234(3)(c).]

DESCRIPTION FOR THE PURPOSES OF SECTIONS 105(4A) AND 234(3)(C)(II) OF THE INHERITANCE TAX ACT

6 For the purposes of section 105(4A) of the Inheritance Tax Act 1984 the description of a business is a business in an EEA State other than the United Kingdom which–

(a) holds itself out at all normal times, in compliance with the rules of a regulated market which has been notified to the European Commission, as willing to buy and sell securities, stocks and shares at a price specified by it, and

(b) is recognised as doing so by that regulated market.

7 For the purposes of section 234(3)(c)(ii) of the Inheritance Tax Act 1984 the description of a company is a company in an EEA State other than the United Kingdom which–

(a) holds itself out at all normal times, in compliance with the rules of a regulated market which has been notified to the European Commission, as willing to buy and sell securities, stocks and shares at a price specified by it, and

(b) is recognised as doing so by that regulated market.

VISITING FORCES AND INTERNATIONAL MILITARY HEADQUARTERS (EU SOFA) (TAX DESIGNATION) ORDER 2012

(SI 2012/3070)

Made on 12 December 2012 at the Court at Buckingham Palace, in exercise of the powers conferred upon Her Majesty by s. 303 of the Income Tax (Earnings and Pensions) Act 2003, s. 833 of the Income Tax Act 2007, s. 155 of the Inheritance Tax Act 1984. Operative in accordance with art. 1(2).

CITATION AND COMMENCEMENT

1(1) This Order may be cited as the Visiting Forces and International Military Headquarters (EU SOFA) (Tax Designation) Order 2012.

1(2) This Order shall come into force immediately after the coming into force of the EU SOFA in respect of the United Kingdom.

INTERPRETATION

2 In this Order–

"the EU SOFA" means the Agreement between the member states of the European Union concerning the status of military and civilian staff seconded to the institutions of the European Union, of the headquarters and forces which may be made available to the European Union in the context of the preparation and execution of the tasks referred to in Article 17(2) of the Treaty on European Union, including exercises, and of the military and civilian staff of the member states put at the disposal of the European Union to act in this context;

"the Treaty on European Union" means the Treaty on European Union signed at Maastricht on 7 February 1992 (as amended by the Treaty of Lisbon).

DESIGNATION

3 For the purpose of giving effect to Article 16 of the EU SOFA, each of the countries specified in the First Schedule to this Order, and the international military headquarters specified in the Second Schedule to this Order, are hereby designated for the purposes of–

(a) section 303 of the Income Tax (Earnings and Pensions) Act 2003;

(b) section 833 of the Income Tax Act 2007; and

(c) section 155 of the Inheritance Tax Act 1984.

SCHEDULE 1 – DESIGNATED COUNTRIES

Article 3

Austria, Belgium, Bulgaria, Cyprus, Czech Republic, Denmark, Estonia, Finland, France, Germany, Greece, Hungary, Ireland, Italy, Latvia, Lithuania, Luxembourg, Malta, Netherlands, Poland, Portugal, Romania, Slovakia, Slovenia, Spain, Sweden.

SCHEDULE 2 – DESIGNATED INTERNATIONAL MILITARY HEADQUARTERS

Article 3

The European Union Operational Headquarters at Northwood.

VISITING FORCES AND INTERNATIONAL MILITARY HEADQUARTERS (NATO AND PFP) (TAX DESIGNATION) ORDER 2012

(SI 2012/3071)

Made on 12 December 2012 at the Court at Buckingham Palace, in exercise of the powers conferred upon Her Majesty by s. 74A of the Finance Act 1960, s. 155 of the Inheritance Tax Act 1984, s. 303 of the Income Tax (Earnings and Pensions) Act 2003 and s. 833 of the Income Tax Act 2007. Operative in accordance with art. 1(2).

CITATION AND COMMENCEMENT

1(1) This Order may be cited as the Visiting Forces and International Military Headquarters (NATO and PfP) (Tax Designation) Order 2012.

1(2) This Order shall come into force on the day after the date on which it is made.

REVOCATIONS

2 The Orders in Schedule 1 are revoked.

INTERPRETATION

3 In this Order–

"NATO" means the North Atlantic Treaty Organisation based on the North Atlantic Treaty dated 4th April 1949;

"the NATO SOFA" means the Agreement regarding the Status of Forces of Parties to the North Atlantic Treaty dated 19th June 1951;

"the Paris Protocol" means the Protocol on the Status of International Military Headquarters set up pursuant to the North Atlantic Treaty dated 28th August 1952;

"PfP" means the Partnership for Peace programme of practical bilateral cooperation between individual Partner countries and NATO;

"the PfP SOFA" means the Agreement among the State Parties to the North Atlantic Treaty and the Other States Participating in the Partnership for Peace regarding the Status of their Forces dated 19th June 1995.

NATO DESIGNATION

4 For the purpose of giving effect to Article X of the NATO SOFA and Article VII of the Paris Protocol each of the countries specified in the Second Schedule to this Order, and each of the headquarters specified in the Fourth Schedule to this Order, is hereby designated for the purposes of section 74A of the Finance Act 1960, section 155 of the Inheritance Tax Act 1984, section 303 of the Income Tax (Earnings and Pensions) Act 2003 and section 833 of the Income Tax Act 2007.

PFP DESIGNATION

5 For the purpose of giving effect to Article I of the PfP SOFA each of the countries specified in the Third Schedule to this Order is hereby designated for the purposes of section 74A of the Finance Act 1960, section 155 of the Inheritance Tax Act 1984, section 303 of the Income Tax (Earnings and Pensions) Act 2003 and section 833 of the Income Tax Act 2007.

SCHEDULE 1 – DESIGNATION ORDERS REVOKED

Article 2

Orders revoked	*References*
The Visiting Forces and Allied Headquarters (Income Tax and Death Duties) (Designation) Order 1961	S.I. 1961/580
The Visiting Forces and Allied Headquarters (Stamp Duties) (Designation) Order 1961	S.I. 1960/581
The Visiting Forces and Allied Headquarters (Income Tax and Capital Gains Tax) (Designation) Order 1998	S.I. 1998/1513

Orders revoked	*References*
The Visiting Forces (Income Tax and Capital Gains Tax) (Designation) Order 1998	S.I. 1998/1514
The Visiting Forces and Allied Headquarters (Inheritance Tax) (Designation) Order 1998	S.I. 1998/1515
The Visiting Forces (Inheritance Tax) (Designation) Order 1998	S.I 1998/1516
The Visiting Forces and Allied Headquarters (Stamp Duties) (Designation) Order 1998	S.I. 1998/1517
The Visiting Forces (Stamp Duties) (Designation) Order 1998	S.I. 1998/1518

SCHEDULE 2 – DESIGNATED NATO COUNTRIES

Article 4

Albania, Belgium, Bulgaria, Canada, Croatia, Czech Republic, Denmark, Estonia, France, Germany, Greece, Hungary, Iceland, Italy, Latvia, Lithuania, Luxembourg, Netherlands, Norway, Poland, Portugal, Romania, Slovakia, Slovenia, Spain, Turkey, United States of America.

SCHEDULE 3 – DESIGNATED PFP COUNTRIES

Article 5

Armenia, Austria, Azerbaijan, Belarus, Bosnia and Herzegovina, Finland, Georgia, Ireland, Kazakhstan, Kyrgyz Republic, Malta, Moldova, Montenegro, Russia, Serbia, Sweden, Switzerland, Tajikistan, the former Yugoslav Republic of Macedonia, Turkmenistan, Ukraine, Uzbekistan.

SCHEDULE 4 – DESIGNATED HEADQUARTERS

Article 4

Headquarters of the Supreme Allied Commander Transformation (HQ SACT)

Supreme Headquarters Allied Powers Europe (SHAPE)

Maritime Component Command Headquarters Northwood (CC-MAR HQ Northwood)

Commander Submarines Allied Naval Forces North (COMSUBNORTH)

NATO Airborne Early Warning and Control Force (NAEW&CF)

NATO Joint Electronic Warfare Core Staff (NATO JEWCS)

Headquarters United Kingdom–Netherlands Amphibious Force (UKNLAF)

Headquarters United Kingdom–Netherlands Landing Force (UKNLLF)

The European Air Group (EAG)

The Intelligence Fusion Centre (IFC)

Headquarters Allied Rapid Reaction Corps (HQ ARRC)

PROMOTERS OF TAX AVOIDANCE SCHEMES (PRESCRIBED CIRCUMSTANCES UNDER SECTION 235) REGULATIONS 2015

(SI 2015/130)

Made on 6 February 2015 by the Commissioners for Her Majesty's Revenue and Customs in exercise of the powers conferred upon them by s. 235(6) and (7) and 283(1) of the Finance Act 2014. Operative from 2 March 2015.

CITATION, COMMENCEMENT AND EFFECT

1(1) These Regulations may be cited as the Promoters of Tax Avoidance Schemes (Prescribed Circumstances under Section 235) Regulations 2015 and come into force on 2nd March 2015.

1(2) Regulations 2 and 3 have effect from 17th July 2014.

COMPANY IN SAME GROUP NOT PROMOTER

2(1) A company ("C") is not a promoter to the extent that–

(a) C carries on a business within the meaning of section 235(1);

(b) the other person (or each of the other persons) to whom C provides services in connection with the relevant proposal or relevant arrangements is a company in the same group as C; and

(c) C has not during the previous three years provided services of that kind to a person other than a company which is in the same group as C.

2(2) If C at any subsequent time provides services of that kind to a person other than a company which is in the same group as C, paragraph (1) will be deemed not to have applied during the previous three years.

2(3) A company cannot rely on paragraph (1) whilst a conduct notice or a monitoring notice has effect in relation to it.

2(4) For the purposes of this regulation companies are members of the same group if one is the 51% subsidiary of the other, or both are 51% subsidiaries of a third company.

2(5) In this regulation **"51% subsidiary"** has the same meaning as it does for the purposes of the Corporation Tax Acts.

PERSONS NOT PROMOTERS – SPECIAL CASES

3(1) A person ("P") is not a promoter on account of section 235(2)(a), or by virtue of being responsible to any extent for the design of arrangements within the meaning of section 235(3)(b), where any of the following conditions are met.

3(2) P does not provide any tax advice in connection with the respective proposed arrangements or arrangements.

3(3) P could not reasonably be expected to know that the proposed arrangements, or arrangements, are a relevant proposal or relevant arrangements respectively.

FINANCE ACT 2014 (SCHEDULE 34 PRESCRIBED MATTERS) REGULATIONS 2015

(SI 2015/131)

Made on 6 February 2015 by the Commissioners for Her Majesty's Revenue and Customs in exercise of the powers conferred upon them by s. 283(1) of, and para. 8(1), 8(3) and 9(2) of Sch. 34 to, the Finance Act 2014. Operative from 2 March 2015.

CITATION AND COMMENCEMENT

1 These Regulations may be cited as the Finance Act 2014 (Schedule 34 Prescribed Matters) Regulations 2015 and come into force on 2nd March 2015.

PRESCRIBED MISCONDUCT

2(1) Prescribed misconduct for the purposes of paragraph 8(1)(a) of Schedule 34 to the Finance Act 2014 means any conduct by a person–

(a) which a professional body describes as misconduct, or

(b) which is a breach of a rule or condition imposed by a professional body,

and is relevant to the provision of tax advice or tax related services.

PRESCRIBED ACTION

3 Prescribed action for the purposes of paragraph 8(1)(b) of Schedule 34 to the Finance Act 2014 means any action by a professional body which results in any claim of misconduct being referred to–

(a) a disciplinary process which determines–

(i) the seriousness of the misconduct, and

(ii) the level of any penalty to be imposed; or

(b) a conciliation, arbitration or similar settlement process (however described) which determines the seriousness of the misconduct and the level of any penalty to be imposed.

PRESCRIBED PENALTY

4 A penalty is prescribed for the purposes of paragraph 8(1)(c) of Schedule 34 to the Finance Act 2014 where it is imposed by a professional body and results in one or more of the following in relation to a person–

(a) a fine or financial penalty greater than £5,000;

(b) a condition or restriction on, or attached to, a certificate or licence required to practice under the professional body;

(c) suspension, withdrawal or non-renewal of a certificate or licence required to practice under the professional body;

(d) suspension, expulsion or exclusion from membership of the professional body, however described (including removal from a membership register, striking off), whether temporary or permanent.

PRESCRIBED PROFESSIONAL BODIES

5 The following are prescribed professional bodies for the purposes of paragraph 8(3)(l) of Schedule 34 to the Finance Act 2014–

(a) the Chartered Institute of Taxation;

(b) Chartered Accountants Ireland.

PRESCRIBED RELEVANT SANCTION

6(1) In paragraph 9 of Schedule 34 to the Finance Act 2014 a sanction is prescribed under sub-paragraph (2)(b) if a regulatory authority imposes one or more of the following in relation to a person–

(a) a fine or financial penalty;

(b) a suspension of an approval issued by the regulatory authority to perform any function to which the approval relates;

(c) the imposition of limitations or other restrictions in relation to the performance of any function to which any approval issued by the regulatory authority relates;

(d) the imposition of any conditions in relation to any approval issued by the regulatory authority.

6(2) A sanction is also prescribed in relation to a person if a regulatory authority publishes a statement of misconduct by that person.

FINANCE ACT 2014 (HIGH RISK PROMOTERS PRESCRIBED INFORMATION) REGULATIONS 2015

(SI 2015/549)

Made on 5 March 2015 by the Commissioners for Her Majesty's Revenue and Customs in exercise of the powers conferred upon them by s. 249(3), (10) and (11), 253(2) and (4), 257(2), 259(9), 260(7), 261(2), 268(1), 282(4) and 283(1) of the Finance Act 2014. Operative from 27 March 2015.

CITATION, COMMENCEMENT AND INTERPRETATION

1(1) These Regulations may be cited as the Finance Act 2014 (High Risk Promoters Prescribed Information) Regulations 2015 and come into force on 27th March 2015.

1(2) In these Regulations–

"accounting period" for the purposes of corporation tax has the same meaning as that given in sections 9 to 12 of the Corporation Tax Act 2009 and **"beginning of accounting period"** and **"end of accounting period"** shall be construed accordingly;

"the Act" means the Finance Act 2014;

"audiovisual formats" means any method of presenting information that uses an audible and visible format including broadcasting by electronic means or transmission over, or publication on, the internet; **"chargeable period"** shall be construed–

(a) for the purposes of annual tax on enveloped dwellings, in accordance with section 94(8) of the Finance Act 2013;

(b) for the purposes of petroleum revenue tax, in accordance with section 1(3) of the Oil Taxation Act 1975;

"effective date" has the meaning given by section 119 of the Finance Act 2003;

"tax year" means a year beginning on 6th April and ending on the following 5th April;

PRESCRIBED PUBLICATION OR CORRESPONDENCE

2(1) The following publications and correspondence are prescribed for the purposes of subsection (10) of section 249 of the Act (publication by monitored promoter)–

(a) any publication or correspondence that–

(i) with the exception of correspondence with HMRC, contains information about any relevant arrangements or any relevant proposal offered or promoted by the monitored promoter;

(ii) is shown, given or sent to clients or prospective clients in relation to any relevant arrangements or any relevant proposal (whether or not the relevant arrangements or relevant proposal is provided by the monitored promoter);

(iii) is shown, given or sent to intermediaries or prospective intermediaries in relation to any relevant arrangements or any relevant proposal (whether or not the relevant arrangements or relevant proposal is provided by the monitored promoter);

(b) any correspondence with–

(i) a professional body referred to in paragraph 8(3) of Schedule 34 to the Act of which the monitored promoter is a member, prospective member or former member and which concerns any relevant arrangements or any relevant proposal;

(ii) a regulatory authority referred to in paragraph 9(3) of Schedule 34 to the Act which the monitored promoter is regulated by and which concerns the monitored promoter's conduct in respect of any relevant arrangements or any relevant proposal.

2(2) In paragraph (1)–

(a) **"correspondence"** includes correspondence in writing or by electronic means;

(b) **"publication"** means publication in any format (including audiovisual formats).

INFORMATION PUBLICISED BY A MONITORED PROMOTER

3(1) For the purposes of subsection (11) of section 249 of the Act (publication by monitored promoter), the prescribed form and manner is as set out in paragraphs (2), (3) and (4).

3(2) Notification given under subsection (1) of section 249 must–

(a) be in writing;

(b) set out clearly and precisely the information required to be stated under paragraphs (a) and (b) of section 249(1) of the Act so that–

(i) in respect of the information required by section 249(1)(a) of the Act, it is clear that the promoter is being monitored by HMRC because it breached a condition or conditions of a conduct notice identified under section 249(1)(b) of the Act, and

(ii) in respect of the information required by section 249(1)(b) of the Act, the specific details of each of the conditions which it has been determined that the person has failed to comply with.

3(3) In respect of subsection (3) of section 249 of the Act, the monitored promoter shall publish on the internet the information mentioned in paragraph (a) and (b) of section 249(1) of the Act. The published information must–

(a) appear in a prominent position on the monitored promoter's or other websites promoting, or providing information on, the activities of the promoter;

(b) if in writing, be legible;

(c) if in an audiovisual format, be clearly audible or visible;

(d) not in any way be concealed;

(e) be specifically referred to or included in any promotional material (of whatever kind or format);

(f) not be presented in a way that it promotes the activity of tax avoidance.

3(4) The information to be provided under subsection (10) of section 249 of the Act and regulation 2 to these Regulations (prescribed publication or correspondence) must–

(a) be prominent and not in any way be concealed;

(b) if in writing, be legible;

(c) if in an audiovisual format, be clearly audible or visible;

(d) not be presented in a way that promotes the activity of tax avoidance.

DUTY OF PERSONS TO NOTIFY THE COMMISSIONERS: PRESCRIBED INFORMATION

4(1) The following information is prescribed for the purposes of paragraphs 2(b) and 4(b) of section 253 of the Act (duty of persons to notify the Commissioners)–

(a) the full name and address (including postcode) of the person reporting the promoter reference number;

(b) the promoter reference number which is the subject of the report;

(c) the type of tax in respect of which the person expects to obtain a tax advantage;

(d) the unique identifier (as to the meaning of which see paragraph (3)(a));

(e) the relevant date of the transaction(s) (as to the meaning of which see paragraph (3)(b));

(f) a declaration that the information provided is correct and complete to the best of the knowledge and belief of the person making the report;

(g) the signature of the person making the report;

(h) the full name of the person signing the report;

(i) the date on which the report is made.

4(2) For relevant arrangements involving annual tax on enveloped dwellings, stamp duty land tax or stamp duty reserve tax transactions under regulation 4 of the Stamp Duty Reserve Tax Regulations 1986 (notice of charge and payment), the unique identifier in sub-paragraph (1)(d) is to be replaced by the following additional prescribed information–

(a) for annual tax on enveloped dwellings–

(i) title number or numbers of the dwelling associated with the relevant arrangements;

(ii) full address of the dwelling including the postcode sufficient to be able to identify it;

(b) for stamp duty land tax–

(i) the unique transaction reference number (if a land transaction return has been submitted to HMRC at the time the prescribed information is provided);

(ii) title number or numbers of the land associated with the relevant arrangements;

(iii) full address or situation of the land including (where available) the postcode, or information sufficient that the land can be uniquely identified;

(c) for stamp duty reserve tax transactions a full description of the shares or securities associated with the relevant arrangements, including the–

(i) number of shares or securities;

(ii) class or classes of the shares;

(iii) name of the company or other body to which the shares relate;

(iv) nominal value;

(v) consideration paid.

4(3) For the purposes of paragraph (1)–

(a) **"unique identifier"** is to be construed as follows–

(i) where the promoter reference number is not reported in a tax return for an individual, the national insurance number and unique tax reference number of the person making the report;

(ii) where the promoter reference number is not reported in a tax return for a trust or company, the unique tax reference number for the trust or company (as the case may be);

(iii) for inheritance tax purposes, the unique tax reference number and any inheritance tax reference previously allocated by HMRC to the person making the report;

(iv) for stamp duty reserve tax transactions authorised by different arrangements under regulation 4A of the Stamp Duty Reserve Tax Regulations 1986, the unique transaction reference provided by the reporting system under the authorised arrangements;

(b) **"relevant date of the transaction(s)"** means–

(i) in respect of capital gains tax or income tax, the date on which the tax year, in which the relevant arrangements enable or seek to enable a tax advantage to be obtained, ends;

(ii) in respect of corporation tax, with the exception of partnerships where one or more of the partners is a company, either the date on which the accounting period, in which the relevant arrangements enable or seek to enable a tax advantage to be obtained, ends, or, where the company does not have an accounting period, the date of the first transaction forming part of the relevant arrangements;

(iii) in respect of corporation tax in relation to partnerships, including where one or more of the partners is a company, the date on which the tax year in which the relevant arrangements enable or seek to enable a tax advantage to be obtained, ends;

(iv) in respect of annual tax on enveloped dwellings, the date on which the chargeable period, in which the relevant arrangements enable or seek to enable a tax advantage to be obtained, ends;

(v) in respect of inheritance tax, the date of the first transaction forming part of the relevant arrangements;

(vi) in respect of stamp duty land tax, the effective date of the land transaction that forms part of the relevant arrangements that enable a tax advantage to be obtained;

(vii) in respect of stamp duty reserve tax, the date of the transaction that forms part of the relevant arrangements that enable a tax advantage to be obtained;

(viii) in respect of petroleum revenue tax, the end of each chargeable period within which a tax advantage may arise.

REPORT OF PROMOTER REFERENCE NUMBER: PRESCRIBED FORM AND MANNER

5(1) The report made under paragraphs 2(b) and 4(b) of section 253 of the Act (duty of persons to notify the Commissioners) must be made in the form prescribed in Schedule 1 to these Regulations. A separate report must be made for each tax which the relevant arrangements enable or seek to enable an advantage to be obtained.

5(2) The completed report must be sent by post to one of the addresses listed in Schedule 2 to these Regulations.

REPORT OF PROMOTER REFERENCE NUMBER: PRESCRIBED TIME

6(1) A report under section 253 of the Act (duty of persons to notify the Commissioners) must be made by the deadlines set out in paragraphs (2), (3) and (4).

6(2) Where a tax return for an individual, partnership, trustee, company or a return for the purposes of the annual tax on enveloped dwellings is not submitted by the date in section 253(3)(a) or (b) of the Act in relation to the period within which a tax advantage may arise, the report must be made by the end of the fifth working day following the date on which the return was required to be submitted.

6(3) Where there is no tax return covering the period within which a tax advantage may arise, then the report must be made–

(a) in the case of an individual, partnership or trustee, by 31st January following the end of each tax year within which a tax advantage may arise;

(b) in the case of a company, not later than 12 months from the end of each accounting period within which a tax advantage may arise;

(c) in the case of an annual tax on enveloped dwellings return, not later than 30 days from the first day of the chargeable period in which the person is within the charge or would have been within the charge but for the relevant arrangements, for each period within which a tax advantage may arise.

6(4) For the purposes of inheritance tax, stamp duty land tax, stamp duty reserve tax, and petroleum revenue tax, the report must be made–

(a) for inheritance tax, not later than the sixth month after the end of the month which the first transaction under the relevant arrangements was entered into;

(b) for stamp duty land tax, not later than 30 days from the effective date of each land transaction which forms part of the relevant arrangements within which a tax advantage may arise;

(c) for stamp duty reserve tax–

(i) in respect of transactions under regulation 4 of the Stamp Duty Reserve Tax Regulations 1986, not later than the time that the notice of the charge to tax is due to be made to HMRC (the accountable date), or

(ii) where a transaction is authorised by different arrangements under regulation 4A of the Stamp Duty Reserve Tax Regulations 1986, not later than the seventh day of the month after the month in which the charge to tax occurred or would have occurred but for the relevant arrangements;

(d) for petroleum revenue tax, not later than 7 days from the end of each chargeable period within which a tax advantage may arise.

6(5) Where a company does not have an accounting period, the report must be made not later than 24 months from the date of the first transaction which forms part of the relevant arrangements and annually thereafter for any period within which a tax advantage arises.

6(6) For the purposes of paragraph (2), **"working day"** means a day that is not a Saturday or Sunday, Christmas Day, Good Friday or any day that is a bank holiday under the Banking and Finance Dealings Act 1971.

ONGOING DUTY TO PROVIDE INFORMATION: PRESCRIBED INFORMATION AND DOCUMENTS

7(1) The following information is prescribed for the purposes of section 257(2) of the Act (ongoing duty to provide information following HMRC notice)–

(a) the name or names by which the monitored promoter refers to the monitored arrangements or monitored proposal;

(b) a summary description of the monitored arrangements or monitored proposal and how they are intended to result in a tax advantage;

(c) a detailed description of each part of the monitored arrangements or monitored proposal and the details of how they are intended to result in a tax advantage;

(d) the legislative provisions (whether in primary legislation, secondary legislation or both) that the person identified in section 257(1) contends provide the basis for the intended tax advantage under the monitored arrangements or monitored proposal;

(e) any reference number allocated under section 311 of the Finance Act 2004 (arrangements to be given reference number);

(f) if the monitored arrangements or monitored proposal have not been disclosed under Part 7 of the Finance Act 2004 (disclosure of tax avoidance schemes), an explanation as to why the monitored arrangements or monitored proposal have not been disclosed;

(g) if the monitored arrangements or monitored proposal are funded by or will require funding from third parties, the names and addresses of the third parties, the level of funding required and the date on which the third parties agreed to provide funding;

(h) the name and address of any person (including any legal advisers) consulted in respect of the monitored arrangements or monitored proposal;

(i) the name and address of any person otherwise involved in planning, organising or operating the monitored arrangements and detailed information on the involvement and role of that person;

IHT Statutory Instruments

(j) a list of each and every fee paid or to be paid by clients to use or participate in the monitored arrangements with a description of what each fee is charged for or will be charged for;

(k) if not included in (b), (c) or (d) above, a list of all taxes in respect of which it is expected to obtain a tax advantage.

7(2) The following are prescribed documents for the purposes of section 257(2) of the Act–

(a) standard letters and templates of documents to be sent to clients regarding the monitored arrangements and monitored proposals;

(b) documentation which is designed or intended to be used in the operation of the monitored arrangements and monitored proposals;

(c) copies of all documents used to market, promote or advertise the monitored arrangements and monitored proposals;

(d) all correspondence which has been sent to, or received from, a client or prospective client or other person involved in the monitored arrangements and monitored proposals and which concerns the arrangements or the proposal;

(e) all correspondence which has been sent to, or received from, any other person which concerns the monitored arrangements and monitored proposals or matters related to the monitored arrangements and monitored proposals;

(f) any agreement signed or otherwise entered into by each client in respect of the monitored arrangements and monitored proposals.

7(3) **"Prescribed documents"** in paragraph (2) includes documents produced in writing or by electronic means.

MONITORED PROMOTERS: PRESCRIBED CLIENT INFORMATION

8 The following information is prescribed for the purposes of section 259(9)(b) of the Act (monitored promoters: duty to provide information about clients)–

(a) where C is an individual, the national insurance number and unique tax reference number identifying C;

(b) where C is a trust, partnership or company, the unique tax reference number identifying C;

(c) in compliance with subsection (3) of section 265 of the Act (duty to provide information to monitored promoter), where C has not provided the information in sub-paragraph (a) or (b), whether or not C has informed the monitored promoter that C has neither a national insurance number nor a unique tax reference number;

(d) the date on which C became a client of the monitored promoter within the meaning of section 259(5) of the Act;

(e) the date on which C entered into transactions referred to in subsection (7) of section 259 of the Act;

(f) the date on which C informed the monitored promoter of the information required by section 265(2) or 265(3) of the Act or, if provided to the monitored promoter earlier, the earlier date;

(g) whether C was a direct client of the monitored promoter, or was acting through an intermediary ("I") and the name and address of I;

(h) the fee or commission paid or payable by C to I in respect of the monitored arrangements or monitored proposals.

INTERMEDIARIES: PRESCRIBED CLIENT INFORMATION

9 The following information about the person ("C") is prescribed for the purposes of section 260(7)(b) of the Act (intermediaries: duty to provide information about clients)–

(a) where the intermediary knows the national insurance number, unique tax reference number or both which identify C, those numbers;

(b) the name, address and the promoter reference number of the monitored promoter in respect of the monitored proposals referred to in section 260(1);

(c) the name and address of any other intermediary from which, or to which, C has been referred in relation to the monitored proposals;

(d) the date on which the information referred to in section 260(5) was communicated;

(e) any fee or commission paid or payable to I in respect of the monitored proposals.

ENQUIRY FOLLOWING PROVISION OF CLIENT INFORMATION: PRESCRIBED INFORMATION

10(1) The information set out in paragraphs (2), (3) and (4) is prescribed for the purposes of section 261(2) of the Act (enquiry following provision of client information).

10(2) Where the authorised officer's suspicion referred to in section 261(1)(b) of the Act is that information has not been provided in respect of a person under section 259 of the Act, the prescribed information under section 261(2) of the Act is–

(i) the information prescribed by regulation 8;

(ii) the reason or reasons why the prescribed information in regulation 8 was not provided as required by section 259.

10(3) Where the authorised officer's suspicion referred to in section 261(1)(b) of the Act is that information has not been provided in respect of a person under section 260 of the Act, the prescribed information under section 261(2) of the Act is–

(a) the information prescribed by regulation 9;

(b) the date of any transaction under section 261(2) of the Act implementing the relevant arrangements or relevant proposal;

(c) the reason or reasons why the prescribed information in regulation 9 was not provided as required by section 260 of the Act.

COPY DOCUMENTS: PRESCRIBED CONDITIONS OR EXCEPTIONS

11(1) The following conditions are prescribed for the purposes of section 268(1) of the Act (production of documents: compliance)–

(a) the copy document must be an exact copy of the original document, without any amendments, corrections or deletions;

(b) the original document must be retained by the person as required;

(c) the person required to produce the document must not alter the original document or allow it to be altered.

11(2) Subject to other provisions in the Tax Acts on the retention of records and documents, the original document under paragraph (1)(b) shall be retained–

(i) for the purposes of sections 255 and 257 of the Act until such time as the monitoring notice or replacement monitoring is withdrawn under section 245 of the Act;

(ii) for the purposes of section 262 of the Act, until such time as the conduct notice or replacement conduct notice is withdrawn under section 240 of the Act or expires at the end of the period under section 241(2) of the Act.

11(3) Nothing in paragraph (1)(a) prevents a person from redacting information in a copy document which is privileged information within the meaning given in section 271 of the Act.

SCHEDULE 1 – REPORT OF PROMOTER REFERENCE NUMBERS

Regulation 5(1)

HM Revenue & Customs

Report of promoter reference number

When to use this form

Please fill in this form if you have been given a promoter reference number (PRN) and you expect to get a tax advantage from one of the promoter's tax avoidance schemes. It is important that you report the PRN to HM Revenue & Customs (HMRC). If you fail to report a PRN to HMRC we will ask you to pay a penalty.

Details about the promoter reference number

If you complete a personal, trust partnership, company or Annual Tax on Enveloped Dwellings (ATED) tax return, you usually have to report the PRN in your tax return.

If your tax return is late you will need to report the PRN on this form within 5 working days of the date the return was due.

If there is no return covering the period, you will need to make the report by:

- 31 January following the end of the tax year for which you expect to get a tax advantage
- 12 months after the end of the accounting period for which you expect to get a tax advantage
- 30 days of the first day in the chargeable period for which you expect to get a tax advantage on which you were within the charge to the ATED

If exceptionally, you are a company and do not have an accounting period, you will need to report the PRN within 24 months of the first transaction forming part of the tax avoidance scheme (and annually thereafter).

When to report the PRN

You will need to use this form to report the PRN if the tax advantage is expected to arise for:

- Inheritance Tax - within 6 months of the end of the month in which the first transaction forming part of the tax avoidance scheme took place
- Petroleum Revenue Tax - within 7 days of the end of the half-year chargeable period in which you expect to get a tax advantage
- Stamp Duty Land Tax - within 30 days of the transaction forming part of the tax avoidance scheme or for which you expect to get a tax advantage
- Stamp Duty Reserve Tax - where the transaction is not settled through CREST, with the notice of the charge to tax but no later than 7 days from the end of the month in which the transaction took place
- Stamp Duty Reserve Tax - within 7 days of the end of the month in which the transaction took place where the transaction is settled through CREST

For details on where to submit this form, please read 'Where to send this form' on page 3.

Your details

1 Full name use capital letters

2 Full address

Postcode

Your promoter reference number

3 Promoter reference number (PRN)

About the tax advantage

4 Which tax do you expect to get a tax advantage?
Please tick 1 box and provide the relevant details in box 5 below. Enter:

Annual Tax on Enveloped Dwellings	the title number or numbers and the full address of the property (if the property does not have a postcode you must provide sufficient detail to allow us to identify the property)
Capital Gains Tax	your Unique Taxpayer Reference (UTR) and National Insurance number (for trustees or partnerships, enter the UTR for the trust or partnership)
Corporation Tax	the UTR of the company (or if the form is being sent by a partnership the UTR of the partnership)
Income Tax	your UTR and National Insurance number (for trustees or partnerships, enter the UTR for the trust or partnership)
Inheritance Tax	your UTR and any Inheritance Tax reference previously allocated to you by HM Revenue & Customs
Petroleum Revenue Tax	the name of the oil field for which you expect to get a tax advantage and your participator's reference for that field
Stamp Duty Land Tax	the title number or numbers, full address of the property (if the property does not have a postcode you must provide sufficient detail to allow us to identify the property) and the Unique Transaction Reference number
Stamp Duty Reserve Tax	(if the transaction is not settled through CREST) a full description of the shares or securities, including number, class, nominal value, the name of the company to which the shares relate and consideration paid (if the transaction is settled through CREST) the CREST transaction reference ID

5 Unique identifier details – include reference number(s), names and addresses as explained in question 4 above

IHT Statutory Instruments

Details of transaction

Consider when you expect to get a tax advantage and enter the end of the accounting period or transaction date for:

- Annual Tax on Enveloped Dwellings – the end of the chargeable period
- Capital Gains Tax, Income Tax and trustees and partnerships – the end of the tax year
- Corporation Tax – the end of the accounting period unless exceptionally there is no accounting period – then enter the date of the first transaction
- Inheritance Tax – the date of the first transaction
- Petroleum Revenue Tax – the end of the half-year chargeable period
- Stamp Duty Land Tax or Stamp Duty Reserve Tax – the date of the transaction

6 Date of transaction DD MM YYYY or End of period DD MM YYYY

Declaration

The information I have given on this form is correct and complete to the best of my knowledge and belief.

Full name of signatory use capital letters

Signature

Date DD MM YYYY

Where to send this form

Please return your completed form to:

HM Revenue & Customs
Counter Avoidance Directorate
CA Intelligence S0528
PO Box 194
BOOTLE
L69 9AA

In the case of Stamp Duty Reserve Tax where the transaction is not settled through CREST, send this form to:

HM Revenue & Customs
SDRT Compliance Team
9th Floor, City Centre House
30 Union Street
BIRMINGHAM
B2 4AB

SCHEDULE 2 – ADDRESSES TO SEND THE PROMOTER REFERENCE NUMBER REPORTS

Regulation 5(2)

In respect of arrangements involving stamp duty reserve tax transactions under regulation 4 of the Stamp Duty Reserve Tax Regulations (1986), the completed report under section 253 must be sent to–

HM Revenue and Customs
SDRT Compliance Team
9th Floor, City Centre House
30 Union Street
BIRMINGHAM
B2 4AR

For all other reports made under section 253 (including those involving stamp duty reserve tax transactions under regulation 4A of the Stamp Duty Reserve Tax Regulations (1986)), the completed report must be sent to–

HM Revenue and Customs
Counter Avoidance Directorate
CA Intelligence S0528
PO Box 194
BOOTLE
L69 9AA

INHERITANCE TAX (ELECTRONIC COMMUNICATIONS) REGULATIONS 2015

(SI 2015/1378)

Made on 9 June 2015 by the Commissioners for Her Majesty's Revenue and Customs in exercise of the powers conferred upon them by s. 132 of the Finance Act 1999. Operative from 6 July 2015.

CITATION, COMMENCEMENT AND INTERPRETATION

1(1) These Regulations may be cited as the Inheritance Tax (Electronic Communications) Regulations 2015 and come into force on 6th July 2015.

1(2) In these Regulations–

"approved" means approved, for the purposes of these Regulations and for the time being, by means of a general or specific direction given by HMRC;

"HMRC" means the Commissioners for Her Majesty's Revenue and Customs;

"IHTA 1984" means the Inheritance Tax Act 1984;

"information delivered by means of electronic communications" includes information delivered to a secure mailbox; and

"official computer system" means a computer system maintained by or on behalf of HMRC–

(a) to send or receive information or payments; or

(b) to process or store information.

1(3) In paragraph (2) **"secure mailbox"** means a facility or feature which–

(a) forms part of an official computer system; and

(b) can be accessed by an individual permitted to use electronic communications by an authorisation given by means of a direction by HMRC.

1(4) References in these Regulations to information and to the delivery of information shall be construed in accordance with section 132(8) of the Finance Act 1999.

SCOPE OF THESE REGULATIONS

2(1) Subject to paragraph (2), these Regulations apply to–

(a) the delivery of information, to or by HMRC, the delivery of which is authorised or required by or under IHTA 1984; and

(b) the making of any payment or repayment of tax or other sums in connection with the operation of IHTA 1984.

2(2) These Regulations do not apply to the delivery of information which is authorised or required by or under sections 222 to 223I of IHTA 1984.

USE OF ELECTRONIC COMMUNICATIONS

3(1) HMRC may only use electronic communications in connection with the matters referred to in regulation 2(1) if–

(a) the recipient has consented to HMRC using electronic communications in connection with those matters; and

(b) HMRC have not been notified that the consent has been withdrawn.

3(2) HMRC may specify by specific or general direction the manner in which the consent may be provided and withdrawn, including the time from which the consent and withdrawal is to take effect.

3(3) A person other than HMRC may only use electronic communications in connection with the matters referred to in regulation 2(1) if the conditions specified in paragraphs (4) to (7) are satisfied.

3(4) The first condition is that the person is for the time being permitted to use electronic communications for the purpose in question by an authorisation given by means of a direction given by HMRC.

3(5) The second condition is that the person uses–

(a) an approved method for authenticating the identity of the sender of the communication;

(b) an approved method of electronic communications; and

(c) an approved method for authenticating any information delivered by means of electronic communications.

3(6) The third condition is that any information or payment sent by means of electronic communications is in a form approved for the purpose of these Regulations, and Extensible Business Reporting Language

(XBRL), Inline XBRL and other electronic data handling techniques are among the forms that may be so approved.
Here **"form"** includes the manner in which the information is presented.

3(7) The fourth condition is that the person maintains such records in written or electronic form as may be specified in a general or specific direction given by HMRC.

Cross references – HMRC Direction of 31 July 2015: partly made under reg. 3(2), (4) to (7).
HMRC Direction of 23 and 26 October 2015: partly made under reg. 3(5).
HMRC Direction of 29 April 2016: made under reg. 3(2) and (5).

USE OF INTERMEDIARIES

4 HMRC may use intermediaries in connection with–

(a) the delivery of information or the making of payments or repayments by means of electronic communications in connection with the matters referred to in regulation 2(1), and

(b) the authentication or security of anything transmitted by such means,

and may require other persons to use intermediaries in connection with those matters.

EFFECT OF DELIVERING INFORMATION BY MEANS OF ELECTRONIC COMMUNICATIONS

5(1) Information to which these Regulations apply, and which is delivered by means of electronic communications, shall be treated as having been delivered, in the manner or form required by or under IHTA 1984 if, but only if, all the conditions imposed by–

(a) these Regulations,

(b) any other applicable enactment (except to the extent that the condition thereby imposed is incompatible with these Regulations), and

(c) any specific or general direction given by HMRC,

are satisfied.

5(2) Information delivered by means of electronic communications shall be treated as having been delivered on the day on which the last of the conditions imposed as mentioned in paragraph (1) is satisfied. This is subject to paragraphs (3) and (4).

5(3) HMRC may by a general or specific direction provide for information to be treated as delivered upon a different date (whether earlier or later) than that given by paragraph (2).

5(4) Information shall not be taken to have been delivered to an official computer system by means of electronic communications unless it is accepted by the system to which it is delivered.

PROOF OF CONTENT

6(1) A document certified by an officer of HMRC to be a printed-out version of any information delivered by means of electronic communications under these Regulations on any occasion shall be evidence, unless the contrary is proved, that that information–

(a) was delivered by means of electronic communications on that occasion; and

(b) constitutes the entirety of what was delivered on that occasion.

6(2) A document purporting to be a certificate given in accordance with paragraph (1) shall be presumed to be such a certificate unless the contrary is proved.

PROOF OF SENDER OR RECIPIENT

7 The identity of–

(a) the sender of any information delivered to an official computer system by means of electronic communications under these Regulations, or

(b) the recipient of any information delivered by means of electronic communications from an official computer system,

shall be presumed, unless the contrary is proved, to be the person recorded as such on an official computer system.

INFORMATION DELIVERED ELECTRONICALLY ON ANOTHER'S BEHALF

8 Any information delivered by an approved method of electronic communications on behalf of any person ("P") shall be deemed to have been delivered by P unless P proves that it was delivered without P's knowledge or connivance.

INFORMATION DELIVERED JOINTLY BY MORE THAN ONE PERSON

9(1) Where an enactment to which these Regulations apply permits or requires information to be delivered jointly by more than one person ("the relevant persons") any one of the relevant persons may deliver the information by means of electronic communications also on behalf of one or more other relevant persons but only if the condition in paragraph (2) is met.

9(2) The condition is that the relevant person delivering the information has prescribed authorisation from each of the other relevant persons on whose behalf he is delivering that information.

9(3) In this regulation **"prescribed authorisation"** means authorisation prescribed for this purpose by means of a specific or general direction given by HMRC.

Cross references – HMRC Direction of 31 July 2015: partly made under reg. 9(3).
HMRC Direction of 23 and 26 October 2015: partly made under reg. 9(3).

PROOF OF DELIVERY OF INFORMATION AND PAYMENTS

10(1) The use of an approved method of electronic communications shall be presumed, unless the contrary is proved, to have resulted in the making of a payment or the delivery of information–

(a) in the case of information falling to be delivered, or a payment falling to be made, to HMRC, if the making of the payment or the delivery of the information has been recorded on an official computer system; and

(b) in the case of information falling to be delivered, or a payment falling to be made, by HMRC, if the despatch of that payment or information has been recorded on an official computer system.

10(2) The use of an approved method of electronic communications shall be presumed, unless the contrary is proved, not to have resulted in the making of a payment, or the delivery of information–

(a) in the case of information falling to be delivered, or a payment falling to be made, to HMRC, if the making of the payment or the delivery of the information has not been recorded on an official computer system; and

(b) in the case of information falling to be delivered, or a payment falling to be made, by HMRC, if the despatch of that payment or information has not been recorded on an official computer system.

10(3) The time of receipt of any information or payment sent by an approved means of electronic communications shall be presumed, unless the contrary is proved, to be that recorded on an official computer system.

USE OF UNAUTHORISED METHODS OF ELECTRONIC COMMUNICATIONS

11(1) Paragraph (2) applies to information which is permitted or required to be delivered to HMRC in connection with the matters mentioned in regulation 2(1).

11(2) The use of a means of electronic communication, for the purpose of delivering any information to which this paragraph applies, shall be conclusively presumed not to have resulted in the delivery of that information, unless–

(a) that means of electronic communications is for the time being approved for the delivery of information of that kind; and

(b) the sender is approved, if necessary, for the use of that means of electronic communications in relation to information of that kind.

ENFORCEMENT BY DEDUCTION FROM ACCOUNTS (PRESCRIBED INFORMATION) REGULATIONS 2015

(SI 2015/1986)

Made on 8 December 2015 by the Commissioners for Her Majesty's Revenue and Customs in exercise of the powers conferred upon them by para. 3(2), 8(2)(a), 8(2)(c), 8(2)(d), 8(4)(b) and 23(1) of Sch. 8 to the Finance (No.2) Act 2015. Operative from 25 January 2016.

CITATION, COMMENCEMENT AND EXTENT

1(1) These Regulations may be cited as the Enforcement by Deduction from Accounts (Prescribed Information) Regulations 2015 and come into force on 25th January 2016.

1(2) These Regulations extend to England and Wales and Northern Ireland only.

INTERPRETATION

2 In these Regulations–

"account details" in respect of an account held by P means–

(a) any account number;

(b) any roll number;

(c) any sort code;

(d) the type of account, including whether or not it is a joint account;

(e) the account balance (in the currency in which the account is held);

(f) whether interest is payable in respect of amounts standing to the credit of the account and, if so, the rate of interest payable;

(g) any minimum balance required to keep the account open;

(h) any contractual term by virtue of which an account holder or interested third party may suffer economic loss where a hold notice or deduction notice is, or has been, given;

(i) specified information about–

(i) any account holder other than P;

(ii) any person (not falling within paragraph (i)) who is an interested third party in relation to the account;

(iii) any person who, in respect of the account, has power of attorney;

"P" means the person in respect of whom HMRC has given an information notice or, as the case may be, hold notice;

"Schedule 8" means Schedule 8 to the Finance (No. 2) Act 2015;

"specified information" in respect of a person means–

(a) name and address;

(b) national insurance number;

(c) all email addresses;

(d) all telephone numbers;

(e) in respect of an account which is a joint account, the proportion of the balance of that joint account to which the person is entitled.

INFORMATION

3(1) Information is only prescribed under these Regulations if it–

(a) is in the possession of, or immediately available to, a deposit-taker at the time the deposit-taker is given an information notice or, as the case may be, a hold notice, and

(b) describes the account, or, as the case may be, person, at the relevant time.

3(2) The relevant time for the purposes of regulation 3(1)(b) is–

(a) in the case of the information prescribed by regulations 5(1)(f) and 5(1)(g), immediately after the deposit-taker has complied with the hold notice, and

(b) in any other case, immediately before the deposit-taker complies with the information notice, or, as the case may be, hold notice.

PRESCRIBED INFORMATION IN RESPECT OF AN INFORMATION NOTICE

4 The following information is prescribed for the purposes of paragraph 3(2) of Schedule 8 (information notice)–

(a) account details for each account P holds with the deposit-taker;

(b) specified information in relation to P.

PRESCRIBED INFORMATION IN RESPECT OF A HOLD NOTICE WHERE AN ACCOUNT IS AN AFFECTED ACCOUNT

5(1) The following information is prescribed for the purposes of paragraph 8(2) of Schedule 8 (duty to notify HMRC and account-holders etc)–

(a) account details for each account P holds with the deposit-taker;

(b) specified information in relation to P;

(c) confirmation of which of the accounts that P holds with the deposit-taker is an affected account;

(d) the date on which the deposit-taker complied with paragraph 6(1) of Schedule 8 (effect of hold notice);

(e) confirmation that the deposit-taker understands the effect of paragraph 14(1)(g) of Schedule 8 (penalties);

(f) the total of all held amounts notified by the deposit-taker under paragraph 8(2)(b) of Schedule 8 in response to a hold notice;

(g) in respect of each account which P holds with the deposit-taker, the amount standing to the credit of the account which is not subject to action taken by the deposit-taker under paragraph 6(3) of Schedule 8;

(h) a description of any economic loss suffered by an account holder or interested third party as a result of any contractual term specified in the definition of **"account details"** in regulation 2 at sub-paragraph (h).

5(2) In this regulation **"held amounts"** is to be read in accordance with paragraph 7 of Schedule 8.

PRESCRIBED INFORMATION IN RESPECT OF A HOLD NOTICE WHERE AN ACCOUNT IS NOT AFFECTED ACCOUNT

6(1) The following information is prescribed for the purposes of paragraph 8(4)(b) of Schedule 8.

6(2) The information which the deposit-taker has taken into account to determine that there are no affected accounts.

ENFORCEMENT BY DEDUCTION FROM ACCOUNTS (IMPOSITION OF CHARGES BY DEPOSIT-TAKERS) REGULATIONS 2016

(SI 2016/44)

Made on 18 January 2016 by the Commissioners for Her Majesty's Revenue and Customs in exercise of the powers conferred upon them by para. 20(2)(e) of Sch. 8 to the Finance (No. 2) Act 2015. Operative from 10 February 2016.

CITATION, COMMENCEMENT AND EXTENT

1(1) These Regulations may be cited as the Enforcement by Deduction from Accounts (Imposition of Charges by Deposit-takers) Regulations 2016 and come into force on 10th February 2016.

1(2) These Regulations extend to England and Wales and Northern Ireland only.

INTERPRETATION

2 In these Regulations **"administrative costs"** means the administrative costs incurred by a deposit-taker in complying with an obligation under Schedule 8 to the Finance (No. 2) Act 2015 to which a final payment required under paragraph 13(11)(b)(ii) of that Schedule relates.

IMPOSITION OF CHARGES

3 A deposit-taker may impose a charge upon an account holder in respect of administrative costs only where–

(a) there is an agreement between it and the account holder (or, as the case may be, account holders), which provides that the deposit-taker may charge a fee in respect of those costs,

(b) the deposit taker–

 (i) has made the final payment required by paragraph 13(11)(b)(ii), and

 (ii) has not previously imposed a charge in respect of those costs, and

(c) the amount of the charge imposed does not exceed the amount specified in regulation 4.

AMOUNT THAT CAN BE CHARGED FOR ADMINISTRATIVE COSTS

4 The amount specified in this regulation is the lesser of–

(a) the amount of those administrative costs reasonably incurred by the deposit-taker, and

(b) £55.

ASSET-BASED PENALTY FOR OFFSHORE INACCURACIES AND FAILURES (REDUCTIONS FOR DISCLOSURE AND CO-OPERATION) REGULATIONS 2017

(SI 2017/334)

Made on 9 March 2017 by the Treasury in exercise of the powers conferred upon them by para. 8(3) and (4) of Sch. 22 to the Finance Act 2016. Operative from 1 April 2017.

CITATION AND COMMENCEMENT

1 These Regulations may be cited as the Asset-based Penalty for Offshore Inaccuracies and Failures (Reductions for Disclosure and Co-operation) Regulations 2017 and come into force on 1st April 2017.

MAXIMUM AMOUNT OF REDUCTION OF THE STANDARD AMOUNT OF THE ASSET-BASED PENALTY FOR DISCLOSURE AND CO-OPERATION

2 The maximum amount by which the standard amount of the asset-based penalty determined in accordance with paragraph 7 of Schedule 22 to the Finance Act 2016 (standard amount of asset-based penalty) may be reduced as required by paragraph 8 of that Schedule (reductions for disclosure and co-operation) is–

(a) 50% of the standard amount in a case involving only unprompted disclosures, and

(b) 20% of the standard amount in a case involving prompted disclosures.

PENALTIES RELATING TO OFFSHORE MATTERS AND OFFSHORE TRANSFERS (ADDITIONAL INFORMATION) REGULATIONS 2017

(SI 2017/345)

Made on 9 March 2017 by the Treasury in exercise of the powers conferred upon them by para. 9(1C) of Sch. 24 to the Finance Act 2007, para. 12(2C) of Sch. 41 to the Finance Act 2008 and para. 14(2C) of Sch. 55 to the Finance Act 2009. Operative from 1 April 2017.

CITATION AND COMMENCEMENT

1 These Regulations may be cited as the Penalties Relating to Offshore Matters and Offshore Transfers (Additional Information) Regulations 2017 and come into force on 1st April 2017.

INTERPRETATION

2 In these Regulations–

"asset" has the meaning given in section 21(1) of the Taxation of Capital Gains Act 1992, but also includes sterling;

"document" includes part of a document.

ADDITIONAL INFORMATION FOR THE PURPOSES OF PARAGRAPH 9(1B)(D) OF SCHEDULE 24 TO THE FINANCE ACT 2007, PARAGRAPH 12(2B)(D) OF SCHEDULE 41 TO THE FINANCE ACT 2008AND PARAGRAPH 14(2B)(D) OF SCHEDULE 55 TO THE FINANCE ACT 2009

3 The additional information required for the purposes of paragraph 9(1B)(d) of Schedule 24 to the Finance Act 2007, paragraph 12(2B)(d) of Schedule 41 to the Finance Act 2008 and paragraph 14(2B)(d) of Schedule 55 to the Finance Act 2009, is that a person ("P") must–

(a) tell HMRC whether or not regulations 4 or 5 (or both) apply to P; and

(b) provide HMRC with the information specified in relation to those regulations set out in regulations 6 and 7 (as appropriate).

4 This regulation applies to P if there is a person ("the enabler") who encouraged, assisted or otherwise facilitated the conduct by P giving rise to the penalty in question.

5 This regulation applies to P if–

(a) P is the sole or a joint beneficial owner of an asset ("the asset") situated or held in a territory outside the United Kingdom; and

(b) the person holding the asset ("the asset holder") is not P.

ADDITIONAL INFORMATION TO BE PROVIDED TO HMRC WHERE REGULATION 4 APPLIES TO P

6 The additional information to be provided to HMRC where regulation 4 applies to P is–

(a) the name and address of the enabler;

(b) a description of the enabler's conduct that encouraged, assisted or otherwise facilitated the conduct by P giving rise to the penalty in question;

(c) a description of how the first contact between P and the enabler was made and how the contact was maintained during the times when the enabler's conduct encouraged, assisted or otherwise facilitated the conduct by P giving rise to the penalty in question; and

(d) a description of all documents held by P relating to the enabler's conduct that encouraged, assisted or otherwise facilitated the conduct by P giving rise to the penalty in question.

ADDITIONAL INFORMATION TO BE PROVIDED TO HMRC WHERE REGULATION 5 APPLIES TO P

7 The additional information to be provided to HMRC where regulation 5 applies to P is–

(a) the name and address of any other joint beneficial owner of the asset;

(b) the extent of P's share of the beneficial ownership of the asset;

(c) a description of all documents of title or other documents indicating P's beneficial ownership of the asset;

(d) details of where the asset is situated or held;

(e) details of when and how P became a beneficial owner of the asset (including a description of all documents held by P relating to the acquisition of P's beneficial ownership of the asset);

(f) a description of all changes in the arrangements for the ownership of the asset since P became a beneficial owner of it (including the date of any change in the arrangements and a description of all documents held by P relating to such changes);

(g) the names and last known addresses of all persons who have been asset holders of the asset during P's beneficial ownership of it; and

(h) in relation to an asset holder who is not an individual, the name and business address (if known) of any director, senior manager, employee or agent of the asset holder who has advised or assisted P in relation to P's beneficial ownership of the asset.

8(1) A description of a document provided in accordance with regulations 6 or 7 must (as far as it is reasonably practicable to do so) state in relation to the document–

(a) the latest of the date when the document was made, prepared or, if appropriate, signed or executed;

(b) the person who made or prepared it (and the person on whose behalf it was made or prepared if different);

(c) the person who signed or executed the document (if appropriate);

(d) the person to whom the document was given or sent (if appropriate);

(e) a summary of its contents or the information recorded in the document;

(f) the location of the document or where it may be inspected.

8(2) The requirement to provide a description of a document in accordance with regulations 6 or 7 may be met by the provision of the document in question to HMRC or a suitable copy of it.

8(3) The provision of a document (or a copy of it) to HMRC as described in paragraph (2) is without prejudice to any requirement to produce the document in question to HMRC or power of HMRC to require the production of the document.

PENALTIES FOR ENABLERS OF DEFEATED TAX AVOIDANCE (LEGALLY PRIVILEGED COMMUNICATIONS DECLARATIONS) REGULATIONS 2017

(SI 2017/1245)

Made on 11 December 2017 by the Treasury in exercise of the powers conferred upon them by para. 44(4) of Sch. 16 to the Finance Act (No. 2) 2017. Operative from 2 January 2018.

CITATION AND COMMENCEMENT

1 These Regulations may be cited as the Penalties for Enablers of Defeated Tax Avoidance (Legally Privileged Communications Declarations) Regulations 2017 and come into force on 2nd January 2018.

INTERPRETATION

2 In these Regulations a reference to a numbered paragraph is a reference to the paragraph in Schedule 16 to the Finance (No. 2) Act 2017 which is so numbered.

THE DECLARATION

3 A declaration under paragraph 44 must satisfy Conditions A, B and C.

CONDITION A

4 Condition A is that the declaration must contain sufficient information as might reasonably be expected to enable HMRC to identify–

(a) the person who would rely on the declaration for the purpose of establishing that that person is not liable to a penalty under paragraph 1;

(b) the relevant lawyer making the declaration;

(c) the relevant lawyers whose legally privileged communications would otherwise be relied upon to establish that the person referred to in paragraph (a) is not a person who enabled the arrangements for the purposes of paragraph 1; and

(d) the arrangements (and, where appropriate, the proposal which was implemented by the arrangements) to which the declaration relates.

CONDITION B

5 Condition B is that the declaration must contain the confirmations set out in regulations 6 to 10 which must be made by the relevant lawyer making the declaration.

DESIGNER OF ARRANGEMENTS (PARAGRAPH 8)

6 In relation to whether the person referred to in regulation 4(a) is a designer of arrangements falling within paragraph 8, the confirmation is that the person–

(a) was not, in the course of a business carried on by that person, responsible to any extent for the design of the arrangements or a proposal which was implemented by the arrangements; or

(b) was responsible to an extent for such design because of having provided advice but–

(i) the advice provided is not relevant advice within the meaning of paragraph 8(3); or

(ii) the knowledge condition in paragraph 8(4) is not met.

MANAGERS OF ARRANGEMENTS (PARAGRAPH 9)

7(1) In relation to whether the person referred to in regulation 4(a) is a manager of the arrangements falling within paragraph 9(1), the confirmation is that–

(a) the person was not, in the course of a business carried on by that person, to any extent responsible for the organisation or management of the arrangements; or

(b) if the person was so responsible for the organisation or management of the arrangements, the condition set out in paragraph 9(1)(b) is not met.

7(2) Where the person referred to in regulation 4(a) is not a manager of the arrangements because of paragraph 9(2), the confirmation is that the person referred to in regulation 4(a) meets the condition set out in paragraph 9(2)(b).

MARKETERS OF ARRANGEMENTS (PARAGRAPH 10)

8 In relation to whether the person referred to in regulation 4(a) marketed arrangements to T so as to fall within paragraph 10, the confirmation is that the person did not in the course of a business carried on by that person–

(a) make available for implementation by T a proposal which has since been implemented, in relation to T, by the arrangements; or

(b) communicate information to T or another person about a proposal which has since been implemented, in relation to T, by the arrangements with a view to T entering into the arrangements or transactions forming part of the arrangements.

ENABLING PARTICIPANTS (PARAGRAPH 11)

9 In relation to whether the person referred to in regulation 4(a) is an enabling participant falling within paragraph 11, the confirmation is that–

(a) the person is not a person (other than T) who entered into the arrangements or a transaction forming part of the arrangements; or

(b) if the person did enter into the arrangements or a transaction forming part of the arrangements, the condition set out in paragraph 11(c) is not met.

FINANCIAL ENABLERS (PARAGRAPH 12)

10 In relation to whether the person referred to in regulation 4(a) is a financial enabler falling within paragraph 12, the confirmation is that–

(a) the person did not in the course of a business carried on by that person, provide a financial product (directly or indirectly) to a relevant party within the meaning of paragraph 12; or

(b) to the extent that the person did provide a financial product, the condition set out in paragraph 12(1)(c) is not met.

CONDITION C

11 Condition C is that the declaration must contain–

(a) a certificate that the information provided by the relevant lawyer making the declaration is correct to the best of their knowledge and belief; and

(b) a statement that the relevant lawyer making the declaration understands that any of the persons referred to in regulation 4 may have to pay financial penalties as set out in paragraphs 1 and 45 and that any relevant lawyer named in the declaration may face prosecution for providing false information should that declaration prove to be incorrect.

MULTIPLE IMPLEMENTATIONS OF A PROPOSAL

12 Where a proposal for arrangements was implemented more than once by arrangements which are substantially similar, the declaration may contain a statement that this is the case and that the involvement of the person referred to in regulation 4(a) in relation to those arrangements was such that all the things stated in the declaration are equally true in relation to those arrangements.

HMRC DIRECTIONS

Table of Contents

DIRECTIONS BY THE COMMISSIONERS FOR HM REVENUE AND CUSTOMS

HMRC DIRECTIONS

DIRECTIONS UNDER REGULATIONS 3(5) AND 9(3) OF THE INHERITANCE TAX (ELECTRONIC COMMUNICATIONS) REGULATIONS 2015 (S.I. 2015/1378) [HMRC, 23 October 2015]

These Directions apply in relation to the delivery of information by and to the Commissioners for Her Majesty's Revenue and Customs in relation to the matters referred to by regulation 2(1) of the Inheritance Tax (Electronic Communications) Regulations 2015.

Authenticating the identity of the sender

The Commissioners for Her Majesty's Revenue and Customs hereby direct that the method approved by them for authenticating the identity of the person sending information to HMRC is the use of a User ID and password issued by the Government Gateway service for Income Tax Self-Assessment.

Authenticating information delivered by means of electronic communications

The Commissioners for Her Majesty's Revenue and Customs hereby direct that the method approved by them for authenticating any information delivered by means of electronic communications is as follows:

Information delivered by an agent

An agent delivering information on behalf of another person confirms that the following procedure has been completed before the information is submitted:

(i) the agent makes a copy (electronic or paper) of the information, and

(ii) the agent obtains, from the person on whose behalf the information is sent, approval that the information is correct and complete to the best of the knowledge and belief of that person.

The approval mentioned in paragraph (ii) must be in writing, but may be given in electronic or non-electronic form.

Commencement and revocation of previous directions

(a) These Directions have effect from 2 November 2015.

(b) The Commissioners of Her Majesty's Revenue and Customs hereby direct that from 2 November 2015 the following provisions of the Directions under regulations 3(2), (4) to (7) and 9(3) of the Inheritance Tax (Electronic Communications) Regulations 2015 (5.1. 2015/1378) made on 31 July 2015 shall cease to have effect:

  (i) Direction 4;

  (ii) Direction 6, in so far as it applies to an agent delivering information on behalf of another person.

DIRECTIONS UNDER REGULATION 3(2) AND (5) OF THE INHERITANCE TAX (ELECTRONIC COMMUNICATIONS) REGULATIONS 2015 (S.I. 2015/1378) (AUTHENTICATING SENDER'S IDENTITY AND WITHDRAWING CONSENT TO USE IHT ONLINE) [HMRC, 29 April 2016]

The Commissioners for Her Majesty's Revenue and Customs (the Commissioners) make the following Directions under regulation 3(2) and (5) of the Inheritance Tax (Electronic Communications) Regulations 2015 in relation to the delivery of information referred to in regulation 2(1)(a) of those Regulations.

These Directions have effect from 9 May 2016

1. Authenticating the identity of the sender

The method approved for authenticating the identity of the person sending information to HMRC is that the person:

(i) enters a User ID and password issued by the Government Gateway service;

(ii) enters an access code sent to the person's mobile phone; and

(iii) on first registration only, answers a series of identity verification questions.

2. Withdrawing consent

(a) A person may withdraw consent to the Commissioners using electronic communications to deliver information, by writing to HMRC Inheritance Tax, Trusts and Pensions, Ferrers House, Castle Meadow Road, Nottingham NG2 1BB giving notice of the withdrawal of consent.

(b) Withdrawal of consent will take effect 5 days after the day on which HMRC receives the notice.

3. Revocation of previous directions

The following Directions shall cease to have effect from 9 May 2016:

(a) Direction 2 of the Directions under regulations 3(2), (4) to (7) and 9(3) of the Inheritance Tax (Electronic Communications) Regulations 2015 made on 31 July 2015;

(b) Direction 1 of the Directions under regulations 3(5) and 9(3) of the Inheritance Tax (Electronic Communications) Regulations 2015 made on 26 October 2015.

EUROPEAN MATERIAL

Table of Contents

RECOMMENDATION

RECOMMENDATION 2011/856
Regarding relief for double taxation of inheritances

(15 December 2011, OJ 2011 L336/81)

The European Commission,

Having regard to the Treaty on the Functioning of the European Union, and in particular Article 292 thereof,

Whereas:

(1) Most Member States apply taxes upon the death of a person, notably inheritance and estate taxes while some Member States may tax inheritances and estates under other tax headings, such as income. All taxes applied upon the death of a person are hereafter called inheritance taxes.

(2) Most Member States that apply inheritance taxes also apply taxes to gifts between living persons.

(3) Member States may tax inheritances on the basis of varying "connecting" factors. They may do so on the basis of a personal link such as the residence, domicile or nationality of the deceased, or the residence, domicile or nationality of the heir, or both. Some Member States may apply more than one of these factors or may apply anti-abuse measures that entail an extended concept of domicile or residence for tax purposes.

(4) In addition to taxing on the basis of a personal link, Member States may apply inheritance tax to assets located in their jurisdictions. Tax may be applied on this basis even if neither the deceased nor the heir has a personal link with the country of location.

(5) Increasing numbers of citizens of the Union are moving during their lifetimes from one country to another within the Union to live, study, work and retire, and are purchasing property and investing in assets in countries other than their home countries.

(6) If these cases result in inheritances across borders upon the death of an individual, more than one Member State may have the right to apply inheritance taxes to those bequests.

(7) Member States have few bilateral conventions to relieve double or multiple taxation of inheritances.

(8) Most Member States provide, through legislation or administrative practices adopted unilaterally at national level, for double taxation relief for foreign inheritance taxes.

(9) However, those national systems of relief for foreign inheritance tax generally have limitations. In particular they may have a limited scope as regards the taxes and persons covered. They may not allow credit for previously paid gift taxes on the same inheritance or for taxes applied at local or regional rather than national level, or for all taxes levied by other countries upon death. They may only grant relief for foreign taxes paid on certain foreign property. They may not grant relief in respect of foreign tax on a property situated in a country other than that of the heir or deceased. They may exclude foreign tax on assets located within the territory of the Member State granting relief. The national systems of relief may also fail because they do not have regard to mismatches with inheritance tax rules in other Member States, particularly regarding what is to be considered as a local compared to a foreign asset, and regarding the timing of the transfer of assets and the date when tax is due. Finally, tax relief may be subject to the discretion of the competent authority and may not, therefore, be guaranteed.

(10) The absence of appropriate ways of relieving cumulative taxation of inheritances may lead to overall levels of taxation that are appreciably higher than those applicable in situations that are purely internal to one or other of the Member States involved.

(11) This may hinder EU citizens from benefiting fully from their right to move and operate freely across borders within the Union. It may also create difficulties for the transfer of small businesses on the death of owners.

(12) While revenues from inheritance taxes represent a relatively low share of the overall tax revenue of Member States, and cross-border cases alone account for far less, double taxation of inheritances may have a major impact on the individuals affected.

(13) Double taxation of inheritances is not currently being resolved comprehensively at national or bilateral level, or on the basis of Union law. In order to ensure the smooth functioning of the internal market a more comprehensive system for granting relief for double inheritance tax in cross-border cases should be encouraged.

(14) An order of priority of taxing rights or, conversely, of granting relief should be provided in cases where two or more Member States apply inheritance taxes to the same inheritance.

(15) As a general rule, and in line with the practice predominantly followed at international level, Member States in which immovable property and business property of a permanent establishment is situated should, as the State with the closest link, have the primary right to apply inheritance tax to such property.

(16) Since movable property that is not the business property of a permanent establishment can easily shift location, its link to the Member State where it happens to be located at the time of death is, in general,

considerably less close than the personal links that the deceased or the heir may have with another Member State. The Member State where such movable property is situated should, therefore, exempt the property from its inheritance taxation if such taxation is applied by the Member State with which the deceased and/or the heir has a personal link.

(17) Inheritances have often been accumulated over the lifetime of the deceased. Moreover, the assets contained in an inheritance are more likely to be located in the Member State to which the deceased has personal links than in the Member State to which the heir has such links, if different. When taxing inheritances on the basis of personal links to their territory, a majority of Member States refers to the links of the deceased rather than to those of the heir, albeit several also or only tax if the heir has a personal link to their territory. Because of the said nature and importance of the personal links of the deceased as well as for practical reasons, double taxation due to the fact that the deceased and the heir have personal links to different Member States should be relieved by the Member State to which the heir has personal links.

(18) Conflicts of personal links to several Member States could be solved on the basis of a mutual agreement procedure involving tie-breaker rules to determine the closest personal link.

(19) Since the timing for the application of inheritance tax may differ in the Member States involved and cases with cross-border elements may take significantly longer to be resolved compared to domestic inheritance tax cases due to the necessity of dealing with more than one legal and/or tax system, Member States should allow claims for tax relief for a reasonable period of time.

(20) This Recommendation promotes the fundamental rights recognised in particular by the Charter of Fundamental Rights of the European Union, such as the right to property (Article 17), which specifically guarantees the right to bequeath lawfully acquired possession, freedom to conduct business (Article 16) and EU citizens' freedom to move freely within the EU (Article 45),

has adopted this Recommendation:

ART. 1 Subject matter

1(1) This Recommendation sets out how Member States can apply measures, or improve existing measures, to relieve double or multiple taxation caused by the application of inheritance taxes by two or more Member States (hereinafter "double taxation").

1(2) This Recommendation relates by analogy to gift taxes, where gifts are taxed under the same or similar rules as inheritances.

ART. 2 Definitions

2 For the purpose of this Recommendation the following definitions apply:

(a) **"inheritance tax"** means any tax levied at national, federal, regional, or local level upon death, irrespective of the name of the tax, of the manner in which the tax is levied and of the person to whom the tax is applied, including in particular estate tax, inheritance tax, transfer tax, transfer duty, stamp duty, income and capital gains tax;

(b) **"tax relief"** means a provision contained in legislation and/or general administrative instructions or guidance whereby a Member State grants relief for inheritance tax paid in another Member State, by crediting the foreign tax against tax due in that Member State, by exempting the inheritance or parts of it from taxation in that Member State in recognition of the foreign tax paid or by otherwise refraining from the imposition of inheritance tax;

(c) **"assets"** means any movable and/or immovable property and/or rights that are subject to inheritance tax;

(d) **"personal link"** refers to the link of a deceased or heir with a Member State, which may be based on domicile, residence, permanent home, centre of vital interests, habitual abode, nationality or centre of effective management;

For the purposes of point (a) previously paid gift tax on the same asset is considered as inheritance tax for the purposes of granting tax credit.

The terms **"permanent establishment"**, **"immovable property"**, **"movable property"**, **"resident"**, **"domicile/domiciled"**, **"national/nationality"**, **"habitual abode"**, and **"permanent home"** have the meaning applicable under the domestic law of the Member State applying the term.

ART. 3 General objective

3 *The recommended measures* aim at resolving cases of double taxation, so that the overall level of tax on a given inheritance is no higher than the level that would apply if only the Member State with the highest tax level among the Member States involved had tax jurisdiction over the inheritance in all its parts.

ART. 4 Provision of tax relief

4 When applying inheritance taxes, Member States should grant tax relief in accordance with points 4.1 to 4.4.

4(1) Tax relief in respect of immovable property and movable property of a permanent establishment

When applying inheritance taxes, a Member State should allow tax relief for inheritance tax applied by another Member State on the following assets:

(a) immovable property situated in that other Member State;

(b) movable property which is the business property of a permanent establishment situated in that other Member State.

4(2) Tax relief in respect of other kinds of movable property

In respect of movable property other than business property as referred to in paragraph 4.1(b), a Member State with which neither the deceased nor the heir has a personal link should refrain from applying inheritance tax provided that such tax is applied by another Member State by reason of the personal link of the deceased and/or the heir to that other Member State.

4(3) Tax relief in cases where the deceased had a personal link to a Member State other than that to which the heir has a personal link

Subject to paragraph 4.1, in cases where more than one Member State can apply taxation to an inheritance on the basis that a deceased had personal links with one Member State and the heir has personal links with another Member State, then the second Member State should give tax relief for the tax paid on the inheritance in the Member State with which the deceased had personal links.

4(4) Tax relief in cases of multiple personal links of a single person

Where, on the basis of provisions of different Member States, a person is deemed to have a personal link with more than one taxing Member State, then the competent authorities of the Member States concerned should determine through mutual agreement, in accordance with the procedure set out in point 6 or otherwise, the Member State that should grant tax relief if inheritance tax is applied in a State with which the person has a closer personal link.

4.4.1 A closer personal link of an individual could be determined as follows:

(a) he could be deemed to have a closer personal link with the Member State in which he has a permanent home available to him;

(b) if the Member State referred to in (a) does not tax or if the individual has a permanent home available to him in more than one Member State, he could be deemed to have a closer personal link with the Member State with which his personal and economic relations are closer (centre of vital interests);

(c) if the Member State referred to in (b) does not tax or if the Member State in which the individual has his centre of vital interests cannot be determined, or if he has not a permanent home available to him in any Member State, he could be deemed to have a closer personal link with the Member State in which he has an habitual abode.

(d) if the Member State referred to in (c) does not tax or if the individual has an habitual abode in more than one Member State or in no Member State, he could be deemed to have a closer personal link with the Member State of which he is a national.

4.4.2 In the case of a person other than an individual, such as a charity, its closer personal link could be deemed to be with the Member State in which its place of effective management is situated.

ART. 5 Timing of application of the tax relief

5 Member States should allow tax relief for a reasonable period of time, e.g. 10 years from the time limit by which inheritance taxes that they apply have to be paid.

ART. 6 Mutual agreement procedure

6 Where necessary in order for the general objective set out in point 3 to be attained, Member States should operate a mutual agreement procedure to deal with any disputes connected with double taxation, including conflicting definitions of movable and immovable property or of the location of assets or the determination of the Member State which should provide tax relief in a given case.

ART. 7 Follow-up

7(1) Member States should continue working on possible ways to improve the cooperation of tax authorities, including at local and regional level, in order to assist taxpayers who are subject to double taxation.

7(2) Member States should also adopt a coordinated position in discussions at the Organisation for Economic Cooperation and Development (OECD) on inheritance taxes.

7(3) The Commission will follow up on the Recommendation with Member States and publish a report on the state of play of cross-border relief for inheritance taxes within the Union three years after the adoption of the Recommendation.

ART. 8 Addresses

8 This Recommendation is addressed to the Member States.

INHERITANCE TAX EXTRA-STATUTORY MATERIAL

Table of Contents

Page

This list of HMRC extra-statutory concessions in respect of inheritance tax and capital transfer tax is based on the current HMRC information at www.hmrc.gov.uk/specialist/esc.pdf. Those concessions which have to do with both inheritance tax and capital transfer tax are classified "F", and those few which apply only to capital transfer tax are grouped under "J".

The statements of practice follow HMRC's own classification, which separates those statements issued before 18 July 1978 (E1–E18) from those issued subsequently (the "SP" series). The collection in this work is based on the current HMRC Statements of Practice (information at www.hmrc.gov.uk/practitioners/sop.pdf).

Following the statements of practice is a selection of other important extra-statutory material, such as HMRC Briefs and Tax Bulletin articles.

Note: for material relating to taxes other than inheritance tax/capital transfer tax, see the relevant divisions.

Entries in italics are those which have been classified by HM Revenue and Customs as obsolete.

EXTRA-STATUTORY CONCESSIONS

F. Concessions relating to inheritance tax (also applicable where tax charged is capital transfer tax)

continued over

STATEMENTS OF PRACTICE

Statements of practice issued before 18 July 1978

E. Inheritance Tax (also applicable where tax charged is capital transfer tax)

Statements of practice issued after 18 July 1978

HMRC BRIEFS

TAX BULLETIN

Interpretations

continued over

IHT Extra-statutory Material

Clearances

OTHER MATERIAL

Miscellaneous

EXTRA-STATUTORY CONCESSIONS

HMRC's Extra-Statutory Concessions as at 6 April 2017 (as published on 21 September 2017) contained the following caveat:

> "The concessions described within are of general application, but it must be borne in mind that in a particular case there may be special circumstances which will require to be taken into account in considering the application of the concession. A concession will not be given in any case where an attempt is made to use it for tax avoidance."

Every Extra-Statutory Concession is to be read as if this caveat is part of each Concession. This principle was confirmed in the case of *R v HMIT, ex parte Fulford-Dobson* [1987] BTC 158 where McNeill J stated that:

> "In my judgment, the [caveat] is effectively part of each concession. It loses none of its force by being given a special and early place in the booklet: indeed, perhaps, it gains force from that."

The House of Lords' decision in *R v IR Commrs, ex parte Wilkinson* made it clear that the scope of HMRC's administrative discretion to make concessions that depart from the strict application of the letter of the law is not as wide as had previously been supposed. In the light of that decision HMRC are reviewing their concessions. The indications are that most concessions will be able to continue in their current form as they are within the scope of HMRC's administrative discretion, although concessions will continue to be withdrawn where they appear to be obsolete. Where an existing concession exceeds the scope of HMRC's discretion and it is deemed appropriate to preserve its effect, this will be achieved by legislation if possible. If it is not possible put the effect of the concession on a legislative basis, the concession will join obsolete concessions and need to be withdrawn. HMRC have confirmed that no extra-statutory concession will be withdrawn retrospectively and that they will generally offer an appropriate period of notice before a concessionary treatment formally comes to an end.

HMRC's Extra-Statutory Concessions as at 6 April 2017 (as published on 21 September 2017) contained the following text:

> "The Civil Partnership Act (CPA) received Royal Assent on 18/11/2004 and became effective from 5 December 2005. The Government's commitment is that, for all tax purposes, same-sex couples who form a civil partnership will be treated the same as married couples.
>
> As part of this commitment to tax parity, from 5 December 2005 all Extra Statutory Concessions (ESCs) or Statements of Practice (SoPs) should be taken as extended to apply equally to civil partners and married couples."

F. CONCESSIONS RELATING TO INHERITANCE TAX (ALSO APPLICABLE WHERE TAX CHARGED IS CAPITAL TRANSFER TAX)

F5 DEATHS OF MEMBERS OF THE POLICE SERVICE OF NORTHERN IRELAND

[Obsolete – Legislated FA 2015, s. 75.]

F6 BLOCKED FOREIGN ASSETS

Where, because of restrictions imposed by the foreign government, executors who intend to transfer to this country sufficient of the deceased's foreign assets for the payment of the inheritance tax attributable to them cannot do so immediately, they are given the option of deferring payment until the transfer can be effected. If the amount in sterling that the executors finally succeed in bringing to this country is less than this tax, the balance is waived.

F8 ACCUMULATION AND MAINTENANCE SETTLEMENTS

[Obsolete (withdrawn with effect from 6 April 2015 (HMRC Technical Note of 31 January 2014 *Withdrawal of extra statutory concessions*, p. 15)).]

F10 PARTNERSHIP ASSURANCE POLICIES

A partnership assurance scheme under which each partner effects a policy on his own life in trust for the other partners is not regarded as a settlement for inheritance tax purposes if the following conditions are fulfilled:

(a) the premiums paid on the policy fall within Section 10, IHTA 1984 (exemption for dispositions not intended to confer a gratuitous benefit to any person);

(b) the policy was effected prior to 15 September 1976 and has not been varied on or after that date (but the exercise of a power of appointment under a "discretionary" trust policy would not be regarded as a variation for this purpose); and

(c) the trusts of the policy are governed by English law or by Scots law, provided that in the latter case the policy does not directly or indirectly involve a partnership itself as a separate persona.

F11 PROPERTY CHARGEABLE ON THE CEASING OF AN ANNUITY

[Obsolete (withdrawn with effect from 6 April 2015 (HMRC Technical Note of 31 January 2014 *Withdrawal of extra statutory concessions*, p. 16)).]

F12 DISPOSITION FOR MAINTENANCE OF DEPENDENT RELATIVE

[Obsolete (withdrawn with effect from 6 April 2015 (HMRC Technical Note of 31 January 2014 *Withdrawal of extra statutory concessions*, p. 17)).]

F13 SUBSEQUENT DEVOLUTIONS OF PROPERTY UNDER THE WILLS OF PERSONS DYING BEFORE 12 MARCH 1952 WHOSE ESTATES WERE WHOLLY EXEMPTED FROM ESTATE DUTY UNDER SECTION 8(1) FA 1894

Where a person died before 12 March 1952 and his estate was wholly exempted from estate duty as the property of a common seaman, marine or soldier who died in the service of the Crown and under his will he left a limited interest to someone who dies on or after 12 March 1975, inheritance tax is not charged on any property exempted on the original death which passes under the terms of the will on the termination of the limited interest.

F15 WOODLANDS

[Obsolete, enacted in FA 1986, Sch. 19, para. 46 by SI 2017/495, art. 2, with effect in relation to transfers of value made on or after 6 April 2017.]

F16 AGRICULTURAL PROPERTY AND FARM COTTAGES

On a transfer of agricultural property which includes a cottage occupied by a retired farm employee or their widow(er), the condition in Sections 117 and 169 IHTA 1984 concerning occupation for agricultural purposes is regarded as satisfied with respect to the cottage if either

- the occupier is a statutorily protected tenant, or
- the occupation is under a lease granted to the farm employee for his/her life and that of any surviving spouse as part of the employee's contract of employment by the landlord for agricultural purposes.

F17 RELIEF FOR AGRICULTURAL PROPERTY

On a transfer of tenanted agricultural land, the condition in Section 116(2)(a) IHTA 1984 is regarded as satisfied where the transferor's interest in the property either

- carries a right to vacant possession within 24 months of the date of the transfer, or
- is, notwithstanding the terms of the tenancy, valued at an amount broadly equivalent to the vacant possession value of the property.

F18 TREATMENT OF INCOME TAX IN CANADA ON CAPITAL GAINS DEEMED TO ARISE ON A PERSON'S DEATH

[Obsolete (withdrawn with effect from 6 April 2015 (HMRC Technical Note of 31 January 2014 *Withdrawal of extra statutory concessions*, p. 18)).]

F20 LATE COMPENSATION FOR WORLD WAR II CLAIMS

[Obsolete, enacted in IHTA 1984, s. 153ZA and Sch. 5A by FA 2016, s. 95, with effect in relation to deaths occurring on or after 1 January 2015.]

STATEMENTS OF PRACTICE

HMRC's Extra-Statutory Concessions as published on 30 January 2012 contained the following text:

"The Civil Partnership Act (CPA) received Royal Assent on 18/11/2004 and became effective from 5 December 2005. The Government's commitment is that, for all tax purposes, same-sex couples who form a civil partnership will be treated the same as married couples.

As part of this commitment to tax parity, from 5 December 2005 all Extra Statutory Concessions (ESCs) or Statements of Practice (SoPs) should be taken as extended to apply equally to civil partners and married couples."

STATEMENTS OF PRACTICE ISSUED BEFORE 18 JULY 1978

E. INHERITANCE TAX (ALSO APPLICABLE WHERE TAX CHARGED IS CAPITAL TRANSFER TAX) AND ESTATE DUTY

SP E1 POWERS OF APPOINTMENT

1. It is not necessary for the interests of individual beneficiaries to be defined. They can for instance be subject to powers of appointment. In any particular case the exemption will depend on the precise terms of the trust and power concerned, and on the facts to which they apply. In general, however, the official view is that the conditions do not restrict the application of Section 71 IHTA 1984 to settlements where the interests of individual beneficiaries are defined and indefeasible.

2. The requirement of Section 71(1)(a) IHTA 1984 is that one or more persons will, on or before attaining a specified age not exceeding twenty five, become beneficially entitled to, or to an interest in possession in, the settled property or part of it. It is considered that settled property would meet this condition if at the relevant time it must vest for an interest in possession in some member of an existing class of potential beneficiaries on or before that member attains 25. The existence of a special power of appointment would not of itself exclude Section 71 if neither the exercise nor the release of the power could break the condition. To achieve this effect might, however, require careful drafting.

3. The inclusion of issue as possible objects of a special power of appointment would exclude a settlement from the benefit of Section 71 if the power would allow the trustees to prevent any interest in possession in the settled property from commencing before the beneficiary concerned attained the age specified. It would depend on the precise words of the settlement and the facts to which they had to be applied whether a particular settlement satisfied the conditions of Section 71(1). In many cases the rules against perpetuity and accumulations would operate to prevent an effective appointment outside those conditions. However the application of Section 71 is not a matter for a once-for-all decision. It is a question that needs to be kept in mind at all times when there is settled property in which no interest in possession subsists.

4. Also, a trust which otherwise satisfies the requirement of Section 71(1)(a) would not be disqualified by the existence of a power to vary or determine the respective shares of members of the class (even to the extent of excluding some members altogether) provided the power is exercisable only in favour of a person under 25 who is a member of the class.

Annex to SP E1

Practical illustrations of Section 71 IHTA 1984. The examples set out below are based on a settlement for the children of X contingently on attaining 25, the trustees being required to accumulate the income so far as it is not applied for the maintenance of X's children.

Example A

The settlement was made on X's marriage and he has as yet no children.

Section 71 IHTA 1984 will not apply until a child is born and that event will give rise to a charge for tax under Section 65 IHTA 1984.

Example B

The trustees have power to apply income for the benefit of X's unmarried sister.

Section 71 IHTA 1984 does not apply because the conditions of subsection (1)(b) are not met.

IHT Extra-statutory Material

Example C

X has power to appoint the capital not only among his children but also among his remoter issue.

Section 71 IHTA 1984 does not apply (unless the power can be exercised only in favour of persons who would thereby acquire interests in possession on or before attaining age 25). A release of the disqualifying power would give rise to a charge for tax under Section 65 IHTA 1984. Its exercise would also give rise to a charge under Section 65 IHTA 1984.

Example D

The trustees have an overriding power of appointment in favour of other persons.

Section 71 IHTA 1984 does not apply (unless the power can be exercised only in favour of persons who would thereby acquire interests in possession on or before attaining age 25). A release of the disqualifying power would give rise to a charge for tax under Section 65 IHTA 1984. Its exercise would give rise to a charge under Section 65 IHTA 1984.

Example E

The settled property has been revocably appointed to one of the children contingently on his attaining 25 and the appointment is now made irrevocable.

If the power to revoke prevents Section 71 IHTA 1984 from applying (as it would for example, if the property thereby became made subject to a power of appointment as at C or D above), tax will be chargeable under Section 65 IHTA 1984 when the appointment is made irrevocable.

Example F

The trust to accumulate income is expressed to be during the life of the settlor.

As the settlor may live beyond the 25th birthday of any of his children the trust does not satisfy the condition in subsection (1)(a) and Section 71 IHTA 1984 does not apply.

Notes – The text of SP E1 is as it appears in HMRC's Statements of Practice as published on 30 January 2012.

SP E3 SUPERANNUATION SCHEMES

1. This Statement clarifies the inheritance tax liability of benefits payable under pension schemes.

2. No liability to inheritance tax arises in respect of benefits payable on a person's death under a normal pension scheme except in the circumstances explained immediately below. Nor does a charge to inheritance tax arise on payments made by the trustees of a superannuation scheme within Section 151 IHTA 1984 in direct exercise of a discretion to pay a lump sum death benefit to any one or more of a member's dependants. It is not considered that pending the exercise of the discretion the benefit should normally be regarded as relevant property comprised in a settlement so as to bring it within the scope of IHTA 1984 Part III. The protection of Section 151 IHTA 1984 would not of course extend further if the trustees themselves then settled the property so paid.

3. Benefits are liable to inheritance tax if:

(a) they form part of the freely disposable property passing under the will or intestacy of a deceased person. This applies only if the executors or administrators have a legally enforceable claim to the benefits: if they were payable to them only at the discretion of the trustees of the pension fund or some similar persons they are not liable to inheritance tax;

or

(b) the deceased had the power, immediately before the death, to nominate or appoint the benefits to any person including his dependants.

4. In these cases the benefits should be included in the personal representatives' account (schedule of the deceased's assets) which has to be completed when applying for a grant of probate or letters of administration. The inheritance tax (if any) which is assessed on the personal representatives' account has to be paid before the grant can be obtained.

5. On some events other than the death of a member information should be given to the appropriate office of IR Capital Taxes. They are:

(i) the payment of contributions to a scheme which has not been approved for income tax purposes;

(ii) the making of an irrevocable nomination or the disposal of a benefit by a member in his or her *lifetime (otherwise than in* favour of a spouse) which reduces the value of his or her estate (e.g. the surrender of part of the pension or lump sum benefit in exchange for a pension for the life of another);

(iii) the decision by a member to postpone the realisation of any of his or her retirement benefits.

6. If inheritance tax proves to be payable the IR Capital Taxes will communicate with the persons liable to pay the tax.

7. See also:

- Statement of Practice 10/86; and
- *Tax Bulletin* No. 2 of February 1992; the article "INHERITANCE TAX – Retirement Benefits Under Private Pension Contracts: Section 3(3) Inheritance Tax Act 1984" [TB02/92-3].

Notes – The text of SP E3 is as it appears in HMRC's Statements of Practice as published on 30 January 2012.

SP E4 ASSOCIATED OPERATIONS

Life assurance policies and annuities are regarded as not being affected by the associated operations rule if, first, the policy was issued on full medical evidence and, second, it would have been issued on the same terms if the annuity had not been bought.

Notes – The text of SP E4 is as it appears in HMRC's Statements of Practice as published on 30 January 2012.

SP E5 CLOSE COMPANIES

The Commissioners for Her Majesty's Revenue and Customs consider that the general intention of Section 101 IHTA 1984 is to treat the participators as beneficial owners for all the purposes of that Act. Consequently, the conditions of Sections 52(2) and 53(2) IHTA 1984 are regarded as satisfied where it is the company that in fact becomes entitled to the property or disposes of the interest.

Notes – The text of SP E5 is as it appears in HMRC's Statements of Practice as published on 30 January 2012.

SP E6 POWER TO AUGMENT INCOME

This statement sets out the effect for inheritance tax of the exercise by trustees of a power to augment a beneficiary's income out of capital.

In the normal case, where the beneficiary concerned is life tenant of the settled property this will have no immediate consequences for inheritance tax. The life tenant already has an interest in possession and under the provisions of Section 49(1) IHTA 1984 is treated as beneficially entitled to the property. The enlargement of that interest to an absolute interest does not change this position (Section 53(2) IHTA 1984 and it is not affected by the relationship of the beneficiary to the testator.

In the exceptional case, where the beneficiary is not the life tenant, or in which there is no subsisting interest in possession, the exercise of the power would give rise to a charge for tax under Section 52(1) IHTA 1984, although on or after 17 March 1987 this may be a potentially exempt transfer, or a charge under Section 65(1)(a) IHTA 1984. But if the life tenant is the surviving spouse of a testator who died before November 13 1974, exemption might be available under paragraph 2 Schedule 6 IHTA 1984.

The exercise of the power would be regarded as distributing the settled property rather than as reducing its value, so that Sections 52(3) and 65(1)(b) IHTA 1984 would not be in point.

Notes – The text of SP E6 is as it appears in HMRC's Statements of Practice as published on 30 January 2012.

SP E7 PROTECTIVE TRUSTS

In the Commissioners for Her Majesty's Revenue and Customs' view, the reference to trusts "to the like effect as those specified in Section 33(1) of the Trustee Act 1925" – contained in Sections 73 and 88 IHTA 1984 – is a reference to trusts which are not materially different in their tax consequences.

The Commissioners for Her Majesty's Revenue and Customs would not wish to distinguish a trust by reason of a minor variation or additional administrative duties or powers. The extension of the list of potential beneficiaries to, for example, brothers and sisters is not regarded as a minor variation.

Notes – The text of SP E7 is as it appears in HMRC's Statements of Practice as published on 30 January 2012.

SP E9 EXCLUDED PROPERTY

Property is regarded, for the purposes of Section 48(3) IHTA 1984, as becoming comprised in a settlement when it, or other property which it represents, is introduced by the settlor.

Notes – The text of SP E9 is as it appears in HMRC's Statements of Practice as published on 30 January 2012.

SP E11 EMPLOYEE TRUSTS

This statement clarifies the application of Section 13(1) IHTA 1984, where employees of a subsidiary company are included in the trust.

The Commissioners for Her Majesty's Revenue and Customs regard Section 13(1) IHTA 1984 as requiring that where the trust is to benefit employees of a subsidiary of the company making the provision, those eligible to benefit must include all or most of the employees and officers of the subsidiary and the employees and officers of the holding company taken as a single class. So it would be possible to exclude all of the officers and employees of the holding company without losing the exemption if they comprised only a minority of the combined class. But the exemption would not be available for a contribution to a fund for the sole benefit of the employees of a small subsidiary. This is because it would otherwise have been easy to create such a situation artificially in order to benefit a favoured group of a company's officeholders or employees. But even where the participators outnumber the other employees the exemption is not irretrievably lost. The requirement to exclude participators and those connected with them from benefit is modified by Section 13(3) IHTA 1984. This limits the meaning of "a participator" for this purpose to those having a substantial stake in the assets being transferred and makes an exception in favour of income benefits. So even where most of the employees are also major participators or their relatives, an exempt transfer could be made if the trust provided only for income benefits and for the eventual disposal of the capital away from the participators and their families.

This restriction does not affect the exemptions offered by Section 86 IHTA 1984 from tax charges during the continuance of a trust for employees which meets the conditions of that section.

Notes – The text of SP E11 is as it appears in HMRC's Statements of Practice as published on 30 January 2012.

SP E13 CHARITIES

1. Sections 23 and 24 IHTA 1984 exempt from inheritance tax certain gifts to charities and political parties to the extent that the value transferred is attributable to property given to a charity etc. Section 25 IHTA 1984 exempts certain gifts for national purposes and for the public benefit.

2. Where the value transferred (i.e. the loss to transferor's estate as a result of the disposition) exceeds the value of the gift in the hands of a charity, etc., the Commissioners for Her Majesty's Revenue and Customs take the view that the exemption extends to the whole value transferred.

Notes – The text of SP E13 is as it appears in HMRC's Statements of Practice as published on 30 January 2012.

SP E14 POOLS ETC SYNDICATES

No liability to inheritance tax arises on winnings by a football pool, National Lottery or similar syndicate provided that the winnings are paid out in accordance with the terms of an agreement drawn up before the win.

Where for example football winnings are paid out, in accordance with a pre-existing enforceable arrangement, among the members of a syndicate in proportion to the share of the stake money each has provided, each member of the syndicate receives what already belongs to him or her. There is therefore no "gift" or "chargeable transfer" by the person who, on behalf of the members, receives the winnings from the pools promoter.

Members of a pool syndicate may think it wise to record in a written, signed and dated statement, the existence and terms of the agreement between them. But HM Revenue and Customs cannot advise on the wording or legal effect of such a statement, nor do they wish copies of such statements to be sent to them for approval or registration. Where following a pools win the terms of an agreement are varied or part of the winnings are distributed to persons who are not members of the syndicate, an IHT liability may be incurred. The same principles apply to premium bonds syndicates and other similar arrangements.

Notes – The text of SP E14 is as it appears in HMRC's Statements of Practice as published on 30 January 2012.

SP E15 CLOSE COMPANIES: GROUP TRANSFERS

This statement clarifies the position concerning dividend payments and transfers of assets from a subsidiary company to a parent or sister company as appropriate.

Whether or not a disposition is a transfer of value for capital transfer tax or inheritance tax purposes has to be determined by reference to Section 3(1), (2) IHTA 1984, and Section 10 provides that a disposition is not a transfer of value if it was not intended to confer any gratuitous benefit on any person, subject to the other provisions of that subsection.

In the Commissioners for Her Majesty's Revenue and Customs' view, the effect is that a dividend paid by a subsidiary company to its parent is not a transfer of value and so Section 94 IHTA 84 does not start to operate in relation to such dividends. Nor do the Commissioners for Her Majesty's Revenue and Customs feel that they can justifiably treat a transfer of assets between a wholly-owned subsidiary and its parent or between two wholly-owned subsidiaries as a transfer of value.

Notes – The text of SP E15 is as it appears in HMRC's Statements of Practice as published on 30 January 2012.

SP E18 PARTIAL DISCLAIMERS OF RESIDUE

Under Scots law there are certain circumstances in which a residuary legatee can make a partial disclaimer. Where this is possible the Commissioners for Her Majesty's Revenue and Customs accept[s] that the provisions of Section 142 IHTA 1984, which deal with disclaimers, apply.

Notes – The text of SP E18 is as it appears in HMRC's Statements of Practice as published on 30 January 2012.

STATEMENTS OF PRACTICE ISSUED AFTER 18 JULY 1978

SP 10/79 POWER FOR TRUSTEES TO ALLOW A BENEFICIARY TO OCCUPY A DWELLING HOUSE [15 August 1979]

Many wills and settlements contain a clause empowering the trustees to permit a beneficiary to occupy a dwelling house which forms part of trust property as they think fit. The Commissioners for Her Majesty's Revenue and Customs do not regard the existence of such a power as excluding any interest in possession in the property.

When there is no interest in possession in the property in question the Commissioners for Her Majesty's Revenue and Customs do not regard the exercise of the power as creating one if the effect is merely to allow non-exclusive occupation or to create a contractual tenancy for full consideration. The Commissioners for Her Majesty's Revenue and Customs also take the view that no interest in possession arises on the creation of a lease for a term or a periodic tenancy for less than full consideration, though this will normally give rise to a charge for tax under Section 65(1)(b) IHTA 1984. On the other hand, if the power is drawn in terms wide enough to cover the creation of an exclusive or joint residence, albeit revocable, for a definite or indefinite period, and is exercised with the intention of providing a particular beneficiary with a permanent home, the Revenue will normally regard the exercise of the power as creating an interest in possession. And if the trustees in exercise of their powers grant a lease for life for less than full consideration, this will be regarded as creating an interest in possession in view of Sections 43(3) and 50(6) IHTA 1984.

A similar view will be taken where the power is exercised over property in which another beneficiary had an interest in possession up to the time of the exercise.

Notes – The above text is as it appears in HMRC's Statements of Practice as published on 30 January 2012.

SP 12/80 BUSINESS PROPERTY RELIEF: "BUY AND SELL" AGREEMENTS [13 October 1980]

The Commissioners for Her Majesty's Revenue and Customs understand that it is sometimes the practice for partners or shareholder directors of companies to enter into an agreement (known as a "Buy and Sell" Agreement) whereby in the event of the death before retirement of one of them, the deceased's personal representatives are obliged to sell and the survivors are obliged to purchase the deceased's business interest or shares, funds for the purchase being frequently provided by means of appropriate life assurance policies. In the Commissioners for Her Majesty's Revenue and Customs' view such an agreement, requiring as it does a sale and purchase and not merely conferring an option to sell or buy, is a binding contract for sale within Section 113 IHTA 1984. As a result the inheritance tax business property relief will not be due on the business interest or shares. (Section 113 IHTA 1984 provides that where any property would be relevant business property for the purpose of business property relief in relation to a transfer of value but a binding contract for its sale has been entered into at the time of the transfer, it is not relevant business property in relation to that transfer).

Notes – The above text is as it appears in HMRC's Statements of Practice as published on 30 January 2012.

SP 1/82 THE INTERACTION OF INCOME TAX AND INHERITANCE TAX ON ASSETS PUT INTO SETTLEMENTS [6 April 1982]

1. For many years the tax code has contained legislation to prevent a person avoiding higher rate income tax by making a settlement, while still retaining some rights to enjoy the income or capital of the settlement. This legislation, which is embodied in Pt. XV of the Taxes Act 1988 (from 6 April 2005, Chapter 5, Part 5 ITTOIA 2005), provides in general terms that the income of a settlement shall, for income tax purposes, be treated as that of the settlor in all circumstances where the settlor might benefit directly or indirectly from the settlement.

2. If the trustees have power to pay or do in fact pay inheritance tax due on assets which the settlor puts into the settlement HM Revenue and Customs have taken the view that the settlor has thereby an interest in the income or property of the settlement, and that the income of the settlement should be treated as his for income tax purposes under Pt. XV ICTA 1988 (from 6 April 2005, Chapter 5, Part 5 ITTOIA 2005).

3. The inheritance tax legislation (Section 199, IHTA) however, provides that **both** the settlor **and** the trustees are liable for any inheritance tax payable when a settlor puts assets into a settlement. The Commissioners for Her Majesty's Revenue and Customs have therefore decided that they will no longer, in these circumstances, treat the income of the settlement as that of the settlor for income tax purposes solely because the trustees have power to pay or do in fact pay inheritance tax on assets put into settlements.

4. This change of practice applies to settlement income for 1981–1982 et seq.

Notes – The above text is as it appears in HMRC's Statements of Practice as published on 30 January 2012.

SP 11/84 ESTATE DUTY: CALCULATION OF DUTY PAYABLE ON A CHARGEABLE EVENT AFFECTING HERITAGE OBJECTS PREVIOUSLY GRANTED CONDITIONAL EXEMPTION [3 May 1984]

Under the estate duty provisions, an object which in the opinion of the Treasury was of national, scientific, historic or artistic interest could be exempt from duty if undertakings were given to preserve it and keep it in the United Kingdom. If an object which had been exempted from duty was subsequently sold (unless the purchaser was a national institution or similar body), or if the undertaking was broken, duty became chargeable, generally either on the sale proceeds or on the value of the object at the date of the charge. These "clawback" charges may still apply now in relation to objects which have previously been exempted from estate duty.

Estate duty applied not only to property passing on death but also to property given away by the deceased within a certain period before his death. In these latter cases the duty chargeable could be reduced by a taper relief (Section 64 of the Finance Act 1960). The exemption described in the preceding paragraph could also apply to an object which came within the charge to duty because it was the subject of an inter vivos gift. The Commissioners for Her Majesty's Revenue and Customs have been advised that in these circumstances taper relief under Section 64 is not available to reduce the amount liable to the clawback charge, and that the amount chargeable to duty is the full value or sale proceeds.

Notes – The above text is as it appears in HMRC's Statements of Practice as published on 30 January 2012.

SP 8/86 TREATMENT OF INCOME OF DISCRETIONARY TRUSTS [10 November 1986]

This statement sets out the Board's practice concerning the inheritance tax treatment of income of discretionary trusts.

The Commissioners for Her Majesty's Revenue and Customs take the view that:

– undistributed and unaccumulated income should not be treated as a taxable trust asset; and
– for the purposes of determining the rate of charge on accumulated income, the income should be treated as becoming a taxable asset of the trust on the date when the accumulation is made.

This practice applies from 10 November 1986 to all new cases and to existing cases where the tax liability has not been settled.

Notes – The above text is as it appears in HMRC's Statements of Practice as published on 30 January 2012.

SP 10/86 DEATH BENEFITS UNDER SUPERANNUATION ARRANGEMENTS [6 July 1986]

The Commissioners for Her Majesty's Revenue and Customs confirm that their previous practice (see SP E3) of not charging capital transfer tax on death benefits that are payable from tax-approved occupational pension and retirement annuity schemes under discretionary trusts also applies to inheritance tax.

The practice extends to tax under the "gifts-with-reservation" rules as well as to tax under the ordinary inheritance tax rules.

Notes – The above text is as it appears in HMRC's Statements of Practice as published on 30 January 2012.

SP 6/87 ACCEPTANCE OF PROPERTY IN LIEU OF INHERITANCE TAX, CAPITAL TRANSFER TAX AND ESTATE DUTY [8 April 1987]

1. The Commissioners for Her Majesty's Revenue and Customs, with the agreement of the Secretary of State for Culture, Media and Sport (and, where appropriate, other Ministers), accept heritage property in whole or part satisfaction of an inheritance tax, capital transfer tax or estate duty debt and any interest payable on the tax.

2. No capital tax is payable on property that is accepted in lieu of tax. The amount of tax satisfied is determined by agreeing a special price. This price is found by establishing an agreed value for the item and deducting a proportion of the tax given up on the item itself, using an agreement known as the "douceur". The terms on which property is accepted are a matter for negotiation.

3. Sections 60 FA 1987 and 97 F(No 2)A 1987 provide that, where the special price is based on the value of the item at a date earlier than the date on which it is accepted, interest on the tax which is being satisfied may cease to accrue from that earlier date.

4. The persons liable for the tax which is to be satisfied by an acceptance in lieu can choose between having the special price calculated from the value of the item when they offer it or when the Commissioners *for Her Majesty's Revenue and* Customs accept it. Since most offers are made initially on the basis of the current value of the item, HM Revenue and Customs considers them on the basis of the value at the "offer date", unless the offeror notifies them that he wishes to adopt the "acceptance date" basis of valuation. The offeror's option will normally remain open until the item is formally accepted. But this will be subject to review if more than 2 years elapse from the date of the offer without the terms being settled. The

Commissioners for Her Majesty's Revenue and Customs may then give 6 months notice that they will no longer be prepared to accept the item on the "offer date" basis.

5. Where the "offer date" option remains open and is chosen, interest on the tax to be satisfied by the item will cease to accrue from that date.

Notes – The above text is as it appears in HMRC's Statements of Practice as published on 30 January 2012.

SP 7/87 DEDUCTION FOR REASONABLE FUNERAL EXPENSES [15 July 1987]

The Commissioners for Her Majesty's Revenue and Customs take the view that the term "funeral expenses" in Section 172 IHTA 1984 allows a deduction from the value of a deceased's estate for the cost of a tombstone or gravestone.

Notes – The above text is as it appears in HMRC's Statements of Practice as published on 30 January 2012.

SP 2/93 INHERITANCE TAX: THE USE OF SUBSTITUTE FORMS [13 January 1993]

Introduction

1. This Statement explains the Commissioners for Her Majesty's Revenue and Customs' approach towards the acceptance of facsimiles of inheritance tax forms as substitutes for officially produced printed forms.

Legislative context

2. Section 257(1) IHTA 1984 says that all accounts and other documents required for the purposes of the Act shall be in such form and shall contain such particulars as the Board may prescribe. The Commissioners for Her Majesty's Revenue and Customs are satisfied that an accurate facsimile of an official Account or other required document will satisfy the requirements of the Section.

What will be considered an accurate facsimile

3. For any substitute inheritance tax form to be acceptable, it must show clearly to the taxpayer the information which the Commissioners for Her Majesty's Revenue and Customs have determined shall be before him or her when he or she signs the declaration that the form is correct and complete to the best of his or her knowledge. In other words, the facsimile must accurately reproduce the words and layout of the official form. It need not, however, be colour printed.

4. The facsimile must also be readily recognisable as an inheritance tax form when it is received by HM Revenue and Customs Capital Taxes, and the entries must be distinguishable from the background text. Where a facsimile is submitted instead of a previously supplied official form it is important that it bears the same reference as appeared on the official form. It is equally important that if no official form was supplied the taxpayer's reference should be inserted on the facsimile.

5. Advances in printing technology now mean that accurate facsimile forms can be produced. The Commissioners for Her Majesty's Revenue and Customs will accept such forms if approval by the Capital Taxes Offices of their wording and design has been obtained before they are used. Any substitute which is produced with approval will need to bear an agreed unique imprint so that its source can be readily identified at all times.

Applications for approval

6. Applications for approval should be made to:

In England, Wales and Northern Ireland

The Customer Service Manager
HM Revenue and Customs
Capital Taxes Office
Ferrers House
PO Box 38
Castle Meadow Road
NOTTINGHAM
NG2 1BB
or
DX 701201 Nottingham 4

or in Scotland

The Customer Service Manager
HM Revenue and Customs
Mulberry House
16 Picardy Place
EDINBURGH
EH1 3NB
or
DX ED305 Edin 1

All applications will be considered as quickly as possible.

Further information available

7. A set of guidelines giving further details on the production of substitute forms is available on application to the appropriate office at the above address.

Notes – The above text is as it appears in HMRC's Statements of Practice as published on 30 January 2012.
See also SP 5/87 for the use of substitute forms in relation to income tax, corporation tax and capital gains tax.

SP 6/95 LEGAL ENTITLEMENT AND ADMINISTRATIVE PRACTICES [31 March 1995]

Where an assessment has been made, and this shows a repayment due to the taxpayer, repayment is invariably made of the full amount…

For Inheritance Tax (and Capital Transfer Tax), assessments that lead to repayments of sums overpaid are not initiated automatically by the Capital Taxes Office if the amount involved is £25 or less.

The aim of these tolerances is to minimise work which is highly cost-effective; they cannot operate to deny a repayment to a taxpayer who claims it.

Notes – The above text is as it appears in HMRC's Statements of Practice as published on 30 January 2012.
Only the IHT-relevant parts of this SP have been reproduced here.

HMRC BRIEFS

BRIEFS

HMRCBrf 71/07 INHERITANCE TAX AND THE VALUATION OF PROPERTY OWNED JOINTLY BY SPOUSES OR CIVIL PARTNERS [HMRC Brief 71/07, November 2007]

Background

In general terms Section 161 Inheritance Tax Act 1984 provides that, when valuing a share of property for inheritance tax where the spouse or civil partner also has an interest in the same property, the spouse's or civil partner's interest is taken into account. The effect is broadly to reduce the level of discount that smaller, un-aggregated shares of property can attract when valued. The precise basis on which this is done was the subject of litigation during 2004 and resulted in the High Court decision Arkwright and another v Inland Revenue Commissioners [2004] EWHC 1720 (Ch) [[2004] BTC 8,082].

The appeal had earlier been considered by the Special Commissioners who found that the Revenue could not rely on section 161(4) in the case of incorporeal shares of land. Section 161(4) requires the aggregate value to be apportioned in accordance with the proportion the smaller number of shares are held to the total held by both spouses/civil partners. The Special Commissioner found that whilst the measure could apply to property which had a distinct or individual existence as a unit, such as unit trusts or a set of furniture (for example twelve dining chairs), it did not apply to fractions of units. The Revenue did not pursue this point when its appeal was heard by the High Court.

HMRC treatment of existing and future cases

The High Court decided that the question of the open market valuation was, in the absence of agreement between HMRC and the personal representatives, a matter for the Lands Tribunal.

In the course of seeking to reach agreement HMRC has received legal advice that section 161(4) may, in fact, apply to fractional shares of units.

Future cases

Accordingly, HMRC will apply section 161(4) when valuing shares of land as related property in any inheritance tax case where the account is received by HMRC after the publication date of this Brief. We will consider litigation in appropriate cases.

Existing cases

It is now not possible to have further judicial consideration of the section 161(4) point in the context of the Arkwright decision. Any existing cases in which section 161(4) is considered in point will therefore be dealt with on the basis of the Special Commissioners' decision in the Arkwright case as it relates to the interpretation of section 161(4).

HMRC will, when so requested, also reconsider any cases involving land valuations which were concluded after the Arkwright decision was handed down on 16 July 2004 and determined on the basis that section 161(4) applied.

If you believe a valuation was concluded on this basis and wish to have the matter reconsidered, you should write to

HMRC Inheritance
Tax Ferrers House
P O Box 38
Castle Meadow Road
Nottingham
NG2 1BB

Please state the name of the deceased, transferor or settlement and quote the official reference. To assist us, please also refer to this Brief in the heading to your letter.

Discounted Gifts Schemes

We will review the guidance we give about valuation of joint settlor schemes in the Technical Note and make appropriate changes in the light of any future developments. Until then we will continue to value schemes on the basis of the guidance in the note.

HMRCBrf 23/08 INHERITANCE TAX AND VALUATION OF GIFTS INVOLVING A DISCOUNTED GIFT SCHEME [HMRC Brief 23/08, April 2008]

HM Revenue & Customs (HMRC) has given notice of appeal to the High Court against the decision of Special Commissioner in the case of the Executors of the Estate of Mrs Marjorie Edna Bower (deceased) and the Commissioners for HMRC [(2008) Sp C 665].

This brief sets out how, pending the outcome of the appeal, HMRC will deal with cases involving a gift for Inheritance Tax (IHT) purposes involving a Discounted Gift Scheme (DGS) where the settlor is older than 90 next birthday (actual or deemed) or is considered to be uninsurable as at the date of the gift. HMRC published a Technical Note [http://www.hmrc.gov.uk/cto/dgs-tech-note.pdf] in May 2007 confirming its long held practice.

When an IHT chargeable event arises, the value of any gift element of a DGS is considered by the Actuarial Team of HMRC. Open cases already being considered by the Actuarial Team will remain under review pending the outcome of the current litigation.

New cases will continue to be dealt with in accordance with the May 2007 Technical Note. Where the Actuarial Team consider (in calculating the value of the gift element) that the value of retained rights is only nominal (because of age of the donor or because the donor is considered to be uninsurable) we will advise those liable for the IHT accordingly, explain that we will not press for payment of the additional IHT for the time being, and suggest they consider putting an appropriate sum on account to stop (further) interest accruing on any IHT due.

This will enable cases to be progressed as far as possible pending the final outcome of the litigation, while safeguarding the position of taxpayers.

If you have any questions related to this matter please refer them to:

Phil Oxlade
Board's Actuarial Officer
Charity, Assets and Residency
Actuarial Group
Ferrers House
PO Box 38
Castle Meadow Road
Nottingham
NG2 1BB

HMRCBrf 25/08 EXTENSION OF NON-STATUTORY CLEARANCES SERVICE FOR HM REVENUE & CUSTOMS (HMRC) BUSINESS CUSTOMERS [HMRC Brief 25/08, May 2008]

Who should read this business brief?

All businesses, business owners and those acting on behalf of business.

Background

At Budget 2006, the Chancellor of the Exchequer announced a review, led by Sir David Varney, of the relationship between large business and HMRC.

The review team consulted with over 140 large businesses and trade and representative bodies and identified four key outcomes that would benefit both large business and HMRC:

- greater certainty
- an efficient risk based approach to dealing with tax matters
- speedy resolution of issues
- clarity through effective consultation and dialogue

The "Review of Links with Large Business" report published in November 2006 outlined 14 key proposals that would together deliver these outcomes.

One of the proposals related to non-statutory clearances. A non-statutory clearance is written confirmation of our view of the application of tax law to a specific transaction or event.

At Pre-Budget Report 2007, we announced an extension of the non-statutory clearances we provide to all our business customers from April 2008. Further details on the extended non-statutory clearances service *that was implemented on 1 April 2008* can be found in Revenue and Customs Brief 20/08.

Today we start a trial of a further extension of the non-statutory clearances we provide to business owners in the area of inheritance tax business property relief.

Changes affecting business and business owners

From 1 May 2008, for a trial period of six months, clearances will be provided to business owners on the availability of inheritance tax business property relief (IHT-BPR) where there is material uncertainty over the interpretation of the law. For inheritance tax legislation older than the last four Finance Acts, there is a further requirement that the uncertainty relates to a commercially significant issue.

We will aim to respond to clearance applications within 28 calendar days, though in complex cases this may take longer.

As part of the extended clearances service from 1 May 2008, we will publish new guidance on IHT-BPR clearances for business owners on the HMRC website (link to be incorporated).

Guidance for businesses seeking clearances on issues other than IHT-BPR can be found on the HMRC website.

Who do I contact?

All business owners and those acting on their behalf should send their applications relating to inheritance tax business property relief to:

IHT-BPR Clearances Team
Ferrers House
PO Box 38
Castle Meadow Road
Nottingham
NG2 1BB
Email: IHT-BPR Clearances Team

Other business clearance applications should continue to be sent to a Client Relationship Manager or the HMRC Clearances Team as set out in Revenue and Customs Brief 20/08.

Comments on the guidance and the extended service can be sent to:

Emma Bailey
Tax Administration Policy
Central Policy
100 Parliament Street
London
SW1A 2BQ

Other guidance on information and advice

Code of Practice 10 (COP10) and Notice 700/6 VAT rulings will remain in place for our customers who are not covered by the new clearances process to provide guidance on how to seek information and advice from HMRC. We will be reviewing these documents over the next year to provide more consistent guidance on the information and advice available to our customers.

HMRCBrf 17/09 RESIDENCE, DOMICILE AND THE REMITTANCE BASIS: OPERATIONAL CHANGES (EXTRACT) [HMRC Brief 17/09, March 2009]

Notes – HMRC Brief 17/09 is superseded in part by HMRC Brief 34/10, with effect for dispositions made after 24 August 2010.

Domicile and inheritance tax

Where an individual who is not domiciled in the UK settles non-UK assets into a non-UK resident trust then assets in that trust will not be subject to inheritance tax. Following the release of the new HMRC guidance on domicile most settlors should now be able to decide for themselves whether or not they are UK domiciled.

An individual setting up a non-resident trust who, having taken account of the new HMRC guidance, considers they are non-UK domiciled is not obliged to submit an Inheritance Tax account to HMRC. If the settlor is non-UK domiciled then no Inheritance Tax is due. But if an Inheritance Tax account is submitted in these circumstances, HMRC will continue its existing practice and only open an enquiry into that return if the amounts of Inheritance Tax at stake make such an enquiry cost effective to carry out. At present that limit is £10,000.

As is currently the case, where HMRC has expressed an opinion on the domicile status of a settlor for Inheritance Tax purposes we will not normally seek to reconsider that opinion unless new information becomes available that indicates our initial opinion was incorrect or there has been a material change in the circumstances of the settlor. However, when we make a decision it applies only to the date of the transaction concerned. So if circumstances change, the individual returns to the UK for example, that individual's domicile may need to be considered again at another point in time. Domicile is not a static thing, it can change as people's circumstances and intentions change.

Enquiries into domicile status

…

Where HMRC has expressed a view on an individual's domicile status for income tax or capital gains tax purposes, as a result of an enquiry, then that view will also apply for Inheritance Tax purposes at that time. Likewise a HMRC view expressed for Inheritance Tax purposes, following a Part VIII IHTA enquiry, will also apply for income tax and capital gains purposes at that time. However, it is important to remember that each decision on domicile will be made at a certain point in time, if circumstances have changed since the time of the relevant decision, the domicile of the taxpayer may also have changed.

Notes – The full text of HMRC Brief 17/09 is reproduced in vol. 1E.

HMRCBrf 21/09 INHERITANCE TAX AND VALUATION OF GIFTS INVOLVING A DISCOUNTED GIFT SCHEME [HMRC Brief 21/09, April 2009]

The appeal referred to in Revenue & Customs Brief 23/08 was heard on 5 November 2008. In its decision (2008) EWHC 3105 (Ch) reported at [2009] BTC 8,106, the High Court found in favour of HM Revenue & Customs (HMRC) and the appeal is now final. The decision therefore confirms as correct the basis on which HMRC values the retained rights in DGS where the settlor is older than 90 next birthday (actual age or deemed age following underwriting) or where the settlor is considered to be uninsurable per se as at the transfer date. This means that only a nominal value is to be attributed to the retained rights and the value transferred by the gift (ie the amount given by the settlor less the nominal value of the retained rights) will extend to a sum adjacent to the whole amount invested in the scheme. Furthermore there is nothing in the Inheritance Tax legislation which allows any withdrawals actually taken between the gift date and the date of death of the settlor to be offset against the sum invested.

Now that the above case has been settled HMRC will begin to process those cases which have been on hold, as explained in Revenue & Customs Brief 23/08. In some cases, no tax has been paid, whereas in others tax has been paid on account to prevent interest accruing.

HMRC will be contacting executors and/or their agents in the near future in order to bring matters to a conclusion. Where (correct) sums have been placed on account no further Inheritance Tax should be payable and if there are no other outstanding matters clearance letters can be issued. Where no such payment on account has been made an Inheritance Tax calculation will be issued for payment of additional Inheritance Tax and interest. New cases will be dealt with in accordance with the Inheritance Tax Technical Note published in May 2007 in the light of the High Court decision.

If you have any questions related to this matter please refer them to:

Phil Oxlade
Board's Actuarial Officer
Charity, Assets and Residency
Actuarial Group
Ferrers House
PO Box 38
Castle Meadow Road
Nottingham
NG2 1BB
Tel: 0115 974 2950

HMRCBrf 49/09 INHERITANCE TAX ON CONTRIBUTIONS TO EMPLOYEE BENEFIT TRUSTS [HMRC Brief 49/09, 11 August 2009]

[Withdrawn and replaced by HMRC Brief 61/09.]

HMRCBrf 61/09 INHERITANCE TAX ON CONTRIBUTIONS TO EMPLOYEE BENEFIT TRUSTS [HMRC Brief 61/09, 12 October 2009]

[This Brief replaced HMRC Brief 49/09. It has now been replaced by HMRC Brief 18/11.]

HMRCBrf 34/10 DOMICILE AND INHERITANCE TAX [HMRC Brief 34/10, 24 August 2010]

This Revenue & Customs Brief details changes to the circumstances in which HM Revenue & Customs (HMRC) will consider an individual's domicile and decide whether to make a determination of Inheritance Tax based on that. These changes are being made because in HMRC experience the existing guidelines were not working well for the customer and HMRC. In future, by adopting a wider risk-based approach HMRC will ensure that resources are deployed in the most cost effective way.

Revenue & Customs Brief 17/09 issued on 25 March 2009 described changes to procedures following the changes to the remittance basis rules and the residence rules made by the Finance Act 2008. The relevant sections are in Appendix A below and these are superseded by the revised guidance below.

Revised guidance

The revised guidance applies to dispositions made after the issue of this Revenue & Customs Brief.

In future HMRC will consider opening an enquiry where domicile could be an issue, or making a determination of Inheritance Tax in such cases, only where there is a significant risk of loss of UK tax.

The significance of the risk will be assessed by HMRC using a wide range of factors. The factors will depend very much on the individual case but will include, for example:

- a review of the information available to HMRC about the individual on HMRC databases
- whether there is a significant amount of tax (all taxes and duties not just Inheritance Tax) at risk

HMRC does not consider it appropriate to state an amount of tax that would be considered significant, as the amount of tax at stake is only one factor. It should be borne in mind that HMRC will take into account the potential costs involved in pursuing an enquiry, and also those of potential litigation should the enquiry not result in agreement between HMRC and the individual; clearly such costs can be substantial.

Where HMRC does open an Inheritance Tax enquiry in any of these cases, it will keep the factors in view and may stop the enquiry at any stage if it considers the continuation of the enquiry is not cost effective. The outcome of such an enquiry may be that HMRC does not consider it appropriate to make a determination of the Inheritance Tax.

Individuals should also bear in mind that enquiries into domicile involve a detailed inquiry into all of the relevant facts and HMRC is likely to require considerable personal information and extensive documentary evidence about the taxpayer and the taxpayer's close family.

Appendix A: Extract from Revenue & Customs Brief 17/09 superseded by Revenue & Customs Brief 34/2010 issued on 24 August 2010

> "Where an individual who is not domiciled in the UK settles non-UK assets into a non-UK resident trust then assets in that trust will not be subject to Inheritance Tax. Following the release of the new HMRC guidance on domicile most settlors should now be able to decide for themselves whether or not they are UK domiciled."
>
> "An individual setting up a non-resident trust who, having taken account of the new HMRC guidance, considers they are non-UK domiciled is not obliged to submit an Inheritance Tax account to HMRC. If the settlor is non-UK domiciled then no Inheritance Tax is due. But if an Inheritance Tax account is submitted in these circumstances, HMRC will continue its existing practice and only open an enquiry into that return if the amounts of Inheritance Tax at stake make such an enquiry cost effective to carry out. At present that limit is £10,000."

HMRCBrf 14/11 PENALTY FOR FAILURE TO DISCLOSE OFFSHORE INCOME OR GAINS
[HMRC Brief 14/11, 6 April 2011]

Introduction

This brief explains how legislation in Schedule 10 to 2010 Finance Act allows for a higher penalty rate where income or gains that arise outside the UK are underdeclared. People who do not declare income or gains arising offshore could face penalties that are up to 200 per cent of the tax owed.

The new penalties for offshore non-compliance came into force on 6 April and will apply for the 2011–12 tax year onwards to Income Tax and Capital Gains Tax.

Background

The offshore penalties legislation is part of the continuing review of HMRC's powers, deterrents and safeguards [http://www.hmrc.gov.uk/about/powers-appeal.htm] which aims to align and modernise the framework for the taxes HM Revenue & Customs (HMRC) administers.

The offshore penalty

The new offshore penalty is an enhancement of three existing penalties for:

- failure to notify – where you fail to tell us that you have a source of income or a capital gain that may be taxable
- inaccuracy on a return – where your Self Assessment tax return is incorrect
- failure to file a tax return on time – where you send your tax return late

Schedule 10 to Finance Act 2010 introduced a new link between these penalties and the tax transparency of the territory in which the undeclared income or gain arises. Where it is harder for us to get information from another country, the penalties for failing to declare income or gains arising in that country will be higher.

Each territory has been placed into one of three categories. The criteria used [http://www.hmrc.gov.uk/news/offshore-faqs.pdf] and the list of territories [http://www.hmrc.gov.uk/news/territories-category.htm] are on the HMRC website.

There will be three new levels of penalty:

- Category 1 territories: the penalty rate is the same as for existing penalties, up to 100 per cent of the tax due.
- Category 2 territories: the penalty is 1.5 times the existing penalties, up to 150 per cent of tax due.
- Category 3 territories: the penalty is double the existing penalties, up to 200 per cent of tax due.

All existing safeguards will still apply. There will be no penalty if a person can demonstrate they have taken reasonable care to get their tax right or have a reasonable excuse for a failure to notify taxable income or gains.

Where penalties are due, HMRC can reduce them depending on how helpful the individual is in assisting us to establish the correct amount of tax due. The largest reductions will be for unprompted disclosures. Unprompted means when you tell us about a tax issue you have no reason to believe we have discovered or are about to discover it.

The existing penalties

A full explanation of these penalties, and the percentage rates attached to each type of behaviour and disclosure, is available on the HMRC website using the links below.

[More information]

HMRCBrf 15/11 PENALTIES: CHANGE TO HMRC'S VIEW OF THE OPERATION OF THE DELAYED TAX PROVISIONS FOR INACCURACY PENALTIES [HMRC Brief 15/11, 6 April 2011]

Introduction

The purpose of this brief is to explain a change in how HM Revenue & Customs (HMRC) views the operation of the "delayed tax" provision of the new penalties for inaccuracies, introduced in paragraph 8 of Schedule 24 to the Finance Act 2007.

Who needs to read this?

Customers who have been charged a penalty for an inaccuracy on a return that would have been automatically reversed in a subsequent return, but for a compliance check by HMRC.

Background

Under the 2007 Finance Act, new penalties were introduced for inaccuracies on returns or other documents. Under these penalties, if a return contains an inaccuracy that relates to a timing error which is automatically reversed in a subsequent tax period, the penalty is not calculated on the full amount of tax underpaid in the first period, but on a reduced amount to take account of the timing error.

For example, if someone reclaims £100,000 VAT on a purchase in period 1 when it should have been reclaimed in period 2, they claim £100,000 too much in the first period but £100,000 too little in the second. Any penalty for the overclaim in period 1 is not calculated on the £100,000 but on a reduced amount to take account of the automatic reversal of the inaccuracy in period 2.

Current position

HMRC's approach to date has been that in order for the penalty to be calculated in this way, the customer had to have submitted both the return containing the initial inaccuracy, and the one containing the automatic reversal of the inaccuracy in a later period. This means that in some cases HMRC has charged a penalty on the full amount because they acted to correct the inaccuracy on the first return before the second return could be submitted, thereby preventing the inaccuracy from being reversed.

Revised position

HMRC is changing its approach for cases where HMRC intervened to correct the inaccuracy before the second return was received, preventing the inaccuracy from being reversed. When HMRC are satisfied that, but for their intervention, the inaccuracy would have been automatically corrected in a subsequent return, customers will receive the reduced penalty based on the rules for delayed tax. HMRC will shortly update our guidance to reflect this.

What you should do

If you have been charged a penalty for an inaccuracy on a return and you believe that, had HMRC not intervened before a subsequent return could be submitted, the inaccuracy would have been automatically reversed in a subsequent period, you should contact HMRC to request that the penalty is reviewed. You should refer to this Revenue and Customs Brief when making your request.

Remember this only applies to timing inaccuracies, those that are automatically reversed in a subsequent period after they are made without you having to do anything more. It does not apply to the VAT Error Correction procedure nor to compensating but unrelated inaccuracies.

Further details

For information about how to ask us to review a penalty, please follow the link below.

Complaints & appeals [http://www.hmrc.gov.uk/complaints-appeals/]

HMRCBrf 18/11 EMPLOYEE BENEFIT TRUSTS: INHERITANCE TAX AND INCOME TAX ISSUES [HMRC Brief 18/11, 4 April 2011]

Introduction

Employment Benefit Trusts are discretionary trusts which seek to reward employees by making payments that favour employees or their families.

This brief sets out HM Revenue & Customs' (HMRC's) current view on Inheritance Tax issues associated with Employee Benefit Trusts. It supersedes and amplifies Revenue & Customs Brief 61/09.

It also includes material on various matters not previously addressed including ongoing Inheritance Tax liabilities of the trust and any sub-trusts it created and the taxation of income arising in offshore Employee Benefit Trusts.

This brief is aimed at agents advising on the Inheritance Tax and trust taxation liabilities of Employee Benefit Trusts.

Existing cases will be taken forward by HMRC on the basis of the views set out in this brief.

All statutory references are to Inheritance Tax Act 1984 unless otherwise stated.

Part 1 – Entry charges payable by a close company when it makes a contribution to a s86 employee benefit trust

1.1 Employee benefit trust

This part of the brief assumes that the Employee Benefit Trust qualifies as a s86 Employee Benefit Trust in that it is a trust where the funds are held at the trustees' discretion to be applied for the benefit of "all or most of the persons employed or holding office with the body concerned" (s86(3)(a)).

1.2 Charge on participators (s94)

Where a Close Company (s102(1)) makes a transfer of value (s3) to an Employee Benefit Trust an Inheritance Tax charge arises under s94 unless, broadly, the disposition:

- is not a transfer of value under sections 10, 12 or 13
- is eligible for relief

1.3 Transfers of value

Where there is a transfer of value it is apportioned between the individual participators according to their respective rights and interest in the company immediately before the contribution to the Employee Benefit Trust is made. There is an immediate charge of 20 per cent on the value transferred (the contribution) in excess of the participator's unused nil rate band.

The liability for the charge to Inheritance Tax that arises under s94 is the company's or, so far as the tax remains unpaid, the participator's (s202).

Inheritance Tax arising under s94 is due six months after the end of the month in which the contribution is made or at the end of April in the year following a contribution made between 6 April and 30 September inclusive. Interest is charged on any unpaid tax from the due date.

IHT Extra-statutory Material

1.3.1 Dispositions not intended to confer gratuitous benefit (s10)

A disposition is not a transfer of value when the terms of s10 are met. There is both a subjective test and an objective test; and both tests must be met to satisfy section 10.

1.3.1.1 Subjective test – no intention to confer gratuitous intent

The test is not met if there is the slightest possibility of gratuitous intent at the date the contribution is made.

1.3.1.2 Objective test – arm's length transaction

To meet the terms of s10 the transaction must either:

- have been made at arm's length between persons not connected with each other (as defined in s270)
- was such as might be expected to be made in a transaction at arm's length between persons not connected with each other

An Employee Benefit Trust is a discretionary trust and to satisfy the conditions of s86 the trustees' discretion must remain unfettered. Given that the potential beneficiaries under an Employee Benefit Trust normally include the participators themselves; the employees or former employees; and/or the wives, husbands, civil partners, widows, widowers, surviving civil partners and children and step children under the age of 18 of such employees and former employees; it will normally be difficult to show that the conditions of s10 are met.

1.3.2 Dispositions allowable in computing profits for corporation tax (s12)

1.3.2.1 Overview

A disposition by a person is not a transfer of value when the terms of s12 are met: broadly, that the disposition is allowable for the purposes of calculating that person's Corporation Tax.

The relieving effect cannot be given provisionally while waiting to see whether the contribution will become allowable for Corporation Tax purposes; and is only available to the extent that a deduction is allowable to the company for the tax year in which the contribution is made.

A deduction in the Corporation Tax accounts can be permanently disallowed by the following:

- capital expenditure disallowed by s74(1)(f) ICTA 1988/s53 CTA 2009
- expenditure not wholly and exclusively incurred under s74(1)(a) ICTA 1988/s54 CTA 2009

Also the timing of a deduction can be deferred to a later period by the following:

- generally accepted accounting practice (UITF32) which capitalises Employee Benefit Trust contributions by showing them as an asset on the company's balance sheet until and to the extent that the assets transferred to the intermediary vest unconditionally in identified beneficiaries
- expenditure subject to s43 FA 1989 (the Dextra decision) – see below
- post 27 November 2002 expenditure subject to Sch24 FA 2003/s1290(2)(3) CTA 2009 – see below

If expenditure is not allowable for any of these reasons then s12 does not apply.

1.3.2.2 Impact of MacDonald (HMIT) v Dextra (2005) UKHL 47 ("Dextra")

The Dextra decision applies to contributions made before 27 November 2002.

In that case, the trust deed gave the trustee wide discretion to pay money and other benefits to beneficiaries and power to lend them money. The potential beneficiaries of the trust included past, present and future employees and officers of the participating companies in the Dextra group and their close relatives and dependants. The trustee did not make payments of emoluments out of the funds in the Employee Benefit Trust during the periods concerned. Instead the trustee made loans to various individuals who were beneficiaries under the terms of the Employee Benefit Trust.

The point at issue was whether the company's contributions to the Employee Benefit Trust were "potential emoluments" within the meaning of s43(11)(a) FA 1989, being amounts "held by an intermediary with a view to their becoming relevant emoluments".

The House of Lords held that the contributions by the company to the Employee Benefit Trust were potential emoluments as there was a "realistic possibility" that the trustee would use the trust funds to pay emoluments. This meant that the company's deductions were restricted. The company could only have a deduction for the amount of emoluments paid by the trustee within nine months of the end of the period of account for which the deduction would otherwise be due. Relief for the amount disallowed would be given in the period of accounting in which emoluments were paid.

1.3.2.3 Restriction of deductions for employee benefit contributions (Sch24 FA 2003)

Section 143 and Schedule 24 to the Finance Act 2003 applies to contributions made after 27 November 2002 and prevents a deduction for Corporation Tax purposes until the contribution made for employee benefits is spent by a payment that has been subjected to both PAYE and National Insurance contributions. The position already established in Dextra is therefore effectively formalised by legislation for events on or after 27 November 2002.

1.3.3 Dispositions by close companies for benefit of employees (s13)

A disposition is not a transfer of value when the terms of s13 are met.

However, this exclusion does not apply where (amongst other things):

- the contributions by the Close Company are made to an Employee Benefit Trust that does not satisfy s86
- the participators (s102(1)) in the company and any person connected with them are not excluded from benefit under the terms of the Employee Benefit Trust and so s13(2) applies

1.4 Relief from inheritance tax – business property relief (s104)

Usually, sections 10, 12 or 13 will not be met and the contribution by the Close Company will be a transfer of value as a result of a reduction in the value of its estate – the aggregate of the property beneficially owned by the company.

Relief from Inheritance Tax may, however, be available where the value transferred is attributable to relevant business property (s105).

The company's estate is capable of being relevant business property if it is "property consisting of a business" (s105(1)(a)). However, the availability of business property relief is conditional on whether the transfer meets all the other requirements in Part V, Chapter 1. This means, in particular that:

- the business is not an excluded one, for example a company the business of which consists wholly or mainly of making or holding investments (s105(3))
- the value of the relevant business property transferred is not attributable to any excepted assets (s112)

Business property relief will, Therefore, not apply on a transfer of value made by a Close Company that is an investment company.

Part 2 – Flat rate exit charge (s72) when property leaves a s86 employee benefit trust

This part describes charges to Inheritance Tax that can arise in any s86 Employee Benefit Trust; **even where the original disposition into the trust was not made by a Close Company or individual.**

The charge arises where a payment is made from the Employee Benefit Trust into a sub-trust that is not itself a qualifying s86 Employee Benefit Trust (as outlined at 1.1 above). The charge is a flat rate charge and is dependant on the length of time the property was held subject to the terms of the s86 Employee Benefit Trust. Business property relief will not apply to the flat rate exit charge in these circumstances.

In addition, where there is a non-commercial loan to a participator then an exit charge may arise under s72(2)(b).

Part 3 – Ten year and exit charges in respect of any sub-trusts

In general, sub-trusts are not s86 Employee Benefit Trusts and are, therefore, relevant property trusts for Inheritance Tax purposes (s58). (Full details of "relevant property trusts" can be found in the Inheritance Tax Manual at page IHTM 42001+.)

Relevant property trusts pay Inheritance Tax on two key occasions:

- on the ten year anniversary of the commencement of the trust (s64) (and every subsequent ten year anniversary)
- when property leaves the relevant property trust or when it ceases to be relevant property (s65)

For both of these occasions a calculation is required in order to establish the Inheritance Tax liability but this charge will not exceed 6 per cent of the value of the trust assets concerned.

For the purposes of the ten year anniversary charge, the anniversary is calculated from the date on which the property became settled (s81), that is, the date the s86 Employee Benefit Trust commenced. However, property can only be treated as relevant property when it leaves the qualifying Employee Benefit Trust.

Where the trustees of a sub-trust decide to bring the trust to an end an exit charge will arise under s65.

The basis of valuation for a charge arising under either s64 or s65 will be an open market value (s160) and will include the value of loans and any accrued interest.

Part 4 – Payment of ongoing inheritance tax liabilities

Section 201(1) (Settled Property) outlines the persons liable for Inheritance Tax on chargeable transfers arising in respect of trusts, including proportionate charges (s65) and ten year anniversary charges (s64) as well as the flat rate charge (s72) (property leaving employee trusts). Where the transfer is made during the life of the settlor and the trustees are not resident in the UK then the settlor is liable for the ongoing trust Inheritance Tax liabilities (s201(1)(d)).

The settlor of an Employee Benefit Trust will usually be the company, whether or not it is a Close Company.

In addition, where a participator has benefited then s201(1)(c) means that they are liable for the ongoing trust Inheritance Tax liabilities.

Part 5 – Income tax assessable under the transfer of asset (ToA) legislation on income arising in offshore employee benefit trusts

5.1 Overview

It is common for the trust vehicle used as the Employee Benefit Trust to be situated in an offshore jurisdiction and this will potentially give rise to additional liabilities where income arises within the trust. The ToA legislation was amended by FA 2006 and the legislation applicable following this amendment can be found at s714 ITA 2007, onwards. It came into effect from 6 April 2007. The pre-FA 2006 legislation is contained in s739 ICTA 1988, onwards. There are two potential charges that arise under the ToA legislation – the so-called "income charge" (s739 ICTA 1988/s720 ITA 2007) and the "benefits charge" (s740 ICTA 1988/s732 ITA 2007). Each of these are considered in turn.

5.1.1 Income charge

The income charge provisions apply to prevent the avoidance of a liability to Income Tax by individuals who are ordinarily resident in the UK where the following conditions apply:

- there is a transfer of assets by virtue or in consequence of which, either alone or in conjunction with associated operations, income becomes payable to a person abroad
- the transferor has the power to enjoy the income

For the income charge provisions to apply the individual on whom the charge arises must be the person who transfers the assets or procures the transfer. If the offshore Employee Benefit Trust is a normal commercial arrangement by a company to reward its employees, the transferor is the employer company; and in such circumstances the income charge is unlikely to be applicable as the transferor and beneficiaries are different people. However, it may be that the employee has transferred a right to receive a bonus into the offshore Employee Benefit Trust and is therefore the transferor. If this is the case the ToA legislation may apply and the employee will be liable to tax on any income arising in the trust.

If the employer company is controlled by its shareholder/directors and the offshore Employee Benefit Trust was formed solely for their benefit, the director/shareholders may have procured the transfer into the offshore Employee Benefit Trust and could be considered transferors for the purposes of the income charge. Whether or not the ToA income charge is then applied will depend on the facts of each case.

5.1.2 Benefit charge

Where the company, not the employee is the transferor the benefit charge may apply. The benefit charge matches any income arising within the Employee Benefit Trust with any benefits received by the employee. The test is effectively the same as s739 ICTA 1988/s720 ITA 2007 in that where by virtue or in consequence of a transfer income becomes payable to a person abroad, s740(1)(b) ICTA 1988/s732(1)(d) ITA 2007 applies the charge to individuals not liable to tax under the income charge. If a person receives a benefit provided out of assets available for the purpose as a consequence of the transfer, and the trustees are in receipt of income, any benefit provided to a beneficiary is potentially chargeable. The amount of the benefit charged to tax is up to the maximum of either the income or benefit. The benefit charge could, therefore, catch any income arising in the offshore Employee Benefit Trust if it is not caught by the income charge and there are actual distributions by the trustees which are not otherwise chargeable to Income Tax.

Part 6 – Income tax in relation to UK source income of offshore employment benefit trusts

If an offshore Employment Benefit Trust receives UK source income then, subject to s811 ITA 2007, the income will be chargeable to tax in the UK and the trustees should make a return of this income to HMRC. *Section 811 ITA 2007 limits the* scope of the liability to Income Tax of a non-UK resident trust provided that none of the trust's beneficiaries are resident in the UK. As Employee Benefit Trusts are discretionary trusts the trustees will be chargeable to tax at the trust rate under s479 ITA 2007. If the trustees make a discretionary payment out of the trust income to a beneficiary this is treated as untaxed income of the

UK resident beneficiary. It does not matter that the trustees have suffered tax on the trust income. The beneficiary returns the income received and can claim relief under Extra Statutory Concession B18.

The trustees of the offshore Employee Benefit Trust or sub-trusts may have advanced interest bearing loans to beneficiaries. If the beneficiaries are resident in the UK then depending on the particular circumstances of each beneficiary the interest will be UK source income in the hands of the trustees and should be reported as such. It is also likely that in such circumstances tax should be deducted at source by the beneficiary paying the interest under s874 ITA 2007.

Where it is contended that the interest is not UK source income, the circumstances surrounding the payment of interest will be closely examined by HMRC.

If the beneficiary does not pay the interest, but the interest is rolled up by the trustees, no immediate tax charge will arise; however, if the interest is subsequently paid or capitalised it is likely that an Income Tax charge will accrue on payment or capitalisation.

Part 7 – Payment of ongoing trust income tax liabilities

To the extent that income continues to arise within an offshore Employee Benefit Trust and is caught by the transfer of assets legislation the income charge and benefits charge will continue to apply. Likewise if the trustees continue to receive UK source income they will have an ongoing liability to Income Tax and should continue to complete Trust Returns.

Part 8 – Contact details and legal references

8.1 Contact details

If you wish to notify the Trusts and Estates business within HMRC of the existence of an Employee Benefit Trust; or, if you wish to discuss settlement of any Inheritance Tax and non-resident trust liabilities that have arisen in respect of an Employee Benefit Trust, then please contact HMRC Trusts & Estates via this link [ebtiht.settlementmailbox@hmrc.gsi.gov.uk].

Further information can be obtained by contacting the Helpline on Tel 0845 30 20 900.

8.2 Legal references

Corporation tax

For accounting periods ending on or after 1 April 2009:

- references to Schedule 24 Finance Act 2003 should be taken to be references to Sections 1290 to 1297 Corporation Tax Act 2009
- references to s74(1)(a) ICTA 1988 should be taken to be references to s54 Corporation Tax Act 2009
- references to s74(1)(f) ICTA 1988 should be taken to be references to s53 Corporation Tax Act 2009

Income tax

For tax years 2005–06 onwards:

- references to Schedule 24 Finance Act 2003 should be taken to be references to Section 38 to 44 Income Tax (Trading and Other Income) Act 2005
- references to s74(1)(a) ICTA 1988 should be taken to be references to s34 Income Tax (Trading and Other Income) Act 2005
- references to s74(1)(f) ICTA 1988 should be taken to be references to s33 Income Tax (Trading and Other Income) Act 2005
- reference to s739 ICTA 1988 should be taken to be references to s720 ITA 2007
- reference to s740 ICTA 1988 should be taken to be references to s731 ITA 2007.

HMRCBrf 22/13 DISCOUNTED GIFT SCHEMES: TEN YEAR ANNIVERSARY VALUES FOR INHERITANCE TAX AND UPDATED GUIDANCE ON THE CALCULATION OF TRANSFER VALUES WHEN DISCOUNTED GIFT SCHEMES ARE EFFECTED [HMRC Brief 22/13, 6 August 2013]

This brief sets out HM Revenue & Customs' (HMRC's) view on how to calculate the value that will be subject to Inheritance Tax for a Discounted Gift Scheme held in a relevant property trust when the ten year anniversary charge arises for the trust. It also provides updated guidance on how the transfer value is to be calculated when a Discounted Gift Scheme is effected including providing clarification and revisions to the assumptions underlying the valuation.

This brief is aimed at the trustees of a relevant property trust which holds a Discounted Gift Scheme and who are responsible for delivering an Inheritance Tax account for the ten year anniversary. It is also aimed at the providers of Discounted Gift Schemes who may wish to provide relevant values to their customers both when a Discounted Gift Scheme is effected and at subsequent Ten Year Anniversaries.

The intention of this brief is to provide certainty for taxpayers and Discounted Gift Scheme providers in that a valuation prepared in accordance with this brief will be acceptable to HMRC.

All statutory references are to Inheritance Tax Act 1984 unless otherwise stated.

1. The Ten Year Anniversary Charge

Following changes to the taxation of trusts for Inheritance Tax purposes in the Finance Act 2006, most types of trust used for Discounted Gift Schemes created on or after 22 March 2006 are relevant property trusts and subject to Inheritance Tax under Part III, Chapter III Inheritance Tax Act 1984. Under s.64 a charge to Inheritance Tax arises on the value of the relevant property held in the trust every ten years at which time the trustees are required to report the value of the relevant property to HMRC.

1.1 Valuation

Under a Discounted Gift Scheme the settlor will typically have settled a bond or a series of policies from which they have retained the right to either pre-determined regular withdrawals or to a succession of maturing reversions. The bond or policies are relevant property. However, the settlor's retained rights are normally held on bare trust for the settlor and as such, these rights are not relevant property for Inheritance Tax purposes. At the ten year anniversary, the value of the relevant property needs to be established for the purpose of calculating the charge that arises under s.64. The value of the relevant property is its open market value as required by s.160, but it does not include the value of the rights retained by the settlor.

The open market purchaser of the relevant property would be purchasing the right to receive the whole value of the underlying bond following the death of the settlor. The open market purchaser will take account of the fund value at the valuation date and will have to allow for

- the expected withdrawals to be received by the settlor between the valuation date and the settlor's date of death, and
- the expected delay between the valuation date and the eventual death of the settlor.

The closest equivalent asset which is sold in the open market is considered to be an interest in reversion. In the case of the purchase of an interest in reversion, analysis of sales indicates that open market purchasers take a prudent approach and they do not factor in any growth in the capital value of the asset. In addition, analysis indicates that an open market purchaser of a reversion takes no account of the interim income payable to the life tenant.

However, under a Discounted Gift Scheme the rights retained by the settlor are not precisely identical to the rights of a life tenant entitled to income. The retained benefits are not limited to any income produced by, or growth on, the fund. It is possible for the settlor's retained rights to exceed the growth generated by the fund itself so that the fund is depleted over time. Equally the growth on the fund may exceed the sums due to the settlor under the retained rights, so that the fund value increases over time. HMRC takes the view that an open market purchaser would take a prudent approach when taking these possibilities into account in the price he or she is prepared to pay.

1.2 Valuation methodology

The asset to be valued is the total fund, less the value of the rights retained by the settlor, payable on the death of the settlor. The actual valuation will be slightly different depending on whether the retained rights are structured as a series of withdrawals of pre-determined amounts or are based on the value of a series of funds payable on fixed future dates. In either case it is considered that the open market purchaser would not allow for any growth in the fund value, but would discount the current value to account for the delay until the fund will be available, being on the death of the settlor.

Where the retained rights are of pre-determined regular withdrawals, the total fund value is discounted to the expected date of death of the settlor. From this value is to be deducted the present value of the expected future withdrawals to be taken by the settlor based on their life expectancy and discounting those payments to the date that each payment is to be made.

Where the retained rights are based on the value of a series of funds payable on fixed future dates the value of the funds that are expected to mature after the death of the settlor are discounted to the expected date of death of the settlor.

There are a number of approaches that can be taken to these calculations that will produce virtually the same values, provided the same mortality and interest rate assumptions are used.

1.3 Health of the Settlor at the Ten Year Anniversary

The open market purchaser of an interest payable only on the death of an individual, such as a reversion, will assume normal life expectancy for the life of that individual unless there is clear evidence that they are terminally ill, for example in the viatical market for life policies. The risk to the open market purchaser is that if the individual survives longer than expected the purchaser has to wait longer to realise his or her investment. This open market practice leads to the view that the age to be used in the valuation is the age next birthday of the settlor with no adjustment for their state of health.

This approach would, however, understate the value, possibly substantially, in cases where the settlor was terminally ill at the date of the ten year anniversary. The rate of tax payable at the ten year anniversary, which is dependent on the value of the relevant property at that date, determines the tax payable under s.65 on property in the settlement which ceases to be relevant property, for example on the distribution of the funds following the death of the settlor. There is therefore a risk that tax will be lost if the valuation at the ten year anniversary is based on the actual age next birthday of the settlor where, in fact, the settlor was terminally ill.

Three options to overcome this risk are:

- To obtain evidence of the settlor's state of health at the ten year anniversary in all cases. This would add both an administrative and a financial burden on the trustees and would require an assessment of the medical evidence obtained, presumably by the provider preparing the valuation, adding to their costs. In most cases the outcome would be that the settlor was not terminally ill and therefore that the valuation should be based on the actual age next birthday of the settlor. The advantage of this approach, however, is that there would be certainty for the trustees that the value at the ten year anniversary was finalised and it would remove the risk to HMRC of loss of tax on any distributions in the following ten years.
- To complete the valuation at the ten year anniversary on the basis of the settlor's actual age next birthday but, where the settlor dies within two years of the ten year anniversary, for HMRC to review the position at the ten year anniversary to satisfy itself as to whether the value needs revision. This would reduce the administrative burden at the ten year anniversary, but would not provide certainty for the trustees that the tax position was settled. There would also be practical difficulties in some cases in obtaining the relevant evidence of the settlor's state of health at the ten year anniversary retrospectively.
- To complete the valuation at the ten year anniversary on the basis of the settlor's rated age next birthday when the Discounted Gift Scheme was effected, plus an addition of 10 years for each ten year anniversary. This has the advantage of simplicity. The settlor's life will, in almost all cases, have been fully underwritten at the outset and no further medical evidence will be required. It would also provide certainty to the trustees that the tax position at the ten year anniversary was finalised and that HMRC would not review that position in the event that the settlor died within the next two years.

HMRC consider that the third option provides a practical approach to the valuation. It places the minimum administrative burden on trustees or product providers whilst at the same time protecting HMRC from potential loss of tax. The majority of settlors effecting Discounted Gift Schemes have no rating added to their age based on medical underwriting when the Discounted Gift Scheme is set up and therefore they would continue to have no rating applied at each ten year anniversary.

Where no underwriting was completed on the original transfer it may be necessary for HMRC to review the original transfer value if this has not previously been reported. Alternatively it may be necessary to obtain evidence of the settlor's state of health at the ten year anniversary to complete the valuation.

1.4 Valuation Basis

The valuation is required to be carried out on an open market basis in accordance with s.160 and it is not possible to predict what open market practice will be by the time these valuations are required, with the first valuations expected to be required in March 2016. The open market valuation would need to reflect current market practice on the mortality assumptions being applied to reversionary interests as well as the rates of return then required by purchasers.

In order to provide some certainty as to the valuations that will be acceptable, HMRC will accept valuations that are calculated using the same mortality basis as is then in use in valuing the transfer when a Discounted Gift Scheme is effected, replacing select with ultimate mortality. This does not preclude the use of alternative valuation approaches to establish open market values, but is intended to provide certainty for valuations provided in accordance with this approach. HMRC will publish any changes to its valuation basis at least three months before the changes are to take effect to give providers time to update their systems.

1.5 Example

The examples below show how the value of the relevant property is calculated. The mortality and interest rate basis used is that set out in paragraph 2.2 below.

1.5.1 Example 1

The first example assumes that the settlor was a woman aged 75 next birthday when the Discounted Gift Scheme was effected with no addition to age based on medical underwriting. At the ten year anniversary the underlying value of the bond is £1,000,000. The withdrawals retained by the settlor are equal to 5% of the original £500,000 investment, payable monthly in arrears.

Calculation

The open market value equals

The fund value at the ten year anniversary × $\overline{A}_x$, less

The annual rate of withdrawals × $a_x^{(p)}$, where

> $\overline{A}_x$ is an immediate assurance factor, payable immediately on the death of a life aged × next birthday, and
>
> $a_x^{(p)}$ is an annuity factor for an annuity payable in arrears at a frequency of p times per year for the term of a life aged × next birthday.

A deduction is made from this value to represent the purchaser's costs associated with the legal formalities connected with completing the purchase. The figures are:

£1,000,000 × $\overline{A}_{85}$ = £1,000,000 × 0.70301 = £703,010, less

£25,000 × $a_{85}^{(12)}$ = £25,000 × 6.710 = £167,750

Which gives a value of £535,260.

From this value a deduction of approximately £1,000 is made in respect of the purchaser's costs, to give a net value of £534,260.

1.5.2 Example 2

The facts are as in example 1, except that an age addition of 4 years was made based on medical underwriting when the Discounted Gift Scheme was effected.

Calculation

As the settlor was aged 75 next birthday when the Discounted Gift Scheme was effected and an age addition of 4 years was applied, the effective age to be used at the ten year anniversary is 89 next birthday. The calculations become:

£1,000,000 × $\overline{A}_{89}$ = £1,000,000 × 0.76160 = £761,600, less

£25,000 × $a_{89}^{(12)}$ = £25,000 × 5.379 = £134,475

Which gives a value of £627,125.

From this value a deduction of approximately £1,000 is made in respect of the purchaser's costs, to give a net value of £626,125.

1.5.3 Example 3

The facts are as example 1, except that the settlor was a man aged 83 when the Discounted Gift Scheme was effected. No age addition was made as a result of medical underwriting.

Calculation

As the settlor was aged 83 next birthday when the Discounted Gift Scheme was effected, the calculations are based on an age next birthday of 93 at the ten year anniversary. The calculations are:

£1,000,000 × $\overline{A}_{93}$ = £1,000,000 × 0.81385 = £813,850, less

£25,000 × $a_{93}^{(12)}$ = £25,000 × 4.192 = £104,800

Which gives a value of £709,050.

From this value a deduction of approximately £1,000 is made in respect of the purchaser's costs, to give a net value of £708,050.

1.6 Jointly effected Discounted Gift Schemes

Many Discounted Gift Schemes are effected jointly by two settlors with the retained rights payable until the death of the survivor of both settlors. Section 44(2) provides that where more than one person is the settlor in relation to a settlement then, for purposes including a ten year anniversary charge, the property is treated as being comprised in separate settlements. The value of the fund will be divided between the separate settlements in the proportion that the original funds were provided by each settlor, usually equally. The valuation of the fund needs to take into account that the fund will not be available to the open market purchaser until after the death of both settlors. The valuation of the expected withdrawals will need to take into account whether or not the full payments continue until the death of the survivor of both settlors.

1.6.1 Example

A husband age 78 and his wife aged 75 each put £500,000 into a Discounted Gift Scheme from which withdrawals of £50,000 per year, paid monthly in arrears, are to be made until the death of the survivor. At the ten year anniversary the fund is worth £2,000,000.

The overall settlement will be treated as two separate settlements in view of s.44(2). The £2,000,000 is apportioned equally between the two settlements. For **each** settlement the calculations are:

$$£1{,}000{,}000 \times \overline{A}_{\overline{8885}} = £1{,}000{,}000 \times 0.63642 = £636{,}420\text{, less}$$

$$£25{,}000 \times a^{(12)}_{\overline{8885}} = £25{,}000 \times 8.223 = £205{,}575$$

Which gives a value of £430,845.

From this value a deduction of approximately £1,000 is made in respect of the purchaser's costs, to give a net value of £429,845.

1.7 Ten Year Anniversary reporting requirements

An account is required to be submitted to HMRC by the trustees of a relevant property settlement where a charge to tax arises under Part III, Chapter III of the Inheritance Tax Act 1984. The reporting requirements are relaxed in connection with Excepted Settlements, the definition of which are set out in the Inheritance Tax (Delivery of Accounts) (Excepted Settlements) Regulations 2008 SI2008/606. For the purpose of establishing whether the transfer exceeds the 80% limit specified in Regulation 4(4), it is the value of the relevant property calculated in accordance with this brief that should be used.

2. Updated guidance on the calculation of transfer values when a Discounted Gift Scheme is effected

In May 2007 HMRC issued a Technical Note setting out the inheritance tax treatment of Discounted Gift Schemes (PDF 45K). That note dealt with the transfer of value that arises when a Discounted Gift Scheme is effected. It also set out the valuation basis that HMRC considered appropriate in establishing the value transferred. Subsequent to that note amendments to the valuation rate of interest have been made which are summarised in the inheritance tax manual at IHTM 20656.

Following a European Court of Justice decision in March 2011 (the "Test-Achats" case) the use of gender as a factor in setting insurance premiums is no longer permissible from 21 December 2012. As one of the main factors used to establish the value transferred when a Discounted Gift Scheme is effected is the cost of insuring the life of the individual who has effected the Scheme, the valuation basis needs to be changed to reflect this significant change in how life assurance premiums are calculated.

The position at the date of a Ten Year Anniversary is somewhat different. At a Ten Year Anniversary the open market purchaser would not be concerned to insure the life of the settlor. Rather the purchaser's concern would be in establishing the settlor's life expectancy. This would be affected by the settlor's age, gender and state of health at that time and would use a different valuation basis from that used for valuing the retained rights when a Discounted Gift Scheme is effected.

In order to try to minimise the administrative burden around providing Discounted Gift Scheme valuations, HMRC will accept Ten Year Anniversary valuations which are calculated using the same mortality and interest rate basis as is then in force for calculating the transfer value when a Discounted Gift Scheme is effected. This is set out in paragraph 2.2 below. This does not preclude valuations being submitted using alternative methods or valuation assumptions, but is intended to provide assurance that valuations calculated in accordance with this brief will be accepted by HMRC.

2.1 Valuation basis of the retained rights

As set out in the 2007 Technical Note, the value transferred is calculated as the difference between the total amount invested in the Discounted Gift Scheme and the open market value of the retained rights. The formula used to calculate the open market value of the retained rights is

$(1 - p) \div (p + i)$ where

p is an annual whole life premium per £1 sum assured, expressed as a decimal, and
i is the open market purchaser's required rate of return on his investment.

2.2 Mortality and interest rate basis

Following the removal of gender as a factor in setting life assurance premiums the mortality basis used by HMRC needs to be altered to reflect this change in open market premium rates. At the same time it is an appropriate time to reconsider the current interest rate assumption within the calculation. The revised mortality and interest rate basis is

Mortality: 80% of AFC00 select mortality (Permanent assurances for females, combined rates from Continuous Mortality Investigation table "00" series published in the CMI Working Papers number 21 on 1 August 2006)

Interest rate of 4.5% p.a.

This revised basis will be applied to all transfers or Ten Year Anniversaries which occur on or after 1 December 2013.

2.3 Further clarification – withdrawals in excess of 5% per year

HMRC has been asked to clarify the valuation approach it takes when withdrawals under a Discounted Gift Scheme exceed 5% per year.

Where the retained rights under a Discounted Gift Scheme derived from regular partial withdrawals from an investment bond do not exceed 5% per year, no personal income tax liabilities are taken into account in the valuation of those retained rights. Where the withdrawals in such circumstances exceed 5% per year, or where the cumulative 5% allowances are exhausted, the personal income tax liabilities of the open market purchaser need to be factored in to the valuation of the retained rights. In HMRC's view the open market purchaser of the retained rights will account for income tax at 40% on the excess over 5% per year. Where the bonds are onshore the assumption is that a 20% non-refundable tax credit will be taken into account so that the excess over 5% per year is reduced by 20% net rather than by 40% for offshore bonds.

TAX BULLETIN

INTERPRETATIONS

IRInt. 1001 INHERITANCE TAX: GIFTS WITH RESERVATION [HMRC Tax Bulletin 9, November 1993]

Under Section 102 Finance Act 1986, any property given away on or after 18 March 1986 subject to a reservation is, on the death of the donor, treated as forming part of the donor's estate immediately before his death. Gifts with reservation (GWRs) are defined as gifts where either:

- the donee does not assume bona fide possession and enjoyment of the property at the date of the gift or 7 years before the donor's death, if later; or
- at any time in the period ending with the donor's death and beginning 7 years before that date or, if later, from the date of gift, the property is not enjoyed to the entire exclusion or virtually to the entire exclusion of the donor.

This note provides some guidance on the Revenue's interpretation of the de minimis rule which is expressed as "virtually to the entire exclusion" and comments on the exclusion from the GWR provisions where the donor pays full consideration for any use of the property. The note also clarifies the position of the annual exemption under Section 19 IHTA 84 where a reservation of benefit ceases.

Interpretation of de minimis rule

The word "virtually" in the de minimis rule in Section 102(1)(b) is not defined and the statute does not give any express guidance about its meaning. However, the shorter OED defines it as, amongst other things, "to all intents" and "as good as". Our interpretation of "virtually to the entire exclusion" is that it covers cases in which the benefit to the donor is insignificant in relation to the gifted property.

It is not possible to reduce this test to a single crisp proposition. Each case turns on its own unique circumstances and the questions are likely to be ones of fact and degree. We do not operate Section 102(1)(b) in such a way that donors are unreasonably prevented from having limited access to property they have given away and a measure of flexibility is adopted in applying the test.

Some examples of situations in which we consider that Section 102(1)(b) permits limited benefit to the donor without bringing the GWR provisions into play are given below to illustrate how we apply the de minimis test:

- a house which becomes the donee's residence but where the donor subsequently
  - stays, in the absence of the donee, for not more than 2 weeks each year, or
  - stays with the donee for less than one month each year;
- social visits, excluding overnight stays made by a donor as a guest of the donee, to a house which he had given away. The extent of the social visits should be no greater than the visits which the donor might be expected to make to the donee's house in the absence of any gift by the donor;
- a temporary stay for some short term purpose in a house the donor had previously given away, for example
  - while the donor convalesces after medical treatment,
  - while the donor looks after a donee convalescing after medical treatment,
  - while the donor's own home is being redecorated;
- visits to a house for domestic reasons, for example baby-sitting by the donor for the donee's children;
- a house together with a library of books which the donor visits less than 5 times in any year to consult or borrow a book;
- a motor car which the donee uses to give occasional (i.e. less than 3 times a month) lifts to the donor;
- land which the donor uses to walk his dogs or for horse riding provided this does not restrict the donee's use of the land.

It follows, of course, that if the benefit to the donor is, or becomes, more significant, the GWR provisions are likely to apply. Examples of this include gifts of:

- a house in which the donor then stays most weekends, or for a month or more each year;
- a second home or holiday home which the donor and the donee both then use on an occasional basis;
- a house with a library in which the donor continues to keep his own books, or which the donor uses on a regular basis, for example because it is necessary for his work;
- a motor car which the donee uses every day to take the donor to work.

Exclusion of benefit where full consideration paid for use of property

The GWR provisions do not apply where an interest in land is given away and the donor pays full consideration for future use of the property (FA 1986, Schedule 20, para. 6(1)(a)). While we take the view that such full consideration is required throughout the relevant period – and therefore consider that the rent paid should be reviewed at appropriate intervals to reflect market changes – we do recognise that there is no single value at which consideration can be fixed as “full”. Rather, we accept that what constitutes full consideration in any case lies within a range of values reflecting normal valuation tolerances, and that any amount within that range can be accepted as satisfying the para. 6(1)(a) test.

Termination of reserved benefits and the annual exemption

Where a reservation ceases, the donor is treated by Section 102(4) Finance Act 1986 as having made a potentially exempt transfer (PET) at that time. In that event the PET will only be taxable if the donor dies within the next 7 years but the value of the PET cannot be reduced by any available annual exemption under Section 19 IHTA 1984. The Statement in paragraph 3.4 of the IHT1 booklet, which indicates that the annual exemption may apply if the reservation ceases to exist in the donor’s lifetime and a PET is treated as made at that time, is incorrect. This will be corrected in IHT1 when it is next updated.

A typical outright gift to an individual of an amount exceeding the available annual exemption is partly exempt, with the balance above the available annual exemption being a PET. But a PET itself cannot qualify for the annual exemption. The reason is that a PET is a transfer which, but for the provisions of Section 3A IHTA 1984, would be an immediately chargeable transfer. By definition a chargeable transfer is a transfer of value which is not an exempt transfer: Section 2(1) IHTA 1984. So a PET cannot be an exempt transfer at the time it is made. The PET will, of course, escape a charge to IHT if the donor survives the statutory period after making it.

The annual exemption is not necessarily lost by the taxpayer. For example, suppose he makes a gift of his home in August 1991 but continues to reside there. In May 1992 he finally leaves the gifted house and the reservation ceases. In October 1992 he makes a gift into a discretionary trust (an immediately chargeable transfer). He is treated as making a PET of his residence in May 1992: the annual £3,000 exemption does not reduce its value. But the £3,000 exemption is available for setting off against the immediately chargeable transfer in October, and so is any unused exemption carried forward from the previous year.

IRInt. 1002 INHERITANCE TAX: BUSINESS & AGRICULTURAL RELIEF [HMRC Tax Bulletin 14, December 1994]

The inheritance tax (IHT) legislation provides relief for transfers of agricultural property and for business property. We have been asked for our views on the availability of relief

- where agricultural property is replaced by business property (or vice versa) shortly before the owner’s death; and
- on the donor’s death, where the donee of a potentially exempt transfer of agricultural property has sold it and reinvested the proceeds in a non-agricultural business (or vice versa).

A “potentially exempt transfer” (PET) is a lifetime transfer which only becomes chargeable to IHT if the donor dies within seven years of the transfer.

All statutory references in this article are to the Inheritance Tax Act (IHTA) 1984.

IHT business and agricultural relief reduces the value of relevant business property, or the agricultural value of agricultural property, by either 50 or 100 per cent. The rate of relief depends on the nature of the property and interest held.

The qualifying conditions for the relief include requirements of a minimum period of ownership and, in the case of agricultural property, of occupation of the property for agricultural purposes immediately before the transfer. If, and to the extent that, the same property may qualify for relief as both agricultural property and business property, Section 114 prevents double relief.

There are also rules which allow for the sale and replacement of qualifying property. The replacement is qualifying property only if it, and the original qualifying property, have together been owned (and, in the case of agricultural property, occupied) for a combined minimum period.

In the Revenue’s view, where agricultural property which is a farming business is replaced by non-agricultural business property, the period of ownership of the original property will be relevant for applying the minimum ownership condition to the replacement property. Business property relief will be available on the replacement if all the conditions for that relief are satisfied. Where non-agricultural business property is replaced by a farming business, and the latter is not eligible for agricultural property relief, Section 114(1) does not exclude business property relief if the conditions for that relief are satisfied.

There could be cases where, for example, agricultural land is not part of a farming business, so any replacement could only qualify for business property relief if it satisfied the minimum ownership conditions in its own right. However, our experience suggests such cases are likely to be exceptional.

Where the donee of a PET of a farming business sells the business, and replaces it with a non-agricultural business, the effect of Section 124A(1) is to deny agricultural property relief on the value transferred by the PET. Consequently, Section 114(1) does not exclude business property relief if the conditions for that relief are satisfied; and, in the reverse situation, the farming business acquired by the donee can be "relevant business property" for the purposes of Section 113B(3)(c).

[Part V Chapters I & II IHTA 1984, as amended by Section 73 Finance (No. 2) Act 1992 and Section 247 Finance Act 1994.]

IRInt. 1003 INHERITANCE TAX: VARIATION OF INHERITANCES FOLLOWING A DEATH [HMRC Tax Bulletin 15, February 1995]

The beneficiaries of a deceased person's estate may wish to alter their entitlements under the estate, by changing the terms under which the original inheritance arose, whether by the deceased's Will, the laws of intestacy or otherwise. For example, a daughter inheriting under her father's Will may want to pass the inheritance onto her own child.

Not surprisingly everyone who would lose out as a result of the change – called a variation – must agree to it.

There are special rules concerning the IHT consequences of variations in Section 142 Inheritance Tax Act (IHTA) 1984. The main ones are set out below:

If a variation is made **by the parties affected by it**:

- in a written instrument **that includes a statement that section 142 IHT is to apply to the variation**; and
- within two years of the relevant death; and
- where the variation means that additional IHT is payable, the personal representatives of the deceased **are also parties to the instrument**,

then the estate will be taxed as if the variation had been made by the deceased at the time of his/her death. In other words IHT will be calculated on the basis of the varied entitlements, not the original ones.

We have recently been asked for guidance in two areas relating to IHT and instruments of variation.

Marshall v Kerr

In June 1994 the House of Lords, in the case of *Marshall v Kerr* [1994] BTC 258, found that those provisions of Section 62 Taxation of Chargeable Gains Act 1992 which apply where there is a variation and election, did not mean that the variation of the terms of a deceased person's Will was to be treated for all purposes of capital gains tax (CGT) as made by the deceased. We have been asked whether variations which meet the conditions in Section 142 IHTA 1984 will still be treated for IHT purposes as made by the deceased and not by the beneficiary or beneficiaries.

Our view is that, as the relevant IHT legislation differs from the CGT provisions which were considered in Marshall v Kerr, that decision has no application to IHT. Variations which meet all the statutory conditions will continue to be treated for IHT purposes as having been made by the deceased.

Variation of inheritances following the death of an original beneficiary within the statutory two-year period

As explained above, for Section 142 IHTA 1984 to apply, all the beneficiaries affected by the variation must join in a written **instrument effecting the variation**. We have been asked how this requirement should be interpreted when one of the beneficiaries dies before a variation is made.

Our view is that the legal personal representatives of a beneficiary (the second deceased) may enter into a variation.

If the variation will reduce the entitlements of the beneficiaries of the second deceased then they, as well as the legal personal representatives of the second deceased, must agree to the variation. The Revenue will require evidence of the consent of the beneficiaries of the second deceased to the variation. If they are not themselves parties to the variation, other written evidence of their consent will be sought.

This view applies for CGT purposes also.

[Section 142 IHTA 1984; Section 62 TGCA 1992]

History – This interpretation shows the text as amended by Tax Bulletin, Issue 74 – see TB12/04-6. The changes made are shown in bold.

IRInt. 1004 INHERITANCE TAX: VALUATION OF ASSETS AT THE DATE OF DEATH [HMRC Tax Bulletin 16, April 1995]

Where the value of an asset is ascertained for Inheritance Tax (IHT) purposes on the owner's death, this is also taken as the beneficiary's acquisition value for capital gains tax (CGT) purposes. We have been asked to say whether the Revenue will ascertain the value of the estate assets using the IHT principles, where either:

- the asset is wholly exempt or relieved from IHT; or
- no IHT is payable on the deceased's estate,

in order to provide a value for any other Revenue purpose, in particular the CGT acquisition value.

The value of an asset for IHT purposes is usually the price it would realise if sold in the open market. In certain circumstances special rules may apply to give a different value. For example, under the related property provisions of Section 161 Inheritance Tax Act 1984, property held jointly by husband and wife is treated as a single unit in arriving at the value of their respective interests.

IHT is charged on the assets in a person's estate on death if their value together with the value of any chargeable lifetime gifts exceeds the IHT "threshold" (£154,000 for deaths and other chargeable events occurring on or after 6 April 1995). There are various exemptions and reliefs. These include the exemption for assets given to a surviving spouse and up to 100 per cent relief for agricultural or business property.

If an asset is wholly exempt or relieved from IHT, neither the personal representatives of the deceased nor the Revenue can require the value of that asset to be ascertained for IHT purposes.

Where it is evident that any possible increase or decrease in the value of the chargeable assets of the estate, as included in an Inland Revenue Account, will leave the total value of the estate below the IHT threshold, it will not be necessary to ascertain the value of all the individual assets for IHT purposes. In some cases, particularly where the estate is close to the threshold, values may be considered but not necessarily "ascertained".

For example, the value included in the Inland Revenue Account for a holding of shares in an unquoted company might appear to the Revenue's Shares Valuation Division (SVD) to be too high. In this situation, as no IHT is at stake, SVD is unlikely to negotiate an ascertained value for IHT. On the other hand if the value included seems, on the face of it, too low, SVD may negotiate an ascertained value if the likely amount of IHT at stake warrants this.

If the value of an asset is not ascertained for IHT, the normal rules of Section 272 Taxation of Chargeable Gains Act 1992 will apply to determine the CGT acquisition value of the beneficiary.

We have also been asked how the Revenue will approach the valuation of a holding of shares in an unquoted company where not all of the company's assets qualify for IHT business property relief, so that the shares are not wholly relieved. Again, SVD's approach will depend very much upon whether in any event IHT is payable and, if so, the amount of tax involved. SVD is unlikely to negotiate an ascertained value for the holding if very little or no tax is at stake.

IRInt. 1006 INHERITANCE TAX (IHT): POST-DEATH VARIATION OF INHERITANCE BY SURVIVORSHIP [HMRC Tax Bulletin 19, October 1995]

Beneficiaries of the estate of a deceased person – whether under the will, relating to intestacy or otherwise – may wish to change their inheritances. There are special IHT rules for changes or variation made within 2 years after the deceased's death.

If a variation made within the 2-year period satisfies certain other conditions, IHT is charged on the death as though the deceased person had made the variation and the beneficiaries do not have to pay tax on any gift of their inheritance. The main conditions are that the variation is made in writing and that the **variation contains a statement that** the IHT rules **are intended** to apply.

Similar rules apply for certain purposes of capital gains tax (CGT).

Recently, we have seen suggestions that these rules do not apply to a variation of the deceased's interest in jointly held assets, which passed on the death to the surviving joint owner(s).

For example, the family home was owned by a mother and her son as beneficial joint tenants and on the mother's death, her interest passed by survivorship to the son who then became the sole owner of the property. It has been suggested that, in this example, the son cannot, for IHT/CGT purposes, vary his inheritance of his mother's interest by redirecting it to his children.

We do not share this view.

Both IHT and CGT rules apply not only to dispositions/inheritances arising under will or the law of intestacy but also to those effected "otherwise". In our view, the words "or otherwise" bring within the rules the automatic inheritance of a deceased owner's interest in jointly held assets by the surviving joint owner(s).

[Section 142 IHT Act 1984 and Section 62(6)–(9) Taxation of Chargeable Gains Act 1992.]

History – This interpretation shows the text as amended by Tax Bulletin, Issue 74 – see TB12/04-6. The amendments made are shown in bold.

IRInt. 1007 INHERITANCE TAX (IHT): EXCLUDED PROPERTY SETTLEMENTS BY PEOPLE DOMICILED OVERSEAS [HMRC Tax Bulletin 27, February 1997]

We have been asked how the IHT provisions on excluded property apply to the assets of a settlement made by a person domiciled overseas where:

- all, or only some, of the settled assets are situated outside the UK when a chargeable event occurs; or
- a person domiciled in the UK has also provided property or funds for the purposes of that settlement.

References in this article are to Sections of the Inheritance Tax Act 1984.

Excluded property

For persons domiciled abroad, IHT generally applies only to their UK assets; it treats their overseas assets as excluded property, that is: not within the charge to IHT – S 6(1)). For assets owned outright, it is the owner's domicile at the time of a tax charge that is relevant in deciding whether or not the assets are excluded property.

Slightly different rules apply to property held in a settlement. An asset is excluded property if it is situated abroad when a chargeable event occurs and if the settlor (defined in s 44) was domiciled outside the UK *at the time the settlement was made* – S 48(3).

However, an "excluded" asset is not always completely irrelevant for the purposes of IHT. So:

- an "excluded" asset in a person's estate may still affect the valuation of another asset in the estate, for example, an "excluded" holding of shares in an unquoted company may affect the value of a similar holding in the estate which is not "excluded";
- the value of an "excluded" asset at the time the asset becomes comprised in a settlement may be relevant in determining the rate of any tax charge arising in respect of the settlement under the IHT rules concerning trusts without interests in possession – Sections 68(5), 66(4) and 69(3).

Domicile is a concept of general law but, in certain circumstances (S 267), a person with a general law domicile abroad can be treated as having a UK domicile for IHT purposes.

Settlor adds assets to his/her existing settlement

In the light of the definitions of "settlement" and "settled property" in S 43, our view is that a settlement in relation to any particular asset is made at the time when that asset is transferred to the settlement trustees to hold on the declared trusts. Thus, assets added to a settlor's own settlement made at an earlier time when the settlor was domiciled abroad will not be "excluded", wherever they may be situated, if the settlor has a UK domicile at the time of making the addition.

In determining the tax treatment of particular assets held in the same settlement it may, therefore, be necessary to consider the settlor's domicile at times other than when the settlement was first made. And if assets added at different times have become mixed, any dealings with the settled fund after the addition(s) may also need to be considered.

Several persons contribute to a single settlement

There are rules (S44(2)) which provide that assets contributed to a "single" settlement by more than one settlor are to be treated as comprised in separate settlements for IHT purposes if "the circumstances so require". There is no definition of "required circumstances" or statutory guidance on how the assets in the single, actual settlement are to be attributed to the deemed separate settlements.

However, the provision is similar in terms to paragraph 1(8) of Schedule 5 Finance Act 1975, which was considered by Chadwick J. in *Hatton v IRC* [1992] BTC 8,024. In the light of the decision in that case we take the view

- that the determination of the extent to which overseas assets in a settlement are excluded property by reason of the settlor's domicile is a relevant "required circumstance"; and
- that
  - where a clear, or reasonably sensible, attribution of settled property between the contributions made by several settlors is possible, there will be a separate settlement, with its own attributed assets, for each contributor for IHT purposes;
  - if such an attribution is not feasible, each separate settlement will comprise all the assets of the single, actual settlement.

Trust records

It follows from the comments above that the trustees of a settlement should keep adequate records to enable any necessary attribution of the settled property to be made if either

- the settlor has added further assets to the settlement after it was made; or
- two or more persons have contributed funds for the purposes of the settlement.

[Sections 43, 44 and 48 IHTA 1984 *Hatton v IRC* [1992] BTC 8,024.]

IRInt. 1008 BOOKMAKERS' PITCHES AND CAPITAL GAINS TAX (EXTRACT) [HMRC Tax Bulletin 43, October 1999]

Inherited pitches

Where a pitch has been acquired by inheritance after the October 1998 changes to the rules came into effect, however, we consider that the position will be different. Section 62(1) TCGA provides that:

> "The assets of which a deceased person was competent to dispose (a) shall be deemed to be acquired on his death by the personal representatives or other persons on whom they devolve for a consideration equal to their market value at the date of death."

Clearly a particular pitch will now have a market value and as it was an asset "of which the deceased was competent to dispose" would fall within Section 62(1).

A pitch will also be "property to which (the deceased) is beneficially entitled", Section 5(1) Inheritance Tax Act 1984 (IHTA), and where it formed part of the deceased's business, its value may qualify for Inheritance Tax business property relief at 100% if the statutory conditions are met, Sections 103–114 IHTA.

If a member of the family acquires a pitch through inheritance then where its value has been "ascertained" for Inheritance Tax purposes, this will also be their acquisition cost, Section 274 TCGA.

History – The full text of this interpretation is reproduced in Volume 1F.

ARTICLES

TB02/92-3 INHERITANCE TAX: RETIREMENT BENEFITS UNDER PRIVATE PENSION CONTRACTS – SECTION 3(3) INHERITANCE TAX ACT 1984[HMRC Tax Bulletin 2, February 1992]

Background

Many pension scheme benefits are written under trust on terms which provide that the retirement benefit (that is, the pension) continues to be for the policyholder and the death benefit is assigned, normally to members of the family. The two benefits are mutually exclusive: once the retirement benefit is taken, the death benefit lapses.

A common feature of these schemes is that from a specified age – from fifty upwards depending on the type of scheme – the policyholder can elect to take the retirement benefit. There are cases where policyholders do not elect to take the benefit at the specified age and have still not done so when they die (so that the death benefit becomes payable). In such cases the Capital Taxes Offices (CTO) take the view that, in certain circumstances, the failure to exercise the right to take the retirement benefit before death can give rise to a lifetime charge to inheritance tax under Section 3(3).

The Association of British Insurers asked the CTO to clarify the circumstances in which a Section 3(3) claim might arise with these pension arrangements. The CTO set out their view in correspondence with the Association. It is summarised here.

The scope for a section 3(3) claim

In practice, the overwhelming majority of pension arrangements are not affected. The CTO expect to see very few cases where a claim would even be considered. This is because

- the vast majority of policyholders exercise their right to take retirement benefits during their lifetime or survive to the age beyond which they cannot defer taking the retirement benefit. All these cases fall outside the scope of a potential claim
- the chargeable estate of many policyholders will be below the inheritance tax threshold. If no tax is actually payable CTO would naturally not pursue a claim
- any claims that do arise are likely to be limited to retirement annuity contracts or personal pension schemes. Only exceptionally would claims involve occupational pension schemes
- there is no question of a claim being raised in cases of **genuine** pension arrangements, that is, where it is clear that the policyholder's primary intention is to provide for his or her own retirement benefit.

CTO would consider raising a claim in such cases as remain only where there was evidence that the policyholder's intention in failing to take up retirement benefits was to **increase the estate of someone else** (the beneficiaries of the death benefit) rather than to benefit himself or herself.

To this end, CTO will look closely at certain pension arrangements where the policyholder became aware that he or she was suffering from a terminal illness, or was in such poor health that his or her life was uninsurable, and **at or after that time** the policyholder

- took out a new policy and assigned the death benefit on trust, or
- assigned on trust the death benefit of an existing policy, or
- paid further contributions to a single premium policy or enhanced contributions to a regular premium policy where the death benefit had been previously assigned on trust, or
- deferred the date for taking retirement benefits.

In these circumstances it would be difficult to argue that the actions of the policyholder were intended to make provision for his or her own retirement given the prospect of an early death. Even then CTO would not pursue the claim where the death benefit was paid to the policyholder's spouse and/or dependents (that is, any individuals financially dependent on the policyholder). In addition, a claim would not normally be pursued where the policyholder survived for two years or more after making **any of these arrangements** but the CTO reserve the right to examine each case individually.

For the avoidance of doubt, CTO would adopt a similar approach in cases involving

- personal pension schemes set up under deed poll under the Superannuation Funds Office or Integrated Model rules, or
- buy-out policies under trust, approved under Section 591(2)(g) ICTA 1988 (commonly known as "Section 32 policies" after the original legislation).

TB12/95-7 INHERITANCE TAX: "HERITAGE" PROPERTY: SECTION 30 IHTA 1984 [HMRC Tax Bulletin 20, December 1995]

The Capital Taxes Office (CTO) no longer requires to see, at the pre-grant stage, Inland Revenue Accounts in which a claim for conditional exemption is made.

Inheritance tax is essentially a self-assessed tax and legal personal representatives should be able to justify their claim during the post-grant examination of the account. It will assist the CTO if the following question is answered when the account is complete:

> "*Did the deceased own or have an interest in possession in any "heritage" property which was given exemption from Capital Taxes on an earlier chargeable occasion for IHT/CTT/ED/CGT? If so, please provide full details and the CTO reference, if known.*"

(This question will be incorporated in future versions of Accounts.)

TB04/98-1 BUILDING SOCIETY AND OTHER WINDFALLS: FREE SHARES & CASH BONUSES [HMRC Tax Bulletin 34, April 1998]

We have been asked to set out our views on the tax treatment of so-called "windfall" pay-outs which are made as a result of the de-mutualisation of a building society or similar mutual society. These pay-outs will generally take the form of shares in the successor company, referred to here as the "free shares", or cash payments, referred to here as the "cash bonus".

A number of fundamental changes to the structure of Capital Gains Tax were proposed by the Chancellor in his Budget. This article **does not** address the effects of these changes on the treatment of such pay-outs following a de-mutualisation on or after 6 April 1998. We will cover these in a further Tax Bulletin article later this summer once the Finance Bill has been enacted by Parliament.

So far as **building societies** are concerned, the details of the pay-out will depend on the terms of the particular de-mutualisation. This article is therefore written in **general** terms. However, building society de-mutualisations are regulated by the Building Societies Act 1986 (BSA 1986) and the Building Societies Commission, so we would expect that the treatment set out in this article will also apply to any of these de-mutualisations.

As far as other de-mutualisations, such as **insurance companies**, are concerned, these are not subject to the same regulatory regime as the building societies and our experience of these is limited. This article is therefore restricted to the two cases for which we have sufficient information to be **specific** about these de-mutualisations.

Building society de-mutualisations

Sections 97–102 BSA 1986 allow building societies to become banks by converting from their existing mutual status to that of a limited company. That de-mutualisation may take place in conjunction with a take-over or on its own. In either event, the building society has to secure the agreement of its members to the proposed de-mutualisation by obtaining a majority vote in favour at an extraordinary general meeting. As a result, it has become customary for members to be offered financial incentives to vote in favour of the proposals. These may be in the form of:

- a right to free shares in the successor company, or
- a right to a cash bonus.

Details of the proposed incentives have to be supplied to members in advance of the meeting. Normally they will be included in the "Transfer Document" which also sets out the background to the proposed de-mutualisation; details on voting etc. Assuming that the majority of members vote in favour, then the society will transfer its business and assets to the successor company on a specified date, referred to as "vesting day". (Although they are not relevant to this article, there are special Capital Gains Tax rules in Section 216 Taxation of Chargable Gains Act (TCGA) 1992 regarding the transfer of the business.)

Capital gains tax

General Points

For Capital Gains Tax purposes, there are certain general points which apply to all investors in a building society who receive either free shares or a cash bonus on de-mutualisation. An investor who has a share account with a building society is a member of that society and their share account is an asset for Capital Gains Tax purposes, Section 21(1) TCGA 1992. The acquisition cost of that asset is the balance of funds remaining in the account on vesting day when the de-mutualisation takes place.

On the de-mutualisation of a society, the investor ceases to be a member and becomes a depositor with the successor bank. They will have a deposit account opened with an amount equal to the closing balance in their share account on vesting day, Section 100(2)(a) BSA 1986.

The Special Commissioners' decision in the case of *Foster & Horan v Williams,* (1997) SpC 133, established that, on vesting day, the investor disposes of the asset, in the form of their share account, in return for the deposit account with the successor bank plus either a cash bonus or a right to free shares. The decision also established that no Capital Gains Tax charge arises where a cash bonus is paid in respect of a deposit account with a building society. As announced in our Press Release of 27 March 1997, PR47/97, we accepted both parts of the decision and this article is **not** therefore concerned with pay-outs received in respect of building society deposit accounts.

The basic Capital Gains Tax consequences of the decision so far as share accounts are concerned are as follows:

- The acquisition cost of the asset is the net closing balance in the share account on vesting day.
- The consideration for the disposal of the asset is the opening balance in the deposit account plus either the cash bonus or the right to free shares.
- When a cash bonus is paid, then a chargeable gain arises on the disposal but indexation allowance, Section 53 TCGA 1992, is due. This is calculated by reference to the dates when amounts were lodged in or withdrawn from the share account. If local Tax Offices or Tax Enquiry Centres are asked for help by investors who are unable to supply computations with their SA Returns, they will offer to prepare these computations using one of our computer programs.
- When free shares are to be issued, as Section 217 TCGA 1992 treats the right to these as an option having no value, no chargeable gain arises on the disposal and indexation allowance is not due. When the free shares are issued, Section 217 treats the investor as acquiring these at nil cost. The normal Capital Gains Tax rules apply when the shares are disposed of.

Specific Points

There are a number of specific points which will only apply to some investors in a building society who receive either free shares or a cash bonus on de-mutualisation.

Multiple Accounts

Where an investor has more than one share account with the society, then each account is treated as a separate asset for Capital Gains Tax purposes. This means that a separate calculation is required for each account where cash bonuses are paid. Where free shares are issued, however, these shares will then be subject to the pooling rules in Section 104 TCGA 1992.

Free Shares Sold Immediately

Investors entitled to free shares may arrange for these to be sold immediately on their behalf by the successor bank, usually through an internal share dealing service. Instead of receiving a share certificate, the investor simply receives the net proceeds of sale. This does not mean, as has been suggested to us, that the investor should be treated as receiving a cash bonus rather than shares. Even if the shares are sold immediately, the investor has still acquired the beneficial interest in those shares on vesting day. When the shares are sold by the successor bank on the investor's behalf, that represents a disposal of that beneficial interest. The proceeds the investor receives come from the sale of the shares and should be treated accordingly.

Statutory Bonuses

On the de-mutualisation of a building society any investor who did not have a share account open for more than two years may not have been entitled to vote on the de-mutualisation resolution. Nor will they, normally, be entitled to anything more than a deposit account with the successor bank and a statutory cash bonus, Section 100(2)(a)(b) BSA 1986. This cash bonus is treated in exactly the same way as any other cash bonus.

Joint etc. Accounts: Capital Gains Tax

A building society is required to regard only the first-named holder of a share account as the member for the purposes of a de-mutualisation, paragraph 7(2) Schedule 2 BSA 1986. Taken together with the terms of the Transfer Document, this generally means that it is only the first-named account holder who has a right to vote on the de-mutualisation resolution. That person is also normally the only one entitled to receive any cash bonus or the right to be allotted free shares. This means that their name will be the only one which appears on any share certificate which may be issued. However, this does not necessarily mean that the first-named account holder is treated as being the recipient, or the only recipient, of the cash or shares for Capital Gains Tax purposes.

In many cases, the first-named account holder receiving the cash or shares will acquire these wholly or partly on behalf of others. The following comments will apply to this type of case generally but local Tax Offices or Tax Enquiry Centres will always have regard to the facts of the particular case they are dealing with. We are, for example, aware that certain societies may be making specific arrangements in respect of nominee accounts which will enable cash payments to be made to all the account holders, not just the first-named.

- Where the building society account which gave rise to the receipt of the cash bonus or free shares was a joint account, e.g. one held between spouses, then beneficial ownership would rest with both spouses. When the cash bonus is paid or the free shares are issued, we will treat them as being received or acquired equally by both spouses.
- Where the building society account which gave rise to the receipt of the cash bonus or free shares was a child account, e.g. one held by a parent or guardian on behalf of a minor child, then beneficial ownership would rest with the child. When the cash bonus is paid or the free shares are issued, we will treat them as being received or acquired wholly by that child.
- Where the building society account which gave rise to the receipt of the cash bonus or free shares was a nominee account, e.g. one held by a carer on behalf of an aged or incapacitated person, then beneficial ownership would rest with the aged or incapacitated person. When the cash bonus is paid or the free shares are issued, we will treat them as received or acquired wholly by that person.
- Where the building society account which gave rise to the receipt of the free shares or the cash bonus was a client account, e.g. one held by a solicitor on behalf of a particular client, then beneficial ownership would rest with the client. When the cash bonus is paid or the free shares are issued, we will treat them as being received or acquired wholly by that client.
- Where the building society account which gave rise to the receipt of the cash bonus or free shares was a partnership account, e.g. one held by a named partner on behalf of themselves and all the other partners, then beneficial ownership would rest with all the partners. When the cash bonus is paid or the free shares are issued, we will treat them as being received or acquired by all the partners in accordance with their fractional shares in the partnership, Section 59 TCGA 1992 and Statement of Practice D12.

Joint etc. Accounts: Income Tax

For income tax, as for capital gains tax, beneficial entitlement is the key to the tax treatment in most cases. It therefore follows that, in the case of a dividend paid on free shares received by the first-named holder of a joint account in which both account holders have an equal beneficial interest, for example, each party should be treated as if they were an individual account holder in respect of their share of the dividend.

This general rule does not apply where parents/guardians hold an account for a minor child. If the parents have provided the capital in the account the dividends will usually be treated as the income of the parents in the proportions in which they have provided the capital so long as the child is under 18 and unmarried.

PIBS

Certain building societies offer what are known as PIBS. These are treated as Qualifying Corporate Bonds, Section 117(4)(5) TCGA 1992, and, as such, there is no chargeable gain on their disposal. Where an investor in a building society had a share account in the form of a PIBS, any cash bonus received in respect of that account does not give rise to a chargeable gain.

This does not apply to cash bonuses in respect of PIBS accounts held by corporate investors received on or after 1 April 1996. These accounts are no longer treated as Qualifying Corporate Bonds, Section 117(A1) TCGA 1992.

Deceased investors

As there may be both Capital Gains Tax and Inheritance Tax consequences where an investor in a mutual building society dies before its de-mutualisation, this topic is dealt with in some detail.

Introduction

Where an investor in a mutual building society dies after the issue of the relevant Transfer Document or Prospectus and before vesting day, there may be Inheritance Tax or Capital Gains Tax consequences in respect of their entitlement to receive either free shares or a cash bonus on de-mutualisation.

Following the death others may become entitled to any free shares or cash bonus due in respect of the account held by the deceased. The precise consequences for both taxes depend on a number of factors, including the rules of the particular society, the terms of the Transfer Document covering the de-mutualisation and whether the deceased was the sole or first-named holder of the account.

Accordingly, this article sets out the basic positions as we understand them.

Sole Account Holders

Inheritance Tax Included in the Estate

Most societies make special provisions in their Transfer Documents to preserve the entitlement of those qualifying members who die before vesting day. Under those special provisions, the qualifying member's personal representatives, as the **qualifying successors**, generally receive the free shares or cash bonus **in that capacity** for the benefit of the estate.

For Inheritance Tax purposes, a person's estate is the aggregate of all the property to which that person is beneficially entitled, Section 5(1) IHTA 1984. The value of that property is the price which it might reasonably be expected to fetch if sold on the open market at that time, Section 160 IHTA 1984.

Inheritance Tax is not charged on the cash bonus or free shares which may be received by the deceased investor's personal representatives (i.e. their executors or administrators) some time after the date of death. However, if the investor died after the particular society had formally announced its plans to de-mutualise by issuing a Transfer Document or Prospectus, but before the completion on vesting day, the anticipated or preserved rights retained for the benefit of their estate should be fully reflected in the estate valuation.

This is because members of a mutual society who invest in its business by acquiring paid up shares, or some other interest, generally have a claim on the society to the amount of their share, or other interest, and a right to participate in any profits. Once a society formally announces its intention to de-mutualise with the issue of a Transfer Document or Prospectus, the value of a qualifying member's share, or other interest, increases significantly. This increase in value reflects the awareness of qualifying members that, subject to the approval of the voting members, they will become entitled to the proceeds of the sale of their business. Included in those proceeds are any cash bonus or free shares which may accrue to them.

Clearly, no prudent investor would consider abandoning their right to either a cash bonus or free shares by ceasing to be a qualifying member before the dates on which such benefits vest. Whatever the terms of the de-mutualisation might be, that non-severable right is property to which they are beneficially entitled and which increases the open market value of their share or other interest with the society at the relevant time.

That open market value of the qualifying member's share, or other interest, in the society, falls to be included as part of their estate and should reflect any entitlements under the terms of the Transfer Document at the date of death.

Valuing the Estate

The valuation of the deceased's share, or other interest, is not directly concerned with the actual amount of cash received or the value of free shares received by their successors on or after vesting day. Rather, it is a matter of determining the value by reference only to the information that was available at the date of death. This is generally the information provided to the qualifying members in the Transfer Document or Prospectus.

Each Transfer Document or Prospectus provides:

- an anticipated price per share of the free shares, or
- details of the proposed cash bonuses

calculated by reference to the amounts involved.

These anticipated prices, or proposed amounts, are the starting point for determining the gross value of the qualifying member's share or other interest at the relevant time. A discount is then applied to reflect any uncertainty or delay. For example, if a qualifying member died after the issue of the Transfer Document but before the extraordinary general meeting at which the de-mutualisation was formally approved by the voting members, the discount would be greater than if the member died after the extraordinary general meeting but before vesting day.

In the interests of consistency, a Valuation Table is provided at the end of this article to help taxpayers and their agents calculate the open market value of the deceased member's share, or other interest, in a mutual society where they died before vesting day. As explained below, this value is also relevant for Capital Gains Tax purposes and local Tax Offices and Tax Enquiry Centres have also been provided with a similar Table.

Capital Gains Tax

Where the deceased investor was the sole holder of a building society share account, then this passes to the personal representatives/beneficiaries who acquire it at the balance standing at the date of death, Section 62(1) TCGA 1992.

If the deceased investor would have been entitled to free shares on the de-mutualisation, then the personal representatives/beneficiaries may also have the right to those free shares. If they have, then they are entitled to have the acquisition cost of the shares, which would otherwise be nil, (Section 217 TCGA 1992), increased to take account of the value of the right to those shares. If they acquire such a right from a deceased investor, who died on or after the date on which the building society announced the de-mutualisation, then that right will have a value as part of the deceased's estate. This value will depend on the length of the period between the date of death and the subsequent date on which the free shares are issued.

If the deceased investor would have been entitled to receive a cash bonus on the de-mutualisation, then the personal representatives/beneficiaries may also be entitled to receive this bonus. If they are, then where the investor died on or after the date on which the building society announced the de-mutualisation, this will increase the value of the share account. The increase in value will depend on the length of the period between the date of death and the subsequent date on which the cash bonus is paid. We have to take account of that increase in establishing the personal representatives/beneficiaries' acquisition cost of the share account (which would otherwise be the balance at the date of death).

Where the Capital Taxes Office has ascertained the value of a building society share account for Inheritance Tax purposes, then, as described above, this may include an increase in value over the balance at the date of death in respect of the deceased's right to free shares or an entitlement to a cash bonus. If it does, then the value so ascertained has to be applied in establishing the personal representatives/beneficiaries' acquisition cost for Capital Gains Tax purposes (Section 274 TCGA 1992).

In cases involving deceased sole account holders who were entitled to free shares or a cash bonus, local Tax Offices or Tax Enquiry Centres will ask the personal representatives/beneficiaries whether they have been in touch with the Capital Taxes Office regarding the value of the estate and if so, what the outcome was. Local Offices have been provided with guidance on taking the case forward from this point using the equivalent of the Valuation Table at the end of this article. This guidance will be published in the Capital Gains Tax Manual in due course.

Joint Account Holders

Where the deceased investor was the first-named holder of a joint account, then we would not normally expect their share of the account to pass to the personal representatives/beneficiaries. Most joint accounts, especially those held between spouses, are such that the survivor will take over the whole account on the death of the first-named holder. Where the deceased investor would have been entitled to free shares or a cash bonus on the de-mutualisation, the surviving account holder may also have the right to those free shares or the cash bonus.

For Inheritance Tax purposes, we take the view that there is generally no charge in respect of either the right to free shares allotted to, or a cash bonus paid to, the surviving account holder(s) when the first-named, or any other, account holder dies before vesting day.

For Capital Gains Tax purposes, the surviving account holder's right to free shares is treated as an option acquired at nil cost (Section 217 TCGA 1992). When the free shares are issued, then the surviving account holder is also treated as acquiring these at nil.

IHT Extra-statutory Material

Where the surviving account holder is entitled to the cash bonus, then the acquisition cost of the share account, which would normally be the surviving account holder's share on vesting day, will be increased by the deceased's share at the date of death.

Insurance Company De-mutualisations

A number of other types of mutual organisation have recently converted from their original mutual status to that of a limited company or have announced their intention to do so. These include insurance companies and sports clubs. However, these organisations are not subject to the same regulatory regime as building societies so direct analogies are not always appropriate. The Capital Gains Tax treatment of "windfall" payments made to members of these types of organisation will depend on the facts of the particular case. Because these facts can vary very significantly from one case to another, it is only in cases where the de-mutualisation has taken place and we have been provided with full information and documentation that we can comment on the appropriate Capital Gains Tax treatment. As a result, this article is confined to the treatment of two recent de-mutualisations which have generated the greatest interest, the de-mutualisation of Norwich Union and the take-over of Scottish Amicable. We may be able to provide guidance on other individual de-mutualisations in due course. If so, this will be included in the published Capital Gains Tax Manual.

Norwich Union

The Norwich Union Life Insurance Society converted to a public company on 16 June 1997. Members who held a life policy with the society at 18 April 1997 were entitled to at least 150 free shares in the successor company. They were also entitled to purchase additional shares at a discount. In the Norwich Union case policy holders had formally to consent to being recognised as members and the date on which a member gave this consent will affect the date on which shares were unconditionally allotted to them and the Capital Gains Tax treatment of those shares. The Capital Gains Tax treatment of the free shares depends on whether or not they were unconditionally allotted on 15 June 1997. If there is any doubt on this point in a particular case, then the taxpayer concerned should ask Norwich Union for the date on which the shares were unconditionally allotted.

Shares Unconditionally Allotted on 15 June 1997

Where policy holders had agreed by the necessary date to be recognised as members and as a consequence had free shares unconditionally allotted on 15 June 1997, then they are treated under the provisions of Section 136 TCGA 1992 as having exchanged their membership rights for the free shares without this giving rise to a disposal for Capital Gains Tax purposes. As their membership rights had a nil acquisition cost, the free shares also have a nil acquisition cost. If they subsequently exercised their right to purchase additional shares, then the pooling rules in Section 104 TCGA 1992 apply. The normal rules apply when the shares are disposed of.

Shares Unconditionally Allotted After 15 June 1997

Where a policy holder only agreed after the necessary date to be recognised as a member and had free shares unconditionally allotted to them after 15 June 1997, then there are two points to consider. These are the disposal of rights in the pre-demutualisation society and the acquisition of the free shares.

- The issue of the free shares is treated for Capital Gains Tax purposes as a disposal of rights in the pre-de-mutualisation society. The consideration for that disposal is the value of those shares and as nothing was paid to acquire the rights, there is a chargeable gain equal to that value.
- The market value of the free shares will also be the acquisition cost of the free shares and a Capital Gains Tax liability may arise on their disposal. The normal rules will apply to any such disposal.

Certain policy holders may receive a cash payment rather than an allocation of free shares. In such cases there is a chargeable gain equal to the full amount of the receipt.

Scottish Amicable

Scottish Amicable was taken over by Prudential Insurance on 30 September 1997. Members of Scottish Amicable holding with-profits life insurance policies which were taken out before 25 March 1997 qualified for two types of payments, a cash amount paid immediately and additions to the value of their with-profits life policies.

Cash Payments

These comprised a "fixed cash payment" of £250 plus a "variable cash payment" calculated as a percentage of the value of the "with-profits" policies held. These payments are treated for Capital Gains Tax purposes as received for the disposal of the membership rights held by the policyholder in Scottish Amicable. As nothing was paid for these rights, a chargeable gain equal to the full amount of those payments will arise.

Special Bonuses

The additions to the value of policies by way of "special bonuses" were made in a stated amount given on 1 October 1997 and an indeterminate further amount when the policy matures. These additions are treated in the same way as the normal annual bonuses which accrue on a with-profits life assurance policy. They are not chargeable to Capital Gains Tax either at the time they are added or when the policyholder is paid out on maturity of the policy, Section 210 TCGA 1992.

De-mutualisation Shares and Personal Equity Plans (PEPS)

Where shares are allotted or allocated to the investor, as a member, employee, former employee or pensioner of a building society or mutual insurance company, on the transfer of the business of the building society or mutual insurance company to a company on de-mutualisation

- in priority to other persons,
- for a consideration of an amount or value lower than the market price of the shares, or
- free

they may be transferred into a PEP at the price, if any, paid by the investor provided the shares are otherwise eligible for such a transfer. The price paid for the shares will count towards the subscription limit.

Investors must, within 42 calendar days (including the day of allotment or allocation), transfer the shares or letters of allotment to their plan manager. Where investors do not receive their share certificates or letters of allotment within those 42 days they must ensure the plan manager is in receipt, within the 42 day period, of all the necessary documentation to effect the transfer pending receipt of the share certificate or letter of allotment. Necessary documentation includes an application to subscribe and share transfer document.

Shares acquired by, or appropriated to, an individual who is an employee of the building society or mutual insurance company in accordance with the provisions of an approved all-employee savings related share option and/or profit-sharing scheme cannot be transferred into a general PEP. But such shares can be transferred into a single company PEP.

Investors can directly transfer de-mutualisation shares into a PEP, only where the shares are:

- allotted in their name,
- allotted in their capacity as an individual, and
- in their sole beneficial ownership.

So shares which are:

- allotted to a bare trustee,
- allotted to a guardian for a child,
- allotted to a personal representative of a deceased's estate, or
- allocated to the first named in a joint account

cannot be directly transferred into a PEP.

The legal ownership of some or all of the shares lies solely with the person in whose name they were allotted even though beneficial ownership of some or all of the shares rests with another person. Where shares are allotted to the first named in a joint account (and so are in the beneficial ownership of that investor and another person), the investor can transfer the shares into a PEP provided they have sole beneficial ownership of the shares before transfer.

A transfer of beneficial ownership from one person to another is a disposal for capital gains tax purposes. However, where the account is held by spouses, a transfer of ownership from one spouse to the other is not a chargeable disposal (Section 58(1) TCGA 1992).

Notes on the Valuation Table

The discount rates offered are not intended to be prescriptive but are a guide to an acceptable valuation for the qualifying member's share, or interest, in the society at the date of death. The amount of any discount will be lower the closer that date is to vesting day.

Society	Vesting day	Date of death between	Percentage discount	Anticipated share price/Cash bonus
Cheltenham & Gloucester	1.8.1995	10.8.1994–31.3.1995 1.4.1995–31.7.1995	35%–25% 10%–0%	Cash bonus £500 + 13.3%
National & Provincial	6.8.1996	28.2.1996–11.4.1996 12.4.1996–5.8.1996	27.5%–25% 10%–0%	£500 in Abbey National shares
Alliance & Leicester	22.4.1997	28.10.1996–10.12.1996 11.12.1996–21.4.1997	27.5%–25% 10%–0%	£3.97 per share

Society	Vesting day	Date of death between	Percentage discount	Anticipated share price/Cash bonus
Halifax	3.6.1997	11.1.1997–24.2.1997 25.2.1997–2.6.1997	30%–25% 7.5%–0%	11.1.1997–28.4.1997 £4.05 per share 29.4.1997–2.6.1997 £5.30 per share
Woolwich	8.7.1997	6.1.1997–11.2.1997 12.2.1997–7.7.1997	27.5%–25% 12.5–0%	£1.81 per share
Northern Rock	2.10.1997	17.2.1997–15.4.1997 16.4.1997–1.10.1997	27.5%–25% 12.5%–0%	£2.68 per share
Bristol & West	26.8.1997	27.2.1997–15.4.1997 16.4.1997–25.8.1997	30%–25% 10%–0%	Cash bonus 6.5% or £250 in Bank of Ireland shares
Greenwich	30.7.1997	13.5.1997–17.6.1997 18.6.1997–29.7.1997	27.5%–25% 5%–0%	Cash bonus 5%
Norwich Union	16.6.1997	18.4.1997–15.6.1997	5%–0%	£2.31 per share
Scottish Amicable	30.9.1997	27.5.1997–26.6.1997 27.6.1997–29.9.1997	27.5%–25% 7.5%–0%	Cash payment £550; immediate bonus £430; bonus on maturity £450
Colonial Mutual	23.5.1997	24.9.1996–10.11.1996 11.11.1996–22.5.1997	28%–25% 17.5%–0%	£1.30 per share

TB12/00-6 INHERITANCE TAX: ACCUMULATION & MAINTENANCE TRUSTS [HMRC Tax Bulletin 50, December 2000]

Most practitioners will be familiar with the inheritance tax (IHT) provisions for "Accumulation and Maintenance" trusts AMTs). Among other things, these provide exemption from the periodic IHT charge on discretionary trusts either:

- so long as all beneficiaries are grandchildren of a common grandparent (or a surviving spouse of such a grandchild);

  or

- in other cases, for a maximum period of 25 years since the test for AMTs were first satisfied.

The second category includes a significant class of trusts which were already in place when these rules for AMTs were finalised in 1976. So for all those which are still subject to this test, the grace period **ran** out on the same date 25 years on, at the close of 15 April 2001. Practitioners responsible for pre-75 AMTs may want to note that a charge potentially **arose** at this point. More generally, they will want to take note that IHT charges at the 25-year point will arise from then on for other trusts set up or modified since the mid-70s, at the particular anniversary dates appropriate to each trust.

In more detail

Trusts are liable to an IHT charge once they fail to qualify under Section 71 of the Inheritance Tax Act 1984 (IHTA) because they no longer meet the conditions for grandparent/ grandchildren or a 25 year period has elapsed.

The 25-year period runs from the latest of:

- 15 April 1976;
- the date the settlement commenced; and
- the date of attainment of accumulation and maintenance status.

Settlements *not* affected are those set up by a common grandparent for grandchildren, whether or not with contingency provision for the widow or widower of any grandchild who dies before becoming entitled to the property.

For those settlements which are affected, IHT is calculated at a flat rate (Section 71(5)) which tapers over time on property which ceases to be held on AMTs or when the trustees make a disposition which reduces *the value of the property*.

- 0.25% for each of the first 40 complete successive quarters in the relevant period;
- 0.20% for each of the next 40 complete successive quarters in the relevant period;
- 0.15% for each of the next 40 complete successive quarters in the relevant period.

Thereafter the normal rules for ten-yearly and proportionate charges for discretionary trusts apply to these settlements.

History – This interpretation shows the text as amended by Tax Bulletin, Issue 74 – see TB12/04-6. The amendments made are shown in bold.

TB10/01-3 INHERITANCE TAX: ACCUMULATION & MAINTENANCE TRUSTS [HMRC Tax Bulletin 55, October 2001]

An article in Tax Bulletin Issue 50 (December 2000) reminded practitioners that after the relevant period of 25 years has elapsed a settlement will only qualify under S71 of the Inheritance Tax Act 1984 so long as all beneficiaries are grandchildren of a common grandparent (or are a surviving spouse or child of such a grandchild).

We have been asked whether the mere existence of a power to appoint (which does not offend the conditions of S71(1)(a)) in favour of beneficiaries who are not grandchildren of a common grandparent will take the settlement outside the common grandparent rule. We have said that in our opinion the mere existence of such a power, as opposed to its actual exercise, does not take a trust outside the common grandparent category.

SPECIAL EDITION

SPECIAL EDITION JUNE 2005: SINGLE PAYMENT SCHEME [HMRC Tax Bulletin, Special Edition, June 2005]

This is an extract from this Special Edition relating directly to inheritance tax. The full text is reproduced in the income, corporation and capital gains tax section.

Introduction

This article sets out our views on the main points arising from the Single Payment Scheme. It has been prepared with the benefit of input from the National Farmers Union, the Institute of Chartered Accountants in England and Wales, the Institute of Chartered Accountants of Scotland, the Country Land and Business Association, the Agricultural Law Association and the Scottish Rural Property & Business Association. After giving briefly the background and an overview of the Scheme it deals in turn with:

- income tax charges
- the corporate intangible assets regime
- capital gains tax
- inheritance tax
- value added tax

There is a glossary of the main terms used in the article at Appendix 1. Appendix 2 reproduces, with permission, guidance on accounting issues arising from the Single Payment Scheme.

During the process of analysing the EU regulations for the purposes of this article we had to contend with a reform that was still evolving and indeed is continuing to do so. As a consequence this article represents our view as at May 2005. In future months the most up to date position will be available within HMRC published guidance material as indicated at the commencement of each section.

Background

The Common Agriculture Policy (CAP) of the European Union (EU) has undergone many changes in its lifetime. The latest reform package was finally agreed on 26 June 2003. The most notable change is the introduction of full decoupling (see below). At the time of writing the decoupled Single Payment Scheme (SPS) will replace all of the following direct aid schemes but it is possible others will be added as time goes by:

i. Arable Area Payments Scheme
ii. Beef Special Premium
iii. Dairy additional payments
iv. Dairy Premium
v. Extensification Payment Scheme
vi. Hops Income Aid
vii. Seed Production Aid
viii. Sheep Annual Premium Scheme
ix. Suckler Cow Premium Scheme

x. Slaughter Premium Scheme

xi. Veal Calf Slaughter Premium Scheme

It is worth noting that farmers who claim SP can also participate in other schemes including a range of agri-environmental schemes as well as new production linked schemes for energy crops, proteins and nuts.

Overview of the reforms

Direct payments to farmers are no longer linked to production, hence the term "decoupled". In effect this means that a farmer can cease to produce agricultural products altogether and still receive financial support. However, in order to receive the full Single Payment (SP) farmers must comply with a series of standards, collectively called Cross Compliance conditions, that include a range of existing statutory management requirements in areas such as environmental, public, animal and plant health and animal welfare as well as aspects that cover good farming and environmental practice. Failure to comply can result in penalties ranging from nominal amounts to 100% of the SP in serious or deliberate cases.

There is a one off opportunity in 2005 to receive payment entitlement (PE). Subject to other conditions being satisfied, PE is expected to provide income support for the next 8 years. After 2005 anyone who has not established entitlement but wishes to receive SP will have to buy, lease or otherwise acquire PE from another farmer. PE will be fully tradable but only within a region (of which there are 6 within the UK, England having been divided into three separate regions).

Each single payment covers a calendar year. It is funded from savings made from the disbanded schemes and payments are subject to a number of reductions (modulation, national reserve, and financial discipline), the overall effect of which will likely increase over the period and hence result in a decrease in the annual value of the SP. While the basic governance of the scheme is found in EU regulations there is sufficient latitude within these to allow for regional variations in its implementation. The differences do not in our view affect the tax treatment. But for completeness and to aid understanding the UK variations are mentioned below:

The Welsh system is based solely on claims in the reference period. In other words, the claims that each farmer made during the reference period divided by the number of hectares (ha) declared in 2005 form the basis of the amount the farmer is entitled to per ha. As a result each farmer will have bespoke PE values. Scotland adopted the same approach but reduced the SP of those that were beef producers in the reference period by 10%. This money will be used to fund the Scottish Beef Calf Scheme. This is a production related scheme but is subject to the same cross compliance conditions as the SP.

In England a flat rate payment system was selected, though its full implementation will be delayed until 2012. In the meantime there will be a sliding scale where an ever reducing part of the SP will consist of an historic component. Additionally, England has been divided into 3 regions, broadly corresponding to moorland, hill land and lowland with a different flat rate component paid in each. Farmers that have a claims history in the reference period and register in 2005 receive both a historic and a flat rate component to the SP. Those with no history and no national reserve entitlement that register a holding in 2005 will receive a SP consisting of the flat rate component only, though because of the sliding scale this will increase year on year until by 2012 this will be the whole of the SP.

Finally in Northern Ireland the system adopted is known as the "static vertical hybrid model". In short, the SP here consists of a historic and a flat rate component that will remain in the same proportions throughout.

The SPS has a number of features that mean payments may go to people other than those traditionally regarded as farmers. For example:

- PE are tradable. Original allocations will generally go to tenants but landlords will, in principle be able to acquire them from tenants; and
- the EU definition of farmer would allow someone to claim SP for grazing horses even though this may not be a farm in the traditionally accepted sense of the word.

There are a number of different types of PE that may be allocated to farmers. These include:

- Ordinary PE to which are attached the basic terms and conditions.
- Set aside entitlements: In addition to ordinary conditions, land must be set aside. These entitlements must be used before ordinary entitlements can be used.
- Special entitlements: different conditions apply, notably there must be a continuing level of livestock production.
- Authorised entitlements: allow farmers to grow negative list crops, broadly (soft) fruit, vegetables and potatoes.

To receive SP the farmer must first hold PE and then match each against an eligible hectare of land that is at the farmer's disposal for a minimum consecutive period of 10 months. To secure full payment the farmer must also comply with a series of cross compliance conditions. With the exception of PE that was allocated from the national reserve as a result of special circumstances (in which case tighter restrictions apply) if PE is not used within 3 years it is taken to the national reserve.

It is worth noting that PE is not permanently linked to the land. For those with land it is one of the components that allow entry to the SPS. For example the PE may be matched against land owned by the farmer in year one and a different parcel of land in year 2, which could even be land rented in. If a farmer had more PEs than eligible hectares the farmer can keep all the PEs by rotating them as long as they are used at least once every 3 years. PEs may be sold or otherwise traded with or without land (the latter subject to certain restrictions). Note there is a requirement that when PE is being leased it is leased with land. But if the land were rented for 11 months at a time, the actual PEs leased with a particular field could change from year to year.

…

Inheritance tax (IHT)

General

The permanent HMRC guidance on this topic will be incorporated in the IHT manual.

As with CGT, PE is subject to the normal IHT rules. So the following references to "transfers" include the most common occasion when an IHT charge arises, i.e. the transfer that is deemed to take place on death, where the value transferred at that time for IHT purposes is equivalent to the value of the deceased's estate immediately before death.

Transfers before 1 January 2005 of a farming business, or an interest in a farming business, whose value reflects the expectation of future PE should be valued for IHT purposes with the benefit of that expectation. Transfers of PE on or after 1 January 2005 (whether before or after actual establishment) are liable to IHT as any other asset.

Agricultural property relief (APR)

APR can apply to "agricultural property" only. This is defined in section 115(2) IHTA 1984 as agricultural land or pasture (including woodland and certain agricultural buildings). So PE itself, being an asset which is separate from land, cannot qualify for APR. (This will of course not affect the availability of APR for any other asset which does qualify as "agricultural property".)

APR applies to agricultural property which has been either occupied by the transferor for agricultural purposes for the two years immediately before the transfer, or owned by the transferor throughout the seven years immediately before the transfer and throughout that period has been occupied for agricultural purposes whether by the transferor or by another (section 117 IHTA).

Agricultural land which is taken out of production can still qualify for APR (including GAEC land) because section 117 IHTA does not require the land to be in production either continuously or at a specific time (though there must be an intention or expectation that the land will be back in production at some time in the future). So, for example, agricultural land set aside to rotational, or even permanent, fallow can still qualify as agricultural property within the definition of section 115(2) IHTA 1984 and as occupied for the purposes of agriculture within the meaning of section 117 IHTA.

Land used for grazing leisure horses does not satisfy the "occupied for the purposes of agriculture" test and so cannot qualify for APR.

Business property relief (BPR)

Land which formerly qualified for APR but which no longer does so (for example, because it ceases to be occupied for agricultural purposes) may nonetheless qualify for BPR if it is an asset of a trading business which satisfies the normal conditions of the relief.

BPR is available for transfers of "relevant business property" which the transferor has owned as such throughout the two years immediately before the transfer. "Relevant business property", which can qualify for BPR at 100 per cent, includes certain categories of business (or an interest in a business, for example a partnership interest) and some types of shares and securities. So in the normal case where the transferor is a farmer who has been farming for at least two years, PE (whether in expectancy pre-1/1/05, or on or after that date regardless of whether PE has actually been established) will qualify for 100 per cent BPR as an asset of the business, on the assumption, which will normally be the case, that the resulting payment will be used in the business or be required for future use in the business. PE will still qualify for BPR where the owner has put farmland out of production, for example into set-aside in order to receive SP, provided the farmer is still carrying on a business on a commercial basis, and provided the nature of the business remains essentially that of a trading concern rather than one that consists of dealing in land or making or holding investments.

As with any asset, the transfer of PE by someone who is not carrying on a trading business will not qualify for BPR. Similarly, the transfer of PE as an individual asset, rather than the business itself, or an interest in the business, will not qualify for BPR.

…

Appendix 1

Glossary of terms

Agricultural Property. Agricultural land or pasture and includes woodland and any building used in connection with intensive rearing of livestock or fish if the woodland or building is occupied with agricultural land or pasture and the occupation is ancillary to that of the agricultural land or pasture; and also includes such cottages, farm buildings and farmhouses, together with the land occupied with them, as are of a character appropriate to the property.

Cross Compliance Conditions. These set out standards and requirements that farmers have to meet as a condition of receiving their Single Payment. They are divided into:

- Statutory Management Requirements (SMR), involving compliance with a range of European regulatory requirements covering the environment, food safety, animal and plant health and animal welfare, and
- Good Agricultural and Environmental Conditions (GAEC). These are a set of requirements developed by individual member states and vary slightly between England, Scotland, Wales and Northern Ireland.

Farmer. For SP purposes this is defined in Regulation (EC) No 1782/03 as someone who exercises an agricultural activity and this covers all the usual farming activities but also keeping the land in good agricultural and environmental condition. The definition should also be taken to include growers of fruit and vegetables.

Farming. For income tax purposes this is defined as the occupation of land wholly or mainly for the purposes of husbandry, but does not include market gardening which has a separate definition.

Financial Discipline. The process by which from 2007 EU Farm Ministers will determine what percentage reductions are required to keep EU spending within budget.

Historic Basis. The method used to compute the value of PE based on the average of actual claims during the reference period of the person farming.

Modulation. The mechanism whereby a percentage of direct aid (subject to a lower threshold limit) is removed and recycled into Rural Development spending. UK regions will be subject to EU compulsory and member state voluntary modulation.

National Envelope. Is a sum of money taken from the reference amount and set aside to support a particular sector of farming. The only region to use the national envelope is Scotland and it is used there to support the beef industry

National Reserve. As a consequence of the transition to the Single Payment, farmers in certain situations may find themselves at a disadvantage for a variety of reasons. The National Reserve, funded by a percentage cut in all farmers' PE is a fund used to supplement PE to those disadvantaged or allocate PE to new entrants.

Negative list crops. The negative list crops are strictly the products referred to in Article 1(2) of Regulation (EC) No 2200/96 and potatoes, other than those intended for manufacture of potato starch. In this article the term has been used to denote fruit, vegetables and potatoes (fvp).

Payment Entitlement (PE). PEs are a requirement to participate in the SPS. They do not grant any automatic right to payment. A farmer with PE applying to join the SPS is further obliged to satisfy certain conditions before payment can be made and indeed full payment is subject to cross compliance. There a number of different types or "flavours" of entitlement. The basic or ordinary PE is amended to become:

- **Set aside entitlement**. Must be used before other entitlement. Land used to meet set aside entitlement must be withdrawn from agricultural production, including grazing for the duration of the set-aside period and be managed in accordance with the set-aside management rules. Organic farmers are exempted.
- **Special entitlement**. Are given to farmers with no eligible land or if the PE (arising from certain of the historic schemes) is more than 5000 euros. Unlike ordinary entitlements, special entitlements *have a production criterion.*
- **Authorised entitlements**. Are allocated to farmers who have grown negative list crops in the reference period and allow SP to be paid when land is used for growing fvp.

Reference Period. The 3 year period consisting of calendar years 2000 to 2002.

Region. A geographical area within the EU within which the SPS is administered. There are 6 in the UK. Scotland, Wales and N. Ireland are one each and England has been divided into 3. Land already categorised as severely disadvantaged (SDA) above the moor line, SDA below the moor line and the rest.

Regional Average or Flat Rate basis. The method used to compute the value of PE based on the average of claims made by all farmers within a member state in the reference period divided into the total area registered in 2005.

Single Payment (SP). A payment to farmers under the Single Payment Scheme.

Single Payment Scheme (SPS). The Single Payment Scheme introduced by EU regulation 1782/2003.

…

Region. A geographical area within the EU within which the SPS is administered. There are 6 in the UK. Scotland, Wales and N. Ireland are one each and England has been divided into 3. Land already categorised as severely disadvantaged (SDA) above the moor line, SDA below the moor line and the rest.

Regional Average or Flat Rate basis. The method used to compute the value of PE based on the average of claims made by all farmers within a member state in the reference period divided into the total area registered in 2005.

Single Payment (SP). A payment to farmers under the Single Payment Scheme.

Single Payment Scheme (SPS). The Single Payment Scheme introduced by EU regulation 1782/2003.

OTHER HMRC MATERIAL

PRESS RELEASES

12/2/76 INHERITANCE TAX: SETTLED PROPERTY – INTEREST IN POSSESSION [Press release, 12 February 1976]

The Board of Inland Revenue are aware that doubts have been expressed in the legal press and elsewhere concerning the precise scope of the term "interest in possession" as used in the Inheritance Tax Act 1984 (formerly FA 1975, Pt. III) and in particular about its application where an interest in settled property is subject to a discretion or power to accumulate the income of the property or to divert it elsewhere.

The Board therefore feel it appropriate, in view of the importance of the expression in IHTA 1984, Pt. III (formerly FA 1975, Sch. 5) to make known their understanding of the meaning of the expression. This is that an interest in possession in settled property exists where the person having the interest has the immediate entitlement (subject to any prior claim by the trustees for expenses or other outgoings properly payable out of income) to any income produced by that property as the income arises; but that a discretion or power, in whatever form, which can be exercised after income arises so as to withhold it from that person negatives the existence of an interest in possession. For this purpose a power to accumulate income is regarded as a power to withhold it, unless any accumulations must be held solely for the person having the interest or his personal representatives.

On the other hand the existence of a mere power of revocation or appointment, the exercise of which would determine the interest wholly or in part (but which, so long as it remains unexercised, does not affect the beneficiary's immediate entitlement to income) does not in the Board's view prevent the interest from being an interest in possession.

HMRC FACTSHEETS

CC/FS1a GENERAL INFORMATION ABOUT COMPLIANCE CHECKS [HMRC, January 2018]

We've given you this factsheet because we've started a compliance check. This factsheet contains important information. Please take the time to read it and keep it safe – you may need to refer to it during our check.

This factsheet is one of a series. For the full list of factsheets in the series, go to www.gov.uk and search for "Compliance checks factsheets".

What is a compliance check

We carry out checks into returns or other documents to make sure that our customers pay the right amount of tax at the right time and receive the right allowances and tax reliefs. We call these checks "compliance checks".

We carry out some checks over the phone. If we phone you, you can ask us to write to you instead. Some types of check can only be done within a certain time limit. The officer dealing with the check can explain these time limits to you. If we find something wrong we may extend our check, for example, we may check earlier periods.

What happens during a compliance check

We'll always tell you what we're checking. If we find that we need to extend the scope of our check, we'll tell you.

If you've appointed a representative, you can ask us to deal directly with them during our check. We may also tell them that we've started a check. We'll only give your representative details of the check if it relates to taxes that you've authorised us to contact them about. Information about how you can authorise a representative is on page 4 of this factsheet.

We'll ask you to give us any information or documents that we may need during the check. In some cases, we'll ask to visit your business premises, if you have any. We normally only ask to visit you at home if you run your business from there.

If you aren't sure why we're asking for something, please speak to the officer dealing with the check and they will explain why we need it. If you can't do what we ask, or if you think that something we have asked for is unreasonable or not relevant to the check, please tell the officer dealing with the check. They will consider your reasons carefully and if they still think they need it, they will tell you why.

If you have any questions at any stage of our check, please contact the officer dealing with the check.

What if you need more time to do something we've asked you to do

If you need more time to do something we've asked you to do, please tell us. If we think it's reasonable to do so, we'll allow you more time. You can also ask us to postpone the check if you have a good reason, for example, if you're seriously ill or someone close to you has died.

The benefits of helping us with a check

Helping us with our check can have benefits for you. It will allow us to complete the check as quickly as possible and reduce any inconvenience that it may cause you.

We may not find anything wrong. But if there's something wrong, helping us with our check will also reduce the amount of any penalty we may charge.

If we do find something wrong, we'll work with you to put it right. We'll also tell you about any additional tax and late payment interest that is due, and about any penalty that we may charge.

You can reduce the amount of any penalty by giving us assistance throughout our check. We call this assistance the "quality of disclosure" or "telling, helping and giving".

We measure the quality of disclosure by considering how much:

- you tell us about what is wrong
- help you give us to work out what is wrong
- access you give us to your records

If we ask you for either of the following:

- information or documents and you don't provide these when we ask for them
- to visit your business premises to inspect your business records, assets or premises or to visit your premises to carry out a valuation and you refuse

this may affect our view on the quality of disclosure, and the amount by which we reduce any penalty.

How to qualify for the maximum penalty reduction if something is wrong

If you know or suspect that there's something wrong, you must:

- tell us everything you know about what's wrong as soon as we tell you that we've started a check
- work with us to calculate the right amount of tax

If we've found something wrong that you didn't know about, you must:

- have given us as much assistance as we needed up to that point
- as soon as we tell you that there is something wrong, tell the officer dealing with the check everything about it, let them see any additional records they need and help them to work out the right amount of tax

We'll reduce the penalty by the maximum amount possible if we agree that you've done everything you could to assist us.

When we work out the quality of disclosure, we'll take into account how long it has taken for you to tell us about the inaccuracy. If you've taken a significant period (normally 3 years) to correct or disclose the inaccuracy, we'll normally restrict the amount of reduction given for disclosure.

We'll restrict the penalty range by 10 percentage points above the minimum to reflect the time taken, before working out the reductions for telling, helping and giving.

You can find more information about penalties and penalty reductions in our penalty factsheets. Go to www.gov.uk and search for "Compliance checks factsheets". In some circumstances we can publish the details of people who have deliberately got their tax affairs wrong, as well as charging them a penalty. We can't publish their details if they qualify for the maximum penalty reduction. You can find more information about this below.

What if you think we should stop the check

If you think we should stop the check, please tell us why. If we don't agree, you may in some cases be able to ask the independent tribunal that deals with tax matters to decide whether we should stop the check.

What happens if something is wrong

If something is wrong, we'll explain why and work with you to put it right. Where relevant, we'll also tell *you how to prevent it happening again.* We may also ask you to sign a certificate confirming that you've told us about all relevant facts relating to our check.

If you're due to pay us some money, we'll tell you how to pay. You may also have to pay interest and any penalty that we charge. If we owe you some money, we'll normally repay you or credit your account. In some cases, we'll also pay you interest.

What happens if you've deliberately done something wrong

We may carry out a criminal investigation with a view to prosecution if you:

- give us information that you know to be untrue, whether verbally or in a document
- dishonestly misrepresent your liability to tax or claim payments to which you aren't entitled

Managing Serious Defaulters

If you've deliberately got your tax affairs wrong, we may need to monitor your tax affairs more closely. We've an enhanced monitoring programme called Managing Serious Defaulters. You can find more information about this in factsheet CC/FS14, "Managing Serious Defaulters". Go to www.gov.uk and search for "CC/FS14".

Publishing details of deliberate defaulters

In certain circumstances we may publish your details if you've deliberately got your tax affairs wrong. We can't publish your details if you qualify for the maximum penalty reduction. You can find more information in factsheet CC/FS13, "Publishing details of deliberate defaulters". Go to www.gov.uk and search for "CC/FS13".

What happens at the end of a check

We'll finish our check by either sending you one or more "decision notices" or by agreeing a contract settlement with you.

A decision notice can be:

- an assessment or amendment to an assessment
- a penalty notice if a penalty is due
- a letter setting out what the final position is

A contract settlement is a legally binding agreement, where you offer to pay everything that is due as a result of our check, and we agree not to use our formal powers to recover that amount. You can only pay through a contract settlement if both you and we agree to this and to the terms of the contract. We can't enter into a contract settlement for any VAT or VAT penalties that are due.

What if you can't pay what you owe

If you think you may have problems paying, please tell the officer dealing with the check.

What to do if you disagree

If there's something that you don't agree with, you should tell us.

If we make a decision that you can appeal against we'll write to you to explain the decision and tell you what to do if you disagree. You'll usually have 3 options. Within 30 days you can:

- send new information to the officer you've been dealing with and ask them to take it into account
- have your case reviewed by an HMRC officer who hasn't been involved in the matter
- arrange for your appeal to be heard by an independent tribunal, who'll decide the matter

Whichever you choose, you may also be able to ask for an HMRC specialist officer to act as a neutral facilitator to help resolve the dispute. This process is known as Alternative Dispute Resolution (ADR).

ADR is only available for disputes relating to some of the taxes and other areas that we administer. The officer dealing with your check will tell you if ADR is available for the matter that you're disputing.

You can find more information in:

- HMRC1, "HM Revenue & Customs decisions – what to do if you disagree", for appeals and reviews
- CC/FS21, "Alternative Dispute Resolution", for ADR
- Go to www.gov.uk and search for "HMRC1" and "CC/FS21".

Your principal rights and obligations

You have:

- the right to be represented – you can appoint anyone to act on your behalf, including professional advisers, friends or relatives
- the right to consult your adviser – we'll allow a reasonable amount of time for you to do so
- an obligation to take care to get things right – if you have an adviser, you must still take reasonable care to make sure that any returns, documents or details they send us on your behalf are correct

"Your Charter" explains what you can expect from us and what we expect from you. For more information, go to www.gov.uk/hmrc/your-charter

Your rights when we're considering penalties

If there's something wrong and we're considering penalties, we'll tell you. The European Convention on Human Rights gives you certain rights when we're considering penalties. You can find full details about these rights in factsheet CC/FS9, "The Human Rights Act and penalties". Go to www.gov.uk and search for "CC/FS9".

Authorising a representative

You can authorise someone to deal with us on your behalf. This includes professional tax advisers, friends or relatives. They can deal with us just for a compliance check, or more permanently for your day-to-day tax affairs. If you want to authorise a professional tax adviser, they will give you a form to complete and send to us. If you want to authorise someone other than a professional tax adviser, you'll need to write to tell us who you want to authorise and what you want them to deal with for you.

This factsheet relates to compliance checks into any of the following:

Aggregates Levy
Annual Tax on Enveloped Dwellings
Apprenticeship Levy**
Bank Payroll Tax
Capital Gains Tax
Climate Change Levy
Construction Industry Scheme
Corporation Tax
Income Tax
Inheritance Tax
Insurance Premium Tax
Landfill Tax
Machine Games Duty
National Insurance Classes 1, 1A* and 4
Pay As You Earn (PAYE)
Petroleum Revenue Tax
Stamp Duty Tax
Stamp Duty Reserve Tax
VAT

* For Class 1A National Insurance, this factsheet only relates to P11D(b) returns for tax years starting on or after 6 April 2010.

** For Apprenticeship Levy, this factsheet relates to returns for tax years starting on or after 6 April 2017.

More information

HMRC may observe, monitor, record and retain internet data which is available to anyone. This is known as "open source" material and includes news reports, internet sites, Companies House and Land registry records, blogs and social networking sites where no privacy settings have been applied.

Our personal information charter sets out the standards you can expect from us when we request or hold information about you, go to www.gov.uk/government/organisations/hm-revenue-customs/about/personal-information-charter

Customers with particular needs

If there's anything about your health or personal circumstances that may make it difficult for you to deal with this check, please tell the officer that is carrying out the check. Telling them will mean that they can help you in the most appropriate way. For more details go to www.gov.uk/dealing-hmrc-additional-needs

Don't stop sending returns or making payments. During the compliance check, please carry on sending returns and making payments when they are due.

Benefits, fees, grants and tax credits

If you're receiving any benefits, fees or grants that are based on your income, and your income changes as a result of this check, you'll need to tell the organisation that is paying you. If you're receiving tax credits and your income changes as a result of this check, you must tell the Tax Credit Office. You can phone 0345 300 3900 or write to us, marking your envelope "Change of circumstances", to:

Tax Credit Office
PRESTON
PR1 4AT

What if you're unhappy with our service

If you're unhappy with our service, please tell the person or office you've been dealing with. They will try to put things right. If you're still unhappy, they will tell you how to complain.

CC/FS1b GENERAL INFORMATION ABOUT CHECKS BY CAMPAIGNS AND PROJECTS [HMRC, January 2018]

We've given you this factsheet because we've started a compliance check. This factsheet contains important information. Please take the time to read it and keep it safe – you may need to refer to it during our check.

This factsheet is one of a series. For the full list of the factsheets in the series, go to www.gov.uk and search for "Compliance checks factsheets".

What is a compliance check

We carry out checks into returns or other documents to make sure that our customers pay the right amount of tax at the right time and receive the right allowances and tax reliefs. We call these checks "compliance checks".

We carry out some checks over the phone. If we phone you, you can ask us to write to you instead. Some types of check can only be done within a certain time limit. Please ask us if you would like us to explain these time limits to you. If we find something wrong we may extend our check, for example, we may check earlier periods.

What happens during a compliance check

We'll always tell you what we're checking. If we find that we need to extend the scope of our check, we'll tell you.

If you've appointed a representative, you can ask us to deal directly with them during our check. We may also tell them that we've started a check. We'll only give your representative details of the check if it relates to taxes that you've authorised us to contact them about. Information about how you can authorise a representative is on page 4 of this factsheet.

We'll ask you to give us any information or documents that we may need during our check

If you're not sure why we're asking for something, please ask us and we'll explain why we need it. If you can't do what we ask, or if you think that something we've asked for is unreasonable or not relevant to the check, please tell us. We'll consider your reasons carefully and if we still think we need it, we'll tell you why. If you have any questions at any stage of our check, please tell us.

The benefits of helping us with a check

Helping us with our check can have benefits for you. It will allow us to complete the check as quickly as possible and reduce any inconvenience that it may cause you.

We may not find anything wrong with the return or document we're checking. But if there is something wrong, helping us with our check will also reduce the amount of any penalty we may charge.

If we do find something wrong, we'll work with you to put it right. We'll also tell you about any additional tax and "late payment" interest that is due, and about any penalty we may charge.

You can reduce the amount of any penalty by giving us assistance throughout our check. We call this assistance the "quality of disclosure" or "telling, helping and giving".

We measure the quality of disclosure by considering how much:

- you tell us about what is wrong
- help you give us to work out what is wrong
- access you give us to your records

If we ask you for information or documents and you don't provide these when we ask for them, this may affect the amount by which we reduce any penalty.

How to qualify for the maximum penalty reduction if something is wrong

If you know or suspect that there's something wrong, you must:

- tell us everything you know about what's wrong as soon as we tell you that we've started a check
- work with us to calculate the right amount of tax

If we've found something wrong that you didn't know about, you must:

- have given us as much help as we needed up to that point
- as soon as we tell you that there is something wrong, tell us everything about it, let us see any additional records we need and help us to work out the right amount of tax

We'll reduce the penalty by the maximum amount possible if we agree that you've done everything you could to help us.

When we work out the quality of disclosure, we'll take into account how long it has taken you to tell us about the inaccuracy. If you've taken a significant period (normally 3 years) to correct or disclose the inaccuracy, we'll normally restrict the amount of reduction given for disclosure.

We'll restrict the penalty range by 10 percentage points above the minimum to reflect the time taken, before working out the reductions for telling, helping and giving.

You can find more information about penalties and penalty reductions in our penalty factsheets. Go to www.gov.uk and search for "Compliance checks factsheets".

In some circumstances we can publish the details of people who have deliberately got their tax affairs wrong, as well as charging them a penalty. We can't publish their details if they qualify for the maximum penalty reduction.

You can find more information about this below.

What if you need more time to do something we've asked you to do

If you need more time to do something we've asked you to do, please tell us. If we think it's reasonable to do so, we'll allow you more time. You can also ask us to postpone the check if you have a good reason, for example, if you're seriously ill or someone close to you has died.

What if you think we should stop the check

If you think we should stop the check, please tell us why. If we don't agree, you may in some cases be able to ask the independent tribunal that deals with tax matters to decide whether we should stop the check.

What happens if something is wrong

If something's wrong, we'll explain why and work with you to put it right. Where relevant, we'll also tell you how to prevent it happening again. If you're due to pay us some money, we'll tell you how to pay. You may also have to pay interest and any penalty that we charge. If we owe you some money, we'll normally repay you or credit your account. In some cases we'll also pay you interest.

What happens if you've deliberately done something wrong

We may carry out a criminal investigation with a view to prosecution if you:

- give us information that you know to be untrue, whether verbally or in a document
- dishonestly misrepresent your liability to tax or claim payments to which you aren't entitled

Managing Serious Defaulters

If you've deliberately got your tax affairs wrong, we may need to monitor your tax affairs more closely.

We've an enhanced monitoring programme called Managing Serious Defaulters. You can find more information about this in factsheet CC/FS14, "Managing Serious Defaulters". Go to www.gov.uk and search for "CC/FS14".

Publishing details of deliberate defaulters

In certain circumstances, we may publish your details if you've deliberately got your tax affairs wrong. We can't publish your details if you qualify for the maximum penalty reduction. You can find more information in factsheet CC/FS13, "Publishing details of deliberate defaulters"Go to www.gov.uk and search for "CC/FS13".

What happens at the end of a check

We'll finish our check by sending you one or more "decision notices". A decision notice can be:

- an assessment or amendment to an assessment
- a penalty notice if a penalty is due
- a letter setting out what the final position is

What if you can't pay what you owe

If you think you may have problems paying, please tell the officer dealing with the check.

What to do if you disagree

If there's something that you don't agree with, you should tell us.

If we make a decision that you can appeal against we'll write to you to explain the decision and tell you what to do if you disagree. You'll usually have 3 options. Within 30 days you can:

- send new information to the officer you've been dealing with and ask them to take it into account
- have your case reviewed by an HMRC officer who hasn't been involved in the matter
- arrange for your appeal to be heard by an independent tribunal, who will decide the matter

Whichever you choose, you may also be able to ask for an HMRC specialist officer to act as a neutral facilitator to help resolve the dispute. This process is known as "Alternative Dispute Resolution" (ADR). ADR is only available for disputes relating to some of the taxes and other areas that we administer.

The officer dealing with your check will tell you if ADR is available for the matter that you are disputing.

You can find more information in:

- HMRC1, "HM Revenue & Customs decisions – what to do if you disagree", for appeals and reviews
- CC/FS21, "Alternative Dispute Resolution", for ADR

Go to www.gov.uk and search for "HMRC1" and "CC/FS21".

Your principal rights and obligations

You have:

- the right to be represented – you can appoint anyone to act on your behalf, this includes professional advisers, friends or relatives
- the right to consult your adviser – we'll allow a reasonable amount of time for you to do so
- an obligation to take care to get things right – if you have an adviser, you must still take reasonable care to make sure that any returns, documents or details they send us on your behalf are correct

"Your Charter" explains what you can expect from us and what we expect from you. For more information, go to www.gov.uk/hmrc/your-charter

Your rights when we're considering penalties

If there's something wrong and we're considering penalties, we'll tell you. The European Convention on Human Rights gives you certain rights when we're considering penalties. You can find full details about these rights in factsheet CC/FS9, "The Human Rights Act and penalties". Go to www.gov.uk and search for "CC/FS9".

Authorising a representative

You can authorise someone to deal with us on your behalf. This includes professional tax advisers, friends or relatives. They can deal with us just for a compliance check, or more permanently for your day-to-day tax affairs.

If you want to authorise a professional tax adviser, they will give you a form to complete and send to us. If you want to authorise someone other than a professional tax adviser, you'll need to write to tell us who you want to authorise and what you want them to deal with for you.

This factsheet relates to compliance checks into any of the following:

Aggregates Levy	Insurance Premium Tax
Annual Tax on Enveloped Dwellings	Landfill Tax
Apprenticeship Levy**	Machine Games Duty
Bank Payroll Tax	National Insurance Classes 1, 1A* and 4
Capital Gains Tax	Pay As You Earn (PAYE)
Climate Change Levy	Petroleum Revenue Tax
Construction Industry Scheme	Stamp Duty Land Tax
Corporation Tax	Stamp Duty Reserve Tax
Income Tax	VAT
Inheritance Tax	

* For Class 1A National Insurance, this factsheet only relates to P11D(b) returns for tax years starting on or after 6 April 2010.

** For Apprenticeship Levy, this factsheet only relates to returns for the tax years starting on or after 6 April 2017

More information

HMRC may observe, monitor, record and retain internet data which is available to anyone. This is known as "open source" material and includes news reports, internet sites, Companies House and Land registry records, blogs and social networking sites where no privacy settings have been applied.

Our personal information charter sets out the standards you can expect from us when we request or hold information about you, go to www.gov.uk/government/organisations/hm-revenue-customs/about/personal-information-charter

Customers with particular needs

If there's anything about your health or personal circumstances that may make it difficult for you to deal with this check, please tell the officer that's carrying out the check. Telling them will mean that they can help you in the most appropriate way. For more details go to www.gov.uk/dealing-hmrc-additional-needs

Don't stop sending returns or making payments

During the compliance check, please carry on sending returns and making payments when they're due.

Benefits, fees, grants and tax credits

If you're receiving any benefits, fees or grants that are based on your income, and your income changes as a result of this check, you'll need to tell the organisation that is paying you. If you're receiving tax credits and your income changes as a result of this check, you must tell the Tax Credit Office. You can phone 0345 300 3900 or write, marking your envelope "change of circumstances", to:

HM Revenue and Customs
Tax Credit Office
PRESTON
PR1 4AT

What if you're unhappy with our service

If you're unhappy with our service, please tell the person or office you have been dealing with. They will try to put things right. If you're still unhappy, they will tell you how to complain.

CC/FS1c GENERAL INFORMATION ABOUT COMPLIANCE CHECKS INTO CERTAIN LARGE AND COMPLEX BUSINESSES [HMRC, January 2018]

This factsheet gives you general information about compliance checks into businesses that have been allocated a HMRC Customer Compliance Manager (CCM) because of their size or the complexity of their tax affairs. This factsheet contains important information. Please take the time to read it and keep it safe – you may need to refer to it during our check.

This factsheet is one of a series. For the full list of the factsheets in the series, go to www.gov.uk and search for "Compliance checks factsheets".

How we work with these large and complex businesses

The tax affairs of the largest and most complex businesses are looked after by the Large Business part of HMRC. Each is allocated a CCM who manages HMRC's compliance activities and the relationship between the business and HMRC across all taxes and duties. Our CCMs work with these large business customers to identify, check and manage tax risk.

Our approach aims to build a transparent and trusting relationship with these businesses. We want to ensure quicker resolution of issues and proportionate use of resources in addressing tax risks, to keep compliance costs down. To do this, we'll:

- be open and transparent in our interactions with you
- expect that you'll interact openly and transparently with us
- work with you to explore tax risks that we, or you, identify
- discuss those risks with you in the first instance, before considering the use of formal powers

We may however need to use our formal powers or issue an assessment notice under certain circumstances. Examples include:

- if you prefer a formal approach
- a time limit for making an assessment is approaching
- where we've been unable to resolve an issue and need to formally request information from you
- where the issue is likely to be taken before an independent appeal tribunal for a decision

About compliance checks

We carry out checks into returns or other documents to make sure that our customers pay the right amount of tax at the right time and receive the right allowances and tax reliefs. We call these checks "compliance checks". Before we start a compliance check, we'll normally discuss our concerns with you.

If we start a check, we'll tell you what we're checking. We'll ask you to give us any information or documents that we may need. If you aren't sure why we're asking for something, please tell us and we'll explain why we need it. If you can't do what we ask, or if you think that something we've asked for is unreasonable or not relevant to the check, please tell us. We'll consider your reasons carefully and if we still think that we need it, we'll tell you why.

The benefits of helping us with a check

If there's something wrong, we'll work with you to put it right and to determine the amount of any additional tax, "late payment" interest and penalties that may be due. Working with us will reduce the amount of any penalties that we may charge.

When we're considering penalties, we refer to the assistance that you give us as the "quality of disclosure", or "telling, helping and giving".

We measure the quality of disclosure by considering how much:

- you tell us about what is wrong
- help you give us to work out what is wrong
- access you give us to your records

If we ask you for either of the following:

- information or documents and you don't provide these when we ask for them
- to visit your business premises to inspect your business records, assets or premises, or to visit your premises to carry out a valuation and you refuse

this may affect our view on the quality of disclosure, and the amount by which we reduce any penalty.

How to qualify for the maximum penalty reduction if something is wrong

If you know or suspect that there's something wrong, you must:

- tell us everything you know about what's wrong straightaway
- work with us to calculate the right amount of tax

If we've found something wrong that you didn't know about, you must:

- have given us as much help as we needed up to that point
- as soon as we tell you that there is something wrong, tell us everything about it, let us see any additional records we need and help us to work out the right amount of tax

We'll reduce the penalty by the maximum amount possible if we agree that you've done everything you could to assist us.

When we work out the quality of disclosure, we'll take into account how long it has taken you to tell us about the inaccuracy. If you've taken a significant period (normally 3 years) to correct or disclose the inaccuracy, we'll normally restrict the amount of reduction given for disclosure.

We'll restrict the penalty range by 10 percentage points above the minimum to reflect the time taken, before working out the reductions for telling, helping and giving.

If you delay telling us, you may still be entitled to a reduction but it will be smaller. You can find more information about penalties and penalty reductions in our penalty factsheets. Go to www.gov.uk and search for "Compliance checks factsheets".

In some circumstances we can publish the details of people who have deliberately got their tax affairs wrong, as well as charging them a penalty. We can't publish their details if they qualify for the maximum penalty reduction. You can find more information about this below.

What if you need more time to do something we've asked you to do

If you need more time to do something we've asked you to do, please tell us. If we think it's reasonable to do so, we'll allow you more time.

What happens if you've deliberately done something wrong

We may carry out a criminal investigation with a view to prosecution if you:

- give us information that you know to be untrue, whether verbally or in a document
- dishonestly misrepresent your liability to tax or claim payments to which you aren't entitled

Managing Serious Defaulters

If you've deliberately got your tax affairs wrong, we may need to monitor your tax affairs more closely. We've an enhanced monitoring programme called Managing Serious Defaulters. You can find more information about this in factsheet CC/FS14, "Managing Serious Defaulters". Go to www.gov.uk and search for "CC/FS14".

Publishing details of deliberate defaulters

In certain circumstances, we may publish your details if you've deliberately got your tax affairs wrong. We can't publish your details if you qualify for the maximum penalty reduction. You can find more information in factsheet CC/FS13, "Publishing details of deliberate defaulters". Go to www.gov.uk and search for "CC/FS13".

What to do if you disagree

If there's something that you don't agree with, you should tell us.

If we make a decision that you can appeal against we'll write to you to explain the decision and tell you what to do if you disagree. You'll usually have 3 options. Within 30 days you can:

- send new information to your CCM and ask them to take it into account
- have your case reviewed by an HMRC officer who hasn't been involved in the matter
- arrange for your appeal to be heard by an independent tribunal, who'll decide the matter

Whichever you choose, you may also be able to ask for a HMRC specialist officer to act as a neutral facilitator to help resolve the dispute. This process is known as "Alternative Dispute Resolution" (ADR). In most Large Business cases you should expect the CCM to work with you to resolve disputes.

ADR is only available for disputes relating to some of the taxes and other areas that we administer. Your CCM will tell you if ADR is available for the matter that you're disputing.

You can find more information in:

- HMRC1, "HM Revenue & Customs decisions – what to do if you disagree", for appeals and reviews
- CC/FS21, "Alternative Dispute Resolution", for ADR
- Go to www.gov.uk and search for "HMRC1" and "CC/FS21".

Your principal rights and obligations

You have:

- the right to be represented – you can appoint anyone to act on your behalf including professional advisers
- the right to consult your adviser – we'll allow a reasonable amount of time for you to do so
- an obligation to take care to get things right – if you have an adviser, you must still take reasonable care to make sure that any returns, documents or details they send us on your behalf are correct

"Your Charter" explains what you can expect from us and what we expect from you. For more information, go to www.gov.uk/hmrc/your-charter

Your rights when we're considering penalties

If there's something wrong and we're considering penalties, we'll tell you. The European Convention on Human Rights gives you certain rights when we're considering certain penalties. You can find full details about these rights in factsheet CC/FS9, "The Human Rights Act and penalties". Go to www.gov.uk and search for "CC/FS9".

This factsheet relates to compliance checks into any of the following:

Aggregates Levy	Income Tax
Air Passenger Duty	Inheritance Tax
Alcoholic Liquor Duties	Insurance Premium Tax
Amusement Machine Licence Duty	Landfill Tax
Annual Tax on Enveloped Dwellings	Lottery Duty
Apprenticeship Levy**	Machine Games Duty
Bank Payroll Tax	National Insurance Classes 1,1a* and 4
Bingo Duty	Pay As You Earn (PAYE)
Capital Gains Tax	Petroleum Revenue Tax
Climate Change Levy	Pool Betting Duty
Construction Industry Scheme	Remote Gaming Duty
Corporation Tax	Stamp Duty Land Tax

Excise Duties (Holding and Movements)
Gaming Duty
General Betting Duty
Hydrocarbon Oils Duty
Stamp Duty Reserve Tax
Tobacco Products Duty
VAT

* For Class 1A National Insurance this factsheet only relates to P11D(b) returns for tax years starting on or after 6 April 2010.

** For Apprenticeship Levy, this factsheet relates to returns for tax year years starting on or after 6 April 2017.

More information

HMRC may observe, monitor, record and retain internet data which is available to anyone. This is known as "open source" material and includes news reports, internet sites, Companies House and Land registry records, blogs and social networking sites where no privacy settings have been applied.

Our Personal information charter sets out the standards you can expect from us when we request or hold information about you, go to www.gov.uk/government/organisations/hm-revenue-customs/about/personal-information-charter

What if you're unhappy with our service

If you're unhappy with our service, please tell your CCM. They will try to put things right. If you're still unhappy, they will tell you how to complain.

CC/FS3 VISITS – BY AGREEMENT OR WITH ADVANCE NOTICE [HMRC, December 2017]

As part of a compliance check, we may ask to visit your business premises if you have any. This is so that we can look at your records or business assets and find out more about how your business operates. We only visit if we think it's necessary. A visit can help us complete the check more quickly and effectively.

How we arrange a visit

We normally carry out visits with your agreement. We'll contact you by phone or letter to arrange a date and time for the visit. We'll usually give you at least 7 days notice. If you need to change the appointment, please tell us as soon as possible.

If we've not been able to get your agreement to a visit, we may still need to visit your business premises to carry out an inspection. If we do, we'll normally give you advance notice. We'll also give you a notice of inspection. This is a legal document that allows us to inspect your business premises, assets and statutory records. Statutory records are the records that tax laws say a person must keep.

In some circumstances we may carry out an inspection without giving advance notice or seeking agreement. You can find more information about this in factsheet CC/FS4, "Unannounced visits for inspections" and CC/FS5, "Unannounced visits for inspections approved by the tribunal". You can get a copy of these factsheets online. Go to www.gov.uk and search for "Compliance checks factsheets".

If you don't think we should visit, please tell us why. We'll explain why we want to visit you and why we think a visit is the best way to carry out our check. There may be other ways for us to get the information we need.

About the visit

You don't have to be present at the visit, but it'll be helpful if you are. This will allow us to ask you any questions we may have about your business and how it operates, and discuss the outcome of the visit with you. This will also help us complete the check as quickly as possible and reduce any inconvenience that it may cause you.

If you can't be there, someone else must be there to give us access to any assets or records that we need to see. We'll normally tell you in advance what records or assets we need to see. If we've given you a notice of inspection, this will give you details of what we need to inspect and when.

If you have an adviser we may contact them to tell them about our check. You can ask your adviser to be there when we visit. If you prefer, we may be able to look at your records in your adviser's office or in our office. Please tell us if this is the case.

A visit can take anything from a few hours to a few days. This will depend on the size of the business and the complexity of the matters we're looking at. When we arrange the visit, we'll let you know how long we expect it to take.

We don't usually need to talk to people who work for you about our check. However, we may ask to speak to the people who keep your records up to date, such as payroll and finance records. We may also need to speak to some of the people who work for you if we're looking at their employment status. If you don't want them to know about our visit, please tell us.

We may need to take some of your records away to check in our own office. If we do, we'll explain why. We'll give you a receipt for your records, keep them secure and return them to you as soon as we can. If you need them back sooner, we'll make copies in our office and give these to you.

If you have any business assets that are kept somewhere other than the premises we're visiting (for example, if you have more than one premises), we may need to arrange a further visit to see them.

If you run your business from home

We'll normally only ever ask to visit you at home if you run your business from there. We may, however, need to value your private premises to check your Income Tax or Corporation Tax liability. We may also need to value property in your private premises. This is to check your liability to Stamp Duty Land Tax, Stamp Duty Reserve Tax or Inheritance Tax, or to check any liabilities that relate to Capital Gains Tax.

Please tell us in advance if your business premises are also your home, or if you keep any stock or other assets at home. The visiting officer will only be able to enter those parts of your home which are used for business purposes unless you invite them in or we're carrying out a valuation. If we visit you at your home without knowing in advance that it's your home, we'll only come in if you give your permission.

If we've given you a notice of inspection and you fail to comply with it

If we give you a notice of inspection and you don't allow us to carry out the inspection, we may ask an independent tribunal to approve an inspection. If they approve an inspection and you still don't allow us to carry it out, we'll charge you a £300 penalty. You might also have to pay further penalties of up to £60 a day until you allow us to carry out the inspection.

If you have a reasonable excuse for not allowing us to carry out an inspection that's been approved by the tribunal, we won't charge you a penalty. Please tell us straightaway if you think you have a reasonable excuse.

A reasonable excuse is something that stopped you from meeting a tax obligation on time which you took reasonable care to meet. It might be due to circumstances outside your control or a combination of events. Once the reasonable excuse has ended, you must put things right without any unnecessary delay.

Whether you have a reasonable excuse depends upon the particular circumstances in which the failure occurred and your particular circumstances and abilities. This may mean that what is a reasonable excuse for one person may not be a reasonable excuse for someone else. If you think you have a reasonable excuse please tell us. If we accept that you have a reasonable excuse, we won't charge you a penalty.

Examples of reasonable excuse may include, when:

- you have been seriously ill
- someone close to you has died
- you have had a flood or a fire

The Human Rights Act and your privacy

Article 8 of the Human Rights Act gives you the right to respect for your private and family life, your home and your correspondence. We've the right to carry out an inspection in a reasonable and proportionate way even when it conflicts with your rights. If you think our inspection is not reasonable and proportionate, tell us why.

Concealing, destroying or otherwise disposing of documents

We may charge you a penalty if you or another person acting on your behalf conceals, destroys, or disposes of any document that we:

- have asked for in an information notice
- told you that we intend to ask for in an information notice

It's a criminal offence to conceal, destroy or otherwise dispose of any of document that we:

- have asked for in an information notice that has been approved by the tribunal
- told you that we intend to ask for in an information notice that has been approved by the tribunal

We may carry out a criminal investigation with a view to prosecution if you or someone acting on your behalf commits this offence.

What happens if you give us information that you know to be untrue

We may carry out a criminal investigation with a view to prosecution if you:

- give us information that you know to be untrue, whether verbally or in a document
- dishonestly misrepresent your liability to tax or claim payments to which you're not entitled

CC/FS4 UNANNOUNCED VISITS FOR INSPECTIONS [HMRC, December 2017]

We're visiting you to carry out an inspection as part of our check of your tax affairs. We've decided that an unannounced visit is the best way to carry out our inspection.

Please take the time to read this factsheet as it gives you important information about this visit and your rights.

About unannounced visits or inspections

As well as giving you this factsheet, our officer will:

- show you their identification
- give you a notice of inspection
- give you a copy of the relevant "General information" factsheet, which tells you about our compliance checks

The notice of inspection is a legal authorisation that allows us to carry out the inspection. It's been authorised by a senior HMRC officer. Before they authorised the inspection, they'll have considered whether we could have got the information we need in another way.

You have the right to seek advice about the inspection, but we won't delay carrying out our inspection while you do this.

Do you have to allow this inspection to take place

If you don't let us carry out the inspection, we can ask an independent tribunal to approve the inspection. If they approve it and you still refuse to let us carry it out, we'll charge you a £300 penalty. You might also have to pay further penalties of up to £60 a day until you let us carry out the inspection.

If this visit is at an inconvenient time, in some circumstances we may agree to visit you at another time.

If you have a reasonable excuse for not allowing the inspection to take place

If you have a reasonable excuse for not allowing us to carry out an inspection, we won't charge you a penalty. Please tell us straightaway if you think you have a reasonable excuse.

A reasonable excuse is something that stopped you from meeting a tax obligation on time which you took reasonable care to meet. It might be due to circumstances outside your control or a combination of events. Once the reasonable excuse has ended, you must put things right without any unnecessary delay.

Whether you have a reasonable excuse depends upon the particular circumstances in which the failure occurred and your particular circumstances and abilities. This may mean that what is a reasonable excuse for one person may not be a reasonable excuse for someone else.

If you run your business from home

We'll normally only visit you at home if you run your business from there. If your business premises are also your home, or if you keep any stock or other assets at home, the visiting officers will only be able to enter those parts of your home which are used for business purposes. This is unless you invite them in or they're carrying out a valuation.

If we're checking your Income Tax or Corporation Tax liability we may need to value your private premises if it's relevant to our check. We may also need to value property in your private premises. This is if we're checking your liability to Stamp Duty Land Tax, Stamp Duty Reserve Tax or Inheritance Tax, or to check any liabilities that relate to Capital Gains Tax.

About the notice of inspection

The notice of inspection tells you:

- the names of the inspecting officers
- when the inspection will take place
- what the officers are authorised to inspect during the visit

The Human Rights Act and your privacy

Article 8 of the Human Rights Act gives you the right to respect for your private and family life, your home and your correspondence. We have the right to carry out an inspection in a reasonable and proportionate way even when it conflicts with your rights. If you think our inspection isn't reasonable and proportionate, please tell us why.

General information about visits

A visit to a small business may take a few hours, but if your business is large or complex, or if the matters we're looking at are complex, it may take several days.

We don't usually need to talk to people who work for you about our check. However, we may ask to speak to the people who keep your records up to date, such as payroll and finance records. We may also need to speak to some of the people who work for you if we're looking at their employment status. If you don't want them to know about our visit, please tell us.

We may ask to take some records away to check in our own office. We'll explain why we want to do this at the visit.

We have the right to remove any records that you produce during our inspection or that our notice of inspection says we're authorised to inspect. If we do take any records away we'll give you a receipt, keep the records securely and return them to you as soon as we can. If you need them back sooner, we'll make copies in our office and give these to you.

Concealing, destroying or otherwise disposing of documents

We may charge you a penalty if you or another person acting on your behalf conceals, destroys, or disposes of any document that we:

- have asked for in an information notice
- told you that we intend to ask for in an information notice

It's a criminal offence to conceal, destroy or otherwise dispose of any of document that we:

- have asked for in an information notice that has been approved by the tribunal
- told you that we intend to ask for in an information notice that has been approved by the tribunal

We may carry out a criminal investigation with a view to prosecution if you or someone acting on your behalf commits this offence.

What happens if you give us information that you know to be untrue

We may carry out a criminal investigation with a view to prosecution if you:

- give us information that you know to be untrue, whether verbally or in a document
- dishonestly misrepresent your liability to tax or claim payments to which you're not entitled

CC/FS7a PENALTIES FOR INACCURACIES IN RETURNS AND DOCUMENTS [HMRC, December 2017]

This factsheet contains information about penalties we may charge if you've sent us an inaccurate return or other document.

This factsheet is one of a series. For the full list of the factsheets in our compliance checks series, go to www.gov.uk and search "factsheets".

When we may charge you a penalty for an inaccuracy

We may charge you a penalty if you send us a return or other document that contains an inaccuracy, and the inaccuracy:

- results in tax being unpaid, understated or over-claimed and
- was careless, deliberate or deliberate and concealed (we refer to these as "behaviours" which are explained later in this factsheet)

If you ask someone else, such as an employee or adviser, to do something on your behalf, you must do as much as you can to make sure that an inaccuracy doesn't occur. If you don't do this, we may charge you a penalty.

When we won't charge you a penalty for an inaccuracy

We won't charge you a penalty for an inaccuracy if you took reasonable care to get things right but your return or document was still wrong. Some of the ways you can show that you took reasonable care include:

- keeping accurate records
- checking with a tax adviser or with us if you aren't sure about anything

Disclosing an inaccuracy before we find it

If you tell us about an inaccuracy before you've any reason to believe that we are about to find it, we call this an "unprompted disclosure". If you tell us about an inaccuracy at any other time, we call it a "prompted disclosure". Once we've started a check, a disclosure can only be unprompted if, exceptionally:

- it is about an unrelated inaccuracy, and
- you had no reason to believe that we could have found it during our check

The minimum penalty for an unprompted disclosure is lower than the minimum penalty for a prompted one.

If you send us a return or document that you believe is correct and you later find that it contains a careless inaccuracy, we may be able to reduce the penalty to nil if you make an unprompted disclosure.

What you can do to reduce any penalty we may charge

We can reduce the amount of any penalty we charge you depending on our view of how much assistance you gave us. We refer to this assistance as the **"quality of disclosure"** or as "telling, helping and giving".

Examples of telling, helping and giving include:

- telling us about, or agreeing that there is something wrong and how and why it happened
- telling us everything you can about the extent of what is wrong as soon as you know about it
- telling and helping us by answering our questions in full
- helping us to understand your accounts or records
- helping us by replying to our letters quickly
- helping us by agreeing to attend any meetings, or visits at a mutually convenient time
- helping us by checking your own records to identify the extent of the inaccuracy
- helping us by using your private records to identify sales or income not included in your tax return
- giving us access to documents we've asked for without unnecessary delay
- giving us access to documents we may not know about, as well as those that we ask to see

We'll reduce the penalty by the maximum amount possible if you:

- tell us everything you can about any inaccuracy as soon as you know about it or you believe we're about to find it
- do everything you can to help us correct it

If you delay telling us, you may still be entitled to a reduction but it will be smaller. If we don't need any extra assistance from you we'll give you the full reduction that the law allows for telling, helping and giving.

Letting us know about any special circumstances

If there are any special circumstances that you believe the officer dealing with the check should take into consideration when calculating the penalty, you should let them know straightaway.

How we work out the amount of a penalty

There are 8 stages in working out the amount of any penalty. Each stage is explained in more detail below.

1 Working out the amount of the potential lost revenue (PLR)

The penalty is a percentage of what we call the "potential lost revenue". PLR is the amount that arises as a result of correcting an inaccuracy in a return or document, an incorrect repayment or an incorrect claim. The officer dealing with the check will explain how this is worked out. There are different rules about calculating the PLR where there are group relief, losses, repayments, or accounting timing issues resulting in delayed tax. If you need to know more, please ask the officer dealing with the check.

2 Determining our view of the "behaviour"

When there is an inaccuracy, we'll work with you to find out what caused it. We refer to this as the "behaviour". The type of behaviour will affect whether we charge a penalty and the amount of the penalty. There are 4 different types of behaviour.

Reasonable care

Everyone has a responsibility to take reasonable care over their tax affairs. What "reasonable care" is will depend on each customer's abilities and circumstances.

If there was anything about your health or personal circumstances that made it difficult for you to take reasonable care, please tell the officer that is carrying out the check. Telling them will mean that they can take this into account when considering whether you took reasonable care.

If you took reasonable care to get things right but your return or document still contained an inaccuracy, we won't charge you a penalty.

Some of the ways you can take reasonable care include:

- keeping enough records to make accurate tax returns
- keeping those records safe
- asking us or a tax adviser if you are not sure about anything and following any advice given

Careless

This is where you failed to take reasonable care to get things right.

Deliberate

This is where you knew that a return or document was inaccurate when you sent it to us. Examples of deliberate inaccuracies include deliberately:

- overstating your business expenses
- understating your income
- paying wages without accounting for Pay As You Earn and National Insurance contributions

Deliberate and concealed inaccuracies

This is where you knew that a return or document was inaccurate and you took active steps to hide the inaccuracy from us, either before or after you sent it to us. An example of taking active steps to conceal an inaccuracy is where you create a false invoice to cover a non-existent stock purchase.

3 Deciding whether the disclosure was unprompted or prompted

This determines the minimum penalty percentage that we can charge. This is explained in more detail in the section of this factsheet titled "Disclosing an inaccuracy before we find it".

4 Deciding the range that the penalty falls within

The penalty percentage falls into one of 6 ranges. The range it falls into depends on the type of behaviour and whether it was a "prompted" or "unprompted" disclosure. The following table shows the 6 penalty ranges.

Type of behaviour	Unprompted disclosure	Prompted disclosure
Reasonable care	No penalty	No penalty
Careless	0% to 30%	15% to 30%
Deliberate	20% to 70%	35% to 70%
Deliberate and concealed	30% to 100%	50% to 100%

5 Working out the reductions for the quality of disclosure (also referred to as "telling, helping and giving")

The quality of disclosure (telling, helping and giving), determines where the penalty will fall within the penalty range. The reduction we give depends on how much assistance you give us. For:

- telling we give up to 30%
- helping we give up to 40%
- giving access to records we give up to 30%

6 Working out the penalty percentage rate

The penalty percentage rate is determined by the penalty range and the reduction for the quality of disclosure.

Example

We found a careless inaccuracy that the customer hadn't told us about before we started our check. When we told them about the inaccuracy, they agreed with us. This was a prompted disclosure.

The penalty range for a careless inaccuracy with a prompted disclosure is 15% to 30% of the potential lost revenue (PLR).

The reduction for quality of disclosure (telling, helping and giving) was 70%.

Steps	Calculation example
To work out the penalty percentage rate, we first work out the difference between the minimum and maximum penalty percentages.	30% minus 15% = 15
We then take off the percentage reduction from the maximum penalty percentage we can charge.	15 × 70% = 10.5%
This gives us the penalty percentage rate.	30% minus 10.5% = 19.5%

7 Working out the amount of the penalty

To work out the amount of the penalty, we multiply the potential lost revenue (PLR) by the penalty percentage rate. For example, if the PLR in the example above was £3,000, and there were no other reductions, the penalty would be £585 (£3,000 × 19.5% = £585).

8 Considering other reductions

After working out the amount of the penalty, we then take into account any other reductions that are necessary. For example, where we've already charged another penalty on the same tax or duty. This then gives the amount of penalty that we'll charge.

How we can suspend a penalty

We can suspend a penalty for a careless inaccuracy if we:

- can set conditions to help you avoid penalties in the future
- believe you can meet these conditions

We can suspend a penalty for up to a maximum of 2 years. Normally the suspension period will be as short as possible to allow you to meet the conditions. If we suspend your penalty, you won't have to pay it if you meet the conditions, unless we charge you another inaccuracy penalty during the suspension period.

You can find more information about this in factsheet CC/FS10, "Suspending penalties for careless inaccuracies in returns or documents". Go to www.gov.uk and search "CC/FS10". We can't suspend penalties for any other type of behaviour.

How we tell you about a penalty

We'll write to you to tell you how much the penalty is and how we've worked it out. If there is anything about the penalty that you don't agree with, or if you think there is any information we haven't already taken into account, you should tell us straightaway.

After taking account of anything you've told us, we'll then either:

- send you a penalty assessment notice
- invite you to enter into a contract with us to pay the penalty, together with the tax and interest

In certain circumstances you may also have to pay interest on the penalty if you don't pay it on time.

When a company officer may have to pay some or all of a company's penalty for a deliberate inaccuracy

A company officer may have to pay some or all of the company's penalty if the penalty is due to their actions, and one or more of the following applies:

- they have gained, or attempted to gain, personally from a deliberate inaccuracy
- the company is, or we believe it is, about to become insolvent – even if the officer didn't gain personally from the deliberate inaccuracy

If the company pays the penalty, we won't ask the individual officers to pay.

A company officer is a director, shadow director, company secretary or manager of a company, or a member of a limited liability partnership.

What happens if you've deliberately done something wrong

If you:

- give us information that you know to be untrue, whether verbally or in a document, or
- dishonestly misrepresent your liability to tax or claim payments to which you aren't entitled

we may carry out a criminal investigation with a view to prosecution.

Managing Serious Defaulters

If you've deliberately got your tax affairs wrong, we may need to monitor your tax affairs more closely. We've an enhanced monitoring programme called Managing Serious Defaulters. You can find more information about this in factsheet CC/FS14, "Managing Serious Defaulters". Go to www.gov.uk and search "CC/FS14".

Publishing details of deliberate defaulters

In certain circumstances, we may publish your details if you've deliberately got your tax affairs wrong. We **cannot** publish your details if you qualify for the maximum penalty reduction. You can find more information in factsheet CC/FS13, "Publishing details of deliberate defaulters". Go to www.gov.uk and search "CC/FS13".

What to do if you disagree

If there is something that you don't agree with, you should tell us.

If we make a decision that you can appeal against we'll write to you to explain the decision and tell you what to do if you disagree. You'll usually have 3 options. Within 30 days you can:

- send new information to the officer you've been dealing with and ask them to take it into account
- have your case reviewed by an HMRC officer who hasn't been involved in the matter
- arrange for your appeal to be heard by an independent tribunal, who will decide the matter

Whichever you choose, you may also be able to ask for an HMRC specialist officer to act as a neutral facilitator to help resolve the dispute. This process is known as "Alternative Dispute Resolution" (ADR).

ADR is only available for disputes relating to some of the taxes and other areas that we administer. The officer dealing with your check will tell you if ADR is available for the matter that you are disputing.

Go to www.gov.uk and search "HMRC1" and "CC/FS21" to find more information about:

- appeals and reviews in factsheet HMRC1, "HM Revenue & Customs decisions – what to do if you disagree".
- ADR in factsheet CC/FS21, "Alternative Dispute Resolution"

Your rights when we're considering penalties

The European Convention on Human Rights gives you certain important rights. If we're considering penalties, we'll tell you. We'll also tell you that these rights apply and ask you to confirm that you understand them. These rights are that:

- if we ask you any questions to help us decide whether to charge you a penalty, you've the right not to answer them. The amount of help that you give us when we are considering penalties is entirely a matter for you to decide
- when deciding whether to answer our questions, you may want to get advice from a professional adviser – particularly if you don't already have one
- if you disagree with us about the tax or any penalties we believe are due, you can appeal. If you appeal about both tax and penalties, you've the right to ask for both appeals to be considered together
- you've the right to apply for funded legal assistance for dealing with any appeal against certain penalties
- you're entitled to have the matter of penalties dealt with without unreasonable delay

You can find full details about these rights in factsheet CC/FS9 "The Human Rights Act and penalties". Go to www.gov.uk and search "CC/FS9".

Which taxes and tax periods these penalty rules apply to:

These penalty rules apply to the following taxes for returns or documents that were due to be sent to us on or after 1 April 2009, and relate to a tax period beginning on or after 1 April 2008.

Capital Gains Tax	Income Tax (including Self Assessment)
Construction Industry Schemes	National Insurance Classes 1 and 4
Corporation Tax	Pay As You Earn (PAYE)
	VAT

These penalty rules apply to the following taxes for returns or documents that were due to be sent to us on or after 1 April 2010, and relate to a tax period beginning on or after 1 April 2009.

Aggregates Levy	Inheritance Tax
Air Passenger Duty	Insurance Premium Tax
Alcohol Duty	Landfill Tax
Amusement Machine Licence Duty (up to 31 January 2013)	Lottery Duty
Bank Payroll Tax	Machine Games Duty (from 1 February 2013)
Bingo Duty	Petroleum Revenue Tax
Climate Change Levy	Pool Betting Duty
Excise duties (Holding and Movements)	Remote Gaming Duty
Gaming Duty	Stamp Duty Land Tax
Hydrocarbon Oils Duty	Stamp Duty Reserve Tax
	Tobacco Duty

These penalty rules apply to the following taxes for returns or documents that relate to the following periods.

National Insurance Class 1A for P11D(b) (returns for the tax year ended 5 April 2011 and later years)

Machine Games Duty (for tax periods beginning on or after 1 February 2013)

Annual Tax on Enveloped Dwellings (for tax periods beginning on or after 1 April 2013)

Apprenticeship Levy (for tax years starting on or after 6 April 2017)

CC/FS17 HIGHER PENALTIES FOR OFFSHORE MATTERS [HMRC, January 2018]

This factsheet gives you detailed information about the higher penalties that we may charge for Income Tax, Capital Gains Tax and Inheritance Tax when an offshore matter is involved.

This factsheet is one of a series. For the full list of factsheets in the series, go to www.gov.uk and search "Compliance checks factsheets".

When we may charge a higher penalty

We may charge a penalty of more than 100% for:

- an inaccuracy in a return or document
- a failure to notify chargeability to tax
- the deliberate withholding of information where a tax return is more than 12 months late

when it involves offshore matters in certain categories of "territory". Otherwise, the maximum penalty we may charge is 100%.

What we mean by an "offshore matter" and "territory" is explained later in this factsheet.

You can find more information about penalties in the following factsheets:

- CC/FS7a, "Penalties for inaccuracies in returns and documents"
- CC/FS11, "Penalties for failure to notify"
- CC/FS18a, "Penalties for failure to file annual and occasional returns and documents on time (including Self Assessment tax returns for Income Tax)"

We'll give you whichever of those factsheets is relevant to you and explain why. Please note that the penalty percentages in those factsheets don't apply to offshore matters for territories in categories 2 and 3. These categories and the higher rates that apply to them are explained on page 2.

We may also charge you an:

- offshore asset move penalty
- offshore asset based penalty

There is more information about these penalties later in this factsheet.

Offshore matters

An offshore matter is an inaccuracy, failure to notify or deliberate withholding of information that leads to a loss of revenue that is charged on or relates to:

- income arising from a source in a territory outside the United Kingdom (UK)
- assets situated or held in a territory outside the UK
- activities carried on wholly or mainly in a territory outside the UK

Offshore transfers

An offshore transfer takes place when there is a deliberate error or failure (whether concealed or not) that doesn't involve an onshore matter and:

- taxable income is received in a territory outside the UK
- taxable income is transferred to a territory outside of the UK before the statutory filing date
- disposal proceeds giving rise to a charge to Capital Gains Tax are received in a territory outside the UK
- disposal proceeds giving rise to a change in Capital Gains Tax are transferred to a territory outside of the UK before the statutory filing date
- assets that give rise to a charge to Inheritance Tax are transferred outside of the UK before the statutory filing date

Additional information requirements for offshore matters

You should provide additional information to us about:

- anyone who encouraged, assisted or facilitated you to carry out offshore tax evasion or non-compliance
- assets you hold in any county outside the UK and any other persons or entities you engaged to hold those assets on your behalf

After the relevant date we take this information into account when calculating the penalty and reduction we'll give you for the quality of disclosure. The relevant date for providing this additional information for:

- Income tax and Capital Gains Tax is tax years starting on or after 6 April 2017
- Inheritance Tax is transfers of value made on or after 1 April 2017

Examples of additional information we need could include:

- name and address of the enabler
- a description of what the enabler did to encourage, assist or facilitate you
- a description of the how you and the enabler first made contact and how you maintained contact
- a description of all documents you hold regarding their behaviour
- name and address of any other joint beneficial owner of the asset
- the extent of your share of the beneficial ownership of the asset
- a description of all documents of title or other documents showing your beneficial ownership
- details of where the asset is situated or held
- details of when and how the you became a beneficial owner of the asset
- a description of all changes in the arrangements for the ownership of the asset since you became a beneficial owner
- the names and last known addresses of all persons who have been asset holders of the asset during your beneficial ownership of it
- in relation to an asset holder who is not an individual, the name and business address (if known) of any director, senior manager, employee or agent of the asset holder who has advised or assisted you in relation to their beneficial ownership of the asset.

If you didn't involve an enabler or you've no assets located outside the UK held by another person, then by telling us this you've met the requirement to provide additional information.

How we work out the amount of the penalty

The penalty percentage range is determined by the place where the income or gains arose. For Inheritance Tax it's the place where the asset was located. We call this place the "territory". Territories are divided into 3 categories.

Category 1

These are generally territories that have agreed to exchange information with us automatically. The maximum penalty is 100% of the tax.

Category 2

These are generally territories that will exchange information with us but only if we ask them to. The maximum penalty is 150% of the tax.

Category 3

These are generally territories that haven't agreed to share information with us. The maximum penalty is 200% of the tax.

You can find a list of the territories and the categories on our website. Go to www.gov.uk and search for "Territory Categorisation for offshore matters".

Inaccuracies

Category of territory	Careless	Deliberate	Deliberate and concealed
1 Unprompted	0%–30%	20%–70%	30%–100%
Prompted	15%–30%	35%–70%	50%–100%
2 Unprompted	0%–45%	30%–105%	45%–150%
Prompted	22.5%–45%	52.5%–105%	75%–150%

Category of territory	Careless	Deliberate	Deliberate and concealed
3 Unprompted	0%–60%	40%–140%	60%–200%
Prompted	30%–60%	70%–140%	100%–200%

From the tax year 2016–17 the minimum penalty for "deliberate" and "deliberate and concealed" increase by 10%. For Inheritance Tax this relates to transfers on or after 1 April 2017.

Failure to notify for Income Tax and Capital Gains Tax only

Category of territory	Non-deliberate	Deliberate	Deliberate and concealed
1 Unprompted			
Failure disclosed more than 12 months after the tax becomes unpaid	10%–30%	20%–70%	30%–100%
Failure disclosed within 12 months of the tax becoming unpaid	0%–30%	20%–70%	30%–100%
1 Prompted			
Failure disclosed more than 12 months after the tax becomes unpaid	20%–30%	35%–70%	50%–100%
Failure disclosed within 12 months of the tax becoming unpaid	10%–30%	35%–70%	50%–100%
2 Unprompted			
Failure disclosed more than 12 months after the tax becomes unpaid	15%–45%	30%–105%	45%–150%
Failure disclosed within 12 months of the tax becoming unpaid	0%–45%	30%–105%	45%–150%
2 Prompted			
Failure disclosed more than 12 months after the tax becomes unpaid	30%–45%	52.5%–105%	75%–150%
Failure disclosed within 12 months of the tax becoming unpaid	15%–45%	52.5%–105%	75%–150%
3 Unprompted			
Failure disclosed more than 12 months after the tax becomes unpaid	20%–60%	40%–140%	60%–200%
Failure disclosed within 12 months of the tax becoming unpaid	0%–60%	40%–140%	60%–200%
3 Prompted			
Failure disclosed more than 12 months after the tax becomes unpaid	40%–60%	70%–140%	100%–200%
Failure disclosed more than 12 months after the tax becomes unpaid	20%–60%	70%–140%	100%–200%

From the tax year 2016–17 the minimum penalty for "deliberate" and "deliberate and concealed" increase by 10%. For inheritance tax this relates to transfers on or after 1 April 2017.

Withholding of information

Category of territory	Deliberate	Deliberate and concealed
1 Unprompted	20%–70%	30%–100%
Prompted	35%–70%	50%–100%
2 Unprompted	30%–105%	45%–150%
Prompted	52.5%–105%	75%–150%
3 Unprompted	52.5%–105%	60%–200%
Prompted	70%–140%	100%–200%

From the tax year 2016–17 the minimum penalty for "deliberate" and "deliberate and concealed" increase by 10%.

For inheritance tax this relates to transfers on or after 1 April 2017. For penalty percentages in category 1 for Inheritance Tax prior to 1 April 2017 read factsheet CC/FS7a, "Penalties for inaccuracies in returns and documents". Go to www.gov.uk and search for "CC/FS7a".

Taxes and tax periods these penalty rules apply to

The higher penalty rates for categories 2 and 3 only apply to Income Tax, Capital Gains Tax and Inheritance Tax.

The penalty rules in this factsheet apply to:

- inaccuracies in returns or other documents which relate to the tax year 2011–12 or later, and are given to us on or after 6 April 2011
- failures to notify that arise on or after 6 April 2012
- deliberate withholding of information when a return for the tax year 2011–12 or later is more than 12 months late

For Inheritance Tax this factsheet applies to inaccuracies in returns submitted for deaths and chargeable events on or after 1 April 2016.

Offshore asset move penalties

You may be liable to an offshore asset move penalty where both:

- an earlier penalty has been charged for a failure to comply with certain Income Tax, Capital Gains Tax or Inheritance Tax obligations – this is the underlying penalty
- a related offshore asset moves from a specified to a non-specified territory, or if there is a change in ownership of the asset resulting in the beneficial owner prior to the move remaining the beneficial owner afterwards

The following conditions must apply:

- the underlying penalty must involve a deliberate failure and the person is liable to a deliberate penalty under
  - paragraph 1 of Schedule 24 Finance Act 2007, where the tax at stake is Income Tax, Capital Gains Tax or Inheritance Tax
  - paragraph 1 of Schedule 41 Finance Act 2008, where there is an obligation to notify for Income Tax or Capital Gains Tax
  - paragraph 6 Schedule 55 Finance Act 2009, where tax at stake is Income Tax, Capital Gains Tax or Inheritance Tax
- the tax at stake in relation to the underlying penalty is Income Tax, Capital Gains Tax or Inheritance Tax
- there is a relevant offshore asset move made after the relevant time connected to the underlying penalty
- the relevant offshore asset move occurred after 26 March 2015
- the main purpose or one of the main purposes of moving the asset to another territory was to prevent or delay discovery by HMRC of the failure that led to the underlying penalty

Relevant time

The relevant time:

- for Schedule 24 penalties
  - for Income Tax and Capital Gains Tax is the beginning of the tax year for which a penalty was charged for an inaccuracy
  - for Inheritance Tax is the time when the liability for the tax at stake first arises
- for Schedule 55 penalties (Income Tax or Capital Gains Tax) is the start of the year the return relates to
- for Schedule 41 penalties, (Income Tax or Capital Gains Tax), is the start of the tax year where the obligation to notify relates to

Amount of the penalty

The offshore asset move penalty is 50% of the amount of the underlying penalty and is in addition to that penalty.

Offshore asset based penalties

You may be liable to an asset based penalty where:

- you made an inaccuracy in your tax return, failed to notify a charge to tax, or failed to make a return on time and we've charged you a penalty (this is the underlying penalty) in respect of that inaccuracy or failure under
  - Schedule 24 Finance Act 2007
  - Schedule 41 Finance Act 2008
  - Schedule 55 Finance Act 2009
- the inaccuracy or failure relates to an offshore matter or offshore transfer
- the behaviour that led to the failure or inaccuracy is deliberate (whether concealed or not)
- the income, gain or transfer of value that relates to the inaccuracy has a clear link to the underlying asset
- potential lost revenue threshold in relation to the offshore matter exceeds £25,000

We can only charge an asset based penalty in respect of income tax and assets listed in the relevant section in the Income Tax (Trade and Other Income) Act 2005 (ITTOIA).

1 Working out the amount of the asset based penalty

The standard amount of the asset based penalty is the lower of:

- 10% of the value of the asset
- 10 × the offshore potential lost revenue (PLR)

If the potential penalty involves both offshore and domestic matters this is called a "combined penalty". The officer you are dealing with will explain the special rules for combined penalties.

The offshore PLR is the total for the year of either the:

- PLR used to calculate the underlying penalty charged under Schedule 24 Finance Act 2007 or Schedule 41 Finance Act 2008
- liability to tax used to calculate the underlying penalty charged under Schedule 55 FA 2009

2 Deciding whether the disclosure was unprompted or prompted

This determines the minimum penalty percentage that we can charge.

The maximum amount of reduction depends on whether the disclosure is prompted or unprompted. This is based on the underlying penalty.

If you make an unprompted disclosure we may reduce the penalty to a lower amount than if you make a prompted disclosure.

The penalty will fall into one of the ranges below depending on whether the disclosure is prompted or unprompted.

Disclosure	Range Minimum	Range Maximum
Unprompted	50% of the standard penalty	100% of the standard penalty
Prompted	80% of the standard penalty	100% of the standard penalty

When calculating penalties we'll take account of how long it has taken you to come forward. If you've taken a significant period (normally 3 years) to tell us about the offshore asset then you won't normally receive the full reduction for disclosure. We consider the earliest date you could have told us about the asset to the actual date you did tell us.

3 Working out the quality of disclosure reduction

We'll reduce the amount of the asset-based penalty where you:

- make a disclosure of the inaccuracy or failure relating to the underlying penalty
- provide us with a reasonable valuation of the asset
- provide give us with information or access to records that we need to value the asset

The quality of disclosure (timing, nature and extent of information you give), determines where the penalty will fall within the penalty range. The reduction we give you depends on how much assistance you give us.

4 Considering other reductions

After working out the amount of the penalty we then take into account any special circumstances that you've told us about. These will be uncommon or exceptional circumstances that we haven't already considered when working out the quality of disclosure.

What happens if you give us information that you know to be untrue

We may carry out a criminal investigation with a view to a prosecution if you:

- give us information that you know to be untrue, whether verbally or in a document
- dishonestly declare the wrong amount of duty or claim payments to which you aren't entitled.

CC/FS17a PENALTIES FOR ENABLERS OF OFFSHORE TAX EVASION OR NON-COMPLIANCE [HMRC, October 2017]

This factsheet gives you detailed information about the enabler penalty that we may charge a person who enabled another person to carry out offshore tax evasion or non-compliance. This is where the tax at stake is income tax, capital gains tax or inheritance tax.

This factsheet is one of a series. For the full list of factsheets in the series, go to www.gov.uk and search "Compliance checks factsheets".

When we may charge an enabler penalty

You may be liable to an enabler penalty if you've encouraged, assisted or otherwise facilitated another person to carry out offshore tax evasion or non-compliance and both of conditions A and B are met:

Condition A is met if you knew that your actions enabled, or were likely to enable, another person to carry out offshore tax evasion or non-compliance. A person carries out offshore tax evasion or non-compliance if either:

- they commit a relevant offence
- their actions make them liable to a relevant civil penalty relating to income tax, capital gains tax or inheritance tax

Condition B is met when the person carrying out the offshore tax evasion or non-compliance either:

- has been convicted of a relevant offence and the conviction is final
- is liable to a relevant penalty and the penalty is final

Condition B is also met if HMRC has entered into and agreed a contract settlement with the person carrying out the offshore tax evasion or non-compliance. This is in place of assessing a penalty or taking proceedings to recover such a penalty.

Relevant offences

The relevant offences are:

- cheating the public revenue involving offshore activity
- fraudulent evasion of income tax involving offshore activity
- being chargeable to income tax or capital gains tax on or by reference to offshore income, assets or liabilities, where the person has:
  - failed to give notice of being chargeable to tax
  - failed to deliver a return
  - made an inaccurate return

Relevant penalties

A relevant penalty is a penalty under:

- paragraph 1 of Schedule 24 Finance Act 2007 for inaccuracies in a document involving an offshore activity
- paragraph 1 of Schedule 41 Finance Act 2008 for a failure to notify liability to tax in involving an offshore activity
- paragraph 6 of Schedule 55 Finance Act 2009 for a failure to file a tax return on time involving an offshore activity
- paragraph 1 of Schedule 21 Finance Act 2015 for a relevant offshore asset move.

You can find more information about these penalties in the following factsheets:

- CC/FS7a, "Penalties for inaccuracies in returns and documents"
- CC/FS11, "Penalties for failure to notify"
- *CC/FS17 "Higher penalties for offshore matters"*
- CC/FS18a, "Penalties for failure to file annual and occasional returns and documents on time - including Self Assessment tax returns for Income Tax"

What we mean by "offshore activity"

A person has carried out an offshore activity if it involves:

- an offshore matter
- an offshore transfer
- a relevant offshore asset move

Our factsheet CC/FS17 "Higher penalties for offshore matters" contains more information about offshore activity.

How we calculate the penalty

Maximum penalty for all cases except where the enabler penalty relates to an offshore asset move

To calculate the penalty we use the original amount of Potential Lost Revenue (PLR) used to apply a penalty to the person who carried out the offshore tax evasion or non-compliance.

The maximum penalty is the higher of either:

- 100% of the PLR
- £3,000

Maximum penalty where the enabler penalty relates to an offshore asset move

To calculate the additional penalty for enabling an offshore asset move we use 50% of the original amount of PLR. This is the PLR used to apply a penalty to the person who carried out the offshore tax evasion or non-compliance.

The maximum penalty for an enabler of an offshore asset move is the higher of either:

- 50% of the PLR
- £3,000

Where offences include offshore tax evasion and an offshore asset move, an enabler may be charged both types of penalty shown above. This means they may be charged a standard penalty for enabling another person to carry out offshore tax evasion or non-compliance and also a separate offshore asset move penalty.

How we reduce the amount of penalty we may charge

We may reduce the penalty depending on:

- whether the disclosure is prompted or unprompted
- the quality of the disclosure
- whether a special reduction is due.

Disclosing an offshore activity

If you tell us about the offshore activity before you've any reason to believe that we've discovered, or are about to discover the offshore tax evasion that you've enabled, we call this an "unprompted disclosure". If you tell us about this activity at any other time, we call it a "prompted disclosure".

The timing of the disclosure relates to the original evasion or non-compliance.

When calculating penalties we'll take account of how long it's taken you to come forward since the inaccuracy or failure occurred.

If you make an unprompted disclosure we may reduce the penalty to a lower amount than if you make a prompted disclosure.

The penalty will fall into one of the ranges below depending on whether the disclosure is prompted or unprompted.

Reduction for disclosure in all cases except where the enabler penalty relates to an offshore asset move

Disclosure	Range Minimum	Range Maximum
Unprompted	Higher of 10% of the PLR or £1,000	Higher of 100% of the PLR or £3,000
Prompted	Higher of 30% of the PLR or £3,000	Higher of 100% of the PLR or £3,000

Reduction for disclosure where the enabler penalty relates to an offshore asset move

Disclosure	Range Minimum	Range Maximum
Unprompted	Higher of 10% of the PLR or £1,000	Higher of 50% of the PLR or £3,000
Prompted	Higher of 30% of the PLR or £3,000	Higher of 50% of the PLR or £3,000

What you can do to reduce any penalty we may charge

We can reduce the amount of any penalty we charge you depending on our view of how much assistance you gave us. We refer to this assistance as the "quality of disclosure" or as "telling, helping and giving".

Examples of telling, helping and giving include:

- telling us about any or all matters which have led to an inaccuracy in a document, a supply of false information or failure to disclose an under-assessment
- telling us about what you did to enable another person to carry out a relevant offence
- helping us by encouraging that person to co-operate with us
- helping us to calculate that person's liability to a penalty
- giving us access to records we've asked for without unnecessary delay
- giving us access to records we may not know about, as well as those that we ask to see
- telling and helping us by answering our questions in full

The quality of disclosure (telling, helping and giving), determines the amount of the penalty we'll charge. The reduction we give depends on how much assistance you give us. If you delay telling us, you may still be entitled to a reduction but it'll be smaller.

Letting us know about any special circumstances

If there are any special circumstances that you believe the officer dealing with the check should take into consideration when calculating the penalty, you should let them know straightaway. These will be uncommon or exceptional circumstances that we haven't already considered when working out the quality of disclosure.

How we work out the amount of a penalty

There are 6 stages in working out the amount of any penalty. Each stage is explained in more detail below.

1 Work out the amount of the maximum penalty

This is the maximum amount worked out as shown on page 2 (amount A).

2 Deciding whether the disclosure was unprompted or prompted

This determines the minimum penalty percentage that we can charge. This is explained in more detail in the section of this factsheet titled "Disclosing an offshore activity".

The penalty falls into one of the ranges shown in the tables on page 3 depending on whether the disclosure is prompted or unprompted.

3 Working out the reductions for the quality of disclosure (also referred to as "telling, helping and giving")

The quality of disclosure (telling, helping and giving), determines where the penalty will fall within the penalty range shown above on page 3. The reduction we give depends on how much assistance you give us. For:

- telling we give up to 30%
- helping we give up to 40%
- giving access to records we give up to 30%

4 Working out the penalty percentage rate

The penalty percentage rate is determined by the penalty range shown on page 3 and the reduction for *quality of disclosure percentage.*

To work out the penalty percentage rate, we first work out the difference between the minimum (amount D) and maximum (amount C) penalty percentages to give us the maximum penalty percentage we can charge (amount E).

We then take off the percentage reduction from the maximum penalty percentage we can charge. This gives us the penalty percentage rate (amount G).

5 Working out the amount of the penalty

To work out the amount of the penalty, we multiply the potential lost revenue (PLR) by the penalty percentage rate.

For example: a prompted disclosure, where the quality and timing of the disclosure had been minimal.

Step 1

The PLR is £5,255,700 (amount A)

Step 2

The penalty range for a prompted disclosure is 30% to 100% of the PLR

Step 3

The percentage reduction for quality of disclosure (telling, helping and giving) was 7% (amount B).

Step 4

The maximum penalty (C) is 100% and the minimum penalty (D) is 30%.

So the maximum penalty percentage we can charge (E) is 100 – 30 = 70%.

The actual reduction percentage for disclosure (F) is 7% × 70 = 4.9% (say 5%).

Penalty percentage to be charged (G) is 100% – 5% = 95%.

Step 5

The penalty to be charged is £5,255,700 × 95% = £4,992,915.

6 Considering other reductions

After working out the amount of the penalty, we then take into account any other reductions that are necessary. This then gives the amount of penalty that we'll charge.

How we tell you about a penalty

We'll write to you to tell you how much the penalty is and how we've worked it out. If there's anything about the penalty that you don't agree with, or if you think there is any information we haven't already taken into account, you should tell us straightaway.

After taking account of anything you've told us, we'll either:

- send you a penalty assessment notice
- invite you to enter into a contract with us to pay the penalty, together with the tax and interest

In certain circumstances you may also have to pay interest on the penalty if you don't pay it on time.

What to do if you disagree

If there's something that you don't agree with, you should tell us.

If we make a decision that you can appeal against we'll write to you to explain the decision and tell you what to do if you disagree. You'll usually have 3 options. Within 30 days you can:

- send new information to the officer you've been dealing with and ask them to take it into account
- have your case reviewed by an HMRC officer who hasn't been involved in the matter
- arrange for your appeal to be heard by an independent tribunal, who'll decide the matter

Your rights when we are considering penalties

The European Convention on Human Rights gives you certain important rights. If we're considering penalties, we'll tell you. We'll also tell you the following that these rights apply and ask you to confirm that you understand them. These rights are that:

- if we ask you any questions to help us decide whether to charge you a penalty, you've the right not to answer them
- the amount of help that you give us when we're considering penalties is entirely a matter for you to decide
- when deciding whether to answer our questions, you may want to get advice from a professional adviser – particularly if you don't already have one
- if you disagree with us about any penalties we believe are due, you can appeal
- you've the right to apply for funded legal assistance for dealing with any appeal against certain penalties
- you're entitled to have the matter of penalties dealt with without unreasonable delay

You can find full details about these rights in factsheet CC/FS9 "The Human Rights Act and penalties". Go to www.gov.uk and search for "CC/FS9".

What happens if you give us information that you know to be untrue

If you:

- give us information that you know to be untrue, whether verbally or in a document
- dishonestly declare the wrong amount of duty or claim payments to which you aren't entitled

we may carry out a criminal investigation and you may be prosecuted.

CC/FS23 THIRD PARTY INFORMATION NOTICES [HMRC, April 2017]

We have given you this factsheet because:

- we've given you a third party information notice, or
- we intend to ask the independent tribunal that deals with tax to approve our request to give you a third party information notice

What is a third party information notice

A third party information notice is a document that legally requires a person to give us certain information and/or documents to help us check another person's tax position.

We refer to the person whose tax position we're checking as the "first party" and we refer to the person we want information and/or documents from as the "third party". So, in respect of this factsheet and our third party information notice, you are the third party.

When we use third party information notices

Sometimes, when we're checking a person's tax position (the first party), we may need information from a third party. This could be because:

- the first party has not been able to give us information that we need or has refused to, or
- we need to independently check business or financial transactions that have taken place

We may ask for the information we need to be sent to us voluntarily, or we may use an information notice if we need to, or if the third party prefers us to.

When we need permission to use a third party notice

When we need information and/or documents from a third party, we'll usually ask the first party to agree to us sending an information notice to a third party. Sometimes we'll ask the independent tax tribunal to approve the issue of a third party notice.

If we intend to ask an independent tribunal to approve the issue of a third party notice, we'll normally give both the first party and the third party the opportunity to tell us about any problem the third party may have in giving us the information and/or documents we intend to request. For example, we'll give both parties the opportunity to tell us if they believe that it would be unduly onerous to comply with a requirement in the notice. If either party expresses any concerns, we'll bring them to the attention of the tribunal so that they can take them into consideration when deciding whether to approve the issue of the notice.

When a third party information notice asks for business records that the third party is required by tax law to keep, we do not need the agreement of the first party, or approval from the tribunal, before issuing a third party information notice for them.

Different rules apply when we're checking the Income or Capital Gains Tax position of 1 or more partners in a partnership. If these rules apply we'll explain them to you.

What the third party information notice will tell you

If we send you a third party information notice, it will tell you:

- the name of the person to whom it relates (unless the tribunal has decided it doesn't need to)
- which documents and/or information you must give us
- how and when to give us what we need
- about any appeal rights

What information and documents we can ask for in a third party information notice

We can ask for information and/or documents if we believe they're relevant to our check of the first party's tax position, and that it's reasonable to ask for them.

What information and documents we cannot ask for in an information notice

We cannot use an information notice to ask a third party to give us information or documents:

- that are not in their possession and they cannot get the documents, or copies from whoever holds them
- that relate to the tax position of a person who died more than 4 years before the notice is issued
- that have been created as part of the preparation for a tax appeal
- that are concerned exclusively with a person's physical, mental, spiritual or personal welfare
- that are privileged communications between lawyers and clients for the purpose of getting or giving legal advice
- if the third party is an auditor, tax adviser or journalist and the information or documents have been created for the purposes of their profession
- if the third party is the subject of journalistic material and the information or documents have been created by a journalist for the purposes of their profession

The rules about what information and documents fall into these categories, especially personal or privileged communications, can be complicated. If you think that anything we've asked for may fall into 1 or more of these categories, please discuss this with the officer who gave you this factsheet.

What happens before we ask an independent tribunal to approve our request to issue a third party notice

We only need to ask a tribunal to approve a third party information notice when:

- the information or documents we need are not statutory records that relate to the supply of services or the acquisition of goods and services, and
- the person whose tax position we're checking has not given us permission to give the third party an information notice

Before we ask an independent tribunal to approve a notice, we'll normally give both the first party and the third party the opportunity to make representations to the tribunal about the information or documents we intend to request. The first party or the third party cannot however attend the tribunal hearing.

If we've written to you to tell you that we intend to ask the tribunal to approve our request to give you a third party notice, we'll have sent you a copy of this factsheet. If you want to make representations, for example, because you believe that it would be unduly onerous to comply with a requirement in the notice, please let us have your reasons by the date in our letter. If however it is more convenient for you to provide us with the information and/or documents on a voluntary basis before we ask the tribunal to approve the information notice, please send the information and/or documents we need to the HM Revenue and Customs (HMRC) officer who wrote to you.

What to do if you disagree with a third party information notice

If we send you an information notice and you think that the request is unreasonable, and we don't agree, you may be able to appeal to the independent tribunal that deals with tax appeals. We'll tell you how to do this when we give you the notice.

You cannot appeal against a third party information notice that has either been approved by an independent tribunal or is a request for statutory records that relate to any of the following:

- the supply of goods or services
- the acquisition of goods from another member state
- the importation of goods from a place outside the member states in the course of carrying on a business

You can only appeal against a third party information notice that has been approved by the first party when it would be unduly onerous to comply with the notice or a requirement in the notice.

What happens if you fail to comply with a third party information notice

To comply with the notice, you must give us everything that the notice asks for, by the date stated in the notice – or by a later date if we've agreed one with you. If you don't comply with the notice, we may charge you a penalty of £300. If you still haven't complied with the notice by the time we've charged you the £300 penalty, we may then charge you daily penalties of up to £60 a day for each day that you don't comply.

Any information you give us must be correct as far as you know. If you give us information or documents that you know are wrong without telling us what is wrong, then you may have to pay a penalty up to a maximum of £3,000.

If you conceal, destroy or otherwise dispose of any document we've asked for in a tribunal approved notice, or arrange for it to be concealed, destroyed or disposed of, you may have to pay a penalty or you may be prosecuted. If we charge you a penalty it will be a penalty of £300. We'll then charge you daily penalties of up to £60 a day for each day you fail to comply with the notice by concealing a document.

For the most serious cases the upper-tier independent tribunal can also impose a further penalty based on the tax that is put at risk by the failure to comply with the notice, concealment, disposal or destruction of the document.

If we agree that you have a reasonable excuse for not giving us information or documents, we will not charge you a penalty but we'll still ask you to provide the information, documents (or replacement documents) within an agreed amount of time.

A reasonable excuse is something that stopped you from meeting a tax obligation on time which you took reasonable care to meet. It might be due to circumstances outside your control or a combination of events. Once the reasonable excuse has ended, you must put things right without any unnecessary delay.

Whether you have a reasonable excuse depends upon the particular circumstances in which the failure occurred and your particular circumstances and abilities. This may mean that what is a reasonable excuse for one person may not be a reasonable excuse for someone else. If you think you have a reasonable excuse please tell us.

Examples of reasonable excuse may include, when:

- you have been seriously ill
- someone close to you has died
- you have lost the documents in a fire or flood

Other types of third party information notices

Third party information notices when the identity of the first party is unknown

This type of notice requires a third party to provide us with information and/or documents about either:

- a person whose identity is not known to us
- a class of persons whose individual identities are not known to us

Normally, this type of notice can only be considered where there are reasonable grounds for believing that failure by a person or persons unknown to comply with the tax law may seriously prejudice the assessment or collection of tax. There are a few exceptions to this rule that relate to, pension matters, subsidiaries, partners, and involved third parties. If these do apply we'll tell you and explain what the exceptions mean. This type of notice must be approved by an independent tribunal and issued by a specialist officer of HMRC.

Identification notices

This type of notice requires a third party to provide us with information that will help us identify a first party from other information that we hold, for example an invoice or credit card number. The information we can ask for using this type of notice is restricted to the person's name, address and date of birth (if known).

This type of notice must be issued by a specialist officer of HMRC. We do not need approval from an independent tribunal to issue this type of notice.

Your principal rights and obligations

You have:

- the right to be represented – you can appoint anyone to act on your behalf, including professional advisers, friends or relatives
- the right to consult your adviser – we'll allow a reasonable amount of time for you to do so
- an obligation to take care to get things right – if you have an adviser, you must still take reasonable care to make sure that any returns, documents or details they send us on your behalf are correct

"Your Charter" explains what you can expect from us and what we expect from you. For more information, go to gov.uk/government/publications/your-charter

This factsheet relates to compliance checks into any of the following:

Aggregates Levy	Insurance Premium Tax
Annual Tax on Enveloped Dwellings	Landfill Tax
Bank Payroll Tax	Machine Games Duty
Capital Gains Tax	National Insurance Classes 1, 1A* and 4
Climate Change Levy	Pay As You Earn (PAYE)
Construction Industry Scheme	Petroleum Revenue Tax
Corporation Tax	Stamp Duty Land Tax
Income Tax	Stamp Duty Reserve Tax
Inheritance Tax	VAT

*For Class 1A National Insurance, this factsheet only relates to P11D(b) returns for tax years starting on or after 6 April 2010.

More information

Dealing with HMRC if you have additional needs

If there is anything about your health or personal circumstances that may make it difficult for you to deal with this check, please tell the officer that is carrying out the check. Telling them will mean that they can help you in the most appropriate way. For more details, go to www.gov.uk/dealing-hmrc-additional-needs

CC/FS30a TAX AVOIDANCE SCHEMES – PENALTIES FOR FOLLOWER NOTICES [HMRC, October 2016]

This factsheet contains information about the penalty we'll charge you if we've sent you a follower notice and you've not taken the necessary corrective action on time. Where this factsheet refers to tax, this includes National Insurance contributions (NICs).

This factsheet is one of a series. For the full list of factsheets in the series, go to **www.gov.uk** and search for "Compliance checks factsheets". This factsheet is for:

- non-partnership cases where the tax avoidance scheme is for any of the taxes or NICs listed on page 6
- partnership cases where the tax avoidance scheme is for Stamp Duty Land Tax or Annual Tax on Enveloped Dwellings

If you're a member of a partnership that has used a tax avoidance scheme for another tax or NICs, you may also need to read factsheet CC/FS30b, "Tax avoidance schemes – penalties for partnership follower notices".

When we'll charge a penalty for not taking corrective action on time

We'll charge you a penalty if we've sent you a follower notice and you've not taken corrective action on time. The follower notice explains what corrective action you need to take.

The amount of the penalty

The penalty for not taking corrective action is equal to 50% of the value of the denied advantage. However, we can reduce the penalty percentage rate if you've co-operated with us. There's more information about reduction and co-operation later in this factsheet.

How we tell you about the penalty

When we've decided the amount of the penalty that we're going to charge, we'll send you a notice of penalty assessment.

Before we send a notice of penalty assessment, we'll normally write to tell you how we've worked out the amount of the penalty. If we do this and you think there's something you have done to co-operate that we haven't taken into account, you'll be able to tell us so we can consider whether it affects the penalty. Once we've allowed time for this to happen, we'll send you the notice of penalty assessment as soon as we can.

When you receive the notice of penalty assessment, you'll be able to appeal if you disagree with it. You'll be able to appeal whether or not we wrote to you about the penalty before we sent the notice of penalty assessment. You can find more about this in the section headed "Appealing against the penalty if you disagree" on page 5.

What's the deadline for us sending the notice of penalty assessment to you

There's a deadline for us sending the notice of penalty assessment to you. If the follower notice relates to a compliance check or relevant contributions dispute, the latest day on which we can send you a notice of penalty assessment is 90 days from the date on which the compliance check is completed or relevant contributions dispute is settled. If the follower notice relates to an appeal or a further appeal, the latest day on which we can send you a notice of penalty assessment is 90 days from the earliest of the following dates. The date on which:

- you took corrective action
- the final ruling was made in respect of your appeal or further appeal
- the appeal or further appeal was abandoned or otherwise disposed of before it was determined by the court or tribunal

The tax legislation that deals with follower notices refers to compliance checks and relevant contributions disputes as "tax enquiries".

How you can help us reduce the penalty

You can help us reduce the penalty by co-operating with us.

We can reduce the penalty percentage rate if you've co-operated with us **before** we send you the notice of penalty assessment. You've co-operated with us if you've done one or more of the following. You've:

- provided us with reasonable help in working out the amount of the tax advantage
- counteracted the denied advantage but after you have become liable to a penalty (or relinquished the denied advantage if your follower notice relates to an appeal)
- given us information that enables us to take corrective action
- given us information that enables us to enter into an agreement with you to counteract the denied advantage
- given us access to tax records so that we can make sure that the denied advantage is fully counteracted

We can't reduce the penalty percentage rate to less than 10%.

The examples of co-operation shown at the 5 bullets above, and later in this factsheet, refer to items (a) to (e) of section 210(3) of the Finance Act 2014, which is the legislation that sets out these reductions.

How we work out the penalty percentage rate

There are 4 stages in working out the penalty percentage rate. Each stage is explained below.

Stage 1: Identifying the penalty range

The penalty range is the difference between the maximum and minimum penalty percentages that we can charge. The maximum is 50 and the minimum is 10, which gives us a penalty range of 40. The maximum and minimum penalty percentages are set out in sections 209 and 210 of the Finance Act 2014.

Stage 2: Working out the reduction to the penalty range for the quality of co-operation

We use the term "quality of co-operation" to describe the level of co-operation given. We can reduce the penalty range of 40 by anything up to 100% for the quality of co-operation. However, the penalty percentage rate that we charge can never be less than 10% – even if we reduce the penalty range by 100%. We take into account all co-operation given up to the point at which we send the notice of penalty assessment.

When working out the quality of your co-operation, we'll consider what we needed you to do in respect of the denied advantage and how much of it you've done. We take into account the timing, nature and extent of what you've done. This means whether you:

- acted as soon as you reasonably could (timing)
- acted in a proactive and collaborative manner (nature)
- did all that you reasonably could have done (extent)

Once we've considered the types of co-operation shown in the table on page 3, and decided the percentage reduction for each, this gives us the reduction to the penalty range for the quality of co-operation. The reductions shown in the table are a guide.

Type of co-operation	Reduction to the penalty range if the follower notice relates to an appeal case	Reduction to the penalty range if the follower notice relates to a compliance check case
Providing us with reasonable help in working out the amount of the tax advantage. (Item (a) of section 210(3) of the Finance Act 2014.)	Not relevant	Up to 20%
Counteracting the denied advantage (this will be described as "relinquishing" the denied advantage if your follower notice relates to an appeal). (Item (b) of section 210(3) of the Finance Act 2014.)	Up to 90%	Up to 50%
Giving us information that enables us to take corrective action. (Item (c) of section 210(3) of the Finance Act 2014.)	Not relevant	Up to 10%
Giving us information that enables us to enter into an agreement with you to counteract (or "relinquish") the denied advantage. (Item (d) of section 210(3) of the Finance Act 2014.)	Up to 10%	Up to 10%
Giving us access to tax records so that we can make sure that the denied advantage is fully counteracted. (Item (e) of section 210(3) of the Finance Act 2014.)	Not relevant	Up to 10%

Follower notices that relate to an appeal

If a follower notice relates to an appeal, we will not normally need to consider allowing any reduction for co-operation for items (a), (c) and (e) above. This is because, in most cases where the follower notice relates to an appeal, all the person will need to do is relinquish the denied advantage. However if, exceptionally, we believe that any one or more of items (a), (c) or (e) are relevant, then we'll take them into account.

Stage 3: Reducing the maximum penalty percentage

Once we've worked out the reduction for the quality of co-operation, we apply this to the penalty range of 40. This gives us the figure by which we will reduce the maximum penalty percentage. For example, if the reduction for quality of co-operation is 70%, the amount by which we reduce the maximum penalty percentage will be 28 (40 × 70% = 28).

Stage 4: Working out the penalty percentage rate

To work out the penalty percentage rate that we'll charge, we deduct the figure established at stage 3 from the maximum penalty percentage. For example, if the amount established at stage 3 was 28, the penalty percentage rate will be 22% (50 less 28 = 22). The example below shows the 4 stages.

Example

The deadline for taking corrective action had passed. Before we issued the notice of penalty assessment, Mr B had co-operated with us. Taking into account the timing, nature and extent of that co-operation, we gave a reduction to the penalty range of 70%.

Stage 1: Identify the penalty range	50 to 10 = 40
Stage 2: Work out the reduction to the penalty range for the quality of co-operation	70%
Stage 3: Work out amount by which we reduce the maximum penalty percentage	40 × 70% = 28
Stage 4: Work out the penalty percentage rate	50 less 28 = 22%

How we work out the amount of your penalty

To work out the amount of your penalty, we multiply the value of the denied advantage by the penalty percentage rate.

The "value of the denied advantage" is calculated by reference to the amount of the tax advantage on which your return, claim or appeal was made, but which would be denied if the principles of the relevant ruling are applied to your return, claim or appeal.

For example, if the value of the denied advantage in the example above was £250,000 the penalty would be £55,000 (£250,000 × 22% = £55,000).

If you've taken corrective action for part of the denied advantage, the penalty will be charged on the remainder that is still in dispute. We'll tell you how we've calculated the value of the denied advantage when we write to you about your penalty.

Restriction for other penalties

After working out the amount of the penalty for not taking corrective action on time, we take into account any other "relevant" penalties that you've incurred that are calculated by reference to the same tax and/or National Insurance contributions (NICs). The legislation refers to this as "aggregate penalties".

A **"relevant"** penalty in this context is one charged under one or more of the following penalty provisions:

- Schedule 24 to the Finance Act 2007 – penalties for inaccuracies
- Schedule 41 to the Finance Act 2008 – penalties for failure to notify
- Schedule 55 to the Finance Act 2009 – penalties for failure to make a return
- section 98A of Taxes Management Act 1970 – special penalties in the case of certain returns (NICs only)
- any penalty in respect of relevant contributions specified in regulations made by the Treasury

If you incur a penalty for not taking corrective action in response to a follower notice, and you also incur one or more of the "relevant" penalties listed above, then the total amount of the penalties we charge (the "aggregate amount") must not exceed the higher of:

- the "relevant percentage" of the amount of tax and/or NICs
- £300 where one of the penalties incurred is under paragraph 5(2)(b), 6(3)(b), 6(4)(b) or 6(5)(b) of Schedule 55 to the Finance Act 2009

The "relevant percentage" is the higher of the following:

- 100%
- the maximum percentage chargeable under the other penalty provision(s) (depending on the specific type of the other penalty, the maximum percentage chargeable can be up to 200%)

Example

Mrs C has incurred a penalty for not taking corrective action. She has also incurred a penalty under Paragraph 5(2)(b) of Schedule 55 to the Finance Act 2009. The amount of tax is £100,000 and the relevant percentage is 100%.

The total amount of the penalties that we charge Mrs C in relation to that £100,000 must not exceed the higher of:

- £100,000 (the amount of tax £100,000 × the relevant percentage 100%)
- £300

So, in this case the aggregate amount of the penalties that we can charge Mrs C must not exceed £100,000.

After taking into account other penalties, this gives the amount of penalty that we'll charge.

The rules about aggregate penalties are set out in section 212 of the Finance Act 2014 and paragraph 15 of Schedule 2 to the National Insurance Contributions Act 2015.

Interest for paying the penalty late

If we charge you a penalty and you don't pay it on time, we may charge you late payment interest on the amount of the penalty.

Stamp Duty Land Tax: partnerships and joint purchasers

For Stamp Duty Land Tax, each responsible partner or joint purchaser is responsible for paying the amount of penalty due. This is known as "joint and several liability", or sometimes referred to as being "jointly and severally liable". What this means in practice is that any one or more of the responsible partners or joint purchasers can be required to pay the penalty for not taking corrective action on time.

Annual Tax on Enveloped Dwellings: partnerships

For Annual Tax on Enveloped Dwellings, each responsible partner is responsible for paying the amount of penalty due. This is known as "joint and several liability", or sometimes referred to as being "jointly and severally liable". What this means in practice is that any one or more of the responsible partners can be required to pay the penalty for not taking corrective action on time.

Appealing against the penalty if you disagree

If we charge you a penalty for not taking corrective action, you'll be able to appeal against it if you disagree.

You can appeal against the amount of the penalty. You can also appeal against the penalty if you believe that one or more of the following applies:

- condition A, B or D hasn't been met in relation to the follower notice (we explained those conditions in the follower notice)
- the final court or tribunal ruling specified in the follower notice isn't relevant to the tax avoidance scheme that you used
- you received the follower notice after the deadline for us sending it to you
- it was reasonable, in all the circumstances, for you to have not taken the necessary corrective action

If you appeal you must do so in writing. You must make sure that your appeal reaches us within 30 days of the date that you receive the notice of penalty assessment. When you write to us, please:

- give us as much information as possible about what you disagree with
- send copies of any documentary evidence that supports your appeal

If your tax liability is settled on the basis that you:

- achieve the tax advantage, then we'll cancel the penalty
- don't achieve the tax advantage, then you'll have to pay the penalty unless you've successfully appealed against it

You can find more information about appeals in factsheet HMRC1, "HM Revenue and Customs decisions – what to do if you disagree". You can get a copy online, go to **www.gov.uk** and search for "HMRC1".

The Human Rights Act and follower notice penalties

Article 6 of the European Convention on Human Rights gives you certain rights when we're considering charging penalties that are based on a maximum of 70%, or more, of the relevant tax. Although penalties for not taking corrective action on time in response to a follower notice are not covered by Article 6, we will administer them in precisely the same way as penalties that are covered by Article 6.

We always welcome your co-operation in taking corrective action, and in providing information about the tax advantage. The amount of penalty we charge will depend on the degree to which you co-operate with us. This is explained earlier in this factsheet.

We also welcome any help that you give us when establishing the amount of the penalty for not taking corrective action on time. When we're considering penalties you have the right not to answer our questions. The degree to which you help us is entirely your choice. In making a decision about how much you're going to help, you have the right to consult an adviser. If you don't already have an adviser, you may want to consider consulting one.

You have the right to have the matter of penalties dealt with without unreasonable delay. We'll tell you how much penalty is due when we've established the full extent of the co-operation that you've given, and the amount of the tax advantage. If you disagree with the penalty you can appeal.

You can apply for publicly funded legal assistance or Legal Aid. In some circumstances, funding may be available to help you bring certain appeals before the tribunal. If you intend to appeal against the amount of the penalty, you may want to check whether your case qualifies for legal assistance and the type of help that may be available. We're not involved in decisions about whether or not your case will qualify for legal assistance. The way you can check what help is available and the qualifying conditions depend on where you live in the United Kingdom (UK). You can find more information from Citizens Advice or you can apply for funded legal assistance or Legal Aid through a solicitor anywhere in the UK.

If there's anything you don't understand about these rights or what they mean for you, please tell the officer who gave you this factsheet straightaway.

The taxes and NICs to which these penalty rules apply

These penalty rules apply to follower notices for the taxes and NICs shown below:

- Annual Tax on Enveloped Dwellings
- Capital Gains Tax
- Class 1, 1A and 1B NICs through PAYE
- certain Class 2 NICs
- Class 4 NICs
- Corporation Tax
- Income Tax (Self Assessment)

- Inheritance Tax
- Income Tax (through PAYE)
- Stamp Duty Land Tax

CC/FS34a COMPLIANCE CHECKS: INFORMATION ABOUT THE GENERAL ANTI-ABUSE RULE – CC/FS34a [HMRC, December 2017]

You will need to read this factsheet if you've used arrangements that we consider the general anti-abuse rule (GAAR) may apply to. This factsheet tells you about the GAAR and contains important information. You may need to refer to it later.

Where this factsheet refers to **"tax"**, this means the taxes, levies and contributions to which the GAAR applies. These are listed at the end of this factsheet.

This factsheet is one of a series of compliance checks factsheets (https://www.gov.uk/government/collections/hm-revenue-and-customs-compliance-checks-factsheets).

About the general anti-abuse rule

The GAAR helps to make sure that people pay the right amount of tax by enabling us to tackle "abusive" tax arrangements. The GAAR legislation sets out what "abusive" tax arrangements are, and what we can do to counteract the tax advantages that people try to gain from using such arrangements. The GAAR also aims to deter people from entering into abusive tax arrangements.

The GAAR enables us to make "just and reasonable" adjustments that counteract the tax advantage that a person has tried to gain from using abusive tax arrangements.

The GAAR came into force on 17 July 2013 and applies to arrangements entered into on or after that date. It was extended to cover National Insurance contributions with effect from 13 March 2014. Further amendments were made to the GAAR on 15 September 2016, which:

- allow us to give provisional counteraction notices
- introduce the concepts of "pooling", "binding" and "generic referrals" where we're applying opinions obtained from the GAAR Advisory Panel to users of equivalent arrangements
- introduce penalties for people who entered into abusive tax arrangements on or after 15 September 2016

If "pooling", "binding" or "generic referrals" apply to your arrangements, we'll give you information about that separately.

You can find more information about the GAAR Advisory Panel later in this factsheet.

What tax arrangements are

Arrangements are "tax arrangements" if, considering all the circumstances, it would be reasonable to conclude that the main purpose, or one of the main purposes of the arrangements was to obtain a tax advantage.

When tax arrangements are considered to be abusive

The GAAR states that tax arrangements are abusive if they are arrangements, the entering into or carrying out of which, can't reasonably be regarded as a reasonable course of action in relation to the relevant tax provisions – taking into account all the circumstances. This is often referred to as the **"double reasonableness test"**. The circumstances that will be taken into account include the following:

- the principles and policy objectives of those tax provisions
- whether the results of the arrangements are consistent with the principles on which those tax provisions are based
- whether the way in which those results are obtained involves one or more contrived or abnormal steps
- whether the arrangements are intended to exploit any shortcomings in those tax provisions
- whether the arrangements produce a tax loss which is significantly greater than the economic loss, or a taxable profit or gain which is significantly smaller than the economic profit or gain
- whether the arrangements enable a claim to be made for a repayment or credit in respect of tax, that has not been paid
- *whether the arrangements* are consistent with established practice that had been accepted by HM Revenue and Customs (HMRC)

You can find more information about when tax arrangements may be considered abusive in Parts A and B of our current GAAR guidance (https://www.gov.uk/government/publications/tax-avoidance-general-anti-abuse-rules).

The GAAR Advisory Panel

The GAAR Advisory Panel is a committee of independent tax specialists, whose purpose is to provide a safeguard for our customers. Their role includes giving us an independent opinion on certain matters. No HMRC staff are on the panel.

We refer tax arrangements to the panel so it can give us its opinion. We ask the panel whether it considers the entering into and carrying out of those tax arrangements is a reasonable course of action in relation to the relevant tax provisions. If different panel members have different opinions, the panel will give us all the opinions. We then take into account the panel's opinion, or opinions when we decide what action to take under the GAAR, if any.

The panel's opinion, or opinions will be relevant to the particular tax arrangements that we referred to the panel, and, where appropriate, to other equivalent arrangements.

We'll give you more information, and tell you what we mean by "equivalent arrangements", if this applies to you.

GAAR Advisory Panel (https://www.gov.uk/government/groups/general-anti-abuse-rule-advisory-panel) gives more information about how the panel considers cases.

General information

Customers with particular needs

If there is anything about your health or personal circumstances that may make it difficult for you to deal with this matter, please let us know. Telling us will mean that we can help you in the most appropriate way. There's more information at Dealing with HMRC if you have additional needs (https://www.gov.uk/dealing-hmrc-additional-needs).

The taxes, levies and contributions to which the GAAR relates

Unless otherwise stated below, the GAAR has effect for any tax arrangements entered into on or after 17 July 2013 for the following:

- Annual Tax on Enveloped Dwellings
- Apprenticeship Levy (with effect from 15 September 2016)
- Capital Gains Tax
- Corporation Tax (including any amount chargeable as if it were Corporation Tax, or treated as if it were Corporation Tax)
- Diverted Profits Tax (on profits arising from 1 April 2015)
- Income Tax (including Income Tax collected through the PAYE system)
- Inheritance Tax
- National Insurance contributions
- Petroleum Revenue Tax
- Stamp Duty Land Tax

The GAAR relates to National Insurance contributions (NICs) with effect from 13 March 2014 in relation to arrangements entered into on or after that date. This includes NICs collected through the PAYE system, Class 4 NICs that are collected through Self Assessment and, from the tax year 6 April 2015 to 5 April 2016 it also includes most Class 2 NICs that are collected through Self Assessment.

CC/FS38 COMPLIANCE CHECKS: SERIAL TAX AVOIDANCE WARNING NOTICES [HMRC, March 2017]

This factsheet tells you about the "serial tax avoidance" legislation, and warning notices given under that legislation. You should read this factsheet if you've used a tax avoidance scheme, or if a tax avoidance scheme has been used by a:

- partnership that you're a member of
- company within your group of companies
- person who is an associate of yours

The factsheet explains that HM Revenue and Customs (HMRC) may give you a warning notice after we've defeated a scheme that you've used. We explain what we mean by **"used"** and **"defeated"** later in this factsheet.

The serial tax avoidance legislation doesn't apply to schemes where you entered into the scheme before 15 September 2016 and we defeated the scheme before 6 April 2017.

Where this factsheet refers to **"tax"**, this means the taxes, levies and contributions to which the serial tax avoidance legislation applies. These are listed at the end of this factsheet. Where this factsheet refers to **"scheme"** it also includes **"arrangements"** or **"tax arrangements"**, which are expressions used in tax avoidance legislation.

This factsheet is one of a series of compliance checks factsheets (https://www.gov.uk/government/collections/hm-revenue-and-customs-leaflets-factsheets-and-booklets).

1. Serial tax avoidance legislation – how it works

The serial tax avoidance legislation was introduced on 15 September 2016. It's designed to deter people from using tax avoidance schemes.

Once we've defeated a tax avoidance scheme that you've used, we'll give you a warning notice. That warning notice will remain in place for 5 years. This period is known as the "warning period". During a warning period, you'll have to give us detailed information about any tax avoidance schemes you've used during that period.

If you're already in a warning period and we give you another warning notice, then we'll extend your warning period by up to a further 5 years.

If we defeat a tax avoidance scheme that you've used during a warning period, we may impose certain sanctions. However, we can't impose these sanctions if you entered into the scheme before 15 September 2016.

If we've defeated a tax avoidance scheme on or after 6 April 2017 and you entered into that scheme before 15 September 2016, we won't take that defeat into account for the purposes of the serial tax avoidance legislation if you've done one of the following before 6 April 2017:

- fully disclosed details of the scheme to us
- told us that you'll fully disclose details of the scheme to us and you then do so within the time limit that we've set

2. What a tax avoidance scheme is and what we mean by "used"

For the serial tax avoidance legislation, a tax avoidance scheme is one of the following:

- arrangements that are disclosable under the disclosure of tax avoidance schemes (DOTAS) legislation
- a scheme that is disclosable, or has been disclosed, under the VAT Avoidance Disclosure Regime (VADR) legislation
- tax arrangements for which we've given you a follower notice
- tax arrangements where we've given you a notice of final decision, telling you that the tax advantages arising from the scheme are to be counteracted under the General AntiAbuse Rule (GAAR)

You've used a tax avoidance scheme if you've done one or more of the following:

- sent us a tax return or claim that relies on a tax avoidance scheme to reduce your liability to tax, or to increase tax reliefs
- failed to meet your tax obligations as a result of a tax avoidance scheme for example, by not registering for VAT when you should have

3. When a tax avoidance scheme is defeated

If you've used one of the types of tax avoidance scheme described above, we may counteract the tax advantages claimed by you. How we'd counteract them would depend on the type of tax and the tax avoidance scheme you've used. Counteracting the tax advantages would involve you or us making adjustments to your tax position, which may also mean you'll have to pay additional tax.

Your tax avoidance scheme would be defeated when the counteraction becomes final. It would become final when the adjustments made to your tax position, and any additional tax resulting from those adjustments, can no longer be varied – either on appeal or otherwise.

Adjustments to your tax position would normally involve us doing one of the following:

- telling you about adjustments that you're required to make to your tax returns or claims
- making adjustments to your tax returns or claims
- giving you one or more tax assessments, decision notices or determinations for the additional tax that you have to pay

4. If we defeat your scheme

If we defeat your scheme and the serial tax avoidance legislation applies to the defeat, we'll give you a warning notice. That warning notice will remain in place for a period of 5 years, although this warning period may be extended if we defeat other schemes that you've used. We explain this in more detail below.

During the warning period you'll have to send us the following each year:

- details of any tax avoidance scheme that you've used during that year, and which is disclosable under DOTAS
- details of any tax avoidance scheme that you've used during that year which is disclosable, or has been disclosed, under VADR
- explanations of why you think the scheme or schemes you've used achieve the intended tax advantage, or avoid an obligation in relation to tax that you would otherwise have
- details of how much tax would be payable to us if you hadn't used the scheme, or the scheme doesn't achieve the tax advantage that it tries to achieve whichever applies

If you're already in a warning period and we defeat another tax avoidance scheme that you've used, we'll give you a new warning notice. That notice will extend your existing warning period by up to 5 years. If we defeat a tax avoidance scheme after a warning period has ended, we'll give you a new notice, which will start a new 5-year warning period.

Also, if we defeat one or more tax avoidance schemes where both of the following apply, you:

- entered into the scheme on or after 15 September 2016 (this is referred to as a **"new scheme"**)
- used the scheme during a warning period including an extended warning period

then we may impose one or more sanctions under the serial tax avoidance legislation. These sanctions are explained below.

4.1 Charge you a penalty

If we defeat one or more new schemes that you've used during a warning period, we'll charge you a penalty. We've explained above what we mean by **"new scheme"**. The penalty will be calculated as a percentage of the counteracted advantage. The counteracted advantage is normally the additional tax due, but we would tell you more about this at the time. After the:

- first defeat of a new scheme used in the warning period, we'll charge you a penalty equal to 20% of the value of the counteracted advantage
- second defeat of a new scheme used in the warning period, we'll charge you a penalty equal to 40% of the value of the counteracted advantage
- third and any subsequent defeats of new schemes used in the warning period, we'll charge you a penalty equal to 60% of the value of the counteracted advantage

4.2 Publish your name

If we defeat 3 new schemes that you've used, and you've used them all during the same warning period, we may publish your name and other details to identify you as a serial tax avoider.

4.3 Stop you from claiming tax reliefs

If we defeat 3 new schemes that you've used during a warning period, and each of those schemes involves the misuse of direct tax reliefs, we'll stop you from claiming, or making use of direct tax reliefs for 3 years. If this happens, we'll give you a "relief restriction notice". The direct taxes to which the serial tax avoidance legislation applies are listed under the heading General information.

5. Benefits of disclosing your DOTAS or VADR scheme before we start a check of your tax affairs

If you want to settle your tax affairs on the basis that you no longer want to use one or more of your avoidance schemes, you can do so and the defeat won't count for the purposes of the serial tax avoidance legislation. That means we won't give you a warning notice for it, or extend an existing warning period for it. This can only apply if:

- you have no reason to believe that we've started, or are about to start, a check of your tax affairs
- the arrangements aren't afterwards counteracted under the GAAR
- we haven't sent you a follower notice for the arrangements

If you want to settle on this basis, you need to contact us straightaway. When you do, you'll need to make a full disclosure of the details of the scheme and its use, and tell us the additional amount of tax.

A check of your tax affairs might be referred to as a compliance check, enquiry, investigation, review or other similar term.

6. Partnerships, groups of companies, and associates

Special rules apply for:

- members of a partnership that has used an avoidance scheme that we've defeated
- companies in a group of companies, where one of the companies has used an avoidance scheme that we've defeated
- associates of a person who has used an avoidance scheme that we've defeated

In these circumstances, as well as giving a warning notice to you when we've defeated a scheme you've used, we'll give a warning notice to those linked to you through partnership, company group membership, or by being associates.

For the serial tax avoidance legislation, 2 persons are associates if one of them is a body corporate (for example, a company) controlled by the other, or if they're both bodies corporate under common control.

The rules about sanctions are different depending on whether the link between persons is from being in a partnership, being part of a group of companies, or by being associates.

6.1 Partnerships

If we defeat a new avoidance scheme that was used in a partnership tax return, we may publish the names of all partners in the partnership. We may also restrict their direct tax reliefs. We may only charge a penalty on the partners whose tax position was affected by the defeat. However, for all partners, the defeat will count towards the number of defeats they've had when we're considering charging them penalties and restricting their direct tax reliefs.

6.2 Groups of companies

If we give a warning notice to other companies in the group, we may also publish the name of those companies.

Although those warning notices can't result directly in us charging the other companies penalties, or stopping them from claiming or using direct tax reliefs, they'll count towards the number of warning notices they've had when we're considering those matters.

6.3 Associates

The warning notices that we give to associates can't result directly in us publishing the names of those associates. However, they'll count towards the 2 warning notices required before we can publish their names. These warning notices don't count towards the number of defeats for the associates where we're considering penalties or direct tax reliefs.

7. Your rights when we're considering penalties and relief restriction

You can't appeal against our decision to give you a warning notice. However, you can appeal to an independent tribunal if we charge you a penalty, or give you a relief restriction notice, and you disagree with our decision.

8. Your rights when we're considering publishing your name

We'll let you know if we're considering publishing your name and other details to identify you as a serial tax avoider. And we'll give you the opportunity to make representations about whether or not the information should be published.

9. If we've charged you a penalty and you think you have a reasonable excuse

If you use a new scheme during a warning period and we defeat it, you'll be liable to pay a penalty. This is explained in the section headed If we defeat your scheme.

When we're considering penalties, your use of the scheme we've defeated is considered to be a failure to meet a tax obligation.

If you have a reasonable excuse for failing to meet that tax obligation, we won't charge you a penalty for it. Also, that defeat won't count if we're considering penalties for defeats of other new schemes that you've used during that warning period.

A reasonable excuse is something that has stopped a person from meeting a tax obligation on time, which they took reasonable care to meet. This might be due to circumstances outside their control, or a combination of events. Once the reasonable excuse has ended, the person must put things right without any unnecessary delay.

Whether a person has a reasonable excuse depends on the particular circumstances in which they failed to meet the tax obligation, and their particular circumstances and abilities. This may mean that what is a reasonable excuse for one person may not be a reasonable excuse for someone else.

It is not a reasonable excuse if the failure to meet the tax obligation was because:

- of a lack of funds – unless it's attributable to events outside your control
- you had relied on another person to do something – unless you took reasonable care to avoid the failure
- you were acting on advice, unless that advice was addressed to you and took account of your circumstances relying on general advice given to a group of people or advice addressed to another person or which takes no account of your individual circumstances won't count as a reasonable excuse

10. General information

10.1 Customers with particular needs

If there's anything about your health or personal circumstances that may make it difficult for you to deal with this matter, please let us know. Telling us will mean that we can help you in the most appropriate way. There is more information at Dealing with HMRC if you have additional needs (https://www.gov.uk/dealing-hmrc-additional-needs).

10.2 Taxes, levies and contributions to which the serial tax avoidance legislation relates

The direct taxes are:

- Annual Tax on Enveloped Dwellings
- Apprenticeship Levy
- Capital Gains Tax
- Corporation Tax (including any amount chargeable as if it were Corporation Tax, or treated as if it were Corporation Tax)
- Diverted Profits Tax
- Income Tax
- Inheritance Tax
- National Insurance contributions
- Petroleum Revenue Tax
- Stamp Duty Land Tax

The indirect tax is Value Added Tax (VAT).

CC/FS38a – SERIAL TAX AVOIDANCE REGIME – GENERAL INFORMATION [HMRC, March 2018]

The Serial Tax Avoidance Regime (STAR) is designed to deter people from using tax avoidance schemes. A tax avoidance scheme is a set of arrangements that try to use the tax legislation to gain a tax advantage that isn't intended by the legislation. In some parts of this factsheet we use the term arrangements because that's the term used in the STAR legislation, and in other tax avoidance legislation.

You should read this factsheet if you've personally used a tax avoidance scheme, or if a tax avoidance scheme has been used by a person linked to you. Persons are linked if they're both one of the following:

- companies in the same group of companies
- associates
- members of a partnership when it used a tax avoidance scheme in a Partnership Tax Return

You can find more information about the special rules that apply when a person is linked to you in the section "Partnerships, groups of companies, and associates in STAR" on page 6 of this factsheet. We explain what we mean by "used" on that page too.

The term "tax" in this factsheet means the taxes, levies and contributions to which STAR applies. These are listed on page 6 of this factsheet.

This factsheet is one of a series. For the full list of factsheets in the series, go to www.gov.uk and search for "Compliance checks factsheets".

When STAR applies

The STAR only applies to the defeat of tax avoidance schemes in the circumstances shown below. It applies to any arrangements:

- that are disclosable under the disclosure of tax avoidance schemes (DOTAS) legislation – we refer to these as DOTAS arrangements

- that are disclosable, or have been disclosed, under the VAT disclosure regime (VADR) – we refer to these as VADR arrangements
- that are disclosable under the disclosure of tax avoidance schemes – VAT and other indirect taxes (DASVOIT) legislation – we refer to these as DASVOIT arrangements
- for which we've given a follower notice, and the denied advantage to which that follower notice relates has been counteracted and is final – we give a follower notice if there's been a court ruling in another person's case, and we believe that ruling is also relevant to the arrangements to which the follower notice relates
- for which we've given a notice of final decision, stating that the tax advantages arising from those arrangements are to be counteracted under the general anti-abuse rule (GAAR)

The STAR will apply to the defeat if the tax avoidance scheme was entered into:

- on or after 15 September 2016
- before 15 September 2016, and we defeat it on or after 6 April 2017 – except if the person who entered into it did one of the following before 6 April 2017
  - fully disclosed to us details of their use of the scheme
  - contacted us to commit to fully disclosing details of their use of the scheme, and then did so within the time limit that we set

We explain what we mean by "defeated" on page 5, and what we mean by "tax advantage" on page 2.

How STAR works

Once we've defeated a tax avoidance scheme that you've used, or that was used by a person linked to you, we'll write to tell you that we've put you into the STAR and give you a warning notice. We have to give you the warning notice within the period of 90 days beginning with the day of the defeat of a tax avoidance scheme that STAR applies to.

The warning notice and warning period

The warning notice will tell you that you're in a 5-year warning period. Being in a warning period means that you'll have to give us information about certain tax avoidance schemes that you've personally used in that period. To do this you'll have to send us written notices, which are known as information notices.

We'll split the 5-year warning period into shorter periods, known as reporting periods. You'll have to give us an information notice for each reporting period.

Your warning notice will tell you:

- when your warning period starts and ends
- when each of your reporting periods starts and ends
- what details you'll need to give us in each of your information notices

Your warning notice will also tell you that we can impose certain sanctions on you if you personally use another tax avoidance scheme while you're in a warning period, and we defeat it. You can find more about these in the section "Sanctions under STAR".

Your warning period will be extended if we give you another warning notice during that period.

Information notices

You'll need to send each of your information notices to us no later than 30 calendar days after the end of the reporting period to which it relates. If we don't receive your information notice on time, or if it's inaccurate or incomplete, we may extend the warning period by up to a further 5 years.

In each information notice you'll have to tell us about DOTAS, VADR or DASVOIT arrangements that you've personally used to achieve a tax advantage:

- on returns, or in claims, elections, declarations or applications for approval, that you sent us in the reporting period
- by failing to meet an obligation that you would otherwise have had in the reporting period – for example, you needed to register for VAT, but you thought that, by using VADR arrangements, you didn't need to

You'll have to explain how the arrangements enable you to achieve the tax advantage including, if relevant, *how they mean you don't* have an obligation to do something. You'll also have to tell us the amount of the tax advantage that your use of the arrangements enables you to obtain.

When you send your information notice, you'll also have to tell us if you failed to make a return that was due in the period. If a return is due in the warning period, but you don't send it to us until after the warning period has ended, you'll still have to tell us about any arrangements you use on that return. We may ask you to do this on a supplementary information notice.

Tax advantage

In general terms, a tax advantage is the difference between the amount of tax that would be payable with and without the use of the tax avoidance scheme. Depending on the tax avoidance scheme that you've used it may not be as straightforward as that.

Sanctions under STAR

If you're in a warning period, and you personally use a new scheme that we defeat, we'll consider imposing sanctions on you. A new scheme is a tax avoidance scheme that's been entered into on or after 15 September 2016. For sanctions, it doesn't matter whether or not the defeat happened during the warning period, as long as you used the new scheme during the warning period.

We may impose any or all of the following sanctions:

- charging you a penalty
- publishing your details to identify you as a serial tax avoider
- stopping you from claiming certain direct tax reliefs

We explain these sanctions in more detail in the next section.

Which sanctions we'll consider

If you use a new scheme while you're in a warning period, the sanctions that we may impose will depend on why you're already in that warning period.

If you're in that warning period because we've given you a warning notice for a scheme used by any of the following:

- you personally
- persons linked to you in your capacity as a partner or as a group company

then we may impose any one or more of the sanctions, which are charging you a penalty, publishing your details and stopping you from claiming certain direct tax reliefs.

However, if you're in that warning period because we've given you a warning notice for a scheme used by a person linked to you in your capacity as an associate, then the only sanction we can consider is publishing your details.

Prior warning notices when we're considering sanctions

If we're considering imposing sanctions on you, we'll look at how many other warning notices we've given you for defeats of new schemes that either:

- you personally used during the warning period
- were used, during the same warning period, by persons linked to you

We refer to such notices as prior warning notices. The prior warning notices we'll take into account will depend on the sanction we're considering. If we're considering:

- publishing your details to identify you as a serial tax avoider, we'll take into account all prior warning notices we've given to you
- charging you a penalty or stopping you from claiming certain direct tax reliefs, we'll take into account prior warning notices we've given you for schemes used by any of the following:
  - you personally
  - persons linked to you in your capacity as a partner or as a group company

Where a prior warning notice covers 2 or more defeats, we'll treat this as if we'd given separate warning notices for each defeat.

When we may charge you a penalty

If you personally use a new scheme during a warning period and we defeat it, we'll give you a warning notice for that defeat and charge you a penalty. The penalty will be calculated as a percentage of the counteracted advantage. The counteracted advantage is normally the additional tax due for the defeat that the penalty relates to, but we'll tell you more about this at the time.

The penalty percentage rate will depend on how many prior warning notices we've given you, either for schemes you've used or for schemes used by persons linked to you in your capacity as a partner or as a group company. We'll charge a penalty of 20% if we've not given you a prior warning notice. The penalty rate rises to 40% if we've given you one prior warning notice, or to 60% if we've given you 2 or more.

When we may publish your details

We'll consider publishing your details if both of the following apply during your warning period:

- you personally used a new scheme during your warning period, and we've given you a warning notice for the defeat of that scheme
- we've given you 2 or more prior warning notices

The information we publish can include:

- your name and address (including any trading name, previous name or other name that you use)
- the nature of your business, if you have one
- the amount of tax you've tried to avoid, and the amount of any penalty that we've charged you under STAR
- the period or periods for which you used the tax avoidance schemes
- any other details we think are necessary to clearly identify you

If we publish details about a company that's part of a group of companies, we may also publish the names, addresses and nature of the business of other members of the group, and the trading name of the group. If we publish details about a person carrying on a trade or business in partnership, we may also publish names and addresses of the other partners, and the trading name of the partnership.

When we may stop you from claiming direct tax reliefs

Direct tax reliefs are those reliefs relating to direct taxes. The direct taxes to which STAR applies are listed under the section "General information" on page 6 of this factsheet.

We'll give you a relief restriction notice that will stop you from claiming or making use of direct tax reliefs for 3 years, if all of the following apply:

- you personally used a new scheme during your warning period, and we've given you a warning notice for the defeat of that scheme
- we've given you at least 2 prior warning notices, either for schemes you've used or for schemes used by persons linked to you in your capacity as a partner or a group company
- the new scheme that you used, and the new schemes for which at least 2 of the prior warning notices were given, all involved the misuse of direct tax reliefs
- for the new scheme that you used, and the new schemes for which the 2 prior warning notices were given, one of the following applies:
  - the arrangements were counteracted on the basis of a particular avoidance related rule
  - the misused relief was a loss relief

An avoidance-related rule is any tax rule, however worded, that refers to either of the following:

- the purpose or expected benefit of a transaction, act or other element of a scheme being tax avoidance, or to obtain a tax advantage
- a transaction, act or other element of a scheme having or not having a commercial purpose

"Loss relief" means any Income Tax loss relief (under Part 4 of the Income Tax Act 2007) or Corporation Tax loss relief and group relief (under Parts 4 and 5 of the Corporation Tax Act 2010).

You can find full details of the types of reliefs that we can stop people from claiming or using in Part 4 of Schedule 18 to the Finance Act 2016. Future changes to tax legislation may mean that we need to change the types of direct tax reliefs that we can stop people from claiming or using.

Extending the restricted period for direct tax reliefs if we defeat another scheme

If you're already in a restricted period and we defeat another new scheme that you've used during the same warning period involving the misuse of direct tax reliefs, we'll extend your restricted period by 3 years beginning with the day of the new defeat.

Your rights when we're considering sanctions

You can't appeal against our decision to give you a warning notice. However, you can appeal to an independent tribunal if we charge you a penalty under STAR, or give you a relief restriction notice, and you disagree with our decision.

We'll let you know if we're considering publishing your details to identify you as a serial tax avoider. At the same time, we'll give you the opportunity to make representations about whether or not we should publish the information, but you wouldn't have any right to appeal against our decision to publish your details.

If you think you have a reasonable excuse

When we're considering charging you a penalty under STAR or stopping you from claiming direct tax reliefs, your use of the scheme we've defeated is considered to be a failure to meet a tax obligation.

If you have a reasonable excuse for this failure, we won't charge you a penalty under STAR, or stop you from claiming direct tax reliefs in respect of your use of the defeated scheme.

A reasonable excuse is something that has stopped you from meeting a tax obligation on time, which you took reasonable care to meet. This might be due to circumstances outside your control, or a combination of events. Once the reasonable excuse has ended, you must put things right without unnecessary delay.

Whether you have a reasonable excuse depends on the particular circumstances of your case. This is because what is a reasonable excuse for one person may not be a reasonable excuse for someone else.

It would **not** be a reasonable excuse if the failure was because:

- of a lack of funds – unless it's attributable to events outside your control
- you had relied on someone else to do something – unless you took reasonable care to avoid the failure
- you had acted on general advice given to a group of people, or advice addressed to someone else, or advice which took no account of your own individual circumstances

Benefits of coming out of, or settling, your tax avoidance schemes

You may be able to adjust or settle your tax affairs for DOTAS, VADR or DASVOIT arrangements that you've used – without them being counted as a defeat for the purposes of the STAR. To do this you'd need to correct your tax position. However, you can only do this if:

- you have no reason to believe that we've started, or are about to start, a check of your tax affairs for the tax that the arrangements affect – this might be referred to as a compliance check, enquiry, investigation, review or similar term
- the arrangements are not counteracted under the GAAR
- we haven't sent you a follower notice for the arrangements

If you want to correct your tax position, you should adjust your return or claim, if you can. If you can't – for example because the time limit has passed for amending your return – then contact us straightaway and we'll tell you what information we need to be able to adjust it for you. If you don't provide that information, and we later defeat the arrangements, that defeat will still count for the purposes of the STAR.

If you've used DOTAS, VADR or DASVOIT arrangements but you can't come out of them in the way described above – for example, because we've started a check of your tax affairs – then you can still settle now. Settling your affairs is a defeat for the purposes of the STAR, so we'd still have to give you a warning notice. But if you've used more than one scheme and you settle everything at once, we can give you all the warning notices at the same time. This means we don't have to keep extending your warning period.

If you don't settle all your schemes at once, we'll give you another warning notice for each defeat. If the defeats happen while you're in warning period, we'll keep extending your warning period for each defeat. If you want to settle, please contact us straightaway. Settling would involve you agreeing that your use of the arrangements doesn't enable you to obtain the tax advantage.

What we mean by "used" and "defeated"

A tax avoidance scheme is "used" if a person has done one or more of the following:

- sent us a tax return, claim or election that relies on a tax avoidance scheme to reduce their liability to tax, or to increase tax reliefs or rights to repayments of tax
- sent us a Partnership Tax Return that relies on a tax avoidance scheme to reduce the partners' liability to tax, or to increase tax reliefs or rights to repayments of tax
- failed to meet their tax obligations as a result of a tax avoidance scheme, for example, by not registering for VAT when they should have

A tax avoidance scheme is "defeated" when the tax advantage has been counteracted and the counteraction has become final. It's been counteracted when either:

- we've made adjustments to the person's tax position to remove the tax advantage
- the person has made adjustments to their own tax position
- we've entered into a contract settlement with the person
- a tribunal or court makes adjustments to the person's tax position to remove the tax advantage

A counteraction becomes final when the adjustments, and any additional tax resulting from those adjustments, can no longer be varied – either on appeal or otherwise. If we make adjustments to a person's tax position, it would normally involve us doing one of the following:

- making adjustments to the person's tax returns or claims
- giving the person one or more tax assessments, decision notices or determinations that show the adjustments and the additional tax that results from the adjustments

If we give a person a follower notice for a scheme they've used, the tax advantage is counteracted when they take corrective action in response to that follower notice. If they don't take corrective action and we, or a tribunal or court, make (or have already made) adjustments to their tax position, the tax advantage is counteracted once that adjustment becomes final.

Partnerships, groups of companies, and associates in STAR

Partnerships

When we've defeated a partner's use of tax arrangements that were used on a Partnership Tax Return, we'll look at those who were partners during the period covered by the return. All those who were partners during this period will be given a warning notice and put into the STAR, if they're not already in it and haven't already settled or fully disclosed. But the timing of these other warning notices will depend on whether or not they tried to obtain a tax advantage from the use of the arrangements. For partners who:

- didn't try to obtain a tax advantage we'll give the warning notice when one partner's use is defeated
- did try to obtain a tax advantage we'll give the warning notice when we defeat their use of the scheme

We'll also require the partnership to give us "partnership information notices". We'll nominate a partner, known as the "appropriate partner", to do this and we'll tell them what they need to do. A partnership includes a limited liability partnership. A Partnership Tax Return is one that's made under section 12AA of the Taxes Management Act 1970.

Groups of companies

For the STAR, 2 companies are members of the same group of companies if one is a 75% subsidiary of the other, or both are 75% subsidiaries of a third company.

If we give a warning notice to a company in a group, we also have to give a warning notice to all the companies in the group. However, instead of giving a separate warning notice to each company, we may give a single warning notice that applies to the whole group. Also, we may allow a group to give us one information notice for each reporting period that combines the information for the whole group.

If we've given a warning notice to a company before it joins a group, and it's still in the warning period when it joins, that warning period will only apply to that company – not to the other companies in the group. However, if we later give a warning notice to another company in the group, or another warning notice to the company that joined the group, the warning notice given to the company before it joined the group will be counted as a prior warning notice for all the companies in the group when we're considering sanctions.

If a company is only in a warning period because another company in the same group used a tax avoidance scheme that we defeated, that company's warning period will end if it leaves the group.

There are special rules for VAT group registrations. For the STAR, a VAT group is treated as if it were a single person. And a defeat of a tax avoidance scheme used on a VAT group's VAT return is treated separately from any defeats of schemes used on other types of returns by individual companies within the group. This is the case even if the membership of the VAT and corporate group is the same. If this applies to you, we'll tell you.

Associates

For the STAR, 2 persons are associates if one of them is a body corporate (for example, a company) controlled by the other, or if they're both bodies corporate under common control. Two bodies corporate are under common control if they're both controlled in one of the following ways:

- by one person
- by 2 or more, but fewer than 6, individuals
- by any number of individuals carrying on a business in partnership
- companies that are in the same group will not be treated as associates.

If we've given a warning notice to a person because we've defeated their use of tax arrangements, we'll also give warning notices to those persons who, at the time we give that notice, are their associates.

General information

Customers with particular needs

If there's anything about your health or personal circumstances that may make it difficult for you to deal with this matter, please let us know. Telling us will mean that we can help you in the most appropriate way. For more details go to www.gov.uk/dealing-hmrc-additional-needs

Taxes, levies and contributions to which STAR relates

Direct taxes – Annual Tax on Enveloped Dwellings; Apprenticeship Levy; Capital Gains Tax; Corporation Tax (CT) (including any amount chargeable as if it were CT, or treated as if it were CT); Diverted Profits Tax; Income Tax; Inheritance Tax; National Insurance contributions; Petroleum Revenue Tax, and Stamp Duty Land Tax.

Indirect taxes – Value Added Tax (VAT), Insurance Premium Tax, General Betting Duty, Pool Betting Duty, Remote Gaming Duty, Machine Games Duty, Gaming Duty, Lottery Duty, Bingo Duty, Air Passenger Duty, Hydrocarbon Oils Duty, Tobacco Products Duty, duties on spirits, beer, wine, made-wine and cider, Soft Drinks Industry Levy, Aggregates Levy, Landfill Tax, Climate Change Levy, customs duties

HMRC1 HM REVENUE AND CUSTOMS (HMRC) DECISIONS – WHAT YOU CAN DO IF YOU DISAGREE [HMRC, January 2017]

Disagreeing with an HMRC decision

This factsheet tells you what you can do if you don't agree with one of our tax decisions and about appealing to the independent tax tribunal. It applies to tax decisions made on or after 1 April 2009.

This factsheet only relates to tax decisions. If your decision relates to:

- tax credits, you should go to www.gov.uk/tax-credits-appeals-complaints
- Child Benefit, you should go to www.gov.uk/social-security-child-support-tribunal
- Child Trust Fund, you should go to www.gov.uk/child-trust-funds/overview
- restoration of seized goods, you should go to www.gov.uk/customs-seizures

Tell us now if you disagree

When we make a decision which you can appeal against, we'll write and tell you. We'll also explain how we arrived at the decision and tell you about your rights of appeal. If you don't agree with the decision, write and tell us straightaway, but in any event, within 30 days of the decision. For direct tax matters, this is known as an "appeal to HMRC". You don't have to do this yourself. An accountant or other adviser can do this for you.

If you have more information or you think we've missed something, please tell us. If you do, we'll tell you if this information changes our decision or if it doesn't change our decision, we'll explain why. We find that most disagreements are resolved by discussing them with us. In some circumstances, you may be able to resolve your disagreement with us using Alternative Dispute Resolution (ADR). You can find more details about ADR in factsheet CC/FS21, "Compliance Checks – Alternative Dispute Resolution". Go to www.gov.uk and search for "CC/FS21".

What you can do if we can't reach agreement

If you are not satisfied with the outcome of our discussions, you can:

- have your case reviewed by a different officer from the one who made the decision
- have your case heard by an independent tax tribunal

If you opt to have your case reviewed you'll still be able to appeal to the tribunal if you disagree with the outcome of that review.

How a review works

You can choose whether or not to have a review. Either:

- we'll offer you a review (in which case you'll have 30 days to tell us if you want one)
- if we haven't offered you a review, you can ask us to carry one out at any stage during our discussion about the dispute

If you tell us that you want a review for indirect tax matters, we'll complete it within 45 days unless we agree another time with you. For direct tax matters, we'll complete it within 45 days from the date we confirm our view of the matter that you are appealing unless we agree another time with you.

Reviews are carried out by our staff not previously involved in the matter that you are disputing. You'll have a chance to provide further information about your case. You can't ask the tribunal to hear your case until the time limit has expired or we've told you the outcome of the review.

Once the review is complete, we'll write and tell you the outcome, and explain our reasons. (If we can't complete our review within 45 days, or any time we agreed with you, we'll write and tell you.) You then have 30 days to ask the tribunal to hear your case.

Appealing to the tribunal

If you don't want a review, or you don't agree with the review conclusion, you can appeal to a tribunal. The tribunal is independent and independently appointed expert tax judges and/or panel members will hear your case. The tribunal is administered by the HM Courts and Tribunals Service (the Tribunal Service), which is part of the Ministry of Justice.

To appeal to the tribunal you must normally write to the Tribunals Service within 30 days of our decision letter. Or, if you've asked for a review, within 30 days of our letter telling you of the outcome of our review. To do this, you can:

- complete a Tribunals Service appeal form available from the Tribunals Service website
- phone the Tribunals Service for a copy
- write to the Tribunals Service

The Tribunals Service will either arrange a hearing to decide your appeal in more straightforward cases, or decide the appeal on the basis of information sent by you and us without the need for a hearing. If you want to appeal to the tribunal, please make sure you attach to your notice of the appeal a copy of the assessment letter, or other notice that you want to appeal against. If you don't then the tribunal may not accept it.

More information about tribunals and tribunal hearings is available from the Tribunals Service website. See "More help" below.

If you want the tribunal to hear your case and it is a direct tax case, you must have appealed to us first.

Payment of tax during reviews and appeals

If the decision is about a direct tax matter, you can usually ask us to postpone part or all of the tax in dispute until the appeal is settled. An appeal may be resolved by being settled by agreement between you and us or decided by the tribunal. You must then pay the tax due in line with the tribunal's decision or the agreed settlement. Interest will continue to accrue on any postponed amount and unpaid tax that is found to be due when the appeal is settled or the tribunal has made its decision.

If the decision relates to an indirect tax matter (except for Customs matters), we will not collect the disputed tax while we carry out a review of our decision.

But normally you must pay the disputed tax before the tribunal can hear any appeal. If paying the tax would cause you hardship, you may ask us not to collect it until the tribunal has decided the matter. If you think this applies to you, please tell us. Interest will continue to accrue on any disputed tax and any unpaid tax that is found to be due when the tribunal has made its decision. Once the tribunal has made its decision, you'll have to pay any tax due in line with the decision, even if there is an appeal against it. We'll pay you any amounts due in line with the tribunal decision and where appropriate, with interest.

If you appeal against the tribunal's decision in an indirect tax matter, you may ask us not to collect the tax due if paying it would put you in a position of financial extremity. For example, by resulting in your bankruptcy or liquidation. If there is an appeal against the tribunal's decision and we think that there is a risk to the revenue, we can ask the Upper Tribunal or court for permission not to pay or repay any amount due to you or to require security before we do so.

More help

For more information about reviews and your appeal rights, go to www.gov.uk/tax-appeals

For more information about the HM Courts and Tribunals Service see:

- First-tier Tribunal, go to **www.gov.uk/courts-tribunals/first-tier-tribunal-tax** or phone them on **0300 123 1024**
- Upper Tribunal, go to **www.gov.uk/courts-tribunals/upper-tribunal-tax-and-chancery-chamber** or phone them on **020 7612 9730**

If you prefer to speak to us, or you want a printed copy of any of our guidance, please phone the helpline phone number on your tax return or letter we have sent you.

Dealing with HMRC if you have additional needs

Go to **www.gov.uk/dealing-hmrc-additional-needs** or contact our helplines for a range of services such as:

- wheelchair access to nearly all appointment venues
- help with filling in forms
- Text Relay and induction loops which are available for people with hearing difficulties

We can arrange additional support, such as:

- services of an interpreter
- sign language interpretation
- leaflets in Braille, audio and large print

For guidance and forms in Welsh please phone:

- 0300 200 1900 for "direct tax"
- 0300 200 3705 for "indirect tax"

Putting things right

If you are unhappy with the way we've handled your tax affairs, for example, because of delays or mistakes, please tell the person or office you have been dealing with. If they are unable to sort things out to your satisfaction, ask for your case to be referred to the Complaints Manager. For more information, you should go to **www.gov.uk** and search for "Complain to HMRC" or contact us. You'll find us in The Phone Book under "HM Revenue & Customs".

In this factsheet "direct tax" includes

- Annual Tax on Enveloped Dwellings (ATED)
- Capital Gains Tax
- Corporation Tax
- Employee related Share Schemes
- Income Tax
- Inheritance Tax
- National Insurance contributions
- Petroleum Revenue Tax
- Stamp Duty Land Tax
- Stamp Duty Reserve Tax
- Statutory payments
- Student Loan repayments
- Tax avoidance schemes (penalty decisions relating to follower notices and accelerated payments)

"Direct tax" in this factsheet also includes tax collected under Pay As You Earn (PAYE) and the Construction Industry Scheme.

In this factsheet "indirect tax" includes

- Aggregates Levy
- Air Passenger Duty
- Alcoholic Liquor duties
- Alcohol Wholesaler Registration Scheme (from October 2015)
- Amusement Machine Licence Duty
- Bingo Duty
- Climate Change Levy
- Counter-Terrorism decisions
- Customs Duty
- Gaming Duty
- General Betting Duty
- Hydrocarbon Oils Duties
- Insurance Premium Tax
- Landfill Tax
- Lottery Duty
- Machine Games Duty
- Money laundering decisions
- Pool Betting Duty

- Remote Gaming Duty
- Tobacco Products Duty
- Value Added Tax (VAT)

Appeals against certain information notices and against penalties for not complying with them follow the direct tax process.

This factsheet doesn't include decisions about the refusal to restore seized goods or agreement to restore goods, whether subject to a condition or not.

MISCELLANEOUS

Misc. 102 INHERITANCE TAX: ASSOCIATED OPERATIONS – ANNUAL EXEMPTION [Inland Revenue letter published in the Law Society's Gazette, 1 March 1978]

You wrote on 7 November to say that you had received enquiries about the application of IHTA 1984, s. 268 (formerly FA 1975, s. 44) (associated operations) to what I may perhaps loosely describe as schemes designed to maximise the advantage of the inheritance tax [£3,000] annual exemption. I am sorry I have not been able to reply earlier.

Your first example concerned the case where A sold an asset to B but left the price outstanding on loan, part of which was written off each year. We will obviously need to consider any actual case of this kind in the light of the full facts but on the facts as given in the example it seems clear that the sale of the asset and the writing off of the loans are associated with each other as a single arrangement and, prima facie, we would consider s. 268 relevant, whether or not interest was payable on the loan. If s. 268 does apply it may well follow that under s. 268(3) we would have to look at the value of the asset at the date of the release of the last part of the debt.

Your second example involved a gift of shares on terms that the son would pay the inheritance tax by instalments, the father subsequently making further gifts of cash to the son. In this case we agree that s. 268 does not apply; the mere fact that the father made later gifts within the annual exemption to enable the son to pay the tax would not therefore require the value transferred by the original gift to be reviewed.

Misc. 107 INHERITANCE TAX: LIABILITY OF PERSONAL REPRESENTATIVES [Letter from the Inland Revenue published in the Law Society's Gazette, 13 March 1991]

The Law Society is concerned about personal representatives made liable under IHTA 1984, s. 199(2) for inheritance tax on lifetime transfers made by a deceased person in the seven years before death. The point was raised again with the Inland Revenue at the meeting on 9 January 1991 to discuss the two Law Society's budget representations.

It may be helpful if I say that the capital taxes offices will not usually pursue for inheritance tax personal representatives who:

- after making the fullest enquiries that are reasonably practicable in the circumstances to discover lifetime transfers, and so
- having done all in their power to make full disclosure of them to the board of Inland Revenue

have obtained a certificate of discharge and distributed the estate before a chargeable lifetime transfer comes to light.

This statement of the board's position is made without prejudice to the application in an appropriate case of IHTA 1984, s. 199(2).

I am writing in similar terms to the Law Society of Scotland.

DY Pitts

Director Capital and Valuation Division, Inland Revenue.

Misc. 118 MCDONALD (HMIT) V DEXTRA ACCESSORIES LTD & ORS [HM Revenue and Customs, 15 July 2005]

In a unanimous verdict, the House of Lords have upheld the decision of the Court of Appeal in favour of the Inland Revenue in the case of Macdonald (HMIT) v Dextra Accessories Ltd & Others.

What were the facts?

Dextra Accessories Ltd and 5 other group companies made contributions to an Employee Benefit Trust (EBT), set up by the holding company of the group. They deducted these contributions in computing their taxable profits for the accounting period in which the contributions were made.

The trust deed gave the trustee wide discretion to pay money and other benefits to beneficiaries and a power to lend them money. The potential beneficiaries of the trust included past, present and future employees and officers of the participating companies in the Dextra group, and their close relatives and dependants.

The trustee did not make payments of emoluments out of the funds in the EBT during the periods concerned, instead the trustee made loans to various individuals who were beneficiaries under the terms of the EBT.

What was the point at issue?

The question was whether the companies' contributions to the EBT were "potential emoluments" within the meaning of section 43(11)(a) Finance Act 1989, being amounts "held by an intermediary, with a view to their becoming relevant emoluments".

What was the decision?

The House of Lords held that the contributions by the companies to the EBT were potential emoluments within section 43(11)(a) as there was a "realistic possibility" that the trustee would use the trust funds to pay emoluments. The Court of Appeal, agreeing with the High Court, had said that it was "rightly accepted" that the trustee was an intermediary. "With a view to" did not mean the sole purpose (as the Special Commissioners had held) or the principal or dominant purpose (as the High Court had held).

This meant that the companies' deductions were restricted. The companies could only have a deduction up to the amount of emoluments paid by the trustee within nine months of the end of the period of account for which the deduction would otherwise be due. Relief for the amount disallowed will be given in later periods of account in which emoluments are paid.

Is the case of wider interest?

The case is of wider importance as contributions to EBTs have been a feature of a number of marketed tax avoidance schemes. The treatment set out below sets out the HMRC view of when relief is available, in light of this decision, for contributions to EBTs before the introduction of Schedule 24 Finance Act 2003.

What EBTs will be affected?

The decision applies to all EBTs where there is a "realistic possibility" under the terms of the trust deed that funds will be used to pay emoluments, however wide the discretion given to the trustees.

It does not apply to contributions made on or after 27/11/2002, which would otherwise be deductible for periods ending on or after that date. Relief for these is governed by Schedule 24 Finance Act 2003.

Implications for inheritance tax (IHT)

Where the company making the contributions to an EBT is a close company, the outcome of this litigation is likely to have implications for IHT.

The effect of section 13 Inheritance Tax Act 1984 (IHTA) is that an IHT charge under section 94 IHTA on transfers of capital by a close company will arise where:

- a close company transfers capital to an EBT which satisfies s86 IHTA;
- the participators in that company are not excluded from benefit under the EBT, and
- the contributions are not allowable in terms of section 12 IHTA in computing its profits for CT purposes.

In these circumstances the transfers of capital by the company will be transfers of value for IHT purposes.

In terms of section 94 IHTA, HMRC then look through the close company and apportion the transfer of value between the participators "according to their respective rights and interests in the company immediately before the transfer". Any IHT charge therefore falls on the participators as individuals and will be at the current lifetime tax rate of 20% rising to 40% in the event that the participator dies within 3 years of the transfer (section 7 IHTA).

Notes – Only material relating to IHT has been reproduced here.

Misc. 120 DISCOUNTED GIFT SCHEMES: (DGSs) [HMRC technical note, 1 May 2007]

A technical note from HMRC

Background

Following recent press interest, this is an opportune moment to set out HMRC's approach to Discounted Gift Schemes (DGS) and their interaction with the Inheritance Tax (IHT) legislation. This note is particularly about valuation of lifetime transfers and the underlying valuation methodology. We are also taking this opportunity to set out the approach we will adopt in joint settlor cases, which, in some cases, will be more precise than that adopted up to now. It is emphasised that this note sets out HMRC's practice and is not seeking to prescribe the approach that must be taken to establish the chargeable value for IHT. Alternative approaches may be used to arrive at broadly similar results and HMRC continue to be open to considering and agreeing alternative valuation bases that achieve that aim.

HMRC has not made any fundamental change to its overall approach towards DGSs. But, as indicated at the end of this note, we are proposing to make a change to one element of the basis of valuation that we use to reflect current market conditions.

IHT treatment of DGSs

Essentially a DGS involves a gift of a bond from which a set of rights are retained, typically withdrawals or a set of successively maturing reversions. The retained rights are sufficiently well defined to preclude the gift being regarded as a gift with reservation (GWR) for IHT purposes.

The gift is a transfer of value for IHT purposes whose value is determined by the loss to the estate principle. This is set out in s. 3(1) Inheritance Tax Act 1984 (IHTA), and quantified by the difference between the amount invested by the settlor and the open market value (OMV) – s. 160 IHTA refers – of the retained rights.

Valuation issues

The OMV of the retained rights will depend on, inter alia, the settlor's sex, age, health and thereby insurability, as at the gift date. If the settlor were to be uninsurable, for any reason, as at the gift date the OMV of the retained rights would be nominal and the gift would be close to the whole amount invested by the settlor. This is because s160 IHTA 1984 provides that, in valuing the retained rights, we assume that a sale of them takes place.

The logic behind that premise is based upon sound open market evidence and fully endorsed by leading counsel from whom HMRC has taken advice. We have looked for evidence to sales of assets similar in nature to the retained rights, for example life interests or contingent reversions which are dependent upon the survival of the relevant life to a series of predetermined dates. This indicates that such rights are not saleable unless life assurance can be effected on that life by the open market purchaser (OMP) or it comes as part of the sale. If it cannot be effected market evidence shows that those assets will not sell. Without life cover being in place the OMP is at risk of anything up to the total loss of his investment should an early death of the settlor occur. We consider it to be fundamental that the open market valuation of the retained rights should be carried out having regard to what market evidence is available. Additionally we have been unable to find any evidence that it is possible to effect cover on lives older than 90 next birthday. HMRC therefore regard lives older than that, true or equivalent (mortality rated), as being uninsurable with the resultant ramifications in respect of the gift value.

Position where there are joint settlors

To date HMRC has taken a pragmatic approach to calculating the value transferred where there are joint settlors, usually husband and wife or civil partners. This approach has been to value the retained rights in their entirety and deduct this amount from the total sum invested. The value of the transfer has then been apportioned between the settlors in the proportions in which they provided the sum invested.

Example of HMRC's "old" approach:

> Husband (H) aged 80 and wife (W) aged 80 invest £100,000 equally in a DGS with monthly withdrawals of £416.67 payable until the death of the last to die of H and W.
>
> Open market value (OMV) of the retained rights calculated as £46,300.
>
> Transfer of value calculated as £100,000 – £46,300 = £53,700.
>
> Of this, £26,850 is attributable to H and £26,850 attributable to W.
>
> In practice, where the joint settlors are of similar ages and in similar states of health the results of this pragmatic approach do not differ dramatically from the results where the value of each settlor's retained rights are considered individually.
>
> Following the changes brought about by the Finance Act 2006, HMRC has seen a number of cases where DGSs have been taken out where there is a significant age difference between the joint settlors or where one of the joint settlors is in very poor health or even uninsurable. In such cases the pragmatic approach does not achieve a reasonable result. We have also been asked to clarify the correct method of valuation in these circumstances as different providers are calculating the transfer values using different methods, resulting in a lack of consistency. This also means that taxpayers and their advisers are unclear as to which approach is correct. In the light of this uncertainty we are setting out below what we consider to be the correct valuation approach. We intend to follow this approach for **all** DGSs where the transfer takes place after 1 June 2007. We will also use this

method where a transfer has taken place before that date and the pragmatic approach would provide an unreasonable valuation of the settlor's retained rights and substantial sums are involved.

In HMRC's view, the correct approach is to value the retained rights in their entirety and to apportion this value between the joint settlors by reference to the OMV of each settlor's retained rights. In the case of joint settlors who are married or in a civil partnership, the related property provisions of s. 161 IHTA are to be taken into account in this valuation. The application of s. 161 IHTA has been considered in some detail in *Arkwright and anor v IRC* [2004] EWHC 1720 (Ch) – [2004] BTC 8,082.

The impact of this on the above example is as follows:

OMV of H's retained rights = £16,400

OMV of W's retained rights = £19,900

OMV of the total retained rights = £46,300

(The calculations of retained rights reflect the age, state of health and insurability of H and W respectively.)

The OMV of H's retained rights, calculated in accordance with s. 161 IHTA is

$$\frac{£16,400}{(£16,400 + £19,900)} \times £46,300 = £20,900$$

The OMV of W's retained rights, calculated in accordance with s. 161 IHTA is

$$\frac{£19,900}{(£16,400 + £19,900)} \times £46,300 = £25,400$$

So the values transferred by H and W are:

Value transferred by H = £50,000 – £20,900 = £29,100

Value transferred by W = £50,000 – £25,400 = £24,600

It is recognised that where there are significant differences in the ages of the settlors (whether their actual ages or their effective ages for insurance purposes) it is technically possible for the value of the retained rights to be calculated as a negative amount using the above approach. It is also technically possible to calculate the value of the retained rights as exceeding the contribution of the settlor. The value of the lifetime transfer is calculated, in accordance with section 3(1) IHTA, as the loss to the transferor's estate. If the value of the retained rights is negative the loss to the transferor's estate cannot exceed the amount contributed, i.e. there cannot be a negative 'discount'. If the value of the retained rights exceeds the settlor's contribution, there would be no loss to the estate and therefore no transfer of value.

We do not propose to re-open cases where the values transferred have been accepted in accordance with our previously adopted approach.

Underwriting approach

As far as DGS contracts are concerned, it is clear that insurance companies adopt differing practices with regard to underwriting the settlor's life ranging from no underwriting through the so-called "sealed-envelope" to full underwriting. HMRC's preference is that full underwriting should be carried out prior to the DGS being effected.

The open-market based valuation method requires that evidence of the settlor's health exists at the transfer date that is sufficient for the settlor's life to be underwritten to the standards required for whole of life assurance. If no evidence of health has been obtained at the outset, HMRC take the view that a discount is not justified unless medical evidence sufficient to underwrite the settlor's life to the standards required for whole of life assurance was already in existence and can be produced, should it be necessary to quantify the gift at a later date.

HMRC adopt this stance because problems can and do arise if no evidence of health has been obtained at the outset **and** therefore is **not** reflected in the estimate of the value of the gift. On the death of a settlor, for example, where no evidence has been obtained HMRC will often need to ask the settlor's personal representatives to obtain evidence about the settlor's health at the time the gift was made. We recognise that this is undesirable as the surviving family may face intrusive and upsetting enquiries at a difficult time. This can be avoided if the information is obtained in advance. Problems also arise where medical evidence is not collected until after the transfer occurs and it then becomes apparent that up to date medical details are not held. This would be insufficient evidence on which to underwrite to the standards required for whole of life assurance and would therefore result in no discount. Additionally survivors may not have been party to the transaction entered into by the settlor. They may feel entitled to particular treatment based on expectations given by financial advisors and then feel aggrieved when HMRC begin investigating.

HMRC's current basis of valuation

The retained rights fall to be valued on an open market basis in accordance with s160 IHTA 1984. In investing in the retained rights the open market purchaser (OMP) will need to take account of the rate of return he requires and the cost of insuring the settlor(s) life.

The annual amount to be paid under the retained rights, net of any income tax liability that the purchaser may suffer, is multiplied by a purchase factor generated from a suitable formula e.g. a Jellicoe formula (see for example "*Actuarial Valuations of Interests in Settled Property*" – Beard FIA & Prevett FIA Institute of Actuaries 1973 page 15).

$$1 - p / p + i \quad \text{where}$$

p is the annual premium expressed as a decimal and
i is the OMP's rate of return also expressed as a decimal.

The present value of the retained rights is arrived at from the product of the net annual amount of the retained rights and the purchase factor. The OMV is 97% of that present value (rounded to the nearest £50) to reflect the OMP's costs of say 3%.

As mentioned at the start of this note, the aim is to set out HMRC's practice, not to prescribe the approach that **must** be taken to establish the chargeable value for IHT. Alternative approaches may be used to arrive at broadly similar results and HMRC continue to be open to considering and agreeing alternative valuation bases that achieve that aim. HMRC's current mortality and interest rate basis is

- Mortality: 70% of AM / AF 80 Mortality (reflecting the improvement over the table for assured lives for males and females published by the Continuous Mortality Investigation Bureau in 1990 reference CMIR 10)
- Interest rate: 5.25% pa
- Open market purchaser's costs: 3% (as a deduction from the present value of the retained rights).

HMRC has recently reviewed its interest rate basis. In the light of recent rises in interest rates, HMRC are proposing to change that basis with effect from 1 June 2007 when a valuation rate of interest of 6% pa will be adopted. Our analysis indicates clearly that such a rise in that rate is warranted and reintroduces the differential over base rate and corresponds to a 1% differential over short term Gilts as at 2 April 2007. The valuation basis is kept under review to ensure that it continues to reflect open market conditions. It is our intention to publish details of any future changes to our valuation basis on the HMRC website.

Any enquiries concerning this note should be directed to:

P Oxlade
Board's Actuarial Officer
Charity, Assets & Residence Actuarial Group
Ferrers House
PO Box 38
Castle Meadow Road
Nottingham
NG2 1BB

Telephone 0115 974 2950

Ian Hempstead
Assistant Actuarial Officer
Charity, Assets & Residence Actuarial Group
Ferrers House
PO Box 38
Castle Meadow Road
Nottingham
NG2 1BB

Telephone 0115 974 2939

Misc. 122 DIRECT PAYMENT SCHEME [HMRC, Website]

What is the direct payment scheme?

You can pay some or all of the inheritance tax (IHT) that is due on delivery of form IHT200 by arranging to have money transferred from the deceased's bank or building society accounts directly to us using the IHT direct payment scheme.

Are all banks taking part in this scheme?

Many banks and building societies are part of this scheme, but you should check with the deceased's bank or building society before going any further.

Can I use funds held in a joint account?

No, the scheme only applies to accounts in the deceased's sole name.

What if there are funds in one account, but an overdraft on another?

If the deceased held more than one account of any sort with the same bank or building society, and one account is overdrawn whilst another is in credit, the bank or building society may wish to repay the overdraft from the funds in credit, leaving only the balance available to pay the IHT.

Will there be fees to pay?

Withdrawal of funds will be subject to normal banking rules applying to accounts. For example, if the account is a "notice" account, there may be a fee to pay or loss of interest. You should check with the bank or building society concerned whether this applies to the deceased's accounts.

We suggest that you also ask whether the bank or building society will charge a fee for this service.

What do I need to do?

If you wish to use this scheme you should identify yourself to the banks or building societies to which you expect to give instruction to transfer money and prove that you are an appropriate personal representative. Contact each organisation to find out what their requirements are for you to do this. We recommend that you do this well before you intend to apply for a grant of representation to avoid unnecessary delays later on.

You should then apply for an Inheritance Tax reference number. You can do this by applying for an IHT reference online, or by using the form D21 Application for an Inheritance Tax reference (PDF 40K). You should apply for a reference in good time because you will need to put the reference number on the direct payment scheme application form.

When we receive your reference request we will send you, by post, a note of your reference number. You can then fill in the application form.

Which form should I fill in?

You should fill in Form D20 (PDF 58K) "Application to transfer funds to pay inheritance tax". Use a separate form for each bank or building society that will be making the transfer of funds. Form D20 is a supplementary page to the form IHT 200.

Then you should

1. Write the reference number on the form D20.
2. When you have filled in the form IHT200, complete the rest of the form D20 by following the instructions in the D20(notes)
3. When you have completed the form D20 and you are ready to apply for a grant you should send
   - form D20 to the banks or building societies that will be making the transfers
   - form IHT200, the relevant supplementary pages, form D18 and any other supporting documents to us.

What happens next?

The bank or building society will transfer the money to us. They will be able to tell you how long it will normally take them to make the transfer. Once we receive notification of the payment, we will link the payment to form IHT200 and provided all is in order, we will stamp and return the form D18.

Misc. 123 TRANSFER OF NIL RATE BAND [HMRC, 9 October 2007]

Guidance

1. In his Pre-Budget Report, the Chancellor of the Exchequer announced that from 9th October 2007, it will be possible for spouses and civil partners to transfer their nil-rate band allowances so that any part of the nil-rate band that was not used when the first spouse or civil partner died can be transferred to the individual's surviving spouse or civil partner for use on their death.

2. HMRC will issue more detailed guidance shortly; what follows explains the basics of the scheme. Detailed guidance on other aspects of the IHT rules is available from the HMRC website as usual and should be read in conjunction with this document.

Commencement

3. The transferable allowance will be available to all survivors of a marriage or civil partnership who die on or after 9th October 2007, no matter when the first partner died/dies

4. The claim to transfer unused nil-rate band must be made by the accountable persons when the surviving spouse or civil partner dies and not when the first spouse or civil partner dies. So if you are dealing with the estate of the first spouse or civil partner to die, there is nothing you need do now in terms of making a claim. However you will need to record the proportion of the nil-rate band that goes unused, and the detailed guidance will explain what sort of records will need to be kept in order to support a claim when the surviving spouse or civil partner dies.

5. If you are dealing with the estate of the surviving spouse or civil partner, you can make a claim to transfer the unused nil-rate band from the estate of the first spouse or civil partner to die. To make a claim, you will need to fill in a claim form, which will be available from the HMRC website shortly.

6. The form will ask for information about the estate of the first spouse or civil partner to die that is necessary to calculate the amount of the nil-rate band that was unused. You can then calculate the extent to which the nil-rate band available to the survivor may be increased (see paragraph 9 below) and use that revised nil-rate band to calculate the inheritance tax payable on the survivor's estate.

7. You should send the form to HMRC, together with the documents requested (for example, the death certificate of the first spouse or civil partner to die, a copy of their Will and the marriage certificate) at the same time as you send form IHT200 for the estate of the survivor to HMRC.

8. The increased nil-rate band does not replace the single nil-rate band available to the survivor that determines whether or not their estate is an excepted estate (see paragraph 17 below).

How the transfer will work

9. Where a valid claim to transfer unused nil-rate band is made, the nil-rate band that is available when the surviving spouse or civil partner dies will be increased by the proportion of the nil-rate band unused on the first death. For example, if on the first death the chargeable estate is £150,000 and the nil-rate band is £300,000, 50% of the nil-rate band would be unused. If the nil-rate band when the survivor dies is £325,000, then that would be increased by 50% to £487,500.

10. The amount of the nil-rate band that can be transferred does not depend on the value of the first spouse or civil partner's estate. Whatever proportion of the nil-rate band is unused on the first death is available for transfer to the survivor.

11. It is important to remember that even if all the assets passing under the Will are left to the surviving spouse or civil partner, there may be other components of the aggregate chargeable "estate" on death for IHT purposes (such as assets in trust, or gifts to other people made within 7 years of death). If present, these may use up some or all of the nil-rate band in the normal way, and so reduce the amount of unused nil-rate band that may be available for transfer.

12. The rules apply in the same way whether the first spouse or civil partner to die leaves a Will or dies intestate.

13. The rules allow unused nil-rate band to be transferred from more than one deceased spouse or civil partner, up to a limit of one additional nil-rate band. So if someone has survived more than one spouse or civil partner, then on their death the accountable persons may be able to claim additional nil-rate band from more than one of the relevant estates. A separate claim form should be completed for each spouse or civil partner who died before the deceased. However the total additional nil-rate band accumulated for this purpose is limited to a maximum of the amount of the nil-rate band in force at the relevant time. Below are some examples showing how the scheme works.

Existing Wills

14. The new rules will not change the effect of existing Wills. So people who have, for example, a nil-rate band trust written into their Will do not have to take any action as a result of this measure. But if someone wants to change their Will to take account of the new rules, that change can usually be made by a Codicil, rather than having to rewrite the Will.

15. Where someone dies with a nil-rate band discretionary trust in their Will, an appointment of the trust assets in favour of the surviving spouse or civil partner (before the second anniversary of the death, but not within the three months immediately following the death) would normally be treated for IHT purposes as if the assets had simply been left to the surviving spouse or civil partner outright. Ending the trust in this way would mean that the nil-rate band was not used on the first death, and so the amount available for eventual transfer to the surviving spouse or civil partner would be increased accordingly.

Immediate Post Death Interests

16. Where individuals leave assets on trust with a life interest for their surviving spouse or civil partner, with the remainder passing on their spouse or civil partner's death to someone else (for example their children), there is no IHT to pay on the first death because spouse or civil partner exemption applies. So if the entire estate is left in trust to the surviving spouse or civil partner, the nil-rate band would be available for transfer to the estate of the survivor on their eventual death in the same way as if the estate had been left to them absolutely.

Link with reporting "excepted estates"

17. Any additional nil-rate band is only relevant in establishing whether or not any tax is payable on the estate of the survivor – it does not replace the individual nil-rate band amount that determines the excepted estate limit for reporting purposes. If when the survivor dies, their gross estate exceeds the individual nil-rate band amount applicable at the time of their death, the estate cannot qualify as an excepted estate. The accountable persons will still need to deliver form IHT200 and make their claim for the transferable nil-rate band on the death of the survivor.

First death before 18 March 1986

18. Inheritance tax was introduced with effect from 18 March 1986, but before this date other estate taxes (Capital Transfer Tax and Estate Duty) applied. Where a surviving spouse dies on or after 9 October 2007 and their spouse died before the introduction of the current inheritance tax provisions, a claim may still be made for the nil-rate band of the surviving spouse to be increased by reference to unused allowances of their spouse.

19. We will shortly publish details of the tax-free bands that applied for Estate Duty and Capital Transfer Taxes. But if you need this information in the meantime, please contact the Inheritance Tax & Probate Helpline on 0845 3020900.

20. Examples of how the new rules will work

A. A dies on 14 April 2007 with an estate of £400,000, which he leaves entirely to his spouse, B. B dies on 17 June 2009 leaving an estate of £600,000 equally between her two children. When B dies the nil-rate band is £325,000. As 100% of A's nil-rate band was unused, the nil-rate band on B's death is doubled to £650,000. As B's estate is £600,000 there is no IHT to pay on B's death.

B. J dies on 27 May 2007, with an estate of £300,000. She leaves legacies of £40,000 to each of her three children with the remainder to her spouse K. The nil-rate band when J dies is £300,000. K dies on 15 September 2009 leaving his estate of £500,000 equally to his three children; the nil-rate band when K dies is £325,000. J used up 40% of her nil-rate band when she died, which means 60% is available to transfer to K on his death. So K's nil-rate band of £325,000 is increased by 60% to £520,000. As K's estate is only £500,000 there is no IHT to pay on K's death.

C. R dies on 14 April 2007 with an estate of £450,000, which he leaves entirely to his spouse, S. S dies on 17 June 2009 leaving an estate of £675,000 which she leaves equally between her two children. When S dies the nil-rate band is £325,000. As 100% of R's nil-rate band was unused, the nil-rate band on S's death is doubled to £650,000. This leaves £25,000 chargeable to IHT on S's death.

D. X dies on 14 April 2007 with an estate of £250,000, leaving £120,000 to his son Y and the remainder to his spouse Z. The nil-rate band when X dies is £300,000 so 60% of his nil-rate band is unused. Z later marries W who dies on 14 May 2008 and also leaves 60% of his nil-rate band unused. Z dies on 14 June 2009 with an estate of £700,000 when the individual nil-rate band is £325,000. Z's nil-rate band is increased to reflect the transfer from X and W, but the amount of increase is limited to 100% of the nil-rate band in force at the time. So Z's nil-rate band is £650,000, leaving £50,000 chargeable to IHT on Z's death.

Misc. 124 TRANSFERABLE NIL RATE BAND – FREQUENTLY ASKED QUESTIONS [HMRC, 23 October 2007]

The Basics

What do you mean by a transferable nil rate band?

A transferable nil rate band arises when one party to a marriage or civil partnership dies and the amount of their estate that is chargeable to IHT does not use up all of the nil rate band they are entitled to. Where this happens, the unused part can now be transferred to the surviving spouse or civil partner when they die.

How does that work then?

Everyone is entitled to a nil rate band for IHT. Assets that pass from one spouse or civil partner to another are exempt from IHT. So if on death, someone leaves everything they own to their spouse or civil partner, it is exempt from IHT and they have not used any part of their nil rate band. That unused nil rate band can now be transferred to their surviving spouse or civil partner and used in working out the IHT liability on their estate when they die.

Does it matter when the deaths occurred?

Yes – this applies where the surviving spouse or civil partner died on or after 9th October 2007. But it does not matter how long before them their spouse or civil partner died. (Note: see paragraphs at the end of this Q&A about the impact for Capital Transfer Tax & Estate Duty).

What if both deaths occurred before 9th October 2007?

Where both spouses or civil partners have died before 9th October 2007, no allowance may be transferred.

How much is the nil rate band?

For 2007–08 the nil rate band is £300,000 – rising to £312,000 in 2008/09.

So you mean that if I inherited all the assets from my spouse or civil partner, my executors could add their nil rate band to the nil rate band that applies when I die?

Essentially yes – but it works by looking at what proportion of the nil rate band that was unused when your spouse or civil partner died and uprating the nil rate band available when you die by that same proportion.

What do you mean by uprating the nil rate band available by the same proportion?

The amount to be transferred is worked out by taking the proportion of the nil rate band that was unused on the first death and applying that to the nil rate band available when you die. So if your spouse or civil partner left assets worth £150,000 to your children with everything else to you and the nil rate band on their death was £300,000; one-half of their nil rate band is unused and is available for transfer. If, when you die, the nil rate band had increased to £325,000, the amount available for transfer would be 50% of £325,000 or £162,500 giving your estate a nil rate band of £325,000 + £162,500, or £487,500 in total.

What if my spouse or civil partner's estate was only worth £100,000, so that they did not need all of their nil rate band. Is the amount that can be transferred tied to the amount that they actually left to me?

No – it doesn't matter what the size of first estate was, whatever proportion of the nil rate band is unused may be transferred to you. If your spouse or civil partner's estate was worth only £100,000 and they left everything to you, they will not have used any part of their nil rate band. So 100% of the nil rate band is available for transfer when you die.

What about any gifts my spouse or civil partner may have made in the 7 years before they died; or any other assets that were chargeable when they died?

Gifts and any other assets that are chargeable on the first death (say assets in trust or assets owned jointly with a son or daughter) all eat into the nil rate band in the normal way and so reduce the amount that may be available for transfer. (Note: see paragraphs toward the end of this Q&A about the impact for Capital Transfer Tax & Estate Duty).

Low value estates

How does the transferable nil rate band affect whether the estate of the surviving spouse or civil partner qualifies as an excepted estate?

At present, the excepted estate rules remain as they are; so if the surviving spouse or civil partner's estate exceeds the single nil rate band at their death (and assuming surviving spouse or civil partner exemption and charity exemption is not available), the estate cannot qualify as an excepted estate even though there may be no tax to pay because of transferred nil rate band. So for the time being at least the surviving spouse or civil partner's personal representatives must deliver form IHT200 and make a claim to transfer the unused nil rate band.

I'm going to leave all my estate to my spouse or civil partner; but between us our estates do not exceed one nil rate band; what should I do?

On your death your executors should still work out how much of your nil rate band is available for transfer as the circumstances of your spouse or civil partner may change before they die. But if, when they die, their estate remains below a single nil rate band and provided they have not remarried or entered into a new civil partnership, there is no need for their personal representatives to make a claim to transfer unused nil rate band.

The process & recording keeping

How is the transfer made?

When the surviving spouse or civil partner dies, their personal representatives will make a claim to transfer the unused nil rate band available from the first death. They will need to fill in a claim form that will help them to work out how much of the nil rate band is available for transfer. They will also need to provide certain documents to support their claim such as

- the death certificate for the first person to die,
- the marriage certificate or civil partnership certificate for the couple,
- if the spouse or civil partner left a Will, a copy of it,
- a copy of the grant of probate/Confirmation, and
- if a Deed of Variation or other similar document was executed to change the people who inherited the estate of the spouse or civil partner, a copy of it.

The personal representatives should send the claim form and the supporting documents to HMRC when they send in the form IHT200 on the death of the surviving spouse or civil partner.

How long do the personal representatives have to make a claim?

The claim must be made within 24 months from the end of the month in which the surviving spouse or civil partner dies.

How will the personal representatives of the surviving spouse or civil partner know how much to claim?

When the estate of the first person to die is settled, their personal representatives will need to work out how much of the nil rate band is transferable. They will then need to make sure the surviving spouse or civil partner knows what that amount is. They will need to let the surviving spouse or civil partner have sufficient documents and information so that when the surviving spouse or civil partner dies, their personal representatives can make a claim to transfer the unused nil rate band. Where this happens people may want to consider keeping this information with their Will in a safe place.

What sort of documents and information do you have in mind?

So far as the person's own assets are concerned, the personal representatives for the first spouse or civil partner to die should let the surviving spouse or civil partner have

- a copy of the HMRC return (form IHT205 or IHT200; in Scotland, forms C1 & C5)
- a copy of the deceased's Will (if any)
- a copy of any documents, such as a Deed of Variation, executed after the death of the first spouse or civil partner, that changes who benefits from their estate,
- any valuation(s) of assets that pass under Will or intestacy other than to the surviving spouse or civil partner,
- any evidence to support the availability of relief (such as agricultural or business relief) where the relievable assets pass to someone other than to the surviving spouse or civil partner.

But there can be other assets that are chargeable when someone dies such as

- assets owned jointly with another person,
- assets held in trust from which the first to die was entitled to benefit and which are treated as forming part of their estate on death,
- any lifetime gifts made by the first to die in the 7 years before their death,

IHT Extra-statutory Material

- any gifts made by the first to die where they did not give up possession and use of the assets, or where they retained a right to use the asset through an arrangement (a gift with reservation of benefit), and
- where the first to die was over 75, any alternatively secured pension fund from which they received a pension.

If any of these apply to the estate of the first person to die, the personal representatives will need to pass on information about these assets as well, for example

- details of the assets concerned and evidence of their values,
- details about any exemptions and/or relief taken into account in arriving at the chargeable values.

We did not know about the need to keep records when the first person died and we do not have papers relating to that death – how can we make a claim?

The personal representatives will be able to obtain copies of some of the documents you need from public records bodies:

- Copies of a grants of representation or Confirmation and copies of Wills are available from the Court Service (for England & Wales, www.hmcourts-service.gov.uk, for Scotland www.scotcourts.gov.uk, and for Northern Ireland www.courtsni.gov.uk), and
- Copies of death certificates and marriage certificates are available from the General Register Office (for England & Wales www.gro.gov.uk, for Scotland www.gro-scotland.gov.uk, and for Northern Ireland www.groni.gov.uk).

These will give you the value of the first estate that was declared for Probate/Confirmation and will also provide information about who inherited the assets that passed under the deceased's Will or intestacy. However, it will not provide any information about other assets that are chargeable when someone dies (list above). The personal representatives will need to make enquiries of those who inherited the first estate to see if they can recall whether or not there may have been other assets that were chargeable on the first death. If values are known, they should be included on the claim form; if values are not known, the personal representatives should complete the claim form to the best of their ability and explain the position to HMRC when they make they claim. If there is no evidence that any other assets were chargeable, the personal representatives can make their claim based on the information they have from the documents already mentioned.

What happens if the surviving spouse or civil partner loses the documents and information?

The information and documents about the claim could be very valuable to the second estate and it will be important to keep them safe. If the material is lost, the personal representatives will need to obtain copies of the documents required to substantiate the claim.

But suppose they are stolen, or destroyed in a fire?

Where something happens that is beyond the control of the surviving spouse or civil partner or their personal representatives, again the personal representatives will need to obtain copies of the documents required to substantiate the claim.

So there is nothing to do when the first person dies?

Not quite. It is important to work out what the transferable amount is and make sure that the surviving spouse or civil partner is given sufficient documents and information to support the claim their personal representatives will need to make. You should not contact HMRC to establish and agree the transferable amount when the first person dies.

What happens about agreeing values of assets like houses or household goods; and what about agreeing whether a relief such as agricultural or business relief applies?

It will only be necessary to agree values where such assets pass to chargeable beneficiaries on the first death (i.e. someone other than the surviving spouse or civil partner). This will be done when the surviving spouse or civil partner dies, but only where it is necessary to do so because the amount of the unused nil rate band may affect the amount of IHT to pay on the second death. Similarly, if a farm is left to, say, a son and the personal representatives of the first death consider that agricultural relief is due against the whole property, the extent to which the relief is due will be established, if it is necessary, on the second death.

So what does this mean as far as information and documents left with the surviving spouse or civil partner is concerned?

The personal representatives of the estate of the first person to die will need to make sure that they take appropriate steps to value assets that pass to chargeable beneficiaries and to make sure that they give sufficient evidence to the surviving spouse or civil partner to support the values used and any relief that is considered due.

Isn't it easier to provide all this information and documents to HMRC on the first death and to agree values and the extent to which relief may be due at that time?

There is no telling how the circumstances of the surviving spouse or civil partner may change during the years before their death. It is possible that when they die, their estate is such that their personal representatives do not need to claim a transfer of unused nil rate band (for example, it is covered by their own nil rate band). In those circumstances, all the work done at the first death in agreeing the amount available for transfer will have been wasted. It is only sensible to defer this work until we know that it is actually relevant for IHT purposes on the second death.

Jointly owned assets

What do I do if all of the deceased's assets were jointly owned and so pass automatically to the surviving spouse or civil partner without the need to take out a grant of representation or Confirmation (in Scotland) on the first death?

Provided there were no other assets chargeable to IHT or Capital Transfer Tax on the deceased's death, the whole of the nil rate band is unused and can be transferred to the surviving spouse or civil partner's estate. The personal representatives can make a claim to transfer the unused nil rate band. Any other assets chargeable on death, such as gifts made within 7 years of the death, will start to use up the nil rate band. Where the deceased died before 13th November 1974, personal representatives will need to bear in mind that there was at that time only limited, or no, spouse exemption for transfers from one spouse to the other. (Note: see paragraphs at the end of this Q&a about the impact for Estate Duty).

What do I do if some of the deceased's assets were jointly owned and so pass to people other than surviving spouse or civil partner without the need to take out a grant of representation or Confirmation (in Scotland) on the first death?

It will be very important for the surviving spouse or civil partner to keep information about any assets (that they know about) that pass to others by survivorship, because the value of those assets will affect the proportion of nil rate band that their personal representatives will be able to claim. The same applies to any other assets that are chargeable to IHT on the deceased's death such as gifts made within 7 years that are not covered by one or other of the exemptions. Without all this information, it will be very difficult for the surviving spouse or civil partner's personal representatives to make a claim to transfer unused nil rate band.

Timing issues

Both parties to a marriage or civil partnership have died one shortly after the other. I want to apply for grants of probate, what should I do?

You should fill in the appropriate forms to apply for a grant in the estate of the first person to die in the normal way. This will allow you to establish how much of the nil rate band is unused on the first death. You should then work out the size of the second estate by adding together the value of that person's own assets and any assets they inherited from the estate of the first spouse to die.

If this does not exceed single nil rate band available to the estate of the second spouse or civil partner to die, there is no need to worry about transferring unused nil rate band from the first death. Provided the other conditions are satisfied, you will be able to apply for a grant as an excepted estate.

If this does exceed the single nil rate band, you will need to fill in form IHT200 for the estate of the second spouse or civil partner to die. You should also make a provisional claim to transfer the unused nil rate band which should be based on the information available to you at the time you make your claim. You should indicate on the claim form that the value is an estimate and you should tell us what the final figure is once it is known. The estimated amount of the nil rate band that can be transferred can be used to work out the tax payable on the second death.

What is the position when husband & wife or civil partners die at the same time?

Although the rules that govern what happens when spouses or civil partners die at the same time are complex, the same basic principle applies – if there is any nil rate band unused on death of one spouse or civil partner, it can be transferred to the estate of the other, if required.

What happens when there has been more than one marriage?

My first husband died whilst we were still married; I subsequently remarried but am now divorced, can my personal representatives make a claim to transfer any unused nil rate band from my first husband's estate?

Yes, any unused nil rate band from your first husband's estate can be transferred to your estate as a result of a claim made by your personal representatives.

What happens if my surviving spouse or civil partner remarries or enters into another civil partnership and they die before their new spouse or civil partner?

Where this happens, the nil rate band available to your spouse or civil partner will be increased by any unused amount of your nil rate band that their personal representatives wish to claim. If your surviving spouse or civil partner dies first and decides to leave all their assets to their new spouse or civil partner, then again, the full amount of the nil rate band on their death is available for transfer to their new spouse or civil partner. But the maximum that can be added to anyone's own nil rate band is 100% of the nil rate band applicable to their death.

Existing nil rate band trusts

My spouse or civil partner has died before me and a nil rate band discretionary trust was set up under their Will. What can we do to make their nil rate band available for transfer now?

The first thing to say is that if the nil rate band was fully used when your spouse died and your estate exceeds the nil rate band when you die, then between you, you will have made full use of the two nil rate bands that are available to you. If, however, you would rather "undo" the nil rate band trust

- if your spouse or civil partner died more than two years ago, unfortunately, there is nothing that can be done. Any changes to the trust may give rise to a separate charge to inheritance tax on the trust itself. You may want to speak to a solicitor or accountant about this.
- if your spouse or civil partner died less than two years ago, an appointment of the trust assets in your favour (before the second anniversary of their death, but not within the three months immediately following the death) would normally be treated for IHT purposes as if the assets had simply been left to you outright. Ending the trust in this way would mean that the nil-rate band was not used on the first death, and so the amount available for eventual transfer to your estate would be increased as appropriate.

My spouse or civil partner has died before me and left their entire estate to me. I executed an Instrument of Variation to create a nil rate band discretionary trust and used up the nil rate band on their death. What can I do to make their nil rate band available for transfer now?

The position is the same as above – if your spouse or civil partner died less than two years ago, an appointment of the trust assets in your favour (before the second anniversary of their death, but not within the three months immediately following the death) would normally be treated for IHT purposes as if the assets had simply been left to you outright. Ending the trust in this way would mean that the nil-rate band was not used on the first death. An appointment made in this way after the Instrument of Variation which created the trust is valid and will not be barred as a subsequent variation.

Miscellaneous

I want to change my Will in the light of these new rules, do I have to have the whole Will rewritten?

Not necessarily, it is possible to change parts of a Will by making a Codicil to the Will. This can revoke existing clauses and insert new ones. You may wish to speak to a solicitor about this.

How does the idea of a transferable nil rate band work where there is conditionally exempt property?

It all depends on whether the surviving spouse or civil partner dies before the conditional exemption ceases. Where the conditional exemption ceases before the surviving spouse or civil partner dies, the charge on cessation of the exemption will apply in the usual way – and if this exhausts the nil rate band, there will then be nothing left to transfer to the surviving spouse or civil partner. If, however, the surviving spouse or civil partner dies first and their personal representatives transfer the unused nil rate band, the amount transferred will not be available for use when the conditional exemption ceases. Nevertheless, if this is some considerable time after the surviving spouse or civil partner dies, the charge on cessation of the exemption will still reflect any increase in the nil rate band that has occurred between death and cessation.

I know that my spouse did not use up all their nil rate band when they died and the unused portion is available for transfer to me. I want to make a lifetime gift that will give rise to an immediate liability to IHT, can I transfer the unused nil rate band against this gift?

No, the unused nil rate band can only be transferred to be used against your estate when you die. If you were to die within 7 years of making the immediately chargeable lifetime transfer, so that additional tax is payable on the gift as a result of your death, the transferred nil rate band will be used in the normal way and may reduce any additional tax due as a result of your death – but you cannot transfer the unused nil rate band against the tax due on a lifetime transfer at the time the transfer is made.

What's the position where my spouse or civil partner is domiciled outside the UK so relief for assets passing to them is restricted to £55,000?

This restriction may mean that bequests from you to your surviving spouse or civil partner will use up some of the nil rate band available on your death; but anything unused remains available for transfer and can be claimed by the personal representatives of the surviving spouse or civil partner when they die.

How does this work if the first death occurred during Capital Transfer Tax or Estate Duty?

The same basic principles apply in that if there was no Capital Transfer Tax or Estate Duty payable on the first death because the estate was less than the amount on which tax or duty was charged at 0%, the nil rate band that applies on the surviving spouse's death can be increased by the proportion that was not used. Personal representatives wishing to make a claim to transfer unused nil rate band where the first spouse died before 13th November 1974 will need to bear in mind that under the Estate Duty rules then in force there was no unlimited exemption for transfers between spouses. For deaths after 21st March 1972 (but before 13th November 1974), the relief was capped at £15,000; and for deaths on or before 21st March 1972 there was no relief at all. Unlimited spouse exemption only applied to Estate Duty for deaths after 12th November 1974 until 12th March 1975.

Example 1: The first spouse died in 1970 (when the nil rate band was £10,000) leaving an estate of £5,000 wholly to the surviving spouse. There was no spouse exemption in place in 1970, so the transfer to the surviving spouse will have used up half of the Estate Duty nil-rate band at that time. Consequently the IHT nil rate band available on the surviving spouse's death can only be increased by 50%.

Example 2: The first spouse died in 1973 (when the nil rate band was £15,000) leaving an estate of £24,000 wholly to the surviving spouse. The first £15,000 of the transfer would have been covered by the limited spouse exemption then in force and the balance of £9,000 would have used up 60% of the Estate Duty nil rate band at that time. Consequently the IHT nil rate band available on the surviving spouse's death can be increased by 40%.

As a general rule of thumb, if some Estate Duty (or Capital Transfer Tax, or IHT) was paid on the first death, there will have been no unused nil rate band available for transfer for use when the surviving spouse dies.

Were the rules about the assets that were chargeable on death any different for CTT & ED?

Again the basic principles remained the same, but there were some differences

- for CTT, initially, all the gifts made during an individual's lifetime were to be taken into account when they died, although this was limited to gifts within 7 years of the death during the first 7 years of CTT and this was subsequently cut from an unlimited cumulation to a period of 10 years in 1981.
- for Estate Duty, settled property in which the deceased had a life interest was not always aggregable with the estate on death.

If the first spouse died prior to 18 March 1986 and the question of other chargeable assets is relevant, and you are not sure what to include in your claims, please discuss the position with us first.

I am divorced and my ex-husband has died without remarrying, can my personal representatives claim to transfer his unused nil rate band to my estate when I die?

No, in order for your personal representatives to be able to make a claim to transfer unused nil rate band, you must have still been married to your husband when he died.

I am an IFA with a range of products designed to make use of the nil rate band, how will these be affected?

There will be no effect on these products, they will continue to work in exactly the same way as before.

Misc. 124A IHT (INHERITANCE TAX) CLEARANCE SERVICE FOR BUSINESS OWNERS

This guidance is for the use of the business owners who make clearance applications in relation to Inheritance Tax business property relief (IHT-BPR). Guidance for the use of business customers who wish to apply for a non-statutory clearance can be found on the HMRC website. The current service for other non-business customers continues. Non-business customers should continue to refer to the existing guidance at Code of Practice 10 or VAT Notice 700/6 VAT rulings. (Please note that as a result of the extension of clearances for business customers COP10 and VAT Notice 700/6 are being revised. Further announcements will be available on the "What's new" section of the HMRC website in due course.)

Clearances: Mission Statement

In developing the new Clearance Service we wanted to provide a facility that was as useful as possible for UK businesses as a whole. To do this within our resources, we have focused our efforts on where the benefit is greatest. There are a wide range of potential applications, from issues that are clearly new to those which are almost without doubt. HM Revenue and Customs (HMRC) wants therefore to work in partnership with businesses and their representatives to ensure that as far as possible those issues brought forward for clearance are the ones that have the greatest impact on the business concerned. Developing a common understanding on this will be an ongoing process between HMRC and the users of the service.

The purpose of the new Clearance Service is:

- to provide certainty for businesses operating in the UK, as a useful practical service at a level whereby speed of response from HMRC can be reasonably assured

We will therefore aim to provide clearances:

- within 28 days as the norm
- on areas of material uncertainty arising within four Finance Acts of the introduction of any new legislation
- on legislation older than last four Finance Acts where there is material uncertainty around the tax outcome of a real issue of commercial significance to the business itself, determined by reference to the scale of the business and the impact of the issue upon it

HMRC and users of the Clearances Service will:

- recognise the need for proportionality from all sides so that applications are relevant, focused and within scope, thus avoiding overload of the service to the detriment of all concerned

Applications for clearances

This guidance sets out what you need to do to make an IHT-BPR clearance application, and what information you need to provide. It includes information for business owners in relation to IHT-BPR that was previously set out in Code of Practice 10.

Guidance on non-statutory clearances for business customers can be found on the HMRC website. Customers who would like advice on other personal tax issues should continue to refer to Code of Practice 10.

Non-statutory clearances

A non-statutory clearance is written confirmation of our view of the application of inheritance tax law and the business property relief provisions, in relation to the tax position following a specific business transaction or event, that you can rely on in most circumstances, as our view of the tax consequences of this transaction.

We will provide clearances in relation to inheritance tax business property relief, regardless of the age of the legislation, where you have demonstrated that:

- there is material uncertainty over the application of the law
- that the issue is commercially significant to the business itself

We will aim to send you our view within 28 calendar days, though in complex cases this may take longer.

We will provide non-statutory clearances both:

- pre-transaction where evidence is supplied that the transaction is genuinely contemplated
- post-transaction

We will also provide our view of the tax consequences of a transfer of value that involves a change of ownership of a business (succession) where this transfer, leaving aside the application of business property relief, would result in an immediate inheritance tax charge. Valuations are not included in the clearance service so we will apply some flexibility in borderline taxpaying cases. Evidence must be provided that the transfer is commercially significant and is genuinely contemplated.

Clearances in these succession cases will only remain valid for a limited period of six months. Applicants should recognize that the clearance service cannot be used for general confirmation of the business property relief position in the absence of a commercial transaction.

Clearances do not alter the tax treatment but simply give you HMRC's view of what the correct tax treatment is.

You may wish to apply for clearance in relation to both business tax and inheritance tax. It is helpful if your applications are submitted separately to speed up the handling of these, but, if you prefer to write a joint application letter, you should send copies of the application to both clearance teams and ensure that it is clear from your letter which teams you have sent copies to.

Statutory clearances

There are a few statutes where tax law provides that HMRC will give a clearance relating to a specific point. These are referred to as 'statutory clearances' and they are outside the scope of this guidance.

For contact details and a comprehensive list of statutory clearances, please see the contact list [available at www.hmrc.gov.uk/cap/statutory-clearances.pdf]. It is helpful if applications for non-statutory clearances are submitted separately to statutory clearances, to speed up the handling of your applications.

You may wish to write one clearance application letter to cover both non-statutory and statutory clearance applications, but you should ensure that copies are sent to all relevant teams. Where you choose to do this, please ensure it is clear at the front of your letter which teams copies of your letter have been sent to.

Statutory approvals

A statutory approval is different from a statutory clearance. Approval can be required in advance for a particular tax treatment to apply to a particular issue that can have wide reaching consequences, and the tax treatment changes according to whether an approval has been given or not. For example, statutory approval for the beneficial tax treatment of certain employee share schemes. For contact details on statutory approvals, please see the contact list [available at www.hmrc.gov.uk/cap/statutory-clearances.pdf].

When and where to apply for a non-statutory clearance

Customers who can use this service

Clearance applications will be accepted from business owners and their advisers where there is demonstrable material uncertainty about the inheritance tax consequences of transaction affecting their business. We do not intend this to encompass applications which clearly fall within other areas of personal taxation or routine product endorsements. Business owners may include individuals or trustees who will become business owners as a consequence of the transaction that is the subject of the clearance application.

The current service for other non-business customers continues. These customers should refer to the existing guidance at Code of Practice 10 or VAT Notice 700/6.

When you may choose to apply for an IHT-BPR non-statutory clearance

We aim to make the guidance that accompanies our taxes legislation as clear as possible. If you feel that the guidance does not make clear how the legislation will apply in a particular situation you can make a non-statutory clearance application.

Please read our guidance on the legislation before applying for an IHT-BPR non-statutory clearance, and then read through the checklist in Annex A . The checklist will help you consider all the information that could be relevant to your particular application and to arrange the information so that we can progress your application as quickly as possible. Please attach the checklist, completed as appropriate, with your application.

To discuss your tax affairs or get tax information, including a wide range of leaflets that explain different aspects of the tax system, please see the information contained in the Contact Us area of our website.

In addition to non-statutory clearances HMRC makes available a wide range of information and advice to our customers. These are set out at Annex B. You may also wish to speak to your adviser.

Where to send your IHT-BPR non-statutory clearance

Applications should be sent to:

HMRC
Trusts & Estates Technical Team (Clearances)
Ferrers House
Castle Meadow Road
Nottingham
NG2 1BB
Email: IHT Technical team (Clearances) [mailpoint.e@hmrc.gsi.gov.uk]

IHT Extra-statutory Material

It will help us if you quote the reference BP102/P1/08E.

We will be able to process your application more efficiently if you send your clearance application by email. Attachments to emails should be no larger than 2 MB. Please don't send self-extracting zip files as our software will block them.

Using email

- HMRC cannot guarantee the security of emails you send to us or we send to you over the internet. Any information you send us by email is at your own risk.
- It is important that you have assessed the risks of using email to send information or to receive it from us.
- We will not generally be able to reply by e-mail. If you would like us to reply by email, please tell us so and confirm that you understand and accept the risks involved in using email.
- Information about market/price sensitive matters or well known individuals should not be sent by email. Courier or post should be used for such sensitive information.
- If you have any doubt about the authenticity of an email you receive which claims to come from the clearances team, please call us to check.

Please attach the checklist in Annex A, completed as appropriate, along with the information and any supporting documents that explain your clearance application. If you do not email your application to us, please print the checklist as a cover page and send all the documents to your designated contact above.

We recognise that many clearance applications contain commercially sensitive information and we will handle all information included in clearance applications securely and in accordance with our legal obligations. Whether you send us information electronically or on paper we will keep it secure, and not disclose it to anyone unless they are authorised to see it.

For an application that you consider particularly sensitive you may wish to notify us in advance, so that we can agree about how best to submit your application to us. Please e-mail IHT Technical Team (Clearances) with a contact name and telephone number and we will contact you.

Information you need to provide with your application

For a clearance to be binding on us you must provide us, at the time the clearance is sought, with the full facts and context of the transaction, and set out the legislative uncertainty in question. The courts have said that the customer must "put all of their cards face upwards on the table" (See Note 1). You are responsible for ensuring the information is correct, accurate and complete.

The information that you provide will depend on the circumstances of the clearance application. You need to decide what information is relevant to your application. Please include a heading to your clearance application that includes the name and address of the business owner and ensure that your application is clearly headed as a non-statutory business clearance application.

The checklist at Annex A and the guidance in this section will help you decide what to provide so that we have the relevant information we need to process your application quickly. The guidance sets out guidelines as to the information to provide. We do not expect that all the information we list will be available or relevant for every clearance application. It minimizes the burden for you and for us if you provide summaries of the relevant information, rather than a large volume of supporting documents.

Please supplement this with more detailed explanations, drawing attention to the relevant paragraphs in any supporting documents you provide.

Information about the applicant

Please set out this information at the start of your clearance application.

We will need to understand who is carrying on the business, including:

- the name and address of the individual or trustee business owner
- if different, the name and address of the business
- the relevant business identification number in full, eg Unique Taxpayer Reference and Company Registration Number
- details of the interest held by the individual or trustee in the business
- contact details
- if you are an adviser acting on a client's behalf, your contact details and statement on whose behalf you are acting – normally we require the full authority for you to act from your client

Information about the transaction(s)

It helps us to handle the application efficiently if you set out the nature of your clearance request at the start – for example, in the heading or first paragraph. Please follow this with:

- details of when the transaction occurred and the parties involved, and any other details of the transaction, eg what assets were acquired or disposed of
- the proposed date if the transaction has not yet happened, and supporting information, such as a draft contract where it is available, so that we have an understanding of the timeframes under which you are working and can verify that the transaction is genuinely contemplated
- any details of the transaction that are contingent, for instance, on future events or the consent of other parties

Please note that if the request relates to one specific part of a series of connected transactions we expect you to provide a summary of the series of transactions as part of the facts about your transaction.

Information about the commercial background

Please explain the context of the transaction and the reasons you are undertaking it, providing details of any connected transactions as appropriate. Please also:

- explain the significance to the business owner of the tax result in achieving the desired outcome, including the consequences of any alternative legal interpretations you have considered
- where you have considered different forms of the transaction explain why you chose the proposed form of transaction over alternatives that could achieve the same commercial result
- where your uncertainty arises from the interpretation of legislation older than the last four Finance Acts, you should also provide details of the commercial significance to the business of the transaction that leads you to make the clearance application
- provide accounts for the business for a representative period up to the date of the transaction including detailed profit and loss accounts together with any other relevant financial information.

Information about legal points

Please set out your view of the tax consequences of the particular transaction, with a summarised explanation of your reasoning, and the full details of the question and issue on which you want a response. Please:

- summarise the specific legislation at issue, any case law considered and guidance consulted that are relevant to the point of doubt on which you have made your clearance application
- demonstrate why you believe there is uncertainty about the way the legislation applies
- explain different ways it might apply that you have considered, paying particular attention to those aspects of the transaction that are critical to the legal analysis
- state any previous advice you have or, where you are an adviser, your client has, received from HMRC (or its predecessor departments) that is relevant to your clearance application, quoting any HMRC (or predecessor) references where known and explaining why this advice does not go far enough to resolve your uncertainty
- consider disclosing any advice, or parts of it, you have received, for example from your professional advisers or tax counsel. You are not obliged to provide this but by doing so we may better understand your request for advice

Note 1: The quote originates from R v IR Commrs (ex parte MFK Underwriting Agencies Ltd) [[1989] BTC 561].

Information about the disclosure of a tax avoidance scheme that covers all or part of the transaction

When submitting a Non-Statutory Business Clearance application for a transaction for which there is also the disclosure of an avoidance scheme which covers all or part of the transaction, it is important that explicit mention is made of any related disclosures, preferably by including a copy of the disclosure or, where available, by reporting the allocated DOTAS scheme reference number.

How and when we will respond

If your application for a clearance is accepted

We will acknowledge your application on receipt and send our full response within 28 calendar days as the norm. Our response will either:

- accept your interpretation of the legislation
- reject your interpretation of the legislation

- request further information that we need before we can give you an answer

Where we reject your interpretation we will set out reasons for this. Once we have provided our response, you are entitled to act on the basis of our view, or on the basis of your own view of the appropriate tax treatment.

Very occasionally we may not be able to send our full response within 28 calendar days. This may be, for example, because the application is very complex and requires advice from a number of specialists within HMRC. Where this is the case we will tell you, and work with you to provide a response as soon as we can.

Sometimes we may need to ask you to provide more information before we can send you a full reply. If we need to ask you for more information, we will suspend the handling time for your application until you are able to provide us with the information we have requested. We may wish to contact you by telephone for clarification, and it helps us if you can provide a regular contact point during the period of your application.

If your application for a clearance is not accepted

We will, as soon as possible after receipt of your application, either:

- respond by referring you to the relevant guidance
- return your request setting out clearly why we are not responding to it

Circumstances when we will not accept your clearance application

We will not accept your application:

- where you ask us to give, or comment on, tax planning advice – in particular, we do not "approve" tax planning arrangements
- where you submit an application that is a minor variation of your previous one for the same client on the same transaction (minor variation does not include where you notify us of a change in the facts of the transaction that is the subject of an ongoing pre-transaction clearance application)
- where we take the view that the arrangements are primarily to gain a tax advantage rather than primarily commercially motivated. We will consider each case on its own merits and in accordance with our published risk guidance
- in response to applications where there is not, in fact, any uncertainty – where the point is covered by our published guidance we will instead refer you to the specific part of relevant publications and indicate its relevance to the issues raised in your clearance application
- where we have already opened an enquiry into the transaction that is the subject of your clearance application; or where an enquiry into an Inheritance Tax return has already been opened
- on issues that do not involve the interpretation of tax law or its application to particular circumstances, for instance asset valuations
- in relation to the tax consequences of executing trust deeds or settlements, and whether Chapter 5 Part 5 Income Tax (Trading and Other Income) Act (ITTOIA) applies
- in cases where the disposition of property under a will is conditional on the availability of business property relief

Where you are not happy about the way we handled your application

We aim to send clear responses to the questions raised in your clearance application. We recognise that sometimes you may not agree with the response you receive from us, or you may not be happy with the service we have provided.

If you believe that we have failed to take account of some of the material facts set out in your application please contact the officer who dealt with your case (the details will be on the correspondence we have sent you) and ask that they look at your application again. If you remain unhappy you can ask to be referred to the complaints manager.

If you are unhappy with the way we have handled your affairs, for example because of delays or mistakes, please tell the person or office you have been dealing with. If they are unable to sort things out, ask for your case to be referred to the complaints manager.

Interest and penalties where you asked us for a clearance

If you have applied for a non-statutory clearance, but have not received it by the time that an IHT account is due to be submitted, then the account must still be sent in before the time limit. If that happens you should complete the account according to your own view of the correct tax treatment of the particular transaction. The normal interest and penalty rules will apply if an account is incorrect, whether or not the transactions have been the subject of a clearance.

If you disagree with the clearance that we gave you and complete the account in accordance with your own view of the proper tax treatment, then it may turn out that you have not declared nor paid enough tax at the right time. Regardless of whether you had applied for a post transaction clearance or whether we had given a clearance by the due date, any unpaid or undeclared tax carries interest in the normal way. Similarly, any overpaid tax carries repayment interest from the date it was paid wherever this is usually the case.

Appeals against clearances

There is no general right of appeal against advice or clearances given by HM Revenue & Customs except where rights to appeal are set out in statute. For example, there is a right to appeal to the independent tax tribunal under Section 83 of the VAT Act 1994 about the amount of VAT chargeable on a specific supply of goods or services. An appeal under this section can only be made if the supply has taken place.

If you disagree with any appealable decision you have been given you should write to us and tell us within 30 days. You can ask for the appealable decision you have been given to be reviewed or can appeal direct to the independent tax tribunal. More information on your rights to review and appeal are set out in the HMRC factsheet HMRC1: HM Revenue & Customs decisions – what to do if you disagree [available at www.hmrc.gov.uk/factsheets/hmrc1.pdf].

When you can rely on a clearance

General principles

A clearance applies:

- to the applicant (even where the application has been made by the applicant's adviser, the adviser cannot apply that clearance to other similar cases)
- to the particular transaction that was the subject of the clearance application

We aim to provide clearances that will give certainty to business owners as to the IHT-BPR consequences of their transactions. Our starting point is therefore that you should be able to rely on any clearance we provide. However for a clearance to be considered binding on HMRC, you must set out all the relevant facts and draw attention to all the issues in your application. We expect businesses to interpret this relatively broadly, for example, by providing information on related transactions where relevant.

In most cases, inheritance tax does not arise as a consequence of the commercial transaction itself but of a later event if that event is a transfer of value. In these circumstances, our view of the application of inheritance tax law to the availability of business property relief for a business, an interest in a business, certain shares and securities or certain business assets applies to the facts and circumstances existing at the date of the commercial transaction. HMRC will not be bound by a clearance we have given if there is a change in circumstances between the date of the commercial transaction and a later transfer of value. A change of circumstances includes a change in the nature of the business or the structure of the business, a change in the nature of the interest held by the person to whom the application applies or a change in the legislation relating to business property relief.

In cases where the commercial transaction is a change in the business ownership, any clearance given will be valid only for a period of six months from the date of the clearance letter.

Under our existing powers of 'collection and management' (See Note 2), the principles of administrative law apply and the Courts will ultimately determine if we are bound by a clearance we have given. The underlying principle is that HMRC has a duty to collect the correct amount of tax as required by statute. In the vast majority of cases a clearance we give will be correct in law and therefore binding on HMRC. However there are some circumstances in which our primary duty to collect tax according to the statute may mean that we can no longer be bound by a clearance we have given. For example this may occur where:

- For a pre-transaction clearance, the nature of the transaction changes in a way that has a material impact on the transaction as a whole.
- You provided incorrect or incomplete information when you made the clearance application.
- A Court or Tribunal judgment changes the prevailing interpretation of the law on which the clearance was based and liability to tax has not been finalised – for example, where a return has not yet been submitted or if you have submitted a return where the opportunity to amend that return remains. A clearance will be based on the prevailing understanding of the law at the time it is given. Where the courts change the prevailing interpretation of the law, subject to the principle of legitimate expectation, we are required to collect the correct amount of tax as required by the new interpretation of the law.
- The statutory law relevant to the transaction for which the clearance was given changes. If this change is retrospective we will not be bound by any pre- or post-transaction clearance we have previously given. This situation occurs very infrequently. If the new statute is enacted pre-transaction

and is prospective, any previously given clearance relating to the transaction will not be considered to be binding. HMRC has a duty to collect the correct amount of tax as required by statute at the time the transaction takes place. It remains your responsibility to take account of changes in the law.

Note 2: Section 5 of the Commissioners for Revenue and Customs Act 2005.

Where HMRC makes an incorrect statement

There may be a small number of cases where we provide a clearance that is incorrect in law. Where this happens, we will be bound by such advice provided that it is clear, unequivocal and explicit and you can demonstrate that:

- you reasonably relied upon the advice
- where appropriate you made full disclosure of all the relevant facts
- the application of the statute would result in your financial detriment

Where this is the case, to apply the statute may be so unfair that it could amount to an abuse of power. But, where we have given an incorrect clearance, our primary duty will always remain to collect the correct amount of tax as required by the law and therefore there will be some circumstances when we would not be bound by the advice we have given.

Where we provide you with an erroneous clearance that is binding on us and subsequently notify you that it is incorrect, the established legal position (See note 3) is that you will only be required to start accounting for tax on the correct basis from the date of notification. For Inheritance Tax, this means that any transfer of value falling after an erroneous clearance has been corrected must be accounted for on the correct basis.

Note 3: See for example F & I Financial Services Ltd [[2001] BVC 347] and Al Fayed and others v Advocate General for Scotland [[2002] BTC 428].

Annex A – checklist for non-statutory clearance applications

Please use the checklist for non-statutory clearance applications (PDF 21K) when deciding which document to attach to your email application, or print and include as a cover sheet where you do not send it electronically.

Check that you have included information that is relevant and available for your clearance application and indicate with a tick items that are included. It helps us if you follow the order set out below in your clearance application letter and follow the same order in grouping any supporting documents.

Annex B – other help and advice available from HMRC

In addition to non-statutory clearances HMRC makes available a wide range of information and advice to our customers.

To discuss your tax affairs or get tax information, including a wide range of leaflets that explain different aspects of the tax system, please see the information contained in the Contact Us area of this website.

For general advice on VAT, Excise and Customs, please ring our National Advice Service (NAS) on Tel 0845 010 9000.

For general queries on IR35 intermediaries legislation, please contact Tel 0845 303 3535.

For general advice on other matters, please ring the Client Relationship Manager (CRM) or Customer Manager (CM) that handles your tax affairs. If you do not have an established contact within HMRC, then please visit the Contact Us area for the number of an appropriate helpline. You will find it helpful if you prepare for the call by having to hand a clear explanation of your question and relevant details.

General advice on specialist technical areas of taxation

Please check the contact details provided.

Statutory approvals

Please check the contact details provided.

Statutory clearances

Please see a list of all our statutory clearances and contact details [available at http://www.hmrc.gov.uk/cap/index.htm].

Statements of Practice

Non routine publications that explain our interpretation of legislation and the way we apply the law in practice.

Extra-statutory concessions
Relaxations of the law that give a reduction in tax liability that you would not be entitled to under the strict letter of the law.

News releases
Published on the Government News Network to announce proposed changes in the law or in our practice, or any other changes or initiatives of interest to the public.

Public Notices
A range of publications in relation to VAT, Customs and Excise.

Revenue & Customs Briefs
Regular publications which include announcements advising of policy changes resulting from legislation, litigation or internal policy reviews.

Guidance manuals
The internal guidance manuals our staff use.

Misc. 125 EXTENSION OF CLEARANCES HM REVENUE & CUSTOMS PROVIDE TO BUSINESS OWNERS [HMRC, 23 January 2009]

At Pre-Budget Report 2007, as part of the review of links with Large Business, we announced that from April 2008 HM Revenue & Customs (HMRC) would provide business with our view of the tax consequences of significant commercial issues wherever there is uncertainty, regardless of when the legislation was enacted. We also committed to responding to clearance applications within 28 days as the norm.

On 1 May 2008, we commenced a six month trial extension of the service to business owners in relation to inheritance tax business property relief where there was a significant commercial issue or transaction of the business itself.

Today [23 January 2009] we announce that the inheritance tax business property relief clearance service for business owners will continue and will include an extension to the scope of the service

Please see the guidance on the clearances process and how to apply [http://www.hmrc.gov.uk/cap/clearanceiht.htm].

For all business owners

As with other clearances we will:

- remove the four Finance Act restrictions that inheritance tax clearance applications are subject to under Code of Practice 10 (COP10) where the application relates to the availability of business property relief
- expect applicants to demonstrate the commercial significance of the transaction that causes genuine uncertainty
- expect them to identify what aspect of the law or HMRC practice they consider to be uncertain
- respond within 28 calendar days, as the norm

Extension

From today [23 January 2009] we will also provide our view of the tax consequences of a transfer of value that involves a change of ownership of a business where this transfer, leaving aside the application of business property relief, would result in an immediate inheritance tax charge and provided that the other conditions are met. Clearances in these change of ownership cases will remain valid for a limited period of six months.

An applicant who has previously had an application rejected because it fell outside the scope of the trial service, but the circumstances are such that it would be included in the scope of the extended service, may request a review of the original application.

Contacts

All business owners and those acting on their behalf should send their applications relating to inheritance tax business property relief to:

IHT Technical Team (Clearances)
Ferrers House
Castle Meadow Road

Nottingham
NG2 1BB
Email: mailpoint.e@hmrc.gsi.gov.uk

Misc. 126 BRADFORD & BINGLEY – INHERITANCE TAX RELIEF [HMRC, 2 April 2009]

Questions and answers

Q. Who does this apply to?

A. It applies potentially to the personal representatives of estates where

- The deceased died in the 12 months prior to 29 September 2008; **and**
- The deceased owned shares in Bradford & Bingley when they died; **and**
- The personal representatives still held the shares when they were taken into public ownership on 29 September 2008.

Q. How am I, as executor of such an estate, affected?

A. The treatment effectively means that for the purpose of making a claim for IHT "loss on sale" relief, a holding of Bradford & Bingley shares can be treated as if they had been sold for £1.

Q. Does that mean I'm due a refund of IHT?

A. That depends on whether there is a net loss from *all* the sales of qualifying shares (i.e. shares listed on a recognised stock exchange) by the personal representatives *including* the deemed loss on transfer of the Bradford & Bingley shares.

Q. How does the "loss on sale" relief work?

A. If qualifying shares (shares listed on a recognised stock exchange) are sold (or can be treated as sold) within one year of the date of death for less than the value on which IHT was paid, you may be able to claim relief for loss on sale of shares using form IHT35 (http://www.hmrc.gov.uk/cto/forms/iht35.pdf). Full instructions for making the claim are given on the form.

Q. The concessionary treatment would have applied except that I actually sold the Bradford & Bingley shares before 29 September 2008: can I substitute the £1 deemed sale proceeds for the actual sale proceeds?

A. No. If you had already sold the shares before 29 September 2008, you must use the actual sale proceeds when you are completing the IHT35 claim form.

Q. Why does the concessionary treatment apply only where the deceased died within the 12 months prior to 29 September 2008?

A. Where the deceased died more than 12 months before 29 September 2008, the full 12 month period during which the "loss on sale" relief applies will have expired before Bradford & Bingley shares were taken into public ownership. And where the deceased died on or after 29 September 2008, the estate of the deceased will not include shares in Bradford & Bingley, but a right to compensation.

Q. Will the IHT "loss on sale" relief calculation be revised once the Bradford & Bingley compensation has been fixed?

A. No.

Q. Will HMRC be reviewing their records to ascertain which estates contained holdings of Bradford & Bingley shares?

A. HMRC's records do not enable estates that included a holding of Bradford & Bingley shares to be identified. So Personal Representatives will need to apply for relief on form IHT 35, as stated above.

Q. I have already claimed "loss on sale" relief for sales of other qualifying shares and received an IHT refund. Can I now make a claim for the Bradford & Bingley shares?

A. Yes (assuming of course that the Bradford & Bingley shares were still held by the personal representatives immediately before 29 September 2008). You should use the IHT 35, as stated above.

Q. Following the Treasury's acquisition of Bradford & Bingley shares, I made a claim for relief, which HMRC rejected because the shares had not actually been sold. Will HMRC automatically review my case?

A. HMRC's records do not enable cases where a claim may have been made in respect of Bradford & Bingley shares, and rejected, to be identified. So you should write to the HMRC Inheritance Tax office that dealt with the original claim and ask for the claim to be reviewed.

If you have any further queries, you should contact the IHT and Probate helpline on 0845 30 20 900.

Misc. 128 SPOTLIGHT 5: USING TRUSTS AND SIMILAR ENTITIES TO REWARD EMPLOYEES [HMRC, 21 August 2009]

…

In addition our view is that an Inheritance Tax charge may arise on the participators of a close company. Unless the participators are excluded beneficiaries and have not had funds applied for their benefit, such as the receipt of a loan, a charge to Inheritance Tax arises on participators of close companies at the time the funds are paid to the trustee by the close company. Relief is only available to the extent that a deduction is allowable to the company for the year in which the contribution is made. Later payments of earnings out of the trust that may trigger a deduction to the company would not qualify for relief.

Participators affected by this may need to self-assess a liability to Inheritance Tax [http://www.hmrc.gov.uk/trusts/iht/iht100.htm]. There is further technical advice on Inheritance Tax on Contributions to Employee Benefit Trusts on the HMRC Internet site [http://www.hmrc.gov.uk/briefs/inheritance-tax/brief4909.htm]. We are actively challenging examples of such arrangements and considering legislative options to end further usage of these schemes.

Misc. 129 VALUATION FOR INHERITANCE TAX PURPOSES OF RIGHT TO RECEIVE COMPENSATION IN RESPECT OF SHARES IN BRADFORD & BINGLEY (B&B) [HMRC, 27 July 2010]

The following guidance reflects HM Revenue & Customs (HMRC) understanding that:

- the Independent Valuer announced on 5 July 2010 that former investors should receive no compensation for their shares
- nearly all B&B shareholders had holdings of less than 1,000 shares

For the purposes of completing Inheritance Tax accounts, on a without prejudice basis, HMRC is now prepared to accept that:

For deaths on or after 5 July 2010, the right to receive compensation in respect of B&B shares may be included at a nil value.

For deaths occurring before 5 July 2010, where the holding is of 1,000 shares or less, the right to receive compensation in respect of B&B shares may be included at a nil value.

For deaths occurring before 5 July 2010, where the holding is of more than 1,000 shares, executors or others liable for Inheritance Tax should contact the Shares and Assets Valuation Helpline on 0115 974 2222 for advice on the appropriate value to be included for Inheritance Tax purposes.

Misc. 130 GUIDANCE: DISCLOSURE OF TAX AVOIDANCE SCHEMES – INCOME TAX, CORPORATION TAX, CAPITAL GAINS TAX, NATIONAL INSURANCE CONTRIBUTIONS, STAMP DUTY LAND TAX AND INHERITANCE TAX

[Reproduced in Vol. 1F (Income Tax, Corporation Tax and Capital Gains Tax) OTHER HMRC MATERIALS – HMRC BOOKLETS as Disclosure of tax avoidance schemes (DOTAS), February 2018.]

Misc. 134 INHERITANCE TAX ON MAIN RESIDENCE NIL-RATE BAND AND DOWNSIZING PROPOSALS: TECHNICAL NOTE [HMRC, October 2015]

1. Introduction

At Summer Budget 2015, the government announced it will phase in a new residence nil-rate band (RNRB) from 6 April 2017 when a residence is passed on death to a direct descendant.

It will be:

- £100,000 in 2017 to 2018
- £125,000 in 2018 to 2019
- £150,000 in 2019 to 2020
- £175,000 in 2020 to 2021

It will then rise in line with the Consumer Price Index (CPI) from 2021 to 2022. This will reduce the burden of Inheritance Tax for most families by making it easier to pass on the family home to direct descendants without a tax charge.

Further details about the measure are available in the tax information and impact note (https://www.gov.uk/government/publications/inheritance-tax-main-residence-nil-rate-band-and-the-existing-nil-rate-band). The relevant legislation is included in clause 9 [http://www.publications.parliament.uk/pa/bills/cbill/2015-2016/0057/cbill_2015-20160057_en_2.htm#pt2-pb1-l1g9] of the Finance Bill (2) 2015.

The government also announced that legislation would be included in Finance Bill 2016 to make sure that those who wish to downsize to a less valuable property or cease to own their own home are not discouraged from doing so.

This technical note provides further detail on the proposals, and asks whether the details need further clarification. It also seeks views on the issues and practical difficulties in implementing the proposals. The note and the comments received will inform the legislation that will be presented in the draft 2016 Finance Bill.

2. Policy aim

The government recognises that individuals may wish to downsize to a smaller and often less valuable property later in life. Others may have to sell their home for a variety of reasons, for example, because they need to go into residential care. This may mean that they would lose some, or all, of the benefit of the available RNRB. However, the government intends that the new RNRB should not be introduced in such a way as to disincentivise an individual from downsizing or selling their property.

Consequently, the government announced that where part or all of the RNRB might be lost because the deceased had downsized to a less valuable residence or had ceased to own a residence the lost RNRB will still be available – provided that the qualifying conditions were met. The RNRB would apply where the residence is sold (or is no longer owned) on or after 8 July 2015. This proposal will ensure there is no disincentive to downsize or sell a home from the date the RNRB was announced at the Summer Budget.

3. Policy design

The proposal would apply to situations where the deceased:

- downsized to a less valuable residence and that residence, together with assets of an equivalent value to the "lost" RNRB, has been left to direct descendants
- sold their only residence, and the sale proceeds, or other assets of an equivalent value, have been left to direct descendants
- has otherwise ceased to own their only residence, and other assets of an equivalent value have been left to direct descendants

The broad intention is that an estate would be eligible for the proportion of the RNRB that is foregone as a result of downsizing or disposal of the property as an addition to the RNRB that can be used on death. For the purposes of this note this will be referred to as the "additional RNRB".

The qualifying conditions for the additional RNRB would be broadly the same as those for the RNRB, that is the:

- individual dies on or after 6 April 2017
- property disposed of must have been owned by the individual and it would have qualified for the RNRB had the individual retained it
- less valuable property, or other assets of an equivalent value if the property has been disposed of, are in the deceased's estate (this would also include assets which are deemed to be part of a person's estate)
- less valuable property, and any other assets of an equivalent value, are inherited by the individual's direct descendants on that person's death – direct descendants are the same as those in relation to the RNRB

In addition, the following conditions would also apply:

- the downsizing or the disposal of the property occurs after 8 July 2015
- subject to the condition above, there would be no time limit on the period in which the downsizing or the disposals took place before death
- there could be any number of downsizing moves between 8 July 2015 and the date of death of the individual
- downsizing would also include disposing of part of a property (including land occupied and used as a garden or grounds) or a share in it
- where a property is given away, assets of an equivalent value to the value of the property when the gift was made must be left to direct descendants
- the value of the property would be the net value i.e. after deducting any mortgage or other debts charged on the property
- the additional RNRB would be tapered away in the same way as the RNRB if the value of the estate at death is above £2m

- the additional RNRB would be applied together with the available RNRB but the total for the two would still be capped so that they would not exceed the limit of the total available RNRB for a particular year
- a claim would have to be made for the additional RNRB in a similar way that a claim is made to transfer any unused RNRB to the estate of a surviving spouse or civil partner

4. Examples

The following examples illustrate how the additional RNRB would apply and how it would be calculated.

Example 1

A widow sells a home worth £400,000 in August 2020 and moves to a home worth £210,000. At the time of the sale the available RNRB is £350,000 as, had she died at that time, her executors would be able to make a claim to transfer all the unused RNRB from her late husband. By downsizing, she has potentially lost the chance to use £140,000 or 40% of the available RNRB which could have applied had the more valuable home not been sold.

When the widow later dies in October 2020, the home is worth £225,000 and is left to her children together with £500,000 of other assets. The estate can use an RNRB of £225,000. However, the widow was eligible for an RNRB of £350,000 had she not downsized. The estate can therefore claim an additional RNRB of 40% of the available RNRB (40% x £350,000) or £140,000. This would give a total RNRB of £365,000 (£225,000 + £140,000). But this is more than the maximum available RNRB (£350,000) so the additional RNRB is restricted to £125,000 to ensure that the total amount used does not exceed the maximum available.

In addition, the existing nil-rate band together with any transferable nil-rate band claimed from her late husband's estate can be applied to the remaining assets in the estate.

Example 2

A husband sells a home worth £300,000 in July 2020 and moves to a home worth £140,000. At the time the available RNRB is £175,000. He has potentially lost the chance to use £35,000 or 20% of the available RNRB which could have applied had the more valuable home not been sold.

When he dies in December 2020, the home is worth £175,000 and is left to his son with the remainder of the estate passing to his wife. The estate can use the RNRB of £175,000 to the full and since the RNRB was fully used on death, there is none to transfer to the widow. However, none of the existing nil-rate band has been used, so it can be transferred and will be available on the widow's death along with her own RNRB.

Example 3

A widower gives away his home worth £400,000 to his children in May 2020 and moves into rented "later living" accommodation. At the time of the gift the available RNRB is £350,000. He has potentially lost the chance to use £350,000 or 100% of the available RNRB which could have applied had he not given away his home.

When he dies in February 2021, within 7 years of the gift, his estate is worth £600,000 and is split between his four children. As there is no qualifying residence in his estate, it cannot use RNRB directly. But the estate is eligible for additional RNRB up to the maximum 100% of the available RNRB at his death or £350,000.

The position for the gift of the house is considered first. RNRB only applies to the assets in the estate, so it is not available in respect of the gift of the house. However, the estate can claim the full transferable nil-rate band (TNRB) of £650,000 so there is no tax to pay on the gift of £400,000. The balance of £250,000 TNRB remains available to be set against the estate.

RNRB is applied first against the estate of £600,000, leaving a remainder of £250,000. The balance of TNRB from his late wife's estate is applied to this amount so no tax is payable as a result of the death.

5. Questions

HM Revenue and Customs (HMRC) would welcome views from representative bodies, individuals, practitioners, solicitors, and other professional advisors who have an interest in the proposals.

Question 1

Do any of the policy design details above or conditions need further clarification? Please illustrate the problem using examples if possible.

Question 2

What are the issues and practical difficulties which might arise when implementing the proposal and complying with the conditions?

6. Responses

Please send responses to the questions above by email to ihtandtrustsconsult.car@hmrc.gsi.gov.uk. HMRC is also willing to meet interested groups to discuss the proposals. Please send an email to the address above if you would like HMRC to set up a meeting.

Alternatively, you can write to:

Assets and Residence Policy
Room G47
100 Parliament Street
London
SW1A 2BQ

The deadline for receiving responses is 16 October 2015.

Misc. 135 INHERITANCE TAX: ADDITIONAL THRESHOLD (RNRB) [HMRC, April 2017]

Introduction

This guide explains how to apply the additional threshold to an estate for most circumstances. But there are some basic rules (https://www.gov.uk/guidance/check-if-you-can-get-an-additional-inheritance-tax-threshold) to follow to see if an estate qualifies for the additional threshold, which is sometimes known as the residence nil rate band or RNRB.

HM Revenue and Customs (HMRC) can't:

- give tax planning advice
- comment on what someone should do to take advantage of the additional threshold
- explain what someone's entitlement to the additional threshold or tax position will be in the future

In some less straightforward situations you may want to get professional advice (https://www.gov.uk/tax-help) about:

- how to work out the additional threshold
- the effect of the additional threshold on the Inheritance Tax (IHT) liability
- what action you need to take to make sure that an estate qualifies for the additional threshold

  You can also use the additional threshold calculator (https://www.tax.service.gov.uk/calculate-additional-inheritance-tax-threshold) to work out how much additional threshold the estate may be entitled to.

When the additional threshold applies

An estate will be entitled to the additional threshold if:

- the person dies on or after 6 April 2017
- the person owns a home, or a share of one, so that it's included in their estate
- their direct descendants such as children or grandchildren inherit the home, or a share of it

For estates valued at more than £2 million, the additional threshold (and any transferred additional threshold) will be gradually withdrawn or tapered away.

An estate may also be entitled to the additional threshold when an individual has downsized to a less valuable home or sold, or given away their home after 7 July 2015.

Additional threshold amounts

The maximum available amount of the additional threshold will increase yearly.

For deaths in the following tax years it will be:

- £100,000 in 2017 to 2018
- £125,000 in 2018 to 2019
- £150,000 in 2019 to 2020
- £175,000 in 2020 to 2021

For later years, the maximum additional threshold will increase in line with inflation (based on the Consumer Prices Index).

Unused additional threshold

Any unused additional threshold when someone dies can be transferred to the deceased's spouse or civil partner's estate. This can also be done if the first of the couple died before 6 April 2017, even though the additional threshold wasn't available at that time.

Although you don't need to make a formal claim for the additional threshold, you'll need to give details of the amount due and supporting information on the IHT return following a death. You'll need to make a claim to transfer any unused additional threshold from the estate of a late spouse or civil partner. You'll also need to make a claim for any additional threshold as a result of downsizing or disposal of the home before death.

The additional threshold only applies to the estate of a person who's died. It doesn't apply to gifts or other transfers made during a person's lifetime. This includes gifts that become taxable because they've been made within 7 years of a donor's death.

Where someone gives away their home and continues to benefit from it, for example, by living in the property, HMRC treats that home as being included in the estate. So the additional threshold may be available for that home if it's given away to a direct descendant.

How to calculate and apply the additional threshold

The additional threshold applies in addition to the basic Inheritance Tax threshold (https://www.gov.uk/guidance/inheritance-tax-transfer-of-threshold) (sometimes known as nil rate band or NRB and currently it's £325,000) if the individual and estate meet the qualifying conditions. The additional threshold doesn't mean that the home is exempt for IHT purposes but that could be the result of the new rules in some cases.

The amount of the additional threshold due for an estate will be the lower of:

- the value of the home, or share, that's inherited by direct descendants
- the maximum additional threshold available for the estate when the individual died

You should add any transferred additional threshold from a late spouse's or civil partner's estate to the amount of the additional threshold due for an estate. You set the combined additional threshold against the value of the estate first.

You then set the basic Inheritance Tax threshold (and any transferred basic threshold) against the remaining value of the estate. In many cases the order that you apply the additional threshold and basic Inheritance Tax threshold will make no difference. But in some cases it will affect the amount of any unused additional threshold or basic threshold available for transfer to a spouse or civil partner's estate.

Case study 1 (https://www.gov.uk/government/case-studies/inheritance-tax-residence-nil-rate-band-case-studies) shows how the additional threshold and basic Inheritance Tax threshold applies to an estate.

The value of the home that direct descendants inherit doesn't have to be more than the existing basic threshold or transferred basic threshold, for the additional threshold to apply. You apply the additional threshold to the whole taxable estate, not just to the value of the home, so the benefit of the additional threshold is shared across the whole estate.

If the value of the home is less than the maximum available additional threshold, the unused amount of additional threshold can't be set against the other assets in the estate. But, the unused additional threshold would be available to transfer to the deceased's spouse or civil partner's estate when they die and leave a home to their direct descendants.

Case study 2 (https://www.gov.uk/government/case-studies/inheritance-tax-residence-nil-rate-band-case-studies) shows how the additional threshold applies in these situations.

Gifts and other transfers made during a person's lifetime (lifetime transfers)

Unlike the existing basic Inheritance Tax threshold (https://www.gov.uk/guidance/inheritance-tax-transfer-of-threshold) the additional threshold doesn't apply to any lifetime transfers, such as:

- transfers into trusts
- the value of any gifts made within 7 years of a donor's death which then become taxable

Case Study 3 (https://www.gov.uk/government/case-studies/inheritance-tax-residence-nil-rate-band-case-studies) shows how the basic Inheritance Tax threshold applies to lifetime transfers, and how that affects how you apply the additional threshold. The basic Inheritance Tax threshold applies to any lifetime transfers and any gifts made within 7 years of the donor's death, but the additional threshold doesn't. So the basic Inheritance Tax threshold could be completely used up by those transfers and gifts, but any additional threshold would still be available to reduce the IHT charge on the estate at death.

Case Study 4 (https://www.gov.uk/government/case-studies/inheritance-tax-residence-nil-rate-band-case-studies) shows how the basic Inheritance Tax threshold is used separately from the additional threshold.

For married couples and civil partners, you look at the position for each person's estate separately on each death. This would include each person's share of the home if it's owned jointly.

Transfer of any unused additional threshold

For married couples and civil partners any unused additional threshold can be transferred when the surviving spouse or civil partner dies after 5 April 2017. It doesn't matter when the first of the couple died, even if the death occurred before the additional threshold was available. The additional threshold can't be transferred to a "partner" who's not the spouse or civil partner of the deceased. This is still true even if they lived together and jointly owned the home.

If the additional threshold wasn't fully used when the first of the couple died, the unused percentage can be transferred to the surviving spouse or civil partner's estate. This is transferred in a similar way to the existing basic Inheritance Tax threshold.

Where the first of the couple died before 6 April 2017 their estate wouldn't have used any of the additional threshold as it wasn't available. So 100% of the additional threshold will be available for transfer unless the value of their estate exceeded £2 million and the additional threshold is tapered away. It's the unused percentage of the additional threshold that's transferred, not the unused amount. This makes sure that if the maximum amount of additional threshold increases over time, the survivor's estate will benefit from that increase.

You calculate the actual amount that's transferred to the surviving spouse or civil partner's estate in 2 steps:

Step 1. Work out the percentage of additional threshold that wasn't used on the first death. You do this by dividing the unused amount of additional threshold by the total additional threshold that was available on the first death and multiplying the result by 100. If the first death occurred before 6 April 2017 the unused additional threshold and total available additional threshold are both deemed to be £100,000 so the unused percentage is 100%.

Step 2. Multiply the percentage of additional threshold that was unused on the first death by the maximum additional threshold available at the time of the survivor's death. This gives the sum available to transfer.

Case study 5 (https://www.gov.uk/government/case-studies/inheritance-tax-residence-nil-rate-band-case-studies) shows an example of how the additional threshold is transferred.

The personal representatives of the surviving spouse or civil partner must make a claim to transfer the unused additional threshold within 2 years of the end of the month in which the person dies. This can be extended in some circumstances.

The additional threshold and basic Inheritance Tax threshold aren't linked so the percentages transferred can be different. For example, if the estate of the first of the couple to die used up all of the basic Inheritance Tax threshold leaving none to transfer, but there's unused additional threshold, you can still transfer the unused additional threshold.

The percentage of transferred additional threshold will be limited to 100%. This means that if an individual has had more than one spouse or civil partner and they make a claim to transfer the unused additional threshold from each one, the total transferred additional threshold can't be more than 100% of the maximum available amount.

The home that the surviving spouse or civil partner leaves to their direct descendants doesn't have to be the same home that they lived in with their late spouse or civil partner to either qualify for the additional threshold or transfer it.

The surviving spouse or civil partner doesn't have to have previously owned the home with their late spouse or civil partner, or inherited it from them. It can be any home as long as the surviving spouse or civil partner lived in it at some stage before they died and the home is included in their estate when they die.

The additional threshold and any transferred additional threshold is only available if:

- the surviving spouse or civil partner leaves a home to their direct descendants
- the home of the surviving spouse or civil partner is included in their estate

But, if the surviving spouse or civil partner disposed of their home after 7 July 2015 and leaves other assets to their direct descendants when they die, the additional threshold may still be available under the downsizing rules.

Couples who aren't married or in a civil partnership, or who've divorced, will still be able to benefit from the additional threshold individually if they leave a home to their direct descendants. But they won't be able to transfer any unused additional threshold to each other.

Direct descendants

For additional threshold purposes, a direct descendant of a person is:

- a child, grandchild or other lineal descendant of that person
- a spouse or civil partner of a lineal descendant (including their widow, widower or surviving civil partner)

In addition, a person's direct descendant is:

- a child who is, or was at any time, that person's stepchild
- an adopted child of that person
- a child who was fostered at any time by that person
- a child where that person is appointed as a guardian or special guardian for that child when they're under 18

In this context, the child who inherits the home doesn't have to be under 18. A person's stepchild is limited to someone whose parent is, or was, the spouse or civil partner of that person.

Direct descendants don't include nephews, nieces, siblings and other relatives who aren't included in the list above.

One or more direct descendants of the deceased can inherit a home, or a share of it.

To be eligible for the additional threshold, the home, or the share of it, must be left to a person's direct descendants so that it becomes part of the beneficiaries' estate as a result of the person's death.

If a home is left to beneficiaries who are a mixture of direct descendants and other relatives or individuals, the value of the home must be apportioned according to the share of the property the direct descendants inherit.

Case study 6 (https://www.gov.uk/government/case-studies/inheritance-tax-residence-nil-rate-band-case-studies) explains this.

The home

The additional threshold only applies to one home where it's both:

- included in the deceased's estate
- lived in at some stage by the deceased before their death

If the deceased downsized or disposed of their home before they died, the additional threshold only applies if the former home would have been included in their estate before the downsizing or disposal.

If the deceased owned more than one home, the personal representatives can nominate which one should qualify for the additional threshold.

The home doesn't have to be a person's main home or have been lived in, or owned, for a minimum period. It can be any property that the deceased lived in as long as it's included in their estate on death. A property that the deceased owned, but never lived in, such as a buytolet property, won't be eligible for the additional threshold.

The value of the home for additional threshold purposes will be the open market value of the property less any liabilities secured on it such as a mortgage. The home doesn't have to be worth more than a certain minimum value (for example, more than £325,000 or above the maximum available additional threshold). If the value of the home, or share of it, being inherited by direct descendants is below the maximum available additional threshold, the amount of the additional threshold is limited accordingly.

The whole of the home doesn't have to be left to direct descendants. If only a share of the home is inherited by the deceased's direct descendants, the value of the home must be apportioned. The additional threshold is calculated on the basis of that apportioned value.

Case Study 6 (https://www.gov.uk/government/case-studies/inheritance-tax-residence-nil-rate-band-case-studies) shows how the additional threshold is calculated when a share of the home is left to direct descendants.

The home doesn't have to be in the UK but it does have to be within the scope of IHT and it must be included in a person's estate. This may depend on the deceased's domicile and the location of the home. UK domiciled individuals are subject to IHT on their worldwide assets so it doesn't matter where the home is located. NonUK domiciled individuals are only subject to IHT on their assets in the UK, so the home must be located in the UK to be within the scope of IHT and within their estate. In these cases, the home will only qualify for the additional threshold if it's in the UK.

Inheriting the home

For additional threshold purposes, a person's direct descendants inherit a home if it's left to them:

- on death in the deceased's will

- under the rules of intestacy
- by some other legal means as a result of the person's death

The home doesn't have to be specifically mentioned in the deceased's will. It can be inherited as part of the residue of the estate. Where the home is included in the residue and that residue passes to a number of different people, HMRC treat each as inheriting a proportion of the home.

The direct descendants will only inherit the property for additional threshold purposes if they become entitled to it on the death of the deceased. If the will has a condition that the deceased's grandchildren have to reach a certain age before they can inherit the home which means the property is held in a trust subject to a contingency, the additional threshold wouldn't apply. This is because the grandchildren don't inherit the home on the death of their grandparent.

If the home is held in trust before death and it stays in trust, the home will only qualify for the additional threshold if it becomes part of the direct descendant's estate for IHT purposes following the death.

The actual home doesn't have to end up in the hands of the deceased's direct descendants. An estate could still be eligible for the additional threshold if the deceased's personal representatives sell the home as part of the administration of the estate and pass the sale proceeds to the direct descendants.

In the same way, once the direct descendants have inherited the home, there are no restrictions on what they have to do with it. An estate will still qualify for the additional threshold even if the direct descendants decide to sell the home after they've inherited it.

Case study 7 (https://www.gov.uk/government/case-studies/inheritance-tax-residence-nil-rate-band-case-studies) shows how the additional threshold applies when the home is sold after a death.

The direct descendants can also inherit the home if it's left to them as a result of amending the deceased's will by a deed of variation (https://www.gov.uk/alter-a-will-after-a-death). The terms of a will would effectively be superseded by the deed of variation so the outcome of the deed has to be considered, rather than the wording of the will.

Trusts

A home, or a share of one, can be held in a trust before an individual's death. Or it can be transferred to a trust on their death.

The availability of the additional threshold will depend on the type of trust. This is because the type of trust will affect whether HMRC treat the home as part of a person's estate for IHT purposes. It will also affect whether HMRC treat that person's direct descendants as inheriting the home.

Because this is complicated, the information given below is only a general guide. Where a home, or a share of one, is held in a trust or transferred to a trust, you should discuss how the additional threshold applies with a solicitor or other professional adviser who knows about trust law.

The additional threshold won't apply to transfers of the home or any other assets into a trust during a person's lifetime. This applies even if the beneficiary is a direct descendant of the transferor, or if they're entitled to the assets in the trust.

Trusts included in a person's estate

If a home is held in a trust for a person's benefit before their death, it'll usually be included in that person's estate for IHT purposes if the trust gives the person (the beneficiary) the right to use or occupy the property. This right is often called an interest in possession.

This can happen when a person is given a right to live in the family home following the death of their spouse or civil partner. The home is held in a trust for the lifetime of the survivor (or life tenant) and is included in their estate for IHT purposes. When the survivor dies, their estate will be eligible for the additional threshold if their direct descendants then inherit their home.

If a home is put into a trust on an individual's death, the additional threshold will available if both the:

- person who benefits from the trust (the beneficiary) is a direct descendant of the deceased
- type of trust, is one that means the home is included in the beneficiary's estate for IHT purposes

If the beneficiary isn't a direct descendant of the deceased, the estate won't qualify for the additional threshold. In that case the unused additional threshold would be available to transfer to a surviving spouse or civil partner's estate.

Case study 8 (https://www.gov.uk/government/case-studies/inheritance-tax-residence-nil-rate-band-case-*studies) shows how the additional* threshold is transferred when a home is put into a trust for a surviving spouse.

The home will no longer be in the beneficiary's estate if the trust comes to an end during the beneficiary's lifetime. This could happen, for example, when the surviving spouse remarries and the home then passes to their direct descendants. In this situation the surviving spouse's estate wouldn't qualify for the additional threshold when they die because the home isn't inherited by their direct descendants on death. But the transfer of the home may still qualify as a disposal for downsizing purposes.

Trusts not included in a person's estate

If a home is held in a discretionary trust, the home wouldn't normally form part of a person's estate. In these circumstances, their estate wouldn't be eligible for the additional threshold even if the home goes to the beneficiary's direct descendants when the beneficiary dies.

If a home is put into a discretionary trust on death, the deceased's estate won't qualify for the additional threshold even if the beneficiaries are direct descendants of the deceased. Whether the beneficiaries are entitled to use the home is at the discretion of the trustees, so the home won't form part of any beneficiary's estate and they'll not be treated as inheriting the home.

The estate may still qualify for the additional threshold if the trust meets certain conditions. For example, if the trust has been set up for:

- a disabled beneficiary
- orphaned children under 18
- any children under 25

You should discuss how the additional threshold applies in these situations with a solicitor or other professional adviser.

Tapering away the additional threshold

The additional threshold will be gradually withdrawn, or tapered away, for an estate valued at more than £2 million even if a home is left to direct descendants. The additional threshold will be reduced by £1 for every £2 that the value of the estate is more than the £2 million taper threshold.

This threshold may increase in line with inflation after the tax year 2020 to 2021.

Case study 9 (https://www.gov.uk/government/case-studies/inheritance-tax-residence-nil-rate-band-case-studies) shows how the additional threshold is tapered away for an estate worth more than £2 million.

To work out whether the taper applies, the value of the estate is the total of all the assets in the estate less any debts or liabilities. When you work out the value of the estate for taper purposes you don't take off any:

- exemptions such as spouse exemption
- reliefs such as agricultural or business property relief

You ignore assets that are specifically excluded from IHT (excluded property).

Tapering can also reduce the amount of additional threshold available to transfer to a surviving spouse or civil partner, even if no additional threshold is used when the first of the couple dies. You calculate the amount of transferred additional threshold that the survivor's estate can claim using the percentage of additional threshold that was unused on the earlier death. If the estate of the first of the couple to die is worth more than £2 million, tapering will reduce the amount of the unused additional threshold in that estate. This also in turn reduces the amount of additional threshold that can be transferred to the surviving spouse or civil partner's estate.

Case study 10 (https://www.gov.uk/government/case-studies/inheritance-tax-residence-nil-rate-band-case-studies) shows how the additional threshold available for transfer is reduced by tapering.

Downsizing

If an estate doesn't qualify for the full amount of additional threshold, the estate may be entitled to an additional amount of additional threshold, known as a downsizing addition if all these conditions apply:

- the deceased disposed of a former home and either downsized to a less valuable home, or ceased to own a home, on or after 8 July 2015
- the former home would have qualified for the additional threshold if it had been kept until death
- at least some of the estate is inherited by the deceased's direct descendants

The amount of the downsizing addition will generally be equal to the additional threshold that's been lost because the former home is no longer in the estate. It will also depend on the value of the other assets in the estate that are left to direct descendants. But the downsizing addition can't exceed the maximum amount of additional threshold that would have been available if the disposal or downsizing hadn't happened.

The deceased's personal representatives must make a claim for the downsizing addition within 2 years of the end of the month in which the person dies. The time limit can be extended in some circumstances.

HMRC doesn't have to be told when the downsizing move or disposal of the former home takes place. The deceased's personal representatives can make the claim for the additional threshold and any downsizing addition as part of completing the IHT returns. But, it may be helpful to make a note of the details of the move or disposal so that personal representatives are aware of it and have the information available to make the claim accordingly.

Only one disposal of a former home can be taken into account for the downsizing addition. If the deceased disposed of more than one home between 8 July 2015 and their date of death, the personal representatives can choose which disposal is taken into account to calculate the downsizing addition.

Calculating the lost additional threshold

There are 5 steps to work out the amount of additional threshold that's been lost:

Step 1. Work out the additional threshold that would have been available when the disposal of the former home took place. This figure is made up of the maximum additional threshold due at the date of disposal (or £100,000 if the disposal occurred before 6 April 2017) on any transferred additional threshold which is available at the date of death.

Step 2. Divide the value of the former home at the date of disposal by the figure in step 1 and multiply the result by 100 to get a percentage. If the value of the former home is greater than the figure in step 1 the percentage will be limited to 100%. If the value of the home disposed of is less than the figure in step 1, the percentage will be between 0% and 100%.

Step 3. If there is a home in the estate on death, divide the value of the home on death by the additional threshold that would be available at the date of death (including any transferred additional threshold). Multiply the result by 100 to get a percentage (again this percentage can't exceed 100%). If there's no home in the estate at death this percentage will be 0%.

Step 4. Deduct the percentage in step 3 from the percentage in step 2.

Step 5. Multiply the additional threshold that would be available at the date of death by the figure from step 4. This gives the amount of the lost additional threshold.

Case study 11 (https://www.gov.uk/government/case-studies/inheritance-tax-residence-nil-rate-band-case-studies) shows how the lost additional threshold is calculated.

The effect of step 3 is that there'll be a different amount of lost additional threshold depending on whether the deceased has either:

- downsized to a less valuable home
- disposed of a home If the percentage in step 3 is the same as, or greater than, the percentage in step 2 there's no loss of additional threshold and there'll be no downsizing addition.

Downsizing to a less valuable home

There may be some lost additional threshold where the deceased downsized to a less valuable home but still has a home in their estate on death. This will only happen when the value of the home at death is below the maximum additional threshold available to the estate.

The downsizing rules won't apply if either:

- there's no loss of the additional threshold because the value of any home at death is equal to, or more than the maximum available additional threshold
- the additional threshold isn't available because although there is a home in the estate on death, the home isn't left to a direct descendant

To see if the downsizing addition applies, you don't just look at whether the estate qualifies for the maximum additional threshold. Instead you have to work out whether the value of any home still in the estate at death is too low to qualify for the maximum additional threshold if it was left to direct descendants.

Case study 12 (https://www.gov.uk/government/case-studies/inheritance-tax-residence-nil-rate-band-case-studies) gives an example of when a downsizing addition wouldn't be due.

Where the deceased downsized and still had a home when they died, the additional threshold for the estate will be made up of both:

- the additional threshold on the home included in the estate
- any downsizing addition due for the former home

The downsizing addition will generally be the lower of:

- the amount of additional threshold that's been lost as a result of the downsizing move
- the value of the other assets in the estate left to direct descendants

Case study 13 (https://www.gov.uk/government/case-studies/inheritance-tax-residence-nil-rate-band-case-studies) shows how the downsizing addition and additional threshold are worked out.

If only part of the home in the estate is left to direct descendants, that part is used to work out the additional threshold. This may also affect the total additional threshold for the estate in downsizing situations.

Case study 14 (https://www.gov.uk/government/case-studies/inheritance-tax-residence-nil-rate-band-case-studies) shows how the downsizing addition and additional threshold are worked out where only a part of the home is left to direct descendants.

Where the downsizing occurs before 6 April 2017, HMRC treat the maximum available additional threshold at that time as £100,000.

Case study 15 (https://www.gov.uk/government/case-studies/inheritance-tax-residence-nil-rate-band-case-studies) shows how the downsizing addition is worked out in these situations.

If the deceased had downsized but had never lived in the less valuable property, that property is not a home and isn't included in the estate for additional threshold purpose. This means that the position is the same as if the former home had been disposed of.

Disposing of a home

Where the deceased sold or disposed of a former home so there's no longer any home in their estate, the additional threshold for the estate will be equal to the downsizing addition in respect of the former home.

You calculate the downsizing allowance in these situations differently because there's no home in the estate that could qualify for any additional threshold on death. When you work out the lost additional threshold, the percentage at step 3 will always be 0% and the result at step 4 will always be the same as the figure at step 2. So, steps 3 and 4 can be missed out.

The amount of additional threshold that's been lost will depend only on the value of the former property and the maximum additional threshold available at that time. Again, if the disposal took place on or after 8 July 2015 but before 6 April 2017, HMRC will treat the maximum additional threshold available as £100,000.

If the value of the former home is equal to or more than the maximum available additional threshold at the time of the disposal, HMRC will treat the lost additional threshold as 100% of the maximum additional threshold available at the date of death.

Where there's no home in the estate at death, the downsizing addition will generally be the lower of:

- the amount of additional threshold that's been lost as a result of the disposal
- the value of the other assets in the estate that the direct descendants inherit

Case study 16 (https://www.gov.uk/government/case-studies/inheritance-tax-residence-nil-rate-band-case-studies) shows how the downsizing addition is worked out if there is no home in the estate at death.

If the value of the home in the person's estate is less than the maximum additional threshold at the time of the disposal, the lost additional threshold is worked out as a percentage of that maximum additional threshold. You then apply that percentage to the maximum additional threshold at the date of death.

Case study 17 (https://www.gov.uk/government/case-studies/inheritance-tax-residence-nil-rate-band-case-studies) shows how the downsizing addition is worked out if the home is worth less than the maximum available additional threshold.

Downsizing where there is transferred additional threshold

Where additional threshold is transferred following the death of a spouse or civil partner, you calculate the downsizing allowance in largely the same way. The difference is that the maximum additional threshold available at both the date of death and the date of disposal is increased to include the amount of transferred additional threshold.

Case study 18 (https://www.gov.uk/government/case-studies/inheritance-tax-residence-nil-rate-band-case-studies) shows how the downsizing addition is worked out when additional threshold has been transferred from a spouse or civil partner's estate.

Downsizing and trusts

The downsizing rules apply where a person disposes of a home that's included in their estate. Property held in certain trusts is included within a person's estate for IHT purposes and so the downsizing rules apply in these circumstances too.

Where a home is held in such a trust, the trustees might be able to dispose of it or they may change it to a less valuable one. This is treated the same as if the deceased had downsized or disposed of the home themselves. Where a person's right to occupy a home held in a trust ceases, for example on remarriage, this is also treated as a disposal for the purposes of the downsizing rules.

A person can have more than one interest in a home. For example, they may own half of a house outright while the other half is held in a trust for their benefit. These would be two separate interests in the same home.

If a person disposes of more than one interest in a single home at the same time, for example, because they sell the whole house, all those interests can be taken into account for downsizing purposes. But, if a person disposes of different interests at different times, the deceased's personal representatives can only nominate one of those disposals to be taken into account to work out any downsizing addition.

The downsizing rules can be complicated where the additional threshold is transferred or trusts are involved. Whilst this guide explains the basic rules, it can't cover more complex situations. You should get professional advice about how to work out the additional threshold in these situations.

CLEARANCES

CL2 – NON-STATUTORY CLEARANCE SERVICE GUIDANCE [HMRC, October 2017]

Guidance on the non-statutory clearance service offered by HM Revenue and Customs for all customers and their advisers.

Introduction

Before using HM Revenue and Customs (HMRC) clearance service you should have first:

- checked that your transaction isn't covered by a more appropriate clearance or approval route
- considered HMRC's guidance to see if this answers your question

Further guidance is available on all clearance and approval routes.

When HMRC will provide advice under this service

You can ask HMRC for further guidance or advice if you:

- have fully considered the relevant guidance and/or contacted the relevant helpline
- have not been able to find the information you need
- remain uncertain about HMRC's interpretation of tax legislation

HMRC will then set out their advice in writing.

When HMRC will not provide advice under this service

If you ask for advice and HMRC doesn't provide it, they will tell you why. For example:

- you haven't provided all the necessary information – see the checklists at Annex A, B, C, D or E for details of what you need to provide
- HMRC doesn't think that there are genuine points of uncertainty – they will explain why they think this and direct you to the relevant online guidance
- you're asking HMRC to give tax planning advice, or to "approve" tax planning products or arrangements
- your application is about treatment of transactions which, in HMRC's view, are for the purposes of avoiding tax
- HMRC is checking your tax position for the period in question, in which case you'll need to contact the officer dealing with the check
- any related return for the period in question is final (except if you're making a clearance application in connection with an offshore disclosure being made via HMRC's Digital Disclosure Service)
- there's a statutory clearance applicable to your transaction
- HMRC won't give clearances or advice in respect of the application of the "settlements legislation" in Chapter 5 Part 5 Income Tax (Trading and Other Income) Act 2005 or the tax consequences of executing non-charitable trust deeds or settlements

What information you need to provide

To help you decide what information is relevant to your application when you write to HMRC you should use the checklist at:

- Annex A for all transactions other than Business Investment Relief, Business Property Relief and VAT (see below) – please head your letter "Clearance service"
- Annex B for advance assurance on Business Investment Relief for non-domiciled persons taxed on the remittance basis – please head your letter "Advance Assurance for Business Investment Relief"
- Annex C for Inheritance Tax Business Property Relief clearances
- Annex D for VAT clearances
- Annex E for post transaction clearances connected to an offshore disclosure

HMRC asks for this information to make sure that they understand the background to your request and where your uncertainty lies. This helps to process your application more quickly.

When you write to HMRC you must be satisfied that the information you give is, to the best of your knowledge and belief, accurate and correct.

Where you should send your application

If your application is in relation to an offshore disclosure, you should send it to the address shown in Annex E.

If you have a customer relationship manager or are already in contact with an HMRC clearance team, please send your application directly to them.

In all other cases, you should send your application to the appropriate address in Annex A, B, C or D.

When HMRC will reply

HMRC will usually reply within 28 days. But where difficult or complicated issues are involved it may take longer to reply. If this is the case, HMRC will acknowledge your request and tell you when you can expect a full reply. Due to current demand, the usual 28 day response time for VAT non-statutory clearance requests is not being met. Replies to clearance requests are currently taking approximately 8 weeks to process.

Sometimes HMRC may need to ask you to provide more information before they can send you a full reply. If so, they will suspend the handling time for your application until you're able to provide them with the additional information that they have requested. HMRC may wish to contact you by telephone for clarification, so it helps if you can provide a day time contact number.

Time limits, interest and penalties

HMRC's advice doesn't affect the date by which you have to pay your tax or send in returns. You may have to pay interest and late payment penalties on any tax that you pay late, for whatever reason.

If you've asked for advice after a transaction has taken place, but not received this by the time your return (or for Business Property Relief clearances – an Inheritance Tax account) is due to be submitted, then you should still send your completed return in on time. If you send HMRC your return on time you won't be liable to penalties for failing to make a return. When you receive HMRC's response you can, if necessary, amend your tax return as long as you're within the normal time limits to do so.

If you're seeking advance assurance that a proposed investment will meet the requirements of Business Investment Relief, the time limit within which qualifying investment needs to be made remains unaffected.

If you disagree with HMRC's view of your transaction and complete your return and pay tax in accordance with your own view of the proper tax treatment, then you may not have paid the right amount of tax at the right time. In such circumstances, if your return contains a careless or deliberate error which results in a loss of tax or an inflated claim to repayment of tax, then you may be liable to interest and penalties.

When you can rely on information or advice provided by HMRC

Provided the information you have supplied is accurate and complete, and you carry out the proposed transactions exactly as you describe them, you will generally be able to rely on HMRC's advice.

What you can do if you disagree

HMRC aims to give you a clear reply to your questions; they recognise that sometimes you may not agree with what they say, or you may not be happy with the service they have provided.

If you disagree with HMRC's advice you may complete your return in accordance with your own view of the proper tax treatment, but you should draw HMRC's attention to the particular entry in your return and explain what you have done.

If you believe that HMRC has failed to take account of some of the material facts set out in your request, please contact the officer who dealt with your application (their details will be on the letter HMRC sent you), explain what facts you feel were overlooked and ask them to look at your request again. If you remain unhappy you can ask for the request to be referred to another officer.

If you're unhappy with the way HMRC has handled your request, please tell the person or office you have been dealing with. If they're unable to resolve the issue, ask for your case to be referred to the complaints manager.

Whether you can appeal

There's no general right of appeal against advice expressed by HMRC, except where rights to appeal are set out in statute. Rather, appeal rights are usually against decisions HMRC take, such as issuing an assessment for underpaid tax or a penalty.

However, some VAT related decisions are classed as "appealable decisions" by statute. The letter HMRC sends you will explain whether you're able to appeal and tell you what to do if you disagree with a VAT decision.

Annex C – Business Property Relief checklist

The Business Property Relief clearance service is available where there is an immediate Inheritance Tax charge, such as transfers into and out of a trust. It is not available for gifts to individuals, 10 year anniversary charges, conditional disposition of property under a will, and deeds of variation. The tax consequences of executing a trust deed, the application of Chapter 5 part 5 Income Tax (Trading and Other Income) Act (ITTOIA), valuations, and requests for general confirmation of the status of businesses for Business Property Relief are also not included.

For Business Property Relief applications involving a change of ownership of a business (succession), any clearance given will remain valid for a limited period of six months.

Use this checklist if you want to ask HMRC to give you their view on the application of the Inheritance Tax Business Property Relief provisions. It helps us if you follow the order set out in the checklist in your clearance application and use the numbering on any supporting documents.

How to send us your request

By email: Send your request to Trusts & Estates Technical Team (Clearances).

Please quote reference BP102/P1/08E

By post: Send your request to:

HMRC

SO842

Fitzroy House First Floor

Inheritance Tax Technical (Clearances)

Central Mail Unit

Newcastle

NE98 1ZZ

We will be able to process your application more efficiently if you send your clearance application by email. Attachments to emails should be no larger than 2 MB. Please don't send self-extracting zip files as our software will block them.

Using email

- HMRC cannot guarantee the security of emails you send to us or we send to you over the internet. Any information you send us by email is at your own risk.
- It is important that you have assessed the risks of using email to send information or to receive it from us.
- If you would like us to reply by email, please tell us so and confirm that you understand and accept the risks involved in using email. We will not always be able to reply by email.

1. Information about the applicant and your application:	Check
1.1 Name and address of the individual or trustee applicant and any existing IHT reference number	□
1.2 Name and address of the business and relevant business identification number, eg. Company Registration Number, Self Assessment Unique Taxpayer Reference (UTR)	□
1.3 Details of the interest held by the individual or trustee in the business eg number and nature of shares held	□
1.4 Your contact details (if you are acting on behalf of a client) and authority to act for the client	□
1.5 A brief indication of the subject of the application. Fuller details should be provided under the appropriate headings below	□
1.6 Accounts for the business for two full accounting years prior to the transaction or proposed transaction including a detailed profit and loss account and any other relevant financial information	□

2. Information about the transaction(s):	Check
2.1 The reasons why the business is undertaking the transaction	□
2.2 The relevant facts about the transaction, set out chronologically as transaction steps, so that we have enough information to provide the clearance response	□
2.3 Set out your view of the tax consequences of the transaction and the issues you want us to consider	□
2.4 The proposed date of the transaction if it has not yet happened, and supporting information, such as a draft contract where available	□
2.5 Any details that are contingent eg. on future events or the consent of others	□
3. Information about legal points:	Check
3.1 Outline the specific legislation in point	□
3.2 Explain why you believe the application of the legislation is open to different possible interpretations, provide a summary of those different interpretations, and explain why the tax consequences are uncertain, including reference to our published guidance and/or to case law	□
3.3 Provide copies of any legal advice you have already received which	□
you are content to disclose	□
3.4 Provide details of any other relevant advice you are seeking or have previously sought from HMRC to include related clearances (statutory or otherwise).	□
4. Declarations: Please include with your request a declaration that	Check
4.1 To the best of your knowledge and belief you have told HMRC about all of the facts relevant to the advice sought and that these are correct.	□
5. Tax avoidance schemes:	Check
5.1 If there is an avoidance scheme which covers all or part of the transaction provide details of the arrangement and/or any disclosure made to HMRC with the allocated DOTAS scheme reference number, if applicable	□

OTHER MATERIAL

MISCELLANEOUS

Misc. 101 INHERITANCE TAX: ASSOCIATED OPERATIONS – SPOUSE EXEMPTION [HC Debates vol. 888 col. 56, 10 March 1975]

The Chief Secretary to the Treasury (Mr Joel Barnett)

I want to explain the reason for IHTA 1984, s. 268 (formerly FA 1975, s. 44). As I said in Committee, it is reasonable for a husband to share capital with his wife when she has no means of her own. If she chooses to make gifts out of the money she has received from her husband, there will be no question of using the associated operation provisions to treat them as gifts made by the husband and taxable as such.

In a blatant case, where a transfer by a husband to a wife was made on condition that the wife should at once use the money to make gifts to others, a charge on a gift by the husband might arise under the section. The Hon Gentleman fairly recognised that.

I want to give an example of certain circumstances that could mean the section having to be invoked. There are complex situations involving transactions between husband and wife and others where, for example, a controlling shareholder with a 60 per cent holding in a company wished to transfer his holding to his son. If he gave half to his son, having first transferred half to his wife, and later his wife transferred her half share to the son, the effect would be to pass a controlling shareholding from father to son. The Revenue would then use the associated operations provisions to ensure that the value of a controlling holding was taxed.

There are ordinary, perfectly innocent transfers between husband and wife. For example, where a husband has the money and the wife has no money – or the other way round, which happens from time to time – and the one with the money gives something to the other to enable the spouse to make a gift to a son or a daughter on marriage, that transaction would not be caught by the clause. It would be a reasonable thing to do. I have made that clear in Committee upstairs, and I make it clear again now.

Misc. 103 PUBLIC ACCESS TO HERITAGE PROPERTY [Written answer by the Financial Secretary to the Treasury, Hansard, 9 February 1987]

Requirements will differ from case to case but, outstanding chattels apart (for which different arrangements apply), these will normally comprise some or all of the following.

(a) Owner to inform the British Tourist Authority (the Scottish Tourist Board and the Highlands and Islands Development Board in Scotland) of the opening arrangements and subsequent changes.

(b) Owner to advertise the opening arrangements in one or more suitable publications with national circulation.

(c) Owner to display a notice outside the property giving details of the opening arrangements.

(d) Owner to agree that the advisory body or bodies (or its/or their agents), which confirmed the property's eligible quality and with whom the terms of the detailed management agreement will have been negotiated, can divulge the access arrangements to anyone who enquires about them.

(e) Owner to agree to such other publicity as the advisory body, or bodies, consider to be appropriate. This could include displaying a notice in some public place in the locality (e.g. the local post office, local library, local tourist office or town hall) or in a local preservation society's newsletter.

The management agreement would also normally provide scope for additional measures to be agreed, if appropriate, between the owner and the advisory body or bodies at a later stage.

Misc. 108 INHERITANCE TAX: EXECUTION OF DOCUMENTS [Law Society's Gazette, 18 December 1991]

The purpose of this article is to serve as a reminder that the Inland Revenue will not accept the validity of certain transactions (which may be carried out for tax planning purposes) unless the transactions are evidenced by deed. It is not intended to be a general guide to the executions of documents by deed, but it is the case that if there is no consideration to support a contractual arrangement, then execution by deed can become vital.

Loans

It has recently been brought to the attention of the revenue law committee that the Capital Taxes Office will not accept that a loan made between individuals has been waived by the lender, so the estate of the lender is reduced, for inheritance tax purposes, by the amount of the loan released – unless the waiver was effected by deed.

Letters and circumstantial evidence clearly indicating an intention to absolve the beneficiary of the loan from any liability to repay will be insufficient.

The Revenue has quoted in support of its contention that a waiver is ineffective unless made by deed *Pinnell* (1602) 5 Co Rep 117a, and *Edwards v Walters* (1896) 2 ChD 157 CA.

Importance of deeds

In the revenue law committee's view, although the Revenue's contention is not unassailable, unless and until the contention is confirmed or rejected by judicial authority, it must be prudent to advise all clients that any inheritance tax planning strategy involving the making of a loan, and subsequent waiver, should be effected by deed in order to ensure the estate of the lender is reduced accordingly.

For alterations of dispositions taking effect on death, s. 142 of the *Inheritance Tax Act* 1984 does not require execution of a deed, but simply "an instrument in writing", though in practice as a prudent precaution, a deed is normally used.

Clearly it is not necessary to effect every single transaction carried out as part of an estate planning exercise by deed (e.g. loans can be repaid and a gift made by exchange of cheques), but members should be aware of the danger of a transaction being defeated by the Revenue unless it has been evidenced by a duly executed deed.

Misc. 110 INHERITANCE TAX: EXEMPT WORKS OF ART: CONSEQUENCES OF DESTRUCTION OR THEFT [*Hansard*, 30 June 1993]

The Minister of State, Department of Transport (The Earl of Caithness)

The theft or loss of a conditionally exempt item will generally not constitute a chargeable occasion for inheritance tax or capital transfer tax, whether or not insurance moneys are received, provided that the owner has taken reasonable steps to preserve the object. Further details are given in paragraph 7.12 of the Inland Revenue's booklet IR67 *Capital Taxation and the National Heritage*.

Misc. 111 PUBLIC ACCESS ARRANGEMENTS REGARDING PRE-1976 CONDITIONALLY EXEMPT WORKS OF ART [*Hansard*, 27 July 1993]

The Minister of State, Department of Transport (The Earl of Caithness)

Conditional exemption may be claimed on the death of the owner of a work of art exempted on a previous occasion before 1976. If conditional exemption is sought and granted the new owner will have to preserve the object, keep it in the UK and provide reasonable public access to it. The old exemption will then lapse. If conditional exemption is not granted on the death of the pre-1976 owner, inheritance tax will be chargeable in the normal way. In addition, if the original exemption was given under the estate duty rules, any undertakings given for the estate duty exemption will either remain in force or, where undertakings were given after 5th August 1965, will have to be renewed. A subsequent sale of the object or failure to observe or, where appropriate, renew any old undertakings will lead to an estate duty charge.

Reasonable access for members of the public is required for all works of art granted conditional exemption on a transfer made after 6th April 1976. Where the last chargeable transfer of the work of art was between 29th July 1950 and 6th April 1976, the owner has to provide access only to researchers. For earlier transfers, there is no right of access to researchers or to the public.

Misc. 113 CAPITAL TAXES OFFICE PRACTICE NOTE: LOSS ON SALE RELIEF: S191 IHTA 1984 [Law Society's Gazette, 12 January 1994]

Loss on sale relief cannot be formally granted until four months have elapsed from the date of the last sale of qualifying property, assuming all the other conditions are satisfied.

In many estates there is one property and it has to be sold to give effect to the terms of the deceased's will. There is no prospect of a re-investment of the proceeds of sale in another property.

The Capital Taxes Office (CTO) has received representations that having sometimes waited one or two years to achieve a sale it is unreasonable to compel personal representatives to wait another four months before lodging an application for loss on sale relief. The CTO has responded by changing its procedures. The CTO will now accept and process a claim and, where appropriate, it will make a provisional repayment *of inheritance tax*.

Formal clearance on form Cap 30 will not be issued until the legal personal representatives have confirmed (after four months have elapsed from the sale) that there have been no changes to the information contained in their original application.

Misc. 114 BUSINESS AND AGRICULTURAL RELIEF: ACCRUER ARRANGEMENTS
[Correspondence between Institute of Taxation and Revenue, 11 May 1994]

The Institute of Taxation wrote to the Revenue in the following terms on 16 December 1993:

"One of our members has pointed out that there seems to be some uncertainty as to whether the existence of an accruer arrangement in a partnership agreement infringes, in relation to transfers made on death, the requirement in IHTA 1984, s. 113 that if property is to be relevant business property for purposes of business relief that property must not be subject to a binding contract for sale. There is, of course, a similar requirement in relation to agricultural relief.

As you will appreciate, this is important to partnerships all over the country.

In *The Law Society's Gazette* of May 6, 1981 an article accompanied by a table appeared indicating business relief was not prevented from being available by an arrangement under which on a partner's death the partnership continued and his share accrued to the other partners, his estate being entitled to a payment from them. This was the situation illustrated in the fourth example in the table published in that article. It was not clear whether the statement had been agreed or accepted by the Revenue, but it was relied on by practitioners without, it seems any challenge from the Revenue.

However, on July 5, 1982, in a letter to the accountancy bodies, the Revenue stated that the 1981 article

"correctly states the general position since it is only in the final case that a binding contract exists."

In TR557 the ICAEW published a further table which gave as an example the following circumstances (b):

"on the death in service or retirement of a partner his share is to accrue to the surviving partners who shall pay an annuity to the partner or his widow as appropriate."

The Revenue's response to this in its letter of July 5, 1982 was

"…on death in service there would again be no business relief…".

There appears to be a clear contradiction between this statement and the statement that the 1981 article in the *Law Society's Gazette* correctly states the general position…

Paragraph 24.739 in *Dymond* suggests that the "official view" is that the existence of an accruer arrangement prevents business relief from being available.

The view of the Institute is that the existence of an accruer arrangement does not prevent business relief or agricultural relief from being available under s. 113 or s. 124.

The Institute takes this view because:

(a) the relevant contract is made at the time the parties enter into the accruer agreement;

(b) the consideration provided by the parties to the contract are reciprocal promises which are to be given effect at some time in the future on the happening of certain events which events may or may not happen, e.g., partner A may predecease partners B and C, or vice-versa.

(c) the effect of inter alia *Coats (J and P) v IRC* [1897] 1 QB 778 and *Littlewoods Mail Order Stores Ltd v IRC* [1963] is that there can be a contract for sale only where there is a consideration in money and not, e.g. where, as in the case of an accruer arrangement, there is a consideration in money's worth;

(d) on the death of a partner, a pre-existing obligation under a contract which is not a contract for sale is performed. On the one hand, by virtue of the agreement which predated the death, the deceased partner's share automatically accrues to the surviving partners. The consideration for this transfer is the earlier undertaking given by the other partners; it is not the payment by the continuing partners. On the other hand, also by virtue of the agreement which predated the death, the surviving partners pay over to the deceased partner's estate whatever sum may be due by virtue of the pre-existing contact. The consideration for this payment is the earlier undertaking given by the deceased partner; it is not the posthumous transfer of his share.

The Institute would very much appreciate the Capital Taxes Office's confirming that they share the Institute's analysis and its conclusion that the existence prevent business or agricultural relief from being available."

Mr Draper of the Revenue's share valuation division replied on the 11 May 1994 in the following terms:

"The Law Society's *Gazette* article (of May 6, 1981) was not in fact approved by the Revenue before issue.

But I can confirm that the Law Society's table is considered to reflect the general position.

As you are aware, the starting point in considering whether s. 113 will serve to deny business relief depends upon whether there is a binding contract for sale, and that obviously depends on the precise wording of the document.

Both the examples in the Law Society's table and the CCAB letter were in much abbreviated form, without consideration of any particular documents. In replying to the CCAB it was thought right at the time to warn of the possibility that example (d) could amount to a contract for sale.

It is accepted that this will not necessarily be the case. The availability of BR turns upon the question of whether there is a binding contract for sale. We would seek to restrict the availability of relief if the deceased's partnership interest was clearly required to be sold in return for the payment of an annuity. I do of course accept that there is no automatic distinction to be drawn between the provision of an annuity and the provision of a cash sum.

I am sorry that confusion has arisen.

I note your points (a) to (d) but I hope you will not mind too much if I do not comment on them. I am reluctant to do so on a theoretical basis when as I have sought to emphasise it is the construction of the particular document which is vital.

However as you will have noted I am quite happy to agree with your conclusion that the existence of an accruer arrangement does not necessarily prevent business or agricultural relief from being available."

Other material – See also Misc. 117 Inheritance Tax: Business Property Relief and Partnerships.

Misc. 117 INHERITANCE TAX: BUSINESS PROPERTY RELIEF AND PARTNERSHIPS [Law Society's *Gazette*, 4 September 1996]

The Inheritance Tax Act 1984, s. 105, provides that property consisting of a business or interest in a business, e.g. a share in a partnership, is relevant business property for the purposes of pt. V c.l of that Act and would be eligible for relief from inheritance tax at the rate of 100%.

S. 113 of the Act provides that property will not qualify for relief if, at the time of the transfer of the property – whether during lifetime or on death, it is subject to a binding contract for sale.

Statement of practice 12/80 gives the view of the board of the Inland Revenue on "buy and sell" agreements. If a partnership agreement provides that, in the event of death before retirement of a partner, the deceased's personal representatives are obliged to sell, and the surviving partners are obliged to purchase the deceased's partnership share, the Revenue's view is that this will require a sale and purchase rather than merely conferring an option to buy or sell. The arrangement would constitute a binding contract for sale within s. 113 so that business property relief would not be available on the partnership share. An article appeared in the *Gazette*, [1981] 6 May, giving examples of various types of partnership agreements dealing with the devolution of a partnership share on death, and how these would be treated for inheritance tax purposes, i.e. whether or not business property relief would be available. The article indicated that where, on the death of a partner, the partnership continued with the share of the deceased partner accruing to surviving partners and the estate being entitled to payment, either on valuation or using a formula, the provisions of s. 113 would not apply and there would be no preclusion of business property relief.

There has recently been concern that the Revenue's attitude on this point had changed, and that where an agreement provided for an accruer of a partnership share on death as outlined above, relief would not be available.

There was also concern that in some circumstances, the decision in *Spiro v Glencrown* [1991] 1 All ER 680 was being interpreted as providing authority for an option to constitute a binding contract for sale, so that where a partnership agreement provided for continuation on death, with the partnership share falling into the deceased's estate but with the option for other partners to acquire the share, business property relief would not be available. At a recent meeting, Revenue representatives were able to confirm that there had been no change in their view on buy and sell agreements and that the *Gazette* article could still be relied upon. Business property relief would be available on a partnership share passing under the type of accruer provision described above. It was also confirmed that the *Spiro v Glencrown* decision would not be cited as authority for an option constituting a binding contract for sale unless the option had been exercised at the time of death, or other transfer where material.

Misc. 119 QUESTIONS BY STEP/CIOT AND ANSWERS FROM HMRC TO SCHEDULE 20 FINANCE ACT 2006 [Revised April 2007 and further updated on 6 August 2008 and 3 October 2008]

A. Transitional serial interests (TSI)

1. Condition 1 contains the requirement that "immediately before 22 March 2006, the property then comprised in the settlement was property in which B, or some other person, was beneficially entitled to an interest in possession ("the prior interest")".

2. Can it be confirmed that this requirement will be satisfied where B, or some other person, has a beneficial interest in possession in some of the property then comprised in the settlement but not all the property so comprised.

Example 1

Under a trust there are two funds. In Fund A, Mr Smith has an interest in possession. In Fund B, Mr Jones has an interest in possession.

Question 1

Will Condition 1 be satisfied separately in relation to Fund A and/or Fund B?

HMRC Answer

We can confirm that condition 1 can be satisfied separately in relation to both funds.

The new s. 49C starts from the point of the view of the "current interest" – a beneficial interest in settled property. Given the wide definition of that term in s. 43 IHTA, it seems that the beneficial IIP referred to in s. 49C(1) can quite easily be in a fund or in property that was previously part of a larger disposition or settlement – and there is nothing to suggest that there must have been a single beneficiary.

Moreover, there is no requirement that the settlement must have been wholly IIP in nature (question 2 below) or that it must have come to an end in its entirety (question 3).

If one can then accept that the property referred to in s.49C(1) is also the property referred to in s. 49C(2), and in which the "prior interest" (s. 49C(2) & (3)) existed, the concerns raised in questions 1 to 4 fall away.

Question 2

Can it be confirmed that Condition 1 will be satisfied in relation to Fund A where Fund B is held not on trusts giving Mr Jones an interest in possession but on discretionary trusts? There is nothing in the wording of s49C to suggest that the pre-Budget 2006 interest in possession must subsist in the entire fund.

HMRC Answer

We agree.

3. Section 49C(3) provides that Condition 2 requires the prior interest to come to an end at a time on or after 22 March 2006 but before 6 October 2008.

Question 3

Will Condition 2 be satisfied where the prior interest comes to an end in that period in part only of the settled property in which that interest subsists?

HMRC Answer

Yes – see the response to question 1 above.

Example 2

In the example given above, if Mr Smith's interest in possession in Fund A comes to an end in 60% of Fund A and is replaced by an interest in possession in favour of Mr Smith's daughter, but Mr Smith's interest in possession continues in relation to the remaining 40% of Fund A, can it be confirmed that the interest in possession in favour of the daughter will be a transitional serial interest?

HMRC Answer

We can confirm this – for the reasons given immediately below.

While it has been suggested that Condition 2 requires that the prior interest comes to an end in all the property in which the interest subsists, Condition 2 does not state this and given the definition of current interest it appears that Condition 2 must be construed as referring to the prior interest coming to an end in the settled property concerned in which B takes a current interest but not necessarily in all the settled property of a particular settlement. The "current interest" is merely defined as an interest in possession in settled property and does not in any way require all the settled property comprised in the settlement to be a current interest.

Question 4

Please also confirm that the remaining 40% of Fund A continues to satisfy Condition 1 so that a transitional serial interest could be created in that 40% prior to 6th October 2008.

HMRC Answer

We can confirm this.

Question 5(1)

Please also confirm that in the above example if 40% of Mr Smith's pre-2006 interest in possession is ended as to half for his daughter and half for his son, both son and daughter take transitional serial interests in their respective shares.

HMRC Answer

We can confirm this.

Question 5(2)

If later the trustees wished to appropriate assets between the two funds for son and daughter and the assets were of the same value as the assets previously contained in each fund, do HMRC accept that such appropriation does not represent the termination of any qualifying interest in possession and therefore does not result in an inheritance tax charge?

HMRC Answer

We agree.

4. We would be grateful for your views on the circumstances in which the prior interest would be considered to have come to an end and have been replaced by a current interest. This is relevant because if a prior interest is considered to have come to an end and have been replaced by a current interest (in favour of the same beneficiary) there will be no possibility of the interest being replaced by a transitional serial interest later and the point is particularly important in relation to spousal relief because spouse exemption will not be available if a spouse of a life tenant who already has a transitional serial interest takes an interest in possession on the death of that life tenant.

Example 3

Under a pre-Budget 2006 trust a beneficiary A is entitled to the capital contingently on attaining the age of 30 years. A was 21 on 22 March 2006 and had been entitled to an interest in possession under section 31 of the Trustee Act 1925 from the age of 18. The interest is therefore an interest in possession which subsisted on 22 March 2006. Before 2008 the trustees exercise their [enlarged] powers of advancement under section 32 of the Trustee Act 1925 to defer the vesting of the capital from the age of 30 to the age of 45 and A's interest in possession in the fund will therefore continue until age 45. Clearly A reaches 30 after 2008 in the above example.

Question 6

There are two possible interpretations of the above and we should be grateful if HMRC could confirm which view they take.

Option 1. The exercise of the trustees' powers in this way creates a new interest in possession for A immediately on exercise of the power of advancement which therefore takes effect as the "current interest" or "transitional serial interest". Any successive interest in possession after A's interest in possession has ended cannot then be a transitional serial interest. The property will be taxed as part of A's estate on his death if he dies with the transitional serial interest. He continues to have a transitional serial interest until termination at 45 or earlier death.

Option 2: A's new interest only arises when A attains the age of 30. Until then he has a pre-Budget 2006 qualifying interest in possession.

The new interest cannot take effect as a transitional serial interest at all since on the above facts it will *arise after October 2008.* Until 30 A will have a pre-Budget interest in possession on the basis that nothing has changed until he reaches 30. Only from 30 will he take a new non-qualifying interest so the settled property will then become relevant property. There will not be an entry charge for A at 30 of 20% due to s53(2) IHTA.

If A dies before reaching 30, then on this analysis his pre-Budget 2006 interest will not previously have ended and therefore if his spouse takes an interest in possession this is a transitional serial interest or if his children take interests in possession before 2008 these will be transitional serial interests.

Does the answer to whether option 1 or option 2 applies depend on whether the advancement is drafted in such a way that it extends the interest in possession from 30 without restating A's existing interest in possession until then? Or would any variation of A's interest in possession be regarded as a transitional serial interest from the date of the variation even if the variation only took effect in the future.

HMRC Answer

We consider that A's original IIP (until 30) will have "come to an end" when the trustees exercised their power of advancement and been replaced by a new IIP (until 45), which will therefore qualify as a TSI. A's interest is expressed as an entitlement to capital contingent on his attaining 30. It seems reasonable to regard the exercise of the s.32 Trustee Act power as immediately bringing this interest to an end and replacing it with a new one.

NB: As regards HMRC's view on whether a charge arises on the creation of the TSI (or other interest in possession) in these circumstances see warning posted on STEP website on 24th September 2007 and see also section 140 of Finance Act 2008 which has now removed any suggestion that there could be a charge where A is given a new IIP before 6 October 2008. Note also that there is a third view i.e. that no new IIP arises at all if A's entitlement to capital is deferred because his entitlement to income is not as such affected. Much may depend on how the power is exercised and whether it is an advancement or an appointment.

5. An interest in possession might also subsist as follows:

Example 4

Under a trust A has a life interest with remainder to his children. The trustees have a power of advancement and exercise such a power to provide that subject to A's existing life interest A's spouse takes a life interest on A's death with remainder to the children at the age of 25. A's interest in possession is not in any way altered.

Question 7

Can HMRC please confirm that the exercise of a power of advancement to create an interest in possession for the spouse, which is expressly made subject to A's existing life interest and does not in any way alter that interest but merely comes into effect on his death, will be a transitional serial interest. Similarly, if spouse predeceases A and the advancement on interest in possession trusts for A's children is made subject to A's interest and takes effect before 2008 (e.g. A surrenders his interest) presumably these trusts could also be transitional serial interests.

HMRC Answer

Assuming that A's present IIP existed before 22 March 2006, we can confirm that the spouse's IIP – whether or not it arises before or after 6 October 2008 – will qualify as a TSI provided that it arises on the death of A and that A is at the date of his *death* still entitled to a pre-budget 2006 interest in possession. Any IIP taken by A's children on the death or earlier termination of A's IIP will also be a transitional serial interest provided that this occurs before 6 October 2008. If A's pre-Budget 2006 interest in possession terminates inter vivos in favour of the spouse then the spouse will only take a TSI if this termination occurs before 6th October 2008.

If, however, A's interest was in any way amended (e.g. the trustees exercised powers of revocation and reappointment restating A's interest in possession albeit in the same terms and then declaring interests in possession for A's spouse or for children if she has predeceased), presumably the interests for spouse and children could never be transitional serial interests because A's interest is a transitional serial interest?

HMRC Answer

We agree.

6. Can it be confirmed that an interest in possession can be a transitional serial interest where the interest arises under a different settlement to that in which the original interest subsisted?

Example 5

Under Trust A Mr Smith has an interest in possession and subject to that, the capital passes to Mr Jones absolutely. Mr Jones on 30 December 2006 assigns his reversionary interest into Trust B set up in December 2006 under which his children have interests in possession. Mr Smith's interest in possession then comes to an end on 30 November 2007 at which time the settled property in Trust A passes to Trust B.

IHT Extra-statutory Material

Question 8

Will the interest in possession of Mr Jones' children qualify as a transitional serial interest bearing in mind that the interests arise in relation to the same settled property even though not under the trusts of the original settlement? A similar situation could arise where there is technically a different settlement under which the successive life interest arises due to the exercise of the trustees' powers of appointment in the wider form (as referred to in *Bond v Pickford* [[1983] BTC 313]).

HMRC Answer

Taken with question 9 below.

Question 9

If the difficulty is that Condition 1 is not satisfied because the second settlement is "made" post Budget 2006 does it make any difference if the second settlement was made pre-Budget 2006 and the interests in the first settlement fall into the second settlement before 2008 to be held on interest in possession trusts. This is a very common situation where there are "trusts over" and there appears nothing in the conditions to prevent this.

HMRC Answer

We do not consider that the IIPs of Mr Jones's children will qualify as TSIs whether the second settlement was made before or after Budget 2006.

As we said earlier, s.49C begins from the point of view of the "current interest". Condition 1 requires that "the settlement" in which that interest subsists "commenced" before 22 March 2006.

It goes on to require that, immediately before that date, the property "then comprised" in the settlement – i.e. the same settlement – was subject to the "prior interest".

The IIPs of Mr Jones's children arise under a different settlement (albeit one which happens to hold, following Mr Smith's death, the property that comprised the earlier one) and will not, therefore, qualify as TSIs – and it will make no difference when the settlement was made.

For the same reasons, the exercise of powers of appointment in such a way that assets are removed from one settlement and subjected to the trusts of another will not give rise to TSIs.

Note: where the second settlement was set up prior to 22 March 2006 and the reversionary interest of Mr Jones was assigned into an IIP trust prior to that date STEP/CIOT do not accept that on the death of the life tenant Mr Smith the property then comprised in the second trust (formerly the reversionary interest and now the settled property originally in trust 1) is not subject to a qualifying pre March 2006 IIP. It is however accepted that a TSI cannot arise if property is appointed from one IIP trust to another whenever they were set up.

7. **Question 10**

What is the position if the beneficiary holding the pre-Budget 2006 interest in possession assigns that interest in possession to another person? Does the assignee's interest qualify as a transitional serial interest? The concern here is that the original interest in possession is not "terminated" by virtue of the assignment, and so the precise terms of the legislation do not appear to have been met.

HMRC Answer

We consider that the assignee's interest can be a TSI in this case because the assignor's IIP will have "come to an end" for the purposes of s. 49C(3). (The interest will be in the original settlement, so the problem outlined in our response to question 9 will not be an issue).

B Administration of estates

8. **Question 11**

Can it be confirmed that where a will provides that a beneficiary has an interest in possession in residue, that interest in possession will be treated as commencing on the date of death of the deceased and not only when the administration of the estate is completed. This appears to be the case by virtue of Section 91 IHTA 1984.

HMRC Answer

We can confirm this.

9. **Question 12**

Can it be confirmed that the position will be the same as in Question 11 above where the interest in possession is in a settled legacy of specific assets not forming part of residue. It seems that this should be the case: *IRC v Hawley* [1929] 1 KB 578.

HMRC Answer

We agree.

This is important for two reasons:

- in order for an interest in possession to satisfy Condition 2 in section 49A for an Immediate Post-Death Interest (IPDI), L must have become beneficially entitled to the interest on the death of the testator or intestate;
- in determining whether an interest in possession is one which subsisted prior to 22 March 2006 where the deceased died before 22 March 2006 but the completion of the administration of the estate was on or after 22 March 2006 there would be difficulties if the pre-Budget 2006 interest in possession was not regarded as commencing on the death of the deceased.

10. **Question 13**

Many wills include a provision which provides that a beneficiary will only take if he survives the testator by a period of time. Please confirm that such a provision would not by itself prevent an IPDI arising.

HMRC Answer

We can confirm this. We consider that s. 92 IHTA removes any doubt here.

C IPDIs generally

11. **Question 14**

Can it be confirmed that if on the death of X a discretionary trust set up in his Will (e.g. a nil rate band legacy trust) is funded by a share in property, and the trustees allow the surviving spouse L to occupy it on an exclusive basis albeit at their discretion along the lines that occurred in *Judge & anor (Representatives of Walden deceased)* (2005) Sp C 506, this will not automatically be an IPDI but it will depend on the terms on which she occupies.

HMRC Answer

We agree.

There is a 3 month requirement for reading back under s144 in respect of appointments of absolute interests but this does not apply to appointments of IPDIs. Therefore if the trustees immediately on the death of X or subsequently, conferred exclusive rights of occupation on L this could indeed be an IPDI.

HMRC Answer

We agree.

It appears to us unlikely that mere exclusivity of occupation could in itself be a problem because as Judge confirms a person can occupy exclusively but not have rights which constitute an interest in possession. Indeed if the surviving spouse merely continued in occupation on the same terms as before X's death without the trustees' doing anything positive either way to affect her occupation it would appear they have not exercised their powers so as to give her any IPDI anyway.

HMRC Answer

We agree.

(Indeed it is doubtful that they have any ability under the Trusts of Land and Appointment of Trustees Act 1996 to disturb her occupation if she already owns a half share in the property personally and therefore the trustees have not exercised any power to confer her a present right to present enjoyment which could constitute an immediate post death interest.)

It would be helpful (given how common this situation is) if HMRC could give some guidance on the various scenarios in which they would or would not regard the surviving spouse as taking an IPDI in a property left on nil rate band discretionary trusts in the will if she is already in occupation.

HMRC Answer

This will depend on the precise terms of the testator's will or any deed of appointment exercised by the trustees after the testator's death, and we will continue to examine each case on its particular facts.

12. **Question 15**

Can it be confirmed that where a settlement (including a settlement created by will) includes a general power of appointment and that power is exercised by will giving an immediate interest in possession, the interest created over the trust property will qualify as an IPDI?

HMRC Answer

We can confirm this.

13. **Question 16**

Can it be confirmed that HMRC takes the view that if an individual (I) leaves by will a gift to a person's estate, when the assets in the estate are held on trusts which qualify as trusts for bereaved minors or age 18-to-25 trusts, the property added pursuant to I's will would also be treated as being held on trusts which qualify as trusts for bereaved minors or 18-to-25 trusts.

HMRC Answer

We have assumed that the scenario envisaged here is: I dies leaving a legacy in their will to P; P dies after I but before the legacy has been paid; P's estate is held on trusts that meet s.71A or s.71D. We agree that, in those circumstances, the legacy from I's estate would qualify under those provisions, also.

Example 6

I leaves his estate to his widow for life with remainder to his son S if alive at I's death. S survives I but predeceases the widow leaving a Will under which his estate passes to his children on trusts which qualify as trusts for bereaved minors. The widow dies when the children are aged 10 and 12, so that I's estate falls to be held on the trusts of S's Will. Will the property in I's estate benefit from trusts for bereaved minors status? I is the grandparent but the property is passing according to S's Will.

HMRC Answer

We consider that the property added pursuant to I's will in this example would also fall within s. 71A.

14. **Question 17**

If a property is left outright to someone by a will and they disclaim within two years of the deceased's death such that an interest in possession trust takes effect, can HMRC confirm that the trust will qualify as an IPDI?

HMRC Answer

We can confirm this.

15. **Question 18**

Can it be confirmed whether, when a will leaves property to an existing settlement (whether funded or unfunded) and under that settlement a beneficiary takes an immediate interest in possession, that interest will qualify as an IPDI. Such arrangements are common for US and other foreign domiciliaries in order to avoid complex probate issues. It might be argued that the interest in possession in the existing settlement does not arise under the will of the deceased. However, there are two arguments against this.

First, HMRC's own analysis is that additions by individuals to existing settlements should be treated as new settlements. Hence the addition by will to an existing settlement is a new settlement set up by virtue of the will.

Secondly, the wording in section 49A Condition 1 refers to "the settlement was effected by will or under the law of intestacy". The question though is what "the settlement" refers to. It would seem that it refers not as such to "the settlement" in the sense of a document but rather to the settlement into trust of the settled property which certainly is effected by will. The same wording is used on deeds of variation under section 142 IHTA and HMRC have always accepted that where property is added by will to a pre-existing settlement there is no reason why the beneficiary of that settlement cannot vary his entitlement.

HMRC Answer

We can confirm that the IIP in this scenario would qualify as an IPDI. We agree that "settlement" in this context relates to the contribution of property into the settlement rather than the document under which it will become held.

D Trusts for bereaved minors, 18–25 trusts and modified section 71 trusts: Section 71A and section 71D

16. **Question 19**

Can it be confirmed that trusts otherwise satisfying the requirements of section 71A or section 71D will be regarded as satisfying those conditions where the trusts were appointed under powers contained in the will and were not provided in the will itself at the outset.

HMRC Answer

We can confirm this – where the trusts are set up as a result of the exercise of a special power of appointment. We consider the position is different with general powers, on the basis, broadly speaking, that having a general power of appointment is tantamount to owning the property.

Example 7

H dies in 2007. His Will leaves an IPDI for his surviving spouse and subject thereto on discretionary trusts for issue of H. The trustees exercise their overriding powers of appointment to create s71A trusts for the children of H. It would appear that the s71A provisions do not need to be incorporated within the Will Trust from the start to qualify for relief but it would be helpful to have this confirmed. Presumably the presence of overriding powers of appointment over capital in favour of surviving spouse would not be treated as breaching the s71A conditions while the s71A interest was a remainder interest.

HMRC Answer

We agree (subject to our comments at question 19).

17. **Question 20**

Can it be further confirmed that the analysis in 16 above will apply both where the prior interest in possession is an IPDI arising after 21 March 2006 and also where there is an interest in possession arising under the will of a person who died prior to 22 March 2006.

HMRC Answer

We can confirm this.

18. **Question 21**

Can it be confirmed that, where a will contains a gift "to such of my children as reach 18 and if more than one in equal shares" or "to such of my children as reach 25 and if more than one in equal shares" all the interests will qualify as trusts for bereaved minors (or as age 18-to-25 trusts) even though one or more of the children might die after the testator but before the capital vests (so that their shares are divided between their siblings).

HMRC Answer

We can confirm this. We consider that each child while alive and under 18/25 has a presumptive share that is held for his or her benefit, and one can apply s. 71A or s. 71D child by child and presumptive share by presumptive share.

Question 21A

On conversion of an existing pre-Budget 2006 a&m trust to s71D status does the class need to close *ab initio* from the date the trust was converted or is it sufficient to say that until someone else is born, the trusts for "B" do qualify as section 71D trusts but not actually close the class?

HMRC Answer

We consider that a trust in the position where anyone (whether unborn or not) who is not currently benefiting can nevertheless become entitled would not meet the requirements of s.71D(6), since it could not be said for certain that "B" will become absolutely entitled to the settled property etc. in due course or that no income will be applied for any other person in the meantime. So we take the view that it will be necessary to close the class of beneficiaries for s. 71D to apply.

19. **Question 22**

Can it be confirmed that the answer to Question 21 is not affected by a gift over provision that substitutes the children (if any) of a deceased child who attain a certain age, so that the increase of the siblings' shares is dependent upon whether the child dies childless.

HMRC Answer

We can confirm this: the siblings' presumptive shares simply increase (or not) when one of their number dies, depending on whether or not the deceased child had any children of their own.

20. **Question 23**

Can it be confirmed that agricultural property relief (apr) and business property relief (bpr) will apply to charges arising under section 71E. It would appear that these reliefs should be applicable as the charges under section 71D (by reference to section 71E) are charges under Chapter III or Part III IHTA and the reliefs are expressly extended to events of charge under this Chapter (section 103(1) IHTA in relation to bpr and section 115(1) in relation to apr). Further, the formula for calculating the charge under section 71F is similar, in principle, to the charges as calculated under section 65 and section 68 IHTA in relation to exit charges for relevant property generally. Can HMRC confirm this analysis is agreed?

HMRC Answer

We agree – for the reasons given.

21. **Question 24**

Section 71E(4) provides that there will be no event of charge where a transaction is entered into by trustees as a result of which the assets held subject to the 18-to-25 trusts are diminished in value, where the disposition by the trustees would not have been a transfer of value under section 10 or section 16 IHTA if they had been beneficially entitled to the trust assets. There is a further exemption in section 71E(3). There are no similar provisions in relation to actions by trustees concerning assets which are held on trusts qualifying under section 71A. Can it be confirmed that in practice HMRC would apply similar principles in relation to events of charge under section 71B for section 71A trusts?

HMRC Answer

The provisions in s.71E that the question refers to are not reproduced in s.71B because the charge there arises under s.70 – and s.70 already includes identical provisions at subsections (3) and (4). S.71B(3) says:

> "Subsections (3) to (8) and (10) of section 70 apply for the purposes of this section as they apply for the purposes of that section …"

22. **Question 25**

Can HMRC confirm that trusts which are held for beneficiaries as a class (e.g. on trust for such of my children as attain the age of 25 and if more than one in equal shares) will qualify as age 18-to-25 trusts under section 71D(3) and (4) notwithstanding that the class could be diminished by reason of the death of members of the class under the age of 25. While it might be said that the class gift does not fall within the strict wording of section 71D(6)(a) it might be said that nonetheless the assets are held on trust, for the time being, for each child being under the age of 25. HMRC are requested to confirm their view in relation to the continued application of 71D to class gifts where a beneficiary (B) dies before reaching 25 and the assets pass to the other beneficiaries under 25 on s71D trusts. (This is a separate point from the situation where in relation to existing inter vivos a&m trusts the class increases as a result of future beneficiaries being born before the eldest reaches 25.)

HMRC Answer

We can confirm this. CIOT/STEP note: further queries were raised with HMRC on the class closing rules and the application of s71D generally and these were posted on the websites separately.

23. **Question 26**

HMRC is asked to confirm that section 71A and section 71D will apply to trusts for a class of children whether or not the assets have been appropriated to each child's share.

HMRC Answer

We can confirm this.

24. **Question 27**

There will be a number of circumstances where different sets of beneficiaries under one accumulation and maintenance settlement may require to be treated differently (for example, a settlement for grandchildren where they differ widely in age). Can HMRC please confirm that trusts will qualify as 18–25 trusts or modified section 71 trusts (capital vesting at age 18) if those trusts exist in only part of the settled property. Thus, a settlement might be divided into two sub-funds, one for A's children who are approaching adulthood and for whom an 18–25 trust is appropriate and another for B's children who are very young and where the trustees value retaining flexibility so that that sub-fund will be allowed to fall within the relevant property regime with effect from 6 April 2008 (or be converted into an 18 trust).

HMRC Answer

We can confirm this.

25. **Question 28**

There has been some confusion about the interaction of s71D(3) and (4) with s71D(1) and (2). Please confirm that existing A&M trusts set up before the Budget where the settlor may still be alive (and the beneficiary's parent has not died) can qualify for 18–25 status if converted before April 2008 if this occurs immediately after the funds cease to qualify under s71.

HMRC Answer

We can confirm that s.71D can apply to existing A&M trusts if the conversion occurs before the funds cease to qualify under s.71 – for the reasons set out in example 8 below.

Further that there is no inheritance tax charge on conversion of an existing accumulation and maintenance trust to a s71D trust. i.e. that para 3(3) schedule 20 protects all pre-Budget accumulation and maintenance trusts so that there is no inheritance tax entry charge either under s71 or otherwise, at the point the trust starts to qualify for s71D status (or indeed enters the relevant property regime).

HMRC Answer

We can confirm this.

Example 8

U sets up an accumulation and maintenance trust for his two nieces S and T in 1999. On 22 March 2006 neither has an interest in possession. Currently the nieces take capital at 30 and income at 21. S becomes 21 in January 2007. T becomes 21 in January 2011.

The trustees exercise their powers to ensure that the trusts qualify for 18–25 status in February 2007 i.e. after S has attained entitlement to income (albeit this is not a qualifying interest in possession post Budget). They provide that each child takes capital outright at 25 in a fixed half share. In these circumstances it would appear that S's share cannot qualify for 18–25 status because immediately after the property ceased to be subject to s71 it did not then fall within s71D. T's interest could however qualify under s71D. There is no inheritance tax charge in February 2007 on S's part although there would be a ten year charge in 2009 on her share because this share is now within the relevant property regime and there would be an exit charge when she reaches 25. There are no ten year or entry or exit charges on T's interest until she reaches 25 at which point her share is subject to tax at 4.2%. (This assumes that she does not die before reaching 25).

It would be helpful if this could be spelt out in the guidance notes because trustees need to be aware of the requirement to act swiftly if beneficiaries are about to take entitlement to income. It would also be helpful if examples could be given as to how 18–25 trusts work in practice and their main advantages i.e. to avoid the ten year anniversary charge.

HMRC Answer

We agree with the consequences set out in the example and will incorporate them in guidance.

26. **Question 29**

It would appear that on the death of a child before 18 on a bereaved minor trust or on an 18–25 trust there is no inheritance tax charge even if they are entitled to income (albeit there is a base cost capital gains tax uplift if they are entitled to income).

HMRC Answer

We agree – by virtue of s.71B(2)(b) or s. 71E(2)(b) and new s. 5(1)(a)(i).

It would appear that after a child reaches 18 there is an exit charge on an 18–25 trust if the property ceases to be held on 18–25 trusts but no base cost uplift for capital gains tax purposes whether or not the child has a right to income. Please confirm.

HMRC Answer

We can confirm this.

Question 30

It would appear that, if a child reaches 18 and on his death his share of the trust fund remains on 18–25 trusts for his siblings under cross-accruer provisions, there will be no exit charge at that time. Please confirm.

HMRC Answer

We can confirm this.

27. **Question 31**

In the HMRC Customer Guide to Inheritance Tax recently published HMRC state under the heading of "What is an age 18 to 25 trust?"

> "If the terms of the trust are not rewritten before 6 April 2008 and the trust has not come to an end then existing accumulation and maintenance trusts will automatically become relevant property trusts on the 18th birthday of the beneficiary."

What is the statutory justification for this view. First it is surely the case that an existing A&M trust can become subject to the relevant property regime before 6th April 2008 if a beneficiary takes a post-Budget 2006 interest in possession.

HMRC Answer

We agree and will amend the Customer Guide.

Second our understanding is that such trusts will become relevant property trusts on the 6th April 2008 or the beneficiary becoming entitled to an interest in possession before that date unless the trust meets the requirements of a s71D trust. If nothing has been done by April 2008 and a beneficiary is not entitled to an interest in possession then the trust falls within the relevant property regime from that date whether or not the beneficiary is a minor. This point needs to be clarified urgently and the information amended.

HMRC Answer

We agree. S. 71D(5)(b) provides that s. 71D does not apply to property to which s. 71 applies. A&M treatment will therefore continue up to an including 5 April 2008 if the trusts of the settlement meet s.71, and will fall away on 6 April 2008. If the trusts provide for absolute entitlement at 18 or 25, the settlement will then fall within s. 71A or s. 71D as appropriate; if they do not, the settlement will be "relevant property" from that date.

28. **Question 32**

Please also confirm whether or not hold over relief will be available if assets are distributed within 3 months of a beneficiary's 18th birthday under an 18–25 trust. There will be no inheritance tax charge as there will be no complete quarters since the 18th birthday. In these circumstances is hold over relief denied?

HMRC Answer

No. The distribution is still an occasion on which IHT is chargeable – it is just that the charge will be nil. There is no provision in s.71F along the lines of s. 65(4).

E Absolute interests

29. Where assets are held by a person on bare trusts for minor children section 31 of the Trustee Act is implied in most cases without express reference and will apply unless expressly excluded.

30. It might be said that the application of the section will cause the property concerned to be settled property within section 43(2)(b) in view of the provisions for the accumulation of income under section 31(2) of the Trustee Act. However, the contrary argument is that the accumulations of income are held for the absolute benefit for the minor concerned and would pass to his estate if he died under 18 (the minor not being able to give a good receipt) and the assets are therefore not held in any real sense subject to any contingency or provision for the diversion of income from the minor. This latter view seems to be in line with the analysis in the IHT Manual which contemplates that section 43(2)(b) deals with the position where there is relevant property held on discretionary trusts (paragraph 4602). The statement in the Inland Revenue letter of 12 February 1976 where, in the last sentence of the second paragraph, it is stated that a provision to accumulate income will not prevent there being an interest in possession if the accumulations are held for the absolute benefit of the beneficiary, supports the view that section 31 of the Trustee Act will *not in these circumstances* cause the relevant property regime to apply.

30. **Question 33**

Can HMRC confirm that the application of section 31 of the Trustee Act 1925 to assets held on a bare trust for a minor will not result in the assets being settled property within the meaning of section 43 IHTA?

HMRC Answer

We confirm that our view is that where assets are held on an absolute trust (ie a bare trust) for a minor the assets so held will not be settled property within the meaning of section 43 IHTA 1984 and that this will be the case whether or not the provisions of section 31 Trustee Act 1925 have been excluded.

32. There appear to be new and unforeseen capital gains tax problems now where *Crowe v Appleby* [1975 (STC 502)] applies on settled property. The position is complex albeit common and can best be illustrated by example.

Example 9

In February 2006 Andrew set up a trust for his children Charlotte and Luke. They each become entitled to one half of the income and capital on reaching 25. Charlotte becomes 25 in 2007 and Luke becomes 25 in 2009. They do not take interests in possession until reaching 25. The trust only holds one piece of land.

When Charlotte reaches 25 in 2007 she becomes absolutely entitled for inheritance tax purposes since Crowe v Appleby has no application for IHT purposes. The trusts over her share end for inheritance tax purposes before April 6 2008 so there is no exit charge since she is within the transitional regime. She is treated from 2007 as entitled to the half share in the property and if she died after that date it would form part of her estate for inheritance tax purposes and hence be potentially taxable.

There is a further problem. For capital gains tax purposes Charlotte does not become absolutely entitled to one half of the land. Until the land is sold or Luke reaches 25 and becomes absolutely entitled (whichever is the earlier) there is no disposal made by the trustees.

There is no inheritance tax change on 6 April 2008 but from that date Luke's share is no longer within A&M trust protection but is taxed as an 18–25 trust. There is no ten year anniversary charge before Luke reaches 25 but if he dies before then there is an inheritance tax charge (likely to be less than 4.2%). As noted above, there is no base cost uplift for capital gains tax purposes.

On Luke reaching 25 in 2009 there is an exit charge on Luke's share of 4.2%.

HMRC Answer

(Note: we do not consider this is quite right. We assume that the 4.2% is referred to on the basis of 7/10ths × 6%. However, the charge will not be based on the 7 years from Luke's 18th birthday. S. 71F(5)(a) provides that the starting date for calculating the relevant fraction is his 18th birthday "or, if later, the day on which the property became property to which section 71D above applies" – in this case, 6 April 2008). If the land has not yet been sold there will at that point be a disposal of all the land by the trustees for capital gains tax purposes because both beneficiaries become absolutely entitled. Hold over relief is available on Luke's part under s260 TCGA 1992 but not on Charlotte's part since there is no exit charge. In summary, the trustees will have to pay capital gains tax on any gain on Charlotte's share in 2009 and cannot hold over the gain on that share.

Question 34

Prior to the Finance Act 2006, Charlotte would have been treated as having a qualifying interest in possession in her share of the trust assets. If she died before Luke reached 25, there would have been a charge to inheritance tax on her death but because she had a qualifying interest in possession, for capital gains tax purposes, there would be an uplift in base cost on her share of the land under s72(1) TCGA 1992.

Post the Finance Act 2006, if Charlotte dies before Luke reaches 25 there will be a charge to inheritance tax but s72(1) TCGA 1992 does not seem to be applicable because Charlotte does not appear to have a qualifying interest in possession which qualifies her for the uplift. Hence she is subject to inheritance tax on her death with no uplift for capital gains tax.

Will HMRC regard her as having a qualifying interest in possession within section 72 for these purposes?

HMRC Answer

No – with the result, as stated, that there would be no CGT uplift under s. 72(1) TCGA.

Question 35

If Charlotte attained 25 in say June 2015 and Luke only reached 25 in 2017 there would be an exit charge on both Luke and Charlotte's shares when each becomes 25 (rate = 4.2%) but hold over relief is only available on Luke's share when the disposal of the land takes place for capital gains tax purposes.

Prior to the Finance Act 2006 there would have been no exit charge when Charlotte reached 25. However, the effect of the new rules is that on reaching 25 Charlotte will now suffer an exit charge but without any entitlement to hold-over the gain which arises when the land is distributed to her when Luke reaches 25. Will HMRC in these circumstances allow hold over relief on both shares?

HMRC Answer

No – hold-over relief will be due on Luke's share only.

F Disabled trusts

33. Section 89A(2) appears to conflict with s89A(3). Condition 1 states that if any of the settled property is applied for A it is applied for the benefit of A but Condition 2 envisages that capital *could* be paid to A or another person on the termination of A's interest during his life provided that the other person became absolutely entitled.

Question 36

Is HMRC's view that capital can be appointed to someone else on the termination of the trust only if it can be demonstrated that it is for the benefit of A?

HMRC Answer

No – we do not consider that that condition is in point.

Otherwise why does s89A(3) Condition 2 refer to other persons at all?

HMRC Answer

We do not agree with the proposition that there is a conflict between s. 89A(2) and (3). Condition 1 refers to the application of "settled property" – i.e. to property that is held on the trusts referred to in s. 89A(1)(c). Condition 2, however, is applying conditions that are effective in the event of such trusts being brought to an end.

G General points

34. **Question 37(1)**

New sections 46A(4) and 46B(5) provide that additions (by way of payment of further premiums) to a pre-Budget 2006 interest in possession or A&M trust which holds an insurance policy would not result either in a chargeable transfer or in any part of the trust falling within the relevant property regime.

It is understood that HMRC believe that additions of cash or other property to existing pre-Budget 2006 interest in possession settlements are subject to the new rules in Schedule 20.

There are other payments which are often made by settlors or beneficiaries on behalf of a trust. For example, buildings insurance premiums and general maintenance costs, payments to cover trust, administration and taxation expenses.

It is noted that for the purposes of TCGA 1992 Sch 5 para 9(3) the payment of expenses relating to administration and taxation of a trust are not be treated as the addition of property to the trust. In SP 5/92 the costs of acquiring, enhancing and disposing of a trust asset are not regarded as expenses relating to administration but other property expenses appear to fall within the definition and therefore are not treated as the addition of property to the trust. Would HMRC maintain that the addition of cash or other property to a settlement which may be used either to enhance trust property (eg payment of costs relating to the building of an extension to property) or to purchase other property will be treated as additions but accept that the payment of other trustee expenses (eg trustee fees, buildings insurance premiums and general maintenance costs) will not be treated as chargeable additions?

HMRC Answer

Schedule 5 TCGA is a statutory provision relating to certain, specific circumstances. There is no legal basis on which payments of "other trustee expenses" should not be treated as chargeable additions for IHT purposes.

Question 37(2)

If any of the additions do bring the trust within the new rules, what property within the trust will be caught and how will it be valued? For example, if an addition of cash was made which was then spent by the trustees and HMRC regard this addition as within the relevant property regime (eg an addition to pay expenses or improve properties), how would the proportion of the settled property subject to the new rules be calculated? Would a valuation be needed of the property before and after the improvement? In HMRC's view, do all subsequent post Budget additions need to be kept physically segregated?

HMRC Answer

[If a payment of cash was made and then spent immediately on, say, a tax liability or another administration expense, then that short period will be the extent of its time as "relevant property" and there will be no question of having to consider what proportion of the existing settled property represents it going forward. If a payment was made towards the improvement of a property, then this would appear to require "with" and "without" valuations when there is a chargeable event.] Note added 6 August 2008: HMRC have indicated that they are actively reconsidering this response with a view to producing further guidance shortly.

It is clearly up to trustees to decide whether to keep post-Budget 2006 additions separate from the rest of the trust fund. We think that it may be sensible to do so – or, at least, to keep good records of additions. (The trustees of discretionary trusts already need to do this, of course, in order for the 10-year anniversary value of each addition to be identified correctly in light of the relief in s. 66(2) IHTA for property that has not been "relevant property" for a full 10-year period).

35. **Question 38**

It is understood that additions to a trust which fall within the normal expenditure out of income exemption will not need to be reported as and when they are made as, following the normal rules, it is not necessary to report exempt transactions? Please confirm.

HMRC Answer

We can confirm this.

36. **Question 39**

It is not unknown for wills to include a gift of an annuity. Some wills give the executors sufficient powers to enable them to choose how best to satisfy the annuity. In such a case there are typically four methods which executors may use to deal with an annuity.

- Pay the annuity out of residue. In such a case the executors delay the completion of the administration of the estate until the annuitant dies.
- Create an appropriated annuity fund. In such a case the executors appropriate a capital fund of sufficient size to pay the annuity.
- Purchase an annuity. The executors purchase an annuity from an insurance office or life company.
- Commute the annuity. The executors pay the annuitant a cash sum sufficient to allow him to purchase the annuity personally.

The first two options create settled property. Will HMRC confirm that a provision in a will conferring the payment of an annuity upon a person (eg to make a gift of an annuity of £x for life) which the executors satisfy by one of the first two options outlined above will be treated as the creation of an IPDI in favour of the annuitant?

HMRC Answer

We can confirm this.

Under s50(2), where a person is entitled to a specified amount (such as an annuity) for any period his interest is taken to subsist in that part of the property that produces that amount in that period. The property in which his interest subsists may therefore vary over time.

Example 10

Say A is entitled to an annuity of £1,000 and the executors set aside a fund of £40,000 to pay this annuity. In year 1 the income from the £40,000 is £2,000 and half is paid to the annuitant. In year 2 the income from the £40,000 is £1,000 and all the income is paid to A. In year 3 (the year in which the annuitant dies) the income from the £40,000 is £4,000 and a quarter is paid to A. Please could HMRC confirm what property would fall within A's estate on his death (assuming he is treated as having an IPDI) and the basis upon which this has been calculated?

HMRC Answer

We would follow the existing principles set out in s.50(2) to s.50(5) IHTA at the date of A's death. (As Dymond, at 16.611, points out, s.50(2) does not give any guidance as to the period over which the income of the settled property should be computed. But the learned authors suggest that looking at the income in the year immediately before the chargeable occasion would normally be a reasonable approach and we would agree.)

H Deeds of variation

Questions have arisen as to the effect of deeds of variation post-Budget 2006.

37.

Example 11

Testator dies pre-Budget 2006 leaving everything outright to X. His will is varied by X and an election made under s 142 to treat the variation as made by the will.

Question 40

Any trust established by the variation will be treated as having been established pre-Budget 2006 whether or not the variation is actually made pre- or post-Budget 2006. If an interest in possession trust is established under such a variation by X, we assume it will be a qualifying interest in possession given it is deemed to be set up prior to the Budget by the deceased and not by X for inheritance tax purposes and further that it will be possible to create a transitional serial interest in relation to this trust before 6 October 2008. Please confirm.

HMRC Answer

We can confirm this.

38.

Example 12

Testator dies post-Budget 2006 leaving everything outright to Y. His will is varied to establish ongoing trusts and an election made under s 142 to read the variation back into the will.

Question 41

Assuming that the terms of the trusts are appropriate, it is possible to establish IPDIs, 18–25 trusts and BMTs by way of such a variation made by Y. Please confirm. As in question 40 it is assumed that for inheritance tax purposes the settlor is the deceased rather than Y.

HMRC Answer

We can confirm this.

39.

Example 13

The testator is not domiciled in the UK at his death leaving everything outright to Z. His will dealing with property outside the UK is varied to establish trusts and an election made under s 142 to read the variation back into the will.

Question 42

Any trusts established by the variation holding non-UK property will be excluded property trusts whatever the domicile status of Z (the beneficiary making the variation) and whatever the terms of the new trusts. This will be the case whether or not the testator died pre- or post-Budget. Please confirm.

HMRC Answer

We can confirm this.

40. Section 54A IHTA contains certain anti-avoidance provisions that arise where a settlor settles assets into a qualifying interest in possession trust by PET and then the life interest is terminated so that discretionary trusts arise within 7 years. In effect the settlor rather than the life tenant can be treated as having made the chargeable transfer if this yields more tax. S54A(1A) states that where a person becomes beneficially entitled on or after 22 March 2006 to a disabled person's interest or a TSI, s54(1)(b) applies. So if the disabled person or the holder of the TSI dies and relevant property trusts arise, the anti-avoidance provision potentially applies. Nothing is said though in respect of inter vivos terminations of the TSI or disabled person's interest when relevant property trusts arise and the termination occurs within 7 years of the original PET made by the settlor.

Question 43

Is it intended that s54A should only apply to interests in possession arising on or after 22 March 2006 if the disabled person's interest or TSI terminates on death rather than inter vivos?

HMRC Answer

Section 54A applies both to lifetime terminations of a TSI or disabled person's interest where the other conditions of s54A are satisfied as well as a termination on the death of the life tenant. The fact that s54A(1)(A) refers expressly to death and not to lifetime terminations does not mean that s54A did not cover both scenarios because s54A(1) covered lifetime terminations. We believe s54A can apply to both inter vivos and terminations on death because s.54A(1)(a) refers back to s.52, where s.52(2A) already provides that, where the person becomes beneficially entitled to the interest in possession on or after 22 March 2006, there will only be a charge under s.52(1) – and so s.54A will only potentially apply – if the interest is:

- an immediate post-death interest,
- a disabled person's interest, or
- a transitional serial interest.

Misc. 121 FINANCE ACT 2006SCHEDULE 20: PRE-EXISTING INTERESTS IN POSSESSION AND RELATED MATTERS [29 May 2007]

We are writing about a number of situations (set out in the questions below) where a person (A) was beneficially entitled to an interest in possession in settled property before 22 March 2006. Doubt has been expressed as to whether section 49(1) of the Inheritance Tax Act 1984 will continue to apply in the future, notwithstanding that A will throughout be entitled to the income of the settled property. We consider that, in all those situations, section 49(1) will continue to apply, notwithstanding section 49(1A) which (with exceptions) disapplies that sub-section where the interest in possession is one to which a person becomes beneficially entitled on or after 22 March 2006.

It has been suggested that A will, after that date, become entitled to a different proprietary interest in the settled property. As the Revenue argued in *Pearson v IRC* [1981] AC 753, and all the members of the House of Lords appear to have accepted, for inheritance tax purposes the expression "interest in possession" must be construed as a single phrase. Pearson decided that it means a present right to present enjoyment of the settled property, ie the right to the income from that property as it arises. And in each of the relevant situations, A became entitled to that right before 22 March 2006. Section 49(1A) does not, therefore, in our view, apply.

If we are right about this, then it means that the IHT treatment of the relevant situations will not depend on the accident of the particular drafting technique adopted, with settlements being treated differently notwithstanding that A's rights are the same and without any possible policy justification that we have been able to identify.

We would emphasise that, in each of the examples below, the trustees have not exercised any dispositive powers post-March 2006: the interest taken by A remains throughout merely an entitlement to income and, moreover, an entitlement which is defined under the terms of the settlement prior to March 2006.

We hope that you will be able to confirm that section 49(1) will continue to apply and, therefore, that the same pre-Budget interest in possession will continue to subsist in each of the following examples.

Example 1

(1) Settled property is held on trust to pay the income to A for life contingently on A attaining the age of 25. The trust carries the intermediate income.

(2) A attained the age of 18 on 1 January 2006 and thereupon became entitled to an interest in possession by virtue of section 31 of the Trustee Act 1925. Section 49(1) applies.

(3) In our view, it will continue to apply after age 25, when the express trust to pay income to him comes into effect. On any footing, A has only one interest, being the present right to present enjoyment, brought into possession earlier than would otherwise be the case by section 31.

Question 1 – do HMRC agree?

HMRC Answer to Question 1 – yes

Example 2

(1) Under a pre-Budget 2006 trust, A is entitled to capital contingently on attaining the age of 25 years. The clause goes on to provide that the trusts carry the intermediate income and section 31 of the Trustee Act is to apply.

(2) The same clause provides that the capital should not vest absolutely on A attaining the age of 25 but should be retained on trust:

a. to pay the income to A for life, and then

b. for A's children after A's death,

(3) A attained the age of 18 on 1 January 2006. Section 49(1) applies.

(4) In our view, it will continue to apply after A attains the age of 25 on 1 January 2013, when the "engrafted" trust to pay income to A comes into effect.

Question 2 – do HMRC agree?

HMRC Answer to Question 2 – yes

Example 3

The facts are the same as example 3, except that the engrafted trusts are contained in a separate clause. In our view, the position is the same, and section 49(1) will continue to apply after A attains the age of 25.

Question 3 – do HMRC agree?

HMRC Answer to Question 3 – yes

Example 4

(1) A became entitled to income at 25 in January 2006 and section 49(1) applies.

(2) A is contingently entitled to capital at the age of 35, but the trustees retain overriding powers of appointment exercisable during his lifetime. He therefore attains only a defeasible interest in capital in 2016, and the capital remains settled property until his death.

(3) In our view, section 49(1) will continue to apply after A attains the age of 35, notwithstanding that his contingent interest in capital is replaced by a vested but defeasible interest in capital.

Question 4 – do HMRC agree?

HMRC Answer to question 4 – yes

Example 5

Presumably, where a transitional serial interest (TSI) arose after 21 March 2006 but before 6 April 2008 (e.g. a pre-22 March 06 Budget life tenant's interest was ended in 2007 and A the new life tenant takes an immediate interest in possession and capital at 35 but that capital entitlement is defeasible being subject to any exercise of the overriding powers), HMRC would agree that section 49C continues to apply to A after he attains the age of 35 for the same reasons, ie that his transitional serial interest entitlement continues following his 35th birthday.

Question 5 – do HMRC agree?

HMRC Answer to Question 5 – yes

In all the above examples, A's interest arises under the terms of the Settlement, and not from the exercise of the trustees' powers. We think these examples can be distinguished from the case where a beneficiary is absolutely entitled to capital on reaching a specified age and the trustees positively exercise their powers to defer that absolute entitlement and maintain the interest in possession, where we understand that different issues may arise as set out in the previous reply to queries on Schedule 20 – see questions revised in April 2007 and in particular Question 6

HMRC Answer – agreed

Interest in possession which continues after death of life tenant

In some circumstances, an interest in possession may continue after the death of the person entitled to the interest up until their death. HMRC have confirmed that a lifetime assignment of an interest in possession will qualify as a TSI (assuming the other requirements are satisfied - Question 10 of Schedule 20 letter) on the basis that the interest in possession will have "come to an end" within the meaning of section 49C(3), presumably on the basis of IHTA section 51(1). There is no equivalent provision to IHTA section 51(1) in relation to transfers on death of an autre vie, but the entitlement of the prior beneficiary who is holding an interest pur autre vie will have come to an end, even though the interest itself will not have done so. This may arise, for example, where the will of the deceased life tenant leaves their residuary estate, which would include their remaining entitlement to the interest pur autre vie, to their surviving spouse.

Question 6

Do HMRC consider that, when a pre-Budget interest in possession beneficiary who holds the pur autre vie dies, any interest in possession in such property then taken by his spouse (or any other person if that occurs *before 6 April 2008) will qualify as a transitional serial interest?*

HMRC Answer to Question 6 – Yes. In the circumstances outlined, it would seem that the death of the beneficiary holding a pur autre vie interest must bring "the prior interest" within the terms of s. 49C IHTA to an end.

IHTA 1984 section 46B

We should be grateful if you would confirm your view in relation to pre-Budget 2006 settled life policies, where a policy is held on section 71 accumulation and maintenance trusts and the trusts are then converted into trusts within section 71D IHTA. Insurance premiums continue to be paid on the policy.

It is clear that the continued payment of the insurance premiums will be potentially exempt transfers under section 46B(5).

Question 7

Are the added rights arising from the payment of the premiums settled property within section 71D, or are they separate settled property which is within the relevant property regime?

There is no equivalent provision in relation to section 71D trusts to section 46B(2), which applies for section 71 trusts where premiums continue to be paid on or after 22 March 2006. Section 46B(2) provides that the rights arising by reference to the payment of the further premiums shall also be within section 71 if they would be but for section71(1A).

The rights arising from the payment of premiums on policies held on trusts where the payments are made after such trust has been converted to section 71D status do not appear to be strictly within section 71D(3), which is necessary for those rights to be held on trusts within section 71D. Section 46B(1) in relation to section 71 trusts refers to sections 46B(2) and (5), but section 46B(3) in relation to section 71D trusts only refers to section 46B(5).

Do HMRC accept that the policy held on section 71D trusts is, in reality, the same asset as that previously held on section 71 trusts and that, in effect, no new rights become comprised in the settlement so that all the policy and its proceeds would be within section 71D?

We would be grateful for HMRC's views on this.

HMRC Answer to question 7 – we do accept that any added rights from the payment of additional premiums would constitute settled property within s71D. If a premium paid once the policy has become property to which s71D applies gives rise to an addition to the settled property the addition will, in our view, automatically become property to which s71D applies.

Section 200

Finally, we note that, under section 200(1)(c), a person with a non-qualifying interest in possession can become personally liable for the tax charged on death, with his liability limited only by reference to the value of the settled property (not the value of his actuarial interest). This seems a somewhat draconian provision, given that the beneficiary is no longer treated as beneficially entitled to the capital. Surely the liability should be limited to the property or income he actually receives? Similarly, in section 201(1)(b), the liability seems anomalous, given that most interests in possession will now be non-qualifying. Why should a beneficiary with a non-qualifying interest in possession have a greater personal liability than a discretionary beneficiary? Can we press for these sections to be reviewed?

HMRC Answer – we do not accept that there is an anomaly here. Although an IIP holder whose interest arose before 22.3.06 has been regarded as owning the underlying property for inheritance tax purposes, in reality he has only ever owned a limited interest. The FA 2006 changes do not alter the IIP owner's real position.

Misc. 122 DETERMINING A DOTAS IHT SCHEME – THE TESTS

A proposal or arrangement is notifiable under DOTAS as an IHT scheme if:

- there are arrangements which are expected to provide an IHT advantage
- this advantage is expected to be one of the main benefits of the arrangements and
- the arrangements fall within one of three hallmarks which apply for IHT

The Inheritance Tax Avoidance Schemes (Prescribed Description of Arrangements) Regulations 2017 (SI 1172/2017) give the description, or IHT hallmark, of arrangements that have to be notified. These regulations take effect from 1st April 2018 and replace the previous IHT hallmark prescribed in The Inheritance Tax Avoidance Schemes (Prescribed Description of Arrangements) Regulations 2011 (SI 170/2011).

The 2011 IHT hallmark included "grandfathering" provisions to except from disclosure arrangements that were first made available before 6th April 2011 or which were substantially the same as arrangements first made available before that date. These "grandfathering" provisions cease to apply from 1st April 2018 when the new IHT hallmark takes effect. This means that arrangements that would have been excepted from disclosure before 1st April 2018 under the 2011 hallmark will, from 1st April 2018, have to be tested against the new IHT hallmark.

In addition to the specific IHT hallmark, the confidentiality and premium fee hallmarks were extended to cover IHT with effect from 23rd February 2016. Guidance on the application of those hallmarks can be found in paragraphs 7.3 to 7.3.6 and 7.5 to 7.5.3 above. Neither the grandfathering exception described in the previous paragraph nor that described below in relation to the new hallmark apply to an IHT scheme which is disclosable under either the confidentiality or the premium fee hallmark.

The IHT hallmark and how it works

The IHT hallmark provides that an arrangement is notifiable if it would be reasonable to expect an informed observer, who has studied the arrangements and had regard to all relevant circumstances, to conclude that conditions 1 and 2 are met. "Arrangements" takes it meaning from section 318 of Finance Act 2004 and includes any scheme, transaction or series of transactions.

The "informed observer" test is crucial as this provides the context in which the conditions are to be judged.

The informed observer is to be contrasted with an "uninformed observer", but isn't an expert or necessarily a tax practitioner.

The informed observer is independent, has all the relevant information about the scheme and has sufficient knowledge to understand both the scheme and the relevant statutory context.

The informed observer is assumed to have the appropriate knowledge and skillset to reach the conclusions that the hallmark requires.

While the promoter isn't an informed observer for this purpose, the informed observer should be presumed to have access to all of the information that is available to the promoter of the scheme.

The scope of "all relevant circumstances" will vary according to the nature of the arrangements, but circumstances which may be relevant for the informed observer to take into account include:

- The non-tax benefits that are expected to arise from the arrangements
- The overall effect or consequences of the arrangements
- The terms of the documentation and the substance of the arrangements, and
- HMRC guidance and published statements

The promoter or other person with a potential duty to notify HMRC about the scheme is required to consider whether an informed observer, who has studied the arrangements and taken all relevant circumstances into account, could reasonably be expected to conclude that:

- the main purpose, or one of the main purposes, of the arrangements is to obtain one of the tax advantages listed in condition 1, and
- the arrangements involve the use of one or more contrived or abnormal steps without which the tax advantage could not be obtained.

The hallmark conditions

The IHT hallmark has two conditions. Both conditions have to be met for the arrangement to be notifiable.

Condition 1

Condition 1 is that the main purpose, or one of the main purposes, of the arrangements is to enable a person to obtain an advantage in relation to inheritance tax set out in one or more of sub-paragraphs (a) to (d).

In most cases it should be clear whether the main purpose, or one of the main purposes, of the arrangements is to secure one of the listed tax advantages, or whether the tax advantage arises inadvertently as a by-product of the arrangements. As this has to be determined by reference to how an "informed observer" would view the arrangements, this test should be relatively straightforward.

Condition 1 focuses on areas of highest risk and greatest concern to HMRC. The tax advantages listed under condition 1 are:

(a) **the avoidance or reduction of a relevant property entry charge**

This imports the wording from the 2011 IHT hallmark. Arrangements, the main purpose, or one of the main purposes, of which is to reduce or avoid the charge which would otherwise arise when property becomes relevant property are within (a).

(b) **the avoidance or reduction of a charge to inheritance tax under section 64, 65, 72 and 94 of IHTA 1984**

This focuses on the avoidance or reduction of the charge on relevant property at the ten-year anniversary – s.64; the charge on relevant property at any other time – s.65; the charge arising on property leaving employee or newspaper trusts – s.72; and the charge arising in connection with close company transfers – s.94.

(c) **the avoidance or reduction of a charge to inheritance tax arising from the application of section 102, 102ZA, 102A, or 102B of the Finance Act 1986 in circumstances where there is also no charge to income tax under Schedule 15 to the Finance Act 2004 (charge to income tax on benefits received by former owner of property)**

This relates to arrangements that seek to avoid the inheritance tax implications of being a gift with reservation of benefit, but where there is also no pre-owned asset income tax charge under Schedule 15 to the Finance Act 2004.

(d) **a reduction in the value of the person's estate without giving rise to a chargeable transfer or potentially exempt transfer.**

This relates to arrangements where a person removes value from their estate without that reduction giving rise to either a chargeable transfer or a potentially exempt transfer. A reduction in the value of a person's estate other than an arm's length bargain will usually give rise to a transfer of value under section 3 IHTA 1984.

While condition 1 identifies arrangements that reduce or avoid the charges to inheritance tax set out in paragraphs (a) to (d) above, these arrangements are only notifiable if they ***also*** meet condition 2. There will be many commonly used tax planning arrangements that fall within one or more of (a) to (d) above, but which will not cause condition 2 to be met and which are therefore ***not*** notifiable.

Condition 2

Condition 2 is that the arrangements involve one or more contrived or abnormal steps without which the tax advantage could not be obtained.

When considering this condition, it is the arrangements that must be reviewed to conclude whether they involve one or more contrived or abnormal steps and then to consider whether those contrived or abnormal steps are necessary to achieve the tax advantage.

For example, the use of trusts is not itself contrived or abnormal. A gift into a discretionary trust would not, on its own, meet condition 2. The gift would be an immediately chargeable transfer and the fact that the gift was to a discretionary trust would not, on its own, mean that the arrangements by way of which the gift is made include a contrived or abnormal step.

If a more complex trust structure was used instead, for example for added protection of the trust assets, the additional complexity might lead an informed observer to conclude that those additional steps are "contrived or abnormal" in the sense that it was unusual to go to those lengths and levels of complexity. However, condition 2 will only be met if the steps that are contrived or abnormal are required to achieve a tax advantage.

To an "uninformed observer" the creation of a trust might seem like an unusual and therefore abnormal thing to do. Equally the idea of creating a trust and then making a loan to the trustees of that trust might seem contrived to an uninformed observer.

However, whether arrangements are contrived or abnormal, or involve contrived or abnormal steps, has to be considered from the point of view of an "informed observer". A straightforward trust arrangement is not contrived or abnormal in this context. Nor is the making of a loan to trustees of a trust that an individual has set up, or to a company to which the individual has a connection. Equally, choosing to invest money into assets which will qualify for relief from inheritance tax may or may not be commonplace, but in the context of the "informed observer" such an investment, on its own, would be neither contrived nor abnormal.

The inclusion of the words "contrived or abnormal" and the requirement for them to be considered by the hypothetical informed observer mean that normal and straightforward inheritance tax planning will not be notifiable. Inheritance tax planning that requires greater complexity or contrivance to achieve the intended tax advantages though is likely to be notifiable. In particular it can be helpful to consider whether the economic consequences are as expected. Making a gift presupposes that the donor no longer beneficially owns the gifted property. If the donor is able to enjoy the gifted property in broadly the same way as previously this might well be an indicator of a disclosable scheme.

The "established practice" exception

The new hallmark takes effect from 1st April 2018, so a proposal which was made available before that date would not have been notifiable at that time. However, where that proposal is implemented again on or after 1st April 2018 a duty to notify would arise under s.308(3) FA04. The established practice exception is intended to ensure that such a duty does not arise if the conditions in the exception are met.

Arrangements are excepted from being prescribed, i.e. they will not be notifiable, if they:

(a) implement a proposal which has been implemented by related arrangements, and

(b) are substantially the same as the related arrangements.

"Related arrangements" are defined as arrangements which:

(a) were entered into before 1st April 2018, and

(b) at the time they were entered into, accorded with established practice of which HMRC had indicated their acceptance.

This provision is designed to remove from the scope of the hallmark established IHT planning schemes whose workings are well understood and agreed. Such schemes are excepted if:

- that scheme has been sold and implemented at least once before the new hallmark takes effect
- HMRC has indicated its acceptance that it achieves that well understood tax outcome, and
- it is sold and implemented again without being changed after the hallmark takes effect

The proposal or scheme

The first stage is to establish whether the proposal or scheme in question, which is being implemented by the present arrangements, was implemented in the same form before 1st April 2018. If that proposal has not been implemented before 1st April 2018 the exception does not apply. Even if the exception does apply, it is still necessary to test the proposal or arrangements against the premium fee and confidentiality hallmarks, which means the proposal or scheme may be notifiable by virtue only of one or both of those hallmarks.

For the exception to apply the present arrangements must implement a proposal which has previously been implemented by related arrangements. It is therefore important to identify the proposal which the present arrangements are implementing.

The proposal is the specific combination of elements or steps which are designed to achieve the intended tax advantage and which is being made available to a potential user. While there may be a number of very similar proposals in existence which are designed to achieve the same tax advantage, for example different companies offering their own versions of a tax saving scheme, each would be a separate proposal.

The exception applies to arrangements which implement a proposal which has been implemented by related arrangements. It follows that the proposal which is being implemented by the present arrangements has to be the same proposal that was implemented by the related arrangements before 1st April 2018. The exception does not apply to arrangements which implement a different proposal. That other proposal must be considered on its own merits.

By way of example, Insurance Co have offered their clients a Discounted Gift Trust v1.0 since 2010. This proposal was first implemented in 2010 and continues to be offered in April 2018 in exactly the same way. The implementation of this proposal by arrangements entered into after 1st April 2018 would be the implementation of a proposal that has previously been implemented before 1st April 2018 and which, subject to satisfying the established practice requirements, would be within the exception. The arrangements would still have to be tested against the confidentiality and premium fee hallmarks but if they accord with established practice they would seem likely not to be notifiable under the IHT hallmark

However, suppose Insurance Co decide that they want to make changes to the elements or steps which are required to achieve the intended tax advantage and after 1st April 2018 offer their clients what amounts to Discounted Gift Trust v.1.1 (notwithstanding that they may choose not to change the name or version number). This is a new proposal, even though it may be "substantially the same" as Discounted Gift Trust v1.0. This proposal and any arrangements that implement it are not excepted, and must be tested by reference to the new IHT hallmark as well as the confidentiality and premium fee hallmarks.

Changes to a proposal or scheme which do not affect the elements or steps that are required to achieve the intended tax advantage would not result in this being a new proposal. For example, changes to the name of the scheme or the entity making the proposal, or changes for other regulatory reasons that do not affect the elements or steps which lead to the intended tax advantage, would not give rise to a new proposal.

If the proposal had previously been implemented before 1st April 2018, the next step is to consider whether the previously implemented arrangements are "related arrangements".

Related arrangements

In order to be "related arrangements", the earlier arrangements must:

- have been entered into before 1 April 2018, and
- at the time they were entered into those arrangements, have accorded with established practice of which HMRC had indicated their acceptance

Established practice and HMRC's acceptance of that practice

There are two elements to this requirement. The first is to consider whether the arrangements "accord with established practice", and secondly whether HMRC has indicated acceptance of that established practice.

Taking the "established practice" first, this is not defined in the legislation and therefore takes its ordinary meaning.

Established practice may be demonstrated by reference to published material (whether from HMRC, or text books or articles in journals) or by other written evidence of what had become a common practice by the relevant time (that is, when the arrangements were entered into).

It is then necessary to consider whether the arrangements actually carried out were the same as those identified as established practice, or whether there were any significant differences between the actual arrangement in question and those that were commonly carried out. If, for example, the particular difference between the actual arrangement and the "normal" arrangement was the introduction of some feature which was designed to achieve a particular tax advantage, then it is doubtful that the actual arrangement accorded with established practice.

The second requirement is that HMRC had, at the time the arrangements were entered into, indicated its acceptance of the established practice. This may have been through published material such as guidance or other means. For example, HMRC may have made a clear statement in its published tax bulletins, or its internal manuals, or in correspondence with some representative body (such as Society of Trust & Estate Practitioners, the Chartered Institute of Taxation, or other similar body).

Substantially the same

Having determined that the current arrangements implement a proposal that had previously been implemented by related arrangements but which would not have been notifiable as it pre-dates the 2018 IHT hallmark, the final criteria for arrangements to be within the exception is that they must be "substantially the same" as the current arrangements.

It is therefore useful to set out what is meant by "substantially the same" in this context.

It is important to bear in mind that the "substantially the same" requirement relates to the arrangements being implemented and the related arrangements, not to the proposal that the arrangements are implementing. For the exception to apply the current arrangements have to implement the same proposal as was implemented by the "related arrangements".

Minor changes, for example to reflect the different personal details of users, will not stop arrangements from being substantially the same. For example, a retail discounted gift product would provide for the user to specify the sum of money being placed into the product, the chosen beneficiaries, the amount and frequency of the payments that the user is to carve out for their own benefit and so on. These differences in personal details do not change the underlying proposal, so that, for example, an implementation of Discounted Gift Trust v1.0 by arrangements entered into by Ms Jones, investing £250,000 and retaining withdrawals of £1,041.66 per month, would be substantially the same as the implementation of Discounted Gift Trust v1.0 by Mr Smith, investing £1 million and retaining withdrawals of £75,000 per annum.

However, where the arrangements being implemented are altered beyond merely making the necessary changes to effect the proposal for that individual, the arrangements will no longer be "substantially the same" and will not be capable of being related arrangements.

Examples of arrangements which are not notifiable

As set out above, the hallmark does not catch straightforward inheritance tax planning. The examples below show how some of these arrangements (which could include proposals) would be tested against the hallmark. Bear in mind however, that arrangements must always be tested against all relevant hallmarks, which, for IHT, includes confidentiality and premium fee.

Ordinary outright gifts are not notifiable, even where they are exempt

Example 1: A lifetime gift to a spouse or civil partner

Condition 1	Such a gift is caught by condition 1(d) as at least a main purpose of the gift is to reduce the value of the person's estate without giving rise to a chargeable transfer or a potentially exempt transfer. Instead the reduction gives rise to an exempt transfer.

But to be notifiable condition 2 must also be met

Condition 2	It is not reasonable to expect that an informed observer would conclude a straightforward gift or transfer of assets to a spouse or civil partner includes either contrived or abnormal steps. This is simply the use of an exemption provided for by the legislation.

Although condition 1 is met, condition 2 is not, so these arrangements are not notifiable under this hallmark.

Example 2: Regular gifts out of income

Condition 1 — If these are gifts to an individual, they may be caught by condition 1(d) as a main purpose of the gifts is to reduce the value of the person's estate without giving rise to a chargeable transfer or a potentially exempt transfer – they give rise to a series of exempt transfers.

If these are gifts into trust, they may also be caught by condition 1(a) in that they avoid or reduce a relevant property entry charge.

Again, although condition 1 may be met, to be notifiable condition 2 must also be met

Condition 2 — It is not reasonable to expect that an informed observer would conclude it is either contrived or abnormal for a person to make regular gifts to those the person wants to benefit from their generosity where they are straightforward gifts to an individual or gifts into trust. This would just be the use of an exemption provided for by the legislation.

In some cases the person intending to make such gifts may be advised to record their intention or commitment in writing before making the gifts. Such a step might seem contrived or abnormal in the sense that unilateral gifts are commonly made without being pre-ordained, so that the pre-ordination appears abnormal. But in the context of the exemption for regular gifts out of income, which have to be part of the transferor's normal expenditure, recording this commitment in advance is simply a step in demonstrating that the exemption is due. Recording the commitment does not secure the exemption, but it may help to establish that the exemption is due based on the subsequent transfers.

Although condition 1 is met, condition 2 is not, so these arrangements are not notifiable under this hallmark.

Example 3: Transfers of value equal to the available nil rate band into trust, which may be repeated every seven years

Condition 1 — These gifts are chargeable but within the available nil rate band, so they are taxed at zero per cent. There is no reduction or avoidance of any charge set out in condition 1, so condition 1 is not met.

Condition 2 — Even if the arrangements met condition 1, it would not be reasonable to expect an informed observer to conclude a gift of a sum equal to the available nil rate band on its own was either contrived or abnormal, or contained contrived or abnormal steps.

Neither condition 1 nor condition 2 is met, so these arrangements are not notifiable under this hallmark.

Example 4: Making a lifetime transfer to a bare trust for a minor beneficiary

Condition 1 — The transfer is a gift into a bare trust from which the donor cannot benefit. Although the transfer reduces the value of the transferor's estate, it gives rise to a potentially exempt transfer. Condition 1(d) is therefore not met and the arrangement does not give rise to any of the other tax advantages set out in condition 1. This analysis would apply whether or not the trustees were able to defer actual payments to the beneficiary beyond the age of 18.

As condition 1 is not met there is no need to consider condition 2.

Executing a will, deed of variation or disclaimer which gives rise to exemption from inheritance tax

Example 5: Executing a will that leaves property to an exempt beneficiary such as the spouse or a charity

Condition 1 — Executing a will does not meet any of the elements of condition 1. Although a will may be executed to reduce or avoid the IHT charge on death by use of exemptions, the will does not reduce the person's estate. Rather the will determines how the estate devolves on death and it is this devolution which secures any IHT exemption. As there is no reduction in the person's estate without giving rise to a chargeable transfer, condition 1(d) is not met.

As condition 1 is not met there is no need to consider condition 2.

Example 6: Executing a deed of variation to which s.142 IHTA 1984 applies to transfer assets on death to an exempt beneficiary

Condition 1 Executing a deed of variation may reduce the inheritance tax charge on a person's death, but it does not meet any of the elements of condition 1 with regard to the person who has died as their estate is not reduced

A deed of variation is a lifetime transfer by the donor (the beneficiary) who originally inherited the property on the death. The property is treated as never being comprised in the donor's estate, so there is no reduction in the donor's estate and condition 1(d) is not met with respect to the donor.

This is not therefore a notifiable arrangement under this hallmark.

As condition 1 is not met there is no need to consider condition 2.

Example 7: Disclaiming an entitlement under a will to which s.142 IHTA 1984 applies where there is an exempt residuary beneficiary

Condition 1 Disclaiming an entitlement under a will where there is an exempt residuary beneficiary may reduce the inheritance tax charge on a person's death, but it does not meet any of the elements of condition 1 with regard to the person who has died.

The beneficiary who makes the disclaimer is making a lifetime transfer of the property, but the property is treated as never being comprised in the beneficiary's estate, so there is no reduction in the value of the beneficiary's estate and condition 1(d) is not met.

This is not therefore a notifiable arrangement under this hallmark.

As condition 1 is not met there is no need to consider condition 2.

Acquisition of property which qualifies for a statutory relief or a transfer which is specifically provided for in the inheritance tax legislation

Example 8: Purchase of shares which will qualify for business property relief after they have been owned for two years

Condition 1 The purchase of shares does not reduce the value of a person's estate. If it becomes available, business property relief only has the effect of reducing the value transferred by a transfer of value, it does not remove the value of the shares from the estate. The act of purchasing shares in order to qualify for business property relief after two years does not, on its own, meet condition 1. It is not therefore a notifiable arrangement under this hallmark.

As condition 1 is not met there is no need to consider condition 2.

Example 9: Gift of land where the donor continues to use that land but pays full consideration for their use

Condition 1 The gift of land which the donor continues to occupy or use would normally be a gift with reservation of benefit, but the payment by the donor of full consideration in money or money's worth for that use prevents section 102 FA 1986 applying. It would be reasonable to expect an informed observer to conclude that at least a main purpose of this arrangement is to reduce or avoid a charge to inheritance tax as a gift with reservation of benefit. As there is also no pre-owned assets income tax charge under Schedule 15 Finance Act 2004, this arrangement meets condition 1(c).

Condition 2 Even though condition 1 is met, the gift of land followed by payment of full consideration for use of that land would not, on its own, be regarded as contrived or abnormal, or involving contrived or abnormal steps. Sale and leaseback arrangements are not unusual in either the commercial world or for individuals (equity release).

Example 10: Gift of an undivided share of property which is subsequently used by both the donor and donee

Condition 1 The gift of land from which the donor continues to enjoy the benefit of occupation would be a gift with reservation of benefit, but where the donee has taken up possession and enjoyment of the property by occupying the property with the donor, section 102B Finance Act 1986 prevents this being a gift with reservation of benefit. There is no pre-owned assets income tax charge under Schedule 15 Finance Act 2004. Depending on all the relevant circumstances it is likely that an informed observer would conclude that obtaining the inheritance tax advantage was the main reason, or one of the main reasons for the arrangements. It would therefore be reasonable to expect an informed observer to conclude that condition 1(c) was met.

Condition 2 If condition 1 was met, the gift of a share in land followed by the donee occupying that land with the donor could not be said to be contrived or abnormal. The analysis might be different where the donor only retained a very small proportion of the property in comparison to their level of occupation.

Example 11: A non-UK domiciled individual who is not UK resident transfers funds from a sterling denominated UK bank account into a US dollar denominated UK bank account, so that the bank account is left out of account under section 157 IHTA 1984

Condition 1 The transfer reduces the value of the person's estate that will be subject to inheritance tax on death, as the US dollar account will be ignored at that time. But the account remains part of the person's estate, so there is no actual reduction in the value of that person's estate and condition 1(d) is not met.

As condition 1 is not met there is no need to consider condition 2.

Example 12: A non-UK domiciled individual transfers non-UK situs property into a trust just before they become deemed domiciled in the UK. The individual can benefit from the trust

Condition 1 The transfer reduces the value of the person's estate, but this reduction does not give rise to a chargeable transfer or potentially exempt transfer due to section 3(2) IHTA 1984. It is likely that an informed observer would conclude that obtaining the inheritance tax advantage was the main reason, or one of the main reasons for the arrangements, so condition 1(d) is met.

Condition 2 A transfer into a discretionary trust, on its own, is not contrived or abnormal. Although this arrangement is entered into to obtain an inheritance tax advantage, it is making use of the excluded property provisions. The transfer is not within condition 2 and is not a notifiable arrangement under this hallmark.

Example 13: Immediately before a ten-year anniversary a distribution is made from a relevant property settlement to reduce the charge on the subsequent ten-year anniversary

Condition 1 This arrangement meets condition 1(b) if it is reasonable to expect an informed observer to conclude that the main purpose, or one of the main purposes, of making the distribution is to reduce the charge at the ten-year anniversary. It would follow that condition 1(b) is met.

Condition 2 This arrangement does not contain any contrived or abnormal steps. The inheritance tax legislation applies a tax charge in respect of the distribution and another tax charge at the ten-year anniversary. The choice of making the distribution before the ten-year anniversary may be to achieve a lower overall inheritance tax bill, but the trustees choosing to exercise their powers to make a distribution is, on its own, neither contrived nor abnormal. It would not therefore be reasonable to expect an informed observer to conclude that condition 2 was met.

Arrangements which may not result in a reduced inheritance tax liability, but which cap the value subject to inheritance tax

Example 14: Gift and Loan Trusts/Loan Trusts

Gift and loan trusts involve the creation of a trust by a person by way of gift, followed by the person making an interest free loan to the trustees which is repayable on demand. The settlor is excluded from benefiting from the trust. Loan trusts are similar except that the trust is established by the granting of the interest free loan without the separate initial gift. The trustees invest the borrowed money. The person may or may not require repayment of some or all of the loan in their lifetime. Any part of the loan which has not been repaid by the person's death is included within their estate.

Condition 1 — The person's estate is not reduced by the granting of the loan, so condition 1(d) is not met. The arrangement does not meet any of conditions 1(a) to (c). The hoped for inheritance tax saving arises only if the value of the investment rises, but if it falls no inheritance tax saving is achieved.

As condition 1 is not met there is no need to consider condition 2.

Example 15: Loans to companies or other entities from which the lender cannot benefit

Condition 1 — The granting of a loan which is repayable on demand, or on which a commercial rate of interest is charged, does not reduce the value of the lender's estate, so condition 1(d) is not met. The granting of such a loan, without any further steps, would not meet any of conditions 1(a) to (c) either.

As condition 1 is not met there is no need to consider condition 2.

Examples of arrangements that might be notifiable

Because conditions 1 and 2 have to be evaluated taking all relevant circumstances of those particular arrangements, or that proposal for arrangements, into account, there will be some arrangements and proposals where it is difficult to be definitive about whether they are notifiable. Where arrangements include multiple steps in order to achieve the intended tax advantage however, there becomes an increased likelihood that they may be notifiable, either by reason of the IHT hallmark or because they fall within the confidentiality or premium fee hallmarks.

Example 16: Arrangement to gift shares which qualify for business property relief into trust and subsequently sell the shares back to the transferor

Condition 1 — In isolation the transfer of shares qualifying for business property relief into a trust, or the sale of trust assets by the trustees, would not meet condition 1. Where arrangements are entered into with the intention that all of these steps take place, the arrangements have the effect of placing cash into a relevant property trust, but without incurring a relevant property entry charge. As one of the main purposes of these arrangements is to reduce or avoid a relevant property entry charge it would be reasonable to expect an informed observer to conclude that condition 1(a) is met.

This can be contrasted to a situation where, for example, family company shares are transferred into trust for succession planning purposes, at which time there is no intention of the trustees selling those shares. If the trustees later took an independent decision to sell the shares it is unlikely that an informed observer would conclude these separate steps form part of a single overall arrangement, or to conclude that condition 1(a) was met.

Condition 2 — It would not normally be possible to transfer cash into a relevant property trust without incurring a relevant property entry charge, which is what has been achieved. To achieve this outcome and to gain this tax advantage, contrived steps are necessary, that is the transfer or shares qualifying for relief followed by their sale back to the transferor rather than the simple transfer of cash which would be the non-contrived way of achieving the same result. Without these contrived steps the tax advantage would not arise. It would therefore be reasonable to expect an informed observer to conclude, considering the arrangements as a whole, that condition 2 was met.

Examples of notifiable arrangements

Where new proposals for arrangements involve contrived or abnormal steps in order to obtain the inheritance tax advantages set out in condition 1 these proposals will be notifiable.

As explained in the introduction, the "grandfathering" provisions in the 2011 regulations cease to apply from 1 April 2018. This means that arrangements which would have previously been excepted from disclosure will be notifiable if the two conditions in the new hallmark are met.

Example 17: Creation of a reversionary lease

A person owning a freehold grants a lease to a trust or to their children. The lease starts in 21 years' time, longer than the person expects to survive. The person continues to live in the property until the sub-lease begins.

Condition 1	The arrangements avoid or reduce a charge to inheritance tax arising from the application of the gift with reservation of benefit rules. The person continues to benefit from the property, but the whole value of the property is no longer in the estate. If, in addition, no charge arises under Schedule 15 Finance Act 2004, it would be reasonable to expect an informed observer to conclude that this arrangement meets condition 1(c).
Condition 2	The creation of a lease which only takes effect several years in the future and which in the meantime allows the owner of the property to continue in occupation at no cost is a contrived and/or abnormal step. The tax advantage would not be achieved without this contrived or abnormal step. It is therefore reasonable to expect an informed observer to conclude that this arrangement meets condition 2 and is notifiable under this hallmark.

Example 18: Employee benefit trusts (EBTs)

A person owns an investment company with two part-time employees. The directors are that person and his two children. He is the sole shareholder and wishes to transfer the company to his children on his death. He creates an employee benefit trust and settles the shares on that trust. The trust excludes him and his children while he is alive and satisfies section 86 IHTA. His children can benefit after his death.

Condition 1	The arrangements result in a reduction in the value of the person's estate which does not give rise to a chargeable transfer or a potentially exempt transfer. It is reasonable to expect an informed observer to conclude that obtaining this tax advantage was the main purpose, or one of the main purposes, of these arrangements and therefore that condition 1(d) is met.
Condition 2	The use of an EBT in these circumstances is a contrived step. The purpose is to transfer the company shares to the children, but the tax advantage is obtained by using an EBT to achieve that outcome. The tax advantage could not be achieved without this contrived step. It is therefore reasonable to expect an informed observer to conclude that condition 2 is met and this arrangement is notifiable under this hallmark.

INHERITANCE TAX

The consolidated provision referred to in the destination column is the *Inheritance Tax Act* 1984 (IHTA 1984).

Finance Act 1975

Former Provision		Destination
s. 19(1)	Capital transfer tax	s. 1
s. 20(2), (3)	Transfers and chargeable transfers	s. 3(1), (2)
s. 20(4)		s. 10(1), (2), (3), 55(2)
s. 20(5)		s. 2(1), (2), 66(5), 67(3), (4), 68(4)
s. 20(6)		s. 2(1), (2)
s. 20(7)		s. 3(3), 10(3)
s. 22(1)	Transfer on death	s. 4(1)
s. 22(2)		s. 54(1), (3)
s. 22(3)		s. 54(2)
s. 22(4)		Sch. 6, para. 2
s. 22(9)		s. 4(2), 54(4)
s. 23(1), (2)	Meaning of estate	s. 5(1), (2)
s. 23(3)		s. 55(1)
s. 24(2)	Excluded property	s. 6(1)
s. 24(3)		s. 48(1)
s. 25(1)	Liability for Tax	s. 205
s. 25(2)		s. 199(1)
s. 25(3)		s. 201(1)
s. 25(4)		s. 199(2), 201(2)
s. 25(5)		s. 200(1), (3)
s. 25(6)		s. 199(4), 200(4)
s. 25(8)		s. 203(1)
s. 25(9)		s. 199(1), 201(5)
s. 25(10)		s. 199(5), 200(4), 201(6)
s. 26(1)	Exceptions from liability	s. 199(3), 200(2)
s. 26(2)		s. 202(4)
s. 26(3)		s. 206
s. 26(4)		s. 209(1)
s. 27(1)–(7)	Limitation of liability	s. 204(1)–(7)
s. 28(1)	Burden of tax	s. 211(1), (2)
s. 28(1A)		s. 211(3)
s. 28(2)		s. 213
s. 28(3)–(5)		s. 212(1)–(3)
s. 28(6), (7)		s. 214(1), (2)
s. 28(8)		s. 211(4), 212(4), 214(3)
s. 31(2)	Conditional exemption for certain objects on death	Sch. 5, para. 5(1)
s. 31(3)		Sch. 5, para. 5(3)
s. 32(1)	Charge on failure of condition of exemption	s. 207(4), Sch. 5, para. 1(1)
s. 32(2)		s. 207(5), Sch. 5, para. 1(2)
s. 32(3), (4)		Sch. 5, para. 1(3), (4)
s. 33(1)	Amount and effect of charge under section 32	Sch. 5, para. 2(1)
s. 33(3)–(5)		Sch. 5, para. 2(2)–(4)
s. 34(2)	Conditional exemption for certain buildings etc., on death	Sch. 5, para. 5(2)
s. 34(3)		s. 207(4)
s. 34(4)		s. 207(5), Sch. 5, para. 3(2)
s. 34(5), (6)		Sch. 5, para. 3(3), (4)
s. 34(8)		Sch. 5, para. 4
s. 34(9)		Sch. 5, para. 3(5)
s. 37(1)	Rate of tax	s. 7(1)
s. 37(2)		s. 7(2)
s. 37(3)		s. 7(3), Sch. 1
s. 38(1)	Valuation	s. 160
s. 39(1)	Close companies	s. 94(1)
s. 39(2)		s. 94(2)
s. 39(3)		s. 202(1)–(3)

Former Provision		Destination
Finance Act 1975		
s. 39(4)		s. 94(4)
s. 39(5)		s. 98(1)
s. 39(6)		s. 98(2), 102(1)
s. 39(6A)		s. 94(3)
s. 39(8)		s. 102(2)
s. 39(8A)		s. 96
s. 39(8B), (8C)		s. 97(1), (2)
s. 39(8D)		s. 95
s. 39(9)		s. 94(1)
s. 40	Tax chargeable in certain cases of future payments, etc.	s. 262
s. 42	Annuity purchased in conjunction with life policy	s. 263
s. 43(1)	Chargeable transfers affecting more than one property	s. 265
s. 43(2)–(5)		s. 266(1)–(4)
s. 44	Associated operations	s. 268
s. 45(1)	Persons treated as domiciled in the United Kingdom	s. 267(1), (3)
s. 45(2)		s. 267(4)
s. 46(1)–(4)	Disposition for maintenance of family	s. 11(1)–(4)
s. 46(5)		s. 11(5), 51(2)
s. 46(6)		s. 11(6)
s. 47(1A), (1AA)	Deeds of family arrangement, etc.	s. 144
s. 47(1B)		s. 17, 143
s. 47(3)		s. 17, 145
s. 47(4)		s. 93
s. 49(5)	Abolition of estate duty and transitional provisions	Sch. 6, para. 1
s. 51(1)	Interpretation	s. 47, 272
s. 51(2)		s. 3(4)
s. 51(2A)		s. 2(3)
s. 51(4)		s. 270
s. 51(5)		s. 271
Sch. 4, para. 1	Administration and collection of capital transfer tax	s. 215
Sch. 4, para. 2(1)		s. 216(1)
Sch. 4, para. 2(2)		s. 216(3)
Sch. 4, para. 2(2A)		s. 216(2)
Sch. 4, para. 2(3)		s. 216(4)
Sch. 4, para. 2(4)		s. 216(5)
Sch. 4, para. 2(5)		s. 216(6)
Sch. 4, para. 2(7)		s. 216(7)
Sch. 4, para. 3		s. 217
Sch. 4, para. 4		s. 218
Sch. 4, para. 5		s. 219
Sch. 4, para. 6		s. 221
Sch. 4, para. 7		s. 222
Sch. 4, para. 8		s. 223
Sch. 4, para. 9		s. 224
Sch. 4, para. 10(1)–(6)		s. 225(1)–(6)
Sch. 4, para. 11		s. 220
Sch. 4, para. 12		s. 226
Sch. 4, para. 13(1)		s. 227(1), (2), (3), 228(1)
Sch. 4, para. 13(2)		s. 228(2)
Sch. 4, para. 13(3)		s. 228(3)
Sch. 4, para. 13(4)		s. 227(4)
Sch. 4, para. 13(5)		s. 227(1)
Sch. 4, para. 13(6)		s. 227(3), (5), 228(1), (3)
Sch. 4, para. 13(7)		s. 269
Sch. 4, para. 13(8)		s. 228(4)
Sch. 4, para. 14(1)		s. 227(1), (2), (3)
Sch. 4, para. 14(2)		s. 227(7)
Sch. 4, para. 14(3)		s. 227(4), (6)
Sch. 4, para. 14(4)		s. 227(1)
Sch. 4, para. 14(5)		s. 227(3), (5)

Former Provision		Destination
Finance Act 1975		
Sch. 4, para. 14(6)		s. 227(7)
Sch. 4, para. 15		s. 229
Sch. 4, para. 16(1)–(3)		s. 234(1)–(3)
Sch. 4, para. 17		s. 230
Sch. 4, para. 18(1)		s. 231(1)
Sch. 4, para. 18(2)		s. 231(3)
Sch. 4, para. 19(1)		s. 233(1), (2)
Sch. 4, para. 19(2)		s. 236(1)
Sch. 4, para. 19(3)		s. 235(1)
Sch. 4, para. 19(4)		s. 233(3), 235
Sch. 4, para. 19(5)		s. 233(4)
Sch. 4, para. 19(6)		s. 230(1), 231(2)
Sch. 4, para. 20		s. 237
Sch. 4, para. 21(1)–(4)		s. 238(1)–(3)
Sch. 4, para. 22		s. 242
Sch. 4, para. 22A		s. 243
Sch. 4, para. 22B		s. 244
Sch. 4, para. 23		s. 240
Sch. 4, para. 24		s. 241
Sch. 4, para. 25		s. 239
Sch. 4, para. 26		s. 255
Sch. 4, para. 27		s. 232
Sch. 4, para. 28		s. 245
Sch. 4, para. 29		s. 246
Sch. 4, para. 30		s. 247
Sch. 4, para. 31		s. 248
Sch. 4, para. 32		s. 249
Sch. 4, para. 33		s. 250
Sch. 4, para. 34		s. 252
Sch. 4, para. 35		s. 251
Sch. 4, para. 36		s. 254(1)
Sch. 4, para. 36A		s. 254(2)
Sch. 4, para. 37		s. 253
Sch. 4, para. 39		s. 257
Sch. 4, para. 40		s. 261
Sch. 4, para. 41		s. 258
Sch. 4, para. 42(1)		s. 260
Sch. 4, para. 42(2)		s. 259
Sch. 5, para. 1(1)–(5)	Settled property	s. 43(1)–(4)
Sch. 5, para. 1(6)		s. 44(1)
Sch. 5, para. 1(7)		s. 45
Sch. 5, para. 1(8)		s. 44(2), 201(4)
Sch. 5, para. 1(9)		s. 46
Sch. 5, para. 1(10)		s. 43(5)
Sch. 5, para. 2(1)		s. 48(3)
Sch. 5, para. 2(2)		s. 267(3)
Sch. 5, para. 3(1)		s. 49(1)
Sch. 5, para. 3(2)–(4)		s. 50(1)–(4)
Sch. 5, para. 3(5), (6)		s. 50(5), (6)
Sch. 5, para. 3(7)		s. 50(4)
Sch. 5, para. 4(1)		s. 51(1)
Sch. 5, para. 4(2)		s. 52(1)
Sch. 5, para. 4(3)		s. 53(2)
Sch. 5, para. 4(4)		s. 52(2)
Sch. 5, para. 4(5)		s. 53(3), (5)
Sch. 5, para. 4(6)		s. 53(4), (5)
Sch. 5, para. 4(7)		Sch. 6, para. 2

Former Provision		Destination
Finance Act 1975		
Sch. 5, para. 4(9)		s. 52(3)
Sch. 5, para. 4(10)		s. 51(3), 52(4)
Sch. 5, para. 4(11)		s. 53(1)
Sch. 5, para. 16(1), (2)		s. 151(1), (2)
Sch. 5, para. 16(3)		s. 151(3), 210
Sch. 5, para. 16(4)		s. 151(4)
Sch. 5, para. 16(6)		s. 151(5)
Sch. 5, para. 17(1)		s. 86(1)
Sch. 5, para. 17(1A)		s. 86(2)
Sch. 5, para. 17(2)		s. 86(3)
Sch. 5, para. 17(3)		s. 86(4)
Sch. 5, para. 17(4A)		s. 86(5)
Sch. 5, para. 17A		s. 87
Sch. 5, para. 18		s. 88
Sch. 5, para. 19(1)		s. 74(1), 89(1)
Sch. 5, para. 19(2), (3)		s. 89(2), (3)
Sch. 5, para. 19(4)		s. 74(4), 89(4)
Sch. 5, para. 19A		s. 90
Sch. 5, para. 22		s. 91
Sch. 5, para. 22A(1), (2)		s. 92
Sch. 5, para. 23		Sch. 6, para. 3
Sch. 5, para. 24(1)		s. 99(1), 202(1)
Sch. 5, para. 24(2), (3)		s. 99(2), (3)
Sch. 5, para. 24(5)		s. 101(1)
Sch. 5, para. 24(5A)		s. 101(2)
Sch. 5, para. 24(6)		s. 102(1)
Sch. 6, para. 1(1), (2)	Exempt transfers	s. 18(1), (2)
Sch. 6, para. 2(1), (2), (3)		s. 19(1)–(4)
Sch. 6, para. 4(1), (2)		s. 20(1), (2)
Sch. 6, para. 5(1)–(3)		s. 21(1)–(4)
Sch. 6, para. 6		s. 22(1)–(5)
Sch. 6, para. 8		s. 19(5), 20(3), 21(5), 22(6), 94(5)
Sch. 6, para. 10(1)		s. 23(1)
Sch. 6, para. 10(3)		s. 23(6)
Sch. 6, para. 11(1), (2)		s. 24(1), (2)
Sch. 6, para. 12		s. 25(1), Sch. 3
Sch. 6, para. 13(1)–(6)		s. 26(1)–(6)
Sch. 6, para. 13(7)		s. 26(8), (9), 76(2)
Sch. 6, para. 13(8)		s. 26(8), (9)
Sch. 6, para. 15(1), (2)		s. 18(3), 23(2), 24(3), 25(2), 26(7)
Sch. 6, para. 15(2A)		s. 56(1)
Sch. 6, para. 15(3)(a)		s. 23(2), 24(3), 25(2), 26(7)
Sch. 6, para. 15(3)(b)		s. 23(3), 24(3), 25(2), 26(7)
Sch. 6, para. 15(3)(ba)		s. 56(3)
Sch. 6, para. 15(3)(bb)		s. 23(4), 24(3), 25(2), 26(7)
Sch. 6, para. 15(3)(bc)		s. 23(4), 24(3), 25(2), 26(7)
Sch. 6, para. 15(3)(c)		s. 23(5), 24(3), 25(2), 26(7)
Sch. 6, para. 15(4)		s. 23(2), (3), (4), 24(3), 25(2), 26(7)
Sch. 6, para. 15(4A)		s. 56(2)

Former Provision		Destination
Finance Act 1975		
Sch. 6, para. 15(4B)		s. 56(3), (4)
Sch. 6, para. 15(5)		s. 18(4), 23(6), 24(4), 25(2), 26(7)
Sch. 6, para. 16		s. 36
Sch. 6, para. 17		s. 37(1)
Sch. 6, para. 18		s. 37(2)
Sch. 6, para. 19(1)–(3)		s. 38(1)–(3)
Sch. 6, para. 19(3A)		s. 38(4)
Sch. 6, para. 19(3B)		s. 38(5)
Sch. 6, para. 19(4)		s. 38(6)
Sch. 6, para. 20		s. 39
Sch. 6, para. 21		s. 40
Sch. 6, para. 22		s. 41
Sch. 6, para. 22A(1), (2), (4)		s. 42(4)
Sch. 6, para. 23(1)–(3)		s. 42(1)–(3)
Sch. 7, para. 1(1), (2)	Miscellaneous exemptions and reliefs	s. 154(1), (2)
Sch. 7, para. 2		s. 152
Sch. 7, para. 3(1)		s. 6(2), 48(4)
Sch. 7, para. 3(2)		s. 48(4)
Sch. 7, para. 3(2A)		s. 48(5)
Sch. 7, para. 3(2AA)		s. 48(6)
Sch. 7, para. 3(3)		s. 267(2)
Sch. 7, para. 3(4)		s. 48(7)
Sch. 7, para. 4		s. 153
Sch. 7, para. 5(1)		s. 6(3)
Sch. 7, para. 5(2)		s. 267(2)
Sch. 7, para. 6(1)		s. 6(4), 155(1)
Sch. 7, para. 6(2)		s. 155(1)
Sch. 7, para. 6(3)–(7)		s. 155(2)–(6)
Sch. 7, para. 6(8), (9)		s. 155(7)
Sch. 7, para. 7(1)–(5)		s. 158(1)–(5)
Sch. 7, para. 7(6)		s. 158(6), 267(2)
Sch. 7, para. 8		s. 159
Sch. 9, para. 1(1)	Relief for woodlands	s. 125(1), (2)
Sch. 9, para. 1(2)		s. 125(3)
Sch. 9, para. 2(1)		s. 126(1)
Sch. 9, para. 2(2)		s. 208
Sch. 9, para. 2(3), (4)		s. 126(2), (3)
Sch. 9, para. 3(1)		s. 127(1), 128
Sch. 9, para. 3(2)		s. 127(2)
Sch. 9, para. 4		s. 129
Sch. 9, para. 5(1)		s. 125(1)
Sch. 9, para. 6		s. 130
Sch. 10, para. 1(1)	Valuation	s. 5(3)
Sch. 10, para. 1(2)		s. 5(4), 162(3)
Sch. 10, para. 1(3)		s. 5(5)
Sch. 10, para. 1(4)		s. 162(2)
Sch. 10, para. 1(5)		s. 162(1)
Sch. 10, para. 2		s. 162(4)
Sch. 10, para. 3		s. 162(5)
Sch. 10, para. 4(1)		s. 165(1)
Sch. 10, para. 4(2)		s. 165(2)

Former Provision		Destination
Finance Act 1975		
Sch. 10, para. 5		s. 163
Sch. 10, para. 6		s. 164
Sch. 10, para. 7		s. 161
Sch. 10, para. 8		s. 170
Sch. 10, para. 9(1)(a)		s. 171(1)
Sch. 10, para. 9(1)(b)		s. 172
Sch. 10, para. 9(1)(c)		s. 175
Sch. 10, para. 9(1)(d)		s. 173
Sch. 10, para. 9(1)(e)		s. 174(1)
Sch. 10, para. 9(1)(f)		s. 174(1)
Sch. 10, para. 9(2)		s. 171(2)
Sch. 10, para. 9(2A)		s. 174(2)
Sch. 10, para. 9A		s. 176
Sch. 10, para. 10		s. 166
Sch. 10, para. 11(1)		s. 167(1)
Sch. 10, para. 12		s. 169
Sch. 10, para. 13		s. 168
Sch. 10, para. 14(1)		s. 178(1)
Sch. 10, para. 14(2)		s. 178(3)
Sch. 10, para. 15		s. 179(1)
Sch. 10, para. 16		s. 179(2)
Sch. 10, para. 17		s. 180(1)
Sch. 10, para. 18(1)		s. 180(2)
Sch. 10, para. 18(2)		s. 180(3), 185(3)
Sch. 10, para. 19		s. 178(4)
Sch. 10, para. 20		s. 179(3)
Sch. 10, para. 21		s. 178(5)
Sch. 10, para. 22		s. 189
Sch. 10, para. 23		s. 186
Sch. 10, para. 24		s. 184
Sch. 10, para. 25		s. 181
Sch. 10, para. 26		s. 182
Sch. 10, para. 27		s. 183
Sch. 10, para. 28		s. 185
Sch. 10, para. 29		s. 187
Sch. 10, para. 30		s. 188
Sch. 10, para. 31(1)		s. 190(1)
Sch. 10, para. 31(2)		s. 190(3)
Sch. 10, para. 32(1)–(3)		s. 191
Sch. 10, para. 32(4)		s. 190(2)
Sch. 10, para. 33		s. 193
Sch. 10, para. 34		s. 194
Sch. 10, para. 35		s. 195
Sch. 10, para. 36		s. 196
Sch. 10, para. 37		s. 192
Sch. 10, para. 38		s. 197
Sch. 10, para. 39		s. 190(4)
Sch. 10, para. 40		s. 198
Sch. 12, para. 1	Consequential amendments	Sch. 6, para. 1

Finance Act 1976

s. 75	Relief for woodlands	s. 130(2)
s. 76(1)–(4)	Conditionally exempt transfers	s. 30
s. 77	Designation and undertakings	s. 31
s. 78(1)	Chargeable events	s. 32(1)
s. 78(2)		s. 32(2), 207(1)
s. 78(3)		s. 32(3), 207(1), (2)
s. 78(4)–(7)		s. 32(4)–(7)
s. 79(1)	Amount of charge under s. 78	s. 33(1)

Former Provision		Destination
Finance Act 1975		
s. 79(3), (4)		s. 33(3), (4)
s. 79(7)		s. 33(7)
s. 80(1)–(4)	Reinstatement of transferor's cumulative total	s. 34(1)–(4)
s. 81(1)–(3)	Conditionally exempt distributions	s. 78(1)–(3)
s. 81(4)		s. 78(6)
s. 82(1)–(5)	Exemption from periodic charge	s. 79(1)–(5)
s. 82(6)		s. 63, 79(6)
s. 82(7)		s. 79(7)
s. 82(8)		s. 207(3)
s. 82(9), (10)		s. 79(8), (9)
s. 82(11)		s. 61(1)
s. 82A(1)–(3)	Relevant person; and appropriate Table	s. 33(5), 78(3)
s. 82A(4)		s. 33(6), 78(3)
s. 82A(5)		s. 33(2), 78(4)
s. 82A(6)		s. 78(5)
s. 82A(7)		s. 61(1), 78(4)
s. 83(2)	Transfers on or before 6 April 1976	Sch. 5, para. 2(2), 4, 6
s. 83(3)		s. 35(2)
s. 83(3A)		s. 78(3), Sch. 6, para. 4(2)
s. 83(4)		s. 35(3), 79(10)
s. 83(5)		s. 233(1)
s. 83(6)		Sch. 6, para. 4(1)
s. 83(7)		Sch. 6, para. 4(2), (3)
s. 83(8), (9)		Sch. 6, para. 4(4), (5)
s. 86(1)–(4)	Mutual transfers; exemption for donee's gift	s. 148(1)–(4)
s. 86(6)		s. 148(5)
s. 86(7)		s. 167(2)
s. 87(1)–(5A)	Mutual transfers: relief for donor's gift	s. 149(1)–(6)
s. 87(5B)		s. 167(2)
s. 87(6)		s. 149(7)
s. 87(7)		s. 236(3)
s. 87(8), (9)		s. 149(8), (9)
s. 88(1), (2)	Voidable transfers	s. 150
s. 88(3)		s. 236(3)
s. 89(1)–(5)	Dispositions allowable for income tax or conferring retirement benefits	s. 12
s. 90(1)	Dispositions on trust for benefit of employees	s. 13(1)
s. 90(3)–(5)		s. 13(2)–(5)
s. 91(1), (2)	Waiver of remuneration	s. 14
s. 92(1)	Waiver of dividends	s. 15
s. 99(1)	Transfers within three years before death	s. 131(1)
s. 99(2), (3)		s. 131(2)
s. 99(4)		s. 132(1)
s. 99(5)		s. 140(2)
s. 99(6)		s. 131(3)
s. 99(7)		s. 132(2)
s. 104	Sales of certain securities within twelve months after a death	s. 178(2)
s. 114	Transfers reported late	s. 264
s. 117(1)	Modifications of exemptions for loans	s. 29(1), 56(6)
s. 117(2)–(5)		s. 29(2)–(5)
s. 117(6)		s. 29(2), (5), 56(6)
s. 118(2), (3)	Close companies	s. 100
s. 119	Liability for tax in respect of transfer by spouse	s. 203
s. 122(1)–(7A)	Inheritance (Provision for Family and Dependants) Act 1975	s. 146(1)–(8)
s. 122(8)		s. 236(2), (3)
s. 122(8A)		s. 146(9), 236(2)
s. 123(1)	Legitim	s. 147(1)
s. 123(2)		s. 147(2), 236(4)
s. 123(3)		s. 147(3)
s. 123(4)		s. 147(4), 236(4)
s. 123(5)		s. 209(2), (3)

Former Provision		Destination
Finance Act 1975		
s. 123(6)		s. 17
s. 123(7)–(11)		s. 147(5)–(9)
Sch. 10, para. 1	Relief for business property	s. 103(1)
Sch. 10, para. 2		s. 104
Sch. 10, para. 3(1)		s. 103(3), 105(1)
Sch. 10, para. 3(1A)		s. 105(2)
Sch. 10, para. 3(2), (3)		s. 105(3), (4)
Sch. 10, para. 3(4)		s. 113
Sch. 10, para. 3(5)		s. 105(5)
Sch. 10, para. 3(6)		s. 105(6)
Sch. 10, para. 4(1)		s. 106, 107(1)
Sch. 10, para. 4(2), (3)		s. 107(2), (3)
Sch. 10, para. 4(4)		s. 108
Sch. 10, para. 4(5)		s. 107(4)
Sch. 10, para. 5		s. 109
Sch. 10, para. 6		s. 110
Sch. 10, para. 7		s. 111
Sch. 10, para. 8		s. 112
Sch. 10, para. 10		s. 114(1)
Sch. 10, para. 11		s. 114(2)
Sch. 10, para. 13(1)		s. 103(2)
Sch. 10, para. 13(2)		s. 269
Sch. 12, para. 1	Transfers within three years before death	s. 140(1)
Sch. 12, para. 2		s. 133
Sch. 12, para. 3		s. 134
Sch. 12, para. 4		s. 135
Sch. 12, para. 5		s. 136
Sch. 12, para. 6		s. 137
Sch. 12, para. 7		s. 138
Sch. 12, para. 8		s. 139(1)–(3)
Sch. 12, para. 9		s. 139(4)
Sch. 14, para. 20	Settled property	s. 201(3)

Finance Act 1978

s. 66(1), (2)	Definition of control of company	s. 269(4)
s. 67(1)–(6)	Employee trusts	s. 28
s. 68(1)	Alteration of dispositions taking effect on death	s. 17, 142(1)
s. 68(2), (3)		s. 142(2), (3)
s. 68(4)		s. 142(4), (7)
s. 68(5)		s. 142(5), (6)
s. 68(6)		s. 239(4)
s. 69(1)	Sales of interests under settlements	s. 54(3)
s. 69(4)		s. 56(2)
s. 69(5)		s. 56(3)
s. 69(6)		s. 53(6), 54(3), 56(5)
s. 69(7)		s. 49(2)
s. 69(8)		s. 53(7), (8), 56(7), (8)

The Capital Transfer Tax (Northern Ireland Consequential Amendment) Order 1979 (SI 1979/927)

(SI 1979/927)	s. 146(9), 236(2)

Administration of Estates (Northern Ireland) Order 1979 (SI 1979/1575)

(SI 1979/1575)	s. 257(3)

Former Provision		Destination
	Finance Act 1980	
s. 85(3)	Reduction of tax	s. 9
s. 94(1)–(3)	Delivery of accounts	s. 256(1)–(3)
s. 94(9)		s. 256(4)
Sch. 15, para. 1–7	Reduction of capital transfer tax: transitional provisions	Sch. 2, para. 1–7
	Finance Act 1981	
s. 94(3)–(6)	Exemptions	s. 57(1)–(4)
s. 97(1), (2)	Grant of tenancies of agricultural property	s. 16
s. 98(1)	Scottish agricultural leases: fixed terms	s. 177(1), (3)
s. 101(1)–(7)	Relief for successive charges	s. 141
Sch. 14, para. 1(1)–(3)	Relief for agricultural property	s. 115(1)–(3)
Sch. 14, para. 1(4)		s. 115(5)
Sch. 14, para. 2		s. 116
Sch. 14, para. 3		s. 117
Sch. 14, para. 4		s. 118
Sch. 14, para. 5		s. 119
Sch. 14, para. 6		s. 120(2)
Sch. 14, para. 7		s. 120(1)
Sch. 14, para. 8		s. 121
Sch. 14, para. 9		s. 122(1), (2)
Sch. 14, para. 10		s. 122(3)
Sch. 14, para. 11		s. 123(1)
Sch. 14, para. 12		s. 123(2)–(4)
Sch. 14, para. 13		s. 123(5)
Sch. 14, para. 14		s. 124
Sch. 14, para. 15		s. 269
	Finance Act 1982	
s. 91(1)–(4)	Indexation of rate bands	s. 8
s. 91(5)		s. 9
s. 93(1)	Maintenance funds: Treasury directions	Sch. 4, para. 1(1)
s. 93(2)		Sch. 4, para. 2(1)
s. 93(3)		Sch. 4, para. 3(1)
s. 93(4), (5)		Sch. 4, para. 4
s. 93(6)–(8)		Sch. 4, para. 5–7
s. 93(9)		Sch. 4, para. 1(2)
s. 94(1)	Provisions supplementary to section 93	Sch. 4, para. 2(2), (3)
s. 94(2)–(4)		Sch. 4, para. 3(2)–(4)
s. 94(5)		Sch. 4, para. 1(3)
s. 94(6)		Sch. 4, para. 3(5)
s. 95(1)	Maintenance funds: exempt tranfers	s. 27, 57(5)
s. 95(2)		s. 27, 56(1), (3), (4)
s. 95(3)		s. 36
s. 96(1)–(5)	Non-residents' bank accounts	s. 157
s. 97(1)	Scottish agricultural leases	s. 177(2), (3)
s. 97(2)		s. 177(4)
s. 100	Apsley House	s. 156
s. 102(1), (2)	Relevant property	s. 58(1), (2)
s. 103	Qualifying interest in possession	s. 59
s. 104	Commencement of settlement	s. 60
s. 105	Ten-year anniversary	s. 61
s. 106	Related settlements	s. 62
s. 107	Charge at ten-year anniversary	s. 64
s. 108(1)–(7)	Charge at other times	s. 65(1)–(7)
s. 108(8)		s. 65(8), 267(3)
s. 108(9)		s. 65(9)
s. 109(1)–(5)	Rate of ten-yearly charge	s. 66(1)–(5)
s. 110(1)–(3)	Added property etc.	s. 67(1)–(3)

Former Provision		Destination
Finance Act 1982		
s. 110(4)–(6)		s. 67(5)–(7)
s. 110(7)		s. 66(6)
s. 111	Rate before first ten-year anniversary	s. 68(1)–(5)
s. 112	Rate between ten-year anniversaries	s. 69
s. 113	Property leaving temporary charitable trusts	s. 70
s. 114	Accumulation and maintenance trusts	s. 71
s. 115	Property becoming subject to employee trusts	s. 75
s. 116	Property leaving employee trusts and newspaper trusts	s. 72
s. 118(1)(a)	Protective trusts and trusts for disabled persons	s. 73(1)
s. 118(1)(b)		s. 74(1)
s. 118(2)		s. 73(2), 74(2)
s. 118(3)		s. 73(3), 74(3)
s. 118(4)		s. 73(2), 74(2)
s. 119	Property becoming held for charitable purposes or by exempt bodies	s. 76
s. 120	Initial interest of settlor or spouse	s. 80
s. 121	Property moving between settlements	s. 81
s. 122(1)–(3)	Excluded property	s. 82
s. 122(4)		s. 267(3)
s. 123	Property becoming settled on death	s. 83
s. 124	Income applied for charitable purposes	s. 84
s. 125	Annual charges under Finance Act 1975	s. 85
s. 126(1)	Minor interpretative provisions	s. 63
s. 126(2)		s. 58(3)
Sch. 15, para. 2	Settlements commencing before 27 March 1974	s. 66(6)
Sch. 15, para. 3		s. 67(4)
Sch. 15, para. 4(1), 5		s. 68(6)
Sch. 16, para. 1	Maintenance funds for historic buildings	Sch. 4, para. 16–18
Sch. 16, para. 2–9		Sch. 4, para. 8–15

The Capital Transfer Tax (Interest on Unpaid Tax) Order 1982 (SI 1982/1585)

(SI 1982/1585)		s. 233(2)

Finance (No. 2) Act 1983

s. 9(2)	Gifts to charities	s. 29(5)
s. 10(1)	Relief for business and agricultural property	s. 104(1)
s. 10(2)		s. 116(2), (4)
s. 11(1)	Payment of tax by instalments	s. 227(1), 229
s. 11(2)		s. 228(3)
s. 13(1)	Burden of tax	s. 211(1), (2), (3)
s. 13(2)		s. 211(4), 212(4), 214(3)

Finance Act 1984

s. 96(8)	Charge to income or corporation tax of offshore income gain	s. 174(1)
s. 101	Reduction of tax	Sch. 1
s. 102(1)	Special discretionary trusts: excluded property	s. 70(7)
s. 102(2)		s. 70(8)
s. 103	Discretionary trusts: distributions made within two years of testator's death	s. 144
s. 104(1)	Property moving between settlements	s. 81(3)
s. 104(2)		s. 48(6)
s. 105(1)	Adjustment of tax	s. 240(3)
s. 106(1)	Recovery of tax	s. 243, 244
s. 106(2)		s. 254(2)
s. 107(1)	Relief for stud farms	s. 115(2), (4)
s. 107(2)		s. 169(2)
s. 107(3)		s. 16(2)
s. 127(2)	Special and General Commissioners	s. 225(7)
Sch. 9, para. 14	Deep discount securities: charge to tax	s. 174(1)
Sch. 14, para. 16	*Beneficiary's liability to tax on gains of non-resident trustees*	s. 165(3)
Sch. 21, para. 1	Capital transfer tax: pre-consolidation amendments	Sch. 6, para. 2

Former Provision	Destination
Finance Act 1984	
Sch. 21, para. 3(b)	s. 202(4)
Sch. 21, para. 4	s. 267(1)
Sch. 21, para. 5(b)	s. 272
Sch. 21, para. 6	s. 221(6)
Sch. 21, para. 7	s. 227(7)
Sch. 21, para. 10	s. 44(2)
Sch. 21, para. 11	Sch. 6, para. 2
Sch. 21, para. 12	s. 86(4)
Sch. 21, para. 13	s. 91(1)
Sch. 21, para. 14(2)	s. 99(1), 202(1)
Sch. 21, para. 14(3)	s. 101(1)
Sch. 21, para. 15	s. 153(2)
Sch. 21, para. 16	s. 5(3)
Sch. 21, para. 17	s. 163(1)
Sch. 21, para. 22	s. 236(4)
Sch. 21, para. 23	Sch. 2, para. 3, 5, 6
Sch. 21, para. 25	s. 80(1), 81, 83
Sch. 21, para. 26	s. 82(1), 84

INDEX TO INHERITANCE TAX

For a list of abbreviations used in this Index see p. xi.

IHT Indexes

For a list of abbreviations used in this Index see p. xi.

For a list of abbreviations used in this Index see p. xi.

IHT Indexes

For a list of abbreviations used in this Index see p. xi.

For a list of abbreviations used in this Index see p. xi.

For a list of abbreviations used in this Index see p. xi.

For a list of abbreviations used in this Index see p. xi.

For a list of abbreviations used in this Index see p. xi.

For a list of abbreviations used in this Index see p. xi.

For a list of abbreviations used in this Index see p. xi.

IHT Indexes

For a list of abbreviations used in this Index see p. xi.

For a list of abbreviations used in this Index see p. xi.

For a list of abbreviations used in this Index see p. xi.

For a list of abbreviations used in this Index see p. xi.

For a list of abbreviations used in this Index see p. xi.

For a list of abbreviations used in this Index see p. xi.

IHT Indexes

For a list of abbreviations used in this Index see p. xi.

For a list of abbreviations used in this Index see p. xi.

IHT Indexes

For a list of abbreviations used in this Index see p. xi.

For a list of abbreviations used in this Index see p. xi.

IHT Indexes

For a list of abbreviations used in this Index see p. xi.

For a list of abbreviations used in this Index see p. xi.

IHT Indexes

For a list of abbreviations used in this Index see p. xi.

For a list of abbreviations used in this Index see p. xi.

IHT Indexes

For a list of abbreviations used in this Index see p. xi.

IHT Indexes

For a list of abbreviations used in this Index see p. xi.

For a list of abbreviations used in this Index see p. xi.

IHT Indexes

For a list of abbreviations used in this Index see p. xi.

INHERITANCE TAX LIST OF DEFINITIONS AND MEANINGS

For a list of abbreviations used in this Index see p. xi.

IHT Indexes

IHT Indexes

PETROLEUM REVENUE TAX

Table of Contents

PRT STATUTES

Table of Contents

continued over

FINANCE ACT 1973

(1973 Chapter 51)

[*25th July 1973*]

ARRANGEMENT OF SECTIONS

PART III – INCOME TAX, CORPORATION TAX AND CAPITAL GAINS TAX

SCHEDULES

PART III – INCOME TAX, CORPORATION TAX AND CAPITAL GAINS TAX

38 Territorial extension of charge to income tax, capital gains tax and corporation tax

38 [Omitted by TIOPA 2010, s. 371 and Sch. 7, para. 7 and repealed by TIOPA 2010, s. 378 and Sch. 10, Pt. 12.]

History – Omitted by TIOPA 2010, s. 371 and Sch. 7, para. 7 and repealed by TIOPA 2010, s. 378 and Sch. 10, Pt. 12, with effect for corporation tax purposes for accounting periods ending on or after 1 April 2010, for income tax and capital gains tax purposes for the tax year 2010–11 and subsequent tax years and for petroleum revenue tax purposes for chargeable periods beginning on or after 1 July 2010.

Notes – S. 38(2) rewritten as TIOPA 2010, Sch. 7, para. 4.

SCHEDULES

SCHEDULE 15 – TERRITORIAL EXTENSION OF CHARGE TO TAX – SUPPLEMENTARY PROVISIONS

Section 38

[Omitted by TIOPA 2010, s. 371 and Sch. 7, para. 8 and repealed by TIOPA 2010, s. 378 and Sch. 10, Pt. 12.]

History – Sch. 15, para. 2 omitted (so far as it continued to have effect – see TIOPA 2010, s. 381) by FA 2011, s. 86 and Sch. 23, para. 52, with effect from 1 April 2012, subject to transitional provisions in FA 2011, Sch. 23, para. 65.
Omitted by TIOPA 2010, s. 371 and Sch. 7, para. 8 and repealed by TIOPA 2010, s. 378 and Sch. 10, Pt. 12, with effect for corporation tax purposes for accounting periods ending on or after 1 April 2010, for income tax and capital gains tax purposes for the tax year 2010–11 and subsequent tax years and for petroleum revenue tax purposes for chargeable periods beginning on or after 1 July 2010.

Notes – Sch. 15 rewritten as follows:
para. 2: TIOPA 2010, Sch. 7, para. 4;
para. 4(1): TIOPA 2010, Sch. 7, para. 2, 3 and 4;
para. 4(2): TIOPA 2010, Sch. 7, para. 2;
para. 4(3): TIOPA 2010, Sch. 7, para. 2;
para. 4A(1): TIOPA 2010, Sch. 7, para. 2;
para. 4A(2): TIOPA 2010, Sch. 7, para. 2;
para. 5: TIOPA 2010, Sch. 7, para. 2 and 3;
para. 6: TIOPA 2010, Sch. 7, para. 2;
para. 7: TIOPA 2010, Sch. 7, para. 3;
para. 7A(1): TIOPA 2010, Sch. 7, para. 3;
para. 7A(2): TIOPA 2010, Sch. 7, para. 3;
para. 7A(3): TIOPA 2010, Sch. 7, para. 2 and 3;
para. 7A(4): TIOPA 2010, Sch. 7, para. 3;
para. 8: TIOPA 2010, Sch. 7, para. 3;
para. 8A(1): TIOPA 2010, Sch. 7, para. 2 and 3;
para. 8A(2): TIOPA 2010, Sch. 7, para. 4;
para. 8A(3): TIOPA 2010, Sch. 7, para. 2;
para. 8A(4): TIOPA 2010, Sch. 7, para. 2 and 3.

OIL TAXATION ACT 1975

(1975 Chapter 22)

[*8th May 1975*]

ARRANGEMENT OF SECTIONS

PART I – PETROLEUM REVENUE TAX

PART III – MISCELLANEOUS AND GENERAL

SCHEDULES

PART I – PETROLEUM REVENUE TAX

Cross references – FA 1980, Sch. 17: to be construed as one with OTA 1975, Pt. 1 (FA 1980, Sch. 17, para. 2) in relation to a transfer of any interest in an oil field, by a participator, after 1 August 1980.

FA 1993, s. 185: petroleum revenue tax not charged in respect of profits from oil won from a field granted development consent on or after 16 March 1993 (a “non-taxable field”) or from tariff receipts or disposal receipts attributable to such a field.

FA 1999, s. 95–97: construed as one with OTA 1975, Pt. 1 (FA 1999, s. 97(7)), generally in relation to disposals of assets on or after 9 March 1999 (FA 1999, s. 97(9), (10)).

FA 2001, s. 102(5)–(10) construed as one with Pt. I of OTA 1975, by virtue of FA 2001, s. 102(11) which came into force on 11 May 2001.

FA 2001, Sch. 32 construed as one with Pt. I of OTA 1975, by virtue of FA 2001, s. 101(4) and Sch. 32, para. 11 which are deemed to have come into force on 7 March 2001.

FA 2011, Sch. 23, para. 23(b): the responsible person in relation to an oil field within the meaning of Pt. 1 is a relevant data-holder for the purposes of FA 2011, Sch. 23 (data-gathering powers).

1 *Petroleum revenue tax*

1(1) A tax, to be known as petroleum revenue tax, shall be charged in accordance with this Part of this Act in respect of profits from oil won under the authority of a licence granted under either Part I of the Petroleum Act 1998 or the Petroleum (Production) Act (Northern Ireland) 1964; and in this Part of this Act

"oil" means any substance so won or capable of being so won other than methane gas won in the course of operations for making and keeping mines safe.

1(2) For each oil field which is a taxable field the tax shall, in the case of each participator, be charged at the rate of 0 per cent on the assessable profit accruing to him in any chargeable period from that field, as reduced under section 7 of this Act by any allowable losses and under section 8 of this Act by reference to his share, if any, of the oil allowance for that period, subject however to the limit imposed in his case by section 9 of this Act.

1(3) In relation to any oil field–

(a) the **"first chargeable period"** is the period ending at the end of the critical half year (including an unlimited time prior to the beginning of that half year); and

(b) each subsequent half year is a **"chargeable period"**.

1(4) In this section–

"the critical half year", in relation to an oil field means the first half year ending after 12th November 1974 at the end of which the total amount of oil ever won and saved from the field exceeds 1,000 metric tonnes (counting 1,100 cubic metres of gas at a temperature of 15 degrees centigrade and pressure of one atmosphere as equivalent to one metric tonne);

"half year" means a period of six months ending at the end of June or December.

1(5) Schedule 1 to this Act shall have effect with respect to the determination of oil fields, and Schedule 2 to this Act shall have effect with respect to the management and collection of the tax; and this Part of this Act shall have effect subject to the further provisions in Schedule 3 to this Act and, in connection with certain gas sold to the British Gas Corporation, to section 10 of this Act.

History – In s. 1(1), the words "Part I of the Petroleum Act 1998" substituted for the words "the Petroleum (Production) Act 1934" by the Petroleum Act 1998, Sch. 4, para. 7 with effect from 15 February 1999 (SI 1999/161 art. 2).
In s. 1(2), "0" substituted for "35" by FA 2016, s. 140(1), with effect with respect to chargeable periods ending after 31 December 2015.
In s. 1(2) "35" substituted for "50" by FA 2015, s. 52(2), with effect with respect to chargeable periods ending after 31 December 2015.
S. 1(2) amended by FA 1993, s. 185(4)(a), by inserting "which is a taxable field". In s. 1(2), the rate of 50 per cent substituted for 75 per cent by FA 1993, s. 186(1), with respect to chargeable periods ending after 30 June 1993.
In s. 1(2), the words "75 per cent" substituted by FA 1982, s. 132(1), in relation to chargeable periods ending after 31 December 1982.
S. 1(4) amended by F(No. 2)A 1979, s. 21(2), in relation to chargeable periods and half years ending after 31 December 1978.

Cross references – S. 2(5)(c), s. 12(1), Sch. 3, para. 4, 7: oil which is not charged to PRT.
OTA 1975, s. 10: excluded oil.
FA 1980, s. 108; FA 1981, s. 121: gas banking schemes.
FA 1982, s. 135(1): Pt. I of this Act applies to oil won from an oil field before the date of its determination as an oil field, where such determination is made after 31 December 1981.
OTA 1983, s. 12(5): definition of "oil" extended to substance won from foreign field for purposes of charge of receipts attributable to UK use of foreign field asset and received or receivable after 30 June 1982.
OTA 1983, Sch. 1, para. 1(4): similar extension of meaning of "oil" in relation to allowable expenditure on "associated assets" used in connection with "external field".
OTA 1983, Sch. 4, para. 9: provisions of Sch. 2(1) and TMA 1970 extended to assessable profit or allowable loss of participator in foreign field.
FA 1993, s. 185(1): a "non-taxable field" is an oil field granted development consent by the Secretary of State on or after 16 March 1993, and a "taxable field" is an oil field which is not a non-taxable field.
FA 1999, s. 954)(a) and s. 97(2)(c): "the applicable rate of tax", which is used to calculate the cap of allowable expenditure in certain sale and leaseback arrangements, is equal to the rate of tax charged that is stated in s. 1(2).

2 Assessable profits and allowable losses

Notes – The text of s. 2 which follows reflects the provisions of s. 2 as they apply in relation to chargeable periods ending after 31 December 1993. Those amendments introduced by FA 1994, Sch. 23 do not have effect as a result of FA 1994, s. 236(2) in relation to any light gases if, before 1 January 1994, an election was made under FA 1982, s. 134 (alternative valuation of certain ethane) or FA 1986, s. 109 (alternative valuation of certain light gases) and the election applies to those gases. See the text of the History note where appropriate.

2(1) For the purposes of the tax the assessable profit or allowable loss accruing to a participator in any chargeable period from an oil field shall be computed in accordance with the following provisions of this section.

2(2) The **"assessable profit"** or **"allowable loss"** so accruing in the period is the difference (if any) between the sum of the positive amounts for the period and the sum of the negative amounts for the period; and that difference (if any) is an assessable profit if the sum of the positive amounts is greater than the sum of the negative amounts, and is otherwise an allowable loss.

2(3) For the period–

(a) the **"positive amounts"** for the purposes of this section are the following (as defined in this section), namely the gross profit (if any) accruing to the participator in the period, his licence credit (if any) for the period, and any amount to be credited to him for the period in respect of expenditure; and

(b) the **"negative amounts"** for those purposes are the following (as so defined) namely the gross loss (if any) so accruing, his licence debit (if any) for the period, and any amount to be debited to him for the period in respect of expenditure.

2(4) For the purposes of the tax (including advance petroleum revenue tax) the **"gross profit or loss"** (if any) accruing to the participator in the period is the difference (if any) between–

(a) the aggregate of the amounts mentioned in subsection (5) below; and

(b) one-half of the market value, on the last business day of the preceding chargeable period, of so much of his share of oil won from the field as he had at the end of that period either–

(i) not disposed of and not relevantly appropriated; or

(ii) disposed of but not delivered,

and the difference (if any) is a gross profit if the said aggregate is greater than one-half of the said market value, and is otherwise a gross loss.

2(5) Subject to subsections (5A) and (5B) below the amounts referred to in subsection (4)(a) above are–

(a) the price received or receivable for so much of any oil won from the field and disposed of by him crude in sales at arm's length as was delivered by him in the period (excluding oil delivered before 13th November 1974);

(b) the aggregate market value, ascertained in accordance with Schedule 3 to this Act, of so much of any oil (not being light gases) so won and disposed of by him crude otherwise than in sales at arm's length as was delivered by him in the period (excluding oil delivered before 13th November 1974);

(c) the aggregate market value, ascertained in accordance with Schedule 3 to this Act, of so much of any oil (not being light gases) so won as was relevantly appropriated by him in the period without being disposed of (excluding oil so appropriated before 13th November 1974); and

(ca) the market value, ascertained in accordance with paragraph 3A of Schedule 3 to this Act, of so much of any light gases so won and disposed of by him otherwise than in sales at arm's length as was delivered by him in the period; and

(cb) the market value, ascertained in accordance with paragraph 3A of Schedule 3 to this Act, of so much of any light gases so won as was relevantly appropriated by him in the period without being disposed of; and

(d) one-half of the market value, on the last business day of the period, of so much of his share of oil so won as he had at the end of that period either–

(i) not disposed of and not relevantly appropriated; or

(ii) disposed of but not delivered; and

(e) the excess of the nominated proceeds for that period, as defined in section 61 of the Finance Act 1987.

2(5A) In any case where oil is disposed of in a sale at arm's length and the terms of the contract are such that the seller is required to transport the oil from a place on land in the United Kingdom or another country, or from its place of extraction (where that is in the territorial sea of the United Kingdom or a designated area), for delivery at another place in or outside the United Kingdom or to meet some or all of the costs of or incidental to its transportation from and to such places then, for the purposes of this Part of this Act–

(a) the price received or receivable for the oil shall be deemed to be that for which it would have been sold, and

(b) the oil shall be deemed to be delivered at the time it would have been delivered,

if the terms of the contract did not require the seller to meet any such costs as are mentioned above but did require the oil to be delivered–

(i) in the case of oil extracted in the United Kingdom, at the place of extraction; or

(ii) in the case of oil extracted from strata in the sea bed and subsoil of the territorial sea of the United Kingdom or of a designated area, at the place in the United Kingdom or, in the case of oil first landed in another country, at the place in that or any other country at which the seller could reasonably be expected to deliver it or, if there is more than one such place, the one nearest to the place of extraction.

2(5B) The Board may by regulations make provision for the purposes of subsection (5)(a) to (c) for determining to which fields and in what proportions blended oil to which subsection (5C) applies is attributable.

2(5C) This section applies to blended oil within the meaning of section 63(1A) of the Finance Act 1987 (other than light gases) which–

(a) is not *gaseous at a temperature* of 15 degrees Centigrade and a pressure of one atmosphere, and

(b) is not normally disposed of crude by deliveries in quantities of 25,000 metric tonnes or less.

2(5D) Regulations under subsection (5B)–

(a) may apply generally or only to specified cases or circumstances,

(b) may make different provision for different cases or circumstances,

(c) may make incidental, consequential, or transitional provision,
(d) shall be made by statutory instrument, and
(e) may not be made unless a draft has been laid before and approved by resolution of the House of Commons.

2(6) The participator's **"licence debit or credit"** (if any) for the period is the difference (if any) between–
(a) the sum of the amounts mentioned in subsection (7) below; and
(b) the sum of–
(i) the amount taken into account under paragraph (a) of that subsection in computing his licence debit or credit for the preceding chargeable period; and
(ii) the amount of any royalty repaid to the participator in the period in respect of the field;

and that difference (if any) is a licence debit if the sum mentioned in paragraph (a) above is greater than the sum mentioned in paragraph (b) above, and is otherwise a licence credit.

2(7) The amounts referred to in subsection (6)(a) above are–
(a) the amount shown in the return for the period made under paragraph 2 of Schedule 2 to this Act as the amount of royalty payable for the period in respect of the participator's share of oil won from the field;
(b) the amount of royalty paid in the period in respect of that share; and
(c) any amount paid in the period in respect of any periodic payment payable to the OGA under any relevant licence otherwise than by way of royalty.

2(8) The amount (if any) to be debited or credited to the participator for the period in respect of expenditure is the sum of the amounts mentioned in subsection (9) below.

2(9) Subject to section 192 of the Finance Act 1993, the amounts referred to in subsection (8)(a) above are–
(a) [omitted by FA 2009, s. 89 and Sch. 43, para. 3(3);]
(b) the participator's share, as determined on a claim under Schedule 5 to this Act, of the aggregate of–
(i) any expenditure allowable under section 3 or 4 of this Act for the field which has been allowed on such a claim before the Board have made an assessment to tax or a determination on or in relation to him for the period in respect of the field; and
(ii) an amount equal to 35 per cent of so much of that expenditure as has been so allowed on such a claim as qualifying for supplement under this sub-paragraph by virtue of subsection (5) of the said section 3,

so far as that share has not been taken into account in any previous assessment to tax or determination;
(c) the aggregate of–
(i) any expenditure allowable in the case of the participator under section 3 or 4 of this Act which has, on a claim made by him under Schedule 6 to this Act, been allowed before the Board have made an assessment to tax or a determination on or in relation to him for the period in respect of the field; and
(ii) an amount equal to 35 per cent of so much of that expenditure as has been so allowed on such a claim as qualifying for supplement under this sub-paragraph by virtue of subsection (5) of the said section 3,

so far as that expenditure and amount have not been taken into account in any previous assessment to tax or determination;
(d) any abortive exploration expenditure allowable in the case of the participator under section 5 of this Act which on a claim made by him under Schedule 7 to this Act has been allowed under that Schedule before the Board have made an assessment to tax or a determination on or in relation to him for the period in respect of the field, so far as that expenditure has not been taken into account in any previous assessment to tax or determination; and
(e) any unrelievable field losses allowable in the case of the participator under section 6 of this Act which on a claim made by him under Schedule 8 to this Act have been allowed under that Schedule before the Board have made an assessment to tax or a determination on or in relation to him for the period in respect of the field, so far as those losses have not been taken into account in any previous assessment to tax or determination; and
(f) any exploration and appraisal expenditure allowable in the case of the participator under section 5A of this Act which, on a claim made by him under Schedule 7 to this Act, has been allowed under that Schedule before the Board have made an assessment to tax or a determination on or in relation

PRT Statutes

to him for the period in respect of the field, so far as that expenditure has not been taken into account in any previous assessment to tax or determination, and

(g) any research expenditure allowable in the case of the participator under section 5B of this Act which, on a claim made by him under Schedule 7 of this Act, has been allowed under that Schedule before the Board have made an assessment to tax or a determination on or in relation to him for the period in respect of the field, so far as that expenditure has not been taken into account in any previous assessment to tax or determination.

2(10) [Omitted by FA 2009, s. 89 and Sch. 43, para. 3(3).]

2(11) [Omitted by FA 2009, s. 89 and Sch. 43, para. 3(3).]

History – In s. 2(4)(b) the words "on the last business day" substituted for "in the last calendar month" by FA 2006, s. 146, and Sch. 18, para. 2(2), with effect in relation to oil delivered or appropriated on or after 1 July 2006, subject to provisions of FA 2006, s. 147(2)–(8).
In s. 2(5) the words "subsections (5A) and (5B)" substituted for "subsection (5A)" by FA 2006, s. 148(1), with effect from 1 July 2006.
In former s. 2(4), the words "in the last calendar month" and "at the end of that period" substituted by FA 1987, s. 62(2)(a), with respect to chargeable periods ending after 31 December 1986; and the words "For the purposes of the tax (including advance petroleum revenue tax)" inserted by FA 1982, s. 139(1), (6) and Sch. 19, para. 18, in respect of chargeable periods ending after 31 December 1982.
In s. 2(5)(d) the words "on the last business day" substituted for "in the last calendar month" by FA 2006, s. 146, and Sch. 18, para. 2(3), with effect in relation to oil delivered or appropriated on or after 1 July 2006, subject to provisions of FA 2006, s. 147(2)–(8).
In s. 2(5)(b), and (c), the words "(not being light gases)" inserted by FA 1994, s. 236 and Sch. 23, para. 1(1). See also Note at head of section.
S. 2(5)(ca) and (cb) inserted by FA 1994, s. 236 and Sch. 23, para. 1(1). See also Note at head of section.
In s. 2(5)(e) and the word "and" immediately preceding it inserted by FA 1987, s. 61(5), effective for each calendar month in a chargeable period beginning with March 1987; the words "in the last calendar month" and "at the end of that period" substituted in para. (d) by FA 1987, s. 62(2)(b), with respect to chargeable periods ending after 31 December 1986; and the words "Subject to subsection (5A) below" inserted by FA 1982, s. 133(1), with respect to chargeable periods ending after 31 December 1981.
In s. 2(5A) the words ", or from its place of extraction (where that is in the territorial sea of the United Kingdom or a designated area)," inserted by FA 2006, s. 146, and Sch. 18, para. 2(4), with effect in relation to oil delivered or appropriated on or after 1 July 2006, subject to provisions of FA 2006, s. 147(2)–(8).
In s. 2(5A), the words "did not require" substituted to the end of the subsection for the words "required the gas to be delivered as mentioned in paragraph 2(2)(b) of Schedule 3 to this Act and did not require the seller to meet any such costs as are mentioned above." by F(No. 2)A 1992, s. 74 and Sch. 15, with effect in accordance with the provisions of F(No. 2)A 1992, s. 74(5).
In s. 2(5A), the word "oil" (on everyoccasion where it occurs) substituted by FA 1994, s. 235(1)(a), (b), in relation to chargeable periods ending after 31 December 1993.
In s. 2(5A), the words "or another country for delivery at another place in or" substituted by FA 1994, s. 235(1)(c), in relation to chargeable periods ending after 31 December 1993.
In s. 2(5A)(ii), the words "or, in the case of … or any other country" inserted by FA 1994, s. 235(1)(d), in relation to chargeable periods ending after 31 December 1993.
S. 2(5A) inserted by FA 1982, s. 133(1), with respect to chargeable periods ending after 31 December 1981.
S. 2(5B) inserted by FA 2006, s. 148(2), with effect from 1 July 2006.
S. 2(5C) inserted by FA 2006, s. 148(2), with effect from 1 July 2006.
S. 2(5D) inserted by FA 2006, s. 148(2), with effect from 1 July 2006.
In s. 2(7)(c), the word "OGA" substituted for the words "Secretary of State" by SI 2016/898, reg. 4(2), with effect from 1 October 2016 (as the 21st day after being made on 10 September 2016).
S. 2(8) substituted by FA 2009, s. 89 and Sch. 43, para. 3(2), with effect in relation to chargeable periods beginning after 30 June 2009 (subject to Sch. 43, para. 4). Former s. 2(8) read as follows:
"**2(8)** The amount (if any) to be debited or credited to the participator for the period in respect of expenditure is the difference (if any) between–
(a) the sum of the amounts mentioned in subsection (9) below; and
(b) subject to subsection (10) below, any amount taken into account under paragraph (a) of the said subsection (9) in computing the assessable profit or allowable loss accruing to the participator in the last but one preceding chargeable period;
and that difference (if any) is an amount to be debited as aforesaid if the sum mentioned in paragraph (a) above is greater than the amount mentioned in paragraph (b) above, and is otherwise an amount to be credited as aforesaid."
S. 2(9)(a) omitted by FA 2009, s. 89 and Sch. 43, para. 3(3), with effect in relation to chargeable periods beginning after 30 June 2009 (subject to Sch. 43, para. 4). Former s. 2(9)(a) read as follows:
"(a) subject to subsection (11) below, an amount equal to 5 per cent of the aggregate of–
(i) the sum of the amounts which, in the participator's return under paragraph 2 of Schedule 2 to this Act for the period, are, in the case of deliveries falling within sub-paragraph (2)(a) of that paragraph, stated to be the price received for the oil, its market value as determined in accordance with Schedule 3 to this Act for each of the deliveries or (in the case of light gases) its market value as determined in accordance with paragraph 3A of that Schedule, as the case may require; and
(ii) the sum of the amounts which, in that return, are, in the case of appropriations falling within sub-paragraph (2)(b) of that paragraph, stated to be the market value of the oil as determined in accordance with Schedule 3 to this Act for each of the appropriations or (in the case of light gases) the market value as determined in accordance with paragraph 3A of that Schedule;".
In s. 2(9)(a)(i) the words "as determined in accordance with Schedule 3 to this Act for each of the deliveries" substituted for "in the calendar month in which the delivery was made" by FA 2006, s. 146, and Sch. 18, para. 2(5)(a), in relation to oil delivered or appropriated on or after 1 July 2006, subject to provisions of FA 2006, s. 147(2)–(8).
In s. 2(9)(a)(i) the words "that Schedule" substituted for "Schedule 3 to this Act" by FA 2006, s. 146, and Sch. 18, para. 2(5)(b), with effect in relation to oil delivered or appropriated on or after 1 July 2006, subject to provisions of FA 2006, s. 147(2)–(8).
In s. 2(9)(a)(i) and (ii), words which occurred before the words "in the calendar month" in both places omitted by FA 1987, s. 62(1)(a) and Sch. 16, Pt. X, effective with respect to chargeable periods ending after 31 December 1986.
In s. 2(9)(a)(i), the words "or, as the case may be" omitted by FA 1994, s. 236 and Sch. 23, para. 1(2)(a). See also Note at head of section.
In s. 2(9)(a)(i), the words "or (in the case … as the case may require" inserted by FA 1994, s. 236 and Sch. 23, para. 1(2)(b). See also Note at head of section.
In s. 2(9)(a)(ii) the words "as determined in accordance with Schedule 3 to this Act for each of the appropriations" substituted for "in the calendar month in which the appropriation was made" by FA 2006, s. 146, and Sch. 18, para. 2(6)(a), with effect in relation to oil delivered or appropriated on or after 1 July 2006, subject to provisions of FA 2006, s. 147(2)–(8).
In s. 2(9)(a)(ii) the words "that Schedule" substituted for "Schedule 3 to this Act" by FA 2006, s. 146, and Sch. 18, para. 2(6)(b), with effect in relation to oil delivered or appropriated on or after 1 July 2006, subject to provisions of FA 2006, s. 147(2)–(8).

this Act in connection with any oil field but where expenditure allowable under section 5A or section 5B of this Act has been allowed on a claim under Schedule 7 to this Act, nothing in this subsection shall prevent a claim being made for an allowance under this section in respect of the same expenditure unless the person making the claim is the participator who made the claim under that Schedule.

3(4) The expenditure allowable under this section for any oil field does not include–

(a) expenditure in respect of interest or any other pecuniary obligation incurred in obtaining a loan or any other form of credit; or

(b) the cost of acquiring any land or interest in land, other than the cost of making to the OGA any payment falling within subsection (1)(b) above; or

(c) the cost of acquiring or erecting any building or structure on land, except–

(i) a structure to be subsequently placed on the sea bed; or

(ii) a building or structure used or to be used wholly in the process of winning oil from strata in or under land or of measuring the quantity of oil won or to be won from such strata; or

(iii) a building or structure used or to be used for initial treatment or initial storage of oil; or

(iv) a building or structure used or to be used for transporting such oil as is mentioned in subsection (1)(f) above from the place where it is first landed to the place in the United Kingdom or, in the case of oil first landed in another country, to the place in that or any other country (other than the United Kingdom) at which the seller in a sale at arm's length could reasonably be expected to deliver it or, if there is more than one place at which he could reasonably be expected to deliver it, the one nearest to the place of extraction; or

(d) any expenditure wholly or partly depending on or determined by reference to the quantity, value or proceeds of, or the profits from, oil won from the field;

(e) any payment made for the purpose of obtaining a direct or indirect interest in oil won or to be won from the field, other than a payment made to the OGA; or

(f) any payment made in pursuance of a notice under section 77C of the Taxes Management Act 1970 (notice requiring licence-holder to pay unpaid tax assessed on non-UK resident);

but nothing in paragraph (e) above shall be taken to apply to a payment made by a participator in pursuance of a contract whereby expenditure incurred for any of the purposes mentioned in subsection (1) above is to be shared between that participator and any of the other participators in the field.

3(5) Subject to subsection (5A) below expenditure allowable under this section for an oil field qualifies for supplement under section 2(9)(b)(ii) or (c)(ii) of this Act if and to the extent that it is incurred for one or more of the following purposes, namely–

(a) bringing about the commencement of the winning of oil from the field or the commencement of the transporting of oil won from it to the United Kingdom or another country;

(b) ascertaining (whether before or after the determination of the field under Schedule 1 to this Act) any of the matters mentioned in subsection (1)(c) above;

(c) carrying out works for, acquiring an asset or an interest in an asset to be used for the purpose of, substantially improving the rate at which oil can be won or transported to the United Kingdom or another country from the field, or preventing or substantially reducing a decline in that rate; or

(d) providing any installation for the initial treatment or initial storage of oil won from the field;

but expenditure incurred in hiring an asset shall not so qualify unless the asset is used in carrying out works for a purpose mentioned in paragraph (a), (b) or (c) above or works for the provision of any such installation as is mentioned in paragraph (d) above.

3(5A) Where expenditure incurred in relation to an asset is incurred–

(a) in part for one of the purposes specified in subsection (5) above (or for what would be one of those purposes if section 10(2) below were disregarded), and

(b) in part for the purpose of enabling the asset to be used in a way giving rise to tariff receipts within the meaning of the Oil Taxation Act 1983,

then, to the extent that the expenditure is incurred for the purpose mentioned in paragraph (b) above, it shall be treated for the purposes of this Part of this Act as incurred for one of the purposes specified in subsection (5) above.

3(5B) Expenditure incurred by a participator in an oil field shall be taken to be incurred for the purpose mentioned in paragraph (hh) of subsection (1) above if, and only if,–

(a) it consists of fees, commission or incidental costs incurred wholly and exclusively for the purposes of obtaining an abandonment guarantee; and

(b) the abandonment guarantee is obtained in order to comply with a term of a relevant agreement relating to that field under which the participator is required to provide security (whether or not specifically in the form of an abandonment guarantee) in respect of his liabilities to contribute to field abandonment costs;

and expressions used in this subsection shall be construed in accordance with section 104 of the Finance Act 1991.

3(6) Without prejudice to any apportionment under subsections (1C) and (1D) above for the purposes of subsections (1) and (5) above other than paragraph (hh) of subsection (1) expenditure incurred partly for one or more of the purposes there mentioned and partly not shall subject to subsection (7) below be apportioned in such manner as is just and reasonable and where, in the case of oil won as mentioned in paragraph (f) of subsection (1) above, expenditure is incurred in transporting–

(a) oil first landed in the United Kingdom to a place in the United Kingdom which is not the nearest place referred to in sub-paragraph (ii) of that paragraph, or

(b) oil first landed in another country to a place in that or any other country (other than the United Kingdom) which is not the nearest place so referred to,

so much of that expenditure as does not exceed what would have been the expenditure incurred in transporting it to that nearest place shall be regarded as falling within the said paragraph (f).

3(7) In any case where–

(a) expenditure which is incurred by any person as mentioned in subsection (6) above is so incurred in connection with a long-term asset, and

(b) the long-term asset gives rise to receipts which, for the purposes of the Oil Taxation Act 1983, are tariff receipts of that person attributable to the field for which any of that expenditure is so allowable,

then, so far as relates to that field, in making in accordance with subsection (6) above any apportionment for the purposes of either or both of subsections (1) and (5) above, the whole of the relevant expenditure shall be apportioned to one or more of the purposes mentioned in that subsection or, as the case may be, those subsections.

3(8) In subsection (7) above–

(a) **"long-term asset"** means an asset whose useful life continues after the end of the claim period for which a claim is first made for an allowance in respect of expenditure incurred in connection with the asset; and

(b) **"relevant expenditure"** means that portion of the expenditure in connection with the asset which is reasonably attributable to the use of the asset which gives rise to the receipts referred to in subsection (7)(b) above.

History – In s. 3(1)(a), the word "OGA" substituted for the words "Secretary of State" by SI 2016/898, reg. 4(3), with effect from 1 October 2016 (as the 21st day after being made on 10 September 2016).

S. 3(1)(f) amended by F(No. 2)A 1992, s. 74 and Sch. 15, para. 2(1), inserting "(i)" after the words "transporting it" and substituting "or (ii) to the place … (other than the United Kingdom)". The amendments have effect in accordance with the provisions of F(No. 2) A 1992, s. 74(5).

S. 3(1)(hh), s. 3(1A)–(1D), s. 3(5B) and the references in s. 3(6) to s. 3(1C), (1D), and to s. 3(1)(hh), inserted, and s. 3(1)(i), (j) substituted for former s. 3(1)(i), by FA 1991, s. 103. In so far as these amendments relate to the insertion of s. 3(1)(hh), they have effect with respect to expenditure incurred on or after 19 March 1991 and, subject to that, they have effect with respect to expenditure incurred after 30 June 1991.

In s. 3(1), the words "subject to subsection (7) below" inserted by OTA 1983, s. 5(1)(a), with respect to expenditure incurred after 30 June 1982. S. 3(1)(f) was amended by F(No. 2)A 1979, s. 20(1), in relation to expenditure claimed after 31 December 1978.

In s. 3(1C)(b) the words "for a qualifying purpose" substituted for the words "in connection with the field" by FA 2009, s. 87 and Sch. 41, para. 1(2), with effect in relation to chargeable periods beginning after 30 June 2009.

In s. 3(1D) the words "for a qualifying purpose" substituted for the words "in connection with the field" by FA 2009, s. 87 and Sch. 41, para. 1(3), with effect in relation to chargeable periods beginning after 30 June 2009.

S. 3(1DA) inserted by FA 2009, s. 87 and Sch. 41, para. 1(4), with effect in relation to chargeable periods beginning after 30 June 2009.

In s. 3(1DB)(b), the words "the definition of "oil-related activities" in section 274 of CTA 2010" substituted for the words "section 492(1) of the Income and Corporation Taxes Act 1988" by CTA 2010, s. 1177 and Sch. 1, para. 161(2), with effect for corporation tax purposes for accounting periods ending on or after 1 April 2010, and for income tax and capital gains tax purposes for the tax year 2010–11 and subsequent tax years.

S. 3(1DB) inserted by FA 2009, s. 87 and Sch. 41, para. 1(4), with effect in relation to chargeable periods beginning after 30 June 2009.

S. 3(1DC) inserted by FA 2009, s. 87 and Sch. 41, para. 1(4), with effect in relation to chargeable periods beginning after 30 June 2009.

S. 3(1C)–(1E) substituted for former s. 3(1C) and (1D) by FA 2001, s. 102(1), which applies to expenditure incurred on or after 7 March 2001.

Former s. 3(1D) amended by FA 1993, s. 185(4)(b) by substituting "a taxable field" in both places for "an oil field".

In s. 3(2), the words "section 16 of ITTOIA 2005 or section 279 of CTA 2010 … would have so consisted if those sections" substituted for the words "subsection (1) of section 492 of the Taxes Act or by virtue of section 16 of ITTOIA 2005 consists of activities carried on by him that fall within paragraph (a) or (b) of that subsection or within the definition of **"oil-related activities"** in section 16(2) of ITTOIA 2005 or which would have so consisted if that subsection or section" and the words "(as defined by section 1119 of CTA 2010)" substituted for the words "(within the meaning of the Taxes Acts)" by CTA 2010, s. 1177 and Sch. 1, para. 161(3), with effect *for corporation tax purposes for* accounting periods ending on or after 1 April 2010, and for income tax and capital gains tax purposes for the tax year 2010–11 and subsequent tax years.

In s. 3(2) the words "under subsection (2) of section 579 of the Taxes Act or" and "that subsection or" omitted (and repealed by CTA 2009, s. 1326 and Sch. 3, Pt. 1) and the words "or section 77 of the Corporation Tax Act 2009" inserted by CTA 2009, s. 1322 and

Sch. 1, para. 314, with effect, for corporation tax purposes, for accounting periods ending on or after 1 April 2009 and, for income tax and capital gains tax purposes, for the tax year 2009–10 and subsequent years.
In s. 3(2) the words "or under section 77 of the Income Tax (Trading and Other Income) Act 2005 ("ITTOIA 2005")", "or that section", "or by virtue of section 16 of ITTOIA 2005", "or within the definition of "oil-related activities" in section 16(2) of ITTOIA 2005" and "or section" inserted and the words "less the amount of the rebate recoverable (within the meaning of that subsection)" omitted (and repealed by s. 884 and Sch. 3) by ITTOIA 2005, s. 882(1) and Sch. 1, para. 392; effective for income tax purposes for 2005–06 onwards and for corporation tax purposes for accounting periods ending after 5 April 2005 (ITTOIA 2005, s. 883(1)).
See ICTA 1988, s. 844 and Sch. 29, para. 32 for substitution of former reference to that Act in s. 3(2).
In s. 3(3), the words "or section 5B" inserted by FA 1987, Sch. 13, Pt. II, para. 2; and the words "but where expenditure allowable ... under that Schedule" inserted by FA 1983, s. 37(2) and Sch. 8, Pt. II, para. 2, with effect from 13 May 1983.
In s. 3(4)(a) and (e), the word "OGA" substituted for the words "Secretary of State" by SI 2016/898, reg. 4(3), with effect from 1 October 2016 (as the 21st day after being made on 10 September 2016).
S. 3(4)(f) substituted by TIOPA 2010, s. 371 and Sch.7, para. 10, with effect for corporation tax purposes for accounting periods ending on or after 1 April 2010, for income tax and capital gains tax purposes for the tax year 2010–11 and subsequent tax years, and for petroleum revenue tax purposes for chargeable periods beginning on or after 1 July 2010.
In s. 3(4)(c)(i), words which appeared after the word "landed" repealed by F(No. 2)A 1992, s. 74 and Sch. 15, para. 2(2)(a), s. 82 and Sch. 18, Pt. VIII. The repeal has effect in accordance with F(No. 2)A 1992, s. 74(5).
S. 3(4)(c)(iv) inserted by FA 1981, s. 119(1), in relation to any expenditure claimed after 31 December 1978; and s. 3(4)(f) and the word "or" preceding it inserted by FA 1984, s. 124(7), 128(6) and Sch. 23, Pt. XIV (which also repealed the word "or" at the end of s. 3(4)(d)).
S. 3(4)(c)(iv) amended by F(No. 2)A 1992, s. 74 and Sch. 15, para. 2(2)(b), substituting "to the place ... (other than the United Kingdom)", to have effect in accordance with F(No. 2)A 1992, s. 74(5).
In s. 3(5), the words "Subject to subsection (5A)" below inserted by OTA 1983, s. 5(1)(b), with respect to expenditure incurred after 30 June 1982.
In s. 3(5)(a) and (c), the words "or another country" inserted by F(No. 2)A 1992, s. 74 and Sch. 15, para. 2(3), to have effect in accordance with F(No. 2)A 1992, s. 74(5).
S. 3(5A), the words in s. 3(6) "subject to subsection (7) below", s. 3(7), (8) inserted by OTA 1983, s. 5, with respect to expenditure incurred after 30 June 1982.
In s. 3(6), the words "subsections (1C) and (1D)" substituted for the words "subsection (1C) or subsection (1D)" by FA 2001, s. 102(2), which applies to expenditure incurred on or after 7 March 2001.
In s. 3(6), the words " and where ... said paragraph (f)" added by F(No. 2)A 1992, s. 74 and Sch. 15, para. 2(4).

Cross references – Sch. 5, para. 2A: allowance of expenditure by participator in meeting defaulter's field abandonment expenditure under s. 3(1)(i), (j).
FA 1980, s. 109(9): fractionation expenditure incurred in chargeable periods ending after 31 December 1979.
FA 1981, s. 118(2)(a): exclusion of payment under s. 3(1)(b) from definition of "chargeable sum" and "allowable sum" paid by or to the Secretary of State.
OTA 1983, s. 3(6): any reference in OTA 1975, Pt. I to s. 4 is to be construed as including a reference to OTA 1983, s. 3, 4 and Sch. 1.
FA 1986, s. 108(1), (2): construction of references to "subsoil", "territorial sea" and "United Kingdom" on or after 1 April 1986.
FA 1987, s. 65 and Sch. 14: cross-field allowance of certain expenditure allowable under s. 3 in respect of new fields.
FA 1991, s. 62(1): expenditure incurred in obtaining abandonment guarantee (s. 3(1)(hh)) deductible in computing participator's ring fence income.
FA 1991, s. 104: interpretation – "abandonment guarantee", "relevant agreement" (s. 3(5B)), "field abandonment costs."
F(No. 2)A 1992, s. 74(3): meaning of a country other than the UK.
FA 1993, s. 185(1): a "non-taxable field" is an oil field granted development consent by the Secretary of State on or after 16 March 1993 and a "taxable field" is an oil field which is not a non-taxable field.
FA 1993, s. 185(6): treatment of allowable expenditure incurred on or after 16 March 1993 and apportionable between two or more oil fields, at least one of which is a non-taxable field.
FA 1994, s. 232(4): expenditure incurred after 30 November 1993 and before election by reference to pipe-line usage.
FA 1994, s. 234(2)(b): expenditure relief provisions and election by reference to pipe-line usage.
FA 1994, s. 234(4)(b): expenditure incurred under s. 3(1) and election by reference to pipe-line usage.
FA 1999, s. 95(2): cap on allowable expenditure associated with sale (on or after 9 March 1999) and leaseback of certain assets.

4 Allowance of expenditure on long-term assets

Notes – The text of s. 4 printed below is the modified version enacted by OTA 1983, s. 1(2) which applies with respect to expenditure incurred after 30 June 1982 in acquiring, bringing into existence or enhancing the value of a mobile asset which is not dedicated to the oil field referred to in s. 4(1). (OTA 1983, s. 13 and Sch. 5, now spent, contained transitional provisions in respect of expenditure incurred during claim periods ending not later than 31 December 1983.)

4(1) Subject to subsection (13) below, and section 1 of the Oil Taxation Act 1983, this section applies to expenditure (whether or not of a capital nature) which is incurred by a person at or before the time when he is a participator in an oil field, being expenditure incurred in acquiring, bringing into existence, or enhancing the value of an asset which is to be or is subsequently used in connection with the field and which, at the end of the first relevant claim period, is or is expected to be a long-term asset as defined in section 3(8) of the Oil Taxation Act 1983:

Provided that this section shall not apply to expenditure incurred as aforesaid in any case where the Board consider that its application to that expenditure would have only a negligible effect on the total expenditure allowable under this Part of this Act for the field and so notify the responsible person.

4(2) The following provisions of this section are subject to Schedules 4, 5 and 6 to this Act.

4(3) [Omitted by OTA 1983, s. 1(2)(b).]

4(4) [Omitted by OTA 1983, s. 1(2)(b).]

4(5) Subject to the following provisions of this section, a proportion of the expenditure shall be allowable under this section on a claim for the first relevant claim period, and that proportion is the proportion which the time during which the asset has been used in that connection in the period between the incurring of the expenditure or the asset's first use in connection with the field (whichever is later) and the end of the first relevant claim period bears to the time between the incurring of the expenditure and the date when the asset's useful life is reasonably likely to end:

PRT Statutes

Provided that, where the asset was not used for any purpose in the period between the incurring of the expenditure and the asset's first use in connection with the field, the expenditure shall for the purposes of this subsection be treated as having been incurred on the date when the asset was first used in connection with the field.

4(6) [Omitted by OTA 1983, s. 1(2)(d).]

4(7) For each claim period subsequent to the first relevant claim period and up to and including that in which use of the asset in connection with the field permanently ceases, the proportion of the expenditure allowable under this section for the relevant period shall be computed by applying the provisions of subsection (5) above with the omission of the words "on a claim" (wherever occurring) and the substitution of references to the relevant period for references to the first relevant claim period.

For the purposes of this subsection **"the relevant period"**, in relation to a claim period, means the period consisting of that claim period and each earlier claim period back to and including that in which the expenditure was incurred.

4(8) If, as computed under subsection (7) above for any claim period, the proportion of the expenditure allowable for the relevant period exceeds the amount thereof which (taking into account any previous adjustments made under the following subsection) has been allowed on claims made for earlier claim periods falling within the relevant period, the excess shall be allowable under this section on a claim for that claim period.

4(9) If, as computed under subsection (7) above for any claim period, the proportion of the expenditure allowable to the relevant period is exceeded by the amount thereof which (taking into account any previous adjustments made under this subsection) has been allowed on claims made for earlier claim periods falling within the relevant period, the total amount of expenditure allowable under this and the preceding section on a claim for the first-mentioned claim period shall be reduced by an amount equal to the excess.

4(10) Subsections (3) to (5) of section 3 of this Act shall apply for the purposes of this section as they apply for the purposes of that section; and where in accordance with subsection (9) above the total amount of the expenditure allowable under this and the preceding section on a claim for any claim period is reduced, the amount falling to be taken into account under section 2(9)(b)(ii) or (c)(ii) of this Act by reference to that expenditure shall be reduced by a proportion equal to the proportion by which the total amount of that expenditure is so reduced.

4(11) For the purposes of subsection (5) above (including that subsection as it applies under subsection (7) above) an asset which is throughout any period of time simultaneously used partly in connection with the field and partly otherwise shall be treated as being used in connection with the field for a proportion of that period equal to the proportion which the extent of its use in the period in that connection bears to the extent of its use in the period in that connection and otherwise.

4(12) For the purposes of this section–

(a) the asset is a **"brought-in asset"** if, between the time when it was acquired or brought into existence and its first use in connection with the field, the asset was used otherwise than in connection with the field; and

(b) **"the first relevant claim period"**–

(i) in the case of expenditure incurred in acquiring or bringing into existence a brought-in asset, means the claim period in which the asset was first used in connection with the field; and

(ii) in the case of any other expenditure, means the claim period in which the expenditure was incurred.

4(13) The preceding provisions of this section, and any other provisions in this Part of this Act as to which it is provided that this subsection applies, shall, with any necessary modification, apply in relation to expenditure incurred by a person in acquiring an interest in an asset, or in bringing into existence an asset in which he is to have an interest, or in enhancing the value of an asset in which he has an interest, as the provisions in question apply in relation to expenditure incurred by a person in acquiring, bringing into existence, or enhancing the value of an asset, as the case may be.

History – See the Note at the head of the section.

Cross references – FA 1980, s. 109(10): date on which fractionation expenditure treated as incurred; Sch. 17: transfer of unused relief where there is a transfer of interests in an oil field.

OTA 1983, s. 3(5)(b): "relevant claim period" for bought-in assets; and s. 3(7): extended application of s. 4(13) to OTA 1983, s. 1–3 and Sch. 1.

FA 1994, s. 234(2)(b): election by reference to pipe-line usage.

FA 1999, s. 95(2): cap on allowable expenditure associated with sale (on or after 9 March 1999) and leaseback of certain assets.

5 Allowance of abortive exploration expenditure

5(1) Subject to the following provisions of this section and Schedule 7 to this Act, the abortive exploration expenditure allowable in the case of a person who is a participator in an oil field is any expenditure (whether or not of a capital nature) incurred on or after 1st January 1960 and before 16th March 1983 which–

(a) was incurred by that person or, if that person is a company, by that company or a company associated with it in respect of the expenditure; and

(b) was incurred wholly and exclusively for the purpose of searching for oil in the United Kingdom, the territorial sea thereof or a designated area; and

(c) is not, and is unlikely to become, allowable under section 3 or 4 of this Act for any oil field,

but so that any expenditure to which subsection (2) below applies shall not be allowable under this section except to the extent that it falls by virtue of that subsection to be treated as incurred wholly and exclusively for the purpose mentioned in paragraph (b) above.

5(2) Where any person has incurred expenditure in acquiring, bringing into existence, or enhancing the value of an asset which is subsequently used by him for the purpose mentioned in paragraph (b) of subsection (1) above, then–

(a) subject to paragraph (b) below, if the useful life of the asset continues after the end of the twelve months beginning with the day on which he acquired the asset or brought it into existence, he shall be treated for the purposes of that subsection as having incurred wholly and exclusively for that purpose a fraction of that expenditure on each day after the expenditure was incurred on which the asset is used by him wholly and exclusively for that purpose, and that fraction is the fraction of which the numerator is 1 and the denominator is the number of days in the period beginning with the day on which he incurred that expenditure and ending with the day on which the asset's useful life is reasonably likely to end;

(b) if a subsequent disposal of the asset by that person otherwise than to a person connected with him gives rise to the receipt of a sum that falls to be taken into account under subsection (6) below, being a sum not less than the price which the asset might reasonably have been expected to fetch if sold in the open market at the time of the disposal, paragraph (a) above shall apply with the substitution, for the reference to the day on which the asset's useful life is reasonably likely to end, of a reference to the day on which the disposal was made.

Section 4(13) of this Act applied to the preceding provisions of this subsection.

5(2A) For the purpose only of determining under paragraph (c) of subsection (1) above whether expenditure is or is likely to become allowable for any oil field, it shall be assumed that any oil field which, apart from this subsection, would be a non-taxable field is or, as the case may be, will be a taxable field and, accordingly, that section 185(4)(e) of the Finance Act 1993 (no expenditure allowable for non-taxable fields) does not apply.

5(3) Expenditure is not allowable under this section in connection with an oil field if, or to the extent that, it has been allowed under Schedule 7 to this Act in connection with any oil field.

5(4) Subsection (4) of section 3 of this Act shall apply for the purposes of this section with the following modifications, that is to say–

(a) in paragraph (c) the words from "except" to the end of subparagraph (iii) shall be omitted;

(b) paragraph (d) shall be omitted;

(c) in paragraph (e), the reference to oil won or to be won from the field shall be read as a reference to oil won or to be won from any area whatsoever.

5(5) Paragraph 2 of Schedule 4 to this Act shall apply in relation to this section as it applies in relation to sections 3 and 4 of this Act.

5(6) Where any expenditure which would otherwise be allowable under this section gives rise to the receipt of any sum (whether or not of a capital nature) by the person who incurred the expenditure or any person connected with him, that expenditure shall for the purposes of this section be reduced by an amount equal to that sum.

5(7) For the purposes of this section–

(a) **"company"** means any body corporate;

(b) section 1122 of CTA 2010 (**"connected persons"**) shall apply; and

(c) a company which is a participator in an oil field is **"associated"** with another company in respect of expenditure incurred by the other company if–

  (i) throughout that part of the relevant period in which both were in existence, one was a 51 per cent subsidiary of the other and the other was not a 51 per cent subsidiary of any company; or

  (ii) each of them was, throughout that part of the relevant period in which it was in existence, a 51 per cent subsidiary of a third company which was not itself a 51 per cent subsidiary of any company.

5(8) For the purposes of subsection (7)(c) above–

(a) **"the relevant period"** is the period beginning immediately before the expenditure was incurred and ending with the end of whichever of the following periods ends later, that is to say–

(i) the earliest chargeable period in which the company which is a participator in the oil field in question was a participator in that field; and

(ii) the chargeable period (for that field) in which the expenditure was incurred, (or, if they are the same period, with the end of that period); and

(b) Chapter 3 of Part 24 of CTA 2010 (**"subsidiaries"**) shall apply.

History – In s. 5(1), the words "and before 16th March 1983" were inserted by FA 1983, s. 37(2) and Sch. 8, Pt. II.
S. 5(2A) inserted by FA 1994, s. 237(1), and deemed to have come into force on 27 July 1993.
S. 5(5) amended by FA 1980, s. 122 and Sch. 20, Pt. XIII, with effect from 1 August 1980.
In s. 5(7)(b), the words "section 1122 of CTA 2010" substituted for the words "section 839 of the Taxes Act" by CTA 2010, s. 1177 and Sch. 1, para. 162(2), with effect for corporation tax purposes for accounting periods ending on or after 1 April 2010, and for income tax and capital gains tax purposes for the tax year 2010–11 and subsequent tax years.
In s. 5(8)(b), the words "Chapter 3 of Part 24 of CTA 2010" substituted for the words "section 838 of the Taxes Act" by CTA 2010, s. 1177 and Sch. 1, para. 162(3), with effect for corporation tax purposes for accounting periods ending on or after 1 April 2010, and for income tax and capital gains tax purposes for the tax year 2010–11 and subsequent tax years.
See ICTA 1988, s. 844 and Sch. 29, para. 32 for substitution of former references to that Act.

Cross references – FA 1980, Sch. 17, para. 16: transfer of unused relief where there is a transfer of interests in an oil field.
FA 1983, s. 37(3) and Sch. 8, Pt. III: set-off of sums received after 15 March 1983.
OTA 1983, s. 3(6): any reference in OTA 1975, Pt. I to s. 4 is to be construed as including a reference to OTA 1983, s. 3, 4 and Sch. 1.
FA 1984, s. 113: no account to be taken of expenditure incurred before a participator's "qualifying date" in determining whether expenditure under s. 5 is allowable.
FA 1986, s. 108(1), (2): construction of references to "territorial sea" and "United Kingdom".
FA 1987, Sch. 13, Pt. III: receipts to be set off against expenditure allowable under s. 5B below.

5A Allowance of exploration and appraisal expenditure

5A(1) The exploration and appraisal expenditure which, subject to the provisions of this section and Schedule 7 to this Act, is allowable in the case of a person who is a participator in an oil field is any expenditure (whether or not of a capital nature) which–

(a) is incurred after 15th March 1983 by that person or, if that person is a company, by that company or a company associated with it in respect of the expenditure; and

(aa) either is incurred before 16th March 1993 or is incurred within the period of two years beginning on that date and is expenditure to which that person or, if that person is a company, that company or a company associated with it in respect of the expenditure, is committed immediately before that date; and

(b) is so incurred wholly and exclusively for one or more of the purposes specified in subsection (2) below; and

(c) at the time it is so incurred, does not relate to a field for which a development decision has previously been made.

5A(1A) For the purposes of subsection (1)(aa) above, in respect of expenditure incurred on or after 16th March 1993, a person is to be regarded as **"committed to that expenditure"** immediately before that date if–

(a) he has an obligation under an exploration and appraisal contract entered into before that date to incur the expenditure; or

(b) the expenditure is incurred wholly and exclusively for the same purpose as that for which the contract referred to in paragraph (a) above was entered into and is so incurred pursuant to an obligation under an exploration and appraisal contract entered into on or after 16th March 1993 and before 16th June 1993.

5A(1B) In considering whether a person has at any time such a contractual obligation as is referred to in paragraph (a) or paragraph (b) of subsection (1A) above in respect of any expenditure,

(a) if the contract contains a power (however exercisable) by virtue of which the person concerned, or a company associated with him in respect of the expenditure, is able to bring any contractual obligations to an end, he shall not be regarded as committed to any expenditure which, if the power were to be exercised, would not be incurred; and

(b) if the person concerned (or a company associated with him in respect of the expenditure) has an option (however described) which was not exercised before 16th March 1993 but the exercise of which would increase his expenditure under the contract, he shall not be regarded as committed to any expenditure which would be incurred only as a result of the exercise of the option.

5A(1C) For the purposes of subsection (1A) above a contract is an **"exploration and appraisal contract"** if it is a contract for the provision of any services or other business facilities or assets for any of the purposes specified in subsection (2) below.

5A(2) The purposes referred to in subsections (1) to (1C) above are–

(a) the purpose of searching for oil in the territorial sea of the United Kingdom or a designated area;

(b) the purpose of ascertaining the extent or characteristics of any oil-bearing area in the territorial sea of the United Kingdom or a designated area,

(c) the purpose of ascertaining what are the reserves of oil of any such oil-bearing area; and

(d) subject to subsection (3) below, the purpose of making to the OGA any payment under or for the purpose of obtaining a licence (not being a payment by way of royalty or other periodic payment).

5A(2A) Any reference in subsection (2) above to a **"designated area"** does not include a sector which, by virtue of subsection (3)(b) of section 107 of the Finance Act 1980 (transmedian fields), is deemed to be a designated area.

5A(3) Expenditure incurred for the purpose mentioned in subsection (2)(d) above is not allowable under this section unless, at the time the allowance is claimed,–

(a) the licence to which the expenditure related has expired or has been determined or revoked; or

(b) part of the licensed area has been surrendered;

and where paragraph (b) above applies only that proportion of the expenditure which corresponds to the proportion of the licensed area which has been surrendered is expenditure falling within subsection (1) above.

5A(4) Subject to subsection (5) below, subsections (2) and (4) to (8) of section 5 of this Act apply for the purposes of this section as they apply for the purposes of that section.

5A(5) In the application for the purposes of this section of the provisions of section 5 of this Act referred to in subsection (4) above,–

(a) any reference in subsection (2) of section 5 to the purpose mentioned in subsection (1)(b) of that section shall be construed as a reference to any of the purposes specified in subsection (2) of this section;

(b) the reference in subsection (2)(a) of section 5 to subsection (1) of that section shall be construed as a reference to subsection (1) of this section; and

(c) the reference in subsection (6) of section 5 to a sum received–

(i) includes a reference to a sum received, or treated by virtue of subsection (5A) below as received, from the disposal of oil won in the course of operations carried out for any of the purposes in paragraphs (a) to (c) of subsection (2) of this section; but

(ii) does not include a reference to a sum received for the assignment of any of the rights conferred by a licence or of any interest in a licensed area.

5A(5A) Subsection (5B) below applies in any case where–

(a) oil which is won as mentioned in paragraph (c)(i) of subsection (5) above is either disposed of otherwise than in sales at arm's length or appropriated to refining or to any use except for production purposes of an oil field, and

(b) if that oil had been disposed of in a sale at arm's length, then, by virtue of section 5(6) of this Act as applied by subsection (5) above, certain expenditure would have been reduced by reference to the receipt of a sum from that disposal.

5A(5B) Where this subsection applies, the oil concerned shall be treated for the purposes of subsection (5)(c)(i) above and section 5(6) of this Act as having been disposed of for a sum equal to its market value determined in accordance with Schedule 3 to this Act for the disposal or appropriation mentioned in subsection (5A)(a) above and, accordingly, for those purposes–

(a) a sum equal to that market value shall be treated as having been received from that disposal; and

(b) no account shall be taken of any sum actually received from the disposal of any of that oil.

5A(5C) In the application of Schedule 3 to this Act for the purpose of ascertaining the **"market value"** of oil as mentioned in subsection (5B) above,–

(a) [omitted by FA 2006, s. 146, and Sch. 18, para. 3(4) and repealed by s. 178 and Sch. 26, Pt. 5(1);]

(b) sub-paragraph (4) of paragraph 2 shall be omitted;

(c) any reference in paragraphs 2 and 2A to oil being relevantly appropriated shall be construed as a reference to its being appropriated as mentioned in subsection (5A)(a) above; and

(d) any reference in paragraph 2 to the notional delivery day for the actual oil shall be construed as a reference to the day on which the oil is disposed of or appropriated as mentioned in subsection (5A)(a) above.

5A(6) Expenditure is not allowable under this section in connection with an oil field if, or to the extent that, it has been allowed under Schedule 5, Schedule 6 or Schedule 7 to this Act in connection with any oil field.

5A(7) For the purposes of subsection (1)(c) above, a development decision is made when–

(a) consent for development is granted to a licensee by the OGA in respect of the whole or part of an oil field; or

(b) a programme of development is served on a licensee or approved by the OGA for the whole or part of an oil field;

and subsections (4) and (5) of section 36 of the Finance Act 1983 (meaning of development etc.) apply in relation to this subsection as they apply in relation to subsections (2) and (3) of that section.

5A(8) If, at the time when it is incurred, expenditure relates to an area–

(a) which is not then an oil field, but

(b) in respect of which notice of a proposed determination has previously been given under paragraph 2(a) of Schedule 1 to this Act,

that area shall be treated for the purposes of this section as having become an oil field at the time the notice was given unless, when the actual determination is made, the area is not included in an oil field.

History – S. 5A(1)(aa), (1A)–(1C), and reference to subsections (1A) to (1C) in s. 5(2), inserted by FA 1993, s. 188.
In s. 5A(2)(a), (b), the words "the territorial sea of the United Kingdom" substituted by FA 1985, s. 90(2), in respect of expenditure incurred on or after 1 April 1986.
In s. 5A(2)(d), the word "OGA" substituted for the words "Secretary of State" by SI 2016/898, reg. 4(4), with effect from 1 October 2016 (as the 21st day after being made on 10 September 2016).
S. 5A(2A) inserted by FA 1980, s. 90(3), s. 5A(5)(c)(i), (ii) substituted by FA 1980, s. 90(4), and s. 5A(5A), (5B), (5C) inserted by FA 1985, s. 90(5), in respect of expenditure incurred on or after 19 March 1985.
In s. 5A(5B) the words "determined in accordance with Schedule 3 to this Act for the disposal or appropriation mentioned" substituted for "in the calendar month in which it was disposed of or appropriated as mentioned" by FA 2006, s. 146, and Sch. 18, para. 3(2), with effect in relation to oil delivered or appropriated on or after 1 July 2006, subject to provisions of FA 2006, s. 147(2)–(8).
In s. 5A(5B), the former words "at the material time" between "its market value" and "in the calendar month" omitted by FA 1987, s. 62(1)(b) and Sch. 16, Pt. X.
S. 5A(5C)(a) omitted by FA 2006, s. 146, and Sch. 18, para. 3(4) and repealed by s. 178 and Sch. 26, Pt. 5(1), with effect in relation to oil delivered or appropriated on or after 1 July 2006, subject to provisions of FA 2006, s. 147(2)–(8).
In former s. 5A(5C)(a), "(f)" substituted by FA 1987, s. 62 and Sch. 11, para. 4.
In s. 5A(5C)(b) words "sub-paragraph (4)" substituted for "sub-paragraphs (3) and (4)" by FA 2006, s. 146, and Sch. 18, para. 3(5), with effect in relation to oil delivered or appropriated on or after 1 July 2006, subject to provisions of FA 2006, s. 147(2)–(8).
In s. 5A(5C)(b) the word "and" repealed by FA 2006 s. 178 and Sch. 26, Pt. 5(1), with effect in relation to oil delivered or appropriated on or after 1 July 2006, subject to provisions of FA 2006, s. 147(2)–(8).
S. 5A(5C)(d) inserted by FA 2006, s. 146, and Sch. 18, para. 3(6), with effect in relation to oil delivered or appropriated on or after 1 July 2006, subject to provisions of FA 2006, s. 147(2)–(8).
In s. 5A(7), the word "OGA" substituted for the words "Secretary of State" (in each place) by SI 2016/898, reg. 4(4), with effect from 1 October 2016 (as the 21st day after being made on 10September 2016).
S. 5A inserted by FA 1983, s. 37(1) and Sch. 8, Pt. I, with effect from 13 May 1983.

Cross references – OTA 1983, s. 8(3) and Sch.1, para. 6(1) (use of qualifying asset in connection with more than one oil field) and FA 1981, s. 111(1) (restriction of expenditure supplement by reference to net profit period): extended application of s. 5A(7).
FA 1984, s. 113: no account is to be taken of expenditure incurred before a participator's "qualifying date" in determining whether expenditure under this section is allowable.
FA 1986, s. 108(1), (2): construction of references to "territorial sea" and "United Kingdom".
FA 1987, s. 65(2)(d): expenditure falling within s. 5A(1) does not qualify for cross-field allowance under FA 1987, s. 65(2)(d) and Sch. 14.

5B Allowance of research expenditure

5B(1) Subject to the following provisions of this section and Schedule 7 to this Act, the research expenditure which is allowable in the case of a person who is a participator in an oil field is any expenditure (whether or not of a capital nature) which–

(a) is incurred by him on or after 17th March 1987; and

(b) at the expiry of the period of three years from the time at which it was incurred, has not become allowable under section 3 or section 4 of this Act or section 3 of the Oil Taxation Act 1983; and

(c) was not incurred for purposes relating to a particular oil field; and

(d) was not incurred wholly and exclusively for one or more of the purposes which, subject to subsection (2) below, are specified in section 5A(2) of this Act; and

(e) was incurred for the purpose of research of such a description that, if it had been incurred by the participator in relation to a particular field, it would have been allowable for that field under section 3 or section 4 of this Act or section 3 of the Oil Taxation Act 1983; and

(f) was incurred wholly or partly for United Kingdom purposes.

5B(2) For the purposes only of subsection (1)(d) above, any reference in section 5A(2) of this Act to the **"territorial sea of the United Kingdom"** shall be taken to include reference to the United Kingdom itself.

5B(3) Where expenditure falling within paragraphs (a) to (e) of subsection (1) above is incurred partly for United Kingdom purposes and partly for other purposes, only such part of the expenditure as it is just and reasonable to apportion to United Kingdom purposes shall be allowable by virtue of this section.

5B(4) In subsections (1)(f) and (3) above, **"United Kingdom purposes"** means purposes relating to the United Kingdom, the territorial sea thereof or designated areas, excluding any sector which, by virtue of subsection (3)(b) of section 107 of the Finance Act 1980 (transmedian fields), is deemed to be a designated area.

5B(5) Expenditure is not allowable under this section if, or to the extent that, it has been allowed under Schedule 5, Schedule 6 or Schedule 7 to this Act for or in connection with an oil field.

5B(6) To the extent that it is reasonable to assume that expenditure which, apart from this subsection, would be allowable under this section has been incurred for purposes relating to excluded oil, within the meaning of section 10(1) of this Act or for purposes relating to non-taxable fields, that expenditure is not allowable under this section.

5B(7) Subject to subsection (3) above, subsections (2) and (6) of section 5 of this Act apply for the purposes of this section as they apply for the purposes of that section except that–

(a) any reference in subsection (2) of section 5 to the purpose mentioned in subsection (1)(b) of that section shall be construed as a reference to the purpose referred to in subsection (1)(e) of this section;

(b) the reference in paragraph (a) of subsection (2) to subsection (1) of that section shall be construed as a reference to subsection (1) of this section; and

(c) where any expenditure falls to be apportioned under subsection (3) of this section, any receipt to which it gives rise shall be similarly apportioned in the application of subsection (6) of section 5.

5B(8) Paragraph 2 of Schedule 4 to this Act applies in relation to this section as it applies in relation to sections 3 and 4 of this Act.

History – S. 5B(6) amended by FA 1993, s. 185(4)(c) by inserting "or for purposes relating to non-taxable fields".
S. 5B inserted by FA 1987, s. 64 and Sch. 13, Pt. I.

Cross references – FA 1993, s. 185(1): a "non-taxable field" is an oil field granted development consent by the Secretary of State on or after 16 March 1993, and a "taxable field" is an oil field which is not a non-taxable field.
FA 1993, s. 185(6): treatment of allowable expenditure incurred on or after 16 March 1993 and apportionable between two or more oil fields, at least one of which is a non-taxable field.

6 Allowance of unrelievable loss from abandoned field

6(1) In the case of a participator in an oil field, an allowable unrelievable field loss is the unrelievable portion of an allowable loss falling within subsection (1B) below.

6(1A) Subsection (1) above is subject to subsections (5) to (9) below and Schedule 8 to this Act and paragraph 6 of Schedule 20B to the Finance Act 1993.

6(1B) An allowable loss falls within this subsection if–

(a) the loss accrued in any chargeable period from another field (**"the abandoned field"**),

(b) the person to whom the loss accrued is–

(i) the participator, or

(ii) if the participator is a company, a company associated with the participator in respect of the loss (see subsection (3) below),

(c) the loss accrued to that person as a participator in the abandoned field, and

(d) the winning of oil from the abandoned field has permanently ceased.

6(1C) The **"unrelievable portion"** of an allowable loss falling within subsection (1B) above is so much of that loss as cannot under the provisions of section 7 of this Act be relieved against assessable profits accruing from the abandoned field to the person to whom the loss accrued.

6(1D) Subsection (1C) above is subject to Schedule 31 to the Finance Act 2001 (determination of unrelievable portion where Parts II and III of Schedule 17 to the Finance Act 1980 did not apply to transfer of interest in abandoned field).

6(2) In determining for the purposes of this section whether an allowable loss has accrued as mentioned in subsection (1B) above from an oil field from which the winning of oil permanently ceased before the total amount of oil ever won and saved from it reached the amount by reference to which the critical half year is defined in section 1(4) of this Act, the first chargeable period for that field shall be taken to have been the period ending at the end of the half year in which the winning of oil from the field so ceased (including an unlimited time prior to the beginning of that half year).

In this subsection **"half year"** has the same meaning as in section 1 of this Act.

6(3) For the purposes of this section–

(a) **"company"** means any body corporate; and

(b) a company which is a participator in an oil field is associated with another company in respect of an allowable loss which accrued to that other company in a chargeable period from another oil field if–

(i) throughout that part of the relevant period in which both were in existence one was a 51 per cent subsidiary of the other and the other was not a 51 per cent subsidiary of any company; or

(ii) each of them was, throughout that part of the relevant period in which it was in existence, a 51 per cent subsidiary of a third company which was not itself a 51 per cent subsidiary of any company;

and in this section and Schedule 8 to this Act any reference to the **"winning of oil from an oil field permanently ceasing"** includes a reference to the permanent cessation of operations for the winning of oil from the field.

6(4) For the purposes of subsection (3)(b) above–

(a) the **"relevant period"** is the period beginning with the chargeable period in which the allowable loss accrued to the other company referred to in that paragraph and ending with the end of whichever of the following period ends later, that is to say–

(i) the earliest chargeable period in which the company which is a participator in the oil field in question was a participator in that field; and

(ii) the chargeable period in which the allowable loss accrued, (or, if they are the same period, with the end of that period); and

(b) Chapter 3 of Part 24 of CTA 2010 (subsidiaries) shall apply.

6(4A) For the purposes of this section and Schedule 8 to this Act, the winning of oil from an oil field shall not be regarded as having permanently ceased until all the oil wells in the field have been permanently abandoned.

6(5) Subsections (6) to (9) below apply if–

(a) a claim is made for the allowance of an unrelievable field loss; and

(b) the person to whom the loss accrued made a claim or election for the allowance of any expenditure unrelated to that field; and

(c) that claim or election was received by the Board on or after 29th November 1994; and

(d) the whole or a part of the expenditure to which the claim or election relates is allowed and, accordingly, falls to be taken into account under section 2(8)(a) of this Act for a chargeable period (whether beginning before or after 29th November 1994).

6(6) Subject to subsection (7) below, where this subsection applies, from the amount which, apart from this subsection, would be the amount of the unrelievable field loss referred to in paragraph (a) of subsection (5) above there shall be deducted an amount equal to so much of any expenditure unrelated to the field as is allowed on a claim or election as mentioned in paragraph (d) of that subsection.

6(7) If–

(a) claims are made for the allowance of more than one unrelievable field loss derived from the same abandoned field, and

(b) the person to whom the loss accrued is the same in respect of each of the unrelievable field losses,

subsection (6) above shall have effect as if the deduction referred to in that subsection fell to be made from the aggregate amount of those losses.

6(8) Where subsection (7) above applies, the deduction shall be set against the unrelievable field losses in the order in which the claims for the allowance of each of those losses were received by the Board.

6(9) In subsections (5) and (6) above, **"expenditure unrelated to the field"** means–

(a) expenditure allowable under any of sections 5, 5A and 5B of this Act;

(b) expenditure allowable under this section (derived from a different abandoned field); or

(c) expenditure falling within section 65 of the Finance Act 1987 which is accepted by the Board as allowable in accordance with Schedule 14 to that Act;

and, in relation to expenditure falling within section 65 of the Finance Act 1987, **"election"** means an election under Part I of Schedule 14 to that Act.

History – S. 6(1) and (1A)–(1D) substituted for former s. 6(1) and (1A) by FA 2001, s. 101(1) which is deemed to have come into force on 7 March 2001.

In former s. 6(1), the words "subsections (5) to (9) below and" added by FA 1995, s. 146(1).

In s. 6(1A) the words "paragraph 6" substituted for the words "paragraph 5" by F(No. 2)A 2017, s. 44(2), with effect from 23 November 2016.

In s. 6(1A) the words "Schedule 20B" substituted for the words "Schedule 20A" by FA 2009, s. 91 and Sch. 45, para. 3(2)(a), with effect from 21 July 2009.

In s. 6(1A) the words "and paragraph 5 of Schedule 20A to the Finance Act 1993" inserted by FA 2008, s. 107 and Sch. 33, para. 2, with effect from 21 July 2008.

Former s. 6(1A) inserted by FA 1995, s. 146(2) and (3).

In s. 6(2), the words "subsection (1B) above" substituted for the words "subsection (1) above" by FA 2001, s. 101(2) which is deemed to have come into force on 7 March 2001.

In s. 6(4)(b), the words "Chapter 3 of Part 24 of CTA 2010" substituted for the words "section 838 of the Taxes Act" by CTA 2010, s. 1177 and Sch. 1, para. 163, with effect for corporation tax purposes for accounting periods ending on or after 1 April 2010, and for income tax and capital gains tax purposes for the tax year 2010–11 and subsequent tax years.
S. 6(4A) inserted by FA 2007, s. 104(1) with effect from 1 July 2007, FA 2007, s. 104(2).
S. 6(5)–(9) inserted by FA 1995, s. 146(2) and (3).
See ICTA 1988, Sch. 29, para. 32, for substitution of former reference to that Act in s. 6(4)(b).

Cross references – FA 1984, s. 113(2): restriction on allowance of unrelievable field losses where the cessation of the winning of oil from the field falls on or after the participator's "qualifying date".
FA 1987, s. 65: cross-field allowance of certain expenditure incurred as new fields.
FA 1987, Sch. 14: elections for cross-field allowance.
FA 2001, Sch. 32, para. 5: application in place of s. 6(1C).

7 Relief for allowable losses

7(1) Where the Board have determined under Schedule 2 to this Act that an allowable loss has accrued to a participator in a chargeable period from an oil field, then, subject to the following provisions of this section, the assessable profit accruing to him from the field in any succeeding chargeable period shall be treated as reduced by the amount of that allowable loss, or by so much of that amount as cannot, under this subsection or on a claim (if made) under subsection (2) below, be relieved against the assessable profit accruing to him from the field in any earlier chargeable period.

7(2) Where the Board have determined under Schedule 2 to this Act that an allowable loss has accrued to a participator in a chargeable period from an oil field, the participator may make a claim requiring that the loss be in the first instance set against any assessable profit which accrued to him from the field in any preceding chargeable period; and the assessable profit which so accrued to him in any such period shall then be treated as reduced by the amount of the loss, or by so much of that amount as cannot be relieved under this subsection against any assessable profit accruing to him from the field in a later chargeable period.

7(3) Where–

(a) the Board have determined under Schedule 2 to this Act that an allowable loss has accrued to a participator in a chargeable period from an oil field; and

(b) the winning of oil from that field has permanently ceased,

then so much of that allowable loss as cannot under subsection (1) or (2) above be relieved against assessable profits accruing to the participator from the field shall be relieved under this subsection by treating the assessable profit accruing to him from the field in any chargeable period as reduced by the amount of the loss, or by so much of that amount as cannot be relieved under this section against the assessable profit so accruing to him in a later chargeable period.

Cross references – FA 1980, Sch. 17, para. 14, 15: transfer of loss relief where there is a transfer of interests in an oil field after 1 August 1980.

8 Oil allowance

8(1) Subject to the provisions of this section and paragraphs 10 and 11 of Schedule 3 to this Act, where a participator in an oil field would, apart from this section and section 9 of this Act, be chargeable to tax for any chargeable period on an amount (**"the said amount"**) consisting of the assessable profit accruing to him in the period from the field or that profit as reduced under section 7 of this Act by any allowable losses, then for the purpose of determining his liability, if any, to tax for that period, the said amount shall be treated as reduced or further reduced as follows, that is to say–

(a) if the said amount exceeds the cash equivalent of his share of the oil allowance for the field for that period, to an amount equal to the excess; or

(b) if the said amount does not exceed the cash equivalent of his share of that allowance, to nil.

8(2) The oil allowance for an oil field is, for each chargeable period, 250,000 metric tonnes, and shall be divided between the participators in shares proportionate to their shares of the oil won and saved from the field during the period.

8(3) For the purposes of this section the **"cash equivalent of a participator's share"** of the oil allowance for an oil field for a chargeable period is (subject to subsection (4) below) the amount given by the formula–

$$£\left(A \times \frac{B}{C}\right)$$

where–

A is the gross profit accruing to him in the period or, if a gross loss (or neither a gross profit nor a gross loss) accrues to him in the period, nil (in which case the cash equivalent itself will be nil);

B is his share of the allowance, in metric tonnes; and

C is his share, exclusive of excluded oil within the meaning of section 10 of this Act, of the oil won and saved from the field during the period, in metric tonnes.

PRT Statutes

8(4) If a participator in an oil field so elects by notice in writing given to the Board at the time when he makes his return under paragraph 2 of Schedule 2 to this Act for a chargeable period, then the cash equivalent of his share of the oil allowance for the field for that period shall be determined under subsection (3) above–

(a) to the extent that his share of that oil allowance does not exceed his share of the oil (other than gas) won and saved from the field in the period, as if–

(i) in computing the gross profit or gross loss accruing to him in the period all amounts relating to gas fell to be disregarded, and

(ii) in the definition of C, for "the oil won and saved" there were substituted "the oil (other than gas) won and saved"; and

(b) to the extent, if any, that his share of that oil allowance exceeds his share of the oil (other than gas) so won and saved, as if–

(i) in computing the gross profit or gross loss so accruing all amounts relating to oil other than gas fell to be disregarded, and

(ii) in the definition of C, for "the oil won and saved" there were substituted "the gas won and saved".

8(5) For the purposes of this section the amount of the oil allowance for an oil field utilised by a participator in any chargeable period is–

(a) if in his case a reduction is made for that period under subsection (1)(a) above, an amount in metric tonnes equal to his share of the oil allowance for the field for that period;

(b) if in his case a reduction is made for that period under subsection (1)(b) above, the amount in metric tonnes arrived at by multiplying his share of the oil allowance for the field for that period (in metric tonnes) by the fraction of which the numerator is the amount of that reduction and the denominator is the cash equivalent of his share of the said oil allowance;

(c) in any other case, nil.

8(6) The total oil allowance for an oil field shall not exceed 5 million metric tonnes, and accordingly–

(a) for each chargeable period there shall be determined the aggregate of the amounts of the oil allowance for the field utilised by the participators in that period; and

(b) as regards the earliest chargeable period such that the sum of the aggregate determined under paragraph (a) above for that period and the aggregates so determined for each earlier chargeable period would, apart from this subsection, exceed 5 million metric tonnes, the necessary restriction shall be apportioned between the participators in such manner as may be notified to the Board by the responsible person or, in default of such notification, as may be determined by the Board.

In this subsection **"the necessary restriction"** means the restriction necessary to secure that the aggregate determined under paragraph (a) above for the chargeable period to which paragraph (b) above applies will, when added to the sum of the aggregates so determined for each earlier chargeable period, produce a total of 5 million metric tonnes.

8(7) For the purpose of this section 1,100 cubic metres of oil consisting of gas at the temperature and pressure mentioned in section 1(4) of this Act shall be counted as equivalent to one metric tonne of oil other than gas.

8(8) Any reduction to be made under subsection (1) above shall be made before applying the provisions of section 9 of this Act.

History – S. 8(4)(a) and (b) substituted by SI 2009/730, art. 15(2), with effect in relation to chargeable periods ending on or after 6 April 2009.

S. 8(2), (3), (5)–(7) amended by F(No. 2)A 1979, s. 21(1), in relation to chargeable periods and half years ending after 31 December 1978.

Cross references – FA 1980, Sch. 17, para 17: restriction on transfer of oil allowance during first three chargeable periods where there is a transfer of interests in an oil field.

OTA 1983, Sch. 4, para. 9(2): reduction under s. 8(1) does not apply to assessable profit accruing to participator in foreign field for any chargeable period.

FA 1983, s. 36 increased oil allowance (s. 8(2)) to 500,000 metric tonnes, and the total oil allowance (s. 8(6)) to 10m metric tonnes, for "all relevant new fields" as defined by s. 36(2).

FA 1988, s. 138(1), (2): in relation to chargeable periods ending after 30 June 1988, the amount of the oil allowance (s. 8(2)) for every "relevant Southern Basin or onshore field" is 125,000 metric tonnes, and the total oil allowance (s. 8(6)) for every such field is 2.5m metric tonnes.

9 Limit on amount payable by participator

9(1) The tax payable by a participator in an oil field for any chargeable period to which this subsection applies shall not exceed 80 per cent of the amount (if any) by which his adjusted profit for that period (as defined in this section) exceeds 15 per cent of his accumulated capital expenditure at the end of that period (as so defined).

9(1A) Subsection (1) above applies to–

(a) any chargeable period from the first chargeable period up to and including the period which is the participator's net profit period for the field for the purposes of section 111 of the Finance Act 1981 or where section 113 of that Act applies, up to and including the earlier of the periods mentioned in subsection (2) of that section; and

(b) any subsequent chargeable period up to such number of periods as is equal to half the number of chargeable periods which are included in paragraph (a) above and in which the amount of oil won and saved from the field exceeds 1,000 metric tonnes (counting any resulting fraction of a period as a whole period)

and for the purposes of paragraph (b) above 1,100 cubic metres of gas at a temperature of 15 degrees centigrade and pressure of one atmosphere shall be counted as equivalent to one metric tonne.

9(2) The **"adjusted profit of a participator in an oil field"** for any chargeable period shall be determined as follows–

(a) there shall be ascertained–

(i) the assessable profit (without any reduction under section 7 or 8 of this Act) or allowable loss accruing to him in that period; and

(ii) the total amount taken into account under section 2(9)(b), (c), (d), (e), (f) and (g) of this Act in computing that profit or loss, excluding expenditure so taken into account under section 2(9)(b)(i) or (c)(i) which was not allowed as qualifying for supplement under section 2(9)(b)(ii) or (c)(ii);

(b) if there is a profit under paragraph (a)(i) above, the sum of that profit and the total ascertained under paragraph (a)(ii) above is his adjusted profit for the period;

(c) if there is a loss under paragraph (a)(i) above smaller than the total ascertained under paragraph (a)(ii) above, the difference is his adjusted profit for the period.

9(3) The **"accumulated capital expenditure of a participator"** in an oil field at the end of any chargeable period is the total amount of expenditure taken into account under section 2(9)(b)(i) and (c)(i) of this Act in computing the assessable profit or allowable loss accruing to him in that period and all earlier chargeable periods excluding all expenditure so taken into account which was not allowed as qualifying for supplement under section 2(9)(b)(ii) or (c)(ii).

9(4) [Omitted by FA 2009, s. 91 and Sch. 45, para. 1(3).]

History – S. 9(1A)(b) was substituted and the words following it were inserted by FA 1985, s. 91(1), with respect to any oil field in respect of which the first chargeable period ends after 30 June 1985.

In s. 9(2)(a)(ii), the words "(f) and (g)" were substituted by FA 1987, s. 64 and Sch. 13, Pt. II, para. 3. That sub-paragraph was previously amended by FA 1983, s. 37(2) and Sch. 8, Pt. II, para. 4.

S. 9(4) omitted by FA 2009, s. 91 and Sch. 45, para. 1(3), with effect in relation to chargeable periods beginning after 30 June 2009.

S. 9 substituted by FA 1981, s. 114(1), with effect whether the net profit period ends before or after the passing of that Act. Marginal heading altered by Croner-i to reflect amended content.

Cross references – FA 1980, Sch. 17, para. 18: accumulated capital expenditure where interests in oil field transferred.

FA 1981, s. 111: restriction of expenditure supplement.

FA 1981, s. 113: restriction of expenditure supplement: loss following net profit period.

OTA 1983, s. 7(6)(b): reduction of expenditure qualifying for supplement where there are disposal receipts in claim period.

FA 1987, Sch. 13, Pt. III, para. 12(3): set-off of receipts against expenditure allowable under s. 5B – excess deducted from total ascertained under s. 9(2)(a)(ii).

FA 1987, Sch. 14, para. 13 (cross-field allowance): expenditure allowed under that Schedule taken into account as an addition to total amount mentioned in s. 9(2)(a)(ii).

FA 1999, s. 95(4) and s. 97(2)(e): application of safeguard relief in chargeable periods where sale and leaseback occurs.

9A Operating expenditure incurred while section 9 applies

9A(1) Subsections (2) and (3) below apply where–

(a) operating expenditure is incurred by a participator in an oil field during a chargeable period to which section 9(1) of this Act applies ("the relevant chargeable period");

(b) a claim for the allowance of the expenditure is made under Schedule 5 or 6 for the claim period which coincides with the relevant chargeable period ("the relevant claim period"); and

(c) the claim is made more than four months after the end of the relevant claim period.

9A(2) The Board shall not allow the expenditure except to such extent (if any) as they consider necessary to secure that the participator's overall liability to tax is no greater than it would have been if the claim had been allowed before the Board had made an assessment to tax or a determination on or in relation to the participator in respect of the field for the relevant chargeable period.

9A(3) Any amounts of oil allowance which, if the claim had been allowed before the Board had made an assessment to tax or a determination on or in relation to the participator in respect of the field for the relevant chargeable period, would not have been utilised by him in that period, or any subsequent chargeable period, shall be disregarded for the purposes of section 8(6) of this Act.

9A(4) Where–

(a) the participator transfers the whole or part of his interest in the oil field to another person; and

(b) Parts II and III of Schedule 17 to the Finance Act 1980 apply to the transfer,

subsections (2) and (3) above shall have effect as if references to the participator included references to that other person.

9A(5) In this section–

"acquisition", in relation to an asset, includes acquisition of an interest in the asset;

"capital expenditure" means expenditure on the acquisition or construction of an asset which is to be used for any of the following purposes–

(a) for ascertaining the extent or characteristics of any oil-bearing area wholly or partly included in the field, or what the reserves of oil of any such oil-bearing area are;

(b) for winning oil from the field;

(c) for transporting oil won from the field, whether to a place in the United Kingdom or to a place in another country; or

(d) or the initial treatment or initial storage of oil won from the field;

"operating expenditure" means any expenditure other than capital expenditure.

9A(6) Where a claim period is a period of twelve months, this section shall have effect as if–

(a) that period were two separate claim periods of six months each;

(b) any claim for that period under Schedule 5 or 6 were two separate claims, one for each of those separate periods; and

(c) the operating expenditure to which that claim relates were apportioned between those separate periods and those separate claims in such manner as may be just and reasonable.

History – S. 9A inserted by FA 2000, s. 139(1), with effect in relation to expenditure incurred on or after 21 March 2000.

10 Modifications of Part I in connection with certain gas sold to British Gas Corporation

10(1) In computing under section 2 of this Act the gross profit or loss (if any) accruing to a participator in any chargeable period from an oil field–

(a) any oil consisting of gas sold to the British Gas Corporation under a contract made before the end of June 1975 shall be disregarded; and

(b) if at the end of that chargeable period the participator's share, exclusive of oil falling within paragraph (a) above or used for production purposes, of the total amount of oil ever won and saved from the field does not exceed 5 per cent of his share of the total amount of oil so falling which was ever so won and saved, his share of the oil won and saved from the field but not so falling shall also be disregarded;

and in the following provisions of this section any oil which falls to be disregarded under this subsection is referred to as "excluded oil".

10(2) Excluded oil shall be deemed not to be oil for the purposes of the following provisions of this Act, namely section 2(7) and (9), section 3 (except paragraphs (a) to (c) and (hh), (i) and (j) of subsection (1) and subsections (1C) and (1D) and section 4 (including, in the case of any expression used in any of those provisions which is defined elsewhere, its definition so far as it has effect for the purpose of that provision); and in computing under section 2 of this Act the licence debit or credit (if any) of a participator in an oil field for any chargeable period, any royalty repaid to him in the period in respect of excluded oil shall be disregarded.

10(3) Subsections (3A) to (3H) below apply where, in the case of any taxable field, the oil–

(a) won and saved from the field, or

(b) expected to be won and saved from the field,

includes oil falling within subsection (1)(a) above.

10(3A) Any expenditure allowable under section 3 of this Act for the field by virtue of any of paragraphs (a) to (c) of section 3(1) of this Act shall be a proportion of what it would otherwise have been.

10(3B) The proportion mentioned in subsection (3A) above is that which, according to estimates submitted to the OGA after the end of June 1975 and approved by it as reasonable, the field's original reserves of oil exclusive of oil falling within subsection (1)(a) above bear to the field's original reserves of oil inclusive of oil so falling.

10(3C) Until estimates have been submitted and approved for the purpose of subsection (3B) above, the expenditure allowable for the field under section 3 of this Act by virtue of section 3(1)(a), (b) or (c) of this Act shall be deemed to be nil.

10(3D) Any expenditure allowable under section 3 of this Act for the field by virtue of section 3(1)(hh) of this Act shall be a portion of what it would otherwise have been.

10(3E) That portion is determined in accordance with the following rules–

1. Identify the abandonment guarantee (within the meaning given by section 104 of the Finance Act 1991) on the obtaining of which the expenditure was incurred.
2. Identify the liabilities covered by the guarantee.
3. Identify which of those liabilities relate to qualifying assets.
4. Identify the portion of the expenditure that it is just and reasonable to apportion to the liabilities identified under rule 3.
5. Identify the qualifying assets to which the liabilities identified under rule 3 relate.
6. Identify the use of those qualifying assets that has been (or is expected to be) non-excluded use.
7. Assume that expenditure is incurred on the provision of those qualifying assets and identify the proportion of the hypothetical expenditure that it would be just and reasonable to apportion to the use of those assets identified under rule 6.
8. The portion mentioned in subsection (3D) above is then determined by multiplying–
   (i) the portion identified under rule 4, by
   (ii) the proportion (expressed as a fraction) identified under rule 7.

10(3F) Any expenditure allowable under section 3 of this Act for the field by virtue of section 3(1)(i) or (j) of this Act shall be a portion of what it would otherwise have been.

10(3G) That portion is determined in accordance with the following rules–

1. Identify the qualifying asset that is relevant to the incurring of the expenditure.
2. Identify the use of that qualifying asset that has been non-excluded use.
3. Assume that expenditure is incurred on the provision of that qualifying asset and identify the proportion of the hypothetical expenditure that it would be just and reasonable to apportion to the use of that asset identified under rule 2.
4. The portion mentioned in subsection (3F) above is then determined by multiplying–
   (i) the expenditure, by
   (ii) the proportion (expressed as a fraction) identified under rule 3.

10(3H) In subsections (3E) and (3G) above–

"non-excluded use" means–

(a) use in connection with the winning and saving of oil, other than excluded oil, from the field, or

(b) use giving rise to receipts that, for the purposes of the Oil Taxation Act 1983, are tariff receipts attributable to a participator in the field;

"qualifying asset" has the same meaning as it has for the purposes of the Oil Taxation Act 1983 (see section 8 of that Act).

10(4) A return made under paragraph 2 of Schedule 2 to this Act by a participator in an oil field need not, in the case of oil falling within subsection 1(a) above, state the price received or receivable for the oil.

10(5) For the purposes of this section 1,100 cubic metres of oil consisting of gas at the temperature and pressure mentioned in section 1(4) of this Act shall be counted as equivalent to one metric tonne of oil other than gas.

History – In s. 10(2), the words "subsections (1C) and (1D)" substituted for the words "subsection (1D)" by FA 2001, s. 102(3), which applies to expenditure incurred on or after 7 March 2001.
S. 10(2) and former s. 10(3) (see History note below) amended by FA 1991, s. 103(7), by substituting references to s. 3(1)(hh), (i), (j), effective in so far as the amendments relate to s. 3(1)(hh), with respect to expenditure incurred on or after 19 March 1991, and subject to that, with respect to expenditure incurred after 30 June 1991.
S. 10(3)–(3H) substituted for former s. 10(3) by FA 2001, s. 103(1), which applies to expenditure incurred on or after 7 March 2001.
In s. 10(3B), the word "OGA" substituted for the words "Secretary of State" and the word "it" substituted for the word "him" by SI 2016/898, reg. 4(5), with effect from 1 October 2016 (as the 21st day after being made on 10 September 2016).

Cross references – FA 1980, Sch. 17, para. 9: treatment of excluded oil where there are transfers of interests in oil fields.
FA 1981, s. 118(2)(d): excludes payment or repayment of royalty in respect of excluded oil from computation of "chargeable sum" and "allowable sum" paid by or to Secretary of State.
OTA 1983, s. 3(6): any reference in OTA 1975, Pt. I to s. 4 is to be construed as including a reference to OTA 1983, s. 3, 4 and Sch. 1.
FA 1999, s. 94(2): a replacement contract, made after the end of June 1975, for sales to the British Gas Corporation or its successors; treated the same as the old contract, unless the rights and liabilities of the new contract are so different as to be a different contract, for the purposes of the disregard in s. 10(1)(a).

11 Application of Provisional Collection of Taxes Act 1968

11 Section 1 of the Provisional Collection of Taxes Act 1968 shall apply to petroleum revenue tax; and accordingly, in subsection (1) of that section after the words "income tax" there shall be inserted the words "petroleum revenue tax".

12 Interpretation of Part I

12(1) In this Part of this Act–

"business day" has the same meaning as in the Bills of Exchange Act 1882;

"calendar month" (where those words are used) means a month of the calendar year;

"Category 1 oil" and **"Category 2 oil"** have the meaning given by paragraph 2(1B) of Schedule 3 to this Act;

"chargeable period", in relation to an oil field, has the meaning given by section 1(3) of this Act;

"claim period", in relation to an oil field, has the meaning given by paragraph 1 of Schedule 5 to this Act;

"crude", where the reference is to oil being disposed of or appropriated crude, refers to its being so dealt with without having been refined (whether or not it has previously undergone initial treatment);

"determination", in a context relating to an assessment or determination on or in relation to a participator, means a determination under Schedule 2 to this Act that a loss is allowable to him or that neither an assessable profit nor an allowable loss has accrued to him;

"initial storage", in relation to oil won from an oil field, means the storage of a quantity of oil won from the field not exceeding, in the case of storage in the United Kingdom or another country, a quantity equal to ten times the maximum daily production rate of oil for the field as planned or achieved (whichever is the greater), but does not include–

(a) the storing of oil as part of or in conjunction with the operation of an oil refinery; or

(b) deballasting; or

(c) conveying oil in a pipe-line;

"initial treatment", in relation to oil from an oil field, means the doing, at any place, of any the following things, that is to say–

(a) subjecting oil won from the field to any process of which the sole purpose is to enable the oil to be safely stored, safely loaded into a tanker or safely accepted by an oil refinery; or

(b) separating oil so won and consisting of gas from other oil so won; or

(c) separating oil so won and consisting of gas of a kind that is transported and sold in normal commercial practice from other oil so won and consisting of gas; or

(d) liquifying oil so won and consisting of gas of such a kind as aforesaid for the purpose of transporting it; or

(e) subjecting oil so won to any process of which the purpose is to secure that oil disposed of crude has the quality that is normal for oil so disposed of from the field,

but does not include–

(i) the storing of oil even where this involves the doing to the oil of things within any of paragraphs (a) to (e) of this definition or

(ii) any activity carried on as part of, or in association with, the refining of oil not consisting of gas or any activity the sole or main purpose of which is to achieve a chemical reaction in respect of oil consisting of gas; or

(iii) deballasting;

"land" includes land in the United Kingdom or another country covered with water;

"licence" means a licence under Part I of the Petroleum Act 1998 or the Petroleum (Production) Act (Northern Ireland) 1964 authorising the winning of oil, and

"licensed area" shall be construed accordingly;

"licensee" means–

(a) the person entitled to the benefit of a licence or, where two or more persons are entitled to the benefit of a licence, each of those persons; and

(b) a person who has rights under an agreement which is approved by the Board and is certified by–

(ai) the Scottish Ministers, where the rights relate to oil in the Scottish onshore area, as defined in section 8A of the Petroleum Act 1998,

(i) the Welsh Ministers, where the rights relate to oil in the Welsh onshore area (as defined in section 8A of the Petroleum Act 1998), or

(ii) the OGA, where the rights relate to oil elsewhere,

to confer on that person rights which are the same as, or similar to, those conferred by a licence;

"light gases", except in relation to an election under section 134 of the Finance Act 1982 or section 109 of the Finance Act 1986, means oil consisting of gas of which the largest component by volume over any chargeable period, measured at a temperature of 15 degrees centigrade and a pressure of one atmosphere, is methane or ethane or a combination of those gases;

"the OGA" means the Oil and Gas Authority;

"oil" has the meaning given by section 1(1) of this Act;

"oil field" shall be construed in accordance with Schedule 1 to this Act (which also includes provision about areas that are to be treated as continuing to be oil fields) and **"taxable field"** and **"non-taxable field"** have the same meaning as in Part III of the Finance Act 1993;

"participator" (except in paragraph 4 of Schedule 2 to this Act) means, in relation to an oil field and a chargeable period ("the relevant chargeable period")–

(a) a person who is or was at any time in the relevant chargeable period a licensee in respect of any licensed area then wholly or partly included in the field; and

(aa) a person who is no longer a licensee in respect of any licensed area wholly or partly included in the field, but who–

(i) was such a licensee at any time in any chargeable period preceding the relevant chargeable period, and

(ii) ceased to be such a licensee because of a cessation event; and

(b) a person who is no longer a licensee in respect of any licensed area wholly or partly included in the field (and who does not fall within paragraph (aa) of this definition), but who was such a licensee at any time in either of the two chargeable periods preceding the relevant chargeable period; and

(c) a person who is no longer a licensee in respect of any licensed area wholly or partly included in the field (and who does not fall within paragraph (aa) or (b) of this definition), but who has or had at any time in the relevant chargeable period a share of oil won (whether or not in that period) from the field, being a share with respect to any part of which either of the following conditions is or was satisfied at that time, that is to say–

(i) he has or had neither disposed of that part nor relevantly appropriated it; or

(ii) he has or had disposed of, but not delivered, that part;

(d) a former participator to whom an amount is attributed under paragraph 2A(2) of Schedule 5 in respect of a default payment made in relation to the field in the relevant chargeable period; and

(e) a former participator to whom an amount was attributed under paragraph 2A(2) of Schedule 5 in respect of a default payment made in relation to the field in either of the two chargeable periods preceding the relevant chargeable period; and

(f) a person who–

(i) made a default payment in relation to the field (whether the person was then a current participator or former participator),

(ii) is not a participator during the relevant chargeable period under any of paragraphs (a) to (e) of this definition, and

(iii) receives, in the relevant chargeable period, reimbursement expenditure (within the meaning of section 108(1)(c) of the Finance Act 1991) in respect of the default payment; and

(g) a person who–

(i) made a default payment in relation to the field (whether the person was then a current participator or former participator),

(ii) is not a participator during the relevant chargeable period under any of paragraphs (a) to (f) of this definition, and

(iii) received, in either of the two chargeable periods preceding the relevant chargeable period, reimbursement expenditure (within the meaning of section 108(1)(c) of the Finance Act 1991) in respect of the default payment;

"pipe-line" means a pipe-line as defined in section 65 of the Pipe-lines Act 1962;

"production purposes", in relation to an oil field, means any of the following purposes, that is to say–

(a) carrying on drilling or production operations within the field; or

(b) in the case of oil won from the field that was so won from strata in the sea bed and subsoil of either the territorial sea of the United Kingdom or a designated area, pumping it to the place where it is first landed in the United Kingdom or to the place in the United Kingdom or another country at which the seller in a sale at arm's length could reasonably be expected to deliver it or, if there is more than one place at which he could reasonably be expected to deliver it, the one nearest to the place of extraction; or

(c) the initial treatment of oil won from the field;

"refining", in relation to oil, does not include subjecting it to initial treatment and **"refined"** and **"refinery"** shall be construed accordingly;

"relevant licence", in relation to a participator in an oil field, means any licence held or previously held by him in respect of a licensed area wholly or partly included in the field;

"relevantly appropriated", in relation to oil won from an oil field, means appropriated to refining or to any use except use for production purposes in relation to that or any other oil field, and **"relevant appropriation"** shall be construed accordingly;

"the responsible person", in relation to an oil field, has the meaning given by paragraph 4 of Schedule 2 to this Act;

"royalty", in relation to a participator in an oil field, means royalty payable (but not, it is hereby declared, oil delivered) to the Secretary of State under any relevant licence;

"tax" or **"the tax"** means petroleum revenue tax.

12(1A) In the definition of "participator" in subsection (1)–

(a) **"cessation event"**, in relation to an oil field to which a licence relates, means any of the following–

(i) determination of the licence by the licensee,

(ii) revocation of the licence by the OGA, the Scottish Ministers, the Welsh Ministers or a Northern Ireland Department,

(iii) expiry of the licence at the end of its term,

(iv) the licensed area ceasing to include any relevant area whatsoever, by reason of the licensee surrendering the licence so far as it relates to the whole of the relevant area, and

(v) the licence ceasing to apply to the oil field by reason of the operation of the licence;

and for the purposes of sub-paragraph (iv) **"relevant area"** means an area which is, or combination of areas each of which is, included in the oil field (whether or not such an area falls partly outside the oil field);

(b) **"current participator"**, **"former participator"** and **"default payment"** have the same meanings as in paragraph 2A of Schedule 5.

12(2) In this Part of this Act any reference to the **"use of an asset"** in connection with an oil field is a reference to its use in connection with that field for one or more of the purposes mentioned in section 3(1) of this Act (excluding section 3(1)(b)).

12(3) In this Part of this Act any reference (however worded) to the **"doing of anything in a chargeable period"** in connection with an oil field or with oil won from an oil field shall be construed as including the doing of that thing in connection with the area of the field as subsequently determined under Schedule 1 to this Act or, as the case may be, with oil won from that area.

12(4) In so far as a person is a participator in an oil field by virtue of a licence under the Petroleum (Production) Act (Northern Ireland) 1964, references in this Part of this Act to the Secretary of State or the OGA (except references in Schedule 1) shall be construed in his case as references to the Department of Commerce for Northern Ireland.

History – In s. 12(1), in the definition of "licensee", para. (b)(ai) inserted by SI 2018/79, reg. 8, with effect from 1 October 2018 (immediately after the commencement of WA 2017, Sch. 6, Pt. 2 (SI 2017/1179).

In s. 12(1), in the definition of "licensee", para. (b)(i) and (ii) substituted for the words "the OGA" by WA 2017, s. 69(1) and Sch. 6, para. 19(2), with effect from 1 October 2018 (SI 2017/1179, reg. 4(b)).

In s. 12(1), in para. (b) of the definition of "licensee", the word "OGA" substituted for the words "Secretary of State" by SI 2016/898, reg. 4(6)(a)(i), with effect from 1 October 2016 (as the 21st day after being made on 10 September 2016).

In s. 12(1) the definitions of "business day", "Category 1 oil" and "Category 2 oil" inserted by FA 2006, s. 146 and Sch. 18, para. 4(2), with effect in relation to oil delivered or appropriated on or after 1 July 2006, subject to provisions of FA 2006, s. 147(2)–(8).

In s. 12(1) definition of "calendar month" substituted by FA 2006, s. 146 and Sch. 18, para. 4(3), with effect in relation to oil delivered or appropriated on or after 1 July 2006, subject to provisions of FA 2006, s. 147(2)–(8). The former definition read as follows:

""**calendar month**" (where those words are used) has the meaning given by paragraph 3(2) of Schedule 3 to this Act;"

In s. 12(1), in the definitions of "initial storage" and "initial treatment" the words "in the United Kingdom, the territorial sea thereof or a designated area" were repealed by F(No. 2)A 1992, s. 74 and Sch. 15, para. 3(a), s. 82 and Sch. 18, Pt. VIII, with effect in accordance with s. 74(5) of that Act.

In s. 12(1), in the definitions of "initial storage", "land" and "production purposes" the words "or another country" were inserted by F(No. 2)A 1992, s. 74 and Sch. 15, para. 3(b)–(d), with effect in accordance with s. 74(5) of that Act.

In s. 12(1), in the definition of "licence", the words "Part I of the Petroleum Act 1998" substituted for the words "the Petroleum (Production) Act 1934" by the Petroleum Act 1998, Sch. 4, para. 7 with effect from 15 February 1999 (SI 1999/161 art. 2).
In s. 12(1), the definition of "light gases" was inserted by FA 1994, s. 236(4).
In s. 12(1), the definition of "the OGA" inserted by SI 2016/898, reg. 4(6)(a)(ii), with effect from 1 October 2016 (as the 21st day after being made on 10 September 2016).
In s. 12(1), in the definition of "oil field", the words "(which also includes provision about areas that are to be treated as continuing to be oil fields)" inserted by FA 2009, s. 88 and Sch. 42, para. 6, with effect in relation to areas that cease to be oil fields, or parts of oil fields, in chargeable periods that begin after 30 June 2009.
In s. 12(1), in the definition of "oil field", the references to "taxable field" and "non-taxable field" were inserted by FA 1993, s. 185(5).
In s. 12(1), in the definition of "participator", the word "a" substituted for the word "any", para. (aa), in para. (b) the words "(and who does not fall within paragraph (aa) of this definition)" and in para. (c) the words "(aa) or" inserted and the following words which appeared at the end omitted by FA 2009, s. 88 and Sch. 42, para. 2(2), with effect in relation to persons who cease to be licencees because of cessation events occurring in chargeable periods that begin after 30 June 2009:
"and for the purposes of paragraphs (f)(i) and (g)(i), **"current participator"**, **"former participator"** and **"default payment"** have the same meaning as in paragraph 2A of Schedule 5;"
In s. 12(1), in the definition of "participator":
- in the words before para. (a) the words "("the relevant chargeable period")" inserted;
- in para (a), (b) and (c) the words "the relevant chargeable period" substituted for the words "that chargeable period"; and
- para. (d)–(g) inserted,

all by FA 2008, s. 102, with effect in relation to expenditure incurred after 30 June 2008.
S. 12(1) amended by FA 1980, s. 109(2)–(5) in relation to chargeable periods ending after 31 December 1979, by F(No. 2)A 1979, s. 20(1) in relation to expenditure claimed after 31 December 1978 and by FA 1983, s. 39 for chargeable periods ending after 31 December 1977.
In s. 12(1A)(a)(ii), the words ", the Welsh Ministers" inserted (after the words "Scottish Ministers") by WA 2017, s. 69(1) and Sch. 6, para. 19(3), with effect from 1 October 2018 (SI 2017/1179, reg. 4(b)).
In s. 12(1A)(a)(ii), the words ", the Scottish Ministers" inserted after the words "Secretary of State" by SCA 2016, s. 48(19), with effect from 9 February 2018 (SI 2018/163, reg. 2(b)).
In s. 12(1A)(a)(ii), the word "OGA" substituted for the words "Secretary of State" by SI 2016/898, reg. 4(6)(b), with effect from 1 October 2016 (as the 21st day after being made on 10 September 2016).
S. 12(1A) inserted by FA 2009, s. 88 and Sch. 42, para. 2(3), with effect in relation to persons who cease to be licencees because of cessation events occurring in chargeable periods that begin after 30 June 2009.
In s. 12(3), words between "oil field shall" and "be construed as" were repealed by FA 1982, s. 135(4), 157 and Sch. 22, Pt. IX, in relation to determinations made after 31 December 1981.
In s. 12(4), the words "or the OGA" inserted by SI 2016/898, reg. 4(6)(c), with effect from 1 October 2016 (as the 21st day after being made on 10 September 2016).
Cross references – ICTA 1988, s. 502: definitions for the purposes of ICTA 1988, Ch. V – Petroleum extraction activities.
SI 1982/846 (NI 11): the Department of Commerce for Northern Ireland is to be construed as the Department of Economic Development.
OTA 1983, Sch. 2, para. 12(2)(b): application of "relevantly appropriated" to oil purchased at place of extraction.
FA 1982, s. 134: alternative valuation of ethane used for petrochemical purposes.
FA 1986, s. 108(1), (2): construction of references to "territorial sea" and "United Kingdom" on or after 1 April 1986.
FA 1986, s. 109: alternative valuation of certain light gases.
TCGA 1992, s. 196(5): application of definitions of "oil", "licence" and cognate expressions for certain allowances in respect of tax on chargeable gains from disposals of oil licences relating to undeveloped areas.
TCGA 1992, s. 197(1): application of s. 12 to the ring fence in respect of net chargeable gains or losses.
SI 2018/79, reg. 3: modification of reg. 12(1), definition of "licensee", para. (b) until 31 October 2018 (the commencement of WA 2017, Sch. 6, Pt. 2).

12A Date of delivery or appropriation: shipped oil not sold at arm's length

12A(1) This section has effect for the purpose of determining the date on which any oil to which it applies is to be regarded for the purposes of this Part as delivered or relevantly appropriated.

12A(2) This section applies to–

(a) oil (not being light gases) won from a field and disposed of crude by a participator otherwise than in sales at arm's length, and

(b) oil (not being light gases) so won and relevantly appropriated by a participator,

if the condition in subsection (3)(a) or (b) below is met.

12A(3) The condition is that the oil is or has been, or is to be,–

(a) transported by ship from the place of extraction to a place in the United Kingdom or elsewhere, or

(b) transported by pipeline to a place in the United Kingdom and loaded on to a ship there.

12A(4) The date on which the oil is to be taken to be delivered, or (as the case may be) relevantly appropriated, by the participator is–

(a) the date of completion of load, in a case where the condition in subsection (3)(a) above is met,

(b) the date of the bill of lading, in a case where the condition in subsection (3)(b) above is met.

History – S. 12A inserted by FA 2006, s. 146 and Sch. 18, para. 5(1), with effect from 1 July 2006, in relation to oil which would (apart from this paragraph) fall to be regarded for the purposes of Part 1 of OTA 1975 as delivered or appropriated on a date after 30 June 2006.

PART III – MISCELLANEOUS AND GENERAL

21 Citation, interpretation and construction

21(1) This Act may be cited as the Oil Taxation Act 1975.

21(2) In this Act–

"the Board" means the Commissioners for Her Majesty's Revenue and Customs;

"CTA 2010" means the Corporation Tax Act 2010;

"designated area" means an area designated by Order in Council under section 1(7) of the Continental Shelf Act 1964;

21(3) Parts II and III of this Act, so far as they relate to income tax, shall be construed as one with the Income Tax Acts and, so far as they relate to corporation tax, shall be construed as one with the Corporation Tax Acts.

21(4) Except so far as the context otherwise requires, any reference in this Act to any enactment shall be construed as a reference to that enactment as applied, by or under any other enactment, including this Act.

History – In s. 21(2), the definition of "CTA 2010" inserted and the definition of "the Taxes Act" omitted by CTA 2010, s. 1177 and Sch. 1, para. 164 (and repealed by CTA 2010, s. 1181 and Sch. 3, Pt. 1), with effect for corporation tax purposes for accounting periods ending on or after 1 April 2010, and for income tax and capital gains tax purposes for the tax year 2010–11 and subsequent tax years.
In s. 21(2) definition of "the Board" substituted by FA 2006, s. 146 and Sch. 18, para. 6(2) with effect from 19 July 2006.
S. 21(5) repealed by the Petroleum Act 1998, Sch. 4, para. 7 with effect from 15 February 1999 (SI 1999/161 art. 2).
See ICTA 1988, s. 844 and Sch. 29, para. 32 for substitution of former reference to that Act in s. 21(2).

Statutory instruments – SI 2006/3313: partly made under s. 21(2).

SCHEDULES

SCHEDULE 1 – DETERMINATION OF OIL FIELDS

Section 1

Cross references – FA 1994, Sch. 22, para. 1(2): oil field includes any area which an electing participator expects might be determined as an oil field.

Notes – FA 1982, s. 135 provides that OTA 1975, Pt. I (except Sch. 7) applies to oil won before the date of determination where such determination is made or varied after 31 December 1981.

AREAS THAT ARE OIL FIELDS

History – The heading preceding para. 1 inserted by FA 2009, s. 88 and Sch. 42, para. 7(2), with effect in relation to areas that cease to be oil fields, or parts of oil fields, in chargeable periods that begin after 30 June 2009.

1(1) For the purposes of this Part of this Act an **"oil field"** is any area which the appropriate authority may determine to be an oil field, being an area of which every part is, or is part of, a licensed area.

1(2) For the purposes of this Schedule the **"appropriate authority"**, in relation to any area–

(a) is the OGA if the area is such that licences can be granted by the OGA for all of it under Part I of the Petroleum Act 1998;

(aa) is the Scottish Ministers if the area is such that licences can be granted by the Scottish Ministers for all of it under Part 1 of the Petroleum Act 1998;

(ab) is the OGA and the Scottish Ministers acting jointly if the area is such that licences can be granted for part of it by the OGA and for part of it by the Scottish Ministers;

(ac) is the Welsh Ministers if the area is such that licences can be granted by the Welsh Ministers for all of it under Part 1 of the Petroleum Act 1998;

(ad) is the OGA and the Welsh Ministers acting jointly if the area is such that licences can be granted for part of it by the OGA and for part of it by the Welsh Ministers;

(b) is the Department of Commerce for Northern Ireland if the area is such that licences can be granted for all of it under the Petroleum (Production) Act (Northern Ireland) 1964; and

(c) is the OGA and that Department acting jointly if the area is such that licences can be granted for part of it under one and for part of it under the other of those Acts;

and any reference in this Schedule to the making of representations to the appropriate authority is, in a case falling within (c) above, a reference to the making of them to either the OGA or the said Department.

History – In para. 1(2)(a), the words "by the Secretary of State" inserted after the word "granted" by SCA 2016, s. 48(20)(a), with effect from 9 February 2018 (SI 2018/163, reg. 2(b)).
In para. 1(2)(a) and (c), the word "OGA" substituted for the words "Secretary of State" by SI 2016/898, reg. 4(7), with effect from 1 October 2016 (as the 21st day after being made on 10 September 2016).
In para. 1(2)(a), the words "Part I of the Petroleum Act 1998" substituted for the words "the Petroleum (Production) Act 1934" by the Petroleum Act 1998, Sch. 4, para. 7 with effect from 15 February 1999 (SI 1999/161 art. 2).
Para. 1(2)(aa) and (ab) inserted by SCA 2016, s. 48(20)(b), with effect from 9 February 2018 (SI 2018/163, reg. 2(b)).
Para. 1(2)(ac) and (ad) inserted by WA 2017, s. 69(1) and Sch. 6, para. 20, with effect from 1 October 2018 (SI 2017/1179, reg. 4(b)).

2 Before determining an area to be an oil field the appropriate authority–

(a) shall give notice in writing of the proposed determination to every person who is a licensee in respect of a licensed area wholly or partly included in that area and to any other licensee whose interests appear to the authority to be affected; and

(b) shall consider any representations in writing which a person to whom a notice under this paragraph has been given may make to the authority within sixty days of receiving the notice, and the determination may be made either as proposed or with such modifications as appear to the authority to be appropriate after considering any representations made to the authority in accordance with this paragraph.

3 A determination under this Schedule shall be in such form as the appropriate authority thinks fit and shall for purposes of identification assign to the field to which it relates a distinguishing number or other designation.

4 The appropriate authority shall give notice of any determination made by the authority under this Schedule to each of the persons to whom notice of the proposed determination was given.

5 A determination under this Schedule may from time to time be varied by a new determination thereunder made by the appropriate authority, and paragraphs 2 to 4 above shall apply to any such new determination.

AREAS TREATED AS CONTINUING TO BE OIL FIELDS

6(1) This paragraph applies if an area has ceased to be–

(a) an oil field within the meaning of paragraph 1(1), or

(b) part of such an oil field.

6(2) The area is to be treated as continuing to be–

(a) the oil field, or

(b) the part of the oil field,

that it actually was.

6(3) Accordingly, whilst the area is treated in accordance with sub-paragraph (2), any reference to an oil field is to include a reference to the area.

6(4) Sub-paragraph (2) ceases to apply to the area–

(a) in accordance with sub-paragraph (5), and

(b) if or to the extent that it has not ceased to apply in accordance with sub-paragraph (5), in accordance with sub-paragraph (6).

6(5) Sub-paragraph (2) ceases to apply to the area if, or to the extent that, it again becomes–

(a) an oil field within the meaning of paragraph 1(1), or

(b) part of such an oil field.

6(6) Sub-paragraph (2) ceases to apply to the area at the end of the second chargeable period that falls after the chargeable period in which the area is decommissioned.

History – Para. 6 inserted by FA 2009, s. 88 and Sch. 42, para. 7(3), with effect in relation to areas that cease to be oil fields, or parts of oil fields, in chargeable periods that begin after 30 June 2009.

7(1) A relevant area is decommissioned for the purposes of paragraph 6 if all qualifying assets of the relevant area are decommissioned.

7(2) If, and to the extent that, a UK offshore decommissioning regime applies to qualifying assets of the relevant area, those assets are decommissioned if–

(a) the OGA has approved one or more abandonment programmes under the regime in relation to those assets, and

(b) those programmes have been carried out to the satisfaction of the OGA.

7(3) If, and to the extent that, a UK offshore decommissioning regime does not apply to qualifying assets of the relevant area, those assets are decommissioned if the Board are satisfied that they have been decommissioned.

7(4) For the purposes of sub-paragraph (3), the Board must have regard to any obligations to decommission the qualifying assets which arise under the law applicable to those qualifying assets (whether the law of any part of the United Kingdom or of any other state or territory), including any obligations imposed by an authority having functions under that law in respect of such decommissioning.

7(5) If sub-paragraph (3) applies (to any extent) to any qualifying assets, the Board must give the responsible person notice of any decision the Board make under that sub-paragraph.

7(6) The responsible person may appeal against such a decision by notice in writing given to the Board within three months of the responsible person receiving the notice under sub-paragraph (5).

7(7) An appeal under sub-paragraph (6) may, before it is notified to the tribunal, be abandoned by notice in writing given to the Board by the responsible person.

7(8) The provisions of paragraphs 14A to 14I of Schedule 2 apply to appeals under sub-paragraph (6) subject to any necessary modifications.

7(9) In this paragraph–

"qualifying assets" means assets that are qualifying assets within the meaning of OTA 1983;

"relevant area" means an area that is treated as being an oil field, or part of an oil field, under paragraph 6;

"UK offshore decommissioning regime" means–

(a) Part 4 of the Petroleum Act 1998, and

(b) Part 1 of the Petroleum Act 1987.

History – In para. 7(2), the word "OGA" substituted for the words "Secretary of State" (in each place) by SI 2016/898, reg. 4(7), with effect from 1 October 2016 (as the 21st day after being made on 10 September 2016).
In para. 7(4), the words "those qualifying assets" substituted for the words "the relevant area" by FA 2011, s. 61(1), with effect in relation to chargeable periods that begin after 30 June 2009.
Para. 7 inserted by FA 2009, s. 88 and Sch. 42, para. 7(3), with effect in relation to areas that cease to be oil fields, or parts of oil fields, in chargeable periods that begin after 30 June 2009.

SCHEDULE 2 – MANAGEMENT AND COLLECTION OF PETROLEUM REVENUE TAX

Section 1

Cross references – OTA 1983, Sch. 4, para. 9(1) (application to assessable profit or allowable loss of participator in a foreign field) and para. 14 (tax chargeable only by virtue of the provisions of OTA 1983, s. 12 and Sch. 4 (charge of receipts attributable to UK use of foreign field assets)).

MANAGEMENT OF TAX

1(1) The tax shall be under the care and management of the Board; and the provisions of the Taxes Management Act 1970 specified in the first column of the following Table shall apply in relation to the tax as they apply in relation to a tax within the meaning of that Act, subject to any modifications specified in the second column of that Table and with the substitution, for references to Part IX of that Act or to the Taxes Acts, of references to this Part of this Act and, for references to chargeable periods within the meaning of that Act, of references to chargeable periods within the meaning of this Part of this Act.

TABLE

Provisions applied	*Modifications*
Section	
1(3)...	–
47C...	–
48...	–
49...	–
56...	–
60...	In subsection (1), omit the words following "charged therewith".
61...	In subsection (1), omit the words from "distrain upon" to "is charged or".
62(1)...	Omit "or which are payable for the year in which the seizure is made" and for "one year" and "one whole year" substitute "two chargeable periods".
(2)...	For "one whole year" substitute "two chargeable periods".
63...	–
64(1)...	For "one year" and "one whole year" substitute "two chargeable periods".
(2)...	For "one whole year" substitute "two chargeable periods".
66...	–
67...	–
68...	–
69...	In paragraph (a), substitute a reference to section 68 as applied by this paragraph for the reference to the sections there specified.
90...	–
100C...	In subsection (1) omit the words after "penalty"
101...	For the reference to income or chargeable gains substitute a reference to assessable profits.
102...	–
103(1)... ...	For the words from the beginning to "court –" substitute "Where the amount of a penalty is to be ascertained by reference to tax payable by a person for any period, proceedings for the penalty may be commenced before the tribunal –"

Provisions applied	*Modifications*
Section	
(4)...	For the words from the beginning to "court," substitute "Proceedings for a penalty to which subsection (1) above does not apply may be commenced before the tribunal".
104...	–
105...	–
107(1)–(3)... ...	–
108...	In subsection (2), for the words from the beginning to "Acts" substitute "The tax chargeable".
112...	In subsection (1), after "assessment to tax" and "the assessment" insert "or determination" and after "duplicate of assessment to tax" and "duplicate of assessment" insert "or of determination".
113(1A)...	–
(3)...	After "assessment" insert "determination" and after "notice of assessment" insert "notice of determination".
114...	After "assessment" wherever occurring insert "or determination".
115(1)–(3)... ...	–
118(1)...	–
(2)...	–

1(2) Any expression to which a meaning is given in this Part of this Act which is used in a provision of the Taxes Management Act 1970 applied by this paragraph shall, in that provision as so applied, have the same meaning as in this Part of this Act.

History – The entry relating to s. 4 omitted by SI 2009/56, art. 3 and Sch. 1, para. 70(2), with effect from 1 April 2009, subject to transitional and saving provisions in SI 2009/56, Sch. 3.
The entry relating to s. 33 omitted by F(No. 3)A 2010, s. 28 and Sch. 12, para. 7, with effect in relation to claims made on or after 1 April 2011.
The entries relating to s. 34 and 36 omitted by FA 2009, s. 99 and Sch. 51, para. 18(3), with effect from 1 April 2011 (SI 2010/867).
The entry relating to s. 46A omitted by SI 2009/56, art. 3 and Sch. 1, para. 70(2), with effect from 1 April 2009, subject to transitional and saving provisions in SI 2009/56, Sch. 3. That entry formerly inserted by F(No. 2)A 1992, s. 76 and Sch. 16, para. 6(2).
The entry relating to s. 47C inserted by SI 2009/56, art. 3 and Sch. 1, para. 70(3), with effect from 1 April 2009, subject to transitional and saving provisions in SI 2009/56, Sch. 3.
In the entry relating to s. 49(1) the "(1)" omitted by SI 2009/56, art. 3 and Sch. 1, para. 70(4), with effect from 1 April 2009, subject to transitional and saving provisions in SI 2009/56, Sch. 3.
The entries relating to s. 50(1)–(5), 51, 52, 56 omitted by SI 1994/1813, Sch. 1, para. 18(a) and Sch. 2, Pt. I, with effect from 1 September 1994.
The entry relating to s. 53 omitted by SI 2009/56, art. 3 and Sch. 1, para. 70(2), with effect from 1 April 2009, subject to transitional and saving provisions in SI 2009/56, Sch. 3.
The entry relating to s. 56A changed to "s. 56" by SI 2009/56, art. 3 and Sch. 1, para. 70(5), with effect from 1 April 2009, subject to transitional and saving provisions in SI 2009/56, Sch. 3.
The entry relating to s. 56B, 56C and 56D omitted by SI 2009/56, art. 3 and Sch. 1, para. 70(2), with effect from 1 April 2009, subject to transitional and saving provisions in SI 2009/56, Sch. 3.
The entry relating to s. 56A–56D inserted by F(No. 2)A 1992, s. 76 and Sch. 16, para. 6(3).
The entry relating to s. 58(2B), (2C) omitted by SI 2009/56, art. 3 and Sch. 1, para. 70(2), with effect from 1 April 2009, subject to transitional and saving provisions in SI 2009/56, Sch. 3. Those entries were substituted for s. 58(2) by SI 1994/1813, Sch. 1, para. 18(b), with effect from 1 September 1994.
The entry relating to s. 58(3) omitted by SI 2009/56, art. 3 and Sch. 1, para. 70(2), with effect from 1 April 2009, subject to transitional and saving provisions in SI 2009/56, Sch. 3. In that former entry the words "Omit the references to section 59 and," were repealed by FA 1988, s. 148 and Sch. 14, Pt. IX, with effect from 3 April 1989 (SI 1989/473 (C 17)).
The entries relating to s. 70(1) and (2) omitted by FA 2008, s. 138 and Sch. 44, para. 2, with effect from 21 July 2008. Note that the legislation actually requires this amendment to be made to the Table in para. 2(1) but as no such table exists Croner-i has assumed that the amendment should be made here (i.e. the Table in para. 1(1)).
The entry relating to s. 89 (repealed) repealed by FA 1989, s. 187 and Sch. 17, Pt. X.
The entry relating to s. 98 omitted by SI 1994/1813, Sch. 1, para. 18(c), with effect from 1 September 1994.
The entry relating to s. 99 omitted by FA 2012, s. 223 and Sch. 38, para. 51, with effect from 1 April 2013 (SI 2013/279, art. 2).
The entry relating to s. *100C changed* to "s. 100" and the words in the second column changed to "In subsection (1) omit the words after "penalty"" from "For the words from "General"" to the end substitute "Special Commissioners for any penalty"." and entries for s. 100C(2)–(5) omitted by SI 2009/56, art. 3 and Sch. 1, para. 70(6) and (7), with effect from 1 April 2009, subject to transitional and saving provisions in SI 2009/56, Sch. 3. The entries for s. 100C formerly substituted for those relating to "s. 100" by FA 1991, s. 109(2).
In the entry relating to s. 103(1) and (4) the word "tribunal" substituted for the words "Special Commissioners" by SI 2009/56, art. 3 and Sch. 1, para. 70(8), with effect from 1 April 2009, subject to transitional and saving provisions in SI 2009/56, Sch. 3. That entry was substituted by FA 1991, s. 109(3).

Cross references – FA 1982, s. 135(1)(b), (3): chargeable period where actual date of determination is later than the winning of oil from the field (deemed determination).

RETURNS BY PARTICIPATORS

2(1) Every participator in a taxable field shall, for each chargeable period, prepare and, within two months after the end of the period or within such longer period as the Board may allow, deliver to the Board a return complying with the following provisions of this paragraph; but nothing in this sub-paragraph shall require a participator to deliver a return under this paragraph before 31st August 1975.

2(2) A return under this paragraph for a chargeable period shall give the following information in relation to oil which is or was included in the participator's share of any oil won from the taxable field (whether or not in that period), that is to say–

(a) in the case of each delivery (other than one made before 13th November 1974) in the period of oil disposed of by him crude (other than oil delivered as mentioned in (c) of this sub-paragraph), the return shall–

(i) state the quantity of oil delivered;

(ii) state the person to whom the oil was disposed of;

(iii) in the case of oil disposed of in a sale at arm's length, state the price received or receivable for the oil or, in the case of oil disposed of otherwise than in a sale at arm's length, state the market value of the oil as determined in accordance with Schedule 3 to this Act in the case of the delivery or (in the case of light gases) the market value as determined in accordance with paragraph 3A of Schedule 3 to this Act; and

(iv) contain such other particulars of or relating to the disposal as the Board may prescribe;

(b) in the case of each relevant appropriation of crude oil (other than one made before 13th November 1974) in the period (not being oil disposed of by him), the return shall–

(i) state the quantity of oil appropriated;

(ii) state the market value of the oil as determined in accordance with Schedule 3 to this Act in the case of the appropriation or (in the case of light gases) the market value as determined in accordance with paragraph 3A of Schedule 3 to this Act; and

(iii) contain such other particulars of or relating to the appropriation as the Board may prescribe;

(c) in the case of crude oil delivered to the OGA in the period under the terms of a licence granted under Part I of the Petroleum Act 1998, the return shall state the total quantity of the oil;

(d) in the case of crude oil which, at the end of the period, has either not been disposed of and not relevantly appropriated or has been disposed of but not delivered, the return shall–

(i) state the quantity of the oil;

(ii) state the market value of the oil on the last business day of the period, and

(iii) contain such other particulars relating to the oil as the Board may prescribe.

2(2A) Every participator in a taxable field shall, in the first return under this paragraph which he makes for that field, state whether any and, if any, how much expenditure to which section 5A or section 5B of this Act applies and which relates to, or to a licence for, any part of the field has been claimed under Schedule 7 to this Act–

(a) by him, or

(b) by a company associated with him in respect of that expenditure, or

(c) if he or such a company is the new participator, within the meaning of Schedule 17 to the Finance Act 1980, by the old participator, within the meaning of that Schedule, or by a company associated with him in respect of that expenditure,

and subsection (7) of section 5 of this Act applies for the purposes of this sub-paragraph as it applies for the purposes of that section.

2(3) A return under this paragraph for a chargeable period shall state–

(a) the amount of royalty payable by the participator for that period in respect of his share of oil won from the field as shown in the return or returns made by him to the Secretary of State under the relevant licence or licences;

(b) the amount of royalty paid by the participator in that period in respect of that share;

(c) the amount of any royalty paid under any relevant licence in respect of the field which was repaid to the participator in that period; and

(d) the amount of any periodic payment made by the participator to the OGA in that period under each relevant licence otherwise than by way of royalty.

2(3A) A return under this paragraph for a chargeable period shall–

(a) state the amount (if any) which, in the case of the participator, is to be brought into account for that period in accordance with section 2(5)(e) of this Act;

(b) contain such particulars as the Board may prescribe (whether before or after the passing of the Finance Act 1987) with respect to any nominated transaction under Schedule 10 to that Act–
 (i) the effective volume of which forms part of the participator's aggregate effective volume (construing those terms in accordance with that Schedule) for any calendar month comprised in that chargeable period; and
 (ii) which has not led to deliveries of oil or relevant appropriations of which particulars are included in the return by virtue of sub-paragraph (2) above; and

(c) contain such other particulars as the Board may prescribe (as mentioned above) in connection with the application of section 61 and Schedule 10 to the Finance Act 1987.

2(4) A return under this paragraph shall be in such form as the Board may prescribe and shall include a declaration that the return is correct and complete.

2(5) The power of the Board to allow an extension of time under sub-paragraph (1) above shall include power–

(a) to allow an extension for an indefinite period; and

(b) to provide for the period of any extension to end at such time as may be stipulated in a notice given by the Board.

History – In para. 2(1) the words "or within such longer period as the Board may allow" inserted by FA 1999, s. 102(1)(a), with effect for chargeable periods ending on or after 30 June 1999.
In para. 2(1), (2), (2A), "a taxable field" and "the taxable field" substituted by FA 1993, s. 187(1). The meaning of "taxable field" is set out in FA 1993, s. 185(1) – see Cross Reference note below.
In para. 2(2)(a)(iii) the words "as determined in accordance with Schedule 3 to this Act in the case of the delivery" substituted for "in the calendar month in which the delivery was made" by FA 2006, s. 146 and Sch. 18, para. 7(2), with effect in relation to oil delivered or appropriated on or after 1 July 2006, subject to provisions of FA 2006, s. 147(2)–(8).
In para. 2(2)(a)(iii) and (b)(ii), the words "or (in the case of … to this Act" inserted by FA 1994, s. 236 and Sch. 23, para. 2. The words inserted may be disregarded by virtue of FA 1994, s. 236(2) if, before 1 January 1994, an election was made under FA 1982, s. 134 (alternative valuation of certain ethane) or FA 1986, s. 109 (alternative valuation of certain light gases) and the election applies to those gases.
In para. 2(2)(b)(ii) the words "as determined in accordance with Schedule 3 to this Act in the case of the appropriation" substituted for "in the calendar month in which the delivery was made" by FA 2006, s. 146 and Sch. 18, para. 7(3), with effect in relation to oil delivered or appropriated on or after 1 July 2006, subject to provisions of FA 2006, s. 147(2)–(8).
In para. 2(2)(c), the word "OGA" substituted for the words "Secretary of State" (in each place) by SI 2016/898, reg. 4(8), with effect from 1 October 2016 (as the 21st day after being made on 10 September 2016).
In para. 2(2)(c), the words "Part I of the Petroleum Act 1998" substituted for the words "the Petroleum (Production) Act 1934" by the Petroleum Act 1998, Sch. 4, para. 7 with effect from 15 February 1999 (SI 1999/161 art. 2).
In para. 2(2)(d)(ii) the words "on the last business day" substituted for "in the last calendar month" by FA 2006, s. 146 and Sch. 18, para. 7(4), with effect in relation to oil delivered or appropriated on or after 1 July 2006, subject to provisions of FA2006, s. 147(2)–(8).
Para. 2(2A) inserted by FA 1983, s. 37(2) and Sch. 8, Pt. II, para. 5, with effect from 13 May 1983, and the words "expenditure to which section 5A or section 5B" substituted by FA 1987, s. 64 and Sch. 13, Pt. II, para. 4.
In para. 2(3)(d), the word "OGA" substituted for the words "Secretary of State" (in each place) by SI 2016/898, reg. 4(8), with effect from 1 October 2016 (as the 21st day after being made on 10 September 2016).
Para. 2(3A) inserted by FA 1987, s. 61 and Sch. 10, para. 13.
Para. 2(5) inserted by FA 1999, s. 102(1)(b), with effect for chargeable periods ending on or after 30 June 1999.

Cross references – PRTA 1980, s. 1: payment of tax with returns for chargeable periods ending on or after 31 December 1979.
FA 1981, s. 118(4): return to include statement of chargeable or allowable sums paid by or to the Secretary of State.
FA 1982, s. 135(3): where there is a variation of determination under Sch. 1, para. 5, period for filing returns extended until later determination. Also s. 135(1)(b): chargeable period where actual date of determination later than the winning of oil from the field (deemed determination).
OTA 1983, s. 10(1)–(3): returns relating to tariff and disposal receipts.
FA 1984, s. 114(7): returns are to include information about oil "deemed to be delivered" by virtue of s. 114(4), (6) (sales of gas).
FA 1986, Sch. 21, para. 6: filing of returns where an election for alternative valuation of light gases is in force.
FA 1987, s. 62(4)–(9): obligation to furnish details of certain "relevant" sales of oil (sales at arm's length); and Sch. 13, Pt. III: obligation to furnish details of receipts to be set against expenditure allowable under s. 5B.
FA 1993, s. 185(1): a "non-taxable field" is an oil field granted development consent by the Secretary of State on or after 16 March 1993, and a "taxable field" is an oil field which is not a non-taxable field.
FA 2009, Sch. 55: penalty for failure to make returns etc.

3(1) If a participator fails to deliver a return within the time allowed for doing so under paragraph 2(1) above he shall be liable, subject to sub-paragraph (3) below–

(a) to a penalty not exceeding, except in the case mentioned in sub-paragraph (2) below, £500; and

(b) if the failure continues after it has been declared by the court or the tribunal before which proceedings for the penalty have been commenced, to a further penalty not exceeding £100 for each day on which the failure so continues.

3(2) If the failure continues after the end of six months from the time by which the return ought to have been delivered, the penalty under sub-paragraph (1)(a) above shall be an amount not exceeding the aggregate or £500 and the total amount of the tax with which the participator is charged for the chargeable period in question.

3(3) Except in the case mentioned in sub-paragraph (2) above, the participator shall not be liable to any penalty incurred under this paragraph for failure to deliver a return if the failure is remedied before proceedings for the recovery of the penalty are commenced.

History – In para. 3(1)(b) the words "tribunal before which" substituted for the words "Commissioners before whom" by SI 2009/56, art. 3 and Sch. 1, para. 71, with effect from 1 April 2009, subject to transitional and saving provisions in SI 2009/56, Sch. 3.

APPOINTMENT OF RESPONSIBLE PERSON FOR EACH OIL FIELD

4(1) For each oil field a body corporate or partnership shall be appointed in accordance with this paragraph as the responsible person for that field to perform, in relation to the field, any functions conferred on it as such by this Part of this Act; and the body or partnership which for the time being holds that appointment is in this Part of this Act referred to as **"the responsible person"**.

4(2) No body corporate shall be eligible for appointment as the responsible person for a taxable field unless it is resident in the United Kingdom, and no partnership shall be so eligible unless all its members are resident there.

4(3) The participators in a taxable field shall, by notice in writing to the Board within the initial period, nominate a body corporate or a partnership for appointment as the responsible person for that oil field and, if the Board approve the nomination, the Board shall appoint that body or partnership as the responsible person and give it notice that it has been so appointed.

4(4) If–

(a) the participators have made no nomination within the initial period; or

(b) the Board do not appoint the body or partnership nominated under sub-paragraph (3) above,

the Board shall appoint one of the participators in the taxable field as the responsible person for the field and shall give notice to that participator that he has been so appointed.

4(5) For the purposes of the preceding provisions of this paragraph, the **"initial period"** is the period of thirty days beginning with the latest date on which notice of determination of the taxable field is given to any of the participators under paragraph 4 of Schedule 1 to this Act.

4(6) The Board may at any time, on the application of all the participators in a taxable field, appoint a body corporate or partnership nominated by the participators as the responsible person for that field in place of the body corporate or partnership which is the responsible person at that time, and shall give the body or partnership so appointed notice that it has been so appointed.

4(7) The Board may, by notice in writing to the body corporate or partnership which is for the time being the responsible person for a taxable field, revoke the appointment of that body or partnership as the responsible person for that field; and where they do so the Board shall appoint one of the participators in the taxable field as the responsible person for that field and shall give notice to the participator that he has been so appointed.

4(8) In this paragraph **"participator"**, in relation to a taxable field, means a person who is a licensee in respect of any licensed area wholly or partly included in the field.

History – In para. 4, in each place where they occur, "a taxable field" substituted for "an oil field", and "the taxable field" substituted for "the oil field", by FA 1993, s. 187(1).

Cross references – OTA 1983, Sch. 4, para. 13: appointment of responsible person in respect of UK use of foreign field.
FA 1993, s. 185(1): a "non-taxable field" is an oil field granted development consent by the Secretary of State on or after 16 March 1993, and a "taxable field" is an oil field which is not a non-taxable field.

RETURNS BY THE RESPONSIBLE PERSON

5(1) The responsible person for a taxable field shall, for each chargeable period, prepare and, within one month after the end of the period or within such longer period as the Board may allow, deliver to the Board a return for that period complying with sub-paragraphs (2) and (3) below; but nothing in this sub-paragraph shall require the responsible person to deliver a return under this paragraph before 31st July 1975.

5(2) A return under this paragraph for a chargeable period shall–

(a) state the quantity of oil won and saved from the taxable field during the period;

(b) state the respective interests of the participators in the field in that oil;

(c) state what, in accordance with those interests, is each participator's share of that oil; and

(d) contain such other particulars of or relating to the field as the Board may require.

5(2A) The reference in sub-paragraph (2)(d) above to particulars of or relating to the field includes a reference to particulars required for determining the amount by which any qualifying tariff receipts, within the meaning of section 9 of the Oil Taxation Act 1983, are to be treated as reduced by virtue of that section.

5(2B) If in any chargeable period oil won from the taxable field is mixed as mentioned in section 63 of the Finance Act 1987 so as to give rise to blended oil, within the meaning of that section, then, as respects that chargeable period, for paragraph (a) of sub-paragraph (2) above there shall be substituted the following paragraph–

"(a) state the total of the shares of the participators in the taxable field of the oil won from the field during the period less so much of the oil won from the field as is not saved."

5(3) A return under this paragraph shall be in such form as the Board may prescribe and shall include a declaration that the return is correct and complete.

5(4) The power of the Board to allow an extension of time under sub-paragraph (1) above shall include power–

(a) to allow an extension for an indefinite period; and

(b) to provide for the period of any extension to end at such time as may be stipulated in a notice given by the Board.

History – In para. 5, wherever occurring, "a taxable field", and "the taxable field" substituted, by FA 1993, s. 187(1).
In para. 5(1), the words "or within such longer period as the Board may allow" inserted by FA 1999, s. 102(2)(a), with effect for chargeable periods ending on or after 30 June 1999.
Para. 5(2A) inserted by OTA 1983, s. 10(4), with respect to chargeable periods ending after 1 December 1983.
Para. 5(2B) inserted by F(No. 2)A 1987, s. 101(4), with respect to chargeable periods ending after 1 January 1987.
Para. 5(4) inserted by FA 1999, s. 102(2)(b), with effect for chargeable periods ending on or after 30 June 1999.

Cross references – FA 1993, s. 185(1): a "non-taxable field" is an oil field granted development consent by the Secretary of State on or after 16 March 1993, and a "taxable field" is an oil field which is not a non-taxable field.

6(1) If the responsible person fails to deliver a return within the time allowed for doing so under paragraph 5(1) above he shall be liable–

(a) to a penalty not exceeding £500, and

(b) if the failure continues after it has been declared by the court or tribunal before which proceedings for the penalty have been commenced, to a further penalty not exceeding £100 for each day on which the failure so continues.

6(2) The responsible person shall not be liable to any penalty incurred under sub-paragraph (1) above for failure to deliver a return if the failure is remedied before proceedings for the recovery of the penalty are commenced.

History – In para. 6(1)(b) the words "tribunal before which" substituted for the words "Commissioners before whom" by SI 2009/56, art. 3 and Sch. 1, para. 72, with effect from 1 April 2009, subject to transitional and saving provisions in SI 2009/56, Sch. 3.

PRODUCTION OF ACCOUNTS, BOOKS AND OTHER INFORMATION

7 [Repealed by FA 1993, s. 187(1), 213 and Sch. 23, Pt. IV, and superseded by FA 1993, s. 187(2)–(8).]

INCORRECT RETURNS, ACCOUNTS, ETC.

8 [Omitted by FA 2008, s. 122 and Sch. 40, para. 21(a).]

History – Para. 8 omitted by FA 2008, s. 122 and Sch. 40, para. 21(a), with effect from 1 April 2009 (SI 2009/571, art. 2 but subject to transitional provisions at SI 2009/571, art. 6 and 7). Former para. 8 read as follows:

"**8(1)** Where a participator in a taxable field fraudulently or negligently–
(a) delivers an incorrect return under paragraph 2 above; or
(b) makes any incorrect statement or declaration in connection with any claim under this Part of this Act for the allowance of any expenditure or for any relief in respect of the tax; or
(c) submits to the Board or the tribunal any incorrect accounts in connection with the ascertainment of the participator's liability to the tax,
the participator shall be liable to a penalty not exceeding the aggregate of–
(i) £50, and
(ii) the amount or, in the case of fraud, twice the amount, of the difference specified in sub-paragraph (2) below.

8(2) The difference is that between–
(a) the amount of tax payable by the participator–
(i) for the chargeable period to which the return relates; or
(ii) for the next chargeable period ending after the allowance of the claim; or
(iii) for the chargeable period or periods against which the relief is claimed; or
(iv) for the chargeable period or periods for which the accounts are relevant,
as the case may be; and
(b) the amount which would have been the amount so payable if the return, statement, declaration or accounts as made or submitted by him had been correct.

8(3) Where the responsible person for a taxable field fraudulently or negligently–
(a) delivers an incorrect return under paragraph 5 above; or
(b) makes any incorrect statement or declaration in connection with any claim under this Part of this Act for the allowance of any expenditure,
the responsible person shall be liable to a penalty not exceeding £2,500 or, in the case of fraud on his part, £5,000.

History – In para. 8(1)(c) the word "tribunal" substituted for the words "Special Commissioners" by SI 2009/56, art. 3 and Sch. 1, para. 73, with effect from 1 April 2009, subject to transitional and saving provisions in SI 2009/56, Sch. 3.
In para. 8(1), (3), "a taxable field" substituted, by FA 1993, s. 187(1)(a).

Cross references – *FA 1982, Sch. 18, para. 10*: penalty provisions extended to inaccurate information contained in an election, books, accounts etc.
FA 1993, s. 185(1): a "non-taxable field" is an oil field granted development consent by the Secretary of State on or after 16 March 1993, and a "taxable field" is an oil field which is not a non-taxable field.
FA 2004, s. 313(4)(b): a person is not liable to a penalty under OTA 1975, Sch. 2, para. 8 by reason of any failure to include in any return or account any reference number or other information required by virtue of subsection (3)(a) (but see TMA 1970, s. 98C for the penalty for failure to comply with this section)."

9 [Omitted by FA 2008, s. 122 and Sch. 40, para. 21(a).]

History – Para. 9 omitted by FA 2008, s. 122 and Sch. 40, para. 21(a), with effect from 1 April 2009 (SI 2009/571, art. 2 but subject to transitional provisions at SI 2009/571, art. 6 and 7). Former para. 9 read as follows:

"**9(1)** Where any such return, statement, declaration or accounts as are mentioned in paragraph 8 above were made or submitted by any person neither fraudulently nor negligently and it comes to his notice that they were incorrect, then, unless the error is remedied without unreasonable delay, the return, statement, declaration or accounts shall be treated as having been negligently made or submitted by the first-mentioned person.

9(2) Where any such return, statement, declaration or accounts were made or submitted by the responsible person for a taxable field neither fraudulently nor negligently and it comes to the notice of any person who subsequently becomes the responsible person for that field that they were incorrect, then, unless the error is remedied without unreasonable delay, the return, statement, declaration or accounts shall be treated as having been negligently made or submitted by the responsible person to whose notice the incorrectness came.

9(3) For the purposes of paragraph 8 above, any accounts submitted on behalf of any person shall be deemed to have been submitted by that person unless he proves that they were submitted without his consent or connivance.

History – In para. 9(2), "a taxable field" substituted by FA 1993, s. 187(1)(a).

Cross references – FA 1993, s. 185(1): a "non-taxable field" is an oil field granted development consent by the Secretary of State on or after 16 March 1993, and a "taxable field" is an oil field which is not a non-taxable field."

ASSESSMENTS TO TAX AND DETERMINATIONS OF LOSS, ETC.

10(1) Where it appears to the Board that, in accordance with the provisions of this Part of this Act, an assessable profit has accrued to a participator in a chargeable period from a taxable field, they shall make an assessment to tax on the participator and shall give him notice of the assessment.

10(1A) An assessment under sub-paragraph (1) may be made at any time not more than 4 years after the end of the chargeable period to which it relates (subject to paragraphs 12A and, 12B and 13E).

10(2) Where it appears to the Board that, in accordance with those provisions, an allowable loss has accrued to a participator in a chargeable period from a taxable field, they shall make a determination that the loss is allowable to the participator and shall give him notice of the determination.

10(3) Where it appears to the Board that, in accordance with those provisions, neither an assessable profit nor an allowable loss has accrued to a participator in a chargeable period, they shall make a determination to that effect and shall give him notice of the determination.

10(4) A notice of assessment for a chargeable period shall state the amount of any allowable losses which, in accordance with those provisions, have been set against the assessable profit for that period.

10(5) A notice of assessment or determination shall state that the participator may appeal against the assessment or determination in accordance with paragraph 14 below.

10(6) After the service of the notice of assessment or the notice of determination the assessment or determination, as the case may be, shall not be altered except in accordance with the express provisions of this Part of this Act (including the provisions applied by paragraph 1 above).

History – In para. 10(1), (2) "a taxable field" substituted by FA 1993, s. 187(1)(a).
In para. 10(1A), ", 12B and 13E" substituted for "and 12B" by F(No. 3)A 2010, s. 28 and Sch. 12, para. 8, with effect in relation to claims made on or after 1 April 2011.
Para. 10(1A) inserted by FA 2009, s. 99 and Sch. 51, para. 19, with effect from 1 April 2011 (SI 2010/867).

Cross references – FA 1980, Sch. 17, para. 14: determination of losses where there is a transfer of interests in an oil field after 1 August 1980.
FA 1993, s. 185(1): a "non-taxable field" is an oil field granted development consent by the Secretary of State on or after 16 March 1993, and a "taxable field" is an oil field which is not a non-taxable field.

11(1) Where a participator has under paragraph 2 above delivered to the Board a return for a chargeable period and the Board are satisfied that the information given in the return is correct in so far as it is material for the purpose of computing his assessable profit or allowable loss (if any) for that period, the Board shall (in so far as the computation falls to be made by reference to the matters dealt with in the return) make the assessment or determination under paragraph 10 above in accordance with the return.

11(2) Where the Board are not so satisfied in relation to a participator's return or a participator fails to deliver to the Board a return for a chargeable period as required by paragraph 2 above, the Board shall, in so far as the computation of his assessable profit or allowable loss (if any) for that period falls to be made by reference to the matters which were dealt with in the return or, as the case may be, ought to have been dealt with in a return, make the assessment or determination under paragraph 10 above to the best of their judgment.

11(3) Nothing in sub-paragraph (2) above or in paragraph 5 above shall be taken, in a case where the participator has delivered a return as to which the Board are not satisfied as mentioned in sub-paragraph (1) above, to prevent the Board from basing their assessment or determination on the participator's having had an interest in oil won and saved from the field different from that on which he based his return.

Cross references – FA 2009, Sch. 56: penalty for failure to make payments on time.

12(1) Where it appears to the Board–

(a) that the assessable profit charged to tax by or stated in an assessment ought to be or to have been larger or smaller; or

(b) that the allowable loss stated in an assessment or a determination of loss ought to be or to have been larger or smaller; or

(c) that, where they made a determination that neither an assessable profit nor an allowable loss accrued in a chargeable period, they ought to have made an assessment to tax or a determination of loss for that period, or

(d) that for any chargeable period they ought to have made an assessment to tax instead of a determination of loss or a determination of loss instead of an assessment to tax;

the Board may make such assessments or determinations or such amendments of assessments or determinations as may be necessary; and where the Board exercise any of their powers under this paragraph in relation to a chargeable period, they may make such assessments or determinations or amendments of assessments or determinations for other chargeable periods as may be necessary in consequence of the exercise of those powers.

12(1A) An assessment (or an amendment of an assessment) under sub-paragraph (1) may be made at any time not more than 4 years after the end of the chargeable period to which the assessment relates (subject to sub-paragraph (1B) and paragraphs 12A and 12B).

12(1B) The time limits in sub-paragraph (1A) and paragraphs 12A and 12B do not apply to an amendment of an assessment where the amendment is made in consequence (directly or indirectly) of–

(a) the granting of relief under section 7(2) or (3) to any participator for allowable losses accruing in any chargeable period,

(aa) a claim under paragraph 13A (see paragraph 13E), or

(b) a notice of variation served under paragraph 9 of Schedule 5 on any responsible person in respect of a claim for any claim period.

12(2) Where under sub-paragraph (1) above it appears to the Board that the assessable profit for a chargeable period ought to have been larger and that the deficiency resulted from an excessive allowable loss accruing in a subsequent period having been set against the profit for that period, the Board may make a further assessment by virtue of sub-paragraph (1) above at any time not later than 4 years after the end of the chargeable period in which the allowable loss accrued (subject to paragraphs 12A and 12B).

12(3) Where under this paragraph the Board make an assessment or determination or amend an assessment or determination they shall give notice thereof to the participator concerned; and sub-paragraphs (4), (5) and (6) of paragraph 10 above shall apply in relation to any such assessment, determination or amendment as they apply in relation to an assessment or determination under that paragraph.

History – Para. 12(1) amended by FA 1976, s. 130(2), with effect from 29 July 1976.
Para. 12(1A) inserted by FA 2009, s. 99 and Sch. 51, para. 20(2), with effect from 1 April 2011 (SI 2010/867).
Para. 12(1B)(aa) inserted (and the "or" at the end of para. 12(1B)(a) omitted) by F(No. 3)A 2010, s. 28 and Sch. 12, para. 9, with effect in relation to claims made on or after 1 April 2011.
Para. 12(1B) inserted by FA 2009, s. 99 and Sch. 51, para. 20(2), with effect from 1 April 2011 (SI 2010/867).
In para. 12(2), the words "(notwithstanding anything in section 34 of the Taxes Management Act 1970 (ordinary time limit for assessment))" omitted, and the words "4 years" substituted for the words "six years", and the words "(subject to paragraphs 12A and 12B)" inserted, by FA 2009, s. 99 and Sch. 51, para. 20(3), with effect from 1 April 2011 (SI 2010/867).
Para. 12(3) inserted by FA 1976, s. 130(3), (4), with effect from 29 July 1976.

12A(1) Where–

(a) the Board has extended the period for the delivery of any return that is required under paragraph 2 of this Schedule to be delivered for any chargeable period, and

(b) the relevant time falls more than one year after the end of the chargeable period,

the period within which the Board may make an assessment under this Schedule for that chargeable period shall not expire before the end of the period of 4 years beginning with the relevant time.

12A(1A) An assessment (or an amendment of an assessment) under sub-paragraph (1) may be made at any time not more than 4 years after the end of the chargeable period to which the assessment relates (subject to sub-paragraph (1B) and paragraphs 12A and 12B).

12A(1B) The time limits in sub-paragraph (1A) and paragraphs 12A and 12B do not apply to an amendment of an assessment where the amendment is made in consequence (directly or indirectly) of–

(a) the granting of relief under section 7(2) or (3) to any participator for allowable losses accruing in any chargeable period, or

(b) a notice of variation served under paragraph 9 of Schedule 5 on any responsible person in respect of a claim for any claim period.

12A(2) In this paragraph

"the relevant time" means the earlier of–

(a) the time which, as a result of the extension, is the latest time for the delivery of the return; and

(b) the time when the return is delivered.

History – In para. 12A(1) the words "4 years" substituted for the words "five years" by FA 2009, s. 99 and Sch. 51, para. 21, with effect from 1 April 2011 (SI 2010/867).
Para. 12A(1A) and (1B) inserted by FA 2009, s. 99 and Sch. 51, para. 21, with effect from 1 April 2011 (SI 2010/867).
Para. 12A inserted by FA 1999, s. 102(3), with effect for chargeable periods ending on or after 30 June 1999.

12B(1) In a case involving a relevant situation brought about carelessly by a participator (or a person acting on behalf of a participator), an assessment (or an amendment of an assessment) under this Schedule on the participator may be made at any time not more than 6 years after the end of the relevant chargeable period (subject to sub-paragraph (2) and (2A)).

12B(2) In a case involving a relevant situation brought about deliberately by a participator (or a person acting on behalf of a participator), an assessment (or an amendment of an assessment) on the participator may be made at any time not more than 20 years after the end of the relevant chargeable period.

12B(2A) In a case involving a relevant situation brought about by arrangements which were expected to give rise to a tax advantage in respect of which a participator (or a person acting on behalf of a participator) was under an obligation to notify the Board under section 253 of the Finance Act 2014 (duty to notify Commissioners of promoter reference number) but failed to do so, an assessment (or an amendment of an assessment) on the participator may be made at any time not more than 20 years after the end of the relevant chargeable period.

12B(3) **"Relevant situation"** means a situation in which–

(a) there is a loss of tax,

(b) the assessable profit charged to tax by or stated in an assessment for a chargeable period ought to be or to have been larger,

(c) the allowable loss stated in an assessment or a determination of loss for a chargeable period ought to be or to have been smaller, or

(d) an assessment to tax should have been made for a chargeable period but was not made.

12B(4) **"Relevant chargeable period"** means–

(a) in the case of a further assessment under paragraph 12(2), the chargeable period in which the excessive allowable loss accrued, and

(b) in any other case, the chargeable period to which the assessment relates.

12B(5) Where the participator carried on a trade or business with one or more other persons at any time in the chargeable period for which the assessment under sub-paragraph (1), (2) or (2A) is made, an assessment to tax in respect of the profits of that trade or business may also be made on any of the participator's partners.

12B(6) In determining the amount of the tax to be charged on a person for a chargeable period in an assessment in a case mentioned in sub-paragraph (1), (2) or (2A) (including an assessment under sub-paragraph (5)), effect must be given to any relief or allowance to which that person would have been entitled for that period if a valid claim or application had been made.

12B(7) Sub-paragraph (6) only applies if the person on whom the assessment is made so requires.

12B(8) Subsections (5) to (7) of section 118 of the Taxes Management Act 1970 (losses and situations brought about carelessly or deliberately) apply for the purposes of this paragraph as they apply for the purposes of that Act.

12B(9) In subsection (6)(b) of that section (as it applies for the purposes of this paragraph), the reference to the person who provides the information has effect as if it included any person who becomes the responsible person for the oil field after the information is provided.

History – In para. 12B(1), "and (2A)" inserted by FA 2014, s. 277(2)(a), with effect from 17 July 2014.
Para. 12B(2A) inserted by FA 2014, s. 277(2)(b), with effect from 17 July 2014.
In para. 12B(5), ", (2) or (2A)" substituted for "or (2)" by FA 2014, s. 277(2)(c), with effect from 17 July 2014.
In para. 12B(6), ", (2) or (2A)" substituted for "or (2)" by FA 2014, s. 277(2)(d), with effect from 17 July 2014.
Para. 12B inserted by FA 2009, s. 99 and Sch. 51, para. 22, with effect from 1 April 2011 (SI 2010/867).

PAYMENT OF TAX

13 Subject to paragraph 14 below, the tax charged in an assessment made on a participator for any chargeable period and payable shall be due within six months after the end of that chargeable period or, if later, thirty days after the date of issue of the notice of assessment; but no tax shall be payable by virtue of this paragraph before 30th April 1976.

History – In para. 13, the words "and payable shall be due within six months" were substituted by FA 1982, s. 139(6) and Sch. 19, para. 19, with respect to chargeable periods ending on or after 30 June 1983.
Para. 13 previously amended by PRTA 1980, s. 1(4), in relation to chargeable periods ending on or after 31 December 1979.

CLAIM FOR RELIEF FOR OVERPAID TAX ETC

13A(1) This paragraph applies where–

(a) a participator has paid an amount by way of tax but believes that the tax was not due, or

(b) a participator has been assessed as liable to pay an amount by way of tax but believes that the tax is not due.

13A(2) The participator may make a claim to the Commissioners for Her Majesty's Revenue and Customs ("HMRC") for repayment or discharge of the amount.

13A(3) Paragraph 13B makes provision about cases in which HMRC are not liable to give effect to a claim under this paragraph.

13A(4) Paragraphs 13C to 14I make further provision about making and giving effect to claims under this paragraph.

13A(5) Paragraph 13F makes provision about the application of this paragraph and paragraphs 13B to 13E to amounts paid under contract settlements.

13A(6) HMRC are not liable to give relief in respect of a case described in sub-paragraph (1)(a) or (b) except as provided–

(a) by this Schedule (following a claim under this paragraph), or

(b) by or under another provision of the Oil Taxation Acts.

13A(7) For the purposes of this paragraph and paragraphs 13B to 13F, an amount paid by one person on behalf of another is treated as paid by the other person.

13A(8) In this paragraph and paragraphs 13B to 13F, **"the Oil Taxation Acts"** means–

(a) Parts 1 and 3 of this Act,

(b) the Oil Taxation Act 1983, and

(c) any other enactment relating to petroleum revenue tax.

History – Para. 13A and the heading before it inserted by F(No. 3)A 2010, s. 28 and Sch. 12, para. 10, with effect in relation to claims made on or after 1 April 2011.

CASES IN WHICH HMRC NOT LIABLE TO GIVE EFFECT TO A CLAIM

13B(1) HMRC are not liable to give effect to a claim under paragraph 13A if or to the extent that the claim falls within a case described in this paragraph.

13B(2) Case A is where the amount paid, or liable to be paid, is excessive by reason of–

(a) a mistake in a claim, election or notice or a nomination under Schedule 10 to FA 1987, or

(b) a mistake consisting of making or giving, or failing to make or give, a claim, election or notice or a nomination under Schedule 10 to FA 1987.

13B(3) Case B is where the participator–

(a) has or could have sought relief by making a claim for expenditure to be allowed under section 3 or 4 (allowance of expenditure), or

(b) is or will be able to seek relief by taking other steps under the Oil Taxation Acts.

13B(4) Case C is where the participator–

(a) could have sought relief by taking such steps within a period that has now expired, and

(b) knew, or ought reasonably to have known, before the end of that period that such relief was available.

13B(5) Case D is where the claim is made on grounds that–

(a) have been put to a court or tribunal in the course of an appeal by the participator relating to the amount paid or liable to be paid, or

(b) have been put to HMRC in the course of an appeal by the participator relating to that amount that is treated as having been determined by a tribunal (by virtue of paragraph 14(9) (settling of appeals by agreement)).

13B(6) Case E is where the participator knew, or ought reasonably to have known, of the grounds for the claim before the latest of the following–

(a) the date on which an appeal by the participator relating to the amount paid, or liable to be paid, in the course of which the ground could have been put forward (a "relevant appeal") was determined by a court or tribunal (or is treated as having been so determined),

(b) the date on which the participator withdrew a relevant appeal to a court or tribunal, and

(c) the end of the period in which the participator was entitled to make a relevant appeal to a court or tribunal.

13B(7) Case F is where the amount in question was paid or is liable to be paid–

(a) in consequence of proceedings enforcing the payment of that amount brought against the participator by HMRC, or

(b) in accordance with an agreement between the participator and HMRC settling such proceedings.

13B(8) Case G is where–

(a) the amount paid, or liable to be paid, is excessive by reason of a mistake in calculating the participator's liability to tax, and

(b) liability was calculated in accordance with the practice generally prevailing at the time.

13B(9) Case G does not apply where the amount paid, or liable to be paid, is tax which has been charged contrary to EU law.

13B(10) For the purposes of sub-paragraph (9), an amount of tax is charged contrary to EU law if, in the circumstances in question, the charge to tax is contrary to–

(a) the provisions relating to the free movement of goods, persons, services and capital in Titles II and IV of Part 3 of the Treaty on the Functioning of the European Union, or

(b) the provisions of any subsequent treaty replacing the provisions mentioned in paragraph (a).

History – Para. 13B(9) and (10) inserted by FA 2013, s. 231(2), with effect in relation to any claim (in respect of overpaid tax, excessive assessment etc) made after the end of the six month period beginning with 17 July 2013 (Royal Assent).

Para. 13B and the heading before it inserted by F(No. 3)A 2010, s. 28 and Sch. 12, para. 10, with effect in relation to claims made on or after 1 April 2011.

MAKING A CLAIM

13C(1) A claim under paragraph 13A may not be made more than 4 years after the end of the relevant chargeable period.

13C(2) In relation to a claim made in reliance on paragraph 13A(1)(a), the relevant chargeable period is–

(a) where the amount paid, or liable to be paid, is excessive by reason of a mistake in a return or returns under paragraph 2 or 5, the chargeable period to which the return (or, if more than one, the first return) relates, and

(b) otherwise, the chargeable period in respect of which the amount was paid.

13C(3) In relation to a claim made in reliance on paragraph 13A(1)(b), the relevant chargeable period is–

(a) where the amount liable to be paid is excessive by reason of a mistake in a return or returns under paragraph 2 or 5, the chargeable period to which the return (or, if more than one, the first return) relates, and

(b) otherwise,

the chargeable period to which the assessment relates.

13C(4) A claim under paragraph 13A must be in such form as the HMRC may prescribe.

History – Para. 13C(3)(a) and (b) (and the "–" before them) inserted by FA 2013, s. 232(2), with effect in relation to any claim (in respect of overpaid tax, excessive assessment etc) made after the end of the six month period beginning with 17 July 2013 (Royal Assent).

Para. 13C and the heading before it inserted by F(No. 3)A 2010, s. 28 and Sch. 12, para. 10, with effect in relation to claims made on or after 1 April 2011.

DECISION ON CLAIM

13D HMRC must–

(a) make a decision on the claim, and

(b) by notice inform the participator of their decision.

History – Para. 13D and the heading before it inserted by F(No. 3)A 2010, s. 28 and Sch. 12, para. 10, with effect in relation to claims made on or after 1 April 2011.

ASSESSMENT OF CLAIMANT IN CONNECTION WITH CLAIM

13E(1) This paragraph applies where–

(a) a claim is made under paragraph 13A,

(b) the grounds for giving effect to the claim also provide grounds for making an assessment or determination under paragraph 10 or 12, or an amendment of such an assessment or determination, on the participator in respect of any accounting period, and

(c) such an assessment, determination or amendment could be made but for the expiry of a time limit in paragraph 10(1A), 12(1A), 12A or 12B.

13E(2) Where this paragraph applies–

(a) the time limit does not apply, and

(b) the assessment, determination or amendment is not out of time if it is made before the final determination of the claim.

13E(3) A claim is not finally determined until it, or the amount to which it relates, can no longer be varied (whether on appeal or otherwise).

History – Para. 13E and the heading before it inserted by F(No. 3)A 2010, s. 28 and Sch. 12, para. 10, with effect in relation to claims made on or after 1 April 2011.

CONTRACT SETTLEMENTS

13F(1) In paragraph 13A(1)(a) the reference to an amount paid by a participator by way of tax includes an amount paid by a person under a contract settlement in connection with tax believed to be due.

13F(2) Sub-paragraphs (3) to (6) apply if the person who paid the amount under the contract settlement ("the payer") and the person from whom the tax was due ("the taxpayer") are not the same person.

13F(3) In relation to a claim under paragraph 13A in respect of that amount–

(a) the references to the participator in paragraph 13B(5) to (7) (Cases D, E and F) have effect as if they included the taxpayer,

(b) the reference to the participator in paragraph 13B(8) (Case G) has effect as if it were a reference to the taxpayer, and

(c) the reference to the participator in paragraph 13E(1)(b) has effect as if it were a reference to the taxpayer.

13F(4) Sub-paragraph (5) applies where the grounds for giving effect to a claim by the payer in respect of the amount also provide grounds for making an assessment or determination under paragraph 10 or 12, or an amendment of such an assessment or determination, on the taxpayer in respect of any chargeable period.

13F(5) HMRC may set any amount repayable to the payer by virtue of the claim against any amount payable by the taxpayer by virtue of the assessment, determination or amendment.

13F(6) The obligations of HMRC and the taxpayer are discharged to the extent of any set-off under sub-paragraph (5).

13F(7) **"Contract settlement"** means an agreement made in connection with any person's liability to make a payment to HMRC under or by virtue of an enactment.

History – Para. 13F and the heading before it inserted by F(No. 3)A 2010, s. 28 and Sch. 12, para. 10, with effect in relation to claims made on or after 1 April 2011.

APPEALS

14(1) A participator may appeal against an assessment or determination or an amendment of an assessment or determination made on or in relation to him by notice of appeal in writing given to HMRC within thirty days after the date of issue of the notice of assessment or determination or of the notice of the amendment.

14(1A) A participator who has made a claim under paragraph 13A may appeal from the decision on the claim by notice in writing given to HMRC within 30 days after the date of issue of the notice of the decision.

14(2) The notice of appeal must specify the grounds of appeal.

14(3) A participator who has given notice of appeal under sub-paragraph (1) above against an assessment charging him with any tax for a chargeable period may, if he delivered a return for that period as required by paragraph 2 above, withhold, until the determination or abandonment of the appeal, so much of the tax charged in the assessment as is the smaller of–

(a) the amount of the tax so charged; and

(b) tax on the difference between–

(i) the aggregate of the consideration received or receivable for oil as stated in the participator's return in pursuance of sub-paragraph (2) of that paragraph and, subject to sub-paragraph (4) below, the market value of oil as so stated; and

(ii) the aggregate of the corresponding consideration and value as included in the assessment.

14(4) Subject to sub-paragraph (5) below, where the market value of all the oil for which a market value is stated in the participator's return is, as stated in that return, less than the value which is produced for that oil by applying to it the average price mentioned in sub-paragraph (6) below, sub-paragraph (3) above shall have effect as if, for the reference to the market value of oil as so stated, there were substituted a reference to the value which is so produced for that oil.

14(5) The comparison of values and the substitution required by sub-paragraph (4) above shall, in the case of an appeal by a participator whose return relates both to gas and to other oil, be made separately for the gas and for the other oil.

14(6) The **"average price"** referred to in sub-paragraph (4) above is the average price at which all oil included in the relevant returns as oil delivered in the period covered by the returns and disposed of in sales at arm's length was so disposed of.

14(7) The **"relevant returns"** for the purposes of sub-paragraph (6) above are all the returns of all the participators in all oil fields which–

(a) were made for the chargeable period preceding that to which the appeal relates; and

(b) were delivered before the end of the chargeable period to which the appeal relates.

14(8) The participator may at any time, if HMRC do not object to his doing so, abandon an appeal instituted by him; and for this purpose he shall notify his desire to do so to HMRC who may, within thirty days after being so notified, object by notice in writing to the participator.

14(9) Where, at any time between–

(a) the giving of a notice of appeal against the assessment determination or amendment or from a decision of HMRC on a claim under paragraph 13A, and

(b) the determination of the appeal by the tribunal,

HMRC and the participator agree on how the assessment, determination, amendment or decision should be varied or on what assessment or determination should be substituted in relation to the chargeable period in question, the same consequences shall ensue as if the tribunal had determined the appeal to that effect.

14(10) If an appeal under sub-paragraph (1) is notified to the tribunal and it appears to the tribunal that the assessment, determination or amendment is wrong–

(a) because no, or a smaller, assessable profit or a, or a larger, allowable loss has accrued for the chargeable period in question; or

(b) because a, or a larger, assessable profit or no, or a smaller, allowable loss has accrued for that period,

the tribunal shall vary the assessment, determination or amendment in such manner, or substitute such assessment or determination, as may be required; and it shall be for the participator to satisfy the tribunal as to any matter within paragraph (a) above.

14(10A) If an appeal under sub-paragraph (1A) is notified to the tribunal and it appears to the tribunal that the decision is wrong, the tribunal shall substitute such decision as may be required.

14(11) When an appeal is notified to the tribunal, the decision of the tribunal on the appeal is final and conclusive.

14(12) But sub-paragraph (11) is subject to–

(a) sections 9 to 14 of the Tribunals, Courts and Enforcement Act 2007,

(b) Tribunal Procedure Rules, and

(c) any provision of this Schedule.

History – In para. 14(1) the words "to the Special Commissioners" omitted and the word "HMRC" substituted for the words "the Board" by SI 2009/56, art. 3 and Sch. 1, para. 74(2), with effect from 1 April 2009, subject to transitional and saving provisions in SI 2009/56, Sch. 3.

Para. 14(1A) inserted by F(No. 3)A 2010, s. 28 and Sch. 12, para. 11(2), with effect in relation to claims made on or after 1 April 2011.

Para. 14(2) substituted by SI 2009/56, art. 3 and Sch. 1, para. 74(3), with effect from 1 April 2009, subject to transitional and saving provisions in SI 2009/56, Sch. 3. Former para. 14(2) read as follows:

"**14(2)** The notice of appeal shall specify the grounds of appeal, but on the hearing of the appeal the Commissioners may allow the appellant to put forward any ground not specified in the notice, and may take it into consideration if satisfied that the omission was not wilful or unreasonable."

In para. 14(8) the word "HMRC" substituted for the words "the Board" twice by SI 2009/56, art. 3 and Sch. 1, para. 74(4), with effect from 1 April 2009, subject to transitional and saving provisions in SI 2009/56, Sch. 3.

In para. 14(9), "paragraph 13A" substituted for the words "section 33 of the Taxes Management Act 1970 as applied by paragraph 1 above" by F(No. 3)A 2010, s. 28 and Sch. 12, para. 11(3), with effect in relation to claims made on or after 1 April 2011.

In para. 14(9) the word "HMRC" substituted for the words "the Board" twice, the word "tribunal" substituted for the words "Special Commissioners" and the word "Commissioners" by SI 2009/56, art. 3 and Sch. 1, para. 74(5), with effect from 1 April 2009, subject to transitional and saving provisions in SI 2009/56, Sch. 3.

In para. 14(10), the words "an appeal under sub-paragraph (1)" substituted for the words "the appeal that" by F(No. 3)A 2010, s. 28 and Sch. 12, para. 11(4), with effect in relation to claims made on or after 1 April 2011.

In para. 14(10) the words "the appeal that is notified to the tribunal and" substituted for the words ", on the appeal,", the words "the tribunal" substituted for the words "a majority of the Commissioners present at the hearing" and the word "tribunal" substituted for the word "Commissioners" twice by SI 2009/56, art. 3 and Sch. 1, para. 74(6), with effect from 1 April 2009, subject to transitional and saving provisions in SI 2009/56, Sch. 3.

Para. 14(10A) inserted by F(No. 3)A 2010, s. 28 and Sch. 12, para. 11(5), with effect in relation to claims made on or after 1 April 2011.

Para 14(11) and (12) substituted for former para. 14(11) by SI 2009/777, art. 2, with effect from 1 April 2009. Former para. 14(11), which was substituted with effect from 1 April 2009 by SI 2009/56, art. 3 and Sch. 1, para. 74(7) (itself omitted by SI 2009/730, art. 7 with effect from the same date), must be taken never to have taken effect, but read as follows:

"**14(11)** Notwithstanding the provisions of sections 11 and 13 of the TCEA 2007 the decision of the tribunal shall be final and conclusive.".

Former para. 14(11) substituted by SI 2009/56, art. 3 and Sch. 1, para. 74(7), with effect from 1 April 2009, subject to transitional and saving provisions in SI 2009/56, Sch. 3. Former para. 14(11) read as follows:

"**14(11)** Save as otherwise provided by this Schedule (including the provisions applied by paragraph 1 above), the determination by the Special Commissioners of any appeal under this Part of this Act shall be final and conclusive."

Para. 14(1), (9) and (11) amended by FA 1976, s. 130(3)–(5), (7), and s. 130(6) substituted by FA 1976, s. 130(6), with effect from 29 July 1976.

Cross references – PRTA 1980, s. 1(5): repayment of excess of payment on account of overpayment of tax which cannot be withheld pending outcome of appeal under para. 14(3).

FA 1987, s. 66(8) and Sch. 12, para. 3(2)(d): para. 14(2), (8) and (11) apply in relation to appeals concerning allocations of blended oil *and apportionments of oil allowance in final periods.*

FA 1994, Sch. 22, para. 4(5): appeal against notice rejecting an election by reference to pipe-line usage.

APPEAL: HMRC REVIEW OR DETERMINATION BY TRIBUNAL

14A(1) This paragraph applies if notice of appeal has been given to HMRC.

14A(2) In such a case–

(a) the participator may notify HMRC that the participator requires HMRC to review the matter in question (see paragraph 14B),

(b) HMRC may notify the participator of an offer to review the matter in question (see paragraph 14C), or

(c) the participator may notify the appeal to the tribunal (see paragraph 14D).

14A(3) See paragraph 14G and 14H for provision about notifying appeals to the tribunal after a review has been required by the participator or offered by HMRC.

14A(4) This paragraph does not prevent the matter in question from being dealt with in accordance with paragraph 14(9).

History – Para. 14A inserted by SI 2009/56, art. 3 and Sch. 1, para. 75, with effect from 1 April 2009, subject to transitional and saving provisions in SI 2009/56, Sch. 3.

PARTICIPATOR REQUIRES REVIEW BY HMRC

14B(1) Sub-paragraphs (2) and (3) apply if the participator notifies HMRC that the participator requires HMRC to review the matter in question.

14B(2) HMRC must, within the relevant period, notify the participator of HMRC's view of the matter in question.

14B(3) HMRC must review the matter in question in accordance with paragraph 14E.

14B(4) The participator may not notify HMRC that the participator requires HMRC to review the matter in question and HMRC shall not be required to conduct a review if–

(a) the participator has already given a notification under this paragraph in relation to the matter in question,

(b) HMRC have given a notification under paragraph 14C in relation to the matter in question, or

(c) the participator has notified the appeal to the tribunal under paragraph 14D.

14B(5) In this paragraph **"relevant period"** means–

(a) the period of 30 days beginning with the day on which HMRC receive the notification from the participator, or

(b) such longer period as is reasonable.

History – Para. 14B inserted by SI 2009/56, art. 3 and Sch. 1, para. 75, with effect from 1 April 2009, subject to transitional and saving provisions in SI 2009/56, Sch. 3.

HMRC OFFER REVIEW

14C(1) Sub-paragraphs (2) to (5) apply if HMRC notify the participator of an offer to review the matter in question.

14C(2) When HMRC notify the participator of the offer, HMRC must also notify the participator of HMRC's view of the matter in question.

14C(3) If, within the acceptance period, the participator notifies HMRC of acceptance of the offer, HMRC must review the matter in question in accordance with paragraph 14E.

14C(4) If the participator does not give HMRC such a notification within the acceptance period, HMRC's view of the matter in question is to be treated as if it were contained in an agreement in writing under paragraph 14(9) for the settlement of that matter.

14C(5) Sub-paragraph (4) does not apply to the matter in question if, or to the extent that, the participator notifies the appeal to the tribunal under paragraph 14H.

14C(6) HMRC may not notify the participator of an offer to review the matter in question (and, accordingly, HMRC shall not be required to conduct a review) if–

(a) HMRC have already given a notification under this paragraph in relation to the matter in question,

(b) the participator has given a notification under paragraph 14B in relation to the matter in question, or

(c) the participator has notified the appeal to the tribunal under paragraph 14D.

14C(7) In this paragraph **"acceptance period"** means the period of 30 days beginning with the date of the document by which HMRC notify the participator of the offer to review the matter in question.

History – Para. 14C inserted by SI 2009/56, art. 3 and Sch. 1, para. 75, with effect from 1 April 2009, subject to transitional and saving provisions in SI 2009/56, Sch. 3.

NOTIFYING APPEAL TO THE TRIBUNAL

14D(1) This paragraph applies if notice of appeal has been given to HMRC.

14D(2) The participator may notify the appeal to the tribunal.

14D(3) If the participator notifies the appeal to the tribunal, the tribunal is to decide the matter in question.

14D(4) Sub-paragraphs (2) and (3) do not apply in a case where–

(a) HMRC have given a notification of their view of the matter in question under paragraph 14B, or

(b) HMRC have given a notification under paragraph 14C in relation to the matter in question.

14D(5) In a case falling within sub-paragraph (4)(a) or (b), the participator may notify the appeal to the tribunal, but only if permitted to do so by paragraph 14G or 14H.

History – Para. 14D inserted by SI 2009/56, art. 3 and Sch. 1, para. 75, with effect from 1 April 2009, subject to transitional and saving provisions in SI 2009/56, Sch. 3.

NATURE OF REVIEW ETC

14E(1) This paragraph applies if HMRC are required by paragraph 14B or 14C to review the matter in question.

14E(2) The nature and extent of the review are to be such as appear appropriate to HMRC in the circumstances.

14E(3) For the purpose of sub-paragraph (2), HMRC must, in particular, have regard to steps taken before the beginning of the review–

(a) by HMRC in deciding the matter in question, and

(b) by any person in seeking to resolve disagreement about the matter in question.

14E(4) The review must take account of any representations made by the participator at a stage which gives HMRC a reasonable opportunity to consider them.

14E(5) The review may conclude that HMRC's view of the matter in question is to be–

(a) upheld,

(b) varied, or

(c) cancelled.

14E(6) HMRC must notify the participator of the conclusions of the review and their reasoning within–

(a) the period of 45 days beginning with the relevant day, or

(b) such other period as may be agreed.

14E(7) In sub-paragraph (6) **"relevant day"** means–

(a) in a case where the participator required the review, the day when HMRC notified the participator of HMRC's view of the matter in question,

(b) in a case where HMRC offered the review, the day when HMRC received notification of the participator's acceptance of the offer.

14E(8) Where HMRC are required to undertake a review but do not give notice of the conclusions within the time period specified in sub-paragraph (6), the review is to be treated as having concluded that HMRC's view of the matter in question (see paragraphs 14B(2) and 14C(2)) is upheld.

14E(9) If sub-paragraph (8) applies, HMRC must notify the participator of the conclusion which the review is treated as having reached.

History – Para. 14E inserted by SI 2009/56, art. 3 and Sch. 1, para. 75, with effect from 1 April 2009, subject to transitional and saving provisions in SI 2009/56, Sch. 3.

EFFECT OF CONCLUSIONS OF REVIEW

14F(1) This paragraph applies if HMRC give notice of the conclusions of a review (see paragraph 14E(6) and (9)).

14F(2) The conclusions are to be treated as if they were an agreement in writing under paragraph 14(9) for the settlement of the matter in question.

14F(3) Sub-paragraph (2) does not apply to the matter in question if, or to the extent that, the participator notifies the appeal to the tribunal under paragraph 14G.

History – Para. 14F inserted by SI 2009/56, art. 3 and Sch. 1, para. 75, with effect from 1 April 2009, subject to transitional and saving provisions in SI 2009/56, Sch. 3.

NOTIFYING APPEAL TO TRIBUNAL AFTER REVIEW CONCLUDED

14G(1) This paragraph applies if–

(a) HMRC have given notice of the conclusions of a review in accordance with paragraph 14E, or

(b) the period specified in paragraph 14E(6) has ended and HMRC have not given notice of the conclusions of the review.

14G(2) The participator may notify the appeal to the tribunal within the post-review period.

14G(3) If the post-review period has ended, the participator may notify the appeal to the tribunal only if the tribunal gives permission.

14G(4) If the participator notifies the appeal to the tribunal, the tribunal is to determine the matter in question.

14G(5) In this paragraph **"post-review period"** means–

(a) in a case falling within sub-paragraph (1)(a), the period of 30 days beginning with the date of the document in which HMRC give notice of the conclusions of the review in accordance with paragraph 14E(6), or

(b) in a case falling within sub-paragraph (1)(b), the period that–

(i) begins with the day following the last day of the period specified in paragraph 14E(6), and

(ii) ends 30 days after the date of the document in which HMRC give notice of the conclusion of the review in accordance with paragraph 14E(9).

History – Para. 14G inserted by SI 2009/56, art. 3 and Sch. 1, para. 75, with effect from 1 April 2009, subject to transitional and saving provisions in SI 2009/56, Sch. 3.

NOTIFYING APPEAL TO TRIBUNAL AFTER REVIEW OFFERED BUT NOT ACCEPTED

14H(1) This paragraph applies if–

(a) HMRC have offered to review the matter in question (see paragraph 14C), and

(b) the participator has not accepted the offer.

14H(2) The participator may notify the appeal to the tribunal within the acceptance period.

14H(3) But if the acceptance period has ended, the participator may notify the appeal to the tribunal only if the tribunal gives permission.

14H(4) If the participator notifies the appeal to the tribunal, the tribunal is to determine the matter in question.

14H(5) In this paragraph **"acceptance period"** has the same meaning as in paragraph 14C.

History – Para. 14H inserted by SI 2009/56, art. 3 and Sch. 1, para. 75, with effect from 1 April 2009, subject to transitional and saving provisions in SI 2009/56, Sch. 3.

INTERPRETATION OF PARAGRAPHS 14A TO 14H

14I(1) In paragraphs 14A to 14H–

(a) **"matter in question"** means the matter to which an appeal relates;

(b) a reference to a notification is a reference to a notification in writing.

14I(2) In paragraphs 14A to 14H, a reference to the participator includes a person acting on behalf of the participator except in relation to–

(a) notification of HMRC's view under paragraphs 14B(2);

(b) notification by HMRC of an offer of review (and of their view of the matter) under paragraph 14C;

(c) notification of the conclusions of a review under paragraph 14E(6); and

(d) notification of the conclusions of a review under paragraph 14E(9).

14I(3) But if a notification falling within sub-paragraph (2) is given to the participator, a copy of the notification may also be given to a person acting on behalf of the participator.

History – Para. 14I inserted by SI 2009/56, art. 3 and Sch. 1, para. 75, with effect from 1 April 2009, subject to transitional and saving provisions in SI 2009/56, Sch. 3.

INTEREST ON TAX

15(1) Subject to sub-paragraph (2) below, tax charged in an assessment for a chargeable period shall carry interest at the rate applicable under section 178 of the Finance Act 1989 from two months after the end of the period until payment.

15(2) Nothing in sub-paragraph (1) shall authorise or require interest to be charged from any time before 30th April 1976.

15(3) Where, under paragraph 14(3) above, tax may be withheld until the determination or abandonment of an appeal, the interest on that tax may also be withheld until the determination or abandonment of the appeal.

History – In para. 15(1), the words "rate applicable … 1989" were substituted by FA 1989, s. 179(1)(a)(v), for periods beginning on or after 18 August 1989 (SI 1989/1298 (C 44)), and the words "two months" substituted by PRTA 1980, s. 2, in relation to tax charged for any period ending on or after 31 December 1979.

16 Subject to paragraph 17 below, where any amount of tax charged by an assessment to tax or paid on account of tax so charged becomes repayable under any provision of this Part of this Act that amount shall carry interest at the rate applicable under section 178 of the Finance Act 1989 from–

(a) two months after the end of the chargeable period for which the assessment was made; or

(b) the date on which it was paid,

whichever is the later, until the order for repayment is issued.

History – The reference to para. 17 was added by FA 1990, s. 121(1), (2).
The words "rate applicable … 1989" were substituted by FA 1989, s. 179(1)(a)(v) for periods beginning on or after 18 August 1989 (SI 1989/1298 (C 44)).
Para. 16 amended by PRTA 1980, s. 2 in relation to tax charged for any period ending on or after 31 December 1979.
The reference to the issuing of the order for repayment inserted retrospectively by FA 1989, s. 180.

17(1) This paragraph applies where–

(a) an assessment made on a participator for a chargeable period or an amendment of such an assessment (in this paragraph referred to as **"the relevant assessment or amendment"**) gives effect to relief under subsection (2) or subsection (3) of section 7 of this Act for one or more allowable losses accruing in a later chargeable period (in this paragraph referred to, in relation to the relevant assessment or amendment, as **"the relief for losses carried back"**); and

(b) the later chargeable period referred to in paragraph (a) above ends after 30th June 1991; and

(c) an amount of tax becomes repayable to the participator by virtue of the relevant assessment or amendment (whether wholly or partly by reason of giving effect to the relief for losses carried back).

17(2) In the following provisions of this paragraph, so much of the repayment of tax referred to in sub-paragraph (1)(c) above as is attributable to giving effect to the relief for losses carried back is referred to as **"the appropriate repayment"** and, in relation to the appropriate repayment, the chargeable period for which the relevant assessment or amendment is made is referred to as **"the repayment period"**.

17(3) For the purpose of determining the amount of the appropriate repayment in a case where the relevant assessment or amendment not only gives effect to the relief for losses carried back but also takes account of any other matter (whether a relief or not) which goes to reduce the assessable profit of the period in question or otherwise to reduce the tax payable for that period, the amount of the repayment which is attributable to the relief for losses carried back is the difference between–

(a) the total amount of tax repayable by virtue of the relevant assessment or amendment; and

(b) the amount of tax (if any) which would have been so repayable if no account had been taken of the relief for losses carried back.

17(4) Subject to sub-paragraph (6) below, where this paragraph applies, the amount of interest which, by virtue of paragraph 16 above, is carried by the appropriate repayment shall not exceed the difference between–

(a) the relevant percentage of the amount of the allowable loss or losses referred to in sub-paragraph (1)(a) above which is treated as reducing the assessable profit of the repayment period; and

(b) the amount of the appropriate repayment.

17(5) For the purposes of sub-paragraph (4)(a) above–

(a) where the repayment period ends on or before 30th June 1993, the relevant percentage, in relation to the amount of the loss or losses which is treated as reducing the assessable profit accruing to the participator for that period is 85 per cent; and

(b) in relation to the amount of the loss or losses which is treated as reducing the assessable profit accruing to the participator for any later repayment period, the relevant percentage is 60 per cent.

17(6) If, in order to give effect to the relief for losses carried back, a repayment of APRT falls, or will on the making of a claim fall, to be made with respect to a chargeable period which is the repayment period in relation to the appropriate repayment, the reference in sub-paragraph (4)(b) above to the appropriate repayment shall be construed as a reference to the aggregate of that repayment and the repayment of APRT.

17(7) In sub-paragraph (6) above **"APRT"** means advance petroleum revenue tax paid under Chapter II of Part VI of the Finance Act 1982.

History – In para. 17(5)(b), the words " if that later repayment period ends on or before 31 December 2015, and 45 per cent if it ends after 31 December 2015" omitted by FA 2016, s. 140(2), with effect from 15 September 2016 (Royal Assent).

In para. 17(5)(b) the words "if that later repayment period ends on or before 31 December 2015, and 45 per cent if it ends after 31 December 2015" inserted by FA 2015, s. 52(3), with effect from 26 March 2015 (Royal Assent).
Para. 17 amended by FA 1993, s. 186(2)–(4) as follows:
- words at end of para. 17(2) from "and, in relation to …" added;
- in para. 17(4), "Subject to sub-paragraph (6) below" inserted, "the relevant percentage of the amount" substituted and words after "above" in para. 17(4)(a) inserted;
- para. 17(5)–(7) added.

Para. 17 inserted by FA 1990, s. 121(1), (3).
Cross references – ICTA 1988, s. 500(5): corporation tax treatment of "appropriate repayment" under para. 17(2).

SCHEDULE 3 – PETROLEUM REVENUE TAX: MISCELLANEOUS PROVISIONS

Section 1

Notes – The text of Sch. 3 which follows includes certain amendments introduced by FA 1994, s. 236 and Sch. 23. These amendments do not have effect in relation to any light gases if, before 1 January 1994, an election was made under FA 1982, s. 134 (alternative valuation of certain ethane) or FA 1986, s. 109 (alternative valuation of certain light gases) and the election applies to those gases. See the text of the History note for any omitted or substituted wording where appropriate.

DEFINITION OF SALE OF OIL AT ARM'S LENGTH

1(1) For the purposes of this Part of this Act a sale of any oil is a **"sale at arm's length"** if, but only if, the following conditions are satisfied with respect to the contract of sale, that is to say–

(a) the contract price is the sole consideration for the sale;

(b) the terms of the sale are not affected by any commercial relationship (other than that created by the contract itself) between the seller or any person connected with the seller and the buyer or any person connected with the buyer; and

(c) neither the seller nor any person connected with him has, directly or indirectly, any interest in the subsequent resale or disposal of the oil or any product derived therefrom.

1(2) Section 1122 of CTA 2010 (connected persons) shall apply for the purposes of the preceding sub-paragraph.

History – In para. 1(2), the words "Section 1122 of CTA 2010" substituted for the words "Section 839 of the Taxes Act" by CTA 2010, s. 1177 and Sch. 1, para. 165(2), with effect for corporation tax purposes for accounting periods ending on or after 1 April 2010, and for income tax and capital gains tax purposes for the tax year 2010–11 and subsequent tax years.
See ICTA 1988, Sch. 29, para. 32 for substitution of former reference to that Act in para. 1(2).

DETERMINATION OF MARKET VALUE: THE NOTIONAL DELIVERY DAY FOR A QUANTITY OF OIL

1A(1) This paragraph has effect for determining, for the purposes of this Schedule, the day which is the **"notional delivery day"** in the case of any particular quantity of oil of any particular kind whose market value falls to be determined in accordance with the provisions of this Schedule in the case of any chargeable period.

1A(2) The notional delivery day need not be a day in the chargeable period.

1A(3) In the case of a quantity of oil which, at the end of the chargeable period,–

(a) has neither been disposed of nor relevantly appropriated in the period, or

(b) has been disposed of but not delivered in the period,

the notional delivery day is the last business day of the chargeable period.

1A(4) In the case of–

(a) a quantity of oil won and disposed of which is delivered on a day in the chargeable period, or

(b) a quantity of oil–

  (i) relevantly appropriated on a day in the chargeable period, but

  (ii) not disposed of in the chargeable period,

the notional delivery day is to be determined in accordance with sub-paragraphs (5) to (7) below.

1A(5) If that oil is–

(a) oil transported by ship from the place of extraction to a place in the United Kingdom or elsewhere, or

(b) oil transported by pipeline to a place in the United Kingdom and loaded on to a ship there,

and there is a loading slot for it (see sub-paragraph (8)), the notional delivery day is the middle day of the loading slot.

PRT Statutes

1A(6) If sub-paragraph (5) above does not apply to that oil, then–

(a) if it is oil delivered on a day in the chargeable period, the notional delivery day is the date of the delivery, or

(b) if it is oil relevantly appropriated on a day in the chargeable period, the notional delivery day is the date of the appropriation.

1A(7) The Treasury may by regulations make provision for or in connection with substituting as the notional delivery day in such circumstances as may be prescribed–

(a) in the case of oil transported by ship from the place of extraction to a place in the United Kingdom or elsewhere, the date of completion of load, or

(b) in the case of oil transported by pipeline to a place in the United Kingdom and loaded on to a ship there, the date of the bill of lading.

1A(8) The "loading slot" for any oil is the period of three days within which the loading of the oil on to the ship is or was to take place–

(a) as duly published by the operator of the facility at which that loading is or was to take place (unless paragraph (b) below applies), or

(b) as subsequently finally duly varied to give effect to any modifications duly notified to that operator by the participator concerned.

1A(9) In sub-paragraph (8) above, **"duly"** means in accordance with the arrangements for the time being governing the time and manner of–

(a) publication, or variation, of the final loading schedule for the calendar month in which loading is or was to take place, or

(b) notification of modifications to that schedule,

and, in any case, before the end of the calendar month immediately preceding that in which loading is to take place.

1A(10) If the Treasury consider that, for the purpose of defining "loading slot", any period of days for the time being specified by or under this Act as the period of days within which loading of oil on to a ship is to take place, is, or is to be, no longer appropriate, they may by regulations make provision for, or in connection with,–

(a) varying the number of days in the period,

(b) determining the day that is to be the notional delivery day if the number, as varied, is an even number.

The power conferred by this sub-paragraph includes power to make amendments to, or modifications of, this Schedule.

History – Para. 1A inserted by FA 2006, s. 146(1), with effect from 1 July 2006 in relation to oil delivered or appropriated on or after that date, subject to the provisions of FA 2006, s. 147(2)–(8).

DEFINITION OF MARKET VALUE OF OIL

2(1) Except in the case of light gases the market value of any particular quantity of oil of any kind on any day shall be determined for the purposes of this Part of this Act in accordance with this paragraph and, accordingly, references in the following provisions of this paragraph to **"oil"** do not apply to light gases.

2(1A) This paragraph makes different provision according to whether the oil is–

(a) Category 1 oil of any kind, or

(b) Category 2 oil of any kind.

2(1B) For the purposes of this Act–

(a) Category 1 oil is oil of any of one or more kinds specified as such in regulations made for the purpose by the Board;

(b) Category 2 oil is oil of any other kind.

2(1C) The Board may specify oil of any particular kind as Category 1 oil only if they are satisfied that reports of prices for sales of oil of that kind are published and widely available (whether or not on payment of a fee).

2(2) The market value of any particular quantity of Category 1 oil of any kind is the price for which that quantity of oil of that kind might reasonably have been expected to be sold under a contract of sale that *meets the following conditions*–

(a) the contract is for the sale of the oil at arm's length to a willing buyer;

(b) the contract is for delivery of a single standard cargo of the oil;

(c) the contract specifies a period of three days within which loading of the oil is to take place and that period includes the notional delivery day for the actual oil;

(d) the contract requires the oil to have been subjected to appropriate initial treatment before delivery;

(e) the contract requires the oil to be delivered–

(i) in the case of oil extracted in the United Kingdom, at the place of extraction; or

(ii) in the case of oil extracted from strata in the sea bed and subsoil of the territorial sea of the United Kingdom or of a designated area, at the place in the United Kingdom or another country at which the seller could reasonably be expected to deliver it or, if there is more than one such place, the one nearest to the place of extraction.

The terms as to payment which are to be implied in the contract are those which are customarily contained in contracts for the sale at arm's length of oil of the kind in question.

2(2AA) The market value of any particular quantity of Category 2 oil of any kind is the price for which that quantity of oil of that kind might reasonably have been expected to be sold under a contract of sale that meets the following conditions–

(a) the contract is for the sale of the oil at arm's length to a willing buyer;

(b) the contract provides for delivery of the oil on the notional delivery day for the actual oil or within such period that includes that day as is normal under a contract at arm's length for the sale of oil of that kind (or, if there is more than one such period, the shortest of them);

(c) the contract is made on a date such that the period between that date and the notional delivery day for the actual oil is the normal period between contract and delivery in the case of a contract at arm's length for the sale of oil of that kind (or, if there is more than one such period, the shortest of them);

(d) the contract requires the oil to have been subjected to appropriate initial treatment before delivery;

(e) the contract requires the oil to be delivered–

(i) in the case of oil extracted in the United Kingdom, at the place of extraction; or

(ii) in the case of oil extracted from strata in the sea bed and subsoil of the territorial sea of the United Kingdom or of a designated area, at the place in the United Kingdom or another country at which the seller could reasonably be expected to deliver it or, if there is more than one such place, the one nearest to the place of extraction.

The terms as to payment which are to be implied in the contract are those which are customarily contained in contracts for the sale at arm's length of oil of the kind in question.

2(2A) [Effectively repealed by FA 2006, s. 146(6).]

2(2B) [Effectively repealed by FA 2006, s. 146(6).]

2(2C) [Effectively repealed by FA 2006, s. 146(6).]

2(2D) [Effectively repealed by FA 2006, s. 146(6).]

2(2E) For the purposes of sub-paragraph (2) or (2AA) above, the price of any quantity of Category 1 or Category 2 oil of any kind shall be determined in such manner, on the basis of such information, and by reference to such factors, as may be prescribed for oil of that Category and kind in regulations made by the Board.

2(2F) The provision that may be made by regulations under subsection (2E) above includes provision for or in connection with any or all of the following–

(a) determining the price by reference to prices, or an average of prices, for sales of oil (whether or not oil of the Category or kind in question, and whether the prices are prices under actual contracts, prices that are published and widely available (whether on payment of a fee or otherwise) or prices ascertained or determined in some other way);

(b) the prices to be taken into account;

(c) the descriptions of contracts to be taken into account;

(d) the method to be used for determining an average of prices;

(e) the day or days, or period or periods, by reference to which prices, or any average of prices, is to be determined;

(f) the application of a prescribed price differential, in cases where the price of oil of one kind falls to be determined in whole or in part by reference to prices for oil of some other kind.

2(2G) Sub-paragraph (2I) below has effect if, or in so far as, the Board are satisfied that it is impracticable or inappropriate to determine for the purposes of sub-paragraph (2) or (2AA) above the price of any oil in accordance with the provisions of regulations for the time being in force under sub-paragraph (2E) above.

2(2H) For that purpose it is immaterial whether the impracticability or inappropriateness is by virtue of–

(a) an insufficiency of contracts or published prices that satisfy the conditions,

(b) an insufficiency of information relating to such contracts or published prices, or

(c) the nature of the market for oil of the kind in question,

or for any other reason.

2(2I) Where this sub-paragraph has effect, the price is to be determined–

(a) so far as it is practicable and appropriate to do so by reference to other contracts or published prices (whether or not relating to oil of the same kind) and in accordance with the principles set out in the regulations for determining an average of prices; and

(b) so far as it is not practicable or appropriate to determine it as mentioned in paragraph (a) above, in such other manner as appears to the Board to be appropriate in the circumstances.

2(3) [Omitted by FA 2006, s. 146(7) and repealed by s. 178 and Sch. 26, Pt. 5(1).]

2(3A) Where all or any of the oil whose market value falls to be ascertained in accordance with sub-paragraph (1) and sub-paragraph (2) or (2AA) above has been subjected to initial treatment before being disposed of or relevantly appropriated, the appropriate initial treatment referred to in sub-paragraph (2)(d) or (2AA)(d) above shall, as respects that oil, include the whole of that treatment.

2(4) The provisions of sub-paragraphs (2) and (2AA) above shall apply for the ascertainment of the market value of oil in any case mentioned in paragraph 2(2) of Schedule 2 to this Act as they apply in relation to the corresponding case mentioned in those provisions.

2(5) In this paragraph **"prescribed"** means specified in, or determined in accordance with, regulations.

History – In para. 2(1) the words "any particular quantity of oil of any kind on any day" substituted for "any oil in any calendar month" by FA 2006, s. 146(3), with effect from 1 July 2006 in relation to oil delivered or appropriated on or after that date, subject to the provisions of FA 2006, s. 147(2)–(8).

In para. 2(1), the words "Except in the case of light gases" and the words "and, accordingly, references … to light gases" inserted by FA 1994, s. 236 and Sch. 23, para. 3(1). See also the Note at the head of this Schedule.

Para. 2(1) substituted by FA 1987, s. 62 and Sch. 11, para. 1(2), with respect to chargeable periods ending after 31 December 1986.

Para. 2(1A) inserted by FA 2006, s. 146(4), with effect from 1 July 2006 in relation to oil delivered or appropriated on or after that date, subject to the provisions of FA 2006, s. 147(2)–(8).

Para. 2(1B) inserted by FA 2006, s. 146(4), with effect from 1 July 2006 in relation to oil delivered or appropriated on or after that date, subject to the provisions of FA 2006, s. 147(2)–(8).

Para. 2(1C) inserted by FA 2006, s. 146(4), with effect from 1 July 2006 in relation to oil delivered or appropriated on or after that date, subject to the provisions of FA 2006, s. 147(2)–(8).

Para. 2(2) and (2AA) substituted for para. 2(2) by FA 2006, s. 147(5), with effect from 1 July 2006 in relation to oil delivered or appropriated on or after that date, subject to the provisions of FA 2006, s. 147(2)–(8). Former para. 2(2) read as follows:

"**2(2)** Subject to the following provisions of this paragraph, the market value of any oil in a calendar month (in this paragraph referred to as "the relevant month") is the price at which oil of that kind might reasonably have been expected to be sold under a contract of sale satisfying the following conditions–

(a) the contract is for the sale of the oil at arm's length to a willing buyer;

(b) the contract is for the delivery of the oil at a time in the relevant month;

(c) the contract is entered into within the period beginning at the beginning of the month preceding the relevant month and ending on the middle day of the relevant month or, if the Treasury by order so direct, within such other period as may be specified in the order;

(d) the contract requires the oil to have been subjected to appropriate initial treatment before delivery;

(e) the contract requires the oil to be delivered–

(i) in the case of oil extracted in the United Kingdom, at the place of extraction; or

(ii) in the case of oil extracted from strata in the sea bed and subsoil of the territorial sea of the United Kingdom or of a designated area, at the place in the United Kingdom or another country at which the seller could reasonably be expected to deliver it or, if there is more than one such place, the one nearest to the place of extraction;

(f) in the case of oil whose market value falls to be ascertained as in a particular month for the purposes of paragraph (b) of section 2(4) or paragraph (d) of section 2(5) of this Act or, subject to sub-paragraph (3) below, under paragraph 3 below for the purposes of paragraph (b) or (c) of the said section 2(5), the contract is for the sale of the whole quantity of oil whose market value falls to be ascertained as in that month for the purposes of the paragraph in question, and of no other oil and, for the avoidance of doubt, it is hereby declared that the terms as to payment which are to be implied in the contract shall be those which are customarily contained in contracts for the sale at arm's length of oil of the kind in question and, for the purposes of paragraph (c) above, the middle day of a month containing an even number of days shall be taken to be the last day of the first half of the month, and the power to make an order under that paragraph shall be exercisable by statutory instrument which shall be subject to annulment in pursuance of a resolution of the Commons House of Parliament."

In former para. 2(2), the words from the beginning to "to be delivered" in para. (e) were substituted, para. (c) was changed to para. (f), the words in para. (f) "as in a particular month" and "as at a particular time" were substituted, and the words "and, for the purposes of paragraph (c)" to the end were inserted by FA 1987, s. 62 and Sch. 11, para. 1(3)–(5), with respect to chargeable periods ending after 31 December 1986. The words in para. (f) (formerly in para. (c)) "and, for the avoidance…in question" were inserted by FA 1983, s. 38, with effect from 13 May 1983.

In former para. 2(2)(e)(ii), the words "or another country" were inserted by F(No. 2)A 1992, s. 74 and Sch. 15, para. 4(1), effective in accordance with s. 74(5) of that Act.

Para. 2(2E)–(2I) substituted for para. 2(2A)–(2D) by FA 2006, s. 146(6), with effect from 1 July 2006 in relation to oil delivered or appropriated on or after that date, subject to the provisions of FA 2006, s. 147(2)–(8). Former para. 2(2A)–(2D) read as follows:

"**2(2A)** For the purpose of sub-paragraph (2) above, the price of any oil in a calendar month shall be determined, subject to sub-paragraphs (2B) and (2C) below, by taking the average of the prices under actual contracts for the sale of oil of that kind–

(a) which are contracts for the sale of oil by a participator in an oil field or by a company which, for the purposes of section 115(2) of the Finance Act 1984, is associated with such a participator; and

(b) which, subject to sub-paragraph (2B) below, satisfy the conditions in paragraphs (a) to (e) of sub-paragraph (2) above; and

(c) which do not contain terms as to payment which differ from those customarily contained in contracts for the sale at arm's length of oil of the kind in question.

2(2B) For the purposes of sub-paragraph (2A)(b) above, a contract shall be treated as fulfilling the condition in paragraph (c) of sub-paragraph (2) above if it contains provisions under which the price for oil to be delivered in the relevant month either is determined or subject to review in the period relevant for the purposes of that paragraph or is determined by reference to other prices which are themselves determined in that period, being prices for oil to be delivered in the relevant month.

2(2C) The average referred to in sub-paragraph (2A) above shall be determined–

(a) by establishing an average price for oil of the kind in question for each business day within the period relevant for the purposes of sub-paragraph (2)(c) above; and

(b) by taking the arithmetic mean of the average prices so established;

and in this sub-paragraph "business day" has the same meaning as in the Bills of Exchange Act 1882.

2(2D) If or in so far as the Board are satisfied that it is impracticable or inappropriate to determine for the purposes of sub-paragraph (2) above the price of any oil in a calendar month as mentioned in sub-paragraph (2A) above (whether by virtue of an insufficiency of contracts satisfying the conditions or of information relating to such contracts or by virtue of the nature of the market for oil of the kind in question or for any other reason), that price shall be determined,–

(a) so far as it is practicable and appropriate to do so by reference to such other contracts (whether or not relating to oil of the same kind) and in accordance with the principles in sub-paragraph (2C) above; and

(b) so far as it is not practicable or appropriate to determine it as mentioned in paragraph (a) above, in such other manner as appears to the Board to be appropriate in the circumstances."

Former para. 2(2A)–(2D) were inserted by FA 1987, s. 62 and Sch. 11, para. 1(6), with respect to chargeable periods ending after 31 December 1986.

Para. 2(3) omitted by FA 2006, s. 146(7) and repealed by FA 2006, s. 178 and Sch. 26, Pt. 5(1), with effect from 1 July 2006 in relation to oil delivered or appropriated on or after that date, subject to the provisions of FA 2006, s. 147(2)–(8).

In former para. 2(3), the words "as in a particular month" "to (2D)", "as in that month" and "(2)(e)" were substituted, words between "the market value" and "of so much of that oil" were omitted, and the words "in that month" after "was disposed of" were inserted, by FA 1987, s. 62 and Sch. 11, para. 1(7) and Sch. 16, Pt. X, with respect to chargeable periods ending after 31 December 1986.

In former para. 2(3), the words "(2)(f)" substituted by FA 1994, s. 235(2) in relation to chargeable periods ending after 31 December 1994.

In para. 2(3A) the words "sub-paragraph (1) and sub-paragraph (2) or (2AA) above" substituted for "sub-paragraphs (1) and (2) above" and "sub-paragraph (2)(d) or (2AA)(d) above" substituted for "sub-paragraph (2)(a) above" by FA 2006, s. 146(8), with effect from 1 July 2006 in relation to oil delivered or appropriated on or after that date, subject to the provisions of FA 2006, s. 147(2)–(8).

Para. 2(3A) was inserted by FA 1980, s. 109(6), in relation to chargeable periods ending after 31 December 1979.

In para. 2(4) the words "sub-paragraphs (2) and (2AA)" substituted for "sub-paragraphs (2) and (3)" by FA 2006, s. 146(9), with effect from 1 July 2006 in relation to oil delivered or appropriated on or after that date, subject to the provisions of FA 2006, s. 147(2)–(8).

Para. 2(5) inserted by FA 2006, s. 146(9), with effect from 1 July 2006 in relation to oil delivered or appropriated on or after that date, subject to the provisions of FA 2006, s. 147(2)–(8).

Cross references – FA 1982, s. 134 and Sch. 18: alternative valuation of ethane used for petrochemical purposes.
FA 1984, s. 115: information relating to sales at arm's length and market value of oil.
FA 1986, s. 108(1), (2): construction of references to "subsoil", "territorial sea" and "United Kingdom" on or after 1 April 1986.
FA 1986, s. 109 and Sch. 21: alternative valuation of light gases other than ethane.
FA 2006, s. 147(7), (8): provisions in relation to powers to make regulations under amendments made by FA 2006, s. 147 or Sch. 18.

Statutory instruments – SI 2006/3313: partly made under para. 2(1B), (1C), (2E) and (2F).

Statements of practice – 14/93: circumstances in which HMRC will exercise discretion under para. 2(2D)(b) to set a different method of valuation.

2A(1) Paragraph 2 above shall have effect in accordance with this paragraph where the oil whose market value falls to be ascertained at any time in accordance with sub-paragraph (1) to (2I) of that paragraph, consists of or includes gas.

2A(1A) Sub-paragraphs (2) and (3) below also apply where the market value of any light gases falls to be ascertained under paragraph 3A below.

2A(2) Sub-paragraph (2)(d) or (as the case may be) (2AA)(d) of paragraph 2 above or, as the case may require, sub-paragraph (2)(b) of paragraph 3A below shall not apply to so much of the oil as consists of gas unless–

(a) it has been subjected to initial treatment before being disposed of or relevantly appropriated; or

(b) it has, after being disposed of or relevantly appropriated, been subjected to initial treatment by or on behalf of the participator in question or by or on behalf or a person who is connected with him within the meaning of section 1122 of CTA 2010;

and where oil consisting of gas has, whether before or after being disposed of or relevantly appropriated, been subjected to initial treatment by or on behalf of the participator in question or by or on behalf of a person who is connected with him as aforesaid the appropriate initial treatment referred to in sub-paragraph (2) or (2AA)(d) of paragraph 2 above or, as the case may require, sub-paragraph (2)(b) of paragraph 3A below shall include the treatment to which it has been so subjected.

2A(3) Where the initial treatment mentioned in sub-paragraph (2) or (2AA) above includes treatment in order to separate gas of one or more kinds which are transported and sold in normal commercial practice, the market value of the gas of each such kind which is separated shall be ascertained in accordance with sub-paragraphs (1) to (2I) of paragraph 2 or, as the case may require, in accordance with paragraph 3A below as if that were the only oil whose market value fell to be ascertained at the time in question.

2A(4) [Omitted by FA 1994, s. 236 and Sch. 23, para. 3(5). See also the Note at the head of this Schedule.]

History – In para. 2A(1) "(2I)" substituted for "(2D)" by FA 2006, s. 146 and Sch. 18, para. 8(2)(a), with effect in relation to oil delivered or appropriated on or after 1 July 2006, subject to provisions of FA 2006, s. 147(2)–(8).

In para. 2A(1) the words ", or in accordance with those sub-paragraphs as modified by sub-paragraph (3) of that paragraph," omitted by *FA 2006, s. 146 and Sch. 18, para. 8(2)(b)* and repealed by s. 178 and Sch. 26, Pt. 5(1), with effect in relation to oil delivered or appropriated on or after 1 July 2006, subject to provisions of FA 2006, s. 147(2)–(8).

In para. 2A(1), the words "to (2D)", in para. 2A(2), the words "(2)(d)" in each place, and in para. 2A(3), the words "to (2D)" and "(2)(e)", were substituted by FA 1987, s. 62 and Sch. 11, para. 2, with respect to chargeable periods ending after 31 December 1986.

Para. 2A(1A) inserted by FA 1994, s. 236 and Sch. 23, para. 3(2). See also the Note at the head of this Schedule.

In para. 2A(2)(b), the words "section 1122 of CTA 2010" substituted for the words "section 839 of the Taxes Act" by CTA 2010, s. 1177 and Sch. 1, para. 165(3), with effect for corporation tax purposes for accounting periods ending on or after 1 April 2010, and for income tax and capital gains tax purposes for the tax year 2010–11 and subsequent tax years.

In para. 2A(2) the words "Sub-paragraph (2)(d) or (as the case may be) (2AA)(d) of paragraph 2 above" substituted for "Sub-paragraph (2)(d) of paragraph 2 above" and the words "or (2AA)" inserted by FA 2006, s. 146 and Sch. 18, para. 8(3), with effect in relation to oil delivered or appropriated on or after 1 July 2006, subject to provisions of FA 2006, s. 147(2)–(8).

In para. 2A(2), the words "or, as the case ... paragraph 3A below", inserted in each place by FA 1994, s. 236 and Sch. 23, para. 3(3). See also the Note at the head of this Schedule.

In para. 2A(3) the words "or (2AA)" inserted by FA 2006, s. 146 and Sch. 18, para. 8(4)(a), with effect in relation to oil delivered or appropriated on or after 1 July 2006, subject to provisions of FA 2006, s. 147(2)–(8).
In para. 2A(3) "(2I)" substituted for "(2D)" by FA 2006, s. 146 and Sch. 18, para. 8(4)(b), with effect in relation to oil delivered or appropriated on or after 1 July 2006, subject to provisions of FA 2006, s. 147(2)–(8).
In para. 2A(3) the words "(with sub-paragraphs (2)(f) of paragraph 2 applying accordingly)" omitted at theend by FA 2006, s. 146 and Sch. 18, para. 8(4)(c) and repealed by s. 178 and Sch. 26, Pt. 5(1), with effect in relation to oil delivered or appropriated on or after 1 July 2006, subject to provisions of FA 2006, s. 147(2)–(8).
In para. 2A(3), the words "or, as the case … paragraph 3A below", inserted by FA 1994, s. 236 and Sch. 23, para. 3(4). See also the Note at the head of this Schedule.
In para. 2A(3), the words "(2)(f)" substituted for "(2)(e)" by FA 1994, s. 235(2), in relation to chargeable periods ending after 31 December 1994.
Para. 2A(4) omitted by FA 1994, s. 236 and Sch. 23, para. 3(5). See also the Note at the head of this Schedule. Para. 2A(4) formerly read as follows:
"2A(4) Where the oil consists of or includes natural gas within the meaning of the Energy Act 1976, it shall be assumed for the purposes of paragraph 2–
(a) that any consent given under section 29 of the Gas Act 1972 for the supply of the gas applies to the supply of the gas under the contract mentioned in sub-paragraph (2) of that paragraph; and
(b) that no consent is required under that section for that supply if no such consent would be required if that contract were in fact made by the participator in question.".
Para. 2A(4) was previously variously amended by the Oil and Gas (Enterprise) Act 1982, s. 37 and Sch. 3, para. 22, Sch. 4 and SI 1982/1059, with effect from 18 August 1982.
See ICTA 1988, s. 844 and Sch. 29, para. 32 for substitution of former reference to that Act in s. 2A(2)(b).
Para. 2A inserted by FA 1980, s. 109(7), in relation to chargeable periods ending after 31 December 1979.
Cross references – FA 1982, s. 134 and Sch. 18: alternative valuation of ethane used for petrochemical purposes.
FA 1986, s. 109 and Sch. 21: alternative valuation of light gases other than ethane.

AGGREGATE MARKET VALUE OF OIL FOR PURPOSES OF SECTION 2(5)

3(1) For the purposes of subsection (5) of section 2 of this Act, the aggregate market value of any oil falling within paragraph (b) or (c) of that subsection is arrived at as follows.

3(2) In the case of oil falling within paragraph (b) of that subsection and delivered as there mentioned in the chargeable period in question–

(a) for each delivery, find (in accordance with paragraph 2 above (read, where applicable, with paragraph 2A above)) the market value of the quantity of oil delivered, and

(b) aggregate the market values so found.

In the case of oil falling within paragraph (c) of that subsection and appropriated as there mentioned in the chargeable period in question–

(a) for each appropriation, find (in accordance with paragraph 2 above (read, where applicable, with paragraph 2A above)) the market value of the quantity of oil appropriated, and

(b) aggregate the market values so found.

History – Para. 3 substituted by FA 2006, s. 146 and Sch. 18, para. 9, with effect in relation to oil delivered or appropriated on or after 1 July 2006, subject to provisions of FA 2006, s. 147(2)–(8). Former para. 3 read as follows:
"3(1) For the purposes of subsection (5) of section 2 of this Act the aggregate market value of any oil falling within paragraph (b) or (c) of that subsection shall be arrived at by ascertaining, for each calendar month in the chargeable period in question, the market value of so much, if any, of that oil as was–
(a) in the case of oil falling within the said paragraph (b), delivered as there mentioned in that month;
(b) in the case of oil falling within the said paragraph (c), appropriated as there mentioned in that month,
and, in either case, aggregating the market values so ascertained.
3(2) In this paragraph and elsewhere in this Part of this Act **"calendar month"** (where those words are used) means a month of the calendar year.".
Words were omitted from original para. 3(1), and the former definition of "the material time" was omitted from para. 3(2), by FA 1987, s. 62 and Sch. 11, para. 3 and s. 72 and Sch. 16, Pt. X, with respect to chargeable periods ending after 31 December 1986.
Cross references – FA 1982, s. 134 and Sch. 18: alternative valuation of ethane.
FA 1986, s. 109 and Sch. 21: alternative valuation of light gases other than ethane.

DEFINITION OF MARKET VALUE OF LIGHT GASES

3A(1) The market value of any light gases for the purposes of this Part of this Act is the price at which, having regard to all the circumstances relevant to the disposal or appropriation in question, light gases of that kind might reasonably have been expected to be sold under a contract of sale satisfying the conditions specified in sub-paragraph (2) below.

3A(2) The conditions referred to in sub-paragraph (1) above are that–

(a) the contract is for the sale of the gases at arm's length to a willing buyer;

(b) the contract requires the gases to have been subjected to appropriate initial treatment before delivery; and

(c) the contract requires the gases to be delivered–

(i) in the case of gases extracted in the United Kingdom, at the place of extraction; or

(ii) in the case of gases extracted from strata in the sea bed and subsoil of the territorial sea of the United Kingdom or of a designated area, at the place in the United Kingdom or another country at which the seller could reasonably be expected to deliver the gases or, if there is more than one such place, the one nearest to the place of extraction.

3A(3) If the circumstances referred to in sub-paragraph (1) above are such that the price referred to in that sub-paragraph might reasonably be expected to include–

(a) any such payments as are referred to in subsection (2) of section 114 of the Finance Act 1984 (treatment of certain payments relating to gas sales), or

(b) any capacity payments, as defined in subsection (5) of that section,

section 114 of the Finance Act 1984 shall apply accordingly in relation to the notional contract specified in sub-paragraph (1) above as it applies in relation to an actual contract.

3A(3A) The circumstances referred to in sub-paragraph (1) above include–

(a) the timing of the making, and of any subsequent variations, of the actual contract or other arrangements under which the disposal or appropriation was made;

(b) the terms of that contract or, as the case may be, of those arrangements, and the terms of any such variations; and

(c) the extent to which the circumstances to which regard is to be had by virtue of paragraphs (a) and (b) above are circumstances that might reasonably have been expected to exist in the case of a contract satisfying the conditions specified in sub-paragraph (2) above.

3A(4) This paragraph has effect subject to sub-paragraphs (2) and (3) of paragraph 2A above.

History – Para. 3A(3A) inserted by FA 1998, s. 152(1) and this insertion is deemed always to have had effect.
Para. 3A inserted by FA 1994, s. 236 and Sch. 23, para. 4. See also the Note at the head of this Schedule.

Cross references – S. 2: assessable profits and allowable losses.
ICTA 1988, s. 493(6): valuation of oil disposed of or appropriated in certain circumstances.

OIL DELIVERED IN PLACE OF ROYALTIES TO BE DISREGARDED FOR CERTAIN PURPOSES

4 Oil delivered to the OGA under the terms of a licence granted under Part I of the Petroleum Act 1998 shall be disregarded for the purposes of section 2(5) of this Act and for the purposes of the references in section 8(3) and (4) of this Act to a participator's share of the oil won and saved from an oil field in a chargeable period.

History – In para. 4, the word "OGA" substituted for the words "Secretary of State" by SI 2016/898, reg. 4(9), with effect from 1 October 2016 (as the 21st day after being made on 10 September 2016).
The words "Part I of the Petroleum Act 1998" substituted for the words "the Petroleum (Production) Act 1934" by the Petroleum Act 1998, Sch. 4, para. 7 with effect from 15 February 1999 (SI 1999/161 art. 2).

EFFECT OF TRANSFER TO AN ASSOCIATED COMPANY OF PARTICIPATOR'S RIGHTS ETC. IN CONNECTION WITH AN OIL FIELD OR RELEVANT LICENCE

5(1) This paragraph applies to any agreement or other arrangement between a participator in an oil field and a company associated with the participator whereby–

(a) ownership of all or any of the participator's share of the oil won and saved from the field is transferred to the company; and

(b) the company obtains or assumes all or any of the participator's other rights, interests and obligations in connection with the field or any relevant licence.

5(2) As regards any chargeable period in which a participator in an oil field is a party to an arrangement to which this paragraph applies, the other party to the arrangement shall be treated for all purposes of this Part of this Act (except this paragraph) and for the purposes of sections 299 to 301 of CTA 2010 as having been a participator in the field at all times when the actual participator was such a participator (including times before the arrangement was made), and shall be assessable and chargeable to tax and entitled to make any claim under this Part of this Act, and any deduction or claim under sections 299 to 301 of CTA 2010 accordingly.

5(3) Where a participator in an oil field is or has been a party to an arrangement to which this paragraph applies then for all purposes of this Part of this Act–

(a) anything done by or in relation to the participator in connection with the field or any relevant licence shall be treated as being or having been done by or, as the case may be, in relation to the other party to the arrangement; and

(b) all rights, interests or obligations of the participator in connection with the field or any relevant licence shall be treated as being or having been rights, interests or obligations of the other party.

5(4) Where a participator in an oil field is or has been a party to an arrangement to which this paragraph applies, then, if any tax or interest payable under this Part of this Act by the other party to the arrangement is not paid within thirty days after the date on which it becomes payable, the Board may be notice in writing require the participator to pay that tax on interest; and where such a notice is served on the participator, the tax or interest in question shall be payable by him forthwith, but without prejudice to the Board's right to recover it from the other party.

5(5) For the purposes of this paragraph **"company"** means any body corporate, and a participator in an oil field and another company are **"associated"** with one another if–

(a) the participator has control over or is under the control of the other company; or

(b) the participator and the other company are both under the control of the same person or persons;

and in this sub-paragraph **"control"** has the meaning given by section 1124 of CTA 2010.

History – In para. 5(2), the words "sections 299 to 301 of CTA 2010" substituted twice for the words "section 500 of the Taxes Act" by CTA 2010, s. 1177 and Sch. 1, para. 165(4), with effect for corporation tax purposes for accounting periods ending on or after 1 April 2010, and for income tax and capital gains tax purposes for the tax year 2010–11 and subsequent tax years.
The former references in para. 5(2) to ICTA 1988, s. 500 were substituted by FA 1990, s. 89 and Sch. 14, para. 16, effective as though made by ICTA 1988.
In para. 5(5), the words "section 1124 of CTA 2010" substituted for the words "section 840 of the Taxes Act" by CTA 2010, s. 1177 and Sch. 1, para. 165(5), with effect for corporation tax purposes for accounting periods ending on or after 1 April 2010, and for income tax and capital gains tax purposes for the tax year 2010–11 and subsequent tax years.
See ICTA 1988, s. 844 and Sch. 29, para. 32 for substitution of former reference to that Act in para. 5(5).

Cross references – FA 1984, s. 113(4): "qualifying date" for the purposes of that section (restriction on PRT reliefs) means, inter alia, the date on which an arrangement to which this paragraph applies was first made, or the date on which the other company first qualified in respect of any licensed area wholly or partly included in the field.

OIL OWNED BY A PERSON OTHER THAN A PARTICIPATOR IN THE OIL FIELD FROM WHICH IT WAS WON

6(1) Where a proportion of a participator's share in the oil won and saved from an oil field (as distinct from a specific quantity of oil comprised in that share) is owned by a person (in this paragraph referred to as **"the owner"**) who is not a participator and who acquired it (whether directly or indirectly) under an agreement to which paragraph 5 above does not apply, the following provisions of this paragraph shall have effect.

6(2) For the purposes of this Part of this Act the oil acquired by the owner under the agreement shall be treated in every case as having been disposed of to him by the participator otherwise than in a sale at arm's length.

6(3) Where any oil which the owner owns in right of the agreement is in pursuance of the agreement–

(a) delivered to the owner by the participator; or

(b) delivered to a third person by the participator acting on behalf of the owner,

the delivery shall for the purposes of this Part of this Act be regarded as a delivery by the participator although he does not own the oil.

6(4) This sub-paragraph applies to all such oil (if any) as, being owned by the owner in right of the agreement, is in any chargeable period delivered by the participator as mentioned in the preceding sub-paragraph and would accordingly, apart from the following sub-paragraph, fall to be brought into account under section 2(5)(b) of this Act in computing the assessable profit or allowable loss accruing to the participator in that period (in the following sub-paragraph referred to as **"the relevant period"**).

6(5) If on a claim made by the participator within two months after the end of the relevant period–

(a) it is shown that some or all of the oil to which sub-paragraph (4) above applies has been disposed of by or on behalf of the owner crude in sales at arm's length; and

(b) the Board are satisfied that the oil with respect to which it is so shown includes the whole of so much of the oil to which that sub-paragraph applies as has been so disposed of,

then, in computing the assessable profit or allowable loss accruing to the participator in the relevant period, the oil with respect to which it is so shown shall be brought into account by reference to the price received or receivable for it by the owner instead of by reference to its market value.

History – Para. 6(1) amended by FA 1977, s. 54(2), with effect from 29 July 1977.

EFFECT OF CERTAIN TRANSACTIONS BETWEEN PARTICIPATORS

6A Where the whole or part of the share of a participator (**"the transferor"**) of oil won from an oil field became the share, or part of the share, of another participator (**"the transferee"**) in pursuance of an agreement between them under which the transferor undertook to remain responsible for carrying out the transferee's obligations in connection with the field so far as they relate to the transferred share or part, then, for the purposes of this Part of this Act–

(a) the shares of the transferor and the transferee of oil won from the field shall be taken to be the same as they would have been if the transfer had not occurred, and

(b) any oil comprised in the transferred share or part and taken up by or on the authority of the transferee in pursuance of the agreement shall be regarded as being disposed of and delivered to him by the transferor at the time when it is taken up.

History – Para. 6A inserted by FA 1977, s. 54, with effect from 29 July 1977.

EXCLUSION FROM SECTION 2(4)(b) AND (5)(d) OF OFFSHORE OIL IN TRANSIT TO PLACE OF FIRST LANDING

7 In computing the assessable profit or allowable loss accruing to a participator in a chargeable period from an oil field, the market value of any oil won as mentioned in section 3(1)(f) of this Act–

(a) shall not be taken into account under section 2(4)(b) of this Act if and to the extent that at the end of the preceding chargeable period the oil was in the course of being transported to the place where it was first landed in the United Kingdom or to the place referred to in section 3(1)(f)(ii) of this Act; and

(b) shall not be taken into account under section 2(5)(d) of this Act if and to the extent that at the end of the first-mentioned chargeable period the oil was in the course of being so transported.

History – In heading, the words "United Kingdom" repealed by F(No. 2)A 1992, s. 74 and Sch. 15, para. 4(2)(a), s. 82 and Sch. 18, Pt. VIII, taking effect in accordance with F(No. 2)A 1992, s. 74(5).
In para. 7(a), the words "or to the place referred to in section 3(1)(f)(ii) of this Act" were inserted by F(No. 2)A 1992, s. 74 and Sch. 15, para. 4(2)(b) and take effect in accordance with s. 74(5) of that Act.

CERTAIN SUBSIDISED EXPENDITURE TO BE DISREGARDED

8(1) Expenditure shall not be regarded for any of the purposes of this Part of this Act as having been incurred by any person in so far as it has been or is to be met directly or indirectly by the Crown or by any government or public or local authority, whether in the United Kingdom or elsewhere, or by any person other than the first-mentioned person.

8(1A) But sub-paragraph (1) above does not apply to any expenditure for which the relevant participator is liable that has been or is to be met directly or indirectly out of a payment made by the guarantor under an abandonment guarantee.

8(1B) In sub-paragraph (1A) above–

"abandonment guarantee" has the same meaning as it has for the purposes of section 3 of this Act (see section 104 of the Finance Act 1991), and

"the guarantor" and **"the relevant participator"** have the same meaning as in section 104 of that Act.

8(2) In considering, for the purposes of this paragraph, how far any expenditure has been or is to be met directly or indirectly by the Crown or by any authority or person other than the person incurring the expenditure, there shall be left out of account any insurance or compensation payable in respect of the loss or destruction of any asset.

History – Para. 8(1A) and (1B) inserted by FA 2013, s. 89 and Sch. 31, para. 3, with effect in relation to expenditure incurred on or after 17 July 2013 (Royal Assent).
The former words at the end of para. 8(1), which provided an exception in the case of grants made under the Industry Act 1972, Pt. I, and corresponding Northern Ireland grants, were repealed by FA 1982, s. 137(1), (7), 157(6) and Sch. 19, Pt. IX, in respect of relevant expenditure incurred after 9 March 1982 where the grant concerned is paid after that date.

Cross references – FA 1981, s. 118(5): "chargeable sum" paid to participator by Secretary of State after 31 December 1980 to be left out of account for purposes of para. 8(1).
FA 1991, s. 108(7): incurring of reimbursement expenditure by defaulter in respect of abandonment costs not to be regarded by virtue of para. 8 as the meeting of the expenditure of the qualifying participator in making the default payment.

ELECTION TO HAVE AMOUNTS MENTIONED IN SECTION 2(9)(B) AND (C) SPREAD

9 [Omitted by FA 2009, s. 91 and Sch. 45, para. 1(2).]

History – Para. 9 omitted by FA 2009, s. 91 and Sch. 45, para. 1(2), with effect in relation to chargeable periods beginning after 30 June 2009.

10 [Omitted by FA 2009, s. 91 and Sch. 45, para. 1(2).]

History – Para. 10 omitted by FA 2009, s. 91 and Sch. 45, para. 1(2), with effect in relation to chargeable periods beginning after 30 June 2009.

RESTRICTION OF AMOUNT OF REDUCTION UNDER SECTION (8)(1)

11 Where–

(a) a claim under Schedule 5 or 6 to this Act is made after the relevant time; and

(b) the reduction which would, apart from this paragraph, fall to be made under subsection (1) of section 8 of this Act for any chargeable period is greater than it would have been if the expenditure and other amounts allowed on the claim had been claimed before and allowed at the relevant time,

then, if the Board so direct, the reduction made under that sub-section for that chargeable period shall be only what it would have been if the expenditure and other amounts allowed on the claim had been claimed before and allowed at the relevant time.

In this paragraph **"the relevant time"** means the end of twelve months from the end of the claim period to which the claim mentioned in sub-paragraph (a) above relates.

POWER TO MAKE REGULATIONS UNDER THIS SCHEDULE

12(1) Any power to make regulations under this Schedule is exercisable by statutory instrument.

12(2) A statutory instrument containing regulations under this Schedule may not be made unless a draft of the instrument has been laid before, and approved by a resolution of, the House of Commons.

12(3) Any power to make regulations under this Schedule includes power–

(a) to make different provision for different Categories or kinds of oil or for different cases, or

(b) to make incidental, consequential, supplemental, or transitional provision or savings.

History – Para. 12 inserted by FA 2006, s. 146 and Sch. 18, para. 10, with effect in relation to oil delivered or appropriated on or after 1 July 2006, subject to provisions of FA 2006, s. 147(2)–(8).

SCHEDULE 4 – PROVISIONS SUPPLEMENTARY TO SECTIONS 3 AND 4

Sections 3 and 4

RESTRICTIONS ON EXPENDITURE ALLOWABLE UNDER SECTION 3 OR 4

1(1) Expenditure incurred by any person in the acquisition of an asset is now allowable under section 3 or 4 of this Act for an oil field if expenditure previously incurred by another person in acquiring, bringing into existence, or enhancing the value of that asset is allowable under that section for that field.

Section 4(13) of this Act applies to the preceding provisions of this sub-paragraph.

1(2) Sub-paragraph (1) above shall, with any necessary modifications, have effect in relation to expenditure incurred by a person–

(a) in renting or hiring an asset or any interest in an asset; or

(b) for the provision of services or other business facilities of whatever kind; or

(c) for the grant or transfer to him of any right, licence or interest (other than an interest in an asset),

as it has effect in relation to expenditure incurred in the acquisition of, or of an interest in, an asset.

Cross references – OTA 1983, s. 3(6): any reference to s. 4 is to be construed as including a reference to OTA 1983, s. 3, 4, and Sch. 1.

2(1) Where, in a transaction to which this paragraph applies, a person has incurred expenditure in acquiring, bringing into existence or enhancing the value of an asset, he shall at any time be treated for the purposes of–

(a) sections 3 and 4 of this Act, and

(b) sections 3 and 4 and Schedule 1 to the Oil Taxation Act 1983,

as having incurred that expenditure only to the extent that it does not exceed the lowest of the amounts described in sub-paragraph (1ZA) below which is applicable in the particular case.

2(1ZA) Those amounts are–

(a) the amount of expenditure (other than loan expenditure) incurred up to the time mentioned in sub-paragraph (1) above in a transaction to which this paragraph does not apply (or, if there has been more than one such transaction, the later or latest of them) in acquiring, bringing into existence, or enhancing the value of, the asset;

(b) the amount of the open market consideration for the acquisition, bringing into existence, or enhancement of the value, of the asset;

(c) in a case where the other party to the transaction is a participator in a taxable field and in the case of that participator either–

(i) an amount is brought into account under section 2 of this Act in accordance with section 7(1) of the Oil Taxation Act 1983 as disposal receipts in respect of the transaction, or

(ii) no amount is so brought into account by reason of reductions falling to be made in the amount that would have been so brought into account apart from those reductions,

the amount so brought into account or, as the case may be, nil;

(d) in a case where the other party to the transaction is not a participator in a taxable field but–

(i) the transaction is the latest in a series of transactions in respect of the asset (or in respect of an asset or assets in which the asset was comprised),

(ii) those transactions are transactions to which this paragraph applies,

(iii) in the case of at least one of those transactions, there is a party who is a participator in an oil field, and

(iv) in the case of any such party, an amount either is brought into account as mentioned in paragraph (c)(i) above in respect of the transaction or would have been so brought into account but for such reductions as are mentioned in paragraph (c)(ii) above,

so much of the amount so brought into account in respect of that transaction (or, where there are two or more such transactions, the later or latest of them) as is justly and reasonably referable to the asset mentioned in sub-paragraph (1) above (taking that amount as being nil in the case of any transaction where no amount is so brought into account by reason of any such reductions).

2(1A) Subsections (1) to (3) of section 191 of the Finance Act 1993 apply to determine for the purposes of this paragraph what expenditure has at any time been incurred under a transaction to which this paragraph does not apply, as they apply in relation to expenditure for the allowance of which a claim is received by the Board after 16th March 1993.

2(1B) In sub-paragraph (1ZA)(a) above **"loan expenditure"** means expenditure in respect of interest or any other pecuniary obligation incurred in obtaining a loan or any other form of credit.

2(1C) The reference in sub-paragraph (1ZA)(b) above to the open market consideration for the acquisition, bringing into existence, or enhancement of the value, of an asset is a reference to the consideration which might reasonably have been given for the acquisition, bringing into existence, or enhancement of the value, of the asset (whatever the nature of the acquisition, bringing into existence or enhancement of the value) had it been made in a transaction to which this paragraph does not apply.

2(2) This paragraph applies to any transaction between connected persons and to any transaction made otherwise than at arm's length; and for the purposes of this paragraph a person is connected with another person if they are connected within the meaning of section 1122 of CTA 2010.

2(3) The preceding provisions of this section shall, with any necessary modification, apply in relation to expenditure incurred by any person in acquiring an interest in an asset or in bringing into existence an asset in which he is to have an interest, or in enhancing the value of an asset in which he has an interest, as those provisions apply in relation to expenditure incurred by a person in acquiring, bringing into existence, or enhancing the value of an asset, as the case may be.

2(4) The provisions of sub-paragraphs (1) to (2) above shall, with any necessary modification, apply in relation to expenditure incurred by any person in respect of–

(a) the use of an asset (including expenditure on renting or hiring), or

(b) the provision of services or other business facilities of whatever kind in connection with the use, otherwise than by that person, of an asset,

as they have effect in relation to expenditure incurred in the acquisition of, or of an interest in, an asset.

History – In para. 2(1) the words "as having incurred that expenditure only to the extent that it does not exceed the lowest of the amounts described in sub-paragraph (1ZA) below which is applicable in the particular case." substituted for "as having incurred that expenditure only to the extent that it does not exceed expenditure (other than loan expenditure) incurred up to that time in a transaction to which this paragraph does not apply (or, if there has been more than one such transaction, the later or latest of them) in acquiring, bringing into existence or enhancing the value of, that asset." by FA 2004, s. 287(2), with effect in relation to expenditure incurred on or after 17 March 2004.

Para. 2(1ZA) inserted by FA 2004, s. 287(3), with effect in relation to expenditure incurred on or after 17 March 2004.

In para. 2(1B) "(1ZA)(a)" substituted for "(1)" by FA 2004, s. 281(4), with effect in relation to expenditure incurred on or after 17 March 2004.

Para. 2(1)–(1B) substituted for former para. 2(1), and para. 2(3), (4) substituted for former para. 2(3), by FA 1993, s. 191(4), (5), with effect where the transaction to which para. 2 applies takes place on or after 16 March 1993.

Para. 2(1C) inserted by FA 2004, s. 287(5), with effect in relation to expenditure incurred on or after 17 March 2004.

In para. 2(2), the words "section 1122 of CTA 2010" substituted for the words "section 839 of the Taxes Act" by CTA 2010, s. 1177 and Sch. 1, para. 166(2), with effect for corporation tax purposes for accounting periods ending on or after 1 April 2010, and for income tax and capital gains tax purposes for the tax year 2010–11 and subsequent tax years.

See ICTA 1988, s. 844 and Sch. 29, para. 32 for substitution of former reference to that Act in para. 2(2).

Cross references – OTA 1983, Sch. 2, para. 5: application of para. 2 to transactions in which a participator disposes of a qualifying asset to another participator and the disposal gives rise to tariff or disposal receipts.

FA 1993, s. 191(1): time when expenditure treated as incurred where claim for allowance received by Board after 16 March 1993.

3 [Omitted by FA 2009, s. 91 and Sch. 45, para. 1(4).]

History – Para. 3 omitted by FA 2009, s. 91 and Sch. 45, para. 1(4), with effect in relation to chargeable periods beginning after 30 June 2009.

DISPOSAL OF LONG-TERM ASSET FORMERLY USED IN CONNECTION WITH AN OIL FIELD

4(1) Where an asset is used in connection with an oil field in circumstances such that section 4 of this Act applies to any expenditure incurred in acquiring, bringing into existence, or enhancing the value of the asset, then if–

(a) the asset is disposed of for valuable consideration while in use in that connection or not more than two years after its use in that connection permanently ceases;

(b) the person making the disposal is either a participator in the field or a person connected with a participator;

(c) the person to whom the disposal is made is not a person connected with a participator; and

(d) the amount or value of the consideration received or receivable for the disposal is not less than the price which the asset might reasonably have been expected to fetch if sold in the open market at the time of the disposal,

sub-paragraphs (2) to (4) below shall have effect.

4(2) If the disposal occurs without the asset permanently ceasing to be used in connection with the field, its use in that connection shall for the purposes of section 4 of this Act and the following provisions of this paragraph be deemed to have permanently ceased at the time of the disposal.

4(3) If the disposal takes place not later than the end of the claim period in which the use of the asset in connection with the field permanently ceases, the proportion of the expenditure allowable under section 4 of this Act for the relevant period (that is to say the period which, in relation to that claim period, is the relevant period for the purposes of subsection (7) of that section) or, if the claim period in question is the first relevant claim period (as defined in that section), the proportion of the expenditure so allowable for that claim period shall be computed under that section subject to the provisions of sub-paragraph (5) below.

4(4) If the disposal takes place after the end of the claim period in which the use of the asset in connection with the field permanently ceases, then, as regards the claim period in which the disposal takes place–

(a) subsection (7) of section 4 of this Act shall have effect in relation to the asset as if its use in that connection had permanently ceased in that claim period (but so that for the purposes of subsections (5) and (6) of that section as applied by the said subsection (7) the asset shall not be treated as having been used in that connection at any time when it was not so used); and

(b) the proportion of the expenditure allowable under that section for the relevant period (that is to say the period which, in relation to that claim period is the relevant period for the purposes of the said subsection (7)) shall be computed under that section subject to the provisions of sub-paragraph (5) below.

4(5) For the purposes of the computation mentioned in sub-paragraph (3) or (4) above, as the case may be–

(a) the amount of the expenditure incurred in acquiring, bringing into existence, or enhancing the value of the asset which would otherwise fall to be taken into account shall be treated as reduced by the amount or value of the consideration received or receivable for the disposal (or, if equal to or smaller than the amount or value of that consideration, as reduced to nil); and

(b) the asset's useful life shall be treated as having ended at the time of the disposal or, if the asset permanently ceased to be used in connection with the field before that time and was neither used nor available for use by anyone in the interval between its permanently ceasing to be so used and the time of the disposal, at the time when it permanently ceased to be so used.

4(6) In any case where, for different parts of the expenditure incurred in the case of an asset as mentioned in sub-paragraph (1) above, different proportions thereof would be allowable under section 4 of this Act apart from sub-paragraph (5)(a) above (including a case where, for some but not all of that expenditure, the proportion thereof so allowable would be 100 per cent), the amount of value of the consideration received or receivable for the disposition shall for the purposes of this paragraph be treated as referable to those different parts in such proportions as may be just and reasonable.

4(7) Section 4(13) of this Act applies to the preceding provisions of this paragraph; and those provisions shall, with any necessary modifications, apply in relation to a disposal of an interest in an asset as they apply in relation to a disposal of an asset.

4(8) Section 1122 of CTA 2010 (connected persons) shall apply for the purposes of this paragraph.

History – In para. 4(8), the words "Section 1122 of CTA 2010" substituted for the words "Section 839 of the Taxes Act" by CTA 2010, s. 1177 and Sch. 1, para. 166(3), with effect for corporation tax purposes for accounting periods ending on or after 1 April 2010, and for income tax and capital gains tax purposes for the tax year 2010–11 and subsequent tax years.
See ICTA 1988, s. 844 and Sch. 29, para. 32 for substitution of former reference to that Act in para. 4(8).

Cross references – OTA 1983, s. 1(4): para. 4 does not apply to any disposal of an asset after 30 June 1982 unless the asset is a non-dedicated mobile asset.
OTA 1983, s. 5(7): despite OTA 1983, s. 3(6), references in para. 4 to OTA 1975, s. 4 do not include references to OTA 1983, s. 3, 4 and Sch. 1.

LONG-TERM ASSETS USED IN CONNECTION WITH MORE THAN ONE OIL FIELD

5 [Repealed by OTA 1983, s. 15(6) and Sch. 6, with effect from 1 December 1983.]

PROVISIONS SUPPLEMENTARY TO SECTION 4(9) OF THIS ACT AND PARAGRAPH 5(2) ABOVE

6(1) Where in the case of an oil field, the total amount of the expenditure allowable under sections 3 and 4 of this Act on a claim for a claim period–

(a) is, under one or more of the relevant provisions, reduced to nil; and

(b) would, under one or more of those provisions, have fallen to be reduced by a further amount if the total amount of that expenditure had been sufficient to enable the maximum reduction thereunder to be made,

that further amount shall be apportioned between the participators in proportions corresponding to what for that claim period would be their respective shares of any expenditure falling within section 2(9)(b)(i) of this Act; and in computing the assessable profit or allowable loss accruing to any participator in the earliest chargeable period which ends after the end of that claim period, the aggregate mentioned in section 2(4)(a) of this Act shall be increased by an amount equal to the amount apportioned to him under this paragraph.

6(2) In this paragraph **"the relevant provisions"** means section 4(9) of this Act and paragraph 5(2) above.

Cross references – OTA 1983, s. 3(6): any reference to s. 4 is to be construed as including a reference to OTA 1983, s. 3, 4 and Sch. 1.

INSURANCE OR COMPENSATION IN RESPECT OF LOSS OR DESTRUCTION OF LONG-TERM ASSET FORMERLY USED IN CONNECTION WITH OIL FIELD

7(1) Where, in consequence of the loss or destruction at any time within the period mentioned in sub-paragraph (1) of paragraph 4 above of such an asset as is mentioned in that sub-paragraph, any insurance or compensation in respect of the loss or destruction is receivable by a participator in the field or a person connected with a participator, paragraphs 4 and 6 above shall apply as if at that time the person by whom the insurance or compensation is receivable had disposed of the asset or his interest in it for an amount equal to the insurance or compensation.

7(2) Section 1122 of CTA 2010 (connected persons) shall apply for the purposes of this paragraph.

History – In para. 7(2), the words "Section 1122 of CTA 2010" substituted for the words "Section 839 of the Taxes Act" by CTA 2010, s. 1177 and Sch. 1, para. 166(4), with effect for corporation tax purposes for accounting periods ending on or after 1 April 2010, and for income tax and capital gains tax purposes for the tax year 2010–11 and subsequent tax years.
See ICTA 1988, s. 844 and Sch. 29, para. 32 for substitution of former reference to that Act.

ASSETS ACQUIRED JOINTLY BY PARTICIPATORS IN DIFFERENT OIL FIELDS

8 Where an asset was acquired jointly by persons who are participators in two or more different oil fields (whether or not any one of those persons is a participator in more than one of those fields), then in determining for the purposes of section 4 of this Act, in the case of any one of those fields, the use which has been, or which it is reasonable to assume will be, made of the asset otherwise than in connection with that field, no regard shall be had to its use or possible use in connection with any other of those fields.

Cross references – OTA 1983, s. 3(6): any reference to s. 4 is to be construed as including a reference to OTA 1983, s. 3, 4 and Sch. 1.

SCHEDULE 5 – ALLOWANCE OF EXPENDITURE (OTHER THAN ABORTIVE EXPLORATION EXPENDITURE)

Sections 3 and 4

Cross references – FA 1994, s. 231: election by reference to pipe-line usage.
FA 1999, s. 95(8): expenditure, which was allowable by virtue of a claim made under this Schedule, shall remain allowable, despite a downward revision of the capped amount because of further information becoming available.

CLAIM PERIODS AND CLAIMS

1(1) In relation to any oil field–

(a) the first claim period is whichever of the following periods the responsible person elects, namely the period ending at the end of June following the determination of the field or the period ending at the end of December following that determination (including, in either case, an unlimited time prior to that determination);

(b) each subsequent claim period is whichever of the following periods the responsible person elects, namely the period of six months or the period of twelve months from the end of the preceding claim period:

Provided that unless and until the responsible person elects the period of six months from the end of any particular claim period, the claim period next after that claim period shall be taken to be the period of twelve months from the end of it.

1(2) An election under this paragraph must be made by notice in writing to the Board.

2(1) A claim under this Schedule for the allowance of any expenditure allowable under section 3 or 4 of this Act for an oil field must be made by the responsible person to the Board and, subject to the provisions of this Part of this Act, must be made in a claim or claims for the claim period in which the expenditure is incurred, but may not be made before the determination of the field or more than 4 years after the end of the claim period in which the expenditure is incurred.

2(2) A claim under this Schedule for the allowance of any expenditure allowable under section 3 or 4 of this Act for an oil field which was incurred by a person before he became a participator in the field must be made in a claim for the claim period in which he became a participator.

2(3) A claim under this Schedule shall not include any expenditure allowable under section 3 or 4 of this Act which has been included in a claim under Schedule 6 to this Act.

2(4) A claim must state–

(a) what part (if any) of the expenditure is claimed as qualifying for supplement under section 2(9)(b)(ii) of this Act; and

(b) subject to paragraph 2A below the shares in which, in accordance with their respective interests in the oil field, the participators propose to divide between them, for the purposes of paragraph (b) of section 2(9) of this Act, the expenditure allowed on the claim and the amount which will arise under sub-paragraph (ii) of that paragraph if some or all of that expenditure is allowed on the claim as so qualifying.

2(5) Where a claim for the allowance of any expenditure under section 4 of this Act for an oil field was made in relation to any asset for the claim period which, in the case of that asset, is the first relevant claim period (as defined in that section), then any claim with respect to that field made under this Schedule for any subsequent claim period must give all such information as is relevant for the purpose of enabling the Board to carry into effect the provisions of that section in relation to that asset.

2(6) A claim must be in such form as the Board may prescribe and must include a declaration that all statements contained in it are correct to the best of the knowledge and belief of the person making the claim.

2(7) Where–

(a) the claim period in which any expenditure allowable under section 3 or 4 of this Act for an oil field is incurred coincides with or includes a chargeable period, and

(b) the Board has extended the period for the delivery of the return that is required under paragraph 5 of Schedule 2 to this Act to be delivered for that chargeable period by the responsible person, and

(c) the relevant time falls more than 2 years after the end of the claim period,

sub-paragraph (1) above shall have effect as if the reference to 4 years after the end of the claim period in which the expenditure is incurred were a reference to two years after the relevant time.

2(8) In sub-paragraph (7) above **"the relevant time"** means the earlier of–

(a) the time which, as a result of the extension mentioned in that sub-paragraph, is the latest time for the delivery of the return there mentioned; and

(b) the time when that return is delivered.

History – In para. 2(1) the words "4 years" substituted for the words "six years" by FA 2009, s. 99 and Sch. 51, para. 23(2), with effect from 1 April 2011 (SI 2010/867).

In para. 2(4)(b), reference to para. 2A inserted by FA 1991, s. 107(1).

In para. 2(7) the words "2 years" and "4 years" substituted for the words "four years" and "six years" respectively by FA 2009, s. 99 and Sch. 51, para. 23(3), with effect from 1 April 2011 (SI 2010/867).

Para. 2(7) and 2(8) inserted by FA 1999, s. 102(4), with effect for chargeable periods ending on or after 30 June 1999.

Cross references – F(No. 2)A 1979, s. 19(4): expenditure qualifying for supplement at different percentage rates to be distinguished in making claim.

FA 1981, s. 111(6): necessity for claims where expenditure supplement restricted after end of net profit period.

FA 1982, s. 135(1)(c): application of para. 2(1) where actual date of determination is later than the end of a claim period – winning of oil before determination of a field.
OTA 1983, s. 3(6): any reference to OTA 1975, s. 4 is to be construed as including a reference to OTA 1983, s. 3, 4 and Sch. 1, except (OTA 1983, s. 5(7)) in the case of para. 2(5).
FA 1993, s. 192(1): where claim received by Board after 16 March 1993, expenditure not to be brought into account to determine assessable profit or allowable loss of any chargeable period ending earlier than the last day of the claim period in which expenditure incurred.

2A(1) This paragraph applies if–

(a) a current participator (“the defaulter”) has defaulted on a liability under–
  (i) a relevant agreement, or
  (ii) an abandonment programme,
  to make a payment towards abandonment expenditure, and
(b) a current or former participator (“the contributing participator”) pays an amount in or towards meeting the whole or part of the default (“a default payment”).

2A(2) If a claim is made under this Schedule for the allowance of the abandonment expenditure, the amount of the default payment is to be attributed to the contributing participator for the purposes of paragraphs 2(4)(b) and 3(1)(c).

2A(3) But the amount attributed under sub-paragraph (2) may not exceed–

(a) so much of the sum in default as the contributing participator is required to meet in accordance with–
  (i) the relevant agreement, or
  (ii) the abandonment programme, or
(b) such other amount as the participator may be required to meet in accordance with a direction given under Part 4 of the Petroleum Act 1998.

2A(4) Sub-paragraph (2) is subject to paragraph 2B.

2A(5) In determining the amount which is to be attributed to the contributing participator under sub-paragraph (2), account shall be taken of the whole of the defaulter’s interest in the relevant oil field.

2A(6) But in determining the share of the abandonment expenditure to be attributed to the defaulter under paragraph 2(4)(b), the amount which would be attributed by reference to the defaulter’s interest in the relevant oil field is to be reduced or (as the case may be) extinguished by the deduction of the aggregate of–

(a) the amount attributed to the contributing participator under sub-paragraph (2), and
(b) any other amounts attributed under sub-paragraph (2) to other current or former participators who make default payments in respect of the defaulter’s default.

History – Para. 2A–2C substituted for former para. 2A by FA 2008, s. 103(1), with effect in relation to expenditure incurred after 30 June 2008. Former para. 2A read as follows:

“2A(1) This paragraph applies where–
(a) a claim is made under this Schedule for the allowance of any expenditure which is incurred after 30th June 1991 and is allowable for an oil field by virtue of paragraph (i) or paragraph (j) of subsection (1) of section 3 of this Act (in this paragraph referred to as **“the abandonment expenditure”**);
(b) a participator (in this paragraph referred to as **“the defaulter”**) has defaulted on his liability under a relevant agreement to make a payment towards the abandonment expenditure;
(c) at the end of the claim period for which the claim is made, the defaulter still has an interest in the oil field which falls to be taken into account in determining, under paragraph 2(4)(b) above, the shares of each of the participators in the abandonment expenditure;
(d) the participators (other than any who have defaulted as mentioned in paragraph (b) above) have taken all reasonable steps by way of legal remedy to secure that the defaulter meets the whole of the liability referred to in paragraph (b) above and to enforce any guarantee or other security provided in respect of that liability; and
(e) one or more of those participators has paid an amount in or towards meeting the whole or any part of the payment for which the defaulter was liable as mentioned in paragraph (b) above.

2A(2) For the purposes of this paragraph, a participator is to be regarded as **“defaulting”** on his liability to make a payment as mentioned in sub-paragraph (1)(b) above if he has failed to make the payment in full on the date on which it becomes due under the relevant agreement and either–
(a) on the sixtieth day after that due date any of the payment remains unpaid; or
(b) before that sixtieth day the participator’s interest in a relevant licence becomes liable under the relevant agreement to be sold or forfeited, in whole or in part, by reason of his failure to meet his liability.

2A(3) In this paragraph–
(a) **“relevant agreement”** has the meaning given by section 104(5)(a) of the Finance Act 1991;
(b) **“the sum in default”** means so much of the payment referred to in sub-paragraph (1)(b) above as has neither been paid by the defaulter nor met by virtue of any such guarantee or security as is referred to in sub-paragraph (1)(d) above;
(c) the **“default payment”** means the amount which the qualifying participator has paid as mentioned in sub-paragraph (1)(e) above; and
(d) a **“qualifying participator”** means a participator who falls within sub-paragraph (1)(e) above and who is not connected with the defaulter, applying section 839 of the Taxes Act (connected persons) for the purposes of this paragraph.

2A(4) For the purposes of paragraphs 2(4)(b) and 3(1)(c) of this Schedule, there shall be attributed to a qualifying participator (as an addition to the share of the abandonment expenditure referable to his own interest in the oil field) whichever is the less of–
(a) the default payment; and
(b) subject to sub-paragraph (5) below, that portion of the sum in default which, in accordance with the relevant agreement, the qualifying participator is required to meet in the event of a failure by the defaulter to meet his liability to pay in full the payment referred to in sub-paragraph (1)(b) above.

PRT Statutes

2A(5) If, in the case of any oil field, there are only two participators and one of them is the defaulter, the portion referred to in sub-paragraph (4)(b) above is the whole.

2A(6) Where this paragraph applies, account shall, in the first instance, be taken under paragraph 2(4)(b) above of the whole of the defaulter's interest in the oil field in determining the share of the abandonment expenditure which, apart from sub-paragraph (4) above, is to be attributed to each of the other participators; but the amount of the abandonment expenditure which, apart from this paragraph, would be attributed to the defaulter by reference to his interest in the oil field shall be reduced (or, as the case may be, extinguished) by deducting therefrom any expenditure attributed to the other participators under sub-paragraph (4) above."

Former para 2A inserted by FA 1991, s. 107(2).

2B(1) No amount is to be attributed to a contributing participator under paragraph 2A(2) unless the following conditions are all met.

2B(2) The first condition is that the contributing participator is not connected with the defaulter, applying section 1122 of CTA 2010 (connected persons) for the purposes of this sub-paragraph.

2B(3) The second condition is that, at the end of the claim period for which the claim is made, the defaulter still has an interest in the relevant oil field which, under paragraph 2(4)(b), falls to be taken into account in determining the shares in the abandonment expenditure.

2B(4) The third condition is that the relevant participators have taken all reasonable steps by way of legal remedy–

(a) to secure that the defaulter meets the whole of the liability referred to in paragraph 2A(1)(a), and

(b) to enforce any guarantee or other security provided in respect of that liability.

2B(5) In sub-paragraph (4) **"relevant participators"** means–

(a) each current participator (other than the defaulter), and

(b) each former participator who makes a default payment in respect of the defaulter's default.

History – In para. 2B(2), the words "section 1122 of CTA 2010" substituted for the words "section 839 of the Taxes Act" by CTA 2010, s. 1177 and Sch. 1, para. 167, with effect for corporation tax purposes for accounting periods ending on or after 1 April 2010, and for income tax and capital gains tax purposes for the tax year 2010–11 and subsequent tax years.

Para. 2A–2C substituted for former para. 2A by FA 2008, s. 103(1), with effect in relation to expenditure incurred after 30 June 2008. Former para. 2A is reproduced in the History note to current para. 2A.

2C(1) An amount attributed under paragraph 2A(2) is–

(a) in the case of a current participator, to be an addition to the share of the abandonment expenditure referable to the current participator's interest in the oil field, or

(b) in the case of a former participator, to be the share of the abandonment expenditure referable to the former participator's interest in the oil field.

2C(2) In paragraphs 2A and 2B and this paragraph–

"abandonment expenditure" means expenditure which is allowable for an oil field by virtue of section 3(1)(i) or (j);

"abandonment programme" means an abandonment programme approved under Part 4 of the Petroleum Act 1998 (including any such programme as revised);

"current participator" means a person who is, by virtue of paragraph (a), (aa), (b) or (c) of the definition in section 12, a participator in the relevant oil field in the chargeable period in which the abandonment expenditure is incurred;

"former participator" means a person who–

(a) is not a current participator, but

(b) was, by virtue of paragraph (a), (aa), (b) or (c) of the definition in section 12, a participator in the relevant oil field in any chargeable period before the chargeable period in which the abandonment expenditure is incurred;

"relevant agreement" has the meaning given by section 104(5)(a) of the Finance Act 1991;

"relevant oil field" means the oil field to which the abandonment expenditure relates;

"sum in default" means the amount of the payment which the defaulter is liable to make as mentioned in paragraph 2A(1)(a), less so much of that payment as has been made by the defaulter.

2C(3) For the purposes of paragraph 2A, a current participator is to be regarded as defaulting on a liability to make a payment towards abandonment expenditure if the following conditions are met.

2C(4) The first condition is that the current participator has failed to make the payment in full on the due day.

2C(5) The second condition is that–

(a) any of the payment remains unpaid on the sixtieth day after the due day, or

(b) before that sixtieth day, the current participator's interest in a relevant licence becomes liable under the relevant agreement to be sold or forfeited, in whole or in part, by reason of the failure to meet the liability.

2C(6) In sub-paragraphs (4) and (5) **"due day"** means the day on which the payment towards abandonment expenditure becomes due under the relevant agreement or the abandonment programme.

History – In para. 2C(2), in the definition of "current participator", "(aa)," inserted by FA 2009, s. 88 and Sch. 42, para. 3(a), with effect in relation to persons who cease to be licencees because of cessation events occurring in chargeable periods that begin after 30 June 2009.
In para. 2C(2), in the definition of "former participator", "(aa)," inserted by FA 2009, s. 88 and Sch. 42, para. 3(a), with effect in relation to persons who cease to be licencees because of cessation events occurring in chargeable periods that begin after 30 June 2009.
In para. 2C(2), in the definition of "sum in default", the words "less so much of that payment as has been made by the defaulter" substituted for the words "less the aggregate of– (a) so much of that payment as has been made by the defaulter, and (b) so much of that payment as has been met by virtue of any guarantee or security provided in respect of the defaulter's liability" by FA 2013, s. 89 and Sch. 31, para. 4, with effect in relation to expenditure incurred on or after 17 July 2013 (Royal Assent).
Para. 2A–2C substituted for former para. 2A by FA 2008, s. 103(1), with effect in relation to expenditure incurred after 30 June 2008. Former para. 2A is reproduced in the History note to current para. 2A.

3(1) The Board shall by notice in writing to the responsible person inform him of their decision on the claim, stating in the notice–

(a) the amount of the expenditure allowed by them on the claim;

(b) the amount, if any, of that expenditure allowed by them on the claim as qualifying for supplement under section 2(9)(b)(ii) of this Act; and

(c) the shares determined by the Board to be the shares in which, in the opinion of the Board, the amount stated under (a) above or, as the case may be, the aggregate of that amount and an amount equal to the relevant percentage of the amount stated under (b) above, is divisible between the participators for the purposes of section 2(9)(b) of this Act;

and where the decision relates to part only of the expenditure claimed, or claimed as so qualifying, the Board shall give a further notice or notices in relation to the remainder.

3(2) In this paragraph **"the relevant percentage"** means the percentage mentioned in the said section 2(9)(b)(ii).

Cross references – F(No. 2)A 1979, s. 19(4): expenditure qualifying for supplement at different percentage rates to be distinguished in making a claim.
FA 1981, s. 111(6): necessity for claims where expenditure supplement restricted after end of net profit period.

4 If, in a case where sub-paragraph (5) of paragraph 2 above requires a claim made for a particular claim period to give all such information as is relevant for the purpose there mentioned in relation to an asset, a claim satisfying the requirements of that sub-paragraph is not made within twelve months after the end of that period, then, in carrying into effect the provisions of section 4 of this Act in relation to that asset for that claim period, the Board may proceed accordingly to the best of their judgment, and may make any adjustments under any of the provisions mentioned in paragraph 6(2) of Schedule 4 to this Act accordingly.

Cross references – OTA 1983, s. 5(7): notwithstanding OTA 1983, s. 3(6), any reference in para. 4 to OTA 1975, s. 4 does not include a reference to s. 3, 4 and Sch. 1 of the 1983 Act.

APPEALS

5(1) If–

(a) the amount or total of the amounts stated under sub-paragraph (1)(a) of paragraph 3 above in the notice or notices given by the Board under that paragraph on a claim, or the amount or total of the amounts so stated under sub-paragraph (1)(b) of that paragraph, is less than the amount claimed; or

(b) the shares so stated under sub-paragraph (1)(c) of that paragraph in the notice or latest of the notices so given differ from the shares stated under paragraph 2(4)(b) above in the claim,

the responsible person may appeal by notice in writing given to the Board not more than three years after the making of the claim; but the bringing of an appeal under this paragraph shall not affect the operation of any notice so given by the Board.

5(2) On an appeal that is notified to the tribunal against a decision on a claim brought on the ground mentioned in sub-paragraph (1)(b) above, and in any proceedings arising out of such an appeal, any participator in the oil field to which the claim relates shall be entitled to be a party.

5(3) An appeal against a decision on a claim may at any time before it is notified to the tribunal be abandoned by a notice in writing given to the Board by the responsible person.

5(4) On an appeal that is notified to the tribunal against a decision on a claim, the tribunal may vary the decision appealed against whether or not the variation is to the advantage of all or any of the participators in the oil field to which the claim relates.

5(5) The provisions of paragraphs 14A to 14I of Schedule 2 shall apply to appeals under this paragraph subject to any necessary modifications.

History – In para. 5(1) the word "appeal" inserted and the words "appeal to the Special Commissioners" omitted by SI 2009/56, art. 3 and Sch. 1, para. 77(2), with effect from 1 April 2009, subject to transitional and saving provisions in SI 2009/56, Sch. 3.
In para. 5(2) the words "that is notified to the tribunal" inserted and the words "be a party" substituted for the words "appear and be heard" by SI 2009/56, art. 3 and Sch. 1, para. 77(3), with effect from 1 April 2009, subject to transitional and saving provisions in SI 2009/56, Sch. 3.

In para. 5(3) the words "before it is notified to the tribunal" inserted by SI 2009/56, art. 3 and Sch. 1, para. 77(4), with effect from 1 April 2009, subject to transitional and saving provisions in SI 2009/56, Sch. 3.
In para. 5(4) the words "that is notified to the tribunal" inserted and the word "tribunal" substituted for the words "Special Commissioners" by SI 2009/56, art. 3 and Sch. 1, para. 77(5), with effect from 1 April 2009, subject to transitional and saving provisions in SI 2009/56, Sch. 3.
Para. 5(5) inserted by SI 2009/56, art. 3 and Sch. 1, para. 77(6), with effect from 1 April 2009, subject to transitional and saving provisions in SI 2009/56, Sch. 3.

Cross references – F(No. 2)A 1979, s. 19(4): expenditure qualifying for supplement at different percentage rates to be distinguished in making claim.

6(1) Where the responsible person gives notice of appeal against a decision on a claim on one or both of the grounds mentioned in paragraph 5(1)(a) above and, before the appeal is determined by the tribunal, the Board and the responsible person agree on–

(a) the amount of the expenditure that ought to be allowed on the claim; or

(b) the amount, if any, of the expenditure claimed which ought to be so allowed as qualifying for supplement under section 2(9)(b)(ii) of this Act;

the appropriate amount (if any) of the expenditure claimed or, as the case may be, claimed as so qualifying shall be treated for the purposes of this Part of this Act as having been allowed by the Board on the claim, and as having been so allowed on the date on which the notice of appeal was given.

For the purposes of this sub-paragraph the **"appropriate amount"** (if any) of the expenditure claimed or, as the case may be, claimed as so qualifying, is an amount thereof equal to the excess, if any, of the amount so agreed on over the corresponding amount or the total of the corresponding amounts allowed by the notice or notices previously given by the Board under paragraph 3 above.

6(2) Where the responsible person gives notice of appeal against a decision on a claim on the ground mentioned in paragraph 5(1)(b) above and, before the appeal is determined by the tribunal, the Board and the responsible person agree on the shares in which the amount of any expenditure allowed on the claim, or so allowed as qualifying for supplement under section 2(9)(b)(ii) of this Act, ought to be divided between the participators for the purposes of section 2(9)(b) of this Act, the shares so agreed on shall be deemed to be the shares stated in any notice previously given by the Board under paragraph 3 above on the claim, and shall apply in the case of any part of the expenditure claimed, or claimed as so qualifying, which is by virtue of this or the following paragraph treated as having been allowed on the claim.

6(3) Where the Board and the responsible person agree on the matter mentioned in sub-paragraph (1)(a), sub-paragraph (1)(b) or sub-paragraph (2) above in the circumstances there mentioned, the corresponding ground of appeal shall be treated as having been abandoned; and where by virtue of this sub-paragraph all the grounds of the appeal fall to be so treated, the appeal itself shall be treated as having been abandoned.

History – In para. 6(1) the word "tribunal" substituted for the words "Special Commissioners" by SI 2009/56, art. 3 and Sch. 1, para. 78, with effect from 1 April 2009, subject to transitional and saving provisions in SI 2009/56, Sch. 3.
In para. 6(2) the word "tribunal" substituted for the words "Special Commissioners" by SI 2009/56, art. 3 and Sch. 1, para. 78, with effect from 1 April 2009, subject to transitional and saving provisions in SI 2009/56, Sch. 3.

Cross references – F(No. 2)A 1979, s. 19(4): expenditure qualifying for supplement at different percentage rates to be distinguished in making claim.

7(1) Where, on an appeal under paragraph 5 above that is notified to the tribunal, the tribunal determines that any amount or part of an amount in dispute is allowable under section 3 or 4 of this Act or qualifies for supplement under section 2(9)(b)(ii) of this Act, the following provisions of this paragraph shall apply.

7(2) Subject to paragraph 8(2) below, the said amount or part shall be treated for the purposes of this Part of this Act as having been allowed on the claim to which the appeal relates, and as having been so allowed on the date on which the notice of appeal was given.

7(3) There shall be made in any computation made under section 2 of this Act, and in any assessment to tax or determination, all such adjustments as are necessary in consequence of the determination of the tribunal.

History – In para. 7(1) a comma inserted after the word "Where" and the words "that is notified to the tribunal, the tribunal determines" substituted for the words "the Special Commissioners determine" by SI 2009/56, art. 3 and Sch. 1, para. 79(2), with effect from 1 April 2009, subject to transitional and saving provisions in SI 2009/56, Sch. 3.
In para. 7(3) the word "tribunal" substituted for the words "Special Commissioners" by SI 2009/56, art. 3 and Sch. 1, para. 79(3), with effect from 1 April 2009, subject to transitional and saving provisions in SI 2009/56, Sch. 3.

Cross references – F(No. 2)A 1979, s. 19(4): expenditure qualifying for supplement at different percentage rates to be distinguished in making claim.
OTA 1983, s. 3(6): any reference to s. 4 is to be construed as including a reference to OTA 1983, s. 3, 4 and Sch. 1.

8(1) Where–

(a) an appeal is made against a determination by the tribunal on an appeal under paragraph 5 above; and

(b) in the proceedings on the appeal so made or in any proceedings arising out of those proceedings, any matter which was determined by the tribunal on the appeal under paragraph 5 above is finally determined otherwise than in accordance with their determination on that appeal,

the following provisions of this paragraph shall apply.

8(2) Any expenditure allowable under section 3 or 4 of this Act, which, if the decision of the Board on the claim to which the appeal under paragraph 5 above related had been in accordance with the final determination of that matter, would have been allowed by that decision, or allowed by it as qualifying for supplement under section 2(9)(b)(ii) of this Act, shall be treated for the purposes of this Part of the Act as having been allowed by the Board on the claim to the extent that it has not been previously allowed on the claim, and as having been so allowed to that extent on the date on which the original notice of appeal was given under paragraph 5 above.

8(3) There shall be made in any computation made under section 2 of this Act and in any assessment to tax or determination all such adjustments or further adjustments as are necessary in consequence of the final determination.

8(4) Any tax which becomes payable in consequence of any adjustment made under sub-paragraph (3) above in an assessment for a chargeable period shall carry interest at the rate applicable under section 178 of the Finance Act 1989 from two months after the end of that period to the date of payment.

8(5) For the purposes of this paragraph a matter shall not be deemed to be **"finally determined"** in any such proceedings as are mentioned in sub-paragraph (1)(b) above until a determination thereof made in any such proceedings can no longer be varied or overruled by the order of any court or the tribunal.

History – Para. 8(1)(a) substituted and in para. 8(1)(b) the word "tribunal" substituted for the words "Special Commissioners" by SI 2009/56, art. 3 and Sch. 1, para. 80(2) and (3), with effect from 1 April 2009, subject to transitional and saving provisions in SI 2009/56, Sch. 3. Former para. 8(1)(a) read as follows:

"(a) an appeal is made under section 56A of the Taxes Management Act 1970 (as applied by paragraph 1 of Schedule 2 to this Act) against a determination by the Special Commissioners on an appeal under paragraph 5 above; and"

In para. 8(1)(a), the words "an appeal is made … Schedule 2 to this Act) against" substituted by SI 1994/1813, Sch. 1, para. 19(a), with effect from 1 September 1994.

In para. 8(1)(b), the words "appeal so made" and "the appeal under paragraph 5 above" substituted by SI 1994/1813, Sch. 1, para. 19(b), with effect from 1 September 1994.

In para. 8(4), the words "rate applicable … 1989" were substituted by FA 1989, s. 179(1)(a)(v), for periods beginning on and after 18 August 1989 (SI 1989/1298 (C 4)).

In para. 8(5) the words "or the tribunal" inserted by SI 2009/56, art. 3 and Sch. 1, para. 80(4), with effect from 1 April 2009, subject to transitional and saving provisions in SI 2009/56, Sch. 3.

Cross references – F(No. 2)A 1979, s. 19(4): expenditure qualifying for supplement at different percentage rates to be distinguished in making claim.

OTA 1983, s. 3(6): any reference to s. 4 is to be construed as including a reference to OTA 1983, s. 3, 4 and Sch. 1.

9(1) If it appears to the Board that the relevant amount was incorrectly stated in a notice of a decision under paragraph 3 above given to the responsible person for an oil field, the Board may before the expiry of the permitted period serve on the responsible person a notice stating what appears to the Board to be the correct amount (referred to below as **"the notice of variation"**).

9(1A) [Omitted by FA 2009, s. 99 and Sch. 51, para. 24(3).]

9(1B) [Omitted by FA 2009, s. 99 and Sch. 51, para. 24(3).]

9(1C) [Omitted by FA 2009, s. 99 and Sch. 51, para. 24(3).]

9(2) In this paragraph **"the relevant amount"**, in relation to a notice of a decision on a claim under paragraph 3 above, means any one or more of the following–

(a) the amount of expenditure allowed on the claim;

(b) the amount of that expenditure allowed as qualifying for supplement under section 2(9)(b)(ii) of this Act;

(c) where different percentages were stated in that notice to apply to different parts of that expenditure for the purpose of calculating the supplement, each of those parts of that expenditure.

9(2A) [Omitted by FA 2009, s. 99 and Sch. 51, para. 24(3).]

9(2B) In this paragraph **"permitted period"** means the period of 4 years beginning with the date on which the notice of the decision under paragraph 3 was given (but see sub-paragraph (2C)).

9(2C) Where the relevant amount was overstated in the notice of decision as a result of an inaccuracy in a statement or declaration made by the responsible person (or a person acting on behalf of the responsible person) in connection with the claim–

(a) if the inaccuracy was careless, the permitted period is extended to 6 years, and

(b) if the inaccuracy was deliberate, the permitted period is extended to 20 years.

9(3) The responsible person may, by notice in writing given to the Board not more than thirty days after the notice of variation was served on him, appeal against the notice of variation.

9(4) A notice of appeal under sub-paragraph (3) shall state the grounds on which the appeal is brought.

9(5) An appeal under this paragraph may at any time before it is notified to the tribunal be abandoned by notice in writing given to the Board by the responsible person.

9(6) A notice of variation may be withdrawn at any time before it becomes effective.

9(7) In any case where–

(a) the responsible person gives notice of appeal against a notice of variation, and

(b) before the appeal is determined by the tribunal, the Board and the responsible person agree as to what the relevant amount ought to be,

the notice of variation shall have effect subject to such modifications as may be necessary to give effect to that agreement; and thereupon the appeal shall be treated as having been abandoned.

9(8) On an appeal that is notified to the tribunal against a notice of variation the tribunal may vary the notice, quash the notice or dismiss the appeal; and the notice may be varied whether or not the variation is to the advantage of all or any of the participators in the oil field in question.

9(9) Where a notice of variation relating to a decision on a claim becomes effective, the relevant amount shall be taken for the purposes of this Part of this Act as having been reduced or increased, as the case may require, on the date on which notice of the decision was given, by such amount as may be necessary to give effect to that notice, and the Board may make such computations under section 2 of this Act and such assessments or determinations of such amendments of assessments or determinations as may be necessary in consequence of that reduction or increase.

9(10) A notice of variation becomes effective for the purposes of this paragraph either–

(a) on the expiry of the period during which notice of appeal against the notice of variation may be given under sub-paragraph (3) above without such notice of appeal being given; or

(b) where such notice of appeal is given, when the notice of variation can no longer be varied or quashed by the tribunal or by the order of any court.

9(11) [Omitted by FA 2009, s. 99 and Sch. 51, para. 24(5).]

9(12) For the purposes of this section, an inaccuracy in a statement or declaration made by the responsible person (or a person acting on behalf of the responsible person) is careless if it is due to a failure by the person to take reasonable care.

9(13) An inaccuracy in a statement or declaration made by the responsible person (or a person acting on behalf of the responsible person) is to be treated as careless if–

(a) the responsible person, the person who acted on behalf of the responsible person or any person who becomes the responsible person for the oil field after the statement or declaration is made discovers the inaccuracy some time after it is made, and

(b) that person fails to take reasonable steps to inform Her Majesty's Revenue and Customs.

History – In para. 9(1) the words ", within the period of three years commencing with the date on which notice of a decision of the Board under paragraph 3 above was given to the responsible person for an oil field," omitted and the words "in a notice of a decision under paragraph 3 above given to the responsible person for an oil field" substituted for the words "in the notice", and the words "the permitted period" substituted for the words "that period", by FA 2009, s. 99 and Sch. 51, para. 24(2), with effect from 1 April 2011 (SI 2010/867).

Para. 9(1A)–(1C) and (2A) omitted by FA 2009, s. 99 and Sch. 51, para. 24(3), with effect from 1 April 2011 (SI 2010/867).

Para. 9(1A)–(1C) and (2A) inserted by FA 1990, s. 122(1)–(3); and para. 9(11) substituted by s. 122(1), (4).

Para. 9(2B) and (2C) inserted by FA 2009, s. 99 and Sch. 51, para. 24(4), with effect from 1 April 2011 (SI 2010/867).

In para. 9(3) the words "to the Special Commissioners" omitted by SI 2009/56, art. 3 and Sch. 1, para. 81(2), with effect from 1 April 2009, subject to transitional and saving provisions in SI 2009/56, Sch. 3.

In para. 9(5) the words "before it is notified to the tribunal" inserted by SI 2009/56, art. 3 and Sch. 1, para. 81(3), with effect from 1 April 2009, subject to transitional and saving provisions in SI 2009/56, Sch. 3.

In para. 9(7) the word "tribunal" substituted for the words "Special Commissioners" by SI 2009/56, art. 3 and Sch. 1, para. 81(4), with effect from 1 April 2009, subject to transitional and saving provisions in SI 2009/56, Sch. 3.

In para. 9(8) the words "that is notified to the tribunal" inserted and the word "tribunal" substituted for the words "Special Commissioners" by SI 2009/56, art. 3 and Sch. 1, para. 81(5), with effect from 1 April 2009, subject to transitional and saving provisions in SI 2009/56, Sch. 3.

In para. 9(10)(a) the words "to the Special Commissioners" omitted by SI 2009/56, art. 3 and Sch. 1, para. 81(6), with effect from 1 April 2009, subject to transitional and saving provisions in SI 2009/56, Sch. 3.

In para. 9(10)(b) the word "tribunal" substituted for the words "Special Commissioners" by SI 2009/56, art. 3 and Sch. 1, para. 81(7), with effect from 1 April 2009, subject to transitional and saving provisions in SI 2009/56, Sch. 3.

Para. 9(11) omitted by FA 2009, s. 99 and Sch. 51, para. 24(5), with effect from 1 April 2011 (SI 2010/867).

Para. 9(12) and (13) inserted by FA 2009, s. 99 and Sch. 51, para. 24(6),with effect from 1 April 2011 (SI 2010/867).

Para. 9 inserted by FA 1983, s. 40(1), with effect from 13 May 1983.

Cross references – OTA 1983, s. 14: re-opening of decisions on claims for periods ending on or after 30 June 1982.

FA 1987, Sch. 14, Pt. IV: notice of variation reducing or increasing expenditure qualifying for supplement – effect on cross-field allowance in respect of new fields from 17 March 1987.

FA 1994, s. 231: notice of variation of election by reference to pipe-line usage.

10 In this Schedule **"tribunal"** means the First-tier Tribunal or, where determined by or under Tribunal Procedure Rules, the Upper Tribunal.

History – Para. 10 inserted by SI 2009/56, art. 3 and Sch. 1, para. 82, with effect from 1 April 2009, subject to transitional and saving provisions in SI 2009/56, Sch. 3.

SCHEDULE 6 – ALLOWANCE OF EXPENDITURE (OTHER THAN ABORTIVE EXPLORATION EXPENDITURE) ON CLAIM BY PARTICIPATOR

Sections 3 and 4

Cross references – FA 1999, s. 95(8): expenditure, which was allowable by virtue of a claim made under this Schedule, shall remain allowable, despite a downward revision of the capped amount because of further information becoming available.
FA 1994, s. 231: election by reference to pipe-line usage.

1(1) A claim for the allowance of any expenditure allowable under section 3 or 4 of this Act for an oil field may be made to the Board under this Schedule by the participator who incurred it (instead of under Schedule 5 to this Act by the responsible person for that field) if the participator satisfies the Board that, for reasons of trade secrecy, it would be unreasonable for him to have to provide the responsible person with the information necessary for the making of a claim under that Schedule.

1(2) A claim by a participator under this Schedule for the allowance of any such expenditure incurred by him must, subject to the provisions of this Part of this Act, be made in a claim or claims for the claim period in which the expenditure is incurred, but may not be made before the determination of the field or more than 4 years after the end of the claim period in which the expenditure is incurred.

1(3) A claim by a participator under this Schedule for the allowance of any such expenditure incurred by him before he became a participator in the field must be made in a claim for the claim period in which he became a participator.

History – In para. 1(2) the words "4 years" substituted for the words "six years" by FA 2009, s. 99 and Sch. 51, para. 25(2), with effect from 1 April 2011 (SI 2010/867).

Cross references – FA 1982, s. 135(1)(c): application of para. 1(2) where actual date of determination is later than the end of a claim period; winning of oil before determination of field.
OTA 1983, s. 3(6): any reference to s. 4 is to be construed as including a reference to OTA 1983, s. 3, 4 and Sch. 1.
FA 1991, s. 108(6): claim by defaulter for allowance of reimbursement expenditure in respect of certain abandonment costs to be made under Sch. 6; modification of para. 1 in respect thereto.
FA 1993, s. 192(1): where claim received by Board after 16 March 1993, expenditure not to be brought into account to determine assessable profit or allowable loss of any chargeable period ending earlier than the last day of the claim period in which expenditure incurred.

2 The provisions of Schedule 5 to this Act specified in the first column of the following Table shall apply in relation to a claim under this Schedule as they apply in relation to a claim under that Schedule subject to any modifications specified in the second column of that Table and with the substitution, for references to the responsible person, of references to the participator by whom the claim under this Schedule is made and, for references to section 2(9)(b)(ii) of this Act, of references to section 2(9)(c)(ii) of this Act.

TABLE

Provisions applied **Paragraph**	*Modifications*
2(3)...	For the reference to this Schedule substitute a reference to Schedule 5 to this Act.
2(4)...	Omit paragraph (b).
2(5)...	–
2(6)...	–
2(7)...	For the reference to paragraph 5 of Schedule 2 to this Act substitute a reference to paragraph 2 of that Schedule; for the reference to paragraph 2(1) of Schedule 5 to this Act substitute a reference to paragraph 1(2) of this Schedule.
2(8)...	–
3(1)...	Omit paragraph (c).
4...	–
5(1)...	Omit paragraph (b).
5(3)...	–
5(4)...	For the reference to all or any of the participators substitute a reference to the participator by whom the claim is made.
5(5)...	–
6(1)...	–

PRT Statutes

Provisions applied	*Modifications*
Paragraph	
6(3)… … …	Omit the reference to paragraph 6(2).
7… … …	–
8… … …	–
9… … …	–

History – In para. 2, the entry for para. 9 amended by FA 2009, s. 99 and Sch. 51, para. 25(3), with effect from 1 April 2011 (SI 2010/867).
"9" added to the first column by FA 1983, s. 40(2), with effect from 13 May 1983.
The modification of para. 9 added to the second column by FA 1990, s. 122(5).
"2(7)" inserted into the first column and the two corresponding modifications inserted into the second column by FA 1999, s. 102(5), with effect for chargeable periods ending on or after 30 June 1999.
"2(8)" added to the first column by FA 1999, s. 102(5), with effect for chargeable periods ending on or after 30 June 1999.
"5(5)" added by SI 2009/56, art. 3 and Sch. 1, para. 83, with effect from 1 April 2009, subject to transitional and saving provisions in SI 2009/56, Sch. 3.

SCHEDULE 7 – ALLOWANCE OF ABORTIVE EXPLORATION EXPENDITURE

Section 5

1(1) A claim for the allowance, in connection with an oil field,

(a) of any abortive exploration expenditure allowable under section 5 of this Act, or

(b) of any exploration and appraisal expenditure allowable under section 5A of this Act, or

(c) of any research expenditure allowable under section 5B of this Act

in the case of a participator in that field must be made by the participator to the Board.

1(2) Where a claim under this Schedule has been made and the participator by whom it was made subsequently discovers that an error or mistake has been made in the claim, he may make a supplementary claim.

1(3) The provisions of Schedule 5 to this Act specified in the first column of the following Table shall apply in relation to a claim under this Schedule as they apply in relation to a claim under that Schedule, subject to any modifications specified in the second column of that Table and with the substitution, for references to the responsible person, of references to the participator by whom the claim under this Schedule is made and, for references to section 3 or 4 of this Act, of references to section 5 or, as the case may be, section 5A or section 5B of this Act.

TABLE

Provisions applied	*Modifications*
Paragraph	
2(6)… … …	–
3(1)… … …	Omit paragraphs (b) and (c).
5(1)… … …	Omit the words from "or the amount" to "(1)(b) of that paragraph" and paragraph (b).
5(3)… … …	–
5(4)… … …	For the reference to all or any of the participators substitute a reference to the participator by whom the claim is made.
5(5)… … …	–
6(1)… … …	For "one or both of the grounds" substitute "the ground", and omit paragraph (b) and the words "or, as the case may be, claimed as so qualifying" (wherever occurring).
6(3)… … …	Omit "sub-paragraph (1)(b) or sub-paragraph (2)", and for the words from "the *corresponding*" to "itself" substitute "the appeal".
7… … …	In sub-paragraph (1), omit the words from "or qualifies" to "2(9)(b)(ii) of this Act".

Provisions applied Paragraph	*Modifications*
8...	In sub-paragraph (2) omit the words from "or allowed by it" to "section 2(9)(b)(ii) of this Act".
9...	In sub-paragraph (2) omit paragraphs (b) and (c), in sub-paragraph (8) for the reference to all or any of the participators substitute a reference to the participator by whom the claim is made.

History – Para. 1(1)(c) and the word "or" immediately preceding it inserted by FA 1987, s. 64 and Sch. 13, Pt. II, para. 5(1).
Para. 1(1)(b) inserted by FA 1983, s. 37(2) and Sch. 8, Pt. II, para. 6(1), with effect from 13 May 1983.
In para. 1(1), (2), FA 1983, s. 37(4), 48(5) and Sch. 10, Pt. III, repealed words deemed always to have been omitted.
In para. 1(3), the entry for para. 9 amended by FA 2009, s. 99 and Sch. 51, para. 26, with effect from 1 April 2011 (SI 2010/867).
In para. 1(3), the words "or section 5B" inserted by FA 1987, s. 64 and Sch. 13, Pt. II, para. 5(2), and "or, as the case may be, section 5A" by FA 1983, s. 37(2) and Sch. 8, Pt. II, para. 6(2).
In the Table "5(5)" added by SI 2009/56, art. 3 and Sch. 1, para. 84, with effect from 1 April 2009, subject to transitional and saving provisions in SI 2009/56, Sch. 3.
In the Table, the modifications of para. 9 relating to para. 9(1C)(c), (2A) inserted by FA 1990, s. 122(6), and the remaining modifications inserted by FA 1987, s. 67.

Cross references – FA 1993, s. 192(2): where claim for allowance of expenditure incurred after 31 March 1993 is allowed, expenditure may not be brought into account to determine assessable profit or allowable loss of any chargeable period which ends before the date on which expenditure incurred.

SCHEDULE 8 – ALLOWANCE OF UNRELIEVABLE FIELD LOSS

Section 6

REFERENCE AND DETERMINATION OF QUESTION OF ABANDONMENT OF OIL FIELD

1 Where it appears to the responsible person for an oil field that the winning of oil from the field has permanently ceased he may by notice in writing given to the Board refer to them for their decision the question whether the winning of oil from that field has permanently ceased.

2(1) The Board shall, by notice in writing given to the responsible person, inform him of their decision on the question and, if their decision is that the winning of oil has so ceased, shall state the date which they are satisfied is that on which the winning of oil from the field in question ceased.

2(2) The responsible person shall, within one month of his receiving a notice under sub-paragraph (1) above informing him of the Board's decision, furnish a copy of that notice to every person who was at any time a participator in the field in question.

3(1) The responsible person may appeal against the Board's decision by notice in writing given to the Board within three months of his receiving the notice under paragraph 2(1) above informing him thereof.

3(2) An appeal under sub-paragraph (1) above may at any time before it is notified to the tribunal be abandoned by notice in writing given to the Board by the responsible person.

3(3) The provisions of paragraphs 14A to 14I of Schedule 2 shall apply to appeals under this paragraph subject to any necessary modifications.

History – In para. 3(1) the words "to the Special Commissioners" omitted by SI 2009/56, art. 3 and Sch. 1, para. 85(2), with effect from 1 April 2009, subject to transitional and saving provisions in SI 2009/56, Sch. 3.
In para. 3(2) the words "before it is notified to the tribunal" inserted by SI 2009/56, art. 3 and Sch. 1, para. 85(3), with effect from 1 April 2009, subject to transitional and saving provisions in SI 2009/56, Sch. 3.
Para. 3(3) inserted by SI 2009/56, art. 3 and Sch. 1, para. 85(4), with effect from 1 April 2009, subject to transitional and saving provisions in SI 2009/56, Sch. 3.

CLAIMS BY PARTICIPATORS FOR ALLOWANCE OF UNRELIEVABLE FIELD LOSSES

4(1) A claim for the allowance, in connection with an oil field, of any unrelievable field loss allowable under section 6 of this Act in the case of a participator in that field must be made by the participator to the Board at any time after the date of the decision (whether of the Board or on appeal from the Board) that the winning of oil from the oilfield in the case of which the loss accrued has permanently ceased.

4(2) Where a claim under this Schedule has been made and the participator by whom it was made subsequently discovers that an error or mistake has been made in the claim, he may make a supplementary claim.

4(3) The provisions of Schedule 5 to this Act specified in the first column of the Table set out in paragraph 1(3) of Schedule 7 to this Act shall apply in relation to a claim under this Schedule as they apply in relation to a claim under the said Schedule 5, subject to any modifications specified in the second column of that Table and with the substitution, for references to the responsible person, of references to the participator by whom the claim under this Schedule is made, for references to the claiming or allowance of expenditure, of references to the claiming or allowance of an unrelievable field loss and, for references to section 3 or 4 of this Act, of references to section 6 of this Act.

History – Para. 4 amended by FA 1995, s. 147, 162 and Sch. 29, Pt. IX, in relation to claims made on or after 1 May 1995, by substituting, in para. 4(1), the words "at any time after" for the former words "and must be made within six years of the later of the following dates, that is to say", by omitting from the end of para. 4(1) the words ", and the date of the determination under Schedule 1 to this Act of the last-mentioned field", and by omitting from the end of para. 4(2) the words "within the time allowed for making the original claim".

Cross references – FA 1984, s. 113(7): date on which the winning of oil from a field has permanently ceased for the purpose of determining a participator's "qualifying date".

FINANCE (NO. 2) ACT 1979

(1979 Chapter 47)

[*26th July 1979*]

ARRANGEMENT OF SECTIONS

PART III – PETROLEUM REVENUE TAX

PART IV – MISCELLANEOUS AND SUPPLEMENTARY

PART III – PETROLEUM REVENUE TAX

19 Reduction of uplift for allowable expenditure

19(1) [Amends OTA 1975, s. 2.]

19(2) Subject to subsection (3) below, subsection (1) above has effect in relation to expenditure incurred in pursuance of a contract entered into on or after 1st January 1979.

19(3) Where expenditure is incurred in pursuance of a contract entered into before the said 1st January but is attributable to a request for an alteration or addition made, or other instruction given, on or after that date by or on behalf of the person incurring the expenditure to another party to the contract, subsection (1) above shall have effect in relation to that expenditure as if the percentage to be substituted for 75 per cent were 662/3; per cent.

19(4) Where under paragraph 2(4)(a) of Schedule 5 to the said Act of 1975 or that paragraph as applied by Schedule 6 to that Act (claims for allowable expenditure) a claim states that any expenditure is claimed as qualifying for supplement under section 2(9)(b)(ii) or (c)(ii) of that Act, then, if by virtue of this section those provisions have effect in relation to different parts of that expenditure with different percentages–

(a) the claim shall distinguish between those parts;

(b) in paragraphs 3(1)(b), 6(1)(b),6(2),7(1) and 8(2) of that Schedule, and in those paragraphs as applied by the said Schedule 6, references to expenditure allowed or which ought to be allowed as qualifying for supplement or to expenditure which does so qualify shall be construed as referring separately to each of those parts; and

(c) in paragraph 5(1)(a) of that Schedule, and in that paragraph as so applied, the reference to the amount or total of the amounts stated under the said paragraph 3(1)(b) shall be construed as a reference to any amount so stated by virtue of paragraph (b) above.

19(5) Where by virtue of subsection (4) above different amounts are stated under paragraph 3(1)(b) of the said Schedule 5 the reference in paragraph 3(1)(c) of that Schedule to an amount equal to the relevant percentage of the amount stated under paragraph 3(1)(b) shall be construed as a reference to an amount arrived at by applying the appropriate percentage to each of those amounts and aggregating the result

20 Extension of allowable expenditure

20 [Amends OTA 1975, s. 3 and Sch. 4, para. 2.]

21 Reduction of oil allowance and metrication of measurements

21 [Amends OTA 1975, s. 1, 8 and 10.]

22 Taxation of British National Oil Corporation

22(1) Section 9(1) of the Petroleum and Submarine Pipe-lines Act 1975 (exemption of British National Oil Corporation and its wholly owned subsidiaries from petroleum revenue tax) shall not have effect in relation to chargeable periods ending after 30th June 1979; and the provisions of subsections (2) and (3) below, being transitional provisions, shall have effect–

(a) in the case of subsection (2), for the purpose of computing the assessable profit or allowable loss accruing from any oil field to that Corporation or any company which is or has been one of those subsidiaries; and

(b) in the case of subsection (3), for the purpose of computing the assessable profit or allowable loss accruing from any oil field to any of the following persons (in this section referred to as **"relevant persons"**) that is to say, that Corporation, any such company and any person having an interest in an oil field, being an interest the whole or part of which in any chargeable period ending before 1st July 1979 constituted the interest in that oil field of that Corporation or one of those subsidiaries.

22(2) [Amends OTA 1975, s. 2.]

22(3) If for any chargeable period–

(a) there is an amount to be taken into account by virtue of paragraph (b) or (c) of subsection (9) of the said section 2 (allowable expenditure) or both those paragraphs; and

(b) the whole or any part of that amount is attributable to expenditure incurred before 1st July 1979,

that amount or, as the case may be, that part (including so much of it as is so taken into account by virtue of sub-paragraph (ii) of the said paragraph (b) or (c)) shall be deemed for the purposes of that Act, except section 9, to be reduced by the relevant amount or, as the case may be, by so much of the relevant amount as has not been taken into account under this subsection in computing the assessable profit or allowable loss accruing to the relevant person in question or any other person in an earlier chargeable period.

22(4) In this section **"the relevant amount"**, in relation to an oil field, means the aggregate gross profit, as defined in section 2(4) of the Oil Taxation Act 1975, accruing in chargeable periods ending before 1st July 1979 in respect of so much of the interest of the relevant person in question in that oil field as in any of those chargeable periods constituted the interest in that oil field of the British National Oil Corporation or one of its wholly owned subsidiaries; and in this subsection **"wholly owned subsidiary"** has the same meaning as in the Petroleum and Submarine Pipe-lines Act 1975.

Cross references – OTA 1975, s. 2: assessable profits and allowable losses.

PART IV – MISCELLANEOUS AND SUPPLEMENTARY

25 Short title, interpretation, construction and repeals

25(1) This Act may be cited as the Finance (No. 2) Act 1979.

25(2), (3) [Not relevant to petroleum revenue tax.]

25(4) Part III of this Act shall be construed as one with Part I of the Oil Taxation Act 1975.

PETROLEUM REVENUE TAX ACT 1980

(1980 Chapter 1)

[*31st January 1980*]

ARRANGEMENT OF SECTIONS

1 Payments on account of tax

1(1) Every participator in an oil field shall, at the time when he delivers to the Board the return for a chargeable period required by paragraph 2 of Schedule 2 to the Oil Taxation Act 1975–

(a) deliver to the Board a statement showing whether any, and if so what, amount of tax is payable by him in accordance with the Schedule to this Act for that period in respect of the field; and

(b) pay to the Board a sum equal to the amount of tax if any, shown in the statement less an amount equal to his APRT credit for that chargeable period in respect of that oil field.

1(2) The statement under subsection (1)(a) above shall be in such form as the Board may prescribe.

1(3) The sum paid under subsection (1)(b) above shall constitute a payment on account of the tax charged in any assessment made on the participator in respect of the assessable profit accruing to him for the chargeable period from the oil field; and if the payment on account exceeds the tax so charged less the amount of the APRT credit deducted in accordance with subsection (1)(b) above from the tax shown in the statement the excess shall be repaid to the participator.

1(3A) In subsections (1) and (3) above **"APRT credit"** has the meaning given by section 139(4) of the Finance Act 1982.

1(3B) Paragraphs 3 of Schedule 2 of the principal Act (penalties for failure to make returns under paragraph 2 of that Schedule) shall apply in relation to statements required to be made under subsection (1)(a) above as they apply in relation to returns required to be made under paragraph 2 of that Schedule.

1(4) [Amends OTA 1975, Sch. 2, para. 13.]

1(5) Where a participator gives notice of appeal under paragraph 14 of the said Schedule 2 against an assessment charging tax in respect of which he has made a payment on account, the amount, if any, to be repaid under subsection (3) above shall be calculated as if the tax charged in the assessment were limited to the tax which he would not be entitled to withhold under sub-paragraph (3) of that paragraph.

1(6) Certificates of tax deposit issued by the Treasury under section 12 of the National Loans Act 1968 on terms published on or before 14th May 1979 may be used for making payments on account under this section; and for that purpose those terms shall have effect with the necessary modifications and as if the tax in or towards the payment of which a certificate is used were due two months after the end of the chargeable period to which it relates.

History – In s. 1(1), the words "less an amount equal to … that oil field", and in s. 1(3), the words "less the amount of … in the statement" and s. 1(3A), (3B) all inserted by FA 1982, s. 139(1), (6) and Sch. 19, para. 21, for chargeable periods ending after 31 December 1982. APRT (advance petroleum revenue tax) ceased to apply in chargeable periods ending after 31 December 1986 (FA 1982, s. 139(1)(b)).
S. 1(3A) inserted by FA 1982, s. 139(6) and Sch. 19, para. 21.
In s. 1(3B), the words ", 8 and 9" omitted by FA 2008, s. 122 and Sch. 40, para. 21(b), with effect from 1 April 2009.
S. 1(3B) inserted by FA 1982, s. 139(6) and Sch. 19, para. 21.

Cross references – FA 1982, s. 135(3)(c): s. 1 does not apply to returns containing particulars required by determination of oil field varying an earlier determination.
FA 2009, Sch. 55: penalty for failure to make returns etc.

2 Interest on tax and on repayments

2(1) [Amends OTA 1975, Sch. 2, para. 15(1) and Sch. 5, para. 8(4).]

2(2) [Amends OTA 1975, Sch. 2, para. 16.]

2(3) [Repealed by FA 1989, s. 187 and Sch. 17, Pt. X.]

History – S. 2(3) repealed by FA 1989, s. 187 and Sch. 17, Pt. X with effect in relation to any period for which s. 178(1) of that Act has effect by virtue of s. 178(7) (i.e. with effect from 18 August 1989 by virtue of SI 1989/1298).

3 Short title, construction and commencement

3(1) This Act may be cited as the Petroleum Revenue Tax Act 1980.

3(2) This Act shall be construed as one with Part I of the Oil Taxation Act 1975.

3(3) Section 1 above has effect in relation to chargeable periods ending on or after 31st December 1979, section 2(1) and (2) above have effect in relation to tax charged for any such period and section 2(3) above has effect from 1st January 1980.

SCHEDULE – COMPUTATION OF PAYMENT ON ACCOUNT

Section 1(1)(a)

1 For the purposes of section 1(1)(a) of this Act the tax payable by a participator for any chargeable period in respect of an oil field shall be determined as provided in the following provisions of this Schedule; and references in those provisions to any section or Schedule is a reference to that section or Schedule in the Oil Taxation Act 1975.

2(1) There shall first be determined whether a computation made in accordance with section 2 as modified by the following provisions of this paragraph would result in an assessable profit, an allowable loss or neither an assessable profit or allowable loss and, if it would result in an assessable profit or allowable loss, the amount of that profit or loss.

2(2) The market value, price and amounts referred to in section 2(5), (6)(b)(ii) and (7)(b) and (c) shall be taken from the particulars included in the return in pursuance of paragraph 2(2) and (3) of Schedule 2.

2(2A) The amount of any tariff or disposal receipts, within the meaning of the Oil Taxation Act 1983, shall be taken from the particulars included in the return referred to in sub-paragraph (2) above, and any amount by which any of those tariff receipts are to be treated as reduced under section 9 of that Act shall be determined accordingly.

2(3) The amount referred to in section 2(8)(b) shall be treated as nil and section 2(9)(a), (10) and (11) shall be omitted.

2(4) Any expenditure in respect of which a claim has been made under Schedule 5, 6 or 7 and in respect of which the Board have not notified their decision under that Schedule may be treated for the purposes of section 2(9)(b), (c), (d), (f) or (g), –

(a) as having been allowed; and

(b) in the case of expenditure claimed as qualifying for supplement under section 2(9)(b)(ii) or (c)(ii), as having been allowed as so qualifying.

2(5) The participator's share of any expenditure which by virtue of sub-paragraph (4) above is treated as having been allowed on a claim under Schedule 5 shall be the share proposed in the claim in pursuance of paragraph 2(4)(b) of that Schedule.

2(6) Any loss in respect of which a claim has been made under Schedule 8 and in respect of which the Board have not notified their decision under that Schedule may be treated for the purposes of section 2(9)(e) as having been allowed.

2(7) No expenditure or loss shall be taken into account under sub-paragraph (4), (5) or (6) above in relation to more than one chargeable period or more than one oil field.

History – Para. 2(2A) inserted by OTA 1983, s. 10(6), with effect from 1 December 1983.
In para. 2(4), the words ", (f) or (g)" substituted by FA 1987, s. 64 and Sch. 13, Pt. II, para. 6, and "(d) [or (f)]" by FA 1983, s. 37(2) and Sch. 8, Pt. II, para. 7.

Cross references – FA 1981, s. 111(6): restriction of expenditure supplement.
OTA 1983, Sch. 4, para. 15: modification of para. 2(2A) for receipts attributable to UK use of foreign field assets.

3 The amount of any assessable profit resulting from the computation under paragraph 2 above may be reduced by any allowable loss in accordance with section 7(1) and shall be reduced in accordance with section 8 by reference to the participator's share, if any, of the oil allowance for the chargeable period.

4(1) The tax payable shall be arrived at by–

(a) calculating the tax on the amount of assessable profit resulting from the computation under paragraph 2 above as reduced under paragraph 3 above; and

(b) applying the limit imposed by section 9.

4(2) In applying section 9 under this paragraph–

(a) the assessable profit or allowable loss referred to in subsection (2)(a)(i) of that section shall be computed as provided in paragraph 2 above; and

(b) the expenditure to be excluded under subsection (2)(a)(ii) and (3) of that section from the expenditure *taken into account* in computing the assessable profit or allowable loss for that period shall not include any expenditure treated under paragraph 2(4)(b) above as having been allowed as qualifying for supplement.

History – In para. 4(2) words after "this paragraph" repealed by FA 1981, s. 139 and Sch. 19, Pt. 8, effective from 27 July 1981.

FINANCE ACT 1980

(1980 Chapter 48)

[*1st August 1980*]

ARRANGEMENT OF SECTIONS

PART VI – OIL TAXATION

PART VIII – MISCELLANEOUS AND SUPPLEMENTARY

SCHEDULES

PART VI – OIL TAXATION

104 Increase of petroleum revenue tax

104(1) [Amends OTA 1975, s. 1(2).]

104(2) This section has effect in relation to chargeable periods ending after 31st December 1979.

106 Transfers of interests in oil fields

106 Schedule 17 to this Act shall have effect for supplementing and modifying Part I of the Oil Taxation Act 1975 where after the passing of this Act a participator in an oil field transfers the whole or part of his interest in the field.

107 Transmedian fields

107(1) The Oil Taxation Acts shall have effect in accordance with this section where provision is made by an agreement between the government of the United Kingdom and the government of another country for–

(a) the exploitation as a single unit of oil in strata in the sea bed and subsoil of an area consisting of–

(i) an oil field within the meaning of Part I of the Oil Taxation Act 1975; and

(ii) a sector under the jurisdiction of the other country; and

(b) the apportionment of the oil between–

(i) the participators in that field; and

(ii) the persons who are, or have rights, interests or obligations of, licensees in respect of that sector under the law of the other country.

107(2) The share of a participator in the oil won from the oil field shall be determined as if the oil won from the field consisted of so much of the oil won from the area as a whole as is apportioned to the participators in accordance with the agreement; and in section 10(3)(b) of the said Act of 1975 (restriction of allowable expenditure) and paragraphs 5(2)(a) and 7 of Schedule 2 to that Act (returns and information as to oil won from the field) references to oil won from the field shall be construed as references to so much of the oil won from the area as a whole as is so apportioned.

107(3) Subject to subsection (2) above–

(a) the oil field shall be deemed to include the sector mentioned in subsection (1)(a)(ii) above;

(b) that sector shall be deemed to be a designated area; and

(c) references to oil shall include references to any substance that would be oil within the meaning of the said Act of 1975 if the enactments mentioned in section 1(1) extended to that sector;

PRT Statutes

but paragraph (a) above does not affect section 10(3)(a) of that Act or paragraph 4 of Schedule 2 to that Act (appointment of responsible person), and paragraph (b) above does not affect section 5(1)(b) of that Act (abortive exploration expenditure) or operate so as to apply section 38(4) of the Finance Act 1973 (taxation of non-residents engaged in activities in designated areas) to the persons referred to in subsection (1)(b)(ii) above.

107(4) Where under the agreement there is a re-determination of the apportionment mentioned in subsection (1)(b) above and in consequence thereof the participators in the field receive a repayment in respect of expenditure which has been allowed for the field under section 3 of the said Act of 1975, the total amount of expenditure allowable under that section and section 4 of that Act for the field in the claim period in which the repayment is received shall be reduced by the amount of the repayment; and paragraph 6 of Schedule 4 to that Act (recovery of deductions from allowable expenditure) shall have effect as if the foregoing provisions of this subsection were relevant provisions within the meaning of that paragraph.

107(5) [Repealed by OTA 1983, s. 15(6) and Sch. 6.]

107(6) In subsection (4) above references to a **"repayment"** include references to a credit or set-off.

107(7) In this section **"the Oil Taxation Acts"** means the Oil Taxation Act 1975, any other enactment relating to petroleum revenue tax and the provisions of the Income Tax Acts and Corporation Tax Acts in their application to oil extraction activities and oil rights within the meaning of Part 8 of the Corporation Tax Act 2010 or Chapter 16A of Part 2 of the Income Tax (Trading and Other Income) Act 2005.

107(8) This section has effect whether the agreement mentioned in subsection (1) above is made before or after the passing of this Act and applies in relation to a chargeable period ending before the coming into force of this Act as well as to a chargeable period ending later.

History – S. 107(5), and the reference to it in s. 107(6), were repealed by OTA 1983, s. 15(6) and Sch. 6, with effect from 1 August 1980.
In s. 107(7) the words "Chapter 16A of Part 2 of the Income Tax (Trading and Other Income) Act 2005" substituted for the words "Chapter V of Part XII of the Taxes Act 1988" by TIOPA 2010, s. 374 and Sch. 8, para. 176, with effect for corporation tax purposes for accounting periods ending on or after 1 April 2010, for income tax and capital gains tax purposes for the tax year 2010–11 and subsequent tax years, and for petroleum revenue tax purposes for chargeable periods beginning on or after 1 July 2010.
In s. 107(7), the words "Part 8 of the Corporation Tax Act 2010 or" inserted by CTA 2010, s. 1177 and Sch. 1, para. 171, with effect for corporation tax purposes for accounting periods ending on or after 1 April 2010, and for income tax and capital gains tax purposes for the tax year 2010–11 and subsequent tax years.
See ICTA 1988, Sch. 29, para. 32 for substitution of former reference to that Act in s. 107(7).

Cross references – OTA 1983, s. 6A(6) (Tax-exempt tariffing receipts): for the purposes of s. 6A, in the case of an oil field which, by virtue of FA 1980, s. 107, is deemed to include the sector mentioned in s. 107 (1)(a)(ii), that sector shall be treated as a foreign field, and the remainder of that field shall be treated as a separate oil field.
OTA 1983, s. 7(3) (repayment under s. 107(4) treated as a disposal receipt).
OTA 1983, s. 9(6) (tariff receipts allowance for transmedian fields).
OTA 1983, s. 12(3) (receipts attributable to UK use of foreign field asset: foreign sector of transmedian field).

108 Gas banking schemes

108(1) Subject to the provisions of this section, the Board may by regulations made by statutory instrument modify the operation of the Oil Taxation Acts in their application to cases where–

(a) a gas banking scheme is in force between the participators in two or more oil fields; and

(b) the participators in those fields elect that the modifications prescribed by the regulations shall apply.

108(2) Subject to subsection (3)(a) below, **"a gas banking scheme"** for the purposes of this section is any scheme which provides for the transfer of oil consisting of gas won from one of the oil fields to which the scheme applies to or to the order of the participators in another of those fields in consideration wholly or mainly of the subsequent transfer of oil consisting of gas won from the other field to or to the order of the participators in the first-mentioned field.

108(3) Regulations under this section may–

(a) prescribe additional conditions required to be satisfied for a scheme to constitute a gas banking scheme, including conditions requiring the gas to be of a description specified in the regulations;

(b) prescribe conditions subject to which, and the manner in which, an election may be made under this section and the time for which any such election is to continue in force; and

(c) contain such incidental, supplementary or transitional provisions as appear to the Board to be necessary or expedient.

108(4) The foregoing provisions of this section shall apply to an international gas banking scheme as they apply to a gas banking scheme within the meaning of those provisions except that only the participators in *the oil field* or *oil fields* to which the scheme applies need make the election referred to in subsection (1)(b) above; and for the purposes of this section an international gas banking scheme is any scheme which–

(a) applies to areas that include both one or more oil fields and one or more areas under the jurisdiction of a country other than the United Kingdom; and

(b) would be a gas banking scheme within the meaning of the foregoing provisions if all the areas were oil fields and all the persons who are, or have rights, interests or obligations of, licensees in respect of those areas were participators.

108(5) Regulations under this section may be made so as to apply only to gas banking schemes other than international gas banking schemes or so as to apply only to the latter; and regulations applying to a scheme of either description may differ from those applying to the other.

108(6) No regulations shall be made under this section unless a draft of the regulations has been laid before, and approved by a resolution of, the House of Commons.

108(7) In this section **"the Board"**, **"oil"**, **"oil field"** and **"participator"** have the same meaning as in Part I of the Oil Taxation Act 1975 and **"the Oil Taxation Acts"** has the same meaning as in section 107 above.

Cross references – FA 1981, s. 121: power to make regulations under this section with retrospective effect.
OTA 1983, s. 9(10): treatment of gas transferred to a user field for purposes of tariff receipts allowance.
Statutory instruments – SI 1982/92: made under s. 108(6).

109 Fractionation

109(1)–(7) [Amends OTA 1975, s. 2 and Sch. 13, para. 2 and 2A.]

109(8) Subject to the following provisions of this section, this section has effect–

(a) as respects Part I of the Oil Taxation Act 1975, in relation to chargeable periods (within the meaning of that Part) ending after 31st December 1979; and

(b) as respects Chapter V of Part XII of the Taxes Act 1988, in relation to chargeable periods (within the meaning of that Part) ending after that date.

109(9) Expenditure shall not by virtue of this section be allowable under section 3 of the said Act of 1975 unless it was incurred after the said 31st December or would have been allowable under section 4 of that Act but for the proviso to subsection (1) of that section.

109(10) For the purposes of section 4 of the said Act of 1975 expenditure incurred in acquiring, bringing into existence or enhancing the value of an asset which before the passing of this Act was used for the purpose of any process which, if this Act had been in force, would by virtue of this section have constituted initial treatment of oil won from an oil field shall be treated as having been incurred on the date when the asset was first so used; and for the purposes of that section (but not of the foregoing provisions of this subsection) the use of the asset in connection with the field shall be treated as having begun–

(a) on 1st January 1980; or

(b) the date on which the asset was first used for that purpose,

whichever is the later.

Subsection (13) of the said section 4 shall apply for the purposes of this subsection.

109(11) [Repealed by ICTA 1988, s. 844 and Sch. 31.]

History – In s. 109(8), the reference to ICTA 1988 was substituted by FA 1988, s. 146 and Sch. 13, para. 20, 25, with effect for 1988–89 and subsequent years of assessment, and for companies' accounting periods ending after 5 April 1988.
S. 109(11) repealed by ICTA 1988, s. 844 and Sch. 31, with effect in relation to tax for 1988–89 and later years of assessment, and for companies' accounting periods ending after 5 April 1988.
Notes – The substance of the former s. 109(11) is reflected in ICTA 1988, s. 502(2)(b).

PART VIII – MISCELLANEOUS AND SUPPLEMENTARY

122 Short title, interpretation, construction and repeals

122(1) This Act may be cited as the Finance Act 1980.

122(2) In this Act **"the Taxes Act"** means the Income and Corporation Taxes Act 1970 and **"the Taxes Act 1988"** means the Income and Corporation Taxes Act 1988.

History – Definition of "the Taxes Act 1988" inserted by ICTA 1988, s. 844 and Sch. 29, para. 32.

SCHEDULE 17 – TRANSFERS OF INTERESTS IN OIL FIELDS

Section 106

Cross references – FA 1999, s. 97(3): transfers of interests in oil fields covered by FA 1999, s. 96 to be construed in accordance with Sch. 17
FA 1981, s. 112: restriction of expenditure supplement following transfers of interests.
CAA 1990, s. 64: restriction of capital allowances on plant and machinery following transfers of interests.

Part I – Preliminary

Cross references – FA 1994, Sch. 22, para. 11(1): transfers of interest and election by reference to pipe-line usage.

INTERPRETATION

1(1) For the purposes of this Schedule a participator in an oil field transfers the whole or part of this interest in the field whenever as a result of a transaction or event other than–

(a) the making of an agreement or arrangement of the kind mentioned in paragraph 5 of Schedule 3 to the Oil Taxation Act 1975; or

(b) a re-determination under a unitisation agreement,

the whole or part of his share in the oil to be won and saved from the field becomes the share or part of the share of another person who is or becomes a participator in the field.

1(2) In sub-paragraph (1) above a **"unitisation agreement"** means an agreement for the exploitation of–

(a) an oil field falling within two or more licensed areas; or

(b) any such area as is mentioned in subsection (1)(a) of section 107 of this Act,

and a **"re-determination"** means, in a case within paragraph (a) above, a re-determination of the apportionment of oil from the field as between the different licensed areas and, in a case within paragraph (b) above, a re-determination of the apportionment mentioned in subsection (1)(b) of that section.

1(3) In this Schedule **"the old participator"** means the participator whose interest is wholly or partly transferred, **"the new participator"** means the person to whom it is transferred and **"the transfer period"** means the chargeable period in which the transfer takes place.

History – In para. 1(3), the words "the transfer period" to the end were substituted by FA 1981, s. 114(2)(a), with effect whether the participator's net profit period ends before or after the passing of that Act.

Cross references – TCGA 1992, s. 197(1): application of para. 1 to the construction of "the transfer by a participator in an oil field of the whole or part of his interest in the field" in relation to the ring fence in respect of net chargeable gains or losses.
FA 2001, Sch. 32, para. 4(2): application of para. 1(2).

2 This Schedule shall be construed as one with Part I of the said Act of 1975, and any reference in this Schedule to a section or Schedule not otherwise identified is a reference to that section or Schedule of that Act.

NOTICE OF TRANSFER

3(1) The old and new participators shall within two months after the end of the transfer period deliver to the Board a notice in such form and containing such particulars with respect to the transfer as the Board may prescribe.

3(2) Where as a result of the same transaction or event–

(a) the whole or part of the interest of two or more persons in an oil field becomes the interest or part of the interest of another person; or

(b) parts of a participator's interest in an oil field are transferred to two or more other persons,

a single notice relating to all the transfers shall be given under this paragraph by all the old participators and new participators, and in relation to any such notice references in paragraphs 4 and 5 below to the old and new participators shall be construed accordingly.

Cross references – FA 1982, s. 135(3)(a): extension of time allowed following variation of determination of oil field.

EXCLUSION OF TRANSFER RULES

4(1) Parts II and III of this Schedule shall not apply in relation to a transfer if the old and new participators make an application in that behalf in the notice under paragraph 3 above and the Board consider that those provisions would not materially affect the total tax chargeable in respect of the field.

4(2) The Board shall give notice of their decision under this paragraph to the old and new participators.

PARTIAL TRANSFERS

5(1) Where the transfer is of part of the old participator's interest in the field the notice under paragraph 3 above shall state what the old and new participators propose should be the corresponding part of the amounts to be transferred to the new participator under paragraphs 6, 7 and 8 below and of the old participator's share of oil to be treated as that of the new participator under paragraph 9 below; and subject to the following provisions of this paragraph, the corresponding part shall for the purposes of those provisions be taken to be such part as is determined by the Board and specified in a notice given to the old and new participators.

5(2) If the corresponding part determined by the Board differs from that proposed by the old and new participators they or any of them may appeal by notice in writing given to the Board not more than three months after the notice given by the Board under sub-paragraph (1) above; but the bringing of an appeal shall not affect the operation of the notice given by the Board.

5(3) The old participator or the new participator shall, whether or not himself the appellant, be entitled to be a party to the appeal and in any proceedings arising out of it.

5(4) An appeal may be abandoned before it is notified to the tribunal by notice in writing to the Board; and if before an appeal is determined the old and new participators agree with the Board on what should be the corresponding part referred to above the Board's notice under subsection (1) above shall have effect as if that were the part specified in it.

5(5) Where the corresponding part referred to above as specified in the Board's notice under sub-paragraph (1) is varied on appeal, the Board's notice shall have effect as if the varied part had been specified in it; and all such assessments or determinations or adjustments shall be made as are necessary in consequence of the variation.

5(6) The provisions of paragraphs 14A to 14I of Schedule 2 to the Oil Taxation Act 1975 shall apply to appeals under this paragraph subject to any necessary modifications.

History – In para. 5(2) the words "may appeal by notice" substituted for the words "may by notice" and the words "appeal to the Special Commissioners" omitted by SI 2009/56, art. 3 and Sch. 1, para. 95(2), with effect from 1 April 2009, subject to transitional and saving provisions in SI 2009/56, Sch. 3.

In para. 5(3) the words "be a party to" substituted for the words "appear and be heard on" by SI 2009/56, art. 3 and Sch. 1, para. 95(3), with effect from 1 April 2009, subject to transitional and saving provisions in SI 2009/56, Sch. 3.

In para. 5(4) the words "before it is notified to the tribunal" inserted by SI 2009/56, art. 3 and Sch. 1, para. 95(4), with effect from 1 April 2009, subject to transitional and saving provisions in SI 2009/56, Sch. 3.

Para. 5(6) inserted by SI 2009/56, art. 3 and Sch. 1, para. 95(5), with effect from 1 April 2009, subject to transitional and saving provisions in SI 2009/56, Sch. 3.

Part II – Transfer of Old Participator's Expenditure Relief, Losses and Exemptions

UNUSED EXPENDITURE RELIEF

6(1) There shall be transferred to the new participator the whole or, if the transfer is of part of the old participator's interest in the field, a corresponding part of any amount which–

(a) would, apart from this paragraph, fall to be taken into account under section 2(9)(b) in computing the assessable profit or allowable loss accruing to the old participator from the field in the transfer period or a later chargeable period; and

(b) is attributable to expenditure allowed to the old participator under Schedule 5 in accordance with his interest in the field before the transfer.

6(2) If the whole of the old participator's interest in the field is transferred in the transfer period (whether to one new participator or partly to one and partly to another or others) there shall be transferred to the new participator the whole or, as the case may be, to each of them a corresponding part, of any amount which–

(a) would, apart from this paragraph, fall to be taken into account under section 2(9)(c) in computing the assessable profit or allowable loss accruing to the old participator from the field in the transfer period or a later chargeable period; and

(b) is attributable to expenditure incurred by the old participator before the transfer and allowed to him under Schedule 6.

6(3) Any amount transferred to the new participator under this paragraph shall, instead of being taken into account as mentioned in sub-paragraph (1)(a) or (2)(a) above, be taken into account in computing the assessable profit or allowable loss accruing to the new participator from the field.

Cross references – FA 1994, Sch. 22, para. 10(1)(a): transfers of interests and election by reference to pipe-line usage.

UNUSED LOSSES

7(1) There shall be transferred to the new participator the whole or, if the transfer is of part of the old participator's interest in the field, a corresponding part of any loss which the Board have determined under Schedule 2 has accrued to the old participator from the field in the transfer period or any earlier chargeable period to the extent that it has not been relieved against assessable profits accruing to him in the transfer period or an earlier chargeable period.

7(2) Subject to the following provisions of this paragraph any amount of a loss transferred to the new participator under this paragraph may be relieved under section 7 against assessable profits accruing to the new participator in the transfer period or a later chargeable period and shall not be set off against assessable profits of the old participator and, for the purposes of effecting such relief, subsection (1) of section 7 shall have effect as if the word "succeeding" were omitted.

7(3) If, in the case of a transfer of the whole or part of an interest on or after 29th November 1994,–

(a) the old participator made a claim or election for the allowance of any expenditure unrelated to the field, and

(b) the claim or election was received by the Board on or after that date, and

(c) the expenditure allowed on the claim or election fell to be taken into account in computing the assessable profit or allowable loss of the old participator for the transfer period or any earlier chargeable period,

then, from the sum which, apart from this sub-paragraph, would be the aggregate of all the losses transferred to the new participator under this paragraph there shall be deducted (subject to sub-paragraphs (5) and (6) below) so much of the expenditure referred to in paragraph (a) above as is allowed on the claim or election (and, accordingly, the amount so deducted shall not fall to be transferred to the new participator under this paragraph).

7(4) In this paragraph **"expenditure unrelated to the field"** means expenditure allowable under any of the following provisions–

(a) section 5 (abortive exploration expenditure);

(b) section 5A (exploration and appraisal expenditure);

(c) section 5B (research expenditure);

(d) section 6 (unrelievable loss from abandoned field); and

(e) section 65 of the Finance Act 1987 (cross-field allowance of certain expenditure incurred on new fields);

and, in relation to any such expenditure, **"claim"** means a claim under Schedule 7 or Schedule 8 and **"election"** means an election under Part I of Schedule 14 to the Finance Act 1987 and, in relation to such an election, expenditure shall be regarded as allowed if it is accepted by the Board as allowable in accordance with that Schedule.

7(5) Where, in accordance with sub-paragraph (1) above, only a part of a loss (corresponding to the part of the interest transferred) falls to be transferred under this paragraph, only a corresponding part of the expenditure referred to in sub-paragraph (3) above shall be deducted under that sub-paragraph.

7(6) Where the amount of the deduction under sub-paragraph (3) above equals or exceeds the sum from which it is to be deducted, no part of any loss shall be transferred to the new participator under this paragraph.

History – In para. 7(1), the words "in the transfer period or any earlier chargeable period" were substituted by FA 1983, s. 41, in relation to transfer periods ending after 31 December 1982.

In para. 7(2), the words "Subject to the following provisions of this paragraph" were added by FA 1995, s. 148(2) with effect from 1 May 1995.

In para. 7(2), the words "and for the purposes … were omitted" were inserted by FA 1983, s. 41, in relation to transfer periods ending after 31 December 1982.

Para. 7(3)–(6) added by FA 1995, s. 148(3) with effect from 1 May 1995.

ACCUMULATED CAPITAL EXPENDITURE

8(1) There shall be transferred to the new participator the whole or, if the transfer is of part of the old participator's interest in the field, a corresponding part of the amount which under section 9(3) is the old participator's accumulated capital expenditure at the end of the last chargeable period before the transfer period.

8(2) Subject to paragraph 18 below, any amount transferred under this paragraph shall be treated for the purposes of section 9(3) as, or as part of, the new participator's accumulated capital expenditure at the end of the transfer period and later chargeable periods and not as, or as part of, the old participator's accumulated capital expenditure at the end of any such period.

History – In para. 8(1), the words "the last chargeable period before the transfer period" substituted by FA 1981, s. 114(2)(b).

In para. 8(2),the words "period" and "chargeable periods" substituted by FA 1981, s. 114(2)(c).

Both these amendments have effect whether the participator's net profit period ends before or after the passing of FA 1981.

Cross references – FA 1994, Sch. 22, para. 11(3): reduction in amount which would otherwise be the accumulated capital expenditure – transfer of correspondingly reduced amount to electing participator.

EXCLUDED OIL

9 For the purpose of determining under section 10(1)(b) what oil is to be disregarded in computing a participator's gross profit or loss attributable to oil won from the field after the transfer there shall be treated as if it were the new participator's, and not the old participator's, the whole or, if the transfer is of part of the old participator's interest in the field, a corresponding part of the old participator's share of oil won and saved from the field before the transfer.

SUCCESSIVE TRANSFERS

10(1) Where the old participator transfers the whole or part of his interest in a field in which he has himself acquired an interest by a previous transfer, the amounts to be taken into account in determining what is to be transferred to the new participator under paragraphs 6, 7 and 8 above and what is to be the share of oil treated as the new participator's under paragraph 9 above shall include–

(a) any amount which falls to be transferred to the old participator under paragraph 6 or 7 above by reference to the previous transfer and has not been taken into account or relieved in relation to him under paragraph 6(3) or 7(2) above; and

(b) any amount or share which falls to be transferred to the old participator or treated as his under paragraph 8 or 9 above by reference to the previous transfer.

10(2) Where the old participator makes successive transfers of parts of his interest, the amounts to be transferred to the new participator under paragraphs 6, 7 and 8 above and the share of oil to be treated as the new participator's under paragraph 9 above by reference to each transfer shall be that amount or share after deducting any of it which falls to be so transferred or treated by reference to a previous transfer.

Part III – Other Rules

11 [Omitted by FA 2009, s. 89 and Sch. 43, para. 3(4).]

History – Para. 11 (and the heading preceding it) omitted by FA 2009, s. 89 and Sch. 43, para. 3(4), with effect in relation to chargeable periods beginning after 30 June 2009 (subject to Sch. 43, para. 4).

ROYALTY PAYMENTS

12(1) Where at the end of the transfer period the old participator has no interest in the field–

(a) any licence debit or credit which, apart from this paragraph, would fall to be taken into account under subsection (6) of section 2 in computing the assessable profit or allowable loss accruing to him from the field in any later chargeable period in which he has no such interest shall not be so taken into account; but

(b) that subsection shall have effect in relation to the transfer period as if the amount of–

 (i) any such licence debit or credit as is mentioned in paragraph (a) above; and

 (ii) any licence debit or credit that would have fallen to be taken into account as there mentioned for a later chargeable period if the old participator were still a participator,

were an amount to be included in the sum referred to in paragraph (a) or, as the case may be, paragraph (b) of that subsection.

12(2) Sub-paragraph (1) above does not affect the amount of any loss transferred under paragraph 7 above.

12(3) Notwithstanding anything in section 34 of the Taxes Management Act 1970 (ordinary time limit for assessments) any further assessment or determination or amendment of an assessment or determination required in consequence of sub-paragraph (1) above may be made at any time not later than six years after the end of the later chargeable period referred to in sub-paragraph (1)(a) or (b)(ii) above.

PAYMENTS ON ACCOUNT AND ADVANCE PAYMENTS

13(1) For the purpose of computing under the Schedule to the Petroleum Revenue Tax Act 1980 (computation of payment on account) whether any, and if so what, amount of tax is payable under that Act by the old participator and the new participator for the transfer period or any later chargeable period–

(a) it shall be assumed that any application or proposal made in relation to the transfer under paragraph 4 or 5(1) above and in respect of which the Board have not notified their decision will be accepted by the Board; and

(b) the computation under that Schedule shall be made as if paragraph 6 above applied in relation to expenditure which under paragraph 2(4) of that Schedule is treated as having been allowed under Schedule 5 or 6 as well as to expenditure which has been so allowed.

13(2) [Spent.]

13(3) The old participator shall not be entitled to interest under subsection (7) of that section by reason of any such excess as is there mentioned for the transfer period or either of the next two chargeable periods if he and the new participator are connected within the meaning of section 1122 of the Corporation Tax Act 2010.

History – In para. 13(3), the words "section 1122 of the Corporation Tax Act 2010" substituted for the words "section 839 of the Taxes Act 1988" by CTA 2010, s. 1177 and Sch. 1, para. 172(2), with effect for corporation tax purposes for accounting periods ending on or after 1 April 2010, and for income tax and capital gains tax purposes for the tax year 2010–11 and subsequent tax years.
See ICTA 1988, s. 844 and Sch. 29, para. 32 for substitution of former reference to that Act.

LOSSES OF NEW PARTICIPATOR

14(1) Where the Board have determined under Schedule 2 that an allowable loss has accrued to the new participator from the field in the transfer period or a later chargeable period, then, if–

(a) the loss has been computed by reference to an amount taken into account by virtue of paragraph 6 above; and

(b) the old participator has no interest in the field at the end of the transfer period,

the old and new participators may jointly elect that the loss shall be surrendered to the old participator to the extent that it does not exceed whichever is the lesser of the amount referred to in paragraph (a) above and the total assessable profits as reduced under section 7 that accrued to the old participator from the field in chargeable periods up to and including the chargeable period after the transfer period.

14(2) Where any amount of a loss is surrendered under this paragraph it shall be treated–

(a) in relation to the old participator, as an allowable loss accruing to him in the chargeable period next but one after the transfer period; and

(b) in relation to the new participator, as if it has been relieved against assessable profits accruing to him from the field in chargeable periods before that in which it accrued.

TERMINAL LOSSES

15(1) This paragraph applies in any case where–

(a) such an allowable loss as falls to be relieved under section 7(3) accrues to the new participator from the field in a chargeable period ending after 17th March 2004, but

(b) some or all of the loss cannot be relieved under section 7(3) against assessable profits accruing to him from the field.

15(2) So much of the loss as cannot be so relieved ("the remaining loss") shall be regarded as an allowable unrelievable field loss in relation to the new participator ("the loss-maker") only to the extent that–

(a) so much of it as cannot be relieved in accordance with sub-paragraphs (3) to (6) below,

exceeds

(b) the aggregate of any relevant previous participators' expenditure unrelated to the field (see sub-paragraphs (10) and (11) below).

15(3) The remaining loss shall be treated as an allowable loss which falls to be relieved under section 7(3) against so much of any assessable profits accruing to the old participator from the field as is attributable to his represented interest (see sub-paragraphs (9) and (12) below).

15(4) Where a person is the new participator in relation to two or more old participators–

(a) the remaining loss shall be apportioned between those old participators in such manner as is just and reasonable having regard to the interests respectively transferred by them to the new participator,

(b) sub-paragraph (3) above shall have effect separately in relation to each of them (and the part of the remaining loss apportioned to him).

15(5) Any relief by virtue of sub-paragraph (3) above shall be given against the assessable profits accruing to the old participator in an earlier chargeable period only to the extent to which it cannot be given against the assessable profits accruing to him in a later chargeable period.

15(6) If–

(a) the old participator acquired some or all of his interest in the field by a previous transfer in relation to which he was the new participator,

(b) Parts 2 and 3 of this Schedule applied in relation to that previous transfer, and

(c) some or all of the part of the remaining loss treated as an allowable loss of his cannot be relieved in accordance with sub-paragraph (3) above,

sub-paragraphs (3) to (5) above shall apply in relation to so much of that part of the remaining loss as cannot be so relieved as they apply in relation to the remaining loss, but construing the references in those sub-paragraphs to the new participator and the old participator by reference to that previous transfer and the parties to it, and then applying this sub-paragraph accordingly (and so on).

15(7) But where–

(a) the person who is the old participator in relation to a transfer made before 17th March 2004 ("the *later transfer*") is also the new participator in relation to a previous transfer, and

(b) Parts 2 and 3 of this Schedule applied in relation to both of those transfers,

sub-paragraph (3) above shall not apply by virtue of sub-paragraph (6) above in relation to so much of the assessable profits of the person who is the old participator in relation to that previous transfer as is attributable to so much of his interest as constitutes the whole or part of his represented interest by virtue of the later transfer.

15(8) Where losses accruing to each of two or more participators fall to be relieved by virtue of sub-paragraph (3) above against the same assessable profits, a loss accruing to the person who last had an interest representing the whole or part of the transferred interest at an earlier time shall be so relieved before one accruing to a person who last had such an interest at a later time.

In this sub-paragraph **"the transferred interest"** means the interest transferred by the person against whose assessable profits the losses fall to be relieved.

15(9) In determining for the purposes of this paragraph the assessable profits of a participator that are attributable to his represented interest, the assessable profits shall be apportioned between–

(a) the represented interest, and

(b) the remainder of the participator's interest, using such method as is just and reasonable, having regard to the respective sizes of those interests.

15(9A) This paragraph is subject to paragraph 6 of Schedule 20B to the Finance Act 1993.

15(10) For the purposes of this paragraph **"relevant previous participators' expenditure unrelated to the field"** means so much of each relevant previous participator's allowed expenditure unrelated to the field as is referable to his represented interest, other than excepted old expenditure.

15(11) For the purposes of sub-paragraph (10) above–

"allowed expenditure unrelated to the field", in relation to a participator, is expenditure unrelated to the field which is allowed on a claim or election made by the participator;

"excepted old expenditure" is expenditure which has been allowed in pursuance of a claim or election for its allowance received by the Board before 17th March 2004;

"relevant previous participator" means a participator against any of whose assessable profits relief is given in accordance with sub-paragraphs (3) to (6) above;

and sub-paragraph (9) above shall apply in relation to allowed expenditure unrelated to the field as it applies in relation to assessable profits.

15(12) In this paragraph–

"expenditure unrelated to the field" has the meaning given by section 6(9);

"the loss-maker" shall be construed in accordance with sub-paragraph (2) above;

"previous owner" means a person from whom the loss-maker directly or indirectly derives his title to the whole or any part of his interest;

"represented interest", in the case of a previous owner, means so much of the interest which that previous owner transferred, by a transfer to which Parts 2 and 3 of this Schedule apply, as is represented in the loss-maker's interest by virtue only of–

(a) that transfer, or

(b) that transfer and one or more subsequent transfers to which those Parts apply,

making, for the purposes of paragraph (b) above, such apportionments as are just and reasonable, having regard to the interests transferred by each of the transferors.

History – In para. 15(9A), the words "paragraph 6" substituted for the words "paragraph 5" by F(No. 2)A 2017, s. 44(3), with effect from 23 November 2016.

In para. 15(9A), the words "Schedule 20B" substituted for the words "Schedule 20A" by FA 2009, s. 91 and Sch. 45, para. 3, with effect from 21 July 2009 (Royal Assent).

Para. 15(9A) inserted by FA 2008, s. 107 and Sch. 33, para. 3, with effect from 21 July 2008.

Para. 15 substituted by FA 2004, s. 288(2), with effect in relation to losses accruing in chargeable periods ending after 17 March 2004.

Cross references – FA 2013, s. 84(2): disapplication of para. 15 in relation to losses accruing by virtue of another's default.

ABORTIVE EXPLORATION EXPENDITURE

16(1) Subject to sub-paragraph (2) below, there shall be allowed under section 5 in the case of the new participator, in connection with any field in which an interest is transferred to him by the old participator, any expenditure incurred–

(a) by the old participator; or

(b) if the old participator is a company, by a company which is within the meaning of that section associated with the old participator in respect of the expenditure,

if no claim in respect of it has been made under Schedule 7 by the old participator or any such company and the expenditure would be allowable under that section in the case of the new participator if he had himself incurred it.

16(2) Sub-paragraph (1) above–

(a) does not apply so long as the old participator or, if the old participator is a company, any company associated with the old participator has an interest in a licence; and

(b) applies to the new participator only if the transfer to him was the last transfer made by the old participator.

16(3) For the purposes of sub-paragraph (2) above a company is **"associated"** with the old participator if–

(a) one is a 51 per cent subsidiary of the other and the other is not a 51 per cent subsidiary of any company; or

(b) each of them is a 51 per cent subsidiary of a third company which is not itself a 51 per cent subsidiary of any company;

and Chapter 3 of Part 24 of the Corporation Tax Act 2010 (subsidiaries) shall apply for the purposes of this sub-paragraph.

16(4) This paragraph is without prejudice to the application of section 5 in cases where the old participator is a company and the new participator is within the meaning of that section a company associated with the old participator in respect of the expenditure in question.

History – In para. 16(3), the words "Chapter 3 of Part 24 of the Corporation Tax Act 2010" substituted for the words "section 838 of the Taxes Act 1988" by CTA 2010, s. 1177 and Sch. 1, para. 172(3), with effect for corporation tax purposes for accounting periods ending on or after 1 April 2010, and for income tax and capital gains tax purposes for the tax year 2010–11 and subsequent tax years. See ICTA 1988, s. 844 and Sch. 29, para. 32 for substitution of former reference to that Act.

Cross references – FA 1984, s. 113(6): restriction of PRT reliefs.

EXPLORATION AND APPRAISAL EXPENDITURE

16A In relation to exploration and appraisal expenditure to which section 5A applies, paragraph 16 above has effect as if any reference therein to section 5 were a reference to section 5A.

History – Para. 16A inserted by FA 1983, s. 37(2) and Sch. 8, Pt. II, para. 8, with effect from 13 May 1983.

RESEARCH EXPENDITURE

16B In relation to research expenditure to which section 5B applies, paragraph 16 above has effect as if any reference therein to section 5 were a reference to section 5B.

History – Para. 16B inserted by FA 1987, s. 64 and Sch. 13, Pt. II, para. 7.

OIL ALLOWANCE

17 If the transfer period is one of the first three chargeable periods of the field section 8 shall not apply to the old participator for that period or any earlier period.

LIMIT ON TAX PAYABLE IN TRANSFER YEAR

18(1) For the purposes of section 9 in its application to the transfer period, the accumulated capital expenditure at the end of that period of the old participator and the new participator respectively shall be treated as equal to the aggregate of–

(a) the pre-transfer fraction of what (apart from this paragraph) would be the amount of his accumulated capital expenditure for the purposes of that section at the end of that period if any transfer from or to him under paragraph 6 or 8 above were disregarded; and

(b) the post-transfer fraction of what (apart from this paragraph) would be that amount having regard to any transfer from or to him in that period under those paragraphs.

18(2) For the purposes of this paragraph the **"pre-transfer"** and **"post-transfer fractions"** are respectively the fractions of the period (reckoned in days) which elapse before and begin with the date of the transfer; and if there are two or more transfers in the period those fractions shall be determined–

(a) for a participator who is the old participator as respects any of the transfers, by reference to the first transfer as respects which he is the old participator;

(b) for a participator who is the new participator as respects any of the transfers, by reference to the last transfer as respects which he is the new participator;

(c) for a participator who is the old participator as respects one or more of the transfers and the new participator as respects another or others, by reference to whichever results in the smallest amount of accumulated capital expenditure under this paragraph.

History – In para. 18(1), (2), the word "period" in each place was substituted by FA 1981, s. 114(2)(d), with effect whether the participator's net profit period ends before or after the passing of that Act.

DISPOSAL OF LONG-TERM ASSETS

19(1) Neither paragraph 4 of Schedule 4 nor section 7 of the Oil Taxation Act 1983 shall apply to the disposal of an asset used in connection with an oil field if the disposal is by the old participator (or a person connected with him) to the new participator (or a person connected with him) and the disposal is in pursuance of the transfer by the old participator to the new participator of an interest in the field.

19(2) Section 839 of the Taxes Act 1988 (connected persons) shall apply for the purposes of this paragraph.

History – In para. 19(1), the word "Neither" was inserted, and the words "nor section 7 of the Oil Taxation Act 1983 shall" were substituted, by OTA 1983, Sch. 2, para. 6, with effect from 1 December 1983.
See ICTA 1988, s. 844 and Sch. 29, para. 32 for substitution of reference to that Act in para. 19(2).

TRANSFERS OF OIL

20 Where in pursuance of the transfer of the whole or part of his interest in the field the old participator transfers his right to any oil already won from the field to the new participator, that oil–

(a) shall not be taken into account under section 2(5) in computing the old participator's assessable profit or allowable loss in the transfer period; but

(b) shall be taken into account under section 2(5) in computing the new participator's assessable profit or allowable loss as if it were included in his share of the oil won from the field.

Cross references – OTA 1975, s. 2: assessable profits and allowable losses.

RETENTION OF SHARE OF OIL

21 Where the old participator retains a share of the oil won from the field in pursuance of an agreement between him and the new participator under which the latter undertakes to be responsible for carrying out the old participator's obligations in connection with the field so far as they relate to that share–

(a) that share shall be taken to belong to the new participator; and

(b) any oil comprised in that share shall be treated as oil acquired by the old participator under an agreement to which paragraph 6 of Schedule 3 applies.

FINANCE ACT 1981

(1981 Chapter 35)

[*27th July 1981*]

ARRANGEMENT OF SECTIONS

PART VII – PETROLEUM REVENUE TAX

PART X – MISCELLANEOUS AND SUPPLEMENTARY

PART VII – PETROLEUM REVENUE TAX

111 Restriction of expenditure supplement

111(1) Expenditure taken into account under section 2(9)(b)(i) or (c)(i) of the Oil Taxation Act 1975 (**"the principal Act"**) in computing the assessable profit or allowable loss accruing to a participator in a chargeable period from an oil field shall not qualify for supplement under section 2(9)(b)(ii)or (c)(ii) of that Act if it is incurred after the end of the chargeable period (**"the net profit period"**) which is the earliest chargeable period ending after a development decision has been made for the field in which–

(a) the amount of oil won and saved from the field exceeds 1,000 metric tonnes (counting 1,100 cubic metres of gas at a temperature of 15 degrees centigrade and pressure of one atmosphere as equivalent to one metric tonne); and

(b) a net profit from the field accrues to the participator;

and subsection (7) of section 5A of the principal Act (time when development decision is made) shall apply for the purposes of this subsection as it applies for the purposes of subsection (1)(c) of that section.

111(2) Subject to subsections (3) and (4) below, a net profit shall be treated as having accrued to a participator from an oil field in a chargeable period when the total assessable profits (without any reduction under section 7 or 8 of the principal Act) that have accrued to him from the field in chargeable periods up to and including that period exceed the aggregate of the total allowable losses that have so accrued to him and the total amount of advance petroleum revenue tax paid by him in respect of that field for chargeable periods up to and including that period.

111(2A) [Spent.]

111(3) In determining for the purposes of subsection (2) above whether any, and if so what, assessable profit or allowable loss has accrued to a participator from an oil field in a chargeable period–

(a) there shall be excluded from its computation any expenditure allowed under Schedule 7 and any loss allowed under Schedule 8 to the principal Act;

(b) any election under paragraph 9(1) of Schedule 3 to that Act (spreading of allowable expenditure) shall be disregarded; and

(c) in the case of the last chargeable period taken into account in deciding what is the net profit period there shall be included in that computation any amount which, by reason of an adjustment under *section 4(9) of that* Act (long-term assets) for a claim period ending not later than that period, will fall to be taken into account under paragraph 6 of Schedule 4 to that Act for the next chargeable period; and

(d) if any qualifying tariff receipts, within the meaning of section 9 of the Oil Taxation Act 1983, are received or receivable by the participator for that period, any amount by which those receipts are treated as reduced by virtue of that section shall be brought into account in that computation as an addition to the positive amounts referred to in section 2(3)(a) of the principal Act.

111(4) A net profit shall not by virtue of subsection (2) above be treated as having accrued to a participator from an oil field in a chargeable period if–

(a) after an assessment or determination has been made in respect of that period under paragraph 10 of Schedule 2 to the principal Act any expenditure incurred before the end of that period is allowed on a claim under Schedule 5 or Schedule 6 to that Act; and

(b) a net profit would not have accrued to the participator from the field in that period if that expenditure (or, as respects expenditure allowed under Schedule 5, his share of it) had been taken into account in the assessment or determination together with any amount falling to be taken into account under section 2(9)(b)(ii) or (c)(ii) of the principal Act by reference to (or, as the case may be, to his share of) that expenditure.

111(5) The expenditure referred to in subsection (4) above does not include expenditure allowed for any claim period beginning after the chargeable period in respect of which the assessment or determination was made.

111(6) In the following provisions, that is to say–

(a) paragraphs 2(4)(a) and 3(1)(b) of Schedule 5 to the principal Act (claims for and determination of expenditure qualifying for supplement), including those paragraphs as applied by Schedule 6 to that Act; and

(b) paragraph 2(4)(b) of the Schedule to the Petroleum Revenue Tax Act 1980 (computation of payment on account),

references to expenditure qualifying for supplement shall include references to expenditure that would so qualify apart from this section; but the responsible person need not make a claim under paragraph 2(4)(a) of the said Schedule if it appears to him that none of the expenditure is likely to qualify because of this section.

111(7) This section applies whether the net profit period ends before or after the passing of this Act but subsection (1) above shall not disqualify any expenditure which was incurred before 1st January 1981 or which is incurred before 1st January 1983 in pursuance of a contract entered into before 1st January 1981.

History – In s. 111(1), the words from "which is the earliest chargeable period" to the end substituted by FA 1985, s. 91(3), in respect of chargeable periods ending after 30 June 1985.
In s. 111(2), the words "exceed the aggregate … that period" substituted by FA 1982, s. 139(6) and Sch. 19, para. 16(2), effective from 30 July 1982.
S. 111(2A) inserted by FA 1982, s. 139(6) and Sch. 19, para. 16(2), effective from 30 July 1982.
In s. 111(3)(a), words which followed "the principal Act" repealed by FA 1987, s. 64 and Sch. 13, Pt. II, para. 8 and s. 72 and Sch. 16, Pt. X.
S. 111(3)(d) inserted by OTA 1983, s. 9(8), to have effect with respect to chargeable periods ending after 1 July 1982.

Cross references – OTA 1983, Sch. 1, para. 2(4): circumstances in which expenditure incurred on remote associated asset to be disregarded in determining whether net profit period shall not have accrued under s. 111(4).
FA 1987, s. 65(4)(c): expenditure allowable under that section (cross-field allowance) excluded in determining assessable profit or allowable loss under s. 111(2).
FA 1994, s. 234(3)(b): net profit period and election for pipe-line usage.

Notes – Advance petroleum revenue tax (APRT) ceased to apply to any chargeable period ending after 31 December 1986 (FA 1983, s. 35). S. 111(2A) dealt with APRT.

112 Restriction of expenditure supplement: transfers of interest

112(1) Section 111 above shall have effect in accordance with this section where a participator in an oil field has acquired the whole or part of his interest in the field as a result of one or more transfers to him within the meaning of Schedule 17 to the Finance Act 1980, and in this section **"the new participator"** and **"the old participator"** mean respectively the first-mentioned participator and any participator from whom he has acquired the whole or part of his interest.

112(2) The new participator's net profit period shall be whichever is the earlier of–

(a) his own net profit period as determined in accordance with section 111 above and subsections (3) and (4) below; or

(b) subject to subsection (5) below, the chargeable period which is the net profit period of the old participator or, if there are two or more old participators, of whichever of them has the earliest net profit period.

112(3) Where the old participator has transferred the whole of his interest in the field to the new participator, the net profit period of the new participator shall be determined by treating as if they were his the total assessable profits and allowable losses of the old participator as determined for the purposes of section 111 above.

PRT Statutes

112(4) Where the old participator has transferred part of his interest in the field to the new participator, the net profit period of the old and new participators shall be determined by treating as if they were the new participator's and not the old participator's such part of the total assessable profits and allowable losses of the old participator (as determined for the purposes of section 111 above) as may be just and reasonable.

112(4A) Subsections (2) and (2A) of section 111 shall have effect as if references to the amount of advance petroleum revenue tax paid by the new participator or repaid to him included references to the amount of that tax paid by or repaid to the old participator or, where the old participator has transferred part of his interest, such part of that amount as is just and reasonable.

112(5) The net profit period of an old participator shall not be taken into account under subsection (2)(b) above if the new participator's own net profit period, as determined without reference under subsection (3) or (4) above to the old participator's assessable profits or allowable losses, fell before the chargeable period in which the new participator acquired the whole or part of the old participator's interest.

History – S. 112(4A) inserted by FA 1982, s. 139(6) and Sch. 19, para. 16(3), effective from 30 July 1982.

113 Restriction of expenditure supplement: loss following net profit period

113(1) This section has effect where the aggregate of–

(a) the total allowable losses that have accrued to a participator from an oil field in chargeable periods up to and including a chargeable period ending not more than three years after his net profit period, and

(b) the amount of advance petroleum revenue tax paid by him in respect of that field for those periods less any such tax repaid to him before the end of those periods or repaid subsequently under section 142(1) of the Finance Act 1982 or paragraph 9 of Schedule 19 to that Act,

exceeds the total assessable profits (without any reduction under section 7 or 8 of the principal Act) that have so accrued to him.

113(2) Section 111(1) above shall not disqualify for supplement under section 2(9)(b)(ii) or (c)(ii) of the principal Act expenditure which is incurred up to the end of–

(a) the last chargeable period in the three years mentioned in subsection (1) above; or

(b) the chargeable period in which a net profit next accrues to the participator from the field after the chargeable period mentioned in that subsection,

whichever is the earlier.

113(3) Subsection (3) of section 111 above shall apply for the purposes of subsection (1) above as it applies for the purposes of subsection (2) of that section and subsections (3), (4) and (5) of that section shall apply for the purposes of subsection (2)(b) above as they apply for the purposes of subsection (2) of that section.

History – S. 113(1) substituted by FA 1982, s. 139(6) and Sch. 19, para. 16(4), effective from 30 July 1982.

Cross references – No account taken of s. 113 for FA 1994, s. 231 election by reference to pipe-line usage.

114 Restriction of limit on amount of tax payable

114(1) [Amends OTA 1975, s. 9.]

114(2) [Amends FA 1980, Sch. 17, para. 1, 8 and 18.]

114(3) This section applies whether the net profit period ends before or after the passing of this Act.

115 Contracts with deferred payment

115(1) Expenditure incurred in pursuance of a contract to which this section applies shall not qualify for supplement under section 2(9)(b)(ii) or (c)(ii) of the principal Act.

115(2) This section applies to any contract which is entered into after 1st July 1980 unless–

(a) the amount required to be paid under it by the person incurring the expenditure is less than £10 million; or

(b) it is reasonable to expect, at the time when the contract is entered into–

(i) that not less than 90 per cent of that amount will be paid within nine months of the date on which the other party begins to perform the contract; or

(ii) that a payment or payments in respect of that amount will be made which comply with *subsection (3)* below;

and for the purposes of paragraph (a) above there may be disregarded any provision of the contract allowing for variations in the amount payable to take account of changes in costs or design.

115(3) The payment or payments referred to in subsection (2)(b)(ii) above must be such that the amount to be paid up to any time after the date on which the other party to the contract begins to perform it is equal to not less than 75 per cent of the amount that would have become payable up to that time if–

(a) the payments required to be made under the contract were such that the first of them was payable within six months after that date and each subsequent one within six months after the previous one; and

(b) the first of the payments were required to be of an amount proportionate to the extent to which the contract has been performed by that party since that date and each subsequent one to be of an amount proportionate to the extent to which the contract has been so performed since the previous payment was required to be made.

115(4) Where a contract requires a payment in respect of any period or in respect of the completion of any stage in the performance of the contract to be made within three months after the end of that period or within three months after the completion of that stage the amount to be paid up to any time shall be determined for the purposes of subsection (3) above as if the payment were required to be made at the end of that period or on completion of that stage.

115(5) Where a contract provides for payments in respect of the completion of stages in the performance of separate parts of the work specified in the contract, the payments under the contract shall be treated as complying with subsection (3) above if the payments attributable to each part of the contract would have complied with that subsection if that part had been the subject of a separate contract.

116 Spreading of capital expenditure

116 [Amends OTA 1975, Sch. 3, para. 9 and 10, in relation to any chargeable period ending after 31 December 1979.]

117 Spreading of capital expenditure: transitional provisions

117(1) Where allowable losses have accrued to a participator from an oil field in chargeable periods ending before 1 January 1980 he may by notice in writing given to the Board elect that so much of those losses as would, apart from this section, be available for set-off under section 7 of the principal Act against assessable profits accruing to him from the field in chargeable periods beginning on or after that date shall instead be treated as an amount of relief for supplemented expenditure which, subject to any election under paragraph 9 of Schedule 3 to that Act, falls to be taken into account in computing the assessable profit or allowable loss accruing to him from the field in the chargeable period ending on 30 June 1980.

117(2) The amount to which an election under this section applies shall not exceed the total amount of relief for supplemented expenditure taken into account in computing the assessable profits or allowable losses accruing to the participator in chargeable periods ending before 1 January 1980.

117(3) Any notice under this section shall be in such form as the Board may prescribe and shall be given before 1 April 1982; and–

(a) any notice under paragraph 9 of Schedule 3 to the principal Act in respect of a chargeable period ending before that date shall not be out of time if given before that date;

(b) any tax charged or repayable in respect of any such chargeable period in consequence of an election under that paragraph shall not carry interest under paragraph 15 or 16 of Schedule 2 to that Act in respect of any period before the date of the election.

117(4) In section 111(3)(b) above and in section 9(4) of, and paragraph 10 of Schedule 3 to, the principal Act references to an election under paragraph 9(1) of that Schedule shall include references to an election under this section.

117(5) This section shall be construed as one with Part I of the principal Act and paragraph 9(7) of Schedule 3 to that Act shall apply for the interpretation of subsections (1) and (2) above.

118 Licence payments other than royalties

118(1) For the purpose of computing under section 2 of the principal Act the assessable profit or allowable loss accruing to a participator in any chargeable period from an oil field–

(a) there shall be included as a positive amount any allowable sum paid to the participator in the period by the Secretary of State or the OGA;

(b) there shall be included as a negative amount any allowable sum paid by the participator in the period to the OGA.

118(2) In this section **"chargeable sum"** and **"allowable sum"** mean any sum which after 31st December 1980 is paid to a participator by the Secretary of State or the OGA or, as the case may be, by the participator to the OGA by reference to a relevant licence except–

(a) any sum falling to be taken into account under section 2(6) of the principal Act (licence debit or credit) or section 3(1)(b) of that Act (payment under or for the purpose of obtaining a relevant licence);

(b) any sum consisting of interest on a sum payable to or by the or the OGA;

(c) any repayment by the Secretary of State under section 6(1) of the Petroleum Act 1998 (repayment of royalty for facilitating or maintaining the development of United Kingdom petroleum resources); and

(d) any payment or repayment of royalty in respect of excluded oil (as defined in section 10 of the principal Act) and any other payment attributable to such oil.

118(3) Where the relevant licence by reference to which a chargeable sum or allowable sum is paid relates to a licensed area comprising the whole or part of two or more oil fields, that sum shall for the purposes of this section be apportioned between all or any of those fields, or attributed wholly to one of them, as may be just and reasonable.

118(4) A return under paragraph 2 of Schedule 2 to the principal Act shall include a statement of the chargeable sums and allowable sums, if any, paid to or by the participator in the chargeable period to which the return relates.

118(5) In considering for the purposes of paragraph 8(1) of Schedule 3 to the principal Act (subsidised expenditure) how far any expenditure has been or is to be met directly or indirectly by the Crown or by any authority or person other than the person incurring the expenditure, any chargeable sum shall be left out of account.

118(6) This section shall be construed as one with Part I of the principal Act.

Prospective amendments – In s. 118(1)(a) the words "or the OGA" inserted after the words "Secretary of State" and in s. 118(1)(b) the word "OGA" substituted for the words "Secretary of State" by SI 2016/898, reg. 5(2), with effect immediately after the commencement of SCA 2016, s. 48.

In s. 118(2) the words "or the OGA" inserted after the words "Secretary of State" (first occurrence), the word "OGA" substituted for the words "Secretary of State" (second occurrence) and in s. 118(2)(b) the word "OGA" substituted for the words "Secretary of State" by SI 2016/898, reg. 5(3), with effect immediately after the commencement of SCA 2016, s. 48.

History – In s. 118(1)(a), the words "or the OGA" inserted by SI 2016/898, reg. 5(2)(a), with effect from 1 October 2016 (as the 21st day after being made on 10 September 2016).

In s. 118(1)(b), the word "OGA" substituted for the words "Secretary of State" by SI 2016/898, reg. 5(2)(b), with effect from 1 October 2016 (as the 21st day after being made on 10 September 2016).

In s. 118(2), the words "or the OGA" inserted and the word "OGA" substituted for the words "Secretary of State" by SI 2016/898, reg. 5(3), with effect from 1 October 2016 (as the 21st day after being made on 10 September 2016).

In s. 118(2)(b), the word "OGA" substituted for the words "Secretary of State" by SI 2016/898, reg. 5(3)(c), with effect from 1 October 2016 (as the 21st day after being made on 10 September 2016).

In s. 118(2)(c), the words "section 6(1) of the Petroleum Act 1998" substituted for the words "section 41(3) of the Petroleum and Submarine Pipe-lines Act 1975" by the Petroleum Act 1998, s. 50 and Sch. 4, para 16 with effect from 15 February 1999 (SI 1999/161, art 2).

119 Transportation costs for off-shore oil

119 [Amends OTA 1975, s. 3, in relation to claims after 31 December 1978.]

121 Gas banking schemes

121 Regulations under section 108 of the Finance Act 1980 (gas banking schemes) may provide for the modifications made by them to have effect from a date before the regulations are made and for any election made under that section to have effect from a date before the election is made.

PART X – MISCELLANEOUS AND SUPPLEMENTARY

139 Short title, interpretation, construction and repeals

139(1) This Act may be cited as the Finance Act 1981.

139(2)–(4) [Not relevant to petroleum revenue tax.]

139(5) In Parts VII and VIII of this Act **"the principal Act"** means the Oil Taxation Act 1975.

FINANCE ACT 1982

(1982 Chapter 39)

[*30th July 1982*]

ARRANGEMENT OF SECTIONS

PART VI – OIL TAXATION

CHAPTER I – GENERAL

CHAPTER II – ADVANCED PETROLEUM REVENUE TAX

PART VII – MISCELLANEOUS AND SUPPLEMENTARY

SCHEDULES

PART VI – OIL TAXATION

Chapter I – General

132 Increase of petroleum revenue tax and ending of supplementary petroleum duty

132 [Amends OTA 1975, s. 1 and FA 1981, s. 122.]

133 Export sales of gas

133 [Amends OTA 1975, s. 2 and FA 1981, s. 122, effective with respect to chargeable periods ending after 31 December 1981.]

134 Alternative valuation of ethane used for petrochemical purposes

134(1) Where an election is made under this section and accepted by the Board, the market value for taxation purposes of any ethane to which the election applies shall be determined, not in accordance with paragraphs 2, 2A and 3 of Schedule 3 to the principal Act (value under a notional contract), but in accordance with a price formula specified in the election; and, in relation to any such ethane, any reference to market value in any other provision of the principal Act, in Part 8 of the Corporation Tax Act 2010 or in Chapter 16A of Part 2 of the Income Tax (Trading and Other Income) Act 2005 shall be construed accordingly.

134(2) Subject to subsection (3) below, an election under this section must be made before 1st January 1994 and applies only to ethane–

Chapter II – Advanced Petroleum Revenue Tax

139 Liability for APRT and credit against liability for petroleum revenue tax

139(1) For each of the following chargeable periods, namely–

(a) the first chargeable period ending after 31st December 1982 and before 1st January 1987 in which, subject to sections 140 and 141 below, a gross profit accrues to a participator from an oil field, and

(b) every one out of the immediately succeeding chargeable periods (if any) which ends before 1st January 1987 and in which, subject to those sections, a gross profit accrues to him from that field,

the participator shall be liable to pay an amount of petroleum revenue tax (to be known as "advance petroleum revenue tax" and in this Chapter referred to as "APRT") in accordance with this section.

139(2) Subject to sections 140 and 141 below, APRT shall be payable on the gross profit accruing to the participator in the chargeable period in question and shall be payable

(a) for the chargeable period ending on 30th June 1983, at the rate of 20 per cent.;

(b) for subsequent chargeable periods ending on or before 31st December 1984, at the rate of 15 per cent.;

(c) for chargeable periods ending in 1985, at the rate of 10 per cent.; and

(d) for chargeable periods ending in 1986, at the rate of 5 per cent.

139(3) The aggregate of–

(a) any APRT which is payable and paid by a participator in respect of any chargeable period and not repaid, and

(b) any APRT which is carried forward from the previous chargeable period by virtue of subsection (4) below,

shall be set against the participator's liability for petroleum revenue tax charged in any assessment made on him in respect of the assessable profit accruing to him in the period referred to in paragraph (a) above from the oil field in question (which liability is in this Chapter referred to as his liability for petroleum revenue tax for a chargeable period) and shall, accordingly, discharge a corresponding amount of that liability.

139(4) If, for any chargeable period, the aggregate of–

(a) any APRT which is payable and paid by a participator for that period and not repaid, and

(b) any APRT carried forward from the previous chargeable period by virtue of this subsection,

exceeds the participator's liability for petroleum revenue tax for that period, the excess shall be carried forward as an accretion to any APRT paid (and not repaid) for the next chargeable period; and any reference in this Chapter to a participator's APRT credit for a chargeable period is a reference to the aggregate of any APRT paid for that period and not repaid and any APRT carried forward from the previous chargeable period by virtue of this subsection.

139(5) The references in section 1 of the Provisional Collection of Taxes Act 1968 to petroleum revenue tax include a reference to APRT.

139(6) The provisions of Schedule 19 to this Act shall have effect for supplementing this section and, accordingly, section 105 of the Finance Act 1980 (advance payments of petroleum revenue tax) shall cease to have effect with respect to chargeable periods ending after 30th June 1983.

139(7) This Chapter shall be included in the Oil Taxation Acts for the purposes of sections 107 and 108 of the Finance Act 1980 (transmedian fields and gas banking schemes).

History – In s. 139(1), the words "and before 1st January 1987" inserted and the words "immediately succeeding chargeable periods (if any) which ends before 1st January 1987" substituted by FA 1983, s. 35(1).
S. 139(2)(a)–(d) substituted by FA 1983, s. 35(2).
In s. 139(3)(a), the words "any APRT which is payable and paid" substituted by FA 1983, s. 35(3).
In s. 139(4)(a), the words "any APRT which is payable and paid" and the words "any APRT paid" (twice) substituted by FA 1983, s. 35(3)(a).
In s. 139(4)(a), the words "any APRT paid" substituted (three times) by FA 1983, s. 35(3)(b).

140 Increase of gross profit by reference to royalties in kind

140(1) This section applies where part of a participator's share of the oil won and saved from an oil field is delivered by him in a chargeable period to the OGA pursuant to a requirement imposed under the terms of a licence granted under the Petroleum (Production) Act 1934.

140(2) In determining for the purposes of APRT the gross profit accruing to the participator from the field in the chargeable period the aggregate of the amounts mentioned in paragraphs (a), (b) and (c) of subsection (5) of section 2 of the principal Act shall be increased by multiplying it by a fraction of which–

(a) the numerator is the total of the quantity of oil won from the field which is delivered or relevantly appropriated by him in the period including the oil delivered to the OGA; and

(b) the denominator is that total excluding the oil delivered to the OGA.

140(3) Where oil is delivered pursuant to a requirement which relates to oil of one or more kinds but not to others, subsection (2) above shall apply only in relation to oil of the kind or kinds to which the requirement relates; and where oil is delivered pursuant to a requirement which specifies different proportions in relation to different kinds of oil, that subsection shall apply separately in relation to each of those kinds.

140(4) For the purposes of subsection (5) of section 2 of the principal Act as it applies in determining for the purposes of APRT the gross profit accruing to a participator, the exclusion by paragraph 4 of Schedule 3 to that Act of oil delivered to the OGA under the terms of a licence granted under the said Act of 1934 shall be deemed to extend to oil which is inadvertently delivered to him in excess of the amount required; and oil so delivered shall be treated for the purposes of this section as delivered pursuant to a requirement imposed under the terms of such a licence.

140(5) Any reference in this section or in section 141 below to the purposes of APRT includes a reference to the purpose of determining whether APRT is payable for a chargeable period by virtue of section 139(1) above.

Prospective amendments – In s. 140 the word "OGA" substituted for the words "Secretary of State" in each place by SI 2016/898, reg. 6(2), with effect immediately after the commencement of SCA 2016, s. 48.

History – In s. 140, the word "OGA" substituted for the words "Secretary of State" (in each place) by SI 2016/898, reg. 6(2), with effect from 1 October 2016 (as the 21st day after being made on 10 September 2016).

141 Reduction of gross profit by reference to exempt allowance

141(1) For the purposes of APRT there shall be for each oil field in each chargeable period an exempt allowance of 500,000 metric tonnes of oil divided between the participators in shares proportionate to their shares of the oil won and saved from the field during the period.

141(2) If the gross profit accruing to a participator in a chargeable period from a field exceeds the cash equivalent of his share of the exempt allowance, the gross profit shall be reduced to an amount equal to the excess.

141(3) If the gross profit accruing to a participator in a chargeable period from a field does not exceed the cash equivalent of his share of the exempt allowance, the gross profit shall be reduced to nil.

141(4) Subject to subsection (5) below, the cash equivalent of a participator's share of the exempt allowance for an oil field for a chargeable period shall be equal to such proportion of the gross profit accruing to him from the field in that period (before any reduction under this section) as his share of the exempt allowance bears to his share, exclusive of excluded oil within the meaning of section 10 of the principal Act, of the oil won and saved from the field during the period.

141(5) If a participator in an oil field so elects by notice in writing given to the Board at the time when he makes his return under paragraph 2 of Schedule 2 to the principal Act for a chargeable period, the cash equivalent of his share of the exempt allowance for the field for that period shall be determined under subsection (4) above–

(a) to the extent that his share of that exempt allowance does not exceed his share of the oil (other than gas) won and saved from the field in the period, as if in computing the gross profit accruing to him in the period all amounts relating to gas fell to be disregarded; and

(b) to the extent, if any, that his share of that allowance exceeds his share of the oil (other than gas) so won and saved, as if in computing the gross profit so accruing all amounts relating to oil other than gas fell to be disregarded.

141(6) In this section references to a participator's share of the oil won and saved from a field are to his share as expressed in metric tonnes and for that purpose 1,100 cubic metres of oil consisting of gas at a temperature of 15 degrees centigrade and pressure of one atmosphere shall be counted as equivalent to one metric tonne of oil other than gas.

142 Consequences of crediting APRT against liability for petroleum revenue tax

142(1) If it appears to the Board–

(a) that any amount of APRT credit which has been set off against a participator's assessed liability to petroleum revenue tax for any chargeable period ought not to have been so set off, or that the amount so set off has become excessive, or

(b) that, disregarding any liability to or credit for APRT, a participator is entitled to a repayment of petroleum revenue tax for any chargeable period, then, for the purpose of securing that the liabilities of the participator to petroleum revenue tax and APRT (including interest on unpaid tax) for the chargeable period in question are what they ought to have been, the Board may make such assessments to, and shall make such repayments of, petroleum revenue tax and APRT as in their judgment are necessary in the circumstances.

142(2) In a case falling within paragraph (a) of subsection (1) above, any necessary assessment to petroleum revenue tax may, where the revised amount of set off is ascertained as a result of an appeal, be made at any time before the expiry of the period of six years beginning at the end of the chargeable period in which the appeal is finally determined; and in a case falling within paragraph (b) of that subsection any necessary assessment to APRT may be made at any time before the expiry of the period of six years beginning at the end of the chargeable period in which the participator became entitled as mentioned in that paragraph.

142(3) [Repealed by FA 1987, s. 72(7) and Sch. 16, Pt. VII.]

142(4) [Repealed by FA 1987, s. 72(7) and Sch. 16, Pt. VII.]

142(5) Paragraphs 13, 14 and 15 of Schedule 2 to the principal Act (payment of tax, appeals and interest on tax) apply in relation to an assessment to petroleum revenue tax under subsection (1) above as they apply to an assessment under that Schedule.

History – S. 142(3) and (4) repealed by FA 1987, s. 72(7) and Sch. 16, Pt. VII.,

PART VII – MISCELLANEOUS AND SUPPLEMENTARY

157 Short title, interpretation, construction and repeals

157(1) This Act may be cited as the Finance Act 1982.

157(2)–(4) [Not relevant to petroleum revenue tax.]

157(5) Part VI of this Act shall be construed as one with Part I of the Oil Taxation Act 1975 and references in Part VI to the principal Act are references to that Act.

History – Words in s. 157(5), between "1975" and "the references" repealed by ICTA 1988, s. 844 and Sch. 31. See now ICTA 1988, Pt. XII, Ch. V.

SCHEDULES

SCHEDULE 18 – ALTERNATIVE VALUATION OF ETHANE USED FOR PETROCHEMICAL PURPOSES

Section 134

Cross references – FA 1986, Sch. 21: modifications of Sch. 18 in relation to elections under FA 1986, s. 109 (election for alternative valuation of light gases other than ethane used for petrochemical purposes).

THE ELECTION

1(1) An election shall be made–

(a) in so far as it is to apply to ethane which is relevantly appropriated, by the participator alone; and

(b) in so far as it is to apply to ethane which is disposed of, by the participator and the person to whom it is disposed of.

1(2) An election shall be made in such form as may be prescribed by the Board and shall–

(a) identify, by reference to volume, chemical composition and initial treatment, the ethane to which the election is to apply;

(b) specify the period, beginning on or after the date of the election and not exceeding fifteen years, which is covered by the election;

(c) specify the price formula which is to apply for determining the market values of ethane during that period;

(d) specify the petrochemical purposes for which ethane to which the election applies will be used; and

(e) specify the place to or at which any such ethane is to be delivered or appropriated.

1(3) The reference in sub-paragraph (2)(a) above to **"initial treatment"** is a reference to such initial treatment (if any) as the ethane will have been subjected to before it is disposed of or relatively appropriated.

CONDITIONS FOR ACCEPTANCE OF AN ELECTION

2(1) Subject to sub-paragraphs (2) and (3) below, the Board shall accept an election if they are satisfied that, under a relevant contract (as defined in paragraph 3 below) for the sale at arm's length of the ethane to which the election applies, the contract prices would not differ materially from the market values determined in accordance with the price formula specified in the election; and if the Board are not so satisfied they shall reject the election.

2(2) The Board shall reject an election if they are not satisfied that the price formula specified in the election is such that the market value of ethane disposed of or relevantly appropriated at any time during the period covered by the election will be readily ascertainable either by reference to the price formula alone or by reference to that formula and to information–

(a) which is, or is expected to be at that time, publicly available; and

(b) which is not related or dependent, in whole or to any substantial degree, to or on the activities of the person or persons making the election or any person connected or associated with him or them.

2(3) The Board shall reject an election if, after receiving notice in writing from the Board, the person or, as the case may be, either of the persons by whom the election was made–

(a) fails to furnish to the Board, before the appropriate date, any information which the Board may reasonably require for the purpose of determining whether the election should be accepted; or

(b) fails to make available for inspection, before the appropriate date, by an officer authorised by the Board any books, accounts or documents in his possession or power which contain any information relevant for that purpose.

2(4) In sub-paragraph (3) above **"the appropriate date"** means such date as may be specified in the notice concerned, being a date not earlier than one month after the date on which the notice was given.

2(5) Any notice under sub-paragraph (3) above shall be given within the period of three months beginning on the date of the election in question.

3(1) In paragraph 2 above **"relevant contract"** means a contract which is entered into,–

(a) if the price formula specified in the election is derived from an actual contract which is identified in the election and was entered into not more than two years before the date of the election, at the time at which that contract was entered into, and

(b) in any other case, at the time of the election in question,

and which incorporates the terms specified in sub-paragraph (2) below, but is not necessarily a contract for the sale of ethane for petrochemical purposes.

3(2) The terms referred to in sub-paragraph (1) above are–

(a) that the ethane is required to be delivered at the place in the United Kingdom or another country at which the seller could reasonably be expected to deliver it or, if there is more than one such place, the one nearest to the place of extraction; and

(b) that the price formula may be varied only in the event of a substantial and lasting change in the economic circumstances surrounding or underlying the contract and that any such variation may not take place before the expiry of the period of five years beginning on the date of the first delivery of ethane during the period covered by the election.

History – In para. 3(2), the words "or another country" inserted by F(No. 2)A 1992, s. 74 and Sch. 15, para. 5, with effect in accordance with s. 74(5) of that Act.

NOTICE OF ACCEPTANCE OR REJECTION

4(1) Notice of the acceptance or rejection of an election shall be given to the party or, as the case may be, each of the parties to the election before the expiry of the period of three months beginning on–

(a) the date of the election, or

(b) if a notice has been given under paragraph 2(3) above relating to the election, the date or, as the case may be, the last date which is the appropriate date, as defined in paragraph 2(4) above, in relation to such a notice.

4(2) If no such notice of acceptance or rejection is so given, the Board shall be deemed to have accepted the election and to have given notice of their acceptance on the last day of the period referred to in sub-paragraph (1) above.

4(3) After notice of the acceptance of an election has been given under this paragraph, a change in the identity of the participator or, where appropriate, of the person to whom the ethane in question is disposed of shall not, of itself, affect the continuing operation of the election.

MARKET VALUE CEASING TO BE READILY ASCERTAINABLE

5(1) In any case where–

(a) it appears to the Board that, at some time during the period covered by an election, the market value of ethane to which the election applies has ceased or is ceasing to be readily ascertainable as mentioned in paragraph 2(2) above, and

(b) the Board give notice of that fact to the party or, as the case may be, each of the parties to the election and in that notice specify a date for the purposes of this paragraph (which may be a date earlier than that on which the notice is given),

then, subject to sub-paragraph (2) below, on the date so specified the election shall cease to have effect.

5(2) If–

(a) within the period of three months beginning on the date of a notice under sub-paragraph (1)(b) above, the party or parties to the election by notice in writing given to the Board specify a new price formula, and

(b) the new price formula is accepted by the Board in accordance with paragraph 7 below,

the election shall continue to have effect and, subject to paragraph 9 below, for the purpose of determining the market value, on and after the date specified in the notice under sub-paragraph (1)(b) above, of ethane to which the election applies, section 134 of this Act shall have effect as if the new price formula were the formula specified in the election.

PRICE FORMULA CEASING TO GIVE REALISTIC MARKET VALUES

6(1) If, at any time after the expiry of the period of five years beginning on the date of the first delivery or relevant appropriation of ethane during the period covered by an election,–

(a) it appears to the party or parties to the election or, as the case may be, to the Board that, by reason of any substantial and lasting change in any economic circumstances which were relevant at the time referred to in paragraph 3(1) above, the market values determined in accordance with the price formula specified in the election are no longer realistic; and

(b) the party or parties to the election give notice of that fact to the Board, or the Board give notice of that fact to the party or, as the case may be, each of the parties to the election,

then, subject to the following provisions of this paragraph, sub-paragraph (2) below shall apply.

6(2) Where this sub-paragraph applies, the election shall not have effect with respect to any chargeable period beginning after the date of the notice under sub-paragraph (1)(b) above.

6(3) Before the expiry of the period of three months beginning on the date on which a notice under sub-paragraph (1)(b) above given by the party or parties to the election is received by the Board, the Board shall give notice of acceptance or rejection of that notice to the party or parties concerned; and

(a) if the Board give notice of rejection, sub-paragraph (2) above shall not apply; and

(b) if no notice of acceptance or rejection is in fact given as required by this sub-paragraph, the Board shall be deemed to have given notice of acceptance on the last day of the period of three months referred to above.

6(4) If a notice under sub-paragraph (1)(b) above which has been given by the party or parties to the election contains a new price formula, the Board shall first consider the notice without regard to that formula and if, following upon that consideration, the Board give a notice of acceptance under sub-paragraph (3) above, they shall then proceed to consider the new price formula.

6(5) In any case where–

(a) sub-paragraph (4) above applies and the new price formula contained in the notice under sub-paragraph (1)(b) above is accepted by the Board in accordance with paragraph 7 below, or

(b) within the period of three months beginning on the date of a notice given by the Board under sub-paragraph (1)(b) above, the party or parties to the election by notice in writing given to the Board specify a new price formula which is accepted by the Board in accordance with paragraph 7 below,

sub-paragraph (2) above shall not apply and for the purpose of determining, for any chargeable period beginning after the date of the notice under sub-paragraph (1)(b) above, the market value of ethane to which the election applies, section 134 of this Act shall have effect as if the new price formula were the formula specified in the election.

6(6) *If, by virtue of sub-paragraph* (5) above or an appeal under paragraph 8 below, a new price formula has effect for determining the market value of ethane to which an election applies, sub-paragraph (1) above shall thereafter have effect in relation to the market value of any such ethane as if–

(a) the reference therein to the date of the first delivery or relevant appropriation of ethane during the period covered by the election, and

(b) the reference therein to the time referred to in paragraph 3(1) above,
were each a reference to the beginning of the first chargeable period for which the new price formula has effect.

ACCEPTANCE OR REJECTION OF NEW PRICE FORMULA

7(1) Subject to sub-paragraph (3) below, the Board shall accept a new price formula specified in a notice under paragraph 5(2) above if they are satisfied that the new formula provides for readily ascertainable market values which correspond, so far as practicable, with those which were intended to be provided for under the original price formula; and if the Board are not so satisfied they shall reject such a new price formula.

7(2) Subject to sub-paragraph (3) below, sub-paragraphs (1) and (2) of paragraph 2 above and paragraph 3 above shall apply to determine whether the Board shall accept–

(a) a new price formula contained in a notice under paragraph 6(1)(b) above which has been accepted by the Board under paragraph 6(3) above, or

(b) if the Board have given notice under paragraph 6(1)(b) above, a new price formula specified in a notice under paragraph 6(5)(b) above,

as if the new price formula were specified in an election made at the time the notice under paragraph 6(1)(b) above was given.

7(3) The Board shall reject such a new price formula as is referred to in sub-paragraph (1) or sub-paragraph (2) above if, after receiving notice in writing from the Board, the party or, as the case may be, either of the parties to the election–

(a) fails to furnish to the Board, before the appropriate date, any information which the Board may reasonably require for the purpose of determining whether the new formula should be accepted in accordance with sub-paragraph (1) or, as the case may be, sub-paragraph (2) above, or

(b) fails to make available for inspection, before the appropriate date, by an officer authorised by the Board any books, accounts or documents in his possession or power which contain information relevant for that purpose.

7(4) Sub-paragraph (4) of paragraph 2 above applies in relation to sub-paragraph (3) above as it applies in relation to sub-paragraph (3) of that paragraph.

7(5) Notice of the acceptance or rejection of a new price formula–

(a) specified in a notice under paragraph 5(2) or paragraph 6(5)(b) above, or

(b) contained in a notice under paragraph 6(1)(b) above which has been accepted by the Board by a notice under paragraph 6(3) above,

shall be given to the party or, as the case may be, each of the parties to the election concerned before the expiry of the period of three months beginning on the relevant date (as defined in sub-paragraph (6) below), and if no notice of acceptance or rejection is in fact given as required by this sub-paragraph, the Board shall be deemed to have accepted the formula and to have given notice of their acceptance on the last day of that period.

7(6) In sub-paragraph (5) above **"the relevant date"** means–

(a) if a notice has been given under sub-paragraph (3) above relating to the price formula in question, the date or, as the case may be, the last date which is the appropriate date, within the meaning of that sub-paragraph, in relation to such a notice; and

(b) if no such notice has been given, then–

(i) in relation to a new price formula, falling within paragraph (a) of sub-paragraph (5) above, the date on which the notice referred to in that paragraph was received by the Board; and

(ii) in relation to a new price formula falling within paragraph (b) of that sub-paragraph, the date of the notice from the Board under paragraph 6(3) above.

8(1) Where the Board give notice to any person or persons–

(a) under paragraph 4 above, rejecting an election; or

(b) under paragraph 5 above, that the value of any ethane has ceased or is ceasing to be readily ascertainable; or

(c) under paragraph 6(1)(b) above, that a price formula is no longer realistic; or

(d) under paragraph 6(3) above, rejecting a notice given under paragraph 6(1)(b) above; or

(e) under paragraph 7(5) above, rejecting a new price formula;

that person or, as the case may be, those persons acting jointly may appeal against the notice.

8(2) An appeal under sub-paragraph (1) above shall be made by notice in writing given to the Board within thirty days after the date of the notice in respect of which the appeal is brought.

8(3) Where at any time after the giving of notice of appeal under this paragraph and before the determination of the appeal by the tribunal, the Board and the appellant agree that the notice in respect of which the appeal is brought should be accepted or withdrawn or varied, the same consequences shall ensue as if the tribunal had determined the appeal to that effect.

8(4) If an appeal under this paragraph is notified to the tribunal and the tribunal determines that the appeal should be allowed it shall allow the appeal and–

(a) where the appeal is against a notice of rejection of an election or proposed new price formula, the tribunal shall substitute a notice of acceptance of the election or price formula without modification or with such modifications as the tribunal think fit;

(b) where the appeal is against a notice under paragraph 5 or paragraph 6(1)(b) above, the tribunal may direct that the price formula in question shall continue to have effect as if the notice had not been given; and

(c) where the appeal is against a notice under paragraph 6(3) above rejecting a notice under paragraph 6(1)(b) above, the tribunal shall substitute a notice of acceptance.

8(5) Sub-paragraphs (2), (8) and (11) of paragraph 14 of Schedule 2 to the principal Act, and paragraphs 14A to 14I of that Schedule shall apply in relation to an appeal against any such notice as is referred to in sub-paragraph (1) above as they apply in relation to an appeal against an assessment or determination made under the principal Act, but with the substitution, for any reference to the participator, of a reference to the person or persons who gave notice of appeal under sub-paragraph (2) above and, in the case of paragraphs 14A to 14I of Schedule 2, with such other modifications as may be necessary.

8(6) Where notice of appeal is duly given against a notice given by the Board under paragraph 5 or paragraph 6(1)(b) above, the period of three months referred to in paragraph 5(2)(a) or, as the case may be, paragraph 6(5)(b) above shall not begin to run until the appeal is withdrawn or finally determined.

8(7) Any reference in section 134 of this Act or the preceding provisions of this Schedule to an **"election accepted"** by the Board shall be construed as including a reference to an election accepted in pursuance of an appeal under this paragraph.

History – In para. 8(1) the words "to the Special Commissioners" omitted by SI 2009/56, art. 3 and Sch. 1, para. 101(2), with effect from 1 April 2009, subject to transitional and saving provisions in SI 2009/56, Sch. 3.

In para. 8(3) the word "tribunal" substituted for the word "Commissioners" twice by SI 2009/56, art. 3 and Sch. 1, para. 101(3), with effect from 1 April 2009, subject to transitional and saving provisions in SI 2009/56, Sch. 3.

In para. 8(4), in words preceding para. (a) the words "If an appeal under this paragraph is notified to the tribunal and the tribunal determines" substituted for the words "If, on a hearing of an appeal under this paragraph it appears to the majority of the Commissioners present at the hearing" and the word "it" substituted for the word "they"; in para. (a) the words "the tribunal shall" substituted for the words "they shall" and the words "the tribunal thinks" substituted for the words "they think"; in para. (b) the words "the tribunal may direct" substituted for the words "they may direct"; in para. (c) the word "tribunal" substituted for the word "Commissioners" by SI 2009/56, art. 3 and Sch. 1, para. 101(4), with effect from 1 April 2009, subject to transitional and saving provisions in SI 2009/56, Sch. 3.

In para. 8(5) the words ", and paragraphs 14A to 14I of that Schedule" and "and, in the case of paragraphs 14A to 14I of Schedule 2, with such other modifications as may be necessary" inserted by SI 2009/56, art. 3 and Sch. 1, para. 101(5), with effect from 1 April 2009, subject to transitional and saving provisions in SI 2009/56, Sch. 3.

RETURNS

9 In any case where a notice under paragraph 5(1)(b) above or paragraph 6(1)(b) above relating to an election has been given to a party to the election or to the Board then, unless the notice has been withdrawn (whether in pursuance of an appeal or otherwise) or a price formula different from that to which the notice referred has effect as if specified in the election, any party to the election, in making a return under paragraph 2 of Schedule 2 to the principal Act with respect to ethane to which that election applies or which by virtue of that election falls within section 134(3) of this Act–

(a) where the notice was given under paragraph 5 above, may include the market value on and after the date specified in the notice of any such ethane determined on such basis as appears to him to be the best practical alternative to that provided by the price formula to which the notice referred; and

(b) where the notice was given under paragraph 6 above, shall include the market value of any such ethane determined in accordance with the price formula to which the notice referred.

PENALTIES FOR INCORRECT INFORMATION ETC.

10(1) Schedule 24 to the Finance Act 2007 (which penalises inaccurate documents and is in this paragraph referred to as "the penalty provisions") shall apply, in accordance with sub-paragraph (2) or sub-paragraph (3) below, in relation to inaccurate information–

(a) contained in an election; or

(b) furnished pursuant to a notice under paragraph 2(3) or paragraph 7(3) above; or

(c) contained in any books, accounts or documents made available as mentioned in paragraph 2(3)(b) or paragraph 7(3)(b) above.

10(2) Where the inaccurate information is provided by a participator, the penalty provisions shall apply–

(a) as they apply in relation to an incorrect return under paragraph 2 of Schedule 2 to the principal Act; and

(b) [repealed by SI 2009/571, art. 8 and Sch. 1, para. 1 and 8.]

10(3) Where the incorrect information is provided by a person other than a participator, the penalty provisions shall apply–

(a) as they apply to an incorrect return under paragraph 5 of Schedule 2 to the principal Act; and

(b) as if that person were the responsible person for an oil field.

History – In para. 10(1), the words "Schedule 24 to the Finance Act 2007 (which penalises inaccurate documents and is in this paragraph referred to as "the penalty provisions")" substituted for words "Paragraphs 8 and 9 of Schedule 2 to the principal Act (which penalise inaccurate returns etc and are in this paragraph referred to as "the penalty provisions")" by SI 2009/571 art. 8 and Sch. 1 para. 1 and 8, with effect from 1 April 2009.
Para. 10(2)(b) repealed, by SI 2009/571 art. 8 and Sch. 1 para. 1 and 8, with effect from 1 April 2009.

INTERPRETATION

11(1) Subsection (6) of section 134 of this Act has effect in relation to this Schedule as it has effect in relation to the preceding provisions of that section.

11(2) In this Schedule, any reference to an **"election"** is a reference to an election under section 134 of this Act; and any reference to the date on which the election (made as mentioned in paragraph 1 above) is received by the Board.

11(3) Any reference in the preceding provisions of this Schedule to the **"party to an election"** is relevant only to an election applying to ethane which is relevantly appropriated and is a reference to the participator by whom the ethane is for the time being so appropriated.

11(4) Any reference in the preceding provisions of this Schedule to the **"parties to an election"** is relevant only to an election applying to ethane which is disposed of as mentioned in section 134(2)(a) of this Act and is a reference to the participator by whom and the person to whom the ethane is for the time being so disposed of.

SCHEDULE 19 – SUPPLEMENTARY PROVISIONS RELATING TO APRT

Section 139

Notes – To the extent that Sch. 19 relates to APRT, it is spent, APRT having ceased to be payable from 1 January 1987, and therefore not reproduced. The provisions set out below relate to the payment of PRT by instalments.

Part I – Collection of Tax

PAYMENT OF TAX

1(1) APRT which a participator is liable to pay in respect of any chargeable period for an oil field shall be due on the date on which the return for that period and that field is made by the participator in accordance with paragraph 2 of Schedule 2 to the principal Act or, if a return is not so made, on the last day of the second month following that period; and APRT which is due shall be payable without the making of an assessment.

1(2) Subject to sub-paragraph (3) below, every participator in an oil field shall, at the time when he delivers to the Board the return for a chargeable period required by paragraph 2 of Schedule 2 to the principal Act–

(a) deliver to the Board a statement showing whether any, and if so what, amount of APRT is payable by him for that chargeable period in respect of the field; and

(b) subject to the following provisions of this Schedule, pay to the Board the amount of APRT, if any, shown in the statement.

1(3) In relation to any oil field, sub-paragraph (2) above does not apply with respect to any chargeable period after the last of the chargeable periods referred to in section 139(1)(b) of this Act.

1(4) The statement under sub-paragraph (2)(a) above shall be in such form as the Board may prescribe.

1(5) Paragraphs 3, 8 and 9 of Schedule 2 to the principal Act shall apply in relation to statements required to be made under this paragraph as they apply in relation to returns required to be made under paragraph 2 of that Schedule.

History – In para. 1(3), words repealed by FA 1983, s. 35, 48 and Sch. 7, para. 1, and Sch. 10, Pt. III.

2(1) Subject to sub-paragraph (2) below, if for any chargeable period for an oil field ending on or after 30th June 1983–

(a) an amount of APRT is shown to be payable by the participator in the statement delivered by him in accordance with paragraph 1 above in respect of that period and that field; or

(b) an amount is payable by the participator on account of petroleum revenue tax in accordance with section 1 of the Petroleum Revenue Tax Act 1980 in respect of that period and that field; or

(c) both such amounts are so payable by the participator,

then the participator shall pay to the Board six monthly instalments commencing in the second month of the next chargeable period each equal to one-eighth of the amount referred to in paragraph (a) or paragraph (b) above or, where paragraph (c) applies, of the aggregate of those amounts.

2(2) With respect to any chargeable period ending on or after 31st December 1984 sub-paragraph (1) above shall have effect as if–

(a) for paragraphs (a) to (c) there were substituted the words "an amount of tax is shown to be payable in the statement delivered in respect of that period in accordance with section 1(1)(a) of the Petroleum Revenue Tax Act 1980"; and

(b) for the words from "the amount referred to in paragraph (a)" onwards there shall be substituted the words "that amount".

2(3) Instalments paid in accordance with sub-paragraph (1) above shall be regarded as being paid in respect of the next chargeable period referred to in that sub-paragraph.

2(4) The aggregate amount paid by a participator in accordance with sub-paragraph (1) above in respect of a chargeable period for an oil field–

(a) to the extent that it is equal to or less than his liability, if any, to pay an amount of APRT under paragraph 1 above in respect of that oil field for that chargeable period shall be deemed to be an amount of APRT paid by him in respect of that field for that period; and

(b) to the extent that it exceeds any such liability of his to pay an amount of APRT and is equal to or less than his liability, if any, to pay an amount in respect of that field for that period in accordance with paragraph (b) of subsection (1) of section 1 of the Petroleum Revenue Tax Act 1980 (payments on account of petroleum revenue tax), shall be deemed to be an amount paid by him under that paragraph.

2(4A) In sub-paragraph (1) the reference to any chargeable period for an oil field ending on or after 30th June 1983 does not include a chargeable period ending on 31st December 2015.

History – In para. 2(2), the words "any chargeable period ending on or after 31st December 1984" substituted by FA 1983, s. 35 and Sch. 7, para. 2, effective from 13 May 1983.
Para. 2(4A) inserted by FA 2016, s. 140(3), with effect from 15 September 2016 (Royal Assent).

3(1) Subject to sub-paragraph (1A) below, if in any month (the relevant month) a participator in an oil field–

(a) has not delivered (otherwise than to the OGA) any of the oil which has been won from the field and disposed of by him at any time in or before that month; and

(b) has not relevantly appropriated any of the oil which has been so won by him at any such time,

he shall be entitled to withhold the instalment due, under paragraph 2 above, for that field in the following month.

3(1A) Sub-paragraph (1) above does not apply if the relevant month is a month in which any consideration (whether in the nature of income or capital) is received or receivable by the participator in respect of any such matter as is mentioned in paragraph (a) or (b) of section 6(2) of the Oil Taxation Act 1983 (chargeable tariff receipts).

3(2) An instalment shall not be withheld by virtue of the conditions in sub-paragraph (1) above being fulfilled in any month unless a notice to that effect, in such form as the Board may prescribe, is given to the Board before the end of the following month and–

(a) where the Board are not satisfied with any such notice, the powers conferred by paragraph 7 of Schedule 2 to the principal Act (production of accounts etc.) shall be exercisable as if the notice were a return under paragraph 2 of that Schedule; and

(b) paragraph 8 of that Schedule (penalties) shall apply to an incorrect notice as it applies to an incorrect return under paragraph 2.

Prospective amendments – In para. 3(1)(a) the word "OGA" substituted for the words "Secretary of State" by SI 2016/898, reg. 6(3), *with effect immediately after the commencement of SCA 2016, s. 48.*

History – In para. 3(1)(a), the word "OGA" substituted for the words "Secretary of State" by SI 2016/898, reg. 6(2), with effect from 1 October 2016 (as the 21st day after being made on 10 September 2016).
In para. 3(1), the words "Subject to sub-paragraph (1A) below," and "(the relevant month)" inserted by FA 1999, s. 99(1)(a), for the purpose of determining whether instalments are payable in respect of chargeable periods ending on or after 31 December 1999.
Para. 3(1A) inserted by FA 1999, s. 99(1)(b), for the purpose of determining whether instalments are payable in respect of chargeable periods ending on or after 31 December 1999.

Extra-statutory concessions – ESC I5: participator entitled, on giving notice to the Board, to withhold the instalment for a month if in the previous or an earlier month, oil actually ceased to be won from the field as a result of some sudden catastrophic loss or damage.

4 Certificates of tax deposit issued by the Treasury under section 12 of the National Loans Act 1968 on terms published on or before 14th May 1979 may be used for making payments of APRT and of instalments under paragraph 2 above; and for that purpose those terms shall have effect with the necessary modifications and as if the tax in or towards the payment of which a certificate is used were due–

(a) in the case of APRT payable under paragraph 1 above, two months after the end of the chargeable period to which it relates;

(b) in the case of an instalment payable under paragraph 2 above, at the end of the month in which the instalment is required to be paid.

ASSESSMENTS AND APPEALS

5(1) Where it appears to the Board that any APRT payable in accordance with paragraph 1 above has not been paid on the due date they may make an assessment to tax on the participator and shall give him notice of any such assessment.

5(2) APRT due under an assessment under this paragraph shall be due within thirty days of the issue of the notice of assessment.

5(3) A notice of assessment shall state that the participator may appeal against the assessment in accordance with paragraph 7 below.

5(4) After the service of a notice of assessment the assessment shall not be altered except in accordance with the express provisions of this Part of this Schedule or any of the provisions of the Taxes Management Act 1970 which apply by virtue of paragraph 1 of Schedule 2 to the principal Act in relation to the assessment.

6(1) Where it appears to the Board that any gross profit charged to tax on a participator for any chargeable period in respect of an oil field by an assessment under paragraph 5 above ought to have been larger or smaller or that no gross profit accrued to the participator from that oil field during that chargeable period, they may make such amendments to the assessment or withdraw the assessment, as the case may require.

6(2) Where the Board amend an assessment under sub-paragraph (1) above they shall give notice to the participator of the amendment; and sub-paragraphs (2) to (4) of paragraph 5 above shall apply in relation to a notice of assessment under paragraph 5.

7(1) A participator may appeal against an assessment or amendment of an assessment under paragraph 5 or paragraph 6 above by notice of appeal in writing to the Board given within thirty days of the date of issue of the notice of the assessment or amendment of assessment.

7(2) Sub-paragraphs (2) to (11) of paragraph 14 of and paragraphs 14A to 14I of Schedule 2 to the principal Act shall apply in relation to an appeal under this paragraph as they apply in relation to an appeal under sub-paragraph (1) of that paragraph except that–

(a) for each reference in paragraph 14(3) to tax there shall be substituted a reference to APRT;

(b) where in determining the gross profit accruing to a participator from a field in a chargeable period the aggregate of the amounts mentioned in paragraphs (a) to (c) of subsection (5) of section 2 of the principal Act falls to be increased under section 140 of this Act (whether as respects all oil or as respects a particular kind or kinds of oil), the difference mentioned in paragraph 14(3)(b) (or as the case may be, the difference so far as relating to oil of the particular kind or kinds in question) shall be increased by multiplying it by the fraction mentioned in subsection (2) of section 140;

(c) for each reference in paragraph 14(10) to an assessable profit there shall be substituted a reference to a gross profit;

(d) any reference in paragraph 14(10) to an allowable loss shall be omitted; and

(e) in the case of paragraphs 14A to 141 of Schedule 2, with such modifications as may be necessary.

History – In para. 7(1) the words"to the Special Commissioners" omitted by SI 2009/56, art. 3 and Sch. 1, para. 102(2), with effect from 1 April 2009, subject to transitional and saving provisions in SI 2009/56, Sch. 3.
In para. 7(2), in the words preceding para. (a) the words "and paragraphs 14A to 14I of" inserted; in para. (a) the words "paragraph 14(3)" substituted for the words "sub-paragraph (3)"; in para. (b) the words "paragraph 14(3)(b)" substituted for the words "sub-paragraph (3)(b)"; in para. (c) the word "and" omitted; in para. (c) and (d) the words "paragraph 14(10)" substituted for the words "sub-paragraph 10"; para. (e) and word "and" preceding it inserted by SI 2009/56, art. 3 and Sch. 1, para. 102(3), with effect from 1 April 2009, subject to transitional and saving provisions in SI 2009/56, Sch. 3.

8 Paragraphs 5(2) to (4) and 7 above shall apply in relation to an assessment to APRT under section 142(1) of this Act as if it were an assessment under paragraph 5.

OVERPAYMENT OF TAX

9(1) Where in respect of any oil field a participator has paid an amount of APRT for a chargeable period which exceeds the amount of APRT payable therefor the amount of that excess shall be repaid to him.

9(2) Where in respect of any oil field the amount paid for any chargeable period by a participator by way of instalments under paragraph 2 above exceeds the aggregate of his liabilities mentioned in sub-paragraph (4) of that paragraph, the amount of that excess shall be repaid to him.

INTEREST

10(1) APRT payable for a chargeable period but not paid before the end of the second month after the end of that period shall carry interest from the end of that month until payment.

10(2) Any amount payable by a participator as an instalment in respect of a chargeable period for a field and not paid by him in the month in which it ought to be paid shall carry interest from the end of that month until–

(a) payment of the amount, or

(b) two months after the end of that period,

whichever is the earlier.

10(3) [Spent.]

10(4) Where an amount of APRT or an amount paid by way of instalment becomes repayable, that amount shall carry interest from–

(a) two months after the end of the chargeable period in respect of which the APRT or the instalment was paid, or

(b) the date on which the amount was paid,

whichever is the later, until the order for repayment is issued.

10(5) For the purposes of sub-paragraph (2) above a payment on account of an overdue instalment shall, so far as possible, be attributed to the earliest month for which an instalment is overdue; and for the purposes of sub-paragraph (4) above any instalment or part of an instalment that becomes repayable shall, so far as possible, be regarded as consisting of the instalment most recently paid.

10(6) In its application (by virtue of paragraph 1 of Schedule 2 to the principal Act) to interest payable under sub-paragraph (1) or sub-paragraph (2) above, section 69 of the Taxes Management Act 1970 shall have effect with the omission of the words "charged and due and payable under the assessment to which it relates".

10(7) [Omitted by CTA 2010, s. 1177 and Sch. 1, para. 178 and by TIOPA 2010, s. 374 and Sch. 8, para. 179 and repealed by TIOPA 2010, s. 378 and Sch. 10, Pt. 6.]

10(8) Any reference in this paragraph to **"interest"** is a reference to interest at the rate applying under paragraph 15 of Schedule 2 to the principal Act.

History – Para. 10(7) omitted by TIOPA 2010, s. 374 and Sch. 8, para. 178 and repealed by TIOPA 2010, s. 378 and Sch. 10, Pt. 6, with effect for corporation tax purposes for accounting periods ending on or after 1 April 2010, for income tax and capital gains tax purposes for the tax year 2010–11 and subsequent tax years, and for petroleum revenue tax purposes for chargeable periods beginning on or after 1 July 2010.

Para. 10(7) omitted by CTA 2010, s. 1177 and Sch. 1, para. 178 and repealed by CTA 2010, s. 1181 and Sch. 3, Pt. 2 (for corporation tax purposes only), with effect for accounting periods ending on or after 1 April 2010.

In para. 10(4) the words "the order for repayment is issued" substituted for the word "repayment " by FA 1989, s. 180(2) and was deemed always to have had effect.

Cross references – TMA 1970, s. 69: interest on tax.

Notes – Para. 10(7) rewritten for corporation tax purposes at CTA 2010, s. 302(2) and (3).
Para. 10(7) rewritten for other purposes at TIOPA 2010, Sch. 1, para. 2.

TRANSITIONAL PROVISIONS

11(1) In any case where, by virtue of section 105 of the Finance Act 1980, a sum is paid by a participator as an advance payment of tax in respect of an oil field for the chargeable period ending on 30 June 1983 then,–

(a) to the extent that the sum so paid does not exceed his liability to APRT for that period, it shall be deemed to be a payment of APRT for that period; and

(b) subsection (5) of that section (treatment of advance payments) shall apply to any such sum only to the extent that it exceeds that liability to APRT.

11(2) In subsection (7) of that section the reference to tax assessed on a participator in respect of a field for a chargeable period shall include, for the chargeable period ending on 30 June 1983, a reference to the amount (if any) of APRT payable by him in respect of that field for that period.

12(1) Every participator in an oil field shall in March 1983 and in each of the four succeeding months pay to the Board an amount equal to one-fifth of the amount, if any, shown in the statement delivered by the participator under paragraph 10(1)(a) of Schedule 16 to the Finance Act 1981 as supplementary petroleum duty payable by him in respect of the field for the chargeable period ending on 31 December 1982.

12(2) Paragraphs 2(4) and 9 above shall apply in relation to any payment made by the participator under sub-paragraph (1) above as if it were an instalment under paragraph 2 above paid in respect of the chargeable period ending on 30 June 1983; but for the purposes of this sub-paragraph the amount of the participator's liability to pay any APRT as mentioned in paragraph 2(4) above shall be reduced by the amount of any APRT deemed to have been paid by him in accordance with paragraph 11 above.

12(3) Paragraphs 3, 4 and 10 above shall apply in relation to a payment under sub-paragraph (1) above as if it were an instalment under paragraph 2 above.

13(1) If, in respect of the chargeable period ending on 30 June 1983, any sum is payable by a participator in accordance with section 1 of the Petroleum Revenue Tax Act 1980, then, so far as the net amount of that sum is concerned, only one-fifth shall become payable at the time specified in that section and the remaining four-fifths shall be paid in four equal monthly instalments in the months of September to December 1983, inclusive.

13(2) The reference in sub-paragraph (1) above to the net amount of any sum payable in accordance with section 1 of the Petroleum Revenue Tax Act 1980 is a reference to the sum specified in paragraph (b) of subsection (1) of that section less any amount which is treated as (or deemed to be) paid as part of that sum–

(a) by virtue of section 105(5) of the Finance Act 1980, as applied by paragraph 11(1)(b) above; or

(b) by virtue of paragraph 2(4)(b) above, as applied by paragraph 12(2) above.

13(3) Any amount payable by a participator as an instalment by virtue of sub-paragraph (1) above and not paid by him in the month in which it ought to be paid shall carry interest from the end of that month until payment.

13(4) Paragraph 15 of Schedule 2 to the principal Act (interest on assessed tax) shall not apply in relation to so much of the tax charged in an assessment on the participator for the chargeable period referred to in sub-paragraph (1) above (excluding any APRT so charged) as is equal to or less than the net amount referred to in that sub-paragraph and payable by him, and in relation to so much if any of that tax as exceeds that net amount paragraph 15 shall apply with the substitution for the words "two months after the end of the period" of the words "the end of October 1983".

13(5) If, in respect of the chargeable period referred to in sub-paragraph (1) above, any amount of tax charged by an assessment to tax or paid on account of tax so charged becomes repayable under any provision of Part I of the principal Act, paragraph 16 of Schedule 2 to the principal Act (interest on such repayments) shall have effect in relation to that amount with the substitution for the words following "per annum" of the words "from the end of October 1983 until repayment".

13(6) Sub-paragraphs (5) to (8) of paragraph 10 above shall apply for the purposes of sub-paragraphs (3) and (5) above as they apply for the purposes of sub-paragraphs (2) and (4) of paragraph 10.

Part II – Miscellaneous

REPAYMENT OF APRT

14(1) If a participator in an oil field has an excess of APRT credit for the ninth chargeable period following the first chargeable period referred to in section 139(1)(a) of this Act, then, on the making of a claim the amount of that excess shall be repaid to him.

14(2) For the purposes of this paragraph there is an excess of APRT credit for the ninth chargeable period referred to in sub-paragraph (1) above if any of that credit would, apart from this paragraph, fall to be carried forward to the next chargeable period in accordance with section 139(4) of this Act; and the amount of the excess is the amount of the credit which would fall to be so carried forward.

14(3) A claim under sub-paragraph (1) above shall be made not earlier than two months after the expiry of the ninth chargeable period referred to in that sub-paragraph.

14(4) In any case where–

(a) a claim is made under sub-paragraph (1) above before an assessment is made for the ninth chargeable period referred to in that sub-paragraph, and

(b) the APRT credit for that period exceeds the amount of tax which, in the statement delivered under section 1(1)(a) of the Petroleum Revenue Tax Act 1980, is shown to be payable by the participator concerned in accordance with the Schedule to that Act for that period in respect of the oil field in question, the amount of the excess shall be repaid to the participator and that repayment shall be regarded as a payment on account of any amount which may fall to be repaid to him by virtue of sub-paragraph (1) above.

14(5) Paragraph 10(4) above shall not apply to any amount of APRT which is repayable only on the making of a claim under sub-paragraph (1) above.

14(6) Amounts repaid to a participator by virtue of this paragraph shall be disregarded in computing his income for the purposes of income tax or corporation tax.

History – In para. 14(2), (3) and (4)(a) words substituted by FA 1983, s. 35 and Sch. 7, para. 3 and 4.

TRANSFER OF INTEREST IN FIELDS

15(1) This paragraph has effect in a case where Part I of Schedule 17 to the Finance Act 1980 applies (transfer of interests in oil fields) and expressions used in the following provisions in this paragraph have the same meaning as in that Schedule.

15(2) For the purpose of determining whether the new participator is liable to pay an amount of APRT, but for no other purpose, subsection (1) of section 139 of this Act shall apply as if any gross profit which at any time before the transfer had accrued to the old participator from the field had accrued at that time to the new participator or, if the transfer is of part of the old participator's interest in the field, as if a corresponding part of that gross profit had at that time accrued to the new participator.

15(3) There shall be treated as the APRT credit of the new participator the whole or, if the transfer is of part of the old participator's interest in the field, a corresponding part of so much, if any, of the old participator's APRT credit in respect of that field for the transfer period as exceeds his liability for petroleum revenue tax for that period.

15(4) For the purposes of computing whether any, and if so what, amount of APRT is payable by the old participator and the new participator for the transfer period or any later chargeable period it shall be assumed that any application or proposal made in relation to the transfer under paragraph 4 or paragraph 5(1) of Schedule 17 to the Finance Act 1980 and in respect of which the Board have not notified their decision will be accepted by the Board.

NET PROFIT PERIODS

16(1) For the purposes of sections 111, 112 and 113 of the Finance Act 1981 (determination of net profit periods etc) the total assessable profits which have accrued to a participator from an oil field at the end of a chargeable period may in addition to being set against allowable losses be set against the APRT paid by the participator in respect of that oil field for chargeable periods up to and including that period and accordingly those sections shall have effect subject to the following modifications.

16(2)–(4) [Amends FA 1981, s. 111(2A), 112(4A) and 113(1).]

ABANDONED FIELDS

17(1) The provisions of this paragraph apply where–

(a) the responsible person for an oil field has given notice under paragraph 1 of Schedule 8 to the principal Act that the winning of oil from the field has permanently ceased;

(b) he has been notified of a decision (whether of the Board or on appeal from the Board) that the winning of oil has so ceased; and

(c) the date stated in that decision as the date on which the winning of oil from the field ceased is earlier than the expiry of the ninth chargeable period following the first chargeable period referred to in section 139(1)(a) of this Act.

17(2) Where a participator in the field in question has an amount of APRT credit–

(a) which cannot be set against a liability for petroleum revenue tax under section 139(3) of this Act, and

(b) which is not repayable by virtue of any other provision of this Schedule,

then, on the making of a claim, that amount shall be repaid to him.

17(3) Paragraph 10(4) above shall not apply to any amount of APRT which is repayable only on the making of a claim under sub-paragraph (2) above.

17(4) Any claim under sub-paragraph (2) above shall be made before any claim for any unrelievable field loss allowance under section 6 of the principal Act; and any amount of APRT which is repayable by virtue of such a claim shall be left out of account in determining the amount of any such loss.

17(5) Amounts repaid to a participator under this paragraph shall be disregarded in computing his income for the purposes of income tax and corporation tax.

History – In para. 17(1)(c) words substituted by FA 1983, s. 35 and Sch. 7, para. 3 and 4.

Part III – Amendments

18 [Amends OTA 1975, s. 2.]

19 [Amends OTA 1975, Sch. 2, para. 13.]

20 In sub-paragraph (2) and (4) of paragraph 5 of Schedule 3 to the principal Act (liability for petroleum revenue tax and interest in the case of transfers to associated companies) the references to tax and to interest payable under Part I of that Act shall include references to APRT and to interest payable under paragraph 10 or paragraph 13 above.

21 [Amends PRTA 1980, s. 1(1), (3), (3A), (3B).]

FINANCE ACT 1983

(1983 Chapter 28)

[*13th May 1983*]

ARRANGEMENT OF SECTIONS

PART III – OIL TAXATION

PART IV – MISCELLANEOUS AND SUPPLEMENTARY

SCHEDULES

PART III – OIL TAXATION

35 Phasing out of APRT

35 [Amends FA 1982, s. 139(1)–(4) and Sch. 19.]

36 Increased oil allowance for certain new fields

36(1) For all relevant new fields, as defined in subsection (2) below, section 8 of the principal Act (the oil allowance) shall have effect subject to the following modifications–

(a) in subsection (2) (the amount of the allowance for each chargeable period) for "250,000 metric tonnes" there shall be substituted "500,000 metric tonnes"; and

(b) in subsection (6) (the total allowance for a field) for "5 million metric tonnes" there shall be substituted "10 million metric tonnes".

36(2) Subject to subsection (3) below, in this section **"relevant new field"** means an oil field–

(a) no part of which lies in a landward area, within the meaning of the Petroleum (Production) Regulations 1982 or in an area to the East of the United Kingdom and between latitudes 52° and 55° North; and

(b) for no part of which consent for development has been granted to the licensee by the Secretary of State before 1st April 1982; and

(c) for no part of which a programme of development had been served on the licensee or approved by the Secretary of State before that date.

36(3) In determining, in accordance with subsection (2) above, whether an oil field (in this subsection referred to as **"the new field"**) is a relevant new field, no account shall be taken of a consent for development granted before 1st April 1982 or a programme of development served on the licensee or approved by the Secretary of State before that date if–

(a) in whole or in part that consent or programme related to another oil field for which a determination *under Schedule 1 to the principal* Act was made before the determination under that Schedule for the new field; and

(b) on or after 1st April 1982, a consent for development is or was granted or a programme of development is or was served on the licensee or approved by the OGA and that consent or programme relates, in whole or in part, to the new field.

36(4) In subsections (2) and (3) above **"development"** means–

(a) the erection or carrying out of permanent works for the purpose of getting oil from the field or for the purpose of conveying oil won from the field to a place on land; or

(b) winning oil from the field otherwise than in the course of searching for oil or drilling wells;

and **"consent for development"** does not include consent which is limited to the purpose of testing the characteristics of an oil-bearing area and does not relate to the erection or carrying out of permanent works.

36(5) In subsection (4) above **"permanent works"** means any structures or other works whatsoever which are intended by the licensee to be permanent and are neither designed to be moved from place to place without major dismantling nor intended by the licensee to be used only for searching for oil.

Prospective amendments – In s. 36(3)(b) the word "OGA" substituted for the words "Secretary of State" by SI 2016/898, reg. 7, with effect immediately after the commencement of SCA 2016, s. 48.

History – In s. 36(3)(b), the word "OGA" substituted for the words "Secretary of State" by SI 2016/898, reg. 7, with effect from 1 October 2016 (as the 21st day after being made on 10 September 2016).

Cross references – S. 36(4), (5) has effect to define development for the purposes of TCGA 1992, s. 196(3) (certain capital gains tax allowances in respect of the disposal of licences relating to undeveloped areas).

37 Reliefs for exploration and appraisal expenditure etc.

37(1) The section set out in Part I of Schedule 8 to this Act shall be inserted in the principal Act after section 5 for the purpose of setting up a new allowance by virtue of which a participator in an oil field may obtain relief for certain expenditure which is incurred otherwise than in connection with that field.

37(2) For the purpose of giving effect to, and in consequence of, the new allowance, the enactments specified in Part II of Schedule 8 to this Act shall have effect subject to the amendments there specified.

37(3) Part III of Schedule 8 to this Act shall have effect with respect to sums received after 15th March 1983 and falling to be set off against expenditure which would otherwise be allowable under section 5 of the principal Act or under the new section set out in Part I of that Schedule.

37(4) [Amendments to OTA 1975, Sch. 7, para. 1, omitting words deemed always to have been omitted.]

38 Terms of payment to be implied in determining market value

38 [Repealed by FA 2006, s. 178 and Sch. 26, Pt. 5(1).]

History – S. 38 repealed by FA 2006, s. 178 and Sch. 26, Pt. 5(1) with effect in relation to oil delivered or appropriated on or after 1 July 2006, but subject to the provisions of FA 2006, s. 147(2)–(8). Former s. 38 amended OTA 1975, Sch. 3, para. 2.

39 Exclusion of oil appropriated for production purposes in other fields

39 [Amends OTA 1975, s. 12, in respect of chargeable periods ending after 31 December 1977.]

40 Variation of decisions on claims for allowable expenditure

40 [Inserts OTA 1975, Sch. 5, para. 9; amendment to OTA 1975, Sch. 6, para. 2.]

41 Transfers of interest in oil fields

41 [Amends FA 1980, Sch. 17, para. 7, in relation to transfer periods ending after 31 December 1982.]

PART IV – MISCELLANEOUS AND SUPPLEMENTARY

48 Short title, interpretation, construction and repeals

48(1) This Act may be cited as the Finance Act 1983.

48(2), (3) [Not relevant to petroleum revenue tax.]

48(4) Part III of this Act shall be construed as one with Part I of the Oil Taxation Act 1975 and references in Part III to the principal Act are references to that Act.

SCHEDULES

SCHEDULE 7 – APRT: MODIFICATIONS OF FA 1982, SCHEDULE 19

Section 35

[Amends FA 1982, Sch. 19, para. 1(3), 2(2), 14(1)–(3) and 17(1)(c).]

SCHEDULE 8 – RELIEFS FOR EXPLORATION AND APPRAISAL EXPENDITURE ETC.

Section 37

Part I – Section to be Inserted After Section 5 of the Principal Act

[Inserts OTA 1975, s. 5A.]

Part II – Amendments Relating to the New Allowance

1–9 [Amends OTA 1975, s. 2, 3, 5, 9, Sch. 2, para. 2 and Sch. 7, para. 1 and PRTA 1980, Schedule, para. 2; Insertion of FA 1980, Sch. 17, para. 16A; Amendment to FA 1981, s. 111. Para. 9 repealed by FA 1987, s. 72 and Sch. 16, Pt. X.]

Part III – Receipts to be Set Against Allowable Expenditure

10 In this Part of this Schedule–

"allowable expenditure" means expenditure which, in accordance with section 5 or section 5A of the principal Act, is allowable on a claim made by a participator under Schedule 7 to that Act; and

"qualifying receipt" means a sum the amount of which falls, by virtue of subsection (6) of section 5 of the principal Act, to be applied by way of reduction in the amount of expenditure which would otherwise be allowable expenditure.

11(1) A return made by a participator for a chargeable period under paragraph 2 of Schedule 2 to the principal Act shall give details of any qualifying receipt (whether received by him or by a person connected with him) of which details have not been given in a return made by him for an earlier chargeable period.

11(2) Section 1122 of the Corporation Tax Act 2010 (connected persons) applies for the purposes of this paragraph.

History – In s. 134(1), the words "Section 1122 of the Corporation Tax Act 2010" substituted for the words "Section 839 of the Income and Corporation Taxes Act 1988" by CTA 2010, s. 1177 and Sch. 1, para. 179, with effect for corporation tax purposes for accounting periods ending on or after 1 April 2010, and for income tax and capital gains tax purposes for the tax year 2010–11 and subsequent tax years.
See ICTA 1988, Sch. 29, para. 32 for substitution of former reference to that Act.

12(1) This paragraph applies where–

(a) a claim for allowable expenditure has been made by a participator under Schedule 7 to the principal Act; and

(b) as a result of the receipt (whether before or after the making of the claim) of a qualifying receipt, the amount allowed by way of allowable expenditure on the claim exceeds what it should have been.

12(2) In determining, in a case where this paragraph applies, the assessable profit or allowable loss accruing to the participator in the chargeable period in which the qualifying receipt is received, the amount of the excess referred to in sub-paragraph (1)(b) above shall be taken into account under section 2 of the principal Act as an amount which is to be included among the positive amounts referred to in subsection (3)(a) of that section.

12(3) In the application of section 9 of the principal Act (limit on amount of tax payable) to a chargeable period in respect of which sub-paragraph (2) above applies, the amount of the excess referred to in sub-paragraph (1)(b) above shall be deducted from the amount which would otherwise be the total ascertained under subsection (2)(a)(ii) of that section and, if the amount of that excess is greater than the amount which would otherwise be that total, that total shall be a negative amount equal to the difference.

OIL TAXATION ACT 1983

(1983 Chapter 56)

[*1st December 1983*]

ARRANGEMENT OF SECTIONS

RELIEFS FOR EXPENDITURE

1 Expenditure incurred on non-dedicated mobile assets

1(1) Subject to subsection (3) below, with respect to expenditure which is or was incurred after 30th June 1982 in acquiring, bringing into existence or enhancing the value of an asset, section 4 of the principal Act (allowance of expenditure on long-term assets) shall apply only where–

(a) the asset is a mobile asset which is not dedicated to the oil field referred to in subsection (1) of that section; or

(b) the expenditure is incurred as mentioned in section 13(1)(b) below.

1(2) Where section 4 of the principal Act applies as mentioned in subsection (1)(a) above, it shall so apply with the following modifications:–

(a) in subsection (1), after the words "subsection (13) below" there shall be inserted the words "and section 1 of the Oil Taxation Act 1983" and for the words from "whose useful life" to "used" there shall be substituted the words "which, at the end of the first relevant claim period, is or is expected to be a long-term asset as defined in section 3(8) of the Oil Taxation Act 1983";

(b) subsections (3) and (4) shall be omitted;

PRT Statutes

(c) in subsection (5), paragraph (a) and the words "in any other case" in paragraph (b) shall be omitted and, in paragraph (b), for the words "that connection" there shall be substituted the words "connection with the field";

(d) subsection (6) shall be omitted;

(e) in subsection (7), for the words from the beginning to "each subsequent claim period" there shall be substituted the words "For each claim period subsequent to the first relevant claim period and" and for the words "subsections (5) and (6)" there shall be substituted the words "subsection (5)"; and

(f) in subsection (11) for the words from "subsections (5)" to "they apply" there shall be substituted the words "subsection (5) above (including that subsection as it applies".

1(3) If the asset referred to in subsection (1)(a) above becomes dedicated to the oil field referred to in subsection (1) of section 4 of the principal Act or is or becomes dedicated to another oil field,–

(a) expenditure incurred as mentioned in subsection (1) above shall not be allowable under section 4 of the principal Act for a claim period for which it is allowable under section 3 below nor, subject to paragraph (b) below, for a claim period which falls wholly or partly within a claim period of another field to which the asset is or becomes dedicated, being a claim period for which the expenditure is allowable; and

(b) where expenditure incurred in relation to the asset becomes allowable under section 3 below, no part of that expenditure shall be allowable under section 4 of the principal Act for any claim period ending less than six months before the end of a claim period for which the expenditure is allowable under section 3 below.

1(4) Paragraph 4 of Schedule 4 to the principal Act (reduction of allowable expenditure on disposal of long-term asset formerly used in connection with an oil field) does not apply to any disposal of an asset after 30th June 1982 unless the asset is a mobile asset which is not dedicated to the oil field referred to in section 4(1) of the principal Act.

Cross references – FA 1993, s. 190(1): disallowance or partial disallowance under s. 4 of the principal Act of expenditure incurred on non-dedicated mobile assets where, during claim period, asset becomes dedicated to a non-taxable field within FA 1993, s. 185(1).

2 Dedicated mobile assets

2(1) For the purposes of this Act and Part I of the principal Act a mobile asset becomes **"dedicated"** to a particular oil field in a claim period if–

(a) the asset is used in connection with that field during the whole or part of that claim period; and

(b) the asset was not, at the beginning of that period, already dedicated to that field; and

(c) at the end of that period it is reasonable to make the assumptions in subsection (2) below.

2(2) The assumptions referred to in paragraph (c) of subsection (1) above are–

(a) that during the whole or substantially the whole of the relevant period, the asset will be used in connection with the field referred to in that subsection (whether or not that use will be exclusive to that field); and

(b) that the main use of the asset during the whole of the relevant period will be in connection with that field or with two or more oil fields of which that field is one.

2(3) In any case where–

(a) at or before the time when he is a participator in an oil field, a person incurs expenditure in bringing into existence a mobile asset, and

(b) that expenditure is so incurred in a claim period for that field which is earlier than that in which the asset is first used by that person in connection with that field, and

(c) at the end of that claim period, it is reasonable to make the assumptions in subsection (2) above, and

(d) the circumstances are such that the asset is not a brought-in asset, as defined in section 4(12)(a) of the principal Act, then, as respects any claim for the allowance of the expenditure referred to in paragraph (a) above which is made before the asset is first used as mentioned in paragraph (b) above, the asset shall be regarded for the purposes of this Act and Part I of the principal Act as becoming dedicated to the oil field in question in the claim period referred to in paragraphs (b) and (c) above.

2(4) In subsection (2) above **"the relevant period"** means the period beginning at the end of the claim period referred to in subsection (1) above or, where subsection (3) above applies, at the end of the claim period in which it can reasonably be expected that the asset will be first used, and ending–

(a) at the end of the useful life of the asset, or

(b) when the winning of oil from the field in question permanently ceases,

whichever first occurs.

2(5) If, in the case of a mobile asset which would not be dedicated to a particular oil field but for the provisions of subsection (3) above, it becomes apparent at any time that it is no longer reasonable to make the assumptions in subsection (2) above, then the asset concerned shall be regarded for the purposes of this Act and Part I of the principal Act as never having been dedicated to that field; and the provisions of paragraph 9 of Schedule 5 to the principal Act (variations of decisions on claims for allowable expenditure) shall have effect accordingly.

Cross references – FA 1993, s. 190(2): modification of s. 2 in determining whether an asset becomes at any time dedicated to a non-taxable field for purposes of identifying expenditure to be disallowed under s. 4 of the principal Act.

3 Expenditure incurred on long-term assets other than non-dedicated mobile assets

3(1) Subject to section 13 below, this section applies to expenditure (whether or not of a capital nature) which is or was incurred by a person after 30th June 1982 and at or before the time when he is or was a participator in an oil field, being expenditure incurred, subject to subsection (2) below, in acquiring, bringing into existence, or enhancing the value of an asset–

(a) which, at the end of the relevant claim period, is being or is expected to be used in connection with the field; and

(b) which, at the end of the relevant claim period, is or is expected to be a long-term asset; and

(c) which either is not a mobile asset or is a mobile asset which became dedicated to that field in the relevant claim period or in any earlier claim period.

3(2) This section does not apply to expenditure incurred as mentioned in subsection (1) above in any case where the Board consider that its application to that expenditure would have only a negligible effect on the total expenditure allowable under Part I of the principal Act for the field and so notify the responsible person.

3(3) Part I of Schedule 1 to this Act shall have effect for the purpose of allowing relief for certain expenditure which would not otherwise fall within this section or, as the case may be, section 3 of the principal Act.

3(4) Except as provided by subsections (6) and (7) and sections 3A and 4 below and Part II of Schedule 1 to this Act, the whole of any expenditure to which this section applies shall be allowable on a claim under Schedule 5 or Schedule 6 to the principal Act for the relevant claim period.

3(5) The **"relevant claim period"** referred to in subsections (1) and (4) above is–

(a) the claim period which is appropriate under paragraph 2 of Schedule 5 or, as the case may be, paragraph 1 of Schedule 6 to the principal Act; or

(b) if the asset is a brought-in asset, as defined in section 4(12)(a) of the principal Act, and the expenditure has not already been allowable for an earlier claim period by virtue of paragraph (a) above, the claim period in which the asset is first used in connection with the field in question, discounting, in the case of a mobile asset, any claim period in which it was not dedicated to that field; or

(c) if the asset is a mobile asset and paragraph (b) above does not apply and the expenditure has not already been allowable for an earlier claim period by virtue of paragraph (a) above, the claim period in which the asset became dedicated to the field in question.

3(6) Subsections (3) to (5A) of section 3 of the principal Act apply for the purposes of this section and Schedule 1 to this Act as they apply for the purposes of that section; and, except in so far as section 5 below provides to the contrary, any reference to section 4 of the principal Act (but not a reference to any specific provision of that section) in–

(a) Part I of that Act,

(b) any enactment, other than this Act, which is to be construed as one with that Part, or

(c) section 107 of the Finance Act 1980 (transmedian fields),

shall be construed as including a reference to this section, section 4 below and Schedule 1 to this Act.

3(7) Section 4(13) of the principal Act (interests in assets) applies to the preceding provisions of this section and the provisions of Schedule 1 to this Act; and those provisions are subject to paragraph 2 of Schedule 4 and to Schedules 5 and 6 to the principal Act.

3(8) In this section **"long-term asset"** means an asset the useful life of which continues after the end of the claim period in which it is first used in connection with the oil field in question.

History – In s. 3(4) "sections 3A and 4" substituted for "section 4" by FA 2004, s. 285 and Sch. 37, para. 2(2), with effect in relation to expenditure incurred on or after 1 January 2004. Transitional provisions are contained in FA 2004, Sch. 37, Pt. 2.

Cross references – OTA 1975, s. 5B: relief for research expenditure incurred on or after 17 March 1987 which does not relate to any particular field.
FA 1987, s. 65 and Sch. 14: cross-field allowance of certain expenditure incurred on or after 17 March 1987.
FA 1994, s. 231: election by reference to pipe-line usage.
FA 1999, s. 95(2): cap on allowable expenditure associated with sale (on or after 9 March 1999) and leaseback of certain assets.

3A Exclusion from section 3(4) of expenditure on assets giving rise to tax-exempt tariffing receipts

3A(1) This section applies where–

(a) expenditure incurred on or after 1st January 2004 falls within section 3(1) above, but

(b) some of the use (or expected use) of the asset in relation to which the expenditure was incurred is used in a way that gives rise to tax-exempt tariffing receipts (see section 6A(2) below).

3A(2) In any such case, such part of the expenditure as it is just and reasonable to apportion to the use mentioned in subsection (1)(b) above shall be excluded from the expenditure which is allowable as mentioned in section 3(4) above.

History – S. 3A inserted by FA 2004, s. 285 and Sch. 37, para. 3, with effect in relation to expenditure incurred on or after 1 January 2004. Transitional provisions are contained in FA 2004, Sch. 37, Pt. 2.

4 Expenditure related to exempt gas and deballasting

4(1) In any case where expenditure falls within section 3(1) above, but by reason of section 10(2) of the principal Act (exempt gas) some of the use (or expected use) of the asset is not use in connection with an oil field, such part of that expenditure as it is just and reasonable to apportion to that use (or expected use) shall be excluded from the expenditure which is allowable as mentioned in section 3(4) above.

4(2) In any case where expenditure–

(a) falls within section 3(1) above, or

(b) by virtue of any provision of Part I of Schedule 1 to this Act, falls within section 3 of the principal Act,

but some of the use (or expected use) of the asset is use for deballasting, such part of that expenditure as it is just and reasonable to apportion to that use (or expected use) shall be excluded from the expenditure which is allowable as mentioned in section 3(4) above or, as the case may be, from the expenditure which is allowable under section 3 of the principal Act.

4(3) In any case where–

(a) expenditure does not fall within section 3(1) above or section 3 of the principal Act by reason only of section 10(2) of that Act (exempt gas), but

(b) the asset in relation to which the expenditure was incurred is or is expected to be used in a way which gives rise to tariff receipts,

then, so far as relates to so much of that expenditure as it is just and reasonable to apportion to the use referred to in paragraph (b) above, that use of the asset shall be treated for the purposes of section 3 above, Schedule 1 to this Act and section 3 of the principal Act as use in connection with the field from which the excluded oil, within the meaning of section 10 of the Act, is won.

4(4) References in subsection (3) above to the **"use of an asset"** (other than the final reference to use in connection with a field) include references to the provision, in connection with the use of the asset, of services or other business facilities of any kind.

4(5) In any case where–

(a) expenditure is incurred in enhancing the value of an asset with a view to the subsequent disposal of it or of an interest in it, and

(b) by reason only of section 10(2) of the principal Act (exempt gas), the expenditure does not fall within section 3(1) above or section 3 of that Act, and

(c) the subsequent disposal of, or of an interest in, the asset gives or is expected to give rise to disposal receipts,

then, such part of the use of the asset as it is just and reasonable to apportion to the expenditure referred to in paragraph (a) above shall be treated for the purposes of section 3 above, Schedule 1 to this Act and section 3 of the principal Act as use in connection with the field from which the excluded oil, within the meaning of section 10 of that Act, is won.

4(6) But where–

(a) expenditure would (apart from this subsection) fall within paragraph (a) of subsection (5) above, and

(b) the asset has, at any time in the period of 6 years ending with the date on which the expenditure was incurred, been used in a way that gives rise to tax-exempt tariffing receipts,

the expenditure shall not be regarded for the purposes of that subsection as expenditure incurred in enhancing the value of the asset with a view to the subsequent disposal of the asset, or of an interest in it, to the extent that the amount of the expenditure falls to be reduced in accordance with subsection (7) below.

4(7) The reduction is to be made by applying section 7A below in relation to the expenditure as it applies in relation to disposal receipts in respect of a disposal, but with the substitution–

(a) for references to the disponor, of references to the person incurring the expenditure ("the relevant participator"),

(b) for references to the amount or value (apart from that section) of any disposal receipts of the disponor in respect of the disposal, of references to the amount which would, apart from subsection (6) above, be the amount of the expenditure incurred by the relevant participator with a view to the subsequent disposal of the asset or of an interest in it,

(c) for references to the interest disposed of, of references to the asset or interest whose subsequent disposal gives or is expected to give rise to disposal receipts,

(d) for references to the date of the disposal, of references to the date on which the expenditure was incurred,

and taking the reference in subsection (6)(b) of that section to a reduction made by virtue of that section as a reference to a reduction made by virtue of that section for the purposes of section 7(9) of this Act.

History – S. 4(6) inserted by FA 2004, s. 285 and Sch. 37, para. 4(2), with effect in relation to expenditure incurred on or after 1 January 2004. Transitional provisions are contained in FA 2004, Sch. 37, Pt. 2.
S. 4(7) inserted by FA 2004, s. 285 and Sch. 37, para. 4(2), with effect in relation to expenditure incurred on or after 1 January 2004. Transitional provisions are contained in FA 2004, Sch. 37, Pt. 2.

5 Miscellaneous amendments relating to reliefs

5(1)–(3) [Amends OTA 1975, s. 3, in respect of expenditure incurred after 30 June 1982.]

5(4) Paragraph 1 of Schedule 4 to the principal Act (expenditure not allowable under section 3 or section 4 of that Act if relief already allowable for another person) does not apply to any expenditure which–

(a) consists of a payment made to a participator or a person connected with him; and

(b) constitutes a tariff receipt or disposal receipt of the participator.

5(5) Subsections (1) to (4) above apply with respect to expenditure which is or was incurred after 30th June 1982.

5(6) [Amends OTA 1975, Sch. 4, para. 2, in relation to expenditure incurred on or after 1 April 1983.]

5(7) Notwithstanding anything in section 3(6) above, any reference to section 4 of the principal Act in–

(a) paragraph 4 of Schedule 4 to that Act (disposal of certain long-term assets), or

(b) paragraph 2(5) or paragraph 4 of Schedule 5 to that Act (claims and appeals relating to allowance of expenditure),

does not include a reference to sections 3 and 4 above or Schedule 1 to this Act.

5(8) Paragraph 5 of Schedule 4 to the principal Act (treatment of payments for hire of assets) shall not apply in any case where the payments are or were received after 30th June 1982 (whenever the expenditure was incurred).

CHARGE OF RECEIPTS

6 Chargeable tariff receipts

6(1) In computing under section 2 of the principal Act the assessable profit or allowable loss accruing to a participator from an oil field in any chargeable period ending after 30th June 1982, the positive amounts for the purposes of that section (as specified in subsection (3)(a) thereof) shall be taken to include any tariff receipts of the participator attributable to that field for that period.

6(2) Subject to the provisions of this section and section 6A below, for the purposes of this Act the **"tariff receipts"** of a participator in an oil field which are attributable to that field for any chargeable period are the aggregate of the amount or value of any consideration (whether in the nature of income or capital) received or receivable by him in that period (and after 30th June 1982) in respect of–

(a) *the use of a qualifying asset*; or

(b) the provision of services or other business facilities of whatever kind in connection with the use, otherwise than by the participator himself, of a qualifying asset.

6(3) Any reference in this Act to the asset to which any **"tariff receipts"** are referable is a reference to the qualifying asset referred to in paragraph (a) or, as the case may be, paragraph (b) of subsection (2) above.

6(4) Notwithstanding anything in subsection (2) above, any amount which–

(a) is, in relation to the person giving it, expenditure in respect of interest or any other pecuniary obligation incurred in obtaining a loan or any other form of credit, or

(b) is referable to the use of an asset for, or the provision of services or facilities in connection with, deballasting, or

(c) is referable to other use of an asset, except use wholly or partly for an oil purpose,

does not constitute a **"tariff receipt"** for the purposes of this Act; and, accordingly, any consideration which includes such an amount shall be apportioned in such manner as is just and reasonable.

6(4A) In this section the reference to use of an asset for an oil purpose is a reference to–

(a) use in connection with an oil field, and

(b) use for any other purpose (apart from a purpose falling within section 3(1)(b) of the principal Act) of a separate trade consisting of activities falling within the definition of "oil-related activities" in section 274 of the Corporation Tax Act 2010.

6(4B) In subsection (4A) the reference to use in connection with an oil field includes use giving rise to receipts which, for the purposes of this Act, are tariff receipts.

6(5) Schedule 2 to this Act shall have effect for supplementing the provisions of this section and of sections 7 and 8 below.

History – In s. 6(2) "and section 6A below" inserted by FA 2004, s. 285(2), with effect from 22 July 2004.
S. 6(4)(c) and the word "or" at end of para. (b) inserted by FA 2009, s. 87 and Sch. 41, para. 2(2), with effect in relation to chargeable periods beginning after 30 June 2009.
In s. 6(4A)(b), the words "the definition of "oil-related activities" in section 274 of the Corporation Tax Act 2010" substituted for the words "section 492(1) of the Income and Corporation Taxes Act 1988" by CTA 2010, s. 1177 and Sch. 1, para. 181, with effect for corporation tax purposes for accounting periods ending on or after 1 April 2010, and for income tax and capital gains tax purposes for the tax year 2010–11 and subsequent tax years.
S. 6(4A) inserted by FA 2009, s. 87 and Sch. 41, para. 2(3), with effect in relation to chargeable periods beginning after 30 June 2009.
S. 6(4B) inserted by FA 2009, s. 87 and Sch. 41, para. 2(3), with effect in relation to chargeable periods beginning after 30 June 2009.
Cross references – FA 1982, Sch. 19, para. 3(1A): PRT instalments.

6A Tax-exempt tariffing receipts

6A(1) An amount which is a tax-exempt tariffing receipt (see subsection (2) below) does not constitute a tariff receipt for the purposes of the Oil Taxation Acts.

6A(2) An amount is a "tax-exempt tariffing receipt" for the purposes of the Oil Taxation Acts if–

(a) it would, apart from this section, be a tariff receipt of a participator in an oil field,

(b) it is received or receivable by the participator in a chargeable period ending on or after 30th June 2004 under a contract entered into on or after 9th April 2003, and

(c) it is in respect of tax-exempt business (see subsection (3) below).

6A(3) For the purposes of this section an amount is in respect of tax-exempt business if it is an amount received or receivable by a participator in an oil field in respect of–

(a) the use of a qualifying asset, or

(b) the provision of services or other business facilities of whatever kind in connection with the use, otherwise than by the participator himself, of a qualifying asset,

and that use of the qualifying asset falls within subsection (4) below.

6A(4) Use of a qualifying asset falls within this subsection if it is–

(a) use in relation to a new field (see subsection (5) below) or oil won from such a field, or

(b) use in relation to a qualifying existing field (see subsection (5) below) or oil won from such a field or

(c) use in relation to a UK recommissioned field (see subsection (5) below) or oil won from such a field.

6A(5) In this section–

"existing field" means any oil field or foreign field which is not a new field;

"foreign field" means, subject to subsection (6) below (treatment of transmedian fields), any hydrocarbon accumulation which is not under the jurisdiction of the government of the United Kingdom;

"licensee," in relation to a foreign field, means a person who has rights, interests or obligations in respect of the foreign field under a licence or other authority granted by the government of a country other than the United Kingdom;

"new field" means–

(a) an oil field for no part of which had–

(i) *consent* for development been granted to a licensee by the Secretary of State before 9th April 2003; or

(ii) a programme of development been served on a licensee or approved by the Secretary of State before that date; or

(b) a foreign field for no part of which had–
  (i) any consent for development been granted to a licensee by the government of a country other than the United Kingdom before 9th April 2003; or
  (ii) a programme of development been served on a licensee or approved by such a government before that date;

and subsections (4) and (5) of section 36 of the Finance Act 1983 (which define "development" for the purposes of subsections (2) and (3) of that section) shall apply also for the purposes of this definition;

"the Oil Taxation Acts" means–

(a) Parts 1 and 3 of the principal Act;

(b) this Act; and

(c) any other enactment relating to petroleum revenue tax;

"qualifying existing field" means an existing field as respects which the condition in section 6B(1) below is satisfied.

"UK recommissioned field" means any oil field which is not a new field or qualifying existing field but as respects which the conditions in section 185(1A) of the Finance Act 1993 are satisfied (fields recommissioned after earlier decommissioning).

6A(6) For the purposes of this section, in the case of an oil field which, by virtue of section 107 of the Finance Act 1980 (transmedian fields), is deemed to include the sector mentioned in subsection (1)(a)(ii) of that section–

(a) that sector shall be treated as a foreign field, and

(b) the remainder of that field shall be treated as a separate oil field.

6A(7) In the application of provisions of the Oil Taxation Acts relating to tax-exempt tariffing receipts, references to oil, in relation to a foreign field, are references to any substance that would be oil within the meaning of the principal Act if the enactments mentioned in section 1(1) of that Act extended to the foreign field.

6A(8) This section is subject to the transitional provisions in Part 2 of Schedule 35 to the Finance Act 2004 (expenditure incurred between 9th April and 31st December 2003: treatment of initial portion of tax-exempt tariffing receipts as tariff receipts).

History – S. 6A(4)(c), and the word "or" immediately preceding it, inserted by FA 2007, s. 103(2) with effect from 1 July 2007, FA 2007, s. 103(4).
In s. 6A(5) the definition of "UK recommissioned field" inserted by FA 2007, s. 103(3) with effect from 1 July 2007, FA 2007, s. 103(4).
S. 6A inserted by FA 2004, s. 285(3), with effect from 22 July 2004.

6B The condition for being a qualifying existing field

6B(1) The condition for an existing field to be a qualifying existing field for the purposes of section 6A above is that at no time in the period of 6 years ending with 8th April 2003 ("the 6 year period") was there–

(a) any use of a disqualifying asset (see subsection (2) below) in a UK area (see subsection (11) below) in relation to the field or oil won from it, or

(b) any provision of any services or other business facilities of whatever kind in connection with the use of a disqualifying asset in a UK area in relation to the field or oil won from it.

6B(2) For the purposes of subsection (1) above **"disqualifying asset"**, in relation to an existing field and any time in the 6 year period, means an asset which at that time–

(a) was a qualifying asset in relation to a participator in an oil field; and

(b) was not an excepted asset (see subsection (3) below).

6B(3) For the purposes of subsection (2) above **"excepted asset"**, in relation to an existing field and any time in the 6 year period, means any of the following–

(a) any asset (other than a tanker) which at that time was wholly situated in the existing field;

(b) any tanker which at that time was a non-dedicated tanker (see subsection (10) below) being used for transporting from the existing field oil which had been won from that field;

(c) any asset which at that time was being used in relation to oil which had been won from the existing field and transported from that field by a non-dedicated tanker;

(d) if the existing field is an oil field and is expected not to be a tanker loading field (see subsection (7) below)–
  (i) any tanker which at that time was a dedicated tanker (see subsection (9) below) being used for transporting from the existing field oil which had been won from that field;

PRT Statutes

(ii) any asset which at that time was being used in relation to oil which had been won from the existing field and transported from that field by a dedicated tanker;

(iii) any asset which at that time was being used to transport from the existing field oil consisting of gas won from that field to another oil field for the purpose of enabling that oil to be used for assisting the extraction of oil from that other field;

(e) if at that time the existing field was not a taxable field, any asset by reference to which an election under section 231 of the Finance Act 1994 (election by reference to asset with excess capacity) was at that time in operation with respect to an oil field.

6B(4) Where any use of an asset is, by virtue of subsection (3) above, use of an excepted asset, the provision of any services or other business facilities of whatever kind in connection with that use of that asset accordingly falls to be disregarded for the purposes of subsection (1)(b) above.

6B(5) Where an asset in a UK area–

(a) is a qualifying asset in relation to a participator in such an oil field as is mentioned in section 107 of the Finance Act 1980 (a "participator in the UK sector"), and

(b) is also, by virtue of paragraph 3 of Schedule 4 to this Act, a chargeable asset in relation to a participator in a foreign field (a "participator in the foreign sector"),

subsection (6) below applies in relation to use of the asset in relation to the existing field or oil won from it.

6B(6) Where this subsection applies, then, in determining for the purposes of subsection (1) above whether there has been any use of a disqualifying asset in relation to the existing field or oil won from it, any use of the asset in relation to that field or oil won from it shall be treated–

(a) as use of a qualifying asset in relation to a participator in an oil field, if or to the extent that the use is attributable, on a just and reasonable basis, to a participator in the UK sector, or

(b) as use of an asset which was not a qualifying asset in relation to a participator in an oil field, if or to the extent that the use is attributable, on a just and reasonable basis, to a participator in the foreign sector.

6B(7) For the purposes of subsection (3) above, the existing field is expected not to be a tanker loading field if, at the time when the relevant contract is entered into, it is expected that all (or virtually all) of the oil (other than oil consisting of gas) to be won from that field and transported from it after the beginning of the operational period will be so transported otherwise than by tanker.

6B(8) For the purposes of subsection (7) above–

(a) **"the relevant contract"** means the contract mentioned in section 6A(2)(b) above; and

(b) **"the beginning of the operational period"** means the time at which the qualifying asset to which that contract relates begins to be used under that contract in relation to the existing field or oil won from that field.

6B(9) For the purposes of subsection (3) above a tanker is a dedicated tanker at any time if–

(a) the existing field mentioned in that subsection is an oil field, and

(b) at that time the tanker is a mobile asset dedicated to that oil field (see section 2 above).

6B(10) For the purposes of subsection (3) above a tanker is a non-dedicated tanker–

(a) at any time, if the existing field mentioned in that subsection is not an oil field, or

(b) where that field is an oil field, at any time when the tanker is not a mobile asset dedicated to that oil field.

6B(11) In this section **"UK area"** means each of the following–

(a) the United Kingdom;

(b) the territorial sea of the United Kingdom;

(c) a designated area, to the extent that it does not fall to be treated by virtue of section 6A(6) above as a foreign field.

6B(12) This section shall be construed as one with section 6A above.

History – S. 6B inserted by FA 2004, s. 285(3), with effect from 22 July 2004.

7 Chargeable receipts from disposals

7(1) In computing under section 2 of the principal Act the assessable profit or allowable loss accruing to a participator from an oil field in any chargeable period ending after 30th June 1982, the positive amounts for the purposes of that section (as specified in subsection (3)(a) thereof) shall be taken to include any disposal receipts of the participator attributable to that field for that period.

7(2) Subject to the provisions of this section, for the purposes of this Act the disposal receipts of a participator in an oil field which are attributable to that field for any chargeable period are the aggregate of the amount or value of any consideration received or receivable by him in respect of the disposal in that period of a qualifying asset or of an interest in such an asset.

7(3) Where there is such a redetermination as is mentioned in subsection (4) of section 107 of the Finance Act 1980 (transmedian fields) and in consequence thereof the participators in the field receive a repayment, credit or set-off in respect of expenditure which was incurred in acquiring, bringing into existence or enhancing the value of a qualifying asset or an interest in it, the repayment shall be regarded as consideration received as mentioned in subsection (2) above in respect of the disposal of an interest in the asset.

7(4) No account shall be taken under subsection (2) above of any disposal of, or of an interest in, a qualifying asset which takes place more than two years after the time at which the asset–

(a) ceases to be used in connection with any oil field whatsoever, or

(b) ceases to give rise to tariff receipts of the participator referred to in that subsection, or

(c) ceases to give rise to tax-exempt tariffing receipts of that participator,

whichever is the latest.

7(5) Notwithstanding anything in subsection (2) or subsection (3) above, any amount which, in relation to the person paying it,–

(a) is expenditure in respect of interest or any other pecuniary obligation incurred in obtaining a loan or any other form of credit, or

(b) is a payment made for the purpose of obtaining a direct or indirect interest in oil won or to be won from an oil field,

does not constitute a disposal receipt for the purposes of this Act; and accordingly, any consideration which includes such an amount shall be apportioned in such manner as is just and reasonable.

7(6) If in any claim period a qualifying asset gives rise to disposal receipts of a participator and any expenditure incurred by the participator is expenditure which in that period qualifies for supplement under paragraph (b)(ii) or paragraph (c)(ii) of subsection (9) of section 2 of the principal Act, then, except in so far as it is expenditure falling within section 111(7) of the Finance Act 1981 (certain expenditure incurred before 1st January 1983),–

(a) the amount which, apart from this subsection, would in his case be taken into account under either or both of those paragraphs shall be reduced by deducting therefrom a fraction thereof determined under subsection (7) below or, if that fraction exceeds unity, shall be taken to be nil; and

(b) references in subsections (2) and (3) of section 9 of the principal Act (limit on amount of tax payable) to expenditure which was not allowed as qualifying for supplement under section 2(9)(b)(ii) or (c)(ii) shall be construed accordingly.

7(7) For the claim period referred to in subsection (6) above, the fraction referred to in paragraph (a) of that subsection is that of which–

(a) the numerator, subject to subsection (8) below, is the disposal receipts of the participator in question for that period in respect of the qualifying asset referred to in subsection (6) above or, if it is less, the expenditure allowed or allowable to the participator in respect of that asset under section 3 above or section 4 of the principal Act; and

(b) the denominator is so much of the total amount of expenditure allowable for the field on a claim for the claim period referred to in subsection (6) above as, in the case of the participator in question, falls to be taken into account under paragraphs (b)(i) and (c)(i) of subsection (9) of section 2 of the principal Act;

and in paragraph (b) above **"allowable"** means allowable under section 3 or section 4 of the principal Act or under section 3 above.

7(8) If the disposal receipts in question relate to a disposal of an interest in the asset, rather than the asset itself, then the reference in subsection (7)(a) above to certain expenditure shall be construed as a reference to such proportion only of that expenditure as it is just and reasonable to apportion to the interest disposed of.

7(9) In determining the amount or value of the disposal receipts of the participator in question in a case where the qualifying asset has been used in a way that gives rise to tax-exempt tariffing receipts, the amount or value (apart from this subsection) of any disposal receipts of his in respect of the disposal shall be reduced in accordance with section 7A below.

History – In s. 7(4) "or" inserted at the end of para. (b), and para. (c) inserted, and in the closing words "latest" substituted for "later" by FA 2004, s. 285 and Sch. 37, para. 5(2), with effect in relation to disposals in chargeable periods ending on or after 30 June 2004. Transitional provisions are contained in FA 2004, Sch. 37, Pt. 2.

S. 7(9) inserted by FA 2004, s. 285 and Sch. 37, para. 5(3), with effect in relation to disposals in chargeable periods ending on or after 30 June 2004. Transitional provisions are contained in FA 2004, Sch. 37, Pt. 2.

Cross references – FA 1980, Sch. 17, para. 19: s. 7 does not apply to disposals in pursuance of transfers of interests in fields.

Notes – FA 1999, s. 98(3)(c): qualifying assets where s. 7 does not apply to the disposal.

7A Reduction of disposal receipts: use giving rise to tax-exempt tariffing receipts

7A(1) Where this section applies, the amount or value (apart from this section) of any disposal receipts of the participator (**"the disponor"**) in respect of the disposal shall be reduced in accordance with the following provisions of this section.

7A(2) The reduction is to be made by multiplying that amount or value by the fraction that is equal to–

$$1 - \frac{T}{A}$$

7A(3) In that formula–

T is the aggregate of the tax-exempt tariffing use of the asset in the reference period by–

(a) the disponor, so far as referable to the interest disposed of, and

(b) each of the previous owners, so far as referable to that previous owner's represented interest, and

A is the aggregate of all use of the asset in the reference period by–

(a) the disponor, so far as referable to the interest disposed of, and

(b) each of the previous owners, so far as referable to that previous owner's represented interest,

but only taking into account for this purpose use of the asset by a person at a time when he is or was a participator in a taxable field.

7A(4) For the purposes of this section–

"the interest disposed of" means the asset, or the interest in an asset, the disposal of which gives rise to the disposal receipts mentioned in sub-section (1) above;

"previous owner" means any person from whom the disponor directly or indirectly derives his title to the whole or any part of the interest disposed of;

"the reference period" means the shorter of the following periods ending with the date of the disposal–

(a) the period of 6 years; or

(b) the period beginning with the bringing into existence of the asset;

"represented interest", in the case of a previous owner, means so much of the interest which that previous owner had in the asset as is represented in the interest disposed of;

"tax-exempt tariffing use", in relation to an asset, means use of the asset in a way that gives rise to tax-exempt tariffing receipts.

7A(5) Any apportionment that falls to be made for the purpose of determining a previous owner's represented interest shall be made using a method which is just and reasonable, having regard to–

(a) the proportion of any person's interest that was acquired from any particular person, and

(b) the proportion of any person's interest that was transferred to any particular person.

7A(6) Where–

(a) the disponor or any previous owner acquired the asset or an interest in the asset from another person, and

(b) on that other person's corresponding disposal of the asset or interest a reduction was made by virtue of this section,

use of the asset shall not be brought into account in determining T or A in the formula in subsection (2) above to the extent that it was so brought into account in relation to that corresponding disposal.

7A(7) Where paragraph 9 of Schedule 2 to this Act (reduction of disposal receipts in respect of brought-in assets) applies in relation to an asset, no account shall be taken for the purposes of this section of any use of the asset during the initial period.

In this subsection **"the initial period"**, in relation to an asset, has the same meaning as it has in relation to that asset in paragraph 7 of Schedule 1 to this Act (restriction on allowable expenditure on brought-in asset).

7A(8) For the purposes of this section, the amount of use of an asset–

(a) where the use is in relation to oil, is to be determined by reference to the volume of oil in relation *to which the asset is used*, and

(b) where the use is otherwise than in relation to oil, is to be determined on a just and reasonable basis.

7A(9) For the purposes of this section, the extent to which use of an asset is referable to–

(a) the interest disposed of, or

(b) the represented interest of a previous owner,

shall be determined on a just and reasonable basis, having regard to the size of the interest in question and the size from time to time of the whole interest in the asset of the disponor or, as the case may be, that previous owner.

History – S. 7A inserted by FA 2004, s. 285 and Sch. 37, para. 5(4), with effect in relation to disposals in chargeable periods ending on or after 30 June 2004. Transitional provisions are contained in FA 2004, Sch. 37, Pt. 2.

8 Qualifying assets

8(1) Subject to paragraph 4 of Schedule 2 to this Act, for the purposes of this Act a **"qualifying asset"**, in relation to a participator in an oil field, means, subject to subsection (1A) below, an asset–

(a) which either is not a mobile asset or is a mobile asset dedicated to that oil field; and

(b) in respect of which expenditure incurred by the participator is allowable, or has been allowed, for that field under section 3 above, section 4 of the principal Act or, subject to subsection (2) below, section 3 of that Act.

8(1A) Notwithstanding anything in subsection (1) above, the following assets are not qualifying assets for the purposes of this Act, namely,–

(a) land or an interest in land; and

(b) a building or structure which is situated on land and which does not fall within any of sub-paragraphs (i) to (iv) of paragraph (c) of subsection (4) of section 3 of the principal Act.

8(2) If, in respect of any asset, the only expenditure which falls within subsection (1)(b) above is expenditure allowable or allowed under section 3 of the principal Act, the asset shall not be a qualifying asset unless, at the time the expenditure was incurred, it was expected that the useful life of the asset would continue after the end of the claim period in which the asset was to be first used in a way which would constitute use in connection with an oil field for the purposes of that section.

8(3) Subject to subsection (4) below, the oil field to which are attributable tariff receipts or disposal receipts referable to a qualifying asset is that field for which the expenditure referred to in subsection (1)(b) above is allowable; and, if there is more than one such field, then,–

(a) in the case of a mobile asset, no account shall be taken of a field to which it is not dedicated; and

(b) no account shall be taken of a field in relation to which the asset is a qualifying asset by virtue only of paragraph 1 of Schedule 1 to this Act; and

(c) subject to paragraphs (a) and (b) above and subsection (3A) below, it is that one of those fields in relation to which a development decision was first made;

and subsection (7) of section 5A of the principal Act (time when development decision is made) shall have effect for the purposes of paragraph (c) above and subsection (3A) below as it has effect for the purposes of subsection (1)(c) of that section.

8(3A) If development decisions were first made in relation to two or more oil fields on the same day, then, for the purposes of subsection (3)(c) above, it shall be conclusively presumed that the first of those decisions was made in relation to that one of those fields in connection with which it appeared–

(a) at the time of the decision, or

(b) if it is later, at the time the asset was acquired or brought into existence by the participator in question for use in connection with an oil field,

that the participator in question would make the most use of the asset.

8(4) In the case of an asset which, in relation to the participator in question, is a qualifying asset by virtue only of paragraph 1 of Schedule 1 to this Act, the oil field to which are attributable tariff receipts or disposal receipts referable to the asset is that to which (in accordance with subsection (3) above) those receipts would be attributable if they were referable to the other asset referred to in sub-paragraph (1)(d) of that paragraph (that is to say, the asset in association with which the first asset is, or is expected to be, used).

8(5) In relation to a qualifying asset or the tariff receipts or disposal receipts referable to it, in this Act **"chargeable field"** means the field referred to in subsection (3) or, as the case may be, subsection (4) above.

History – In s. 8(1), the words "subject to subsection (1A) below", and s. 8(1A), were inserted by FA 1985, s. 92(1), (2), in respect of consideration received or receivable after 19 March 1985. In s. 8(3), the words "and subsection 3A below" in both places, and s. 8(3A), were inserted by FA 1986, s. 110(2), (3), with retrospective effect.

Cross references – FA 1999, s. 98(1) and (3): qualifying assets.

9 Tariff receipts allowance

9(1) Subject to the provisions of this section and Schedule 3 to this Act if, in computing the assessable profit or allowable loss accruing to a participator from an oil field (in this section referred to as **"the principal field"**) in any chargeable period, account would be taken, apart from this section, of an amount of qualifying tariff receipts received or receivable by him for that period from a user field, then, for the purpose of determining his liability (if any) to tax for that period, the amount of those qualifying tariff receipts shall be treated as reduced as follows, that is to say,–

(a) if that amount exceeds the cash equivalent of his share of the tariff receipts allowance in respect of that user field for that period, to an amount equal to the excess; or

(b) if that amount equals the cash equivalent of his share of that allowance, to nil.

9(2) Subject to subsection (4) below, for the participators in the principal field there shall be, for each chargeable period, a separate tariff receipts allowance of 250,000 metric tonnes in respect of each user field.

9(3) [Omitted by FA 2009, s. 91 and Sch. 45, para. 2(2).]

9(4) Schedule 3 to this Act shall have effect–

(a) for determining for the purposes of this section the cash equivalent of a participator's share of the tariff receipts allowance in respect of a user field for a chargeable period; and

(b) generally for supplementing subsections (1) and (2) above.

9(5) Any reference in this section or in Schedule 3 to this Act to a **"user field"** is a reference–

(a) to an oil field other than–

(i) the principal field, or

(ii) an oil field that is a non-taxable field by virtue of section 185(1) or (1A) of the Finance Act 1993.

(b) to an area which is not under the jurisdiction of the government of the United Kingdom but which, by an order made by statutory instrument by the Secretary of State for the purposes of this Act, is specified as a foreign field.

9(5A) No order may be made under subsection (5)(b) above on or after 1st July 1993.

9(6) In this section–

(a) **"qualifying tariff receipts"** means tariff receipts in relation to which the principal field is the chargeable field and which are attributable to, or to the provision of services or other business facilities in connection with, the use of any asset for extracting, transporting, initially treating or initially storing oil won otherwise than from the principal field; and

(b) any reference to **"qualifying tariff receipts received from a user field"** is a reference to any of those receipts which are received from a participator in the user field in respect of the use of an asset for extracting, transporting, initially treating or initially storing oil won from that field or the provision of services or other business facilities in connection with that use;

and, for the purposes of this section and Schedule 3 to this Act, an oil field which, by virtue of section 107 of the Finance Act 1980 (transmedian fields), is deemed to include the sector mentioned in subsection (1)(a)(ii) of that section, shall be treated as two separate oil fields, one being that sector and the other being the rest of the field.

9(7) In relation to any user field which is not an oil field within the meaning of the principal Act,–

(a) references to **"oil"** are references to any substance that would be oil within the meaning of that Act if the enactments mentioned in section 1(1) thereof extended to the user field; and

(b) references to a **"participator"** are references to a person who is, or has rights, interests or obligations of, a licensee in respect of the user field under the law of a country outside the United Kingdom.

9(8) [Amendments to FA 1981, s. 111, with respect to chargeable periods ending after 1st July 1982.]

9(9) For the purposes of this section and Schedule 3 to this Act 1,100 cubic metres of oil consisting of gas at the temperature and pressure mentioned in section 1(4) of the principal Act shall be counted as equivalent to one metric tonne of oil other than gas.

9(10) In any case where there is in force a scheme which, for the purposes of section 108 of the Finance Act 1980 (gas banking schemes) is either a gas banking scheme or an international gas banking scheme, then, whether or not an election is made under that section, in determining for the purposes of this section and Schedule 3 to this Act what oil is won from a particular user field, oil consisting of gas which is transferred to a user field pursuant to the scheme shall be treated as won from that field.

History – In s. 9(2), the words "subsection (4)" substituted for the words "subsections (3) and (4)" by FA 2009, s. 91 and Sch. 45, para. 2(23)(a), with effect from 21 July 2009.

S. 9(3) omitted by FA 2009, s. 91 and Sch. 45, para. 2(2), with effect from 21 July 2009.

In s. 9(4)(b), the words "subsections (1) and (2)" substituted for the words "subsections (1) to (3)" by FA 2009, s. 91 and Sch. 45, para. 2(23)(b), with effect from 21 July 2009.

In s. 9(5)(a), the words "other than–" and sub-paragraphs (i) and (ii) substituted for the words "other than the principal field or a non-taxable field; or" by FA 2008, s. 107 and Sch. 33, para. 4, with effect from 21 July 2008.

In s. 9(5)(a), words "or a non-taxable field" inserted by FA 1993, s. 193(1).

S. 9(5A), inserted by FA 1993, s. 193(1).

Cross references – FA 1981, s. 111(3)(d): restriction of expenditure supplement where qualifying tariff receipts received.
FA 1993, s. 185(1): a "non-taxable field" is an oil field granted development consent by the Secretary of State on or after 16 March 1993, and a "taxable field" is an oil field which is not a non-taxable field.
FA 1993, s. 193(2): disallowance of expenditure which, in the hands of the recipient, constitutes tariff receipts or disposal receipts of a participator in a non-taxable field.
Statutory instruments – SI 1986/1644: made under s. 9(5).
SI 1986/1645: made under s. 9(5).
SI 1987/545: made under s. 9(5).
SI 1989/2384: made under s. 9(5).
SI 1991/1982: made under s. 9(5).
SI 1991/1983: made under s. 9(5).
SI 1991/1984: made under s. 9(5).
SI 1993/1408: made under s. 9(5).
SI 1993/1566: made under s. 9(5).
Extra-statutory concessions – I4: s. 9(5) tariff receipts allowance in respect of foreign "user" fields.

10 Returns relating to tariff and disposal receipts

10(1) A return made by a participator in an oil field under paragraph 2 of Schedule 2 to the principal Act shall contain the following particulars–

(a) a statement of the amount or value and the source of any tariff receipts or disposal receipts of the participator which are attributable to that field for the chargeable period to which the return relates; and

(b) a statement of the assets to which any such tariff receipts or disposal receipts are referable; and

(c) such other particulars as the Board may prescribe with respect to any such tariff receipts or disposal receipts.

10(2) In any case where,–

(a) before the commencement of this Act, a participator in an oil field has made a return under paragraph 2 of Schedule 2 to the principal Act in respect of a chargeable period, and

(b) if subsection (1) above had been in force at the time that the return was made, the return would have been required to contain the particulars referred to in paragraphs (a) to (c) of that subsection,

the participator shall prepare and before 30th June 1984 deliver to the Board a supplementary return for that chargeable period identifying it and containing those particulars.

10(3) Paragraphs 2(4) and 3 of Schedule 2 to the principal Act shall apply in relation to a supplementary return under subsection (2) above with the substitution of a reference to that subsection for the reference in paragraph 3(1) to paragraph 2(1) of that Schedule.

10(4) [Amends OTA 1975, Sch. 2, para. 5, with respect to chargeable periods ending after 1 December 1983.]

10(5) In the return under paragraph 5 of Schedule 2 to the principal Act for the chargeable period ending on 30th June 1984, the Board may require the responsible person to include particulars required for determining the amount by which any qualifying tariff receipts, within the meaning of section 9 above, are to be treated as reduced by virtue of that section for earlier chargeable periods.

10(6) [Amends PRTA 1980, Schedule.]

12 Charge of receipts attributable to UK use of foreign field asset

12(1) The provisions of Schedule 4 to this Act have effect for the purpose of bringing into charge to tax the amount or value of certain consideration (whether in the nature of income or capital) which is received or receivable after 30th June 1982 by a participator in a foreign field–

(a) in respect of the United Kingdom use of a field asset; or

(b) in respect of the provision, in connection with the United Kingdom use of a field asset, of services or other business facilities of whatever kind; or

(c) in respect of the disposal of a field asset or an interest in such an asset where either the asset has already been in United Kingdom use or it is reasonable to expect that, after the disposal, the asset will be in United Kingdom use.

12(2) In this section and Schedule 4 to this Act–

(a) **"foreign field"** means, subject to subsection (3) below, an area which is not under the jurisdiction of the government of the United Kingdom but which, by an order made by statutory instrument by the Secretary of State for the purposes of this Act, is specified as a foreign field; and

(b) in relation to a foreign field, **"participator"** means a person who is, or has rights, interests or obligations of, a licensee in respect of the foreign field under the law of a country outside the United Kingdom.

12(3) For the purposes of this section and Schedule 4 to this Act, in the case of an oil field which is a taxable field and which, by virtue of section 107 of the Finance Act 1980 (transmedian fields) is deemed to include the sector mentioned in subsection (1)(a)(ii) of that section–

(a) that sector shall be treated as a foreign field; and

(b) the remainder of that field shall be treated as a separate oil field.

12(3A) No order may be made under subsection (2)(a) above on or after 1st July 1993.

12(4) In this section and Schedule 4 to this Act–

(a) **"field asset"**, in relation to a foreign field, means an asset which–

(i) is not a mobile asset, and

(ii) is situated in the United Kingdom, the territorial sea thereof or a designated area, and

(iii) subject to subsection (6) below, is, has been or is expected to be used in a way which, on the assumptions in subsection (5) below, would be use in connection with the foreign field; and

(b) **"United Kingdom use"**, in relation to a field asset, means the use of the asset in connection with the exploration or exploitation of so much of the seabed and subsoil and their natural resources as is situated in the territorial sea of the United Kingdom or a designated area.

12(5) The assumptions referred to in subsection (4)(a) above are–

(a) that every foreign field is situated in a designated area and is an oil field within the meaning of Part I of the principal Act; and

(b) that references in Part I of the principal Act to **"oil"** are references to any substance that would be oil if the enactments mentioned in section 1(1) thereof extended to the foreign field.

12(6) For the purposes of this section and Schedule 4 to this Act an asset which falls within sub-paragraphs (i) and (ii) of paragraph (a) of subsection (4) above but does not fall within sub-paragraph (iii) of that paragraph is nevertheless a field asset if–

(a) its use gives rise or is expected to give rise to consideration which, assuming the asset to be a field asset, would fall within subsection (1) above; and

(b) its useful life continues, or is expected to continue, for more than six months after the time at which the consideration referred to in paragraph (a) above is first received or receivable; and

(c) it is, or is expected to be, used in association with another asset which is a field asset.

12(7) For the purposes of subsection (6)(c) above, an asset shall not be regarded as used in association with a field asset unless it is so used in a way which constitutes use in connection with an oil field or would constitute such use but for section 10(2) of the principal Act (exempt gas).

History – In s. 12(3), words "which is a taxable field and" inserted by FA 1993, s. 193(4).
S. 12(3A) inserted by FA 1993, s. 193(5).

Cross references – FA 1986, s. 108(1), (2): construction of references to "subsoil", "territorial sea" and "United Kingdom" on or after 1 April 1986.
FA 1993, s. 185(1): a "non-taxable field" is an oil field granted development consent by the Secretary of State on or after 16 March 1993, and a "taxable field" is an oil field which is not a non-taxable field.
FA 1993, s. 193(2): disallowance of expenditure which, in the hands of the recipient, constitutes tariff receipts or disposal receipts of a participator in a non-taxable field.
FA 1993, s. 194(1): modified application of ICTA 1988, s. 788 in giving double taxation relief from charge to PRT of receipts attributable to UK use of foreign field assets.

Statutory instruments – SI 1986/1644: made under s. 12(2).
SI 1986/1645: made under s. 12(2).
SI 1987/545: made under s. 12(2).
SI 1989/2384: made under s. 12(2).
SI 1991/1982: made under s. 12(2).
SI 1991/1983: made under s. 12(2).
SI 1991/1984: made under s. 12(2).
SI 1993/1408: made under s. 12(2).
SI 1993/1566: made under s. 12(2).

SUPPLEMENTARY

14 Re-opening of decisions for periods before the passing of this Act

14 In any case where, before the passing of this Act,–

(a) notice has been given of a decision on a claim for a claim period which is, or is subsequent to, the transitional claim period, as defined in Schedule 5 to this Act, and

(b) if this Act had been in force at the beginning of that claim period, the decision would have been different,

then, for the purpose of giving effect to the provisions of this Act, paragraph 9 of Schedule 5 to the principal Act (variation of decisions on claims for allowable expenditure) shall have effect whether or not notice of the decision of the Board was given as mentioned in sub-paragraph (11) of that paragraph.

15 Short title, interpretation, construction and repeals

15(1) This Act may be cited as the Oil Taxation Act 1983.

15(2) In this Act **"the principal Act"** means the Oil Taxation Act 1975.

15(3) In this Act–

"chargeable field" shall be construed in accordance with section 8(5) above;

"disposal receipts" shall be construed in accordance with section 7(2) above;

"qualifying asset" shall be construed in accordance with section 8 above; and

"tariff receipts" shall be construed, subject to Schedule 5 to this Act, in accordance with section 6(2) above.

15(4) Section 1122 of the Corporation Tax Act 2010 (**"connected persons"**) applies for the purposes of this Act.

15(5) This Act shall be construed as one with Part I of the principal Act.

History – In s. 15(3), the words "section 8" were substituted by FA 1985, s. 92(3).
In s. 15(4), the words "Section 1122 of the Corporation Tax Act 2010" substituted for the words "Section 839 of the Taxes Act" by CTA 2010, s. 1177 and Sch. 1, para. 182, with effect for corporation tax purposes for accounting periods ending on or after 1 April 2010, and for income tax and capital gains tax purposes for the tax year 2010–11 and subsequent tax years.
See ICTA 1988, s. 844 and Sch. 29, para. 32 for substitution of former reference to that Act in s. 15(4).

SCHEDULES

SCHEDULE 1 – ALLOWABLE EXPENDITURE

Section 3

Part I – Extensions of Allowable Expenditure for Assets Generating Receipts

ASSOCIATED ASSETS

1(1) This paragraph applies where, after 30th June 1982, a participator in an oil field (in this paragraph referred to as **"the principal field"**) incurs or incurred expenditure in acquiring, bringing into existence or enhancing the value of an asset–

(a) which is not a mobile asset and which, apart from this paragraph, does not fall within subsection (1)(a) of section 3 of this Act; and

(b) the use of which gives rise, or is expected to give rise, to receipts which, assuming the asset to be a qualifying asset, would be tariff receipts; and

(c) the useful life of which continues, or is expected to continue, after the end of the first chargeable period in which the receipts referred to in paragraph (b) above arise; and

(d) which is, or is expected to be, used in association with another asset which itself is, has been, or is expected to be, used in connection with the principal field;

and, where this paragraph applies, the asset on which the expenditure is or was incurred is in the following provisions of this paragraph referred to as **"the associated asset"**.

1(2) Subject to section 4(2) of this Act, for the purposes of section 3 of this Act, Part II below and section 3 of the principal Act, the use of the associated asset to give rise to the receipts referred to in sub-paragraph (1)(b) above shall be assumed to be use in connection with the principal field.

1(3) For the purposes of this paragraph, an asset shall not be regarded as **"used in association with another asset"** which is, has been or is expected to be used in connection with the principal field unless it is used in a way–

(a) which constitutes use in connection with another oil field; or

(b) which would constitute such use but for section 10(2) of the principal Act (exempt gas); or

(c) which, on the assumptions in sub-paragraph (4) below, would constitute use in connection with an external field;

and for the purposes of paragraph (c) above, an **"external field"** is an area which is not under the jurisdiction of the government of the United Kingdom.

1(4) The assumptions referred to in sub-paragraph (3)(c) above are–

(a) that every external field is situated in a designated area and is an oil field within the meaning of Part I of the principal Act; and

(b) that references in Part I of the principal Act to **"oil"** are references to any substance that would be oil if the enactments mentioned in section 1(1) thereof extended to the external field;

(c) [Repealed by F(No. 2)A 1992, s. 74 and Sch. 15, para. 6, s. 82 and Sch. 18, Pt. VIII.]

History – In para. 1(4)(b), the word "and", and para. 1(4)(c), repealed by F(No. 2)A 1992, s. 74 and Sch. 15, para. 6 and by s. 82 and Sch. 18, Pt. VIII, in accordance with s. 74(5) of that Act.

RESTRICTION OF RELIEF FOR REMOTE ASSOCIATED ASSETS

2(1) The provisions of this paragraph apply where some part of the associated asset is situated more than 100 metres from the nearest part of another asset–

(a) in association with which the associated asset is or is expected to be used; and

(b) which is, has been or is expected to be used in a way which, otherwise than by virtue of paragraph 1 above, constitutes use in connection with the principal field;

and sub-paragraphs (3) and (4) of paragraph 1 above have effect for the purposes of this sub-paragraph as they have effect for the purposes of that paragraph.

2(2) In sub-paragraph (1) above,–

(a) **"the associated asset"** has the meaning assigned to it by sub-paragraph (1) of paragraph 1 above;

(b) **"the principal field"** has the same meaning as in that paragraph;

and where the associated asset falls within sub-paragraph (1) above it is in the following provisions of this paragraph referred to as **"the remote asset"**.

2(3) For the purpose of determining, in accordance with subsection (8) of section 2 of the principal Act, the amount to be debited or credited to a participator for a chargeable period in respect of expenditure, where any expenditure which is or was incurred by the participator in respect of the remote asset–

(a) is expenditure to which section 3 of this Act or section 3 of the principal Act applies by virtue only of paragraph 1 above, and

(b) has been allowed on a claim under Schedule 5 or Schedule 6 to the principal Act before the Board have made an assessment to tax or a determination on or in relation to the participator for a chargeable period earlier than that referred to in sub-paragraph (5) below,

the expenditure shall be treated for the purposes of paragraph (b) or paragraph (c) of subsection (9) of the said section 2 as having been allowed immediately before the Board made an assessment to tax or a determination on or in relation to the participator for the period specified in sub-paragraph (5) below and not at any earlier time.

2(4) In determining under subsection (4) of section 111 of the Finance Act 1981 (restriction of expenditure supplement) whether, if account were to be taken of certain expenditure, a net profit would not have accrued to a participator in a chargeable period, expenditure which–

(a) is or was incurred by the participator in respect of the remote asset, and

(b) is expenditure to which section 3 of this Act or section 3 of the principal Act applies by virtue only of paragraph 1 above,

shall be disregarded unless the chargeable period in question is, or is later than, the period specified in sub-paragraph (5) below.

2(5) The chargeable period referred to in sub-paragraphs (3) and (4) above is the first in which either–

(a) by virtue of section 6(1) of this Act, the positive amounts for the purposes of section 2 of the principal Act include (after taking account of any reduction under section 9 of this Act) an amount of tariff receipts derived, in whole or in part, from the remote asset; or

(b) by virtue of section 7(1) of this Act, the positive amounts for the purposes of section 2 of the principal Act include an amount of disposal receipts in respect of the disposal of, or of an interest in, that asset.

2(6) For any chargeable period in which expenditure incurred by a participator in respect of the remote asset falls to be brought into account under paragraph (b) or paragraph (c) of subsection (9) of section 2 of the principle Act the amount of that expenditure which is to be so brought into account shall not exceed the aggregate of–

(a) the amount of the tariff receipts (if any) which are derived, in whole or in part, from the remote asset, and

(b) the amount of the disposal receipts (if any) in respect of the disposal of, or of an interest in, the remote asset,

which (after taking account of any reduction under section 9 of this Act) are included in the positive amounts for that chargeable period for the purposes of that section.

2(7) In any case where–

(a) for any chargeable period the positive amounts for the purposes of section 2 of this Act include an amount (in this sub-paragraph referred to as **"the reduced amount"**) which represents an amount of qualifying tariff receipts which were received from one user field and which have been reduced by virtue of section 9 of this Act, and

(b) those qualifying tariff receipts include tariff receipts which are derived, in whole or in part, from the remote asset as well as other tariff receipts,

the portion of the reduced amount which is to be regarded for the purpose of the preceding provisions of this paragraph as tariff receipts derived, in whole or in part, from the remote asset shall bear to the whole of the reduced amount the same proportion as, before the reduction, the tariff receipts so derived bore to the whole of the qualifying tariff receipts in question.

2(8) For the purpose of the preceding provisions of this paragraph a tariff receipt is derived, in whole or in part, from the remote asset if it consists of or includes consideration in respect of–

(a) the use of the remote asset; or

(b) the provision of services or other business facilities of whatever kind in connection with the use of that asset;

and subsection (6) of section 9 of this Act shall have effect for the purposes of sub-paragraph (7) above as it has effect for the purposes of that section.

ASSETS NO LONGER IN USE FOR THE PRINCIPAL FIELD

3(1) This paragraph applies where–

(a) a participator in an oil field (in this paragraph referred to as **"the principal field"**) incurs expenditure in enhancing the value of or otherwise in connection with an asset which is not a mobile asset; and

(b) before the expenditure was incurred the asset had already been used or was expected to be used in connection with the principal field (and, accordingly, is a qualifying asset); and

(c) at the end of the claim period in which the expenditure is incurred, the asset is no longer being, and is not expected to be, used in connection with the principal field; and

(d) either the use of the asset gives rise or is expected to give rise to tariff receipts or the expenditure is incurred with a view to the subsequent disposal of the asset or of an interest in it.

3(2) For the purposes of section 3 of this Act, Part II below and section 3 of the principal Act,–

(a) the use of the asset referred to in sub-paragraph (1) above to give rise to tariff receipts shall be assumed to be use in connection with the principal field; and

(b) if the subsequent disposal of, or of an interest in, the asset gives or is expected to give rise to disposal receipts, the asset shall be assumed to be being used in connection with the principal field throughout the claim period in which the expenditure is incurred.

3(2A) But where–

(a) the expenditure would (apart from this sub-paragraph) be regarded as incurred with a view to the subsequent disposal of the asset or of an interest in it, and

(b) the asset has, at any time in the period of 6 years ending with the date on which the expenditure was incurred, been used in a way that gives rise to tax-exempt tariffing receipts,

the expenditure shall not be regarded for the purposes of this paragraph as expenditure incurred with a view to the subsequent disposal of the asset or of an interest in it, to the extent that the amount of the expenditure falls to be reduced in accordance with sub-paragraph (2B) below.

3(2B) The reduction is to be made by applying section 7A of this Act in relation to the expenditure as it applies in relation to disposal receipts in respect of a disposal, but with the substitution–

(a) for references to the disponor, of references to the participator incurring the expenditure (**"the relevant participator"**),

(b) for references to the amount or value (apart from that section) of any disposal receipts of the disponor in respect of the disposal, of references to the amount which would, apart from sub-paragraph (2A) above, be the amount of the expenditure incurred by the relevant participator with a view to the subsequent disposal of the asset or of an interest in it,

(c) for references to the interest disposed of, of references to the asset or interest whose subsequent disposal gives or is expected to give rise to disposal receipts,

(d) for references to the date of the disposal, of references to the date on which the expenditure was incurred,

and taking the reference in subsection (6)(b) of that section to a reduction made by virtue of that section as a reference to a reduction made by virtue of that section for the purposes of section 7(9) of this Act.

3(3) References in sub-paragraphs (1) and (2) above to **"use in connection with the principal field"** include references to use which would constitute use in connection with that field but for section 10(2) of the principal Act (exempt gas).

History – In para. 3(1), the words "or otherwise in connection with" in para. (a) and "the expenditure" in para. (d) inserted, and the words "either the use of the asset" in para. (d) were substituted, by FA 1988, s. 139, with respect to expenditure incurred on or after 15 March 1988.

Para. 3(2A) inserted by FA 2004, s. 285 and Sch. 37, para. 6(2), with effect in relation to expenditure incurred on or after 1 January 2004. Transitional provisions are contained in FA 2004, Sch. 37, Pt. 2.

Para. 3(2B) inserted by FA 2004, s. 285 and Sch. 37, para. 6(2), with effect in relation to expenditure incurred on or after 1 January 2004. Transitional provisions are contained in FA 2004, Sch. 37, Pt. 2.

Part II – Special Rules as to Expenditure Allowable in Respect of Fixed Assets and Dedicated Mobile Assets

Cross references – FA 1994, Sch. 22, para. 9(2): allowable expenditure and election by reference to pipe-line usage.

INTERPRETATION

4 In this Part of this Schedule–

"allowable expenditure" means expenditure which, subject to the provisions of this Part, is allowable as mentioned in subsection (4) of the principal section;

"the new asset" means the asset referred to in subsection (1) of the principal section which was acquired or brought into existence, or the value of which was enhanced, as a result of the incurring of the allowable expenditure;

"the principal section" means section 3 of this Act;

"the purchaser" means the person referred to in subsection (1) of the principal section as the person incurring the allowable expenditure; and

"the relevant claim period", in relation to any allowable expenditure, has the same meaning as, by virtue of subsection (5) of the principal section, it has for the purposes of subsection (1) of that section.

ASSETS ACQUIRED ETC. FOR TWO OR MORE FIELDS

5(1) Subject to sub-paragraphs (2) and (3) below, where the purchaser is a participator in two or more oil fields (in this paragraph referred to as **"the purchaser's fields"**) and, at the end of the relevant claim period, it appears that the new asset is or is expected to be used in connection with two or more of those fields then, unless it seems just and reasonable to attribute all of the allowable expenditure relevant to the new asset to only one of those fields, that expenditure shall be apportioned, in such manner as may be just and reasonable, between those of the purchaser's fields in connection with which the new asset is or is expected to be used.

5(2) If, in a case falling within sub-paragraph (1) above, the use of the new asset in connection with one of the purchaser's fields (in this paragraph referred to as **"the paying field"**) gives, or is at the end of the relevant claim period expected to give, rise to receipts which, by virtue of section 8 of this Act, are to be attributed to another of those fields, as being the chargeable field, so much (if any) of the allowable expenditure as, apart from this sub-paragraph, would be apportioned to the paying field and as is reasonably attributable to the use of the new asset which gives rise to the receipts shall be apportioned to the chargeable field.

5(3) If, in a case falling within sub-paragraph (1) above, it appears, at the end of the relevant claim period, that the new asset also is or is expected to be used otherwise than in connection with a field in which the purchaser is a participator, then–

(a) in the apportionment made by virtue of sub-paragraph (1) above, such a percentage of the allowable expenditure as is just and reasonable shall be apportioned to that use; and

(b) for the purpose of any claim for an allowance in respect of any of the allowable expenditure, the percentage of that expenditure which under paragraph (a) above was apportioned to that use shall be added to the percentage of that expenditure which, under sub-paragraph (1) above, was apportioned to that one of the purchaser's fields which, in relation to the new asset, is the chargeable field.

5(4) If, in relation to the allowable expenditure, the relevant claim periods of the purchaser's fields are not the same, references in the preceding provisions of this paragraph to the end of the relevant claim period are references to the end of that relevant claim period which ends earlier or earliest.

Cross references – FA 1994, Sch. 22, para. 9(3): apportionment of expenditure between fields.

6(1) In any case where–

(a) the new asset is or is expected to be used in connection with two or more oil fields, and

(b) no apportionment of the allowable expenditure falls to be made by virtue of paragraph 5 above, the allowable expenditure shall be treated as wholly attributable to the use of the asset in connection with that field in which the purchaser is a participator or, if there is more than one such field, that one of them in relation to which a development decision is or was first made.

6(2) Subsection (7) of section 5A of the principal Act (time when development decision is made) shall have effect for the purposes of sub-paragraph (1) above as it has effect for the purposes of subsection (1)(c) of that section.

6(3) Subsection (3A) of section 8 of this Act applies for the purposes of sub-paragraph (1) above as it applies for the purposes of subsection (3)(c) of that section.

History – Para. 6(3) inserted with retrospective effect by FA 1986, s. 110(4).

BROUGHT-IN ASSETS

7(1) The provisions of this paragraph apply where–

(a) the allowable expenditure is (in whole or in part) referable to the use of the new asset in connection with an oil field which is not an exempt field; and

(b) the allowable expenditure was incurred at a time before the new asset was first used in connection with that oil field, discounting, in the case of a mobile asset, any use in a claim period when it was not dedicated to that oil field; and

(c) during the period (in this paragraph referred to as **"the initial period"**) between the time when the new asset was acquired or brought into existence and that first use, the new asset was used.

(i) otherwise than in connection with a taxable field, or

(ii) in connection with a taxable field in a way that gives rise to tax-exempt tariffing receipts,

by the purchaser or a person connected with him.

7(2) In any case where–

(a) at some time during the initial period the new asset was used in a way which, disregarding section 10(2) of the principal Act (exempt gas), would be use in connection with an exempt field, and

(b) at the beginning of the initial period it was not reasonable to expect that the asset would be used in connection with an oil field,

the amount which, apart from this sub-paragraph, would be the amount of the allowable expenditure in respect of the expected use referred to in sub-paragraph (1)(a) above, shall be reduced to nil.

7(3) In determining whether the condition in sub-paragraph (2)(b) above is fulfilled, no account shall be taken of use which, by virtue only of subsection (3) or subsection (5) of section 4 of this Act, is treated as use in connection with an exempt field.

7(4) In a case where sub-paragraph (2) above does not apply, the amount which, apart from this sub-paragraph, would be the amount of the allowable expenditure shall be reduced by multiplying it by the fraction of which–

(a) the numerator is a reasonable estimate of so much of the useful life of the asset as remains after the date on which it was first used as mentioned in sub-paragraph (1)(b) above; and

(b) the denominator is the aggregate of that reasonable estimate and the initial period.

7(5) In this paragraph an **"exempt field"** means an oil field from which all the oil won is excluded oil, as defined in section 10(1) of the principal Act.

History – In para. 7(1)(c) "(i)" inserted after "was used", "or" inserted after "otherwise than in connection with a taxable field,", and sub-para. (ii) inserted by FA 2004, s. 285 and Sch. 37, para. 7(2), with effect in relation to expenditure incurred on or after 1 January 2004. Transitional provisions are contained in FA 2004, Sch. 37, Pt. 2.
In para. 7(1)(c), "a taxable field" substituted for FA 1993, s. 190(3).

Cross references – FA 1993, s. 185(1): a "non-taxable field" is an oil field granted development consent by the Secretary of State on or after 16 March 1993, and a "taxable field" is an oil field which is not a non-taxable field.

SUBSEQUENT USE OF NEW ASSET OTHERWISE THAN IN CONNECTION WITH A TAXABLE FIELD

8(1) Subject to sub-paragraph (3) below,–

(a) if at any time the new asset ceases to be used by the purchaser in a way which either constitutes use for a qualifying purpose or would constitute such use but for section 10(2) of the principal Act (exempt gas), and

(b) thereafter, the new asset is or is expected to be used otherwise than for a qualifying purpose and is not disposed of in circumstances giving rise to disposal receipts,

the amount which, apart from this paragraph, would be the amount of the allowable expenditure shall be taken to be reduced by multiplying it by the fraction specified in sub-paragraph (2) below.

8(2) The fraction referred to in sub-paragraph (1) above is that of which–

(a) the numerator is a reasonable estimate of the period beginning when the purchaser first used the asset in connection with a taxable field or, if it was earlier, when the asset first gave rise to tariff receipts of the purchaser and ending when the asset is or is expected to be first used as mentioned in paragraph (b) of sub-paragraph (1) above after the cessation referred to in paragraph (a) of that sub-paragraph; and

(b) the denominator is a reasonable estimate of the useful life of the asset or, where sub-paragraph (4) of paragraph 7 above applies, of so much of that useful life as falls after the date on which the asset was first used as mentioned in sub-paragraph (1)(a) of that paragraph.

8(2A) In sub-paragraph (1) a reference to use for a qualifying purpose is a reference to–

(a) use in connection with a taxable field, and

(b) other use in–

(i) the United Kingdom,

(ii) the territorial sea of the United Kingdom, or

(iii) a designated area,

except use wholly or partly for an ineligible oil purpose.

8(2B) In this Act a reference to use of an asset for an ineligible oil purpose is a reference to–

(a) use in connection with an oil field that is not a taxable field, and

(b) use for any other purpose (apart from a purpose falling within section 3(1)(b) of the principal Act) of a separate trade consisting of activities falling within the definition of "oil-related activities" in section 274 of the Corporation Tax Act 2010.

8(2C) In sub-paragraphs (2A) and (2B) a reference to use in connection with a taxable field or other oil field includes use giving rise to receipts which, for the purposes of this Act, are tariff receipts.

8(3) If and so long as an asset gives rise to

(a) tariff receipts of the purchaser attributable to a taxable field, or

(b) tax-exempt tariffing receipts which, if they were tariff receipts (and expenditure were or had been allowable accordingly), would be tariff receipts of the purchaser attributable to a taxable field,

the asset shall be treated, for the purposes of sub-paragraph (1) above, as if it were used by him in connection with a taxable field.

8(4) If, in any case where the amount of any expenditure falls to be reduced under sub-paragraph (1) above, so much of the expenditure as has been previously allowed on a claim for any claim period exceeds the reduced allowable expenditure, an amount equal to the excess shall be treated (otherwise than for the purposes of paragraph (b) of that sub-paragraph) as disposal receipts of the purchaser arising from the asset in the chargeable period in which the asset ceased to be used as mentioned in paragraph (a) of that sub-paragraph.

8(5) In the case of an asset which has been used in connection with two or more oil fields for which any of the purchaser's allowable expenditure is or has been allowed or allowable, the chargeable period referred to in sub-paragraph (4) above shall be determined in relation to that one of those fields–

(a) in connection with which the asset was last used by the purchaser; or

(b) if it is later, in respect of which the asset last gave rise to tariff receipts of the purchaser; or

(c) if it is later than paragraph (a) and (where otherwise applicable) paragraph (b) above, in respect of which the asset would have last given rise to tariff receipts of the purchaser had tax-exempt tariffing receipts of the purchaser been tariff receipts of his (and if expenditure were or had been allowable accordingly);

and the reference in that sub-paragraph to **"disposal receipts"** shall accordingly be construed as a reference to disposal receipts attributable to that field.

8(6) In any case where–

(a) at a time before the new asset is brought into use by the purchaser in such a way as is mentioned in sub-paragraph (1)(a) above, it ceases to be expected to be used in such a way, and

(b) thereafter the new asset is or is expected to be used otherwise than in connection with a taxable field and is not disposed of in circumstances giving rise to disposal receipts,

the amount which, apart from this paragraph, would be the amount of the allowable expenditure shall be taken to be reduced to *nil*.

8(7) In any case where the amount of any expenditure falls to be reduced to nil under sub-paragraph (6) above, an amount equal to so much of the expenditure as has been previously allowed on a claim for any claim period shall be treated (otherwise than for the purposes of paragraph (b) of that sub-paragraph) as disposal receipts of the purchaser arising from the asset in the chargeable period in which the asset ceased to be expected to be used in such a way as is mentioned in sub-paragraph(1)(a) above.

History – In para. 8(1)(a) and (b) the words "for a qualifying purpose" substituted for the words "in connection with a taxable field" by FA 2009, s. 87 and Sch. 41, para. 3(2), with effect in relation to chargeable periods beginning after 30 June 2009.
In para. 8(1)–(3), (6), "a taxable field" substituted in each place for "an oil field" by FA 1993, s. 190(4).
Para. 8(2A) inserted by FA 2009, s. 87 and Sch. 41, para. 3(3), with effect in relation to chargeable periods beginning after 30 June 2009.
In para. 8(2B)(b), the words "the definition of "oil-related activities" in section 274 of the Corporation Tax Act 2010" substituted for the words "section 492(1) of the Income and Corporation Taxes Act 1988" by CTA 2010, s. 1177 and Sch. 1, para. 183, with effect for corporation tax purposes for accounting periods ending on or after 1 April 2010, and for income tax and capital gains tax purposes for the tax year 2010–11 and subsequent tax years.
Para. 8(2B) inserted by FA 2009, s. 87 and Sch. 41, para. 3(3), with effect in relation to chargeable periods beginning after 30 June 2009.
Para. 8(2C) inserted by FA 2009, s. 87 and Sch. 41, para. 3(3), with effect in relation to chargeable periods beginning after 30 June 2009.
In para. 8(3) "(a)" inserted after "gives rise to ", "or" inserted after "attributable to a taxable field,", and para. (b) inserted by FA 2004, s. 285 and Sch. 37, para. 8(2), with effect in relation to expenditure incurred on or after 1 January 2004. Transitional provisions are contained in FA 2004, Sch. 37, Pt. 2.
In para. 8(5) "or" inserted at the end of para. (b), and para. (c) inserted by FA 2004, s. 285 and Sch. 37, para. 8(3), with effect in relation to expenditure incurred on or after 1 January 2004. Transitional provisions are contained in FA 2004, Sch. 37, Pt. 2.

Cross references – FA 1993, s. 185(1): a "non-taxable field" is an oil field granted development consent by the Secretary of State on or after 16 March 1993, and a "taxable field" is an oil field which is not a non-taxable field.

MOBILE ASSETS BECOMING DEDICATED ASSETS

9(1) Subject to sub-paragraph (2) below, where any expenditure in connection with a mobile asset has been allowed or is allowable under section 4 of the principal Act and the asset becomes dedicated to an oil field, the expenditure which would otherwise be allowable under the principal section shall be reduced by so much of that expenditure as has been allowed or is allowable under the said section 4.

9(2) Sub-paragraph (1) above does not apply in any case where–

(a) paragraph 7 above applies; and

(b) sub-paragraph (4) of that paragraph applies to reduce the amount of expenditure which is allowable expenditure.

SCHEDULE 2 – SUPPLEMENTAL PROVISIONS AS TO RECEIPTS FROM QUALIFYING ASSETS

Sections 6–8

Cross references – Sch. 4, para. 5: Sch. 2 applies, with modifications, in relation to Sch. 4 of this Act (receipts attributable to UK use of foreign field assets).

INTERPRETATION

1(1) Any reference in this Schedule to the **"use of an asset"** includes a reference to the provision, in connection with that use, of services or other business facilities of whatever kind.

1(2) Any reference in this Schedule to the **"disposal of an asset"** includes a reference to the disposal of an interest in it.

CONSIDERATION RECEIVED BY CONNECTED PERSONS UNDER AVOIDANCE SCHEMES

2(1) This paragraph applies if consideration in respect of the use or disposal of an asset which, in relation to a participator or two or more participators in an oil field, is a qualifying asset is received or receivable–

(a) by a person in relation to whom the asset is not a qualifying asset but who is connected with the participator or, as the case may be, with each of them; and

(b) under or in consequence of a scheme or arrangements the main purpose or one of the main purposes of which is the avoidance of petroleum revenue tax or corporation tax.

2(2) In relation to the participator or, as the case may be, each of the participators referred to in sub-paragraph (1) above, any reference in section 6 or section 7 of this Act or in the following provisions of this Schedule to consideration received or receivable by him in respect of the use or disposal of the asset referred to in that sub-paragraph includes, subject to sub-paragraph (3) below, a reference to the consideration referred to in sub-paragraph (1) above or, if there is more than one participator, such portion of that consideration as it is just and reasonable to apportion to the participator in question.

2(3) In any case where–

(a) the tariff receipts or disposal receipts of a participator in respect of the use or disposal of a qualifying asset include consideration which is received or receivable from a person who is connected with the participator, and

PRT Statutes

(b) consideration is received or receivable from a person who is not connected with the participator by a person who is so connected (whether the person referred to in paragraph (a) above or not), and

(c) apart from this sub-paragraph, the consideration referred to in paragraph (b) above or (where there is more than one connected participator) a portion of that consideration would, by virtue of sub-paragraph (2) above, be included in the tariff receipts or disposal receipts of the participator which are referable to the use or disposal of the qualifying asset concerned,

only so much of the consideration or, as the case may be, of the portion of it referred to in paragraph (b) above as exceeds the consideration referred to in paragraph (a) above shall be included (by virtue of sub-paragraph (2) above) in the tariff receipts or, as the case may be, the disposal receipts of the participator.

APPORTIONMENT OF CONSIDERATION IN RESPECT OF USE OR DISPOSAL

3 In any case where–

(a) consideration received or receivable by a participator in an oil field in respect of the use or disposal of a qualifying asset includes an element that is unquantified but which does not constitute a tariff receipt or disposal receipt of his, and

(b) the consideration does not fall to be apportioned by virtue of section 6(4) or section 7(5) of this Act,

the portion of the consideration which constitutes a tariff receipt or disposal receipt of the participator shall be determined in such manner as is just and reasonable.

CASES WHERE ALL THE OIL IS DISREGARDED UNDER SECTION 10 OF THE PRINCIPAL ACT

4(1) This paragraph applies in any case where, in computing under section 2 of the principal Act the gross profit or loss accruing to a participator in any chargeable period from the chargeable field, all the oil which, apart from section 10 of that Act (exempt gas), would be taken into account falls to be disregarded under subsection (1) of that section.

4(2) In any case where this paragraph applies, subsection (1) of section 8 of this Act shall have effect in relation to the participator as if–

(a) in paragraph (a) the word “either” and the words “or is a mobile asset dedicated to that oil field” were omitted; and

(b) in paragraph (b) for the words “is allowable, or has” there were substituted the words “would, apart from section 10(2) of the principal Act, be allowed or have”;

and, in relation to the participator, tariff receipts and disposal receipts shall be construed accordingly.

4(2A) In any case where this paragraph applies, paragraph (b) of subsection (1A) of section 8 of this Act shall have effect in relation to the participator as if–

(a) for the words “does not” there were substituted “would not”; and

(b) at the end there were added the words “even if section 10(2) of the principal Act were disregarded”.

4(3) Subsections (6) to (8) of section 7 of this Act shall not apply where the asset is a qualifying asset by reason only of sub-paragraph (2) above.

History – Para. 4(2A) inserted by FA 1985, s. 92(4), in respect of consideration received or receivable after 19 March 1985.

ACQUISITION OTHERWISE THAN AT ARM’S LENGTH: LIMIT ON TARIFF AND DISPOSAL RECEIPTS

5(1) In any case where–

(a) in a transaction to which paragraph 2 of Schedule 4 to the principal Act applies (restriction on allowable expenditure where asset acquired in a transaction not at arm’s length) a participator in a taxable field makes a disposal of a qualifying asset, and

(b) the disposal gives rise to what would, apart from this paragraph, be tariff receipts or disposal receipts of the participator for a chargeable period, and

(c) those receipts are received from a person who is also a participator in a taxable field (whether the same field or not), and

(d) the use of the asset will be wholly by that person in connection with a taxable field in which he is a participator (and accordingly, and in particular, there will be no one giving rise to tariff receipts),

the receipts referred to in paragraphs (b) and (c) above shall not be regarded as tariff receipts or disposal receipts if and to the extent that their aggregate in the period beginning with the transaction and ending with the end of that chargeable period exceeds relevant expenditure.

5(2) In this paragraph **"relevant expenditure"** means expenditure (other than expenditure in respect of interest or any other pecuniary obligation incurred in obtaining a loan or any other form of credit) incurred by the participator referred to in sub-paragraph (1)(a) above or by another person in acquiring, bringing into existence, or enhancing the value of the asset in a transaction to which paragraph 2 of Schedule 4 to the principal Act does not apply (or, if there has been more than one such transaction, the later or latest of them).

5(3) In any case where–

(a) in a transaction to which paragraph 2 of Schedule 4 to the principal Act applies, a participator in a taxable field makes a disposal of a qualifying asset, and

(b) the disposal does not fall within sub-paragraph (1) above, and

(c) the disposal either gives rise to tariff receipts or disposal receipts of the participator for a chargeable period or is made for no consideration,

the disposal shall be treated as giving rise to disposal receipts or tariff receipts (according to the nature of the disposal) equal to the open market consideration for the disposal and any actual receipts falling within paragraph (c) above shall be disregarded.

5(4) Without prejudice to paragraph 1(2) above, in this paragraph **"disposal"**, in relation to a qualifying asset, includes the hiring of it or any similar transaction by which the use of the asset gives rise, or might reasonably be expected to give rise, to receipts (whether in the nature of income or capital).

5(5) The reference in sub-paragraph (3) above to the **"open market consideration for a disposal"** is a reference to the consideration which might reasonably have been obtained for the disposal in question (whatever its nature) had it been made in a transaction to which paragraph 2 of Schedule 4 to the principal Act does not apply.

History – In para. 5(1)(a), (c), "a taxable field" substituted; para. 5(1)(d) added; in para. 5(3)(a), "a taxable field" substituted and in para. 5(3)(b), words "a taxable field or," to "a non-taxable field" substituted by FA 1993, s. 190(5).

In para. 5(1)(d), the whole sub-paragraph was substituted by FA 1994, s. 238(2), with respect to disposals made after 30 November 1993.

In para. 5(1), the words "the receipts referred to in paragraph (b) and (c) above" substituted by FA 1994, s. 238(2), with respect to disposals made after 30 November 1993.

In para. 5(3)(b), the whole sub-paragraph was substituted by FA 1994, s. 238(3), with respect to disposals made after 30 November 1993.

Cross references – FA 1993, s. 185(1): a "non-taxable field" is an oil field granted development consent by the Secretary of State on or after 16 March 1993, and a "taxable field" is an oil field which is not a non-taxable field.

FA 1994, s. 233(3): sum received or receivable includes a tariff receipt or disposal receipt.

TRANSFERS OF INTERESTS IN FIELDS

6 [Amends FA 1980, Sch. 17, para. 19.]

INSURANCE AND COMPENSATION PAYMENTS

7 Any payment by way of insurance or compensation in respect of the loss or destruction of an asset which, in relation to a participator in an oil field, is a qualifying asset, shall be brought into account for the purposes of section 7 of this Act and this Schedule as consideration in respect of a disposal of the asset taking place at the time the payment is received or receivable.

DEDICATED MOBILE ASSETS CEASING TO BE USED IN CONNECTION WITH PARTICIPATOR'S OIL FIELD

8(1) This paragraph applies in any case where–

(a) a mobile asset which, in relation to a participator in an oil field, is a qualifying asset gives rise to receipts which, apart from the provisions of this paragraph, would be tariff receipts of the participator; and

(b) the asset has ceased to be used in connection with any oil field whatsoever in which the participator or a person connected with him is a participator.

8(2) In any case where this paragraph applies, so much of what would, apart from this paragraph, be tariff receipts of the participator arising from the asset and which are neither–

(a) received or receivable before the end of the chargeable period in which falls the second anniversary of the date on which the asset ceased to be used as mentioned in sub-paragraph (1)(b) above, nor

(b) received or receivable after the end of that chargeable period in respect of the use of the asset before the end of that period,

shall not form part of the tariff receipts of the participator for any chargeable period in which the asset is not used as mentioned in sub-paragraph (1)(b) above.

PRT Statutes

DISPOSAL RECEIPTS IN RESPECT OF BROUGHT-IN ASSETS

9 If paragraph 7(4) of Schedule 1 to this Act applies to reduce the allowable expenditure, within the meaning of Part II of that Schedule, in respect of an asset and any disposal receipt is received or receivable in respect of the asset, the amount which, apart from this paragraph, would be the amount of that receipt shall be taken to be reduced by multiplying it by the same fraction as, by virtue of the said paragraph 7(4), was applied to that allowable expenditure.

DISPOSAL RECEIPTS: ASSETS USED FOR DEBALLASTING

10 In any case where–

(a) section 4(2) of this Act applies to reduce the expenditure allowable as mentioned in section 3(4) of this Act in respect of an asset, and

(b) any disposal receipt is received or receivable in respect of the asset,

the amount which, apart from this paragraph, would be the amount of that receipt shall be taken to be reduced in the proportion in which the expenditure so allowable was reduced by virtue of section 4(2) of this Act.

USE BY CONNECTED OR ASSOCIATED PERSON: AVOIDANCE DEVICES

11(1) This paragraph applies in any case where–

(a) any consideration in respect of the use of an asset is received or receivable by a person (in this paragraph referred to as **"the recipient"**) in relation to whom the asset is not a qualifying asset; and

(b) the asset is at any time used in connection with an oil field by a person (in this paragraph referred to as **"the user"**) who is connected or associated with the recipient and who is a participator in that or any other oil field; and

(c) the consideration is so received or receivable under or in consequence of a scheme or arrangements the main purpose or one of the main purposes of which is the avoidance of petroleum revenue tax or corporation tax.

11(2) Subject to sub-paragraphs (5) and (6) below, the user shall be treated for the purposes of this Act and Part I of the principal Act and sections 299 to 301 of the Corporation Tax Act 2010 as if–

(a) any consideration arising from the use of the asset and received or receivable at any time by the recipient or a person connected or associated with him, other than consideration received or receivable from the user himself, had been received or receivable at that time by the user; and

(b) such proportion of any expenditure incurred by the recipient at any time in connection with the asset as it is just and reasonable to apportion to the use which gives rise to the consideration had been incurred at that time by the user for the purpose for which it was in fact incurred by the recipient.

11(3) For the purposes of this paragraph, a participator in an oil field is **"associated"** with another person if the participator, by acting together with a person who is, or two or more persons each of whom is, a participator in that oil field or in any other relevant field, would be able to secure or exercise control of that other person, and for this purpose–

(a) **"control"** shall be construed in accordance with sections 450 and 451 of the Corporation Tax Act 2010; and

(b) **"relevant field"** means an oil field in connection with which the asset referred to in sub-paragraph (1)(a) above has been, is, or is expected to be, used.

11(4) For the purposes of sub-paragraph (3) above–

(a) a foreign field, within the meaning of section 12 of this Act, shall be treated as an oil field, and

(b) an asset is used in connection with a relevant field which is a foreign field if it is used in a way which, on the assumptions set out in subsection (5) of that section, would be use in connection with the foreign field,

and, in relation to a relevant field which is a foreign field, the reference in sub-paragraph (3) above to a **"participator"** shall be construed in accordance with section 12(2)(b) of this Act.

11(5) If, in relation to the recipient, there is more than one person who is the user, any consideration or expenditure falling within paragraph (a) or paragraph (b) of sub-paragraph (2) above shall be apportioned between those persons in such manner as is just and reasonable.

11(6) Sub-paragraph (2)(b) above does not apply if the asset is a mobile asset which is not dedicated to an oil field.

History – In para. 11(2), the words "sections 299 to 301 of the Corporation Tax Act 2010" substituted for the words "section 500 of the Taxes Act" by CTA 2010, s. 1177 and Sch. 1, para. 184(2), with effect for corporation tax purposes for accounting periods ending on or after 1 April 2010, and for income tax and capital gains tax purposes for the tax year 2010–11 and subsequent tax years.

In para. 11(3)(a), the words "sections 450 and 451 of the Corporation Tax Act 2010" substituted for the words "section 416 of the Taxes Act" by CTA 2010, s. 1177 and Sch. 1, para. 184(2), with effect for corporation tax purposes for accounting periods ending on or after 1 April 2010, and for income tax and capital gains tax purposes for the tax year 2010–11 and subsequent tax years.
See ICTA 1988, s. 844 and Sch. 29, para. 32 for substitution of former references to that Act.

PURCHASE AT PLACE OF EXTRACTION

12(1) Subject to sub-paragraphs (4) to (6) below, in any case where–

(a) a participator in an oil field or any person connected with him purchases any oil, otherwise than in pursuance of such an agreement as is mentioned in paragraph 6A of Schedule 3 to the principal Act (transactions between participators), and takes delivery of that oil at the place of extraction, and

(b) any of that oil is transported, initially treated or initially stored (or subjected to any two or more of those operations) by means of any asset which is a qualifying asset in relation to that field, and

(c) when the oil is disposed of or relevantly appropriated by the participator or the person connected with him, the selling price of the oil exceeds the price paid for it on the purchase referred to in paragraph (a) above,

the participator shall be treated for the purposes of this Act and Part I of the principal Act and sections 299 to 301 of the Corporation Tax Act 2010 as having received an amount equal to that excess as tariff receipts which arise in the chargeable period in which the selling price falls to be determined and are attributable to the use of the asset for carrying out the operation or operations referred to in paragraph (b) above.

12(2) In this paragraph **"selling price"**, in relation to any oil, means the aggregate of the amounts determined in relation to that oil in accordance with paragraphs (a) to (cb) of subsection (5) of section 2 of the principal Act; and for the purpose of the application of those paragraphs and of determining whether any oil falling within sub-paragraph (1) above is relevantly appropriated,–

(a) a person who is connected with the participator and who purchases oil as mentioned in sub-paragraph (1)(a) above shall be deemed to be a participator; and

(b) oil falling within sub-paragraph (1) above shall be treated, for the purposes of section 2(5) of the principal Act and the definition of **"relevantly appropriated"** in section 12 of that Act as if it were oil won from the field referred to in paragraph (a) of that sub-paragraph.

12(3) A person who takes delivery of oil before it has been transported–

(a) to the place at which it is first landed in the United Kingdom; or

(b) to the place referred to in section 3(1)(f)(ii) of the principal Act,

shall be treated for the purposes of sub-paragraph (1)(a) above as having taken delivery of the oil at the place of extraction.

12(4) Sub-paragraph (1) above does not apply to oil if, at a time before the participator's selling price for that oil falls to be determined as mentioned in sub-paragraph (2) above, the oil is either–

(a) stored in the field referred to in paragraphs (a) and (b) of sub-paragraph (1) above; or

(b) used for the purpose of assisting the extraction of oil from that field.

12(5) Sub-paragraph (1) above does not apply to oil if, by virtue of section 2(5)(b) or (ca) of the principal Act (oil disposed of otherwise than in sales at arm's length), the market value of the oil is taken into account in calculating the gross profit and loss (if any) accruing to a participator from an oil field in any chargeable period.

12(6) In any chargeable period ending on or after 30th June 2004, sub-paragraph (1) above does not apply to oil in a case where–

(a) had the operation or operations to which the oil was subjected as mentioned in paragraph (b) of that sub-paragraph been carried out under a contract entered into on or after 9th April 2003, and

(b) had an amount been received or receivable under the contract in that chargeable period by the participator, that amount would have been a tax-exempt tariffing receipt.

History – In para. 12(1), the words "sections 299 to 301 of the Corporation Tax Act 2010" substituted for the words "section 500 of the Taxes Act" by CTA 2010, s. 1177 and Sch. 1, para. 184(2), with effect for corporation tax purposes for accounting periods ending on or after 1 April 2010, and for income tax and capital gains tax purposes for the tax year 2010–11 and subsequent tax years.
In para. 12(1) "Subject to sub-paragraphs (4) to (6)" substituted for "Subject to sub-paragraphs (4) and (5)" by FA 2004, s. 285(4)(a), with effect from 22 July 2004.
Para. 12(2) amended by FA 1998, s. 152(2)(a) by substituting the words "paragraphs (a) to (cb)", with effect in relation to light gases disposed of or appropriated at any time on or after 3 May 1994.
Para. 12(3) amended by F(No. 2)A 1992, s. 74 and Sch. 15, para. 7 by substituting the words "before it has been transported … the principal Act", with effect in accordance with F(No. 2)A 1992, s. 74(5).
Para. 12(5) amended by FA 1998, s. 152(2)(b) by substituting the words "2(5)(b) or (ca) of the principal Act (oil disposed of otherwise than in sales at arm's length", with effect in relation to light gases disposed of or appropriated at any time on or after 3 May 1994.
Para. 12(6) inserted by FA 2004, s. 285(4)(b), with effect from 22 July 2004.
See ICTA 1988, Sch. 29, para. 32 for substitution of former reference to that Act in para. 12(1).

SCHEDULE 3 – TARIFF RECEIPTS ALLOWANCE

Section 9

THE PARTICIPATOR'S SHARE

1(1) In this Schedule–

"the principal section" means section 9 of this Act;

"receipts from existing contracts" means qualifying tariff receipts under a contract or contracts made as mentioned in subsection (3) of the principal section;

and other expressions have the same meaning as in the principal section.

1(2) In relation to a user field, any reference in the following provisions of this Schedule to the **"oil to which any qualifying tariff receipts which are received or receivable"** in a chargeable period relate is a reference to the oil won from that user field which, in that chargeable period, is extracted, transported, initially treated or initially stored (or subjected to two or more of those operations) by means of the asset to which the qualifying tariff receipts are referable.

2(1) Subject to paragraphs 3 and 6 below, where an amount of qualifying tariff receipts received or receivable by a participator in a chargeable period from a user field falls to be treated, for the purpose mentioned in subsection (1) of the principal section, as reduced in accordance with paragraph (a) or paragraph (b) of that subsection, the cash equivalent of his share of the tariff receipts allowance in respect of that user field for that period is the amount given, subject to sub-paragraph (2) below, by the formula:–

$$£\left(A \times \frac{B}{C}\right)$$

where–

A is the amount of those qualifying tariff receipts;

B is the tariff receipts allowance in respect of that user field, expressed in metric tonnes; and

C is the amount, in metric tonnes, of the oil to which those qualifying tariff receipts relate.

2(2) If, apart from this sub-paragraph, the fraction B/C in the formula in sub-paragraph (1) above would exceed unity, it shall be treated as unity for the purposes of this Schedule.

3 [Omitted by FA 2009, s. 91 and Sch. 45, para. 2(2).]

History – Para. 3 omitted by FA 2009, s. 91 and Sch. 45, para. 2(2), with effect from 21 July 2009.

QUALIFYING TARIFF RECEIPTS REFERABLE TO DIFFERENT PERIODS

4(1) This paragraph applies if any qualifying tariff receipts which are received or receivable by a participator for a chargeable period from a user field are referable to the use of a qualifying asset for a period (in this paragraph and paragraph 5 below referred to as **"the period of use"**) which is not wholly comprised in that chargeable period.

4(2) If, apart from this sub-paragraph, the period of use would exceed ten years, it shall be treated for the purposes of the following provisions of this paragraph as ending immediately before the tenth anniversary of the first day of the period.

4(3) In a case where this paragraph applies, the qualifying tariff receipts referred to in sub-paragraph (1) above shall be treated for the purpose mentioned in subsection (1) of the principal section as reduced in accordance with paragraph 5 below and not in accordance with paragraph (a) or paragraph (b) of that subsection.

4(4) For the purpose of determining the amount of the reduction under paragraph 5 below,–

(a) the qualifying tariff receipts shall be regarded as wholly received in the period of use; and

(b) if the period of use is not wholly comprised in a chargeable period, a portion of those receipts shall be regarded as received in each chargeable period which, in whole or in part, is comprised in the period of use;

and any chargeable period which, in whole or in part, is comprised in the period of use is in the following provisions of this paragraph and paragraph 5 below referred to as a **"relevant chargeable period"**.

4(5) For the relevant chargeable period or, as the case may be, for each of them, there shall be determined the amount of oil won from the user field in question which is expected to be qualifying oil for that period; and in this paragraph and paragraph 5 below **"qualifying oil"**, in relation to a chargeable period, means oil which in that period is extracted, transported, initially treated or initially stored by means of any asset or assets giving rise to the qualifying tariff receipts referred to in sub-paragraph (1) above.

4(6) In a case falling within paragraph (b) of sub-paragraph (4) above, the portion of the qualifying tariff receipts which is to be regarded as received in each of the relevant chargeable periods shall bear to each of those receipts the same proportion as the amount of the qualifying oil for that period bears to the total of the qualifying oil for all the relevant chargeable periods.

4(7) In any case where, apart from this sub-paragraph, it is not practicable to determine for the purpose of sub-paragraph (5) above how much of the oil won from a user field is for any period expected to be qualifying oil, such a determination shall be made on the assumption that any asset which gives rise to qualifying tariff receipts falling within that sub-paragraph will at all times be used to the full extent which, by reference to the receipts, is available for the extraction, transport, initial treatment or initial storage of oil won from the user field in question.

5(1) For the purpose of calculating the reduction referred to in paragraph 4(3) above, there shall be determined, in accordance with paragraphs 2 and 3 above and sub-paragraphs (2) and (3) below, the amount which would be the cash equivalent of the participator's share of the tariff receipts allowance in respect of the user field in question for the relevant chargeable period or, if there is more than one such period, for each of them.

5(2) For a relevant chargeable period, the determination referred to in sub-paragraph (1) above shall be made on the basis–

(a) that "A" in the formula in paragraph 2 above is the amount of the qualifying tariff receipts determined for the period under sub-paragraph (6) of paragraph 4 above or, if that sub-paragraph does not apply, the whole of the qualifying tariff receipts referred to in sub-paragraph (1) of that paragraph; and

(b) that "C" in the formula in paragraph 2 above is the amount of the qualifying oil for that period.

5(3) If, on the determination under sub-paragraph (1) above, the cash equivalent of the participator's share of the tariff receipts allowance in respect of the user field in question would, apart from this sub-paragraph, exceed the qualifying tariff receipts for that period (as calculated under sub-paragraph (2) above) then, for the purposes of this paragraph, the amount of that cash equivalent shall be taken to be reduced to an amount equal to those qualifying tariff receipts.

5(4) The amount of the reduction referred to in paragraph 4(3) above shall be an amount equal to the cash equivalent of the participator's share of the tariff receipts allowance in respect of the user field in question for the relevant chargeable period, as determined under this paragraph, or, if there is more than one relevant chargeable period, the aggregate of the cash equivalents as so determined for each of the relevant chargeable periods.

6(1) In any case where–

(a) there are normal qualifying tariff receipts from a user field for a chargeable period which, for the purpose of determining the amount of a reduction under paragraph 5 above in an amount of straddling qualifying tariff receipts from that field, was a relevant chargeable period as defined in paragraph 4(4) above, and

(b) those normal qualifying tariff receipts relate to oil to which the straddling qualifying tariff receipts do not relate,

the amount which, apart from this paragraph, would be the cash equivalent of the participator's share of the tariff receipts allowance in respect of that user field for that chargeable period shall be varied in accordance with the following provisions of this paragraph.

6(2) In the first instance, the cash equivalent of the participator's share of the tariff receipts allowance for the chargeable period in question shall be determined, in accordance with paragraphs 2 and 3 above, on the basis that–

(a) there is to be added to the normal qualifying tariff receipts for that period that portion of the straddling qualifying tariff receipts which, in accordance with sub-paragraph (6) of paragraph 4 above, is to be regarded as received in that period or, if that sub-paragraph does not apply, the whole of those receipts; and

(b) there is to be added to the oil referred to in sub-paragraph (1)(b) above the oil which, by reference to the straddling qualifying tariff receipts, is qualifying oil for that chargeable period for the purposes of paragraphs 4 and 5 above.

6(3) The cash equivalent of the participator's share referred to in sub-paragraph (1) above shall be the amount produced by deducting from the cash equivalent of that share, as determined under sub-paragraph (2) above, the amount of the cash equivalent of his share for the period in question as determined under paragraph 5 above.

6(4) For the purposes of this paragraph, qualifying tariff receipts are **"normal"** if they fall to be treated as reduced in accordance with paragraph (a) or paragraph (b) of subsection (1) of the principal section and **"straddling"** if they fall to be treated as reduced in accordance with paragraph 5 above.

SCHEDULE 4 – RECEIPTS ATTRIBUTABLE TO UNITED KINGDOM USE OF FOREIGN FIELD ASSETS

Section 12

INTERPRETATION

1 In this Schedule–

(a) **"the principal section"** means section 12 of this Act;

(b) **"the relevant assumptions"** means–

(i) those specified in subsection (5) of the principal section; and

(ii) the assumption that a participator in a foreign field is a participator within the meaning of Part I of the principal Act;

(c) **"United Kingdom field"** means an oil field within the meaning of Part I of the principal Act.

CHARGEABLE RECEIPTS

2 A participator in a foreign field is chargeable to tax in accordance with this Schedule in respect of consideration falling within subsection (1) of the principal section if, and only if–

(a) the field asset which gives rise to that consideration is, in accordance with paragraph 3 below, a chargeable asset in relation to him; and

(b) the consideration constitutes, in accordance with paragraph 4 below, a receipt for which he is accountable;

and, where the conditions in paragraphs (a) and (b) above are fulfilled, the consideration is in this Schedule referred to as a chargeable receipt of the participator.

3(1) Subject to sub-paragraph (2) below, a field asset is a chargeable asset in relation to a participator in a foreign field if, on the relevant assumptions, expenditure incurred by the participator in respect of the asset would be or would have been allowable for that foreign field–

(a) under section 3 of this Act or section 4 of the principal Act, or

(b) in the case of an asset the useful life of which was, at the time the expenditure was incurred, expected to exceed six months, under section 3 of the principal Act.

3(2) An asset which is a field asset by virtue of subsection (6) of the principal section is a chargeable asset in relation to that participator in that foreign field in relation to whom and to which the asset referred to in paragraph (c) of that subsection is a chargeable asset.

4(1) Consideration falling within subsection (1) of the principal section constitutes a receipt for which a participator in a foreign field is accountable if, and only if,–

(a) on the relevant assumptions, and

(b) on the further assumption that the field asset which gives rise to the consideration is a qualifying asset,

the consideration would constitute, for the purposes of this Act, a tariff receipt or disposal receipt of the participator attributable to the foreign field.

4(2) In applying section 7 of this Act to determine whether any consideration falling within subsection (1)(c) of the principal section would, on the assumptions in sub-paragraph (1) above, constitute a disposal receipt, the reference in section 7(4)(b) of this Act to tariff receipts of the participator shall be construed as a reference to consideration falling within paragraph (a) or paragraph (b) of subsection (1) of the principal section which, on those assumptions, would constitute a tariff receipt of his.

5(1) Schedule 2 to this Act, except paragraphs 4 and 6 to 8, applies in relation to chargeable receipts on the relevant assumptions and also on the further assumptions–

(a) that any reference in that Schedule to **"tariff receipts"** or **"disposal"** receipts includes a reference to chargeable receipts;

(b) that, except in paragraphs 5 and 11(3), any reference in that Schedule to an **"oil field"** or a **"participator"** applies only to a foreign field or, as the case may be, a participator in a foreign field; and

(c) that any reference in that Schedule to a **"qualifying asset"** is a reference to a field asset which, in accordance with paragraph 3 above, is a chargeable asset.

5(2) In Schedule 2 to this Act, as applied by sub-paragraph (1) above, any reference to any of the provisions specified in sub-paragraph (2) of paragraph 8 below shall be construed as a reference to that provision as it has effect by virtue of that sub-paragraph.

5(3) In its application by virtue of sub-paragraph (1) above, paragraph 2 of Schedule 2 to this Act shall have effect as if the reference in sub-paragraph (2) of that paragraph to section 6 or section 7 of this Act included a reference to the principal section.

5(4) Notwithstanding anything in paragraph (a) of sub-paragraph (1) above, paragraph 9 of Schedule 2 to this Act, in its application by virtue of that sub-paragraph, shall have effect as if the reference in that paragraph to any disposal receipt were a reference to any chargeable receipt falling within paragraph (c) of subsection (1) of the principal section.

5(5) In its application by virtue of sub-paragraph (1) above, paragraph 10 of Schedule 2 to this Act shall have effect as if,–

(a) notwithstanding anything in paragraph (a) of that sub-paragraph, the reference in that paragraph to any disposal receipt were a reference to any chargeable receipt falling within paragraph (c) of subsection (1) of the principal section; and

(b) in the application of paragraph 4 above for the purposes of paragraph 10 below, section 6(4)(b) of this Act were disregarded.

5(6) In its application by virtue of sub-paragraph (1) above, paragraph 11 of Schedule 2 to this Act shall have effect as if sub-paragraph (4) of that paragraph were omitted.

6(1) Subject to sub-paragraph (2) below, the chargeable receipts of a participator in a foreign field are attributable to that field for which expenditure incurred by him in respect of the field asset concerned would be or would have been allowable as mentioned in paragraph 3(1) above; and if there is more than one such foreign field, then the receipts are attributable to that one of those fields in connection with which, on the relevant assumptions, the field asset would have been first used.

6(2) The foreign field to which are attributable chargeable receipts referable to an asset which is a field asset by virtue of subsection (6) of the principal section is that field to which are attributable chargeable receipts referable to the field asset referred to in paragraph (c) of that subsection.

THE CHARGE TO TAX

7(1) In relation to a foreign field, every half year beginning on or after 1st July 1982 shall be taken to be a chargeable period.

7(2) In this paragraph **"half year"** has the same meaning as in section 1 of the principal Act.

7(3) Any reference in this Schedule to the **"chargeable period"** to which any chargeable receipts of a participator in a foreign field are attributable is,–

(a) in the case of chargeable receipts falling within paragraph (c) of subsection (1) of the principal section, a reference to the chargeable period in which the disposal referred to in that paragraph occurs; and

(b) in any other case, a reference to the chargeable period in which the receipts are received or receivable by him.

8(1) For each chargeable period of a foreign field beginning with that in which a participator in that field has chargeable receipts, there shall be determined, subject to the following provisions of this Schedule but otherwise in accordance with section 2 of the principal Act, what is the assessable profit or allowable loss accruing to the participator from the foreign field on the basis that–

(a) the positive amounts for the purposes of section 2 of the principal Act consist of any chargeable receipts of his attributable to that field for that period; and

(b) the negative amounts for those purposes are any amounts referred to in paragraphs (b), (c) and (f) of subsection (9) of that section.

8(2) For the purpose of the determination referred to in sub-paragraph (1) above, the provisions of Part I of the principal Act and sections 3 and 4 of and Part II of Schedule 1 to this Act shall have effect–

(a) on the relevant assumptions; and

(b) on the further assumption that any reference in those provisions to an **"oil field"** or a **"participator"** applies only to a foreign field or, as the case may be, a participator in a foreign field.

8(3) Without prejudice to sub-paragraph (2) above, in computing the assessable profit or allowable loss accruing to a participator in a foreign field, section 9 of and Schedule 3 to this Act shall apply–

(a) on the relevant assumptions; and

(b) on the further assumption that any chargeable receipts of his, other than those falling within subsection (1)(c) of the principal section, are tariff receipts.

8(4) In any case where, apart from this sub-paragraph, the whole or any part of any consideration which constitutes a chargeable receipt of a participator in a foreign field would also fall to be treated, by virtue of paragraph 2 or paragraph 11 of Schedule 2 to this Act, as a tariff or disposal receipt of a participator in a United Kingdom field, it shall not be so treated.

8(5) In any case where, apart from this sub-paragraph, the whole or any part of any consideration which constitutes a tariff or disposal receipt of a participator in a United Kingdom field would also fall to be treated, by virtue of paragraph 2 or paragraph 11 of Schedule 2 to this Act, as applied by paragraph 5(1) above, as a chargeable receipt of a participator in a foreign field, it shall not be so treated.

9(1) Subject to sub-paragraph (2) below,–

(a) the principal Act, and

(b) the provisions of the Taxes Management Act 1970 which are applied by paragraph 1 of Schedule 2 to the principal Act,

shall have effect in relation to any assessable profit or allowable loss of a participator in a foreign field determined for a chargeable period under paragraph 8(1) above as if it were such an assessable profit or allowable loss as is referred to in section 1(2) of the principal Act.

9(2) No reduction shall be made by virtue of section 8 of the principal Act (oil allowance) in the assessable profit accruing to a participator in a foreign field for any chargeable period.

EXPENDITURE RELIEF

10(1) For the purpose of the determination referred to in sub-paragraph (1) of paragraph 8 above, no expenditure shall be allowable, by virtue of paragraph (b) of that sub-paragraph, under section 3 of the principal Act or section 3 of this Act unless–

(a) the expenditure relates to a field asset which is a chargeable asset which gives rise, or is expected to give rise, to chargeable receipts; and

(b) the expenditure is incurred either for the purpose of enabling the asset to be used in a way which gives rise, or is expected to give rise, to chargeable receipts falling within paragraph (a) or paragraph (b) of subsection (1) of the principal section, or for the purpose of enhancing the value of the asset with a view to the subsequent disposal of it or of an interest in it.

10(2) Where expenditure falling within paragraph (a) of sub-paragraph (1) above is incurred partly for one or both of the purposes referred to in paragraph (b) of that sub-paragraph and partly for other purposes, only so much of that expenditure as it is just and reasonable to apportion to a purpose referred to in that paragraph shall be regarded as falling within those paragraphs.

10(3) References in the preceding provisions of this paragraph to the use of an asset in a way which gives rise, or is expected to give rise, to chargeable receipts include references to the provision, in connection with the use of that asset, of services or other business facilities of any kind which give rise, or are expected to give rise, to chargeable receipts.

10(4) To the extent only that expenditure falls within paragraphs (a) and (b) of sub-paragraph (1) above, the field asset to which the expenditure relates shall be regarded for the purposes of section 3 of the principal Act and section 3 of this Act as used in connection with the foreign field.

11(1) In the following provisions of this Schedule expenditure which falls within paragraphs (a) and (b) of sub-paragraph (1) of paragraph 10 above is referred to as **"qualifying expenditure"**.

11(2) In relation to qualifying expenditure, references in section 3 of the principal Act to tariff receipts shall be construed as references to chargeable receipts falling within paragraph (a) or paragraph (b) of subsection (1) of the principal section.

11(3) If, on the relevant assumptions, expenditure which was incurred in relation to a field asset but which is not qualifying expenditure would have qualified for supplement as mentioned in subsection (5) of section 3 of the principal Act, then, in relation to qualifying expenditure which relates to that field asset, subsection (5A) of that section shall have effect with the omission of paragraph (a).

11(4) [Repealed by F(No. 2)A 1992, s. 74 and Sch. 15, para. 8(b), s. 82 and Sch. 18, Pt. VIII.]

11(5) In relation to qualifying expenditure which is allowable expenditure within the meaning of Part II of Schedule 1 to this Act, in paragraph 8 of that Schedule–

(a) any reference to disposal receipts shall be construed as a reference to chargeable receipts falling within subsection (1)(c) of the principal section; and

(b) any reference to tariff receipts shall be construed as a reference to other descriptions of chargeable receipts.

History – In para. 11(3), the words "and on the further assumption set out in sub-paragraph (4) below" which appeared after "assumptions", and para. 11(4), were repealed by F(No. 2)A 1992, s. 74 and Sch. 15, para. 8, s. 82 and Sch. 18, Pt. VIII, in accordance with s. 74(5) of that Act.

CLAIMS FOR EXPENDITURE RELIEF

12 In relation to a claim for the allowance of any qualifying expenditure, and in relation to the foreign field in connection with which, by virtue of paragraph 10(4) above, the field asset concerned is to be regarded as used, the first claim period shall be the period ending on 30th June 1982 and each subsequent claim period shall be the period of six months from the end of the preceding claim period.

THE RESPONSIBLE PERSON

13 In relation to a foreign field, paragraph 4 of Schedule 2 to the principal Act shall have effect as if–

(a) for sub-paragraphs (1) to (5) there were substituted the following sub-paragraph–

"**4(1)** For each oil field the Board may, by notice in writing given to him, appoint one of the participators in the field as the responsible person for that field, to perform in relation to the field, any functions conferred on the responsible person as such by this Part of this Act; and the participator who for the time being holds that appointment is in this Part of this Act referred to as "the responsible person";"

(b) in sub-paragraphs (6) and (7) for any reference to a body corporate or partnership there were substituted a reference to a participator; and

(c) sub-paragraph (8) (which varies the definition of "participator" in relation to a United Kingdom field) were omitted.

MANAGEMENT AND COLLECTION

14(1) In its application to tax chargeable only by virtue of the provisions of the principal section and this Schedule, Schedule 2 to the principal Act (in this paragraph referred to as **"Schedule 2"**) shall have effect as if–

(a) any reference in that Schedule to an oil field or a participator were a reference only to a foreign field or, as the case may be, a participator in a foreign field, and

(b) any reference in that Schedule to a chargeable period (within the meaning of Part I of the principal Act) were a reference only to a chargeable period within the meaning of this Schedule to which there are attributable any chargeable receipts of a participator in a foreign field,

and subject to the modifications made in the following provisions of this paragraph.

14(2) Notwithstanding anything in sub-paragraph (2) of paragraph 1 of Schedule 2, sub-paragraph (1) above shall have effect in relation to those provisions of the Taxes Management Act 1970 which are applied by that paragraph as it has effect in relation to Schedule 2 itself.

14(3) Paragraph 2 of Schedule 2 shall have effect as if for sub-paragraphs (2) and (3) there were substituted the following sub-paragraph–

"**2(2)** A return under this paragraph for a chargeable period shall contain the following particulars–

(a) a statement of the amount or value and the source of any receipts which are, within the meaning of Schedule 4 to the Oil Taxation Act 1983, chargeable receipts of the participator attributable to the chargeable period to which the return relates; and

(b) a statement of the assets giving rise to any such receipts; and

(c) such other particulars as the Board may prescribe with respect to any such receipts;"

and accordingly subsections (1) to (3) of section 10 of this Act shall not apply in relation to a return made under that paragraph by virtue of this Schedule.

14(4) Paragraph 5 of Schedule 2 shall have effect as if for sub-paragraphs (2) and (2A) there were substituted the following sub-paragraph–

"**5(2)** A return under this paragraph shall contain such particulars of or relating to the oil field as the Board may require for the purpose of determining the amount by which any chargeable receipts, within the meaning of Schedule 4 to the Oil Taxation Act 1983, are to be treated as reduced by virtue of section 9 of that Act, as applied by paragraph 8(3) of that Schedule."

14(5) Paragraph 7(1) of Schedule 2 shall have effect with the omission of the words "or to oil won therefrom", in both places where they occur.

14(6) Paragraph 14 of Schedule 2 shall have effect as if for sub-paragraphs (i) and (ii) of paragraph (b) of sub-paragraph (3) there were substituted the following sub-paragraphs–

"(i) the aggregate of the receipts as stated in the participator's return in pursuance of sub-paragraph (2)(a) of that paragraph; and

(ii) the aggregate of the corresponding receipts as included in the assessment;"

and with the omission of sub-paragraphs (4) to (7).

PAYMENT ON ACCOUNT

15 In its application to tax chargeable only as mentioned in paragraph 14(1) above, paragraph 2 of the Schedule to the Petroleum Revenue Tax Act 1980 shall have effect as if, in place of the sub-paragraph (2A) set out in section 10(6) of this Act, there were substituted the following sub-paragraph–

> "**2(2A)** The amount of any chargeable receipts, within the meaning of Schedule 4 to the Oil Taxation Act 1983, shall be taken from the particulars included in the return referred to in sub-paragraph (2) above, and any amount by which any of those receipts are to be treated as reduced under section 9 of that Act, as applied by paragraph 8(3) of that Schedule, shall be determined accordingly."

INCOME AND CORPORATION TAXES

16(1) Section 11 of this Act shall have effect as if–

(a) any reference therein to an oil field included a reference to a foreign field; and

(b) any reference therein to a participator were to be construed, in relation to a foreign field, in accordance with subsection (2)(b) of the principal section; and

(c) any reference therein to a tariff receipt included a reference to a chargeable receipt consisting of consideration received or receivable as mentioned in paragraph (a) or paragraph (b) of subsection (1) of the principal section.

16(2) Paragraphs (a) and (b) of sub-paragraph (1) above apply in relation to paragraph 11(3) of Schedule 2 to this Act in so far as that paragraph has effect for the purposes of section 11 of this Act by virtue of subsection (4) thereof.

FINANCE ACT 1984

(1984 Chapter 43)

[*26th July 1984*]

ARRANGEMENT OF SECTIONS

PART V – OIL TAXATION

PART VI – MISCELLANEOUS AND SUPPLEMENTARY

PART V – OIL TAXATION

113 Restriction on PRT reliefs

113(1) Subject to subsection (3) below, in determining whether any expenditure is allowable in the case of a participator in an oil field under section 5 or section 5A or section 5B of the principal Act, no account shall be taken of any expenditure incurred before his qualifying date.

113(2) Subject to subsection (3) below, in determining whether any unrelievable field losses are allowable in the case of a participator in an oil field under section 6 of that Act, no account shall be taken of any allowable loss falling within subsection (1B) of that section unless the date on which the winning of oil from the abandoned field permanently ceased fell on or after his qualifying date.

113(3) Subsections (1) and (2) above do not apply in the case of a participator in an oil field if his qualifying date falls before 14th September 1983 or before the end of the first chargeable period in relation to the field.

113(4) In this section **"qualifying date"**, in relation to a participator in an oil field, means (subject to subsection (6) below) whichever of the following dates is applicable in his case or (if there is more than one) the earliest of them–

(a) the date on which the participator first qualified in respect of any licensed area, being an area which is wholly or partly included in the field;

(b) if the participator is a company, the date on which another company first satisfied both of the following conditions, that is to say–

(i) it qualified in respect of any licensed area, being an area which is wholly or partly included in the field; and

(ii) it was connected with the participator; and

(c) if he is a participator in the field by reason of an arrangement between him and another company, being an arrangement to which paragraph 5 of Schedule 3 to the principal Act applies (transfer of rights etc. to associated company), the date on which the arrangement was made or, if later, the date on which that other company first qualified in respect of any licensed area, being an area which is wholly or partly included in the field.

113(5) For the purposes of subsection (4) above, a person qualifies in respect of a licensed area when, in respect of that area–

(a) he is, or is one of those, entitled to the benefit of a licence, or

(b) he enjoys rights under an agreement, being an agreement which has been approved by the Board and certified by the OGA to confer on him rights which are the same as, or similar to, those conferred by a licence.

113(6) Where (apart from this section) expenditure would be allowable under section 5 or section 5A or section 5B of the principal Act in the case of a participator in an oil field (in this subsection referred to as **"the new participator"**) by virtue only of paragraphs 16 to 16B of Schedule 17 to the Finance Act 1980 (transfers of interests in oil fields) then, for the purpose of determining whether the expenditure is allowable in his case in accordance with this section, the date which was the qualifying date in relation to the old participator (within the meaning of that Schedule), rather than the date given by subsection (4) above, shall be taken to be the qualifying date in relation to the new participator.

113(7) For the purposes of subsection (2) above the date on which the winning of oil from an oil field has permanently ceased is the date stated in a decision (whether of the Board or on appeal from the Board) under Schedule 8 to the principal Act to be that date.

113(8) For the purposes of this section, one company is **connected** with another if–

(a) one is a 51 per cent subsidiary of the other and the other is not a 51 per cent subsidiary of any company; or

(b) each of them is a 51 per cent subsidiary of a third company which is not itself a 51 per cent subsidiary of any company;

and Chapter 3 of Part 24 of the Corporation Tax Act 2010 (subsidiaries) applies for the purposes of this subsection.

113(9) In this section–

(a) **"company"** means any body corporate; and

(b) any reference to the **winning of oil from an oil field permanently ceasing** includes a reference to the permanent cessation of operations for the winning of oil from the field.

113(10) This section shall have effect in relation to any expenditure or losses in respect of which a claim is made after 13th September 1983.

Prospective amendments – In s. 113(5)(b) the word "OGA" substituted for the words "Secretary of State" in each place by SI 2016/898, reg. 6(2), with effect immediately after the commencement of SCA 2016, s. 48.

History – In s. 113(1), the words "or section 5B" were inserted, and words between "determining whether any" and "expenditure is allowable" were omitted by FA 1987, s. 64 and Sch. 13, Pt. II, para. 9(1) and s. 72 and Sch. 16, Pt. X.

In s. 113(2), the words "falling within subsection (1B)" substituted for the words "which, in the case of any other oil field from which the winning of oil has permanently ceased, has accrued as mentioned in subsection (1) " and the words "from the abandoned field" substituted for the words "from that other field" by FA 2001, s. 101(3)(a), (b) which is deemed to have come into force on 7 March 2001.

In s. 113(4), the words "(subject to subsection (6) below)" inserted, and in s. 113(6), the words ", rather than the date given … in relation to the new participator" substituted by FA 1997, s. 107 in relation to any expenditure in respect of which a claim is made on or after 23 July 1996.

In s. 113(5)(b), the word "OGA" substituted for the words "Secretary of State" by SI 2016/898, reg. 8, with effect from 1 October 2016 (as the 21st day after being made on 10 September 2016).

In s. 113(6), the words "or section 5B" were inserted, and "paragraphs 16 to 16B" were substituted by FA 1987, s. 64 and Sch. 13, Pt. II, para. 9(2).

In s. 113(8), the words "Chapter 3 of Part 24 of the Corporation Tax Act 2010" substituted for the words "section 838 of the Taxes Act 1988" by CTA 2010, s. 1177 and Sch. 1, para. 186, with effect for corporation tax purposes for accounting periods ending on or after 1 April 2010, and for income tax and capital gains tax purposes for the tax year 2010–11 and subsequent tax years.

See ICTA 1988, s. 844 and Sch. 29, para. 32 for substitution of former reference to that Act in s. 113(8).

114 Sales of gas: treatment of certain payments

114(1) This section applies only in relation to oil consisting of gas and references in the following provisions of this section to oil shall be construed accordingly.

114(2) In any case where, under a contract for the sale of oil won from an oil field, the consideration includes any sum–

(a) which is payable by the buyer in respect of a quantity of oil to be delivered at a specified time or in a specified period, and

(b) which is payable whether or not the buyer takes delivery of the whole of the oil at that time or in that period, and

(c) which, in the event that the buyer does not take delivery of the whole of the oil, entitles the buyer to delivery of oil free of charge at a later time or in a later period,

then, to the extent that the sum is payable in respect of oil which is not delivered at the time or in the period in question, the sum shall be treated for the purposes of the principal Act as an advance payment for the oil to be delivered free of charge and, accordingly, that oil shall be treated for those purposes as sold for a price which (subject to any additional element arising under the following provisions of this section) is equal to that advance payment.

114(3) Where, in a case falling within subsection (2) above, an amount of oil is delivered free of charge in pursuance of the entitlement referred to in paragraph (c) of that subsection, the proportion of the advance payment referred to in that subsection which is to be attributed to that amount of oil shall be that which that amount of oil bears to the total quantity of oil of which the buyer is entitled to delivery free of charge by virtue of the payment of the sum in question.

114(4) In any case where–

(a) by virtue of subsection (2) above a sum falls to any extent to be treated as an advance payment for oil to be delivered free of charge, but

(b) at the latest date at which oil could be delivered free of charge in pursuance of the entitlement referred to in paragraph (c) of that subsection, the whole or any part of the oil to which that entitlement relates has not been so delivered,

then at that latest date, one tonne of oil shall be deemed to be delivered as mentioned in paragraph (b) above and so much of the advance payment as has not, under subsection (3) above, been attributed to oil actually delivered shall be attributed to that one tonne.

114(5) Where, under a contract for the sale of oil won from an oil field, the consideration includes any sums (in this section referred to as **"capacity payments"**)–

(a) which are payable by the buyer at specified times or in respect of specified periods, and

(b) which, though they may vary in amount by reference to deliveries of oil or other factors, are payable whether or not oil is delivered under the contract at particular times or in particular periods, and

(c) which do not, under the terms of the contract or by virtue of subsection (2) above, fall to be treated, in whole or in part, as advance payments for oil to be delivered at some time after the times or periods at or in respect of which the sums are payable,

then, in so far as they would not do so apart from this subsection, the capacity payments shall be treated for the purposes of the principal Act as an additional element of the price received or receivable for the oil sold under the contract.

114(6) For the purpose of determining, in a case where there are capacity payments under a contract for the sale of oil won from an oil field, the assessable profit or allowable loss accruing in a particular chargeable period to the participator by whom oil is sold under the contract, each capacity payment shall be treated as an additional element of the price received or receivable for the oil delivered by him under the contract in the chargeable period in which the capacity payment is paid or payable; and if no oil is in fact so delivered in a chargeable period in which a capacity payment is paid or payable, one tonne of oil shall be deemed to be so delivered in that period and, accordingly, the capacity payment shall be treated for the purposes of the principal Act as the price for which that tonne is sold.

114(7) If, by virtue of subsection (4) or subsection (6) above, one tonne of oil is deemed to be delivered in any chargeable period of the oil field referred to in subsection (2) or, as the case may be, subsection (5) above, a return for that period by the participator concerned under paragraph 2 of Schedule 2 to the principal Act shall give the like information in relation to that tonne as in relation to any other oil falling within sub-paragraph (2)(a) of that paragraph.

Cross references – OTA 1975, Sch. 3, para. 3A: definition of market value of light gases.
FA 1986, Sch. 21, para. 4, 6: treatment of "take or pay" and "capacity" payments under election for alternative valuation of light gases.

115 Information relating to sales at arm's length and market value of oil

115(1) The Board may, by notice in writing given to a company which is or has been a participator in an oil field, require that company to give to the Board, within such time (not being less than thirty days) as may be specified in the notice, such particulars (which may include details of relevant documents) as may be so specified of any related transaction which appears to the Board to be relevant for the purpose of–

(a) determining whether a disposal of any oil is a sale at arm's length, or

(b) ascertaining the market value of any oil.

115(2) For the purposes of a notice under subsection (1) above a transaction is a **related transaction** if, but only if, it is one to which the company to whom the notice is given or a company associated with that company was a party; and for the purposes of this subsection two companies are **associated** with one another if–

(a) one is under the control of the other; or

(b) both are under the control of the same person or persons;

and in this subsection **"control"** has the meaning given by section 1124 of the Corporation Tax Act 2010.

115(3) In any case where a company (in this subsection and subsection (4) below referred to as **"the participator company"**) is or has been a participator in an oil field and–

(a) the participator company is a 51 per cent subsidiary of another company, or

(b) another company is a 51 per cent subsidiary of the participator company, or

(c) the participator company and another company are both 51 per cent subsidiaries of a third company,

the Board may, by notice in writing given to any company referred to in paragraphs (a) to (c) above which is resident in the United Kingdom, require it to make available for inspection any relevant books, accounts or other documents or records whatsoever of the company itself, or, subject to subsection (5) below, of any other company which is its 51 per cent subsidiary.

115(4) In subsection (3) above **"relevant"** means relating to any transaction which is relevant for the purpose of–

(a) determining whether a disposal of any oil by the participator company is a sale at arm's length; or

(b) ascertaining the market value of oil won by the participator company.

115(5) In any case where–

(a) under subsection (3) above a company is by notice required to make available for inspection any books, accounts, documents or records of one of its 51 per cent subsidiaries which is resident outside the United Kingdom, and

(b) it appears to the Board, on the application of the company, that the circumstances are such that the requirement ought not to have effect,

the Board shall direct that the company need not comply with the requirement.

115(6) If, on an application under subsection (5) above, the Board refuse to give a direction under that subsection, the company concerned may appeal, by notice in writing given to the Board within thirty days after the refusal, and, where such an appeal is notified to the tribunal, the tribunal, if satisfied that the requirement in question ought in the circumstances not to have effect, may determine accordingly.

115(6A) The provisions of paragraphs 14A to 14I of Schedule 2 to the principal Act shall apply to appeals under this paragraph subject to any necessary modifications.

115(7) In this section– **"company"** means any body corporate; and **"51 per cent subsidiary"** shall be construed in accordance with Chapter 3 of Part 24 of the Corporation Tax Act 2010 (subsidiaries).

History – In s. 115(2), the words "section 1124 of the Corporation Tax Act 2010" substituted for the words "section 840 of the Taxes Act 1988" by CTA 2010, s. 1177 and Sch. 1, para. 187(2), with effect for corporation tax purposes for accounting periods ending on or after 1 April 2010, and for income tax and capital gains tax purposes for the tax year 2010–11 and subsequent tax years.
In s. 115(6) the words "may appeal, by notice" substituted for the words "may, by notice" and the words "and, where such an appeal is notified to the tribunal, the tribunal" substituted for the words "appeal to the Special Commissioners who" by SI 2009/56, art. 3 and Sch. 1, para. 104(2), with effect from 1 April 2009, subject to transitional and saving provisions in SI 2009/56, Sch. 3.
S. 115(6A) inserted by SI 2009/56, art. 3 and Sch. 1, para. 104(3), with effect from 1 April 2009, subject to transitional and saving provisions in SI 2009/56, Sch. 3.
In s. 115(7), the words "Chapter 3 of Part 24 of the Corporation Tax Act 2010" substituted for the words "section 838 of the Taxes Act 1988" by CTA 2010, s. 1177 and Sch. 1, para. 187(3), with effect for corporation tax purposes for accounting periods ending on or after 1 April 2010, and for income tax and capital gains tax purposes for the tax year 2010–11 and subsequent tax years.
See ICTA 1988, Sch. 29, para. 32 for substitution of former references to that Act.

116 Offences relating to section 115

116(1) Where a company has been required by notice under subsection (1) or subsection (3) of section 115 above to give any particulars or, as the case may be, to make available for inspection any books, accounts, documents or records and fails to comply with the notice, the company shall be liable, subject to subsection (3) below–

(a) to a penalty not exceeding £500; and

(b) if the failure continues after it has been declared by the court or the tribunal before whom proceedings for the penalty have been commenced, to a further penalty not exceeding £100 for each day on which the failure so continues.

116(2) Where a company fraudulently or negligently furnishes, gives, produces or makes any incorrect information, document or record of a kind mentioned in subsection (1) or subsection (3) of section 115 above, the company shall be liable to a penalty not exceeding £2,500 or, in the case of fraud on its part, £5,000.

116(3) A company shall not be liable to any penalty incurred under subsection (1) above for failure to comply with a notice if the failure is remedied before proceedings for the recovery of the penalty are commenced.

116(4) In this section **"company"** has the same meaning as in section 115 above.

History – In s. 116(1)(b) the word "tribunal" substituted for the word "Commissioners" by SI 2009/56, art. 3 and Sch. 1, para. 105, with effect from 1 April 2009, subject to transitional and saving provisions in SI 2009/56, Sch. 3.

PART VI – MISCELLANEOUS AND SUPPLEMENTARY

128 Short title, interpretation, construction and repeals

128(1) This Act may be cited as the Finance Act 1984.

128(2) In this Act **"the Taxes Act"** means the Income and Corporation Taxes Act 1970; and **"the Taxes Act 1988"** means the Income and Corporation Taxes Act 1988.

128(5) Part V of this Act shall be construed as one with Part I of the Oil Taxation Act 1975 and references in Part V of this Act to the principal Act are references to that Act.

History – See ICTA 1988, s. 844 and Sch. 29, para. 32 for insertion of reference to that Act in s. 128(2).

FINANCE ACT 1985

(1985 Chapter 54)

[*25th July 1985*]

ARRANGEMENT OF SECTIONS

PART IV – OIL TAXATION

PART V – MISCELLANEOUS AND SUPPLEMENTARY

PART IV – OIL TAXATION

90 Limitations on relief for exploration and appraisal expenditure

90 [Amends OTA 1975, s. 5(A), with respect to expenditure incurred on or after 1 April 1986 in the case of amendments to s. 5A(2), and 19 March 1985 in all other cases.]

91 Chargeable periods relevant to limit on tax payable and expenditure supplement

91 [Amends OTA 1975, s. 9, in respect of new oil fields whose first chargeable period ends after 30 June 1985, and to FA 1981, s. 111, with respect to chargeable periods ending after 30 June 1985.]

92 Qualifying assets: exclusion of land and certain buildings etc.

92 [Amends OTA 1983, s. 8, 15 and Sch. 2, para. 4, in respect of consideration received or receivable after 19 March 1985.]

PART V – MISCELLANEOUS AND SUPPLEMENTARY

98 Short title, interpretation, construction and repeals

98(1) This Act may be cited as the Finance Act 1985.

98(5) Part IV of this Act shall be construed as one with Part I of the Oil Taxation Act 1975.

FINANCE ACT 1986

(1986 Chapter 41)

[*25th July 1986*]

ARRANGEMENT OF SECTIONS

PART VI – OIL TAXATION

PART VII – MISCELLANEOUS AND SUPPLEMENTARY

SCHEDULES

PART VI – OIL TAXATION

108 The on-shore/off-shore boundary

108(1) For the purposes of the enactments relating to oil taxation, land lying between the landward boundary of the territorial sea and the shoreline of the United Kingdom (as defined below) shall be treated as part of the bed of the territorial sea of the United Kingdom and any reference in those enactments to the territorial sea or the subsoil beneath it shall be construed accordingly.

108(2) Any reference to the **United Kingdom** in the enactments relating to oil taxation, where that reference is a reference to a geographical area, shall be treated as a reference to the United Kingdom exclusive of the land referred to in subsection (1) above and of any waters for the time being covering that land.

108(3) In this section–

(a) **"the landward boundary of the territorial sea"** means the line for the time being ordered by Her Majesty in Council to be the baseline from which the breadth of the territorial sea is measured; and

(b) **"the shoreline of the United Kingdom"** means, subject to subsection (4) below, the high-water line along the coast, including the coast of all islands comprised in the United Kingdom.

108(4) In the case of waters adjacent to a bay, as defined in the Territorial Waters Order in Council 1964, the shoreline means–

(a) if the bay has only one mouth and the distance between the high-water lines of the natural entrance points of the bay does not exceed 5,000 metres, a straight line joining those high-water lines;

(b) if, because of the presence of islands, the bay has more than one mouth and the distances between the high-water lines of the natural entrance points of each mouth added together do not exceed 5,000 metres, a series of straight lines across each of the mouths drawn so as to join those high-water lines; and

(c) if neither paragraph (a) nor paragraph (b) above applies, a straight line 5,000 metres in length drawn from high-water line to high-water line within the bay in such a manner as to enclose the maximum area of water that is possible with a line of that length.

108(5) If, by virtue of this section, it becomes necessary at any time to establish the high-water line at any place, it shall be taken to be the line which, on the current Admiralty chart showing that place, is depicted as "the coastline"; and for this purpose,–

(a) an Admiralty chart means a chart published under the superintendence of the Hydrographer of the Navy;

(b) if there are two or more Admiralty charts of different scales showing the place in question and depicting the coastline, account shall be taken only of the largest scale chart; and

(c) subject to paragraph (b) above, the current Admiralty chart at any time is that most recently published before that time.

108(6) In this section **"the enactments relating to oil taxation"** means Part I of the Oil Taxation Act 1975 and any enactment which is to be construed as one with that Part.

108(7) This section shall be deemed to have come into force on 1st April 1986.

Cross references – F(No. 2)A 1992, s. 74(2): oil exported direct from offshore fields: an oil field is offshore if the whole of it is situated outside the geographical area of the UK, as determined under s. 108.

Notes – Territorial Sea Act 1987, s. 1: breadth of territorial sea is 12 nautical miles.

109 Alternative valuation of light gases

109(1) Where an election is made under this section before 1st January 1994 and accepted by the Board, the market value for the purposes of the Oil Taxation Acts of any light gases to which the election applies shall be determined, not in accordance with paragraphs 2, 2A and 3 of Schedule 3 to the principal Act (value under a notional contract), but by reference to a price formula specified in the election; and in relation to any such light gases, any reference to market value in any other provision of the Oil Taxation Acts shall be construed accordingly.

109(2) No election may be made under this section in respect of light gases which are "ethane" as defined in subsection (6)(a) of section 134 of the Finance Act 1982 (alternative valuation of ethane used for petrochemical purposes) if the principal purpose for which the gases are being or are to be used is that specified in subsection (2)(b) of the said section 134 (use for petrochemical purposes).

109(3) Subject to subsection (4) below, an election under this section applies only to light gases–

(a) which, during the period covered by the election, are either disposed of otherwise than in sales at arm's length or relevantly appropriated; and

(b) which are not subject to fractionation between the time at which they are so disposed of or appropriated and the time at which they are applied or used for the purposes specified in the election.

109(4) In any case where–

(a) at a time during the period covered by an election, a market value falls to be determined for light gases to which subsection (4)(b) or (5)(d) of section 2 of the principal Act applies (oil stocks at the end of chargeable periods), and

(b) after the expiry of the chargeable period in question, the light gases are disposed of or appropriated as mentioned in subsection (3) above,

the market value of those light gases at the time referred to in paragraph (a) above shall be determined as if they were gases to which the election applies.

109(5) Schedule 18 to the Finance Act 1982 (which applies to elections under section 134 of that Act relating to ethane used or to be used for petrochemical purposes) shall have effect for supplementing this section but subject to the modifications in Schedule 21 to this Act (in which **"the 1982 Schedule"** means the said Schedule 18).

109(6) This section shall be construed as one with Part I of the principal Act and in this section–

(a) **"light gases"** means oil consisting of gas of which the largest component by volume over any chargeable period is methane or ethane or a combination of those gases and which–

 (i) results from the fractionation of gas before it is disposed of or appropriated as mentioned in subsection (3)(a) above, or

 (ii) before being so disposed of or appropriated, is not subjected to initial treatment or is subjected to initial treatment which does not include fractionation;

(b) **"the principal Act"** means the Oil Taxation Act 1975; and

(c) **"the Oil Taxation Acts"** means Part I of the principal Act and any enactment which is to be construed as one with that Part.

109(7) In this section **"fractionation"** means the treatment of gas in order to separate gas of one or more kinds as mentioned in paragraph 2A(3) of Schedule 3 to the principal Act; and for the purposes of subsection (6)(a) above,–

(a) the proportion of methane, ethane or a combination of the two in any gas shall be determined at a temperature of 15°C and at a pressure of one atmosphere; and

(b) any component other than methane, ethane or liquified petroleum gas shall be disregarded.

History – In s. 109(1), the words "before 1st January 1994" inserted by FA 1994, s. 236(3)(b).

Cross references – FA 1994, s. 236(2), (3): valuation of certain light gases.

110 Attribution of certain receipts and expenditure between oil fields

110(1) Section 8 of the Oil Taxation Act 1983 (qualifying assets) shall have effect, and be deemed always to have had effect, subject to the amendments in subsections (2) and (3) below.

110(2) [Amends OTA 1983, s. 8(3).]

110(3) [Inserts OTA 1983, s. 8(3A).]

110(4) [Inserts OTA 1983, Sch. 1, para. 6(3), to be deemed always to have had effect.]Pt. VII

PART VII – MISCELLANEOUS AND SUPPLEMENTARY

114 Short title, interpretation, construction and repeals

114(1) This Act may be cited as the Finance Act 1986.

114(2) [Not relevant to petroleum revenue tax.]

114(3) [Not relevant to petroleum revenue tax.]

114(4) [Not relevant to petroleum revenue tax.]

114(5) [Not relevant to petroleum revenue tax.]

114(6) The enactments and Orders specified in Schedule 23 to this Act are hereby repealed to the extent specified in the third column of that Schedule, but subject to any provision at the end of any Part of that Schedule.

SCHEDULE 21 – MODIFICATIONS OF FINANCE ACT 1982, SCHEDULE 18 IN RELATION TO ELECTIONS UNDER SECTION 109 OF THIS ACT

Section 109

GENERAL MODIFICATIONS

1(1) For any reference in the 1982 Schedule to ethane there shall be substituted a reference to light gases, as defined in section 109 of this Act.

1(2) Except as provided below, any reference in the 1982 Schedule to section 134 of the Finance Act 1982 shall be construed as a reference to section 109 of this Act.

SPECIFIC MODIFICATIONS

2(1) In paragraph 1 (provisions as to the election) in sub-paragraph (2)(b) for the words "and not exceeding fifteen years" there shall be substituted "or in the case of an election made before 31st December 1986, beginning on 1st July 1986" and, for sub-paragraph (2)(d) there shall be substituted–

"(d) specify the purposes for which the light gases to which the election applies will be applied or used,".

2(2) At the end of that paragraph there shall be inserted the following sub-paragraph–

"**1(4)** If an election relates to light gases, then, in addition to the matters referred to in sub-paragraph (2) above the election shall contain–

(a) a description of the characteristics of the supply by which the disposal or appropriation is intended to be effected; and

(b) if that supply is of such a description that, if it were under a contract at arm's length, it is reasonable to expect that the price of the gas would vary with the level of the supply, a description of the pattern of supply which the party or parties to the election consider most probable."

3(1) In paragraph 2 (conditions for acceptance of an election) in sub-paragraph (1) after the words "and (3)" there shall be inserted "and paragraph 2A".

3(2) In sub-paragraph (2) of that paragraph, after the words "such that" there shall be inserted "subject to paragraphs 2A and 3A below".

4 After paragraph 2 there shall be inserted the following paragraph–

"**2A(1)** The provisions of this paragraph apply if, having regard to the pattern of supply described in an election as mentioned in paragraph 1(4)(b) above, it is reasonable to assume that, under a contract for the sale at arm's length of the light gases to which the election applies, the consideration would include–

(a) any such payments as are referred to in subsection (2) of section 114 of the Finance Act 1984 ("take or pay" payments), or

(b) any capacity payments, as defined in subsection (5) of that section.

2A(2) The relevant contract–

(a) shall be assumed to be for the delivery of gas according to the pattern of supply described in the election; and

(b) shall be assumed to contain provision for such of the payments referred to in sub-paragraph (1) above as are appropriate to that pattern of supply.

2A(3) Sub-paragraph (1) of paragraph 2 above shall have effect as if for the words following "sale at arm's length" there were substituted "of the light gases to which the election applies, the total sums payable under the contract in respect of deliveries of gas in any chargeable period would not differ materially from the sums determined in accordance with the price formula specified in the election for gases disposed of or appropriated in that period; and if the Board are not so satisfied they shall reject the election".

2A(4) The price formula specified in the election shall contain provisions for determining sums corresponding to such of the payments referred to in sub-paragraph (1) above as, by virtue of sub-paragraph (2) above, are assumed to be provided for by the relevant contract."

5(1) In paragraph 3 (definition of "the relevant contract") in sub-paragraph (1) in paragraph (a) after the word "and", in the first place where it occurs, there shall be inserted the words "which, subject to sub-paragraph (3) below" and in the words following paragraph (b) for the words from "is not" onwards, there shall be substituted "which, subject to paragraph 2A(2) above, is not necessarily a contract for the sale of light gases for the purposes specified in the election".

5(2) At the end of that paragraph there shall be added the following sub-paragraphs–

"**3(3)** In the case of an election which relates to light gases which are 'excluded oil', as defined in section 10(1) of the principal Act, sub-paragraph (1)(a) above shall have effect with the omission of the words from 'and which' to 'date of the election'.

3(4) Sub-paragraph (4) of paragraph 2A of Schedule 3 to the principal Act (assumptions as to consents in determining price under an arm's length contract) shall apply for the purposes of paragraphs 2 and 2A above as it applies for the purposes of paragraph 2 of that Schedule, substituting a reference to a relevant contract (as defined above) for any reference to the contract mentioned in paragraph 2(2) of that Schedule."

History – In para. 5(1), the words "in sub-paragraph (1)" were inserted by F(No. 2)A 1992, s. 74 and Sch. 15, para. 9, in accordance with s. 74(5).

6 After paragraph 3 there shall be inserted the following paragraph–

"MARKET VALUE WHERE PARAGRAPH 2A APPLIES

3A(1) Where an election is accepted by the Board and the price formula contains provision for the determination of sums as mentioned in paragraph 2A(4) above, then, for the purpose of determining the market value of gas to which the election applies, section 114 of the Finance Act 1984 (which deals with the treatment of such payments as are referred to in paragraph 2A(1) above) shall have effect in relation to those sums and that gas as if–

(a) those sums were part of the consideration under a contract for the sale of gas to which the election applies, and

(b) that contract provided for delivery of the gas according to the pattern of supply described in the election; and where the said section 114 has effect by virtue of this sub-paragraph, subsections (4), (6) and (7) of that section (which provide for and relate to the deemed delivery of one tonne of oil in certain periods) shall be treated for the purposes of the principal Act as providing for and relating to the deemed disposal or appropriation of one tonne of gas to which the election applies.

3A(2) Where sub-paragraph (1) above applies, the market value of the gas to which the election applies which is disposed of or appropriated in any chargeable period shall consist of–

(a) such amount (if any) as is determined in accordance with the price formula by reference to the quantity of gas disposed of or appropriated in that chargeable period; and

(b) any sums which, by virtue of sub-paragraph (1) above, either are treated as payments for gas supplied free of charge in that period or are treated as an additional element of the price received or receivable for gas disposed of or appropriated in that period.

3A(3) Where the market value of gas is determined as mentioned in sub-paragraph (2) above, any reference in the following provisions of this Schedule (however expressed) to the market value determined in accordance with the price formula is a reference to that value determined as mentioned in that sub-paragraph (that is to say, in accordance with the formula and section 114 of the Finance Act 1984 as applied by sub-paragraph (1) above).

3A(4) Where the market value of light gases to which an election applies is determined for a chargeable period as mentioned in sub-paragraph (2) above then, as respects a return for that period under paragraph 2 of Schedule 2 to the principal Act which is made by the participator who is the party or one of the parties to the election,–

(a) sub-paragraphs (2)(a)(iii) and (2)(b)(ii) of that paragraph (which require information with respect to each delivery or relevant appropriation of oil in the period) shall not apply in relation to the light gases to which the election applies; and

(b) there shall be included in his return a statement of the market value (determined as mentioned in sub-paragraph (2) above) of the light gases relevantly appropriated or disposed of by him in that period.

3A(5) Notwithstanding that, under sub-paragraph (2) above, a market value is determined for all the gas disposed of or appropriated in a particular chargeable period, for the purposes of determining–

(a) the market value referred to in section 2(5)(d) of the principal Act (stocks at the end of a period), and

(b) the market value referred to in subsection (1) or, as the case may be, subsection (2) of section 14 of that Act (valuation for corporation tax purposes of oil disposed of or appropriated), then, except in a case where the only gas disposed of or appropriated in a particular chargeable period is a single tonne which, by virtue of sub-paragraph (1) above, is treated as being disposed of or appropriated, the market value determined as mentioned in sub-paragraph (2) above shall be apportioned rateably to each quantity of gas disposed of or appropriated in that period."

7 After paragraph 6 there shall be inserted the following paragraph–

"PRICE FORMULA NO LONGER APPROPRIATE FOR PATTERN OF SUPPLY ETC.

6A(1) In any case where it appears to the Board–

(a) that light gases to which an election applies are being disposed of or appropriated in a manner, to an extent or by a pattern of supply which is different from that which was taken into consideration in the acceptance of the election, and

(b) that if, at the time the Board were considering whether the election should be accepted, they had taken into account as a probability the manner, extent or pattern of supply by which the gases are in fact being disposed of, they would have rejected the election, then, subject to sub-paragraph (4) below, the election shall not have effect with respect to any chargeable period beginning after the date on which the Board give notice under this paragraph to each of the parties to the election.

6A(2) Without prejudice to the generality of sub-paragraph (1) above, if at any time in a chargeable period the extent to which gases to which an election applies are disposed of or relevantly appropriated (including the case where none is so disposed of or appropriated) is such that, if the gas were being delivered under a contract at arm's length–

(a) the seller would be likely to incur financial penalties by reason of a failure to meet requirements arising from the pattern of supply described in the election, and

(b) those penalties would not be insubstantial, that shall be a ground for the Board to give notice under this paragraph.

6A(3) A notice under this paragraph shall state that, by reason of the matters referred to in sub-paragraph (1) above, the Board are no longer satisfied that the price formula specified in the election is appropriate to the disposals or appropriations actually being made of gases to which the election applies.

6A(4) If, within the period of three months beginning on the date of a notice under this paragraph, the party or parties to the election give notice in writing to the Board–

(a) specifying a new price formula taking account of the manner, extent or pattern of supply by which the gases to which the election applies are being disposed of or appropriated, and

(b) containing, if appropriate, a description of the changed pattern of supply which at the time of the notice, the party or parties to the election consider most probable, then, if that new price formula is accepted by the Board in accordance with paragraph 7 below, so much of sub-paragraph (1) above as provides that the election shall not have effect with respect to certain periods shall not apply.

61(4A) For each month in which a participator makes a relevant delivery, his monthly excess is the sum of his excesses (if any) calculated in accordance with subsection (3).

61(4B) For each chargeable period of an oil field **"the excess of nominated proceeds for the period"** means, in relation to a participator in the oil field, that proportion of the sum of his monthly excesses for the chargeable period (if any) which is attributable to the field.

61(5) [Inserts OTA 1975, s. 2(5)(e).]

61(6) [Omitted by FA 2006, s. 149(4).]

61(7) [Omitted by FA 2006, s. 149(4).]

61(8) The Board may by regulations made by statutory instrument make provision, including provision having effect with respect to things done on or after 1st July 2006–

(a) as to oil which is excluded from this section, as mentioned in subsection (2) above; and

(b) for any purpose for which regulations, other than those described as "Treasury regulations", may be made under Schedule 10 to this Act;

and regulations made by virtue of paragraph (a) above may amend paragraph (a) and (b) of subsection (2) above.

61(9) A statutory instrument made in the exercise of the power conferred by subsection (8) above shall (unless otherwise expressly provided) be subject to annulment in pursuance of a resolution of the Commons House of Parliament.

History – In s. 61(1) words ", supplies and appropriations" omitted by FA 2006, s. 150(2) and repealed by FA 2006, s. 178 and Sch. 26, Pt. 5(2), with effect in relation to chargeable periods ending on or after 1 July 2006.
S. 61(3)–(4B) substituted for former s. 61(3) and (4) by FA 2006, s. 149(3), with effect in relation to chargeable periods ending on or after 1 July 2006.
S. 61(6) and (7) omitted by FA 2006, s. 149(4) and repealed by FA 2006, s. 178 and Sch. 26, Pt. 5(2), with effect in relation to chargeable periods ending on or after 1 July 2006.
In s. 61(8) the words "1st July 2006" substituted for the words "9th February 1987" by FA 2006, s. 149(5), with effect in relation to chargeable periods ending on or after 1 July 2006.
In s. 61(9) the words "subsection (7) or" which preceded "subsection (8)" omitted (and repealed by FA 2006, s. 178 and Sch. 26, Pt. 5(2)) and the words "(unless otherwise expressly provided)" inserted by FA 2006, s. 149(6), with effect in relation to chargeable periods ending on or after 1 July 2006.

Cross references – OTA 1975, s. 2: assessable profits and allowable losses.

Statutory instruments – SI 1987/1338: partly made under s. 61(8).

62 Market value of oil to be determined on a monthly basis

62(1) [Amends OTA 1975, s. 2(9)(a)(i) and (ii), 5A(5B), 14(4), (4A)(b).]

62(2) [Amends OTA 1975, s. 2(4)(b), (5)(d) and Sch. 2, para. 2(2)(d). Partly repealed by FA 2006, s. 178 and Sch. 26, Pt. 5(1).]

62(3) In Schedule 3 to the principal Act (miscellaneous provisions relating to petroleum revenue tax) paragraphs 2, 2A and 3 (market value of oil) shall be amended in accordance with Part I of Schedule 11 to this Act; and the consequential amendments of the principal Act in Part II of that Schedule shall have effect.

62(3A) Subsection (4) applies to a participator in an oil field in any case where–

(a) paragraph 2 of Schedule 2 to the principal Act requires the participator to make a return for any chargeable period (including cases where the latest time for the delivery of that return is deferred), and

(b) there are any relevant sales of Category 2 oil (as defined in subsection (6) below).

62(4) In such a case, that participator shall also be required, not later than the end of the second month after the end of that chargeable period, to deliver to the Board a return of all relevant sales of Category 2 oil stating–

(a) the date of the contract of sale;

(b) the name of the seller;

(c) the name of the buyer;

(d) the quantity of Category 2 oil actually sold and, if it is different, the quantity of Category 2 oil contracted to be sold;

(e) the price receivable for that Category 2 oil;

(f) the date which, under the contract, was the date or, as the case may be, the latest date for delivery of the Category 2 oil and the date on which the Category 2 oil was actually delivered; and

(g) such other particulars as the Board may prescribe.

62(5) Where two or more companies which are participators in the same oil field are members of the same group of companies, within the meaning of section 413(3) of the Taxes Act, a return made for the

PRT Statutes

purposes of subsection (4) above by one of them and expressed also to be made on behalf of the other or others shall be treated for the purposes of this section as a return made by each of them.

62(6) For the purposes of the return required by subsection (4) above from a participator in an oil field, **a relevant sale of Category 2 oil** is a contract for the sale of Category 2 oil at arm's length to which the participator or any company which is resident in the United Kingdom and associated with the participator for the purposes of section 115(2) of the Finance Act 1984 is a party (as seller, buyer or otherwise), being a sale of Category 2 oil–

(a) for delivery at any time during the chargeable period referred to in subsection (3A) above; and

(b) details of which are not included in a return for the period under paragraph 2 of Schedule 2 to the principal Act which is delivered to the Board at the same time as the return required by subsection (4) above or which was delivered to them previously; and

(c) which is for the delivery of at least 500 metric tonnes of Category 2 oil;

(d) [omitted by FA 2008, s. 106(5).]

62(7) A return under subsection (4) above shall be in such form as the Board may prescribe and shall include a declaration that the return is correct and complete; and if a participator fails to delivery a return under that subsection he shall be liable–

(a) to a penalty not exceeding £500; and

(b) if the failure continues after it has been declared by the court or the tribunal before which proceedings for the penalty have been commenced, to a further penalty not exceeding £100 for each day on which the failure so continues;

except that a participator shall not be liable to a penalty under this subsection if the failure is remedied before proceedings for the recovery of the penalty are commenced.

62(8) Where a participator fraudulently or negligently delivers an incorrect return under subsection (4) above, he shall be liable to a penalty not exceeding £2,500 or, in the case of fraud, £5,000.

62(8A) For provision about the meaning of **"Category 2 oil"**, see paragraph 2 of Schedule 3 to the principal Act (which applies by virtue of section 72(6) below).

62(9) This section has effect with respect to chargeable periods ending after 31st December 1986.

History – S. 62(2)(c) repealed by FA 2006, s. 178 and Sch. 26, Pt. 5(1), with effect in relation to oil delivered or appropriated on or after 1 July 2006, subject to the provisions of FA 2006, s. 147(2)–(8).
S. 62(3A) inserted by FA 2008, s. 106(2), with effect in relation to chargeable periods ending on or after 30 June 2008.
In s. 62(4) the words before para. (a) substituted by FA 2008, s. 106(3), with effect in relation to chargeable periods ending on or after 30 June 2008.
In s. 62(4)(d), (e) and (f) the words "Category 2 oil" substituted for the word "oil" by FA 2008, s. 106(4), with effect in relation to chargeable periods ending on or after 30 June 2008.
In s. 62(4), the words from the beginning of the subsection to "deliver to the Board a return" substituted by FA 1999, s. 102(6) for chargeable periods ending on or after 30 June 1999.
In s. 62(6) the words "Category 2 oil" substituted for the word "oil" twice, in para. (a) the words "subsection (3A)" substituted for the words "subsection (4)", in para. (c) the words "Category 2 oil" substituted for the word "oil" and para. (d) and the word "and" preceding it omitted by FA 2008, s. 106(5), with effect in relation to chargeable periods ending on or after 30 June 2008.
S. 62(6)(b) substituted by FA 1999, s. 102(7) for chargeable periods ending on or after 30 June 1999.
In s. 62(6), the words "at arm's length" and, in former s. 62(6)(b), the words "or otherwise" inserted by F(No. 2)A 1987, s. 101(2) as modifications, with respect to chargeable periods ending after 1 January 1987.
In s. 62(7)(b) the words "tribunal before which" substituted for the words "Commissioners before whom" by SI 2009/56, art. 3 and Sch. 1, para. 127, with effect from 1 April 2009, subject to transitional and saving provisions in SI 2009/56, Sch. 3.
S. 62(8A) inserted by FA 2008, s. 106(6), with effect in relation to chargeable periods ending on or after 30 June 2008.
See ICTA 1988, s. 844 and Sch. 29, para. 32 for substitution of reference to that Act in s. 62(5).

63 Blends of oil from two or more fields

63(1) This section applies if, at any time before its disposal or relevant appropriation, oil won from an oil field ("the relevant field") in a chargeable period ("the relevant period") is mixed with oil won from one or more other oil fields.

63(2) A relevant participator's share of oil won from the relevant field in the relevant period is to be taken to be the amount of the blended oil that it is just and reasonable (for the purposes of the oil taxation legislation) to allocate to the participator in respect of the relevant period.

63(3) In making the allocation regard must be had (in particular) to the quantity and quality of the oil derived from each of the originating fields.

63(4) If the participators in the originating fields select a method for making the allocation, that method is to be used to determine that allocation.

63(5) But that is subject to Schedule 12.

63(6) If the participators in the originating fields fail to select a method for making the allocation, HMRC may select a method.

63(7) In a case where only some oil won from the relevant field in the relevant period is, before its disposal or relevant appropriation, mixed with oil won from one or more other fields, subsection (2) has effect for the purpose of determining the amount of the blended oil that is to be taken to be included in a relevant participator's share of oil won from the relevant field.

63(8) Schedule 12 contains provision supplementing this section.

63(9) In this section and Schedule 12–

"blended oil" means oil that consists of oil from two or more oil fields that has been mixed;

"foreign field" means an area which is a foreign field for the purposes of section 12 of the Oil Taxation Act 1983;

"oil" includes any substance which would be oil if the enactments mentioned in section 1(1) of the principal Act extended to a foreign field;

"oil field" includes a foreign field;

"oil taxation legislation" means Part 1 of the principal Act and any enactment construed as one with that Part;

"originating fields", in relation to any blended oil, means the oil fields from which oil which has been mixed as mentioned in subsection (1);

"relevant participator" means a person who is a participator in the relevant field at any time in the relevant period.

History – S. 63 substituted by FA 2009, s. 85 and Sch. 39, para. 2, with effect in relation to chargeable periods beginning after 30 June 2009.

64 Relief for research expenditure

64(1) The section set out in Part I of Schedule 13 to this Act shall be inserted in the principal Act after section 5A for the purpose of setting up a new allowance by virtue of which a participator in an oil field may obtain relief for certain research expenditure which is incurred otherwise than in connection with that field.

64(2) For the purpose of giving effect to, and in consequence of, the new allowance, the enactments specified in Part II of Schedule 13 to this Act shall have effect subject to the amendments there specified.

64(3) Part III of Schedule 13 to this Act shall have effect with respect to sums falling to be set off against expenditure which would otherwise be allowable under the new section set out in Part I of that Schedule.

65 Cross-field allowance of certain expenditure incurred on new fields

65(1) Where an election is made by a participator in an oil field (in this section referred to as **"the receiving field"**), up to ten per cent of certain expenditure incurred on or after 17th March 1987 in connection with another field, being a field which is for the purposes of this section a relevant new field, shall be allowable in accordance with this section in respect of the receiving field; and in the following provisions of this section the relevant new field in connection with which the expenditure was incurred is referred to as **"the field of origin"**.

65(2) An election under this section may be made only in respect of expenditure which–

(a) was incurred by the participator making the election or, if that participator is a body corporate, by an associated company; and

(b) as regards the field of origin, is allowable under section 3 or section 4 of the principal Act or section 3 of the Oil Taxation Act 1983; and

(c) as regards the field of origin, has been allowed as qualifying for supplement under section 2(9)(b)(ii) or (c)(ii) of the principal Act (in the following provisions of this section referred to as **"supplement"**); and

(d) is not expenditure falling within subsection (1) of section 5A of the principal Act (allowance of exploration and appraisal expenditure);

and Part I of Schedule 14 to this Act shall have effect with respect to elections under this section.

65(3) A participator may not make an election under this section in respect of expenditure which was incurred before the date which is his qualifying date, within the meaning of section 113 of the Finance Act 1984 (restriction of PRT reliefs), in relation to the receiving field unless that date falls before the end of the first chargeable period in relation to that field.

65(4) Where, by virtue of an election by a participator under this section, an amount of expenditure is allowable in respect of the receiving field, it shall be allowable as follows–

(a) it shall be taken into account in that assessment to tax or determination relating to a chargeable period of the receiving field which is specified in Part II of Schedule 14 to this Act; and

(b) it shall be so taken into account under subsection (8) of section 2 of the principal Act (allowable expenditure etc.) as if, for the chargeable period in question, it were an addition to the sum mentioned in paragraphs (a) of that subsection; and

(c) it shall be excluded in determining for the purposes of section 111(2) of the Finance Act 1981 (restriction of expenditure supplement) whether any, and if so what, assessable profit or allowable loss accrues to the participator in any chargeable period of the receiving field.

65(5) Where, by virtue of an election by a participator under this section, an amount of expenditure is allowable in respect of the receiving field, that amount shall be disregarded in determining, as regards the field of origin, the amounts referred to (in relation to the participator or the associated company, as the case may be) in paragraph (b) or paragraph (c) of subsection (9) of section 2 of the principal Act (allowable expenditure and supplement thereon).

65(6) In Schedule 14 to this Act–

(a) Part III has effect to determine for the purposes of this section what is a relevant new field and who is an associated company of a participator making an election;

(b) Part IV contains provisions supplemental to and consequential upon the allowance of expenditure by virtue of an election under this section, including provisions applicable where a notice of variation is served in respect of expenditure which is already the subject of such an election;

(c) **"the receiving field"** and **"the field of origin"** have the meaning assigned by subsection (1) above;

(d) **"the principal section"** means this section;

(e) **"election"** means an election under this section; and

(f) **"supplement"** has the meaning assigned by subsection (2)(c) above.

Cross references – OTA 1975, s. 6(9)(c): set-off of unrelievable field loss against expenditure falling within s. 65 which is allowable in accordance with Sch. 14

OTA 1983, s. 3: expenditure incurred on long-term assets other than non-dedicated mobile assets.

66 Oil allowance: adjustment for final periods

66(1) For the purposes of this section–

(a) **"the final allocation period"**, in relation to an oil field, means the chargeable period of that field in which section 8(6)(b) of the principal Act applies (the earliest chargeable period in which oil allowance is subject to "the necessary restriction" in order to confine it within the overall maximum); and

(b) **"the penultimate period"**, in relation to an oil field, means the chargeable period of that field which immediately precedes the final allocation period;

and any reference in this section to **the final periods** is a reference to the final allocation period and the penultimate period.

66(2) The following provisions of this section apply if the responsible person gives notice to the Board (in this section referred to as an **"apportionment notice"**) specifying the manner in which the oil allowance for the field is to be apportioned between the participators in each of the two final periods, being a manner designed–

(a) to produce, so far as practicable, the result specified in subsection (4) below, being a result which, in the circumstances of the case, could not be achieved under section 8(6)(b) of the principal Act; and

(b) to secure that adjustments in a participator's share of the oil allowance are made in the final allocation period in preference to the penultimate period.

66(3) An apportionment notice shall be of no effect unless–

(a) it is given not later than six months after the expiry of the final allocation period; and

(b) not later than the date of the notice the responsible person notifies the Board in accordance with paragraph (b) of subsection (6) of section 8 of the principal Act of the manner in which the necessary restriction, as defined in that subsection, is to be apportioned between the participators; and

(c) it specifies a period for each of paragraphs (a) and (b) of subsection (4) below; and

(d) it contains such information as the Board may prescribe for the purpose of showing how, or to what extent, the apportionment of the oil allowance achieves the result specified in subsection (4) below.

66(4) The result referred to in subsection (2) above is that the respective shares of the oil allowance utilised by each of two or more participators specified in the apportionment notice bear to each other the same proportion as their respective shares in oil won and saved from the field and, for this purpose–

(a) *a participator's share of the oil allowance* means the total amount of the allowance utilised by him over the period specified for the purpose of this paragraph in the apportionment notice; and

(b) a participator's share in oil won and saved from the field means the total of the oil included in his share of oil won and saved from the field (as specified in returns under Schedule 2 to the principal

Act) over the period specified for the purposes of this paragraph in the apportionment notice, being a period which includes that specified for the purposes of paragraph (a) above.

66(5) If the Board are satisfied that an apportionment notice complies with subsections (2) to (4) above, they shall give notice to the responsible person accepting the apportionment notice and, on the giving of that notice–

(a) the apportionment specified in the apportionment notice shall, as respects the two final periods, have effect as if it were the apportionment resulting from section 8(2) of the principal Act; and

(b) all such amendments of assessments to tax and determinations shall be made as may be necessary in consequence of paragraph (a) above.

66(6) If the Board are not satisfied that an apportionment notice complies with subsections (2) to (4) above, they shall give notice to the responsible person rejecting the apportionment notice and, where the Board give such a notice, the responsible person may, by notice in writing given to the Board within thirty days after the date of the notice of rejection, appeal against the notice.

66(7) Where notice of appeal is given under subsection (6) above–

(a) if, at any time after the giving of the notice and before the determination of the appeal by the tribunal, the Board and the appellant agree that the apportionment notice should be accepted or withdrawn or varied, the same consequences shall ensue as if the tribunal had determined the appeal to that effect;

(b) if the appeal is notified to the tribunal and it appears to [the] tribunal that the apportionment notice should be accepted, with or without modifications, the tribunal shall allow the appeal and, where appropriate, make such modifications of the apportionment specified in the notice as the tribunal thinks fit; and

(c) where the appeal is allowed, subsection (5) above shall apply as if the apportionment notice (subject to any modifications made by the tribunal) had been accepted by the Board.

66(8) Paragraphs 14(2), (8) and (11) and 14A to 14I of Schedule 2 to the principal Act shall apply in relation to an appeal under subsection (6) as they apply in relation to an appeal against an assessment or determination made under that Act subject to the following modifications–

(a) any reference in those paragraphs to a participator is to be construed as a reference to the responsible person by whom notice of appeal is given;

(b) any reference to an agreement under paragraph 14(9) shall be construed as a reference to an agreement under subsection (7)(a) above;

(c) any other modifications that are necessary.

66(9) This section applies where the final allocation period ends on or after 30th June 1987.

History – In s. 66(6) the words "to the Special Commissioners" omitted by SI 2009/56, art. 3 and Sch. 1, para. 129(2), with effect from 1 April 2009, subject to transitional and saving provisions in SI 2009/56, Sch. 3.

In s. 66(7)(a) the word "tribunal" substituted for the word "Commissioners"; in para. (b) the words "the appeal is notified to the tribunal and" substituted for the words ", on the hearing of the appeal,", the word "tribunal" (presumably should read "the tribunal") substituted for the words "the majority of Commissioners present at the hearing", the words "the tribunal shall" substituted for the words "they shall" and the words "the tribunal thinks" substituted for the words "they think"; in para. (c) the word "tribunal" substituted for the word "Commissioners" by SI 2009/56, art. 3 and Sch. 1, para. 129(3), with effect from 1 April 2009, subject to transitional and saving provisions in SI 2009/56, Sch. 3.

S. 66(8) substituted by SI 2009/56, art. 3 and Sch. 1, para. 129(4), with effect from 1 April 2009, subject to transitional and saving provisions in SI 2009/56, Sch. 3. Former s. 66(8) read as follows:

"**66(8)** Sub-paragraphs (2), (8) and (11) of paragraph 14 of Schedule 2 to the principal Act shall apply in relation to an appeal against a notice of rejection under subsection (6) above as they apply in relation to an appeal against an assessment or determination made under that Act, construing any reference in those provisions to the participator as a reference to the responsible person by whom notice of appeal is given."

67 Variation of decisions on claims for allowable expenditure

67 [Amends table in OTA 1975, Sch. 7, para. 1(3).]

PART VI – MISCELLANEOUS AND SUPPLEMENTARY

72 Short title, interpretation, construction and repeals

72(1) This Act may be cited as the Finance Act 1987.

72(2) In this Act **"the Taxes Act"** means the Income and Corporation Taxes Act 1988.

72(6) Part V of this Act shall be construed as one with Part I of the Oil Taxation Act 1975 and in that Part **"the principal Act"** means that Act.

History – See ICTA 1988, s. 844 and Sch. 29, para. 32 for substitution of reference to that Act.

SCHEDULE 10 – NOMINATION SCHEME FOR DISPOSALS AND APPROPRIATIONS

Section 61

Statutory instruments – SI 1987/1338: partly made under Sch. 10.

INTERPRETATION

1(1) In this Schedule–

"month" means calendar month;

"nominal volume" shall be construed in accordance with paragraph 7 below;

"nominated price" shall be construed in accordance with paragraph 6 below;

"nomination" means a nomination made in such manner as may be prescribed by regulations made by the Board;

"proposed sale", shall be construed in accordance with paragraph (a) of sub-paragraph (1) of paragraph 2 below;

"proposed delivery month" shall be construed in accordance with paragraph 12A below;

"proposed transaction" means one falling within paragraph 2(1) below;

"regulations made by the Board" means regulations under section 61(7) of this Act; and

"Treasury regulations" means regulations under section 61(7) of this Act.

1(2) [Omitted by FA 2006, s. 150(2)(b).]

1(3) Where an amount of oil is required to be delivered to the OGA pursuant to a notice served by it, any oil which is inadvertently delivered to him in excess of the amount required shall be treated for the purposes of sub-paragraph (2) above as delivered pursuant to the notice.

Prospective amendments – In s. 1(3) the word "OGA" substituted for the words "Secretary of State" and the words "it" substituted for the word "him" by SI 2016/898, reg. 9(2), with effect immediately after the commencement of SCA 2016, s. 48.

History – In para. 1(1) words "proposed supply" and "proposed appropriation" omitted (and repealed by FA 2006, s. 178 and Sch. 26, Pt. 5(2)), the words "paragraph 12A below" substituted for "paragraph 3 below", and the words "paragraph (a)" substituted for "paragraphs (a) to (c)" by FA 2006, s. 150(2)(a) with effect from 1 July 2006, in relation to a transaction whenever proposed, but not for a proposed transaction with a transaction base date on or before 30 June 2006 (FA 2006, s. 150(14)).

Para. 1(2) omitted by FA 2006, s. 151(2)(b) and repealed by FA 2006, s. 178 and Sch. 26, Pt. 5(2), with effect from 1 July 2006, in relation to a transaction whenever proposed, but not for a proposed transaction with a transaction base date on or before 30 June 2006 (FA 2006, s. 150(14)).

In para. 1(3), the word "OGA" substituted for the words "Secretary of State" and the word "it" substituted for the word "him" by SI 2016/898, reg. 9(2), with effect from 1 October 2016 (as the 21st day after being made on 10 September 2016).

Para. 1(3) added by F(No. 2)A 1987, s. 101 and Sch. 8, para. 1, with respect to calendar months in chargeable periods beginning with March 1987.

TRANSACTIONS WHICH MAY BE NOMINATED

2(1) The proposed transactions which may be nominated by a participator in an oil field for the purposes of this Schedule are–

(a) proposed sales at arm's length by the participator of specified quantities of oil for delivery from that oil field; and

(b) [omitted by FA 2006, s. 150(3);]

(c) [omitted by FA 2006, s. 150(3);]

(d) [omitted by FA 2006, s. 150(3).]

2(2) Where a proposed sale is nominated before a contract of sale comes into being, any reference in this Schedule to the contract of sale is a reference to the subsequent contract for the sale of oil in accordance with the terms of the nomination; and, accordingly, if no such contract of sale comes into being, the nomination of the proposed sale shall be of no effect.

2(3) A participator may not nominate a proposed sale if–

(a) under the terms of the contract of sale as originally entered into, the party undertaking to sell the oil is someone other than the participator; or

(b) it is a description prescribed for the purposes of this sub-paragraph by regulations made by the Board.

History – *Para. 2(1)(b)–(d) and the words following sub-para. (d) omitted by FA 2006, s. 150(3) and repealed by FA 2006, s. 178 and* Sch. 26, Pt. 5(2), with effect from 1 July 2006, in relation to a transaction whenever proposed, but not for a proposed transaction with a transaction base date on or before 30 June 2006 (FA 2006, s. 150(14)).

Notes – In para. 2(1)(a) at the end the word "and" remains following the omission of sub-para. (b)–(d), this is presumably an oversight.

PERIOD FOR WHICH NOMINATION HAS EFFECT

3 [Omitted by FA 2006, s. 150(4) and repealed by FA 2006, s. 178 and Sch. 26, Pt. 5(2).]

History – Para. 3 omitted by FA 2006, s. 150(4) and repealed by FA 2006, s. 178 and Sch. 26, Pt. 5(2), with effect from 1 July 2006, in relation to a transaction whenever proposed, but not for a proposed transaction with a transaction base date on or before 30 June 2006 (FA 2006, s. 150(14)).

TIMING OF NOMINATIONS

4(1) If a nomination is made during business hours it shall be effective only if–

(a) it is made within the period of two hours beginning with the transaction base time, and

(b) it satisfies the requirements of paragraph 5.

4(1A) If a nomination is made outside business hours it shall be effective only if–

(a) it is made within the period of two hours beginning with the transaction base time, and

(b) it satisfies the requirements of paragraph 5 or 5A.

4(1B) For the purposes of this paragraph–

(a) the transaction base time of a proposed transaction is such time on such date as the Board shall prescribe by regulations, and

(b) **"business hours"** means the period beginning with 09.00 and ending with 17.00 (UK time) on a business day (within the meaning of the Bills of Exchange Act 1882 (c. 61)).

4(2) [Omitted by FA 2006, s. 150(5)(b) and repealed by FA 2006, s. 178 and Sch. 26, Pt. 5(2).]

4(2A) [Omitted by FA 2006, s. 150(5)(b) and repealed by FA 2006, s. 178 and Sch. 26, Pt. 5(2).]

4(3) The transaction base time prescribed for a proposed sale may be a time earlier than the time on which a legally binding agreement for the sale of the oil in question comes into being but may not be later than the time on which there is an agreed price at which any oil which is to be delivered pursuant to the contract of sale will be sold.

4(4) [Omitted by FA 2006, s. 150(5)(d) and repealed by FA 2006, s. 178 and Sch. 26, Pt. 5(2).]

History – Para. 4(1), (1A) and (1B) substituted for para. 4(1) by FA 2006, s. 150(5)(a), with effect from 1 July 2006, in relation to a transaction whenever proposed, but not for a proposed transaction with a transaction base date on or before 30 June 2006 (FA 2006, s. 150(14)). See cross reference below in relation to para. 4(1B).

In former para. 4(1), the words "sub-paragraphs (2) and (2A)" substituted by FA 1994, s. 235(3)(a), with respect to chargeable periods ending after 31 December 1993.

Para. 4(2) omitted by FA 2006, s. 150(5)(b) and repealed by FA 2006, s. 178 and Sch. 26, Pt. 5(2), with effect from 1 July 2006, in relation to a transaction whenever proposed, but not for a proposed transaction with a transaction base date on or before 30 June 2006 (FA 2006, s. 150(14)).

Para. 4(2A) omitted by FA 2006, s. 151(5)(b) and repealed by FA 2006, s. 178 and Sch. 26, Pt. 5(2), with effect from 1 July 2006, in relation to a transaction whenever proposed, but not for a proposed transaction with a transaction base date on or before 30 June 2006 (FA 2006, s. 150(14)).

Former Para. 4(2A) inserted by FA 1994, s. 235(3)(b), with effect for transactions having a base date later than 31 December 1993.

In para. 4(3) the words "transaction base time" substituted for the words "transaction base date" and the words "time" substituted for the words "date" in each place by FA 2006, s. 150(5)(c) with effect from 1 July 2006, in relation to a transaction whenever proposed, but not for a proposed transaction with a transaction base date on or before 30 June 2006 (FA 2006, s. 150(14)).

Para. 4(4) omitted by FA 2006, s. 150(5)(d) and repealed by FA 2006, s. 178 and Sch. 26, Pt. 5(2), with effect from 1 July 2006, in relation to a transaction whenever proposed, but not for a proposed transaction with a transaction base date on or before 30 June 2006 (FA 2006, s. 150(14)).

Cross references – FA 2006, s. 150(15): regulations under para. 4(1B) may have retrospective effect.
SI 1987/1338, 7 and 8: transaction base date in respect of proposed sales, supplies and relevant appropriations.

CONTENT OF NOMINATION

5(1) The requirements of this paragraph for a nomination in respect of a proposed transaction are–

(a) the name of the participator;

(b) the name of the person to whom the oil is to be sold;

(c) the field from which the oil is to be delivered;

(d) the nominated price of the oil to be delivered;

(e) the nominal volume of that oil;

(f) the proposed delivery month;

(g) the transaction base time; and

(h) such other information as may be prescribed by the Board.

5(2) A nomination made under this paragraph shall include a declaration that it is correct and complete and, in the case of a nomination of a proposed sale which is made before the contract of sale comes into being, shall also include a declaration that, to the best of the knowledge and belief of the participator making the nomination, a contract of sale will come into being in accordance with the terms of the nomination.

5(3) Where a participator fraudulently or negligently furnishes any incorrect information or makes any incorrect declaration in or in connection with a nomination made under this paragraph he shall be liable to a penalty not exceeding £50,000 or, in the case of fraud, £100,000, and the nomination shall not be effective.

History – In para. 5(1) the words "The requirements of this paragraph for a nomination in respect of a proposed transaction are" substituted for the words "A nomination of a proposed transaction shall not be effective unless it specifies, in respect to that transaction" by FA 2006, s. 150(6)(a) with effect from 1 July 2006, in relation to a transaction whenever proposed, but not for a proposed transaction with a transaction base date on or before 30 June 2006 (FA 2006, s. 150(14)).
In para. 5(1)(b) the words "in the case of a proposed sale" omitted by FA 2006, s. 150(6)(b) and repealed by FA 2006, s. 178 and Sch. 26, Pt. 5(2), with effect from 1 July 2006, in relation to a transaction whenever proposed, but not for a proposed transaction with a transaction base date on or before 30 June 2006 (FA 2006, s. 150(14)).
In para. 5(1)(b), the former words "in the case of a proposed sale" and "sold" substituted and, in para. 5(3), the words "and the nomination shall not be effective" added by F(No. 2)A 1987, s. 101 and Sch. 8, para. 2, with respect to calendar months in chargeable periods beginning with March 1987.
In para. 5(1)(c) and (d) the words "or relevantly appropriated" omitted by FA 2006, s. 150(6)(c) and repealed by FA 2006, s. 178 and Sch. 26, Pt. 5(2), with effect from 1 July 2006, in relation to a transaction whenever proposed, but not for a proposed transaction with a transaction base date on or before 30 June 2006 (FA 2006, s. 150(14)).
In para. 5(1)(d) the word "delivered" substituted for the word "supplied" by FA 2006, s. 150(6)(d) with effect from 1 July 2006, in relation to a transaction whenever proposed, but not for a proposed transaction with a transaction base date on or before 30 June 2006 (FA 2006, s. 150(14)).
Para. 5(1)(g) substituted by FA 2006, s. 150(6)(e) with effect from 1 July 2006, in relation to a transaction whenever proposed, but not for a proposed transaction with a transaction base date on or before 30 June 2006 (FA 2006, s. 150(14)). Former para. 5(1)(g) read as follows:

"(g) the transaction base date; and"

In para. 5(2) the words "made under this paragraph" inserted by FA 2006, s. 150(6)(f), with effect from 1 July 2006, in relation to a transaction whenever proposed, but not for a proposed transaction with a transaction base date on or before 30 June 2006 (FA 2006, s. 150(14)).
In para. 5(3) words "made under this paragraph" inserted by FA 2006, s. 150(6)(g), with effect from 1 July 2006, in relation to a transaction whenever proposed, but not for a proposed transaction with a transaction base date on or before 30 June 2006 (FA 2006, s. 150(14)).

Cross references – SI 1987/1338, reg. 6: content of composite nominations.
SI 1987/1338, reg. 20(5): para. 5(1)(c) does not apply in the case of nomination of a proposed transaction in blended oil.

5A(1) The requirements of this paragraph for a nomination in respect of a proposed transaction are–

(a) the name of the participator or of the group of which the participator is a member;

(b) the name of the person to whom the oil is to be sold, or the name of the group of which that person is a member;

(c) the blend or grade of oil to be delivered;

(d) the nominated price of the oil to be delivered;

(e) the nominal volume of the oil;

(f) the proposed delivery month;

(g) the transaction base time; and

(h) such other information as may be prescribed by the Board.

5A(2) In sub-paragraph (1) **"group"** has the meaning given by section 53 of the Companies Act 1989.

History – Para. 5A inserted by FA 2006, s. 150(7) with effect from 1 July 2006, in relation to a transaction whenever proposed, but not for a proposed transaction with a transaction base date on or before 30 June 2006 (FA 2006, s. 150(14)).

5B(1) A nomination of a transaction shall not be effective unless oil is delivered pursuant to a contract at arm's length the terms of which incorporate the information specified in the nomination in accordance with paragraph 5(1) or 5A(1).

5B(2) But–

(a) a contract need not refer to the transaction base time, and

(b) the nomination shall be effective whether or not delivery takes place in the proposed delivery month specified in the nomination and the contract.

History – Para. 5B inserted by FA 2006, s. 150(7), with effect from 1 July 2006, in relation to a transaction whenever proposed, but not for a proposed transaction with a transaction base date on or before 30 June 2006 (FA 2006, s. 150(14)).

NOMINATED PRICE

6(1) In the case of a proposed sale, the **"nominated price"**, in relation to the oil which is to be delivered pursuant to the sale, is the price specified in the contract of sale (expressed as a unit price) or, as the case may be, the formula under which, in accordance with the contract, the price for that oil (as so expressed) is to be determined.

6(2) [Omitted by FA 2006, s. 150(8) and repealed by FA 2006, s. 178 and Sch. 26, Pt. 5(2).]

6(3) [Omitted by FA 2006, s. 150(8) and repealed by FA 2006, s. 178 and Sch. 26, Pt. 5(2).]

History – In para. 6(1) the words "Subject to sub-paragraph (3) below," which appeared at the start omitted by FA 2006, s. 150(8)(a) and repealed by FA 2006, s. 178 and Sch. 26, Pt. 5(2), with effect from 1 July 2006, in relation to a transaction whenever proposed, but not for a proposed transaction with a transaction base date on or before 30 June 2006 (FA 2006, s. 150(14)).

Para. 6(2) omitted by FA 2006, s. 150(8)(b) and repealed by FA 2006, s. 178 and Sch. 26, Pt. 5(2), with effect from 1 July 2006, in relation to a transaction whenever proposed, but not for a proposed transaction with a transaction base date on or before 30 June 2006 FA 2006, s. 150(14)).
Para. 6(3) omitted by FA 2006, s. 150(8)(b) and repealed by FA 2006, s. 178 and Sch. 26, Pt. 5(2), with effect from 1 July 2006, in relation to a transaction whenever proposed, but not for a proposed transaction with a transaction base date on or before 30 June 2006 (FA 2006, s. 150(14)).

Cross references – SI 1987/1338, reg. 18: conversion of nominated price into sterling.

NOMINAL VOLUME

7(1) Subject to sub-paragraph (3) below, in the case of a proposed sale, the **nominal volume** means the quantity of oil which it is proposed should be delivered under the contract of sale in the proposed delivery month.

7(2) [Omitted by FA 2006, s. 150(9).]

7(3) In the case of any proposed transaction, the nominal volume means the quantity of oil expressed in such manner as may be prescribed by regulations made by the Board.

7(4) In any case where–

(a) apart from this sub-paragraph, the nominal volume in any proposed transaction would be expressed as a specific volume of oil, plus or minus a particular tolerance, and

(b) that tolerance exceeds the limits prescribed for the purposes of this Schedule by regulations made by the Board,

the nominal volume shall for those purposes be taken to be the specific volume referred to in paragraph (a) above, plus or minus the maximum tolerance permitted by the regulations.

7(5) [Omitted by FA 2006, s. 150(9).]

7(6) The Board may by regulations prescribe that in specified circumstances the nominal volume in relation to a delivery shall be treated as greater or less than the nominal volume ascertained in accordance with the preceding provisions of this paragraph.

7(7) Regulations under sub-paragraph (6)–

(a) shall be made by statutory instrument, and

(b) may not be made unless a draft has been laid before and approved by resolution of the House of Commons.

History – Para. 7(2) omitted by FA 2006, s. 150(9) with effect from 1 July 2006, in relation to a transaction whenever proposed, but not for a proposed transaction with a transaction base date on or before 30 June 2006 (FA 2006, s. 150(14)).
Para. 7(5) omitted by FA 2006, s. 150(9) with effect from 1 July 2006, in relation to a transaction whenever proposed, but not for a proposed transaction with a transaction base date on or before 30 June 2006 (FA 2006, s. 150(14)).
Para. 7(6) inserted by FA 2006, s. 150(10) with effect from 1 July 2006, in relation to a transaction whenever proposed, but not for a proposed transaction with a transaction base date on or before 30 June 2006 (FA 2006, s. 150(14)).
Para. 7(7) inserted by FA 2006, s. 150(10) with effect from 1 July 2006, in relation to a transaction whenever proposed, but not for a proposed transaction with a transaction base date on or before 30 June 2006 (FA 2006, s. 150(14)).

Cross references – SI 1987/1338, reg. 9: expression of nominal volume.
SI 1987/1338, reg. 10: maximum tolerance prescribed – five per cent.

REVISION OF NOMINATIONS

8 [Omitted by FA 2006, s. 150(11).]

History – Para. 8 omitted by FA 2006, s. 150(11) and repealed by FA 2006, s. 178 and Sch. 26, Pt. 5(2), with effect from 1 July 2006, in relation to a transaction whenever proposed, but not for a proposed transaction with a transaction base date on or before 30 June 2006 (FA 2006, s. 150(14)).

EFFECTIVE VOLUME FOR NOMINATED TRANSACTIONS

9 [Omitted by FA 2006, s. 150(11).]

History – Para. 9 omitted by FA 2006, s. 150(11) and repealed by FA 2006, s. 178 and Sch. 26, Pt. 5(2), with effect from 1 July 2006, in relation to a transaction whenever proposed, but not for a proposed transaction with a transaction base date on or before 30 June 2006 (FA 2006, s. 150(14)).

AGGREGATE EFFECTIVE VOLUME FOR A MONTH

10 [Omitted by FA 2006, s. 150(11).]

History – Para. 10 omitted by FA 2006, s. 150(11) and repealed by FA 2006, s. 178 and Sch. 26, Pt. 5(2), with effect from 1 July 2006, in relation to a transaction whenever proposed, but not for a proposed transaction with a transaction base date on or before 30 June 2006 (FA 2006, s. 150(14)).

AGGREGATE NOMINATED PROCEEDS FOR A MONTH

11 [Omitted by FA 2006, s. 150(11).]

History – Para. 11 omitted by FA 2006, s. 150(11) and repealed by FA 2006, s. 178 and Sch. 26, Pt. 5(2), with effect from 1 July 2006, in relation to a transaction whenever proposed, but not for a proposed transaction with a transaction base date on or before 30 June 2006 (FA 2006, s. 150(14)).

BLENDED OIL

12(1) If a person is a participator in two or more oil fields which, in relation to any blended oil, are or are included among the originating fields, then, in accordance with regulations made by the Board, he may make a nomination, having effect with respect to all the originating fields in which he is a participator, of a proposed sale of the blended oil; and the preceding provisions of this Schedule shall have effect in relation to such a nomination subject to such modifications as may be prescribed by regulations made by the Board.

12(2) In sub-paragraph (1) above **"blended oil"** and **"the originating fields"** have the same meaning as in section 63 of this Act.

History – In para. 12(1) the words ", supply or appropriation" which followed "of a proposed sale" omitted by FA 2006, s. 150(12) and repealed by FA 2006, s. 178 and Sch. 26, Pt. 5(2), with effect from 1 July 2006, in relation to a transaction whenever proposed, but not for a proposed transaction with a transaction base date on or before 30 June 2006 (FA 2006, s. 150(14)).
In para. 12, the words "12(1) If a person is … of the blended oil" substituted and para. 12(2) added by F(No. 2)A 1987, s. 101 and Sch. 8, para. 6, with respect to calendar months in chargeable periods beginning with March 1987.

INTERPRETATION

12A For the purposes of section 61 and this Schedule–

(a) a reference to the proposed delivery month in relation to a proposed transaction is a reference to the month in which delivery is to take place,

(b) **"relevant delivery"** means a delivery of oil under a contract made at arm's length in respect of which there has been no effective nomination, and

(c) **"delivery proceeds"** means the price received for a relevant delivery.

History – Para. 12A inserted by FA 2006, s. 150(13) with effect from 1 July 2006, in relation to a transaction whenever proposed, but not for a proposed transaction with a transaction base date on or before 30 June 2006 (FA 2006, s. 150(14)).

RETURNS

13 [Inserts OTA 1975, Sch. 2, para. 2(3A).]

SCHEDULE 11 – MARKET VALUE OF OIL

Section 62

Part I – Amendments of Paragraphs 2, 2A and 3 of Schedule 3 to Principal Act

1 [Substitutes OTA 1975, Sch. 3, para. 2(1); partly repealed by FA 2006, s. 178 and Sch. 26, Pt. 5(1).]

2 [Amends OTA 1975, Sch. 3, para. 2A(1)–(3).]

3 [Repealed by FA 2006, s. 178 and Sch. 26, Pt. 5(1).]

History – Para. 1(3)–(7) repealed by FA 2006, s. 178 and Sch. 26, Pt. 5(1), with effect in relation to oil delivered or appropriated on or after 1 July 2006, subject to the provisions of FA 2006, s. 147(2)–(8).
Para. 3 repealed by FA 2006, s. 178 and Sch. 26, Pt. 5(1), with effect in relation to oil delivered or appropriated on or after 1 July 2006, subject to the provisions of FA 2006, s. 147(2)–(8).

Part II – Consequential Amendments of Principal Act

4 [Repealed by FA 2006, s. 178 and Sch. 26, Pt. 5(1).]

History – Para. 4 repealed by FA 2006, s. 178 and Sch. 26, Pt. 5(1), with effect in relation to oil delivered or appropriated on or after 1 July 2006, subject to the provisions of FA 2006, s. 147(2)–(8).

5 [Repealed by FA 2006, s. 178 and Sch. 26, Pt. 5(1).]

History – Para. 5 repealed by FA 2006, s. 178 and Sch. 26, Pt. 5(1), with effect in relation to oil delivered or appropriated on or after *1 July 2006, subject to the provisions of FA 2006, s. 147(2)–(8).*

SCHEDULE 12 – SUPPLEMENTARY PROVISIONS AS TO BLENDED OIL

Section 63

INTERPRETATION

1(1) In this Schedule–

"HMRC" means Her Majesty's Revenue and Customs;

"method of allocation" means a method for making an allocation of blended oil for the purposes of section 63 that has been selected by the participators in the originating fields (including such a method that has been amended in accordance with this Schedule).

1(2) In this Schedule a reference to a suitable method of allocation is a reference to a method which secures that allocation of blended oil is just and reasonable (for the purposes of the oil taxation legislation).

History – Para. 1 substituted by FA 2009, s. 85 and Sch. 39, para. 3(2), with effect in relation to chargeable periods beginning after 30 June 2009.

METHOD OF ALLOCATION NOT SUITABLE

2(1) This paragraph applies if it appears to HMRC that–

(a) a method of allocation that has been used in respect of a chargeable period was not suitable, or

(b) a method of allocation that is proposed to be used in respect of a chargeable period would not be suitable.

2(2) HMRC may give notice to each of the participators in the originating fields–

(a) informing the participators of what appears to HMRC to be the case, and

(b) proposing amendments to the method of allocation.

2(3) If HMRC give notice, the allocation of the blended oil for the purposes of section 63 in respect of the chargeable period is to be redetermined, or determined, using the method of allocation as amended in accordance with the notice.

2(4) Sub-paragraph (3) is subject to–

(a) the following provisions of this Schedule,

(b) any subsequent notice given under this paragraph, and

(c) any amendment to the method of allocation made by the participators in the originating fields.

History – Para. 2 substituted by FA 2009, s. 85 and Sch. 39, para. 3(2), with effect in relation to chargeable periods beginning after 30 June 2009.

APPEALS

3(1) Where HMRC give notice to the participators in the originating fields under paragraph 2(2) above, any of those participators may appeal against the notice by giving notice in writing to HMRC within thirty days after the date of the notice given by HMRC.

3(2) Where notice of appeal is given under sub-paragraph (1) above–

(a) HMRC shall give notice in writing to all those participators in the originating fields who have not given notice of appeal and they shall, by virtue of that notice, become parties to the appeal;

(b) if, before the determination of the appeal by the tribunal, HMRC and the participators in the originating fields agree that the method of allocation concerned should not be amended or should have effect with particular amendments, the same consequences shall ensue as if the tribunal had determined the appeal to that effect;

(c) if, on an appeal notified to the tribunal, it appears to the tribunal that the method of allocation concerned is satisfactory, with or without modifications, for the purposes of the oil taxation legislation the tribunal shall allow the appeal and, where appropriate, shall amend the method of allocation accordingly for those purposes; and

(d) paragraphs 14(2), (8) and (11) and 14A to 14I of Schedule 2 to the principal Act shall apply in relation to the appeal as they apply in relation to an appeal against an assessment or determination made under that Act subject to the following modifications–

(i) any reference to an agreement under paragraph 14(9) shall be construed as a reference to an agreement under sub-paragraph (2)(b) above;

(ii) any other modifications that are necessary.

3(3) If the method of allocation is amended in accordance with this paragraph, the allocation of the blended oil for the purposes of section 63 in respect of the chargeable period is to be redetermined, or determined, using the method of allocation as so amended.

3(4) Sub-paragraph (3) is subject to–

(a) any subsequent notice given under this paragraph, and

(b) any amendment to the method of allocation made by the participators in the originating fields.

History – In para. 3(1) "HMRC" substituted for "the Board" (three times) and the words" paragraph 2(2)" substituted for the words "paragraph 2(a)" by FA 2009, s. 85 and Sch. 39, para. 3(3), with effect in relation to chargeable periods beginning after 30 June 2009.
In para. 3(1) the words "to the Special Commissioners" omitted by SI 2009/56, art. 3 and Sch. 1, para. 130(2), with effect from 1 April 2009, subject to transitional and saving provisions in SI 2009/56, Sch. 3.
In para. 3(2) "HMRC" substituted for "the Board" (twice) by FA 2009, s. 85 and Sch. 39, para. 3(4), with effect in relation to chargeable periods beginning after 30 June 2009.
In para. 3(2)(a) the words "and be entitled to appear accordingly" omitted and in para. (b) the word "tribunal" substituted for the words "Special Commissioners" and "Commissioners" by SI 2009/56, art. 3 and Sch. 1, para. 130(3), with effect from 1 April 2009, subject to transitional and saving provisions in SI 2009/56, Sch. 3.
In para. 3(2)(c) the words "if, on an appeal notified to the tribunal, it appears to the tribunal" substituted for the words "if, on the hearing of the appeal, it appears to the majority of the Commissioners present" and the word "the tribunal" substituted for the words "they" by SI 2009/56, art. 3 and Sch. 1, para. 130(4), with effect from 1 April 2009, subject to transitional and saving provisions in SI 2009/56, Sch. 3.
Para. 3(2)(d) substituted by SI 2009/56, art. 3 and Sch. 1, para. 130(5), with effect from 1 April 2009, subject to transitional and saving provisions in SI 2009/56, Sch. 3. Former para. 3(2)(d) read as follows:

"(d) sub-paragraphs (2), (8) and (11) of paragraph 14 of Schedule 2 to the principal Act shall apply in relation to the appeal as they apply in relation to an appeal against an assessment or determination made under that Act."

Para. 3(3) inserted by FA 2009, s. 85 and Sch. 39, para. 3(5), with effect in relation to chargeable periods beginning after 30 June 2009.
Para. 3(4) inserted by FA 2009, s. 85 and Sch. 39, para. 3(5), with effect in relation to chargeable periods beginning after 30 June 2009.

4 [Omitted by FA 2009, s. 85 and Sch. 39, para. 3(6).]

History – Para. 4 omitted by FA 2009, s. 85 and Sch. 39, para. 3(6), with effect in relation to chargeable periods beginning after 30 June 2009.

SCHEDULE 13 – RELIEF FOR RESEARCH EXPENDITURE

Section 64

Part I – Section to be Inserted after Section 5A of the Principal Act

[Inserts OTA 1975, s. 5B.]

Part II – Amendments Relating to the New Allowance

THE PRINCIPAL ACT

1 [Inserts OTA 1975, s. 2(9)(g).]

2 [Amends OTA 1975, s. 3(3).]

3 [Amends OTA 1975, s. 9(2)(a)(ii).]

4 [Amends OTA 1975, sch. 2, para. 2(2A).]

5 [Amends OTA 1975, Sch. 7, para. 1(1), (3).]

THE PETROLEUM REVENUE TAX ACT 1980

6 [Amends PRTA 1980, Schedule, para. 2(4).]

THE FINANCE ACT 1980

7 [Inserts FA 1980, Sch. 17, para. 16B.]

THE FINANCE ACT 1981

8 [Amends FA 1981, s. 111(3)(a).]

THE FINANCE ACT 1984

9 [Amends FA 1984, s. 113(1), (6).]

Part III – Receipts to be Set Against Allowable Expenditure

10 In this Part of this Schedule–

"allowable expenditure" means expenditure which, in accordance with section 5B of the principal Act, is allowable on a claim made by a participator under Schedule 7 to that Act; and

"qualifying receipt" means a sum the amount of which falls, by virtue of subsection (6) of section 5 of the principal Act, to be applied by way of reduction in the amount of expenditure which would otherwise be allowable expenditure.

11(1) A return made by a participator for a chargeable period under paragraph 2 of Schedule 2 to the principal Act shall give details of any qualifying receipt (whether received by him or by a person connected with him) of which details have not been given in a return made by him for an earlier chargeable period.

11(2) Section 1122 of the Corporation Tax Act 2010 (connected persons) applies for the purposes of this paragraph.

History – In para. 11(2), the words "Section 1122 of the Corporation Tax Act 2010" substituted for the words "Section 839 of the Taxes Act" by CTA 2010, s. 1177 and Sch. 1, para. 204, with effect for corporation tax purposes for accounting periods ending on or after 1 April 2010, and for income tax and capital gains tax purposes for the tax year 2010–11 and subsequent tax years.
See ICTA 1988, s. 844 and Sch. 29, para. 32 for substitution of former reference to that Act in para. 11(2).

12(1) This paragraph applies where–

(a) a claim for allowable expenditure has been made by a participator under Schedule 7 to the principal Act; and

(b) as a result of the receipt (whether before or after the making of the claim) of a qualifying receipt, the amount allowed by way of allowable expenditure on the claim exceeds what it should have been.

12(2) In determining, in a case where this paragraph applies, the assessable profit or allowable loss accruing to the participator in the chargeable period in which the qualifying receipt is received, the amount of the excess referred to in sub-paragraph (1)(b) above shall be taken into account under section 2 of the principal Act as an amount which is to be included among the positive amounts referred to in subsection (3)(a) of that section.

12(3) In the application of section 9 of the principal Act (limit on amount of tax payable) to a chargeable period in respect of which sub-paragraph (2) above applies, the amount of the excess referred to in sub-paragraph (1)(b) above shall be deducted from the amount which would otherwise be the total ascertained under subsection (2)(a)(ii) of that section and, if the amount of that excess is greater than the amount which would otherwise be that total, that total shall be a negative amount equal to the difference.

SCHEDULE 14 – CROSS-FIELD ALLOWANCE

Section 65

Part I – Elections

GENERAL

1(1) An election shall be made in such form as may be prescribed by the Board.

1(2) Without prejudice to sub-paragraph (1) above, an election shall specify–

(a) the expenditure in respect of which it is made and the amount of that expenditure (in this Part of this Schedule referred to as **"the elected amount"**), which shall not exceed 10 per cent, which is to be allowable under the principal section;

(b) the field of origin and the receiving field;

(c) the notice, agreement or determination which, under paragraph 2 below, determines the earliest date on which the election could be made;

(d) in a case where the elected amount is to be allowable in respect of more than one receiving field, the proportions in which that amount is to be apportioned between those fields; and

(e) in the case of expenditure incurred by a company which is an associated company of the participator for the purposes of the principal section, the name of that company.

1(3) An election shall be irrevocable.

EARLIEST DATE FOR AN ELECTION

2(1) No election may be made in respect of an amount of expenditure until a final decision as to supplement has been made on a claim in respect of that amount under Schedule 5 or Schedule 6 to the principal Act.

2(2) For the purposes of this paragraph, a final decision as to supplement is made in relation to an amount of expenditure when–

(a) the Board give to the responsible person or, as the case may be, the participator notice under paragraph 3 of Schedule 5 to the principal Act stating that amount of expenditure as an amount qualifying for supplement; or

(b) after notice of appeal has been given against a decision on a claim, an agreement is made as mentioned in sub-paragraph (1) of paragraph 6 of Schedule 5 to the principal Act and that amount of expenditure is, for the purposes of that sub-paragraph, the appropriate amount of the expenditure claimed as qualifying for supplement; or

(c) on an appeal against a decision on a claim, there is a determination by the tribunal or the court by virtue of which that amount of expenditure falls (under paragraph 7(2) or paragraph 8(2) of Schedule 5 to the principal Act) to be treated for the purposes of Part I of that Act as qualifying for supplement.

2(3) Nothing in Schedule 5 to the principal Act relating to the date on which an amount of expenditure is to be treated as having been allowed as qualifying for supplement applies for the purposes of sub-paragraph (2) above.

History – In para. 2(2)(c) the word "tribunal" substituted for the words "Special Commissioners" by SI 2009/56, art. 3 and Sch. 1, para. 131, with effect from 1 April 2009, subject to transitional and saving provisions in SI 2009/56, Sch. 3.

LATEST DATE FOR ELECTION

3(1) Subject to sub-paragraph (2) below, an election by a participator in respect of a particular amount of expenditure may be made at any time before–

(a) the Board make, for a chargeable period of the field of origin, an assessment or determination which takes account of that amount of expenditure as qualifying for supplement; and

(b) notice of that assessment or determination is given to the participator or, as the case may be, the associated company, under paragraph 10 of Schedule 2 to the principal Act.

3(2) Where the earliest date for the making of an election in respect of a particular amount of expenditure is a date determined under paragraph 2(2)(b) or paragraph 2(2)(c) above, such an election may be made at any time before notice is given as mentioned in sub-paragraph (1)(b) above or, if it is later, before the expiry of the period of thirty days beginning on the day following that earliest date.

TWO OR MORE ELECTIONS RELATING TO SAME EXPENDITURE

4 Where more than one election is made in respect of the same amount of expenditure–

(a) the maximum of 10 per cent specified in paragraph 1(2)(a) above shall be cumulative; and

(b) if the elected amount specified in a second or subsequent election is such that, when aggregated with the elected amount or amounts specified in the earlier election or elections, it would exceed 10 per cent, that second or subsequent election shall have effect as if it specified such an elected amount as would, when so aggregated, be equal to 10 per cent of the expenditure concerned; and

(c) an election shall be of no effect if it is made after one or more earlier elections have specified (or been treated by paragraph (b) above as having specified) an elected amount or an aggregate of elected amounts equal to 10 per cent.

Part II – Effect on Receiving Field

5(1) In relation to an election, the assessment to tax or determination referred to in subsection 4(a) of the principal section is that which is first made after the relevant date on or in relation to the participator by whom the election is made.

5(2) Subject to paragraphs 6 and 7 below, the relevant date for the purposes of sub-paragraph (1) above is the date of the election.

6 In any case where–

(a) an election is made in the period of thirty days beginning on the day following that on which the Board give notice under paragraph 3 of Schedule 5 to the principal Act stating the expenditure in respect of which the election is made as expenditure qualifying for supplement,

(b) after *the date of that notice* but on or before the date of the election, an assessment to tax or determination for the receiving field is made on or in relation to the participator making the election,

the **relevant date** for the purposes of paragraph 5(1) above is the date of the notice referred to in paragraph (a) above; and the assessment or determination referred to in paragraph (b) above shall be amended accordingly.

7 In any case where, following the giving of a notice of appeal, an election is made in respect of expenditure which (under paragraph 6(1), paragraph 7(2) or paragraph 8(2) of Schedule 5 to the principal Act) is treated for the purposes of Part I of that Act as having been allowed as qualifying for supplement on the date on which the notice of appeal was given, the relevant date for the purposes of paragraph 5(1) above is the date on which that notice was given; and in any assessment to tax or determination (relating to the field of origin or the receiving field) all such adjustments or further adjustments shall be made as are necessary in consequence of the election.

Part III – Relevant New Fields and Associated Companies

RELEVANT NEW FIELDS

8(1) For the purposes of the principal section **"relevant new field"** means, subject to sub-paragraph (2) below, an oil field–

(a) no part of which lies in a landward area, within the meaning of the Petroleum (Production) Regulations 1982 or in an area to the East of the United Kingdom and between latitudes 52° and 55° North; and

(b) for no part of which consent for development has been granted to the licensee by the Secretary of State before 17th March 1987; and

(c) for no part of which a programme of development had been served on the licensee or approved by the Secretary of State before that date.

8(2) In determining, in accordance with sub-paragraph (1) above, whether an oil field (in this sub-paragraph referred to as **"the new field"**) is a relevant new field, no account shall be taken of a consent for development granted before 17th March 1987 or a programme of development served on the licensee or approved by the Secretary of State before that date if–

(a) in whole or in part that consent or programme related to another oil field for which a determination under Schedule 1 to the principal Act was made before the determination under that Schedule for the new field; and

(b) on or after 17th March 1987 a consent for development is or was granted or a programme of development is or was served on the licensee or approved by the OGA and that consent or programme relates, in whole or in part, to the new field.

Prospective amendments – In para. 8(2)(b) the word "OGA" substituted for the words "Secretary of State" by SI 2016/898, reg. 9(3), with effect immediately after the commencement of SCA 2016, s. 48.

History – In para. 8(2)(b), the word "OGA" substituted for the words "Secretary of State" by SI 2016/898, reg. 9(3), with effect from 1 October 2016 (as the 21st day after being made on 10 September 2016).

9(1) In paragraph 8 above **"development"** means–

(a) the erection or carrying out of permanent works for the purpose of getting oil from the field or for the purpose of conveying oil won from the field to a place on land; or

(b) winning oil from the field otherwise than in the course of searching for oil or drilling wells;

and consent for development does not include consent which is limited to the purpose of testing the characteristics of an oil-bearing area and does not relate to the erection or carrying out of permanent works.

9(2) In sub-paragraph (1) above **"permanent works"** means any structures or other works whatsoever which are intended by the licensee to be permanent and are neither designed to be moved from place to place without major dismantling nor intended by the licensee to be used only for searching for oil.

ASSOCIATED COMPANIES

10(1) For the purposes of the principal section, a company is an **associated company** of a participator (being itself a company) making an election under that section if–

(a) throughout that part of the relevant period in which both were in existence one was a 51 per cent subsidiary of the other and the other was not a 51 per cent subsidiary of any company; or

(b) each of them was, throughout that part of the relevant period in which it was in existence, a 51 per cent subsidiary of a third company which was not itself a 51 per cent subsidiary of any company.

10(2) In this paragraph **"company"** means any body corporate and Chapter 3 of Part 24 of the Corporation Tax Act 2010 (subsidiaries) applies for the purposes of this paragraph.

10(3) For the purposes of this paragraph the **relevant period** ends on the date on which the election in question is made and begins–

(a) in the case of an election relating to expenditure incurred in the first claim period of the field of origin, on the date on which any part of that field was first determined under Schedule 1 to the principal Act; and

(b) in the case of an election relating to expenditure incurred in any other claim period of the field of origin, at the beginning of that claim period.

History – In para. 10(2), the words "Chapter 3 of Part 24 of the Corporation Tax Act 2010" substituted for the words "section 838 of the Taxes Act" by CTA 2010, s. 1177 and Sch. 1, para. 205, with effect for corporation tax purposes for accounting periods ending on or after 1 April 2010, and for income tax and capital gains tax purposes for the tax year 2010–11 and subsequent tax years.
See ICTA 1988, s. 844 and Sch. 29, para. 32 for substitution of reference to that Act in para. 10(2).

Part IV – Supplemental and Consequential Provisions

NOTICE OF VARIATION REDUCING EXPENDITURE QUALIFYING FOR SUPPLEMENT

11(1) This paragraph applies in any case where–

(a) an amount of expenditure is allowed as qualifying for supplement as regards the field of origin; and

(b) one or more elections is made in respect of that expenditure; and

(c) a notice of variation is served under paragraph 9 of Schedule 5 to the principal Act; and

(d) on that notice of variation becoming effective for the purposes of the said paragraph 9, the amount of the expenditure referred to in paragraph (a) above is taken for the purposes of Part I of the principal Act as having been reduced.

11(2) In sub-paragraph (3) below–

(a) **"the original expenditure"** means the amount of expenditure referred to in sub-paragraph (1)(a) above, disregarding the effect of the notice of variation;

(b) **"the reduced expenditure"** means the amount of that expenditure after the notice of variation became effective for the purposes of paragraph 9 of Schedule 5 to the principal Act; and

(c) **"the expenditure originally allowable"** means the amount of the original expenditure which, having regard to the election or elections in respect of that expenditure but disregarding the effect of the notice of variation, was allowable in accordance with the principal section.

11(3) If the expenditure originally allowable exceeds 10 per cent of the reduced expenditure, the principal section shall have effect as if the election or elections had specified an amount of that expenditure equal (or equal in the aggregate) to 10 per cent of the reduced expenditure and, where there was more than one election, paragraph 4 above shall be taken to have applied accordingly.

11(4) Such amendments of assessments to tax or determinations (relating to the field of origin or the receiving field) shall be made as may be necessary in consequence of the preceding provisions of this paragraph.

ELECTIONS FOLLOWING VARIATION INCREASING EXPENDITURE QUALIFYING FOR SUPPLEMENT

12(1) In any case where–

(a) an amount of expenditure is allowed as qualifying for supplement as regards the field of origin, and

(b) one or more elections is made in respect of that expenditure, and

(c) a notice of variation is served under paragraph 9 of Schedule 5 to the principal Act, and

(d) on that notice of variation becoming effective for the purposes of the said paragraph 9, the amount of the expenditure referred to in paragraph (a) above is taken for the purposes of Part I of the principal Act as having been increased,

an election may be made in respect of the amount of the increase as if it were a separate amount of expenditure.

12(2) In the circumstances referred to in sub-paragraph (1) above an election may be made by the participator in question at any time before–

(a) notice is given to the participator or, as the case may be, the associated company of the making of that assessment or determination or that amendment of an assessment or determination which takes account of the increase resulting from the notice of variation; or

(b) if it is later, the expiry of the period of 30 days beginning on the date on which the notice of variation becomes effective for the purposes of paragraph 9 of Schedule 5 to the principal Act.

12(3) Where an election is made by a participator in the circumstances referred to in sub-paragraph (1) above–

(a) paragraph 1(2)(c) above shall have effect as if it referred to the notice of variation;

(b) subsection (4)(a) of the principal section shall not apply; and

(c) the expenditure allowable as a result of the election shall be taken into account in the first assessment to tax or determination relating to a chargeable period of the receiving field which is made on or in relation to the participator after the date of the decision to which the notice of variation relates.

12(4) Such amendments of assessments to tax or determinations (relating to the field of origin or the receiving field) shall be made as may be necessary in consequence of the preceding provisions of this paragraph.

LIMIT ON AMOUNT OF TAX PAYABLE IN RESPECT OF RECEIVING FIELD

13(1) Where an election has been made by a participator, this paragraph has effect with respect to the determination under section 9 of the principal Act (limit on amount of tax payable) of the adjusted profit of the participator in respect of the receiving field.

13(2) For the chargeable period in which the amount of expenditure allowable by virtue of the election is taken into account as mentioned in subsection (4) of the principal section, that amount shall also be taken into account as if it were an addition to the total amount mentioned in section 9(2)(a)(ii) of the principal Act.

FINANCE (NO. 2) ACT 1987

(1987 Chapter 51)

[*23rd July 1987*]

ARRANGEMENT OF SECTIONS

SCHEDULES

PART III – MISCELLANEOUS AND SUPPLEMENTARY

101 Oil taxation

101(1) Schedule 10 to the Finance Act 1987 (nomination scheme for disposals and appropriations of oil) shall have effect subject to the amendments in Schedule 8 to this Act.

101(2) [Amends FA 1987, s. 62(6). Partly repealed by FA 1999, s. 139 and Sch. 20, Pt. IV(1).]

101(3) [Amends FA 1987, s. 63(1); inserts s. 63(1A).]

101(4) [Inserts OTA 1975, Sch. 2, para. 5(2B).]

101(5) Subsections (2) to (4) above have effect with respect to chargeable periods ending after 1st January 1987 and Schedule 8 to this Act has effect with respect to calendar months in chargeable periods beginning with March 1987.

101(6) [Repealed by FA 2006, s. 178 and Sch. 26, Pt. 5(1).]

History – S. 101(2)(b) and the word "and" which immediately preceded it were repealed by FA 1999, s. 139 and Sch. 20, Pt. IV(1), with effect in relation to any chargeable period ending on or after 30 June 1999.

In s. 101(5) the words ", subject to subsection (6) below" which preceded "Schedule 8", repealed by FA 2006, s. 178 and Sch. 26, Pt. 5(1), with effect in relation to oil delivered or appropriated on or after 1 July 2006, but subject to the provisions of FA 2006, s. 147(2)–(8).

S. 101(6) repealed by FA 2006, s. 178 and Sch. 26, Pt. 5(1), with effect in relation to oil delivered or appropriated on or after 1 July 2006, but subject to the provisions of FA 2006, s. 147(2)–(8).

104 Short title, interpretation, construction and repeals

104(1) This Act may be cited as the Finance (No. 2) Act 1987.

SCHEDULE 8 – AMENDMENTS OF SCHEDULE 10 TO FINANCE ACT 1987

Section 101

1 [Inserts FA 1987, Sch. 10, para. 1(3).]

2 [Amends FA 1987, Sch. 10, para. 5(1)(b), (3).]

3(1) [Inserts FA 1987, Sch. 10, para. 8(2A)–(2C).]

3(2)–(4) [Amends FA 1987, Sch. 10, para. 8(3)–(5) respectively.]

4 [Amends FA 1987, Sch. 10, para. 9.]

5 [Repealed by FA 2006, s. 146 and Sch. 18, para. 11(2); s. 178 and Sch. 26, Pt. 5(1).]

History – Para. 5 omitted by FA 2006, s. 146 and Sch. 18, para. 11(2) and repealed by s. 178 and Sch. 26, Pt. 5(1) with effect for chargeable periods beginning on or after 1 July 2006.

6 [Amends FA 1987, Sch. 10, para. 12.]

FINANCE ACT 1988

(1988 Chapter 39)

[*29th July 1988*]

ARRANGEMENT OF SECTIONS

PART IV – MISCELLANEOUS AND GENERAL

SCHEDULES

PART IV – MISCELLANEOUS AND GENERAL

PETROLEUM REVENUE TAX

138 Reduced oil allowance for certain Southern Basin and onshore fields

138(1) For every relevant Southern Basin or onshore field, as defined in subsection (2) below, section 8 of the Oil Taxation Act 1975 (the oil allowance) shall have effect subject to the following modifications–

(a) in subsection (2) (the amount of the allowance for each chargeable period) for "250,000 metric tonnes" there shall be substituted "125,000 metric tonnes"; and

(b) in subsection (6) (the total allowance for a field) for "5 million metric tonnes" there shall be substituted "2.5 million metric tonnes".

138(2) Subject to subsection (3) below, for the purposes of this section a **"relevant Southern Basin or onshore field"** is any oil field other than one–

(a) which is a relevant new field for the purposes of section 36 of the Finance Act 1983 (increased oil allowance for certain new fields); or

(b) for any part of which consent for development was granted to the licensee by the Secretary of State before 1st April 1982; or

(c) for any part of which a programme of development was served on the licensee or approved by the Secretary of State before that date.

138(3) In determining, in accordance with subsection (2) above, whether an oil field (in this subsection referred to as **"the field in question"**) is a relevant Southern Basin or onshore field, no account shall be taken of a consent for development granted before 1st April 1982 or a programme of development served on the licensee or approved by the Secretary of State before that date if–

(a) in whole or in part that consent or programme related to another oil field for which a determination under Schedule 1 to the Oil Taxation Act 1975 was made before the determination under that Schedule for the field in question; and

(b) on or after 1st April 1982, a consent for development is or was granted or a programme of development is or was served on the licensee or approved by the OGA and that consent or programme relates, in whole or in part, to the field in question.

138(4) Subsections (4) and (5) of section 36 of the Finance Act 1983 (which define "development" for the purposes of subsections (2) and (3) of that section) shall apply also for the purposes of subsections (2) and (3) of this section.

138(5) This section shall have effect in relation to chargeable periods ending after 30th June 1988.

138(6) This section shall be construed as one with Part I of the Oil Taxation Act 1975.

Prospective amendments – In s. 138(3)(b) the word "OGA" substituted for the words "Secretary of State" by SI 2016/898, reg. 10, with effect immediately after the commencement of SCA 2016, s. 48.

History – In s. 138(3)(b), the word "OGA" substituted for the words "Secretary of State" by SI 2016/898, reg. 10, with effect from 1 October 2016 (as the 21st day after being made on 10 September 2016).

139 Assets generating tariff receipts: extension of allowable expenditure

139(1) In Part I of Schedule 1 to the Oil Taxation Act 1983 (extensions of allowable expenditure for assets generating receipts) paragraph 3 (expenditure on enhancing the value of assets no longer in use for the principal field) shall be amended as follows–

(a) in sub-paragraph (1)(a) after the words "enhancing the value of" there shall be inserted "or otherwise in connection with";

(b) in sub-paragraph (1)(d) for the words "the expenditure" there shall be substituted "either the use of the asset" and after the words "tariff receipts or" there shall be inserted "the expenditure".

139(2) This section shall have effect with respect to expenditure incurred on or after 15th March 1988.

MISCELLANEOUS

149 Short title

149 This Act may be cited as the Finance Act 1988.

SCHEDULES

SCHEDULE 13 – POST CONSOLIDATION AMENDMENTS

Section 146

PART II – AMENDMENTS OF OTHER ENACTMENTS

20 [Amends FA 1980, s. 109(8)(b).]

21 [Amends FA 1984, s. 80.]

25 The amendments made by paragraphs 16 to 23 of this Schedule shall be treated for the purposes of their commencement as if they had been made by the Taxes Act 1988.

FINANCE ACT 1989

(1989 Chapter 26)

[*27th July 1989*]

ARRANGEMENT OF SECTIONS

PART III – MISCELLANEOUS AND GENERAL

PART III – MISCELLANEOUS AND GENERAL

INTEREST ETC.

178 Setting of rates of interest

178(1) The rate of interest applicable for the purposes of an enactment to which this section applies shall be the rate which for the purposes of that enactment is provided for by regulations made by the Treasury under this section.

178(2) This section applies to–

(aa) [not relevant to petroleum revenue tax,]

(a) [not relevant to petroleum revenue tax,]

(b) [not relevant to petroleum revenue tax,]

(c) [not relevant to petroleum revenue tax,]

(d) [not relevant to petroleum revenue tax,]

(e) [repealed by Land Registration Act 2002, s. 135 and Schedule 13,]

(f) [not relevant to petroleum revenue tax,]

(g) [not relevant to petroleum revenue tax,]

(ga) [not relevant to petroleum revenue tax,]

(gg) [not relevant to petroleum revenue tax,]

(gh) [not relevant to petroleum revenue tax,]

(h) paragraphs 15 and 16 of Schedule 2, and paragraph 8 of Schedule 5, to the Oil Taxation Act 1975,

(i) [not relevant to petroleum revenue tax,]

(j) [not relevant to petroleum revenue tax,]

(k) [not relevant to petroleum revenue tax,]

(l) [not relevant to petroleum revenue tax,]

(m) [not relevant to petroleum revenue tax,]

(n) [repealed by FA 1995, s. 153 and Sch. 29, Pt. XII, and]

(o) [not relevant to petroleum revenue tax,]

(p) [not relevant to petroleum revenue tax,]

(q) [not relevant to petroleum revenue tax,]

(r) [not relevant to petroleum revenue tax,]

(s) [not relevant to petroleum revenue tax,]

(t) [not relevant to petroleum revenue tax,]

(u) [not relevant to petroleum revenue tax,]

(v) [not relevant to petroleum revenue tax.]

178(3) Regulations under this section may–

(a) make different provision for different enactments or for different purposes of the same enactment,

(b) either themselves specify a rate of interest for the purposes of an enactment or make provision for any such rate to be determined by reference to such rate or the average of such rates as may be referred to in the regulations,

(c) provide for rates to be reduced below, or increased above, what they otherwise would be by specified amounts or by reference to specified formulae,

(d) provide for rates arrived at by reference to averages to be rounded up or down,

(e) provide for circumstances in which alteration of a rate of interest is or is not to take place, and

(f) provide that alterations of rates are to have effect for periods beginning on or after a day determined in accordance with the regulations in relation to interest running from before that day as well as from or from after that day.

178(4) The power to make regulations under this section shall be exercisable by statutory instrument which shall be subject to annulment in pursuance of a resolution of the House of Commons.

178(5) [Omitted by FA 2009, s. 105(6)(a).]

178(6) [Repealed by CTA 2010, s. 1181 and Sch. 3, Pt. 1.]

178(7) Subsection (1) shall have effect for periods beginning on or after such day as the Treasury may by order made by statutory instrument appoint and shall have effect in relation to interest running from before that day as well as from or from after that day; and different days may be appointed for different enactments.

History – S. 178(5) omitted by FA 2009, s. 105(6)(a), with effect from 21 July 2009.
S. 178(6) repealed by CTA 2010, s. 1181 and Sch. 3, Pt. 1, with effect for corporation tax purposes for accounting periods ending on or after 1 April 2010, and for income tax and capital gains tax purposes for the tax year 2010–11 and subsequent tax years. Former s. 178(6) amended ICTA 1988, s. 828(2).

Cross references – ICTA 1988, s. 826A: interest on payments of corporation tax at the rate applicable under s. 178

GENERAL

188 Short title

188 This Act may be cited as the Finance Act 1989.

FINANCE ACT 1990

(1990 Chapter 29)

[*26th July 1990*]

ARRANGEMENT OF SECTIONS

PART III – MISCELLANEOUS AND GENERAL

PETROLEUM REVENUE TAX

MISCELLANEOUS

PART III – MISCELLANEOUS AND GENERAL

PETROLEUM REVENUE TAX

121 Limit on PRT repayment interest where loss carried back

121(1) Schedule 2 to the Oil Taxation Act 1975 (management and collection of PRT) shall be amended as follows.

121(2) [Amends Sch. 2, para. 16.]

121(3) [Inserts Sch. 2, para. 17.]

122 Variation, on account of fraudulent or negligent conduct, of decision on expenditure claim etc.

122 [Omitted by FA 2009, s. 99 and Sch. 51, para. 43(a).]

History – S. 122 omitted by FA 2009, s. 99 and Sch. 51, para. 43(a), with effect from 1 April 2010 (SI 2010/867).

MISCELLANEOUS

133 Short title

133 This Act may be cited as the Finance Act 1990.

FINANCE ACT 1991

(1991 Chapter 31)

[*25th July 1991*]

ARRANGEMENT OF SECTIONS

PART III – OIL TAXATION

ABANDONMENT ETC.

PENALTIES

PART V – MISCELLANEOUS AND GENERAL

GENERAL

PART III – OIL TAXATION

ABANDONMENT ETC.

103 Allowance of certain expenditure relating to abandonment, decommissioning assets, etc.

103(1) Section 3 of the principal Act (allowance of certain expenditure) shall be amended in accordance with subsections (2) to (6) below.

103(2) [Inserts OTA 1975, s. 3(1)(hh).]

103(3) [Substitutes OTA 1975, s. 3(i) and (j).]

103(4) [Inserts OTA 1975, s. 3(1A), (1B), (1C) and (1D).]

103(5) [Inserts OTA 1975, s. 3(5B).]

103(6) [Amends OTA 1975, s. 3(6).]

(a) [Amends OTA 1975, s. 10(2).]

(b)–(c) [Repealed by FA 2001, s. 110 and Sch. 33, Pt. 3(2).]

103(8) So far as they relate to the paragraph (hh) inserted by subsection (2) above, the amendments in subsections (5) to (7) above have effect with respect to expenditure incurred on or after 19th March 1991 and, subject to that, the amendments in subsections (4) to (7) above have effect with respect to expenditure incurred after 30th June 1991.

History – S. 103(7)(b) and (c) (which amended OTA 1975, s. 10(3)) repealed by FA 2001, s. 110 and Sch. 33, Pt. 3(2), the repeal applying to expenditure incurred on or after 7 March 2001.

104 Abandonment guarantees

104(1) Subject to subsection (2) below, for the purposes of section 3 of the principal Act, an abandonment guarantee is a contract under which a person (**"the guarantor"**) undertakes to make good any default by a participator in an oil field (**"the relevant participator"**) in meeting the whole or any part of those liabilities of his which–

(a) arise under a relevant agreement relating to that field; and

(b) are liabilities to contribute to field abandonment costs;

and such a contract is an **abandonment guarantee** regardless of the form of the undertaking of the guarantor and, in particular, whether or not it is expressed as a guarantee or arises under a letter of credit, a performance bond or any other instrument.

104(2) For the purposes of section 3 of the principal Act a contract is not an **abandonment guarantee**–

(a) unless it is entered into in good faith and on terms reasonably appropriate to the nature and extent of the guarantee; or

(b) if the guarantor undertakes any liability beyond that of making good any such default as is referred to in subsection (1) above; or

(c) if it can be revoked by the guarantor otherwise than on account of some fraud, misrepresentation or other fault on the part of the relevant participator occurring prior to the making of the contract; or

(d) if, subject to subsection (3) below, the guarantor is, or is a person connected with, a participator in one or more oil fields.

104(3) Paragraph (d) of subsection (2) above does not apply if–

(a) the main business carried on by the guarantor is such that it is in the ordinary course of that business to provide guarantees; and

(b) the relevant participator is not connected with the guarantor;

and section 839 of the Taxes Act 1988 (connected persons) applies for the purposes of this subsection and subsection (2) above.

104(4) Without prejudice to the generality of paragraph (a) of subsection (2) above, a contract shall not be regarded as entered into in good faith if, as a result of any arrangement, the liability to make good any such default as is referred to in subsection (1) above will be met, directly or indirectly, by such a person that, if he were the guarantor under the contract, the contract could not be an abandonment guarantee by virtue of paragraph (d) of subsection (2) above.

104(5) In this section and in section 3(5B) of the principal Act–

(a) in relation to an oil field, a **"relevant agreement"** means a joint operating agreement, a unitisation agreement (within the meaning of paragraph 1(1) of Schedule 17 to the Finance Act 1980) or an agreement entered into by some or all of the parties to a joint operating agreement or such a unitisation agreement; and

(b) in relation to an oil field, **"field abandonment costs"** means costs incurred in closing down the field or any part of it, together with any costs incurred in discharging any continuing liabilities resulting directly from that closure.

History – In s. 104(1), the words "and sections 105 and 106 below" omitted by FA 2013, s. 89 and Sch. 31, para. 11(2), with effect in relation to expenditure incurred on or after 17 July 2013 (Royal Assent).
In s. 104(2), the words "and section 106 (but not section 105) below" omitted by FA 2013, s. 89 and Sch. 31, para. 11(3), with effect in relation to expenditure incurred on or after 17 July 2013 (Royal Assent).

Cross references – OTA 1975, s. 3: allowance of expenditure (other than expenditure on long-term assets and abortive exploration expenditure).

105 Restriction of expenditure relief by reference to payments under abandonment guarantees

105 [Omitted by FA 2013, s. 89 and Sch. 31, para. 5(2).]

History – S. 105 omitted by FA 2013, s. 89 and Sch. 31, para. 5(2), with effect in relation to expenditure incurred on or after 17 July 2013 (Royal Assent). Former s. 105 read as follows:

"105 Restriction of expenditure relief by reference to payments under abandonment guarantees

105(1) If, under an abandonment guarantee, a payment is made by the guarantor on or after 19th March 1991, then, to the extent that any expenditure for which the relevant participator is liable is met, directly or indirectly, out of the payment, that expenditure shall not be regarded for any of the purposes of the principal Act as having been incurred by the relevant participator or any other participator in the oil field concerned.

105(2) In any case where–

(a) a payment made by the guarantor under an abandonment guarantee is not immediately applied in meeting any expenditure, and

(b) the payment is for any period invested (either specifically or together with payments made by persons other than the guarantor) so as to be represented by, or by part of, the assets of a fund or account, and

(c) at a subsequent time, any expenditure for which the relevant participator is liable is met out of the assets of the fund or account,

any reference in subsection (1) above or section 106 below to expenditure which is met, directly or indirectly, out of the payment shall be construed as a reference to so much of the expenditure for which the relevant participator is liable as is met out of those assets of the fund or account which, at the subsequent time referred to in paragraph (c) above, it is just and reasonable to attribute to the payment.

105(3) In subsections (1) and (2) above **"the guarantor"** and **"the relevant participator"** have the same meaning as in subsection (1) of section 104 above.".

106 Relief for reimbursement expenditure under abandonment guarantees

106 [Omitted by FA 2013, s. 89 and Sch. 31, para. 5(3).]

History – S. 106 omitted by FA 2013, s. 89 and Sch. 31, para. 5(3), with effect in relation to expenditure incurred on or after 17 July 2013 (Royal Assent). Former s. 106 read as follows:

"106 Relief for reimbursement expenditure under abandonment guarantees

106(1) This section applies in any case where–

(a) on or after 19th March 1991 a payment (in this section referred to as **"the guarantee payment"**) is made by the guarantor under an abandonment guarantee; and

(b) by virtue of the making of the guarantee payment, the relevant participator becomes liable under the terms of the abandonment guarantee to pay any sum or sums to the guarantor; and

(c) in any claim period (in this section referred to as **"the relevant period"**) expenditure is incurred, or consideration in money's worth is given, by the relevant participator in or towards meeting that liability.

106(2) In any case where the whole of the guarantee payment or, as the case may require, of the assets which, under section 105(2) above, are attributed to the guarantee payment is not applied in meeting liabilities of the relevant participator which fall within paragraphs (a) and (b) of subsection (1) of section 104 above and a sum representing the unapplied part of the guarantee payment or of those assets is repaid, directly or indirectly, to the guarantor,–

(a) any liability of the relevant participator to repay that sum shall be excluded in determining the total liability of the relevant participator which falls within subsection (1)(b) above; and

(b) the repayment to the guarantor of that sum shall not be regarded as expenditure incurred by the relevant participator as mentioned in subsection (1)(c) above.

106(3) In the following provisions of this section **"reimbursement expenditure"** means expenditure incurred as mentioned in subsection (1)(c) above or consideration (or, as the case may require, the value of consideration) given as so mentioned; and any reference to the incurring of reimbursement expenditure shall be construed accordingly.

106(4) So much of any reimbursement expenditure as, in accordance with subsection (5) below, is qualifying expenditure shall be treated for the purposes of the principal Act as if it were expenditure incurred by the relevant participator for the purpose of obtaining an abandonment guarantee.

106(5) Subject to subsection (6) below, of the reimbursement expenditure which is incurred in the relevant period, the amount which constitutes qualifying expenditure shall be determined by the formula–

$$A \times \frac{B}{C}$$

where–

A is the reimbursement expenditure incurred in the relevant period;

B is so much of the expenditure represented by the guarantee payment as, if it had been incurred by the relevant participator, would have constituted expenditure allowable under section 3 of the principal Act; and

C is the total of the sums which, at or before the end of the relevant period, the participator is or has become liable to pay to the guarantor as mentioned in subsection (1)(b) above.

106(6) In relation to the guarantee payment, the total of the reimbursement expenditure (whether incurred in one or more claim periods) which constitutes qualifying expenditure shall not exceed whichever is the less of "B" and "C" in the formula in subsection (5) above; and any limitation on qualifying expenditure arising by virtue of this subsection shall be applied to the expenditure of a later in preference to an earlier claim period.

106(7) For the purposes of this section, the expenditure represented by the guarantee payment is any expenditure–

(a) for which the relevant participator is liable; and

(b) which is met, directly or indirectly, out of the guarantee payment (and which, accordingly, by virtue of section 105 above is not to be regarded as expenditure incurred by the relevant participator).

106(8) In this section **"the guarantor"** and **"the relevant participator"** have the same meaning as in subsection (1) of section 104 above.".

107 Allowance of expenditure of participator meeting defaulter's field abandonment expenditure

107(1) [Amends OTA 1975, Sch. 5, para. 2(4)(b).]

107(2) [Inserts OTA 1975, Sch. 5, para. 2A.]

108 Reimbursement by defaulter in respect of certain abandonment expenditure

108 [Omitted by FA 2013, s. 89 and Sch. 31, para. 8.]

History – S. 108 omitted by FA 2013, s. 89 and Sch. 31, para. 8, with effect in relation to expenditure incurred on or after 17 July 2013 (Royal Assent). Former s. 108 read as follows:

"108 Reimbursement by defaulter in respect of certain abandonment expenditure

108(1) This section applies in any case where–

(a) paragraph 2A of Schedule 5 to the principal Act applies; and

(b) an amount is attributed to a contributing participator under paragraph 2A(2) of Schedule 5 to the principal Act; and

(c) expenditure is incurred, or consideration in money's worth is given, by the defaulter in reimbursing the contributing participator in respect of, or otherwise making good to him, the whole or any part of the default payment;

and expressions used in this section have the same meaning as in the said paragraph 2A.

108(2) In the following provisions of this section **"reimbursement expenditure"** means expenditure incurred as mentioned in *subsection (1)(c) above or consideration* (or, as the case may require, the value of consideration) given as so mentioned; and any reference to the incurring of reimbursement expenditure shall be construed accordingly.

108(3) Subject to subsection (5) below, in relation to the defaulter, reimbursement expenditure shall be treated for the purposes of the principal Act as if it were expenditure incurred by the defaulter for purposes falling within paragraph (i) of subsection (1) of section 3 of that Act.

108(4) Subject to subsection (5) below, in computing under section 2 of the principal Act the assessable profit or allowable loss accruing to the contributing participator from the oil field concerned in any chargeable period, the positive amounts for the purposes of that section (as specified in subsection (3)(a) thereof) shall be taken to include any reimbursement expenditure received by the contributing participator in that period.

108(5) In relation to a particular default payment, reimbursement expenditure incurred at any time–

(a) shall be treated as mentioned in subsection (3) above, and

(b) shall be taken to be included as mentioned in subsection (4) above,

only to the extent that, when aggregated with any reimbursement expenditure previously incurred in respect of that default payment, it does not exceed so much of the default payment as falls to be attributed to the contributing participator as mentioned in subsection (1)(b) above.

108(6) A claim by the defaulter for the allowance of reimbursement expenditure by virtue of subsection (3) above shall be made under Schedule 6 to the principal Act (instead of under Schedule 5); and, for this purpose only, Schedule 6 to that Act shall have effect as if, in sub-paragraph (1) of paragraph 1, the words from "if the participator" onwards were omitted.

108(7) The incurring of reimbursement expenditure shall not be regarded, by virtue of paragraph 8 of Schedule 3 to the principal Act (certain subsidised expenditure to be disregarded), as the meeting of the expenditure of the contributing participator in making the default payment.".

In former s. 108(1)(a), the words "(as set out in section 107 above)" omitted by FA 2008, s. 105(2), with effect in relation to expenditure incurred after 30 June 2008.

Former s. 108(1)(b), substituted by FA 2008, s. 105(3), with effect in relation to expenditure incurred after 30 June 2008.

In former s. 108(1)(c), the words "contributing participator" substituted for the words "qualifying participator" by FA 2008, s. 105(4), with effect in relation to expenditure incurred after 30 June 2008.

In former s. 108(4), the words "contributing participator" substituted for the words "qualifying participator" twice by FA 2008, s. 105(5), with effect in relation to expenditure incurred after 30 June 2008.

In former s. 108(5), the words "contributing participator" substituted for the words "qualifying participator" by FA 2008, s. 105(6), with effect in relation to expenditure incurred after 30 June 2008.

In former s. 108(7), the words "contributing participator" substituted for the words "qualifying participator" by FA 2008, s. 105(7), with effect in relation to expenditure incurred after 30 June 2008.

PENALTIES

109 PRT: proceedings for penalties

109(1) In Schedule 2 to the principal Act (management and collection of petroleum revenue tax) the Table in paragraph 1(1) shall be amended as follows.

109(2) [Substitutes entries relating to TMA 1970, s. 100C(1)–(5) in OTA 1975, Sch. 2, para. 1(1).]

109(3) [Substitutes entries relating to TMA 1970, s. 103(1) and (4) in OTA 1975, Sch. 2, para. 1(1).]

PART V – MISCELLANEOUS AND GENERAL

GENERAL

122 Interpretation etc.

122(1) In this Act **"the Taxes Act 1988"** means the Income and Corporation Taxes Act 1988.

122(2) Part II of this Act, so far as it relates to capital gains tax, shall be construed as one with the Capital Gains Tax Act 1979.

122(3) Part III of this Act shall be construed as one with Part I of the Oil Taxation Act 1975 and in that Part of this Act **"the principal Act"** means that Act.

124 Short title

124 This Act may be cited as the Finance Act 1991.

FINANCE (NO. 2) ACT 1992

(1992 Chapter 48)

[*16th July 1992*]

ARRANGEMENT OF SECTIONS

PART III – MISCELLANEOUS AND GENERAL

PETROLEUM REVENUE TAX

GENERAL

SCHEDULES

PART III – MISCELLANEOUS AND GENERAL

PETROLEUM REVENUE TAX

74 Oil exported direct from United Kingdom off-shore fields

74(1) The enactments specified in Schedule 15 to this Act (being enactments relating to oil taxation) shall have effect subject to the amendments in that Schedule, being amendments–

(a) which take account, for the purpose of determining assessable profits and allowable losses, of certain cases where oil which is won from an off-shore oil field is, or could reasonably be expected to be, first landed in a country other than the United Kingdom; or

(b) which are consequential upon, or incidental to, the amendments referred to in paragraph (a) above.

74(2) For the purposes of subsection (1)(a) above an oil field is an **off-shore oil field** if the whole of it is situated outside the geographical area of the United Kingdom (as determined under section 108 of the Finance Act 1986 – the on-shore/off-shore boundary).

74(3) In the amendments in Schedule 15 to this Act, any reference to a country other than the United Kingdom shall be treated as a reference to the geographical area of that country exclusive of any land (or waters) to the seaward side of the high-water line along the coast of that country, including the coast of all islands comprised in that country.

74(4) For the purpose of subsection (3) above, section 108(5) of the Finance Act 1986 (which provides a means of determining the high-water line at any place in the United Kingdom) shall, with any necessary modifications, apply to determine the high-water line at any place in a country other than the United Kingdom.

74(5) Except in so far as they have effect in relation to corporation tax or income tax, the amendments in Schedule 15 to this Act take effect as follows–

(a) in so far as they relate to expenditure incurred, they take effect for claim periods ending after 27th November 1991; and

(b) in so far as they relate to any other matter, they take effect for chargeable periods ending after 30th June 1992.

74(6) This section shall be construed as one with Part I of the Oil Taxation Act 1975.

Cross references – FA 1986, s. 108 defines the on-shore/off-shore boundary.

76 *Miscellaneous*

76 [Omitted by SI 2009/56, art. 3 and Sch. 1, para. 186.]

History – S. 76 and the cross-heading which preceded it omitted by SI 2009/56, art. 3 and Sch. 1, para. 186, with effect from 1 April 2009, subject to transitional and saving provisions in SI 2009/56, Sch. 3. Former s. 76 and the heading read as follows:

"GENERAL AND SPECIAL COMMISSIONERS

76 Miscellaneous

76 Schedule 16 to this Act (which makes provision in relation to the remuneration, jurisdiction, practice and procedure of the General Special Commissioners etc.) shall have effect."

GENERAL

83 Short Title

83 This Act may be cited as the Finance (No. 2) Act 1992.

SCHEDULES

SCHEDULE 15 – AMENDMENTS RELATING TO OIL EXPORTED DIRECTLY FROM OFF-SHORE FIELDS

Section 74

THE OIL TAXATION ACT 1975

1 [Amends OTA 1975, s. 2(5A).]

2(1) [Amends OTA 1975, s. 3(1)(f).]

2(2) [Amends OTA 1975, s. 3(4)(c).]

2(3) [Amends OTA 1975, s. 3(5)(a), (c).]

2(4) [Amends OTA 1975, s. 3(6)(f).]

3 [Amends OTA 1975, s. 12(1).]

4(1) [Repealed by FA 2006, s. 178 and Sch. 26, Pt. 5(1).]

4(2) [Amends OTA 1975, Sch. 3, para. 7.]

History – Para. 4(1) repealed by FA 2006, s. 178 and Sch. 26, Pt. 5(1), with effect in relation to oil delivered or appropriated on or after 1 July 2006, but subject to the provisions of FA 2006, s. 147(2)–(8).

THE FINANCE ACT 1982

5 [Amends FA 1982, Sch. 18, para. 3(2)(a).]

THE OIL TAXATION ACT 1983

6 [Amends OTA 1983, Sch. 1, para. 1(4).]

7 [Amends OTA 1983, Sch. 2, para. 12(3).]

8 [Amends OTA 1983, Sch. 4, para. 11.]

THE FINANCE ACT 1986

9 [Amends FA 1986, Sch. 21, para. 5(1).]

SCHEDULE 16 – GENERAL AND SPECIAL COMMISSIONERS

Section 76

[Omitted by SI 2009/56, art. 3 and Sch. 1, para. 186.]

History – Sch. 16 omitted by SI 2009/56, art. 3 and Sch. 1, para. 186, with effect from 1 April 2009, subject to transitional and saving provisions in SI 2009/56, Sch. 3. Former Sch. 16, para. 6 amended Schedule 2 to the Oil Taxation Act 1975 (management and collection of petroleum revenue tax) the Table in paragraph 1(1).
Former para. 7 read as follows:
"7 The Revenue Appeals Order 1987 shall have effect (subject to its revocation or amendment) as if any reference to section 56 of the Taxes Management Act 1970 included a reference to that section as applied by paragraph 1 of Schedule 2 to the Oil Taxation Act 1975."

FINANCE ACT 1993

(1993 Chapter 34)

[*27th July 1993*]

ARRANGEMENT OF SECTIONS

PART III – OIL TAXATION

SCHEDULES

PART III – OIL TAXATION

185 Abolition of PRT for oil fields with development consents on or after 16th March 1993

185(A1) In this Part of this Act–

"non-taxable oil field" means an oil field which meets the conditions in subsection (1), (1ZA) or (1A), and

"taxable oil field" means an oil field which is not a non-taxable field.

185(1) An oil field meets the conditions in this subsection if it is an oil field–

(a) for no part of which consent for development was granted to a licensee by the Secretary of State before 16th March 1993; and

(b) for no part of which a programme of development was served on a licensee or approved by the Secretary of State before that date.

185(1ZA) An oil field meets the conditions in this subsection if–

(a) the field does not meet the conditions in subsection (1), and

(b) an election under Schedule 20B that the field is to be non-taxable is in effect.

185(1A) An oil field meets the conditions in this subsection if–

(za) the field does not meet the conditions in subsection (1),

(a) the Secretary of State has at any time approved one or more abandonment programmes under Part 4 of the Petroleum Act 1998 (or Part 1 of the Petroleum Act 1987) in relation to all assets of the field which are relevant assets;

(b) those programmes have been carried out to the satisfaction of the Secretary of State;

(c) a development decision is made in relation to the field; and

(d) that decision is made on or after 16th March 1993 and after those programmes have been so carried out.

185(1B) For the purposes of subsection (1A)(a) above, an asset is a relevant asset of an oil field if–

(a) *it has at any time been* a qualifying asset (within the meaning of the 1983 Act) in relation to any participator in the field; and

(b) it has at any time been used for the purpose of winning oil from the field.

185(1C) For the purposes of subsection (1A)(c) and (d) above, a development decision is made in relation to an oil field when–

(a) consent for development is granted to a licensee by the appropriate authority in respect of the whole or part of the field; or

(b) a programme of development is served on a licensee or approved by the appropriate authority for the whole or part of the field.

185(2) For the purposes of subsection (1) above, no account shall be taken, in relation to an oil field, of a consent for development granted before 16th March 1993 or a programme of development served on a licensee or approved by the Secretary of State before that date if–

(a) in whole or in part that consent or programme related to another oil field for which a determination under Schedule 1 to the principal Act was made before the determination under that Schedule for the field in question; and

(b) on or after 16th March 1993, a consent for development is or was granted or a programme of development is or was served on a licensee or approved by the appropriate authority and that consent or programme relates, in whole or in part, to the field in question.

185(2A) In subsections (1C) and (2), **"the appropriate authority"** means–

(za) in relation to a field that is wholly within the Scottish onshore area, as defined in section 8A of the Petroleum Act 1998, the Scottish Ministers;

(a) in relation to a field that is wholly within the Welsh onshore area (as defined in section 8A of the Petroleum Act 1998), the Welsh Ministers;

(b) otherwise, the OGA.

185(3) Petroleum revenue tax shall not be charged in accordance with the Oil Taxation Acts in respect of–

(a) profits from oil won from a non-taxable field under the authority of such a licence as is referred to in section 1(1) of the principal Act; or

(b) any receipts accruing to a participator in a non-taxable field which, in the case of a taxable field, would be tariff receipts or disposal receipts attributable to the field for any period.

185(4) Without prejudice to the generality of subsection (3) above–

(a) [amends OTA 1975, s. 1(2);]

(b) [amends OTA 1975, s. 3(1D);]

(c) [amends OTA 1975, s. 5B;]

(d) no computation shall be made under the Oil Taxation Acts of the assessable profit or allowable loss accruing to a participator in any period from a non-taxable field; and

(e) no expenditure shall be regarded as allowable (or allowed) for a non-taxable field under the Oil Taxation Acts.

185(5) [Amends OTA 1975, s. 12(1).]

185(6) Subject to paragraphs (b) and (c) of subsection (4) above, where, apart from this section, expenditure incurred on or after 16th March 1993 would fall to be apportioned (as being allowable expenditure) between two or more oil fields, at least one of which is a non-taxable field, the apportionment shall be made as if all the fields were taxable fields, but subsection (4)(e) above shall then apply to any amount of expenditure apportioned to a non-taxable field.

185(7) In this section above **"development"**, in relation to an oil field, means–

(a) the erection or carrying out of permanent works for the purpose of getting oil from the field or for the purpose of conveying oil won from the field to a place on land; or

(b) winning oil from the field otherwise than in the course of searching for oil or drilling wells;

and consent for development does not include consent which is limited to the purpose of testing the characteristics of an oil-bearing area and does not relate to the erection or carrying out of permanent works.

185(8) In subsection (7) above **"permanent works"** means any structures or other works whatsoever which are intended by the licensee to be permanent and are neither designed to be moved from place to place without major dismantling nor intended by the licensee to be used only for searching for oil.

Prospective amendments – In s. 185(1C)(a) and (b), the word "OGA" substituted for the words "Secretary of State" by SI 2016/898, reg. 11, with effect immediately after the commencement of SCA 2016, s. 48.

In s. 185(2)(b) the word "OGA" substituted for the words "Secretary of State" by SI 2016/898, reg. 12, with effect immediately after the commencement of SCA 2016, s. 48.

S. 185(2A)(za) inserted by SI 2018/79, reg. 10, with effect from 1 October 2018 (immediately after the commencement of WA 2017, Sch. 6, Pt. 2 (SI 2017/1179)).

History – S. 185(A1) inserted by FA 2008, s. 107(2), with effect from 21 July 2008.
In s. 185(1) the words before para. (a) inserted by FA 2008, s. 107(3)(a), with effect from 21 July 2008.
In s. 185(1) the words after para. (b) omitted by FA 2008, s. 107(3)(b), with effect from 21 July 2008.
In s. 185(1) the words from "or an oil field" to "(1A) below" inserted by FA 2007, s. 102(2) with effect on or after 1 July 2007, FA 2007, s. 101(5).
In s. 185(1ZA)(b), the words "Schedule 20B" substituted for the words "Schedule 20A" by FA 2009, s. 91 and Sch. 45, para. 3(2)(c), with effect from 21 July 2009 (Royal Assent).
S. 185(1ZA) inserted by FA 2008, s. 107(4), with effect from 21 July 2008.
S. 185(1A)(za) inserted by FA 2008, s. 107(5), with effect from 21 July 2008.
S. 185(1A), (1B) and (1C) inserted by FA 2007, s. 101(3) with effect on or after 1 July 2007. See FA 2007, s. 102(5).
In s. 185(1C)(a) and (b), the words "appropriate authority" substituted for the word "OGA" by WA 2017, s. 69(1) and Sch. 6, para. 22(2), with effect from 1 October 2018 (SI 2017/1179, reg. 4(b)).
In s. 185(1C)(a) and (b), the word "OGA" substituted for the words "Secretary of State" by SI 2016/898, reg. 12, with effect from 1 October 2016 (as the 21st day after being made on 10 September 2016).
In s. 185(2)(b), the words "appropriate authority" substituted for the words "OGA" by WA 2017, s. 69(1) and Sch. 6, para. 22(3), with effect from 1 October 2018 (SI 2017/1179, reg. 4(b)).
In s. 185(2)(b), the word "OGA" substituted for the words "Secretary of State" by SI 2016/898, reg. 12, with effect from 1 October 2016 (as the 21st day after being made on 10 September 2016).
S. 185(2A)(za) inserted by SI 2018/79, reg. 10, with effect from 1 October 2018 (immediately after the commencement of WA 2017, Sch. 6, Pt. 2 (SI 2017/1179)).
S. 185(2A) inserted by WA 2017, s. 69(1) and Sch. 6, para. 22(4), with effect from 1 October 2018 (SI 2017/1179, reg. 4(b)).
In s. 185(7) the words "this section" substituted for "subsections (1) and (2)" by FA 2007, s. 102(4) with effect on or after 1 July 2007. See FA 2007, s. 102(5).

Cross references – OTA 1975, s. 5: allowance of abortive exploration expenditure.
SI 2018/79, reg. 5: modification of s. 185 until 1 October 2018 (and the commencement of WA 2017, Sch. 6, Pt. 2).

186 Reduction of rates of PRT and interest repayments for taxable oil fields

186(1) [Amends OTA 1975, s. 1(2), with respect to chargeable periods ending after 30 June 1993.]

186(2) [Amends OTA 1975, Sch. 2, para. 17(2).]

186(3) [Amends OTA 1975, Sch. 2, para. 17(4).]

186(4) [Adds OTA 1975, Sch. 2, para. 17(5)–(7).]

187 Returns and information

187(1) [Amends OTA 1975, Sch. 2 and omits OTA 1975, Sch. 2, para. 7.]

187(2)–(8) [Omitted by SI 2009/3054, art. 3 and Schedule, para. 5(a).]

History – S. 187(2)–(8) omitted by SI 2009/3054, art. 3 and Schedule, para. 5(a), with effect from 1 April 2010, except that s. 187(2) and (6) continue to apply in relation to a notice given under s. 187 before 1 April 2010 (SI 2009/3054, art. 5). Former s. 187(2)–(8) read as follows:
"**187(2)** The Board may by notice in writing require a person–
(a) to deliver to a named officer of the Board such documents as are in the person's possession or power and as (in the Board's reasonable opinion) contain, or may contain, information relevant to–
(i) any tax liability to which that person is or may be subject, or
(ii) the amount of any such liability; or
(b) to furnish to a named officer of the Board such particulars as the Board may reasonably require as being relevant to, or to the amount of, any such liability.
187(3) The Board may, for the purpose of enquiring into the tax liability of any person (**"the taxpayer"**), by notice in writing require any other person to deliver to or, if the person to whom the notice is given so elects, to make available for inspection by, a named officer of the Board, such documents–
(a) as are in his possession or power; and
(b) as (in the Board's reasonable opinion) contain, or may contain, information relevant to–
(i) any tax liability to which the taxpayer is or may be or may have been subject; or
(ii) the amount of any such liability.
187(4) Subject to subsection (5) below, a notice under subsection (3) above shall name the taxpayer with whose liability the Board is concerned; and (for the avoidance of doubt) a company which has ceased to exist may be so named.
187(5) If, on an application made by the Board, the tribunal consents, the Board may give such a notice as is mentioned in subsection (3) above but without naming the taxpayer to whom the notice relates; but such a consent shall not be given unless the tribunal is satisfied–
(a) that the notice relates to a taxpayer whose identity is not known to the Board or to a class of taxpayers whose individual identities are not so known;
(b) that there are reasonable grounds for believing that the taxpayer or any of the class of taxpayers to whom the notice relates may have failed or may fail to comply with any provision of the Oil Taxation Acts;
(c) that any such failure is likely to have led or to lead to serious prejudice to the proper assessment or collection of tax; and
(d) that the information which is likely to be contained in any documents to which the notice relates is not readily available from another source.
187(6) A person to whom a notice is given under subsection (5) above may, by notice in writing given to the Board within thirty days after the date of the notice under that subsection, object to that notice on the ground that it would be onerous for him to comply with it; and, if the matter is not resolved by agreement, it shall be referred to the tribunal which may confirm, vary or cancel that notice.
187(7) Subsections (2) to (6) above (which, in relation to petroleum revenue tax, contain provisions similar to those of section 20 of the Taxes Management Act 1970) shall have effect subject to Part I of Schedule 21 to this Act (which contains provisions similar to those of section 20B of that Act); and the provisions of Part II of that Schedule relating to the meaning of "documents" (which are derived from provisions of sections 20 and 20D of that Act) shall have effect.
187(8) Section 98 of the Taxes Management Act 1970 (penalties, etc. in relation to special returns) shall have effect as if, in the first column of the Table in that section, there were included a reference to subsections (2) to (6) above.".
In former s. 187(5), the words "the tribunal consents" substituted for the words "a Special Commissioner gives his consent" and the word "tribunal" substituted for the words "Special Commissioner" by SI 2009/56, art. 3(1) and Sch. 1, para. 193(2), operative from 1 April 2009, subject to transitional and saving provisions in SI 2009/56, Sch. 3.

In former s. 187(6), the words "tribunal which" substituted for the words "Special Commissioners who" by SI 2009/56, art. 3(1) and Sch. 1, para. 193(3), operative from 1 April 2009, subject to transitional and saving provisions in SI 2009/56, Sch. 3.
Cross references – Sch. 21: supplementary provisions about information.
SI 2009/275, art. 3(e): any decision under s. 187(5) or (6) is an excluded decision for the purposes of TCEA 2007, s. 11(1) and 13(1).

188 Exploration and appraisal expenditure

188(1) [Inserts OTA 1975, s. 5A(1)(aa).]

188(2) [Inserts OTA 1975, s. 5A(1A)–(1C).]

188(3) [Amends OTA 1975, s. 5A(2).]

189 Transitional relief for certain exploration and appraisal expenditure

189(1) This section applies in any case where–

(a) a participator in an oil field or an associate incurs expenditure on or after 16th March 1993 and before 1st January 1995; and

(b) apart from this section, that expenditure would not be allowable under section 5A of the principal Act (as amended by section 188 above); and

(c) if section 188 above had not been enacted, the expenditure would be allowable in the case of the participator under section 5A of the principal Act; and

(d) on 16th March 1993 the participator or the associate was a licensee in respect of the area to which the expenditure related.

189(2) In the following provisions of this section–

(a) expenditure falling within subsection (1) above is referred to as **"transitional E and A expenditure"**; and

(b) the participator in whose case that expenditure would be allowable as mentioned in paragraph (c) of that subsection is referred to as **"the claimant"**.

189(3) Subject to the following provisions of this section, so much of the transitional E and A expenditure incurred by the claimant or an associate as does not in the aggregate exceed £10 million shall be allowable in the case of the claimant under section 5A of the principal Act (as exploration and appraisal expenditure).

189(4) In subsections (1) to (3) above any reference to an **associate of a participator** applies only where the participator is a company and is a reference to another company–

(a) which on 16th March 1993 was a member of the same group of companies as the participator; and

(b) with which the participator is associated in respect of expenditure incurred by the other company;

and subsections (7) and (8) of section 5 of the principal Act (companies and associates etc.) apply for the purposes of this section as they apply for the purposes of that section.

189(5) Where–

(a) the claimant is a company, and

(b) on 16th March 1993 the claimant was a member of a group of companies, and

(c) at least one other company which was a member of the group on that date was then a participator in an oil field, and

(d) that other company is also the claimant in relation to an amount of transitional E and A expenditure,

subsection (3) above shall have effect as if references therein to the claimant were references to the aggregate of all those companies which on that date were members of the group and are the claimants in relation to any transitional E and A expenditure.

189(6) In this section, a **group of companies** means a company which is not a 51 per cent subsidiary of any other company, together with each company which is its 51 per cent subsidiary; and section 838 of the Taxes Act 1988 (subsidiaries) applies for the purposes of this section as it applies for the purposes of the Tax Acts (within the meaning of that Act).

190 Allowance of expenditure on certain assets limited by reference to taxable field use

190(1) Where, in the case of expenditure incurred as mentioned in section 1(1) of the 1983 Act (expenditure incurred on non-dedicated mobile assets),–

(a) the expenditure would, apart from this subsection, be allowable under section 4 of the principal Act for a claim period of a taxable field, and

(b) during that claim period, the asset becomes dedicated to a non-taxable field,

PRT Statutes

that proportion of the expenditure which is equal to the proportion of the claim period during which the asset is dedicated to a non-taxable field shall not be allowable as mentioned in paragraph (a) above.

190(2) For the purpose of determining whether an asset becomes at any time **dedicated to a non-taxable field**, it shall be assumed that, in relation to a non-taxable field, any reference in section 2 of the 1983 Act (dedicated mobile assets) to a claim period is a reference to–

(a) the period ending at the end of December following the determination of the field; or

(b) the period of twelve months ending at the end of December in any later year.

190(3) In paragraph 7 of Schedule 1 to the 1983 Act (brought-in assets) in sub-paragraph (1)(c) (which requires that during the initial period the asset should have been used otherwise than in connection with an oil field) for the words "an oil field" there shall be substituted "a taxable field".

190(4) In paragraph 8 of that Schedule (subsequent use of new asset otherwise than in connection with an oil field) in the heading and in sub-paragraphs (1) to (3) and (6) for the words "an oil field" there shall be substituted "a taxable field".

190(5) In paragraph 5 of Schedule 2 to the 1983 Act (acquisition otherwise than at arm's length: limit on tariff and disposal receipts)–

(a) [amends FA 1993, Sch. 2, para. 5(1)(a) and (b);]

(b) [repealed by FA 1994, s. 258 and Sch. 26, Pt. VI;]

(c) [amends FA 1993, Sch. 2, para. 5(3)(a);]

(d) [amends FA 1993, Sch. 2, para. 5(3)(b).]

History – S. 190(5)(b) repealed by FA 1994, s. 258 and Sch. 26, Pt. VI, with respect to disposals made after 30 November 1993.

191 Time when expenditure is incurred

191(1) Subject to the following provisions of this section, where a claim is made under the principal Act for the allowance of any expenditure and the claim is received by the Board after 16th March 1993, an amount of expenditure is to be taken to be incurred for the purposes of the Oil Taxation Acts on the date on which the obligation to pay that amount becomes unconditional (whether or not there is a later date on or before which the whole or any part of that amount is required to be paid).

191(2) Subject to subsection (3) below, where the amount of any expenditure incurred by any person at any time after 16th March 1993 under a contract–

(a) for the acquisition from any other person of, or of an interest in, an asset, or

(b) for the provision by any other person of services or other business facilities of whatever kind (whether in connection with the use of an asset or not), or

(c) for the grant or transfer to that person by any other person of any right, licence or interest (other than an interest in an asset)

is disproportionate to the extent to which that other person has, at or before that time, performed his obligations under the contract then, for the purposes of the Oil Taxation Acts, only so much of the expenditure shall be taken to have been incurred at that time as is proportionate to those obligations which have been so performed.

191(3) If, in the case of a contract entered into after 16th March 1993 and falling within paragraph (a) or paragraph (b) of subsection (2) above–

(a) the expenditure referred to in that subsection is incurred before 1st July 1993, and

(b) the other person referred to in paragraph (a) or paragraph (b) (**"the contractor"**) has performed his obligations by entering into one or more further contracts,

the contractor shall be treated for the purposes of subsection (2) above as having at any time performed his obligations under the contract only to the extent that, at that time, the asset or interest in question has been acquired by, or, as the case may be, the services or other business facilities have been provided to, the person incurring the expenditure.

191(4) [Amends OTA 1975, Sch. 4, para. 2.]

191(5) [Amends OTA 1975, Sch. 4, para. 2.]

191(6) The amendments made by subsections (4) and (5) above have effect where the transaction to which paragraph 2 of Schedule 4 to the principal Act applies takes place on or after 16th March 1993.

Cross references – FA 1994, Sch. 22, para. 13(2): obligations treated as performed at the time asset etc. was acquired – election by *reference to pipe-line usage.*

192 Chargeable periods in which expenditure may be brought into account

192(1) Where a claim which–

(a) is made under Schedule 5 or Schedule 6 to the principal Act for the allowance of any expenditure, and

(b) is received by the Board after 16th March 1993,

has been allowed, the expenditure shall not be brought into account in determining the assessable profit or allowable loss of any chargeable period which ends earlier than the last day of the claim period in which the expenditure was incurred.

192(2) Where a claim has been made under Schedule 7 to the principal Act for the allowance of any expenditure incurred after 31st March 1993 and that claim has been allowed, the expenditure shall not be brought into account in determining the assessable profit or allowable loss of any chargeable period which ends before the date on which the expenditure was incurred.

192(3) The preceding provisions of this section have effect notwithstanding anything in subsection (9) of section 2 of the principal Act (under which expenditure which had been allowed might in certain cases be taken into account in earlier chargeable periods) and, accordingly, at the beginning of that subsection there shall be inserted "Subject to section 192 of the Finance Act 1993".

193 Tariff receipts etc.

193(1) [Amends OTA 1983, s. 9(5)(a) and inserts s. 9(5A).]

193(2) Where a participator in a taxable field incurs any expenditure and,–

(a) apart from this subsection, the expenditure would be taken into account in determining the assessable profit or allowable loss accruing to that participator from the taxable field in any chargeable period, and

(b) in the hands of the recipient, the expenditure would, on the relevant assumptions, constitute tariff receipts or disposal receipts of a participator in a non-taxable field attributable to that field for any period, and

(c) at the time the expenditure is incurred, the participator referred to in paragraph (a) above is or is connected with a participator in the non-taxable field referred to in paragraph (b) above,

the expenditure shall be disregarded in determining the assessable profit or allowable loss referred to in paragraph (a) above.

193(3) For the purposes of subsection (2) above, the relevant assumptions are–

(a) that the non-taxable field is a taxable field; and

(b) that the asset which gives rise to the expenditure (by virtue of its use, the provision of services or other business facilities in connection with its use or its disposal) is a qualifying asset in relation to the participator in question.

193(4) [Amends OTA 1983, s. 12(3).]

193(5) [Inserts OTA 1983, s. 12(3A).]

193(6) In this section **"disposal receipts"**, **"qualifying asset"** and **"tariff receipts"** have the same meaning as in the 1983 Act; and section 1122 of the Corporation Tax Act 2010 (connected persons) applies for the purposes of subsection (2)(c) above.

History – In s. 193(6), the words "section 1122 of the Corporation Tax Act 2010" substituted for the words "section 839 of the Taxes Act 1988" by CTA 2010, s. 1177 and Sch. 1, para. 278, with effect for corporation tax purposes for accounting periods ending on or after 1 April 2010, and for income tax and capital gains tax purposes for the tax year 2010–11 and subsequent tax years.

194 Double taxation relief in relation to petroleum revenue tax

194 [Omitted by TIOPA 2010, s. 374 and Sch. 8, para. 49 and TIOPA 2010, s. 378 and Sch. 10, Pt. 1.]

History – S. 194 omitted by TIOPA 2010, s. 374 and Sch. 8, para. 49 and TIOPA 2010, s. 378 and Sch. 10, Pt. 1, with effect for corporation tax purposes for accounting periods ending on or after 1 April 2010, for income tax and capital gains tax purposes for the tax year 2010–11 and subsequent tax years, and for petroleum revenue tax purposes for chargeable periods beginning on or after 1 July 2010.

Notes – S. 194 rewritten in TIOPA 2010 as follows:
s. 194(1): TIOPA 2010, s. 2(1), (2), (3), 3(1), (2), (3), 6(4), 124(1), 125(1);
s. 194(3): TIOPA 2010, s. 6(4);
s. 194(4): TIOPA 2010, Sch. 8, para. 7;
s. 194(5): TIOPA 2010, s. 129(1), (2), (3), (4).

195 Interpretation of Part III and consequential amendments of assessments etc.

195(1) In this Part–

(a) **"the principal Act"** means the Oil Taxation Act 1975;

(b) **"the 1983 Act"** means the Oil Taxation Act 1983;

(c) **"the Oil Taxation Acts"** means Parts I and III of the principal Act, the 1983 Act and any other enactment relating to petroleum revenue tax; and

(d) **"taxable field"** and **"non-taxable field"** shall be construed in accordance with section 185 above.

195(2) The Board may make all such amendments of assessments or determinations or of decisions on claims as may be necessary in consequence of the provisions of this Part.

195(3) This Part shall be construed as one with Part I of the principal Act.

History – In s. 195(3), the words ", other than section 194," (which followed the words "This Part") omitted by TIOPA 2010, s. 374 and Sch. 8, para. 49 and TIOPA 2010, s. 378 and Sch. 10, Pt. 1, with effect for corporation tax purposes for accounting periods ending on or after 1 April 2010, for income tax and capital gains tax purposes for the tax year 2010–11 and subsequent tax years, and for petroleum revenue tax purposes for chargeable periods beginning on or after 1 July 2010.

SCHEDULE 20B – PRT: ELECTIONS FOR OIL FIELDS TO BECOME NON-TAXABLE

History – Sch. 20B renumbered (previously Sch. 20A) by FA 2009, s. 91 and Sch. 45, para. 3(1), with effect from 21 July 2009 (Royal Assent).
Sch. 20B inserted (as Sch. 20A) by FA 2008, s. 107(6) and Sch. 33, para. 1, with effect from 21 July 2008.

ELECTION BY RESPONSIBLE PERSON

1(1) The responsible person for a taxable field may make an election that the field is to be non-taxable.

1(2) An election is irrevocable.

1(3) The responsible person may not make an election unless each person who is a participator at the time the election is made agrees to the election being made.

1(4) If the responsible person makes an election, the Commissioners may assume that each participator agrees to the election being made (unless it appears to the Commissioners that a participator does not agree).

METHOD OF ELECTION

History – The heading before para. 2 substituted by F(No. 2)A 2017, s. 44(1), with effect as having come into force on 23 November 2016. Former para. 2 heading read as "DECISION BY COMMISSIONERS".

2 An election must be made in writing.

History – Para. 2 substituted by F(No. 2)A 2017, s. 44(1), with effect as having come into force on 23 November 2016. Former para. 2 read as follows:

"**2(1)** If an election is made, the Commissioners must decide whether or not the field is no longer taxable.

2(2) For the purposes of this paragraph, the field is no longer taxable if it appears to the Commissioners that one or other of the following conditions is met in relation to each future chargeable period.

2(3) Condition A is that no assessable profit will accrue to any participator in the field in that period.

2(4) Condition B is that the assessable profit accruing to each participator in the field in that period will be equal to, or smaller than, the cash equivalent of that participator's share of the oil allowance for the field in that period.

2(5) The responsible person must give the Commissioners such information as the Commissioners may reasonably require in connection with their making a decision under sub-paragraph (1).

2(6) The Commissioners may make such assumptions as they think appropriate for the purposes of making a decision under this paragraph (including assumptions about what, if any, participators there will be in the field in future chargeable periods).

2(7) In this paragraph–

"assessable profit" means assessable profit before any reduction under section 7 of OTA 1975 (relief for allowable losses);

"future chargeable period", in relation to a decision by the Commissioners under this paragraph, means a chargeable period that falls at any time after the chargeable period in which the Commissioners make that decision."

3 An election must be notified to the Commissioners.

History – Para. 3 substituted by F(No. 2)A 2017, s. 44(1), with effect as having come into force on 23 November 2016. Former para. 3 read as follows:

"**3(1)** The Commissioners must give the responsible person notice of their decision under paragraph 2(1).

3(2) Within one month of being given notice by the Commissioners of their decision, the responsible person must give copies of the notice to each person who is a participator, or a former participator, at the time the Commissioners' notice is given.

3(3) But the responsible person is not required to give notice to any person to whom it would be impracticable to give notice."

4 An election is deemed to have been made on the date on which notification of the election was sent to the Commissioners.

History – Para. 4 substituted (and the heading before it effectively omitted) by F(No. 2)A 2017, s. 44(1), with effect as having come into force on 23 November 2016. Former para. 4 read as follows:

"WHEN ELECTION HAS EFFECT

4(1) An election does not have effect unless the Commissioners decide under paragraph 2(1) that the field is no longer taxable.

4(2) In such a case, the election has effect from the start of the first chargeable period to begin after the Commissioners give notice under paragraph 3.

4(3) The election then continues to have effect indefinitely (unless cancelled in accordance with paragraph 6)."

EFFECT OF ELECTION

5 If an election is made, the field ceases to be taxable with effect from the start of the first chargeable period to begin after the election is made.

History – Para. 5 (and the heading before it) substituted by F(No. 2)A 2017, s. 44(1), with effect as having come into force on 23 November 2016. Former para. 5 read as follows:

"NO UNRELIEVABLE FIELD LOSSES FROM FIELD

5 For as long as the election has effect, no allowable loss that accrues from the oil field is an allowable unrelievable field loss for the purposes of petroleum revenue tax."

NO UNRELIEVABLE FIELD LOSSES FROM FIELD

6 From the start of the first chargeable period to begin after an election is made, no allowable loss that accrues from the oil field is an allowable unrelievable field loss for the purposes of petroleum revenue tax.

History – Para. 6 (and the heading before it) substituted by F(No. 2)A 2017, s. 44(1), with effect as having come into force on 23 November 2016. Former para. 6 read as follows:

"CANCELLATION OF ELECTION BY COMMISSIONERS

6(1) The Commissioners may cancel an election if, within 3 years of their giving notice under paragraph 3, it appears to them that–

(a) information that the responsible person gave the Commissioners in connection with the election was inaccurate or incomplete at the time it was given, and

(b) if the information had not been inaccurate or incomplete,

the Commissioners would not have made the decision that they made under paragraph 2.

6(2) For the purposes of sub-paragraph (1) it does not matter whether or not the Commissioners required the information to be given."

INTERPRETATION

7(1) In this Schedule–

"Commissioners" means the Commissioners for Her Majesty's Revenue and Customs;

"participator", in relation to a particular time, means a person who is a participator in the chargeable period which includes that time.

7(2) Expressions used in this Schedule and in Part 1 of the Oil Taxation Act 1975 have the same meaning in this Schedule as in Part 1 of that Act.

History – Para. 7 substituted by F(No. 2)A 2017, s. 44(1), with effect as having come into force on 23 November 2016. Former para. 7 read as follows:

"7(1) If the Commissioners cancel an election, they must give notice of the cancellation–

(a) to the person who made the election, or

(b) if it is impracticable to give notice to that person, to a person who is a participator at the time the election is cancelled, or

(c) if it is impracticable to give notice to any such person, to a person who is a former participator at the time the election is cancelled;

but the Commissioners are not required to give notice to a person falling within paragraph (c) if it would be impracticable to give notice to any such person.

7(2) Within one month of being given notice by the Commissioners under sub-paragraph (1), the person must give copies of the notice to each person who is a participator, or a former participator, at the time the Commissioners' notice is given.

7(3) But that person is not required to give notice to any person to whom it would be impracticable to give notice."

EFFECT OF CANCELLATION

8 [Effectively omitted by F(No. 2)A 2017, s. 44(1).]

History – Para. 8 (and the heading before it) effectively omitted by F(No. 2)A 2017, s. 44(1), with effect as having come into force on 23 November 2016. Former para. 8 read as follows:

"EFFECT OF CANCELLATION

8(1) If the Commissioners cancel an election under paragraph 6, the election is to be treated as though it had never had effect.

8(2) But that does not make a person liable for anything that the person did, or did not do, in consequence of the election having effect before its cancellation.

8(3) If the Commissioners cancel an election, the enactments relating to petroleum revenue tax apply to the oil field subject to sub-paragraphs (4) to (7).

8(4) The Commissioners may specify the periods within which PRT returns for the relevant chargeable periods must be delivered.

8(5) If the Commissioners specify the period within which a PRT return must be delivered, the provisions of OTA 1975 set out in sub-paragraph (6) apply to the specified period as if it were a period for the delivery of a PRT return that has been extended under paragraph 2 or 5 of Schedule 2 to OTA 1975.

8(6) The provisions of OTA 1975 referred to in sub-paragraph (5) are–

(a) paragraph 12A of Schedule 2, and

(b) paragraph 2(7) and (8) of Schedule 5 (including those provisions as applied to Schedule 6 to OTA 1975 by paragraph 2 of Schedule 6).

8(7) For the purposes of paragraph 4 of Schedule 2 to OTA 1975, the "initial period" is the period of thirty days beginning with the date on which the Commissioners give notice in accordance with paragraph 6 of this Schedule.

8(8) The Commissioners may by regulations make transitional provision (including provision modifying enactments) applicable to cases where elections are made and subsequently cancelled under this Schedule.

8(9) Regulations under sub-paragraph (8)–

(a) are to be made by statutory instrument, and

(b) are subject to annulment in pursuance of a resolution of the House of Commons.

8(10) In this paragraph–

"PRT return" means a return under paragraph 2 or 5 of Schedule 2 to OTA 1975;

"relevant chargeable periods", in relation to a cancelled election, means the series of consecutive chargeable periods that–

(a) begins with the chargeable period from the start of which the election had effect, and

(b) ends with the chargeable period during which the election is cancelled."

APPEALS

9 [Effectively omitted by F(No. 2)A 2017, s. 44(1).]

History – Para. 9 (and the heading before it) effectively omitted by F(No. 2)A 2017, s. 44(1), with effect as having come into force on 23 November 2016. Former para. 9 read as follows:

"APPEALS

9(1) The responsible person may appeal against a decision of the Commissioners under paragraph 2(1).

9(2) Any such appeal must be made within 3 months of the Commissioners giving notice under paragraph 3 of their decision to the responsible person."

10 [Effectively omitted by F(No. 2)A 2017, s. 44(1).]

History – Para. 10 effectively omitted by F(No. 2)A 2017, s. 44(1), with effect as having come into force on 23 November 2016. Former para. 10 read as follows:

"**10(1)** A person who is a participator, or a former participator, at the time the Commissioners cancel an election under paragraph 6 may appeal against the cancellation.

10(2) Any such appeal must be made within 3 months of the Commissioners giving notice under paragraph 7 of the cancellation (whether or not the notice was given to the person making the appeal)."

11 [Effectively omitted by F(No. 2)A 2017, s. 44(1).]

History – Para. 11 effectively omitted by F(No. 2)A 2017, s. 44(1), with effect as having come into force on 23 November 2016. Former para. 11 read as follows:

"**11(1)** Any appeal under paragraph 9 or 10 must be made to the Commissioners–

(a) by notice in writing, or

(b) in any other form authorised by direction of the Commissioners.

11(2) [Omitted by SI 2009/56, art. 3(1) and Sch. 1, para. 194(2).]

11(3) The provisions of paragraphs 14A to 14I of Schedule 2 to OTA 1975 shall apply in relation to an appeal under paragraphs 9 or 10 above as they apply in relation to an appeal against an assessment or determination made under that Act, subject to any necessary modifications.

History – Para. 11(2) omitted by SI 2009/56, art. 3(1) and Sch. 1, para. 194(2), operative from 1 April 2009, subject to transitional and saving provisions in SI 2009/56, Sch. 3. Former para. 11(2) read as follows:

"**11(2)** Any appeal under paragraph 9 or 10 is to be determined by the Special Commissioners.".

Para. 11(3) inserted by SI 2009/56, art. 3(1) and Sch. 1, para. 194(3), operative from 1 April 2009, subject to transitional and saving provisions in SI 2009/56, Sch. 3."

INTERPRETATION

12 [Effectively omitted by F(No. 2)A 2017, s. 44(1).]

History – Para. 12 (and the heading before it) effectively omitted by F(No. 2)A 2017, s. 44(1), with effect as having come into force on 23 November 2016. Former para. 12 read as follows:

"INTERPRETATION

12(1) In this Schedule–

"Commissioners" means the Commissioners for Her Majesty's Revenue and Customs;

"election" means an election in writing, or in any other form authorised by direction of the Commissioners, made to the Commissioners;

"former participator", in relation to a particular time, means a person who–

(a) is not a participator in the chargeable period which includes that time, but

(b) was a participator in any earlier chargeable period;

"OTA 1975" means the Oil Taxation Act 1975;

"participator", in relation to a particular time, means a person who is a participator in the chargeable period which includes that time.

12(2) Expressions used in this Schedule and in Part 1 of OTA 1975 have the same meaning in this Schedule as in that Part of OTA 1975.

History – In para. 12(1), in the entry for "Commissioners", the words "(except in the expression "Special Commissioners")" omitted by SI 2009/56, art. 3(1) and Sch. 1, para. 194(4), operative from 1 April 2009, subject to transitional and saving provisions in SI 2009/56, Sch. 3."

SCHEDULE 21 – OIL TAXATION: SUPPLEMENTARY PROVISIONS ABOUT INFORMATION

Section 187

[Omitted by SI 2009/3054, art. 3 and Schedule, para. 5(b).]

History – Sch. 21 omitted by SI 2009/3054, art. 3 and Schedule, para. 5(b), with effect from 1 April 2010.

FINANCE ACT 1994

(1994 Chapter 9)

[*3rd May 1994*]

ARRANGEMENT OF SECTIONS

PART V – OIL TAXATION

CHAPTER I – ELECTION BY REFERENCE TO PIPE-LINE USAGE

CHAPTER II – MISCELLANEOUS

SCHEDULES

PART V – OIL TAXATION

Chapter I – Election by Reference to Pipe-Line Usage

231 Election by reference to pipe-line with excess capacity

231(1) The provisions of this Chapter apply where, on or before 1st January 1996, a participator in a taxable field makes, in accordance with Part I of Schedule 22 to this Act, an election with respect to that field by reference to a pipe-line–

(a) which is a qualifying asset;

(b) which is used or intended to be used for transporting oil in circumstances which give rise or are expected to give rise to tariff receipts;

(c) which, at the date of the election, is at least 25 kilometres in length; and

(d) for which the initial usage fraction does not exceed one-half.

231(2) A participator may not make an election–

(a) unless the field to which the election applies is (or, as the case may be, is intended to be) the chargeable field in relation to the tariff receipts referred to in subsection (1)(b) above; or

(b) if the first chargeable period of that field ended on or before 30th June 1982; or

(c) if the participator's net profit period with respect to that field ended on or before 30th June 1993;

and for the purposes of paragraph (c) above no account shall be taken of the operation of section 113 of the Finance Act 1981 (loss following net profit period).

231(3) If there is more than one pipe-line by reference to which the electing participator could, apart from this subsection, make an election (with respect to the same field) he may make an election only by reference to that pipe-line which is the longer or longest.

231(4) In this Chapter, in relation to a pipe-line or an election made by reference to a pipe-line, **"the initial usage fraction"** means the fraction of which–

PRT Statutes

(a) the numerator is the daily contracted and production throughput of oil in relation to the pipe-line on 16th March 1993; and

(b) the denominator is the design capacity of the pipe-line, expressed on a daily basis.

231(5) Subject to subsection (6) below, where an election is in operation it shall apply to all those assets which, by reference to the field to which the election applies, are at the date of the election or subsequently become–

(a) qualifying assets in relation to the electing participator; and

(b) assets to which are or are expected to be referable any tariff receipts of the electing participator attributable to that field.

231(6) If the electing participator specifies in his election that the election is to be limited to oil which is, or is expected to be, transported by the pipe-line by reference to which the election is made, the election shall apply only to such of the assets referred to in subsection (5) above as, in whole or in part, are or subsequently become used in connection with that oil.

231(7) For the purposes of this Chapter, unless it is just and reasonable to determine some other quantity of oil, the **daily contracted and production throughput of oil** in relation to a pipe-line on 16th March 1993 is the aggregate of–

(a) the maximum daily capacity specified in contracts then in force for the use of the pipe-line (whether at that date or in the future) for transporting oil won from any taxable field (including the field to which the election applies); and

(b) the maximum expected daily throughput, otherwise than pursuant to such contracts, of oil transported by the pipe-line and won from the field to which the election applies or any other taxable field, being the throughput ascertained by reference to what was at that date the most recent development plan applicable to the field to which the election applies or, as the case may be, the other taxable field.

231(8) For the purposes of this Chapter, unless it is just and reasonable to determine some other capacity, the **design capacity of a pipe-line** is that which is specified for the pipe-line as a whole in what was, on 16th March 1993, the most recent development plan applicable to the field to which the election applies or, as the case may be, the pipe-line itself.

232 Restriction on electing participator's allowable expenditure on elected assets

232(1) This section has effect in relation to expenditure which is incurred on an asset to which an election applies; and in this section **"allowable or allowed"**, in relation to any expenditure, means allowable or allowed under any of the expenditure relief provisions.

232(2) Subject to the following provisions of this section, in the case of expenditure incurred before the date of the election, the amount which, apart from this section, would be allowable or allowed in the case of the electing participator shall be reduced by multiplying it by the initial usage fraction.

232(3) Subject to subsection (5) below, in the case of expenditure incurred on or after the date of the election, the amount which, apart from this section, would be allowable or allowed in the case of the electing participator shall be reduced to nil.

232(4) Where, after 30th November 1993 and before the date of the election, expenditure was incurred on an asset to which the election applies and–

(a) apart from this section, that expenditure would have qualified for supplement by virtue of paragraph (c) or paragraph (d) of subsection (5) of section 3 of the principal Act, and

(b) the effect of the expenditure is to increase the maximum capacity of the pipe-line by reference to which the election was made above its design capacity or to increase the capacity of any asset used or to be used for the initial treatment or initial storage of oil transported by the pipe-line above its development plan capacity,

that expenditure shall be treated for the purposes of the application of subsections (2) and (3) above as if it had been incurred after the date of the election.

232(5) Where, at the date of the election, an asset to which the election applies is for the time being leased or hired under a contract which was entered into before 16th March 1993, any expenditure–

(a) which is incurred on or after the date of the election on the leasing or hiring of the asset under the contract, and

(b) which is not of a description falling within paragraphs (a) and (b) of subsection (4) above,

shall be treated for the purposes of the application of subsections (2) and (3) above as if it had been incurred before the date of the election.

232(6) For the purposes of subsection (4)(b) above, the **development plan capacity** of any asset used or to be used for the initial treatment or initial storage of oil transported by a pipe-line is–

(a) the maximum capacity of that asset as specified in what, on 16th March 1993, was the most recent development plan applicable to the field to which the election applies or, as the case may be, to the asset itself; or

(b) if no such maximum capacity was so specified in relation to an asset, its actual maximum capacity on that date or, if there was no such capacity on that date, nil.

232(7) Where a claim under Schedule 5 or Schedule 6 to the principal Act relates to the allowance of any expenditure to which subsection (2) above applies, the amount claimed shall take account of the operation of that subsection; and where subsection (3) above applies to any expenditure, no such claim shall be made with respect to it.

232(8) Where a claim has been made under Schedule 5 or Schedule 6 to the principal Act with respect to any expenditure and, subsequently, an election is made which has the effect of altering the amount of expenditure which is allowable or allowed,–

(a) a notice of variation such as is mentioned in paragraph 9 of Schedule 5 to the principal Act may be served after the end of the period referred to in sub-paragraph (1) of that paragraph if it is served before the expiry of the period of three years beginning on the date of the election; and

(b) if the effect of such a notice is that the net profit period with respect to the field to which the election applies is changed, the change shall not (by virtue of section 231(2) above) affect the validity of the election.

232(9) Nothing in this section affects the determination of the question whether an asset is a qualifying asset for the purposes of the 1983 Act and, accordingly, for that purpose, the preceding provisions of this section shall be disregarded in determining whether any expenditure is allowable or allowed.

233 Tax relief for certain receipts of an electing participator

233(1) If any sum–

(a) is received or receivable by the electing participator on or after the date of an election, and

(b) is so received or receivable from any person in respect of the use, otherwise than in connection with a taxable field, of an asset to which the election applies or the provision of services or other business facilities of whatever kind in connection with that use, and

(c) would, apart from this section, constitute a tariff receipt attributable to the field to which the election applies,

that sum shall not be regarded as a tariff receipt for the purposes of the Oil Taxation Acts.

233(2) If any sum–

(a) is received or receivable by the electing participator on or after the date of an election, and

(b) is so received or receivable in respect of the disposal of an asset to which the election applies or of an interest in such an asset, and

(c) constitutes a disposal receipt of the electing participator attributable to the field to which the election applies,

that sum shall, for the purposes of the Oil Taxation Acts, be taken to be reduced in accordance with subsection (4) below.

233(3) Any reference in subsection (1) or subsection (2) above to a **sum received or receivable** includes a reference to an amount which (apart from this section) would be treated as a tariff receipt or disposal receipt by virtue of paragraph 5 of Schedule 2 to the 1983 Act (acquisition and disposal of qualifying assets otherwise than at arm's length).

233(4) Unless it is just and reasonable to make a different reduction, the reduction referred to in subsection (2) above shall be determined by reference to that applicable under subsection (2) or subsection (3) of section 232 above to the expenditure incurred on the asset concerned so that if, for the purposes of determining under those subsections the amount of that expenditure which was allowed or allowable,–

(a) the whole or any part of that expenditure was reduced by multiplying it by the initial usage fraction, or

(b) the whole or any part of that expenditure was reduced to nil,

a similar reduction shall apply to the whole or, as the case may require, to each correspondingly proportionate part of any sum falling within subsection (2) above.

233(5) In this section **"the Oil Taxation Acts"** means Parts I and III of the principal Act, the 1983 Act and any other enactment relating to petroleum revenue tax.

History – In s. 233(1)(b), the words "any person" and "otherwise than in connection with a taxable field" substituted by FA 1999, s. 101(1)(a), (b) in respect of sums received or receivable in chargeable periods ending on or after 31 December 1999.

234 Interpretation of Chapter and supplementary provisions

234(1) In this Chapter **"the 1983 Act"** means the Oil Taxation Act 1983 and expressions used in this Chapter have the same meaning as in that Act.

234(2) In this Chapter–

(a) **"election"** means an election under section 231 above and **"electing participator"** means a participator who makes or has made an election;

(b) **"the expenditure relief provisions"** means sections 3 and 4 of the principal Act and section 3 of the 1983 Act; and

(c) **"the initial usage fraction"** shall be construed in accordance with section 231(4) above.

234(3) In this Chapter–

(a) any reference to the **assets to which an election applies** is a reference to the pipe-line by reference to which the election is made together with the assets determined in accordance with subsections (5) and (6) of section 231 above;

(b) any reference to the **net profit period** is a reference to the chargeable period which is the net profit period for the purposes of section 111 of the Finance Act 1981 (restriction of expenditure supplement); and

(c) any reference to a **development plan** is a reference to a consent for, or programme of, development granted, served or approved by the Secretary of State.

234(4) Any reference in this Chapter to **expenditure incurred on an asset** is a reference to expenditure (whether or not of a capital nature) which–

(a) is incurred in acquiring, bringing into existence or enhancing the value of the asset, or

(b) is incurred (for any of the purposes mentioned in section 3(1) of the principal Act) by reference to the use of the asset in connection with a taxable field,

other than expenditure which, in the hands of the recipient, constitutes a tariff receipt.

234(5) For the purpose of this Chapter–

(a) an election is **"in operation"** if it has been accepted by the Board; and

(b) the date of an election which is in operation is the date on which the election was received by the Board.

234(6) The provisions of Part II of Schedule 22 to this Act shall have effect for supplementing the preceding provisions of this Chapter.

234(7) The Board may make all such amendments of assessments or determinations or of decisions on claims as may be necessary in consequence of the provisions of this Chapter.

Chapter II – Miscellaneous

235 Valuation of oil

235(1) [Amends OTA 1975, s. 2(5A). Para. (d) repealed by FA 2006, s. 178 and Sch. 26, Pt.5(1).]

235(2) [Repealed by FA 2006, s. 178 and Sch. 26, Pt. 5(1).]

235(3) [Amends FA 1987, Sch. 10, para. 4(1); inserts para. 4(2A).]

235(4) [Amends FA 1987, Sch. 10, para. 11(2); inserts para. 11(2B).]

History – S. 235(1)(d) and (2) repealed by FA 2006, s. 178 and Sch. 26, Pt. 5(1) with effect in relation to oil delivered or appropriated on or after 1 July 2006, but subject to the provisions of FA 2006, s. 147(2)–(8).

236 Valuation of certain light gases

236(1) Subject to subsection (2) below, the principal Act shall have effect subject to the amendments in Schedule 23 to this Act, being–

(a) amendments altering the rules for determining the market value of certain light gases for the purposes of petroleum revenue tax; and

(b) amendments consequential upon, or incidental to, those amendments.

236(2) The amendments in Schedule 23 to this Act do not have effect in relation to any light gases if, *before 1st January* 1994, an election was made under section 134 of the Finance Act 1982 (alternative valuation of certain ethane) or section 109 of the Finance Act 1986 (alternative valuation of certain light gases) and the election applies to those gases.

236(3) No election may be made after 31st December 1993 under section 134 of the Finance Act 1982 or section 109 of the Finance Act 1986; and, accordingly–

(a) [amends FA 1982, s. 134(2); and]

(b) [amends FA 1986, s. 109(1).]

236(4) [Inserts definition of "light gases" into OTA 1975, s. 12.]

237 Abortive exploration expenditure

237(1) [Inserts OTA 1975, s. 5(2A).]

237(2) Subsection (1) above shall be deemed to have come into force at the same time as Part III of the Finance Act 1993 (27th July 1993).

237(3) The Board may make all such amendments of assessments or determinations or of decisions on claims as may be necessary in consequence of the preceding provisions of this section.

238 Disposals of assets producing tariff receipts

238(1) With respect to disposals made after 30th November 1993, paragraph 5 of Schedule 2 to the Oil Taxation Act 1983 (acquisition and disposal of qualifying assets otherwise than at arm's length: limit on tariff and disposal receipts) shall be amended in accordance with subsections (2) and (3) below; and in this subsection **"disposal"** has the same meaning as in that paragraph.

238(2) [Inserts OTA 1983, Sch. 2, para. 5(1)(d); amends para. 5(1).]

238(3) [Substitutes OTA 1983, Sch. 2, para. 5(3)(b).]

238(4) The Board may make all such amendments of assessments or determinations or of decisions on claims as may be necessary in consequence of the preceding provisions of this section.

SCHEDULES

SCHEDULE 22 – SUPPLEMENTARY PROVISIONS AS TO ELECTIONS BY REFERENCE TO PIPE-LINE USAGE

Sections 231 and 234

Part I – Procedure for and in Connection with an Election

THE ELECTION

1(1) An election shall be made by serving it on the Board, shall be in such form as may be prescribed by the Board and shall contain such information as the Board may reasonably require with respect to–

(a) the oil field to which the election is to apply, the pipe-line by reference to which the election is being made and whether the election is to be limited in accordance with subsection (6) of section 231 of this Act;

(b) all other assets which, if the election were to be accepted, would at the date of the election be assets to which the election applies;

(c) the electing participator's interest in those assets;

(d) the sums to which, if the election is accepted, it is reasonable to expect that section 233 of this Act will apply and the sources, quantities and descriptions of oil which will give rise to those sums;

(e) any other oil field (whether taxable or non-taxable) in connection with which any of the assets referred to in paragraph (b) above is or is expected to be used or in respect of which services or other business facilities in connection with that use are or are expected to be provided; and

(f) the initial usage fraction and the amounts which make up the numerator and the denominator of that fraction.

1(2) The reference in sub-paragraph (1)(e) above to an **oil field** includes a reference to any area which the electing participator expects might be determined as an oil field under Schedule 1 to the principal Act.

1(3) An election shall include a declaration that it is correct and complete to the best of the knowledge and belief of the electing participator.

1(4) An election shall be irrevocable.

CONDITIONS FOR ACCEPTANCE OF AN ELECTION

2(1) The Board shall reject an election if they are not satisfied–

(a) that the conditions relating to the pipe-line in paragraphs (a) to (d) of subsection (1) or in subsection (3) of section 231 of this Act are fulfilled; or

(b) that the conditions relating to the oil field or the participator in subsection (2) of that section are fulfilled; or

(c) that, if the election were to be accepted, the assets to which the election would apply (having regard to any limitation under subsection (6) of that section) have the capacity and characteristics, and are otherwise suitable, to handle the quantities and descriptions of oil specified in accordance with paragraph 1(1)(d) above.

2(2) Subject to sub-paragraph (3) below, the Board shall also reject an election if it appears to them–

(a) that any of the information required to be contained in the election by virtue of paragraph 1(1) above is incorrect; or

(b) that, after receiving notice in writing from the Board, the electing participator has failed to furnish to the Board on or before the specified date any information which the Board have reasonably required either with respect to the matters specified in paragraph 1(1) above or for the purpose of satisfying themselves as to the matters referred to in sub-paragraph (1) above.

2(3) Before rejecting an election under sub-paragraph (2)[(1)](a) above the Board may, if they think fit, by notice in writing give the electing participator an opportunity to correct any error in the information and, if he does so, the information shall then be treated as having been provided in the correct form.

2(4) In sub-paragraph (2)[(1)](b) above **"the specified date"** means such date as may be specified in the notice concerned, being a date not earlier than one month after the date on which the notice was given.

2(5) A notice under sub-paragraph (2)[(1)](b) above shall be given within the period of three months beginning on the date on which the election was received by the Board.

NOTICE OF ACCEPTANCE OR REJECTION

3(1) Notice of the acceptance or rejection of an election shall be served on the electing participator before the expiry of the period of three months beginning on whichever of the following dates is the later or latest–

(a) the date on which the election was received by the Board;

(b) if a notice was given under paragraph 2(2)(b) above relating to the election, the date or, as the case may be, the last date which is the specified date, as defined in paragraph 2(4) above, in relation to such a notice;

(c) if a notice was given under paragraph 2(3) above relating to the election, the date on which that notice was given.

3(2) If no such notice of acceptance or rejection is so served, the Board shall be deemed to have accepted the election and to have served notice of their acceptance on the last day of the period referred to in sub-paragraph (1) above.

APPEALS

4(1) Where the Board serve notice on an electing participator under paragraph 3 above rejecting an election, he may appeal against the notice.

4(2) An appeal under sub-paragraph (1) above shall be made by notice of appeal served on the Board within thirty days beginning on the date of the notice in respect of which the appeal is brought.

4(3) Where, at any time after the service of notice of appeal under this paragraph and before the determination of the appeal by the tribunal, the Board and the appellant agree that the notice in respect of which the appeal is brought should stand or that the election to which it related should be accepted with or without modification, the same consequences shall ensue as if the tribunal had determined the appeal to that effect.

4(4) On the hearing of an appeal under this paragraph, the tribunal shall either dismiss the appeal or allow it; and if the tribunal allows the appeal, the tribunal shall direct either–

(a) that the election shall be accepted; or

(b) that the election shall have effect subject to such modifications as may be specified in the direction and shall be accepted in its modified form.

4(5) In an appeal under sub-paragraph (1)–

(a) paragraphs 14(2), (8) and (11) and 14A to 14I of Schedule 2 to the principal Act shall apply as they apply in relation to an appeal against an assessment or determination made under that Act subject to any necessary modifications including the following;

(b) any reference in those paragraphs to an agreement under paragraph 14(9) shall be construed as a reference to an agreement under sub-paragraph (3) above.

4(6) Any reference in this Chapter to an **election accepted by the Board** shall be construed as including a reference to an election accepted in pursuance of an appeal under this paragraph.

History – In para. 4(1), the words "to the Special Commissioners", which appeared after the words "may appeal", omitted by SI 2009/56, art. 3(1) and Sch. 1, para. 211(2), operative from 1 April 2009, subject to transitional and saving provisions in SI 2009/56, Sch. 3.

In para. 4(3), the word "tribunal" substituted for the word "Commissioners" (twice) by SI 2009/56, art. 3(1) and Sch. 1, para. 211(3), operative from 1 April 2009, subject to transitional and saving provisions in SI 2009/56, Sch. 3.

In para. 4(4), the word "tribunal" (where it first appears) substituted for the word "Commissioners", the words "tribunal allows" substituted for the words "Commissioners allow", and the words "the tribunal shall" substituted for the words "they shall" by SI 2009/56, art. 3(1) and Sch. 1, para. 211(4), operative from 1 April 2009, subject to transitional and saving provisions in SI 2009/56, Sch. 3.

Para. 4(5) substituted by SI 2009/56, art. 3(1) and Sch. 1, para. 211(5), operative from 1 April 2009, subject to transitional and saving provisions in SI 2009/56, Sch. 3. Former para. 4(5) read as follows:

"**4(5)** Sub-paragraphs (2), (8) and (11) of paragraph 14 of Schedule 2 to the principal Act shall apply in relation to an appeal against a notice under paragraph 3 above rejecting an election as they apply in relation to an appeal against an assessment or determination made under the principal Act.".

INFORMATION TO THE RESPONSIBLE PERSON

5(1) Within thirty days of the relevant date, the electing participator shall furnish to the responsible person for the field to which the election applies (or would apply if the election were accepted) a copy of–

(a) any election made by him; and

(b) any notice under paragraph 3 above accepting or rejecting the election.

5(2) For the purposes of sub-paragraph (1) above, the **relevant date** is–

(a) in the case of an election made by the electing participator, the date on which it was served on the Board; and

(b) in the case of a notice under paragraph 3 above, the date on which the electing participator received it.

5(3) In a case where paragraph 9 below applies (or would apply if an election were accepted) sub-paragraphs (1) and (2) above shall require the electing participator additionally to furnish copies of the same documents to the responsible person for any non-chargeable field mentioned in sub-paragraph (3) of that paragraph.

5(4) In a case where paragraph 11 below applies (or would apply if an election were accepted) sub-paragraphs (1) and (2) above shall require the electing participator additionally to furnish copies of the same documents to the old participator referred to in that paragraph.

PENALTIES FOR INCORRECT INFORMATION

6 Where a participator fraudulently or negligently furnishes any incorrect information or makes any incorrect declaration in or in connection with an election he shall be liable to a penalty not exceeding–

(a) in the case of negligence, £50,000, and

(b) in the case of fraud, £100,000.

RE-OPENING ELECTION DECISIONS ON GROUNDS OF INCORRECT INFORMATION

7(1) Without prejudice to paragraph 6 above, this paragraph applies if, at any time after notice of the acceptance of an election has been served by the Board, it appears to the Board that, as a result of an error in the information furnished to the Board, the election should not have been accepted.

7(2) If, in a case where this paragraph applies, either–

(a) the error was attributable, in whole or in part, to the fraudulent or negligent conduct of the electing participator or a person acting on his behalf, or

(b) on the error coming to the notice of the electing participator, or a person acting on his behalf, the error was not remedied without unreasonable delay,

the Board may serve on the electing participator and on the responsible person for the field to which the election applies a notice rescinding the acceptance and stating what appears to the Board to be the correct position.

PRT Statutes

7(3) When a notice under sub-paragraph (2) above becomes effective, the election shall be treated as having been rejected in accordance with paragraph 3 above.

7(4) If, in a case where this paragraph applies,–

(a) neither of the conditions in sub-paragraph (2) above is fulfilled, and

(b) the Board are of the opinion that, if the correct information had been furnished, the election could have been accepted,

the election shall be treated as having been made and accepted subject to such modifications (being modifications to correct the effect of the error) as the Board may direct, by notice served on the electing participator and on the responsible person for the field to which the election applies.

7(5) A notice served under sub-paragraph (2) or sub-paragraph (4) above shall become effective either–

(a) on the expiry of the period during which notice of appeal against the notice may be served on the Board under paragraph 8 below without such notice of appeal being served; or

(b) where such notice of appeal is served, when the notice can no longer be varied or quashed by the tribunal or by the order of any court.

History – In para. 7(5)(b), the word "tribunal" substituted for the words "Special Commissioners" by SI 2009/56, art. 3(1) and Sch. 1, para. 212, operative from 1 April 2009, subject to transitional and saving provisions in SI 2009/56, Sch. 3.

APPEALS AGAINST RE-OPENING NOTICES

8(1) This paragraph applies where the Board serve notice under sub-paragraph (2) or sub-paragraph (4) of paragraph 7 above; and in the following provisions of this paragraph such a notice is referred to as a **"re-opening notice"**.

8(2) The electing participator may, by notice of appeal served on the Board within thirty days beginning on the date of the re-opening notice, appeal against the re-opening notice.

8(3) A notice of appeal under sub-paragraph (2) above shall state the grounds on which the appeal is brought.

8(4) An appeal under this paragraph may at any time before it is notified to the tribunal be abandoned by notice served on the Board by the electing participator.

8(5) A re-opening notice may be withdrawn at any time before it becomes effective.

8(6) In any case where–

(a) the electing participator serves notice of appeal against a re-opening notice served under sub-paragraph (4) of paragraph 7 above, and

(b) before the appeal is determined by the tribunal, the Board and the electing participator agree as to the modifications necessary to correct the effect of the error concerned,

the re-opening notice shall take effect subject to such modifications as may be necessary to give effect to that agreement; and thereupon the appeal shall be treated as having been abandoned.

8(7) Subject to sub-paragraph (8) below, on an appeal against a re-opening notice the tribunal may vary the notice, quash the notice or dismiss the appeal; and the notice may be varied whether or not the variation is to the advantage of the electing participator.

8(8) The provisions relating to the variation of a re-opening notice referred to in sub-paragraph (7) above shall not apply in respect of any such notice served under sub-paragraph (2) of paragraph 7 above.

8(9) In an appeal under sub-paragraph (2)–

(a) paragraphs 14A to 14I of Schedule 2 to the principal Act shall apply as they apply in relation to an appeal against an assessment or determination made under that Act subject to any necessary modifications including the following;

(b) any reference in those paragraphs to an agreement under paragraph 14(9) shall be construed as a reference to an agreement under sub-paragraph (6) above.

History – In para. 8(2), the words "to the Special Commissioners" (which appeared before the word "against") omitted by SI 2009/56, art. 3(1) and Sch. 1, para. 213(2), operative from 1 April 2009, subject to transitional and saving provisions in SI 2009/56, Sch. 3.
In para. 8(4), the words "before it is notified to the tribunal" inserted by SI 2009/56, art. 3(1) and Sch. 1, para. 213(3), operative from 1 April 2009, subject to transitional and saving provisions in SI 2009/56, Sch. 3.
In para. 8(6)(b), the word "tribunal" substituted for the words "Special Commissioners" by SI 2009/56, art. 3(1) and Sch. 1, para. 213(4), operative from 1 April 2009, subject to transitional and saving provisions in SI 2009/56, Sch. 3.
In para. 8(7), the word "tribunal" substituted for the words "Special Commissioners" by SI 2009/56, art. 3(1) and Sch. 1, para. 213(4), operative from 1 April 2009, subject to transitional and saving provisions in SI 2009/56, Sch. 3.
Para. 8(9) inserted by SI 2009/56, art. 3(1) and Sch. 1, para. 213(5), operative from 1 April 2009, subject to transitional and saving *provisions in SI 2009/56, Sch. 3.*

Part II – Supplementary Provisions

ASSETS USED IN CONNECTION WITH MORE THAN ONE TAXABLE FIELD

9(1) The provisions of this paragraph apply where–

(a) an election is in operation; and

(b) any of the assets to which the election applies is used or expected to be used in connection with two or more taxable fields.

9(2) Any reference in this paragraph to **allowable expenditure** has the same meaning as in Part II of Schedule 1 to the 1983 Act and is a reference to expenditure incurred on an asset to which the election applies.

9(3) Sub-paragraph (4) below applies if, by virtue of paragraph 5 of Schedule 1 to the 1983 Act (which, in a case falling within this paragraph, provides for the apportionment of allowable expenditure between two or more fields), any part of the allowable expenditure is apportioned to a taxable field (a **"non-chargeable field"**) other than the field to which the election applies.

9(4) Where this sub-paragraph applies, then, so far as concerns the electing participator (as a participator in a non-chargeable field), section 232 of this Act shall apply in relation to that part of the allowable expenditure which is apportioned to the non-chargeable field as it applies in relation to the part apportioned to the field to which the election applies.

TRANSFER OF INTERESTS

10(1) If, while an election is in operation, the electing participator (or a person who is treated as an electing participator by virtue of this paragraph) transfers the whole or part of his interest in the field to which the election applies, then, so far as concerns that interest or part, the new participator shall thereafter be treated as the electing participator for the purposes of this Chapter, other than paragraph 11 below, and, in particular,–

(a) any restriction on the amount of expenditure allowed or allowable by virtue of section 232 of this Act shall continue to apply to any expenditure relief transferred to the new participator under paragraph 6 of Schedule 17 to the Finance Act 1980; and

(b) any relief from tax under section 233 of this Act shall apply in relation to the new participator as it applied in relation to the old participator.

10(2) If, in a case where paragraph 9 above applies, the electing participator, as a participator in the non-chargeable field (within the meaning of that paragraph) transfers the whole or part of his interest in that field, sub-paragraph (1) above (except paragraph (b)) shall apply in relation to that transfer as if–

(a) any reference to the **field to which the election applies** were a reference to the non-chargeable field; and

(b) any reference to the **electing participator** were a reference to him in his capacity as a participator in the non-chargeable field.

10(3) In sub-paragraph (1) above the expressions **"the old participator"** and **"the new participator"** have the same meaning as in Schedule 17 to the Finance Act 1980.

11(1) This paragraph applies in any case where–

(a) the electing participator acquired the whole or any part of his interest in the field to which the election applies as a result of a transfer to which Part I of Schedule 17 to the Finance Act 1980 applies (so that the electing participator is the new participator); and

(b) some or all of the relief in respect of any expenditure incurred (before the transfer) on any asset to which the election applies did not fall to be transferred to the electing participator (whether by virtue of paragraph 6 or paragraph 7 of that Schedule).

11(2) With regard to so much of the expenditure referred to in sub-paragraph (1)(b) above as falls to be taken into account under paragraph (b)(i) or paragraph (c)(i) of subsection (9) of section 2 of the principal Act in computing, for any chargeable period ending before the transfer period, the assessable profit or allowable loss accruing to the old participator or any predecessor of his, section 232 of this Act shall apply in the case of the old participator or, as the case may be, his predecessor as it is expressed to apply in the case of the electing participator.

11(3) If, as a result of the operation of sub-paragraph (2) above, there is a reduction in the amount which would otherwise be the accumulated capital expenditure of the old participator at the end of the last chargeable period before the transfer period, paragraph 8 of Schedule 17 to the Finance Act 1980 shall be taken to have transferred a correspondingly reduced amount to the electing participator.

11(4) In this paragraph–

(a) the expressions **"the old participator"**, **"the new participator"** and **"the transfer period"** have the same meaning as in Schedule 17 to the Finance Act 1980; and

(b) any reference to a **predecessor of the old participator** is a reference to a person who (before the transfer referred to in sub-paragraph (1)(a) above) transferred the whole or part of his interest in the field to which the election applies either to the old participator or to another person who is a predecessor in title of the old participator in respect of that interest or part.

TRANSFER OF ELECTED ASSETS

12(1) This paragraph applies if there is a disposal of an asset which, immediately before the disposal or at an earlier time, was an asset to which an election applies; and in this paragraph–

(a) **"the asset transferred"** means the asset so disposed of;

(b) **"the vendor"** means the electing participator or other person by whom the asset is disposed of.

12(2) Where a person has incurred expenditure on the acquisition of a transferred asset, he shall be treated for the purposes of the expenditure relief provisions as having incurred that expenditure only to the extent that it does not exceed the amount which, having regard to section 232 of this Act or the previous operation of this paragraph, was (in the case of the vendor) allowable under those provisions immediately before the disposal in respect of his expenditure on the asset.

12(3) Any expenditure incurred on the asset after the disposal shall be left out of account for the purposes of the expenditure relief provisions.

RESTRICTION OF RELIEF FOR EXPENDITURE INCURRED AFTER 30TH NOVEMBER 1993 AND BEFORE THE DATE OF AN ELECTION

13(1) This paragraph applies if, after 30th November 1993 and before the date of an election, expenditure was incurred by the electing participator under a contract–

(a) for the acquisition from any other person of, or of an interest in, an asset to which the election applies; or

(b) for the provision by any other person of services or other business facilities of whatever kind in connection with the use of an asset to which the election applies.

13(2) If, in a case where this paragraph applies, the other person referred to in paragraph (a) or paragraph (b) of sub-paragraph (1) above (**"the contractor"**) has performed his obligations by entering into one or more further contracts, the contractor shall be treated for the purposes of subsection (2) of section 191 of the Finance Act 1993 (time when expenditure is incurred) as having performed his obligations under the contract only to the extent that, at that time, the asset or interest in question has been acquired by or, as the case may be, the services or other business facilities have been provided to, the electing participator.

SCHEDULE 23 – AMENDMENTS OF THE PRINCIPAL ACT RELATING TO VALUATION OF LIGHT GASES

Section 236

1(1) [Inserts OTA 1975, s. 2(5)(ca), (cb); amends s. 2(5)(b), (c).]

1(2) [Amends OTA 1975, s. 2(9)(a).]

2 [Amends OTA 1975, Sch. 2, para. 2(2).]

3(1) [Amends OTA 1975, Sch. 3, para. 2(1).]

3(2) [Inserts OTA 1975, Sch. 3, para. 2A(1A).]

3(3) [Amends OTA 1975, Sch. 3, para. 2A(2).]

3(4) [Amends OTA 1975, Sch. 3, para. 2A(3).]

3(5) [Repeals OTA 1975, Sch. 3, para. 2A(4).]

4 [Inserts OTA 1975, Sch. 3, para. 3A.]

FINANCE ACT 1995

(1995 Chapter 4)

[*1st May 1995*]

ARRANGEMENT OF SECTIONS

PART IV – PETROLEUM REVENUE TAX

PART IV – PETROLEUM REVENUE TAX

146 Restriction of unrelievable field losses

146(1) [Repealed by FA 2001, s. 110 and Sch. 33, Pt. 3(2).]

146(2) [Repealed by FA 2001, s. 110 and Sch. 33, Pt. 3(2).]

146(3) [Inserts OTA 1975 s. 6(5)–(9).]

History – S. 146(1) and (2) repealed by FA 2001, s. 110 and Sch. 33, Pt. 3(2), the repeal being deemed to come into force on 7 March 2001.

147 Removal of time limits for claims for unrelievable field losses

147(1) [Amends OTA 1975, Sch. 8, para. 4(1), (2).]

147(2) This section applies to claims made on or after the day on which this Act is passed.

148 Transfer of interests in fields: restriction of transferred losses

148(1) In Schedule 17 to the Finance Act 1980 (transfer of interests in oil fields) paragraph 7 (transfer of unused losses from the old to the new participator) shall be amended as follows.

148(2) [Amends FA 1980, Sch. 17, para. 7(2).]

148(3) [Inserts FA 1980, Sch. 17, para. 7(3)–(6).]

FINANCE ACT 1996

(1996 Chapter 8)

[*29th April 1996*]

ARRANGEMENT OF SECTIONS

PART VII – MISCELLANEOUS AND SUPPLEMENTAL

MISCELLANEOUS: DIRECT TAXATION

SCHEDULES

PART VII – MISCELLANEOUS AND SUPPLEMENTAL

MISCELLANEOUS: DIRECT TAXATION

199 Quotation or listing of securities

199 Schedule 38 to this Act (which contains amendments of enactments referring to the quotation or listing of securities) shall have effect.

SCHEDULE 38 – QUOTATION FOR LISTING OF SECURITIES

Section 189

THE FINANCE ACT 1973

1(1) [Amends FA 1973, s. 38(2)(c).]

1(2) This paragraph has effect in relation to disposals of shares on or after 1st April 1996.

2–12 [Not relevant to petroleum revenue tax.]

FINANCE ACT 1997

(1997 Chapter 16)

[*19th March 1997*]

ARRANGEMENT OF SECTIONS

PART VIII – MISCELLANEOUS AND SUPPLEMENTAL

MISCELLANEOUS

PART VIII – MISCELLANEOUS AND SUPPLEMENTAL

MISCELLANEOUS

107 Petroleum revenue tax: non-field expenditure

107(1) [Amends FA 1984, s. 113.]

107(2) [Amends FA 1984, s. 113(4).]

107(3) [Amends FA 1984, s. 113(6).]

107(4) This section has effect in relation to any expenditure in respect of which a claim is made on or after 23rd July 1996.

FINANCE ACT 1998

(1998 Chapter 36)

[*31st July 1998*]

ARRANGEMENT OF SECTIONS

PART V – OTHER TAXES

PETROLEUM REVENUE TAX ETC.

PART V – OTHER TAXES

PETROLEUM REVENUE TAX ETC.

152 Gas valuation

152(1) [Amends OTA 1975, Sch. 3, para. 3A with the insertion of sub-para. (3A).]

152(2) [Amends OTA 1983, Sch. 2, para. 12(2) and (5).]

152(3) [Repealed by CTA 2010, s. 1181 and Sch. 3, Pt. 2 and TIOPA 2010, s. 378 and Sch. 10, Pt. 6.]

History – S. 152(3) repealed by CTA 2010, s. 1181 and Sch. 3, Pt. 2, with effect for accounting periods ending on or after 1 April 2010 and TIOPA 2010, s. 378 and Sch. 10, Pt. 6, with effect for corporation tax purposes for accounting periods ending on or after 1 April 2010, for income tax and capital gains tax purposes for the tax year 2010–11 and subsequent tax years, and for petroleum revenue tax purposes for chargeable periods beginning on or after 1 July 2010.

166 Short title

166 This Act may be cited as the Finance Act 1998.

FINANCE ACT 1999

(1999 Chapter 16)

[*27th July 1999*]

ARRANGEMENT OF SECTIONS

PART IV – OIL TAXATION

PART VIII – SUPPLEMENTAL

MISCELLANEOUS AND SUPPLEMENTAL

PART IV – OIL TAXATION

94 Excluded oil

94(1) This section applies where–

(a) a contract ("the old contract") provides for the sale by a person ("A") of oil consisting of gas to the British Gas Corporation or one of its successors ("the purchaser");

(b) the old contract is a contract made, or treated (by virtue of this section) as made, before the end of June 1975;

(c) the old contract is replaced by a contract ("the new contract") for the sale of oil consisting of gas to the purchaser made after the end of June 1975; and

(d) any of the rights and liabilities which, under the old contract, were rights and liabilities of A are, under the new contract, rights and liabilities of another person ("B").

94(2) The new contract shall be treated for the purposes of section 10(1)(a) of the Oil Taxation Act 1975 as the same contract as the old contract unless the rights and liabilities of B under the new contract are so different from those of A under the old contract that a contract conferring those rights and imposing those liabilities on A could not have been regarded as the same contract as the old contract.

94(3) For the purposes of subsection (1) above, the successors of the British Gas Corporation are–

(a) British Gas plc; and

(b) British Gas Trading Limited.

94(4) This section shall be deemed always to have had effect.

95 Sale and lease-back

95(1) This section applies to a lease ("the lease in question") of an asset ("the relevant asset") where–

(a) a person ("the seller") who is a participator in an oil field ("the seller's oil field") has made a disposal in a chargeable period of the relevant asset or an interest in it;

(b) the relevant asset was a qualifying asset in relation to the seller and the seller's oil field is the chargeable field in relation to it;

(c) the relevant asset is used in connection with an oil field ("the lessee's oil field") by a participator in that field ("the lessee") under the lease in question;

(d) the seller, or a person connected with him at any time in the relevant period, is the lessee; and

(e) the lessee uses the relevant asset before the end of the period of two years beginning with the disposal.

PRT Statutes

95(2) Subject to subsection (8) below, to the extent that the expenditure falling within subsection (3) below exceeds the amount of the cap, that expenditure shall not be allowable under section 3 or 4 of the principle Act or section 3 of the Oil Taxation Act 1983 for the lessee's oil field.

95(3) That expenditure is the aggregate of the following–

(a) the total expenditure, excluding operating expenditure, incurred by the lessee under the lease in question; and

(b) if at any time after the disposal he acquires the relevant asset or an interest in it, the total expenditure (not falling within paragraph (a) above) incurred by him in acquiring the asset or interest.

95(4) Subject to subsections (5) to (7) below–

(a) if the period in which the disposal was made is one in which the seller has benefitted from safeguard relief, the amount of the cap is the smaller of–

(i) the amount given by dividing the marginal tax on the disposal receipts by the applicable rate of tax; and

(ii) the amount of the disposal receipts; and

(b) in any other case the amount of the cap is the amount of the disposal receipts.

95(5) Subject to subsection (7) below, where at the relevant time there are, in relation to the relevant asset, two or more leases to which this section applies, the amount of the cap for the lease in question shall be the appropriate proportion of the cap found by applying subsection (4) above.

95(6) For the purposes of subsection (5) above the appropriate proportion is the proportion given by the formula–

$$\frac{A}{B}$$

where–

A is the proportion of the total use of the relevant asset during the term of the lease in question that is expected to be use under the lease; and

B is–

(a) in a case where the seller disposed of the whole of the relevant asset, one; and

(b) in any other case, the proportion that the value of the interest disposed of by him bore to the total value of the relevant asset.

95(7) Where at the relevant time the relevant asset is used, or is expected to be used, by the lessee under the lease in question in connection with two or more oil fields, the amount of the cap for each of the fields shall be so much of the cap found by applying subsections (4) to (6) above as accords with the proportion of the use of the asset under the lease that is expected, at that time, to be–

(a) use in connection with that field; or

(b) use giving rise to tariff receipts of the lessee attributable to that field.

95(8) Where–

(a) expenditure falling within subsection (3) above has been allowed for the lessee's oil field, on a claim under Schedule 5 or 6 to the principal Act, on the basis that the cap was of a particular amount;

(b) information later becomes available to the Board which establishes that the cap is not of that amount; and

(c) the amount that was allowed exceeds the amount (if any) of the expenditure falling within that subsection that would have been allowed on the claim if the information had been available when the expenditure was allowed,

the excess shall continue to be allowable.

95(9) Subject to subsection (10) below, this section and sections 96 and 97 below apply to assets, or interests in assets, disposed of on or after 9th March 1999.

95(10) This section and those sections do not apply to assets, or interests in assets, disposed of pursuant to an agreement made before that date if–

(a) the agreement is not conditional; or

(b) the agreement is conditional and the condition is satisfied before that date.

96 Transfer of field interest

96(1) This section applies where–

(a) section 95 above has applied to a lease;

(b) the lessee has transferred the whole or part of his interest in the lessee's oil field; and

(c) pursuant to the transfer, the relevant asset is used in connection with that oil field under a lease ("the new participator's lease") by the person who is the new participator in relation to the transfer.

96(2) Subject to subsection (4) below, section 95 above shall have effect as if the new participator were the lessee and the new participator's lease were the lease in question.

96(3) The reference in subsection (1)(b) above to the lessee includes a reference to a successor of his; and subject to subsection (4) below, the expenditure that the new participator is treated by virtue of subsection (2) above as having incurred includes–

(a) any expenditure, excluding operating expenditure, incurred by the lessee or a successor of his under the lease in question or a lease of the relevant asset; and

(b) any expenditure (not falling within paragraph (a) above) incurred by the lessee or a successor of his after the disposal mentioned in section 95(1)(a) above in acquiring the relevant asset or an interest in it.

96(4) Where the transfer mentioned in subsection (1)(b) above, or any antecedent transfer, was a transfer of part of the transferor's interest in the lessee's oil field–

(a) the amount of the cap which is applicable by virtue of subsection (2) above shall be so much of the cap that would be applicable apart from this subsection as accords with the proportion of the lessee's interest in the field that is represented by the new participator's interest in the field; and

(b) the expenditure incurred (as mentioned in subsection (3) above) by the lessee or any successor of his that is treated, by virtue of subsection (2) above, as expenditure incurred by the new participator shall be so much of the expenditure incurred (as so mentioned) by the person concerned as accords with the proportion of that person's interest in the field that is represented by the new participator's interest in the field.

96(5) A person is a successor of the lessee for the purposes of this section if and only if–

(a) this section has applied to an earlier transfer by the lessee or a successor of his of the whole or part of his interest in the lessee's oil field; and

(b) that person was the new participator in relation to the earlier transfer and used the relevant asset under the lease in connection with that oil field.

96(6) In this section **"antecedent transfer"** means a transfer (other than the transfer mentioned in subsection (1)(b) above) by the lessee or a successor of his of the whole or part of his interest in the lessee's oil field, pursuant to which the relevant asset was used as mentioned in subsection (1)(c) above.

97 Provisions supplementary to ss. 95 and 96

97(1) For the purposes of section 95 above the marginal tax on the disposal receipts is the difference between–

(a) the amount of tax to which the seller is chargeable on the assessable profit accruing to him from the seller's oil field in the period in which the asset or interest was disposed of; and

(b) the amount of tax to which the seller would have been so chargeable if the amount or value of the consideration received or receivable by him in respect of the disposal in that period of the asset or interest had been nil.

97(2) For the purposes of that section–

(a) any question whether a person is connected with the seller shall be determined in accordance the provisions of section 1122 of the Corporation Tax Act 2010;

(b) the relevant period is the period beginning with the time of the disposal of the asset or interest and ending with the time when the first claim is made for the allowance, for the lessee's oil field, of expenditure incurred by the lessee or a successor of his under the lease in question or a lease of the relevant asset (and in this paragraph the reference to the lessee includes a reference to a person who is treated as the lessee by virtue of section 96 above);

(c) the applicable rate of tax is the rate at which tax is charged under section 1(2) of the principal Act at the time of the disposal of the asset or interest;

(d) the amount of the disposal receipts is the aggregate of the amount or value of any consideration received or receivable by the seller in respect of the disposal of the asset or interest;

(e) a chargeable period is a period in which the seller benefits from safeguard relief if and only if the tax payable by the seller for that period is less than it would have been if section 9 of the principal Act (safeguard relief) had not been enacted;

(f) the relevant time is the end of the earliest claim period for which a claim such as is mentioned in paragraph (b) above is made; and

(g) tariff receipts of the lessee shall be taken to be attributable to an oil field if and only if they are attributable to the field for any chargeable period for the purposes of the Oil Taxation Act 1983.

97(3) In section 96 above references–

(a) to the transfer by a person of the whole or part of his interest in the lessee's oil field; or

(b) in relation to a transfer, to the new participator,

shall be construed in accordance with Schedule 17 to the Finance Act 1980.

97(4) The expenditure which for the purposes of sections 95 and 96 above shall be taken to be operating expenditure shall be so much of the expenditure incurred by the lessee or, as the case may be, a successor of his under the lease concerned as appears, on a just and reasonable estimate, to be operating expenditure.

97(5) References in this section to a successor of the lessee shall be construed in accordance with section 96(5) above.

97(6) In this section and sections 95 and 96 above–

"the chargeable field" has the same meaning as in the Oil Taxation Act 1983;

"lease", in relation to an asset, has the same meaning as in Chapter 3 of Part 19 of CTA 2010 (see section 868);

"the lease in question", **"the lessee"**, **"the lessee's oil field"**, **"the relevant asset"**, **"the seller"** and **"the seller's oil field"** shall be construed in accordance with section 95(1) above;

"operating expenditure" means expenditure (for example, in respect of the provision of staff or crew or the maintenance or operation of the relevant asset) of such a nature that the lessee or, as the case may be, his successor would or might have incurred it, otherwise than under any arrangements to finance his ownership, if he had been the owner of the asset;

"the new participator's lease" shall be construed in accordance with section 96(1) above;

"the principal Act" means the Oil Taxation Act 1975;

"qualifying asset" has the same meaning as in the Oil Taxation Act 1983; and

"tariff receipts" has the same meaning as in that Act.

97(7) This section and sections 95 and 96 above shall be construed as one with Part I of the principal Act.

History – In s. 97(2)(a), the words "section 1122 of the Corporation Tax Act 2010" substituted for the words "section 839 of the Taxes Act 1988" by CTA 2010, s. 1177 and Sch. 1, para. 301, with effect for corporation tax purposes for accounting periods ending on or after 1 April 2010, and for income tax and capital gains tax purposes for the tax year 2010–11 and subsequent tax years.
In s. 97(6), in the definition of "lease", the words "Chapter 3 of Part 19 of CTA 2010 (see section 868)" substituted for the words "sections 781 to 784 of the Taxes Act 1988" by TIOPA 2010, s. 374 and Sch. 8, para. 248, with effect for corporation tax purposes for accounting periods ending on or after 1 April 2010, for income tax and capital gains tax purposes for the tax year 2010–11 and subsequent tax years, and for petroleum revenue tax purposes for chargeable periods beginning on or after 1 July 2010.

98 Qualifying assets

98(1) Subsection (2) below applies where–

(a) an asset which is not a mobile asset is a qualifying asset for the purposes of the Oil Taxation Act 1983 in relation to a person ("the taxpayer") who is a participator in an oil field ("the field");

(b) tariff receipts, tax-exempt tariffing receipts or disposal receipts of the taxpayer which are referable to the asset are attributable to the field for a chargeable period ("the earlier period");

(c) receipts of the taxpayer which are referable to the asset for a subsequent chargeable period ("the later period") would not, apart from this section, be tariff receipts, tax-exempt tariffing receipts or disposal receipts attributable to the field for that period as a result of–

(i) the taxpayer's ceasing to be a participator in the field; or

(ii) his becoming a participator in another oil field; and

(d) not more than two chargeable periods intervene between the earlier period and the later period.

98(2) The Oil Taxation Acts shall have effect, in relation to the later period and any subsequent chargeable period, as if–

(a) receipts of the taxpayer which are referable to the asset for the period concerned were tariff receipts, tax-exempt tariffing receipts or disposal receipts attributable to the field for that period; and

(b) in a case falling within subsection (1)(c)(i) above, the taxpayer continued to be a participator in the field.

98(3) Subsection (4) below applies where–

(a) an asset which is not a mobile asset is a qualifying asset for the purposes of the Oil Taxation Act 1983 in relation to a person ("the taxpayer") who is a participator in an oil field ("the field");

(b) tariff receipts, tax-exempt tariffing receipts or disposal receipts of the taxpayer which are referable to the asset are attributable to the field for a chargeable period ("the earlier period");

(c) in a subsequent chargeable period ("the later period") the taxpayer disposes of–

(i) the asset; or

(ii) an interest in the asset,

to another person ("the transferee") in circumstances such that section 7 of the Oil Taxation Act 1983 does not apply to the disposal; and

(d) not more than two chargeable periods intervene between the earlier period and the later period.

98(4) The Oil Taxation Acts shall have effect, in relation to the later period and any subsequent chargeable period, as if–

(a) receipts of the transferee which are referable to the asset for the period concerned were tariff receipts, tax-exempt tariffing receipts or disposal receipts attributable to the field for that period; and

(b) the transferee were a participator in the field.

98(5) Subject to subsection (6) below, any reference in this section to receipts of any person which are referable to the asset for a period is a reference to any sums which–

(a) are received or receivable by that person in that period in respect of the use of the asset, or the provision of services or other business facilities of whatever kind in connection with its use; or

(b) are received or receivable by that person in respect of the disposal in that period of the asset, or an interest in the asset.

98(6) In a case falling within subsection (3)(c)(ii) above–

(a) any sums which are received or receivable by the transferee otherwise than by virtue of his acquisition of the interest shall not be regarded for the purposes of subsection (4) above as receipts of his which are referable to the asset for any period; and

(b) for the purposes of paragraph (a) above, such apportionments shall be made as may be just and reasonable.

98(6A) In relation to tax-exempt tariffing receipts, any reference in this section–

(a) to being attributable to a field for a period, or

(b) to being referable to an asset,

shall be construed as if tax-exempt tariffing receipts were tariff receipts (and expenditure were or had been allowable accordingly).

98(7) This section shall be construed as one with Part I of the Oil Taxation Act 1975; and in this section **"the Oil Taxation Acts"** means–

(a) the enactments relating to petroleum revenue tax (including this section);

(aa) Part 8 of the Corporation Tax Act 2010 (oil activities); and

(ba) Chapter 16A of Part 2 of the Income Tax (Trading and Other Income) Act 2005 (oil activities).

98(8) Nothing in this section shall be taken to affect the meaning of **"participator"** in paragraph 4 of Schedule 2 to the principal Act.

98(9) Subject to subsection (11) below, subsection (1) above applies where–

(a) the disposal by virtue of which the taxpayer ceased to be a participator in the field; or

(b) the acquisition by virtue of which he became a participator in the other oil field,

was made on or after 1st July 1999.

98(10) Subject to subsection (11) below, subsection (3) above applies where the asset, or the interest in the asset, was disposed of on or after that date.

98(11) Neither subsection (1) nor subsection (3) above applies where the disposal or acquisition concerned was made pursuant to an agreement which was made before 1st July 1999 and either–

(a) the agreement was not conditional; or

(b) the agreement was conditional and the condition was satisfied before that date.

History – S. 98(7)(aa) inserted by CTA 2010, s. 1177 and Sch. 1, para. 302 with effect for corporation tax purposes for accounting periods ending on or after 1 April 2010, and for income tax and capital gains tax purposes for the tax year 2010–11 and subsequent tax years.

S. 98(7)(ba) substituted for former s. 98(7)(b) and (c) by TIOPA 2010, s. 374 and Sch. 8, para. 188, with effect for corporation tax purposes for accounting periods ending on or after 1 April 2010, for income tax and capital gains tax purposes for the tax year 2010–11 and subsequent tax years, and for petroleum revenue tax purposes for chargeable periods beginning on or after 1 July 2010.

In s. 98 the words", tax-exempt tariffing receipts" inserted in each place by FA 2004, s. 285 and Sch. 37, para. 12(2), with effect in relation to chargeable periods, within the meaning of ICTA 1988, s. 98, ending on or after 30 June 2004.

S. 98(6A) inserted by FA 2004, s. 285 and Sch. 37, para. 12(3), with effect in relation to chargeable periods, within the meaning of ICTA 1988, s. 98, ending on or after 30 June 2004.

99 PRT instalments

99(1) [Amends FA 1982, Sch. 19, para. 3(1) and inserts FA 1982, Sch. 19, para. 3(1A).]

99(2) Subsection (1) above applies for the purpose of determining whether instalments are payable in respect of chargeable periods ending on or after 31st December 1999.

101 Pipe-line elections

101(1) [Amends FA 1994, s. 233(1)(b).]

101(2) Subsection (1) above applies to sums received or receivable in any chargeable period ending on or after 31st December 1999.

102 PRT returns

102(1) [Amends OTA 1975, Sch. 2, para. 2(1) and inserts para. 2(5).]

102(2) [Amends OTA 1975, Sch. 2, para. 5(1) and inserts para. 5(4).]

102(3) [Inserts OTA 1975, Sch. 2, para. 12A.]

102(4) [Inserts OTA 1975, Sch. 5, para. 2(7) and (8).]

102(5) [Amends the Table in OTA 1975, Sch. 6, para. 2.]

102(6) [Amends FA 1987, s. 62(4).]

102(7) [Substitutes FA 1987, s. 62(6)(b).]

102(8) The preceding provisions of this section apply in relation to chargeable periods ending on or after 30th June 1999.

PART VIII – SUPPLEMENTAL

MISCELLANEOUS AND SUPPLEMENTAL

138 Interpretation

138 In this Act **"the Taxes Act 1988"** means the Income and Corporation Taxes Act 1988.

140 Short title

140 This Act may be cited as the Finance Act 1999.

FINANCE ACT 2000

(2000 Chapter 17)

[*28th July 2000*]

PART V – OTHER TAXES

PETROLEUM REVENUE TAX

139 Operating expenditure incurred while safeguard relief applies

139(1) [Inserts OTA 1975, s. 9A.]

139(2) This section has effect in relation to expenditure incurred on or after 21st March 2000.

FINANCE ACT 2001

(2001 Chapter 9)

[*11th May 2001*]

ARRANGEMENT OF SECTIONS

PART 4 – OTHER TAXES

PETROLEUM REVENUE TAX

PART 5 – MISCELLANEOUS AND SUPPLEMENTARY PROVISIONS

SUPPLEMENTARY

SCHEDULES

PART 4 – OTHER TAXES

PETROLEUM REVENUE TAX

101 PRT: unrelievable field losses

101(1) [Amends OTA 1975, s. 6.]

101(2) [Amends OTA 1975, s. 6.]

101(3) [Amends FA 1984, s. 113(2).]

101(4) Schedule 32 to this Act has effect.

101(5) The provisions of this section shall be deemed to have come into force on 7th March 2001.

102 PRT: allowable decommissioning expenditure

102(1) [Amends OTA 1975, s. 3.]

102(2) [Amends OTA 1975, s. 3.]

102(3) [Amends OTA 1975, s. 10(2).]

102(4) The amendments made by subsections (1) to (3) apply to expenditure incurred on or after 7th March 2001.

102(5) Subsections (6) to (8) apply where–

(a) on or after 7th March 2001 a participator in a taxable field (**"the transitional participator"**) incurs expenditure that falls to be apportioned under the new provision,

(b) the transitional participator was a participator in the field both immediately before, and at the beginning of, 7th March 2001,

(c) the qualifying asset that is relevant to the incurring of the expenditure was, at both of the times mentioned in paragraph (b), a qualifying asset in relation to the transitional participator and the field, and

(d) at a time before 7th March 2001–

(i) a person was a participator in two or more oil fields, and

(ii) the asset was a qualifying asset in relation to that person and each of at least two of those fields.

102(6) If there would be no apportionment of the expenditure under the old provision, for the purpose of applying the new provision to the expenditure **"the relevant portion"** of the expenditure is the taxable field portion.

102(7) If the expenditure would be apportioned between two or more oil fields under the old provision, for the purpose of applying the new provision to the expenditure **"the relevant portion"** of the expenditure is the portion of the taxable field portion which it is just and reasonable to apportion to use of the asset in connection with the field.

102(8) In carrying out that apportionment of the taxable field portion, ignore use of the asset in connection with an oil field that is not one of the oil fields between which the expenditure would be apportioned under the old provision.

102(9) In subsections (6) to (8) **"the taxable field portion"** means the portion of the expenditure that it is just and reasonable to apportion to use of the asset in connection with a taxable field.

102(10) In subsections (5) to (8)–

"the new provision" means section 3(1C) of the Oil Taxation Act 1975 (c. 22) as substituted by subsection (1);

"the old provision" means section 3(1C) of that Act as it would have effect apart from the amendments made by subsections (1) to (3);

"qualifying asset" has the same meaning as it has for the purposes of the Oil Taxation Act 1983 (c. 56) (see section 8 of that Act).

102(11) Subsections (5) to (10) shall be construed as one with Part 1 of the Oil Taxation Act 1975.

103 PRT: expenditure in certain gas-producing fields

103(1) [Amends OTA 1975, s. 10(3) and inserts OTA 1975, s. 10(3A)–(3H).]

103(2) The amendments made by this section apply to expenditure incurred on or after 7th March 2001.

PART 5 – MISCELLANEOUS AND SUPPLEMENTARY PROVISIONS

SUPPLEMENTARY

109 Interpretation

109 In this Act **"the Taxes Act 1988"** means the Income and Corporation Taxes Act 1988 (c. 1).

111 Short title

111 This Act may be cited as the Finance Act 2001.

SCHEDULES

SCHEDULE 32 – PETROLEUM REVENUE TAX: UNRELIEVABLE FIELD LOSSES

Section 101

SCHEDULE APPLIES WHERE THERE HAS BEEN A TRANSFER TO WHICH PARTS 2 AND 3 OF SCHEDULE 17 TO THE FINANCE ACT 1980 DO NOT APPLY

1(1) This Schedule applies where–

(a) there has been a transfer of the whole or part of the interest in an oil field of a participator in the field (see paragraph 4),

(b) the transfer is an excluded transfer (see paragraph 2), and

(c) an allowable loss has accrued from the field to–

(i) the old participator,

(ii) the new participator, or

(iii) a subsequent new owner (see paragraph 3).

1(2) In this Schedule–

"the loss-maker" means the person to whom the allowable loss accrues;

"the old participator" means the person whose interest is wholly or partly transferred by the transfer and **"the new participator"** means the person to whom the interest or part is transferred by the transfer;

"the transferred interest" means–

(a) where the transfer is of the whole of the old participator's interest in the field, that interest, and

(b) where the transfer is of part of the old participator's interest in the field, that part.

MEANING OF "EXCLUDED TRANSFER"

2 For the purposes of this Schedule, a transfer of the whole or part of the interest in an oil field of a participator in the field is an **"excluded transfer"** if–

(a) Parts 2 and 3 of Schedule 17 to the Finance Act 1980 (c. 48) do not apply to the transfer, and

(b) either–

(i) the transfer is made pursuant to an agreement made on or after 7th March 2001, or

(ii) the transfer is made pursuant to a conditional agreement made before 7th March 2001 and the condition is satisfied on or after 7th March 2001.

MEANING OF "SUBSEQUENT NEW OWNER"

3 For the purposes of this Schedule, a **"subsequent new owner"** is any participator in the field who has the transferred interest, or any part of the transferred interest, as a result of–

(a) a transfer by the new participator of the whole or part of the transferred interest, or

(b) the combination of such a transfer as is mentioned in paragraph (a) and–

(i) a transfer by a subsequent new owner of the whole or part of the transferred interest, or

(ii) two or more such transfers as are mentioned in sub-paragraph (i).

TRANSFERS OF INTERESTS IN OIL FIELDS: INTERPRETATION

4(1) For the purposes of this Schedule, a participator in an oil field transfers the whole or part of his interest in the field whenever as a result of a transaction or event other than–

(a) the making of an agreement or arrangement of the kind mentioned in paragraph 5 of Schedule 3 to the Oil Taxation Act 1975 (agreement or arrangement for transfer of participator's rights to associated company), or

(b) a re-determination under a unitisation agreement,

the whole or part of his share in the oil to be won and saved from the field becomes the share or part of the share of another person who is or becomes a participator in the field.

4(2) Paragraph 1(2) of Schedule 17 to the Finance Act 1980 (meaning of **"unitisation agreement"** and **"re-determination"**) applies for the purposes of sub-paragraph (1) above as for those of paragraph 1(1) of that Schedule.

SCHEDULE APPLIES IN PLACE OF SECTION 6(1C) OF THE OIL TAXATION ACT 1975

5 Where this Schedule makes provision for determining the unrelievable portion of an allowable loss, that portion is determined in accordance with the provisions of this Schedule instead of in accordance with the provisions of section 6(1C) of the Oil Taxation Act 1975.

GENERAL RULE FOR DETERMINATIONS UNDER THIS SCHEDULE OF "UNRELIEVABLE PORTION" OF LOSS

6(1) The unrelievable portion of the allowable loss is so much of the intermediate unrelieved loss as cannot be relieved under paragraph 7 against relevant profits.

6(2) In this Schedule–

"the intermediate unrelieved loss" is so much of the allowable loss as cannot be relieved under section 7 of the Oil Taxation Act 1975 against assessable profits accruing from the field to the loss-maker;

"relevant profits" means assessable profits–

(a) accruing from the field to any participator in the field other than the loss-maker,

(b) computed as if the amounts mentioned in section 2(8)(a) of that Act did not include expenditure unrelated to the field except where it has been allowed in pursuance of a claim or election for its allowance received by the Board before 29th November 1994, and

(c) reduced (after being so computed) under section 7 of that Act.

6(3) In sub-paragraph (2) **"expenditure unrelated to the field"** has the meaning given by section 6(9) of that Act.

LOSS TO BE RELIEVED AGAINST OTHER PARTICIPATORS' PROFITS

7(1) The intermediate unrelieved loss shall (but only for the purposes of determinations under this Schedule) be relieved against relevant profits accruing to a different owner.

7(2) The provisions of paragraphs 8 to 10 apply for the purposes of relieving the intermediate unrelieved loss under this paragraph.

7(3) In this paragraph and paragraph 8, a **"different owner"** means any participator in the field who–

(a) has the loss-maker's interest at any time (whether before or after the transfer) when the loss-maker does not have that interest, or

(b) has a part of the loss-maker's interest at any time (whether before or after the transfer) when the loss-maker does not have that part.

7(4) In sub-paragraph (3) **"the loss-maker's interest"** means–

(a) if the loss-maker is the old participator or the new participator, the transferred interest;

(b) if the loss-maker is a subsequent new owner and at any time (whether before or after the transfer) has the whole of the transferred interest, that interest; and

(c) if the loss-maker is a subsequent new owner and paragraph (b) does not apply, the aggregate of each part of the transferred interest that at any time (whether before or after the transfer) is a part that the loss-maker has.

EXTENT TO WHICH LOSSES TO BE RELIEVED

8(1) Where the interest in the field of a different owner is the transferred interest, the intermediate unrelieved loss is to be relieved against the whole of any relevant profits accruing to the different owner.

8(2) Where the interest in the field of a different owner is part of the transferred interest, the corresponding part (but only that part) of the intermediate unrelieved loss is to be relieved against the whole of any relevant profits accruing to the different owner.

8(3) Where–

(a) a different owner's interest in the field includes the transferred interest, but

(b) the transferred interest is only part of the different owner's interest in the field,

the intermediate unrelieved loss is to be relieved against the corresponding part (but no other part) of any relevant profits accruing to the different owner.

8(4) Sub-paragraph (5) applies where–

(a) a different owner's interest in the field includes part only of the transferred interest ("the owned part of the transferred interest"), and

(b) the owned part of the transferred interest is only part of the different owner's interest in the field.

8(5) Only the part of the intermediate unrelieved loss corresponding to the owned part of the transferred interest is to be relieved, and it is to be relieved against (but only against) the part of any relevant profits accruing to the different owner that corresponds to the part which the owned part of the transferred interest forms of the different owner's interest in the field.

PROFITS NOT TO BE UTILISED MORE THAN ONCE

9 The intermediate unrelieved loss may not be relieved against relevant profits to the extent that those profits have already been utilised for the purposes of paragraph 7.

RELIEVING DIFFERENT LOSSES AGAINST THE SAME PROFITS

10(1) Where intermediate unrelieved losses accruing to each of two or more persons fall to be relieved under paragraph 7 against the same relevant profits, such a loss accruing to a person who last had the transferred interest (or part of it) at an earlier time shall be so relieved before one accruing to a person who last had the interest (or part) at a later time.

10(2) Where–

(a) two or more persons each last had a part of the transferred interest at the same time, and

(b) intermediate unrelieved losses accruing to each of them fall to be relieved under paragraph 7 against the same relevant profits,

those losses shall be so relieved in such a manner as ensures that the same proportion of each is so relieved.

10(3) In this paragraph, references to an intermediate unrelieved loss accruing to a person are to the intermediate unrelieved loss in respect of an allowable loss accruing to the person.

CONSTRUCTION AS ONE WITH PART 1 OF THE OIL TAXATION ACT 1975

11 This Schedule shall be construed as one with Part 1 of the Oil Taxation Act 1975.

FINANCE ACT 2004

(2004 Chapter 12)

[*22nd July 2004*]

ARRANGEMENT OF SECTIONS

PRT Statutes

PART 5 – OIL

Notes – As they do not relate directly to petroleum revenue tax, s. 286 in this Part (and Sch. 38 which it introduces) are reproduced in the Income, Corporation and Capital Gains Taxes statutes in Croner-i *Tax Statutes and Statutory Instruments* (in Vol. 1B of the print edition).

285 Certain receipts not to be tariff receipts

285(1) The Oil Taxation Act 1983 (c. 56) is amended as follows.

285(2) [Amends OTA 1983, s. 6(2).]

285(3) [Inserts OTA 1983, s. 6A–6B.]

285(4) [Amends OTA 1983, Sch. 2, para. 12.]

285(5) Schedule 37 to this Act has effect; and in that Schedule–

Part 1 makes amendments to the Oil Taxation Act 1983 (c. 56) relating to allowable expenditure and disposal receipts;

Part 2 makes transitional provision;

Part 3 makes amendments to the Taxes Act 1988;

Part 4 makes amendments to other enactments.

285(6) In Part 1 of Schedule 37 to this Act–

(a) the amendments made by paragraph 5 (which relate to disposal receipts) have effect in relation to disposals in chargeable periods ending on or after 30th June 2004, and

(b) the other amendments made by that Part have effect in relation to expenditure incurred on or after 1st January 2004.

285(7) [Repealed by CTA 2010, s. 1181 and Sch. 3, Pt. 2; also repealed by TIOPA 2010, s. 378 and Sch. 10, Pt. 6.]

285(8) The amendments made by Part 4 of that Schedule have effect in relation to chargeable periods (within the meaning of section 98 of the Finance Act 1999 (c. 16)) ending on or after 30th June 2004.

History – S. 285(7) repealed by CTA 2010, s. 1181 and Sch. 3, Pt. 2, for corporation tax purposes only, with effect for accounting periods ending on or after 1 April 2010. S. 285(7) also repealed by TIOPA 2010, s. 378 and Sch. 10, Pt. 6, with effect for corporation tax purposes for accounting periods ending on or after 1 April 2010, for income tax and capital gains tax purposes for the tax year 2010–11 and subsequent tax years, and for petroleum revenue tax purposes for chargeable periods beginning on or after 1 July 2010.

286 Petroleum extraction activities: exploration expenditure supplement

286 [See note below.]

Notes – As they do not relate directly to petroleum revenue tax, s. 286 in this Part (and Sch. 38 which it introduces) are reproduced in the Income, Corporation and Capital Gains Taxes statutes in Croner-i *Tax Statutes and Statutory Instruments* (in Vol. 1B of the print edition).

287 Restrictions on expenditure allowable

287(1) In Schedule 4 to the Oil Taxation Act 1975 (c. 22), paragraph 2 (restrictions on expenditure allowable where acquisition etc from connected person or otherwise not at arm's length) is amended as follows.

287(2) [Amends OTA 1975, Sch. 4, para. 2(1).]

287(3) [Inserts OTA 1975, Sch. 4, para. 2(1ZA).]

287(4) [Amends OTA 1975, Sch. 4, para. 2(1B).]

287(5) [Inserts OTA 1975, Sch. 4, para. 2(1C).]

287(6) The amendments made by this section have effect in relation to expenditure incurred on or after 17th March 2004.

288 Terminal losses

288(1) Schedule 17 to the Finance Act 1980 (c. 48) (transfers of interests in oil fields) is amended as follows.

288(2) [Substitutes FA 1980, Sch. 17, para. 15.]

288(3) The amendment made by this section has effect in relation to losses accruing in chargeable periods ending after 17th March 2004.

PART 7 – DISCLOSURE OF TAX AVOIDANCE SCHEMES

Cross references – SI 2004/1863: prescribed descriptions of arrangements, where the main benefit which might be expected to arise is the obtaining of a tax advantage, resulting in the promoter's duty to notify HMRC.
SI 2004/1864: details of the information that must be provided to HMRC – entered into force on 1 August 2004, but which generally do not impose a requirement to provide information relating to proposals or arrangements where the "relevant date" (see s. 308(2)) is before 22 July 2004).
SI 2004/1865: circumstances in which a person is not to be regarded as a promoter in relation to tax avoidance schemes for the purposes of s. 307.
SI 2007/785: provisions corresponding to Pt. 7, other than s. 314.

306 Meaning of "notifiable arrangements" and "notifiable proposal"

306(1) In this Part **"notifiable arrangements"** means any arrangements which–
(a) fall within any description prescribed by the Treasury by regulations,
(b) enable, or might be expected to enable, any person to obtain an advantage in relation to any tax that is so prescribed in relation to arrangements of that description, and
(c) are such that the main benefit, or one of the main benefits, that might be expected to arise from the arrangements is the obtaining of that advantage.

306(2) In this Part **"notifiable proposal"** means a proposal for arrangements which, if entered into, would be notifiable arrangements (whether the proposal relates to a particular person or to any person who may seek to take advantage of it).

Statutory instruments – SI 2006/1543: made under s. 306(1)(a) and (b).
SI 2004/1863: made under s. 306(1)(a) and (b).

Other material – M04/2006: HMRC guidance on the disclosure of tax avoidance schemes.

306A Doubt as to notifiability

306A(1) HMRC may apply to the tribunal for an order that–
(a) a proposal is to be treated as notifiable, or
(b) arrangements are to be treated as notifiable.

306A(2) An application must specify–
(a) the proposal or arrangements in respect of which the order is sought, and
(b) the promoter.

306A(3) On an application the tribunal may make the order only if satisfied that HMRC–
(a) have taken all reasonable steps to establish whether the proposal or arrangements are notifiable, and
(b) have reasonable grounds for suspecting that the proposal or arrangements may be notifiable.

306A(4) Reasonable steps under subsection (3)(a) may (but need not) include taking action under section 313A or 313B.

306A(5) Grounds for suspicion under subsection (3)(b) may include–
(a) the fact that the relevant arrangements fall within a description prescribed under section 306(1)(a);
(b) an attempt by the promoter to avoid or delay providing information or documents about the proposal or arrangements under or by virtue of section 313A or 313B;
(c) the promoter's failure to comply with a requirement under or by virtue of section 313A or 313B in relation to another proposal or other arrangements.

306A(6) Where an order is made under this section in respect of a proposal or arrangements, the prescribed period for the purposes of section 308(1) or (3) in so far as it applies by virtue of the order–
(a) shall begin after a date prescribed for the purpose, and
(b) may be of a different length than the prescribed period for the purpose of other applications of section 308(1) or (3).

306A(7) An order under this section in relation to a proposal or arrangements is without prejudice to the possible application of section 308, other than by virtue of this section, to the proposal or arrangements.

History – In s. 306A*(1)* and *(3)*, *"tribunal"* substituted for "Special Commissioners" by SI 2009/56, art. 3(1) and Sch. 1, para. 429, operative from 1 April 2009, subject to transitional and saving provisions in SI 2009/56, Sch. 3.
S. 306A inserted by FA 2007, s. 108(2) with effect from 19 July 2007.

Cross references – SI 2009/275, art. 3(i): any decision under s. 306A is an excluded decision for the purposes of TCEA 2007, s. 11(1) and 13(1).
SI 2007/3104: where a penalty is imposed under TMA 1970, s. 98C(1) following an order under FA 2004, s. 306A, or s. 314A the amount specified in s. 98C(1)(b) is increased to £5,000.

Other material – M04/2006: HMRC guidance on the disclosure of tax avoidance schemes.

307 Meaning of "promoter"

307(1) For the purposes of this Part a person is a promoter–

(a) in relation to a notifiable proposal, if, in the course of a relevant business, the person ("P")–

(i) is to any extent responsible for the design of the proposed arrangements,

(ii) makes a firm approach to another person ("C") in relation to the notifiable proposal with a view to P making the notifiable proposal available for implementation by C or any other person, or

(iii) makes the notifiable proposal available for implementation by other persons, and

(b) in relation to notifiable arrangements, if he is by virtue of paragraph (a)(ii) or (iii) a promoter in relation to a notifiable proposal which is implemented by those arrangements or if, in the course of a relevant business, he is to any extent responsible for–

(i) the design of the arrangements, or

(ii) the organisation or management of the arrangements.

307(1A) For the purposes of this Part a person is an introducer in relation to a notifiable proposal if the person makes a marketing contact with another person in relation to the notifiable proposal.

307(2) In this section **"relevant business"** means any trade, profession or business which–

(a) involves the provision to other persons of services relating to taxation, or

(b) is carried on by a bank, as defined by section 1120 of the Corporation Tax Act 2010, or by a securities house, as defined by section 1009(3) of that Act.

307(3) For the purposes of this section anything done by a company is to be taken to be done in the course of a relevant business if it is done for the purposes of a relevant business falling within subsection (2)(b) carried on by another company which is a member of the same group.

307(4) Section 170 of the Taxation of Chargeable Gains Act 1992 has effect for determining for the purposes of subsection (3) whether two companies are members of the same group, but as if in that section–

(a) for each of the references to a 75 per cent subsidiary there were substituted a reference to a 51 per cent subsidiary, and

(b) subsection (3)(b) and subsections (6) to (8) were omitted.

307(4A) For the purposes of this Part a person makes a firm approach to another person in relation to a notifiable proposal if the person makes a marketing contact with the other person in relation to the notifiable proposal at a time when the proposed arrangements have been substantially designed.

307(4B) For the purposes of this Part a person makes a marketing contact with another person in relation to a notifiable proposal if–

(a) the person communicates information about the notifiable proposal to the other person,

(b) the communication is made with a view to that other person, or any other person, entering into transactions forming part of the proposed arrangements, and

(c) the information communicated includes an explanation of the advantage in relation to any tax that might be expected to be obtained from the proposed arrangements.

307(4C) For the purposes of subsection (4A) proposed arrangements have been substantially designed at any time if by that time the nature of the transactions to form part of them has been sufficiently developed for it to be reasonable to believe that a person who wished to obtain the advantage mentioned in subsection (4B)(c) might enter into–

(a) transactions of the nature developed, or

(b) transactions not substantially different from transactions of that nature.

307(5) A person is not to be treated as a promoter or introducer for the purposes of this Part by reason of anything done in prescribed circumstances.

307(6) In the application of this Part to a proposal or arrangements which are not notifiable, a reference to a promoter or introducer is a reference to a person who would be a promoter or introducer under subsections (1) to (5) if the proposal or arrangements were notifiable.

History – In s. 307(1)(a), the words from "business, the person ("P")–" to "makes" (in s. 307(1)(a)(iii)) substituted for the former words by FA 2010, s. 56 and Sch. 17, para. 2(2), with effect from 1 January 2011 (2010/3019).

In s. 307(1)(b), "or (iii)" inserted after "(a)(ii)" by FA 2010, s. 56 and Sch. 17, para. 2(3), with effect from 1 January 2011 (SI 2010/3019).

S. 307(1A) inserted by FA 2010, s. 56 and Sch. 17, para. 2(4), with effect from 1 January 2011 (SI 2010/3019).

In s. 307(2)(b), the words "section 1120 of the Corporation Tax Act 2010" substituted for the words "section 840A of the Taxes Act 1988", and the words "section 1009(3)" substituted for the words "section 209A(4)", by CTA 2010, s. 1177 and Sch. 1, para. 429, with effect for corporation tax purposes for accounting periods ending on or after 1 April 2010, and for income tax and capital gains tax purposes for the tax year 2010–11 and subsequent tax years.

S. 307(4A) inserted by FA 2010, s. 56 and Sch. 17, para. 2(5), with effect from 1 January 2011 (SI 2010/3019).

S. 307(4B) inserted by FA 2010, s. 56 and Sch. 17, para. 2(5), with effect from 1 January 2011 (SI 2010/3019).
S. 307(4C) inserted by FA 2010, s. 56 and Sch. 17, para. 2(5), with effect from 1 January 2011 (SI 2010/3019).
In s. 307(5), the words "or introducer" inserted after "promoter" by FA 2010, s. 56 and Sch. 17, para. 2(6), with effect from 1 January 2011 (SI 2010/3019).
In s. 307(6), the words "or introducer" inserted after "promoter" in both places by FA 2010, s. 56 and Sch. 17, para. 2(7), with effect from 1 January 2011 (SI 2010/3019).
S. 307(6) inserted by FA 2007, s. 108(3) with effect from 19 July 2007.

Cross references – SI 2004/1865.

Statutory instruments – SI 2004/1865: made under s. 307(5).

Other material – M04/2006: HMRC guidance on the disclosure of tax avoidance schemes.

308 Duties of promoter

308(1) A person who is a promoter in relation to a notifiable proposal must, within the prescribed period after the relevant date, provide the Board with prescribed information relating to the notifiable proposal.

308(2) In subsection (1) **"the relevant date"** means the earliest of the following–

(za) the date on which the promoter first makes a firm approach to another person in relation to a notifiable proposal,

(a) the date on which the promoter makes the notifiable proposal available for implementation by any other person, or

(b) the date on which the promoter first becomes aware of any transaction forming part of notifiable arrangements implementing the notifiable proposal.

308(3) A person who is a promoter in relation to notifiable arrangements must, within the prescribed period after the date on which he first becomes aware of any transaction forming part of the notifiable arrangements, provide the Board with prescribed information relating to those arrangements, unless those arrangements implement a proposal in respect of which notice has been given under subsection (1).

308(4) Subsection (4A) applies where a person complies with subsection (1) in relation to a notifiable proposal for arrangements and another person is–

(a) also a promoter in relation to the notifiable proposal or is a promoter in relation to a notifiable proposal for arrangements which are substantially the same as the proposed arrangements (whether they relate to the same or different parties), or

(b) a promoter in relation to notifiable arrangements implementing the notifiable proposal or notifiable arrangements which are substantially the same as notifiable arrangements implementing the notifiable proposal (whether they relate to the same or different parties).

308(4A) Any duty of the other person under subsection (1) or (3) in relation to the notifiable proposal or notifiable arrangements is discharged if–

(a) the person who complied with subsection (1) has notified the identity and address of the other person to HMRC or the other person holds the reference number allocated to the proposed notifiable arrangements under section 311, and

(b) the other person holds the information provided to HMRC in compliance with subsection (1).

308(4B) Subsection (4C) applies where a person complies with subsection (3) in relation to notifiable arrangements and another person is–

(a) a promoter in relation to a notifiable proposal for arrangements which are substantially the same as the notifiable arrangements (whether they relate to the same or different parties), or

(b) also a promoter in relation to the notifiable arrangements or notifiable arrangements which are substantially the same (whether they relate to the same or different parties).

308(4C) Any duty of the other person under subsection (1) or (3) in relation to the notifiable proposal or notifiable arrangements is discharged if–

(a) the person who complied with subsection (3) has notified the identity and address of the other person to HMRC or the other person holds the reference number allocated to the notifiable arrangements under section 311, and

(b) the other person holds the information provided to HMRC in compliance with subsection (3).

308(5) Where a person is a promoter in relation to two or more notifiable proposals or sets of notifiable arrangements which are substantially the same (whether they relate to the same parties or different parties), he need not provide information under subsection (1) or (3) if he has already provided information under either of those subsections in relation to any of the other proposals or arrangements.

308(6) [Not relevant to petroleum revenue tax.]

History – In s. 308(1), the words "A person who is a promoter in relation to a notifiable proposal" substituted for the words "The promoter", and the word "the" substituted for the word "any" (before "notifiable"), by FA 2008, s. 116 and Sch. 38, para. 2, with effect from 1 November 2008, for purposes other than stamp duty land tax (by virtue of SI 2008/1935).
In s. 308(2), the word "earliest" substituted for the word "earlier" by FA 2010, s. 56 and Sch. 17, para. 3(2), with effect from 1 January 2011 (SI 2010/3019).

S. 308(2)(za) inserted by FA 2010, s. 56 and Sch. 17, para. 3(3), with effect from 1 January 2011 (SI 2010/3019).
In s. 308(2)(a), the word "the" substituted for the word "a" (before "notifiable"), by FA 2008, s. 116 and Sch. 38, para. 3, with effect from 1 November 2008, for purposes other than stamp duty land tax (by virtue of SI 2008/1935).
In s. 308(3), the words "A person who is a promoter in relation to notifiable arrangements" substituted for the words "The promoter", and the words "the notifiable" substituted for the words "any notifiable", by FA 2008, s. 116 and Sch. 38, para. 4, with effect from 1 November 2008, for purposes other than stamp duty land tax (by virtue of SI 2008/1935).
S. 308(4), (4A), (4B) and (4C) substituted for former s. 308(4) by FA 2008, s. 116 and Sch. 38, para. 5, with effect from 1 November 2008, for purposes other than stamp duty land tax (by virtue of SI 2008/1935).

Cross references – SI 2004/1864.
SI 2004/1865.

Statutory instruments – SI 2004/1864: made under s. 308(1) and (3).

Other material – M04/2006: HMRC guidance on the disclosure of tax avoidance schemes.

308A Supplemental information

308A(1) This section applies where–

(a) a promoter (P) has provided information in purported compliance with section 308(1) or (3), but

(b) HMRC believe that P has not provided all the prescribed information.

308A(2) HMRC may apply to the tribunal for an order requiring P to provide specified information about, or documents relating to, the notifiable proposal or arrangements.

308A(3) The tribunal may make an order under subsection (2) in respect of information or documents only if satisfied that HMRC have reasonable grounds for suspecting that the information or documents–

(a) form part of the prescribed information, or

(b) will support or explain the prescribed information.

308A(4) A requirement by virtue of subsection (2) shall be treated as part of P's duty under section 308(1) or (3).

308A(5) In so far as P's duty under section 308(1) or (3) arises out of a requirement by virtue of subsection (2) above, the prescribed period shall begin after a date prescribed for the purpose.

308A(6) In so far as P's duty under section 308(1) or (3) arises out of a requirement by virtue of subsection (2) above, the prescribed period–

(a) may be of a different length than the prescribed period for the purpose of other applications of section 308(1) or (3), and

(b) may be extended by HMRC by direction.

History – In s. 308A(2) and (3), "tribunal" substituted for "Special Commissioners" by SI 2009/56, art. 3(1) and Sch. 1, para. 430, operative from 1 April 2009, subject to transitional and saving provisions in SI 2009/56, Sch. 3.
S. 308A inserted by FA 2007, s. 108(4) with effect from 19 July 2007.

Cross references – SI 2009/275, art. 3(i): any decision under s. 308A is an excluded decision for the purposes of TCEA 2007, s. 11(1) and 13(1).

Other material – M04/2006: HMRC guidance on the disclosure of tax avoidance schemes.

309 Duty of person dealing with promoter outside United Kingdom

309(1) Any person ("the client") who enters into any transaction forming part of any notifiable arrangements in relation to which–

(a) a promoter is resident outside the United Kingdom, and

(b) no promoter is resident in the United Kingdom,

must, within the prescribed period after doing so, provide the Board with prescribed information relating to the notifiable arrangements.

309(2) Compliance with section 308(1) by any promoter in relation to the notifiable arrangements discharges the duty of the client under subsection (1).

Cross references – SI 2004/1864.

Statutory instruments – SI 2004/1864 made under s. 309(1).

Other material – M04/2006: HMRC guidance on the disclosure of tax avoidance schemes.

310 Duty of parties to notifiable arrangements not involving promoter

310 Any person who enters into any transaction forming part of notifiable arrangements as respects which neither he nor any other person in the United Kingdom is liable to comply with section 308 (duties of promoter) or section 309 (duty of person dealing with promoter outside the United Kingdom) must at the prescribed time provide the Board with prescribed information relating to the notifiable arrangements.

Cross references – SI 2004/1864.

Statutory instruments – SI 2004/1864 made under s. 310.

Other material – M04/2006: HMRC guidance on the disclosure of tax avoidance schemes.

312A Duty of client to notify parties of number

312A(1) This section applies where a person (a "client") to whom a person who is a promoter in relation to notifiable arrangements or a notifiable proposal is providing (or has provided) services in connection with the notifiable arrangements or notifiable proposal receives prescribed information relating to the reference number allocated to the notifiable arrangements or proposed notifiable arrangements.

312A(2) The client must, within the prescribed period, provide prescribed information relating to the reference number to any other person–

(a) who the client might reasonably be expected to know is or is likely to be a party to the arrangements or proposed arrangements, and

(b) who might reasonably be expected to gain a tax advantage in relation to any relevant tax by reason of the arrangements or proposed arrangements.

312A(2A) Where the client–

(a) is an employer, and

(b) by reason of the arrangements or proposed arrangements, receives or might reasonably be expected to receive an advantage, in relation to any relevant tax, in relation to the employment of one or more of the client's employees,

the client must, within the prescribed period, provide to each of the client's relevant employees prescribed information relating to the reference number.

312A(3) For the purposes of this section–

(a) a tax is a **"relevant tax"**, in relation to arrangements or arrangements proposed in a proposal of any description, if it is prescribed in relation to arrangements or proposals of that description by regulations under section 306;

(b) **"relevant employee"** means an employee in relation to whose employment the client receives or might reasonably be expected to receive the advantage mentioned in subsection (2A);

(c) **"employee"** includes a former employee;

(d) a reference to employment includes holding an office (and references to "employee" and "employer" are to be construed accordingly).

312A(4) HMRC may give notice that, in relation to notifiable arrangements or a notifiable proposal specified in the notice, persons are not under one or both of the duties under this section after the date specified in the notice.

312A(5) The duty under subsection (2) or (2A) does not apply in prescribed circumstances.

History – S. 312A(2A) inserted by FA 2015, s. 117 and Sch. 17, para. 5(2), with effect from 26 March 2015 subject to the transitional provisions at Sch. 17, para. 20.
S. 312A(3) substituted by FA 2015, s. 117 and Sch. 17, para. 5(3), with effect from 26 March 2015 subject to the transitional provisions at Sch. 17, para. 20. Former s. 312A(3) read as follows:
"**312A(3)** For the purposes of subsection (1) a tax is a **"relevant tax"** in relation to arrangements or arrangements proposed in a proposal of any description if it is prescribed in relation to arrangements or proposals of that description by regulations under section 306."
In s. 312A(4) the words "one or both of the duties under this section" substituted for the words "the duty under subsection (2)" by FA 2015, s. 117 and Sch. 17, para. 5(4), with effect from 26 March 2015 subject to the transitional provisions at Sch. 17, para. 20.
In s. 312A(5) the words "or (2A)" inserted by FA 2015, s. 117 and Sch. 17, para. 5(5), with effect from 26 March 2015 subject to the transitional provisions at Sch. 17, para. 20.
S. 312A (together with s. 312) substituted for former s. 312 by FA 2008, s. 116 and Sch. 38, para. 4, with effect from 1 November 2008, for purposes other than stamp duty land tax (by virtue of SI 2008/1935).

Cross references – SI 2004/1864: prescribed information under s. 312.

Statutory instruments – SI 2004/1864: made under s. 312.

Other material – M04/2006: HMRC guidance on the disclosure of tax avoidance schemes.

312B Duty of client to provide information to promoter

312B(1) This section applies where a person who is a promoter in relation to notifiable arrangements has provided a person ("the client") with the information prescribed under section 312(2) (duty of promoter to notify client of reference number).

312B(2) The client must, within the prescribed period, provide the promoter with prescribed information relating to the client.

312B(3) The duty under subsection (2) is subject to any exceptions that may be prescribed.

History – S. 312B inserted by FA 2013, s. 223(2), with effect from 17 July 2013 (Royal Assent).

313 Duty of parties to notifiable arrangements to notify Board of number, etc.

313(1) Any person who is a party to any notifiable arrangements must provide the Board with prescribed information relating to–

(a) any reference number notified to him, and

(b) the time when he obtains or expects to obtain by virtue of the arrangements an advantage in relation to any relevant tax.

313(2) For the purposes of subsection (1) a tax is a **"relevant tax"** in relation to any notifiable arrangements if it is prescribed in relation to arrangements of that description by regulations under section 306.

313(3) Regulations made by HMRC may–

(a) in prescribed cases, require the information prescribed under subsection (1) to be included in any return or account which the person is required by or under any enactment to deliver to the Board, and

(b) in prescribed cases, require the information prescribed under subsection (1) and such other information as is prescribed to be provided separately to the Board at the prescribed time or times.

313(4) A person is not liable to a penalty under–

(a) any provision relating to incorrect or uncorrected returns made under section 98 of the Finance Act 1986 (administration of stamp duty reserve tax),

(b) Schedule 24 to the Finance Act 2007 (penalties for errors), or

(c) any other prescribed provision,

by reason of any failure to include in any return or account any reference number or other information required by virtue of subsection (3)(a) (but see section 98C of the Taxes Management Act 1970 for the penalty for failure to comply with this section).

313(5) HMRC may give notice that, in relation to notifiable arrangements specified in the notice, persons are not under the duty under subsection (1) after the date specified in the notice.

313(6) The duty under subsection (1) does not apply in prescribed circumstances.

History – S. 313(4)(a)–(c) substituted for former s. 313(4(a)–(g) by SI 2009/571, art. 8 and Sch. 1, para. 36, with effect from 1 April 2009.

In s. 313(1)(a), the words "under section 311 by the Board or under section 312 by the promoter", which followed "notified to him", omitted by FA 2008, s. 116 and Sch. 38, para. 5(2), with effect from 1 November 2008, for purposes other than stamp duty land tax (by virtue of SI 2008/1935).

In s. 313(3), the words "made by HMRC" substituted for the words "under subsection (1)" by FA 2008, s. 116 and Sch. 38, para. 5(3)(a), with effect from 1 November 2008, for purposes other than stamp duty land tax (by virtue of SI 2008/1935).

In s. 313(3)(a), the words "information prescribed under subsection (1)" substituted for the words "number and other information" by FA 2008, s. 116 and Sch. 38, para. 5(3)(b), with effect from 1 November 2008, for purposes other than stamp duty land tax (by virtue of SI 2008/1935).

In s. 313(3)(b), the words "information prescribed under subsection (1) and such other information as is prescribed" substituted for the words "number and other information" by FA 2008, s. 116 and Sch. 38, para. 5(3)(c), with effect from 1 November 2008, for purposes other than stamp duty land tax (by virtue of SI 2008/1935).

S. 313(5) inserted by FA 2008, s. 116 and Sch. 38, para. 5(4), with effect from 1 November 2008, for purposes other than stamp duty land tax (by virtue of SI 2008/1935).

S. 313(6) inserted by FA 2015, s. 117 and Sch. 17, para. 6, with effect from 26 March 2015.

Cross references – SI 2004/1864.

Statutory instruments – SI 2004/1864: made under s. 313(1), (3) and (4)(g).

Other material – M04/2006: HMRC guidance on the disclosure of tax avoidance schemes.

313ZA Duty to provide details of clients

313ZA(1) This section applies where a person who is a promoter in relation to notifiable arrangements is providing (or has provided) services to any person ("the client") in connection with the notifiable arrangements and either–

(a) the promoter is subject to the reference number information requirement, or

(b) the promoter has failed to comply with section 308(1) or (3) in relation to the notifiable arrangements (or the notifiable proposal for them) but would be subject to the reference number information requirement if a reference number had been allocated to the notifiable arrangements.

313ZA(2) For the purposes of this section **"the reference number information requirement"** is the requirement under section 312(2) to provide to the client prescribed information relating to the reference number allocated to the notifiable arrangements.

313ZA(3) The promoter must, within the prescribed period after the end of the relevant period, provide HMRC with prescribed information in relation to the client.

313ZA(4) In subsection (3) **"the relevant period"** means such period during which the promoter is or would be subject to the reference number information requirement as is prescribed.

313ZA(5) The promoter need not comply with subsection (3) in relation to any notifiable arrangements at any time after HMRC have given notice under section 312(6) in relation to the notifiable arrangements.

History – S. 313ZA inserted by FA 2010, s. 56 and Sch. 17, para. 6, with effect from 1 January 2011 (SI 2010/3019).

313ZB Enquiry following disclosure of client details

313ZB(1) This section applies where–

(a) a person who is a promoter in relation to notifiable arrangements has provided HMRC with information in relation to a person ("the client") under section 313ZA(3) (duty to provide client details), and

(b) HMRC suspect that a person other than the client is or is likely to be a party to the arrangements.

313ZB(2) HMRC may by written notice require the promoter to provide prescribed information in relation to any person other than the client who the promoter might reasonably be expected to know is or is likely to be a party to the arrangements.

313ZB(3) The promoter must comply with a requirement under or by virtue of subsection (2) within–

(a) the prescribed period, or

(b) such longer period as HMRC may direct.

History – S. 313ZB inserted by FA 2013, s. 223(3), with effect from 17 July 2013 (Royal Assent).

313ZC Duty of employer to notify HMRC of details of employees etc

313ZC(1) This section applies if conditions A, B and C are met.

313ZC(2) Condition A is that a person who is a promoter in relation to notifiable arrangements or a notifiable proposal is providing (or has provided) services in connection with the notifiable arrangements or notifiable proposal to a person ("the client").

313ZC(3) Condition B is that the client receives information under section 312(2) or as mentioned in section 312(5).

313ZC(4) Condition C is that the client is an employer in circumstances where, as a result of the notifiable arrangement or proposed notifiable arrangement–

(a) one or more of the client's employees receive, or might reasonably be expected to receive, in relation to their employment, an advantage in relation to any relevant tax, or

(b) the client receives or might reasonably be expected to receive such an advantage in relation to the employment of one or more of the client's employees.

313ZC(5) Where an employee is within subsection (4)(a), or is an employee mentioned in subsection (4)(b), the client must provide HMRC with prescribed information relating to the employee at the prescribed time or times.

313ZC(6) The client need not comply with subsection (5) in relation to any notifiable arrangements at any time after HMRC have given notice under section 312(6) or 313(5) in relation to the notifiable arrangements.

313ZC(7) The duty under subsection (5) does not apply in prescribed circumstances.

313ZC(8) Section 312A(3) applies for the purposes of this section as it applies for the purposes of that section.

History – S. 313ZC inserted by FA 2015, s. 117 and Sch. 17, para. 9, with effect from 26 March 2015.

313A Pre-disclosure enquiry

313A(1) Where HMRC suspect that a person (P) is the promoter or introducer of a proposal, or the promoter of arrangements, which may be notifiable, they may by written notice require P to state–

(a) whether in P's opinion the proposal or arrangements are notifiable by P, and

(b) if not, the reasons for P's opinion.

313A(2) A notice must specify the proposal or arrangements to which it relates.

313A(3) For the purpose of subsection (1)(b)–

(a) it is not sufficient to refer to the fact that a lawyer or other professional has given an opinion,

(b) the reasons must show, by reference to this Part and regulations under it, why P thinks the proposal or arrangements are not notifiable by P, and

(c) in particular, if P asserts that the arrangements do not fall within any description prescribed under section 306(1)(a), the reasons must provide sufficient information to enable HMRC to confirm the assertion.

313A(4) P must comply with a requirement under or by virtue of subsection (1) within–

(a) the prescribed period, or

(b) such longer period as HMRC may direct.

History – In s. 313A(1), the words "or introducer of a proposal, or the promoter of arrangements," substituted for the words "of a proposal or arrangements" by FA 2010, s. 56 and Sch. 17, para. 4, with effect from 1 January 2011 (SI 2010/3019).
S. 313A inserted by FA 2007, s. 108(5) with effect from 19 July 2007.

Other material – M04/2006: HMRC guidance on the disclosure of tax avoidance schemes.

313B Reasons for non-disclosure: supporting information

313B(1) Where HMRC receive from a person (P) a statement of reasons why a proposal or arrangements are not notifiable by P, HMRC may apply to the tribunal for an order requiring P to provide specified information or documents in support of the reasons.

313B(2) P must comply with a requirement under or by virtue of subsection (1) within–

(a) the prescribed period, or

(b) such longer period as HMRC may direct.

313B(3) The power under subsection (1)–

(a) may be exercised more than once, and

(b) applies whether or not the statement of reasons was received under section 313A(1)(b).

History – In s. 313B(1), "tribunal" substituted for "Special Commissioners" by SI 2009/56, art. 3(1) and Sch. 1, para. 431, operative from 1 April 2009, subject to transitional and saving provisions in SI 2009/56, Sch. 3.
S. 313B inserted by FA 2007, s. 108(5) with effect from 19 July 2007.

Other material – M04/2006: HMRC guidance on the disclosure of tax avoidance schemes.

313C Provision of information to HMRC by introducers

History – The heading for former wording "Information provided to introducers" by FA 2015, s. 117 and Sch. 17, para. 12(4), with effect from 26 March 2015.

313C(1) This section applies where HMRC suspect–

(a) that a person ("P") is an introducer in relation to a proposal, and

(b) that the proposal may be notifiable.

313C(1A) HMRC may by written notice require P to provide HMRC with one or both of the following–

(a) prescribed information in relation to each person who has provided P with any information relating to the proposal;

(b) prescribed information in relation to each person with whom P has made a marketing contact in relation to the proposal.

313C(2) A notice must specify the proposal to which it relates.

313C(3) P must comply with a requirement under subsection (1A) within–

(a) the prescribed period, or

(b) such longer period as HMRC may direct.

History – S. 313C(1) and (1A) substituted for former s. 313C(1) by FA 2015, s. 117 and Sch. 17, para. 12(2), with effect from 26 March 2015.
In s. 313C(3) the words "subsection (1A)" substituted for the words "or by virtue of subsection (1)" by FA 2015, s. 117 and Sch. 17, para. 12(3), with effect from 26 March 2015.
S. 313C inserted by FA 2010, s. 56 and Sch. 17, para. 9, with effect from 1 January 2011 (SI 2010/3019).

314 Legal professional privilege

314(1) Nothing in this Part requires any person to disclose to the Board any privileged information.

314(2) In this Part **"privileged information"** means information with respect to which a claim to legal professional privilege, or, in Scotland, to confidentiality of communications, could be maintained in legal proceedings.

Cross references – SI 2004/1865, reg. 6: persons not to be treated as promoters if information to be provided is subject wholly or partly subject to legal professional privilege.

Other material – M04/2006: HMRC guidance on the disclosure of tax avoidance schemes.

314A Order to disclose

314A(1) HMRC may apply to the tribunal for an order that–

(a) a proposal is notifiable, or

(b) arrangements are notifiable.

314A(2) An application must specify–

(a) the proposal or arrangements in respect of which the order is sought, and

(b) the promoter.

314A(3) On an application the tribunal may make the order only if satisfied that section 306(1)(a) to (c) applies to the relevant arrangements.

History – In s. 314A(1) and (3), "tribunal" substituted for "Special Commissioners" by SI 2009/56, art. 3(1) and Sch. 1, para. 432, operative from 1 April 2009, subject to transitional and saving provisions in SI 2009/56, Sch. 3.
S. 314A inserted by FA 2007, s. 108(6) with effect from 19 July 2007.

Cross references – SI 2009/275, art. 3(i): any decision under s. 314A is an excluded decision for the purposes of TCEA 2007, s. 11(1) and 13(1).
SI 2007/3104: where a penalty is imposed under TMA 1970, s. 98C(1) following an order under FA 2004, s. 306A, or s. 314A the amount specified in s. 98C(1)(b) is increased to £5,000.

Other material – M04/2006: HMRC guidance on the disclosure of tax avoidance schemes.

315 Penalties

315(1) [Inserts TMA 1970, s. 98C.]

315(2) [Amends TMA 1970, s. 100(2).]

315(3) [Inserts TMA 1970, s. 100C(1A).]

316 Information to be provided in form and manner specified by HMRC

316(1) HMRC may specify the form and manner in which information required to be provided by any of the information provisions must be provided if the provision is to be complied with.

316(2) The "information provisions" are sections 308(1) and (3), 309(1), 310, 310A, 310C, 312(2), 312A(2) and (2A), 313(1) and (3), 313ZA(3) and 313ZC(5).

History – In s. 316(2) the words ", 313ZA(3) and 313ZC(5)" substituted for the words "and 313ZA(3)" by FA 2015, s. 117 and Sch. 17, para. 10, with effect from 26 March 2015.
In s. 316(2) the words "and (2A)" inserted by FA 2015, s. 117 and Sch. 17, para. 7, with effect from 26 March 2015.
In s. 316(2) the words "310C," inserted by FA 2015, s. 117 and Sch. 17, para. 2, with effect from 26 March 2015.
In s. 316(2), "310A," inserted by FA 2014, s. 284(3) with effect from 17 July 2014.
In s. 316, the words ", 313(1) and (3) and 313ZA(3)" substituted for the words "and 313(1) and (3)" by FA 2010, s. 56 and Sch. 17, para. 7, with effect from 1 January 2011 (SI 2010/3019).
S. 316 substituted by FA 2008, s. 116 and Sch. 38, para. 6, with effect from 1 November 2008, for purposes other than stamp duty land tax (by virtue of SI 2008/1935).

Other material – M04/2006: HMRC guidance on the disclosure of tax avoidance schemes.

316A Duty to provide additional information

316A(1) This section applies where a person is required to provide information under section 312(2) or 312A(2) or (2A).

316A(2) HMRC may specify additional information which must be provided by that person to the recipients under section 312(2) or 312A(2) or (2A) at the same time as the information referred to in subsection (1).

316A(3) HMRC may specify the form and manner in which the additional information is to be provided.

316A(4) For the purposes of this section **"additional information"** means information supplied by HMRC which relates to notifiable proposals or notifiable arrangements in general.

History – S. 316A inserted by FA 2015, s. 117 and Sch. 17, para. 14, with effect from 26 March 2015.

316B Confidentiality

316B No duty of confidentiality or other restriction on disclosure (however imposed) prevents the voluntary disclosure by any person to HMRC of information or documents which the person has reasonable grounds for suspecting will assist HMRC in determining whether there has been a breach of any requirement imposed by or under this Part.

History – S. 316B inserted by FA 2015, s. 117 and Sch. 17, para. 16, with effect from 26 March 2015.

316C Publication by HMRC

316C(1) HMRC may publish information about–

(a) any notifiable arrangements, or proposed notifiable arrangements, to which a reference number is allocated under section 311;

(b) any person who is a promoter in relation to the notifiable arrangements or, in the case of proposed notifiable arrangements, the notifiable proposal.

316C(2) The information that may be published is (subject to subsection (4))–

(a) any information relating to arrangements within subsection (1)(a), or a person within subsection (1)(b), that is prescribed information for the purposes of section 308, 309 or 310;

(b) any ruling of a court or tribunal relating to any such arrangements or person (in that person's capacity as a promoter in relation to a notifiable proposal or arrangements);

(c) the number of persons in any period who enter into transactions forming part of notifiable arrangements within subsection (1)(a);

PRT Statutes

(d) whether arrangements within subsection (1)(a) are APN relevant (see subsection (7));

(e) any other information that HMRC considers it appropriate to publish for the purpose of identifying arrangements within subsection (1)(a) or a person within subsection (1)(b).

316C(3) The information may be published in any manner that HMRC considers appropriate.

316C(4) No information may be published under this section that identifies a person who enters into a transaction forming part of notifiable arrangements within subsection (1)(a).

316C(5) But where a person who is a promoter within subsection (1)(b) is also a person mentioned in subsection (4), nothing in subsection (4) is to be taken as preventing the publication under this section of information so far as relating to the person's activities as a promoter.

316C(6) Before publishing any information under this section that identifies a person as a promoter within subsection (1)(b), HMRC must–

(a) inform the person that they are considering doing so, and

(b) give the person reasonable opportunity to make representations about whether it should be published.

316C(7) Arrangements are **"APN relevant"** for the purposes of subsection (2)(d) if HMRC has indicated in a publication that it may exercise (or has exercised) its power under section 219 of the Finance Act 2014 (accelerated payment notices) by virtue of the arrangements being DOTAS arrangements within the meaning of that section.

History – S. 316C inserted by FA 2015, s. 117 and Sch. 17, para. 17, with effect from 26 March 2015 subject to the transitional provisions at Sch. 17, para. 21.

316D Section 316C: subsequent judicial rulings

316D(1) This section applies if–

(a) information about notifiable arrangements, or proposed notifiable arrangements, is published under section 316C,

(b) at any time after the information is published, a ruling of a court or tribunal is made in relation to tax arrangements, and

(c) HMRC is of the opinion that the ruling is relevant to the arrangements mentioned in paragraph (a).

316D(2) A ruling is **"relevant"** to the arrangements if–

(a) the principles laid down, or reasoning given, in the ruling would, if applied to the arrangements, allow the purported advantage arising from the arrangements in relation to tax, and

(b) the ruling is final.

316D(3) HMRC must publish information about the ruling.

316D(4) The information must be published in the same manner as HMRC published the information mentioned in subsection (1)(a) (and may also be published in any other manner that HMRC considers appropriate).

316D(5) A ruling is **"final"** if it is–

(a) a ruling of the Supreme Court, or

(b) a ruling of any other court or tribunal in circumstances where–

(i) no appeal may be made against the ruling,

(ii) if an appeal may be made against the ruling with permission, the time limit for applications has expired and either no application has been made or permission has been refused,

(iii) if such permission to appeal against the ruling has been granted or is not required, no appeal has been made within the time limit for appeals, or

(iv) if an appeal was made, it was abandoned or otherwise disposed of before it was determined by the court or tribunal to which it was addressed.

316D(6) Where a ruling is final by virtue of sub-paragraph (ii), (iii) or (iv) of subsection (5)(b), the ruling is to be treated as made at the time when the sub-paragraph in question is first satisfied.

316D(7) In this section **"tax arrangements"** means arrangements in respect of which it would be reasonable to conclude (having regard to all the circumstances) that the obtaining of an advantage in relation to tax was the main purpose, or one of the main purposes.

History – S. 316D inserted by FA 2015, s. 117 and Sch. 17, para. 17, with effect from 26 March 2015.

317 Regulations under Part 7

317(1) Any power of the Treasury or the Board to make regulations under this Part is exercisable by statutory instrument.

317(2) Regulations made by the Treasury or the Board under this Part may make different provision for different cases and may contain transitional provisions and savings.

317(3) A statutory instrument containing regulations made by the Treasury or the Board under any provision of this Part is subject to annulment in pursuance of a resolution of the House of Commons.

History – In s. 317(2), the words "make different provision for different cases and may" inserted by FA 2010, s. 56 and Sch. 17, para. 8, with effect from 1 January 2011 (SI 2010/3019).

Statutory instruments – SI 2004/1864: made under s. 317(2).

Other material – M04/2006: HMRC guidance on the disclosure of tax avoidance schemes.

317A Special Commissioners: procedure

317A [Omitted by SI 2009/56, art. 3(1) and Sch. 1, para. 433.]

History – S. 317A omitted by SI 2009/56, art. 3(1) and Sch. 1, para. 433, operative from 1 April 2009, subject to transitional and saving provisions in SI 2009/56, Sch. 3. Former s. 317A read as follows:

"317A Special Commissioners: procedure

317A Sections 56B to 56D of the Taxes Management Act 1970 (procedure) shall apply (with any necessary modifications) to applications under this Part as to appeals.".

Former s. 317A inserted by FA 2007, s. 108(7) with effect from 19 July 2007.

Other material – M04/2006: HMRC guidance on the disclosure of tax avoidance schemes.

318 Interpretation of Part 7

318(1) In this Part–

"advantage", in relation to any tax, means–

(a) relief or increased relief from, or repayment or increased repayment of, that tax, or the avoidance or reduction of a charge to that tax or an assessment to that tax or the avoidance of a possible assessment to that tax,

(b) the deferral of any payment of tax or the advancement of any repayment of tax, or

(c) the avoidance of any obligation to deduct or account for any tax;

"arrangements" includes any scheme, transaction or series of transactions;

"company" has the meaning given by section 1121 of the Corporation Tax Act 2010;

"corporation tax" includes any amount which, by virtue of any of the provisions mentioned in paragraph 1 of Schedule 18 to the Finance Act 1998 (c. 36) (company tax returns, assessments and related matters) is assessable and chargeable as if it were corporation tax;

"HMRC" means the Commissioners for Her Majesty's Revenue and Customs;

"introducer", in relation to a notifiable proposal, has the meaning given by section 307;

"make a firm approach" has the meaning given by section 307(4A);

"make a marketing contact" has the meaning given by section 307(4B);

"notifiable arrangements" has the meaning given by section 306(1);

"notifiable proposal" has the meaning given by section 306(2);

"prescribed", except in section 306, means prescribed by regulations made by the Board;

"promoter", in relation to notifiable arrangements or a notifiable proposal, has the meaning given by section 307;

"reference number", in relation to notifiable arrangements, has the meaning given by section 311(3);

"tax" means–

(a) income tax,

(b) capital gains tax,

(c) corporation tax,

(d) petroleum revenue tax,

(da) apprenticeship levy,

(e) inheritance tax,

(f) stamp duty land tax, or

(g) stamp duty reserve tax.

"trade" includes every venture in the nature of trade.

"tribunal" means the First-tier tribunal, or where determined by or under Tribunal Procedure Rules, the Upper Tribunal.

"working day" means a day which is not a Saturday or a Sunday, Christmas Day, Good Friday or a bank holiday under the Banking and Financial Dealings Act 1971 in any part of the United Kingdom.

318(2) [Omitted by TIOPA 2010, s. 374 and Sch. 8, para. 302(3) and repealed by TIOPA 2010, s. 378 and Sch. 10, Pt. 13.]

History – In s. 318(1), the definition of "working day" inserted by FA 2014, s. 284(4), with effect from 17 July 2014.
In s. 318(1), the definition of "company" inserted by TIOPA 2010, s. 374 and Sch. 8, para. 302(2)(a), with effect for corporation tax purposes for accounting periods ending on or after 1 April 2010, for income tax and capital gains tax purposes for the tax year 2010–11 and subsequent tax years, and for petroleum revenue tax purposes for chargeable periods beginning on or after 1 July 2010.
In s. 318(1), definitions of "introducer", "make a firm approach" and "make a marketing contact" inserted by FA 2010, s. 56 and Sch. 17, para. 5, with effect from1 January 2011 (SI 2010/3019).
In s. 318(1), in the definition of "tax", para. (da) inserted by FA 2016, s. 104(1), with effect from 15 September 2016 (Royal Assent).
In s. 318(1), the definition of "trade" inserted by TIOPA 2010, s. 374 and Sch. 8, para. 302(2)(b), with effect for corporation tax purposes for accounting periods ending on or after 1 April 2010, for income tax and capital gains tax purposes for the tax year 2010–11 and subsequent tax years, and for petroleum revenue tax purposes for chargeable periods beginning on or after 1 July 2010.
In s. 318(1), the definition of "the Special Commissioners" omitted by SI 2009/56, art. 3(1) and Sch. 1, para. 434(2), operative from 1 April 2009, subject to transitional and saving provisions in SI 2009/56, Sch. 3.
In s. 318(1), the definition of "tribunal" inserted by SI 2009/56, art. 3(1) and Sch. 1, para. 434(3), operative from 1 April 2009, subject to transitional and saving provisions in SI 2009/56, Sch. 3.
In s. 318(1), the definitions of "HMRC" and "the Special Commissioners" inserted by FA 2007, s. 108(8) with effect from 19 July 2007.
S. 318(2) omitted by TIOPA 2010, s. 374 and Sch. 8, para. 302(3) and repealed by TIOPA 2010, s. 378 and Sch. 10, Pt. 13, with effect for corporation tax purposes for accounting periods ending on or after 1 April 2010, for income tax and capital gains tax purposes for the tax year 2010–11 and subsequent tax years, and for petroleum revenue tax purposes for chargeable periods beginning on or after 1 July 2010.

Statutory instruments – SI 2004/1864: made under s. 318(1).
SI 2004/1865: made under s. 318(1).

Other material – M04/2006: HMRC guidance on the disclosure of tax avoidance schemes.

Notes – S. 318(2) not rewritten, as its effect is preserved in the amendments made in s. 318(1) by TIOPA 2010, Sch. 8, para. 302.

319 Part 7: commencement and savings

319(1) The following provisions of this Part come into force on the passing of this Act–

sections 306 to 315, so far as is necessary for enabling the making of any regulations for which they provide, and

sections 317 and 318 and this section.

319(2) Except as provided by subsection (1), the provisions of this Part come into force on 1st August 2004.

319(3) Section 308 does not apply to a promoter in the case of–

(a) any notifiable proposal as respects which the relevant date, as defined by subsection (2) of that section, fell before 18th March 2004,

(b) any notifiable arrangements which implement such a proposal, or

(c) any notifiable arrangements which include any transaction entered into before 18th March 2004.

319(4) Sections 309 and 310 do not apply in relation to notifiable arrangements which include any transaction entered into before 23rd April 2004.

319(5) Section 313 does not apply in relation to any notifiable arrangements in respect of which, by virtue of subsection (3) or (4), none of the duties imposed by sections 308 to 310 arises.

Other material – M04/2006: HMRC guidance on the disclosure of tax avoidance schemes.

SCHEDULES

SCHEDULE 37 – OIL TAXATION: TAX-EXEMPT TARIFFING RECEIPTS AND ASSETS PRODUCING THEM

Section 285

Part 1 – Amendments of the Oil Taxation Act 1983 Relating to Allowable Expenditure and Disposal Receipts

INTRODUCTORY

1 The Oil Taxation Act 1983 (c. 56) is amended in accordance with the following provisions of this Part.

EXPENDITURE INCURRED ON LONG-TERM ASSETS OTHER THAN NON-DEDICATED MOBILE ASSETS

2(1) Section 3 (expenditure incurred on long-term assets other than non-dedicated mobile assets) is amended as follows.

2(2) [Amends OTA 1983, s. 3(4).]

SCHEDULE 38 – SCHEDULE TO BE INSERTED AS SCHEDULE 19B TO THE TAXES ACT 1988

[See note below.]

Notes – As they do not relate directly to petroleum revenue tax, s. 286 in this Part (and Sch. 38 which it introduces) are reproduced in the Income, Corporation and Capital Gains Taxes statutes in Croner-i *Tax Statutes and Statutory Instruments* (in Vol. 1B of the print edition).

INCOME TAX (TRADING AND OTHER INCOME) ACT 2005

(2005 Chapter 5)

[*24th March 2005*]

SCHEDULES

SCHEDULE 1 – CONSEQUENTIAL AMENDMENTS

OIL TAXATION ACT 1975 (c. 22)

391 The Oil Taxation Act 1975 is amended as follows.

392 [Amends OTA 1975, s. 3(2).]

FINANCE ACT 2006

(2006 Chapter 25)

[19th July 2006]

ARRANGEMENT OF SECTIONS

PART 5 – OIL

PART 5 – OIL

NEW BASIS FOR DETERMINING MARKET VALUE

146 New basis for determining the market value of oil

146(1) [Inserts OTA 1975, Sch. 3, para. 1A.]

146(2) Paragraph 2 of that Schedule (definition of market value of oil) is amended as follows.

146(3) [Amends OTA 1975, Sch. 3, para. 2(1).]

146(4) [Inserts OTA 1975, Sch. 3, para. 2(1A)–(1C).]

146(5) [Substitutes OTA 1975, Sch. 3, para. 2(2) and (2AA) for (2).]

146(6) [Substitutes OTA 1975, Sch. 3, para. 2(2E)–(2I) for (2A)–(2D).]

146(7) [Omits OTA 1975, Sch. 3, para. 2(3).]

146(8) [Amends OTA 1975, Sch. 3, para. 2(3A).]

146(9) [Amends OTA 1975, Sch. 3, para. 2(4).]

146(10) [Inserts OTA 1975, Sch. 3, para. 2(5).]

146(11) Schedule 18 (which makes minor and consequential amendments) has effect.

147 Section 147: commencement and transitional provisions

147(1) The amendments made by section 147 and Schedule 18 have effect in relation to oil delivered or appropriated on or after 1st July 2006 (disregarding section 12A of that Act).

147(2) Those amendments also have effect for the purpose of determining for any chargeable period ending on or after 31st December 2006–

(a) the value to be brought into account under section 2(4)(b) of OTA 1975 by reference to a previous chargeable period ending on or after 30th June 2006, and

(b) the value to be brought into account under section 2(5)(d) of that Act.

PRT Statutes

147(3) Subsections (1) and (2) are subject to any express provision in Schedule 18 as to the commencement or application of any provision of that Schedule.

147(4) In the following provisions of this section–

(a) **"the last old period"** means the chargeable period that ends on 30th June 2006, and

(b) **"the first new period"** means the chargeable period that ends on 31st December 2006.

147(5) Subsection (6) applies in relation to oil which was won from an oil field before 1st July 2006 and which–

(a) was loaded on to a ship before 1st July 2006 and transported from the place of extraction to a place in the United Kingdom or elsewhere, or

(b) was transported by pipeline from the place of extraction to a place in the United Kingdom and there loaded on to a ship before that date.

147(6) If the oil is or was disposed of crude by a participator in sales otherwise than at arm's length, but the market value of the oil–

(a) does not fall to be brought into account for the purposes of section 2(5)(b) of OTA 1975 for the last old period by reason only that the oil was not delivered in that period, and

(b) would not (apart from this subsection) fall to be brought into account for the purposes of that provision in the first new period by reason only that the date on which the oil is to be regarded by virtue of section 12A of that Act as delivered falls in the last old period,

the date on which the oil is to be taken for the purposes of section 2(5)(b) of that Act to have been delivered is instead to be the first business day of the first new period.

147(7) Any power to make regulations that is conferred under or by virtue of any of the amendments made by section 147 or Schedule 18 includes power to make regulations having effect for, or in relation to,–

(a) the first new period, or

(b) for the purpose mentioned in subsection (2), the last old period,

notwithstanding that the period in question has begun or ended before the making of the regulations.

147(8) Any regulations made by virtue of subsection (7) must be made before 31st December 2006.

Statutory instruments – SI 2006/3313: partly made under s. 147(4) and (7).

ATTRIBUTION OF BLENDED CRUDE OIL

148 Crude oil: power to make regulations

148(1) [Amends OTA 1975, s. 2(5).]

148(2) [Inserts OTA 1975, s. 2(5B)–(5D).]

148(3) Regulations under section 2(5B) of OTA 1975 (inserted by subsection (2) above) may have effect for the purpose of calculating profits in relation to a chargeable period ending at any time on or after 1st July 2006.

Statutory instruments – SI 2006/3312: partly made under s. 148(3).

NOMINATION SCHEME

149 Nomination scheme

149(1) Section 61 of FA 1987 (oil taxation: nominations) shall be amended as follows.

149(2) [Amends FA 1987, s. 61(1).]

149(3) [Substitutes FA 1987, s. 61(3)–(4B) for (3) and (4).]

149(4) [Repeals FA 1987, s. 61(6) and (7).]

149(5) [Amends FA 1987, s. 61(8).]

149(6) [Amends FA 1987, s. 61(9).]

149(7) This section shall have effect in relation to chargeable periods ending on or after 1st July 2006.

150 Amendment of Schedule 10 to FA 1987

150(1) *Schedule 10 to FA 1987* (oil taxation: nominations) shall be amended as follows.

150(2) [Amends FA 1987, Sch. 10, para. 1.]

150(3) [Amends FA 1987, Sch. 10, para. 2.]

150(4) [Omits FA 1987, Sch. 10, para. 3.]

150(5) [Amends FA 1987, Sch. 10, para. 4.]

150(6) [Amends FA 1987, Sch. 10, para. 5.]

150(7) [Inserts FA 1987, Sch. 10, para. 5A and 5B.]

150(8) [Amends FA 1987, Sch. 10, para. 6.]

150(9) [Omits FA 1987, Sch. 10, para. 7(2) and (5).]

150(10) [Inserts FA 1987, Sch. 10, para. 7(6) and (7).]

150(11) [Omits FA 1987, Sch. 10, para. 8–11.]

150(12) [Amends FA 1987, Sch. 10, para. 12(1).]

150(13) [Inserts FA 1987, Sch. 10, para. 12A.]

150(14) This section shall have effect in relation to a transaction whenever proposed, but shall not have effect in relation to a proposed transaction with a transaction base date (within the meaning given by regulations under paragraph 4 of Schedule 10 to FA 1987) on or before 30th June 2006.

150(15) Regulations under paragraph 4(1B) of Schedule 10 to FA 1987 (inserted by subsection (5) above) may have retrospective effect.

Statutory instruments – SI 2006/3089: partly made under s. 150(15).

PART 10 – SUPPLEMENTARY PROVISIONS

178 Repeals

178(1) The enactments mentioned in Schedule 26 (which include provisions that are spent or of no practical utility) are repealed to the extent specified.

178(2) The repeals specified in that Schedule have effect subject to the commencement provisions and savings contained or referred to in the notes set out in that Schedule.

179 Interpretation

179 In this Act–

"ALDA 1979" means the Alcoholic Liquor Duties Act 1979 (c. 4);

"CAA 2001" means the Capital Allowances Act 2001 (c. 2);

"CTA 2009" means the Corporation Tax Act 2009;

"FA", followed by a year, means the Finance Act of that year;

"F(No. 2)A", followed by a year, means the Finance (No. 2) Act of that year;

"HODA 1979" means the Hydrocarbon Oil Duties Act 1979 (c. 5);

"ICTA" means the Income and Corporation Taxes Act 1988 (c. 1);

"IHTA 1984" means the Inheritance Tax Act 1984 (c. 51);

"ITEPA 2003" means the Income Tax (Earnings and Pensions) Act 2003 (c. 1);

"ITTOIA 2005" means the Income Tax (Trading and Other Income) Act 2005 (c. 5);

"OTA 1975" means the Oil Taxation Act 1975 (c. 22);

"TCGA 1992" means the Taxation of Chargeable Gains Act 1992 (c. 12);

"TMA 1970" means the Taxes Management Act 1970 (c. 9);

"VATA 1994" means the Value Added Tax Act 1994 (c. 23);

"VERA 1994" means the Vehicle Excise and Registration Act 1994 (c. 22).

History – In s. 179, the definition of "CTA 2009" inserted by CTA 2009, s. 1322 and Sch. 1, para. 692, with effect for corporation tax purposes for accounting periods ending on or after 1 April 2009, and for income tax and capital gains tax purposes for the tax year 2009–10 and subsequent tax years.

180 Short title

180 This Act may be cited as the Finance Act 2006.

SCHEDULES

SCHEDULE 18 – OIL TAXATION: MARKET VALUE OF OIL

Section 147

Part 1 – Amendments of the Oil Taxation Act 1975

INTRODUCTORY

1 OTA 1975 is amended as follows.

ASSESSABLE PROFITS AND ALLOWABLE LOSSES

2(1) Section 2 is amended as follows.

2(2) [Amends OTA 1975, s. 2(4)(b).]

2(3) [Amends OTA 1975, s. 2(5)(d).]

2(4) [Amends OTA 1975, s. 2(5A).]

2(5) [Amends OTA 1975, s. 2(9)(a)(i).]

2(6) [Amends OTA 1975, s. 2(9)(a)(ii).]

ALLOWANCE OF EXPLORATION AND APPRAISAL EXPENDITURE

3(1) Section 5A is amended as follows.

3(2) [Amends OTA 1975, s. 5A(5B).]

3(3) Amend subsection (5C) (application of Schedule 3 with modifications for ascertaining market value for the purposes of subsection (5B)) as follows.

3(4) [Omits OTA 1975, s. 5A(5C)(a).]

3(5) [Amends OTA 1975, s. 5A(5C)(b).]

3(6) [Amends OTA 1975, s. 5A(5C)(c).]

INTERPRETATION

4(1)–(3) [Amends OTA 1975, s. 12(1).]

DATE OF DELIVERY OR APPROPRIATION FOR SHIPPED OIL NOT DISPOSED OF IN SALES AT ARM'S LENGTH

5(1) [Inserts OTA 1975, s. 12A.]

5(2) The amendment made by this paragraph has effect in relation to oil which would (apart from this paragraph) fall to be regarded for the purposes of Part 1 of OTA 1975 as delivered or appropriated on a date after 30th June 2006.

"THE BOARD"

6(1) In section 21 (citation, interpretation and construction of the Act) subsection (2) is amended as follows.

6(2) [Substitutes definition of "the Board" in OTA 1975, s. 21(2).]

6(3) The amendment made by this paragraph comes into force on the day on which this Act is passed.

RETURNS BY PARTICIPATORS

7(1) In Schedule 2 (management and collection) paragraph 2 is amended as follows.

7(2) *[Amends OTA 1975, Sch. 2, para. 2(2)(a)(iii).]*

7(3) [Amends OTA 1975, Sch. 2, para. 2(2)(b)(ii).]

7(4) [Amends OTA 1975, Sch. 2, para. 2(2)(d)(ii).]

GAS FRACTIONATION

8(1) In Schedule 3 (petroleum revenue tax: miscellaneous provisions) paragraph 2A (market value of oil that consists of or includes gas) is amended as follows.

8(2) [Amends OTA 1975, Sch. 3, para. 2A(1).]

8(3) [Amends OTA 1975, Sch. 3, para. 2A(2).]

8(4) [Amends OTA 1975, Sch. 3, para. 2A(3).]

AGGREGATE MARKET VALUE OF OIL FOR PURPOSES OF SECTION 2(5)

9 [Amends OTA 1975, Sch. 3, paragraph 3.]

POWER TO MAKE REGULATIONS

10 [Inserts OTA 1975, Sch. 3, para. 12.]

Part 2 – Amendments of Other Enactments

FINANCE (NO. 2) ACT 1987

The designated fraction for the month

11(1) Schedule 8 to F(No. 2)A 1987 (amendments of Schedule 10 to FA 1987) is amended as follows.

11(2) [Omits FA 1987, Sch. 8, para. 5.]

11(3) The amendment made by this paragraph has effect for chargeable periods beginning on or after 1st July 2006.

FINANCE ACT 2007

(2007 Chapter 11)

[19th July 2007]

ARRANGEMENT OF SECTIONS

PART 6 – INVESTIGATION, ADMINISTRATION ETC

OTHER ADMINISTRATION

97 Penalties for errors

97(1) Schedule 24 contains provisions imposing penalties on taxpayers who–

(a) make errors in certain documents sent to HMRC, or

(b) unreasonably fail to report errors in assessments by HMRC.

97(2) That Schedule comes into force in accordance with provision made by the Treasury by order.

97(3) An order–

(a) may commence a provision generally or only for specified purposes,

(b) may make different provision for different purposes, and

(c) may include incidental, consequential or transitional provision.

97(4) The power to make an order is exercisable by statutory instrument.

PART 7 – MISCELLANEOUS

PETROLEUM REVENUE TAX

102 Abolition of PRT for fields recommissioned after earlier decommissioning

102(1) Section 185 of FA 1993 (abolition of PRT for oil fields with development consents on or after 16th March 1993) is amended as follows.

102(2) [Amends FA 1993, s. 185(1).]

102(3) [Inserts FA 1993, s. 185(1A)–(1C).]

102(4) [Amends FA 1993, s. 185(7).]

102(5) An oil field which meets the conditions in subsection (1A) of section 185 of FA 1993 (as inserted by subsection (3) above) becomes a non-taxable field for the purposes of any enactment relating to petroleum revenue tax–

(a) in any case where the development decision is made before 1st July 2007, on that date, and

(b) in any other case, on the date on which the development decision is made.

103 Tax-exempt tariffing receipts

103(1) Section 6A of the Oil Taxation Act 1983 (c. 56) (tax-exempt tariffing receipts) is amended as follows.

103(2) [Amends OTA 1983, s. 6A(4).]

103(3) [Amends OTA 1983, s. 6A(5).]

103(4) The amendments made by this section are deemed to have come into force on 1st July 2007.

104 Allowance of unrelievable loss from abandoned field

104(1) [Inserts OTA 1975, s. 6(4A).]

104(2) The amendment made by subsection (1) is deemed to have come into force on 1st July 2007.

PART 8 – FINAL PROVISIONS

114 Repeals

114 Schedule 27 contains repeals.

115 Short title

115 This Act may be cited as the Finance Act 2007.

SCHEDULES

SCHEDULE 24 – PENALTIES FOR ERRORS

Section 97

Commencement Date – Sch. 24 has effect as follows by virtue of SI 2008/568, art. 2:

- 1 April 2008 in relation to relevant documents relating to tax periods commencing on or after that date;
- 1 April 2008 in relation to assessments falling within paragraph 2 for tax periods commencing on or after that date;
- 1 April 2009 in relation to documents relating to all other claims for repayments of relevant tax made on or after 1 April 2009 which are not related to a tax period; and
- in any other case, 1 April 2009 in relation to documents given where a person's liability to pay relevant tax arises on or after that date.

However, no person will be liable to a penalty under Sch. 24 in respect of any tax period for which a return is required to be made before 1 April 2009.

Cross references – FA 2009, s. 94: Publishing details of deliberate tax defaulters.

Other material – HMRC Brief 14/11: Penalty for failure to disclose offshore income or gains.

Notes – This is an edited version of Sch. 24, containing only the provisions that are relevant to petroleum revenue tax.

Part 1 – Liability for Penalty

ERROR IN TAXPAYER'S DOCUMENT

1(1) A penalty is payable by a person (P) where–

(a) P gives HMRC a document of a kind listed in the Table below, and

(b) Conditions 1 and 2 are satisfied.

1(2) Condition 1 is that the document contains an inaccuracy which amounts to, or leads to–

(a) an understatement of a liability to tax,

(b) a false or inflated statement of a loss, or

(c) a false or inflated claim to repayment of tax.

1(3) Condition 2 is that the inaccuracy was careless (within the meaning of paragraph 3) or deliberate on P's part.

1(4) Where a document contains more than one inaccuracy, a penalty is payable for each inaccuracy.

Tax	Document
Petroleum revenue tax	Return under paragraph 2 of Schedule 2 to the Oil Taxation Act 1975.
Petroleum revenue tax	Statement or declaration in connection with a claim under paragraph 13A of Schedule 2 to the Oil Taxation Act 1975.
Petroleum revenue tax	Statement or declaration in connection with a claim under Schedule 5, 6, 7 or 8 to the Oil Taxation Act 1975.
Petroleum revenue tax	Statement under section 1(1)(a) of the Petroleum Revenue Tax Act 1980.
Any of the taxes mentioned above	Any document which is likely to be relied upon by HMRC to determine, without further inquiry, a question about– (a) P's liability to tax, (b) payments by P by way of or in connection with tax, (c) any other payment by P (including penalties), or (d) repayments, or any other kind of payment or credit, to P.

1(5) In relation to a return under paragraph 2 of Schedule 2 to the Oil Taxation Act 1975 or a statement or declaration under paragraph 13A of that Schedule, references in this Schedule to P include any person who, after the giving of the return for a taxable field (within the meaning of that Act), becomes the responsible person for the field (within the meaning of that Act).

Commencement Date – See headnote to Sch. 24.

History – In para. 1(2)(a) the word "a" substituted for the word "P's" and in para. (b) the words "by P" omitted by FA 2008, s. 122 and Sch. 40, para. 2(2), with effect from 1 April 2009 (SI 2009/571, art. 2).
In para. 1(3), the words "careless (within the meaning of paragraph 3) or deliberate on P's part" substituted for the words "careless or deliberate (within the meaning of paragraph 3)" by FA 2008, s. 122 and Sch. 40, para. 2(3), with effect from 1 April 2009 (SI 2009/571, art. 2).
In para. 1(4), the second entry relating to petroleum revenue tax inserted by F(No. 3)A 2010, s. 28 and Sch. 12, para. 12(2), with effect in relation to claims made on or after 1 April 2011.
In para. 1(4), in the Table, the entries for petroleum revenue tax inserted by FA 2008, s. 122 and Sch. 40, para. 2(4), with effect from 1 April 2009 (SI 2009/571, art. 2) but subject to the provisions of SI 2009/571, art. 3–5. (Note that the Table as reproduced here shows only those entries relevant to petroleum revenue tax. The Table as it relates to other taxes is reproduced in the version of para. 1 for those other taxes in the relevant division of this publication).
In para. 1(4), in the Table, in the last entry the words "Any of the taxes mentioned above" in column 1 substituted for the words "Income tax, capital gains tax, corporation tax or VAT" by FA 2008, s. 122 and Sch. 40, para. 2(6), with effect from 1 April 2009 (SI 2009/571, art. 2) but subject to the provisions of SI 2009/571, art. 3–5.
In para. 1(5), the words "or a statement or declaration under paragraph 13A of that Schedule" inserted by F(No. 3)A 2010, s. 28 and Sch. 12, para. 12(3), with effect in relation to claims made on or after 1 April 2011.
Para. 1(5) inserted by FA 2008, s. 122 and Sch. 40, para. 2(7), with effect from 1 April 2009 (SI 2009/571, art. 2).

Cross references – FA 2009, s. 94(2)(a): Publishing details of deliberate tax defaulters.

ERROR IN TAXPAYER'S DOCUMENT ATTRIBUTABLE TO ANOTHER PERSON

1A(1) A penalty is payable by a person (T) where–

(a) another person (P) gives HMRC a document of a kind listed in the Table in paragraph 1,

(b) the document contains a relevant inaccuracy, and

(c) the inaccuracy was attributable to T deliberately supplying false information to P (whether directly or indirectly), or to T deliberately withholding information from P, with the intention of the document containing the inaccuracy.

1A(2) A **"relevant inaccuracy"** is an inaccuracy which amounts to, or leads to–

(a) an understatement of a liability to tax,

(b) a false or inflated statement of a loss, or

(c) a false or inflated claim to repayment of tax.

1A(3) A penalty is payable under this paragraph in respect of an inaccuracy whether or not P is liable to a penalty under paragraph 1 in respect of the same inaccuracy.

History – Para. 1A inserted by FA 2008, s. 122 and Sch. 40, para. 3, with effect from 1 April 2009 (SI 2009/571, art. 2).

Cross references – FA 2009, s. 94(2)(b): Publishing details of deliberate tax defaulters.

UNDER-ASSESSMENT BY HMRC

2(1) A penalty is payable by a person (P) where–

(a) an assessment issued to P by HMRC understates P's liability to a relevant tax, and

(b) P has failed to take reasonable steps to notify HMRC, within the period of 30 days beginning with the date of the assessment, that it is an under-assessment.

2(2) In deciding what steps (if any) were reasonable HMRC must consider–

(a) whether P knew, or should have known, about the under-assessment, and

(b) what steps would have been reasonable to take to notify HMRC.

2(3) In sub-paragraph (1) **"relevant tax"** means any tax mentioned in the Table in paragraph 1.

2(4) In this paragraph (and in Part 2 of this Schedule so far as relating to this paragraph)–

(a) **"assessment"** includes determination, and

(b) accordingly, references to an under-assessment include an under-determination.

Commencement Date – See headnote to Sch. 24.

History – In para. 2(1)(a) the words "a relevant tax" substituted for the word "tax" by FA 2008, s. 122 and Sch. 40, para. 4(2), with effect from 1 April 2009 (SI 2009/571, art. 2).
Para. 2(3) substituted by FA 2008, s. 122 and Sch. 40, para. 4(3), with effect from 1 April 2009 (SI 2009/571, art. 2).
Para. 2(4) inserted by FA 2009. s. 109 and Sch. 57, para. 2, with effect from 21 July 2009.

DEGREES OF CULPABILITY

3(1) For the purposes of a penalty under paragraph 1, inaccuracy in a document given by P to HMRC is–

(a) **"careless"** if the inaccuracy is due to failure by P to take reasonable care,

(b) **"deliberate but not concealed"** if the inaccuracy is deliberate on P's part but P does not make arrangements to conceal it, and

(c) **"deliberate and concealed"** if the inaccuracy is deliberate on P's part and P makes arrangements to conceal it (for example, by submitting false evidence in support of an inaccurate figure).

3(2) An inaccuracy in a document given by P to HMRC, which was neither careless nor deliberate on P's part when the document was given, is to be treated as careless if P–

(a) discovered the inaccuracy at some later time, and

(b) did not take reasonable steps to inform HMRC.

Commencement Date – See headnote to Sch. 24.

History – In para. 3(1) the words "For the purposes of a penalty under paragraph 1, inaccuracy in" substituted for the words "Inaccuracy in" and the words "on P's part" inserted twice by FA 2008, s. 122 and Sch. 40, para. 5(2), with effect from 1 April 2009 (SI 2009/571, art. 2).
In para. 3(2) the words "on P's part" inserted by FA 2008, s. 122 and Sch. 40, para. 5(3), with effect from 1 April 2009 (SI 2009/571, art. 2).

ERRORS RELATED TO AVOIDANCE ARRANGEMENTS

3A(1) This paragraph applies where a document of a kind listed in the Table in paragraph 1 is given to HMRC by a person ("P") and the document contains an inaccuracy which–

(a) falls within paragraph 1(2), and

(b) arises because the document is submitted on the basis that particular avoidance arrangements (within the meaning of paragraph 3B) had an effect which in fact they did not have.

3A(2) It is to be presumed that the inaccuracy was careless, within the meaning of paragraph 3, unless–

(a) the inaccuracy was deliberate on P's part, or

(b) P satisfies HMRC or (on an appeal notified to the tribunal) the tribunal that P took reasonable care to avoid inaccuracy.

3A(3) In considering whether P took reasonable care to avoid inaccuracy, HMRC and (on an appeal notified to the tribunal) the tribunal must take no account of any evidence of any reliance by P on advice where the advice is disqualified.

3A(4) Advice is **"disqualified"** if any of the following applies–

(a) the advice was given to P by an interested person;

(b) the advice was given to P as a result of arrangements made between an interested person and the person who gave the advice;

(c) the person who gave the advice did not have appropriate expertise for giving the advice;

(d) the advice took no account of P's individual circumstances;

(e) the advice was addressed to, or given to, a person other than P;

but this is subject to sub-paragraphs (5) and (7).

3A(5) Where (but for this sub-paragraph) advice would be disqualified under any of paragraphs (a) to (c) of sub-paragraph (4), the advice is not disqualified under that paragraph if at the relevant time P–

(a) has taken reasonable steps to find out whether the advice falls within that paragraph, and

(b) reasonably believes that it does not.

3A(6) In sub-paragraph (4) **"an interested person"** means–

(a) a person, other than P, who participated in the avoidance arrangements or any transaction forming part of them, or

(b) a person who for any consideration (whether or not in money) facilitated P's entering into the avoidance arrangements.

3A(7) Where (but for this sub-paragraph) advice would be disqualified under paragraph (a) of sub-paragraph (4) because it was given by a person within sub-paragraph (6)(b), the advice is not disqualified under that paragraph if–

(a) the person giving the advice had appropriate expertise for giving it,

(b) the advice took account of P's individual circumstances, and

(c) at the time when the question whether the advice is disqualified arises–

 (i) Condition E in paragraph 3B(5) is met in relation to the avoidance arrangements, but

 (ii) none of Conditions A to D in paragraph 3B(5) is or has at any time been met in relation to them.

3A(8) If the document mentioned in sub-paragraph (1) is given to HMRC by P as a personal representative of a deceased person ("D")–

(a) sub-paragraph (4) is to be read as if–

 (i) the references in paragraphs (a) and (b) to P were to P or D;

 (ii) the reference in paragraph (d) to P were to D, and

 (iii) the reference in paragraph (e) to a person other than P were to a person who is neither P nor D,

(b) sub-paragraph (6) is to be read as if–

 (i) the reference in paragraph (a) to P were a reference to the person to whom the advice was given, and

 (ii) the reference in paragraph (b) to P were to D (or, where P also participated in the avoidance arrangements, P or D), and

(c) sub-paragraph (7) is to be read as if the reference in paragraph (b) to P were to D.

3A(9) In this paragraph–

"arrangements" includes any agreement, understanding, scheme, transaction or series of transactions (whether or not legally enforceable);

"the relevant time" means the time when the document mentioned in sub-paragraph (1) is given to HMRC;

"the tribunal" has the same meaning as in paragraph 17 (see paragraph 17(5A)).

History – Para. 3A inserted by F(No. 2)A 2017, s. 64(2), with effect in relation to any document of a kind listed in the Table in para. 1 which is given to HMRC on or after 16 November 2017 (Royal Assent) and relates to a tax period that begins on or after 6 April 2017 and ends on or after 16 November 2017 (Royal Assent).

3B(1) In paragraph 3A **"avoidance arrangements"** means, subject to sub-paragraph (3), arrangements which fall within sub-paragraph (2).

3B(2) Arrangements fall within this sub-paragraph if, having regard to all the circumstances, it would be reasonable to conclude that the obtaining of a tax advantage was the main purpose, or one of the main purposes, of the arrangements.

3B(3) Arrangements are not avoidance arrangements for the purposes of paragraph 3A if (although they fall within sub-paragraph (2))–

(a) they are arrangements which accord with established practice, and

(b) HMRC had, at the time the arrangements were entered into, indicated its acceptance of that practice.

3B(4) If, at any time, any of Conditions A to E is met in relation to particular arrangements–

(a) for the purposes of this Schedule the arrangements are to be taken to fall within (and always to have fallen within) sub-paragraph (2), and

(b) in relation to the arrangements, sub-paragraph (3) (and the reference to it in sub-paragraph (1)) are to be treated as omitted.

This does not prevent arrangements from falling within sub-paragraph (2) other than by reason of one or more of Conditions A to E being met.

3B(5) Conditions A to E are as follows–

(a) Condition A is that the arrangements are DOTAS arrangements within the meaning given by section 219(5) and (6) of FA 2014;

(b) Condition B is that the arrangements are disclosable VAT arrangements or disclosable indirect tax arrangements for the purposes of Schedule 18 to FA 2016 (see paragraphs 8A to 9A of that Schedule);

(c) Condition C is that both of the following apply–

(i) P has been given a notice under a provision mentioned in sub-paragraph (6) stating that a tax advantage arising from the arrangements is to be counteracted, and

(ii) that tax advantage has been counteracted under section 209 of FA 2013;

(d) Condition D is that a follower notice under section 204 of FA 2014 has been given to P by reference to the arrangements (and not withdrawn) and–

(i) the necessary corrective action for the purposes of section 208 of FA 2014 has been taken in respect of the denied advantage, or

(ii) the denied advantage has been counteracted otherwise than as mentioned in sub-paragraph (i);

(e) Condition E is that a tax advantage asserted by reference to the arrangements has been counteracted (by an assessment, an amendment of a return or claim, or otherwise) on the basis that an avoidance-related rule applies in relation to P's affairs.

3B(6) The provisions referred to in sub-paragraph (5)(c)(i) are–

(a) paragraph 12 of Schedule 43 to FA 2013 (general anti-abuse rule: notice of final decision);

(b) paragraph 8 or 9 of Schedule 43A to that Act (pooled or bound arrangements: notice of final decision);

(c) paragraph 8 of Schedule 43B to that Act (generic referrals: notice of final decision).

3B(7) In sub-paragraph (5)(d) the reference to giving a follower notice to P includes giving a partnership follower notice in respect of a partnership return in relation to which P is a relevant partner; and for the purposes of this sub-paragraph–

(a) **"relevant partner"** has the meaning given by paragraph 2(5) of Schedule 31 to FA 2014;

(b) a partnership follower notice is given "in respect of" the partnership return mentioned in paragraph 2(2)(a) or (b) of that Schedule.

3B(8) For the purposes of sub-paragraph (5)(d) it does not matter whether the denied advantage has been dealt with–

(a) wholly as mentioned in one or other of sub-paragraphs (i) and (ii) of sub-paragraph (5)(d), or

(b) partly as mentioned in one of those sub-paragraphs and partly as mentioned in the other;

and **"the denied advantage"** has the same meaning as in Chapter 2 of Part 4 of FA 2014 (see section 208(3) of and paragraph 4(3) of Schedule 31 to that Act).

3B(9) For the purposes of sub-paragraph (5)(e) a tax advantage has been **"asserted by reference to"** the arrangements if a return, claim or appeal has been made by P on the basis that the tax advantage results from the arrangements.

3B(10) In this paragraph–

"arrangements" has the same meaning as in paragraph 3A;

"avoidance-related rule" has the same meaning as in Part 4 of Schedule 18 to FA 2016 (see paragraph 25 of that Schedule);

a **"tax advantage"** includes–

(a) relief or increased relief from tax,

(b) repayment or increased repayment of tax,

(c) avoidance or reduction of a charge to tax or an assessment to tax,

(d) avoidance of a possible assessment to tax,

(e) deferral of a payment of tax or advancement of a repayment of tax,

(f) avoidance of an obligation to deduct or account for tax, and

(g) in relation to VAT, anything which is a tax advantage for the purposes of Schedule 18 to FA 2016 under paragraph 5 of that Schedule.

History – Para. 3B inserted by F(No. 2)A 2017, s. 64(2), with effect in relation to any document of a kind listed in the Table in para. 1 which is given to HMRC on or after 16 November 2017 (Royal Assent) and relates to a tax period that begins on or after 6 April 2017 and ends on or after 16 November 2017 (Royal Assent).

Part 2 – Amount of Penalty

STANDARD AMOUNT

4(1) This paragraph sets out the penalty payable under paragraph 1.

4(2) If the inaccuracy is in category 1, the penalty is–

(a) for careless action, 30% of the potential lost revenue,

(b) for deliberate but not concealed action, 70% of the potential lost revenue, and

(c) for deliberate and concealed action, 100% of the potential lost revenue.

4(3) If the inaccuracy is in category 2, the penalty is–

(a) for careless action, 45% of the potential lost revenue,

(b) for deliberate but not concealed action, 105% of the potential lost revenue, and

(c) for deliberate and concealed action, 150% of the potential lost revenue.

4(4) If the inaccuracy is in category 3, the penalty is–

(a) for careless action, 60% of the potential lost revenue,

(b) for deliberate but not concealed action, 140% of the potential lost revenue, and

(c) for deliberate and concealed action, 200% of the potential lost revenue.

4(5) Paragraph 4A explains the 3 categories of inaccuracy.

Commencement Date – See headnote to Sch. 24 for commencement date of former para. 4.

Prospective amendments – Para. 4(1A) inserted by FA 2015, s. 120 and Sch. 20, para. 2(2), with effect from a day to be appointed under FA 2015, s. 120(2).

In para. 4(2)(a) "37.5%" substituted for "30%", in para. 4(2)(b) "87.5%" substituted for "70%" and in para. 4(2)(c) "125%" substituted for "100%" by FA 2015, s. 120 and Sch. 20, para. 2(3), with effect from a day to be appointed under FA 2015, s. 120(2).

In para. 4(2)(a) "4" substituted for "3" by FA 2015, s. 120 and Sch. 20, para. 2(4), with effect from a day to be appointed under FA 2015, s. 120(2).

History – Para. 4, 4A, 4B, 4C and 4D substituted for former para. 4 by FA 2010, s. 35 and Sch. 10, para 2, with effect from 6 April 2011, but the substitution does not have effect in relation to documents given to HMRC and assessments issued by HMRC in relation to a tax period (as defined in para. 28(g)) commencing on or before 5 April 2011 (SI 2011/975). Former para. 4 read as follows:

"**4(1)** The penalty payable under paragraph 1 is–

(a) for careless action, 30% of the potential lost revenue,

(b) for deliberate but not concealed action, 70% of the potential lost revenue, and

(c) for deliberate and concealed action, 100% of the potential lost revenue.

4(1A) The penalty payable under paragraph 1A is 100% of the potential lost revenue.

4(2) The penalty payable under paragraph 2 is 30% of the potential lost revenue.

4(3) Paragraphs 5 to 8 define "potential lost revenue".".

Former para. 4(1A) inserted by FA 2008, s. 122 and Sch. 40, para. 6, with effect from 1 April 2009 (SI 2009/571, art. 2).

4A(1) An inaccuracy is in category 1 if–

(a) it involves a domestic matter, or

(b) it involves an offshore matter and–

(i) the territory in question is a category 1 territory, or

(ii) the tax at stake is a tax other than income tax or capital gains tax.

4A(2) An inaccuracy is in category 2 if–

(a) it involves an offshore matter or an offshore transfer,

(b) the territory in question is a category 2 territory, and

(c) the tax at stake is income tax, capital gains tax or inheritance tax.

4A(3) An inaccuracy is in category 3 if–

(a) it involves an offshore matter or an offshore transfer,

(b) the territory in question is a category 3 territory, and

(c) the tax at stake is income tax, capital gains tax or inheritance tax.

4A(4) An inaccuracy **"involves an offshore matter"** if it results in a potential loss of revenue that is charged on or by reference to–

(a) income arising from a source in a territory outside the UK,

(b) assets situated or held in a territory outside the UK,

(c) activities carried on wholly or mainly in a territory outside the UK, or

(d) anything having effect as if it were income, assets or activities of a kind described above.

4A(4A) Where the tax at stake is inheritance tax, assets are treated for the purposes of sub-paragraph (4) as situated or held in a territory outside the UK if they are so situated or held immediately after the transfer of value by reason of which inheritance tax becomes chargeable.

4A(4B) An inaccuracy **"involves an offshore transfer"** if–

(a) it does not involve an offshore matter,

(b) it is deliberate (whether or not concealed) and results in a potential loss of revenue,

(c) the tax at stake is income tax, capital gains tax or inheritance tax, and

(d) the applicable condition in paragraph 4AA is satisfied.

4A(5) An inaccuracy **"involves a domestic matter"** if it results in a potential loss of revenue and does not involve either an offshore matter or an offshore transfer.

4A(6) If a single inaccuracy is in more than one category (each referred to as a "relevant category")–

(a) it is to be treated for the purposes of this Schedule as if it were separate inaccuracies, one in each relevant category according to the matters or transfers that it involves, and

(b) the potential lost revenue is to be calculated separately in respect of each separate inaccuracy.

4A(7) **"Category 1 territory"**, **"category 2 territory"** and **"category 3 territory"** are defined in paragraph 21A.

4A(8) **"Assets"** has the meaning given in section 21(1) of TCGA 1992, but also includes sterling.

Prospective amendments – Para. 4A(1A) and (1) substituted for para. 4A(1) by FA 2015, s. 120 and Sch. 20, para. 3(2), with effect from a day to be appointed under FA 2015, s. 120(2).

In para. 4A(7) the words "Category 0 territory", "category 1" substituted for the words "Category 1" by FA 2015, s. 120 and Sch. 20, para. 3(8), with effect from a day to be appointed under FA 2015, s. 120(2).

History – In para. 4A(2)(a) the words "or an offshore transfer" inserted and in para. 4A(2)(c) the words ", capital gains tax or inheritance tax" substituted for the words "or capital gains tax" by FA 2015, s. 120 and Sch. 20, para. 3(3), with effect from 1 April 2016 (in relation to documents given to HMRC relating to a transfer of value made on or after that date for the purposes of inheritance tax; and a tax year commencing on or after 6 April 2016 for the purposes of income tax and capital gains tax) (SI 2016/456, art. 3).

In para. 4A(3)(a) the words "or an offshore transfer" inserted and in para. 4A(3)(c) the words ", capital gains tax or inheritance tax" substituted for the words "or capital gains tax" by FA 2015, s. 120 and Sch. 20, para. 3(4), with effect from 1 April 2016 (in relation to documents given to HMRC relating to a transfer of value made on or after that date for the purposes of inheritance tax; and a tax year commencing on or after 6 April 2016 for the purposes of income tax and capital gains tax) (SI 2016/456, art. 3).

Para. 4A(4A) and (4B) inserted by FA 2015, s. 120 and Sch. 20, para. 3(5), with effect from 1 April 2016 (in relation to documents given to HMRC relating to a transfer of value made on or after that date for the purposes of inheritance tax; and a tax year commencing on or after 6 April 2016 for the purposes of income tax and capital gains tax) (SI 2016/456, art. 3).

In para. 4A(5) the words "and does not involve either an offshore matter or an offshore transfer" substituted for the words "that is charged on or by reference to anything not mentioned in sub-paragraph (4)(a) to (d)" by FA 2015, s. 120 and Sch. 20, para. 3(6), with effect from 1 April 2016 (in relation to documents given to HMRC relating to a transfer of value made on or after that date for the purposes of inheritance tax; and a tax year commencing on or after 6 April 2016 for the purposes of income tax and capital gains tax) (SI 2016/456, art. 3).

In para. 4A(6)(a) the words "or transfers" inserted by FA 2015, s. 120 and Sch. 20, para. 3(7), with effect from 1 April 2016 (in relation to documents given to HMRC relating to a transfer of value made on or after that date for the purposes of inheritance tax; and a tax year commencing on or after 6 April 2016 for the purposes of income tax and capital gains tax) (SI 2016/456, art. 3).

Para. 4, 4A, 4B, 4C and 4D substituted for former para. 4 by FA 2010, s. 35 and Sch. 10, para 2, with effect from 6 April 2011, but the substitution does not have effect in relation to documents given to HMRC and assessments issued by HMRC in relation to a tax period (as defined in para. 28(g)) commencing on or before 5 April 2011 (SI 2011/975).

4AA(1) This paragraph makes provision in relation to offshore transfers.

4AA(2) Where the tax at stake is income tax, the applicable condition is satisfied if the income on or by reference to which the tax is charged, or any part of the income–

(a) is received in a territory outside the UK, or

(b) is transferred before the filing date to a territory outside the UK.

4AA(3) Where the tax at stake is capital gains tax, the applicable condition is satisfied if the proceeds of the disposal on or by reference to which the tax is charged, or any part of the proceeds–

(a) are received in a territory outside the UK, or

(b) are transferred before the filing date to a territory outside the UK.

4AA(4) Where the tax at stake is inheritance tax, the applicable condition is satisfied if–

(a) the disposition that gives rise to the transfer of value by reason of which the tax becomes chargeable involves a transfer of assets, and

(b) after that disposition but before the filing date the assets, or any part of the assets, are transferred to a territory outside the UK.

4AA(5) In the case of a transfer falling within sub-paragraph (2)(b), (3)(b) or (4)(b), references to the income, proceeds or assets transferred are to be read as including references to any assets derived from or representing the income, proceeds or assets.

4AA(6) In relation to an offshore transfer, the territory in question for the purposes of paragraph 4A is the highest category of territory by virtue of which the inaccuracy involves an offshore transfer.

4AA(7) **"Filing date"** means the date when the document containing the inaccuracy is given to HMRC.

4AA(8) **"Assets"** has the same meaning as in paragraph 4A.

History – Para. 4AA inserted by FA 2015, s. 120 and Sch. 20, para. 4, with effect from 1 April 2016 (in relation to documents given to HMRC relating to a transfer of value made on or after that date for the purposes of inheritance tax; and a tax year commencing on or after 6 April 2016 for the purposes of income tax and capital gains tax) (SI 2016/456, art. 3).

4B The penalty payable under paragraph 1A is 100% of the potential lost revenue.

History – Para. 4, 4A, 4B, 4C and 4D substituted for former para. 4 by FA 2010, s. 35 and Sch. 10, para 2, with effect from 6 April 2011, but the substitution does not have effect in relation to documents given to HMRC and assessments issued by HMRC in relation to a tax period (as defined in para. 28(g)) commencing on or before 5 April 2011 (SI 2011/975).

4C The penalty payable under paragraph 2 is 30% of the potential lost revenue.

History – Para. 4, 4A, 4B, 4C and 4D substituted for former para. 4 by FA 2010, s. 35 and Sch. 10, para 2, with effect from 6 April 2011, but the substitution does not have effect in relation to documents given to HMRC and assessments issued by HMRC in relation to a tax period (as defined in para. 28(g)) commencing on or before 5 April 2011 (SI 2011/975).

4D Paragraphs 5 to 8 define **"potential lost revenue"**.

History – Para. 4, 4A, 4B, 4C and 4D substituted for former para. 4 by FA 2010, s. 35 and Sch. 10, para. 2, with effect from 6 April 2011, but the substitution does not have effect in relation to documents given to HMRC and assessments issued by HMRC in relation to a tax period (as defined in para. 28(g)) commencing on or before 5 April 2011 (SI 2011/975).

POTENTIAL LOST REVENUE: NORMAL RULE

5 [Not relevant to petroleum revenue tax.]

POTENTIAL LOST REVENUE: MULTIPLE ERRORS

6(1) Where P is liable to a penalty under paragraph 1 in respect of more than one inaccuracy, and the calculation of potential lost revenue under paragraph 5 in respect of each inaccuracy depends on the order in which they are corrected–

(a) careless inaccuracies shall be taken to be corrected before deliberate inaccuracies, and

(b) deliberate but not concealed inaccuracies shall be taken to be corrected before deliberate and concealed inaccuracies.

6(2) In calculating potential lost revenue where P is liable to a penalty under paragraph 1 in respect of one or more understatements in one or more documents relating to a tax period, account shall be taken of any overstatement in any document given by P which relates to the same tax period.

6(3) In sub-paragraph (2)–

(a) **"understatement"** means an inaccuracy that satisfies Condition 1 of paragraph 1, and

(b) **"overstatement"** means an inaccuracy that does not satisfy that condition.

6(4) For the purposes of sub-paragraph (2) overstatements shall be set against understatements in the following order–

(a) understatements in respect of which P is not liable to a penalty,

(b) careless understatements,

(c) deliberate but not concealed understatements, and

(d) deliberate and concealed understatements.

6(5) In calculating for the purposes of a penalty under paragraph 1 potential lost revenue in respect of a document given by or on behalf of P no account shall be taken of the fact that a potential loss of revenue from P is or may be balanced by a potential over-payment by another person (except to the extent that an enactment requires or permits a person's tax liability to be adjusted by reference to P's).

Commencement Date – See headnote to Sch. 24.

History – In para. 6(1) the words "under paragraph 1" inserted by FA 2008, s. 122 and Sch. 40, para. 8(2), with effect from 1 April 2009 (SI 2009/571, art. 2).

In para. 6(2) the words "under paragraph 1" inserted by FA 2008, s. 122 and Sch. 40, para. 8(2), with effect from 1 April 2009 (SI 2009/571, art. 2).

In para. 6(5) the words "for the purposes of a penalty under paragraph 1" inserted by FA 2008, s. 122 and Sch. 40, para. 8(3), with effect from 1 April 2009 (SI 2009/571, art. 2).

POTENTIAL LOST REVENUE: LOSSES

7(1) Where an inaccuracy has the result that a loss is wrongly recorded for purposes of direct tax and the loss has been wholly used to reduce the amount due or payable in respect of tax, the potential lost revenue is calculated in accordance with paragraph 5.

7(2) Where an inaccuracy has the result that a loss is wrongly recorded for purposes of direct tax and the loss has not been wholly used to reduce the amount due or payable in respect of tax, the potential lost revenue is–

(a) the potential lost revenue calculated in accordance with paragraph 5 in respect of any part of the loss that has been used to reduce the amount due or payable in respect of tax, plus

(b) 10% of any part that has not.

7(3) Sub-paragraphs (1) and (2) apply both–

(a) to a case where no loss would have been recorded but for the inaccuracy, and

(b) to a case where a loss of a different amount would have been recorded (but in that case sub-paragraphs (1) and (2) apply only to the difference between the amount recorded and the true amount).

7(4) Where an inaccuracy has the effect of creating or increasing an aggregate loss recorded for a group of companies–

(a) the potential lost revenue shall be calculated in accordance with this paragraph, and

(b) in applying paragraph 5 in accordance with sub-paragraphs (1) and (2) above, group relief may be taken into account (despite paragraph 5(4)(a)).

7(5) The potential lost revenue in respect of a loss is nil where, because of the nature of the loss or P's circumstances, there is no reasonable prospect of the loss being used to support a claim to reduce a tax liability (of any person).

Commencement Date – See headnote to Sch. 24.

POTENTIAL LOST REVENUE: DELAYED TAX

8(1) Where an inaccuracy resulted in an amount of tax being declared later than it should have been ("the delayed tax"), the potential lost revenue is–

(a) 5% of the delayed tax for each year of the delay, or

(b) a percentage of the delayed tax, for each separate period of delay of less than a year, equating to 5% per year.

8(2) This paragraph does not apply to a case to which paragraph 7 applies.

Commencement Date – See headnote to Sch. 24.

Other material – HMRC Brief 15/11: change in HMRC's view of the operation of the delayed tax provisions for inaccuracy penalties.

REDUCTIONS FOR DISCLOSURE

9(A1) Paragraph 10 provides for reductions in penalties–

(a) under paragraph 1 where a person discloses an inaccuracy that involves a domestic matter,

(b) under paragraph 1A where a person discloses a supply of false information or withholding of information, and

(c) under paragraph 2 where a person discloses a failure to disclose an under-assessment.

9(A2) Paragraph 10A provides for reductions in penalties under paragraph 1 where a person discloses an inaccuracy that involves an offshore matter or an offshore transfer.

9(A3) Sub-paragraph (1) applies where a person discloses–

(a) an inaccuracy that involves a domestic matter,

(b) a careless inaccuracy that involves an offshore matter,

(c) a supply of false information or withholding of information, or

(d) a failure to disclose an under-assessment.

9(1) A person discloses the matter by–

(a) telling HMRC about it,

(b) giving HMRC reasonable help in quantifying the inaccuracy, the inaccuracy attributable to the supply of false information or withholding of information, or the under-assessment, and

(c) allowing HMRC access to records for the purpose of ensuring that the inaccuracy, the inaccuracy attributable to the supply of false information or withholding of information, or the under-assessment is fully corrected.

9(1A) Sub-paragraph (1B) applies where a person discloses–

(a) a deliberate inaccuracy (whether concealed or not) that involves an offshore matter, or

(b) an inaccuracy that involves an offshore transfer.

9(1B) A person discloses the inaccuracy by–

(a) telling HMRC about it,

(b) giving HMRC reasonable help in quantifying the inaccuracy,

(c) allowing HMRC access to records for the purpose of ensuring that the inaccuracy is fully corrected, and

(d) providing HMRC with additional information.

9(1C) The Treasury must make regulations setting out what is meant by **"additional information"** for the purposes of sub-paragraph (1B)(d).

9(1D) Regulations under sub-paragraph (1C) are to be made by statutory instrument.

9(1E) An instrument containing regulations under sub-paragraph (1C) is subject to annulment in pursuance of a resolution of the House of Commons.

9(2) Disclosure–

(a) is "unprompted" if made at a time when the person making it has no reason to believe that HMRC have discovered or are about to discover the inaccuracy, the supply of false information or withholding of information, or the under assessment, and

(b) otherwise, is "prompted".

9(3) In relation to disclosure **"quality"** includes timing, nature and extent.

9(4) Paragraph 4A(4) to (5) applies to determine whether an inaccuracy involves an offshore matter, an offshore transfer or a domestic matter for the purposes of this paragraph.

Commencement Date – See headnote to Sch. 24.

History – Para. 9(A1)–(A3) substituted for (A1) by FA 2016, s. 163(1) and Sch. 21, para. 2(2), with effect from 1 April 2017 for all purposes and has effect for inheritance tax purposes (in relation to transfers of value on or after that date) and for income tax and capital gains tax purposes (in relation to any tax year commencing on or after 6 April 2016) (SI 2017/259, reg. 2). Former para. 9(A1) read as follows:

"**9(A1)** Paragraph 10 provides for reductions in penalties under paragraphs 1, 1A and 2 where a person discloses an inaccuracy, a supply of false information or withholding of information, or a failure to disclose an under-assessment.".

Para. 9(A1) inserted by FA 2008, s. 122 and Sch. 40, para. 9(2), with effect from 1 April 2009 (SI 2009/571, art. 2).

In para. 9(1), the words "the matter" substituted for the words "an inaccuracy, a supply of false information or withholding of information, or a failure to disclose an under-assessment" by FA 2016, s. 163(1) and Sch. 21, para. 2(3), with effect from 1 April 2017 for all purposes and has effect for inheritance tax purposes (in relation to transfers of value on or after that date) and for income tax and capital gains tax purposes (in relation to any tax year commencing on or after 6 April 2016) (SI 2017/259, reg. 2).

In para. 9(1)(b), the words "supply of false information" substituted for "supply or false information" by FA 2009, s. 109 and Sch. 57, para. 4, with effect from 21 July 2009.

In para. 9(1)(c), the words "supply of false information" substituted for "supply or false information" by FA 2009, s. 109 and Sch. 57, para. 4, with effect from 21 July 2009.

In para. 9(1), the words ", a supply of false information or withholding of information," inserted and in para. (b) and (c) the words ", the inaccuracy attributable to the supply or false information or withholding of information, or the" substituted for the word "or" by FA 2008, s. 122 and Sch. 40, para. 9(3), with effect from 1 April 2009 (SI 2009/571, art. 2).

Para. 9(1A) to (1E) inserted by FA 2016, s. 163(1) and Sch. 21, para. 2(4), with effect from 8 March 2017 for the purpose of making the regulations and from 1 April 2017 for all purposes and has effect for inheritance tax purposes (in relation to transfers of value on or after that date) and for income tax and capital gains tax purposes (in relation to any tax year commencing on or after 6 April 2016) (SI 2017/259, reg. 2 and 3).

In para. 9(2)(a) the words ", the supply of false information or withholding of information, or the under assessment" substituted for the word "or under-assessment" by FA 2008, s. 122 and Sch. 40, para. 9(3), with effect from 1 April 2009 (SI 2009/571, art. 2).

Para. 9(4) inserted by FA 2016, s. 163(1) and Sch. 21, para. 2(5), with effect from 1 April 2017 for all purposes and has effect for inheritance tax purposes (in relation to transfers of value on or after that date) and for income tax and capital gains tax purposes (in relation to any tax year commencing on or after 6 April 2016) (SI 2017/259, reg. 2).

10(1) If a person who would otherwise be liable to a penalty of a percentage shown in column 1 of the Table (a "standard percentage") has made a disclosure, HMRC must reduce the standard percentage to one that reflects the quality of the disclosure.

10(2) But the standard percentage may not be reduced to a percentage that is below the minimum shown for it–

(a) in the case of a prompted disclosure, in column 2 of the Table, and

(b) in the case of an unprompted disclosure, in column 3 of the Table.

Standard %	*Minimum % for prompted disclosure*	*Minimum % for unprompted disclosure*
30%	15%	0%
70%	35%	20%
100%	50%	30%

Commencement Date – See headnote to Sch. 24 for commencement of former para. 10.

Prospective amendments – The Table in para. 10(2) amended by FA 2015, s. 120 and Sch. 20, para. 5, with effect from a day to be appointed under FA 2015, s. 120(2).

History – The Table in para. 10(2) substituted by FA 2016, s. 163(1) and Sch. 21, para. 3, with effect from 1 April 2017 for all purposes and has effect for inheritance tax purposes (in relation to transfers of value on or after that date) and for income tax and capital gains tax purposes (in relation to any tax year commencing on or after 6 April 2016) (SI 2017/259, reg. 2). Former table read as follows:

Standard %	*Minimum % for prompted disclosure*	*Minimum % for unprompted disclosure*
30%	15%	0%
45%	22.5%	0%
60%	30%	0%
70%	35%	20%
105%	52.5%	30%
140%	70%	40%
100%	50%	30%
150%	75%	45%
200%	100%	60%.

Para. 10 substituted by FA 2010, s. 35 and Sch. 10, para. 3, with effect from 6 April 2011, but the substitution does not have effect in relation to documents given to HMRC and assessments issued by HMRC in relation to a tax period (as defined in para. 28(g)) commencing on or before 5 April 2011 (SI 2011/975). Former para. 10 read as follows:
"**10(1)** Where a person who would otherwise be liable to a 30% penalty has made an unprompted disclosure, HMRC shall reduce the 30% to a percentage (which may be 0%) which reflects the quality of the disclosure.
10(2) Where a person who would otherwise be liable to a 30% penalty has made a prompted disclosure, HMRC shall reduce the 30% to a percentage, not below 15%, which reflects the quality of the disclosure.
10(3) Where a person who would otherwise be liable to a 70% penalty has made an unprompted disclosure, HMRC shall reduce the 70% to a percentage, not below 20%, which reflects the quality of the disclosure.
10(4) Where a person who would otherwise be liable to a 70% penalty has made a prompted disclosure, HMRC shall reduce the 70% to a percentage, not below 35%, which reflects the quality of the disclosure.
10(5) Where a person who would otherwise be liable to a 100% penalty has made an unprompted disclosure, HMRC shall reduce the 100% to a percentage, not below 30%, which reflects the quality of the disclosure.
10(6) Where a person who would otherwise be liable to a 100% penalty has made a prompted disclosure, HMRC shall reduce the 100% to a percentage, not below 50%, which reflects the quality of the disclosure.".

Cross references – FA 2009, s. 94(10)(a): no information may be published if the amount of the penalty is reduced to the full extent permitted.

10A(1) If a person who would otherwise be liable to a penalty of a percentage shown in column 1 of the Table (a "standard percentage") has made a disclosure, HMRC must reduce the standard percentage to one that reflects the quality of the disclosure.

10A(2) But the standard percentage may not be reduced to a percentage that is below the minimum shown for it–

(a) in the case of a prompted disclosure, in column 2 of the Table, and

(b) in the case of an unprompted disclosure, in column 3 of the Table.

Standard %	*Minimum % for prompted disclosure*	*Minimum % for unprompted disclosure*
30%	15%	0%
37.5%	18.75%	0%
45%	22.5%	0%
60%	30%	0%
70%	45%	30%
87.5%	53.75%	35%
100%	60%	40%
105%	62.5%	40%
125%	72.5%	50%
140%	80%	50%
150%	85%	55%
200%	110%	70%

History – Para. 10A inserted by FA 2016, s. 163(1) and Sch. 21, para. 4, with effect from 1 April 2017 for all purposes and has effect for inheritance tax purposes (in relation to transfers of value on or after that date) and for income tax and capital gains tax purposes (in relation to any tax year commencing on or after 6 April 2016) (SI 2017/259, reg. 2).

SPECIAL REDUCTION

11(1) If they think it right because of special circumstances, HMRC may reduce a penalty under paragraph 1, 1A or 2.

11(2) In sub-paragraph (1) **"special circumstances"** does not include–

(a) ability to pay, or

(b) the fact that a potential loss of revenue from one taxpayer is balanced by a potential over-payment by another.

11(3) In sub-paragraph (1) the reference to reducing a penalty includes a reference to–

(a) staying a penalty, and

(b) agreeing a compromise in relation to proceedings for a penalty.

Commencement Date – See headnote to Sch. 24.

History – In para. 11(1) ", (1A)" inserted by FA 2008, s. 122 and Sch. 40, para. 10, with effect from 1 April 2009 (SI 2009/571, art. 2).

INTERACTION WITH OTHER PENALTIES AND LATE PAYMENT SURCHARGES

History – In above heading the words "AND LATE PAYMENT SURCHARGES" inserted by FA 2008, s. 122 and Sch. 40, para. 11(4), with effect from 1 April 2009 (SI 2009/571, art. 2).

12(1) The final entry in the Table in paragraph 1 excludes a document in respect of which a penalty is payable under section 98 of TMA 1970 (special returns).

12(2) The amount of a penalty for which P is liable under paragraph 1 or 2 in respect of a document relating to a tax period shall be reduced by the amount of any other penalty incurred by P, or any surcharge for late payment of tax imposed on P, if the amount of the penalty or surcharge is determined by reference to the same tax liability.

12(2A) In sub-paragraph (2) **"any other penalty"** does not include a penalty under Part 4 of FA 2014 (penalty where corrective action not taken after follower notice etc) or Schedule 22 to FA 2016 (asset-based penalty).

12(3) In the application of section 97A of TMA 1970 (multiple penalties) no account shall be taken of a penalty under paragraph 1 or 2.

12(4) Where penalties are imposed under paragraphs 1 and 1A in respect of the same inaccuracy, the aggregate of the amounts of the penalties must not exceed the relevant percentage of the potential lost revenue.

12(5) The relevant percentage is–

(a) if the penalty imposed under paragraph 1 is for an inaccuracy in category 1, 100%,

(b) if the penalty imposed under paragraph 1 is for an inaccuracy in category 2, 150%, and

(c) if the penalty imposed under paragraph 1 is for an inaccuracy in category 3, 200%.

Commencement Date – See headnote to Sch. 24.

Prospective amendments – Para. 12(5)(za) inserted and in para. 12(5)(a) "125%" substituted for "100%" amended by FA 2015, s. 120 and Sch. 20, para. 6, with effect from a day to be appointed under FA 2015, s. 120(2).

History – In para. 12(2) the words "incurred by P, or any surcharge for late payment of tax imposed on P, if the amount of the penalty or surcharge is determined by reference to the same tax liability." substituted for the words "which P has incurred and the amount of which is determined by reference to P's tax liability for that period." by FA 2008, s. 122 and Sch. 40, para. 11(2), with effect from 1 April 2009 (SI 2009/571, art. 2).

In para. 12(2A), the words "or Schedule 22 to FA 2016 (asset-based penalty)" inserted by FA 2016, s. 165(1) and Sch. 22, para. 20(3), with effect for inheritance tax purposes, in relation to transfers of value made on or after 1 April 2017 and for income tax and capital gains tax purposes, in relation to tax years commencing on or after 6 April 2016 (SI 2017/277, reg. 2).

Para. 12(2A) inserted by FA 2014, s. 233 and Sch. 33, para. 3, with effect from 17 July 2014.

Para. 12(4) and (5) substituted for former para. 12(4) by FA 2010, s. 35 and Sch. 10, para. 4, with effect from 6 April 2011, but the substitution does not have effect in relation to documents given to HMRC and assessments issued by HMRC in relation to a tax period (as defined in para. 28(g)) commencing on or before 5 April 2011 (SI 2011/975). Former para. 12(4) read as follows:

"**12(4)** Where penalties are imposed under paragraphs 1 and 1A in respect of the same inaccuracy, the aggregate of the amounts of the penalties must not exceed 100% of the potential lost revenue.".

Former para. 12(4) inserted by FA 2008, s. 122 and Sch. 40, para. 11(2), with effect from 1 April 2009 (SI 2009/571, art. 2).

Part 3 – Procedure

ASSESSMENT

13(1) Where a person becomes liable for a penalty under paragraph 1, 1A or 2 HMRC shall–

(a) assess the penalty,

(b) notify the person, and

(c) state in the notice a tax period in respect of which the penalty is assessed (subject to sub-paragraph (1ZB)).

13(1ZA)–(1ZD) [Not relevant to petroleum revenue tax.]

13(1A) A penalty under paragraph 1, 1A or 2 must be paid before the end of the period of 30 days beginning with the day on which notification of the penalty is issued.

13(2) An assessment–

(a) shall be treated for procedural purposes in the same way as an assessment to tax (except in respect of a matter expressly provided for by this Act),

(b) may be enforced as if it were an assessment to tax, and

(c) may be combined with an assessment to tax.

13(3) An assessment of a penalty under paragraph 1 or 1A must be made before the end of the period of 12 months beginning with–

(a) the end of the appeal period for the decision correcting the inaccuracy, or

(b) if there is no assessment to the tax concerned within paragraph (a), the date on which the inaccuracy is corrected.

13(4) An assessment of a penalty under paragraph 2 must be made before the end of the period of 12 months beginning with–

(a) the end of the appeal period for the assessment of tax which corrected the understatement, or

(b) if there is no assessment within paragraph (a), the date on which the understatement is corrected.

13(5) For the purpose of sub-paragraphs (3) and (4) a reference to an appeal period is a reference to the period during which–

(a) an appeal could be brought, or

(b) an appeal that has been brought has not been determined or withdrawn.

13(6) Subject to sub-paragraphs (3) and (4), a supplementary assessment may be made in respect of a penalty if an earlier assessment operated by reference to an underestimate of potential lost revenue.

13(7) In this Part of this Schedule references to an assessment to tax, in relation to inheritance tax and stamp duty reserve tax, are to a determination.

Commencement Date – See headnote to Sch. 24.

History – In para. 13(1) the words "Where a person" substituted for the words "Where P", ", (1A)" inserted and the words "notify the person" substituted for the words "notify P" by FA 2008, s. 122 and Sch. 40, para. 12(2), with effect from 1 April 2009 (SI 2009/571, art. 2).

In para. 13(1)(c), the words "(subject to sub-paragraph (1ZB))" inserted by FA 2013, s. 230 and Sch. 50, para. 1(2), with effect in relation to any assessment of a penalty under Sch. 24 made on or after 17 July 2013 (Royal Assent).

Para. 13(1ZA)–(1ZD) inserted by FA 2013, s. 230 and Sch. 50, para. 1(3), with effect in relation to any assessment of a penalty under Sch. 24 made on or after 17 July 2013 (Royal Assent).

Para. 13(1A) inserted by FA 2008, s. 122 and Sch. 40, para. 12(3), with effect from 1 April 2009 (SI 2009/571, art. 2).

In para. 13(3) "or (1A)" inserted, the words "before the end of the" substituted for the words "within the" and the words "to the tax concerned" inserted by FA 2008, s. 122 and Sch. 40, para. 12(4), with effect from 1 April 2009 (SI 2009/571, art. 2).

In para. 13(4) the words from "before the end" to the end substituted for the words "within the period of 12 months beginning with the end of the appeal period for the assessment of tax which corrected the understatement." by FA 2008, s. 122 and Sch. 40, para. 12(5), with effect from 1 April 2009 (SI 2009/571, art. 2).

Para. 13(7) inserted by FA 2009, s. 109 and Sch. 57, para. 5, with effect from 21 July 2009.

SUSPENSION

14(1) HMRC may suspend all or part of a penalty for a careless inaccuracy under paragraph 1 by notice in writing to P.

14(2) A notice must specify–

(a) what part of the penalty is to be suspended,

(b) a period of suspension not exceeding two years, and

(c) conditions of suspension to be complied with by P.

14(3) HMRC may suspend all or part of a penalty only if compliance with a condition of suspension would help P to avoid becoming liable to further penalties under paragraph 1 for careless inaccuracy.

14(4) A condition of suspension may specify–

(a) action to be taken, and

(b) a period within which it must be taken.

14(5) On the expiry of the period of suspension–

(a) if P satisfies HMRC that the conditions of suspension have been complied with, the suspended penalty or part is cancelled, and

(b) otherwise, the suspended penalty or part becomes payable.

14(6) If, during the period of suspension of all or part of a penalty under paragraph 1, P becomes liable for another penalty under that paragraph, the suspended penalty or part becomes payable.

Commencement Date – See headnote to Sch. 24.

APPEAL

15(1) A person may appeal against a decision of HMRC that a penalty is payable by the person.

15(2) A person may appeal against a decision of HMRC as to the amount of a penalty payable by the person.

15(3) A person may appeal against a decision of HMRC not to suspend a penalty payable by the person.

15(4) A person may appeal against a decision of HMRC setting conditions of suspension of a penalty payable by the person.

Commencement Date – See headnote to Sch. 24.

History – In para. 15 the words "A person may" substituted for the words "P may" (four times) and the words "by the person" substituted for the words "by P" (four times) by FA 2008, s. 122 and Sch. 40, para. 13, with effect from 1 April 2009 (SI 2009/571, art. 2).

16(1) An appeal under this Part of this Schedule shall be treated in the same way as an appeal against an assessment to the tax concerned (including by the application of any provision about bringing the appeal by notice to HMRC, about HMRC review of the decision or about determination of the appeal by the First-tier Tribunal or Upper Tribunal).

16(2) Sub-paragraph (1) does not apply–

(a) so as to require P to pay a penalty before an appeal against the assessment of the penalty is determined, or

(b) in respect of any other matter expressly provided for by this Act.

Commencement Date – See headnote to Sch. 24.

History – Para. 16(2) substituted by FA 2009, s. 109 and Sch. 57, para. 6, with effect from 21 July 2009.
Para. 16 substituted by SI 2009/56, art. 3(1) and Sch. 1, para. 466, operative from 1 April 2009, subject to transitional and saving provisions in SI 2009/56, Sch. 3.
Para. 16 also substituted by FA 2008, s. 122 and Sch. 40, para. 14, with effect from 1 April 2009 (SI 2009/571, art. 2). The version of para. 16 inserted by FA 2008 reads as follows:
"**16(1)** An appeal is to be brought to the First-tier tribunal.
16(2) An appeal shall be treated for procedural purposes in the same way as an appeal against an assessment to the tax concerned (except in respect of a matter expressly provided for by this Act)."
Before these substitutions para. 16 read as follows:
"**16** An appeal may be brought to–
(a) the General Commissioners, in so far as the penalty relates to direct tax, or
(b) a VAT and duties tribunal, in so far as the penalty relates to VAT.".

17(1) On an appeal under paragraph 15(1) the tribunal may affirm or cancel HMRC's decision.

17(2) On an appeal under paragraph 15(2) the tribunal may–

(a) affirm HMRC's decision, or

(b) substitute for HMRC's decision another decision that HMRC had power to make.

17(3) If the tribunal substitutes its decision for HMRC's, the appellate tribunal may rely on paragraph 11–

(a) to the same extent as HMRC (which may mean applying the same percentage reduction as HMRC to a different starting point), or

(b) to a different extent, but only if the appellate tribunal thinks that HMRC's decision in respect of the application of paragraph 11 was flawed.

17(4) On an appeal under paragraph 15(3)–

(a) the tribunal may order HMRC to suspend the penalty only if it thinks that HMRC's decision not to suspend was flawed, and

(b) if the tribunal orders HMRC to suspend the penalty–

(i) P may appeal against a provision of the notice of suspension, and

(ii) the tribunal may order HMRC to amend the notice.

17(5) On an appeal under paragraph 15(4) the tribunal–

(a) may affirm the conditions of suspension, or

(b) may vary the conditions of suspension, but only if the tribunal thinks that HMRC's decision in respect of the conditions was flawed.

17(5A) In this paragraph **"tribunal"** means the First-tier Tribunal or Upper Tribunal (as appropriate by virtue of paragraph 16(1)).

17(6) In sub-paragraphs (3)(b), (4)(a) and (5)(b) **"flawed"** means flawed when considered in the light of the principles applicable in proceedings for judicial review.

17(7) Paragraph 14 (see in particular paragraph 14(3)) is subject to the possibility of an order under this paragraph.

Commencement Date – See headnote to Sch. 24.

History – In para. 17(1), (2) and (3), the word "appellate", which appeared before the word "tribunal", omitted by SI 2009/56, art. 3(1) and Sch. 1, para. 467(2), operative from 1 April 2009, subject to transitional and saving provisions in SI 2009/56, Sch. 3.
In para. 17(4)(a) and (b), the word "appellate", which appeared before the word "tribunal", omitted by SI 2009/56, art. 3(1) and Sch. 1, para. 467(3)(a) and (b)(i), operative from 1 April 2009, subject to transitional and saving provisions in SI 2009/56, Sch. 3.
In para. 17(4)(b)(i), the words "to the appellate tribunal", which appeared after the word "appeal", omitted by SI 2009/56, art. 3(1) and Sch. 1, para. 467(3)(b)(ii), operative from 1 April 2009, subject to transitional and saving provisions in SI 2009/56, Sch. 3.
In para. 17(4)(b)(ii), the word "appellate", which appeared before the word "tribunal", omitted by SI 2009/56, art. 3(1) and Sch. 1, para. 467(3)(b)(iii), operative from 1 April 2009, subject to transitional and saving provisions in SI 2009/56, Sch. 3.
In para. 17(5), the word "appellate", which appeared before the word "tribunal" in each place, omitted by SI 2009/56, art. 3(1) and Sch. 1, para. 467(4), operative from 1 April 2009, subject to transitional and saving provisions in SI 2009/56, Sch. 3.
Para. 17(5A) inserted by SI 2009/56, art. 3(1) and Sch. 1, para. 467(5), operative from 1 April 2009, subject to transitional and saving provisions in SI 2009/56, Sch. 3.

Part 4 – Miscellaneous

AGENCY

18(1) P is liable under paragraph 1(1)(a) where a document which contains a careless inaccuracy (within the meaning of paragraph 3) is given to HMRC on P's behalf.

18(2) In paragraph 2(1)(b) and (2)(a) a reference to P includes a reference to a person who acts on P's behalf in relation to tax.

18(3) Despite sub-paragraphs (1) and (2), P is not liable to a penalty under paragraph 1 or 2 in respect of anything done or omitted by P's agent where P satisfies HMRC that P took reasonable care to avoid inaccuracy (in relation to paragraph 1) or unreasonable failure (in relation to paragraph 2).

18(4) In paragraph 3(1)(a) (whether in its application to a document given by P or, by virtue of sub-paragraph (1) above, in its application to a document given on P's behalf) a reference to P includes a reference to a person who acts on P's behalf in relation to tax.

18(5) In paragraph 3(2) a reference to P includes a reference to a person who acts on P's behalf in relation to tax.

18(6) Paragraph 3A applies where a document is given to HMRC on behalf of P as it applies where a document is given to HMRC by P (and in paragraph 3B(9) the reference to P includes a person acting on behalf of P).

Commencement Date – See headnote to Sch. 24.

History – In para. 18(3) the words "under paragraph 1 or 2" inserted by FA 2008, s. 122 and Sch. 40, para. 15, with effect from 1 April 2009 (SI 2009/571, art. 2).
Para. 18(6) inserted by F(No. 2)A 2017, s. 64(3), with effect in relation to any document of a kind listed in the Table in para. 1 which is given to HMRC on or after 16 November 2017 (Royal Assent) and relates to a tax period that begins on or after 6 April 2017 and ends on or after 16 November 2017 (Royal Assent).

COMPANIES: OFFICERS' LIABILITY

19(1) Where a penalty under paragraph 1 is payable by a company for a deliberate inaccuracy which was attributable to an officer of the company, the officer is liable to pay such portion of the penalty (which may be 100%) as HMRC may specify by written notice to the officer.

(a) the officer as well as the company shall be liable to pay the penalty, and

(b) HMRC may pursue the officer for such portion of the penalty (which may be 100%) as they may specify by written notice to the officer.

19(2) Sub-paragraph (1) does not allow HMRC to recover more than 100% of a penalty.

19(3) In the application of sub-paragraph (1) to a body corporate other than a limited liability partnership **"officer"** means–

(a) a director (including a shadow director within the meaning of section 251 of the Companies Act 2006 (c. 46)),

(aa) a manager, and

(b) a secretary.

19(3A) In the application of sub-paragraph (1) to a limited liability partnership **"officer"** means a member.

19(4) In the application of sub-paragraph (1) in any other case **"officer"** means–

(a) a director,

(b) a manager,

(c) a secretary, and

(d) any other person managing or purporting to manage any of the company's affairs.

19(5) Where HMRC have specified a portion of a penalty in a notice given to an officer under sub-paragraph (1)–

(a) paragraph 11 applies to the specified portion as to a penalty,

(b) the officer must pay the specified portion before the end of the period of 30 days beginning with the day on which the notice is given,

(c) paragraph 13(2), (3) and (5) apply as if the notice were an assessment of a penalty,

(d) a further notice may be given in respect of a portion of any additional amount assessed in a supplementary assessment in respect of the penalty under paragraph 13(6),

(e) paragraphs 15(1) and (2), 16 and 17(1) to (3) and (6) apply as if HMRC had decided that a penalty of the amount of the specified portion is payable by the officer, and

(f) paragraph 21 applies as if the officer were liable to a penalty.

19(6) In this paragraph **"company"** means any body corporate or unincorporated association, but does not include a partnership, a local authority or a local authority association.

Commencement Date – See headnote to Sch. 24.

History – In para. 19(1) the words "of the company, the officer is liable to pay such portion of the penalty (which may be 100%) as HMRC" substituted for the following words by FA 2008, s. 122 and Sch. 40, para. 16(2), with effect from 1 April 2009 (SI 2009/571, art. 2).

In para. 19(3), the words "other than a limited liability partnership" inserted by FA 2009, s. 109 and Sch. 57, para. 7(2)(a), with effect from 21 July 2009.

In para. 19(3)(a), the word "or" at the end omitted by FA 2009, s. 109 and Sch. 57, para. 7(2)(b), with effect from 21 July 2009.

Para. 19(3)(aa) inserted by FA 2009, s. 109 and Sch. 57, para. 7(2)(c), with effect from 21 July 2009.

Para. 19(3A) inserted by FA 2009, s. 109 and Sch. 57, para. 7(3), with effect from 21 July 2009.

Para. 19(6) inserted by FA 2009, s. 109 and Sch. 57, para. 7(4), with effect from 21 July 2009.

Para. 19(5) substituted by FA 2008, s. 122 and Sch. 40, para. 16(3), with effect from 1 April 2009 (SI 2009/571, art. 2).

PARTNERSHIPS

20(1) This paragraph applies where P is liable to a penalty under paragraph 1 for an inaccuracy in or in connection with a partnership return.

20(2) Where the inaccuracy affects the amount of tax due or payable by a partner of P, the partner is also liable to a penalty ("a partner's penalty").

20(3) Paragraphs 4 to 13 and 19 shall apply in relation to a partner's penalty (for which purpose a reference to P shall be taken as a reference to the partner).

20(4) Potential lost revenue shall be calculated separately for the purpose of P's penalty and any partner's penalty, by reference to the proportions of any tax liability that would be borne by each partner.

20(5) Paragraph 14 shall apply jointly to P's penalty and any partner's penalties.

20(6) P may bring an appeal under paragraph 15 in respect of a partner's penalty (in addition to any appeal that P may bring in connection with the penalty for which P is liable).

Commencement Date – See headnote to Sch. 24.

DOUBLE JEOPARDY

21 A person is not liable to a penalty under paragraph 1, 1A or 2 in respect of an inaccuracy or failure in respect of which the person has been convicted of an offence.

Commencement Date – See headnote to Sch. 24.

History – In para. 21 the words "A person is" substituted for the words "P is", ", 1A" inserted and the words "the person has" substituted for the words "P has" by FA 2008, s. 122 and Sch. 40, para. 17, with effect from 1 April 2009 (SI 2009/571, art. 2).

21ZA(1) A person is not liable to a penalty under paragraph 1 in respect of an inaccuracy if–

(a) the inaccuracy involves a claim by the person to exercise or rely on a VAT right (in relation to a supply) that has been denied or refused by HMRC as mentioned in subsection (4) of section 69C of VATA 1994, and

(b) the person has been assessed to a penalty under that section (and the assessment has not been successfully appealed against or withdrawn).

21ZA(2) In sub-paragraph (1)(a) **"VAT right"** has the same meaning as in section 69C of VATA 1994.

History – Para. 21ZA inserted by F(No. 2)A 2017, s. 68(6), with effect from 16 November 2017 (Royal Assent).

Part 5 – General

CLASSIFICATION OF TERRITORIES

21A(1) A category 1 territory is a territory designated as a category 1 territory by order made by the Treasury.

21A(2) A category 2 territory is a territory that is neither–

(a) a category 1 territory, nor

(b) a category 3 territory.

21A(3) A category 3 territory is a territory designated as a category 3 territory by order made by the Treasury.

21A(4) In considering how to classify a territory for the purposes of this paragraph, the Treasury must have regard to–

(a) the existence of any arrangements between the UK and that territory for the exchange of information for tax enforcement purposes,

(b) the quality of any such arrangements (in particular, whether they provide for information to be exchanged automatically or on request),

(c) the benefit that the UK would be likely to obtain from receiving information from that territory, were such arrangements to exist with it,

(d) the existence of any other arrangements between the UK and that territory for co-operation in the area of taxation, and

(e) the quality of any such other arrangements (in particular, the extent to which the co-operation provided for in them assists or is likely to assist in the protection of revenue raised from taxation in the UK).

21A(5) An order under this paragraph is to be made by statutory instrument.

21A(6) Subject to sub-paragraph (7), an instrument containing an order under this paragraph is subject to annulment in pursuance of a resolution of the House of Commons.

21A(7) If the order is–

(a) the first order to be made under sub-paragraph (1), or

(b) the first order to be made under sub-paragraph (3),

it may not be made unless a draft of the instrument containing it has been laid before, and approved by a resolution of, the House of Commons.

21A(8) An order under this paragraph does not apply to inaccuracies in a document given to HMRC (or, in a case within paragraph 3(2), inaccuracies discovered by P) before the date on which the order comes into force.

Prospective amendments – Para. 21A(A1) inserted by FA 2015, s. 120 and Sch. 20, para. 7(2), with effect from a day to be appointed under FA 2015, s. 120(2).
Para. 21A(2) substituted by FA 2015, s. 120 and Sch. 20, para. 7(3), with effect from a day to be appointed under FA 2015, s. 120(2).
Para. 21A(7) substituted by FA 2015, s. 120 and Sch. 20, para. 7(4), with effect from a day to be appointed under FA 2015, s. 120(2).
History – In para. 21A(4)(b), the word "and" at the end omitted by FA 2012, s. 219(a), with effect from 17 July 2012.
Para. 21A(4)(d) inserted by FA 2012, s. 219(b), with effect from 17 July 2012.
Para. 21A(4)(e) inserted by FA 2012, s. 219(b), with effect from 17 July 2012.
Para. 21A and the heading before it inserted by FA 2010, s. 35 and Sch. 10, para. 5, with effect from 6 April 2011, but the insertion does not have effect in relation to documents given to HMRC and assessments issued by HMRC in relation to a tax period (as defined in para. 28(g)) commencing on or before 5 April 2011 (SI 2011/975).
Statutory instruments – SI 2011/976: made under para. 21A(1)–(4).

LOCATION OF ASSETS ETC

21B(1) The Treasury may by regulations make provision for determining for the purposes of paragraph 4A where–

(a) a source of income is located,

(b) an asset is situated or held, or

(c) activities are wholly or mainly carried on.

21B(1A) The Treasury may by regulations make provision for determining for the purposes of paragraph 4AA where–

(a) income is received or transferred,

(b) the proceeds of a disposal are received or transferred, or

(c) assets are transferred.

21B(2) Different provision may be made for different cases and for income tax, capital gains tax and inheritance tax.

21B(3) Regulations under this paragraph are to be made by statutory instrument.

21B(4) An instrument containing regulations under this paragraph is subject to annulment in pursuance of a resolution of the House of Commons.

History – Para. 21B(1A) inserted by FA 2015, s. 120 and Sch. 20, para. 8(2), with effect from 1 April 2016 (in relation to documents given to HMRC relating to a transfer of value made on or after that date for the purposes of inheritance tax; and a tax year commencing on or after 6 April 2016 for the purposes of income tax and capital gains tax) (SI 2016/456, art. 3).
In para. 21B(2) the words ", capital gains tax and inheritance tax" substituted for the words "and capital gains tax" by FA 2015, s. 120 and Sch. 20, para. 8(3), with effect from 1 April 2016 (in relation to documents given to HMRC relating to a transfer of value made on or after that date for the purposes of inheritance tax; and a tax year commencing on or after 6 April 2016 for the purposes of income tax and capital gains tax) (SI 2016/456, art. 3).
Para. 21B and the heading before it inserted by FA 2010, s. 35 and Sch. 10, para. 5, with effect from 6 April 2011, but the insertion does not have effect in relation to documents given to HMRC and assessments issued by HMRC in relation to a tax period (as defined in para. 28(g)) commencing on or before 5 April 2011 (SI 2011/975).

TREATMENT OF CERTAIN PAYMENTS ON ACCOUNT OF TAX

21C In paragraphs 1(2) and 5 references to "tax" are to be interpreted as if amounts payable under section 59AA(2) of TMA 1970 (non-resident CGT disposals: payments on account of capital gains tax) were tax.

Prospective amendments – In para. 21C, the words "and amounts payable on account of apprenticeship levy" inserted (after the words "capital gains tax)") by FA 2016, s. 113(4), with effect in accordance with regulations made under FA 2016, s. 113(16).

History – Para. 21C inserted by FA 2015, s. 37 and Sch. 7, para. 56(3), with effect in relation to disposals made on or after 6 April 2015.

INTERPRETATION

22 Paragraphs 23 to 27 apply for the construction of this Schedule.

Commencement Date – See headnote to Sch. 24.

History – In para. 22 "27" substituted for "26" by FA 2008, s. 122 and Sch. 40, para. 18, with effect from 1 April 2009 (SI 2009/571, art. 2).

23 HMRC means Her Majesty's Revenue and Customs.

Commencement Date – See headnote to Sch. 24.

23A **"Tax"**, without more, includes duty.

History – Para. 23A inserted by FA 2008, s. 122 and Sch. 40, para. 19, with effect from 1 April 2009 (SI 2009/571, art. 2).

23B **"UK"** means the United Kingdom, including the territorial sea of the United Kingdom.

History – Para. 23B inserted by FA 2010, s. 35 and Sch. 10, para. 6, with effect from 6 April 2011, but the insertion does not have effect in relation to documents given to HMRC and assessments issued by HMRC in relation to a tax period (as defined in para. 28(g)) commencing on or before 5 April 2011 (SI 2011/975).

24–27 [Not relevant to petroleum revenue tax.]

28 In this Schedule–

(a) [not relevant to petroleum revenue tax.]

(b) [not relevant to petroleum revenue tax.]

(c) [not relevant to petroleum revenue tax.]

(d) [not relevant to petroleum revenue tax.]

(da) [omitted by FA 2009, s. 109 and Sch. 57, para. 8,]

(e) [not relevant to petroleum revenue tax.]

(f) a reference to repayment of tax includes a reference to allowing a credit against tax or to a payment of a corporation tax credit,

(fa) [not relevant to petroleum revenue tax.]

(g) **"tax period"** means a tax year, accounting period or other period in respect of which tax is charged,

(h) a reference to giving a document to HMRC includes a reference to communicating information to HMRC in any form and by any method (whether by post, fax, email, telephone or otherwise),

(i) a reference to giving a document to HMRC includes a reference to making a statement or declaration in a document,

(j) a reference to making a return or doing anything in relation to a return includes a reference to amending a return or doing anything in relation to an amended return, and

(k) a reference to action includes a reference to omission.

Commencement Date – See headnote to Sch. 24.

History – Para. 28(da) omitted by FA 2009, s. 109 and Sch. 57, para. 8, with effect from 21 July 2009.

FINANCE ACT 2008

(2008 Chapter 9)

[*21st July 2008*]

ARRANGEMENT OF SECTIONS

PART 6 – OIL

PETROLEUM REVENUE TAX

102 Meaning of "participator"

102(1) In section 12 of OTA 1975 (interpretation of Part 1), the definition of "participator" is amended as follows.

102(2)–(4) [Amends OTA 1975, s. 12.]

102(5) The amendments made by this section have effect in relation to expenditure incurred after 30 June 2008.

103 Abandonment expenditure: default by participator met by former participator

103(1) [Substitutes OTA 1975, Sch. 5, para. 2A.]

103(2) The amendment made by subsection (1) has effect in relation to expenditure incurred after 30 June 2008.

105 Abandonment expenditure: former participator reimbursed by defaulter

105 [Omitted by FA 2013, s. 89 and Sch. 31, para. 12.]

History – S. 105 omitted by FA 2013, s. 89 and Sch. 31, para. 12, with effect in relation to expenditure incurred on or after 17 July 2013 (Royal Assent). Former s. 105 amended FA 1991, s. 108(1)(a), (4), (5) and (7), and substituted FA 1991, s. 108(1)(b) and (c).

106 Returns of relevant sales of oil

106(1) Section 62 of FA 1987 (returns of relevant sales of oil) is amended as follows.

106(2) [Inserts FA 1997, s. 62(3).]

106(3) [Amends FA 1997, s. 62(4).]

106(4) [Amends FA 1997, s. 62(4).]

106(5) [Amends FA 1997, s. 62(6).]

106(6) [Inserts FA 1997, s. 62(8A).]

106(7) The amendments made by this section have effect in relation to chargeable periods ending on or after 30 June 2008.

107 Elections for oil fields to become non-taxable

107(1) Section 185 of FA 1993 is amended as follows.

107(2) [Inserts FA 1993, s. 185(A1).]

107(3) [Amends FA 1993, s. 185(1).]

107(4) [Inserts FA 1993, s. 185(1ZA).]

107(5) [Inserts FA 1993, s. 185(1A)(za).]

107(6) [Inserts FA 1993, Sch. 20A.]

107(7) Part 2 of Schedule 33 contains other amendments relating to the amendments made by this section.

PART 7 – ADMINISTRATION

Chapter 1 – Information etc

NEW INFORMATION ETC POWERS

113 Information and inspection powers

113(1) Schedule 36 contains provision about the powers of officers of Revenue and Customs to obtain information and to inspect businesses.

113(2) That Schedule comes into force on such day as the Treasury may by order made by statutory instrument appoint.

113(3) An order under subsection (2) may contain transitional provision and savings.

POWER TO OBTAIN INFORMATION AND DOCUMENTS FROM THIRD PARTY

2(1) An officer of Revenue and Customs may by notice in writing require a person–

(a) to provide information, or

(b) to produce a document,

if the information or document is reasonably required by the officer for the purpose of checking the tax position of another person whose identity is known to the officer ("the taxpayer").

2(2) A third party notice must name the taxpayer to whom it relates, unless the tribunal has approved the giving of the notice and disapplied this requirement under paragraph 3.

2(3) In this Schedule, **"third party notice"** means a notice under this paragraph.

APPROVAL ETC OF TAXPAYER NOTICES AND THIRD PARTY NOTICES

3(1) An officer of Revenue and Customs may not give a third party notice without–

(a) the agreement of the taxpayer, or

(b) the approval of the tribunal.

3(2) An officer of Revenue and Customs may ask for the approval of the tribunal to the giving of any taxpayer notice or third party notice (and for the effect of obtaining such approval see paragraphs 29, 30 and 53 (appeals against notices and offence)).

3(2A) An application for approval under this paragraph may be made without notice (except as required under sub-paragraph (3)).

3(3) The tribunal may not approve the giving of a taxpayer notice or third party notice unless–

(a) an application for approval is made by, or with the agreement of, an authorised officer of Revenue and Customs,

(b) the tribunal is satisfied that, in the circumstances, the officer giving the notice is justified in doing so,

(c) the person to whom the notice is to be addressed has been told that the information or documents referred to in the notice are required and given a reasonable opportunity to make representations to an officer of Revenue and Customs,

(d) the tribunal has been given a summary of any representations made by that person, and

(e) in the case of a third party notice, the taxpayer has been given a summary of the reasons why an officer of Revenue and Customs requires the information and documents.

3(4) Paragraphs (c) to (e) of sub-paragraph (3) do not apply to the extent that the tribunal is satisfied that taking the action specified in those paragraphs might prejudice the assessment or collection of tax.

3(5) Where the tribunal approves the giving of a third party notice under this paragraph, it may also disapply the requirement to name the taxpayer in the notice if it is satisfied that the officer has reasonable grounds for believing that naming the taxpayer might seriously prejudice the assessment or collection of tax.

COPYING THIRD PARTY NOTICE TO TAXPAYER

4(1) An officer of Revenue and Customs who gives a third party notice must give a copy of the notice to the taxpayer to whom it relates, unless the tribunal has disapplied this requirement.

4(2) The tribunal may not disapply that requirement unless–

(a) an application for approval is made by, or with the agreement of, an authorised officer of Revenue and Customs, and

(b) the tribunal is satisfied that the officer has reasonable grounds for believing that giving a copy of the notice to the taxpayer might prejudice the assessment or collection of tax.

POWER TO OBTAIN INFORMATION AND DOCUMENTS ABOUT PERSONS WHOSE IDENTITY IS NOT KNOWN

5(1) An authorised officer of Revenue and Customs may by notice in writing require a person–

(a) to provide information, or

(b) to produce a document,

if the condition in sub-paragraph (2) is met.

5(2) That condition is that the information or document is reasonably required by the officer for the purpose of checking the tax position of–

(a) a person whose identity is not known to the officer, or

(b) a class of persons whose individual identities are not known to the officer.

5(3) An officer of Revenue and Customs may not give a notice under this paragraph without the approval of the tribunal.

5(3A) An application for approval under this paragraph may be made without notice.

5(4) The tribunal may not approve the giving of a notice under this paragraph unless it is satisfied that–

(a) the notice would meet the condition in sub-paragraph (2),

(b) there are reasonable grounds for believing that the person or any of the class of persons to whom the notice relates may have failed or may fail to comply with any provision of the law (including the law of a territory outside the United Kingdom) relating to tax,

(c) any such failure is likely to have led or to lead to serious prejudice to the assessment or collection of tax, and

(d) the information or document to which the notice relates is not readily available from another source.

5(5) [Omitted by FA 2011, s. 86 and Sch. 24, para. 2(4).]

History – In para. 5(2), "UK" omitted by FA 2011, s. 86 and Sch. 24, para. 2(2), with effect from 1 April 2012 in relation to tax regardless of when the tax became due (whether before, on or after that date).

In para. 5(4)(b), the words "the law (including the law of a territory outside the United Kingdom) relating to tax," substituted for the words "the Taxes Acts, or any other enactment relating to UK tax," by FA 2011, s. 86 and Sch. 24, para. 2(3)(a), with effect from 1 April 2012 in relation to tax regardless of when the tax became due (whether before, on or after that date).

In para. 5(4)(b), the words "or any other enactment relating to UK tax" substituted for the words ", VATA 1994 or any other enactment relating to value added tax charged in accordance with that Act" by FA 2009, s. 96 and Sch. 48, para. 2 with effect from 1 April 2010, by virtue of SI 2009/3054.

In para. 5(4)(c), "UK" omitted by FA 2011, s. 86 and Sch. 24, para. 2(3)(b), with effect from 1 April 2012 in relation to tax regardless of when the tax became due (whether before, on or after that date).

Para. 5(5) omitted by FA 2011, s. 86 and Sch. 24, para. 2(4), with effect from 1 April 2012 in relation to tax regardless of when the tax became due (whether before, on or after that date).

POWER TO OBTAIN INFORMATION ABOUT PERSONS WHOSE IDENTITY CAN BE ASCERTAINED

5A(1) An authorised officer of Revenue and Customs may by notice in writing require a person to provide relevant information about another person ("the taxpayer") if conditions A to D are met.

5A(2) Condition A is that the information is reasonably required by the officer for the purpose of checking the tax position of the taxpayer.

5A(3) Condition B is that–

(a) the taxpayer's identity is not known to the officer, but

(b) the officer holds information from which the taxpayer's identity can be ascertained.

5A(4) Condition C is that the officer has reason to believe that–

(a) the person will be able to ascertain the taxpayer's identity from the information held by the officer, and

(b) the person obtained relevant information about the taxpayer in the course of carrying on a business.

5A(5) Condition D is that the taxpayer's identity cannot readily be ascertained by other means from the information held by the officer.

5A(6) **"Relevant information"** means all or any of the following–

(a) name,

(b) last known address, and

(c) date of birth (in the case of an individual).

5A(7) This paragraph applies for the purpose of checking the tax position of a class of persons as for the purpose of checking the tax position of a single person (and references to "the taxpayer" are to be read accordingly).

History – Para. 5A inserted by FA 2012, s. 224(2), with effect from 17 July 2012, subject to the transitional provisions in FA 2012, s. 224(7).

NOTICES

6(1) In this Schedule, **"information notice"** means a notice under paragraph 1, 2, 5 or 5A.

6(2) An information notice may specify or describe the information or documents to be provided or produced.

12(2) This sub-paragraph is satisfied if–

(a) the occupier of the premises has been given at least 7 days' notice of the time of the inspection (whether in writing or otherwise), or

(b) the inspection is carried out by, or with the agreement of, an authorised officer of Revenue and Customs.

12(3) An officer of Revenue and Customs seeking to carry out an inspection under sub-paragraph (2)(b) must provide a notice in writing as follows–

(a) if the occupier of the premises is present at the time the inspection is to begin, the notice must be provided to the occupier,

(b) if the occupier of the premises is not present but a person who appears to the officer to be in charge of the premises is present, the notice must be provided to that person, and

(c) in any other case, the notice must be left in a prominent place on the premises.

12(4) The notice referred to in sub-paragraph (3) must state the possible consequences of obstructing the officer in the exercise of the power.

12(5) If a notice referred to in sub-paragraph (3) is given in respect of an inspection approved by the tribunal (see paragraph 13), it must state that the inspection has been so approved.

History – In para. 12(1), the words "paragraph 10, 10A or 11" substituted for the words "this Part of this Schedule" by FA 2009, s. 96 and Sch. 48, para. 4(2) with effect from 1 April 2010, by virtue of SI 2009/3054.

POWERS TO INSPECT PROPERTY FOR VALUATION ETC

12A(1) An officer of Revenue and Customs may enter and inspect premises for the purpose of valuing the premises if the valuation is reasonably required for the purpose of checking any person's position as regards income tax or corporation tax.

12A(2) An officer of Revenue and Customs may enter premises and inspect–

(a) the premises, and

(b) any other property on the premises,

for the purpose of valuing, measuring or determining the character of the premises or property.

12A(3) Sub-paragraph (2) only applies if the valuation, measurement or determination is reasonably required for the purpose of checking any person's position as regards–

(a) capital gains tax,

(b) corporation tax in respect of chargeable gains,

(c) inheritance tax,

(d) stamp duty land tax,

(e) stamp duty reserve tax, or

(f) annual tax on enveloped dwellings.

12A(4) A person who the officer considers is needed to assist with the valuation, measurement or determination may enter and inspect the premises or property with the officer.

History – Para. 12A(3)(f) (and the ", or" before it) inserted (and the "or" after (d) omitted) by FA 2013, s. 164 and Sch. 34, para. 2, with effect from 17 July 2013 (Royal Assent).
Para. 12A inserted by FA 2009, s. 96 and Sch. 48, para. 5, with effect from 1 April 2010, by virtue of SI 2009/3054.

CARRYING OUT INSPECTIONS UNDER PARAGRAPH 12A

12B(1) An inspection under paragraph 12A may be carried out only if condition A or B is satisfied.

12B(2) Condition A is that–

(a) the inspection is carried out at a time agreed to by a relevant person, and

(b) the relevant person has been given notice in writing of the agreed time of the inspection.

12B(3) **"Relevant person"** means–

(a) the occupier of the premises, or

(b) if the occupier cannot be identified or the premises are vacant, a person who controls the premises.

12B(4) Condition B is that–

(a) the inspection has been approved by the tribunal, and

(b) any relevant person specified by the tribunal has been given at least 7 days' notice in writing of the time of the inspection.

12B(5) A notice under sub-paragraph (4)(b) must state the possible consequences of obstructing the officer in the exercise of the power.

12B(6) If a notice is given under this paragraph in respect of an inspection approved by the tribunal (see paragraph 13), it must state that the inspection has been so approved.

12B(7) An officer of Revenue and Customs seeking to carry out an inspection under paragraph 12A must produce evidence of authority to carry out the inspection if asked to do so by–

(a) the occupier of the premises, or

(b) any other person who appears to the officer to be in charge of the premises or property.

History – Para. 12B inserted by FA 2009, s. 96 and Sch. 48, para. 5, with effect from 1 April 2010, by virtue of SI 2009/3054.

APPROVAL OF TRIBUNAL

13(1) An officer of Revenue and Customs may ask the tribunal to approve an inspection under this Part of this Schedule (and for the effect of obtaining such approval see paragraph 39 (penalties)).

13(1A) An application for approval under this paragraph may be made without notice (except as required under sub-paragraph (2A)).

13(2) The tribunal may not approve an inspection under paragraph 10, 10A or 11unless–

(a) an application for approval is made by, or with the agreement of, an authorised officer of Revenue and Customs, and

(b) the tribunal is satisfied that, in the circumstances, the inspection is justified.

13(2A) The tribunal may not approve an inspection under paragraph 12A unless–

(a) an application for approval is made by, or with the agreement of, an authorised officer of Revenue and Customs,

(b) the person whose tax position is the subject of the proposed inspection has been given a reasonable opportunity to make representations to the officer of Revenue and Customs about that inspection,

(c) the occupier of the premises has been given a reasonable opportunity to make such representations,

(d) the tribunal has been given a summary of any representations made, and

(e) the tribunal is satisfied that, in the circumstances, the inspection is justified.

13(2B) Paragraph (c) of sub-paragraph (2A) does not apply if the tribunal is satisfied that the occupier of the premises cannot be identified.

13(3) A decision of the tribunal under this paragraph is final (despite the provisions of sections 11 and 13 of the Tribunals, Courts and Enforcement Act 2007).

History – In para. 13(1), the words "(and for the effect of obtaining such approval see paragraph 39 (penalties))" inserted by FA 2009, s. 96 and Sch. 48, para. 6(2), with effect from 1 April 2010, by virtue of SI 2009/3054.
In para. 13(2), the words "under paragraph 10, 10A or 11" inserted by FA 2009, s. 96 and Sch. 48, para. 6(4), with effect from 1 April 2010, by virtue of SI 2009/3054.
Para. 13(2A) and (2B) inserted by FA 2009, s. 96 and Sch. 48, para. 6(5), with effect from 1 April 2010, by virtue of SI 2009/3054.

RESTRICTIONS AND SPECIAL CASES

14 This Part of this Schedule has effect subject to Parts 4 and 6 of this Schedule.

Part 3 – Further Powers

POWER TO COPY DOCUMENTS

15 Where a document (or a copy of a document) is produced to, or inspected by, an officer of Revenue and Customs, such an officer may take copies of, or make extracts from, the document.

POWER TO REMOVE DOCUMENTS

16(1) Where a document is produced to, or inspected by, an officer of Revenue and Customs, such an officer may–

(a) remove the document at a reasonable time, and

(b) retain it for a reasonable period,

if it appears to the officer to be necessary to do so.

16(2) *Where* a document is removed in accordance with sub-paragraph (1), the person who produced the document may request–

(a) a receipt for the document, and

(b) if the document is reasonably required for any purpose, a copy of the document,

and an officer of Revenue and Customs must comply with such a request without charge.

16(3) The removal of a document under this paragraph is not to be regarded as breaking any lien claimed on the document.

16(4) Where a document removed under this paragraph is lost or damaged, the Commissioners are liable to compensate the owner of the document for any expenses reasonably incurred in replacing or repairing the document.

16(5) In this paragraph, references to a document include a copy of a document.

POWER TO MARK ASSETS AND TO RECORD INFORMATION

17 The powers under Part 2 of this Schedule include–

(a) power to mark business assets, and anything containing business assets, for the purpose of indicating that they have been inspected, and

(b) power to obtain and record information (whether electronically or otherwise) relating to the premises, property, goods, assets and documents that have been inspected.

History – In para. 17(b), the words "property, goods," inserted by FA 2009, s. 96 and Sch. 48, para. 7 with effect from 1 April 2010, by virtue of SI 2009/3054.

Part 4 – Restrictions on Powers

DOCUMENTS NOT IN PERSON'S POSSESSION OR POWER

18 An information notice only requires a person to produce a document if it is in the person's possession or power.

TYPES OF INFORMATION

19(1) An information notice does not require a person to provide or produce–

(a) information that relates to the conduct of a pending appeal relating to tax or any part of a document containing such information,

(aa) information that relates to the conduct of a pending appeal under the Savings (Government Contributions) Act 2017 or any part of a document containing such information, or

(b) journalistic material (as defined in section 13 of the Police and Criminal Evidence Act 1984 (c. 60)) or information contained in such material.

19(2) An information notice does not require a person to provide or produce personal records (as defined in section 12 of the Police and Criminal Evidence Act 1984) or information contained in such records, subject to sub-paragraph (3).

19(3) An information notice may require a person–

(a) to produce documents, or copies of documents, that are personal records, omitting any information whose inclusion (whether alone or with other information) makes the original documents personal records ("personal information"), and

(b) to provide any information contained in such records that is not personal information.

Prospective amendments – Para. 19(4) and (5) inserted by Investigatory Powers Act 2016, s. 12(1) and Sch. 2, para. 10, with effect from such day as the Secretary of State may by regulations appoint. Para. 19(4) and (5) to read:

"**19(4)** An information notice does not require a telecommunications operator or postal operator to provide or produce communications data.

19(5) In sub-paragraph (4) **"communications data"**, **"postal operator"** and **"telecommunications operator"** have the same meanings as in the Investigatory Powers Act 2016 (see sections 261 and 262 of that Act)."

History – Para. 19(1)(aa) inserted by SGCA 2017, s. 3(1), with effect from 17 January 2017.

OLD DOCUMENTS

20 An *information notice* may not require a person to produce a document if the whole of the document originates more than 6 years before the date of the notice, unless the notice is given by, or with the agreement of, an authorised officer.

TAXPAYER NOTICES FOLLOWING TAX RETURN

History – In the heading to para. 21, the words "following tax return" inserted by FA 2009, s. 96 and Sch. 48, para. 8(3), with effect from 1 April 2010, by virtue of SI 2009/3054.

21(1) Where a person has made a tax return in respect of a chargeable period under section 8, 8A or 12AA of TMA 1970 (returns for purpose of income tax and capital gains tax), a taxpayer notice may not be given for the purpose of checking that person's income tax position or capital gains tax position in relation to the chargeable period.

21(2) Where a person has made a tax return in respect of a chargeable period under paragraph 3 of Schedule 18 to FA 1998 (company tax returns), a taxpayer notice may not be given for the purpose of checking that person's corporation tax position in relation to the chargeable period.

21(3) Sub-paragraphs (1) and (2) do not apply where, or to the extent that, any of conditions A to D is met.

21(4) Condition A is that a notice of enquiry has been given in respect of–

(a) the return, or

(b) a claim or election (or an amendment of a claim or election) made by the person in relation to the chargeable period in respect of the tax (or one of the taxes) to which the return relates ("relevant tax"),

and the enquiry has not been completed so far as relating to the matters to which the taxpayer notice relates.

21(5) In sub-paragraph (4), **"notice of enquiry"** means a notice under–

(a) section 9A or 12AC of, or paragraph 5 of Schedule 1A to, TMA 1970, or

(b) paragraph 24 of Schedule 18 to FA 1998.

21(6) Condition B is that, as regards the person, an officer of Revenue and Customs has reason to suspect that–

(a) an amount that ought to have been assessed to relevant tax for the chargeable period may not have been assessed,

(b) an assessment to relevant tax for the chargeable period may be or have become insufficient, or

(c) relief from relevant tax given for the chargeable period may be or have become excessive.

21(7) Condition C is that the notice is given for the purpose of obtaining any information or document that is also required for the purpose of checking the person's position as regards any tax other than income tax, capital gains tax or corporation tax.

21(8) Condition D is that the notice is given for the purpose of obtaining any information or document that is required (or also required) for the purpose of checking the person's position as regards any deductions or repayments of tax or withholding of income referred to in paragraph 64(2) or (2A) (PAYE etc).

21(9) In this paragraph, references to the person who made the return are only to that person in the capacity in which the return was made.

Prospective amendments – In para. 21(1) the words ", or regulations under paragraph 10 of Schedule A1 to," inserted after the words "12AA of" by F(No. 2)A 2017, s. 61 and Sch. 14, para. 38(2), with effect from a day to be appointed under F(No. 2)A 2017, s. 61(6).

History – In para. 21(4) the words "so far as relating to the matters to which the taxpayer notice relates" inserted by F(No. 2)A 2017, s. 63 and Sch. 15, para. 36, with effect from 16 November 2017 (Royal Assent).

In para. 21(7), the words "position as regards any tax other than income tax, capital gains tax or corporation tax" substituted for the words "VAT position" by FA 2009, s. 96 and Sch. 48, para. 8(2), with effect from 1 April 2010, by virtue of SI 2009/3054.

TAXPAYER NOTICES FOLLOWING NRCGT RETURN

21ZA [Not relevant to petroleum revenue tax.]

TAXPAYER NOTICES FOLLOWING LAND TRANSACTION RETURN

21A(1) Where a person has delivered a land transaction return under section 76 of FA 2003 (returns for purposes of stamp duty land tax) in respect of a transaction, a taxpayer notice may not be given for the purpose of checking that person's stamp duty land tax position in relation to that transaction.

21A(2) Sub-paragraph (1) does not apply where, or to the extent that, any of conditions A to C is met.

21A(3) Condition A is that a notice of enquiry has been given in respect of–

(a) the return, or

(b) a claim (or an amendment of a claim) made by the person in connection with the transaction,

and the enquiry has not been completed.

21A(4) In sub-paragraph (3) **"notice of enquiry"** means a notice under paragraph 12 of Schedule 10, or paragraph 7 of Schedule 11A, to FA 2003.

21A(5) *Condition B is that*, as regards the person, an officer of Revenue and Customs has reason to suspect that–

(a) an amount that ought to have been assessed to stamp duty land tax in respect of the transaction may not have been assessed,

(b) an assessment to stamp duty land tax in respect of the transaction may be or have become insufficient, or

(c) relief from stamp duty land tax in respect of the transaction may be or have become excessive.

21A(6) Condition C is that the notice is given for the purpose of obtaining any information or document that is also required for the purpose of checking that person's position as regards a tax other than stamp duty land tax.

History – Para. 21A inserted by FA 2009, s. 96 and Sch. 48, para. 9, with effect from 1 April 2010, by virtue of SI 2009/3054.

ANNUAL TAX ON ENVELOPED DWELLINGS: TAXPAYER NOTICES FOLLOWING RETURN

21B(1) Where a person has delivered, for a chargeable period with respect to a single-dwelling interest–

(a) an annual tax on enveloped dwellings return, or

(b) a return of the adjusted chargeable amount,

a taxpayer notice may not be given for the purpose of checking the person's annual tax on enveloped dwellings position as regards the matters dealt with in that return.

21B(2) Sub-paragraph (1) does not apply where, or to the extent that, any of conditions A to C is met.

21B(3) Condition A is that notice of enquiry has been given in respect of–

(a) the return, or

(b) a claim (or an amendment of a claim) made by the person in relation to the chargeable period,

and the enquiry has not been completed.

21B(4) In sub-paragraph (3) **"notice of enquiry"** means a notice under paragraph 8 of Schedule 33 to FA 2013 or paragraph 7 of Schedule 11A to FA 2003 (as applied by paragraphs 28(2) and 31(3) of Schedule 33 to FA 2013).

21B(5) Condition B is that, as regards the person, an officer of Revenue and Customs has reason to suspect that–

(a) an amount that ought to have been assessed to annual tax on enveloped dwellings for the chargeable period may not have been assessed,

(b) an assessment to annual tax on enveloped dwellings for the chargeable period may be or have become insufficient, or

(c) relief from annual tax on enveloped dwellings for the chargeable period may be or have become excessive.

21B(6) Condition C is that the notice is given for the purpose of obtaining any information or document that is also required for the purpose of checking that person's position as regards a tax other than annual tax on enveloped dwellings.

21B(7) In this Schedule references to a **"single-dwelling interest"** are to be read in accordance with section 108 of FA 2013.

History – Para. 21B inserted by FA 2013, s. 164 and Sch. 34, para. 3, with effect from 17 July 2013 (Royal Assent).

DECEASED PERSONS

22 An information notice given for the purpose of checking the tax position of a person who has died may not be given more than 4 years after the person's death.

PRIVILEGED COMMUNICATIONS BETWEEN PROFESSIONAL LEGAL ADVISERS AND CLIENTS

23(1) An information notice does not require a person–

(a) to provide privileged information, or

(b) to produce any part of a document that is privileged.

23(2) For the purpose of this Schedule, information or a document is privileged if it is information or a document in respect of which a claim to legal professional privilege or, (in Scotland) to confidentiality of communications as between client and professional legal adviser, could be maintained in legal proceedings.

23(3) The Commissioners may by regulations make provision for the resolution by the tribunal of disputes as to whether any information or document is privileged.

23(4) The regulations may, in particular, make provision as to–

(a) the custody of a document while its status is being decided,

(b) [omitted by SI 2009/56, art. 3(1) and Sch. 1, para. 471(6)(b).]

Cross references – SI 2009/1916: resolution of disputes as to privileged communications.

Statutory instruments – SI 2009/1916: made under para. 23(3) and (4).

AUDITORS

24(1) An information notice does not require a person who has been appointed as an auditor for the purpose of an enactment–

(a) to provide information held in connection with the performance of the person's functions under that enactment, or

(b) to produce documents which are that person's property and which were created by that person or on that person's behalf for or in connection with the performance of those functions.

24(2) Sub-paragraph (1) has effect subject to paragraph 26.

TAX ADVISERS

25(1) An information notice does not require a tax adviser–

(a) to provide information about relevant communications, or

(b) to produce documents which are the tax adviser's property and consist of relevant communications.

25(2) Sub-paragraph (1) has effect subject to paragraph 26.

25(3) In this paragraph–

"relevant communications" means communications between the tax adviser and–

(a) a person in relation to whose tax affairs he has been appointed, or

(b) any other tax adviser of such a person,

the purpose of which is the giving or obtaining of advice about any of those tax affairs, and

"tax adviser" means a person appointed to give advice about the tax affairs of another person (whether appointed directly by that person or by another tax adviser of that person).

AUDITORS AND TAX ADVISERS: SUPPLEMENTARY

26(1) Paragraphs 24(1) and 25(1) do not have effect in relation to–

(a) information explaining any information or document which the person to whom the notice is given has, as tax accountant, assisted any client in preparing for, or delivering to, HMRC, or

(b) a document which contains such information.

26(2) In the case of a notice given under paragraph 5, paragraphs 24(1) and 25(1) do not have effect in relation to–

(a) any information giving the identity or address of a person to whom the notice relates or of a person who has acted on behalf of such a person, or

(b) a document which contains such information.

26(3) Paragraphs 24(1) and 25(1) are not disapplied by sub-paragraph (1) or (2) if the information in question has already been provided, or a document containing the information in question has already been produced, to an officer of Revenue and Customs.

27(1) This paragraph applies where paragraph 24(1) or 25(1) is disapplied in relation to a document by paragraph 26(1) or (2).

27(2) An information notice that requires the document to be produced has effect as if it required any part or parts of the document containing the information mentioned in paragraph 26(1) or (2) to be produced.

CORRESPONDING RESTRICTIONS ON INSPECTION OF DOCUMENTS

History – In the heading before para. 28, the word "business" (which appeared before the word "documents") omitted by FA 2009, s. 96 and Sch. 48, para. 10, with effect from 1 April 2010, by virtue of SI 2009/3054.

28 An officer of Revenue and Customs may not inspect a document under Part 2 of this Schedule if or to the extent that, by virtue of this Part of this Schedule, an information notice given at the time of the inspection to the occupier of the premises could not require the occupier to produce the document.

History – In para. 28, the word "business" (which appeared before the word "document") omitted by FA 2009, s. 96 and Sch. 48, para. 10, with effect from 1 April 2010, by virtue of SI 2009/3054.

Part 5 – Appeals Against Information Notices

RIGHT TO APPEAL AGAINST TAXPAYER NOTICE

29(1) Where a taxpayer is given a taxpayer notice, the taxpayer may appeal against the notice or any requirement in the notice.

29(2) Sub-paragraph (1) does not apply to a requirement in a taxpayer notice to provide any information, or produce any document, that forms part of the taxpayer's statutory records.

29(3) Sub-paragraph (1) does not apply if the tribunal approved the giving of the notice in accordance with paragraph 3.

RIGHT TO APPEAL AGAINST THIRD PARTY NOTICE

30(1) Where a person is given a third party notice, the person may appeal against the notice or any requirement in the notice on the ground that it would be unduly onerous to comply with the notice or requirement.

30(2) Sub-paragraph (1) does not apply to a requirement in a third party notice to provide any information, or produce any document, that forms part of the taxpayer's statutory records.

30(3) Sub-paragraph (1) does not apply if the tribunal approved the giving of the notice in accordance with paragraph 3.

RIGHT TO APPEAL AGAINST NOTICE GIVEN UNDER PARAGRAPH 5 OR 5A

31 Where a person is given a notice under paragraph 5 or 5A, the person may appeal against the notice or any requirement in the notice on the ground that it would be unduly onerous to comply with the notice or requirement.

History – In para. 31, in the heading, the words "or 5A" inserted by FA 2012, s. 222(5), with effect from 17 July 2012, subject to the transitional provisions in FA 2012, s. 222(7).
In para. 31, the words "or 5A" inserted by FA 2012, s. 222(4), with effect from 17 July 2012, subject to the transitional provisions in FA 2012, s. 222(7).

PROCEDURE

32(1) Notice of an appeal under this Part of this Schedule must be given–

(a) in writing,

(b) before the end of the period of 30 days beginning with the date on which the information notice is given, and

(c) to the officer of Revenue and Customs by whom the information notice was given.

32(2) Notice of an appeal under this Part of this Schedule must state the grounds of appeal.

32(3) On an appeal that is notified to the tribunal, the tribunal may–

(a) confirm the information notice or a requirement in the information notice,

(b) vary the information notice or such a requirement, or

(c) set aside the information notice or such a requirement.

32(4) Where the tribunal confirms or varies the information notice or a requirement, the person to whom the information notice was given must comply with the notice or requirement–

(a) within such period as is specified by the tribunal, or

(b) if the tribunal does not specify a period, within such period as is reasonably specified in writing by an officer of Revenue and Customs following the tribunal's decision.

32(5) Notwithstanding the provisions of sections 11 and 13 of the Tribunals, Courts and Enforcement Act 2007 a decision of the tribunal on an appeal under this Part of this Schedule is final.

32(6) Subject to this paragraph, the provisions of Part 5 of TMA 1970 relating to appeals have effect in relation to appeals under this Part of this Schedule as they have effect in relation to an appeal against an assessment to income tax.

SPECIAL CASES

33 This Part of this Schedule has effect subject to Part 6 of this Schedule.

Part 6 – Special Cases

SUPPLY OF GOODS OR SERVICES ETC

34(1) This paragraph applies to a taxpayer notice or third party notice that refers only to information or documents that form part of any person's statutory records and relate to–

(a) the supply of goods or services,

(b) the acquisition of goods from another member State, or

(c) the importation of goods from a place outside the member States in the course of carrying on a business.

34(2) Paragraph 3(1) (requirement for consent to, or approval of, third party notice) does not apply to such a notice.

34(3) Where a person is given such a notice, the person may not appeal against the notice or any requirement in the notice.

34(4) Sections 5, 11 and 15 of, and Schedule 4 to, VATA 1994, and any orders made under those provisions, apply for the purposes of this paragraph as if it were part of that Act.

INVOLVED THIRD PARTIES

34A [Omitted by FA 2011, s. 86 and Sch. 23, para. 62(2).]

History – Para. 34A omitted by FA 2011, s. 86 and Sch. 23, para. 62(2), with effect from 1 April 2012, subject to transitional provisions in FA 2011, Sch. 23, para. 65. Former para. 34A read as follows:

"**34A(1)** This paragraph applies to a third party notice or a notice under paragraph 5 if–

(a) it is given to an involved third party (see paragraph 61A),

(b) it is given for the purpose of checking the position of a person, or a class of persons, as regards the relevant tax, and

(c) it refers only to relevant information or relevant documents.

34A(2) In relation to such a third party notice–

(a) paragraph 3(1) (approval etc of third party notices) does not apply,

(b) paragraph 4(1) (copying third party notices to taxpayer) does not apply, and

(c) paragraph 30(1) (appeal) has effect as if it permitted an appeal on any grounds.

34A(3) In relation to such a notice under paragraph 5–

(a) sub-paragraphs (3) and (4) of that paragraph (approval of tribunal) have effect as if they permitted, but did not require, an authorised officer of Revenue and Customs to obtain the approval of the tribunal, and

(b) paragraph 31 (appeal) has effect as if it permitted an appeal on any grounds.

34A(4) The involved third party may not appeal against a requirement in the notice to provide any information, or produce any document, that forms part of the involved third party's statutory records.

34A(5) In relation to an involved third party, **"relevant documents"**, **"relevant information"** and **"relevant tax"** are defined in paragraph 61A.".

Former para. 34A inserted by FA 2009, s. 96 and Sch. 48, para. 11, with effect from 1 April 2010, by virtue of SI 2009/3054.

REGISTERED PENSION SCHEMES ETC

34B(1) This paragraph applies to a third party notice or a notice under paragraph 5 if it refers only to information or documents that relate to any pensions matter.

34B(2) **"Pensions matter"** means any matter relating to–

(a) a registered pension scheme,

(b) an annuity purchased with sums or assets held for the purposes of a registered pension scheme or a pre-2006 pension scheme, or

(c) an employer-financed retirement benefits scheme.

34B(3) In relation to such a third party notice–

(a) paragraph 3(1) (approval etc of third party notices) does not apply,

(b) paragraph 4(1) (copying third party notices to taxpayer) does not apply, and

(c) paragraph 30(1) (appeal) has effect as if it permitted an appeal on any grounds.

34B(4) In relation to such a notice under paragraph 5–

(a) sub-paragraphs (3) and (4) of that paragraph (approval of tribunal) have effect as if they permitted, but did not require, an authorised officer of Revenue and Customs to obtain the approval of the tribunal, and

(b) paragraph 31 (appeal) has effect as if it permitted an appeal on any grounds.

34B(5) A person may not appeal against a requirement in the notice to provide any information, or produce any document, that forms part of any person's statutory records.

34B(6) Where the notice relates to a matter within sub-paragraph (2)(a) or (b), the officer of Revenue and Customs who gives the notice must give a copy of the notice to the scheme administrator in relation to the pension scheme.

(e) in paragraph 30(2) (no appeal in relation to taxpayer's statutory recor[…] the reference to the taxpayer has effect as if it were a reference to the parent undertaking or any o[…] subsidiary undertakings.

35(5) Where a notice is given under paragraph 5 to the parent undertaking fo[…] purpose of checking the tax position of one or more subsidiary undertakings whose identities are not […] to the officer giving the notice–

(a) sub-paragraphs (3) and (4) of that paragraph (approval of tribunal) have ef[…] they permitted, but did not require, the officer to obtain the approval of the tribunal, and

(b) paragraph 31 (appeal) has effect as if it permitted an appeal on any gro[…] the parent undertaking may not appeal against a requirement in the notice to produce any d[…] hat forms part of the statutory records of the parent undertaking or any of its subsidiary un[…]

35(6) [Omitted by FA 2009, s. 95 and Sch. 47, para. 10(5).]

35(7) In this paragraph, **"parent undertaking"**, **"subsidiary undertaking"** and **"unde[…]** the same meaning as in the Companies Acts (see sections 1161 and 1162 of, and Sche[…] Companies Act 2006 (c. 46)).

History – In para. 35(4A)(c), the words "paragraphs 21 and 21A" substituted for the words "paragraph 21" and the […] substituted for the word "applies" by FA 2009, s. 96 and Sch. 48, para. 12, with effect from 1 April 2010, by virtue of SI […]

CHANGE OF OWNERSHIP OF COMPANIES

36 [Not relevant to petroleum revenue tax.]

PARTNERSHIPS

37(1) This paragraph applies where a business is carried on by two or more persons in partnership.

37(2) Where, in respect of a chargeable period, any of the partners has–

(a) made a tax return under section 12AA of TMA 1970 (partnership returns), or

(b) made a claim or election in accordance with section 42(6)(b) of TMA 1970 (partnership claims and elections),

paragraph 21 (restrictions where taxpayer has made tax return) has effect as if that return, claim or election had been made by each of the partners.

37(2A) Where, in respect of a transaction entered into as purchaser by or on behalf of the members of the partnership, any of the partners has–

(a) delivered a land transaction return under Part 4 of FA 2003 (stamp duty land tax), or

(b) made a claim under that Part of that Act,

paragraph 21A (restrictions where taxpayer has delivered land transaction return) has effect as if that return had been delivered, or that claim had been made, by each of the partners.

37(2B) Where, in respect of a single-dwelling interest (see paragraph 21B(7)) to which one or more companies are or were entitled as members of a partnership, any member of the partnership has–

(a) delivered an annual tax on enveloped dwellings return or a return of the adjusted chargeable amount under Part 3 of FA 2013, or

(b) made a claim under that Part of that Act,

paragraph 21B (restrictions where taxpayer has delivered return) has effect as if that return had been delivered, or that claim had been made, by each member of the partnership.

37(3) Where a third party notice is given for the purpose of checking the tax position of more than one of the partners (in their capacity as such)–

(a) paragraph 2(2) only requires the notice to state this and give a name in which the partnership is registered for any purpose, and

(b) the references in paragraph 3(5) to naming the taxpayer are to making that statement and naming the partnership.

37(4) In relation to such a notice given to a person other than one of the partners–

(a) in paragraphs 3 and 4 (approval etc of notices and copying third party notices to taxpayer), the references to the taxpayer have effect as if they were references to at least one of the partners, and

(b) in paragraph 30(2) (no appeal in relation to taxpayer's statutory records), the reference to the taxpayer has effect as if it were a reference to any of the partners in the partnership.

37(5) In relation to a third party notice given to one of the partners for the purpose of checking the tax position of one or more of the other partners (in their capacity as such)–

(a) in paragraph 3 (approval etc of notices), sub-paragraphs (1) and (3)(e) do not apply,

(b) paragraph 4(1) (copying third party notices to taxpayer) does not apply,

CONCEALING, DESTROYING ETC DOCUMENTS FOLLOWING INFORMATION NOTICE

42(1) A person must not conceal, destroy or otherwise dispose of, or arrange for the concealment, destruction or disposal of, a document that is the subject of an information notice addressed to the person (subject to sub-paragraphs (2) and (3)).

42(2) Sub-paragraph (1) does not apply if the person acts after the document has been produced to an officer of Revenue and Customs in accordance with the information notice, unless an officer of Revenue and Customs has notified the person in writing that the document must continue to be available for inspection (and has not withdrawn the notification).

42(3) Sub-paragraph (1) does not apply, in a case to which paragraph 8(1) applies, if the person acts after the expiry of the period of 6 months beginning with the day on which a copy of the document was produced in accordance with that paragraph unless, before the expiry of that period, an officer of Revenue and Customs made a request for the original document under paragraph 8(2)(b).

CONCEALING, DESTROYING ETC DOCUMENTS FOLLOWING INFORMAL NOTIFICATION

43(1) A person must not conceal, destroy or otherwise dispose of, or arrange for the concealment, destruction or disposal of, a document if an officer of Revenue and Customs has informed the person that the document is, or is likely, to be the subject of an information notice addressed to that person (subject to sub-paragraph (2)).

43(2) Sub-paragraph (1) does not apply if the person acts after–

(a) at least 6 months has expired since the person was, or was last, so informed, or

(b) an information notice has been given to the person requiring the document to be produced.

FAILURE TO COMPLY WITH TIME LIMIT

44 A failure by a person to do anything required to be done within a limited period of time does not give rise to liability to a penalty under paragraph 39 or 40 if the person did it within such further time, if any, as an officer of Revenue and Customs may have allowed.

REASONABLE EXCUSE

45(1) Liability to a penalty under paragraph 39 or 40 does not arise if the person satisfies HMRC or (on an appeal notified to the tribunal) the tribunal that there is a reasonable excuse for the failure or the obstruction of an officer of Revenue and Customs.

45(2) For the purposes of this paragraph–

(a) an insufficiency of funds is not a reasonable excuse unless attributable to events outside the person's control,

(b) where the person relies on any other person to do anything, that is not a reasonable excuse unless the first person took reasonable care to avoid the failure or obstruction, and

(c) where the person had a reasonable excuse for the failure or obstruction but the excuse has ceased, the person is to be treated as having continued to have the excuse if the failure is remedied, or the obstruction stops, without unreasonable delay after the excuse ceased.

ASSESSMENT OF PENALTY

46(1) Where a person becomes liable for a penalty under paragraph 39, 40 or 40A,–

(a) HMRC may assess the penalty, and

(b) if they do so, they must notify the person.

46(2) An assessment of a penalty under paragraph 39 or 40 must be made within the period of 12 months beginning with the date on which the person became liable to the penalty, subject to sub-paragraph (3).

46(3) In a case involving an information notice against which a person may appeal, an assessment of a penalty under paragraph 39 or 40 must be made within the period of 12 months beginning with the latest of the following–

(a) the date on which the person became liable to the penalty,

(b) the end of the period in which notice of an appeal against the information notice could have been given, and

(c) if notice of such an appeal is given, the date on which the appeal is determined or withdrawn.

46(4) An assessment of a penalty under paragraph 40A must be made–

(a) within the period of 12 months beginning with the date on which the inaccuracy first came to the attention of an officer of Revenue and Customs, and

(b) within the period of 6 years beginning with the date on which the person became liable to the penalty.

RIGHT TO APPEAL AGAINST PENALTY

47 A person may appeal against any of the following decisions of an officer of Revenue and Customs–

(a) a decision that a penalty is payable by that person under paragraph 39, 40 or 40A, or

(b) a decision as to the amount of such a penalty.

PROCEDURE ON APPEAL AGAINST PENALTY

48(1) Notice of an appeal under paragraph 47 must be given–

(a) in writing,

(b) before the end of the period of 30 days beginning with the date on which the notification under paragraph 46 was issued, and

(c) to HMRC.

48(2) Notice of an appeal under paragraph 47 must state the grounds of appeal.

48(3) On an appeal under paragraph 47(a), that is notified to the tribunal, the tribunal may confirm or cancel the decision.

48(4) On an appeal under paragraph 47(b), the First-tier Tribunal may–

(a) confirm the decision, or

(b) substitute for the decision another decision that the officer of Revenue and Customs had power to make.

48(5) Subject to this paragraph and paragraph 49, the provisions of Part 5 of TMA 1970 relating to appeals have effect in relation to appeals under this Part of this Schedule as they have effect in relation to an appeal against an assessment to income tax.

ENFORCEMENT OF PENALTY

49(1) A penalty under paragraph 39, 40 or 40A must be paid–

(a) before the end of the period of 30 days beginning with the date on which the notification under paragraph 46 was issued, or

(b) if a notice of an appeal against the penalty is given, before the end of the period of 30 days beginning with the date on which the appeal is determined or withdrawn.

49(2) A penalty under paragraph 39, 40 or 40A may be enforced as if it were income tax charged in an assessment and due and payable.

INCREASED DAILY DEFAULT PENALTY

49A(1) This paragraph applies if–

(a) a penalty under paragraph 40 is assessed under paragraph 46 in respect of a person's failure to comply with a notice under paragraph 5,

(b) the failure continues for more than 30 days beginning with the date on which notification of that assessment was issued, and

(c) the person has been told that an application may be made under this paragraph for an increased daily penalty to be imposed.

49A(2) If this paragraph applies, an officer of Revenue and Customs may make an application to the tribunal for an increased daily penalty to be imposed on the person.

49A(3) If the tribunal decides that an increased daily penalty should be imposed, then for each applicable day (see paragraph 49B) on which the failure continues–

(a) *the person is not liable* to a penalty under paragraph 40 in respect of the failure, and

(b) the person is liable instead to a penalty under this paragraph of an amount determined by the tribunal.

49A(4) The tribunal may not determine an amount exceeding £1,000 for each applicable day.

49A(5) But subject to that, in determining the amount the tribunal must have regard to–
(a) the likely cost to the person of complying with the notice,
(b) any benefits to the person of not complying with it, and
(c) any benefits to anyone else resulting from the person's non-compliance.

49A(6) Paragraph 41 applies in relation to the sum specified in sub-paragraph (4) as it applies in relation to the sums mentioned in paragraph 41(1).

History – Para. 49A and the heading before it inserted by FA 2011, s. 86 and Sch. 24, para. 4(1), with effect in relation to failures to comply with a notice under para. 5 that begin on or after 1 April 2012.

49B(1) If a person becomes liable to a penalty under paragraph 49A, HMRC must notify the person.

49B(2) The notification must specify the day from which the increased penalty is to apply.

49B(3) That day and any subsequent day is an **"applicable day"** for the purposes of paragraph 49A(3).

History – Para. 49B inserted by FA 2011, s. 86 and Sch. 24, para. 4(1), with effect in relation to failures to comply with a notice under para. 5 that begin on or after 1 April 2012.

49C(1) A penalty under paragraph 49A must be paid before the end of the period of 30 days beginning with the date on which the notification under paragraph 49B is issued.

49C(2) A penalty under paragraph 49A may be enforced as if it were income tax charged in an assessment and due and payable.

History – Para. 49C inserted by FA 2011, s. 86 and Sch. 24, para. 4(1), with effect in relation to failures to comply with a notice under para. 5 that begin on or after 1 April 2012.

TAX-RELATED PENALTY

50(1) This paragraph applies where–
(a) a person becomes liable to a penalty under paragraph 39,
(b) the failure or obstruction continues after a penalty is imposed under that paragraph,
(c) an officer of Revenue and Customs has reason to believe that, as a result of the failure or obstruction, the amount of tax that the person has paid, or is likely to pay, is significantly less than it would otherwise have been,
(d) before the end of the period of 12 months beginning with the relevant date, an officer of Revenue and Customs makes an application to the Upper Tribunal for an additional penalty to be imposed on the person, and
(e) the Upper Tribunal decides that it is appropriate for an additional penalty to be imposed.

50(2) The person is liable to a penalty of an amount decided by the Upper Tribunal.

50(3) In deciding the amount of the penalty, the Upper Tribunal must have regard to the amount of tax which has not been, or is not likely to be, paid by the person.

50(4) Where a person becomes liable to a penalty under this paragraph, HMRC must notify the person.

50(5) Any penalty under this paragraph is in addition to the penalty or penalties under paragraph 39 or 40.

50(6) In the application of the following provisions, no account shall be taken of a penalty under this paragraph–
(a) section 97A of TMA 1970 (multiple penalties),
(b) paragraph 12(2) of Schedule 24 to FA 2007 (interaction with other penalties), and
(c) paragraph 15(1) of Schedule 41 (interaction with other penalties).

50(7) In sub-paragraph (1)(d) **"the relevant date"** means–
(a) in a case involving an information notice against which a person may appeal, the latest of–
  (i) the date on which the person became liable to the penalty under paragraph 39,
  (ii) the end of the period in which notice of an appeal against the information notice could have been given, and
  (iii) if notice of such an appeal is given, the date on which the appeal is determined or withdrawn, and
(b) in any other case, the date on which the person became liable to the penalty under paragraph 39.

History – In para. 50(1)(d), the words "(within the meaning of paragraph 46)", which appeared after the words "relevant date", omitted by FA 2011, s. 86 and Sch. 24, para. 5(2), with effect where a person becomes liable to a penalty under para. 39 on or after 19 July 2011.
Para. 50(7) inserted by FA 2011, s. 86 and Sch. 24, para. 5(3), with effect where a person becomes liable to a penalty under para. 39 on or after 19 July 2011.

ENFORCEMENT OF TAX-RELATED PENALTY

51(1) A penalty under paragraph 50 must be paid before the end of the period of 30 days beginning with the date on which the notification of the penalty is issued.

51(2) A penalty under paragraph 50 may be enforced as if it were income tax charged in an assessment and due and payable.

DOUBLE JEOPARDY

52 A person is not liable to a penalty under this Schedule in respect of anything in respect of which the person has been convicted of an offence.

Part 8 – Offence

CONCEALING ETC DOCUMENTS FOLLOWING INFORMATION NOTICE

53(1) A person is guilty of an offence (subject to sub-paragraphs (2) and (3)) if–

(a) the person is required to produce a document by an information notice,

(b) the tribunal approved the giving of the notice in accordance with paragraph 3 or 5, and

(c) the person conceals, destroys or otherwise disposes of, or arranges for the concealment, destruction or disposal of, that document.

53(2) Sub-paragraph (1) does not apply if the person acts after the document has been produced to an officer of Revenue and Customs in accordance with the information notice, unless an officer of Revenue and Customs has notified the person in writing that the document must continue to be available for inspection (and has not withdrawn the notification).

53(3) Sub-paragraph (1) does not apply, in a case to which paragraph 8(1) applies, if the person acts after the expiry of the period of 6 months beginning with the day on which a copy of the document was so produced unless, before the expiry of that period, an officer of Revenue and Customs made a request for the original document under paragraph 8(2)(b).

CONCEALING ETC DOCUMENTS FOLLOWING INFORMAL NOTIFICATION

54(1) A person is also guilty of an offence (subject to sub-paragraph (2)) if the person conceals, destroys or otherwise disposes of, or arranges for the concealment, destruction or disposal of a document after the person has been informed by an officer of Revenue and Customs in writing that–

(a) the document is, or is likely, to be the subject of an information notice addressed to that person, and

(b) an officer of Revenue and Customs intends to seek the approval of the tribunal to the giving of the notice under paragraph 3 or 5 in respect of the document.

54(2) A person is not guilty of an offence under this paragraph if the person acts after–

(a) at least 6 months has expired since the person was, or was last, so informed, or

(b) an information notice has been given to the person requiring the document to be produced.

FINE OR IMPRISONMENT

55 A person who is guilty of an offence under this Part of this Schedule is liable–

(a) on summary conviction, to a fine not exceeding the statutory maximum, and

(b) on conviction on indictment, to imprisonment for a term not exceeding 2 years or to a fine, or both.

Part 9 – Miscellaneous Provisions and Interpretation

APPLICATION OF PROVISIONS OF TMA 1970

56 Subject to the provisions of this Schedule, the following provisions of TMA 1970 apply for the purposes of this Schedule as they apply for the purposes of the Taxes Acts–

(a) section 108 (responsibility of company officers),

(b) section 114 (want of form), and

(c) section 115 (delivery and service of documents).

REGULATIONS UNDER THIS SCHEDULE

57(1) Regulations made by the Commissioners or the Treasury under this Schedule are to be made by statutory instrument.

57(2) A statutory instrument containing regulations under this Schedule is subject to annulment in pursuance of a resolution of the House of Commons.

GENERAL INTERPRETATION

58 In this Schedule–

"checking" includes carrying out an investigation or enquiry of any kind,

"the Commissioners" means the Commissioners for Her Majesty's Revenue and Customs,

"document" includes a part of a document (except where the context otherwise requires),

"enactment" includes subordinate legislation (within the meaning of the Interpretation Act 1978 (c. 30)),

"HMRC" means Her Majesty's Revenue and Customs,

"premises" includes–

(a) any building or structure,

(b) any land, and

(c) any means of transport,

"the Taxes Acts" means–

(a) TMA 1970,

(b) the Tax Acts, and

(c) TCGA 1992 and all other enactments relating to capital gains tax

"taxpayer", in relation to a taxpayer notice or a third party notice, has the meaning given in paragraph 1(1) or 2(1) (as appropriate), and

"tribunal" means the First-tier Tribunal or, where determined by or under Tribunal Procedure Rules, the Upper Tribunal.

AUTHORISED OFFICER OF REVENUE AND CUSTOMS

59 A reference in a provision of this Schedule to an authorised officer of Revenue and Customs is a reference to an officer of Revenue and Customs who is, or is a member of a class of officers who are, authorised by the Commissioners for the purpose of that provision.

BUSINESS

60(1) In this Schedule (subject to regulations under this paragraph), references to carrying on a business include–

(a) the letting of property,

(b) the activities of a charity, and

(c) the activities of a government department, a local authority, a local authority association and any other public authority.

60(2) In sub-paragraph (1)–

"local authority" has the meaning given in section 999 of ITA 2007, and

"local authority association" has the meaning given in section 1000 of that Act.

60(3) The Commissioners may by regulations provide that for the purposes of this Schedule–

(a) the carrying on of an activity specified in the regulations, or

(b) the carrying on of such an activity (or any activity) by a person specified in the regulations,

is or is not to be treated as the carrying on of a business.

History – In para. 60(2), the definition of "charity" omitted by FA 2010, s. 30 and Sch. 6, para. 24, with effect from 1 April 2012 (SI 2012/736, art. 19).

CHARGEABLE PERIOD

61 In this Schedule, **"chargeable period"** means–

(a) in relation to income tax or capital gains tax, a tax year, and

(b) in relation to corporation tax, an accounting period.

INVOLVED THIRD PARTIES

61A(1) In this Schedule, **"involved third party"** means a person described in the first column of the Table below.

61A(2) In this Schedule, in relation to an involved third party, **"relevant information"**, **"relevant document"** and **"relevant tax"** have the meaning given in the corresponding entries in that Table.

	Involved third party	*Relevant documents*	*Relevant tax*
1.	A body approved by an officer of Revenue and Customs for the purpose of paying donations within the meaning of Part 12 of ITEPA 2003 (donations to charity: payroll giving) (see section 714 of that Act)	Documents relating to the donations	Income tax
2.	A plan manager (see section 696 of ITTOIA 2005 (managers of individual investment plans))	Documents relating to the plan, including investments which are or have been held under the plan	Income tax
3.	An account provider in relation to a child trust fund (as defined in section 3 of the Child Trust Funds Act 2004)	Documents relating to the fund, including investments which are or have been held under the fund	Income tax
4.	A person who is or has been registered as a managing agent at Lloyd's in relation to a syndicate of underwriting members of Lloyd's	Documents relating to, and to the activities of, the syndicate	Income tax Capital gains tax Corporation tax
5.	A person involved (in any capacity) in an insurance business (as defined for the purposes of Part 3 of FA 1994)	Documents relating to contracts of insurance entered into in the course of the business	Insurance premium tax
6.	A person who makes arrangements for persons to enter into contracts of insurance	Documents relating to the contracts	Insurance premium tax
7.	A person who– (a) is concerned in a business that is not an insurance business (as defined for the purposes of Part 3 of FA 1994), and (b) has been involved in the entry into a contract of insurance providing cover for any matter associated with that business	Documents relating to the contracts	Insurance premium tax
8.	A person who, in relation to a charge to stamp duty reserve tax on an agreement, transfer, issue, appropriation or surrender, is an accountable person (as defined in regulation 2 of the Stamp Duty Reserve Tax Regulations S.I. 1986/1711 (as amended from time to time))	Documents relating to the agreement, transfer, issue, appropriation or surrender	Stamp duty reserve tax

	Involved third party	*Relevant documents*	*Relevant tax*
9.	A responsible person in relation to an oil field (as defined for the purposes of Part 1 of OTA 1975)	Documents relating to the oil field	Petroleum revenue tax
10.	A person involved (in any capacity) in subjecting aggregate to exploitation in the United Kingdom (as defined for the purposes of Part 2 of FA 2001) or in connected activities	Documents relating to matters in which the person is or has been involved	Aggregates levy
11.	A person involved (in any capacity) in making or receiving supplies of taxable commodities (as defined for the purposes of Schedule 6 to FA 2000) or in connected activities	Documents relating to matters in which the person is or has been involved	Climate change levy
12.	A person involved (in any capacity) with any landfill disposal (as defined for the purposes of Part 3 of FA 1996)	Documents relating to the disposal	Landfill tax.

History – In para. 61A(2), the words "“relevant information”," omitted by FA 2011, s. 86 and Sch. 23, para. 62(3)(a), with effect from 1 April 2012, subject to transitional provisions in FA 2011, Sch. 23, para. 65.
In para. 61A(2), in each entry in the second column of the Table, the word “Documents” substituted for the words “Information and documents” by FA 2011, s. 86 and Sch. 23, para. 62(3)(b), with effect from 1 April 2012, subject to transitional provisions in FA 2011, Sch. 23, para. 65.
In para. 61A(2), in the heading to the second column of the Table, the words “information and relevant” omitted by FA 2011, s. 86 and Sch. 23, para. 62(3)(c), with effect from 1 April 2012, subject to transitional provisions in FA 2011, Sch. 23, para. 65.
In para. 61A(2), in the first column of item 11 of the Table, the words “supplies of” inserted by FA 2011, s. 86 and Sch. 24, para. 6, with effect from 19 July 2011.
Para. 61A inserted by FA 2009, s. 96 and Sch. 48, para. 14 with effect from 1 April 2010, by virtue of SI 2009/3054.

STATUTORY RECORDS

62(1) For the purposes of this Schedule, information or a document forms part of a person’s statutory records if it is information or a document which the person is required to keep and preserve under or by virtue of–

(a) the Taxes Acts, or

(b) any other enactment relating to a tax,

subject to the following provisions of this paragraph.

62(2) To the extent that any information or document that is required to be kept and preserved under or by virtue of the Taxes Acts–

(a) does not relate to the carrying on of a business, and

(b) is not also required to be kept or preserved under or by virtue of any other enactment relating to a tax,

it only forms part of a person’s statutory records to the extent that the chargeable period or periods to which it relates has or have ended.

62(3) Information and documents cease to form part of a person’s statutory records when the period for which they are required to be preserved by the enactments mentioned in sub-paragraph (1) has expired.

History – *Para. 62(1)(b) substituted by FA 2009, s. 96 and Sch. 48, para. 15(2) with effect from 1 April 2010, by virtue of SI 2009/3054.*
In para. 62(2)(b), the words “any other enactment relating to a tax” substituted for the words “VATA 1994 or any other enactment relating to value added tax” by FA 2009, s. 96 and Sch. 48, para. 15(3), with effect from 1 April 2010, by virtue of SI 2009/3054.

TAX

63(1) In this Schedule, except where the context otherwise requires, **“tax”** means all or any of the following–

(a) income tax,

(b) capital gains tax,

(c) corporation tax,

(ca) diverted profits tax,
(cb) apprenticeship levy,
(d) VAT,
(e) insurance premium tax,
(f) inheritance tax,
(g) stamp duty land tax,
(h) stamp duty reserve tax,
(ha) annual tax on enveloped dwellings,
(i) petroleum revenue tax,
(j) aggregates levy,
(k) climate change levy,
(l) landfill tax, and
(m) relevant foreign tax,

and references to **"a tax"** are to be interpreted accordingly.

63(2) In this Schedule, **"corporation tax"** includes any amount assessable or chargeable as if it were corporation tax.

63(3) In this Schedule, **"VAT"** means–

(a) value added tax charged in accordance with VATA 1994,
(b) value added tax charged in accordance with the law of another member State, and
(c) amounts listed in sub-paragraph (3A).

63(3A) Those amounts are–

(a) any amount that is recoverable under paragraph 5(2) of Schedule 11 to VATA 1994 (amounts shown on invoices as VAT), and
(b) any amount that is treated as VAT by virtue of regulations under section 54 of VATA 1994 (farmers etc).

63(4) In this Schedule, **"relevant foreign tax"** means–

(a) a tax of a member State, other than the United Kingdom, which is covered by the provisions for the exchange of information under Council Directive 2011/16/EU of 15 February 2011 on administrative cooperation in the field of taxation (as amended from time to time), and
(b) any tax or duty which is imposed under the law of a territory in relation to which arrangements having effect by virtue of section 173 of FA 2006 (international tax enforcement arrangements) have been made and which is covered by the arrangements.

Prospective amendments – Para. 63(1)(ia) inserted by FA 2017, s. 56 and Sch. 11, para. 1(3), with effect from a day to be appointed under FA 2017, s. 61(1). Para. 63(1)(ia) to read as follows:

"(ia) soft drinks industry levy,"

History – Para. 63(1)(ca) inserted by FA 2015, s. 105(2), with effect in relation to accounting periods beginning on or after 1 April 2015 (subject to the provisions of FA 2015, s. 116(2)–(5)).
Para. 63(1)(cb) inserted by FA 2016, s. 112, with effect from 15 September 2016 (Royal Assent).
Para. 63(1)(e)–(m) substituted for former s. 63(1)(e) (and the "and" before it) by FA 2009, s. 96(1), with effect from 1 April 2010, by virtue of SI 2009/3054. The wording of former s. 63(1)(e) was "relevant foreign tax".
Para. 63(1)(ha) inserted by FA 2013, s. 164 and Sch. 34, para. 5, with effect from 17 July 2013 (Royal Assent).
In para. 63(4), the words "Council Directive 2011/16/EU of 15 February 2011 on administrative cooperation in the field of taxation" substituted for the words "the Directive of the Council of the European Communities dated 19 December 1977 No. 77/799/EEC" by SI 2012/3062, reg. 6(1), with effect from 1 January 2013.

TAX POSITION

64(1) In this Schedule, except as otherwise provided, **"tax position"**, in relation to a person, means the person's position as regards any tax, including the person's position as regards–

(a) past, present and future liability to pay any tax,
(b) penalties and other amounts that have been paid, or are or may be payable, by or to the person in connection with any tax, and
(c) claims, elections, applications and notices that have been or may be made or given in connection with the person's liability to pay any tax,

and references to a person's position as regards a particular tax (however expressed) are to be interpreted accordingly.

64(2) References in this Schedule to a person's tax position include, where appropriate, a reference to the person's position as regards any deductions or repayments of tax, or of sums representing tax, that the person is required to make–

(a) under PAYE regulations,

(b) under Chapter 3 of Part 3 of FA 2004 or regulations made under that Chapter (construction industry scheme), or

(c) by or under any other provision of the Taxes Acts.

64(2A) References in this Schedule to a person's tax position also include, where appropriate, a reference to the person's position as regards the withholding by the person of another person's PAYE income (as defined in section 683 of ITEPA 2003).

64(3) References in this Schedule to the tax position of a person include the tax position of–

(a) a company that has ceased to exist, and

(b) an individual who has died.

64(4) References in this Schedule to a person's tax position are to the person's tax position at any time or in relation to any period, unless otherwise stated.

Part 10 – Consequential Provisions

TMA 1970

65 TMA 1970 is amended as follows.

66 [Omits TMA 1970, s. 19A.]

67 [Omits TMA 1970, s. 20.]

68(1) Section 20B (restrictions on powers to call for documents under ss20 and 20A) is amended as follows.

68(2) [Amends heading to TMA 1970, s. 20B.]

68(3) [Amends TMA 1970, s. 20B(1).]

68(4) [Omits TMA 1970, s. 20B(1A), (1B).]

68(5) [Amends TMA 1970, s. 20B(2).]

68(6) [Amends TMA 1970, s. 20B(3).]

68(7) [Omits TMA 1970, s. 20B(4).]

68(8) [Omits TMA 1970, s. 20B(5), (6), (7).]

68(9) [Amends TMA 1970, s. 20B(8).]

68(10) [Omits TMA 1970, s. 20B(9)–(14).]

69(1) Section 20BB (falsification etc. of documents) is amended as follows.

69(2) [Amends TMA 1970, s. 20BB(1)(a).]

69(3) [Amends TMA 1970, s. 20BB(2)(b).]

70(1) Section 20D (interpretation) is amended as follows.

70(2) [Amends TMA 1970, s. 20D(2).]

70(3) [Omits TMA 1970, s. 20D(3).]

71 [Amends TMA 1970, s. 29(6)(c).]

72 [Omits TMA 1970, s. 97AA.]

73 [Amends TMA 1970, s. 98.]

74 [Omitted by FA 2009, s. 109 and Sch. 57, para. 14(a).]

75(1) Section 107A (relevant trustees) is amended as follows.

75(2) [Amends TMA 1970, s. 107A(2)(a).]

75(3) [Omits TMA 1970, s. 107A(3)(a).]

76 [Amends TMA 1970, s. 118.]

77 [Amends TMA 1970, Sch. 1A, para. 6, 6A.]

NATIONAL SAVINGS BANK ACT 1971 (C. 29)

78 [Amends National Savings Bank Act 1971, s. 12(3).]

ICTA

79 ICTA is amended as follows.

80 [Repealed by CTA 2010, s. 1181 and Sch. 3, Pt. 1.]

History – Para. 80 repealed by CTA 2010, s. 1181 and Sch. 3, Pt. 1, with effect for corporation tax purposes for accounting periods ending on or after 1 April 2010, and for income tax and capital gains tax purposes for the tax year 2010–11 and subsequent tax years.

81 [Omits ICTA 1988, s. 767C.]

82 [Repealed by CTA 2010, s. 1181 and Sch. 3, Pt. 1.]

History – Para. 82 repealed by CTA 2010, s. 1181 and Sch. 3, Pt. 1, with effect for corporation tax purposes for accounting periods ending on or after 1 April 2010, and for income tax and capital gains tax purposes for the tax year 2010–11 and subsequent tax years.

FA 1990

83 [Amends FA 1990, s. 125(1), (2), (3), (4), (6); partially omitted by SI 2009/2035, art. 2 and Sch., para. 60(p).]

SOCIAL SECURITY ADMINISTRATION ACT 1992 (C. 5)

84 [Amends SSAA 1992, s. 110ZA.]

SOCIAL SECURITY ADMINISTRATION (NORTHERN IRELAND) ACT 1992 (C. 8)

85 [Amends Social Security (Northern Ireland) Act 1992, s. 104ZA.]

F(NO. 2)A 1992

86 [Omits F(No. 2)A 1992, s. 28(1)–(3).]

VATA 1994

87 [Amends VATA 1994, Sch. 11, para. 7, 10.]

FA 1998

88 [Omits FA 1998, Sch. 18, para. 27, 28, 29.]

FA 1999

89 [Omits FA 1990, s. 13(5)(c).]

TAX CREDITS ACT 2002 (C. 21)

90 [Omits TCA 2002, s. 25(3), (4).]

FA 2006

91 [Omits FA 2006, s. 174.]

OTHER REPEALS

92 In consequence of the preceding provisions of this Part of this Schedule, omit the following–

(a) [omits FA 1988, s. 126;]

(b) [omits FA 1989, s. 142(2), (3), (4), (6)(a), (7), (8), (9) and 144(3), (5), (7);]

(c) [omits FA 1994, s. 187, 255, Sch. 19, para. 29;]

(d) [omits Civil Evidence Act 1995, Sch. 1, para. 6;]

(e) [omits FA 1996, Sch. 3, para. 17, Sch. 19, para. 3 and Sch. 22, para. 2;]

(f) [omits FA 1998, s. 115, Sch. 19, para. 36, 42(6), (7);]

(g) [omits FA 1999, s. 15(3);]

(h) [omits FA 2001, Sch. 29, para. 21, 38(4);]
(i) [omits FA 2006, s. 20;]
(j) [omits ITA 2007, Sch. 1, para. 350.]

SCHEDULE 38 – DISCLOSURE OF TAX AVOIDANCE SCHEMES

Section 116

Commencement Date – The day appointed for the amendments made by Sch. 38 is 1 November 2008, for purposes other than stamp duty land tax (SI 2008/1935).

AMENDMENTS OF PART 7 OF FA 2004

1 Part 7 of FA 2004 (disclosure of tax avoidance schemes) is amended as follows.
Commencement Date – See headnote to Sch. 38.

2(1) Section 308 (duties of promoter) is amended as follows.
2(2) [Amends FA 2004, s. 308(1).]
2(3) [Amends FA 1998, s. 308(2)(a).]
2(4) [Amends FA 1998, s. 308(3).]
2(5) [Substitutes FA 1998, s. 308(4), (4A), (4B), (4C).]
Commencement Date – See headnote to Sch. 38.

3 [Amends FA 2004, s. 311(1).]
Commencement Date – See headnote to Sch. 38.

4 [Substitutes FA 2004, s. 312, 312A.]
Commencement Date – See headnote to Sch. 38.

5(1) Section 313 (duty of parties to notifiable arrangements to notify HMRC of number etc) is amended as follows.
5(2) [Amends FA 2004, s. 313(1)(a).]
5(3) [Amends FA 2004, s. 313(3).]
5(4) [Inserts FA 2004, s. 313(5).]
Commencement Date – See headnote to Sch. 38.

6 [Substitutes FA 2004, s. 316.]
Commencement Date – See headnote to Sch. 38.

AMENDMENTS OF TMA 1970

7(1) Section 98C of TMA 1970 (penalties for failure to comply with duties under Part 7 of FA 2004) is amended as follows.
7(2) [Amends TMA 1970, s. 98C(2).]
7(3) [Amends FA 1998, s. 98C(3).]
7(4) [Amends TMA 1970, s. 98C(4).]
Commencement Date – See headnote to Sch. 38.

SCHEDULE 39 – TIME LIMITS FOR ASSESSMENTS, CLAIMS ETC.

Section 118

Commencement Date – Sch. 39, para. 66 came into effect on 1 April 2010 (SI 2009/403, art. 2 subject to transitional rules at SI 2009/403, art. 3–10).

SAVING

66 [Omitted by FA 2009, s. 99 and Sch. 51, para. 42.]
History – Para. 66 omitted by FA 2009, s. 99 and Sch. 51, para. 42, with effect from 1 April 2010 (SI 2010/867).

SCHEDULE 40 – PENALTIES: AMENDMENTS OF SCHEDULE 24 TO FA 2007

Section 122

Commencement Date – Sch. 40 came into effect on 1 April 2009 (SI 2009/571, art. 2–5 subject to transitional rules at SI 2009/571, art. 6 and 7).

1 Schedule 24 to FA 2007 (penalties for errors) is amended as follows.

2(1) Paragraph 1 (error in taxpayer's document) is amended as follows.

2(2) [Amends FA 2007, Sch. 24, para. 1(2).]

2(3) [Amends FA 2007, Sch. 24, para. 1(3).]

2(4) [Amends FA 2007, Sch. 24, para. 1, Table.]

2(5) [Amends FA 2007, Sch. 24, para. 1, Table.]

2(6) [Amends FA 2007, Sch. 24, para. 1, Table.]

2(7) [Inserts FA 2007, Sch. 24, para. 1(5).]

3 [Inserts FA 2007, Sch. 24, para. 1A.]

4(1) Paragraph 2 (under-assessment by HMRC) is amended as follows.

4(2) [Amends FA 2007, Sch. 24, para. 2(1).]

4(3) [Substitutes FA 2007, Sch. 24, para. 1(3).]

5(1) Paragraph 3 (degrees of culpability) is amended as follows.

5(2) [Amends FA 2007, Sch. 24, para. 3(1).]

5(3) [Amends FA 2007, Sch. 24, para. 3(2).]

6 [Inserts FA 2007, Sch. 24, para. 4(1A).]

7 [Amends FA 2007, Sch. 24, para. 5(1).]

8(1) Paragraph 6 (potential lost revenue: multiple errors) is amended as follows.

8(2) [Amends FA 2007, Sch. 24, para. 6(1), (2).]

8(3) [Amends FA 2007, Sch. 24, para. 6(5).]

9(1) Paragraph 9 (reductions for disclosure) is amended as follows.

9(2) [Inserts FA 2007, Sch. 24, para. 9(A1).]

9(3) [Amends FA 2007, Sch. 24, para. 9(1).]

9(4) [Amends FA 2007, Sch. 24, para. 9(2)(a).]

10 [Amends FA 2007, Sch. 24, para. 11(1).]

11(1) Paragraph 12 (interaction with other penalties) is amended as follows.

11(2) [Amends FA 2007, Sch. 24, para. 12(2).]

11(3) [Inserts FA 2007, Sch. 24, para. 12(4).]

11(4) [Amends heading before FA 2007, Sch. 24, para. 12.]

12(1) Paragraph 13 (assessment) is amended as follows.

12(2) [Amends FA 2007, Sch. 24, para. 13(1).]

12(3) [Inserts FA 2007, Sch. 24, para. 13(1A).]

12(4) [Amends FA 2007, Sch. 24, para. 13(3).]

12(5) [Amends FA 2007, Sch. 24, para. 13(4).]

13 [Amends FA 2007, Sch. 24, para. 15.]

14 [Omitted by SI 2009/56, art. 3(1) and Sch. 1, para. 472.]

History – Para. 14 omitted by SI 2009/56, art. 3(1) and Sch. 1, para. 472, operative from 1 April 2009, subject to transitional and saving provisions in SI 2009/56, Sch. 3. Former para. 14 read as follows:

"**14** For paragraph 16 substitute–

"**16(1)** An appeal is to be brought to the First-tier tribunal.

16(2) An appeal shall be treated for procedural purposes in the same way as an appeal against an assessment to the tax concerned (except in respect of a matter expressly provided for by this Act).""".

15 [Amends FA 2007, Sch. 24, para. 18(3).]

16(1) Paragraph 19 (companies: officers' liability) is amended as follows.

16(2) [Amends FA 2007, Sch. 24, *para. 19(1).]*

16(3) [Substitutes FA 2007, Sch. 24, para. 19(5).]

17 [Amends FA 2007, Sch. 24, para. 21.]

18 [Amends FA 2007, Sch. 24, para. 22.]

19 [Inserts FA 2007, Sch. 24, para. 23.]

20(1) Paragraph 28 (interpretation) is amended as follows.

20(2) [Amends FA 2007, Sch. 24, para. 28(c).]

20(3) [Omitted by FA 2009, s. 109 and Sch. 57, para. 14(b).]

20(4) [Amends FA 2007, Sch. 24, para. 28(f).]

20(5) [Inserts FA 2007, Sch. 24, para. 28(fa).]

History – Para. 20(3) omitted by FA 2009, s. 109 and Sch. 57, para. 14(b), with effect from 21 July 2009.

21 In consequence of this Schedule the following provisions are omitted–

(a) [omits OTA 1975, Sch. 2, para. 8 and 9,]

(b) [omits words in PRTA 1980, s. 1(3B),]

(c) [not relevant to petroleum revenue tax,]

(d) [not relevant to petroleum revenue tax,]

(e) [not relevant to petroleum revenue tax,]

(f) [not relevant to petroleum revenue tax,]

(g) [not relevant to petroleum revenue tax,]

(h) [not relevant to petroleum revenue tax,]

(i) [not relevant to petroleum revenue tax,]

(j) [not relevant to petroleum revenue tax,]

(k) [not relevant to petroleum revenue tax,]

(l) [not relevant to petroleum revenue tax.]

SCHEDULE 44 – CERTIFICATES OF DEBT: CONSEQUENTIAL PROVISION

Section 138

OTA 1975

2 [Amends OTA 1975, Sch. 2, para. 1(1), Table.]

FINANCE ACT 2009

(2009 Chapter 10)

[*21st July 2009*]

ARRANGEMENT OF SECTIONS

PART 6 – OIL

85 Blended oil

85 Schedule 39 contains provision about the treatment of blended oil for the purposes of petroleum revenue tax.

87 Oil assets put to other uses

87 Schedule 41 contains provision about oil production assets put to certain other uses.

88 Former licensees and former oil fields

88 Schedule 42 contains provision about the treatment of certain former licensees and former oil fields for the purposes of petroleum revenue tax.

89 Abolition of provisional expenditure allowance

89 Schedule 43 contains provision abolishing provisional expenditure allowance.

91 Miscellaneous amendments

91 Schedule 45 contains miscellaneous amendments relating to oil taxation.

PART 7 – ADMINISTRATION

STANDARDS AND VALUES

94 Publishing details of deliberate tax defaulters

94(1) The Commissioners may publish information about any person if–

(a) in consequence of an investigation conducted by the Commissioners, one or more relevant tax penalties is found to have been incurred by the person, and

(b) the potential lost revenue in relation to the penalty (or the aggregate of the potential lost revenue in relation to each of the penalties) exceeds £25,000.

94(2) A **"relevant tax penalty"** is–

(a) a penalty under paragraph 1 of Schedule 24 to FA 2007 (inaccuracy in taxpayer's document) in respect of a deliberate inaccuracy on the part of the person,

(b) a penalty under paragraph 1A of that Schedule (inaccuracy in taxpayer's document attributable to deliberate supply of false information or deliberate withholding of information by person),

(c) a penalty under paragraph 1 of Schedule 41 to FA 2008 (failure to notify) in respect of a deliberate failure on the part of the person, or

(d) a penalty under paragraph 2 (unauthorised VAT invoice), 3 (putting product to use attracting higher duty etc) or 4 (handling goods subject to unpaid excise duty) of that Schedule in respect of deliberate action by the person.

94(3) **"Potential lost revenue"**, in relation to a penalty, has the meaning given by–

(a) paragraphs 5 to 8 of Schedule 24 to FA 2007, or

(b) paragraphs 7 to 11 of Schedule 41 to FA 2008,

in relation to the inaccuracy, failure or action to which the penalty relates.

94(4) The information that may be published is–

(a) the person's name (including any trading name, previous name or pseudonym),

(b) the person's address (or registered office),

(c) the nature of any business carried on by the person,

(d) the amount of the penalty or penalties and the potential lost revenue in relation to the penalty (or the aggregate of the potential lost revenue in relation to each of the penalties),

(e) the periods or times to which the inaccuracy, failure or action giving rise to the penalty (or any of the penalties) relates, and

(f) any such other information as the Commissioners consider it appropriate to publish in order to make clear the person's identity.

94(4A) Subsection (4B) applies where a person who is a body corporate or a partnership has incurred–

(a) a penalty under paragraph 1 of Schedule 24 to FA 2007 in respect of a deliberate inaccuracy which involves an offshore matter or an offshore transfer (within the meaning of paragraph 4A of that Schedule), or

PRT Statutes

(b) a penalty under paragraph 1 of Schedule 41 to FA 2008 in respect of a deliberate failure which involves an offshore matter or an offshore transfer (within the meaning of paragraph 6A of that Schedule).

94(4B) The Commissioners may publish the information mentioned in subsection (4) in respect of any individual who–

(a) controls the body corporate or the partnership (within the meaning of section 1124 of CTA 2010), and

(b) has obtained a tax advantage as a result of the inaccuracy or failure.

94(4C) Subsection (4D) applies where one or more trustees of a settlement have incurred–

(a) a penalty under paragraph 1 of Schedule 24 to FA 2007 in respect of a deliberate inaccuracy which involves an offshore matter or an offshore transfer (within the meaning of paragraph 4A of that Schedule), or

(b) a penalty under paragraph 1 of Schedule 41 to FA 2008 in respect of a deliberate failure which involves an offshore matter or an offshore transfer (within the meaning of paragraph 6A of that Schedule).

94(4D) The Commissioners may publish the information mentioned in subsection (4) in respect of any trustee who is an individual and who has obtained a tax advantage as a result of the inaccuracy or failure.

94(5) The information may be published in any manner that the Commissioners consider appropriate.

94(6) Before publishing any information about a person under subsection (1), the Commissioners–

(a) must inform the person that they are considering doing so, and

(b) afford the person reasonable opportunity to make representations about whether it should be published.

94(6A) Before publishing any information about an individual under subsection (4B) or (4D), the Commissioners–

(a) must inform the individual that they are considering doing so, and

(b) afford the individual reasonable opportunity to make representations about whether it should be published.

94(7) No information may be published before the day when the penalty becomes final (or the latest day when any of the penalties becomes final).

94(8) No information may be published for the first time after the end of the period of one year beginning with that day (or that latest day).

94(9) No information may be published (or continue to be published) after the end of the period of one year beginning with the day on which it is first published.

94(10) No information may be published if the amount of the penalty is reduced under–

(a) paragraph 10 of Schedule 24 to FA 2007,

(aa) paragraph 10A of that Schedule to the full extent permitted following an unprompted disclosure,

(b) paragraph 13 of Schedule 41 to FA 2008, or

(c) paragraph 13A of that Schedule to the full extent permitted following an unprompted disclosure.

(reductions for disclosure) to the full extent permitted.

94(11) For the purposes of this section, a penalty becomes final–

(a) if it has been assessed, when the time for any appeal or further appeal relating to it expires or, if later, any appeal or final appeal relating to it is finally determined, or

(b) if a contract is made between the Commissioners and the person under which the Commissioners undertake not to assess the penalty or (if it has been assessed) not to take proceedings to recover it, at the time when the contract is made.

94(12) The Treasury may by order vary the amount for the time being specified in subsection (1).

94(13) This section comes into force on a day appointed by order made by the Treasury.

94(14) Orders under this section are to be made by statutory instrument.

94(15) A statutory instrument containing an order under subsection (12) is subject to annulment in pursuance of a resolution of the House of Commons.

94(16) In this section–

"the Commissioners" means the Commissioners for Her Majesty's Revenue and Customs;

"tax advantage" has the meaning given by section 208 of FA 2013.

History – S. 94(4A)–(4D) inserted by FA 2016, s. 164(2), with effect from 1 April 2017 (SI 2017/261, reg. 2).
In s. 94(6), the words "about a person under subsection (1)," inserted by FA 2016, s. 164(3), with effect from 1 April 2017 (SI 2017/261, reg. 2).
S. 94(6A) inserted by FA 2016, s. 164(4), with effect from 1 April 2017 (SI 2017/261, reg. 2).

S. 94(10)(aa) inserted (and the "or" after (a) omitted) by FA 2016, s. 164(5)(a), with effect from 1 April 2017 (SI 2017/261, reg. 2).
S. 94(10)(c) (and the ", or" before it) inserted by FA 2016, s. 164(5)(b), with effect from 1 April 2017 (SI 2017/261, reg. 2).
S. 94(16) substituted by FA 2016, s. 164(6), with effect from 1 April 2017 (SI 2017/261, reg. 2). Former s. 94(16) read as follows:
"94(16) In this section **"the Commissioners"** means the Commissioners for Her Majesty's Revenue and Customs.".

INFORMATION ETC

96 Extension of information and inspection powers to further taxes

96(1) [Amends FA 2008, Sch. 36, para. 63(1).]

96(2) Schedule 48 contains further amendments of that Schedule.

96(3) The amendments made by this section and Schedule 48 come into force on such day as the Treasury may by order appoint.

96(4) An order under subsection (3) may–

(a) appoint different days for different purposes, and

(b) contain transitional provision and savings.

96(5) The Treasury may by order make any incidental, supplemental, consequential, transitional or transitory provision or saving which appears appropriate in consequence of, or otherwise in connection with, this section and Schedule 48.

96(6) An order under subsection (5) may–

(a) make different provision for different purposes, and

(b) make provision amending, repealing or revoking an enactment or instrument (whenever passed or made).

96(7) An order under this section is to be made by statutory instrument.

96(8) A statutory instrument containing an order under subsection (5) is subject to annulment in pursuance of a resolution of the House of Commons.

Commencement Date – SI 2009/3054 sets 1 April 2010 as the appointed day for the amendments made by s. 96 and Sch. 48 and contains savings provisions.
Statutory instruments – SI 2009/3054: made under s. 96(3)–(6).

ASSESSMENTS, CLAIMS ETC

99 Time limits for assessments, claims etc

99(1) Schedule 51 contains provision about time limits for assessments, claims etc.

99(2) The amendments made by that Schedule come into force on such day as the Treasury may by order made by statutory instrument appoint.

99(3) An order under subsection (2)–

(a) may make different provision for different purposes, and

(b) may include transitional provision and savings.

INTEREST

101 Late payment interest on sums due to HMRC

Prospective amendments – S. 101 to apply to petroleum revenue tax from a day to be appointed by Treasury order, by virtue of the omission of s. 101(2)(b) by F(No. 3)A 2010, s. 25 and Sch. 9, para. 14 (see note below).

101(1) This section applies to any amount that is payable by a person to HMRC under or by virtue of an enactment.

101(2) But this section does not apply to–

(a) [not relevant to petroleum revenue tax,]

(b) an amount of petroleum revenue tax, or

(c) an amount of any description specified in an order made by the Treasury.

101(3) An amount to which this section applies carries interest at the late payment interest rate from the late payment interest start date until the date of payment.

101(4) The late payment interest start date in respect of any amount is the date on which that amount becomes due and payable.

101(5) In Schedule 53–

(a) Part 1 makes special provision as to the amount on which late payment interest is calculated,

(b) Part 2 makes special provision as to the late payment interest start date,

(c) Part 3 makes special provision as to the date to which late payment interest runs, and

(d) Part 4 makes provision about the effect that the giving of a relief has on late payment interest.

101(6) Subsection (3) applies even if the late payment interest start date is a non-business day within the meaning of section 92 of the Bills of Exchange Act 1882.

101(7) Late payment interest is to be paid without any deduction of income tax.

101(8) Late payment interest is not payable on late payment interest.

101(9) For the purposes of this section any reference to the payment of an amount to HMRC includes a reference to its being set off against an amount payable by HMRC (and, accordingly, the reference to the date on which an amount is paid includes a reference to the date from which the set-off takes effect).

Commencement Date – The day appointed as the day on which s. 101 comes into force for the purposes of penalties assessed under FA 2012, Sch. 38, Pt. 3–5 (tax agents dishonest conduct) is 1 April 2013 (SI 2013/280).

Prospective amendments – S. 101(2)(b) omitted by F(No. 3)A 2010, s. 25 and Sch. 9, para. 14, with effect from a day to be appointed by Treasury order.

Cross references – SI 2010/1879, reg. 3: sets late payment interest rate for the purposes of s. 101.

102 Repayment interest on sums to be paid by HMRC

Prospective amendments – S. 102 to apply to petroleum revenue tax from a day to be appointed by Treasury order, by virtue of the omission of s. 102(2)(b) by F(No. 3)A 2010, s. 25 and Sch. 9, para. 15 (see note below).

102(1) This section applies to–

(a) any amount that is payable by HMRC to any person under or by virtue of an enactment, and

(b) a relevant amount paid by a person to HMRC that is repaid by HMRC to that person or to another person.

102(2) But this section does not apply to–

(a) [not relevant to petroleum revenue tax,]

(b) an amount constituting a repayment of petroleum revenue tax, or

(c) an amount of any description specified in an order made by the Treasury.

102(3) An amount to which this section applies carries interest at the repayment interest rate from the repayment interest start date until the date on which the payment or repayment is made.

102(4) In Schedule 54–

(a) Parts 1 and 2 define the repayment interest start date, and

(b) Part 3 makes supplementary provision.

102(5) Subsection (3) applies even if the repayment interest start date is a non-business day within the meaning of section 92 of the Bills of Exchange Act 1882.

102(6) Repayment interest is not payable on an amount payable in consequence of an order or judgment of a court having power to allow interest on the amount.

102(7) Repayment interest is not payable on repayment interest.

102(8) For the purposes of this section–

(a) **"relevant amount"** means any sum that was paid in connection with any liability (including any purported or anticipated liability) to make a payment to HMRC under or by virtue of an enactment, and

(b) any reference to the payment or repayment of an amount by HMRC includes a reference to its being set off against an amount owed to HMRC (and, accordingly, the reference to the date on which an amount is paid or repaid by HMRC includes a reference to the date from which the set-off takes effect).

Prospective amendments – S. 102(2)(b) omitted by F(No. 3)A 2010, s. 25 and Sch. 9, para. 15, with effect from a day to be appointed by Treasury order.

Cross references – SI 2010/1879, reg. 4: sets repayment interest rate for the purposes of s. 102.

103 Rates of interest

Prospective amendments – S. 103 to apply to petroleum revenue tax from a day to be appointed by Treasury order, by virtue of the omission of s. 101(2)(b) and s. 102(2)(b) by F(No. 3)A 2010, s. 25 and Sch. 9, para. 14 and 15.

103(1) The late payment interest rate is the rate provided for in regulations made by the Treasury under this subsection.

103(2) The repayment interest rate is the rate provided for in regulations made by the Treasury under this subsection.

103(3) Regulations under subsection (1) or (2)–

(a) may make different provision for different purposes,

(b) may either themselves specify a rate of interest or make provision for such a rate to be determined (and to change from time to time) by reference to such rate, or the average of such rates, as may be referred to in the regulations,

(c) may provide for rates to be reduced below, or increased above, what they otherwise would be by specified amounts or by reference to specified formulae,

(d) may provide for rates arrived at by reference to averages to be rounded up or down,

(e) may provide for circumstances in which alteration of a rate of interest is or is not to be take place, and

(f) may provide that alterations of rates are to have effect for periods beginning on or after a day determined in accordance with the regulations in relation to interest running from before that day as well as from or from after that day.

Commencement Date – S. 103 came into force generally on 6 October 2011 (SI 2011/2401).

Cross references – F(No. 2)A 2015, s. 52(3), (4), (5): application of late payment interest rate provided for in regulations made under s. 103(1) (in substitution for the rate specified in section 17(1) of the Judgments Act 1838 and any other rate specified in an order under section 74 of the County Courts Act 1984) in relation to tax-related judgment debts payable to the Commissioners.

Statutory instruments – SI 2010/1879: made under s. 103.

103A Further provision as to late payment interest and repayment interest

103A [Not relevant to petroleum revenue tax.]

104 Supplementary

Prospective amendments – S. 104 to apply to petroleum revenue tax from a day to be appointed by Treasury order, by virtue of the omission of s. 101(2)(b) and s. 102(2)(b) by F(No. 3)A 2010, s. 25 and Sch. 9, para. 14 and 15.

104(1) In sections 101 to 103–

"HMRC" means Her Majesty's Revenue and Customs;

"late payment interest" means interest payable under section 101;

"repayment interest" means interest payable under section 102;

"revenue" has the meaning given in section 5(4) of CRCA 2005.

104(2) A reference to the date on which an amount becomes due and payable is a reference to the date (however described) on or before which the amount must be paid.

104(3) Sections 101 to 103 come into force on such day as the Treasury may by order appoint.

104(4) An order under subsection (3)–

(a) may commence a provision generally or only for specified purposes, and

(b) may appoint different days for different provisions or for different purposes.

104(5) The Treasury may by order make any incidental, supplemental, consequential, transitional, transitory or saving provision which may appear appropriate in consequence of, or otherwise in connection with, those sections.

104(6) An order under subsection (5) may include provision amending, repealing or revoking any provision of any Act or subordinate legislation whenever passed or made (including this Act and any Act amended by it).

104(7) An order under subsection (5) may make different provision for different purposes.

104(8) The following are to be made by statutory instrument–

(a) orders under section 101(2) or 102(2),

(b) regulations under section 103(1) or (2), and

(c) orders under subsection (3) or (5).

104(9) A statutory instrument containing–

(a) an order under section 101(2) or 102(2),

(b) regulations under section 103(1) or (2),

(c) an order under subsection (5) which includes provision amending or repealing any provision of an Act,

is subject to annulment in pursuance of a resolution of the House of Commons.

Prospective amendments – In s. 104(1), "103A (and Schedules 53 to 54A)" substituted for "103" by F(No. 3)A 2010, s. 25 and Sch. 9, para. 5, with effect from a day to be appointed by Treasury order.

105 Miscellaneous amendments

105(1) [Not relevant to petroleum revenue tax.]

105(2) [Not relevant to petroleum revenue tax.]

105(3) [Not relevant to petroleum revenue tax.]

105(4) [Not relevant to petroleum revenue tax.]

105(5) [Not relevant to petroleum revenue tax.]

105(6) [Omits FA 1989, s. 178(5).]

PENALTIES

106 Penalties for failure to make returns etc

106(1) Schedule 55 contains provision for imposing penalties on persons in respect of failures to make returns and other documents relating to liabilities for tax.

106(2) That Schedule comes into force on such day as the Treasury may by order appoint.

106(3) An order under subsection (2)–

(a) may commence a provision generally or only for specified purposes, and

(b) may appoint different days for different provisions or for different purposes.

106(4) The Treasury may by order make any incidental, supplemental, consequential, transitional, transitory or saving provision which may appear appropriate in consequence of, or otherwise in connection with, Schedule 55.

106(5) An order under subsection (4) may include provision amending, repealing or revoking any provision of any Act or subordinate legislation whenever passed or made (including this Act and any Act amended by it).

106(6) An order under subsection (4) may make different provision for different purposes.

106(7) An order under this section is to be made by statutory instrument.

106(8) A statutory instrument containing an order under subsection (4) which includes provision amending or repealing any provision of an Act is subject to annulment in pursuance of a resolution of the House of Commons.

107 Penalties for failure to pay tax

107(1) Schedule 56 contains provision for imposing penalties on persons in respect of failures to comply with obligations to pay tax.

107(2) That Schedule comes into force on such day as the Treasury may by order appoint.

107(3) An order under subsection (2)–

(a) may commence a provision generally or only for specified purposes, and

(b) may appoint different days for different provisions or for different purposes.

107(4) The Treasury may by order make any incidental, supplemental, consequential, transitional, transitory or saving provision which may appear appropriate in consequence of, or otherwise in connection with, Schedule 56.

107(5) An order under subsection (4) may include provision amending, repealing or revoking any provision of any Act or subordinate legislation whenever passed or made (including this Act and any Act amended by it).

107(6) An order under subsection (4) may make different provision for different purposes.

107(7) An order under this section is to be made by statutory instrument.

107(8) A statutory instrument containing an order under subsection (4) which includes provision amending or repealing any provision of an Act is subject to annulment in pursuance of a resolution of the House of Commons.

SCHEDULES

SCHEDULE 39 – PRT: BLENDED OIL

Section 85

1 Part 5 of FA 1987 (oil taxation) is amended as follows.

2 [Substitutes FA 1987, s. 63.]

3(1) Schedule 12 (supplementary provisions as to blended oil) is amended as follows.

3(2) [Substitutes FA 1987, Sch. 12, para. 1 and 2.]

3(3) [Amends FA 1987, Sch. 12, para. 3(1).]

3(4) [Amends FA 1987, Sch. 12, para. 3(2).]

3(5) [Inserts FA 1987, Sch. 12, para. 3(3) and (4).]

3(6) [Inserts FA 1987, Sch. 12, para. 4.]

4 The amendments made by this Schedule have effect in relation to chargeable periods beginning after 30 June 2009.

SCHEDULE 41 – OIL ASSETS PUT TO OTHER USES

Section 87

Part 1 – Petroleum Revenue Tax

ALLOWANCE OF DECOMMISSIONING AND RESTORATION EXPENDITURE

1(1) Section 3 of OTA 1975 (allowance of expenditure) is amended as follows.

1(2) [Amends OTA 1975, s. 3(1C)(b).]

1(3) [Amends OTA 1975, s. 3(1D).]

1(4) [Inserts OTA 1975, s. 3(1DA)–(1DC).]

AMOUNTS WHICH ARE NOT CHARGEABLE TARIFF RECEIPTS

2(1) Section 6 of OTA 1983 (amounts which are not chargeable tariff receipts) is amended as follows.

2(2) [Amends OTA 1983, s. 6(4).]

2(3) [Inserts OTA 1983, s. 6(4A).]

NO REDUCTION OF ALLOWABLE EXPENDITURE

3(1) Paragraph 8 of Schedule 1 to OTA 1983 (allowable expenditure: use of new asset otherwise than in connection with taxable field) is amended as follows.

3(2) [Amends OTA 1983, Sch. 1, para. 8(1)(a) and (b).]

3(3) [Inserts OTA 1983, Sch. 1, para. 8(2A)–(2C).]

COMMENCEMENT

4 The amendments made by this Part have effect in relation to chargeable periods beginning after 30 June 2009.

SCHEDULE 42 – PRT: FORMER LICENSEES AND FORMER OIL FIELDS

Section 88

Part 1 – Persons Who Cease to be Licensees Because of Cessation Events

1 OTA 1975 is amended as follows.

2(1) Section 12 (interpretation of Part 1) is amended as follows.

2(2) [Amends OTA 1975, s. 12(1).]

2(3) [Inserts OTA 1975, s. 12(1A).]

3 [Amends OTA 1975, Sch. 5, para. 2C(2).]

4 The amendments made by this Part have effect in relation to persons who cease to be licensees because of cessation events occurring in chargeable periods that begin after 30 June 2009.

Part 2 – Areas Treated as Continuing to be Oil Fields

5 OTA 1975 is amended as follows.

6 [Amends OTA 1975, s. 12(1).]

7(1) Schedule 1 (determination of oil fields) is amended as follows.

7(2) [Amends OTA 1975, Sch. 1, para. 1.]

7(3) [Inserts OTA 1975, Sch. 1, para. 6 and 7.]

8 The amendments made by this Part have effect in relation to areas that cease to be oil fields, or parts of oil fields, in chargeable periods that begin after 30 June 2009.

SCHEDULE 43 – PRT: ABOLITION OF PROVISIONAL EXPENDITURE ALLOWANCE

Section 89

INTERPRETATION

1 In this Schedule–

"future chargeable period" means a chargeable period beginning after 30 June 2009;

"provisional expenditure allowance" means an amount calculated under section 2(9)(a) of OTA 1975.

ABOLITION OF ALLOWANCE

2 No provisional expenditure allowance is to be calculated in respect of a future chargeable period.

AMENDMENTS CONSEQUENTIAL ON ABOLITION

3(1) Section 2 of OTA 1975 (assessable profits and allowable losses) is amended as follows.

3(2) [Substitutes OTA 1975, s. 2(8).]

3(3) [Omits OTA 1975, s. 2(9)(a), (10) and (11).]

3(4) [Omits FA 1980, Sch. 17, para. 11.]

3(5) This paragraph has effect in relation to future chargeable periods.

3(6) But this paragraph is subject to paragraph 4.

SAVINGS

4(1) This paragraph applies if provisional expenditure allowance has been calculated in respect of a pre-abolition chargeable period ("the relevant allowance").

4(2) The saved provisions continue to have effect in future chargeable periods in relation to the relevant allowance and the relevant participator as if those provisions had not been amended by paragraph 3.

4(3) In this paragraph–

"pre-abolition chargeable period" means a chargeable period that begins before 30 June 2009;

"relevant participator" means the participator in respect of which the relevant allowance has been calculated;

"the saved provisions" means–

(a) section 2(8) and (10) of OTA 1975, and

(b) paragraph 11 of Schedule 17 to FA 1980.

SCHEDULE 45 – OIL: MISCELLANEOUS AMENDMENTS

Section 91

OTA 1975

1(1) OTA 1975 is amended as follows.

1(2) [Omits OTA 1975, Sch. 3, para. 9 and 10.]

1(3) [Omits OTA 1975, s. 9(4).]

1(4) [Omits OTA 1975, Sch. 4, para. 3.]

1(5) The repeals made by this paragraph have effect in relation to chargeable periods beginning after 30 June 2009.

OTA 1983

2(1) OTA 1983 is amended as follows.

2(2) [Omits OTA 1983, s. 9(3) and Sch. 3, para. 3.]

2(3) In consequence of the omission of subsection (3) of section 9–

(a) [amends OTA 1983, s. 9(2),]

(b) [amends OTA 1983, s. 9(4)(b).]

2(4) [Omits OTA 1983, s. 13 and 14 and Sch. 5.]

FA 1993

3(1) [Renumbers FA 1993, Sch. 20A as Sch. 20B.]

3(2) [Amends OTA 1975, s. 6(1A), FA 1980, Sch. 17, para. 15(9A) and FA 1993, s. 185(1ZA)(b).]

SCHEDULE 48 – EXTENSION OF INFORMATION AND INSPECTION POWERS

Section 96

Commencement Date – SI 2009/3054 sets 1 April 2010 as the appointed day for the amendments made by s. 96 and Sch. 48 and contains savings provisions.

[This Schedule amends FA 2008, Sch. 36 which is reproduced in full in the Income Tax, Corporation Tax and Capital Gains Tax section (Vol. 1C in print).]

SCHEDULE 51 – TIME LIMITS FOR ASSESSMENTS, CLAIMS ETC

Section 99

Commencement Date – Sch. 51 as it applies to petroleum revenue tax comes into force on 1 April 2011, except for para. 43, which came into force on 1 April 2010 (SI 2010/867).

PETROLEUM REVENUE TAX

17 OTA 1975 is amended as follows.

18(1) The Table in paragraph 1(1) of Schedule 2 (applying provisions of TMA 1970 in relation to management and collection of petroleum revenue tax) is amended as follows.

18(2) [Omitted by F(No. 3)A 2010, s. 28 and Sch. 12, para. 13(a),]

18(3) [Amends Table in OTA 1975, Sch. 2, para. 1(1).]

History – Para. 18(2) omitted by F(No. 3)A 2010, s. 28 and Sch. 12, para. 13(a), with effect in relation to claims made on or after 1 April 2011.

19 [Inserts OTA 1975, Sch. 2, para. 10(1A).]

20(1) Paragraph 12 of Schedule 2 (further assessments and determinations) is amended as follows.

20(2) [Inserts OTA 1975, Sch. 2, para. 12(1A) and (1B).]

20(3) [Amends OTA 1975, Sch. 2, para. 12(2).]

21 [Amends OTA 1975, Sch. 2, para. 12A(1).]

22 [Inserts OTA 1975, Sch. 2, para. 12B.]

23(1) Paragraph 2 of Schedule 5 (allowance of expenditure other than abortive exploration expenditure: claim period) is amended as follows.

23(2) [Amends OTA 1975, Sch. 5, para. 2(1).]

23(3) [Amends OTA 1975, Sch. 5, para. 2(7).]

24(1) Paragraph 9 of Schedule 5 (allowance of expenditure other than abortive exploration expenditure: notice of variation) is amended as follows.

24(2) [Amends OTA 1975, Sch. 5, para. 9(1).]

24(3) [Omits OTA 1975, Sch. 5, para 9(1A) to (1C) and (2A).]

24(4) [Inserts OTA 1975, Sch. 5, para 9(2B) and (2C).]

24(5) [Omits OTA 1975, Sch. 5, para. 9(11).]

24(6) [Inserts OTA 1975, Sch. 5, para. 9(12) and (13).]

25(1) Schedule 6 (allowance of expenditure (other than abortive exploration expenditure) on claim by participator) is amended as follows.

25(2) [Amends OTA 1975, Sch. 6, para. 1(2).]

25(3) [Amends the Table in OTA 1975, Sch. 6, para. 2.]

26 [Amends the Table in OTA 1975, Sch. 7, para. 1(3).]

MINOR AND CONSEQUENTIAL PROVISION

43 In consequence of the amendments made by this Schedule, omit–

(a) [omits FA 1990, s. 122,]

(b) [not relevant to petroleum revenue tax.]

SCHEDULE 52 – RECOVERY OF OVERPAID TAX ETC

Section 100

Part 1 – Income Tax and Capital Gains Tax

SAVING FOR PETROLEUM REVENUE TAX

11 [Omitted by F(No. 3)A 2010, s. 28 and Sch. 12, para. 13(b).]

History – Para. 11 omitted by F(No. 3)A 2010, s. 28 and Sch. 12, para. 13(b), with effect in relation to claims made on or after 1 April 2011.

SCHEDULE 53 – LATE PAYMENT INTEREST

Section 101

Prospective amendments – Sch. 53 to apply to petroleum revenue tax with effect from a day to be appointed by Treasury order, by virtue of the omission of s. 101(2)(b) by F(No. 3)A 2010, s. 25 and Sch. 9, para. 14.

The day appointed as the day on which s. 101 and Sch. 53 comes into force for the purposes of penalties assessed under FA 2012, Sch. 38, Pt. 3–5 (tax agents dishonest conduct) is 1 April 2013 (SI 2013/280).

Part 2 – Special Provision: Late Payment Interest Start Date

INSTALMENTS OF PETROLEUM REVENUE TAX

11A [Prospectively inserted by F(No. 3)A 2010, s. 25 and Sch. 9, para. 17.]

Prospective amendments – Para. 11A and the heading before it inserted by F(No. 3)A 2010, s. 25 and Sch. 9, para. 17, with effect from a day to be appointed by Treasury order. Para. 11A to read as follows:

"**11A** The late payment interest start date in respect of an instalment of petroleum revenue tax payable under paragraph 2 of Schedule 19 to FA 1982 (payment for tax) is the last day of the month in which that instalment is payable.".

OTHER AMOUNTS OF PETROLEUM REVENUE TAX

11B [Prospectively inserted by F(No. 3)A 2010, s. 25 and Sch. 9, para. 17.]

Prospective amendments – Para. 11B and the heading before it inserted by F(No. 3)A 2010, s. 25 and Sch. 9, para. 17, with effect from a day to be appointed by Treasury order. Para. 11B to read as follows:

"**11B** The late payment interest start date in respect of any other amount of petroleum revenue tax is the date falling two months after the end of the chargeable period in respect of which the amount is due.".

Part 3 – Special Provision: Date to Which Late Payment Interest Runs

INSTALMENTS OF PETROLEUM REVENUE TAX

14A [Prospectively inserted by F(No. 3)A 2010, s. 25 and Sch. 9, para. 18.]

Prospective amendments – Para. 14A and the heading before it inserted by F(No. 3)A 2010, s. 25 and Sch. 9, para. 18, with effect from a day to be appointed by Treasury order. Para. 14A to read as follows:

"**14A(1)** An instalment of petroleum revenue tax payable under paragraph 2 of Schedule 19 to FA 1982 (payment for tax) carries late payment interest until the earlier of–

(a) the date on which the instalment is paid, and

(b) the date falling two months after the end of the chargeable period in respect of which the instalment is due.

14A(2) An instalment which remains unpaid after the date mentioned in sub-paragraph (1)(b) carries interest as an amount payable on account under section 1 of PRTA 1980.

14A(3) For the purposes of determining the date on which an overdue instalment is paid, a payment on account of one or more such instalments is to be attributed, so far as possible, to the earliest month for which an instalment is overdue.".

SCHEDULE 54 – REPAYMENT INTEREST

Section 102

Prospective amendments – Sch. 54 to apply to petroleum revenue tax with effect from a day to be appointed by Treasury order, by virtue of the omission of s. 102(2)(b) by F(No. 3)A 2010, s. 25 and Sch. 9, para. 15.

Part 1 – Repayment Interest Start Date: General Rule

INTRODUCTORY

Prospective amendments – Para. 1 to apply to petroleum revenue tax with effect from a day to be appointed by Treasury order, by virtue of the omission of s. 102(2)(b) by F(No. 3)A 2010, s. 25 and Sch. 9, para. 15.

1(1) This Part sets out the general rule for determining the repayment interest start date.

1(2) The general rule is subject to the special provision made by Part 2.

REPAYMENT OF AMOUNTS PAID TO HMRC

Prospective amendments – Para. 2–4 to apply to petroleum revenue tax with effect from a day to be appointed by Treasury order, by virtue of the omission of s. 102(2)(b) by F(No. 3)A 2010, s. 25 and Sch. 9, para. 15.

2 In the case of an amount which has been paid to HMRC, the repayment interest start date is the later of date A and (where applicable) date B.

3 Date A is the date on which the amount was paid to HMRC.

4 Date B is, in the case of an amount which–

(a) has been paid in connection with a liability to make a payment to HMRC, and

(b) is to be repaid by them,

the date on which the payment became due and payable to HMRC.

PAYMENT OF AMOUNTS ON RETURN OR CLAIM

Prospective amendments – Para. 5 to apply to petroleum revenue tax with effect from a day to be appointed by Treasury order, by virtue of the omission of s. 102(2)(b) by F(No. 3)A 2010, s. 25 and Sch. 9, para. 15.

5(1) In the case of an amount which–

(a) has not been paid to HMRC, and

(b) is payable by virtue of a return having been filed or a claim having been made,

the repayment interest start date is the later of the dates mentioned in sub-paragraph (2).

5(2) The dates are–

(a) the date (if any) on which the return was required to be filed or the claim was required to be made, and

(b) the date on which the return was in fact filed or the claim was in fact made.

Part 2 – Special Provision as to Repayment Interest Start Date

PETROLEUM REVENUE TAX

12A [Prospectively inserted by F(No. 3)A 2010, s. 25 and Sch. 9, para. 19.]

Prospective amendments – Para. 12A and the heading before it inserted by F(No. 3)A 2010, s. 25 and Sch. 9, para. 19, with effect from a day to be appointed by Treasury order. Para. 12A to read as follows:

"**12A(1)** The repayment interest start date in respect of any amount of petroleum revenue tax is the later of–

(a) the date falling two months after the end of the chargeable period in respect of which the amount was paid, and

(b) the date on which the amount was paid.

12A(2) Sub-paragraph (1) is subject to paragraph 12B (limit on amount of repayment interest carried by certain repayments generated by carry back reliefs).

12A(3) For the purposes of this paragraph any instalment or part of an instalment that becomes repayable is to be regarded, so far as possible, as consisting of the instalment most recently paid.".

12B [Prospectively inserted by F(No. 3)A 2010, s. 25 and Sch. 9, para. 19.]

Prospective amendments – Para. 12B inserted by F(No. 3)A 2010, s. 25 and Sch. 9, para. 19, with effect from a day to be appointed by Treasury order. Para. 12B to read as follows:

"**12B(1)** This paragraph applies where–

(a) an assessment for a chargeable period ("the earlier period") gives effect to relief under section 7(2) or (3) of OTA 1975 for one or more allowable losses accruing in a later chargeable period, and

(b) by virtue of that assessment, an amount of tax becomes repayable to the participator in question (whether wholly or partly by reason of giving effect to that relief).

12B(2) The amount of repayment interest carried by the appropriate repayment is not to exceed the difference between–

(a) 60% of the amount of the allowable loss or losses which is treated as reducing the assessable profit of the earlier period, and

(b) the amount of the appropriate repayment.

12B(3) In this paragraph **"the appropriate repayment"** means so much of the repayment as is attributable to giving effect to the relief (but this is subject to sub-paragraphs (4) and (5)).

12B(4) Sub-paragraph (5) applies where the assessment (as well as giving effect to the relief mentioned in sub-paragraph (1)) takes account of any other matter, whether a relief or not, which goes–

(a) to reduce the assessable profit of the earlier period, or

(b) otherwise to reduce the tax payable for that period.

12B(5) The appropriate repayment is to be taken to be the difference between–

(a) the total amount of tax repayable by virtue of the assessment, and

(b) the amount of tax (if any) which would have been repayable if no account had been taken of that relief.

12B(6) If the earlier period ends on or before 30 June 1993, sub-paragraph (2) has effect as if the percentage specified in paragraph (a) were 85%.

12B(7) In this paragraph references to an assessment include an amendment of an assessment.".

SCHEDULE 55 – PENALTY FOR FAILURE TO MAKE RETURNS ETC

Section 106

Other material – HMRC Brief 14/11: Penalty for failure to disclose offshore income or gains.

Notes – This is an edited version of Sch. 55 containing only provisions relevant for petroleum revenue tax.

PENALTY FOR FAILURE TO MAKE RETURNS ETC

1(1) A penalty is payable by a person ("P") where P fails to make or deliver a return, or to deliver any other document, specified in the Table below on or before the filing date.

1(2) Paragraphs 2 to 13 set out–

(a) the circumstances in which a penalty is payable, and

(b) subject to paragraphs 14 to 17, the amount of the penalty.

1(3) If P's failure falls within more than one paragraph of this Schedule, P is liable to a penalty under each of those paragraphs (but this is subject to paragraph 17(3)).

1(4) In this Schedule–

"filing date", in relation to a return or other document, means the date by which it is required to be made or delivered to HMRC;

"penalty date", in relation to a return or other document falling within any of items 1 to 3 and 5 to 13 in the Table, means the date on which a penalty is first payable for failing to make or deliver it (that is to say, the day after the filing date).

1(4A) [Not relevant to petroleum revenue tax.]

1(5) In the provisions of this Schedule which follow the Table–

(a) any reference to a return includes a reference to any other document specified in the Table, and

(b) any reference to making a return includes a reference to delivering a return or to delivering any such document.

	Tax to which return etc relates	*Return or other document*
12	Petroleum revenue tax	Return under paragraph 2 of Schedule 2 to OTA 1975
13	Petroleum revenue tax	Statement under section 1(1)(a) of PRTA 1980

Prospective amendments – In para. 1(2), "13J" substituted for "13" by F(No. 3)A 2010, s. 26 and Sch. 10, para. 2(2), with effect from a day to be appointed by Treasury order.

In para. 1(4), in the definition of "penalty date", "13A" substituted for "13" by FA 2017, s. 56 and Sch. 11, para. 4(2), with effect from a day to be appointed under FA 2017, s. 61(1).

In para. 1(4), in the definition of "filing date", the words "(or, in the case of a return mentioned in item 7AA or 7AB of the Table, to the tax authorities to whom the return is required to be delivered)" inserted (at the end) by F(No. 3)A 2010, s. 26 and Sch. 10, para. 2(2A) (as inserted by FA 2014, s. 103 and Sch. 22, para. 2(a)), with effect from a date to be appointed under F(No. 3)A 2010, s. 26(2).

History – In para. 1(4), in the definition of "penalty date", the words "falling within any of items 1 to 3 and 5 to 13 in the Table" inserted by FA 2013, s. 230 and Sch. 50, para. 3(a), with effect for the tax year 2014–15 and subsequent tax years in relation to failures to make returns with a filing date (as defined in para. 1(4)) on or after 6 April 2014.

Para. 1(4A) inserted by FA 2013, s. 230 and Sch. 50, para. 3, with effect for the tax year 2014–15 and subsequent tax years in relation to failures to make returns with a filing date (as defined in para. 1(4)) on or after 6 April 2014.

AMOUNT OF PENALTY: OCCASIONAL RETURNS AND ANNUAL RETURNS

2 Paragraphs 3 to 6 apply in the case of a return falling within any of items 1 to 3, 5 and 7 to 13 in the Table.

Prospective amendments – Para. 2 and the heading before it substituted by F(No. 3)A 2010, s. 26 and Sch. 10, para. 3, with effect from *a day to be appointed by Treasury order. The substituted text reads as follows:*

"AMOUNT OF PENALTY: OCCASIONAL RETURNS AND RETURNS FOR PERIODS OF 6 MONTHS OR MORE

2(1) Paragraphs 3 to 6 apply in the case of–

(a) a return falling within any of items 1 to 5, 7 and 8 to 13 in the Table,

(b) [not relevant to petroleum revenue tax,]

(c) [not relevant to petroleum revenue tax.]

2(2) [Not relevant to petroleum revenue tax.]".

History – In para. 2, the words "1 to 3, 5" substituted for the words "1 to 5" by FA 2013, s. 230 and Sch. 50, para. 5, with effect for the tax year 2014–15 and subsequent tax years in relation to failures to make returns with a filing date (as defined in para. 1(4)) on or after 6 April 2014.

3 P is liable to a penalty under this paragraph of £100.

4(1) P is liable to a penalty under this paragraph if (and only if)–

(a) P's failure continues after the end of the period of 3 months beginning with the penalty date,

(b) HMRC decide that such a penalty should be payable, and

(c) HMRC give notice to P specifying the date from which the penalty is payable.

4(2) The penalty under this paragraph is £10 for each day that the failure continues during the period of 90 days beginning with the date specified in the notice given under sub-paragraph (1)(c).

4(3) The date specified in the notice under sub-paragraph (1)(c)–

(a) may be earlier than the date on which the notice is given, but

(b) may not be earlier than the end of the period mentioned in sub-paragraph (1)(a).

5(1) P is liable to a penalty under this paragraph if (and only if) P's failure continues after the end of the period of 6 months beginning with the penalty date.

5(2) The penalty under this paragraph is the greater of–

(a) 5% of any liability to tax which would have been shown in the return in question, and

(b) £300.

6(1) P is liable to a penalty under this paragraph if (and only if) P's failure continues after the end of the period of 12 months beginning with the penalty date.

6(2) Where, by failing to make the return, P withholds information which would enable or assist HMRC to assess P's liability to tax, the penalty under this paragraph is determined in accordance with sub-paragraphs (3) and (4).

6(3) If the withholding of the information is deliberate and concealed, the penalty is the greater of–

(a) 100% of any liability to tax which would have been shown in the return in question, and

(b) £300.

6(4) If the withholding of the information is deliberate but not concealed, the penalty is the greater of–

(a) 70% of any liability to tax which would have been shown in the return in question, and

(b) £300.

6(5) In any case not falling within sub-paragraph (2), the penalty under this paragraph is the greater of–

(a) 5% of any liability to tax which would have been shown in the return in question, and

(b) £300.

Prospective amendments – In para. 6(2), after "P" in the first place it occurs, the word "deliberately" inserted by F(No. 3)A 2010, s. 26 and Sch. 10, para. 4(2), with effect from a day to be appointed by Treasury order.

In para. 6(3)(a), the words "the relevant percentage" substituted for "100%" by FA 2010, s. 35 and Sch. 10, para. 11(2), with effect from a date to be appointed.

Para. 6(3A)(za) inserted and in para. 6(3A)(a) "125%" substituted for "100%" by FA 2015, s. 120 and Sch. 20, para. 15(2), with effect from a day to be appointed under FA 2015, s. 120(2).

Para. 6(3A) inserted by FA 2010, s. 35 and Sch. 10, para. 11(3), with effect from a date to be appointed. Para. 6(3A) reads:

"6(3A) For the purposes of sub-paragraph (3)(a), the relevant percentage is–

(a) for the withholding of category 1 information, 100%,

(b) for the withholding of category 2 information, 150%, and

(c) for the withholding of category 3 information, 200%."

In para. 6(4)(a), the words "the relevant percentage" substituted for "70%" by FA 2010, s. 35 and Sch. 10, para. 11(4), with effect from a date to be appointed.

Para. 6(4A)(za) inserted and in para. 6(3A)(a) "87.5%" substituted for "70%" by FA 2015, s. 120 and Sch. 20, para. 15(3), with effect from a day to be appointed under FA 2015, s. 120(2).

Para. 6(4A) inserted by FA 2010, s. 35 and Sch. 10, para. 11(5), with effect from a date to be appointed. Para. 6(4A) reads:

"6(4A) For the purposes of sub-paragraph (4)(a), the **relevant percentage** is–

(a) for the withholding of category 1 information, 70%,

(b) for the withholding of category 2 information, 105%, and

(c) for the withholding of category 3 information, 140%."

In para. 6(5), the words "any case not falling within sub-paragraph (2)" substituted for the words "any other case" by F(No. 3)A 2010, s. 26 and Sch. 10, para. 4(3), with effect from a day to be appointed by Treasury order.

In para. 6(6) "4" substituted for "3" by FA 2015, s. 120 and Sch. 20, para. 15(4), with effect from a day to be appointed under FA 2015, s. 120(2).

Para. 6(6) inserted by FA 2010, s. 35 and Sch. 10, para. 11(6), with effect from a date to be appointed. Para. 6(6) reads:

"6(6) Paragraph 6A explains the 3 categories of information."

Notes – The amendments by FA 2010, Sch. 10, para. 10 to 14 were brought into effect from 6 April 2011 but only in relation to items 1, 2 or 3 in the Table in para. 1 (which relate to income tax, capital gains tax and corporation tax) (SI 2011/975).

The amendments by F(No. 3)A 2010, s. 27 and Sch. 10, para. 4, were brought into effect from 6 April 2011 in relation to items 1, 2 or 3 in the Table in para. 1 (which relate to income tax, capital gains tax and corporation tax) and from 1 April 2011 in relation to a return under FA 2004, s. 254 (pension schemes; accounting for tax) (SI 2011/703).

6A [Para. 6A prospectively inserted by FA 2010, s. 35 and Sch. 10, para. 12.]

Prospective amendments – Para. 6A inserted by FA 2010, s. 35 and Sch. 10, para. 12, with effect from a date to be appointed. Para. 6A (as amended by FA 2015, s. 120 and Sch. 20, para. 16(3) to (9) (see history notes below)) reads:

"**6A(1)** Information is **category 1** information if–

(a) it involves a domestic matter, or

(b) it involves an offshore matter and–

(i) the territory in question is a category 1 territory, or

(ii) it is information which would enable or assist HMRC to assess P's liability to a tax other than income tax or capital gains tax.

6A(2) Information is **category 2** information if–

(a) it involves an offshore matter or an offshore transfer,

(b) the territory in question is a category 2 territory, and

(c) it is information which would enable or assist HMRC to assess P's liability to income tax, capital gains tax or inheritance tax.

6A(3) Information is **category 3** information if–

(a) it involves an offshore matter or an offshore transfer,

(b) the territory in question is a category 3 territory, and

(c) it is information which would enable or assist HMRC to assess P's liability to income tax, capital gains tax or inheritance tax.

6A(4) Information **"involves an offshore matter"** if the liability to tax which would have been shown in the return includes a liability to tax charged on or by reference to–

(a) income arising from a source in a territory outside the UK,

(b) assets situated or held in a territory outside the UK,

(c) activities carried on wholly or mainly in a territory outside the UK, or

(d) anything having effect as if it were income, assets or activities of a kind described above.

6A(4A) If the liability to tax which would have been shown in the return is a liability to inheritance tax, assets are treated for the purposes of sub-paragraph (4) as situated or held in a territory outside the UK if they are so situated or held immediately after the transfer of value by reason of which inheritance tax becomes chargeable.

6A(4B) Information **"involves an offshore transfer"** if–

(a) it does not involve an offshore matter,

(b) it is information which would enable or assist HMRC to assess P's liability to income tax, capital gains tax or inheritance tax,

(c) by failing to make the return, P deliberately withholds the information (whether or not the withholding of the information is also concealed), and

(d) the applicable condition in paragraph 6AA is satisfied.

6A(5) Information **"involves a domestic matter"** if it does not involve an offshore matter or an offshore transfer.

6A(6) If the information which P withholds falls into more than one category–

(a) P's failure to make the return is to be treated for the purposes of this Schedule as if it were separate failures, one for each category of information according to the matters or transfers which the information involves, and

(b) for each separate failure, the liability to tax which would have been shown in the return in question is taken to be such share of the liability to tax which would have been shown in the return mentioned in paragraph (a) as is just and reasonable.

6A(7) For the purposes of this Schedule–

(a) paragraph 21A of Schedule 24 to FA 2007 (classification of territories) has effect, but

(b) an order under that paragraph does not apply to a failure if the filing date is before the date on which the order comes into force.

6A(8) [Omitted by FA 2015, s. 120 and Sch. 20, para. 16(8).]

6A(9) In this paragraph and paragraph 6AA–

"assets" has the meaning given in section 21(1) of TCGA 1992, but also includes sterling;

"UK" means the United Kingdom, including the territorial sea of the United Kingdom."

Para. 6A(A1) and (1) substituted for former para. 6A(1) by FA 2015, s. 120 and Sch. 20, para. 16(2), with effect from a day to be appointed under FA 2015, s. 120(2).

History – In para. 6A(2)(a) the words "or an offshore transfer" inserted and in para. 6A(2)(c) the words ", capital gains tax or inheritance tax" substituted for the words "or capital gains tax" by FA 2015, s. 120 and Sch. 20, para. 16(3), with effect from 6 April 2016 (and the amendments have effect in relation to a return or other document which: is required to be made or delivered to HMRC in relation to a tax year commencing on or after 6 April 2016; and falls within item 1, 2 or 3 of the Table in para. 1(5)) (SI 2016/456, art. 5).

In para. 6A(3)(a) the words "or an offshore transfer" inserted and in para. 6A(3)(c) the words ", capital gains tax or inheritance tax" substituted for the words "or capital gains tax" by FA 2015, s. 120 and Sch. 20, para. 16(4), with effect from 6 April 2016 (and the amendments have effect in relation to a return or other document which: is required to be made or delivered to HMRC in relation to a tax year commencing on or after 6 April 2016; and falls within item 1, 2 or 3 of the Table in para. 1(5)) (SI 2016/456, art. 5).

Para. 6A(4A) and (4B) inserted by FA 2015, s. 120 and Sch. 20, para. 16(5), with effect from 6 April 2016 (and the amendments have effect in relation to a return or other document which: is required to be made or delivered to HMRC in relation to a tax year commencing on or after 6 April 2016; and falls within item 1, 2 or 3 of the Table in para. 1(5)) (SI 2016/456, art. 5).

In para. 6A(5) the words "it does not involve an offshore matter or an offshore transfer" substituted for the words "the liability to tax which would have been shown in the return includes a liability to tax charged on or by reference to anything not mentioned in sub-paragraph (4)(a) to (d)" by FA 2015, s. 120 and Sch. 20, para. 16(6), with effect from 6 April 2016 (and the amendments have effect in relation to a return or other document which: is required to be made or delivered to HMRC in relation to a tax year commencing on or after 6 April 2016; and falls within item 1, 2 or 3 of the Table in para. 1(5)) (SI 2016/456, art. 5).

In para. 6A(6)(a) the words "or transfers" inserted by FA 2015, s. 120 and Sch. 20, para. 16(7), with effect from 6 April 2016 (and the amendments have effect in relation to a return or other document which: is required to be made or delivered to HMRC in relation to a tax year commencing on or after 6 April 2016; and falls within item 1, 2 or 3 of the Table in para. 1(5)) (SI 2016/456, art. 5).

Para. 6A(8) omitted by FA 2015, s. 120 and Sch. 20, para. 16(8), with effect from 6 April 2016 (and the amendments have effect in relation to a return or other document which: is required to be made or delivered to HMRC in relation to a tax year commencing on or after 6 April 2016; and falls within item 1, 2 or 3 of the Table in para. 1(5)) (SI 2016/456, art. 5).

In para. 6A(9) the words "and paragraph 6AA" insertedby FA 2015, s. 120 and Sch. 20, para. 16(9), with effect from 6 April 2016 (and the amendments have effect in relation to a return or other document which: is required to be made or delivered to HMRC in relation to a tax year commencing on or after 6 April 2016; and falls within item 1, 2 or 3 of the Table in para. 1(5)) (SI 2016/456, art. 5).

Notes – The amendments by FA 2010, Sch. 10, para. 10 to 14 were brought into effect from 6 April 2011 but only in relation to items 1, 2 or 3 in the Table in para. 1 (which relate to income tax, capital gains tax and corporation tax) (SI 2011/975).

The amendments by FA 2015, Sch. 20, para. 16(3) to (9) were brought into effect from 6 April 2016 in relation to a return or other document which is required to be made or delivered to HMRC in relation to a tax year commencing on or after 6 April 2016; and falls within item 1, 2 or 3 of the Table in para. 1(5) (SI 2016/456, art. 5).

6AA [Not relevant to petroleum revenue tax.]

History – Para. 6AA inserted by FA 2015, s. 120 and Sch. 20, para. 17, with effect from 6 April 2016 (in relation to a return or other document which: is required to be made or delivered to HMRC in relation to a tax year commencing on or after 6 April 2016; and falls within item 1, 2 or 3 of the Table in para. 1(5)) (SI 2016/456, art. 5).

6AB Regulations under paragraph 21B of Schedule 24 to FA 2007 (location of assets etc) apply for the purposes of paragraphs 6A and 6AA of this Schedule as they apply for the purposes of paragraphs 4A and 4AA of that Schedule.

History – Para. 6AB inserted by FA 2015, s. 120 and Sch. 20, para. 17, with effect from 6 April 2016 (in relation to a return or other document which: is required to be made or delivered to HMRC in relation to a tax year commencing on or after 6 April 2016; and falls within item 1, 2 or 3 of the Table in para. 1(5)) (SI 2016/456, art. 5).

AMOUNT OF PENALTY: REAL TIME INFORMATION FOR PAYE AND APPRENTICESHIP LEVY

History – In heading before para. 6B, the words "and apprenticeship levy" inserted by FA 2016, s. 113(8), with effect from 15 September 2016 (Royal Assent).

6B–6D [Not relevant to petroleum revenue tax.]

AMOUNT OF PENALTY: CIS RETURNS

7–13 [Not relevant to petroleum revenue tax.]

AMOUNT OF PENALTY: RETURNS FOR PERIODS OF BETWEEN 2 AND 6 MONTHS

13A–13E [Not relevant to petroleum revenue tax.]

AMOUNT OF PENALTY: RETURNS FOR PERIODS OF 2 MONTHS OR LESS

13F–13J [Not relevant to petroleum revenue tax.]

REDUCTIONS FOR DISCLOSURE

14(A1) In this paragraph, **"relevant information"** means information which has been withheld by a failure to make a return.

14(1) Paragraph 15 provides for reductions in the penalty under paragraph 6(3) or (4) where P discloses relevant information that involves a domestic matter or 11(3) or (4) where P discloses relevant information.

14(1A) Paragraph 15A provides for reductions in the penalty under paragraph 6(3) or (4) where P discloses relevant information that involves an offshore matter or an offshore transfer.

14(1B) Sub-paragraph (2) applies where–

(a) P is liable to a penalty under paragraph 6(3) or (4) and P discloses relevant information that involves a domestic matter, or

(b) P is liable to a penalty under any of the other provisions mentioned in sub-paragraph (1) and P discloses relevant information.

14(2) P discloses relevant information by–

(a) telling HMRC about it,

(b) giving HMRC reasonable help in quantifying any tax unpaid by reason of its having been withheld, and

(c) allowing HMRC access to records for the purpose of checking how much tax is so unpaid.

14(2A) Sub-paragraph (2B) applies where P is liable to a penalty under paragraph 6(3) or (4) and P discloses relevant information that involves an offshore matter or an offshore transfer.

14(2B) P discloses relevant information by–

(a) telling HMRC about it,

(b) giving HMRC reasonable help in quantifying any tax unpaid by reason of its having been withheld,

(c) allowing HMRC access to records for the purpose of checking how much tax is so unpaid, and

(d) providing HMRC with additional information.

14(2C) The Treasury must make regulations setting out what is meant by **"additional information"** for the purposes of sub-paragraph (2B)(d).

14(2D) Regulations under sub-paragraph (2C) are to be made by statutory instrument.

14(2E) An instrument containing regulations under sub-paragraph (2C) is subject to annulment in pursuance of a resolution of the House of Commons.

14(3) Disclosure of relevant information–

(a) is **"unprompted"** if made at a time when P has no reason to believe that HMRC have discovered or are about to discover the relevant information, and

(b) otherwise, is **"prompted"**.

14(4) In relation to disclosure **"quality"** includes timing, nature and extent.

14(5) Paragraph 6A(4) to (5) applies to determine whether relevant information involves an offshore matter, an offshore transfer or a domestic matter for the purposes of this paragraph.

Prospective amendments – In para. 14(1), ", 11(3) or (4), 13E(3) or (4) or 13J(3) or (4)" substituted for "or 11(3) or (4)" by F(No. 3)A 2010, s. 26 and Sch. 10, para. 8, with effect from a day to be appointed by Treasury order.

History – Para. 14(A1) inserted by FA 2016, s. 163(1) and Sch. 21, para. 10(2), with effect from 1 April 2017 for all purposes and has effect for inheritance tax purposes (in relation to transfers of value on or after that date) and for income tax and capital gains tax purposes (in relation to any tax year commencing on or after 6 April 2016) (SI 2017/259, reg. 2).
In para. 14(1), the words "where P discloses relevant information that involves a domestic matter" inserted and the words "relevant information" substituted for the words "information which has been withheld by a failure to make a return ("relevant information")" by FA 2016, s. 163(1) and Sch. 21, para. 10(3), with effect from 1 April 2017 for all purposes and has effect for inheritance tax purposes (in relation to transfers of value on or after that date) and for income tax and capital gains tax purposes (in relation to any tax year commencing on or after 6 April 2016) (SI 2017/259, reg. 2).
Para. 14(1A) and (1B) inserted by FA 2016, s. 163(1) and Sch. 21, para. 10(4), with effect from 1 April 2017 for all purposes and has effect for inheritance tax purposes (in relation to transfers of value on or after that date) and for income tax and capital gains tax purposes (in relation to any tax year commencing on or after 6 April 2016) (SI 2017/259, reg. 2).
Para. 14(2A)–(2E) inserted by FA 2016, s. 163(1) and Sch. 21, para. 10(5), with effect from 8 March 2017 for the purpose of making the regulations and from 1 April 2017 for all purposes and has effect for inheritance tax purposes (in relation to transfers of value on or after that date) and for income tax and capital gains tax purposes (in relation to any tax year commencing on or after 6 April 2016) (SI 2017/259, reg. 2 and 3).
Para. 14(5) inserted by FA 2016, s. 163(1) and Sch. 21, para. 10(6), with effect from 1 April 2017 for all purposes and has effect for inheritance tax purposes (in relation to transfers of value on or after that date) and for income tax and capital gains tax purposes (in relation to any tax year commencing on or after 6 April 2016) (SI 2017/259, reg. 2).

15(1) Where a person who would otherwise be liable to a 100% penalty has made an unprompted disclosure, HMRC must reduce the 100% to a percentage, not below 30%, which reflects the quality of the disclosure.

15(2) Where a person who would otherwise be liable to a 100% penalty has made a prompted disclosure, HMRC must reduce the 100% to a percentage, not below 50%, which reflects the quality of the disclosure.

15(3) Where a person who would otherwise be liable to a 70% penalty has made an unprompted disclosure, HMRC must reduce the 70% to a percentage, not below 20%, which reflects the quality of the disclosure.

15(4) Where a person who would otherwise be liable to a 70% penalty has made a prompted disclosure, HMRC must reduce the 70% to a percentage, not below 35%, which reflects the quality of the disclosure.

15(5) But HMRC must not under this paragraph–

(a) reduce a penalty under paragraph 6(3) or (4) below £300, or

(b) reduce a penalty under paragraph 11(3) or (4) below the amount set by paragraph 11(3)(b) or (4)(b) (as the case may be).

Prospective amendments – Para. 15(1) substituted by FA 2010, s. 35 and Sch. 10, para. 13(2), with effect from a date to be appointed. Para. 15(1) reads:
"15(1) If a person who would otherwise be liable to a penalty of a percentage shown in column 1 of the Table (a "standard percentage") has made a disclosure, HMRC must reduce the standard percentage to one that reflects the quality of the disclosure."
The Table in para. 15(2) amended by FA 2015, s. 120 and Sch. 20, para. 18, with effect from a day to be appointed under FA 2015, s. 120(2).
Para. 15(2) substituted by FA 2010, s. 35 and Sch. 10, para. 13(2), with effect from a date to be appointed. Para. 15(2) (as amended by by FA 2016, s. 163(1) and Sch. 21, para. 11 (see history notes below)) reads:
"15(2) But the standard percentage may not be reduced to a percentage that is below the minimum shown for it–
(a) in the case of a prompted disclosure, in column 2 of the Table, and
(b) in the case of an unprompted disclosure, in column 3 of the Table.

Standard %	*Minimum % for prompted disclosure*	*Minimum % for unprompted disclosure*
70%	35%	20%
100%	50%	30%"

Para. 15(3) omitted by FA 2010, s. 35 and Sch. 10, para. 13(3), with effect from a date to be appointed.
Para. 15(4) omitted by FA 2010, s. 35 and Sch. 10, para. 13(3), with effect from a date to be appointed.
In para. 15(5), the words "sub-paragraph (3) or (4) of any of paragraphs 11, 13E and 13J" substituted for the words "paragraph 11(3) or (4)" by F(No. 3)A 2010, s. 26 and Sch. 10, para. 9(a), with effect from a day to be appointed by Treasury order.
In para. 15(5), the words "paragraph (b) of that sub-paragraph" substituted for the words "paragraph 11(3)(b) or (4)(b) (as the case may be)" by F(No. 3)A 2010, s. 26 and Sch. 10, para. 9(b), with effect from a day to be appointed by Treasury order.

History – The Table in para. 15(2) substituted by FA 2016, s. 163(1) and Sch. 21, para. 11, with effect from 1 April 2017 for all purposes and has effect for inheritance tax purposes (in relation to transfers of value on or after that date) and for income tax and capital gains tax purposes (in relation to any tax year commencing on or after 6 April 2016) (SI 2017/259, reg. 2).

Notes – The amendments by FA 2010, Sch. 10, para. 10 to 14 were brought into effect from 6 April 2011 but only in relation to items 1, 2 or 3 in the Table in para. 1 (which relate to income tax, capital gains tax and corporation tax) (SI 2011/975).

15A(1) If a person who would otherwise be liable to a penalty of a percentage shown in column 1 of the Table (a "standard percentage") has made a disclosure, HMRC must reduce the standard percentage to one that reflects the quality of the disclosure.

15A(2) *But the standard percentage* may not be reduced to a percentage that is below the minimum shown for it–

(a) in the case of a prompted disclosure, in column 2 of the Table, and

(b) in the case of an unprompted disclosure, in column 3 of the Table.

Standard %	*Minimum % for prompted disclosure*	*Minimum % for unprompted disclosure*
70%	45%	30%
87.5%	53.75%	35%
100%	60%	40%
105%	62.5%	40%
125%	72.5%	50%
140%	80%	50%
150%	85%	55%
200%	110%	70%

15A(3) But HMRC must not under this paragraph reduce a penalty below £300.

History – Para. 15A inserted by FA 2016, s. 163(1) and Sch. 21, para. 12, with effect from 1 April 2017 for all purposes and has effect for inheritance tax purposes (in relation to transfers of value on or after that date) and for income tax and capital gains tax purposes (in relation to any tax year commencing on or after 6 April 2016) (SI 2017/259, reg. 2).

SPECIAL REDUCTION

16(1) If HMRC think it right because of special circumstances, they may reduce a penalty under any paragraph of this Schedule.

16(2) In sub-paragraph (1) **"special circumstances"** does not include–

(a) ability to pay, or

(b) the fact that a potential loss of revenue from one taxpayer is balanced by a potential over-payment by another.

16(3) In sub-paragraph (1) the reference to reducing a penalty includes a reference to–

(a) staying a penalty, and

(b) agreeing a compromise in relation to proceedings for a penalty.

INTERACTION WITH OTHER PENALTIES AND LATE PAYMENT SURCHARGES

17(1) Where P is liable for a penalty under any paragraph of this Schedule which is determined by reference to a liability to tax, the amount of that penalty is to be reduced by the amount of any other penalty incurred by P, if the amount of the penalty is determined by reference to the same liability to tax.

17(2) In sub-paragraph (1) the reference to **"any other penalty"** does not include–

(a) a penalty under any other paragraph of this Schedule, or

(b) a penalty under Schedule 56 (penalty for late payment of tax), or

(c) a penalty under Part 4 of FA 2014 (penalty where corrective action not taken after follower notice etc), or.

(d) a penalty under Schedule 22 to FA 2016 (asset-based penalty).

17(3) Where P is liable for a penalty under more than one paragraph of this Schedule which is determined by reference to a liability to tax, the aggregate of the amounts of those penalties must not exceed 100% of the liability to tax.

Prospective amendments – In para. 17(3), the words "the relevant percentage" substituted for "100%" by FA 2010, s. 35 and Sch. 10, para. 14(a), with effect from a day to be appointed.

Para. 17(4)(ba) (and the word "and" immediately after it) inserted and the words "and" at the end of para. (b) omitted by FA 2015, s. 120 and Sch. 20, para. 19, with effect from a day to be appointed under FA 2015, s. 120(2).

Para. 17(4) inserted by FA 2010, s. 35 and Sch. 10, para. 14(b), with effect from a day to be appointed. Para. 17(4) reads:

"**17(4)** The **relevant percentage** is–

(a) if one of the penalties is a penalty under paragraph 6(3) or (4) and the information withheld is category 3 information, 200%,

(b) if one of the penalties is a penalty under paragraph 6(3) or (4) and the information withheld is category 2 information, 150%, and

(c) in all other cases, 100%."

History – Para. 17(2)(c) (and the ", or" before it) inserted by FA 2014, s. 233 and Sch. 33, para. 5, with effect from 17 July 2014.

Para. 17(2)(d) (and the ", or" before it) inserted by FA 2016, s. 165(1) and Sch. 22, para. 20(5), with effect for inheritance tax purposes, in relation to transfers of value made on or after 1 April 2017 and for income tax and capital gains tax purposes, in relation to tax years commencing on or after 6 April 2016 (SI 2017/277, reg. 2).

Notes – The amendments by FA 2010, Sch. 10, para. 10 to 14 were brought into effect from 6 April 2011 but only in relation to items 1, 2 or 3 in the Table in para. 1 (which relate to income tax, capital gains tax and corporation tax) (SI 2011/975).

CANCELLATION OF PENALTY

17A [Not relevant to petroleum revenue tax.]

17B [Not relevant to petroleum revenue tax.]

ASSESSMENT

18(1) Where P is liable for a penalty under any paragraph of this Schedule HMRC must–

(a) assess the penalty,

(b) notify P, and

(c) state in the notice the period in respect of which the penalty is assessed.

18(2) A penalty under any paragraph of this Schedule must be paid before the end of the period of 30 days beginning with the day on which notification of the penalty is issued.

18(3) An assessment of a penalty under any paragraph of this Schedule–

(a) is to be treated for procedural purposes in the same way as an assessment to tax (except in respect of a matter expressly provided for by this Schedule),

(b) may be enforced as if it were an assessment to tax, and

(c) may be combined with an assessment to tax.

18(4) A supplementary assessment may be made in respect of a penalty if an earlier assessment operated by reference to an underestimate of the liability to tax which would have been shown in a return.

18(5) Sub-paragraph (6) applies if–

(a) an assessment in respect of a penalty is based on a liability to tax that would have been shown in a return, and

(b) that liability is found by HMRC to be excessive.

18(6) HMRC may by notice to P amend the assessment so that it is based upon the correct amount.

18(7) An amendment under sub-paragraph (6)–

(a) does not affect when the penalty must be paid;

(b) may be made after the last day on which the assessment in question could have been made under paragraph 19.

History – Para. 18(5), (6) and (7) substituted for para. 18(5) by FA 2013, s. 230 and Sch. 50, para. 7, with effect for the tax year 2014–15 and subsequent tax years in relation to failures to make returns with a filing date (as defined in para. 1(4)) on or after 6 April 2014.

Notes – Para. 18(5) was inserted by F(No. 3)A 2010, s. 27 and Sch. 10, para. 10, which was brought into effect from 6 April 2011 in relation to items 1, 2 or 3 in the Table in para. 1 (which relate to income tax, capital gains tax and corporation tax) and from 1 April 2011 in relation to a return under FA 2004, s. 254 (pension schemes; accounting for tax) (SI 2011/703), and from 6 October 2011 in relation to item 6 (CIS returns) (SI 2011/2391) but remained prospective for other purposes. As a consequence of the substitution of para. 18(5)–(7) by FA 2013, s. 230 and Sch. 50, para. 7 (see history note above) (which applies for all purposes), F(No. 3)A 2010, Sch. 10, para. 10 was repealed by FA 2013, s. 230 and Sch. 50, para. 15, with effect for the tax year 2014–15 and subsequent tax years in relation to failures to make returns with a filing date (as defined in para. 1(4)) on or after 6 April 2014.

19(1) An assessment of a penalty under any paragraph of this Schedule in respect of any amount must be made on or before the later of date A and (where it applies) date B.

19(2) Date A is–

(a) [not relevant to petroleum revenue tax,]

(b) [not relevant to petroleum revenue tax,]

(c) in any other case, the last day of the period of 2 years beginning with the filing date.

19(3) Date B is the last day of the period of 12 months beginning with–

(a) the end of the appeal period for the assessment of the liability to tax which would have been shown in the return or returns (as the case may be in relation to penalties under section 6C or 6D), or

(b) if there is no such assessment, the date on which that liability is ascertained or it is ascertained that the liability is nil.

19(4) In sub-paragraph (3)(a) **"appeal period"** means the period during which–

(a) an appeal could be brought, or

(b) an appeal that has been brought has not been determined or withdrawn.

19(5) Sub-paragraph (1) does not apply to a re-assessment under paragraph 24(2)(b).

History – In para. 19(2), the words " — (a) in the case of an assessment of a penalty under paragraph 6C, the last day of the period of *2 years beginning with the end of the tax month* in respect of which the penalty is payable, (b) in the case of an assessment of a penalty under paragraph 6D, the last day of the period of 2 years beginning with the filing date for the relevant extended failure (as defined in paragraph 6D(10)), and (c) in any other case," inserted by FA 2013, s. 230 and Sch. 50, para. 8(2), with effect for the tax year 2014–15 and subsequent tax years in relation to failures to make returns with a filing date (as defined in para. 1(4)) on or after 6 April 2014.
In para. 19(3)(a), the words "or returns (as the case may be in relation to penalties under section 6C or 6D)" inserted by FA 2013, s. 230 and Sch. 50, para. 8(3), with effect for the tax year 2014–15 and subsequent tax years in relation to failures to make returns with a filing date (as defined in para. 1(4)) on or after 6 April 2014.

APPEAL

20(1) P may appeal against a decision of HMRC that a penalty is payable by P.

20(2) P may appeal against a decision of HMRC as to the amount of a penalty payable by P.

21(1) An appeal under paragraph 20 is to be treated in the same way as an appeal against an assessment to the tax concerned (including by the application of any provision about bringing the appeal by notice to HMRC, about HMRC review of the decision or about determination of the appeal by the First-tier Tribunal or Upper Tribunal).

21(2) Sub-paragraph (1) does not apply–

(a) so as to require P to pay a penalty before an appeal against the assessment of the penalty is determined, or

(b) in respect of any other matter expressly provided for by this Act.

22(1) On an appeal under paragraph 20(1) that is notified to the tribunal, the tribunal may affirm or cancel HMRC's decision.

22(2) On an appeal under paragraph 20(2) that is notified to the tribunal, the tribunal may–

(a) affirm HMRC's decision, or

(b) substitute for HMRC's decision another decision that HMRC had power to make.

22(3) If the tribunal substitutes its decision for HMRC's, the tribunal may rely on paragraph 16–

(a) to the same extent as HMRC (which may mean applying the same percentage reduction as HMRC to a different starting point), or

(b) to a different extent, but only if the tribunal thinks that HMRC's decision in respect of the application of paragraph 16 was flawed.

22(4) In sub-paragraph (3)(b) **"flawed"** means flawed when considered in the light of the principles applicable in proceedings for judicial review.

22(5) In this paragraph **"tribunal"** means the First-tier Tribunal or Upper Tribunal (as appropriate by virtue of paragraph 21(1)).

REASONABLE EXCUSE

23(1) Liability to a penalty under any paragraph of this Schedule does not arise in relation to a failure to make a return if P satisfies HMRC or (on appeal) the First-tier Tribunal or Upper Tribunal that there is a reasonable excuse for the failure.

23(2) For the purposes of sub-paragraph (1)–

(a) an insufficiency of funds is not a reasonable excuse, unless attributable to events outside P's control,

(b) where P relies on any other person to do anything, that is not a reasonable excuse unless P took reasonable care to avoid the failure, and

(c) where P had a reasonable excuse for the failure but the excuse has ceased, P is to be treated as having continued to have the excuse if the failure is remedied without unreasonable delay after the excuse ceased.

Prospective amendments – Para. 23(1) substituted by F(No. 3)A 2010, s. 26 and Sch. 10, para. 11, with effect from a day to be appointed by Treasury order. The substituted para. 23(1) to read as follows:

"**23(1)** If P satisfies HMRC or (on appeal) the First-tier Tribunal or Upper Tribunal that there is a reasonable excuse for a failure to make a return–

(a) liability to a penalty under any paragraph of this Schedule does not arise in relation to that failure, and

(b) [not relevant to petroleum revenue tax.]"

DETERMINATION OF PENALTY GEARED TO TAX LIABILITY WHERE NO RETURN MADE

24(1) References to a liability to tax which would have been shown in a return are references to the amount which, if a complete and accurate return had been delivered on the filing date, would have been shown to be due or payable by the taxpayer in respect of the tax concerned for the period to which the return relates.

24(2) In the case of a penalty which is assessed at a time before P makes the return to which the penalty relates–

(a) HMRC is to determine the amount mentioned in sub-paragraph (1) to the best of HMRC's information and belief, and

(b) if P subsequently makes a return, the penalty must be re-assessed by reference to the amount of tax shown to be due and payable in that return (but subject to any amendments or corrections to the return).

24(3) In calculating a liability to tax which would have been shown in a return, no account is to be taken of any relief under section 458 of CTA 2010 (relief in respect of repayment etc of loan) which is deferred under subsection (5) of that section.

History – In para. 24(3), the words "section 458 of CTA 2010" substituted for the words "subsection (4) of section 419 of ICTA" and the words "subsection (5)" substituted for the words "subsection (4A)" by CTA 2010, s. 1177 and Sch. 1, para. 723, with effect for corporation tax purposes for accounting periods ending on or after 1 April 2010, and for income tax and capital gains tax purposes for the tax year 2010–11 and subsequent tax years.

PARTNERSHIPS

25 [Not relevant to petroleum revenue tax.]

DOUBLE JEOPARDY

26 P is not liable to a penalty under any paragraph of this Schedule in respect of a failure or action in respect of which P has been convicted of an offence.

INTERPRETATION

27(1) This paragraph applies for the construction of this Schedule.

27(2) The withholding of information by P is–

(a) **"deliberate and concealed"** if P deliberately withholds the information and makes arrangements to conceal the fact that the information has been withheld, and

(b) **"deliberate but not concealed"** if P deliberately withholds the information but does not make arrangements to conceal the fact that the information has been withheld.

27(2A) **"The Commissioners"** means the Commissioners for Her Majesty's Revenue and Customs.

27(3) **"HMRC"** means Her Majesty's Revenue and Customs.

27(3A) **"Tax month"** means the period beginning with the 6th day of a month and ending with the 5th day of the following month.

27(4) References to a liability to tax, in relation to a return falling within item 6 in the Table (construction industry scheme), are to a liability to make payments in accordance with Chapter 3 of Part 3 of FA 2004.

27(5) References to an assessment to tax, in relation to inheritance tax and stamp duty reserve tax, are to a determination.

History – Para. 27(2A) inserted by FA 2013, s. 230 and Sch. 50, para. 9(2), with effect for the tax year 2014–15 and subsequent tax years in relation to failures to make returns with a filing date (FA 2009, Sch. 55, para. 1(4)) on or after 6 April 2014.
Para. 27(3A) inserted by FA 2013, s. 230 and Sch. 50, para. 9(3), with effect for the tax year 2014–15 and subsequent tax years in relation to failures to make returns with a filing date (FA 2009, Sch. 55, para. 1(4)) on or after 6 April 2014.

Notes – This is an edited version of Sch. 55 containing only provisions relevant for petroleum revenue tax.

SCHEDULE 56 – PENALTY FOR FAILURE TO MAKE PAYMENTS ON TIME

Section 107

Notes – This is an edited version of Sch. 56 containing only provisions relevant for petroleum revenue tax.

PENALTY FOR FAILURE TO PAY TAX

1(1) A penalty is payable by a person ("P") where P fails to pay an amount of tax specified in column 3 of the Table below on or before the date specified in column 4.

1(2) Paragraphs 3 to 8 set out–

(a) the circumstances in which a penalty is payable, and

(b) subject to paragraph 9, the amount of the penalty.

1(3) If P's failure falls within more than one provision of this Schedule, P is liable to a penalty under each of those provisions.

1(4) In the following provisions of this Schedule, the **"penalty date"**, in relation to an amount of tax, means the day after the date specified in or for the purposes of column 4 of the Table in relation to that amount.

1(5) [Not relevant to petroleum revenue tax.]

Tax to which payment relates	*Amount of tax payable*	*Date after which penalty is incurred*
	PRINCIPAL AMOUNTS	
11 Petroleum revenue tax	Amount charged in an assessment under paragraph 11(1) of Schedule 2 to OTA 1975	The date falling 30 days after the date determined in accordance with paragraph 13 of Schedule 2 to OTA 1975 as the date by which the amount must be paid
	AMOUNTS PAYABLE IN DEFAULT OF A RETURN BEING MADE	
16 Petroleum revenue tax	Amount charged in an assessment made where participator fails to deliver return for a chargeable period	The date falling 6 months and 30 days after the end of the chargeable period
	AMOUNTS SHOWN TO BE DUE IN OTHER ASSESSMENTS, DETERMINATIONS, ETC	
22 Petroleum revenue tax	Amount charged in an assessment, or an amendment of an assessment, made in circumstances other than those set out in items 11 and 16	The date falling 30 days after– (a) the date by which the amount must be paid, or (b) the date on which the assessment or amendment is made, whichever is later

Prospective amendments – In para. 1(2), "8J" substituted for "8" by F(No. 3)A 2010, s. 27 and Sch. 11, para. 2(2), with effect from a day to be appointed by Treasury order.

History – In para. 1(4), the words "the day after the date specified in or for the purposes of column 4 of the Table in relation to that amount." substituted for the words "the date on which a penalty is first payable for failing to pay the amount (that is to say, the day after the date specified in or for the purposes of column 4 of the Table)." by FA 2013, s. 230 and Sch. 50, para. 11, with effect for defaults made in relation to the tax year 2014–15 and subsequent tax years (see FA 2009, Sch. 56, para. 6(2) as to when a default is made in relation to a tax year).

Para. 1(5) inserted by F(No. 3)A 2010, s. 27 and Sch. 11, para. 2(3), with effect from 25 January 2011 (SI 2011/132, art. 2(a)).

ASSESSMENTS AND DETERMINATIONS IN DEFAULT OF RETURN

2 [Not relevant to petroleum revenue tax.]

DIFFERENT PENALTY DATE FOR CERTAIN PAYE PAYMENTS

2A [Not relevant to petroleum revenue tax.]

AMOUNT OF PENALTY: OCCASIONAL AMOUNTS AND AMOUNTS IN RESPECT OF PERIODS OF 6 MONTHS OR MORE

3(1) This paragraph applies in the case of–

(a) a payment of tax falling within any of items 1, 3 and 7 to 24 in the Table,

(aa) [not relevant to petroleum revenue tax,]

(b) [not relevant to petroleum revenue tax,]

(c) [not relevant to petroleum revenue tax,]

(ca) [not relevant to petroleum revenue tax.]

3(2) P is liable to a penalty of 5% of the unpaid tax.

3(3) If any amount of the tax is unpaid after the end of the period of 5 months beginning with the penalty date, P is liable to a penalty of 5% of that amount.

3(4) If any amount of the tax is unpaid after the end of the period of 11 months beginning with the penalty date, P is liable to a penalty of 5% of that amount.

Prospective amendments – In para. 3(1)(a), "1A," inserted (after the words "items 1,") by FA 2016, s. 167(1) and Sch. 23, para. 9(3), with effect from a day to be appointed under FA 2016, s. 167(3)

In para. 3(1)(a), "items 1, 3, 6B, 7 to 11 and 12 to 24" substituted for "items 1, 3 and 7 to 24" by F(No. 3)A 2010, s. 27 and Sch. 11, para. 5(3), with effect from a day to be appointed by Treasury order.

Para. 3(1)(d) inserted by F(No. 3)A 2010, s. 27 and Sch. 11, para. 5(5), with effect from a day to be appointed by Treasury order. Para. 3(1)(d) is not relevant to petroleum revenue tax.

Para. 3(1A) inserted by F(No. 3)A 2010, s. 27 and Sch. 11, para. 5(6), with effect from a day to be appointed by Treasury order. Para. 3(1A) relates to VAT and will not be reproduced here.

History – Para. 3(1)(aa) inserted by FA 2015, s. 104(3), with effect in relation to accounting periods beginning on or after 1 April 2015 (subject to FA 2015, s. 116(2)–(5)).

4 [Not relevant to petroleum revenue tax.]

AMOUNT OF PENALTY: PAYE AND CIS AMOUNTS ETC.

History – In the heading before para. 5, the word "ETC." inserted by FA 2016, s. 113(15), with effect from 15 September 2016 (Royal Assent).

5–8 [Not relevant to petroleum revenue tax.]

AMOUNT OF PENALTY: AMOUNTS IN RESPECT OF PERIODS OF BETWEEN 2 AND 6 MONTHS

8A–8J [Not relevant to petroleum revenue tax.]

CALCULATION OF UNPAID VAT: TREATMENT OF PAYMENTS ON ACCOUNT

8K [Prospectively inserted (see note below).]

Prospective amendments – Para. 8K inserted by F(No. 3)A 2010, s. 27 and Sch. 11, para. 8, with effect from a day to be appointed. Para. 8K relates to VAT and will not be reproduced here.

SPECIAL REDUCTION

9(1) If HMRC think it right because of special circumstances, they may reduce a penalty under any paragraph of this Schedule.

9(2) In sub-paragraph (1) **"special circumstances"** does not include–

(a) ability to pay, or

(b) the fact that a potential loss of revenue from one taxpayer is balanced by a potential over-payment by another.

9(3) In sub-paragraph (1) the reference to reducing a penalty includes a reference to–

(a) staying a penalty, and

(b) agreeing a compromise in relation to proceedings for a penalty.

INTERACTION WITH OTHER PENALTIES AND LATE PAYMENT SURCHARGES

9A In the application of the following provisions, no account shall be taken of a penalty under this Schedule–

(a) [not relevant to petroleum revenue tax,]

(b) paragraph 12(2) of Schedule 24 to FA 2007 (interaction with other penalties), and

(c) [not relevant to petroleum revenue tax,]

History – Para. 9A inserted by FA 2013, s. 230 and Sch. 50, para. 13, with effect for defaults made in relation to the tax year 2014–15 and subsequent tax years (see FA 2009, Sch. 56, para. 6(2) as to when a default is made in relation to a tax year).

SUSPENSION OF PENALTY DURING CURRENCY OF AGREEMENT FOR DEFERRED PAYMENT

10(1) This paragraph applies if–

(a) P fails to pay an amount of tax when it becomes due and payable,

(b) P makes a request to HMRC that payment of the amount of tax be deferred, and

(c) HMRC agrees that payment of that amount may be deferred for a period ("the deferral period").

10(2) If P would (apart from this sub-paragraph) become liable, between the date on which P makes the request and the end of the deferral period, to a penalty under any paragraph of this Schedule for failing to pay that amount, P is not liable to that penalty.

10(3) But if–

(a) P breaks the agreement (see sub-paragraph (4)), and

(b) HMRC serves on P a notice specifying any penalty to which P would become liable apart from sub-paragraph (2),

P becomes liable, at the date of the notice, to that penalty.

10(4) P breaks an agreement if–

(a) P fails to pay the amount of tax in question when the deferral period ends, or

(b) the deferral is subject to P complying with a condition (including a condition that part of the amount be paid during the deferral period) and P fails to comply with it.

10(5) If the agreement mentioned in sub-paragraph (1)(c) is varied at any time by a further agreement between P and HMRC this paragraph applies from that time to the agreement as varied.

ASSESSMENT

11(1) Where P is liable for a penalty under any paragraph of this Schedule HMRC must–
(a) assess the penalty,
(b) notify P, and
(c) state in the notice the period in respect of which the penalty is assessed.

11(2) A penalty under any paragraph of this Schedule must be paid before the end of the period of 30 days beginning with the day on which notice of the assessment of the penalty is issued.

11(3) An assessment of a penalty under any paragraph of this Schedule–
(a) is to be treated for procedural purposes in the same way as an assessment to tax (except in respect of a matter expressly provided for by this Schedule),
(b) may be enforced as if it were an assessment to tax, and
(c) may be combined with an assessment to tax.

11(4) A supplementary assessment may be made in respect of a penalty if an earlier assessment operated by reference to an underestimate of an amount of unpaid tax.

11(5) [Omitted by FA 2013, s. 230 and Sch. 50, para. 14(3).]

Prospective amendments – In para. 11(4), the words "tax which was due or payable" substituted for the words "unpaid tax" by F(No. 3)A 2010, s. 27 and Sch. 11, para. 9(2), with effect from a day to be appointed by Treasury order.
Former para. 11(4A) inserted by F(No. 3)A 2010, s. 27 and Sch. 11, para. 9(3), with effect from a day to be appointed by Treasury order. Para. 11(4A), as amended by FA 2013, s. 230 and Sch. 50, para. 14(2), to read as follows:
"**11(4A)** If an assessment in respect of a penalty is based on an amount of tax due or payable that is found by HMRC to be excessive, HMRC may by notice to P amend the assessment so that it is based upon the correct amount.
11(4B) An amendment made under sub-paragraph (4A)–
(a) does not affect when the penalty must be paid;
(b) may be made after the last day on which the assessment in question could have been made under paragraph 12.".

History – Para. 11(4A) and (4B) substituted for para. 11(4A) by FA 2013, s. 230 and Sch. 50, para. 14(2) with effect for defaults made in relation to the tax year 2014–15 and subsequent tax years (see FA 2009, Sch. 56, para. 6(2) as to when a default is made in relation to a tax year).
Para. 11(5) omitted by FA 2013, s. 230 and Sch. 50, para. 14(3) with effect for defaults made in relation to the tax year 2014–15 and subsequent tax years (see FA 2009, Sch. 56, para. 6(2) as to when a default is made in relation to a tax year).

Notes – The amendments made by F(No. 3)A 2010, s. 27 and Sch. 11, para. 9(2) and (3), were brought into effect from 6 April 2011 for the purposes of items 1, 12, 18 or 19 of the Table in para. 1 (income tax self assessment) (and insofar as the tax falls within item 1 of that Table, item 17, 23 or 24 of that Table) (SI 2011/703, art. 3).

12(1) An assessment of a penalty under any paragraph of this Schedule in respect of any amount must be made on or before the later of date A and (where it applies) date B.

12(2) Date A is the last day of the period of 2 years beginning with the date specified in or for the purposes of column 4 of the Table (that is to say, the last date on which payment may be made without incurring a penalty).

12(3) Date B is the last day of the period of 12 months beginning with–
(a) the end of the appeal period for the assessment of the amount of tax in respect of which the penalty is assessed, or
(b) if there is no such assessment, the date on which that amount of tax is ascertained.

12(4) In sub-paragraph (3)(a) **"appeal period"** means the period during which–
(a) an appeal could be brought, or
(b) an appeal that has been brought has not been determined or withdrawn.

APPEAL

13(1) P may appeal against a decision of HMRC that a penalty is payable by P.

13(2) P may appeal against a decision of HMRC as to the amount of a penalty payable by P.

14(1) An appeal under paragraph 13 is to be treated in the same way as an appeal against an assessment to the tax concerned (including by the application of any provision about bringing the appeal by notice to HMRC, about HMRC review of the decision or about determination of the appeal by the First-tier Tribunal or Upper Tribunal).

14(2) Sub-paragraph (1) does not apply–
(a) so as to require P to pay a penalty before an appeal against the assessment of the penalty is determined, or
(b) in respect of any other matter expressly provided for by this Act.

15(1) On an appeal under paragraph 13(1) that is notified to the tribunal, the tribunal may affirm or cancel HMRC's decision.

15(2) On an appeal under paragraph 13(2) that is notified to the tribunal, the tribunal may–

(a) affirm HMRC's decision, or

(b) substitute for HMRC's decision another decision that HMRC had power to make.

15(3) If the tribunal substitutes its decision for HMRC's, the tribunal may rely on paragraph 9–

(a) to the same extent as HMRC (which may mean applying the same percentage reduction as HMRC to a different starting point), or

(b) to a different extent, but only if the tribunal thinks that HMRC's decision in respect of the application of paragraph 9 was flawed.

15(4) In sub-paragraph (3)(b) **"flawed"** means flawed when considered in the light of the principles applicable in proceedings for judicial review.

15(5) In this paragraph **"tribunal"** means the First-tier Tribunal or Upper Tribunal (as appropriate by virtue of paragraph 14(1)).

REASONABLE EXCUSE

16(1) Liability to a penalty under any paragraph of this Schedule does not arise in relation to a failure to make a payment if P satisfies HMRC or (on appeal) the First-tier Tribunal or Upper Tribunal that there is a reasonable excuse for the failure.

16(2) For the purposes of sub-paragraph (1)–

(a) an insufficiency of funds is not a reasonable excuse unless attributable to events outside P's control,

(b) where P relies on any other person to do anything, that is not a reasonable excuse unless P took reasonable care to avoid the failure, and

(c) where P had a reasonable excuse for the failure but the excuse has ceased, P is to be treated as having continued to have the excuse if the failure is remedied without unreasonable delay after the excuse ceased.

Prospective amendments – Para. 16(1) substituted by F(No. 3)A 2010, s. 27 and Sch. 11, para. 10, with effect from a day to be appointed by Treasury order. The substituted para. 16(1) to read as follows:

"**16(1)** If P satisfies HMRC or (on appeal) the First-tier Tribunal or Upper Tribunal that there is a reasonable excuse for a failure to make a payment–

(a) liability to a penalty under any paragraph of this Schedule does not arise in relation to that failure, and

(b) the failure does not count as a default for the purposes of paragraphs 6, 8B, 8C, 8G and 8H."

Notes – The substitution of para. 16(1) by F(No. 3)A 2010, s. 27 and Sch. 11, para. 10 was brought into effect from 25 January 2011 for the purposes of item 2 (PAYE regulations), item 3 (returns under FA 2004, s. 254(1)) and item 4 (FA 2004, s. 62) of the Table in para. 1 and items 17, 23 and 24 but only insofar as the tax falls within any of items 2, 3 or 4 (SI 2011/132, art. 3).

DOUBLE JEOPARDY

17 P is not liable to a penalty under any paragraph of this Schedule in respect of a failure or action in respect of which P has been convicted of an offence.

INTERPRETATION

18(1) This paragraph applies for the construction of this Schedule.

18(2) **"HMRC"** means Her Majesty's Revenue and Customs.

18(3) References to tax include construction industry deductions under Chapter 3 of Part 3 of FA 2004.

18(4) References to a determination, in relation to an amount payable under PAYE regulations or under Chapter 3 of Part 3 of FA 2004, include a certificate.

18(5) References to an assessment to tax, in relation to inheritance tax and stamp duty reserve tax, are to a determination.

FINANCE ACT 2010

(2010 Chapter 13)

[*8th April 2010*]

ARRANGEMENT OF SECTIONS

PART 2 – ANTI-AVOIDANCE AND REVENUE PROTECTION

PART 3 – OTHER PROVISIONS

SCHEDULES

PART 2 – ANTI-AVOIDANCE AND REVENUE PROTECTION

CHARITIES ETC

30 Charities and community amateur sports clubs: definitions

30 Schedule 6 contains provision about the meaning of **"charity"** (and related expressions) and **"community amateur sports club"**.

OTHER INTERNATIONAL MATTERS

35 Penalties: offshore income etc

35(1) Schedule 10 contains provision about penalties in respect of offshore income etc.

35(2) Schedule 10 comes into force on such day as the Treasury may by order appoint.

35(3) An order under subsection (2)–

(a) may make different provision for different purposes, and

(b) may include transitional provisions and savings.

35(4) The Treasury may by order make any incidental, supplemental, consequential, transitional or transitory provision or saving that appears appropriate in consequence of, or otherwise in connection with, Schedule 10.

35(5) An order under subsection (4) may–

(a) make different provision for different purposes, and

(b) make provision amending, repealing or revoking an enactment or instrument (whenever passed or made).

35(6) An order under this section is to be made by statutory instrument.

35(7) A statutory instrument containing an order under subsection (4) is subject to annulment in pursuance of a resolution of the House of Commons.

Statutory instruments – SI 2011/975 (not reproduced): made under s. 35(2) and (3).

ADMINISTRATION

56 Disclosure of tax avoidance schemes

56 Schedule 17 contains amendments of the provisions relating to the disclosure of tax avoidance schemes.

PART 3 – OTHER PROVISIONS

FINAL PROVISIONS

69 Interpretation

69(1) In this Act–

"ALDA 1979" means the Alcoholic Liquor Duties Act 1979;

"BGDA 1981" means the Betting and Gaming Duties Act 1981;

"CAA 2001" means the Capital Allowances Act 2001;

"CTA 2009" means the Corporation Tax Act 2009;

"CTA 2010" means the Corporation Tax Act 2010;

"FISMA 2000" means the Financial Services and Markets Act 2000;

"HODA 1979" means the Hydrocarbon Oil Duties Act 1979;

"ICTA" means the Income and Corporation Taxes Act 1988;

"IHTA 1984" means the Inheritance Tax Act 1984;

"ITA 2007" means the Income Tax Act 2007;

"ITEPA 2003" means the Income Tax (Earnings and Pensions) Act 2003;

"ITTOIA 2005" means the Income Tax (Trading and Other Income) Act 2005;

"TCGA 1992" means the Taxation of Chargeable Gains Act 1992;

"TIOPA 2010" means the Taxation (International and Other Provisions) Act 2010;

"TMA 1970" means the Taxes Management Act 1970;

"TPDA 1979" means the Tobacco Products Duty Act 1979;

"VATA 1994" means the Value Added Tax Act 1994;

"VERA 1994" means the Vehicle Excise and Registration Act 1994.

69(2) In this Act–

"FA", followed by a year, means the Finance Act of that year;

"F(No. 2)A", followed by a year, means the Finance (No. 2) Act of that year.

70 Short title

70 This Act may be cited as the Finance Act 2010.

SCHEDULES

SCHEDULE 6 – CHARITIES AND COMMUNITY AMATEUR SPORTS CLUBS: DEFINITIONS

Section 30

Part 1 – Definition of "Charity", "Charitable Company" and "Charitable Trust"

DEFINITION OF "CHARITY" ETC

1(1) For the purposes of the enactments to which this Part applies **"charity"** means a body of persons or trust that–

(a) is established for charitable purposes only,

(b) meets the jurisdiction condition (see paragraph 2),

(c) meets the registration condition (see paragraph 3), and

(d) meets the management condition (see paragraph 4).

1(2) For the purposes of the enactments to which this Part applies–

"charitable company" means a charity that is a body of persons;

"charitable trust" means a charity that is a trust.

1(3) Sub-paragraphs (1) and (2) are subject to any express provision to the contrary.

1(4) For the meaning of **"charitable purpose"**, see section 2 of the Charities Act 2011 (which–

(a) applies regardless of where the body of persons or trust in question is established, and

(b) for this purpose forms part of the law of each part of the United Kingdom (see sections 7 and 8 of that Act)).

History – In para. 1(4), the words "see section 2 of the Charities Act 2011" substituted for the words "see section 2 of the Charities Act 2006" by Charities Act 2011, s. 354 and Sch. 7, para. 143(2)(a), with effect from the end of the period of 3 months beginning with 14 December 2011.

In para. 1(4)(b), the words "(see sections 7 and 8 of that Act)" substituted for the words "(see section 80(3) to (6) of that Act)" by Charities Act 2011, s. 354 and Sch. 7, para. 143(2)(b), with effect from the end of the period of 3 months beginning with 14 December 2011.

JURISDICTION CONDITION

2(1) A body of persons or trust meets the jurisdiction condition if it falls to be subject to the control of–

(a) a relevant UK court in the exercise of its jurisdiction with respect to charities, or

(b) any other court in the exercise of a corresponding jurisdiction under the law of a relevant territory.

2(2) In sub-paragraph (1)(a) **"a relevant UK court"** means–

(a) the High Court,

(b) the Court of Session, or

(c) the High Court in Northern Ireland.

2(3) In sub-paragraph (1)(b) **"a relevant territory"** means–

(a) a member State other than the United Kingdom, or

(b) a territory specified in regulations made by the Commissioners for Her Majesty's Revenue and Customs.

2(4) Regulations under this paragraph are to be made by statutory instrument.

2(5) A statutory instrument containing regulations under this paragraph is subject to annulment in pursuance of a resolution of the House of Commons.

REGISTRATION CONDITION

3(1) A body of persons or trust meets the registration condition if–

(a) in the case of a body of persons or trust that is a charity within the meaning of section 10 of the Charities Act 2011, condition A is met, and

(b) in the case of any other body of persons or trust, condition B is met.

3(2) Condition A is that the body of persons or trust has complied with any requirement to be registered in the register of charities kept under section 29 of the Charities Act 2011.

3(3) Condition B is that the body of persons or trust has complied with any requirement under the law of a territory outside England and Wales to be registered in a register corresponding to that mentioned in sub-paragraph (2).

History – In para. 3(1)(a), the words "within the meaning of section 10 of the Charities Act 2011" substituted for the words "within the meaning of the Charities Act 1993" by Charities Act 2011, s. 354 and Sch. 7, para. 143(3), with effect from the end of the period of 3 months beginning with 14 December 2011.

In para. 3(2), the words "section 29 of the Charities Act 2011" substituted for the words "section 3 of the Charities Act 1993" by Charities Act 2011, s. 354 and Sch. 7, para. 143(4), with effect from the end of the period of 3 months beginning with 14 December 2011.

MANAGEMENT CONDITION

4(1) A body of persons or trust meets the management condition if its managers are fit and proper persons to be managers of the body or trust.

4(2) In this paragraph **"managers"**, in relation to a body of persons or trust, means the persons having the general control and management of the administration of the body or trust.

PERIODS OVER WHICH MANAGEMENT CONDITION TREATED AS MET

5(1) This paragraph applies in relation to any period throughout which the management condition is not met.

5(2) The management condition is treated as met throughout the period if the Commissioners for Her Majesty's Revenue and Customs consider that–

(a) the failure to meet the management condition has not prejudiced the charitable purposes of the body or trust, or

(b) it is just and reasonable in all the circumstances for the condition to be treated as met throughout the period.

PUBLICATION OF NAMES AND ADDRESSES OF BODIES OR TRUSTS REGARDED BY HMRC AS CHARITIES

6 Her Majesty's Revenue and Customs may publish the name and address of any body of persons or trust that appears to them to meet, or at any time to have met, the definition of a charity in paragraph 1.

ENACTMENTS TO WHICH THIS PART APPLIES

7 The enactments to which this Part applies are the enactments relating to–

(a) income tax

(b) capital gains tax,

(c) corporation tax,

(d) value added tax,

(e) inheritance tax,

(f) stamp duty,

(g) stamp duty land tax,

(h) stamp duty reserve tax,

(i) annual tax on enveloped dwellings, and

(j) diverted profits tax.

History – Para. 7(i) (and the word ", and" before it) inserted (and the word "and" formerly at end of para. 7(g) omitted) by FA 2013, s. 168 and Sch. 35, para. 3, with effect from 17 July 2013 (Royal Assent).

Para. 7(j) (and the word ", and" before it) inserted (and the word "and" formerly at end of para. 7(h) omitted) by FA 2015, s. 115(2), with effect in relation to accounting periods beginning on or after 1 April 2015.

Part 2 – Repeals of Superseded Definitions and Other Consequential Amendments

Notes – *Only paragraphs relating to petroleum revenue are tax reproduced here.*

FA 2008

24 [Amends FA 2008, Sch. 36, para. 60(2).]

POWER TO MAKE FURTHER CONSEQUENTIAL PROVISION

29(1) The Commissioners for Her Majesty's Revenue and Customs may by order make such further consequential, incidental, supplemental, transitional or transitory provision or saving as appears appropriate in consequence of, or otherwise in connection with, Part 1.

29(2) An order under this paragraph may–

(a) make different provision for different purposes, and

(b) make provision repealing, revoking or otherwise amending any enactment or instrument (whenever passed or made).

29(3) An order under this paragraph is to be made by statutory instrument.

29(4) A statutory instrument containing an order under this paragraph is subject to annulment in pursuance of an order of the House of Commons.

Part 4 – Commencement

COMMENCEMENT OF PART 1

33(1) Part 1 is treated as having come into force on 6 April 2010.

33(2) But the definitions of **"charity"**, **"charitable company"** and **"charitable trust"** in that Part do not apply for the purposes of an enactment in relation to which, on that date, another definition applies until such time as that other definition ceases to have effect on the coming into force of provision made by or under Part 2.

33(3) For provision about the coming into force of provision made by that Part, see paragraph 34.

COMMENCEMENT OF PART 2

34(1) The repeal of the definition of **"charity"** in section 989 of ITA 2007 made by paragraph 23(6) above has effect–

(a) so far as it applies for the purposes of Chapter 2 of Part 8 of that Act (gift aid), in relation to gifts made on or after 6 April 2010, and

(b) so far as it applies for other purposes, in accordance with such provision as the Treasury may make by order.

34(2) The other amendments made by Part 2 come into force in accordance with such provision as the Treasury may make by order.

34(3) An order under this paragraph may–

(a) make different provision for different purposes, and

(b) include transitional provision and savings.

34(4) An order under this paragraph is to be made by statutory instrument.

SCHEDULE 10 – PENALTIES: OFFSHORE INCOME ETC

Section 35

Other material – HMRC Brief 14/11: Penalty for failure to disclose offshore income or gains.

SCHEDULE 24 TO FA 2007

1 Schedule 24 to FA 2007 (penalties for errors) is amended as follows.

2 [Substitutes FA 2007, Sch. 24, para. 4, 4A, 4B, 4C, 4D.]

3 [Substitutes FA 2007, Sch. 24, para. 10.]

4 [Substitutes FA 2007, Sch. 24, para. 12(4), (5).]

5 [Inserts FA 2007, Sch. 24, para. 21A, 21B.]

6 [Inserts FA 2007, Sch. 24, para. 23B.]

SCHEDULE 55 TO FA 2009

10 Schedule 55 to FA 2009 (penalties for failure to make returns etc) is amended as follows.

11(1) Paragraph 6 (amount of penalty if failure continues more than 12 months) is amended as follows.

11(2) [Amends FA 2009, Sch. 55, para. 6(3)(a).]

11(3) [Inserts FA 2009, Sch. 55, para. 6(3A).]

11(4) [Amends FA 2009, Sch. 55, para. 6(4)(a).]

11(5) [Inserts FA 2009, Sch. 55, para. 6(4A).]

11(6) [Inserts FA 2009, Sch. 55, para. 6(6).]

12 [Inserts FA 2009, Sch. 55, para. 6A.]

13(1) Paragraph 15 (reductions for disclosure) is amended as follows.

13(2) For sub-paragraphs (1) and (2) substitute–

"**15(1)** If a person who would otherwise be liable to a penalty of a percentage shown in column 1 of the Table (a "standard percentage") has made a disclosure, HMRC must reduce the standard percentage to one that reflects the quality of the disclosure.

15(2) But the standard percentage may not be reduced to a percentage that is below the minimum shown for it–

(a) in the case of a prompted disclosure, in column 2 of the Table, and

(b) in the case of an unprompted disclosure, in column 3 of the Table.

Standard %	*Minimum % for prompted disclosure*	*Minimum % for unprompted disclosure*
70%	35%	20%
105%	52.5%	30%
140%	70%	40%
100%	50%	30%
150%	75%	45%
200%	100%	60%".

13(3) Omit sub-paragraphs (3) and (4).

14 In paragraph 17 (interaction with other penalties)–

(a) in sub-paragraph (3), for "100%" substitute "the relevant percentage", and

(b) after that sub-paragraph insert–

"**17(4)** The relevant percentage is–

(a) if one of the penalties is a penalty under paragraph 6(3) or (4) and the information withheld is category 3 information, 200%,

(b) if one of the penalties is a penalty under paragraph 6(3) or (4) and the information withheld is category 2 information, 150%, and

(c) in all other cases, 100%."

SCHEDULE 17 – DISCLOSURE OF TAX AVOIDANCE SCHEMES

Section 56

INTRODUCTION

1 Part 7 of FA 2004 (disclosure of tax avoidance schemes) is amended as follows.

INITIAL MARKETING

2(1) Section 307 (meaning of **"promoter"**) is amended as follows.

2(2) [Amends FA 2004, s. 307(1)(a).]

2(3) [Amends FA 2004, s. 307(1)(b).]

2(4) [Inserts FA 2004, s. 307(1A).]

2(5) [Inserts FA 2004, s. 307(4A), (4B) and (4C).]

2(6) [Amends FA 2004, s. 307(5).]

2(7) [Amends FA 2004, s. 307(6).]

3(1) Section 308(2) (duties of promoter) is amended as follows.

3(2) [Amends FA 2004, s. 308(2).]

3(3) [Inserts FA 2004, s. 308(2)(za).]

4 [Amends FA 2004, s. 313A(1).]

5 [Amends FA 2004, s. 318(1).]

PROMOTERS TO PROVIDE CLIENT LISTS

6 [Inserts FA 2004, s. 313ZA.]

7 [Amends FA 2004, s. 316.]

8 [Amends FA 2004, s. 317(2).]

INFORMATION PROVIDED TO INTRODUCERS

9 [Inserts FA 2004, s. 313C.]

PENALTIES

10(1) Section 98C of TMA 1970 (penalties for failures to comply with duties relating to disclosure of tax avoidance schemes) is amended as follows.

10(2) [Amends TMA 1970, s. 98C(1)(a).]

10(3) In subsection (2)–

(a) [amends TMA 1970, s. 98C(2)(da),]

(b) [inserts TMA 1970, s. 98C(2)(db),]

(c) [inserts TMA 1970, s. 98C(2)(f).]

10(4) [Inserts TMA 1970, s. 98C(2ZA), (2ZB), (2ZC), (2ZD) and (2ZE).]

10(5) [Amends TMA 1970, s. 98C(2A).]

10(6) [Amends TMA 1970, s. 98C(2B).]

10(7) [Amends TMA 1970, s. 98C(2C)(b).]

10(8) [Amends TMA 1970, s. 98C(2D).]

10(9) [Amends TMA 1970, s. 98C(2E).]

10(10) In subsection (2F)–

(a) [amends TMA 1970, s. 98C(2C),]

(b) [amends TMA 1970, s. 98C(2C)(c).]

COMMENCEMENT

11(1) The amendments made by this Schedule come into force on such day as the Treasury may by order made by statutory instrument appoint.

11(2) An order may appoint different days for different provisions or for different purposes.

Statutory instruments – SI 2010/3019 (not reproduced): appoints 1 January 2011 as the commencement day for the amendments made by Sch. 17.

FINANCE (NO. 3) ACT 2010

(2010 Chapter 33)

[*16th December 2010*]

ARRANGEMENT OF SECTIONS

PART 3 – ADMINISTRATION

PART 5 – FINAL PROVISIONS

SCHEDULES

PART 3 – ADMINISTRATION

25 Interest: corporation tax and petroleum revenue tax

25(1) Schedule 9 contains amendments of FA 2009 relating to late payment interest and repayment interest on amounts of corporation tax and petroleum revenue tax.

25(2) That Schedule comes into force on such day as the Treasury may by order appoint.

25(3) An order under subsection (2)–

(a) may commence a provision generally or only for specified purposes, and

(b) may appoint different days for different provisions or for different purposes.

25(4) The Treasury may by order make any incidental, supplemental, consequential, transitional, transitory or saving provision which appears appropriate in consequence of, or otherwise in connection with, that Schedule.

25(5) An order under subsection (4) may–

(a) make different provision for different purposes, and

(b) make provision amending, repealing or revoking any Act or subordinate legislation whenever passed or made (including this Act and any Act amended by it).

25(6) An order under this section is to be made by statutory instrument.

25(7) A statutory instrument containing an order under subsection (4) which includes provision amending or repealing any provision of an Act is subject to annulment in pursuance of a resolution of the House of Commons.

26 Penalties for failure to make returns etc

26(1) Schedule 10 contains provision amending Schedule 55 to FA 2009 (penalties in respect of failures to make returns and other documents relating to liabilities for tax).

26(2) *Schedule 10 comes into force on such day as the Treasury may by order appoint.*

26(3) An order under subsection (2)–

(a) may commence a provision generally or only for specified purposes, and

(b) may appoint different days for different provisions or for different purposes.

26(4) The Treasury may by order make any incidental, supplemental, consequential, transitional, transitory or saving provision which appears appropriate in consequence of, or otherwise in connection with, that Schedule.

26(5) An order under subsection (4) may–

(a) make different provision for different purposes, and

(b) make provision amending, repealing or revoking any Act or subordinate legislation whenever passed or made (including this Act and any Act amended by it).

26(6) An order under this section is to be made by statutory instrument.

26(7) A statutory instrument containing an order under subsection (4) which includes provision amending or repealing any provision of an Act is subject to annulment in pursuance of a resolution of the House of Commons.

27 Penalties for failure to pay tax

27(1) Schedule 11 contains provision amending Schedule 56 to FA 2009 (penalties in respect of failures to comply with obligations to pay tax).

27(2) Schedule 11 comes into force on such day as the Treasury may by order appoint.

27(3) An order under subsection (2)–

(a) may commence a provision generally or only for specified purposes, and

(b) may appoint different days for different provisions or for different purposes.

27(4) The Treasury may by order make any incidental, supplemental, consequential, transitional, transitory or saving provision which appears appropriate in consequence of, or otherwise in connection with, that Schedule.

27(5) An order under subsection (4) may–

(a) make different provision for different purposes, and

(b) make provision amending, repealing or revoking any Act or subordinate legislation whenever passed or made (including this Act and any Act amended by it).

27(6) An order under this section is to be made by statutory instrument.

27(7) A statutory instrument containing an order under subsection (4) which includes provision amending or repealing any provision of an Act is subject to annulment in pursuance of a resolution of the House of Commons.

28 Recovery of overpaid stamp duty land tax and petroleum revenue tax etc

28(1) Schedule 12 contains–

(a) provision amending Part 4 of FA 2003 (stamp duty land tax) in respect of the recovery of overpaid tax etc, and

(b) provision amending Schedule 2 to OTA 1975 (management and collection of petroleum revenue tax) in respect of the recovery of overpaid tax etc.

28(2) The amendments made by Schedule 12 have effect in relation to claims made on or after 1 April 2011.

28(3) The Treasury may by order make any incidental, supplemental, consequential, transitional, transitory or saving provision which appears appropriate in consequence of, or otherwise in connection with, that Schedule.

28(4) An order under this section may–

(a) make different provision for different purposes, and

(b) make provision amending, repealing or revoking any Act or subordinate legislation whenever passed or made (including this Act and any Act amended by it).

28(5) An order under this section is to be made by statutory instrument.

28(6) A statutory instrument containing an order under this section which includes provision amending or repealing any provision of an Act is subject to annulment in pursuance of a resolution of the House of Commons.

PART 5 – FINAL PROVISIONS

32 Interpretation

32(1) In this Act–

"BGDA 1981" means the Betting and Gaming Duties Act 1981;

"CAA 2001" means the Capital Allowances Act 2001;

"CTA 2009" means the Corporation Tax Act 2009;

"CTA 2010" means the Corporation Tax Act 2010;

"HODA 1979" means the Hydrocarbon Oil Duties Act 1979;

"ICTA" means the Income and Corporation Taxes Act 1988;

"IHTA 1984" means the Inheritance Tax Act 1984;

"ITA 2007" means the Income Tax Act 2007;

"ITEPA 2003" means the Income Tax (Earnings and Pensions) Act 2003;

"ITTOIA 2005" means the Income Tax (Trading and Other Income) Act 2005;

"OTA 1975" means the Oil Taxation Act 1975;

"TCGA 1992" means the Taxation of Chargeable Gains Act 1992;

"TIOPA 2010" means the Taxation (International and Other Provisions) Act 2010;

"TMA 1970" means the Taxes Management Act 1970;

"TPDA 1979" means the Tobacco Products Duty Act 1979;

"VATA 1994" means the Value Added Tax Act 1994;

"VERA 1994" means the Vehicle Excise and Registration Act 1994.

32(2) In this Act–

"FA", followed by a year, means the Finance Act of that year;

"F(No. 2)A", followed by a year, means the Finance (No. 2) Act of that year.

33 Short title

This Act may be cited as the Finance (No. 3) Act 2010.

SCHEDULES

SCHEDULE 9 – INTEREST

Section 25

Part 1 – Corporation Tax

AMENDMENTS OF SECTIONS 101 TO 104

1 FA 2009 is amended as follows.

2 In section 101 (late payment interest on sums due to HMRC), omit subsection (2)(a).

3(1) Section 102 (repayment interest on sums to be paid by HMRC) is amended as follows.

3(2) Omit subsection (2)(a).

3(3) [Not relevant to petroleum revenue tax.]

5 In section 104(1), for "103" substitute "103A (and Schedules 53 to 54A)".

Part 2 – Petroleum Revenue Tax

13 FA 2009 is amended as follows.

14 In section 101 (late payment interest on sums due to HMRC), omit subsection (2)(b).

15 In section 102 (repayment interest on sums to be paid by HMRC), omit subsection (2)(b).

16 *Schedule 53 (late payment interest)* is amended as follows.

17 After paragraph 11 insert–

"INSTALMENTS OF PETROLEUM REVENUE TAX

11A The late payment interest start date in respect of an instalment of petroleum revenue tax payable under paragraph 2 of Schedule 19 to FA 1982 (payment for tax) is the last day of the month in which that instalment is payable.

OTHER AMOUNTS OF PETROLEUM REVENUE TAX

11B The late payment interest start date in respect of any other amount of petroleum revenue tax is the date falling two months after the end of the chargeable period in respect of which the amount is due."

18 After paragraph 14 insert–

"INSTALMENTS OF PETROLEUM REVENUE TAX

14A(1) An instalment of petroleum revenue tax payable under paragraph 2 of Schedule 19 to FA 1982 (payment for tax) carries late payment interest until the earlier of–

(a) the date on which the instalment is paid, and

(b) the date falling two months after the end of the chargeable period in respect of which the instalment is due.

14A(2) An instalment which remains unpaid after the date mentioned in sub-paragraph (1)(b) carries interest as an amount payable on account under section 1 of PRTA 1980.

14A(3) For the purposes of determining the date on which an overdue instalment is paid, a payment on account of one or more such instalments is to be attributed, so far as possible, to the earliest month for which an instalment is overdue."

19 In Schedule 54 (repayment interest), after paragraph 12 insert–

"PETROLEUM REVENUE TAX

12A(1) The repayment interest start date in respect of any amount of petroleum revenue tax is the later of–

(a) the date falling two months after the end of the chargeable period in respect of which the amount was paid, and

(b) the date on which the amount was paid.

12A(2) Sub-paragraph (1) is subject to paragraph 12B (limit on amount of repayment interest carried by certain repayments generated by carry back reliefs).

12A(3) For the purposes of this paragraph any instalment or part of an instalment that becomes repayable is to be regarded, so far as possible, as consisting of the instalment most recently paid.

12B(1) This paragraph applies where–

(a) an assessment for a chargeable period ("the earlier period") gives effect to relief under section 7(2) or (3) of OTA 1975 for one or more allowable losses accruing in a later chargeable period, and

(b) by virtue of that assessment, an amount of tax becomes repayable to the participator in question (whether wholly or partly by reason of giving effect to that relief).

12B(2) The amount of repayment interest carried by the appropriate repayment is not to exceed the difference between–

(a) 60% of the amount of the allowable loss or losses which is treated as reducing the assessable profit of the earlier period, and

(b) the amount of the appropriate repayment.

12B(3) In this paragraph **"the appropriate repayment"** means so much of the repayment as is attributable to giving effect to the relief (but this is subject to sub-paragraphs (4) and (5)).

12B(4) Sub-paragraph (5) applies where the assessment (as well as giving effect to the relief mentioned in sub-paragraph (1)) takes account of any other matter, whether a relief or not, which goes–

(a) to reduce the assessable profit of the earlier period, or

(b) otherwise to reduce the tax payable for that period.

12B(5) The appropriate repayment is to be taken to be the difference between–

(a) the total amount of tax repayable by virtue of the assessment, and

(b) the amount of tax (if any) which would have been repayable if no account had been taken of that relief.

12B(6) If the earlier period ends on or before 30 June 1993, sub-paragraph (2) has effect as if the percentage specified in paragraph (a) were 85%.

12B(7) In this paragraph references to an assessment include an amendment of an assessment."

SCHEDULE 10 – PENALTY FOR FAILURE TO MAKE RETURNS ETC

Section 26

1 Schedule 55 to FA 2009 (penalty for failure to make returns etc) is amended as follows.

2(1) Paragraph 1 (penalty for failure) is amended as follows.

2(2) In sub-paragraph (2), for "13" substitute "13J".

2(3) The Table is amended as follows.

2(4) [Not relevant to petroleum revenue tax.]

2(5) [Not relevant to petroleum revenue tax.]

3 For paragraph 2 (amount of penalty for occasional or annual returns) and the italic heading preceding it substitute–

"AMOUNT OF PENALTY: OCCASIONAL RETURNS AND RETURNS FOR PERIODS OF 6 MONTHS OR MORE

2(1) Paragraphs 3 to 6 apply in the case of–

(a) a return falling within any of items 1 to 5, 7 and 8 to 13 in the Table,

(b) a return falling within any of items 7A, 7B and 14 to 28 which relates to a period of 6 months or more, and

(c) a return falling within item 7A which relates to a transitional period for the purposes of the annual accounting scheme.

2(2) In sub-paragraph (1)(c), a transitional period for the purposes of the annual accounting scheme is a prescribed accounting period (within the meaning of section 25(1) of VATA 1994) which–

(a) ends on the day immediately preceding the date indicated by the Commissioners for Her Majesty's Revenue and Customs in a notification of authorisation under regulation 50 of the Value Added Tax Regulations 1995 (S.I. 1995/2518) (admission to annual accounting scheme), or

(b) begins on the day immediately following the end of the last period of 12 months for which such an authorisation has effect."

4(1) Paragraph 6 (amount of penalty for occasional returns and annual returns) is amended as follows.

4(2) In sub-paragraph (2), after "P" in the first place it occurs insert "deliberately".

4(3) In sub-paragraph (5), for "any other case" substitute "any case not falling within sub-paragraph (2)".

8 In paragraph 14(1) (reductions for disclosure), for "or 11(3) or (4)" substitute ", 11(3) or (4), 13E(3) or (4) or 13J(3) or (4)".

9 In paragraph 15(5) (reductions for disclosure not below certain amounts)–

(a) for "paragraph 11(3) or (4)" substitute "sub-paragraph (3) or (4) of any of paragraphs 11, 13E and 13J", and

(b) for "paragraph 11(3)(b) or (4)(b) (as the case may be)" substitute "paragraph (b) of that sub-paragraph".

10 [Repealed by FA 2013, s. 230 and Sch. 50, para. 15.]

History – Para. 10 repealed by FA 2013, s. 230 and Sch. 50, para. 15, with effect for the tax year 2014–15 and subsequent tax years in relation to failures to make returns with a filing date (as defined in FA 2009, Sch. 55, para. 1(4)) on or after 6 April 2014. Former para. 10 inserted *FA 2009, Sch. 55, para. 18(5).*

11 For paragraph 23(1) (no liability where there is reasonable excuse for failure) substitute–

"**23(1)** If P satisfies HMRC or (on appeal) the First-tier Tribunal or Upper Tribunal that there is a reasonable excuse for a failure to make a return–

(a) liability to a penalty under any paragraph of this Schedule does not arise in relation to that failure, and

(b) the failure does not count for the purposes of paragraphs 13B(2), 13C, 13G(2) and 13H."

SCHEDULE 11 – PENALTY FOR FAILURE TO MAKE PAYMENTS ON TIME

Section 27

1 Schedule 56 to FA 2009 (penalty for failure to make payments on time) is amended as follows.

2(1) Paragraph 1 (penalty for failure) is amended as follows.

2(2) In sub-paragraph (2), for "8" substitute "8J".

2(3) [Not relevant to petroleum revenue tax.]

2(4) [Not relevant to petroleum revenue tax.]

2(5) [Not relevant to petroleum revenue tax.]

2(6) [Not relevant to petroleum revenue tax.]

2(7) [Not relevant to petroleum revenue tax.]

2(8) [Not relevant to petroleum revenue tax.]

2(9) [Not relevant to petroleum revenue tax.]

2(10) [Not relevant to petroleum revenue tax.]

2(11) [Not relevant to petroleum revenue tax.]

2(12) [Not relevant to petroleum revenue tax.]

2(13) [Not relevant to petroleum revenue tax.]

2(14) [Not relevant to petroleum revenue tax.]

5(1) Paragraph 3 (amount of penalty for occasional amounts and amounts due for periods of 6 months or more) is amended as follows.

5(2) Sub-paragraph (1) is amended as follows.

5(3) In paragraph (a), for "items 1, 3 and 7 to 24" substitute "items 1, 3, 6B, 7 to 11 and 12 to 24".

5(4) [Not relevant to petroleum revenue tax.]

5(5) [Not relevant to petroleum revenue tax.]

5(6) [Not relevant to petroleum revenue tax.]

9(1) Paragraph 11 (assessment) is amended as follows.

9(2) In sub-paragraph (4), for "unpaid tax" substitute "tax which was due or payable".

9(3) After sub-paragraph (4) insert–

"**11(4A)** A replacement assessment may be made in respect of a penalty if an earlier assessment operated by reference to an overestimate of an amount of tax which was due or payable."

10 For paragraph 16(1) (no liability where there is reasonable excuse for failure) substitute–

"**16(1)** If P satisfies HMRC or (on appeal) the First-tier Tribunal or Upper Tribunal that there is a reasonable excuse for a failure to make a payment–

(a) liability to a penalty under any paragraph of this Schedule does not arise in relation to that failure, and

(b) the failure does not count as a default for the purposes of paragraphs 6, 8B, 8C, 8G and 8H."

SCHEDULE 12 – RECOVERY OF OVERPAID TAX ETC

Section 28

Part 2 – Petroleum Revenue Tax

CLAIMS FOR RECOVERY OF OVERPAID TAX ETC

6 Schedule 2 to OTA 1975 (management and collection of petroleum revenue tax) is amended as follows.

7 [Amends the Table in OTA 1975, Sch. 2, para. 1(1).]

8 [Amends OTA 1975, Sch. 2, para. 10(1A).]

9 [Amends OTA 1975, Sch. 2, para. 12(1B).]

10 [Inserts OTA 1975, Sch. 2, paras. 13A–13F.]

11(1) Paragraph 14 (appeals) is amended as follows.

11(2) [Inserts OTA 1975, Sch. 2, para. 14(1A).]

11(3) [Amends OTA 1975, Sch. 2, para. 14(9).]

11(4) [Amends OTA 1975, Sch. 2, para. 14(10).]

11(5) [Inserts OTA 1975, Sch. 2, para. 14(10A).]

CONSEQUENTIAL AMENDMENTS

12(1) Schedule 24 to FA 2007 (penalties for errors) is amended as follows.

12(2) [Amends the table in FA 2007, Sch. 24, para. 1.]

12(3) [Amends FA 2007, Sch. 24, para. 1(5).]

13 In FA 2009–

(a) [omits FA 2009, Sch. 51, para. 18(2),]

(b) [omits FA 2009, Sch. 52, para. 11.]

FINANCE ACT 2011

(2011 Chapter 11)

[*19th July 2011*]

ARRANGEMENT OF SECTIONS

PART 3 – OIL

61 PRT: areas treated as continuing to be oil fields

61(1) [Amends OTA 1975, Sch. 1, para. 7(4).]

61(2) The amendment made by this section has effect in relation to chargeable periods that begin after 30 June 2009.

PART 7 – ADMINISTRATION ETC

86 Data-gathering powers

86(1) Schedule 23 contains provision for officers of Revenue and Customs to obtain data from data-holders.

86(2) Schedule 24 contains amendments of Schedule 36 to FA 2008 (information and inspection powers).

PART 9 – FINAL PROVISIONS

92 Interpretation

92(1) In this Act–

"ALDA 1979" means the Alcoholic Liquor Duties Act 1979,

"BGDA 1981" means the Betting and Gaming Duties Act 1981,

"CAA 2001" means the Capital Allowances Act 2001,

"CRCA 2005" means the Commissioners for Revenue and Customs Act 2005,

"CTA 2009" means the Corporation Tax Act 2009,

"CTA 2010" means the Corporation Tax Act 2010,

"FISMA 2000" means the Financial Services and Markets Act 2000,

PRT Statutes

"HODA 1979" means the Hydrocarbon Oil Duties Act 1979,
"ICTA" means the Income and Corporation Taxes Act 1988,
"IHTA 1984" means the Inheritance Tax Act 1984,
"ITA 2007" means the Income Tax Act 2007,
"ITEPA 2003" means the Income Tax (Earnings and Pensions) Act 2003,
"ITTOIA 2005" means the Income Tax (Trading and Other Income) Act 2005,
"OTA 1975" means the Oil Taxation Act 1975,
"PRTA 1980" means the Petroleum Revenue Tax Act 1980,
"TCGA 1992" means the Taxation of Chargeable Gains Act 1992,
"TIOPA 2010" means the Taxation (International and Other Provisions) Act 2010,
"TMA 1970" means the Taxes Management Act 1970,
"TPDA 1979" means the Tobacco Products Duty Act 1979,
"VATA 1994" means the Value Added Tax Act 1994, and
"VERA 1994" means the Vehicle Excise and Registration Act 1994.

92(2) In this Act–
"FA", followed by a year, means the Finance Act of that year;
"F(No. 2)A", followed by a year, means the Finance (No. 2) Act of that year.

93 Short title

93 This Act may be cited as the Finance Act 2011.

SCHEDULES

SCHEDULE 23 – DATA-GATHERING POWERS

Section 86(1)

Part 1 – Power to Obtain Data

POWER TO GIVE NOTICE

1(1) An officer of Revenue and Customs may by notice in writing require a relevant data-holder to provide relevant data.

1(2) Part 2 of this Schedule sets out who is a relevant data-holder.

1(3) In relation to a relevant data-holder, **"relevant data"** means data of a kind specified for that type of data-holder in regulations made by the Treasury.

1(4) The data that a relevant data-holder may be required to provide–
(a) may be general data or data relating to particular persons or matters, and
(b) may include personal data (such as names and addresses of individuals).

1(5) A notice under this paragraph is referred to as a data-holder notice.

PURPOSE OF POWER

2(1) The power in paragraph 1(1) is exercisable to assist with the efficient and effective discharge of HMRC's tax functions–
(a) whether a particular function or more generally, and
(b) whether involving a particular taxpayer or taxpayers generally.

2(2) It is additional to and is not limited by other powers that HMRC may have to obtain data (for example, in Schedule 36 to FA 2008).

2(3) But it may not be used (in place of the power in paragraph 1 of that Schedule) to obtain data required for the purpose of checking the relevant data-holder's own tax position.

2(4) *Sub-paragraph (3) does not prevent* use of the power in paragraph 1(1) of this Schedule to obtain data about a matter mentioned in paragraph 14(3)(a) (beneficial ownership of certain payments etc).

2(5) Nothing in this paragraph limits the use that may be made of data that have been obtained under this Schedule (see section 17(1) of CRCA 2005).

MONEY SERVICE BUSINESSES

13D(1) A person is a relevant data-holder if the person–

(a) carries on any of the activities in sub-paragraph (2) by way of business,

(b) is a relevant person within the meaning of regulation 8(1) of the Money Laundering, Terrorist Financing and Transfer of Funds (Information on the Payer) Regulations 2017 (S.I. 2017/692), and

(c) is not an excluded credit institution.

13D(2) The activities referred to in sub-paragraph (1)(a) are–

(a) operating a currency exchange office;

(b) transmitting money (or any representation of monetary value) by any means;

(c) cashing cheques which are made payable to customers.

13D(3) An excluded credit institution is a credit institution which has permission to carry on the regulated activity of accepting deposits–

(a) under Part 4A of the Financial Services and Markets Act 2000 (permission to carry on regulated activities), or

(b) resulting from Part 2 of Schedule 3 to that Act (exercise of passport rights by EEA firms).

13D(4) Sub-paragraph (3) is to be read with section 22 of and Schedule 2 to the Financial Services and Markets Act 2000, and any order under that section (classes of regulated activities).

13D(5) In this paragraph **"credit institution"** has the meaning given by Article 4.1(1) of Regulation (EU) No 575/2013 of the European Parliament and of the Council of 26 June 2013 on prudential requirements for credit institutions and investment firms.

History – Para. 13D inserted by F(No. 2)A 2017, s. 69(1), with effect in relation to relevant data with a bearing on any period whether before, on or after 16 November 2017 (Royal Assent).

PETROLEUM ACTIVITIES

23 Each of the following is a relevant data-holder–

(a) the holder of a licence granted under Part 1 of the Petroleum Act 1998, and

(b) the responsible person in relation to an oil field (within the meaning of Part 1 of OTA 1975).

Cross references – SI 2012/847, reg. 21: relevant data.

Part 3 – Appeals Against Data-Holder Notices

RIGHT OF APPEAL

28(1) The data-holder may appeal against a data-holder notice, or any requirement in such a notice, on any of the following grounds–

(a) it is unduly onerous to comply with the notice or requirement,

(b) the data-holder is not a relevant data-holder, or

(c) data specified in the notice are not relevant data.

28(2) Sub-paragraph (1)(a) does not apply to a requirement to provide data that form part of the data-holder's statutory records.

28(3) Sub-paragraph (1) does not apply if the tribunal approved the giving of the notice in accordance with paragraph 5.

PROCEDURE FOR APPEAL

29(1) Notice of an appeal under paragraph 28 must be given–

(a) in writing,

(b) before the end of the period of 30 days beginning with the date on which the data-holder notice was given, and

(c) to the officer of Revenue and Customs by whom the data-holder notice was given.

29(2) It must state the grounds of appeal.

29(3) On an appeal that is notified to the tribunal, the tribunal may confirm, vary or set aside the data-holder notice or a requirement in it.

29(4) If the tribunal confirms or varies the notice or a requirement in it, the data-holder must comply with the notice or requirement–

(a) within such period as is specified by the tribunal, or

(b) if the tribunal does not specify a period, within such period as is reasonably specified in writing by an officer of Revenue and Customs following the tribunal's decision.

29(5) A decision by the tribunal under this Part is final (despite the provisions of sections 11 and 13 of the Tribunals, Courts and Enforcement Act 2007).

29(6) Subject to this paragraph, the provisions of Part 5 of TMA 1970 relating to appeals have effect in relation to appeals under paragraph 28 as they have effect in relation to an appeal against an assessment to income tax.

Part 4 – Penalties

PENALTIES FOR FAILURE TO COMPLY

30(1) If the data-holder fails to comply with a data-holder notice, the data-holder is liable to a penalty of £300.

30(2) A reference in this Schedule to failing to comply with a data-holder notice includes–

(a) concealing, destroying or otherwise disposing of a material document, or

(b) arranging for any such concealment, destruction or disposal.

30(3) A document is a material document if, at the time when the data-holder acts–

(a) the data-holder has received a data-holder notice requiring the data-holder to provide the document or data contained in the document, or

(b) the data-holder has not received such a notice but has been informed by an officer of Revenue and Customs that the data-holder will do so or is likely to do so.

30(4) A document is not a material document by virtue of sub-paragraph (3)(a) if the data-holder notice has already been complied with, unless–

(a) the data-holder has been notified in writing by an officer of Revenue and Customs that the data-holder must continue to preserve the document, and

(b) the notification has not been withdrawn.

30(5) A document is not a material document by virtue of sub-paragraph (3)(b) if more than 6 months have elapsed since the data-holder was (or was last) informed.

DAILY DEFAULT PENALTIES FOR FAILURE TO COMPLY

31 If–

(a) a penalty under paragraph 30 is assessed, and

(b) the failure in question continues after the data-holder has been notified of the assessment,

the data-holder is liable to a further penalty, for each subsequent day on which the failure continues, of an amount not exceeding £60 for each such day.

PENALTIES FOR INACCURATE INFORMATION OR DOCUMENTS

32(1) This paragraph applies if–

(a) in complying with a data-holder notice, the data-holder provides inaccurate data, and

(b) condition A, B or C is met.

32(2) Condition A is that the inaccuracy is–

(a) due to a failure by the data-holder to take reasonable care, or

(b) deliberate on the data-holder's part.

32(3) Condition B is that the data-holder knows of the inaccuracy at the time the data are provided but does not inform HMRC at that time.

32(4) Condition C is that the data-holder–

(a) discovers the inaccuracy some time later, and

(b) fails to take reasonable steps to inform HMRC.

32(5) If this paragraph applies, the data-holder is liable to a penalty not exceeding £3,000.

FAILURE TO COMPLY WITH TIME LIMIT

33 A failure to do anything required to be done within a limited period of time does not give rise to liability under paragraph 30 or 31 if the thing was done within such further time (if any) as an officer of Revenue and Customs may have allowed.

REASONABLE EXCUSE

34(1) Liability to a penalty under paragraph 30 or 31 does not arise if the data-holder satisfies HMRC or (on an appeal notified to the tribunal) the tribunal that there is a reasonable excuse for the failure.

34(2) For the purposes of this paragraph–

(a) an insufficiency of funds is not a reasonable excuse unless attributable to events outside the data-holder's control,

(b) if the data-holder relies on another person to do anything, that is not a reasonable excuse unless the data-holder took reasonable care to avoid the failure,

(c) if the data-holder had a reasonable excuse for the failure but the excuse has ceased, the data-holder is to be treated as having continued to have the excuse if the failure is remedied without unreasonable delay after the excuse ceased.

ASSESSMENT OF PENALTIES

35(1) If the data-holder becomes liable to a penalty under paragraph 30, 31 or 32, HMRC may assess the penalty.

35(2) If they do so, they must notify the data-holder.

35(3) An assessment of a penalty under paragraph 30 or 31 must be made within the period of 12 months beginning with the latest of the following–

(a) the date on which the data-holder became liable to the penalty,

(b) the end of the period in which notice of an appeal against the data-holder notice (or a requirement in it) could have been given, and

(c) if notice of such an appeal is given, the date on which the appeal is determined or withdrawn.

35(4) An assessment of a penalty under paragraph 32 must be made–

(a) within the period of 12 months beginning with the date on which the inaccuracy first came to the attention of an officer of Revenue and Customs, and

(b) within the period of 6 years beginning with the date on which the data-holder became liable to the penalty.

RIGHT TO APPEAL AGAINST PENALTY

36(1) The data-holder may appeal against a decision by an officer of Revenue and Customs–

(a) that a penalty is payable under paragraph 30, 31 or 32, or

(b) as to the amount of such a penalty.

36(2) But sub-paragraph (1)(b) does not give a right of appeal against the amount of an increased daily penalty payable by virtue of paragraph 38.

History – Para. 36(1) created from existing text by FA 2016, s. 177(5), with effect from 15 September 2016 (Royal Assent). Para. 36(2) inserted by FA 2016, s. 177(5), with effect from 15 September 2016 (Royal Assent).

PROCEDURE ON APPEAL AGAINST PENALTY

37(1) Notice of an appeal under paragraph 36 must be given–

(a) in writing,

(b) before the end of the period of 30 days beginning with the date on which notification under paragraph 35 was given, and

(c) to HMRC.

37(2) It must state the grounds of appeal.

37(3) On an appeal under paragraph 36(a) that is notified to the tribunal, the tribunal may confirm or cancel the decision.

37(4) On an appeal under paragraph 36(b) that is notified to the tribunal, the tribunal may–

(a) confirm the decision, or

(b) substitute for the decision another decision that the officer of Revenue and Customs had power to make.

37(5) Subject to this paragraph and paragraph 40, the provisions of Part 5 of TMA 1970 relating to appeals have effect in relation to appeals under paragraph 36 as they have effect in relation to an appeal against an assessment to income tax.

INCREASED DAILY DEFAULT PENALTY

38(1) This paragraph applies if–

(a) a penalty under paragraph 31 is assessed under paragraph 35,

(b) the failure in respect of which that assessment is made continues for more than 30 days beginning with the date on which notification of that assessment is given, and

(c) the data-holder has been told that an application may be made under this paragraph for an increased daily penalty to be assessable.

38(2) If this paragraph applies, an officer of Revenue and Customs may make an application to the tribunal for an increased daily penalty to be assessable on the data-holder.

38(3) If the tribunal decides that an increased daily penalty should be assessable–

(a) the tribunal must determine the day from which the increased daily penalty is to apply and the maximum amount of that penalty ("the new maximum amount");

(b) from that day, paragraph 31 has effect in the data-holder's case as if "the new maximum amount" were substituted for "£60".

38(4) The new maximum amount may not be more than £1,000.

38(5) But subject to that, in determining the new maximum amount the tribunal must have regard to–

(a) the likely cost to the data-holder of complying with the data-holder notice,

(b) any benefits to the data-holder of not complying with it, and

(c) any benefits to anyone else resulting from the data-holder's non-compliance.

History – In para. 38(1)(c) and (2), the word "assessable" substituted for the word "imposed" by FA 2016, s. 177(2)(a), with effect from 15 September 2016 (Royal Assent).

Para. 38(3) and (4) substituted by FA 2016, s. 177(2)(b), with effect from 15 September 2016 (Royal Assent). Former para. 38(3) and (4) read as follows:

"**38(3)** If the tribunal decides that an increased daily penalty should be imposed, then for each applicable day (see paragraph 39) on which the failure continues–

(a) the data-holder is not liable to a penalty under paragraph 31 in respect of the failure, and

(b) the data-holder is liable instead to a penalty under this paragraph of an amount determined by the tribunal.

38(4) The tribunal may not determine an amount exceeding £1,000 for each applicable day.".

In para. 38(5), the words "the new maximum amount" substituted for the words "the amount" by FA 2016, s. 177(2)(c), with effect from 15 September 2016 (Royal Assent).

39(1) If the tribunal makes a determination under paragraph 38, HMRC must notify the data-holder.

39(2) The notification must specify [the] new maximum amount and the day from which it applies.

39(3) [Omitted by FA 2016, s. 177(3)(c).]

History – In para. 39(1), the words "the tribunal makes a determination" substituted for the words "a data-holder becomes liable to a penalty" by FA 2016, s. 177(3)(a), with effect from 15 September 2016 (Royal Assent).

In para. 39(2), the words "[the] new maximum amount and the day from which it applies" (the word in square brackets inserted by Croner-i) substituted for the words "the day from which the increased penalty is to apply" by FA 2016, s. 177(3)(b) with effect from 15 September 2016 (Royal Assent).

Para. 39(3) omitted by FA 2016, s. 177(3)(c), with effect from 15 September 2016 (Royal Assent). Former para. 39(3) read as follows: "**39(3)** That day and any subsequent day is an **"applicable day"** for the purposes of paragraph 38(3).".

ENFORCEMENT OF PENALTIES

40(1) A penalty under this Schedule must be paid before the end of the period of 30 days beginning with the date mentioned in sub-paragraph (2).

40(2) That date is–

(a) the date on which notification under paragraph 35 is given in respect of the penalty, or

(b) if (in the case of a penalty under paragraph 30, 31 or 32) a notice of appeal under paragraph 36 is given, the date on which the appeal is finally determined or withdrawn.

40(3) A penalty under this Schedule may be enforced as if it were income tax charged in an assessment and due and payable.

History – In para. 40(2)(a), the words "or 39" (which appeared after the words "paragraph 35") omitted by FA 2016, s. 177(4), with effect from 15 September 2016 (Royal Assent).

POWER TO CHANGE AMOUNT OF PENALTIES

41(1) If it appears to the Treasury that there has been a change in the value of money since the last relevant date, they may by regulations substitute for the sums for the time being specified paragraphs 30(1), 31, 32(5) and 38(4) such other sums as appear to them to be justified by the change.

41(2) **"Relevant date"**, in relation to a specified sum, means–

(a) the day on which this Act is passed, and

(b) each date on which the power conferred by sub-paragraph (1) has been exerc relation to that sum.

41(3) Regulations under this paragraph do not apply to–

(a) a failure which began before the date on which they come into force, or

(b) an inaccuracy in any data or document provided to HMRC before that date.

DOUBLE JEOPARDY

42 The data-holder is not liable to a penalty under this Schedule in respect of anythi of which the data-holder has been convicted of an offence.

Part 5 – Miscellaneous Provision and Interpretat

APPLICATION OF PROVISIONS OF TMA 1970

43 Subject to the provisions of this Schedule, the following provisions of TMA 1970 a purposes of this Schedule as they apply for the purposes of the Taxes Acts–

(a) section 108 (responsibility of company officers),

(b) section 114 (want of form), and

(c) section 115 (delivery and service of documents).

REGULATIONS

44(1) Regulations under this Schedule are to be made by statutory instrument.

44(2) The first regulations to be made under paragraph 1(3) may not be made unless the instrument containing them has been laid in draft before, and approved by a resolution of, the House of Commons.

44(3) Subject to sub-paragraph (2), a statutory instrument containing regulations under this Schedule is subject to annulment in pursuance of a resolution of the House of Commons.

Statutory instruments – SI 2012/847: made under para. 44(2).

TAX

45(1) In this Schedule **"tax"** means any or all of the following–

(a) [not relevant to petroleum revenue tax,]

(b) [not relevant to petroleum revenue tax,]

(c) [not relevant to petroleum revenue tax,]

(ca) [not relevant to petroleum revenue tax,]

(d) [not relevant to petroleum revenue tax,]

(e) [not relevant to petroleum revenue tax,]

(f) [not relevant to petroleum revenue tax,]

(g) [not relevant to petroleum revenue tax,]

(h) [not relevant to petroleum revenue tax,]

(i) petroleum revenue tax,

(j) [not relevant to petroleum revenue tax,]

(k) [not relevant to petroleum revenue tax,]

(l) [not relevant to petroleum revenue tax,]

(m) relevant foreign tax.

45(2) [Not relevant to petroleum revenue tax.]

45(3) [Not relevant to petroleum revenue tax.]

45(4) "Relevant forig tax" means–

(a) a tax of a m r State, other than the United Kingdom, which is covered by the provisions for the exchan information under the Council Directive 2011/16/EU of 15 February 2011 on administra ooperation in the field of taxation (as amended from time to time), and

(b) any tax y which is imposed under the law of a territory in relation to which arrangements havin by virtue of section 173 of FA 2006 (international tax enforcement arrangements) have bee nd which is covered by the arrangements.

History – a) inserted by FA 2015, s. 105(1), with effect in relation to accounting periods beginning on or after 1 April 2015 (subject ons of FA 2015, s. 116(2)-(5)).

In para ords "Council Directive 2011/16/EU of 15 February 2011 on administrative cooperation in the field of taxation" substi words "Directive of the Council of the European Communities No 77/799/EEC" by SI 2012/3062, reg. 6(2), with effe ry 2013.

STATUTORY RECORDS

the purposes of this Schedule data form part of a data-holder's statutory records if they are data ta-holder is required to keep and preserve under or by virtue of any enactment relating to tax.

ata cease to form part of a data-holder's statutory records when the period for which the data are to be preserved under or by virtue of that enactment has expired.

GENERAL INTERPRETATION

In this Schedule–

"address" includes an electronic address;

"body of persons" has the same meaning as in TMA 1970;

"chargeable period" means a tax year, accounting period or other period for which a tax is charged;

"charity" has the meaning given by paragraph 1(1) of Schedule 6 to FA 2010;

"the Commissioners" means the Commissioners for Her Majesty's Revenue and Customs;

"company" has the meaning given by section 288(1) of TCGA 1992;

"data" includes information held in any form;

"the data-holder", in relation to a data-holder notice, means the person to whom the notice is addressed;

"data-holder notice" is defined in paragraph 1;

"dividend" includes any kind of distribution;

"document" includes a copy of a document (see also section 114 of FA 2008);

"employment", **"employee"** and **"employer"** have the same meaning as in Parts 2 to 7 of ITEPA 2003 (see, in particular, sections 4 and 5 of that Act);

"HMRC" means Her Majesty's Revenue and Customs;

"local authority" has the meaning given in section 999 of ITA 2007;

"provide" includes make available for inspection;

"specify" includes describe;

"securities" includes–

(a) shares and stock,

(b) debentures, including debenture stock, loan stock, bonds, certificates of deposit and other instruments creating or acknowledging indebtedness, and

(c) warrants or other instruments entitling the holder to subscribe for or otherwise acquire anything within paragraph (a) or (b),

issued by or on behalf of a person resident in, or a government or public or local authority of, any country (including a country outside the United Kingdom);

"shares" is to be construed in accordance with sections 99 of TCGA 1992;

"tax functions" means functions relating to tax;

"the tribunal" means the First-tier Tribunal or, where determined by or under the Tribunal Procedure Rules, the Upper Tribunal.

History – *In para. 47, the words "section 99" substituted for the words "sections 99 and 103A" by SI 2017/1204, reg. 15, with effect from 1 January 2018.*

48 A reference in this Schedule to providing data includes–

(a) preparing and delivering a return, statement or declaration, and

(b) providing documents.

FINANCE ACT 2012

(2012 Chapter 14)

[*17th July 2012*]

ARRANGEMENT OF SECTIONS

PART 9 – MISCELLANEOUS MATTERS

PART 9 – MISCELLANEOUS MATTERS

INTERNATIONAL MATTERS

219 Penalties: offshore income etc

219 [Amends FA 2007, Sch. 24, para. 21A(4).]

ADMINISTRATION

223 Tax agents: dishonest conduct

223(1) Schedule 38 contains provision about tax agents who engage in dishonest conduct.

223(2) That Schedule comes into force on such day as the Treasury may by order appoint.

223(3) An order under subsection (2)–

(a) may make different provision for different purposes, and

(b) may include transitional provision and savings.

223(4) The Treasury may by order make any incidental, supplemental, consequential, transitional or saving provision in consequence of Schedule 38.

223(5) An order under subsection (4) may–

(a) make different provision for different purposes, and

(b) make provision amending, repealing or revoking any provision made by or under an Act (whenever passed or made).

223(6) An order under this section is to be made by statutory instrument.

223(7) A statutory instrument containing an order under subsection (4) is subject to annulment in pursuance of a resolution of the House of Commons.

Commencement Date – The day appointed as the day on which Sch. 38 comes into force is 1 April 2013 (SI 2013/279, made under s. 223(2) and (3)).

224 Information powers

224(1) Schedule 36 to FA 2008 (information and inspection powers) is amended as follows.

224(2) [Inserts FA 2008, Sch. 36, para. 5A.]

224(3) [Amends FA 2008, Sch. 36, para. 6(1).]

224(4) [Amends FA 2008, Sch. 36, para. 31.]

224(5) [Amends heading to FA 2008, Sch. 36, para. 31.]

224(6) [Amends TMA 1970, s. 18D(1).]

224(7) The amendments made by subsections (1) to (5) apply for the purpose of checking the tax position of a taxpayer as regards periods or tax liabilities whenever arising (whether before, on or after the day on which this Act is passed).

224(8) The amendment made by subsection (6) is treated as having come into force on 1 April 2012.

PART 10 – FINAL PROVISIONS

228 Interpretation

228(1) In this Act–

"ALDA 1979" means the Alcoholic Liquor Duties Act 1979,
"BGDA 1981" means the Betting and Gaming Duties Act 1981,
"CAA 2001" means the Capital Allowances Act 2001,
"CEMA 1979" means the Customs and Excise Management Act 1979,
"CRCA 2005" means the Commissioners for Revenue and Customs Act 2005,
"CTA 2009" means the Corporation Tax Act 2009,
"CTA 2010" means the Corporation Tax Act 2010,
"F(No. 3)A 2010" means the Finance (No. 3) Act 2010,
"HODA 1979" means the Hydrocarbon Oil Duties Act 1979,
"ICTA" means the Income and Corporation Taxes Act 1988,
"IHTA 1984" means the Inheritance Tax Act 1984,
"ITA 2007" means the Income Tax Act 2007,
"ITEPA 2003" means the Income Tax (Earnings and Pensions) Act 2003,
"ITTOIA 2005" means the Income Tax (Trading and Other Income) Act 2005,
"OTA 1975" means the Oil Taxation Act 1975,
"PRTA 1980" means the Petroleum Revenue Tax Act 1980,
"TCGA 1992" means the Taxation of Chargeable Gains Act 1992,
"TIOPA 2010" means the Taxation (International and Other Provisions) Act 2010,
"TMA 1970" means the Taxes Management Act 1970,
"TPDA 1979" means the Tobacco Products Duty Act 1979,
"VATA 1994" means the Value Added Tax Act 1994, and
"VERA 1994" means the Vehicle Excise and Registration Act 1994.

228(2) In this Act–

"FA", followed by a year, means the Finance Act of that year;
"F(No. 2)A", followed by a year, means the Finance (No. 2) Act of that year.

229 Short title

229 This Act may be cited as the Finance Act 2012.

SCHEDULES

SCHEDULE 38 – TAX AGENTS: DISHONEST CONDUCT

Section 223

Commencement Date – The day appointed as the day on which Sch. 38 comes into force is 1 April 2013 (SI 2013/279).
Other material – HMRC Factsheet TA/FS1: Tax agents: dishonest conduct.

Part 1 – Introduction

OVERVIEW

1 This Schedule is arranged as follows–

(a) this Part explains who is a tax agent and what it means to engage in dishonest conduct,

(b) Part 2 sets out the process for establishing whether someone is engaging in or has engaged in dishonest conduct,

(c) Part 3 confers power on HMRC to obtain relevant documents,

(d) Part 4 sets out sanctions for engaging in dishonest conduct,

(e) Part 5 provides for assessment of and appeals against penalties, and

(f) Parts 6 and 7 contain miscellaneous provisions and consequential amendments.

TAX AGENT

2(1) A **"tax agent"** is an individual who, in the course of business, assists other persons ("clients") with their tax affairs.

2(2) Individuals can be tax agents even if they (or the organisations for which they work) are appointed–

(a) indirectly, or

(b) at the request of someone other than the client.

2(3) Assistance with a client's tax affairs includes–

(a) advising a client in relation to tax, and

(b) acting or purporting to act as agent on behalf of a client in relation to tax.

2(4) Assistance with a client's tax affairs also includes assistance with any document that is likely to be relied on by HMRC to determine a client's tax position.

2(5) Assistance given for non-tax purposes counts as assistance with a client's tax affairs if it is given in the knowledge that it will be, or is likely to be, used by a client in connection with the client's tax affairs.

DISHONEST CONDUCT

3(1) An individual **"engages in dishonest conduct"** if, in the course of acting as a tax agent, the individual does something dishonest with a view to bringing about a loss of tax revenue.

3(2) It does not matter whether a loss is actually brought about.

3(3) Nor does it matter whether the individual is acting on the instruction of clients.

3(4) A loss of tax revenue would be brought about for these purposes if clients were to–

(a) account for less tax than they are required to account for by law,

(b) obtain more tax relief than they are entitled to obtain by law,

(c) account for tax later than they are required to account for it by law, or

(d) obtain tax relief earlier than they are entitled to obtain it by law.

3(5) **"Tax"** is defined in Part 6 of this Schedule.

3(6) **"Tax relief"** includes–

(a) any exemption from or deduction or credit against or in respect of tax, and

(b) any repayment of tax.

3(7) A reference in this paragraph to doing something dishonest includes–

(a) dishonestly omitting to do something, and

(b) advising or assisting a client to do something that the individual knows to be dishonest.

Part 2 – Establishing Dishonest Conduct

CONDUCT NOTICE

4(1) This paragraph applies if HMRC determine that an individual is engaging in or has engaged in dishonest conduct.

4(2) An authorised officer (or an officer of Revenue and Customs with the approval of an authorised officer) may notify the individual of that determination.

4(3) The notice must state the grounds on which the determination was made.

4(4) For the effect of notifying the individual, see paragraphs 7(2) and 29(2).

4(5) A notice under this paragraph is referred to as a **"conduct notice"**.

4(6) In relation to a conduct notice, a reference to **"the determination"** is to the determination forming the subject of the notice.

APPEAL AGAINST DETERMINATION

5(1) An individual to whom a conduct notice is given may appeal against the determination.

5(2) Notice of appeal must be given–

(a) in writing to the officer who gave the conduct notice, and

(b) within the period of 30 days beginning with the day on which the conduct notice was given.

5(3) It must state the grounds of appeal.

5(4) On an appeal that is notified to the tribunal, the tribunal may confirm or set aside the determination.

5(5) Subject to this paragraph, the provisions of Part 5 of TMA 1970 relating to appeals have effect in relation to an appeal under this paragraph as they have effect in relation to an appeal against an assessment to income tax.

5(6) Setting aside a determination does not prevent a further conduct notice being given in respect of the same conduct if further evidence emerges.

OFFENCE OF CONCEALMENT ETC IN CONNECTION WITH CONDUCT NOTICE

6(1) A person ("P") commits an offence if, after a relevant event has occurred, P–

(a) conceals, destroys or otherwise disposes of a material document, or

(b) arranges for the concealment, destruction or disposal of a material document.

6(2) A **"relevant event"** occurs if–

(a) a conduct notice is given to an individual, or

(b) an individual is informed by an officer of Revenue and Customs that a conduct notice will be or is likely to be given to the individual.

6(3) A **"material document"** is any document that could be sought under paragraph 8 as a result of the giving of the conduct notice.

6(4) If P acts after the event described in sub-paragraph (2)(a), no offence is committed if P acts–

(a) after the determination has been set aside,

(b) more than 4 years after the conduct notice was given, or

(c) without knowledge of that event.

6(5) If P acts before that event but after the event described in sub-paragraph (2)(b), no offence is committed if P acts–

(a) more than 2 years after the individual was, or was last, so informed, or

(b) without knowledge of the event described in sub-paragraph (2)(b).

6(6) P acts without knowledge of an event if P–

(a) is not the individual with respect to whom the event has occurred, and

(b) does not know, and could not reasonably be expected to know, that the event has occurred.

6(7) A person guilty of an offence under this paragraph is liable–

(a) *on summary conviction*, to a fine not exceeding the statutory maximum, and

(b) on conviction on indictment, to imprisonment for a term not exceeding 2 years or to a fine, or both.

PRIVILEGED COMMUNICATIONS BETWEEN PROFESSIONAL LEGAL ADVISERS AND CLIENTS

17(1) A file access notice does not require the document-holder to provide any part of a document that is privileged.

17(2) For the purposes of this paragraph a document is privileged if it is a document in respect of which a claim to legal professional privilege, or (in Scotland) to confidentiality of communications between client and professional legal adviser, could be maintained in legal proceedings.

17(3) Regulations under paragraph 23 of Schedule 36 to FA 2008 (information powers: privileged communications) apply (with any necessary modifications) to disputes under this paragraph as to whether a document is privileged.

POWER TO COPY DOCUMENTS

18 If a document is provided pursuant to a file access notice, an officer of Revenue and Customs may take copies of or make extracts from the document.

POWER TO RETAIN DOCUMENTS

19(1) If a document is provided pursuant to a file access notice, HMRC may retain the document for a reasonable period if an officer of Revenue and Customs thinks it necessary to do so.

19(2) While a document is retained–

(a) the document-holder may, if the document is reasonably required for any purpose, request a copy of it, and

(b) an officer of Revenue and Customs must comply with such a request without charge.

19(3) The retention of a document under this paragraph is not to be regarded as breaking any lien claimed on the document.

19(4) If a document retained under this paragraph is lost or damaged, the Commissioners are liable to compensate the owner of the document for any expenses reasonably incurred in replacing or repairing the document.

APPEAL AGAINST FILE ACCESS NOTICE

20(1) If the document-holder is a person other than the tax agent, the document-holder may appeal against the file access notice, or any requirement in it, on the ground that it would be unduly onerous to comply with the notice or requirement.

20(2) Notice of appeal must be given–

(a) in writing to the officer by whom the file access notice was given, and

(b) within the period of 30 days beginning with the day on which the file access notice was given.

20(3) It must state the grounds of appeal.

20(4) On an appeal that is notified to the tribunal, the tribunal may confirm, vary or set aside the file access notice or a requirement in it.

20(5) If the tribunal confirms or varies the notice or a requirement in it, the document-holder must comply with the notice or requirement–

(a) within such period as is specified by the tribunal, or

(b) if the tribunal does not specify a period, within such period as is reasonably specified in writing by an officer of Revenue and Customs following the tribunal's decision.

20(6) A decision by the tribunal under this paragraph is final (despite the provisions of sections 11 and 13 of the Tribunals, Courts and Enforcement Act 2007).

20(7) *Subject to this paragraph*, the provisions of Part 5 of TMA 1970 relating to appeals have effect in relation to an appeal under this paragraph as they have effect in relation to an appeal against an assessment to income tax.

OFFENCE OF CONCEALMENT ETC IN CONNECTION WITH FILE ACCESS NOTICE

21(1) A person ("P") commits an offence if P–

(a) conceals, destroys or otherwise disposes of a required document, or

(b) arranges for the concealment, destruction or disposal of a required document.

21(2) A **"required document"** is a document within sub-paragraph (3) or sub-paragraph (4).

21(3) A document is within this sub-paragraph if at the time when P acts–

(a) P is required to provide the document by a file access notice, and

(b) either–

(i) the notice has not been complied with, or

(ii) it has been complied with, but P has been notified in writing by an officer of Revenue and Customs that P must continue to preserve the document (and the notification has not been withdrawn).

21(4) A document is within this sub-paragraph if at the time when P acts–

(a) P is not required to provide the document by a file access notice,

(b) P has been informed by an officer of Revenue and Customs that P will be or is likely to be so required, and

(c) no more than 6 months have elapsed since P was, or was last, so informed.

21(5) A person guilty of an offence under this paragraph is liable–

(a) on summary conviction, to a fine not exceeding the statutory maximum, and

(b) on conviction on indictment, to imprisonment for a term not exceeding 2 years or to a fine, or both.

PENALTY FOR FAILURE TO COMPLY

22(1) A person who fails to comply with a file access notice is liable to a penalty of £300.

22(2) Failing to comply with a file access notice also includes–

(a) concealing, destroying or otherwise disposing of a required document, or

(b) arranging for any such concealment, destruction or disposal.

22(3) **"Required document"** has the same meaning as in paragraph 21.

DAILY PENALTY FOR FAILURE TO COMPLY

23 If the failure continues after notification of a penalty under paragraph 22 has been issued, the person is liable to a further penalty, for each subsequent day on which the failure continues, of an amount not exceeding £60 for each such day.

FAILURE TO COMPLY WITH TIME LIMIT

24 A failure to do anything required to be done within a limited period of time does not give rise to liability to a penalty under paragraph 22 or 23 if the thing was done within such further time (if any) as an officer of Revenue and Customs may have allowed.

REASONABLE EXCUSE

25(1) Liability to a penalty under paragraph 22 or 23 does not arise if the person satisfies HMRC or (on an appeal notified to the tribunal) the tribunal that there is a reasonable excuse for the failure.

25(2) For the purposes of this paragraph–

(a) an insufficiency of funds is not a reasonable excuse unless attributable to events outside the person's control,

(b) if the person relies on another person to do anything, that is not a reasonable excuse unless the first person took reasonable care to avoid the failure,

(c) if the person had a reasonable excuse for the failure but the excuse has ceased, the person is to be treated as having continued to have the excuse if the failure is remedied without unreasonable delay after the excuse ceased.

Part 4 – Sanctions for Dishonest Conduct

PENALTY FOR DISHONEST CONDUCT

26(1) *An individual* who engages in dishonest conduct is liable to a penalty.

26(2) Subject to paragraph 27, the penalty to which the individual is liable is to be–

(a) no less than £5,000, and

(b) no more than £50,000.

26(3) In assessing the amount of the penalty, regard must be had to–

(a) whether the individual disclosed the dishonest conduct,

(b) whether that disclosure was prompted or unprompted,

(c) the quality of that disclosure, and

(d) the quality of the individual's compliance with any file access notice in connection with the dishonest conduct.

26(4) An individual **"discloses"** dishonest conduct by–

(a) telling HMRC about it,

(b) giving HMRC reasonable help in identifying the client or clients concerned and in quantifying the loss of tax revenue (if any) brought about by it, and

(c) allowing HMRC access to records for the purpose of ensuring that any such loss is recovered or otherwise properly accounted for.

26(5) A disclosure is **"unprompted"** if it is made at a time when the individual has no reason to believe that HMRC have discovered or are about to discover the dishonest conduct.

26(6) Otherwise, a disclosure is **"prompted"**.

26(7) In relation to disclosure or compliance, **"quality"** includes timing, nature and extent.

SPECIAL REDUCTION

27(1) This paragraph applies if HMRC propose to assess an individual to a penalty under paragraph 26 of £5,000.

27(2) If they think it right because of special circumstances, HMRC may take one or more of the following steps–

(a) reduce the penalty to an amount below £5,000 (which may be nil),

(b) stay the penalty, or

(c) agree a compromise in relation to proceedings for the penalty.

27(3) **"Special circumstances"** does not include–

(a) ability to pay, or

(b) the fact that a loss of tax revenue from a client is balanced by an overpayment by another person (whether or not a client).

POWER TO PUBLISH DETAILS

28(1) The Commissioners may publish information about an individual if the individual incurs a penalty under paragraph 26.

28(2) The information that may be published is–

(a) the individual's name (including any trading name, previous name or pseudonym),

(b) the individual's address,

(c) the nature of any business carried on by the individual,

(d) the amount of the penalty,

(e) the periods or times to which the dishonest conduct relates,

(f) any other information the Commissioners consider it appropriate to publish in order to make clear the individual's identity, and

(g) the link (if there is one) between the dishonest conduct and any inaccuracy, failure or action as a result of which information is published under section 94 of FA 2009 (which relates to deliberate tax defaulters).

28(3) No information may be published under this paragraph if the penalty incurred by the individual is £5,000 or less.

28(4) Subsections (5) to (9) and (11) of section 94 of FA 2009 apply to publishing information about an individual under this paragraph as they apply to publishing information about a person under that section.

28(5) If, in acting as a tax agent, the individual works or worked for an organisation, sub-paragraph (2)(f) includes power to publish such information about that organisation as the Commissioners consider appropriate in order to make clear the individual's identity.

28(6) Before publishing information about the organisation, the Commissioners must–

(a) inform the organisation that they are considering doing so, and

(b) afford the organisation reasonable opportunity to make representations about whether it should be published.

Part 5 – Penalties: Assessment etc

ASSESSMENT OF PENALTIES

29(1) If a person becomes liable to a penalty under Part 3 or 4 of this Schedule, HMRC may assess the penalty.

29(2) But, in the case of a penalty under Part 4, they may only do so if a conduct notice has been given to the person and either–

(a) the time allowed for giving notice of appeal against the determination has expired without notice of appeal being given, or

(b) notice of appeal against the determination was given within the time allowed, but the appeal has been withdrawn or the determination confirmed.

29(3) Paragraph 7(4) applies for the purposes of sub-paragraph (2)(b).

29(4) If HMRC assess a penalty, they must notify the person.

30(1) HMRC may not assess a penalty under this Schedule after the applicable deadline.

30(2) For a penalty under Part 3, the applicable deadline is the end of the period of 12 months beginning with the day on which the person became liable to the penalty.

30(3) For a penalty under Part 4, the applicable deadline is the end of the period of 12 months beginning with the later of–

(a) the first day on which HMRC may assess the penalty (see paragraph 29(2)), and

(b) day X.

30(4) If a loss of tax revenue is brought about by the dishonest conduct, day X is–

(a) the day immediately following the end of the appeal period for the assessment or determination of the tax revenue lost (or, if more than one client is involved, the end of the last such period), or

(b) if there is no such assessment or determination, the day on which the amount of tax revenue lost is ascertained.

30(5) Otherwise, day X is the day on which HMRC ascertain that no loss of tax revenue has been brought about by the dishonest conduct.

30(6) In sub-paragraph (4), **"appeal period"** means the period during which–

(a) an appeal could be brought, or

(b) an appeal that has been brought has not been withdrawn or determined.

APPEAL AGAINST PENALTY

31(1) A person may appeal against a decision of HMRC–

(a) that a penalty is payable under Part 3 of this Schedule, or

(b) as to the amount of a penalty payable under Part 3 or 4 of this Schedule.

31(2) Notice of appeal must be given–

(a) in writing to HMRC, and

(b) before the end of the period of 30 days beginning with the day on which notification of the penalty was issued.

31(3) It must state the grounds of appeal.

31(4) On an appeal under sub-paragraph (1)(a) that is notified to the tribunal, the tribunal may confirm or cancel the decision.

31(5) On an appeal under sub-paragraph (1)(b) that is notified to the tribunal, the tribunal may–

(a) confirm the decision, or

(b) substitute for the decision another decision that HMRC had power to make.

31(6) If, in the case of an appeal against a penalty under Part 4, the tribunal substitutes its decision for HMRC's, the tribunal may rely on paragraph 27 (special reduction)–

(a) to the same extent as HMRC (which may mean applying the same reduction as HMRC to a different starting point), or

(b) to a different extent, but only if the tribunal thinks that HMRC's decision in respect of the application of that paragraph was flawed (when considered in the light of the principles applicable in proceedings for judicial review).

31(7) Subject to this paragraph and paragraph 32, the provisions of Part 5 of TMA 1970 relating to appeals have effect in relation to an appeal under this paragraph as they have effect in relation to an appeal against an assessment to income tax.

ENFORCEMENT OF PENALTY

32(1) A penalty under this Schedule must be paid–

(a) before the end of the period of 30 days beginning with the day on which notification of the penalty was issued, or

(b) if a notice of appeal under paragraph 31 is given, before the end of the period of 30 days beginning with the day on which the appeal is withdrawn or determined.

32(2) A penalty under this Schedule may be enforced as if it were income tax charged in an assessment and due and payable.

DOUBLE JEOPARDY

33 A person is not liable to a penalty under this Schedule in respect of anything in respect of which the person has been convicted of an offence.

34(1) A person is not liable to a penalty under this Schedule in respect of anything in respect of which the person is personally liable to a penalty under–

(a) Schedule 24 to FA 2007 (penalties for errors),

(b) Schedule 41 to FA 2008 (penalties for failure to notify etc), or

(c) Schedule 55 to FA 2009 (penalties for failure to make a return etc).

34(2) Sub-paragraph (1) applies where, for example, the person is personally liable by virtue of section 48(3) of VATA 1994 (VAT representatives).

POWER TO CHANGE AMOUNT OF PENALTIES

35(1) If it appears to the Treasury that there has been a change in the value of money since the last relevant day, they may by regulations substitute for the sums for the time being specified in paragraphs 22(1), 23, 26(2), 27(1) and (2)(a) and 28(3) such other sums as appear to them to be justified by the change.

35(2) **"Relevant day"**, in relation to a specified sum, means–

(a) the day on which this Act is passed, and

(b) each day on which the power conferred by sub-paragraph (1) has been exercised in relation to that sum.

35(3) Regulations under this paragraph do not apply to a failure or conduct that began before the day on which they come into force.

35(4) The power to make regulations under this paragraph is exercisable by statutory instrument.

35(5) A statutory instrument containing regulations under this paragraph is subject to annulment in pursuance of a resolution of the House of Commons.

Part 6 – Miscellaneous Provision and Interpretation

APPLICATION OF PROVISIONS OF TMA 1970

36 Subject to the provisions of this Schedule, the following provisions of TMA 1970 apply for the purposes of this Schedule as they apply for the purposes of the Taxes Acts–

(a) section 108 (responsibility of company officers),

(b) section 114 (want of form), and

(c) section 115 (delivery and service of documents).

TAX

37(1) **"Tax"** means–

(a) income tax,

(b) capital gains tax,

(c) corporation tax,

(d) construction industry deductions,

(e) VAT,
(f) insurance premium tax,
(g) inheritance tax,
(h) stamp duty land tax,
(i) stamp duty reserve tax,
(j) petroleum revenue tax,
(k) aggregates levy,
(l) climate change levy,
(la) apprenticeship levy,
(m) landfill tax, and
(n) any duty of excise other than vehicle excise duty.

37(2) **"Construction industry deductions"** means construction industry deductions under Chapter 3 of Part 3 of FA 2004.

37(3) **"Corporation tax"** includes an amount assessable or chargeable as if it were corporation tax.

37(4) **"VAT"** means–

(a) value added tax charged in accordance with VATA 1994,
(b) amounts recoverable under paragraph 5(2) of Schedule 11 to that Act (amounts shown on invoices as VAT), and
(c) amounts treated as VAT by virtue of regulations under section 54 of that Act (farmers etc).

History – S. 37(1)(la) inserted by FA 2016, s. 115, with effect from 15 September 2016 (Royal Assent).

GENERAL INTERPRETATION

38 In this Schedule–

"appointed" includes engaged;

"client" (except in paragraph 17)–

(a) has the meaning given in paragraph 2(1), and
(b) in relation to a particular tax agent, means a client of that tax agent;

"the Commissioners" means the Commissioners for Her Majesty's Revenue and Customs;

"conduct notice" has the meaning given in paragraph 4;

"the document-holder" has the meaning given in paragraph 8;

"document" includes a copy of a document (see also section 114 of FA 2008);

"file access notice" has the meaning given in paragraph 8;

"HMRC" means Her Majesty's Revenue and Customs;

"organisation" includes any person or firm carrying on a business;

"specify" includes describe;

"tax period" means a tax year, accounting period or other period in respect of which tax is charged;

"the tribunal" means the First-tier Tribunal or, where determined by or under the Tribunal Procedure Rules, the Upper Tribunal.

39(1) A reference in this Schedule to clients of a tax agent (or to a tax agent's clients) is a reference to the persons whom the agent assists with their tax affairs.

39(2) Sub-paragraph (1) applies even if–

(a) the agent works for an organisation, and
(b) it is the organisation that is appointed to give the assistance.

40 A loss of tax revenue is taken for the purposes of this Schedule to be (or to be capable of being) brought about by dishonest conduct despite the fact that the loss can be recovered or properly accounted for (following discovery of the conduct or otherwise).

41 A reference in this Schedule to working for an organisation includes being a partner or member of an organisation.

42 A reference in a provision of this Schedule to an authorised officer is to an officer of Revenue and Customs who is, or is a member of a class of officers who are, authorised by the Commissioners for the purposes of that provision.

RELATIONSHIP WITH OTHER ENACTMENTS

43 Nothing in this Schedule limits–

(a) any liability a person may have under any other enactment in respect of conduct in respect of which a person is liable to a penalty under this Schedule, or

(b) any power a person may have under any other enactment to obtain relevant documents.

Part 7 – Consequential Provisions

OTA 1975

51 [Omits entry in table in OTA 1975, Sch. 2, para. 1(1).]

FINANCE ACT 2013

(2013 Chapter 29) [*17th July 2013*]

ARRANGEMENT OF SECTIONS

PART 2 – OIL

DECOMMISSIONING RELIEF AGREEMENTS

DECOMMISSIONING EXPENDITURE ETC

ADMINISTRATION AND PAYMENT OF TAX

PART 5 – GENERAL ANTI-ABUSE RULE

PART 6 – OTHER PROVISIONS

DISCLOSURE

PAYMENT

PART 7 – FINAL PROVISIONS

SCHEDULES

31. MISCELLANEOUS AMENDMENTS RELATING TO DECOMMISSIONING
Part 1 – Abandonment Guarantees and Abandonment Expenditure
Part 3 – Commencement
34. ANNUAL TAX ON ENVELOPED DWELLINGS: INFORMATION AND ENFORCEMENT
Part 1 – Information and Inspection Powers
43. GENERAL ANTI-ABUSE RULE: PROCEDURAL REQUIREMENTS
43A. PROCEDURAL REQUIREMENTS: POOLING NOTICES AND NOTICES OF BINDING
43B. PROCEDURAL REQUIREMENTS: GENERIC REFERRAL OF TAX ARRANGEMENTS
43C. PENALTY UNDER SECTION 212A: SUPPLEMENTARY PROVISION
50. PENALTIES: LATE FILING, LATE PAYMENT AND ERRORS

PART 2 – OIL

DECOMMISSIONING RELIEF AGREEMENTS

80 Decommissioning relief agreements

80(1) There are to be paid out of money provided by Parliament any sums which a Minister of the Crown is liable to pay under a decommissioning relief agreement.

80(2) A **"decommissioning relief agreement"** is an agreement which–

(a) is made between a Minister of the Crown and a qualifying company, and

(b) provides that, in such circumstances as are specified in the agreement, if the amount of tax relief in respect of any decommissioning expenditure incurred by that or another qualifying company is less than an amount determined in accordance with the agreement ("the reference amount"), the difference is payable to the company that incurred the expenditure.

80(3) **"Qualifying company"** means–

(a) any company that has at any time carried on a ring fence trade,

(b) any company that is associated with a company carrying on a ring fence trade,

(c) any company that has at any time been associated with a company that was carrying on a ring fence trade at that time, and

(d) in the case of decommissioning expenditure incurred in connection with any plant or machinery, or any land, situated in the UK sector of a cross-boundary field, any company that is a party to a joint operating agreement or unitisation agreement in relation to that field.

80(4) For the purposes of subsection (2)(b) the amount of tax relief in respect of any decommissioning expenditure is to be determined in accordance with the agreement; and in making such a determination tax relief in respect of expenditure incurred by the qualifying company that is not decommissioning expenditure may, in such circumstances as are specified in the agreement, be treated as if it were tax relief in respect of decommissioning expenditure.

80(5) A payment made to a company under a decommissioning relief agreement is not to be regarded as income or a gain of the company for any purpose of the Tax Acts.

80(6) Section 18(1) of CRCA 2005 (restriction on disclosure by Revenue and Customs officials) does not prevent–

(a) disclosure to a Minister of the Crown for the purpose of enabling the Minister of the Crown to determine the extent of any liability under a decommissioning relief agreement, or

(b) disclosure to a company that has rights under a decommissioning relief agreement for the purpose of enabling the company to determine the reference amount.

80(7) In this section–

"company" has the meaning given by section 1121 of CTA 2010,

"cross-boundary field" has the meaning given by section 10(9) of the Petroleum Act 1998,

"decommissioning expenditure" has the meaning given by section 81,

"Minister of the Crown" includes the Treasury,

"ring fence trade" has the same meaning as in Part 8 of CTA 2010 (see section 277 of that Act),

"the UK sector of a cross-boundary field" means that part of a cross-boundary field lying within the UK marine area (as defined by section 42 of the Marine and Coastal Access Act 2009), and

"unitisation agreement" has the meaning given by paragraph 1(2) of Schedule 17 to FA 1980.

80(8) Subsections (8) to (9) of section 30 of the Petroleum Act 1998 (which specifies when one body corporate is associated with another) apply for the purposes of this section as they apply for the purposes of that section.

81 Meaning of "decommissioning expenditure"

81(1) In section 80 **"decommissioning expenditure"** means expenditure incurred in connection with–

(a) demolishing any plant or machinery,

(b) preserving any plant or machinery pending its reuse or demolition,

(c) preparing any plant or machinery for reuse,

(d) arranging for the reuse of any plant or machinery, or

(e) the restoration of any land.

81(2) It is immaterial for the purposes of subsection (1)(b) whether the plant or machinery is reused, is demolished or is partly reused and partly demolished.

81(3) It is immaterial for the purposes of subsection (1)(c) and (d) whether the plant or machinery is in fact reused.

81(4) In subsection (1)(e) **"restoration"** includes landscaping.

81(5) The Treasury may by order amend this section.

81(6) An order under subsection (5) may include transitional provision and savings.

81(7) The power to make an order under subsection (5) is exercisable by statutory instrument.

81(8) A statutory instrument containing an order under subsection (5) is subject to annulment in pursuance of a resolution of the House of Commons.

82 Annual report

82(1) For each financial year the Treasury must prepare a report containing the information in subsection (2).

82(2) The information is–

(a) the number of decommissioning relief agreements entered into in that year,

(b) the total number of decommissioning relief agreements in force at the end of that year,

(c) the number of payments made under any decommissioning relief agreements during that year, and the amount of each payment,

(d) the total number of payments that have been made under any decommissioning relief agreements as at the end of that year, and the total amount of those payments, and

(e) an estimate of the maximum amount liable to be paid under any decommissioning relief agreements.

82(3) The report for a financial year must be laid before the House of Commons as soon as is reasonably practicable after the end of that year.

82(4) In this section **"decommissioning relief agreement"** has the same meaning as in section 80.

82(5) This section has effect in relation to financial years ending on or after 31 March 2014.

83 Effect of claim on PRT

83(1) This section applies where a sum is payable to a company ("the claimant") under a decommissioning relief agreement.

83(2) Subsection (3) applies where the reference amount is calculated by reference to what the claimant's assessable profit in any chargeable period would be if any expenditure incurred by it were used to reduce its profit in a particular way (rather than in any way that it has in fact been used).

83(3) For the purposes of petroleum revenue tax–

(a) the expenditure is treated as having been used to reduce the claimant's profit in that way (rather than in any way that it has in fact been used), and

(b) the claimant is treated as if it had received the tax relief it would receive if its profit were reduced in that way (so no repayment of tax is to be made by virtue of this subsection).

83(4) Subsection (5) applies where the reference amount is calculated by reference to what any other company's assessable profit in any chargeable period would be if any expenditure incurred by the claimant–

(a) had been incurred by the other company, and

(b) were used to reduce the other company's profit in a particular way.

83(5) For the purposes of petroleum revenue tax–

(a) the expenditure is treated as incurred by the other company (and not the claimant),

(b) the expenditure is treated as having been used by the other company to reduce its profit in that way, and

(c) the other company is treated as if it had received the tax relief it would receive if its profit were reduced in that way (so no repayment of tax is to be made by virtue of this subsection).

83(6) In this section–

"assessable profit" and **"chargeable period"** have the same meaning as in Part 1 of OTA 1975,

"company" has the meaning given by section 1121 of CTA 2010,

"decommissioning relief agreement" has the same meaning as in section 80, and

"the reference amount" means the reference amount (within the meaning of that section) that relates to the sum mentioned in subsection (1).

84 Terminal losses accruing by virtue of another's default

84(1) This section applies where–

(a) a company defaults on a liability under–

(i) a relevant agreement, or

(ii) an abandonment programme,

to make a payment towards decommissioning expenditure in respect of an oil field,

(b) in consequence of the default, another company ("the other company") that has rights under a decommissioning relief agreement at the time of the default incurs decommissioning expenditure in respect of that oil field, and

(c) but for paragraph 15 of Schedule 17 to FA 1980 (terminal losses), a sum (or a sum of a greater amount) would be payable to the other company under the decommissioning relief agreement.

84(2) Paragraph 15 of Schedule 17 to FA 1980 does not apply in relation to any allowable loss accruing to the other company from that oil field.

84(3) Any allowable unrelievable field loss (within the meaning of section 6 of OTA 1975) that–

(a) consists of the unrelieved portion of an allowable loss within subsection (2), and

(b) would (in the absence of this subsection) arise as a result of subsection (2),

is not to be regarded as arising.

84(4) Nothing in this section affects the operation of section 83(3) or (5).

84(5) In this section–

"abandonment programme" means an abandonment programme approved under Part 4 of the Petroleum Act 1998 (including such a programme as revised),

"company" has the meaning given by section 1121 of CTA 2010,

"decommissioning expenditure" has the same meaning as in section 80,

"decommissioning relief agreement" has the same meaning as in that section,

"oil field" has the same meaning as in OTA 1975,

"relevant agreement" has the meaning given by section 104(5)(a) of FA 1991, and

"unrelieved portion", in relation to an allowable loss, is to be read in accordance with section 6 of OTA 1975.

85 Claims under agreement not to affect oil allowance

85(1) This section applies where–

(a) a company defaults on a liability under–

(i) a relevant agreement, or

(ii) an abandonment programme,

to make a payment towards decommissioning expenditure in respect of an oil field,

(b) in consequence of the default, another company that has rights under a decommissioning relief agreement at the time of the default incurs decommissioning expenditure in respect of that oil field, and

(c) by virtue of section 83, any expenditure incurred by that company (whether or not that decommissioning expenditure) is treated as having been used by that company or any other company ("the affected company") to reduce its assessable profit in a chargeable period in a particular way.

85(2) If, in the absence of section 83, the assessable profit accruing to the affected company from an oil field in that chargeable period would be reduced under section 8(1) of OTA 1975, the amount of the oil allowance for the oil field utilised by the affected company in that chargeable period for the purposes of section 8 of that Act is to be determined as if section 83 did not apply.

85(3) In this section–

"abandonment programme" means an abandonment programme approved under Part 4 of the Petroleum Act 1998 (including such a programme as revised),

"company" has the meaning given by section 1121 of CTA 2010,

"decommissioning expenditure" has the same meaning as in section 80,

"decommissioning relief agreement" has the same meaning as in that section,

"oil field" has the same meaning as in OTA 1975, and

"relevant agreement" has the meaning given by section 104(5)(a) of FA 1991.

DECOMMISSIONING EXPENDITURE ETC

89 Miscellaneous amendments relating to decommissioning

89(1) Part 1 of Schedule 31 contains provision about expenditure on and under abandonment guarantees and abandonment expenditure.

89(2) [Not relevant to petroleum revenue tax.]

PART 3 – ANNUAL TAX ON ENVELOPED DWELLINGS

ADMINISTRATION AND PAYMENT OF TAX

164 Information and enforcement

164 In Schedule 34–

(a) Part 1 contains provision about information and inspection powers, and

(b) [Not relevant to petroleum revenue tax.]

PART 5 – GENERAL ANTI-ABUSE RULE

Other material – Misc. 02/2015: HMRC general anti-abuse rule (GAAR) guidance.

206 General anti-abuse rule

206(1) This Part has effect for the purpose of counteracting tax advantages arising from tax arrangements that are abusive.

206(2) The rules of this Part are collectively to be known as "the general anti-abuse rule".

206(3) The general anti-abuse rule applies to the following taxes–

(a) income tax,

(b) corporation tax, including any amount chargeable as if it were corporation tax or treated as if it were corporation tax,

(c) capital gains tax,

(d) petroleum revenue tax,

(da) diverted profits tax,

(db) apprenticeship levy,

(e) inheritance tax,

(f) stamp duty land tax, and

(g) annual tax on enveloped dwellings.

History – S. 206(3)(da) inserted by FA 2015, s. 115(1), with effect in relation to accounting periods beginning on or after 1 April 2015 (subject to provisions of FA 2015, s. 116(2)–(5)).
S. 206(3)(db) inserted by FA 2016, s. 104(2), with effect from 15 September 2016 (Royal Assent).

207 Meaning of "tax arrangements" and "abusive"

207(1) Arrangements are **"tax arrangements"** if, having regard to all the circumstances, it would be reasonable to conclude that the obtaining of a tax advantage was the main purpose, or one of the main purposes, of the arrangements.

207(2) Tax arrangements are **"abusive"** if they are arrangements the entering into or carrying out of which cannot reasonably be regarded as a reasonable course of action in relation to the relevant tax provisions, having regard to all the circumstances including–

(a) whether the substantive results of the arrangements are consistent with any principles on which those provisions are based (whether express or implied) and the policy objectives of those provisions,

(b) whether the means of achieving those results involves one or more contrived or abnormal steps, and

(c) whether the arrangements are intended to exploit any shortcomings in those provisions.

207(3) Where the tax arrangements form part of any other arrangements regard must also be had to those other arrangements.

207(4) Each of the following is an example of something which might indicate that tax arrangements are abusive–

(a) the arrangements result in an amount of income, profits or gains for tax purposes that is significantly less than the amount for economic purposes,

(b) the arrangements result in deductions or losses of an amount for tax purposes that is significantly greater than the amount for economic purposes, and

(c) the arrangements result in a claim for the repayment or crediting of tax (including foreign tax) that has not been, and is unlikely to be, paid,

but in each case only if it is reasonable to assume that such a result was not the anticipated result when the relevant tax provisions were enacted.

207(5) The fact that tax arrangements accord with established practice, and HMRC had, at the time the arrangements were entered into, indicated its acceptance of that practice, is an example of something which might indicate that the arrangements are not abusive.

207(6) The examples given in subsections (4) and (5) are not exhaustive.

208 Meaning of "tax advantage"

208 A **"tax advantage"** includes–

(a) relief or increased relief from tax,

(b) repayment or increased repayment of tax,

(c) avoidance or reduction of a charge to tax or an assessment to tax,

(d) avoidance of a possible assessment to tax,

(e) deferral of a payment of tax or advancement of a repayment of tax, and

(f) avoidance of an obligation to deduct or account for tax.

209 Counteracting the tax advantages

209(1) If there are tax arrangements that are abusive, the tax advantages that would (ignoring this Part) arise from the arrangements are to be counteracted by the making of adjustments.

209(2) The adjustments required to be made to counteract the tax advantages are such as are just and reasonable.

209(3) The adjustments may be made in respect of the tax in question or any other tax to which the general anti-abuse rule applies.

209(4) The adjustments that may be made include those that impose or increase a liability to tax in any case where (ignoring this Part) there would be no liability or a smaller liability, and tax is to be charged in accordance with any such adjustment.

209(5) Any adjustments required to be made under this section (whether by an officer of Revenue and Customs or the person to whom the tax advantage would arise) may be made by way of an assessment, the modification of an assessment, amendment or disallowance of a claim, or otherwise.

209(6) But–

(a) no steps may be taken by an officer of Revenue and Customs by virtue of this section unless the procedural requirements of Schedule 43, 43A or 43B have been complied with, and

(b) the power to make adjustments by virtue of this section is subject to any time limit imposed by or under any enactment other than this Part.

209(7) Any adjustments made under this section have effect for all purposes.

209(8) Where a matter is referred to the GAAR Advisory Panel under paragraph 5 or 6 of Schedule 43, the taxpayer (as defined in paragraph 3 of that Schedule) must not make any GAAR-related adjustments in relation to the taxpayer's tax affairs in the period (the "closed period") which–

(a) begins with the 31st day after the end of the 45 day period mentioned in paragraph 4(1) of that Schedule, and

(b) ends immediately before the day on which the taxpayer is given the notice under paragraph 12 of Schedule 43 (notice of final decision after considering opinion of GAAR Advisory Panel).

209(9) Where a person has been given a pooling notice or a notice of binding under Schedule 43A in relation to any tax arrangements, the person must not make any GAAR-related adjustments in the period ("the closed period") that–

(a) begins with the 31st day after that on which that notice is given, and

(b) ends–

(i) in the case of a pooling notice, immediately before the day on which the person is given a notice under paragraph 8(2) or 9(2) of Schedule 43A, or a notice under paragraph 8(2) of Schedule 43B, in relation to the tax arrangements (notice of final decision after considering opinion of GAAR Advisory Panel), or

(ii) in the case of a notice of binding, with the 30th day after the day on which the notice is given.

209(10) In this section **"GAAR-related adjustments"** means–

(a) for the purposes of subsection (8), adjustments which give effect (wholly or in part) to the proposed counteraction set out in the notice under paragraph 3 of Schedule 43;

(b) for the purposes of subsection (9), adjustments which give effect (wholly or partly) to the proposed counteraction set out in the notice of pooling or binding (as the case may be).

History – In s. 209(6)(a), the words ", 43A or 43B" inserted by FA 2016, s. 157(4), with effect in relation to tax arrangements (within the meaning of FA 2013, Pt. 5) entered into at any time (whether before or on or after 15 September 2016).
S. 209(8)–(10) inserted by FA 2016, s. 158(4), with effect in relation to tax arrangements (within the meaning of FA 2013, Pt. 5) entered into on or after 15 September 2016.

209A Effect of adjustments specified in a provisional counteraction notice

209A(1) Adjustments made by an officer of Revenue and Customs which–

(a) are specified in a provisional counteraction notice given to a person by the officer (and have not been cancelled: see sections 209B to 209E),

(b) are made in respect of a tax advantage that would (ignoring this Part) arise from tax arrangements that are abusive, and

(c) but for section 209(6)(a), would have effected a valid counteraction of that tax advantage under section 209,

are treated for all purposes as effecting a valid counteraction of the tax advantage under that section.

209A(2) A **"provisional counteraction notice"** is a notice which–

(a) specifies adjustments (the "notified adjustments") which the officer reasonably believes may be required under section 209(1) to counteract a tax advantage that would (ignoring this Part) arise to the person from tax arrangements;

(b) specifies the arrangements and the tax advantage concerned, and

(c) notifies the person of the person's rights of appeal with respect to the notified adjustments (when made) and contains a statement that if an appeal is made against the making of the adjustments–

(i) no steps may be taken in relation to the appeal unless and until the person is given a notice referred to in section 209F(2), and

(ii) the notified adjustments will be cancelled if HMRC fails to take at least one of the actions mentioned in section 209B(4) within the period specified in section 209B(2).

209A(3) It does not matter whether the notice is given before or at the same time as the making of the adjustments.

209A(4) In this section **"adjustments"** includes adjustments made in any way permitted by section 209(5).

History – S. 209A inserted by FA 2016, s. 156(1), with effect in relation to tax arrangements (within the meaning of FA 2013, Pt. 5) entered into at any time (whether before or on or after 15 September 2016).

209B Notified adjustments: 12 month period for taking action if appeal made

209B(1) This section applies where a person (the "taxpayer") to whom a provisional counteraction notice has been given appeals against the making of the notified adjustments.

209B(2) The *notified adjustments* are to be treated as cancelled with effect from the end of the period of 12 months beginning with the day on which the provisional counteraction notice is given unless an action mentioned in subsection (4) is taken before that time.

209B(3) For the purposes of subsection (2) it does not matter whether the action mentioned in subsection (4)(c), (d) or (e) is taken before or after the provisional counteraction notice is given (but if that action is taken before the provisional counteraction notice is given subsection (5) does not have effect).

209B(4) The actions are–

(a) an officer of Revenue and Customs notifying the taxpayer that the notified adjustments are cancelled;

(b) an officer of Revenue and Customs giving the taxpayer written notice of the withdrawal of the provisional counteraction notice (without cancelling the notified adjustments);

(c) a designated HMRC officer giving the taxpayer a notice under paragraph 3 of Schedule 43 which–

(i) specifies the arrangements and the tax advantage which are specified in the provisional counteraction notice, and

(ii) specifies the notified adjustments (or lesser adjustments) as the counteraction that the officer considers ought to be taken (see paragraph 3(2)(c) of that Schedule);

(d) a designated HMRC officer giving the taxpayer a notice of binding under paragraph 1 of Schedule 43A which–

(i) specifies the arrangements and the tax advantage which are specified in the provisional counteraction notice, and

(ii) specifies the notified adjustments (or lesser adjustments) as the counteraction that the officer considers ought to be taken (see paragraph 1(4)(c) of that Schedule);

(e) a designated HMRC officer giving the taxpayer a notice under paragraph 1(2) of Schedule 43B which–

(i) specifies the arrangements and the tax advantage which are specified in the provisional counteraction notice, and

(ii) specifies the notified adjustments (or lesser adjustments) as the counteraction that the officer considers ought to be taken.

209B(5) In a case within subsection (4)(c), (d) or (e), if–

(a) the notice under paragraph 3 of Schedule 43, or

(b) the pooling notice or notice of binding, or

(c) the notice under paragraph 1(2) of Schedule 43B,

(as the case may be) specifies lesser adjustments the officer must modify the notified adjustments accordingly.

209B(6) The officer may not take the action in subsection (4)(b) unless the officer was authorised to make the notified adjustments otherwise than under this Part.

209B(7) In this section **"lesser adjustments"** means adjustments which assume a smaller tax advantage than was assumed in the provisional counteraction notice.

History – S. 209B inserted by FA 2016, s. 156(1), with effect in relation to tax arrangements (within the meaning of FA 2013, Pt. 5) entered into at any time (whether before or on or after 15 September 2016).

209C Notified adjustments: case within section 209B(4)(c)

209C(1) This section applies if the action in section 209B(4)(c) (notice to taxpayer of proposed counteraction of tax advantage) is taken.

209C(2) If the matter is not referred to the GAAR Advisory Panel, the notified adjustments are to be treated as cancelled with effect from the date of the designated HMRC officer's decision under paragraph 6(2) of Schedule 43 unless the notice under paragraph 6(3) of Schedule 43 states that the adjustments are not to be treated as cancelled under this section.

209C(3) A notice under paragraph 6(3) of Schedule 43 may not contain the statement referred to in subsection (2) unless HMRC would have been authorised to make the adjustments if the general anti-abuse rule did not have effect.

209C(4) If the taxpayer is given a notice under paragraph 12 of Schedule 43 which states that the specified tax advantage is not to be counteracted under the general anti-abuse rule, the notified adjustments are to be treated as cancelled unless that notice states that those adjustments are not to be treated as cancelled under this section.

209C(5) A notice under paragraph 12 of Schedule 43 may not contain the statement referred to in subsection (4) unless HMRC would have been authorised to make the adjustments if the general anti-abuse rule did not have effect.

209C(6) If the taxpayer is given a notice under paragraph 12 of Schedule 43 stating that the specified tax advantage is to be counteracted–

(a) the notified adjustments are confirmed only so far as they are specified in that notice as adjustments required to give effect to the counteraction, and

(b) so far as they are not confirmed, the notified adjustments are to be treated as cancelled.

History – S. 209C inserted by FA 2016, s. 156(1), with effect in relation to tax arrangements (within the meaning of FA 2013, Pt. 5) entered into at any time (whether before or on or after 15 September 2016).

209D Notified adjustments: case within section 209B(4)(d)

209D(1) This section applies if the action in section 209B(4)(d) (notice of binding) is taken.

209D(2) If the taxpayer is given a notice under paragraph 8(2) or 9(2) of Schedule 43A which states that the specified tax advantage is not to be counteracted under the general anti-abuse rule, the notified adjustments are to be treated as cancelled, unless that notice states that those adjustments are not to be treated as cancelled under this section.

209D(3) A notice under paragraph 8(2) or 9(2) of Schedule 43A may not contain the statement referred to in subsection (2) unless HMRC would have been authorised to make the adjustments if the general anti-abuse rule did not have effect.

209D(4) If the taxpayer is given a notice under paragraph 8(2) or 9(2) of Schedule 43A stating that the specified tax advantage is to be counteracted–

(a) the notified adjustments are confirmed only so far as they are specified in that notice as adjustments required to give effect to the counteraction, and

(b) so far as they are not confirmed, the notified adjustments are to be treated as cancelled.

History – S. 209D inserted by FA 2016, s. 156(1), with effect in relation to tax arrangements (within the meaning of FA 2013, Pt. 5) entered into at any time (whether before or on or after 15 September 2016).

209E Notified adjustments: case within section 209B(4)(e)

209E(1) This section applies if the action in section 209B(4)(e) (notice of proposal to make generic referral) is taken.

209E(2) If the notice under paragraph 1(2) of Schedule 43B is withdrawn, the notified adjustments are to be treated as cancelled unless the notice of withdrawal states that the adjustments are not to be treated as cancelled under this section.

209E(3) The notice of withdrawal may not contain the statement referred to in subsection (2) unless HMRC was authorised to make the notified adjustments otherwise than under this Part.

209E(4) If the taxpayer is given a notice under paragraph 8(2) of Schedule 43B, which states that the specified tax advantage is not to be counteracted under the general anti-abuse rule, the notified adjustments are to be treated as cancelled, unless that notice states that those adjustments are not to be treated as cancelled under this section.

209E(5) A notice under paragraph 8(2) of Schedule 43B may not contain the statement referred to in subsection (4) unless HMRC was authorised to make the adjustments otherwise than under this Part.

209E(6) If the taxpayer is given a notice under paragraph 8(2) of Schedule 43B stating that the specified tax advantage is to be counteracted–

(a) the notified adjustments are confirmed only so far as they are specified in that notice as adjustments required to give effect to the counteraction, and

(b) so far as they are not confirmed, the notified adjustments are to be treated as cancelled.

History – S. 209E inserted by FA 2016, s. 156(1), with effect in relation to tax arrangements (within the meaning of FA 2013, Pt. 5) entered into at any time (whether before or on or after 15 September 2016).

209F Appeals against provisional counteractions: further provision

209F(1) Subsections (2) to (5) have effect in relation to an appeal by a person ("the taxpayer") against the making of adjustments which are specified in a provisional counteraction notice.

209F(2) No steps after the initial notice of appeal are to be taken in relation to the appeal unless and until the taxpayer is given–

(a) a notice under section 209B(4)(b),

(b) a notice under paragraph 6(3) of Schedule 43 (notice of decision not to refer matter to GAAR advisory panel) containing the statement described in section 209C(2) (statement that adjustments are not to be treated as cancelled),

(c) a notice under paragraph 12 of Schedule 43, or

(d) a notice under paragraph 8(2) or 9(2) of Schedule 43A,

(e) a notice under paragraph 8 of Schedule 43B,

in respect of the tax arrangements concerned.

209F(3) The taxpayer has until the end of the period mentioned in subsection (4) to comply with any requirement to specify the grounds of appeal.

209F(4) The period mentioned in subsection (3) is the 30 days beginning with the day on which the taxpayer receives the notice mentioned in subsection (2).

209F(5) In subsection (2) the reference to **"steps"** does not include the withdrawal of the appeal.

History – S. 209F inserted by FA 2016, s. 156(1), with effect in relation to tax arrangements (within the meaning of FA 2013, Pt. 5) entered into at any time (whether before or on or after 15 September 2016).

210 Consequential relieving adjustments

210(1) This section applies where–

(a) the counteraction of a tax advantage under section 209 is final, and

(b) if the case is not one in which notice of the counteraction was given under paragraph 12 of Schedule 43, paragraph 8 or 9 of Schedule 43A or paragraph 8 of Schedule 43B, HMRC have been notified of the counteraction by the taxpayer.

210(2) A person has 12 months, beginning with the day on which the counteraction becomes final, to make a claim for one or more consequential adjustments to be made in respect of any tax to which the general anti-abuse rule applies.

210(3) On a claim under this section, an officer of Revenue and Customs must make such of the consequential adjustments claimed (if any) as are just and reasonable.

210(4) Consequential adjustments–

(a) may be made in respect of any period, and

(b) may affect any person (whether or not a party to the tax arrangements).

210(5) But nothing in this section requires or permits an officer to make a consequential adjustment the effect of which is to increase a person's liability to any tax.

210(6) For the purposes of this section–

(a) if the claim relates to income tax or capital gains tax, Schedule 1A to TMA 1970 applies to it;

(b) if the claim relates to corporation tax, Schedule 1A to TMA 1970 (and not Schedule 18 to FA 1998) applies to it;

(c) if the claim relates to petroleum revenue tax, Schedule 1A to TMA 1970 applies to it, but as if the reference in paragraph 2A(4) of that Schedule to a year of assessment included a reference to a chargeable period within the meaning of OTA 1975 (see section 1(3) and (4) of that Act);

(d) if the claim relates to inheritance tax it must be made in writing to HMRC and section 221 of IHTA 1984 applies as if the claim were a claim under that Act;

(e) if the claim relates to stamp duty land tax or annual tax on enveloped dwellings, Schedule 11A to FA 2003 applies to it as if it were a claim to which paragraph 1 of that Schedule applies.

210(7) Where an officer of Revenue and Customs makes a consequential adjustment under this section, the officer must give the person who made the claim written notice describing the adjustment which has been made.

210(8) For the purposes of this section the counteraction of a tax advantage is final when the adjustments made to effect the counteraction, and any amounts arising as a result of those adjustments, can no longer be varied, on appeal or otherwise.

210(9) Any adjustments required to be made under this section may be made–

(a) by way of an assessment, the modification of an assessment, the amendment of a claim, or otherwise, and

(b) despite any time limit imposed by or under any enactment other than this Part.

210(10) In this section **"the taxpayer"**, in relation to a counteraction of a tax advantage under section 209, means the person to whom the tax advantage would have arisen.

History – In s. 210(1)(b), the words "paragraph 8 or 9 of Schedule 43A or paragraph 8 of Schedule 43B," inserted by FA 2016, s. 157(5), with effect in relation to tax arrangements (within the meaning of FA 2013, Pt. 5) entered into at any time (whether before or on or after 15 September 2016).

211 Proceedings before a court or tribunal

211(1) In proceedings before a court or tribunal in connection with the general anti-abuse rule, HMRC must show–

(a) that there are tax arrangements that are abusive, and

(b) that the adjustments made to counteract the tax advantages arising from the arrangements are just and reasonable.

211(2) In determining any issue in connection with the general anti-abuse rule, a court or tribunal must take into account–

(a) HMRC's guidance about the general anti-abuse rule that was approved by the GAAR Advisory Panel at the time the tax arrangements were entered into, and

(b) any opinion of the GAAR Advisory Panel given–

(i) under paragraph 11 of Schedule 43 about the arrangements or any tax arrangements which are, as a result of a notice under paragraph 1 or 2 of Schedule 43A, the referred or (as the case may be) counteracted arrangements in relation to the arrangements, or

(ii) under paragraph 6 of Schedule 43B in respect of a generic referral of the arrangements.

211(3) In determining any issue in connection with the general anti-abuse rule, a court or tribunal may take into account–

(a) guidance, statements or other material (whether of HMRC, a Minister of the Crown or anyone else) that was in the public domain at the time the arrangements were entered into, and

(b) evidence of established practice at that time.

History – S. 211(2)(b)(i) and (ii) and the words "Panel given–" before them substituted for the words "Panel about the arrangements (see paragraph 11 of Schedule 43)." by FA 2016, s. 157(6), with effect in relation to tax arrangements (within the meaning of FA 2013, Pt. 5) entered into at any time (whether before or on or after 15 September 2016).

212 Relationship between the GAAR and priority rules

212(1) Any priority rule has effect subject to the general anti-abuse rule (despite the terms of the priority rule).

212(2) A **"priority rule"** means a rule (however expressed) to the effect that particular provisions have effect to the exclusion of, or otherwise in priority to, anything else.

212(3) Examples of priority rules are–

(a) the rule in section 464, 699 or 906 of CTA 2009 (priority of loan relationships rules, derivative contracts rules and intangible fixed assets rules for corporation tax purposes), and

(b) the rule in section 6(1) of TIOPA 2010 (effect to be given to double taxation arrangements despite anything in any enactment).

212A Penalty

212A(1) A person (P) is liable to pay a penalty if–

(a) (P) has been given a notice under

(i) paragraph 12 of Schedule 43,

(ii) paragraph 8 or 9 of Schedule 43A, or

(iii) paragraph 8 of Schedule 43B,

stating that a tax advantage arising from particular tax arrangements is to be counteracted,

(b) a tax document has been given to HMRC on the basis that the tax advantage arises to P from those arrangements,

(c) that document was given to HMRC–

(i) by P, or

(ii) by another person in circumstances where P knew, or ought to have known, that the other person gave the document on the basis mentioned in paragraph (c), and

(d) the tax advantage has been counteracted by the making of adjustments under section 209.

212A(2) The penalty is 60% of the value of the counteracted advantage.

212A(3) Schedule 43C–

(a) gives the meaning of **"the value of the counteracted advantage"**, and

(b) makes other provision in relation to penalties under this section.

212A(4) In this section **"tax document"** means any return, claim or other document submitted in compliance (or purported compliance) with any provision of, or made under, an Act.

212A(5) In this section the reference to giving a tax document to HMRC is to be interpreted in accordance with paragraph 11(g) and (h) of Schedule 43C.

History – S. 212A inserted by FA 2016, s. 158(2). with effect in relation to tax arrangements (within the meaning of FA 2013, Pt. 5) entered into on or after *15 September 2016*.

214 Interpretation of Part 5

214(1) In this Part–

"abusive", in relation to tax arrangements, has the meaning given by section 207(2) to (6);

"arrangements" includes any agreement, understanding, scheme, transaction or series of transactions (whether or not legally enforceable);

"the Commissioners" means the Commissioners for Her Majesty's Revenue and Customs;

"designated HMRC officer" has the meaning given by paragraph 2 of Schedule 43;

"the GAAR Advisory Panel" has the meaning given by paragraph 1 of Schedule 43;

"the general anti-abuse rule" has the meaning given by section 206;

"HMRC" means Her Majesty's Revenue and Customs;

"notice of binding" has the meaning given by paragraph 2(2) of Schedule 43A;

"notified adjustments", in relation to a provisional counteraction notice, has the meaning given by section 209A(2);

"pooling notice" has the meaning given by paragraph 1(4) of Schedule 43A;

"provisional counteraction notice" has the meaning given by section 209A(2);.

"tax advantage" has the meaning given by section 208;

"tax appeal" has the meaning given by paragraph 1A of Schedule 43;

"tax arrangements" has the meaning given by section 207(1).

"tax enquiry" has the meaning given by section 202(2) of FA 2014.

214(2) In this Part references to any **"opinion of the GAAR Advisory Panel"** about any tax arrangements are to be interpreted in accordance with paragraph 11(5) of Schedule 43.

214(3) In this Part references to tax arrangements which are **"equivalent"** to one another are to be interpreted in accordance with paragraph 11 of Schedule 43A.

History – In s. 214(1), definitions of "notified adjustments" and "provisional counteraction notice" inserted by FA 2016, s. 156(2), with effect in relation to tax arrangements (within the meaning of FA 2013, Pt. 5) entered into at any time (whether before or on or after 15 September 2016).

In s. 214(1), definitions of "designated HMRC officer", "notice of binding", "pooling notice", "tax appeal" and "tax enquiry" inserted by FA 2016, s. 157(9), with effect in relation to tax arrangements (within the meaning of FA 2013, Pt. 5) entered into at any time (whether before or on or after 15 September 2016).

S. 214(1) created from existing text by FA 2016, s. 157(8), with effect in relation to tax arrangements (within the meaning of FA 2013, Pt. 5) entered into at any time (whether before or on or after 15 September 2016).

S. 214(2) and (3) inserted by FA 2016, s. 157(10), with effect in relation to tax arrangements (within the meaning of FA 2013, Pt. 5) entered into at any time (whether before or on or after 15 September 2016).

215 Commencement and transitional provision

215(1) The general anti-abuse rule has effect in relation to any tax arrangements entered into on or after the day on which this Act is passed.

215(2) Where the tax arrangements form part of any other arrangements entered into before that day those other arrangements are to be ignored for the purposes of section 207(3), subject to subsection (3).

215(3) Account is to be taken of those other arrangements for the purposes of section 207(3) if, as a result, the tax arrangements would not be abusive.

PART 6 – OTHER PROVISIONS

DISCLOSURE

223 Disclosure of tax avoidance schemes

223(1) Part 7 of FA 2004 (disclosure of tax avoidance schemes) is amended in accordance with subsections (2) and (3).

223(2) [Inserts FA 2004, s. 312B.]

223(3) [Inserts FA 2004, s. 313ZB.]

223(4) [Not relevant to petroleum revenue tax.]

PAYMENT

230 Penalties: late filing, late payment and errors

230 Schedule 50 contains provision for, and in connection with, penalties for late filing, late payment and errors.

231 Overpayment relief: generally prevailing practice exclusion and EU law

231(1) [Inserts TMA 1970, Sch. 1AB, para. 2(9A) and (9B).]

231(2) [Inserts OTA 1975, Sch. 2, para. 13B(9) and (10).]

231(3) [Inserts FA 1998, Sch. 18, para. 51A(9) and (10).]

231(4) [Inserts FA 2003, Sch. 10, para. 34A(9) and (10).]

231(5) The amendments made by this section have effect in relation to any claim (in respect of overpaid tax, excessive assessment etc) made after the end of the six month period beginning with the day on which this Act is passed.

232 Overpayment relief: time limit for claims

232(1) [Not relevant to petroleum revenue tax.]

232(2) [Amends OTA 1975, Sch. 2, para. 13C(3).]

232(3) [Not relevant to petroleum revenue tax.]

232(4) The amendments made by this section have effect in relation to any claim (in respect of overpaid tax, excessive assessment etc) made after the end of the six month period beginning with the day on which this Act is passed.

PART 7 – FINAL PROVISIONS

235 Interpretation

235(1) In this Act–

"ALDA 1979" means the Alcoholic Liquor Duties Act 1979,

"BGDA 1981" means the Betting and Gaming Duties Act 1981,

"CAA 2001" means the Capital Allowances Act 2001,

"CEMA 1979" means the Customs and Excise Management Act 1979,

"CRCA 2005" means the Commissioners for Revenue and Customs Act 2005,

"CTA 2009" means the Corporation Tax Act 2009,

"CTA 2010" means the Corporation Tax Act 2010,

"F(No. 3)A 2010" means the Finance (No. 3) Act 2010,

"HODA 1979" means the Hydrocarbon Oil Duties Act 1979,

"ICTA" means the Income and Corporation Taxes Act 1988,

"IHTA 1984" means the Inheritance Tax Act 1984,

"ITA 2007" means the Income Tax Act 2007,

"ITEPA 2003" means the Income Tax (Earnings and Pensions) Act 2003,

"ITTOIA 2005" means the Income Tax (Trading and Other Income) Act 2005,

"OTA 1975" means the Oil Taxation Act 1975,

"TCGA 1992" means the Taxation of Chargeable Gains Act 1992,

"TIOPA 2010" means the Taxation (International and Other Provisions) Act 2010,

"TMA 1970" means the Taxes Management Act 1970,

"TPDA 1979" means the Tobacco Products Duty Act 1979,

"VATA 1994" means the Value Added Tax Act 1994, and

"VERA 1994" means the Vehicle Excise and Registration Act 1994.

235(2) In this Act–

"FA", followed by a year, means the Finance Act of that year;

"F(No. 2)A", followed by a year, means the Finance (No. 2) Act of that year.

236 Short title

236 This Act may be cited as the Finance Act 2013.

SCHEDULES

SCHEDULE 31 – MISCELLANEOUS AMENDMENTS RELATING TO DECOMMISSIONING

Section 89

Part 1 – Abandonment Guarantees and Abandonment Expenditure

EXPENDITURE ON ABANDONMENT GUARANTEES

1 [Not relevant to petroleum revenue tax.]

2 [Not relevant to petroleum revenue tax.]

EXPENDITURE UNDER ABANDONMENT GUARANTEES

3 [Inserts OTA 1975, Sch. 3, para. 8(1A) and (1B).]

4 [Amends OTA 1975, Sch. 5, para. 2C(2).]

5(1) Part 3 of FA 1991 (oil taxation) is amended as follows.

5(2) [Omits FA 1991, s. 105.]

5(3) [Omits FA 1991, s. 106.]

6 [Not relevant to petroleum revenue tax.]

7 [Not relevant to petroleum revenue tax.]

REIMBURSEMENT BY DEFAULTER IN RESPECT OF ABANDONMENT EXPENDITURE

8 [Omits FA 1991, s. 108.]

9 [Not relevant to petroleum revenue tax.]

10 [Not relevant to petroleum revenue tax.]

CONSEQUENTIAL AMENDMENTS

11(1) Section 104 of FA 1991 is amended as follows.

11(2) [Amends FA 1991, s. 104(1).]

11(3) [Amends FA 1991, s. 104(2).]

12 [Omits FA 2008, s. 105.]

13 [Not relevant to petroleum revenue tax.]

14 [Not relevant to petroleum revenue tax.]

15 [Not relevant to petroleum revenue tax.]

16 [Not relevant to petroleum revenue tax.]

17 [Not relevant to petroleum revenue tax.]

18 [Not relevant to petroleum revenue tax.]

19 [Not relevant to petroleum revenue tax.]

20 [Not relevant to petroleum revenue tax.]

Part 3 – Commencement

23 The amendments made by this Schedule have effect in relation to expenditure incurred on or after the day on which this Act is passed.

SCHEDULE 34 – ANNUAL TAX ON ENVELOPED DWELLINGS: INFORMATION AND ENFORCEMENT

Section 164

Part 1 – Information and Inspection Powers

1 Schedule 36 to FA 2008 (information and inspection powers) is amended as follows.

2 [Inserts FA 2008, Sch. 36, para. 12A(3)(f).]

3 [Inserts FA 2008, Sch. 36, para. 21B.]

4 [Inserts FA 2008, Sch. 36, para. 37(2B).]

5 [Inserts FA 2008, Sch. 36, para. 63(1)(ha).]

SCHEDULE 43 – GENERAL ANTI-ABUSE RULE: PROCEDURAL REQUIREMENTS

Section 209

Other material – HMRC guidance: the general anti-abuse rule.

THE GAAR ADVISORY PANEL

1(1) In this Part **"the GAAR Advisory Panel"** means the panel of persons established by the Commissioners for the purposes of the general anti-abuse rule.

1(2) In this Schedule **"the Chair"** means any member of the GAAR Advisory Panel appointed by the Commissioners to chair it.

MEANING OF "TAX APPEAL"

1A In this Part **"tax appeal"** means–

(a) an appeal under section 31 of TMA 1970 (income tax: appeals against amendments of self-assessment, amendments made by closure notices under section 28A or 28B of that Act, etc), including an appeal under that section by virtue of regulations under Part 11 of ITEPA 2003 (PAYE),

(b) an appeal under paragraph 9 of Schedule 1A to TMA 1970 (income tax: appeals against amendments made by closure notices under paragraph 7(2) of that Schedule, etc),

(c) an appeal under section 705 of ITA 2007 (income tax: appeals against counteraction notices),

(d) an appeal under paragraph 34(3) or 48 of Schedule 18 to FA 1998 (corporation tax: appeals against amendment of a company's return made by closure notice, assessments other than self-assessments, etc),

(e) an appeal under section 750 of CTA 2010 (corporation tax: appeals against counteraction notices),

(f) an appeal under section 222 of IHTA 1984 (appeals against HMRC determinations) other than an appeal made by a person against a determination in respect of a transfer of value at a time when a tax enquiry is in progress in respect of a return made by that person in respect of that transfer,

(g) an appeal under paragraph 35 of Schedule 10 to FA 2003 (stamp duty land tax: appeals against amendment of self-assessment, discovery assessments, etc),

(h) an appeal under paragraph 35 of Schedule 33 to FA 2013 (annual tax on enveloped dwellings: appeals against amendment of self-assessment, discovery assessments, etc),

(i) an appeal under paragraph 14 of Schedule 2 to the Oil Taxation Act 1975 (petroleum revenue tax: appeal against assessment, determination etc),

(j) an appeal under section 102 of FA 2015 (diverted profits tax: appeal against charging notice etc),

(k) an appeal under section 114 of FA 2016 (apprenticeship levy: appeal against an assessment), or

(l) an appeal against any determination of–

(i) an appeal within paragraphs (a) to (k), or

(ii) an appeal within this paragraph.

History – Para. 1A (and the heading before it) inserted by FA 2016, s. 158(6) with effect in relation to tax arrangements (within the meaning of FA 2013, Pt. 5) entered into on or after 15 September 2016.

MEANING OF "DESIGNATED HMRC OFFICER"

2 In this Schedule a **"designated HMRC officer"** means an officer of Revenue and Customs who has been designated by the Commissioners for the purposes of the general anti-abuse rule.

NOTICE TO TAXPAYER OF PROPOSED COUNTERACTION OF TAX ADVANTAGE

3(1) If a designated HMRC officer considers–

(a) that a tax advantage has arisen to a person ("the taxpayer") from tax arrangements that are abusive, and

(b) that the advantage ought to be counteracted under section 209,

the officer must give the taxpayer a written notice to that effect.

3(2) The notice must–

(a) specify the arrangements and the tax advantage,

(b) explain why the officer considers that a tax advantage has arisen to the taxpayer from tax arrangements that are abusive,

(c) set out the counteraction that the officer considers ought to be taken,

(d) inform the taxpayer of the period under paragraph 4 for making representations, and

(e) explain the effect of–

(i) paragraphs 5 and 6, and

(ii) sections 209(8) and (9) and 212A.

3(3) The notice may set out steps that the taxpayer may take to avoid the proposed counteraction.

History – Para. 3(2)(e)(i) and (ii) and the word "of–" before them substituted for the words "of paragraphs 5 and 6" by FA 2016, s. 158(7), with effect in relation to tax arrangements (within the meaning of FA 2013, Pt. 5) entered into on or after 15 September 2016.

4(1) If a notice is given to the taxpayer under paragraph 3, the taxpayer has 45 days beginning with the day on which the notice is given to send written representations in response to the notice to the designated HMRC officer.

4(2) The designated officer may, on a written request made by the taxpayer, extend the period during which representations may be made.

CORRECTIVE ACTION BY TAXPAYER

4A(1) If the taxpayer takes the relevant corrective action before the beginning of the closed period mentioned in section 209(8), the matter is not to be referred to the GAAR Advisory Panel.

4A(2) For the purposes of this Schedule the **"relevant corrective action"** is taken if (and only if) the taxpayer takes the steps set out in sub-paragraphs (3) and (4).

4A(3) The first step is that–

(a) the taxpayer amends a return or claim to counteract the tax advantage specified in the notice under paragraph 3, or

(b) if the taxpayer has made a tax appeal (by notifying HMRC or otherwise) on the basis that the tax advantage specified in the notice under paragraph 3 arises from the tax arrangements specified in that notice, the taxpayer takes all necessary action to enter into an agreement with HMRC (in writing) for the purpose of relinquishing that advantage.

4A(4) The second step is that the taxpayer notifies HMRC–

(a) that the taxpayer has taken the first step, and

(b) of any additional amount which has or will become due and payable in respect of tax by reason of the first step being taken.

4A(5) Where the taxpayer takes the first step described in sub-paragraph (3)(b), HMRC may proceed as if the taxpayer had not taken the relevant corrective action if the taxpayer fails to enter into the written agreement.

4A(6) In determining the additional amount which has or will become due and payable in respect of tax for the purposes of sub-paragraph (4)(b), it is to be assumed that, where P takes the necessary action as mentioned in sub-paragraph (3)(b), the agreement is then entered into.

4A(7) No enactment limiting the time during which amendments may be made to returns or claims operates to prevent P taking the first step mentioned in sub-paragraph (3)(a) before the tax enquiry is closed (whether or not before the specified time).

4A(8) No appeal may be brought, by virtue of a provision mentioned in sub-paragraph (9), against an amendment made by a closure notice in respect of a tax enquiry to the extent that the amendment takes into account an amendment made by the taxpayer to a return or claim in taking the first step mentioned in sub-paragraph (3)(a).

4A(9) The provisions are–

(a) section 31(1)(b) or (c) of TMA 1970,

(b) paragraph 9 of Schedule 1A to TMA 1970,

(c) paragraph 34(3) of Schedule 18 to FA 1998,

(d) paragraph 35(1)(b) of Schedule 10 to FA 2003, and

(e) paragraph 35(1)(b) of Schedule 33 to FA 2013.

History – Para. 4A (and the heading before it) inserted by FA 2016, s. 158(8), with effect in relation to tax arrangements (within the meaning of FA 2013, Pt. 5) entered into on or after 15 September 2016.

REFERRAL TO GAAR ADVISORY PANEL

4B Paragraphs 5 and 6 apply if the taxpayer does not take the relevant corrective action (see paragraph 4A) by the beginning of the closed period mentioned in section 209(8).

History – Para. 4B inserted by FA 2016, s. 158(9), with effect in relation to tax arrangements (within the meaning of FA 2013, Pt. 5) entered into on or after 15 September 2016.

5 If no representations are made in accordance with paragraph 4, a designated HMRC officer must refer the matter to the GAAR Advisory Panel.

6(1) If representations are made in accordance with paragraph 4, a designated HMRC officer must consider them.

6(2) If, after considering them, the designated HMRC officer considers that the tax advantage ought to be counteracted under section 206, the officer must refer the matter to the GAAR Advisory Panel.

6(3) The officer must, as soon as reasonably practicable after deciding whether or not the matter is to be referred to the GAAR Advisory Panel, give the taxpayer written notice of the decision.

History – Para. 6(3) inserted by FA 2016, s. 157(11), with effect in relation to tax arrangements (within the meaning of FA 2013, Pt. 5) entered into at any time (whether before or on or after 15 September 2016).

7 If the matter is referred to the GAAR Advisory Panel, the designated HMRC officer must at the same time provide it with–

(a) a copy of the notice given to the taxpayer under paragraph 3,

(b) a copy of any representations made in accordance with paragraph 4 and any comments that the officer has on those representations, and

(c) a copy of the notice given to the taxpayer under paragraph 8.

8 If the matter is referred to the GAAR Advisory Panel, the designated HMRC officer must at the same time give the taxpayer a notice which–

(a) specifies that the matter is being referred,

(b) is accompanied by a copy of any comments provided to the GAAR Advisory Panel under paragraph 7(b), and

(c) informs the taxpayer of the period under paragraph 9 for making representations, and of the requirement under that paragraph to send any representations to the officer.

9(1) The taxpayer has 21 days beginning with the day on which a notice is given under paragraph 8 to send the GAAR Advisory Panel written representations about–

(a) the notice given to the taxpayer under paragraph 3, or

(b) any comments provided under paragraph 7(b).

9(2) The GAAR Advisory Panel may, on a written request made by the taxpayer, extend the period during which representations may be made.

9(3) The taxpayer must send a copy of any representations to the designated HMRC officer at the same time as the representations are sent to the GAAR Advisory Panel.

9(4) If no representations were made in accordance with paragraph 4, the designated HMRC officer–

(a) may provide the GAAR Advisory Panel with comments on any representations made under this paragraph, and

(b) if comments are provided, must at the same time send a copy of them to the taxpayer.

DECISION OF GAAR ADVISORY PANEL AND OPINION NOTICES

10(1) If the matter is referred to the GAAR Advisory Panel, the Chair must arrange for a sub-panel consisting of 3 members of the GAAR Advisory Panel (one of whom may be the Chair) to consider it.

10(2) The sub-panel may invite the taxpayer or the designated HMRC officer (or both) to supply the sub-panel with further information within a period specified in the invitation.

10(3) Invitations must explain the effect of sub-paragraph (4) or (5) (as appropriate).

10(4) If the taxpayer supplies information to the sub-panel under this paragraph, the taxpayer must at the same time send a copy of the information to the designated HMRC officer.

10(5) If the designated HMRC officer supplies information to the sub-panel under this paragraph, the officer must at the same time send a copy of the information to the taxpayer.

11(1) Where the matter is referred to the GAAR Advisory Panel, the sub-panel must produce–

(a) one opinion notice stating the joint opinion of all the members of the sub-panel, or

(b) two or three opinion notices which taken together state the opinions of all the members.

11(2) The sub-panel must give a copy of the opinion notice or notices to–

(a) the designated HMRC officer, and

(b) the taxpayer.

11(3) An opinion notice is a notice which states that in the opinion of the members of the sub-panel, or one or more of those members–

(a) the entering into and carrying out of the tax arrangements is a reasonable course of action in relation to the relevant tax provisions–

(i) having regard to all the circumstances (including the matters mentioned in subsections (2)(a) to (c) and (3) of section 207), and

(ii) taking account of subsections (4) to (6) of that section, or

(b) the entering into or carrying out of the tax arrangements is not a reasonable course of action in relation to the relevant tax provisions having regard to those circumstances and taking account of those subsections, or

(c) it is not possible, on the information available, to reach a view on that matter,

and the reasons for that opinion.

11(4) For the purposes of the giving of an opinion under this paragraph, the arrangements are to be assumed to be tax arrangements.

11(5) In this Part, a reference to any opinion of the GAAR Advisory Panel about any tax arrangements is a reference to the contents of any opinion notice about the arrangements.

NOTICE OF FINAL DECISION AFTER CONSIDERING OPINION OF GAAR ADVISORY PANEL

12(1) A designated HMRC officer who has received a notice or notices under paragraph 11 must, having considered any opinion of the GAAR Advisory Panel about the tax arrangements, give the taxpayer a written notice setting out whether the tax advantage arising from the arrangements is to be counteracted under the general anti-abuse rule.

12(2) If the notice states that a tax advantage is to be counteracted, it must also set out–

(a) the adjustments required to give effect to the counteraction, and

(b) if relevant, any steps that the taxpayer is required to take to give effect to it.

NOTICES MAY BE GIVEN ON ASSUMPTION THAT TAX ADVANTAGE DOES ARISE

13(1) A designated HMRC officer may give a notice, or do anything else, under this Schedule where the officer considers that a tax advantage might have arisen to the taxpayer.

13(2) Accordingly, any notice given by a designated HMRC officer under this Schedule may be expressed to be given on the assumption that the tax advantage does arise (without agreeing that it does).

SCHEDULE 43A – PROCEDURAL REQUIREMENTS: POOLING NOTICES AND NOTICES OF BINDING

History – Sch. 43A inserted by FA 2016, s. 157(2), with effect in relation to tax arrangements (within the meaning of FA 2013, Pt. 5) entered into at any time (whether before or on or after 15 September 2016).

POOLING NOTICES

1(1) This paragraph applies where a person has been given a notice under paragraph 3 of Schedule 43 in relation to any tax arrangements (the "lead arrangements") and the condition in sub-paragraph (2) is met.

1(2) The condition is that the period of 45 days mentioned in paragraph 4(1) of Schedule 43 has expired but no notice under paragraph 12 of Schedule 43 or paragraph 8 of Schedule 43B has yet been given in respect of the matter.

1(3) If a designated HMRC officer considers–

(a) that a tax advantage has arisen to a person ("R") from tax arrangements (other than the lead arrangements) that are abusive,

(b) that those tax arrangements ("R's arrangements") are equivalent to the lead arrangements, and

(c) that the advantage ought to be counteracted under section 209,

the officer may give R a notice (a "pooling notice") to that effect.

1(3A) For the purposes of this Schedule and Schedule 43B, all the tax arrangements in relation to which pooling notices have been served in respect of the same lead arrangements are to be regarded as being in a "pool" together.

1(4) [Omitted by SI 2017/1090, reg. 3(4).]

1(5) [Omitted by SI 2017/1090, reg. 3(4).]

1(6) The officer may not give R a pooling notice if R has been given in respect of R's arrangements a notice under paragraph 3 of Schedule 43.

History – In para. 1(3)(a), the word "a" substituted for the word "another" and the words "(other than the lead arrangements)" inserted by SI 2017/1090, reg. 3(2)(a), with effect from 5 December 2017.
In para. 1, the words "to that effect" substituted for the words "which places R's arrangements in a pool with the lead arrangements." by SI 2017/1090, reg. 3(2)(b), with effect from 5 December 2017.
Para. 1(3A) inserted by SI 2017/1090, reg. 3(3), with effect from 5 December 2017.
Para. 1(4) and (5) omitted by SI 2017/1090, reg. 3(4), with effect from 5 December 2017.

NOTICE OF PROPOSAL TO BIND ARRANGEMENTS TO COUNTERACTED ARRANGEMENTS

2(1) This paragraph applies where a counteraction notice has been given to a person in relation to any tax arrangements (the "counteracted arrangements").

2(2) If a designated HMRC officer considers–

(a) that a tax advantage has arisen to a person ("R") from tax arrangements (other than the counteracted arrangements) that are abusive,

(b) that those tax arrangements ("R's arrangements") are equivalent to the counteracted arrangements, and

(c) that the advantage ought to be counteracted under section 209,

the officer may give R a notice (a "notice of binding") in relation to R's arrangements.

2(3) The officer may not give R a notice of binding if R has been given in respect of R's arrangements a notice under–

(a) paragraph 1, or

(b) paragraph 3 of Schedule 43.

2(4) In this paragraph **"counteraction notice"** means a notice such as is mentioned in sub-paragraph (2) of paragraph 12 of Schedule 43 or sub-paragraph (3) of paragraph 8 of Schedule 43B (notice of final decision to counteract).

History – In para. 2(1), the words "which are in a pool created under paragraph 1" (which appeared after the words "(the "counteracted arrangements")") omitted by SI 2017/1090, reg. 4(2), with effect from 5 December 2017.
In para. 2(2)(a), the word "a" substituted for the word "another" and the words "(other than the counteracted arrangements)" inserted by SI 2017/1090, reg. 4(3), with effect from 5 December 2017.

3(1) The decision of a designated HMRC officer whether or not to give R a pooling notice or notice of binding must be taken, and any notice must be given, as soon as is reasonably practicable after the officer becomes aware of the relevant facts.

3(2) A pooling notice or notice of binding must–

(a) specify the tax arrangements in relation to which the notice is given and the tax advantage,

(b) explain why the officer considers R's arrangements to be equivalent to the lead arrangements or the counteracted arrangements (as the case may be),

(c) explain why the officer considers that a tax advantage has arisen to R from tax arrangements that are abusive,

(d) set out the counteraction that the officer considers ought to be taken, and

(e) explain the effect of–

 (i) paragraphs 4 to 10,

 (ii) subsection (9) of section 209, and

(iii) section 212A.

3(3) A pooling notice or notice of binding may set out steps that R may (subject to subsection (9) of section 209) take to avoid the proposed counteraction.

History – In para. 3(1), the words "of a designated HMRC officer" inserted and the words "the officer" substituted for the word "HMRC" by SI 2017/1090, reg. 5, with effect from 5 December 2017.

CORRECTIVE ACTION BY A NOTIFIED TAXPAYER

4(1) If a person to whom a pooling notice or notice of binding has been given takes the relevant corrective action in relation to the tax arrangements and tax advantage specified in the notice before the beginning of the closed period mentioned in section 209(9), the person is to be treated for the purposes of paragraphs 6 to 8 and 9 and Schedule 43B (generic referral of tax arrangements) as not having been given the notice in question (and accordingly the tax arrangements in question are no longer in the pool).

4(2) For the purposes of this Schedule the **"relevant corrective action"** is taken if (and only if) the person takes the steps set out in sub-paragraphs (3) and (4).

4(3) The first step is that–

(a) the person amends a return or claim to counteract the tax advantage specified in the pooling notice or notice of binding, or

(b) P takes all necessary action to enter into an agreement with HMRC (in writing) for the purpose of relinquishing that advantage.

4(4) The second step is that the person notifies HMRC–

(a) that the first step has been taken, and

(b) of any additional amount which has or will become due and payable in respect of tax by reason of the first step being taken.

4(5) Where a person takes the first step described in sub-paragraph (3)(b), HMRC may proceed as if the person had not taken the relevant corrective action if the person fails to enter into the written agreement.

4(6) In determining the additional amount which has or will become due and payable in respect of tax for the purposes of sub-paragraph (4)(b), it is to be assumed that, where P takes the necessary action as mentioned in sub-paragraph (3)(b), the agreement is then entered into.

4(7) No enactment limiting the time during which amendments may be made to returns or claims operates to prevent P taking the first step mentioned in sub-paragraph (3)(a) before the tax enquiry is closed.

4(8) No appeal may be brought, by virtue of a provision mentioned in sub-paragraph (9), against an amendment made by a closure notice in respect of a tax enquiry to the extent that the amendment takes into account an amendment made by the taxpayer to a return or claim in taking the first step mentioned in sub-paragraph (3)(a).

4(9) The provisions are–

(a) paragraph 35(1)(b) of Schedule 33,

(b) section 31(1)(b) or (c) of TMA 1970,

(c) paragraph 9 of Schedule 1A to TMA 1970,

(d) paragraph 34(3) of Schedule 18 to FA 1998, and

(e) paragraph 35(1)(b) of Schedule 10 to FA 2003.

History – In para. 4(1), the words "6 to" inserted by SI 2017/1090, reg. 6(2), with effect from 5 December 2017.
In para. 4(3)(b), the words "if the person has made a tax appeal (by notifying HMRC or otherwise) on the basis that the tax advantage specified in the pooling notice or notice of binding arises from the tax arrangements specified in that notice," (which appeared before the words "P takes all ") omitted by SI 2017/1090, reg. 6(3), with effect from 5 December 2017.

CORRECTIVE ACTION BY LEAD TAXPAYER

5 [Omitted by SI 2017/1090, reg. 7.]

History – Para. 5 omitted by SI 2017/1090, reg. 7, with effect from 5 December 2017.

OPINION NOTICES AND RIGHT TO MAKE REPRESENTATIONS

6(1) Sub-paragraph (2) applies where–

(a) a pooling notice is given to a person in relation to any tax arrangements, and

(b) an opinion notice (or opinion notices) under paragraph 11(2) of Schedule 43 aboutanother set of tax arrangements in the pool or the lead arrangements ("the referred arrangements") is subsequently given to a designated HMRC officer.

6(2) The officer must give the person a pooled arrangements opinion notice.

6(3) No more than one pooled arrangements opinion notice may be given to a person in respect of the same tax arrangements.

6(4) Where a designated HMRC officer gives a person a notice of binding, the officer must, at the same time, give the person a bound arrangements opinion notice.

History – In para. 6(1)(b), the words "or the lead arrangements" inserted by SI 2017/1090, reg. 8, with effect from 5 December 2017.

7(1) In relation to a person who is, or has been, given a pooling notice, **"pooled arrangements opinion notice"** means a written notice which–

(a) sets out a report prepared by HMRC of any opinion of the GAAR Advisory Panel about the referred arrangements,

(b) explains the person's right to make representations falling within sub-paragraph (3), and

(c) sets out the period in which those representations may be made.

7(2) In relation to a person who is given a notice of binding **"bound arrangements opinion notice"** means a written notice which–

(a) sets out a report prepared by HMRC of any opinion of the GAAR Advisory Panel about the counteracted arrangements (see paragraph 2(1)),

(b) explains the person's right to make representations falling within sub-paragraph (3), and

(c) sets out the period in which those representations may be made.

7(3) A person who is given a pooled arrangements opinion notice or a bound arrangements opinion notice has 30 days beginning with the day on which the notice is given to make representations in any of the following categories–

(a) representations that no tax advantage has arisen to the person from the arrangements to which the notice relates;

(b) representations as to why the arrangements to which the notice relates are or may be materially different from–

(i) the referred arrangements (in the case of a pooled arrangements opinion notice), or

(ii) the counteracted arrangements (in the case of a bound arrangements opinion notice).

7(4) In sub-paragraph (3)(b) references to **"arrangements"** include any circumstances which would be relevant in accordance with section 207 to a determination of whether the tax arrangements in question are abusive.

NOTICE OF FINAL DECISION

8(1) This paragraph applies where–

(a) further to a pooling notice given under paragraph 1(3), a set of tax arrangements is in a pool relating to any lead arrangements, and

(b) a designated HMRC officer has given a notice under paragraph 12 of Schedule 43 in relation to any other arrangements in the pool or the lead arrangements (the "referred arrangements").

8(2) The officer must, having considered any opinion of the GAAR Advisory Panel about the referred arrangements and any representations made under paragraph 7(3) in relation to the arrangements mentioned in sub-paragraph (1)(a), give the person a written notice setting out whether the tax advantage arising from those arrangements is to be counteracted under the general anti-abuse rule.

History – Para. 8(1)(a) substituted by SI 2017/1090, reg. 9(a), with effect from 5 December 2017.
In para. 8(1)(b), the words "or the lead arrangements " inserted by SI 2017/1090, reg. 9(b), with effect from 5 December 2017.

9(1) This paragraph applies where–

(a) a person has been given a notice of binding under paragraph 2, and

(b) the period of 30 days for making representations under paragraph 7(3) has expired.

9(2) A designated HMRC officer must, having considered any opinion of the GAAR Advisory Panel about the counteracted arrangements and any representations made under paragraph 7(3) in relation to the arrangements specified in the notice of binding, give the person a written notice setting out whether the tax advantage arising from the arrangements specified in the notice of binding is to be counteracted under the general anti-abuse rule.

10 If a notice under paragraph 8(2) or 9(2) states that a tax advantage is to be counteracted, it must also set out–

(a) the adjustments required to give effect to the counteraction, and

(b) if relevant, any steps the person concerned is required to take to give effect to it.

"EQUIVALENT ARRANGEMENTS"

11(1) For the purposes of paragraph 1, tax arrangements are **"equivalent"** to one another if they are substantially the same as one another having regard to–

(a) their substantive results,

(b) the means of achieving those results, and

(c) the characteristics on the basis of which it could reasonably be argued, in each case, that the arrangements are abusive tax arrangements under which a tax advantage has arisen to a person.

NOTICES MAY BE GIVEN ON ASSUMPTION THAT TAX ADVANTAGE DOES ARISE

12(1) A designated HMRC officer may give a notice, or do anything else, under this Schedule where the officer considers that a tax advantage might have arisen to the person concerned.

12(2) Accordingly, any notice given by a designated HMRC officer under this Schedule may be expressed to be given on the assumption that a tax advantage does arise (without conceding that it does).

HMRC OFFICERS

12A Anything that may or must be done by a given designated HMRC officer under this Schedule may be done instead by any other designated HMRC officer.

History – Para. 12A inserted by SI 2017/1090, reg. 10, with effect from 5 December 2017.

POWER TO AMEND

13(1) The Treasury may by regulations amend this Schedule (apart from this paragraph).

13(2) Regulations under sub-paragraph (1) may include–

(a) any amendment of this Part that is appropriate in consequence of an amendment by virtue of sub-paragraph (1);

(b) transitional provision.

13(3) Regulations under sub-paragraph (1) are to be made by statutory instrument.

13(4) A statutory instrument containing regulations under sub-paragraph (1) is subject to annulment in pursuance of a resolution of the House of Commons.

SCHEDULE 43B – PROCEDURAL REQUIREMENTS: GENERIC REFERRAL OF TAX ARRANGEMENTS

History – Sch. 43B inserted by FA 2016, s. 157(3), with effect in relation to tax arrangements (within the meaning of FA 2013, Pt. 5) entered into at any time (whether before or on or after 15 September 2016).

NOTICE OF PROPOSAL TO MAKE GENERIC REFERRAL OF TAX ARRANGEMENTS

1(1) Sub-paragraph (2) applies if–

(a) further to pooling notices given under paragraph 1(3) of Schedule 43A, two or more sets of tax arrangements are in a pool relating to any lead arrangements,

(b) the person to whom the notice mentioned in paragraph 1(1) of Schedule 43A was given takes the relevant corrective action (as defined in paragraph 4A of Schedule 43) before–

(i) the end of the period of 75 days beginning with the day on which that notice was given, or

(ii) such later time as that person and HMRC may agree, and

(c) no referral under paragraph 5 or 6 of Schedule 43 has been made in respect of any arrangements in the pool.

1(2) A designated HMRC officer may determine that, in respect of each of the tax arrangements that are in the pool, there is to be given (to the person to whom the pooling notice in question was given) a written notice of a proposal to make a generic referral to the GAAR Advisory Panel in respect of the arrangements in the pool.

1(3) Only one determination under sub-paragraph (2) may be made in relation to any one pool.

1(4) The persons to whom those notices are given are **"the notified taxpayers"**.

1(5) A notice given to a person ("T") under sub-paragraph (2) must–

(a) specify the arrangements (the "specified arrangements") and the tax advantage (the "specified advantage") to which the notice relates,

(b) inform T of the period under paragraph 2 for making a proposal.

History – Para. 1(1)(a) and (b) substituted by SI 2017/1090, reg. 12(2), with effect from 5 December 2017.

2(1) T has 30 days beginning with the day on which the notice under paragraph 1 is given to propose to HMRC that it–

(a) should give T a notice under paragraph 3 of Schedule 43 in respect of the arrangements to which the notice under paragraph 1 relates, and

(b) should not proceed with the proposal to make a generic referral to the GAAR Advisory Panel in respect of those arrangements.

2(2) If a proposal is made in accordance with sub-paragraph (1) a designated HMRC officer must consider it.

GENERIC REFERRAL

3(1) This paragraph applies where a designated HMRC officer has given notices to the notified taxpayers in accordance with paragraph 1(2).

3(2) If none of the notified taxpayers has made a proposal under paragraph 2 by the end of the 30 day period mentioned in that paragraph, the officer must make a referral to the GAAR Advisory Panel in respect of the notified taxpayers and the arrangements which are specified arrangements in relation to them.

3(3) If at least one of the notified taxpayers makes a proposal in accordance with paragraph 2, the designated HMRC officer must, after the end of that 30 day period, decide whether to–

(a) give a notice under paragraph 3 of Schedule 43 in respect of one set of tax arrangements in the relevant pool in relation to which such a proposal has been made, or

(b) make a referral to the GAAR Advisory Panel in respect of the tax arrangements in the relevant pool.

3(3A) If under sub-paragraph (3)(a) a notice is given under paragraph 3 of Schedule 43 in respect of one set of tax arrangements but (by virtue of paragraph 4A of that Schedule) the matter is not referred to the GAAR Advisory Panel, a designated officer must make a referral to the GAAR Advisory Panel in respect of the notified taxpayers and the arrangements which are specified arrangements in relation to them.

3(4) A referral under this paragraph is a **"generic referral"**.

History – In para. 3(3)(a), the words " in relation to which such a proposal has been made" inserted by SI 2017/1090, reg. 13(2), with effect from 5 December 2017.

Para. 3(3A) inserted by SI 2017/1090, reg. 13(3), with effect from 5 December 2017.

4(1) If a generic referral is made to the GAAR Advisory Panel, the designated HMRC officer must at the same time provide it with–

(a) a general statement of the material characteristics of the specified arrangements, and

(b) a declaration that–

(i) the statement under paragraph (a) is applicable to all the specified arrangements, and

(ii) as far as HMRC is aware, nothing which is material to the GAAR Advisory Panel's consideration of the matter has been omitted.

4(2) The general statement under sub-paragraph (1)(a) must–

(a) contain a factual description of the tax arrangements;

(b) set out HMRC's view as to whether the tax arrangements accord with established practice (when the arrangements were entered into);

(c) explain why it is the designated HMRC officer's view that a tax advantage of the nature described in the statement and arising from tax arrangements having the characteristics described in the statement would be a tax advantage arising from arrangements that are abusive;

(d) set out any matters the designated officer is aware of which may suggest that any view of HMRC or the designated HMRC officer expressed in the general statement is not correct;

(e) set out any other matters which the designated officer considers are required for the purposes of the exercise of the GAAR Advisory Panel's functions under paragraph 6.

5 If a generic referral is made the designated HMRC officer must at the same time give each of the notified taxpayers a notice which–

(a) specifies that a generic referral is being made, and

(b) is accompanied by a copy of the statement given to the GAAR Advisory Panel in accordance with paragraph 4(1)(a).

DECISION OF GAAR ADVISORY PANEL AND OPINION NOTICES

6(1) If a generic referral is made to the GAAR Advisory Panel under paragraph 3, the Chair must arrange for a sub-panel consisting of 3 members of the GAAR Advisory Panel (one of whom may be the Chair) to consider it.

6(2) The sub-panel must produce–

(a) one opinion notice stating the joint opinion of all the members of the sub-panel, or

(b) two or three opinion notices which taken together state the opinions of all the members.

6(3) The sub-panel must give a copy of the opinion notice or notices to the designated HMRC officer.

6(4) An opinion notice is a notice which states that in the opinion of the members of the sub-panel, or one or more of those members–

(a) the entering into and carrying out of tax arrangements such as are described in the general statement under paragraph 4(1)(a) is a reasonable course of action in relation to the relevant tax provisions,

(b) the entering into or carrying out of such tax arrangements is not a reasonable course of action in relation to the relevant tax provisions, or

(c) it is not possible, on the information available, to reach a view on that matter,

and the reasons for that opinion.

6(5) In forming their opinions for the purposes of sub-paragraph (4) members of the sub-panel must–

(a) have regard to all the matters set out in the statement under paragraph 4(1)(a),

(b) assume (unless the contrary is stated in the statement under paragraph 4(1)(a)) that the tax arrangements do not form part of any other arrangements,

(c) have regard to the matters mentioned in paragraphs (a) to (c) of section 207(2), and

(d) take account of subsections (4) to (6) of section 207.

6(6) For the purposes of the giving of an opinion under this paragraph, the arrangements are to be assumed to be tax arrangements.

6(7) In this Part, a reference to any opinion of the GAAR Advisory Panel in respect of a generic referral of any tax arrangements is a reference to the contents of any opinion notice given in relation to a generic referral in respect of the arrangements.

NOTICE OF RIGHT TO MAKE REPRESENTATIONS

7(1) Where a designated HMRC officer is given an opinion notice (or opinion notices) under paragraph 6, the officer must give each of the notified taxpayers a copy of the opinion notice (or notices) and a written notice which–

(a) explains the notified taxpayer's right to make representations falling within sub-paragraph (2), and

(b) sets out the period in which those representations may be made.

7(2) A notified taxpayer ("T") who is given a notice under sub-paragraph (1) has 30 days beginning with the day on which the notice is given to make representations in any of the following categories–

(a) representations that no tax advantage has arisen from the specified arrangements;

(b) representations that T has already been given a notice under paragraph 6 of Schedule 43A in relation to the specified arrangements;

(c) representations that any matter set out in the statement under paragraph 4(1)(a) is materially inaccurate as regards the specified arrangements (having regard to all circumstances which would be relevant in accordance with section 207 to a determination of whether the tax arrangements in question are abusive).

NOTICE OF FINAL DECISION AFTER CONSIDERING OPINION OF GAAR ADVISORY PANEL

8(1) A designated HMRC officer who has received a notice or notices under paragraph 6(3) in respect of a generic referral must consider the case of each notified taxpayer in accordance with sub-paragraph (2).

8(2) The officer must, having considered–

(a) any opinion of the GAAR Advisory Panel about the matters referred to it, and

(b) any representations made by the notified taxpayer under paragraph 7,

give to the notified taxpayer a written notice setting out whether the specified advantage is to be counteracted under the general anti-abuse rule.

8(3) If the notice states that a tax advantage is to be counteracted, it must also set out–

(a) the adjustments required to give effect to the counteraction, and

(b) if relevant, any steps that the taxpayer is required to take to give effect to it.

NOTICES MAY BE GIVEN ON ASSUMPTION THAT TAX ADVANTAGE DOES ARISE

9(1) A designated HMRC officer may give a notice, or do anything else, under this Schedule where the officer considers that a tax advantage might have arisen to the person concerned.

9(2) Accordingly, any notice given by a designated HMRC officer under this Schedule may be expressed to be given on the assumption that a tax advantage does arise (without conceding that it does).

HMRC OFFICERS

9A Anything that may or must be done by a given designated HMRC officer under this Schedule may be done instead by any other designated HMRC officer.

History – Para. 9A inserted by SI 2017/1090, reg. 14, with effect from 5 December 2017.

POWER TO AMEND

10(1) The Treasury may by regulations amend this Schedule (apart from this paragraph).

10(2) Regulations under sub-paragraph (1) may include–

(a) any amendment of this Part that is appropriate in consequence of an amendment by virtue of sub-paragraph (1);

(b) transitional provision.

10(3) Regulations under sub-paragraph (1) are to be made by statutory instrument.

10(4) A statutory instrument containing regulations under sub-paragraph (1) is subject to annulment in pursuance of a resolution of the House of Commons.

SCHEDULE 43C – PENALTY UNDER SECTION 212A: SUPPLEMENTARY PROVISION

History – Sch. 43C inserted by FA 2016, s. 158(3), with effect in relation to tax arrangements (within the meaning of FA 2013, Pt. 5) entered into on or after 15 September 2016.

VALUE OF THE COUNTERACTED ADVANTAGE: INTRODUCTION

1 Paragraphs 2 to 4 set out how to calculate the **"value of the counteracted advantage"** for the purposes of section 212A.

VALUE OF THE COUNTERACTED ADVANTAGE: BASIC RULE

2(1) The **"value of the counteracted advantage"** is the additional amount due or payable in respect of tax as a result of the counteraction mentioned in section 212A(1)(c).

2(2) The reference in sub-paragraph (1) to the additional amount due and payable includes a reference to–

(a) an amount payable to HMRC having erroneously been paid by way of repayment of tax, and

(b) an amount which would be repayable by HMRC if the counteraction were not made.

2(3) The following are ignored in calculating the value of the counteracted advantage–

(a) group relief, and

(b) any relief under section 458 of CTA 2010 (relief in respect of repayment etc of loan) which is deferred under subsection (5) of that section.

2(4) For the purposes of this paragraph consequential adjustments under section 210 are regarded as part of the counteraction in question.

2(5) If the counteraction affects the person's liability to two or more taxes, the taxes concerned are to be considered together for the purpose of determining the value of the counteracted advantage.

2(6) This paragraph is subject to paragraphs 3 and 4.

VALUE OF COUNTERACTED ADVANTAGE: LOSSES

3(1) To the extent that the tax advantage mentioned in section 212A(1)(b) ("the tax advantage") resulted in the wrong recording of a loss for the purposes of direct tax and the loss has been wholly used to reduce the amount due or payable in respect of tax, the value of the counteracted advantage is determined in accordance with paragraph 2.

3(2) To the extent that the tax advantage resulted in the wrong recording of a loss for purposes of direct tax and the loss has not been wholly used to reduce the amount due or payable in respect of tax, the value of the counteracted advantage is–

(a) the value under paragraph 2 of so much of the tax advantage as results (or would in the absence of the counteraction result) from the part (if any) of the loss which was used to reduce the amount due or payable in respect of tax, plus

(b) 10% of the part of the loss not so used.

3(3) Sub-paragraphs (1) and (2) apply both–

(a) to a case where no loss would have been recorded but for the tax advantage, and

(b) to a case where a loss of a different amount would have been recorded (but in that case sub-paragraphs (1) and (2) apply only to the difference between the amount recorded and the true amount).

3(4) To the extent that the tax advantage creates or increases (or would in the absence of the counteraction create or increase) an aggregate loss recorded for a group of companies–

(a) the value of the counteracted advantage is calculated in accordance with this paragraph, and

(b) in applying paragraph 2 in accordance with sub-paragraphs (1) and (2), group relief may be taken into account (despite paragraph 2(3)).

3(5) To the extent that the tax advantage results (or would in the absence of the counteraction result) in a loss, the value of it is nil where, because of the nature of the loss or the person's circumstances, there was no reasonable prospect of the loss being used to support a claim to reduce a tax liability (of any person).

VALUE OF COUNTERACTED ADVANTAGE: DEFERRED TAX

4(1) To the extent that the tax advantage mentioned in section 212A is a deferral of tax, the value of the counteracted advantage is–

(a) 25% of the amount of the deferred tax for each year of the deferral, or

(b) a percentage of the amount of the deferred tax, for each separate period of deferral of less than a year, equating to 25% per year,

or, if less, 100% of the amount of the deferred tax.

4(2) This paragraph does not apply to a case to the extent that paragraph 3 applies.

ASSESSMENT OF PENALTY

5(1) Where a person is liable for a penalty under section 212A, HMRC must assess the penalty.

5(2) Where HMRC assess the penalty, HMRC must–

(a) notify the person who is liable for the penalty, and

(b) state in the notice a tax period in respect of which the penalty is assessed.

5(3) A penalty under this paragraph must be paid before the end of the period of 30 days beginning with the day on which notification of the penalty is issued.

5(4) An assessment–

(a) is to be treated for procedural purposes as if it were an assessment to tax,

(b) may be enforced as if it were an assessment to tax, and

(c) may be combined with an assessment to tax.

5(5) An assessment of a penalty under this paragraph must be made before the end of the period of 12 months beginning with–

(a) the end of the appeal period for the assessment which gave effect to the counteraction mentioned in section 212A(1)(b), or

(b) if there is no assessment within paragraph (a), the date (or the latest of the dates) on which that counteraction becomes final.

5(6) The reference in sub-paragraph (5)(b) to the counteraction becoming final is to be interpreted in accordance with section 210(8).

ALTERATION OF ASSESSMENT OF PENALTY

6(1) After notification of an assessment has been given to a person under paragraph 5(2), the assessment may not be altered except in accordance with this paragraph or paragraph 7, or on appeal.

6(2) A supplementary assessment may be made in respect of a penalty if an earlier assessment operated by reference to an underestimate of the value of the counteracted advantage.

6(3) An assessment may be revised as necessary if it operated by reference to an overestimate of the value of the counteracted advantage.

REVISION OF ASSESSMENT FOLLOWING CONSEQUENTIAL RELIEVING ADJUSTMENT

7(1) Sub-paragraph (2) applies where a person–

(a) is notified under section 210(7) of a consequential adjustment relating to a counteraction under section 209, and

(b) an assessment to a penalty in respect of that counteraction of which the person has been notified under paragraph 5(2) does not take account of that consequential adjustment.

7(2) HMRC must make any alterations of the assessment that appear to HMRC to be just and reasonable in connection with the consequential amendment.

7(3) Alterations under this paragraph may be made despite any time limit imposed by or under an enactment.

AGGREGATE PENALTIES

8(1) Sub-paragraph (3) applies where–

(a) two or more penalties are incurred by the same person and fall to be determined by reference to an amount of tax to which that person is chargeable,

(b) one of those penalties is incurred under section 212A, and

(c) one or more of the other penalties are incurred under a relevant penalty provision.

8(2) But sub-paragraph (3) does not apply if section 212(2) of FA 2014 (follower notices: aggregate penalties) applies in relation to the amount of tax in question.

8(3) The aggregate of the amounts of the penalties mentioned in subsection (1)(b) and (c), so far as determined by reference to that amount of tax, must not exceed–

(a) the relevant percentage of that amount, or

(b) in a case where at least one of the penalties is under paragraph 5(2)(b) of, or sub-paragraph (3)(b), (4)(b) or (5)(b) of paragraph 6 of, Schedule 55 to FA 2009, £300 (if greater).

8(4) In the application of section 97A of TMA 1970 (multiple penalties) no account shall be taken of a penalty under section 212A.

8(5) **"Relevant penalty provision"** means–

(a) Schedule 24 to FA 2007 (penalties for errors),

(b) Schedule 41 to FA 2008 (penalties: failure to notify etc),

(c) Schedule 55 to FA 2009 (penalties for failure to make returns etc), or

(d) Part 5 of Schedule 18 to FA 2016 (penalty under serial tax avoidance regime).

8(6) **"The relevant percentage"** means–

(a) 200% in a case where at least one of the penalties is determined by reference to the percentage in–

(i) paragraph 4(4)(c) of Schedule 24 to FA 2007,

(ii) paragraph 6(4)(a) of Schedule 41 to FA 2008, or

(iii) paragraph 6(3A)(c) of Schedule 55 to FA 2009,

(b) 150% in a case where paragraph (a) does not apply and at least one of the penalties is determined by reference to the percentage in–

(i) paragraph 4(3)(c) of Schedule 24 to FA 2007,

(ii) paragraph 6(3)(a) of Schedule 41 to FA 2008, or

(iii) paragraph 6(3A)(b) of Schedule 55 to FA 2009,

(c) 140% in a case where neither paragraph (a) nor paragraph (b) applies and at least one of the penalties is determined by reference to the percentage in–

(i) paragraph 4(4)(b) of Schedule 24 to FA 2007,

(ii) paragraph 6(4)(b) of Schedule 41 to FA 2008, or

(iii) paragraph 6(4A)(c) of Schedule 55 to FA 2009,

(d) 105% in a case where at none of paragraphs (a), (b) and (c) applies and at least one of the penalties is determined by reference to the percentage in–

(i) paragraph 4(3)(b) of Schedule 24 to FA 2007,

(ii) paragraph 6(3)(b) of Schedule 41 to FA 2008, or

(iii) paragraph 6(4A)(b) of Schedule 55 to FA 2009, and

(e) in any other case, 100%.

Prospective amendments – Para. 8(6)(ba) inserted by FA 2015, s. 120 and Sch. 20, para. 20(2), with effect from a day to be appointed under s. 120(2).
In para. 8(6)(c), the words "none of paragraphs (a) to (ba) applies" substituted for the words "neither paragraph (a) nor paragraph (b) applies" by FA 2015, s. 120 and Sch. 20, para. 20(3), with effect from a day to be appointed under s. 120(2).
In para. 8(6)(d), the words "none of paragraphs (a) to (c) applies" substituted for the words "none of paragraphs (a), (b) and (c) applies" by FA 2015, s. 120 and Sch. 20, para. 20(4), with effect from a day to be appointed under s. 120(2).

APPEAL AGAINST PENALTY

9(1) A person may appeal against–

(a) the imposition of a penalty under section 212A, or

(b) the amount assessed under paragraph 5.

9(2) An appeal under sub-paragraph (1)(a) may only be made on the grounds that the arrangements were not abusive or there was no tax advantage to be counteracted.

9(3) An appeal under sub-paragraph (1)(b) may only be made on the grounds that the assessment was based on an overestimate of the value of the counteracted advantage (whether because the estimate was made by reference to adjustments which were not just and reasonable or for any other reason).

9(4) An appeal under this paragraph must be made within the period of 30 days beginning with the day on which notification of the penalty is given under paragraph 5(2).

9(5) An appeal under this paragraph is to be treated in the same way as an appeal against an assessment to the tax concerned (including by the application of any provision about bringing the appeal by notice to HMRC, about HMRC's review of the decision or about determination of the appeal by the First-tier Tribunal or Upper Tribunal).

9(6) Sub-paragraph (5) does not apply–

(a) so as to require a person to pay a penalty before an appeal against the assessment of the penalty is determined, or

(b) in respect of any other matter expressly provided for by this Part.

9(7) On an appeal against the penalty the tribunal may affirm or cancel HMRC's decision.

9(8) On an appeal against the amount of the penalty the tribunal may–

(a) affirm HMRC's decision, or

(b) substitute for HMRC's decision another decision that HMRC has power to make.

9(9) In this paragraph **"tribunal"** means the First-tier Tribunal or Upper Tribunal (as appropriate by virtue of sub-paragraph (5)).

MITIGATION OF PENALTIES

10(1) The Commissioners may in their discretion mitigate a penalty under section 212A, or stay or compound any proceedings for such a penalty.

10(2) They may also, after judgment, further mitigate or entirely remit the penalty.

INTERPRETATION

11 In this Schedule–

(a) a reference to an **"assessment"** to tax is to be interpreted, in relation to inheritance tax, as a reference to a determination;

(b) **"direct tax"** means–

(i) income tax,

(ii) capital gains tax,

(iii) corporation tax (including any amount chargeable as if it were corporation tax or treated as corporation tax), and

(iv) petroleum revenue tax;

(v) diverted profits tax;

(c) a reference to a loss includes a reference to a charge, expense, deficit and any other amount which may be available for, or relied on to claim, a deduction or relief;

(d) a reference to a repayment of tax includes a reference to allowing a credit against tax or to a payment of a corporation tax credit;

(e) **"corporation tax credit"** means–

(i) an R&D tax credit under Chapter 2 or 7 of Part 13 of CTA 2009,

(ii) an R&D expenditure credit under Chapter 6A of Part 3 of CTA 2009,

(iii) a land remediation tax credit or life assurance company tax credit under Chapter 3 or 4 respectively of Part 14 of CTA 2009,

(iv) a film tax credit under Chapter 3 of Part 15 of CTA 2009,

(v) a television tax credit under Chapter 3 of Part 15A of CTA 2009,

(vi) a video game tax credit under Chapter 3 of Part 15B of CTA 2009,

(vii) a theatre tax credit under section 1217K of CTA 2009,

(viii) an orchestra tax credit under Chapter 3 of Part 15D of CTA 2009, or

(ix) a first-year tax credit under Schedule A1 to CAA 2001;

(f) **"tax period"** means a tax year, accounting period or other period in respect of which tax is charged;

(g) a reference to giving a document to HMRC includes a reference to communicating information to HMRC in any form and by any method (whether by post, fax, email, telephone or otherwise),

(h) a reference to giving a document to HMRC includes a reference to making a statement or declaration in a document.

SCHEDULE 50 – PENALTIES: LATE FILING, LATE PAYMENT AND ERRORS

Section 230

AMENDMENTS TO SCHEDULE 24 TO FA 2007: PENALTIES FOR ERRORS

1(1) In Schedule 24 to FA 2007 (penalties for errors), paragraph 13 (procedure: assessment) is amended as follows.

1(2) [Amends FA 2007, Sch. 24, para. 13(1)(c).]

1(3) [Inserts FA 2007, Sch. 24, para. 13(1ZA)–(1ZD).]

AMENDMENTS TO SCHEDULE 55 TO FA 2009: PENALTY FOR FAILURE TO MAKE RETURNS

2 Schedule 55 (penalty for failure to make returns etc) to FA 2009 is amended in accordance with paragraphs 3 to 9.

3 In paragraph 1 (returns etc in respect of which penalties are to be paid under that Schedule)–

(a) [amends FA 2009, Sch. 55, para. 1;]

(b) [inserts FA 2009, Sch. 55, para. 1(4A).]

4 [Not relevant to petroleum revenue tax.]

5 [Amends FA 2009, Sch. 55, para. 2.]

6 [Not relevant to petroleum revenue tax.]

7 [Substitutes FA 2009, Sch. 55, para. 18(5)–(7).]

8(1) Paragraph 19 (assessment) is amended as follows.

8(2) [Amends FA 2009, Sch. 55, para. 19(2).]

8(3) [Amends FA 2009, Sch. 55, para. 19(3)(a).]

9(1) Paragraph 27 (interpretation) is amended as follows.

9(2) [Inserts FA 2009, Sch. 55, para. 27(2A).]

9(3) [Inserts FA 2009, Sch. 55, para. 27(3A).]

AMENDMENTS TO SCHEDULE 56 TO FA 2009: PENALTY FOR FAILURE TO MAKE PAYMENTS ON TIME

10 Schedule 56 (penalty for failure to make payments on time) to FA 2009 is amended in accordance with paragraphs 11 to 14.

11 [Amends FA 2009, Sch. 56, para. 1(4).]

12 [Not relevant to petroleum revenue tax.]

13 [Inserts FA 2009, Sch. 56, para. 9A.]

14(1) Paragraph 11 (assessment of penalty) is amended as follows.

14(2) [Substitutes FA 2009, Sch. 56, para. 11(4A) and (4B).]

14(3) [Omits FA 2009, Sch. 56, para. 11(5).]

CONSEQUENTIAL AMENDMENT

15 [Repeals F(No. 3)A 2010, Sch. 10, para. 10.]

COMMENCEMENT

16(1) The amendments made by paragraph 1 have effect in relation to any assessment of a penalty under Schedule 24 to FA 2007 made on or after the day on which this Act is passed.

16(2) The amendments made by paragraphs 2 to 9 and 15 have effect for the tax year 2014–15 and subsequent tax years in relation to failures to make returns with a filing date (as defined in paragraph 1(4) of Schedule 55 to FA 2009) on or after 6 April 2014.

16(3) The amendments made by paragraphs 10 to 14 have effect for defaults made in relation to the tax year 2014–15 and subsequent tax years (see paragraph 6(2) of Sch. 56 to FA 2009 (as amended by paragraph 12(3) of this Schedule) as to when a default is made in relation to a tax year).

FINANCE ACT 2014

(2014 Chapter 26) [*17th July 2014*]

ARRANGEMENT OF SECTIONS

PART 4 – FOLLOWER NOTICES AND ACCELERATED PAYMENTS

CHAPTER 4 – MISCELLANEOUS AND GENERAL PROVISION

CONSEQUENTIAL AMENDMENTS

PART 5 – PROMOTERS OF TAX AVOIDANCE SCHEMES

INTRODUCTION

CONDUCT NOTICES

DEFEAT NOTICES

MONITORING NOTICES: PROCEDURE AND PUBLICATION

ALLOCATION AND DISTRIBUTION OF PROMOTER REFERENCE NUMBER

OBTAINING INFORMATION AND DOCUMENTS

PART 4 – FOLLOWER NOTICES AND ACCELERATED PAYMENTS

Chapter 4 – Miscellaneous and General Provision

CONSEQUENTIAL AMENDMENTS

233 Consequential amendments

233 Schedule 33 contains consequential amendments.

PART 5 – PROMOTERS OF TAX AVOIDANCE SCHEMES

INTRODUCTION

234 Meaning of "relevant proposal" and "relevant arrangements"

234(1) **"Relevant proposal"** means a proposal for arrangements which (if entered into) would be relevant arrangements (whether the proposal relates to a particular person or to any person who may seek to take advantage of it).

234(2) Arrangements are **"relevant arrangements"** if–

(a) they enable, or might be expected to enable, any person to obtain a tax advantage, and

(b) the main benefit, or one of the main benefits, that might be expected to arise from the arrangements is the obtaining of that advantage.

234(3) **"Tax advantage"** includes–

(a) relief or increased relief from tax,

(b) repayment or increased repayment of tax,

(c) avoidance or reduction of a charge to tax or an assessment to tax,

(d) avoidance of a possible assessment to tax,

(e) deferral of a payment of tax or advancement of a repayment of tax, and

(f) avoidance of an obligation to deduct or account for tax.

234(4) **"Arrangements"** includes any agreement, scheme, arrangement or understanding of any kind, whether or not legally enforceable, involving a single transaction or two or more transactions.

235 Carrying on a business "as a promoter"

235(1) A person carrying on a business in the course of which the person is, or has been, a promoter in relation to a relevant proposal or relevant arrangements carries on that business "as a promoter".

235(2) A person is a **"promoter"** in relation to a relevant proposal if the person–

(a) is to any extent responsible for the design of the proposed arrangements,

(b) makes a firm approach to another person in relation to the relevant proposal with a view to making the proposal available for implementation by that person or any other person, or

(c) makes the relevant proposal available for implementation by other persons.

235(3) A person is a **"promoter"** in relation to relevant arrangements if the person–

(a) is by virtue of subsection (2)(b) or (c), a promoter in relation to a relevant proposal which is *implement*ed by the arrangements, or

(b) is responsible to any extent for the design, organisation or management of the arrangements.

235(4) For the purposes of this Part a person makes a firm approach to another person in relation to a relevant proposal if–

(a) the person communicates information about the relevant proposal to the other person at a time when the proposed arrangements have been substantially designed,

(b) the communication is made with a view to that other person or any other person entering into transactions forming part of the proposed arrangements, and

(c) the information communicated includes an explanation of the tax advantage that might be expected to be obtained from the proposed arrangements.

235(5) For the purposes of subsection (4) proposed arrangements have been substantially designed at any time if by that time the nature of the transactions to form them (or part of them) has been sufficiently developed for it to be reasonable to believe that a person who wished to obtain the tax advantage mentioned in subsection (4)(c) might enter into–

(a) transactions of the nature developed, or

(b) transactions not substantially different from transactions of that nature.

235(6) A person is not a promoter in relation to a relevant proposal or relevant arrangements by reason of anything done in prescribed circumstances.

235(7) Regulations under subsection (6) may contain provision having retrospective effect.

Statutory instruments – SI 2015/130: partly made under s. 235(6) and (7).

236 Meaning of "intermediary"

236 For the purposes of this Part a person ("A") is an intermediary in relation to a relevant proposal if–

(a) A communicates information about the relevant proposal to another person in the course of a business,

(b) the communication is made with a view to that other person, or any other person, entering into transactions forming part of the proposed arrangements, and

(c) A is not a promoter in relation to the relevant proposal.

CONDUCT NOTICES

237 Duty to give conduct notice

237(1) Subsections (5) to (9) apply if an authorised officer becomes aware at any time that a person ("P") who is carrying on a business as a promoter–

(a) has, in the period of 3 years ending with that time, met one or more threshold conditions, and

(b) was carrying on a business as a promoter when P met that condition.

237(1A) Subsections (5) to (9) also apply if an authorised officer becomes aware at any time ("the relevant time") that–

(a) a person has, in the period of 3 years ending with the relevant time, met one or more threshold conditions,

(b) at the relevant time another person ("P") meets one or more of those conditions by virtue of Part 2 of Schedule 34 (meeting the threshold conditions: bodies corporate and partnerships), and

(c) P is, at the relevant time, carrying on a business as a promoter.

237(2) Part 1 of Schedule 34 sets out the threshold conditions and describes how they are met.

237(3) Part 2 of that Schedule contains provision about when a person is treated as meeting a threshold condition.

237(4) See also Schedule 36 (which contains provision about the meeting of threshold conditions and other conditions by partnerships).

237(5) The authorised officer must determine–

(a) in a case within subsection (1), whether or not P's meeting of the condition mentioned in subsection (1)(a) (or, if more than one condition is met, the meeting of all of those conditions, taken together) should be regarded as significant in view of the purposes of this Part, or

(b) in a case within subsection (1A), whether or not–

(i) the meeting of the condition by the person as mentioned in subsection (1A)(a) (or, if more than one condition is met, the meeting of all of those conditions, taken together), and

(ii) P's meeting of the condition (or conditions) as mentioned in subsection (1A)(b),

should be regarded as significant in view of those purposes.

237(6) Subsection (5) does not apply if a conduct notice or a monitoring notice already has effect in relation to P.

237(7) If the authorised officer determines under subsection (5)(a) that P's meeting of the condition or conditions in question should be regarded as significant, the officer must give P a conduct notice, unless subsection (8) applies.

237(7A) If the authorised officer determines under subsection (5)(b) that both–

(a) the meeting of the condition or conditions by the person as mentioned in subsection (1A)(a), and

(b) P's meeting of the condition or conditions as mentioned in subsection (1A)(b),

should be regarded as significant, the officer must give P a conduct notice, unless subsection (8) applies.

237(8) This subsection applies if the authorised officer determines that, having regard to the extent of the impact that P's activities as a promoter are likely to have on the collection of tax, it is inappropriate to give P a conduct notice.

237(9) The authorised officer must determine under subsection (5) that the meeting of the condition (or all the conditions) should be regarded as significant if the condition (or any of the conditions) is in any of the following paragraphs of Schedule 34–

(a) paragraph 2 (deliberate tax defaulters);

(b) paragraph 3 (breach of Banking Code of Practice);

(c) paragraph 4 (dishonest tax agents);

(d) paragraph 6 (persons charged with certain offences);

(e) paragraph 7 (opinion notice of GAAR Advisory Panel).

237(10) If, as a result of subsection (1A), subsections (5) to (9) apply to a person, this does not prevent the giving of a conduct notice to the person mentioned in subsection (1A)(a).

History – S. 237(1A) inserted by FA 2015, s. 119 and Sch. 19, para. 2(2), with effect for the purposes of determining whether a person meets a threshold condition in a period of three years ending on or after 26 March 2015 (Royal Assent).

In s. 237(3) the words "when a person is treated as meeting a threshold condition" substituted for the words "the meeting of threshold conditions by bodies corporate" by FA 2015, s. 119 and Sch. 19, para. 2(3), with effect for the purposes of determining whether a person meets a threshold condition in a period of three years ending on or after 26 March 2015 (Royal Assent).

S. 237(5) substituted by FA 2015, s. 119 and Sch. 19, para. 2(4), with effect for the purposes of determining whether a person meets a threshold condition in a period of three years ending on or after 26 March 2015 (Royal Assent). Former s. 237(5) read as follows:

"**237(5)** The authorised officer must determine whether or not P's meeting of the condition mentioned in subsection (1)(a) (or, as the case requires, P's meeting of all those conditions, taken together) should be regarded as significant in view of the purposes of this Part."

In s. 237(7) the words "subsection (5)(a)" substituted for the words "subsection (5)" by FA 2015, s. 119 and Sch. 19, para. 2(5), with effect for the purposes of determining whether a person meets a threshold condition in a period of three years ending on or after 26 March 2015 (Royal Assent).

S. 237(7A) inserted by FA 2015, s. 119 and Sch. 19, para. 2(6), with effect for the purposes of determining whether a person meets a threshold condition in a period of three years ending on or after 26 March 2015 (Royal Assent).

In s. 237(9) the words "mentioned in subsection (1)(a)" omitted by FA 2015, s. 119 and Sch. 19, para. 2(7), with effect for the purposes of determining whether a person meets a threshold condition in a period of three years ending on or after 26 March 2015 (Royal Assent).

S. 237(10) inserted by FA 2015, s. 119 and Sch. 19, para. 2(8), with effect for the purposes of determining whether a person meets a threshold condition in a period of three years ending on or after 26 March 2015 (Royal Assent).

237A Duty to give conduct notice: defeat of promoted arrangements

237A(1) If an authorised officer becomes aware at any time ("the relevant time") that a person ("P") who is carrying on a business as a promoter meets any of the conditions in subsections (11) to (13), the officer must determine whether or not P's meeting of that condition should be regarded as significant in view of the purposes of this Part.

But see also subsection (14).

237A(2) An authorised officer must make the determination set out in subsection (3) if the officer becomes aware at any time ("the section 237A(2) relevant time") that–

(a) a person meets a condition in subsection (11), (12) or (13), and

(b) at the section 237A(2) relevant time another person ("P"), who is carrying on a business as a promoter, meets that condition by virtue of Part 4 of Schedule 34A (meeting the section 237A conditions: bodies corporate and partnerships).

237A(3) The authorised officer must determine whether or not–

(a) the meeting of the condition by the person as mentioned in subsection (2)(a), and

(b) P's meeting of the condition as mentioned in subsection (2)(b),

should be regarded as significant in view of the purposes of this Part.

237A(4) Subsections (1) and (2) do not apply if a conduct notice or monitoring notice already has effect in relation to P.

237A(5) Subsection (1) does not apply if, at the relevant time, an authorised officer is under a duty to make a determination under section 237(5) in relation to P.

237A(6) Subsection (2) does not apply if, at the section 237A(2) relevant time, an authorised officer is under a duty to make a determination under section 237(5) in relation to P.

237A(7) But in a case where subsection (1) does not apply because of subsection (5), or subsection (2) does not apply because of subsection (6), subsection (5) of section 237 has effect as if–

(a) the references in paragraph (a) of that subsection to "subsection (1)", and "subsection (1)(a)" included subsection (1) of this section, and

(b) in paragraph (b) of that subsection the reference to "subsection (2)(a)" included a reference to subsection (2)(a) of this section and the reference to subsection (2)(b) included a reference to subsection (2)(b) of this section.

237A(8) If the authorised officer determines under subsection (1) that P's meeting of the condition in question should be regarded as significant, the officer must give P a conduct notice, unless subsection (10) applies.

237A(9) If the authorised officer determines under subsection (3) that–

(a) the meeting of the condition by the person as mentioned in subsection (2)(a), and

(b) P's meeting of the condition as mentioned in subsection (2)(b),

should be regarded as significant in view of the purposes of this Part, the officer must give P a conduct notice, unless subsection (10) applies.

237A(10) This subsection applies if the authorised officer determines that, having regard to the extent of the impact that P's activities as a promoter are likely to have on the collection of tax, it is inappropriate to give P a conduct notice.

237A(11) The condition in this subsection is that in the period of 3 years ending with the relevant time at least 3 relevant defeats have occurred in relation to P.

237A(12) The condition in this subsection is that at least two relevant defeats have occurred in relation to P at times when a single defeat notice under section 241A(2) or (6) had effect in relation to P.

237A(13) The condition in this subsection is that at least one relevant defeat has occurred in relation to P at a time when a double defeat notice under section 241A(3) had effect in relation to P.

237A(14) A determination that the condition in subsection (12) or (13) is met cannot be made unless–

(a) the defeat notice in question still has effect when the determination is made, or

(b) the determination is made on or before the 90th day after the day on which the defeat notice in question ceased to have effect.

237A(15) Schedule 34A sets out the circumstances in which a **"relevant defeat"** occurs in relation to a person and includes provision limiting what can amount to a further relevant defeat in relation to a person (see paragraph 6).

History – S. 237A inserted by FA 2016, s. 160(2), with effect from 15 September 2016 (Royal Assent).

Cross references – FA 2016, s. 160(20)– (25): defeats treated as not having occurred.

237B Duty to give further conduct notice where provisional notice not complied with

237B(1) An authorised officer must give a conduct notice to a person ("P") who is carrying on a business as a promoter if–

(a) a conduct notice given to P under section 237A(8)–

(i) has ceased to have effect otherwise than as a result of section 237D(2) or 241(3) or (4), and

(ii) was provisional immediately before it ceased to have effect,

(b) the officer determines that P had failed to comply with one or more conditions in the conduct notice,

(c) the conduct notice relied on a Case 3 relevant defeat,

(d) since the time when the conduct notice ceased to have effect, one or more relevant defeats falling within subsection (2) have occurred in relation to–

(i) P, and

(ii) any arrangements to which the Case 3 relevant defeat also relates, and

(e) had that relevant defeat or (as the case may be) those relevant defeats, occurred before the conduct notice ceased to have effect, an authorised officer would have been required to notify the person under section 237C(3) that the notice was no longer provisional.

237B(2) A relevant defeat falls within this subsection if it occurs by virtue of Case 1 or Case 2 in Schedule 34A.

237B(3) Subsection (1) does not apply if the authorised officer determines that, having regard to the extent of the impact that the person's activities as a promoter are likely to have on the collection of tax, it is inappropriate to give the person a conduct notice.

237B(4) Subsection (1) does not apply if a conduct notice or monitoring notice already has effect in relation to the person.

237B(5) For the purposes of this Part a conduct notice **"relies on a Case 3 relevant defeat"** if it could not have been given under the following condition.

The condition is that paragraph 9 of Schedule 34A had effect with the substitution of "100% of the tested arrangements" for "75% of the tested arrangements".

History – S. 237B inserted by FA 2016, s. 160(2), with effect from 15 September 2016 (Royal Assent).

237C When a conduct notice given under section 237A(8) is "provisional"

237C(1) This section applies to a conduct notice which–

(a) is given to a person under section 237A(8), and

(b) relies on a Case 3 relevant defeat.

237C(2) The notice is **"provisional"** at all times when it has effect, unless an authorised officer notifies the person that the notice is no longer provisional.

237C(3) An authorised officer must notify the person that the notice is no longer provisional if subsection (4) or (5) applies.

237C(4) This subsection applies if–

(a) the condition in subsection (5)(a) is not met, and

(b) a full relevant defeat occurs in relation to P.

237C(5) This subsection applies if–

(a) two, or all three, of the relevant defeats by reference to which the conduct notice is given would not have been relevant defeats if paragraph 9 of Schedule 34A had effect with the substitution of "100% of the tested arrangements" for "75% of the tested arrangements", and

(b) the same number of full relevant defeats occur in relation to P.

237C(6) A **"full relevant defeat"** occurs in relation to P if–

(a) a relevant defeat occurs in relation to P otherwise than by virtue of Case 3 in paragraph 9 of Schedule 34A, or

(b) circumstances arise which would be a relevant defeat in relation to P by virtue of paragraph 9 of Schedule 34A if that paragraph had effect with the substitution of "100% of the tested arrangements" for "75% of the tested arrangements".

237C(7) In determining under subsection (6) whether a full relevant defeat has occurred in relation to P, assume that in paragraph 6 of Schedule 34A (provision limiting what can amount to a further relevant defeat in relation to a person) the first reference to a **"relevant defeat"** does not include a relevant defeat by virtue of Case 3 in paragraph 9 of Schedule 34A.

History – S. 237C inserted by FA 2016, s. 160(2), with effect from 15 September 2016 (Royal Assent).

237D Judicial ruling upholding asserted tax advantage: effect on conduct notice which is provisional

237D(1) Subsection (2) applies if at any time–

(a) a conduct notice which relies on a Case 3 relevant defeat (see section 237B(5)) is provisional, and

(b) a court or tribunal upholds a corresponding tax advantage which has been asserted in connection with any of the related arrangements to which that relevant defeat relates (see paragraph 5(2) of Schedule 34A).

237D(2) The conduct notice ceases to have effect when that judicial ruling becomes final.

237D(3) An authorised officer must give the person to whom the conduct notice was given a written notice stating that the conduct notice has ceased to have effect.

237D(4) For the purposes of this section, a tax advantage is **"asserted"** in connection with any arrangements if a person makes a return, claim or election on the basis that the tax advantage arises from those arrangements.

In relation to the arrangements mentioned in paragraph (b) of subsection (1) **"corresponding tax advantage"** means a tax advantage corresponding to any tax advantage the counteraction of which contributed to the relevant defeat mentioned in that paragraph.

237D(5) For the purposes of this section a court or tribunal **"upholds"** a tax advantage if–

(a) the court or tribunal makes a ruling to the effect that no part of the tax advantage is to be counteracted, and

(b) that judicial ruling is final.

237D(6) For the purposes of this Part of this Act a judicial ruling is **"final"** if it is–

(a) a ruling of the Supreme Court, or

(b) a ruling of any other court or tribunal in circumstances where–

(i) no appeal may be made against the ruling,

(ii) if an appeal may be made against the ruling with permission, the time limit for applications has expired and either no application has been made or permission has been refused,

(iii) if such permission to appeal against the ruling has been granted or is not required, no appeal has been made within the time limit for appeals, or

(iv) if an appeal was made, it was abandoned or otherwise disposed of before it was determined by the court or tribunal to which it was addressed.

237D(7) In this section references to **"counteraction"** include anything referred to as a counteraction in any of Conditions A to F in paragraphs 11 to 16 of Schedule 34A.

History – S. 237D inserted by FA 2016, s. 160(2), with effect from 15 September 2016 (Royal Assent).

238 Contents of a conduct notice

238(1) A conduct notice is a notice requiring the person to whom it has been given ("the recipient") to comply with conditions specified in the notice.

238(2) Before deciding on the terms of a conduct notice, the authorised officer must give the person to whom the notice is to be given an opportunity to comment on the proposed terms of the notice.

238(3) A notice may include only conditions that it is reasonable to impose for any of the following purposes–

(a) to ensure that the recipient provides adequate information to its clients about relevant proposals, and relevant arrangements, in relation to which the recipient is a promoter;

(b) to ensure that the recipient provides adequate information about relevant proposals in relation to which it is a promoter to persons who are intermediaries in relation to those proposals;

(c) to ensure that the recipient does not fail to comply with any duty under a specified disclosure provision;

(d) to ensure that the recipient does not discourage others from complying with any obligation to disclose to HMRC information of a description specified in the notice;

(e) to ensure that the recipient does not enter into an agreement with another person ("C") which relates to a relevant proposal or relevant arrangements in relation to which the recipient is a promoter, on terms which–

(i) impose a contractual obligation on C which falls within paragraph 11(2) or (3) of Schedule 34 (contractual terms restricting disclosure), or

(ii) impose on C obligations within both paragraph 11(4) and (5) of that Schedule (contractual terms requiring contribution to fighting funds and restricting settlement of proceedings);

(f) to ensure that the recipient does not promote relevant proposals or relevant arrangements which rely on, or involve a proposal to rely on, one or more contrived or abnormal steps to produce a tax advantage;

(g) to ensure that the recipient does not fail to comply with any stop notice which has effect under paragraph 12 of Schedule 34.

238(4) References in subsection (3) to ensuring that adequate information is provided about proposals or arrangements include–

(a) ensuring the adequacy of the description of the arrangements or proposed arrangements;

(b) ensuring that the information includes an adequate assessment of the risk that the arrangements or proposed arrangements will fail;

(c) ensuring that the information does not falsely state, and is not likely to create a false impression, that HMRC have (formally or informally) considered, approved or expressed a particular opinion in relation to the proposal or arrangements.

238(5) In subsection (3)(c) **"specified disclosure provision"** means a disclosure provision that is specified in the notice; and for this purpose **"disclosure provision"** means any of the following–

(a) section 308 of FA 2004 (disclosure of tax avoidance schemes: duties of promoter);

(b) section 312 of FA 2004 (duty of promoter to notify client of number);

(c) sections 313ZA and 313ZB of FA 2004 (duties to provide details of clients and certain others);

(d) Part 1 of Schedule 36 to FA 2008 (duties to provide information and produce documents).

238(6) In subsection (4)(b) **"fail"**, in relation to arrangements or proposed arrangements, means not result in a tax advantage which the arrangements or (as the case may be) proposed arrangements might be expected to result in.

238(7) The Treasury may by regulations amend the definition of **"disclosure provision"** in subsection (5).

239 Section 238: supplementary

239(1) In section 238 the following expressions are to be interpreted as follows.

239(2) **"Adequate"** means adequate having regard to what it might be reasonable for a client or (as the case may be) an intermediary to expect; and **"adequacy"** is to be interpreted accordingly.

239(3) A person ("C") is a "client" of a promoter, if at any time when a conduct notice has effect, the promoter–

(a) makes a firm approach to C in relation to a relevant proposal with a view to the promoter making the proposal available for implementation by C or another person;

(b) makes a relevant proposal available for implementation by C;

(c) takes part in the organisation or management of relevant arrangements entered into by C.

239(4) The recipient of a conduct notice **"promotes"** a relevant proposal if it–

(a) takes part in designing the proposal,

(b) makes a firm approach to a person in relation to the proposal with a view to making the proposal available for implementation by that person or another person, or

(c) makes the proposal available for implementation by persons (other than the recipient).

239(5) The recipient of a conduct notice **"promotes"** relevant arrangements if it takes part in designing, organising or managing the arrangements.

240 Amendment or withdrawal of conduct notice

240(1) This section applies where a conduct notice has been given to a person.

240(2) An authorised officer may at any time amend the notice.

240(3) An authorised officer–

(a) may withdraw the notice if the officer thinks it is not necessary for it to continue to have effect, and

(b) in considering whether or not that is necessary must take into account the person's record of compliance, or failure to comply, with the conditions in the notice.

241 Duration of conduct notice

241(1) A conduct notice has effect from the date specified in it as its commencement date.

241(2) A conduct notice ceases to have effect–

(a) at the end of the period of two years beginning with its commencement date, or

(b) if an earlier date is specified in it as its termination date, at the end of that day.

241(3) A conduct notice ceases to have effect if withdrawn by an authorised officer under section 240.

241(4) A conduct notice ceases to have effect in relation to a person when a monitoring notice takes effect in relation to that person.

241(5) See also section 237D(2) (provisional conduct notice affected by judicial ruling).

History – S. 241(5) inserted by FA 2016, s. 160(6), with effect from 15 September 2016 (Royal Assent).

DEFEAT NOTICES

History – Heading inserted by FA 2016, s. 160(3), with effect from 15 September 2016 (Royal Assent).

241A Defeat notices

241A(1) This section applies in relation to a person ("P") only if P is carrying on a business as a promoter.

241A(2) An authorised officer, or an officer of Revenue and Customs with the approval of an authorised officer, may give P a notice if the officer concerned has become aware of one (and only one) relevant defeat which has occurred in relation to P in the period of 3 years ending with the day on which the notice is given.

241A(3) An authorised officer, or an officer of Revenue and Customs with the approval of an authorised officer, may give P a notice if the officer concerned has become aware of two (but not more than two) relevant defeats which have occurred in relation to P in the period of 3 years ending with the day on which the notice is given.

241A(4) A notice under this section must be given by the end of the 90 days beginning with the day on which the matters mentioned in subsection (2) or (as the case may be) (3) come to the attention of HMRC.

241A(5) Subsection (6) applies if–

(a) a single defeat notice which had been given to P (under subsection (2) or (6)) ceases to have effect as a result of section 241B(1), and

(b) in the period when the defeat notice had effect a relevant defeat ("the further relevant defeat") occurred in relation to P.

241A(6) An authorised officer or an officer of Revenue and Customs with the approval of an authorised officer may give P a notice in respect of the further relevant defeat (regardless of whether or not it occurred in the period of 3 years ending with the day on which the notice is given).

241A(7) In this Part–

(a) **"single defeat notice"** means a notice under subsection (2) or (6);

(b) **"double defeat notice"** means a notice under subsection (3);

(c) **"defeat notice"** means a single defeat notice or a double defeat notice.

241A(8) A defeat notice must–

(a) set out the dates on which the look-forward period for the notice begins and ends;

(b) in the case of a single defeat notice, explain the effect of section 237A(12);

(c) in the case of a double defeat notice, explain the effect of section 237A(13).

241A(9) HMRC may specify what further information must be included in a defeat notice.

241A(10) **"Look-forward period"**–

(a) in relation to a defeat notice under subsection (2) or (3), means the period of 5 years beginning with the day after the day on which the notice is given;

(b) in relation to a defeat notice under subsection (6), means the period beginning with the day after the day on which the notice is given and ending at the end of the period of 5 years beginning with the day on which the further relevant defeat mentioned in subsection (6) occurred in relation to P.

241A(11) A defeat notice has effect throughout its look-forward period unless it ceases to have effect earlier in accordance with section 241B(1) or (4).

History – S. 241A inserted by FA 2016, s. 160(3), with effect from 15 September 2016 (Royal Assent).

Cross references – FA 2016, s. 160(20)–(25): defeats treated as not having occurred.

241B Judicial ruling upholding asserted tax advantage: effect on defeat notice

241B(1) If the relevant defeat to which a single defeat notice relates is overturned (see subsection (5)), the notice has no further effect on and after the day on which it is overturned.

241B(2) Subsection (3) applies if one (and only one) of the relevant defeats in respect of which a double defeat notice was given is overturned.

241B(3) The notice is to be treated for the purposes of this Part (including this section) as if it had always been a single defeat notice given (in respect of the other of the two relevant defeats) on the date on which the notice was in fact given.

The look-forward period for the notice is accordingly unchanged.

241B(4) If both the relevant defeats to which a double defeat notice relates are overturned (on the same date), that notice has no further effect on and after that date.

241B(5) A relevant defeat specified in a defeat notice is **"overturned"** if–

(a) the notice could not have specified that relevant defeat if paragraph 9 of Schedule 34A had effect with the substitution of "100% of the tested arrangements" for "75% of the tested arrangements", and

(b) at a time when the notice has effect a court or tribunal upholds a corresponding tax advantage which has been asserted in connection with any of the related arrangements to which the relevant defeat relates (see paragraph 5(2) of Schedule 34A).

Accordingly the relevant defeat is overturned on the day on which the judicial ruling mentioned in paragraph (b) becomes final.

241B(6) If a defeat notice ceases to have effect as a result of subsection (1) or (4) an authorised officer, or an officer of Revenue and Customs with the approval of an authorised officer, must notify the person to whom the notice was given that it has ceased to have effect.

241B(7) If subsection (3) has effect in relation to a defeat notice, an authorised officer, or an officer of Revenue and Customs with the approval of an authorised officer, must notify the person of the effect of that subsection.

241B(8) For the purposes of this section, a tax advantage is **"asserted"** in connection with any arrangements if a person makes a return, claim or election on the basis that the tax advantage arises from those arrangements.

241B(9) In relation to the arrangements mentioned in paragraph (b) of subsection (5) **"corresponding tax advantage"** means a tax advantage corresponding to any tax advantage the counteraction of which contributed to the relevant defeat mentioned in that paragraph.

241B(10) For the purposes of this section a court or tribunal **"upholds"** a tax advantage if–

(a) the court or tribunal makes a ruling to the effect that no part of the tax advantage is to be counteracted, and

(b) that judicial ruling is final.

241B(11) In this section references to **"counteraction"** include anything referred to as a counteraction in any of Conditions A to F in paragraphs 11 to 16 of Schedule 34A.

History – S. 241B inserted by FA 2016, s. 160(3), with effect from 15 September 2016 (Royal Assent).

MONITORING NOTICES: PROCEDURE AND PUBLICATION

242 Monitoring notices: duty to apply to tribunal

242(1) If–

(a) a conduct notice has effect in relation to a person who is carrying on a business as a promoter, and

(b) an authorised officer determines that the person has failed to comply with one or more conditions in the notice,

the authorised officer must apply to the tribunal for approval to give the person a monitoring notice.

242(2) An application under subsection (1) must include a draft of the monitoring notice.

242(3) Subsection (1) does not apply if–

(a) the condition (or all the conditions) mentioned in subsection (1)(b) were imposed under subsection (3)(a), (b) or (c) of section 238, and

(b) the authorised officer considers that the failure to comply with the condition (or all the conditions, taken together) is such a minor matter that it should be disregarded for the purposes of this section.

242(4) Where an authorised officer makes an application to the tribunal under subsection (1), the officer must at the same time give notice to the person to whom the application relates.

242(5) The notice under subsection (4) must state which condition (or conditions) the authorised officer has determined under subsection (1)(b) that the person has failed to comply with and the reasons for that determination.

242(6) At a time when a notice given under section 237A is provisional, no determination is to be made under subsection (1) in respect of the notice.

242(7) If a promoter fails to comply with conditions in a conduct notice at a time when the conduct notice is provisional, nothing in subsection (6) prevents those failures from being taken into account under subsection (1) at any subsequent time when the conduct notice is not provisional.

History – S. 242(6) inserted by FA 2016, s. 160(4), with effect from 15 September 2016 (Royal Assent).
S. 242(7) inserted by FA 2016, s. 160(4), with effect from 15 September 2016 (Royal Assent).

243 Monitoring notices: tribunal approval

243(1) On an application under section 242, the tribunal may approve the giving of a monitoring notice only if–

(a) the tribunal is satisfied that, in the circumstances, the authorised officer would be justified in giving the monitoring notice, and

(b) the person to whom the monitoring notice is to be given ("the affected person") has been given a reasonable opportunity to make representations to the tribunal.

243(2) The tribunal may amend the draft notice included with the application under section 242.

243(3) If the representations that the affected person makes to the tribunal include a statement that in the affected person's view it was not reasonable to include the condition mentioned in section 242(1)(b) in the conduct notice, the tribunal must refuse to approve the giving of the monitoring notice if it is satisfied that it was not reasonable to include that condition (but see subsection (4)).

243(4) If the representations made to the tribunal include the statement described in subsection (3) and the determination under section 242(1)(b) is a determination that there has been a failure to comply with more than one condition in the conduct notice–

(a) subsection (3) does not apply, but

(b) in deciding whether or not to approve the giving of the monitoring notice, the tribunal is to assume, in the case of any condition that the tribunal considers it was not reasonable to include in the conduct notice, that there has been no failure to comply with that condition.

244 Monitoring notices: content and issuing

244(1) Where the tribunal has approved the giving of a monitoring notice, the authorised officer must give the notice to the person to whom it relates.

244(2) A monitoring notice given under subsection (1) or paragraph 9 or 10 of Schedule 36 must–

(a) explain the effect of the monitoring notice and specify the date from which it takes effect;

(b) inform the recipient of the right to request the withdrawal of the monitoring notice under section 245.

244(3) In addition, a monitoring notice must–

(a) if given under subsection (1), state which condition (or conditions) it has been determined the person has failed to comply with and the reasons for that determination;

(b) if given under paragraph 9 or 10 of Schedule 36, state the date of the original monitoring notice and name the partnership to which that notice was given.

244(4) The date specified under subsection (2)(a) must not be earlier than the date on which the monitoring notice is given.

244(5) In this Part, a person in relation to whom a monitoring notice has effect is called a "monitored promoter".

245 Withdrawal of monitoring notice

245(1) A person in relation to whom a monitoring notice has effect may, at any time after the end of the period of 12 months beginning with the end of the appeal period, request that the notice should cease to have effect.

245(2) The **"appeal period"** means–

(a) the period during which an appeal could be brought against the approval by the tribunal of the giving of the monitoring notice, or

(b) where an appeal mentioned in paragraph (a) has been brought, the period during which that appeal has not been finally determined, withdrawn or otherwise disposed of.

245(3) A request under this section is to be made in writing to an authorised officer.

245(4) Where a request is made under this section, an authorised officer must within 30 days beginning with the day on which the request is received determine either–

(a) that the monitoring notice is to cease to have effect, or

(b) that the request is to be refused.

245(5) The matters to be taken into account by an authorised officer in making a determination under subsection (4) include–

(a) whether or not the person subject to the monitoring notice has, since the time when the notice took effect, engaged in behaviour of a sort that conditions included in a conduct notice in accordance with section 238(3) could be used to regulate;

(b) whether or not it appears likely that the person will in the future engage in such behaviour;

(c) the person's record of compliance, or failure to comply, with obligations imposed on it under this Part, since the time when the monitoring notice took effect.

245(6) An authorised officer–

(a) may withdraw a monitoring notice if the officer thinks it is not necessary for it to continue to have effect, and

(b) in considering whether or not that is necessary, the officer must take into account the matters in paragraphs (a) to (c) of subsection (5).

245(7) If the authorised officer makes a determination under subsection (4)(a), or decides to withdraw a monitoring notice under subsection (6), the officer must also determine that the person is, or is not, to be given a follow-on conduct notice.

245(8) **"Follow-on conduct notice"** means a conduct notice taking effect immediately after the monitoring notice ceases to have effect.

245(9) Where the monitoring notice mentioned in subsection (1) is a replacement monitoring notice–

(a) in subsection (1) the reference to the end of the appeal period is to be read as a reference to whichever is the later of the end of the appeal period for the original monitoring notice and the date the replacement monitoring notice takes effect, and

(b) in subsection (5)(a) and (c) the time referred to is to be read as the time when the original monitoring notice (see paragraph 11(2) of Schedule 36) took effect.

246 Notification of determination under section 245

246(1) Where an authorised officer makes a determination under section 245(4), that officer, or an officer of Revenue and Customs with that officer's approval, must notify the person who made the request of the determination.

246(2) If the determination is that the monitoring notice is to cease to have effect, the notice must–

(a) specify the date from which the monitoring notice is to cease to have effect, and

(b) inform the person of the determination made under section 245(7).

246(3) If the determination is that the request is to be refused, the notice must inform the person who made the request–

(a) of the reasons for the refusal, and

(b) of the right to appeal under section 247.

247 Appeal against refusal to withdraw monitoring notice

247(1) A person may appeal against a refusal by an authorised officer of a request that a monitoring notice should cease to have effect.

247(2) Notice of appeal must be given–

(a) in writing to the officer who gave the notice of the refusal under section 245, and

(b) within the period of 30 days beginning with the day on which notice of the refusal was given.

247(3) The notice of appeal must state the grounds of appeal.

247(4) On an appeal that is notified to the tribunal, the tribunal may–

(a) confirm the refusal, or

(b) direct that the monitoring notice is to cease to have effect.

247(5) Subject to this section, the provisions of Part 5 of TMA 1970 relating to appeals have effect in relation to an appeal under this section.

248 Publication by HMRC

248(1) An authorised officer may publish the fact that a person is a monitored promoter.

248(2) Publication under subsection (1) may also include the following information about the monitored promoter–

(a) its name;

(b) its business address or registered office;

(c) the nature of the business mentioned in section 242(1)(a);

(d) any other information that the authorised officer considers it appropriate to publish in order to make clear the monitored promoter's identity.

248(3) The reference in subsection (2)(a) to the monitored promoter's name includes any name under which it carries on a business as a promoter and any previous name or pseudonym.

248(4) Publication under subsection (1) may also include a statement of which of the conditions in a conduct notice it has been determined that the person (or, in the case of a replacement monitoring notice, the person to whom the original monitoring notice was given) has failed to comply with.

248(5) Publication may not take place before the end of the appeal period (or, in the case of a replacement monitoring notice, the appeal period for the original monitoring notice).

248(6) The ***"appeal period"***, in relation to a monitoring notice, means–

(a) the period during which an appeal could be brought against the approval by the tribunal of the giving of the notice, or

(b) where an appeal mentioned in paragraph (a) has been brought, the period during which that appeal has not been finally determined, withdrawn or otherwise disposed of.

248(7) Publication under this section is to be in such manner as the authorised officer thinks fit; but see subsection (8).

248(8) If an authorised officer publishes the fact that a person is a monitored promoter and the monitoring notice is withdrawn, the officer must publish the fact of the withdrawal in the same way as the officer published the fact that the person was a monitored promoter.

249 Publication by monitored promoter

249(1) A person who is given a monitoring notice ("the monitored promoter") must give the persons mentioned in subsection (6) a notice stating–

(a) that it is a monitored promoter, and

(b) which of the conditions in a conduct notice it has been determined that it (or, if the monitoring notice is a replacement monitoring notice, the person to whom that notice was given) has failed to comply with.

249(2) If the monitoring notice is a replacement monitoring notice, the notice under subsection (1) must also identify the original monitoring notice.

249(3) If regulations made by the Commissioners so require, the monitored promoter must publish on the internet–

(a) the information mentioned in paragraph (a) and (b) of subsection (1), and

(b) its promoter reference number (see section 250).

249(4) Subsection (1) and any duty imposed under subsection (3) or (10) do not apply until the end of the period of 10 days beginning with the end of the appeal period (and also see subsection (9)).

249(5) The **"appeal period"** means–

(a) the period during which an appeal could be brought against the approval by the tribunal of the giving of the monitoring notice, or

(b) where an appeal mentioned in paragraph (a) has been brought, the period during which that appeal has not been finally determined, withdrawn or otherwise disposed of.

249(6) The notice under subsection (1) must be given–

(a) to any person who becomes a client of the monitored promoter while the monitoring notice has effect, and

(b) (except in a case where the monitoring notice is a replacement monitoring notice) any person who is a client of the monitored promoter at the time the monitoring notice takes effect.

249(7) A person ("C") is a client of a monitored promoter at the time a monitoring notice takes effect if during the period beginning with the date the conduct notice mentioned in subsection (1)(b) takes effect and ending with that time the promoter–

(a) made a firm approach to C in relation to a relevant proposal with a view to the promoter making the proposal available for implementation by C or another person;

(b) made a relevant proposal available for implementation by C;

(c) took part in the organisation or management of relevant arrangements entered into by C.

249(8) A person becomes a client of a monitored promoter if the promoter does any of the things mentioned in paragraph (a) to (c) of subsection (7) in relation to that person.

249(9) In the case of a person falling within subsection (6)(a), notice under subsection (1) may be given within the period of 10 days beginning with the day on which the person first became a client of the monitored promoter if that period would expire at a later date than the date on which notification would otherwise be required by virtue of subsection (4).

249(10) A monitored promoter must also include in any prescribed publication or prescribed correspondence–

(a) the information mentioned in paragraph (a) and (b) of subsection (1), and

(b) its promoter reference number (see section 250).

249(11) Notification under subsection (1), publication under subsection (3) or inclusion of the information required by subsection (10) is to be in such form and manner as is prescribed.

249(12) Where the monitoring notice mentioned in subsection (1) is a replacement monitoring notice, the reference in subsection (4) to the end of the appeal period is to be read as a reference to whichever is the later of the end of the appeal period for the original monitoring notice and the date the replacement monitoring notice takes effect.

Statutory instruments – SI 2015/549: partly made under s. 249(3), (10), and (11).

ALLOCATION AND DISTRIBUTION OF PROMOTER REFERENCE NUMBER

250 Allocation of promoter reference number

250(1) Where a monitoring notice is given to a person ("the monitored promoter") HMRC must as soon as practicable after the end of the appeal period–

(a) allocate the monitored promoter a reference number, and

(b) notify the relevant persons of that number.

250(2) **"Relevant persons"** means–

(a) the monitored promoter, and

(b) if the monitored promoter is resident outside the United Kingdom, any person who HMRC know is an intermediary in relation to a relevant proposal of the monitored promoter.

250(3) The **"appeal period"** means–

(a) the period during which an appeal could be brought against the approval by the tribunal of the giving of the monitoring notice, or

(b) where an appeal mentioned in paragraph (a) has been brought, the period during which that appeal has not been finally determined, withdrawn or otherwise disposed of.

250(4) The duty in subsection (1) does not apply if the monitoring notice is set aside following an appeal.

250(5) A number allocated to a person under this section is referred to in this Part as a "promoter reference number".

250(6) Where the monitoring notice mentioned in subsection (1) is a replacement monitoring notice–

(a) in subsection (1) the reference to the end of the appeal period is to be read as a reference to whichever is the later of the end of the appeal period for the original monitoring notice and the date the replacement monitoring notice takes effect, and

(b) in subsection (4) the reference to the monitoring notice is to be read as a reference to the original monitoring notice.

251 Duty of monitored promoter to notify clients and intermediaries of number

251(1) This section applies where a person who is a monitored promoter ("the monitored promoter") is notified under section 250 of a promoter reference number.

251(2) The monitored promoter must, within the relevant period, notify the promoter reference number to–

(a) any person who has become its client at any time in the period beginning with the day on which the monitoring notice in relation to the monitored promoter took effect and ending with the day on which the monitored promoter was notified of that number,

(b) any person who becomes its client after the end of the period mentioned in paragraph (a) but while the monitoring notice has effect,

(c) any person who the monitored promoter could reasonably be expected to know falls within subsection (4), and

(d) any person who the monitored promoter could reasonably be expected to know is a relevant intermediary in relation to a relevant proposal of the monitored promoter.

251(3) A person ("C") becomes a client of a monitored promoter if the promoter does any of the following in relation to C–

(a) makes a firm approach to C in relation to a relevant proposal with a view to the promoter making the proposal available for implementation by C or another person;

(b) makes a relevant proposal available for implementation by C;

(c) takes part in the organisation or management of relevant arrangements entered into by C.

251(4) A person falls within this subsection if during the period beginning with the date the conduct notice took effect and ending with the date on which the monitoring notice took effect the person has entered into transactions forming part of relevant arrangements and those arrangements–

(a) enable, or are likely to enable, the person to obtain a tax advantage during the time a monitoring notice has effect, and

(b) are either relevant arrangements in relation to which the monitored promoter is or was a promoter or implement a relevant proposal in relation to which the monitored promoter was a promoter.

251(5) A person is a relevant intermediary in relation to a relevant proposal of a monitored promoter if the person meets the conditions in section 236(a) to (c) (meaning of "intermediary") at any time while the monitoring notice in relation to the monitored promoter has effect.

251(6) The **"relevant period"** means–

(a) in the case of a person falling within subsection (2)(a), the period of 30 days beginning with the day of the notification mentioned in subsection (1),

(b) in the case of a person falling within subsection (2)(b), the period of 30 days beginning with the day on which the person first became a client in relation to the monitored promoter,

(c) in the case of a person falling within subsection (2)(c), the period of 30 days beginning with the later of the day of the notification mentioned in subsection (1) and the first day on which the monitored promoter could reasonably be expected to know that the person fell within subsection (4), and

(d) in the case of a person falling within subsection (2)(d), the period of 30 days beginning with the later of the day of the notification mentioned in subsection (1) and the first day on which the monitored promoter could reasonably be expected to know that the person was a relevant intermediary in relation to a relevant proposal of the monitored promoter.

251(7) In this section **"the conduct notice"** means the conduct notice that the monitored promoter failed to comply with which resulted in the monitoring notice being given to the monitored promoter.

251(8) Subsection (2)(c) is to be ignored in a case where the monitoring notice is a replacement monitoring notice.

252 Duty of those notified to notify others of promoter's number

252(1) In this section **"notified client"** means–

(a) a person who is notified of a promoter reference number under section 250 by reason of being a person falling within subsection (2)(b) of that section, and

(b) a person who is notified of a promoter reference number under section 251.

252(2) A notified client must, within 30 days of being notified as described in subsection (1), provide the promoter reference number to any other person who the notified client might reasonably be expected to know has become, or is likely to have become, a client in relation to the monitored promoter concerned at a time when the monitoring notice in relation to that monitored promoter had effect.

252(3) A person ("C") becomes a client of a monitored promoter if the promoter does any of the following in relation to C–

(a) makes a firm approach to C in relation to a relevant proposal with a view to the promoter making the proposal available for implementation by C or another person;

(b) makes a relevant proposal available for implementation by C;

(c) takes part in the organisation or management of relevant arrangements entered into by C.

252(4) Where the notified client is an intermediary in relation to a relevant proposal of the monitored promoter concerned, the notified client must also, within 30 days, provide the promoter reference number to–

(a) any person to whom the notified client has, since the monitoring notice in relation to the monitored promoter concerned took effect, communicated in the course of a business information about a relevant proposal of the monitored promoter, and

(b) any person who the notified client might reasonably be expected to know has, since that monitoring notice took effect, entered into, or is likely to enter into, transactions forming part of relevant arrangements in relation to which that monitored promoter is a promoter.

252(5) Subsection (2) or (4) does not impose a duty on a notified client to notify a person of a promoter reference number if the notified client reasonably believes that the person has already been notified of the promoter reference number (whether as a result of a duty under this section or as a result of any of the other provision of this Part).

253 Duty of persons to notify the Commissioners

253(1) If a person ("N") is notified of a promoter reference number under section 250, 251 or 252, N must report the number to the Commissioners if N expects to obtain a tax advantage from relevant arrangements in relation to which the monitored promoter to whom the reference number relates (whether that is N or another person) is the promoter.

253(2) A report under this section–

(a) must be made in (or, if prescribed circumstances exist, submitted with) each tax return made by N for a period that is or includes a period for which the arrangements enable N to obtain a tax advantage (whether in relation to the tax to which the return relates or another tax);

(b) if no tax return falls within paragraph (a), or in the case mentioned in subsection (3), must contain such information, and be made in such form and manner and within such time, as is prescribed.

253(3) The case is that the tax return in which the report would (apart from this subsection) have been made is not submitted–

(a) by the filing date, or

(b) if there is no filing date in relation to the tax return concerned, by such other time that the tax return is required to be submitted by or under any enactment.

253(4) Where N expects to obtain the tax advantage referred to in subsection (1) in respect of inheritance tax, stamp duty land tax, stamp duty reserve tax or petroleum revenue tax–

(a) subsection (2) does not apply in relation to that tax advantage, and

(b) a report under this section in respect of that tax must be in such form and manner and contain such information and be made within such time as is prescribed.

253(5) Where the relevant arrangements referred to in subsection (1) give rise to N making a claim under section 261B of TCGA 1992 (treating trade loss as CGT loss) or for loss relief under Part 4 of ITA 2007 and that claim is not contained in a tax return, a report under this section must also be made in that claim.

253(6) In this section **"tax return"** means any of the following–

(a) a return under section 8 of TMA 1970 (income tax and capital gains tax: personal return);

(b) a return under section 8A of TMA 1970 (income tax and capital gains tax: trustee's return);

(c) a return under section 12AA of TMA 1970 (income tax and corporation tax: partnership return);

(d) a company tax return under paragraph 3 of Schedule 18 to the FA 1998 (company tax return);

(da) a return under regulations made under section 105 of FA 2016 (apprenticeship levy);

(e) a return under section 159 or 160 of FA 2013 (returns and further returns for annual tax on enveloped dwellings).

Prospective amendments – In s. 253(6)(c) the words ", or regulations under paragraph 10 of Schedule A1 to," inserted after the words "section 12AA of" by F(No. 2)A 2017, s. 61 and Sch. 14, para. 44, with effect from a day to be appointed under F(No. 2)A 2017, s. 61(6).

History – S. 253(6)(da) inserted by FA 2016, s. 104(7), with effect from 15 September 2016 (Royal Assent).

Statutory instruments – SI 2015/549: partly made under s. 253(2) and (4).

OBTAINING INFORMATION AND DOCUMENTS

254 Meaning of "monitored proposal" and "monitored arrangements"

254(1) For the purposes of this Part a relevant proposal in relation to which a person ("P") is a promoter is a "monitored proposal" in relation to P if any of the following dates fell on or after the date on which a monitoring notice took effect–

(a) the date on which P first made a firm approach to another person in relation to the relevant proposal;

(b) the date on which P first made the relevant proposal available for implementation by any other person;

(c) the date on which P first became aware of any transaction forming part of the proposed arrangements being entered into by any person.

254(2) For the purposes of this Part relevant arrangements in relation to which a person ("P") is a promoter are "monitored arrangements" in relation to P if–

(a) P was by virtue of section 235(2)(b) or (c) a promoter in relation to a relevant proposal which was implemented by the arrangements and any of the following fell on or after the date on which the monitoring notice took effect–

  (i) the date on which P first made a firm approach to another person in relation to the relevant proposal;

  (ii) the date on which P first made the relevant proposal available for implementation by any other person;

  (iii) the date on which P first became aware of any transaction forming part of the proposed arrangements being entered into by any person,

(b) the date on which P first took part in designing, organising or managing the arrangements fell on or after the date on which a monitoring notice took effect, or

(c) the arrangements enable, or are likely to enable, the person who has entered into transactions forming them to obtain the tax advantage by reason of which they are relevant arrangements, at any time on or after the date on which a monitoring notice took effect.

255 Power to obtain information and documents

255(1) An authorised officer, or an officer of Revenue and Customs with the approval of an authorised officer, may by notice in writing require any person ("P") to whom this section applies–

(a) to provide information, or

(b) to produce a document,

if the information or document is reasonably required by the officer for any of the purposes in subsection (3).

255(2) This section applies to–

(a) any person who is a monitored promoter, and

(b) any person who is a relevant intermediary in relation to a monitored proposal of a monitored promoter,

and in either case that monitored promoter is referred to below as "the relevant monitored promoter".

255(3) The purposes mentioned in subsection (1) are–

(a) considering the possible consequences of implementing a monitored proposal of the relevant monitored promoter for the tax position of persons implementing the proposal,

(b) checking the tax position of any person who the officer reasonably believes has implemented a monitored proposal of the relevant monitored promoter, or

(c) checking the tax position of any person who the officer reasonably believes has entered into transactions forming monitored arrangements of the relevant monitored promoter.

255(4) A person is a **"relevant intermediary"** in relation to a monitored proposal if the person meets the conditions in section 236(a) to (c) (meaning of "intermediary") in relation to the proposal at any time after the person has been notified of a promoter reference number of a person who is a promoter in relation to the proposal.

255(5) In this section **"checking"** includes carrying out an investigation or enquiry of any kind.

255(6) In this section **"tax position"**, in relation to a person, means the person's position as regards any tax, including the person's position as regards–

(a) past, present and future liability to pay any tax,

(b) penalties and other amounts that have been paid, or are or may be payable, by or to the person in connection with any tax,

(c) claims, elections, applications and notices that have been or may be made or given in connection with the person's liability to pay any tax,

(d) deductions or repayments of tax, or of sums representing tax, that the person is required to make–

(i) under PAYE regulations, or

(ii) by or under any other provision of the Taxes Acts, and

(e) the withholding by the person of another person's PAYE income (as defined in section 683 of ITEPA 2003).

255(7) In this section the reference to the tax position of a person–

(a) includes the tax position of a company that has ceased to exist and an individual who has died, and

(b) is to the person's tax position at any time or in relation to any period.

255(8) A notice under subsection (1) which is given for the purpose of checking the tax position of a person mentioned in subsection (3)(b) or (c) may not be given more than 4 years after the person's death.

255(9) A notice under subsection (1) may specify or describe the information or documents to be provided or produced.

255(10) *Information or a document required* as a result of a notice under subsection (1) must be provided or produced within–

(a) the period of 10 days beginning with the day on which the notice was given, or

(b) such longer period as the officer who gives the notice may direct.

256 Tribunal approval for certain uses of power under section 255

256(1) An officer of Revenue and Customs may not, without the approval of the tribunal, give a notice under section 255 requiring a person ("A") to provide information or produce a document which relates (in whole or in part) to a person who is neither A nor an undertaking in relation to which A is a parent undertaking.

256(2) An officer of Revenue and Customs may apply to the tribunal for the approval required by subsection (1); and an application for approval may be made without notice.

256(3) The tribunal may approve the giving of the notice only if–

(a) the application for approval is made by, or with the agreement of, an authorised officer,

(b) the tribunal is satisfied that, in the circumstances, the officer giving the notice is justified in doing so,

(c) the person to whom the notice is to be given has been informed that the information or documents referred to in the notice are required and given a reasonable opportunity to make representations to an officer of Revenue and Customs, and

(d) the tribunal has been given a summary of any representations made by that person.

256(4) Where a notice is given under section 255 with the approval of the tribunal, it must state that it is given with that approval.

256(5) Paragraphs (c) and (d) of subsection (3) do not apply to the extent that the tribunal is satisfied that taking the action specified in those paragraphs might prejudice the assessment or collection of tax.

256(6) In subsection (1) **"parent undertaking"** and **"undertaking"** have the same meaning as in the Companies Acts (see section 1161 and 1162 of, and Schedule 7 to, the Companies Act 2006).

256(7) A decision of the tribunal under this section is final (despite the provisions of sections 11 and 13 of the Tribunals, Courts and Enforcement Act 2007).

257 Ongoing duty to provide information following HMRC notice

257(1) An authorised officer, or an officer of Revenue and Customs with the approval of an authorised officer, may give a notice to a person ("P") in relation to whom a monitoring notice has effect.

257(2) A person to whom a notice is given under subsection (1) must provide prescribed information and produce prescribed documents relating to–

(a) all the monitored proposals and all the monitored arrangements in relation to which the person is a promoter at the time of the notice, and

(b) all the monitored proposals and all the monitored arrangements in relation to which the person becomes a promoter after that time.

257(3) The duty under subsection (2)(b) does not apply in relation to any proposals or arrangements in relation to which the person first becomes a promoter after the monitoring notice ceases to have effect.

257(4) A notice under subsection (1) must specify the time within which information must be provided or a document produced and different times may be specified for different cases.

Statutory instruments – SI 2015/549: partly made under s. 257(2).

258 Duty of person dealing with non-resident monitored promoter

258(1) This section applies where a monitored promoter who is resident outside the United Kingdom has failed to comply with a duty under section 255 or 257 to provide information about a monitored proposal or monitored arrangements.

258(2) An authorised officer, or an officer of Revenue and Customs with the approval of an authorised officer, may give a notice to a relevant person which–

(a) specifies or describes the information which the monitored promoter has failed to provide, and

(b) requires the person to provide the information.

258(3) A **"relevant person"** means–

(a) any person who is an intermediary in relation to the monitored proposal concerned, and

(b) any person ("A") to whom the monitored promoter has made a firm approach in relation to the monitored proposal concerned with a view to making the proposal available for implementation by a person other than A.

258(4) If an authorised officer is not aware of any person to whom a notice could be given under subsection (2) the authorised officer, or an officer of Revenue and Customs with the approval of the authorised officer, may give a notice to any person who has implemented the proposal which–

(a) specifies or describes the information which the monitored promoter has failed to provide, and

(b) requires the person to provide the information.

258(5) If the duty mentioned in subsection (1) relates to monitored arrangements an authorised officer, or an officer of Revenue and Customs with the approval of an authorised officer, may give a notice to any person who has entered into any transaction forming part of the monitored arrangements concerned which–

(a) specifies or describes the information which the monitored promoter has failed to provide, and
(b) requires the person to provide the information.

258(6) A notice under this section may be given only if the officer giving the notice reasonably believes that the person to whom the notice is given is able to provide the information requested.

258(7) Information required as a result of a notice under this section must be provided within–
(a) the period of 10 days beginning with the day on which the notice was given, or
(b) such longer period as the officer who gives the notice may direct.

259 Monitored promoters: duty to provide information about clients

259(1) An authorised officer, or an officer of Revenue and Customs with the approval of an authorised officer, may give notice to a person in relation to whom a monitoring notice has effect ("the monitored promoter").

259(2) A person to whom a notice is given under subsection (1) must, for each relevant period, give the officer who gave the notice the information set out in subsection (9) in respect of each person who was its client with reference to that relevant period (see subsections (5) to (8)).

259(3) Each of the following is a **"relevant period"**–
(a) the calendar quarter in which the notice under subsection (1) was given but not including any time before the monitoring notice takes effect,
(b) the period (if any) beginning with the date the monitoring notice takes effect and ending immediately before the beginning of the period described in paragraph (a), and
(c) each calendar quarter after the period described in paragraph (a) but not including any time after the monitoring notice ceases to have effect.

259(4) Information required as a result of a notice under subsection (1) must be given–
(a) within the period of 30 days beginning with the end of the relevant period concerned, or
(b) in the case of a relevant period within subsection (3)(b), within the period of 30 days beginning with the day on which the notice under subsection (1) was given if that period would expire at a later time than the period given by paragraph (a).

259(5) A person ("C") is a client of the monitored promoter with reference to a relevant period if–
(a) the promoter did any of the things mentioned in subsection (6) in relation to C at any time during that period, or
(b) the person falls within subsection (7).

259(6) Those things are that the monitored promoter–
(a) made a firm approach to C in relation to a relevant proposal with a view to the promoter making the proposal available for implementation by C or another person;
(b) made a relevant proposal available for implementation by C;
(c) took part in the organisation or management of relevant arrangements entered into by C.

259(7) A person falls within this subsection if the person has entered into transactions forming part of relevant arrangements and those arrangements–
(a) enable the person to obtain a tax advantage either in that relevant period or a later relevant period, and
(b) are either relevant arrangements in relation to which the monitored promoter is or was a promoter, or implement a relevant proposal in relation to which the monitored promoter was a promoter.

259(8) But a person is not a client of the monitored promoter with reference to a relevant period if–
(a) the person has previously been a client of the monitored promoter with reference to a different relevant period,
(b) the promoter complied with the duty in subsection (2) in respect of the person for that relevant period, and
(c) the information provided as a result of complying with that duty remains accurate.

259(9) The information mentioned in subsection (2) is–
(a) the person's name and address, and
(b) such other information about the person as may be prescribed.

259(10) Where the monitoring notice mentioned in subsection (1) is a replacement monitoring notice, subsection (5)(b) does not impose a duty on the monitored promoter concerned to provide information about a person who has entered into transactions forming part of relevant arrangements (as described in subsection (7)) if the monitored promoter reasonably believes that information about that person has, in relation to those arrangements, already been provided under the original monitoring notice.

Statutory instruments – SI 2015/549: partly made under s. 259(9).

260 Intermediaries: duty to provide information about clients

260(1) An authorised officer, or an officer of Revenue and Customs with the approval of an authorised officer, may give notice to a person ("the intermediary") who is an intermediary in relation to a relevant proposal which is a monitored proposal of a person in relation to whom a monitoring notice has effect ("the monitored promoter").

260(2) A person to whom a notice is given under subsection (1) must, for each relevant period, give the officer who gave the notice the information set out in subsection (7) in respect of each person who was its client with reference to that relevant period (see subsections (5) to (6)).

260(3) Each of the following is a **"relevant period"**–

(a) the calendar quarter in which the notice under subsection (1) was given but not including any time before the intermediary was first notified under section 250, 251 or 252 of the promoter reference number of the monitored promoter,

(b) the period (if any) beginning with the date of the notification under section 250, 251 or 252 and ending immediately before the beginning of the period described in paragraph (a), and

(c) each calendar quarter after the period described in paragraph (a) but not including any time after the monitoring notice mentioned in subsection (1) ceases to have effect.

260(4) Information required as a result of a notice under subsection (1) must be given–

(a) within the period of 30 days beginning with the end of the relevant period concerned, or

(b) in the case of a relevant period within subsection (3)(b), within the period of 30 days beginning with the day on which the notice under subsection (1) was given if that period would expire at a later time than the period given by paragraph (a).

260(5) A person ("C") is a client of the intermediary with reference to a relevant period if during that period–

(a) the intermediary communicated information to C about a monitored proposal in the course of a business, and

(b) the communication was made with a view to C, or any other person, entering into transactions forming part of the proposed arrangements.

260(6) But a person is not a client of the intermediary with reference to a relevant period if–

(a) the person has previously been a client of the intermediary with reference to a different relevant period,

(b) the intermediary complied with the duty in subsection (2) in respect of the person for that relevant period, and

(c) the information provided as a result of complying with that duty remains accurate.

260(7) The information mentioned in subsection (2) is–

(a) the person's name and address, and

(b) such other information about the person as may be prescribed.

Statutory instruments – SI 2015/549: partly made under s. 260(7).

261 Enquiry following provision of client information

261(1) This section applies where–

(a) a person ("the notifying person") has provided information under section 259 or 260 about a person who was a client of the notifying person with reference to a relevant period (within the meaning of the section concerned) in connection with a particular relevant proposal or particular relevant arrangements, and

(b) an authorised officer suspects that a person in respect of whom information has not been provided under section 259 or 260–

(i) has at any time been, or is likely to be, a party to transactions implementing the proposal, or

(ii) is a party to a transaction forming (in whole or in part) particular relevant arrangements.

261(2) The authorised officer may by notice in writing require the notifying person to provide prescribed information in relation to any person whom the notifying person might reasonably be expected to know–

(a) has been, or is likely to be, a party to transactions implementing the proposal, or

(b) is a party to a transaction forming (in whole or in part) the relevant arrangements.

261(3) But a notice under subsection (2) does not impose a requirement on the notifying person to provide information which the notifying person has already provided to an authorised officer under section 259 or 260.

261(4) The notifying person must comply with a requirement under subsection (2) within–

(a) 10 days of the notice, or

(b) such longer period as the authorised officer may direct.

Statutory instruments – SI 2015/549: partly made under s. 261(2).

262 Information required for monitoring compliance with conduct notice

262(1) This section applies where a conduct notice has effect in relation to a person.

262(2) An authorised officer, or an officer of Revenue and Customs with the approval of an authorised officer, may (as often as is necessary for the purpose mentioned below) by notice in writing require the person–

(a) to provide information, or

(b) to produce a document,

if the information or document is reasonably required for the purpose of monitoring whether and to what extent the person is complying with the conditions in the conduct notice.

263 Duty to notify HMRC of address

263 If, on the last day of a calendar quarter, a monitoring notice has effect in relation to a person ("the monitored promoter") the monitored promoter must within 30 days of the end of the calendar quarter inform an authorised officer of its current address.

264 Failure to provide information: application to tribunal

264(1) This section applies where–

(a) a person ("P") has provided information or produced a document in purported compliance with section 255, 257, 258, 259, 260, 261 or 262, but

(b) an authorised officer suspects that P has not provided all the information or produced all the documents required under the section concerned.

264(2) The authorised officer, or an officer of Revenue and Customs with the approval of the authorised officer, may apply to the tribunal for an order requiring P to–

(a) provide specified information about persons who are its clients for the purposes of the section to which the application relates,

(b) provide specified information, or information of a specified description, about a monitored proposal or monitored arrangements,

(c) produce specified documents relating to a monitored proposal or monitored arrangements.

264(3) The tribunal may make an order under subsection (2) in respect of information or documents only if satisfied that the officer has reasonable grounds for suspecting that the information or documents–

(a) are required under section 255, 257, 258, 259, 260, 261 or 262 (as the case may be), or

(b) will support or explain information required under the section concerned.

264(4) A requirement by virtue of an order under subsection (2) is to be treated as part of P's duty under section 255, 257, 258, 259, 260, 261 or 262 (as the case may be).

264(5) Information or a document required as a result of subsection (2) must be provided, or the document produced, within the period of 10 days beginning with the day on which the order under subsection (2) was made.

264(6) An authorised officer may, by direction, extend the 10 day period mentioned in subsection (5).

265 Duty to provide information to monitored promoter

265(1) This section applies where a person has been notified of a promoter reference number–

(a) under section 250 by reason of being a person falling within subsection (2)(b) of that section, or

(b) under section 251 or 252.

265(2) The person notified ("C") must within 10 days notify the person whose promoter reference number it is of–

(a) C's national insurance number (if C has one), and

(b) C's unique tax reference number (if C has one).

265(3) If C has neither a national insurance number nor a unique tax reference number, C must within 10 days inform the person whose promoter reference number it is of that fact.

265(4) A unique tax reference number is an identification number allocated to a person by HMRC.

265(5) Subsection (2) or (3) does not impose a duty on C to provide information which C has already provided to the person whose promoter reference number it is.

OBTAINING INFORMATION AND DOCUMENTS: APPEALS

266 Appeals against notices imposing information etc requirements

266(1) This section applies where a person is given a notice under section 255, 257, 258, 259, 260, 261 or 262.

266(2) The person to whom the notice is given may appeal against the notice or any requirement under the notice.

266(3) Subsection (2) does not apply–

(a) to a requirement to provide any information or produce any document that forms part of the person's statutory records, or

(b) if the tribunal has approved the giving of the notice under section 256.

266(4) For the purposes of this section, information or a document forms part of a person's statutory records if it is information or a document which the person is required to keep and preserve under or by virtue of–

(a) the Taxes Acts, or

(b) any other enactment relating to a tax.

266(5) Information and documents cease to form part of a person's statutory records when the period for which they are required to be preserved by the enactments mentioned in subsection (4) has expired.

266(6) Notice of appeal must be given–

(a) in writing to the officer who gave the notice, and

(b) within the period of 30 days beginning with the day on which the notice was given.

266(7) The notice of appeal must state the grounds of the appeal.

266(8) On an appeal that is notified to the tribunal, the tribunal may–

(a) confirm the notice or a requirement under the notice,

(b) vary the notice or such a requirement, or

(c) set aside the notice or such a requirement.

266(9) Where the tribunal confirms or varies the notice or a requirement, the person to whom the notice was given must comply with the notice or requirement–

(a) within such period as is specified by the tribunal, or

(b) if the tribunal does not specify a period, within such period as is reasonably specified in writing by an officer of Revenue and Customs following the tribunal's decision.

266(10) A decision of the tribunal on an appeal under this section is final (despite the provisions of sections 11 and 13 of the Tribunals, Courts and Enforcement Act 2007).

266(11) Subject to this section, the provisions of Part 5 of TMA 1970 relating to appeals have effect in relation to an appeal under this section.

OBTAINING INFORMATION AND DOCUMENTS: SUPPLEMENTARY

267 Form and manner of providing information

267(1) The Commissioners may specify the form and manner in which information required to be provided or documents required to be produced by sections 255 to 264 must be provided or produced if the provision is to be complied with.

267(2) The Commissioners may specify that a document must be produced for inspection–

(a) at a place agreed between the person and an officer of Revenue and Customs, or

(b) at such place (which must not be a place used solely as a dwelling) as an officer of Revenue and Customs may reasonably specify.

267(3) The production of a document in compliance with a notice under this Part is not to be regarded as breaking any lien claimed on the document.

268 Production of documents: compliance

268(1) Where the effect of a notice under section 255, 257 or 262 is to require a person to produce a document, the person may comply with the requirement by producing a copy of the document, subject to any conditions or exceptions that may be prescribed.

268(2) Subsection (1) does not apply where–

(a) the effect of the notice is to require the person to produce the original document, or

(b) an authorised officer, or an officer of Revenue and Customs with the approval of an authorised officer, subsequently makes a request in writing to the person for the original document.

268(3) Where an officer requests a document under subsection (2)(b), the person to whom the request is made must produce the document–

(a) within such period, and

(b) at such time and by such means,

as is reasonably requested by the officer.

Statutory instruments – SI 2015/549: partly made under s. 268(1).

269 Exception for certain documents or information

269(1) Nothing in this Part requires a person to provide or produce–

(a) information that relates to the conduct of a pending appeal relating to tax or any part of a document containing such information,

(b) journalistic material (as defined in section 13 of the Police and Criminal Evidence Act 1984) or information contained in such material, or

(c) personal records (as defined in section 12 of the Police and Criminal Evidence Act 1984) or information contained in such records (but see subsection (2)).

269(2) A notice under this Part may require a person–

(a) to produce documents, or copies of documents, that are personal records, omitting any information whose inclusion (whether alone or with other information) makes the original documents personal records ("personal information"), and

(b) to provide any information contained in such records that is not personal information.

270 Limitation on duty to produce documents

270 Nothing in this Part requires a person to produce a document–

(a) which is not in the possession or power of that person, or

(b) if the whole of the document originates more than 6 years before the requirement to produce it would, if it were not for this section, arise.

271 Legal professional privilege

271(1) Nothing in this Part requires any person to disclose to HMRC any privileged information.

271(2) **"Privileged information"** means information with respect to which a claim to legal professional privilege by the person who would (ignoring the effect of this section) be required to disclose it, could be maintained in legal proceedings.

271(3) In the case of legal proceedings in Scotland, the reference in subsection (2) to legal professional privilege is to be read as a reference to confidentiality of communications.

272 Tax advisers

272(1) This section applies where a notice is given under section 258(4) or (5) and the person to whom the notice is given is a tax adviser.

272(2) The notice does not require a tax adviser–

(a) to provide information about relevant communications, or

(b) to produce documents which are the tax adviser's property and consist of relevant communications.

272(3) Subsection (2) does not have effect in relation to–

(a) information explaining any information or document which the person to whom the notice is given has, as tax accountant, assisted any person in preparing for, or delivering to, HMRC, or

(b) a document which contains such information.

272(4) But subsection (2) is not disapplied by subsection (3) if the information in question has already been provided, or a document containing the information has already been produced, to an officer of Revenue and Customs.

272(5) In this section–

"relevant communications" means communications between the tax adviser and–

(a) a person in relation to whose tax affairs the tax adviser has been appointed, or

(b) any other tax adviser of such a person,

the purpose of which is the giving or obtaining of advice about any of those tax affairs, and

"tax adviser" means a person appointed to give advice about the tax affairs of another person (whether appointed directly by that person or by another tax adviser of that person).

273 Confidentiality

273(1) No duty of confidentiality or other restriction on disclosure (however imposed) prevents the voluntary disclosure by a relevant client or a relevant intermediary to HMRC of information or documents about–

(a) a monitored promoter, or

(b) relevant proposals or relevant arrangements in relation to which a monitored promoter is a promoter.

273(2) **"Relevant client"** means a person in relation to whom the monitored promoter mentioned in subsection (1)(a) or (b)–

(a) has made a firm approach in relation to a relevant proposal with a view to making the proposal available for implementation by that person or another person;

(b) has made a relevant proposal available for implementation by that person;

(c) took part in the organisation or management of relevant arrangements entered into by that person.

273(3) **"Relevant intermediary"** means a person who is an intermediary in relation to a relevant proposal in relation to which the monitored promoter mentioned in subsection (1)(a) or (b) is a promoter.

273(4) The relevant proposal or relevant arrangements mentioned in subsection (2) or (3) need not be the relevant proposals or relevant arrangements to which the disclosure relates.

PENALTIES

274 Penalties

274 Schedule 35 contains provision about penalties for failure to comply with provisions of this Part.

275 Failure to comply with Part 7 of the Finance Act 2004

275 [Inserts TMA 1970, s. 98C(2EA)–(2EB).]

276 Limitation of defence of reasonable care

276 [Omitted by F(No. 2)A 2017, s. 64(4).]

History – Omitted by F(No. 2)A 2017, s. 64(4), with effect in relation to any document of a kind listed in the Table at FA 2007, Sch. 24, para. 1 which is given to HMRC on or after 16 November 2017 (Royal Assent) and relates to a tax period that begins on or after 6 April 2017 and ends on or after 16 November 2017 (Royal Assent). Former s. 276 read as follows:

"276 Limitation of defence of reasonable care

276(1) Subsection (2) applies where–

(a) a person gives HMRC a document of a kind listed in the Table in paragraph 1 of Schedule 24 to FA 2007 (penalties for providing inaccurate documents to HMRC), and

(b) the document contains an inaccuracy.

276(2) In determining whether or not the inaccuracy was careless for the purposes of paragraph 3(1)(a) of Schedule 24 to FA 2007, reliance by the person on legal advice relating to relevant arrangements in relation to which a monitored promoter is a promoter is to be disregarded if the advice was given or procured by a person who was a monitored promoter in relation to the arrangements."

277 Extended time limit for assessment

277(1) [Not relevant to PRT.]

277(2) In paragraph 12B of Schedule 2 to OTA 1975 (extended time limits for assessment of petroleum revenue tax)–

(a) [amends OTA 1975, Sch. 2, para. 12B(1),]

(b) [inserts OTA 1975, Sch. 2, para. 12B(2A),]

(c) [amends OTA 1975, Sch. 2, para. 12B(5),]

(d) [amends OTA 1975, Sch. 2, para. 12B(6).]

277(3) [Not relevant to petroleum revenue tax.]
277(4) [Not relevant to petroleum revenue tax.]
277(5) [Not relevant to petroleum revenue tax.]
277(6) [Not relevant to petroleum revenue tax.]

OFFENCES

278 Offence of concealing etc documents

278(1) A person is guilty of an offence if–

(a) the person is required to produce a document by a notice given under section 255,
(b) the tribunal approved the giving of the notice under section 256, and
(c) the person conceals, destroys or otherwise disposes of, or arranges for the concealment, destruction or disposal of, that document.

278(2) Subsection (1) does not apply if the person acts after the document has been produced to an officer of Revenue and Customs in accordance with section 255, unless the officer has notified the person in writing that the document must continue to be available for inspection (and has not withdrawn the notification).

278(3) Subsection (1) does not apply, in a case to which section 268(1) applies, if the person acts after the end of the expiry of 6 months beginning with the day on which a copy of the document was produced in accordance with that section unless, before the expiry of that period, an officer of Revenue and Customs makes a request for the original document under section 268(2)(b).

279 Offence of concealing etc documents following informal notification

279(1) A person is guilty of an offence if the person conceals, destroys or otherwise disposes of, or arranges for the concealment, destruction or disposal of, a document after an officer of Revenue and Customs has informed the person in writing that–

(a) the document is, or is likely, to be the subject of a notice under section 255, and
(b) the officer of Revenue and Customs intends to seek the approval of the tribunal to the giving of the notice.

279(2) A person is not guilty of an offence under this section if the person acts after–

(a) at least 6 months has expired since the person was, or was last, informed as described in subsection (1), or
(b) a notice has been given to the person under section 255, requiring the document to be produced.

280 Penalties for offences

280(1) A person who is guilty of an offence under section 278 or 279 is liable–

(a) on summary conviction, to–
  (i) in England and Wales, a fine, or
  (ii) in Scotland or Northern Ireland, a fine not exceeding the statutory maximum, or
(b) on conviction on indictment, to imprisonment for a term not exceeding 2 years or to a fine or both.

280(2) In relation to an offence committed before section 85(1) of the Legal Aid, Sentencing and Punishment of Offenders Act 2012 comes into force, subsection (1)(a)(i) has effect as if the reference to "a fine" were a reference to "a fine not exceeding the statutory maximum".

SUPPLEMENTAL

281 Partnerships

281 *Schedule 36 contains provision about the application of this Part to partnerships.*

281A VAT and other indirect taxes

History – In the heading to s. 281A the words "and other indirect taxes" inserted by F(No. 2)A 2017, s. 66 and Sch. 17, para. 53(2), with effect so far as necessary for enabling the making of regulations under that Schedule from 16 November 2017 (Royal Assent) and from 1 January 2018 for all other purposes.

281A [Not relevant to petroleum revenue tax.]

History – S. 281A inserted by FA 2016, s. 160(7), with effect from 15 September 2016 (Royal Assent).

282 Regulations under this Part

282(1) Regulations under this Part are to be made by statutory instrument.

282(2) Apart from an instrument to which subsection (3) applies, a statutory instrument containing regulations made under this Part is subject to annulment in pursuance of a resolution of the House of Commons.

282(3) A statutory instrument containing (whether alone or with other provision) regulations made under–

(a) section 238(7),

(b) paragraph 14 of Schedule 34,

(ba) paragraph 31 of Schedule 34A,

(c) paragraph 5(1) of Schedule 35, or

(d) paragraph 21 of Schedule 36,

may not be made unless a draft of the instrument has been laid before and approved by a resolution of the House of Commons.

282(4) Regulations under this Part–

(a) may make different provision for different purposes;

(b) may include transitional provision and savings.

History – S. 282(3)(ba) inserted by FA 2016, s. 160(8), with effect from 15 September 2016 (Royal Assent).
Statutory instruments – SI 2015/549: partly made under s. 282(4).

283 Interpretation of this Part

283(1) In this Part–

"arrangements" has the meaning given by section 234(4);

"the Commissioners" means the Commissioners for Her Majesty's Revenue and Customs;

"calendar quarter" means a period of 3 months beginning with 1 January, 1 April, 1 July or 1 October;

"conduct notice" means a notice of the description in section 238 that is given under–

(a) section 237(7) or (7A),

(aa) section 237A(8),

(ab) section 237B(1),

(b) section 245(7), or

(c) paragraph 8(2) or (3) or 10(3)(a) or (4)(a) of Schedule 36;

"contract settlement" means an agreement in connection with a person's liability to make a payment to the Commissioners under or by virtue of an enactment;

"defeat", in relation to arrangements, has the meaning given by paragraph 10 of Schedule 34A;

"defeat notice" has the meaning given by section 241A(7);

"double defeat notice" has the meaning given by section 241A(7);

"final", in relation to a judicial ruling, is to be interpreted in accordance with section 237D(6);

"HMRC" means Her Majesty's Revenue and Customs;

"firm approach" has the meaning given by section 235(4);

"judicial ruling" means a ruling of a court or tribunal on one or more issues;

"look-forward period", in relation to a defeat notice, has the meaning given by section 241A(10);

"monitored promoter" has the meaning given by section 244(5);

"monitored proposal" and **"monitored arrangements"** have the meaning given by section 254;

"monitoring notice" means a notice given under section 244(1) or paragraph 9(2) or (3) or 10(3)(b) or (4)(b) of Schedule 36;

"the original monitoring notice" has the meaning given by paragraph 11(2) of Schedule 36;

"prescribed" means prescribed, or of a description prescribed, in regulations made by the Commissioners;

"promoter reference number" has the meaning given by section 250(5);

"provisional", in relation to a conduct notice given under section 237A(8), is to be interpreted in accordance with section 237C;

"related", in relation to arrangements, is to be interpreted in accordance with paragraph 2 of Schedule 34A;

"relevant arrangements" has the meaning given by section 234(2);
"relevant defeat", in relation to a person, is to be interpreted in accordance with Schedule 34A;
"relevant proposal" has the meaning given by section 234(1);
"relies on a Case 3 relevant defeat" is to be interpreted in accordance section 237B(5);
"replacement conduct notice" has the meaning given by paragraph 11(1) of Schedule 36;
"replacement monitoring notice" has the meaning given by paragraph 11(1) of Schedule 36;
"single defeat notice" has the meaning given by section 241A(7).
"tax" (except in provisions to which section 281A applies) means–
(a) income tax,
(b) capital gains tax,
(c) corporation tax,
(d) petroleum revenue tax,
(da) apprenticeship levy,
(e) inheritance tax,
(f) stamp duty land tax,
(g) stamp duty reserve tax, or
(h) annual tax on enveloped dwellings;
"tax advantage" has the meaning given by section 234(3) (but see also section 281A);
"Taxes Acts" has the same meaning as in TMA 1970 (see section 118(1) of that Act);
"the tribunal" means the First-tier Tribunal or, where determined by or under Tribunal Procedure Rules, the Upper Tribunal.

283(2) A reference in a provision of this Part to an authorised officer is to an officer of Revenue and Customs who is, or is a member of a class of officers who are, authorised by the Commissioners for the purposes of that provision.

283(3) A reference in a provision of this Part to meeting a threshold condition is to meeting one of the conditions described in paragraphs 2 to 12 of Schedule 34.

History – In s. 283(1), in the definition of "conduct notice", para. (aa) and (ab) inserted by FA 2016, s. 160(9)(a), with effect from 15 September 2016 (Royal Assent).
In s. 283(1), in the definition of "conduct notice", the words "or (7A)" inserted by FA 2015, s. 119 and Sch. 19, para. 3, with effect for the purposes of determining whether a person meets a threshold condition in a period of three years ending on or after 26 March 2015 (Royal Assent).
In s. 283(1), definitions of "contract settlement", "defeat", "defeat notice", "double defeat notice", "final", "judicial ruling", "look-forward period", "provisional", "relevant defeat", "related", "relies on a Case 3 relevant defeat" and "single defeat notice" inserted by FA 2016, s. 160(9)(d), with effect from 15 September 2016 (Royal Assent).
In s. 283(1), in the definition of "tax", the words "(except in provisions to which section 281A applies)" inserted by FA 2016, s. 160(9)(b), with effect from 15 September 2016 (Royal Assent).
In s. 283(1), in the definition of "tax", para. (da) inserted by FA 2016, s. 104(8), with effect from 15 September 2016 (Royal Assent).
In s. 283(1), in the definition of "tax advantage", the words "(but see also section 281A)" inserted by FA 2016, s. 160(9)(c), with effect from 15 September 2016 (Royal Assent).

Statutory instruments – SI 2015/130: partly made under s. 283(1).
SI 2015/131: partly made under s. 283(1).
SI 2015/549: partly made under s. 283(1).

PART 6 – OTHER PROVISIONS

ANTI-AVOIDANCE

284 Disclosure of tax avoidance schemes: information powers

284(1) Part 7 of FA 2004 (disclosure of tax avoidance schemes) is amended as set out in subsections (2) to (4).

284(2) [*Inserts FA 2004, s. 310A and 310B.*]

284(3) [Amends FA 2004, s. 316(2).]

284(4) [Amends FA 2004, s. 318(1).]

284(5) [Not relevant to petroleum revenue tax.]

284(6) [Not relevant to petroleum revenue tax.]

284(7) [Not relevant to petroleum revenue tax.]

284(8) [Not relevant to petroleum revenue tax.]

284(9) [Not relevant to petroleum revenue tax.]

284(10) [Not relevant to petroleum revenue tax.]

284(11) Section 310A of FA 2004 applies to a person who provides the prescribed information about notifiable proposals or arrangements in compliance or purported compliance with section 308, 309 or 310 on or after the day on which this Act is passed.

PART 7 – FINAL PROVISIONS

301 Power to update indexes of defined terms

301(1) The Treasury may by order amend any index of defined expressions contained in an Act relating to taxation, so as to make amendments consequential on any enactment.

301(2) In this section–

"enactment" means any provision made by or under an Act (whether before or after the passing of this Act);

"index of defined expressions" means a provision contained in an Act relating to taxation which lists where expressions used in the Act, or in a particular part of the Act, are defined or otherwise explained.

301(3) The power to make an order under this section is exercisable by statutory instrument.

301(4) An order under this section is subject to annulment in pursuance of a resolution of the House of Commons.

302 Interpretation

302(1) In this Act–

"ALDA 1979" means the Alcoholic Liquor Duties Act 1979,

"BGDA 1981" means the Betting and Gaming Duties Act 1981,

"CAA 2001" means the Capital Allowances Act 2001,

"CEMA 1979" means the Customs and Excise Management Act 1979,

"CRCA 2005" means the Commissioners for Revenue and Customs Act 2005,

"CTA 2009" means the Corporation Tax Act 2009,

"CTA 2010" means the Corporation Tax Act 2010,

"F(No.3)A 2010" means the Finance (No. 3) Act 2010,

"IHTA 1984" means the Inheritance Tax Act 1984,

"ITA 2007" means the Income Tax Act 2007,

"ITEPA 2003" means the Income Tax (Earnings and Pensions) Act 2003,

"ITTOIA 2005" means the Income Tax (Trading and Other Income) Act 2005,

"OTA 1975" means the Oil Taxation Act 1975,

"TCGA 1992" means the Taxation of Chargeable Gains Act 1992,

"TIOPA 2010" means the Taxation (International and Other Provisions) Act 2010,

"TMA 1970" means the Taxes Management Act 1970,

"TPDA 1979" means the Tobacco Products Duty Act 1979,

"VATA 1994" means the Value Added Tax Act 1994, and

"VERA 1994" means the Vehicle Excise and Registration Act 1994.

302(2) In this Act–

"FA", followed by a year, means the Finance Act of that year, and

"F(No. 2)A", followed by a year, means the Finance (No. 2) Act of that year.

303 Short title

303 This Act may be cited as the Finance Act 2014.

SCHEDULE 33 – PART 4: CONSEQUENTIAL AMENDMENTS

Section 233

FINANCE ACT 2007

3 [Inserts FA 2007, Sch. 24, para. 12(2A).]

FINANCE ACT 2009

5 [Inserts FA 2009, Sch. 55, para. 17(2)(c).]

SCHEDULE 34 – PROMOTERS OF TAX AVOIDANCE SCHEMES: THRESHOLD CONDITIONS

Section 237

Part 1 – Meeting the Threshold Conditions: General

MEANING OF "THRESHOLD CONDITION"

1 Each of the conditions described in paragraphs 2 to 12 is a "threshold condition".

DELIBERATE TAX DEFAULTERS

2 A person meets this condition if the Commissioners publish information about the person in reliance on section 94 of FA 2009 (publishing details of deliberate tax defaulters).

BREACH OF THE BANKING CODE OF PRACTICE

3 A person meets this condition if the person is named in a report under section 285 as a result of the Commissioners determining that the person breached the Code of Practice on Taxation for Banks by reason of promoting arrangements which the person cannot have reasonably believed achieved a tax result which was intended by Parliament.

DISHONEST TAX AGENTS

4 A person meets this condition if the person is given a conduct notice under paragraph 4 of Schedule 38 to FA 2012 (tax agents: dishonest conduct) and either–

(a) the time period during which a notice of appeal may be given in relation to the notice has expired, or

(b) an appeal against the notice has been made and the tribunal has confirmed the determination referred to in sub-paragraph (1) of paragraph 4 of that Schedule.

NON-COMPLIANCE WITH PART 7 OF FA 2004

5(1) A person meets this condition if the person fails to comply with any of the following provisions of Part 7 of FA 2004 (disclosure of tax avoidance schemes)–

(a) section 308(1) and (3) (duty of promoter in relation to notifiable proposals and notifiable arrangements);

(b) section 309(1) (duty of person dealing with promoter outside the United Kingdom);

(c) section 310 (duty of parties to notifiable arrangements not involving promoter);

(d) section 313ZA (duty of promoter to provide details of clients).

5(2) For the purposes of sub-paragraph (1), a person ("P") fails to comply with a provision mentioned in that sub-paragraph if and only if any of conditions A to C are met.

5(3) Condition A is met if–

(a) the tribunal has determined that P has failed to comply with the provision concerned,

(b) the appeal period has ended, and

(c) the determination has not been overturned on appeal.

5(4) Condition B is met if–

(a) the tribunal has determined for the purposes of section 118(2) of TMA 1970 that P is to be deemed not to have failed to comply with the provision concerned as P had a reasonable excuse for not doing the thing required to be done,

(b) the appeal period has ended, and

(c) the determination has not been overturned on appeal.

5(5) Condition C is met if P has admitted in writing to HMRC that P has failed to comply with the provision concerned.

5(6) The **"appeal period"** means–

(a) the period during which an appeal could be brought against the determination of the tribunal, or

(b) where an appeal mentioned in paragraph (a) has been brought, the period during which that appeal has not been finally determined, withdrawn or otherwise disposed of.

History – Para. 5(2)–(6) substituted for former para. 5(2) by FA 2015, s. 119 and Sch. 19, para. 6, with effect for the purposes of determining whether a person meets a threshold condition in a period of three years ending on or after 26 March 2015 (Royal Assent). Former para. 5(2) read as follows:

"**5(2)** For the purposes of sub-paragraph (1), failure to comply includes cases (despite section 118(2) of TMA 1970) where a person had a reasonable excuse for not doing the thing required to be done."

CRIMINAL OFFENCES

6(1) A person meets this condition if the person is charged with a relevant offence.

6(2) The fact that a person has been charged with an offence is disregarded for the purposes of this paragraph if–

(a) the person has been acquitted of the offence, or

(b) the charge has been dismissed or the proceedings have been discontinued.

6(3) An acquittal is not taken into account for the purposes of sub-paragraph (2) if an appeal has been brought against the acquittal and has not yet been disposed of.

6(4) **"Relevant offence"** means any of the following–

(a) an offence at common law of cheating in relation to the public revenue;

(b) in Scotland, an offence at common law of–

(i) fraud;

(ii) uttering;

(c) an offence under section 17(1) of the Theft Act 1968 or section 17 of the Theft Act (Northern Ireland) 1969 (c. 16 (N.I.)) (false accounting);

(d) an offence under section 106A of TMA 1970 (fraudulent evasion of income tax);

(e) an offence under section 107 of TMA 1970 (false statements: Scotland);

(f) an offence under any of the following provisions of CEMA 1979–

(i) section 50(2) (improper importation of goods with intent to defraud or evade duty);

(ii) section 167 (untrue declarations etc);

(iii) section 168 (counterfeiting documents etc);

(iv) section 170 (fraudulent evasion of duty);

(v) section 170B (taking steps for the fraudulent evasion of duty);

(g) an offence under any of the following provisions of VATA 1994–

(i) section 72(1) (being knowingly concerned in the evasion of VAT);

(ii) section 72(3) (false statement etc);

(iii) section 72(8) (conduct involving commission of other offence under section 72);

(h) an offence under section 1 of the Fraud Act 2006 (fraud);

(i) an offence under any of the following provisions of CRCA 2005–

(i) section 30 (impersonating a Commissioner or officer of Revenue and Customs);

(ii) section 31 (obstruction of officer of Revenue and Customs etc);

(iii) section 32 (assault of officer of Revenue and Customs);

(j) *an offence under regulation 86(1)* of the Money Laundering, Terrorist Financing and Transfer of Funds (Information on the Payer) Regulations 2017;

(k) an offence under section 49(1) of the Criminal Justice and Licensing (Scotland) Act 2010 (asp 13) (possession of articles for use in fraud).

History – In para. 6(4)(j), the words "regulation 86(1) of the Money Laundering, Terrorist Financing and Transfer of Funds (Information on the Payer) Regulations 2017" substituted for the words "regulation 45(1) of the Money Laundering Regulations 2007 (S.I. 2007/2157)" by SI 2017/692, Sch. 7, para. 10, with effect from 26 June 2017.

OPINION NOTICE OF GAAR ADVISORY PANEL

7 A person meets this condition if–

(a) arrangements in relation to which the person is a promoter–

(i) have been referred to the GAAR Advisory Panel under Schedule 43 to FA 2013 (referrals of single schemes),

(ii) are in a pool in respect of which a referral has been made to that Panel under Schedule 43B to that Act (generic referrals), or

(iii) have been referred to that Panel under paragraph 26 of Schedule 16 to F(No. 2)A 2017 (referrals in relation to penalties for enablers of defeated tax avoidance),

(b) one or more opinion notices are given in respect of the referral under (as the case may be)–

(i) paragraph 11(3)(b) of Schedule 43 to FA 2013,

(ii) paragraph 6(4)(b) of Schedule 43B to that Act, or

(iii) paragraph 34(3)(b) of Schedule 16 to F(No. 2)A 2017,

(opinion of sub-panel of GAAR Advisory Panel that arrangements are not reasonable), and

(c) the notice, or the notices taken together, either–

(i) state the joint opinion of all the members of the sub-panel arranged under that Schedule, or

(ii) state the opinion of two or more members of that sub-panel.

History – Para. 7(a)(i)–(iii) (and the "–" preceding them) substituted for the words "have been referred to the GAAR Advisory Panel under Schedule 43 to FA 2013, (referrals of single schemes) or are in a pool in respect of which a referral has been made to that Panel under Schedule 43B to that Act (generic referrals)," by F(No. 2)A 2017, s. 65 and Sch. 16, para. 61(a), with effect in relation to arrangements entered into on or after 16 November 2017 (Royal Assent).

In para. 7(a), the words "(referrals of single schemes) or are in a pool in respect of which a referral has been made to that Panel under Schedule 43B to that Act (generic referrals)," inserted by FA 2016, s. 157(29)(a), with effect in relation to tax arrangements (within the meaning of FA 2013, Pt. 5) entered into at any time (whether before or on or after 15 September 2016).

Para. 7(b)(i)–(iii) (and the "under (as the case may be)–" preceding them and the end words after them) substituted for the words "under paragraph 11(3)(b) or (as the case may be) 6(4)(b) of that Schedule (opinion of sub-panel of GAAR Advisory Panel that arrangements are not reasonable), and" by F(No. 2)A 2017, s. 65 and Sch. 16, para. 61(b), with effect in relation to arrangements entered into on or after 16 November 2017 (Royal Assent).

In para. 7(b), the words "in respect of the referral" substituted for the words "in relation to the arrangements" and the words "or (as the case may be) 6(4)(b)" inserted by FA 2016, s. 157(29)(b), with effect in relation to tax arrangements (within the meaning of FA 2013, Pt. 5) entered into at any time (whether before or on or after 15 September 2016).

In para. 7(c), the words "paragraph 10 of" (which appeared before the words "that Schedule") omitted by FA 2016, s. 157(29)(c), with effect in relation to tax arrangements (within the meaning of FA 2013, Pt. 5) entered into at any time (whether before or on or after 15 September 2016).

DISCIPLINARY ACTION AGAINST A MEMBER OF A TRADE OR PROFESSION

History – In the heading the words "AGAINST A MEMBER OF A TRADE OR PROFESSION" substituted for the words "BY A PROFESSIONAL BODY" by FA 2015, s. 119 and Sch. 19, para. 7(3), with effect for the purposes of determining whether a person meets a threshold condition in a period of three years ending on or after 26 March 2015 (Royal Assent).

8(1) A person who carries on a trade or profession that is regulated by a professional body meets this condition if all of the following conditions are met–

(a) the person is found guilty of misconduct of a prescribed kind,

(b) action of a prescribed kind is taken against the person in relation to that misconduct, and

(c) a penalty of a prescribed kind is imposed on the person as a result of that misconduct.

8(2) Misconduct may only be prescribed for the purposes of sub-paragraph (1)(a) if it is misconduct other than misconduct in matters (such as the payment of fees) that relate solely or mainly to the person's relationship with the professional body.

8(3) A **"professional body"** means–

(a) the Institute of Chartered Accountants in England and Wales;

(b) the Institute of Chartered Accountants of Scotland;

(c) the General Council of the Bar;

(d) the Faculty of Advocates;

(e) the General Council of the Bar of Northern Ireland;

(f) the Law Society;

(g) the Law Society of Scotland;

(h) the Law Society of Northern Ireland;

(i) the Association of Accounting Technicians;

(j) the Association of Chartered Certified Accountants;

(k) the Association of Taxation Technicians;

(l) any other prescribed body with functions relating to the regulation of a trade or profession.

History – Para. 8(1) substituted by FA 2015, s. 119 and Sch. 19, para. 7(2), with effect for the purposes of determining whether a person meets a threshold condition in a period of three years ending on or after 26 March 2015 (Royal Assent). Former para. 8(1) read as follows:

"**8(1)** A person meets this condition if a professional body–

(a) determines that the person is guilty of misconduct of a kind prescribed for the purposes of this paragraph, and

(b) takes in relation to that misconduct action of a kind so prescribed, and

(c) imposes on the person a penalty of a kind so prescribed."

In para. 8(3)(h) the word "of" substituted for the word "for" by FA 2015, s. 119 and Sch. 19, para. 7(2)4 with effect for the purposes of determining whether a person meets a threshold condition in a period of three years ending on or after 26 March 2015 (Royal Assent).

Statutory instruments – SI 2015/131: partly made under para. 8(1) and (3).

DISCIPLINARY ACTION BY A REGULATORY AUTHORITY

9(1) A person meets this condition if a regulatory authority imposes a relevant sanction on the person.

9(2) A **"relevant sanction"** is a sanction which is–

(a) imposed in relation to misconduct other than misconduct in matters (such as the payment of fees) that relate solely or mainly to the person's relationship with the regulatory authority, and

(b) prescribed.

9(3) The following are regulatory authorities for the purposes of this paragraph–

(a) the Financial Conduct Authority;

(b) the Financial Services Authority;

(c) any other authority that may be prescribed.

9(4) Only authorities that have functions relating to the regulation of financial institutions may be prescribed under sub-paragraph (3)(c).

Statutory instruments – SI 2015/131: partly made under para. 9(2).

EXERCISE OF INFORMATION POWERS

10(1) A person meets this condition if the person fails to comply with an information notice given under any of paragraphs 1, 2, 5 and 5A of Schedule 36 to FA 2008.

10(2) For the purposes of section 237, the failure to comply is taken to occur when the period within which the person is required to comply with the notice expires (without the person having complied with it).

RESTRICTIVE CONTRACTUAL TERMS

11(1) A person ("P") meets this condition if P enters into an agreement with another person ("C") which relates to a relevant proposal or relevant arrangements in relation to which P is a promoter, on terms which–

(a) impose a contractual obligation on C which falls within sub-paragraph (2) or (3), or

(b) impose on C both obligations within sub-paragraph (4) and obligations within sub-paragraph (5).

11(2) A contractual obligation falls within this sub-paragraph if it prevents or restricts the disclosure by C to HMRC of information relating to the proposals or arrangements, whether or not by referring to a wider class of persons.

11(3) A contractual obligation falls within this sub-paragraph if it requires C to impose on any tax adviser to whom C discloses information relating to the proposals or arrangements a contractual obligation which prevents or restricts the disclosure of that information to HMRC by the adviser.

11(4) A contractual obligation falls within this sub-paragraph if it requires C to–

(a) meet (in whole or in part) the costs of, or contribute to a fund to be used to meet the costs of, any proceedings relating to arrangements in relation to which P is a promoter (whether or not implemented by C), or

(b) take out an insurance policy which insures against the risk of having to meet the costs connected with proceedings relating to arrangements which C has implemented and in relation to which P is a promoter.

11(5) A contractual obligation falls within this paragraph if it requires C to obtain the consent of P before–

(a) entering into any agreement with HMRC regarding arrangements which C has implemented and in relation to which P is a promoter, or

(b) withdrawing or discontinuing any appeal against any decision regarding such arrangements.

11(6) In sub-paragraph (5)(b), the reference to withdrawing or discontinuing an appeal includes any action or inaction which results in an appeal being discontinued.

11(7) In this paragraph–

"proceedings" includes any sort of proceedings for resolving disputes (and not just proceedings in court), whether commenced or contemplated;

"tax adviser" means a person appointed to give advice about the tax affairs of another person (whether appointed directly by that person or by another tax adviser of that person).

CONTINUING TO PROMOTE CERTAIN ARRANGEMENTS

12(1) A person ("P") meets this condition if P has been given a stop notice and after the end of the notice period P–

(a) makes a firm approach to another person ("C") in relation to an affected proposal with a view to making the affected proposal available for implementation by C or another person, or

(b) makes an affected proposal available for implementation by other persons.

12(2) **"Affected proposal"** means a relevant proposal that is in substance the same as the relevant proposal specified in the stop notice in accordance with sub-paragraph (4)(c).

12(3) An authorised officer may give a person ("P") a notice (a "stop notice") if each of these conditions is met–

(a) a person has been given a follower notice under section 204 (circumstances in which a follower notice may be given) in relation to particular relevant arrangements;

(b) P is a promoter in relation to a relevant proposal that is implemented by those arrangements;

(c) 90 days have elapsed since the follower notice was given and–

(i) the follower notice has not been withdrawn, and

(ii) if representations objecting to the follower notice were made under section 207 (representations about a follower notice), HMRC have confirmed the follower notice.

12(4) A stop notice must–

(a) specify the arrangements which are the subject of the follower notice mentioned in sub-paragraph (3)(a),

(b) specify the judicial ruling identified in that follower notice,

(c) specify a relevant proposal in relation to which the condition in sub-paragraph (3)(b) is met, and

(d) explain the effect of the stop notice.

12(5) An authorised officer may determine that a stop notice given to a person is to cease to have effect.

12(6) If an authorised officer makes a determination under sub-paragraph (5) the officer must give the person written notice of the determination.

12(7) The notice must specify the date from which it takes effect, which may be earlier than the date on which the notice is given.

12(8) In this paragraph–

"the notice period" means the period of 30 days beginning with the day on which a stop notice is given;

"judicial ruling" means a ruling of a court or tribunal.

Part 2 – Meeting the Threshold Conditions: Bodies Corporate and Partnerships

History – In the heading the words "and Partnerships" inserted by FA 2015, s. 119 and Sch. 19, para. 4(2), with effect for the purposes of determining whether a person meets a threshold condition in a period of three years ending on or after 26 March 2015 (Royal Assent).

13 [Substituted for para. 13A–13D by FA 2015, s. 119 and Sch. 19, para. 4(3).]

History – Para. 13 substituted by former para 13A–13D by FA 2015, s. 119 and Sch. 19, para. 4(3), with effect for the purposes of determining whether a person meets a threshold condition in a period of three years ending on or after 26 March 2015 (Royal Assent). Former para. 13 read as follows:

PRT Statutes

"**13(1)** Sub-paragraph (2) applies where–
(a) a relevant threshold condition is met by a person ("P") at a time ("the earlier time") when P has control of a body corporate,
(b) a determination under section 237 is made at a later time in relation to the body corporate, and
(c) P has control of the body corporate at the time of the determination.
13(2) The body corporate is regarded as having met the threshold condition at the earlier time.
13(3) **"Relevant threshold condition"** means a threshold condition specified in any of the following paragraphs of Schedule 34–
(a) paragraph 2 (deliberate tax defaulters);
(b) paragraph 4 (dishonest tax agents);
(c) paragraph 6 (criminal offences);
(d) paragraph 7 (opinion notice of GAAR advisory panel);
(e) paragraph 8 (disciplinary action by professional body);
(f) paragraph 9 (disciplinary action by regulatory authority);
(g) paragraph 10 (failure to comply with information notice).
13(4) For the purposes of this paragraph a person ("P") has control of a body corporate ("B") if P has power to secure–
(a) by means of the holding of shares or the possession of voting power in relation to B or any other body corporate, or
(b) as a result of any powers conferred by the articles of association or other document regulating B or any other body corporate,
that the affairs of B are conducted in accordance with P's wishes."

INTERPRETATION

13A(1) This paragraph contains definitions for the purposes of this Part of this Schedule.

13A(2) Each of the following is a **"relevant body"**–
(a) a body corporate, and
(b) a partnership.

13A(3) **"Relevant time"** means the time referred to in section 237(1A) (duty to give conduct notice to person treated as meeting threshold condition).

13A(4) **"Relevant threshold condition"** means a threshold condition specified in any of the following paragraphs of this Schedule–
(a) paragraph 2 (deliberate tax defaulters);
(b) paragraph 4 (dishonest tax agents);
(c) paragraph 6 (criminal offences);
(d) paragraph 7 (opinion notice of GAAR advisory panel);
(e) paragraph 8 (disciplinary action against a member of a trade or profession);
(f) paragraph 9 (disciplinary action by regulatory authority);
(g) paragraph 10 (failure to comply with information notice).

13A(5) A person controls a body corporate if the person has power to secure that the affairs of the body corporate are conducted in accordance with the person's wishes–
(a) by means of the holding of shares or the possession of voting power in relation to the body corporate or any other relevant body,
(b) as a result of any powers conferred by the articles of association or other document regulating the body corporate or any other relevant body, or
(c) by means of controlling a partnership.

13A(6) Two or more persons together control a body corporate if together they have the power to secure that the affairs of the body corporate are conducted in accordance with their wishes in any way specified in sub-paragraph (5)(a) to (c).

13A(7) A person controls a partnership if the person is a member of the partnership and–
(a) has the right to a share of more than half the assets, or more than half the income, of the partnership, or
(b) directs, or is on a day-to-day level in control of, the management of the business of the partnership.

13A(8) Two or more persons together control a partnership if they are members of the partnership and together they–
(a) have the right to a share of more than half the assets, or of more than half the income, of the partnership, or
(b) direct, or are on a day-to-day level in control of, the management of the business of the partnership.

13A(9) Paragraph 19(2) to (5) of Schedule 36 (connected persons etc) applies to a person referred to in sub-paragraph (7) or (8) as if references to "P" were to that person.

13A(10) A *person* has significant influence over a body corporate or partnership if the person–
(a) does not control the body corporate or partnership, but
(b) is able to, or actually does, exercise significant influence over it (whether or not as the result of a legal entitlement).

13A(11) Two or more persons together have significant influence over a body corporate or partnership if together those persons–

(a) do not control the body corporate or partnership, but

(b) are able to, or actually do, exercise significant influence over it (whether or not as the result of a legal entitlement).

13A(12) References to a person being a promoter are to the person carrying on business as a promoter.

History – Para. 13A(6)–(12) substituted for para. 13(6)–(8), by FA 2017, s. 24(1), with effect for the purposes of determining whether a person meets a threshold condition in a period of three years ending on or after 8 March 2017. Former para. 13A(6)–(8) read as follows:
"**13A(6)** A person controls a partnership if the person is a controlling member or the managing partner of the partnership.
13A(7) **"Controlling member"** has the same meaning as in Schedule 36 (partnerships).
13A(8) **"Managing partner"**, in relation to a partnership, means the member of the partnership who directs, or is on a day-to-day level in control of, the management of the business of the partnership.".
Para. 13A–13D substituted for former para 13 by FA 2015, s. 119 and Sch. 19, para. 4(3), with effect for the purposes of determining whether a person meets a threshold condition in a period of three years ending on or after 26 March 2015 (Royal Assent).

RELEVANT BODIES CONTROLLED ETC BY OTHER PERSONS TREATED AS MEETING A THRESHOLD CONDITION

13B(1) A relevant body is treated as meeting a threshold condition at the relevant time if any of Conditions A to C is met.

13B(2) Condition A is that–

(a) a person met the threshold condition at a time when the person was a promoter, and

(b) the person controls or has significant influence over the relevant body at the relevant time.

13B(3) Condition B is that–

(a) a person met the threshold condition at a time when the person controlled or had significant influence over the relevant body,

(b) the relevant body was a promoter at that time, and

(c) the person controls or has significant influence over the relevant body at the relevant time.

13B(4) Condition C is that–

(a) two or more persons together controlled or had significant influence over the relevant body at a time when one of those persons met the threshold condition,

(b) the relevant body was a promoter at that time, and

(c) those persons together control or have significant influence over the relevant body at the relevant time.

13B(5) Where the person referred to in sub-paragraph (2)(a) or (3)(a) or (4)(a) as meeting a threshold condition is an individual, sub-paragraph (1) only applies if the threshold condition is a relevant threshold condition.

13B(6) For the purposes of sub-paragraph (2) it does not matter whether the relevant body existed at the time referred to in sub-paragraph (2)(a).

History – Para. 13B substituted by FA 2017, s. 24(2), with effect for the purposes of determining whether a person meets a threshold condition in a period of three years ending on or after 8 March 2017. Former para. 13B read as follows:

"TREATING PERSONS UNDER ANOTHER'S CONTROL AS MEETING A THRESHOLD CONDITION

13B(1) A relevant body ("RB") is treated as meeting a threshold condition at the relevant time if–
(a) the threshold condition was met by a person ("C") at a time when–
(i) C was carrying on a business as a promoter, or
(ii) RB was carrying on a business as a promoter and C controlled RB, and
(b) RB is controlled by C at the relevant time.
13B(2) Where C is an individual sub-paragraph (1) applies only if the threshold condition mentioned in sub-paragraph (1)(a) is a relevant threshold condition.
13B(3) For the purposes of determining whether the requirements of sub-paragraph (1) are met by reason of meeting the requirement in sub-paragraph (1)(a)(i), it does not matter whether RB existed at the time when the threshold condition was met by C.".
Para. 13A and former para. 13B–13D substituted for former para. 13 by FA 2015, s. 119 and Sch. 19, para. 4(3), with effect for the purposes of determining whether a person meets a threshold condition in a period of three years ending on or after 26 March 2015 (Royal Assent).

PERSONS WHO CONTROL ETC A RELEVANT BODY TREATED AS MEETING A THRESHOLD CONDITION

13C(1) If at a time when a person controlled or had significant influence over a relevant body–

(a) the relevant body met a threshold condition, and

(b) the relevant body, or another relevant body which the person controlled or had significant influence over, was a promoter,

the person is treated as meeting the threshold condition at the relevant time.

13C(2) It does not matter whether any relevant body referred to sub-paragraph (1) exists at the relevant time.

History – Para. 13C substituted by FA 2017, s. 24(2), with effect for the purposes of determining whether a person meets a threshold condition in a period of three years ending on or after 8 March 2017. Former para. 13C read as follows:

"TREATING PERSONS IN CONTROL OF OTHERS AS MEETING A THRESHOLD CONDITION

13C(1) A person other than an individual is treated as meeting a threshold condition at the relevant time if–

(a) a relevant body ("A") met the threshold condition at a time when A was controlled by the person, and

(b) at the time mentioned in paragraph (a) A, or another relevant body ("B") which was also at that time controlled by the person, carried on a business as a promoter.

13C(2) For the purposes of determining whether the requirements of sub-paragraph (1) are met it does not matter whether A or B (or neither) exists at the relevant time.".

Para. 13A and former para. 13B–13D substituted for former para. 13 by FA 2015, s. 119 and Sch. 19, para. 4(3), with effect for the purposes of determining whether a person meets a threshold condition in a period of three years ending on or after 26 March 2015 (Royal Assent).

RELEVANT BODIES CONTROLLED ETC BY THE SAME PERSON TREATED AS MEETING A THRESHOLD CONDITION

13D(1) If–

(a) a person controlled or had significant influence over a relevant body at a time when it met a threshold condition, and

(b) at that time that body, or another relevant body which the person controlled or had significant influence over, was a promoter,

any relevant body which the person controls or has significant influence over at the relevant time is treated as meeting the threshold condition at the relevant time.

13D(2) If–

(a) two or more persons together controlled or had significant influence over a relevant body at a time when it met a threshold condition, and

(b) at that time that body, or another relevant body which those persons together controlled or had significant influence over, was a promoter,

any relevant body which those persons together control or have significant influence over at the relevant time is treated as meeting the threshold condition at the relevant time.

13D(3) It does not matter whether–

(a) a relevant body referred to in sub-paragraph (1)(a) or (b) or (2)(a) or (b) exists at the relevant time, or

(b) a relevant body existing at the relevant time existed at the time referred to in sub-paragraph (1)(a) or (2)(a).

History – Para. 13D substituted by FA 2017, s. 24(2), with effect for the purposes of determining whether a person meets a threshold condition in a period of three years ending on or after 8 March 2017. Former para. 13D read as follows:

"TREATING PERSONS CONTROLLED BY THE SAME PERSON AS MEETING A THRESHOLD CONDITION

13D(1) A relevant body ("RB") is treated as meeting a threshold condition at the relevant time if–

(a) RB or another relevant body met the threshold condition at a time ("time T") when it was controlled by a person ("C"),

(b) at time T, there was a relevant body controlled by C which carried on a business as a promoter, and

(c) RB is controlled by C at the relevant time.

13D(2) For the purposes of determining whether the requirements of sub-paragraph (1) are met it does not matter whether–

(a) RB existed at time T, or

(b) any relevant body (other than RB) by reason of which the requirements of sub-paragraph (1) are met exists at the relevant time.".

Para. 13A and former para. 13B–13D substituted for former para. 13 by FA 2015, s. 119 and Sch. 19, para. 4(3), with effect for the purposes of determining whether a person meets a threshold condition in a period of three years ending on or after 26 March 2015 (Royal Assent).

Part 3 – Power to Amend

14(1) The Treasury may by regulations amend this Schedule.

14(2) An amendment made by virtue of sub-paragraph (1) may, in particular–

(a) vary or remove any of the conditions set out in paragraphs 2 to 12;

(b) add new conditions.

(c) vary any of the circumstances described in paragraphs 13B to 13D in which a person is treated as meeting a threshold condition (including by amending paragraph 13A);

(d) add new circumstances in which a person will be so treated.

14(3) Regulations under sub-paragraph (1) may include any amendment of this Part of this Act that is appropriate in consequence of an amendment made by virtue of sub-paragraph (1).

History – Para. 14(2)(c) and (d) inserted by FA 2015, s. 119 and Sch. 19, para. 8 with effect from 26 March 2015 (Royal Assent).

SCHEDULE 34A – PROMOTERS OF TAX AVOIDANCE SCHEMES: DEFEATED ARRANGEMENTS

History – Sch. 34A inserted by FA 2016, s. 160(5), with effect from 15 September 2016 (Royal Assent).

Part 1 – Introduction

1 In this Schedule–

(a) Part 2 is about the meaning of **"relevant defeat"**;

(b) Part 3 contains provision about when a relevant defeat is treated as occurring in relation to a person;

(c) Part 4 contains provision about when a person is treated as meeting a condition in subsection (11), (12) or (13) of section 237A;

(d) Part 5 contains definitions and other supplementary provisions.

Part 2 – Meaning of "Relevant Defeat"

"RELATED" ARRANGEMENTS

2(1) For the purposes of this Part of this Act, separate arrangements which persons have entered into are **"related"** to one another if (and only if) they are substantially the same.

2(2) Sub-paragraphs (3) to (6) set out cases in which arrangements are to be treated as being **"substantially the same"** (if they would not otherwise be so treated under sub-paragraph (1)).

2(3) Arrangements to which the same reference number has been allocated under Part 7 of FA 2004 (disclosure of tax avoidance schemes) are treated as being substantially the same.

For this purpose arrangements in relation to which information relating to a reference number has been provided in compliance with section 312 of FA 2004 are treated as arrangements to which that reference number has been allocated under Part 7 of that Act.

2(4) Arrangements to which the same reference number has been allocated under paragraph 9 of Schedule 11A to VATA 1994 (disclosure of avoidance schemes) or paragraph 22 of Schedule 17 to F[(No. 2)]A 2017 (disclosure of avoidance schemes: VAT and other indirect taxes) are treated as being substantially the same.

2(5) Any two or more sets of arrangements which are the subject of follower notices given by reference to the same judicial ruling are treated as being substantially the same.

2(6) Where a notice of binding has been given in relation to any arrangements ("the bound arrangements") on the basis that they are, for the purposes of Schedule 43A to FA 2013, equivalent arrangements in relation to another set of arrangements (the "lead arrangements")–

(a) the bound arrangements and the lead arrangements are treated as being substantially the same, and

(b) the bound arrangements are treated as being substantially the same as any other arrangements which, as a result of this sub-paragraph, are treated as substantially the same as the lead arrangements.

History – In para. 2(4) the words "or paragraph 22 of Schedule 17 to FA 2017 (disclosure of avoidance schemes: VAT and other indirect taxes)" inserted by F(No. 2)A 2017, s. 66 and Sch. 17, para. 54(2), with effect so far as necessary for enabling the making of regulations under that Schedule from 16 November 2017 (Royal Assent) and from 1 January 2018 for all other purposes.

"PROMOTED ARRANGEMENTS"

3(1) For the purposes of this Schedule arrangements are **"promoted arrangements"** in relation to a person if–

(a) they are relevant arrangements or would be relevant arrangements under the condition stated in sub-paragraph (2), and

(b) the person is carrying on a business as a promoter and–

(i) the person is or has been a promoter in relation to the arrangements, or

(ii) that would be the case if the condition in sub-paragraph (2) were met.

3(2) That condition is that the definition of **"tax"** in section 283 includes, and has always included, value added tax.

RELEVANT DEFEAT OF SINGLE ARRANGEMENTS

4(1) A defeat of arrangements (entered into by any person) which are promoted arrangements in relation to a person ("the promoter") is a **"relevant defeat"** in relation to the promoter if the condition in sub-paragraph (2) is met.

4(2) The condition is that the arrangements are not related to any other arrangements which are promoted arrangements in relation to the promoter.

4(3) For the meaning of **"defeat"** see paragraphs 10 to 16.

RELEVANT DEFEAT OF RELATED ARRANGEMENTS

5(1) This paragraph applies if arrangements (entered into by any person) ("Set A")–

(a) are promoted arrangements in relation to a person ("P"), and

(b) are related to other arrangements which are promoted arrangements in relation to P.

5(2) If Case 1, 2 or 3 applies (see paragraphs 7 to 9) a relevant defeat occurs in relation to P and each of the related arrangements.

5(3) **"The related arrangements"** means Set A and the arrangements mentioned in sub-paragraph (1)(b).

LIMIT ON NUMBER OF SEPARATE RELEVANT DEFEATS IN RELATION TO THE SAME, OR RELATED, ARRANGEMENTS

6 In relation to a person, if there has been a relevant defeat of arrangements (whether under paragraph 4 or 5) there cannot be a further relevant defeat of–

(a) those particular arrangements, or

(b) arrangements which are related to those arrangements.

CASE 1: COUNTERACTION UPHELD BY JUDICIAL RULING

7(1) Case 1 applies if–

(a) any of Conditions A to E is met in relation to any of the related arrangements, and

(b) in the case of those arrangements the decision to make the relevant counteraction has been upheld by a judicial ruling (which is final).

7(2) In sub-paragraph (1) **"the relevant counteraction"** means the counteraction mentioned in paragraph 11(d), 12(1)(b), 13(1)(d), 14(1)(d) or 15(1)(d) (as the case requires).

CASE 2: JUDICIAL RULING THAT AVOIDANCE-RELATED RULE APPLIES

8 Case 2 applies if Condition F is met in relation to any of the related arrangements.

CASE 3: PROPORTION-BASED RELEVANT DEFEAT

9(1) Case 3 applies if–

(a) at least 75% of the tested arrangements have been defeated, and

(b) no final judicial ruling in relation to any of the related arrangements has upheld a corresponding tax advantage which has been asserted in connection with any of the related arrangements.

9(2) In this paragraph **"the tested arrangements"** means so many of the related arrangements (as defined in paragraph 5(3)) as meet the condition in sub-paragraph (3) or (4).

9(3) Particular arrangements meet this condition if a person has made a return, claim or election on the basis that a tax advantage results from those arrangements and–

(a) there has been an enquiry or investigation by HMRC into the return, claim or election, or

(b) HMRC assesses the person to tax on the basis that the tax advantage (or any part of it) does not arise, or

(c) a GAAR counteraction notice has been given in relation to the tax advantage or part of it and the arrangements.

9(4) Particular arrangements meet this condition if HMRC takes other action on the basis that a tax advantage which might be expected to arise from those arrangements, or is asserted in connection with them, does not arise.

9(5) For the purposes of this paragraph a tax advantage has been **"asserted"** in connection with particular *arrangements* if a person has made a return, claim or election on the basis that the tax advantage arises from those arrangements.

9(6) In sub-paragraph (1)(b) **"corresponding tax advantage"** means a tax advantage corresponding to any tax advantage the counteraction of which is taken into account by HMRC for the purposes of sub-paragraph (1)(a).

9(7) For the purposes of this paragraph a court or tribunal **"upholds"** a tax advantage if–

(a) the court or tribunal makes a ruling to the effect that no part of the tax advantage is to be counteracted, and

(b) that judicial ruling is final.

9(8) In this paragraph references to **"counteraction"** include anything referred to as a counteraction in any of Conditions A to F in paragraphs 11 to 16.

9(9) In this paragraph **"GAAR counteraction notice"** means–

(a) a notice such as is mentioned in sub-paragraph (2) of paragraph 12 of Schedule 43 to FA 2013 (notice of final decision to counteract),

(b) a notice under paragraph 8(2) or 9(2) of Schedule 43A to that Act (binding of arrangements to lead arrangements) stating that the tax advantage is to be counteracted under the general anti-abuse rule, or

(c) a notice under paragraph 8(2) of Schedule 43B to that Act (generic referrals) stating that the tax advantage is to be counteracted under the general anti-abuse rule.

"DEFEAT" OF ARRANGEMENTS

10 For the purposes of this Part of this Act a **"defeat"** of arrangements occurs if any of Conditions A to F (in paragraphs 11 to 16) is met in relation to the arrangements.

11 Condition A is that–

(a) a person has made a return, claim or election on the basis that a tax advantage arises from the arrangements,

(b) a notice given to the person under paragraph 12 of Schedule 43 to, paragraph 8(2) or 9(2) of Schedule 43A to or paragraph 8(2) of Schedule 43B to FA 2013 stated that the tax advantage was to be counteracted under the general anti-abuse rule,

(c) the tax advantage has been counteracted (in whole or in part) under the general anti-abuse rule, and

(d) the counteraction is final.

12(1) Condition B is that a follower notice has been given to a person by reference to the arrangements (and not withdrawn) and–

(a) the person has complied with subsection (2) of section 208 of FA 2014 by taking the action specified in subsections (4) to (6) of that section in respect of the denied tax advantage (or part of it), or

(b) the denied tax advantage has been counteracted (in whole or in part) otherwise than as mentioned in paragraph (a) and the counteraction is final.

12(2) In this paragraph **"the denied tax advantage"** is to be interpreted in accordance with section 208(3) of FA 2014.

12(3) In this Schedule **"follower notice"** means a follower notice under Chapter 2 of Part 4 of FA 2014.

13(1) Condition C is that–

(a) the arrangements are DOTAS arrangements,

(b) a person ("the taxpayer") has made a return, claim or election on the basis that a relevant tax advantage arises,

(c) the relevant tax advantage has been counteracted, and

(d) the counteraction is final.

13(2) For the purposes of sub-paragraph (1) **"relevant tax advantage"** means a tax advantage which the arrangements might be expected to enable the taxpayer to obtain.

13(3) For the purposes of this paragraph the relevant tax advantage is **"counteracted"** if adjustments are made in respect of the taxpayer's tax position on the basis that the whole or part of that tax advantage does not arise.

14(1) Condition D is that–

(a) the arrangements are disclosable VAT or other indirect tax arrangements to which a person is a party,

(b) the person has made a return or claim on the basis that a relevant tax advantage arises,

(c) the relevant tax advantage has been counteracted, and

(d) the counteraction is final.

PRT Statutes

14(2) For the purposes of sub-paragraph (1) **"relevant tax advantage"** means a tax advantage which the arrangements might be expected to enable the person to obtain.

14(3) For the purposes of this paragraph the relevant tax advantage is **"counteracted"** if adjustments are made in respect of the person's tax position on the basis that the whole or part of that tax advantage does not arise.

History – In para. 14(1)(a) the words "or other indirect tax" inserted by F(No. 2)A 2017, s. 66 and Sch. 17, para. 54(3)(a), with effect so far as necessary for enabling the making of regulations under that Schedule from 16 November 2017 (Royal Assent) and from 1 January 2018 for all other purposes.

In para. 14(1)(a) and (b) the word "taxable" (which appeared before the word "person") omitted by F(No. 2)A 2017, s. 66 and Sch. 17, para. 54(3)(b), with effect so far as necessary for enabling the making of regulations under that Schedule from 16 November 2017 (Royal Assent) and from 1 January 2018 for all other purposes.

In para. 14(2) the word "taxable" (which appeared before the word "person") omitted by F(No. 2)A 2017, s. 66 and Sch. 17, para. 54(3)(b), with effect so far as necessary for enabling the making of regulations under that Schedule from 16 November 2017 (Royal Assent) and from 1 January 2018 for all other purposes.

In para. 14(3) the word "taxable" (which appeared before the word "person") omitted by F(No. 2)A 2017, s. 66 and Sch. 17, para. 54(3)(b), with effect so far as necessary for enabling the making of regulations under that Schedule from 16 November 2017 (Royal Assent) and from 1 January 2018 for all other purposes.

15(1) Condition E is that the arrangements are disclosable VAT arrangements to which a taxable person ("T") is a party and–

(a) the arrangements relate to the position with respect to VAT of a person other than T ("S") who has made supplies of goods or services to T,

(b) the arrangements might be expected to enable T to obtain a tax advantage in connection with those supplies of goods or services,

(c) the arrangements have been counteracted, and

(d) the counteraction is final.

15(2) For the purposes of this paragraph the arrangements are **"counteracted"** if–

(a) HMRC assess S to tax or take any other action on a basis which prevents T from obtaining (or obtaining the whole of) the tax advantage in question, or

(b) adjustments are made on a basis such as is mentioned in paragraph (a).

16(1) Condition F is that–

(a) a person has made a return, claim or election on the basis that a relevant tax advantage arises,

(b) the tax advantage, or part of the tax advantage would not arise if a particular avoidance-related rule (see paragraph 25) applies in relation to the person's tax affairs,

(c) it is held in a judicial ruling that the relevant avoidance-related rule applies in relation to the person's tax affairs, and

(d) the judicial ruling is final.

16(2) For the purposes of sub-paragraph (1) **"relevant tax advantage"** means a tax advantage which the arrangements might be expected to enable the person to obtain.

Part 3 – Relevant Defeats: Associated Persons

ATTRIBUTION OF RELEVANT DEFEATS

17(1) Sub-paragraph (2) applies if–

(a) there is (or has been) a person ("Q"),

(b) arrangements ("the defeated arrangements") have been entered into,

(c) an event occurs such that either–

(i) there is a relevant defeat in relation to Q and the defeated arrangements, or

(ii) the condition in sub-paragraph (i) would be met if Q had not ceased to exist,

(d) at the time of that event a person ("P") is carrying on a business as a promoter (or is carrying on what would be such a business under the condition in paragraph 3(2)), and

(e) Condition 1 or 2 is met in relation to Q and P.

17(2) The event is treated for all purposes of this Part of this Act as a relevant defeat in relation to P and the defeated arrangements (whether or not it is also a relevant defeat in relation to Q, and regardless of whether or not P existed at any time when those arrangements were promoted arrangements in relation to Q).

17(3) Condition 1 is that–
(a) P is not an individual,
(b) at a time when the defeated arrangements were promoted arrangements in relation to Q–
(i) P was a relevant body controlled by Q, or
(ii) Q was a relevant body controlled by P, and
(c) at the time of the event mentioned in sub-paragraph (1)(c)–
(i) Q is a relevant body controlled by P,
(ii) P is a relevant body controlled by Q, or
(iii) P and Q are relevant bodies controlled by a third person.

17(4) Condition 2 is that–
(a) P and Q are relevant bodies,
(b) at a time when the defeated arrangements were promoted arrangements in relation to Q, a third person ("C") controlled Q, and
(c) C controls P at the time of the event mentioned in sub-paragraph (1)(c).

17(5) For the purposes of sub-paragraphs (3)(b) and (4)(b), the question whether arrangements are promoted arrangements in relation to Q at any time is to be determined on the assumption that the reference to **"design"** in paragraph (b) of section 235(3) (definition of "promoter" in relation to relevant arrangements) is omitted.

DEEMED DEFEAT NOTICES

18(1) This paragraph applies if–
(a) an authorised officer becomes aware at any time ("the relevant time") that a relevant defeat has occurred in relation to a person ("P") who is carrying on a business as a promoter,
(b) there have occurred, more than 3 years before the relevant time–
(i) one third party defeat, or
(ii) two third party defeats, and
(c) conditions A1 and B1 (in a case within paragraph (b)(i)), or conditions A2 and B2 (in a case within paragraph (b)(ii)), are met.

18(2) Where this paragraph applies by virtue of sub-paragraph (1)(b)(i), this Part of this Act has effect as if an authorised officer had (with due authority), at the time of the time of the third party defeat, given P a single defeat notice under section 241A(2) in respect of it.

18(3) Where this paragraph applies by virtue of sub-paragraph (1)(b)(ii), this Part of this Act has effect as if an authorised officer had (with due authority), at the time of the second of the two third party defeats, given P a double defeat notice under section 241A(3) in respect of the two third party defeats.

18(4) Section 241A(8) has no effect in relation to a notice treated as given as mentioned in subsection (2) or (3).

18(5) Condition A1 is that–
(a) a conduct notice or a single or double defeat notice has been given to the other person (see sub-paragraph (9)) in respect of the third party defeat,
(b) at the time of the third party defeat an authorised officer would have had power by virtue of paragraph 17 to give P a defeat notice in respect of the third party defeat, had the officer been aware that it was a relevant defeat in relation to P, and
(c) so far as the authorised officer mentioned in sub-paragraph (1)(a) is aware, the conditions for giving P a defeat notice in respect of the third party defeat have never been met (ignoring this paragraph).

18(6) Condition A2 is that–
(a) a conduct notice or a single or double defeat notice has been given to the other person (see sub-paragraph (9)) in respect of each, or both, of the third party defeats,
(b) at the time of the second third party defeat an authorised officer would have had power by virtue of paragraph 17 to give P a double defeat notice in respect of the third party defeats, had the officer been aware that either of the third party defeats was a relevant defeat in relation to P, and
(c) so far as the authorised officer mentioned in sub-paragraph (1)(a) is aware, the conditions for giving P a defeat notice in respect of those third party defeats (or either of them) have never been met (ignoring this paragraph).

18(7) Condition B1 is that, had an authorised officer given P a defeat notice in respect of the third party defeat at the time of that relevant defeat, that defeat notice would still have effect at the relevant time (see sub-paragraph (1)).

18(8) Condition B2 is that, had an authorised officer given P a defeat notice in respect of the two third party defeats at the time of the second of those relevant defeats, that defeat notice would still have effect at the relevant time.

18(9) In this paragraph **"third party defeat"** means a relevant defeat which has occurred in relation to a person other than P.

MEANING OF "RELEVANT BODY" AND "CONTROL"

19(1) In this Part of this Schedule **"relevant body"** means–

(a) a body corporate, or

(b) a partnership.

19(2) For the purposes of this Part of this Schedule a person controls a body corporate if the person has power to secure that the affairs of the body corporate are conducted in accordance with the person's wishes–

(a) by means of the holding of shares or the possession of voting power in relation to the body corporate or any other relevant body,

(b) as a result of any powers conferred by the articles of association or other document regulating the body corporate or any other relevant body, or

(c) by means of controlling a partnership.

19(3) For the purposes of this Part of this Schedule a person controls a partnership if the person is a controlling member or the managing partner of the partnership.

19(4) In this paragraph **"controlling member"** has the same meaning as in Schedule 36 (partnerships).

19(5) In this section **"managing partner"**, in relation to a partnership, means the member of the partnership who directs, or is on a day-to-day level in control of, the management of the business of the partnership.

Part 4 – Meeting Section 237A Conditions: Bodies Corporate and Partnerships

RELEVANT BODIES CONTROLLED ETC BY OTHER PERSONS TREATED AS MEETING SECTION 237A CONDITION

20(1) A relevant body is treated as meeting a section 237A condition at the section 237A(2) relevant time if any of Conditions A to C is met.

20(2) Condition A is that–

(a) a person met the section 237A condition at a time when the person was a promoter, and

(b) the person controls or has significant influence over the relevant body at the section 237A(2) relevant time.

20(3) Condition B is that–

(a) a person met the section 237A condition at a time when the person controlled or had significant influence over the relevant body,

(b) the relevant body was a promoter at that time, and

(c) the person controls or has significant influence over the relevant body at the section 237A(2) relevant time.

20(4) Condition C is that–

(a) two or more persons together controlled or had significant influence over the relevant body at a time when one of those persons met the section 237A condition,

(b) the relevant body was a promoter at that time, and

(c) those persons together control or have significant influence over the relevant body at the section 237A(2) relevant time.

20(5) Sub-paragraph (1) does not apply where the person referred to in sub-paragraph (2)(a), (3)(a), or (4)(a) as meeting a section 237A condition is an individual.

20(6) For the purposes of sub-paragraph (2) it does not matter whether the relevant body existed at the time referred to in sub-paragraph (2)(a).

History – Para. 20 substituted by FA 2017, s. 24(3), with effect for the purposes of determining whether a person meets a FA 2014, s. 237A condition in a period of three years ending on or after 8 March 2017. Former para. 20 read as follows:

"TREATING PERSONS UNDER ANOTHER'S CONTROL AS MEETING SECTION 237A CONDITION

20(1) A relevant body ("RB") is treated as meeting a section 237A condition at the section 237A(2) relevant time if–

(a) that condition was met by a person ("C") at a time when–

(i) C was carrying on a business as a promoter, or

(ii) RB was carrying on a business as a promoter and C controlled RB, and

(b) RB is controlled by C at the section 237A(2) relevant time.

20(2) Sub-paragraph (1) does not apply if C is an individual.

20(3) For the purposes of determining whether the requirements of sub-paragraph (1) are met by reason of meeting the requirement in sub-paragraph (1)(a)(i), it does not matter whether RB existed at the time when C met the section 237A condition.".

PERSONS WHO CONTROL ETC A RELEVANT BODY TREATED AS MEETING A SECTION 237A CONDITION

21(1) If at a time when a person controlled or had significant influence over a relevant body–

(a) the relevant body met a section 237A condition, and

(b) the relevant body, or another relevant body which the person controlled or had significant influence over, was a promoter,

the person is treated as meeting the section 237A condition at the section 237A(2) relevant time.

21(2) It does not matter whether any relevant body referred to sub-paragraph (1) exists at the section 237A(2) relevant time.

History – Para. 21 substituted by FA 2017, s. 24(3), with effect for the purposes of determining whether a person meets a FA 2014, s. 237A condition in a period of three years ending on or after 8 March 2017. Former para. 21 read as follows:

"TREATING PERSONS IN CONTROL OF OTHERS AS MEETING SECTION 237A CONDITION

21(1) A person other than an individual is treated as meeting a section 237A condition at the section 237A(2) relevant time if–

(a) a relevant body ("A") met the condition at a time when A was controlled by the person, and

(b) at the time mentioned in paragraph (a) A, or another relevant body ("B") which was also at that time controlled by the person, carried on a business as a promoter.

21(2) For the purposes of determining whether the requirements of sub-paragraph (1) are met it does not matter whether A or B (or neither) exists at the section 237A(2) relevant time.".

RELEVANT BODIES CONTROLLED ETC BY THE SAME PERSON TREATED AS MEETING A SECTION 237A CONDITION

22(1) If–

(a) a person controlled or had significant influence over a relevant body at a time when it met a section 237A condition, and

(b) at that time that body, or another relevant body which the person controlled or had significant influence over, was a promoter,

any relevant body which the person controls or has significant influence over at the section 237A(2) relevant time is treated as meeting the section 237A condition at the section 237A(2) relevant time.

22(2) If–

(a) two or more persons together controlled or had significant influence over a relevant body at a time when it met a section 237A condition, and

(b) at that time that body, or another relevant body which those persons together controlled or had significant influence over, was a promoter,

any relevant body which those persons together control or have significant influence over at the section 237A(2) relevant time is treated as meeting the section 237A condition at the section 237A(2) relevant time.

22(3) It does not matter whether–

(a) a relevant body referred to in sub-paragraph (1)(a) or (b) or (2)(a) or (b) exists at the section 237A(2) relevant time, or

(b) a relevant body existing at the section 237A(2) relevant time existed at the time referred to in sub-paragraph (1)(a) or (2)(a).

History – Para. 22 substituted by FA 2017, s. 24(3), with effect for the purposes of determining whether a person meets a FA 2014, s. 237A condition in a period of three years ending on or after 8 March 2017. Former para. 22 read as follows:

"TREATING PERSONS CONTROLLED BY THE SAME PERSON AS MEETING SECTION 237A CONDITION

22(1) A relevant body ("RB") is treated as meeting a section 237A condition at the section 237A(2) relevant time if–

(a) another relevant body met that condition at a time ("time T") when it was controlled by a person ("C"),

(b) at time T, there was a relevant body controlled by C which carried on a business as a promoter, and

(c) RB is controlled by C at the section 237A(2) relevant time.

22(2) For the purposes of determining whether the requirements of sub-paragraph (1) are met it does not matter whether–

(a) RB existed at time T, or

(b) any relevant body (other than RB) by reason of which the requirements of sub-paragraph (1) are met exists at the section 237A(2) relevant time.".

INTERPRETATION

23(1) In this Part of this Schedule–

"control" and **"significant influence"** have the same meanings as in Part 4 of Schedule 34 (see paragraph 13A(5) to (11));

references to a person being a promoter are to the person carrying on business as a promoter;

"relevant body" has the same meaning as in Part 3 of this Schedule;

"section 237A(2) relevant time" means the time referred to in section 237A(2);

"section 237A condition" means any of the conditions in section 237A(11), (12) and (13).

23(2) For the purposes of paragraphs 20 to 22, the condition in section 237A(11) (occurrence of 3 relevant defeats in the 3 years ending with the relevant time) is taken to have been met by a person at any time if at least 3 relevant defeats have occurred in relation to the person in the period of 3 years ending with that time.

History – In para. 23(1), definition of "control" substituted by FA 2017, s. 24(4)(a), with effect for the purposes of determining whether a person meets a FA 2014, s. 237A condition in a period of three years ending on or after 8 March 2017.
In para. 23(2), the words "20 to 22" substituted for the words "20(1)(a), 21(1)(a) and 22(1)(a)" by FA 2017, s. 24(4)(b), with effect for the purposes of determining whether a person meets a FA 2014, s. 237A condition in a period of three years ending on or after 8 March 2017.

Part 5 – Supplementary

"ADJUSTMENTS"

24 In this Schedule **"adjustments"** means any adjustments, whether by way of an assessment, the modification of an assessment or return, the amendment or disallowance of a claim, the entering into of a contract settlement or otherwise (and references to **"making"** adjustments accordingly include securing that adjustments are made by entering into a contract settlement).

MEANING OF "AVOIDANCE-RELATED RULE"

25(1) In this Schedule **"avoidance-related rule"** means a rule in Category 1 or 2.

25(2) A rule is in Category 1 if–

(a) it refers (in whatever terms) to the purpose or main purpose or purposes of a transaction, arrangements or any other action or matter, and

(b) to whether or not the purpose in question is or involves the avoidance of tax or the obtaining of any advantage in relation to tax (however described).

25(3) A rule is also in Category 1 if it refers (in whatever terms) to–

(a) expectations as to what are, or may be, the expected benefits of a transaction, arrangements or any other action or matter, and

(b) whether or not the avoidance of tax or the obtaining of any advantage in relation to tax (however described) is such a benefit.

For the purposes of paragraph (b) it does not matter whether the reference is (for instance) to the **"sole or main benefit"** or **"one of the main benefits"** or any other reference to a benefit.

25(4) A rule falls within Category 2 if as a result of the rule a person may be treated differently for tax purposes depending on whether or not purposes referred to in the rule (for instance the purposes of an actual or contemplated action or enterprise) are (or are shown to be) commercial purposes.

25(5) For example, a rule in the following form would fall within Category 1 and within Category 2–

"Example rule

Section X does not apply to a company in respect of a transaction if the company shows that the transaction meets Condition A or B.

Condition A is that the transaction is effected–

(a) for genuine commercial reasons, or

(b) in the ordinary course of managing investments.

Condition B is that the avoidance of tax is not the main object or one of the main objects of the *transaction*."

"DOTAS ARRANGEMENTS"

26(1) For the purposes of this Schedule arrangements are **"DOTAS arrangements"** at any time if at that time a person–

(a) has provided, information in relation to the arrangements under section 308(3), 309 or 310 of FA 2004, or

(b) has failed to comply with any of those provisions in relation to the arrangements.

26(2) But for the purposes of this Schedule **"DOTAS arrangements"** does not include arrangements in respect of which HMRC has given notice under section 312(6) of FA 2004 (notice that promoters not under duty to notify client of reference number).

26(3) For the purposes of sub-paragraph (1) a person who would be required to provide information under subsection (3) of section 308 of FA 2004–

(a) but for the fact that the arrangements implement a proposal in respect of which notice has been given under subsection (1) of that section, or

(b) but for subsection (4A), (4C) or (5) of that section,

is treated as providing the information at the end of the period referred to in subsection (3) of that section.

DISCLOSABLE VAT OR OTHER INDIRECT TAX ARRANGEMENTS

26A(1) For the purposes of this Schedule arrangements are **"disclosable VAT or other indirect tax arrangements"** at any time if at that time–

(a) the arrangements are disclosable Schedule 11A arrangements, or

(b) sub-paragraph (2) applies.

26A(2) This sub-paragraph applies if a person–

(a) has provided information in relation to the arrangements under paragraph 12(1), 17(2) or 18(2) of Schedule 17 to F[(No. 2)]A 2017, or

(b) has failed to comply with any of those provisions in relation to the arrangements.

26A(3) But for the purposes of this Schedule arrangements in respect of which HMRC have given notice under paragraph 23(6) of that Schedule (notice that promoters not under duty to notify client of reference number) are not to be regarded as disclosable VAT or other indirect tax arrangements.

26A(4) For the purposes of sub-paragraph (2) a person who would be required to provide information under paragraph 12(1) of that Schedule–

(a) but for the fact that the arrangements implement a proposal in respect of which notice has been given under paragraph 11(1) of that Schedule, or

(b) but for paragraph 13, 14 or 15 of that Schedule,

is treated as providing the information at the end of the period referred to in paragraph 12(1).

History – Para. 26A inserted by F(No. 2)A 2017, s. 66 and Sch. 17, para. 54(4), with effect so far as necessary for enabling the making of regulations under that Schedule from 16 November 2017 (Royal Assent) and from 1 January 2018 for all other purposes.

"DISCLOSABLE SCHEDULE 11A VAT ARRANGEMENTS"

History – In the heading the words "Schedule 11A" inserted by F(No. 2)A 2017, s. 66 and Sch. 17, para. 54(5), with effect so far as necessary for enabling the making of regulations under that Schedule from 16 November 2017 (Royal Assent) and from 1 January 2018 for all other purposes.

27 For the purposes of paragraph 26 arrangements are **"disclosable Schedule 11A VAT arrangements"** at any time if at that time–

(a) a person has complied with paragraph 6 of Schedule 11A to VATA 1994 in relation to the arrangements (duty to notify Commissioners),

(b) a person under a duty to comply with that paragraph in relation to the arrangements has failed to do so, or

(c) a reference number has been allocated to the scheme under paragraph 9 of that Schedule (voluntary notification of avoidance scheme which is not a designated scheme).

History – In para. 27 the words "paragraph 26A" substituted for the words "this Schedule" and the words "Schedule 11A" inserted by F(No. 2)A 2017, s. 66 and Sch. 17, para. 54(6), with effect so far as necessary for enabling the making of regulations under that Schedule from 16 November 2017 (Royal Assent) and from 1 January 2018 for all other purposes.

PARAGRAPHS 26 TO 27: SUPPLEMENTARY

History – In the heading the words "to 27" substituted for the words "and 27" by F(No. 2)A 2017, s. 66 and Sch. 17, para. 54(7), with effect so far as necessary for enabling the making of regulations under that Schedule from 16 November 2017 (Royal Assent) and from 1 January 2018 for all other purposes.

28(1) A person **"fails to comply"** with any provision mentioned in paragraph 26(1)(a), 26A(2)(a) or 27(b) if and only if any of the conditions in sub-paragraphs (2) to (4) is met.

28(2) The condition in this sub-paragraph is that–

(a) the tribunal has determined that the person has failed to comply with the provision concerned,

(b) the appeal period has ended, and

(c) the determination has not been overturned on appeal.

28(3) The condition in this sub-paragraph is that–

(a) the tribunal has determined for the purposes of section 118(2) of TMA 1970 that the person is to be deemed not to have failed to comply with the provision concerned as the person had a reasonable excuse for not doing the thing required to be done,

(b) the appeal period has ended, and

(c) the determination has not been overturned on appeal.

28(4) The condition in this sub-paragraph is that the person admitted in writing to HMRC that the person has failed to comply with the provision concerned.

28(5) In this paragraph **"the appeal period"** means–

(a) the period during which an appeal could be brought against the determination of the tribunal, or

(b) where an appeal mentioned in paragraph (a) has been brought, the period during which that appeal has not been finally determined, withdrawn or otherwise disposed of.

History – In para. 28(1) the words ", 26A(2)(a)" (the comma assumed by Croner-i) inserted by F(No. 2)A 2017, s. 66 and Sch. 17, para. 54(8), with effect so far as necessary for enabling the making of regulations under that Schedule from 16 November 2017 (Royal Assent) and from 1 January 2018 for all other purposes.

"FINAL" COUNTERACTION

29 For the purposes of this Schedule the counteraction of a tax advantage or of arrangements is **"final"** when the assessment or adjustments made to effect the counteraction, and any amounts arising as a result of the assessment or adjustments, can no longer be varied, on appeal or otherwise.

INHERITANCE TAX, STAMP DUTY RESERVE TAX, VAT AND PETROLEUM REVENUE TAX

30(1) In this Schedule, in relation to inheritance tax, each of the following is treated as a return–

(a) an account delivered by a person under section 216 or 217 of IHTA 1984 (including an account delivered in accordance with regulations under section 256 of that Act);

(b) a statement or declaration which amends or is otherwise connected with such an account produced by the person who delivered the account;

(c) information or a document provided by a person in accordance with regulations under section 256 of that Act;

and such a return is treated as made by the person in question.

30(2) In this Schedule references to an assessment to tax, in relation to inheritance tax, stamp duty reserve tax and petroleum revenue tax, include a determination.

30(3) In this Schedule an expression used in relation to VAT has the same meaning as in VATA 1994.

POWER TO AMEND

31(1) The Treasury may by regulations amend this Schedule (apart from this paragraph).

31(2) An amendment by virtue of sub-paragraph (1) may, in particular, add, vary or remove conditions or categories (or otherwise vary the meaning of "avoidance-related rule").

31(3) Regulations under sub-paragraph (1) may include any amendment of this Part of this Act that is appropriate in consequence of an amendment made by virtue of sub-paragraph (1).

SCHEDULE 35 – PROMOTERS OF TAX AVOIDANCE SCHEMES: PENALTIES

Section 274

INTRODUCTION

1 In this Schedule a reference to an **"information duty"** is to a duty arising under any of the following provisions to provide information or produce a document–

(a) section 255 (duty to provide information or produce document);
(b) section 257 (ongoing duty to provide information);
(c) section 258 (duty of person dealing with non-resident promoter);
(d) section 259 (monitored promoter: duty to provide information about clients);
(e) section 260 (intermediaries: duty to provide information about clients);
(f) section 261 (duty to provide information about clients following enquiry);
(g) section 262 (information required for monitoring compliance with conduct notice);
(h) section 263 (information about monitored promoter's address).

PENALTIES FOR FAILURE TO COMPLY

2(1) A person who fails to comply with a duty imposed by or under this Part mentioned in column 1 of the Table is liable to a penalty not exceeding the amount shown in relation to that provision in column 2 of the Table.

Table

Column 1 **Provision**	Column 2 **Maximum penalty (£)**
Section 249(1) (duty to notify clients of monitoring notice)	5,000
Section 249(3) (duty to publicise monitoring notice)	1,000,000
Section 249(10) (duty to include information on correspondence etc)	1,000,000
Section 251 (duty of promoter to notify clients and intermediaries of reference number)	5,000
Section 252 (duty of those notified to notify others of promoter's number)	5,000
Section 253 (duty to notify HMRC of reference number)	the relevant amount (see sub-paragraph (3))
Section 255 (duty to provide information or produce document)	1,000,000
Section 257 (ongoing duty to provide information or produce document)	1,000,000
Section 258 (duty of person dealing with non-resident promoter)	1,000,000
Section 259 (monitored promoter: duty to provide information about clients)	5,000
Section 260 (intermediaries: duty to provide information about clients)	5,000
Section 261 (duty to provide information about clients following an enquiry)	10,000
Section 262 (duty to provide information required to monitor compliance with conduct notice)	5,000
Section 263 (duty to provide information about address)	5,000
Section 265 (duty to provide information to promoter)	5,000

2(2) In relation to a failure to comply with section 249(1), 251, 252, 259 or 260 the maximum penalty specified in column 2 of the Table is a maximum penalty which may be imposed in respect of each person to whom the failure relates.

PRT Statutes

2(3) In relation to a failure to comply with section 253, the **"relevant amount"** is–

(a) £5,000, unless paragraph (b) or (c) applies;

(b) £7,500, where a person has previously failed to comply with section 253 on one (and only one) occasion during the period of 36 months ending with the date on which the current failure occurred;

(c) £10,000, where a person has previously failed to comply with section 253 on two or more occasions during the period mentioned in paragraph (b).

2(4) The amount of a penalty imposed under sub-paragraph (1) is to be arrived at after taking account of all relevant considerations, including the desirability of setting it at a level which appears appropriate for deterring the person, or other persons, from similar failures to comply on future occasions having regard (in particular)–

(a) in the case of a penalty imposed for a failure to comply with section 255 or 257, to the amount of fees received, or likely to have been received, by the person in connection with the monitored proposal, arrangements implementing the monitored proposal or monitored arrangements to which the information or document required as a result of section 255 or 257 relates;

(b) in the case of a penalty imposed in relation to a failure to comply with section 258(4) or (5), to the amount of any tax advantage gained, or sought to be gained, by the person in relation to the monitored arrangements or the arrangements implementing the monitored proposal.

DAILY DEFAULT PENALTIES FOR FAILURE TO COMPLY

3(1) If the failure to comply with an information duty continues after a penalty is imposed under paragraph 2(1), the person is liable to a further penalty or penalties not exceeding the relevant sum for each day on which the failure continues after the day on which the penalty under paragraph 2(1) was imposed.

3(2) In sub-paragraph (1) **"the relevant sum"** means–

(a) £10,000, in a case where the maximum penalty which could have been imposed for the failure was £1,000,000;

(b) £600, in cases not falling within paragraph (a).

PENALTIES FOR INACCURATE INFORMATION AND DOCUMENTS

4(1) If–

(a) in complying with an information duty, a person provides inaccurate information or produces a document that contains an inaccuracy, and

(b) condition A, B or C is met,

the person is liable to a penalty not exceeding the relevant sum.

4(2) Condition A is that the inaccuracy is careless or deliberate.

4(3) An inaccuracy is careless if it is due to a failure by the person to take reasonable care.

4(4) For the purpose of determining whether or not a person who is a monitored promoter took reasonable care, reliance on legal advice is to be disregarded if either–

(a) the advice was not based on a full and accurate description of the facts, or

(b) the conclusions in the advice that the person relied on were unreasonable.

4(5) For the purpose of determining whether or not a person who complies with a duty under section 258 took reasonable care, reliance on legal advice is to be disregarded if the advice was given or procured by the monitored promoter mentioned in subsection (1) of that section.

4(6) Condition B is that the person knows of the inaccuracy at the time the information is provided or the document produced but does not inform HMRC at that time.

4(7) Condition C is that the person–

(a) discovers the inaccuracy some time later, and

(b) fails to take reasonable steps to inform HMRC.

4(8) The **"relevant sum"** means–

(a) £1,000,000, where the information is provided or document produced in compliance with a duty under section 255, 257 or 258;

(b) £10,000, where the information is provided in compliance with a duty under section 261;

(c) £5,000, where the information is provided or document produced in compliance with a duty under section 259, 260, 262 or 263.

4(9) If the information or document contains more than one inaccuracy, one penalty is payable under this paragraph whatever the number of inaccuracies.

POWER TO CHANGE AMOUNT OF PENALTIES

5(1) If it appears to the Treasury that there has been a change in the value of money since the last relevant date, they may by regulations substitute for the sums for the time being specified in paragraph 2, 3 or 4 such other sums as appear to them to be justified by the change.

5(2) Regulations under sub-paragraph (1) may include any amendment of paragraph 10(b) that is appropriate in consequence of an amendment made by virtue of sub-paragraph (1).

5(3) The **"relevant date"**, in relation to a specified sum, means–

(a) the date on which this Act is passed, and

(b) each date on which the power conferred by sub-paragraph (1) has been exercised in relation to that sum.

CONCEALING, DESTROYING ETC DOCUMENTS FOLLOWING IMPOSITION OF A DUTY TO PROVIDE INFORMATION

6(1) A person must not conceal, destroy or otherwise dispose of, or arrange for the concealment, destruction or disposal of, a document which is subject to a duty under section 255, 257 or 262.

6(2) Sub-paragraph (1) does not apply if the person acts after the document has been produced to an officer of Revenue and Customs in accordance with the duty, unless the officer has notified the person in writing that the document must continue to be available for inspection (and has not withdrawn the notification).

6(3) Sub-paragraph (1) does not apply, in a case to which section 268(1) applies, if the person acts after the expiry of the period of 6 months beginning with the day on which a copy of the document was produced in accordance with that section unless, before the expiry of that period, an officer of Revenue and Customs makes a request for the original document under section 268(2)(b).

6(4) A person who conceals, destroys or otherwise disposes of, or arranges for the concealment, destruction or disposal of, a document in breach of sub-paragraph (1), is taken to have failed to comply with the duty to produce the document under the provision concerned (but see sub-paragraph (5)).

6(5) If a person conceals, destroys or otherwise disposes of, or arranges for the concealment, destruction or disposal of, a document which is subject to a duty under more than one of the provisions mentioned in sub-paragraph (1) then–

(a) in a case where a duty under section 255 applies, the person will be taken to have failed to comply only with that provision, or

(b) in a case where a duty under section 255 does not apply, the person will be taken to have failed to comply only with section 257.

CONCEALING, DESTROYING ETC DOCUMENTS FOLLOWING INFORMAL NOTIFICATION

7(1) A person must not conceal, destroy or otherwise dispose of, or arrange for the concealment, destruction or disposal of, a document if an officer of Revenue and Customs has informed the person in writing that the person is, or is likely, to be given a notice under 255, 257 or 262 the effect of which will, or is likely to, require the production of the document.

7(2) Sub-paragraph (1) does not apply if the person acts–

(a) at least 6 months after the person was, or was last, informed as described in sub-paragraph (1), or

(b) after the person becomes subject to a duty under 255, 257 or 262 which requires the document to be produced.

7(3) A person who conceals, destroys or otherwise disposes of, or arranges for the concealment, destruction or disposal of, a document in breach of sub-paragraph (1), is taken to have failed to comply with the duty to produce the document under the provision concerned (but see sub-paragraph (4)).

7(4) If a person conceals, destroys or otherwise disposes of, or arranges for the concealment, destruction or disposal of, a document which is subject to a duty under more than one of the provisions mentioned in sub-paragraph (1) then–

(a) in a case where a duty under section 255 applies, the person will be taken to have failed to comply only with that provision, or

(b) in a case where a duty under section 255 does not apply, the person will be taken to have failed to comply only with section 257.

FAILURE TO COMPLY WITH TIME LIMIT

8 A failure to do anything required to be done within a limited period of time does not give rise to liability to a penalty under this Schedule if the person did it within such further time, if any, as an officer of Revenue and Customs or the tribunal may have allowed.

REASONABLE EXCUSE

9(1) Liability to a penalty under this Schedule does not arise if there is a reasonable excuse for the failure.

9(2) For the purposes of this paragraph–

(a) an insufficiency of funds is not a reasonable excuse unless attributable to events outside the person's control,

(b) if the person relies on any other person to do anything, that is not a reasonable excuse unless the first person took reasonable care to avoid the failure,

(c) if the person had a reasonable excuse for the failure but the excuse has ceased, the person is to be treated as having continued to have the excuse if the failure is remedied without unreasonable delay after the excuse ceased,

(d) reliance on legal advice is to be taken automatically not to constitute a reasonable excuse where the person is a monitored promoter if either–

(i) the advice was not based on a full and accurate description of the facts, or

(ii) the conclusions in the advice that the person relied on were unreasonable, and

(e) reliance on legal advice is to be taken automatically not to constitute a reasonable excuse in the case of a penalty for failure to comply with section 258, if the advice was given or procured by the monitored promoter mentioned in subsection (1) of that section.

ASSESSMENT OF PENALTY AND APPEALS

10 Part 10 of TMA 1970 (penalties, etc) has effect as if–

(a) the reference in section 100(1) to the Taxes Acts were read as a reference to the Taxes Acts and this Schedule,

(b) in subsection (2) of section 100, there were inserted a reference to a penalty under this Schedule, other than a penalty under paragraph 3 of this Schedule in respect of which the relevant sum is £600.

INTEREST ON PENALTIES

11(1) A penalty under this Schedule is to carry interest at the rate applicable under section 178 of FA 1989 from the date it is determined until payment.

11(2) [Inserts FA 1989, s. 178(2)(u).]

DOUBLE JEOPARDY

12 A person is not liable to a penalty under this Schedule in respect of anything in respect of which the person has been convicted of an offence.

OVERLAPPING PENALTIES

13 A person is not liable to a penalty under–

(a) Schedule 24 to the FA 2007 (penalties for errors),

(b) Part 7 of FA 2004, or

(c) any other provision which is prescribed,

by reason of any failure to include in any return or account a reference number required by section 253.

SCHEDULE 36 – PROMOTERS OF TAX AVOIDANCE SCHEMES: PARTNERSHIPS

Section 281

Part 1 – Partnerships as Persons

"PERSON" INCLUDES A PARTNERSHIP

1(1) Persons carrying on a business in partnership–

(a) are regarded as a person for the purposes of this Part of this Act;

(b) are referred to in this Part as a **"partnership"**.

1(2) But in this Part of this Act **"partnership"** does not include a body of persons forming a legal person that is distinct from themselves (and paragraphs 2 to 21 may accordingly be disregarded in applying this Part of this Act to such a body of persons).

1(3) In the references in this Part to carrying on a business in partnership, **"partnership"** has the same meaning as in the Partnership Act 1890.

CONTINUITY OF PARTNERSHIPS

2 A partnership is regarded for the purposes of this Part of this Act as continuing to be the same partnership (and the same person) regardless of a change in membership, provided that a person who was a member before the change remains a member after the change.

MEETING OF CONDITIONS

3(1) Accordingly, for the purposes of this Part of this Act a partnership is taken–

(a) to have done any act that bound the members, and

(b) to have failed to comply with any obligation of the firm which the members failed to comply with;

but see sub-paragraph (3).

3(2) In sub-paragraph (1), **"the members"** means those who were the members of the partnership or (in the case of a limited partnership) the general partners of the partnership at the time when the act was done or the failure to comply occurred.

3(3) Where a member of a partnership ("M") has done, or failed to do, an act at any time ("the earlier time"), the partnership is not treated at any later time as having done, or failed to do, that act unless–

(a) M, or

(b) another person who was a member of the partnership at the earlier time,

is a member of the partnership at the later time.

3(4) In this paragraph **"firm"** has the same meaning as in the Partnership Act 1890.

THRESHOLD CONDITIONS: ACTIONS OF PARTNERS IN A PERSONAL CAPACITY

4 [Omitted by FA 2015, s. 119 and Sch. 19, para. 5(a).]

History – Para. 4 (and the heading before it) omitted by FA 2015, s. 119 and Sch. 19, para. 5(a), with effect for the purposes of determining whether a person meets a threshold condition in a period of three years ending on or after 26 March 2015 (Royal Assent). Former para. 4 read as follows:

"**4(1)** Sub-paragraph (2) applies where–

(a) a relevant threshold condition is met by a person ("P") at a time ("the earlier time") when P is a controlling member, or managing partner, of a partnership,

(b) a determination under section 237 is made at a later time in relation to the partnership, and

(c) P is a controlling member, or managing partner, of the partnership at the time of the determination.

4(2) The partnership is regarded as having met the threshold condition at the earlier time (regardless of whether or not the partnership was bound by the act or omission as a result of which P met the threshold condition).

4(3) **"Relevant threshold condition"** means a threshold condition specified in any of the following paragraphs of Schedule 34–

(a) paragraph 2 (deliberate tax defaulters);

(b) paragraph 4 (dishonest tax agents);

(c) paragraph 6 (criminal offences);

(d) paragraph 7 (opinion notice of GAAR advisory panel);

(e) paragraph 8 (disciplinary action by a professional body);

(f) paragraph 9 (disciplinary action by a regulatory authority);

(g) paragraph 10 (failure to comply with information notice)."

Part 2 – Conduct Notices and Monitoring Notices

DEFEAT NOTICES

4A A defeat notice that is given to a partnership must state that it is a partnership defeat notice.

History – Para. 4A (and the heading before it) inserted by FA 2016, s. 160(11), with effect from 15 September 2016 (Royal Assent).

CONDUCT NOTICES

5(1) A conduct notice that is given to a partnership must state that it is a partnership conduct notice.

5(2) In accordance with paragraphs 1 and 2, where the person to whom a conduct notice is given is a partnership, section 238 authorises the imposition of conditions relating to–

(a) the persons who are members of the partnership when the conduct notice is given, and

(b) any person who becomes a member of the partnership after the conduct notice is given.

MONITORING NOTICES

6 A monitoring notice that is given to a partnership must state that it is a partnership monitoring notice.

PERSON CONTINUING TO CARRY ON PARTNERSHIP BUSINESS AS A SOLE TRADER

7(1) This paragraph applies where–

(a) a person or persons have ceased to be members of a partnership,

(b) immediately before the cessation, a defeat notice, conduct notice or monitoring notice had effect in relation to the partnership, and

(c) immediately after the cessation, a person who was a member of the partnership immediately before the cessation is carrying on the business of the partnership, but not in partnership.

7(2) Where this paragraph applies, the defeat notice, conduct notice or monitoring notice continues (despite paragraphs 1 and 2) to have effect in relation to the person mentioned in sub-paragraph (1)(c) (but, in relation to times when the business is not being carried on in partnership, the notice is not regarded for the purposes of this Part of this Act as a notice that has been given to a partnership.)

History – In para. 7(1)(b), the words "defeat notice," inserted by FA 2016, s. 160(12), with effect from 15 September 2016 (Royal Assent).

In para. 7(2), the words "defeat notice," inserted by FA 2016, s. 160(13), with effect from 15 September 2016 (Royal Assent).

PERSONS LEAVING PARTNERSHIP: DEFEAT NOTICES

7A(1) Sub-paragraphs (2) and (3) apply where–

(a) a person ("P") who was a controlling member of a partnership at the time when a defeat notice ("the original notice") was given to the partnership has ceased to be a member of the partnership,

(b) the defeat notice had effect in relation to the partnership at the time of that cessation, and

(c) P is carrying on a business as a promoter.

7A(2) An authorised officer may give P a defeat notice.

7A(3) If P is carrying on a business as a promoter in partnership with one or more other persons and is a controlling member of that partnership ("the new partnership"), an authorised officer may give a defeat notice to the new partnership.

7A(4) A defeat notice given under sub-paragraph (3) ceases to have effect if P ceases to be a member of the new partnership.

7A(5) A notice under sub-paragraph (2) or (3) may not be given after the original notice has ceased to have effect.

7A(6) A defeat notice given under sub-paragraph (2) or (3) is given in respect of the relevant defeat or relevant defeats to which the original notice relates.

History – Para. 7A (and the heading before it) inserted by FA 2016, s. 160(14), with effect from 15 September 2016 (Royal Assent).

PERSONS LEAVING A PARTNERSHIP: CONDUCT NOTICES

8(1) Sub-paragraphs (2) and (3) apply where–

(a) a person ("P") who was a controlling member of a partnership at the time when a conduct notice ("the original notice") was given to the partnership has ceased to be a member of the partnership,

(b) the conduct notice had effect in relation to the partnership at the time of that cessation, and

(c) P is carrying on a business as a promoter.

8(2) An authorised officer may give P a conduct notice.

8(3) If P is carrying on a business as a promoter in partnership with one or more other persons and is a controlling member of that partnership ("the new partnership"), an authorised officer may give a conduct notice to the new partnership.

8(4) A conduct notice given under sub-paragraph (3) ceases to have effect if P ceases to be a member of the new partnership.

8(5) A notice under sub-paragraph (2) or (3) may not be given after the termination date of the original notice (under section 241(2)(a) or (b)).

PERSONS LEAVING A PARTNERSHIP: MONITORING NOTICES

9(1) Sub-paragraphs (2) and (3) apply where–

(a) a person ("P") who was a controlling member of a partnership at the time when a monitoring notice was given to the partnership has ceased to be a member of the partnership,

(b) the monitoring notice had effect in relation to the partnership at the time of that cessation, and

(c) P is carrying on a business as a promoter.

9(2) An authorised officer may give P a monitoring notice.

9(3) If P is carrying on a business as a promoter in partnership with one or more other persons, and is a controlling member of that partnership ("the new partnership"), an authorised officer may give a monitoring notice to the new partnership.

9(4) A monitoring notice given under sub-paragraph (3) ceases to have effect if P ceases to be a member of the new partnership.

DIVISION OF PARTNERSHIP BUSINESS

10(1) This paragraph applies if–

(a) a person ("a departing partner") who has been carrying on a business in partnership ceases to carry on the business in partnership,

(b) a defeat notice, conduct notice or monitoring notice had effect in relation to the partnership immediately before the departing partner ceased to carry on the business in partnership, and

(c) the departing partner is continuing to carry on part (but not the whole) of the business ("the transferred part").

10(2) The notice mentioned in sub-paragraph (1)(b) is referred to in this paragraph as "the original notice".

10(3) An authorised officer may give the departing partner–

(za) a defeat notice (if the original notice is a defeat notice);

(a) a conduct notice (if the original notice is a conduct notice);

(b) a monitoring notice (if the original notice is a monitoring notice).

10(4) If the departing partner is itself carrying on the transferred part of the business in partnership, the authorised officer may give that partnership ("the new partnership")–

(za) a defeat notice (if the original notice is a defeat notice);

(a) a conduct notice (if the original notice is a conduct notice);

(b) a monitoring notice (if the original notice is a monitoring notice).

10(5) A notice given under sub-paragraph (4) ceases to have effect if the departing partner ceases to be a member of the new partnership.

10(5A) A notice under sub-paragraph (3)(za) or (4)(za) may not be given after the end of the look-forward period of the original notice.

10(6) A notice under sub-paragraph (3)(a) or (4)(a) may not be given after the termination date of the original notice (under section 241(2)(a) or (b)).

10(7) It does not matter whether one, some or all of the persons who were carrying on the business in partnership are departing partners by virtue of sub-paragraph (1).

History – In para. 10(1)(b), the words ", defeat notice, conduct notice or" substituted for the words "conduct notice or a" by FA 2016, s. 160(15)(a), with effect from 15 September 2016 (Royal Assent).
Para. 10(3)(za) inserted by FA 2016, s. 160(15)(b), with effect from 15 September 2016 (Royal Assent).
Para. 10(4)(za) inserted by FA 2016, s. 160(15)(c), with effect from 15 September 2016 (Royal Assent).
Para. 10(5A) inserted by FA 2016, s. 160(15)(d), with effect from 15 September 2016 (Royal Assent).

NOTICES UNDER PARAGRAPHS 8 TO 10: GENERAL

11(1) In this Part of this Act–

"replacement conduct notice" means a notice under paragraph 8(2) or (3) or 10(3)(a) or (4)(a);

"replacement monitoring notice" means a notice given under paragraph 9(2) or (3) or 10(3)(b) or (4)(b).

11(2) In this Part of this Act, **"the original monitoring notice"** means–

(a) in relation to a replacement monitoring notice given under paragraph 9(2), the monitoring notice mentioned in paragraph 9(1), and

(b) in relation to a replacement monitoring notice given under paragraph 10(3)(b) or (4)(b), the monitoring notice mentioned in paragraph 10(2),

and that original monitoring notice is also the **"original monitoring notice"** in relation to any monitoring notice that (under paragraph 9(2) or (3) or 10(3)(b) or (4)(b)) replaces a replacement monitoring notice.

11A The look-forward period for a notice under paragraph 7A(2) or (3) or 10(3)(za) or (4)(za)–

(a) begins on the day after the day on which the notice is given, and

(b) continues to the end of the look-forward period for the original notice (as defined in paragraph 7A(1)(a) or 10(2), as the case may be).

History – Para. 11A inserted by FA 2016, s. 160(16), with effect from 15 September 2016 (Royal Assent).

12 A notice under paragraph 8(2) or (3) or 10(3)(a) or (4)(a)–

(a) has no effect after the termination date of the original notice;

(b) must state that that date is its termination date.

13 An authorised officer may not give a replacement conduct notice or replacement monitoring notice to a person if a conduct notice or monitoring notice previously given to the person still has effect in relation to the person.

PUBLICATION UNDER SECTION 248

14 Where the monitored promoter referred to in section 248(2) is a partnership, paragraphs (a), (b) and (d) of that subsection are to be read as referring to details of the partnership (for instance, the name under which the business of the partnership is carried on), not to details of particular partners.

Part 3 – Responsibility of Partners

RESPONSIBILITY OF PARTNERS

15(1) A notice given to a partnership under this Part of this Act has effect, at any time, in relation to the persons who are members of the partnership at that time ("the responsible partners").

15(2) Sub-paragraph (1) does not affect any liability of a person who has ceased to be a member of a partnership in respect of things that the responsible partners did or failed to do before that person ceased to be a member of the partnership.

15(3) Anything required to be done by the responsible partners under or by virtue of a provision of this Part of this Act is required to be done by all the responsible partners (but see paragraph 18).

15(4) In relation to any right (such as a right of appeal) conferred by this Part of this Act references to a person have the meaning that is appropriate in consequence of sub-paragraphs (1) to (3).

JOINT AND SEVERAL LIABILITY OF RESPONSIBLE PARTNERS

16(1) Where the responsible partners are liable to a penalty under this Part of this Act, or to interest on such a penalty, their liability is joint and several.

16(2) No amount may be recovered under sub-paragraph (1) from a person who did not become a responsible partner until after the relevant time.

16(3) **"The relevant time"** means–

(a) in relation to so much of the penalty as is payable in respect of any day, or to interest on so much of a penalty as is so payable, the beginning of that day;

(b) in relation to any other penalty, or interest on such a penalty, the time when the act or omission occurred that caused the penalty to become payable.

SERVICE OF NOTICES

17(1) Any notice given to a partnership by an officer of Revenue and Customs under this Part of this Act must be served either–

(a) on all the persons who are members of the partnership when the notice is given, or

(b) on a representative partner.

17(2) **"Representative partner"** means–

(a) a nominated partner, or

(b) if no partner has been nominated under paragraph 18(2), a partner designated by an authorised officer as a representative partner.

17(3) A designation under sub-paragraph (2), or the revocation of such a designation, has effect only when notice of the designation, or revocation, has been given to the partnership by an authorised officer.

NOMINATED PARTNERS

18(1) Anything required to be done by the responsible partners under this Part of this Act may instead be done by any nominated partner.

18(2) **"Nominated partner"** means a partner nominated by a majority of the partners to act as the representative of the partnership for the purposes of this Part of this Act.

18(3) A nomination under sub-paragraph (2), or the revocation of such a nomination, has effect only after notice of the nomination, or revocation, has been given to an authorised officer.

Part 4 – Interpretation

MEANING OF "CONTROLLING MEMBER"

19(1) For the purposes of this Schedule a person ("P") is a **"controlling member"** of a partnership at any time when the person has a right to a share of more than half the assets, or of more than half the income, of the partnership.

19(2) For that purpose there are to be attributed to P any interests or rights of–

(a) any individual who is connected with P (if P is an individual), and

(b) any body corporate that P controls.

19(3) An individual is **"connected"** with P if the individual is–

(a) P's spouse or civil partner;

(b) a relative of P;

(c) the spouse or civil partner of a relative of P;

(d) a relative of P's spouse or civil partner, or

(e) the spouse or civil partner of a relative of P's spouse or civil partner.

19(4) In sub-paragraph (3) **"relative"** means brother, sister, ancestor or lineal descendant.

19(5) P controls a body corporate ("B") if P has power to secure–

(a) by means of the holding of shares or the possession of voting power in relation to B or any other body corporate, or

(b) as a result of any powers conferred by the articles of association or other document regulating that or any other body corporate,

that the affairs of B are conducted in accordance with P's wishes.

MEANING OF "MANAGING PARTNER"

20 [Omitted by FA 2015, s. 119 and Sch. 19, para. 5(b).]

History – Para. 20 (and the heading before it) omitted by FA 2015, s. 119 and Sch. 19, para. 5(b), with effect for the purposes of determining whether a person meets a threshold condition in a period of three years ending on or after 26 March 2015 (Royal Assent). Former para. 20 read as follows:

"**20** In this Schedule **"managing partner"**, in relation to a partnership, means a member of the partnership who directs or is on a day-to-day level in control of, the management of the business of the partnership."

POWER TO AMEND DEFINITIONS

21(1) The Treasury may by regulations amend paragraph 19.

21(2) Regulations under sub-paragraph (1) may include any amendment of this Schedule that is necessary in consequence of any amendment made by virtue of sub-paragraph (1).

History – In para. 21 the words "or 20" omitted by FA 2015, s. 119 and Sch. 19, para. 5(c), with effect for the purposes of determining whether a person meets a threshold condition in a period of three years ending on or after 26 March 2015 (Royal Assent).

FINANCE ACT 2015

(2015 Chapter 11)

[*26th March 2015*]

ARRANGEMENT OF SECTIONS

PART 2 – EXCISE DUTIES AND OTHER TAXES

PETROLEUM REVENUE TAX

52 Reduction in rate of petroleum revenue tax

52(1) OTA 1975 is amended as follows.

52(2) In section 1(2) (rate of petroleum revenue tax) for “50” substitute “35”.

52(3) In paragraph 17(5)(b) of Schedule 2 (relevant percentage in relation to the amount of loss which is treated as reducing assessable profit) after “60 per cent” insert “if that later repayment period ends on or before 31 December 2015, and 45 per cent if it ends after 31 December 2015”.

52(4) The amendment made by subsection (2) has effect with respect to chargeable periods ending after 31 December 2015.

PART 4 – OTHER PROVISIONS

ANTI-AVOIDANCE

117 Disclosure of tax avoidance schemes

117 Schedule 17 contains amendments relating to the disclosure of tax avoidance schemes.

119 Promoters of tax avoidance schemes

119 Schedule 19 contains provision about promoters of tax avoidance schemes.

120 Penalties in connection with offshore matters and offshore transfers

120(1) Schedule 20 contains provisions amending–

(a) Schedule 24 to FA 2007 (penalties for errors),

(b) Schedule 41 to FA 2008 (penalties for failure to notify),

(c) Schedule 55 to FA 2009 (penalties for failure to make returns etc), and

(d) Schedule 43C to FA 2013 (as amended by FA 2016).

120(2) That Schedule comes into force on such day as the Treasury may by order appoint.

120(3) An order under subsection (2)–

(a) may commence a provision generally or only for specified purposes, and

(b) may appoint different days for different provisions or for different purposes.

120(4) The power to make an order under this section is exercisable by statutory instrument.

History – S. 120(1)(d) (and the ", and" before it) inserted (and the "and" after (b) omitted) by FA 2016, s. 158(13), with effect in relation to tax arrangements (within the meaning of FA 2013, Pt. 5) entered into on or after 15 September 2016 (Royal Assent).

PART 5 – FINAL PROVISIONS

126 Interpretation

126(1) In this Act–

"ALDA 1979" means the Alcoholic Liquor Duties Act 1979,

"CAA 2001" means the Capital Allowances Act 2001,

"CTA 2009" means the Corporation Tax Act 2009,

"CTA 2010" means the Corporation Tax Act 2010,

"IHTA 1984" means the Inheritance Tax Act 1984,

"ITA 2007" means the Income Tax Act 2007,

"ITEPA 2003" means the Income Tax (Earnings and Pensions) Act 2003,

"ITTOIA 2005" means the Income Tax (Trading and Other Income) Act 2005,

"OTA 1975" means the Oil Taxation Act 1975,

"TCGA 1992" means the Taxation of Chargeable Gains Act 1992,

"TIOPA 2010" means the Taxation (International and Other Provisions) Act 2010,

"TMA 1970" means the Taxes Management Act 1970,

"TPDA 1979" means the Tobacco Products Duty Act 1979,

"VATA 1994" means the Value Added Tax Act 1994, and

"VERA 1994" means the Vehicle Excise and Registration Act 1994.

126(2) In this Act **"FA"**, followed by a year, means the Finance Act of that year.

127 Short title

127 This Act may be cited as the Finance Act 2015.

SCHEDULES

SCHEDULE 7 – DISPOSALS OF UK RESIDENTIAL PROPERTY INTERESTS BY NON-RESIDENTS ETC

Section 37

Part 2 – Other Amendments

56(1) In FA 2007, Schedule 24 (penalties for errors) is amended as follows.

56(2) [Not relevant to petroleum revenue tax.]

56(3) [*Inserts* FA 2007, Sch. 24, para. 21C.]

Part 3 – Commencement

60 The amendments made by this Schedule have effect in relation to disposals made on or after 6 April 2015.

SCHEDULE 17 – DISCLOSURE OF TAX AVOIDANCE SCHEMES

Section 117

REQUIREMENT TO UPDATE DOTAS INFORMATION

1 [Inserts FA 2004, s. 310C.]

2 [Amends FA 2004, s. 316(2).]

3 [Not relevant to petroleum revenue tax.]

ARRANGEMENTS TO BE GIVEN REFERENCE NUMBER

4 [Amends FA 2004, s. 311(1)(a).]

NOTIFICATION OF EMPLOYEES

5(1) Section 312A of FA 2004 (duty of client to notify parties of number) is amended as follows.

5(2) [Inserts FA 2004, s. 312A(2A).]

5(3) [Substitutes FA 2004, s. 312A(3).]

5(4) [Amends FA 2004, s. 312A(4).]

5(5) [Amends FA 2004, s. 312A(5).]

6 [Inserts FA 2004, s. 313(6).]

7 [Amends FA 2004, s. 316(2).]

8 [Not relevant to petroleum revenue tax.]

EMPLOYERS' DUTY OF DISCLOSURE

9 [Inserts FA 2004, s. 313ZC.]

10 [Amends FA 2004, s. 316(2).]

11 [Not relevant to petroleum revenue tax.]

IDENTIFYING SCHEME USERS

12(1) Section 313C of FA 2004 (information provided to introducers) is amended as follows.

12(2) [Substitutes FA 2004, s. 313C(1) and inserts (1A).]

12(3) [Amends FA 2004, s. 313C(3).]

12(4) [Amends heading to FA 2004, s. 313C.]

13 [Not relevant to petroleum revenue tax.]

ADDITIONAL INFORMATION

14 [Inserts FA 2004, s. 316A.]

15 [Not relevant to petroleum revenue tax.]

PROTECTION OF PERSONS MAKING VOLUNTARY DISCLOSURES

16 [Inserts FA 2004, s. 316B.]

PUBLICATION OF DOTAS INFORMATION

17 [Inserts FA 2004, s. 316C and 316D.]

INCREASE IN PENALTIES FOR FAILURE TO COMPLY WITH SECTION 313 OF FA 2004

18 [Not relevant to petroleum revenue tax.]

TRANSITIONAL PROVISIONS

19(1) Section 310C of FA 2004 applies in relation to notifiable arrangements, or proposed notifiable arrangements, only if a reference number under section 311 of that Act is allocated to the arrangements on or after the day on which this Act is passed.

19(2) But section 310C of FA 2004 does not apply in relation to notifiable arrangements, or proposed notifiable arrangements, where prescribed information relating to the arrangements was provided to HMRC before that day in compliance with section 308 of that Act.

20 Any notice given by HMRC under section 312A(4) of FA 2004 (notice that section 312A(2) duty does not apply) before the day on which this Act is passed is treated on and after that day as given also in relation to the duty under section 312A(2A) of that Act.

21(1) Section 316C of FA 2004 applies in relation to notifiable arrangements, or proposed notifiable arrangements, only if a reference number under section 311 of that Act is allocated to the arrangements on or after the day on which this Act is passed.

21(2) But section 316C of FA 2004 does not apply in relation to notifiable arrangements, or proposed notifiable arrangements, where prescribed information relating to the arrangements was provided to HMRC before that day in compliance with section 308, 309 or 310 of that Act.

21(3) Section 316C(2)(b) of FA 2004 applies in relation to a ruling of a court or tribunal only if the ruling is given on or after the day on which this Act is passed.

SCHEDULE 19 – PROMOTERS OF TAX AVOIDANCE SCHEMES

Section 119

1 Part 5 of FA 2014 (promoters of tax avoidance schemes) is amended as follows.

TREATING PERSONS AS MEETING A THRESHOLD CONDITION

2(1) Section 237 (duty to give conduct notice) is amended as follows.

2(2) [Inserts FA 2014, s. 237(1A).]

2(3) [Amends FA 2014, s. 237(3).]

2(4) [Substitutes FA 2014, s. 237(5).]

2(5) [Amends FA 2014, s. 237(7).]

2(6) [Inserts FA 2014, s. 237(7A).]

2(7) [Amends FA 2014, s. 237(9).]

2(8) [Inserts FA 2014, s. 237(10).]

3 [Amends FA 2014, s. 283.]

4(1) Part 2 of Schedule 34 (meeting the threshold conditions) is amended as follows.

4(2) [Amends heading to FA 2014, Sch. 34, Pt. 2.]

4(3) [Substitutes FA 2014, Sch. 34, para. 13A to 13D.]

5 In Schedule 36 (partnerships)–

(a) [omits FA 2014, Sch. 36, para. 4,]

(b) [omits FA 2014, Sch. 36, para. 20,]

(c) [amends FA 2014, Sch. 36, para. 21.]

FAILURE TO COMPLY WITH PART 7 OF FA 2004

6 [Substitutes FA 2014, Sch. 34, para. 5(2)–(6).]

DISCIPLINARY ACTION IN RELATION TO PROFESSIONALS ETC

7(1) In Schedule 34 (threshold conditions), paragraph 8 (disciplinary action: professionals etc) is amended as follows.

7(2) [Substitutes FA 2014, Sch. 34, para. 8(1).]

7(3) [Amends heading to FA 2014, Sch. 34, para. 8.]

7(4) [Amends FA 2014, Sch. 34, para. 8(3).]

POWER TO AMEND SCHEDULE 34

8 [Inserts FA 2014, Sch. 34, para. 14(2)(c) and (d).]

COMMENCEMENT

9 The amendments made by paragraphs 2 to 7 have effect for the purposes of determining whether a person meets a threshold condition in a period of three years ending on or after the day on which this Act is passed.

SCHEDULE 20 – PENALTIES IN CONNECTION WITH OFFSHORE MATTERS AND OFFSHORE TRANSFERS

Section 120

Commencement Date – 1 April 2016 is the day appointed for the coming into force of Sch. 20, para. 3(3)–3(7), 4 and 8 and 6 April 2016 is the day appointed for the coming into force of Sch. 20, para. 16(3)–16(9) and 17 (SI 2016/456).

PENALTIES FOR ERRORS

1 Schedule 24 to FA 2007 is amended as follows.

2(1) Paragraph 4 (penalties payable under paragraph 1) is amended as follows.

2(2) After sub-paragraph (1) insert–

"**4(1A)** If the inaccuracy is in category 0, the penalty is–

(a) for careless action, 30% of the potential lost revenue,

(b) for deliberate but not concealed action, 70% of the potential lost revenue, and

(c) for deliberate and concealed action, 100% of the potential lost revenue."

2(3) In sub-paragraph (2)–

(a) in paragraph (a), for "30%" substitute "37.5%",

(b) in paragraph (b), for "70%" substitute "87.5%", and

(c) in paragraph (c), for "100%" substitute "125%".

2(4) In sub-paragraph (5), for "3" substitute "4".

3(1) Paragraph 4A (categorisation of inaccuracies) is amended as follows.

3(2) For sub-paragraph (1) substitute–

"**4A(A1)** An inaccuracy is in category 0 if–

(a) it involves a domestic matter,

(b) it involves an offshore matter or an offshore transfer, the territory in question is a category 0 territory and the tax at stake is income tax, capital gains tax or inheritance tax, or

(c) it involves an offshore matter and the tax at stake is a tax other than income tax, capital gains tax or inheritance tax.

4A(1) An inaccuracy is in category 1 if–

(a) it involves an offshore matter or an offshore transfer,

(b) the territory in question is a category 1 territory, and

(c) the tax at stake is income tax, capital gains tax or inheritance tax."

3(3) [Amends FA 2007, Sch. 24, para. 4A(2)(a) and (c).]

3(4) [Amends FA 2007, Sch. 24, para. 4A(3)(a) and (c).]

3(5) [Inserts FA 2007, Sch. 24, para. 4A(4A) and (4B).]

3(6) [Amends FA 2007, Sch. 24, para. 4A(5).]

3(7) [Amends FA 2007, Sch. 24, para. 4A(6)(a).]

3(8) In sub-paragraph (7), for "Category 1" substitute "Category 0 territory", "category 1".

Commencement Date – 1 April 2016 is the appointed day for the coming into force of para. 3(3)–(7) (and the amendments have effect in relation to documents given to HMRC relating to: a transfer of value made on or after that date for the purposes of inheritance tax; and a tax year commencing on or after 6 April 2016 for the purposes of income tax and capital gains tax) (SI 2016/456, art. 3).

4 [Inserts FA 2007, Sch. 24, para. 4AA.]

Commencement Date – 1 April 2016 is the appointed day for the coming into force of para. 4 (and the amendments have effect in relation to documents given to HMRC relating to: a transfer of value made on or after that date for the purposes of inheritance tax; and a tax year commencing on or after 6 April 2016 for the purposes of income tax and capital gains tax) (SI 2016/456, art. 3).

5 In paragraph 10 (standard percentage reductions for disclosure), in the Table in sub-paragraph (2), at the appropriate places insert–

"37.5%	18.75%	0%",
"87.5%	43.75%	25%", and
"125%	62.5%	40%".

6 In paragraph 12(5) (interaction with other penalties and late payment surcharges: the relevant percentage)–

(a) before paragraph (a) insert–

"(za) if the penalty imposed under paragraph 1 is for an inaccuracy in category 0, 100%,", and

(b) in paragraph (a), for "100%" substitute "125%".

7(1) Paragraph 21A (classification of territories) is amended as follows.

7(2) Before sub-paragraph (1) insert–

"**21A(A1)** A category 0 territory is a territory designated as a category 0 territory by order made by the Treasury."

7(3) For sub-paragraph (2) substitute–

"**21A(2)** A category 2 territory is a territory that is not any of the following–

(a) a category 0 territory;

(b) a category 1 territory;

(c) a category 3 territory."

7(4) For sub-paragraph (7) substitute–

"**21A(7)** An instrument containing (whether alone or with other provisions) the first order to be made under sub-paragraph (A1) may not be made unless a draft of the instrument has been laid before, and approved by a resolution of, the House of Commons."

8(1) Paragraph 21B (location of assets etc) is amended as follows.

8(2) [Inserts FA 2007, Sch. 24, para. 21B(1A).]

8(3) [Amends FA 2007, Sch. 24, para. 21B(2).]

Commencement Date – 1 April 2016 is the appointed day for the coming into force of para. 8 (and the amendments have effect in relation to documents given to HMRC relating to: a transfer of value made on or after that date for the purposes of inheritance tax; and a tax year commencing on or after 6 April 2016 for the purposes of income tax and capital gains tax) (SI 2016/456, art. 3).

PENALTIES FOR FAILURE TO MAKE RETURNS ETC

14 Schedule 55 to FA 2009 is amended as follows.

15(1) Paragraph 6 (penalty for failure continuing 12 months after penalty date) is amended as follows.

15(2) In sub-paragraph (3A)–

(a) before paragraph (a) insert–

"(za) for the withholding of category 0 information, 100%,", and

(b) in paragraph (a), for "100%" substitute "125%".

15(3) In sub-paragraph (4A)–

(a) before paragraph (a) insert–

"(za) for the withholding of category 0 information, 70%,", and

(b) in paragraph (a), for "70%" substitute "87.5%".

15(4) In sub-paragraph (6), for "3" substitute "4".

16(1) Paragraph 6A (categorisation of information) is amended as follows.

16(2) For sub-paragraph (1) substitute–

"**6A(A1)** Information is category 0 information if–

(a) it involves a domestic matter,

(b) it involves an offshore matter or an offshore transfer, the territory in question is a category 0 territory and it is information which would enable or assist HMRC to assess P's liability to income tax, capital gains tax or inheritance tax, or

(c) it involves an offshore matter and it is information which would enable or assist HMRC to assess P's liability to a tax other than income tax, capital gains tax or inheritance tax.

6A(1) Information is category 1 information if–

(a) it involves an offshore matter or an offshore transfer,

(b) the territory in question is a category 1 territory, and

(c) it is information which would enable or assist HMRC to assess P's liability to income tax, capital gains tax or inheritance tax."

16(3) [Amends FA 2009, Sch. 55, para. 6A(2)(a) and (c).]

16(4) [Amends FA 2009, Sch. 55, para. 6A(3)(a) and (c).]

16(5) [Inserts FA 2009, Sch. 55, para. 6A(4A) and (4B).]

16(6) [Amends FA 2009, Sch. 55, para. 6A(5).]

16(7) [Amends FA 2009, Sch. 55, para. 6A(6)(a).]

16(8) [Omits FA 2009, Sch. 55, para. 6A(8).]

16(9) [Amends FA 2009, Sch. 55, para. 6A(9).]

Commencement Date – 6 April 2016 is the day appointed for the coming into force of para. 16(3)–16(9) (and the amendments have effect in relation to a return or other document which: is required to be made or delivered to HMRC in relation to a tax year commencing on or after that date; and falls within item 1, 2 or 3 of the Table in Sch. 55, para. 1(5) (penalty for failure to make returns etc)) (SI 2016/456, art. 5).

17 [Inserts FA 2009, Sch. 55, para. 6AA and 6AB.]

Commencement Date – 6 April 2016 is the day appointed for the coming into force of para. 17 (and the amendments have effect in relation to a return or other document which: is required to be made or delivered to HMRC in relation to a tax year commencing on or after that date; and falls within item 1, 2 or 3 of the Table in Sch. 55, para. 1(5) (penalty for failure to make returns etc)) (SI 2016/456, art. 5).

18 In paragraph 15 (standard percentage reductions for disclosure), in the Table in sub-paragraph (2), at the appropriate places insert–

"87.5%	43.75%	25%", and
"125%	62.5%	40%".

19 In paragraph 17(4) (interaction with other penalties and late payment surcharges), omit the "and" at the end of paragraph (b) and after that paragraph insert–

"(ba) if one of the penalties is a penalty under paragraph 6(3) or (4) and the information withheld is category 1 information, 125%, and".

GENERAL ANTI-ABUSE RULE: AGGREGATE PENALTIES

20(1) In Schedule 43C to FA 2013 (general anti-abuse rule: supplementary provision about penalty), sub-paragraph (6) of paragraph 8 is amended as follows.

20(2) After paragraph (b) insert–

"(ba) 125% in a case where neither paragraph (a) nor paragraph (b) applies and at least one of the penalties is determined by reference to the percentage in–

(i) paragraph 4(2)(c) of Schedule 24 to FA 2007,

(ii) paragraph 6(2)(a) of Schedule 41 to FA 2008,

(iii) paragraph 6(3A)(a) of Schedule 55 to FA 2009,".

20(3) In sub-paragraph (c) for "neither paragraph (a) nor paragraph (b) applies" substitute "none of paragraphs (a) to (ba) applies".

20(4) In sub-paragraph (d) for "none of paragraphs (a), (b) and (c) applies" substitute "none of paragraphs (a) to (c) applies".

History – Para. 20 (and the heading before it) inserted by FA 2016, s. 158(14), with effect in relation to tax arrangements (within the meaning of FA 2013, Pt. 5) entered into on or after 15 September 2016.

FINANCE (NO. 2) ACT 2015

(2015 Chapter 33)

[18th November 2015]

ARRANGEMENT OF SECTIONS

PART 6 – ADMINISTRATION AND ENFORCEMENT

PART 7 – FINAL

PART 6 – ADMINISTRATION AND ENFORCEMENT

52 Rate of interest applicable to judgment debts etc in taxation matters

52(1) This section applies if a sum payable to or by the Commissioners under a judgment or order given or made in any court proceedings relating to a taxation matter (a "tax-related judgment debt") carries interest as a result of a relevant enactment.

52(2) The **"relevant enactments"** are–

(a) section 17 of the Judgments Act 1838 (judgment debts to carry interest), and

(b) any order under section 74 of the County Courts Act 1984 (interest on judgment debts etc).

52(3) The relevant enactment is to have effect in relation to the tax-related judgment debt as if for the rate specified in section 17(1) of the Judgments Act 1838 and any other rate specified in an order under section 74 of the County Courts Act 1984 there were substituted–

(a) in the case of a sum payable to the Commissioners, the late payment interest rate provided for in regulations made by the Treasury under section 103(1) of FA 2009, and

(b) in the case of a sum payable by the Commissioners, the special repayment rate.

52(4) Subsection (3) does not affect any power of the court under the relevant enactment to prevent any sum from carrying interest or to provide for a rate of interest which is lower than (and incapable of exceeding) that for which the subsection provides.

52(5) If section 44A of the Administration of Justice Act 1970 (interest on judgment debts expressed otherwise than in sterling), or any corresponding provision made under section 74 of the County Courts Act 1984 in relation to the county court, applies to a tax-related judgment debt–

(a) subsection (3) does not apply, but

(b) the court may not specify in an order under section 44A of the Administration of Justice Act 1970, or under any provision corresponding to that section which has effect under section 74 of the County Courts Act 1984, an interest rate which exceeds (or is capable of exceeding)–

(i) in the case of a sum payable to the Commissioners, the rate mentioned in subsection (3)(a), or

(ii) in the case of a sum payable by the Commissioners, the special repayment rate.

52(6) The **"special repayment rate"** is the percentage per annum given by the formula–

$$BR + 2$$

where BR is the official Bank rate determined by the Bank of England Monetary Policy Committee at the operative meeting.

52(7) **"The operative meeting"**, in relation to the special repayment rate applicable in respect of any day, means the most recent meeting of the Bank of England Monetary Policy Committee apart from any meeting later than the 13th working day before that day.

52(8) The Treasury may by regulations made by statutory instrument–

(a) repeal subsections (6) and (7), and

(b) provide that the **"special repayment rate"** for the purposes of this section is the rate provided for in the regulations.

52(9) Regulations under subsection (8)–

(a) may make different provision for different purposes,

(b) may either themselves specify a rate of interest or make provision for such a rate to be determined (and to change from time to time) by reference to such rate, or the average of such rates, as may be referred to in the regulations,

(c) may provide for rates to be reduced below, or increased above, what they would otherwise be by specified amounts or by reference to specified formulae,

(d) may provide for rates arrived at by reference to averages to be rounded up or down,

(e) may provide for circumstances in which the alteration of a rate of interest is or is not to take place, and

(f) may provide that alterations of rates are to have effect for periods beginning on or after a day determined in accordance with the regulations ("the effective date") regardless of–

(i) the date of the judgment or order in question, and

(ii) whether interest begins to run on or after the effective date, or began to run before that date.

52(10) A statutory instrument containing regulations under subsection (8) is subject to annulment in pursuance of a resolution of the House of Commons.

52(11) To the extent that a tax-related judgment debt consists of an award of costs to or against the Commissioners, the reference in section 24(2) of the Crown Proceedings Act 1947 (which relates to interest on costs awarded to or against the Crown) to the rate at which interest is payable upon judgment debts due from or to the Crown is to be read as a reference to the rate at which interest is payable upon tax-related judgment debts.

52(12) This section has effect in relation to interest for periods beginning on or after 8 July 2015, regardless of–

(a) the date of the judgment or order in question, and

(b) whether interest begins to run on or after 8 July 2015, or began to run before that date.

52(13) Subsection (14) applies where, at any time during the period beginning with 8 July 2015 and ending immediately before the day on which this Act is passed ("the relevant period")–

(a) a payment is made in satisfaction of a tax-related judgment debt, and

(b) the payment includes interest under a relevant enactment in respect of any part of the relevant period.

52(14) The court by which the judgment or order in question was given or made must, on an application made to it under this subsection by the person who made the payment, order the repayment of the amount by which the interest paid under the relevant enactment in respect of days falling within the relevant period exceeds the interest payable under the relevant enactment in respect of those days in accordance with the provisions of this section.

52(15) In this section–

"the Commissioners" means the Commissioners for Her Majesty's Revenue and Customs;

"taxation matter" means anything the collection and management of which is the responsibility of the Commissioners (or was the responsibility of the Commissioners of Inland Revenue or Commissioners of Customs and Excise);

"working day" means any day other than a non-business day as defined in section 92 of the Bills of Exchange Act 1882.

52(16) This section extends to England and Wales only.

History – In s. 52(15), in the definition of "taxation matter", the words ", other than national insurance contributions," (which appeared after the words "means anything") omitted by FA 2016, s. 172(1), with effect (in England and Wales only) in relation to interest for periods beginning on or after 15 September 2016, regardless of— (a) the date of the judgment or order in question, and (b) whether interest begins to run on or after 15 September 2016, or began to run before that date

PART 7 – FINAL

53 Interpretation

53 In this Act–

"CAA 2001" means the Capital Allowances Act 2001,

"CTA 2009" means the Corporation Tax Act 2009,

"CTA 2010" means the Corporation Tax Act 2010,

"FA", followed by a year, means the Finance Act of that year,

"IHTA 1984" means the Inheritance Tax Act 1984,

"ITA 2007" means the Income Tax Act 2007,

"ITEPA 2003" means the Income Tax (Earnings and Pensions) Act 2003,

"ITTOIA 2005" means the Income Tax (Trading and Other Income) Act 2005,

"TCGA 1992" means the Taxation of Chargeable Gains Act 1992,

"TIOPA 2010" means the Taxation (International and Other Provisions) Act 2010,

"TMA 1970" means the Taxes Management Act 1970,

"VATA 1994" means the Value Added Tax Act 1994, and

"VERA 1994" means the Vehicle Excise and Registration Act 1994.

54 Short title

54 This Act may be cited as the Finance (No. 2) Act 2015.

FINANCE ACT 2016

(2016 Chapter 24)

[*15th September 2016*]

ARRANGEMENT OF SECTIONS

PART 6 – APPRENTICESHIP LEVY

ANTI-AVOIDANCE

104 Application of other regimes to apprenticeship levy

104(1) [Amends FA 2004, s. 318(1).]

104(2) [Inserts FA 2013, s. 206(3)(db).]

104(3)–(5) [Not relevant to petroleum revenue tax.]

104(6) Part 5 of FA 2014 (promoters of tax avoidance schemes) is amended in accordance with subsections (7) and (8).

104(7) [Inserts FA 2014, s. 253(6)(da).]

104(8) [Inserts FA 2014, s. 283(1)(da).]

INFORMATION AND PENALTIES

112 Information and inspection powers

112 [Inserts FA 2008, Sch. 36, para. 63(1)(cb).]

113 Penalties

113(1) Schedule 24 to FA 2007 (penalties for errors) is amended in accordance with subsections (2) to (4).

113(2) [Not relevant to petroleum revenue tax.]

113(3) [Not relevant to petroleum revenue tax.]

113(4) [Amends FA 2007, Sch. 24, para. 21C.]

113(5)–(15) [Not relevant to petroleum revenue tax.]

113(16) The amendments made by subsections (1) to (4) of this section come into force in accordance with provision made by the Treasury by regulations.

113(17) In subsections (2) and (4) of section 106 of FA 2009 (penalties for failure to make returns: commencement etc) references to Schedule 55 to that Act have effect as references to that Schedule as amended by subsections (5) to (8) of this section.

113(18) Schedule 56 to FA 2009, as amended by this section, is taken to come into force for the purposes of apprenticeship levy on the date on which this Act is passed.

Commencement Date – S. 113(1) to (4) comes into force on 6 April 2017 (SI 2017/355, reg. 2).

GENERAL

115 Tax agents: dishonest conduct

115 [Inserts FA 2012, Sch. 38, para. 37(1)(la).]

PART 9 – OTHER TAXES AND DUTIES

PETROLEUM REVENUE TAX

140 Petroleum revenue tax: rate

140(1) [Amends OTA 1975, s. 1(2).]

140(2) [Amends OTA 1975, Sch. 2, para. 17(5)(b).]

140(3) [Inserts FA 1982, Sch. 19, para. 2(4A).]

140(4) The amendment made by subsection (1) has effect with respect to chargeable periods ending after 31 December 2015.

PART 10 – TAX AVOIDANCE AND EVASION

GENERAL ANTI-ABUSE RULE

156 General anti-abuse rule: provisional counteractions

156(1) [Inserts FA 2013, s. 209A to 209F.]

156(2) [Amends FA 2013, s. 214(1).]

156(3) The amendments made by this section have effect in relation to tax arrangements (within the meaning of Part 5 of FA 2013) entered into at any time (whether before or on or after the day on which this Act is passed).

157 General anti-abuse rule: binding of tax arrangements to lead arrangements

157(1) Part 5 of FA 2013 (general anti-abuse rule) is amended in accordance with subsections (2) to (11).

157(2) [Inserts FA 2013, Sch. 43A.]

157(3) [Inserts FA 2013, Sch. 43B.]

157(4) [Amends FA 2013, s. 209(6)(a).]

157(5) [Inserts FA 2013, s. 210(1)(b).]

157(6) [Substitutes FA 2013, s. 211(2)(b).]

157(7) Section 214 (interpretation of Part 5) is amended in accordance with subsections (8) to (10).

157(8) [Amends FA 2013, s. 214(1).]

157(9) [Amends FA 2013, s. 214(1).]

157(10) [Inserts FA 2013, s. 214(2) and (3).]

157(11) [Inserts FA 2013, Sch. 43, para. 6(3).]

157(12)–(28) [Not relevant to petroleum revenue tax.]

157(29) In Schedule 34 to FA 2014 (promoters of tax avoidance schemes: threshold conditions), in paragraph 7–

(a) [amends FA 2014, Sch. 34, para. 7(a);]

(b) [amends FA 2014, Sch. 34, para. 7(b);]

(c) [amends FA 2014, Sch. 34, para. 7(c).]

157(30) The amendments made by this section have effect in relation to tax arrangements (within the meaning of Part 5 of FA 2013) entered into at any time (whether before or on or after the day on which this Act is passed).

158 General anti-abuse rule: penalty

158(1) Part 5 of FA 2013 (general anti-abuse rule) is amended as follows.

158(2) [Inserts FA 2013, s. 212A.]

158(3) [Inserts FA 2013, Sch. 43C.]

158(4) [Inserts FA 2013, s. 209(8)–(10).]

158(5) Schedule 43 (general anti-abuse rule: procedural requirements) is amended in accordance with subsections (6) to (9).

158(6) [Inserts FA 2013, Sch. 43, para. 1A.]

158(7) [Amends FA 2013, Sch. 43, para. 3(2)(e).]

158(8) [Inserts FA 2013, Sch. 43, para. 4A.]

158(9) [Inserts FA 2013, Sch. 43, para. 4B.]

158(10) [Not relevant to petroleum revenue tax.]

158(11) [Not relevant to petroleum revenue tax.]

158(12) FA 2015 is amended in accordance with subsections (13) and (14).

158(13) [Inserts FA 2015, s. 120(1)(d).]

158(14) [Inserts FA 2015, Sch. 20, para. 20.]

158(15) The amendments made by this section have effect in relation to tax arrangements (within the meaning of Part 5 of FA 2013) entered into on or after the day on which this Act is passed.

TACKLING FREQUENT AVOIDANCE

160 Promoters of tax avoidance schemes

160(1) Part 5 of FA 2014 (promoters of tax avoidance schemes) is amended as follows.

160(2) [Inserts FA 2014, s. 237A–237D.]

160(3) [Inserts FA 2014, s. 241A and 241B.]

160(4) [Inserts FA 2014, s. 242(6) and (7).]

160(5) [Inserts FA 2014, Sch. 34A.]

160(6) [Inserts FA 2014, s. 241(5).]

160(7) [Inserts FA 2014, s. 281A.]

160(8) [Inserts FA 2014, s. 282(3)(ba).]

160(9) [Amends FA 2014, s. 283(1).]

160(10) Schedule 36 (promoters of tax avoidance schemes: partnerships) is amended in accordance with subsections (11) to (16).

160(11) [Inserts FA 2014, Sch. 36, para. 4A.]

160(12) [Amends FA 2014, Sch. 36, para. 7(1)(b).]

160(13) [Amends FA 2014, Sch. 36, para. 7(2).]

160(14) [Inserts FA 2014, Sch. 36, para. 7A.]

160(15) In paragraph 10–

(a) [amends FA 2014, Sch. 36, para. 10(1)(b);]

(b) [inserts FA 2014, Sch. 36, para. 10(3)(za);]

(c) [inserts FA 2014, Sch. 36, para. 10(4)(za);]

(d) [inserts FA 2014, Sch. 36, para. 10(5A).]

160(16) [Inserts FA 2014, Sch. 36, para. 11A.]

160(17)–(19) [Not relevant to petroleum revenue tax.]

160(20) For the purposes of sections 237A and 241A of FA 2014, a defeat (by virtue of any of Conditions A to F in Schedule 34A to that Act) of arrangements is treated as not having occurred if–

(a) there has been a final judicial ruling on or before the day on which this Act is passed as a result of which the counteraction referred to in paragraph 11(d), 12(1)(b), 13(1)(d), 14(1)(d) or 15(1)(d) (as the case may be) is final for the purposes of Schedule 34A of that Act, or

(b) (in the case of a defeat by virtue of Condition F in Schedule 34A) the judicial ruling mentioned in paragraph 16(1)(d) of that Schedule becomes final on or before the day on which this Act is passed.

160(21) Subsection (20) does not apply in relation to a person (who is carrying on a business as a promoter) if at any time after 17 July 2014 that person or an associated person takes action as a result of which the person taking the action–

(a) becomes a promoter in relation to the arrangements, or arrangements related to those arrangements, or

(b) would have become a promoter in relation to arrangements mentioned in paragraph (a) had the person not already been a promoter in relation to those arrangements.

160(22) For the purposes of sections 237A and 241A of FA 2014, a defeat of arrangements is treated as not having occurred if it would (ignoring this sub-paragraph) have occurred–

(a) on or before the first anniversary of the day on which this Act is passed, and

(b) by virtue of any of Conditions A to E in Schedule 34A to FA 2014, but otherwise than as a result of a final judicial ruling.

160(23) For the purposes of subsection (21) a person ("Q") is an **"associated person"** in relation to another person ("P") at any time when any of the following conditions is met–

(a) P is a relevant body which is controlled by Q;

(b) Q is a relevant body, P is not an individual and Q is controlled by P;

(c) P and Q are relevant bodies and a third person controls P and Q.

160(24) In subsection (23) **"relevant body"** and **"control"** are to be interpreted in accordance with paragraph 19 of Schedule 34A to FA 2014.

160(25) In subsections (20) to (22) expressions used in Part 5 of FA 2014 (as amended by this section) have the same meaning as in that Part.

161 Large businesses: tax strategies and sanctions for persistently unco-operative behaviour

161(1) Schedule 19 contains provisions relating to–

(a) the publication of tax strategies by bodies which are or are part of a large business,

(b) the imposition of sanctions for such bodies where there has been persistent unco-operative behaviour.

161(2) That Schedule, so far as relating to the publication of a tax strategy for a financial year of a relevant body or other entity, has effect only where the financial year begins on or after the day on which this Act is passed.

161(3) An officer of HMRC may not give a warning notice under Part 3 of that Schedule to a relevant body or other entity before the beginning of its first financial year beginning on or after the day on which this Act is passed.

161(4) In this section and Schedule 19 **"HMRC"** means Her Majesty's Revenue and Customs.

OFFSHORE ACTIVITIES

163 Penalties in connection with offshore matters and offshore transfers

163(1) Schedule 21 contains provisions amending–

(a) Schedule 24 to FA 2007 (penalties for errors in tax returns etc),

(b) Schedule 41 to FA 2008 (penalties for failure to notify etc), and

(c) Schedule 55 to FA 2009 (penalties for failure to make return etc).

163(2) That Schedule comes into force on such day as the Treasury may by regulations made by statutory instrument appoint.

163(3) Regulations under this section may–

(a) commence a provision generally or only for specified purposes,

(b) appoint different days for different provisions or for different purposes, and

(c) make supplemental, incidental and transitional provision.

164 Offshore tax errors etc: publishing details of deliberate tax defaulters

164(1) Section 94 of FA 2009 (publishing details of deliberate tax defaulters) is amended as follows.

164(2) [Inserts FA 2009, s. 94(4A)–(4D).]

164(3) [Amends FA 2009, s. 94(6).]

164(4) [Inserts FA 2009, s. 94(6A).]

164(5) [Inserts FA 2009, s. 94(10)(aa) and (c).]

164(6) [Substitutes FA 2009, s. 94(16).]

164(7) The amendments made by this section come into force on such day as the Treasury may by regulations made by statutory instrument appoint.

Commencement Date – 1 April 2017 is the appointed day for the coming into force of amendments made by s. 164 (SI 2017/261, reg. 2).

165 Asset-based penalties for offshore inaccuracies and failures

165(1) Schedule 22 contains provision imposing asset-based penalties on certain taxpayers who have been charged a penalty for deliberate offshore inaccuracies and failures.

165(2) That Schedule comes into force on such day as the Treasury may by regulations made by statutory instrument appoint.

165(3) Regulations under subsection (2) may–

(a) commence a provision generally or only for specified purposes,

(b) appoint different days for different provisions or for different purposes, and

(c) make supplemental, incidental and transitional provision.

PART 11 – ADMINISTRATION, ENFORCEMENT AND SUPPLEMENTARY POWERS

ASSESSMENT AND RETURNS

167 Simple assessments

167(1) Schedule 23 contains provisions about simple assessments by HMRC.

167(2) Paragraphs 1 to 8 of that Schedule have effect in relation to the 2016–17 tax year and subsequent years.

167(3) Paragraph 9 of that Schedule comes into force on such day as the Treasury may appoint by regulations made by statutory instrument.

167(4) Regulations under subsection (3) may–

(a) commence paragraph 9 generally or only for specified purposes, and

(b) appoint different days for different purposes.

JUDGMENT DEBTS

170 Rate of interest applicable to judgment debts etc: Scotland

170(1) This section applies if–

(a) a sum is payable to or by the Commissioners under a decree or extract issued in any court proceedings relating to a taxation matter (a "tax-related judgment debt"), and

(b) interest in relation to the tax-related judgment debt is included in or payable under the decree or extract.

170(2) In a case where the rate of interest in relation to the tax-related judgment debt is stated in the decree or extract, the rate stated in relation to that debt may not exceed (and may not be capable of exceeding)–

(a) in the case of a sum payable to the Commissioners, the late payment interest rate, and

(b) in the case of a sum payable by the Commissioners, the special repayment rate.

170(3) In a case where the rate of interest in relation to the tax-related judgment debt is not stated in the decree or extract but provided for by an enactment or rule of court (whenever passed or made), that enactment or rule is to have effect in relation to the debt as if for the rate for which it provides there were substituted–

(a) in the case of a sum payable to the Commissioners, the late payment interest rate, and

(b) in the case of a sum payable by the Commissioners, the special repayment rate.

170(4) This section has effect in relation to interest for periods beginning on or after the day on which this Act is passed, regardless of–

(a) the date of the decree or extract in question, and

(b) whether interest begins to run on or after the day on which this Act is passed, or began to run before that date.

170(5) In this section–

"the Commissioners" means the Commissioners for Her Majesty's Revenue and Customs;

"enactment" includes an Act of the Scottish Parliament or an instrument made under such an Act;

"late payment interest rate" means the rate provided for in regulations made by the Treasury under section 103(1) of FA 2009;

"special repayment rate" has the same meaning as in section 52 of F(No. 2)A 2015 (and subsections (7) to (10) of that section apply for the purposes of this section as they apply for the purposes of that section);

"taxation matter" means anything the collection and management of which is the responsibility of the Commissioners (or was the responsibility of the Commissioners of Inland Revenue or Commissioners of Customs and Excise);

"working day" means any day other than a non-business day as defined in section 92 of the Bills of Exchange Act 1882.

170(6) This section extends to Scotland only.

171 Rate of interest applicable to judgment debts etc: Northern Ireland

171(1) This section applies if a sum payable to or by the Commissioners under a judgment or order given or made in any court proceedings relating to a taxation matter (a "tax-related judgment debt") carries interest.

171(2) In a case where the rate of interest is specified in the judgment (in the case of the High Court) or directed by the judge (in the case of a county court), the rate specified or directed in relation to that debt may not exceed (and may not be capable of exceeding)–

(a) in the case of a sum payable to the Commissioners, the late payment interest rate, and

(b) in the case of a sum payable by the Commissioners, the special repayment rate.

171(3) In a case where the rate of interest in relation to the tax-related judgment debt is not specified in the judgment or directed by the judge but provided for by an enactment or rule of court (whenever passed or made), that enactment or rule is to have effect in relation to the debt as if for the rate for which it provides there were substituted–

(a) in the case of a sum payable to the Commissioners, the late payment interest rate, and

(b) in the case of a sum payable by the Commissioners, the special repayment rate.

171(4) This section has effect in relation to interest for periods beginning on or after the day on which this Act is passed, regardless of–

(a) the date of the judgment or order in question, and

(b) whether interest begins to run on or after the day on which this Act is passed, or began to run before that date.

171(5) In this section–

"the Commissioners" means the Commissioners for Her Majesty's Revenue and Customs;

"enactment" includes Northern Ireland legislation or an instrument made under such legislation;

"late payment interest rate" means the rate provided for in regulations made by the Treasury under section 103(1) of FA 2009;

"special repayment rate" has the same meaning as in section 52 of F(No. 2)A 2015 (and subsections (7) to (10) of that section apply for the purposes of this section as they apply for the purposes of that section);

"taxation matter" means anything the collection and management of which is the responsibility of the Commissioners (or was the responsibility of the Commissioners of Inland Revenue or Commissioners of Customs and Excise);

"working day" means any day other than a non-business day as defined in section 92 of the Bills of Exchange Act 1882.

171(6) This section extends to Northern Ireland only.

172 Rate of interest applicable to judgment debts etc: England and Wales

172(1) [*Amends F(No. 2)A 2015, s. 52(15).*]

172(2) This section has effect in relation to interest for periods beginning on or after the day on which this Act is passed, regardless of–

(a) the date of the judgment or order in question, and

(b) whether interest begins to run on or after the day on which this Act is passed, or began to run before that date.

172(3) This section extends to England and Wales only.

ENFORCEMENT POWERS

176 Data-gathering powers: providers of payment or intermediary services

176(1) [Inserts FA 2011, Sch. 23, para. 13B and 13C.]

176(2) This section applies in relation to relevant data with a bearing on any period (whether before, on or after the day on which this Act is passed).

177 Data-gathering powers: daily penalties for extended default

177(1) Part 4 of Schedule 23 to FA 2011 (data-gathering powers: penalties) is amended as follows.

177(2) In paragraph 38 (increased daily default penalty)–

(a) [amends FA 2011, Sch. 23, para. 38(1)(c) and (2);]

(b) [substitutes FA 2011, Sch. 23, para. 38(3) and (4);]

(c) [amends FA 2011, Sch. 23, para. 38(5).]

177(3) In paragraph 39–

(a) [amends FA 2011, Sch. 23, para. 39(1);]

(b) [amends FA 2011, Sch. 23, para. 39(2);]

(c) [omits FA 2011, Sch. 23, para. 39(3).]

177(4) [Amends FA 2011, Sch. 23, para. 40(2)(a).]

177(5) [Inserts FA 2011, Sch. 23, para. 36(2).]

PART 13 – FINAL

190 Interpretation

190 In this Act–

"ALDA 1979" means the Alcoholic Liquor Duties Act 1979;

"CAA 2001" means the Capital Allowances Act 2001;

"CEMA 1979" means the Customs and Excise Management Act 1979;

"CTA 2009" means the Corporation Tax Act 2009;

"CTA 2010" means the Corporation Tax Act 2010;

"FA", followed by a year, means the Finance Act of that year;

"F(No. 2)A", followed by a year means the Finance (No. 2) Act of that year;

"F(No. 3)A", followed by a year, means the Finance (No. 3) Act of that year;

"HODA 1979" means the Hydrocarbon Oil Duties Act 1979;

"ICTA" means the Income and Corporation Taxes Act 1988;

"IHTA 1984" means the Inheritance Tax Act 1984;

"ITA 2007" means the Income Tax Act 2007;

"ITEPA 2003" means the Income Tax (Earnings and Pensions) Act 2003;

"ITTOIA 2005" means the Income Tax (Trading and Other Income) Act 2005;

"OTA 1975" means the Oil Taxation Act 1975;

"TCGA 1992" means the Taxation of Chargeable Gains Act 1992;

"TIOPA 2010" means the Taxation (International and Other Provisions) Act 2010;

"TMA 1970" means the Taxes Management Act 1970;

"TPDA 1979" means the Tobacco Products Duty Act 1979;

"VATA 1994" means the Value Added Tax Act 1994;

"VERA 1994" means the Vehicle Excise and Registration Act 1994.

191 Short title

191 This Act may be cited as the Finance Act 2016.

"DISCLOSABLE SCHEDULE 11A VAT ARRANGEMENTS"

History – In the heading the words "SCHEDULE 11A" inserted by F(No. 2)A 2017, s. 66 and Sch. 17, para. 55(4) with effect so far as is necessary for enabling the making of regulations under that Schedule on 16 November 2017 (Royal Assent) and on 1 January 2018 for all other purposes.

8A [Not relevant to petroleum revenue tax.]

History – Para. 8A inserted by F(No. 2)A 2017, s. 66 and Sch. 17, para. 55(3) with effect so far as is necessary for enabling the making of regulations under that Schedule on 16 November 2017 (Royal Assent) and on 1 January 2018 for all other purposes.

9 [Not relevant to petroleum revenue tax.]

DISCLOSABLE INDIRECT TAX ARRANGEMENTS

9A [Not relevant to petroleum revenue tax.]

History – Para. 9A inserted by F(No. 2)A 2017, s. 66 and Sch. 17, para. 55(6) with effect so far as is necessary for enabling the making of regulations under that Schedule on 16 November 2017 (Royal Assent) and on 1 January 2018 for all other purposes.

PARAGRAPHS 8 TO 9A: "FAILURE TO COMPLY"

History – In the heading the words "TO 9A" substituted for the words "AND 9" by F(No. 2)A 2017, s. 66 and Sch. 17, para. 55(7) with effect so far as is necessary for enabling the making of regulations under that Schedule on 16 November 2017 (Royal Assent) and on 1 January 2018 for all other purposes.

10(1) A person **"fails to comply"** with any provision mentioned in paragraph 8(1), 8A(2)(c), 9(a) or 9A(1)(c) if and only if any of the conditions in sub-paragraphs (2) to (4) is met.

10(2) The condition in this sub-paragraph is that–

(a) the tribunal has determined that the person has failed to comply with the provision concerned,

(b) the appeal period has ended, and

(c) the determination has not been overturned on appeal.

10(3) The condition in this sub-paragraph is that–

(a) the tribunal has determined for the purposes of section 118(2) of TMA 1970 that the person is to be deemed not to have failed to comply with the provision concerned as the person had a reasonable excuse for not doing the thing required to be done,

(b) the appeal period has ended, and

(c) the determination has not been overturned on appeal.

10(4) The condition in this sub-paragraph is that the person admitted in writing to HMRC that the person has failed to comply with the provision concerned.

10(5) In this paragraph **"the appeal period"** means–

(a) the period during which an appeal could be brought against the determination of the tribunal, or

(b) where an appeal mentioned in paragraph (a) has been brought, the period during which that appeal has not been finally determined, withdrawn or otherwise disposed of.

10(6) In this paragraph **"the tribunal"** means the First-tier tribunal or, where determined by or under Tribunal Procedure Rules, the Upper Tribunal.

History – In para. 10(1) the words ", 8A(2)(c), 9(a) or 9A(1)(c)" substituted for the words "or 9(a)" by F(No. 2)A 2017, s. 66 and Sch. 17, para. 55(8) with effect so far as is necessary for enabling the making of regulations under that Schedule on 16 November 2017 (Royal Assent) and on 1 January 2018 for all other purposes.

"RELEVANT DEFEAT"

11(1) A person ("P") incurs a **"relevant defeat"** in relation to arrangements if any of Conditions A to F is met in relation to P and the arrangements.

11(2) The relevant defeat is incurred when the condition in question is first met.

History – In para. 11(1) "F" substituted for "E" by F(No. 2)A 2017, s. 66 and Sch. 17, para. 55(9) with effect so far as is necessary for enabling the making of regulations under that Schedule on 16 November 2017 (Royal Assent) and on 1 January 2018 for all other purposes.

CONDITION A

12(1) Condition A is that–

(a) P has been given a notice under paragraph 12 of Schedule 43 to FA 2013 (general anti-abuse rule: notice of final decision), paragraph 8 or 9 of Schedule 43A to that Act (pooled arrangements: notice of final decision) or paragraph 8 of Schedule 43B to that Act (generic referrals: notice of final decision)stating that a tax advantage arising from the arrangements is to be counteracted,

(b) that tax advantage has been counteracted under section 209 of FA 2013, and

(c) the counteraction is final.

12(2) For the purposes of this paragraph the counteraction of a tax advantage is **"final"** when the adjustments made to effect the counteraction, and any amounts arising as a result of those adjustments, can no longer be varied, on appeal or otherwise.

CONDITION B

13(1) Condition B is that (in a case not falling within Condition A above) a follower notice has been given to P by reference to the arrangements (and not withdrawn) and–

(a) the necessary corrective action for the purposes of section 208 of FA 2014 has been taken in respect of the denied advantage, or

(b) the denied advantage has been counteracted otherwise than as mentioned in paragraph (a) and the counteraction of the denied advantage is final.

13(2) In sub-paragraph (1) the reference to giving a follower notice to P includes a reference to giving a partnership follower notice in respect of a partnership return in relation to which P is a relevant partner (as defined in paragraph 2(5) of Schedule 31 to FA 2014).

13(3) For the purposes of this paragraph it does not matter whether the denied advantage has been dealt with–

(a) wholly as mentioned in one or other of paragraphs (a) and (b) of sub-paragraph (1), or

(b) partly as mentioned in one and partly as mentioned in the other of those paragraphs.

13(4) In this paragraph **"the denied advantage"** has the same meaning as in Chapter 2 of Part 4 of FA 2014 (see section 208(3) of and paragraph 4(3) of Schedule 31 to that Act).

13(5) For the purposes of this paragraph the counteraction of a tax advantage is **"final"** when the adjustments made to effect the counteraction, and any amounts arising as a result of those adjustments, can no longer be varied, on appeal or otherwise.

13(6) In this Schedule **"follower notice"** means a follower notice under Chapter 2 of Part 4 of FA 2014.

13(7) For the purposes of this paragraph a partnership follower notice is given **"in respect of"** the partnership return mentioned in paragraph (a) or (b) of paragraph 2(2) of Schedule 31 to FA 2014.

CONDITION C

14(1) Condition C is that (in a case not falling within Condition A or B)–

(a) the arrangements are DOTAS arrangements,

(b) P has relied on the arrangements (see sub-paragraph (2))–

(c) the arrangements have been counteracted, and

(d) the counteraction is final.

14(2) For the purposes of sub-paragraph (1), P **"relies on the arrangements"** if–

(a) P makes a return, claim or election, or a partnership return is made, on the basis that a relevant tax advantage arises, or

(b) P fails to discharge a relevant obligation ("the disputed obligation") and there is reason to believe that P's failure to discharge that obligation is connected with the arrangements.

14(3) For the purposes of sub-paragraph (2) **"relevant tax advantage"** means a tax advantage which the arrangements might be expected to enable P to obtain.

14(4) For the purposes of sub-paragraph (2) an obligation is a **"relevant obligation"** if the arrangements might be expected to have the result that the obligation does not arise.

14(5) For the purposes of this paragraph the arrangements are **"counteracted"** if–

(a) adjustments, other than taxpayer emendations, are made in respect of P's tax position–

  (i) on the basis that the whole or part of the relevant tax advantage mentioned in sub-paragraph (2)(a) does not arise, or

  (ii) on the basis that the disputed obligation does (or did) arise, or

(b) an assessment to tax other than a self-assessment is made, or any other action is taken by HMRC, on the basis mentioned in paragraph (a)(i) or (ii) (otherwise than by way of an adjustment).

14(6) For the purposes of this paragraph a counteraction is **"final"** when the assessment, adjustments or action in question, and any amounts arising from the assessment, adjustments or action, can no longer be varied, on appeal or otherwise.

14(7) For the purposes of sub-paragraph (1) the time at which it falls to be determined whether or not the arrangements are DOTAS arrangements is when the counteraction becomes final.

14(8) The following are **"taxpayer emendations"** for the purposes of sub-paragraph (5)–

(a) an adjustment made by P at a time when P had no reason to believe that HMRC had begun or were about to begin enquiries into P's affairs relating to the tax in question;

(b) an adjustment (by way of an assessment or otherwise) made by HMRC with respect to P's tax position as a result of a disclosure made by P which meets the conditions in sub-paragraph (9).

For the purposes of paragraph (a) a payment in respect of a liability to pay national insurance contributions is not an adjustment unless it is a payment in full.

14(9) The conditions are that the disclosure–

(a) is a full and explicit disclosure of an inaccuracy in a return or other document or of a failure to comply with an obligation, and

(b) was made at a time when P had no reason to believe that HMRC were about to begin enquiries into P's affairs relating to the tax in question.

14(10) For the purposes of this paragraph a contract settlement which HMRC enters into with P is treated as an assessment to tax (other than a self-assessment); and in relation to contract settlements references in sub-paragraph (5) to the basis an which any assessment or adjustments are made, or any other action is taken, are to be read with any necessary modifications.

CONDITION D

15 [Not relevant to petroleum revenue tax.]

CONDITION E

16 [Not relevant to petroleum revenue tax.]

CONDITION F

16A [Not relevant to petroleum revenue tax.]

History – Para. 16A inserted by F(No. 2)A 2017, s. 66 and Sch. 17, para. 55(10) with effect so far as is necessary for enabling the making of regulations under that Schedule on 16 November 2017 (Royal Assent) and on 1 January 2018 for all other purposes.

Part 3 – Annual Information Notices and Naming

ANNUAL INFORMATION NOTICES

17(1) A person ("P") who has been given a warning notice under this Schedule must give HMRC a written notice (an "information notice") in respect of each reporting period in the warning period (see sub-paragraph (11)).

17(2) An information notice must be given not later than the 30th day after the end of the reporting period to which it relates.

17(3) An information notice must state whether or not P–

(a) has in the reporting period delivered a return, or made a claim, election, declaration or application for approval, on the basis that a relevant tax advantage arises, or has since the end of the reporting period delivered on that basis a return which P was required to deliver before the end of that period,

(b) has in the reporting period failed to take action which P would be required to take under or by virtue of an enactment relating to tax but for particular disclosable arrangements to which P is a party,

(c) has in the reporting period become a party to arrangements which–

  (i) relate to the position with respect to VAT of another person ("S") who has made supplies of goods or services to P, and

  (ii) might be expected to enable P to obtain a relevant tax advantage ("the expected tax advantage") in connection with those supplies of goods or services,

(d) has failed to deliver a return which P was required to deliver by a date falling in the reporting period.

17(4) In this paragraph **"relevant tax advantage"** means a tax advantage which particular disclosable arrangements enable, or might be expected to enable, P to obtain.

17(5) If P has, in the reporting period concerned, made a return, claim, election, declaration or application for approval on the basis mentioned in sub-paragraph (3)(a) or failed to take action as mentioned in sub-paragraph (3)(b) the information notice must–

(a) explain (on the assumptions made by P in so acting or failing to act) how the disclosable arrangements enable P to obtain the tax advantage, or (as the case may be) have the result that P is not required to take the action in question, and

(b) state (on the same assumptions) the amount of the relevant tax advantage mentioned in sub-paragraph (3)(a) or (as the case may be) the amount of any tax advantage which arises in connection with the absence of a requirement to take the action mentioned in sub-paragraph (3)(b).

17(6) If P has, in the reporting period, become a party to arrangements such as are mentioned in sub-paragraph (3)(c), the information notice–

(a) must state whether or not it is P's view that the expected tax advantage arises to P, and

(b) if that is P's view, must explain how the arrangements enable P to obtain the tax advantage and state the amount of the tax advantage.

17(7) If the time by which P must deliver a return falls within a reporting period and P fails to deliver the return by that time, HMRC may require P to give HMRC a written notice (a "supplementary information notice") setting out any matters which P would have been required to set out in an information notice had P delivered the return in that reporting period.

17(8) A requirement under sub-paragraph (7) must be made by a written notice which states the period within which P must comply with the notice.

17(9) If P fails to comply with a requirement of (or imposed under) this paragraph HMRC may by written notice extend the warning period to the end of the period of 5 years beginning with–

(a) the day by which the information notice or supplementary information notice should have been given (see sub-paragraphs (2) and (8)) or, as the case requires,

(b) the day on which P gave the defective information notice or supplementary information notice to HMRC,

or, if earlier, the time when the warning period would have expired but for the extension.

17(10) HMRC may permit information notices given by members of the same group of companies (as defined in paragraph 46(9)) to be combined.

17(11) For the purposes of this paragraph–

(a) the first reporting period in any warning period begins with the first day of the warning period and ends with a day specified by HMRC ("the specified day"),

(b) the remainder of the warning period is divided into further reporting periods each of which begins immediately after the end of the preceding reporting period and is twelve months long or (if that would be shorter) ends at the end of the warning period.

17(12) In this paragraph **"disclosable arrangements"** means any of the following–

(a) DOTAS arrangements,

(b) disclosable VAT arrangements, and

(c) disclosable indirect tax arrangements.

History – In para. 17(3)(a) the words ", election, declaration or application for approval," (initial comma assumed by Croner-i) substituted for the words "or election," by F(No. 2)A 2017, s. 66 and Sch. 17, para. 55(11)(a) with effect so far as is necessary for enabling the making of regulations under that Schedule on 16 November 2017 (Royal Assent) and on 1 January 2018 for all other purposes.
In para. 17(3)(b) the words "disclosable" (initial comma assumed by Croner-i) substituted for the words "DOTAS arrangements or [disclosable] VAT" by F(No. 2)A 2017, s. 66 and Sch. 17, para. 55(11)(b) with effect so far as is necessary for enabling the making of regulations under that Schedule on 16 November 2017 (Royal Assent) and on 1 January 2018 for all other purposes.
In para. 17(4) the words "disclosable" (initial comma assumed by Croner-i) substituted for the words "DOTAS arrangements or [disclosable] VAT" by F(No. 2)A 2017, s. 66 and Sch. 17, para. 55(11)(b) with effect so far as is necessary for enabling the making of regulations under that Schedule on 16 November 2017 (Royal Assent) and on 1 January 2018 for all other purposes.
In para. 17(5)(a) the words "disclosable" (initial comma assumed by Croner-i) substituted for the words "DOTAS arrangements or [disclosable] VAT" by F(No. 2)A 2017, s. 66 and Sch. 17, para. 55(11)(b) with effect so far as is necessary for enabling the making of regulations under that Schedule on 16 November 2017 (Royal Assent) and on 1 January 2018 for all other purposes.
In para. 17(5) the words ", election, declaration or application for approval" (initial comma assumed by Croner-i) substituted for the words "or election" by F(No. 2)A 2017, s. 66 and Sch. 17, para. 55(11)(c) with effect so far as is necessary for enabling the making of regulations under that Schedule on 16 November 2017 (Royal Assent) and on 1 January 2018 for all other purposes.
Para. 17(12) inserted by F(No. 2)A 2017, s. 66 and Sch. 17, para. 55(11)(d) with effect so far as is necessary for enabling the making of regulations under that Schedule on 16 November 2017 (Royal Assent) and on 1 January 2018 for all other purposes.

NAMING

18(1) The Commissioners may publish information about a person if the person–

(a) incurs a relevant defeat in relation to arrangements which the person has used in a warning period, and

(b) has been given at least two warning notices in respect of other defeats of arrangements which were used in the same warning period.

18(2) Information published for the first time under sub-paragraph (1) must be published within the 12 months beginning with the day on which the most recent of the warning notices falling within that sub-paragraph has been given to the person.

18(3) No information may be published (or continue to be published) after the end of the period of 12 months beginning with the day on which it is first published.

18(4) The information that may be published is–

(a) the person's name (including any trading name, previous name or pseudonym),

(b) the person's address (or registered office),

(c) the nature of any business carried on by the person,

(d) information about the fiscal effect of the defeated arrangements (had they not been defeated), for instance information about total amounts of tax understated or total amounts by which claims, or statements of losses, have been adjusted,

(e) the amount of any penalty to which the person is liable under paragraph 30 in respect of the relevant defeat of any defeated arrangements,

(f) the periods in which or times when the defeated arrangements were used, and

(g) any other information the Commissioners may consider it appropriate to publish in order to make clear the person's identity.

18(5) If the person mentioned in sub-paragraph (1) is a member of a group of companies (as defined in paragraph 46(9)), the information which may be published also includes–

(a) any trading name of the group, and

(b) information about other members of the group of the kind described in sub-paragraph (4)(a), (b) or (c).

18(6) If the person mentioned in sub-paragraph (1) is a person carrying on a trade or business in partnership, the information which may be published also includes–

(a) any trading name of the partnership, and

(b) information about other members of the partnership of the kind described in sub-paragraph (4)(a) or (b).

18(7) The information may be published in any manner the Commissioners may consider appropriate.

18(8) Before publishing any information the Commissioners–

(a) must inform the person that they are considering doing so, and

(b) afford the person reasonable opportunity to make representations about whether or not it should be published.

18(9) Arrangements are **"defeated arrangements"** for the purposes of sub-paragraph (4) if the person used them in the warning period mentioned in sub-paragraph (1) and a warning notice specifying the defeat of those arrangements has been given to the person before the information is published.

18(10) If a person has been given a single warning notice in relation to two or more relevant defeats, the person is treated for the purposes of this paragraph as having been given a separate warning notice in relation to each of those relevant defeats.

18(11) Nothing in this paragraph prevents the power under sub-paragraph (1) from being exercised on a subsequent occasion in relation to arrangements used by the person in a different warning period.

Part 4 – Restriction of Reliefs

DUTY TO GIVE A RESTRICTION RELIEF NOTICE

19(1) HMRC must give a person a written notice (a "restriction of relief notice") if–

(a) the person incurs a relevant defeat in relation to arrangements which the person has used in a warning period,

(b) the person has been given at least two warning notices in respect of other relevant defeats of arrangements which were used in that same warning period, and

(c) the defeats mentioned in paragraphs (a) and (b) meet the conditions in sub-paragraph (2).

19(2) The conditions are–

(a) that each of the relevant defeats is by virtue of Condition A, B or C,

(b) that each of the relevant defeats relates to the misuse of a relief (see sub-paragraph (5)), and

(c) in the case of each of the relevant defeats, either–
(i) that the relevant counteraction (see sub-paragraph (7)) was made on the basis that a particular avoidance-related rule applies in relation to a person's affairs, or
(ii) that the misused relief is a loss relief.

19(3) In sub-paragraph (2)(c)–
(a) the **"misused relief"** means the relief mentioned in sub-paragraph (5), and
(b) **"loss relief"** means any relief under Part 4 of ITA 2007 or Part 4 or 5 of CTA 2010.

19(4) A restriction of relief notice must–
(a) explain the effect of paragraphs 20, 21 and 22, and
(b) set out when the restricted period is to begin and end.

19(5) For the purposes of this Part of this Schedule, a relevant defeat by virtue of Condition A, B or C **"relates to the misuse of a relief"** if–
(a) the tax advantage in question, or part of the tax advantage in question, is or results from (or would but for the counteraction be or result from) a relief or increased relief from tax, or
(b) it is reasonable to conclude that the making of a particular claim for relief, or the use of a particular relief, is a significant component of the arrangements in question.

19(6) In sub-paragraph (5) **"the tax advantage in question"** means–
(a) in relation to a defeat by virtue of Condition A, the tax advantage mentioned in paragraph 12(1)(a),
(b) in relation to a defeat by virtue of Condition B, the denied advantage (as defined in paragraph 13(4)), or
(c) in relation to a defeat by virtue of Condition C–
(i) the tax advantage mentioned in paragraph 14(2)(a), or, as the case requires,
(ii) the absence of the relevant obligation (as defined in paragraph 14(4)).

19(7) In this paragraph **"the relevant counteraction"**, in relation to a relevant defeat means–
(a) in the case of a defeat by virtue of Condition A, the counteraction referred to in paragraph 12(1)(c);
(b) in the case of a defeat by virtue of Condition B, the action referred to in paragraph 13(1);
(c) in the case of a defeat by virtue of Condition C, the counteraction referred to in paragraph 14(1)(d).

19(8) If a person has been given a single warning notice in relation to two or more relevant defeats, the person is treated for the purposes of this paragraph as having been given a separate warning notice in relation to each of those relevant defeats.

RESTRICTION OF RELIEF

20(1) Sub-paragraphs (2) to (15) have effect in relation to a person to whom a relief restriction notice has been given.

20(2) The person may not, in the restricted period, make any claim for relief.

20(3) Sub-paragraph (2) does not have effect in relation to–
(a) a claim for relief under Schedule 8 to FA 2003 (stamp duty land tax: charities relief);
(b) a claim for relief under Chapter 3 of Part 8 of ITA 2007 (gifts of shares, securities and real property to charities etc);
(c) a claim for relief under Part 10 of ITA 2007 (special rules about charitable trusts etc);
(d) a claim for relief under double taxation arrangements;
(e) an election under section 426 of ITA 2007 (gift aid: election to treat gift as made in previous year).

20(4) Claims under the following provisions in Part 4 of FA 2004 (registered pension schemes: tax reliefs etc) do not count as claims for relief for the purposes of this paragraph–

section 192(4) (increase of basic rate limit and higher rate limit);
section 193(4) (net pay arrangements: excess relief);
section 194(1) (relief on making of a claim).

20(5) The person may not, in the restricted period, surrender group relief under Part 5 of CTA 2010.

20(6) No deduction is to be made under section 83 of ITA 2007 (carry forward against subsequent trade profits) in calculating the person's net income for a relevant tax year.

20(7) No deduction is to be made under section 118 of ITA 2007 (carry-forward property loss relief) in calculating the person's net income for a relevant tax year.

20(8) The person is not entitled to relief under section 448 (annual payments: relief for individuals) or 449 (annual payments: relief for other persons) of ITA 2007 for any payment made in the restricted period.

20(9) No deduction of expenses referable to a relevant accounting period is to be made under section 1219(1) of CTA 2009 (expenses of management of a company's investment business).

20(10) No reduction is to be made under section 45(4) of CTA 2010 (carry-forward of trade loss relief) in calculating the profits for a relevant accounting period of a trade carried on by the person.

20(11) In calculating the total amount of chargeable gains accruing to a person in a relevant tax year (or part of a relevant tax year), no losses are to be deducted under subsections (2) to (2B) of section 2 of TCGA 1992 (persons and gains chargeable to capital gains tax, and allowable losses).

20(12) In calculating the total amount of ATED-related chargeable gains accruing to a person in a relevant tax year, no losses are to be deducted under subsection (3) of section 2B of TCGA 1992 (persons chargeable to capital gains tax on ATED-related gains).

20(13) In calculating the total amount of chargeable NRCGT gains accruing to a person in a relevant tax year on relevant high value disposals, no losses are to be deducted under subsection (2) of section 14D of TCGA 1992 (persons chargeable to capital gains tax on NRCGT gains).

20(14) If the person is a company, no deduction is to be made under section 62 of CTA 2010 (relief for losses made in UK property business) from the company's total profits of a relevant accounting period.

20(15) No deduction is to be made under regulation 18 of the Unauthorised Unit Trusts (Tax) Regulations 2013 (S.I. 2013/2819) (relief for deemed payments by trustees of an exempt unauthorised unit trust) in calculating the person's net income for a relevant tax year.

20(16) In this paragraph **"relevant tax year"** means any tax year the first day of which is in the restricted period.

20(17) In this paragraph **"relevant accounting period"** means an accounting period the first day of which is in the restricted period.

20(18) In this paragraph **"double taxation arrangements"** means arrangements which have effect under section 2(1) of TIOPA 2010 (double taxation relief by agreement with territories outside the UK).

THE RESTRICTED PERIOD

21(1) In paragraphs 19 and 20 (and this paragraph) **"the restricted period"** means the period of 3 years beginning with the day on which the relief restriction notice is given.

21(2) If during the restricted period (or the restricted period as extended under this sub-paragraph) the person to whom a relief restriction notice has been given incurs a further relevant defeat meeting the conditions in sub-paragraph (4), HMRC must give the person a written notice (a "restricted period extension notice").

21(3) A restricted period extension notice extends the restricted period to the end of the period of 3 years beginning with the day on which the further relevant defeat occurs.

21(4) The conditions mentioned in sub-paragraph (2) are that–

(a) the relevant defeat is incurred by virtue of Condition A, B or C in relation to arrangements which the person used in the warning period mentioned in paragraph 19(1)(a), and

(b) the warning notice given to the person in respect of the relevant defeat relates to the misuse of a relief.

21(5) If the person to whom a relief restriction notice has been given incurs a relevant defeat which meets the conditions in sub-paragraph (4) after the restricted period has expired but before the end of a concurrent warning period, HMRC must give the person a restriction of relief notice.

21(6) In sub-paragraph (5) **"concurrent warning period"** means a warning period which at some time ran concurrently with the restricted period.

REASONABLE EXCUSE

22(1) If a person who has incurred a relevant defeat satisfies HMRC or, on an appeal under paragraph 24, the First-tier Tribunal or Upper Tribunal that the person had a reasonable excuse for the matters to which that relevant defeat relates, then–

(a) for the purposes of paragraph 19(1)(a) and 21(2) and (5), the person is treated as not having incurred that relevant defeat, and

(b) for the purposes of paragraph 19(1)(b) and (c) any warning notice given to the person which relates to that relevant defeat is treated as not having been given to the person.

22(2) For the purposes of this paragraph, in the case of a person ("P")–

(a) an insufficiency of funds is not a reasonable excuse unless attributable to events outside P's control,

(b) where P relies on another person to do anything, that is not a reasonable excuse unless P took reasonable care to avoid the relevant failure, and

(c) where P had reasonable excuse for the relevant failure but the excuse had ceased, P is to be treated as having continued to have the excuse if the failure is remedied without unreasonable delay after the excuse ceased.

22(3) In determining for the purposes of this paragraph whether or not a person ("P") had a reasonable excuse for any action, failure or inaccuracy, reliance on advice is to be taken automatically not to constitute a reasonable excuse if the advice is addressed to, or was given to, a person other than P or takes no account of P's individual circumstances.

22(4) In this paragraph **"relevant failure"**, in relation to a relevant defeat, is to be interpreted in accordance with sub-paragraphs (2) to (7) of paragraph 43.

MITIGATION OF RESTRICTION OF RELIEF

23(1) The Commissioners may mitigate the effects of paragraph 20 in relation to a person ("P") so far as it appears to them that there are exceptional circumstances such that the operation of that paragraph would otherwise have an unduly serious impact with respect to the tax affairs of P or another person.

23(2) For the purposes of sub-paragraph (1) the Commissioners may modify the effects of paragraph 20 in any way they think appropriate, including by allowing P access to the whole or part of a relief to which P would otherwise not be entitled as a result of paragraph 20.

APPEAL

24(1) A person may appeal against–

(a) a relief restriction notice, or

(b) a restricted period extension notice.

24(2) An appeal under this paragraph must be made within the period of 30 days beginning with the day on which the notice is given.

24(3) An appeal under this paragraph is to be treated in the same way as an appeal against an assessment to income tax (including by the application of any provision about bringing the appeal by notice to HMRC, about HMRC's review of the decision or about determination of the appeal by the First-tier Tribunal or Upper Tribunal).

24(4) On an appeal the tribunal may–

(a) cancel HMRC's decision, or

(b) affirm that decision with or without any modifications in accordance with sub-paragraph (5).

24(5) On an appeal the tribunal may rely on paragraph 23 (mitigation of restriction of relief)–

(a) to the same extent as HMRC (which may mean applying the same mitigation as HMRC to a different starting point), or

(b) to a different extent, but only if the tribunal thinks that HMRC's decision in respect of the application of paragraph 23 was flawed.

24(6) In this paragraph **"tribunal"** means the First-tier Tribunal or Upper Tribunal (as appropriate by virtue of sub-paragraph (3)).

MEANING OF "AVOIDANCE-RELATED RULE"

25(1) In this Part of this Schedule **"avoidance-related rule"** means a rule in Category 1 or 2.

25(2) A rule is in Category 1 if it refers (in whatever terms)–

(a) to the purpose or main purpose or purposes of a transaction, arrangements or any other action or matter, and

(b) to whether or not the purpose in question is or involves the avoidance of tax or the obtaining of any advantage in relation to tax (however described).

25(3) A *rule is also in* Category 1 if it refers (in whatever terms) to–

(a) expectations as to what are, or may be, the expected benefits of a transaction, arrangements or any other action or matter, and

(b) whether or not the avoidance of tax or the obtaining of any advantage in relation to tax (however described) is such a benefit.

For the purposes of paragraph (b) it does not matter whether the reference is (for instance) to the "sole or main benefit" or "one of the main benefits" or any other reference to a benefit.

25(4) A rule falls within Category 2 if as a result of the rule a person may be treated differently for tax purposes depending on whether or not purposes referred to in the rule (for instance the purposes of an actual or contemplated action or enterprise) are (or are shown to be) commercial purposes.

25(5) For example, a rule in the following form would fall within Category 1 and within Category 2–

"Example rule

Section X does not apply to a company in respect of a transaction if the company shows that the transaction meets Condition A or B.

Condition A is that the transaction is effected–

(a) for genuine commercial reasons, or

(b) in the ordinary course of managing investments.

Condition B is that the avoidance of tax is not the main object or one of the main objects of the transaction."

MEANING OF "RELIEF"

26 The following are **"reliefs"** for the purposes of this Part of this Schedule–

(a) any relief from tax (however described) which must be claimed, or which is not available without making an election,

(b) relief under section 1219 of CTA 2009 (expenses of management of a company's investment business),

(c) any relief (not falling within paragraph (a)) under Part 4 of ITA 2007 (loss relief) or Part 4 or 5 of CTA 2010 (loss relief and group relief), and

(d) any relief (not falling within paragraph (a) or (b)) under a provision listed in section 24 of ITA 2007 (reliefs deductible at Step 2 of the calculation of income tax liability).

"CLAIM" FOR RELIEF

27 In this Part of this Schedule **"claim for relief"** includes any election or other similar action which is in substance a claim for relief.

VAT AND INDIRECT TAXES

History – In the heading the words "and indirect taxes" inserted by F(No. 2)A 2017, s. 66 and Sch. 17, para. 55(12) with effect so far as is necessary for enabling the making of regulations under that Schedule on 16 November 2017 (Royal Assent) and on 1 January 2018 for all other purposes.

28 In this Part of this Schedule **"tax"** does not include VAT or any other indirect tax.

History – In para. 28 the words "or any other indirect tax" inserted by F(No. 2)A 2017, s. 66 and Sch. 17, para. 55(13) with effect so far as is necessary for enabling the making of regulations under that Schedule on 16 November 2017 (Royal Assent) and on 1 January 2018 for all other purposes.

POWER TO AMEND

29(1) The Treasury may by regulations amend–

(a) amend paragraph 20;

(b) amend paragraph 26.

29(2) Regulations under sub-paragraph (1)(a) may, in particular, alter the application of paragraph 20 in relation to any relief, exclude any relief from its application or extend its application to further reliefs.

29(3) Regulations under sub-paragraph (1)(b) may amend the meaning of "relief" in any way (including by extending or limiting the meaning).

29(4) Regulations under this paragraph may–

(a) make supplementary, incidental and consequential provision;

(b) make transitional provision.

29(5) Regulations under this paragraph are to be made by statutory instrument.

29(6) A statutory instrument containing regulations under this Part may not be made unless a draft of the instrument has been laid before and approved by a resolution of the House of Commons.

Part 5 – Penalty

PENALTY

30(1) A person is liable to pay a penalty if the person incurs a relevant defeat in relation to any arrangements which the person has used in a warning period.

30(2) The penalty is 20% of the value of the counteracted advantage if neither sub-paragraph (3) nor sub-paragraph (4) applies.

30(3) The penalty is 40% of the value of the counteracted advantage if before the relevant defeat is incurred the person has been given, or become liable to be given, one (but not more than one) relevant prior warning notice.

30(4) The penalty is 60% of the value of the counteracted advantage if before the current defeat is incurred the person has been given, or become liable to be given, two or more relevant prior warning notices.

30(5) In this paragraph **"relevant prior warning notice"** means a warning notice in relation to the defeat of arrangements which the person has used in the warning period mentioned in sub-paragraph (1).

30(6) For the meaning of "the value of the counteracted advantage" see paragraphs 32 to 37.

SIMULTANEOUS DEFEATS ETC

31(1) If a person incurs simultaneously two or more relevant defeats in relation to different arrangements, sub-paragraphs (2) to (4) of paragraph 30 have effect as if the relevant defeat with the lowest value was incurred last, the relevant defeat with the next lowest value immediately before it, and so on.

31(2) For this purpose the **"value"** of a relevant defeat is taken to be equal to the value of the counteracted advantage.

31(3) If a person has been given a single warning notice in relation to two or more relevant defeats, the person is treated for the purposes of paragraph 30 as having been given a separate warning notice in relation to each of those relevant defeats.

VALUE OF THE COUNTERACTED ADVANTAGE: BASIC RULE FOR TAXES OTHER THAN VAT

32(1) In relation to a relevant defeat incurred by virtue of Condition A, B, C or F, the **"value of the counteracted advantage"** is–

(a) in the case of a relevant defeat incurred by virtue of Condition A, the additional amount due or payable in respect of tax as a result of the counteraction mentioned in paragraph 12(1)(c);

(b) in the case of a relevant defeat incurred by virtue of Condition B, the additional amount due or payable in respect of tax as a result of the action mentioned in paragraph 13(1);

(c) in the case of a relevant defeat incurred by virtue of Condition C, the additional amount due or payable in respect of tax as a result of the counteraction mentioned in paragraph 14(1)(d);

(d) in the case of a relevant defeat incurred by virtue of Condition F, the additional amount due or payable in respect of tax as a result of the counteraction mentioned in paragraph 16A(1)(d).

32(2) The reference in sub-paragraph (1) to the additional amount due and payable includes a reference to–

(a) an amount payable to HMRC having erroneously been paid by way of repayment of tax, and

(b) an amount which would be repayable by HMRC if the counteraction mentioned in paragraph (a), (c) or (d) of sub-paragraph (1) were not made or the action mentioned in paragraph (b) of that sub-paragraph were not taken (as the case may be).

32(3) The following are ignored in calculating the value of the counteracted advantage–

(a) group relief, and

(b) any relief under section 458 of CTA 2010 (relief in respect of repayment etc of loan) which is deferred under subsection (5) of that section.

32(4) This paragraph is subject to paragraphs 33 and 34.

History – In para. 32(1) the words ", C or F" (comma assumed by Croner-i) substituted for the words "or C" and para. 32(1)(d) inserted by F(No. 2)A 2017, s. 66 and Sch. 17, para. 55(14)(a) with effect so far as is necessary for enabling the making of regulations under that Schedule on 16 November 2017 (Royal Assent) and on 1 January 2018 for all other purposes.

In para. 32(2)(b) the words ", (c) or (d)" (comma assumed by Croner-i) substituted for the words "or (c)" and para. 32(1)(d) inserted by F(No. 2)A 2017, s. 66 and Sch. 17, para. 55(14)(b) with effect so far as is necessary for enabling the making of regulations under that Schedule on 16 November 2017 (Royal Assent) and on 1 January 2018 for all other purposes.

VALUE OF COUNTERACTED ADVANTAGE: LOSSES FOR PURPOSES OF DIRECT TAX

33(1) This paragraph has effect in relation to relevant defeats incurred by virtue of Condition A, B or C.

33(2) To the extent that the counteracted advantage (see paragraph 35) has the result that a loss is wrongly recorded for the purposes of direct tax and the loss has been wholly used to reduce the amount due or payable in respect of tax, the value of the counteracted advantage is determined in accordance with paragraph 32.

33(3) To the extent that the counteracted advantage has the result that a loss is wrongly recorded for purposes of direct tax and the loss has not been wholly used to reduce the amount due or payable in respect of tax, the value of the counteracted advantage is–

(a) the value under paragraph 32 of so much of the counteracted advantage as results from the part (if any) of the loss which is used to reduce the amount due or payable in respect of tax, plus

(b) 10% of the part of the loss not so used.

33(4) Sub-paragraphs (2) and (3) apply both–

(a) to a case where no loss would have been recorded but for the counteracted advantage, and

(b) to a case where a loss of a different amount would have been recorded (but in that case sub-paragraphs (2) and (3) apply only to the difference between the amount recorded and the true amount).

33(5) To the extent that a counteracted advantage creates or increases an aggregate loss recorded for a group of companies–

(a) the value of the counteracted advantage is calculated in accordance with this paragraph, and

(b) in applying paragraph 32 in accordance with sub-paragraphs (2) and (3), group relief may be taken into account (despite paragraph 32(3)).

33(6) To the extent that the counteracted advantage results in a loss, the value of it is nil where, because of the nature of the loss or the person's circumstances, there is no reasonable prospect of the loss being used to support a claim to reduce a tax liability (of any person).

VALUE OF COUNTERACTED ADVANTAGE: DEFERRED TAX

34(1) To the extent that the counteracted advantage (see paragraph 35) is a deferral of tax (other than VAT), the value of that advantage is–

(a) 25% of the amount of the deferred tax for each year of the deferral, or

(b) a percentage of the amount of the deferred tax, for each separate period of deferral of less than a year, equating to 25% per year,

or, if less, 100% of the amount of the deferred tax.

34(2) This paragraph does not apply to a case to the extent that paragraph 33 applies.

MEANING OF "THE COUNTERACTED ADVANTAGE" IN PARAGRAPHS 33 AND 34

35(1) In paragraphs 33 and 34 **"the counteracted advantage"** means–

(a) in relation to a relevant defeat incurred by virtue of Condition A, the tax advantage mentioned in paragraph 12(1)(b);

(b) in relation to a relevant defeat incurred by virtue of Condition B, the denied advantage in relation to which the action mentioned in paragraph 13(1) is taken;

(c) in relation to a relevant defeat incurred by virtue of Condition C, means any tax advantage in respect of which the counteraction mentioned in paragraph 14(1)(c) is made;

(d) in relation to a relevant defeat incurred by virtue of Condition F, means any tax advantage in respect of which the counteraction mentioned in paragraph 16A(1)(c) is made.

35(2) In sub-paragraph (1)(c) **"counteraction"** is to be interpreted in accordance with paragraph 14(5).

History – Para. 35(1)(d) inserted by F(No. 2)A 2017, s. 66 and Sch. 17, para. 55(15) with effect so far as is necessary for enabling the making of regulations under that Schedule on 16 November 2017 (Royal Assent) and on 1 January 2018 for all other purposes.

VALUE OF THE COUNTERACTED ADVANTAGE: CONDITIONS D AND E

36 [Not relevant to petroleum revenue tax.]

VALUE OF COUNTERACTED ADVANTAGE: DELAYED VAT

37 [Not relevant to petroleum revenue tax.]

ASSESSMENT OF PENALTY

38(1) Where a person is liable for a penalty under paragraph 30, HMRC must assess the penalty.

38(2) Where HMRC assess the penalty, HMRC must–

(a) notify the person who is liable for the penalty, and

(b) state in the notice a tax period in respect of which the penalty is assessed.

38(3) A penalty under this paragraph must be paid before the end of the period of 30 days beginning with the day on which the person is notified of the penalty under sub-paragraph (2).

38(4) An assessment–

(a) is to be treated for procedural purposes as if it were an assessment to tax,

(b) may be enforced as if it were an assessment to tax, and

(c) may be combined with an assessment to tax.

38(5) An assessment of a penalty under this paragraph must be made before the end of the period of 12 months beginning with the date of the defeat mentioned in paragraph 30(1).

ALTERATION OF ASSESSMENT OF PENALTY

39(1) After notification of an assessment has been given to a person under paragraph 38(2), the assessment may not be altered except in accordance with this paragraph or on appeal.

39(2) A supplementary assessment may be made in respect of a penalty if an earlier assessment operated by reference to an underestimate of the value of the counteracted advantage.

39(3) An assessment may be revised as necessary if operated by reference to an overestimate of the value of the counteracted advantage.

AGGREGATE PENALTIES

40(1) The amount of a penalty for which a person is liable under paragraph 30 is to be reduced by the amount of any other penalty incurred by the person, or any surcharge for late payment of tax imposed on the person, if the amount of the penalty or surcharge is determined by reference to the same tax liability.

40(2) In sub-paragraph (1) **"any other penalty"** does not include a penalty under section 212A of FA 2013 (GAAR penalty) or Part 4 of FA 2014 (penalty where corrective action not taken after follower notice etc).

40(3) In the application of section 97A of TMA 1970 (multiple penalties) no account shall be taken of a penalty under paragraph 30.

APPEAL AGAINST PENALTY

41(1) A person may appeal against a decision of HMRC that a penalty is payable under paragraph 30.

41(2) A person may appeal against a decision of HMRC as to the amount of a penalty payable by P under paragraph 30.

41(3) An appeal under this paragraph must be made within the period of 30 days beginning with the day on which notification of the penalty is given under paragraph 38.

41(4) An appeal under this paragraph is to be treated in the same way as an appeal against an assessment to the tax concerned (including by the application of any provision about bringing the appeal by notice to HMRC, about HMRC's review of the decision or about determination of the appeal by the First-tier Tribunal or Upper Tribunal).

41(5) Sub-paragraph (4) does not apply–

(a) so as to require a person to pay a penalty before an appeal against the assessment of the penalty is determined, or

(b) in respect of any other matter expressly provided for by this Part of this Schedule.

41(6) *On an appeal under sub-*paragraph (1) or (2) the tribunal may–

(a) affirm HMRC's decision, or

(b) substitute for HMRC's decision another decision that HMRC has power to make.

41(7) In this paragraph **"tribunal"** means the First-tier Tribunal or Upper Tribunal (as appropriate by virtue of sub-paragraph (4)).

PENALTIES: REASONABLE EXCUSE

42(1) A person is not liable to a penalty under paragraph 30 in respect of a relevant defeat if the person satisfies HMRC or (on appeal) the First-tier Tribunal or Upper Tribunal that the person had a reasonable excuse for the relevant failure to which that relevant defeat relates (see paragraph 43).

42(2) Sub-paragraph (3) applies if–

(a) a person has incurred a relevant defeat in respect of which the person is liable to a penalty under paragraph 30, and

(b) before incurring that defeat the person had been given, or become liable to be given, an excepted warning notice.

42(3) The person is treated for the purposes of sub-paragraphs (2) to (4) of paragraph 30 (rate of penalty) as not having been given, and not having become liable to be given, the excepted notice (so far as it relates to the relevant defeat in respect of which the person had a reasonable excuse).

42(4) A warning notice is **"excepted"** for the purposes of this paragraph if the person was not liable to a penalty in respect of the defeat specified in it because the person had a reasonable excuse for the relevant failure in question.

42(5) For the purposes of this paragraph, in the case of a person ("P")–

(a) an insufficiency of funds is not a reasonable excuse unless attributable to events outside P's control,

(b) where P relies on another person to do anything, that is not a reasonable excuse unless P took reasonable care to avoid the relevant failure, and

(c) where P had a reasonable excuse for the relevant failure but the excuse had ceased, P is to be treated as having continued to have the excuse if the failure is remedied without unreasonable delay after the excuse ceased.

42(6) In determining for the purposes of this paragraph whether or not a person ("P") had a reasonable excuse for any action, failure or inaccuracy, reliance on advice is to be taken automatically not to constitute a reasonable excuse if the advice is addressed to, or was given to, a person other than P or takes no account of P's individual circumstances.

PARAGRAPH 42: MEANING OF "THE RELEVANT FAILURE"

43(1) In paragraph 42 **"the relevant failure"**, in relation to a relevant defeat, is to be interpreted in accordance with sub-paragraphs (2) to (7).

43(2) In relation to a relevant defeat incurred by virtue of Condition A, **"the relevant failure"** means the failures or inaccuracies as a result of which the counteraction under section 209 of FA 2013 was necessary.

43(3) In relation to a relevant defeat incurred by virtue of Condition B, **"the relevant failure"** means the failures or inaccuracies in respect of which the action mentioned in paragraph 13(1) was taken.

43(4) In relation to a relevant defeat incurred by virtue of Condition C, **"the relevant failure"** means the failures of inaccuracies as a result of which the adjustments, assessments, or other action mentioned in paragraph 14(5) are required.

43(5) In relation to a relevant defeat incurred by virtue of Condition D, **"the relevant failure"** means the failures or inaccuracies as a result of which the adjustments, assessments or other action mentioned in paragraph 15(5) are required.

43(6) In relation to a relevant defeat incurred by virtue of Condition E, **"the relevant failure"** means P's actions (and failures to act), so far as they are connected with matters in respect of which the counteraction mentioned in paragraph 16(1) is required.

43(7) In sub-paragraph (6) **"counteraction"** is to be interpreted in accordance with paragraph 16(2).

43(8) In relation to a relevant defeat incurred by virtue of Condition F, **"the relevant failure"** means the failures or inaccuracies as a result of which the adjustments, assessments, or other actions mentioned in paragraph 16A(5) are required.

History – Para. 43(8) inserted by *F(No. 2)A 2017*, s. 66 and Sch. 17, para. 55(16) with effect so far as is necessary for enabling the making of regulations under that Schedule on 16 November 2017 (Royal Assent) and on 1 January 2018 for all other purposes.

MITIGATION OF PENALTIES

44(1) The Commissioners may in their discretion mitigate a penalty under paragraph 30, or stay or compound any proceedings for such a penalty.

44(2) They may also, after judgment, further mitigate or entirely remit the penalty.

Part 6 – Corporate Groups, Associated Persons and Partnerships

REPRESENTATIVE MEMBER OF A VAT GROUP

45 [Not relevant to petroleum revenue tax.]

CORPORATE GROUPS

46(1) Sub-paragraphs (2) and (3) apply if HMRC has a duty under paragraph 2 to give a warning notice to a company ("C") which is a member of a group.

46(2) That duty has effect as a duty to give a warning notice to each current group member (see sub-paragraph (8)).

46(3) Any warning notice which has been given (or is treated as having been given) previously to any current group member is treated as having been given to each current group member (and any provision in this Schedule which refers to a **"warning period"** in relation to a person is to be interpreted accordingly). But see sub-paragraphs (4) and (5).

46(4) In relation to a company which incurs a relevant defeat, paragraph 19(1) (duty to give relief restriction notice) does not have effect unless the warning period mentioned in that sub-paragraph would be a warning period in relation to the company regardless of sub-paragraph (3).

46(5) A company which incurs a relevant defeat is not liable to pay a penalty under paragraph 30 unless the warning period mentioned in sub-paragraph (1) of that paragraph would be a warning period in relation to the company regardless of sub-paragraph (3).

46(6) HMRC may discharge any duty to give a warning notice to a current group member in accordance with sub-paragraph (2) by delivering the notice to C (and if it does so may combine one or more warning notices in a single notice).

46(7) If a company ceases to be a member of a group, and–

(a) immediately before it ceases to be a member of the group, a warning period has effect in relation to the company, but

(b) no warning period would have effect in relation to the company at that time but for sub-paragraph (2) or (3),

that warning period ceases to have effect in relation to the company when it ceases to be a member of that group.

46(8) In this paragraph **"current group member"** means a company which is a member of the group concerned at the time when the warning notice mentioned in sub-paragraph (1) is given.

46(9) For the purposes of this paragraph two companies are members of the same group of companies if–

(a) one is a 75% subsidiary of the other, or

(b) both are 75% subsidiaries of a third company.

46(10) In this paragraph **"75% subsidiary"** has the meaning given by section 1154 of CTA 2010.

46(11) In this paragraph **"company"** has the same meaning as in the Corporation Tax Acts (see section 1121 of CTA 2010).

ASSOCIATED PERSONS TREATED AS INCURRING RELEVANT DEFEATS

47(1) Sub-paragraph (2) applies if a person ("P") incurs a relevant defeat in relation to any arrangements (otherwise than by virtue of this paragraph).

47(2) Any person ("S") who is associated with P at the relevant time is also treated for the purposes of paragraphs 2 (duty to give warning notice) and 3(2) (warning period) as having incurred that relevant defeat in relation to those arrangements (but see sub-paragraph (3)).
For the meaning of "associated" see paragraph 48.

47(3) Sub-paragraph (2) does not apply if P and S are members of the same group of companies (as defined in paragraph 46(9)).

47(4) In relation to a warning notice given to S by virtue of sub-paragraph (2), paragraph 2(4)(c) (certain information to be included in warning notice) is to be read as referring only to paragraphs 3, 17 and 18.

47(5) A warning notice which is given to a person by virtue of sub-paragraph (2) is treated for the purposes of paragraphs 19(1) (duty to give relief restriction notice) and 30 (penalty) as not having been given to that person.

52(2) For the purposes of paragraph 14 (Condition C: counteraction of DOTAS arrangements), the partner is treated as having at that time amended–

(a) the partner's return under section 8 or 8A of TMA 1970, or

(b) the partner's company tax return,

so as to give effect to the amendments of the partnership return.

52(3) Sub-paragraph (4) applies if a partnership return is amended at any time by HMRC as a result of a disclosure made by the representative partner or that person's successor on a basis that–

(a) results in an increase or decrease in, or

(b) otherwise affects the calculation of,

any amount stated under subsection (1)(b) of section 12AB (partnership statement) as the share of a particular partner (P) of any income, loss, consideration, tax or credit for any period.

52(4) If the conditions in sub-paragraph (5) are met, P is treated for the purposes of paragraph 14 as having at that time amended–

(a) P's return under section 8 or 8A of TMA 1970, or

(b) P's company tax return,

so as to give effect to the amendments of the partnership return.

52(5) The conditions are that the disclosure–

(a) is a full and explicit disclosure of an inaccuracy in the partnership return, and

(b) was made at a time when neither the person making the disclosure nor P had reason to believe that HMRC was about to begin enquiries into the partnership return.

Prospective amendments – In para. 52(1) the words "section 12AB(1)(b) of that Act or under equivalent provision made by regulations under paragraph 10 of Schedule A1 to that Act (partnership statement)" substituted for the words "subsection (1)(b) of section 12AB of that Act (partnership statement)" by F(No. 2)A 2017, s. 61 and Sch. 14, para. 48(3)(a), with effect from a day to be appointed under F(No. 2)A 2017, s. 61(6).

In para. 52(3)(a) the words "(in the case of a section 12AA partnership return) or the nominated partner (in the case of a Schedule A1 partnership return)" inserted after the words "that person's successor" and in the end words to para. 52(3) the words "section 12AB(1)(b) of TMA 1970 or under equivalent provision made by regulations under paragraph 10 of Schedule A1 to that Act (partnership statement)" substituted for the words "subsection (1)(b) of section 12AB of TMA 1970 (partnership statement)" by F(No. 2)A 2017, s. 61 and Sch. 14, para. 48(3)(b), with effect from a day to be appointed under F(No. 2)A 2017, s. 61(6).

SUPPLEMENTARY PROVISION RELATING TO PARTNERSHIPS

53(1) In paragraphs 49 to 52 and this paragraph–

"partnership" is to be interpreted in accordance with section 12AA of TMA 1970 (and includes a limited liability partnership);

"the representative partner", in relation to a partnership return, means the person who was required by a notice served under or for the purposes of section 12AA(2) or (3) of TMA 1970 to deliver the return;

"successor", in relation to a person who is the representative partner in the case of a partnership return, has the same meaning as in TMA 1970 (see section 118(1) of that Act).

53(2) For the purposes of this Part of this Act a partnership is treated as the same partnership notwithstanding a change in membership if any person who was a member before the change remains a member after the change.

Prospective amendments – In para. 53(1), in the definition of "the representative partner" the words "section 12AA" inserted after the words "in relation to a" by F(No. 2)A 2017, s. 61 and Sch. 14, para. 48(4)(a), with effect from a day to be appointed under F(No. 2)A 2017, s. 61(6).

In para. 53(1) the definition of "the nominated partner" inserted by F(No. 2)A 2017, s. 61 and Sch. 14, para. 48(4)(b), with effect from a day to be appointed under F(No. 2)A 2017, s. 61(6).

Part 7 – Supplemental

MEANING OF "ADJUSTMENTS"

54(1) In this Schedule **"adjustments"** means any adjustments, whether by way of an assessment, the modification of an assessment or return, amendment or disallowance of a claim, a payment, the entering into of a contract settlement, or otherwise (and references to "making" adjustments accordingly include securing that adjustments are made by entering into a contract settlement).

54(2) **"Adjustments"** also includes a payment in respect of a liability to pay national insurance contributions.

TIME OF "USE" OF DEFEATED ARRANGEMENTS

55(1) With reference to a particular relevant defeat incurred by a person in relation to arrangements, the person is treated as having "used" the arrangements on the dates set out in this paragraph.

55(2) If the person incurs the relevant defeat by virtue of Condition A, the person is treated as having **"used"** the arrangements on the following dates–

(a) the filing date of any return made by the person on the basis that the tax advantage mentioned in paragraph 12(1)(a) arises from the arrangements;

(b) the date on which the person makes any claim or election on that basis;

(c) the date of any relevant failure by the person to comply with an obligation.

55(3) For the purposes of sub-paragraph (2) a failure to comply with an obligation is a **"relevant failure"** if the whole or part of the tax advantage mentioned in paragraph 12(1)(b) arose as a result of, or in connection with, that failure.

55(4) If the person incurs the relevant defeat by virtue of Condition B, the person is treated as having **"used"** the arrangements on the following dates–

(a) the filing date of any return made by the person on the basis that the asserted advantage (see section 204(3) of FA 2014) results from the arrangements,

(b) the date on which any claim is made by the person on that basis,

(c) the date of any failure by the person to comply with a relevant obligation.

In this sub-paragraph **"relevant obligation"** means an obligation which would not have fallen on the person (or might have been expected not to do so), had the denied advantage arisen (see section 208(3) of FA 2014).

55(5) If the person incurs the relevant defeat by virtue of Condition C, the person is treated as having **"used"** the arrangements on the following dates–

(a) the filing date of any return made by the person on the basis mentioned in paragraph 14(2)(a);

(b) the date on which the person makes any claim or election on that basis;

(c) the date of any failure by the person to comply with a relevant obligation (as defined in paragraph 14(4)).

55(6) If the person incurs the relevant defeat by virtue of Condition D, the person is treated as having **"used"** the arrangements on the following dates–

(a) the filing date of any return made by the person on the basis mentioned in paragraph 15(2)(a);

(b) the date on which the person makes any claim on that basis;

(c) the date of any failure by the person to comply with a relevant obligation (as defined in paragraph 15(4)).

55(7) If the person incurs the relevant defeat by virtue of Condition E, the person is treated as having **"used"** the arrangements on the following dates–

(a) the filing date of any return made by S to which the counteraction mentioned in paragraph 16(1)(c) relates;

(b) the date on which S made any claim to which that counteraction relates;

(c) the date of any relevant failure by S to which that counteraction relates.

55(8) In sub-paragraph (7) **"relevant failure"** means a failure to comply with an obligation relating to VAT.

55(8A) If the person incurs the relevant defeat by virtue of Condition F, the person is treated as having **"used"** the arrangements on the following dates–

(a) the filing date of any return made by the person on the basis mentioned in paragraph 16A(2)(a);

(b) the date on which the person makes any claim, declaration or application for approval;

(c) the date of any failure by the person to comply with a relevant obligation (as defined in paragraph 16A(4)).

55(9) In this paragraph **"filing date"**, in relation to a return, means the earlier of–

(a) the day on which the return is delivered, or

(b) the last day of the period within which the return must be delivered.

55(10) References in this *paragraph to the date* on which a person fails to comply with an obligation are *to the date* on which the person is first in breach of the obligation.

History – Para. 55(8A) inserted by F(No. 2)A 2017, s. 66 and Sch. 17, para. 55(17) with effect so far as is necessary for enabling the making of regulations under that Schedule on 16 November 2017 (Royal Assent) and on 1 January 2018 for all other purposes.

INHERITANCE TAX

56 [Not relevant to petroleum revenue tax.]

NATIONAL INSURANCE CONTRIBUTIONS

57 [Not relevant to petroleum revenue tax.]

GENERAL INTERPRETATION

58(1) In this Schedule–

"arrangements" has the meaning given by paragraph 2(6);

"the Commissioners" means the Commissioners for Her Majesty's Revenue and Customs;

"contract settlement" means an agreement in connection with a person's liability to make a payment to the Commissioners under or by virtue of an enactment;

"disclosable indirect tax arrangements" is to be interpreted in accordance with paragraph 9A;

"disclosable Schedule 11A VAT arrangements" is to be interpreted in accordance with paragraph 9;

"disclosable VAT arrangements" is to be interpreted in accordance with paragraph 8A;

"DOTAS arrangements" is to be interpreted in accordance with paragraph 8 (and see also paragraph 57(2));

"follower notice" has the meaning given by paragraph 13(6);

"HMRC" means Her Majesty's Revenue and Customs;

"indirect tax" has the meaning given by paragraph 4(2);

"national insurance contributions" means contributions under Part 1 of the Social Security Contributions and Benefits Act 1992 or Part 1 of the Social Security Contributions and Benefits (Northern Ireland) Act 1992;

"net income" has the meaning given by section 23 of ITA 2007 (see Step 2 of that section);

"partnership follower notice" has the meaning given by paragraph 2(2) of Schedule 31 to FA 2014;

"partnership return" means a return under section 12AA of TMA 1970;

"relevant contributions" means the following contributions under Part 1 of the Social Security Contributions and Benefits Act 1992 or Part 1 of the Social Security Contributions and Benefits (Northern Ireland) Act 1992–

(a) Class 1 contributions;

(b) Class 1A contributions;

(c) Class 1B contributions;

(d) Class 2 contributions which must be paid but in relation to which section 11A of the Act in question (application of certain provisions of the Income Tax Acts in relation to Class 2 contributions under section 11(2) of that Act) does not apply;

"relevant defeat" is to be interpreted in accordance with paragraph 11;

"tax" has the meaning given by paragraph 4(1);

"tax advantage" has the meaning given by paragraph 7;

"warning notice" has the meaning given by paragraph 2.

58(2) In this Schedule an expression used in relation to VAT has the same meaning as in VATA 1994.

58(3) In this Schedule (except where the context requires otherwise) references, however expressed, to a person's affairs in relation to tax include the person's position as regards deductions or repayments of, or of sums representing, tax that the person is required to make by or under an enactment.

58(4) For the purposes of this Schedule a partnership return is regarded as made on the basis that a particular tax advantage arises to a person from particular arrangements if–

(a) it is made on the basis that an increase or reduction in one or more of the amounts mentioned in section 12AB(1) of TMA 1970 (amounts in the partnership statement in a partnership return) results from those arrangements, and

(b) that increase or reduction results in that tax advantage for the person.

Prospective amendments – In para. 58(1) the definition of "partnership return" substituted by F(No. 2)A 2017, s. 61 and Sch. 14, para. 48(5), with effect from a day to be appointed under F(No. 2)A 2017, s. 61(6).

History – In para. 58(1) the definition of "disclosable indirect tax arrangements" inserted by F(No. 2)A 2017, s. 66 and Sch. 17, para. 55(18)(a) with effect so far as is necessary for enabling the making of regulations under that Schedule on 16 November 2017 (Royal Assent) and on 1 January 2018 for all other purposes.

In para. 58(1) the definition of "disclosable Schedule 11A VAT arrangements" inserted by F(No. 2)A 2017, s. 66 and Sch. 17, para. 55(18)(a) with effect so far as is necessary for enabling the making of regulations under that Schedule on 16 November 2017 (Royal Assent) and on 1 January 2018 for all other purposes.

In para. 58(1) the definition of "indirect tax" inserted by F(No. 2)A 2017, s. 66 and Sch. 17, para. 55(18)(b) with effect so far as is necessary for enabling the making of regulations under that Schedule on 16 November 2017 (Royal Assent) and on 1 January 2018 for all other purposes.

In para. 58(1), in the definition of "disclosable VAT arrangements", "8A" substituted for "9" by F(No. 2)A 2017, s. 66 and Sch. 17, para. 55(18)(c) with effect so far as is necessary for enabling the making of regulations under that Schedule on 16 November 2017 (Royal Assent) and on 1 January 2018 for all other purposes.

In para. 58(1), in the definition of "tax", "4(1)" substituted for "4" by F(No. 2)A 2017, s. 66 and Sch. 17, para. 55(18)(d) with effect so far as is necessary for enabling the making of regulations under that Schedule on 16 November 2017 (Royal Assent) and on 1 January 2018 for all other purposes.

CONSEQUENTIAL AMENDMENTS

59 [Not relevant to petroleum revenue tax.]

60 [Inserts FA 2014, s. 212(4)(d).]

61 [Not relevant to petroleum revenue tax.]

62 [Not relevant to petroleum revenue tax.]

COMMENCEMENT

63 Subject to paragraphs 64 and 65, paragraphs 1 to 62 of this Schedule have effect in relation to relevant defeats incurred after the day on which this Act is passed.

64(1) A relevant defeat is to be disregarded for the purposes of this Schedule if it is incurred before 6 April 2017 in relation to arrangements which the person has entered into before the day on which this Act is passed.

64(2) A relevant defeat incurred on or after 6 April 2017 is to be disregarded for the purposes of this Schedule if–

(a) the person entered into the arrangements concerned before the day on which this Act is passed, and

(b) before 6 April 2017–

(i) the person incurring the defeat fully discloses to HMRC the matters to which the relevant counteraction relates, or

(ii) that person gives HMRC notice of a firm intention to make a full disclosure of those matters and makes such a full disclosure within any time limit set by HMRC.

64(3) In sub-paragraph (2) **"the relevant counteraction"** means–

(a) in a case within Condition A, the counteraction mentioned in paragraph 12(1)(c);

(b) in a case within Condition B, the action mentioned in paragraph 13(1);

(c) in a case within Condition C, the counteraction mentioned in paragraph 14(1)(c);

(d) in a case within Condition D, the counteraction mentioned in paragraph 15(1)(d);

(e) in a case within Condition E, the counteraction mentioned in paragraph 16(1)(c).

64(4) In sub-paragraph (3)–

(a) in paragraph (c) **"counteraction"** is to be interpreted in accordance with paragraph 14(5);

(b) in paragraph (d) **"counteraction"** is to be interpreted in accordance with paragraph 15(5);

(c) in paragraph (e) **"counteraction"** is to be interpreted in accordance with paragraph 16(2).

64(5) See paragraph 11(2) for provision about when a relevant defeat is incurred.

65(1) A warning notice given to a person is to be disregarded for the purposes of–

(a) paragraph 18 (naming), and

(b) Part 4 of this Schedule (restriction of reliefs),

if the relevant defeat specified in the notice relates to arrangements which the person has entered into before the day on which this Act is passed.

65(2) Where a person has entered into any arrangements before the day on which this Act is passed–

(a) a relevant defeat incurred by a person in relation to the arrangements, and

(b) any warning notice specifying such a relevant defeat,

is to be disregarded for the purposes of paragraph 30 (penalty).

SCHEDULE 19 – LARGE BUSINESSES: TAX STRATEGIES AND SANCTIONS

Section 161

Part 1 – Interpretation

PURPOSE OF PART 1

1 This Part defines terms for the purposes of this Schedule.

"RELEVANT BODY"

2(1) **"Relevant body"** means a UK company or any other body corporate (wherever incorporated), but does not include a limited liability partnership.

2(2) A relevant body is a **"foreign"** relevant body (or member of a group or subgroup) if it is incorporated outside the United Kingdom.

"UK COMPANY"

3(1) **"UK company"** means a company which is (or is treated as if it is) formed and registered under the Companies Act 2006, unless it falls within sub-paragraph (2).

3(2) The term **"UK company"** does not include a company which is–

(a) an open-ended investment company within the meaning of section 613 of CTA 2010, or

(b) an investment trust within the meaning of section 1158 of CTA 2010.

"UK PERMANENT ESTABLISHMENT"

4(1) **"UK permanent establishment"** means a permanent establishment in the United Kingdom of a foreign relevant body.

4(2) In sub-paragraph (1) **"permanent establishment"** has the same meaning as it has for the purposes of the Corporation Tax Acts (see section 1141 to 1144 of CTA 2010).

"QUALIFYING COMPANY"

5(1) A UK company is a **"qualifying company"** in any financial year (subject to any regulations under sub-paragraph (5)) if sub-paragraph (2) or (3) applies to it.

5(2) This sub-paragraph applies to the company if, at the end of the previous financial year–

(a) it satisfied the qualification test for a UK company, and

(b) was not a member of a UK group or a UK sub-group.

5(3) This sub-paragraph applies to the company if, at the end of the previous financial year–

(a) it was a member of a foreign group,

(b) the group met the qualification test for a group, and

(c) it was not a member of a UK sub-group of that foreign group.

5(4) The qualification test for a UK company is that the company satisfied either or both of the following conditions (by reference to the previous financial year)–

1. The company's turnover	More than £200 million
2. The company's balance sheet total	More than £2 billion.

5(5) The Treasury may by regulations provide that a company of a description specified in the regulations is not a qualifying company for the purposes of this Schedule (or any such purpose specified in the regulations).

5(6) For the purposes of this paragraph a UK permanent establishment of a foreign relevant body is to be treated as if it were–

(a) a UK company, and

(b) if the foreign relevant body is a member of a UK group or a UK subgroup, a member of that group or sub-group.

"GROUP" AND RELATED EXPRESSIONS

6(1) **"Group"** means two or more relevant bodies which together constitute–

(a) an MNE Group (see paragraph 7), or

(b) a group other than an MNE group (see paragraph 8).

6(2) **"UK group"** means a group whose head is a relevant body incorporated in the United Kingdom.

6(3) **"Foreign group"** means a group whose head is a foreign relevant body.

6(4) For the purposes of sub-paragraphs (2) and (3) it is immaterial where other members of the group are incorporated.

7(1) **"MNE Group"** has the same meaning (subject to sub-paragraph (2) below) as in the OECD Model Legislation in the OECD Country-by-Country Reporting Implementation Package as contained in the OECD's Guidance on Transfer Pricing Documentation and Country-by-Country Reporting published in 2014.

7(2) Paragraph (ii) (excluded MNE Group) of the Implementation Package is not part of the definition applied by sub-paragraph (1) above for the purposes of this Schedule.

7(3) In sub-paragraph (1) **"OECD"** means the Organisation for Economic Cooperation and Development.

8(1) A **"group other than an MNE group"** means a group consisting of two or more relevant bodies–

(a) each of which is a member of the group by virtue of sub-paragraph (3) or (4),

(b) at least two of which are UK companies,

which is not an MNE Group.

8(2) For the purposes of the condition in sub-paragraph (1)(b) a UK permanent establishment of a foreign member of a group is to be treated as if it were a UK company and a member of the group.

8(3) A relevant body is a member of a group if–

(a) another relevant body is its 51% subsidiary, or

(b) it is a 51% subsidiary of another relevant body.

8(4) Two relevant bodies are members of the same group if–

(a) one is a 51% subsidiary of the other, or

(b) both are 51% subsidiaries of another relevant body.

8(5) Chapter 3 of Part 24 of CTA 2010 (meaning of 51% subsidiary) applies for the purposes of this Schedule as it applies for the purposes of the Corporation Tax Acts (but with the modification in sub-paragraph (6)).

8(6) It applies as if references to a body corporate were references to a relevant body.

9 A group is headed by whichever relevant body within the group is not a 51% subsidiary of another relevant body within the group (and **"head"**, in relation to the group, means that body).

"QUALIFYING GROUP"

10(1) A group is a **"qualifying group"** in any financial year if, at the end of the previous financial year–

(a) in the case of a group other than an MNE Group, the group satisfied the qualification test for such a group (subject to any regulations under sub-paragraph (6)), or

(b) in the case of an MNE Group–

(i) there was a mandatory reporting requirement in respect of the group under regulations made under section 122 of FA 2015 (country-by-country reporting), or

(ii) there would have been such a requirement if the head of the group were resident in the United Kingdom for tax purposes.

10(2) The qualification test for a group other than an MNE Group is that the group satisfied either or both of the following conditions (by reference to the previous financial year)–

1. Group turnover	More than £200 million
2. Group balance sheet total	More than £2 billion.

10(3) In sub-paragraph (2)–

(a) **"group turnover"** means the aggregate turnover of the UK companies that are members of the group at the end of the previous financial year, and

(b) **"group balance sheet total"**, means the aggregate balance sheet totals for all those UK companies.

10(4) Where the financial year of a UK company within in the group does not end on the same day as the previous financial year of the head of the group, the figures from the company that are to be included in the aggregate figures are those for the company's financial year ending last before the end of the previous financial year of the head of the group.

10(5) For the purposes of assessing the turnover or balance sheet total of the group, sub-paragraphs (3) and (4) apply as if a UK permanent establishment of a foreign member of the group were a UK company and a member of the group.

10(6) The Treasury may by regulations provide–

(a) that a group other than an MNE Group which is of a specified description is not a qualifying group for the purposes, or any specified purpose, of this Schedule, or

(b) that a relevant body, or a UK permanent establishment, of a specified description is to be disregarded in determining whether the qualification test is satisfied by a group other than an MNE Group;

and in this sub-paragraph **"specified"** means specified in the regulations.

10(7) In this paragraph **"financial year"**, in relation to a group, means a financial year of the head of the group.

"UK SUB-GROUP" AND "HEAD" (IN RELATION TO A UK SUB-GROUP)

11(1) A **"UK sub-group"** consists of two or more relevant bodies that would be a UK group, but for the fact that they are members of a larger group headed by a relevant body incorporated outside the United Kingdom.

11(2) A UK sub-group is headed by the company or other relevant body incorporated in the United Kingdom that is not a 51% subsidiary of another member of the UK sub-group (and **"head"**, in relation to the sub-group, means that company or body).

"UK PARTNERSHIP", "QUALIFYING PARTNERSHIP" AND "REPRESENTATIVE PARTNER"

12(1) **"UK partnership"** means a body of any of the following descriptions which is carrying on a trade, business or profession with a view to profit–

(a) a partnership within the meaning of the Partnership Act 1890,

(b) a limited partnership registered under the Limited Partnerships Act 1907, or

(c) a limited liability partnership incorporated in the United Kingdom.

12(2) A UK partnership is a **"qualifying partnership"** in a financial year, if it satisfied the qualification test for a UK partnership at the end of the previous financial year (subject to any regulations under sub-paragraph (4)).

12(3) The qualification test for a UK partnership is that the partnership satisfied either or both of the following conditions (by reference to the previous financial year)–

1. The partnership's turnover	More than £200 million
2. The partnership's balance sheet total	More than £2 billion.

12(4) The Treasury may by regulations provide that a UK partnership of a description specified in the regulations is not a qualifying partnership for the purposes of this Schedule (or any such purpose specified in the regulations).

12(5) **"Representative partner"**, in relation to a UK partnership, means the partner who is required by a notice served under or by virtue of section 12AA(2) or (3) of TMA 1970 to make and deliver returns to an officer of HMRC.

Prospective amendments – Para. 12(5)(a) created from existing text and para. 12(5)(b) (and the word ", or" preceding it) inserted by F(No. 2)A 2017, s. 61 and Sch. 14, para. 49(2), with effect from a day to be appointed under F(No. 2)A 2017, s. 61(6).

"FINANCIAL YEAR"

13 "Financial year"–

(a) in relation to a UK company, has the meaning given by the Companies Act 2006 (see section 390 of that Act),

(b) in relation to any other relevant body, means any period in respect of which a profit and loss account for the body's undertaking is required to be made up (whether by its constitution or by the law under which it is established), whether that period is a year or not,

(c) in relation to a UK partnership, means any period of account for which its representative partner has provided or is required to provide a partnership statement under a return issued under section 12AB TMA 1970.

Prospective amendments – In para. 13(c) the words "within the meaning of" substituted for the words "under a return issued under section 12AB" by F(No. 2)A 2017, s. 61 and Sch. 14, para. 49(3), with effect from a day to be appointed under F(No. 2)A 2017, s. 61(6).

"TURNOVER" AND "BALANCE SHEET TOTAL"

14(1) "Turnover"–

(a) in relation to a UK company, has the same meaning as in Part 15 of the Companies Act 2006 (see section 474 of that Act), and

(b) in relation to a UK partnership or a UK permanent establishment, has a corresponding meaning.

14(2) "Balance sheet total", in relation to a UK company, UK partnership or UK permanent establishment and a financial year, means the aggregate of the amounts shown as assets in its balance sheet at the end of the financial year.

"UK TAXATION"

15(1) "UK taxation" means–

(a) income tax,

(b) corporation tax, including any amount assessable or chargeable as if it were corporation tax or treated as if it were corporation tax,

(c) value added tax,

(d) amounts for which the company is accountable under PAYE regulations,

(e) diverted profits tax,

(f) insurance premium tax,

(g) annual tax on enveloped dwellings,

(h) stamp duty land tax,

(i) stamp duty reserve tax,

(j) petroleum revenue tax;

(k) customs duties,

(l) excise duties,

(m) national insurance contributions.

15(2) In relation to a tax strategy required to be published by Part 2, **"UK taxation"** refers to the taxes or duties mentioned above so far as relating to or affecting the bodies or body to which the required tax strategy relates.

Part 2 – Publication of Tax Strategies

QUALIFYING UK GROUPS: DUTY TO PUBLISH A GROUP TAX STRATEGY

16(1) This paragraph applies in relation to a UK group which is a qualifying group in any financial year ("the current financial year").

16(2) The head of the group must ensure that a group tax strategy for the group, containing the information required by paragraph 17, is prepared and published on behalf of the group in accordance with this paragraph.

16(3) The group tax strategy–

(a) must be published before the end of the current financial year, and

(b) if the group was a qualifying group in the previous financial year, must not be published more than 15 months after the day on which its previous group tax strategy was published.

16(4) The group tax strategy–
(a) must be published on the internet by any of the UK companies that are members of the group so as to be accessible to the public free of charge (whether or not it is also published in any other way), and
(b) may be published as a separate document or as a self-contained part of a wider document.

16(5) The head of the group must ensure that the group tax strategy published on the internet remains accessible to the public free of charge–
(a) if a group tax strategy for the group's next financial year is required by this paragraph to be published, until that tax strategy is published, or
(b) if paragraph (a) does not apply, for at least one year.

16(6) For the purposes of this paragraph–
(a) a group tax strategy is published when it is first published on the internet as mentioned in paragraph (4)(a),
(b) the identity of the group is not to be regarded as altered by any change in its membership during the current financial year resulting from a relevant body–
  (i) becoming a 51% subsidiary of a member of the group, or
  (ii) ceasing to be a 51% subsidiary of another member of the group; and
(c) if the group becomes a UK sub-group of a foreign group during the current financial year, it is to be treated for the rest of that year as if it were still a UK group.

16(7) In this paragraph and paragraph 17 **"financial year"**, in relation to a UK group, means a financial year of the head of the group.

CONTENT OF GROUP TAX STRATEGY

17(1) A group tax strategy required to be published on behalf of a UK group by paragraph 16 must set out–
(a) the approach of the group to risk management and governance arrangements in relation to UK taxation,
(b) the attitude of the group towards tax planning (so far as affecting UK taxation),
(c) the level of risk in relation to UK taxation that the group is prepared to accept, and
(d) the approach of the group towards its dealings with HMRC.

17(2) The group tax strategy may–
(a) include other information relating to taxation (whether UK taxation or otherwise), and
(b) deal with a matter mentioned in sub-paragraph (1) by reference to the group as a whole or to individual members of the group (or to both).

17(3) The information required by sub-paragraph (1) to be included in the group tax strategy does not include any information about activities of any member of the group that consists of the provision of tax advice or related professional services to persons who are not members of the group.

17(4) The publication of information as the group tax strategy does not constitute publication of the strategy for the purposes of paragraph 16 unless the UK company publishing it makes clear (in a way that will be readily apparent to anyone accessing the information online) that the company regards its publication as complying with the duty under paragraph 16(2) in the current financial year.

17(5) For the purposes of this paragraph a UK permanent establishment of a foreign member of the group is to be treated as if it were a member of the group.

17(6) The Treasury may by regulations require the group tax strategy to include a country-by-country report.

17(7) In this paragraph **"country-by-country report"** has the meaning given by the Taxes (Base Erosion and Profit Shifting) (Country-by-Country Reporting) Regulations 2016.

PENALTY FOR NON-COMPLIANCE WITH PARAGRAPH 16

18(1) This paragraph applies where paragraph 16 requires a group tax strategy to be published for a UK group in any financial year of the head of the UK group.

18(2) The head of the group is liable to a penalty of £7,500 if–
(a) there is a failure to publish a group tax strategy for the group that complies with paragraph 16(2), or
(b) where a group tax strategy has been published, there is a failure to comply with paragraph 16(5).

18(3) Subject to sub-paragraph (5) the head of the group is only liable to one penalty by virtue of sub-paragraph (2) in respect of a group tax strategy required for the financial year in question.

18(4) Sub-paragraph (5) applies where–

(a) the head of the group is liable to a penalty under this paragraph in respect of a failure mentioned in sub-paragraph (2)(a), and

(b) no group tax strategy for the group that complies with paragraph 16(2) (disregarding paragraph 16(3)) is published within the period of 6 months after the last day on which the duty under paragraph 16(2) could have been complied with.

18(5) At the end of that period, the head of the group–

(a) is liable to a further penalty of £7,500, and

(b) where the failure mentioned in sub-paragraph (4)(b) continues, is liable to a further penalty of £7,500 at the end of each subsequent month in which no such group tax strategy is published.

UK SUB-GROUPS: DUTY TO PUBLISH A SUB-GROUP TAX STRATEGY

19(1) This paragraph applies to a UK sub-group of a foreign group if in any financial year ("the current financial year") the foreign group is a qualifying group.

19(2) The head of the sub-group must ensure that a sub-group tax strategy for the sub-group, giving the information required by paragraph 20, is prepared and published in accordance with this paragraph.

19(3) The sub-group tax strategy–

(a) must be published before the end of the current financial year, and

(b) if the group of which the sub-group is part was a qualifying group in the previous financial year, must not be published more than 15 months after the day on which its sub-group tax strategy for that year was published;

19(4) The sub-group tax strategy–

(a) must be published on the internet by any of the UK companies that are members of the foreign group so as to be accessible to the public free of charge (whether or not it is also published in any other way), and

(b) may be published as a separate document or as a self-contained part of a wider document.

19(5) The head of the sub-group must ensure that the sub-group tax strategy published on the internet remains accessible to the public free of charge–

(a) if a sub-group tax strategy for the sub-group's next financial year is required by this paragraph to be published, until that tax strategy is published, or

(b) if paragraph (a) does not apply, for at least one year.

19(6) For the purposes of this paragraph–

(a) a sub-group tax strategy is published when it is first published on the internet as mentioned in sub-paragraph (4)(a),

(b) the identity of the sub-group is not affected by any change in its membership in the current financial year resulting from a relevant body becoming or ceasing to be a 51% subsidiary of a member of the sub-group, and

(c) if the sub-group becomes a UK sub-group of another foreign group during the current financial year, for the rest of that year it is to be treated as if it were still a UK sub-group of the original foreign group (but only a UK company within the sub-group may publish a subgroup tax strategy for the sub-group after that change).

19(7) In this paragraph **"financial year"**, in relation to a UK sub-group, means a financial year of the head of the group of which it is a sub-group.

CONTENT OF A SUB-GROUP TAX STRATEGY

20(1) Paragraph 17 applies in relation to a sub-group tax strategy required to be published on behalf of a UK sub-group by paragraph 19 as it applies to a group tax strategy required to be published by a qualifying UK group.

20(2) In the application of paragraph 17 to a sub-group tax strategy, references to the group or members *of the group are to be read as references to the UK sub-group or members of the UK sub-group.*

20(3) In the application of paragraph 17 as modified by this paragraph to a subgroup tax strategy, a UK permanent establishment of a foreign member of the UK sub-group is to be treated as if it were a member of the sub-group.

PENALTY FOR NON-COMPLIANCE WITH REQUIREMENTS OF PARAGRAPH 19

21(1) This paragraph applies where paragraph 19 requires a sub-group tax strategy to be published for a UK sub-group in any financial year of the head of the sub-group.

21(2) The head of the sub-group is liable to a penalty of £7,500 if–

(a) there is a failure to publish a sub-group tax strategy for the subgroup that complies with paragraph 19(2), or

(b) where a sub-group tax strategy has been published, there is a failure to comply with paragraph 19(5).

21(3) Subject to sub-paragraph (5), the head of the sub-group is only liable to one penalty by virtue of sub-paragraph (2) in respect of a sub-group tax strategy required for the financial year in question.

21(4) Sub-paragraph (5) applies where–

(a) the head of the sub-group is liable to a penalty under this paragraph in respect of a failure mentioned in sub-paragraph (2)(a), and

(b) no sub-group tax strategy for the sub-group that complies with paragraph 19(2) (disregarding paragraph 19(3)) is published within the period of 6 months after the last day on which the duty under paragraph 19(2) could have been complied with.

21(5) At the end of that period, the head of the sub-group is liable–

(a) to a further penalty of £7,500, and

(b) where the failure mentioned in sub-paragraph (4)(b) continues, to a further penalty of £7,500 at the end of each subsequent month in which no such sub-group tax strategy is published.

QUALIFYING COMPANIES: DUTY TO PUBLISH A COMPANY TAX STRATEGY

22(1) This paragraph applies in relation to a UK company which in any financial year ("the current financial year") is a qualifying company.

22(2) The company must prepare and publish a company tax strategy, containing the information required by paragraph 23, in accordance with this paragraph.

22(3) The duty under sub-paragraph (2) applies even if the company becomes a member of a UK group or a UK sub-group during the current financial year.

22(4) The company tax strategy–

(a) must be published by the company before the end of the current financial year, and

(b) if the company was a qualifying company in the previous financial year, must not be published more than 15 months after the day on which its company tax strategy was published in the previous financial year.

22(5) The company tax strategy–

(a) must be published on the internet so as to be accessible to the public free of charge (whether or not published in any other way), and

(b) may be published as a separate document or a self-contained part of a wider document.

22(6) The company must ensure that the company tax strategy published on the internet remains accessible to the public free of charge–

(a) if a company tax strategy for the next financial year is required by this paragraph to be published, until that tax strategy is published, or

(b) if paragraph (a) does not apply, for at least one year.

22(7) For the purposes of this paragraph a company tax strategy is published when it is first published as mentioned in sub-paragraph (5)(a).

22(8) A UK permanent establishment which in any financial year is by virtue of paragraph 5(6) to be treated as a qualifying company is to be treated for the purposes of this paragraph and paragraphs 23 and 24 as if it were a UK company which in that financial year is a qualifying company.

CONTENT OF A COMPANY TAX STRATEGY

23(1) The company tax strategy must set out–

(a) the company's approach to risk management and governance arrangements in relation to UK taxation,

(b) the company's attitude towards tax planning (so far as affecting UK taxation),

(c) the level of risk in relation to UK taxation that the company is prepared to accept,

(d) the company's approach towards its dealings with HMRC.

23(2) The company tax strategy may include other information relating to taxation (whether UK taxation or otherwise).

23(3) The information required by sub-paragraph (1) to be included in a company tax strategy does not include any information about activities of the company that consist of the provision of tax advice or related professional services to other persons.

23(4) The publication of information as a company tax strategy does not constitute publication of the strategy for the purposes of paragraph 22 unless the company makes clear (in a way that will be readily apparent to anyone accessing the information online) that the company regards its publication as complying with the duty under paragraph 22(2) in the current financial year.

PENALTY FOR NON-COMPLIANCE WITH PARAGRAPH 22

24(1) This paragraph applies where paragraph 22 requires a company tax strategy to be published for a UK company in any financial year.

24(2) The company is liable to a penalty of £7,500 if–

(a) there is a failure to publish a company tax strategy for the company that complies with paragraph 22(2), or

(b) where a company tax strategy has been published, there is a failure to comply with paragraph 22(6).

24(3) Subject to sub-paragraph (5), the company is only liable to one penalty by virtue of sub-paragraph (2) in respect of a company tax strategy required for the financial year in question.

24(4) Sub-paragraph (5) applies where–

(a) a penalty is imposed under this paragraph in respect of a failure mentioned in sub-paragraph (2)(a), and

(b) no company tax strategy that complies with paragraph 22(2) (disregarding paragraph 22(4)) is published within the period of 6 months after the last day on which the duty under paragraph 22(2) could have been complied with.

24(5) At the end of that period, the company is liable–

(a) to a further penalty of £7,500, and

(b) where the failure mentioned in sub-paragraph (4)(b) continues, to a further penalty of £7,500 at the end of each subsequent month in which no such company tax strategy is published.

QUALIFYING PARTNERSHIPS: DUTY TO PUBLISH A PARTNERSHIP TAX STRATEGY

25(1) Paragraphs 22 to 24 apply in relation to a UK partnership which is (in any financial year of the partnership) a qualifying partnership as they apply to a UK company which is (in any financial year of the company) a qualifying company.

25(2) Those paragraphs have effect in their application to a qualifying partnership–

(a) with the omission of paragraph 22(3) and (8),

(b) as if for "company tax strategy" (in each place) there were substituted "partnership tax strategy", and

(c) as if for "company" and "company's" (in each place) there were substituted respectively "partnership" and "partnership's".

PENALTIES UNDER THIS PART: GENERAL PROVISIONS

26(1) Paragraphs 27 to 33 apply in relation to the liability of any person to a penalty under this Part and, accordingly, in those paragraphs–

"failure", in relation to a liability for a penalty, means a failure which could give rise to that liability,

"liability to a penalty" means a liability under paragraph 18, 21 or 24 (including paragraph 24 as applied to a qualifying UK partnership), and

"penalty" means a penalty under any of those paragraphs.

26(2) In those paragraphs **"tribunal"** means the First-tier Tribunal or, where determined by or under the Tribunal Procedure Rules, the Upper Tribunal.

FAILURE TO COMPLY WITH A TIME LIMIT

27 A failure to do anything required by this Part to be done within a limited period of time goes not give rise to liability to a penalty if it is done within such further time (if any) as an officer of Revenue and Customs may have allowed.

REASONABLE EXCUSE

28(1) Liability to a penalty for a failure does not arise if the person who would otherwise be liable to that penalty satisfies HMRC or (on an appeal notified to the tribunal) the tribunal that the person had a reasonable excuse for that failure.

28(2) For the purposes of this paragraph–

(a) an insufficiency of funds is not a reasonable excuse unless attributable to events outside the person's control,

(b) where the person relies on another person to do anything, that cannot be a reasonable excuse–

(i) unless the first person took reasonable care to avoid the failure, or

(ii) if the first person is a UK group or UK sub-group, where the person relied on is another member of the group or subgroup,

(c) where the person had a reasonable excuse but the excuse has ceased, the person is to be treated as having continued to have the excuse if the failure is remedied without unreasonable delay after the excuse ceased.

ASSESSMENT OF PENALTIES

29(1) Where a person becomes liable to a penalty–

(a) HMRC may assess the penalty, and

(b) if they do so, HMRC must notify the person of the assessment.

29(2) An assessment of a penalty may not be made–

(a) more than 6 months after the failure first comes to the attention of an officer of Revenue and Customs, or

(b) more than 6 years after the end of the financial year in which the tax strategy to which the failure relates was (or was originally) required to be published.

APPEAL

30(1) A person may appeal against a decision of HMRC that a penalty is payable by that person.

30(2) Notice of an appeal must be given–

(a) in writing,

(b) before the end of the period of 30 days beginning with the date on which the notification under paragraph 29(1)(b) was issued,

30(3) Notice of an appeal must state the grounds of appeal.

30(4) On an appeal that is notified to the tribunal, the tribunal may confirm or cancel the decision.

30(5) Subject to this paragraph and paragraph 31, the provisions of Part 5 of TMA 1970 relating to appeals have effect in relation to appeals under this Schedule as they have effect in relation to an appeal against an assessment to income tax.

ENFORCEMENT

31(1) A penalty must be paid–

(a) before the end of the period of 30 days beginning with the date on which the notification under paragraph 29(1)(b) was issued, or

(b) if a notice of appeal is given, before the end of 30 days beginning with the day on which the appeal is determined or withdrawn.

31(2) A penalty may be enforced as if it were corporation tax charged in an assessment and due and payable.

POWER TO CHANGE AMOUNT OF PENALTIES

32(1) If it appears to the Treasury that there has been a change in the value of money since the last relevant date, they may by regulations substitute for any sums for the time being specified in paragraph 18, 21 or 24 such other sum as appear to them to be justified by the change.

32(2) In sub-paragraph (1) **"relevant date"** means–

(a) the date on which this Act is passed, and

(b) each date on which the power conferred by that sub-paragraph has been exercised.

32(3) Regulations under this paragraph do not apply to a failure that occurs in respect of a financial year (of the body or partnership responsible for the failure) that begins before the date on which they come into force.

APPLICATION OF PROVISIONS OF TMA 1970

33 Subject to the provisions of this Part, the following provisions of TMA 1970 apply for the purposes of this Part as they apply for the purposes of the Taxes Acts–

(a) section 108 (responsibility of company officers),

(b) section 114 (want of form), and

(c) section 115 (delivery and service of documents).

MEANING OF "TAX STRATEGY"

34 In this Part **"tax strategy"** means–

(a) a group tax strategy (see paragraphs 16 to 18),

(b) a sub-group tax strategy (see paragraphs 19 to 21),

(c) a company tax strategy (see paragraphs 22 to 24), or

(d) a partnership tax strategy (see paragraph 25).

Part 3 – Sanctions for Persistently Unco-operative Large Businesses

LARGE GROUPS FALLING WITHIN PART 3

35 A UK group falls within this Part of this Schedule ("this Part") if–

(a) the group has persistently engaged in unco-operative behaviour (see paragraphs 36 to 38),

(b) some or all of the unco-operative behaviour has caused there to be, or contributed to there being, two or more significant tax issues in respect of the group or members of the group which are unresolved (see paragraph 39), and

(c) there is a reasonable likelihood of further instances of the group engaging in unco-operative behaviour in a manner which causes there to be, or contributes to there being, significant tax issues in respect of the group or members of the group.

36(1) A UK group has **"engaged in unco-operative behaviour"** if–

(a) a member of the group has satisfied either or both of the conditions listed in sub-paragraph (2), or

(b) two or more of the members of the group, taken together, have satisfied either or both of those conditions.

36(2) Those conditions are–

(a) the behaviour condition (see paragraph 37);

(b) the arrangements condition (see paragraph 38).

36(3) A UK group has engaged in unco-operative behaviour **"persistently"** if–

(a) a member of the group has done so persistently, or

(b) two or more members of the group, taken together, have done so persistently.

36(4) References in this Part to doing something **"persistently"** include doing it on a sufficient number of occasions for it to be clear that it represents a pattern of behaviour.

37(1) A member of a UK group has, or two or more members of a UK group (taken together) have, **"satisfied the behaviour condition"** if it has, or they have, behaved in a manner which has delayed or otherwise hindered HMRC in the exercise of their functions in connection with determining the liability to UK taxation of the group or a member of the group.

37(2) Factors which may indicate that a member of a UK group has behaved as described in sub-paragraph (1) include–

(a) the extent to which HMRC have used statutory powers to obtain information relating to the UK group or members of the group;

(b) the reasons why those powers have been used;

(c) the number and seriousness of inaccuracies in, and omissions from, documents given to HMRC by or on behalf of the UK group or members of the group;

(d) the extent to which, in dealings with HMRC, members of the group (or people acting on their behalf) have relied on interpretations of legislation relating to UK taxation which, at the time, are speculative.

37(3) An interpretation of legislation relating to UK taxation is **"speculative"** if it is likely that a court or tribunal would disagree with it.

38(1) A member of a UK group has **"satisfied the arrangements condition"** if it is a party to a tax avoidance scheme.

38(2) **"Tax avoidance scheme"** means–

(a) arrangements in respect of which a notice of final decision has been given under–

(i) paragraph 12 of Schedule 43 to FA 2013,

(ii) paragraph 5 or 6 of Schedule 43A to FA 2013, or

(iii) paragraph 9 of Schedule 43B to FA 2013,

stating that a tax advantage arising from the arrangements is to be counteracted;

(b) arrangements which are notifiable arrangements for the purposes of Part 7 of FA 2004 (disclosure of tax avoidance schemes), other than arrangements in relation to which HMRC have given notice under section 312(6) of FA 2004 (notice that promoters not under duty to provide clients with prescribed information);

(c) a scheme which is a notifiable scheme for the purposes of Schedule 11A to VATA 1994 (disclosure of avoidance schemes).

39(1) There is a significant tax issue in respect of a UK group or a member of a UK group where–

(a) there is a disagreement between HMRC and a member of the group about an issue affecting the amount of the liability of the group or a member of the group to UK taxation,

(b) the issue has been, or could be, referred to a court or tribunal to determine, and

(c) as regards the amount of the liability, the difference between HMRC's view and the view of the member is, or is likely to be, not less than £2 million.

39(2) The reference in sub-paragraph (1)(a) to circumstances in which there is a disagreement include circumstances in which there is a reasonable likelihood of a disagreement.

39(3) The Treasury may by regulations substitute a higher amount for the amount for the time being specified in sub-paragraph (1)(c).

40 The references in paragraphs 36 to 39 to things done by a member of a UK group ("the group in question")–

(a) include acts and omissions of a relevant body that is not a member of the group in question if they took place at a time when the relevant body was a member of a group headed by the body that is the head of the group in question;

(b) do not include acts or omissions of a relevant body that is a member of the group in question if they took place at a time when the relevant body was not a member of a group headed by the body that is the head of the group in question.

WARNING NOTICES

41(1) A designated HMRC officer may give the head of a UK group a notice under this paragraph (a "warning notice") if the officer considers that the group is a qualifying group that falls within this Part.

41(2) The notice must set out the reasons why the officer considers that the group falls within this Part.

41(3) The notice–

(a) may be withdrawn by a designated HMRC officer at any time by giving a further notice to the head of the group, and

(b) expires (if not previously withdrawn) at the end of the period of 15 months beginning with the day on which it was given.

41(4) Once a warning notice has been given –

(a) it is immaterial for the purposes of this Part whether the group remains a qualifying group,

(b) the identity of the group is not to be regarded as altered by any change in its membership resulting from a relevant body–

(i) becoming a 51% subsidiary of a member of the group, or

(ii) ceasing to be a 51% subsidiary of another member of the group; and

(c) if the group becomes a UK sub-group of a foreign group it is to be treated as if it were still a UK group.

41(5) Sub-paragraph (4) applies while the group is subject to–

(a) the warning notice, or

(b) any other notice under this Part issued as a result of the group having been given the warning notice.

SPECIAL MEASURES NOTICES

42(1) This paragraph applies to a UK group if–

(a) the head of the group has been given a warning notice in relation to the group that has not been withdrawn,

(b) the period of 12 months beginning with the day on which the warning notice was given has elapsed, and

(c) the period of 15 months beginning with that day has not elapsed.

42(2) If a designated HMRC officer considers that the group falls within this Part, the officer may give the head of the group a notice under this paragraph (a "special measures notice").

42(3) When considering whether the group falls within this Part, the officer may take into account any relevant behaviour, whether or not it is mentioned in the warning notice.

42(4) When deciding whether to give a special measures notice, the designated HMRC officer must consider any representations made by a member of the group before the end of the period of 12 months beginning with the day on which the warning notice was given.

42(5) The special measures notice must set out the reasons why the officer considers that the group falls within this Part.

42(6) Paragraph 45 deals with other circumstances in which a UK group may be given a special measures notice.

43(1) A special measures notice–

(a) may be withdrawn by a designated HMRC officer at any time by giving a further notice to the head of the UK group, and

(b) expires, if not previously withdrawn, at the end of the period of 27 months beginning with the relevant day.

43(2) **"The relevant day"** means the later of–

(a) the day on which the special measures notice was given, and

(b) the day on which it was last confirmed under paragraph 44.

44(1) This paragraph applies to a UK group if–

(a) the head of the group has been given a special measures notice in relation to the group which has not been withdrawn,

(b) the period of 24 months beginning with the relevant day has elapsed, and

(c) the period of 27 months beginning with that day has not elapsed.

44(2) If a designated HMRC officer considers that the group falls within this Part, the officer may give the head of the group a notice under this paragraph (a "confirmation notice") confirming the special measures notice given in relation to the group.

44(3) When considering whether the group falls within this Part, the officer may take into account any relevant behaviour, whether or not it is mentioned in the special measures notice which is to be confirmed, in any previous confirmation notice or in the warning notice.

44(4) **"The relevant day"** has the same meaning as in paragraph 43(2).

44(5) The *confirmation notice* must set out the reasons why the officer considers that the group falls within this Part.

44(6) When deciding whether to give a confirmation notice, a designated HMRC officer must consider any representations made by a member of the group before the end of the period of 24 months beginning with the relevant day.

44(7) A confirmation notice–

(a) may be withdrawn by a designated HMRC officer at any time by giving a further notice to the head of the group, and

(b) expires, if not previously withdrawn, at the end of the period of 27 months beginning with the day on which it is given.

45(1) This paragraph applies in relation to a UK group where–

(a) the head of the group has been given a warning notice or a special measures notice in relation to the group, and

(b) that notice has expired.

45(2) A designated HMRC officer may give the head of a UK group a special measures notice if–

(a) it appears to the officer that–

(i) during the period of 6 months beginning with the day on which the notice mentioned in sub-paragraph (1)(a) expired ("the expiry day"), the group has engaged in unco-operative behaviour (see paragraphs 36 to 38), and

(ii) there is a reasonable likelihood that, if it had engaged in the behaviour before the notice expired, a designated HMRC officer would have considered that the group fell within this Part (so that a special measures notice or confirmation notice could have been given to the head of the group),

(b) during the period of 7 months beginning with the expiry day, a designated HMRC officer has notified the head of the group that the power under this paragraph may be exercised in relation to the group, and

(c) the period of 9 months beginning with that day has not elapsed.

45(3) When deciding whether to give a special measures notice under this paragraph, the officer must consider any representations made by a member of the group before the end of the period of 8 months beginning with the expiry day.

CIRCUMSTANCES IN WHICH WARNING AND SPECIAL MEASURES NOTICES ARE TREATED AS HAVING BEEN GIVEN

46(1) Sub-paragraphs (2) and (3) apply where–

(a) a relevant body ("B1") is given a warning notice, and

(b) before the notice ceases to have effect, B1 becomes a member of a group headed by another relevant body ("H1").

46(2) H1 is to be treated as having been given a warning notice on the day on which the warning notice was given to B1.

46(3) A warning notice treated as given under sub-paragraph (2) is valid whether or not, on the day mentioned in that sub-paragraph, H1 was the head of a qualifying UK group that fell within this Part.

46(4) Sub-paragraphs (5) to (7) apply where–

(a) a relevant body ("B2") is given a special measures notice, and

(b) before the notice ceases to have effect, B2 becomes a member of a group headed by another relevant body ("H2").

46(5) H2 is to be treated as having been given a special measures notice on the day on which the special measures notice was given to B2.

46(6) A special measures notice treated as given under sub-paragraph (5) is valid whether or not, on the day mentioned in that sub-paragraph, H2 was the head of a qualifying UK group that fell within this Part.

46(7) Paragraph 47(1) does not by virtue of sub-paragraphs (5) and (6) of this paragraph apply to an inaccuracy in a document given to HMRC by or on behalf of a person–

(a) at a time when the person was a member of a group headed by H2, but

(b) before the day B2 becomes a member of H2.

46(8) Sub-paragraphs (9) and (10) apply where–

(a) a relevant body ("B3") is given a confirmation notice, and

(b) before the notice ceases to have effect, B3 becomes a member of a group headed by another relevant body ("H3").

46(9) H3 is to be treated as having been given a confirmation notice on the day on which the confirmation notice was given to B3.

46(10) A confirmation notice treated as given under sub-paragraph (9) is valid whether or not, on the day mentioned in that sub-paragraph, H3 was the head of a qualifying UK group that fell within this Part.

46(11) The Treasury may by regulations make provision for warning notices, special measures notices and confirmation notices to be treated as having been given to relevant bodies in other circumstances described in the regulations.

46(12) Regulations under this paragraph may, in particular–

(a) make provision about the validity of notices treated as given by virtue of the regulations;

(b) make provision about the effect of paragraph 47(1) in cases involving such notices.

SANCTIONS: LIABILITY FOR PENALTIES FOR ERRORS IN DOCUMENTS GIVEN TO HMRC

47(1) For the purposes of Schedule 24 to FA 2007 (penalties for errors), an inaccuracy in a document given to HMRC by or on behalf of a person is to be treated as being due to failure by the person to take reasonable care if–

(a) the document was given to HMRC at a time when the person was a member of a group subject to a special measures notice, and

(b) the inaccuracy–

(i) relates to a tax avoidance scheme (as defined in paragraph 38) entered into by the person at a time when the person was a member of a group subject to a special measures notice, or

(ii) is, entirely or partly, attributable to an interpretation of legislation relating to UK taxation which, at the time the document was given to HMRC, was speculative.

47(2) A group is **"subject to a special measures notice"** if a special measures notice–

(a) has been given to the head of the group in relation to the group, and

(b) is in force.

47(3) An interpretation of legislation relating to UK taxation is **"speculative"** if it is likely that a court or tribunal would disagree with it.

47(4) Sub-paragraph (1) does not apply to an inaccuracy if–

(a) it is deliberate on the part of the person or someone acting on the person's behalf,

(b) it is in fact due to a failure by the person or someone acting on the person's behalf to take reasonable care, or

(c) it is treated as due to such a failure by virtue of another enactment.

48 In Schedule 24 to FA 2007 (penalties for errors), at the end of paragraph 3 (meaning of "careless" etc) insert–

> "**3(3)** Paragraph 47 of Schedule 19 to FA 2016 (special measures for persistently unco-operative large businesses) provides for certain inaccuracies to be treated, for the purposes of this Schedule, as being due to a failure by P to take reasonable care."

SANCTIONS: COMMISSIONERS PUBLISHING INFORMATION

49(1) If a group is subject to a confirmed special measures notice, the Commissioners for Her Majesty's Revenue and Customs ("the Commissioners") may publish the following information–

(a) the name of the group, including any previous name;

(b) the address or registered office of the head of the group;

(c) any other information that the Commissioners consider it appropriate to publish in order to identify the group;

(d) the fact that the group is subject to a confirmed special measures notice.

49(2) A group is **"subject to a confirmed special measures notice"** if sub-paragraph (3) or (4) is satisfied.

49(3) This sub-paragraph is satisfied if–

(a) a special measures notice has been given to the head of the group and confirmed under paragraph 44, and

(b) the special measures notice is in force.

49(4) This sub-paragraph is satisfied if–

(a) a special measures notice has been given to the head of the group and confirmed under paragraph 44,

(b) that notice has ceased to have effect,

(c) a further special measures notice has been given to the head of the group under paragraph 45 in the period of 9 months beginning with the day on which the special measures notice mentioned in paragraph (a) ceased to have effect, and

(d) that notice is in force.

49(5) Before publishing the information, the Commissioners must–

(a) inform the head of the group that they are considering doing so, and

(b) allow the head of the group a reasonable opportunity to make representations about whether the information should be published.

49(6) If, after information about a group is published under this paragraph, the group ceases to be subject to a confirmed special measures notice, the Commissioners must publish a notice stating that the group is no longer subject to a confirmed special measures notice.

49(7) A notice under sub-paragraph (6) must be published before the end of the period of 30 days beginning with the day on which the special measures notice is withdrawn or has expired.

49(8) The Commissioners may publish information and notices under this paragraph in any manner they consider appropriate.

APPLICATION OF PART 3 TO LARGE UK SUB-GROUPS

50(1) A UK sub-group of a foreign group falls within this Part if–

(a) the sub-group has persistently engaged in unco-operative behaviour (see paragraphs 36 to 38),

(b) some or all of the unco-operative behaviour has caused there to be, or contributed to there being, two or more significant tax issues in respect of the sub-group or members of the sub-group which are unresolved (see paragraph 39), and

(c) there is a reasonable likelihood of further instances of the sub-group engaging in unco-operative behaviour in a manner which causes there to be, or contributes to there being, significant tax issues in respect of the sub-group or members of the sub-group.

50(2) Paragraphs 36 to 40 apply in relation to a UK sub-group as they apply in relation to a UK group.

50(3) Paragraphs 41 to 45 apply in relation to the head of a UK sub-group of a foreign group that is a qualifying group at the material time as they apply in relation to the head of a UK group.

50(4) In the application of paragraph 41 in the case of a UK sub-group, sub-paragraph (4) has effect in relation to a UK sub-group as if for paragraphs (b) and (c) there were substituted–

"(b) the identity of the sub-group is not to be regarded as altered by any change in its membership resulting from a relevant body–

(i) becoming a 51% subsidiary of a member of the sub-group, or

(ii) ceasing to be a 51% subsidiary of another member of the sub-group; and

(c) if the sub-group becomes a UK sub-group of another foreign group, it is to be treated as if it were still a UK subgroup of the original foreign group."

50(5) As applied by this paragraph, paragraphs 36 to 45 have effect as if references to a UK group (including in references to the head of a UK group or members of a UK group) were references to a UK sub-group.

50(6) In paragraphs 40, 41, 46, 47 and 49, references to a group (including in references to the head of a group or members of a group) include a UK sub-group.

50(7) In paragraph 46, references to the head of a UK group include the head of a UK sub-group.

APPLICATION OF PART 3 TO LARGE COMPANIES

51(1) A UK company falls within this Part if–

(a) the company has persistently engaged in unco-operative behaviour (see paragraphs 36 to 38),

(b) some or all of the unco-operative behaviour has caused there to be, or contributed to there being, two or more significant tax issues in respect of the company which are unresolved (see paragraph 39), and

(c) there is a reasonable likelihood of further instances of the company engaging in unco-operative behaviour in a manner which causes there to be, or contributes to there being, significant tax issues in respect of the company.

51(2) Paragraphs 36 to 39 apply in relation to a company as they apply in relation to a UK group.

51(3) Paragraphs 41 to 45 apply in relation to a company as they apply in relation to the head of a UK group.

51(4) As applied by this paragraph, paragraphs 36 to 39 and 41 to 45 have effect as if references to a UK group, the head of a UK group or a member of a UK group were references to a company.

51(5) Paragraph 47 applies in relation to a company as it applies in relation to a member of a group.

51(6) Paragraph 49 applies in relation to a company as it applies in relation to a group.

51(7) As applied by this paragraph, paragraphs 47 and 49 have effect as if references to a group, the head of a group or a member of a group were references to a company.

APPLICATION OF PART 3 TO LARGE PARTNERSHIPS

52(1) A UK partnership falls within this Part if–

(a) the partnership has persistently engaged in unco-operative behaviour (see paragraphs 36 to 38),

(b) some or all of the unco-operative behaviour has caused there to be, or contributed to there being, two or more significant tax issues in respect of the partnership which are unresolved (see paragraph 39), and

(c) there is a reasonable likelihood of further instances of the partnership engaging in unco-operative behaviour in a manner which causes there to be, or contributes to there being, significant tax issues in respect of the partnership.

52(2) Paragraphs 36 to 39 of this Schedule apply in relation to a UK partnership as they apply in relation to a UK group.

52(3) Paragraphs 41 to 45 of this Schedule apply in relation to the representative partner of a UK partnership as they apply in relation to the head of a UK group.

52(4) As applied by this paragraph, paragraphs 36 to 39 and 41 to 45 have effect as if–

(a) references to a UK group were references to a UK partnership;

(b) references to the head of a UK group were references to the representative partner of a UK partnership;

(c) references to a member of a UK group were references to a partner of a UK partnership, acting in the person's capacity as such.

52(5) The Treasury may by regulations make provision for warning notices, special measures notices and confirmation notices to be treated as having been given to the representative partner of a UK partnership in circumstances described in the regulations.

52(6) Paragraph 46(12) applies to regulations under this paragraph.

52(7) Paragraph 47 applies in relation to an inaccuracy in a document given to HMRC by a partner of a UK partnership, acting in the person's capacity as such, as if–

(a) references to a group were references to a partnership;

(b) references to the head of a group were references to the representative partner of a partnership;

(c) references to a member of a group were references to a partner of a partnership.

52(8) Paragraph 47 applies in relation to an inaccuracy in any other document given to HMRC on behalf of a UK partnership as if–

(a) references to a person included a UK partnership;

(b) references to a group, or a member of a group, were references to a UK partnership;

(c) references to the head of a group were references to the representative partner of a UK partnership.

52(9) Paragraph 49 applies in relation to a UK partnership as it applies in relation to a group.

52(10) As applied by this paragraph, paragraph 49 has effect as if–

(a) references to a group were references to a UK partnership;

(b) references to the head of a group were references to the representative partner of a UK partnership.

MEANING OF "DESIGNATED HMRC OFFICER"

53 In this Part **"designated HMRC officer"** means an officer of Revenue and Customs who has been designated by the Commissioners for Her Majesty's Revenue and Customs for the purposes of this Part.

Part 4 – Supplementary

AMENDMENT OF POWER UNDER SECTION 122 OF FA 2015

54 The power to make regulations under section 122(6)(c) of FA 2015 (country-by-country reporting: incidental etc provision that may be included in regulations) includes power to amend paragraph 7 above.

REGULATIONS

55(1) Regulations under this Schedule are to be made by statutory instrument.

55(2) A statutory instrument containing regulations under this Schedule is subject to annulment in pursuance of a resolution of the House of Commons.

Terms defined for purposes of more than one paragraph of this Schedule

Term	*Paragraph*
balance sheet total	paragraph 14(2)
confirmation notice (in Part 3)	paragraph 44
designated HMRC officer (in Part 3)	paragraph 53
engaged in unco-operative behaviour (in Part 3)	paragraph 36
failure (in paragraphs 27 to 33)	paragraph 26(1)
financial year (in relation to a UK group) (in paragraphs 16 and 17)	paragraph 16(7)
foreign (in relation to a relevant body)	paragraph 2(2)
foreign (in relation to a group)	paragraph 6(3)
group	paragraph 6(1)
group other than an MNE Group	paragraph 8
head (in relation to a group)	paragraph 9
head (in relation to a UK sub-group)	paragraph 11(2)
"liability to a penalty" (in paragraphs 27 to 33)	paragraph 26(1)
MNE Group	paragraph 7(1)
member (in relation to a group)	paragraph 8(2) and (3)
penalty (in paragraphs 27 to 33)	paragraph 26(1)
qualifying company	paragraph 5
qualifying group	paragraph 10
qualifying UK partnership	paragraph 12(2)
relevant body	paragraph 2(1)
representative partner	paragraph 12(5)
satisfied the arrangements condition (in Part 3)	paragraph 38
satisfied the behaviour condition (in Part 3)	paragraph 37
special measures notice	paragraphs 42 and 45
tax strategy (in Part 2)	paragraph 34
tribunal (in paragraphs 27 to 33)	paragraph 26(2)
turnover	paragraph 14(1)
UK company	paragraph 3
UK group	paragraph 6(2)
UK partnership	paragraph 12(1)
UK permanent establishment	paragraph 4(1)
UK sub-group	paragraph 11(1)
UK taxation	paragraph 15
warning notice	paragraph 41.

SCHEDULE 21 – PENALTIES RELATING TO OFFSHORE MATTERS AND OFFSHORE TRANSFERS

Section 163

Commencement Date – 1 April 2017 is the day appointed for the coming into force of amendments by Sch. 21 for all purposes except as noted below and the amendments have effect for inheritance tax purposes, in relation to transfers of value made on or after that day; and for income tax and capital gains tax purposes, in relation to any tax year commencing on or after 6 April 2016 (SI 2017/259, reg. 2–3). Excepted commencement dates as follows:

- para. 2(4) comes into force on 8 March 2017 for the purpose of making the regulations required by FA 2007, Sch. 24, para. 9(1C) (penalties for errors);
- para. 10(5) comes into force on 8 March 2017 for the purpose of making the regulations required by FA 2009, Sch. 55, para. 14(2C) (penalty for failure to make returns etc).

AMENDMENTS TO SCHEDULE 24 TO THE FINANCE ACT 2007 (C. 11)

1 Schedule 24 to FA 2007 (penalties for errors) is amended as follows.

2(1) Paragraph 9 (reductions for disclosure) is amended as follows.

2(2) [Substitutes FA 2007, Sch. 24, para. 9(A1) to (A3).]

2(3) [Amends FA 2007, Sch. 24, para. 9(1).]

2(4) [Inserts FA 2007, Sch. 24, para. 9(1A) to (1E).]

2(5) [Inserts FA 2007, Sch. 24, para. 9(4).]

Commencement Date – Para. 2(4) comes into force on 8 March 2017 for the purpose of making the regulations required by FA 2007, Sch. 24, para. 9(1C) (penalties for errors) (SI 2017/259, reg. 3(a)).

3 [Substitutes Table in FA 2007, Sch. 24, para. 10(2).]

4 [Inserts FA 2007, Sch. 24, para. 10A.]

AMENDMENTS TO SCHEDULE 55 TO THE FINANCE ACT 2009 (C.10)

9 Schedule 55 to FA 2009 (penalty for failure to make returns etc) is amended as follows

10(1) Paragraph 14 (reductions for disclosure) is amended as follows.

10(2) [Inserts FA 2009, Sch. 55, para. 14(A1).]

10(3) [Amends FA 2009, Sch. 55, para. 14(1).]

10(4) [Inserts FA 2009, Sch. 55, para. 14(1A) and (1B).]

10(5) [Inserts FA 2009, Sch. 55, para. 14(2A) to (2E).]

10(6) [Inserts FA 2009, Sch. 55, para. 14(5).]

History – Para. 10(5) comes into force on 8 March 2017 for the purpose of making the regulations required by FA 2009, Sch. 55, para. 14(2C) (penalty for failure to make returns etc) (SI 2017/259, reg. 3(c)).

11 [Substitutes Table in FA 2009, Sch. 55, para. 15(2).]

12 [Inserts FA 2009, Sch. 55, para. 15A.]

SCHEDULE 22 – ASSET-BASED PENALTY FOR OFFSHORE INACCURACIES AND FAILURES

Section 165

Commencement Date – Sch. 22 comes into force on 1 April 2017 and has effect for inheritance tax purposes, in relation to transfers of value made on or after 1 April 2017 and for income tax and capital gains tax purposes, in relation to tax years commencing on or after 6th April 2016 (SI 2017/277, reg. 2).

Part 5 – General

CONSEQUENTIAL AMENDMENTS ETC

20(1) [Not relevant to petroleum revenue tax.]

20(2) [Not relevant to petroleum revenue tax.]

20(3) [Amends FA 2007, Sch. 24, para. 12(2A).]

20(4) [Not relevant to petroleum revenue tax.]

20(5) [Inserts FA 2009, Sch. 55, para. 17(2)(d).]

SCHEDULE 23 – SIMPLE ASSESSMENTS

Section 167

9(1) Schedule 56 to FA 2009 (penalty for failure to make payments on time) is amended as follows.

9(2) [Not relevant to petroleum revenue tax.]

9(3) In paragraph 3(1)(a), after “items 1,” insert “1A,”.

FINANCE ACT 2017

(2017 Chapter 10)

[*27th April 2017*]

ARRANGEMENT OF SECTIONS

PART 1 – DIRECT AND INDIRECT TAXES

AVOIDANCE

24 Promoters of tax avoidance schemes: threshold conditions etc

24(1) [Substitutes FA 2014, Sch. 34, para. 13A(6)–(12).]

24(2) [Substitutes FA 2014, Sch. 34, para. 13B–13D.]

24(3) [Substitutes FA 2014, Sch. 34A, para. 20–22.]

24(4) [Substitutes FA 2014, Sch. 34A, para. 23.]

24(5) The amendments made by subsections (1) and (2) have effect for the purposes of determining whether a person meets a threshold condition in a period of three years ending on or after 8 March 2017.

24(6) The amendments made by subsections (3) and (4) have effect for the purposes of determining whether a person meets a section 237A condition in a period of three years ending on or after 8 March 2017.

PART 3 – FINAL

62 Interpretation

62 In this Act the following abbreviations are references to the following Acts.

ALDA 1979	Alcoholic Liquor Duties Act 1979
CAA 2001	Capital Allowances Act 2001
CTA 2009	Corporation Tax Act 2009
CTA 2010	Corporation Tax Act 2010
FA, followed by a year	Finance Act of that year
ICTA	Income and Corporation Taxes Act 1988
IHTA 1984	Inheritance Tax Act 1984
ITA 2007	Income Tax Act 2007
ITEPA 2003	Income Tax (Earnings and Pensions) Act 2003
ITTOIA 2005	Income Tax (Trading and Other Income) Act 2005
TCGA 1992	Taxation of Chargeable Gains Act 1992
TMA 1970	Taxes Management Act 1970
TPDA 1979	Tobacco Products Duty Act 1979
VATA 1994	Value Added Tax Act 1994
VERA 1994	Vehicle Excise and Registration Act 1994

63 Short title

63 This Act may be cited as the Finance Act 2017.

SCHEDULES

SCHEDULE 11 – SOFT DRINKS INDUSTRY LEVY: SUPPLEMENTARY AMENDMENTS

Section 56

HMRC POWERS TO OBTAIN INFORMATION ETC.

1(1) Schedule 36 to FA 2008 (powers to obtain information etc.) is amended as follows.

1(2) In paragraph 10 (power to inspect business premises etc.), at the end insert–

"**10(5)** In sub-paragraph (1), the reference to a person's tax position does not include a reference to a person's position as regards soft drinks industry levy."

1(3) In paragraph 63(1) (meaning of "tax"), after paragraph (i) insert–

"(ia) soft drinks industry levy,".

PENALTIES: FAILURE TO COMPLY WITH REQUIREMENTS RELATING TO RETURNS

4(1) Schedule 55 to FA 2009 (penalty for failure to make returns etc) is amended in accordance with this paragraph.

4(2) In paragraph 1(4), in the definition of "penalty date", for "13" substitute "13A".

4(3) [Not relevant to petroleum revenue tax.]

4(4) In subsections (2) and (4) of section 106 of FA 2009 (penalties for failure to make returns: commencement) references to Schedule 55 to that Act have effect as references to that Schedule as amended by this paragraph.

FINANCE (NO. 2) ACT 2017

(2017 Chapter 32)

[*16th November 2017*]

ARRANGEMENT OF SECTIONS

PART 2 – INDIRECT TAXES

44 Petroleum revenue tax: elections for oil fields to become non-taxable

44(1) [Substitutes FA 1993, Sch. 20B, para 2–7.]

44(2) [Amends OTA 1975, s. 6(1A).]

44(3) [Amends FA 1980, Sch. 17, para. 15(9A).]

44(4) The amendment made by this section is to be treated as having come into force on 23 November 2016.

PART 4 – ADMINISTRATION, AVOIDANCE AND ENFORCEMENT

REPORTING AND RECORD-KEEPING

61 Digital reporting and record-keeping for income tax etc: further amendments

61(1) Schedule 14 contains provision amending TMA 1970 and other Acts.

61(2) The Commissioners for Her Majesty's Revenue and Customs may by regulations amend or modify any provision of the Taxes Acts in consequence of the provision made by section 60 or Schedule 14.

61(3) Regulations under subsection (2) may make transitional, transitory or saving provision.

61(4) Regulations under subsection (2) must be made by statutory instrument.

61(5) A statutory instrument containing regulations under subsection (2) may not be made unless a draft of the instrument has been laid before, and approved by a resolution of, the House of Commons.

61(6) Subsections (1) to (5) and Schedule 14 come into force on such day as the Treasury may by regulations made by statutory instrument appoint.

61(7) Regulations under subsection (6) may appoint different days for different purposes.

ENQUIRIES

63 Partial closure notices

63 Schedule 15 makes provision for partial closure notices in respect of enquiries under sections 9A, 12ZM and 12AC of TMA 1970 and Schedule 18 to FA 1998.

AVOIDANCE ETC

64 Errors in taxpayers' documents

64(1) Schedule 24 to FA 2007 (penalties for errors) is amended as set out in subsections (2) and (3).

64(2) [Inserts FA 2007, Sch. 24, para. 3A and 3B.]

64(3) [Substitutes FA 2007, Sch. 24, para. 18(6).]

64(4) [Omits FA 2014, s. 276.]

64(5) The amendments made by this section have effect in relation to any document of a kind listed in the Table in paragraph 1 of Schedule 24 to FA 2007 which–

(a) is given to HMRC on or after the day on which this Act is passed, and

(b) relates to a tax period that–

  (i) begins on or after 6 April 2017, and

  (ii) ends on or after the day on which this Act is passed.

64(6) In subsection (5) **"tax period"**, and the reference to giving a document to HMRC, have the same meaning as in Schedule 24 to FA 2007 (see paragraph 28 of that Schedule).

65 Penalties for enablers of defeated tax avoidance

65 Schedule 16 makes provision for penalties for persons who enable tax avoidance which is defeated.

66 Disclosure of tax avoidance schemes: VAT and other indirect taxes

66(1) Schedule 17 contains provision about the disclosure of tax avoidance schemes involving VAT or other indirect taxes.

66(2) In consequence of the provision made by Schedule 17, section 58A of, and Schedule 11A to, VATA 1994 (disclosure of VAT avoidance schemes) cease to have effect to require a person to disclose any scheme which–

(a) is first entered into by that person on or after 1 January 2018,

(b) constitutes notifiable *arrangements* under Schedule 17,

(c) implements proposals which are notifiable proposals under Schedule 17.

66(3) No scheme or proposed scheme may be notified to the Commissioners under paragraph 9 of Schedule 11A to VATA 1994 (voluntary notification of schemes) on or after 1 January 2018.

66(4) This section and Schedule 17 come into force–

(a) so far as is necessary for enabling the making of regulations under that Schedule, on the passing of this Act, and

(b) for all other purposes, on 1 January 2018.

68 Penalty for transactions connected with VAT fraud etc

68(6) [Inserts FA 2007, Sch. 24, para. 21ZA.]

INFORMATION

69 Data-gathering from money service businesses

69(1) [Inserts FA 2011, Sch. 23, para. 13D.]

69(2) This section applies in relation to relevant data with a bearing on any period (whether before, on or after the day on which this Act is passed).

PART 5 – FINAL

71 Interpretation

71 In this Act the following abbreviations are references to the following Acts.

CAA 2001	Capital Allowances Act 2001
CEMA 1979	Customs and Excise Management Act 1979
CTA 2009	Corporation Tax Act 2009
CTA 2010	Corporation Tax Act 2010
CT(NI)A 2015	Corporation Tax (Northern Ireland) Act 2015
FA, followed by a year	Finance Act of that year
F(No. 2)A, followed by a year	Finance (No. 2) Act of that year
F(No. 3)A, followed by a year	Finance (No. 3) Act of that year
ICTA	Income and Corporation Taxes Act 1988
IHTA 1984	Inheritance Tax Act 1984
ITA 2007	Income Tax Act 2007
ITEPA 2003	Income Tax (Earnings and Pensions) Act 2003
ITTOIA 2005	Income Tax (Trading and Other Income) Act 2005
OTA 1975	Oil Taxation Act 1975
TCGA 1992	Taxation of Chargeable Gains Act 1992
TIOPA 2010	Taxation (International and Other Provisions) Act 2010
TMA 1970	Taxes Management Act 1970
TPDA 1979	Tobacco Products Duty Act 1979
VATA 1994	Value Added Tax Act 1994

72 Short title

72 This Act may be cited as the Finance (No. 2) Act 2017.

SCHEDULES

SCHEDULE 14 – DIGITAL REPORTING AND RECORD-KEEPING FOR INCOME TAX ETC: FURTHER AMENDMENTS

Section 61

Part 2 – Amendments of Other Acts

FA 2008

38(1) Schedule 36 to FA 2008 (information and inspection powers) is amended as follows.

38(2) In paragraph 21(1) (taxpayer notices) after "12AA of" insert ", or regulations under paragraph 10 of Schedule A1 to,".

38(3) In paragraph 37(2)(a) (partnerships) after "section 12AA of" insert ", or regulations under paragraph 10 of Schedule A1 to,".

FA 2014

43 FA 2014 is amended as follows.

44 In section 253(6)(c) (definition of "tax return") after "section 12AA of" insert ", or regulations under paragraph 10 of Schedule A1 to,".

FA 2016

47 FA 2016 is amended as follows.

48(1) Schedule 18 (serial tax avoidance) is amended as follows.

48(2) In paragraph 51(8)(b) (partnerships: information) after "TMA 1970" insert ", or under equivalent provision made by regulations under paragraph 10 of Schedule A1 to that Act,".

48(3) In paragraph 52 (partnerships: special provision about taxpayer emendations)–

(a) in sub-paragraph (1) for "subsection (1)(b) of section 12AB of that Act (partnership statement)" substitute "section 12AB(1)(b) of that Act or under equivalent provision made by regulations under paragraph 10 of Schedule A1 to that Act (partnership statement)";

(b) in sub-paragraph (3)–

(i) in the words before paragraph (a), after "that person's successor" insert "(in the case of a section 12AA partnership return) or the nominated partner (in the case of a Schedule A1 partnership return)";

(ii) for "subsection (1)(b) of section 12AB of TMA 1970 (partnership statement)" substitute "section 12AB(1)(b) of TMA 1970 or under equivalent provision made by regulations under paragraph 10 of Schedule A1 to that Act (partnership statement)".

48(4) In paragraph 53(1) (supplementary provision relating to partnerships)–

(a) in the definition of "the representative partner" after "in relation to a" insert "section 12AA";

(b) after the definition of "successor" insert–

""**the nominated partner**", in relation to a Schedule A1 partnership return, has the meaning given by paragraph 5 of Schedule A1 to TMA 1970."

48(5) In paragraph 58(1) (general interpretation), for the definition of "partnership return" substitute–

""**partnership return**" means a return–

(a) under section 12AA of TMA 1970 (a "section 12AA partnership return"), or

(b) required by regulations made under paragraph 10 of Schedule A1 to TMA 1970 (a "Schedule A1 partnership return");".

49(1) Schedule 19 (large businesses: tax strategies and sanctions) is amended as follows.

49(2) In paragraph 12(5) (definition of "representative partner")–

(a) the words from "the partner" to the end become paragraph (a);

(b) at the end of that paragraph insert ", or";

(c) after that paragraph insert–

"(b) the nominated partner within the meaning of paragraph 5 of Schedule A1 to TMA 1970."

49(3) In paragraph 13 (definition of "financial year") in paragraph (c) for "under a return issued under section 12AB" substitute "within the meaning of".

SCHEDULE 15 – PARTIAL CLOSURE NOTICES

Section 63

FA 2008

36 [Amends FA 2008, Sch. 36, para. 21(4) and 21ZA(3).]

COMMENCEMENT

44 The amendments made by this Schedule have effect in relation to an enquiry under section 9A, 12ZM or 12AC of TMA 1970 or Schedule 18 to FA 1998 where–

(a) notice of the enquiry is given on or after the day on which this Act is passed, or

(b) the enquiry is in progress immediately before that day.

SCHEDULE 16 – PENALTIES FOR ENABLERS OF DEFEATED TAX AVOIDANCE

Section 65

Part 1 – Liability to Penalty

1 Where–

(a) a person ("T") has entered into abusive tax arrangements, and

(b) T incurs a defeat in respect of the arrangements,

a penalty is payable by each person who enabled the arrangements.

2(1) Parts 2 to 4 of this Schedule define–

"abusive tax arrangements";

a **"defeat in respect of the arrangements"**;

a **"person who enabled the arrangements"**.

2(2) The other Parts of this Schedule make provision supplementing paragraph 1 as follows–

(a) Part 5 makes provision about the amount of a penalty;

(b) Parts 6 to 8 provide for the assessment of penalties, referrals to the GAAR Advisory Panel and appeals against assessments;

(c) Part 9 applies information and inspection powers, and makes provision about declarations relating to legally privileged communications;

(d) Part 10 confers power to publish details of persons who have incurred penalties;

(e) Parts 11 and 12 contain miscellaneous and general provisions.

Part 2 – "Abusive" and "Tax Arrangements": Meaning

3(1) Arrangements are **"tax arrangements"** for the purposes of this Schedule if, having regard to all the circumstances, it would be reasonable to conclude that the obtaining of a tax advantage was the main purpose, or one of the main purposes, of the arrangements.

3(2) Tax arrangements are **"abusive"** for the purposes of this Schedule if they are arrangements the entering into or carrying out of which cannot reasonably be regarded as a reasonable course of action in relation to the relevant tax provisions, having regard to all the circumstances.

3(3) The circumstances to which regard must be had under sub-paragraph (2) include–

(a) whether the substantive results, or the intended substantive results, of the arrangements are consistent with any principles on which the relevant tax provisions are based (whether express or implied) and the policy objectives of those provisions,

(b) whether the means of achieving those results involves one or more contrived or abnormal steps, and

(c) whether the arrangements are intended to exploit any shortcomings in those provisions.

3(4) Where the tax arrangements form part of any other arrangements regard must also be had to those other arrangements.

3(5) Each of the following is an example of something which might indicate that tax arrangements are abusive–

(a) the arrangements result in an amount of income, profits or gains for tax purposes that is significantly less than the amount for economic purposes;

(b) the arrangements result in deductions or losses of an amount for tax purposes that is significantly greater than the amount for economic purposes;

(c) the arrangements result in a claim for the repayment or crediting of tax (including foreign tax) that has not been, and is unlikely to be, paid;

but a result mentioned in paragraph (a), (b) or (c) is to be taken to be such an example only if it is reasonable to assume that such a result was not the anticipated result when the relevant tax provisions were enacted.

3(6) The fact that tax arrangements accord with established practice, and HMRC had, at the time the arrangements were entered into, indicated their acceptance of that practice, is an example of something which might indicate that the arrangements are not abusive.

3(7) The examples given in sub-paragraphs (5) and (6) are not exhaustive.

3(8) In sub-paragraph (5) the reference to income includes earnings, within the meaning of Part 1 of the Social Security Contributions and Benefits Act 1992 or Part 1 of the Social Security Contributions and Benefits (Northern Ireland) Act 1992.

Part 3 – "Defeat" in Respect of Abusive Tax Arrangements

"DEFEAT" IN RESPECT OF ABUSIVE TAX ARRANGEMENTS

4 T (within the meaning of paragraph 1) incurs a **"defeat"** in respect of abusive tax arrangements entered into by T ("the arrangements concerned") if–

(a) Condition A (in paragraph 5) is met, or

(b) Condition B (in paragraph 6) is met.

CONDITION A

5(1) Condition A is that–

(a) T, or a person on behalf of T, has given HMRC a document of a kind listed in the Table in paragraph 1 of Schedule 24 to FA 2007 (returns etc),

(b) the document was submitted on the basis that a tax advantage ("the relevant tax advantage") arose from the arrangements concerned,

(c) the relevant tax advantage has been counteracted, and

(d) the counteraction is final.

5(2) For the purposes of this paragraph the relevant tax advantage has been **"counteracted"** if adjustments have been made in respect of T's tax position on the basis that the whole or part of the relevant tax advantage does not arise.

5(3) For the purposes of this paragraph a counteraction is **"final"** when the adjustments in question, and any amounts arising from the adjustments, can no longer be varied, on appeal or otherwise.

5(4) In this paragraph **"adjustments"** means any adjustments, whether by way of an assessment, the modification of an assessment or return, the amendment or disallowance of a claim, a payment, the entering into of a contract settlement or otherwise.

Accordingly, references to "making" adjustments include securing that adjustments are made by entering into a contract settlement.

5(5) Any reference in this paragraph to giving HMRC a document includes–

(a) communicating information to HMRC in any form and by any method;

(b) making a statement or declaration in a document.

5(6) Any reference in this paragraph to a document of a kind listed in the Table in paragraph 1 of *Schedule 24 to FA 2007 includes–*

(a) a document amending a document of a kind so listed, and

(b) a document which–

(i) relates to national insurance contributions, and

(ii) is a document in relation to which that Schedule applies.

CONDITION B

6(1) Condition B is that (in a case not falling within Condition A)–

(a) HMRC have made an assessment in relation to tax,

(b) the assessment counteracts a tax advantage that it is reasonable to assume T expected to obtain from the arrangements concerned ("the expected tax advantage"), and

(c) the counteraction is final.

6(2) For the purposes of this paragraph an assessment **"counteracts"** the expected tax advantage if the assessment is on a basis which prevents T from obtaining (or obtaining the whole of) the expected tax advantage.

6(3) For the purposes of this paragraph a counteraction is **"final"**–

(a) when a relevant contract settlement is made, or

(b) if no contract settlement has been made, when the assessment in question and any amounts arising from the assessment can no longer be varied, on appeal or otherwise.

6(4) In sub-paragraph (3) a **"relevant contract settlement"** means a contract settlement on a basis which prevents T from obtaining (or obtaining the whole of) the expected tax advantage.

Part 4 – Persons Who "Enabled" the Arrangements

PERSONS WHO "ENABLED" THE ARRANGEMENTS

7(1) A person is a person who **"enabled"** the arrangements mentioned in paragraph 1 if that person is–

(a) a designer of the arrangements (see paragraph 8),

(b) a manager of the arrangements (see paragraph 9),

(c) a person who marketed the arrangements to T (see paragraph 10),

(d) an enabling participant in the arrangements (see paragraph 11), or

(e) a financial enabler in relation to the arrangements (see paragraph 12).

7(2) This paragraph is subject to paragraph 13 (excluded persons).

DESIGNERS OF ARRANGEMENTS

8(1) For the purposes of paragraph 7 a person is a **"designer"** of the arrangements if that person was, in the course of a business carried on by that person, to any extent responsible for the design of–

(a) the arrangements, or

(b) a proposal which was implemented by the arrangements;

but this is subject to sub-paragraph (2).

8(2) Where a person would (in the absence of this sub-paragraph) fall within sub-paragraph (1) because of having provided advice which was used in the design of the arrangements or of a proposal, that person does not because of that advice fall within that sub-paragraph unless–

(a) the advice is relevant advice, and

(b) the knowledge condition is met.

8(3) Advice is **"relevant advice"** if–

(a) the advice or any part of it suggests arrangements or an alteration of proposed arrangements, and

(b) it is reasonable to assume that the suggestion was made with a view to arrangements being designed in such a way that a tax advantage (or a greater tax advantage) might be expected to arise from them.

8(4) The knowledge condition is that, when the advice was provided, the person providing it knew or could reasonably be expected to know–

(a) that the advice would be used in the design of abusive tax arrangements or of a proposal for such arrangements, or

(b) that it was likely that the advice would be so used.

8(5) For the purposes of sub-paragraph (3), advice is not to be taken to "suggest" anything–

(a) which is put forward by the advice for consideration, but

(b) which the advice can reasonably be read as recommending against.

8(6) In sub-paragraph (3)–

(a) the reference in paragraph (a) to arrangements or an alteration of proposed arrangements includes a proposal for arrangements or an alteration of a proposal for arrangements, and

(b) the reference in paragraph (b) to arrangements includes arrangements proposed by a proposal.

8(7) For the purposes of this paragraph–

(a) references to advice include an opinion;

(b) advice is "used" in a design if the advice is taken account of in that design.

MANAGERS OF ARRANGEMENTS

9(1) For the purposes of paragraph 7 a person is a **"manager"** of the arrangements if that person–

(a) was, in the course of a business carried on by that person, to any extent responsible for the organisation or management of the arrangements, and

(b) when carrying out any functions in relation to the organisation or management of the arrangements, knew or could reasonably be expected to know that the arrangements involved were abusive tax arrangements.

9(2) Where–

(a) a person is, in the course of a business carried on by the person, to any extent responsible for facilitating T's withdrawal from the arrangements, and

(b) it is reasonable to assume that the obtaining of a tax advantage is not T's purpose (or one of T's purposes) in withdrawing from the arrangements,

that person is not because of anything done in the course of facilitating that withdrawal to be regarded as to any extent responsible for the organisation or management of the arrangements.

MARKETERS OF ARRANGEMENTS

10 For the purposes of paragraph 7 a person **"marketed"** the arrangements to T if, in the course of a business carried on by that person–

(a) that person made available for implementation by T a proposal which has since been implemented, in relation to T, by the arrangements, or

(b) that person–

(i) communicated information to T or another person about a proposal which has since been implemented, in relation to T, by the arrangements, and

(ii) did so with a view to T entering into the arrangements or transactions forming part of the arrangements.

ENABLING PARTICIPANTS

11 For the purposes of paragraph 7 a person is **"an enabling participant"** in the arrangements if–

(a) that person is a person (other than T) who enters into the arrangements or a transaction forming part of the arrangements,

(b) without that person's participation in the arrangements or transaction (or the participation of another person in the arrangements or transaction in the same capacity as that person), the arrangements could not be expected to result in a tax advantage for T, and

(c) when that person entered into the arrangements or transaction, that person knew or could reasonably be expected to know that what was being entered into was abusive tax arrangements or a transaction forming part of such arrangements.

FINANCIAL ENABLERS

12(1) For the purposes of paragraph 7 a person is a **"financial enabler"** in relation to the arrangements if–

(a) in the course of a business carried on by that person, that person provided a financial product (directly or indirectly) to a relevant party,

(b) it is reasonable to assume that the purpose (or a purpose) of the relevant party in obtaining the financial product was to participate in the arrangements, and

(c) when the financial product was provided, the person providing it knew or could reasonably be expected to know that the purpose (or a purpose) of obtaining it was to participate in abusive tax arrangements.

12(2) In this paragraph **"a relevant party"** means T or an enabling participant in the arrangements within the meaning given by paragraph 11.

12(3) Any reference in this paragraph to a person's providing a financial product to a relevant party includes (but is not limited to) the person's doing any of the following–

(a) providing a loan to a relevant party;

(b) issuing or transferring a share to a relevant party;

(c) entering into arrangements with a relevant party such that–

  (i) the person becomes a party to a relevant contract within the meaning of section 577 of CTA 2009 (derivative contracts);

  (ii) there is a repo in respect of securities within the meaning of section 263A(A1) of TCGA 1992;

  (iii) the person or the relevant party has a creditor repo, creditor quasi-repo, debtor repo or debtor quasi-repo within the meaning of sections 543, 544, 548 and 549 of CTA 2009;

(d) entering into a stock lending arrangement, within the meaning of section 263B(1) of TCGA 1992, with a relevant party;

(e) entering into an alternative finance arrangement, within the meaning of Chapter 6 of Part 6 of CTA 2009 or Part 10A of ITA 2007, with a relevant party;

(f) entering into a contract with a relevant party which, whether alone or in combination with one or more other contracts–

  (i) is in accordance with generally accepted accounting practice required to be treated as a loan, deposit or other financial asset or obligation, or

  (ii) would be required to be so treated by the person if the person were a company to which the Companies Act 2006 applies;

and references to obtaining a financial product are to be read accordingly.

12(4) The Treasury may by regulations amend sub-paragraph (3).

EXCLUDED PERSONS

13(1) A person who–

(a) would (in the absence of this paragraph) be regarded for the purposes of this Schedule as having enabled particular arrangements mentioned in paragraph 1, but

(b) is a person within sub-paragraph (2),

is not to be regarded as having enabled those arrangements.

13(2) The persons within this sub-paragraph are–

(a) T;

(b) where T is a company, any company in the same group as T.

POWERS TO ADD CATEGORIES OF ENABLER AND TO PROVIDE EXCEPTIONS

14(1) The Treasury may by regulations add to the categories of persons who, in relation to arrangements mentioned in paragraph 1, are for the purposes of this Schedule persons who enabled the arrangements.

14(2) The Treasury may by regulations provide that a person who would otherwise be regarded for the purposes of this Schedule as having enabled arrangements is not to be so regarded where conditions prescribed by the regulations are met.

14(3) Regulations under this paragraph may–

(a) amend this Part of this Schedule;

(b) make supplementary, incidental, and consequential provision, including provision amending any other Part of this Schedule;

(c) make transitional provision.

Part 5 – Amount of Penalty

AMOUNT OF PENALTY

15(1) For each person who enabled the arrangements mentioned in paragraph 1, the penalty payable under paragraph 1 is the total amount or value of all the relevant consideration received or receivable by that person ("the person in question").

15(2) Particular consideration is **"relevant"** for the purposes of this paragraph if–

(a) it is consideration for anything done by the person in question which enabled the arrangements mentioned in paragraph 1, and

(b) it has not previously been taken into account in calculating the amount of a penalty payable under paragraph 1.

15(3) For the purposes of this paragraph a thing done by a person **"enabled"** the arrangements mentioned in paragraph 1 if, by doing that thing (alone or with anything else), the person fell within the definition in Part 4 of this Schedule of a person who enabled those arrangements.

16(1) This paragraph applies for the purposes of paragraph 15.

16(2) Where consideration for anything done by a person ("A") is, under any arrangements with A, paid or payable to a person other than A, it is to be taken to be received or receivable by A.

16(3) The **"consideration"** for anything done by a person does not include any amount charged by that person in respect of value added tax.

16(4) Consideration attributable to two or more transactions is to be apportioned on a just and reasonable basis.

16(5) Any consideration given for what is in substance one bargain is to be treated as attributable to all elements of the bargain, even though–

(a) separate consideration is, or purports to be, given for different elements of the bargain, or

(b) there are, or purport to be, separate transactions in respect of different elements of the bargain.

REDUCTION OF PENALTY WHERE OTHER PENALTIES INCURRED

17(1) The amount of a penalty for which a person is liable under paragraph 1 is to be reduced by the amount of any other penalty incurred by the person in respect of conduct for which the person is liable to the penalty under paragraph 1.

17(2) In this paragraph **"any other penalty"** means a penalty–

(a) which is a penalty under a provision other than paragraph 1, and

(b) which has been assessed.

MITIGATION OF PENALTY

18(1) HMRC may in their discretion reduce a penalty under paragraph 1.

18(2) In this paragraph the reference to reducing a penalty includes a reference to–

(a) entirely remitting the penalty, or

(b) staying, or agreeing a compromise in relation to, proceedings for the recovery of a penalty.

Part 6 – Assessment of Penalty

ASSESSMENT OF PENALTY

19(1) Where a person is liable for a penalty under paragraph 1 HMRC must–

(a) assess the penalty, and

(b) notify the person.

19(2) If–

(a) HMRC do not have all the information required to determine the amount or value of the relevant consideration within the meaning of paragraph 15, and

(b) HMRC have taken all reasonable steps to obtain that information,

HMRC may assess the penalty on the basis of a reasonable estimate by HMRC of that consideration.

19(3) This paragraph is subject to–

(a) paragraphs 21 and 22 (limits on when penalty may be assessed); and

(b) Part 7 of this Schedule (requirement for opinion of GAAR Advisory Panel before penalty may be assessed).

20(1) A penalty under paragraph 1 must be paid before the end of the period of 30 days beginning with the day on which notification of the penalty is issued.

20(2) An assessment of a penalty under paragraph 1–

(a) is to be treated for procedural purposes in the same way as an assessment to tax (except in respect of a matter expressly provided for by this Schedule), and

(b) may be enforced as if it were an assessment to tax.

SPECIAL PROVISION ABOUT ASSESSMENT FOR MULTI-USER SCHEMES

21(1) This paragraph applies where–

(a) a proposal for arrangements is implemented more than once, by a number of tax arrangements which are substantially the same as each other ("related arrangements"),

(b) paragraph 1 applies in relation to particular arrangements ("the arrangements concerned") which are one of the number of related arrangements implementing the proposal, and

(c) at the time when the person who entered into the arrangements concerned incurs a defeat in respect of them, the required percentage of relevant defeats has not been reached.

21(2) HMRC may not assess any penalty payable under paragraph 1 in respect of the arrangements concerned until the required percentage of relevant defeats is reached.

21(3) For the purposes of this paragraph the **"required percentage of relevant defeats"** is reached when HMRC reasonably believe that defeats have been incurred in the case of more than 50% of the related arrangements implementing the proposal.

21(4) Sub-paragraph (2) does not apply in relation to a penalty if the person liable to the penalty requests assessment of the penalty sooner than the time allowed by sub-paragraph (2).

TIME LIMIT FOR ASSESSMENT

22(1) An assessment of a person as liable to a penalty under paragraph 1 may not take place after the relevant time.

22(2) In this paragraph **"the relevant time"** means, subject to sub-paragraphs (3) to (6)–

(a) where a GAAR final decision notice within the meaning of paragraph 24(1) has been given in relation to the arrangements to which the penalty relates, the end of 12 months beginning with the date on which T incurs the defeat mentioned in paragraph 1;

(b) where a notice under paragraph 25 has been given to the person mentioned in sub-paragraph (1) above in respect of the arrangements to which the penalty relates, the end of 12 months beginning with the end of the time allowed for making representations in respect of that notice;

(c) where–

(i) a referral has been made under paragraph 26 in respect of the arrangements to which the penalty relates, and

(ii) paragraph (d) does not apply,

the end of 12 months beginning with the date on which the opinion of the GAAR Advisory Panel is given on the referral (within the meaning given by paragraph 34(6));

(d) where a notice under paragraph 35 has been given to the person mentioned in sub-paragraph (1) above in respect of the arrangements to which the penalty relates, the end of 12 months beginning with the end of the time allowed for making representations in respect of that notice.

22(3) Where–

(a) paragraph 21 prevented a penalty from being assessed before the required percentage of relevant defeats was reached, and

(b) the required percentage of relevant defeats (within the meaning of paragraph 21) has been reached, the relevant time in relation to that penalty is whichever is the later of–

(i) the relevant time given by sub-paragraph (2), and

(ii) the end of 12 months beginning with the date on which that required percentage was reached.

22(4) Where under paragraph 21(4) a person requests assessment of a penalty, the relevant time in relation to that penalty is whichever is the later of–

(a) the relevant time given by sub-paragraph (2), and

(b) the end of 12 months beginning with the date on which the request is made,

and sub-paragraph (3) does not apply to the penalty even if the required percentage of relevant defeats is reached.

22(5) Sub-paragraph (6) applies where–

(a) at any time a declaration has been made under paragraph 44 for the purposes of any determination of whether a person is liable to a penalty under paragraph 1 in relation to particular arrangements ("the arrangements concerned"), and

(b) subsequently, facts that in the Commissioners' opinion are sufficient to indicate that the declaration contains a material inaccuracy have come to the Commissioners' knowledge.

22(6) The relevant time in respect of any penalty under paragraph 1 payable by that person in relation to the arrangements concerned is whichever is the later of–

(a) the relevant time given by the preceding provisions of this paragraph, and

(b) the end of 12 months beginning with the date on which such facts came to the Commissioners' knowledge.

Part 7 – GAAR Advisory Panel Opinion, and Representations

REQUIREMENT FOR OPINION OF GAAR ADVISORY PANEL

23(1) A penalty under paragraph 1 may not be assessed unless–

(a) the decision that it should be assessed is taken by a designated HMRC officer, and

(b) either the condition in sub-paragraph (2) or the condition in sub-paragraph (3) is met.

23(2) The condition in this sub-paragraph is that, when the assessment is made–

(a) a GAAR final decision notice has been given in relation to–

(i) the arrangements to which the penalty relates ("the relevant arrangements"), or

(ii) arrangements that are equivalent to the relevant arrangements,

(b) where a notice is required by paragraph 25 to be given to the person liable to the penalty, that notice has been given and the time allowed for making representations under that paragraph has expired, and

(c) a designated HMRC officer has, in deciding whether the penalty should be assessed, considered–

(i) the opinion of the GAAR Advisory Panel which was considered by HMRC in preparing that GAAR final decision notice, and

(ii) any representations made under paragraph 25.

23(3) The condition in this sub-paragraph is that, when the assessment is made–

(a) an opinion of the GAAR Advisory Panel which applies to the relevant arrangements has been given on a referral under paragraph 26,

(b) where a notice is required by paragraph 35 to be given to the person liable to the penalty, that notice has been given and the time allowed for making representations under that paragraph has expired, and

(c) a designated HMRC officer has, in deciding whether the penalty should be assessed, considered–

(i) that opinion of the GAAR Advisory Panel, and

(ii) any representations made under paragraph 35.

23(4) Where a notification of a penalty under paragraph 1 is given, the notification must be accompanied by a report prepared by HMRC of–

(a) if the condition in sub-paragraph (2) is met, the opinion of the GAAR Advisory Panel which was considered by HMRC in preparing the GAAR final decision notice;

(b) if the condition in sub-paragraph (3) is met, the opinion of the GAAR advisory panel mentioned in that sub-paragraph.

23(5) Paragraph 24 contains definitions of terms used in this paragraph.

24(1) In this Schedule a **"GAAR final decision notice"** means a notice under–

(a) paragraph 12 of Schedule 43 to FA 2013 (notice of final decision after considering opinion of GAAR Advisory Panel on referral under Schedule 43),

(b) paragraph 8 or 9 of Schedule 43A to FA 2013 (notice of final decision after considering opinion of GAAR Advisory Panel), or

(c) paragraph 8 of Schedule 43B to FA 2013 (notice of final decision after considering opinion of GAAR Advisory Panel on referral under Schedule 43B).

24(2) For the purposes of this Part of this Schedule, where the GAAR Advisory Panel gives an opinion on a referral under paragraph 26 the arrangements to which the opinion **"applies"** are–

(a) the arrangements in respect of which the referral was made (that is, "the arrangements in question" within the meaning given by paragraph 26(1)), and

(b) any arrangements that are equivalent to those arrangements.

24(3) For the purposes of this Part of this Schedule, arrangements are **"equivalent"** to one another if they are substantially the same as one another having regard to–

(a) their substantive results or intended substantive results,

(b) the means of achieving those results, and

(c) the characteristics on the basis of which it could reasonably be argued, in each case, that the arrangements are abusive tax arrangements.

NOTICE WHERE PANEL OPINION ALREADY OBTAINED IN RELATION TO EQUIVALENT ARRANGEMENTS

25(1) This paragraph applies where a designated HMRC officer is of the view that–

(a) a person is liable to a penalty under paragraph 1 in relation to particular arrangements ("the arrangements concerned"),

(b) no GAAR final decision notice has been given in relation to those arrangements, but those arrangements are equivalent to arrangements in relation to which a GAAR final decision notice has been given ("the GAAR decision arrangements"), and

(c) accordingly, the opinion of the GAAR Advisory Panel which was considered by HMRC in preparing that GAAR final decision notice is relevant to the arrangements concerned.

25(2) A designated HMRC officer must give the person mentioned in sub-paragraph (1) a notice in writing–

(a) explaining that the officer is of the view mentioned there,

(b) specifying the arrangements concerned,

(c) describing the material characteristics of the GAAR decision arrangements,

(d) setting out a report prepared by HMRC of the opinion of the GAAR Advisory Panel which was considered by HMRC in preparing the GAAR final decision notice, and

(e) explaining the effect of sub-paragraphs (3) and (4).

25(3) A person to whom a notice under this paragraph is given has 30 days, beginning with the day on which the notice is given, to send to the designated HMRC officer (in writing) any representations that that person wishes to make as to why the arrangements concerned are not equivalent to the GAAR decision arrangements.

25(4) A designated HMRC officer may, on a written request by that person, extend the period during which representations may be made by that person.

25(5) Paragraph 24 contains definitions of the following terms used in this paragraph–

"GAAR final decision notice";

"equivalent", in relation to arrangements.

REFERRAL TO GAAR ADVISORY PANEL

26(1) A designated HMRC officer may make a referral under this paragraph if–

(a) the officer considers that a person is liable to a penalty under paragraph 1 in relation to particular arrangements ("the arrangements in question"), and

(b) the requirements of paragraph 28 (procedure before making of referral) have been complied with.

26(2) But a referral may not be made under this paragraph if a GAAR final decision notice (within the meaning of paragraph 24(1)) has already been given in relation to–

(a) the arrangements in question, or

(b) arrangements that are equivalent to those arrangements.

26(3) A referral under this paragraph is a referral to the GAAR Advisory Panel of the question whether the entering into and carrying out of tax arrangements such as are described in the referral statement (see paragraph 27) is a reasonable course of action in relation to the relevant tax provisions.

27(1) In this Part of this Schedule **"the referral statement"**, in relation to a referral under paragraph 26, means a statement made by a designated HMRC officer which–

(a) accompanies the referral,

(b) is a general statement of the material characteristics of the arrangements in question (within the meaning given by paragraph 26(1)), and

(c) complies with sub-paragraph (2).

27(2) A statement under this paragraph must–

(a) contain a factual description of the arrangements in question,

(b) set out HMRC's view as to whether those arrangements accord with established practice (as it stood when those arrangements were entered into),

(c) explain why it is the designated HMRC officer's view that a tax advantage of the nature described in the statement and arising from tax arrangements having the characteristics described in the statement would be a tax advantage arising from arrangements that are abusive,

(d) set out any matters the designated HMRC officer is aware of which may suggest that any view of HMRC or the designated HMRC officer expressed in the statement is not correct, and

(e) set out any other matters which the designated HMRC officer considers are required for the purposes of the exercise of the GAAR Advisory Panel's functions under paragraphs 33 and 34.

NOTICE BEFORE DECISION WHETHER TO REFER

28(1) A referral must not be made under paragraph 26 unless–

(a) a designated HMRC officer has given each relevant person a notice under this paragraph,

(b) in the case of each relevant person, the time allowed for making representations has expired, and

(c) in deciding whether to make the referral, a designated HMRC officer has considered any representations made by a relevant person within the time allowed.

28(2) In this paragraph a **"relevant person"** means any person who at the time of the referral is considered by the officer making the referral to be liable to a penalty under paragraph 1 in relation to the arrangements in question (within the meaning given by paragraph 26(1)).

28(3) A notice under this paragraph is a notice in writing which–

(a) explains that the officer giving the notice considers that the person to whom the notice is given is liable to a penalty under paragraph 1 in relation to the arrangements in question (specifying those arrangements),

(b) explains why the officer considers those arrangements to be abusive tax arrangements,

(c) explains that HMRC are proposing to make a referral under paragraph 26 of the question whether the entering into and carrying out of tax arrangements that have the characteristics of the arrangements in question is a reasonable course of action in relation to the relevant tax provisions, and

(d) explains the effect of sub-paragraphs (4) and (5).

28(4) Each person to whom a notice under this paragraph is given has 45 days, beginning with the day on which the notice is given to that person, to send written representations to the designated HMRC officer in response to the notice.

28(5) A designated HMRC officer may, on a written request by a person to whom a notice is given, extend the period during which representations may be made by that person.

NOTICE OF DECISION WHETHER TO REFER

29 Where a designated HMRC officer decides whether to make a referral under paragraph 26, the officer must, as soon as reasonably practicable, give written notice of that decision to each person to whom notice under paragraph 28 was given.

INFORMATION TO ACCOMPANY REFERRAL

30 A referral under paragraph 26 must (as well as being accompanied by the referral statement under paragraph 27) be accompanied by–

(a) a declaration that, as far as HMRC are aware, nothing which is material to the GAAR Advisory Panel's consideration of the matter has been omitted from that statement,

(b) a copy of each notice given under paragraph 28 by HMRC in relation to the referral,

(c) a copy of any representations received under paragraph 28 and any comments that HMRC wish to make in respect of those representations, and

(d) a copy of each notice given under paragraph 31 by HMRC.

NOTICE ON MAKING OF REFERRAL

31(1) Where a referral is made under paragraph 26, a designated HMRC officer must at the same time give to each relevant person a notice in writing which–

(a) notifies the person of the referral,

(b) is accompanied by a copy of the referral statement,

(c) is accompanied by a copy of any comments provided to the GAAR Advisory Panel under paragraph 30(c) in respect of representations made by the person,

(d) notifies the person of the period under paragraph 32 for making representations, and

(e) notifies the person of the requirement under that paragraph to send any representations to the officer.

31(2) In this paragraph **"relevant person"** has the same meaning as in paragraph 28 (see sub-paragraph (2) of that paragraph).

RIGHT TO MAKE REPRESENTATIONS TO GAAR ADVISORY PANEL

32(1) A person who has received a notice under paragraph 31 has 21 days, beginning with the day on which that notice is given, to send to the GAAR Advisory Panel written representations about–

(a) the notice given to the person under paragraph 28, or

(b) any comments provided to the GAAR Advisory Panel under paragraph 30(c) in respect of representations made by the person.

32(2) The GAAR Advisory Panel may, on a written request made by the person, extend the period during which representations may be made.

32(3) If a person sends representations to the GAAR Advisory Panel under this paragraph, the person must at the same time send a copy of the representations to the designated HMRC officer.

32(4) If a person sends representations to the GAAR Advisory Panel under this paragraph and that person made no representations under paragraph 28, a designated HMRC officer–

(a) may provide the GAAR Advisory Panel with comments on that person's representations under this paragraph, and

(b) if such comments are provided, must at the same time send a copy of them to that person.

DECISION OF GAAR ADVISORY PANEL AND OPINION NOTICES

33(1) Where a referral is made to the GAAR Advisory Panel under paragraph 26, the Chair must arrange for a sub-panel consisting of 3 members of the GAAR Advisory Panel (one of whom may be the Chair) to consider it.

33(2) The sub-panel may invite–

(a) any person to whom notice under paragraph 28 was given, or

(b) the designated HMRC officer,

(or both) to supply the sub-panel with further information within a period specified in the invitation.

33(3) Invitations must explain the effect of sub-paragraph (4) or (5) (as appropriate).

33(4) If a person invited under sub-paragraph (2)(a) supplies information to the sub-panel under this paragraph, that person must at the same time send a copy of the information to the designated HMRC officer.

33(5) If a designated HMRC officer supplies information to the sub-panel under this paragraph, the officer must at the same time send a copy of the information to each person to whom notice under paragraph 28 was given.

34(1) The sub-panel must produce–

(a) one opinion notice stating the joint opinion of all the members of the sub-panel, or

(b) two or three opinion notices which taken together state the opinions of all the members.

34(2) The sub-panel must give a copy of the opinion notice or notices to the designated HMRC officer.

34(3) An opinion notice is a notice which states that in the opinion of the members of the sub-panel, or one or more of those members–

(a) the entering into and carrying out of tax arrangements such as are described in the referral statement is a reasonable course of action in relation to the relevant tax provisions,

(b) the entering into or carrying out of such tax arrangements is not a reasonable course of action in relation to the relevant tax provisions, or

(c) it is not possible, on the information available, to reach a view on that matter,

and the reasons for that opinion.

34(4) In forming their opinions for the purposes of sub-paragraph (3) members of the sub-panel must–

(a) have regard to all the matters set out in the referral statement,

(b) have regard to the matters mentioned in paragraphs (a) to (c) of paragraph 3(3) and paragraph 3(4), and

(c) take account of paragraph 3(5) to (7).

34(5) For the purposes of the giving of an opinion under this paragraph, the arrangements are to be assumed to be tax arrangements.

34(6) For the purposes of this Schedule–

(a) an opinion of the GAAR Advisory Panel is to be treated as having been given on a referral under paragraph 26 when an opinion notice (or notices) has been given under this paragraph in respect of the referral, and

(b) any requirement to consider the opinion of the GAAR Advisory Panel given on such a referral is a requirement to consider the contents of the opinion notice (or notices) given on the referral.

NOTICE BEFORE DECIDING THAT ARRANGEMENTS ARE ONES TO WHICH PANEL OPINION APPLIES

35(1) This paragraph applies where–

(a) an opinion of the GAAR Advisory Panel has been given on a referral under paragraph 26,

(b) a designated HMRC officer is of the view that a person is liable to a penalty under paragraph 1 in relation to particular arrangements ("the arrangements concerned") and that that opinion of the GAAR Advisory Panel applies to those arrangements, and

(c) that person is not a person to whom notice under paragraph 28 was given in connection with the referral.

35(2) A designated HMRC officer must give the person mentioned in sub-paragraph (1)(b) a notice in writing–

(a) explaining that the officer is of the view mentioned in that paragraph,

(b) specifying the arrangements concerned,

(c) setting out a report prepared by HMRC of the opinion mentioned in sub-paragraph (1)(a), and

(d) explaining the effect of sub-paragraphs (3) and (4).

35(3) A person to whom a notice under this paragraph is given has 30 days, beginning with the day on which the notice is given, to send the designated HMRC officer (in writing) any representations as to why the opinion does not apply to the arrangements concerned.

35(4) A designated HMRC officer may, on a written request by that person, extend the period during which representations may be made by that person.

35(5) Paragraph 24(2) defines the arrangements that an opinion given on a referral under paragraph 26 "applies to".

REQUIREMENT FOR COURT OR TRIBUNAL TO TAKE PANEL OPINION INTO ACCOUNT

36(1) In this paragraph **"enabler penalty proceedings"** means proceedings before a court or tribunal in connection with a penalty under paragraph 1.

36(2) In determining in enabler penalty proceedings any question whether tax arrangements to which the penalty relates were abusive, the court or tribunal–

(a) must take into account the relevant Panel opinion, and

(b) may also take into account any matter mentioned in sub-paragraph (4).

36(3) In sub-paragraph (2)(a) **"the relevant Panel opinion"** means the opinion of the GAAR Advisory Panel which under this Part of this Schedule was required to be considered by a designated HMRC officer in deciding whether the penalty should be assessed.

36(4) The matters mentioned in sub-paragraph (2)(b) are–

(a) guidance, statements or other material (whether of HMRC, a Minister of the Crown or anyone else) that was in the public domain at the time the arrangements were entered into, and

(b) evidence of established practice at that time.

Part 8 – Appeals

37 A person may appeal against–

(a) a decision of HMRC that a penalty under paragraph 1 is payable by that person, or

(b) a decision of HMRC as to the amount of a penalty under paragraph 1 payable by the person.

38(1) An appeal under paragraph 37 is to be treated in the same way as an appeal against an assessment to the tax to which the arrangements concerned relate (including by the application of any provision about bringing the appeal by notice to HMRC, about HMRC review of the decision or about determination of the appeal by the First-tier Tribunal or Upper Tribunal).

38(2) Sub-paragraph (1) does not apply–

(a) so as to require a person to pay a penalty under paragraph 1 before an appeal against the assessment of the penalty is determined;

(b) in respect of any other matter expressly provided for by this Schedule.

38(3) In this paragraph **"the arrangements concerned"** means the arrangements to which the penalty relates.

39(1) On an appeal under paragraph 37(a) that is notified to the tribunal, the tribunal may affirm or cancel HMRC's decision.

39(2) On an appeal under paragraph 37(b) that is notified to the tribunal, the tribunal may–

(a) affirm HMRC's decision, or

(b) substitute for that decision another decision that HMRC had power to make.

39(3) the tribunal substitutes its decision for HMRC's, the tribunal may rely on paragraph 18–

(a) to the same extent as HMRC (which may mean applying the same percentage reduction as HMRC to a different starting point), or

(b) to a different extent, but only if the tribunal thinks that HMRC's decision in respect of the application of paragraph 18 was flawed.

39(4) In sub-paragraph (3)(b) **"flawed"** means flawed when considered in the light of the principles applicable in proceedings for judicial review.

39(5) In this paragraph **"tribunal"** means the First-tier Tribunal or Upper Tribunal (as appropriate by virtue of paragraph 38(1)).

Part 9 – Information

INFORMATION AND INSPECTION POWERS: APPLICATION OF SCHEDULE 36 TO FA 2008

40(1) Schedule 36 to FA 2008 (information and inspection powers) applies for the purpose of checking a relevant person's position as regards liability for a penalty under paragraph 1 as it applies for checking a person's tax position, subject to the modifications in paragraphs 41 to 43.

40(2) In this paragraph and paragraphs 41 to 43–

"relevant person" means a person an officer of Revenue and Customs has reason to suspect is or may be liable to a penalty under paragraph 1;

"the Schedule" means Schedule 36 to FA 2008.

GENERAL MODIFICATIONS OF SCHEDULE 36 TO FA 2008 AS APPLIED

41 In its application for the purpose mentioned in paragraph 40(1) above, the Schedule has effect as if–

(a) any provisions which can have no application for that purpose were omitted,

(b) references to **"the taxpayer"** were references to the relevant person whose position as regards liability for a penalty under paragraph 1 is to be checked, and references to **"a taxpayer"** were references to a relevant person,

(c) references to a person's **"tax position"** were to the relevant person's position as regards liability for a penalty under paragraph 1,

(d) references to prejudice to the assessment or collection of tax included prejudice to the investigation of the relevant person's position as regards liability for a penalty under paragraph 1, and

(e) references to a *pending* appeal relating to tax were to a pending appeal relating to an assessment of liability for a penalty under paragraph 1.

SPECIFIC MODIFICATIONS OF SCHEDULE 36 TO FA 2008 AS APPLIED

42(1) The Schedule as it applies for the purpose mentioned in paragraph 40(1) above has effect with the modifications in sub-paragraphs (2) to (6).

42(2) Paragraph 10A (power to inspect business premises of involved third parties) has effect as if the reference in sub-paragraph (1) to the position of any person or class of persons as regards a relevant tax were to the position of a relevant person as regards liability for a penalty under paragraph 1.

42(3) Paragraph 47 (right to appeal against penalties under the Schedule) has effect as if after paragraph (b) (but not as part of that paragraph) there were inserted the words "but paragraph (b) does not give a right of appeal against the amount of an increased daily penalty payable by virtue of paragraph 49A."

42(4) Paragraph 49A (increased daily default penalty) has effect as if–

(a) in sub-paragraphs (1)(c) and (2) for "imposed" there were substituted "assessable";

(b) for sub-paragraphs (3) and (4) there were substituted–

"**49A(3)** If the tribunal decides that an increased daily penalty should be assessable–

(a) the tribunal must determine the day from which the increased daily penalty is to apply and the maximum amount of that penalty ("the new maximum amount");

(b) from that day, paragraph 40 has effect in the person's case as if "the new maximum amount" were substituted for "£60".

49A(4) The new maximum amount may not be more than £1,000.";

(c) in sub-paragraph (5) for "the amount" there were substituted "the new maximum amount".

42(5) Paragraph 49B (notification of increased daily default penalty) has effect as if–

(a) in sub-paragraph (1) for "a person becomes liable to a penalty" there were substituted "the tribunal makes a determination";

(b) in sub-paragraph (2) for "the day from which the increased penalty is to apply" there were substituted "the new maximum amount and the day from which it applies";

(c) sub-paragraph (3) were omitted.

42(6) Paragraph 49C is treated as omitted.

43 Paragraphs 50 and 51 are excluded from the application of the Schedule for the purpose mentioned in paragraph 40(1) above.

DECLARATIONS ABOUT CONTENTS OF LEGALLY PRIVILEGED COMMUNICATIONS

44(1) Subject to sub-paragraph (5), a declaration under this paragraph is to be treated by–

(a) HMRC, or

(b) in any proceedings before a court or tribunal in connection with a penalty under paragraph 1, the court or tribunal,

as conclusive evidence of the things stated in the declaration.

44(2) A declaration under this paragraph is a declaration which–

(a) is made by a relevant lawyer,

(b) relates to one or more communications falling within sub-paragraph (3), and

(c) meets such requirements as may be prescribed by regulations under sub-paragraph (4).

44(3) A communication falls within this sub-paragraph if–

(a) it was made by a relevant lawyer (whether or not the one making the declaration),

(b) it is legally privileged, and

(c) if it were not legally privileged, it would be relied on by a person for the purpose of establishing that that person is not liable to a penalty under paragraph 1 (whether or not that person is the person who made the communication or is making the declaration).

44(4) The Treasury may by regulations impose requirements as to the form and contents of declarations under this paragraph.

44(5) Sub-paragraph (1) does not apply where HMRC or (as the case may be) the court or tribunal is satisfied that the declaration contains information which is incorrect.

44(6) In this paragraph **"a relevant lawyer"** means a barrister, advocate, solicitor or other legal representative communications with whom may be the subject of a claim to legal professional privilege or, in Scotland, protected from disclosure in legal proceedings on the grounds of confidentiality of communication.

44(7) For the purpose of this paragraph, a communication is **"legally privileged"** if it is a communication in respect of which a claim to legal professional privilege, or (in Scotland) to confidentiality of communications as between client and professional legal adviser, could be maintained in legal proceedings.

Statutory instruments – SI 2017/1245: made under para. 44(4).

45(1) Where a person carelessly or deliberately gives any incorrect information in a declaration under paragraph 44, the person is liable to a penalty not exceeding £5,000.

45(2) For the purposes of this paragraph, incorrect information is carelessly given by a person if the information is incorrect because of a failure by the person to take reasonable care.

45(3) Paragraphs 19(1), 20, 22(1), 37, 38 and 39(1), (2) and (5) apply in relation to a penalty under this paragraph as they apply in relation to a penalty under paragraph 1, subject to the modifications in sub-paragraphs (4) and (5).

45(4) In its application to a penalty under this paragraph, paragraph 22(1) has effect as if for "the relevant time" there were substituted "the end of 12 months beginning with the date on which facts sufficient to indicate that the person is liable to the penalty came to the Commissioners' knowledge".

45(5) In its application to a penalty under this paragraph, paragraph 38(3) has effect as if the reference to the arrangements to which the penalty relates were to the arrangements to which the declaration under paragraph 44 relates.

45(6) In paragraph 44 any reference to a penalty under paragraph 1 includes a reference to a penalty under this paragraph.

Part 10 – Publishing Details of Persons Who Have Incurred Penalties

POWER TO PUBLISH DETAILS

46(1) The Commissioners may publish information about a person where–

(a) the person has incurred a penalty under paragraph 1,

(b) the penalty has become final, and

(c) either the condition in sub-paragraph (2) or the condition in sub-paragraph (3) is met.

46(2) The condition in this sub-paragraph is that, at the time when the penalty mentioned in sub-paragraph (1) becomes final, 50 or more other penalties which are reckonable penalties have been incurred by the person.

46(3) The condition in this sub-paragraph is that–

(a) the amount of the penalty mentioned in sub-paragraph (1), or

(b) the total amount of that penalty and any other penalties incurred by that person which are reckonable penalties,

is more than £25,000.

46(4) The information that may be published under this paragraph is–

(a) the person's name (including any trading name, previous name or pseudonym),

(b) the person's address (or registered office),

(c) the nature of any business carried on by the person,

(d) the total number of the penalties in question (that is, the penalty mentioned in sub-paragraph (1) and any penalties that are reckonable penalties in relation to that penalty),

(e) the total amount of the penalties in question, and

(f) any other information that the Commissioners consider it appropriate to publish in order to make clear the person's identity.

46(5) The information may be published in any way that the Commissioners consider appropriate.

46(6) For the purposes of this Part of this Schedule a penalty becomes **"final"**–

(a) if the penalty has been assessed and paragraph (b) does not apply, at the time when the period for any appeal or further appeal relating to the penalty expires or, if later, when any appeal or final appeal relating to it is finally determined;

(b) if a contract settlement has been made in relation to the penalty, at the time when the contract is made;

and **"contract settlement"** here means a contract between the Commissioners and the person under which the Commissioners undertake not to assess the penalty or (if it has been assessed) not to take proceedings to recover it.

46(7) **"Reckonable penalty"** has the meaning given by paragraph 47.

46(8) This paragraph is subject to paragraphs 48 to 50.

47(1) A penalty is a **"reckonable penalty"** for the purposes of paragraph 46 if–

(a) it is a penalty under paragraph 1 which becomes final at the same time as, or before, the penalty mentioned in paragraph 46(1),

(b) its entry date and the entry date of the penalty mentioned in paragraph 46(1) are not more than 12 months apart, and

(c) it is not a penalty which under paragraph 48(1) is to be disregarded.

47(2) For the purposes of this paragraph the **"entry date"** of a penalty under paragraph 1 is the date (or, if more than one, the latest date) on which the arrangements concerned or any agreement or transaction forming part of those arrangements was entered into by the taxpayer.

47(3) In sub-paragraph (2)–

"the arrangements concerned" means the arrangements to which the penalty relates, and

"the taxpayer" means the person whose defeat in respect of those arrangements resulted in the penalty being payable.

47(4) For the purposes of this paragraph, the entry date of a penalty is not more than 12 months apart from the entry date of another penalty if–

(a) the entry dates of those penalties are the same, or

(b) the period beginning with whichever of the entry dates is the earlier and ending with whichever of the entry dates is the later is 12 months or less.

RESTRICTIONS ON POWER

48(1) In determining at any time whether or what information may be published in relation to a person under paragraph 46, the following penalties incurred by the person are to be disregarded–

(a) a penalty which has been reduced to nil or stayed;

(b) a penalty by reference to which information has previously been published under paragraph 46;

(c) a penalty where–

(i) the arrangements to which the penalty relates ("the arrangements concerned") are related to other arrangements, and

(ii) the condition in sub-paragraph (3) is not met;

(d) a penalty that relates to arrangements which are related to arrangements that have already been dealt with (within the meaning given by sub-paragraph (4)).

48(2) For the purposes of sub-paragraph (1)(c) and (d) arrangements are **"related to"** each other if they–

(a) implement the same proposal for tax arrangements, and

(b) are substantially the same as each other.

48(3) The condition referred to in sub-paragraph (1)(c) is that HMRC reasonably believe that–

(a) defeats have been incurred in the case of all the arrangements that are related to the arrangements concerned ("the related arrangements"), and

(b) each penalty under paragraph 1 which relates to the arrangements concerned or to any of the related arrangements has become final.

48(4) For the purposes of sub-paragraph (1)(d) arrangements have **"already been dealt with"** if information about the person has already been published under paragraph 46 by reference to a penalty that relates to those arrangements.

49(1) Publication of information under paragraph 46 on the basis of a penalty or penalties incurred by a person may not take place after the relevant time.

49(2) In this paragraph **"the relevant time"** means the end of 12 months beginning with the date on which the penalty became final or, where more than one penalty is involved, the latest date on which any of them became final.

49(3) Sub-paragraph (1) is not to be taken to prevent the re-publishing, or continued publishing, after the relevant time of a set of information published under paragraph 46 before that time.

49(4) Information published under paragraph 46 may not be re-published, or continue to be published, after the end of 12 months beginning with the date on which it was first published.

49(5) Nothing in paragraph 48 applies in relation to determining whether to re-publish (or continue to publish) a set of information already published under paragraph 46.

50 Before publishing information under paragraph 46 the Commissioners must–

(a) inform the person that they are considering doing so, and

(b) afford the person the opportunity to make representations about whether it should be published.

POWER TO AMEND

51 The Treasury may by regulations amend this Part of this Schedule so as to alter any of the following–

(a) the figure for the time being specified in paragraph 46(2);

(b) the sum for the time being specified in paragraph 46(3);

(c) any period for the time being specified in paragraph 47(1)(b) or (4).

Part 11 – Miscellaneous

DOUBLE JEOPARDY

52 A person is not liable to a penalty under paragraph 1 in respect of conduct for which the person has been convicted of an offence.

APPLICATION OF PROVISIONS OF TMA 1970

53 Subject to the provisions of this Schedule, the following provisions of TMA 1970 apply for the purposes of this Schedule as they apply for the purposes of the Taxes Acts–

(a) section 108 (responsibility of company officers),

(b) section 114 (want of form), and

(c) section 115 (delivery and service of documents).

Part 12 – General

MEANING OF "TAX"

54(1) In this Schedule **"tax"** includes any of the following taxes–

(a) income tax,

(b) corporation tax, including any amount chargeable as if it were corporation tax or treated as if it were corporation tax,

(c) capital gains tax,

(d) petroleum revenue tax,

(e) diverted profits tax,

(f) apprenticeship levy,

(g) inheritance tax,

(h) stamp duty land tax, and

(i) annual tax on enveloped dwellings,

and also includes national insurance contributions.

54(2) The Treasury may by regulations amend sub-paragraph (1) so as to–

(a) add a tax to the list of taxes for the time being set out in that sub-paragraph;

(b) remove a tax for the time being set out in that sub-paragraph;

(c) remove the reference to national insurance contributions;

(d) substitute for that reference a reference to national insurance contributions of a particular class or classes;

(e) where provision has been made under paragraph (d)–

(i) add a class or classes of national insurance contributions to those for the time being specified in that sub-paragraph;

(ii) remove a class or classes of national insurance contributions for the time being so specified.

54(3) Regulations under this paragraph may–

(a) make supplementary, incidental, and consequential provision, including provision amending or repealing any provision of this Schedule;

(b) make transitional provision.

MEANING OF "TAX ADVANTAGE"

55 In this Schedule **"tax advantage"** includes–

(a) relief or increased relief from tax,

(b) repayment or increased repayment of tax,

(c) receipt, or advancement of a receipt, of a tax credit,

(d) avoidance or reduction of a charge to tax, an assessment of tax or a liability to pay tax,

(e) avoidance of a possible assessment to tax or liability to pay tax,

(f) deferral of a payment of tax or advancement of a repayment of tax, and

(g) avoidance of an obligation to deduct or account for tax.

OTHER DEFINITIONS

56(1) In this Schedule–

"abusive tax arrangements" has the meaning given by paragraph 3;

"arrangements" includes any agreement, understanding, scheme, transaction or series of transactions (whether or not legally enforceable);

"business" includes any trade or profession;

"the Commissioners" means the Commissioners for Her Majesty's Revenue and Customs;

"company" has the same meaning as in the Corporation Tax Acts (see section 1121 of CTA 2010);

"contract settlement" (except in paragraph 46(6)) means an agreement in connection with a person's liability to make a payment to the Commissioners under or by virtue of an enactment;

"a defeat", in relation to arrangements, is to be read in accordance with paragraph 4;

a **"designated HMRC officer"** means an officer of Revenue and Customs who has been designated by the Commissioners for the purposes of this Schedule;

"the GAAR Advisory Panel" has the meaning given by paragraph 1 of Schedule 43 to FA 2013;

"group" is to be read in accordance with sub-paragraph (2);

"HMRC" means Her Majesty's Revenue and Customs;

"national insurance contributions" means contributions under Part 1 of the Social Security Contributions and Benefits Act 1992 or Part 1 of the Social Security Contributions and Benefits (Northern Ireland) Act 1992;

a **"NICs decision"** means a decision under section 8 of the Social Security Contributions (Transfer of Functions, etc.) Act 1999 or Article 7 of the Social Security Contributions (Transfer of Functions, etc.) (Northern Ireland) Order 1999 (S.I. 1999/671) relating to a person's liability for relevant contributions;

"relevant contributions" means any of the following contributions under Part 1 of the Social Security Contributions and Benefits Act 1992 or Part 1 of the Social Security Contributions and Benefits (Northern Ireland) Act 1992–

(a) Class 1 contributions;

(b) Class 1A contributions;

(c) Class 1B contributions;

(d) Class 2 contributions which must be paid but in relation to which section 11A of the Act in question (application of certain provisions of the Income Tax Acts) does not apply;

"tax" is to be read in accordance with paragraph 54;

"tax advantage" is to be read in accordance with paragraph 55.

56(2) For the purposes of this Schedule two companies are members of the same group if–

(a) one is a 75% subsidiary of the other, or

(b) both are 75% subsidiaries of a third company;

and in this paragraph **"75% subsidiary"** has, subject to sub-paragraph (3), the meaning given by section 1154 of CTA 2010.

56(3) So far as relating to 75% subsidiaries, section 151(4) of CTA 2010 (requirements relating to beneficial ownership) applies for the purposes of this Schedule as it applies for the purposes of Part 5 of that Act.

56(4) In this Schedule references to an assessment to tax, however expressed–

(a) in relation to inheritance tax and petroleum revenue tax, include a determination;

(b) in relation to relevant contributions, include a NICs decision.

REGULATIONS

57(1) Any regulations under this Schedule must be made by statutory instrument.

57(2) A statutory instrument which contains (alone or with other provision) any regulations within sub-paragraph (3) may not be made unless a draft of the instrument has been laid before, and approved by a resolution of, the House of Commons.

57(3) Regulations within this sub-paragraph are–

(a) regulations under paragraph 12;
(b) regulations under paragraph 14(1);
(c) regulations under paragraph 14(2) which amend or repeal any provision of this Schedule;
(d) regulations under paragraph 51;
(e) regulations under paragraph 54.

57(4) A statutory instrument containing only–

(a) regulations under paragraph 14(2) which do not amend or repeal any provision of this Schedule, or
(b) regulations under paragraph 44,

is subject to annulment in pursuance of a resolution of the House of Commons.

CONSEQUENTIAL AMENDMENTS

61 [Amends FA 2014, Sch. 34, para. 7.]

COMMENCEMENT

62(1) Subject to sub-paragraphs (2) and (3), paragraphs 1 to 61 of this Schedule have effect in relation to arrangements entered into on or after the day on which this Act is passed.

62(2) In determining in relation to any particular arrangements whether a person is a person who enabled the arrangements, any action of the person carried out before the day on which this Act is passed is to be disregarded.

62(3) The amendments made by paragraph 61 do not apply in relation to a person who is a promoter in relation to arrangements if by virtue of sub-paragraph (2) above that person is not a person who enabled the arrangements.

PRT STATUTORY INSTRUMENTS

Table of Contents

Those statutory instruments listed below which contain substantive provisions are reproduced in the following pages. Statutory instruments which do no more than amend other instruments are not reproduced; the amendments made by them have been consolidated in the relevant amended regulations. They are, however, listed below for convenience.

continued over

continued over

continued over

continued over

STATUTORY INSTRUMENTS **Page**

ALPHABETICAL LISTING

continued over

continued over

continued over

OIL TAXATION (GAS BANKING SCHEMES) REGULATIONS 1982

(SI 1982/92, as amended by SI 1982/1858 and SI 2009/56)

Made on 29 January 1982 by the Commissioners of Inland Revenue, in exercise of the powers conferred on them by s. 108(6) of Finance Act 1980.

CITATION AND COMMENCEMENT

1 These Regulations may be cited as the Oil Taxation (Gas Banking Schemes) Regulations 1982 and shall come into operation on 1st February 1982.

INTERPRETATION

2 In these Regulations, unless the context otherwise requires:–

"associated gas" means gas found in an oil field in association with oil other than gas, which has been won from the field at a rate dependent on that at which the oil other than gas is so won;

"election" means an election under the principal section;

"gas" means oil consisting of gas;

"gas banking scheme" means such a scheme as is defined in sub-section (2) of the principal section as a gas banking scheme for the purposes of the section;

"the modifications" means the modifications to the operation of the Oil Taxation Acts prescribed by Regulation 3 below;

"the Oil Taxation Acts" has the same meaning as in the principal section;

"the principal section" means section 108 of the Finance Act 1980;

"relevant field" means, in relation to a gas banking scheme, an oil field to which the scheme applies;

"responsible persons" means the bodies corporate or partnerships appointed in accordance with paragraph 4 of Schedule 2 to the Oil Taxation Act 1975 as the responsible persons for the oil fields to which a gas banking scheme applies;

"transferor field" and **"transferee field"** mean, in relation to a transfer of gas won from a relevant field by the participators in that field to the participators in another relevant field under a gas banking scheme, the first-mentioned field and the last-mentioned field respectively;

other expressions have the same meaning as in the Oil Taxation Act 1975.

MODIFICATIONS TO THE OPERATION OF THE OIL TAXATION ACTS

3(1) This Regulation shall apply for the purposes of modifying the operation of the Oil Taxation Acts in their application to cases where–

(a) a gas banking scheme which satisfies the additional conditions contained in Regulation 4 below is in force between the participators in two or more relevant fields;

(b) the participators in those fields have elected under the principal section in the manner prescribed by Regulation 6 below that the modifications prescribed by this Regulation shall apply; and

(c) gas won from a relevant field is transferred by the participators in that field to the participators in another relevant field under the scheme.

3(2) Gas which is transferred in the circumstances described in paragraph (1)(c) above (in this Regulation referred to as **"transferred gas"**) shall be disregarded in determining–

(a) the gross profit or gross loss for the purposes of petroleum revenue tax accruing to a participator from the transferor field in a chargeable period;

(b) the cash equivalent of the share of a participator in a transferor field of the oil allowance referred to in section 8 of the Oil Taxation Act 1975 and the exempt allowance referred to in section 141 of the Finance Act 1982 for that field for a chargeable period; and

(c) the total amount of oil ever won and saved from the transferor field referred to in section 10(1)(b) of the Oil Taxation Act 1975.

3(3) For all the purposes of petroleum revenue tax, transferred gas shall be treated as having been won and saved from the transferee field by the participators in the field in the chargeable period in which it is transferred to them, in shares proportionate to their shares of oil actually won and saved from the field during the period.

3(4) For the purposes of income tax and of the charge of corporation tax on income, transferred gas shall be treated–

(a) as not having been extracted from the transferor field by the participators in the field in the course of oil extraction activities carried on by them nor as having been acquired by those participators by virtue of oil rights held by them; and

(b) as having been extracted from the transferee field by the participators in the field in the course of oil extraction activities carried on by them.

History – In reg. 3(2)(a), (3), the former references to supplementary duty were omitted by SI 1982/1858, with effect from 1 January 1983.
Reg. 3(2)(b) was substituted by SI 1982/1858, with effect from 1 January 1983.

ADDITIONAL CONDITIONS FOR GAS BANKING SCHEMES

4(1) The additional conditions to be satisfied for a scheme to constitute a gas banking scheme are–

(a) that the scheme provides that the transfer of gas won from a relevant field to or to the order of the participators in another relevant field, in consideration for which gas won from the other field is subsequently transferred to or to the order of the participators in the first-mentioned field, is to be transfer of associated gas;

(b) that the scheme provides that gas won from a relevant field and transferred to or to the order of the participators in another relevant field under the scheme is to be of a kind which, after it has been subjected to initial treatment, would be suitable for use by the British Gas Corporation in the National Gas Transmission System; and

(c) that the scheme is a separate scheme constituted by one or more agreements under which it enters into force between the participators in each relevant field as from the same date.

4(2) For the purposes of this Regulation there will be a **separate scheme** whenever the participators in a relevant field who have entered into an agreement constituting a scheme enter into a further agreement with the participator in an oil field to which the first agreement did not apply; but a further agreement which is entered into solely for the purpose of replacing a participator as a party to a scheme by another person or of adding another person as a party to a scheme, on his becoming a participator in a relevant field by virtue of the transfer to him of the first participator's interest in the field, or part of that interest as the case may be, shall not constitute a separate scheme.

CONDITIONS FOR ELECTIONS

5(1) The consent of the Board shall be obtained before an election is made by the participators in the relevant fields that the modifications shall apply in the case of a gas banking scheme.

5(2) An application for the consent of the Board to the making of an election–

(a) shall be made, in such form as the Board may prescribe, jointly by the responsible persons within three months after the end of the chargeable period in which gas is first transferred under the scheme; and

(b) shall be accompanied by the agreement or agreements constituting the scheme, the undertakings referred to in paragraph (5) below and such other documents and information as the Board may require.

5(3) A separate application under paragraph (2) above shall be made on behalf of all the participators in the relevant fields in respect of each scheme that is in force between them.

5(4) If the Board are of the opinion that the documents or information accompanying an application under paragraph (2) above are not sufficient to enable them to decide whether to consent to the making of an election, they shall within three months of the receipt thereof notify in writing to the responsible persons what further documents or information they require for that purpose.

5(5) In connection with an application under paragraph (2) above the participators in each relevant field shall undertake to the Board, in consideration of the Board's consent to the making of an election in respect of the scheme to which the application relates–

(a) that they will, within three months after the making of an election, accept a variation of the provisions of any licence granted under the Petroleum (Production) Act 1934 or the Petroleum (Production) Act (Northern Ireland) 1964 in respect of the licensed area of which the relevant field in which they are participators forms part, in terms proposed by the Secretary of State for Energy or by the Department of Commerce for Northern Ireland as the case may be, to the effect that gas transferred *under the scheme* shall, so long as the election is in force, be–

(i) disregarded in determining the value of petroleum relating to any chargeable period for the purpose of the payment of royalty, and the quantity of petroleum won and saved in any half-year for the purpose of delivery of petroleum to the Minister, under a licence in respect of a licensed area of which a transferor field forms part, and

(ii) taken into account in determining the value of petroleum relating to the chargeable period, and the quantity of petroleum won and saved in the half-year, in which it is so transferred for the purpose of the payment of royalty and delivery of petroleum to the Minister under a licence in respect of a licensed area of which a transferee field forms part; and

(b) that they will each use gas which is transferred to them under the scheme for one or more of the following purposes, and for no purpose other than these, namely–

(i) sale to the British Gas Corporation,

(ii) production purposes in relation to the transferee field on the footing that such gas has been won from the field, or

(iii) in an emergency, flaring or venting at any place outside the transferor field.

5(6) The Board shall not consent to the making of an election in respect of a gas banking scheme unless the participators in each relevant field show to the satisfaction of the Board that they entered into the scheme for *bona fide* commercial reasons.

5(7) The Board shall within three months from the receipt of an application under paragraph (2) above give notice of their decision in writing to the responsible persons consenting to or refusing consent to the making of an election and, subject to paragraph (8) below, if no such notice has been given within the said period of three months, the Board will be deemed to have so consented.

5(8) In any case where the Board have notified to the responsible persons that they require further documents or information in accordance with paragraph (4) above the period of three months referred to in the preceding paragraph shall not commence until the Board have received the further documents or information so required.

5(9) If a participator in a relevant field is in breach of an undertaking given by him to the Board under paragraph (5)(a) above or ceases to be a party to the scheme other than on the transfer of his interest in the field to another person who becomes a party to it or the scheme ceases to be a gas banking scheme, the Board may at any time thereafter by notice in writing to the responsible persons revoke their consent to the making of an election in respect of the scheme and any election which has been made shall thereupon cease to be in force and be treated as if it never was in force and the Board may make such assessments or determinations or such amendments of assessments or determinations in relation to petroleum revenue tax and supplementary petroleum duty and the inspector may make such assessments or adjustments to assessments to income tax or corporation tax (notwithstanding that the assessments concerned may have become final or that the time for making assessments may have expired) as may be necessary in the circumstances.

History – In reg. 5(2)(a), words at the end of the sub-paragraph were repealed by SI 1982/1858, with effect from 1 January 1983.

ELECTION UNDER THE PRINCIPAL SECTION

6(1) On being notified of the decision of the Board consenting to the making of an election, or on the expiration of the period of three months referred to in paragraph (7) of Regulation 5 above, the responsible persons shall forthwith inform the participators in the relevant fields that the Board have, or are to be deemed to have, so consented and the participators in each relevant field may within one month of such notification make an election in the manner prescribed by this Regulation.

6(2) An election shall be made by all the participators in the relevant fields in the form of a notice to the Board signed by each of them stating that they have elected that the modifications shall apply in the case of the scheme.

6(3) Following the making of an election the modifications shall, subject to paragraph (4) below, apply–

(a) for the purposes of petroleum revenue tax, for chargeable periods beginning with that in which gas is first transferred under the scheme, and

(b) for the purposes of income tax and the charge of corporation tax on income, in relation to any gas transferred under the scheme.

6(4) Where gas has been transferred under a gas banking scheme before these Regulations come into operation and an election is subsequently made in accordance with this Regulation the modifications shall apply–

(a) for the purposes of petroleum revenue tax, for chargeable periods before these Regulations came into operation beginning with that in which gas was first transferred under the scheme, and

(b) for the purposes of income tax and the charge of corporation tax on income, in relation to any gas transferred under the scheme whether before or after these Regulations came into operation,

and the Board shall make such assessments and determinations or such amendments of assessments and determinations in relation to petroleum revenue tax and the inspector shall make such assessments or adjustments to assessments to income tax or corporation tax (notwithstanding that the assessments in question may have become final) as may be necessary in the circumstances.

6(5) An election shall continue in force so long as gas is transferred under the gas banking scheme in respect of which the election was made and the Board have not revoked their consent to the making of the election; and any person to whom a participator in a relevant field transfers his interest, or part of his interest, in the field and who is or becomes a participator in that field shall be treated by virtue of the transfer as having joined in the election and as having given the same undertakings to the Board under paragraph (5)(b) of Regulation 5 above as were given by the participators in connection with the application for the Board's consent to the making of the election.

6(6) No election may be made otherwise than in accordance with this Regulation.

History – In reg. 6(3)(a) and (4), references to supplementary petroleum duty were omitted by SI 1982/1858, with effect from 1 January 1983.

APPEALS

7(1) The responsible persons may appeal by notice in writing given to the Board not more than two months after receipt of notice of a decision of the Board refusing or revoking consent to the making of an election in respect of a gas banking scheme; but the bringing of an appeal under this paragraph shall not affect the operation of any revocation of consent under paragraph (9) of Regulation 5 above.

7(2) A participator in a relevant field, whether or not himself an appellant, shall be entitled to appear and be heard on the appeal and any proceedings arising out of it.

7(3) An appeal against a decision of the Board refusing or revoking consent to the making of an election may at any time be abandoned by a notice in writing given to the Board by the appellants.

7(4) On an appeal against a decision of the Board refusing or revoking consent to the making of an election the tribunal may vary the decision appealed against, whether or not the variation is to the advantage of all or any of the participators in the relevant fields, and the provisions of the Taxes Management Act 1970 shall apply in relation to such an appeal as they apply in relation to an appeal under Part I of the Oil Taxation Act 1975.

7(5) The provisions of paragraphs 14A to 14I of Schedule 2 to the Oil Taxation Act 1975 shall apply in relation to appeals under this regulation, subject to any necessary modifications.

History – In reg. 7(1), the word "appeal" inserted after "may" by SI 2009/56, art. 3(2) and Sch. 2, para. 8(2)(a), operative from 1 April 2009 subject to transitional and saving provisions in SI 2009/56, Sch. 3.

In reg. 7(1), the words "appeal to the Special Commissioners", which appeared after "gas banking scheme", omitted by SI 2009/56, art. 3(2) and Sch. 2, para. 8(2)(b), operative from 1 April 2009 subject to transitional and saving provisions in SI 2009/56, Sch. 3.

In reg. 7(4), the word "tribunal" substituted for the words "Special Commissioners" by SI 2009/56, art. 3(2) and Sch. 2, para. 8(3), operative from 1 April 2009 subject to transitional and saving provisions in SI 2009/56, Sch. 3.

Reg. 7(5) inserted by SI 2009/56, art. 3(2) and Sch. 2, para. 8(4), operative from 1 April 2009 subject to transitional and saving provisions in SI 2009/56, Sch. 3.

PAYMENT ON ACCOUNT

8 In computing for the purposes of the statements to be delivered to the Board under section 1(1)(a) of the Petroleum Revenue Tax Act 1980 and paragraph 1(2)(a) of Schedule 19 to the Finance Act 1982 the tax payable for any chargeable period in respect of an oil field, it shall be assumed that the consent of the Board to the making of an election in respect of a gas banking scheme, for which application has been made under paragraph (2) of Regulation 5 above at the time when any such statement is to be delivered, will be forthcoming and that such an election will be made by the participators in the relevant fields in the manner prescribed by Regulation 6.

History – Reg. 8 was substituted by SI 1982/1858, with effect from 1 January 1983.

INTERNATIONAL GAS BANKING SCHEMES

9 These Regulations do not apply to international gas banking schemes as defined for the purposes of the principal section by subsection (4) of the section.

FOREIGN FIELDS (SPECIFICATION) (NO. 1) ORDER 1986

(SI 1986/1644)

Made on 9 September 1986 by the Secretary of State, in exercise of the powers conferred on him by s. 9(5) and 12(2) of the Oil Taxation Act 1983.

1 This Order may be cited as the Foreign Fields (Specification) (No. 1) Order 1986.

2 In this Order the **"Heimdal Field"** means the hydrocarbon accumulation above a depth of 7,200 feet beneath mean sea level within the boundary defined by a set of lines of latitude and longitude joining the surface co-ordinates set out in the Schedule hereto together with any additional hydrocarbon accumulations outside the boundary which are subsequently discovered above the said depth of 7,200 feet and which are not separated from the main accumulation by an aquifer.

3 The Heimdal Field, being an area which is not under the jurisdiction of the government of the United Kingdom, is for the purposes of the Act hereby specified as a foreign field.

SCHEDULES

SCHEDULE – HEIMDAL FIELD CO-ORDINATES

Article 2

Latitude North	*Longitude East*	*Latitude North*	*Longitude East*
59° 38′ 00″	02° 10′ 00″	59° 32′ 00″	02° 16′ 00″
59° 38′ 00″	02° 17′ 00″	59° 32′ 00″	02° 08′ 00″
59° 37′ 00″	02° 17′ 00″	59° 35′ 00″	02° 08′ 00″
59° 37′ 00″	02° 20′ 00″	59° 35′ 00″	02° 09′ 00″
59° 35′ 00″	02° 20′ 00″	59° 37′ 00″	02° 09′ 00″
59° 35′ 00″	02° 17′ 00″	59° 37′ 00″	02° 10′ 00″
59° 34′ 00″	02° 17′ 00″	59° 38′ 00″	02° 10′ 00″
59° 34′ 00″	02° 16′ 00″		

FOREIGN FIELDS (SPECIFICATION) (NO. 2) ORDER 1986

(SI 1986/1645)

Made on 9 September 1986 by the Secretary of State, in exercise of the powers conferred on him by s. 9(5) and 12(2) of the Oil Taxation Act 1983.

1 This Order may be cited as the Foreign Fields (Specification) (No. 2) Order 1986.

2 In this Order the **"North East Frigg Field"** means the hydrocarbon accumulation within the boundary defined by a set of lines of latitude and longitude joining the surface co-ordinates set out in the Schedule hereto.

3 The North East Frigg Field being an area which is not under the jurisdiction of the government of the United Kingdom, is for the purposes of the Act hereby specified as a foreign field.

SCHEDULE – NORTH EAST FRIGG FIELD CO-ORDINATES

Article 2

Latitude North	*Longitude East*	*Latitude North*	*Longitude East*
60° 03′00″	02° 17′15″	59° 58′00″	02° 12′00″
60° 02′45″	02° 17′15″	59° 58′00″	02° 12′15″
60° 02′45″	02° 17′00″	59° 57′45″	02° 12′15″
60° 02′30″	02° 17′00″	59° 57′45″	02° 13′30″
60° 02′30″	02° 16′15″	59° 58′00″	02° 13′30″
60° 02′15″	02° 16′15″	59° 58′00″	02° 14′30″
60° 02′15″	02° 16′00″	59° 58′15″	02° 14′30″
60° 02′00″	02° 16′00″	59° 58′15″	02° 15′15″
60° 02′00″	02° 16′15″	59° 58′30″	02° 15′15″
60° 01′30″	02° 16′15″	59° 58′30″	02° 15′30″
60° 01′30″	02° 16′00″	59° 58′45″	02° 15′30″
60° 01′15″	02° 16′00″	59° 58′45″	02° 16′15″
60° 01′15″	02° 15′45″	59° 59′00″	02° 16′15″
60° 00′45″	02° 15′45″	59° 59′00″	02° 16′45″
60° 00′45″	02° 15′30″	59° 59′15″	02° 16′45″
60° 00′30″	02° 15′30″	59° 59′15″	02° 17′30″
60° 00′30″	02° 15′00″	59° 59′45″	02° 17′30″
60° 00′15″	02° 15′00″	59° 59′45″	02° 17′45″
60° 00′15″	02° 14′45″	60° 00′00″	02° 17′45″
60° 00′00″	02° 14′45″	60° 00′00″	02° 18′45″
60° 00′00″	02° 14′30″	60° 00′15″	02° 18′45″
59° 59′30″	02° 14′30″	60° 00′15″	02° 19′00″
59° 59′30″	02° 13′45″	60° 00′45″	02° 19′00″
59° 59′15″	02° 13′45″	60° 00′45″	02° 18′45″
59° 59′15″	02° 13′30″	60° 01′15″	02° 18′45″
59° 59′00″	02° 13′30″	60° 01′15″	02° 19′15″
59° 59′00″	02° 13′15″	60° 01′45″	02° 19′15″
59° 58′45″	02° 13′15″	60° 01′45″	02° 19′45″
59° 58′45″	02° 13′00″	60° 03′00″	02° 19′45″
59° 58′30″	02° 13′00″	60° 03′00″	02° 17′15″
59° 58′30″	02° 12′00″		

FOREIGN FIELDS (SPECIFICATION) (NO. 1) ORDER 1987

(SI 1987/545)

Made on 18 March 1987 by the Secretary of State, in exercise of the powers conferred on him by s. 9(5) and 12(2) of the Oil Taxation Act 1983.

1 This Order may be cited as the Foreign Fields (Specification) (No. 1) Order 1987.

2 In this Order the **"Ekofisk Area Fields"** means the hydrocarbon accumulations, known as Albuskjell, Cod, Edda, Ekofisk, Eldfisk, Tor and West Ekofisk Fields respectively, the boundaries of which are defined by the sets of lines of latitude and longitude joining the surface co-ordinates set out in the Schedule hereto.

3 Each of the Ekofisk Area Fields being an area which is not under the jurisdiction of the government of the United Kingdom, is for the purposes of the Act hereby specified as a foreign field.

SCHEDULE – EKOFISK AREA FIELDS CO-ORDINATES

ELDFISK FIELD

Latitude North	*Longitude East*	*Latitude North*	*Longitude East*
56° 21′09.8″	03° 16′44.2″	56° 25′22.2″	03° 11′50.1″
56° 21′23.7″	03° 17′14.6″	56° 24′56.8″	03° 12′05.4″
56° 21′51.3″	03° 17′28.8″	56° 24′34.0″	03° 12′25.8″
56° 22′19.8″	03° 17′11.3″	56° 24′07.6″	03° 12′54.4″
56° 22′42.6″	03° 16′45.7″	56° 23′36.2″	03° 13′08.1″
56° 23′09.8″	03° 16′15.6″	56° 23′13.1″	03° 13′06.2″
56° 23′33.7″	03° 15′48.3″	56° 22′49.1″	03° 13′22.3″
56° 24′03.2″	03° 15′34.9″	56° 22′23.9″	03° 13′44.9″
56° 24′37.2″	03° 15′37.2″	56° 22′00.1″	03° 14′13.6″
56° 25′07.6″	03° 15′19.8″	56° 21′38.9″	03° 14′41.3″
56° 25′31.5″	03° 14′42.6″	56° 21′19.0″	03° 15′21.0″
56° 25′43.2″	03° 13′56.4″	56° 21′10.9″	03° 15′58.7″
56° 25′59.8″	03° 13′06.0″	56° 21′07.3″	03° 16′26.4″
56° 26′10.4″	03° 12′17.4″	56° 21′09.4″	03° 16′42.1″
56° 26′07.7″	03° 11′39.9″	56° 21′09.8″	03° 16′44.2″
56° 25′43.9″	03° 11′33.8″		

TOR FIELD

Latitude North	*Longitude East*	*Latitude North*	*Longitude East*
56° 37′32.3″	03° 18′32.9″	56° 39′21.0″	03° 20′28.4″
56° 37′41.3″	03° 19′22.2″	56° 39′26.6″	03° 19′40.4″
56° 37′47.1″	03° 20′01.1″	56° 39′18.9″	03° 18′38.3″
56° 37′58.6″	03° 20′26.0″	56° 39′00.1″	03° 17′48.8″
56° 38′14.5″	03° 21′03.0″	56° 38′48.6″	03° 17′13.7″
56° 38′07.4″	03° 21′56.5″	56° 38′16.9″	03° 16′57.6″
56° 38′23.1″	03° 22′25.3″	56° 37′49.3″	03° 17′19.8″
56° 38′32.6″	03° 22′56.8″	56° 37′47.9″	03° 18′00.6″
56° 38′48.8″	03° 22′53.6″	56° 37′32.2″	03° 18′30.5″
56° 38′52.3″	03° 21′52.8″	56° 37′32.3″	03° 18′32.9″
56° 38′51.9″	03° 21′05.3″		

WEST EKOFISK FIELD

Latitude North	*Longitude East*	*Latitude North*	*Longitude East*
56° 32′ 42.3″	03° 04′ 37.6″	56° 34′ 26.1″	03° 04′ 06.6″
56° 32′ 46.3″	03° 05′ 18.0″	56° 34′ 12.2″	03° 03′ 31.2″
56° 32′ 56.8″	03° 05′ 47.7″	56° 33′ 50.0″	03° 03′ 11.2″
56° 33′ 07.3″	03° 06′ 11.3″	56° 33′ 27.0″	03° 03′ 04.6″
56° 33′ 18.3″	03° 06′ 37.7″	56° 33′ 03.8″	03° 03′ 22.8″
56° 33′ 28.2″	03° 06′ 58.2″	56° 32′ 52.2″	03° 03′ 48.6″
56° 33′ 34.6″	03° 06′ 57.2″	56° 32′ 45.2″	03° 04′ 07.6″
56° 33′ 48.0″	03° 06′ 33.4″	56° 32′ 42.7″	03° 04′ 22.2″
56° 34′ 01.9″	03° 06′ 16.4″	56° 32′ 41.7″	03° 04′ 36.1″
56° 34′ 20.9″	03° 05′ 44.1″	56° 32′ 42.3″	03° 04′ 37.6″
56° 34′ 30.6″	03° 04′ 53.7″		

ALBUSKJELL FIELD

Latitude North	*Longitude East*	*Latitude North*	*Longitude East*
56° 36′ 18.9	03° 06′ 01.0	56° 38′ 14.9	02° 53′ 40.9
56° 36′ 49.6	03° 05′ 44.0	56° 37′ 52.6	02° 54′ 21.0
56° 37′ 12.8	03° 04′ 55.9	56° 37′ 33.7	02° 55′ 18.4
56° 37′ 35.8	03° 03′ 59.1	56° 37′ 17.8	02° 56′ 27.0
56° 37′ 53.2	03° 02′ 59.1	56° 37′ 19.7	02° 57′ 33.4
56° 38′ 12.6	03° 01′ 47.1	56° 37′ 19.6	02° 58′ 30.0
56° 38′ 24.0	03° 00′ 56.2	56° 37′ 14.0	02° 59′ 23.8
56° 38′ 38.7	02° 59′ 52.4	56° 37′ 02.4	03° 00′ 19.1
56° 38′ 49.7	02° 58′ 43.6	56° 36′ 50.1	03° 01′ 19.7
56° 38′ 59.9	02° 57′ 39.7	56° 36′ 38.2	03° 02′ 22.8
56° 39′ 07.8	02° 56′ 42.8	56° 36′ 23.9	03° 03′ 28.5
56° 39′ 16.5	02° 55′ 46.0	56° 36′ 09.0	03° 04′ 33.9
56° 39′ 24.5	02° 54′ 27.6	56° 36′ 06.4	03° 05′ 34.3
56° 39′ 25.2	02° 53′ 27.5	56° 36′ 18.9	03° 05′ 58.5
56° 39′ 12.2	02° 52′ 44.4	56° 36′ 18.9	03° 06′ 01.0
56° 38′ 43.0	02° 52′ 59.8		

COD FIELD

Latitude North	*Longitude East*	*Latitude North*	*Longitude East*
57° 02′ 08.8″	02° 28′ 20.7″	57° 05′ 40.4″	02° 23′ 53.4″
57° 02′ 11.3″	02° 29′ 20.3″	57° 05′ 03.0″	02° 23′ 19.7″
57° 02′ 35.6″	02° 30′ 09.5″	57° 04′ 36.1″	02° 23′ 01.3″
57° 02′ 57.2″	02° 29′ 45.6″	57° 03′ 59.3″	02° 22′ 47.1″
57° 02′ 52.9″	02° 28′ 55.8″	57° 03′ 20.1″	02° 23′ 01.1″
57° 03′ 04.4″	02° 28′ 26.9″	57° 02′ 54.4″	02° 23′ 39.8″
57° 03′ 39.1″	02° 28′ 35.0″	57° 02′ 35.4″	02° 24′ 26.7″
57° 04′ 04.6″	02° 28′ 42.0″	57° 02′ 18.4″	02° 25′ 25.8″
57° 04′ 42.1″	02° 28′ 32.4″	57° 02′ 11.2″	02° 26′ 17.6″
57° 05′ 12.8″	02° 28′ 07.1″	57° 02′ 16.0″	02° 27′ 01.2″

Latitude North	*Longitude East*	*Latitude North*	*Longitude East*
57° 05′33.4″	02° 27′06.4″	57° 02′15.3″	02° 27′42.8″
57° 05′43.2″	02° 26′13.2″	57° 02′09.5″	02° 28′18.9″
57° 05′53.7″	02° 24′59.3″	57° 02′08.8″	02° 28′20.7″

EDDA FIELD

Latitude North	*Longitude East*	*Latitude North*	*Longitude East*
56° 27′33.4″	03° 05′12.9″	56° 29′13.6″	03° 07′03.1″
56° 27′12.2″	03° 06′03.9″	56° 29′12.4″	03° 06′17.9″
56° 27′09.8″	03° 06′56.0″	56° 29′02.5″	03° 05′34.2″
56° 27′15.9″	03° 08′02.7″	56° 28′47.5″	03° 04′54.2″
56° 27′37.4″	03° 08′53.3″	56° 28′23.6″	03° 04′29.4″
56° 27′53.2″	03° 09′27.9″	56° 28′03.8″	03° 04′33.7″
56° 28′11.1″	03° 10′04.9″	56° 27′51.4″	03° 04′50.5″
56° 28′36.2″	03° 10′20.9″	56° 27′44.6″	03° 04′58.6″
56° 28′59.7″	03° 10′11.4″	56° 27′38.7″	03° 05′05.7″
56° 29′11.5″	03° 09′28.8″	56° 27′33.4″	03° 05′12.9″
56° 29′12.4″	03° 08′16.7″		

EKOFISK FIELD

Latitude North	*Longitude East*	*Latitude North*	*Longitude East*
56° 29′30.8″	03° 13′28.4″	56° 34′22.1″	03° 10′44.9″
56° 29′32.1″	03° 14′05.7″	56° 33′50.9″	03° 10′24.1″
56° 29′59.1″	03° 14′17.5″	56° 33′19.3″	03° 10′25.5″
56° 30′29.1″	03° 14′20.7″	56° 32′50.2″	03° 10′21.9″
56° 31′03.5″	03° 14′41.0″	56° 32′17.0″	03° 10′34.6″
56° 31′32.6″	03° 14′58.5″	56° 31′57.5″	03° 10′58.9″
56° 31′52.1″	03° 15′13.4″	56° 31′39.1″	03° 11′22.8″
56° 32′24.5″	03° 15′28.1″	56° 31′20.3″	03° 11′48.7″
56° 32′57.6″	03° 15′39.0″	56° 30′57.5″	03° 12′16.1″
56° 33′31.3″	03° 15′40.5″	56° 30′41.2″	03° 12′35.6″
56° 34′05.4″	03° 15′25.5″	56° 30′20.1″	03° 12′56.4″
56° 34′27.8″	03° 14′59.6″	56° 29′58.5″	03° 13′09.4″
56° 34′44.1″	03° 14′14.8″	56° 29′40.6″	03° 13′17.5″
56° 34′53.2″	03° 13′17.2″	56° 29′31.5″	03° 13′27.7″
56° 34′57.4″	03° 12′16.5″	56° 29′30.8″	03° 13′28.4″
56° 34′46.6″	03° 11′24.9″		

OIL TAXATION (NOMINATION SCHEME FOR DISPOSALS) REGULATIONS 1987

(SI 1987/1338, as amended by SI 1990/2469, SI 1993/2939, SI 1994/939, SI 2000/1072, SI 2003/2155, SI 2006/3089 and SI 2007/1454)

Made on 28 July 1987 by the Commissioners of Inland Revenue in exercise of the powers conferred on them by s. 61(8) of, and Sch. 10 to, the Finance Act 1987.

History – In the heading words "Oil Taxation" substituted for "Petroleum Revenue Tax" and "and Appropriations" omitted by SI 2006/3089, reg. 3, in force from 12 December 2006 and with effect from 1 July 2006 in relation to proposed sales whose transaction base time (SI 2006/3089, reg. 9) is a time on or after that date; and not in relation to proposed transactions with a transaction base date (within the meaning in reg. 7, as that regulation stood prior to SI 2006/3089) before that date.

CITATION AND COMMENCEMENT

1 These Regulations may be cited as the Oil Taxation (Nomination Scheme for Disposals) Regulations 1987 and shall come into force on 22nd August 1987 but shall have effect with respect to things done on or after 9th February 1987.

History – In reg. 1, words "Oil Taxation" substituted for "Petroleum Revenue Tax" and "and Appropriations" omitted by SI 2006/3089, reg. 3, in force from 12 December 2006 and with effect from 1 July 2006 in relation to proposed sales whose transaction base time (SI 2006/3089, reg. 9) is a time on or after that date; and not in relation to proposed transactions with a transaction base date (within the meaning in reg. 7, as that regulation stood prior to SI 2006/3089) before that date.

INTERPRETATION

2 In these Regulations unless the context otherwise requires–

"blended oil" has the meaning given to it by section 63(1A)(c) of the Finance Act 1987;

"the Commissioners" means the Commissioners for Her Majesty's Revenue and Customs;

"the originating fields" has the meaning given to it by section 63(1A)(d) of the Finance Act 1987; and

"Schedule 10" means Schedule 10 to the Finance Act 1987.

History – In reg. 2 the definition of "composite nomination" omitted and the definition of "the Commissioners" substituted for the definition of "the Board" by SI 2006/3089, reg. 4, in force from 12 December 2006 and with effect from 1 July 2006 in relation to proposed sales whose transaction base time (SI 2006/3089, reg. 9) is a time on or after that date; and not in relation to proposed transactions with a transaction base date (within the meaning in reg. 7, as that regulation stood prior to SI 2006/3089) before that date.
In the definitions of "blended oil" and "the originating fields", the reference to s. 63(1A)(c) and (d) substituted by SI 1990/2469, reg. 3(1), in relation to chargeable periods ending after 31 December 1990.

EXCLUDED OIL

2A(1) Oil which forms part of a participator's equity production from an oil field (within the meaning in paragraph 1(2) of Schedule 10, immediately before the coming into force of section 150 of the Finance Act 2006, but omitting references to a month) shall be excluded from section 61 of the Finance Act 1987 if it is sold otherwise than under a Brent-Forties-Oseberg forward contract or a Brent-Forties-Oseberg-Ekofisk forward contract.

2A(2) In paragraph (1) **"a Brent-Forties Oseberg forward contract"** means a contract which provides for settlement, at least 21days after the date on which it is made, by the delivery of a volume of oil comprising, at the seller's election, Brent blend, Forties blend or oil of Oseberg grade, or a cash payment.

2A(3) In paragraph (1) **"a Brent-Forties-Oseberg-Ekofisk forward contract"** means a contract which provides for settlement, at least 21 days after the date on which it is made, by the delivery of a volume of oil comprising, at the seller's election, Brent blend, Forties blend or oil of Oseberg grade or oil of Ekofisk blend, or a cash payment.

History – In reg. 2A(1) the words "or a Brent-Forties-Oseberg-Ekofisk forward contract" inserted by SI 2007/1454, reg. 3(a), with effect from 8 June 2007.
Reg. 2A(3) inserted by SI 2007/1454, reg. 3(b), with effect from 8 June 2007.
Reg. 2A substituted by SI 2006/3089, reg. 5, in force from 12 December 2006 and with effect from 1 July 2006 in relation to proposed sales whose transaction base time (SI 2006/3089, reg. 9) is a time on or after that date; and not in relation to proposed transactions with a transaction base date (within the meaning in reg. 7, as that regulation stood prior to SI 2006/3089) before that date.
Former reg. 2A inserted by SI 1990/2469, reg. 3(2), in relation to chargeable periods ending after 31 December 1990.
Former reg. 2A(1) substituted by SI 1993/2939, reg. 3(1), in relation to chargeable periods ending after 31 December 1993.
In former reg. 2A(2)(c), the words "of the same kind … equity production from" substituted by SI 1993/2939, reg. 3(2), in relation to chargeable periods ending after 31 December 1993.
Former reg. 2A(2)(d) omitted by SI 1993/2939, reg. 3(2), in relation to chargeable periods ending after 31 December 1993.
In former reg. 2A(3), the words "The further condition specified in this paragraph is" substituted by SI 1993/2939, reg. 3(3), in relation to chargeable periods ending after 31 December 1993.
Former reg. 2A(3)(b) omitted by SI 1993/2939, reg. 3(3), in relation to chargeable periods ending after 31 December 1993.
Former reg. 2A(3A) substituted by SI 1994/939, reg. 3(1), with effect from 18 April 1994.
Former reg. 2A(3A) and reg. (3B)–(3D) inserted by SI 1993/2939 reg. 3(4), in relation to chargeable periods ending after 31 December 1993.

In former reg. 2A(3B)(a), the words "or for the next following chargeable period" inserted by SI 2000/1072, reg. 3(2). This insertion has effect in respect of transactions for which the transaction base date prescribed by SI 1987/1338, reg. 7 falls in a chargeable period beginning on or after 1 July 2000.

In former reg. 2A(3C)(a), the words "any one or more of those conditions, or any one or more of those conditions and that further condition," substituted by SI 1994/939, reg. 3(2), with effect from 18 April 1994.

MANNER OF MAKING NOMINATIONS

3(1) This regulation prescribes the manner in which a nomination of a proposed transaction by a participator may be made for the purposes of the scheme established by Schedule 10.

3(2) A nomination shall–

(a) be made in writing–

(i) in the case of a nomination made during business hours, by or on behalf of the participator who is proposing to carry out the sale in respect of which the nomination is made; and

(ii) in the case of a nomination made outside business hours, by or on behalf of the participator, where the participator (or group of which the participator is a member) is proposing to carry out the sale in respect of which the nomination is made; and

(b) be transmitted to the Commissioners–

(i) at the e-mail address published by the Commissioners for the receipt of such nominations, from time to time, by e-mail electronic communications; or

(ii) in the case of disruption of e-mail communications, by telephonic facsimile transmission to the number published by the Commissioners for the receipt of such nominations, from time to time.

3(3) For the purpose of determining whether the nomination is made within the period of two hours mentioned in paragraph 4(1)(a) or (1A)(a) of Schedule 10, the time of sending the transmission is to be used.

3(3A) But transmission shall not be regarded as having been effected for the purposes of paragraph (2) until the nomination is received by the Commissioners at that address or number.

3(4) In paragraph (2) above **"electronic communications"** includes any communications conveyed by means of an electronic communications network.

History – Reg. 3(2), (3) and (3A) substituted for reg. 3(2) and (3) by SI 2006/3089, reg. 6, in force from 12 December 2006 and with effect from 1 July 2006 in relation to proposed sales whose transaction base time (SI 2006/3089, reg. 9) is a time on or after that date; and not in relation to proposed transactions with a transaction base date (within the meaning in reg. 7, as that regulation stood prior to SI 2006/3089) before that date.

In former reg. 3(2)(a), the words "or on behalf of" inserted by SI 1993/2939, reg. 4, in relation to chargeable periods ending after 31 December 1993.

Immediately after reg. 3(2)(c)(iii), the word "or" deleted by SI 2000/1072, reg. 4(2). This removal takes effect in respect of transactions for which the transaction base date prescribed by SI 1987/1338, reg. 7 falls in a chargeable period beginning on or after 1 July 2000.

Immediately after reg. 3(2)(c)(iv), the word "or" inserted by SI 2000/1072, reg. 4(3). This insertion takes effect in respect of transactions for which the transaction base date prescribed by SI 1987/1338, reg. 7 falls in a chargeable period beginning on or after 1 July 2000.

Reg. 3(2)(c)(v) inserted by SI 2000/1072, reg. 4(3). This insertion takes effect in respect of transactions for which the transaction base date prescribed by SI 1987/1338, reg. 7 falls in a chargeable period beginning on or after 1 July 2000.

In reg. 3(4) the definition of "electronic communications" substituted by SI 2003/2155, art. 3 and Sch. 1, para. 23, with effect from 17 September 2003.

In reg. 3(4) the words "(c)(v) above" omitted by SI 2006/3089, reg. 7, in force from 12 December 2006 and with effect from 1 July 2006 in relation to proposed sales whose transaction base time (SI 2006/3089, reg. 9) is a time on or after that date; and not in relation to proposed transactions with a transaction base date (within the meaning in reg. 7, as that regulation stood prior to SI 2006/3089) before that date.

Reg. 3(4) inserted by SI 2000/1072, reg. 4(4). This insertion takes effect in respect of transactions for which the transaction base date prescribed by SI 1987/1338, reg. 7 falls in a chargeable period beginning on or after 1 July 2000.

COMPOSITE NOMINATIONS

4 [Omitted by SI 2006/3089, reg. 8.]

History – Reg. 4 omitted by SI 2006/3089, reg. 8, in force from 12 December 2006 and with effect from 1 July 2006 in relation to proposed sales whose transaction base time (SI 2006/3089, reg. 9) is a time on or after that date; and not in relation to proposed transactions with a transaction base date (within the meaning in reg. 7, as that regulation stood prior to SI 2006/3089) before that date.

5 [Omitted by SI 2006/3089, reg. 8.]

History – Reg. 5 omitted by SI 2006/3089, reg. 8, in force from 12 December 2006 and with effect from 1 July 2006 in relation to proposed sales whose transaction base time (SI 2006/3089, reg. 9) is a time on or after that date; and not in relation to proposed transactions with a transaction base date (within the meaning in reg. 7, as that regulation stood prior to SI 2006/3089) before that date.

6 [Omitted by SI 2006/3089, reg. 8.]

History – Reg. 6 omitted by SI 2006/3089, reg. 8, in force from 12 December 2006 and with effect from 1 July 2006 in relation to proposed sales whose transaction base time (SI 2006/3089, reg. 9) is a time on or after that date; and not in relation to proposed transactions with a transaction base date (within the meaning in reg. 7, as that regulation stood prior to SI 2006/3089) before that date.

TRANSACTION BASE TIME

7(1) This regulation prescribes the transaction base time for a proposed sale for the purposes of paragraph 4 of Schedule 10.

7(2) The transaction base time is the time (and date) at which there is an agreed price (in the form of a unit price or formula for determination of the price) at which oil is to be delivered pursuant to the contract of sale (irrespective of whether or not a legally binding agreement has come into being).

History – Reg. 7 substituted by SI 2006/3089, reg. 9, in force from 12 December 2006 and with effect from 1 July 2006 in relation to proposed sales whose transaction base time (SI 2006/3089, reg. 9) is a time on or after that date; and not in relation to proposed transactions with a transaction base date (within the meaning in reg. 7, as that regulation stood prior to SI 2006/3089) before that date.

8 [Omitted by SI 2006/3089, reg. 9.]

History – Reg. 7 substituted for reg. 7 and 8 by SI 2006/3089, reg. 9, in force from 12 December 2006 and with effect from 1 July 2006 in relation to proposed sales whose transaction base time (SI 2006/3089, reg. 9) is a time on or after that date; and not in relation to proposed transactions with a transaction base date (within the meaning in reg. 7, as that regulation stood prior to SI 2006/3089) before that date.

NOMINAL VOLUME

9(1) This regulation prescribes the manner in which the quantity of oil which it is proposed to deliver under the contract of sale is to be expressed for the purpose of specifying the nominal volume with respect to a proposed transaction.

9(2) The quantity of oil may be expressed for that purpose–

(a) as a specific volume plus or minus a tolerance expressed as a percentage of that specific volume;

(b)–(d) [Omitted by SI 2006/3089, reg. 10(b).]

9(3) [Omitted by SI 2006/3089, reg. 10(c).]

History – In reg. 9(1) words ", or to supply or relevantly appropriate," omitted by SI 2006/3089, reg. 10(a), in force from 12 December 2006 and with effect from 1 July 2006 in relation to proposed sales whose transaction base time (SI 2006/3089, reg. 9) is a time on or after that date; and not in relation to proposed transactions with a transaction base date (within the meaning in reg. 7, as that reg. stood prior to SI 2006/3089) before that date.

In reg. 9(2), subpara. (b)–(d), and the word "or" preceding them omitted by SI 2006/3089, reg. 10(b), in force from 12 December 2006 and with effect from 1 July 2006 in relation to proposed sales whose transaction base time (SI 2006/3089, reg. 9) is a time on or after that date; and not in relation to proposed transactions with a transaction base date (within the meaning in reg. 7, as that regulation stood prior to SI 2006/3089) before that date.

Reg. 9(3) omitted by SI 2006/3089, reg. 10(c), in force from 12 December 2006 and with effect from 1 July 2006 in relation to proposed sales whose transaction base time (SI 2006/3089, reg. 9) is a time on or after that date; and not in relation to proposed transactions with a transaction base date (within the meaning in reg. 7, as that regulation stood prior to SI 2006/3089) before that date.

10 The maximum tolerance prescribed for the purposes of Schedule 10 is 1 per cent of a volume of oil.

History – In reg. 10 figure "1" substituted for "5" by SI 2006/3089, reg. 11, in force from 12 December 2006 and with effect from 1 July 2006 in relation to proposed sales whose transaction base time (SI 2006/3089, reg. 9) is a time on or after that date; and not in relation to proposed transactions with a transaction base date (within the meaning in reg. 7, as that regulation stood prior to SI 2006/3089) before that date.

WITHDRAWAL AND AMENDMENT OF NOMINATIONS – PROPOSED SALES

11 [Omitted by SI 2006/3089, reg. 12.]

History – Reg. 11 omitted by SI 2006/3089, reg. 12, in force from 12 December 2006 and with effect from 1 July 2006 in relation to proposed sales whose transaction base time (SI 2006/3089, reg. 9) is a time on or after that date; and not in relation to proposed transactions with a transaction base date (within the meaning in reg. 7, as that regulation stood prior to SI 2006/3089) before that date.

12 [Omitted by SI 2006/3089, reg. 12.]

History – Reg. 12 omitted by SI 2006/3089, reg. 12, in force from 12 December 2006 and with effect from 1 July 2006 in relation to proposed sales whose transaction base time (SI 2006/3089, reg. 9) is a time on or after that date; and not in relation to proposed transactions with a transaction base date (within the meaning in reg. 7, as that regulation stood prior to SI 2006/3089) before that date.

13 [Omitted by SI 2006/3089, reg. 12.]

History – Reg. 13 omitted by SI 2006/3089, reg. 12, in force from 12 December 2006 and with effect from 1 July 2006 in relation to proposed sales whose transaction base time (SI 2006/3089, reg. 9) is a time on or after that date; and not in relation to proposed transactions with a transaction base date (within the meaning in reg. 7, as that regulation stood prior to SI 2006/3089) before that date.

14 [Omitted by SI 2006/3089, reg. 12.]

History – Reg. 14 omitted by SI 2006/3089, reg. 12, in force from 12 December 2006 and with effect from 1 July 2006 in relation to proposed sales whose transaction base time (SI 2006/3089, reg. 9) is a time on or after that date; and not in relation to proposed transactions with a transaction base date (within the meaning in reg. 7, as that regulation stood prior to SI 2006/3089) before that date.

WITHDRAWAL AND AMENDMENT OF NOMINATIONS – PROPOSED SUPPLIES AND APPROPRIATIONS

15 [Omitted by SI 2006/3089, reg. 12.]

History – Reg. 15 omitted by SI 2006/3089, reg. 12, in force from 12 December 2006 and with effect from 1 July 2006 in relation to proposed sales whose transaction base time (SI 2006/3089, reg. 9) is a time on or after that date; and not in relation to proposed transactions with a transaction base date (within the meaning in reg. 7, as that regulation stood prior to SI 2006/3089) before that date.

16 [Omitted by SI 2006/3089, reg. 12.]

History – Reg. 16 omitted by SI 2006/3089, reg. 12, in force from 12 December 2006 and with effect from 1 July 2006 in relation to proposed sales whose transaction base time (SI 2006/3089, reg. 9) is a time on or after that date; and not in relation to proposed transactions with a transaction base date (within the meaning in reg. 7, as that regulation stood prior to SI 2006/3089) before that date.

17 [Omitted by SI 2006/3089, reg. 12.]

History – Reg. 17 omitted by SI 2006/3089, reg. 12, in force from 12 December 2006 and with effect from 1 July 2006 in relation to proposed sales whose transaction base time (SI 2006/3089, reg. 9) is a time on or after that date; and not in relation to proposed transactions with a transaction base date (within the meaning in reg. 7, as that regulation stood prior to SI 2006/3089) before that date.

CONVERSION OF NOMINATED PRICE INTO STERLING

18 [Omitted by SI 2006/3089, reg. 12.]

History – Reg. 18 omitted by SI 2006/3089, reg. 12, in force from 12 December 2006 and with effect from 1 July 2006 in relation to proposed sales whose transaction base time (SI 2006/3089, reg. 9) is a time on or after that date; and not in relation to proposed transactions with a transaction base date (within the meaning in reg. 7, as that regulation stood prior to SI 2006/3089) before that date.

NOMINATIONS OF PROPOSED TRANSACTIONS IN BLENDED OIL HAVING EFFECT WITH RESPECT TO MORE THAN ONE FIELD

19(1) A person who is a participator in two or more fields which, in relation to any blended oil, are or are included among the originating fields may make a nomination, having effect with respect to all the originating fields in which he is a participator, of a proposed sale of the blended oil in the manner prescribed by regulation 3;

19(2) [Omitted by SI 2006/3089, reg. 13.]

History – In reg. 19(1) "A" substituted for "Subject to paragraph (2) below, a" and ", supply or appropriation" omitted by SI 2006/3089, reg. 13, in force from 12 December 2006 and with effect from 1 July 2006 in relation to proposed sales whose transaction base time (SI 2006/3089, reg. 9) is a time on or after that date; and not in relation to proposed transactions with a transaction base date (within the meaning in reg. 7, as that regulation stood prior to SI 2006/3089) before that date.
In reg. 19(1) words omitted from the end by SI 2006/3089, reg. 13, in force from 12 December 2006 and with effect from 1 July 2006 in relation to proposed sales whose transaction base time (SI 2006/3089, reg. 9) is a time on or after that date; and not in relation to proposed transactions with a transaction base date (within the meaning in reg. 7, as that regulation stood prior to SI 2006/3089) before that date.
Reg. 19(2) omitted by SI 2006/3089, reg. 13, in force from 12 December 2006 and with effect from 1 July 2006 in relation to proposed sales whose transaction base time (SI 2006/3089, reg. 9) is a time on or after that date; and not in relation to proposed transactions with a transaction base date (within the meaning in reg. 7, as that regulation stood prior to SI 2006/3089) before that date.

20 [Omitted by SI 2006/3089, reg. 14.]

History – Reg. 20 omitted by SI 2006/3089, reg. 14, in force from 12 December 2006 and with effect from 1 July 2006 in relation to proposed sales whose transaction base time (SI 2006/3089, reg. 9) is a time on or after that date; and not in relation to proposed transactions with a transaction base date (within the meaning in reg. 7, as that regulation stood prior to SI 2006/3089) before that date.

TAXES (INTEREST RATE) REGULATIONS 1989

(SI 1989/1297, as amended by SI 1991/889, SI 1993/2212, SI 1994/1307, SI 1994/1567, SI 1996/2644, SI 1996/3187, SI 1997/1681, SI 1997/2707, SI 1998/310, SI 1998/3176, SI 1999/1928, SI 1999/2538, SI 1999/2637, SI 2000/893, SI 2001/204, SI 2001/254, SI 2005/2462, SI 2007/684, SI 2008/778, SI 2008/3234, SI 2009/199 and SI 2009/2032)

Made on 27 July 1989 by the Treasury, in exercise of the powers conferred on them by s. 178 of the Finance Act 1989.

CITATION AND COMMENCEMENT

1 These Regulations may be cited as the Taxes (Interest Rate) Regulations 1989 and shall come into force on 18th August 1989.

INTERPRETATION

2(1) In these Regulations unless the context otherwise requires–

"the 1998 Regulations" means the Corporation Tax (Instalment Payments) Regulations 1998;

"established rate" means–

(a) on the coming into force of these Regulations, 14 per cent per annum; and

(b) in relation to any date after the first reference date after the coming into force of these Regulations, the reference rate found on the immediately preceding reference date;

"operative date" means–

(a) the twelfth working day after the reference date, or

(b) where regulation 3ZA or 3BA applies–

(i) where the reference date is the first Tuesday, the day which is the Monday next following the first Tuesday, or

(ii) where the reference date is the second Tuesday, the day which is the Monday next following the second Tuesday;

"reference date" means–

(a) the working day following the day on which the most recent meeting of the Monetary Policy Committee of the Bank of England took place, or

(b) where regulation 3ZA or 3BA applies–

(i) the day which is the Tuesday next following the day on which that meeting took place ("the first Tuesday"), and

(ii) the day which is the Tuesday ("the second Tuesday") occurring two weeks after the first Tuesday;

"section 178" means section 178 of the Finance Act 1989;

"working day" means any day other than a non-business day within the meaning of section 92 of the Bills of Exchange Act 1882.

2(2) In these Regulations the reference rate found on a reference date is the official bank rate determined by the most recent meeting of the Monetary Policy Committee of the Bank of England.

History – In reg. 2(1), in para. (a) of the definition of "operative date", the word "twelfth" substituted for the word "eleventh" by SI 2009/2032, reg. 3(2)(a), with effect from 12 August 2009.
In reg. 2(1), the definition of "operative date" substituted by SI 2008/3234, reg. 2(2)(a), with effect from 7 January 2009.
In reg. 2(1), in para. (a) of the definition of "reference date", the word "second" (which appeared before the word "working") omitted by SI 2009/2032, reg. 3(2)(b), with effect from 12 August 2009.
In reg. 2(1), the definition of "reference date" substituted by SI 2008/3234, reg. 2(2)(b), with effect from 7 January 2009.
In reg. 2(1), definition of "the 1998 Regulations" inserted, words from "or, where regulation 3ZA" to the end added to each of the definitions of "operative date" and "reference date" by SI 1998/3176, reg. 3, and in reg. 2(2), para. (i), (ii) and (iii) substituted for former wording by SI 1998/3176, reg. 4, operative from 7 January 1999.
Reg. 2(2) substituted by SI 2009/2032, reg. 3(3), with effect from 12 August 2009.

APPLICABLE RATE OF INTEREST EQUAL TO ZERO

2A [Omitted by SI 2009/2032, reg. 4.]

History – Reg. 2A omitted by SI 2009/2032, reg. 4, with effect from 12 August 2009.

APPLICABLE RATE OF INTEREST ON UNPAID TAX, TAX REPAID AND REPAYMENT SUPPLEMENT

3 [Not relevant to petroleum revenue tax.]

3AA(1) For the purposes of–

(a)–(b) [Not relevant to petroleum revenue tax.]

(c) paragraphs 15 of Schedule 2, and paragraph 8 of Schedule 5, to the Oil Taxation Act 1975,

(d)–(f) [Not relevant to petroleum revenue tax.]

the rate applicable under section 178 shall, except where regulation 3AC applies and subject to paragraph (2), be–

(i) where paragraph (aa) above applies, 6.5 per cent per annum;

(ii) in all other cases, 6.25 per cent per annum.

3AA(2) Where, on a reference date after 1st January 1997, the reference rate found on that date differs from the established rate, the rate applicable under section 178 for the purposes of the enactments referred to in paragraph (1) shall, on and after the next operative date, be the percentage per annum found by applying the formula specified in paragraph (3).

3AA(3) The formula specified in this paragraph is–

$$RR + 2.5,$$

where RR is the reference rate referred to in paragraph (2).

History – In reg. 3AA(1)(c) the words "and 16" and sub-para. (d) and (f) omitted by SI 2009/2032, reg. 5(2), with effect from 12 August 2009.

In reg. 3AA(1) the words

"be–

(i) where paragraph (aa) above applies, 6.5 per cent per annum;

(ii) in all other cases, 6.25 per cent per annum."

substituted for "be 6.25 per cent per annum" by SI 2001/204, reg. 4, operative from 6 March 2001.

In reg. 3AA(1), words "except where regulation 3AC applies and" inserted by SI 1999/2637, reg. 3, operative from 14 October 1999.

Reg. 3AA(1)(aa) inserted by SI 2001/204, reg. 4, operative from 6 March 2001.

Reg. 3AA(1)(e) omitted by SI 1999/2538, reg. 4, with effect from 1 October 1999.

In reg. 3AA(2) the words "and, if the result is not a multiple of one-quarter, rounding the result down to the nearest amount which is such a multiple" omitted by SI 2009/2032, reg. 5(3), with effect from 12 August 2009.

Reg. 3AA(3) substituted by SI 2009/2032, reg. 5(4), with effect from 12 August 2009.

3AB–6 [Not relevant to petroleum revenue tax.]

FOREIGN FIELDS (SPECIFICATION) ORDER 1989

(SI 1989/2384)

Made on 16 December 1989 by the Secretary of State, in exercise of the powers conferred on him by s. 9(5) and 12(2) of the Oil Taxation Act 1983 (hereinafter referred to as "the Act"), and all other powers enabling him in that behalf.

1 This Order may be cited as the Foreign Fields (Specification) Order 1989.

2 In this Order, the **"Gullfaks Field"** means the hydrocarbon accumulation within the boundary defined by lines of latitude and longitude joining the surface co-ordinates set out in the Schedule hereto.

3 The Gullfaks Field, being an area which is not under the jurisdiction of the government of the United Kingdom, is hereby specified as a foreign field for the purposes of the Act.

SCHEDULE – GULLFAKS FIELD CO-ORDINATES

Article 2

Latitude North	*Longitude East*	*Latitude North*	*Longitude East*
61° 13′12″	2° 9′54″	61° 11′18″	2° 18′12″
61° 13′12″	2° 10′18″	61° 11′18″	2° 18′0″
61° 13′6″	2° 10′18″	61° 11′12″	2° 18′0″
61° 13′6″	2° 10′36″	61° 11′12″	2° 17′48″
61° 13′0″	2° 10′36″	61° 11′6″	2° 17′48″
61° 13′0″	2° 11′6″	61° 11′6″	2° 17′36″
61° 13′18″	2° 11′6″	61° 11′0″	2° 17′36″
61° 13′18″	2° 11′12″	61° 11′0″	2° 17′30″
61° 13′24″	2° 11′12″	61° 10′54″	2° 17′30″
61° 13′24″	2° 11′18″	61° 10′54″	2° 17′18″
61° 13′42″	2° 11′18″	61° 10′48″	2° 17′18″
61° 13′42″	2° 11′24″	61° 10′48″	2° 17′6″
61° 13′54″	2° 11′24″	61° 10′42″	2° 17′6″
61° 13′54″	2° 11′30″	61° 10′42″	2° 16′54″
61° 14′0″	2° 11′30″	61° 10′6″	2° 16′54″
61° 14′0″	2° 11′42″	61° 10′6″	2° 15′48″
61° 14′6″	2° 11′42″	61° 10′12″	2° 15′48″
61° 14′6″	2° 12′18″	61° 10′12″	2° 15′36″
61° 14′12″	2° 12′18″	61° 10′18″	2° 15′36″
61° 14′12″	2° 12′24″	61° 10′18″	2° 15′30″
61° 14′24″	2° 12′24″	61° 10′48″	2° 15′30″
61° 14′24″	2° 12′30″	61° 10′48″	2° 15′6″
61° 14′36″	2° 12′30″	61° 10′36″	2° 15′6″
61° 14′36″	2° 13′6″	61° 10′36″	2° 15′0″
61° 14′24″	2° 13′6″	61° 10′30″	2° 15′0″
61° 14′24″	2° 13′36″	61° 10′30″	2° 14′54″
61° 14′30″	2° 13′36″	61° 10′24″	2° 14′54″
61° 14′30″	2° 14′18″	61° 10′24″	2° 14′42″
61° 14′36″	2° 14′18″	61° 10′18″	2° 14′42″
61° 14′36″	2° 16′12″	61° 10′18″	2° 14′36″
61° 14′30″	2° 16′12″	61° 10′12″	2° 14′36″
61° 14′30″	2° 16′18″	61° 10′12″	2° 14′30″
61° 14′24″	2° 16′18″	61° 10′6″	2° 14′30″

Latitude North	*Longitude East*	*Latitude North*	*Longitude East*
61° 14′24″	2° 16′24″	61° 10′6″	2° 14′0″
61° 14′18″	2° 16′24″	61° 10′0″	2° 14′0″
61° 14′18″	2° 16′36″	61° 10′0″	2° 13′48″
61° 14′6″	2° 16′36″	61° 9′54″	2° 13′48″
61° 14′6″	2° 17′0″	61° 9′54″	2° 13′30″
61° 14′0″	2° 17′0″	61° 9′48″	2° 13′30″
61° 14′0″	2° 17′18″	61° 9′48″	2° 13′18″
61° 13′54″	2° 17′18″	61° 9′36″	2° 13′18″
61° 13′54″	2° 17′30″	61° 9′36″	2° 12′54″
61° 13′48″	2° 17′30″	61° 9′30″	2° 12′54″
61° 13′48″	2° 18′30″	61° 9′30″	2° 10′36″
61° 13′42″	2° 18′30″	61° 9′54″	2° 10′36″
61° 13′42″	2° 18′54″	61° 9′54″	2° 10′24″
61° 13′36″	2° 18′54″	61° 9′48″	2° 10′24″
61° 13′36″	2° 19′6″	61° 9′48″	2° 10′6″
61° 13′30″	2° 19′6″	61° 9′42″	2° 10′6″
61° 13′30″	2° 19′18″	61° 9′42″	2° 9′42″
61° 13′0″	2° 19′18″	61° 9′36″	2° 9′42″
61° 13′0″	2° 19′6″	61° 9′36″	2° 9′30″
61° 12′54″	2° 19′6″	61° 9′30″	2° 9′30″
61° 12′54″	2° 18′54″	61° 9′30″	2° 8′54″
61° 12′48″	2° 18′54″	61° 9′36″	2° 8′54″
61° 12′48″	2° 18′42″	61° 9′36″	2° 8′48″
61° 12′0″	2° 18′42″	61° 9′42″	2° 8′48″
61° 12′0″	2° 18′54″	61° 9′42″	2° 8′30″
61° 11′30″	2° 18′54″	61° 9′48″	2° 8′30″
61° 11′30″	2° 18′42″	61° 9′48″	2° 8′6″
61° 11′24″	2° 18′42″	61° 10′36″	2° 8′6″
61° 11′24″	2° 18′12″	61° 10′36″	2° 8′18″
61° 11′6″	2° 8′18″	61° 11′42″	2° 9′42″
61° 11′6″	2° 8′24″	61° 11′54″	2° 9′42″
61° 11′12″	2° 8′24″	61° 11′54″	2° 9′54″
61° 11′12″	2° 8′30″	61° 12′0″	2° 9′54″
61° 11′18″	2° 8′30″	61° 12′0″	2° 10′0″
61° 11′18″	2° 8′36″	61° 12′6″	2° 10′0″
61° 11′24″	2° 8′36″	61° 12′6″	2° 10′6″
61° 11′24″	2° 8′42″	61° 12′42″	2° 10′6″
61° 11′30″	2° 8′42″	61° 12′42″	2° 10′0″
61° 11′30″	2° 9′30″	61° 12′48″	2° 10′0″
61° 11′42″	2° 9′30″	61° 12′48″	2° 9′54″
		61° 13′12″	2° 9′54″

FOREIGN FIELDS (SPECIFICATION) ORDER 1991

(SI 1991/1982, as amended by SI 1993/1565)

Made on 22 August 1991 by the Secretary of State, in exercise of the powers conferred on him by s. 9(5) and 12(2) of the Oil Taxation Act 1983 (hereinafter referred to as "the Act"), and all other powers enabling him in that behalf.

1 This Order may be cited as the Foreign Fields (Specification) Order 1991.

2 In this Order, **"the Odin Field"** means the hydrocarbon accumulation within the boundary defined by lines of latitude and longitude joining the surface co-ordinates set out in the Schedule hereto.

3 The Odin Field, being an area which is not under the jurisdiction of the government of the United Kingdom, is hereby specified as a foreign field for the purpose of the Act.

SCHEDULES

SCHEDULE – ODIN FIELD CO-ORDINATES

Article 2

Latitude North	*Longitude East*	*Latitude North*	*Longitude East*
60° 5′ 50″	2° 7′ 15″	60° 1′ 50″	2° 11′ 15″
60° 5′ 50″	2° 8′ 10″	60° 1′ 50″	2° 10′ 50″
60° 6′ 0″	2° 8′ 10″	60° 1′ 30″	2° 10′ 50″
60° 6′ 0″	2° 8′ 45″	60° 1′ 30″	2° 10′ 30″
60° 6′ 10″	2° 8′ 45″	60° 0′ 25″	2° 10′ 30″
60° 6′ 10″	2° 9′ 15″	60° 0′ 25″	2° 10′ 10″
60° 6′ 20″	2° 9′ 15″	60° 0′ 10″	2° 10′ 10″
60° 6′ 20″	2° 9′ 35″	60° 0′ 10″	2° 9′ 45″
60° 6′ 30″	2° 9′ 35″	59° 59′ 55″	2° 9′ 45″
60° 6′ 30″	2° 9′ 45″	59° 59′ 55″	2° 9′ 25″
60° 6′ 40″	2° 9′ 45″	59° 59′ 45″	2° 9′ 25″
60° 6′ 40″	2° 9′ 55″	59° 59′ 45″	2° 9′ 05″
60° 6′ 50″	2° 9′ 55″	59° 59′ 5″	2° 9′ 05″
60° 6′ 50″	2° 11′ 15″	59° 59′ 05″	2° 7′ 55″
60° 6′ 40″	2° 11′ 15″	60° 0′ 30″	2° 7′ 55″
60° 6′ 40″	2° 11′ 45″	60° 0′ 30″	2° 8′ 30″
60° 6′ 30″	2° 11′ 45″	60° 0′ 40″	2° 8′ 30″
60° 6′ 30″	2° 12′ 15″	60° 0′ 40″	2° 8′ 50″
60° 5′ 55″	2° 12′ 15″	60° 1′ 55″	2° 8′ 50″
60° 5′ 55″	2° 12′ 00″	60° 1′ 55″	2° 8′ 10″
60° 5′ 40″	2° 12′ 00″	60° 2′ 40″	2° 8′ 10″
60° 5′ 40″	2° 12′ 10″	60° 2′ 40″	2° 9′ 05″
60° 5′ 30″	2° 12′ 10″	60° 2′ 25″	2° 9′ 05″
60° 5′ 30″	2° 12′ 20″	60° 2′ 25″	2° 9′ 30″
60° 5′ 20″	2° 12′ 20″	60° 2′ 40″	2° 9′ 30″
60° 5′ 20″	2° 12′ 30″	60° 2′ 40″	2° 9′ 45″
60° 5′ 10″	2° 12′ 30″	60° 3′ 00″	2° 9′ 45″
60° 5′ 10″	2° 12′ 45″	60° 3′ 00″	2° 9′ 10″
60° 5′ 00″	2° 12′ 45″	60° 3′ 10″	2° 9′ 10″
60° 5′ 00″	2° 12′ 55″	60° 3′ 10″	2° 8′ 50″

Latitude North	*Longitude East*	*Latitude North*	*Longitude East*
60° 4′ 15″	2° 12′ 55″	60° 3′ 20″	2° 8′ 50″
60° 4′ 15″	2° 12′ 45″	60° 3′ 20″	2° 8′ 35″
60° 3′ 55″	2° 12′ 45″	60° 3′ 30″	2° 8′ 35″
60° 3′ 55″	2° 12′ 55″	60° 3′ 30″	2° 8′ 05″
60° 3′ 25″	2° 12′ 55″	60° 3′ 40″	2° 8′ 05″
60° 3′ 25″	2° 12′ 40″	60° 3′ 40″	2° 7′ 50″
60° 3′ 00″	2° 12′ 40″	60° 3′ 50″	2° 7′ 50″
60° 3′ 00″	2° 11′ 35″	60° 3′ 50″	2° 7′ 40″
60° 2′ 05″	2° 11′ 35″	60° 4′ 00″	2° 7′ 40″
60° 2′ 05″	2° 11′ 15″	60° 4′ 00″	2° 7′ 25″
		60° 4′ 10″	2° 7′ 25″
		60° 4′ 10″	2° 7′ 15″
		60° 5′ 50″	2° 7′ 15″

History – Schedule substituted by SI 1993/1565, art. 3 and Schedule, with effect from 18 June 1993.

FOREIGN FIELDS (SPECIFICATION) (NO. 2) ORDER 1991

(SI 1991/1983)

Made on 22 August 1991 by the Secretary of State, in exercise of the powers conferred on him by s. 9(5) and 12(2) of the Oil Taxation Act 1983 (hereinafter referred to as "the Act"), and all other powers enabling him in that behalf.

1 This Order may be cited as the Foreign Fields (Specification) (No. 2) Order 1991.

2 In this Order:

"the East Frigg Alpha Field" means the hydrocarbon accumulation within the boundary defined by lines of latitude and longitude joining the surface co-ordinates set out in Part I of the Schedule hereto; and **"the East Frigg Beta Field"** means the hydrocarbon accumulation within the boundary defined by the lines of latitude and longitude joining the surface co-ordinates set out in Part II of the Schedule hereto.

3 The East Frigg Alpha Field and the East Frigg Beta Field, both being areas which are not under the jurisdiction of the government of the United Kingdom, are hereby specified as foreign fields for the purposes of the Act.

SCHEDULE

Article 2

Part I – East Frigg Alpha Field Co-ordinates

Latitude North	*Longitude East*	*Latitude North*	*Longitude East*
59° 54′ 55″	2° 18′ 10″	59° 55′ 35″	2° 24′ 55″
59° 54′ 55″	2° 18′ 35″	59° 55′ 0″	2° 24′ 55″
59° 55′ 0″	2° 18′ 35″	59° 55′ 0″	2° 23′ 55″
59° 55′ 0″	2° 18′ 45″	59° 55′ 5″	2° 23′ 55″
59° 55′ 25″	2° 18′ 45″	59° 55′ 5″	2° 23′ 35″
59° 55′ 25″	2° 18′ 50″	59° 54′ 50″	2° 23′ 35″
59° 55′ 35″	2° 18′ 50″	59° 54′ 50″	2° 23′ 5″
59° 55′ 35″	2° 19′ 10″	59° 54′ 35″	2° 23′ 5″
59° 55′ 40″	2° 19′ 10″	59° 54′ 35″	2° 23′ 15″
59° 55′ 40″	2° 20′ 40″	59° 54′ 10″	2° 23′ 15″
59° 55′ 45″	2° 20′ 40″	59° 54′ 10″	2° 23′ 0″
59° 55′ 45″	2° 21′ 30″	59° 53′ 55″	2° 23′ 0″
59° 55′ 55″	2° 21′ 30″	59° 53′ 55″	2° 21′ 55″
59° 55′ 55″	2° 22′ 5″	59° 54′ 5″	2° 21′ 55″
59° 56′ 15″	2° 22′ 5″	59° 54′ 5″	2° 21′ 35″
59° 56′ 15″	2° 35′ 35″	59° 54′ 15″	2° 21′ 35″
56° 56′ 20″	2° 22′ 35″	59° 54′ 15″	2° 21′ 10″
59° 56′ 20″	2° 23′ 5″	59° 54′ 25″	2° 21′ 10″
59° 56′ 15″	2° 23′ 5″	59° 54′ 25″	2° 20′ 40″
59° 56′ 15″	2° 24′ 30″	59° 54′ 10″	2° 20′ 40″
59° 56′ 5″	2° 24′ 30″	59° 54′ 10″	2° 20′ 5″
59° 56′ 5″	2° 24′ 50″	59° 54′ 0″	2° 20′ 5″
59° 55′ 50″	2° 24′ 50″	59° 54′ 0″	2° 18′ 10″
59° 55′ 35″	2° 24′ 40″	59° 54′ 55″	2° 18′ 10″

Part II – East Frigg Beta Field Co-ordinates

Latitude North	*Longitude East*	*Latitude North*	*Longitude East*
59° 53′25″	2° 18′50″	59° 53′5″	2° 25′5″
59° 53′25″	2° 19′15″	59° 53′5″	2° 24′30″
59° 53′35″	2° 19′15″	59° 52′55″	2° 24′30″
59° 53′35″	2° 19′25″	59° 52′55″	2° 24′5″
59° 53′45″	2° 19′25″	59° 52′45″	2° 24′5″
59° 53′45″	2° 22′5″	59° 52′45″	2° 21′35″
59° 53′50″	2° 22′5″	59° 52′50″	2° 21′35″
59° 53′50″	2° 23′20″	59° 52′50″	2° 19′10″
59° 53′45″	2° 23′20″	59° 53′0″	2° 19′10″
59° 53′45″	2° 24′25″	59° 53′0″	2° 18′50″
59° 53′40″	2° 24′25″	59° 53′25″	2° 18′50″
59° 53′40″	2° 25′5″		

FOREIGN FIELDS (SPECIFICATION) (NO. 3) ORDER 1991

(SI 1991/1984)

Made on 22 August 1991 by the Secretary of State, in exercise of the powers conferred on him by s. 9(5) and 12(2) of the Oil Taxation Act 1983 (hereinafter referred to as "the Act"), and all other powers enabling him in that behalf.

1 This Order may be cited as the Foreign Fields (Specification) (No. 3) Order 1991.

2 In this Order, **"the Snorre Field"** means the hydrocarbon accumulation within the boundary defined by lines of latitude and longitude joining the surface co-ordinates set out in the Schedule hereto.

3 The Snorre Field, being an area which is not under the jurisdiction of the government of the United Kingdom, is hereby specified as a foreign field for the purposes of the Act.

SCHEDULE – SNORRE FIELD CO-ORDINATES

Article 2

Latitude North	*Longitude East*	*Latitude North*	*Longitude East*
61° 24′ 30″	2° 6′ 00″	61° 35′ 00″	2° 18′ 00″
61° 25′ 00″	2° 6′ 00″	61° 32′ 00″	2° 18′ 00″
61° 25′ 00″	2° 4′ 00″	61° 32′ 00″	2° 17′ 00″
61° 27′ 00″	2° 4′ 00″	61° 29′ 00″	2° 17′ 00″
61° 27′ 00″	2° 5′ 00″	61° 29′ 00″	2° 16′ 00″
61° 28′ 00″	2° 5′ 00″	61° 28′ 00″	2° 16′ 00″
61° 28′ 00″	2° 6′ 00″	61° 28′ 00″	2° 15′ 00″
61° 29′ 00″	2° 6′ 00″	61° 27′ 00″	2° 15′ 00″
61° 29′ 00″	2° 7′ 00″	61° 27′ 00″	2° 13′ 00″
61° 32′ 00″	2° 7′ 00″	61° 26′ 00″	2° 13′ 00″
61° 32′ 00″	2° 10′ 00″	61° 26′ 00″	2° 12′ 00″
61° 34′ 00″	2° 10′ 00″	61° 25′ 00″	2° 12′ 00″
61° 34′ 00″	2° 12′ 00″	61° 25′ 00″	2° 11′ 00″
61° 35′ 00″	2° 12′ 00″	61° 24′ 30″	2° 11′ 00″
		61° 24′ 30″	2° 6′ 00″

FOREIGN FIELDS (SPECIFICATION) ORDER 1993

(SI 1993/1408)

Made on 7 June 1993 by the Secretary of State, in exercise of the powers conferred on him by s. 9(5) and 12(2) of the Oil Taxation Act 1983 and all other powers enabling him in that behalf.

1 This Order may be cited as the Foreign Fields (Specification) Order 1993.

2 In this Order the **"Lille Frigg Field"** means the hydrocarbon accumulation between the depths of 3,570 metres and 3,700 metres beneath mean sea level within the boundary defined by a set of lines of latitude and longitude joining the surface co-ordinates set out in the Schedule hereto.

3 The Lille Frigg Field, being an area which is not under the jurisdiction of the government of the United Kingdom, is for the purposes of the Act hereby specified as a foreign field.

SCHEDULE – LILLE FRIGG CO-ORDINATES

Article 2

Latitude North	*Longitude East*	*Latitude North*	*Longitude East*
59° 59′ 40″	02° 23′ 20″	59° 56′ 10″	02° 22′ 15″
59° 59′ 40″	02° 23′ 40″	59° 56′ 40″	02° 22′ 15″
59° 59′ 05″	02° 23′ 40″	59° 56′ 40″	02° 22′ 25″
59° 59′ 05″	02° 23′ 35″	59° 57′ 00″	02° 22′ 25″
59° 58′ 50″	02° 23′ 35″	59° 57′ 00″	02° 22′ 20″
59° 58′ 50″	02° 23′ 30″	59° 57′ 20″	02° 22′ 20″
59° 58′ 30″	02° 23′ 30″	59° 57′ 20″	02° 22′ 15″
59° 58′ 30″	02° 23′ 35″	59° 57′ 40″	02° 22′ 15″
59° 58′ 25″	02° 23′ 35″	59° 57′ 40″	02° 22′ 25″
59° 58′ 25″	02° 23′ 40″	59° 57′ 55″	02° 22′ 25″
59° 57′ 55″	02° 23′ 40″	59° 57′ 55″	02° 22′ 20″
59° 57′ 55″	02° 23′ 45″	59° 58′ 10″	02° 22′ 20″
59° 57′ 45″	02° 23′ 45″	59° 58′ 10″	02° 22′ 25″
59° 57′ 45″	02° 23′ 50″	59° 58′ 25″	02° 22′ 25″
59° 57′ 40″	02° 23′ 50″	59° 58′ 25″	02° 22′ 35″
59° 57′ 40″	02° 23′ 55″	59° 58′ 30″	02° 22′ 35″
59° 57′ 35″	02° 23′ 55″	59° 58′ 30″	02° 22′ 30″
59° 57′ 35″	02° 24′ 00″	59° 58′ 35″	02° 22′ 30″
59° 57′ 30″	02° 24′ 00″	59° 58′ 35″	02° 22′ 25″
59° 57′ 30″	02° 24′ 05″	59° 58′ 45″	02° 22′ 25″
59° 57′ 25″	02° 24′ 05″	59° 58′ 45″	02° 22′ 30″
59° 57′ 25″	02° 24′ 10″	59° 58′ 55″	02° 22′ 30″
59° 56′ 50″	02° 24′ 10″	59° 58′ 55″	02° 22′ 40″
59° 56′ 50″	02° 24′ 05″	59° 59′ 05″	02° 22′ 40″
59° 56′ 45″	02° 24′ 05″	59° 59′ 05″	02° 22′ 50″
59° 56′ 45″	02° 24′ 00″	59° 59′ 10″	02° 22′ 50″
59° 56′ 35″	02° 24′ 00″	59° 59′ 10″	02° 22′ 55″
59° 56′ 35″	02° 23′ 55″	59° 59′ 15″	02° 22′ 55″
59° 56′ 30″	02° 23′ 55″	59° 59′ 15″	02° 23′ 00″
59° 56′ 30″	02° 23′ 20″	59° 59′ 20″	02° 23′ 00″
59° 56′ 25″	02° 23′ 20″	59° 59′ 20″	02° 23′ 05″
59° 56′ 25″	02° 23′ 00″	59° 59′ 25″	02° 23′ 05″

Latitude North	*Longitude East*	*Latitude North*	*Longitude East*
59° 56′20″	02° 23′00″	59° 59′25″	02° 23′10″
59° 56′20″	02° 22′50″	59° 59′30″	02° 23′10″
59° 56′10″	02° 22′50″	59° 59′30″	02° 23′15″
59° 56′10″	02° 22′45″	59° 59′35″	02° 23′15″
59° 56′05″	02° 22′45″	59° 59′35″	02° 23′20″
59° 56′05″	02° 22′20″	59° 59′40″	02° 23′20″
59° 56′10″	02° 22′20″		

FOREIGN FIELDS (SPECIFICATION) (NO. 2) ORDER 1993

(SI 1993/1566)

Made on 18 June 1993 by the Secretary of State, in exercise of the powers conferred on him by sections 9(5) and 12(2) of the Oil Taxation Act 1983 (hereinafter referred to as "the Act"), and all other powers enabling him in that behalf.

1 This Order may be cited as the Foreign Fields (Specification) (No. 2) Order 1993.

2 In this Order the **"Froy Field"** means the hydrocarbon accumulation between the depths of 2,920 metres and 3,200 metres beneath mean sea level within the boundary defined by a set of lines of latitude and longitude joining the surface co-ordinates set out in the Schedule hereto.

3 The Froy Field, being an area which is not under the jurisdiction of the government of the United Kingdom, is for the purposes of the Act hereby specified as a foreign field.

PETROLEUM REVENUE TAX (ELECTRONIC COMMUNICATIONS) REGULATIONS 2003

(SI 2003/2718)

Made on 23 October 2003 by the Commissioners of Inland Revenue, in exercise of the powers conferred upon them by s. 132 of the Finance Act 1999. Operative from 13 November 2003.

PART 1 – INTRODUCTION

CITATION, COMMENCEMENT AND INTERPRETATION

1(1) These Regulations may be cited as the Petroleum Revenue Tax (Electronic Communications) Regulations 2003 and shall come into force on 13th November 2003.

1(2) In these Regulations–

"the Act" means the Oil Taxation Act 1975 and references, without more, to a numbered section or Schedule are to the section of, or Schedule to, the Act bearing that number;

"approved" means approved, for the purposes of these Regulations and for the time being, by means of a general or specific direction of the Board;

"the Management Act" means the Taxes Management Act 1970;

"the Board" means the Commissioners of Inland Revenue;

"field" means an oil field as defined in Schedule 1;

"official computer system" means a computer system maintained by or on behalf of the Board–

(a) to send or receive information, or

(b) to process or store information;

"participator" has the meaning given in section 12; and

"responsible person" has the meaning given in paragraph 4 of Schedule 2.

1(3) References in these Regulations to information and to the delivery of information shall be construed in accordance with section 132(8) of the Finance Act 1999.

SCOPE

2 These Regulations apply for the purposes of delivering information in, or in connection with, the claims, elections, notices and returns specified in the Schedule to these Regulations.

PART 2 – ELECTRONIC COMMUNICATIONS – GENERAL PROVISIONS

RESTRICTION ON THE USE OF ELECTRONIC COMMUNICATIONS

3(1) The Board may only use electronic communications in connection with the matters referred to in regulation 2 if–

(a) the recipient has indicated that he consents to the Board using electronic communications in connection with those matters; and

(b) the Board have not been informed that that consent has been withdrawn.

3(2) A person other than the Board may only use electronic communications in connection with the matters referred to in regulation 2 if the conditions specified in paragraphs (3) to (6) are satisfied.

3(3) The first condition is that the person is for the time being permitted to use electronic communications for the purpose in question by a general or specific direction of the Board.

3(4) The second condition is that the person uses–

(a) an approved method for authenticating the identity of the sender of the communication;

(b) an approved method of electronic communications; and

(c) an approved method for authenticating any information delivered by means of electronic communications.

3(5) The third condition is that any information sent by means of electronic communications is in a form approved.

Here **"form"** includes the manner in which the information is presented.

3(6) The fourth condition is that the person maintains such records in written or electronic form as may be specified in a general or specific direction of the Board.

Notes – HMRC Direction under reg. 3 of 9 February 2007.

USE OF INTERMEDIARIES

4 The Board may use intermediaries in connection with–

(a) the delivery of information by means of electronic communications in connection with the matters referred to in regulation 2, and

(b) the authentication or security of anything transmitted by such means,

and may require other persons to use intermediaries in connection with those matters.

PART 3 – ELECTRONIC COMMUNICATIONS – EVIDENTIAL PROVISIONS

EFFECT OF DELIVERING INFORMATION BY MEANS OF ELECTRONIC COMMUNICATIONS

5(1) Information to which these Regulations apply, and which is delivered by means of electronic communications, shall be treated as having been delivered, in the manner or form required by any provision of the Act or the Management Act which applies of the purpose of petroleum revenue tax if, but only if, all the conditions imposed by–

(a) these Regulations,

(b) any other applicable enactment (except to the extent that the condition thereby imposed is incompatible with these Regulations), and

(c) any specific or general direction given by the Board,

are satisfied.

5(2) Information delivered by means of electronic communications shall be treated as having been delivered on the day on which the last of the conditions imposed as mentioned in paragraph (1) is satisfied.

This is subject to paragraphs (3) and (4).

5(3) The Board may by a general or specific direction provide for information to be treated as delivered upon a different date (whether earlier or later) than that given by paragraph (2).

5(4) Information shall not be taken to have been delivered to an official computer system by means of electronic communications unless it is accepted by the system to which it is delivered.

PROOF OF CONTENT

6(1) A document certified by an officer of the Board to be a printed-out version of any information delivered by means of electronic communications under these Regulations on any occasion shall be evidence, unless the contrary is proved, that that information–

(a) was delivered by means of electronic communications on that occasion; and

(b) constitutes the entirety of what was delivered on that occasion.

6(2) A document purporting to be a certificate given in accordance with paragraph (1) shall be presumed to be such a certificate unless the contrary is proved.

PROOF OF SENDER OR RECIPIENT

7 The identity of–

(a) the sender of any information delivered to an official computer system by means of electronic communications under these Regulations, or

(b) the recipient of any information delivered by means of electronic communications from an official computer system,

shall be presumed, unless the contrary is proved, to be the person recorded as such on an official computer system.

INFORMATION DELIVERED ELECTRONICALLY ON ANOTHER'S BEHALF

8 Any information delivered by an approved method of electronic communications on behalf of any person shall be deemed to have been delivered by him unless he proves that it was delivered without his knowledge or connivance.

PROOF OF DELIVERY OF INFORMATION

9(1) The use of an authorised method of electronic communications shall be presumed, unless the contrary is proved, to have resulted in the delivery of information–

(a) in the case of information falling to be delivered to the Board, if the delivery of the information has been recorded on an official computer system; and

(b) in the case of information falling to be delivered by the Board, if the despatch of that information has been recorded on an official computer system.

9(2) The use of an authorised method of electronic communications shall be presumed, unless the contrary is proved, not to have resulted in the delivery of information–

(a) in the case of information falling to be delivered to the Board, if the delivery of the information has not been recorded on an official computer system; and

(b) in the case of information falling to be delivered by the Board, if the despatch of that information has not been recorded on an official computer system.

9(3) The time of receipt of any information sent by an authorised means of electronic communications shall be presumed, unless the contrary is proved, to be that recorded on an official computer system.

USE OF UNAUTHORISED MEANS OF ELECTRONIC COMMUNICATIONS

10(1) Paragraph (2) applies to information which is required to be delivered to the Board in connection with the matters mentioned in regulation 2.

10(2) The use of a means of electronic communications, for the purpose of delivering any information to which this paragraph applies, shall be conclusively presumed not to have resulted in the delivery of that information, unless–

(a) that means of electronic communications is for the time being approved for delivery of information of that kind; and

(b) the sender is approved for the use of that means of electronic communications in relation to information of that kind.

SCHEDULE

Regulation 2

Information permitted to be delivered to the Board by means of electronic communications

1 A return by a participator under paragraph 2 of Schedule 2.

2 A return by a responsible person under paragraph 5 of Schedule 2.

3 An election by a responsible person under paragraph 1 of Schedule 5.

4 A claim made by a responsible person for expenditure under paragraph 2 of Schedule 5.

5 A claim made by a participator for expenditure under paragraph 1 of Schedule 6.

6 A claim by a participator for under paragraph 1 of Schedule 7 for the allowance of expenditure of any of the classes mentioned in that paragraph.

7 A notice by a responsible person under paragraph 1 of Schedule 8.

8 A claim by a participator under paragraph 4 of Schedule 8 for the allowance under section 6 of an unrelievable field loss.

9 A statement of tax payable on account under section 1 of the Petroleum Revenue Tax Act 1980.

10 A notice to the Board of the transfer of an interest in a field under paragraph 3 of Schedule 17 to the Finance Act 1980.

11 A return by a participator under section 62(4) of the Finance Act 1987.

12 An election by a participator under section 65 of the Finance Act 1987 for the allowance of expenditure as *mentioned in subsection* (1) of that section.

13 A participator's undertaking under regulation 5(5) of the Oil Taxation (Gas Banking Schemes) Regulations 1982 in connection with an application under regulation regulation 5(2) of those Regulations.

14 An election under regulation 6 of the Oil Taxation (Gas Banking Schemes) Regulations 1982.

For the purpose of this paragraph, regulation 6(2) of the 1982 Regulations shall have effect, in relation to an election which is made electronically, as if for "signed" there were substituted "authenticated in such manner as the Board may approve".

PETROLEUM REVENUE TAX (ATTRIBUTION OF BLENDED CRUDE OIL) REGULATIONS 2006

(SI 2006/3312)

Made on 13 December 2006 by the Commissioners for Her Majesty's Revenue and Customs in exercise of the powers conferred upon them by s. 2(5B)–(5D) of the Oil Taxation Act 1975 and s. 148(3) of the Finance Act 2006. Operative from 14 December 2006.

CITATION AND COMMENCEMENT

1 These Regulations may be cited as the Petroleum Revenue Tax (Attribution of Blended Crude Oil) Regulations 2006, shall come into force on the day following that on which they are made and shall have effect in respect of chargeable periods ending on or after 1st July 2006.

INTERPRETATION

2(1) In these Regulations–

"the Act" means the Finance Act 1987;

"balancing parcel" is the difference between–

(a) the volume of blended oil which a purchaser has notified to the participator as being required under the contract; and

(b) the volume of blended oil actually lifted under that contract;

"blended oil" has the meaning given by section 63(1A) of the Act;

"lifting" is–

(a) the loading of a volume of blended oil onto a tanker from an offshore loading point or an onshore oil terminal, or

(b) the transfer of a volume of blended oil by means of a pipeline to an onshore oil terminal,

and cognate expressions shall be construed accordingly;

"loading schedule" is the schedule produced each month by the terminal operator based upon the projected monthly production entitlement for each participator for the blended oil in question;

"month" is a calendar month and "monthly" shall be construed accordingly;

"nomination excess" is the amount by which the market value of a relevant delivery exceeds the participator's delivery proceeds of that relevant delivery (within the meaning of section 61(3) of the Act);

"opening stock"–

(a) in relation to the first month to which these Regulations apply in relation to a participator's interest in a particular originating field, is so much of the amount found by the latest computation of a participator's production entitlement in that field, used in constructing a loading schedule, as has not been lifted at the start of that month (and which may accordingly be a positive or negative value); and

(b) in relation to any later month to which these Regulations apply in relation to such an interest is–

  (i) the participator's production entitlement in respect of that interest at the start of the preceding month; less

  (ii) the total volume of oil lifted during the previous month and allocated, in accordance with these Regulations to that field;

"originating field" has the meaning given by section 63(1A) of the Act;

"period of entitlement contract" is a contract under which a participator sells its projected oil entitlement over a fixed period to a purchaser in return for regular payment, and under which the purchaser has discretion as to when to lift that oil;

"production entitlement" in relation to an originating field means the sum of–

(a) the participator's opening stock of oil from that field; and

(b) his qualifying production from that field;

"qualifying production" means–

(a) in the case of oil in a blend where oil is normally allocated to an originating field in advance of lifting, the projected production referred to in the loading schedule for the period in question; and

(b) in any other case, the amount of oil actually won by the participator from that field;

"relevant delivery" has the meaning given by paragraph 12A of Schedule 10 to the Act;

"term contract" is a contract for the sale of a volume of oil within a specified period which is subject to more than one delivery.

2(2) Section 839 of the Income and Corporation Taxes Act 1988 (connected persons) applies to determine whether persons are connected with each other for the purposes of these Regulations.

VOLUME OF OIL

3(1) For the purposes of the following provisions of these Regulations references to the volume of oil lifted shall be construed–

(a) if the conditions in paragraph (2) are satisfied, as a reference to the nominated volume; and

(b) in any other case, as a reference to the volume actually lifted.

3(2) The conditions are that–

(a) the contract under which the oil is to be lifted entitles the purchaser to notify the participator of the volume of oil to be lifted under it ("the nominated volume");

(b) the agreement between the participator and the operator of the terminal from which the oil is actually to be lifted entitles the participator to allocate the nominated volume between the participator's field interests and provides for different treatment of the balancing parcel; and

(c) the nominated volume is allocated as mentioned in sub-paragraph (b).

3(3) Regulation 6 (treatment of balancing parcels) applies where the conditions in paragraph (2) are satisfied.

3(4) Any references in these Regulations to a volume of oil is to a volume calculated in barrels. For this purpose a barrel is a volume of 0.158987 cubic metres of oil.

ALLOCATION OF BLENDED OIL LIFTED

4(1) For each lifting of blended oil by a participator in an originating field, the amount to be allocated to each originating field in respect of that lifting is–

$$A \times \frac{B}{C}$$

Here–

A is the volume of blended oil of a particular blend lifted by the participator in that lifting;

B is the total volume of the participator's production entitlement for that blend from the originating field for that month; and

C is the sum of–

(a) the participator's production entitlements from all originating fields for that blend, and

(b) so much of the seller's production entitlement in respect of oil of that blend for that period as the participator is entitled to lift under period of entitlement contracts,

but where an entitlement in respect of an originating field is a negative amount that entitlement shall be treated as zero in computing C.

These definitions are subject to the following qualifications.

4(2) Where oil is lifted under a period of entitlement contract or a term contract regulation 5 applies.

4(3) The final volume produced by application of the formula in paragraph (1) may be adjusted (up or down) by the participator by up to a maximum of 1000 barrels.

But the sum of the adjusted volumes in respect of each allocation must equal the total volume of blended oil lifted.

PERIOD OF ENTITLEMENT CONTRACTS AND TERM CONTRACTS

5(1) Where a participator in an originating field sells blended oil under a period of entitlement contract or a term contract, and the contract relates to oil from more than one field, the following formula applies to determine how much of the volume of oil lifted and sold under the contract must be allocated to each originating field in the blend–

$$A \times \frac{B}{C}$$

Here–

A is the volume of blended oil lifted in the lifting in question;

B is the total volume of the participator's production entitlement for that blend from the originating field for that month under the terms of the contract; and

C is the sum of the participator's production entitlements from that blend from all originating fields for that month under the contract, but where an entitlement in respect of an originating field is a negative amount, that entitlement shall be treated as zero in computing C.

5(2) The final volume produced by application of the formula in paragraph (1) may be adjusted (up or down) by the participator to a maximum of 1000 barrels.

But the sum of the adjusted volumes in respect of each allocation must be equal to the total volume of oil of the particular blend lifted.

BALANCING PARCELS

6(1) Where this regulation applies–

(a) the participator must notify Her Majesty's Revenue and Customs of an originating field ("the receiving field") to which balancing parcels of the particular blend of oil are to be attributed, and

(b) every balancing parcel in respect of that blend must be allocated to the receiving field, but subject to the following provisions of this regulation.

6(2) When a receiving field ceases oil production, the participator must allocate balancing parcels to another originating field ("the substituted field"), and thereafter this regulation applies to the substituted field as it applied to the receiving field.

6(3) Where the allocation, or continuing allocation, of a balancing parcel to a receiving field becomes impossible having regard to the terms of the agreement between the participator and the terminal operator for that field, the participator must notify Her Majesty's Revenue and Customs that another originating field is to be treated as the receiving field while those conditions persist.

6(4) A notice under paragraph (3) must be given before the first allocation of a balancing parcel to the other originating field which is to be treated as the receiving field.

SALE OF FIELD INTERESTS

7(1) If a participator ("the seller") agrees to sell a field interest to an unconnected party ("the buyer") the seller must notify Her Majesty's Revenue and Customs in writing of–

(a) the names of the buyer and seller;

(b) the field interest in question;

(c) the proposed completion date of the sale; and

(d) the cessation date.

7(2) In this regulation **"the cessation date"** means the date after which, in accordance with the contract for the sale of the field interest, the seller will make no further lifting of oil won from that field interest, except as required by the terminal operator, prior to completion of the sale.

7(3) The information must be provided to Her Majesty's Revenue and Customs no later than the first day of the month preceding the month in which the cessation date falls.

7(4) From the later of the cessation date, or the end of the month in which falls the date on which the information specified in paragraph (1) is received by Her Majesty's Revenue and Customs–

(a) any amounts lifted from that field interest ("the separated interest" shall be separated from the seller's other field interests for the purposes of calculating the allocation entitlements for that field; and

(b) the entitlements in respect of the separated interest shall be calculated on the basis of the formula set out in paragraph (5).

7(5) For each lifting of blended oil from the separated interest in a month, the following formula applies to determine the quantity of oil lifted from each of the fields from which the oil is derived–

$$A \times \frac{B}{C}$$

Here–

A is the volume of oil lifted;

B is the total amount of the seller's production entitlement for the separated interest for that month; and

C is the sum of the seller's production entitlement from all his separated interests for that month.

SALE OF FIELD INTEREST – FURTHER PROVISIONS

8(1) This regulation applies when, during a chargeable period–

(a) a field interest, from which oil is used to produce blended crude oil, is sold to a buyer with whom the seller is not connected; and

(b) the seller retains another field interest forming part of the same blend.

8(2) Where this regulation applies, the adjustment to the closing stock is calculated as follows.

Step 1

Find the operational closing stock, that is to say the amount found by the formula E – L.

Here–

E is the sum of–

(a) the participator's operational stock of oil won from that field interest at the start of the month in which the field interest is sold; and

(b) the amount of oil actually won by the participator from that field interest during that month; and

L is the amount of oil actually lifted in that month and won from that field interest.

In paragraph (a) of the definition of E **"operational stock"** is so much of the amount found by the latest computation of a participator's production entitlement in that field, used in constructing a loading schedule, as has not been lifted at the start of that month (and which may accordingly be a positive or negative value).

Step 2

Find the tax closing stock, that is to say the amount found by the formula O + W – A

Here–

O is the opening stock at the start of the month in which the field interest is sold;

W is the amount of oil actually won by the participator from that field interest during that month; and

A is the amount of oil allocated to that field under regulations 4 to 6.

Step 3

Subtract the result of Step 2 from that of Step 1.

8(3) The amount found under Step 3 (whether positive or negative) must be allocated to the other field interests in the blend of which the field interest to be sold is a part, in accordance with regulation 4 but, for the purposes of calculating C in regulation 4(1), the participator's production entitlement for the field interest being sold shall be zero.

SALE OF FIELD INTEREST NOT PROCEEDING

9(1) In the event that it appears to the proposed seller that the sale of a field interest or interests will not proceed, the seller shall notify Her Majesty's Revenue and Customs, no later than the due date for his petroleum revenue tax return for the period in which the seller is first aware of this, that it will not proceed.

9(2) Where a sale does not proceed–

(a) from the beginning of the month following that in which the seller is first aware that the sale will not proceed the separation of the field interest or interests which were the subject matter of the sale will cease; and

(b) thereafter the formula set out in regulation 4 will again apply for the purposes of allocating any lifting from that field or those fields.

ALLOCATION OF NOMINATION EXCESSES

10 Where a participator makes a relevant delivery of blended oil the following provisions apply to determine how much of his nomination excess to attribute to each originating field.

Step 1

Calculate the respective volumes of blended lifted oil to be allocated to individual originating fields applying the formula in regulation 4(1).

Step 2

Establish the total volume of the relevant delivery of blended oil.

Step 3

Divide each of the volumes calculated in Step 1 by the amount found under Step 2.

Step 4

Multiply each result of Step 3 by the nomination excess.

The result is the nomination excess to be allocated to the individual originating field in question.

OIL TAXATION (MARKET VALUE OF OIL) REGULATIONS 2006

(SI 2006/3313)

Made on 13 December 2006 by the Commissioners for Her Majesty's Revenue and Customs in exercise of the powers conferred by s. 21(2) of, and para. 2(1B), (1C), (2E) and (2F) of Sch. 3 to that Act, and s. 147(4) and (7) of the Finance Act 2006. Operative in accordance with regulation 1(1).

INTRODUCTION

Citation, commencement and effect

1(1) These Regulations may be cited as the Oil Taxation (Market Value of Oil) Regulations 2006, and shall come into force on the day after that on which they are made.

1(2) These Regulations have effect in relation to the first new period, within the meaning of section 147(4)(b) of FA 2006 (commencement and transitional provisions for amendments to Schedule 3 to OTA by section 146 of, and Schedule 18 to, FA 2006) and subsequent periods.

Interpretation

2(1) This paragraph gives the meaning of the abbreviated references used in these Regulations–

"FA 2006" means the Finance Act 2006;

"ICTA" means the Income and Corporation Taxes Act 1988; and

"OTA" means the Oil Taxation Act 1975.

2(2) This paragraph gives the meaning of other terms used in these Regulations–

"bank holiday" means a day which is a bank holiday in England and Wales under the Banking and Financial Dealings Act 1971;

"Category 1 oil" is oil of any of the kinds specified in regulation 3;

"relevantly appropriated" has the meaning given by section 12(1) of OTA.

2(3) A sale of oil is at arm's length if (but only if) it satisfies paragraph 1 of Schedule 3 to OTA.

Category 1 oil

3(1) Category 1 oil is oil of any of the following kinds–

(a) Brent blend;

(b) Ekofisk blend;

(c) Flotta blend;

(d) Forties blend;

(e) Statfjord oil.

3(2) In these Regulations–

"Brent blend" means the blend of crude oils landed at Sullom Voe in Shetland via either the Brent or Ninian pipeline systems;

"Ekofisk blend" means the blend of crude oils landed at the Teesside Oil Terminal at Seal Sands via the Norpipe pipeline;

"Flotta blend" means the blend of crude oils landed at the Flotta Oil Terminal in Orkney and originating from the Flotta catchment area;

"Forties blend" means the blend of crude oils landed at Cruden Bay, Aberdeenshire via the Forties pipeline system;

"Statfjord oil" means oil to which article 23 of the Agreement between Her Majesty's Government of the United Kingdom and Northern Ireland and the Government of the Kingdom of Norway relating to the exploitation of the Statfjord Field Reservoirs signed at Oslo on 16th October 1979 applies.

Interpretation – reports and factors used in calculations

4(1) In these Regulations the terms defined in the following paragraphs, which relate to the way in which the market value of a Category 1 oil is determined, have the meanings given there.

4(2) **"The relevant reports"** means–

(a) Argus Crude published by Argus Media Limited, whose registered office is Argus House, St. John Street London EC1V 4LW;

PRT Statutory Instruments

(b) ICIS (the Independent Chemical Information Services' World Crude Report), published by Reed Elsevier Group plc whose registered office is Quadrant House, The Quadrant, Sutton, Surrey, SM2 5AS; and

(c) Platts Oilgram published by Platts, a division of the McGraw-Hill Companies, whose registered office is Two Penn Plaza, 25th Floor, New York, N.Y. 10121-2298.

4(3) **"The reference value"** is the value quoted–

(a) in the case of Argus Crude as "Dated BFO" in the section of the report entitled "Atlantic Basin Crudes, London 16.30 hours, North Sea";

(b) in the case of ICIS, as "Dated BFO" in the North Sea 3rd Update; and

(c) in the case of Platts Oilgram, as "Brent (DTD)" in the International section of the report.

4(4) **"Adjustment factor"** means the differential, upon the day in question, from the reference value–

(a) found, in the case of Brent blend, in accordance with regulation 14;

(b) for any other Category 1 oil, shown–

(i) in the case of Argus Crude, in the report under "Atlantic Basin Crudes, London 16.30 hours North Sea";

(ii) in the case of ICIS, in North Sea 3rd Update; and

(iii) in the case of Platts Oilgram, as the assessment of the spread against forward dated Brent blend (described in the report as "spread vs fwd DTD Brent".

SCOPE

General scope of these Regulations

5 These Regulations apply for the purpose of determining the market value of oil won from a field to which section 2(5)(b) or (c) of OTA applies and which is–

(a) delivered, or relevantly appropriated, on or after 1st July 2006; or

(b) held by a participator and not delivered at the end of a chargeable period.

VALUING CATEGORY 1 OIL

General

6 The method of determining the market value of Category 1 oil to which these Regulations apply is as follows–

(a) find the notional delivery day (see regulations 7 and 8);

(b) find the average reference value for that day (see regulations 9 to 12);

(c) add the adjustment factor (see regulations 13 to 15); and

(d) find the total market value of the oil (see regulation 16).

The notional delivery day: the general rule

7(1) The general rule is that the notional delivery day is found in accordance with paragraph 1A of Schedule 3 to OTA (determination of market value: notional delivery day for a quantity of oil).

7(2) The general rule is subject to regulation 8.

The notional delivery day: additional rule

8(1) Paragraph (2) applies to a delivery of Category 1 oil by way of a sale otherwise than at arm's length if–

(a) during any period of 24 months, beginning on or after 1st July 2006, the total quantity of equity oil of that type disposed of by a participator and persons connected with him is not less than 4,000,000 barrels;

(b) a lower price would fall to be taken into account in determining the participator's gross profit under section 2(1) of OTA for the delivery from that which would have applied if it had been by way of a sale at arm's length;

(c) the reason for that lower price is because the notional delivery day is a day other than that on which the actual delivery takes place;

(d) the whole or main benefit which might reasonably be expected to be obtained from a sale otherwise than at arm's length, when compared with a sale at arm's length, is a tax advantage within the meaning of section 709 of ICTA.

8(2) The notional delivery day is the day specified in paragraph (a) or (b) (as the case requires) of paragraph 1A(7) of Schedule 3 to OTA.

8(3) In this regulation–

"barrel" means a volume of 0.158987 cubic metres of oil; and

"equity oil" means oil forming part of the trading stock of a participator or a person connected with him which has been won by that participator or a person connected with him from a field in the United Kingdom sector of the North Sea.

8(4) Section 839 of ICTA (connected persons) applies for determining whether persons are connected for the purposes of this regulation.

The average reference value: notional delivery day one for which reference values available

9(1) If the notional delivery day is a day for which reference values are available find the daily average of the reference values from each of the three relevant reports for–

(a) each of the two dates immediately preceding the notional delivery day;

(b) the notional delivery day; and

(c) each of the two dates immediately following notional delivery day.

9(2) If any of the relevant reports contains more than one reference value for any of these dates, the result for that report for that date is the arithmetical mean of those values.

9(3) Find the average of the daily averages found for each of the five days referred to in paragraph (1).

9(4) The result is the average reference value for the notional delivery day.

The average reference value: notional delivery day a Saturday, or a Bank Holiday which is not a Monday, and for which reference values not available

10(1) If the notional delivery day is not a day for which reference values are available but is a Saturday, or a bank holiday which is not a Monday, find the daily average of the reference values from each of the three relevant reports for–

(a) each of the three business days immediately preceding the notional delivery day; and

(b) each of the two business days immediately following the notional delivery day.

10(2) If any of the relevant reports contains more than one reference value for any of these dates, the result for that report for that date is the arithmetical mean of those values.

10(3) Find the average of the daily averages found for each of the five days referred to in paragraph (1).

10(4) The result is the average reference value for the notional delivery day.

The average reference value: notional delivery day a Sunday, or a Bank Holiday which is a Monday

11(1) If the notional delivery day is not a day for which reference values are available but is a Sunday, or a bank holiday which is a Monday, find the daily average of the reference values from each of the three relevant reports for–

(a) each of the two business days immediately preceding the notional delivery day; and

(b) each of the three business days immediately following the notional delivery day.

11(2) If any of the relevant reports contains more than one reference value for any of these dates, the result for that report for that date is the arithmetical mean of those values.

11(3) Find the average of the daily averages found for each of the five days referred to in paragraph (1).

11(4) The result is the average reference value for the notional delivery day.

The average reference value: additional provisions

12(1) If in respect of any of the days specified in a provision of regulation 9, 10 or 11 one or two of the relevant reports is not published, that provision has effect as if references to the relevant reports were to such of the relevant reports as are actually published in respect of that day.

12(2) If in respect of any of the days specified in a provision of regulation 9, 10 or 11 other than the notional delivery day, none of the relevant reports is published ("a non-publication day"), that provision has effect as if–

(a) references to a day which is a non-publication day falling before the notional delivery day were to the day falling next before that day on which at least one of the relevant reports is published; and

(b) references to a day which is a non-publication day falling after the notional delivery day were to the day falling next after that day on which at least one of the relevant reports is published.

12(3) If the application of the rule in paragraph (2) would lead to the reports for a day being taken into account more than once, a reference to the day falling next before, or after, the nonpublication day shall be read as a reference to the first day falling next before or after (as the case may be) the non-publication day which would not otherwise be taken into account for the purposes of this regulation.

12(4) In cases where the date of completion of load or the date of the bill of lading is substituted for the notional delivery day under regulation 8, references in this regulation to the notional delivery day are to be read as references to the day substituted under that regulation.

The adjustment factors – general

13(1) The adjustment factor applicable to the Category 1 oil in question must be added to the average reference value.

13(2) The adjustment factor is found–

(a) in accordance with regulation 14 in the case of Brent blend; and

(b) in accordance with regulation 15 in the case of other Category 1 oil.

Adjustment factor – Brent blend

14(1) The adjustment factor for Brent blend is found as follows.

14(2) Find the daily average of the differentials from the reference value quoted in the relevant reports for each of the days–

(a) during the period which begins 21 days, and ends 14 days before the notional delivery day, and

(b) in respect of which at least one such report is produced,

as follows.

14(3) Find the Argus Crude differential for a particular day by taking the value shown as the "Brent" assessment and subtracting from it the value shown as "Dated BFO" in that report.

14(4) Find the ICIS differential for a particular day by taking the value shown as the "Brent" assessment and subtracting from it the value shown as "Dated BFO" in that report.

14(5) Find the Platts differential for a particular day by taking the value for "Brent Assessment 10 – 21 days out" in Platts Crude Oil Marketwire and subtracting from it the value for "North Sea Dated Strip" in that report.

14(6) In this regulation "Platts Crude Oil Marketwire" means the report of that name published by Platts, a division of the McGraw-Hill Companies, whose registered office is Two Penn Plaza, 25th Floor, New York, N.Y. 10121-2298.

14(7) If any of the reports referred to in this regulation contains more than one value for the relevant quote for any of these days, the result for that report for that day is the arithmetical mean of those values.

14(8) Find the average of the daily averages found in accordance with this regulation for each of the days specified in paragraph (2).

14(9) The result is the adjustment factor for Brent blend.

Adjustment factor – other Category 1 oil

15(1) The adjustment factor for a Category 1 oil other than Brent blend is found as follows.

15(2) Find the daily average of the differentials, from reference value, for the Category 1 oil in question quoted in the three relevant reports for each of the days–

(a) during the period which begins 21 days, and ends 14 days before the notional delivery day, and

(b) in respect of which at least one such report is produced.

15(3) If any of the relevant reports contains more than one value for the Category 1 oil in question for any of these days, the result for that report for that day is the arithmetical mean of those values.

15(4) Find the average of the daily averages found by paragraphs (2) and (3) for each of the days specified in paragraph (2).

15(5) The result is the adjustment factor for the relevant Category 1 oil.

The total market value of the oil

16(1) The total market value of a volume of Category 1 oil to which these Regulations apply is found as follows–

(a) take the average reference value for the notional delivery day (see regulations 9 to 12);

(b) add the adjustment factor applicable to the Category 1 oil in question (see regulations 13 to 15); and

(c) multiply the sum found by sub-paragraph (b) by the volume of Category 1 oil in question.

16(2) The result is the total market value of the oil.

VALUING CATEGORY 2 OILS

Market value: Category 2 oils

17 The market value of a quantity of Category 2 oil to which these Regulations apply is found by whichever of the methods in regulation 18 (method 1) or regulations 19 to 23 (method 2) would produce a sum which more closely reflects the price which would normally apply in a sale at arm's length for a similar quantity of that oil on the notional delivery day (found in accordance with paragraph 1A of Schedule 3 to OTA), but subject to the special rules in regulation 24.

Method 1

18 The first method is to find the average unit price for actual sales at arm's length of the relevant Category 2 oil under contracts meeting the conditions set out in paragraphs (a) to (e) of paragraph 2(2AA) of Schedule 3 to OTA.

Method 2: general

19 The second method is as follows–

(a) find the relevant reference oils ("the marker crudes") for the relevant Category 2 oil (see regulation 20);

(b) find the average marker crude price quoted in respect of the relevant Category 2 oil (see regulation 21);

(c) adjust the average marker crude price (see regulation 22);

(d) find the total market value of the oil (see regulation 23).

Finding the relevant reference oils for the Category 2 oil in question

20 Ascertain which crude oils are normally used as marker crudes for the purposes of determining the market value of the relevant Category 2 oil under contracts at arm's length.

Finding the average marker crude price

21(1) Find the average of the prices quoted by the relevant reports for the sale of the marker crudes in respect of trades during the reference period in contracts for the sale at arm's length of the relevant Category 2 oil.

21(2) In paragraph (1) **"the reference period"** means the period ordinarily used to find the market value of oils, by reference to which the price of the oil in question is determined, in a contract for the sale of that oil at arm's length.

Adjusting the average marker crude price

22 Add to the result of regulation 21 differential or combination of differentials normally applied in a contract for the sale at arm's length of the relevant Category 2 oil.

Total value of the Category 2 oil sold or relevantly appropriated

23(1) Multiply the result of regulation 22 by the volume of Category 2 oil to which these Regulations apply in the particular case.

23(2) The product so found is the market value of the Category 2 oil in question.

23(3) This is subject to regulation 24.

Special rules

24(1) If a participator's contracts for the sale of Category 2 oil in sales at arm's length normally provide for the price to be determined–

(a) in the case of oil transported by ship from the place of extraction to a place in the United Kingdom or elsewhere, by reference to the actual date of the completion of the load, or completion of the discharge, of the cargo; or

(b) in the case of oil transported by pipeline to a place in the United Kingdom and loaded on to a ship there, by reference to the date of the bill of lading;

references to the notional delivery day in regulation 17 are to be construed, in relation to that participator as references to the day mentioned in sub-paragraph (a) or (b) (as the case requires).

24(2) The modification in paragraph (1) also applies where Category 2 oil is loaded onto a ship at least 7 days later than the date provided for by the contract for sale by reason of circumstances wholly beyond the control of the parties.

TRANSFER OF TRIBUNAL FUNCTIONS AND REVENUE AND CUSTOMS APPEALS ORDER 2009

(SI 2009/56, as amended by SI 2009/777)

Made on 18 January 2009 by the Lord Chancellor and the Treasury in exercise of the powers conferred by s. 30(1) and (4), 31(1), (2) and (9) and 38 of, and para. 30 of Sch. 5 to, the Tribunals, Courts and Enforcement Act 2007 and s. 124(1)–(7) of the Finance Act 2008. Operative from 1 April 2009.

CITATION AND COMMENCEMENT

1(1) This Order may be cited as the Transfer of Tribunal Functions and Revenue and Customs Appeals Order 2009.

1(2) This Order comes into force on 1st April 2009.

THE EXISTING TRIBUNALS

2 In this Order **"existing tribunals"** means–

(a) the Commissioners for the general purposes of the income tax established under section 2 of the Taxes Management Act 1970;

(b) the Commissioners for the special purposes of the Income Tax Acts established under section 4 of the Taxes Management Act 1970;

(c) [not relevant to petroleum revenue tax;]

(d) [not relevant to petroleum revenue tax;]

(e) [not relevant to petroleum revenue tax.]

TRANSFER OF FUNCTIONS, CONSEQUENTIAL AND OTHER AMENDMENTS

3(1) Schedule 1 contains amendments to primary legislation which–

(a) transfer functions of existing tribunals, and

(b) make consequential and other provision (including provision about reviews of decisions by Her Majesty's Revenue and Customs).

3(2) Schedule 2 contains amendments to secondary legislation which–

(a) transfer functions of existing tribunals, and

(b) make consequential and other provision (including provision about reviews of decisions by Her Majesty's Revenue and Customs).

ABOLITION OF EXISTING TRIBUNALS

4 The existing tribunals (apart from the Commissioners for the general purposes of the income tax) are abolished.

TRANSFER OF MEMBERS OF EXISTING TRIBUNALS

5 A person who, immediately before this Order comes into force, holds an office listed in column 1 of any of the following tables is to hold the office or offices listed in the corresponding entry in column 2 of that table–

THE SPECIAL COMMISSIONERS

1. Office held	2. Office or offices to be held
Commissioner for the special purposes of the Income Tax Acts appointed under section 4 of the Taxes Management Act 1970	Transferred-in judge of the Upper Tribunal
Deputy Commissioner for the special purposes of the Income Tax Acts appointed under section 4A of the Taxes Management Act 1970	Transferred-in judge of the First-tier Tribunal and deputy judge of the Upper Tribunal

TRANSITIONALS AND SAVINGS

6 Schedule 3 contains–

(a) transitional provision, and

(b) saving provision.

SCHEDULES

SCHEDULE 1 – CONSEQUENTIAL AMENDMENTS AND SUPPLEMENTAL PROVISIONS – PRIMARY LEGISLATION

Article 3

OIL TAXATION ACT 1975

68 The Oil Taxation Act 1975 is amended as follows.

69 Schedule 2 (management and collection of petroleum revenue tax) is amended as follows.

70 [Amends the Table in OTA 1975, Sch. 2, para. 1.]

71 [Amends OTA 1975, Sch. 2, para. 3.]

72 [Amends OTA 1975, Sch. 2, para. 6.]

73 [Amends OTA 1975, Sch. 2, para. 3.]

74 [Amends OTA 1975, Sch. 2, para. 14.]

History – Para. 74(7) omitted by SI 2009/777, art. 7, with effect from 1 April 2009.

75 [Inserts OTA 1975, Sch. 2, para. 14A–14I.]

76 Schedule 5 (allowance of expenditure) is amended as follows.

77 [Amends OTA 1975, Sch. 5, para. 5.]

78 [Amends OTA 1975, Sch. 5, para. 6(1) and (2).]

79 [Amends OTA 1975, Sch. 5, para. 7.]

80 [Amends OTA 1975, Sch. 5, para. 8.]

81 [Amends OTA 1975, Sch. 5, para. 9.]

82 [Inserts OTA 1975, Sch. 5, para. 10.]

83(1) Schedule 6 (allowance of expenditure on claim by participator) is amended as follows.

83(2) [Amends the Table in OTA 1975, Sch. 6, para. 2.]

84(1) Schedule 7 (allowance of abortive exploration expenditure) is amended as follows.

84(2) [Amends OTA 1975, Sch. 7, para. 1(3).]

85 [Amends OTA 1975, Sch. 8, para. 3.]

FINANCE ACT 1980

94 The Finance Act 1980 is amended as follows.

95 [Amends FA 1980, Sch. 17, para. 5.]

FINANCE ACT 1982

100 The Finance Act 1982 is amended as follows.

101 [Amends FA 1982, Sch. 18.]

102 [Amends FA 1982, Sch. 19.]

FINANCE ACT 1984

103 The Finance Act 1984 is amended as follows.

104 [Amends FA 1984, s. 115.]

105 [Amends FA 1984, s. 116(1)(b).]

FINANCE ACT 1987

126 The Finance Act 1987 is amended as follows.

127 [Amends FA 1987, s. 62(7)(b).]

128 [Amends FA 1987, s. 63(3)(b).]

129 [Amends FA 1987, s. 66.]

130 [Amends FA 1987, Sch. 12, para. 3.]

131 [Amends FA 1987, Sch. 14, para. 2(2)(c).]

FINANCE ACT 1989

166 The Finance Act 1989 is amended as follows.

167 [Amends FA 1989, s. 182.]

FINANCE ACT 1993

192 The Finance Act 1993 is amended as follows.

193 [Amends FA 1993, s. 187.]

194 [Amends FA 1993, Sch. 20A.]

195 [Amends FA 1993, Sch. 21.]

SCHEDULE 2 – CONSEQUENTIAL AMENDMENTS AND SUPPLEMENTAL PROVISIONS – SECONDARY LEGISLATION

Article 3

OIL TAXATION (GAS BANKING SCHEME) REGULATIONS 1982

8 [Amends SI 1982/92, reg. 7.]

REVOCATIONS

187 The following instruments are revoked–

(a)–(d) [Not relevant to petroleum revenue tax.]

(e) The Special Commissioners (Jurisdiction and Procedure) Regulations 1994.

(f) The General Commissioners (Jurisdiction and Procedure) Regulations 1994.

(h) The Retirement Age of General Commissioners Order 1995.

(i) The Special Commissioners (Jurisdiction and Procedure) (Amendment) Regulations 1999.

(j) The General Commissioners (Jurisdiction and Procedure) (Amendment) Regulations 1999.

(k) The Special Commissioners (Amendment of the Taxes Management Act 1970) Regulations 1999.

(1) The Special Commissioners (Jurisdiction and Procedure) (Amendment) Regulations 2000.

(o) The Referrals to the Special Commissioners Regulations 2001.

(p) The General Commissioners and Special Commissioners (Jurisdiction and Procedure) (Amendment) Regulations 2002.

(q) The Special Commissioners (Jurisdiction and Procedure) (Amendment) Regulations 2003.

(s) The General Commissioners (Jurisdiction and Procedure) (Amendment) Regulations 2005.

(t) The Special Commissioners (Jurisdiction and Procedure) (Amendment) Regulations 2005.

(v) The General Commissioners and Special Commissioners (Jurisdiction and Procedure) (Amendment) Regulations 2007.

SCHEDULE 3 – TRANSITIONAL AND SAVING PROVISIONS

Article 6

GENERAL

1(1) In this Schedule–

"commencement date" means the date on which this Order comes into force;

"enactment" includes subordinate legislation (within the meaning of the Interpretation Act 1978);

"HMRC" means Her Majesty's Revenue and Customs;

"tribunal" means the First-tier Tribunal or, where determined by or under Tribunal Procedure Rules, the Upper Tribunal.

1(2) For the purposes of this Schedule there are "current proceedings" if, before the commencement date–

(a) any party has served notice on an existing tribunal for the purpose of beginning proceedings before the existing tribunal, and

(b) the existing tribunal has not concluded proceedings arising by virtue of that notice.

FORMER VAT AND DUTIES TRIBUNALS MATTERS (EXCEPT VAT)

2(1) This paragraph applies in relation to the following decisions–

(a) any relevant decision which HMRC notify before the commencement date, unless–

(i) the period to require a review of the decision has expired before that date, or

(ii) a review of the decision has been required before that date;

(b) any relevant review decision which HMRC notify before the commencement date unless–

(i) the period to serve notice of appeal against the decision on an existing tribunal has expired before that date, or

(ii) notice of appeal against the decision has been served on an existing tribunal before that date.

2(2) On and after the commencement date, the following enactments continue to apply (subject to sub-paragraphs (3) and (4)) as they applied immediately before that date–

(a) the review and appeal provisions,

(b) rule 4(2) of the Value Added Tax Tribunals Rules 1986, and

(c) any other enactments that apply in relation to relevant decisions or relevant review decisions.

2(3) Those enactments apply subject to Tribunal Procedure Rules.

2(4) Any reference to an existing tribunal is to be substituted with a reference to the tribunal.

2(5) Any time period which has started to run before the commencement date and has not expired will continue to apply.

2(6) In this paragraph–

"relevant decision" means a decision to which a review and appeal provision applies (apart from a relevant review decision);

"relevant review decision" means a decision–

(a) that is made on a review of a relevant decision, and

(b) to which a review and appeal provision applies,

and includes a relevant decision that is treated as having been confirmed under a review and appeal provision.

"review and appeal provisions" means–

(a) sections 14 to 16 of the Finance Act 1994,

(b) sections 59 and 60 of the Finance Act 1994,

(c) sections 54 to 56 of the Finance Act 1996,

(d) paragraphs 121 to 123 of Schedule 6 to the Finance Act 2000,

(e) sections 40 to 42 of the Finance Act 2001,

(f) sections 33 to 37 of the Finance Act 2003,

(g) regulations 9 to 13 of the Export (Penalty) Regulations 2003,

(h) regulations 4 to 7 of the Control of Cash (Penalties) Regulations 2007,

(i) regulations 43 and 44 of the Money Laundering Regulations 2007, and

(j) regulations 12 and 13 of the Transfer of Funds (Information on the Payer) Regulations 2007.

3(1) This paragraph applies in relation to a relevant decision if, before the commencement date–

(a) HMRC have notified the relevant decision, and

(b) a review of the decision has begun under a review and appeal provision (whether or not a relevant review decision has been notified).

3(2) On and after the commencement date the following enactments continue to apply (subject to sub-paragraphs (3) and (4)), as they applied immediately before that date–

(a) the review and appeal provisions,

(b) rule 4(2) of the VAT Tribunals Rules 1986, and

(c) any other enactments that apply in relation to relevant decisions or relevant review decisions.

3(3) Those enactments apply subject to Tribunal Procedure Rules.

3(4) Any reference to an existing tribunal is to be substituted with a reference to the tribunal.

3(5) Any time period which has started to run before the commencement date and has not expired will continue to apply.

3(6) On and after the commencement date, no notification offering or requiring a review may be given under any review and appeal provision or any other enactments that are applicable to the decision as they apply after that date.

3(7) In this paragraph **"review and appeal provision"**, **"relevant decision"** and **"relevant review decision"** have the same meaning as in paragraph 2.

FORMER VAT AND DUTIES TRIBUNALS MATTERS: VAT

4(1) This paragraph applies if, before the commencement date–

(a) HMRC have notified a decision relating to a matter to which section 83 of the Value Added Tax Act 1994 applies, and

(b) no party has served notice on a VAT and duties tribunal for the purpose of beginning proceedings before such a tribunal in relation to that decision.

4(2) On and after the commencement date, the following enactments continue to apply (subject to sub-paragraphs (3) and (4)) as they applied immediately before that date–

(a) the Value Added Tax Act 1994,

(b) rule 4(2) of the VAT Tribunals Rules 1986, and

(c) any other enactments that are applicable to the decision.

4(3) Those enactments apply subject to Tribunal Procedure Rules.

4(4) Any reference to an existing tribunal is to be substituted with a reference to the tribunal.

4(5) Any time period which has started to run before the commencement date and has not expired will continue to apply.

MATTERS FORMERLY HEARD BY EXISTING TRIBUNALS (EXCEPT VAT AND DUTIES TRIBUNALS)

5(1) This paragraph applies if, before the commencement date–

(a) a notice of appeal has been given to HMRC; but

(b) no party has served notice on an existing tribunal for the purpose of beginning proceedings before the existing tribunal in relation to that appeal.

5(2) Where the date on which a review is required or offered falls on or before 31 March 2010, the period for HMRC to give notice of their conclusions for the purposes of the relevant provision is to be 90 days (but without prejudice to any power to agree to a different period).

5(3) In this paragraph–

"review" means a review under–

(a) section 49B or 49C of the Taxes Management Act 1970, or

(b) any other enactment which, as amended by this Order, contains provisions corresponding to section 49B or 49C for review to be required or offered;

"relevant provision" means–

(a) in the case of a review under section 49B or 49C of the Taxes Management Act 1970, section 49E(6) of that Act, or

(b) in the case of a review under any other enactment amended by this Order, the provision that corresponds to section 49E(6) of the Taxes Management Act 1970 in relation to that review.

CURRENT PROCEEDINGS

6 Any current proceedings are to continue on and after the commencement date as proceedings before the tribunal.

7(1) This paragraph applies to current proceedings that are continued before the tribunal by virtue of paragraph 6.

7(2) Where a hearing before an existing tribunal (except for the Commissioners for the general purposes of the income tax) began before the commencement date but was not completed by that date, the tribunal must be comprised for the continuation of that hearing of the person or persons who began it.

7(3) The tribunal may give any direction to ensure that proceedings are dealt with fairly and justly and, in particular, may–

(a) apply any provision in procedural rules which applied to the proceedings before the commencement date; or

(b) disapply any provision of Tribunal Procedure Rules.

7(4) In sub-paragraph (3) **"procedural rules"** means any provision (whether called rules or not) regulating practice or procedure before an existing tribunal.

7(5) Any direction or order made or given in proceedings which is in force immediately before the commencement date remains in force on and after that date as if it were a direction or order of the tribunal relating to proceedings before that tribunal.

7(6) A time period which has started to run before the commencement date and which has not expired will continue to apply.

7(7) An order for costs may only be made if, and to the extent that, an order could have been made before the commencement date (on the assumption, in the case of costs actually incurred after that date, that they had been incurred before that date).

CASES TO BE REMITTED BY COURTS

8 Any case to be remitted by a court on or after the commencement date in relation to an existing tribunal shall be remitted to the tribunal.

DECISIONS OF VAT AND DUTIES TRIBUNALS AND COURTS: INTEREST AND PAYMENT

9(1) This paragraph applies in relation to any decision of a VAT and duties tribunal made before the commencement date.

9(2) On and after that date, the following provisions continue to apply as they applied immediately before that date–

(a) section 84(8) of the Value Added Tax Act 1994 (VAT),

(b) section 60(6) to (8) of the Finance Act 1994 (insurance premium tax),

(c) paragraphs 8 and 10 of Schedule 6 to the Finance Act 1994 (air passenger duty),

(d) section 56(3) to (5) of the Finance Act 1996 (landfill tax),

(e) paragraph 123(4) to (6) of Schedule 6 to the Finance Act 2000 (climate change levy),

(f) section 42(4) to (6) of the Finance Act 2001 (aggregates levy),

(g) paragraph 14(4) of Schedule 3 to the Finance Act 2001 (excise and customs).

10(1) This paragraph applies if an appeal from a decision of a VAT and duties tribunal, or from a court, is made before the commencement date.

10(2) Section 85B of the Value Added Tax Act 1994 does not apply in relation to that decision.

DECISIONS OF EXISTING TRIBUNALS: RIGHTS OF APPEAL, REVIEWS AND IRREGULARITIES

11(1) This paragraph applies to a decision of an existing tribunal if, immediately before the commencement date–

(a) an appeal lies to a court from that decision,

(b) an application may be or has been made to an existing tribunal seeking a review of that decision, or

(c) the existing tribunal wishes to correct an irregularity.

11(2) Except as provided for in sub-paragraph (3), on and after the commencement date such rights of appeal shall lie from the decision as would lie from a decision of the First-tier Tribunal made on or after that date.

11(3) Subject to the modifications specified in sub-paragraphs (4) and (5) the following enactments continue to apply for the purposes of a case to be stated, a review, or for correcting an irregularity in respect of any decision of the Commissioners for the general purposes of the income tax made before the commencement date, as if the amendments in this Order had not been made–

(a) sections 56 and 58 of the Taxes Management Act 1970,

(b) regulations 17 and 20 to 24 of the General Commissioners (Jurisdiction and Procedure) Regulations 1994, and

(c) the General Commissioners of Income Tax (Costs) Regulations 2001.

11(4) Section 56(6) of the Taxes Management Act 1970 is modified so that for "the Commissioners" there is substituted "the tribunal".

11(5) Section 58 of the Taxes Management Act 1970 is modified as follows–

(a) omit subsection (2B); and

(b) in subsection (2C) omit "or on an appeal under section 56A of this Act".

11(6) In article 4 of the Tribunals, Courts and Enforcement Act 2007 (Commencement No. 6 and Transitional Provisions) Order 2008–

(a) for "section 56 of the 1970 Act (statement of case for opinion of the High Court)" substitute "sections 56(3) and (11) and 58 of the 1970 Act (statement of case for opinion of the High Court) and regulations 17 and 20 to 24 of the General Commissioners (Jurisdiction and Procedure) Regulations 1994 (review of tribunal's final determination, stated case procedures and correction of irregularities)"; and

(b) after "commenced" insert ", and the amendments to the 1970 Act and the revocation of the General Commissioners (Jurisdiction and Procedure) Regulations 1994, the General Commissioners (Jurisdiction and Procedure) (Amendment) Regulations 1999, the General Commissioners (Jurisdiction and Procedure) (Amendment) Regulations 2005 and the General Commissioners and Special Commissioners (Jurisdiction and Procedure) (Amendment) Regulations 2007 (as they relate to the General Commissioners) in the Transfer of Tribunal Functions and Revenue and Customs Appeals Order 2009 had not been made".

EXISTING TRIBUNALS – STAFF

12 Staff appointed to the existing tribunals (except to the Commissioners for the general purposes of the income tax) before the commencement date are, on and after that date, to be treated, for the purpose of any enactment, as if they had been appointed by the Lord Chancellor under section 40(1) of the Tribunals, Courts and Enforcement Act 2007 (tribunal staff and services).

TRANSITIONAL: GENERAL

13(1) In so far as appropriate in consequence of this Order, a reference in an enactment, instrument or other document to an existing tribunal, or a member or official of an existing tribunal (however expressed) is to be taken to be a reference to the tribunal.

13(2) Sub-paragraph (1) does not apply to any reference that is amended by Schedule 1 or 2.

FINANCE ACT 2009, SECTION 96 AND SCHEDULE 48 (APPOINTED DAY, SAVINGS AND CONSEQUENTIAL AMENDMENTS) ORDER 2009

(SI 2009/3054)

Made on 19 November 2009 by the Treasury in exercise of the powers conferred by s. 96(3)–(6) of the Finance Act 2009. Operative from 1 April 2010.

CITATION AND COMMENCEMENT

1 This Order may be cited as the Finance Act 2009, Section 96 and Schedule 48 (Appointed Day, Savings and Consequential Amendments) Order 2009 and comes into force on 1st April 2010.

APPOINTED DAY

2 The day appointed as the day on which the amendments made by section 96 of and Schedule 48 to the Finance Act 2009 (extension of information and inspection powers to further taxes) come into force is 1st April 2010.

CONSEQUENTIAL AMENDMENTS

3 The Schedule to this Order contains amendments of enactments in consequence of section 96(1) of and Schedule 48 to the Finance Act 2009.

SAVINGS

4 [Not relevant to petroleum revenue tax.]

5 In section 187 of the Finance Act 1993 (petroleum revenue tax: provision of information etc), in relation to a notice given under that section before 1st April 2010, the following provisions continue to have effect on and after that day despite their repeal by the Schedule to this Order–

(a) subsection (6) (right to object to notice), and

(b) subsection (8) (penalty for failure to comply with notice).

6–8 [Not relevant to petroleum revenue tax.]

SCHEDULE

Article 3

FINANCE ACT 1993

1–4 [Not relevant to petroleum revenue tax.]

5 In the Finance Act 1993, omit–

(a) section 187(2) to (8) (petroleum revenue tax: return and information), and

(b) Schedule 21 (supplementary provisions about information).

6–16 [Not relevant to petroleum revenue tax.]

FIELD ALLOWANCE FOR NEW OIL FIELDS ORDER 2010

(SI 2010/610)

Made on 4 March 2010 by the Commissioners for Her Majesty's Revenue and Customs in exercise of the powers conferred on them by para. 17(1) to (3) of Sch. 44 to the Finance Act 2009. Operative in accordance with art. 1(1).

CITATION, COMMENCEMENT AND INTERPRETATION

1(1) This Order may be cited as The Field Allowance for New Oil Fields Order 2010 and shall come into force on the day after the day on which it is made.

1(2) In this Order–

"pipe-line" means a pipe-line as defined by section 65 of the Pipe-lines Act 1962 (meaning of pipe-line),

"Schedule 44" means Schedule 44 to the Finance Act 2009 (supplementary charge: reduction for certain new oil fields).

1(3) In this Order, where any term is given a definition taken from legislation which is excluded from extension to Northern Ireland, that exclusion shall not be taken into account.

QUALIFYING OIL FIELD

2 A deep water gas field is a qualifying oil field for the purposes of Schedule 44 and paragraph 20 of Schedule 44 (qualifying oil fields) shall be treated as modified accordingly.

DEEP WATER GAS FIELD

3(1) An oil field is a **"deep water gas field"** if all of the following conditions are met.

3(2) The first condition is that–

(a) the material submitted in support of the authorisation of the oil field identifies the planned route for the primary pipe-line (or pipe-lines) for transporting gas from the oil field to the relevant infrastructure, and

(b) the distance gas is to be transported along the planned route is more than 60 kilometres.

3(3) The second condition is that the natural seabed above the oil field must lie below the water surface at a depth of more than 300 metres.

3(4) The third condition is that on the authorisation day of the oil field more than 75 per cent of the reserves of the oil field comprise gas.

RELEVANT INFRASTRUCTURE

4(1) In this Order **"relevant infrastructure"** means any–

(a) pipe-line, or

(b) gas processing facility,

which is being used by, or is planned for use by, another oil field whose development has been authorised before the authorisation day for the deep water gas field.

4(2) In this article **"gas processing facility"** has the same meaning as provided by section 12 of the Gas Act 1995 (acquisition of rights to use gas processing facilities).

WATER DEPTH

5 For the purpose of article 3(3), the depth is to be measured at the lowest astronomical tide from the water surface to the lowest point of the natural seabed at the location of the primary subsea manifold or first development well whichever is the deeper.

RESERVES

6 For the purpose of article 3(4), 1,100 cubic metres of gas at a temperature of 15 degrees Celsius and pressure of one atmosphere is to be counted as equivalent to one tonne of oil.

FIELD ALLOWANCE FOR DEEP WATER GAS FIELD

7 For the purpose of Schedule 44, the total field allowance ("TFA") for a new oil field in the case of a deep water gas field is, subject to article 8, calculated as follows–

$$TFA = Y\left(\frac{D-60}{60}\right)$$

where

(a) "Y" is–

(i) £800,000,000; or

(ii) where there are more than two deep water gas fields authorised on the same day, £1,600,000,000 divided by the number of deep water gas fields authorised on that day; and

(b) "D" is–

(i) the length in kilometres of the distance covered by article 3(2) where that is more than 60 but less than 120; or

(ii) 120 where that length is 120 kilometres or more.

OVERLAPPING CATEGORIES OF QUALIFYING OIL FIELD

8 Where a new oil field falls into two or more of the following categories–

(a) a small oil field,

(b) an ultra heavy oil field,

(c) an ultra high pressure/high temperature oil field,

(d) a deep water gas field;

it is to be treated as being in the category of qualifying oil field that yields the highest total field allowance and paragraph 24 of Schedule 44 (total field allowance for new oil field) is to be treated as modified accordingly.

DATA-GATHERING POWERS (RELEVANT DATA) REGULATIONS 2012

(SI 2012/847, as amended by SI 2016/979 and SI 2017/1171)

Made on 14 March 2012 by the Treasury, in exercise of the power conferred by para. 1(3) of Sch. 23 to the Finance Act 2011. Operative from 1 April 2012.

CITATION, COMMENCEMENT AND INTERPRETATION

1 These Regulations may be cited as the Data-gathering Powers (Relevant Data) Regulations 2012 and come into force on 1st April 2012.

2 In these Regulations–

"company registration number" has the same meaning as "registered number" in section 1066 of the Companies Act 2006;

"identifying information" means information which identifies a person or an account and includes–

(a) any unique or generic identifier or reference number allocated by, or used by, the data-holder for the purposes of identifying a person or account, or classifying the trade of a person or account;

(b) name, address (including email, website, and any other electronic address), and telephone number associated with a person or account;

(c) company registration number or national insurance number, unique taxpayer reference, VAT number, any other unique government-issued identifier associated with a person or account;

(d) in relation to a person, whether that person is an individual, partnership, limited company, or has any other legal status;

"Schedule 23" means Schedule 23 to the Finance Act 2011;

"VAT number" has the same meaning as "registration number" in paragraph (1) of regulation 2 of the Value Added Tax Regulations 1995.

History – Reg. 2 substituted by SI 2016/979, reg. 3, with effect from 1 November 2016. Former reg. 2 read as follows:
"2 In these Regulations **"Schedule 23"** means Schedule 23 to the Finance Act 2011.".

INCOME, ASSETS ETC BELONGING TO OTHERS

11 The relevant data for a data-holder of the type described in paragraph 13 of Schedule 23 are–

(a) information relating to the money or value received; and

(b) the name and address of the beneficial owner of the money or value.

MONEY SERVICE BUSINESSES

11D(1) he relevant data for a data-holder of the type described in paragraph 13D of Schedule 23 are–

(a) records required to be kept by the data-holder under regulation 40 of the Money Laundering, Terrorist Financing and Transfer of Funds (Information on the Payer) Regulations 2017;

(b) the quantity and value of transactions carried out by the data-holder for a customer during any period;

(c) identifying information relating to a customer; and

(d) where, in a transaction carried out by the data-holder for a customer, there is a beneficial owner who is not the customer, identifying information relating to the beneficial owner.

11D(2) In this regulation **"beneficial owner"** has the meaning given by regulations 5 and 6 of the Money Laundering, Terrorist Financing and Transfer of Funds (Information on the Payer) Regulations 2017.

History – Reg. 11D inserted by SI 2017/1175, reg. 3, with effect from 21 December 2017.

PETROLEUM ACTIVITIES

21 The relevant data for a data-holder of the type described in paragraph 23 of Schedule 23 are–

(a) particulars of transactions in connection with any activities authorised by a petroleum licence as a result of which any person is or might be liable to tax by virtue of section 276 of the Taxation of Chargeable Gains Act 1992, section 1313 of the Corporation Tax Act 2009 or section 874 of the Income Tax (Trading and Other Income) Act 2005;

(b) particulars of earnings or money treated as earnings, which constitute employment income (see *section 7(2)(a)* or *(b)* of the Income Tax (Earnings and Pensions) Act 2003) or other payments paid or payable in respect of duties or services performed in an area in which those activities may be carried on under the petroleum licence;

(c) particulars of the persons to whom such earnings, money or other payments were paid and are payable;

(d) information and documents relating to the oil field.

PROMOTERS OF TAX AVOIDANCE SCHEMES (PRESCRIBED CIRCUMSTANCES UNDER SECTION 235) REGULATIONS 2015

(SI 2015/130)

Made on 6 February 2015 by the Commissioners for Her Majesty's Revenue and Customs in exercise of the powers conferred upon them by s. 235(6) and (7) and 283(1) of the Finance Act 2014. Operative from 2 March 2015.

CITATION, COMMENCEMENT AND EFFECT

1(1) These Regulations may be cited as the Promoters of Tax Avoidance Schemes (Prescribed Circumstances under Section 235) Regulations 2015 and come into force on 2nd March 2015.

1(2) Regulations 2 and 3 have effect from 17th July 2014.

COMPANY IN SAME GROUP NOT PROMOTER

2(1) A company ("C") is not a promoter to the extent that–

(a) C carries on a business within the meaning of section 235(1);

(b) the other person (or each of the other persons) to whom C provides services in connection with the relevant proposal or relevant arrangements is a company in the same group as C; and

(c) C has not during the previous three years provided services of that kind to a person other than a company which is in the same group as C.

2(2) If C at any subsequent time provides services of that kind to a person other than a company which is in the same group as C, paragraph (1) will be deemed not to have applied during the previous three years.

2(3) A company cannot rely on paragraph (1) whilst a conduct notice or a monitoring notice has effect in relation to it.

2(4) For the purposes of this regulation companies are members of the same group if one is the 51% subsidiary of the other, or both are 51% subsidiaries of a third company.

2(5) In this regulation **"51% subsidiary"** has the same meaning as it does for the purposes of the Corporation Tax Acts.

PERSONS NOT PROMOTERS – SPECIAL CASES

3(1) A person ("P") is not a promoter on account of section 235(2)(a), or by virtue of being responsible to any extent for the design of arrangements within the meaning of section 235(3)(b), where any of the following conditions are met.

3(2) P does not provide any tax advice in connection with the respective proposed arrangements or arrangements.

3(3) P could not reasonably be expected to know that the proposed arrangements, or arrangements, are a relevant proposal or relevant arrangements respectively.

PRT Statutory Instruments

FINANCE ACT 2014 (SCHEDULE 34 PRESCRIBED MATTERS) REGULATIONS 2015

(SI 2015/131)

Made on 6 February 2015 by the Commissioners for Her Majesty's Revenue and Customs in exercise of the powers conferred upon them by s. 283(1) of, and para. 8(1), 8(3) and 9(2) of Sch. 34 to, the Finance Act 2014. Operative from 2 March 2015.

CITATION AND COMMENCEMENT

1 These Regulations may be cited as the Finance Act 2014 (Schedule 34 Prescribed Matters) Regulations 2015 and come into force on 2nd March 2015.

PRESCRIBED MISCONDUCT

2(1) Prescribed misconduct for the purposes of paragraph 8(1)(a) of Schedule 34 to the Finance Act 2014 means any conduct by a person–

(a) which a professional body describes as misconduct, or

(b) which is a breach of a rule or condition imposed by a professional body,

and is relevant to the provision of tax advice or tax related services.

PRESCRIBED ACTION

3 Prescribed action for the purposes of paragraph 8(1)(b) of Schedule 34 to the Finance Act 2014 means any action by a professional body which results in any claim of misconduct being referred to–

(a) a disciplinary process which determines–

(i) the seriousness of the misconduct, and

(ii) the level of any penalty to be imposed; or

(b) a conciliation, arbitration or similar settlement process (however described) which determines the seriousness of the misconduct and the level of any penalty to be imposed.

PRESCRIBED PENALTY

4 A penalty is prescribed for the purposes of paragraph 8(1)(c) of Schedule 34 to the Finance Act 2014 where it is imposed by a professional body and results in one or more of the following in relation to a person–

(a) a fine or financial penalty greater than £5,000;

(b) a condition or restriction on, or attached to, a certificate or licence required to practice under the professional body;

(c) suspension, withdrawal or non-renewal of a certificate or licence required to practice under the professional body;

(d) suspension, expulsion or exclusion from membership of the professional body, however described (including removal from a membership register, striking off), whether temporary or permanent.

PRESCRIBED PROFESSIONAL BODIES

5 The following are prescribed professional bodies for the purposes of paragraph 8(3)(l) of Schedule 34 to the Finance Act 2014–

(a) the Chartered Institute of Taxation;

(b) Chartered Accountants Ireland.

PRESCRIBED RELEVANT SANCTION

6(1) In paragraph 9 of Schedule 34 to the Finance Act 2014 a sanction is prescribed under sub-paragraph (2)(b) if a regulatory authority imposes one or more of the following in relation to a person–

(a) a fine or financial penalty;

(b) a suspension of an approval issued by the regulatory authority to perform any function to which the approval relates;

(c) the imposition of limitations or other restrictions in relation to the performance of any function to which any approval issued by the regulatory authority relates;

(d) the imposition of any conditions in relation to any approval issued by the regulatory authority.

6(2) A sanction is also prescribed in relation to a person if a regulatory authority publishes a statement of misconduct by that person.

FINANCE ACT 2014 (HIGH RISK PROMOTERS PRESCRIBED INFORMATION) REGULATIONS 2015

(SI 2015/549)

Made on 5 March 2015 by the Commissioners for Her Majesty's Revenue and Customs in exercise of the powers conferred upon them by s. 249(3), (10) and (11), 253(2) and (4), 257(2), 259(9), 260(7), 261(2), 268(1), 282(4) and 283(1) of the Finance Act 2014. Operative from 27 March 2015.

CITATION, COMMENCEMENT AND INTERPRETATION

1(1) These Regulations may be cited as the Finance Act 2014 (High Risk Promoters Prescribed Information) Regulations 2015 and come into force on 27th March 2015.

1(2) In these Regulations–

"accounting period" for the purposes of corporation tax has the same meaning as that given in sections 9 to 12 of the Corporation Tax Act 2009 and **"beginning of accounting period"** and **"end of accounting period"** shall be construed accordingly;

"the Act" means the Finance Act 2014;

"audiovisual formats" means any method of presenting information that uses an audible and visible format including broadcasting by electronic means or transmission over, or publication on, the internet; **"chargeable period"** shall be construed–

(a) for the purposes of annual tax on enveloped dwellings, in accordance with section 94(8) of the Finance Act 2013;

(b) for the purposes of petroleum revenue tax, in accordance with section 1(3) of the Oil Taxation Act 1975;

"effective date" has the meaning given by section 119 of the Finance Act 2003;

"tax year" means a year beginning on 6th April and ending on the following 5th April;

PRESCRIBED PUBLICATION OR CORRESPONDENCE

2(1) The following publications and correspondence are prescribed for the purposes of subsection (10) of section 249 of the Act (publication by monitored promoter)–

(a) any publication or correspondence that–

(i) with the exception of correspondence with HMRC, contains information about any relevant arrangements or any relevant proposal offered or promoted by the monitored promoter;

(ii) is shown, given or sent to clients or prospective clients in relation to any relevant arrangements or any relevant proposal (whether or not the relevant arrangements or relevant proposal is provided by the monitored promoter);

(iii) is shown, given or sent to intermediaries or prospective intermediaries in relation to any relevant arrangements or any relevant proposal (whether or not the relevant arrangements or relevant proposal is provided by the monitored promoter);

(b) any correspondence with–

(i) a professional body referred to in paragraph 8(3) of Schedule 34 to the Act of which the monitored promoter is a member, prospective member or former member and which concerns any relevant arrangements or any relevant proposal;

(ii) a regulatory authority referred to in paragraph 9(3) of Schedule 34 to the Act which the monitored promoter is regulated by and which concerns the monitored promoter's conduct in respect of any relevant arrangements or any relevant proposal.

2(2) In paragraph (1)–

(a) **"correspondence"** includes correspondence in writing or by electronic means;

(b) **"publication"** means publication in any format (including audiovisual formats).

INFORMATION PUBLICISED BY A MONITORED PROMOTER

3(1) For the purposes of subsection (11) of section 249 of the Act (publication by monitored promoter), the prescribed form and manner is as set out in paragraphs (2), (3) and (4).

3(2) Notification given under subsection (1) of section 249 must–

(a) be in writing;

(b) set out clearly and precisely the information required to be stated under paragraphs (a) and (b) of section 249(1) of the Act so that–

(i) in respect of the information required by section 249(1)(a) of the Act, it is clear that the promoter is being monitored by HMRC because it breached a condition or conditions of a conduct notice identified under section 249(1)(b) of the Act, and

(ii) in respect of the information required by section 249(1)(b) of the Act, the specific details of each of the conditions which it has been determined that the person has failed to comply with.

3(3) In respect of subsection (3) of section 249 of the Act, the monitored promoter shall publish on the internet the information mentioned in paragraph (a) and (b) of section 249(1) of the Act. The published information must–

(a) appear in a prominent position on the monitored promoter's or other websites promoting, or providing information on, the activities of the promoter;
(b) if in writing, be legible;
(c) if in an audiovisual format, be clearly audible or visible;
(d) not in any way be concealed;
(e) be specifically referred to or included in any promotional material (of whatever kind or format);
(f) not be presented in a way that it promotes the activity of tax avoidance.

3(4) The information to be provided under subsection (10) of section 249 of the Act and regulation 2 to these Regulations (prescribed publication or correspondence) must–

(a) be prominent and not in any way be concealed;
(b) if in writing, be legible;
(c) if in an audiovisual format, be clearly audible or visible;
(d) not be presented in a way that promotes the activity of tax avoidance.

DUTY OF PERSONS TO NOTIFY THE COMMISSIONERS: PRESCRIBED INFORMATION

4(1) The following information is prescribed for the purposes of paragraphs 2(b) and 4(b) of section 253 of the Act (duty of persons to notify the Commissioners)–

(a) the full name and address (including postcode) of the person reporting the promoter reference number;
(b) the promoter reference number which is the subject of the report;
(c) the type of tax in respect of which the person expects to obtain a tax advantage;
(d) the unique identifier (as to the meaning of which see paragraph (3)(a));
(e) the relevant date of the transaction(s) (as to the meaning of which see paragraph (3)(b));
(f) a declaration that the information provided is correct and complete to the best of the knowledge and belief of the person making the report;
(g) the signature of the person making the report;
(h) the full name of the person signing the report;
(i) the date on which the report is made.

4(2) For relevant arrangements involving annual tax on enveloped dwellings, stamp duty land tax or stamp duty reserve tax transactions under regulation 4 of the Stamp Duty Reserve Tax Regulations 1986 (notice of charge and payment), the unique identifier in sub-paragraph (1)(d) is to be replaced by the following additional prescribed information–

(a) for annual tax on enveloped dwellings–
  (i) title number or numbers of the dwelling associated with the relevant arrangements;
  (ii) full address of the dwelling including the postcode sufficient to be able to identify it;
(b) for stamp duty land tax–
  (i) the unique transaction reference number (if a land transaction return has been submitted to HMRC at the time the prescribed information is provided);
  (ii) title number or numbers of the land associated with the relevant arrangements;
  (iii) full address or situation of the land including (where available) the postcode, or information sufficient that the land can be uniquely identified;
(c) for stamp duty reserve tax transactions a full description of the shares or securities associated with the relevant arrangements, including the–
  (i) number of shares or securities;
  (ii) class or classes of the shares;

(iii) name of the company or other body to which the shares relate;

(iv) nominal value;

(v) consideration paid.

4(3) For the purposes of paragraph (1)–

(a) **"unique identifier"** is to be construed as follows–

(i) where the promoter reference number is not reported in a tax return for an individual, the national insurance number and unique tax reference number of the person making the report;

(ii) where the promoter reference number is not reported in a tax return for a trust or company, the unique tax reference number for the trust or company (as the case may be);

(iii) for inheritance tax purposes, the unique tax reference number and any inheritance tax reference previously allocated by HMRC to the person making the report;

(iv) for stamp duty reserve tax transactions authorised by different arrangements under regulation 4A of the Stamp Duty Reserve Tax Regulations 1986, the unique transaction reference provided by the reporting system under the authorised arrangements;

(b) **"relevant date of the transaction(s)"** means–

(i) in respect of capital gains tax or income tax, the date on which the tax year, in which the relevant arrangements enable or seek to enable a tax advantage to be obtained, ends;

(ii) in respect of corporation tax, with the exception of partnerships where one or more of the partners is a company, either the date on which the accounting period, in which the relevant arrangements enable or seek to enable a tax advantage to be obtained, ends, or, where the company does not have an accounting period, the date of the first transaction forming part of the relevant arrangements;

(iii) in respect of corporation tax in relation to partnerships, including where one or more of the partners is a company, the date on which the tax year in which the relevant arrangements enable or seek to enable a tax advantage to be obtained, ends;

(iv) in respect of annual tax on enveloped dwellings, the date on which the chargeable period, in which the relevant arrangements enable or seek to enable a tax advantage to be obtained, ends;

(v) in respect of inheritance tax, the date of the first transaction forming part of the relevant arrangements;

(vi) in respect of stamp duty land tax, the effective date of the land transaction that forms part of the relevant arrangements that enable a tax advantage to be obtained;

(vii) in respect of stamp duty reserve tax, the date of the transaction that forms part of the relevant arrangements that enable a tax advantage to be obtained;

(viii) in respect of petroleum revenue tax, the end of each chargeable period within which a tax advantage may arise.

REPORT OF PROMOTER REFERENCE NUMBER: PRESCRIBED FORM AND MANNER

5(1) The report made under paragraphs 2(b) and 4(b) of section 253 of the Act (duty of persons to notify the Commissioners) must be made in the form prescribed in Schedule 1 to these Regulations. A separate report must be made for each tax which the relevant arrangements enable or seek to enable an advantage to be obtained.

5(2) The completed report must be sent by post to one of the addresses listed in Schedule 2 to these Regulations.

REPORT OF PROMOTER REFERENCE NUMBER: PRESCRIBED TIME

6(1) A report under section 253 of the Act (duty of persons to notify the Commissioners) must be made by the deadlines set out in paragraphs (2), (3) and (4).

6(2) Where a tax return for an individual, partnership, trustee, company or a return for the purposes of the annual tax on enveloped dwellings is not submitted by the date in section 253(3)(a) or (b) of the Act in relation to the period within which a tax advantage may arise, the report must be made by the end of the fifth working day following the date on which the return was required to be submitted.

6(3) Where there is no tax return covering the period within which a tax advantage may arise, then the report must be made–

(a) in the case of an individual, partnership or trustee, by 31st January following the end of each tax year within which a tax advantage may arise;

(b) in the case of a company, not later than 12 months from the end of each accounting period within which a tax advantage may arise;

(c) in the case of an annual tax on enveloped dwellings return, not later than 30 days from the first day of the chargeable period in which the person is within the charge or would have been within the charge but for the relevant arrangements, for each period within which a tax advantage may arise.

6(4) For the purposes of inheritance tax, stamp duty land tax, stamp duty reserve tax, and petroleum revenue tax, the report must be made–

(a) for inheritance tax, not later than the sixth month after the end of the month which the first transaction under the relevant arrangements was entered into;

(b) for stamp duty land tax, not later than 30 days from the effective date of each land transaction which forms part of the relevant arrangements within which a tax advantage may arise;

(c) for stamp duty reserve tax–

(i) in respect of transactions under regulation 4 of the Stamp Duty Reserve Tax Regulations 1986, not later than the time that the notice of the charge to tax is due to be made to HMRC (the accountable date), or

(ii) where a transaction is authorised by different arrangements under regulation 4A of the Stamp Duty Reserve Tax Regulations 1986, not later than the seventh day of the month after the month in which the charge to tax occurred or would have occurred but for the relevant arrangements;

(d) for petroleum revenue tax, not later than 7 days from the end of each chargeable period within which a tax advantage may arise.

6(5) Where a company does not have an accounting period, the report must be made not later than 24 months from the date of the first transaction which forms part of the relevant arrangements and annually thereafter for any period within which a tax advantage arises.

6(6) For the purposes of paragraph (2), **"working day"** means a day that is not a Saturday or Sunday, Christmas Day, Good Friday or any day that is a bank holiday under the Banking and Finance Dealings Act 1971.

ONGOING DUTY TO PROVIDE INFORMATION: PRESCRIBED INFORMATION AND DOCUMENTS

7(1) The following information is prescribed for the purposes of section 257(2) of the Act (ongoing duty to provide information following HMRC notice)–

(a) the name or names by which the monitored promoter refers to the monitored arrangements or monitored proposal;

(b) a summary description of the monitored arrangements or monitored proposal and how they are intended to result in a tax advantage;

(c) a detailed description of each part of the monitored arrangements or monitored proposal and the details of how they are intended to result in a tax advantage;

(d) the legislative provisions (whether in primary legislation, secondary legislation or both) that the person identified in section 257(1) contends provide the basis for the intended tax advantage under the monitored arrangements or monitored proposal;

(e) any reference number allocated under section 311 of the Finance Act 2004 (arrangements to be given reference number);

(f) if the monitored arrangements or monitored proposal have not been disclosed under Part 7 of the Finance Act 2004 (disclosure of tax avoidance schemes), an explanation as to why the monitored arrangements or monitored proposal have not been disclosed;

(g) if the monitored arrangements or monitored proposal are funded by or will require funding from third parties, the names and addresses of the third parties, the level of funding required and the date on which the third parties agreed to provide funding;

(h) the name and address of any person (including any legal advisers) consulted in respect of the monitored arrangements or monitored proposal;

(i) the name and address of any person otherwise involved in planning, organising or operating the monitored arrangements and detailed information on the involvement and role of that person;

(j) a list of each and every fee paid or to be paid by clients to use or participate in the monitored arrangements with a description of what each fee is charged for or will be charged for;

(k) if not included in (b), (c) or (d) above, a list of all taxes in respect of which it is expected to obtain a tax advantage.

7(2) The following are prescribed documents for the purposes of section 257(2) of the Act–

(a) standard letters and templates of documents to be sent to clients regarding the monitored arrangements and monitored proposals;

(b) documentation which is designed or intended to be used in the operation of the monitored arrangements and monitored proposals;

(c) copies of all documents used to market, promote or advertise the monitored arrangements and monitored proposals;

(d) all correspondence which has been sent to, or received from, a client or prospective client or other person involved in the monitored arrangements and monitored proposals and which concerns the arrangements or the proposal;

(e) all correspondence which has been sent to, or received from, any other person which concerns the monitored arrangements and monitored proposals or matters related to the monitored arrangements and monitored proposals;

(f) any agreement signed or otherwise entered into by each client in respect of the monitored arrangements and monitored proposals.

7(3) **"Prescribed documents"** in paragraph (2) includes documents produced in writing or by electronic means.

MONITORED PROMOTERS: PRESCRIBED CLIENT INFORMATION

8 The following information is prescribed for the purposes of section 259(9)(b) of the Act (monitored promoters: duty to provide information about clients)–

(a) where C is an individual, the national insurance number and unique tax reference number identifying C;

(b) where C is a trust, partnership or company, the unique tax reference number identifying C;

(c) in compliance with subsection (3) of section 265 of the Act (duty to provide information to monitored promoter), where C has not provided the information in sub-paragraph (a) or (b), whether or not C has informed the monitored promoter that C has neither a national insurance number nor a unique tax reference number;

(d) the date on which C became a client of the monitored promoter within the meaning of section 259(5) of the Act;

(e) the date on which C entered into transactions referred to in subsection (7) of section 259 of the Act;

(f) the date on which C informed the monitored promoter of the information required by section 265(2) or 265(3) of the Act or, if provided to the monitored promoter earlier, the earlier date;

(g) whether C was a direct client of the monitored promoter, or was acting through an intermediary ("I") and the name and address of I;

(h) the fee or commission paid or payable by C to I in respect of the monitored arrangements or monitored proposals.

INTERMEDIARIES: PRESCRIBED CLIENT INFORMATION

9 The following information about the person ("C") is prescribed for the purposes of section 260(7)(b) of the Act (intermediaries: duty to provide information about clients)–

(a) where the intermediary knows the national insurance number, unique tax reference number or both which identify C, those numbers;

(b) the name, address and the promoter reference number of the monitored promoter in respect of the monitored proposals referred to in section 260(1);

(c) the name and address of any other intermediary from which, or to which, C has been referred in relation to the monitored proposals;

(d) the date on which the information referred to in section 260(5) was communicated;

(e) any fee or commission paid or payable to I in respect of the monitored proposals.

ENQUIRY FOLLOWING PROVISION OF CLIENT INFORMATION: PRESCRIBED INFORMATION

10(1) The information set out in paragraphs (2), (3) and (4) is prescribed for the purposes of section 261(2) of the Act (enquiry following provision of client information).

10(2) Where the authorised officer's suspicion referred to in section 261(1)(b) of the Act is that information has not been provided in respect of a person under section 259 of the Act, the prescribed information under section 261(2) of the Act is–

(i) the information prescribed by regulation 8;

(ii) the reason or reasons why the prescribed information in regulation 8 was not provided as required by section 259.

10(3) Where the authorised officer's suspicion referred to in section 261(1)(b) of the Act is that information has not been provided in respect of a person under section 260 of the Act, the prescribed information under section 261(2) of the Act is–

(a) the information prescribed by regulation 9;

(b) the date of any transaction under section 261(2) of the Act implementing the relevant arrangements or relevant proposal;

(c) the reason or reasons why the prescribed information in regulation 9 was not provided as required by section 260 of the Act.

COPY DOCUMENTS: PRESCRIBED CONDITIONS OR EXCEPTIONS

11(1) The following conditions are prescribed for the purposes of section 268(1) of the Act (production of documents: compliance)–

(a) the copy document must be an exact copy of the original document, without any amendments, corrections or deletions;

(b) the original document must be retained by the person as required;

(c) the person required to produce the document must not alter the original document or allow it to be altered.

11(2) Subject to other provisions in the Tax Acts on the retention of records and documents, the original document under paragraph (1)(b) shall be retained–

(i) for the purposes of sections 255 and 257 of the Act until such time as the monitoring notice or replacement monitoring is withdrawn under section 245 of the Act;

(ii) for the purposes of section 262 of the Act, until such time as the conduct notice or replacement conduct notice is withdrawn under section 240 of the Act or expires at the end of the period under section 241(2) of the Act.

11(3) Nothing in paragraph (1)(a) prevents a person from redacting information in a copy document which is privileged information within the meaning given in section 271 of the Act.

SCHEDULE 1 – REPORT OF PROMOTER REFERENCE NUMBERS

Regulation 5(1)

HM Revenue & Customs

Report of promoter reference number

When to use this form

Please fill in this form if you have been given a promoter reference number (PRN) and you expect to get a tax advantage from one of the promoter's tax avoidance schemes. It is important that you report the PRN to HM Revenue & Customs (HMRC). If you fail to report a PRN to HMRC we will ask you to pay a penalty.

Details about the promoter reference number

If you complete a personal, trust partnership, company or Annual Tax on Enveloped Dwellings (ATED) tax return, you usually have to report the PRN in your tax return.

If your tax return is late you will need to report the PRN on this form within 5 working days of the date the return was due.

If there is no return covering the period, you will need to make the report by:

- 31 January following the end of the tax year for which you expect to get a tax advantage
- 12 months after the end of the accounting period for which you expect to get a tax advantage
- 30 days of the first day in the chargeable period for which you expect to get a tax advantage on which you were within the charge to the ATED

If exceptionally, you are a company and do not have an accounting period, you will need to report the PRN within 24 months of the first transaction forming part of the tax avoidance scheme (and annually thereafter).

When to report the PRN

You will need to use this form to report the PRN if the tax advantage is expected to arise for:

- Inheritance Tax - within 6 months of the end of the month in which the first transaction forming part of the tax avoidance scheme took place
- Petroleum Revenue Tax - within 7 days of the end of the half-year chargeable period in which you expect to get a tax advantage
- Stamp Duty Land Tax - within 30 days of the transaction forming part of the tax avoidance scheme or for which you expect to get a tax advantage
- Stamp Duty Reserve Tax - where the transaction is not settled through CREST, with the notice of the charge to tax but no later than 7 days from the end of the month in which the transaction took place
- Stamp Duty Reserve Tax - within 7 days of the end of the month in which the transaction took place where the transaction is settled through CREST

For details on where to submit this form, please read 'Where to send this form' on page 3.

Your details

1 Full name use capital letters

2 Full address

Postcode

Your promoter reference number

3 *Promoter reference number (PRN)*

PRT Statutory Instruments

About the tax advantage

4 **Which tax do you expect to get a tax advantage?**

Please tick 1 box and provide the relevant details in box 5 below. Enter:

Annual Tax on Enveloped Dwellings	the title number or numbers and the full address of the property (if the property does not have a postcode you must provide sufficient detail to allow us to identify the property)
Capital Gains Tax	your Unique Taxpayer Reference (UTR) and National Insurance number (for trustees or partnerships, enter the UTR for the trust or partnership)
Corporation Tax	the UTR of the company (or if the form is being sent by a partnership the UTR of the partnership)
Income Tax	your UTR and National Insurance number (for trustees or partnerships, enter the UTR for the trust or partnership)
Inheritance Tax	your UTR and any Inheritance Tax reference previously allocated to you by HM Revenue & Customs
Petroleum Revenue Tax	the name of the oil field for which you expect to get a tax advantage and your participator's reference for that field
Stamp Duty Land Tax	the title number or numbers, full address of the property (if the property does not have a postcode you must provide sufficient detail to allow us to identify the property) and the Unique Transaction Reference number
Stamp Duty Reserve Tax	(if the transaction is not settled through CREST) a full description of the shares or securities, including number, class, nominal value, the name of the company to which the shares relate and consideration paid (if the transaction is settled through CREST) the CREST transaction reference ID

5 **Unique identifier details – include reference number(s), names and addresses as explained in question 4 above**

Details of transaction

Consider when you expect to get a tax advantage and enter the end of the accounting period or transaction date for:

- Annual Tax on Enveloped Dwellings - the end of the chargeable period
- Capital Gains Tax, Income Tax and trustees and partnerships - the end of the tax year
- Corporation Tax - the end of the accounting period unless exceptionally there is no accounting period - then enter the date of the first transaction
- Inheritance Tax - the date of the first transaction
- Petroleum Revenue Tax - the end of the half-year chargeable period
- Stamp Duty Land Tax or Stamp Duty Reserve Tax - the date of the transaction

6 **Date of transaction** DD MM YYYY or **End of period** DD MM YYYY

Declaration

The information I have given on this form is correct and complete to the best of my knowledge and belief.

Full name of signatory use capital letters

Signature

Date DD MM YYYY

Where to send this form

Please return your completed form to:

HM Revenue & Customs
Counter Avoidance Directorate
CA Intelligence S0528
PO Box 194
BOOTLE
L69 9AA

In the case of Stamp Duty Reserve Tax where the transaction is not settled through CREST, send this form to:

HM Revenue & Customs
SDRT Compliance Team
9th Floor, City Centre House
30 Union Street
BIRMINGHAM
B2 4AR

SCHEDULE 2 – ADDRESSES TO SEND THE PROMOTER REFERENCE NUMBER REPORTS

Regulation 5(2)

In respect of arrangements involving stamp duty reserve tax transactions under regulation 4 of the Stamp Duty Reserve Tax Regulations (1986), the completed report under section 253 must be sent to–

HM Revenue and Customs
SDRT Compliance Team
9th Floor, City Centre House
30 Union Street
BIRMINGHAM
B2 4AR

For all other reports made under section 253 (including those involving stamp duty reserve tax transactions under regulation 4A of the Stamp Duty Reserve Tax Regulations (1986)), the completed report must be sent to–

HM Revenue and Customs
Counter Avoidance Directorate
CA Intelligence S0528
PO Box 194
BOOTLE
L69 9AA

PENALTIES FOR ENABLERS OF DEFEATED TAX AVOIDANCE (LEGALLY PRIVILEGED COMMUNICATIONS DECLARATIONS) REGULATIONS 2017

(SI 2017/1245)

Made on 11 December 2017 by the Treasury in exercise of the powers conferred upon them by para. 44(4) of Sch. 16 to the Finance (No. 2) Act 2017. Operative from 2 January 2018.

CITATION AND COMMENCEMENT

1 These Regulations may be cited as the Penalties for Enablers of Defeated Tax Avoidance (Legally Privileged Communications Declarations) Regulations 2017 and come into force on 2nd January 2018.

INTERPRETATION

2 In these Regulations a reference to a numbered paragraph is a reference to the paragraph in Schedule 16 to the Finance Act (No. 2) 2017 which is so numbered.

THE DECLARATION

3 A declaration under paragraph 44 must satisfy Conditions A, B and C.

CONDITION A

4 Condition A is that the declaration must contain sufficient information as might reasonably be expected to enable HMRC to identify–

(a) the person who would rely on the declaration for the purpose of establishing that that person is not liable to a penalty under paragraph 1;

(b) the relevant lawyer making the declaration;

(c) the relevant lawyers whose legally privileged communications would otherwise be relied upon to establish that the person referred to in paragraph (a) is not a person who enabled the arrangements for the purposes of paragraph 1; and

(d) the arrangements (and, where appropriate, the proposal which was implemented by the arrangements) to which the declaration relates.

CONDITION B

5 Condition B is that the declaration must contain the confirmations set out in regulations 6 to 10 which must be made by the relevant lawyer making the declaration.

DESIGNER OF ARRANGEMENTS (PARAGRAPH 8)

6 In relation to whether the person referred to in regulation 4(a) is a designer of arrangements falling within paragraph 8, the confirmation is that the person–

(a) was not, in the course of a business carried on by that person, responsible to any extent for the design of the arrangements or a proposal which was implemented by the arrangements; or

(b) was responsible to an extent for such design because of having provided advice but–

(i) the advice provided is not relevant advice within the meaning of paragraph 8(3); or

(ii) the knowledge condition in paragraph 8(4) is not met.

MANAGERS OF ARRANGEMENTS (PARAGRAPH 9)

7(1) In relation to whether the person referred to in regulation 4(a) is a manager of the arrangements falling within paragraph 9(1), the confirmation is that–

(a) the person was not, in the course of a business carried on by that person, to any extent responsible for the organisation or management of the arrangements; or

(b) if the person was so responsible for the organisation or management of the arrangements, the condition set out in paragraph 9(1)(b) is not met.

7(2) Where the person referred to in regulation 4(a) is not a manager of the arrangements because of paragraph 9(2), the confirmation is that the person referred to in regulation 4(a) meets the condition set out in paragraph 9(2)(b).

MARKETERS OF ARRANGEMENTS (PARAGRAPH 10)

8 In relation to whether the person referred to in regulation 4(a) marketed arrangements to T so as to fall within paragraph 10, the confirmation is that the person did not in the course of a business carried on by that person–

(a) make available for implementation by T a proposal which has since been implemented, in relation to T, by the arrangements; or

(b) communicate information to T or another person about a proposal which has since been implemented, in relation to T, by the arrangements with a view to T entering into the arrangements or transactions forming part of the arrangements.

ENABLING PARTICIPANTS (PARAGRAPH 11)

9 In relation to whether the person referred to in regulation 4(a) is an enabling participant falling within paragraph 11, the confirmation is that–

(a) the person is not a person (other than T) who entered into the arrangements or a transaction forming part of the arrangements; or

(b) if the person did enter into the arrangements or a transaction forming part of the arrangements, the condition set out in paragraph 11(c) is not met.

FINANCIAL ENABLERS (PARAGRAPH 12)

10 In relation to whether the person referred to in regulation 4(a) is a financial enabler falling within paragraph 12, the confirmation is that–

(a) the person did not in the course of a business carried on by that person, provide a financial product (directly or indirectly) to a relevant party within the meaning of paragraph 12; or

(b) to the extent that the person did provide a financial product, the condition set out in paragraph 12(1)(c) is not met.

CONDITION C

11 Condition C is that the declaration must contain–

(a) a certificate that the information provided by the relevant lawyer making the declaration is correct to the best of their knowledge and belief; and

(b) a statement that the relevant lawyer making the declaration understands that any of the persons referred to in regulation 4 may have to pay financial penalties as set out in paragraphs 1 and 45 and that any relevant lawyer named in the declaration may face prosecution for providing false information should that declaration prove to be incorrect.

MULTIPLE IMPLEMENTATIONS OF A PROPOSAL

12 Where a proposal for arrangements was implemented more than once by arrangements which are substantially similar, the declaration may contain a statement that this is the case and that the involvement of the person referred to in regulation 4(a) in relation to those arrangements was such that all the things stated in the declaration are equally true in relation to those arrangements.

SCOTLAND ACT 2016 (ONSHORE PETROLEUM) (CONSEQUENTIAL AMENDMENTS) REGULATIONS 2018

(SI 2018/79)

Made on 19 January 2018 by the Secretary of State for Business, Energy and Industrial Strategy in exercise of the powers conferred upon them by s. 71 of the Scotland Act 2016. Operative in accordance with reg. 1(2).

PART 1 – INTRODUCTORY

CITATION, COMMENCEMENT AND EXTENT

1(1) These Regulations may be cited as the Scotland Act 2016 (Onshore Petroleum) (Consequential Amendments) Regulations 2018.

1(2) Parts 1 and 2 come into force on the twenty-first day after the day on which these Regulations are made.

1(3) Part 3 comes into force immediately after the commencement of Part 2 of Schedule 6 (amendments relating to onshore petroleum consequential on transfer of certain functions under the Petroleum Act 1998 to the Welsh Ministers) to the Wales Act 2017.

1(4) An amendment or modification made by these Regulations has the same extent as the provision to which it relates.

PART 2 – TRANSITIONAL MODIFICATIONS OF TAXATION LEGISLATION HAVING EFFECT UNTIL THE COMMENCEMENT OF PART 2 OF SCHEDULE 6 TO THE WALES ACT 2016

PERIOD FOR WHICH THE MODIFICATIONS MADE BY REGULATIONS 3 TO 7 HAVE EFFECT

2 The modifications specified in regulations 3 to 7 have effect until the commencement of Part 2 of Schedule 6 (amendments relating to onshore petroleum consequential on transfer of certain functions under the Petroleum Act 1998 to the Welsh Ministers) to the Wales Act 2017.

OIL TAXATION ACT 1975

3 In section 12(1) (interpretation of Part 1) of the Oil Taxation Act 1975, in the definition of "licensee", paragraph (b) has effect as if, for "the OGA" there were substituted–

"–

(i) the Scottish Ministers, where the rights relate to oil in the Scottish onshore area, as defined in section 8A of the Petroleum Act 1998, or

(ii) the OGA, where the rights relate to oil elsewhere,"

TAXATION OF CHARGEABLE GAINS ACT 1992

4 Section 196 (interpretation) of the Taxation of Chargeable Gains Act 1992 has effect as if–

(a) in subsection (1), in paragraphs (a) and (b), and subsection (3), for "Oil and Gas Authority" there were substituted "appropriate authority";

(b) in subsection (5), after "section–" there were inserted–

""**appropriate authority**", in relation to a licence under Part 1 of the Petroleum Act 1998–

(a) the Scottish Ministers, in relation to the Scottish onshore area, as defined in section 8A of that Act, or

(b) otherwise, the Oil and Gas Authority;".

FINANCE ACT 1993

5 Section 185 (abolition of petroleum revenue tax for oil fields with development consent on or after 16 March 1993) of the Finance Act 1993 has effect as if–

(a) in subsection (1C), in paragraphs (a) and (b), for "OGA" there were substituted "appropriate authority";

(b) in subsection (2), in paragraph (b), for "OGA" there were substituted "appropriate authority";

(c) after subsection (2) there were inserted–

"**185(2A)** In subsections (1C) and (2), the **"appropriate authority"** means–

(a) in relation to a field that is wholly within the Scottish onshore area, as defined in section 8A of the Petroleum Act 1998, the Scottish Ministers;

(b) otherwise, the OGA.".

CAPITAL ALLOWANCES ACT 2001

6 In section 556(2) of the Capital Allowances Act 2001, paragraph (a) of the definition of "the relevant authority" has effect as if for ", the Oil and Gas Authority" there were substituted–

"

(i) the Scottish Ministers, in relation to the Scottish onshore area, as defined in section 8A of that Act;

(ii) otherwise, the Oil and Gas Authority".

CORPORATION TAX ACT 2010

7(1) Section 356IB (authorisation of development: oil fields) of the Corporation Tax Act 2010 has effect as if, in subsection (2), in the definition of "national authority"–

(a) the word "or" were omitted at the end of paragraph (a);

(b) after paragraph (a) there were inserted–

"(aa) the Scottish Ministers, or".

7(2) Section 356J (authorisation of development: drilling and extraction sites) of that Act has effect as if, in subsection (4), in the definition of "national authority"–

(a) the word "or" were omitted at the end of paragraph (a);

(b) after paragraph (a) there were inserted–

"(aa) the Scottish Ministers, or".

PART 3 – AMENDMENTS TO TAXATION LEGISLATION CONSEQUENTIAL UPON THE TRANSFER OF CERTAIN FUNCTIONS UNDER THE PETROLEUM ACT 1998 TO THE SCOTTISH MINISTERS

OIL TAXATION ACT 1975

8 In section 12(1) (interpretation of Part 1) of the Oil Taxation Act 1975, in the definition of "licensee", in paragraph (b), before sub-paragraph (i) insert–

"(ai) the Scottish Ministers, where the rights relate to oil in the Scottish onshore area, as defined in section 8A of the Petroleum Act 1998,".

TAXATION OF CHARGEABLE GAINS ACT 1992

9 In section 196(5) (interpretation) of the Taxation of Chargeable Gains Act 1992, in paragraph (a) of the definition of "appropriate authority", before sub-paragraph (i) insert–

"(ai) the Scottish Ministers, in relation to the Scottish onshore area, as defined in section 8A of *that Act*;".

FINANCE ACT 1993

10 In section 185 (abolition of petroleum revenue tax for oil fields with development consent on or after 16 March 1993) of the Finance Act 1993, in subsection (2A), before paragraph (a) insert–

"(za) in relation to a field that is wholly within the Scottish onshore area, as defined in section 8A of the Petroleum Act 1998, the Scottish Ministers;".

CAPITAL ALLOWANCES ACT 2001

11 In section 556(2) (minor definitions) of the Capital Allowances Act 2001, in paragraph (a) of the definition of "the relevant authority", before sub-paragraph (i) insert–

"(ai) the Scottish Ministers, in relation to the Scottish onshore area, as defined in section 8A of that Act;".

CORPORATION TAX ACT 2010

12(1) In section 356IB (authorisation of development: oil fields) of the Corporation Tax Act 2010, in subsection (2), in the definition of "national authority", after paragraph (a) insert–

"(aza) the Scottish Ministers,".

12(2) In section 356J (authorisation of development: drilling and extraction sites) of that Act, in subsection (4), in the definition of "national authority", after paragraph (a) insert–

"(aza) the Scottish Ministers,".

HMRC DIRECTIONS

Table of Contents

DIRECTIONS BY THE BOARD OF HM REVENUE AND CUSTOMS RELATING TO THE SUBMISSION OF RETURNS USING THE INTERNET

HMRC DIRECTIONS

DIRECTIONS UNDER REGULATION 3 OF THE PETROLEUM REVENUE TAX (ELECTRONIC COMMUNICATIONS) REGULATIONS 2003 [(SI 2003/2718)]
[Date made 9 February 2007]

Companies – information in, or in connection with, the claims, elections, notices and returns specified in the Schedule to the Petroleum Revenue Tax (Electronic Communications) Regulations 2003

The Commissioners for Her Majesty's Revenue and Customs hereby direct that, on and after 9th February 2007, a company that is required to deliver information in, or in connection with, the claims, elections, notices and returns specified in the Schedule to the Petroleum Revenue Tax (Electronic Communications) Regulations 2003 ("the relevant information") is authorised to do so using e-mail or over the Internet.

The Commissioners further direct that–

(a) the methods approved by them for–

(i) authenticating the identity of the person sending the relevant information,

(ii) delivery of the relevant information, and

(iii) authenticating the relevant information; and

(b) the form approved by them in which the relevant information is to be delivered;

are the methods and form set out, at the time of, and for the purposes of, the delivery of the relevant information, in the terms and conditions for use of e-communication for Petroleum Revenue Tax, on the HM Revenue and Customs website.

Agents acting on behalf of companies – information in, or in connection with, the claims, elections, notices and returns specified in the Schedule to the Petroleum Revenue Tax (Electronic Communications) Regulations 2003.

The Commissioners for Her Majesty's Revenue and Customs hereby direct that on and after 9th February 2007 an agent who delivers information on behalf of a company, which the company is required to deliver in, or in connection with, the claims, elections, notices and returns specified in the Schedule to the Petroleum Revenue Tax (Electronic Communications) Regulations 2003 ("the relevant information"), is authorised to do so using e-mail or over the Internet provided that the following conditions are met.

The first condition is that the agent is authorised to act for the company to which the return relates by means of a form 64-8 signed by a proper officer of the company.

The second condition is that–

(a) the agent makes a copy of the relevant information before it is sent; and

(b) the copy is authenticated by a proper officer of the company, (or other person authorised to make the return of behalf of the company) by means of a signature confirming that the information is correct to the best of his knowledge and belief before the information is sent by the agent.

This second condition will not apply where the agent is a person authorised by the company to make the return on its behalf.

The Commissioners further direct that–

(a) the methods approved by them for–

(i) authenticating the identity of the person sending the relevant information,

(ii) delivery of the relevant information, and

(iii) authenticating the relevant information; and

(b) the form approved by them in which the relevant information is to be delivered;

are the methods and form set out, at the time of, and for the purposes of, the delivery of the relevant information, in the terms and conditions for use of e-communication for Petroleum Revenue Tax, on the HM Revenue and Customs website.

Other communications within the scope of the Petroleum Revenue Tax (Electronic Communications) Regulations 2003

The Commissioners for Her Majesty's Revenue and Customs hereby direct that companies or their agents may use telephonic facsimile for other communications to which the regulations apply.

PRT EXTRA-STATUTORY MATERIAL

Table of Contents

Page

Entries in italics are those which have been classified by HM Revenue and Customs as obsolete and/or have been enacted in other legislation.

EXTRA-STATUTORY CONCESSIONS

I. Concessions relating to Petroleum Revenue Tax

STATEMENTS OF PRACTICE

HMRC BRIEFS

PRT EXTRA-STATUTORY MATERIAL

Table of Contents

EXTRA-STATUTORY CONCESSIONS

HMRC's Extra-Statutory Concessions as published on 6 April 2015 contained the following caveat:

> "The concessions described within are of general application, but it must be borne in mind that in a particular case there may be special circumstances which will require to be taken into account in considering the application of the concession. A concession will not be given in any case where an attempt is made to use it for tax avoidance."

Every Extra-Statutory Concession is to be read as if this caveat is part of each Concession. This principle was confirmed in the case of *R v HMIT, ex parte Fulford-Dobson* [1987] BTC 158 where McNeill J stated that:

> "In my judgment, the [caveat] is effectively part of each concession. It loses none of its force by being given a special and early place in the booklet: indeed, perhaps, it gains force from that."

The House of Lords' decision in *R v IR Commrs, ex parte Wilkinson* made it clear that the scope of HMRC's administrative discretion to make concessions that depart from the strict application of the letter of the law is not as wide as had previously been supposed. In the light of that decision HMRC are reviewing their concessions. The indications are that most concessions will be able to continue in their current form as they are within the scope of HMRC's administrative discretion, although concessions will continue to be withdrawn where they appear to be obsolete. Where an existing concession exceeds the scope of HMRC's discretion and it is deemed appropriate to preserve its effect, this will be achieved by legislation if possible. If it is not possible put the effect of the concession on a legislative basis, the concession will join obsolete concessions and need to be withdrawn. HMRC have confirmed that no extra-statutory concession will be withdrawn retrospectively and that they will generally offer an appropriate period of notice before a concessionary treatment formally comes to an end.

I. CONCESSIONS RELATING TO PETROLEUM REVENUE TAX

I3 PARAGRAPH 9, SCHEDULE 3, OIL TAXATION ACT 1975

[Obsolete.]

I4 SECTION 9(5), OTA 1983: TARIFF RECEIPTS ALLOWANCE IN RESPECT OF FOREIGN "USER" FIELDS

[Obsolete.]

I5 PETROLEUM REVENUE TAX INSTALMENTS

Paragraph 3(1), Schedule 19, Finance Act 1982 entitles a participator, on giving notice to the Board, to withhold the instalment due for a month under paragraph 2 of the Schedule if, in the previous month, he did not deliver or relevantly appropriate any of the oil won from the field. By concession, a participator is also entitled, again on giving notice to the Board, to withhold the instalment for a month if in the previous or an earlier month, oil actually ceased to be won from the field as a result of some sudden catastrophic loss of or damage to production, transportation or initial treatment facilities relating to the field, and has not recommenced.

STATEMENTS OF PRACTICE

SP 6/84 NON-RESIDENT LESSORS – SECTION 830 ICTA 1988 [31 July 1984]

Where mobile drilling rigs, vessels or equipment leased by a non-resident lessor are used in connection with exploration or exploitation activities carried on in the UK or in a designated area, the question of whether the profits or gains arising from the lease constitute income from such activities depends on the facts and circumstances of each particular case. However, the practice of HM Revenue and Customs is not to seek to charge such profits or gains to tax under S. 830 ICTA 1988 if all of the following conditions are satisfied–

(1) the contract is concluded outside the United Kingdom and the designated areas;

(2) the lessor's obligations are limited to the provision of the asset, for example, a rig on "bare-boat" terms, that is to say, if the lessor has not undertaken to provide any facilities, service or personnel;

(3) the lessee takes delivery of the asset outside the designated areas, and is responsible for moving it to the place where it is used, and is not restricted to using it solely in the United Kingdom or a designated area;

(4) the lessee and lessor are not connected persons, and no facilities, services or personnel related to the operation of the asset are provided by any person connected with the lessor.

Notes – The text of SP 6/84 is as it appears in HMRC's Statements of Practice as published on 30 January 2012.

HMRC BRIEFS

BRIEFS

HMRCBrf 14/11 PENALTY FOR FAILURE TO DISCLOSE OFFSHORE INCOME OR GAINS [HMRC – 6 April 2011]

Introduction

This brief explains how legislation in Schedule 10 to 2010 Finance Act allows for a higher penalty rate where income or gains that arise outside the UK are underdeclared. People who do not declare income or gains arising offshore could face penalties that are up to 200 per cent of the tax owed.

The new penalties for offshore non-compliance came into force on 6 April and will apply for the 2011–12 tax year onwards to Income Tax and Capital Gains Tax.

Background

The offshore penalties legislation is part of the continuing review of HMRC's powers, deterrents and safeguards [http://www.hmrc.gov.uk/about/powers-appeal.htm] which aims to align and modernise the framework for the taxes HM Revenue & Customs (HMRC) administers.

The offshore penalty

The new offshore penalty is an enhancement of three existing penalties for:

- failure to notify – where you fail to tell us that you have a source of income or a capital gain that may be taxable
- inaccuracy on a return – where your Self Assessment tax return is incorrect
- failure to file a tax return on time – where you send your tax return late

Schedule 10 to Finance Act 2010 introduced a new link between these penalties and the tax transparency of the territory in which the undeclared income or gain arises. Where it is harder for us to get information from another country, the penalties for failing to declare income or gains arising in that country will be higher.

Each territory has been placed into one of three categories. The criteria used [http://www.hmrc.gov.uk/news/offshore-faqs.pdf] and the list of territories [http://www.hmrc.gov.uk/news/territories-category.htm] are on the HMRC website.

There will be three new levels of penalty:

- Category 1 territories: the penalty rate is the same as for existing penalties, up to 100 per cent of the tax due.
- Category 2 territories: the penalty is 1.5 times the existing penalties, up to 150 per cent of tax due.
- Category 3 territories: the penalty is double the existing penalties, up to 200 per cent of tax due.

All existing safeguards will still apply. There will be no penalty if a person can demonstrate they have taken reasonable care to get their tax right or have a reasonable excuse for a failure to notify taxable income or gains.

Where penalties are due, HMRC can reduce them depending on how helpful the individual is in assisting us to establish the correct amount of tax due. The largest reductions will be for unprompted disclosures. Unprompted means when you tell us about a tax issue you have no reason to believe we have discovered or are about to discover it.

The existing penalties

A full explanation of these penalties, and the percentage rates attached to each type of behaviour and disclosure, is available on the HMRC website using the links below.

More information

Offshore penalties internet page [http://nds.coi.gov.uk/clientmicrosite/Content/Detail.aspx?ClientId=257&NewsAreaId=2&ReleaseID=417695&SubjectId=36

Understanding penalties – agents and advisers [http://www.hmrc.gov.uk/agents/penalties.htm]

Q&A briefing on the offshore penalty [http://www.hmrc.gov.uk/news/offshore-faqs.pdf]

Liechtenstein Disclosure Facility – runs from 1 September 2009 until 31 March 2015 [http://www.hmrc.gov.uk/disclosure/liechtenstein-disclosure.htm]

How to take care and avoid the inaccuracy and failure to notify penalties [http://www.hmrc.gov.uk/about/new-penalties/index.htm]

HMRCBrf 15/11 PENALTIES: CHANGE TO HMRC'S VIEW OF THE OPERATION OF THE DELAYED TAX PROVISIONS FOR INACCURACY PENALTIES [HMRC – 6 April 2011]

Introduction

The purpose of this brief is to explain a change in how HM Revenue & Customs (HMRC) views the operation of the "delayed tax" provision of the new penalties for inaccuracies, introduced in paragraph 8 of Schedule 24 to the Finance Act 2007.

Who needs to read this?

Customers who have been charged a penalty for an inaccuracy on a return that would have been automatically reversed in a subsequent return, but for a compliance check by HMRC.

Background

Under the 2007 Finance Act, new penalties were introduced for inaccuracies on returns or other documents. Under these penalties, if a return contains an inaccuracy that relates to a timing error which is automatically reversed in a subsequent tax period, the penalty is not calculated on the full amount of tax underpaid in the first period, but on a reduced amount to take account of the timing error.

For example, if someone reclaims £100,000 VAT on a purchase in period 1 when it should have been reclaimed in period 2, they claim £100,000 too much in the first period but £100,000 too little in the second. Any penalty for the overclaim in period 1 is not calculated on the £100,000 but on a reduced amount to take account of the automatic reversal of the inaccuracy in period 2.

Current position

HMRC's approach to date has been that in order for the penalty to be calculated in this way, the customer had to have submitted both the return containing the initial inaccuracy, and the one containing the automatic reversal of the inaccuracy in a later period. This means that in some cases HMRC has charged a penalty on the full amount because they acted to correct the inaccuracy on the first return before the second return could be submitted, thereby preventing the inaccuracy from being reversed.

Revised position

HMRC is changing its approach for cases where HMRC intervened to correct the inaccuracy before the second return was received, preventing the inaccuracy from being reversed. When HMRC are satisfied that, but for their intervention, the inaccuracy would have been automatically corrected in a subsequent return, customers will receive the reduced penalty based on the rules for delayed tax. HMRC will shortly update our guidance to reflect this.

What you should do

If you have been charged a penalty for an inaccuracy on a return and you believe that, had HMRC not intervened before a subsequent return could be submitted, the inaccuracy would have been automatically reversed in a subsequent period, you should contact HMRC to request that the penalty is reviewed. You should refer to this Revenue and Customs Brief when making your request.

Remember this only applies to timing inaccuracies, those that are automatically reversed in a subsequent period after they are made without you having to do anything more. It does not apply to the VAT Error Correction procedure nor to compensating but unrelated inaccuracies.

Further details

For information about how to ask us to review a penalty, please follow the link below.

Complaints & appeals [http://www.hmrc.gov.uk/complaints-appeals/]

INDEX TO PETROLEUM REVENUE TAX

For a list of abbreviations used in this Index see p. xi.

For a list of abbreviations used in this Index see p. xi.

For a list of abbreviations used in this Index see p. xi.

For a list of abbreviations used in this Index see p. xi.

For a list of abbreviations used in this Index see p. xi.

PRT Indexes

For a list of abbreviations used in this Index see p. xi.

For a list of abbreviations used in this Index see p. xi.

For a list of abbreviations used in this Index see p. xi.

For a list of abbreviations used in this Index see p. xi.

For a list of abbreviations used in this Index see p. xi.

For a list of abbreviations used in this Index see p. xi.

For a list of abbreviations used in this Index see p. xi.

For a list of abbreviations used in this Index see p. xi.

For a list of abbreviations used in this Index see p. xi.

PETROLEUM REVENUE TAX LIST OF DEFINITIONS AND MEANINGS

For a list of abbreviations used in this Index see p. xi.

PRT Indexes

PRT Indexes